KLINCK MEMORIAL LIBRARY
Concordia College
River Forest, IL 60305

WITHDRAWN

Fiction
1876-1983

KLINCK MEMORIAL LIBRARY
Concordia College
River Forest, IL 60305

This edition of *FICTION 1876–1983: A Bibliography of United States Editions* was prepared by the R.R. Bowker Company's Department of Bibliography in collaboration with the Publications Systems Department.

Senior staff of the Department of Bibliography includes:

Peter Simon, Database Manager
Beverley Lamar, Senior Product Manager

Michael B. Howell, Manager, Systems Development
Philip Pan, Applications Manager

Andrew H. Uszak, Senior Vice President, Data Services/Systems

Gertrude Jennings, Manager, Product Research and Development, Data Services

The R.R. Bowker Company has used its best efforts in collecting and preparing material for inclusion in *FICTION 1876–1983* but does not assume, and hereby disclaims, any liability to any party for any loss or damage caused by errors or omissions in *FICTION 1876–1983* whether such errors or omissions result from negligence, accident, or any other cause.

Fiction 1876–1983

A Bibliography of United States Editions

CLASSIFIED AUTHOR INDEX

MAIN AUTHOR INDEX

TITLE INDEX

KEY TO PUBLISHERS AND DISTRIBUTORS ABBREVIATIONS/

DIRECTORY OF PUBLISHERS AND DISTRIBUTORS

R.R. BOWKER COMPANY

New York & London

Published by R.R. Bowker Company (a Xerox Information Company)
205 East Forty-second Street, New York, N.Y. 10017
Copyright © 1983 by Xerox Corporation
All rights reserved

International Standard Book Number (Set) 0-8352-1726-4
International Standard Book Number (Vol. 1) 0-8352-1880-5
International Standard Book Number (Vol. 2) 0-8352-1881-3

Printed and bound in the
United States of America

Library of Congress Cataloging in Publication Data
Main entry under title:
Fiction, 1876–1983.
   "Prepared by the R.R. Bowker Company's Department
of Bibliography in collaboration with the Publications
Systems Department"—
  Includes index.
  1. Fiction—Bibliography. 2. United States—Imprints.
I. R.R. Bowker Company. Dept. of Bibliography.
II. R.R. Bowker. Publications Systems Dept.
Z5916.F49 1983   [PN3451]   016.80883   83-21376
ISBN 0-8352-1726-4 (set)
ISBN 0-8352-1880-5 (v. 1)
ISBN 0-8352-1881-3 (v. 2)

Contents

FOREWORD VII
PREFACE IX

VOLUME I
Classified Author Index 1
Main Author Index 43

VOLUME 2
Title Index 1055
Key To Publishers' and Distributors Abbreviations/Directory of
    Publishers and Distributors 2127

Foreword

Fiction is, without a doubt, America's most popular literary form. We read it, study it, appreciate it, and collect it. Not surprisingly, we ask a lot of questions about fiction:

- When was the first English translation of *One Hundred Years of Solitude* published in the United States?
- When did John Cheever die, and what is the title of his last anthology of short stories?
- What kind of *fantasy novels* were published between the two world wars?
- Which 20th-century Italian novelists have published in the United States in English language editions?
- Is this copy of Hemingway's *Farewell to Arms* a first edition?
- Where can I find a list of all the novels written by Kurt Vonnegut?

These are just a sampling of typical questions which regularly confront librarians in public and academic libraries. While any given question about fiction can probably be answered by using a variety of reference sources currently available in some libraries, no single, inexpensive, and convenient work was available with a sufficient range of bibliographic resources—until now. *FICTION 1876-1983: A Bibliography of United States Editions* is that long awaited and needed comprehensive, retrospective bibliography. Listing all fiction published in this country from the last quarter of the nineteenth century to the present, this two-volume set and its 170,000 entries cover collections of fiction, anthologies of short stories and novellas, and separately printed novels.

BACKGROUND

A brief examination of the major fiction bibliographies currently available points out the considerable gap which Bowker has filled with its decision to publish *FICTION 1876-1983*.

Clearly the most extensive bibliography of United States fiction to date is Lyle H. Wright's *American Fiction*.[1] This three-volume set is a "standard" tool for research librarians and bookdealers, offering a comprehensive list of fiction by both author and title published between 1774 and 1900. But even this major reference set has important limitations. For example, volume three, which covers the period from 1876 to 1900, cites only first editions published during those twenty-five years. The 1774-1850 volume is the only one of the three with a chronological index, in addition to those for author and title, and no other classified indexes appear in the set. Juvenile literature has been excluded entirely from all three volumes. And, strictly a historical tool, *American Fiction* provides no assistance for the 20th-century.

The very popular *Fiction Catalog*,[2] now in its 10th edition and available in most public and academic libraries, represents the "best fiction" chosen by a panel of veteran public librarians. But this bibliography is intentionally limited to a mere 5,000 carefully chosen, albeit well annotated entries. Although useful as a selection tool for many public libraries, *Fiction Catalog* is unable to answer most bibliographic reference questions posed by library patrons.

For years librarians have consulted the *United States Catalog*[3] and *Cumulative Book Index*[4] for English language literary verifications. Anyone who has had to search volume-by-volume through the many years of either of these tools can attest to the inconvenience. Since the *United States Catalog* and *CBI* together provide a complete record of books published in the United States from 1899 to the present, they cannot be used for early American literature.

Of course, dozens of excellent topical bibliographies of fiction have been published over the years. But each of these has focused on a specific author, a narrow time period, or on a particular literary genre, such as historical fiction or the western novel. Bowker's own *Anatomy of Wonder: A Critical Guide to Science Fiction*[5] is a good example. Clearly these specialized sources are not intended and are unable to provide bibliographic verification for works outside their limited and carefully defined parameters. Only research libraries could or would acquire all of them anyway.

When Bowker began to consider publishing *FICTION*

1876-1983, a marketing survey of potential users was conducted to determine the degree of interest in such an undertaking. Given the paucity of bibliographic tools at this time, the overwhelming majority of the public and academic librarians who were polled in the survey expressed wholehearted support for Bowker's idea. Convenience, price, and the ability to serve in so many varied library functions were the reasons most often expressed for this support. Unlike any other book, *FICTION 1876-1983* would be useful for reference, interlibrary loan, and collection development in libraries patronized by the general public as well as by academia.

SCOPE

Derived from the *Books in Print*[6] and *American Book Publishing Record*[7] databases, this bibliography cites virtually every fiction title published in the United States between 1876 and 1983, and regardless of whether the book is still in print. The *Books in Print* tapes assure an up-to-date list, while comprehensive, retrospective coverage is guaranteed by the *American Book Publishing Record* data. It should be noted that almost one thousand titles dating to as early as 1800 appear in the bibliography because these books were cataloged by the Library of Congress sometime during or after 1876.

ARRANGEMENT

FICTION 1876-1983 has three sections: an author, a title, and a special classified author index. The goal is convenience for both librarian and patron.

AUTHOR INDEX

Each author is listed alphabetically, followed by his or her works, also in alphabetical order. Full bibliographic citations are provided with the following elements if known: author, co-author, editor, co-editor, translator, title, original title, edition, whether a reprint, Library of Congress number, whether illustrated, pagination, date of publication and/or copyright, publisher and distributor (if different), type of binding (if other than cloth over boards), price, ISBN, and imprint. Both hardcover and paperback editions are included; only out-of-print editions of mass-market paperbacks are excluded. Name authority is maintained to guarantee that all titles by the same author appear together.

TITLE INDEX

In this alphabetical listing, complete bibliographic citations (mirror images of those in the author section) are supplied for each entry. In other words, the title index is entirely independent from the author section so that the user is not simply cross-referenced from the title index back to the author index for all the bibliographic information.

CLASSIFIED-AUTHOR INDEX

In this section, a unique feature of *FICTION 1876-1983*, authors are grouped by their nationality and/or literary period. Birth and death dates, as appropriate, follow their names. Headings follow the format of those found in *Library of Congress Subject Headings*.[8]

APPLICATIONS

Many practical uses for this bibliography come immediately to mind. Its power as a general reference source should be obvious, considering the vast sweep of information carried in each citation. The Interlibrary Loan Department can verify incomplete or inaccurate citations. Those of us who read comprehensively now have every conceivable checklist, such as all works by an author, or all translated fiction by authors of a particular nationality. Evaluation of the library's retrospective fiction collection would clearly be facilitated by this bibliography, an almost final arbiter as to whether or not the library has complete holdings by particular authors. Verification of bibliographic information for acquisition purposes should consume less time and effort; ISBN and LC numbers are provided when available as well as other bits of information not always noted in other sources, at least not clearly.

AUDIENCE

FICTION 1876-1983 will certainly be an indispensable tool for public, academic, and all other libraries serving fiction lovers of all ages. Bookdealers and other collectors, especially antiquarian specialists in literature or Americana, will find in this bibliography a timesaving investment.

REFERENCES

[1] Wright, Lyle H. *American Fiction 1774-1850*. 2nd rev ed. San Marino, CA: Huntington Library, 1969.

———. *American Fiction 1851-1875*. San Marino, CA: Huntington Library, 1965.

———. *American Fiction 1876-1900*. San Marino, CA: Huntington Library, 1966.

[2] *Fiction Catalog*. 10th ed. New York: H. W. Wilson, 1980.

[3] *United States Catalog*. 1st ed. New York: H. W. Wilson, 1899.

———. 2nd ed. New York: H. W. Wilson, 1902.

———. 3rd ed. New York: H. W. Wilson, 1912.

———. 4th ed. New York: H. W. Wilson, 1928.

[4] *Cumulative Book Index*. New York: H. W. Wilson, 1933–

[5] Barron, Neil, ed. *Anatomy of Wonder: A Critical Guide to Science Fiction*. 2nd ed. New York: R. R. Bowker Co., 1981.

[6] *Books in Print*. New York: R. R. Bowker Co., 1948–

[7] *American Book Publishing Record*. New York: R. R. Bowker Co., 1960–

[8] *Library of Congress Subject Headings*. 9th ed. 2 vols. Washington, D.C.: Library of Congress, 1980.

Nancy L. Baker, Head, General Reference,
University of Utah, Salt Lake City, Utah 84108

Nancy L. Baker holds the following degrees: B.A. English Literature, University of Connecticut, M.L.S. the University of Michigan, M.A. English Literature, SUNY Binghamton and Graduate Certificate, Public Administration, University of Utah. She has served in the library profession since 1973 as: Assistant Reference Librarian/English Bibliographer, State University of New York (SUNY) at Binghamton, 1973-1976; Senior Reference Librarian, Middlebury College (Vermont), 1976-1978: Head Reference Department, University of Kentucky, 1978-81; and currently as Head, General Reference, University of Utah. Nancy L. Baker's teaching experience includes a number of courses in reference service at University of Kentucky, College of Library Science. She is the author of Library Research Guide for Undergraduate English and American Literature.

Preface

The comprehensive bibliographies published by R.R. Bowker have consistently aimed at serving the needs of librarians, booksellers, scholars and researchers. *FICTION 1876-1983: A Bibliography of United States Editions*, provides full bibliographic information for more than 100 years of world fiction published in the United States. It contains 170,000 titles with over 1000 of these published as early as 1800. Included in this compilation are: novels, novellas, short stories, collections of short stories and anthologies. *FICTION 1876-1983* has two volumes. Volume I includes the Classified Author Index and the Main Author Index. Volume II contains the Title Index and the Key to Publishers' and Distributors Abbreviations/Directory of Publishers and Distributors.

SELECTION OF INFORMATION

FICTION 1876-1983: A Bibliography of United States Editions is compiled from two major Bowker Databases: the extensive BOOKS IN PRINT database of over 800,000 in-print and out-of-print titles and the close to 2,000,000 title AMERICAN BOOK PUBLISHING RECORD database. Virtually every fiction title that appeared in the United States in the period covered will be found in these volumes. Entries for this edition of fiction were selected on the basis of all editions for which Library of Congress cataloging data is available. The BOOKS IN PRINT database was used to add additional titles for which we did not have Library of Congress cataloging. Full acquisitions information for all titles currently available can be found in BOOKS IN PRINT. Both hardcover and paperback editions are included, but out-of-print mass market paperbacks are generally not included.

DESCRIPTION OF CLASSIFIED AUTHOR INDEX

Authors are grouped by their nationality and/or the period in which they wrote. Following their names their birth and death dates are given when available. Headings follow the format of Library of Congress Subject Headings. These are examples of types of entries that will appear.

AUTHORS, AMERICAN—20TH CENTURY
Anderson, Poul 1925–
Baldwin, James 1841-1925
Baldwin, James, 1924–
Oates, Joyce Carol 1934–

AUTHORS, ENGLISH—18TH CENTURY
Kimber, Edward 1719-1769
Richardson, Samuel 1689-1761
Scott, Sarah Robinson 1723-1795

The basis for assigning classification to approximately 80% of the authors found in this index was derived from classification of the authors by Library of Congress, which follows the principle that authors who have written in more than one language or have been citizens of more than one country may be assigned numbers accordingly. Following is a statement by the Library of Congress regarding this:

> [1]. "The principal factors to be considered in determining the location of these numbers are the language in which the author wrote, the author's nationality, and if required, the time period during which the author was productive. The simplest situation encountered in establishing an author's number is the author who wrote in one language only and was a citizen of only one country. For such an author a number would be provided under the literature of the language in which the author wrote, with the possibility of further subarrangement by country and period . . . no effort is made to keep all the works together. (For

---

[1]Chan, Lois Mai. *Immroth's Guide to the Library of Congress Classification.* 3rd ed. Littleton, CO, Libraries Unlimited, 1980

example Vladimir Nabokov wrote works in both Russian and English; his Russian literature is in PG3476.N3 and his English language works are classed with American literature.)...If the author was a citizen of several countries the preferred classification is under the country in which the author's most productive years were spent or under the country usually associated with the author by scholars in the field."

Authors for whom we could not find the information necessary to classify them are not represented in this index.

THE MAIN AUTHOR INDEX

In this index extensive editorial work was done to present the author's name uniformly. The fullest form of an author's name is given when variant forms appeared prior to the editing of the author's names. Likewise, if variant spellings of author's names appeared prior to editing a singular form was chosen. True names are often cross-referenced by pseudonyms.

A full bibliographic entry in author sequence with all the works of one author is filed alphabetically by title under the author's name.

TITLE INDEX

A full bibliographic entry is also presented here in alphabetical sequence.

ENTRY INFORMATION

Entries include the following bibliographic information when available: author, co-author, editor, co-editor, translator, co-translator, title, number of volumes, edition, Library of Congress number, series information, page numbers, whether or not illustrated, year of publication, type of binding other than cloth over boards, price, International Standard Book Number, publisher's order number, imprint and publisher. When an entry includes the prices for both the hardover and paperback editions, the publication date within the entry refers to the hardcover binding; however, when the paperback binding is the only one included in the entry, the publication date is the paperback publication date.

KEY TO PUBLISHERS' AND DISTRIBUTORS ABBREVIATIONS/DIRECTORY OF PUBLISHERS AND DISTRIBUTORS

In *FICTION 1876-1983: A Bibliography of United States Editions*, there will be a variety of forms of publisher names, due to the use of both the BOOKS IN PRINT and AMERICAN BOOK PUBLISHING RECORD databases as sources of information. As a special feature of this edition, two indexes are being included to facilitate the location of publisher information. First the Key to Publishers' and Distributors Abbreviations prepared for this publication which will serve as a guide to most of the abbreviated forms of publisher and distributor names for entries derived from the BOOKS IN PRINT database. Entries in this index are arranged by the abbreviation for publisher or distributor name, and give full information. Secondly, the BOOKS IN PRINT Publisher Authority Database, in the form of the Directory of Publishers and Distributors, provides the most recent name and address information for some 15,000 publishers and distributors in the United States. Names referred to in the Abbreviations Index can be found in this full directory. This listing should prove to be most useful in the location of information on the availability of listed entries. This directory is arranged alphabetically by publisher or distributor name, followed by the abbreviation, when used, from the Key to Abbreviations.

BOWKER SURVEYS INFLUENCE PUBLISHING DECISIONS

For a number of years Bowker has regularly enlisted the aid of librarians, booksellers and other potential users of a reference work in the planning stages. We find that this review of our concept and the additional suggestions and comments from those surveyed enables us to produce databases and publications that better serve the needs of the users.

We ask your opinion of a proposed publication, because we want to publish reference books which satisfy your professional needs. We recognize that you know more about your needs than we do.

The number who responded positively to our pre-published survey on *FICTION 1876-1983* pre-publishing was well above average. We want to thank you for your participation in this effort. Your comments, suggestions and opinions have had a significant influence on our publishing decisions.

These special features of *FICTION 1876-1983* were commended by those surveyed:

- The comprehensive coverage of more than 100 years of United States publishing.
- The standardization of author's names with all titles of an author appearing together.
- The expanse of coverage which provides answers to virtually every reference question covering editors of fiction in English, making it invaluable for public libraries, college and university libraries, scholars, book collectors and rare booksellers.
- The classified list of authors provides a unique approach to fiction.
- *FICTION 1876-1983* will greatly facilitate retrospective reference work in fiction which until now has been difficult and time-consuming since it could involve the use of many volumes of the National Union Catalog.
- *FICTION 1876-1983* will provide professional support for reference work and scholarly research, collection assessment and development, acquisitions and inter-library loan.

We hope that you agree with this assessment of the published work and always welcome your comments.

ACKNOWLEDGEMENTS

Gertrude Jennings, Manager Product Research and Development, is responsible for the concept and design of this bibliography. Working with her to bring this idea to reality—the first edition of *FICTION 1876–1983: A Bibliography of United States Editions* were Peter Simon, Database Manager, and Beverley Lamar, Senior Product Manager. Special thanks to Craig Dietle, Qamar Jaffery, Assistant Editors and Keith Schiffman, Editorial Co-ordinator.

We extend our thanks to Marc Alston, Janet Nelson and Reginald Puryear for their diligent work on this publication.

Our special thanks and appreciation to Michael B. Howell, Manager, Systems Development and Philip Pan, Applications Manager, for their special contributions. Our thanks to Frank McWade, Manager Data Processing, Jack Murphy, Computer Operator Specialist, and Joyce Edwards, Data Processing Control Supervisor, for their support and cooperation in the processing of the data used in this publication.

Beverley Lamar
Senior Product Manager
Department of Bibliography

Gertrude Jennings
Manager, Product Research and Development
Data Services Division

Peter Simon
Database Manager
Data Services Division

Title Index

A

A--100: A Mystery Story. Bruce Harrison. LC 30-22207. E. P. Dutton & Co., Inc.

A: A Novel. Andy Warhol. LC 68-22013. 1968. 10.00. Grove Press.

A B C Affair. Peter Winston. (O.s.i.). (Orig.). 1967. pap. 0.60 o.s.i. (A232X, Award). Univ Pub & Dist.

A. B. C. Murders. Agatha Miller Christie. (Greenway Edition). 1978. 8.95 (ISBN 0-396-07512-6). Dodd.

A. B. C. Murders: A New Poirot Mystery. Agatha Miller Christie. LC 36-271204. 1936. Dodd, Mead & Company.

A Brilliant Future" Life Moves Forward in a Great Department Store. LC 32-162488. 1932. The Vanguard Press.

A. Conan Doyle's The White Company: Abridged and Edited. Arthur Conan Doyle & Edwards, Laura V., Ed. LC 31-10085. (Modern literature series). Ginn and Company.

A Cosmic Fable. Rob Swigart. LC 77-25291. 1978. 8.95 (ISBN 0-395-26306-9) (ISBN 0-395-26384-0). Houghton Mifflin.

A. D. Two Thousand. Alvarado Mortimer Fuller. LC 71-154441. (Utopian Literature Ser). (Illus.). 1971. Repr. of 1890 ed. 22.00 (ISBN 0-405-03524-1). Ayer Co.

A. D. 2000. Alvarado Mortimer Fuller. LC 6-44731. (On cover: The library of choice fiction, no. 8). 1890. Laird & Lee.

A. D. 2050. Electrical Development at Atlantis. John Bachelder. LC 6-5085. 1890. The Bancroft Company.

A. G. Man. William Hansman. 1968. 3.95 o.p. Vantage.

A. Hall & Co. Joseph Crosby Lincoln. LC 38-19636. 1938. D. Appleton-Century Company, Incorporated.

A" Is for Alibi: A Kinsey Millhone Mystery. Sue Grafton. LC 81-7128. (Rinehart suspense novel). 12.95. Holt, Rinehart, and Winston.

A la Cama, Perversa! new ed. Rogelio A. Rios. (Pimienta Collection Ser). 160p. (Span.). 1975. pap. 1.00 (ISBN 0-88473-223-1). Fiesta Pub.

A la Recherche Du Temps Perdu: Selections. Marcel Proust. Ed. by H. F. Brookes & C. E. Fraenkel. 1954. pap. text ed. 3.25x o.p. (ISBN 0-435-37100-2). Heinemann Ed.

A L'Ombre De Tes Soleils. Alix Saint-Val. (Collection Colombine). 192p. 1983. pap. 1.95 (ISBN 0-373-48066-0). Harlequin Bks.

A Long Way from Home, and Other Stories. Vern J Sneider. LC 56-6495. 1956. Putnam.

A Market for an Impulse. William Whittemore Tufts. 1895. Arena Publishing Co.

A. Merritt: The Fox Woman. Hannes Bok: The Blue Pagoda. Abraham Merritt & Bok, Hannes, 1914- The Blue Pagoda. LC 47-15520. 1946. New Collectors Group.

A-18: A Novel. Thomas Taylor. LC 67-26244. 1967. Crown Publishers.

Aamon Always. Dan E L Patch. LC 40-35166. Bica Press.

Aaron in the Wildwoods. Joel Chandler Harris. LC 4-23574. 1897. Houghton, Mifflin and Company.

Aaron Traum. Hyman Cohen & Cohen, Lester, Joint Author. LC 30-877610. 1930. H. Liveright.

Aaron West. John Knittel. LC 22-6516. 2.00. George H. Doran Company.

Aaron's Acre. stories by edward b. golla. ed. Edward B Golla. (Illus.). 1976. 6.95. Rastetter Press.

Aaron's Rod. David Herbert Lawrence. LC 74-170394. (Viking compass book). 1972. 1.85 (ISBN 0-670-00085-X). Viking Press.

Aaron's Rod. David Herbert Lawrence. LC 22-9200. 1922. T. Seltzer.

Abaft the Funnel. Rudyard Kipling. LC 9-28704. 1909. B. W. Dodge & Company.

Abai. M. Auezov. 459p. 1975. 6.95 (ISBN 0-8285-1949-8, Pub. by Progress Pubs USSR). Imported Pubns.

Abandon Hope. Isabel Garland. LC 41-653. 1941. Mystery House.

Abandoned. Jules Verne & Kingston, William Henry Giles, 1814-1880, Tr. LC 41-35146. (Half-title: Everyman's library, ed. by Ernest Rhys. For young people. no. 368). 1915. J. M. Dent & Sons.

Abandoned Farmer. Sydney Herman Preston. LC 1-11796. 1901. C. Scribner's Sons.

Abandoned for Love. Caroline Courtney. LC 82-6048. 1982. 13.95 (ISBN 0-8161-3269-0). G.K. Hall.

Abandoned for Love. Caroline Courtney. 224p. (Orig.). 1981. pap. 1.75 (ISBN 0-446-94607-9). Warner Bks.

Abandoned Room. Charles Wadsworth Camp. LC 17-29177. 1917. Doubleday, Page & Company.

Abandoned Room: A Mystery Story. Charles Wadsworth Camp. LC 42-26490. (International adventure library). W. R. Caldwell & Co.

Abandoned Trails. Helen Barham Shipman. LC 32-9444. 1932. L. MacVeagh, Dial Press, Inc.

Abandoned Woman. Richard Condon. LC 76-56240. (Illus.). 8.95 (ISBN 0-8037-0283-3). Dial Press.

Abandoned Woman. Howard Vincent O'Brien. LC 30-25300. 1930. Doubleday, Doran & Company, Inc.

Abandoned Wood: Translated from the French. Monique Saint-Helier & Whitall, James, 1888- LC 36-6816. Harcourt, Brace and Company.

Abandoned. 1st Ed. Paul Gallico. LC 50-9484. 1950. Knopf.

Abandoning an Adopted Farm. Katherine Abbott Sanborn. LC 8-3752. 1894. D. Appleton and Company.

Abasement. Jean Vandorre. 1971. pap. 0.95 o.p. (B309, BC). Grove.

Abastement of the Northmores see Author of Beltraffio.

Abba. Harry Edgington. 1979. pap. text ed. 1.95 o.s.i. (ISBN 0-89559-185-5). Dale Books Inc.

Abba. Nicholas Michelson. LC 40-16825. 1937. J. J. Augustin.

Abba. Evelyn Underhill. 96p. 1982. pap. 1.65 (ISBN 0-88028-020-4). Forward Movement.

Abba Abba. Anthony Burgess, pseud. LC 78-27141. 4.95 (ISBN 0-316-11652-1). Little, Brown.

Abba, Father. Virginia F. Matson. LC 71-155690. 1971. 4.95. Moody Press.

Abbe Constantin. Ludovic Halevy. LC 41-28181. Homebook Company.

Abbe' Constantin. Ludovic Halevy. LC 4856. W. B. Conkey Company.

Abbe' Constantin. Ludovic Halevy. LC 4-16880. 1902. Dodd, Mead, and Company.

Abbe' Constantin. Ludovic Halevy. LC 23-17383. Translation Publishing Company, Inc.

Abbe' Constantin: A Marriage for Love, and Other Stories. Ludovic Halevy & Ayer, Annie W., Tr. LC 4-316607. (On cover: Burt's home library). 1895. A. L. Burt.

Abbe' Constantin, and A Marriage for Love. Ludovic Halevy. LC 3-6439. (Half-title: A century of French romance. Parisian ed. vol. xvi). D. Appleton & Co.

Abbe' Constantine. Ludovic Halevy & Hazen, Emily H., Tr. LC 6-46314. (On cover: Trans-Atlantic novels v. 15). 1882. G. P. Putnam's Sons.

Abbe Daniel. Andre Theuriet & Dole, Mrs. Helen James (Bennett) Tr. LC 8-27748. Thomas Y. Crowell and Company.

Abbe Mouret's Sin. Tr. from French by Alec Brown. Emile Zola. LC 57-23452. 1964. bds., 3.95. Elek Bks. Dist. Chester Springs, Pa., Dufour.

Abbe Pierre. Jay William Hudson. LC 24-21811. 1924. D. Appleton and Company.

Abbe Pierre's People. Jay William Hudson. LC 28-24278. 1928. D. Appleton & Company.

Abbe' Tigrane. Candidate for the Papal Chair. Ferdinand Fabre. Tr. by Bacon, Leonard Woolsey. LC 6-37855. 1875. J. B. Ford & Company.

Abbess: A Romance. William Henry Ireland. LC 73-22764. (Gothic Novels II). 1974. (ISBN 0-405-06015-7). Arno Press.

Abbess of Crewe. Muriel Spark. LC 74-16161. 1974. 6.95 (ISBN 0-670-10029-3). Viking Press.

Abbess of Crewe. Muriel Spark. LC 77-368588. 1975-1977. 1.95 (ISBN 0-14-004074-9). Penguin.

Abbess of Vlaye. Stanley John Weyman. LC 4-30586. 1904. Longmans, Green, and Co.

Abbey: And Other Tales. Catherine Grace Frances Moody Gore. LC 6-27489. 1840. Lea and Blanchard.

Abbey Court. Marcella Thum. LC 76-3136. 1976. 7.95 (ISBN 0-385-12040-0). Doubleday.

Abbey Murder. Joseph Hatton. (On cover: Lovell's library, no. 1147). 1888. J. W. Lovell Company.

Abbey of Fontenelles. A Legend of the XI Century. Nicolas Alfred De Vervins. LC 8-29984. (On cover: Summerland series, no. 2). 1883. J. E. Heg.

Abbey of St. Asaph: A Novel. Isabella Kelly. LC 77-2041. (Gothic Novels III). 1977. 60.00 (ISBN 0-405-10140-6). Arno Press.

Abbeychurch; The Castle Builders. Charlotte Mary Yonge. LC 75-470. (Victorian Fiction: Novels of Faith and Doubt). 1976. 35.00 (ISBN 0-8240-1548-7). Garland Pub.

Abbeygate. Cecily Crowe. LC 76-50540. 8.95 (ISBN 0-698-10819-1). Coward, McCann & Geoghegan.

Abbeygate. Cecily Crowe. (Kangaroo Book). 1978. 1.75 (ISBN 0-671-81748-5). Pocket Books.

Abbey's Road: Take the Other. Edward Abbey. 1979. 9.95 o.p. (ISBN 0-525-05006-X, 0655-20); pap. 6.95 (ISBN 0-525-03001-8). Dutton.

Abbie. Dane Chandos. LC 46-25226. 1946. G. P. Putnam's Sons.

Abbie in Love. 192p. 1981. pap. 1.95 (ISBN 0-345-29734-2). Ballantine.

Abbot. Walter Scott. LC 8-3023. (English classics for schools). 1893. American Book Company.

Abbot. Walter Scott. Ed. by Lang, Andrew. LC 12-24124. (On cover: Waverley novels). D. Estes & Company.

Abbot. Walter Scott. LC 36-37112. (Half-title: Everyman's library, ed. by Ernest Rhys. Fiction. no. 124). 1924. J. M. Dent & Sons, Ltd.

Abbot: Being a Sequel to The Monastery. Walter Scott. (On cover: Lovell's library, no. 569). 1885. J. W. Lovell Company.

Abbot: Being the Sequel to The Monastery. parker's ed. Walter Scott. (Waverley novels; Library ed. v. 10). 1831. Bazin & Ellsworth.

Abbot: Being the Sequel to The Monastery... parker's ed., rev. and cor., with a general preface, an introduction to each novel, and notes, historical and illustrative, by the author. ed. Walter Scott. (Waverley novels, v. 19-20). 1836. Pub. by S. H. Parker for Desilver, Thomas, and Co., Philadelphia.

Abbot of Montserrat: Or, The Pool of Blood: a Romance. William Child Green. LC 77-2038. (Gothic Novels III). 1977. 35.00 (ISBN 0-405-10137-6). Arno Press.

Abbot. Sequel to "The Monastery.". Walter Scott. (On cover: Seaside library. Pocket ed. no. 292). 1884. G. Munro.

Abbot Sisters. Mary Carter Roberts. LC 51-13378. 1951. Doubleday.

Abbot's House. Dorothy Phoebe Ansle. LC 74-3629. 1974. 5.95 (ISBN 0-8415-0336-2). Saturday Review Press.

Abbot's House. Laura Conway. LC 74-3629. 160p. 1974. 5.95 o.p. (ISBN 0-8415-0336-2). Dutton.

Abby Found Him. William Arthur Neubauer. LC 64-25959. 1964. Arcadia House.

Abby Goes to Washington: By Frances Dean Hancock Pseud. Jeanne Judson. LC 57-12662. 1957. Avalon Books.

ABC Affair. Peter Winston. 160p. 1980. pap. 1.95 (ISBN 0-441-00274-9, Pub. by Charter Bks). Ace Bks.

ABC Murders. Agatha Miller Christie. LC 77-156195. (Greenway edition; 22). 1977. 6.95. Dodd, Mead.

ABCD. David R. Slavitt. LC 72-77005. 264p. 1972. 6.95 o.p. (ISBN 0-385-03634-5). Doubleday.

Abc's of Transistors. 1st Ed. Georg Mann. (O). 1960. Macmillan.

Abdallah: Or, The Four-Leaved Shamrock. Edouard Rene Lefebvre De Laboulaye, pseud. Tr. by Mary Louise Booth. LC 5-34696. The Bobbs-Merrill Company.

Abdeker: Or, The Art of Preserving Beauty. Antoine Le Camus. LC 74-17402. (Flowering of the Novel). 1974. (ISBN 0-8240-1140-6). Garland Pub.

Abdication. Edmund Candler. LC 22-21952. 1922. E. P. Dutton & Company.

Abdication: A Novel. Ruth Wolff. 1974. (pbk.) 1.25. Warner Paperback Library.

Abducted. Michael MacPherson. pap. 1.95 o.p. (0105). Essex Hse.

Abducted Heart. Maxine Patrick. (Signet Book). 1978. 1.50 (ISBN 0-451-08094-7). New American Library.

Abduction. Harrison James. (Illus.). 1975. pap. 1.95 o.p. (ISBN 0-8021-0118-6, GP0118, Dist. by Whirlwind Bk. Co.). Grove.

Abduction. Maxine W Kumin. LC 70-156562. 1971. 6.95 (ISBN 0-06-012472-5). Harper & Row.

Abduction. Charlotte Lamb, pseud. (Harlequin Presents Ser.). 192p. 1981. pap. 1.50 (ISBN 0-373-10435-9, Pub. by Harlequin). PB.

Abduction. Gerd Seeber. LC 81-47465. 1983. 16.50 (ISBN 0-03-059404-9). Holt, Rinehart and Winston.

Abduction: Fiction Before Fact. Ed. by Al Ellenberg. Harrison James. (Dell-Grove book). 1974. (pbk.) 1.50. Dell.

Abduction: Fiction Before Fact. Illus. by Al Ellenberg. 1974. pap. 1.50 o.p. (0281, Dist. by Dell). Grove.

Abduction of Edith Martin. 1972. pap. 1.75 o.s.i. (V1074K, Venus). Grove.

Abduction of Princess Chriemhild: A Romance. La Roy Freese Griffin. LC 6-45431. R. L. Weed Company; Etc., Etc.

Abduction of Virginia Lee. Frank O'Rourke. LC 78-118973. (Illus.). 1970. 4.95. Lippincott.

Abductor. Dolores Birk Hitchens. (Inner sanctum mystery). 1973. 0.75. Curtis Books.

Abductors. Stuart Cloete. LC 66-15655. 1966. 5.95. Trident.

Abductors. Stuart Cloete. (95055). 1967. Pocket Bks.

Abe and Mawruss: Being Further Adventures of Potash and Perlmutter. Montague Marsden Glass. LC 11-264105. 1911. 1.20. Doubleday, Page & Company.

Abe Lincoln at Loafer Station: A Novel Based on Hoosier Legends. Anet Garrison. LC 51-7950. 1951. Exposition Press.

Abe Lincoln of Pigeon Creek: A Novel. William Edward Wilson. LC 49-112166. 1949. Whittlesey House.

Abee Mouret's Sin. Emile Zola. 1957. 12.95 (ISBN 0-236-30808-4, Pub. by Paul Elek). Merrimack Pub Cir.

ABehind the Counter. Handel and Wandel. by f.w. hacklander. from the german, by mary howitt. ed. Friedrich Wilhelm Hacklander & Howitt, Mary (Botham) "Mrs. W. Howitt," 1799-1888, Tr. (seaside library. v. 31, no. 645). 1879. G. Munro.

Abel. Ana Maria Matute. 3.50 o.s.i. French & Eur.

Abel Allnutt. A Novel. LC 42-26104. 1837. E. L. Carey & A. Hart.

Abel Dayton. Flannery Lewis. LC 39-190094. 1939. The Macmillan Company.

Abel Sanchez. Miguel Del Unamuno. 1947. pap. 2.95 o.p. (ISBN 0-03-060390-0). HR&W.

Abel Sanchez. Miguel De Unamuno Y Jugo. (Rinehart Editions). 1948. pap. 2.95 o.p. (ISBN 0-03-060390-0, HoltC). HR&W.

Abel Sanchez & Other Stories. Miguel De Unamuno. Tr. by Anthony Kerrigan. pap. 3.95 (ISBN 0-89526-923-6). Regnery-Gateway.

Abel Sanchez: And Other Stories. Translated and with an Introd. by Anthony Kerrigan. Miguel De Unamuno Y Jugo. LC 56-14025. (Gateway edition, 6034). 1956. Gateway Editions Distributed by H. Regnery Co.

Abel's Daughter. Rachel Maddux. LC 60-5959. 1960. Harper.

Abel's Daughter. Rachel Maddux. 1978. 1.75 (ISBN 0-380-39040-X). Avon Books.

Abeng. Michelle Cliff. 180p. (Orig.). 1983. pap. 6.95 (ISBN 0-930436-18-0). Persephone.

Abeniki Caldwell: A Burlesque Historical Novel. Carolyn Wells. LC 2-30054. 1902. R. H. Russell.

Aberration of Starlight. Gilbert Sorrentino. LC 80-5280. 9.95 (ISBN 0-394-51189-1). Random House.

Aberration of Starlight. Gilbert Sorrentino. LC 80-29457. 1981. 9.95 (ISBN 0-14-005879-6). Penguin Books.

Abhimanyu. K. P. Balaji. 1978. 3.75x (ISBN 0-8364-0226-X); pap. 2.00x (ISBN 0-8364-0227-8). South Asia Bks.

Abide, Joshua: And Other Stories. Edith L. Tiempo. LC 65-439600. 1965. 2.50. A. S. Florentino.

Abide, Joshua & Other Stories. Edith L. Tiempo. 1964. wrps. 4.50x o.p. Cellar.

Abiding of Ume: Ume No Kakurega. Edith Augusta Sawyer. LC 32-35023. 1932. J. L. Pratt.

Abie's Irish Rose: A Novel. Anne Nichols. LC 74-29510. (Modern Jewish Experience). 1975. 20.00 (ISBN 0-405-06736-4). Arno Press.

Abie's Irish Rose: A Novel. Anne Nichols. LC 27-23001. 1927. Harper & Brothers.

Abigail. Mary Louise White Aswell. LC 59-12492. 1959. Crowell.

Abigail. Barbara Corcoran. 160p. (Orig.). 1981. pap. 1.95 (ISBN 0-345-28669-3). Ballantine.

Abigail. Malcolm MacDonald. 1980. pap. 2.95 (ISBN 0-451-09404-2, E9404, Sig). NAL.

Abigail. Emma Louise Mally. LC 56-704124. 1956. Appleton-Century-Crofts.

Abigail: A Novel. Lois T Henderson. LC 80-65429. 8.95 (ISBN 0-915684-62-4). Christian Herald Books.

Abigail: A Novel. Lois T Henderson. LC 82-48397. 6.68 (ISBN 0-06-063865-6). Harper & Row.

Abigail: The Life and Loves of a Victorian Girl. Malcolm MacDonald. LC 79-392. 1979. 11.95 (ISBN 0-394-50492-5). Knopf; Distributed by Random House.

Abijah Beanpole in New York. Detailing the Misfortunes and Mishaps of a Country Storekeeper on a Business Visit to the Great City of New York. Metta Victoria Victor. 1884. G. W. Carleton & Co., Street & Smith.

Abijah Beanpole in New York. Detailing the Misfortunes and Mishaps of a Country Storekeeper on a Business Visit to the Great City of New York. Metta Victoria Victor. (select series. no. 83). 1891. Street & Smith.

Abiku. Goke Ajiboye. 1983. 8.95 (ISBN 0-533-05110-X). Vantage.

Abimelech Pott: The Don Quixote of the Bar, a Novel. Henry Wynans Jessup. LC 29-1676. 1928. W. Neale.

Abingdon's. Michael French. LC 78-55850. 1979. 10.00 (ISBN 0-385-14334-6). Doubleday.

Abingdon's. Michael French. 1980. 2.50 (ISBN 0-425-04479-3). Berkley Pub. Corp.

Abington Abbey: A Novel. Archibald Marshall. LC 17-25863. 1917. Dodd, Mead and Company.

Able Baker, and Others. 1st Ed. Joseph Whitehill. LC 57-5826. 1957. Little, Brown.

Able Company. Douglas John Hollands. LC 56-11059. 1956. Houghton Mifflin.

Able McLaughlins. Margaret Wilson. LC 23-13896. Harper & Brothers.

Able One Four. Lawrence H Kahn. LC 52-6303. 1952. A. Swallow.

Abner Daniel: A Novel. William Nathaniel Harben. LC 2-16923. 1902. Harper & Brothers.

Abner Ferret, the Lawyer Detective. LC 9-2498. J. S. Ogilvie & Company.

Abner Grimes. Watson Lamont. LC 13-1154. 1913. 1.50. Broadway Publishing Co.

Aboard a Flying Saucer. Non-Fiction; a True Story of Personal Experience. Truman Bethurum. LC 54-964246. 1954. De Vorss.

Aboard "the American Duchess,". George L Myers. 1900. G. P. Putnam's Sons.

Aboard the Flying Swan. Stanley Wolpert. LC 54-7920. 1954. Scribner.

Abode of Dead Souls: A Novel. Harry A Gould. LC 56-11462. (Nobel book). 1956. Comet Press Books.

Abode of Life. Lee Corey. 1982. pap. 2.50 (ISBN 0-671-83297-2, Timescape). PB.

Abode of Love: The Conception, Financing, and Daily Routine of an English Harem in the Middle of the 19th Century Described in the Form of a Novel. Aubrey Menen. LC 56-851556. 1956. Scribner.

Abolition of Death. James Anderson. LC 74-21911. 232p. 1975. 6.95 o.p. (ISBN 0-8027-5316-7). Walker & Co.

Abolitionist. Leslie Gladson. (Orig.). 1970. pap. 0.95 o.p. (ISBN 0-447-75123-9). Lancer.

Abolitionist of Clark Gable Place. Charles Richard Webb. LC 74-26887. 1975. 7.95 (ISBN 0-07-068785-4). McGraw-Hill.

Abolitionist of Clark Gable Place. Charles Richard Webb. 1.50 (ISBN 0-445-03171-9). Popular Library.

Abominable Man. Maj Sjowall & Per Wahloo. 1974. (pbk.) 0.95. Bantam Books.

Abominable Man. Maj Sjowall & Per Wahloo. LC 72-3408. 1972. 4.95 (ISBN 0-394-47166-0). Pantheon Books.

Abominable Snow Mad. (Mad Ser.: No. 52). (Illus.). 1979. pap. 1.75 (ISBN 0-446-94446-7). Warner Bks.

Abominations of Yondo. Clark Ashton Smith. LC 60-1535. 1960. Arkham House.

Abondoned. Edwin Silberstang. LC 80-1071. 1981. 10.95 (ISBN 0-385-15978-1). Doubleday.

Abortion. Richard Brautigan. 1971. pap. 2.95 o.p. (ISBN 0-671-20873-X, Touchstone Bks). S&S.

Abortion. Joseph Pillitteri. (Signet book). New American Library.

Abortion: An Historical Romance 1966. Richard Brautigan. LC 78-150949. 1971. 5.95 (ISBN 0-671-20872-1). Simon and Schuster.

About a Marriage. Giles Gordon. LC 72-80764. 1972. 5.95 (ISBN 0-8128-1502-5). Stein and Day.

About Animals. Alfred Sutro. LC 37-4391. Printed by L. Kennedy.

About Catharine De' Medici. Honore De Balzac. Tr. by Clara Courtenay Poynter Bell. Saintsbury, George Edward Bateman, 1845- Ed. LC 8-33160. (Half-title:... Comedie humaine, ed. by George Saintsbury). 1897. J. M. Dent and Co.

About Catherine De Medici. Honore De Balzac. Tr. by Clara Courtenay Poynter Bell. LC 36-37189. (Half-title: Everyman's library, ed. by Ernest Rhys. Fiction. no. 419). 1934. J. M. Dent & Sons, Lts.

About Edwin Drood. Henry Jackson. LC 73-22017. (Illus.). 1974. (ISBN 0-8414-5285-7). Folcroft Library Editions.

About Face. Frank Kane. LC 54-200099. (Ace double novel books, D-33). 1953. Ace Books.

About Face: A Johnny Liddell Mystery. Frank Kane. LC 47-24298. 1947. Pub. for Mystery House by S. Curl.

About Girls: Spicy Sketches Revealing the Choicest Feminine Fads and Fancies. Helen Follett Jameson. LC 6-41422. (On cover: Pastime series. no. 133). 1894. Laird & Lee.

About Harry Towns. Bruce Jay Friedman. LC 73-20762. 1974. 5.95 (ISBN 0-394-48178-X). Knopf.

About Levy. Arthur Calder-Marshall. LC 34-5895. 1934. C. Scribner's Sons.

About Lyddy Thomas. Maritta Martin Wolff. LC 47-11594. 1947. Random House.

About Miss Mattie Morningglory. Lilian Lida Bell. LC 16-8459. 1.35. Rand, McNally & Company.

About Mrs. Leslie. 1st Ed. Vina Delmar. LC 50-6147. 1950. Harcourt, Brace.

About My Father's Business. Austin Miles. LC 1556. The Mershon Company.

About the Murder of a Man Afraid of Women: A Thatcher Colt Detective Mystery. Fulton Oursler. LC 37-6379. Farrar & Rinehart, Incorporated.

About the Murder of a Startled Lady: A Thatcher Colt Detective Mystery. Fulton Oursler. LC 35-31030. Farrar & Rinehart, Incorporated.

About the Murder of a Startled Lady: "a Thatcher Colt Police Mystery". Fulton Oursler. LC 44-990976. (Murder mystery monthly. No. 25). 1944. Avon Book Company.

About the Murder of Geraldine Foster: A Thatcher Colt Detective Mystery. Fulton Oursler. LC 30-32831. Covici-Friede.

About the Murder of the Circus Queen. by anthony abbot pseud. ed. Fulton Oursler. LC 32-33054. Covici, Friede.

About the Murder of the Clergyman's Mistress. Fulton Oursler. LC 31-10175. 1931. Covici-Friede.

About the Murder of the Night Club Lady: A Thatcher Colt Detective Mystery. Fulton Oursler. LC 31-28499. Covici, Friede.

About Us: A Novel. Chester Aaron. LC 67-15035. 1967. McGraw-Hill.

About Us and the Deacon. Clarke Smith. LC 11-14101. The Literary Bureau, Inc.

About Women: A Collection of Short Stories. Ed. by Helene Reed. LC 43-16587. 1943. The World Publishing Company.

About 2 A.M. Charles Francis Coe. LC 31-22898. 1931. Cosmopolitan Book Corporation.

Above Below: Text and Illus. by C. G. Knoblock. Curt George Knoblock. LC 52-20984. 1952.

Above Destiny. Gabriel Richard Mason. LC 57-8229. 1957. Pageant Press.

Above Ground: A Novel, by Jack Ludwig. 1st Ed. Jack Barry Ludwig. LC 67-28227. 1968. bds., 6.95. Little, Brown.

Above Par. John Edwin Hurlbut. LC 13-23880. 1.25. R. G. Badger.

Above Suspicion. Helen MacInnes Highet. LC 41-11684. 1941. Little, Brown and Company.

Above Suspicion. Helen MacInnes. 1978. pap. 2.50 (ISBN 0-449-23833-4, Crest). Fawcett.

Above Suspicion. Helen MacInnes. LC 54-928. 1954. 7.95 o.s.i. (ISBN 0-15-102707-2). HarBraceJ.

Above Suspicion. Isabel Egenton Ostrander. LC 23-414126. 1923. R. M. McBride & Company.

Above Suspicion. Charlotte Eliza Lawson Cowan Riddell. (Seaside library, v. 28, no. 565). 1879. G. Munro.

Above the Clouds. Elizabeth Ashby. 196p. 1979. 12.00 (ISBN 0-88428-046-2); pap. 8.50 (ISBN 0-88428-047-0). Parchment Pr.

Above the Clouds: An Other Tales. Clara Evangeline Smith. LC 6-25173. 1906. Leadville Publishing and Printing Co.

Above the Dark Tumult, an Adventure. Hugh Walpole. LC 31-26748. 1931. Doubleday, Doran & Company, Inc.

Above the Human Landscape: A Social Science Fiction Anthology. Ed. by Willis Everett McNelly. LC 75-184131. (Illus.). 1972. (ISBN 0-87620-003-X) (ISBN 0-87620-002-1). Goodyear Pub. Co.

Above the Rainbow. Anne West Strawbridge. LC 38-5288. Stackpole Sons.

Above the Shame of Circumstances. Gertrude Capen Whitney. LC 13-265567. 1913. Sherman, French & Company.

Above the Stars. Edith Snyder Pedersen. LC 45-8187. 1945. Wm. B. Eerdmans Publishing Company.

Above the Wind & Fire. Donna Comeaux Zide. 512p. (Orig.). 1983. pap. 3.75 (ISBN 0-446-30296-1). Warner Bks.

Abra: A Novel. Joan Barfoot. LC 79-303508. 9.95 (ISBN 0-07-082740-0). McGraw-Hill Ryerson.

Abra-Cadaver. Christopher Monig, pseud. 1971. pap. 0.75 o.p. (ISBN 0-446-64590-7, 64-590). Paperback Lib.

Abracadabra: A Novel. Rosemarie Santini. LC 77-17175. 8.95 (ISBN 0-671-16972-6). Playboy Press.

Abracadaver. Peter Lovesey. LC 77-3686. 1977. 8.95 (ISBN 0-89340-061-0). J. Curley.

Abracadaver. Peter Lovesey. LC 72-3146. (Red badge novel of suspense). 1972. 4.95 (ISBN 0-396-06627-5). Dodd, Mead.

Abracadaver. Peter Lovesey. LC 80-20877. 1981. 2.50 (ISBN 0-14-005803-6). Penguin Books.

Abraham, Father of Nations. 1st Ed. Alan Lake Chidsey. LC 56-12356. Pageant Press.

Abraham, Isaac, Jacob, and Zev: A Novel. Jerry Marcus. LC 81-70363. 1982. 13.95 (ISBN 0-941394-00-X). Brittany Publications.

Abraham of Brooklyn. Didier Decoin. LC 73-7297. 1974. 6.95 (ISBN 0-394-48115-1). Knopf; Distributed by Random House.

Abraham Page, Esq. A Novel... John Saunders Holt. LC 7-5185. 1868. J. B. Lippincott & Company.

Abraham, Prince of Ur. William George Hardy. 1935. Dodd, Mead & Company.

Abraham's Wife. Francis J Thompson. LC 53-108025. 1953. Vanguard Press.

Abram and Sarai. J. SerVaas Williams. LC 80-69805. (Illus.). 12.95 (ISBN 0-938280-01-5). Corinth House.

Abram Force: A Novel of the American Revolution. Arthur Peters. LC 76-352446. 1975. Lee-Howard Co.

Abram: Son of Terah. Florence Anne Marvyne Bauer. LC 48-6197. 1948. Bobbs-Merrill Co.

Abramsky Variations. Morley Torgov. 1978. pap. 1.95 o.p. (ISBN 0-14-004979-7). Penguin.

Abraxas. Arlene Zekowski. LC 64-21951. (Illus.). 1964. pap. 10.00 (ISBN 0-913844-32-2). Am Canadian.

Abraxas. Arlene Zekowski. (Orig.). 1964. pap. 6.00x o.p. (ISBN 0-8150-0140-1). Wittenborn.

Abroad with the Jimmies. Lilian Lida Bell. 1902. L. C. Page & Company.

Absalom: A Novel. 1st Ed. Elinor Gage Babcock. LC 55-11375. Greenwich Book Publishers.

Absalom, Absalom! William Faulkner. LC 51-10393. (Modern library of the world's best books, 271). 1951. Modern Library.

Absalom, Absalom! William Faulkner. LC 72-398. 1972. 1.95 (ISBN 0-394-71780-5). Vintage Books.

Absalom, Absalom! William Faulkner. LC 36-246783. 1936. Random House.

Absence. Uwe Johnson. LC 72-121407. (Cape Editions Ser). 1970. pap. 1.50 o.p. (ISBN 0-670-10085-4, Grossman). Penguin.

Absence of a Cello: A Novel. 1st Ed. Ira Jan Wallach. LC 60-9327. 1960. Little, Brown.

Absence of Bells. Michael Rubin. LC 70-178933. 1971. (ISBN 0-07-054190-6). McGraw-Hill.

Absence of Malice. Kerry Stewart, pseud. 1982. pap. 2.50 (ISBN 0-345-30161-7). Ballantine.

Absent Father: Viriginia Woolf and Walter Pater. Perry Meisel. LC 79-19289. 1980. 22.50 (ISBN 0-300-02401-0). Yale University Press.

Absent in the Spring. Mary Westmacott, pseud. LC 44-7192. 1944. Farrar & Rinehart.

Absent in the Spring. Mary Westmacott. LC 44-7192. 1944. Farrar & Rinehart, Inc.

Absent in the Spring: A Novel of Romance and Suspense. Agatha Miller Christie. LC 70-150379. 1971. 5.95. Arbor House.

Absent Without Leave. Heinrich Boll. Tr. by Leila Vennewitz. (Ger.). 1965. 6.95 o.p. (ISBN 0-07-006404-0, GB). McGraw.

Absent Without Leave: Two Novellas. Boll, Heinrich. LC 65-22594. 1965. McGraw-Hill.

Absent Without Leave: Two Novellas. Heinrich Boll. LC 75-26961. 2.95 (ISBN 0-07-006426-1). McGraw-Hill.

Absentee. Maria Edgeworth. (Harper's handy ser. no. 73). 1886. Harper & Brothers.

Absentee. Maria Edgeworth. LC 12-19568. (Half-title: The English Comedie humaine). 1904. The Century Co.

Absentee. Maria Edgeworth. LC 6-39757. (Half-title: The English Comedie humaine). 1905. The Century Co.

Absentee. Maria Edgeworth. LC 12-195717. (Half-title: The English Comedie humaine). 1906. The Century Co.

Absentee. Maria Edgeworth. LC 78-17962. (Ireland, from the Act of Union, 1800, to the Death of Parnell, 1891). 1979. 32.00 (ISBN 0-8240-3453-8). Garland Pub.

Absentee: A Tale. Maria Edgeworth. LC 6-26308. 1812. W. Cooper.

Absentee. An Irish Story. Maria Edgeworth. (On cover: Seaside library. Pocket ed. no. 788). G. Munro.

Absolute at Large. Karel Capek. LC 75-397. (Garland Library of Science Fiction). 1975. 11.00 (ISBN 0-8240-1403-0). Garland Pub.

Absolute at Large. Karel Capek. LC 73-13248. (Classics of science fiction). 1974. (ISBN 0-88355-104-7) (ISBN 0-88355-133-0). Hyperion Press.

Absolute at Large. Karel Capek. LC 27-12300. 1927. The Macmillan Company.

Absolute Elizabeth. Joanna Dessau. LC 78-69818. 1979. 7.95 (ISBN 0-312-00187-8). St. Martin's Press.

Absolute Zero. Ernest Tidyman. LC 79-150401. 1971. 5.95. Dial Press.

Absolutely Nothing to Get Alarmed About. Charles Stevenson Wright. LC 72-86414. 1973. 6.95 (ISBN 0-374-10036-5). Farrar, Straus and Giroux.

Absolution. Alberta Stedman Eagan. LC 28-14553. The Macaulay Company.

Absorbing Fire: The Byron Legend, by F. W. Kenyon. Frank Wilson Kenyon. LC 66-23214. 1966. 5.95. Dodd.

Abstract Relations. Thomas E Connors. LC 79-50423. (Illus.). 5.00 (ISBN 0-913204-12-9). December Press.

Absurd. Dilip Mukerjee. 1979. 7.50 (ISBN 0-533-03868-5). Vantage.

Abu Wahab Caper. Ross H. Spencer. 1980. pap. 1.95 (ISBN 0-380-76356-7, 76356). Avon.

Abundantly Above. Harold Lindsell. LC 44-4187. 1944. Wm. B. Eerdmans Publishing Company.

Abysmal Brute. Jack London. LC 13-11303. 1913. The Century Co.

Abyss. Jere Cunningham. 1982. 13.95 (ISBN 0-671-61020-1, Wyndham Bks). S&S.

Abyss. Nathan Kussy. LC 16-6059. The Macmillan Company.

Abyss. Manes Sperber. LC 52-6363. 1952. Doubleday.

Abyss. Dorothea Tanning. 1977. pap. 5.00 (ISBN 0-918746-02-7). Standard Edns.

Abyss. Marguerite Yourcenar. LC 76-72. 10.00 (ISBN 0-374-10040-3). Farrar, Straus and Giroux.

Abyss of Wonders: Illustrated by John T. Brooks. With an Introd. by P. Schuyler Miller. 1st Ed. Perley Poore Sheehan. LC 53-10035. (Polaris fantasy library, v.2). 1953. Polaris Press.

Abyss: Two Novellas. Kate Wilhelm. LC 75-131110. 1971. 4.95. Doubleday.

ABZ of Pleasure & Pain. Ed. by A. M. LeDeLuge. pap. 1.95 o.p. (V1035T, Venus). Grove.

Academia Nuts. Charles R Larson. LC 76-46698. 1977. 7.95 (ISBN 0-672-52310-8). Bobbs-Merrill.

Academic Factor. C. A Haddad. LC 79-3410. 9.95 (ISBN 0-06-011814-8). Harper & Row.

Academic Question. Richard H R Smithies. LC 65-153671. bds., 3.95. Horizon.

Academy of Goodbye. Paul Petrie. LC 74-75682. 84p. 1974. text ed. 7.00x (ISBN 0-87451-098-8); pap. text ed. 4.00x (ISBN 0-87451-099-6). U Pr of New Eng.

Acadian Exile. Hugh Finlay Graham. R. G. Badger.

Acapulco. Burt Hirschfeld. (Dell Book). 1977. 1.95 (ISBN 0-440-10402-5). Dell Pub. Co.

Acapulco: A Novel. Burt Hirschfeld. LC 79-169925. 1971. 7.50 (ISBN 0-87795-021-0). Arbor House.

Acapulco Gold. Edwin Corley. LC 72-3145. (Illus.). 1972. 7.95 (ISBN 0-396-06632-1). Dodd, Mead.

Acapulco Nocturne. Barry Devlin. LC 52-68718. 1952. Vixen Press.

Acapulco Passage. Patricia Bird. 1975. 4.95. Avalon Books.

Acapulco Rampage. Don Pendleton. (Executioner Ser.: No. 26). 192p. 1976. pap. 1.95 (ISBN 0-523-41090-5). Pinnacle Bks.

Acapulco Rampage. Don Pendleton. (Executioner Series#26). 1976. (pbk.) 1.25 (ISBN 0-523-00868-6). Pinnacle Books.

Accent on Love: By Joan Sargent Pseud. Sara Lucile Jenkins. LC 56-3498. 1956. Avalon Books.

Accent on Murder: A Captain Heimrich Mystery, by Richard and Frances Lockridge. 1st Ed. Richard Lockridge & Frances Louise Davis Lockridge. LC 58-13628. (Main line mysteries). 1958. Lippincott.

Accent on Sin. Idabel Williams. LC 36-6962. Godwin.

Accent on the Negative: A Novelette. Joseph Noel. LC 47-15740. 1946. Gansevoort Square Publishing Company Reg.

Acceptable Losses: A Novel. Irwin Shaw. LC 82-72056. 14.95 (ISBN 0-87795-437-2). Arbor House.

Acceptance World: A Novel. Anthony Dymoke Powell. LC 56-598895. Farrar. Straus and Cudahy.

Accession to Extinction: The Story of Indian Princes. D. R. Mankekar. 1974. 10.50. Intl Bk Dist.

Accessory. Mary Lockwood. LC 68-28575. 1968. 4.95. Random House.

Accessory After the Fact. William Alfred Hobday. LC 12-6585. The C. M. Clark Publishing Company.

Accessory After the Fact. Lee Thayer. LC 43-4379. 1943. Dodd, Mead & Company.

Accident. Arnold Bennett. LC 29-1802. 1928. Doubleday, Doran & Company, Inc.

Accident. Walt Browder. 1977. pap. 1.75 (ISBN 0-89041-166-2, 3166). Major Bks.

Accident. Elizabeth Janeway. (Perennial lib., P77F). 1965. Harper.

Accident. Elizabeth Janeway. LC 62-14556. 1964. Harper & Row.

Accident. Dexter Masters. LC 54-7198. 1955. Knopf.

Accident. Elie Wiesel. 96p. (Orig.). 1982. pap. 2.50 (ISBN 0-553-22688-6). Bantam.

Accident. Elie Wiesel. Tr. by Anne Borchardt. 1962. 3.50 o.p. (ISBN 0-8090-2310-5). Hill & Wang.

Accident. Hans Heinrich Ziemann. LC 78-19387. 1979. 10.00 (ISBN 0-312-00219-X). St. Martin's Press.

Accident: A Novel 1st Amer. Ed. Nicholas Mosley. LC 66-13125. 1966. 4.00. Coward.

Accident by Design. Edith Caroline Rivett. LC 51-2218. 1951. Published for the Crime Club by Doubleday.

Accident Call. Elizabeth Harrison. 1974. (pbk.) 0.95 (ISBN 0-671-77932-X). Pocket Books.

Accident, Manslaughter or Murder?... Lee Thayer. LC 45-5066. 1945. Dodd, Mead & Company.

Accident of Birth. Edith P. Begner. LC 77-72360. 1977. 1.95 (ISBN 0-380-00990-0). Avon.

Accident of Love. Mary Ellin Barrett. 1974. (pbk.) 1.50. Bantam Books.

Accident of Love: A Novel. Mary Ellin Barrett. LC 73-133597. 1973. 6.95 (ISBN 0-525-05010-8). Dutton.

Accident. Translated from the French by Anne Borchardt. 1st American Ed. Eliezer Wiesel. LC 62-10862. 1962. Hill and Wang.

Accident Ward Mystery. Rhoda Truax. LC 37-166421. 1937. Little, Brown and Company.

Accidental Accomplice. William Andrew Johnston. LC 28-9464. 1928. Doubleday, Doran & Company, Inc.

Accidental Agent. John Goldsmith. LC 78-158884. (O.s.i.). 192p. 1973. pap. 1.25 o.s.i. (532-12166-125). Manor Bks.

Accidental Center. Michael Heller. 1972. 7.50 (ISBN 0-912090-17-0); pap. 2.45 (ISBN 0-912090-16-2). Sumac Mich.

Accidental Death of an Anarchist. Dario Fo. pap. 4.95 (ISBN 0-86104-217-4). Pluto Pr.

Accidental Earth. Leo P. Kelley. 1970. pap. 0.75 o.p. (B75-1088). Belmont-Tower.

Accidental Father. Wanda V Risler. LC 42-15007. 1942. J. Swift, Inc.

Accidental Grace. Irene Mahoney. LC 82-5648. 1982. 14.95 (ISBN 0-312-00223-8). St. Martin's Press.

Accidental Heroine. Eleanor Atterbury. LC 42-20322. 1942. Arcadia House, Inc.

Accidental Honeymoon. by edward stratton holloway. ed. David Potter. 1911. J. B. Lippincott Company.

Accidental Husband. Charles Edward Colahan. LC 34-23851. W. Godwin, Inc.

Accidental Journey. Theodore V. Kundrat. 1978. 22.00x (ISBN 0-88020-089-8). Coach Hse.

Accidental Man. Iris Murdoch. 1973. 1.50 (ISBN 0-446-78013-8). Warner Paperback Lib.

Accidental Man. Iris Murdoch. LC 79-171893. 1971. 7.95 (ISBN 0-670-10208-3). Viking Press.

Accidental Romance: And Other Stories. William Sidney Rossiter. LC 9-1489. 1895. The Republic Press.

Accidental Woman. Richard Neely. LC 80-26126. 12.95 (ISBN 0-03-058623-2). Holt, Rinehart, and Winston.

Accidental Woman. Richard Neely. 1982. 3.50 (ISBN 0-86721-072-9). Playboy Paperbacks.

Accidentals. Helen Gansevoort Edwards Mackay. LC 15-12250. 1915. Duffield & Company.

Accidents Do Happen. Miles Burton. LC 46-306665. 1946. Pub. for the Crime Club by Doubleday & Company, Inc.

Accompanied by His Wife. Mary Burchell. (Presents Ser.). 1974. pap. 1.25 (ISBN 0-373-70567-0, 70567, Pub by Harlequin). PB.

Accomplice. Frederick Trevor Hill. LC 5-13966. 1905. Harper & Borthers.

Accomplice. Darryl Ponicsan. LC 74-5802. 1975. 7.95 (ISBN 0-06-013379-1). Harper & Row.

Accomplice. Darryl Ponicsan. 1976. (pbk.) 1.75. Bantam Books.

Accomplice: A Novel of Suspense. John Edwin Canaday. LC 47-12113. (Inner sanctum suspense special). 1947. Simon and Schuster.

Accomplices. David Fletcher, pseud. LC 77-367235. 1976. 3.50 (ISBN 0-333-19401-2). Macmillan.

Accomplices. Georges Simenon. LC 76-41313. (Harbrace paperbound library; HPL 74). 1977. 2.25 (ISBN 0-15-602670-8). Harcourt Brace Jovanovich.

Accomplished Gentleman. Julian Sturgis. LC 8-16863. (On cover: Appleton's new handy-volume series. no. 30). 1879. D. Appleton and Company.

Accomplished Rake, or Modern Fine Gentleman see Four Before Richardson: Selected English Novels, 1720-1727.

Accomplished Through Sacrifice. Bert Noland Everett. LC 10-14675. 0.50. The Review Press.

Accomplished Woman. Nancy Price. LC 78-12456. 9.95 (ISBN 0-698-10963-5). Coward, McCann & Geoghegan.

Accomplished Woman. Nancy Price. 1980. 2.50 (ISBN 0-451-09115-9). New American Library.

According to Gibson. Denis George Mackail. LC 23-12458. 1923. Houghton Mifflin Company.

According to Her Light. Mercedes Cumming Dana. LC 22-184024. Dorrance.

According to Maria. Anna Eichberg Lane. LC 10-7783. 1910. J. Lane Company; Etc., Etc.

According to Orders. Frederick Britten Austin. LC 19-543090. 1.50. George H. Doran Company.

According to Plato. Frank Frankfort Moore. LC 1-30789. 1901. Dodd, Mead & Company.

According to the Evidence. 1st Ed. Henry Cecil. LC 54-89392. 1954. Harper.

According to the Pattern. Grace Livingston Hill. LC 3-17911. 1903. The Griffith and Rowland Press.

According to the Pattern. Grace Livingston Hill. LC 81-10982. 1981-1982. 15.50 (ISBN 0-89190-016-0). Aeonian Press.

According to the Pattern. Grace Livingston Hill. LC 81-19940. (Hill, Grace Livingston, 1865-1947. Classic Ser.: 6). 5.95 (ISBN 0-8007-1297-8). Revell.

According to Thomas. Gladys Malvern. LC 47-3261. 1947. R. M. McBride & Company.

According to Thomas: An Historical Novel of the First Century. Ivan Fedorovich Nazhivin. Tr. by Burna, Emile. LC 31-350761. Harper & Brothers.

According to Your Faith. Emma Marr Petersen. LC 67-21828. (Illus.). 1967. Bookcraft.

Account of a Battle Between the Ancient & Modern Books in St. James's Library see Tale of a Tub.

Account of a Lady Taken by the Indians in 1777. Abraham Panther. LC 77-18885. (Garland Library of Narratives of North American Indian Captivities; V. 17). 1979. 29.50 (ISBN 0-8240-1641-6). Garland Pub.

Account of the State of Learning in the Empire of Lilliput see Virgin Seducer.

Account Rendered. Edward Frederic Benson. LC 11-5373. 1911. 1.20. Doubleday, Page & Company.

Account Rendered. Vera Mary Brittain. LC 44-40202. 1944. The Macmillan Company.

Account Rendered. Patricia Wentworth. LC 40-12741. J. B. Lippincott Company.

Account Unsettled. Georges Simenon. LC 67-76794. 1966. Penguin in Association with H. Hamilton.

Accounting. Bruce Marshall. LC 57-10785. 1958. Houghton Mifflin.

Accounting for Murder. Emma Lathen, pseud. 1974. (pbk.) 0.95. Pocket Books.

Accrington Pals. Peter Whelan. 48p. 1982. pap. 6.95 (ISBN 0-413-49870-0, NO. 3647). Methuen Inc.

Accursed. Paul Boorstin. (Signet Book). 1977. 1.75 (ISBN 0-451-07745-8). New American Library.

Accursed. Gary Burdick. LC 82-81996. 256p. 1982. pap. 2.95 (ISBN 0-86721-218-7). Playboy Pbks.

Accursed Roccos: A Tale of Dalmatia. David Powell Johnson. LC 13-1897. 1913. 1.50. Broadway Publishing Co.

Accursed: Two Diabolic Tales. Claude Seignolle. 1967. 5.50 o.p. (ISBN 0-698-10001-8). Coward.

Accursed: Two Diabolical Tales. Tr. by Bernard Wall. Foreword by Lawrence Durrell. 1st Amer. Ed. Claude Seignolle & Claude. Malvenue Seignolle. LC 67-16262. 1967. 5.50. Coward.

Accuse the Toff. John Creasey. LC 74-31916. 192p. 1975. 5.95 o.p. (ISBN 0-8027-5319-1). Walker & Co.

Accused. Nina Miller Elliott. LC 13-24448. 1.50. Saxonia Press.

Accused. Jerrold Morgulas. LC 67-19063. 1967. Doubleday.

Accused Nurse. Jane Converse. (Signet book). 1974. (pbk.) 0.95. New American Library.

Ace High. Gus March-Phillipps. LC 39-7078. 1939. E. P. Dutton & Co., Inc.

Ace High: The Frisco Detective; or, The Girl Sport's Double Game. A Story of the Sierra & the Golden Gate City. C E Tripp. LC 49-5017. 1948. Book Club of California.

Ace in the Hole. Gene Curry. (Saddler Ser.: No. 6). (Orig.). 1981. pap. 1.95 (ISBN 0-505-51666-7). Tower Bks.

Ace in the Hole. Jackson Gregory. LC 41-4132. 1941. Dodd, Mead & Company.

Ace in the Hole. Zeke Masters, pseud. (Faro Blake Ser.: No. 8). 176p. pap. 1.95 (ISBN 0-671-42619-2). PB.

Ace-in-the-Hole Haggarty. Robert Maxwell Hankins. 1945. Macrae-Smith-Company.

Ace of Blades. Charles B. Stilson. LC 24-19469. 1924. G. H. Watt.

Ace of Clubs. Jozef Lubomirski. Tr. by De Vere, Meta. LC 7-14752. (On cover: Lovell's series of foreign literature, no. 7). J. W. Lovell Company.

Ace of Danger: An Adventure of the Lothian Coast. Augustus Muir. The Bobbs-Merrill Company.

Ace of Death. Jay Callahan. 1978. pap. 1.95 o.s.i. (ISBN 0-89559-156-1). Dale Books Inc.

Ace of Jades. Stuart Palmer. LC 31-19275. 1931. The Mohawk Press.

Ace of Knaves: The Saint Goes into Action. Leslie Charteris. LC 37-226353. 1937. Pub. for the Crime Club, Inc., by Doubleday, Doran & Company, Inc.

Ace of Knaves: The Saint Goes into Action. Leslie Charteris. LC 39-4770. 1938. The Sun Dial Press, Inc.

Ace of Knaves: The Saint Goes into Action. Leslie Charteris. LC 44-6603. (Murder mystery monthly. No. 22).

Ace of Spades. Henry Holt. 1930. L. MacVeagh, The Dial Press.

Ace of Spades. Dell Shannon. 1970. pap. 0.75 o.p. (T2143). Pyramid Pubns.

Ace of Spades: By Dell Shannon Pseud. Elizabeth Linington. LC 61-5789. 1961. Morrow.

Ace of Spies. Robin Bruce Lockhart. (Leisure books). 1979. 1.75 (ISBN 0-8439-0650-2). Nordon Pubns.

Ace of Spies. Don Von Elsner. (O.s.i.). 1968. pap. 0.60 o.s.i. (A263X, Award). Univ Pub & Dist.

Ace of the Deep. Jim Young. 1.95 (ISBN 0-671-82930-0). Pocket Books.

Ace of the Diamond Deuce. Charles Stanley Strong. LC 44-917. 1943. Phoenix Press.

Aces: A Collection of Short Stories. The Community Workers of the New York Guild for the Jewish Blind, Comp & Fisher, Dorothea Frances (Canfield) LC 24-28960. 1924. G. P. Putnam's Sons.

Aces & Eights. Loren D Estleman. LC 80-2447. 1981. 9.95 (ISBN 0-385-17469-1). Doubleday.

Aces and Eights. Philip Garlington. LC 75-14191. 1975. 7.95 (ISBN 0-87131-191-7). M. Evans.

Aces, Eights & Murder. Mary Violet Heberden. LC 41-15442. 1941. Pub. for the Crime Club by Doubleday, Doran and Co., Inc.

Aces High. William Hughes (ISBN 0-380-00788-6). Avon.

Aces Wild. E. Jefferson Clay. Bd. with Badge for Brazos. 1980. pap. 2.25 (ISBN 0-505-51470-2). Tower Bks.

Aces Wild at Golden Eagle. Jackson Gregory. LC 44-2189. 1944. The Blakiston Company, Distributed by Dodd, Mead & Company, New York.

Achievement. Ernest Charles Temple Thurston. LC 14-172866. 1914. D. Appleton and Company.

Achievement of C. S. Lewis. Thomas Howard. LC 80-14188. 5.95 (ISBN 0-87788-004-2). H. Shaw Publishers.

Achievements in Fiction: A College Anthology. Ed. by Burton L. Cooper. LC 74-148322. 1971. Allyn and Bacon.

Achievements of Luther Trant. Edwin Balmer. LC 10-101862. 1.50. Small, Maynard & Company.

Achiles Absent. Marie Monchen. LC 51-1836. 1951. Vantage Press.

Achilles Affair. Berkely Mather. LC 59-5915. 1959. Scribner.

Achilles His Armour. 1st Ed. in the U. S. A. Peter Green, pseud. LC 67-21408. 1967. 6.95. Doubleday.

Achilles' Stone. Dean Holt. 5.95 o.p. Vantage.

Achilles Stone. 1st. ed. Dean Holt. 1974. 5.95 (ISBN 0-533-00757-7). Vantage.

Achsah: a New-England Life-Study. William Marshall Fitts Round. LC 8-687178. 1876. Lee & Shepard.

Achsah, the Sister of Jairus. Mabel Cronise Jones. LC 11-14751. 1.00. Broadway Publishing Co.

Acid Drop. Sara George. LC 75-10754. 1975. 6.95 (ISBN 0-689-10673-4). Atheneum.

Acid Nightmare. M. E. Chaber, pseud. 1967. 3.50 o.p. (ISBN 0-03-065595-1). HR&W.

Acid Nightmare. Kendell Foster Crossen. 1967. Holt, Rinehart and Winston.

Acid Temple Ball. Mary Sativa. LC 72-9894. (Traveller's companion series). 1969. 1.95. Traveller's Companion, Inc.

Acknowledgment. Ercell H. Hoffman. Ed. by Joseph Lawrence. LC 78-50055. 1978. pap. 3.95 (ISBN 0-89144-051-8). Crescent Pubns.

Ackroyd. Jules Feiffer. 1978. 1.95 (ISBN 0-380-39347-6). Avon Books.

Ackroyd: A Novel. Jules Feiffer. LC 76-58872. 8.95 (ISBN 0-671-22502-2). Simon and Schuster.

Ackroyd of the Faculty. Anna Chapin Ray. LC 7-12975. 1907. Little, Brown, and Company.

Acolyte. Thea Astley. LC 81-454493. 1980. 7.25 (ISBN 0-7022-1540-6). University of Queensland Press.

Acoma. Peter Neill. LC 77-92932. 1978. pap. 3.95 (ISBN 0-918172-03-9). Leetes Isl.

Aconite Murders. Sidney Clark Williams. LC 36-70424. 1936. Dodd, Mead & Company.

Acorn People. Ron Jones. (gr. 7 up). 1977. pap. 1.75 (ISBN 0-553-20243-X). Bantam.

Acquainted with Grief. Carlo Emilio Gadda. LC 69-12804. 1969. 6.95. G. Braziller.

Acquainted with the Night: A Novel. Translated from the German Und Sagte Kein Einziges Wort by Richard Graves. 1st Ed. Heinrich Boll. 1954. Holt.

Acquittal. Graeme Lorimer & Lorimer, Sarah. LC 38-5290. 1938. Little, Brown and Company.

Acquittal. Helen De Guerry Simpson. LC 26-9326. 1925. A. A. Knopf.

Acquittal. John Williams Wainwright. LC 75-26200. 1976. 7.95. St. Martin's Press.

Acquitted! Message from the Cross. Sakae Kubo. LC 74-28685. (Stories That Win Ser.). 1975. pap. 0.95 o.p. (ISBN 0-8163-0190-5, 01070-2). Pacific Pr Pub Assn.

Acre of Grass: A Novel. John Innes Mackintosh Stewart. LC 65-25936. 1966. bds., 4.50. Norton.

Acres & Pains. Sidney J. Perelman. (O.s.i.). 1972. pap. 1.95 o.s.i. (ISBN 0-671-21075-0, Touchstone Bks). S&S.

Acres of Antaeus. Paul Corey. LC 46-6849. 1946. H. Holt and Company.

Acres of Sky. Charles Morrow Wilson. LC 30-357425. 1930. G. P. Putnam's Sons.

Acrobat Admits: A Novel. Alfred Grossman. LC 58-13668. 1959. G. Braziller.

Acrobatic Alpha-Batic Mother Goose ABC Book. Illus. by Star Bellei. (Illus.). 1974. (pbk.) 1.95 (ISBN 0-8331-0512-4). Hubbard Press.

Acrobats: A Novel. Mordecai Richler. LC 54-10488. 1954. Putnam.

Acrophile. Yoram Kaniuk. Tr. by Zeva Shapiro. 1961. 3.50 o.p. Atheneum.

Across a Crowded Room. Lilian Peake. (Harlequin Presents Ser.). 192p. 1981. pap. 1.75 (ISBN 0-373-10474-X). Harlequin Bks.

Across an Ulster Bog. M Hamilton. LC 7-7406. 1896. E. Arnold.

Across Captive Seas, No. 2. Michele DuBarry. (Loves of Angela Carlyle Ser.). 1981. pap. 2.50 (ISBN 0-8439-0932-3). Nordon Pubns.

Across from the Floral Park. Kent Thompson. LC 74-81457. 1974. 7.95. St. Martin's Press.

Across Her Path. Annie S Swan Smith. LC 8-8191. 1890. Cranston and Stowe.

Across One Hundred & Tenth. Wally Ferris. LC 77-105241. 1970. 5.95 o.p. (ISBN 0-06-012934-4, HarpT). Har-Row.

Across One Hundred Tenth. Wally Ferris. 1971. pap. 0.95 o.p. (ISBN 0-446-65612-7, 65-612). Paperback Lib.

Across Paris, and Other Stories. Translated from the French and with an Introd. by Norman Denny. Marcel Ayme. LC 58-12467. Harper.

Across the Arid Zone. Walter Samuel Cramp. LC 11-1857. 1.50. The C. M. Clark Publishing Company.

Across the Bitter Sea. Eilis Dillon. (Fawcett crest book). 1974. (pbk.) 1.75. Fawcett.

Across the Bitter Sea: A Novel. Eilis Dillon. LC 73-8225. 1973. 8.95 (ISBN 0-671-21591-4). Simon and Schuster.

Across the Black Waters. Mulk Raj Anand. (Orient Paperbacks Ser.). 322p. 1980. pap. 5.95 (ISBN 0-86578-081-1). Ind-US Inc.

Across the Board: A Trilogy. Dick Francis. LC 74-15869. 1975. 12.95 (ISBN 0-06-011318-9). Harper & Row.

Across the Board: Three Harper Novels of Suspense. Dick Francis. Incl. Enquiry; Flying Finish; Blood Sport. LC 74-15869. 1975. 14.95 o.p. (ISBN 0-06-011318-9, HarpT). Har-Row.

Across the Campus: A Story of College Life. Caroline Macomber Fuller. LC 99-2656. 1899. C. Scribner's Sons.

Across the Chasm. Julia Magruder. LC 7-20134. 1885. C. Scribner's Sons.

Across the Common. Elizabeth Berridge. LC 65-1980. 1964. Heinemann.

Across the Common: 1st Amer. Ed. Elizabeth Berridge. LC 65-20411. 1965. 3.95. Coward.

Across the Crevasse: A Novel. Rudolph Mellard. LC 65-25795. 4.75. Sage Dist. Swallow.

Across the Dark River: A Novel. Peter Mendelssohn. LC 40-270084. 1939. Doubleday, Doran & Co., Inc.

Across the High Sierra. Robert E. Mills. (Kansan Ser.: No. 2). 1980. pap. 1.75 (ISBN 0-8439-0820-3). Nordon Pubns.

Across the Latitudes. John Fleming Wilson. LC 11-24970. 1911. Little, Brown, and Company.

Across the Mesa. Helen Bagg. LC 22-11296. 1922. The Penn Publishing Company.

Across the Moon. Hamish Macleod. LC 25-11365. 1925. Boni & Liveright.

Across the Pacific. A Novel Founded Upon the Melodrama of the Same Title. Charles E Blaney. LC 33-28370. (On cover: Play book series. no. 43). 1904. J. S. Ogilvie Publishing Company.

Across the Prairie. Dora Aydelotte. LC 41-51732. 1941. D. Appleton-Century Company, Incorporated.

Across the Rio Grande. Jake Logan. LC 75-23640. (John Logan WesternSer.: No. 4). 208p. 1976. pap. 1.50 (ISBN 0-87216-702-X). Playboy Pbks.

Across the Rio Grande. Jake Logan. LC 75-23640. 208p. 1982. pap. 2.25 (ISBN 0-86721-216-0). Playboy Pbks.

Across the River and into the Trees. Ernest Hemingway. LC 50-9370. 1950. Scribner.

Across the River and into the Trees. Ernest Hemingway. LC 75-100353. (Scribner library, SL202. Contemporary classics). 1970. 2.45. Scribner.

Across the Running Tide. Michael J. Cohen. (Illus.). 1979. pap. 6.00 (ISBN 0-89166-010-0). Cobblesmith.

Across the Salt Seas: A Romance of the War of Succession. John Bloundelle- Burton. 1897. H. S. Stone & Co.

Across the Sea of Stars. Arthur C. Clarke. LC 59-10252. 8.95 o.p. (ISBN 0-15-103259-9). HarBraceJ.

Across the Sea of Stars: An Omnibus Containing the Complete Novels of Childhood's End and Earthlight and Eighteen Short Stories. Arthur Charles Clarke. LC 59-10252. 1959. Harcourt, Brace.

Across the Seas. Le Roy Allen. LC 53-22440. 1953. Zondervan Pub. House.

Across the Stream. Edward Frederic Benson. LC 19-8074. 1.50. George H. Doran Company.

Across the Water. Michael Campbell. LC 61-9298. 1961. Orion Press.

Across the Western. Patrick O'Connor. 1976. 7.95 o.p. (ISBN 0-395-24300-9). HM.

Across the Western: A Novel. Patrick O'Connor. LC 76-931. 1976. 7.95 (ISBN 0-395-24300-9). Houghton Mifflin.

Across the Wide Missouri. Bernard De Voto. (Illus.). 608p. 1981. 8.98 (ISBN 0-517-10266-8). Crown.

Across the Years. Emilie Baker Loring. LC 39-245721. 1939. Little, Brown and Company.

Across the Years. Eleanor Hodgman Porter. LC 19-16145. 1919. 1.75. Houghton Mifflin Company.

Across the Zodiac, 2 vols. in 1. Percy Greg. LC 73-13271. (Classics of Science Fiction Ser.). 602p. 1974. 16.50 (ISBN 0-88355-125-X); pap. 5.50 (ISBN 0-88355-154-3). Hyperion Conn.

Across the Zodiac. Percy Greg. (o.s.i). 1978. pap. 1.95 (ISBN 0-445-04299-0). Popular Lib.

Across These Waters. Nora B. Thompson. LC 75-179787. 164p. 1972. 5.95 o.p. (ISBN 0-8059-1638-5). Dorrance.

Across Time. David Grinnell, pseud. LC 57-26954. 1957. Avalon Books.

Across 110th. Wally Ferris. LC 77-105241. 1970. 5.95. Harper & Row.

Act. Tom Raworth. 1973. 8.00 (Pub. by Trigram Pr); pap. 4.50. SBD.

Act in a Backwater. Edward Frederic Benson. LC 3-28962. 1903. D. Appleton and Company.

Act of Anger. Bart Spicer. LC 62-17277. 1962. Atheneum.

Act of Anger. Bart Spicer. 1976. (pbk.) 1.75 (ISBN 0-425-03036-9). Berkley Publishing Corp.

Act of Betrayal. Max Byrd. LC 76-10841. 1976. 1.50. Ballantine Books.

Act of Darkness. John Peale Bishop. LC 35-4217. 1935. C. Scribner's Sons.

Act of Destruction. 1st Ed. Ronald Hardy. LC 62-15694. 1962. Doubleday.

Act of Faith: And Other Stories. Irwin Shaw. LC 46-7547. 1946. Random House.

Act of Faith, & Other Stories. facsimile ed. Irwin Shaw. LC 70-169561. (Short Story Index Reprint Ser.). Repr. of 1946 ed. 15.00 (ISBN 0-8369-4024-5). Ayer Co.

Act of Fear. Michael Collins, pseud. LC 79-89320. (Dan Fortune Novel: No. 5). 192p. 1980. pap. 2.25 (ISBN 0-86721-004-4). Playboy Pbks.

Act of Fear. Michael Collins, pseud. (Red Badge Mystery Ser). 1967. 3.95 o.p. Dodd.

Act of Fear. Willo Davis Roberts. LC 76-42389. 1977. 6.95 (ISBN 0-385-12520-8). Published for the Crime Club by Doubleday.

Act of God. Richard Ashby. 1974. pap. 0.75 o.p. (LB00083). Leisure Bks.

Act of God. Fryniwyd Tennyson Jesse. LC 37-28591. 1937. The Greystone Press.

Act of God. Margaret Kennedy. LC 55-507954. Rinehart.

Act of God: A Novel. Charles Templeton. LC 77-17833. 8.95 (ISBN 0-316-83686-9). Little, Brown.

Act of Love. Celia Dale. LC 69-15720. 1969. 5.95. Walker.

Act of Love. Joe R. Lansdale. 1981. pap. 2.75 (ISBN 0-89083-735-X). Zebra.

Act of Love. Ira Wolfert. LC 48-10610. 1948. Simon and Schuster.

Act of Love: A Completely Retold Version of the Novel. Ira Wolfert. LC 54-5810. 1954. Simon and Schuster.

Act of Loving. Robert Russell. LC 67-19287. 1967. Vanguard Press.

Act of Mercy. Arthur Leonard Bell Thompson. LC 60-11286. 1960. Coward-McCann.

Act of Outrage. Alison Hart. (Girls in Trouble). (Signet Book: Vol. 3). 1976. (pbk.) 1.25. New American Library.

Act of Passion, a Novel. Georges Simenon. LC 52-9542. 1952. Prentice-Hall.

Act of Vengeance. Trevor Armbrister. 1980. pap. 2.75 (ISBN 0-446-85707-6). Warner Bks.

Act of Violence. Edwin Fadiman. LC 57-6915. (Signet book, 1374). 1957. New American Library.

Act of Violence. Basil Heatter. LC 55-223061. (Lion book, 228). 1954. Lion Books.

Act of War. Brian Callison. LC 77-77930. 1977. 7.95 (ISBN 0-525-05023-X). Dutton.

Act of War: A Novel of Love and Treason. Leonard Sanders. LC 81-23229. 14.95 (ISBN 0-671-25610-6). Simon and Schuster.

Actaeon. Laura Daintrey. LC 6-33192. The Empire City Publishing Company.

Actaeon Homeward. Robert Emmett. 212p. 1980. pap. 4.50 (ISBN 0-8040-9010-6). Stonehenge.

Actaeon Homeward. Robert Emmett. 1979. 8.95 o.p.; pap. 4.50 o.p. Writers West.

Actaeon Homeward: A Novel. Robert Emmett. LC 78-60621. 8.95. Writers West Books.

Acte. Lawrence Durrell. (Illus.). 1965. 4.50 o.p. Dutton.

Acte of Corinth: Or, The Convert of St. Paul. A Tale of Greece and Rome. Alexandre Dumas. Tr. by Herbert, Henry William. 1847. E. P. Williams & Co.

Actes and Monuments: Stories. John William Corrington. LC 78-15325. (Illinois short fiction). 7.95. (ISBN 0-252-00716-6) (ISBN 0-252-00715-8). University of Illinois Press.

Action. James L Guetti. LC 78-37447. 1972. 6.95. Dial Press.

Action, and Other Stories. Charles Edward Montague. LC 70-134971. (Short story index reprint series). 1970. Books for Libraries Press.

Action: And Other Stories. Charles Edward Montague. LC 29-8988. 1929. Doubleday, Doran & Company, Inc.

Action and Passion. Percival Christopher Wren. LC 77-364212. 1976. 3.75 (ISBN 0-7278-0161-9). Severn House: Distributed by Hutchinson.

Action and Passion. Percival Christopher Wren. LC 33-25970. 1933. Frederick A. Stokes Company.

Action and the Word: A Novel of New York. Brander Matthews. LC 2116. 1900. Harper & Brothers.

Action at Aquila. Hervey Allen. LC 38-27118. 1938. Farrar & Rinehart.

Action at Arcanum: A Gregory Quist Story. 1st Ed. William Colt MacDonald. LC 58-13180. 1958. Lippincott.

Action at Beecher Island. Dee Alexander Brown. LC 67-22440. 1967. Doubleday.

Action at Boundary Peak: By Stuart Brock Pseud. Louis Trimble. LC 55-13735. Avalon Books.

Action at the Bitterroot. Paul Evan Lehman. 1970. pap. 0.50 o.p. (50-314). Manor Bks.

Action at the Sioux. Philip Morgan. 1958. Avalon Books.

Action at Three Peaks. Frank O'Rourke. LC 48-8241. 1948. Random House.

Action at Thunder Mountain. Owen G Irons. (Avalon Books). 4.95. Thomas Bouregy.

Action at Velasquez. W. G Schreiber. (Avalon Books). 4.95. Thomas Bouregy.

Action at War Bow Valley: By Michael Carder Pseud. Vernon L Fluharty. LC 52-11859. 1952. Macrae Smith.

Action at World's End. Elwyn Whitman Chambers. LC 45-205846. 1945. E. P. Dutton & Company, Inc.

Action Atlantic. Edwyn Gray. 1.25 (ISBN 0-523-00898-8). Pinnacle Books.

Action by Night. Ernest Haycox. LC 43-164. 1943. Little, Brown and Company.

Action by Night. Ernest Haycox. LC 44-21950. 1944. The Sun Dial Press.

Action: Division 3. Kurt Mahr. (Perry Rhodan#94). 1976. (pbk.) 1.25. Ace Books.

Action for Slander: A Novel. Mary Borden. 1937. Harper & Brothers.

Action in Diamonds. Courtney Ryley Cooper. LC 42-23592. 1942. Wm. Penn Pbulishing Corp.

Action in Havana. Elinor Rice. LC 40-14498. Duell, Sloan and Pearce.

Action in the North Atlantic. Guy Gilpatric. LC 43-825115. 1943. E. P. Dutton & Co., Inc.

Action in the Sky: By Arch Whitehouse. 1st Ed. Arthur George Joseph Whitehouse. LC 62-16428. 1962. Duell, Sloan and Pearce.

Action of the Tiger. Thomas Walsh. LC 68-11019. (Inner sanctum mystery). 1968. Simon and Schuster.

Action of the Tiger: A Novel. James Howard Wellard. LC 55-4380. 1955. Macmillan.

Action of the Tiger, a Novel. James Howard Wellard. LC 57-116153. 1957. St. Martin's Press.

Action Stations! Lewis Anselm da Costa Ricci. LC 41-15453. 1941. Little, Brown and Company.

Action Tonight. large type ed. James David Horan. 1966. 4.95 o.s.i.; lib. bdg. 5.34 o.s.i. Large Print.

Actions and Passions: A Novel of the 1960's. Patrick Anderson. LC 73-83610. 1974. 7.95 (ISBN 0-385-00369-2). Doubleday.

Actions and Passions: A Novel of the 1960's. Patrick Anderson. (Kangaroo Book). 1977 (ISBN 0-671-81178-9). Pocket Books.

Actions and Reactions. Rudyard Kipling. LC 9-26138. 1909. Doubleday, Page & Company.

Active Service: A Novel. Stephen Crane. LC 99-46396. Frederick A. Stokes Company.

Active Service: A Novel. Stephen Crane. LC 41-2431. 1901. International Association of Newspapers and Authors.

Actor. Niven Busch. LC 55-6956. 1955. Simon and Schuster.

Actor. Allan Nixon. (Orig.). 1968. pap. 0.75 o.p. (ISBN 0-446-54544-9, 54-544). Paperback Lib.

Actor in Room 931. Cyril Maude & Towne, Charles Hanson, 1877- Joint Author. LC 26-103161. 1926. J. H. Sears & Company, Inc.

Actor-Manager. Leonard Merrick. LC 12-14398. 1912. M. Kennerley.

Actor-Manager. Leonard Merrick. LC 20-23140. (Half-title: The works of Leonard Merrick. vol. iii). 1919. E. P. Dutton and Company.

Actor Named Moliere. Beatrix Dussane. Tr. by Galantiere, Lewis. LC 37-27186. 1937. C. Scribner's Sons.

Actor's Blood. Ben Hecht. LC 36-3538. Covici, Friede.

Actor's Daughter. Aline Frankau Bernstein. LC 40-29646. 1941. A. A. Knopf.

Actress. Bessie Breuer. LC 56-11098. 1957. Harper.

Actress. Henry Denker. LC 78-7243. 9.95 (ISBN 0-671-24129-X). Simon and Schuster.

Actress. Henry Denker. 1979. 2.50 (ISBN 0-671-81958-5). Pocket Books.

Actress. Frank Owen. LC 16-1480. 1.00. Broadway Publishing Co.

Actress: A Novel. Louise Closser Hale. LC 9-5702. 1909. Harper & Brothers.

Actress' Crime: Or, All for Name and Gold. Edna Winfield, pseud. LC 21733. (On cover: Holly library. no. 156). 1900. The Mershon Co.

Actress' Daughter. A Novel. May Agnes Early Fleming. LC 6-39916. 1886. G. W. Carleton & Co.; Etc., Etc.

Actress of Padus: And Other Tales. Richard Penn Smith. LC 8-96251. 1836. E. L. Carey & A. Hart.

Actresses see Sex Goddess.

Acts of Black Night. Kathleen Moore Knight. LC 38-10849. 1938. Pub. for the Crime Club, Inc., by Doubleday, Doran & Company, Inc.

Acts of Black Night. Kathleen Moore Knight. LC 39-16859. 1939. The Sun Dial Press, Inc.

Acts of Kindness. Charlotte Vale Allen. (Signet book). 1979. 1.95 (ISBN 0-451-08690-2). New American Library.

Acts of King Arthur and His Noble Knights: From the Winchester MMS. of Thomas Malory and Other Sources. Thomas Malory & John Steinbeck. LC 76-28210. 10.00 (ISBN 0-374-10085-3). Farrar, Straus and Giroux.
Acts of King Arthur & His Noble Knights. John Steinbeck. 464p. 1980. pap. 2.95 (Del Rey). Ballantine.
Acts of King Arthur & His Noble Knights. John Steinbeck. 364p. 1976. 10.00 (ISBN 0-374-10085-3). FS&G.
Acts of Love. Elia Kazan. LC 77-90939. 1978. 10.95 (ISBN 0-394-42524-3). Knopf.
Acts of Love. Elia Kazan. 1979. 2.75 (ISBN 0-446-95553-1). Warner Books.
Acts of Love: An American Novel. Carol Berge. LC 72-89688. 1973. 6.95 (ISBN 0-672-51780-9). Bobbs-Merrill.
Acts of Mercy. Bill Pronzini & Barry N. Malzberg. LC 77-88405. 8.95 (ISBN 0-399-11996-5). Putnam.
Acts of Theft. Arthur Allen Cohen. LC 79-1818. 10.00 (ISBN 0-15-103334-X). Harcourt Brace Jovanovich.
Acupuncture Murders. Dwight Steward. LC 72-9120. 1973. 5.95 (ISBN 0-06-014122-0). Harper & Row.
Acupuncture Murders. Dwight Steward. 1974. (pbk.) 1.25. Warner Paperback Library.
Ad Astra: A Novel. Iris Vorel. LC 33-165831. Uranian Press, Inc.
Ad for Murder. John Penn. LC 82-10761. 1982. 10.95 (ISBN 0-684-17761-7). Scribner.
Ada Dallas. 1st Ed. Wirt Williams. LC 59-14468. 1959. McGraw-Hill.
Ada or Ardor. Vladimir Vladimirovich Nabokov. 1969. 8.95 o.p. (ISBN 0-07-045720-4, GB). McGraw.
Ada: Or, Ardor: a Family Chronicle. Vladimir Vladimirovich Nabokov. LC 71-79763. 1969. 8.95. McGraw-Hill.
Ada or Ardor: A Family Chronicle. Vladimir Vladimirovich Nabokov. (McGraw-Hill Paperback Ser.). 612p. 1980. pap. 6.95 (ISBN 0-07-045723-9, GB). McGraw.
Ada Vernham: Actress. Richard Marsh. LC 4290. 1900. L. C. Page & Company.
Adalaska: Or, The Strange and Mysterious Family of the Cave of Genreva. George W L Bickley. LC 6-13108. 1853. H. M. Rulison.
Adam. David Langstone Bolt. LC 79-12863. 1979. 5.95 (ISBN 0-87788-018-2). H. Shaw Publishers.
Adam and Caroline: Being a Sequel to Adam of Dublin. Conal O'Connell O'Riordan. LC 22-2311. 1922. Harcourt, Brace and Company.
Adam & Eve. Marcus Von Heller. 1971. 1.75 o.p. (V1007K, Venus). Grove.
Adam and Eve. A Novel. Louisa Taylor Parr. (Seaside library. v. 42, no. 853). 1880. G. Munro.
Adam & Eve & Pinch Me. Alfred Edgar Coppard. LC 24-27983. 1922. A. A. Knopf.
Adam & Eve & Pinch Me: Tales. Alfred Edgar Coppard. LC 70-106274. (Short story index reprint series). 1970. Books for Libraries Press.
Adam and Eve: Though He Knew Better. John Erskine. LC 27-24006. The Bobbs-Merrill Company.
Adam and Evelyn in the Garden of Edenbridge. Cosmo Hamilton. 1936. Dodd, Mead & Company.
Adam & His Women. Sarah Clifford. 1972. pap. 0.95 o.p. (09120). Curtis.
Adam and His Works: Collected Stories. Paul Goodman. LC 68-29394. 1968. 2.45. Vintage Books.
Adam and Some Eves. Concordia Merrel. LC 31-12257. Doubleday, Doran & Company, Inc.
Adam and the Serpent. Vardis Fisher. LC 47-179267. 1947. The Vanguard Press, Inc.
Adam & the Train. Heinrich Boll. Tr. by Leila Vennewitz from Ger. Bd. with Train. LC 71-127920. 288p. 1974. pap. 4.95 (SP). McGraw.
Adam and Two Eves: Strange Story of a Girl Told by Herself. Edith Gyorgy. LC 34-6833. The Macaulay Company.
Adam Bede. George Eliot. (Harcourt library of English and American classics). 1962. Harcourt, Brace & World.
Adam Bede. George Eliot. LC 6-40742. 1859. Harper & Brothers.
Adam Bede. George Eliot. 1860. Harper & Brothers.
Adam Bede. 3d ed. George Eliot. (Seaside library, v. 1, no. 7). 1877. G. Munro.
Adam Bede. George Eliot. LC 1-20006. (Half-title: The works of George Eliot. Foleshill ed. v. 3)). 1900. Little, Brown, and Company.
Adam Bede. George Eliot. LC 2-29062. (English Comedie humaine. 1st series, v. 11). 1902. The Century Co.
Adam Bede. George Eliot. (Half-title: Everyman's library, ed. by Ernest Rhys. Fiction. no. 27). 1906. J. M. Dent & Co.
Adam Bede. George Eliot. LC 27-26102. (International classics). 1926. Dodd, Mead and Company.
Adam Bede. George Eliot. LC 36-37058. (Half-title: Everyman's library ed. by Ernest Rhys. Fiction. no. 27). 1930. J. M. Dent & Sons, Ltd.
Adam Bede. George Eliot. (Rinehart editions, 32). 1919. Rinehart.
Adam Bede. George Eliot. LC 49-4963. 1949. Dodd, Mead.
Adam Bede. George Eliot & Browne, Gordon Frederick 1858- Illus. LC 25-274712. 1925. J. B. Lippincott Company; Etc., Etc.
Adam Bede. George Eliot & Stephen Charles Gill. LC 80-514612. (Penguin English library). 1980. 3.95 (ISBN 0-14-043121-7). Penguin Books.
Adam Bede. George Eliot & Patterson, Samuel White, Ed. LC 23-11824. (Macmillan's pocket American and English classics). 1923. The Macmillan Company.
Adam Bede. George Eliot & Wylie, Laura Johnson, 1853-1932, Ed. LC 17-246973. (Half-title: The modern student's library, ed. by W. D. Howe). C. Scribner's Sons.
Adam Bede. A Novel. George Eliot. (Harper's Franklin square library, no. 489). 1885. Harper & Brothers.
Adam Bede: Biographical Introduction by Esther Wood. George Eliot. LC 1-31171. (personal edition of George Eliot's works). 1901. Doubleday,Page & Co.
Adam Bede: Chapter Notes and Criticism. Text by Carol Z. Rothkopf. Carol Z Rothkopf. (Study master pubn., 257). pap., 1.00. Amer. R.D.M.
Adam Bede. Ed., Introd. by John Paterson. George Eliot. Ed. by John Paterson. (Riverside eds., B109). 1968. pap., 1.75. Houghton.
Adam Bede: With a Teacher's Manual and a Reader's Supplement. George Eliot. (Reader's enrichment ser. RE 700). Washington.
Adam Bede: With an Introd. by Maxwell H. Goldberg. Complete and Unabridged. George Eliot. LC 56-44036. (Pocket library, PL507). 1956. Pocket Books.
Adam Brunskill. 1st American Ed. Thomas Armstrong. LC 52-11348. 1952. Harcourt, Brace.
Adam Cargo. Upton Terrell. LC 35-566141. Reilly & Lee Co.
Adam Chasers. Bertha Muzzy Sinclair. LC 27-15118. 1927. Little, Brown, and Company.
Adam Clarke, a Story of Toilers: Being a Narrative of the Experiences of a Family of British Emigrants to the United States in Cotton Mill, Iron Foundry, Coal Mine, and Other Fields of Labor. Henry Mann. LC 5-58. 1904. Popular Book Company.
Adam Experiment. Geoffrey S. Simmons. LC 77-93098. (F). 1978. 8.95 (ISBN 0-87795-185-3). Arbor Hse.
Adam Experiment: A Novel. Geoffrey S. Simmons. 1979. 2.25 (ISBN 0-425-04492-0). Berkley Publishing Corp.
Adam Gimbel, Pioneer Trader. Helen Wells. LC 55-8997. 1955. D. McKay Co.
Adam Hepburn's Vow: A Tale of Kirk and Covenant. Annie S Swan Smith. (On cover: Cassell's "rainbow" series of original novels, v. 1, no. 15). 1888. Cassell & Company, Limited.
Adam Hepburn's Vow: A Tale of Kirk and Covenant. Annie S Swan Smith. LC 2-20818. Street & Smith.
Adam Homo. Paludan-Muller, Frederik. LC 81-58568. 1981. 49.95 (ISBN 0-936726-01-6) (ISBN 0-936726-02-4). Twickenham Press.
Adam in Moonshine. John Boynton Priestley. LC 27-4637. 1927. Harper & Brothers.
Adam Johnstone's Son. Francis Marion Crawford. LC 8-31066. 1896. Macmillan and Co.
Adam Johnstones's Son. Francis Marion Crawford. LC 6-310672. 1895. Macmillan and Co.
Adam Kent's Choice. A Novel. Humphrey Elliott. (On cover: The ideal series of American copyright novels). A.L. Burt.
Adam Kent's Choice. A Novel. Humphrey Elliott. (On Cover: The Select Series, No. 66). 1890. Street & Smith.
Adam Link, Robot. Eando Binder, pseud. 1968. pap. 0.60 o.p. (53-763). Paperback Lib.
Adam M-1: A Novel, by William C. Anderson. William C Anderson. LC 64-23805. 1964. Crown Publishers.
Adam of Dublin: A Romance of to-Day. Conal O'Connell O'Riordan. 1920. Harcourt, Brace and Howe.
Adam of the Road. Elizabeth Janet Gray. (Seafarer Book). (Illus.). 1973. 1.50 (ISBN 0-670-05080-6). Viking.
Adam Penfeather, Buccaneer, His Early Exploits: Being a Curicous and Intimate Relation of His Tribulations, Joys and Triumphs Taken from Notes of His Journal and Pages from His Ship's Log, and Here Put into Complete Narrative. Jeffery Farnol. LC 41-440741. 1941. Doubleday, Doran and Co., Inc.
Adam Resurrected. Yoram Kaniak. 1978. 4.95 (ISBN 0-06-090620-0). Harper and Ro W.
Adam Resurrected. Yoram Kaniuk. LC 75-124962. 1971. 8.95. Atheneum.
Adam Rush: A Novel. Lynn Roby Meekins. LC 2-25169. 1902. J. B. Lippincott Company.
Adam Sleep. Winfred Van Atta. LC 79-7781. 1980. 7.95 (ISBN 0-385-06897-2). Published for the Crime Club by Doubleday.
Adam Steele: The Bounty Hunter. George G Gilman. (Steele Series,#2). 1975. (pbk.) 1.25 (ISBN 0-523-00713-2). Pinnacle Books.
Adam, Where Art Thou? Translated by Mervyn Savill. 1stAmerican Ed. Heinrich Boll. LC 55-11022. 1955. Criterion Books.
Adamantine Sherlock Holmes: The Adventures in Tibet & India. Hapi. 144p. 1974. pap. 3.95 (ISBN 0-916926-00-1). Kanthaka.
Adamnan. Jack Hirschman. 1972. pap. 3.00 o.p. (ISBN 0-87922-009-0, Pub. by Christopher's Bks). SBD.
Adam's Apple & Other Stories. Marne Breckensiek. LC 70-151148. 1970. pap. 1.25 o.p. (45080). Liguori Pubns.
Adam's Best Fiction. Ed. by Thomas H. Schulz. (Orig.). pap. 0.95 o.p. (88-129). Holloway.
Adam's Breed. Radclyffe Hall. 1926. Cassell and Company, Ltd.
Adam's Breed. Radclyffe Hall. LC 29-26896. 1929. J. Cape & H. Smith.
Adams Child: A Modern Horror Story. Richard Breen. 1978. 1.95 (ISBN 0-440-10917-5). Dell.
Adam's Clay: A Novel. Cosmo Hamilton. 1908. Brentano's.
Adam's Crusade: An Autumn Fantasy. Lyman V. Rutledge. 180p. 1971. 6.00 o.p. (ISBN 0-682-47359-6). Exposition.
Adam's Daughter. Faye Ashley. 496p. (Orig.). 1982. pap. 3.50 (ISBN 0-8439-1071-2, Leisure Bks). Nordon Pubns.
Adam's Daughters. Julia MacNair Wright. American Tract Society.
Adam's Eden. Faith Baldwin. 202p. Repr. of 1977 ed. lib. bdg. 10.05x (ISBN 0-88411-630-1). Amereon Ltd.
Adam's Eden. Faith Baldwin. LC 76-29898. 1977. 7.95 o.p. (ISBN 0-03-018896-2). HR&W.
Adam's Eden. Faith Baldwin Cuthrell. LC 76-29898. 7.95 (ISBN 0-03-018896-2). Holt, Rinehart and Winston.
Adam's Eden. Faith Baldwin Cuthrell. LC 77-15517. 1977. 10.95 (ISBN 0-8161-6533-5). G. K. Hall.
Adam's First Wife. Jane Speller & Speller, Robert, Joint Author. LC 29-154815. The Macaulay Company.
Adam's Garden: A Novel. Nina Wilcox Putnam. LC 16-9267. 1916. 1.25. J. B. Lippincott Company.
Adams of the Bounty. Wilson, Erie. LC 59-8099. 1959. Criterion Books.
Adam's Rest. Sarah Gertrude Liebson Millin. LC 30-24041. H. Liveright.
Adams' Way. William Laurence Coleman. LC 53-10336. 1953. Dutton.
Adaptable Man. Janet Frame, pseud. LC 65-19327. (O.s.i.). 1965. 4.95 o.s.i. (ISBN 0-8076-0302-3). Braziller.
Ada's Trust. Anna Hanson McKenney Dorsey. LC 42-35713. John Murphy Company.
Add a Dash of Pity. Peter Ustinov. LC 59-11098. 1959. Little, Brown.
Add a Pinch of Cyanide. Emma Page. 224p. 1973. 5.95 o.p. (ISBN 0-8027-5291-8). Walker & Co.
Added Upon. A Story. Nephi Anderson. 1898. Deseret News Publishing Company.
Added Upon: A Story. 5th and enl. ed. Nephi Anderson. LC 12-16361. 1912. 0.75. The Deseret News.
Adders on the Heath. Gladys Mitchell. LC 63-22304. 1963. London House & Maxwell.
Addie Pray: A Novel. Joe David Brown. LC 73-154096. 1971. 6.95 (ISBN 0-671-20962-0). Simon and Schuster.
Addie Was a Lady: The Saga of Grandmother Waterbury. John Wilmot Wiley. LC 62-13919. 1962. St. Martin's Press.
Addie's Husband. Bertha M. Clay. LC 1-30004. (Bertha Clay library, no. 49). 1900. Street & Smith.
Addie's Husband: Or, Through Clouds to Sunshine. Harriet Maria Gordon Smythies. LC 8-10193. (On cover: Seaside library. Pocket ed. no. 388). 1885. G. Munro.
Addison. Leon Hale. LC 77-14892. 1979. 7.95 (ISBN 0-385-12911-4). Doubleday.
Addison Broadhurst, Master Merchant: The Intimate History of a Man Who Came up from Failure. Edward Mott Woolley. LC 13-8905. 1913. Doubleday, Page & Company.
Addison Tradition. John Morressy. LC 68-18069. 1968. Doubleday.
Address: Centauri. 1st Ed. Floyd L Wallace. LC 55-6843. 1955. Gnome Press.
Address of Castro, and Other Tales. Marie Henri Beyle. Tr. by Scott-Moncrieff, Charles Kenneth. LC 26-7899. 1926. Boni & Liveright.
Address Unknown. Malcolm Hutton. LC 81-5762. 1981. 9.95 (ISBN 0-312-00427-3). St. Martin's.
Address Unknown. Taylor, Kressmann. LC 39-147905. 1939. Simon and Schuster.
Addsfish. Robert Hugh Benson. LC 14-18880. 1914. Dodd, Mead and Company.
Adela Cathcart. George Macdonald. LC 42-268863. Loring.
Adela Cathcart. George Macdonald. LC 12-18275. 1911. D. McKay.
Adela Cathcart. A Novel. George Macdonald. (Seaside library. v. 71, no. 1439). 1882. G. Munro.
Adela, the Octoroon. Hezekiah L Hosmer. LC 71-39091. (Black Heritage Library Collection). 1972. (ISBN 0-8369-9029-3). Books for Libraries Press.
Adelaide of Brunswick. Donatien Alphonse Francois Sade. LC 72-11856. 1973. 5.00 (ISBN 0-8108-0574-X). Scarecrow Reprint Corp.
Adelaide of Brunswick: Translated by Hobart Ryland from an Unpublished Manuscript Recently Discovered Among the Papers Left by the Marquis De Sade. Donatien Alphonse Francois Sade. LC 54-9027. 1954. Scarecrow Press.
Adela's Ordeal. Florence Alice Price James. LC 7-7423. (On cover: The authors' library, no. 6). The International News Company.
Adele: A Tale. Julia Kavanagh. LC 7-111149. 1858. D. Appleton and Company.
Adele and Co. Cecil William Mercer. LC 77-354414. (Mercer, Cecil William, 1885-1960. Berry Books). (Illus.). 1976. 3.50 (ISBN 0-7063-1677-0). Ward Lock.
Adele & Co. Cecil William Mercer. LC 31-19684. 1931. Minton, Balch & Company.
Adele Dubois: A Story of the Lovely Miramichi Valley, in New Brunswick. William T. Savage. (On cover: Loring's railway library). Loring.
Adele Hamilton. Delia Buford Elliott. LC 7-14586. 1907. The Neale Publishing Company.
Adeline Gray. A Tale. Hampden Burnham. LC 6-19667. Wynkoop & Hallenbeck.
Adeline Mowbray: Or, The Mother and Daughter. A Tale, in Two Volumes. Amelia Alderson Opie. LC 27-22284. 1808. Dinmore and Cooper, Printers.
Adeline Mowbray: Or, The Mother and Daughter. Amelia Alderson Opie. LC 73-22076. (Feminist Controversy in England, 1788-1810). 1974. (3 vols.) 66.00 (ISBN 0-8240-0874-X). Garland Pub.
Adelita. Oakley M Hall. LC 74-9452. (Illus.). 1975. 8.95 (ISBN 0-385-09731-X). Doubleday.
Adell Waltby. William Salisbury. LC 24-8797. 1924. The Independent Publishing Company.
Adept: A Novel. Michael McClure. LC 79-131923. 1971. 5.95. Delacorte Press.
Ade's Fables. George Ade. LC 14-7488. 1914. Doubleday, Page & Company.
Adieu Aux Armes. Ernest Hemingway. 8.50 o.p.; pap. 1.25 pocket ed. o.p. (16). French & Eur.
Adieu Gary Cooper. Romain Gary, pseud. (Coll. Soleil). 13.95. French & Eur.
Adios! Lanier Bartlett & Bartlett, Virginia Stivers. LC 29-12618. 1929. W. Morrow & Company.
Adios, Bandido! E. Jefferson Clay. Bd. with Desparados on the Loose. 1980. pap. 2.25 (ISBN 0-505-51459-1). Tower Bks.
Adios My Love. new ed. Jason Barb. (Popular Stories Ser). 176p. 1973. pap. 1.95 o.s.i. Pyramid Pr.
Adios, O'Shaughnessy: A Novel. Tallman, Robert. LC 50-8219. 1950. Doubleday.
Adios, Scheherazade. Donald E Westlake. LC 77-107262. 1970. 5.50 (ISBN 0-671-20505-6). Simon and Schuster.
Adios, Scheherazade. Donald E. Westlake. LC 77-107262. (O.S.I.). 1970. 5.50 o.s.i. (ISBN 0-671-20505-6). S&S.
Adipose Complex: A Novel. Paul Deutschman. LC 72-5258. 1972. 7.95. Dial Press.
Adirondack Idyl. Lida Ostrom Vanamee. LC 8-30239. C. T. Dillingham & Co.
Adirondack Romance. Caroline Washburn Rockwood. LC 7-39799. New Amsterdam Book Company.
Adirondack Stories. Philander Deming. LC 68-55672. (American short story series, v. 12). 1969. Garrett Press.
Adirondack Stories. Philander Deming. LC 11-10539. 1880. Houghton, Osgood and Company.
Adirondack Stories. Philander Deming. LC 4-15446. 1902. Houghton, Mifflin and Company.
Adirondack Stories. Philander Deming. 1907. Houghton, Mifflin and Company.
Adirondack Stories. John B. Sanford. LC 76-22612. 1976. 10.00. (ISBN 0-88496-065-X) (ISBN 0-88496-066-8). Capra Press.
Adjacent Lives. Ellen Schwamm. 1979. 2.50 (ISBN 0-380-45211-1). Avon Books.
Adjacent Lives: A Novel. Ellen Schwamm. LC 77-19317. 1978. 8.95 (ISBN 0-394-50142-X). Knopf.
Adjustable Halo. Kenneth Anderson. LC 68-31103. 1968. 5.95. Word Books.
Adjustment. Marguerite Bryant. LC 12-4358. 1912. Duffield and Company.
Adlon, Berlin see Adlon Link.

Adlon Link. Hughes Zachary. (Hotel Destiny Ser.: No. 1). Orig. Title: Adlon, Berlin. 320p. (Orig.). 1981. pap. 2.95 (ISBN 0-515-06046-1). Jove Pubns.

Admen: A Novel. Shepherd Mead. LC 58-9041. 1958. Simon and Schuster.

Admirable and Indefatigable Adventures of the Nine Pious Pilgrims. Richard Franck. LC 72-170515. (Foundations of the Novel). 1973. 22.00 ea. (ISBN 0-8240-0523-6). Garland Publishing.

Admirable & Indefatigable Adventures of the Nine Pious Pilgrims... Written in America. Richard Franck. LC 72-170515. (Foundations of the Novel Ser.: Vol. 11). lib. bdg. 50.00 (ISBN 0-8240-0523-6). Garland Pub.

Admirable Crichton. William Harrison Ainsworth. LC 37-31198. (Half-title: Everyman's library, ed. by Ernest Rhys. Fiction. no. 804). 1927. J. M. Dent & Sons, Ltd.

Admirable Tinker: Child of the World. Edgar Jepson. LC 4-7532. 1904. McClure, Phillips & Co.

Admiral: A Novel. Martin Dibner. LC 67-12850. 1967. Doubleday.

Admiral and the Nuns: With Other Stories. Frank Tuohy. LC 63-106366. 1963. 3.50, 1.65 pap. Scribners.

Admiral Hornblower in the West Indies. Cecil Scott Forester. (Hornblower saga, # 10). 1975. (pbk.) 1.50 (ISBN 0-523-00390-0). Pinnacle Books.

Admiral Hornblower in the West Indies see Indomitable Hornblower.

Admiral's Aid: A Story of Life in the New Navy. Henry Howard Clark. LC 2-19997. 1902. Lothrop Publishing Company.

Admiral's Daughter. Victoria Fyodorova & Haskel Frankel. 1980. pap. 2.50 (ISBN 0-440-10366-5). Dell.

Admiral's Daughter. Judith Harkness. (Orig.). 1980. pap. 1.75 (ISBN 0-451-09161-2, E9161, Sig). NAL.

Admiral's Fancy. Showell Styles. LC 58-12521. 1958. Longmans, Green.

Admiral's Lady. Mary Ann Gibbs, pseud. LC 74-23049. 1975. 6.95 (ISBN 0-88405-099-8). Mason/Charter.

Admiral's Lady. Mary Ann Gibbs, pseud. (Fawcett Crest Book). 1975. (pbk.) 1.25. Fawcett.

Admiral's Light. Henry Milner Rideout. 1907. Houghton, Mifflin and Company.

Admirals on Horseback. Geoffrey Willans. LC 55-78893. 1955. Vanguard Press.

Admiral's Ward. Annie French Hector. (On cover: Lovell's library, v. 3, no. 99). 1883. J. W. Lovell Company.

Admiral's Ward. A Novel. Annie French Hector. (On cover: Seaside library. Pocket ed., no. 5). 1883. G. Munro.

Admiral's Ward. A Novel. Annie French Hector. (Seaside library, v. 79, no. 1595). 1883. G. Munro.

Admiral's Wolfpack. Jean Noli. (World at War Ser.). 1978. pap. 2.25 (ISBN 0-89083-362-1). Zebra.

Admirer Unknown. Amy Roberta Ruck. LC 57-6419. 1957. Dodd, Mead.

Admission to the Feast. Gunnell Beckman. 144p. 1973. pap. 1.25 (ISBN 0-440-90312-2, LFL). Dell.

Admistratrix. Emma Ghent Curtis. LC 6-31713. 1889. J. A. Berry & Company.

Admit Desire. Catherine Lanigan. (Avon Romance Ser.). 352p. 1983. pap. 2.95 (ISBN 0-380-81810-8, 81810-8). Avon.

Admit One: A Novel. Laura Beheler. LC 79-100987. 4.95. Harlo.

Admonitory Hippopotamus. Edward Gorey. (Illus.). 1970. 3.50 o.p. (ISBN 0-396-06244-X). Dodd.

Adnah: A Tale of the Time of Christ. John Breckenridge Ellis. LC 2-25933. 1902. G. W. Jacobs & Co.

Adnam's Orchard. Sarah Grand. LC 12-28703. 1913. 1.30. D. Appleton and Company.

Adobe Doorways. Dorothy L Pillsbury. LC 52-11521. (Illus.). 1952. University of New Mexico Press.

Adobe Walls. William Patterson White. LC 33-3221. 1933. Little, Brown, and Company.

Adobe Walls: A Novel of the Last Apache Rising. 1st Ed. William Riley Burnett. LC 53-683854. 1953. Knopf.

Adobeland Stories. Verner Zevola Reed. LC 98-2199. 1899. R. G. Badger & Co.

Adolescence. Tr. by L. E. LaBan. pap. 1.95 o.p. (6022). Brandon.

Adolescence of P-1. Thomas Joseph Ryan. LC 77-12091. 8.95 (ISBN 0-02-606500-2). Macmillan.

Adolescence of P-1. Thomas Joseph Ryan. LC 77-12092. 1977. 4.95 (ISBN 0-02-024880-6). Collier Books.

Adolescence of P-1. Thomas Joseph Ryan. 1979. 2.25 (ISBN 0-441-00360-5). Ace Books.

Adolescence of Zhenya Luvers. Translated by I. Langnas. Boris Leonidovich Pasternak. LC 61-15246. 1961. Philosophical Library.

Adolescent. Fedor Mikhailovich Dostoevskii. LC 74-144260. 1971. 10.00. Doubleday.

Adolescent. Fedor Mikhailovich Dostoevskii. Tr. by Andrew R. MacAndrew. 608p. 1981. pap. 9.95 (ISBN 0-393-00995-5). Norton.

Adolescent. Fedor Mikhailovich Dostoevskii & Andrew Robert MacAndrew. LC 80-29643. (Norton Paperback Edition). 1981. 8.95 (ISBN 0-393-00995-5). W. W. Norton.

Adolphe. Benjamin Constant. (Classiques Larousse). (Illus., Fr.). pap. 2.95 (59). Larousse.

Adolphe. Benjamin Constant. Tr. by L. W. Tancock. (Penguin Classics). 1980. pap. 3.95 (ISBN 0-14-044134-4). Penguin.

Adolphe. Constant De Rebecque, Henri Benjamin & May, James Lewis, 1873- Tr. LC 46-39315. (The International library). 1925. S. Paul & Co., Ltd.

Adolphe: An Anecdote Found Among the Papers of an Unknown Person. Constant De Rebecque, Henri Benjamin & Walker, Alexander, of Edinburgh, Tr. LC 6-27195. 1817. M. Carey and Son.

Adolphe: An Autobiographical Novel. Constant De Rebecque, Henri Benjamin & Barrett, Mrs. Wilhelmina (Lalor) 1862- Tr. LC 33-3746. 1933. L. MacVeagh, Dial Press, Inc.

Adoniram. first ed.... ed. Alexander Tobias Findlay & Patterson, Susie Emily, 1886- LC 27-240111. 1927. Adoniram Publishing Co.

Adonis Garcia: A Picaresque Novel. Luis Zapata. LC 81-4169. 1981. 20.00 (ISBN 0-917342-79-8) (ISBN 0-917342-80-1). Gay Sunshine Press.

Adopted Daughter. Edgar Fawcett. LC 1-30735. (The Hawthorne library). Hurst & Company.

Adopted Face. Alberta Simpson Carter. (Queen-size gothic). 1975. (pbk.) 1.25. Popular Library.

Adopted Husband: Sono Omokage. Shimei Futabatei. LC 70-94609. 1969. (ISBN 0-8371-2693-2). Greenwood Press.

Adopted: Or, The Serpent Bracelet. A Novel. Laura Eugenia Newhall. LC 7-1173. 1886. Golden Era Co.

Adopted Rebel. B. Palmer. (Lori Adams Ser.). pap. 0.95 o.p. Believers Bkshelf.

Adopted Son: A Legend of the Rebellion of Jack Cade. John Yonge Akerman & Pindar, Paul, Gent., Pseud. LC 1-1527. 1842. Wilson & Company.

Adopters. William Hegner. (Pocket books, 78632). 1974. (pbk.) 1.50. Pockett Books.

Adopting an Abandoned Farm. Katherine Abbott Sanborn. 1891. D. Appleton and Company.

Adopting an Abandoner Farm. Katherine Abbott Sanborn. 1892. D. Appleton and Company.

Adora. Bertrice Small. 440p. 1982. pap. 2.95 (ISBN 0-345-30213-3). Ballantine.

Adora. Bertrice Small. (Orig.). 1980. pap. 2.50 (ISBN 0-345-28493-3). Ballantine.

Adorable Dreamer. Elizabeth Kirby. LC 20-159530. George H. Doran Company.

Adrian Bright. Florence Caddy. LC 6-21866. (Harper's Franklin square library, no. 347). 1883. Harper & Brothers.

Adrian Bright. A Novel. Florence Caddy. (On cover: Seaside library, Pocket ed., no 127). 1884. G. Munro.

Adrian Lyle. Issued in England Under the Title of "Gretchen.". Eliza M. J. Humphreys. (On cover: Seaside library. Pocket ed., no. 1215). 1889. G. Munro.

Adrian: Or, The Clouds of the Mind. A Romance. George Payne Rainsford James & Field, Maunsell Bradhurst. LC 7-7971. 1852. D. Appleton & Company.

Adrian Savage: A Novel. Mary St. Leger Kingsley Harrison. LC 11-25436. 1911. Harper & Brothers.

Adrian Vidal. A Novel. William Edward Norris. (Harper's Franklin square library, no. 475). 1885. Harper & Brothers.

Adrian Vidal. A Novel. William Edward Norris. (On cover: Seaside library. Pocket ed. no. 500). 1885. G. Munro.

Adrians. George Dyer. LC 39-7082. 1939. C. Scribner's Sons.

Adriatic Formula. Mira Lederer. 1980. pap. 1.95 (ISBN 0-8439-0829-7). Nordon Pubns.

Adrien: Or, Parent Power. new ed. Annette Marie Maillard. LC 52-467849. (Routledge's original novels). 1857. Routledge.

Adrienne. Mary Lavinia Thompson Hoy. LC 6-46252. 1906. The Neale Publishing Company.

Adrienne. Barbara Levy. LC 60-13227. 1960. Holt, Rinehart and Winston.

Adrienne. Barbara Levy. LC 60-13227. (Berkley medallion book). 1975. (pbk.) 1.50 (ISBN 0-425-02770-8). Berkley Pub. Co.

Adrienne De Portalis: A Novel. Archibald Clavering Gunter. (On cover: The welcome series, no. 54). The Home Publishing Company.

Adrienne Toner. Anne Douglas Sedgwick. LC 22-9191. 1922. Houghton Mifflin Company.

Adrienne Toner: A Novel. Anne Douglas Sedgwick. LC 75-145287. 1970. Scholarly Press.

Adrienne's House. Lari Field Siler. LC 78-13163. (Illus.). 8.95 (ISBN 0-03-044076-9). Holt, Rinehart, and Winston.

Adrietta: Or, Her Grandfather's Heiress. A Novel. Mary Kyle Dallas. LC 6-33183. G. Munro.

Adrift. Sara Ware Bassett. LC 54-6784. 1954. Doubleday.

Adrift. Anna Hanson McKenney Dorsey. LC 6-33715. 1887. J. Murphy & Co.

Adrift. Anna Hanson McKenney Dorsey. LC 44-228443. John Murphy Company.

Adrift. Tristan Jones. 288p. 1983. pap. 2.95 (ISBN 0-380-62455-9, Discus). Avon.

Adrift: A Story of Niagara. Julia Evelyn Ditto Young. LC 9-119986. 1889. J. B. Lippincott Company.

Adrift in a Boneyard. Robert Lewis Taylor. LC 47-30281. 1947. Doubleday & Company, Inc.

Adrift in New York: And The World Before Him. Horatio Alger. Ed. by William Coyle. LC 66-23257. (Popular American fiction). 1966. Odyssey Press.

Adrift in Soho. Colin Wilson. LC 61-15179. 1961. Houghton Mifflin.

Adrift in the Ice-Fields. Charles Winslow Hall. LC 43-26608. 1877. Lee and Shephard.

Adrift in the Pacific. Jules Verne. 3.95. Assoc Bk.

Adrift in the Unknown: Or, Queer Adventures in a Queer Realm. William Wallace Cook. LC 74-15957. (Science Fiction). 1975. 17.00 (ISBN 0-405-06283-4). Arno Press.

Adrift in the Wilds: Or, The Adventures of Two Ship-Wrecked Boys. Edward Sylvester Ellis. (On cover: Boys' home library, v. 1, no. 3). 1887. A. L. Burt.

Adrift on the Black Wild Tide. 2d ed. James Johnson Kane. LC 3-28163. 1879. J. B. Lippincott & Co.

Adrift on the Pacific: A Boys Story of the Sea and Its Perils. Edward Sylvester Ellis. LC 11-9903. (Burt's library of the world's best books). 1.00. A. L. Burt Company.

Adrift Upon the World: A Novel. Bertha N Clay. LC 7-16120. E. A. Weeks Company.

Adrift Upon the World: A Novel. Bertha N Clay. LC 99-1647. (phoenix series. no. 11). 1899. E. A. Weeks Co.

Adrift with a Vengeance: A Tale of Love and Adventure. Kinahan Cornwallis. LC 6-28730. 1870. Carleton; Etc., Etc.

Adrift with a Vengeance: A Tale of Love and Adventure. Kinahan Cornwallis. (On cover: Lovell's library, v. 8, no. 409). 1884. J. W. Lovell Company.

Adrigoole. Peadar O'Donnell. LC 29-16822. 1929. G. P. Putnam's Sons.

Ads Infinitum. T. Wayman. (Orig.). 1971. pap. 0.75 o.p. (07130). Curtis.

Adult Education. Annette Williams Jaffee. LC 80-84834. 12.95 (ISBN 0-86538-007-4). Ontario Review Press.

Adult Education. Annette Williams Jaffee. LC 82-8445. 1982. 6.95 (ISBN 0-446-37192-0). Warner Books.

Adult Western. 1980. pap. 1.95 (ISBN 0-671-83435-5). PB.

Adult Western: Threes Are Wild. Zeke Masters, pseud. 1980. pap. 1.95 (ISBN 0-671-83426-6). PB.

Adulteress. Norah E Dunn. LC 27-152190. The MacGregor Company.

Adulteress. Jean Plaidy. LC 81-15874. (Illus.). 12.95 (ISBN 0-399-12680-5). Putnam.

Adulteress. Jean Plaidy. LC 83-216. 1983. 19.95 (ISBN 0-8161-3513-4). G.K. Hall.

Adultery. John London. LC 95-1073. (Orig.). 1969. pap. 0.95 o.p. (B95-1073). Belmont-Tower.

Adultery Accepted. (Illus.). 4.95 (ISBN 0-910550-26-3). Centurion Pr.

Adultery & Other Choices. Andre Dubus. LC 77-78392. 1977. 8.95 (ISBN 0-87923-213-7). D. R. Godine.

Adultery by Consent. Gerald Summers. pap. 1.95 o.p. (ISBN 0-87056-225-8, 6225). Brandon.

Adultress. Philippa Carr, pseud. 336p. 1982. 12.95 (ISBN 0-399-12680-5). Putnam Pub Group.

Adult's Story. Robert Desmond. 1968. pap. 1.25 o.s.i. (213, Travellers Comp). Olympia.

Advance Agent. Bernard Augustine De Voto. LC 41-28072. 1942. Little, Brown and Company.

Advance Agent. Bernard Augustine De Voto. LC 41-28072. 1942. Little, Brown and Company.

Advanced Wizard. (Fantasy Trip Ser.). 1980. pap. write for info. (ISBN 0-88074-452-9). Metagam.

Advances of Harriet. Phyllis Bottome. LC 33-548450. 1933. Houghton Mifflin Company.

Advancing Paul Newman. Eleanor Bergstein. LC 73-3952. 1973. 7.95 (ISBN 0-670-10518-X). Viking Press.

Advancing Paul Newman. Eleanor Bergstein. 1976. (pbk.) 1.75. Popular Library.

Advancing South. Edwin Mims. 319p. 1979. Repr. of 1927 ed. lib. bdg. 25.00 (ISBN 0-89987-552-1). Darby Bks.

Advantages of Education: Or, The History of Maria Williams. Jane West. LC 73-22104. (Feminist Controversy in England, 1788-1810). (Illus.). 1974. (2 vols.) 44.00 (ISBN 0-8240-0883-9). Garland Pub.

Advent of Frederick Giles. Josiah Bunting. LC 73-18340. 1974. 6.95 (ISBN 0-316-11490-1). Little, Brown.

Adventrues of School-Boys. Coryell, John Russell & Ditto, Margaret Emma. LC 11-8954. 1911. Harper & Brothers.

Adventure. Borden Deal. LC 77-74297. 1978. 8.95 (ISBN 0-385-05227-8). Doubleday.

Adventure. Jack London. LC 11-3945. 1911. 1.50. The Macmillan Company.

Adventure Among the Rosicrucians. Franz Hartmann. LC 7-3657. 1887. Occult Publishing Co.

Adventure and Fomance in the Dells and Vallys of Sweden: Including When Lucifer Kidnapped Kristina from the City of Mora, on Lake Siljan... John S Anderson. LC 59-708156. 1959. Christopher Pub. House.

Adventure Calls. Katharine Woolley. LC 29-9006. 1929. Minton, Balch & Company.

Adventure for Lisa: By Bennie C. Hall. Bennie Caroline Hall. LC 64-7368. 1964. Arcadia House.

Adventure Holidays, Ltd. Leslie Purnell Davies. LC 78-103739. 1970. 3.95. Doubleday.

Adventure in a Model T and Other Dud Dean Stories. Arthur Raymond Macdougall. LC 80-25752. (Illus.). 3.95 (ISBN 0-89621-063-4). Thorndike Press.

Adventure in Diamonds. David Esdaile Walker. LC 56-10084. (Illus.). 1956. W. W. Norton.

Adventure in Exile: A Sentimental Comedy. Richard Duffy. LC 8-33153. 1908. B. W. Dodge & Company.

Adventure in Pyramids: A Novelette. William Hempstead Porterfield. LC 28-113932. 1928. A. & C. Boni.

Adventure in Survival. Maurice Beam. (Illus.). 1967. Putnam.

Adventure in the Night. Francis Warrington Dawson. LC 29-30767. 1924. N. Y., Doubleday, Page & Company.

Adventure in the Rich Port. Gerald Dorset. LC 76-62622. 3.95 (ISBN 0-918258-01-4). New Earth Books.

Adventure in the Sky: By Arch Whitehouse. Arthur George Joseph Whitehouse. 1961. Duell, Sloan and Pearce.

Adventure in Thule. A Story for Young People. William Black. LC 21-13961. (Seaside library, v. 70, no. 1429). 1882. G. Munro.

Adventure in Thule: And Marriage of Moria ! Fergus. William Black. LC 6-12943. (Lovell's library, v. 2, no. 40). J. W. Lovell Company.

Adventure in Time. Ilija Poplasen. LC 76-170934. 1972. 4.50 o.p. (ISBN 0-8059-1605-9). Dorrance.

Adventure in Washington. Leo Calvin Rosten. LC 40-27019. Harcourt, Brace and Company.

Adventure into the Unknown. A. R. Simpson. 2.50 o.p. Carlton.

Adventure of a Prodigal Father. Frank Hobart Cheley. LC 17-2024. 1916. Association Press.

Adventure of Christopher Columin. Sylvia Thompson. LC 39-27056. 1939. Little, Brown and Company.

Adventure of Cobbler's Rune. Ursula K. Le Guin. (Adventures in Kroy: No. 1). (Illus.). 36p. (Orig.). 1982. signed casebound numbered ed. 75.00 (ISBN 0-941826-00-7). Cheap St.

Adventure of Hadrian Hedgehog. Candida L. Green. LC 78-93804. (Illus.). 1970. 3.50 o.p. (ISBN 0-695-85296-5). Follett.

Adventure of "Horse" Barnsby. Philip Duffield Stong. LC 56-8096. 1956. Doubleday.

Adventure of Mr. Mocker. Thornton Burgess. 120p. 1977. Repr. of 1914 ed. lib. bdg. 12.95x (ISBN 0-89966-271-4). Buccaneer Bks.

Adventure of Princess Sylvia. Alice Muriel Livingston Williamson. LC 10-9512. 1909. The Metropolitan Press.

Adventure of the Blue Carbuncle: With an Introd. by Christopher Morley. Arthur Conan Doyle & Smith, Edgar Wadsworth, 1894- Ed. LC 49-1508. 1948. Baker Street Irregulars.

Adventure of the Eleven Cuff-Buttons. James F. Thierry. 1979. pap. 6.50 (ISBN 0-915230-14-3). Rue Morgue.

Adventure of the Eleven Cuff-Buttons: Being One of the Exciting Episodes in the Career of the Famous Detective Hemlock Holmes. James Francis Thierry. 1918. The Neale Publishing Company.

Adventure of the Lost Manuscripts & One Other. Edmund Lester Pearson. LC 75-318798. (Illus.). 1974. 4.00. Aspen Press.

Adventure of the Marked Man and One Other: Two Sherlock Holmes Pastiches & an Introduction. Stuart Palmer. LC 74-170374. (Illus.). 1973. 4.00. Aspen Press.

Adventure of the Orient Express. Illus. by Henry Lauritzen. August William Derleth. LC 65-4729. (His Solar Pons books). pap., 3.00. Candlelight Pr., E. Th St.

Adventure of the Peerless Peer. Philip Jose Farmer. LC 75-314225. 1974. 5.50. Aspen Press.

Adventure of the Six Napoleons. Arthur Conan Doyle. LC 17-24712. P. F. Collier & Son.

Adventure of the Speckled Band & Other Stories of Sherlock Holmes. Conan Doyle. (RL 6). pap. 1.95 (ISBN 0-451-51642-7, CJ1642, Sig Classics). NAL.

Adventure of the Stalwart Companions: Heretofore Unpublished Letters and Papers Concerning a Singular Collaboration Between Theodore Roosevelt and Sherlock Holmes. Harry Paul Jeffers. LC 78-2060. 8.95 (ISBN 0-06-012248-X). Harper & Row.

Adventure of the Unique Dickensians. August William Derleth. LC 68-7901. (Illus.). 1968. 1.50. Mycroft & Moran.

Adventure or Experience: Four Essays on Certain Writers and Readers of Novels. Dorothy Brewster & Burrell, John Angus, Joint Author. LC 31-512. 1930. Columbia University.

Adventure Westward. Eric Acland. (Illus.). 1967. T. Nelson.

Adventure with the Apaches. Louis De Bellemare. LC 1-30696. 1901. Benziger Bros.

Adventure with Women. Sophie Kerr. LC 38-8560. Farrar & Rineheart, Incorporated.

Adventurer. Beverly Byrne. 480p. 1982. pap. 2.95 (ISBN 0-449-14452-6, GM). Fawcett.

Adventurer. Barbara Cartland. 1977. pap. 1.50 o.p. (ISBN 0-515-03987-X). BJ Pub Group.

Adventurer. Rudolf Herzog. LC 12-22874. 1.25. D. Fitz-Gerald, Inc.

Adventurer. Lloyd Osbourne. LC 7-31207. 1907. D. Appleton and Company.

Adventurer. Mika Toimi Waltari. LC 50-9498. 1950. Putnam.

Adventurer in Spain. Samuel Rutherford Crockett. LC 70-106282. (Short story index reprint series). (Illus.). 1970. (ISBN 0-8369-3319-2). Books for Libraries Press.

Adventurer in Spain. Samuel Rutherford Crockett. LC 4-2539. 1904. F. A. Stokes Company.

Adventurer of the North: Being a Continuation of the Histories of "Pierre and His People," and the Latest Existing Records of Pretty Pierre. Gilbert Parker. LC 74-98589. (Short story index reprint series). 1969. Books for Libraries Press.

Adventurer of the North: Being a Continuation of the Histories of "Pierre and His People," and the Latest Existing Records of Pretty Pierre. Gilbert Parker. LC 7-34999. 1895. Stone & Kimball.

Adventurer of the North: Being a Continuation of the Histories of "Pierre and His People," and the Latest Existing Records of Pretty Pierre. Gilbert Parker. LC 4-15147. 1898. The Macmillan Company.

Adventurer of the North: Being a Continuation of the Histories of "Pierre and His People,". Gilbert Parker. LC 44-30998. 1896. Stone & Kimball.

Adventurer of the North: Being a Continuation of the Histories of "Pierre and His People,". Gilbert Parker. LC 45-26388. 1897. Stone & Kimball.

Adventurer: Or, The Wreck on the Indian Ocean. A Land and Sea Tale. Maturin Murray Ballou. LC 6-6096. 1848. F. Gleason.

Adventureras. Luisa Estrella. (Pimienta Collection Ser). 160p. (Span.). 1974. pap. 1.00 (ISBN 0-88473-206-1). Fiesta Pub.

Adventurers. Ernest Haycox. LC 54-5140. 1975. (pbk.) 1.50. New American Library.

Adventurers. Ernest Haycox. LC 76-6515. 1976. (ISBN 0-89190-971-0). Rivercity Press.

Adventurers. Jane Aiken Hodge. LC 65-12819. 4.95. Doubleday.

Adventurers. Jane Aiken Hodge. (AFawcett Crest Book). 1978. 1.95 (ISBN 0-449-23451-7). Fawcett Books.

Adventurers. Harold Robbins. 1977. pap. 3.95 (ISBN 0-671-41707-X). PB.

Adventurers. Harold Robbins. 1966. 5.95 o.p. (01118). Trident.

Adventurers. Harold Rubin. LC 66-16179. 5.95. Trident.

Adventurers see Royal Gamble.

Adventurers: A Story. Adelaide Blenus Collins. LC 28-328. Lakeview Press.

Adventurers. A Story of a Love-Chase. Gustave Aimard & St. John, Percy Bolingbroke, 1821-1889, Ed. 1885. J.W. Lovell Company.

Adventurers: A Tale of Treasure Trove. Henry Brereton Marriott Watson. LC 96-1697. 1899. Harper & Brothers.

Adventurers All. John Buchan. 6.95 o.p. HM.

Adventurers All: Sir Richard Hannay, Sir Edward Leithen and Others... John Buchan. LC 43-6807. 1942. Houghton Mifflin Company.

Adventurers: By Harold Robbins. Harold Rubin. (Cardinal ed., 12501). 1966. pap., 1.25. Pocket Bks.

Adventurers of the Night. LC 21-155079. George H. Doran Company.

Adventurers. 1st Ed. Ernest Haycox. LC 54-5140. 1954. Little, Brown.

Adventures Among the Toroids. 2nd ed. B. M. Stewart. LC 73-14167. 1980. pap. 12.50. B M Stewart.

Adventures and Exploits of the Younger Brothers. Missouri's Most Daring Outlaws... Henry Dale. (Secret service series, no. 32). 1890. Street & Smith.

Adventures & Memoirs of Sherlock Holmes. Arthur Conan Doyle. 1946. 3.95 o.s.i. (ISBN 0-394-60206-4, M206). Modern Lib.

Adventures, Blizzards & Coastal Calamities. Edward R. Snow. LC 78-23316. (Illus.). 1978. 8.95 (ISBN 0-396-07634-3). Dodd.

Adventures by Sea and Land of the Count De Ganay; or: The Devotion and Fidelity of Woman. An Episode of the Colonization of Canada. Henry Emile Chevalier. LC 6-21343. 1863. J. Bradburn.

Adventure's End. John Harris. LC 59-765918. 1959. W. Sloane Associates.

Adventures for Readers, Bks. 1 & 2. Elizabeth C. O'Daly & Egbert W. Nieman. (Adventures in Literature Ser: Olympic Ed). (gr. 7-8). text ed. 3.90 Bk. 1. gr. 7. s.p. o.p.; text ed. 4.08 Bk. 2. gr. 8. o.p.; reading wkshops with tests. 0.90 ea., record albums 1 & 2. 6.00 ea o.p. HarBraceJ.

Adventures in Contentment. Ray Stannard Baker. LC 7-400343. 1907. Doubleday, Page & Company.

Adventures in Contentment. Ray Stannard Baker. LC 33-17489. 1910. Doubleday, Page & Company.

Adventures in Darkness. Derek Gill & Tom Sullivan. 1976. 7.95 o.p. (ISBN 0-679-20377-X). McKay.

Adventures in Friendship. Ary Stannard Baker. LC 10-25879. 1910. Doubleday, Pag & Company.

Adventures in Heaven. Charles Angoff. LC 45-9503. 1945. B. Ackerman, Incorporated.

Adventures in High Fantasy. Jeffery Dillow. 1981. 14.95 (ISBN 0-8359-0165-3); pap. 12.95 (ISBN 0-8359-0164-5). Reston.

Adventures in Mashonaland. R. Blennerhassett & I. Sleeman. (Rhodesiana Reprint Library Ser.: Vol. 8). (Illus.). 1969. Repr. 16.00x (ISBN 0-8426-1170-3). Verry.

Adventures in Oatmeal: By George Vermont Pseud. Donald G Smith. LC 52-11906. 1953. Vantage Press.

Adventures in Sakaeland. Martin Louis Alan Gompertz. LC 77-84226. (Lost Race and Adult Fantasy Fiction). (Illus.). 1978. 40.00 (ISBN 0-405-10978-4). Arno Press.

Adventures in Southern Seas: A Tale of the Sixteenth Century. George Forbes. LC 20-16854. 1920. Dodd, Mead and Company.

Adventures in Story Land: A Collection of Short Stories, with an Intro- Introduction by A.B. De Mille. De Mille., Albun Bertram, 1873- LC 32-16551. (On cover: Aendems classics). Allyn and Bacon.

Adventures in the Land of the Behemoth. Fully Illustrated by Ferat. Jules Verne. LC 1-9779. 1874. H. L. Shepard.

Adventures in the Minds of Men. Lynn Harold Hough. LC 27-24560. The Abingdon Press.

Adventures in the Skin Trade see Collected Prose.

Adventures in the Skin Trade, and Other Stories. Dylan Thomas. LC 55-7367. 1955. New Directions.

Adventures in the Skin Trade, and Other Stories. Dylan Thomas. LC 64-25441. (New Directions paperbook, no. 183). 1964. New Directions Pub. Corp.

Adventures in the West. Jane V. Barker & Sybil Downing. (Colorado Heritage Ser.: Bk. 5). (Illus.). 45p. (gr. 3-4). 1979. pap. text ed. 3.50x (ISBN 0-87108-220-9). Pruett.

Adventures in Time and Space: An Anthology of Modern Science-Fiction Stories. Ed. by Raymond J. Healy. McComas, J. Francis, Joint Ed. LC 46-7121. 1946. Random House.

Adventures in Tomorrow: By Ward Moore and Others. Ed. by Kendell Foster Crossen. LC 51-3719. (Corwin book). 1951. Greenberg.

Adventures in Understanding. Ray Stannard Baker. LC 25-20632. 1925. Doubleday, Page & Company.

Adventures of a Bank-Note. Thomas Bridges. LC 74-34358. (Flowering of the Novel). 1975. 25.00 (ISBN 0-8240-1189-9). Garland Pub.

Adventures of a Bashful Bachelor. Clara Augusta Jones. LC 7-12134. (peerless series, no. 28). 1890. J. S. Ogilvie.

Adventures of a Casket. An Episode of the Invasion of 1814. Just Jean Etienne Roy. LC 8-952. Benziger Brothers.

Adventures of a Cork-Screw. LC 74-26890. (Flowering of the Novel). 1975. (ISBN 0-8240-1206-2). Garland Pub.

Adventures of a Fakir. Vsevolod Viacheslavovich Ivanov. LC 74-10085. 1975. 17.00 (ISBN 0-88355-172-1). Hyperion Press.

Adventures of a Forgotten Man. James S. Doran. 2.00 o.p. Carlton.

Adventures of a Freshman. Jesse Lynch Williams. LC 99-5363. C. Scribner's Sons.

Adventures of a Hackney Coach. the 4th ed. ... ed. LC 5-42181. Reprinted and Sold by Enoch Story, in Strawberry Alley, About Mid-Way.

Adventures of a Jesuit. LC 74-18289. (Flowering of the Novel). 1974. 25.00 (ISBN 0-8240-1193-7). Garland Pub.

Adventures of a Kidnapped Orphan. LC 74-16068. (Flowering of the Novel). 1974. (ISBN 0-8240-1120-1). Garland Pub.

Adventures of a Marquis. Alexandre Dumas. (Seaside library, v. 17, no. 331). G. Munro.

Adventures of a Marquis. A Novel. Alexandre Dumas. LC 24-14942. T. B. Peterson & Brothers.

Adventures of a Medical Student. Robert Douglas. LC 6-35884. 1848. Burgess, Stringer, & Co.

Adventures of a Modest Man. Robert William Chambers. LC 11-2973. 1911. 1.30. D. Appleton and Company.

Adventures of a Naval Officer: A Narrative. Archibald Clavering Gunter. The Home Publishing Company.

Adventures of a Nice Young Man: A Novel. Pseud Aix. LC 8-26194. 1908. Duffield & Company.

Adventures of a Philosopher: A Dun Mule, and a Brindle Dog. Henry C Fox. LC 6-43278. 1888. M. Cullaton & Co.

Adventures of a Runaway. Grundvald Miller. 6.95 o.p. Vantage.

Adventures of a Rustic. Leroy Stoner. LC 8-16292. 1888. Press of Ramsey, Millett & Hudson.

Adventures of a School Boy see New Epicureans.

Adventures of a Seventeen-Year-Old Lad and the Fortunes He Might Have Won. John G. Williams. 1894. Printed for the Author by the Collins Press.

Adventures of a Skeleton. A Tale of Natural Gas. Beecher Wesley Waltermire. (On cover: The peerless series, no. 2). J. S. Ogilvie.

Adventures of a Suburbanite. Ellis Parker Butler. LC 11-288175. 1911. Doubleday, Page & Company.

Adventures of a Supercargo. Louis Becke. LC 27-1856. 1925. J. B. Lippincott Company.

Adventures of a Tenderfoot. Halbert H Sauber. LC 99-5236. 1899. Pub. for the Author by the Whitaker & Ray Company.

Adventures of a Tramp. John Spollon. LC 8-14049. 1897. J. Spollon.

Adventures of a Virginian. Henry Flanders. LC 6-41132. 1881. E. Claxton & Co.

Adventures of a Widow: A Novel. Edgar Fawcett. LC 6-38958. 1884. J. R. Osgood and Comapny.

Adventures of a Young Girl: A Romance. Marion Phelan. LC 14-18305. 0.25. The Vail-Ballou Co.

Adventures of a Young Man. John Dos Passos. LC 39-27434. Harcourt, Brace and Company.

Adventures of a Young Man: Short Stories from Life. John Reed. LC 75-14275. (Series: Seven Seas Books.). 1975. 3.00 (ISBN 0-87286-083-3). City Lights Books.

Adventures of a Young Outlaw. Thomas J Bontly. LC 73-87177. 1974. 6.95 (ISBN 0-399-11248-0). Putnam.

Adventures of a Younger Son. a new ed., with an introd. by edward garnett. london, t. f. unwin; new york, macmillan, 1890. ed. Edward John Trelawny. LC 70-177569. 1973. 18.00 (ISBN 0-404-07448-0). AMS Press.

Adventures of a Younger Son. Edward John Trelawny. LC 74-189509. (Oxford English novels). (Illus.). 1974. 17.75 (ISBN 0-19-255361-5). Oxford University Press.

Adventures of a Younger Son. Edward John Trelawny. LC 33-24664. (Half-title: The world's classics. 288). H. Milford, Oxford University Press.

Adventures of Abel Blow. A Circumstantial Narrative. Nelson Ayers. LC 6-3851. (On cover: Pastime series, no. 170). Laird & Lee.

Adventures of Achilles Jones. (Orig.). 1979. 10.00 (ISBN 0-914476-81-5); pap. 5.00x (ISBN 0-914476-80-7). Thorp Springs.

Adventures of Alli Baba of Ispahan, 2 vols. James Justinian Morier. 1978. Repr. of 1895 ed. lib. bdg. 75.00 set (ISBN 0-8495-3753-3). Arden Lib.

Adventures of Alonso. Thomas Atwood Digges. LC 74-104439. 1970. (ISBN 0-8398-0362-1). Literature House.

Adventures of an Author (Anonymous). LC 74-17295. (Flowering of the Novel). 1974. (ISBN 0-8240-1176-7). Garland Pub.

Adventures of an East-India Rupee. Wherein Are Interspersed, Various Anecdotes Asiatic and European... Helenus Scott. LC 10-3729. 1783. Printed by R. Bell.

Adventures of an Elephant Boy. Leonard Patrick O'Connor Wibberley. LC 68-29613. 1968. 3.95. W. Morrow.

Adventures of an Enthusiast. Ernest Everett Day. 1907. The Tri-State Publishing Co.

Adventures of an Evangelist. A Circumstantial Narrative of Commonplace Events. Nelson Ayers. LC 6-3850. 1892. Laird & Lee.

Adventures of an Officer in the Service of Runjeet Singh. Henry Montgomery Lawrence. LC 75-325332. (Oxford in Asia historical reprints from Pakistan). (Illus.). 1975. 19.50 (ISBN 0-19-577196-6). Oxford University Press.

Adventures of an Old Maid. Belle C Greene. LC 6-45556. J. S. Ogilvie and Company.

Adventures of an Oldtimer, As Told to His Wife. Lela H. Roberts. 3.75 o.p. Vantage.

Adventures of an Ugly Girl. George Corbett. LC 6-30859. (On cover: Once-a-week library, vol. xi, no. 10). 1893. P. F. Collier.

Adventures of Antar. Antar. Ed. by H. T. Norris. (Approaches to Arabic Literature Ser.: No. 3). (Illus.). 254p. 30.00x (ISBN 0-89410-304-0, Pub. by Aris & Phillips England). Three Continents.

Adventures of Antar: An Early Arab Epic. H. T. Norris. (Approaches to Arabic Literature: No. 3). 264p. 1980. text ed. 35.00x (ISBN 0-85668-161-X, Pub. by Aris & Phillips England). Humanities.

Adventures of Antoine. H Collinson Owen. LC 22-9669. The James A. McCann Company.

Adventures of Arnold Adair. American Ace. Laurence La Tourette Driggs. LC 18-9773. 1918. Little, Brown and Company.

Adventures of Arthur Artfully. Peter Patent. 1975. 6.95x o.s.i. (ISBN 0-8277-4122-7). British Bk Ctr.

Adventures of Augie March. Saul Bellow. 1977. pap. 3.50 (ISBN 0-380-00961-7, 54924). Avon.

Adventures of Augie March. Saul Bellow. 1953. 12.95 (ISBN 0-670-10602-X). Viking Pr.

Adventures of Augie March. With an Introd. by Lionel Trilling. Saul Bellow. LC 65-6643. (modern Library of the world's best books). 1965. Modern Libray.

Adventures of Baby Penrose-the Richest Infant in the World: Being the Tales of Life in Silicone City in the Early Nineteen Nineties. 2nd ed. Daniel Dove. (Orig.). 1980. pap. 10.00. Tetragrammaton.

Adventures of Baron Munchausen. Munchausen. English. LC 2-17550. T. Y. Crowell & Co.

Adventures of Baron Munchausen. Munchausen. English. LC 37-1581. 1936. Three Sirens Press.

Adventures of Baron Munchausen. Munchausen. English & Dore, Gustave, 1832-1883, Illus. LC 37-1581. 1931. Three Sirens Press.

Adventures of Baron Munchausen. Munchausen. English & Dore, Gustave, 1832-1883, Illus. LC 44-47224. 1944. Pantheon Books Inc.

Adventures of Blackshirt. Graham Montague Jeffries. LC 29-22049. 1929. Dodd, Mead & Company.

Adventures of Brigadier Gerard. Sir Arthur Conan Doyle. 1976. 1.75. Belmont Tower Books.

Adventures of Brigadier Gerard. Conan A. Doyle. (O.s.i.). 1976. pap. 1.75 o.s.i. (BT51100). Belmont-Tower.

Adventures of Bumpy. first ed. Robert Babbitt. 1974. 4.50 (ISBN 0-682-47830-X). Exposition Press.

Adventures of Buster Bear. Thornton Waldo Burgess. LC 16-9577. (Bedtime story-books). 1916. Little, Brown, and Company.

Adventures of Butch & Pillow. Mary M. Jones. 2.95 o.p. Vantage.

Adventures of Caleb Williams. William Godwin. 1856. Harper & Brothers.

Adventures of Caleb Williams. William Godwin. LC 26-9576. (rogues' bookshelf). 1926. Greenberg.

Adventures of Caleb Williams. William Godwin. LC 43-46670. 1870. Harper & Brothers.

Adventures of Caleb Williams: Or, Things As They Are. William Godwin. LC 7-3513. 1849. J. A. & U. P. James.

Adventures of Caleb Williams, or, Things As They Are. William Godwin. LC 67-71435. 1966. 7.95 (ISBN 0-304-91758-3). Dufour.

Adventures of Caleb Williams or Things As They Are. William Godwin. Ed. by Herbert Van Thal. (First Novel Library). 1969. 4.25 o.p. (ISBN 0-304-91758-3); pap. 2.25 o.p. Dufour.

Adventures of Captain Farrago. Hugh Henry Brackenridge. LC 45-45399. T. B. Peterson and Brothers.

Adventures of Captain Grief. Rev. Ed. Jack London. LC 54-5350. 1954. World Pub. Co.

Adventures of Captain Hatteras. Introd. by Commander Finn Ronne. Jules Verne. LC 51-12857. Didier.

Adventures of Captain Haylestone. Alan Easton. LC 75-320634. (ISBN 0-07-082177-1). McGraw-Hill Ryerson.

Adventures of Captain Horn. Frank Richard Stockton. LC 9-925. 1899. C. Scribner's Sons.

Adventures of Captain Horn. Frank Richard Stockton. LC 4-16109. 1901. C. Scribner's Sons.

Adventures of Captain Horn. Frank Richard Stockton. LC 8-2938. 1907. C. Scribner's Sons.

Adventures of Captain Horn. Frank Richard Stockton. LC 21-13945. 1908. C. Scribner's Sons.

Adventures of Captain Kettle. Charles John Cutcliffe Wright Hyne. LC 98-243. 1898. Doubleday & McClure Company.

Adventures of Captain Kettle. Charles John Cutcliffe Wright Hyne. LC 4-905. G. W. Dillingham Company.

Adventures of Captain McCargo. William Ratigan. LC 56-5213. 1956. Random House.

Adventures of Captain Mago: Or, A Phoenician Expedition, B. C. 1000, by Leon Cahun. Leon I. E. David Leon Cahun. Tr. by Frewer, Ellen Elizabeth. LC 14-22472. 1889. C. Scribner's Sons.

Adventures of Captain O'Shea. Ralph Delahaye Paine. LC 13-19330. 1913. 1.35. C. Scribner's Sons.

Adventures of Captain Simon Suggs. Johnson Jones Hooper. Repr. of 1845 ed. lib. bdg. 9.50x o.p. (ISBN 0-8398-0789-9). Gregg.

Adventures of Captain Simon Suggs, Late of the Tallapoosa Volunteers. Johnson Jones Hooper. LC 77-89949. (Southern literary classics series). (Illus.). 1969. University of North Carolina Press.

Adventures of Charles Edward. Harrison Garfield Rhodes. LC 8-13950. 1908. Little, Brown, and Company.

Adventures of Charlie Bates. James D Houston. LC 75-315463. (Illus.). 1973. 3.75 (ISBN 0-912264-56-X) (ISBN 0-912264-55-1). Capra Press.

Adventures of Chet Blake-Plastic Man. Richard Weekley. LC 75-21445. (Illus.). 1975. (pbk.) 3.95 (ISBN 0-89144-008-9). Crescent.

Adventures of Claudia. Joan Cabot. pap. 1.95 o.p. (ISBN 0-87056-248-7, 6248). Brandon.

Adventures of Col. Gracchus Vanderbomb, of Sloughcreek, in Pursuit of the Presidency: Also the Exploits of Mr. Numerius Plutarch Kipps, His Private Secretary. John Beauchamp Jones. 1852. A. Hart.

Adventures of Colonel Sellers: Being Mark Twain's Share of The Gilded Age; a Novel Which He Wrote with Charles Dudley Warner. Now Published Separately for the First Time and Comprising, in Effect, a New Work. Ed., Introd., Notes by Charles Neider. Samuel Langhorne Clemens. Ed. by Charles Neider. Samuel Langhorne Clemens. 4.95. New York.

Adventures of Colonel Sellers, Being Mark Twain's Share of The Gilded Age 1st Ed., 1st Issue a Novel Which He Wrote with Charles Dudley Warner. Now Published Separately for the First Time and Comprising, in Effect, a New Work. Edited and with an Introd. and Notes by Charles Neider. Samuel Langhorne Clemens. Ed. by Charles Neider. Samuel Langhorne Clemens. LC 65-11053. 1965. Doubleday.

Adventures of Cousin Clemmy. 1st Ed. Gene Deadrick Robinson. LC 56-12204. 1957. Vantage Press.

Adventures of Creighton Holmes. Ned Hubbell. 1.95 (ISBN 0-445-04350-4). Popular Library.

Adventures of Cyrano De Bergerac: Translated from the French of Louis Gallet. Louis Gallet. Tr. by Miller, Hettie E. LC 98-2260. R. F. Fenno & Company.

Adventures of David Grayson Pseud.... Ray Stannard Baker. LC 37-11013. 1937. The Sun Dial Press, Inc.

Adventures of David Grayson Pseud.... Illustrated by Thomas Fogarty. Ray Stannard Baker. LC 26-457. 1925. Doubleday, Page & Company.

Adventures of David Simple. Sarah Fielding. LC 74-17028. (Flowering of the Novel). 1974. (ISBN 0-8240-1113-9). Garland Pub.

Adventures of David Simple: Containing an Account of His Travels Through the Cities of London and Westminster in the Search of a Real Friend. Sarah Fielding. Ed. by Malcolm Kelsall. LC 78-385732. (Oxford English novels). (Illus.). 1969. Oxford U.P.

Adventures of Deerslayer: Adapted from J. Fenimore Cooper's "Deerslayer". Margaret Nanette Haight & Haight, Margaret N. LC 7-33197. (On cover: Electric readings). American Book Company.

Adventures of Dennis. V. Dragunsky. 237p. 1981. 7.00 (ISBN 0-8285-1983-8, Pub. by Progress Pubs USSR). Imported Pubns.

Adventures of Detective Barney. Harvey Jerrold O'Higgins. LC 15-200518. 1915. 1.30. The Century Co.

Adventures of Dr. Burton. Archibald Clavering Gunter. LC 5-33978. The Home Publishing Company.

Adventures of Dr. Whitty. James Owen Hannay. LC 13-94777. Hodder & Stoughton, George H. Doran Company.

Adventures of Dolphin Green. Herbert H. Lieberman. 246p. 1967. 4.95 (ISBN 0-8090-2320-2). Hill & Wang.

Adventures of Dolphin Green: A Novel, by Herbert Lieberman. 1st Ed. Herbert H. Lieberman. LC 67-14649. 1967. 4.95. Hill & Wang.

Adventures of Don Juan. Richard M Gardner. LC 73-17677. (Illus.). 1974. 10.00 (ISBN 0-670-10607-0). Viking Press.

Adventures of Don Juan De Ulloa: In a Voyage to Calecut, Soon After the Discovery of India, by Vasco De Gama... LC 7-1498. 1826. W.B. Gilley.

Adventures of Don Juan De Ulloa: In a Voyage to Calecut, Soon After the Discovery of India. by Vasco De Gama... LC 6-182823. 1833. P. Hill.

Adventures of Don Quixote. abridged. ed. Miguel de Cervantes de Saavedra. LC 66-43290. 1927. Dodd, Mead.

Adventures of Don Quixote. Miguel de Cervantes de Saavedra. Tr. by Daly Dominick. LC 26-23892. 1926. The Macmillian Company.

Adventures of Don Quixote. Miguel de Cervantes de Saavedra. Ed. by Olive Jones. Tr. by J. M. Cohen from Span. LC 79-23512. (Illus.). 1980. 10.95 (ISBN 0-416-87910-1, NO.0189). Methuen Inc.

Adventures of Don Quixote. Miguel de Cervantes de Saavedra & Rich, Edwin Gile. LC 21-16537. Small, Maynard & Company.

Adventures of Don Quixote De la Mancha. Miguel de Cervantes de Saavedra. LC 63-7413. (Great illustrated classics: Titan editions). 1962. Dodd, Mead.

Adventures of Don Quixote De la Mancha. Miguel de Cervantes de Saavedra. Tr. by Jarvis, Charles. LC 6-26728. 1881. The Arundel Print.

Adventures of Don Quixote: Man of la Mancha. Miguel de Cervantes de Saavedra. Tr. by John Ormsby. LC 70-76041. (A G & D classic). (Illus.). 1969. 4.95. Grosset & Dunlap.

Adventures of Don Quixote of La Mancha. Miguel de Cervantes de Saavedra. LC 4-7539. 1902. J. M. Dent & Co.

Adventures of Dunno & His Friends. N. Nosov. 1980. 5.95 (ISBN 0-8285-1911-0, Pub. by Progress Pubs USSR). Imported Pubns.

Adventures of Elder Triptolemus Tub: Comprising Important and Startling Disclosures Concerning Hell; Its Magnitude, Morals, Employments, Climate Etc., All Very Satisfactorily Authenticated. To Which Is Added, The Old Man of the Hill-Side. George Rogers. 1846. A. Tompkins.

Adventures of Elizabeth in Rugen. Mary Annette Beauchamp Russell. 1904. The Macmillan Company.

Adventures of Ellery Queen. Ellery Queen, pseud. LC 40-13894. 1940. Triangle Books.

Adventures of Ellery Queen: Problems in Deduction. Ellery Queen, pseud. LC 34-365511. 1934. Frederick A. Stokes Company.

Adventures of Emmera. Arthur Young. LC 74-23695. (Flowering of the Novel). 1974. (ISBN 0-8240-1179-1). Garland Pub.

Adventures of Emperor Jones, an Independent Cat. Hope R. Kjellerup. 1982. 5.95 (ISBN 0-533-05451-6). Vantage.

Adventures of Eovaai, Princess of Ijaveo. Eliza Fowler Haywood. LC 70-170595. (Foundations of the Novel). 1972. (part of 71 vol. series) 22.00 ea. (ISBN 0-8240-0577-5). Garland Pub.

Adventures of Ephraim Tutt, Attorney and Counsellor-at-Law. Arthur Cheney Train. LC 30-28196. 1930. C. Scribner's Sons.

Adventures of Father Silas - Flesh & Bone. Beauregard De Farniente & Henry Crannach. pap. 1.75 (ISBN 0-87067-148-0, BH148). Holloway.

Adventures of Father Silas (Le Portier Des Chartreux) Beauregard De Farniente. LC 67-29973. 1967. Holloway House Pub. Co.; Distributed by All America Distributors Corp.

Adventures of Ferdinand, Count Fathom. Tobias George Smollett. LC 78-596788. (Oxford English novels). 1971. 2.75 (ISBN 0-19-255321-6). Oxford University Press.

Adventures of Ferdinand: Count Fathom. Tobias George Smollett. LC 26-9628. (rogues' bookshelf). 1926. Greenberg.

Adventures of Ferdinand: Count Fathom. Tobias George Smollett. 1817. William B. Gilley.

Adventures of Ferdinand Count Fathom. Tobias George Smollett. Ed. by Damian Grant. (Oxford English Novels Ser). 1971. 14.95x o.p. (ISBN 0-19-255321-6). Oxford U Pr.

Adventures of Ferdinand Tomasso. Thomas J Holmes. LC 7-5183. 1894. The Irving Co.

Adventures of Finspot. prepublication ed. Zane Grey. LC 74-77788. 1974. (ISBN 0-914556-00-2). D-J Books.

Adventures of Five Englishmen from Pub Condoro, a Factory of the New Company in the East-Indies Who Were Shipwreckt Upon the Little Kingdom of Jehore see Impartial Secret History of Arlus, Fortunatus, & Odolphus, Ministers of State to the Empress Ofgrand-Insula.

Adventures of Francois: Foundling, Thief, Juggler, and Fencing Master During the French Revolution. Silas Weir Mitchell. LC 9-32294. Grosset & Dunlap.

Adventures of Francois: Foundling, Thief, Juggler, and Fencing Master During the French Revolution. Silas Weir Mitchell. LC 16-75454. 1909. The Century Co.

Adventures of Frank Friendless and Elder Webber: Or, The Pirate's Ghost. J Haren. LC 7-2615. 1878. Standard Print, Salem N.J.

Adventures of Galldora. Modwena Sedgwick. pap. 0.95 o.p. (ISBN 0-14-030277-8). Penguin.

Adventures of Geoffrey Mildmay: A Trilogy. Burke Wilkinson. LC 77-76374. 1969. 7.95. R. B. Luce.

Adventures of Gerard. Arthur Conan Doyle. LC 76-376203. 1976. 8.25 (ISBN 0-7195-3226-4). J. Murray.

Adventures of Gerard. Arthur Conan Doyle. LC 3-23517. 1903. McClure, Phillips & Co.

Adventures of Gerard. new ed. Arthur Conan Doyle. 15.95 (ISBN 0-7195-3226-4). Transatlantic.

Adventures of Gil Blas... Alain Rene Le Sage. Tr. by Benjamin Heath Malkin. LC 36-37626. (Half-title: Everyman's library, ed. by Ernest Rhys. Romance. no. 437-438). 1928. J. M. Dent & Sons, Ltd.

Adventures of Gil Blas De Santillana: By Alain-Renee Lesage. Alain Rene Le Sage. Tr. by Tobias George Smollett. Fitzmaurice-Kelly, James, 1858-1923. (Half-title: The world's classics, cix). 1907. H. Frowde.

Adventures of Gil Blas of Santillane. Alain Rene Le Sage. Tr. by Tobias George Smollett. LC 76-48435. (Classics of European Literature; 14). (Hyperion library of world literature). 1977. 14.95. (ISBN 0-88355-566-2) (ISBN 0-88355-567-0). Hyperion Press.

Adventures of Gil Blas of Santillane. Alain Rene Le Sage. Tr. by Benjamin Heath Malkin. LC 26-6698. (Lettered on cover: The lotus lubrary). 1922. Brentano's.

Adventures of Gil Blas of Santillane. Alain Rene Le Sage et al. 1937. Printed for the Limited Editions Club at the University Press.

Adventures of Gil Blas, of Santillane. Abridged. Alain Rene Le Sage. LC 7-13128. 1810. Printed by Salmon Wilder, For Isaiah Thomas, Jun. September.

Adventures of Gil Blas of Santillane. A New Ed., Carefully Rev. Alain Rene Le Sage. Tr. by Tobias George Smollett. LC 37-11057. (On cover: The home library). A. L. Burt Company.

Adventures of Gil Blas of Santillane: Translated from the French of Lesage. Alain Rene Le Sage. Tr. by Tobias George Smollett. LC 8-11003. 1866. G.Routledge and Sons.

Adventures of Gil Blas of Santillane: Tr. from the French of Lesage. Alain Rene Le Sage. Tr. by Tobias George Smollett. LC 24-11851. (Library of early novelists. Picaresque section, ed. by H. Warner Allen. v.2). 1913. G. Routledge and Sons; Limited.

Adventures of God in His Search for the Black Girl. Brigid Brophy. LC 74-6362. (Illus.). 1974. 7.95 (ISBN 0-316-10976-2). Little, Brown.

Adventures of Good Comrade Schweik. Helmut Putz. LC 68-20523. 1968. 5.50. Ungar.

Adventures of Gremlin. DuPre Jones. (Illus.). 1966. 3.95 o.p. (ISBN 0-397-00412-5). Lippincott.

Adventures of Hajji Baba, in Turkey, Persia and Russia. James Justinian Morier. 1855. Lippincott, Grambo & Co.

Adventures of Hajji Baba of Ispahan. James Justinian Morier. LC 48-5553. 1947. Heritage Press.

Adventures of Hajji Baba of Ispahan. James Justinian Morier. (Half-title: Everyman's library, ed. by Ernest Rhys. Fiction. no. 679). J. M. Dent & Sons, Ltd.

Adventures of Hajji Baba of Ispahan. James Justinian Morier. LC 7-25994. 1895. Macmillan and Co.

Adventures of Hajji Baba of Ispahan. James Justinian Morier & Baldridge, Cyrus Le Roy, 1889- Illus. LC 37-39105. 1937. Random House, Inc.

Adventures of Hajji Baba of Ispahan. James Justinian Morier & Limited Editions Club, Inc., New York. LC 47-4714. 1947. For the Members of the Limited Editions Club.

Adventures of Hajji Baba of Ispahan. James Justinian Morier & Stewart, C. W., Ed. LC 23-12439. (Half-title: The World's classics. CCXXXVIII). 1923. H. Milford, Oxford University Press.

Adventures of Harlequin. Francis Lawrance Bickley. LC 25-90252. 1923. E. P. Dutton & Co.

Adventures of Harry Franco. Charles Frederick Briggs. LC 72-8204. 1972. (ISBN 0-8422-8009-X). MSS Information Corp.

Adventures of Harry Franco: A Tale of the Great Panic... Charles Frederick Briggs. 1839. F. Saunders.

Adventures of Harry Franco: A Tale of the Great Panic. Charles Frederick Briggs. 1972. Repr. of 1839 ed. 26.50x (ISBN 0-8422-8010-3). Irvington.

Adventures of Harry Franco: a Tale of the Great Panic. Charles Frederick Briggs. 1976. Repr. 35.00 o.p. (Regency). Scholarly.

Adventures of Harry Marline: Or, Notes from an American Midshipman's Lucky Bag. David Dixon Porter. LC 11-15065. 1885. D. Appleton and Company.

Adventures of Harry Revel. Arthur Thomas Quiller-Couch. LC 3-11157. 1903. C. Scribner's Sons.

Adventures of Harry Richmond. George Meredith. LC 78-88088. (Illus.). 1970. 7.95. University of Nebraska Press.

Adventures of Harry Richmond. new ed. George Meredith. LC 25-155001. 1886. Roberts Brothers.

Adventures of Harry Richmond. rev. ed. George Meredith. LC 1-12771. 1897. C. Scribner's Sons.

Adventures of Hatim Tai. Tr. by Duncan Forbes. 1969. Repr. of 1830 ed. 14.50 o.p. (ISBN 0-8337-1171-7). B Franklin.

Adventures of Hatim Tai: By Dorothy Ensor. Illustrated by Pauline Baynes. 1st American Ed. Hatim Tai (Romance) & Dorothy Ensor. LC 62-650857. 1962. H. Z. Walck.

Adventures of Hawke Travis: Episodes in the Life of a Gunman. Eli Colter. LC 31-512520. 1931. The Macmillan Company.

Adventures of Hercules Hardy: Or, Guiana in 1772. Eugene Sue & Pooley, Thomas, Tr. LC 8-28266. J. Winchester.

Adventures of Herlock Sholmes. Charles Hamilton. LC 76-7154. (Illus.). 1976. 10.00. (ISBN 0-89296-025-6). Mysterious Press.

Adventures of Herlock Sholmes. Peter Todd. LC 76-7154. 1976. 10.00 o.p. (ISBN 0-89296-000-0). Mysterious Pr.

Adventures of Hiram Holliday. Paul Gallico. LC 39-30542. 1939. A. A. Knopf.

Adventures of Holly Hobbie: A Novel. Richard Dubelman. LC 79-17636. (Illus.). 10.95 (ISBN 0-440-00154-4). Delacorte Press/E. Friede.

Adventures of Huckleberry Finn. Samuel Langhorne Clemens. LC 66-30699. (Library of literature, 4). 1967. Bobbs-Merrill.

Adventures of Huckleberry Finn. Samuel Langhorne Clemens. (Washington Square Press Enriched Classics). (Illus.). 1973. (pbk.) 0.75. Pocket Books.

Adventures of Huckleberry Finn. Samuel Langhorne Clemens. Ed. by Peter Coveney. LC 67-92318. (Penguin English library EL 18). (Illus.). 1966. Penguin.

Adventures of Huckleberry Finn. Samuel Langhorne Clemens. LC 71-2795. 1969. 4.95. F. Watts.

Adventures of Huckleberry Finn. Samuel Langhorne Clemens. Ed. by James K. Bowen & Richard Vanderbeets. LC 76-118332. 1970. Scott, Foresman.

Adventures of Huckleberry Finn. penguin ed. reprinted. ed. Samuel Langhorne Clemens. Ed. by Peter Coveney. LC 78-393286. (Penguin English library EL 18). (Illus.). 1968. Penguin.

Adventures of Huckleberry Finn. Samuel Langhorne Clemens. (Macmillan classics, 38). (Illus.). 1962. Macmillan.

Adventures of Huckleberry Finn. Samuel Langhorne Clemens. LC 48-2020. (Illustrated junior library). 1948. Grosset & Dunlap.

Adventures of Huckleberry Finn. Samuel Langhorne Clemens. LC 48-6226. (Illustrated junior library). 1948. Grossett & Dunlap.

Adventures of Huckleberry Finn. Samuel Langhorne Clemens. LC 48-19810. (Illustrated junior library). 1948. Grosset & Dunlap.

Adventures of Huckleberry Finn. Samuel Langhorne Clemens. LC 48-8523. (Rinehart editions, 11). 1948. Rinehart.

Adventures of Huckleberry Finn. Samuel Langhorne Clemens. Ed. by Emily Fanning Barry & Herbert Bascom Bruner. LC 31-17596. (Harper's modern classics). Harper & Brothers.

Adventures of Huckleberry Finn. Samuel Langhorne Clemens. (Rainbow Classics). 1947. World Pub. Co.

Adventures of Huckleberry Finn. Samuel Langhorne Clemens. LC 80-13399. (Classics in Large Print). 1980. 13.95 (ISBN 0-8161-3079-5). G. K. Hall.

Adventures of Huckleberry Finn. Mark Twain. (Illus.). (pbk.) 0.95. New American Library.

Adventures of Huckleberry Finn see Classics Set.

Adventures of Huckleberry Finn see Four Classic American Novels.

Adventures of Huckleberry Finn: A Facsimile of the Manuscript. Mark Twain. LC 82-9192. 1982. 250.00 (ISBN 0-8103-1635-8). Gale Research Co.

Adventures of Huckleberry Finn. A Facsim. of the 1st Ed., Introd. and Bibliography Prepared by Hamlin Hill. Samuel Langhorne Clemens. Ed. by Hamlin Lewis Hill. LC 62-14104. Chandler.

Adventures of Huckleberry Finn: An Annotated Text, Backgrounds and Sources, Essays in Criticism. Samuel Langhorne Clemens. Ed. by Edward Sculley Bradley. LC 62-9571. (Norton critical editions, N304). 1962. Norton.

Adventures of Huckleberry Finn: An Authoritative Text, Backgrounds and Sources, Criticism. 2d ed. Samuel Langhorne Clemens et al. LC 76-30648. (Norton Critical Edition). (Norton critical edition). 12.95 (ISBN 0-393-04454-8). Norton.

Adventures of Huckleberry Finn: By Mark Twain Pseud. Samuel Langhorne Clemens. LC 62-52195. (Riverside literature series, R6). 1962. Houghton Mifflin.

Adventures of Huckleberry Finn: By Mark Twain Pseud. Ed., Introd. by Peter Coveney. Samuel Langhorne Clemens. (Penguin Eng. Lib., EL18). 1966. pap., 1.25. Penguin.

Adventures of Huckleberry Finn: By Mark Twain Pseud. Illustrated by Richard M. Powers. Samuel Langhorne Clemens. LC 54-489222. 1954. Doubleday Classics.

Adventures of Huckleberry Finn: By Mark Twain Pseud. Illustrated by Richard M. Powers. Samuel Langhorne Clemens. LC 54-14320. 1954. Junior Deluxe Editions.

Adventures of Huckleberry Finn: By Mark Twain Pseud. Illustrated by Harold Minton. Samuel Langhorne Clemens. LC 60-263469. (Washington Square Press book, W-242). 1960. Washington Square Press.

Adventures of Huckleberry Finn: By Mark Twain Pseud. Illustrated with Colour Plates and Drawings in the Text by C. Walter Hodges. Samuel Langhorne Clemens. LC 55-1997. (Children's illustrated classics). 1955. Dent.

Adventures of Huckleberry Finn: By Mark Twain. Study Material Prepd. by C. J. Porter. Samuel Langhorne Clemens. Ed. by Cecil J. Porter. LC 67-8737. 1967. 1.60. St. Martin's.

Adventures of Huckleberry Finn (Condensed) Samuel Langhorne Clemens. LC 40-6584. McLoughlin Brothers, Inc.

Adventures of Huckleberry Finn (The) Chapter Notes and Criticism. Text by Claire Spatz Connelly, An Keats. Introd. by Clarence W. Hach. Claire Spatz Connelly & An Keats. (Study master pubn., 206). pap., 1.00. Amer. R.D.M.

Adventures of Huckleberry Finn (Tom Sayer's Comrade) Samuel Langhorne Clemens. LC 23-17472. 1923. Harper & Brothers.

Adventures of Huckleberry Finn: Tom Sawyer's Comrade. Samuel Langhorne Clemens. LC 48-2019. (Harpers modern classics). 1948. Harper.

Adventures of Huckleberry Finn (Tom Sawyer's Comrade)... Samuel Langhorne Clemens. 1885. C. L. Webster and Company.

Adventures of Huckleberry Finn (Tom Sawyer's Comrade)... Samuel Langhorne Clemens. LC 13-76796. 1885. C. L. Webster and Company.

Adventures of Huckleberry Finn (Tom Sawyer's Comrade)... new ed. from new plates. ed. Samuel Langhorne Clemens. LC 3-19534. 1896. Harper & Brothers.

Adventures of Huckleberry Finn (Tom Sawyers's Comrade)... Samuel Langhorne Clemens. LC 15-21857. Harper & Brothers.

Adventures of Huckleberry Finn (Tom Sawyer's Comrade)... Samuel Langhorne Clemens. LC 20-123483. Harper & Brothers.

Adventures of Huckleberry Finn (Tom Sawyer's Comrade)... new ed. from new plates. ed. Samuel Langhorne Clemens. LC 21-414081. Harper & Brothers.

Adventures of Huckleberry Finn (Tom Sawyer's Conrade)... Samuel Langhorne Clemens. LC 15-12853. (Added t.-p.: Harper's modern classics, ed. for educational use by W. T. Brewster). 1918. Harper & Brothers.

Adventures of Huckleberry Finn (Tom Sawyer's Comrade) Samuel Langhorne Clemens. LC 41-5574. 1941. The Saalfield Publishing Company.

Adventures of Huckleberry Finn: Tom Sawyer's Comrade. modern abridged ed. CLemens, Samuel Langhorne. LC 41-178724. Whitman Publishing Company.

Adventures of Huckleberry Finn (Tom Sawyer's Comrade)... Samuel Langhorne Clemens & Kemble, Edward Windsor, 1861- Illus. LC 27-27811. 1927. Harper & Brothers.

Adventures of Huckleberry Finn: Tom Sawyer's Comrade) Mark Twain. LC 80-54137. (Silver Classic). (Illus.). 1982. 2.95 (ISBN 0-382-03438-4). Silver Burdett Co.

Adventures of Huckleberry Finn: Tom Sawyer's Comrade, by Mark Twain Pseud. Illustrated by Paul Frame. Modern Abridged Ed. Samuel Langhorne Clemens. LC 55-30074. (Whitman famous classics). Wis.

Adventures of Huckleberry Finn: Tom Sawyer's Comrade, by Mark Twain Pseud. Illustrated by Paul Frame. Modern Abridged Ed. Samuel Langhorne Clemens. LC 51-8196. (Whitman classic). 1951. Whitman.

Adventures of Huckleberry Finn, Tom Sawyer's Comrade. Scene: The Mississippi Valley; Times: Early Nineteenth Century. Samuel Langhorne Clemens. LC 65-6561. (Signet Classics, CD5). (Perennial classic). 1962. New American Library.

Adventures of Huckleberry Finn. With 16 Full-Page Illus.; Descriptive Captions and Introductory Remarks by Stanley T. Williams. Samuel Langhorne Clemens. LC 53-953872. (Great illustrated classics). 1953. Dodd, Mead.

Adventures of Hugh Trevor. Thomas Holcroft. Ed. by Seamus Deane. LC 73-169418. (Oxford English novels). 1973. 5.00 (ISBN 0-19-255355-0). Oxford University Press.

Adventures of Jack Wander. LC 74-16029. (Flowering of the Novel). 1974. (ISBN 0-8240-1172-4). Garland Publishing.

Adventures of Jimmie Dale. Frank Lucius Packard. LC 17-5814. George H. Doran Company.

Adventures of Joel Pepper. Margaret Sidney. 2.50 o.p.; special ed. 3.50 o.p.; deluxe ed. 4.50 o.p.; comparison lib. ed. 1.25 o.p. G&D.

Adventures of John Pas-Plus. John George Edward Campbell. J. W. Lovell Company.

Adventures of Johnny Bob. Ted Mann. 1979. 10.95 o.s.i. (ISBN 0-88373-097-9); pap. 5.95 o.s.i. (ISBN 0-88373-098-7). Stonehill Pub Co.

Adventures of Jonathan Corncob, Loyal American Refugee, Written by Himself. Noel Perrin. LC 75-43348. (Illus.). 1976. 8.95 (ISBN 0-87923-184-X). D. R. Godine.

Adventures of Jones. Hayden Carruth. LC 6-24221. 1895. Harper & Brothers.

Adventures of Joseph Andrews. Henry Fielding. LC 76-39749. (Hart classics). (Illus.). 8.95 (ISBN 0-8055-1220-9). Hart Pub. Co.

Adventures of Joseph Andrews. Henry Fielding. LC 1-18364. 1852. Stringer & Townsend.

Adventures of Joseph Andrews. Henry Fielding. (Half-title: The World's classics, CCCXXXIV). 1935. H. Milford, Oxford University Press.

Adventures of Joseph Andrews. Henry Fielding & Harper, Henry Howard, 1871- Ed. LC 33-606. 1931. Printed for Members of the Bibliophile Society.

Adventures of Joseph Andrews. Henry Fielding & McCullough, Bruce Welker, Ed. LC 30-6149. (Half-title: The modern student's library). C. Scribner's Sons.

Adventures of Joujou. Edith Macvane. LC 6-34817. 1906. J. B. Lippincott Company.

Adventures of Justin Clay. Telfair. 182p. 1981. pap. 3.95 (ISBN 0-9609502-0-6). Perilous Pr.

Adventures of Kathlyn. Harold MacGrath. LC 14-11354. The Bobbs-Merrill Company.

Adventures of Lady Susan. Cyrus Townsend Brady. LC 8-29649. 1908. Moffat, Yard & Company.

Adventures of Li Chi: A Modern Chinese Legend. Humphrey Evans. LC 67-11362. 1967. Dutton.

Adventures of Lindamira, a Lady of Quality. Bd. with Jilted Bridegroom: The London Coquet. LC 72-170507. LC 79-170506. (Foundations of the Novel Ser.: Vol. 5). lib. bdg. 50.00 o.s.i. (ISBN 0-8240-0517-1). Garland Pub.

Adventures of Lindamira, a Lady of Quality. Ed. by Benjamin Boyce. 1949. 3.00 o.p. U of Minn Pr.

Adventures of Lindamira: A Lady of Quality. Brown, Thomas. Ed. by Boyce, Benjamin. LC 49-898748. 1949. Univ. of Minnesota Press.

Adventures of Lindamira, a Lady of Quality. The Jilted Bridegroom; or, London Coquet. LC 79-170506. (Foundations of the novel). 1972. (ISBN 0-8240-0517-1). Garland Pub.

Adventures of Louis Blake. Louis Becke. LC 26-27688. 1926. J. B. Lippincott Company.

Adventures of M. D'Haricot. Joseph Storer Clouston. LC 2-27938. 1902. Harper and Brothers.

Adventures of Major Alexander MacPherson. John R Hodgson. LC 57-811624. (Nobel book). 1957. Comet Press Books.

Adventures of Major O'Regan. Hugh Henry Brackenridge. LC 45-45398. (With, as issued, his Adventures of Captain Farrago. Philadelphia c1856). T. B. Peterson and Brothers.

Adventures of Mao on the Long March. Frederic Tuten. LC 71-151415. 1971. 5.95 (ISBN 0-8065-0248-7). Citadel Press.

Adventures of Martin Hewitt. Third Series. Arthur Morrison. LC 38-134131. 1896. Ward, Lock & Co., Limited.

Adventures of Mary Jane. John W. Whalen. 3.95 o.p. Vantage.

Adventures of Me An' My Burro. Reni Berry. LC 38-174527. R. S. Berry.

Adventures of Menahem-Mendl. Sholom Aleichem. Tr. by Tamara Kahana. 1970. pap. 0.95 o.p. (ISBN 0-446-65211-3, 65-211). Paperback Lib.

Adventures of Menahem Mendl. Sholom Aleichem. Tr. by Tamara Kahana. (YA) 1969. 6.95 o.p. (ISBN 0-399-10003-2). Putnam.

Adventures of Menahem-Mendl. Shalom Rabinowitz. LC 69-13650. 1969. 5.95. Putnam.

Adventures of Menahem-Mendl. Shalom Rabinowitz. LC 79-13506. (Paragon book). 1979. 4.95 (ISBN 0-399-50396-X). Putnam.

Adventures of Menahem-Mendl. Sholom Aleichem. LC 79-13506. 1979. pap. 4.95 (ISBN 0-399-50396-X, Perige). Putnam Pub Group.

Adventures of Mick Callighin, M. P. A Story of Home Rule; and The De Burghos. A Romance. W R Ancketill. LC 6-2442. 1875. Railroad News Company.

Adventures of Miss Gregory. Perceval Gibbon. LC 13-734002. 1913. G. P. Putnam's Sons.

Adventures of Miss Volney. Ella Wheeler Wilcox. (On cover: The red cover series, no. 29). J. S. Ogilvie.

Adventures of Mr. George Edwards. John Hill. LC 74-23649. (Flowering of the Novel). 1974. (ISBN 0-8240-1133-3). Garland Pub.

Adventures of Mr. Joseph P. Cray. Edward Phillips Oppenheim. LC 27-1103. 1927. Little, Brown, and Company.

Adventures of Mr. Verdant Green. Cuthbert Bede. (Illus.). 1982. pap. 9.95x (ISBN 0-19-281331-5). Oxford U Pr.

Adventures of Mr. Verdant Green. 90th thousand. ed. Edward Bradley. LC 42-26352. 1860. Rudd & Carleton.

Adventures of Mr. Verdant Green: An Oxford Freshman. Edward Bradley. LC 6-15201. (On back of cover: Cuthbert Bede's College stories). 1893. Little, Brown and Company.

Adventures of Monsieur De Mailly. David Lindsay. LC 27-159012. 1926. A. Melrose, Ltd.

Adventures of Mottel the Cantor's Son. Sholom Aleichem. (O.s.i). 1961. pap. 1.25 o.s.i. (01615, Collier). Macmillan.

Adventures of My Cousin Smooth. Charles Adams. LC 20-19330. 1856. Miller, Orton & Mulligan; Etc.,Etc.

Adventures of Napoleon Prince. Helen Marion Edginton. LC 12-20790. 1912. 1.25. Cassell and Company, Ltd.

Adventures of Oliver Twist. Charles Dickens. LC 64-9260. 1962. St Martin's Press.

Adventures of Oliver Twist. Charles Dickens. LC 62-10492. (Rinehart editions, 115). 1962. Holt, Rinehart and Winston.

Adventures of Oliver Twist. Charles Dickens. (On cover: Lovell's library. v. 1, no. 10). 1882. J. W. Lovell Company.

Adventures of Oliver Twist. Charles Dickens. Ed. by Whipple, Edwin Percy. LC 15-231313. (Half-title: Works of Charles Dickens. New illustrated library ed. vol. iv). Houghton Mifflin Company.

Adventures of Oliver Twist. Charles Dickens. Ed. by Dickens, Charles. LC 4-15296. 1897. Macmillan and Co., Limited.

Adventures of Oliver Twist. Charles Dickens. Ed. by Pine, Frank Woodworth. LC 18-6024. (Macmillan's pocket American and English classics). 1918. 0.28. The Macmillan Company.

Adventures of Oliver Twist. Charles Dickens. (golden books). 1930. D. McKay.

Adventures of Oliver Twist. Charles Dickens. Ed. by Pine, Frank Woodworth. Moffett, Harold Young. LC 32-16552. (Half-title: New pocket classics). The Macmillan Company.

Adventures of Oliver Twist. Charles Dickens. LC 40-670. The Heritage Club.

Adventures of Oliver Twist. Charles Dickens & Greenawalt, Lambert, 1890- LC 50-5760. Globe Book Co.

Adventures of Oliver Twist. Charles Dickens & Whipple, Edwin Percy. LC 6-37242. (Half-title: Works... New illustrated library ed. vol. v). 1876. Hurd and Houghton.

Adventures of Oliver Twist. Also, American Notes for General Circulation, and Pictures from Italy. illustrated household ed. Charles Dickens. LC 6-26419. 1870. Fields, Osgood & Co.

Adventures of Oliver Twist. Also, Pictures from Italy, and American Notes for General Circulation. diamond ed. Charles Dickens. LC 6-26421. 1867. Ticknor and Fields.

Adventures of Oliver Twist. Illustrated by Lawrence Beall Smith. Charles Dickens. LC 56-465773. 1956. Junior Deluxe Editions.

Adventures of Oliver Twist: Or, The Parish Boy's Progress. Charles Dickens. (Half-title: The centenary edition of the works of Charles Dickens in 36 volumes). 1910. Chapman & Hall, Ltd.

Adventures of Oliver Twist: Or, The Parish Boy S Progress. With the Original Illus. by George Cruikshank. Charles Dickens & George Cruikshank. LC 66-5544. (Macdonald illus. classics, 6). 1966. 3.50. Macdonald.

Adventures of Oliver Twist: Reissue Illus. by Barnett Freedman. Charles Dickens & Barnett Freedman. LC 40-670. 1966. 6.50. Heritage Pr Dist. Dial.

Adventures of One Terence McGrant. A Brevet Irish Cousin of President Ulisses S. Grant... Who Has Been Having Considerable Trouble About Getting Properly Settled into a Paying Office, Notwithstanding His Relationship... George Wilbur Peck. LC 7-36481. 1871. J. H. Lambert.

Adventures of Oscar Seymore. L. Middleton. 4.00 o.p. (ISBN 0-8062-0567-9). Carlton.

Adventures of Oxymel Classic, Esq. LC 74-16067. (Flowering of the Novel). 1974. (ISBN 0-8240-1181-3). Garland Pub.

Adventures of Pathfinder: Adapted from J. Fenimore Cooper's "Pathfinder". James Fenimore Cooper & Haight, Margaret Nanette. LC 9-22939. (On cover: Electic readings). American Book Company.

Adventures of Peregrine Pickle: In Which Are Included Memoirs of a Lady of Quality by Tobias Smollett. Tobias George Smollett. Ed. by Clifford, James Lowry. LC 64-56171. (Oxford English novels). 1964. Oxford University Press.

Adventures of Peregrine Pickle. In Which Are Included Memoirs of a Lady of Quality. Tobias George Smollett. LC 43-466641. (On cover: Railway library). G. Routledge and Sons.

Adventures of Peter Whiffen. Enid L Meadowcroft. LC 36-24402. Thomas Y. Crowell Company.

Adventures of Philip on His Way Through the World: Showing Who Robbed Him, Who Helped Him, and Who Passed Him by, to Which Is Now Prefixed A Shabby Genteel Story. William Makepeace Thackeray. Caxton Publishing Co.

Adventures of Philip on His Way Through the World: Showing Who Robbed Him, Who Helped Him, and Who Passed Him by. William Makepeace Thackeray. LC 8-27766. 1862. Harper & Brothers.

Adventures of Philip on His Way Through the World: Showing Who Robbed Him, Who Helped Him, and Who Passed Him by; to Which Is Now Prefixed A Shabby Genteel Story. household ed. William Makepeace Thackeray. 1869. Fields, Osgood & Co.

Adventures of Philip on His Way Through the World: Showing Who Robbed Him, and Who Passed Him by; to Which Is Now Prefixed A Shabby Genteel Story. William Makepeace Thackeray. LC 8-7696. (Added t.-p.: The works of William Makepeace Thackeray... V. 10, 1). 1879. Smith, Elder, & Co.

Adventures of Philip, on His Way Through the World: Showing Who Robbed Him. Who Helped Him, and Who Passed Him by. William Makepeace Thackeray. (On cover: Lovell's library. v. 5, no. 235). 1883. J. W. Lovell Company.

Adventures of Philip on His Way Through the World: Showing Who Robbed Him, Who Helped Him, and Who Passed Him by: to Which Is Now Prefixed A Shabby Genteel Story. Catherine: a Story. William Makepeace Thackeray. LC 8-308945. 1887. J. B. Lippincott Company.

Adventures of Philip on His Way Through the World, Showing Who Robbed Him, Who Helped Him, and Who Passed Him by; to Which Is Prefixed A Shabby Genteel Story: By William Makepeace Thackeray; with Illustrations by the Author and Frederick Walker. William Makepeace Thackeray. LC 4-16318. (Half-title: The biographical edition. The works of William Makepeace Thackeray... vol. XI). 1899. Harper & Brothers.

Adventures of Philippe: A Story of Old Kebec. Gwendolyn Bowers. LC 49-866238. 1949. Aladdin Books.

Adventures of Picklock Holes. R. C. Lehmann. (Illus.). 64p. 1975. 10.00 o.p. (ISBN 0-915230-07-0); pap. 5.00 o.p. (ISBN 0-915230-08-9). Rue Morgue.

Adventures of Picklock Holes. R. C. Lehmann. (Illus.). 64p. 1975. 10.00 o.p. (ISBN 0-915230-07-0); pap. 5.00 o.p. (ISBN 0-915230-08-9). Aspen Pr.

Adventures of Pioneer Children: Or, Life in the Wilderness. A Portrayal of the Part Performed by the Children of the Early Pioneers in Establishing Homes in the Wilderness... E Fenwick Colerick. LC 6-25414. 1888. R. Clarke & Co.

Adventures of Pirates and Sea-Rovers. Pyle, Howard, 1853-1911. LC 8-18408. (On cover of t.-p.: Harper's adventure series). 1908. Harper & Brothers.

Adventures of Polydore. Stanley Hart Cauffman. LC 30-7292. The Penn Publishing Company.

Adventures of Private Faust. Hans Hellmut Kirst. LC 73-136442. 1971. 5.95. Coward, McCann & Geoghegan.

Adventures of Remi: From the French of Hector Malot's "Sans Famille". Hector Henri Malot & Allen, Philip Schuyler, 1871- Tr. LC 25-13867. Rand, McNally & Company.

Adventures of Reuben Davidger: Seventeen Years and Four Months Captive Among the Dyaks of Borneo. James Greenwood. LC 45-26343. 1866. Harper & Brothers.

Adventures of Richard Hannay... John Buchan. LC 39-27285. 1939. Houghton Mifflin Company.

Adventures of Richard O'Boy. Benjamin Siegel. 320p. 1980. 10.95i (ISBN 0-690-01860-6). Har-Row.

Adventures of Richard O'Boy: A Novel. Benjamin Siegel. LC 79-25146. 10.95 (ISBN 0-690-01860-6). Lippincott & Crowell.

Adventures of Rivella. Mary De La Riviere Manley & Ambrose Evans. LC 72-7419. (Foundations of the Novel). 1972. 22.00 (ISBN 0-8240-0534-1). Garland Publishing.

Adventures of Rob Roy. James Grant. LC 24-27984. 1865. Crosby and Ainsworth.

Adventures of Robin Day. Robert Montgomery Bird. 1839. Lea & Blanchard.

Adventures of Robin Day. Robert Montgomery Bird. LC 42-267923. 1877. J. Polhemus.

Adventures of Robin Hood. Ed. by Rudy Behlmer & Tino Balio. LC 79-3971. (Wisconsin-Warner Bros. Screenplay Ser.). (Illus.). 1979. 17.50 (ISBN 0-299-07940-6); pap. 6.95 (ISBN 0-299-07944-9). U of Wis Pr.

Adventures of Robinson Crusoe. Daniel Defoe. LC 35-27384. (The Riversied book-shelf). 1931. Houghton Mifflin Company.

Adventures of Robinson Crusoe. Ed. by M. W. & G. Thomas. Illus. by Albrecht Appelhans. Daniel Defoe. Ed. by Maurice Walton Thomas & Gladys Thomas. LC 66-6337. (Shorter classics). 1966. bds., 2.50. Ginn.

Adventures of Roderick Random. Tobias George Smollett. (Half-title: The world's classics. 353). 1930. Oxford University Press, H. Milford.

Adventures of Roderick Random. Tobias George Smollett. LC 78-41108. (Oxford English novels). 1979. 43.50 (ISBN 0-19-255370-4). Oxford University Press.

Adventures of Romney Pringle. Clifford Ashdown. LC 74-18050. 1968. 4.50. O. Train.

Adventures of Sally Ann. Alice Elizabeth Priestland Cooper & British War Relief Society. LC 43-3665. Webb-Linn.

Adventures of Search for Life: A Bunyanic Narrative, As Detailed by Himself. D. J Mandell. LC 7-16802. 1838. S. H. Colesworthy.

Adventures of Sherlock Holmes. Arthur Conan Doyle. LC 65-11926. (Whitman classics library). 1965. Whitman Pub. Co.

Adventures of Sherlock Holmes. Arthur Conan Doyle. LC 66-2946. 1966. Harper & Row.

Adventures of Sherlock Holmes. Arthur Conan Doyle. 1975. (pbk.) 1.25. Popular Library.

Adventures of Sherlock Holmes. Arthur Conan Doyle. 1975. (pbk.) 1.25 (ISBN 0-345-24716-7). Ballantine Books.

Adventures of Sherlock Holmes. Arthur Conan Doyle. LC 75-37008. (Illus.). 1976. 5.95 (ISBN 0-8052-3621-X). Schocken Books.

Adventures of Sherlock Holmes. Arthur Conan Doyle. LC 75-18879. (Illus.). 3.95 (ISBN 0-89104-023-4). A & W Visual Library.

Adventures of Sherlock Holmes. Arthur Conan Doyle. LC 64-15716. (Classics to grow on). 1966. Parents' Magazine's Cultural Institute.

Adventures of Sherlock Holmes. Arthur Conan Doyle. LC 50-11604. (Illus.). 1950. For the Members of the Limited Editions Club.

Adventures of Sherlock Holmes. Arthur Conan Doyle. LC 16-7600. A. L. Burt Company.

Adventures of Sherlock Holmes. Arthur Conan Doyle. LC 12-188096. Harper & Brothers.

Adventures of Sherlock Holmes. Arthur Conan Doyle. LC 21-13709. 1920. A. L. Burt Company.

Adventures of Sherlock Holmes. facsimile ed. Arthur Conan Doyle. (Illus.). 320p. 1975. pap. 3.95 o.p. (ISBN 0-89104-023-4). A & W Pubs.

Adventures of Sherlock Holmes. Arthur Conan Doyle. 288p. 1981. pap. 3.50 (ISBN 0-14-005724-2). Penguin.

Adventures of Sherlock Holmes. Arthur Conan Doyle & Arthur Conan Doyle. LC 21-13700. 1902. Harper & Brothers.

Adventures of Sherlock Holmes. Arthur Conan Doyle & Opdycke, John Baker, 1876- LC 30-4490. (Harper's modern classics). Harper & Brothers.

Adventures of Sherlock Holmes: A Definitive Text, Corrected and Edited by Edgar W. Smith, with an Introd. by Vincent Starrett, and Illustrated with a Selective Collation of the Original Illus. by Frederic Dorr Steele, Sidney Paget and Others. Arthur Conan Doyle. LC 50-14604. 1950. For the Members of the Limited Editions Club.

Adventures of Sherlock Holmes. Adapted by Olive Eckerson, Edited by Wallace R. Murray. Arthur Conan Doyle & Olive Eckerson. LC 50-9949. 1950. Globe Book Co.

Adventures of Sherlock Holmes & Memoirs of Sherlock Holmes. facsimile ed. Arthur Conan Doyle. (Illus.). 616p. 1975. Boxed Set Of 2 Vols. pap. 7.95 o.p. (ISBN 0-89104-025-0). A & W Pubs.

Adventures of Sherlock Holmes: Eight Popular Stories, Espicially Selected and Edited. Illustrated by Cheslie D'Andrea. Arthur Conan Doyle. LC 55-12935. 1955. Whitman Pub. Co.

Adventures of Sherlock Holmes: Illustrated by Richard M. Powers. Arthur Conan Doyle. LC 56-58508. 1956. Junior Deluxe Editions.

Adventures of Shlomele. Drawings by Forrest Jacobs. Saul Davis. LC 56-8957. 1956. T. Yoseloff.

Adventures of Signor McGlusky. A. G. Hales. LC 19-10471. Hodder and Stoughton.

Adventures of Sir Launcelot Greaves: And The History and Adventures of an Atom. Tobias George Smollett. LC 43-39497. G. Routledge and Sons, Limited.

Adventures of Sir Lyon Bouse, Bart., in America During the Civil War. Being Extracts from His Diary. Richard Grant White. 1867. The American News Company.

Adventures of Steve Waterhouse: Or, The Surprising Career of a Texas-Man. Joseph Gallegly. LC 47-11201. 1947. Naylor Co.

Adventures of Steven & Sally Steward. Charles L. Koester. 1976. pap. 2.55 o.p. (ISBN 0-89536-011-X). CSS Pub.

Adventures of Sylvia Hughes. LC 74-26997. (Flowering of the Novel). 1975. (ISBN 0-8240-1155-4). Garland Pub.

Adventures of Tapiola. Robert Nathan. (YA) 1950. 4.50 o.p. Knopf.

Adventures of Telemachus. Francois De Salignac De La Mothe- Fenelon. LC 78-60835. (Series: Novel, 1720-1805.). (Illus.). 1979. 56.00 (ISBN 0-8240-3650-6). Garland Pub.

Adventures of the Black Duse. Josephine Holt Throckmorton. LC 32-943330. Press of Judd & Detweiler, Inc.

Adventures of the Black Girl in Her Search for God. George Bernard Shaw. LC 33-5437. 1933. Dodd, Mead & Company.

Adventures of the Black Girl in Her Search for God. With the Original Illus. by John Farleigh. George Bernard Shaw. LC 59-11379. (Putnam Capricorn book). 1959. Capricorn Books.

Adventures of the Chicano Kid & Other Stories. Max Martinez. LC 81-68069. 120p. (Orig.). 1981. pap. 7.50 (ISBN 0-934770-08-5). Arte Publico.

Adventures of the Comte De la Muette During the Reign of Terror. Bernard Edward Joseph Capes. LC 98-984. 1898. Dodd, Mead and Company.

Adventures of the Five Puce Map Tacks. Paul Nizza. LC 76-6580. (Illus.). 5.00 (ISBN 0-915494-05-1). Fibonacci Corp.

Adventures of the Infallible Godahl. Frederick Irving Anderson. LC 14-5165. 1914. Thomas Y. Crowell Company.

Adventures of the Little Wooden Horse. Ursula Moray Williams. LC 39-21774. J. B. Lippincott Company.

Adventures of the Peerless Peer. Philip Jose Farmer. 1976. 1.25. Dell.

Adventures of the Rev. Samuel Entwhistle: With Illus. by the Author. Thomas Van Braam Barrett. LC 55-9998. 1955. Morehouse-Gorham Co.

Adventures of the S. S. Happiness Crew: Cap'n Joshua's Super Secret: 3rd Adventure. June Dutton. (Illus.). 1982. 5.95 (ISBN 0-915696-50-9). Determined Prods.

Adventures of the S. S. Happiness Crew: Mystery in the Middle of the Ocean: 2nd Adventure. June Dutton & Eric Hill. LC 81-65682. (Illus.). 1981. 5.95 (ISBN 0-915696-48-7). Determined Prods.

Adventures of the Scarlet Pimpernel. Emmuska Orczy. LC 29-25600. 1929. Doubleday, Doran & Company, Inc.

Adventures of the Stainless Steel Rat. Harry Harrison. 1978. 2.25 (ISBN 0-425-03819-X). Berkley Pub. Corp.

Adventures of the White Girl in Her Search for God. Charles Herbert Maxwell & George Bernard Shaw. LC 74-20648. 1974. 5.50 (ISBN 0-8414-5951-7). Folcroft Library Editions.

Adventures of Theodore: A Humorous Extravaganza. 1901. The H. J. Smith & Devereaux Co.

Adventures of Thomas Jefferson Snodgrass. Mark Twain. LC 73-13981. 1928. lib. bdg. 15.00 (ISBN 0-8414-8519-4). Folcroft.

Adventures of Timias Terrystone. Oliver Bell Bunce. LC 6-18680. 1885. D. Appleton and Company.

Adventures of Tom Bombadil. John Ronald Reuel Tolkien. (O.s.i.). 1978. 6.95 o.s.i. (ISBN 0-395-08251-X); pap. 4.95 o.s.i. (ISBN 0-395-26801-X). HM.

Adventures of Tom Bombadil. John Ronald Reuel Tolkien. (Illus.). 1963. 6.95 o.p. (ISBN 0-395-08251-X). HM.

Adventures of Tom Sawyer. Samuel Langhorne Clemens. LC 63-747. 1962. Collier Books.

Adventures of Tom Sawyer. Samuel Langhorne Clemens. LC 65-6769. (Perennial library). 1965. Harper & Row.

Adventures of Tom Sawyer. Samuel Langhorne Clemens. LC 68-56881. (Cambridge Classics Library. "Black & Gold Edition"). (Illus.). 1968. Cambridge Book Co.

Adventures of Tom Sawyer. Samuel Langhorne Clemens. (Macmillan classics, 39). (Illus.). 1962. Macmillan.

Adventures of Tom Sawyer. Samuel Langhorne Clemens. (Great illustrated classics). (Illus.). 1958. Dodd, Mead.

Adventures of Tom Sawyer. Samuel Langhorne Clemens. LC 63-6925. (Illus.). 1964. Heritage Press.

Adventures of Tom Sawyer. Samuel Langhorne Clemens. LC 66-28553. (Bantam pathfinder edition, FP159). 1966. Bantam Books.

Adventures of Tom Sawyer. Samuel Langhorne Clemens. LC 31-35220. 1885. The American Publishing Company.

Adventures of Tom Sawyer. Samuel Langhorne Clemens. 1888. The American Publishing Company.

Adventures of Tom Sawyer. Samuel Langhorne Clemens. 1891. The American Publishing Co.

Adventures of Tom Sawyer. Samuel Langhorne Clemens. LC 24-149403. 1899. The American Publishing Company.

Adventures of Tom Sawyer. Samuel Langhorne Clemens. LC 3-17534. 1903. The American Publishing Company.

Adventures of Tom Sawyer. Samuel Langhorne Clemens. LC 4-224877. 1903. Harper & Brothers.

Adventures of Tom Sawyer. Samuel Langhorne Clemens. LC 16-7550. Harper & Brother.

Adventures of Tom Sawyer. Samuel Langhorne Clemens. LC 10-23132. 1910. Harper & Brothers.

Adventures of Tom Sawyer. Samuel Langhorne Clemens. LC 12-21935. Harper & Brothers.

Adventures of Tom Sawyer. Samuel Langhorne Clemens. LC 17-31034. Harper & Brothers.

Adventures of Tom Sawyer. Samuel Langhorne Clemens. LC 21-4139. Harper & Brothers.

Adventures of Tom Sawyer. Samuel Langhorne Clemens. LC 20-15592. Harper & Brothers.

Adventures of Tom Sawyer. Samuel Langhorne Clemens. LC 20-326259. (Harper's modern classics). Harper & Brothers.

Adventures of Tom Sawyer. Samuel Langhorne Clemens. LC 31-25417. Whitman Publishing Company.

Adventures of Tom Sawyer. Samuel Langhorne Clemens. Ed. by Emily Fanning Barry & Herbert Bascom Bruner. (Harper's modern classics). Harper & Brothers.

Adventures of Tom Sawyer. Samuel Langhorne Clemens. Noble and Noble, Inc.

Adventures of Tom Sawyer. an abridged ed. with 35 illustrations by true williams, reproduced from the original edition of tom sawyer, first published in 1876, cover illustration by milo winter. ed. Samuel Langhorne Clemens. LC 38-29627. Rand. McNally & Company.

Adventures of Tom Sawyer. complete authorized ed. Samuel Langhorne Clemens. LC 40-11334. (Young moderns bookshelf). 1940. The Sun Dial Press.

Adventures of Tom Sawyer. Samuel Langhorne Clemens. LC 46-684521. (Half-title: Rainbow classics). 1946. The World Publishing Company.

Adventures of Tom Sawyer. Samuel Langhorne Clemens. LC 46-22587. (Illustrated junior library). 1946. Grosset & Dunlap.

Adventures of Tom Sawyer. Samuel Langhorne Clemens & Morley, Christopher Darlington, 1890- LC 31-25924. The John C. Winston Company.

Adventures of Tom Sawyer. Mark Twain. LC 80-54138. (Silver classic). (Illus.) (ISBN 0-382-03437-6). Silver Burdett Co.

Adventures of Tom Sawyer. Mark Twain & John C Gerber. LC 81-40324. (Twain, Mark, 1835-1910. Mark Twain Library). 1982. 13.50 (ISBN 0-520-04558-0) (ISBN 0-520-04559-9). University of California Press.

Adventures of Tom Sawyer. Mark Twain & Ted Lewin. LC 81-16074. 1982. 13.50 (ISBN 0-671-43791-7). Wanderer Books.

Adventures of Tom Sawyer: A Complete Edition of the Famous Story, Illustrated. Samuel Langhorne Clemens. LC 31-20404. (Every child's library). The Saalfield Publishing Company.

Adventures of Tom Sawyer: A Facsimile Edition of Mark Twain's Complete Manuscript. Intro. by Paul Baender. 920p. Date not set. lib. bdg. 120.00 (ISBN 0-89093-456-8, Aletheia Bks). U Pubns Amer.

Adventures of Tom Sawyer and Adventures of Huckleberry Finn. Introd. by William Donahey. Illus. by Dave Mink. Samuel Langhorne Clemens. LC 53-132519. 1953. Spencer Press.

Adventures of Tom Sawyer and The Adventures of Huckleberry Finn. Samuel Langhorne Clemens. LC 41-5104. (Half-title: The modern library of the world's best books). 1946. The Modern Library.

Adventures of Tom Sawyer: And The Adventures of Huckleberry Finn by Mark Twain Pseud. With a Special Pref. by Clara Clemens: Tom, Huck, and My Father, Mark Twain. Samuel Langhorne Clemens. LC 60-12428. (Platt & Munk great writers collection). 1960. Platt & Munk.

Adventures of Tom Sawyer: By Mark Twain.Ed. by M. W. and G. Thomas. Illus. by Dick Hart. Samuel Langhorne Clemens. Ed. by Maurice Walton Thomas & Gladys Thomas. LC 66-6593. (Shorter classics). 1965. bds., 2.50. Ginn.

Adventures of Tom Sawyer: By Mark Twain Pseud. Adapted by Erwin H. Schubert, Edited by Delpha Hurlburt. Samuel Langhorne Clemens & Erwin H. Schubert. LC 51-10982. 1951. Globe Book Co.

Adventures of Tom Sawyer. By Mark Twain Pseud. Gen. Eds.: Kenneth S. Lynn, Arno Jewett. Introd. by Walter Blair. Suggestions for Reading and Discussion by Frank H. Townsend. Samuel Langhorne Clemens. (RLS R2). 1.72, 1.20 pap.,. Houghton.

Adventures of Tom Sawyer: By Mark Twain Pseud. Harmondsworth. Samuel Langhorne Clemens. LC 50-8241. (Puffin story books, PS 62). 1950. Penguin Books.

Adventures of Tom Sawyer: By Mark Twain Pseud. Illustrated by John Falter. Afterword by Clifton Fadiman. Samuel Langhorne Clemens. LC 62-19420. (Macmillan classics, 39). 1962. Macmillan.

Adventures of Tom Sawyer: By Mark Twain Pseud. Illustrated with Colour Plates and Drawings in the Text by C. Walter Hodges. Samuel Langhorne Clemens. LC 55-145585. (Children's illustrated classics). 1955. Dent.

Adventures of Tom Sawyer: By Mark Twain (Samuel L. Clemens. Samuel Langhorne Clemens. LC 57-127919. (Children's classics). Winston.

Adventures of Tom Sawyer: Illustrated by Richard Rogers. Samuel Langhorne Clemens. LC 34-4340. Three Sirens Press.

Adventures of Tom Sawyer: Together with The Celebrated Jumping Frog of Calaveras County, and Other Tales. Samuel Langhorne Clemens. LC 48-4717. (World's greatest literature). 1949. Fountain Press.

Adventures of Tom Sawyer: Together with The Celebrated Jumping Frog of Calaveras County and Other Tales. Samuel Langhorne Clemens. LC 37-2571. (Immortal masterpieces of literature. vol. II). The Spencer Press.

Adventures of Tom Stapleton. John M Moore. LC 1-1513. (Brother Jonathan. Extra. no. 25. May 4, 1843). 1843. Wilson and Company.

Adventures of Tom Stapleton: Or, 202 Broadway. John M Moore. LC 1-1514. Garrett & Co.

Adventures of Torqua: Being the Life and Remarkable Adventures of Three Boys, Refugees on the Island of Santa Catalina (Pimugna) in the Eighteenth Century. Charles Frederick Holder. LC 2-23903. 1902. Little, Brown, & Company.

Adventures of Two Wild Injuns: As Fussed About by the Injuns Themselves. Paul Merrick & Davenport, Delbert Essex, 1887- Joint Author. LC 47-158005. 1946. The Geary Publishing Company.

Adventures of Two Yachtmen. Thomas Fleming Day. LC 8-2944. 1907. The Rudder Publishing Company.

Adventures of Una Persson and Catherine Cornelius in the Twentieth Century: A Romance. Michael Moorcock. LC 77-355084. 1976. 3.95 (ISBN 0-7043-2121-1). Quartet Books.

Adventures of una Persson & Catherine Cornelius in the Twentieth Century see Black Corridor.

Adventures of Uncle Jeremiah and Family at the Great Fair: Their Observations and Triumphs. Charles McClellan Stevens. (On cover: The Pastime series, no. 108). 1893. Laird & Lee.

Adventures of Uncle Jeremiah in the South... Charles McClellan Stevens. (On cover: The Enterprise series, no. 48). 1895. E. A. Weeks & Company.

Adventures of Uncle Sam. Frederick A. Fidfaddy. LC 76-104450. 1970. Repr. of 1816 ed. lib. bdg. 8.00x o.p. (ISBN 0-8398-0555-1). Gregg.

Adventures of Wesley Jackson. William Saroyan. LC 46-25168. 1946. Harcourt, Brace and Company.

Adventures of Wesley Jackson: In Saroyan, William, 1908- The Twin Adventures... William Saroyan. LC 50-6550. 1950. Harcourt, Brace.

Adventures of Zeloide and Amanzarifdine. Francois Augustin Paradis De Moncrif. LC 75-172542. 1971. B. Blom.

Adventures of Zeloide and Amanzarifdine. Francois Augustin Paradis De Moncrif. LC 78-178449. (Series: The Broadway Library of XVIII French Literature.). (Short story index reprint series). 1971. (ISBN 0-8369-4050-4). Books for Libraries Press.

Adventures on a Journey to New Holland: And The Lonely Deathbed. Tr. by Rodney Livingstone, Ed., Preface, Notes, by Leslie Bodi. Therese Heyne Forster Huber. Ed. by Leslie Bodi. LC 65-74164. 1966. bds., 7.50. Lansdowne Pr.

Adventures on the Lazy N. Ellen J. Macleod. 1957. 1.50 o.p. (ISBN 0-87508-640-3). Chr Lit.

Adventures, Wanderings and Sufferings of the Merton Family: Or, Life Scenes Among the South American Indians. Anne Bowman. LC 11-355. 1868. Quaker City Publishing House.

Adventures While Preaching the Gospel of Beauty. Nicholas Vachel Lindsay. LC 14-30915. 1914. M. Kennerley.

Adventures While Preaching the Gospel of Beauty. Nicholas Vachel Lindsay. LC 23-26579. 1921. The Macmillan Company.

Adventures with a Lamp: The Story of a Nurse. Ruth Louise Partridge. LC 39-6268. 1939. E. P. Dutton & Company, Inc.

Adventures with My Pets (Histoire De Mes Betes) Alexandre Dumas. 1960. Chilton Co., Book Division.

Adventuress. Coralie Stanton. 1907. T. J. McBride & Son.

Adventuress. Daoma Winston. (O.s.i.). 1978. 11.95 o.s.i. (ISBN 0-671-22888-9). S&S.

Adventuress: A Craig Kennedy Detective Story. Arthur Benjamin Reeve. LC 17-30121. 1917. Harper & Brothers.

Adventuress: A Novel. Rama Rau, Santha. LC 69-15283. 1970. 6.95. Harper & Row.

Adventuress: A Novel. Daoma Winston. LC 77-13767. 10.00 (ISBN 0-671-22888-9). Simon and Schuster.

Adventuring. Raphael Hayes. LC 78-70789. 1979. 1.75 (ISBN 0-515-04804-6). Jove/HBJ.

Adventuring. Tristram Tupper. LC 23-12115. George H. Doran Company.

Adventurous History of Hsi Men & His Six Wives. Chin P'Ing Mei. 1959. 6.50 o.p. Dufour.

Adventurous Lady. John Collis Snaith. LC 20-150663. 1920. D. Appleton and Company.

Adventurous Simplicissimus: Being the Description of the Life of a Strange Vagabond Named Melchior Sternfels Von Fuchshaim. Translated by A. T. S. Goodrick. Hans Jacob Christoffel Von Grimmelshausen. LC 62-8406. (Bison book, BB134). 1962. University of Nebraska Press.

Adversaries. Edward Linn. LC 73-79529. 1973. 10.00 (ISBN 0-8415-0281-1). Saturday Review Press.

Adversary. Bart Spicer. LC 73-82019. 1973. 7.95 (ISBN 0-399-11168-9). Putnam.

Adversary: By H. H. Lynde Pseud. Helen Huntington. LC 57-8850. 1957. Random House.

Adversary: By Jan Widgery. Jeanne Anna Ayres Widgery. LC 66-17402. 5.95. Doubleday.

Adversary in the House. Irving Stone. LC 47-31015. 1947. Doubleday.

Adversary in Tomika. Gilbert Van Tassel Hamilton & Reynolds, Mary, Joint Author. Sears Publishing Company, Inc.

Adverse Alliance. Lucia Curzon, pseud. (Second Chance at Love Ser.: No. 33). 1982. pap. 1.75 (ISBN 0-515-05626-X). Jove Pubns.

Advertised Orgy. (Illus.). pap. 5.00 (ISBN 0-910550-27-1). Centurion Pr.

Advertisement for a Husband. A Novel: in a Series of Letters Between Belinda Blacket, Louise Lenox, and Others. Two Volumes in One. 1799. Printed by Issiah Thomas, Jun.

Advertisements for Myself. Norman Mailer. LC 80-27130. 1981. 6.95 (ISBN 0-399-50538-5). Perigee Books.

Advertising Man. Jack Dillon. 312p. 1972. 6.95 o.p. (ISBN 0-06-122000-0). Harper Mag Pr.

Advertising Man: A Novel. John Dillon. (Fawcett Crest Book). 1973. (pbk.) 1.25. Fawcett.

Advice Limited. Edward Phillips Oppenheim. LC 36-273363. 1936. Little, Brown, and Company.

Advice Limited: A Series of Stories. Edward Phillips Oppenheim. LC 74-134972. (Short story index reprint series). 1970. Books for Libraries Press.

Advice to a Vampire at Puberty. Norman N. McWhinney. 1975. pap. 1.50 o.p. (ISBN 0-916684-02-4). Rook Pr.

Advice to a Young Man on the Choice of a Mistress. Benjamin Franklin. 1978. pap. 1.00 o.p. Loompanics.

Advice to Farm Women. Ed. by Jeanne H. Delgado. (Wisconsin Stories Ser.). 27p. pap. 1.25. State Hist Soc Wis.

Advise and Consent. Allen Drury. LC 77-364865. (Illus.). 1976. Franklin Library.

Advise and Consent. Allen Drury. LC 59-9137. (Illus.). 1959. Doubleday.

Advisory Ben: A Story. Edward Verrall Lucas. LC 24-673896. 2.00. George H. Doran Company.

Advocate. Borden Deal. LC 68-22499. 1968. 5.95. Doubleday.

Advocate: A Novel. Charles Heavysege. LC 74-167082. (Toronto reprint library of Canadian prose and poetry). (Illus.). (ISBN 0-8020-7511-8). University of Toronto Press.

Aegean Adventure. John Lodwick. 1946. Dodd, Mead & Company.

Aegean Affair. Walter Satterthwait. (Orig.). 1982. pap. 2.95 (ISBN 0-440-10076-3). Dell.

Aelian Fragment. George Bartram. LC 75-37113. (YA) 1976. 7.95 o.p. (ISBN 0-399-11625-7). Putnam.

Aelian Fragment. Kenneth M. Cameron. LC 75-37113. 7.95 (ISBN 0-399-11625-7). Putnam.

Aelian Fragment. Kenneth M Cameron. (Illus.). 1977. 1.95 (ISBN 0-445-08587-8). Popular Library.

Aelita. Aleksei Nikolaevich Tolstoi. LC 81-2185. (MacMillan's Best of Soviet Science Fiction). 1981. 11.95 (ISBN 0-02-619200-4). Macmillan.

Aelita or, The Decline of Mars. Aleksei Nikolaevich Tolstoi. Tr. by Leland Fetzer from Rus. 140p. 1983. 15.00; pap. 4.50. Ardis Pubs.

Aeneid. Vergilius Maro, Publius. Tr. by Day, Lewis, Cecil. LC 52-13026. 1952. Oxford University Press.

Aeneid of Virgil: A Verse Translation. Maro Publius Vergilius & Allen Mandelbaum. LC 80-53773. (Illus.). 27.50 (ISBN 0-520-04439-8). University of California Press.

Aeneid of Virgil: Retold by N. B. Taylor. Illus. by Joan Kiddell-Monroe. N. B Taylor. LC 61-16310. (Pt. col.). 3.75, 2.81 lib. ed.,. Walck.

Aerie. J. Sloan McClean. 1975. 5.95 o.p. (ISBN 0-8402-1359-X). Nash Pub.

Aerie: A Gothic Novel. J. Sloan McLean. LC 74-83037. 5.95 (ISBN 0-8402-1359-X). Nash Pub.

Aerodrome. Rex Warner. 1982. pap. 7.95 (ISBN 0-19-281336-6). Oxford U Pr.

Aerodrome, a Love Story. Rex Warner. LC 47-2195. 1946. J. B. Lippincott Company.

Aerodrome: A Love Story Introd. by Angus Wilson. Rex Warner. 1966. bds., 5.95. Little.

Aerospace. Joseph H. Hughes, Jr. & James S. Priamos. LC 77-926280. 1977. pap. 3.25; signed 3.50. Aaron-Jenkins.

Aesop's & Other Fables. Aesop. 1971. Repr. of 1913 ed. 8.95x (ISBN 0-460-00657-6, Evman). Biblio Dist.

Aesop's Fables. (Tempo Classics Ser.). (Illus.). 192p. 1982. pap. 1.95 (ISBN 0-448-16968-1, Pub. by Tempo). Ace Bks.

Aesop's Fables. Valerius Babrius. Tr. by Denison B. Hull from Gr. LC 60-14237. 112p. 1974. pap. 2.95 (ISBN 0-226-03384-8, P577, Phoen). U of Chicago Pr.

Aesop's Fables. Alan Doan. LC 75-122365. (Illus.). 1971. 2.50 o.p. (ISBN 0-87529-115-5). Hallmark.

Afar in the Forest. A Tale of Adventure in North America. William Henry Giles Kingston. LC 46-44335. (On cover: Daring adventure library). 1884. T. Nelson and Sons.

Afersata. Berhane Marian Sahle Sellassie. (African Writers Ser.). 1969. pap. text ed. 3.00x (ISBN 0-435-90052-8). Heinemann Ed.

Affair. Emily Hahn. LC 35-5462. Bobbs-Merrill Company.

Affair. Morton Hunt. 1973. pap. 1.75 (ISBN 0-451-06820-3, E6820, Sig). NAL.

Affair. Derek Monsey. LC 73-168758. 1973. 2.25 (ISBN 0-491-01080-X). W. H. Allen.

Affair. Charles Percy Snow. LC 60-6324. 1960. Scribner.

Affair at Abu Mina. Peter William. LC 44-6839. 1944. Macrae-Smith-Company.

Affair at Flower Acres. Carolyn Wells. LC 23-818298. George H. Doran Company.

Affair at Helen's Court, by Carol Carnac Pseud. 1st Ed. Edith Caroline Rivett. LC 58-77974. 1958. Published for the Crime Club by Doubleday.

Affair at Honey Hill. Berry Fleming. LC 81-65833. 1981. 5.95 (ISBN 0-9604810-2-8). Cotton Lane.

Affair at Islington... Matthew White. LC 8-36620. 1897. F. A. Munsey.

Affair at Lover's Leap: A Tony Hunter Mystery. 1st Ed. Robert George Dean. LC 53-9103. 1953. Published for the Crime Club by Doubleday.

Affair at Palm Springs. Clifford Knight. LC 38-25880. 1938. Dodd, Mead & Company.

Affair at Pine Court: A Tale of the Adirondacks. Nelson Rust Gilbert. LC 7-30455. 1907. J. B. Lippincott Company.

Affair at Quala: A Novel. Thomas Helmore. LC 64-12481. 1964. Simon and Schuster.

Affair at Ritos Bay. Muriel Bradley. LC 47-4638. 1947. Pub. for the Crime Club by Doubleday.

Affair at Royalties. George Baxt. LC 78-37203. 1972. 4.95 (ISBN 0-684-12746-6). Scribner.

Affair at Santa Margarita. Barbara Tori. 1974. (pbk.) 1.50. Avon.

Affair at Santo Escombro. Sherman Oakes. 1974. (pbk.) 1.25. Dell.

Affair at the Boat Landing. Albert Benjamin Cunningham. LC 43-982. 1943. E. P. Dutton & Co., Inc.

Affair at the Grotto. Esther Haven Fonseca. LC 39-3179. 1939. Pub. for the Crime Club, Inc., by Doubleday, Doran & Company, Inc.

Affair at the Inn. Kate Douglas Smith Wiggin. LC 4-18896. 1904. Houghton, Mifflin and Company.

Affair at Tideways. Edith Austin Holton. LC 32-3294. Thomas Y. Crowell Company.

Affair at Timber Lake. Ann Anderson. 1975. (pbk.) 0.95. Dell.

Affair for the Baron. John Creasey. LC 68-17638. 1968. Walker.

Affair for Tomorrow. Bette Ziegler. LC 77-91238. 1978. 1.50. Jove Pubns.

Affair in Arcady. James Howard Wellard. LC 59-12461. 1959. Reynal.

Affair in Death Valley. Clifford Knight. LC 40-340718. 1940. Dodd, Mead & Company.

Affair in Duplex 9 B. William Andrew Johnston. LC 27-3367. George H. Doran Company.

Affair in Hong Kong. Dorothy Daniels. (O.s.i.). 1974. pap. 0.95 o.s.i. (ISBN 0-515-03357-X, N3357). Pyramid Pubns.

Affair in Marakesh. Dorothy Daniels. 1974. pap. 0.95 o.p. (ISBN 0-515-03342-1, N3342). Pyramid Pubns.

Affair of Chief Strongheart. Patrick O'Malley. LC 64-11271. 1964. M. S. Mill Co.; Distributed by Morrow.

Affair of Dishonor. William Frend De Morgan. LC 10-20179. 1910. 1.75. H. Holt and Company.

Affair of Doctors. Frances Rickett. LC 75-11145. 8.95 (ISBN 0-87795-109-8). Arbor House.

Affair of Honor. Robert Wilder. LC 76-81641. 1969. 6.95. Putnam.

Affair of Honour: A Novel. Stephen McKenna. LC 25-8664. 1925. Little, Brown, and Company.

Affair of John Donne. Patrick O'Malley. LC 64-21960. 1964. M. S. Mill Co.

Affair of Jolie Madame. Patrick O'Malley. LC 62-18302. 1963. M. S. Mill Co. and Distributed by Morrow.

Affair of Love. Frank Arthur Swinnerton. 1973. pap. 1.25 o.s.i. (78-720). Lancer.

Affair of Love. 1st Ed. Frank Arthur Swinnerton. LC 52-133797. 1953. Doubleday.

Affair of Men. Errol Brathwaite. LC 62-11112. 1962. St. Martin's Press.

Affair of Nina B. Johannes Mario Simmel. Orig. Title: Affare Nina B. 1978. pap. 1.95 (ISBN 0-445-04160-9). Popular Lib.

Affair of Risk. Jayne Castle. (Candlelight Ecstasy Ser.: No. 55). (Orig.). 1982. pap. 1.95 (ISBN 0-440-10054-2). Dell.

Affair of Sorcerers. George C Chesbro. LC 78-27654. 9.95 (ISBN 0-671-24625-9). Simon and Schuster.

Affair Of Sorcerers. George C Chesbro. (Signet Book). 1979. 2.25 (ISBN 0-451-09243-0). New American Library.

Affair of State. Pat Frank. LC 48-8236. 1948. J. B. Lippincott Co.

Affair of State. Ken John & David Welch. 1971. 5.95 o.p. (ISBN 0-8402-1177-5). Nash Pub.

Affair of State. Ken Johnson & David Welch. LC 76-143009. 1971. 6.95 (ISBN 0-8402-1177-5). Nash Pub.

Affair of State. John Collis Snaith. LC 13-63342. 1913. 1.25. Doubleday, Page & Co.

Affair of Strangers. John Crosby. 1976. 1.95. Warner Books.

Affair of Strangers: A Novel. John Crosby. LC 74-30071. 1975. 8.95 (ISBN 0-8128-1785-0). Stein and Day.

Affair of Swan Lake. Patrick O'Malley. LC 62-9314. 1962. M. S. Mill Co. and W. Morrow.

Affair of the Albatross. Jane Edwards. 1973. pap. 0.75 o.s.i. (01-375). Lancer.

Affair of the Black Sombrero. Clifford Knight. LC 39-9211. 1939. Dodd, Mead & Company.

Affair of the Blood-Stained Egg Cosy. James Anderson. 1978. pap. 2.95 (ISBN 0-380-01919-1, 638266). Avon.

Affair of the Blood-Stained Egg Cosy. James Anderson. (McKay-Washburn Mystery Ser.). 1977. 6.95 o.p. (ISBN 0-679-50727-2). McKay.

Affair of the Bloodstained Egg Cosy: A Novel of Suspense. James Anderson. LC 76-62541. 1976. 6.95 (ISBN 0-679-50727-2). McKay.

Affair of the Blue Pig. Patrick O'Malley. LC 65-22619. bds., 3.50. Mill, Dist. Morrow.

Affair of the Bumbling Briton. Patrick O'Malley. LC 65-18512. bds., 3.50. M. S. Mill; Dist. Morrow.

Affair of the Circus Queen. Clifford Knight. LC 40-7706. 1940. Dodd, Mead & Company.

Affair of the Corpse Escort... Clifford Knight. LC 46-183534. 1946. David McKay Company.

Affair of the Crimson Gull. Clifford Knight. LC 41-5437. 1941. Dodd, Mead & Company.

Affair of the Dead Stranger. Clifford Knight. LC 44-9743. 1944. Dodd, Mead & Company.

Affair of the Exotic Dancer. Ben Benson. LC 58-105694. 1958. M. S. Mill Co. and W. Morrow.

Affair of the Fainting Butler. Clifford Knight. LC 43-152944. 1943. Dodd, Mead & Company.

Affair of the Gallows Tree... Stephen Chalmers. LC 30-20596. 1930. Pub. for The Crime Club, Inc., by Doubleday, Doran & Company, Inc.

Affair of the Ginger Lei. Clifford Knight. LC 38-9726. 1938. Dodd, Mead & Company.

Affair of the Golden Buzzard. Clifford Knight. LC 47-5995. 1946. David McKkay Company.

Affair of the Heart. Margaret Long. LC 52-7131. 1953. Random House.

Affair of the Heart. Jean Potts. LC 73-100646. 1970. 3.95. Scribner.

Affair of the Heart. Joan Smith. 1980. pap. 1.75 (ISBN 0-449-50061-6, Coventry). Fawcett.

Affair of the Heart: A Novel. Joan Smith. (Fawcett Crest Book). 1977. 1.50 (ISBN 0-449-23092-9). Fawcett Publications.

Affair of the Heavenly Voice. Clifford Knight. LC 37-23345. 1937. Dodd, Mead & Company.

Affair of the Jade Monkey. Clifford Knight. LC 43-5354. 1943. Dodd, Mead & Company.

Affair of the Limping Sailor. Clifford Knight. LC 42-10022. 1942. Dodd, Mead & Company.

Affair of the Malacca Stick. Charlton Andrews. LC 36-19837. I. Washburn, Inc.

Affair of the Poisons. Frances Mossiker. 1972. pap. 1.25 o.s.i. (ISBN 0-447-78662-8, 78-711). Lancer.

Affair of the Red Mosaic. Patrick O'Malley. LC 61-13547. 1961. M. S. Mill Co.

Affair of the Scarlet Crab. Clifford Knight. LC 37-329420. 1937. Dodd, Mead & Company.

Affair of the Semiramis Hotel. Alfred Edward Woodley Mason. LC 17-2027. 1917. C. Scribner's Sons.

Affair of the Sixth Button. Clifford Knight. LC 47-12474. (armchair mystery). 1947. D. McKay Co.

Affair of the Skiing Clown. Clifford Knight. LC 41-18112. 1941. Dodd, Mead & Company.

Affair of the Splintered Heart. Clifford Knight. LC 42-22618. 1942. Dodd, Mead & Company.

Affair of the Substitute Doctor. Street, Cecil John Charles. LC 51-11301. (Red badge detective). 1951. Dodd, Mead.

Affair of the Syrian Dagger. Charlton Andrews. LC 37-876098. I. Washburn, Inc.

Affair on the Painted Desert. Clifford Knight. LC 39-259611. 1939. Dódd, Mead & Company.

Affair on the Rhine. Dennis Weber. 1981. pap. 1.95 (ISBN 0-8439-0906-4, Leisure Bks). Nordon Pubns.

Affair to Remember. Owen Aherne. LC 57-3878. (Avon T-182). 1957. Avon Publications.

Affair to Remember. Barbara Cameron. (Candlelight Ecstasy Ser.: No. 124). (Orig.). 1983. pap. 1.95 (ISBN 0-440-11405-5). Dell.

Affair. 1st Ed. Hans Koningsberger. LC 58-6533. 1958. Knopf.

Affairs at the Chateau. Gertrude M. Robins Reynolds. LC 29-19248. 1929. Pub. for The Crime Club, Inc., by Doubleday, Doran & Company, Inc.

Affairs for the Baron. Anthony Morton. 1968. 3.95 o.p. (ISBN 0-8027-5001-X). Walker & Co.

Affairs in Tokyo. Cover Painting by Clark Hulings. John McPartland. LC 54-33174. (Gold medal books, 406). 1954. Fawcett Publications.

Affairs of a Brother & Sister. Thomas H. Hilton. pap. 1.95 o.p. (ISBN 0-87056-202-9, 6202). Brandon.

Affairs of Caroline Cherie, by Cecil Saint-Laurent Pseud. Translated from the French by Coburn Gilman. Jacques Laurent. LC 54-11172. 1954. Crown Publishers.

Affairs of Destiny. Georges Simenon & Gilbert, Stuart, Tr. LC 44-53467. 1944. Harcourt, Brace and Company.

Affairs of Doctor Maurer. Lewis W. Moore. 1970. 2.95 o.p. Vantage.

Affairs of Flavie (Les Heritiers Euffe) Gabriel Chevallier. Tr. by Godefroi, Jocelyn. LC 49-8145. 1949. Doubleday.

Affairs of Gidget. Frederick Kohner. LC 63-10777. 1963. Bantam Books.

Affairs of Gwendolyn. Henry Howard Harper. LC 39-380. 1938.

Affairs of Judge Black. John Mankin. LC 46-22545. 1946. The Hobson Book Press.

Affairs of Love. Glenna Finley, pseud. 1980. pap. 1.95 (ISBN 0-451-11174-5, AJ1174, Sig). NAL.

Affairs of Nicholas Culpeper: A Novel. Mabel Louise Tyrrell. LC 46-3015. 1946. Macrae-Smith-Company.

Affairs of O'Malley. William Briggs MacHarg. LC 40-6340. 1940. The Dial Press.

Affairs of Patricia: A Novel. May Christie. LC 35-29667. Grosset & Dunlap.

Affairs of State. Margot Arnold, pseud. 352p. 1983. pap. 3.50 (ISBN 0-449-12384-7, GM). Fawcett.

Affairs of State: Being an Account of Certain Surprising Adventures Which Befell an American Family in the Land of Windmills. Burton Egbert Stevenson. LC 6-34368. 1906. H. Holt and Company.

Affairs of the Generals. Hans Hellmut Kirst. LC 78-12394. 1979. 9.95 (ISBN 0-698-10923-6). Coward, McCann & Geoghegan.

Affairs of the Generals. Hans Hellmut Kirst. 1980. 1.95 (ISBN 0-449-23897-0). Fawcett Crest Books.

Affairs of the Heart. Nora Powers. 192p. (Orig.). 1980. pap. 1.50 (ISBN 0-671-57003-X, Pub. by Silhouette Bks). S&S.

Affairs of Tom Long: A Novel. LC 46-22507. 1946. The Hobson Book Press.

Affare Nina B. see Affair of Nina B.

Affecting Scenes: Being Passages from the Diary of a Physician... Samuel Warren. LC 15-21833. 1831. J. & J. Harper.

Affectionate Cousins: T. Sturge Moore & Maria Appia. Sylvia Legge. (Illus.). 1980. text ed. 24.50x (ISBN 0-19-211761-0). Oxford U Pr.

Affectionately, Eve. Upton Beall Sinclair. 1971. 3.75 o.p. Twayne.

Affectionately, Eve; a Novel. Upton Beall Sinclair. LC 61-13049. 1961. Twayne Publishers.

Affinities. A Romance of to-Day. Rosa Caroline Murray-Prior Praed. (On cover: Seaside library. Pocket ed. no. 477). 1885. G. Munro.

Affinities: A Short Story Anthology. Ed. by John Tytell. LC 77-107309. 1970. Crowell.

Affinities: A Short Story Anthology: with Headnotes. Ed. by John Tytell. LC 76-375535. 6.00 (ISBN 0-690-05248-0). Crowell.

Affinities: And Other Stories. Mary Roberts Rinehart. LC 20-9275. 1.75. George H. Doran Company.

Affinities: And Other Stories. Mary Roberts Rinehart. LC 30-12330. 1922. A. L. Burt Company.

Affinity. Katherine Hale. LC 78-27623. 1978. 1.95 (ISBN 0-380-40907-0). Avon Books.

Affinity. Harry Angle Raum. LC 8-25997. 1908.

Affirmation. Christopher Priest. LC 81-252. 10.95 (ISBN 0-684-16957-6). Scribner.

Afflicted Man's Companion. Thomas Brooks et al. 1972. 6.00 o.p. (ISBN 0-8254-2224-8, RBDH). Kregel.

Afield and Afloat. Frank Richard Stockton. LC 72-10809. (Short story index reprint series). 1973. (ISBN 0-8369-4230-2). Books for Libraries Press.

Afield and Afloat. Frank Richard Stockton. LC 5157. 1900. C. Scribner's Sons.

Aflame & Afun of Walking Faces. Kenneth Patchen. LC 75-103371. 1970. 5.00 (ISBN 0-8112-0341-7); pap. 1.50 (ISBN 0-8112-0136-8, NDP292). New Directions.

Afloat and Ashore: A Sea Tale. household ed. James Fenimore Cooper. Ed. by Cooper, Susan Fenimore. 1884. Houghton, Mifflin and Company.

Afloat and Ashore: A Sea Tale. James Fenimore Cooper. (On cover: Lovell's library, no. 532). 1885. J. W. Lovell Company.

Afloat and Ashore. A Sea Tale. James Fenimore Cooper. (On cover: Seaside library, Pocket ed. no. 413). 1885. G. Munro.

Afloat and Ashore. A Sea Tale. James Fenimore Cooper. LC 4-15427. (In his Works. Mohawk ed.). 1896. Etc. G. P. Putnam's Sons.

Afloat and Ashore. A Sea Tale. James Fenimore Cooper. LC 4-19553. 1897. D. Appleton and Company.

Afloat and Ashore. Biographical Illus., Pictures of Contemporary Scenes, Drawings Reproduced from Early Eds., with Introd., Captions by Allen Knots, Jr. Reissue. James Fenimore Cooper. (Great illustrated classics). 1965. 4.50. Dodd.

Afloat and Ashore: Or, The Adventures of Miles Walingford. James Fenimore Cooper. LC 4-35653. 1844. The Author.

Afloat and Shore. A Sea Tale. new ed. James Fenimore Cooper. LC 4-31639. 1867. Hurd and Houghton.

Afraid. Sidney Dark. LC 17-2344. 1917. 1.35. John Lane.

Afraid in the Dark: A Novel. Mark Derby. LC 51-14902. 1952. Viking Press.

Afraid in the Dark: A Novel by Mark Derby Pseud. Harry Wilcox. LC 51-14902. 1952. Viking Press.

Afraid of the Dark. Mary Linn Roby. 1974. (pbk.) 0.95 (ISBN 0-523-00311-0). Pinnacle Books.

Afraid of the Dark. Mary Linn Roby. LC 65-20913. (Red badge mystery). 1965. Dodd, Mead.

Afraid of The Dark. Larry G. Stenzel. 187p. (Orig.). 1981. pap. 4.50 (ISBN 0-910021-01-5). Samuel P Co.

Afraid to Love. Marion White. LC 37-12214. M. S. Mill Co., Inc.

Afraja, a Norwegian and Lapland Tale: Or, Life and Love in Norway. Theodor Mugge. Tr. by Morris, Edward Joy. LC 7-26090. 1854. Lindsay & Blakiston.

African. William Farquhar Conton. (African Writers Ser.). 1964. pap. text ed. 3.00x (ISBN 0-435-90012-9). Heinemann Ed.

African. Harold Courlander. 1977. 7.95 (ISBN 0-517-50680-7). Crown.

African: A Novel. William Farquhar Conton. LC 60-5861. 1960. Little, Brown.

African: A Novel. Harold Courlander. LC 67-27026. 1967. Crown Publishers.

African Fabiola: Or, The Church of Carthage in the Days of Tertullian. O'Connell, Joseph P., Tr. LC 5-42992. 1881. D. & J. Sadlier & Co.

African Harvest. Nora Stevenson. LC 29-748530. 1929. I. Washburn.

African Heart-Beat: A Novel. Ida Hurst. LC 48-15982. 1946. J. Long.

African Love Song. Helen Murray. (Orig.). 1980. pap. 1.75 (ISBN 0-8439-8010-9, Tiara Bks). Nordon Pubns.

African Millionaire. Grant Allen. LC 75-32732. (Literature of Mystery and Detection). (Illus.). 1976. 18.00 (ISBN 0-405-07862-5). Arno Press.

African Millionaire: Episodes in the Life of the Illustrious Colonel Clay. Grant Allen. LC 80-65318. (Illus.). 1980. 4.50 (ISBN 0-486-23992-6). Dover Publications.

African Nights Entertainment. Alec John Dawson. LC 3446. 1900. Dodd, Mead and Company.

African Poison Murders. Elspeth Joscelin Grant Huxley. LC 75-44985. (Fifty classics of crime fiction, 1900-1950; 28). 1976. 12.00 (ISBN 0-8240-2377-3). Garland Pub. Co.

African Poison Murders. Elspeth Joscelin Grant Huxley. LC 40-1701. 1940. Harper & Brothers.

African Poison Murders. Elspeth Joscelin Grant Huxley. (Perennial Library.). 1981. 2.25 (ISBN 0-06-080540-4). Harper & Row.

African Preacher: An Authentic Narrative. William Spottswood White. LC 72-3105. (Black Heritage Library Collection). (Illus.). 1972. 9.50 (ISBN 0-8369-9092-7). Books for Libraries Press.

African Preacher. An Authentic Narrative. William Spottswood White. LC 8-36558. Presbyterian Board of Publications.

African Queen. Cecil Scott Forester. LC 77-2868. 1977. 10.00 (ISBN 0-89244-065-1). Queens House.

African Queen. Cecil Scott Forester. LC 35-24933. 1935. Little, Brown, and Company.

African Queen. Cecil Scott Forester. LC 40-27677. (Half-title: The modern library of the world's best books). 1940. The Modern Library.

African Rhythms: Selected Stories and Poems. Ed. by Charlotte Brooks. LC 74-188893. (Illus.). 1974. 1.95 (ISBN 0-671-48758-2). Pocket Books: Distributed by Simon & Schuster.

African Shadows. Ugo Mochi. 1933. Repr. 12.00 o.s.i. Finch Pr.

African Short Stories. Ed. by Charles R. Larson. (African American Library Ser). 1970. pap. 1.50 o.p. (05271, Collier). Macmillan.

African Short Stories: A Collection of Contemporary African Writing. Ed. by Charles R. Larson. LC 70-109450. (American Library). 1970. 1.50. Collier Books.

African Stories. Doris May Lessing. LC 65-23003. bds., 7.95. S. & S.

African Stories. Doris May Lessing. (U7044). 1966. Ballantine.

African Stories. Doris May Lessing. LC 65-230031. 1975. (pbk.) 1.95. Popular Library.

African Stories. Doris May Lessing. LC 81-8915. (Touchstone book). 1981. 9.95 (ISBN 0-671-42809-8). Simon and Schuster.

African Trio: Talatala, Tropic Moon, Aboard the Aquitaine. Georges Simenon. LC 78-22272. 9.95 (ISBN 0-15-103955-0). Harcourt Brace Jovanovich.

African Witch. Joyce Cary. LC 36-21351. 1936. W. Morrow and Company.

Africana. William Harrison. LC 76-49494. 1977. 8.95 (ISBN 0-688-03166-8). Morrow.

Africans. Betty Winston. (Orig.). 1983. pap. 3.95 (ISBN 0-440-00076-9). Dell.

Afrikaans Short Stories. Felix V. Lategan. 1964. 7.95 o.p. Dufour.

Afro-American Literature. Ed. by William Adams. LC 77-12560. (Illus.). Houghton Mifflin.

Afro-American Literature: Fiction. Ed. by William Adams et al. (Afro-American Literature Ser). (gr. 9-12). 1970. pap. 6.08 (ISBN 0-395-01977-X, 2-00204). HM.

After. Robert Woodruff Anderson. LC 72-11439. 1973. 6.95 (ISBN 0-394-48536-X). Random House.

After a Hundred Years... Ruth Eleanor McKee. LC 35-25388. 1935. Doubleday, Doran & Company, Inc.

After a Man's Heart. Louise Platt Nauck. LC 37-21534. 1937. Macrae-Smith-Company.

After a Man's Heart. Jean Randall. LC 37-21534. 1937. Macrae Smith Company.

After: A Novel. Robert Woodruff Anderson. (Fawcett crest book). 1974. (pbk.) 1.50. Fawcett.

After: A Novel. Frederic Pierpont Ladd. LC 18-5499. 1918. 1.50. Duffield & Company.

After All. Mary Cholmondeley. LC 13-23733. 1913. D. Appleton and Company.

After All. George Frederick Hummel. LC 23-9747. Boni and Liveright.

After All. George Frederick Hummel. LC 26-7513. 1925. Boni and Liveright.

After All. A Novel. Lillian Spencer. LC 8-15507. 1885. S. C. Griggs and Company.

After All These Years. Elinor Maxwell. LC 35-5301. Arcadia House.

After All, They're Only Cats. Patricia Moyes. (Orig.). 1973. pap. 0.95 o.p. (09221). Curtis.

After All, This Is England. Robert Muller. LC 78-351650. 1967. Penguin.

After Bread: A Story of Polish Emigrant Life to America. Henryk Sienkiewicz & Hlasko, Vatslaf A., Tr. LC 8-6886. R. F. Fenno & Company.

After Cataclysm: A Romance of the Age to Come. Henry Percy Blanchard. 1909. Cochrane Publishing Company.

After Claude. Harriet Daimler. LC 72-97609. 1973. 6.95 (ISBN 0-374-10131-0). Farrar, Straus and Giroux.

After Claude. Iris Owens. 216p. 1973. 6.95 o.p. (ISBN 0-374-10131-0). FS&G.

After Damien: Dutton, Yankee Soldier at Molokai. Howard E. Crouch & Mary Augustine. LC 81-67534. (Illus.). 144p. (Orig.). 1981. pap. 5.95 (ISBN 0-9606330-0-6). Damien-Dutton Soc.

After Dark. Manly Wade Wellman. LC 80-650. 1980. 8.95 (ISBN 0-385-15604-9). Doubleday.

After Dark, and Other Stories. Wilkie Collins. LC 72-5911. (Short story index reprint series). 1972. (ISBN 0-8369-4204-3). Books for Libraries Press.

After Dark: And Other Stories. Wilkie Collins. LC 6-39307. Harper & Brothers.

After Dark: And Other Stories. Wilkie Collins. LC 3-27791. 1875. Harper & Brothers.

After-Dinner Stories from Balzac. Done into English by Myndart Vereist. With an Introduction by Edgar Saltus... Honore De Balzac & Vereist, Myndart. Pseud., Tr. LC 6-6818. 1886. G. J. Coombes.

After-Dinner Story... Cornell George Hopley-Woolrich. LC 44-8830. 1944. J. B. Lippincott Company.

After Divorce! Charles B Parmer. LC 33-148. 1932. G. H. Watt.

After Doomsday. Poul Anderson. LC 62-2296. (Ballantine books, 579). 1962. Ballantine Books.

After Eli. Terry Kay. LC 80-27577. 1981. 10.95 (ISBN 0-395-30854-2). Houghton Mifflin.

After Experience. W. D. Snodgrass. LC 67-22508. Repr. of 1968 ed. 6.95 o.p. (ISBN 0-06-013947-1, HarpT). Har-Row.

After Five O'clock. Elizabeth Frances Corbett. LC 32-24668. The Century Co.

After Freud. Mary Elsie Robertson. LC 80-20497. 1981. 9.95 (ISBN 0-87395-462-9). State University of New York Press.

After Hard Guns. Eli Mitchell. 272p. (Orig.). 1980. pap. 1.95 (ISBN 0-89083-699-X). Zebra.

After His Kind. John Williamson Palmer. LC 7-35776. (Leisure hour series, no. 184). 1886. H. Holt and Company.

After Hours. William Frederick Feld. LC 16-21263. 1916. 1.00. Loyola University Press.

After Hours. Edwin Torres. LC 79-4114. 9.95 (ISBN 0-8037-0159-4). Dial Press.

After House. Mary Roberts Rinehart. 1975. (pbk.) 0.95. Dell.

After House. Mary Roberts Rinehart. LC 41-13062. 1941. Triangle Books.

After House. Mary Roberts Rinehart. LC 81-306. 1981. 11.95 (ISBN 0-8161-3236-4). G. K. Hall.

After House: A Story of Love, Mystery and a Private Yacht. Mary Roberts Rinehart. LC 14-235593. 1914. Houghton Mifflin Company.

After Innocence. Ian Gordon, pseud. LC 55-8348. (Dell first edition 58). 1955. Dell Pub. Co.

After Julius. Elizabeth Jane Howard. LC 87-47562. 272p. 1982. pap. 2.84i (ISBN 0-06-080626-5, P626, PL). Har-Row.

After Julius. Elizabeth Jane Howard. 1966. 4.95 o.p. (ISBN 0-670-10902-9). Viking Pr.

After Leaving Mr. Mackenzie. Jean Rhys. LC 73-13785. 1974. (pbk.) 1.55 (ISBN 0-394-71024-X). Vintage Books.

After Leaving Mr. Mackenzie. Jean Rhys. LC 79-160658. 1972. 5.95 (ISBN 0-06-013534-4). Harper & Row.

After Leaving Mr. Mackenzie. Jean Rhys. LC 31-16669. 1931. A. A. Knopf.

After London: Or, Wild England. Richard Jefferies. LC 74-16503. (Science Fiction). 1975. 25.00 (ISBN 0-405-06301-6). Arno Press.

After London: Or, Wild England. Richard Jefferies. LC 4-15316. 1885. Cassell & Company, Limited.

After London, or, Wild England, 2 pts. Richard Jefferies. Incl. Pt 1. Relapse into Barbarism; Pt 2. Wild England. LC 74-16503. (Science Fiction Ser). 450p. 1975. Repr. of 1899 ed. 25.00x (ISBN 0-405-06301-6). Ayer Co.

After Long Grief and Pain. Eliza M. J. Humphreys. (On cover: Lovell's library, no. 1149). 1888. J. W. Lovell Company.

After Long Silence... & Other Liberian Stories. R. H. Brown. 1978. 6.95 (ISBN 0-533-03833-2). Vantage.

After Long Silence. 1st Ed. Robert Gutwillig. LC 57-119980. 1958. Little, Brown.

After Long Years: Or, Chedayne of Kotono. A Story of the Early Days of the Republic. Ausburn Towner. LC 8-29831. 1882. Dodd, Mead & Company.

After Love. Jacqueline Briskin. LC 74-3448. 1974. (pbk.) 1.50. Bantam Books.

After Many a Summer Dies the Swan. Aldous Leonard Huxley. LC 65-9705. (Harper perennial classic). 1965. Harper & Row.

After Many a Summer Dies the Swan. Aldous Leonard Huxley. LC 40-27086. 1939. Harper & Brothers.

After Many Days. Joye Hoekzema. LC 46-232. 1945. Zondervan Publishing House.

After Many Days: a Novel. Frances Christine Tiernan. (On cover: Appletons' library of American fiction no. 16). 1877. D. Appleton and Company.

After Many Days; a Novel. Frances Christine Tiernan. LC 5-9716. 1905. D. Appleton and Company.

After Many Days, and Other Stories. Junius Lackland Hempstead. 1897. F. T. Neely.

After Many Years. Robert Boggs. The Authors' Publishing Company.

After Midnight. Irmgard Keun & Clough, James, Tr. LC 38-8825. 1938. A. A. Knopf.

After Midnight. Helen Nielsen. LC 66-17185. 1966. Morrow.

After Midnight Ghost Book. James Hale. LC 81-2963. 1981. 12.95 (ISBN 0-531-09860-5). F. Watts.

After Noon. Susan Ertz. LC 26-9019. 1926. D. Appleton & Company.

After Office Hours. Barbara Black. (O.s.i.). 1974. pap. 0.95 o.s.i. (AN1278, Award). Univ Pub & Dist.

After Our War. John Balaban. LC 73-13313. (Pitt poetry series). 1974. (pbk.) 2.95 (ISBN 0-8229-5247-5). University of Pittsburgh Press.

After Passion. Jerome Shard. LC 36-6963. Godwin.

After Passion. Gladys Sloan. LC 41-5502. Phoenix Press.

After Passion. Leona Slottman. LC 41-5502. 1940. Phoenix Press.

After Pentecost. Richard Bankowsky. 1961. 6.95 o.p. (ISBN 0-394-41436-5). Random.

After Pentecost: An Epistle to the Romans. Richard Bankowsky. LC 61-62490. 1961. Random House.

After Rain. Netta Muskett. 1975. pap. 1.25 o.p. (ISBN 0-515-03759-1). BJ Pub Group.

After Rome, Africa. Brian Glanville. 1977. 6.00 o.p. State Mutual Bk.

After Seven Years. Mary McDonough. LC 51-8661. 1951. Vantage Press.

After Strange Gods. Josephine Weatherly. LC 13-24798. 1913. Broadway Publishing Co.

After Success, What? By Sara Lippincott Pseud. 1st Ed. Sara Lippincott Richards. LC 56-131254. 1956. Pageant Press.

After Such Knowledge. Sallie Bingham. LC 60-7195. 1960. Houghton Mifflin.

After Such Pleasure... Dorothy Rothschild Parker. LC 33-31313. 1932. The Viking Press.

After Sundown. Anne Hampson. (Presents Ser.). 1974. pap. 1.25 (ISBN 0-373-70556-5, 70556, Pub by Harlequin). PB.

After the Act. Winston Graham. (Crest bk., R1087). 1968. Fawcett.

After the Act. 1st Amer. Ed. Winston Graham. LC 66-11739. 1966. 4.95. Doubleday.

After the Afternoon. Arthur MacArthur. LC 41-24078. 1941. D. Appleton-Century Company, Incorporated.

After the Apocalypse. W. Randolph Fox. (Orig.). 1980. pap. 1.95 (ISBN 0-532-23118-X). Woodhill.

After the Ball. a romance of youth today, illustrated with scenes from the photoplay "after the ball" as produced by renco film company, from the widley popular song story of the same name by charles k. harris. ed. James Colwell. LC 25-812. The Time-Mirror Press.

After the Banquet. Yukio Mishima, pseud. LC 80-14686. 1980. 4.95 (ISBN 0-399-50486-9). Perigee Books.

After the Bugles. Elmer Kelton. 160p. (Orig.). 1981. pap. 1.95 (ISBN 0-553-20046-1). Bantam.

After the Crash. rev. ed. Geoffrey Abert. 1982. pap. 3.95 (ISBN 0-451-11869-3, AE1869, Sig). NAL.

After the Day. Robert H Ross Church. LC 65-8528. 1964. Sidgwich and Jackson.

After the Deacon Was Murdered. Cornelia Penfield Lathrop. LC 33-6474. 1933. G. P. Putnam's Sons.
After the Death of Don Juan. Sylvia Townsend Warner. LC 38-29040. 1939. The Viking Press.
After the Divorce: A Romance of Grazia Deledda. Grazia Deledda. Tr. by Lansdale, Maria Hornor. LC 5-7381. 1905. H. Holt and Company.
After the Fall. Ed. by Robert Sheckley. 224p. (Orig.). 1981. pap. 2.25 (ISBN 0-441-00941-7). Ace Bks.
After the Festival. March Cost, pseud. LC 66-28883. (O.s.i.). 1966. 7.95 o.s.i. (ISBN 0-8149-0049-6). Vanguard.
After the Festival. Peggy Morrison, pseud. LC 66-28883. 1966. Vanguard Press.
After the Fine Weather. Michael Francis Gilbert. LC 63-10617. 1963. Harper & Row.
After the Fire. Rose Marie Ferris. (Candlelight Ecstasy Ser.: No. 37). (Orig.). 1982. pap. 1.75 (ISBN 0-440-10036-4). Dell.
After the First Death. Lawrence Block. LC 69-10289. (Cock Robin mystery). 1969. Macmillan.
After the First Death. Donald Taylor. LC 72-93479. 176p. 1973. 5.95 o.p. (ISBN 0-8076-0675-8). Braziller.
After the First Death: A Novel. Donald Taylor. LC 72-93479. 1973. 5.95 (ISBN 0-8076-0675-8). G. Braziller.
After the First Death There Is No Other. Natalie L. M. Petesch. LC 74-8851. 1974. 7.95 (ISBN 0-87745-050-1). University of Iowa Press.
After the Freshet. Edward Augustus Rand. LC 8-217. (V. I. F. series, v. 2). D. Lothrop and Company.
After the Glory. Helen Topping Miller. LC 58-126387. 1958. Appleton-Century-Crofts.
After the Good War: A Love Story. Peter Roger Breggin. LC 72-80344. 1972. 6.95 (ISBN 0-8128-1492-4). Stein and Day.
After the Harvest. Edith Snyder Pedersen. LC 49-8608. 1949. Zondervan Pub. House.
After the Hawk. Richard H. Curtis. (Skymasters Ser.). 320p. 1982. pap. 3.25 (ISBN 0-440-00286-9, Emerald). Dell.
After the Killing. Dudley Randall. (Third World Press Ser). 1973. pap. 1.25. Broadside.
After the Last Race. Dean Koontz. LC 74-77848. 1974. 8.95 (ISBN 0-689-10621-1). Atheneum.
After the Last Race. Dean Koontz. LC 74-77848. (Fawcett Crest Books). 1975. 1.50. Fawcett.
After the Manner of Men. Francis Lynde. LC 16-17656. 1916. C. Scribner's Sons.
After the Night Has Passed. A Novel. Laura Eugenia Newhall. LC 7-1172. (On cover: The pastime series, no. 39). Laird & Lee.
After the Ninth Hour: A Picture of the Dawn of the Christian Era. Marie Reynes-Monlaur. LC 7-1940. 1906. B. Herder.
After the Pardon. Matilde Serao. LC 9-15207. 1909. The Stuyvesant Press.
After the Planners. Robert Goodman. LC 74-154100. 1973. pap. 4.95 o.p. (ISBN 0-671-21530-2, Touchstone Bks). S&S.
After the Prom. Hadden Luce. 1977. pap. 3.50 o.s.i. Vanity.
After the Rain. John Bowen. LC 58-11034. (Ballantine books, an original, 284K). 1959. Ballantine Books.
After the Rapture. Ann Laurie. 3.50 o.p. Carlton.
After the Ruptured Duck. Joseph P. Aulisio. 6.75 o.p. Carlton.
After the Sex Struck: Or, Zugassent's Discovery. George Noyes Miller. (On cover: Copley square series). Arena Publishing Company.
After the Storm. Arlo D Pollock. LC 37-16936. 1937. Home Printing Co.
After the Storm. Claudette Williams. 1979. pap. 1.75 (ISBN 0-449-23928-4, Crest). Fawcett.
After the Storm. Claudette Williams (ISBN 0-449-23081-3). Fawcett Crest.
After the Storm: A Novel. Albert Benjamin Cunningham. LC 49-4132. 1949. E. P. Dutton.
After the Storm: A Novel. Annie Greene Nelson. LC 76-14493. 1976. 12.00 (ISBN 0-87152-243-8). Reprint Co.
After the Storm: A Novel. Annie Greene Nelson. LC 42-14635. 1942. Hampton Publishing Company.
After the Trial: A Novel. 1st Ed. Eric Roman. LC 67-25656. 1968. bds., 4.95. Citadel.
After the Verdict. Anthony Gilbert. (YA) (gr. 9-12). pap. 0.50 o.p. (R1041). Pyramid Pubns.
After the Verdict. Robert Smythe Hichens. LC 24-18269. George H. Doran Company.
After the Verdict. Elizabeth Garver Jordan. LC 39-8348. 1939. D. Appleton-Century Company, Incorporated.
After the Verdict: By Anthony Gilbert Pseud. Lucy Beatrice Malleson. LC 61-12166. (Random House mystery). 1961. Random House.
After the Wake. Brendan Behan. Ed. by Peter Fallon. 160p. 1982. 30.00x (ISBN 0-905140-97-4, Pub. by O'Brien Pr Ireland). State Mutual Bk.
After the War. Herbert R Coursen. LC 81-4241. (Illus.). 1981. 13.95 (ISBN 0-918606-06-3) (ISBN 0-918606-05-5). Heidelberg Graphics.
After the War. Daniel Stern. 1972. pap. 0.95 o.p. (75-300). Lancer.
After the War: A Novel. Daniel Stern. LC 67-15271. 1967. Putnam.
After the Wedding Anniversary. Bettina Linn. LC 64-21825. 1965. A. S. Barnes.
After the Widow Changed Her Mind. Cornelia Penfield Lathrop. LC 33-33685. 1933. G. P. Putnam's Sons.
After the Wind. Eileen Lottman. (Dell Book). 1979. 2.50 (ISBN 0-440-18138-0). Dell Pub. Co.
After They Learn to Dance. Lee Hopkins. LC 75-316450. (Yes! Capra chapbook series; no. 25). (Illus.). 1974. 2.50 (ISBN 0-88496-014-5) (ISBN 0-88496-013-7). Capra Press.
After Things Fell Apart. Ron Goulart. LC 77-4776. (Gregg Press science fiction series). 1977. 10.00 (ISBN 0-8398-2368-1). Gregg Press.
After Thirty. Julian Leonard Street. LC 19-135385. 1919. The Century Co.
After This: A Novel. Ryland Kent. LC 39-297211. 1939. Harper & Brothers.
After to-Morrow and The New Love. Robert Smythe Hichens. LC 7-4757. (On cover: Merriam's voilet series. 5). The Merriman Company.
After Tomorrow. Dref Keric. LC 60-16263. 1960. Forum Pub. Co.
After Tomorrow: By Jennifer Ames Pseud. Maysie Greig. LC 51-11470. 1951. Bouregy & Curl.
After Twelve Thousand Years. Stanton Arthur Coblentz. 5.00; pap. 2.00. Fantasy Pub Co.
After Twelve Thousand Years. Stanton Arthur Coblentz. Ed. by Lester Del Rey. LC 75-398. (Library of Science Fiction). 1975. lib. bdg. 17.50 (ISBN 0-8240-1404-9). Garland Pub.
After Twenty Years: And Other Stories. Julian Sturgis. LC 8-16862. 1892. Longmans, Green, and Co.
After Utopia. Mack Reynolds, pseud. 1977. 1.50 (ISBN 0-441-00958-1). Ace Books.
After War. Arnold Friedrich Vieth von Golsennau. LC 31-6076. 1931. Dodd, Mead & Company.
After Weary Years. Cornelius O'Brien. LC 7-33185. 1885. J. Murphy & Co.
After Worlds Collide. Edwin Balmer & Philip Wylie. LC 34-8579. 1934. Frederick A. Stokes Company.
After Worlds Collide. Philip Wylie & Edwin Balmer. 1970. pap. 0.75 o.p. (ISBN 0-446-64361-0, 64-361). Paperback Lib.
After Worlds Collide: By Edwin Balmer and Philip Wylie. Edwin Balmer & Philip Wylie. LC 51-5074. 1950. Lippincott.
After You with the Pistol. Kyril Bonfiglioli. LC 80-937. 1980. 8.95 (ISBN 0-385-17190-0). Published for the Crime Club by Doubleday.
After 12,000 Years. Stanton Arthur Coblentz. LC 50-12832. 1950. Fantasy Pub. Co.
After 12,000 Years. Stanton Arthur Coblentz. LC 75-398. (Garland Library of Science Fiction). 1975. 11.00 (ISBN 0-8240-1404-9). Garland Pub.
Aftercourse. Ed. by Lou Warner & Joan V. Moran. (People Systems Ser.). 1978. pap. 4.95 (ISBN 0-913502-03-0); pap. 2.25 (ISBN 0-913502-07-3). NELF Pr.
Afterglow. Ruby Mildred Ayres. LC 36-323428. 1936. The Sun Dial Press.
Afterglow. Edward Delavan Disbrow. LC 38-34054. Chapman and Grimes.
Afterglow. George Parsons Lathrop. LC 7-13850. (No name series. 1st series, v. 7). 1877. Roberts Brothers.
Afterglow. Judith Plowden. 1979. pap. 2.25 o.s.i. (ISBN 0-8439-0665-0, Leisure Bks). Nordon Pubns.
Afterglow. Judith Plowden. 320p. 1983. pap. 3.25 (ISBN 0-8439-2028-9, Leisure Bks). Dorchester Pub Co.
Afterglow. Edith Thomson. LC 22-11517. 1922. E. P. Dutton & Company.
Afterglow. Elizabeth Wood. LC 47-28683. 1947. Pellegrini & Cudahy.
Afterglow: A Collection of Short Stories and Poems. W. E Blackhurst. LC 72-80632. (Illus.). 1972. 7.00 (ISBN 0-87012-127-8). McClain Print. Co.
Aftergrowth, and Other Stories. Hayyim Nahman Bialik. Tr. by Lask, I. M. LC 40-4499. 1939. The Jewish Publication Society of American.
Aftermath. James Lane Allen. Repr. of 1906 ed. lib. bdg. 12.50 (ISBN 0-8414-3056-X). Folcroft.
Aftermath. Genevieve Cunningham. LC 79-55687. 3.95 (ISBN 0-935774-01-7). Elgen Pub. Co.
Aftermath. Daingerfield Glass. LC 54-6948. Bruce Humphries.
Aftermath. O. T Jackson. (Leisure book). 1.50 (ISBN 0-8439-0609-X). Nordon Pubns.
Aftermath of Murder. Mary Fitt. LC 41-8541. 1941. Pub. for the Crime Club by Doubleday, Doran and Company, Inc.
Aftermath of Murder. Kathleen Freeman. LC 41-8541. 1941. Published for the Crime Club by Doubleday Doran.
Aftermath of Sabbatino. Ed. by Lyman M. Tondel, Jr. (Orig.). pap. 2.95x o.p. Oceana.
Aftermath. Part Second of "A Kentucky Cardinal". James Lane Allen. LC 1-5113. (On cover: Harper's little novels). 1896. Harper & Brothers.
Aftermath: Part Second of "A Kentucky Cardinal". James Lane Allen. LC 90-5563. 1899. Harper & Brothers.
Aftermath: Part Second of "A Kentucky Cardinal,". James Lane Allen. LC 41-34774. 1927. The Macmillan Company.
Afternoon. Elizabeth Parsons. LC 46-719424. 1946. The Viking Press.
Afternoon, and Other Sketches. Louise De La Ramee. LC 13-2064. (On cover: Seaside library. Pocket ed. no. 128). 1884. G. Munro.
Afternoon and Twilight of Vanda Pinelli. L Steni. LC 29-29425. J. Cape & H. Smith.
Afternoon Chat. George Blankenship. LC 46-17428. 1946. The Hobson Book Press.
Afternoon in March. 1st Ed. Robert Molloy. LC 58-8105. 1958. Doubleday.
Afternoon in the Jungle: The Selected Short Stories of Albert Maltz. Albert Maltz. LC 74-131272. 1970. 5.95 (ISBN 0-87140-525-3). Liveright.
Afternoon Neighbors. Hamlin Garland. Ed. by Donald Pizer. (American Authors Ser). 1934. 27.50 o.s.i. (ISBN 0-512-00270-3). Garrett Pr.
Afternoon Neighbors. Hamlin Garland. Ed. by Donald Pizer. LC 71-96607. (American Authors Ser., Collected Works of Hamlin Garland, 45 Vols). 1969. Repr. of 1934 ed. 24.50 o.s.i. (ISBN 0-512-00270-3). Garrett Pr.
Afternoon Neighbors see Collected Works.
Afternoon of a Faun. Shelby Hearon. LC 82-16301. 1983. 12.95 (ISBN 0-689-11350-1). Atheneum.
Afternoon of a Good Woman. Nina Bawden. LC 77-352849. 1976. 3.50 (ISBN 0-333-21184-7). Macmillan.
Afternoon of a Loser. Tom Pace. LC 76-85971. 1969. 4.95. Harper & Row.
Afternoon of an Author. F. Scott Fitzgerald. 1957. 5.95 o.p. (ISBN 0-684-10149-1, ScribT); pap. 2.95 (ISBN 0-684-12734-2, SL332, ScribT). Scribner.
Afternoon of an Autocrat. Norah Robinson Lofts. LC 56-7946. 1956. Doubleday.
Afternoon of an Autocrat see Deadly Gift.
Afternoon of Mr. Andesmas see Four Novels.
Afternoon to Kill. Shelley Smith. 1979. 11.00x o.p. (Pub. by Ian Henry Pubns England). State Mutual Bk.
Afternoon to Kill. Shelley Smith. 1977. 6.40 o.p. State Mutual Bk.
Afternoon to Kill: By. Nancy Bodington. LC 53-11868. 1954. Harper.
Afternoon Walk. Dorothy Eden. LC 72-8983. 1972. 9.95 (ISBN 0-8161-6057-0). G. K. Hall.
Afternoon Walk. Dorothy Eden. LC 75-159753. 1971. 6.95. Coward, McCann & Geoghegan.
Afternoon Women. Lael Tucker Wertenbaker. LC 66-109835. bds., 4.95. Little.
Afternoon Women. Lael Tucker Wertenbaker. (S3359). 1967. Bantam.
Afternoons of Thereze Lamarck. Juan Ventura Agudiez. LC 68-7759. 1967. Las Americas Pub. Co.
Aftershock. David Howell. 192p. (Orig.). 1981. pap. 2.50 (ISBN 0-515-05454-2). Jove Pubns.
Aftershock. Lillian O'Donnell. LC 76-52435. 7.95 (ISBN 0-399-10005-9). Putnam.
Aftershock. Collin Wilcox. LC 74-23124. 1975. (ISBN 0-394-49235-8). Random House.
Aftershocks: A Tale of Two Victims. David Haward Bain. LC 80-15735. 10.95 (ISBN 0-416-00681-7). Methuen.
Afterward. Mary Harriott Norris. (On cover: The Golden library, no. 2). 1892. The Price-McGill Company.
Afterwards. Emma S Allen. LC 14-145662. E.J. Clode.
Afterwards. Elizabeth Fenwick. LC 50-14132. 1950. Rinehart.
Afterwards. Marie Adelaide Belloc Lowndes. LC 25-108101. 1925. Doubleday, Page & Company.
Afterwards. Kathlyn Rhodes. LC 17-26263. 1917. Duffield and Company.
Afterwards, and Other Stories. John Watson. LC 75-150565. (Short story index reprint series). 1971. (ISBN 0-8369-3863-1). Books for Libraries Press.
Afterwards: And Other Stories. John Watson. LC 98-1280. 1898. Dodd, Mead & Company.
Again: Attan! K. H Scheer. 1974. (pbk.) 0.95. Ace Books.
Again, Dangerous Visions. Harlan Ellison. (Signet book; J5672/5673). (Illus.). 1973. each (pbk) 1.95. New American Library.
Again, Dangerous Visions: 46 Original Stories. Harlan Ellison. LC 70-123689. (Doubleday science fiction). (Illus.). 1972. 12.95. Doubleday.
Again in October. Lilian Van Ness. LC 44-2893. 1944. Doubleday, Doran and Co., Inc.
Again Sanders. Edgar Wallace. LC 31-14183. ("First edition."). Doubleday, Doran & Company, Inc.
Again the Ringer. Edgar Wallace. Orig. Title: Ringer Returns. 192p. 1973. Repr. of 1931 ed. lib. bdg. 5.95 o.s.i. (ISBN 0-85617-360-6). White Lion Pubs.
Again the River. Stella Embree Morgan. LC 39-25557. 1939. Thomas Y. Crowell Company.
Again the Three Just Men. Edgar Wallace. LC 75-130077. (Short story index reprint series). 1970. Books for Libraries Press.
Again the Three Just Men: More Adventures of Edgar Wallace's Most Popular Characters--Manfred, Gonsalez, and Poiccart... Edgar Wallace. LC 33-17284. 1933. Pub. for the Crime Club, Inc., by Doubleday, Doran & Company, Inc.
Again this Rapture. Barbara Cartland. 240p. 1982. pap. 1.95 (ISBN 0-515-06385-1). Jove Pubns.
Again This Rapture. Barbara Cartland. (Hist. Romance Ser.: No. 36). 1975. pap. 1.25 o.p. (V3908). Pyramid Pubns.
Again This Rapture. Barbara Cartland. 1977. pap. 1.50 o.p. (ISBN 0-515-04340-0). BJ Pub Group.
Again to Earth: A Novel. 1st Ed. Elizabeth Hammack Cross. LC 56-7465. 1956. Exposition Press.
Again We Dream. Rosemary Frances Rees. LC 44-1289. 1943. Arcadia House, Inc.
Against a Crooked Sky. Eleanor Lamb & Douglas Stewart. 1976. (pbk.) 1.25. Bantam Books.
Against a Darkening Sky. Janet Lewis, pseud. LC 43-22636. 1943. Doudleday, Doran & Company, Inc.
Against All Enemies. Ervin S Duggan & Wattenberg, Ben J. 1979. 2.50 (ISBN 0-380-41723-5). Avon Books.
Against All Enemies: A Novel. Ervin S Duggan & Ben J. Wattenberg. LC 73-22796. 1977. 10.00 (ISBN 0-385-03768-6). Doubleday.
Against Entropy. Michael Frayn. LC 67-13498. 1967. bds., 4.95. Viking.
Against Heavy Odds: A Tale of Norse Heroism, and A Fearless Trio. Hjalmar Hjorth Boyesen. LC 6-15225. (Norseland series). 1894. C. Scribner's Sons.
Against Heavy Odds: A Tale of Norse Heroism. Hjalmar Hjorth Boyesen. LC 6-15226. 1890. C. Scribner's Sons.
Against Her Will and A Haunted Life. Adah M Howard. (On cover: Lovell's library, v. 20 no. 970). 1887. J. W. Lovell Company.
Against Human Nature: A Novel. Maria Louise Pool. LC 7-38182. 1895. Harper & Brothers.
Against Nature. Joris Karl Huysmans, pseud. LC 59-1598. 1974. (pbk.) 2.50. Penguin Books.
Against Nature. A New Translation of A Rebours, by Robert Baldick. Joris Karl Huysmans. LC 59-159821. (Penguin classics, L86). 1959. Penguin Books.
Against Oods. A Romance of the Midway Plaisance. Emma Murdoch Van Deventer. LC 7-14720. (On cover: Globe library, v. 1, no. 183). 1894. Rand, McNally & Company.
Against the Evidence: By Lesley Egan Pseud. 1st Ed. Elizabeth Linington. LC 62-20128. 1962. Harper & Row.
Against the Fall of Night. Michael P Arnold. LC 72-89292. (Illus.). 1975. 10.00. (ISBN 0-385-05691-5). Doubleday.
Against the Fall of Night. Arthur Charles Clarke. LC 53-9537. 1953. Gnome Press.
Against the Fall of Night see Lion of Comarre.
Against the Grain. Joris Karl Huysmans. LC 56-10484. (Modern library paperbacks, P23). 1956. Random House.
Against the Grain: A Rebours). Joris Karl Huysmans. LC 77-81802. (Illus.). 1969. 2.00. Dover Publications.
Against the Grain A Rebours: By J. K. Huysmans, with an Introduction by Havelock Ellis; Illustrated by Arthur Zaidenberg. Joris Karl Huysmans & Ellis, Havelock. LC 31-34094. Illustrated Edition Company.
Against the Moon. Jane Gilmore Rushing. LC 68-14166. 1968. Doubleday.
Against the Moon. Jane Gilmore Rushing. 1979. 1.95 (ISBN 0-380-42812-1). Avon Books.
Against the Public Interest. Robert Gaines. LC 64-16806. 1964. Walker.
Against the River. Leslie Konnyu. 1961. pap. 2.50 (ISBN 0-911862-02-1). Hungarian Rev.
Against the Season. Jane Rule. LC 70-139525. 1971. 5.95 (ISBN 0-8415-0083-5). McCall Pub. Co.
Against the Seasons. Jane Rule. (OSI). 1971. 5.95 o.s.i. (ISBN 0-8415-0083-5). Sat Rev Pr.
Against the Sky. Konrad Bercovici. LC 32-2658. 1932. Covici, Friede.

Against the Stream. James Hanley. LC 81-82845. (Illus.). 10.95 (ISBN 0-8180-0629-3). Horizon Press.

Against the Stream, No. 68. Barbara Cartland. 1974. pap. 1.25 o.p. (ISBN 0-515-03389-8, V3389). Pyramid Pubns.

Against the Stream, No. 68. Barbara Cartland. 1977. pap. 1.25 o.p. (ISBN 0-515-04277-3). BJ Pub Group.

Against the Stream. The Story of a Heroic Age in England. Elizabeth Rundle Charles. 1873. Dodd & Mead.

Against the Sun. Godfrey Elton Baron Elton. LC 28-24062. 1928. Houghton Mifflin Company.

Against the Tide. Henry Bedford-Jones. LC 24-17127. 1924. Dodd, Mead and Company.

Against the Tide. Muriel Elwood. LC 50-6265. 1950. Bobbs-Merrill.

Against the Tide. Walter M S Lowell. LC 7-14750. 1892. Leonard Publishing Company.

Against the Wall. Kathleen Millay. LC 29-18337. 1929. The Macaulay Company.

Against the Wind. Richard Butler. 1979. 2.25 (ISBN 0-440-10249-9). Dell Pub. Co.

Against the Wind: Stories. Martin Alfred Hansen. LC 78-20926. 10.00 (ISBN 0-8044-2342-3). F. Ungar Pub. Co.

Against the Winds. Kate Jordan. LC 19-7464. 1919. Little, Brown, and Company.

Against the World. Jeannette Ritchie Hadermann Walworth. LC 8-33255. 1873. Shepard and Gill.

Against This Rock. Louis Zara. LC 43-15007. 1943. Creative Age Press, Inc.

Against Time's Arrow, the High Crusade of Poul Anderson. Sandra Miesel. LC 78-14913. (The Milford Ser: Popular Writers of Today, Vol. 18). 1978. lib. bdg. 9.95x (ISBN 0-89370-124-6); pap. 3.95x (ISBN 0-89370-224-2). Borgo Pr.

Against Tomorrow. Illus. by the Author, Foreword by W. Edwin Hemphill. Starnell Kilgore. LC 64-8227. 1964. 4.75. Garrett & Massie.

Agamenticus. Edward Payson Tenney. LC 8-26042. 1878. Lee and Shepard.

Agapito. Cardona-Hine, Alvaro. LC 69-17058. 1969. 4.50. Scribner.

Agatha. Theodor Kowan. 80p. 1983. 7.95 (ISBN 0-89962-317-4). Todd & Honeywell.

Agatha. Augusta L Ord. (On cover: The satchel series, no. 37). W. B. Smith & Co.

Agatha. Kathleen Tynan. LC 78-17508. 1978. 7.95 (ISBN 0-345-27718-X). Ballantine Books.

Agatha and the Shadow: A Novel. Edward Payson Tenney. LC 8-26043. 1887. Roberts Brothers.

Agatha Christie's Detectives: Five Complete Novels. Agatha Miller Christie. LC 82-1765. 1982. 6.98 (ISBN 0-517-37997-X). Avenel Books.

Agatha Crumm, No. 3: Too Mush is Never Enough. Bill Hoest, pseud. 1982. pap. 1.95 (ISBN 0-451-11844-8, AJ1844, Sig). NAL.

Agatha Lee's Inheritance. Mary R Higham. (On cover: Sunday-hour series. v. 2). A. D. F. Randolph & Company.

Agatha Moudio's Son. Francis Bebey. LC 72-96591. 1973. 5.95 (ISBN 0-88208-037-7) (ISBN 0-88208-037-7). L. Hill.

Agatha Page: A Parable. Isaac Henderson. LC 12-24352. 1888. Ticknor and Company.

Agatha Webb. Anna Katharine Green Rohlfs. LC 99-3087. 1899. G. P. Putnam's Sons.

Agatha's Aunt. Harriet Lummis Smith. LC 20-14707. The Bobbs-Merril Company.

Agatha's Friends. Thomas Houser. 224p. 1983. pap. 2.50 (ISBN 0-380-82222-9, 82222-9). Avon.

Agatha's Hard Saying. Rosa Mulholland Gilbert. LC 11-30781. 1912. 1.25. Benziger Brothers.

Agatha's Husband: A Novel. Dinah Maria Mulock Craik. LC 4-16508. 1902. Harper & Brothers.

Age for Fortunes. Walter Hegarty. LC 78-25674. 10.95 (ISBN 0-698-10845-0). Coward, McCann & Geoghegan.

Age for Love. Ernest Pascal. LC 30-8163. Harcourt, Brace and Company.

Age of Blind Revolt. Donald L. Kimball. 300p. 1982. 14.95 (ISBN 0-942698-03-7); pap. 6.95 (ISBN 0-942698-04-5). Trends & Events.

Age of Consent. Norman Lindsay. LC 38-16536. Farrar & Rinehart, Inc.

Age of Consent. Ramona Stewart. LC 74-22344. 1975. 7.95 (ISBN 0-525-05125-2). Dutton.

Age of Consent. Stewart, Ramona. (Signet Book). 1976. (pbk.) 1.50. New American Library.

Age of Death. William Leonard Marshall. LC 73-123028. 1971. 7.50 (ISBN 0-670-10961-4). Viking Press.

Age of Innocence. Edith Newbold Jones Wharton. LC 77-460443. (Illus.). 1976. Franklin Library.

Age of Innocence. Edith Newbold Jones Wharton. LC 68-27785. 1968. 5.95. Scribner.

Age of Innocence. Edith Newbold Jones Wharton. LC 75-318890. (Penguin modern classics). 1974. 0.55 (ISBN 0-14-003784-5). Penguin.

Age of Innocence. Edith Newbold Jones Wharton. LC 20-18615. 1920. D. Appleton and Company.

Age of Innocence. Edith Newbold Jones Wharton. LC 43-51104. (Half-title: The Modern library of the world's best books). 1943. The Modern Library.

Age of Innocence. Edith Newbold Jones Wharton & Lowe, Orton, 1873- Ed. LC 32-1073. (Half-title: Appleton modern literature series). D. Appleton and Company.

Age of Innocence. Edith Newbold Jones Wharton & Lawrence Beall Smith. LC 75-311997. (Illus.). 1973. Printed for the Members of the Limited Editions Club at the Press of the Archer, Mount Vernon, N.Y.

Age of Iron & Other Interludes, Vol. 1. Arlene Zekowski. LC 73-77095. (Archives of Post-Modern Literature). 1973. pap. 10.00 (ISBN 0-913844-01-2). Am Canadian.

Age of Light. Donald Wetzel. LC 52-5672. 1952. Crown Publishers.

Age of Longing. Arthur Koestler. LC 51-9546. 1951. Macmillan.

Age of Noon, a Novel. Henrietta Weigel. LC 47-6042. 1947. E. P. Dutton.

Age of Reason. Philip Hamilton Gibbs. LC 28-18124. 1928. Doubleday, Doran & Company, Inc.

Age of Reason. Jean Paul Sartre. LC 72-4476. 1973. 1.95. Vintage Books.

Age of Reason. Jean Paul Sartre & Sutton, Eric, Tr. LC 47-4526. (His The roads to freedom, 1). 1947. A. A. Knopf.

Age of Reason. Tr. from French by Eric Sutton. Jean Paul Sartre. Tr. by Eric Sutton. (Modern Lib. ML 335). 1963. 1.95. Random.

Age of Reason. Tr. from French by Eric Sutton, Introd. by Henri Peyre. Jean Paul Sartre. (Modern classic, NY4011). 1968. Bantam.

Age of Shrinks. Leonard Blank. LC 79-52476. 10.95. Ewing Publications.

Age of Stoning. Dan Potter. LC 73-151287. 1971. 6.95 (ISBN 0-8128-1386-3). Stein and Day.

Age of the Daughters. Aurora J. Selenian. 110p. 1982. pap. 4.95 spiral bound (ISBN 0-942762-02-9). Daughterayne.

Age of the Fish. Odon Norvath. Ed. by Ruth Nathan. Tr. by R. Wills Thomas. 1978. Repr. 5.95 o.p. (ISBN 0-918732-06-9). Pomerica Pr.

Age of the Fish. Odon Von Horvath. 1979. 2.25 (ISBN 0-445-04368-7). Popular Library.

Age of the Fish: A Novel. Odon Horvath. LC 39-5472. 1939. The Dial Press.

Age of the Pussyfoot. Frederik Pohl. LC 69-13009. 1969. 4.95. Trident Press.

Age of the Pussyfoot. Frederik Pohl. LC 78-7478. (Ballantine Books science fiction). 1969. 0.75. Ballantine Books.

Age of the Tail: Illustrated by Leo Harshfield. 1st Ed. Harry Allen Smith. LC 55-10751. 1955. Little, Brown.

Age of Thunder. Frederic Prokosch. LC 45-2642. 1945. Harper & Brothers.

Age of Wonders. Aron. Appelfeld. LC 81-47318. 1981. 12.50 (ISBN 0-87923-402-4). D.R. Godine, Publisher.

Age of Youth. Arthur Somers Roche. LC 30-7306. Sears Publishing Company, Inc.

Age Without Pity. John Prebble. LC 50-9599. 1950. Holt.

Agency Girls. Matt Stern. pap. 1.95 o.p. (ISBN 0-87056-228-2, 6228). Brandon.

Agency House, Malaya. Susan Yorke. 1962. 3.95 o.p. (ISBN 0-374-10253-8). FS&G.

Agency House, Malaya. Susan Yorke. Orig. Title: Girl in the Cheongsam. pap. 0.60 o.p. (60-380). Manor Bks.

Agency House, Malaya: The Girl in the Cheongsam by Susan Yorke Pseud. Suzette Telenga. LC 62-9220. 1962. Farrar, Straus and Cudahy.

Agent B-7: A Story of the American Secret Service. Ared White. LC 34-379941. 1934. Houghton Mifflin Company.

Agent Counter Agent. Nick Carter. (Nick Carter Ser.). (O.s.i.). 192p. 1975. pap. 1.25 o.s.i. (AQ1477, Award). Univ Pub & Dist.

Agent Extraordinary. Spencer Bayne. LC 42-16142. 1942. E.P. Dutton and Company, Inc.

Agent in Place. Helen MacInnes. LC 75-44165. 8.95 (ISBN 0-15-103967-4). Harcourt Brace Jovanovich.

Agent in Place. Helen MacInnes. LC 76-25598. 1976. 17.95 (ISBN 0-8161-6401-0). G. K. Hall.

Agent in Place: The Wennerstrom Affair. Thomas Whiteside. 160p. 1983. pap. 2.50 (ISBN 0-345-30326-1). Ballantine.

Agent of Chaos. Norman Spinrad. (Orig.). 1970. pap. price not set o.p. (B75-2003). Belmont-Tower.

Agent of Chaos. Norman Spinrad. 1972. pap. 0.75 o.p. (BT40125). Belmont-Tower.

Agent of Entropy. Martin Siegel. 1969. pap. 0.75 o.p. (ISBN 0-447-74573-5). Lancer.

Agent of Love. Jillian Kearny. 1979. 1.75 (ISBN 0-446-94003-8). Warner Books.

Agent of the Terran Empire. Oul Anderson. LC 65-20905. 1965. Chilton Books.

Agent of the Terran Empire. Poul Anderson. LC 65-20905. 3.95. Chilton.

Agent of the Terran Empire. Poul Anderson. LC 79-12946. (Gregg Press science fiction series). 1979. 12.50 (ISBN 0-8398-2528-5). Gregg Press.

Agent of the Unknown. St. Clair, Margaret. LC 56-28855. (Ace double novel books, D-150). 1956. Ace Books.

Agent of Vega. 1st Ed. James H Schmitz. LC 60-10555. 1960. Gnome Press.

Agent on the Other Side. George O'Toole. LC 73-84059. 1973. 5.95 (ISBN 0-679-50410-9). D. McKay Co.

Agent on the Other Side. George O'Toole. 1975. (pbk.) 1.25. Dell.

Agent Out of Place. Irving A. Greenfield. (Illus.). 304p. pap. 3.25 (ISBN 0-441-01027-X, Pub. by Charter Bks). Ace Bks.

Agent Outside. Patrick Wynnton. LC 31-32076. 1931. Longmans, Green and Co.

Agents and Witnesses. Percy Howard Newby. LC 47-4065. 1947. Doubleday & Company, Inc.

Agents of Influence. Palma Harcourt. LC 77-80207. 1978. 7.95 (ISBN 0-8027-5374-4). Walker.

Agents of Love. Rudolf Nassauer. LC 76-382465. 1976. 3.95 (ISBN 0-224-01235-5). Cape.

Ages Ago: Thirty-Seven Tales from the Konjaku Monogatari Collection. Tr. by Susan W. Jones. 1959. 5.50 o.p. (ISBN 0-674-01050-7). Harvard U Pr.

Ages Ago: Thirty-Seven Tales from the Konjaku Monogatari Collection, Translated by S. W. Jones. Konjaku Monogatari & Susan Wilbur - Jones. LC 59-115105. 1959. Harvard University Press.

Aggressive Ways of the Casual Stranger. Rosemary Waldrop. 1972. 5.00 o.p. (ISBN 0-394-47924-6); pap. 1.95 o.p. (ISBN 0-394-70766-4). Random.

Agincourt. A Romance. George Payne Rainsford James. LC 7-7970. (On cover: Library of select novels, no. 44). 1844. Harper & Brothers.

Aging Boy. Julian Claman. LC 63-18200. 1963. Doubleday.

Agitator: A Novel. Clementina Black. LC 6-12421. 1895. Harper & Brothers.

Agnes. Margaret Oliphant Wilson Oliphant. (On cover: Seaside library. Pocket ed., no. 608). 1885. G. Munro.

Agnes: A Handful of Lust. Josiah Pitts Woolfolk & Clinton Campbell. LC 50-19190. 1950. Arco Pub. Co.

Agnes. A Novel. Margaret Oliphant Wilson Oliphant. LC 7-32621. 1866. Harper & Brothers.

Agnes. A Novel. Mary Hayden Green Pike. LC 7-35895. 1858. Phillips, Sampson & Company.

Agnes Farriday: Or, The Harlot's Friend... William Adolphus Clark. LC 6-21459. 1869. F. A. Brady.

Agnes Goodmaid. A Mystery Explained. On the Waves of Ether Space. Konrad Sachaefer. LC 99-5737. 1899.

Agnes Graham: A Novel. Sarah Anne Dorsey. LC 6-33701. 1869. Claxton, Remsen, and Haffelfinger.

Agnes Grey. Anne Bronte & Bronte, Emily Jane, 1818-1848. (Seaside library, v. 54, no. 1098). 1881. G. Munro.

Agnes Grey. An Autobiography. Anne Bronte. LC 7-3543. 1850. T. P. Peterson.

Agnes Hilton: Or, Practical Views of Catholicity. A Tale of Trials and Triumphs. Mary Jane Hoffman. 1864. P. O'Shea.

Agnes Nixon's All My Children: Erica, Bk. II. Rosemarie Santini. 224p. (Orig.). 1980. pap. 2.50 (ISBN 0-515-04895-X). Jove Pubns.

Agnes Nixon's All My Children: The Lovers, Bk. III. Rosemarie Santini. 240p. (Orig.). 1981. pap. 2.50 (ISBN 0-515-04896-8). Jove Pubns.

Agnes of Sorrento. Harriet Elizabeth Beecher Stowe. LC 72-144691. 1971. (ISBN 0-404-06289-X). AMS Press.

Agnes of Sorrento. Harriet Elizabeth Beecher Stowe. 1862. Ticknor and Fields.

Agnes of Sorrento. 21st ed. Harriet Elizabeth Beecher Stowe. LC 8-16280. 1890. Houghton, Mifflin and Company.

Agnes of the Bad Lands. John Breckenridge Ellis. LC 16-18326. 1916. 1.25. The Macaulay Company.

Agnes: Or, The Possessed. A Revelation of Mesmerism. Timothy Shay Arthur. LC 6-2460. T. B. Peterson.

Agnes Serle. A Novel. Ellen Pickering. G. B. Zieber & Co.

Agnes Sorel. George Payne Rainsford James. (Lovell's library, no. 1410). 1889. J. W. Lovell Company.

Agnes Sorel. A Novel. George Payne Rainsford James. LC 7-7593. 1853. Harper & Brothers.

Agnes Sorel. A Novel. George Payne Rainsford James. (On cover: Seaside library. Pocket ed., no. 218). 1884. G. Munro.

Agnes Stanhope: A Tale of English Life. Martha Remick. 1862. J. M. Usher.

Agnes Surriage. Edwin Lassetter Bynner. LC 4-16455. Houghton, Mifflin and Company.

Agnes Surriage. Edwin Lassetter Bynner. LC 11-105505. 1887. Ticknor and Company.

Agnes Surriage. Edwin Lassetter Bynner. LC 23-6498. 1923. Houghton Mifflin Company.

Agnes Wentworth. Sara Hammond Palfrey. LC 7-35786. 1869. J. B. Lippincott & Co.

Agnew, the Unexamined Man: A Political Profile. Robert L. Marsh. LC 70-150797. 224p. 1971. 5.95 (ISBN 0-87131-032-5). M Evans.

Agnostic: A Novel. Guido Negri. LC 29-25615. 1929. The Ruralist Press.

Agnostic Island. Frederick James Gould. LC 75-1536. (Victorian Fiction: Novels of Faith and Doubt; No. 84). 1975. 35.00 (ISBN 0-8240-1608-4). Garland Pub.

Agoak: The Legacy of Agaguk. Yves Theriault. LC 80-455531. 1979. 9.95 (ISBN 0-07-082947-0). McGraw-Hill Ryerson.

Agony & the Ecstasy. Irving Stone. pap. 3.95 (ISBN 0-451-11010-2, AE1010, Sig). NAL.

Agony and the Ectasy: A Novel of Michelangelo. Irving Stone. LC 61-6520. 1961. Doubleday.

Agony Column. Earl Derr Biggers. LC 33-28335. 1926. The Bobbs-Merrill Company.

Agony Column. Earl Derr Biggers. LC 43-736788. Avon Book Company.

Agony Column. Earl Derr Buggers. LC 16-22299. The Bobbs-Merrill Company.

Agony Column Murders: A Secret Service Smith Novel. Reginald Thomas Maitland Scott. LC 46-205505. 1946. E. P. Dutton & Co. Inc.

Agony of Love. Translated by Peter Wiles. Claude Roy. LC 59-8584. 1959. Pantheon Books.

Agotime: Her Legend. Judith Illsley Gleason. LC 73-106299. (Illus.). 1970. 7.95. Grossman.

Agreement Between Us: Stories. John Arthur Hermann. LC 72-95437. (Breakthrough Bks). 124p. 1973. 8.95 (ISBN 0-8262-0141-5); pap. 5.95 (ISBN 0-8262-0140-7). U of Mo Pr.

Agrippa's Daughter. Howard Melvin Fast. LC 64-19262. 1964. Doubleday.

Agrippina: Empress of Depravity. Frederick William Farrar. (Golden Age of Rome Ser.). 1978. pap. 2.50 (ISBN 0-89083-354-0). Zebra.

Aground. Charles Williams. LC 56-11496. (Dell first edition, A114). 1956. Dell Pub. Co.

Agunah. Chaim Grade. Tr. by Curt Leviant from Yiddish. 1978. pap. 3.95 (ISBN 0-932232-00-0). Menorah Pub.

Agunah. Chaim Grade. Tr. by Curt Leviant. 6.00x o.p. Twayne.

Ah, but in Casper. Gil Stevenson. LC 72-81638. 66p. 1972. 3.00 o.p. (ISBN 0-8059-1720-9). Dorrance.

Ah, but in Casper. Gil Stevenson. LC 72-81638. 66p. 1972. 3.00 o.p. (ISBN 0-8059-1720-9). Dorrance.

Ah, but Your Land Is Beautiful. Alan Paton. LC 81-13547. 1982. 12.95 (ISBN 0-684-17336-0). Scribner.

Ah King. William Somerset Maugham. LC 75-26127. (Maugham, William Somerset, 1874-1965. Works. 1976). 1977. 15.00 (ISBN 0-405-09336-5). Arno Press.

Ah King. William Somerset Maugham. LC 33-32416. 1933. Doubleday, Doran & Company, Inc.

Ah King: And Other Romance Stories of the Tropics. William Somerset Maugham. LC 44-47301. (On cover: Avon modern short story monthly. No. 18). 1944. Avon Book Company.

Ah-Ling of Peking: A Romance of Old China. Miriam Harriman. LC 23-13448. George H. Doran Company.

Ah Moy: The Story of a Chinese Girl. Lu Wheat. LC 8-20018. The Grafton Press.

Ah Pook is Here. William S. Burroughs. 1982. pap. 8.95 (ISBN 0-7145-3683-0). Riverrun NY.

Ah Q and Others: Selected Stories of. Shu-Jen Chou & Wang, Chi-Chen, Tr. LC 41-10678. 1941. Columbia University Press.

Ah Q and Others: Selected Stories of Lusin (Chou-Shu-Jen. Shu-Jen Chou. Tr. by Chi-Chen Wang. LC 70-150542. (Short story index reprint series). 1971. (ISBN 0-8369-3839-9). Books for Libraries Press.

Ah Q & Others: Selected Stories of Lusin. Shu-Jen Chou. Tr. by Chi-Chen Wang from Chinese. LC 75-143310. 1971. Repr. of 1941 ed. lib. bdg. 15.00x (ISBN 0-8371-5965-2, CHAQ). Greenwood.

Ah Sin: A Factual Novel of the Hakka Chinese. Sherman A Nagel. LC 42-19688. 1940. Wm. B. Eerdmans Publishing Co.

Ah, the Delicate Passion! Elizabeth Hall Yates. LC 29-5946. The Penn Publishing Company.

Ah... the Endlessly. David Hunter. 1979. pap. 6.95 (ISBN 0-89185-191-7). Anthelion Pr.

Aha! Aleister Crowley, pseud. 7.95 o.p. Weiser.

Ahaz. Constance Head. LC 79-50340. 7.95 (ISBN 0-8054-7309-2). Broadman Press.
Ahead of the Hounds: A Story of to-Day. Lydia Platt Richards. (On verso of t.-p.: Library of progress, no. 31). 1899. C. H. Kerr & Company.
Ahead of Time. Ed. by Harry Harrison & Theodore J. Gordon. LC 74-170797. (Science Fiction Ser.). 1972. 4.95 o.p. (ISBN 0-385-01300-0). Doubleday.
Ahead of Time: Ten Stories of Science Fiction and Fantasy. Henry Kuttner. LC 53-9110. 1953. Ballantine Books.
Ahira, Prince of Naphtali: The Story of the Journey into Canaan. Ella M Noller. LC 47-28683. 1947. W. B. Eerdmans Pub. Co.
Ahmed and the Old Lady. Jon Godden. LC 77-4711. 1977. 10.95 (ISBN 0-8161-6483-5). G. K. Hall.
Ai: A Social Vision. Charles S Daniel. LC 70-154438. (Utopian Literature). 1971. (ISBN 0-405-03521-7). Arno Press.
Ai: A Social Vision. Charles S Daniel. 1893. Arena Publishing Co.
Aia. Evelyn Charles H Vivian. LC 77-84272. (Lost Race and Adult Fantasy Fiction). 1978. 34.00 (ISBN 0-405-11011-1). Arno Press.
Aid-De-Camp: A Romance of the War. James Dabney McCabe. 1863. W. A. J. Smith.
Aid-De-Camp of Napoleon. Being the Conclusion of "The Companion of Jehu.". Alexandre Dumas. LC 13-7653. (On cover: Seaside library. Pocket ed. no. 2060). 1897. G. Munro's Sons.
Aid Man. Robert B. Bradley. 1970. 3.95 o.p. Vantage.
Aida Rocksbege and the White Stone. Today's Problem, a Presbyterial Romance... Presbyterial Home Missionary Society of Freeport Presbytery. Ed. by Holmes, Mary Emilie. LC 7-30563. Calvert Bros.
Aida, the Ethiopian Slave. An Egyptian Legend. Felice Venosta. LC 8-30204. S. French.
Aide to Glory. Louis Devon. LC 52-10035. 1952. Crowell.
Aideen MacLennon: The Story of a Rebel. Robert E Wilson. LC 52-14284. 1952. Fellowship Publications.
Aiglon. Edmond Rostand. (Illus.). 1964. pap. 3.95. French & Eur.
Aileen Rogers. James Lumpp. LC 50-12677. 1950. Gramercy Pub. Co.
Ailieford: a Family History. William Mitchel. LC 7-25321. 1855. Stringer & Townsend.
Ailieford: a Family History. William Wilson. LC 7-25321. 1855. Stringer & Townsend.
Ailsa Paige: A Novel. Robert William Chambers. LC 20-15597. A. L. Burt Company.
Ailsa Paige: A Novel. Robert William Chambers. LC 10-188800. 1910. 1.50. D. Appleton and Company.
Ailsa Paige: A Novel. Robert William Chambers. LC 35-28564. 1912. A. L. Burt Company.
Aim for a Star. Helen Lowrie Marshall. 1966. 4.95 (ISBN 0-385-08258-4). Doubleday.
Aim to Kill. Rosemary Gatenby. LC 68-21002. 1968. W. Morrow.
Aimbe - the Magician. Paulias Matane. 1978. 5.95 o.p. (ISBN 0-533-03180-X). Vantage.
Aimbe, the Pastor: A Novel. Paulias Matane. LC 78-57988. 12.50 (ISBN 0-682-49230-2). Exposition Press.
Aimee. Margaret Lathrop Law. LC 56-10702. 1956. Funk & Wagnalls.
Aimee Villard, Daughter of France. Charles Silvestre & Ilsley, Marjorie Henry, Tr. LC 28-11173. 1928. The Macmillan Company.
Aimez-Vous Brahms. Francoise Quoirez. LC 60-5971. 1974. (pbk.) 0.95. Popular Library.
Aimez-Vous Brahms? Francoise Sagan, pseud. 1963. 13.95. French & Eur.
Aimez-Vous Brahms: By Francoise Sagan Pseud. Translated from the French by Peter Wiles. 1st American Ed. Francoise Quoirez. LC 60-5971. 1960. Dutton.
Aims and Obstacles. A Romance. George Payne Rainsford James. LC 7-7582. (On cover: Library of select novels, no. 162). 1851. Harper & Brothers.
Ainceworth Mystery. Gregory Baxter. LC 30-7101. 1930. D. Appleton and Company.
Ain't Angie Awful!... Gelett Burgess. LC 23-13000. Dorrance & Co.
Ain't I a Wonder & Ain't You a Wonder Too. Jess Lair. 1978. pap. 2.50 (ISBN 0-449-23688-9, Crest). Fawcett.
Air Apparent: A New Boysie Oakes Adventure. John E Gardner. LC 74-136792. 1971. 5.95. Putnam.
Air Bridge: By Hammond Innes Pseud. 1st American Ed. Ralph Hammond-Innes. LC 51-11977. 1952. Knopf.
Air Cage. Per Wastberg. LC 79-37659. 1972. Delacorte Press.
Air Castle Architect. Charles S Wolfe. LC 46-2358. 1946. The Hobson Book Press.
Air Eaters Strike Back. (Fantasy Trip Ser.). 1981. pap. write for info. Metagam.
Air Evac. William E Butterworth. 1967. W. W. Norton.
Air Evac. William E Butterworth. LC 67-18675. 1967. W. W. Norton.
Air Force Girl. Renee Shann. LC 43-14628. 1942. Carlton House.
Air Force; Novelization. John O Watson & Nichols, Dudley. Air Force. 1943. Grosset & Dunlap.
Air Force One. Edwin Corley. (Dell Book). 1979. 2.50 (ISBN 0-440-10063-1). Dell Publishing Co.
Air Force One: A Novel. Edwin Corley. LC 77-82618. 1978. 8.95 (ISBN 0-385-11402-8). Doubleday.
Air Force Surgeon. Abraham Louis Furman. LC 43-13680. 1943. Sheridan House.
Air-Man and the Tramp. Jennette Barbour Perry Lee. LC 18-7290. 1918. C. Scribner's Sons.
Air Mission Red. Frederic Nelson Litten. LC 51-10351. 1951. Rand, McNally.
Air Murders. Richard Howells Watkins. LC 29-10745. 1929. Pub. for The Crime Club, Inc., by Doubleday, Doran & Company, Inc.
Air of Glory. Sarah Neilan. LC 77-1606. 1977. 6.95 (ISBN 0-688-03209-5). Morrow.
Air Pilot: A Modern Love Story. Randall Parrish. LC 13-828327. 1913. 1.25. A. C. McClurg & Co.
Air Pirate. Cyril Arthur Edward Ranger Gull. LC 20-26883. 1920. Harcourt, Brace and Howe.
Air Stewardess. Nellie Graf. LC 38-20987. Gramercy Publishing Co.
Air Stewardess. Vida Hurst. LC 34-36238. Grosset & Dunlap.
Air That Kills. Margaret Millar. LC 57-10024. 1957. Random House.
Air Trust. George Allan England. LC 75-28854. (Classics of science fiction). (Illus.). 1976. 12.95. (ISBN 0-88355-368-6) (ISBN 0-88355-453-4). Hyperion Press.
Air Trust. George Allan England. P. Wagner.
Airesboro Castle. Emma McCloy Layman. LC 74-31248. 1974-1975. 4.95 (ISBN 0-517-52115-6). Lenox Hill Press.
Airing in a Closed Carriage... Joseph Shearing. LC 43-5897. 1943. Harper & Brothers.
Airline Hostess. Natalie Cole. LC 39-25564. Gramercy Publishing Co.
Airman's Odyssey. Antoine De Saint Exupery & Galantiere, Lewis, 1893-Tr. LC 43-51284. 1943. Reynal & Hitchcock.
Airman's Wife. Renee Shann. LC 44-891547. 1944. Random House.
Airmen Who Would Not Die. John G. Fuller. 1980. pap. 2.50 (ISBN 0-425-04273-1). Berkley Pub.
Airport. Arthur Hailey. LC 68-11755. 1968. Doubleday.
Airport Affair. David Toma & Jack Pearl. 1975. (pbk.) 1.25. Dell.
Airport Cop. Charles Miron. (Airport Cop Ser). 192p. 1974. pap. 1.25 o.p. (ISBN 0-532-12242-9). Woodhill.
Airport Cop. Charles Miron. (Airport Cop Ser). 192p. 1974. pap. 1.25 o.p. (ISBN 0-532-12242-9). Manor Bks.
Airport People. Norton J. Hughes. (Inflation Fighter Ser.). 192p. 1982. pap. 1.50 o.s.i. (ISBN 0-8439-1149-2, Leisure Bks). Nordon Pubns.
Airport People. Norton Hughes Jonathan. Orig. Title: Love Merger. 1971. pap. 0.95 o.p. (B95-2103). Belmont-Tower.
Airport People. Norton Hughes Jonathan. 1975. (pbk.) 1.50. Belmont Tower Books.
Airs Above the Ground. Mary Stewart. LC 65-22978. 1965. M. S. Mill Co.; Distributed by Morrow, New York.
Airs from Arcadia & Elsewhere. Henry Cuyer Bunner. 59.95 (ISBN 0-87968-587-5). Gordon Pr.
Air's Nearly Perfect Elasticity. Richard Duerden. 1979. pap. 3.50 (ISBN 0-939180-08-1). Tombouctou.
Airscream. John Bruce. LC 77-13572. 1978. 8.95 (ISBN 0-689-10843-5). Atheneum Publishers.
Airship Cruising from Silver Fox Farm. James Otis Kaler. LC 13-187356. 1.50. Thomas Y. Crowell Company.
Airship Dragon-Fly. William John Hopkins. LC 6-31658. 1906. Doubleday, Page & Company.
Airships. Barry Hannah. LC 77-90938. 1978. 7.95 (ISBN 0-394-50021-0). Knopf: Distributed by Random House.
Airships. Barry Hannah. (Delta Book). 1979. 4.95 (ISBN 0-440-50155-5). Dell Publishing Co.
Airtight Willie & Me. Robert Beck. (Orig.). 1979. pap. 2.25 (ISBN 0-87067-031-X, BH031). Holloway.
Airy Fairy Lilian." A Novel. Margaret Wolfe Hungerford. LC 7-8492. 1882. J. B. Lippincott & Co.
Airy Fairy Lilian." A Novel. Margaret Wolfe Hungerford. LC 9-8350. 1907. J. B. Lippincott Company.
Aissa Saved. Joyce Cary. LC 62-20121. Harper & Row.
AKA: A Novel. Tristan Jones. 224p. 1981. 12.95 (ISBN 0-02-559870-8). Macmillan.
A.K.A. Chip Harrison. Lawrence Block. 380p. 1983. pap. 5.95 (ISBN 0-88150-001-1, Foul Play Pr). Countryman.
A.K.A. Katherine Wilson. Ellen Feldman. 1983. pap. 3.50 (ISBN 0-440-10219-7). Dell.
Ake and His World. Bertil Malmberg & Wenner-Gren, Marguerite (Gauntier) Tr. LC 40-6540. Farrar & Rinehart, Inc.
Akhnaton: King of Egypt. Dmitril Sergieevich Merezhkovskil. Tr. by Duddington, Mathalii Aleksandrovna. LC 27-15520. E. P. Dutton & Company.
Akiba. Marcus Lehmann & Schaffer, Aaron, 1894- Tr. LC 25-14511. Jewish Forum Publishing Co.
Akiba's Children. Geoffrey Hartman. 64p. (Orig.). 1978. pap. 12.50 (ISBN 0-931182-00-X). Iron Mtn Pr.
Akin to Murder: A Mystery Story. 1st Ed. Kathleen Moore Knight. LC 53-503656. 1953. Published for the Crime Club by Doubleday.
Akiviak: A Novel Based on the Life of a Frontier Eskimo. Kare Rodahl. LC 78-24502. (Illus.). 8.95 (ISBN 0-393-01181-X). Norton.
Akka, Dwarf of Syracuse. Agnes Carr Vaughan. LC 40-13054. 1940. Longmans, Green and Co.
Akmens Maize. Ausma Jaunzeme. 1975. pap. 2.75 o.p. Echo Pubs.
Al Alligator, and How He Learned to Play the Banjo. Walter J. Pat Enright. LC 47-31039. 1947. Dodd, Mead.
Al filo del agua see Edge of the Storm.
Al Jaffee: Dead or Alive. Al Jaffee. 1980. pap. 2.25 (ISBN 0-451-12340-9, AE2340, Sig). NAL.
Al Jaffee's Mad Inventions. Al Jaffee. (Illus., Orig.). 1978. pap. 1.75 (ISBN 0-446-94407-6). Warner Bks.
Ala Ka Zot! The Wizard of Id. Brant Parker & Johnny Hart. (Illus.). 1979. pap. 1.75 (ISBN 0-449-14217-5, GM). Fawcett.
Alabam McCall. Walt Huffine. (Alabam La Clare). 1970. pap. 0.60 o.p. (B60-2012). Belmont-Tower.
Alabama Brown. Lorinda Hagen. (Orig.). 1980. pap. 2.25 o.s.i. (ISBN 0-505-51564-4). Tower Bks.
Alabama Empire. Welbourn Kelley. LC 57-5091. 1957. Rinehart.
Alabama Prize Stories, Nineteen Seventy. Ed. by O. B. Emerson. LC 70-119460. 1970. 6.00 (ISBN 0-87397-014-4). Strode.
Alabama Prize Stories, 1970. Ed. by O. B. Emerson. LC 70-119460. 1970. 6.00. Strode Publishers.
Alabama Sketches. Samuel Minturn Peck. LC 72-1528. (Black Heritage Library Collection). 1972. 13.00 (ISBN 0-8369-9043-9). Books for Libraries Press.
Alabama Sketches. Samuel Minturn Peck. LC 2-7627. 1902. A. C. McClurg & Co.
Alabam's. Donald Henderson Clarke. LC 34-87621. The Vanguard Press.
Alabaster Bambino: A Novel. Frank John Pepe. LC 63-21156. 1963. Paesano Press.
Alabaster Box. James Lane Allen. LC 23-16974. 1923. Harper & Brothers.
Alabaster Box. Walter Besant. LC 2-4890. 1900. Dodd, Mead & Co.
Alabaster Box. Mary Eleanor Wilkins Freeman & Kingsley, Florence (Morse) LC 17-9348. 1917. D. Appleton and Company.
Alabaster Chambers. Emily Ellison Hudlow. LC 78-21350. 8.95 (ISBN 0-312-01702-2). St. Martin's Press.
Alabaster Cities. Alex Brodmerkel. 1978. 4.95 o.p. (ISBN 0-533-03704-2). Vantage.
Alabaster Egg. Gillian Freeman. LC 75-141986. 1971. 5.95 (ISBN 0-670-11143-0). Viking Press.
Alabaster Lamps. Margaret Turnbull. LC 25-19112. The Reilly & Lee Co.
Aladale. Shaun Herron. LC 78-31714. 1979. 12.95 (ISBN 0-671-40059-2). Summit Books.
Aladdin & Co. A Romance of Yankee Magic. Herbert Quick. LC 4-9460. 1904. H. Holt and Company.
Aladdin & Co. A Romance of Yankee Magic. Herbert Quick. LC 7-39575. The Bobbs-Merrill Company.
Aladdin from Broadway. Frederic Stewart Isham. LC 13-18719. The Bobbs-Merrill Company.
Aladdin in London: A Romance. Fergus Hume. LC 7-5854. 1892. Houghton, Mifflin and Company.
Aladdin O'Brien. Gouverneur Morris. LC 2-22480. 1902. The Century Co.
Aladdin of London: Or, Lodestar. Max Pemberton. LC 8-10857. Empire Book Company.
Aladore. Henry John Newbolt. LC 75-23080. (Newcastle Forgotten Fantasy classic series; F-104). 1975. 3.95 (ISBN 0-87877-104-2). Newcastle Pub. Co.
Aladore. Henry John Newbolt. LC 80-19114. 1980. 10.95 (ISBN 0-87877-504-8). Borgo Press.
Alain Tanger's Wife. James Henry Yoxall. LC 3-17915. 1903. L. C. Page & Company.
Alamance: Or, The Great and Final Experiment... Calvin Henderson Wiley. LC 8-37022. 1847. Harper & Brothers.
Alameda. K. R. G. Granger. (Orig.). 1978. pap. 2.25 (ISBN 0-89083-429-6). Zebra.
Alamo Soldier: The Story of Peaceful Mitchell. R. L Templeton. LC 77-153947. (ISBN 0-89015-119-9). Nortex Press.
Alamontada, the Galley-Slave. Heinrich Zschokke & Mosher, Ira G., Tr. 1882. D. M. Bennett.
Alamontada, the Galley-Slave. Heinrich Zschokke & Mosher, Ira G., Tr. LC 43-43395. D. M. Bennett.
Alamut Ambush. Anthony Price. LC 72-180098. 1972. 4.95. Published for the Crime Club by Doubleday.
Alan. Edward Frederic Benson. LC 25-6166. 2.00. George H. Doran Company.
Alan Breck Again, Being an Account of the Adventures of Ian MacDonnell, of New York, and His Foster-Brother, Ho-No-We-Na-to, Son to the Onondaga Royaneh: In the Course of a Journey to Scotland in the Year 1755, and of Their Experiences with the Famous Jacobite Agent, Alan Breck Stewart, and the Notorious Spy, Pickle, As Likewise, of Their Attempt to Recover the Loch Arkaig Treasure on Behalf of Prince Charles Stuart, Miscalled the Young Pretender, the Which Narrative Has Been. Arthur Douglas Howden Smith. LC 34-38525. Coward, McCann, Inc.
Alan Thorne. Martha Livingston Moodey. D. Lothrop Company.
Alana & the Dolphins. Wendy Mateja. Orig. Title: Alana, Lady of Light. (Illus.). 16p. (Orig.). 1978. pap. text ed. 4.95 (ISBN 0-9601836-0-4). Magic Unicorn Pubns.
Alana, Lady of Light see Alana & the Dolphins.
Alaric, Galactic Diplomat. Lee Andre. 1974. 6.00 o.p. (ISBN 0-682-47859-8). Exposition.
Alaric, or: The Tyrant's Vault. A Novel. Sylvanus Cobb. (On cover: The popular series, no. 22). 1892. R. Bonner's Sons.
Alarm in the Night: A Marshal Pedley Story. Prentice Winchell. LC 49-11271. 1949. E. P. Dutton.
Alarm of the Black Cat. Dolores Birk Hitchens. LC 42-538. 1942. Pub. for the Crime Club by Doubleday, Doran & Co., Inc.
Alarm of the Black Cat. Dolores Birk Olsen. LC 42-538. 1942. Pub. for the Crime Club by Doubleday, Doran & Co.,Inc.
Alarming Clock. Michael Avallone. (Orig.). 1973. pap. 0.75 o.p. (07303). Curtis.
Alarms & Diversions. James Thurber. LC 80-8401. 367p. 1981. pap. 4.95i (ISBN 0-06-090830-0, CN 830, CN). Har-Row.
Alarum and Excursion. Virginia Perdue. LC 76-381. (Fifty Classics of Crime Fiction, 1900-1950; 41). 1976. 12.00 (ISBN 0-8240-2390-0). Garland Pub.
Alarum and Excursion. Virginia Perdue. LC 44-8143. 1944. Pub. for The Crime Club by Doubleday, Doran and Co., Inc.
Alas: A Novel. Rhoda Broughton. (On cover: Lovell's international series nos. 132). 1890. United States Book Company.
Alas, Babylon: A Novel. Pat Frank. LC 59-5405. 1959. Lippincott.
Alas Poor Father. Joan Margaret Fleming. LC 72-90808. (Red mask mystery). 1973. 4.95 (ISBN 0-399-11089-5). Putnam.
Alas, Poor Father! Joan Margaret Fleming. LC 76-46426. 1977. 8.95 (ISBN 0-89340-056-4). J. Curley & Associates.
Alas, Poor Yorick! Being Three Hitherto Unrecorded Adventures in the Life of the Reverend Laurence Sterne... Alfred Hoyt Bill. LC 71-110180. (Short story index reprint series). (Illus.). 1970. Books for Libraries Press.
Alas, Por Yorick: Being Three Hitherto Unrecorded Adventures in the Life of the Reverend Laurence Sterne, A. Z., Vicar of Coxwold in Yorkshire, Etc., Etc., Author of the Life and Opinions of Tristram Shandy, Gent. Alfred Hoyt Bill. LC 27-20080. 1927. Little, Brown, and Company.
Alas, That Spring! Elinor Mordaunt, pseud. LC 23-13320. Small, Maynard & Company.
Alaska: A Novel. Jana Harris. LC 80-7735. 11.95 (ISBN 0-06-250382-0). Harper & Row.
Alaska & the Job. Paul L. Wilcox. 1975. 9.75 o.p. (ISBN 0-8283-1609-0). Branden.
Alaska Conspiracy. Joseph Rosenberger. (Death Merchant Ser.: No. 33). 1979. pap. 1.50 (ISBN 0-523-40476-X). Pinnacle Bks.
Alaska Snowtrapped. Bailey E Bell. 3.50. Vantage Press.
Alaska Star. Ellen J. Macleod. 1960. 1.50 o.p. (ISBN 0-87508-642-X). Chr Lit.
Alaska Steel. John Benteen. LC 60-1068. (Orig.). 1969. pap. 0.60 o.p. (B60-1068). Belmont-Tower.
Alaska Steel. John Benteen. (O.s.i.). 1971. pap. 0.75 o.s.i. (B75-2137). Belmont-Tower.
Alaska Steel. John Benteen. (Fargo Ser.). (O.s.i.). 1973. pap. 0.75 o.s.i. (BT50550). Belmont-Tower.

Alaska Trail Dogs. Elsie Noble Caldwell. 1945. R. R. Smith.
Alaskan: A Novel. Robert Lund. LC 52-14036. 1953. J. Day Co.
Alaskan: A Novel of the North. James Oliver Curwood. LC 23-11260. 1923. Cosmopolitan Book Corporation.
Alaskan: A Novel of the North. James Oliver Curwood. LC 33-17485. 1926. Grasset & Dunlap.
Alaskan: A Novel of the North. James Oliver Curwood. LC 43-9929. 1943. Triangle Books.
Alaskan Christmas & Other Stories. Nora Young. 150p. 1982. 8.95 (ISBN 0-918270-10-3). That New Pub.
Alaskan Poker Stories. Kenneth Gilbert. LC 58-8803. (Illus.). 1958. R.D. Seal.
Alaskan Summer. Nina Cornett. (Candlelight romance). 1974. (pbk.) 0.75. Dell.
Alban: A Tale of the New World. Jedediah Vincent Huntington. LC 77-11293. (American Catholic Tradition). 1978. 29.00 (ISBN 0-405-10836-2). Arno Press.
Alban. A Tale of the New World. Emma Marshall. LC 44-22009. 1852. The Author.
Albany Starks' Revenge. A Novel. Richard Steel Maurice. Ed. by Sophia L. Presbrey. (On cover: Idle moments series, no. 6). 1891. The Price McGill Company.
Albatross. Evelyn Anthony. LC 82-20456. 240p. 1983. 13.95 (ISBN 0-399-12773-9, Putnam). Putnam Pub Group.
Albatross. Charlotte Armstrong. LC 57-10710. 1957. Coward-McCann.
Albatross. Gladys Skelton. LC 32-1651. 1932. D. Appleton and Company.
Albatross & Other Stories. Susan Hill. LC 75-10082. 1975. 6.95 (ISBN 0-8415-0383-4). Saturday Review Press.
Albatross Murders. Inigo Jones. LC 42-2907. 1941. Mystery House.
Albergo Empedocle, and Other Writings. Edward Morgan Forster. Ed. by George H. Thomson. LC 79-162435. 1971. 7.95 (ISBN 0-87140-540-7). Liveright.
Albert City Caper. Don Buchan. LC 67-9673. 1967.
Albert Gate Mystery, Being Further Adventures of Reginald Brett, Barrister Detective. Louis Tracy. LC 4-30953. 1904. R. F. Fenno & Company.
Albert Goes Through. John Boynton Priestley. LC 33-36722. 1933. Harper & Brothers.
Albert Grope: The Story of a Belated Victorian. Francis Oscar Mann. LC 31-21181. Harcourt, Brace and Company.
Albert Merton, the Farm Hand: A Domestic Story of Life Among Working People. George Dillwyn Hunt. LC 7-11683. 1893. The T. J. Walton Job Printing House.
Albert Savarus. Honore De Balzac. Tr. by Katharine Prescott Wormeley. LC 3-24437. (Half-title: The comedy of human life... Scenes from private life). 1892. Roberts Brothers.
Albert Savarus: A Daughter of Eve. Honore De Balzac. Tr. by George Burnham Ives. The Neale Company.
Albert Sears: A Novel. Millen Brand. LC 47-3784. 1947. Simon and Schuster.
Alberta: Adventuress. Edmond Loutil. Tr. by Hannon, John. LC 18-19729. 1918. Benziger Brothers.
Alberta Alone: 3v. in 1, by Cora Sandel. Tr. from Norwegian by Elizabeth Rokkan. Sara Fabricius. LC 66-19028. 1966. 7.95. Orion Dist. Grossman.
Albert's Victoria. Tyler-Whittle, Michael Sidney. LC 72-79504. (Illus.). 1972. 6.95. St. Martin's Press.
Albigenses: A Romance. Charles Robert Maturin. LC 73-22768. (Gothic Novels). 1974. (ISBN 0-405-06011-4). Arno Press.
Albigenses: A Romance. Charles Robert Maturin. LC 7-17593. 1824. S.F. Bradford and J. Laval.
Albine: Or, The Abbe's Temptation. (La Faute De L'abbe Mouret. Emile Zola & Sherwood, Mrs. Mary (Neal) Tr. LC 9-1339. T. B. Peterson & Brothers.
Albion Walk. Gwendoline Butler. LC 82-7447. 14.95 (ISBN 0-698-11172-9). Coward, McCann & Geoghegan.
Albreeht. Arlo Bates. LC 6-9089. 1890. Roberts Brothers.
Album. Mary Roberts Rinehart. LC 33-13640. Farrar & Rinehart, Incorporated.
Album. Mary Roberts Rinehart. LC 42-17354. 1942. Triangle Books.
Album. Mary Roberts Rinehart. LC 78-24286. (Illus.). 1979. 14.95 (ISBN 0-8161-6640-4). Hall.
Album: A Novel. Victor Jones. LC 65-12350. 1965. 4.00. Lyle Stuart.
Albuquerque. Jeannine D. Van Eperen. 386p. 1980. 15.95 (ISBN 0-937268-02-X); pap. 8.95 (ISBN 0-937268-01-1). Alpha Printing.
Alcalde de Zalamea see La Vida es Sueno.
Alcar, the Captive Creole. facsimile ed. M. Roland Markham. LC 77-170701. (Black Heritage Library Collection). Repr. of 1857 ed. 14.75 (ISBN 0-8369-8891-4). Ayer Co.
Alcatraz. Max Brand. LC 23-2886. 1923. 1.90. G. P. Putnam's Sons.
Alcatraz Incident. Russell O'Neil. LC 70-150064. 1971. 5.95. McKay.
Alchemist. Honore De Balzac. (choice series, no. 25) PZ3.B22Alc3). 1890. R. Bonner's Sons.
Alchemist. Charles Graves. 156p. (Orig.). 1981. pap. 1.95 (ISBN 0-441-01426-7, Pub. by Charter Bks). Ace Bks.
Alchemist. Leslie H. Whitten. LC 73-84079. 1973. 7.95 (ISBN 0-88327-025-0). Charterhouse.
Alchemist: Or, The House of Claes. From the French of. Honore De Balzac. Tr. by Orlando Williams Wight. Goodrich, Frank Boott, 1826-1894, Tr. LC 6-6317. (Half-title: Novels of M. Honore de Balzac. Library ed., v. 3). 1861. Rudd & Carleton.
Alchemist's Secret. Isabel Cecilia Williams. LC 10-105782. P. J. Kenedy & Sons.
Alchemist's Voyage: An Adventure. 1st Ed. Calvin Kentfield. LC 55-10149. 1955. Harcourt, Brace.
Alchemy and Academe: A Collection of Original Stories Concerning Themselves with Transmutations, Mental and Elemental, Alchemical and Academic. Ed. by Anne McCaffrey. LC 73-129892. (Doubleday science fiction). 1970. 4.95. Doubleday.
Alchemy & Academie: A Collection of Original Stories Concerning Themselves with Transmutation, Mental and Elemental, Alchemical and Academic. Ed. by Anne McCaffrey. (Del Rey Book). 1980. 2.25. Ballantine Books.
Alchemy and Finnegans Wake. Barbara DiBernard. LC 79-22809. (Illus.). 24.00 (ISBN 0-87395-388-6). State University of New York Press.
Alchemy Deception. Hans Holzer. (Randy Knowles Series). 1973. (pbk) 0.95. Award Books.
Alchemy Murder. Peter Oldfeld, pseud. LC 29-9002. 1929. I. Washburn.
Alcibiades: Beloved of Gods and Men. Vincenz Brun. LC 36-6659. 1935. G. P. Putnam's Sons.
Aldabra Alone. Tony Beamish. 1970. 7.95 o.p. (ISBN 0-87156-043-7). Sierra.
Aldair Across the Misty Sea. Neal Barrett, Jr. (Science Fiction Ser.). 1980. pap. 1.75 (ISBN 0-87997-525-3, UE1525). Daw Bks.
Aldair in Albion. Neal Barrett. (Daw Science Fiction#195). 1976. (pbk.) 1.25. Daw Books.
Aldair, Master of Ships. Neal Barrett, Jr. 1977. 1.50 (ISBN 0-87997-326-9). DAW Books.
Aldair: The Legion of the Beasts. Neal Barrett, Jr. 1982. pap. 2.25 (ISBN 0-87997-696-9, UE1696). Daw Bks.
Aldeane. A Novel. Louise Palmer Heaven. LC 7-5041. 1868. A. Roman & Company.
Aldeburg Cezanne. John Alexander Graham. LC 70-129071. 1970. 5.95. Little, Brown.
Alden Church. Sophie Bronson Titterington. LC 8-26781. American Baptist Publication Society.
Alder Gulch. Ernest Haycox. LC 42-7196. 1942. Little, Brown and Company.
Alder Gulch. Ernest Haycox. LC 43-18644. 1943. The Sun Dial Press.
Alderman's Wife. Henry E Scott. LC 4-9572. 1904. H. E. Scott.
Aldiss Unbound: The Science Fiction of Brian Aldiss. Richard W. Mathews. LC 77-24582. (Milford Ser.: Popular Writers of Today Vol. 9). 1977. lib. bdg. 9.95x (ISBN 0-89370-113-0); pap. 3.95x (ISBN 0-89370-213-7). Borgo Pr.
Aldringham's Last Chance. Arthur John Rees. LC 33-2224. 1933. Dodd, Mead & Company.
Ale-House Guest: A Novel. Joan Frances Young. LC 27-9455. 1927. Longmans, Green and Co., Ltd.
Alec Forbes of Howglen. George Macdonald. LC 75-1509. (Victorian Fiction: Novels of Faith and Doubt; V. 59). 1975. 35.00 (ISBN 0-8240-1583-5). Garland Pub.
Alec Forbes of Howglen. George Macdonald. LC 12-183203. 1911. D. McKay.
Alec Forbes of Howglen. A Novel. George Macdonald. (Seaside library. v. 38, no. 790). 1880. G. Munro.
Aleck Hormby. Charles Stell. LC 98-1267. E. R. Herrick & Company.
Aleck Maury, Sportsman. Caroline Gordon. LC 74-164531. 1971. (ISBN 0-8154-0400-X). Cooper Square Publishers.
Aleck Maury: Sportsman. Caroline Gordon. LC 34-370838. 1934. C. Scribner's Sons.
Aleck Maury, Sportsman: A Novel. Caroline Gordon. LC 80-14493. (Lost American fiction). 1980. 12.95 (ISBN 0-8093-0972-6) (ISBN 0-8093-0988-2). Southern Illinois University Press.
Aleestis: A Musical Novel... Cornish. LC 6-28733. (Leisure hour series, no. 40). 1874. H. Holt and Company.
Alejandro E Isabel. Jose R. Frontado. 96p. (Span.). 1981. pap. 2.75 (ISBN 0-311-37024-1, Edit Mundo). Casa Bautista.
Aleph & Other Stories Nineteen Thirty-Three to Nineteen Sixty-Nine. Jorge Luis Borges. 1979. pap. 5.95 (ISBN 0-525-45037-8, 0578-170). Dutton.
Aleph and Other Stories, 1933-1969: Together with Commentaries and an Autobiographical Essay. Jorge Luis Borges. LC 77-122797. 1970. 7.95. E. P. Dutton.
Aleph Solution. Sandor Frankel & Webster Mews. LC 78-7172. 1979. 8.95 (ISBN 0-8128-2534-9). Stein and Day.
Aleph, the Chaldean: Or, The Messiah As Seen from Alexandria. Enoch Fitch Burr. LC 6-196609. W. B. Ketcham.
Aletta Laird. Barbara Webb. LC 35-3660. 1935. Doubleday, Doran & Company, Inc.
Alex and the Gypsy. Stanley Elkin. 1976. 1.50 (ISBN 0-671-80744-7). Pocket Books.
Alex & the Raynhams. Iris Bromige. 1972. pap. 0.75 o.p. (94279). Beagle Bks.
Alex Driving South: A Novel. Keith Maillard. LC 79-21779. 8.95 (ISBN 0-8037-0196-9). Dial Press.
Alex: Portrait of a Teenage Prostitute. Rosalyn Drexler. LC 76-56409. 1977. 1.50 (ISBN 0-345-25770-7). Ballantine Books.
Alex the Great. Harry Charles Witwer. LC 19-15221. Small, Maynard & Company.
Alexa. Anne Melville. LC 77-92227. 1979. 10.00 (ISBN 0-385-13501-7). Doubleday.
Alexa. Maggie Osborne. (Signet Book.). 1980. 2.25 (ISBN 0-451-09244-9). New American Library.
Alexander: A Novel of Utopia. Klaus Mann & Saunders, Marion, Tr. II. Title. LC 30-32137. Brewer & Warren, Inc.
Alexander: A Romantic Biography. Konrad Bercovici. LC 28-20224. 1928. Cosmopolitan Book Corporation.
Alexander Botts: Earthworm Tractors. William Hazlett Upson. 1929. Farrar & Rinehart Incorporated.
Alexander Botts: Great Stories from the Saturday Evening Post. William Hazlett Upson. LC 77-90937. 5.95 (ISBN 0-89387-011-0). Curtis Pub. Co.
Alexander Gifford: Or, Vi'let's Boy; a Story of Negro Life. Henry A Merrill. LC 72-1821. (Black heritage library collection). (Illus.). 1972. 15.00 (ISBN 0-8369-9036-6). Books for Libraries Press.
Alexander in Babylon. Jakob Wassermann. LC 49-191623. 1949. Ziff-Davis Pub. Co.
Alexander McBain, B.A. A Prince in Penury. Adeline Margaret Teskey. LC 6-39026. F. H. Revell Company.
Alexander MacKenzie: Lone Courage. Guy Forve. (American Explorers Ser.: No. 12). 320p. (Orig.). 1983. pap. 2.95 (ISBN 0-440-00066-1, Emerald). Dell.
Alexander of Macedon: The Journey to World's End. Harold Lamb. LC 46-4464. 1946. Doubleday & Company, Inc.
Alexander the Glorious: 1st Amer. Ed. Jane Oliver, pseud. LC 65-18475. 4.95. Putnam.
Alexander the God. Pierre Stephen Robert Payne. LC 54-113673. 1954. A. A. Wyn.
Alexander the Great. Nikos Kazantzakis. LC 81-11307. 1982. 17.95 (ISBN 0-8214-0654-X). Ohio University Press.
Alexanderplatz: Berlin, the Story of Franz Biberkopf. Alfred Doblin. Tr. by Jolas, Eugene. LC 31-234679. 1931. The Viking Press.
Alexander's Bridge. Willa Sibert Cather. LC 76-56439. 1977. 2.95 (ISBN 0-8032-5864-X). University of Nebraska Press.
Alexander's Bridge. Willa Sibert Cather. LC 12-9856. 1912. Houghton Mifflin Company.
Alexander's Bridge. new ed. with a preface. ed. Willa Sibert Cather. LC 22-21209. 1922. Houghton Mifflin Company.
Alexander's Feast. John Kelly. LC 49-11293. 1949. Harcourt, Brace.
Alexander's Feast. Arthur R. G Solmssen. LC 79-161856. (Illus.). 1971. 7.95. Little, Brown.
Alexander's Feast: A Novel. Arthur R. G Solmssen. (Illus.). 1973. 1.50 (ISBN 0-671-78579-6). Pocket Bks.
Alexandra. Valerie Martin. LC 79-10243. 8.95 (ISBN 0-374-10264-3). Farrar Straus Giroux.
Alexandra. Gladys Schmitt. LC 47-311034. 1947. Dial Press.
Alexandria Quartet. Lawrence Durrell. Incl. Justine; Balthazar; Mountolive; Clea. 1961. Boxed set. pap. 19.50 (ISBN 0-525-47795-0, 01893-570). Dutton.
Alexandria Quartet: Justine, Balthazar, Mountolive, Clea. Lawrence Durrell. LC 62-53350. 1962. Dutton.
Alexandria, the Ambivalent. Katheryn Kimbrough. (Saga of the Phenwick Women Ser.: No. 36). 256p. 1981. pap. 2.25 (ISBN 0-445-04655-4). Popular Lib.
Alexandrian. Martha Rofheart. 1977. pap. 1.95 o.p. (ISBN 0-515-04404-0, Jove). BJ Pub Group.
Alexandrian: A Novel. Martha Rofheart. LC 76-3659. 8.95 (ISBN 0-690-01148-2). Crowell.
Alexandriana. Le Gette Blythe. LC 40-33695. Stackpole Sons.
Alexandrians. Charles Mills. LC 52-5270. 1952. Putnam.
Alexei the Gangster. IUrii Pavlovich German. LC 74-10084. 1974. 16.00 (ISBN 0-88355-171-3). Hyperion Press.
Alexei the Gangster. Yuri Herman. Tr. by Stephen Garry from Rus. LC 74-10084. (Soviet Literature in English Translation Ser). 288p. 1974. Repr. of 1940 ed. 17.50 (ISBN 0-88355-171-3). Hyperion Conn.
Alexia. Mary Perkins Ives Abbott. LC 5-426078. 1889. A.C. McClurg and Company.
Alexis: A Story of Love and Music. Stuart Maclean. LC 17-22300. 1917. D. Appleton and Company.
Alexis: Or, The Cottage in the Woods. A Novel, from the French. The Manuscript Found on the Banks of the Isere. The 1st American Ed. Ornamented with Handsome Copper Plates. Francois Guillaume Ducray-Daminil. LC 6-15444. From the Press of A. Martin.
Alfanhui. Rafael S. Ferlosio. Tr. by Ruth M. Danald from Sp. LC 74-82791. (Illus.). 156p. 1975. pap. 3.50 (ISBN 0-911198-39-3). Purdue.
Alfanhui: A Translation with Critical Introduction of Rafael Sanchez Ferlosio's Industrias y Andanzas De Alfanhui. Sanchez Ferlosio, Rafael. LC 74-82791. (Illus.). 1975. 3.50 (ISBN 0-911198-39-3). Purdue University Press.
Alfie Darling. Bill Naughton. LC 72-139642. (O.s.i.). 1971. 6.95 o.s.i. (ISBN 0-671-20816-0). S&S.
Alfio Balzani: Or, Extracts from the Diary of a Proscribed Sicilian. J Minelli. LC 7-25459. 1861. Rudd & Carleton.
Alfred & Guinevere. Drawings by Paul Sagsoorian. James Schuyler. LC 58-5920. 1958. Harcourt, Brace.
Alfred Bester. Carolyn Wendell. LC 80-19655. (Starmont Reader's Guides to Contemporary Science Fiction and Fantasy Authors; 6). 1980. 3.95 (ISBN 0-916732-08-8) (ISBN 0-916732-37-1). Starmont House.
Alfred De Rosann: Or, The Adventures of a French Gentleman. George William McArthur Reynolds. LC 7-30596. 1839. Carey and Hart.
Alfred Hagart's Household. Alexander Smith. LC 8-8189. 1865. Ticknor and Fields.
Alfred Hagart's Household. Alexander Smith. LC 7-3052. 1866. A Strahan.
Alfred Hitchcock Presents. Alfred Hitchcock. LC 77-3047. 8.95 (ISBN 0-394-41216-8). Random House.
Alfred Hitchcock Presents: I Want My Mummy. Ed. by Alfred Hitchcock. (Dell Book). 1977. 1.25 (ISBN 0-440-13985-6). Dell Pub. Co.
Alfred Hitchcock Presents: A Month of Mystery. Ed. by Alfred Hitchcock. LC 79-85630. 1969. 6.95. Random House.
Alfred Hitchcock Presents: Dates with Death. Ed. by Alfred Hitchcock. 1.25. Dell.
Alfred Hitchcock Presents More Stories My Mother Never Told Me. Ed. by Alfred Hitchcock. (Dell Book). 1977. 1.25 (ISBN 0-440-15816-8). Dell Pub. Co.
Alfred Hitchcock Presents: More Stories Not for the Nervous. Alfred Joseph Hitchcock. 1973. 0.75. Dell.
Alfred Hitchcock Presents My Favorites in Suspense. Ed. by Alfred Hitchcock. LC 59-10818. 1959. Random House.
Alfred Hitchcock Presents: Scream Along with Me. Ed. by Alfred Hitchcock. (Dell Book). 1977. 1.25 (ISBN 0-440-13633-4). Dell Pub. Co.
Alfred Hitchcock Presents Skeleton Crew. Ed. by Alfred Hitchcock. (Dell Book). 1977. 1.25 (ISBN 0-440-15815-X). Dell Pub. Co.
Alfred Hitchcock Presents Stories My Mother Never Told Me. Ed. by Alfred Hitchcock. LC 63-16155. 1963. Random House.
Alfred Hitchcock Presents Stories Not for the Nervous. Ed. by Alfred Hitchcock. LC 65-21262. 1965. Random House.
Alfred Hitchcock Presents: Stories That Go Bump in the Night. Ed. by Alfred Hitchcock. (Illus.). 1977. 8.95 (ISBN 0-394-41216-8, BYR). Random.
Alfred Hitchcock Presents: Stories That Scared Even Me. Ed. by Alfred Hitchcock. LC 67-22678. 1967. 8.95 o.p. (ISBN 0-394-41231-1, BYR). Random.
Alfred Hitchcock Presents Stories They Wouldn't Let Me Do on TV. Ed. by Alfred Hitchcock. LC 57-7307. 1957. Simon and Schuster.
Alfred Hitchcock Presents Stories to Be Read with the Door Locked. Alfred Hitchcock. LC 75-12992. 1975. 8.95 (ISBN 0-394-49839-9). Random House.

Alfred Hitchcock Presents: Stories to Be Read with the Lights on. Ed. by Alfred Hitchcock. LC 73-5059. 1973. 7.95 (ISBN 0-394-48720-6). Random House.

Alfred Hitchcock Presents: Stories to Be Read with the Door Locked. Ed. by Alfred Hitchcock. 1977. 1.25. Dell Pub. Co.

Alfred Hitchcock Presents: Stories to Stay Awake by. Ed. by Alfred Hitchcock. 1973. (pbk.) 0.95. Dell.

Alfred Hitchcock Presents: Stories to Stay Awake by. Ed. by Alfred Hitchcock. LC 71-159350. 1971. 7.95 (ISBN 0-394-47303-5). Random House.

Alfred Hitchcock Presents: The Master's Choice. Alfred Hitchcock. LC 79-4789. 10.00 (ISBN 0-394-50419-4). Random House.

Alfred Hitchcock Presents 12 Stories for Late at Night. Ed. by Alfred Hitchcock. 1976. 1.50. Dell.

Alfred Hitchcock's Deathreach. Ed. by Cathleen Jordan. 348p. 1982. 12.95 (ISBN 0-385-27777-6). Davis Pubns.

Alfred Hitchcock's Deathreach. Ed. by Cathleen Jordan. 352p. 1982. 12.95 (ISBN 0-385-27777-6). Dial.

Alfred Hitchcock's Fear. Cathleen Jordan. LC 82-214307. (Alfred Hitchcock's Anthology; 12). 1982. (pbk.) 2.95. Davis Publications.

Alfred Hitchcock's Spellbinders in Suspense. Ed. by Alfred Hitchcock. LC 67-20603. (Illus.). 1967. Random House.

Alfred Hitchcock's Tales to Be Read with Caution. Eleanor Sullivan. LC 80-106921. 9.95 (ISBN 0-8037-0343-0). Dial Press.

Alfred Hitchcock's Tales to Fill You with Fear & Trembling. Eleanor Sullivan. 1980. 9.95 o.s.i. (ISBN 0-8037-0392-9). Davis Pubns.

Alfred Hitchcock's Tales to Keep You Spellbound. Eleanor Sullivan. LC 77-358830. 8.95 (ISBN 0-8037-0077-6). Davis Publications: Distributed by Dial Press.

Alfred Hitchcock's Tales to Make You Quake & Quiver. Ed. by Cathleen Jordan. 348p. 1982. 12.95 (ISBN 0-385-27682-6). Davis Pubns.

Alfred Hitchcock's Tales to Make You Quake & Quiver. Ed. by Cathleen Jordan. 348p. 1982. 12.95 (ISBN 0-385-27682-6). Dial.

Alfred Hitchcock's Tales to Make You Weak in the Knees. Alfred Hitchcock. 288p. 1982. 10.95 (ISBN 0-385-27210-3). Dial.

Alfred Hitchcock's Tales to Make You Weak in the Knees. Eleanor Sullivan. 1981. 10.95 (ISBN 0-8037-0103-9). Davis Pubns.

Alfred Hitchcock's Tales to Make Your Blood Run Cold. Eleanor Sullivan. LC 78-108686. 8.95 (ISBN 0-8037-0134-9). Dial Press.

Alfred Hitchcock's Tales to Make Your Hair Stand on End. Eleanor Sullivan. LC 81-152424. (Illus.). 9.95 (ISBN 0-8037-0028-8). Dial Press.

Alfred Hitchcock's Tales to Make Your Teeth Chatter. Alfred Hitchcock & Eleanor Sullivan. LC 81-101612. 9.95 (ISBN 0-8037-0173-X). Dial Press.

Alfred Hitchcock's Tales to Make Your Teeth Chatter. Eleanor Sullivan. 348p. 1980. 9.95 o.s.i. (ISBN 0-8037-0173-X). Davis Pubns.

Alfred Hitchcock's Tales to Scare You Stiff. Eleanor Sullivan & Alfred Joseph Hitchcock. LC 78-113337. 8.95 (ISBN 0-8037-0135-7). Dial Press.

Alfred Hitchcock's Tales to Send Chills Down Your Spine. Eleanor Sullivan. LC 79-110657. 8.95 (ISBN 0-8037-0342-2). Dial Press.

Alfred Hitchcock's Tales to Take Your Breath Away. Eleanor Sullivan. LC 78-301558. 8.95 (ISBN 0-8037-0081-4). Dial Press.

Alfred Hitchcock's Your Share of Fear. Ed. by Cathleen Jordan. 352p. 1982. 12.95 (ISBN 0-385-27773-3). Dial.

Alfred, King of the English. Carola Mary Anima Oman Lenanton, pseud. LC 40-32134. 1939. E.P. Dutton & Co. Inc.

Alfrieda. A Novel. Emma E. H Specht. LC 8-15514. 1890. The Author.

Alf's Button. William Aubrey Darlington. LC 20-12958. Frederick A. Stokes Company.

Algerine Captive: Or, The Life and Adventures of Doctor Updike Underhill, Six Years a Prisoner Among the Algerines. (1797) A Facsimile Reproduction of the London Ed. of 1802, with an Introd. Royall Tyler. Ed. by Jack B. Moore. LC 67-10272. 1967. Scholars' Facsimiles & Reprints.

Algonquin Cat. Val Schaffner & Hilary Knight. LC 80-16866. 9.95 (ISBN 0-440-00073-4). Delacorte Press/E. Friede.

Algonquin Indian Tales: Collected by Egerton R. Young... Egerton Ryerson Young. Eaton & Mains.

Algonquin Maiden: A Romance of the Early Days of Upper Canada. Graeme Mercer Adam & Wetherald, A. Ethelwyn, Joint Author. (On cover: Lovell's library. v. 17, no. 846). J. W. Lovell Company.

Algonquin Project. Frederick W. Nolan. LC 74-8988. 1974. 5.95 (ISBN 0-688-00319-2). Morrow.

Algonquin Project. Frederick W. Nolan. 1976. 1.75 (ISBN 0-515-03752-4). Pyramid Publications.

Algonquin: The Story of a Great Dog. Dion Henderson. LC 53-8977. (Illus.). 1953. Holt.

Algonquin Woods. Bob Callahan. (New World Writing Ser.). (Illus., Orig.). 1978. 10.00 (ISBN 0-913666-26-2); pap. 4.95 (ISBN 0-913666-25-4). Turtle Isl Foun.

Algorithm. Jean Mark Gawron. (Berkley Book). 1978. 1.75 (ISBN 0-425-03751-7). Berkley Pub. Corp.

Alhambra. author's rev. ed. Washington Irving. LC 20-9517. (Half-title: The works of Washington Irving. vol. XV). 1857. G. P. Putnam & Co.

Alhambra. author's rev. ed. Washington Irving. LC 26-251. (Added t.-p.: The works of Washington Irving. v. 15). 1863. G. P. Putnam.

Alhambra. author's rev. ed. Washington Irving. LC 15-14187. 1868. G. P. Putnam and Son.

Alhambra. author's rev. ed. knickerbocker ed. Washington Irving. 1871. J. B. Lippincott & Co.

Alhambra. Washington Irving. LC 44-44309. A. L. Burt.

Alhambra. author's rev. ed. Washington Irving. LC 44-50897. 1883. G. P. Putnam's Sons.

Alhambra. Washington Irving. LC 44-44308. Worthington Co.

Alhambra. Washington Irving. LC 80-13501. 1980. 199.95 (ISBN 0-8490-1409-3). Gordon Press.

Alhambra. Washington Irving & Hitchcock, Alfred Marshall, 1868-1941, Ed. LC 44-50896. (Macmillan's pocket American and English classics). 1912. The Macmillan Company.

Alhambra. Washington Irving & Law, Frederick Houk, 1871- Ed. LC 26-17989. (Academy classics for junior high schools). Allyn and Bacon.

Alhambra. Washington Irving & Pennell, Joseph, 1857-1926, Illus. LC 38-36424. 1896. Macmillan and Co., Ltd.

Alhambra. Washington Irving & Robinson, Edward Kilburn, 1883- Ed. LC 15-27746. Ginn and Company.

Alhambra. Washington Irving & White, Alice H., Ed. LC 44-11039. (On cover: Home and school library). 1902. Ginn & Company.

Alhambra: Palace of Mystery and Splendor. Washington Irving & Williams, Mabel, 1887- Ed. LC 26-16724. (The Macmillan children's classics). 1926. The Macmillan Company.

Alhambra: Tales and Sketches of the Moors and Spaniards. Washington Irving. LC 44-44310. (On cover: The Home library). A. L. Burt Company.

Ali & Nino. Kurban Said. LC 74-143823. 1971. 5.95 (ISBN 0-394-46975-5). Random House.

Ali Baba & the Thieves. Gary Coates & Joyce Sanker. 1982. pap. 3.50. Eldridge Pub.

Ali Baba's Pride & His Failures. John Puoplo. 3.50 o.p. Carlton.

Alias Basil Willing. Helen McCloy. LC 51-10618. 1951. Random House.

Alias Ben Alibi. Irvin Shrewsbury Cobb. LC 25-878933. George H. Doran Company.

Alias Blackshirt. Graham Montague Jeffries. LC 32-15761. 1932. Dodd, Mead & Company.

Alias Blue Mask. John Creasey. LC 39-5468. 1939. J. B. Lippincott Co.

Alias Blue Mask. Anthony Morton, pseud. LC 39-5468. J. B. Lippincott Company.

Alias Butch Cassidy: By Will Henry. Henry Allen, pseud. LC 66-21496. 1968. bds., 4.95. Random.

Alias Dr. Ely: Peter Clancy's New Impersonation. Lee Thayer. LC 27-40598. 1927. Doubleday, Page & Company.

Alias for Death. Barbara Leonard Reynolds. LC 51-9105. (Gargoyle mystery). Coward-McCann.

Alias His Wife: By Steven Ransome Pseud. Frederick Clyde Davis. LC 65-13641. (Red badge detective). bds., 3.50. Dodd.

Alias Jane Smith. Clarence Budington Kelland. 1944. Harper & Brothers.

Alias Kitty Casey: A Novel. Mary Gertrude Williams. LC 11-31893. P. J. Kenedy & Sons.

Alias Man. David Craig. LC 68-9168. (A Stein and Day mystery). 1968. 4.95. Stein and Day.

Alias Miss Saunders, R.N. Large print ed. Jane Converse. LC 81-14529. 266p. 1981. Repr. of 1962 ed. 9.95x (ISBN 0-89621-315-3). Thorndike Pr.

Alias Mr. Death. G Wayman Jones. LC 32-316141. The Fiction League.

Alias Red Ryan. Charles Neville Buck. LC 23-9171. 1923. Doubleday, Page & Company.

Alias Richard Power. William Allison. LC 21-196502. 1921. Doubleday, Page & Company.

Alias the Buffalo Doctor. Jean Cummings. LC 82-79770. (Illus.). 266p. 1981. 11.95 (ISBN 0-8040-0815-9). Swallow.

Alias the Dead. George Harmon Coxe. LC 43-347. 1943. A. A. Knopf.

Alias the Lone Wolf. Louis Joseph Vance. LC 21-193953. 1921. Doubleday, Page & Company.

Alias "the Night Wind" The Story of an Allsweeping Revenge Against False Witness. pseud. ed. Frederic Van Rensselaer Dey. LC 24-149485. M. A. Donohue & Company?

Alias "the Night Wind" The Story of an All-Sweeping Revenge Against False Witnesses. Frederic Van Rensselaer Dey. LC 13-24109. 1.25. G. Dillingham Company.

Alias the Promised Land. Samuel Gordon Gurwit. J. H. Hopkins, Inc.

Alias the Saint. Leslie Charteris. (Saint Ser.). 160p. 1980. pap. 1.95 (ISBN 0-441-01350-3, Pub. by Charter Bks). Ace Bks.

Alias Uncle Hugo. 1st Ed. Manning Coles, pseud. LC 52-10398. 1952. Published for the Crime Club by Doubleday.

Alibaba, the Double Crosser. John Puoplo. 1970. 3.50 o.p. Carlton.

Alibi. John Creasey. LC 72-143931. 1971. 4.95 (ISBN 0-684-12347-9). Scribner.

Alibi. George Allan England. LC 16-10305. Small, Maynard & Company.

Alibi. Frederic Franklyn Van De Water. LC 30-23083. 1930. Pub. for the Crime Club, Inc., by Doubleday, Doran & Company, Inc.

Alibi at Dusk: A Mystery Story. Ben Benson. LC 51-9000. 1951. M. S. Mill Co. and W. Morrow.

Alibi Baby: A Gil Vine Mystery, by Stewart Sterling Pseud. Prentice Winchell. LC 55-1105. 1955. Washburn.

Alibi for a Witch. E. X. Ferrars, pseud. 1971. pap. 0.75 o.p. (07175). Curtis.

Alibi for a Witch: ByE. X. Ferrars Pseud. 1st Ed. Morna Doris MacTaggart Brown. LC 52-11625. 1952. Published for the Crime Club by Doubleday.

Alibi for Isabel. Mary Roberts Rinehart. Repr. lib. bdg. 14.40x (ISBN 0-89190-326-7). Am Repr-Rivercity Pr.

Alibi for Isabel: And Other Stories. Mary Roberts Rinehart. LC 44-6124. 1944. Farrar & Rinehart, Inc.

Alibi in Time. June Thompson. 208p. 1981. pap. text ed. 2.25 (ISBN 0-553-14904-0). Bantam.

Alibi in Time. June Thomson. LC 80-501. 1980. 8.95 (ISBN 0-385-17075-0). Published for the Crime Club by Doubleday.

Alice. Elizabeth Eliot. LC 50-9255. 1950. Duell, Sloan and Pearce.

Alice. Howard Melvin Fast. LC 63-11241. 1963. Doubleday.

Alice. Sandra Wilson. LC 75-10003. 1976. 7.95. St. Martin's Press.

Alice Adams. Booth Tarkington. LC 21-26561. 1921. Doubleday, Page & Company.

Alice and a Family. St. John Greer Ervine. LC 15-8086. 1915. The Macmillan Company.

Alice and Me: A Novel. William Judson. LC 72-94675. 1973. 6.95 (ISBN 0-525-63000-7). A. Fields Books; Distributed by E. P. Dutton.

Alice, and The Lost Novel. Sherwood Anderson. LC 73-5920. (Series: The Woburn Books, No. 10.). 1973. (ISBN 0-8414-1743-1). Folcroft Library Editions.

Alice Ashland: A Romance of the World's Fair. Edith Neville. (On cover: Once a week semi-monthly library. v. 11, no. 4). 1893. P. F. Collier.

Alice Brand. A Romance of the Capital. Albert Gallatin Riddle. LC 7-41430. 1875. D. Appleton and Company.

Alice Brenton: A Tale of Old Newport in Revolutionary Days. Marie Josephine Gale. LC 9-12199. 1909. The C. M. Clark Publishing Company.

Alice Cracks the Looking-Glass. Oscar S Erlandson. LC 51-14067. 1951. Vantage Press.

Alice Devine. Edgar Jepson. LC 16-7664. 1.25. The Bobbs-Merrill Company.

Alice Dies Twice. Ben Grant, pseud. LC 75-17077. 176p. (Orig.). 1975. pap. 1.25 (ISBN 0-89041-025-9, 3025). Major Bks.

Alice Doesn't Live Here Anymore. Robert Getchell. 1975. (pbk.) 1.25 (ISBN 0-446-76634-8). Warner Paperback Library.

Alice-for-Short: A Dichronism. William Frend De Morgan. 1907. H. Holt and Company.

Alice Gordon. Or, The Uses of Orphanage. Joseph Alden. LC 42-26570. (On cover: Harper's Fireside library). 1847. Harper & Brothers.

Alice in Acidland. Thomas Fensch. LC 70-92041. (Illus.). 1970. 5.95. A. S. Barnes.

Alice in Bed: A Novel. Cathleen Schine. LC 82-48721. 1983. 12.95 (ISBN 0-394-52982-0). Knopf.

Alice in Sunderland. Jane Anne Torrey Kendall. LC 9-26666. 1909. 1.00. Cochrane Publishing Co.

Alice in Wonderland. Lewis Carroll. (Illus.). 108p. 1973. o. p 7.95 (ISBN 0-517-50857-5, C N Potter Bks); pap. 3.95 (ISBN 0-517-50858-3, C N Potter). Crown.

Alice in Wonderland. Charles Lutwidge Dodgson. Ed. by Donald J. Gray. LC 72-141586. (Norton critical editions). (Illus.). 1971. 10.00 (ISBN 0-393-04343-6) (ISBN 0-393-09977-6). W. W. Norton.

Alice in Wonderland: Through the Looking Glass, Etc. Charles Lutwidge Dodgson. LC 37-5640. (Half-title: Everyman's library, ed. by Ernest Rhys. For young people. no. 836). 1934. J. M. Dent & Soins, Ltd.

Alice Learmont: Or, A Mother's Love. Dinah Maria Mulock Craik. LC 41-31309. 1859. Mayhew & Baker.

Alice Lee: Or, The Maine Law Triumphant. S. A. Southworth. LC 8-10840. 1855. Hall and Brother.

Alice Lorraine. Richard Doddridge Blackmore. (On cover: Lovell's library, no. 1035). J. W. Lovell Company.

Alice Lorraine. Richard Doddridge Blackmore. A. I. Burt Company.

Alice Lorraine. A Tale of the South Downs. Blackmore, Richard Doddridge. (On cover: Seaside library. Pocket ed. no. 636). G. Munro.

Alice McDonald; or, The Heroine of Principle: A Story of the Early Cumberland Presbyterian Church. rev. ed., ed. J B Logan. LC 1-29526. 1900. C. P. Publishing House.

Alice Mannering: Or The Nobleman's Son. A Tale of London. Emily Appleton. 1845. Gleason's Publishing Hall.

Alice Mansfield's Sin: Or, The Power of a Woman's Love. Joseph Washington Thompson. LC 8-20134. 1908. Thompson Publishing Company.

Alice Moon: Or, A Brother's Crime. Dan M Davidson. LC 98-1492. 1898. Speaker Printing Company.

Alice Murray. A Tale. Mary Jane Hoffman. LC 7-6150. 1869. P. O'Shea.

Alice Norwood: Or, The Winter of the Heart. Rhoby S. Williams. LC 8-36909. 1884. N. Tibbals & Sons.

Alice O'Connor's Surrender. Mary Elizabeth Carey. 1897. Angel Guardian Press.

Alice of Old Vincennes. Maurice Thompson. LC 62-5890. 1961. Vincennes University Press.

Alice of Old Vincennes. Maurice Thompson. LC 78-104578. (Illus.). 1970. Literature House.

Alice of Old Vincennes. Maurice Thompson. LC 55960. The Bowen-Merrill Company.

Alice of Old Vincennes. Maurice Thompson. LC 9-32287. Grosset & Dunlap.

Alice of Old Vincennes. Maurice Thompson. LC 33-7777. The Bowen-Merrill Company.

Alice of Old Vincennes. Maurice Thompson. LC 11-1009. 1908. Grosset & Dunlap.

Alice: Or, The Mysteries. a new edition. ed. Edward George Earle Lytton Bulwer-Lytton Lytton. LC 7-8365. 1879. G. Routledge and Sons.

Alice: Or, the Mysteries. Edward George Earle Lytton Bulwer-Lytton Lytton. LC 8-11033. G. Routledge and Sons.

Alice: Or, The Mysteries. A Sequel to "Ernest Maltravers.". Edward George Earle Lytton Bulwer-Lytton Lytton. LC 7-8362. (On cover: Seaside library. Pocket ed., no. 650). 1885. G. Munro.

Alice: Or, The Mysteries. A Sequel to "Ernest Maltravers.". Edward George Earle Lytton Bulwer-Lytton Lytton. (Half-title: Novels of Sir Edward Bulwer Lytton, Library ed. Novels of life and manners, vol. IX). 1893. Little, Brown, and Company.

Alice: Or, The Mysteries. Being Part II of Ernest Maltravers. Edward George Earle Lytton Bulwer-Lytton Lytton. 1882. J. W. Lovell Company.

Alice: Or, The Wages of Sin. A Novel. Frederic Werden Pangborn. LC 7-35771. 1883. C. T. Dillingham.

Alice Rayden: Or, Weighed in the Balance. Agnes Elnor Albert. LC 10-31005. Broadway Publishing Co.

Alice Singleton: Or, The Fashion of This World Passeth Away. Sara Henderson Smith. 1850. J. Wiley.

Alice Tracy: Or, Faint, Yet Pursuing. A Sketch, from Real Life... Sophronia Currier. LC 6-31718. 1868. E. P. Dutton and Company.

Alice Vale: A Story for the Times. Lois Nichols Waisbrooker. LC 8-32824. 1869. W. White and Company.

Alice Wilde: the Raftman's Daughter. A Forest Romance. Metta Victoria Fuller Victor. LC 43-47576. (Beadle's Dime Novels: No. 4). 1860. I. P. Beadle and Company.

Alice with Golden Hair. Eleanor Hull. 1982. pap. 2.25 (ISBN 0-451-11795-6, AE1795, Sig). NAL.

Alice's Adventures In Jurisprudencia. Peter F. Sloss. (Illus.). 87p. (Orig.). 1982. pap. 4.95 (ISBN 0-9608246-0-X). Borogove Pr.

Alice's Adventures in Wonderland, No. I. Pennyroyal ed. Lewis Carroll. (Illus.). 148p. 1982. 19.95 (ISBN 0-520-04815-6); deluxe ed. 195.00 (ISBN 0-520-04820-2). U of Cal Pr.

Alice's Adventures in Wonderland. Lewis Carroll. LC 75-12604. (Pictorial Treasury Bookshelf Ser.). (Illus.). 144p. 1975. 9.95 o.p. (ISBN 0-690-00984-4). T Y Crowell.

Alice's Adventures in Wonderland. Charles Lutwidge Dodgson. Limited Editions Club, Inc., New York. LC 32-32402. 1932. The Limited Editions Club.

Alice's Adventures in Wonderland. Charles Lutwidge Dodgson & Salvador Dali. LC 74-9873. (Illus.). 1969. Maecenas Press.

Alice's Adventures in Wonderland & Through the Looking Glass see Classics Set.

Alice's Adventures in Wonderland: By Lewis Carroll. 42 Illus. by John Tenniel. Large Type Ed. Charles Lutwidge Dodgson. (Keith Jennison bk.). 1968. 6.95. Watts.

Alice's Adventures in Wonderland: Through the Looking Glass. Lewis Carroll. 1978. Repr. of 1929 ed. text ed. 8.95x (ISBN 0-460-00836-6, Evman). Biblio Dist.

Alice's Restaurant. Venable Herndon & Arthur Penn. 1970. pap. 1.95 o.p. (Anch). Doubleday.

Alicia. Muriel Bennett Pfahler. LC 66-29824. (Illus.). 1967. Dorrance.

Alicia. Elizabeth Walker. (Orig.). 1980. pap. 2.25 (ISBN 0-440-10014-3). Dell.

Alicia: A Tale of the American Navy. John McDowell Leavitt. LC 98-1844. 1898. Bonnell, Silver and Company.

Alicia II. Robert Thurston. LC 77-28897. 10.95. Berkley Pub. Corp.: Distributed by Putnam.

Alicia Two. Robert Thurston. 1979. pap. text ed. 2.25 (ISBN 0-425-04259-6). Berkley Pub.

Alicia's Trump. Joseph Mathewson. 224p. 1980. pap. 2.25 (ISBN 0-380-76521-7, 76521). Avon.

Alida: An Erotic Novel. Edna MacBrayne. LC 81-80486. 1981. 9.00 (ISBN 0-939500-00-0). Parkhurst Press.

Alida Craig. Pauline King. LC 7-12213. 1896. G. H. Richmond & Co.

Alida: Or, Miscellaneous Sketches of Incidents During the Late American War. Founded on Fact. With Poems. 4th ed., with additions, revised and improved. ed. Amelia Stratton Comfield. LC 6-30668. 1849. Printed for the Author by Angell & Engel.

Alida: Or, Miscellaneous Sketches of Occurrences During the Late American War. Founded on Fact. Amelia Stratton Comfield. LC 6-30669. 1841. Printed for the Author.

Alide: An Episode of Goethe's Life. Emma Lazarus. LC 7-132344. 1874. J. B. Lippincott & Co.

Alie Dear. 1st Ed. Arthur J. Barry & Alice Julia Ryan Barry. LC 56-9495. 1956. Pageant Press.

Alien. Leslie Purnell Davies. LC 70-144259. (Doubleday science fiction). 1971. 4.95. Doubleday.

Alien. Alan Dean Foster & Dan O'Bannon. LC 79-111961. 2.25 (ISBN 0-446-82977-3). Warner Books.

Alien. George Leonard. LC 76-49397. 1977. pap. 1.75 o.p. (ISBN 0-87216-378-4, K 16378). Playboy Pr Pbks.

Alien. Edwin Rosskam. LC 64-7806. 1964. Grossman Publishers.

Alien; a Story of Middle Age. Frances Frederica Montresor. LC 1-24656. 1901. D. Appleton and Company.

Alien Abductors. H. U. Bevis. 192p. (OSI). 1972. 3.95 o.s.i. Lenox Hill.

Alien Art & Arcturus Landing. Gordon R. Dickson. 352p. 1981. pap. 2.75 (ISBN 0-441-01685-5). Ace Bks.

Alien Atlas. C. M. Alexander. (Orig.). 1980. pap. 1.95 (ISBN 0-532-23189-9). Woodhill.

Alien Creatures. Richard Siegel & J. C. Suares. LC 77-94830. (Illus.). 1978. 14.95 (ISBN 0-89169-521-4); pap. 6.95 (ISBN 0-89169-501-X). Reed Bks.

Alien Dust. LC 57-13559. (Science fiction). 1957. Avalon Books.

Alien Earth. Ed. by Elwood & Moskowitz. (O.s.i.). pap. 0.75 o.s.i. (532-75219-075). Manor Bks.

Alien Embassy. Ian Watson. 1978. 1.75 (ISBN 0-441-01475-5). Ace Books.

Alien Encounter. Flanna Devin. 1981. pap. 1.95 (ISBN 0-8439-0898-X, Leisure Bks). Nordon Pubns.

Alien Encounters. Jan Howard Finder. LC 81-50227. 1982. 11.95 (ISBN 0-8008-0168-7). Taplinger Pub. Co.

Alien Flesh. Seabury Quinn. LC 78-104711. (Illus.). 1977. 10.00. O. Train.

Alien from Heaven. Nathalia Clara Ruth Crane. LC 29-21201. 1929. Coward-McCann, Inc.

Alien from the Commonwealth: The Romance of an Odd Young Man. Frederic Mayer Bird. LC 8-27022. (Half-title: The Algonquin press library). 1889. Cupples and Hurd.

Alien from the Stars. R. Lionel Fanthorpe. LC 68-1501. 1968. Arcadia House.

Alien Heart. Alice Lent Covert. LC 57-12669. 1957. Avalon Books.

Alien Heart. Catherine Hutter. LC 56-580896. (Signet book, S1337). 1956. New American Library.

Alien Heart. 1st Ed. Catherine Hutter. LC 54-5449. 1954. Holt.

Alien Heat. Michael Moorcock. 1977. 1.50 (ISBN 0-380-01749-0). Avon Books.

Alien Horizons. William F Nolan. 1974. (pbk.) 0.95 (ISBN 0-671-77928-1). Pocket Books.

Alien Light. Crichton Smith, Iain. LC 69-13781. 1969. 4.95. Houghton Mifflin.

Alien Light. Iain C. Smith. 1969. 4.95 o.p. (ISBN 0-395-08202-1). HM.

Alien Minds. Edward Everett Evans. 1976. Repr. of 1955 ed. lib. bdg. 11.95 (ISBN 0-88411-981-5). Amereon Ltd.

Alien Minds. 1st Ed. Edward Everett Evans. LC 55-136285. 1955. Fantasy Press.

Alien Ones. Leo Brett, pseud. 1969. pap. 0.60 o.p. (T060-1). Tower.

Alien Paradise. Lawrence Russell. 1978. saddlestitch 2.00 (ISBN 0-914580-10-8). Angst World.

Alien Perspective. David Houston. 1978. pap. 1.75 o.s.i. (ISBN 0-8439-0574-3, Leisure Bks). Nordon Pubns.

Alien Rice: A Novel. Ichiro Kawasaki. LC 72-96775. 1973. 5.50 (ISBN 0-8048-1054-0). C. E. Tuttle Co.

Alien Seed. E. C Tubb. (Space: 1999#7). 1976. (pbk.) 1.50 (ISBN 0-671-80520-7). Pocket Books.

Alien Skies. Peter Dagmar. LC 67-8712. 1967. Arcadia House.

Alien Souls. Achmed Abdullah. LC 75-121518. (Short story index reprint series). 1970. Books for Libraries Press.

Alien Souls. Achmed Abdullah. LC 22-18853. The James A. McCann Company.

Alien: The Movie Novel. Ed. by Richard J. Anobile. 1979. pap. 8.95 (ISBN 0-380-46631-7, 46631). Avon.

Alien Upstairs. Pamela Sargent. LC 82-45271. 1983. 11.95 (ISBN 0-385-17803-4). Doubleday.

Alien Way. Gordon R Dickson. (Illus.). 1977. 1.75 (ISBN 0-446-84552-3). Warner Books.

Alien World: The Complete Illustrated Guide. crescent 1980 ed. Steven Eisler. LC 79-23746. 6.98 (ISBN 0-517-30560-7). Crescent Books.

Alien Worlds. Ed. by Roger Elwood. 1968. pap. 0.60 o.p. (53-667). Paperback Lib.

Alienation see House on the Canal: Bibliotheca Neerlandica Ser.

Alienation: A Novel on British Gay Movement. Ian Everton. 216p. (Orig.). 1982. pap. 7.50 (ISBN 0-907040-10-1). Gay Mens Pr.

Aliens. William McFee. LC 15-182877. Longmans, Green & Co.

Aliens. William McFee. LC 18-261761. 1918. Doubleday, Page & Company.

Aliens. William McFee. LC 37-306751. 1937. The Sun Dial Press, Inc.

Aliens: A Novel. Henry Francis Keenan. LC 7-11428. 1886. D. Appleton and Company.

Aliens: A Novel. Mary Tappan Wright. LC 2-8242. 1902. C. Scribner's Sons.

Aliens Among Us. James White. 224p. 1981. pap. 2.25 (ISBN 0-345-29171-9, Del Rey). Ballantine.

Aliens Among Us. James White. 1979. lib. bdg. 15.00x (ISBN 0-86025-140-3, Pub. by Ian Henry Pubns England). State Mutual Bk.

Aliens in Space: An Illustrated Guide to the Inhabited Galaxy. Steven Caldwell. LC 79-52716. (Illus.). 3.98 (ISBN 0-517-29223-8). Crescent Books.

Aliens in Their Land: The Aborigine in the Australian Short Story. Ed. by Louise Elizabeth Rorabacher. LC 67-20061. 1968. (aust.) 4.75. Cheshire.

Aliens: Seven Stories of Science Fiction. Robert Silverberg. LC 76-147. 6.95 (ISBN 0-8407-6488-X). T. Nelson.

Aliens: 3 Novellas. Benjamin Bova. LC 78-3958. 1978. 7.95 (ISBN 0-312-01859-2). St. Martin's Press.

Aliette (La Morte) Octave Feuillet & Hager, J. Henry, Tr. 1886. D. Appleton and Company.

Alimony. Faith Baldwin. 1976. Repr. of 1928 ed. 15.70x (ISBN 0-88411-616-6). Amereon Ltd.

Alimony. Faith Baldwin Cuthrell. LC 76-40438. 1976. 6.95 (ISBN 0-88411-616-6). Aeonian Press.

Alimony. Faith Baldwin Cuthrell. LC 28-218933. Dodd, Mead & Company.

Alimony. Faith Baldwin Cuthrell. 1973. (pbk) 0.95. Warner Paperback Lib.

Alimony Jail. Bobbie Meredith. LC 32-16443. Covici, Friede.

Alimony Queens. Vernie E. Connelly. LC 31-16333. Grosset & Dunlap.

Aline. Carole Klein. (Illus.). 1980. pap. 2.95 (ISBN 0-446-93526-3). Warner Bks.

Aline of the Grand Woods: A Story of Louisiana. Nevil Gratiot Henshaw. LC 9-3875. 1909. The Outing Publishing Company.

Alington Inheritance. Patricia Wentworth. LC 58-8671. (Her A Miss Silver mystery). 1958. Lippincott.

Alinor. Roberta Gellis. LC 78-51278. (Roselynde Chronicles: Bk. 2). 560p. 1978. pap. 2.95 (ISBN 0-86721-166-0). Playboy Pbks.

Alinsky's Diamond. Tom McHale. 1975. (pbk.) 1.95 (ISBN 0-397-01018-4). Ballantine Books.

Alinsky's Diamond: A Novel. Tom McHale. LC 74-11007. 1974. 8.95 (ISBN 0-397-01018-4). Lippincott.

Aliscans: Chanson De Geste, Pub. D'apres le Manuscrit De la Bibliotheque De L'Arsenal et a L'aide De Cinque Autres Manuscrits, Par F. Guessard, A. Montaiglon. Paris, A. Franck, 1870. Aliscans. Ed. by Francois Guessard & Anatole De C. De. Montaiglon. (Added t.p.: Les anciens poetes de la France, t.10). 1966. 18.00. Kraus Reprint.

Alise of Astra. Henry Brereton Marriott Watson. LC 10-21633. 1910. Little, Brown, and Company.

Alise of Astra. Henry Brereton Marriott Watson. LC 11-2072. 1911. Little, Brown, and Company.

Alison Blair. Gertrude Crownfield. LC 27-9071. E. P. Dutton & Company.

Alison Vail. Elizabeth Newport Hepburn. LC 26-8189. H. Holt and Company.

Alistair MacLean's Hostage Tower. John Denis. 192p. 1983. pap. 2.50 (ISBN 0-449-20086-8, Crest). Fawcett.

Alive and Dead. E. X Ferrars, pseud. LC 74-14379. 1975. 4.95 (ISBN 0-385-08397-1). Published for the Crime Club by Doubleday.

Alive & Free. Paul J. Kuhwald. 2.95 o.p. Vantage.

Alive in the Brown Stone-Age: By B. A. Henry Pseud. 1st Ed. Henry B. Abrahams. LC 50-7321. 1950. Dutton.

Aliya: A Love Story. Brenda Lesley Segal & Marianne Kanter. LC 77-9217. 8.95 (ISBN 0-312-01865-7). St. Martin's Press.

Alkahest: Or, The House of Claes. Honore De Balzac. Tr. by Katharine Prescott Wormeley. LC 3-28201. (Half-title: The comedy of human life... Philosophical studies). 1887. Roberts Brothers.

Alkahest: Or, The House of Claes. Honore De Balzac. Tr. by Katharine Prescott Wormeley. LC 3-232003. (Half-title: The comedy of human life... Philosophical studies). 1889. Roberts Brothers.

All Aboard for Yesterday. 1979. pap. 9.95 (ISBN 0-89272-053-0). Down East.

All Aboard: Saga of the Romantic River. Irvin Shrewsbury Cobb. LC 28-20336. 1928. Cosmopolitan Book Corporation.

All About Brother Bird. 1st Ed. Catharine Plummer. LC 66-20956. 1966. 4.50. Doubleday.

All About Eileen. Ruth McKenney. LC 52-6445. 1952. Harcourt, Brace.

All About H. Hatterr. rev. ed. Govindas Vishnoodas Desani. LC 77-97137. 1970. 5.95. Farrar, Straus and Giroux.

All About H. Hatterr: A Gesture. Govindas Vishnoodas Desani. LC 51-10898. 1951. Farrar, Straus and Young.

All About Jane. Winifred Mary Scott. LC 34-8978. 1934. Doubleday, Doran & Company, Inc.

All About Jeeves, Vol. 2. 2nd ed. P. G. Wodehouse. 320p. 1976. pap. 1.95 (ISBN 0-532-19118-8). Woodhill.

All About Love. Nadezhda Teffi. Tr. by Darra Goldstein from Rus. 144p. 15.00 (ISBN 0-88233-792-0); pap. 6.50 (ISBN 0-88233-793-9). Ardis Pubs.

All About Lucia: Four Novels by E. F. Benson... Edward Frederic Benson. LC 40-77048. 1940. The Sun Dial Press.

All About Marriage: A Novel. Ethel Powelson Hueston. LC 48-6916. 1948. Bobbs-Merrill Co.

All About Marriage: A Parisian Novel of to-Day. Sibylle Gabrielle Marie Antoinette De Riquetti De Mirabeau Martel De Janville. (Brookside library, no. 384). 1884. F. Tousey.

All About the Emerald Ring. A Fantasy. Charles Francis Carty. (Dillingham's American authors library, no. 32). 1897. G. W. Dillingham Co.

All About the Future: By Poul Anderson and Others Introductions by Robert A. Heinlein and Isaac Asimov. 1st Ed. Ed. by Martin Greenberg. Poul Anderson. LC 54-13101. (Adventures in science fiction series). 1955. Gnome Press.

All About the Merry Tales of Gotham. Alfred Stapleton. LC 77-12726. 1977. 30.00 (ISBN 0-8414-7944-5). Folcroft Library Editions.

All Aces: A Nero Wolfe Omnibus. Rex Stout. LC 58-7182. 1958. Viking Press.

All Alone. A Story. From the French of Andre Theuriet... Andre Theuriet. LC 8-27747. (Appleton's new handy-volume series. v. 65). 1881. D. Appleton and Company.

All Along the River. Mary Elizabeth Braddon Maxwell. LC 7-25591. Cassell Publishing Company.

All Alongshore. Joseph Crosby Lincoln. LC 31-27216. Coward-McCann, Inc.

All Alongshore: Cape Cod Characters. Joseph Crosby Lincoln. LC 41-6656. 1941. Blue Ribbon Books.

All-American Boy. Charles Eastman. (Illus.). 1973. pap. 2.75 o.p. (ISBN 0-374-50922-0, N406). FS&G.

All-American Stud. Martin Burnside. pap. 2.25 o.s.i. (Venus). Grove.

All Angels Cry. Mary Sheppard. LC 77-88211. 7.95 (ISBN 0-87716-085-6). Moore Pub. Co.

All Around Our Town. Charles F. Davis. LC 77-80398. (Illus.). 12.00 (ISBN 0-930000-03-X). Mathom Pub. Co.

All Around the Moon: From the French of Jules Verne. Jules Verne & Roth, Edward, 1826-1911, Tr. 1876. The Catholic Publication Society.

All at Sea: A Fleming Stone Story. Carolyn Wells. LC 27-3374. 1927. J. B. Lippincott Company.

All Brides Are Beautiful. Thomas Bell. LC 36-24948. 1936. Little, Brown, and Company.

All but Impossible! An Anthology of Locked Room & Impossible Crime Stories by Members of the Mystery Writers of America. Edward D. Hoch & Mystery Writers of America. LC 81-8718. 1981. 14.95 (ISBN 0-89919-045-6). Ticknor & Fields.

All But Impossible! An Anthology of Locked Room & Impossible Crime Stories. Mystery Writers of America Members. Ed. by Edward D. Hoch. LC 81-8718. (Joan Kahn Bk). 372p. 1981. 14.95 (ISBN 0-89919-045-6). Ticknor & Fields.

All but the People. G. Wolfskill & J. A. Hudson. (O.s.i.). 1969. 7.95 o.s.i. (ISBN 0-02-630900-9). Macmillan.

All by Wire: A Telegraphic Explanation of a Telepathic Union of Hearts. Frank Palmer Sibley. 1905. J. W. Luce & Company.

All Came by the Sea: A Tale of Early Washington. Michele Cristoforo Strizzi. LC 49-487673. 1949. Dorrance.

All Cats Are Gray. Charles G Givens. LC 37-16647. The Bobbs-Merrill Company.

All Cats Go to Heaven: An Anthology of Stories About Cats. Illustrated by Peggy Bacon. Ed. by Beth Brown. LC 60-51366. 1960. Grosset & Dunlap.

All Concerned Notified. Helen Kieran Reilly. 1968. pap. 0.60 o.p. (60-361). Manor Bks.

All Concerned Notified. Helen Kieran Reilly. 160p. 1974. pap. 0.95 o.p. (532-95355-095). Manor Bks.

All Concerned Notified: An Inspector McKee Story. Helen Kieran Reilly. LC 39-27681. 1939. Pub. for the Crime Club, Inc., by Doubleday, Doran & Company, Inc.

All Concerned Notified: An Inspector McKee Story. Helen Kieran Reilly. LC 40-325652. 1940. The Sun Dial Press.

All-Conference Tackle. Caary Paul Jackson. LC 47-31096. 1947. T. Y. Crowell Co.

All Dames Are Dynamite. Timothy Trent, pseud. LC 35-941. W. Godwin, Inc.

All Darkness Met. Glen Cook. 1980. pap. 1.95 (ISBN 0-425-04539-0). Berkley Pub.

All Dead but One: A Novel. 1st Ed. Stanley F KAsper. LC 55-8379. 1955. Pageant Press.

All Dogs Go to Heaven. Beth Brown. LC 43-22708. 1943. The Arco Company, Distributed by F. Fell, Inc.

All Done by Kindness: A Novel. Doris Langley-Levy Moore. LC 52-10935. 1953-1952. Lippincott.

All Else Confusion. Betty Neels. (Harlequin Romances Ser.). 192p. 1983. pap. 1.75 (ISBN 0-373-02542-4). Harlequin Bks.

All Else in Folly. 1st American Ed. Catherine Gaskin. LC 51-11767. 1951. Harper.

All Evil Shed Away. new ed. Archie Roy. (Falcon's Head Mystery Ser.). 192p. 1972. 5.95 o.p. (ISBN 0-529-04833-7). World Pub.

All Fall Down. Leonard Alfred George Strong. 1944. Pub. for the Crime Club by Doubleday, Doran & Co., Inc.

All Fall Down: A Novel. James Leo Herlihy. 1977. 1.75 (ISBN 0-380-01707-5). Avon Books.

All Fall Down: A Novel. 1st Ed. James Leo Herlihy. LC 60-12090. 1960. Dutton.

All-Fellows and The Cloak of Friendship. Laurence Housman. LC 74-122721. (Short story index reprint series). (Illus.). 1970. Books for Libraries Press.

All Fires the Fire, and Other Stories. Julio Cortazar. LC 73-2937. 1973. 5.95 (ISBN 0-394-46821-X). Pantheon Books.

All Flags Flying: Reminiscences of Frances Parkinson Keyes. Frances Parkinson Wheeler Keyes. LC 70-38971. (Illus.). 1972. 10.00 (ISBN 0-07-034456-6). McGraw-Hill.

All Flesh Is Grass. Clifford D. Simak. (Medallion bk., X1312). 1966. Berkley.

All Flesh Is Grass. Clifford D Simak. LC 65-19926. 1965. Doubleday.

All Fools' Day. Edmund Cooper. LC 66-22503. 1966. bds., 3.50. Walker.

All for a Crown: Or, The Only Love of King Henry the Eighth (Catherine Howard. Henry Llewellyn Williams. LC 3-158132. 1902. Street & Smith.

All for a Scrap of Paper: A Romance of the Present War. 16th ed. Joseph Hocking. LC 18-48895. 1918. Hodder and Stoughton.

All for Her: Or, St. Jude's Assistant. A Novel. 1877. G. W. Carleton & Co.

All for Him. A Novel. By ? Author of "All for Her"... LC 6-505. 1877. G. W. Carleton & Co.; Etc., Etc.

All for Him. Eros and Anteros. Albert Delpit. Tr. by Lyster, Frederic. (On cover: Pollard's popular publications, no. 4). 1890. Pollard Publishing Company.

All for His Country. John Ulrich Giesy. 1915. 0.50. The Macaulay Company.

All for Jack. Jules Claretie. LC 6-25370. (On cover: Rialto ser. no. 43). 1892. Rand, McNally & Company.

All for Love. Jean Crooks Devanny. LC 32-18243. The Macaulay Company.

All for Love. Patricia Gallagher. 400p. 1981. pap. 2.95 (ISBN 0-380-77818-1, 77818). Avon.

All for Love of a Fair Face: Or, A Broken Betrothal. Laura Jean Libbey. (On cover: The library of American authors, no. 14). 1889. G. Munro.

All for Love: Or, The Outlaw's Bride. Eliza Ann Dupuy. LC 11-10524. T. B. Peterson & Brothers.

All for Money. Mary Dwinell Chellis. LC 6-23426. 1876. National Temperance Society and Publication House.

All for Nothing. rev ed. Dirk Vanden. 192p. 1971. pap. 1.95 o.s.i. (T*C515, Travellers Comp). Olympia.

All for One and One for Death. Stanton Forbes, pseud. LC 75-144263. 1971. 4.95. Published for the Crime Club by Doubleday.

All for the Best. Bentz Plagemann. LC 46-37787. 1946. Simon and Schuster.

All for the Love of a Lady. Zenith Jones Brown. LC 44-334529. 1944. C. Scribner's Sons.

All for the Love of a Lady. Elinor Macartney Lane. LC 6-15429. 1906. D. Appleton and Company.

All for the Love of Money. Mary Morrison Chitwood. LC 17-12862. Printed by Combination Card Co.

All for You. Denise Robins. (Beagle romance#38). 1975. (pbk.) 0.95 (ISBN 0-345-26669-2). Ballantine Books.

All Giants Wear Yellow Breeches: A Chronicle of Boyhood. Vernon Patterson. W. R. Scott.

All-Girl Crew. Frank Anvic, pseud. 1973. (pbk.) 1.95 (ISBN 0-87682-362-2). Barclay House.

All Glorious Within.". Jennie Maria Bingham. LC 6-12730. 1889. Hunt & Eaton.

All G.O.D.'s Children. John Craig. LC 75-1256. 1975. 6.95 (ISBN 0-688-02913-2). Morrow.

All G.O.D.'s Children. John Craig. (Signet Book). 1976. 1.75. New American Library.

All God's Children. Arthur Lyons. 1976. (pbk.) 1.50. Ballantine.

All God's Children: A Novel. Alston Anderson. LC 65-21399. bds., 4.50. Bobbs.

All God's Children: A Novel. Arthur Lyons. LC 75-5647. 1975. 6.95 (ISBN 0-88405-109-9). Mason/Charter.

All Good Americans. Jerome Bahr. 1937. C. Scribner's Sons.

All Good Men. Thomas J Fleming. LC 76-6341. (Irish-Americans). 1976. 23.00 (ISBN 0-405-09336-5). Arno Press.

All Grass Isn't Green. A. A. Fair, pseud. 1970. 4.95 o.p. Morrow.

All Grass Isn't Green. Erle Stanley Gardner. LC 72-114698. 1970. 4.95. Morrow.

All Green and White. Caroline Stetson Allen. LC 37-5405. 1937. The Riverside Press.

All Green Shall Perish: And Other Novellas and Stories. Ed., Introd., by John B. Hughes. Tr. from Spanish by the Ed., Others. Eduardo Mallea. LC 66-11113. 1966. 7.95. Knopf.

All Hallows' Eve. Charles Williams. LC 48-8932. 1948. Pellegrini & Cudahy.

All Hallow's Eve. Charles Williams. LC 80-29072. 1981. 5.95 (ISBN 0-8028-1250-3). W. B. Eerdmans Pub. Co.

All He Knew: A Story. John Habberton. LC 6-46687. 1890. Flood and Vincent.

All Heads Turn When the Hunt Goes by. John Farris. LC 77-95544. (ISBN 0-671-16975-0). Playboy Press.

All Heaven in a Rage. Maureen Duffy. LC 72-11019. 1973. 5.95 (ISBN 0-394-48404-5). Knopf.

All Her Men. James Nobel Gifford. LC 44-7025. 1944. Phoenix Press.

All Her Paths Are Peace. Ellis J Swartz. LC 69-16272. 1969. 4.95 (ISBN 0-8158-0018-5). Christopher Pub. House.

All Honorable Men. 1st Ed. David Karp. LC 56-5291. 1956. Knopf.

All Horses Go to Heaven: An Anthology of Stories About Horses. Ed. by Beth Brown. LC 63-8123. 1963. Grosset & Dunlap.

All I Asking for Is My Body. Milton Murayama. LC 75-320701. 1975. 3.00. Supa Press.

All I Could Never Be. Anzia Yezierska. LC 32-20614. 1932. Brewer, Warren & Putnam.

All I Could See from Where I Stood: A Novel. George Christy. LC 63-11629. 1963. Bobbs-Merrill.

All I Survey. facs. ed. Gilbert Keith Chesterton. LC 67-26723. (Essay Index Reprint Ser). 1933. 18.00 (ISBN 0-8369-0293-9). Ayer Co.

All I Want. Howard Rockey. LC 25-5620. The Macaulay Company.

All in a Day... Martin Donisthorpe Armstrong. LC 29-595441. 1929. Harper & Brothers.

All in a Garden Fair. The Simple Story of Three Boys and a Girl. Walter Besant. (On cover: Seaside library. Pocket ed., no. 97). G. Munro.

All in a Garden Fair. The Simple Story of Three Boys and a Girl. Walter Besant. (Harper' Franklin square library, no. 342). 1883. Harper & Brothers.

All in a Twilight. Allen Roy Evans. LC 44-40025. 1944. Doubleday, Doran & Co., Inc.

All in Blue. Douglas Marshall, pseud. LC 45-1020. 1945. Gramercy Publishing Co.

All in Good Time. Marguerite Allis. LC 44-3241. 1944. G. P. Putnam's Sons.

All in Love. Dorothy Frooks. LC 32-657. The Macaulay Company.

All in Our Day, Thirty Stories... Manuel Komroff. LC 42-22719. 1942. Harper & Brothers.

All in the Dark. Joseph Sheridan Le Fanu. LC 76-4046. (Le Fanu, Joseph Sheridan, 1814-1873. Works. 1976). 1976. 38.00 (ISBN 0-405-09191-5). Arno Press.

All in the Family. Michael F. Kael. 192p. pap. 1.95 o.p. (ISBN 0-87682-250-2, 7250). Barclay Hse.

All in the Family. Edwin O'Connor. (N3483). 1967. Bantam.

All in the Family. Edwin O'Connor. LC 66-24017. 1966. Little, Brown.

All in the Family. Burton Wohl. 1976. (pbk.) 1.25. Bantam Books.

All in the Family. 1st Ed. Thelma Wamble. LC 53-23305. 1953. New Voices Pub. Co.

All in the Night's Work. Ethel Watts Mumford Grant & Howard, George Fitzalan Bronson. LC 24-748147. (Famous authors series. no. 37). 1924. Garden City Publishing Co., Inc.

All in the Past, a Novel. 1st Ed. Rafael Aran. LC 55-11052. 1955. Pageant Press.

All in the Racket. William E. Weeks & Hays, Arthur Garfield, 1831- LC 30-217721. 1930. C. Boni.

All Is Bright. Eleanore Browne. LC 37-35651. 1937. Arcadia House.

All Is Grist: A Book of Essays. facs. ed. Gilbert Keith Chesterton. LC 67-22058. (Essay Index Reprint Ser). 1932. 15.00 (ISBN 0-8369-0294-7). Ayer Co.

All Is Not Butter. James B. Wheelwright. LC 54-6875. 1954. Little, Brown.

All Is Not Gold. Rosamond Neal Du Jardin. LC 35-14237. J. B. Lippincott Company.

All Is Not Gold That Glistens. A Sketch. W. L. Stiles. LC 8-15685. 1887.

All Is Right with My World: A Novel. Grace Rogers Hill. LC 53-2243. 1953. Bellevue Books.

All Is Vanity: A Detective Novel. Doris Bell Collier Ball. LC 40-29639. 1940. Longmans, Green and Co.

All Is Vanity: A Detective Novel by Josephine Bell. Josephine Bell. LC 40-296391. 1940. Longmans, Green and Co.

All Is Well. Dirk Vanden. 240p. (Orig.). 1971. pap. 1.95 o.s.i. (T*C512, Travellers Comp). Olympia.

All Judgment Fled. James White. LC 70-86388. 1969. 4.95. Walker.

All Kinds of Loving. David Spencer. (Orig.). pap. 0.95 o.p. (1149). Brandon.

All Kneeling. Anne Parrish. LC 28-21055. 1928. Harper & Brothers.

All Leads Negative. Peter Alding. LC 67-28823. 1967. Harper & Row.

All Lie in Wait. William Samelson. LC 68-9042. 1969. 5.95. Prentice-Hall.

All Manner of Men: Representative Fiction from the American Catholic Press. Ed. by Riley Hughes. LC 56-5748. Kenedy.

All Men Are Brothers - Shui Huchuan, Vol. I. Tr. by Pearl S. Buck. (John Day Bk.). (Vol. 2 10.00 o.p.). 1968. Repr. of 1933 ed. 10.00i (ISBN 0-381-98017-0, A2000, TYC-T). T Y Crowell.

All Men Are Brothers (Shi Hu Chuan) Tr. from the Chinese by Pearl S. Buck. Shui Hu Chuan & Nai-An Shih. Tr. by Pearl Sydenstricker Buck. 1968. 17.50 set. John Day.

All Men Are Brothers: Shui Hu Chuan. Nai-An Shih & Kuan-Chung Lo. Tr. by Pearl Sydenstricker Buck. LC 73-153519. (Illus.). 1968. J. Day Co.

All Men Are Brothers Shui Hu Chuan. Shui Hu Chuan & Buck, Mrs. Pearl (Sydenstricker) 1892- Tr. LC 33-293515. The John Day Company.

All Men Are Brothers: Shui Hu Chuan. Shui Hu Chuan & Buck, Mrs. Pearl (Sydenstricker) 1892- Tr. LC 38-281322. The John Day Company.

All Men Are Enemies: A Romance. Richard Aldington. LC 33-20284. 1933. Doubleday, Doran & Company, Inc.

All Men Are Ghosts. Lawrence Pearsall Jacks. LC 72-125220. (Short story index reprint series). 1970. Books for Libraries Press.

All Men Are Ghosts. Lawrence Pearsall Jacks. 1913. H. Holt and Company.

All Men Are Liars. Dorothy Stockbridge Tillett. LC 48-9110. 1948. Pub. for the Crime Club by Doubleday.

All Men Are Liars;" A Novel. Joseph Hocking. LC 7-4952. Roberts Brothers.

All Men Are Lonely Now. Arthur Leonard Bell Thompson. LC 67-21453. 1967. Coward-McCann.

All Men Are Lonely Now. Arthur Leonard Bell Thompson. LC 70-402353. 1969. 0.85. Readers Book Club in Association with Companion Book Club, London.

All Men Are Lonely Now. Arthur Leonard Bell Thompson. LC 67-21453. 1967. Coward-McCann.

All Men Are Lonely Now: By Francis Clifford. Arthur Leonard Bell Thompson. (60-2337). 1968. Popular Lib.

All Men Are Mad. Philippe Thoby-Marcelin & Pierre Marcelin. LC 73-113780. 1970. 6.75. Farrar, Straus & Giroux.

All Men Are Mariners: A Novel. 1st Ed. Calvin Kentfield. LC 62-17886. 1962. McGraw-Hill.

All Men Are Mortal: A Novel. Translated by Leonard M. Friedman. 1st Ed. Simone De Beauvoir. LC 54-10358. World Pub. Co.

All Men Are Murderers. Ursula Torday. LC 58-12031. 1958. Published for the Crime Club by Doubleday.

All My Children: Book II: Erica. Rosemarie Santini. 224p. pap. 2.50 (ISBN 0-515-06105-0). Jove Pubns.

All My Children: Book III: the Lovers. Rosemarie Santini. 240p. pap. 2.50 (ISBN 0-515-04896-8). Jove Pubns.

All My Children: Book 1: Tara & Philip. Rosemarie Santini. 256p. pap. 2.50 (ISBN 0-515-06058-5). Jove Pubns.

All My Enemies. Stanley Wade Baron. LC 52-14215. 1952. Ballantine Books.

All My Enemies. Rosemary Harris. LC 72-82204. (Simon and Schuster novel of suspense). 1973. 5.95 (ISBN 0-671-21383-0). Simon and Schuster.

All My Enemies. Rosemary Harris. 1973. (pbk.) 1.25 (ISBN 0-671-78322-X). Pocket Books.

All My Fathers. Natala De La Fere. LC 59-10328. 1959. Dutton.

All My Friends Are Going to Be Strangers: A Novel. McMurtry, Larry. 1973. 1.50 (ISBN 0-671-78576-1). Pocket Bks.

All My Friends Are Going to Be Strangers: A Novel. Larry McMurtry. LC 78-179584. 1972. 7.50 (ISBN 0-671-21160-9). Simon and Schuster.

All My Friends Are Going to Be Strangers. Larry McMurtry. LC 81-11652. (Zia book). 1981. 6.95 (ISBN 0-8263-0593-8). University of New Mexico Press.

All My Pretty Ones. 1st Ed. Roger Hall. LC 59-5619. 1959. W. W. Norton.

All My Sins: A Novel of the Life and Loves of Ninon De Lenclos. Norbeart Estey. LC 54-6941. 1954. A. A. Wyn.

All My Sins Remembered. Joe W Haldeman. LC 76-62773. 1977. 7.95 (ISBN 0-312-01977-7). St. Martin's Press.

All My Sins Remembered. Joe W. Haldeman. 1978. 1.95 (ISBN 0-380-39321-2). Avon Books.

All Neat in Black Stockings. Jane Gaskell. 1981. 18.95x (Pub. by Remploy England). State Mutual Bk.

All Night at Mr. Stanyhurst's. Hugh Edwards. LC 63-18594. 1963. Macmillan.

All Night Cowboy. Thomas Shire. 192p. (Orig.). 1972. pap. 1.95 o.p. (ISBN 0-87056-262-2, 6262). Brandon.

All Night Long: A Novel of Guerrilla Warfare in Russia. Erskine Caldwell. LC 42-36397. 1942. Duell, Sloan and Pearce.

All Night Stand. Thom Keyes. (O.S.I.). 1966. 4.95 o.s.i. (ISBN 0-671-01855-8). S&S.

All-Night Visitors. Clarence Major. LC 71-3252. 1969. 3.95. Olympia Press.

All Ocean West of San Andreas. Tom Shoso Nakatsukasa. LC 73-76979. (Illus.). 1972. 2.95 (ISBN 0-8181-0312-4). Pageant-Poseidon.

All-of-a-Sudden Carmen. Gustav Kobbe. LC 17-13315. 1917. 1.35. G. P. Putnam's Sons.

All of Mine for Him. Damon C. Dodd. 1977. pap. 2.25 (ISBN 0-89265-045-1). Randall Hse.

All of Our Aircraft Are Missing. John P. Radford. (Illusionist Ser.: No. 2). 192p. (Orig.). 1974. pap. 1.50 o.p. (ISBN 0-89014-112-6, CB-112). Canyon Bks.

All of Their Lives. Myron Brinig. LC 41-7793. Farrar and Rinehart, Inc.

All on a Summer's Day. John William Wainwright. LC 81-14517. 1982. 10.95 (ISBN 0-312-01983-1). St. Martin's Press.

All on a Summer's Night. Maurice Edelman. LC 79-85578. 1970. 5.95. Random House.

All on the Irish Shore. Edith Anna CEnon Somerville & Violet Florence Martin. LC 70-81275. (Short story index reprint series). (Illus.). 1969. (ISBN 0-8369-3027-4). Books for Libraries Press.

All on the Irish Shore: Irish Sketches. Edith Anna Oenone Somerville & Violet Florence Martin. LC 3-14983. 1903. Longmans, Green and Co.

All One Summer. Elizabeth Fair. LC 53-107957. 1953. Funk & Wagnalls.

All or Nothing. John Davys Beresford. LC 28-8706. The Bobbs-Merrill Company.

All or Nothing. A Novel, After the Russian of Count Nepomuk Czapski. Nepomuk Czapski & De Vere, Meta, Tr. LC 6-32231. (Ledger library. No. 91, August 15, 1898). 1893. R. Bonner's Sons.

All Other Ground: A Novel. 1st Ed. Argye M Briggs. LC 56-128023. 1956. Eerdmans.

All Other Perils. Michael Kirk, pseud. LC 74-12694. 1975. 4.95 (ISBN 0-385-04588-3). Published for the Crime Club by Doubleday.

All Our Hearts Are Trump. Beatrice Keiser. LC 76-1455. 1976. 10.95 (ISBN 0-87716-066-X, Pub. by Moore Pub Co). F Apple.

All Our Secrets. Mary Drayton. 384p. (Orig.). 1981. pap. 2.95 (ISBN 0-449-14391-0, GM). Fawcett.

All Our Secrets Are the Same: New Fiction from Esquire. Gordon Lish. LC 76-40486. 3.95 (ISBN 0-393-08748-4). Norton.

All Our Sons & Daughters. Ed. by John Garvey. 1977. pap. 3.95 (ISBN 0-87243-074-X). Templegate.

All Our Tomorrows. Josephine Lawrence. 1959. Harcourt, Brace.

All Our Tomorrows. Jan MacLean. (Harlequin Romances Ser.). 192p. 1983. pap. 1.75 (ISBN 0-373-02547-5). Harlequin Bks.

All Our Yesterdays. Henry Major Tomlinson. LC 30-8450. 1930. Harper & Brothers.

All Our Yesterdays. Harry Warner, Jr. LC 69-17980. (Pap. ed. 4.50 o.p.). (Illus.). 1970. 10.00 (ISBN 0-911682-00-7). Advent.

All Our Yesterdays. Joseph Weeks. LC 55-7730. 1955. Rinehart.

All Over Again. Ruby Mildred Ayres. LC 34-41054. 1934. Doubleday, Doran & Company, Inc.

All Over Again. Nathaniel Benchley. LC 80-1800. 1981. 12.95 (ISBN 0-385-15859-9). Doubleday.

All Over but the Shooting. Richard Pitts Powell. 1944. Simon and Schuster.

All Over the Town. Ronald Frederick Delderfield. LC 77-24561. 1977. 7.95 (ISBN 0-671-22920-6). Simon and Schuster.

All Papa's Children. Ama A. Aidoo. 113p. (Orig.). (gr. 10-12). 1978. 10.00x (ISBN 0-89410-118-8); pap. 5.00x (ISBN 0-906403-00-6). Three Continents.

All Part of the Game: The Stories of A. P. Gaskell. A. P. Gaskell & R. A Copland. LC 78-323277. (New Zealand fiction; 12). 1978. 15.95 (ISBN 0-19-647964-9). Auckland University Press.

All Passion Spent. Victoria Mary Sackville-West. LC 31-28061. 1931. Doubleday, Doran & Company, Inc.

All Passion Spent. Victoria Mary Sackville-West. LC 32-6666. 1932. Doubleday, Doran & Company, Inc.

All Passion Spent. Victoria Mary Sackville-West. LC 37-1453. 1936. The Sun Dial Press, Inc.

All Passion Spent: A Realistic Novel. Chandler Brossard. LC 55-21026. (Popular library, 626). 1954. Popular Library.

All-Purpose Bodies. Philip McCutchan. LC 77-120863. 1970. 4.50. John Day Co.

All Quiet on the Western Front. Erich Maria Remarque. LC 75-20340. 1975. 7.95 (ISBN 0-316-73992-8). Little, Brown.

All Quiet on the Western Front. Erich Maria Remarque. Tr. by Arthur Wesley Wheen. LC 70-5148. (Illus.). 1969. Printed at the Spiral Press for the Members of the Limited Editions Club.

All Quiet on the Western Front. Erich Maria Remarque. LC 74-194328. 1958. Little, Brown.

All Quiet on the Western Front. Erich Maria Remarque. Tr. by Arthur Wesley Wheen. LC 29-12059. 1929. Little, Brown, and Company.

All Quiet on the Western Front, Translated from the German. Erich Maria Remarque & Wheen, Arthur Wesley, Tr. LC 30-20066. Grosset & Dunlap.

All Right, Everybody off the Planet! A Novel. Bob Ottum. LC 70-159363. 1972. 5.95 (ISBN 0-394-46914-3). Random House.

All Rightee. Douglas Hayes. LC 63-8807. 1963. Abelard-Schuman.

All Roads Lead to Calvary. Jerome Klapka Jerome. LC 19-19056. 1919. Dodd Mead and Company.

All Roads to Sospel. George Bellairs. LC 81-51980. 1981. 9.95 (ISBN 0-8027-5454-6). Walker.

All Sails Set. Edith Austin Holton. LC 42-10937. 1942. H. C. Kinsey & Company, Inc.

All Screwed Up. Troy Conway, pseud. (Coxeman Ser). (Orig.). 1970. pap. 0.75 o.p. (ISBN 0-446-64430-7, 64-430). Paperback Lib.

All She Can Be. Fern Michaels. (Love & Life Romance Ser.). 176p. (Orig.). 1983. pap. 1.75 (ISBN 0-345-30839-5). Ballantine.

All Shot up. Chester B. Himes. (Coffin Ed Johnson and Grave Digger Jones series, #5). 1975. (pbk.) 1.25. New American Library.

All Six Were Lovers. Nard Jones. LC 34-24862. 1934. Dodd, Mead & Company.

All Sons Must Say Goodbye. Michael Amrine. LC 42-21687. 1942. Harper & Brothers.

All Sorts and Conditions of Men. Walter Besant. (On cover: Lovell's library, v. 5, no. 257). 1883. J. W. Lovell Company.

All Sorts and Conditions of Men: An Impossible Story. Walter Besant. LC 78-131632. 1971. (ISBN 0-403-00519-1). Scholarly Press.

All Sorts and Conditions of Men. An Impossible Story. Walter Besant. (Harper's Franklin square library, no. 277). 1882. Harper & Brothers.

All Sorts and Conditions of Men: An Impossible Story. Walter Besant. 1902. Harper & Brothers.

All Sorts and Kinds. Christopher La Farge. LC 49-8258. 1949. Coward-McCann.

All Souls. Geraldine Symons. LC 51-9790. 1950. Longmans, Green.

All Souls: A Family Album. Frances Oliver. LC 76-25527. 8.95. St. Martin's Press.

All Soul's Night. John Kelly. LC 47-3318. 1947. Harcourt, Brace and Company.

All Souls' Night: A Book of Stories. Hugh Walpole. LC 33-14402. 1933. Doubleday, Doran & Company, Inc.

All-Star Cast: A Footlight Anthology. Ed. by Sally Deutsch. LC 47-6576. 1947. Ziff-Davis Pub. Co.

All Star Cast: A Novel. Naomi Guiladys Royde-Smith. LC 36-18149. 1936. The Macmillan Company.

All Strange Away. Samuel Beckett. LC 77-362177. (Gotham Book Mart Master Series; 1). (Illus.). Gotham Book Mart.

All Summer Long. Wilder Hobson. LC 45-8644. 1945. Duell, Sloan and Pearce.

All That Glitters. Noel Bertram Gerson. LC 74-4833. 1975. 6.95 (ISBN 0-385-08503-6). Doubleday.

All That Glitters. Frances Parkinson Wheeler Keyes. LC 43-12352. 1943. The Sun Dial Press.

All That Glitters. Frances Parkinson Wheeler Keyes & Book League of America, Inc. LC 43-4979. The Book League of America.

All That Glitters. Francis Parkinson Wheeler Keyes. LC 41-22518. J. Messner, Inc.

All That Glitters. Francis Parkinson Wheeler Keyes. 1974. (pbk.) 1.75 (ISBN 0-671-78686-5). Pocket Books.

All That Glitters. Jane McCarthy. 1976. 4.95. Avalon Books.

All that Glitters. Elizabeth Powers. 176p. 1983. 2.50 (ISBN 0-380-63883-5). Avon.

All That Glitters: The Case of the Ice-Cold Diamond. Elizabeth Powers. LC 80-1691. 1981. 9.95 (ISBN 0-385-17314-8). Published for the Crime Club by Doubleday.

All That Glitters: The Case of the Ice-Cold Diamond. large print ed. Elizabeth Powers. LC 81-8927. 9.95 (ISBN 0-89621-299-8). Thorndike Press.

All That Glitters. 1st Ed. Manning Coles, pseud. LC 54-527110. 1954. Published for the Crime Club by Doubleday.

All That Heaven Allows: By Edna and Harry Lee. Edna L. Mooney Lee. LC 52-5267. 1952. Putnam.

All That Man Should Be Unto Woman: A Psychic Story, by Susie C. Clark... Susie Champney Clark. LC 10-19620. 1910. The C. M. Clark Publishing Company.

All That Matters. Peter Mendelssohn. LC 38-16094. H. Holt and Company.

All That Matters. Pearl Weymouth. LC 24-10304. 1924. T. Seltzer.

All That Seemed Final. Joan Colebrook. LC 41-213982. 1941. Houghton Mifflin Company.

All That We Share. Barbara Hedworth. LC 44-1213. 1944. Arcardia House, Inc.

All That's Mine. Alice Lent Covert. LC 47-1459. 1946. S. Curl, Inc.

All the Abandoned Children. George Constable. LC 67-19195. 1967. Harcourt, Brace & World.

All the Beautiful People. Richard Dowling. LC 64-15227. 1964. Dial Press.

All the Best People. Sloan Wilson. LC 75-125383. 1970. 7.95. Putnam.

All the Brave Rifles. Clarke Venable. LC 29-9640. The Reilly & Lee Co.

All the Brothers Were Valiant. Ben Ames Williams. LC 29-29441. E. P. Dutton & Co., Inc.

All the Brothers Were Valiant. Ben Ames Williams. 1919. The Macmillan Company.

All the Buffalo Returning. Dorothy M Johnson. LC 78-22425. 7.95 (ISBN 0-396-07668-8). Dodd, Mead.

All the Colors of Darkness. Lloyd Biggle, Jr. 1975. (pbk.) 1.25. Leisure Books.

All the Comforts: A Novel. Joseph Papaleo. (0079). 1968. Dell.

All the Comforts: A Novel. Joseph Papaleo. LC 67-11237. 1967. Little, Brown.

All the Conspirators. Christopher Isherwood. LC 58-12798. 1979. pap. 6.95 (ISBN 0-8112-0725-0, NDP480). New Directions.

All the Days Were Summer. Jack M. Bickham. LC 80-2895. 192p. 1981. 12.95 (ISBN 0-385-17597-3). Doubleday.

All the Dead Are Not Buried. Ben McElveen, Jr. 4.75 o.s.i. (ISBN 0-8181-0049-4). Pageant-Poseidon.

All the Dear Pain. Edna M Reimer Hines. LC 52-3524. 1952. Dorrance.

All the Dogs' Fault. Thomas Bernard Joseph Connery & Coppee, Francois I.E. Francis Edouard Joachim, 1842- (On cover: Once a week library, v. 10, no. 23). 1893. P.F. Collier.

All the Girls We Loved. Prudencio De Pereda. LC 48-772. 1948. Farrar, Straus.

All the Glitters. Anne Gardner, pseud. LC 35-9855. J. H. Hopkins & Son.

All the Golden Doors. Willa Gibbs. LC 57-106006. 1957. Appleton-Century-Crofts.

All the Golden Gifts. Iola Fuller, pseud. LC 66-26639. 1966. Putnam.

All the Good People I've Left Behind. Joyce Carol Oates. LC 78-22110. 1979. 14.00. (ISBN 0-87685-394-7) (ISBN 0-87685-395-5) (ISBN 0-87685-393-9). Black Sparrow Press.

All the Green Gold: An Irish Boyhood. Colm Luibheid. LC 73-123639. 200p. 1970. 5.95 o.p. (ISBN 0-275-25320-1). Praeger.

All the Harvestment. John F. Newber. 3.50 o.p. Carlton.

All the Kingdoms of Earth: A Novel. Hoke Norris. LC 56-9906. 1956. Simon and Schuster.

All the King's Horses. Louis Stevens. LC 28-7329. 1928. The John Day Company.

All the King's Horses. Margaret Widdemer. LC 30-27145. Farrar & Rinehart Incorporated.

All the King's Mem: By Robert Penn Warren... Robert Penn Warren. LC 46-6144. 1946. Harcourt, Brace and Company.

All the King's Men. nd ed. James Leonard Johnson. LC 80-83842. 328p. 1981. pap. 3.25 o.p. (ISBN 0-89081-267-5). Harvest Hse.

All the King's Men. Robert Penn Warren. 448p. (gr. 11 up). 1973. pap. 3.95 (ISBN 0-553-20454-8). Bantam.

All the King's Men. Robert Penn Warren. LC 64-987. (Time reading program special edition). Time, Inc.

All the King's Men. Robert Penn Warren. LC 53-7891. (Modern library of the world's best books, 170). 1953. Modern Library.

All the King's Men. Robert Penn Warren & Bernard Fuchs. LC 77-460445. (Illus.). 1976. Franklin Library.

All the Little Heroes: A Novel. Herbert Wilner. LC 66-18593. 1966. Bobbs-Merrill.

All the Little Live Things. Wallace Earle Stegner. LC 79-13839. 1979. 15.95 (ISBN 0-8032-4110-0) (ISBN 0-8032-9109-4). University of Nebraska Press.

All the Little Live Things: By Wallace Stegner. Wallace Earle Stegner. LC 67-134991. 1967. 5.75. Viking.

All the Little Things. Wallace Earle Stegner. LC 67-13499. 1967. Viking Press.

All the Living: A Novel of One Year in the Life of William Shakespeare. Henrietta Buckmaster, pseud. LC 62-17164. 1962. Random House.

All the Lovely Ladies. John Mack Carter. LC 80-22441. 13.95 (ISBN 0-698-11073-0). Coward, McCann & Geoghegan.

All the Loyal People: A Novel. David Stone. LC 60-8483. 1961. Putnam.

All the Millionaires. Alec Rackowe. LC 67-10444. 1967. Macmillan.

All the Mowgli Stories. Illus. by Richard M. Powers. Rudyard Kipling. LC 56-1339. 1956. Junior Deluxe Editions.

All the Naked Heroes: A Novel. Alan Kapelner. LC 60-5611. 1960. G. Braziller.

All the News... James F Lynch. LC 74-147132. 1971. 6.95 (ISBN 0-396-06333-0). Dodd, Mead.

All the Nice Girls. Agnes Mary Robertson Dunlop. LC 77-366840. 1976. 3.50 (ISBN 0-432-08492-4). P. Davies.

All the Passions. Paula V. Arbose. pap. 2.50 (ISBN 0-87164-034-1). William-F.

All the Pleasures. James Lumpp. LC 42-141182. 1942. Phoenix Press.

All the Queen's Men. Evelyn Anthony. LC 60-9155. 1974. (pbk.) 1.25. New American Library.

All the Queen's Men. Eve Stephens, pseud. LC 60-9155. 1960. Crowell.

All the Rest Have Died. William Gunn. LC 64-13654. 1964. Delacorte Press; Distributed by the Dial Press.

All the Right People. William Wetmore. LC 64-11280. 1964. Doubleday.

All the Rivers Run. Nancy Cato. LC 77-10289. 1978. 10.00 (ISBN 0-312-02021-X). St. Martin's Press.

All the Rivers Run: A Novel. Nancy Cato. (Signet Book). 1979. 2.95 (ISBN 0-451-08693-7). New American Library, Inc.

All the Sad Young Men. Francis Scott Key Fitzgerald. LC 26-861890. 1926. C. Scribner's Sons.

All the Shattered Worlds. Steve Vance. (Orig.). 1979. pap. 1.95 (ISBN 0-532-23154-6). Woodhill.

All the Skeletons in All the Closets. Keith Fowler. LC 34-21155. The Macaulay Company.

All the Summer Days. 1st Ed. Ned Calmer. LC 61-574719. 1961. Little, Brown.

All the Tea in China. Kyril Bonfiglioli. LC 77-88780. 8.95. Pantheon Books.

All the Tea in China. Katharine Topkins. LC 62-19432. 1962. Macmillan.

All the Time There Is. Toby Stein. LC 76-53532. 7.95 (ISBN 0-394-41160-9). Random House.

All the Tomorrows: A Novel by Naomi Lane Babson... Naomi Lane Babson. LC 39-27624. Reynal & Hitchcock.

All the Traps of Earth. Clifford D. Simak. 1979. pap. 2.25 (ISBN 0-380-45500-5, 45500). Avon.

All the Traps of Earth. 2nd ed. Clifford D. Simak. 160p. 1974. pap. 0.95 o.p. (532-95315-095). Manor Bks.

All the Traps of Earth & Other Stories. Clifford D. Simak. 1963. pap. 0.50 o.p. (50-388). Manor Bks.

All the Trumpets. Hazel Iris Addis. LC 38-29165. 1938. M.S. Mill Co., Inc.

All the Trumpets Sounded, Novel Based on the Life of Moses. William George Hardy. LC 42-14356. 1942. Coward-McCann, Inc.

All the Way. Felice Buckvar. (Orig.). 1980. pap. 2.25 (ISBN 0-89083-571-3). Zebra.

All the Way by Water. Elisabeth Stancy Payne. LC 22-11291. 1922. The Penn Publishing Company.

All the Way Home. Jeanne Bowman, pseud. 2.95. Arcadia House.

All the Way Home. Walter Freeman. LC 55-6903. (Signet book, 1186). 1955. New American Library.

All-the-Way Man. Joyce Dingwell. (Harlequin Romances Ser.). 192p. 1981. pap. 1.50 (ISBN 0-373-02432-0). Harlequin Bks.

All the World. Charles Monroe Sheldon. LC 19-104613. George H. Doran Company.

All the World and I. Hepburn Dinwoodie. LC 40-316226. 1940. Little, Brown and Company.

All the World to Nothing. Wyndham Martyn. LC 12-21406. 1912. Little, Brown, and Company.

All the Year Round. Dorothy Keeley Aldis. LC 38-27580. 1938. Houghton Mifflin Company.

All the Year Round: A Book of Stories. Robert Myron Coates. LC 43-157607. 1943. Harcourt, Brace and Company.

All the Years of Her Life. Josephine Lawrence. LC 72-75418. 1972. (ISBN 0-15-104780-4). Harcourt Brace Jovanovich.

All the Young Men. Oliver La Farge. LC 35-13561. 1935. Houghton Mifflin Company.

All the Young Men: Stories. Oliver La Farge. LC 75-41169. 1976. 14.00 (ISBN 0-404-14566-3). AMS Press.

All the Young Summer Days. 1st Ed. Bernice Kavinoky. LC 53-52370. 1953. Bobbs-Merrill.

All Their Children Were Acrobats. Harry Hamilton. LC 36-19840. The Bobbs-Merrill Company.

All Their Kingdoms. Madeleine A Polland. LC 80-19132. 10.95 (ISBN 0-440-00019-X). Delacorte Press.

All Their Kingdoms. Madeline A. Pollard. 1982. pap. 3.25 (ISBN 0-440-10091-7). Dell.

All These Condemned. Cover Painting by James Meese. John Dann MacDonald. LC 54-386632. (Gold medal books, 420). 1954. Fawcett Publications.

All These Earths. F. M Busby. (Berkley Book). 1978. 1.75 (ISBN 0-425-03902-1). Berkley Pub. Corp.

All These Geniuses. John Freda. LC 41-19305. The Dial Press.

All These Splendid Sins. Lee Rogers. (Orig.). 1979. pap. 2.50 (ISBN 0-89083-480-6). Zebra.

All Things Are Possible. Yvonne Duffy. LC 81-83657. (Illus.). 1981. pap. 8.95 (ISBN 0-9607252-0-2). Garvin A J.

All Things Are Possible: A Novel, Dealing with the Psychology of Motherhood and with Religion in Politics. Henry Neil. LC 28-11162. The Bible House.

All Things Are Possible: An Apocryphal Novel. Lewis Browne. 1935. The Macmillan Company.

All Things Are Yours: A Novel. Henry Beetle Hough. LC 42-21650. 1942. Doubleday, Doran and Company, Inc.

All Things Considered. Gilbert Keith Chesterton. 1978. Repr. of 1915 ed. lib. bdg. 20.00 (ISBN 0-8414-0893-9). Folcroft.

All Things Considered, and Other Stories. Elaine Sterne Carrington. LC 39-30336. J. Messner, Inc.

All Things Human. Stuart Benton. LC 49-11835. Sheridan House.

All Things in Their Season. Helen Chappell. (Orig.). 1983. pap. 3.95 (ISBN 0-440-10057-7). Dell.

All Things New. Ann Harvey. LC 41-8171. 1941. Wm. B. Eerdmans Publishing Co.

All This, and Heaven Too. Rachel Lyman Field. LC 38-27858. 1938. The Macmillan Company.

All This, and Heaven Too. Rachel Lyman Field. LC 40-1012. 1939. The Macmillan Company.

All This, and Heaven Too. Rachel Lyman Field. LC 40-10768. 1940. The Macmillan Company.

All This, and Mrs. Calucci Too! Alan Cliburn. LC 78-67934. 3.95 (ISBN 0-89636-011-3). Accent Books.

All This Is Ended: The Life and Times of H. H. the Begum Sumroo of Sardhana. Vera Chatterjee. LC 79-903884. 12.00 (ISBN 0-7069-0719-1). Vikas.

All Through the Day. Guy King. 128p. 1980. pap. 3.95 (ISBN 0-310-41831-3). Zondervan.

All Through the Night. Grace Livingston Hill. LC 75-31588. 1975-1976. 9.95 (ISBN 0-89190-001-2). American Reprint Co.

All Through the Night. Grace Livingston Hill. LC 45-2695. 1945. J. B. Lippincott Company.

All Through the Night. Whit Masterson, pseud. LC 55-9921. (Red badge detective). 1955. Dodd, Mead.

All Through the Night. Playboy Editors. LC 75-9413. 192p. 1975. pap. 1.25 o.p. (ISBN 0-87216-279-6, B16279). Playboy Pr Pbks.

All Through the Night: Stories of the World's Oldest Profession. LC 75-9413. 1975. (pbk.) 1.25. Playboy Press.

All Through the Night: Stories of the World's Oldest Profession. LC 75-9413. 1.25. Playboy Press.

All Through the Night. 1st Ed. Richard Vaughan. LC 57-5341. 1957. Dutton.

All Thy Conquests. Alfred Hayes. LC 46-7864. 1946. Howell, Soskin.

All Time Favorites from Reader's Digest Condensed Books. 1976. (pbk.) 1.95. Bantam Books.

All Times Possible. Gordon Eklund. 1974. (pbk.) 0.95. DAW Books.

All True Lovers. Sarah Aldridge. LC 78-59626. 1978. 6.75 (ISBN 0-930044-10-X). Naiad Press.

All Under Heaven. Pearl Sydenstricker Buck. LC 72-7285. 208p. 1973. 7.95 o.p. (ISBN 0-381-98211-4, A02030). John Day.

All Under Heaven:; a Novel. Pearl Sydenstricker Buck. 1974. (pbk.) 1.50 (ISBN 0-671-78698-9). Pocket Books.

All Under Heaven: A Novel. Pearl Sydenstricker Buck. LC 72-7285. 1973. 7.95 (ISBN 0-381-98211-4). John Day Co.

All Victories Are Alike. Leane Zugsmith. LC 29-839525. Payson & Clarke Ltd.

All Visitors Must Be Announced. Helen Van Slyke. LC 72-76215. 1974. (pbk.) 1.25. Popular Library.

All Was Made Whole. 1st Ed. Eugene C Santor. LC 55-8391. 1955. Vantage Press.

All We Have Built. Evelyn Cowdin. LC 43-3706. 1943. M. S. Mill Co. Inc.

All We Know of Heaven. Dore Mullen. (Orig.). 1980. pap. 2.50 (ISBN 0-440-10178-6). Dell.

All Woman. Matt Harding, pseud. 1970. pap. 0.75 o.p. (75-351). Manor Bks.

All Women Are Fatal. Claude Mauriac. (O.s.i.). 1964. 4.95 o.s.i. (ISBN 0-8076-0261-2). Braziller.

All Women Die. P. J Wolfson. LC 33-2860. The Vanguard Press.

All-Wool Morrison: Time: Today, Place: the United States, Period of Action: Twenty-Four Hours. Holman Francis Day. LC 20-13700. 1920. Harper & Brothers.

All Wrong. A Leaf from a Drama. Annie M Griffen. LC 6-45417. 1877. J. B. Lippincott & Co.

All Ye People. Merle Estes Colby. LC 31-30605. 1931. The Viking Press.

All Your Born Days. Heath Bowman. LC 39-225856. The Bobbs-Merrill Company.

All Your Lovely Words Are Spoken. Mary Linn Roby. 1975. (pbk.) 0.95. Ace Books.

Allah Conspiracy. Christopher Warren. LC 80-27097. 10.95 (ISBN 0-8253-0052-5). Beaufort Books.

Allan and the Holy Flower. Henry Rider Haggard. LC 15-7359. 1915. 1.35. Longmans, Green, and Co.

Allan and the Holy Flower. Illus. by Hookway Cowles. Henry Rider Haggard. LC 66-5436. 1966. bds., 2.95. Macdonald.

Allan and the Ice-Gods: A Tale of Beginnings. Henry Rider Haggard. LC 75-46274. (Supernatural and Occult Fiction). 1976. 18.00 (ISBN 0-405-08132-4). Arno Press.

Allan and the Ice-Gods: A Tale of Beginnings. Henry Rider Haggard. LC 27-12295. 1927. Doubleday, Page & Company.

Allan Dare and Robert le Diable. A Romance. David Dixon Porter. LC 7-37781. 1885. D. Appleton and Company.

Allan Quatermain... Henry Rider Haggard. (On cover: Harper's handy series, no. 139). 1887. Harper & Brothers.

Allan Quatermain. Being an Account of His Adventures with Sir Henry Curtis, Bart., Commander John Good, R. N., and One Umslopogass. Henry Rider Haggard. LC 6-45973. (On cover: The Franklin library. no. 5). 1887. Franklin News Co.

Allan Quatermain: Being an Account of His Further Adventures and Discoveries with Sir Henry Curtis, Bart., Commander John Good, R. N., and One Umslopogaas. Henry Rider Haggard. (On cover: Lovell's library, v. 21, no. 1020). 1887. J. W. Lovell Company.

Allan Quatermain, Being an Account of His Further Adventures and Discoveries in Company with Sir Henry Curtis, Bart., Commander John Good, R. N., and One Umslopogaas: By Sir Rider Haggard... Henry Rider Haggard. LC 17-500. 1914. Longmans, Green and Co.

Allan Quatermain: Being an Account of His Further Adventures and Discoveries in Company with Sir Henry Curtis, Bart., Commander John Good, R.N., and One Umslopogaas. Henry Rider Haggard. LC 80-19297. 1980. 11.95 (ISBN 0-89370-523-3). Borgo Press.

Allan Quatermain. Illus. by Hookway Cowles. Henry Rider Haggard. LC 66-5440. 1966. bds., 2.95. Macdonald.

Allan, Son of a Gunmaker. Harvey Rowell. LC 9-24963. 1909. 1.50. Cochrane Publishing Company.

Allan the Hunter: A Tale of Three Lions and Prince: Another Lion. Henry Rider Haggard. LC 6-45974. Lothrop Publishing Company.

Allan's Wife. Henry Rider Haggard. (On cover: Seaside library. Pocket ed., no. 1248). 1889. G. Munro.

Allan's Wife, with Hunter Quatermain's Story, A Tale of Three Lions, and Long Odds. Henry Rider Haggard. LC 80-10083. (Newcastle Forgotten Fantasy library; 24). 1980. 10.95 (ISBN 0-87877-523-4) (ISBN 0-87877-123-9). Newcastle Pub. Co.

Allan's Wife: With Hunter Quatermain's Story, A Tale of Three Lions, and Long Odds. Henry Rider Haggard & Henry Rider Haggard. LC 66-543912. 1966. bds., 2.95. Macdonald.

Allapattah. Patrick D. Smith. (Orig.). 1979. pap. 1.75 (ISBN 0-532-17240-X). Woodhill.

Allbrights. Archibald Marshall. 1926. Dodd, Mead and Company.

Allee Same". Frances Aymar Mathews. LC 7-22821. T. Y. Crowell & Co.

Alleged Great-Aunt. Henry Kitchell Webster & Fairbank, Mrs. Janet (Ayer) LC 35-27183. The Bobbs-Merrill Company.

Allegiance. Wayne L Green. LC 82-19806. 12.95 (ISBN 0-517-54927-1). Crown.

Allegories. Frederic William Farrar. LC 6-38664. 1898. Longmans, Green and Co.

Allegories of Life. Harriet A Adams. LC 5-42967. 1872. Lee & Shepard.

Allegra. Clare Darcy. LC 74-82400. 1975. 7.95 (ISBN 0-8027-0475-1). Walker.

Allegra. Clare Darcy. (Signet Book). 1976. (pbk.) 1.50. New American Library.

Allegra. Clare Darcy. LC 77-14109. (Regency Romance). 1978. 9.95 (ISBN 0-89340-110-2). J. Curley.

Allegra. Lizzie Allen Harker. LC 20-161. 1920. C. Scribner's Sons.

Allegra. Rosemary Winfield. 1980. pap. 1.95 o.s.i. (ISBN 0-8439-0720-7, Leisure Bks). Nordon Pubns.

Allegra Maud Goldman. Edith Konecky. LC 76-9207. 7.95 (ISBN 0-06-012452-0). Harper & Row.

Allegra's Child. Jennette Dowling Letton. LC 69-18636. 1969. 4.50. M. Smith Co.

Allegro with Passion. Dick Wine, pseud. 1973. pap. 1.50 o.s.i. (71-361). Lancer.

Allen Lucas; the Self-Made Man. Emily Chubbuck Judson. LC 52-56007. 1844. Bennett, Backus, & Hawley.

Allen Prescott; or, The Fortunes of a New-England Boy. Susan Ann Livingston Sedgwick. LC 2-3954. 1834. Harper & Brothers.

Allendale's Choice, a Village Chronicle. Elizabeth Steward Phelps. LC 7-36079. 1895. The Young Churchman Co.

Allenwood Pa: Escape to-from a Possibility of a Nightmare. W. M. Payne. 1977. 4.50 o.p. (ISBN 0-533-02368-8). Vantage.

Allerton and Dreux. Jean Ingelow. LC 75-475. (Victorian Fiction: Novels of Faith and Doubt; V. 29). 1975. 35.00 (ISBN 0-8240-1553-3). Garland Pub.

Allerton Towers. A Novel. Annie Hall Thomas Cudlip. (Harper's Franklin square library, no. 275). 1882. Harper & Brothers.

Alley Cop: A Novel. Josephine Koury. LC 58-10389. 1958. House of Edinboro.

Alley Girl: By Jonathan Craig Pseud. Frank E Smith. LC 54-27802. (Lion book, 206). 1954. Lion Books by Arrangement with Postal Publications.

Alley Jaggers. Paul West. LC 66-13932. 1966. Harper & Row.

Alley of Flashing Spears, and Other Stories. Donn Bryne. LC 34-38189. 1934. D. Appleton-Century Company, Incorporated.

Alley of Flashing Spears: And Other Stories. Donn Byrne. LC 70-103501. (Short story index reprint series). 1969. Books for Libraries Press.

Alley of Flashing Spears & Other Stories. facsimile ed. Donn B. Byrne. LC 70-103501. (Short Story Index Reprint Ser.). 1934. 15.00 (ISBN 0-8369-3243-9). Ayer Co.

Alley Oop. Vincent T. Hamlin. 256p. (Orig.). 1983. pap. 2.50 (ISBN 0-523-49026-7). Pinnacle Bks.

Alleys: A Novel. Ronald Ditz Taylor. LC 80-65066. 3.95 (ISBN 0-931604-07-9). Curbstone Press.

Alleys of Eden. Robert Olen Butler. 256p. 1983. pap. 2.95 (ISBN 0-345-30774-7). Ballantine.

Allie Baird: The Settler's Son. A Weird Tale of the Wilderness. Harland Page Halsey. (Old Sleuth's own no. 95). 1897. Parlor Car Publishing Co.

Allie Winters: The Mountain Girl of the Southland, and Charles Beverley, in a Drama of Life and Love. Charles William Harrington. LC 42-5687. 1942. C. W. Harrington.

Allies in Flight. LaMar Porter. LC 64-18176. 1964. Dorrance.

Allies of Antares. Dray Prescot. (Science Fiction Ser.). 1981. pap. 2.25 (ISBN 0-87997-671-3, U E 1671). DAW Bks.

Alligator. Shelley Katz. (Dell Book). 1977. 1.95. Dell Pub. Co.

Alligator. Shelley Katz. (Dell Book). 1977. 1.95. Dell Pub. Co.

Alligator Gar. Chester L Sullivan. LC 72-96642. 1973. 6.95 (ISBN 0-517-50417-0). Crown Publishers.

Alligator Lamp: A Novel. 1st Ed. John Kellogg. LC 53-9789. 1953. Exposition Press.

Alligator Named Daisy: An Entertainment. 1st American Ed. Charles Terrot. LC 55-5342. 1955. Dutton.

Allingham Case-Book. Margery Allingham. LC 73-91995. 1969. 5.50. Morrow.

Allingham Minibus. Margery Allingham. LC 73-9839. 1973. 5.95 (ISBN 0-688-00178-5). W. Morrow.

Allinghams. May Sinclair. LC 27-6053. 1927. The Macmillan Company.

Alli's Son: A Novel. Magnhild Haalke & Chater, Arthur G., Tr. LC 37-4608. 1937. A. A. Knopf.

Allison's Girl. Theodore Acland Harper. LC 36-16932. 1936. The Viking Press.

Allison's Shadow. Tracy Leddy. LC 82-61020. 124p. (Orig.). 1982. pap. 12.00 (ISBN 0-89142-040-1). Sant Bani Ash.

Allouma and Other Tales. Guy De Maupassant. Tr. by Arthur Hornblow. LC 8-20115. 1895. Holland Publishing Company.

Alloy of Gold. Francis William Sullivan. LC 15-17321. 1915. R. M. McBride & Company.

All's Dross but Love." A Strange Record of Two Reincarnated Souls. Republished from the Christmas Number of the New York Morning Journal. December 16th, 1888. Albert Edmund Lancaster. (On cover: lovell's library, no. 1344). J. W. Lovell Company.

All's Fair. Anne N. Reisser. (Candlelight Ecstasy Ser.: No. 51). (Orig.). 1982. pap. 1.75 (ISBN 0-440-10098-4). Dell.

All's Fair...". Richard Edward Wormser. LC 74-22825. (Labor Movement in Fiction and Non-Fiction). 1976. 10.00 (ISBN 0-404-58484-5). AMS Press.

All's Fair...". Richard Edward Wormser. LC 37-286748. (Modern age books. Blue seal books, no. 2). Modern Age Books, Inc.

All's Fair in Love. Jeanne Andrews. (Sweet Dreams Ser.: No. 41). 160p. 1982. pap. 1.95 (ISBN 0-553-22607-X). Bantam.

All's Fair in Love. Jeanne Judson. LC 53-123344. 1953. Avalon Books.

All's Not Gold That Glitters" Or, The Young Californian. Alice Bradley Haven. LC 14-19351. 1853. D. Appleton & Company.

All's Well; a Story of the Sea. Fred Of San Francisco Harris. LC 53-6473. Vantage Press.

Allward: A Story of Gypsy Life. Ethel Stefana Stevens Drower. LC 15-12884. Dodd, Mead and Company.

Allworth Abbey. Emma Dorothy Eliza Nevitte Southworth. LC 12-38901. T. B. Peterson & Brothers.

Ally of Cortes. Fernando De Alva Ixtlilxochitl. Tr. by Douglass K. Ballentine. (Illus.). 142p. 1970. 5.00 o.p. (ISBN 0-87404-015-9). Tex Western.

Allyson. Jerry B Jenkins. LC 81-9665. 2.50 (ISBN 0-8024-4315-X). Moody Press.

Alma Adentro: Novels. Riobo Caputto. LC 61-29141. 1959. Argentina, Castellvi.

Alma: Or, Otonkah's Daughter; a Story of the 20,000 Sioux. Gay Waters. LC 8-34342. T. S. Denison.

Almansor: A Novel. Sondra Till Robinson. LC 73-83522. 7.95 (ISBN 0-8402-1322-0). Nash Pub.

Almanzar. James Francis Davis. LC 70-144153. (Short story index reprint series). (Illus.). 1971. (ISBN 0-8369-3768-6). Books for Libraries Press.

Almanzar. James Francis Davis. LC 18-19728. 1918. 1.00. H. Holt and Company.

Almanzar Evarts, Hero. James Francis Davis. LC 25-24061. 1925. The J. W. Burke Company.

Alma's Senior Year. Louise Marks Clancy. LC 14-3105. (Her The Hadley hall series) $1.50). 1915. The Page Company.

Almaver's Folly: A Story of an Eastern River. Joseph Conrad. LC 6-30680. 1895. Macmillan and Co.

Almayer's Folly. Joseph Conrad. (Penguin modern classics). 1976. 1.95 (ISBN 0-14-000036-4). Penguin Books.

Almayer's Folly. Joseph Conrad. LC 79-184735. 1971. (ISBN 0-8376-0408-7). R. Bentley.

Almayer's Folly. Joseph Conrad. LC 22-10642. 1921. Doubleday, Page & Company.

Almayer's Folly: A Story of an Eastern River. Joseph Conrad. LC 16-935776. 1915. Doubleday, Page & Company.

Almayer's Folly: And Other Stories. Afterword by Jocelyn Baines. Joseph Conrad. LC 65-997. (Signet classic, CP258) Bibl.). New Amer. Lib.

Almeda: A Tale of the Buellos Madros. E. O Tilburn. (On cover: Globe library, no. 95). 1889. Rand, McNally & Company.

Almetta of Gabriel's Run. Louise R. Saunders Murdoch. 1.25. The Meridian Press.

Almighty. Irving Wallace. LC 82-45567. (Illus.). 416p. 1982. 15.95 (ISBN 0-385-18389-5). Doubleday.

Almirante. A Romance of Old-Time California. George Homer Meyer. LC 6-60. 1890. W. M. Hinton & Co.

Almond-Blossom. Olive Wadsley. LC 21-188046. 1921. Dodd, Mead & Company.

Almond-Eyed. A Story of the Day. Atwell Whitney. LC 22-51493. 1878. Printed for the Author by A. L. Bancroft & Company.

Almond Tree. Grace Zaring Stone. LC 31-28316. The Bobbs-Merrill Company.

Almonds & Raisins. Maisie Mosco. 384p. (Orig.). 1981. pap. cancelled (ISBN 0-553-13913-4). Bantam.

Almonds of Life. Florence Ethel Mills Young. LC 20-232073. George H. Doran Company.

Almoran and Hamet: An Oriental Tale. John Hawkesworth. LC 74-17144. (Flowering of the Novel). 1974. (ISBN 0-8240-1156-2). Garland Pub.

Almoran and Hamet: an Oriental Tale. In Two Volumes. John Hawkesworth. LC 5-41095. 1808. Reynolds and Palmer, Printers.

Almoran & Hamnet: An Oriental Tale 1761, 2 vols. in 1. John Hawkesworth. Ed. by Michael F. Shugrue. (Flowering of the Novel, 1740-1775 Ser: Vol. 57). 1974. lib. bdg. 50.00 (ISBN 0-8240-1156-2). Garland Pub.

Almost. William Bryant. LC 76-80967. 1969. McGraw-Hill.

Almost a Lady. Florence Stonebraker. LC 47-24299. 1947. Phoenix Press.

Almost a Life. Bernard Harper Friedman. LC 75-5569. 1975. 8.95 (ISBN 0-670-11452-9). Viking Press.

Almost.. A Novel. By John S. Shriver...Illustrated by Wilson De Meza, Alfred Gillam and Charles E. Sickels. John Shultz Shriver. 1888. Lombard, Druid & Co.

Almost a Nun. Julia MacNair Wright. LC 9-923. Presbyterian Publication Committee.

Almost a Nun. Julia MacNair Wright. LC 9-922. Presbyterian Board of Publication and Sabbath-School Work.

Almost a Priest. A Tale That Deals in Facts. Julia MacNair Wright. LC 9-921. 1870. McKinney & Martin.

Almost an Angel. Mary M. Friend Harwell. LC 8-23531. 1908. The Neale Publishing Company.

Almost an Englishman. Moses Lewis Scudder. LC 8-3391. 1878. G. P. Putnam's Sons.

Almost Dead. 1st Ed. William Herber. LC 56-11691. (Main line mysteries). 1957. Lippincott.

Almost Everything. Bobbie L. Hawkins. (Illus.). 176p. 1982. 15.00 (ISBN 0-942986-00-8); pap. 7.00 (ISBN 0-942986-01-6). Longriver Bks.

Almost Famous. David Small. LC 81-22407. 13.95 (ISBN 0-393-01525-4). W.W. Norton.

Almost Glory: A Novel by F. Benedict Pseud. Frederick Benedict De Verteuil. LC 50-10010. 1950. Duell, Sloan and Pearce.

Almost Home. Jonathan Schwartz. LC 78-73192. 1979. pap. 5.95 o.p. (ISBN 0-385-15087-3). Doubleday.

Almost Home: Collected Stories. Jonathan Schwartz. LC 75-113987. 1970. 5.95. Doubleday.

Almost Midnight. Martin Caidin. 1971. 5.95 o.p. Morrow.

Almost Midnight: A Novel. Martin Caidin. LC 75-105743. 1971. 5.95. W. Morrow.

Almost Murder. Raymond Hughes. 1979. 8.00 (ISBN 0-682-49437-2). Exposition.

Almost Pagan. John Davys Beresford. The Bobbs-Merrill Company.

Almost Paradise. Luis Spota. LC 63-11232. 1963. Doubleday.

Almost Perfect Murder: A Case Book of Madame Storey. Hulbert Footner. LC 37-14581. 1937. J. B. Lippincott Company.

Almost Persuaded. William Nathaniel Harben. (On cover: Minerva series, no. 37). 1890. The Minerva Publishing Company.

Almost Summer: A Novel. John Minahan. (Dell Book). 1978. 1.95 (ISBN 0-440-10491-2). Dell Publishing Co.

Almost Transparent Blue. Ryu Murakami. Tr. by Nancy Andrew from Japanese. LC 77-75959. 136p. 1977. 10.50x (ISBN 0-87011-305-4); pap. 4.25 (ISBN 0-87011-469-7). Kodansha.

Almost up Devil's Tower. Mae Urbanek. 104p. 3.00x (ISBN 0-940514-00-1); pap. 2.00 (ISBN 0-940514-01-X). Urbanek.

Almuric. Robert E. Howard. (Berkley Medallion Book). (Illus.). 1977. 1.95 (ISBN 0-425-03483-6). Berkley Pub. Corp.

Aloe. Katherine Mansfield. LC 74-16074. 1974. H. Fertig.

Aloha. Robin Moore, pseud. 1977. pap. 1.95 (ISBN 0-532-19133-1). Woodhill.

Aloha, Death. Virginia Nielson. 1973. pap. 0.75 o.s.i. (01-389). Lancer.

Aloha Means Goodbye. Naomi A Hintze. LC 72-37049. 1972. 5.95 (ISBN 0-394-48028-7). Random House.

Aloma of the South Seas. MacBurney Gates & Hymer, John B. LC 26-14519. 1926. Grosset & Dunlap.

ALondon Life. Henry James. LC 57-6531. (Evergreen book, E-58). 1957. Grove Press.

Alone. Eleanor Martin. LC 33-645. 1932. W. Godwin, Inc.

Alone. 5th ed. Mary Virginia Terhune. LC 25-15517. 1854. A. Morris.

Alone. 5th ed. Mary Virginia Terhune. LC 25-15517. 1854. A. Morris.

Alone (a Beautiful Land of Dreams) George Wesley Davis. LC 23-1206. Times-Mirror Press.

Alone Against Tomorrow. Harlan Ellison. 312p. 1972. pap. 3.95 (ISBN 0-02-019780-2, Collier). Macmillan.

Alone Against Tomorrow: Stories of Alienation in Speculative Fiction. Harlan Ellison. LC 78-127465. 1971. Macmillan.

Alone Along a Lonely Road & Other Stories. Roman A. De La Cruz. 1973. 4.50 o.p. Cellar.

Alone Among Men. Marjorie Coryn. LC 47-30572. 1947. D. Appleton-Century Co.

Alone Atop the Mountain. Samuel Sandmel. LC 72-93399. (Illus.). 1973. 5.95 (ISBN 0-385-03877-1). Doubleday.

Alone by the Sea: The Story of Jane Wilkinson Long, Mother of Texas. Effie Missouria Pitchford Moore. LC 51-13342. 1951. Naylor Co.

Alone I Wait. Lynn Vanlandingham. LC 77-121016. 1970. 6.50 o.p. (ISBN 0-87358-051-6). Northland.

Alone in China, and Other Stories. Julian Ralph. LC 70-101819. (Short story index reprint series). (Illus.). 1969. Books for Libraries Press.

Alone in London see Jessica's First Prayer.

Alone in Paris. Barbara Cartland. LC 79-154. 1979. 6.95 (ISBN 0-87272-076-4, Duron Bks). Brodart.

Alone in the World Looking. Elroy Bode. LC 73-76995. 1973. 8.00 (ISBN 0-87404-046-9). Tex Western.

Alone on a Wide, Wide Sea: An Ocean Mystery. William Clark Russell. LC 8-1800. (On cover: Broadway series, no. 9). 1892. J. A. Taylor and Company.

Alone Together. Sherrye Henry. LC 81-43412. 288p. 1982. 14.95 (ISBN 0-385-17958-8). Doubleday.

Alone We Embark. Maura Laverty. LC 44-8165. 1944. Longmans, Green and Co.

Along a Dark Path. Velda Johnston. LC 67-12288. (Red badge mystery). 1967. Dodd, Mead.

Along Came a Stranger. Mary F. Ford. 1973. pap. 0.75 o.s.i. (01-367). Lancer.

Along Came Love. Patty Pierce. 192p. (Orig.). Date not set. pap. cancelled o.p. (ISBN 0-505-51842-2). Tower Bks.

Along Came Romance. Anne Gardner, pseud. LC 36-15376. J. H. Hopkins & Son, Inc.

Along Came the Devil. 1st Ed. Mamie Peters Call. LC 52-22905. 1952. Borden Pub. Co.

Along Came the Other Girl: A Story of Love and Adventure in Pre-Revolutionary Virginia. 1st Ed. Stella Wilson Lambert. LC 61-10294. 1961. American Press.

Along the Anataw. The Record of a Campaign. Mary Ruth Baldwin. LC 6-6855. 1891. Hunt & Eaton.

Along the Arno. Brian Glanville. LC 57-7163. Crowell.

Along the Edges: Special Issue 19. Ray Boxer. pap. 1.00 o.p. The Smith.

Along the King's Highway: Or, The Invisible Route; a Romance of the Southern United States. Martha Caroline Shook. LC 12-12375. Press of Maverick-Clarke Litho Co.

Along the Old Road. Mary Hubbard Howell. LC 7-6620. The American Sunday-School Union.

Along the Raccoon River: Winter. John Kemmerer. LC 77-362173. Kemmerer.

Along the Tallahatchie. Lae Cornell. LC 45-10325. 1945. C. White & Company.

Along the Trail: In Which Marjorie Finds That Everyone Does Not Hurry Past the Rough Places on the Rail !--and Why. Katherine Merritte Yates. LC 14-5164. 1912. Davis & Bond.

Along the Way. William Walker Canfield. LC 9-24449. 1909. 1.50. R. F. Fenno & Company.

Along the Way. Bessie B. Redish. LC 68-19349. (Illus.). 1969. 0.98 o.p. Doubleday.

Along These Streets. Maxwell Struthers Burt. LC 42-568257. 1942. C. Scribner's Sons.

Alongside Night. J. Neil Schulman. 288p. 1982. pap. 2.50 (ISBN 0-441-01768-1, Pub. by Ace Science Fiction). Ace Bks.

Alongside Night: A Novel. J. Neil Schulman. LC 79-13587. 8.95 (ISBN 0-517-53923-3). Crown Publishers.

Alonzo and Melissa: Or The Unfeeling Father. An American Tale... Daniel Jackson. LC 33-17771. 1880. A. Brown.

Alonzo and Melissa; or, The Unfeeling Father. An American Tale... Daniel Jackson. LC 39-4614. 1834.

Alonzo and Melissa; or, The Unfeeling Father. An American Tale. Daniel Jackson & Mitchell, Isaac. LC 3-22390. 1864. J. B. Lippincott & Co.

Aloys. Berthold Auerbach. Tr. by Brooks, Charles Timothy. LC 6-4499. (Leisure hour series, v. 78). 1877. H. Holt and Company.

Alp: A Novel. William Hjortsberg. LC 70-92190. 1969. 4.95. Simon and Schuster.

Alp Murder. Aaron Marc Stein. LC 78-89077. 1970. 4.50. Published for the Crime Club by Doubleday.

Alpha. Imre Balint & Rittenberg, Louis, Tr. LC 27-5685. 1927. Macy-Masius.

Alpha & Omega. Allan Hartley. (Illus.). 1978. pap. 0.69 o.p. (ISBN 0-8007-8534-7, Spire Comics). Revell.

Alpha & Omega: A Revealing & Candid Story of the Last Days. Eva Music. 48p. 1975. 4.00 o.p. (ISBN 0-682-48161-0). Exposition.

Alpha and Omega: Stories. Isaac Rosenfeld. LC 66-15913. bds., 5.95. Viking.

Alpha and Omega: Stories. Isaac Rosenfeld. LC 67-81722. 1966-1967. MacGibbon & Kee.

Alpha and Omega: Stories. Isaac Rosenfeld. LC 66-15913. 1966. Viking Press.

Alpha Beta. Ted Whitehead. 70p. 1982. pap. 5.95 (ISBN 0-571-09974-2). Faber & Faber.

Alpha Centauri. Robert Siegel. 1982. pap. 3.95 (ISBN 0-425-05708-9). Berkley Pub.

Alpha Centauri - or Die! Leigh Brackett. 1976. 1.50. Ace.

Alpha Centauri Symbolism. John C. Wilson. LC 79-64036. 7.95 (ISBN 0-87426-048-5). Whitmore Pub. Co.

Alpha Curse. Walter D. Lee. 1981. 8.95 (ISBN 0-8062-1578-X). Carlton.

Alpha-II. Thomas Hubschman. (Orig.). 1979. pap. 1.95 (ISBN 0-532-23266-6). Woodhill.

Alpha List. Ted Allbeury. LC 80-15257. 9.95 (ISBN 0-416-00771-6). Methuen.

Alpha List. James Anderson. LC 72-80525. 1973. 5.95 (ISBN 0-8027-5257-8). Walker.

Alpha Nine. Robert Silverberg. 1978. pap. 1.75 (ISBN 0-425-03838-6, Medallion). Berkley Pub.

Alpha Raid. Alan Scholefield. LC 76-30288. 1977. 7.95 (ISBN 0-688-03165-X). Morrow.

Alpha Raid. Alan Scholefield. LC 76-379204. 1977. 7.95. Morrow.

Alpha Six. Ed. by Robert Silverberg. 1976. pap. 1.50 (ISBN 0-425-03048-2, Medallion). Berkley Pub.

Alpha Trap. Stuart J. Byrne. LC 75-40779. 176p. 1978. pap. 1.50 (ISBN 0-89041-194-8, 3194). Major Bks.

Alpha Two. Ed. by Robert Silverberg. LC 72-191150. 1971. 0.95 (ISBN 0-345-02419-2). Ballantine Books.

Alpha 4. Ed. by Robert Silverberg. LC 74-162887. 1973. (pbk.) 1.25 (ISBN 0-345-23564-9). Ballantine Books.

Alpha 5. Ed. by Robert Silverberg. LC 74-10768. 1974. 1.25. Ballantine Books.

Alpha 6. Ed. by Robert Silverberg. (Berkley Medallion Book). 1976. (pbk.) 1.50 (ISBN 0-425-03048-2). Berkley Publishing Corp.

Alpha 7. Ed. by Robert Silverberg. (Berkley Medallion Book). 1977. 1.50 (ISBN 0-425-03530-1). Berkley Pub. Co.

Alpha 8. Ed. by Robert Silverberg. (Berkley Medallion Book). 1977. 1.50 (ISBN 0-425-03561-1). Berkley Pub. Co.

Alpha 9. Ed. by Robert Silverberg. 1978. 1.75 (ISBN 0-425-03838-6). Berkley Pub. Corp.

Alphabet Hicks see Sound of Murder.

Alphabet Hicks: A Mystery. Rex Stout. LC 41-27321. Farrar & Rinehart, Inc.

Alphabet Jackson: A Novel. Jack Olsen, pseud. LC 74-82483. 1974. 7.95 (ISBN 0-87223-418-5). Playboy Press.

Alphabet Jackson: A Novel. Jack Olsen, pseud. 1975. (pbk.) 1.75. Bantam Books.

Alphabet of Grace. Frederick Buechner. LC 73-120365. 1970. 3.95. Seabury Press.

Alphabet of Love. A Thrilling Romance, Portraying the Strange Adventures of a Beautiful Young Girl. Laura Jean Libbey. LC 11-15092. 1892. N. L. Munro.

Alphabet of Romance. Minna Bardon. LC 52-9309. 1952. Arcadia House.

Alphabetical Africa. Walter Abish. LC 73-89478. (New Directions book). 1974. 7.95 (ISBN 0-8112-0532-0) (ISBN 0-8112-0532-0). New Directions Pub. Corp.

Alphonse Daudet: An Introduction. Alphonse Daudet. Tr. by Ives, George Burnham. (Little French masterpieces... v). 1903. G. P. Putnam's Sons.

Alphonse Daudet: An Introduction. Alphonse Daudet. Tr. by Ives, George Burnham. LC 41-36682. (Little French masterpieces, ed. by Alexander Jessup v). 1909. G. P. Putnam's Sons.

Alpine Affair. Jean Francois Vignant. LC 76-111918. 1970. 4.95. Chelsea House.

Alpine Encounter. Hester Rowan. LC 79-14123. 1979. 7.95 (ISBN 0-684-16263-6). Scribner.

Alpine Fay: A Romance. Elisabeth Burstenbinder. Tr. by Wister, Annis Lee (Furness) LC 3-6869. 1897. J. B. Lippincott Company.

Alpine Fay: A Romance. Elisabeth Burstenbinder & Annis Lee Furness Wister. LC 3-6868. 1889. J. B. Lippincott Company.

Alps Assignment. Andrew Sugar. (Israeli Commandos Ser.: No. 4). 208p. (Orig.). 1975. pap. 1.25 o.p. Woodhill.

Alps Assignment. Andrew Sugar. (Israeli Commandos Ser.: No. 4). 208p. (Orig.). 1975. pap. 1.25 o.p. Manor Bks.

Alraune. Hanns Heinz Ewers. LC 75-46269. (Supernatural and Occult Fiction). 1976. 19.00 (ISBN 0-405-08130-8). Arno Press.

Alraune: Translated from the German of Hanns Heinz Ewers. Hanns Heinz Ewers. Tr. by Endore, S. Guy. LC 29-23490. 1929. The John Day Company.

Already on the Hills. Lavinia Mansel. 1968. pap. 3.50 ea. signed ed. 50 copies o.p. Anvil Pr.

Alroy. Ixion in Heaven. The Infernal Marriage. Popanilla. new ed. Benjamin Disraeli Beaconsfield. G. Routledge and Sons.

Alroy: Or, The Prince of the Captivity: "a Wondrous Tale". Benjamin Disraeli Beaconsfield. LC 76-12448. (Works of Benjamin Disraeli, Earl of Beaconsfield; v. 7). (Illus.). 1976. 16.50 (ISBN 0-404-08800-7). AMS Press.

Also Ran. Gertrude M. Robins Reynolds. LC 20-19180. George H. Doran Company.

Also the Hills. Frances Parkinson Wheeler Keyes. LC 43-16437. 1943. J. Messner, Inc.

Also the Hills. Frances Parkinson Wheeler Keyes. LC 46-43573. 1943. Jordan Publishing Co., Distributed by J. Messner, Inc.

Also the Hills. Frances Parkinson Wheeler Keyes. LC 46-3632. 1945. The Sun Dial Press.

Also the Hills. Frances Parkinson Wheeler Keyes. 1.95 (ISBN 0-671-80616-5). Pocket Books.

Alsop the Son of Adam Wyngate. Mary Sture-Vasa. LC 52-8410. 1952. McKay.

Alster Case. Rufus Hamilton Gillmore. LC 14-14921. 1914. 1.35. D. Appleton and Company.

Altar & Flame. Amal Kiran. (Illus.). 56p. (Orig.). 1975. 4.95 o.p. (ISBN 0-914182-06-4). ASPIRATION.

Altar and the Crown. Marion Niven. LC 73-175112. 1972. 7.95. University Press.

Altar Boy. S. J. Cassidy. 256p. 1982. pap. 3.25 (ISBN 0-425-05533-7). Berkley Pub.

Altar in the Fields: A Novel. Ludwig Lewisohn. LC 34-3538. 1934. Harper & Brothers.

Altar Mayor. edited by anne harrington... ed. Espina De Serna, Concha & Harrington, Anne, Ed. LC 30-122551. H. Holt and Company.

Altar of Eros. Frazer Ross. LC 72-12069. 1973. 7.95 (ISBN 0-200-04005-7). Abelard-Schuman.

Altar of Evil. Florence Stevenson. (Kitty Telefair Ser.). (O.s.i.). 192p. (Orig.). 1973. pap. 0.95 o.s.i. (AN1107, Award). Univ Pub & Dist.

Altar of Evil. Florence Stevenson. (Kitty Telefair gothic series, #3). 1973. (pbk.) 0.95. Award Books.

Altar of Honour. Ethel May Dell. LC 30-13453. 1930. G. P. Putnam's Sons.

Altar of the Dead. Henry James. 73p. 1980. Repr. of 1915 ed. lib. bdg. 20.00 (ISBN 0-8495-2748-1). Arden Lib.

Altar of the Dead. Henry James. Bd. with Beast in the Jungle; Birthplace; Private Life; Owen Wingrave; Friend of the Friends; Sir Edmund Orme; Real Right Thing; Jolly Corner; Julia Bride. LC 74-158796. (Novels & Tales of Henry James: Vol. 17). xxviii, 541p. Repr. of 1909 ed. 25.00x (ISBN 0-678-02815-X). Kelley.

Altar of the Dead & Other Stories. Henry James. 1909. 7.50 o.p. Scribner.

Altar of Venus. (Venus Bks). 1969. pap. 1.75 o.p. (V1004). Grove.

Altar-Piece: An Edwardian Mystery. Naomi Gwladys Royde-Smith. LC 39-11748. 1939. The Macmillan Company.

Altar Stairs. Charles Josiah Scofield. LC 3-29616. 1903. Christian Century Company.

Altar Steps. Compton Mackenzie. LC 22-18860. 1922. Cassell and Company, Limited.

Altar Steps. Compton Mackenzie. LC 22-20054. George H. Doran Company.

Altars of Brick. Mae Eleanor Edick Frey. LC 44-1737. 1943. Wm. B. Eerdmans Publishing Co.

Altars of the Heart. Richard Lebherz. LC 58-552958. (Evergreen books, E-98). Grove Press.

Altars of the Heart. Limited Ed. Richard Lebherz. LC 58-10959. 1957. Grove Press.

Altars to Mammon. Elizabeth Hyer Neff. LC 8-5884. 1908. F. A. Stokes Company.

Alter Ego. Patrick Watson. LC 78-21613. 1979. 10.95 (ISBN 0-670-11520-7). Viking Press.

Alter Ego. Patrick Watson. 1980. 1.95 (ISBN 0-449-24286-2). Fawcett Crest.

Alter Ego: A Hank & Biff Mystery. Mel Arrighi. 176p. 1983. 11.95 (ISBN 0-312-02144-5). St Martin.

Alteration. Kingsley Amis. LC 76-42233. 1977. 7.95 (ISBN 0-670-11522-3). Viking Press.

Altered Ego. Jerry Sohl. LC 54-6373. 1954. Rinehart.

Altered I. Ursula K. Le Guin. 1978. pap. 3.95 (ISBN 0-425-03849-1, Medallion). Berkley Pub.

Altered States. Paddy Chayefsky. 1979. pap. 2.50 (ISBN 0-553-14737-4). Bantam.

Altered States. Paddy Chayefsky. LC 77-11542. 1978. 12.45i (ISBN 0-06-010727-8, HarpT). Har-Row.

Alternate Heartbeats. Pearl White. 2.95 o.p. Vantage.

Alternating Currents. Frederik Pohl. LC 56-7235. 1956. Ballantine Books.

Alternative. Muriel Morgan Gibbon. LC 21-10025. 1921. Doubleday, Page & Company.

Alternative. Rodney Hyde-Thompson. 179p. 1972. pap. 0.95 o.p. (ISBN 0-446-65904-5). Paperback Lib.

Alternative. George Barr McCutcheon. 1909. Dodd, Mead & Company.

Alternative Lives. R. D. Skillings. (Ithaca House Fiction Ser.). 149p. 1974. 4.95 o.p. (ISBN 0-87886-032-0). Ithaca Hse.

Alternative Society. Kenneth Rexroth. LC 71-116141. 1971. pap. 2.95 o.p. (ISBN 0-8164-9174-7, Continuum Bks). Seabury.

Alternities. Ed. by David Gerrold. 1974. (pbk.) 0.95. Dell.

Altha... A M Freeman. LC 7-298. B. B. Russell.

Althea. J. M. Alonso. LC 76-2875. 1976. 11.95 (ISBN 0-914590-24-3, Dist. by Braziller); pap. 4.95 (ISBN 0-914590-25-1). Fiction Coll.

Althea. Margaret McDonell. LC 51-3969. 1951. Published for the Crime Club by Doubleday.

Althea. Madeleine Robins. (Fawcett Crest Book). 1977. 1.50 (ISBN 0-449-23268-9). Fawcett Pubns.

Althea: And Other Stories. Mildred H Copperwheat. LC 65-28420. 3.00. Dorrance.

Althea, the Divorce of Adam and Eve: A Novel. Juan M. Alonso. LC 76-2875. 11.95. (ISBN 0-914590-24-3) (ISBN 0-914590-25-1). Fiction Collective: Distributed by G. Braziller.

Althea Vernon: Or The Embroidered Handkerchief. To Which Is Added, Henrietta Harrison; or, The Blue Cotton Umbrella. Eliza Leslie. LC 7-14483. 1838. Les & Blanchard.

Althen. Grace Zaring Stone. LC 62-15727. 1962. Harper & Row.

Although He Was a Lord and Other Tales. Colonel Bridges. (On cover: Seaside library. Pocker ed., no. 484). 1885. G. Munro.

Altiora Peto: A Novel. Laurence Oliphant. (Harper's Franklin square library. Duodecimo ed.). 1883. Harper & Brothers.

Altiora Peto. A Novel. Laurence Oliphant. (On cover: Lovell's library, v. 4. no. 196). 1883. J. W. Lovell Company.

Altiora Peto. A Novel. Laurence Oliphant. (On cover: Seaside library. Pocket ed., no. 47). 1883. G. Munro.

Altiora Peto. A Novel. Laurence Oliphant. (Seaside library, v. 85, no. 1712). 1883. G. Munro.

Altogether Now! Kiskaddon Wylie. LC 32-32268. Farrar & Rinehart, Incorporated.

Alton. Irving A Greenfield. 1975. (pbk.) 1.75 (ISBN 0-380-00374-0). Avon.

Alton Locke, Tailor and Poet. Charles Kingsley. LC 7-12161. (Harper's handy series. no. 83). 1886. Harper & Brothers.

Alton Locke, Tailor and Poet. Charles Kingsley. 1910. J. M. Dent & Sons, Ltd.

Alton Locke, Tailor and Poet: An Autobiography. Charles Kingsley. LC 78-145120. 1972. (ISBN 0-403-01056-X). Scholarly Press.

Alton Locke, Tailor and Poet. An Autobiography. Charles Kingsley. LC 7-12246. 1850. Harper & Brothers.

Alton Locke, Tailor and Poet. An Autobiography. Charles Kingsley. (Seaside library. v. 61, no. 1248). 1882. G. Munro.

Alton Locke, Tailor and Poet: An Autobiography. Charles Kingsley. LC 16-7552. 1905. Macmillan and Co., Limited.

Alton Locke, Tailor and Poet. An Autobiography. new ed. Charles Kingsley & Hughes, Thomas, 1829-1898. LC 42-31598. 1886. Macmillan and Co.

Alton of Somasco: A Romance of the Great Northwest. Harold Bindloss. LC 6-10023. 1906. F. A. Stokes Company.

Alton of Somasco: A Romance of the Great Northwest. Harold Bindloss. LC 22-24747. 1915. A. L. Burt Company.

Alton-Thorpe. A Novel. Lucy N Janney. LC 41-405104. 1880. J. B. Lippincott & Co.

Altowan: Or, Incidents of Life and Adventure in the Rocky Mountains. William George Drummond Stewart. Ed. by James Watson Webb. 1846. Harper & Brothers.

Altruist. Louise De La Ramee. F. T. Neely.

Altruist. Louise De La Ramee. LC 1-30723. (On cover: The Hawthorne library). 1901. Hurst & Co.

Altruist, by Ouida Pseud.... Louise De La Ramee. LC 6-33376. 1897. F. T. Neely.

Altruria. Titus K Smith. LC 8-9631. Altruria Publishing Company.

Altrurian Romances. William Dean Howells. LC 68-29522. (His A Selected edition of W. D. Howells, v. 20). (Illus.). 1968. 15.00. Indiana University Press.

Altzar, the Pirate: A Tale of Reincarnation. Wallace Jerome Chambers. LC 44-6868. 1944. Meador Publishing Company.

Aluminum Heart. Royall Smith. LC 46-3218. 1946. Doubleday & Company, Inc.

Aluminum Man. G. C Edmondson. (Berkley medallion book). 1975. (pbk.) 0.95 (ISBN 0-425-02737-6). Berkley Pub. Co.

Aluminum Turtle. Baynard Hardwick Kendrick. LC 60-8441. (Red badge detective). 1960. Dodd, Mead.

Alumni Murders. Paul Ruse. (Orig.). 1980. pap. text ed. 1.95 o.s.i. (ISBN 0-505-51594-6). Tower Bks.

Alva Vine: Or, Art Versus Duty. Henri Gordon. LC 6-27485. The American News Company.

Alvah Bessie's Short Fictions. Alvah Cecil Bessie. LC 82-9739. 7.95 (ISBN 0-88316-546-5). Chandler & Sharp Publishers.

Alvarez Journal. Rex Burns. LC 75-6365. 1975. 6.95 (ISBN 0-06-010576-3). Harper & Row.

Alvin Fernald TV Anchorman: Skylark Ser. Clifford B. Hicks. 144p. 1982. pap. 1.95 (ISBN 0-553-15157-6, Skylark). Bantam.

Alvina Foster. Doris Bell Collier Ball. LC 44-7474. 1943. Longmans, Green and Co.

Alvira: A Story of the War of 1812. Edward Ruben. LC 11-24111. 1911. 1.35. Central Literary Publishing Co.

Alvira, the Heroine of Vesuvius. A Remarkable Sensation of the Seventeenth Century. Founded on Facts Recorded in the Acts of Canonization of St. Francis of Jerome. Augustine J O'Reilly. LC 7-23189. 1877. D. & J. Sadlier & Co.; Etc., Etc.

Always. Trevor Meldal-Johnsen. 1979. pap. 2.50 (ISBN 0-380-41897-5, 41897). Avon.

Always a Catholic. Robert Byrne. 192p. (Orig.). 1981. pap. 2.50 (ISBN 0-523-42035-8). Pinnacle Bks.

Always a River: By Drayton Mayrant Pseud. Katherine Drayton Mayrant Simons. LC 56-6004. 1956. Appleton-Century-Crofts.

Always a Sister. William Arthur Neubauer. LC 50-14691. 1950. Arcadia House.

Always Another Spring. Adelaide Humphries. LC 38-5867. 1938. Arcadia House.

Always Ask a Policeman. Seldon Truss, pseud. LC 52-12354. 1952. Published for the Crime Club by Doubleday.

Always Becoming. Sharalee Lucas. LC 78-58204. 1978. 4.95 o.p. (ISBN 0-914850-32-6); pap. 2.50 o.p. (ISBN 0-914850-36-9). Impact Tenn.

Always Farewell. Esther Houston. 4.95 o.p. Vantage.

Always Fight Back. Andrew MacKenzie. LC 55-31001. (British bloodhound, no. 101). 1955. T. V. Boardman.

Always Forever. B. Pvinsky. 3.75 o.p. Carlton.

Always Go First Class. Laurence Marks. LC 62-8470. 1962. Random House.

Always Hard. Gracie Amber. pap. 1.95 o.p. (8067). Cameo.

Always in August. Ann Head, pseud. LC 61-12529. (Signet book). 1974. (pbk.) 1.25. New American Library.
Always in August. 1st Ed. Ann Head, pseud. LC 61-125295. 1961. Doubleday.
Always in Her Heart. Rob Eden. LC 44-9905. 1944. Gramercy Publishing Company.
Always in Season. Translated from the French by Frances Frenaye. Marie Gisele Landes. LC 60-8694. half cloth, 2.95. Macmillan.
Always Is Not Forever. Helen Van Slyke. LC 76-51990. 1977. 10.00 (ISBN 0-385-11648-9). Doubleday.
Always Is Not Forever. Helen Van Wlyke. 1978. 2.25 (ISBN 0-445-04271-0). Popular Library.
Always Kill a Stranger. Robert L. Fish. (Red Mask Mystery Ser). (YA) 1966. 3.95 o.p. (ISBN 0-399-10017-2). Putnam.
Always Kill a Stranger: A Captain Jose Da Silva Novel, by Robert L. Fish. Robert L Fish. LC 67-10953. (Red mask mystery). 3.95. Putnam.
Always, Lana. Pero & Rovin. 288p. 1982. pap. 3.50 (ISBN 0-553-20805-5). Bantam.
Always Leave 'em Dying. Richard S. Prather. (Orig.). 1970. pap. 0.60 o.p. (R2261, GM). Fawcett World.
Always Leave 'em Dying. Cover Painting by Barye Phillips. Richard S Prather. LC 54-43094. (Gold medal books, 413). 1954. Fawcett Publications.
Always Murder a Friend. Margaret Scherf. LC 48-5141. 1948. Pub. for the Crime Club by Doubleday.
Always, My Love. Dorothy Fletcher. (Orig.). 1979. pap. 2.25 (ISBN 0-89083-517-9). Zebra.
Always New Frontiers. George Pattullo. LC 52-20653. 1951.
Always on Sunday. Glen Chase, pseud. (Cherry Delight Ser). (O.s.i.: No. 19). (Orig.). 1975. pap. 1.25 o.s.i. (LB253ZK, Leisure Bks). Nordon Pubns.
Always on Sunday. Glen Chase, pseud. (Cherry Delight,#20). 1975. (pbk.) 1.25. Leisure Books.
Always Room for One More. 1st Ed. Virginia Julier. LC 60-14685. 1960. Chilton Co., Book Division.
Always Say Thanks: A Novel. Hewes, Margaret. LC 64-749. Exposition Press.
Always the Boss. Victoria Gordon. (Harlequin Romances Ser.). 192p. 1982. pap. 1.50 (ISBN 0-373-02469-X). Harlequin Bks.
Always the Land. Paul Engle. LC 41-3535. Random House.
Always the Need: A Story in Verse. Joseph Joel Keith. LC 48-20602. 1948. Dierkes Press.
Always the River. Katherine Harvey Roger. LC 58-21833. Pelican Pub. Co.
Always to-Morrow. Ruby Mildred Ayres. LC 34-5595. 1934. Doubleday, Doran & Company, Inc.
Always Together, Horses & All. Constance Shepard. 3.00 o.p. Carlton.
Always with Me: A Novel. Margaret Gorman Nichols. LC 45-142111. 1945. Macrae-Smith-Company.
Always Young and Fair. Conrad Richter. LC 47-1679. 1947. A. A. Knopf.
Alyx. Joanna Russ. LC 76-10144. (Gregg Press science fiction series). 1976. 12.50. Gregg Press.
Am I Greedy If I Want More? Fables. Beatrice Chernuchin Schuman. LC 79-87905. (Illus.). 1979. 9.95 (ISBN 0-8119-0329-X). F. Fell.
Am I Not You? Malka Heifetz & Tussman. Tr. by Marcia Falk. pap. 3.00. Tree Bks.
Amabel: A Family History. Elizabeth Wormeley Latimer. LC 41-27430. 1853. G. P. Putnam & Co.
Amabel: A Military Romance. Cathae Macguire. LC 7-20000. (On cover: Rialto series, no. 54). 1893. Rand, McNally & Company.
Amabel Channice. Anne Douglas Sedgwick. LC 8-27496. 1908. The Century Co.
Amabel: Or, Amor Omnia Vincit. A Novel. Elizabeth Wormeley Latimer. LC 7-13859. (Harper's Franklin square library. no. 256). 1882. Harper & Brothers.
Amadis De Gaula. Francis William Pierce. LC 75-25907. (Twayne's world authors series; TWAS 372: Spain). (Illus.). 8.95 (ISBN 0-8057-6220-5). Twayne.
Amadis of Gaul: A Novel of Chivalry of the 14th Century Presumably First Written in Spanish. Rodriquez De Montalvo, Garci & Edwin Bray Place. LC 73-77256. (Studies in Romance Languages; 11). 15.00 (ISBN 0-8131-1304-0). University Press of Kentucky.
Amadis of Gaul: A Novel of Chivalry of the 14th Century Presumably First Written in Spanish, Vol. 2, Bks. 3 & 4. Tr. by Edwin B. Place & Herbert C. Behm. LC 73-77256. (Studies in Romance Languages: No. 11). 752p. 1975. 28.00x (ISBN 0-8131-1313-X). U Pr of Ky.
Amadu's Bundle: Fulani Tales of Love and Djinns. Malum Amadu. Ed. by Gulla Kell. LC 73-165154. (African writers series, 118). (H.E.B. paperback). 1972. (ISBN 0-435-90118-4). Heinemann Educational.
Amadu's Bundle: Fulani Tales of Love and Djinns. Malum Amadu. Ed. by Gulla Kell. LC 73-16514. (African writers series, 118). (H. E. B. paperback). 1972. (ISBN 0-435-90118-4). Heinemann Educational.
Amalia: A Romance of the Argentine. Jose Marmol & Serrano, Mary Jane (Christie) E. P. Dutton & Company.
Amalie of of So. 1 Vang. Anna O Bertinuson. LC 55-13881. 1955. Meador Pub. Co.
Amalie's Story. Julie McDonald. LC 71-128605. 1970. 6.50. Simon and Schuster.
Amanda. Paul Hyde Bonner. LC 57-12060. 1957. Scribner.
Amanda. Paula Christian. LC 81-50052. 1981. 6.95 (ISBN 0-931328-07-1). Timely Books.
Amanda. Pamela Conrad. (Orig.). 1980. pap. 2.25 o.s.i. (ISBN 0-505-51554-7). Tower Bks.
Amanda: A Daughter of the Mennonites. Anna Balmer Myers. LC 21-17620. G. W. Jacobs & Company.
Amanda, a Novel. Winthrop Bushnell Palmer. 1946. The Beechhurst Press, B. Ackerman, Incorporated.
Amanda: A Tale for the Times. William Henry Brisbane. LC 6-182793. 1848. Merrihew & Thompson, Printers.
Amanda in France. Geoffrey Bocca. (Commander Amanda). 224p. 1976. pap. 1.50 (ISBN 0-89083-170-X). Zebra.
Amanda in Spain. Geoffrey Bocca. 1975. pap. 1.50 (ISBN 0-89083-146-7). Zebra.
Amanda of the Mill: A Novel. Marie Van Vorst. LC 5-8736. 1905. Dodd, Mead & Company.
Amanda Said the Grass Was Green. Robert Manson Bunker. LC 48-57833. 1948. Swallow Press.
Amanda's Castle. George Revelli. LC 72-3662. 1972. 1.25. Bantam Books.
Amante Anglaise see English Lover.
Amaranth Club. Joseph Smith Fletcher. LC 26-1535. 1926. A. A. Knopf.
Amarilis. Christine Turner Curtis. LC 27-19413. 1927. Doubleday. Page & Co.
Amarilly in Love. Belle Kanaris Maniates. LC 17-266573. 1917. Little, Brown, and Company.
Amarilly of Clothes-Line Alley. Belle Kanaris Maniates. LC 15-3867. 1915. Little, Brown, and Company.
Amaru: A Romance of the South Seas... Robert Dean Frisbie. LC 45-5483. 1945. Doubleday, Doran & Co., Inc.
Amasque of Exile: A Novel. Martha Sherman Bacon. LC 62-19296. C. N. Potterc.
Amata: From the German of Richard Voss by Roger S. G. Boutell. Richard Voss & Boutell, Roger S. G., Tr. LC 1-23695. 1901. The Neale Publishing Company.
Amateur. Robert Litell. 1982. pap. 3.25 (ISBN 0-440-10119-0). Dell.
Amateur. Charles Gilman Norris. LC 16-6314. 1.35. George H. Doran Company.
Amateur: A Novel. Robert Littell. LC 80-29630. 12.95 (ISBN 0-671-41873-4). Simon and Schuster.
Amateur Bondage. LC 78-58421. (Illus.). Vol. 1. pap. 6.50 (ISBN 0-914646-18-4); Vol. 2. pap. 6.50 (ISBN 0-914646-27-3). Belier Pr.
Amateur Corpse. Simon Brett. LC 77-25462. 7.95 (ISBN 0-684-15571-0). Scribner.
Amateur Corpse. Simon Brett. 1980. 1.95 (ISBN 0-425-04489-0). Berkley Pub. Corp.
Amateur Cracksman. Ernest William Hornung. LC 76-98576. (Short story index reprint series). 1969. Books for Libraries Press.
Amateur Cracksman. Ernest William Hornung. LC 75-38587. 1976. (ISBN 0-8032-0869-3) (ISBN 0-8032-5836-4). University of Nebraska Press.
Amateur Cracksman. Ernest William Hornung. LC 90-11301. 1899. C. Scribner's Sons.
Amateur Cracksman. Ernest William Hornung. LC 36-29322. 1908. C. Scribner's Sons.
Amateur Crime. Anthony Berkeley Cox. LC 28-26640. 1928. Doubleday, Doran & Company, Inc.
Amateur Garden. George W. Cable. Ed. by Donald Pizer. LC 75-96501. (American Authors Ser. - Collected Works of George Washington Cable). 1970. Repr. of 1914 ed. lib. bdg. 14.00 o.s.i. (ISBN 0-512-00081-6). Garrett Pr.
Amateur Garden see Collected Works.
Amateur Gentleman. Jeffery Farnol. LC 13-35198. 1913. Little Brown, and Company.
Amateur Gentleman. Jeffery Farnol. LC 37-18291. A. L. Burt Company.
Amateur Hour: A Novel of Suspense. Robert Hardin. LC 76-46699. 1977. 7.95 (ISBN 0-672-52255-1). Bobbs-Merrill.
Amateur Inn. Albert Payson Terhune. LC 23-16042. George H. Doran Company.
Amateur Man. William Robbins Gaut. LC 18-23225. 1918. Duffield & Company.
Amateur Murderer. Carroll John Daly. LC 33-6572. 1933. I. Washburn.
Amateur People. Andree Connors. LC 76-47836. 8.95. (ISBN 0-914590-30-8) (ISBN 0-914590-31-6). Fiction Collective: Distributed by G. Braziller.
Amateur Performance. Elmer Ellsworth Vinson. LC 9-18367. Broadway Publishing Company.
Amateur Snatch. Ross Kenyon. 1974. (pbk.) 1.95 (ISBN 0-87056-402-1). Brandon Books.
Amateurs. Donald Barthelme. (Kangaroo Book). 1977. 1.95 (ISBN 0-671-81246-7). Pocket Books.
Amateurs. Leo C Kimble. LC 57-8473. 1957. Dorrance.
Amateur's Holiday: The Story of a Holiday with Stringed Instruments by the Sea. Frances Lester Warner. LC 30-294271. 1939. Houghton Mifflin Company.
Amateurs in Arms. F. J Joseph. LC 39-340397. Carrick & Evans, Inc.
Amatory Adventures of a Surgeon see Libertine Reader.
Amaury. Translated from the French of Alexandre Dumas. Alexandre Dumas. Tr. by P., E. Meurice, Paul I. E. Francois Paul. LC 6-42837. 1845. Harper & Brothers.
Amazing Adventures of an Inventor: Being a Partial Account of the Life of Alfred Ingleson, Esq., the American Nonpareil. Embracing Sketches of His Daring Exploits Under Divers Exciting Circumstances, Together with Anecdotes of His Public and Private Life from the Commencement of His Career till the Sad Catastrophe of the "Enchanted Horse." Containing Also a Short Account of the West Point Episodes; Compiled and Collated from Authentic Sources with Footnotes. Arthur Gordon Jones. LC 8-16518. 1908. The J. C. Winston Company.
Amazing Adventures of Flash Gordon, 6 vols. King Features. Incl. Vol. 1 (ISBN 0-448-17240-2); Vol. 2 (ISBN 0-448-17241-0); Vol. 3. 192p (ISBN 0-448-17242-9); Vol. 4 (ISBN 0-448-17155-4); Vol. 5 (ISBN 0-448-17208-9); Vol. 6 (ISBN 0-448-17245-3). (Flash Gordon Cartoon Ser.). 192p. 1980. pap. 1.75 ea. (Tempo). Ace Bks.
Amazing Adventures of Letitia Carberry. Mary Roberts Rinehart. LC 11-303614. 1.25. The Bobbs-Merrill Company.
Amazing Chance. Patricia Wentworth. LC 27-3375. 1927. J. B. Lippincott Company.
Amazing Dope Tales. Stephen Gaskin. (Illus.). 1980. pap. 7.00 (ISBN 0-913990-29-9). Book Pub Co.
Amazing Finale. Ida May Hill Starr. LC 27-854445. The Christopher Publishing House.
Amazing Grace. Alida Baxter. LC 80-13009. 1980. 9.95 (ISBN 0-531-09550-9). D. Elliott Publisher: Distributed by F. Watts.
Amazing Grace. Judith Davis. LC 80-26220. 4.95 (ISBN 0-453-00399-0). New American Library.
Amazing Grace. Robert Drake. LC 65-139246. 3.95. Chilton.
Amazing Grace. Robert Drake. LC 80-16873. 1980. 4.95 (ISBN 0-8028-1852-8). Eerdmans.
Amazing Grace: Who Proves That Virtue Has Its Silver Lining. Kate Trimble Sharber. LC 14-19618. The Bobbs-Merrill Company.
Amazing Guest. Gilbert Watson. LC 24-20722. 1924. Houghton Mifflin Company.
Amazing Inheritance. Frances Roberta Sterrett. LC 22-17148. 1922. D. Appleton and Company.
Amazing Interlude. Mary Roberts Rinehart. LC 18-988447. George H. Doran Company.
Amazing Journey of David Ingram: Being the Story of Three White Men, David Ingram, Richard Twide, and Richard Browne, Who Crossed, in 1568-69, Those Lands of the New World Which Later Became the United States of America. Eric Philbrook Kelly. LC 49-11292. 1949. Lippincott Co.
Amazing Marriage. George Meredith. LC 1-12783. 1895. C. Scribner's Sons.
Amazing Marriage. George Meredith. 1915. C. Scribner's Sons.
Amazing Mrs. Bonaparte. Gladys Bagg Taber. 1972. pap. 0.95 o.p. (09157). Curtis.
Amazing Mrs. Bonaparte: A Novel Based on the Life of Betsy Patterson. Harnett Thomas Kane. LC 62-7650. 1963. Doubleday.
Amazing Mrs. Pollifax. Dorothy Gilman Butters. LC 70-89067. 1970. 4.95. Doubleday.
Amazing Mrs. Pollifax. Dorothy Gilman. LC 70-89067. 1970. 5.95 o.p. (ISBN 0-385-02907-1). Doubleday.
Amazing Mrs. Pollifax. Dorothy Gilman. 1978. pap. 1.95 (ISBN 0-449-23447-9, Crest). Fawcett.
Amazing Mycroft Mysteries: Three Novels. Gerald Heard. LC 80-52557. 14.95 (ISBN 0-8149-0840-3). Vanguard Press.
Amazing Summer: A Novel. Philip Hamilton Gibbs. LC 41-14432. 1941. Doubleday, Doran and Company, Inc.
Amazing Test Match Crime. Adrian Alington. 1981. 18.95x (Pub. by Remploy England). State Mutual Bk.
Amazing Visions of the Endtime. Michael X. 1970. pap. 6.95. G Barker Bks.
Amazing Web. Harry Stephen Keeler. LC 30-5697. E. P. Dutton & Co., Inc.
Amazon. Nick Carter. (Nick Carter Ser.). (O.s.i.). (Orig.). 1969. pap. 0.75 o.s.i. (A928S, Award). Univ Pub & Dist.
Amazon. Franz Dingelstedt. Tr. by Hart, James Morgan. LC 6-36818. 1868. G. P. Putnam and Son.
Amazon. Elliot Harold Paul. LC 30-5337. 1930. H. Liveright Inc.
Amazon. Roy Bernard Sparkia. 384p. (Orig.). 1981. pap. 3.25 (ISBN 0-553-13808-1). Bantam.
Amazon: A Novel. Charles E Ross. LC 43-7233. 1943. B. Humphries, Inc.
Amazon, and Other Stories. Nikolai Semenovich Leskov. LC 76-23884. (Classics of Russian literature). (Hyperion library of world literature). 1977. 11.50. (ISBN 0-88355-495-X). Hyperion Press.
Amazon Factor. William Wise. (Raven House Mysteries). 224p. 1982. pap. 2.25 (ISBN 0-373-63036-0, Pub. by Worldwide). Harlequin Bks.
Amazon of the Desert. Petr Nikolaevich Krasnov. Tr. by Vitall, Olga. LC 29-2244. 1929. Duffield and Company.
Amazon One. Mary F Beal. LC 74-28111. 1975. 7.95 (ISBN 0-316-08466-2). Little, Brown.
Amazon Planet. Mack Reynolds. 1975. (pbk.) 1.25. Ace Books.
Amazon Slaughter. Piers Anthony & Roberto Fuentes. 1976. (pbk.) 1.25 (ISBN 0-425-03090-3). Berkley Publishing Corp.
Amazon Slaughter. Dick Stivers. (Able Team Ser.). 192p. 1983. pap. 1.95 (ISBN 0-373-61204-4, Pub. by Worldwide). Harlequin Bks.
Amazon Woman Defeated. Theodore V. Kundrat. 1978. 42.00x (ISBN 0-88020-086-3). Coach Hse.
Amazon Woman Victorious. Theodore V. Kundrat. 1978. 42.00x (ISBN 0-88020-085-5). Coach Hse.
Amazonian Republic. a facsim. reproduction / with an introd. by joel nydahl. ed. Timothy Savage. LC 76-1998. 1976. 16.00 (ISBN 0-8201-1169-4). Scholars' Facsimiles & Reprints.
Amazonian Republic: Recently Discovered in the Interior of Peru Fictitious Description. Timothy Savage. LC 8-2009. 1842. S. Colman.
Amazons. Ian Ross. (Mind Masters). (Signet Book: Vol. 4). 1976. (pbk.) 1.25. New American Library.
Amazons! Jessica A. Salmonson. (Science Fiction Ser.). (Orig.). 1979. pap. 2.25 (ISBN 0-87997-503-2, UE1503). Daw Bks.
Amazon's Angry Winds. D. S. Hevelhurst. 3.00 o.p. Carlton.
Amazons II. Ed. by Jessica A. Salmonson. 240p. 1982. pap. 2.95 (ISBN 0-87997-736-1, UE1736). DAW Bks.
Ambapali. Vimala Raina. LC 63-2214. Asia Pub. House.
Ambassador. Stephen Longstreet. LC 77-91014. 1978. 1.95 (ISBN 0-380-00938-2). Avon Books.
Ambassador. Morris L. West. LC 65-16571. bds., 4.95. Morrow.
Ambassador. Morris L West. (0097). 1966. Dell.
Ambassador. Morris L. West. LC 65-16571. 1975. (pbk.) 1.75 (ISBN 0-671-78763-2). Pocket Books.
Ambassador and the Spy. Vincent Brome. 1976. 1.75. Dell.
Ambassador and the Spy: A Novel. Vincent Brome. LC 73-84254. 1973. 6.95 (ISBN 0-517-51115-0). Crown Publishers.
Ambassador Extraordinary. Paul Hyde Bonner. LC 62-9947. 1962. Scribner.
Ambassador of Death. Jacob Franz Fishter. LC 38-219435. The Macaulay Company.
Ambassadors. Henry James. LC 58-12046. (Doubleday anchor books, A154). 1958. Doubleday.
Ambassadors. Henry James. LC 60-3458. (APremier world classic, d88). 1960. Fawcett Publications.
Ambassadors. Henry James. LC 64-101215. 1963. Printed for the Members of the Limited Editions Club of the Garamond Press.
Ambassadors. Henry James. LC 75-158800. (Scribner reprint editions). 1971. (ISBN 0-678-02821-4). A. M. Kelley.
Ambassadors. Henry James. LC 75-308111. (Penguin modern classics). 1973. (0.50, 2.75 u.s.) (ISBN 0-14-003499-4). Penguin.
Ambassadors. Henry James. Ed. by Sampson, Martin Wright. LC 30-34411. (Harper's modern classics). Harper & Brothers.
Ambassadors see Bodley Head Henry James.
Ambassadors: A Novel. Henry James. LC 3-28287. 1903. Harper & Brothers.
Ambassadors: An Authoritative Text, the Author on the Novel, Criticism. Henry James. Ed. by Stanford Patrick Rosenbaum. LC 63-8035. (Norton critical editions). 1963. W. W. Norton.
Ambassadors. Edited with an Introd. and Notes by Leon Edel. Henry James. Ed. by Leon Edel. LC 60-51326. (Riverside editions A39). 1960. Houghton Mifflin.

Ambassador's Trunk. George Barton. LC 19-80695. 1919. The Page Company.

Ambassadors. With the Author's Pref. and the Text of the New York Ed. Henry James. LC 60-6495. (Rinehart editions, 104). 1960. Rinehart.

Ambassadors 2 Vols. Henry James. 1909. 7.50 ea. o.p. Scribner.

Ambassadress. William Wriothesley. LC 13-12434. George H. Doran Company.

Amber and Jade. Aceituna Griffin. LC 28-6090. 1928. 2.00. Longmans, Green and Co., Ltd.

Amber Dust. Sanford Aday. LC 52-11934. 1952. Dorrance.

Amber Enchantment. Bonnie Drake. (Candlelight Ecstasy Ser.: No. 101). (Orig.). 1982. pap. 1.95 (ISBN 0-440-10842-X). Dell.

Amber-Eyed Man. Johanna Phillips. (Second Chance at Love Ser.: No. 30). 1982. pap. 1.75 (ISBN 0-515-06280-4). Jove Pubns.

Amber Fire. Elaine Barbieri. (Orig.). 1981. pap. 3.50 (ISBN 0-89083-848-8). Zebra.

Amber Fire. Don Tracy. LC 54-36460. (Pocket book, 1006). 1954. Pocket Books.

Amber Glints. Martha Everts Holden. LC 27-29. 1897. Rand, McNally & Company.

Amber Gods: And Other Stories. Harriet Elizabeth Prescott Spofford. LC 78-101821. (Short story index reprint series). 1969. (ISBN 0-8369-3209-9). Books for Libraries Press.

Amber Gods: And Other Stories. Harriet Elizabeth Prescott Spofford. LC 8-15524. 1863. Ticknor and Fields.

Amber Gods: And Other Stories. Harriet Elizabeth Prescott Spofford. LC 16-191605. (Leisure hour series. no. 123). 1881. H. Holt and Company.

Amber Gods & Other Stories. facsimile ed. Harriet Elizabeth Prescott Spofford. LC 78-101821. (Short Story Index Reprint Ser.). 1863. 22.00 (ISBN 0-8369-3209-9). Ayer Co.

Amber Necklace. Akira. 1974. pap. 2.00. Being Inc.

Amber Nine. John E Gardner. LC 66-15903. 1966. Viking Press.

Amber Princess. Henry Treece. LC 63-9355. 1963. Random House.

Amber Satyr. Roy Catesby Flannagan. LC 32-13057. 1932. Doubleday, Doran & Company, Inc.

Amber Star: And A Fair Half-Dozen. Mary Lowe Dickinson. LC 6-37030. 1886. Phillips & Hunt.

Amber, the Adopted. Harriet Lewis. LC 7-14371. J. S. Ogilvie and Company.

Amber Treasure. Elaine Barbieri. (Orig.). 1983. pap. 3.50 (ISBN 0-8217-1201-2). Zebra.

Amber Witch. Translated from the German. Wilhelm Meinhold. Tr. by Duff-Gordon, Lucie (Austin) LC 7-4439. (Cassell's national library. v. 3, no. 153). 1888. Cassell & Company, Limited.

Amber's Delight. Darrell Fairfield. (Amber Ser.: No. 3). (Orig.). 1982. pap. 2.25 (ISBN 0-440-10040-2). Dell.

Amber's Fancy. Darrell Fairfield. (Amber Ser.: No. 2). (Orig.). 1982. pap. 2.25 (ISBN 0-440-10043-7). Dell.

Amber's Passion. Darrell Fairfield. (Orig.). 1982. pap. 2.25 (ISBN 0-440-10193-X). Dell.

Amber's Pleasure. Darrell Fairfield. 160p. 1982. pap. 2.25 (ISBN 0-440-10195-6). Dell.

Amber's Thrill. Darrell Fairfield. (Orig.). 1982. pap. 2.25 (ISBN 0-440-10208-1). Dell.

Amberstar: An Illustrated Cosmic Odyssey. Bruce Jones. LC 79-13873. 1979. 7.95 (ISBN 0-446-97147-2). Warner Books.

Amberstone. Pamela Bennetts. LC 80-14017. 8.95 (ISBN 0-312-02156-9). St. Martin's Press.

Amberstone. Margaret James. 176p. 1980. 8.95 (ISBN 0-312-02156-9). St Martin.

Amberwell. Dorothy Emily Stevenson. LC 55-8732. 1955. Rinehart.

Amberwood. Kay Richardson. 1974. 4.95 (ISBN 0-517-51567-9). Lenox Hill Press.

Amberwood. Anne Rundle. 1974. (pbk.) 1.25. Bantam Books.

Ambiguous Adventure. Hamidou Kane. LC 63-19200. 1963. Walker.

Ambition. Constance Leonie Caroline Borgstrom Aminoff. LC 23-17722. (Her Torchlight series of Napoleonic romances. ii). 1923. E. P. Dutton & Company.

Ambition. Bernhard Guttman & Lewisohn, Ludwig, 1882- Tr. LC 30-29902. 1930. Harper & Brothers.

Ambition. Arthur Cheney Train. LC 28-6169. 1928. C. Scribner's Sons.

Ambition. Arthur Cheney Train. LC 41-40524. (His Criminal court series, v. 2). C. Scribner's Sons.

Ambition: A Novel. Charles Bonner. LC 46-7562. 1946. Coward-McCann, Inc.

Ambition of Mark Truitt. Henry Russell Miller. LC 13-10988. The Bobbs-Merrill Company.

Ambition: Or, The Launch of a Skiff Upon the Sea of Life. Maggie Roberts. 1876. Lange, Little & Co.

Ambition: Secret Passion. Joseph Epstein. 1982. pap. 4.95 (ISBN 0-14-005986-5). Penguin.

Ambition's Woman. Jeanne Jones. LC 81-9721. 312p. 1981. 11.95 (ISBN 0-87131-359-6). M Evans.

Ambitious Lady. Geoffrey Harwood. LC 33-19963. A. H. King.

Ambitious Man. Ella Wheeler Wilcox. LC 8-37030. E. A. Weeks & Company.

Ambitious Woman: A Novel. Edgar Fawcett. LC 6-38957. 1884. Houston, Mifflin and Company.

Ambitious Women. Barbara E. Wilson. LC 82-80902. (Orig.). 1982. 13.95 (ISBN 0-933216-05-X); pap. 7.95 (ISBN 0-933216-04-1). Spinsters Ink.

Amboy Dukes. Irving Shulman. LC 49-1758. (New Avon library189). 1948. Avon Pub. Co.

Amboy Dukes. Irving Shulman. LC 49-3607. (New Avon library 169). 1949. Avon Pub. Co.

Amboy Dukes. Irving Shulman. LC 47-2664. 1947. Doubleday & Company, Inc.

Ambrose. Tristram Tupper. LC 51-13970. 1951. A. Love Enterprises.

Ambrose and Eleanor: Or, The Disinherited Pair. A Tale of the Revolution. By an Officer... LC 6-509. 1834. J.A. Clussman.

Ambrose Bierce, F. A. Mitchell-Hedges, and the Crystal Skull. Sibley S Morrill. LC 72-79466. (Illus.). 1972. 3.95 (ISBN 0-9600310-3-0). Cadleon Press.

Ambrose Holt and Family. Susan Glaspell. LC 31-26724. 1931. Frederick A. Stokes Company.

Ambrosio De Letinez: Or, The First Texian Novel, Embracing a Description of the Countries Bordering on the Rio Bravo, with Incidents of the War of Independence. LC 7-24122. 1842. C. Francis & Co.

Ambrosio De Letinez: Or, The First Texian Novel, Embracing a Description of the Countries Bordering on the Rio Bravo, with Incidents of the War of Independence. Anthony Ganilh. LC 67-31532. (Illus.). 1967. Steck Co.

Ambrosio: Or, The Monk. A Romance. Matthew Gregory Lewis. LC 7-14496. 1830. J. A. Clussman.

Ambulance. Hugh Miller. LC 75-7659. 1975. 8.95. St. Martin's Press.

Ambulance Call. Elizabeth Harrison. 1974. (pbk.) 0.95 (ISBN 0-671-77734-3). Pocket Books.

Ambulance Call. Nathan A. Shiff. 1970. pap. 0.95 o.p. (ISBN 0-447-75143-3). Lancer.

Ambulance Driver. Rufus Gunn King. 1940. Meador Publishing Company.

Ambuscade. Frank O'Rourke. Bd. with Thunder on the Buckhorn. 1980. pap. 1.75 (ISBN 0-451-09490-5, Sig). NAL.

Ambush. Herbert Edward Read. LC 74-7020. (Series: Criterion Miscellany, No. 16.). 1974. (lib. bdg.) 7.95 (ISBN 0-8383-1996-3). Haskell House.

Ambush. Samuel Alexander White. LC 20-11893. 1920. Doubleday, Page & Company.

Ambush at Adams Crossing. Edwin Booth. 4.95. Avalon Books.

Ambush at Antlers Spring. Will Cook. (O.s.i.). (Orig.). pap. 0.95 o.s.i. (A280, Award). Univ Pub & Dist.

Ambush at Antler's Spring. Will Cook. (O.s.i.). 160p. 1975. pap. 1.25 o.s.i. (AQ1503, Award). Univ Pub & Dist.

Ambush at Bedrock. Gifford Paul Cheshire. LC 69-20057. (Doubleday western). 1969. 4.50. Doubleday.

Ambush at Big Creek Bridge. Donald B. Hobart. (Orig.). 1970. pap. 0.60 o.p. (0502-06113). Curtis.

Ambush at Buffalo Wallow. Cover Painting. by Walter Baumhofer. T. D. Allen, pseud. LC 57-281053. (Crest book, 152). 1956. Fawcett Publications.

Ambush at Coffin Canyon: By Bliss Lomax Pseud. Original Title: The Leather Burners. Rev. Ed. Harry Sinclair Drago. LC 54-31824. 1954. Ace Books.

Ambush at Derati Wells. Peter McCurtin. (Belmont Tower Book). 1977. 1.50 (ISBN 0-505-51153-3). Tower Pubns.

Ambush at Jubilo Junction. Leslie Charles Ernenwein. LC 50-5943. (Dutton Diamond D western). 1950. Dutton.

Ambush at Junction Rock. Robert MacLeod, pseud. 1979. pap. 1.75 (ISBN 0-449-14303-1, GM). Fawcett.

Ambush at Soda Creek. Lewis B Patten. LC 75-25441. 1976. 5.95 (ISBN 0-385-11418-4). Doubleday.

Ambush at Soda Creek. Lewis B Patten. (Signet Book). 1977. 1.25 (ISBN 0-451-07465-3). New American Library.

Ambush at Soda Creek. Lewis B Patten. LC 78-24113. 1979. 10.50 (ISBN 0-8161-6645-5). G. K. Hall.

Ambush at Torture Canyon. Max Brand. LC 76-37949. (Adult Ser.). 1972. Repr. lib. bdg. 8.95 o.p. (ISBN 0-8161-6001-5, Large Print Bks). G K Hall.

Ambush at Torture Canyon. Max Brand. 1981. pap. 1.95 (ISBN 0-671-41557-3). PB.

Ambush at Torture Canyon. Max Brand. 1971. 4.95 o.p. (ISBN 0-396-06324-1). Dodd.

Ambush at Torture Canyon. Frederick Faust. LC 78-158344. 1971. 4.95 (ISBN 0-396-06324-1). Dodd, Mead.

Ambush at Torture Canyon. Frederick Faust. LC 76-37949. (Dodd, Mead silver star westerns). 1971. 8.95 (ISBN 0-8161-6001-5). G. K. Hall.

Ambush at Torture Canyon. Frederick Faust. 1973. 0.75. Pocket Books.

Ambush for Anatol. John Sherwood. LC 52-11620. 1952. Published for the Crime Club by Doubleday.

Ambush for the Hunter. Frederick Lawrence Green. LC 53-6908. 1953. Random House.

Ambush House. Rudolf Kagey. LC 43-5779. 1943. Harcourt, Brace and Company.

Ambush Murders. Ben Bradlee, Jr. 1982. pap. 3.50 (ISBN 0-425-04946-9). Berkley Pub.

Ambush Planet. E. Rew Bixby. 1979. pap. 1.75 (ISBN 0-89041-238-3, 3238). Major Bks.

Ambush Range. Don P. Jenison. 224p. (Orig.). 1980. pap. 1.95 (ISBN 0-89083-696-5). Zebra.

Ambush Rider. Hal George Evarts. 1973. (pbk.) 0.75 (ISBN 0-671-75788-1). Pocket Books.

Ambush Trail. Lee Floren. (O.s.i.). 1976. pap. 0.95 o.s.i. (BT50922). Belmont-Tower.

Ambush Trail: By Lee Thomas Pseud. Lee Floren. LC 52-6505. 1952. Arcadia House.

Ambushers. Donald Hamilton. 1978. pap. 1.95 (ISBN 0-449-14102-0, GM). Fawcett.

Ambushers. Donald Hamilton. (Matt Helm Ser). 1971. pap. 0.75 o.p. (T2249, GM). Fawcett World.

Ame Enchantee, 3 Vols. Romain Rolland. 1963-64. pocket ed. 5.25 o.p. French & Eur.

Amedee see Three Plays.

Amedee's Son: By Harry James Smith. Harry James Smith. LC 8-23927. 1908. Houghton Mifflin Company.

Amedeo. 1st Ed. Daphne Barclay. LC 58-10824. 1958. Dutton.

Amelia. Megan Daniel. 1980. pap. 1.75 (ISBN 0-451-09487-5, E9487, Sig). NAL.

Amelia. Henry Fielding. (Half-title: Everyman's library, ed. by Ernest Rhys. Fiction no. 852 and 853). 1930. J. M. Dent & Sons, Ltd.

Amelia. Henry Fielding & Cruikshank, George, 1792-1878, Illus. LC 12-26507. (On cover: Bohn's libraries). 1892. G. Bell & Sons.

Amelia, a Mid-Nineteenth Century Novel of Kauai. Juliet R. Wichman. LC 79-21726. 1979. pap. 5.95. Kauai Museum.

Amelia: Or, the Faithless Briton. LC 72-78638. 1798. Repr. 9.00 o.p. (ISBN 0-403-03301-2). Somerset Pub.

Amelia, or the Faithless Briton. Ed. by Joseph V. Ridgely. LC 72-93587. (American Fiction Ser). (Illus.). 1970. lib. bdg. 7.50 o.s.i. (ISBN 0-512-00012-3). Garrett Pr.

Amelia: Or, The Faithless Briton. An Original American Novel, Founded Upon Recent Facts. To Which Is Added, Amelia; or, Malevolence Defeated; and Miss Seward's Monody on Major Andre. Anna Seward. LC 6-507. 1798. W. Spotswood, and C.P. Wayne.

Amelia Rankin: A Novel. 1st Ed. Charles O Locke. LC 59-5621. 1959. Norton.

Amelie in France. Maurice Francis Egan. LC 12-27189. H. L. Kilner & Co.

Amelie in Love. Henri Troyat. LC 56-7494. (Seed and the Fruit, v. 1). 1974. (pbk.) 1.25 (ISBN 0-671-78424-2). Pocket Books.

Ameline Du Bourg. A Tale of the Huguenots. Alfred Louis Auguste Franklin & D. J. H., Tr. LC 6-43162. (On cover: Lovell's library, v. 3, no. 122). J. W. Lovell Company.

AMEPIKH, AMEPIKH. Title Transliterated: Amerike, Amerike. Introd. by S. N. Behrman. Elia Kazan. LC 66-29732. (Sightsaver ser.). 1966. pap., 4.95. LargePrint Pubns.

Amergin: An Enigma of the Forest. Sven Berlin. LC 78-314412. (Illus.). 10.95 (ISBN 0-7153-7447-8). David & Charles.

America, America. Elia Kazan. 1974. (pbk.) 1.95. Stein and Day.

America, America. With an Introd. by S. N. Behrman. Elia Kazan. LC 62-200962. Stein and Day.

America Betrayed: Save the Nation. Albert D Nelson. LC 40-31186. 1936. Suttonhouse.

America Bewitched. Daniel Logan. 192p. 1975. pap. 1.50 (ISBN 0-532-15174-7). Woodhill.

America: Glorious and Chaotic Land: Charles Sealsfield Discovers the Young United States. An Account of Our Post-Revolutionary Ancestors by a Contemporary. Emil Leopold Jordan & Charles Sealsfield. LC 69-14473. 1969. 7.95. Prentice-Hall.

America, I Like You. P. G. Wodehouse. (O.S.I.). 1956. 3.50 o.s.i. (ISBN 0-671-01940-6). S&S.

America II: Special Issue 21. Robin White et al. pap. 1.00 o.p. The Smith.

America in the Last Days. Carrie Faye Bridgwater. LC 64-18971. 1964. Christopher Pub. House.

America Made Me. Hans Koning. LC 82-19715. 160p. 1983. 14.95 (ISBN 0-938410-09-1); pap. 8.95 (ISBN 0-938410-08-3). Thunder's Mouth.

America, My Wilderness. Frederic Prokosch. LC 73-182107. 1972. 6.95 (ISBN 0-374-10388-7). Farrar, Straus & Giroux.

America: Or, The Sacrifice, a Romance of the American Revolution. Robert William Chambers. LC 24-8882. Grosset & Dunlap.

America Returns. Anthony York. LC 30-14667. Renaissance Publishers.

America the Beautiful. Ross Drago. (Orig.). 1979. pap. 3.95 o.p. (ISBN 0-89581-003-4). Lancaster-Miller.

America the Beautiful. Ross Drago. (Orig.). 1979. pap. 3.95 o.p. (ISBN 0-89581-003-4). Lancaster-Miller.

America: the Flame of Life. 1st Ed. Carl F Mayer. LC 53-5871. 1952. Pageant Press.

America Through the Short Story. Ed. by Nathan Bryllion Fagin. LC 36-8019. 1936. Little, Brown, and Company.

America, with Love. Kathleen Winson. LC 55-10097. 1957. Putnam.

America: With Love. Kathleen Winsor. LC 55-10097. 1957. Putnam.

Americaca. Tomas Fuentez. write for info o.p. (Pub. by Black Dragon Bks). Panjandrum Pr.

American. Mary C Johnson Dillon. LC 19-4847. 1919. 1.50. The Century Co.

American. Louis Dodge. LC 34-33269. J. Messner, Inc.

American. Howard Melvin Fast. 320p. 1981. pap. 2.75 (ISBN 0-441-01741-X). Ace Bks.

American. Howard Melvin Fast. 1970. pap. 0.95 o.p. (ISBN 0-448-05328-4, Tempo). G&D.

American. Belle Willey Gue. LC 21-13501. R. G. Badger.

American. Henry James. (Classics ser., CL176). 1968. Airmont.

American. Henry James. LC 79-158781. (Scribner reprint editions). 1976. (ISBN 0-678-02802-8). A. M. Kelley.

American. Henry James. LC 71-117437. (Crowell critical library). 1972. (ISBN 0-690-05887-X). Crowell.

American. Henry James. LC 7-7560. 1877. J. R. Osgood and Company.

American. Henry James. LC 4-15460. Mifflin and Company.

American. Henry James & William C Spengemann. LC 81-10714. (Penguin American Library). 1981. 3.95 (ISBN 0-14-039009-X). Penguin.

American see Four Selected Novels of Henry James.

American: A Middle Western Legend. Howard Melvin Fast. LC 46-252202. 1945. Duell, Sloan and Pearce.

American: A Novel. Leslie Waller. LC 78-105591. 1970. 6.95. Putnam.

American Accent: Fourteen Stories by Authors Associated with the Bread Loaf Writers' Conference, with a Foreword by Theodore Morrison. Ed. by Elizabeth Abell. Bread Loaf Writers'conference, Bread Loaf, Vt. LC 54-8215. (Ballantine books, 75). 1954. Ballantine Books.

American Acres. Louise Redfield Peattie. LC 36-185561. 1936. G. P. Putnam's Sons.

American Adventurer. Don Maguire. LC 7-20127. 1879. Trow's Printing and Bookbinding Co.

American Alarm Clock. Glen Wright. LC 72-195880. 1972. 5.95 (ISBN 0-533-00407-1). Vantage Press.

American Ambassador. Lawrence Byrne. LC 17-13818. 1917. 1.35. C. Scribner's Sons.

American Ambassador: A Novel. William Albert Lewis. (Pinkerton series, no. 20). 1894. Laird & Lee.

American and Arabian Love: By Wilfred J. Angers. Wilfred J Angers. LC 28-24702. The Stratford Company.

American Atlas: A Novel. Daniel F. Gerber. LC 73-62. 1973. 5.95 (ISBN 0-13-023879-1). Prentice-Hall.

American: Authoritative Text, Backgrounds and Sources, Criticism. Henry James & James W Tuttleton. LC 77-27622. (Norton critical edition). 11.95 (ISBN 0-393-04476-9). Norton.

American Authors of the East. LC 15-21863. 1893. Belford Publishing Company.

American Authors of the South. LC 15-21862. 1893. Belford Publishing Company.

American Authors of the West. LC 15-128642. 1893. Belford Publishing Company.

American Avenger, No. 3: The Devil's Finger. Robert Emmett. 1982. pap. 2.50 (ISBN 0-451-11458-2, AE1458, Sig). NAL.

American Avenger, No. 5: Trojan Horses. Robert Emmett. 208p. 1982. pap. 2.50 (ISBN 0-451-11825-1, Sig). NAL.

American Baby Abroad: How He Played Cupid to a Kentucky Beauty. Lula Cox Crewdson. LC 10-11641. 1910. 1.50. Little, Brown, and Company.

American Baron. A Novel. James De Mille. LC 9-8346. 1872. Harper & Brothers.

American Baroque. Lamar Herrin. 336p. 1981. pap. 3.50 (ISBN 0-380-77362-7, 77362, Bard). Avon.

American Beauty. Mary Ellin Barrett. LC 80-15142. 10.95 (ISBN 0-525-05285-2). E. P. Dutton.

American Beauty. Edna Ferber. LC 31-28323. 1931. Doubleday, Doran & Company, Inc.

American Beauty. Edna Ferber. LC 31-323459. 1931. Doubleday, Doran & Company, Inc.

American Beauty. Edna Ferber. (Fawcett crest book). 1974. (pbk.) 0.95. Fawcett.

American Beauty. Arthur Meeker. LC 29-359619. 1929. Covici, Friede.

American Beauty: Novel of Two Centuries in the Connecticut Valley. Edna Ferber. 3.95 o.s.i. (ISBN 0-385-04014-8). Doubleday.

American Bee: A Collection of Entertaining Histories, Selected from Different Authors, and Calculated for Amusement and Instructions. the 1st ed. Prentiss, Charles, 1774-1830, Pub. LC 5-42993. 1799. Printed by and for Charles Prentiss.

American Bicentennial Series. John W. Jakes. LC 75-323546. 1.75. Pyramid Books.

American Boys. Steven Phillip Smith. LC 75-305666. 1975. 8.95 (ISBN 0-399-11462-9). Putnam.

American Bred. Franken Meloney. LC 41-2209. Farrar & Rinehart, Inc.

American Captain. Edison Marshall. LC 54-11068. 1954. Farrar, Straus & Young.

American Cardinal. A Novel. John McDowell Leavitt. LC 7-18762. 1871. Dodd & Mead.

American Casanova. Roland Everhard. 192p. pap. 1.95 o.p. (6086). Brandon.

American Casualty. Roy Graves. LC 66-25403. 1967. F. Fell.

American Cavalier: A Novel. William Cadwalader Hudson. LC 7-5650. (On cover: Cassell's Union square library. no. 28). 1897. The Cassell Publishing Co.

American Cavalryman: A Liberian Romance. Henry Francis Downing. LC 78-164784. 1973. 15.00 (ISBN 0-404-00148-3). AMS Press.

American Cavalryman: A Liberian Romance. Henry Francis Downing. LC 75-76100. 1969. McGrath Pub. Co.

American Cavalryman: A Liberian Romance. Henry Francis Downing. LC 17-28079. 1917. The Neale Publishing Company.

American Children. Ann Birstein. LC 79-7665. 1980. 10.00 (ISBN 0-385-15264-7). Doubleday.

American Chrome: A Novel. Edwin Gilbert. LC 65-10853. 5.95. Putnam.

American Citizen a Novel. Madeleine Lucette Ryley. LC 8-1360. 1898. G. W. Dillingham Co.

American City Novel. Blanche H. Gelfant. 1970. Repr. of 1954 ed. 8.95 o.p. (ISBN 0-8061-0293-4). U of Okla Pr.

American Claimant. Samuel Langhorne Clemens. 1981. Repr. lib. bdg. 39.00 (ISBN 0-403-00103-X). Scholarly.

American Claimant. Mark Twain. LC 72-144588. (Illus.). Repr. of 1897 ed. 27.50 (ISBN 0-404-01576-X). AMS Pr.

American Claimant: And Other Stories and Sketches. Samuel Langhorne Clemens. LC 6-21356. 1897. Harper & Brothers.

American Claimant, and Other Stories and Sketches. Samuel Langhorne Clemens. LC 28-4845. 1917. Harper & Brothers.

American Coin: A Novel ... LC 5-42994. (On cover: Appletons' town and country library, no. 31). 1889. D. Appleton and Company.

American Colonel: A Story of Thrilling Times During the Revolution and the Great Rivalry of Aaron Burr and Alexander Hamilton. Jeremiah Clemens. LC 2951. 1900. Wolfe Publishing Co.

American Colony. Charles Brackett. LC 29-16596. 1929. H. Liveright.

American Contemporary. Curtis Zahn. LC 76-369859. 1968. Penguin.

American Contemporary: Short Stories. Curtis Zahn. LC 63-18632. (New Directions-San Francisco review paperbook original, ND139). 1963. New Directions.

American County Fair. Sherwood Anderson. LC 31-8318. 1930. Random House.

American Cowboy. Will James. LC 42-7197. 1942. C. Scribner's Sons.

American Cowboy. Will James. LC 80-26133. (Gregg Press Western Fiction Series). 1981. 13.95 (ISBN 0-8398-2681-8). Gregg Press.

American Cruiser: A Tale of the Last War. George Little. LC 7-16064. 1847. W. J. Reynolds and Company, and Waite, Peirce, and Co.

American Cruiser's Own Book. George Little. LC 7-16063. 1859. J. B. Smith & Co.

American Dad. Tama Janowitz. LC 80-24327. 11.95 (ISBN 0-399-12585-X). Putnam.

American Detective in Russia: Or, "Piping a Conspiracy.". Harlan Fage Halsey. LC 7-1198. (On cover: The calumet series, no. 13). G. Munro.

American Detective Stories. Maurice Richardson. Repr. of 1943 ed. 10.00 (ISBN 0-8414-7433-8). Folcroft.

American Detective Stories. Ed. by Carolyn Wells. LC 27-25421. 1927. Oxford University Press.

American Diary of a Japanese Girl. Yone Noguchi. LC 2-23992. 1902. Frederick A. Stokes Company.

American Disinherited: A Profile in Fiction. Ed. by Abe C. Ravitz. LC 79-103041. 1970. Dickenson Pub. Co.

American Divorce Novel. J. H. Barnett. 59.95 (ISBN 0-87968-597-2). Gordon Pr.

American Don Juan: Or, The Story of a Fashionable Preacher. E P Buffett. (On cover: Columbian library, no. 8). 1890. Columbia Publishing Company.

American Dream: A Novel. Michael Foster. LC 37-27398. 1937. W. Morrow & Company.

American Dream & Zoo Story. Edward Albee. pap. 1.95 (ISBN 0-451-11235-0, AJ1235, Sig). NAL.

American Dream Girl. James Thomas Farrell. LC 50-10661. 1950. Vanguard Press.

American Duchess. Princess De Bourg. LC 6-32896. 1896. G. W. Dillingham Co.

American Duchess. Joan Wolf. 1982. pap. 2.25 (ISBN 0-451-11918-5, AE1918, Sig). NAL.

American Duchess: Or, Cortlandt Laster, Capitalist. Harley Deen. (On cover: Library of choice fiction, no. 6). 1896. Laird & Lee.

American Duchesse. Helen Lewis Croy. LC 32-33155. 1932. R. M. McBride & Company.

American Earth. Erskine Caldwell. LC 51-2726. (uniform edition of the works of Erskine Caldwell). 1950. Duell, Sloan and Pearce.

American Earth. Erskine Caldwell. LC 31-109767. 1931. C. Scribner's Sons.

American Earthquake: A Documentary of the Twenties & Thirties. Edmund Wilson. 1979. pap. 7.95 (ISBN 0-374-51507-7). FS&G.

American Emperor: A Novel. William Salisbury. LC 13-8756. 1913. The Tabard Inn Press.

American Emperor: The Story of the Fourth Empire of France. Louis Tracy. LC 8-29808. 1897. G. P. Putnam's Sons.

American Epic - Virgil - a Story of Love. Daniel Jones. 3.95 o.p. Vantage.

American Epic: Virgil - A Story of Love. Daniel M. Jones. 73p. 1981. 6.95 (ISBN 0-533-01646-0). Vantage.

American Evening Entertainments: Or, Tales of City and Country Life. Jane C Campbell. LC 6-21480. 1856. J. C. Derby.

American Experience: Fiction. Ed. by Marjorie Wescott Barrows & Clarence W. Wachner. LC 68-2751. (Macmillan literary heritage). 1968. Macmillan.

American Experience (The): Fiction: Ed. by Marjorie Wescott Barrows, Others. Ed. by Marjorie Wescott Barrows & Clarence W. Wachner. LC 68-2751. (Macmillan lit. heritage). 1968. pap., 3.00. Macmillan.

American Family. Faith Baldwin. 390p. Repr. of 1934 ed. lib. bdg. 15.40x (ISBN 0-88411-629-8). Amereon Ltd.

American Family. Faith Baldwin. 1972. 6.95 o.p. (ISBN 0-03-001016-0). HR&W.

American Family. new ed. Faith Baldwin Cuthrell. LC 72-78110. 1972. 6.95. Holt, Rinehart and Winston.

American Family. Faith Baldwin Cuthrell. LC 35-44693. Farrar & Rinehart, Incorporated.

American Family: A Novel of to-Day. Henry Kitchell Webster. LC 18-188822. The Bobbs-Merrill Company.

American Family Robinson: Or, The Adventures of a Family Lost in the Great Desert of the West. David W Belisle. LC 6-9421. 1854. W. P. Hazard.

American Fantasy & Science Fiction. Ed. by Marshall Tymn. LC 76-55151. 1979. 14.95x (ISBN 0-913960-23-3); pap. 6.95xx (ISBN 0-913960-15-2). Fax Collect.

American Father. William Reynolds. (gr. 12up). 1980. pap. 2.50 (ISBN 0-671-82776-6). PB.

American Faust. Edward Antonio Paulton. LC 7-33781. (On cover: The Belford American novel series. no. 14). Belford Company.

American Fiction: Edgar Allan Poe, Edward Everett Hale, Washington Irving, Francis Bret Harte, Nathaniel Hawthorne, Mark Twain Pseud.... Poe. Edgar Allan et al. LC 17-17433. (Harvard Classics Shelf of Fiction: 10). P. F. Collier & Son.

American Fiction Series, 47 Vols. Ed. by Joseph V. Ridgely. 1774-1860. Set. lib. bdg. 756.27 o.s.i. (ISBN 0-512-00009-3). Garrett Pr.

American Flaggs. Kathleen Thompson Norris. LC 36-19172. 1936. Doubleday, Doran & Co., Inc.

American Flaggs. Kathleen Thompson Norris. LC 37-20210. 1937. The Sun Dial Press, Inc.

American Folk and Fairy Tales. Rachel Lyman Field. LC 20-28017. 1929. C. Scribner's Sons.

American Genesis. Jeffrey Goodman. 1982. pap. 2.95 (ISBN 0-425-05173-0). Berkley Pub.

American Ghost Stories. Ed. by C. Armitage Harper. LC 28-22958. 1928. Houghton Mifflin Company.

American Gigolo. Timothy Harris & Paul Schrader. LC 78-23736. 8.95 (ISBN 0-440-00218-4). Delacorte Press.

American Girl. Patricia Dizenzo. 1.25 (ISBN 0-380-00863-7). Avon.

American Girl. Patricia Dizenzo. LC 76-138871. 1971. 4.95 (ISBN 0-03-085968-9). Holt, Rinehart & Winston.

American Girl. Tiffany Thayer. LC 33-6258. C. Kendall.

American Girl. John Roberts Tunis. LC 30-192769. 1930. Brewer & Warren Inc.

American Girl and Her Four Years in a Boys' College. Olive San Louis Anderson. LC 6-2455. 1878. D. Appleton and Company.

American Girl at the Durbar. Shelland Bradley. LC 12-230711. 1912. 1.25. John Lane.

American Girl in Korea. Annie Maria Barnes. LC 5-13203. 1905. The Penn Publishing Company.

American Girl in London. Sara Jeanette Duncan Cotes. LC 6-29024. 1891. D. Appleton and Company.

American Girl in London. Sara Jeannette Duncan Cotes. 1908. D. Appleton and Company.

American Girl in Paris. A Novel of Affection and Fashionable Life. From the French of Alexander Dumas the Younger. Alexandre Dumas. Tr. by Williams, Henry Llewellyn, Jr. LC 6-42314. (On cover: The optimus series, no. 8). 1891. Donohue, Henneberry & Co.

American Gold. Ernest Seeman. LC 77-25750. 8.95 (ISBN 0-8037-0349-X). Dial Press.

American Gold. Ernest Seeman. 1979. 2.50 (ISBN 0-380-43679-5). Avon Books.

American Gold. Ernest Seeman. LC 78-24145. 1978. 15.60 (ISBN 0-8161-6637-4). G. K. Hall.

American Gothic. Robert Bloch. LC 73-15485. (Simon and Schuster novel of suspense). 1974. 6.95 (ISBN 0-671-21691-0). Simon and Schuster.

American Government Through Science Fiction. Ed. by Joseph D. Olander. LC 74-5711. 1974-1975. 5.95 (ISBN 0-528-65902-2). Rand McNally College Pub. Co.

American Graffiti. W. Huyck et al. LC 73-17640. 1979. pap. 1.95 (ISBN 0-345-28408-9). Ballantine.

American Gun Mystery. Ellery Queen. 308p. 1976. lib. bdg. 16.95x (ISBN 0-89966-152-1). Buccaneer Bks.

American Gun Mystery Death at the Rodeo: A Problem in Deduction. Ellery Queen, pseud. 1933. Frederick A. Stokes Company.

American Gun Mystery Death at the Rodeo: A Problem in Deduction. Ellery Queen, pseud. LC 40-1154. 1940. Triangle Books.

American Gun Mystery: Death at the Rodeo. Ellery Queen. 1975. (pbk.) 1.25 (ISBN 0-345-24363-3). Ballantine Books.

American Heiress. Dorothy Eden. LC 80-15256. 11.95 (ISBN 0-698-11058-7). Coward, McCann & Geoghegan.

American Heiress. Dorothy Eden. LC 81-922. 1981. 13.95 (ISBN 0-8161-3232-1). G.K. Hall.

American Heritage in Song. Alta Brown Chittenden. LC 73-151012. (Hearthstone book). 1972. 3.75. Carlton Press.

American Hero. Francis Woolsey Bronson. LC 33-19394. Farrar & Rinehart, Inc.

American Historical Novel Series One, 71 Vols. Ed. by Clarence Gohdes. 1941. Set. lib. bdg. 725.00 o.s.i. (ISBN 0-512-00884-1). Garrett Pr.

American House. Virginia Chase Perkins. LC 44-40012. 1944. World Book Company, Distributed by Duell, Sloan and Pearce.

American Hunger. Richard Wright. (Perennial library). 1979. 1.95 (ISBN 0-06-080464-5). Harper & Row.

American in New York: A Novel of to-Day. Opie Percival Read. LC 5-24182. 1905. Thompson & Thomas.

American in Paris: A Biographical Novel of the Franco-Prussian War; the Siege and Commune of Paris, from an American Stand-Point. Eugene Coleman Savidge. LC 8-2015. 1896. J. B. Lippincott Company.

American Indian Life. Ed. by Elsie C. Parsons. LC 22-16158. (Illus.). viii, 419p. 1967. 24.95x (ISBN 0-8032-3651-4); pap. 4.50 (ISBN 0-8032-5148-3, BB 364, Bison). U of Nebr Pr.

American Indian Reader: Literature. Ed. by Jeannette Henry. LC 72-86873. 248p. 1973. pap. 4.50 (ISBN 0-913436-11-9). Indian Hist Pr.

American L'assommoir." A Parody on Zola's "L'assommoir.". Joseph Sydney. LC 8-25589. 1879. T. B. Peterson & Brothers.

American Legend: A Treasury of Our Country's Yesterdays. Ed. by Robert Van Gelder. Van Gelder, Dorothy (Scarborough) Joint Comp. LC 46-4573. 1946. D. Appleton-Century Company, Inc.

American Life: Shtetl Style: Stories & Sketches. Elkanah Schwartz. LC 67-18087. 1967. 5.95. J. David.

American Local-Color Stories. Ed. by Harry Redcay Warfel. Orians, George Harrison, 1809- Joint Ed. LC 41-17552. American Book Company.

American Local-Color Stories. Ed. by Harry Redcay Warfel & George Harrison Orians. LC 72-127599. 1970. Cooper Square Publishers.

American Made. Shylah Boyd. LC 75-5624. 1975. 10.00. Farrar, Straus and Giroux.

American Made. Shylah Boyd. 1976. 1.95. Fawcett Publications.

American Madonna: A Story of Love. by mary ives todd... ed. Mary Van Lennup Ives Todd. LC 9-1583. 1908. The Binghamton Book Mfg., Co.

American Marquis. George Weston. LC 30-29824. 1930. Dodd, Mead & Company.

American Marquis: Or, Detective for Vengeance. A Story of a Masked Bride and a Husband's Quest. George Weston. (On cover: The secret service series, no. 21). 1889. Street & Smith.

American Marriage. Hilary Masters. LC 69-11104. 1969. Macmillan.

American Medley: Stories from American Prefaces. American Prefaces. Ed. by Schramm, Wilbur Lang. LC 38-207982. 1937. The Prairie Press.

American Men at Arms. Ed. by Francis Van Wyck Mason. LC 64-25729. (Illus.). 1964. Little, Brown.

American Men at Arms. F. Van Wyck Mason. 1964. 6.95 o.p. Little.

American Men at Arms: Selected, Introd. by F. Van Wyck Mason. Ed. by Francis Van Wyck Mason. (95018). 1966. Pocket Bks.

American Mischief: A Novel. Alan Lelchuk. LC 74-179792. 1973. 8.95 (ISBN 0-374-10421-2). Farrar, Straus and Giroux.

American Mischief: A Novel. Alan Lelchuk. (Signet book). 1974. (pbk.) 2.25. New American Library.

American Mother, & Other Stories. Mary Lanman Underwood. LC 8-32289. 1898. Van Vechten and Ellis.

American Mystery Stories. Ed. by Carolyn Wells. LC 27-254197. 1927. Oxford University Press.

American Nabob: A Novel. Holmes Moss Alexander. LC 39-174102. 1939. Harper and Brothers.

American Negro Short Stories. Ed. by John Henrik Clarke. LC 66-23863. 1966. Hill and Wang.

American Neo-Classic Sculpture: The Marble Resurrection. William H. Gerdts. (Illus.). 1973. 15.95 o.p. (ISBN 0-670-12002-2, Studio). Viking Pr.

American Nights. William Kimberly Palmer & Fanos, Ernest. LC 19-19243. The New Era Publishing Co.

American Nights' Entertainment: Compiled from Pencilings of a United States Senator: Entitle. A Winter in the Federal City... Talbot Greene. LC 6-45567. 1860. W. A. Sparks & Co., Printers.

American Nobility. Helen Favre de Couvelin. LC 6-29003. 1897. C. Scribner's Sons.

American Nobility: From the French of Pierre De Coulevain Pseud. LC 13-47639. E. P. Dutton & Company.

American Nobleman: A Story of the Canaan Wilderness. William Armstrong. LC 6-2437. F. J. Schulte & Company.

American Nobleman: A Story of the Canaan Wilderness. William Armstrong. 1896. Rand, McNally & Company.

American Novels and Stories of Henry James. Henry James & Matthiessen, Francis Otto, 1902- Ed. LC 47-1392. 1947. A. A. Knopf.

American Omnibus. Georges Simenon. LC 67-16084. 1967. Harcourt, Brace & World.

American Peasant, a Timely Allegory. Thomas H Tibbles & Peattie, Mrs. Elia (Wilkinson) 1862- Joint Author. LC 8-19801. (On cover: The economic library, v. 3, no. 6). 1892. Vincent Bros. Publishing Company.

American Peasant. A Timely Allegory. Thomas H Tibbles & Peattie, Mrs. Elia (Wilkinson) 1862- Joint Author. LC 8-19802. (On cover: The Ariel library, no. 20A). 1892. F. J. Schulte & Company.

American Peeress. Hobart Chatfield Chatfield-Taylor. LC 6-234343. 1894. A. C. McClurg and Company.

American Pep: A Tale of America's Efficiency. A Stone. LC 18-207844. (R. J. S. mystery stories). 1918. The Robert J. Shores Corporation.

American Pescadero. Sherman Welden. 1973. pap. 4.95 (ISBN 0-915572-49-4, Pub by Black Dragon Bks). Panjandrum.

American Politican: A Novel. Francis Marion Crawford. LC 73-111088. 1970. AMS Press.

American Politician. Francis Marion Crawford. LC 32-33609. 1893. Macmillan and Co.

American Politician: A Novel. Francis Marion Crawford. LC 74-8186. Scholarly Press.

American Politician: A Novel. Francis Marion Crawford. LC 3-223697. 1885. Houghton, Mifin and Company.

American POWs. Samuel Kim. LC 77-90036. 9.75 (ISBN 0-8283-1708-9). Branden Press.

American Princess. William Tillinghast Eldridge. 1909. 1.50. Sturgis & Walton Company.

American Princess. Edward Kuhn, Jr. LC 76-139635. (O.s.i.). 1971. 7.95 o.s.i. (ISBN 0-671-20875-6). S&S.

American Princess. William Irwin MacIntyre. LC 26-18511. The Christopher Publishing House.

American Princess: A Novel. Edward Kuhn, Jr. LC 76-139635. 1971. 7.95 (ISBN 0-671-20875-6). Simon and Schuster.

American Prisoner: A Romance of the West Country. Eden Phillpotts. 1903. The Macmillan Company.

American Prisoner: A Romance of the West Country. Eden Phillpotts. LC 4-1644. 1904. The Macmillan Company.

American Prophet. Gerald Green. LC 76-18348. 1977. 8.95 (ISBN 0-385-03709-0). Doubleday.

American Push. Edgar Fawcett. (On Cover: The Ariel library, no. 24). 1892. F. J. Schulte & Company.

American Quartet: A Novel. Warren Adler. LC 81-70030. 1982. 13.95 (ISBN 0-87795-365-1). Arbor House.

American Quartet: A Novel about the Mortal Link between Four Marked Presidents of the United States. Warren Adler. LC 81-70030. 1982. 13.95 (ISBN 0-87795-365-1). Arbor Hse.

American Quest. Bradford Smith. LC 38-24566. The Bobbs-Merrill Company.

American Realism: A Shape for Fiction. Ed. by Jane Benardete. 384p. (YA) 1972. 7.95 o.p. (ISBN 0-399-10903-X). Putnam.

American Remnant. Robert Lee Straus. LC 31-1715. 1930. Bloch Publishing Company.

American Rhythm. Mary Austin. Repr. of 1923 ed. lib. bdg. 20.00 (ISBN 0-8414-1680-X). Folcroft.

American Rivals of Sherlock Holmes. Hugh Greene. LC 76-12938. 8.95 (ISBN 0-394-40921-3). Pantheon Books.

American Rivals of Sherlock Holmes. Hugh Greene. 1978. 2.95 (ISBN 0-14-004697-6). Penguin Books.

American Romance. John Casey. LC 76-50915. 1977. 9.95 (ISBN 0-689-10770-6). Atheneum.

American Romance. John Casey. (Kangaroo Book). 1978. 2.25 (ISBN 0-671-81870-8). Pocket Books.

American Romance. Hans Koningsberger. 1960. 3.50 o.p. (ISBN 0-671-03204-6). S&S.

American Romance: A Novel. Hans Koningsberger. LC 60-8008. 1960. Simon and Schuster.

American Rose: A Novel. Julia Markus. LC 80-20290. 1980. 11.95 (ISBN 0-395-30229-3). Houghton Mifflin.

American Scrapbook. Jerome Charyn. LC 69-18796. 1969. 4.95. Viking Press.

American Scrapbook: Manzanar-Tule Lake, 1942 - 44. Jerome Charyn. 1969. 4.95 o.p. (ISBN 0-670-12015-4). Viking Pr.

American Senator. Anthony Trollope. LC 31-28507. (Half-title: The World's classics.). 1931. H. Milford, Oxford University Press.

American Senator. Anthony Trollope. LC 40-27466. Random House.

American Senator. A Novel. Anthony Trollope. LC 4-19545. (On cover: Library of select novels. no. 487). 1877. Harper & Brothers.

American Sextet. Warren Adler. LC 82-72050. 256p. 1982. 13.95 (ISBN 0-87795-414-3). Arbor Hse.

American Short Fiction: Readings and Criticism. Ed. by James K. Bowen. LC 74-115055. (Illus.). 1970. 3.50. Bobbs-Merrill.

American Short Novels. Ed. by Richard P. Blackmur. LC 60-6314. (American Literary Forms). 1960. Crowell.

American Short Short Story 1982: An Anthology of... New Short Short Stories... Houston, Kenneth. LC 34-241483. The Galleon Press.

American Short Stories. 3d ed. Ed. by Eugene Current-Garcia & Walton R. Patrick. LC 75-35980. 6.50 (ISBN 0-673-15008-9). Scott, Foresman.

American Short Stories. 3d ed. Ed. by Eugene Current-Garcia & Walton R. Patrick. LC 75-35980. (ISBN 0-673-15008-9). Scott, Foresman.

American Short Stories. 4th ed. Ed. by Eugene Current-Garcia & Walton R. Patrick. LC 81-14481. 1981. 9.95 (ISBN 0-673-15570-6). Scott, Foresman.

American Short Stories. Ed. by Douglas Grant. LC 73-150983. (Oxford paperbacks, 274). 1972. 0.90 (ISBN 0-19-281122-3). Oxford University Press.

American Short Stories. Ed. by Douglas Grant. LC 74-505056. (World's classics). 1968. Oxford University Press.

American Short Stories. Cyril M. Gulassa. 1971. pap. 3.95x o.p. (ISBN 0-06-383407-3). Canfield Pr.

American Short Stories. Ed. by Fred Lewis Pattee. LC 25-18773. 1925. Duffield and Company.

American Short Stories. Ed. by James Finch Royster. LC 25-15121. (Lake English classics). Scott, Foresman and Company.

American Short Stories. Ed. by Lewis George Sterner. LC 66-9080. 1966. Globe Book Co.

American Short Stories. Ed. by Ray Benedict West. LC 60-6318. (American literary forms: paperback ser.: Reader's bookshelf of American literature: hardbound ser.). (22.50 in bxd. set of 5) 5.95, pap., 2.75 (13.75 in bxd. set of 5). Crowell.

American Short Stories of the Nineteenth Century. 1967. Repr. of 1930 ed. 9.95x (ISBN 0-460-00840-4, Evman). Biblio Dist.

American Short Stories of the Nineteenth Century. Ed. by Cournos, John. LC 37-31198. (Half-title: Everyman's library, ed by Ernest Elkya. Fiction. no. 840). 1930. J. M. Dent & Sons, Ltd.

American Short Stories of the Nineteenth Century. Ed. by K. A. Preuschen & M. Schulze. 1973. 20.00 o.p.; pap. 10.50 o.p. Adler.

American Short Stories: Selected and Ed. with an Introductory Essay on the Short Story. Ed. by Charles Sears Baldwin. LC 4-23724. (Half-title: The wampum library of American literature, ed. by Brander Matthews). 1904. Longmans, Green, and Co.

American Short Stories Series: 1832-1936, 83 vols. Ed. by Clarence Gohdes. Set. 1000.00 (ISBN 0-8290-0751-2). Irvington.

American Short Stories Since Nineteen Forty-Five. Ed. by John Hollander. LC 68-57375. (Orig.). 1968. pap. 1.95 o.p. (ISBN 0-06-083083-2, P3083, PL). Har-Row.

American Short Stories: 1820 to the Present by Eugene Current-Garcia and Walton R. Patrick. Ed. by Eugene Current-Garcia & Walton R. Patrick. LC 52-815. (Key editions). 1952. Scott, Foresman.

American Short Stories, 1820 to the Present. rev. ed. Ed. by Eugene Current-Garcia & Walton R. Patrick. LC 64-23299. (Key editions). (Illus.). 1964. Scott, Foresman.

American Short Story. Charles Alphonso Smith. LC 12-14129. 1912. Ginn and Company.

American Short Story Series, 87 Vols. Ed. by Clarence Gohdes. 1969. Repr. of 1906 ed. lib. bdg. 1177.70 o.s.i. (ISBN 0-512-00011-5). Garrett Pr.

American Singer in Paris: A Novel. Mary Christiana Sheedy Hanson Workman Workman. LC 8-29732. 1908. The Tribune Printing Co.

American, Sir: A Novel. Corwin Root. 1940. E. P. Dutton & Company, Inc.

American Soldier: A Novel. Michael Lynch. LC 71-91232. 1969. 5.95. Little, Brown.

American Sovereign. James Milford Merrill. LC 10-403. 1909. 1.50. The C. M. Clark Publishing Company.

American Spy, or Freedom's Early Sacrifice: A Tale of the Revolution, Founded Upon Fact. Jeptha Root Simms. LC 8-13066. 1846. Printed by J. Munsell.

American Spy, or Freedom's Early Sacrifice I: A Tale of the Revolution, Founded Upon Fact. Jeptha Root Simms. 1857. J. Munsell.

American Stories. Ed. by Edward Everett Hale. LC 4-52313. (Hawthorne classics). 1903. Globe School Book Company.

American Story: A Novel of Three Lives. Allen Robert Taft. LC 47-31084. 1947. Arco Pub. Co.

American Story-Book. Short Stories from Studies of Life in Southwestern Pennsylvania. Pathetic, Tragic, Humorous, and Grotesque. Frank Cowan. LC 6-31152. 1881.

American Suffragette: A Novel. Isaac Newton Stevens. LC 11-22759. 1911. 1.20. W. Rickey & Company.

American Surrender. Michael Brady. 1980. pap. 2.25 (ISBN 0-440-10469-6). Dell.

American Surrender: A Novel. Michael Brady. LC 79-391. 9.95 (ISBN 0-440-00469-1). Delacorte Press.

American Tableaux, No. L. Sketches of Aboriginal Life... V. V Vide. LC 9-3420. 1846. Buckland & Sumner.

American: The Version of 1877 Revised in Autograph and Typescript for the New York Edition of 1907: Reproduced in Facsimile from the Original in the Houghton Library, Harvard University. Henry James & Harvard University. Library. Houghton Library. LC 77-352086. 1976. 25.00 (ISBN 0-85967-224-7). Scolar Press.

American Thug. Harlan Page Halsey. LC 7-1197. (On cover: The calumet series, no. 33). G. Munro's Sons.

American Tragedy. Theodore Dreiser. (Modern library of the world's best books. Modern library giant, G80). 1956. Modern Library.

American Tragedy. Theodore Dreiser. LC 75-31583. (Illus.). 1971. 10.00. World Pub. Co.

American Tragedy. Theodore Dreiser. LC 48-11678. 1948. World Pub. Co.

American Tragedy. Theodore Dreiser. LC 26-141. 1925. Boni and Liveright.

American Tragedy. Theodore Dreiser. LC 31-105247. 1929. H. Liveright.

American Tragedy. Theodore Dreiser. LC 34-42572. 1934. Garden City Publishing Co., Inc.

American Tragedy. memorial ed.... ed. Theodore Dreiser. LC 46-25177. 1946. The World Publishing Company.

American Tragedy. Theodore Dreiser. LC 78-55741. (Illus.). 1978. 15.00 (ISBN 0-8376-0424-9). R. Bentley.

American Tragedy Notes. Martin Bucco. 1974. (pbk.) 1.50 (ISBN 0-8220-0169-1). Cliffs Notes.

American Tragedy. With an Introd. by Harry Hansen and with Illus. by Reginald Marsh. Theodore Dreiser. LC 55-1359. 1954. Limited Editions Club.

American Tricentennial. Edward Bryant. 1977. pap. 1.95 o.p. (ISBN 0-515-04203-X). BJ Pub Group.

American Triptych: Three 'John Sedges' Novels. Pearl Sydenstricker Buck. LC 58-6808. 1958. J. Day Co.

American Tuesday Blues Cycle. Franklin Haar. LC 70-132516. 1970. pap. 4.95 (ISBN 0-913632-02-3). Am Univ Artforms.

American Utopias; Selected Short Fiction. Ed. by Arthur Orcutt Lewis. LC 77-154448. (Utopian Literature). 1971. (ISBN 0-405-03530-6). Arno Press.

American Vanguard. 1948- ed. Ed. by Wolfe, Don Marton & Glicksberg, Charles Irving. New York. New School for Social Research. LC 48-7128. Cambridge Pub. Co.

American. With an Introd. by Roy Harvey Pearce. Text Established by Matthew J. Bruccoli. Henry James. LC 62-4689. (Riverside editions, A68). 1962. Houghton Mifflin.

American Wives and English Husbands: A Novel. Gertrude Franklin Horn Atherton. LC 21-16820. 1901. International Association of Newspapers and Authors.

American Wives and English Husbands. A Novel by Gertrude Atherton... Gertrude Franklin Horn Atherton. LC 6-4515. 1898. Dodd, Mead and Company.

American Wives and Others. Jerome Klapka Jerome. LC 4-32395. 1904. F. A. Stokes Company.

American Wooing. Florence Drummond. LC 13-815. 1912. Houghton Mifflin Company.

American Years: A Novel. Harold Sinclair. LC 38-27509. 1938. Doubleday, Doran & Co., Inc.

Americana. Don DeLillo. 1973. (pbk.) 1.25 (ISBN 0-671-78321-1). Pocket Books.

Americana. Don DeLillo. LC 78-144079. 1971. 6.95 (ISBN 0-395-12094-2). Houghton Mifflin.

Americana All: Stories of American Life. Benjamin Alexander Heydrick & Thompson, Blanche Jennings. LC 41-23704. 1941. Harcourt, Brace and Company.

Americanization of Emily: A Novel. William Bradford Huie. LC 59-5060. 1959. Dutton.

Americanization of Manuel De Rosas. R. De Villafuerte. 4.50 o.p. Vantage.

Americano. William Murray. LC 68-20117. 1968. New American Library.

Americans. Henry James. pap. 3.50 (ISBN 0-451-51709-1, CE1709, Sig Classics). NAL.

Americans, No. 8. John Jakes. (Kent Family Chronicles). (Orig.). 1980. lib. bdg. 2.95 (ISBN 0-515-05432-1). Jove Pubns.

Americans see Kent Family Chronicles.

Americans All: A Romance of the Great War. John Merritte Driver. LC 11-5644. 1911. Forbes & Company.

Americans All: Stories of American Life of to-Day. Benjamin Alexander Heydrick. LC 20-14759. 1920. Harcourt, Brace and Howe.

Americans All: Stories of American Life of to-Day. Ed. by Benjamin Alexander Heydrick. LC 74-160934. (Short story index reprint series). 1971. (ISBN 0-8369-3913-1). Books for Libraries Press.

Americans All: Stories of American Life of Today. Ed. by Benjamin Alexander Heydrick. LC 45-47545. 1921. Harcourt, Brace and Company.

Americans All: Stories of American Life Today. Benjamin A. Heybrick. 1921. lib. bdg. 7.50 o.p. Folcroft.

Americans and Europe: Selected Tales of Henry James. Introd. by Napier Wilt, John Lucas. Henry James. LC 65-6728. (Riverside eds. A94). 3.00, 1.65 pap.,. Houghton.

Americans at Home: A Novel. Morton D Elevitch. LC 75-36319. 1976. 3.50 (ISBN 0-916452-01-8). First Person.

Americans in America. Minnie T Shores. LC 66-15395. 3.95. Christopher Pub.

Americans in Exile: From the Pictures and Papers of Paul Duane, Ex-Officer of the United States Army. Grace Stuart Reid. F. T. Neely.

Americans in Rome: Or, Paul Errington and His Struggles. A Novel. John McDowell Leavitt. LC 7-18765. 1886. J. R. Barnett & Company.

Americans One and All. Harry Shaw & Davis, Ruth, 1913- Joint Ed. LC 47-30363. 1947. Harper.

America's One Hundred One Most High Falutin', Big Talkin' Knee Slappin', Golly Whoppers & Tall Tales: The Best of the Burlington Liars' Club. Ed. by Robert G. Deindorfer. LC 80-51618. (Illus.). 128p. (Orig.). 1980. pap. 3.95 (ISBN 0-89480-136-8). Workman Pub.

America's Sweetheart. Alan Dubois. LC 33-16068. 1933. W. Godwin, Inc.

America's Sweetheart. Clement Wood. LC 33-16063. 1933. W. Godwin, Inc.

Americathon. Ed. by Fotonovel Publications Staff. (Illus., Orig.). 1979. pap. 2.75. Fotonovel.

Americaville. Minor Watts. LC 70-99156. 1969. 3.95. Olympia Press.

Americus Moor: Or, Life Among the American Freedmen. Edward W Williams. 1886.

Amerika. Franz Kafka. LC 62-10411. (New Directions paperbook, 117). (Illus.). 1962. New Directions.

Amerika. Franz Kafka. Tr. by Muir, Edwin. Mann, Klaus & Brod, Max. 1940. A New Directions Book.

Amerika, a Novel. Franz Kafka. Tr. by Willa Muir & Edwin Muir. LC 62-10411. (Illus.). (YA) (gr. 9 up). 1962. 10.00x (ISBN 0-8052-3002-5); pap. 4.95 (ISBN 0-8052-0417-2). Schocken.

Amerika. Pref. by Klaus Mann. Translation by Edwin Muir. Afterword by Max Brod. Franz Kafka. LC 55-2474. (Doubleday anchor book, A49). 1955. Doubleday.

Amerikai Magyar Irodalom Tortenete. Leslie Konnyu. (Hungarian.). pap. 3.25 (ISBN 0-911862-11-0). Hungarian Rev.

Amerloque: A Novel. Richard Connelly Miller. LC 65-243281. 4.95. Crown.

Ames Narratives: Romances of Rural Life. Iowa State College of Agriculture and Mechanic Arts, Ames. Division of Agriculture. LC 24-88802. 1924. Pub. by J. M. Thurber for Alpha Chapter of Kappa Lambda Alpha.

Amethyst Box. Anna Katharine Green Rohlfs. LC 5-11901. (On cover: The pocket books). The Bobbs-Merrill Company.

Amethyst Quest. Lois A. Sunagel. (YA) 1975. 6.95 (Avalon). Bouregy.

Amethyst Ring. Anatole France, pseud. Tr. by Drillen, Berengere. LC 19-4988. (Half-title: The works of Anatole France in an English translation, ed. by Frederic Chapman). 1919. John Lane.

Amethyst Spectacles. Frances Kirkwood Crane. 1944. Random House.

Amethyst Summer. Claire Cameron. (Adventures in Love Ser.: No. 21). 1982. pap. 1.75 (ISBN 0-451-11469-8, AE1469, Sig). NAL.

Amethyst Tears. Marilyn Ross. (Birthstone Gothic). (Beagle book: Vol.). 1975. (pbk.) 0.95 (ISBN 0-345-26686-2). Ballantine Books.

Ami. Joe Aved. LC 81-51961. 192p. 1981. 10.00 (ISBN 0-88400-077-X). Shengold.

Ami d'enfance de Maigret. Georges Simenon. pap. 3.95. French & Eur.

Amiable Charlatan. Edward Phillips Oppenheim. LC 16-8225. 1916. Little, Brown, and Company.

Amiable Crimes of Dirk Memling. Rupert Hughes. LC 13-6772. 1913. D. Appleton and Company.

Amiable Meddlers. 1st Ed. Josephine Lawrence. LC 61-11908. 1961. Harcourt, Brace & World.

Amid a Place of Stone. Frank Butler. LC 67-12397. 1967. Crowell.

Amiel: A Novel. Myrtle Johnston. LC 41-5577. 1941. D. Appleton-Century Company, Incorporated.

Amigo: A Novel. Elwyn Whitman Chambers. LC 42-3945. 1942. Howell, Soskin, Inc.

Amigo, Amigo. Francis Clifford. 256p. (YA) 1973. 6.95 o.p. (ISBN 0-698-10542-7). Coward.

Amigo, Amigo. Arthur Leonard Bell Thompson. LC 73-78744. 1973. 6.95 (ISBN 0-698-10542-7). Coward, McCann & Geoghegan.

Amigos. Pico Rivera. 1975. (pbk.) 0.95. Dell.

Amindra Gamble. John Sherlock & David Westheimer. LC 81-15130. 12.95 (ISBN 0-698-11100-1). Coward, McCann & Geoghegan.

Amistad One. Ed. by John A. Williams & Charles F. Harris. LC 75-107196. (Orig.). 1971. pap. 1.95 o.p. (ISBN 0-394-70605-6, V660, Vin). Random.

Amityville Curse. Hans Holzer. 2.25 (ISBN 0-505-51676-4). Tower Publications, Inc.

Amityville Horror. Jay Anson. 1979. lib. bdg. 11.95 o.p. (ISBN 0-8161-6709-5, Large Print Bks). G K Hall.

Amityville Horror II. John G. Jones. 400p. (Orig.). 1982. pap. 3.95 (ISBN 0-446-30615-0). Warner Bks.

Ammahabas: A Novel. Bill Hotchkiss. LC 82-14217. 1983. 16.50 (ISBN 0-393-01718-4). Norton.

Ammie, Come Home. Barbara Mertz. LC 68-9528. 1968. 4.95. Meredith Press.

Ammie, Come Home. Barbara Michaels. 1979. pap. 1.95 (ISBN 0-449-23926-8, Crest). Fawcett.

Ammonite. Blaine C Thomsen. LC 78-16788. 9.00 (ISBN 0-8309-0220-1). Herald Pub. House.

Amnesia: A Novel in Three Parts. Anna M Lucas. LC 40-118904. Buechler Publishing Company.

Amo. Alice Denham. LC 74-79697. 1974. 7.95 (ISBN 0-698-10625-3). Coward, McCann & Geoghegan.

Amok. George Fox. 1979. pap. 2.50 (ISBN 0-449-23995-0, Crest). Fawcett.

Amok: A Novel. George Fox. LC 77-29097. 8.95 (ISBN 0-671-22681-9). Simon and Schuster.

Amok: A Novel. George Fox. 1979. 2.50 (ISBN 0-449-23995-0). Fawcett Crest Books.

Amok: A Story. Stefan Zweig & Paul, Eden, 1885- Tr. LC 31-15934. 1931. The Viking Press.

Amokura. June Mitchell. xi, 204p. (Orig.). (gr. 10 up). 1978. pap. 6.00x (ISBN 0-582-71765-5, Pub. by Longman Paul New Zealand). Three Continents.

Amon Re. Marguerite Collins. LC 39-11573. Times-Mirror.

Among a Godly Few. Peter Magliocco. LC 82-81129. (Illus.). 179p. (Orig.). 1982. pap. 6.95 (ISBN 0-88100-003-5). Limited Ed.

Among Friends: The Stories of Five Women. Irene Tiersten. LC 82-5783. 1982. 13.95 (ISBN 0-312-03138-6). St. Martin's Press.

Among Jews. Morris Salmonsen. LC 7-415840. Meyer & Brother.

Among the Cannibals. Jules Verne. 3.95. Assoc Bk.

Among the Carnivores. Daniel Curzon. Ed. by Sylvia Ashton. LC 77-94071. 1979. 12.95 (ISBN 0-87949-124-8). Ashley Bks.

Among the Chosen. Mary S Emerson. (On cover: American novel series. no. 5). 1884. H. Holt and Company.

Among the Cinders: 1st Amer. Ed. Maurice Shadbolt. LC 65-15914. 4.50. Atheneum.

Among the Crags: Or, Legends of the Covenanters ... LC 7-1815. American Tract Society.

Among the Dangs: Ten Short Stories. George P. Elliott. (Compass bk., C194). 1966. pap., 1.45. Viking.

Among the Daughters: A Novel. Angna Enters. LC 54-101433. Coward-McCann.

Among the Dead: And Other Events Leading to the Apocalypse. Edward Bryant. 203p. 1974. pap. 1.25. Macmillan.

Among the Dead, and Other Events Leading up to the Apocalypse. Edward Bryant. LC 72-85764. 1973. 5.95. Macmillan.

Among the Dead, and Other Events Leading up to the Apocalypse. Edward Bryant. 1974. (pbk.) 1.25. Collier Books.

Among the Dunes. Rosamond Dodson Rhone. LC 7-30588. (On cover: Neely's continental library. no. 1). 1897. F. T. Neely.

Among the Dunes. 4th ed. Rosamond Dodson Rhone. Eaton & Mains.

Among the Gnomes: An Occult Tale of Adventure in the Untersberg. Franz Hartmann. Ed. by R. Reginald & Douglas Melville. LC 77-84237. (Lost Race & Adult Fantasy Ser.). (Illus.). 1978. Repr. of 1895 ed. lib. bdg. 17.00x (ISBN 0-405-10985-7). Ayer Co.

Among the Guerrillas. James Roberts Gilmore. 1866. Carleton.

Among the Hunted. Michael Hammonds. LC 72-96241. 1973. 4.95 (ISBN 0-385-01103-2). Doubleday.

Among the Hunted see Marshall of Bitterroot.

Among the Idolmakers. Lawrence Pearsall Jacks. LC 76-125221. (Short story index reprint series). 1970. Books for Libraries Press.

Among the Idolmakers. Lawrence Pearsall Jacks. LC 12-35557. 1912. H. Holt and Company.

Among the Immortals: In the Land of Desire; a Glimpse of the Beyond. Mary Ann Fisher. LC 17-13323. The Shakespeare Press.

Among the Innocent. Elizabeth Borton Trevino. LC 79-6858. 13.95 (ISBN 0-335-13397-9). Doubleday.

Among the Lost People. Conrad Potter Aiken. LC 34-9408. 1934. C. Scribner's Sons.

Among the Maples. Samuel Alexander Jackson. LC 8-18001. 1908. United Presbyterian Board of Publication.

Among the Meadows. Frances Allen Harris. LC 5-42526. 1905. The Neele Publishing Company.

Among the Nihilists: Or, A Plot Against the Czar. John Russell Coryell. (On cover: Magnet detective library. no. 43). 1898. Street & Smith.

Among the Palms. Nina Larrey Smith Duryea. LC 3-5789. 1903. J. F. Taylor & Company.

Among the Pines: Or, South in Secession-Time. James Roberts Gilmore. LC 72-92433. Negro History Press.

Among the Pines: Or, South in Secession-Time. James Roberts Gilmore. LC 78-89436. 1969. Mnemosyne Pub. Co.

Among the Pines: Or, South in Secession-Time. James Roberts Gilmore. LC 79-101142. 1969. (ISBN 0-8383-1219-5). Haskell House Publishers.

Among the Pines: Or, South in Secession-Time. James Roberts Gilmore. LC 6-44715. 1862. J. R. Gilmore Etc.

Among the Pines: Or, South in Secession Times. Edmund Kirke. LC 72-92433. 1862. 19.00 (ISBN 0-403-00167-6). Scholarly.

Among the Quiet Folks. John Cecil Moore. LC 67-10161. 1967. Lippincott.

Among the Quiet Folks: Short Stories. John Moore. 1967. 4.50 o.p. Lippincott.

Among the Shadows: A Novel. Sarah Elizabeth Blacklock. LC 36-21346. Fleming H. Revell Company.

Among the Sourdoughs. Sigurd Jay Simonsen. LC 40-33708. Fortuny's.

Among the Survivors. Tamara Hovey. LC 77-135123. (Orion Press book). 1971. 7.95 (ISBN 0-670-12216-5). Grossman.

Among the Thorns. A Novel. Mary Lowe Dickinson. LC 6-37029. 1880. G. W. Carleton & Co.; Etc., Etc.

Among the Trumpets: Stories of War Horses and Others. Leonard Hastings Nason. LC 32-9035. 1932. Houghton Mifflin Company.

Among Thieves. George Cuomo. LC 68-14169. 1968. Doubleday.

Among Those Absent. Manning Coles, pseud. LC 48-757167. 1948. Pub. for the Crime Club by Doubleday.

Among Those Present. Lois Seyster Montross. LC 77-132121. (Short story index reprint series). 1970. (ISBN 0-8369-3678-7). Books for Libraries Press.

Among Those Present. Lois Seyster Montross. LC 27-5943. George H. Doran Company.

Among Those Present. Arthur Somers Roche. LC 30-166089. Sears Publishing Company, Inc.

Among Women Only. Translated from the Italian by D. D. Paige. Cesare Pavese. LC 59-9454. (Noonday paperbacks, N145). 1959. Noonday Press.

Amor and Psyche: The Psychic Development of the Feminine; a Commentary on the Tale by Apuleius. Apuleius Madaurensis & Erich Neumann. Tr. by Ralph Manheim. LC 74-168015. (Harper torchbooks, TB 2012. The Bollingen library). 1962. 1.25. Harper & Row.

Amor Gemelo. Jorge E. Florian. (Romance Real Ser.). 189p. 1981. pap. 1.50 (ISBN 0-88025-002-X). Roca Pub.

Amor Libre. Gabriel Espada. (Pimienta Collection Ser.). (Span.). 1977. pap. 1.00 (ISBN 0-88473-264-9). Fiesta Pub.

Amor, un Simposia. Beverly Francisca. pap. 2.95 o.p. New Age.

Amor Victor: A Novel of Ephesus and Rome, 95 105 A. D. Russell Kelso Carter. LC 2-15205. 1902. Frederick A. Stokes Company.

Amore. Elizabeth Morrison Boynton Harbert. LC 17-22983. New Era Publishing Co.

Amore,". Elizabeth Morrisson Boynton Harbert. LC 7-1919. Lovell, Gestefeld & Company.

Amorelle. Grace Livingston Hill. LC 34-179751. J. B. Lippincott Company.

Amores y Amorios. S. Alvarez Quintero. Bd. with Galeotes. (Span.). pap. 1.50 o.s.i. French & Eur.

Amorous Adventures of a Japanese Gentleman. Hoyo Nanhomu. 1972. pap. 1.50 o.s.i. (V1068D, Venus). Grove.

Amorous Adventures of Margot. Jean-Louis Fougeret De Monbron. Tr. by Mark Alexander & L. E. La Ban. Bd. with Scarlet Sofa. Orig. Title: Margot la Ravaudeuse. pap. 1.25 o.p. (2030). Brandon.

Amorous Fiammetta. Giovanni Boccaccio. Tr. by Bartholomew Young. Ed. by Edward Hutton. LC 76-98821. 1970. (ISBN 0-8371-3026-3). Greenwood Press.

Amorous Ghost. Translated from the French by Hugh Shelley. Pierre Bessand-Massenet. LC 58-543991. 1958. Abelard-Schuman.

Amorous Philandro. Galli De Bibiena, Jean. LC 48-10852. (New Avon library 171). 1948. Avon Pub. Co.

Amorous Rogue. Raymond Foxall. (Signet Book). 1977. 1.25 (ISBN 0-451-07616-8). New American Library.

Amorous Umbrella. Marvin Kaye. LC 79-8561. 1981. 10.95 (ISBN 0-385-15509-3). Doubleday.

Amos Benevolos. 2nd rev. ed. Enrique A. Laguerre. LC 76-21757. 311p. (Orig., Span.). 1977. pap. 3.75 (ISBN 0-8477-3185-5). U of PR Pr.

Amos Berry: A Novel. Allan Seager. LC 53-6701. 1953. Simon and Schuster.

Amos Flagg: Showdown. Clay Randall, pseud. (Amos Flagg Ser). (Orig.). 1969. pap. 0.50 o.p. (D2098, GM). Fawcett World.

Amos Jackman. Daniel Doan. LC 57-9090. 1957. Beacon Press.

Amos Judd. John Ames Mitchell. 1901. C. Scribner's Sons.

Amos Judd. John Ames Mitchell. LC 16-25048. 1914. C. Scribner's Sons.

Amos Judd. 15th ed. John Ames Mitchell. LC 43-26708. (The Ivory series). 1899. C. Scribner's Sons.

Amos Judd: A Novel. John Ames Mitchell. 1895. C. Scribner's Sons.

Amos Kilbright: His Adscititious Experiences: With Other Stories. Frank Richard Stockton. LC 72-2024. (Black Heritage Library Collection). 1972. 9.00 (ISBN 0-8369-9067-6). Books for Libraries Press.

Amos Kilbright: His Adscititious Experiences; with Other Stories. Frank Richard Stockton. 1888. C. Scribner's Sons.

Amos Meekin's Ghost. Wilbur Morris Stine. LC 24-16570. 1924. The Acorn Press.

Amos the Wanderer. William Babington Maxwell. LC 32-18738. 1932. Dodd, Mead & Company.

Amos Tutuola. Harold Reeves Collins. LC 68-59050. (Twayne's world authors series, 62.). 1969. Twayne Publishers.

Amour--French for Love. Jack Kahane. LC 35-5406. 1934. Liveright Publishing Corporation.

Amouretta Landscape: And Other Stories. Adeline Valentine Adams. LC 79-103486. (Short story index reprint series). 1969. Books for Libraries Press.

Amouretta Landscape: And Other Stories. Adeline Valentine Adams. LC 22-10770. 1922. Houghton Mifflin Company.

Amouretta Landscape & Other Stories. facsimile ed. Adeline Valentine Adams. LC 79-103486. (Short Story Index Reprint Ser.). 1922. 15.00 (ISBN 0-8369-3192-0). Ayer Co.

Amours and Adventures of Two English Gentlemen in Italy. With a Particular Description of the Diversions of the Carnival in Venice. Also the Duels They Fought; the Dangers They Escaped; and Their Safe Arrival in England. LC 17-20604. 1795. Printed and Sold at the Worcester Bookstore.

Amours De Voyage. Clough. Ed. by Patrick Scott. 1974. 14.95x (ISBN 0-7022-0847-7); pap. 8.95x (ISBN 0-7022-0841-8). U of Queensland Pr.

Amours of Aaron Burr: Or, The Story of Margaret Moncrieffe, the Beautiful Spy. Charles Burdett. LC 6-17386. (On cover: Columbian library, no. 2). 1890. Columbian Publishing Company.

Amours of Edward the IV. Elysium; or, The State of Love and Honour in the Superior Regions of Bliss. Giovanni Paolo Marana & Turkish Spy, Author of. LC 73-9525. (Foundations of the Novel). 1973. (ISBN 0-8240-0513-9). Garland Pub.

Amours of Peterkin. Hervey White. LC 33-9098. The Maverick Press.

Amours of Philario and Olinda. The Forced Virgin. Narzanes. The Unparallel'd Impostor. LC 73-170577. (Foundations of the Novel). 1973. 22.00 (ISBN 0-8240-0566-X). Garland Pub.

Ampersand Papers. Michael Innes. (Sir John Appleby Mystery Novel-Red Badge Novel of Suspence Ser.). 1979. 7.95 o.p. (ISBN 0-396-07663-7). Dodd.

Ampersand Papers. Michael Innes. (Penguin Crime Monthly). 1980. pap. 2.95 (ISBN 0-14-005163-5). Penguin.

Ampersand Papers. John Innes Mackintosh Stewart. LC 78-25590. (Red badge novel of suspense). 1979. 7.95 (ISBN 0-396-07663-7). Dodd, Mead.

Ampersand Papers. John Innes Mackintosh Stewart. LC 80-17646. 1980. 2.50 (ISBN 0-14-005163-5). Penguin Books.

Amphigorey. Edward Gorey. 1975. pap. 5.95 (ISBN 0-425-03911-0, Windhover). Berkley Pub.

Amphigorey Too. Edward Gorey. (Illus.). 224p. 1975. 15.00 (ISBN 0-399-11565-X). Putnam Pub Group.

Amphorae Pirates. Lou Cameron. LC 70-102343. 1970. 4.95. Random House.

Ampurias Exchange. Angus Ross. LC 76-57844. 1977. 6.95 (ISBN 0-8027-5364-7). Walker.

Amrita: A Novel. Ruth Prawer Jhabvala. LC 55-13917. 1956. W. W. Norton.

Amrtin Make-Believe: A Romance. Gilbert Frankau. LC 31-2157. 1931. Harper & Brothers.

Amsterdam. Nick Carter. (Nick Carter Espionage Ser). (O.s.i.). (Orig.). 1970. pap. 0.60 o.s.i. (A628X, Award). Univ Pub & Dist.

Amulet. Borland, Hal Glen. LC 57-11947. 1957. Lippincott.

Amulet. Hendrik Conscience. LC 6-28070. 1873. J. Murphy & Co.

Amulet. Michael McDowell. LC 79-550327. 1979. 2.50 (ISBN 0-380-40584-9). Avon Books.

Amulet: A Novel. Mary Noailles Murfree. LC 6-37962. London.

Amulet: A Tale of the Orient. Katharine Treat Blackledge. LC 16-21940. 1916. 1.50. Commercial Printing House.

Amulet of Fortune. Susannah Broome. LC 77-83934. 1978. 8.95 (ISBN 0-385-13317-0). Doubleday.

Amusement Park. Roger Garis. LC 34-19491. 1934. D. Appleton-Century Company, Inc.

Amusement Park. Robert Stuart Nathan. LC 77-22008. 8.95 (ISBN 0-8037-0150-0). Dial Press.

Amusing Companion: Or, Interesting Story Teller. Being a Collection of Moral, Sentimental and Miscellaneous Tales ... Printed by Hohn Lamson, for John W. Folsom, No. , Union-Street, Boston,Mdccxcvii.

Amy. Bess Sprague. LC 32-3489. A. L. Burt Company.

Amy: A Novel. Katherine Wigmore Eyre. LC 62-8504. 1963. Appleton-Century-Crofts.

Amy Denbrook. A Life Drama. Sara A Wentz. LC 8-362369. J. O'Kane.

Amy Ferraby's Daughter: A Novel. Elizabeth Ford. LC 44-3049. 1944. Coward-McCann, Inc.

Amy Go Home. Joe Morgan. LC 64-20368. 1964. D. McKay Co.

Amy Jean. Lorinda Hagen. (Belmont Tower Book). 1.75 (ISBN 0-505-51151-7). Tower Publications.

Amy March in Copenhagen. Sarah Nichols. 1973. pap. 0.75 o.p. (07317). Curtis.

Amy Marsh in London. Sarah Nichols. 1973. pap. 0.75 o.p. (07307). Curtis.

Amy Marsh, Star Nurse. Sarah Nichols. (Orig.). 1972. pap. 0.75 o.p. (07246). Curtis.

Amy Marsh, TV Nurse. Sarah Nichols. (Orig.). 1972. pap. 0.75 o.p. (07226). Curtis.

Amy Oakly: Or, The Reign of the Carpet Bagger. A Story... Florella Meynardie. 1879. Walker, Evans & Cogswell, Printers.

Amy Warren: A Tale of the Bay Shore. Algernon Sydney Logan. LC 2024. 1900. G. W. Dillingham Co.

Amy Warren: A Tale of the Bay Shore. collected ed. Algernon Sydney Logan. LC 34-24492. 1934. National Publishing Company.

Amy Wordsworth's Seekers: No. 4. 1978. pap. 1.25 o.s.i. (ISBN 0-89559-119-7). Dale Books Inc.

Amyas Egerton, Cavalier. Maurice H Hervey. LC 7-4313. 1896. Harper & Brothers.

Amyot Crime. Christopher Nicole. 1974. (pbk.) 1.25. Bantam Books.

Amyot's Cay. Christopher Nicole. 1974. (pbk.) 1.25. Bantam Books.

Amzi, a Novelette. Oliver James Bond. LC 5-54. 1904. Braodway Publishing Company.

Ana Maria: Tu Eres la Paz. Gregorio Martinez Sierra & Crocker, Marion A. "Mrs. Emmons Crocker", Tr. LC 21-21699. R. G. Badger.

Ana Mistral. Selma Olson. LC 75-263. 1975. 6.00 (ISBN 0-915392-00-3). Domina Books.

Anabel at Sea: The Adventure of a Shy but Determined Lady in Search of a Husband. Samuel Merwin. LC 27-177884. 1927. Houghton Mifflin Company.

Anabel's Windows. Agnes Danforth Hewes. LC 49-10971. 1949. Dodd, Mead.

Anaconda. Jerry Bumpus & December. LC 67-16982. 1967.

Anagram Detectives. Norma Schier. LC 78-71278. 1979. 10.00 (ISBN 0-89296-047-7). Mysterious Press.

Anagrams. David R. Slavitt. LC 79-144299. 1971. 6.95 o.p. (ISBN 0-385-00626-8). Doubleday.

Anahid and There Was Light. Frances A Paelian & Garabed Hagop Paelian. LC 56-28862. 1956. De Vorss.

Anais Nin Reader. Ed. by Philip K. Jason. LC 82-73211. 316p. 1973. 10.00 o.p. (ISBN 0-8040-0595-8); pap. 7.95 (ISBN 0-8040-0596-6). Swallow.

Anais Nin Reader. Anais Nin. LC 72-91913. 1973. 8.95 (ISBN 0-8040-0595-8) (ISBN 0-8040-0595-8). Swallow Press.

Anal Artists. Jack Michaels. pap. 1.95 o.p. (ISBN 0-87056-210-X, 6210). Brandon.

Anal Bedtime Story. Ted Hudson. pap. 1.95 o.p. (ISBN 0-87682-255-3, 7255). Barclay Hse.

Anal Cult. J. P. Donaldson. pap. 1.95 o.p. (ISBN 0-87682-235-9, 7235). Barclay Hse.

Anal Daughter. Geoffrey Kyle. 192p. pap. 1.95 o.p. (6154). Brandon.

Anal Daughters. Jack Benjamin. 192p. pap. 1.95 o.p. (7162). Barclay Hse.

Anal Girl. Preston Harriman. 192p. pap. 1.95 o.p. (6151). Brandon.

Anal Girl. Preston Harriman. pap. 1.95 o.p. (ISBN 0-87056-151-0, 6151). Brandon.

Anal Girls. Trina Slade. 192p. pap. 1.95 o.p. (6169). Brandon.

Anal Institute. Jack Michaels. pap. 1.95 o.p. (ISBN 0-87056-203-7, 6203). Brandon.

Anal Lovers. James Z. Muntz, pseud. 192p. pap. 1.95 o.p. (7151). Barclay Hse.

Anal Nieces. Edwards. pap. 1.95 o.p. (ISBN 0-87682-183-2, 7235). Barclay Hse.

Anal Orgies. H. Hadley Williams. 224p. pap. 1.95 o.p. (7131). Barclay Hse.

Anal Sexpots. Edwin Croft. pap. 1.95 o.p. (ISBN 0-87056-189-8, 6189). Brandon.

Anal Sisters. Ward Fulton. pap. 1.95 o.p. (ISBN 0-87682-173-5). Barclay Hse.

Anal Slaves. Mark S. Wolin. 192p. (Orig.). 1972. pap. 1.95 o.p. (ISBN 0-87682-232-4, 7232). Barclay Hse.

Anal Stud. Rex Hardy. pap. 1.95 o.p. (ISBN 0-87056-197-9, 6197). Brandon.

Anal Wives. Jack Benjamin. 224p. pap. 1.95 o.p. (7137). Barclay Hse.
Anal Women. Bannister. pap. 1.95 o.p. (ISBN 0-87682-188-3, 7188). Barclay Hse.
Analism Among the Poor. Preston Harriman. 192p. pap. 1.95 o.p. (7142). Barclay Hse.
Analism Among the Rich. Preston Harriman. 192p. pap. 1.95 o.p. (7153). Barclay Hse.
Analog Bullet. Martin Cruz Smith. 1978. pap. 1.50 o.p. (ISBN 0-505-51220-3). Tower Bks.
Analog Bullet. Martin Cruz Smith. 192p. 1981. pap. 2.50 (ISBN 0-8439-1011-9, Leisure Bks). Nordon Pubns.
Analog Eight. John Wood Campbell. 1971. 5.95 o.p. (ISBN 0-385-02519-X). Doubleday.
Analog Five see Countercommandment.
Analog Nine. Ed. by Ben Bova & Benjamin Bova. LC 63-7719. 264p. 1973. 5.95 o.p. (ISBN 0-385-07190-6). Doubleday.
Analog: Readers' Choice. Ed. by Stanley Schmidt. 288p. 1982. 12.95 (ISBN 0-385-27681-8). Davis Pubns.
Analog Science Fact & Science Fiction: Analog 5; Ed. by John W. Campbell Stories Selected from Analog Magazine. Ed. by John Wood Campbell. LC 63-1137. 1967. 4.95. Doubleday.
Analog Science Fact & Science Fiction Analog. 6 1968- Ed. by John Wood Campbell. LC 63-77198. 4.95. Doubleday.
Analog Seven. John Wood Campbell. LC 63-7719. 1963. 5.95 o.p. Doubleday.
Analog Two. John Wood Campbell. 1971. pap. 0.75 o.p. (ISBN 0-446-64667-9, 64-667). Paperback Lib.
Analog. 1- 1963- Analog Science Fact & Science Fiction & Campbell, John Wood, 1910- Ed. LC 63-7719. 1963. Doubleday.
Analog's Children of the Future. Stanley Schmidt. LC 82-222830. 12.95 (ISBN 0-385-27778-4). Dial Press: Davis Publications.
Analog's Lighter Side. Stanley Schmidt. LC 82-246628. (Illus.). 12.95 (ISBN 0-385-27775-X). Dial Press: Davis Publications.
Analysis of a Slut. Carl Land. pap. 1.95 o.p. (8077). Cameo.
Analyst. Anne Osborne. LC 79-1065. 1979. 9.95 (ISBN 0-688-03478-0). Morrow.
Analyst. Florence Stonebraker. LC 47-15515. 1946. Phoenix Press.
Ananga Ranga of Kalyana Malla. 1969. pap. 0.95 o.p. (151, Cap). Putnam.
Ananias' Daughter. Alice Garden. LC 23-14804. Dorrance.
Anarch Lords. A. Bertram Chandler. (Science Fiction Ser.). 1981. pap. 2.25 (ISBN 0-87997-653-5, UE1653). DAW Bks.
Anarchist: A Story of to-Day. Richard Henry Savage. LC 8-19933. 1894. F. T. Neely.
Anarchist Woman. Hutchins Hapgood. LC 9-12198. 1909. Duffield & Company.
Anarchists: A Picture of Civilization at the Close of the Nineteenth Century. John Henry Mackay. LC 77-185840. (Illus.). 1972. (ISBN 0-87700-059-X). Revisionist Press.
Anarchists: A Picture of Civilization at the Close of the Nineteenth Century. John Henry Mackay & Schumm, George, Tr. LC 7-19986. 1891. B. R. Tucker.
Anarchists' Convention. John Sayles. LC 78-78036. 9.95 (ISBN 0-316-77232-1). Little, Brown.
Anarchist's Convention: & Other Stories. John Sayles. 1980. 3.50 (ISBN 0-671-83020-1). Pocket Books.
Anarchist's Convention & Other Stories. John Sayles. 320p. 1980. pap. 3.50 (ISBN 0-671-83020-1). WSP.
Anarchy of Love. Colin Spencer. LC 67-20365. 1967. Weybright and Talley.
Anarchy Plot. Peter B. Van Osdol. 368p. 1982. pap. 3.25 (ISBN 0-8439-1100-X, Leisure Bks). Nordon Pubns.
Anastasia Arrives. Eleanor G. R Young. LC 73-152966. (Short story index reprint series). (Illus.). 1971. (ISBN 0-8369-3881-X). Books for Libraries Press.
Anastasia Arrives. Eleanor G. R Young. LC 29-204299. G. Sully & Company, Inc.
Anastasia Schultz. Illustrated by Warren Alan Kass. 1st Ed. Todd Hunt. LC 60-13530. 1960. Doubleday.
Anastasia's Daughter. Gale Taylor. LC 55-13907. 1955. Bouregy & Carl.
Anastasius: Or, Memoirs of a Greek. Written at the Close of the Eighteenth Century... Thomas Hope. LC 7-3521. (On cover: Library of select novels. no. vii-viii). 1831. J. & J. Harper.
Anastasius; or, Memoirs of a Greek. Written at the Close of the 18th Century... harper's stereotype ed. Thomas Hope. LC 7-5255. 1832. J. & J. Harper.
Anathema Stone. John Buxton Hilton. LC 79-25352. 8.95 (ISBN 0-312-03351-6). St. Martin's Press.
Anathemata. David Jones. 1972. pap. 9.95 (ISBN 0-571-10127-5). Faber & Faber.
Anatol. Arthur Schnitzler. Tr. by Frank Marcus. 1982. pap. 7.50 (ISBN 0-413-49880-8, NO. 3636). Methuen Inc.
Anatol: A Sequence of Dialogues. Arthur Schnitzler & Granville-Barker, Harley Granville. LC 11-17080. 1911. M. Kennerley.
Anatol: Living Hours: The Green Cockatoo. Arthur Schnitzler. Tr. by Colbron, Grace Isabel. LC 18-4847. (Half-title: The Modern library of the world's best books). Boni and Liveright, Inc.
Anatola. Elizabeth Wade. 1976. pap. 1.25 (ISBN 0-532-12421-9). Woodhill.
Anatolian. Elia Kazan. LC 81-48611. 1982. 15.45 (ISBN 0-394-52560-4). Knopf: Distributed by Random House.
Anatolian Tales. Yashar Kemal. 1969. 4.00 o.p. (ISBN 0-396-05982-1). Dodd.
Anatolian Tales. Yasar Kemal. LC 70-90595. 1969. 4.00. Dodd, Mead.
Anatomist's Dream of Love. Arthur W Epstein. LC 66-2984. 1966. Libra Publishers.
Anatomy Lesson. Evan S. Connell, Jr. 1969. pap. 2.95 o.s.i. (ISBN 0-87465-024-0, Farallon). Pacific Coast.
Anatomy Lesson. Marshall Goldberg. LC 73-87185. 1974. 7.95 (ISBN 0-399-11257-X). Putnam.
Anatomy Lesson, and Other Stories. Evan S Connell. LC 57-8403. 1957. Viking Press.
Anatomy Lesson, and Other Stories. Evan S. Connell. LC 79-38719. (Short story index reprint series). 1972. 8.75 (ISBN 0-8369-4132-2). Books for Libraries Press.
Anatomy of a Crime. Joseph Francis Dinneen. LC 54-6519. 1954. Scribner.
Anatomy of a Killer. Peter Rabe. LC 60-7213. (Raven book). 1960. Abelard-Schuman.
Anatomy of a Murder. A. Traver. 1958. 5.95 o.p. St Martin.
Anatomy of a Murder. Robert Traver. LC 57-13115. 1978. pap. text ed. 1.95 o.s.i. (ISBN 0-89559-009-3, Co-Pub Greenhill Pub). Dale Books Inc.
Anatomy of a Murder. Robert Traver. 2.95 o.p. (ISBN 0-89559-009-3). Green Hill.
Anatomy of A Murder. Robert Traver. 448p. 1983. pap. 7.95 (ISBN 0-312-03356-7). St Martin.
Anatomy of a Murder. John Donaldson Voelker. LC 57-13115. St. Martin's Press.
Anatomy of a Prostitute. Jhan Robbins. (Signet book). 1974. (pbk.) 1.50. New American Library.
Anatomy of an Arsonist. Gene Mahoney. LC 78-53520. 1978. pap. 2.25 o.s.i. (ISBN 0-89516-039-0). Condor Pub Co.
Anatomy of Virtue: A Novel. Vincent Sheean. LC 27-18845. 1927. The Century Co.
Ancestor. Robin Carol. (Orig.). 1968. pap. 0.60 o.p. (ISBN 0-446-63020-9, 63-020). Paperback Lib.
Ancestor. Elissa Landi. LC 34-20028. 1934. Double-Day, Doran & Company, Inc.
Ancestor Jorico. William John Locke. LC 29-24373. 1929. Dodd, Mead & Company.
Ancestors. Gertrude Franklin Horn Atherton. LC 7-30868. 1907. Harper & Brothers.
Ancestors Cry Out. Eugenia Lovett West. LC 78-14686. 1979. 8.95 (ISBN 0-385-14640-X). Doubleday.
Ancestors of Bantan. Maurice B Gardner. LC 76-8105. (Illus.). 1976. T. Gaus' Sons.
Ancestors of Peter Atherly, and Other Tales. Bret Harte. LC 72-12501. (Harte, Bret, 1836-1902. Short Story Index Reprint Ser.: Autograph Edition: Vol. 16). 1973. (ISBN 0-8369-4235-3). Books for Libraries Press.
Ancestral Invasion: And Other Stories. Madeline Yale Wynne. LC 70-152965. (Short story index reprint series). 1971. (ISBN 0-8369-3880-1). Books for Libraries Press.
Ancestral Invasion: And Other Stories. Madeline Yale Wynne & Putnam, Anna Cabot, Ed. LC 20-14763. 1920. The Country Life Press.
Ancestral Voices: An Anthology of Early Science Fiction. Ed. by Douglas Alver Menville. LC 74-16508. (Science Fiction). (Illus.). 1975. 15.00 (ISBN 0-405-06305-9). Arno Press.
Ancestral Voices: An Anthology of Early Science Fiction. Ed. by R. Reginald & Douglas Alver Menville. LC 74-16508. (Science Fiction Ser). 1975. Repr. 15.00x (ISBN 0-405-06305-9). Ayer Co.
Anchor Anthology of Short Fiction of the Seventeenth Century see Short Fiction of the Seventeenth Century.
Anchor Book of Stories. Ed. by Randall Jarrell. LC 58-9383. (Doubleday anchor books, A145). 1958. Doubleday.
Anchor in the Sea; an Anthology of Psychological Fiction: Edited by Alan Swallow. Ed. by Alan Swallow. LC 47-1874. 1947. The Swallow Press and W. Morrow & Company.
Anchor Man. Fannie Heaslip Lea. LC 35-18076. 1935. Dodd, Mead & Company.
Anchorage. Sara Ware Bassett. LC 43-10063. 1943. Doubleday, Doran and Co., Inc.
Anchorage. Florence Olmstead. LC 17-129567. 1917. 1.35. C. Scribner's Sons.
Anchorhold: A Divine Comedy. Enid Maud Dinnis. LC 24-14021. 1923. Sands & Co.
Anchorman. Ned Calmer. LC 72-105615. 1970. 6.95. Doubleday.
Anchors Aweigh. Harriet Ogden Deen Welles. LC 19-3785. 1919. C. Scribner's Sons.
Anchors Aweigh: A Tragedy of the War. Carroll Hampton Francis. LC 30-24242. Dorrance & Company, Inc.
Anchors to Windward. Edith Austin Holton. LC 41-597942. The Penn Publishing Company.
Anchorwoman: A Novel. Albert Morgan. LC 73-81961. 1974. 7.95 (ISBN 0-8128-1644-7). Stein and Day.
Ancient Allan. Henry Rider Haggard. LC 20-5239. 1920. Longmans, Green and Co.
Ancient and Modern. Peter Marshall. LC 70-98281. 1970. 5.95. Bobbs-Merrill.
Ancient Cavern of Dark Nightmares. Scott D. Norte. 209p. (Orig.). 1973. pap. 2.62 o.p. RHS Bk Assn.
Ancient Cities of the Southwest. Buddy Mays. LC 81-21732. (Illus.). 120p. 1982. pap. 7.95 (ISBN 0-87701-191-5). Chronicle Bks.
Ancient City. Fustel De Coulanges. 11.50 (ISBN 0-8446-1960-4). Peter Smith.
Ancient Enemy. Pierre Moinot. LC 65-14001. 1965. Doubleday.
Ancient Enemy. Donald Thompson. 1979. pap. 1.95 (ISBN 0-449-14216-7, GM). Fawcett.
Ancient Evenings. Norman Mailer. LC 82-22839. 1983. 19.95 (ISBN 0-316-54410-8). Little, Brown.
Ancient Fires. Ida Alexa Ross Wylie. LC 24-11877. E. P. Dutton & Company.
Ancient Grudge. Arthur Stanwood Pier. 1905. Houghton, Mifflin and Company.
Ancient Hauntings. Douglas Alver Menville & R Reginald. LC 75-46303. (Supernatural & Occult Fiction). (Illus.). 1976. 26.00 (ISBN 0-405-08163-4). Arno Press.
Ancient Highway: A Novel of High Hearts and Open Roads. James Oliver Curwood. LC 25-138669. 1925. Cosmopolitan Book Corporation.
Ancient Highway: A Novel of High Hearts and Open Roads. James Oliver Curwood. LC 34-377652. 1927. Grosset & Dunlap.
Ancient History: A Paraphase. Joseph McElroy. LC 70-142952. 1971. 6.95 (ISBN 0-394-46925-9). Knopf.
Ancient Hunger. Edwin Granberry. LC 27-3357. The Macaulay Company.
Ancient Indian Fables & Stories. Stanley P. Rice. LC 74-12477. 1974. Repr. of 1924 ed. lib. bdg. 17.50 (ISBN 0-8414-7329-3). Folcroft.
Ancient Irish Tales. Ed. by Tom P. Cross & Clark H. Slover. (Illus.). 1969. Repr. of 1936 ed. 18.50x (ISBN 0-06-480177-2). B&N Imports.
Ancient Landmark: A Kentucky Romance. Elizabeth Cherry Waltz. 1905. McClure, Phillips & Co.
Ancient Law. Ellen Anderson Gholson Glasgow. LC 8-2945. 1908. Doubleday, Page & Company.
Ancient Legends, Mystic Charms, & Superstitions of Ireland. Wilde. 1973. text ed. 17.50x o.p. (ISBN 0-87696-058-1); pap. text ed. 2.50x o.p. (ISBN 0-9504574-0-X). Humanities.
Ancient Lights. Davis Grubb. LC 81-51881. 1982. 25.00 (ISBN 0-670-12262-9). Viking Press.
Ancient Miracle. Jane Grosvenor Cooke. LC 6-32856. 1906. A. S. Barnes & Company.
Ancient, My Enemy. Gordon R Dickson. LC 74-4871. 1974. 6.95 (ISBN 0-385-05202-2). Doubleday.
Ancient, My Enemy. Gordon R Dickson. (DAW Science Fiction#190). 1976. (pbk.) 1.50. DAW Books.
Ancient Mysteries Reader. Peter Haining. LC 74-18802. (Illus.). 1975. 7.95 (ISBN 0-385-09867-7). Doubleday.
Ancient Pond. Courtney Browne. LC 67-10492.
Ancient Sorceries: And Other Stories. Algernon Blackwood. LC 72-400417. 1968. Penguin.
Ancilla DeMontes: Or, One Summer. With Key. Clarence F. Gray. LC 6-45536. 1885. The Author.
And--If Man Triumph... Illustrated by Paul Clowes. George Dixon Snell. LC 38-295516. 1938. The Caxton Printers, Ltd.
And a Few Marines. John William Thomason. LC 58-12516. 1958. Scribner.
And a Few Marines. John William Thomason. LC 43-6821. 1943. C. Scribner's Sons.
And a Woodstock in a Birch Tree. Charles M. Schulz. LC 79-1926. (Peanuts Parade Ser.). 192p. 1979. pap. 3.95 (ISBN 0-03-053291-4). HR&W.
And Abram Journeyed. Harry Simonhoff. LC 67-10814. 1967. T. Yoseloff.
And After Death! The Story of a Woman's Love... Ed Hamilton Cahill. (On cover: The echo series, no. 117). 1890. Pollard & Moss.
And After That. Kenneth Phillips Britton. LC 34-31295. The Bobbs-Merrill Company.
And Afterward, the Dark: Seven Tales. Basil Copper. LC 77-78594. 1977. 7.50 (ISBN 0-87054-079-3). Arkham House.
And All Because. Denise Robins. 1972. pap. 0.75 o.p. (T2613). Pyramid Pubns.
And All Because. Denise Robins. 1977. pap. 1.50 o.p. (ISBN 0-515-04238-2). BJ Pub Group.
And All Points West! William Surrey Hart & Mary E. Hart. LC 70-144156. (Short story index reprint series). (Illus.). 1971. (ISBN 0-8369-3771-6). Books for Libraries Press.
And All Points West! William Surrey Hart & Hart, Mary E. LC 41-1974. The Lacotah Press.
And All the Stars a Stage. James Blish. (Avon Science fiction). 1974. (pbk.) 0.95. Avon.
And All the Stars a Stage. James Blish. LC 77-144250. (Doubleday science fiction). 1971. 4.95. Doubleday.
And Answer None. Alice Lent Covert. LC 46-18489. S. Curl, Inc.
And Be a Villain: A Nero Wolfe Novel. Rex Stout. LC 48-8378. 1948. Viking Press.
And Berry Came Too... Cecil William Mercer. LC 36-7726. G. P. Putnam's Sons.
And Bid Him Sing: A Novel. David Graham DuBois. LC 73-80527. 1975. 8.95 (ISBN 0-87867-041-6). Ramparts Press.
And Both Were Young. Reita Lambert. LC 38-869928. 1938. Lothrop, Lee & Shepard Company.
And Call It Accident. Marie Adelaide Belloc Lowndes. LC 36-31236. 1936. Longmans, Green and Co.
And Chaos Died. Joanna Russ. LC 77-28358. (Gregg Press science fiction series). (Illus.). 1978. 10.00 (ISBN 0-8398-2410-6). Gregg Press.
And Chaos Died. Joanna Russ. 1975. Ace Books.
And China Has Hands... Hsi-Tseng Chiang. 1937. R. Speller.
And Come Out Fighting: A Novel of the Prize Ring. 1st Ed. Fredric Solla. LC 54-9539. 1954. Exposition Press.
And Daddy Came, Too. Sterling Harkins. 192p. (Orig.). 1973. pap. 1.95 o.p. (ISBN 0-87682-306-1, 7306). Barclay Hse.
And Dangerous to Know. A Henry Gamadge Story. Elizabeth Daly. LC 49-10320. (Murray Hill mystery). 1949. Reinhart.
And Death Came Too. Richard Henry Sampson. LC 42-22692. 1942. J. Messner, Inc.
And Death Came Too: By Anthony Gilbert Pseud. Lucy Beatrice Malleson. LC 56-5217. 1956. Random House.
And Die She Did: A Matt Winter Story. Inez Hildagard Oellrichs. LC 45-2691. 1945. Pub. for the Crime Club by Doubleday, Doran and Co., Inc.
And Down the Days. John Louis Bonn. LC 42-10296. 1942. The Macmillan Company.
And Dream of Evil. Tedd Thomey. LC 54-64646. 1954. Abelard-Schuman.
And Faith Renew. Ruth Rosemary Corby. LC 40-311771. 1940. Arcadia House, Inc.
And Finally-- Heaven. 1st Ed. Verna C Green. LC 54-12631. 1955. Vantage Press.
And Forever. Esther Morgan McCullough. LC 36-10499. 1935. Gotham House.
And Four to Go. Rex Stout. 208p. 1981. pap. 2.25 (ISBN 0-553-14452-9). Bantam.
And Four to Go: A Nero Wolfe Foursome. Rex Stout. LC 58-7063. 1958. Viking Press.
And from Such Men: A Historical Novel of the Years 1830 to 1880. Virginia G Scott. LC 72-90679. 1973. 5.95 (ISBN 0-8059-1774-8). Dorrance.
And from That Center. Joyce Borden Balokovic. LC 67-2226. 1966. House of Falmouth.
And Give Me Yesterday. James Noble Gifford. LC 42-24975. 1942. Arcadia House.
And Give Me Yesterday. Warren Howard. LC 42-24975. 1942. Arcadia House, Inc.
And Have Not Love. Margaret Gorman Nichols. LC 48-861049. 1948. Macrae-Smith-Co.
And Have Not Love. Anne Parrish. LC 54-6023. 1954. Harper.
And Having Writ... A Science Fiction Novel. Donald R. Bensen. LC 77-15442. 1978. 8.95 (ISBN 0-672-52078-8). Bobbs-Merrill.
And Heaven Cried. Lawrence James Babin. 1971. deluxe ed. 3.00x; pap. 1.00x (ISBN 0-912492-01-5). Pyquag.
And Her Name Was Lina. Johanna Anderson. LC 54-447235. 1954.
And Here's to Charley Boyd: A Novel by June Rayfield Welch; Ill. by Lynn Guier. June Rayfield Welch. LC 75-13401. (Illus.). 1975. 6.95. G.L.A. Press.
And High Water. Aaron Marc Stein. 1946. Pub. for the Crime Club by Doubleday & Company, Inc.
And Hope to Die. Richard Pitts Powell. 1947. Simon and Schuster.
And I Shall Sleep... Down Where the Moon Is Small.' Richard Llewellyn. LC 66-122050. 5.95. Doubleday.

And I Shall Sleep... Down Where the Moon Is Small. Richard Llewellyn. LC 77-361970. 1976. 1.00 (ISBN 0-450-02932-8). New English Library.

And I Shall Sleep... Down Where the Moon Is Small. Richard Llewellyn. LC 77-887681. 1970 (ISBN 0-14-003095-6). Penguin.

And Incidentally: Murder! B E Lovell. LC 52-10657. (Mystery house). 1952. Bouregy & Curl.

And It Came to Pass: Intimate Stories of the Child of Bethlehem. 2d ed. Karl Heinrich Waggerl. LC 77-76331. (Illus.). 1968. Murray.

And It Came to Pass. Various Episodes. Roman Ivanovitch Zubof. LC 8-37862. (Dillingham's metropolitan library, no. 13). 1896. G. W. Dillingham.

And It Came to Pass. 1st Ed. Olive Webster Roberts. LC 52-14520. 1952. Pageant Press.

And It Was Told of a Certain Potter. Walter Clemow Lanyon. LC 78-163038. (Short story index reprint series). 1971. (ISBN 0-8369-3952-2). Books for Libraries Press.

And Justice for All" A Novel by Robert Grossbach, Based on a Motion Picture Written by Valerie Curtin & Barry Levinson. Robert Grossbach & Valerie Curtin. LC 79-52506. 1979. 2.25 (ISBN 0-345-28268-X). Ballantine Books.

And Ladies of the Club". Helen Hooven Santmyer. LC 81-22401. 35.00 (ISBN 0-8142-0323-X). Ohio State University Press.

And Leffe Was Instead of a Dad. Kerstin Thorvall. LC 74-81694. (Illus.). 1974. 5.95 (ISBN 0-87888-103-4). Bradbury Press.

And Left for Dead. Frances Louise Davis Lockridge & Richard Lockridge. 1962. 2.95 o.p. (ISBN 0-397-00197-5). Lippincott.

And Let the Coffin Pass. Kieran Abbey. LC 42-10294. 1942. C. Scribner's Sons.

And Let the Credit Go. Lloyd Alexander. LC 55-562296. Crowell.

And Life Goes on. Vicki Baum. Tr. by Goldsmith, Margaret Leland. LC 31-28579. 1931.

And Love Survived. R. Chetwynd-Hayes. 1979. pap. 2.25 (ISBN 0-89083-531-4). Zebra.

And Loving It! William Johnston. (Tempo books, T-159). 1967. Grosset & Dunlap.

And Master of None. Ruth Bebermeyer. (Illus.). 1976. 5.00. Impermanent Pr.

And Miss Carter Wore Pink. Helen Bradley. 1972. 6.95 o.p. HR&W.

And Miss Reardon Drinks a Little. Paul Zindel. 1972. 4.95 o.p. (ISBN 0-394-47901-7). Random.

And Mr. Wyke Bond. William Babington Maxwell. LC 35-6275. 1935. D. Appleton-Century Company Incorporated.

And More Also. Elizabeth Carfrae, pseud. LC 37-13863. 1937. G. P. Putnam's Sons.

And Morning. Roland Flint. LC 74-11608. 1975. pap. 4.50 (ISBN 0-931848-02-4). Dryad Pr.

And Mother Makes Six. Clarke Hammond. pap. 1.95 o.p. (ISBN 0-87056-193-6). Brandon.

And Never Been Kissed. Josephine Moore Proffitt. LC 49-7429. 1949. Macmillan Co.

And Never Goodbye. Robert J. Kuhn. LC 47-3662. 1947. D. Appleton-Century Company, Inc.

And Never Said a Word. Heinrich Boll & Leila Vennewitz. LC 77-18123. 8.95 (ISBN 0-07-006428-8). McGraw-Hill.

And Never Yield. Elinor Pryor. LC 42-13267. 1942. The Macmillan Company.

And New Stars Burn. Faith Baldwin Cuthrell. LC 41-303. Farrar & Rinehart, Inc.

And New Stars Burn. Faith Baldwin Cuthrell. (Paperback Lib., 75-036). 1973. 0.95. Warner Paperback Lib.

And No Birds Sing. Pauline Leader. LC 31-16130. The Vanguard Press.

And No Man's Wit. Rose Macaulay. LC 40-32620. 1940. Little, Brown and Company.

And No Regrets. Rosalind Brett. (Presents Ser.). 1974. pap. 1.25 (ISBN 0-373-70571-9, 70571, Pub by Harlequin). PB.

And None Shall Mourn: A Novel. 1st Ed. Richard Margaris. LC 56-10300. 1956. Exposition Press.

And Not for Love. Philip Mechem. LC 42-247691. 1942. Duell, Sloan & Pearce.

And Not Make Dreams Your Master. Stephen Goldin. 224p. (Orig.). 1981. pap. 2.25 (ISBN 0-449-14410-0, GM). Fawcett.

And Not to Yield. James Ramsey Ullman. LC 70-104983. 1970. 6.95. Doubleday.

And Nothing But the Truth. Richard Scariano. (Perspectives II Ser.). (Illus.). 48p. (Orig.). (gr. 7-12). 1982. pap. 2.50 (ISBN 0-87879-316-X). Acad Therapy.

And Now Good-Bye. James Hilton. LC 48-478962. 1948. W. Morrow.

And Now Good-Bye. James Hilton. LC 32-463301. 1932. W. Morrow & Co.

And Now Good-Bye. James Hilton. LC 42-508573. 1942. The Sun Dial Press.

And Now Tomorrow. Rachel Lyman Field. LC 42-36215. 1942. The Macmillan Company.

And Now We'll Play a Man's Game: Montana Stories. Dean Phelps. LC 76-1979. (Illus.). 3.00 (ISBN 0-914974-10-6). Holmgangers Press.

And on the Eighth Day. Ellery Queen, pseud. LC 77-14111. (Ellery Queen mystery.). 1978. 7.95 (ISBN 0-89340-108-0). J. Curley.

And One Cried Murder. Emma Redington Lee Thayer. LC 61-16658. (Red badge detective). 1961. Dodd, Mead.

And One for the Dead. Pierre Audemars. LC 80-54823. 1981. 9.95 (ISBN 0-8027-5440-6). Walker.

And One Was Beautiful. Alice Duer Miller. LC 38-573826. 1938. Dodd, Mead & Company.

And Onward, My Daughter. 1st Ed. Lillian Allen. LC 54-13137. 1955. Vantage Press.

And Other Dirty Stories. Larry L. King. LC 68-18256. 1968. 6.95 o.p. (NAL). Norton.

And Other Stories. John O'Hara. LC 68-28527. 1968. 14.95 (ISBN 0-394-41534-5). Random.

And Points Beyond: A Novel. Percy Marks. LC 37-22216. 1937. Frederick A. Stokes Company.

And Presumed Dead. Lucille Fletcher, pseud. LC 63-8343. 1963. Random House.

And Quiet Flows the Don. Mikhail Aleksandrovich Sholokhov & Garry, Stephen, Tr. LC 42-25901. 1911. A. A. Knopf.

And Quiet Flows the Don. Mikhail Aleksandrovich Sholokov & Garry, Stephen, Tr. LC 34-18837. 1934. A. A. Knopf.

And Quiet Flows the Don. Tr. from Russian by Stephen Garry. Mikhail Aleksandrovich Sholokhov. (Vintage giant, V330). 1966. pap., 2.45. Random.

And Really Frau Blum Would Very Much Like to Meet the Milkman: 21 Short Stories. Peter Bichsel. LC 69-20443. 1969. 4.75. Delacorte Press.

And Ride a Tiger. Robert Wilder. LC 51-13048. 1951. Putnam.

And Ride Forth Singing. Katharine Dunlap. 1949. W. Morrow.

And Ruffians Leap: By Desmond Carolan Pseud. Daniel Anthony Ffrench-Kehoe. LC 53-9838. 1953. Roy Publishers.

And Satan Laughed. Sibyl Johnstone. LC 52-49165. Eytinge Pub. Co.

And Scatter the Proud. Lewis W. Green. LC 78-88672. 1969. 6.95. J. F. Blair.

And Shame the Devil. Sara Woods, pseud. LC 73-161206. (Rinehart suspense novel). 1972. 4.95 (ISBN 0-03-086715-0). Holt, Rinehart, and Winston.

And Shame the Devil. Sara Woods. 1974. (pbk.) 0.95. Dell Book.

And She Got All That!" Woman's Sphere in Life's Battle. Cara Reese. LC 7-30644. 1897. F. H. Revell Company.

And She Had a Little Knife: A Silas Booth Mystery. Alex Watkins. LC 48-8340. 1948. M. S. Mill Co.

And Sleep Until Noon. Gene Lees. LC 66-24833. 1966. Trident Press.

And So--Victoria. William Vaughan Wilkins. LC 37-16216. 1937. The Macmillan Company.

And So Dedicated; an American Novel. Stephen Longstreet. LC 40-5216. Harrison-Hilton Books.

And So Dedicated: An American Novel. Philip Wiener. LC 40-5216. 1940. Harrison-Hilton Books.

And So Forth. Richard Kostelanetz. LC 79-52317. 1979. pap. text ed. 12.00; signed & numbered 1-10 100.00. Future Pr.

And So He Had to Die. Donald Clough Cameron. LC 41-4914. H. Holt and Company.

And So My Heart. Harriett Thurman. LC 39-20437. 1939. Macrae Smith Company.

And So the Irish Built a Church. Charlie Davis. (Illus.). 1975. pap. 6.95 (ISBN 0-930000-07-2). Mathom.

And So They Were Married. Florence Morse Kingsley. LC 8-23918. 1908. Dodd, Mead & Company.

And So to Bed. Edna M Roy. LC 64-18663. 1964. Dorrance.

And So to Murder. John Dickson Carr. LC 40-7588. 1940. W. Morrow & Company.

And Some Had Wine: A Novel. Ann Katherine Gilliland Ritner. LC 39-31532. M. S. Mill Co., Inc.

And Still I Rise. Maya Angelou. LC 78-57118. 6.95 (ISBN 0-394-50252-3). Random House.

And Still They Dream. Ruby Mildred Ayres. LC 38-32632. 1938. Doubleday, Doran & Co., Inc.

And Strange at Ecbatan the Trees: A Novel. Michael Bishop. LC 75-25075. 7.95 (ISBN 0-06-010352-3). Harper & Row.

And Sudden Death. Cleve Franklin Adams. LC 40-310380. 1940. E. P. Dutton & Co., Inc.

And Sudden Death. Joseph Smith Fletcher. LC 38-13111. 1938. Hillman-Curl, Inc.

And Tell of Time. Laura Smith Krey. LC 38-27596. 1938. Houghton Mifflin Company.

And Thats All: A Novel. Eddie Suckle. LC 77-368126. (ISBN 0-88964-006-8) (ISBN 0-88964-007-6). Air Press.

And That's My Final Offer! G. B. Trudeau. LC 80-81272. (Doonesbury Ser.). 128p. (Orig.). 1980. pap. 3.95 (ISBN 0-03-049191-6). HR&W.

And the Angels Won't Blame Him: By Barton Michael Phillips Pseud. Philip Basvic. LC 56-38435. 1955. Story Book Press.

And the Bullets Were Made of Lead. Paul Wheeler. LC 70-76986. 1969. 4.50. Published for the Crime Club by Doubleday.

And the Captain Answered. Alice French. LC 17-28798. 1917. 0.50. The Bobbs-Merrill Company.

And the Darkness Falls. Ed. by Boris Karloff. LC 46-25174. 1946. The World Publishing Company.

And the Deep Blue Sea. Raymond Knotts. LC 44-3162. 1944. Farrar & Rinehart Incorporated.

And the Devil Will Drag You Under. Jack L. Chalker. 1982. pap. 2.50 (Del Rey). Ballantine.

And the Earth Did Not Part.". Tomas Rivera. LC 70-178026. (Illus.). 1971. Quinto Sol Publications.

And the Field in the World. Dola De Jong & Duym, Alfred Van Ameyden Van, Tr. LC 45-9486. 1945. C. Scribner's Sons.

And the Garden Waited: A Novel. Jeanne De Lavigne & Rutherford, Jacques. LC 27-6916. 1926. H. Vinal.

And the Hunter Home. Charlotte Underwood. LC 46-2114. 1946. Harper & Brothers.

And the Master Said. Matilda Churchill. 80p. 1975. pap. 3.00 o.p. (ISBN 0-912760-14-1). Valkyrie Pr.

And the Master Said. Matilda Churchill. 80p. 1975. pap. 3.00 o.p. (ISBN 0-912760-14-1). Valkyrie Pr.

And the Moon Was Full. 1st Ed. in the U. S. A. Hugh McCutcheon. LC 67-16795. 1967. 3.95. Pub. for the Crime Club by Doubleday.

And the Rain My Drink. 1st American Ed. Suyin Han. LC 56-10645. (Atlantic Monthly Press book). 1956. Little, Brown.

And the Roof Leaks. Jean Bodman & Michael Lanzano. 1981. pap. 4.95 (ISBN 0-02-975090-3). Macmillan.

And the Sphinx Spoke. Paul Eldridge. LC 21-15487. The Stratford Company.

And the Stagecoach Tipped Over. Mary P. Vogel. 1970. 4.50 o.p. Vantage.

And the Stars Shall Fall: A Novel of the Life and Times of the Last Tsaritsa. True Bowen. LC 51-10745. 1951. Wyn.

And the Sword Fell. A Novel. Carrie Goldsmith Childs. 1895. Mayflower Publishing Co.

And the Whale Is Ours. Pamela A. Miller. LC 78-58449. (Creative Writing of American Whalemen). (Illus.). 201p. 1979. 15.00 (ISBN 0-87923-252-8). Kendall Whaling.

And the Wife Ran Away. Fay Weldon. LC 68-17655. 1975. (pbk.) 1.50 (ISBN 0-446-78862-7). Warner Books.

And the Wife Ran Away. 1st Amer. Ed. Fay Weldon. LC 68-17655. 1968. bds., 4.50. McKay.

And the Wind Blows Free. Frederick Dilley Glidden. LC 45-4309. 1945. The Macmillan Company.

And the Winds Blew. Hazel Joan Heinecke. LC 57-7132. (Nobel book). 1957. Comet Press Books.

And Then: A Novel. Natsume Soseki. Tr. by Norma Field. LC 77-13175. 1978. 22.50x (ISBN 0-8071-0387-X). La State U Pr.

And Then Came Fear. Marten Cumberland. LC 48-793590. 1948. Pub. for the Crime Club by Doubleday.

And Then Came Jean. Robert Alexander Wason. LC 13-24977. Small, Maynard & Company.

And Then Came Love. Roberta Leigh. (Presents Ser.). 1974. pap. 1.25 (ISBN 0-373-70568-9, 70568, Pub by Harlequin). PB.

And Then Came Spring. John Hargrave. LC 26-16355. 2.00. The Century Co.

And Then Came Spring: A Story of Moods. Edward P Buffet. LC 99-750. 1899. E. R. Herrick & Company.

And Then, Eternity. 1st Ed. Eva Williams Harvey. LC 55-11664. 1957. Vantage Press.

And Then Love Came: By Warren Howard Pseud. James Noble Gifford. LC 52-3395. 1952. Arcadia House.

And Then: Natsume Soseki's a Novel Sorekara. Soseki Natsume. LC 77-13175. (UNESCO Collection of Representative Works: Japanese Series.). 14.95 (ISBN 0-8071-0387-X). Louisiana State University Press.

And Then: Natsume Soseki's Novel Sorekara. Soseki Natsume. LC 81-15390. 1982. 6.95 (ISBN 0-399-50611-X). Putnam.

And Then One Day... Pat Mensch. LC 75-7747. 7.95 (ISBN 0-87949-040-3). Ashley Books.

And Then Put Out the Light. Edith Caroline Rivett. 1950. Published for the Crime Club by Doubleday.

And Then the Dawn. Garnett Ann Schultz. LC 79-188943. 1972. 3.95 (ISBN 0-8059-1682-2). Dorrance.

And Then There Was. Joanie Whitebird. LC 78-63429. (Illus., Orig.). pap. cancelled o.p. (ISBN 0-930138-06-6). Harold Hse.

And Then There Was Georgia. Jane Blackmore. 1975. (pbk.) 1.25. Ace Books.

And Then There Were None. Agatha Miller Christie. (Enriched classics series). (Illus.). 1973. 0.75 (ISBN 0-671-46606-2). Washington Square Pr.

And Then There Were None. Agatha Miller Christie. LC 40-6132. 1940. Dodd, Mead & Company.

And Then There'll Be Fireworks. Suzette Haden Elgin. LC 80-3001. (Elgin, Suzette Haden. Ozark Fantasy Trilogy: Bk. 3). 1981. 10.95 (ISBN 0-385-15878-5). Doubleday.

And Then There'll Be Fireworks: Book Three of the Ozark Fantasy Trilogy. Suzette Haden Elgin. LC 80-3001. (Double D Science Fiction Ser.). 192p. 1981. 10.95 (ISBN 0-385-15878-5). Doubleday.

And Then We Heard the Thunder. John Oliver Killens. LC 62-15560. 1963. Knopf.

And Then We Moved to Rossenarra: Or, The Art of Emigrating. Richard Condon. LC 73-265. (Illus.). 1973. 7.95. Dial Press.

And Then We'll Be Rich. Clare Bell. LC 51-10378. (Illus.). 1951. McGraw-Hill.

And Then We'll Get Him! Gahan Wilson. LC 78-1312. 1978. 12.95 o.s.i. (ISBN 0-399-90003-9, Marek); pap. 5.95 o.s.i. (ISBN 0-399-90014-4). Putnam Pub Group.

And Then You Came: By Ann Bridge Pseud. Mary Dolling Sanders O'Malley. LC 49-8098. Macmillan Co.,

And Then You Wish. John Van Druten. LC 37-1604. 1937. Little, Brown and Company.

And There Were Seven. Ronald Toniutti. LC 51-519. 1950. Exposition Press.

And Thereby Hangs. M. Merwin. pap. 0.95 o.s.i. (75-310). Lancer.

And There's Opal Out There. Ed Waller. LC 70-520520. (Illus.). 1969. 5.50. Lansdowne.

And There's Tomorrow. Alice M Weir. LC 75-6232. Christian Book Club of America.

And These Shall See: A Short Novel. Mary Ann Ballard & Annis, Jere W., Joint Author. LC 62-21708. 1963. Dorrance.

And They Called Him Amos: The Story of John Amos Comenius-a Woodcut in Words. Florence H. Anastasas. LC 73-86540. 1973. 10.00 (ISBN 0-682-47814-8, University). Exposition.

And They Left Their Father Zebedee in the Boat. Robert O Reddish. LC 68-9679. 1968. Rorge Pub. Co.

And They Lived Happily Ever After! Meredith Nicholson. LC 25-26930. 1925. C. Scribner's Sons.

And This Is Laura. Ellen Conford. (Kangaroo Book). 1978. Pocket Books.

And Thou Philip. David P Allison. LC 39-6845. 1939. Wm. B. Eerdmans Publishing Co.

And Thou Shalt Teach Them. Paul Eldridge. LC 47-11281. 1947. Sheridan House.

And Thus He Came: A Christmas Fantasy. Cyrus Townsend Brady. LC 16-21938. 1916. 1.00. G. P. Putnam's Sons.

And Thy Mother. Eula Lawrence. LC 43-11466. 1943. B. Humphries, Inc.

And to My Beloved Husband. Philip Loraine. LC 50-9713. 1950. M. S. Mill Co.

And to My Nephew Albert I Leave the Island What I Won off Fatty Hagan in a Poker Game... David Forrest. LC 69-14998. 1969. 4.95. Morrow.

And Tomorrow-- Michael Scott Stone. LC 38-133988. 1938. Sovereign House.

And Trouble Deaf Heaven. Wayne D Phipps. LC 78-25414. (Illus.). 4.00 (ISBN 0-87108-536-4). Pruett Pub. Co.

And Two Shall Meet. Cover Painting by James Meese. Raymond Mason. LC 54-27001. (Gold medal books, 395). 1954. Fawcett Publications.

And Walk in Love. Henrietta Buckmaster, pseud. 1956. 10.95 o.p. (ISBN 0-394-41524-8). Random.

And Walk in Love: A Novel Based on the Life of the Apostle Paul. Henrietta Buckmaster. LC 56-5223. 1956. Random House.

And Walk in Love: A Novel Based on the Life of the Apostle Paul by Henrietta Buckmaster Pseud. Henrietta Henkle. LC 56-5223. 1956. Random House.

And Walk Now Gently Through the Fire, and Other Science Fiction Stories. Ed. by Roger Elwood. LC 72-8060. 1972. 6.95 (ISBN 0-8019-5701-X). Chilton Book Co.

And We Have to Live (y Tenemos Que Vivir) Argentina D. Lozano. Tr. by Lillian Sears from Span. LC 78-59598. 1978. softcover 6.00 (ISBN 0-89430-032-6). Morgan-Pacific.

And We Were Young: A Novel. Elliott Baker. LC 79-64451. 9.95 (ISBN 0-8129-0862-7). Times Books.

And When She Was Bad She Was Murdered. Richard Starnes. LC 50-5644. (Main line mysteries). 1950. Lippincott.

And Where It Stops Nobody Knows: A Novel. 1st Ed. David Mark. LC 60-7877. 1960. Doubleday.
And Why Not? Vincent Gaspard Malo. LC 59-5112. 1959. Abelard-Schuman.
And Woodstock in a Birch Tree, Vol. 2. Charles M. Schulz. 128p. 1981. pap. 1.75 (ISBN 0-449-24452-0, Crest). Fawcett.
And Wretches Hang: The True and Authentic Story of the Rise and Fall of Matt Brady, Bushranger. Richard Butler. LC 78-60464. (Illus.). 1979. 8.95 (ISBN 0-312-03619-1). St. Martin's Press.
And You'll Wear Diamonds. James Noble Gifford. LC 44-8142. 1944. Phoenix Press.
Andamooka. Wal Watkins. LC 73-163333. 1972. 1.65 (ISBN 0-7260-0034-5). Gold Star Publications.
Ande Trembath: A Tale of Old Cornwall England. Matthew Stanley Kemp. LC 5-27128. 1905. C. M. Clark Publishing Co., Inc.
Anderby Wold. Winifred Holtby. LC 76-381288. 1976. 0.65 (ISBN 0-552-10122-2). Corgi.
Anderson Crow, Detective. George Barr McCutcheon. LC 20-4957. 1920. Dodd, Mead and Company.
Anderson Tapes. Lawrence Sanders. 320p. 1983. pap. 3.50 (ISBN 0-425-05747-X). Berkley Pub.
Anderson Tapes. Lawrence Sanders. (YA) 1970. 5.95 o.p. (ISBN 0-399-10043-1). Putnam.
Anderson Tapes: A Novel. Lawrence Sanders. LC 74-104297. 1970. 5.95. Putnam.
Andersons. Sarah Broom Macnaughtan. LC 11-35356. 1911. E. P. Dutton and Company.
Andersonville. MacKinlay Kantor. LC 66-1394. 1964. New American Library.
Andersonville. MacKinlay Kantor. LC 77-364856. (Illus.). 1976. Franklin Library.
Andersonville. 1st Ed. MacKinlay Kantor. LC 55-8257. 1955. World Pub. Co.
Andivius Hedulio: Adventures of a Roman Nobleman in the Days of the Empire. Edward Lucas White. LC 21-18418. 1921. E. P. Dutton & Company.
Andivius Hedulio: Adventures of a Roman Nobleman in the Days of the Empire. Edward Lucas White. LC 42-47084. 1937. E. P. Dutton & Co., Inc.
Andorra: A Novel. Isabelle Sandy & Monnier, Mathilde, Tr. LC 24-122823. 1924. Houghton Mifflin Company.
Andoshen, Pa. Darryl Ponicsan. LC 72-6134. 1973. 6.95 o.p. D Ponicsan.
Andoshen, Pa. A Novel. Darryl Ponicsan. LC 72-6134. 1973. 6.95. Dial Press.
Andrassy Legacy. Jeffrey Rovin. 368p. (Orig.). 1981. pap. 2.95 (ISBN 0-515-04813-5). Jove Pubns.
Andre Gide, Karl Gjellerup and Paul Heyse. Andre Paul Guillaume Gide & Paul Johann Ludwig Von Heyse. LC 71-29787. (Noble Prize Library). (Illus.). 1971. A. Gregory.
Andre Tom Macgregor. Betty Wilson. LC 76-363605. (ISBN 0-7705-1329-8). Macmillan of Canada.
Andrea. Jo Stewart. 1982. pap. 2.50 (ISBN 0-451-11654-2, AE1654, Sig Vista). NAL.
Andrea Moves in. Frances Nichols Hanna. LC 40-31181. 1940. Arcadia House, Inc.
Andrea: The Tribulations of a Child. Karin Michaelis. Tr. by Laurvik, John Nilsen. LC 4-29188. 1904. McClure, Phillips & Co.
Andrea Thorne. Sylvia Chatfield Bates. LC 25-6857. 1925. 2.00. Duffield & Company.
Andreas Hofer. Klara Muller Mundt. Tr. by Jordan, F. LC 16-1232. (historical romances of Louisa Muhlbach pseud.). D. Appleton and Company.
Andreas Hofer. An Historical Novel. Klara Muller Mundt & Hofer, Andreas. Tr. by Jordan, F. LC 7-31817. 1868. D. Appleton and Company.
Andreas Hofer: An Historical Novel. Klara Muller Mundt & Hofer, Andreas. Tr. by Jordan, F. LC 7-31818. 1393. D. Appleton and Company.
Andree at the North Pole: With Details of His Fate. Leon Lewis. (Dillingham's metropolitan library, no. 48). 1899. G. W. Dillingham Co.
Andree De Taverney: Or, The Downfall of French Monarchy. Alexandre Dumas. LC 6-42141. (American series, no. 319). M. J. Ivers & Co.
Andree De Taverney: Or, The Downfall of French Monarchy. Alexandre Dumas. LC 5-18470. (On cover: Seaside library. Pocket ed., no. 2123). 1895. G. Munro's Sons.
Andree De Taverney: Or, The Downfall of French Monarchy. Alexandre Dumas. (Seaside library, v. 30, no. 622). G. Munro.
Andree De Taverney: Or, The Downfall of French Monarchy. Being the "Fifth Series" of "The Memoirs of a Physician". Alexandre Dumas. Tr. by Williams, Henry Llewellyn. LC 25-155235. 1862. T. B. Peterson & Brothers.
Andree De Taverney: Or, The Downfall of the French Monarchy. Being the Final Conclusion of "The Memoirs of a Physician," "The Queen's Necklace," "Six Years Later," and "Countess of Charny.". Alexandre Dumas. Tr. by Williams, Henry Llewellyn. LC 6-422989. T. B. Peterson & Brothers.
Andrew: A Romance of Conesus Lake. James Hogarth Dennis. LC 13-2076. 1886. Sunday Herald Printing Company.
Andrew and Tobias. John Innes Mackintosh Stewart. LC 80-14910. 10.95 (ISBN 0-393-01405-3). Norton.
Andrew Bentley: Or, How He Retrieved His Honor... A Story of the Civil War Founded on Facts. Walter Scott Browne. LC 4014. A. C. Graw.
Andrew Bride of Paris. Henry Sydnor Harrison. LC 25-187003. 1925. Houghton Mifflin Company.
Andrew Connington: A Novel. Grace Lillian Riwin. LC 58-9545. 1958. Eerdmans.
Andrew the Glad. Maria Thompson Daviess. LC 13-1636. 1.30. The Bobbs-Merrill Company.
Andrew to the Lions: A Story in Three Parts. Harold Webber Freeman. LC 38-24742. 1938. W. Morrow & Co.
Andrew Trayton: A Novel of Modern Life. Albert O Boschen. LC 28-9993. Printed by C. W. Saunders & Sons, Inc.
Andrews' Harvest. Howard Browne. LC 33-22165. 1933. W. Morrow & Co.
Andrews' Harvest. John Evans, pseud. LC 33-22165. 1933. W. Morrow & Co.
Andrew's Wife. Kage Booton. LC 64-13098. 1964. Published for the Crime Club by Doubleday.
Andria: A Novel. Percy White. LC 8-36618. 1897. G. H. Richmond & Co.
Android Planet. John Rankine. (Space: 1999 series). 1.50 (ISBN 0-671-80706-4). Pocket Books.
Androids. Frank Belnap Long. (Orig.). 1969. pap. 0.60 o.p. (T060-3, 43-338). Tower.
Androids Are Coming: Seven Stories of Science Fiction. Robert Silverberg. LC 79-17457. 7.95 (ISBN 0-525-66672-9). Elsevier/Nelson Books.
Androids, Time Machines, and Blue Giraffes: A Panorama of Science Fiction. Ed. by Roger Elwood. LC 72-85580. 1973. 6.95 (ISBN 0-695-80369-7) (ISBN 0-695-80369-7). Follett Pub. Co.
Androids, Time Machines, & Blue Giraffes. Ed. by Roger Elwood & Vic Ghidalia. (O.s.i.). 384p. 1973. 6.95 o.s.i. (ISBN 0-695-80369-7). Follett.
Andromache: Or, The Inadvertent Murder. Hubert Monteilhet. LC 72-116511. (Inner sanctum mystery special). 1970. 5.50 (ISBN 0-671-20662-1). Simon and Schuster.
Andromeda. Jacland Marmur. LC 47-576. 1947. H. Holt and Company.
Andromeda. A Novel. Julian Constance Fletcher. LC 6-41682. 1885. Roberts Brothers.
Andromeda: An Original SF Anthology. Peter Weston. LC 78-21400. (v. 1) 8.95 (ISBN 0-312-03649-3). St. Martin's Press.
Andromeda Assignment. David Lewis. 1976. (pbk.) 1.25 (ISBN 0-523-00816-3). Pinnacle Books.
Andromeda Breakthrough. Fred Hoyle & John Elliot. 1970. pap. 0.75 o.p. (T2357, GM). Fawcett World.
Andromeda Breakthrough: By Fred Hoyle, John Elliot. Fred Hoyle & John Elliot. LC 64-7828. 1965. 3.50. Harper.
Andromeda Gun. John Boyd. LC 74-79640. 1975. 5.95 o.p. (ISBN 0-399-11377-0, Pub. by Berkley Pub). Putnam.
Andromeda Gun. Boyd Upchurch. LC 74-79640. 1974. 5.95 (ISBN 0-399-11377-0). Berkley Pub. Corp.: Distributed by Putnam.
Andromeda Gun. Boyd Upchurch. LC 74-79640. (Berkley Medallion Book). 1975. (pbk.) 0.95 (ISBN 0-425-02878-X). Berkley Pub. Co.
Andromeda Strain. Michael Crichton. LC 69-14731. (Illus.). 1969. 5.95. Knopf; Distributed by Random House.
Andronike: The Heroine of the Greek Revolution. Stephanos Theodoros Xenos & Grosvenor, Edwin Augustus, 1845- Tr. LC 9-3435. 1897. Roberts Brothers.
Andros of Ephesus: A Tale of Early Christianity. John Edwin Copus. LC 10-29750. The M. H. Wiltzius Co.
Andy Adams' Campfire Tales. Andy Adams. Ed. by Wilson M. Hudson. LC 75-29131. (Illus.). xxxii, 296p. 1976. 21.50x (ISBN 0-8032-0870-7); pap. 6.50 (ISBN 0-8032-5835-6, BB 615, Bison). U of Nebr Pr.
Andy Adams' Campfires Tales. Andy Adams & Malcolm Thurgood. LC 75-29131. (Illus.). 1976. 13.50 (ISBN 0-8032-0870-7) (ISBN 0-8032-5835-6). University of Nebraska Press.
Andy Barr. Willis B Hawkins. Lothrop Publishing Company.
Andy Brandt's Ark. Edna Bryner. LC 27-7187. E. P. Dutton & Company.
Andy Claybourne. David Sievert Lavender. LC 46-780338. 1946. Doubleday & Company, Inc.
Andy Dodge: The History of a Scapegrace. Mark Pierce Pendleton. LC 2302. 1900. Lee and Shepard.
Andy Gump: His Life Story. Sidney Smith. LC 24-22569. The Reilly & Lee Co.
Andy Jessup: A Novel. Winston M. Estes. LC 74-28466. 1975. 7.95 (ISBN 0-397-31608-9). Lippincott.
Andy Jessup: A Novel. Winston M Estes. 1978. 1.75 (ISBN 0-380-01852-7). Avon.
Anecdotes of Destiny. Karen Blixen. LC 77-350538. 1976. 4.80 (ISBN 0-226-15295-2). University of Chicago Press.
Anecdotes of Destiny. Karen Blixen. LC 74-5323. 1974. (ISBN 0-394-71177-7). Vintage Books.
Anecdotes of Destiny: By Isak Dinesen Pseud. Karen Blixen. LC 58-13594. 1958. Random House.
Aner's Return: Or, The Migrations of a Soui. An Allegorical Tale. Alto Sebastian Hoermann & Bergrath, Innocent A., Tr. LC 7-6599. 1867. P. O'Shea.
Ange. Florence Marryat Church Lean. LC 7-13239. (On cover: The seaside library. Pocket ed. no. 897). 1886. G. Munro.
Ange. Florence Marryat Church Lean. LC 7-13240. (On cover: Lovell's library. v. 19, no. 945). 1887. J. W. Lovell Company.
Ange Pitou. Alexandre Dumas & Maquet, Auguste. LC 8-26653. 1894. Little, Brown, and Company.
Ange Pitou. Alexandre Dumas & Maquet, Auguste. LC 6-42847. (Half-title: The romances of Alexandre Dumas. Illustrated library ed. vol. xxxii-xxxiii). 1894. Little, Brown, and Company.
Ange Pitou: Or, Taking the Bastile; or, Six Years Later. Alexandre Dumas & Maquet, Auguste. LC 6-42849. (On cover: Seaside library. Pocket ed. no. 2121). G. Munro's Sons.
Angel. Walter Bloch & Robert L. Munger. LC 77-81858. 8.95 (ISBN 0-378-06791-5). Ward Ritchie Press.
Angel. Mark Dunster. 1972. 4.00 (ISBN 0-89642-011-6). Linden Pubs.
Angel. Cyril Arthur Edward Ranger Gull. LC 8-29738. G. W. Dillingham Company.
Angel. David Hanna. 1976. pap. 1.25 o.s.i. (ISBN 0-8439-0376-7, Leisure Bks). Nordon Pubns.
Angel. David Hanna. Leisure Books.
Angel. Samantha Harte, pseud. 320p. (Orig.). 1982. pap. 2.95 (ISBN 0-523-41490-0). Pinnacle Bks.
Angel. Du Bose Heyward. LC 26-17248. George H. Doran Company.
Angel. Frances Rickett. 1972. pap. 0.95 o.p. (09121). Curtis.
Angel. Elizabeth Taylor. LC 57-9583. 1957. Viking Press.
Angel: A Novel Based on the Life of Alexander I of Russia. William James Blech. LC 50-8303. 1950. Doubleday.
Angel: A Sketch in Indian Ink. Bithia Mary Sheppard Croker. LC 1-25426. 1901. Dodd, Mead & Company.
Angel and the Cuckoo. Gerald Kersh. LC 66-18810. bds., 5.95. New Amer. Lib.
Angel and the Demon: A Tale of Modern Spiritualism. Timothy Shay Arthur. LC 6-2461. 1858. J. W. Bradley.
Angel and the Sailor: A Novella and Nine Stories. Calvin Kentfield. LC 57-6399. 1957. McGraw-Hill.
Angel and the Star. Charles William Gordon. LC 8-300183. F. H. Revell Company.
Angel, Angel, Down We Go. William Johnston. (Orig.). 1969. pap. 0.75 o.p. (74-582). Lancer.
Angel Ass. Alastair Galt. pap. 1.95 o.s.i. (OPH-244, Ophelia). Olympia.
Angel at Her Shoulder. Kenneth L. Wilson. 1970. pap. 0.95 o.p. (N2359). Pyramid Pubns.
Angel at the Gate. Wilson Harris. LC 82-11964. 1983. 12.95 (ISBN 0-571-11929-8). Faber & Faber.
Angel Blushed and All Heaven Broke Loose. Audrey Needles. LC 64-23757. 1964. Wake-Brook House.
Angel by Brevet: A Story of Modern New Orleans. Helen Pitkin. LC 4-31056. 1904. J. B. Lippincott Company.
Angel Cake. Pelham Grenville Wodehouse. LC 52-5767. 1952. Doubleday.
Angel Casey. Charles Bonner. LC 41-13493. 1941. A. A. Knopf.
Angel Child: A Novel. Grace Perkins Oursler. LC 28-22146. Rae D. Henkle Co., Inc.
Angel City: A Novel. Patrick D. Smith. LC 78-55491. (Illus.). 8.95 (ISBN 0-912760-71-0). Valkyrie Press.
Angel Dance. Mary F. Beal. LC 77-80959. 1977. pap. 5.00 (ISBN 0-913780-16-2). Daughters.
Angel Dark, Angel Bright. Julia Wherlock. (Orig.). 1981. pap. 2.50 (ISBN 0-505-51692-6). Tower Bks.
Angel Death. Patricia Moyes. LC 80-13196. (Rinehart suspense novel). 1981. 10.95 (ISBN 0-03-057592-3). Holt, Rinehart, and Winston.
Angel Esquire. Edgar Wallace. LC 8-20673. 1908. H. Holt and Company.
Angel Esquire. Edgar Wallace. LC 27-3816. Small, Maynard & Company.
Angel Eyes. Loren D Estleman. LC 81-4664. (Amos Walker mystery). 1981. 11.95 (ISBN 0-395-31558-1). Houghton Mifflin.
Angel Face. Stanley Cohen. LC 81-21555. 14.95 (ISBN 0-312-03659-0). St. Martin's Press.
Angel-Face. Reginald Noton Hincks. LC 22-152031. The Cornhill Publishing Co.
Angel Face. Fan Nichols. 1970. Repr. pap. 0.75 o.p. (75-363). Manor Bks.
Angel Face Leopard. Elsie O Drew. LC 38-6967. Advance Publishing Co.
Angel from Hell. George Boyle. LC 35-391893. W. Godwin, Inc.
Angel in a Web. Julian Ralph. LC 98-2014. 1899. Harper & Brothers.
Angel in Love. William Arthur Neubauer. LC 44-6993. 1944. Grammercy Publishing Company.
Angel in My House. Tobias Palmer, pseud. (Illus.). 28p. 1975. pap. 1.75 o.p. (ISBN 0-912484-03-9). J Nichols.
Angel in the Corner. 1st American Ed. Monica Dickens. LC 57-6199. 1957. Coward-McCann.
Angel in the Flesh. Orson Durand. LC 78-28502. (Traveller's companion series, TC 475). 2.25. Traveller's Companion, Inc.
Angel in the Flesh. Dominick Ricca. 1970. 3.75 o.p. Vantage.
Angel in the House. Kathleen Thompson Norris. LC 75-31900. 1975. 9.95 (ISBN 0-89190-301-1). American Reprint Co.
Angel in the House. Kathleen Thompson Norris. LC 33-25375. 1933. Doubleday, Doran and Company, Inc.
Angel in the Rain. Dorothy Quentin. LC 44-2701. 1944. Arcadia House, Inc.
Angel in the Rigging. Erika Nau. (Berkley Medallion Book). 1977. 1.50 (ISBN 0-425-03479-8). Berkley Pub. Corp.
Angel in the Room. Gerard Hopkins. LC 31-211791. 1931. G. P. Putnam's Sons.
Angel in the Snow. Patricia Welles. (Orig.). 1980. pap. 2.25 (ISBN 0-671-41726-6). PB.
Angel in the Wardrobe. Robert Tallant. LC 48-8507. Doubleday.
Angel Island. Inez H. Gillmore. Ed. by R. Reginald & Douglas Melville. LC 77-84229. (Lost Race & Adult Fantasy Ser.). (Illus.). 1978. Repr. of 1914 ed. lib. bdg. 25.00x (ISBN 0-405-10979-2). Ayer Co.
Angel Island. Inez Haynes Irwin. LC 14-2479. 1914. 1.35. H. Holt and Company.
Angel Island. Inez Haynes Irwin. LC 77-84229. (Lost Race and Adult Fantasy Fiction). (Illus.). 1978. 25.00 (ISBN 0-405-10979-2). Arno Press.
Angel Landing. Alice Hoffman. LC 80-16377. 10.95. Putnam.
Angel Landing. large print ed. Alice Hoffman. LC 81-5335. 1981. 11.95 (ISBN 0-89621-286-6). Thorndike Press.
Angel Loves Nobody. Richard Miles, pseud. LC 67-16397. 1967. 5.95. Prentice.
Angel Loves Nobody. Richard Miles, pseud. (0168). 1968. Dell.
Angel Makers. Gordon Rattray Taylor. 1974. 10.00 o.p. (ISBN 0-525-05480-4). Dutton.
Angel Making Music. Ferenc Molnar. Tr. by Katona, Victor. LC 35-115043. 1935. H. Smith & R. Haas.
Angel Mink: A Novel. Letty M Shaw. LC 57-7023. (Nobel book). 1957. Comet Press Books.
Angel O' Deadman. Guy Fitch Phelps. 1.50. The Standard Publishing Company.
Angel of Christmas: A Vision of to-Day. Stella George Stern Perry. LC 17-24690. Frederick A. Stokes Company.
Angel of Clay. William Ordway Partridge. LC 2558. 1900. G. P. Putnam's Sons.
Angel of Death. Philip Loraine. LC 61-5591. 1961. M.S. Mill Co., and W. Morrow.
Angel of Forgiveness. Rosa Nouchette Carey. LC 7-31281. 1907. J. B. Lippincott Company.
Angel of Gaiety: A Novel. Joseph George Hitrec. LC 51-9286. 1951. Harper.
Angel of Hangtown. Lee D. Willoughby. 368p. (Orig.). 1982. pap. 3.25 (ISBN 0-440-00117-X, Bryans). Dell.
Angel of Hell. Robin Waldron. 96p. 1976. 4.50 o.p. (ISBN 0-682-48405-9). Exposition.
Angel of Hell's Kitchen. Millicent Kent. LC 37-11008. 1937. Godwin.
Angel of His Presence. Grace Livingston Hill. Repr. lib. bdg. 9.95x (ISBN 0-89190-032-2). Am Repr-Rivercity Pr.
Angel of His Presence. Grace Livingston Hill & Bowyer, Mrs. Edith M. (Nicholl) LC 2-25932. 1902. American Bapist Publication Society.
Angel of Light. Hugh McCutcheon. LC 52-34943. 1951. Rich and Cowan.
Angel of Light. Joyce Carol Oates. LC 81-730. 15.05. Dutton.
Angel of Light. Joyce Carol Oates. 1982. 3.95 (ISBN 0-446-30189-2). Warner Books Inc.
Angel of Pain. Edward Frederic Benson. LC 5-24854. 1905. J. B. Lippincott Company.

Angel of Satan. Aaron Stell. 1974. (pbk.) 1.25 (ISBN 0-523-00292-0). Pinnacle Books.
Angel of Terror. Edgar Wallace. LC 22-4237. Small, Maynard & Company.
Angel of the Bells. L'ange Du Bourdon. Fortune Du Boisgobey & Kendall, Laura E., Tr. LC 6-34437. (On cover: Seaside library. Pocket ed. no. 648). G. Munro.
Angel of the Delta. 1st Ed. Edward Francis Murphy. LC 58-5950. 1958. Hanover House.
Angel of the Gila: A Tale of Arizona. Cora Marsland. LC 11-317445. 1.50. R. G. Badger.
Angel of the Night. B. W. Battin. 256p. (Orig.). 1983. pap. 2.95 (ISBN 0-449-12380-4, GM). Fawcett.
Angel of the Pines. Sarah E Phipps. LC 13-1201. 1912. 1.00. Broadway Publishing Co.
Angel of the Revolution. George Chetwynd Griffith. LC 73-13254. (Classics of Science Fiction Ser.). (Illus.). 410p. 1973. 13.95 (ISBN 0-88355-109-8); pap. 4.75 (ISBN 0-88355-138-1). Hyperion Conn.
Angel of the Revolution: A Tale of the Coming Terror. George Chetwynd Griffith. LC 73-13254. (Classics of science fiction). (Illus.). 1974. 11.50 (ISBN 0-88355-110-1) (ISBN 0-88355-110-1). Hyperion Press.
Angel of the Village. Anton Ohorn. Tr. by Mathews. LC 7-32513. 1888. Cupples and Hurd.
Angel of Vengeance. Gerard De Villiers. (Malko series,#5). 1974. (pbk.) 1.25 (ISBN 0-523-00375-7). Pinnacle Books.
Angel on Horseback. Ralph J Burns. LC 46-1633. 1945. Priv. Print, at the Colonial Press Inc.
Angel on Horseback. Ralph Byrne, pseud. LC 46-1633. Priv. Print. at the Colonial Press Inc.
Angel on My Shoulder. Paul Kalmbach. 1977. 7.95 o.p. (ISBN 0-8059-2407-8). Dorrance.
Angel Pavement. John Boynton Priestley. (95-193). 1968. Popular Lib.
Angel Pavement. John Boynton Priestley. LC 67-11214. 1967. Little, Brown.
Angel Pavement. John Boynton Priestley. LC 30-208673. 1930. Harper & Brothers.
Angel Pavement. John Boynton Priestley. LC 42-17389. 1942. The Press of the Readers Club.
Angel Possessed. J. C Conaway. 1974. (pbk.) 0.95. Belmont Tower Books.
Angel Range. John Henry Reese. LC 79-181792. (Doubleday western). 1973. 4.95 (ISBN 0-385-03426-1). Doubleday.
Angel Range. john reese. ed. John Henry Reese. 1976. 1.25. Leisure Books.
Angel Town. Charles Grayson. LC 46-4755. 1946. Doubleday & Company, Inc.
Angel Tracks in the Cabbage Patch. Nell Brasher. LC 73-14381. (O.s.i). 128p. 1972. 4.00 o.s.i. (ISBN 0-88289-006-9). Pelican.
Angel Unawares: A Story of Christmas Eve. Charles Norris Williamson & Alice Muriel Livingston Williamson. LC 16-214008. 1916. Harper & Brothers.
Angel Who Couldn't Sing. Sophia Cleugh. LC 35-153547. 1935. Doubleday, Doran & Company, Inc.
Angel Who Pawned Her Harp. 1st American Ed. Charles Terrot. LC 54-5033. 1954. Dutton.
Angel with a Broom. Elia Wilkinson Peattie. LC 16-4581. 0.50. R. F. Seymour, for the Cordon.
Angel with Spurs: A Novel. Paul Iselin Wellman. LC 42-12034. 1942. J. B. Lippincott Company.
Angel with the Trumpet. Ernest Lothar & Hapgood, Elizabeth Reynolds, Tr. LC 44-3344. 1944. Doubleday, Doran & Co., Inc.
Angel Without Wings. Martha Ellen Wright Shakespeare. LC 43-11461. 1943. Doubleday, Doran and Company, Inc.
Angela. 1974. pap. 1.25 o.p. (LB00172). Leisure Bks.
Angela. Dianne Black. 1975. (pbk.) 1.25. Dell.
Angela. Elizabeth Chater. (Coventry Romance Ser.: No. 167). 224p. 1982. pap. 1.50 (ISBN 0-449-50268-6, Coventry). Fawcett.
Angela. Vida Hurst. LC 39-337463. Gramercy Publishing Co.
Angela. A Novel. Anne Marsh-Caldwell. LC 7-17561. 1848. Harper & Brothers.
Angela: A Salvation Army Lassie. Rosa Meyers Mumma. LC 7-38029. 1907. The Neale Publishing Co.
Angela: A Sketch. Alice Weber. LC 8-36744. 1891. E. P. Dutton & Company.
Angela Comes Home. Margaret Widdemer. LC 42-215161. 1942. Farrar & Rinehart, Inc.
Angela Harpe: The Dream Girl Caper. James D. Lawrence. (Dark Angel Ser.: No. 1). (Orig.). 1975. pap. 1.25 o.p. (ISBN 0-515-03470-3, V3470). BJ Pub Group.
Angela Harpe: The Gilded Snatch Caper. James D. Lawrence. (Dark Angel Ser.: No. 3). (Orig.). 1975. pap. 1.25 o.p. (ISBN 0-515-03713-3). BJ Pub Group.
Angela Harpe: The Godmother Caper. James D. Lawrence. (Dark Angel Ser: No. 4). (Orig.). 1975. pap. 1.25 o.p. (ISBN 0-515-03826-1). Pyramid Pubns.
Angela of Brooks Hill: A Novel. 1st Ed. Mary Mountain Scott. LC 60-16548. Greenwich Book Publishers.
Angela: The Story of a Strange Woman. Jean Blanche. LC 55-18077. Castle Books.
Angela's Business. Henry Sydnor Harrison. 1915. Houghton Mifflin Company.
Angela's Quest. Lilian Lida Bell. LC 10-25578. 1910. Duffield & Co.
Angele: Tr. from the French of Edmond Tarbe. Edmond Tarbe & Bartol, H. W., Tr. LC 17-7814. 1917. J. B. Lippincott Company.
Angele's Fortune. A Story of Real Life. Andre Theurie & Sherwood, Mrs. Mary (Neal) Tr. LC 8-27749. T. B. Peterson & Brothers.
Angeles y Rameras. Harry Gomez. (Pimienta Collection Ser). (Sp.). 1977. pap. 1.00 (ISBN 0-88473-256-8). Fiesta Pub.
Angelic Alpabet. Susan Mernit. pap. 2.50 o.p. Tree Bks.
Angelic Avenger. Isak Dinesen, pseud. LC 75-12973. 1978. pap. 4.95 (ISBN 0-226-15292-8, P765, Phoen). U of Chicago Pr.
Angelic Avengers. Karen Blixen. LC 75-12973. 1975. 8.95 (ISBN 0-226-15290-1). University of Chicago Press.
Angelic Avengers. Karen Blixen. LC 47-30031. 1946. Random House.
Angelic Avengers. Karen Blixen. LC 47-6233. 1947. Random House.
Angelic Avengers. Isak Dinesen, pseud. LC 75-12973. viii, 304p. 1975. Repr. of 1947 ed. 8.95 (ISBN 0-226-15290-1). U of Chicago Pr.
Angelica. Jean Anne Bartlett. (Illus.). 1977. 1.75 (ISBN 0-445-08579-7). Popular Library.
Angelica. Elisabeth Sanxay Holding. LC 23-7527. George H. Doran Company.
Angelica. Samuel Agnew Schreiner, Jr. LC 78-57323. 1978. 9.95 (ISBN 0-87795-194-2). Arbor Hse.
Angelica: A Novel. May Dikeman. LC 74-128358. 1971. 6.95. Little, Brown.
Angeline: A Story of the Franco-Prussian War. Colmar Goltz. Tr. by Safford, Mary Joanna. (On Cover: The Midland Series, Vol. Iv, No. 34). Morrill, Higgins & Co.
Angeline De Montbrun. Felicite Angers. LC 73-82585. (Literature of Canada, poetry and prose in reprint; 14). 1975. 12.50 (ISBN 0-8020-2126-3) (ISBN 0-8020-6234-2). University of Toronto Press.
Angelique see Libertine Reader.
Angelique and the Demon. Anne Golon. LC 73-76154. (Illus.). 1973. 7.95 (ISBN 0-399-11193-X). Putnam.
Angelique and the Demon. Anne Golon. 1975. (pbk.) 1.50. Bantam Books.
Angelique and the Ghosts. Anne Golon & Serge Golon. LC 77-20018. 1978. 8.95 (ISBN 0-399-11981-7). Putnam.
Angelique and the King: By Sergeanne Golon Pseud. Translated from the French by Monroe Stearns. Anne Golon. LC 60-7853. 4.95. Lippincott.
Angelique in Barbary. Anne Golon. LC 61-8691. 1963. Bantam Books.
Angell, Pearl, and Little God. Winston Graham. LC 79-97664. 1969. Doubleday.
Angelo: Or, The Tyrant of Padua. A Drama of Three Days. Victor Marie Hugo. LC 44-24141. 1855. Darcie & Corbyn.
Angelo: Roman. Jean Giono. (Coll. Soleil). 10.50. French & Eur.
Angelo: The Circus Boy. Frank Sewall. LC 28-17905. 1879. J. B. Lippincott & Co.
Angelo's Wife: A Novel. Virginia Myers. LC 48-871290. 1948. Bobbs-Merrill.
Angel's Advocates. Maggi Nolan And Sr. Janet. 2.95 o.p. Vantage.
Angels and Awakenings: Stories of the Miraculous by Great Modern Writers. M. Cameron Grey. LC 79-7111. (Illus.). 1980. 15.95 (ISBN 0-385-15311-2). Doubleday.
Angels & Beasts. Denis Saurat. Repr. of 1947 ed. 15.00 o.p. Folcroft.
Angels and Women: A Revision of the Unique Novel Seola. Ann Eliza Brainerd Smith. LC 25-8125. 1924. A. B. Abac Company.
Angels Are Cowards. David Garth. LC 34-5604. 1934. Dodd, Mead & Company.
Angels Are Painted Fair by Paul Whelton... Paul Whelton. LC 47-665. 1947. J. B. Lippincott Company.
Angels at the Ritz. William Trevor. 1979. pap. 2.95 o.p. (ISBN 0-14-004708-5). Penguin.
Angels at the Ritz and Other Stories. William Trevor. LC 75-30528. 1976. 7.95 (ISBN 0-670-12594-6). Viking Press.
Angels at the Ritz and Other Stories. William Trevor. 1979. 2.95 (ISBN 0-14-004708-5). Penguin Books.
Angels Camp: A Novel. Ray Morrison. LC 49-9145. 1949. W. W. Norton.
Angels Can't Do Better. Peter De Vries. LC 44-7949. 1944. Coward-McCann, Inc.
Angels Come in Pairs. Marjorie Bayley. LC 50-13798. 1950. Gramercy Pub. Co.
Angels Falling. Janice Elliott. LC 73-79324. 1969. 6.95. Knopf.
Angels Fell. Anne Miller Downes. LC 41-20047. 1941. Frederick A. Stokes Company.
Angels Fell. Bruno Fischer. LC 50-6174. (Red badge mystery). 1950. Dodd, Mead.
Angel's Flight. Edward Nils Holstius. LC 47-3016. 1947. Doubleday & Company, Inc.
Angel's Flight. Don Ryan. LC 27-20664. 1927. Boni & Liveright.
Angels Have White Wings. Ethel Anderson Becker. 2.50. Pageant Press, Inc.
Angels in Chains: Based Upon the Script "Angels in Chains" by Robert Earll. Richard Deming. LC 77-6138. (Deming, Richard. Charlie's Angels: No. 4). 1977. 1.50 (ISBN 0-345-27182-3). Ballantine Books.
Angels in Exile. Garland Roark. LC 67-20915. 1967. Doubleday.
Angels in My Oven: A Story Workshop Anthology. John Schultz. LC 75-33527. (Illus.). 1976. 6.50 (ISBN 0-89005-083-X). Columbia College Press of Chicago: Distributed by Ares Publishers.
Angels in Pinafores. Alice Lee Humphreys. LC 53-117645. 1954. John Knox Press.
Angels in the Dust. Zofia Kossak-Szczucka. LC 54-15100. 1951. Hutchinson.
Angels in the Dust: A Novel of the First Crusade. Zofia Kossak-Szczucka. Tr. by Rulka Godlewska Langer. LC 47-12190. 1947. Roy Publishers.
Angels in the Snow. Derek Lambert. LC 69-11062. 1969. 6.95. Coward-McCann.
Angel's Laundromat. Ed. by Lucia Berlin. (New World Writing Ser). (Illus.). 96p. (Orig.). 1981. pap. 4.95. Turtle Isl Foun.
Angels Look the Same. Norman Donald Hunter. 1976. 4.00 o.p. (ISBN 0-682-48470-9). Exposition.
Angels May Weep. Jane Ludlow Drake Abbott. LC 37-23788. J. B. Lippincott Company.
Angels' Metal. Ann Abelson. LC 47-2901. 1947. Harcourt, Brace and Company.
Angels' Mirth. Ethel Cook Eliot. LC 36-29008. 1936. Sheed & Ward.
Angels of Commerce: Or, Thirty Days with the Drummers of Arkansas. George H Briscoe. LC 6-18251. 1891. Press of the Publishers' Printing Co.
Angels of Darkness. Cornell Woolrich, pseud. LC 77-20720. 1978. 10.00 (ISBN 0-89296-037-X); ltd. ed., o.p. 25.00 (ISBN 0-89296-038-8). Mysterious Pr.
Angels of Doom... Leslie Charteris. LC 32-9667. Pub. for the Crime Club, Inc., by Doubleday, Doran & Company, Inc.
Angels of Doom. Leslie Charteris. LC 36-17951. 1936. Doubleday, Doran & Company, Inc.
Angels of Doom: The Saint Meets His Match. Leslie Charteris. LC 42-111153. (Sun dial mysteries). 1941. The Sun Dial Press.
Angels of God. Gildas O. Roberts. LC 73-93509. 1974. 4.95 (ISBN 0-8059-1989-9). Dorrance.
Angels of Messer Ercole: A Tale of Perugia. Duffield Osborne. LC 7-28457. (On cover: Little novels of famous cities). 1907. Frederick A. Stokes Company.
Angels of Mons. The Bowman and Other Legends of the War. Arthur Machen. LC 72-4474. (Short story index reprint series). 1972. (ISBN 0-8369-4183-7). Books for Libraries Press.
Angels of Mons. The Bowmen and Other Legends of the War. Arthur Machen. LC 15-20421. 1915. G. P. Putnam's Sons.
Angels of the Mons, the Bowen, & Other Legends of the War, Vol. 1. Arthur Machen. LC 72-4474. (Short Story Index Reprint Ser). Repr. of 1915 ed. 12.50 o.p. (ISBN 0-8369-4183-7). Ayer Co.
Angels of the Mons, the Bowen, & Other Legends of the War, Vol. 1. Arthur Machen. LC 72-4474. (Short Story Index Reprint Ser). Repr. of 1915 ed. 12.50 o.p. (ISBN 0-8369-4183-7). Arno.
Angels on the Bough. Sam M Steward. 1936. The Caxton Printers, Ltd.
Angels on Toast. Dawn Powell. LC 40-32367. 1940. C. Scribner's Sons.
Angels Over Manilla. Hazel Wilcox. (Daybreak Ser.). 1980. pap. 4.50 (ISBN 0-8163-0349-5). Pacific Pr Pub Assn.
Angel's Ransom. David Dodge. LC 56-5206. 1956. Random House.
Angels' Song: A Christmas Token. Charles Benjamin Tayler. LC 8-20130. (On cover: C. B. Tayler's works). 1851. Stanford and Swords.
Angel's Tear. Jane Blackmore. (Ace gothic). 1974. (pbk.) 0.95. Ace Books.
Angels That Beckon Me: Or, The Costly Glories of the Higher Life. Lincoln Hulley. LC 25-25877. E. O. Painter Printing Co.
Angels Unaware. Lenore Glen Offord. LC 40-6704. 1940. Macrae-Smith-Company.
Angels Unaware. Clarence Prentice Parker. LC 12-11604. 1.25. Press of Geo. G. Fetter Company.
Angels' Visits to My Farm in Florida. William Watkin Hicks. LC 7-4767. United States Book Company.
Angels' Visits to My Farm in Florida. new ed., may, 1913... ed. William Watkin Hicks. LC 13-16138. 1.25. The Sanctury Publishing Company.
Angels Watched Over Him: A Novel of Faith Put to the Test of War. Joseph J Novellino. LC 53-7707. 1953. William- Frederick Press.
Angel's Wickedness: A True Story. Marie Corelli. LC 2-30151. 1903. W. R. Beers.
Angeltread. Kitty Mendenhall. 1978. pap. 1.50 (ISBN 0-532-15302-2). Woodhill.
Angelus of Sunset Hill. Emmet Claire May. LC 25-3091. 1924.
Angelward. Grant Gordon. LC 7-33912. Broadway Publishing Co.
Anger see Hunger & Thirst & Other Plays.
Anger: A Novel. May Sarton. LC 82-7843. 12.95 (ISBN 0-393-01643-9). Norton.
Anger at Innocence. William Gardner Smith. LC 50-10194. 1950. Farrar, Straus.
Anger in the Sky: A Novel. Susan Ertz. LC 43-16484. 1943. Harper & Brothers.
Anger in the Wind. Logan Forster. LC 74-80503. 1974. 7.95 (ISBN 0-679-50464-8). D. McKay Co.
Anger of Fear. Jeffrey Ashford, pseud. (o.s.i.). 1979. 7.95 o.s.i. (ISBN 0-8027-5406-6). Walker & Co.
Anger of Fear. Roderic Jeffries. LC 79-83804. 1979. 7.95 (ISBN 0-8027-5406-6). Walker.
Anger of the Bells. Virginia Rath. LC 37-638372. 1937. Pub. for the Crime Club, Inc., by Doubleday, Doran & Company, Inc.
Angers of Spring. 1st Ed. Joseph Whitehill. LC 59-5930. 1959. Little, Brown.
Angkor Massacre. Loup Durand. LC 82-18818. 1983. 15.95 (ISBN 0-688-00487-3). Morrow.
Angle of Attack. Rex Burns. LC 79-1699. 9.95 (ISBN 0-06-010523-2). Harper & Row.
Angle of Attack. Joseph Landon. LC 52-5535. 1952. Doubleday.
Angle of Repose. Wallace Earle Stegner. (Crest bk., Q1768). 1972. 1.50. Fawcett.
Angle of Repose. Wallace Earle Stegner. LC 72-144301. 1971. Doubleday.
Angle of Repose. limited ed. Wallace Earle Stegner. LC 78-104738. (Illus.). 1978. 1.95. Franklin Library.
Angle of Vision. Thomas R. Coleman. 1970. 4.50 o.p. Vantage.
Anglers All: The Great Fishing Stories of John Taintor Foote. John Taintor Foote. LC 47-12238. 1947. D. Appleton-Century Co.
Angles and Spaceships. Fredric Brown. LC 54-8864. 1954. Dutton.
Angles of Darkness. Hopley-Woolrich, Cornell George. LC 77-20720. 1978. 10.00. (ISBN 0-89296-037-X) (ISBN 0-89296-038-8). Mysterious Press.
Anglo-American Alliance: A Serio-Comic Romance and Forecast of the Future. Gregory Casparian. LC 6-19934. 1906. Mayflower PrSses.
Anglo-Irish of the Nineteenth Century. John Banim. LC 78-16348. (Ireland, from the Act of Union, 1800, to the Death of Parnell, 1891; No. 20). 1978. (3 vol set.) 126.00 (ISBN 0-8240-3469-4). Garland Pub.
Anglo-Saxon Attitudes. Angus Wilson. 1978. pap. 4.95 (ISBN 0-14-001311-3). Penguin.
Anglo-Saxon Attitudes. Angus Wilson. 1960. pap. 1.85 o.p. (ISBN 0-670-00062-0, Comp). Viking Pr.
Anglo-Saxon Attitudes: A Novel. Angus Wilson. LC 56-9740. 1956. Viking Press.
Anglo-Saxons, Onward! A Romance of the Future. Benjamin Rush Davenport. LC 98-137. Hubbell Publishing Company.
Anglomaniacs. Constance Cary Harrison. LC 76-51669. (Recovered Fiction by American Women). 1977. 22.00 (ISBN 0-405-10048-5). Arno Press.
Anglomaniacs. Constance Cary Harrison. LC 7-3003. Cassell Publishing Company.
Anglomaniacs. Constance Cary Harrison. LC 99-5411. 1899. The Century Co.
Anglophile. Egan O'Neill. LC 57-625780. J. Messner.
Anglophile: By Egan O'Neill Pseud. Elizabeth Linington. LC 57-6257. 1957. J. Messner.
Angrey Scar see Journey into Terror.
Angry Angel. Lajos Zilahy. LC 53-5736. 1953. Prentice-Hall.
Angry Atheist. Johnny Giesbrecht. 160p. (Orig.). 1976. 1.50 o.p. (ISBN 0-8024-0223-2). Moody.
Angry Dream. Gil Brewer. LC 57-8733. 1957. Mystery House.
Angry Dust. Dorothy Stockbridge Tillett. LC 46-7944. 1946. Doubleday & Company, Inc.
Angry Dust: A Novel. Clement R Hoopes. LC 67-14999. 1967. Devin-Adair Co.
Angry Flames. George Orwell. 1968. 1.00 o.p. Northwestern U Pr.
Angry Harvest. Hermann Field & Stanislaw Mierzenski. LC 58-5360. 1958. Crowell.
Angry Heart. Leslie Edgley. LC 47-113984. 1947. Pub. for the Crime Club by Doubleday.
Angry Hills. Leon M. Uris. LC 55-10631. 1955. Random House.
Angry Horseman. large type ed. Lewis B. Patten. LC 82-10534. 233p. 1982. Repr. of 1960 ed. 9.95 (ISBN 0-89621-383-8). Thorndike Pr.
Angry Jigsaw: A Novel of the New Left. R. Paul Pipkin. 1968. 3.50 o.p. Vantage.

Angry Land. Samuel Anthony Peeples. LC 58-6831. (Silver star westerns). 1958. Dodd, Mead.

Angry Love. Charles J. McClun. 2.95 o.p. Vantage.

Angry Man. Thomas Theodore Flynn. LC 56-8042. (Dell first edition, 103). 1956. Dell Pub. Co.

Angry Man's Tale. Peter De Polnay. LC 39-11567. 1939. A. A. Knopf.

Angry Millionaire. Selwyn Jepson. LC 68-28231. 1968. 5.95. Harper & Row.

Angry Mountain: By Hammond Innes Pseud. 1st American Ed. Hammond-Innes, Ralph. LC 51-9531. 1951. Harper.

Angry Mountain. 1st American Ed. Hammond Innes, pseud. LC 51-9531. 1951. Harper.

Angry Ocean. Ronald Johnston. LC 69-12039. 1969. Harcourt, Brace & World.

Angry River. Ruskin Bond. (Puffin book). (Illus.). 1974. (pbk.) 0.95 (ISBN 0-14-030648-X). Penguin.

Angry Tide. Winston Graham. LC 77-90809. 1978. 10.00 o.p. (ISBN 0-385-13682-X). Doubleday.

Angry Tide: A Novel of Cornwall, 1789-1799. Winston Graham. LC 77-90809. 1978. 10.95 (ISBN 0-385-13682-X). Doubleday.

Angry Tide: A Novel of Cornwall, 1798-1799. Winston Graham. LC 79-10638. 1979. 19.95 (ISBN 0-8161-6682-X). G. K. Hall.

Angry Time: A Novel. Leonard Bishop. LC 60-6218. 1960. Fell.

Angry Town of Pawnee Bluffs. Lewis B Patten. LC 74-2832. 1974. 4.95 (ISBN 0-385-09602-X). Doubleday.

Angry Wife. John Sedtes. LC 47-31212. 1947. J. Day Co.

Angry Wind. Leslie Ames, pseud. 1970. 3.95 o.p. Lenox Hill.

Angry Wind. Leslie Ames, pseud. 1973. pap. 0.75 o.s.i. (01-383). Lancer.

Angry Woman. James Ronald. LC 48-7770. 1948. J. B. Lippincott Co.

Angry Young Men: A Novel. John Rogers Shuman. LC 53-6480. 1953. Vantage Press.

Anguish. Graciliano Ramos. LC 72-163539. 1972. 11.25 (ISBN 0-8371-6203-3). Greenwood Press.

Anguish. Graciliano Ramos & Kaplan, Lewis C., 1911- Tr. LC 46-1914. 1946. A. A. Knopf.

Anguish & the Triumph. Evelyn Britton. 1965. 2.00 o.p. Vantage.

Angular Stone. Pardo Bazan, Emilia. Tr. by Serrano, Mary Jane (Christie) LC 7-35770. Cassell Publishing Company.

Angus Leslie's Daughter. Lydia L Rouse. LC 8-689. 1888. Phillips & Hunt.

Angus Lost. Marjorie Flack. (Zephyr bk.). (Illus.). 1973. Doubleday.

Anhelli. Juliusz Sowacki & George Rapall Noyes. LC 78-21548. 1979. 13.00 (ISBN 0-313-20828-X). Greenwood Press.

Anie. Hector Henri Malot & Robins, E. P., Tr. LC 7-24365. (On cover: Once a week library. v. 9, no. 7-8). 1892. P. F. Collier.

Anima. Marie Buchanan. LC 79-180760. 1973. (pbk) 1.25. Fawcett.

Anima Vilis: A Tale of the Great Siberian Steppe. Marja Rodziewiczowna & Soissons, Guy Jean Raoul Eugene Charles Emmanuel De Savoie-Carignan, Comte De, 1860- Tr. LC 2136. 1900. Dodd, Mead & Company.

Animal. Jack Jones. LC 75-4815. 228p. 1975. 6.95 o.p. (ISBN 0-688-02923-X). Morrow.

Animal: A Novel. Jack Jones. LC 75-4815. 1975. 6.95 (ISBN 0-688-02923-X). Morrow.

Animal Catchers. Colin D Willock. LC 64-14280. 1964. Doubleday.

Animal City. Ray Staszko. LC 77-353011. 1976. 1.95 (ISBN 0-671-80372-7). Simon & Schuster of Canada.

Animal Crackers. Robert Hendrickson. 1983. pap. 6.95 (ISBN 0-14-006487-7). Penguin.

Animal Doctor. Per Christian Jersild. LC 75-10360. 1975. 7.95 (ISBN 0-394-49464-4). Pantheon Books.

Animal Factory. Edward Bunker. LC 77-4921. 1977. 8.95 (ISBN 0-670-12709-4). Viking Press.

Animal Factory. Edward Bunker. (Dell book). 1979. 1.95. Dell Pub. Co.

Animal Fair. Evelyn West. LC 45-6473. 1945. J. B. Lippincott Company.

Animal Farm. George Orwell. LC 54-11330. (Illus.). 1954. Harcourt, Brace.

Animal Farm. George Orwell. LC 46-629019. 1946. Harcourt, Brace and Company.

Animal Farm; Burmese Days; A Clergyman's Daughter; Coming up for Air; Keep the Aspidistra Flying; Nineteen Eighty-Four. George Orwell. LC 77-364607. 1976. 3.95 (ISBN 0-7064-0567-6). Secker and Warburg: Octopus Books.

Animal Farm: Notes, Including Introduction, Brief Synopsis, List of Characters, Chapter Commentaries, Notes on Main Characters, Critical Review...Rev. by Frank H. Thompson, Jr. Consulting Ed.: James L. Roberts. Frank H Thompson. 1967. pap., 1.00. Cliff's.

Animal Game. Lionel Derrick, pseud. (Penetrator Series; 27). 1978. 1.50 (ISBN 0-523-40180-9). Pinnacle Books.

Animal Game. Frank Tuohy. LC 57-12358. 1957. Scriber.

Animal Ghosts. Raymond Bayless. 1970. 5.95 (ISBN 0-8216-0054-0). Univ Bks.

Animal Hotel. Jean Garrigue. LC 66-23197. 3.95. Eakins Pr.

Animal House. Ivor Cutler & Helen Oxenbury. LC 77-358148. (Illus.). 1976. 2.50 (ISBN 0-434-93353-8). Heinemann.

Animal Kingdom. Mary Fabilli. 1975. pap. 2.50 (Pub. by Oyez). SBD.

Animal Magnetism. Francine Prose. LC 77-28220. 8.95. Putnam.

Animal People. Stanton Arthur Coblentz. Orig. Title: Crimson Capsule. 1970. pap. 0.75 o.p. (B75-2038). Belmont-Tower.

Animal School. Pedling Albert. LC 78-62002. (Orig.). 1978. 5.95 (ISBN 0-9602716-2-7); pap. 2.95 (ISBN 0-9602716-1-9). Paranoid Pubns.

Animal Stories. Phineas Taylor Barnum. Repr. lib. bdg. 14.10x (ISBN 0-89190-447-6). Am Repr-Rivercity Pr.

Animal Stories from Rudyard Kipling. Rudyard Kipling & Tresilian, Stuart, Illus. LC 38-27649. 1938. Doubleday, Doran & Company, Inc.

Animal Street: An Athology. 1st Ed. Ed. by Beth Brown. LC 62-11008. (Collier books, AS184. Original). 1962. Collier Books.

Animal Tales from the Wall Street Journal. Ed. by Michael Gartner. LC 73-82489. 133p. (Orig.). 1973. pap. 2.95 o.p. (ISBN 0-87128-482-0). Dow Jones.

Animalitos Amigables. Paulina G. Patterson. (Illus.). 32p. 1980. pap. 0.95 (ISBN 0-311-03602-3). Casa Bautista.

Animals for Innocents. Maurice L. Sullivan. 1970. 2.95 o.p. Vantage.

Animals of Farthing Wood. Colin Dann. LC 80-14783. 9.95 (ISBN 0-525-66677-X). Elsevier/Nelson Books.

Animals of the Sea. new ed. Marcelle Verite. LC 67-20113. (Adventures in nature and science). (Illus.). 1968. Childrens Press.

Animated Seasons. Maggi Richardson. LC 77-84314. 1977. pap. 3.95 o.s.i. (ISBN 0-89543-002-9). Grossmont Pr.

Anipas, Son of Chuze and Others Whom Jesus Loved. Louise Seymour Houghton. LC 7-7139. A. D. F. Randolph & Co.

Anita. Keith Roberts. LC 77-364676. 1976. 3.50 (ISBN 0-86000-070-2). Millington.

Anita Agrees: A Novel. Theodora Benson. LC 30-7104. 1930. Harper & Brothers.

Anita: or, The Spectre of a Snow-Storm. A Novel. John Walter Scott. LC 8-2912. 1891. G. W. Dillingham, Successor to G. W. Carleton & Co.

Anita, the Cuban Spy. Gilson Willets. (On cover: Neely's imperial library, no. 12). F. T. Neely.

Anitra's Dance. Fannie Hurst. 1974. pap. 1.50 o.p. (ISBN 0-515-03364-2, A3364). Pyramid Pubns.

Ann. Esther Loewen Vogt. LC 77-170594. 1971. 3.95 (ISBN 0-8361-1652-6). Herald Press.

Ann and Her Mother. Anna Buchan. LC 22-27467. 1.75. George H. Doran Company.

Ann and the Hoosier Doctor. Adeline McElfresh. LC 55-14831. 1955. Avalon Books.

Ann Annington. Edgar Jepson. LC 18-6643. 1.50. The Bobbs-Merrill Company.

Ann Arbor Tales. Karl Edwin Harriman. LC 73-86142. (Short story index reprint series). 1969. Books for Libraries Press.

Ann Arbor Tales. Karl Edwin Harriman. LC 2-28292. 1902. G. W. Jacobs and Company.

Ann Bartlett at Bataan: The Adventures of a Navy Nurse. Elisabeth Carelton Lansing. LC 43-9098. 1943. Thomas Y. Crowell Company.

Ann Bartlett in the South Pacific. Elisabeth Carleton Lansing. LC 44-5769. 1944. Thomas Y. Crowell Company.

Ann Bartlett, Navy Nurse. Martha Johnson. LC 41-5876. 1941. Thomas Y. Crowell Company.

Ann Bartlett: Navy Nurse. Elisabeth Carlelton Hubbard Lansing. LC 41-5876. 1941. The Thomas Y. Crowell Company.

Ann Bartlett on Stateside Duty. Elisabeth Carleton Lansing. LC 46-824776. 1946. Thomas Y. Crowell Company.

Ann Bartlett Returns to the Philippines. Elisabeth Carleton Lansing. LC 45-897929. 1945. Thomas Y. Crowell Company.

Ann Boleyn. Margaret Heys. Orig. Title: May Queen. 1972. pap. 0.95 o.p. (95245). Beagle Bks.

Ann Boyd: A Novel. William Nathaniel Harben. 1906. Harper & Brothers.

Ann Boyd: A Novel. William Nathaniel Harben. LC 24-20472. 1911. A.L. Burt Company.

Ann Carmeny. Hoffman Birney. LC 41-8918. G. P. Putnam's Sons.

Ann Decides. Robert Keable. LC 27-56073. 1927. G. P. Putnam's Sons.

Ann Fitzgerald. Elizabeth Donovan Bailly. LC 56-49582. 1956. Blackmore Press.

Ann Foster, Lab Technician. Adeline McElfresh. LC 56-3579. 1956. Avalon Books.

Ann Lee's: & Other Stories. Elizabeth Bowen. LC 70-103497. (Short story index reprint series). 1969. Books for Libraries Press.

Ann Lee's: & Other Stories. Elizabeth Bowen. LC 27-27979. Boni and Liveright.

Ann Lee's & Other Stories. facsimile ed. Elizabeth Bowen. LC 70-103497. (Short Story Index Reprint Ser.). 1926. 16.00 (ISBN 0-8369-3239-0). Ayer Co.

Ann Margret Loves You & Other Psychotopological Diversions. Franz Kamin. LC 80-15325. 1980. 10.00 (ISBN 0-930794-33-8) (ISBN 0-930794-32-X). Station Hill Press.

Ann Marguerite. Sophia Cleugh. LC 32-30790. 1932. Houghton Mifflin Company.

Ann of Cleves. Julia Hamilton, pseud. Orig. Title: Flander Mare. 1972. pap. 0.95 o.p. (95246). Beagle Bks.

Ann of the House of Barlow. Dorothy Alice Bonavia Hunt. LC 26-14797. 1926. Cassell and Company, Ltd.

Ann of Windy Populars, No. 4. Lucy Maud Montgomery. 272p. 1981. pap. 2.25. Bantam.

Ann Singleton. Cid Ricketts. LC 38-574924. 1938. D. Appleton-Century Company, Incorporated.

Ann Singleton: By Cid Rickets. Cid Ricketts Sumner. LC 38-5749. 1938. D. Appelton-Century Company, Incorporated.

Ann Somers: Story of an Unowned Girl. Philip Harrower. LC 40-12735. Wetzel Publishing Co., Inc.

Ann Star at Warm Springs. Adelaide Humphries. LC 47-17973. 1947. Arcadia House.

Ann Star, Nurse. Adelaide Humphries. LC 44-51249. 1944. Arcadia House, Inc.

Ann Star: Senior Nurse. Adelaide Humphries. LC 45-61009. 1945. Arcadia House, Inc.

Ann Star, Staff Nurse. Adelaide Humphries. LC 46-601. 1946. Arcadia House Inc.

Ann, the Gentle. Katheryn Kimbrough, pseud. (Saga of the Phenwick Women: No. 20). 1978. pap. 1.75 (ISBN 0-445-04168-4). Popular Lib.

Ann Thorne Comes to America. Rosamund Bertram. LC 41-1825. 1941. T. Nelson & Sons.

Ann Veronica: A Modern Love Story. Herbert George Wells. LC 9-28269. 1909. Harper & Brothers.

Ann Vickers. Sinclair Lewis. LC 33-270065. 1933. Doubleday, Doran & Companh, Inc.

Ann Zu-Zan: A Chinese Love Story. Louise Jordan Miln. LC 32-7346. 1932. Frederick A. Stokes Company.

Anna. Dagfinn Gronoset. 1977. pap. 1.50 o.s.i. (ISBN 0-8439-0458-5, Leisure Bks). Nordon Pubns.

Anna. Boris Konstantinovich Zaltsev & Duddington, Mrs. Natalia Aleksandrovna (Ertel') Tr. LC 37-29388. H. Holt and Company.

Anna and Her Daughters. Dorothy Emily Stevenson. LC 58-10700. 1958. Rinehart.

Anna Apparent. Nina Bawden. LC 72-79703. 1972. 6.95 (ISBN 0-06-010249-7). Harper & Row.

Anna Archdale: Or, The Lowell Factory Girl. And Other Tales. LC 22-24750. F. Gleason.

Anna Becker: A Novel. Charles William White. LC 37-2464. 1937. Stackpole Sons.

Anna Borden's Career: A Novel. Margarete Anna Adelheid Munsterberg. LC 13-18717. 1913. 1.30. D. Appleton and Company.

Anna-Clara. Hasse Z. LC 71-127423. Orig. Title: Anna-Clara Och Hennes Broder. (Illus.). 1970. 5.95 o.s.i. (ISBN 0-87806-011-1, 87806-011-1). Winter Hse.

Anna-Clara. Hasse Zetterstrom. LC 71-127423. (Illus.). 1970. 5.95. Winter House.

Anna-Clara Och Hennes Broder see Anna-Clara.

Anna Clayton: Or, The Enquirer After Truth. Francis Marion Dimmick. LC 6-36820. 1859. Lindsay & Blakiston.

Anna Clayton: Or, The Mother's Trial. A Tale of Real Life ... LC 6-2051. 1855. J. French and Company.

Anna Clayton: Or, The Mother's Trial. A Tale of Real Life. 9th ed. H. J. Moore. LC 42-393555. 1857. Crown & Co.

Anna Collett. Barbara Lucas, pseud. LC 47-311760. 1947. Houghton Mifflin Co.

Anna Elizabeth. Lucille Long, pseud. 128p. 1975. pap. 1.95 (ISBN 0-87178-040-2). Brethren.

Anna Elizabeth: A Girl of the Plain People. Lucille Long, pseud. 1975. pap. 1.50 o.p. (ISBN 0-515-03817-2). Pyramid Pubns.

Anna Fitzalan. Marguerite Steen. LC 53-7986. 1968. 5.75x o.p. (ISBN 0-7182-0761-0). Intl Pubns Serv.

Anna Fitzalan: 1st Ed. Marguerite Steen. LC 53-7986. 1953. Doubleday.

Anna Hammer: A Tale of Contemporary German Life. Tr. from the German of Temme. Jodocus Donatus Hubertus Temme & Guernsey, Alfred Hudson, 1825-1902, Tr. LC 8-308783. 1852. Harper & Brothers.

Anna Hastings: The Story of a Washington Newspaperperson!: A Novel. Allen Drury. LC 77-4151. 1977. 8.95 (ISBN 0-688-03221-4). Morrow.

Anna Hastings: the Story of a Washington Newspaper Person! A Novel. Allen Drury. 1978. 2.50 (ISBN 0-446-81603-5). Warner Books.

Anna Heritage. Mary Howard, pseud. LC 45-9320. 1945. Arcadia House, Inc.

Anna Karenia; a Novel. Lev Nikolaevich Tolstoi & Garnett, Mrs. Constance (Black) 1862- Tr. LC 11-13361. 1911. John Lane Company.

Anna Karenin... Lev Nikolaevich Tolstoi & Garnett, Mrs. Constance (Black) 1862- Tr. LC 17-17427. (Harvard classics shelf of fiction, selected by C. W. Eliot. 16-17). P. F. Collier & Sons.

Anna Karenina. Lev Nikolaevich Tolstoi. LC 65-24991. (Modern library of the world's best books). 1965. Random House.

Anna Karenina. Lev Nikolaevich Tolstoi. LC 66-14559. (Great illustrated classics: Titan editions). 1966. Dodd, Mead.

Anna Karenina. Lev Nikolaevich Tolstoi. LC 66-6219. 1966. Washington Square Press.

Anna Karenina. Tolstoi, Lev Nikolaevich. LC 58-143837. (Harper's modern classics). 1959. Harper.

Anna Karenina. Lev Nikolaevich Tolstoi. LC 50-11916. (Modern Library college editions, T36). 1950. Modern Library.

Anna Karenina. Lev Nikolaevich Tolstoi. LC 52-854843. 1952. Heritage Press.

Anna Karenina. Lev Nikolaevich Tolstoi. LC 4-16895. 1889. T. Y. Crowell & Co.

Anna Karenina. Lev Nikolaevich Tolstoi. LC 30-263895. (Half-title: The Modern library of the world's best books.). 1930. The Modern Library.

Anna Karenina. Lev Nikolaevich Tolstoi. LC 35-15050. (Universal library). 1931. Grosset & Dunlap.

Anna Karenina. Lev Nikolaevich Tolstoi. LC 77-80238. 1978. 14.95 (ISBN 0-672-52383-3). Bobbs-Merrill.

Anna Karenina. Lev Nikolaevich Tolstoi. Tr. by Joel Carmichael from Russian. (Bantam Classics Ser.). 873p. (Orig.). (gr. 9-12). 1981. pap. 2.75 (ISBN 0-553-21034-3). Bantam.

Anna Karenina. Lev Nikolaevich Tolstoi. 1982. pap. 10.00x (ISBN 0-330-24802-2, Pub. by Pan Bks). State Mutual Bk.

Anna Karenina. Lev Nikolaevich Tolstoi. Ed. by Kent & Berberova. Tr. by Constance Garnett. 9.95 (ISBN 0-394-60448-2). Modern Lib.

Anna Karenina. Lev Nikolaevich Tolstoi. (Orig.). pap. 0.90 o.p. (W1005). WSP.

Anna Karenina. Lev Nikolaevich Tolstoi. (World's Classics Ser: No. 210). 7.95 o.p. (ISBN 0-19-250210-7). Oxford U Pr.

Anna Karenina. Lev Nikolaevich Tolstoi. (Illus.). 968p. cancelled printed linen bdg. o.p. (ISBN 0-89050-277-3). Heritage Conn.

Anna Karenina. Lev Nikolaevich Tolstoi & Dole, Nathan Haskell, 1852-1935, Tr. LC 8-26750. T. Y. Crowell & Co.

Anna Karenina. Lev Nikolaevich Tolstoi & Garnett, Mrs. Constance (Black) 1862- Tr. LC 20-820. 1919. G. W. Jacobs & Company.

Anna Karenina. Lev Nikolaevich Tolstoi & Louise Shanks Maude. LC 79-41037. (World's classics). 1980. 5.95 (ISBN 0-19-251007-X). Oxford University Press.

Anna Karenina. Lev Nikolaevich Tolstoi & Townsend, Rochelle S., Tr. (Half-title: Everyman's library; ed. by Ernest Rhys. Fiction.). J. M. Dent & Sons, Ltd.

Anna Karenina. Lev Nikolavich Tolstoi & Garnett, Constance (Black) 1862- LC 46-8672. (Half-time: The Living library). 1946. The World Publishing Company.

Anna Karenina, Vol. 1. Lev Nikolaevich Tolstoi. 3.95x o.p. (Evman). Dutton.

Anna Karenina. Ed., Introd. by Leonard J. Kent, Nina Berberova. Constance Garnett Tr. Has Been Rev. Throughout by the Eds. Lev Nikolaevich Tolstoi. (Mod. lib. of the world's best bks.) Bibl.). 3.95. Random.

Anna Karenina. Foreword by E. Hudson Long. Lev Nikolaevich Tolstoi. LC 66-145594. (Great illus. classics: Titan eds.). 4.50. Dodd.

Anna Karenine. Lev Nikolaevich Tolstoi & Townsend, A. C., Tr. (On cover: The sovenir series, no. 65). 1892. The F. M. Lupton Publishing Company.

Anna Karenine. Lev Nikolaevich Tolstoi & Townsend, A. C., Tr. LC 40-14086. Illustrated Editions Company.

Anna Lombard. LC 43-39950. Kensington Press.

Anna Luhanna. Esther Chase. LC 46-9491. 1946. Greenberg.

Anna Malleen. George Hugh Brennan. LC 11-18195. 1911. 1.35. M. Kennerley.

Anna Nugent: A Novel. Isabel Constance Clarke. LC 24-8370. 1924. Benziger Brothers.

Anna of the Five Towns. Arnold Bennett. 1903. McClure, Phillips & Co.

Anna of the Five Towns: A Novel. Arnold Bennett. LC 74-5320. (collected works of Arnold Bennett). 1974. (ISBN 0-518-19082-X). Books for Libraries Press.

Anna St Ives. Thomas Holcroft. LC 71-496041. (Oxford English novels). 1970. Oxford U.P.

Anna Teller: By Jo Sinclair Pseud. Ruth Seid. LC 60-7114. 1960. D. Mc-Kay Co.

Anna the Adventuress. Edward Phillips Oppenheim. LC 4-1641. 1904. Little, Brown, & Company.

Anna: The Professor's Daughter... Marie Daal. Tr. by Mueller, Charles. LC 6-32229. 1885. Lee and Shepard.

Anna Zenger, Mother of Freedom. Kent Cooper. LC 46-7863. 1946. Farrar, Straus and Company.

Annabel: A Novel for Young Folks. Suzanne Metcalf. LC 6-32106. The Reilly & Britton Co.

Annabelle. Ann Fairfax. 176p. (Orig.). 1980. pap. 1.75 (ISBN 0-515-05399-6). Jove Pubns.

Annalisa. Christine Hunter, pseud. LC 75-181590. 1972. 3.95 (ISBN 0-8024-0230-5). Moody Press.

Annalisa: A Novel of Suspense. Forbes Rydell, pseud. LC 59-11186. (Torquil book). 1959. Distributed by Dodd, Mead.

Annals of a Baby. Sarah Bridges Stebbins. LC 12-15060. T. B. Peterson & Brothers.

Annals of a Baby. How It Was Named; How It Was Nursed; How It Was a Tyrant; and How Its Nose Got Out of Joint. Also, a Few Words About Its Aunties, Its Grandfathers, Grandmothers, and Other Important Relations. Sarah Bridges Stebbins. LC 8-14277. 1877. G. W. Carleton & Co.; Etc., Etc.

Annals of a Quiet Country Town: Other Sketches from Life. Julia Katherine Barnes. LC 2-26756. 1902. The Abbey Press.

Annals of a Quiet Neighborhood. George Macdonald. (Seaside library. v. 29, no. 595). 1879. G. Munro.

Annals of a Quiet Neighborhood. George Macdonald. LC 7-15850. (On cover: Harper's Franklin square library, no. 759). 1895. Harper & Brothers.

Annals of a Quiet Neighbourhood. George Macdonald. LC 42-26422. 1873. G. Routledge and Sons.

Annals of a Quiet Neighbourhood. George Macdonald. LC 4-16555. G. Routledge & Sons, Limited.

Annals of a Quiet Neighbourhood. George Macdonald. LC 12-18277. 1911. D. McKay.

Annals of a Sportsman. Ivan Sergieevich Turgenev & Abbott, Franklin Pierce, Tr. LC 8-32680. (On cover: Leisure hour series. no. 164). 1885. H. Holt and Company.

Annals of Ann. Kate Trimble Sharber. LC 10-25219. The Bobbs-Merrill Company.

Annals of Innocence and Experience. Herbert Edward Read. LC 74-7019. 1974. (ISBN 0-8383-1993-9). Haskell House Publishers.

Annals of the Parish. John Galt. (Nelson classics). T. Nelson.

Annals of the Parish. John Galt. LC 72-172250. (His Works, v. 1-2). (Illus.). 1968. AMS Press.

Annals of the Parish: And The Ayrshire Legatees. John Galt & Ainger, Alfred. LC 6-44474. 1895. Macmillan and Co.

Annam Jewel. Patricia Wentworth. LC 25-6202. 1924. A. Melrose, Ltd.

Annam Jewel. Patricia Wentworth. LC 25-7939. Small, Maynard & Company.

Annan Water. A Romance. Robert Williams Buchanan. (Harper's Franklin square library, no. 350). 1883. Harper & Brothers.

Annan Water. A Romance. Robert Williams Buchanan. (On cover: Seaside library. Pocket ed., no. 154). 1884. G. Munro.

Annan Water. A Romance. Robert Williams Buchanan. (Lovell's library, no. 1326). J. W. Lovell Company.

Annapolis Misfit. Kurt Schmidt. LC 73-90313. 1974. 5.95 (ISBN 0-517-51435-4). Crown Publishers.

Anna's. Constance Antonina Boyle. LC 25-8371. 1925. T. Seltzer.

Anna's Country. Elizabeth Lang. LC 81-80020. (Illus.). 1981. 6.95 (ISBN 0-930044-19-3). Naiad Press.

Anna's Diary. Joseph Juffo. LC 77-3640. 1977. 1.75 (ISBN 0-345-25406-6). Ballantine Books.

Anna's Story. Betty Hale Hyatt. LC 79-93211. 192p. (Orig.). 1980. pap. 1.95 (ISBN 0-87216-674-0). Playboy Pbks.

Anna's Woods. Audrey Odell. 2.50. Brown Penny Press.

Annd Chaos Died. Joanna Russ. (Berkley book). 1979. 1.95 (ISBN 0-425-04135-2). Berkley Pub. Corp.

Anne. Constance Fenimore Woolson. LC 76-51682. (Recovered Fiction by American Women). 1977. 22.00. Arno Press.

Anne. biographical ed. Constance Fenimore Woolson. 1899. Harper & Brothers.

Anne: A Novel. Olga Hartley. LC 21-1362. 1920. J. B. Lippincott Company.

Anne: A Novel. Constance Fenimore Woolson. LC 4-15185. 1882. Harper & Brothers.

Anne, Actress: The Romance of a Star. Juliet Gilman Sager. LC 13-202010. 1913. Frederick A. Stokes Company.

Anne & Jay. Barbara Bartholmer. 1982. pap. 1.75 (ISBN 0-451-11655-0, AE1655, Sig Vista). NAL.

Anne Belinda. Patricia Wentworth. LC 28-7752. 1928. J. B. Lippincott Company.

Anne Boleyn. Lily Moresby Adams Beck. LC 32-28017. 1932. Doubleday, Doran & Company, Inc.

Anne Boleyn. Reginald Drew. LC 13-627.

Anne Bonny. Chloe Gartner. LC 77-3182. 1977. 8.95 (ISBN 0-688-03208-7). Morrow.

Anne Carmel. Gwendolen Overton. 1903. The Macmillan Company.

Anne Du Rousier. L. Keppel. 1947. 2.00 o.p. Chr Classics.

Anne Feversham. John Collis Snaith. LC 14-18496. 1914. 1.35. D. Appleton and Company.

Anne Furness. A Novel. Frances Eleanor Ternan Trollope. LC 42-27070. 1871. Harper & Brothers.

Anne Furness. A Novel. Frances Eleanor Ternan Trollope. (seaside library. v. 69, no. 1401). 1882. G. Munro.

Anne Grey: A Novel. Thomas Henry Lister. LC 7-16035. 1835. Carey, Lea and Blanchard.

Anne Herrick. John Patrick Lally. LC 34-25929. A. L. Burt Company.

Anne Kempburn, Truthseeker. Marguerite Bryant. LC 10-213031. 1910. Duffield & Company.

Anne Marries Again. Louise Platt Hauck. LC 30-25624. The Penn Publishing Company.

Anne of Argyle: Or, Cavalier and Covenant. George Eyre-Todd. LC 14-193438. (On verso of half-title: West end series). Frederick A. Stokes Company.

Anne of Austria and Her Maids of Honor: A Tale of the Seventeenth Century. Eugene Sue. LC 25-15505. 1849. Stratton & Barnard.

Anne of Avonlea. L. M Montgomery. 1.50 (ISBN 0-553-02816-2). Bantam.

Anne of Avonlea. Lucy Maud Montgomery. LC 9-229413. 1909. 1.50. L. C. Page & Company.

Anne of Avonlea. Lucy Maud Montgomery. LC 20-18843. 1920. The Page Company.

Anne of Destiny House. Wilma Forrest. 1973. pap. 0.75 o.p. (T2721, GM). Fawcett World.

Anne of Geierstein. Walter Scott. LC 36-37113. (Half-title: Everyman's library, ed. by Ernest Rhys. Fiction. no. 125). 1927. J. M. Dent & Sons, Ltd.

Anne of Geierstein: Or, The Maiden of the Mist. Walter Scott. (On cover: Lovell's library, no. 595). 1885. J. W. Lovell Company.

Anne of Geierstein: Or, The Maiden of the Mist. Walter Scott. (Half-title: Everyman's library, ed. by Ernest Rhys. Fiction). 1907. J. M. Dent & Co.

Anne of Geierstein: Or, The Maiden of the Mist... From the Last Rev. Ed., Containing the Author's Final Corrections, Notes, &C. parker's ed. Walter Scott. (Waverley novels: Library ed. v. 22). 1831. Bazin & Ellsworth.

Anne of Geierstein: Or, The Maiden of the Mist. Count Robert of Paris. Walter Scott. LC 42-28858. J. Clarke and Company.

Anne of Green Gables. Lucy Maud Montgomery. LC 8-18572. 1908. L. C. Page & Company.

Anne of Green Gables. Lucy Maud Montgomery. LC 20-18814. 1920. The Page Company.

Anne of Green Gables. Lucy Maud Montgomery. LC 33-34147. 1933. L. C. Page & Company.

Anne of Ingleside. Lucy Maud Montgomery. LC 39-18157. 1939. Frederick A. Stokes Company.

Anne of St. Morven. Deborah Ross. (Candlelight Regency Ser.). (Orig.). Date not set. pap. 1.75 (ISBN 0-440-10052-6). Dell.

Anne of Summer Ho. Clare Rossiter. LC 76-28075. 1977. 7.95. St. Martin's Press.

Anne of the Barricades. Samuel Rutherford Crockett. LC 12-14460. Hodder and Stoughton.

Anne of the Blossom Shop: Or, The Growing up of Anne Carter. Isla May Hawley Mullins. LC 14-15180. 1914. 1.00. The Page Company.

Anne of the Island. Lucy Maud Montgomery. LC 15-15242. 1915. The Page Company.

Anne of Treboul. Marice Rutledge Hale. LC 10-12170. 1910. The Cnetury Co.

Anne of Windy Poplars. Lucy Maud Montgomery. LC 36-15378. 1936. Frederick A. Stokes Company.

Anne, Princess of Everything. Blanche Elizabeth Wade. Sully and Kleinteich.

Anne Scarlett. Mary Imlay Taylor. LC 1-244667. 1901. A. C. McClurg & Co.

Anne Seabury. Caroline Stetson Allen. LC 30-32327. Augustana Book Concern.

Anne Severin. Pauline Marie Armande Aglae Ferron De La Ferronnays Craven. LC 16-7555. Christian Press Association Publishing Company.

Anne Severin. Pauline Marie Armande Aglae Ferron De La Ferronnays Craven. LC 6-31069. 1869. G. P. Putnam and Son.

Anne Severn and the Fieldings. May Sinclair. LC 22-23903. 1922. The Macmillan Company.

Anne, the Rose of Hever. Maureen Peters. 1971. pap. 0.95 o.p. (95116). Beagle Bks.

Anneau d'amethyste. Anatole France, pseud. 1965. pap. 7.95. French & Eur.

Anneau d'Amethyste see Romans et Contes.

Anneti: The Gypsy Artist. Winfield Scott Sly. LC 1-31232. 1901. The Author.

Anneke: A Little Dame of New Netherlands. Elizabeth Williams Champney. LC 6759. (Her Dames and daughters of colonial days, v. 2.). 1900. Dodd, Mead and Company.

Annes. Marion Ames Taggart. LC 21-10016. 1921. Doubleday, Page & Company.

Anne's Bridge. Robert William Chambers. LC 14-20779. 1914. 1.00. D. Appleton and Company.

Anne's Head. Carol Blum. LC 81-9859. 1981. 13.95 (ISBN 0-385-27207-3). Dial Press.

Anne's House of Dreams. (Anne of Green Gables Bks). 6.95 (ISBN 0-448-02549-3, G&D). Putnam Pub Group.

Anne's House of Dreams. Lucy Maud Montgomery. LC 17-22301. Frederick A. Stokes Company.

Anne's Wedding: A Blossom Shop Romance. Isla May Hawley Mullins. LC 16-17729. 1916. 1.25. The Page Company.

Annetta: Or, The Story of a Life. Margie S Hughes. LC 7-5425. 1873. Nelson and Philips.

Annette. Erskine Caldwell. LC 73-80322. 1973. 6.95. New American Library.

Annette. Erskine Caldwell. (Signet book). 1974. (pbk.) 1.25. New American Library.

Annette and Bennett. Gilbert Cannan. LC 23-8359. 1923. T. Seltzer.

Annette: Or, The Chronicles of Bellevue. Charlotte Walsingham. 1875. Claxton, Remsen & Haffelfinger.

Annexation Society. Joseph Smith Fletcher. LC 25-11823. 1925. A. A. Knopf.

Annie. Leonore Fleischer & Carol Sobieski. LC 82-1686. (Illus.). 1982. 2.50 (ISBN 0-345-30451-9). Ballantine Books.

Annie. Gloria Jahoda. LC 60-921561. 1960. Houghton Mifflin.

Annie: A Novel. Paul Smith. LC 74-163585. 1972. 5.95. Dial Press.

Annie Allen. Gwendolyn Brooks. LC 78-138207. 60p. 1972. Repr. of 1949 ed. lib. bdg. 15.00x (ISBN 0-8371-5561-4, BRAA). Greenwood.

Annie: An Old-Fashioned Story. Thomas Meehan & Julia Noonan. LC 80-16335. (Illus.). 14.95. Macmillan.

Annie Besant's Rise to Power in Indian Politics, 1914-1917. Raj Kumar. 190p. 1982. text ed. 15.75x (ISBN 0-391-02492-2, Pub. by Concept India). Humanities.

Annie, Child of the Prairie. Annie Elizabeth Albright Scott & Ethel Etrick Watkins. LC 68-26117. (Illus.). Printed by Prairie Printers.

Annie Cooper's Friends, of "The Do Society" Series. C. B. Howard. LC 7-712828. 1893. Publishing House, Methodist Episcopal Church, South.

Annie Deane. Robert H Adleman. 1973. 1.25. Warner Paperback Lib.

Annie Deane. Robert H. Adleman. LC 75-154008. 1971. 6.95. World Pub. Co.

Annie Grayson: Or, Life in Washington. Nancy Polk Lasselle. LC 7-13847. 1853. H. Lasselle.

Annie Grayson: Or, Life in Washington. Nancy Polk Lasselle. LC 44-14181. 1853. Printed by H. B. Ashmead.

Annie Jordan. Mary Brinker Post. 1981. pap. 2.75 (ISBN 0-441-02332-0). Ace Bks.

Annie Jordan: A Novel of Seattle. Mary Brinker Post. LC 48-6153. 1948. Doubleday.

Annie Kilburn. William Dean Howells. LC 75-104490. 1970. (ISBN 0-8398-0795-3). Literature House.

Annie Kilburn. William Dean Howells. LC 19-147958. (Harper's modern classics). Harper & Brothers.

Annie Kilburn: A Novel. William Dean Howells. LC 72-145096. 1972. 19.50 (ISBN 0-403-01033-0). Scholarly Press.

Annie Kilburn: A Novel. William Dean Howells. LC 7-578283. (On cover: Harper's Franklin square library. new ser. no. 694). 1891. Harper & Brothers.

Annie Laurie Mine: A Story of Love, Economics and Religion. David Nelson Beach. LC 3-13015. 1902. The Pilgrim Press.

Annie Laurie (of the River Aire) Lera. LC 76-4082. 7.95 (ISBN 0-914042-09-2) (ISBN 0-914042-10-6). Coral Reef Publications.

Annie Parsons. Sarah Shears. LC 79-670274. 1979. 10.95 (ISBN 0-236-40135-1). Elek.

Annie Reilly: Or, The Fortunes of an Irish Girl in New York. A Tale Founded on Fact. John McElgun. LC 7-20098. 1873. J. A. McGee.

Annie Reilly: Or, The Fortunes of an Irish Girl in New York. A Tale Founded on Fact. John McElgun. LC 44-481006. 1878. J. A. McGee.

Annie Wallace: Or, The Exile of Penang. A Tale. Harlan Page Halsey. LC 7-1199. 1857. Miller & Holman.

Annie's Captain. 1st Ed. Kathryn Cavarly Hulme. LC 61-5734. 1961. Little, Brown.

Annihilation. Isabel Egenton Ostrander. LC 24-5455. 1924. R. M. McBride & Company.

Annihilator One World. 1979. pap. write for info. (ISBN 0-88074-201-1). Metagam.

Annis Warden: Or, A Story of Real Life. Julia Flander Wheelock. LC 8-36048. 1889. Republican Print.

Anniversaries. John Jenkins Espey. LC 63-8091. 1963. Harcourt, Brace & World.

Anniversaries: From the Life of Gesine Cresspahl. Uwe Johnson. LC 74-20942. 1975. 10.00 (ISBN 0-15-107560-3). Harcourt Brace Jovanovich.

Anniversary. Ludwig Lewisohn. LC 74-156199. 1972. (ISBN 0-8371-5974-1). Greenwood Press.

Anniversary. Ludwig Lewisohn. LC 48-511441. 1948. Farrar, Strauss.

Anniversary Murder... Eden Phillpotts. LC 37-270119. 1936. E. P. Dutton & Co., Inc.

Anno Domini: Three Stories. George Steiner. LC 64-25366. 1964. Atheneum.

Anno Domini: Three Stories. George Steiner. LC 80-15345. 1980. 10.95 (ISBN 0-87951-113-3). Overlook Press.

Annotated Christmas Carol. Charles Dickens & Michael Patrick Hearn. LC 76-21345. (Illus.). 12.95 (ISBN 0-517-52741-3). C. N. Potter: Distributed by Crown Publishers.

Annotated Christmas Carol. Michael P. Hearn. (Illus.). 1976. 15.00 (ISBN 0-517-52741-3, C N Potter Bks). Crown.

Annotated Dracula: Annotated Ed. of Dracula. Bram Stoker. Ed. by Leonard Wolf. LC 75-4544. (Illus.). 1975. (ISBN 0-517-52017-6). C. N. Potter: Distributed by Crown Publishers.

Annotated Frankenstein. Mary Wollstonecraft Godwin Shelley & Leonard Wolf. LC 77-7458. (Illus.). 14.95 (ISBN 0-517-53071-6). C. N. Potter: Distributed by Crown Publishers.

Annotated Gulliver's Travels. Jonathan Swift & Isaac Asimov. LC 80-15032. 19.95 (ISBN 0-517-53949-7). C. N. Potter: Distributed by Crown Publishers.

Annotated Huckleberry Finn: Adventures of Huckleberry Finn. Michael P. Hearn. (Illus.). 352p. 1982. 25.00 (ISBN 0-517-53031-7, C N Potter Bks). Crown.

Annotated Huckleberry Finn: The Adventures of Huckleberry Finn. Mark Twain & Michael Patrick Hearn. LC 81-5904. 25.00 (ISBN 0-517-53031-7). C.N. Potter; Distributed by Crown Publishers.

Annotated Jules Verne, From the Earth to the Moon, Direct in Ninety-Seven Hours and Twenty Minutes. Walter James Miller & Jules Verne. LC 78-3327. (Illus.). 14.95 (ISBN 0-690-01701-4). Crowell.

Annotated Jules Verne, Twenty Thousand Leagues Under the Sea. Walter James Miller. LC 76-10968. 1976. 16.95 (ISBN 0-690-01151-2). Crowell.

Annotated Lolita. Vladimir Vladimirovich Nabokov. Ed. by Alfred Appel. LC 75-95819. 1970. McGraw-Hill.

Annotated Pilgrim's Progress. Warren W. Wiersbe. LC 80-427. 1980. 8.95 (ISBN 0-8024-0229-1). Moody.

Annotated Sherlock Holmes: The Four Novels and the Fifty-Six Short Stories Complete. Arthur Conan Doyle. LC 67-22406. 1967. C. N. Potter: Distributed by Crown Publishers.

Annotated Snark. Martin Gardner. (O.S.I.). 1962. 3.95 o.s.i. (03450). S&S.

Annotated Tales of Edgar Allan Poe. Edgar Allan Poe. Ed. by Stephen Peithman. LC 79-8032. (Illus.). 672p. 1981. 35.00 (ISBN 0-385-14990-5). Doubleday.

Annotated Uncle Tom's Cabin. Harriet Elizabeth Beecher Stowe & Stern, Philip Van Doren, 1900- Ed. LC 64-15781. 1964. P. S. Eriksson.

Annotated Wizard of Oz. Michael P. Hearn. (Illus.). 384p. 1973. 20.00 (ISBN 0-517-50086-8, C N Potter Bks). Crown.

Annouchka: A Tale. by franklin abbott. ed. Ivan Sergieevich Turgenev & Abbott, Franklin Pierce, Tr. 1884. Cupples, Upham and Company.

Announcer. Donald Landels Henderson. LC 45-4044. 1945. Hurst & Blackett, Ltd.

Ann's an Idiot: A Novel. Winifred Mary Scott. LC 23-13007. Frederick A. Stokes Company.

Ann's Crime: Still Another Adventure of "Secret Service Smith". Reginald Thomas Maitland Scott. LC 26-17610. E. P. Dutton & Company.

Annual of the Year's Best Science Fiction, 6th. Ed. by Judith Merril. (O.s.i.). 1961. 3.95 o.s.i. (ISBN 0-671-83601-3). S&S.

Annual of the Year's Best SF. 1st-? 1956- Ed. by Judith Merril. LC 56-8938. Simon and Schuster Etc.

Annulet of Gilt. Phoebe Atwood Taylor. (Asey Mayo Mystery Series). 1968. 4.95 o.p. (ISBN 0-393-08564-3). Norton.

Annulet of Gilt: An Asey Mayo Mystery. Phoebe Atwood Taylor. LC 38-5877. W. W. Norton & Co., Inc.

Annunciation: A Novel. Ellen Gilchrist. LC 83-800. 1983. 13.45 (ISBN 0-316-31302-5). Little, Brown.
Anointing. Martha Mabey. (Orig.). 1982. pap. 2.95 (ISBN 0-440-10033-X). Dell.
Anomalous Phenomena. Jules Verne. 3.95. Assoc Bk.
Anomaly. Jerry Sohl. 1972. pap. 0.75 o.p. (07151). Curtis.
Anome; Durdane: Book I. Jack Vance. 1973. 0.95. Dell.
Anon Eight: The Street Fiction Anthology of Fictions & Poetry. Warren Jay Hecht. 96p. 1974. pap. 3.45 o.p. (ISBN 0-914908-74-X). Street Fiction.
Anon Nine: The Street Fiction Anthology of Prose Fiction. Warren Jay Hecht. LC 75-19942. (Illus.). 1975. pap. 3.95 o.p. (ISBN 0-914908-75-8). Street Fiction.
Anon Ten. Warren Jay Hecht. LC 77-8167. 3.95 (ISBN 0-914908-76-6). Street Fiction Press.
Anonymity of Sacrifice. I. N. C Aniebo. LC 75-321120. (African writers series; 148). (HEB paperback). (Illus.). 1974-1975. 2.00 (ISBN 0-435-90148-6). Heinemann Educational.
Anonymous Footsteps. John Marshall O'Connor. LC 33-485. 1932. Cheshire House.
Anonymous Lover. John Logan. 1973. 5.95 (ISBN 0-87140-564-4); pap. 2.95 (ISBN 0-87140-280-7). Liveright.
Another Bad Girl. Lester L Gotha. LC 36-35995. 1936. Godwin.
Another Beginning. Sian James. LC 81-1459. 1981. 9.95 (ISBN 0-395-30535-7). Houghton Mifflin.
Another Bob: Or, What Father and Mother Sparenot, Uncle Ham and Auntie Hephzibah and Others Had to Say. h. horace romig. ed. Henry Horace Romig. LC 399. 1899. The Milton Printing Co.
Another Caesar: A Novel. Alfred Neumann. Tr. by Paul, Eden. LC 35-1485. 1935. A. A. Knopf.
Another Cat Book. Charles Ortleb & Arthur Howard. 1979. pap. 4.95 (ISBN 0-312-04195-0); prepack 49.50 (ISBN 0-312-04196-9). St Martin.
Another Chance. Med Bridgeforth. LC 73-18569. Repr. of 1951 ed. 12.50 (ISBN 0-404-11379-6). AMS Pr.
Another Chance: A Novel. Med Bridgeforth. LC 51-6674. 1951. Exposition Press.
Another Claudia. Rose Franken. LC 43-4272. 1943. Farrar & Rinehart, Inc.
Another Claudia. Rose Franken. LC 46-20591. 1946. The Sun Dial Press.
Another Country. James B. Baldwin. LC 61-7367. 1962. Dial Press.
Another Cynthia: The Adventures of Cynthia, Lady Ffulkes (1780-1850) Reconstructed from Her Hitherto Unpublished Memoirs. Doris Oppenheim Leslie, pseud. LC 39-27808. 1939. The Macmillan Companu.
Another Day. Jeffery Farnol. 1929. Little, Brown, and Company.
Another Day, Another Death. George Bagby, pseud. 1969. pap. 0.60 o.p. (0502-06006-060). Curtis.
Another Day, Another Death. George Bagby, pseud. 1968. 3.95 o.p. Doubleday.
Another Day, Another Death. Aaron Marc Stein. LC 68-14050. 1968. Published for the Crime Club by Doubleday.
Another Day in Another Way. A Littlefellow. LC 34-40675. D. D. Mangone.
Another Day Toward Dying. Melba Balmat Grimes Marlett. LC 43-251521. 1943. Pub. for the Crime Club by Doubleday, Doran and Company, Inc.
Another Fine Myth. Robert L. Asprin & Polly Freas. LC 78-2630. (Illus.). 1978. 4.95 (ISBN 0-915442-54-X). Starblaze Editions.
Another Front: A Novel of World War II. Mack Leonard. 165p. 1976. 6.95 (ISBN 0-87881-036-6); pap. 2.50 o.p. (ISBN 0-87881-037-4). Mojave Bks.
Another Helen: A Novel. Lane Kauffmann. LC 68-14131. 1968. Lippincott.
Another I, Another You: A Love Story for the Once-Married. Richard Schickel. LC 77-3805. 9.95 (ISBN 0-06-013794-0). Harper & Row.
Another Issue. LC 1-31176. (personal edition of George Eliot's works). Doubleday, Page & Co.
Another Kind. Anthony P West. LC 52-5253. 1952. Houghton Mifflin.
Another Kind of Love. Paula Christian. LC 79-92584. 144p. 1980. pap. 6.95 (ISBN 0-931328-06-3). Timely Bks.
Another Kind of Magic. Allen Charltte Vale. 1.75 (ISBN 0-446-84356-3). Warner Books.
Another Kind of Rain. Gerald W. Barrax. LC 75-117470. (Pitt Poetry Ser). 1970. 7.95 o.p. (ISBN 0-8229-3206-7); pap. 4.50 o.p. (ISBN 0-8229-5218-1). U of Pittsburgh Pr.
Another Kind: Science-Fiction Stories. Chad Oliver. LC 55-116475. 1955. Ballantine Books.
Another Kind: Science-Fiction Stories. Symmes Chadwick Oliver. LC 55-11647. 1955. Ballentine Books.
Another Land. Richard Vasquez. 288p. 1982. pap. 2.75 (ISBN 0-380-79400-4, 79400). Avon.
Another Life. Rosemary Carter. (Harlequin Presents Ser.). 192p. 1981. pap. 1.75 (ISBN 0-373-10469-3). Harlequin Bks.
Another Life. Derek Walcott. 152p. 1973. pap. 3.95 o.p. (ISBN 0-374-51052-0, N443, Noonday). FS&G.
Another Little Death. William Price Turner. LC 77-142840. 1971. 4.95 (ISBN 0-8027-5220-9). Walker.
Another Lonely Voice: The Urdu Short Stories of Saadat Hasan Manto. Leslie A. Flemming. 1979. 10.75 o.p. UC Ctr S&SE Asian.
Another Look at Two Spirits. Jay Pascal. 1977. 5.95 o.p. Vantage.
Another Look at Two Spirits. Jay Pascal. 1973. 5.95 (ISBN 0-533-00458-6). Vantage.
Another Love, Another Spring. B. M Sawdon & Wansbrough, P., Joint Author. LC 47-2031. 1946. S. Curl, Inc.
Another Love, Another Time. Anthony Tuttle. (Orig.). 1979. pap. 2.50 (ISBN 0-89083-486-5). Zebra.
Another Man's Life. John Edwin Canaday. LC 53-1941. (Inner sanctum mystery). 1953. Simon and Schuster.
Another Man's Life. Barbara Noble. LC 51-4408. 1951. Doubleday.
Another Man's Murder. Mignon Good Eberhart. LC 57-10056. 1957. Random House.
Another Man's Poison: A Sheriff Macready Detective Story. Hugh Holman. LC 47-19152. 1947. M. S. Mill Co., Inc.
Another Man's Shoes. Victor Bridges. LC 13-15685. George H. Doran Company, Publishers in America for Hodder & Stoughton.
Another Man's Shoes. 1st Ed. Betsy Beaton. LC 53-8975. 1953. Holt.
Another Man's Wife. Charlotte Mary Brame. (Primrose edition, no, 1). Street & Smith.
Another Man's Wife. Charlotte Mary Brame. (On cover: Street & Smith's select series, no, 101). Street & Smith.
Another Man's Wife. Bertha M. Clay. LC 46-40930. (Primrose edition, no. 1). 1890. Street & Smith.
Another Man's Wife. Bertha M. Clay. LC 44-11671. (On cover: Street & Smith's select series, no. 101). Street & Smith.
Another Man's Wife. Marie Adelaide Belloc Lowndes. LC 34-897723. 1934. Longmans, Green and Co.
Another Man's Wife. Tr. from Spanish by John Marks. 1st Amer Ed. Luca De Tena, Torcuato. LC 64-12325. bds., 5.95. Knopf.
Another Morgue Heard from. 1st Ed. Frederick Clyde Davis. LC 54-9844. 1954. Published for the Crime Club by Doubleday.
Another Morning. Wessel Smitter. LC 41-617812. Harper & Brothers.
Another Mother Tongue: Stories from the Ancient Gay Tradition. Judy Grahn. (Orig.). 1983. pap. price not set (ISBN 0-930436-13-X). Persephone.
Another Mug for the Bier. 1st Ed. Richard Starnes. LC 50-10349. (Main line mysteries). 1950. Lippincott.
Another Mystery in Suva. Frank Arthur. LC 81-47382. (Fifty classics in crime fiction, 1950-1975). 1982. 14.95 (ISBN 0-8240-4989-6). Garland.
Another Night,--Another Day. John Klempner. LC 41-5109. 1941. C. Scribner's Sons.
Another "Odd" Book: Twenty-Five Selected Stories of O. O. McIntyre. Oscar Odd McIntyre. LC 32-13572. 1932. Cosmopolitan Magazine.
Another Ophelia. Edwin Moultrie Lanham. LC 38-5608. 1938. Longmans, Green and Co.
Another Pamela: Or, Virtue Still Rewarded, a Story. Upton Beall Sinclair. LC 50-6910. 1950. Viking Press.
Another Part of the House. Winston M. Estes. LC 70-91674. 1970. 5.95. Lippincott.
Another Part of the House. Winston M Estes. 1978. 1.75 (ISBN 0-380-01959-0). Avon Books.
Another Part of the Wood. Denis George Mackail. LC 29-4533. 1929. Houghton Mifflin Company.
Another Pasture. Mary Elizabeth Osborn. LC 40-2696. B. Humphries, Inc.
Another Roadside Attraction. Tom Robbins. LC 73-144292. 1971. 6.95. Doubleday.
Another Roadside Attraction. Tom Robbins. LC 73-175890. 1973. 2.25 (ISBN 0-491-00804-X). W. H. Allen.
Another Runner in the Night. Robert Granit. LC 80-66265. 9.95 (ISBN 0-89479-074-9). A & W Publishers.
Another Scandal. Cosmo Hamilton. LC 23-12708. 1923. Little, Brown, and Company.
Another Side of the Blues: Seven Stories. Charles Wilder. (Orig.). 1980. pap. 6.00 (ISBN 0-682-49543-3). Exposition.
Another Sky. Naomi Lane Babson. 1956. Harcourt, Brace.
Another Spring. Loula Grace Erdman. LC 66-24270. 1966. Dodd, Mead.
Another Spring. Henry S Maxfield. LC 74-4140. 1974. 6.95 (ISBN 0-316-55120-1). Little, Brown.
Another Spring. Winifred West. LC 58-75887. Avalon Books.
Another Such Victory. Clifton Cuthbert. LC 74-22777. (Labor Movement in Fiction and Non-Fiction). 1976. 17.00 (ISBN 0-404-58417-9). AMS Press.
Another Such Victory. Clifton Cuthbert. LC 37-1664. 1937. Hillman-Curl, Inc.
Another Such Victory. John Downing Weaver. LC 48-6248. 1948. Viking Press.
Another Sun, Another Home. Rupert Croft-Cooke. LC 49-7945. 1949. H. Holt.
Another Three-Act Special: 3 Complete Mystery Novels: False Scent. Scales of Justice. Singing in the Shrouds. Ngaio Marsh. LC 62-9542. 1962. Little, Brown.
Another Three Weeks: Not by El-N-R Gl-N. James Stetson Metcalfe. LC 8-4441. 1908. Life Publishing Company.
Another Time: Another Place. Lenore Coffee. LC 56-11359. 1956. Crown Publishers.
Another Time, Another Voice: A Novel of the Seventeenth Century. Barnet Litvinoff. LC 72-187436. 1971. 2.00 (ISBN 0-491-00357-9). W. H. Allen.
Another Tomorrow. Elinor Maxwell. LC 36-194420. 1936. Arcadia House.
Another Tomorrow. Lois L Smith. LC 56-12650. (Pan Press fiction library book). Pan Press.
Another Tomorrow: A Science Fiction Anthology. Bernard Hollister. LC 74-180292. (Illus.). 1974. (ISBN 0-8278-0037-1). Pflaum Pub.
Another View. Rosamunde Pilcher. LC 73-92055. 1974. 5.95. St. Martin's Press.
Another War - Another World. Duane C. Booth. 226p. 1973. 7.50 o.p. (ISBN 0-682-47701-X). Exposition.
Another Way of Dying. Francis Clifford. (YA) 1969. 4.95 o.p. (ISBN 0-698-10022-0). Coward.
Another Way of Dying. Arthur Leonard Bell Thompson. LC 69-11058. 1969. 4.95. Coward-McCann.
Another Way Out. Eric Tucker. LC 81-85735. 80p. 1983. pap. 4.95 (ISBN 0-86666-057-7). GWP.
Another Way Out: A Thematic Reader. L. A. Michel. LC 73-15807. 1974. pap. text ed. 8.50 o.p. (ISBN 0-03-008156-4, HoltC). HR&W.
Another Way to Die. John Crowe, pseud. LC 77-37034. 224p. 1973. pap. 0.95 o.p. (532-95290-095). Manor Bks.
Another Way to Die. John Crowe, pseud. 1972. 4.95 o.p. (ISBN 0-394-47044-3). Random.
Another Way to Die. Dennis Lynds. LC 77-37034. (Buena Costa County mystery). (Illus.). 1972. 4.95 (ISBN 0-394-47044-3). Random House.
Another Way to Die. John Crowe Lynds. 1973. (pbk.) 0.95. Manor Books.
Another Weeping Woman. Donald Zochert. LC 79-22759. 9.95 (ISBN 0-03-046681-4). Holt, Rinehart and Winston.
Another Weeping Woman. Donald Zochert. LC 83-1955. 1983. 12.95 (ISBN 0-89340-602-3). J. Curley.
Another Woman's House. Mignon Good Eberhart. LC 47-30112. 1947. Random House.
Another Woman's Husband. Charlotte Mary Brame. (On cover: Street & Smith's select series, no. 92). Street & Smith.
Another Woman's Husband. Bertha M. Clay. LC 44-11670. (On cover: Street & Smith's select series, no. 92). Street & Smith.
Another World. James Hanley. LC 72-188191. 1972. 5.95 (ISBN 0-8180-0613-7). Horizon Press.
Another World: A Science Fiction Anthology. Gardner Dozois. LC 76-19885. 7.95. (ISBN 0-695-80695-5) (ISBN 0-695-40695-7). Follett Pub. Co.
Another Year: A Novel. Robert Cedric Sherriff. LC 48-6451. 1948. Macmillan Co.
Another's Crime. From the Diary of Inspector Byrnes. Julian Hawthorne. LC 12-25951. Cassell & Company.
Anouk in Love: A Novel. Christine Arnothy. LC 75-13481. 1975. 7.95 (ISBN 0-385-04065-2). Doubleday.
Anowa. Ama Ata Aidoo. (Sun-Lit Ser.). 64p. 1980. 9.00x o.s.i. (ISBN 0-89410-087-4); pap. 5.00x o.s.i. (ISBN 0-89410-088-2). Three Continents.
Anowa. Ama Ata Aidoo. 1970. pap. text ed. 2.50x o.p. (ISBN 0-582-64031-8). Longman.
ANPAO: An American Indian Odyssey. Jamake Highwater. LC 77-9264. (Illus.). 256p. 1980. pap. 5.95i (ISBN 0-06-090762-2, CN 762, CN). Har-Row.
Anselma: Or, In Spite of All. by arthur d. hall. this story is based upon the famous play of the same name, by victorian sardou. ed. Arthur D Hall & Sardou, Victorien, 1831- Anselma. LC 7-539. 1886. Rand, McNally & Co.
Ansel's Cave. A Story of Early Life in the Western Reserve. Albert Gallatin Riddle. 1893. The Burrows Brothers Company.
Answer. Jeremy Larner. LC 68-12931. 1968. Macmillan.
Answer. Philip Wylie. LC 56-7006. 1956. Rinehart.
Answer As a Man. Taylor Caldwell. LC 80-18187. 12.95 (ISBN 0-399-12566-3). Putnam.
Answer from a Dead Man. George P. Cronin. LC 77-90457. 1978. pap. 1.95 o.s.i. (ISBN 0-89516-021-8). Condor Pub Co.
Answer from Limbo: A Novel. 1st Ed. Brian Moore. LC 62-17946. 1962. Little, Brown.
Answer in the Sky. Dieter Meichsner. LC 53-10793. 1953. Funk & Wagnalls.
Answer in the Tide. Elisabeth Ogilvie. LC 77-26012. 10.95 (ISBN 0-07-047664-0). McGraw-Hill.
Answer in the Tide. Elisabeth Ogilvie. LC 79-17912. 1979. 15.95 (ISBN 0-8161-6751-6). G. K. Hall.
Answer in the Tide. large print ed. Elisabeth Ogilvie. (General Ser.). 1979. lib. bdg. 15.95 (ISBN 0-8161-6751-6, Large Print Bks). G K Hall.
Answer Me! Answer Me! Jeanne Davis Glynn. LC 76-112284. 1970. Bruce Pub. Co.
Answer to a Christmas Prayer. Annie S Swan Smith. (On cover: Once a week library, no. 12). 1894. P. F. Collier.
Answered in Jest. Dora Delmar. (On cover: Library of American authors. no. 61). 1895. G. Munro's Sons.
Answered in the Negative. Mary Platt Parmele. Parmele & Chaffee.
Answerer. Grant Martin Overton. LC 21-18802. 1921. Harcourt, Brace and Company.
Answering Glory. Ray Coryton Hutchinson. LC 32-187298. Farrar & Rinehart, Incorporated.
Answering Message: And Other Naval Stories. Rush M Hoag. LC 12-288. 1.00. Broadway Publishing Co.
Ant and Bee, and Kind Dog: An Alphabetical Story. Angela Banner. LC 63-20114. (Bk. 7). bds. 1.50. Watts.
Ant Heap. Vincent Gaston Dethier. LC 79-52701. (Illus.). 7.95 (ISBN 0-87850-034-0). Darwin Press.
Ant Heap: A Novel. Edward Knoblock. LC 30-12147. 1930. Minton, Balch & Company.
Ant Hills. Hannah Berman. LC 27-2810. Payson & Clarke, Ltd.
Ant Men. Eric North. 1971. pap. 0.75 o.p. (75-443). Manor Bks.
Antagonists. Owen Cameron. LC 46-6908. 1946. Doubleday & Company, Inc.
Antagonists. Richard Clayton. LC 64-21635. 1964. I. Washburn.
Antagonists. Roy Doliner. LC 67-19100. 1967. Doubleday.
Antagonists. Paul Hervey Fox. LC 37-599537. H. Holt and Company.
Antagonists. Ernest Kellogg Gann. LC 70-130472. 1970. 6.95. Simon and Schuster.
Antagonists. William Haggard. 1964. 3.50 o.p. Washburn.
Antagonists. Ernest Temple Thurston. LC 12-212746. 1912. D. Appleton and Company.
Antagonists see Masada.
Antar: A Bedoueen Romance. 1983. Repr. of 1819 ed. 35.00x (ISBN 0-8201-1375-1). Schol Facsimiles.
Antar: A Bedoueen Romance (1819) facsim. reproduction / with an introduction by ben harris mcclary. ed. Terrick Hamilton. LC 81-21401. 1981. 35.00 (ISBN 0-8201-1375-1). Scholars' Facsimiles & Reprints.
Antarctic Mystery. Jules Verne. LC 75-5898. (Gregg Press science fiction series). 1975. 15.00 (ISBN 0-8398-2316-9) (ISBN 0-8398-2316-9) (ISBN 0-8398-2316-9). Gregg Press.
Antarctic Mystery. Translated by Mrs. Cashel Hoey. Jules Verne. LC 56-50474. 1900. Lippincott.
Antarctic Secret. Illus. by Stuart Tresilian. Michael Barrett. LC 65-251516. 1966. bds., 3.50. Roy.
Ante Bellum. Southern Life As It Was. Mary Louise Cook. 1868. J. B. Lippincott & Co.
Ante-Mortem Statement. Edgar Watson Howe. LC 7-7126. (Howe's quarterly series no. 1). 1891. The Globe Publishing Co.
Ante-Mortem Statement see Collected Works.
Antenna Syndrome. Alan Marks. 1979. pap. 1.75 o.s.i. (ISBN 0-505-51343-9). Tower Bks.
Antennae. Hulbert Footner. LC 26-17246. George H. Doran Company.
Anteroom. Kate O'Brien. LC 34-33476. 1934. Doubleday, Doran & Company, Inc.
Anteros. George Alfred Lawrence. LC 44-32800. 1888. G. Routledge and Sons.
Anteros. A Novel. George Alfred Lawrence. LC 41-40512. 1871. Harper & Brothers.
Anthe. Izora Cecilia Chandler. LC 6-23129. 1885. Phillips & Hunt.
Anthea Gordon. Christine Hunter, pseud. LC 81-2308. 3.50 (ISBN 0-8024-0285-2). Moody Press.
Anthem. Noel Bertram Gerson. (M1136). 1968. Fawcett.

Anthem. Noel Bertram Gerson. LC 67-15786. 1967. Published by M. Evans, and Distributed in Association with Lippincott, Philadelphia.
Anthem. Ayn Rand. LC 52-5216. 1953. Caxton Printers.
Anthem. Ayn Rand. LC 47-1578. (Freeman... vol. III, no. I). 1946. Pamphleteers, Inc.
Anthill. Daniel Gilles. 1963. 4.50 o.p. (ISBN 0-8149-0105-0). Vanguard.
Anthology of Another Town see Collected Works.
Anthology of Best Original Short-Shorts. Ed. by Robert Oberfirst. LC 54-336766. (Oberfirst's short-short fiction library.). Oberfirst Publications.
Anthology of Best Short Short Stories. V. 1-1952- LC 54-33676. Etc. F. Fell Etc.
Anthology of Cities. Alice Elinor Bowen Bartlett. 1977. Repr. of 1927 ed. 30.00 (ISBN 0-89984-043-4). Century Bookbindery.
Anthology of Contemporary Chinese Literature: Taiwan: 1949-1974, Short Stories, Vol. 2. Ed. by Pang-Yuan Chi et al. LC 75-42791. 484p. 1976. 17.50 (ISBN 0-295-95503-1, Pub. by Natl Inst Comp Taiwan); pap. 9.50 (ISBN 0-295-95629-1); 2 Vol. Set 35.00. U of Wash Pr.
Anthology of Famous American Stories. Ed. by John Angus Burrell & Bennett Alfred Cerf. LC 53-9916. (Modern library of the world's best books. A Modern library giant, G77). 1953. Modern Library.
Anthology of Famous American Stories. Bennett Alfred Cerf. 1953. 5.95 o.s.i. (ISBN 0-394-60777-5). Modern Lib.
Anthology of Famous British Stories. 4.95 o.p. (G54). Modern Lib.
Anthology of Famous British Stories. Ed. by Bennett Alfred Cerf. LC 52-5878. (Modern library of the world's best books). 1952. Modern Library.
Anthology of Korean Literature: From Early Times to the Nineteenth Century. Ed. by Peter H. Lee. LC 81-69567. 448p. 1981. lib. bdg. 24.00x (ISBN 0-8248-0739-1); pap. text ed. 12.00x (ISBN 0-8248-0756-1). UH Pr.
Anthology of Modern Historical Fiction. Ed. by Frederick James Tickner. LC 39-2167. (Half-title: Modern anthologies; general editor--Richard Wilson... no. 11). 1938. T. Nelson and Sons, Ltd.
Anthology of Modern Prose. Ed. by Arthur James John Ratcliff. LC 38-52532. (Half-title: Modern anthologies; general editor--Richard Wilson... no. 1). 1936. T. Nelson and Sons, Ltd.
Anthology of Modern Short Stories. Ed. by James William Marriott. LC 39-1647. (Half-title: Modern anthologies; general editor--Richard Wilson... no. 10). 1938. T. Enlson and Sons, Ltd.
Anthology of Modern Turkish Short Stories. Fahir Iz. LC 77-89828. (Studies in Middle Eastern Literatures: No. 9). cloth o.p. 20.00x (ISBN 0-88297-021-6); pap. 12.50x (ISBN 0-88297-022-4). Bibliotheca.
Anthology of Mystery and Suspense. 1st Ed. The Reader's Digest. LC 59-13447. 1959. Reader's Digest Association.
Anthology of Pre-Revolutionary Russian Science Fiction. Ed. by L. Fetzer. 370p. 1981. 27.50 (ISBN 0-88233-594-4). Ardis Pubs.
Anthology of Russian Romanticism. Ed. by Christine Rydel. 1983. 25.00 (ISBN 0-88233-741-6). Ardis Pubs.
Anthology of Sinhalese Literature up to 1815. Ed. by C. H. Reynolds. (UNESCO Collection of Representative Works). 377p. 1970. 17.50x o.p. (ISBN 0-8448-0025-2). Crane-Russak Co.
Anthology of Soviet Short Stories. Nikolai Sergeevich Atarov. LC 77-364071. (Progress Soviet authors library). (Illus.). 1976. Progress.
Anthology of the Best Short Short Stories. Vol. 8. Edited by Robert Oberfirst. LC 54-33676. 3.95. Oberfirst Pubns.
Anthology of Yugoslav Short Stories. Indian Council For Cultural Relations. 1969. 8.25 o.p. Verry.
Anthony Adverse. Hervey Allen. LC 74-151896. 1960. Holt, Rinehart and Winston.
Anthony Adverse. Hervey Allen. LC 33-27189. 1933. Farrar and Rinehart, Inc.
Anthony Adverse. Hervey Allen. 1978. 2.50 (ISBN 0-446-81439-3). Warner Books.
Anthony Adverse. Hervey Allen & Wyeth, Newell Convers, 1882-Illus. LC 34-33869. 1934. Farrar and Rinehart, Inc.
Anthony Cuthbert. Richard Bagot. LC 9-19668. 1909. Brentano's.
Anthony Dare. Archibald Marshall. LC 23-151596. 1923. Dodd, Mead and Company.
Anthony Dare's Progress. Archibald Marshall. LC 24-21806. 1924. 2.00. Dodd, Mead and Company.
Anthony in the Nude. Myron Brinig. LC 30-12292. Farrar & Rinehart, Incorporated.
Anthony John. Jerome Klapka Jerome. LC 23-7989. 1923. 2.00. Dodd, Mead and Company.
Anthony John: A Biography. Jerome Klapka Jerome. LC 23-7988. 1923. Cassell and Company, Ltd.
Anthony Melgrave: A Novel. Thomas M'Caleb. LC 7-15275. 1892. G. P. Putnam's Sons.
Anthony Overman. Miriam Michelson. LC 6-27355. 1906. Doubleday, Page & Company.
Anthony the Absolute. Samuel Merwin. LC 14-4459. 1914. 1.35. The Century Co.
Anthony Trant. John Hyatt Downing. LC 41-20723. 1941. G. P. Putnam's Sons.
Anthony Trent: Master Criminal. Wyndham Martyn. LC 18-22364. 1918. Moffat, Yard & Company.
Anthony Tressel. Somers Gill. LC 42-15551. 1942. Rich & Cowan.
Anthracite Country. Jay Parini. LC 81-10588. 68p. 1982. 10.50 (ISBN 0-394-52263-X); pap. 5.95 (ISBN 0-394-70454-1). Random.
Anthrax Mutation. Alan Scott. 1976. (pbk.) 1.50 (ISBN 0-515-03949-7). Pyramid Books.
Anti-Babel: And Other Such Doings. William Henry Bishop. LC 20-6263. 1919. The Neale Publishing Company.
Anti-Death League. Kingsley Amis. LC 66-18822. 5.95. Harcourt.
Anti-Death League. Kingsley Amis. (U6114). 1967. Ballantine.
Anti-Death League. Kingsley Amis. 1975. (pbk.) 2.25 (ISBN 0-14-002803-X). Penguin.
Anti Fanaticism: A Tale of the South. Martha Haines Butt. LC 2-19884. 1853. Lippincott, Grambo, and Co.
Anti-Man. Dean R. Koontz. (Orig.). 1970. pap. 0.60 o.p. (63-384). Paperback Lib.
Anti-Matter. C. M Stanbury. LC 76-30638. (American dust series; no. 7). 1977. 7.95 (ISBN 0-913218-55-3) (ISBN 0-913218-54-5). Dustbooks.
Anti-Social Register. Ed. by Alfred Hitchcock. 1975. (pbk.) 0.95. Dell.
Anti-Story: An Anthology of Experimental Fiction. Ed. by Philip Stevick. LC 78-131596. 1971. Free Press.
Antibodies. Peter Gorton Baker. LC 69-18162. 1969. 6.95. Putnam.
Antic Hay. Aldous Leonard Huxley. LC 23-179246. 1923. George H. Doran Company.
Antic Hay. Aldous Leonard Huxley. LC 33-27026. (Half-title: The modern library of the world's best books). 1933. The Modern Library.
Antic Hay: & The Gioconda Smile. Aldous Leonard Huxley. LC 64-394. 1964. Harper & Row.
Antic Hay and The Gioconda Smile. Aldous Leonard Huxley. LC 56-12646. (Harper's modern classics). 1957. Harper.
Antichrist: A Novel of the Emperor Frederick II. Cecelia Holland. LC 78-103826. 1970. 6.95. Atheneum.
Anticipations. Christopher Priest. LC 78-52223. 8.95 (ISBN 0-684-15634-2). Scribner.
Antifanaticism: a Tale of the South. Martha Haines Butt. LC 78-39571. 1973. 11.00 (ISBN 0-404-04575-8). AMS Press.
Antigone. Sophocles. (Petits Classiques Bordas). (Fr). pap. 2.50. French & Eur.
Antigone, and Other Portraits of Women (Voyageuses). Paul Charles Joseph Bourget. LC 71-150469. (Short story index reprint series). 1971. (ISBN 0-8369-3809-7). Books for Libraries Press.
Antigone: And Other Portraits of Women (Voyageuses) Paul Charles Joseph Bourget. Tr. by William Marchant. LC 98-843. 1898. C. Scribner's Sons.
Antigray: Cosmic Comedies by SF Masters. Philip Strick. LC 75-26328. 1976. 8.50 (ISBN 0-8008-0237-3). Taplinger Pub. Co.
Antigua, Penny, Puce'. Robert Graves. LC 78-377460. 1968. Penguin.
Antigua Stamp. Robert Graves. LC 37-3095. Random House.
Anting-Anting Stories, & Other Strange Tales of the Filipinos. facs. ed. Sargent Kayme. LC 71-81270. (Short Story Index Reprint Ser.). 1901. 15.00 (ISBN 0-8369-3022-3). Ayer Co.
Antinous: A Romance of Ancient Rome. Adolf Hausrath. Tr. by Mary Joanna Safford. LC 7-2603. 1882. W. S. Gottsberger.
Antinous: A Romance of Ancient Rome. Adolf Hausrath & Adolf Hausrath. LC 78-63988. (Gay Experience). Repr. of 1882 ed. 28.50 (ISBN 0-404-61507-4). AMS Pr.
Antioch Actress: A Novel of Pagan Against Christian. Jacob Randolph Perkins. LC 46-2075. 1946. The Bobbs-Merrill Company.
Antiochus. Wilbur K Price & John Gillies. LC 81-16769. 3.95 (ISBN 0-8024-0249-6). Moody Press.
Antiphon. Djuna Barnes. 1958. 3.50 o.p. (ISBN 0-374-10532-4). FS&G.
Antiquary. Walter Scott. (On cover: Lovell's library, no. 629). 1885. J. W. Lovell Company.
Antiquary... Walter Scott. Ed. by Lang, Andrew. LC 8-3020. 1893. Estes and Lauriat.
Antiquary. Walter Scott. (Half-title: Everyman's library, ed. by Ernest Rhys. Fiction). 1907. J. M. Dent & Co.
Antiquary. Walter Scott. LC 45-48716. (His Waverley novels). De Wolfe, Fiske, & Co.
Antiquary... From the Last Rev. Ed., Containing the Author's Final Corrections, Notes, &C. parker's ed. Walter Scott. LC 8-57687. (Waverley novels: Library ed. v. 3). Bazin & Ellsworth.
Antique Man: A Novel. Merrill Joan Gerber. LC 67-20149. 1967. Houghton Mifflin.
Antoine Bloye: A Novel. Paul Nizan. LC 72-92034. 1973. 6.95 (ISBN 0-85345-277-6). Monthly Review Press.
Antoine De Bonneval: A Tale of Paris, in the Days of St. Vincent De Paul. William Henry Anderdon. LC 6-2443. 1867. Kelly and Piet.
Antoinette. A Story. Andre Theurie. (Appletons' new handy-volume series v. 17). 1878. D. Appleton and Company.
Antoinette De Mirecourt: Or, Secret Marrying and Secret Sorrowing; a Canadian Tale. Rosanna Eleanor Mullins Leprohon. LC 74-169296. (Toronto reprint library of Canadian prose and poetry). (ISBN 0-8020-7514-2). University of Toronto Press.
Antoinette: Or, The Marl-Pit Mystery. (La Grande Marniere. Georges Ohnet. Tr. by Bramwell, Remington. (On cover: The world library, no. 2). The Waverly Company.
Anton Chekhov's Three Sisters: A New English Version. Anton Pavlovich Chekhov & Jean Claude Van Itallie. LC 80-121558. 2.25. Dramatists Play Service.
Anton Reiser: A Psychological Novel. Karl Philipp Moritz. LC 76-48443. (Classics of European Literature). (Hyperion library of world literature). 1977. 15.50. (ISBN 0-88355-582-4) (ISBN 0-88355-583-2). Hyperion Press.
Anton Reiser; a Psychological Novel: By Carl Philipp Moritz... Translated by P. E. Matheson... Karl Philipp Moritz & Matheson, Percy Ewing, 1850-Tr. LC 27-261722. (Half-title: The world's classics. CCXCIX). 1926. H. Milford, Oxford University Press.
Anton York, Immortal. Eando Binder, pseud. 1969. pap. 0.60 o.p. (B60-1033). Belmont-Tower.
Antonia. Jessie Perry Van Zile Belden. LC 1-100003. 1901. L. C. Page & Company.
Antonia. A Novel. George Sand & Vaughan, Virginia, Tr. LC 13-17718. 1883. Roberts Brothers.
Antonia. A Novel. Tr. by Virginia Vaughan. Vaughan, Virginia, D. 1913, Tr & Sweat, Mrs. Margaret Jane Mussey, 1823- LC 6-34622. 1870. Roberts Brothers.
Antonina: Or, Fall of Rome. Wilkie Collins. LC 16-7566. Harper & Brothers.
Antonina: Or, The Fall of Rome. Wilkie Collins. LC 3-27277. 1874. Harper & Brothers.
Antonio. Ernest James Oldmeadow. LC 9-19188. 1909. The Century Co.
Antonio, Antonia. Joseph Howatch. LC 76-25010. 1976. 8.95 (ISBN 0-395-24769-1). Houghton Mifflin.
Antonio in Love. Giuseppe Berto. LC 68-12680. 1968. 5.95. Knopf.
Antonio Salazar Is Dead. James L. McManus. (Illus.). 56p. (Orig.). 1980. pap. 3.00 (ISBN 0-9603794-0-1). Syncline.
Antonio's Revenge. John Marston. Ed. by Reavley Gair. (Revels Plays Ser.). 1978. text ed. 14.00 (ISBN 0-8018-2012-X). Johns Hopkins.
Antonita, the Female Contrabandista. A Mexican Tale of Land and Water. Lorry Luff. LC 9-2490. 1848. Williams Brothers.
Antonius and Theodosia: A Romance of Long Ago. Christo Thomas. LC 26-1389. The Novelart Publishing Co.
Antonov Project. Antony Trew. LC 79-3113. 1979. 10.95 (ISBN 0-312-04518-2). St. Martin's Press.
Anton's Angels: A Romance. Anita Trueman. 1900. The Alliance Publishing Co.
Anton's Angel's: A Romance, by Anita Trueman... Anita Trueman Pickett. LC 1-29600. 1900. The Alliance Publishing Co.
Antony Brade. Robert Traill Spence Lowell. LC 7-14746. 1874. Roberts Brothers.
Antony Gray,-- Gardener. Leslie Moore. LC 17-11702. 1917. 1.50. G. P. Putnam's Sons.
Antrobus Trust. Robert Haig. LC 76-364597. (Illus.). 1976. 3.25 (ISBN 0-333-18805-5). Macmillan.
Ants' Nest. Muriel De B Daly. LC 79-37265. (Short story index reprint series). 1971. (ISBN 0-8369-4076-8). Books for Libraries Press.
Ant's Nest. Muriel De B Daly. LC 38-16230. 1938. D. Appleton-Century Company, Incorporated.
Ants of God. W. T Tyler. LC 80-22571. 10.95 (ISBN 0-8037-0270-1). Dial Press.
Anvil. Gustav Frenssen. Tr. by Paterson, Huntley. LC 30-24353. 1930. Houghton Mifflin Company.
Anvil of Adversity. William Stevens. 6.95 o.p. G&D.
Anvil of Chance. Gerald Chittenden. LC 15-21417. 1915. 1.35. Longmans, Green, and Co.
Anvil of the Heart. Bruce T. Holmes. 312p. 1983. 11.95 (ISBN 0-911361-00-6). Haven Corp.
Anxious Conspirator. Michael Underwood. 1979. 15.00x (ISBN 0-86025-054-7, Pub. by Ian Henry Pubns England). State Mutual Bk.
Anxious Conspirator. Michael Underwood. 1977. 10.00 o.p. State Mutual Bk.
Anxious Conspirators: By Michael Underwood. John Michael Evelyn. LC 65-23780. 3.50. Pub. for the Crime Club by Doubleday.
Anxious Days. Philip Hamilton Gibbs. LC 32-32414. 1932. Doubleday, Doran & Company, Inc.
Any Bedtime: A Novel. Bob Goodman. 1973. 5.00 (ISBN 0-682-47706-0). Exposition Pr.
Any Day Now. August William Derleth. LC 39-2608. 1938. Normandie House.
Any Four Can Play. Alec Manning. pap. 1.95 o.s.i. (Venus). Grove.
Any God Will Do. Richard Condon. LC 66-21462. 1966. Random House.
Any Highway Some Night. Charles Adenour. 5.95 (ISBN 0-533-01633-9). Vantage.
Any Love Notes Today? Wilma J. Jacobs. LC 76-48409. 143p. (Orig.). 1976. pap. 4.95 (ISBN 0-89146-002-0). J & J Dist.
Any Minute I Can Split. Judith Rossner. 1981. pap. 2.95 (ISBN 0-671-42739-3). PB.
Any Minute I Can Split. Judith Rossner. LC 72-55. 240p. 1972. 6.95 o.p. (ISBN 0-07-053942-1). McGraw.
Any Minute I Can Split: A Novel. Judith Rossner. 1973. (pbk.) 1.25. Warner Paperback Lib.
Any Minute I Can Split: A Novel. Judith Rossner. LC 72-55. 1972. 6.95 (ISBN 0-07-053942-1). McGraw-Hill.
Any Number Can Die. Morgan Ross. 256p. (Orig.). 1981. pap. 2.25 (ISBN 0-505-51743-4). Tower Bks.
Any Number Can Play. Dennis Bloodworth. LC 72-79865. 1973. 6.95 (ISBN 0-374-10537-5). Farrar, Straus and Giroux.
Any Number Can Play. Edward Harris Heth. LC 45-35209. 1945. Harper & Brothers.
Any Shape or Form. Elizabeth Daly. LC 45-4232. 1945. Farrar & Rinehart, Inc.
Any Smaller Person. Alexander Duffield. LC 35-5613. Loring & Mussey.
Any Two Can Play. Elizabeth Cadell. LC 80-25772. 1981. 9.95 (ISBN 0-688-00454-7). Morrow.
Any Two Can Play. Elizabeth Cadwell. LC 81-13281. 1981. 12.95 (ISBN 0-8161-3322-0). G.K. Hall.
Any Village. Faith Baldwin. LC 77-117283. 1971. 5.95 o.p. (ISBN 0-03-085046-0). HR&W.
Any Village: By Faith Baldwin. Faith Baldwin Cuthrell. LC 77-117283. 1971. 5.95. Holt, Rinehart and Winston.
Any War Will Do. Eric Pace. LC 72-10477. 1973. 5.95 (ISBN 0-394-46172-X). Random House.
Any Woman's Man. Ida M Evans. LC 37-23535. 1937. Hillman-Curl, Inc.
Anya. Joy Davidman. LC 40-12262. 1940. The Macmillan Company.
Anya. Susan Fromberg Schaeffer. 1975. pap. 3.95 (ISBN 0-380-00573-5, 58214, Bard). Avon.
Anya: A Novel. Susan Fromberg Schaeffer. LC 73-20990. 1974. 6.95 (ISBN 0-02-607020-0). Macmillan.
Anya Kovalchuk. Clarence Wilbur Taber. LC 23-15825. 1923. Covici-McGee Co.
Anybody but Anne. Carolyn Wells. LC 14-7281. 1914. J. B. Lippincott Company.
Anybody's Girl. William Arthur Neubauer. LC 49-496192. 1949. Phoenix Press.
Anybody's Pearls. Hulbert Footner. LC 30-643635. 1930. Pub. for The Crime Club, Inc., by Doubleday, Doran & Company, Inc.
Anybody's Plaything. Mildred Thompson. 192p. (Orig.). 1972. pap. 1.95 o.p. (ISBN 0-87977-178-X). Brandon.
Anybody's Property. Willard Mack. LC 17-236444. 1917. 1.25. The Macaulay Company.
Anymoon. Horace William Bleackley. LC 19-10475. 1919. John Lane.
Anyone for Denis? John Wells. 80p. 1982. pap. 5.95 (ISBN 0-571-11920-4). Faber & Faber.
Anyone Got a Match? Max Shulman. LC 64-18082. 1964. Harper & Row.
Anyone's My Name(A Novel. Seymour Shubin. 1953. Simon and Schuster.
Anything Box. Zenna Henderson. LC 65-24001. (Doubleday sci. fic.). 3.95. Doubleday.
Anything but a Hero: A Novel. Rudolf Lorenzen. LC 62-10901. 1962. St. Martin's Press.
Anything but Love. Carolyn Fireside. 336p. 1982. pap. 3.25 (ISBN 0-425-05710-0). Berkley Pub.
Anything but the Truth. Michael Underwood. LC 78-56355. 1978. 7.95 (ISBN 0-312-04522-0). St. Martin's Press.
Anything but the Truth: A Fleming Stone Story. Carolyn Wells. LC 25-5770. 1925. J. B. Lippincott Company.
Anything Can Happen. George Fort Gibbs. LC 36-221873. 1936. D. Appleton-Century Company, Incorporated.
Anything Else. Dorothy I. Rachelle. 1970. 3.75 o.p. Vantage.
Anything for a Friend. Russell F Davis. LC 63-12059. 1963. Crown Publishers.

Anything for a Quiet Life: A Mystery. A. A Avery. LC 42-15001. 1942. Farrar & Rinehart, Inc.

Anything for the Boys. Kenneth Harding. pap. 1.95 o.s.i. (Venus). Grove.

Anything Goes. Bine Strange Petersen. LC 67-27882. (Black circle book). 1967. Grove Press.

Anything Once. Isabel Egenton Ostrander. LC 20-14286. W. J. Watt & Company.

Anything You Can Do. Randall Garrett. 1969. pap. 0.75 o.p. (ISBN 0-447-74532-8). Lancer.

Anything You Can Do... Darrel T Langart. LC 62-7710. (Doubleday science fiction). 1963. Doubleday.

Anytime, Anywhere: A Novel. Martin Caidin. LC 68-25780. 1969. 5.95. Dutton.

Anytime for Love. Tony Trelos, pseud. (Orig.). pap. 0.95 o.p. (1143). Brandon.

Anywhen. James Blish. LC 78-111144. (Doubleday science fiction). 1970. 4.95. Doubleday.

Anywoman. 1st Ed. Fannie Hurst. LC 50-6917. 1950. Harper.

Anzac Day. K. S. Inglis. write for info o.p. (Pub by Melbourne U Pr). Intl Schol Bk Serv.

Anzio-Gamble That Failed. M. Blumenson. 1971. pap. 1.25 o.p. (01022). Curtis.

Apache. James Warner Bellah. LC 51-25331. (Gold medal book, 155). 1951. Fawcett Publications.

Apache. Will Levington Comfort. LC 31-2444. E. P. Dutton & Co., Inc.

Apache. Will Levington Comfort. LC 79-27815. (Series: Gregg Press Western Fiction Series.). 1980. 11.95 (ISBN 0-8398-2678-8). Gregg Press.

Apache Agent: A Western Novel. Hal George Evarts. LC 55-32828. (Popular library, 651). 1955. Popular Library.

Apache Ambush. Will Cook. LC 55-11790. (Dodd, Mead silver start westerns). 1955. Dodd, Mead.

Apache Basin. Ray Jackson Miller. LC 44-51329. 1944. Arcadia House, Inc.

Apache Canyon. Brian Wynne Garfield. 1974. (pbk.) 0.95. Ace Books.

Apache Crossing: By Will Ermine Pseud. 1st Ed. Harry Sinclair Drago. LC 50-8754. (Double D western). 1950. Doubleday.

Apache Death. George G. Gilman, pseud. (Edge Ser. No. 3). 1972. pap. 1.95 (ISBN 0-523-41769-1). Pinnacle Bks.

Apache Desert. Llewellyn Perry Holmes. LC 52-5546. (Double D western). 1952. Doubleday.

Apache Devil. Edgar Rice Burroughs. LC 33-49903. E. R. Burroughs, Inc.

Apache Devil. Edgar Rice Burroughs. LC 78-13061. (Gregg Press Western Fiction Series). 1978. 9.95 (ISBN 0-8398-2454-8). Gregg Press.

Apache: Fast Living, No. 19. William M. James, pseud. 160p. (Orig.). 1981. pap. 1.75 (ISBN 0-523-40696-7). Pinnacle Bks.

Apache Gold. Joseph Alexander Altsheler. 1976. Repr. of 1913 ed. lib. bdg. 18.80x (ISBN 0-88411-941-6). Amereon Ltd.

Apache Gold. J. D. Hardin. 224p. (Orig.). 1983. pap. 2.25 (ISBN 0-425-06152-3). Berkley Pub.

Apache Gold: A Story of the Strange Southwest. Joseph Alexander Altsheler. LC 13-20343. 1913. D. Appleton and Company.

Apache Halfbreed. Glen Blackburn. (Orig.). 1971. pap. 0.75 o.p. (B75-2087). Belmont-Tower.

Apache Hunter. Gordon D Shirreffs. (Gold Medal Book). 1976. (pbk.) 1.25. Fawcett.

Apache Junction. Jack Slade. (Lassiter,#19). 1975. (pbk.) 0.95. Belmont Tower Books.

Apache Kill. William L Hopson. LC 54-35956. 1954. Avalon Books.

Apache Kill. William L. Hopson. (Avalon westerns). 1974. 4.50. Avalon Books.

Apache Landing. Robert J Hogan. LC 51-13655. (Silver star westerns). 1951. Dodd, Mead.

Apache Landing see Bloody Crossing.

Apache Number Fourteen: Born to Die, No. 14. William M. James, pseud. 1979. pap. 1.50 (ISBN 0-523-40357-7). Pinnacle Bks.

Apache Princess: A Tale of the Indian Frontier. Charles King. LC 3-23599. 1903. The Hobart Company.

Apache Raiders, John Benteen. (Belmont Tower book). 1980. 1.75 (ISBN 0-505-51562-8). Tower Publications.

Apache Ransom. Clay Fisher. 1974. (pbk.) 0.75. Bantam Books.

Apache Scout. Roy Wayne. 1981. pap. 6.95 (Avalon). Bouregy.

Apache Tears. Robert MacLeod. 1974. (pbk.) 1.25 (ISBN 0-671-78353-X). Pocket Books.

Apache Thunder. Strong, Charles Stanley. LC 52-14354. 1952. Arcadia House.

Apache Trail. LC 57-7715. 1957. Arcadia House.

Apache Trail. George Brydges Rodney. LC 34-13761. E. J. Clode, Inc.

Apache War. Peter McCurtin. (Sundance Ser.: No. 34). 1980. pap. 1.75 (ISBN 0-8439-0780-0). Nordon Pubns.

Apache War Cry: A Frontier Western Novel. William E Vance. LC 55-42194. (Popular Library eagle book, EB 45). 1955. Popular Library.

Apache Warrior. Steve Mensing. 1981. pap. 2.25 (ISBN 0-89083-836-4). Zebra.

Apache Wars: The Exciting True Saga of the Bloody Conflict Between the White Men and the Apache Indians on the Southwest Frontier by John Conway Pseud. Joseph Chadwick. LC 61-3414. (Monarch Americans book, MA309). 1961. Monarch Books.

Apache Wells. Robert J. Steelman. LC 59-9211. (Ballantine Books, 294D). 1959. Ballantine Books.

Apaches of New York. Alfred Henry Lewis. LC 73-37277. (Short story index reprint series). (Illus.). 1971. (ISBN 0-8369-4088-1). Books for Libraries Press.

Apaches of New York. Alfred Henry Lewis. LC 12-7299. 1.25. G. W. Dillingham Company.

Apalachee Gold. Frank Gill Slaughter. 1974. (pbk.) 0.95 (ISBN 0-671-77924-9). Pocket Books.

Apartamento de Soltero. new ed. Rodolfo David. (Pimienta Collection Ser). 160p. (Span.). 1974. pap. 1.00 o.p. (ISBN 0-88473-198-7). Fiesta Pub.

Apartment for Sex. Jim Conroy. (Orig.). 1968. pap. 1.25 o.p. (2078). Brandon.

Apartment Hotel. Henry Leyford Gates. LC 33-10977. 1933. The Macaulay Company.

Apartment in Athens. Glenway Wescott. LC 76-152617. 1972. (ISBN 0-8371-6052-9). Greenwood Press.

Apartment in Athens. Glenway Wescott. LC 45-2271. 1945. Harper & Brothers.

Apartment Next Door. William Andrew Johnston. LC 19-773. 1919. 1.50. Little, Brown, and Company.

Apartment on K Street. Robert Travers. 1973. (pbk.) 0.95. Popular Lib.

Apartment on K Street. Robert John Travers. 1973. (pbk.) 0.95. Popular Library.

Apartment on K Street. Robert John Travers. LC 72-6439. 1972. 6.95 (ISBN 0-316-85236-8). Little, Brown.

Apartments. Charles Beardsley. (Signet book). 1974. (pbk.) 1.50. New American Library.

Apartments to Let. Norah Hoult. LC 32-4558. 1932. Harper & Borthers.

Apathetic Bookie Joint. Daniel Fuchs. LC 79-15364. 10.00 (ISBN 0-416-00061-4). Methuen.

Ape and Essence. Aldous Leonard Huxley. LC 48-7921. 1948. Harper.

Ape in Velvet: By Rae Foley Pseud. Elinore Denniston. LC 51-11607. (Red badge detective). 1951. Dodd, Mead.

Ape of Heaven. Roy Dixon. LC 36-34166. Mathis, Van Nort & Co.

Ape, the Idiot & Other People. William Chambers Morrow. LC 7-32484. 1897. J. B. Lippincott Company.

Apeland. Paul Allen. LC 76-2743. 1976. 7.95 (ISBN 0-670-12950-X). Viking Press.

Apeman, Spaceman: Anthropological Science Fiction. Ed. by Leon E. Stover. LC 68-14170. 1968. Doubleday.

Apenas un Bolero: Novela. Omar Torres. LC 81-65511. (Coleccion Caniqui Ser.). 95p. (Orig., Span.). 1981. pap. 6.95 (ISBN 0-89729-292-8). Ediciones.

Apes. Eden Phillpotts. LC 30-115021. 1929. The Macmillan Company.

Apes and Angels. Richard Edward Connell. LC 73-106272. (Short story index reprint series). 1970. Books for Libraries Press.

Apes and Angels. Richard Edward Connell. LC 24-114771. 1924. Minton, Balch & Company.

Apes & Husbands. Frank Klock. 6.95 (ISBN 0-87505-212-6). Borden.

Ape's-Face. Marion Fox. LC 14-193631. 1914. 1.25. John Lane.

Apes of God. Wyndham Lewis. LC 32-6433. 1932. R. M. McBride & Company.

Apes of God. Wyndham Lewis. LC 81-7659. (Illus.). 1981. 20.00 (ISBN 0-87685-513-3) (ISBN 0-87685-514-1) (ISBN 0-87685-512-5). Black Sparrow Press.

Apes on a Tissue Paper Bridge. Robert P Davis. LC 63-9514. 1963. Fleet Pub. Corp.

Apex Treasury of Underground Comics. Ed. by Don Donahue & Susan Goodrick. LC 74-78872. (Illus.). 192p. 1974. pap. 5.95 o.p. (ISBN 0-8256-3042-8, Quick Fox). Putnam Pub Group.

Aphrodisiac, Fiction from Christopher Street. LC 81-15406. 1982. 5.95 (ISBN 0-399-50603-9). Putnam.

Aphrodisiac: Fiction from Christopher Street. Ed. by Christopher Street Editors. 324p. 1982. pap. 6.95 (ISBN 0-399-50603-9, Perige). Putnam Pub Group.

Aphrodisiacs & Anti-Aphrodisiacs. John Davenport. (O.s.i.). 1970. pap. 0.95 o.s.i. (A606N, Award). Univ Pub & Dist.

Aphrodite. David Chandler. LC 77-7990. 1977. 8.95 (ISBN 0-688-03228-1). Morrow.

Aphrodite. Pierre Louys. LC 52-40118. 1948.

Aphrodite. Pierre Louys. Tr. by Galantiere, Lewis. LC 32-17945. (Half-title: The modern library of the world's best books). 1933. The Modern Library.

Aphrodite... Pierre Louys. LC 47-21945. (On cover: New Avon library. 113). 1946.

Aphrodite: A Romance of Ancient Hellas. Ernst Eckstein & Safford, Mary Joanna, Tr. LC 6-26323. 1886. W.S. Gottsberger.

Aphrodite Ancient Manners. Pierre Louys. Tr. by Parker, Willis L. LC 32-31587. Illustrated Editions Co.

Aphrodite in Aulia. George Moore. LC 31-4067. 1930. W. Heinemann Ltd.

Aphrodite in Aulis. George Moore. LC 31-3806. 1930. W. Heinemann Ltd.

Aphrodite in Aulis. George Moore. LC 31-6862. Brentano's.

Aphrodite: The Romance of a Sculptor's Masterpiece. Franklin Kent Gifford. 1901. Small, Maynard & Company.

Aphrodite: Translated by Frances Keene. Pierre Louys. LC 60-14436. (Libra collection). Libra.

Aphrodite's Cave. N. Richard Nash. LC 80-1069. 489p. 1980. 15.95 o.p. (ISBN 0-385-14294-3). Doubleday.

Aphrodite's Cave: A Novel. N. Richard Nash. LC 80-1069. 1980. 12.95 (ISBN 0-385-14294-3). Doubleday.

Aphrodite's Caves. N. Richard Nash. 480p. (Orig.). 1982. pap. 3.50 (ISBN 0-380-55970-6, 55970). Avon.

Aphrodite's Legend. Lynn Fairfax. (Second Chance at Love: No. 28). 192p. (Orig.). 1982. pap. 1.75 (ISBN 0-515-06335-5). Jove Pubns.

Aphros. Froma Sand. 1973. 1.50. Dell.

Apocalypse. D. H. Lawrence. 1977. pap. 3.95 (ISBN 0-14-003856-6). Penguin.

Apocalypse Brigade. Alfred Coppel. LC 81-47459. 12.95 (ISBN 0-03-059532-0). Holt, Rinehart and Winston.

Apocalypse U. S. A! Joseph Rosenberger. (Death Merchant Ser.: No. 54). 224p. (Orig.). 1983. pap. 2.25 (ISBN 0-523-41998-8). Pinnacle Bks.

Apocolocyntosis Divi Claudii: The Pumpkinification of Claudius. Lucius Annaeus Seneca. Tr. by Apostolos N. Athanassakis. LC 73-85651. 1973. 5.00 (ISBN 0-87291-061-X). Coronado Press.

Apocryphal Stories. Karel Capek. LC 49-5662. G. Allen and Unwin.

Apocryphal Stories. Tr. from Czech by Dora Round. Karel Capek. 1965. 3.00. G. Allen & Unwin.

Apollo at Go. Jefferson Sutton. LC 63-15577. 1963. Putnam.

Apollo Fountain. Dorothy Daniels. (Paperback Library gothic). 1974. (pbk.) 0.95. Warner Paperback Library.

Apollo Legacy. Albert Barker. (Reefe King Espionage Ser). (O.s.i.). (Orig.). 1970. pap. 0.75 o.s.i. (A719S, Award). Univ Pub & Dist.

Apollo Sleeps. Daphne Shathin. LC 38-476. J. Messner, Inc.

Apollo's Daughter. (Harlequin Romances Ser.). 192p. 1980. pap. 1.25 (ISBN 0-373-02356-1, Pub. by Harlequin). PB.

Apollo's Dream. Claire Evans. 192p. 1982. pap. 1.75. Jove Pubns.

Apollo's Seed. Anne Mather. (Harlequin Presents Ser.). (Orig.). 1980. pap. 1.50 (ISBN 0-373-70835-1, Pub. by Harlequin). PB.

Apollo's Summer Look. Kathleen Conlon. LC 69-13732. 1969. 4.50. Dodd, Mead.

Apologies for Love. Frank A Myers. LC 9-303854. 1909. 1.50. R. G. Badger.

Apology. Max Hampton. LC 72-161246. 1972. 6.50. Bobbs-Merrill.

Apology for a Hero. A. L. Barker. LC 50-6847. 1950. Scribner.

Apology for Heroism. Mulk Raj Anand. (Mayfair Paperbacks Ser.). 203p. 1975. pap. 3.60 (ISBN 0-86578-074-9). Ind-US Inc.

Apology for Rain. Jean Mark Gawron. LC 73-14046. (Doubleday science fiction). 1974. 4.95 (ISBN 0-385-09634-8). Doubleday.

Apology for the Life of Mrs. Shamela Andrews. Edited, with an Introd. and Notes, by Sheridan W. Baker, Jr. Henry Fielding. LC 53-11235. 1953. University of California Press.

Apology for the Life of Mrs. Shamela Andrews. Henry Fielding. LC 72-186987. 1970. Folcroft Press.

Apology for the Life of Mrs. Shamela Andrews (1741) Henry Fielding. LC 74-26835. (Richardsoniana; 3). (Life & times of seven major British writers). 1974. (ISBN 0-8240-1306-9). Garland Pub.

Apology for the Life of Mrs. Shamela Andrews. Henry Fielding. LC 76-7563. 1976. 12.50 (ISBN 0-88305-697-6). Norwood Editions.

Apology for Wonder. Sam Keen. LC 69-17017. 1969. pap. 6.95i (ISBN 0-06-064261-0, RD 58, HarpR). Har-Row.

Apology of Ayliffe. Ellen Warner Olney Kirk. LC 4-21723. 1904. Houghton, Mifflin and Company.

Apoplectic Palm Tree: Or, The Happy Happening Among Blacks and Whites at the Greater Mount Moriah Solid Rock True Happiness Baptist Church and Funeral Parlor; a Novel. William C Anderson. LC 74-86650. 1969. 5.95. Crown Publishers.

Apostate: A Novel. Ernest Daudet. Tr. by Train, Elizabeth Phipps. LC 6-33033. (On cover: Appletons' town and country library). 1889. D. Appleton and Company.

Apostate Heriger. Anthony Shafton. LC 61-11774. 1962. Grove Press.

Apostate Physician. Harvey L Frick. LC 40-8132. House of Field, Inc.

Apostle. Shalom Asch. Tr. by Samuel, Maurice. LC 43-51252. 1943. G. P. Putnam's Sons.

Apostle. Roger Lovin. Ed. by Polly Freas & Kelly Freas. LC 78-15252. (Illus.). 1978. pap. 4.95 o.p. (ISBN 0-915442-61-2, Starblaze). Donning Co.

Apostle & the Wild Ducks. Gilbert Keith Chesterton. Ed. by Dorothy Collins. 1975. 9.95 o.p. (ISBN 0-236-31025-9, Pub. by Paul Elek). Merrimack Pub Cir.

Apostle from Space. Gordon L Harris. LC 78-58860. 1.95 (ISBN 0-88270-281-5). Logos International.

Apostle. Translated by Maurice Samuel. Shalom Asch. LC 57-1080. (Cardinal Giant, GC-88. Fiction, 8). 1957. Pocket Books.

Apostles of Light. Ellen Douglas, pseud. LC 72-5542. 1973. 6.95 (ISBN 0-395-15473-1). Houghton Mifflin.

Apostles of the Southeast. Frank Thomas Bullen. LC 1-25707. 1901. D. Appleton and Company.

Apotheosis of Mr. Tyrawley. Edith Katharine Spicer Jay. LC 7-30119. 1896. Harper & Brothers.

Appalachee Red: A Novel. Raymond Andrews. LC 78-17761. (Illus.). (ISBN 0-8037-0916-1). Dial Press.

Appalachian Dawn. John Foster West. LC 73-77500. (ISBN 0-87716-041-4). Moore Pub. Co.

Appalachian Ghost Stories & Other Tales. James Gay Jones. 1975. 3.50 (ISBN 0-87012-203-7). McClain.

Appalachian Shepherd: A Story of Religion in the Southern Appalachians. Garland A Hendricks. LC 65-26771. Spiritual Life Publishers.

Appaloosa. Robert Parker MacLeod. LC 81-69105. 9.95 (ISBN 0-8027-4004-9). Walker.

Appaloosa Rising: Or, The Legend of the Cowboy Buddha. Gino Sky. LC 79-7810. 1980. 8.95 (ISBN 0-385-15386-4) (ISBN 0-385-15387-2). Doubleday.

Apparition. Ramona Stewart. LC 73-612. 1973. 6.95 (ISBN 0-316-81434-2). Little, Brown.

Appassionata. Fannie Hurst. LC 26-2809. 1926. A. A. Knopf.

Appassionata. Jeanette Salerno. LC 81-3113. 13.95 (ISBN 0-385-27188-3). Dial Press.

Appassionata. A Musician's Story. Elsa de'Esterre Keeling. (choice series. no. 98). R. Bonner's Sons.

Appearance of a Man. George Backer. LC 66-11986. 1966. 5.95. Random.

Appearances of Death. Elizabeth Linington. LC 77-5709. 1977. 7.95 (ISBN 0-688-03238-9). Morrow.

Appearances of Death. Dell Shannon. LC 81-14480. 1981. 9.95 (ISBN 0-89621-319-6). Thorndike Press.

Appearing. Penny Estes Wheeler. LC 79-16298. (Orion Ser.). 1979. pap. 2.95 (ISBN 0-8127-0231-X). Review & Herald.

Appendix A. Hayden Carruth. LC 63-17512. 1963. Macmillan.

Appius and Virginia. Gertrude Eileen Trevelyan. LC 33-134. 1932. G. P. Putnam's Sons.

Applause. Beth Brown. LC 28-21482. 1928. H. Liveright.

Apple a Day. Henry Brinton. LC 59-12253. (Chantecler novel of suspense). 1959. I. Washburn.

Apple a Day: The Story of a Hollywood Doctor. Howard Wilson. LC 39-29832. 1939. G. P. Putnam, Inc.

Apple and Eve. Jo Van Ammers-Kuller. Tr. by Bodde, Charlotte Beatrice (Hodgkinson) LC 33-291966. 1933. Dodd, Mead & Company.

Apple & the Egg. Joseph McHugh & Renee Locks. LC 79-90758. 1980. pap. 4.95 (ISBN 0-89087-261-9). Celestial Arts.

Apple Bay. Paul Williams. 1976. pap. 3.95 (ISBN 0-446-87163-X). Warner Bks.

Apple Blossoms. Ed. by William G. Wilcox. 1976. pap. 2.95 o.p. (ISBN 0-89002-068-X). Northwoods Pr.

Apple-Blossoms. A Novel. Anna Oldfield Wiggs. LC 9-928. 1886. A. E. Davis & Company.

Apple Crunch. Frederic Vincent Huber. LC 80-54520. 10.95 (ISBN 0-87223-687-0). Seaview Books.

Apple Dumpling Gang. Jack M. Bickham. LC 72-144249. 1971. 4.95 o.p. Doubleday.

Apple Falls Not Far. 1st. ed. Moses B. Goldman. LC 67-5754. 1967. Harlo Press.

Apple for Eve. Kathleen Thompson Norris. LC 42-21971. 1942. Doubleday, Doran and Company, Inc

Apple from Eve. Betty Neels. (Harlequin Romances Ser.). 192p. 1982. pap. 1.50 (ISBN 0-373-02463-0). Harlequin Bks.

Apple in the Attic: A Pennsylvania Legend. Mildred A. Jordan. LC 42-20095. 1942. A. A. Knopf.

Apple in the Dark. Tr. from Portuguese, Introd., by Gregory Rabassa. 1st Amer. Ed. Clarice Lispector. LC 66-193862. 1967. 5.95. Knopf.

Apple in the Dark. Translated from the Portuguese, with an Introd., by Gregory Rabassa. 1st American Ed. LC 66-19386. 1967. Knopf.

Apple Must Be Bitten. Frances Bainbridge Colby. LC 44-2183. 1944. C. Scribner's Sons.

Apple of Discord. Earle Ashley Walcott. LC 7-31209. 1907. The Bobbs-Merrill Company.

Apple of Discord: A Novel. Henry Cottrell Rowland. 1913. 1.25. Dodd, Mead and Company.

Apple of Eden. Ernest Temple Thurston. LC 14-169247. 1910. Dodd, Mead & Company.

Apple of His Eye. Gerard Robichaud. LC 65-19859. 4.95. Doubleday.

Apple of His Eye. Gerard Robichaud. (Echo bk., E44). 1967. Doubleday.

Apple of the Eye. Glenway Wescott. LC 24-23494. 1924. L. MacVeagh, The Dial Press.

Apple on a Pear Tree. John Burress. LC 53-10803. 1953. Vanguard Press.

Apple or the Axe. Paul J. Brown. 224p. 1974. 7.50 o.p. (ISBN 0-682-48046-0). Exposition.

Apple Orchard. John Kafka. LC 47-11373. 1947. Coward-McCann.

Apple Spy in the Sky. Marc Lovell, pseud. LC 82-45453. (Crime Club Ser.). 192p. 1983. 11.95 (ISBN 0-385-18308-9). Doubleday.

Apple Tree. John Galsworthy. LC 35-123653. 1934. C. Scribner's Sons.

Apple Tree and Other Tales. John Galsworthy. LC 65-814. (Scribner library books, SL103). 1965. Scribner.

Apple-Tree Cottage. Elinor Macartney Lane. LC 10-10510. 1910. 0.50. Harper & Brothers.

Apple-Tree Girl: The Story of Little Miss Moses, Who Led Herself into the Promised Land. George Weston. LC 18-5644. 1918. J. B. Lippincott Company.

Apple Tree Lean Down. Mary Emily Pearce. LC 75-40802. 10.00. St. Martin's Press.

Apple-Tree Table: And Other Sketches. Herman Melville. LC 70-88907. 1969. Greenwood Press.

Apple Woman of the Klickitat. Anna Van Rensselaer Morris. LC 18-17494. 1918. Duffield & Company.

Appleby File. Michael Innes. 202p. 1976. 5.95 o.p. (ISBN 0-396-07279-8). Dodd.

Appleby File: Detective Stories. John Innes MacKintosh Stewart. LC 75-22398. 1976. (ISBN 0-396-07279-8). Dodd, Mead.

Appleby Intervenes. Michael Innes. Incl. One-Man Show; Comedy of Terrors; Secret Vanguard. 1965. 4.95 o.p. Dodd.

Appleby Intervenes: Three Tales from Scotland Yard by Michael Innes. Pseud. John Innes Mackintosh Stewart. LC 65-244633. bds., 4.95. Dodd.

Appleby on Ararat. John Innes Mackintosh Stewart. LC 70-106676. 1971. (ISBN 0-8371-3377-7). Greenwood Press.

Appleby on Ararat. John Innes Mackintosh Stewart. LC 41-17617. 1941. Dodd Mead & Company.

Appleby Talking: Twenty-Three Detective Stories. John Innes Mackintosh Stewart. LC 74-166793. 1973. 0.30 (ISBN 0-14-003423-4). Penguin.

Appleby Talks Again. John Innes Mackintosh Stewart. LC 56-11889. Dodd, Mead,

Appleby Talks Again: Eighteen Detective Stories. John Innes Mackintosh Stewart. LC 77-81277. (Short story index reprint series). 1969. (ISBN 0-8369-3029-0). Books for Libraries Press.

Appleby's Answer. Michael Innes. (Red Badge Mystery Series). 224p. 1973. 4.95 o.p. (ISBN 0-396-06744-1). Dodd.

Appleby's Answer. John Innes Mackintosh Stewart. LC 73-1651. (Red badge novel of suspense). 1973. 4.95 (ISBN 0-396-06744-1). Dodd, Mead.

Appleby's End. Michael Innes, pseud. LC 82-48813. 224p. 1983. pap. text ed. 2.84i (ISBN 0-06-080649-4, P 649, PL). Har-Row.

Appleby's End. Michael Innes, pseud. 1965. pap. 0.95 o.p. (02117, Collier). Macmillan.

Appleby's End. Michael Innes. 1975. (pbk.) 1.25 (ISBN 0-345-24409-5). Ballantine Books.

Appleby's End. John Innes Mackintosh Stewart. LC 74-106677. 1970. (ISBN 0-8371-3376-9). Greenwood Press.

Appleby's End. John Innes Mackintosh Stewart. 1945. Dodd, Mead & Company.

Appleby's Other Story. Michael Innes, pseud. 1974. 4.95 o.p. (ISBN 0-396-06715-8). Dodd.

Appleby's Other Story. John Innes Mackintosh Stewart. LC 74-683. (Red badge novel of suspense). 1974. 4.95 (ISBN 0-396-06715-8). Dodd, Mead.

Appledore Farm. Katharine Sarah Gadsden Macquoid. LC 7-20292. Lovell, Coryell & Company.

Appledore Farm. Katharine Sarah Gadsden Macquoid. LC 7-20291. (On cover: The premier series, no. 2). National Book Company.

Applegreen Cat. Frances Kirkwood Crane. LC 43-18118. 1943. J. B. Lippincott Company.

Apples Be Ripe. Llewelyn Powys. LC 30-18869. 1930. Longmans, Green and Co.

Apples Be Ripe. Llewelyn Powys. LC 30-14008. Harcourt, Brace and Company.

Apples from Eden: And Other Stories. Robert E Horton. LC 38-30797. The Christopher Publishing House.

Apples of Paradise: And Other Stories. Frederick Feikema Manfred. LC 68-14287. 1968. Trident Press.

Apples of Sodom: A Story of Mormon Life. Rosetta Luce Gilchrist. LC 6-44057. 1883. W. W. Williams.

Applesauce. June Arnold. LC 66-28828. 1967. McGraw-Hill.

Applesauce. June Arnold. LC 77-80961. 1977. 5.00. Daughters Pub. Co.

Appleshaw. Christine Damien. LC 75-22384. 1975. 1.25 (ISBN 0-345-24614-4). Ballantine Books.

Appletons of Herne: A Family Chronicle. Archibald Marshall. LC 31-28128. 1931. Dodd, Mead and Company.

Appointed: An American Novel. Walter H. Stowers & Anderson, William H., 1858- Joint Author. LC 8-30872. 1894. Detroit Law Printing Co.

Appointed: An American Novel. Walter H. Stowers & William H. Anderson. LC 70-158255. 1977. 18.00 (ISBN 0-404-00001-0). AMS Press.

Appointed Date. Joseph Jefferson Farjeon. LC 30-277536. 1929. L. MacVeagh, The Dial Press.

Appointed Paths: A Novel. Annie Stevens Perkins. LC 7-36347. 1896. J. H. Earle.

Appointed Way: A Tale of the Seventh-Day Adventists. Anna Johnson. LC 5-32392. 1905. The Griffith & Rowland Press.

Appointment at Bloodstar. E. E. Smith & Stephen Goldin. (Family D'Alembert Ser: No. 5). 1978. pap. 1.50 (ISBN 0-515-04005-3). Jove Pubns.

Appointment at Bloodstar. E. E. Smith & Stephen Goldin. (Family d'Alembert Ser.: No. 5). 192p. 1983. pap. 2.25 (ISBN 0-425-05821-2). Berkley Pub.

Appointment at Nine. Doris Miles Disney. LC 47-2408. 1947. Pub. for the Crime Club by Doubleday & Company, Inc.

Appointment in Andalusia. May Mackintosh. 1973. (pbk.) 0.95. Dell.

Appointment in Andalusia. May Mackintosh. LC 72-5327. 1972. Delacorte Press.

Appointment in Budapest: An Autobiographical Novel. Eva Kennedy. LC 68-18548. 1968. McGraw-Hill.

Appointment in Haiphong. Nick Carter. (Illus.). 224p. 1982. pap. 2.50 (ISBN 0-441-02592-7, Pub. by Charter Bks). Ace Bks.

Appointment in Manila. Elinor Chamberlain. LC 45-9485. 1945. Dodd, Mead & Company.

Appointment in Samarra. John O'Hara. LC 53-5341. (Modern library of the world's best books, 42). 1953. Modern Library.

Appointment in Samarra. John O'Hara. LC 82-4840. 1982. 3.95 (ISBN 0-394-71192-0). Vintage Books.

Appointment in Samarra; BUtterfield 8; Hope of Heaven. John O'Hara. LC 75-333017. 1968. Random House.

Appointment in Samarra: A Novel. John O'Hara. LC 34-25527. Harcourt, Brace and Company.

Appointment in Samarra: A Novel. John O'Hara. LC 35-11507. 1935. Harcourt, Brace and Company.

Appointment in Samarra: A Novel. John O'Hara. LC 46-30071. 1936. Grosset & Dunlap.

Appointment in Tibet: A Novel. 1st American Ed. William Hutchinson Murray. LC 59-12005. 1959. Putnam.

Appointment with Death. Agatha Miller Christie. 1975. (pbk.) 0.95. Dell.

Appointment with Death. Pamela Frankau. LC 40-3031. E. P. Dutton & Co., Inc.

Appointment with Death: A Poirot Mystery. Agatha Miller Christie. LC 38-27744. 1938. Dodd, Mead & Company.

Appointment with Fear. Donald Hubert Stokes. LC 50-9540. (Gargoyle mystery). 1950. Coward-McCann.

Appointment with Fortune: A Novel. Marius Hansome. LC 54-11892. 1955. Vantage Press.

Appointment with Yesterday. Frank Dorn. 1978. pap. 1.50 (ISBN 0-532-15379-0). Woodhill.

Appointment with Yesterday. Celia Fremlin, pseud. LC 77-39761. 1972. (ISBN 0-397-00873-2). Lippincott.

Appraiser. Jack Mayfield. 416p. (Orig.). 1981. pap. 2.95 (ISBN 0-441-02595-1). Ace Bks.

Apprehensive Dag. Henry Christopher Bailey. 1942. Published for the Crime Club by Doubleday, Doran & Co., Inc.

Apprentice. Arun Joshi. LC 74-175112. 1974. 4.50 (ISBN 0-210-40558-9). Asia Pub. House.

Apprentice: A Historical Novel. Richard E. Early. LC 78-300731. 1977. 9.75 (ISBN 0-7100-8692-X). Routledge and Kegan Paul.

Apprentice Bastard: By Bendict and Nancy Freedman. Benedict Freedman & Nancy Mars Freedman. LC 66-24828. 1966. 6.50. Trident.

Apprentice Bastard: By Benedict and Nancy Freedman. Benedict Freedman & Nancy Mars Freedman. (75251). 1967. Pocket Bks.

Apprentice Gay. Walter Febick. 192p. (Orig.). 1974. pap. 2.25 o.s.i. (ISBN 0-89053-106-4). Lambda Pr.

Apprentice in Terror. Paulette Warren. (Berkley Medallion) (ISBN 0-425-03205-1). Berkley.

Apprentice to Truth. Helen Manchester Gates Granville-Barker. LC 10-5218. 1910. 1.50. G. P. Putnam's Sons.

Apprentices to Destiny. Lily Augusta Long. LC 7-15150. Merrill & Baker.

Apprenticeship of Duddy Kravitz. Mordecai Richler. 1974. (pbk.) 1.50. Ballantine Books.

Approach to Kings. Patrick Anderson. LC 78-123683. 1970. 6.95. Doubleday.

Approaches to Science Fiction Selected by Donald L. Lawler. Donald L Lawler. LC 77-77995. 7.95 (ISBN 0-395-25496-5). Houghton Mifflin.

Approaching Oblivion: Road Signs on the Treadmill Toward Tomorrow: Eleven Uncollected Stories. Harlan Ellison. LC 75-309113. 1974. 7.95. Walker.

Approaching Oblivion: Road Signs on the Treadmill Toward Tomorrow: Eleven Uncollected Stories. Harlan Ellison. (Signet Book). 1976. (pbk.) 1.25. New American Library.

Approximation. Hans Joachim Schadlich. LC 78-22271. 10.00. Harcourt Brace Jovanovich.

Apricot Sky. 1st American Ed. Ruby Ferguson. LC 52-10948. Little, Brown.

April: A Fable of Love. Vardis Fisher. LC 37-3793. 1937. The Caxton Printers, Ltd.

April Afternoon. Philip Wylie. LC 38-33006. Farrar & Rinehart, Incorporated.

April and Sally June. Margaret Rebecca Piper Chalmers. The Penn Publishing Company.

April Day. A Novel. Philippa Prittie Jephson. LC 7-10322. (Harper's Franklin square library, no. 351). Harper & Brothers.

April Day. A Novel. Philippa Prittie Jephson. LC 7-103212. (On cover: Seaside library. Pocket ed. no. 176). G. Munro.

April Evil. John MacDonald. LC 56-60095. (Dell first edition, 86). 1956. Dell Pub. Co.

April Evil. John Dann MacDonald. LC 56-6009. (Dell first edition, 85). 1956. Dell Pub. Co.

April Fools: A Comedy of Bad Manners. Compton Mackenzie. LC 30-19715. 1930. Doubleday, Doran and Company, Inc.

April Girl. Iris Bromige. 1971. pap. 0.75 o.p. (94119). Beagle Bks.

April Gold. Grace Livingston Hill. LC 36-4984. 1936. J. B. Lippincott Company.

April Grasses. Marion Vera Cuthbert. LC 36-8483. The Womans Press.

April Harvest. Lillian Budd. LC 59-555833. 1959. Duell, Sloan and Pearce.

April Harvest. Lillian Budd. 1980. 2.25. Avon Books.

April Has Wings. Phyllis Yahnke. LC 55-118781. 1955. Arcadia House.

April Heart. Peggy Gaddis, pseud. (Starlight Romance Ser.). 176p. 1973. pap. 0.75 o.p. (532-00487-075). Manor Bks.

April Heart. Peggy Gaddis. 1972. 0.75. Manor Books.

April Hopes. William Dean Howells. LC 4-15120. 1888. Harper & Brothers.

April Hopes. William Dean Howells & Kermit Vanderbilt. LC 75-184525. (selected edition of W. D. Howells, v. 15). 1974. 17.50 (ISBN 0-253-30770-8). Indiana University Press.

April in Arcadia. Bennie Caroline Hall. LC 57-7724. 1957. Arcadia House.

April in Chains. Paul Roan. pap. 1.95 o.p. (ISBN 0-87977-153-4, DDB153). Dansk Blue Bk.

April Is the Cruelest Month. Michael J Quigley. LC 78-100690. (Illus.). 1969. Kendall/Hunt Pub. Co.

April, June, and November. Frederic Raphael. LC 76-11614. 1976. 10.00. Bobbs-Merrill.

April Lady. 2d american ed. Georgette Heyer. LC 72-97296. 1973. 6.95 (ISBN 0-399-11136-0). Putnam.

April Lady. 1st American Ed Georgette Heyer. LC 57-11140. 1957. Putnam.

April Luck. James Woods Morrison. LC 32-8312. 1932. G. P. Putnam's Sons.

April Morning. Howard Melvin Fast. (gr. 6 up). 1962. pap. 2.25 (ISBN 0-553-13962-2, Y13381-0). Bantam.

April Morning. Howard Melvin Fast. (YA) 1961. 8.95 (ISBN 0-517-50681-5). Crown.

April Morning. Howard Melvin Fast. Ed. by Virginia F. Allen & Dora F. Pantell. (Falcon Bks: Classroom Lib. B). (RL 3-5). 1970. Set Of 7 Copies. pap. 37.50 set o.p. (ISBN 0-8372-9637-4); tchrs' notes avail. o.p. (ISBN 0-8372-8941-6). Bowmar-Noble.

April Morning: A Novel. Howard Melvin Fast. LC 61-10306. 1961. Crown Publishers.

April Panhasard. Muriel Hine Coxon. LC 13-115373. 1913. 1.35. John Lane Company.

April Princess. Anne Constance Smedley Maxwell Armfield Armfield. LC 3-25884. 1903. Dodd, Mead and Company.

April Promise: By Bette Allan Pseud. Elizabeth Ashbey. LC 50-8998. 1950. Gramercy Pub. Co.

April Robin Murders. Craig Rice & McBain, Ed. (Signet Book). 1.50 (ISBN 0-451-07794-6). New American Library.

April Robin Murders: By Craig Rice and Ed McBain. Craig Rice & Ed McBain. LC 58-986936. (Random House mystery). 1958. Random House.

April Serenade. Ruth Rosemary Corby. LC 38-5866. 1938. Arcadia House.

April Showers. Gloria Goddard. LC 36-19439. Phoenix Press.

April Snow. Lillian Budd. LC 51-3029. 1951. Lippincott.

April Thirtieth. St. James, Bernard, pseud. LC 78-2069. 8.95 (ISBN 0-06-013707-X). Harper & Row.

April to Remember. Helen Topping Miller. LC 55-762024. 1955. Appleton-Century-Crofts.

April Twilights. Willa Sibert Cather. (O.s.i.). 1933. 4.50 o.s.i. (ISBN 0-394-40306-1). Knopf.

April Was When It Began. Barry Benefield. LC 39-19013. 1939. Reynal & Hitchcock.

April's Grave. Susan Howatch. LC 73-88401. 1974. 6.95 (ISBN 0-8128-1647-1). Stein and Day.

April's Lady. Jeanne Violet Dussap. Tr. by Safford, Mary Joanna. LC 11-9971. 1911. 1.25. Dodd, Mead and Company.

April's Lady. Margaret Wolfe Hungerford. LC 7-9369. (Lovell's International Ser.). (On cover: Lovell's international series. 90: 90). 1890. J. W. Lovell Company.

April's Sowing. Gertrude Hall Brownell. LC 1-29052. 1900. McClure, Phillips & Co.

April's Sowing. Rosemary Frances Rees. LC 37-771921. 1936. Arcadia House.

April's There. Robert Simpson. LC 73-4157. 1973. 6.95 (ISBN 0-06-013888-2). Harper & Row.

Aprocryphal Stories. Karel Capek. Tr. by D. Round. 1949. 3.00 o.p. Verry.

Apron Strings. May Frend Dickenson. LC 28-17205. The Macaulay Company.

Apron-Strings. Eleanor Gates. LC 17-29731. 1917. Sully and Kleinteich.

Apropos of Dolores. Herbert George Wells. LC 38-29001. 1938. C. Scribner's Sons.

Apuleius and The Golden Ass. James Tatum. LC 78-74220. (Illus.). 1979. 12.50 (ISBN 0-8014-1163-7). Cornell University Press.

Apuleius' The Golden Ass. Robert Graves. 293p. 1951. pap. 6.25 (ISBN 0-374-50532-2). FS&G.

Aqua. Asgar Schnack. 32p. 1982. pap. 3.50 (ISBN 0-915306-34-4). Curbstone.

Aquarian Pioneers: Adventure and Romance on the High Sea. Theo Nyland. LC 27-21617. 1927. A. Wagner Publishing Co.

Aquarius Curse. Marilyn Ross. (Orig.). 1970. pap. 0.75 o.p. (64-437). Paperback Lib.

Aquarius Transfer. Robert F. Joseph. 288p. 1982. pap. 2.95 (ISBN 0-449-14467-4, GM). Fawcett.

Aquis Submersus. Theodor Storm. Ed. by Patricia M. Boswell. (Blackwell's German Text Ser.). 102p. 1974. pap. 9.95x (ISBN 0-631-01920-0, Pub. by Basil Blackwell). Biblio Dist.

Arab. Hans Ruesch. 1974. (pbk.) 1.50. Ballantine.

Arab Crisis: Why and How- Oscar M. Olsen. LC 80-53657. 7.95 (ISBN 0-533-04859-1). Vantage Press.

Arab Wife. A Romance of the Polynesian Seas. LC 6-2056. (On cover: Appletons' new handy-volume series. 13). 1878. D. Appleton and Company.

Arabella. 2d american ed. Georgette Heyer. LC 77-163532. 1971. 5.95. Putnam.

Arabella. Georgette Heyer. LC 49-9142. 1949. G.P. Putnam's Sons.

Arabella and Araminta Stories. 5th ed. Gertrude Smith. LC 4-18028. 1902. Small, Maynard & Company.

Arabelle: A Romantic Novel. Edith Montgomery. LC 54-9029. 1954. Vantage Press.

Arabesque. Theresa De Kerpely. LC 75-37817. 300p. 1976. 10.00 o.s.i. (ISBN 0-8128-1938-1). Stein & Day.

Arabesque. Geoffrey Household. LC 48-5976. 1948. Liitle, Brown.

Arabesque. Eleanor Mercein Kelly. LC 33-4984. 1933. Harper & Brothers.

Arabesque. Theresa De Kerpely. LC 75-37817. 1976. 9.95 (ISBN 0-8128-1938-1). Stein and Day.

Arabesque. Theresa De Kerpely. (Signet Book). 1977. 1.95 (ISBN 0-451-07424-6). New American Library.

Arabesque. Yolande Langworthy. LC 31-24138. 1931. Lewis Copeland Company.

Arabesques. Nikolai Vasilevich Gogol. LC 81-14854. 1981. 17.50 (ISBN 0-88233-435-2). Ardis Publishers.

Arabesques: Monare. Apollyona. Domitia. Ombra. Sarah Dana Loring Greenough. LC 6-44860. 1872. Roberts Brothers.

Arabia Without Sultans. Fred Halliday. 1975. cancelled o.p. (ISBN 0-394-49398-2). Random.

Arabian Bird: A Novel. Constantine Fitz Gibbon. LC 48-1508. 1948. Rinhart.

Arabian Delights. Margaret J. Philippou. 1969. 4.50 o.p. Intl Pubns Serv.

Arabian Fires. Forest S. Slaugh. 4.50 o.p. Carlton.

Arabian Nights. (Tempo Classics Ser.). (Illus.). 320p. 1982. pap. 1.95 (ISBN 0-448-16984-3, Pub. by Tempo). Ace Bks.

Arabian Nights. Hawthorne, Hildegarde, Ed & Sterrett, Virginia Frances, Illus. LC 28-20227. C.

Arabian Nights Murder. John Dickson Carr. LC 36-631329. 1936. Harper & Brothers.

Araby. Hutten Zum Stolzenberg, Betsy (Riddle) LC 4-16171. 1904. The Smart Set Publishing Co.

Arachne: A Historical Romance. Georg Moritz Ebers. Tr. by Mary Joanne Stafford. LC 6-43722. 1898. D. Appleton and Company.

Arafat Is Next! Dudley Barker. LC 74-29318. 1975. 7.95 (ISBN 0-8128-1761-3). Stein and Day.

Arafat Is Next. Lionel Black. LC 74-29318. 1975. 25.00 o.s.i. (ISBN 0-8128-1761-3). Stein & Day.

Araminta. John Collis Snaith. LC 9-4191. 1909. Moffat, Yard and Company.

Araminta. John Collis Snaith. LC 23-12870. 1923. D. Appleton and Company.

Araminta and the Automobile. Charles Battell Loomis. LC 7-21370. T. Y. Crowell & Co.

Aransas. Stephen Harrigan. 256p. 1981. pap. 2.50 (ISBN 0-380-54866-6, 54866). Avon.

Aransas: A Novel. Stephen Harrigan. LC 79-21083. 1980. 9.95 (ISBN 0-394-50624-3). Knopf: Distributed by Random House.

Araphel: Or, The Falling Stars of 1833; a Story of Evolution. Robert Haskins Crozier. LC 6-31949. 1884. Presbyterian Publishing Co.

Ararat. 3d ed. Elgin Earl Groseclose. LC 77-78493. 2.95 (ISBN 0-89191-078-6). David C. Cook Pub. Co.

Ararat. Elgin Earl Groseclose. LC 39-276550. Carrick & Evans, Inc.

Ararat. Elgin Earl Groseclose. 1974. (pbk.). 1.50 (ISBN 0-671-78694-6). Pocket Books.

Ararat. Robert Houston. 400p. 1982. pap. 3.50 (ISBN 0-380-80937-0, 80937). Avon.

Ararat. D. M Thomas. LC 82-17397. 1983. 13.50 (ISBN 0-670-13009-5). Viking Press.

Ararat: A Collection of Hungarian-Jewish Short Stories. Andrew Handler. LC 75-5244. 10.00 (ISBN 0-8386-1733-6). Fairleigh Dickinson University Press.

Ararat. 1st Ed. Stella Wilchek. LC 62-791761. 1962. Harper.

Arbaugh Affair. Darrell Garwood. LC 70-108860. 1970. 5.95. Macrae Smith.

Arbiter of Your Fate: Sequel to The Pastor's Son and The Doctor's Daughter. William Wilfred Walter. LC 11-269553. W. W. Walter.

Arbor House Celebrity Book of Horror Stories. Ed. by Martin Harry Greenberg. 600p. 1982. 20.95 (ISBN 0-87795-373-2, Pub. by Priam); pap. 9.95 (ISBN 0-87795-400-3). Arbor Hse.

Arbor House Celebrity Book of Horror Stories. Charles Waugh & Martin Harry Greenberg. LC 81-71667. 9.95 (ISBN 0-87795-400-3). Arbor House.

Arbor House Celebrity Book of the Greatest Stories Ever Told. Ed. by Martin Harry Greenberg & Charles G. Waugh. 512p. 1983. 15.95 (ISBN 0-87795-448-8); pap. 8.95 (ISBN 0-87795-449-6). Arbor Hse.

Arbor House Necropolis. Bill Pronzini. LC 81-66969. (Priam books). 1981. 11.50 (ISBN 0-87795-338-4). Arbor House.

Arbor House Treasure of Detective & Mystery Stories from the Great Pulps. Ed. by Bill Pronzini. 356p. 1983. 15.95 (ISBN 0-87795-451-8); pap. 8.95 (ISBN 0-87795-452-6). Arbor Hse.

Arbor House Treasury of Great Science Fiction Short Novels. Robert Silverberg & Martin Harry Greenberg. LC 80-66764. (Priam books). 19.95 (ISBN 0-87795-284-1) (ISBN 0-87795-295-7). Arbor House.

Arbor House Treasury of Great Western Stories. Ed. by Bill Pronzini. Martin H. Greenberg. LC 82-72052. 1982. 17.95 (ISBN 0-87795-439-9, Priam); pap. 8.95 (ISBN 0-87795-410-0). Arbor Hse.

Arbor House Treasury of Horror and the Supernatural. Bill Pronzini & Barry N Malzberg. LC 80-70220. (Priam books). 8.95 (ISBN 0-87795-319-8) (ISBN 0-87795-309-0). Arbor House.

Arbor House Treasury of Modern Science Fiction. Ed. by Martin Harry Greenberg & Robert Silverberg. LC 79-54005. (Sf). 1980. 19.95 (ISBN 0-87795-246-9); pap. 8.95 (ISBN 0-87795-266-3). Arbor Hse.

Arbor House Treasury of Modern Science Fiction. Robert Silverberg & Martin Harry Greenberg. LC 79-54005. (Priam books). 19.95 (ISBN 0-87795-284-1). Arbor House: Distributed by Dutton.

Arbor House Treasury of Mystery and Suspense. Bill Pronzini & Barry N Malzberg. LC 81-67525. 9.95 (ISBN 0-87795-348-1) (ISBN 0-87795-349-X). Arbor House.

Arbor House Treasury of Mystery & Suspense. Ed. by Bill Pronzini & Barry N. Malzberg. LC 81-67525. 1982. 20.95 (ISBN 0-87795-349-X); pap. 9.95 (ISBN 0-87795-348-1). Arbor Hse.

Arcane Seventeen. Andre Breton. 9.95; pap. 3.95. French & Eur.

"Arch Adept" of the "First Degree," The Hindu's "Astral Bell," the Curse, the Doom of Major General J. B. Heatherstone, "The Mystery of Cloomber,". Arthur Conan Doyle. Ed. by Lauron William De Laurence. LC 11-776307. 1910. De Laurence, Scott & Co.

Arch Bishop: Or, Romanism in the United States. 4th ed. Orvilla S Belisle. LC 6-9420. 1855. W. W. Smith.

Arch of Stars. Clifford Lindsey Alderman. LC 50-7920. 1950. Appleton-Century-Crofts.

Arch of Triumph. Erich Maria Remarque. Tr. by Walter Sorell. Lindley, Denver, 1901- Joint Tr. LC 45-9381. 1945. D. Appleton Century Company, Inc.

Arch-Satirist. Frances De Wolfe Fenwick. LC 10-9255. 1910. Lothrop, Lee & Shepard Co.

Archangel. Keith Korman. LC 82-10858. 1983. 15.95 (ISBN 0-670-14317-0). Viking Press.

Archangel. Gerald Seymour. LC 82-72434. 14.95 (ISBN 0-525-24129-9). Dutton.

Archangel House. Esther Morgan McCullough. LC 40-1221. 1939. Gotham House.

Archbishop. Clay Blair. LC 70-124276. 1970. 7.95. World Pub. Co.

Archbishop and the Lady. Mary Bradford Crowninshield. LC 6609. 1900. McClure, Phillips & Co.

Archbishop's Unguarded Moment and Other Stories. Oscar Fay Adams. LC 99-3488. 1899. L. C. Page and Company (Incorporated).

Archdeacon. Lucy Bethia Colquhoun Walford. LC 8-32819. 1899. Longmans, Green & Co.

Archdeacon Prettyman in Politics. Norma Bertha Hardin. LC 21-15947. The Stratford Company.

Archduke. Michael P Arnold. LC 67-10352. 1967. Doubleday.

Archduke: By Michael Arnold. Michael P Arnold. (V2245). 1968. Avon.

Archeologist and the Princess: A Novel. 1st Ed. Walter W Leight. LC 57-14140. 1957. Exposition Press.

Archer at Large. Kenneth Millar. LC 72-106620. 1970. 7.95. Knopf.

Archer in Hollywood. Ross Macdonald. (YA) 1967. 7.95 o.p. (1113). Knopf.

Archer in Hollywood: Three Exciting Novels: The Moving Target, The Way Some People Die and The Barbarous Coast. Kenneth Millar. LC 67-11128. 1967. Knopf.

Archer in Jeopardy. Ross Macdonald. LC 79-63807. 1979. 14.95 (ISBN 0-394-50804-1). Knopf.

Archer Pilgrim... Donald Dean Jackson. LC 42-14391. 1942. Dodd, Mead & Company.

Archers at Home. Katinka Loeser. LC 68-8371. 1968. 4.95. Atheneum.

Archetypal Themes in the Modern Story. Ed. by Jack Matthews. LC 72-95904. 1973. 3.95. St. Martin's Press.

Archibald. Frederick William Wheldon. LC 30-24627. 1930. Brewer and Warren Inc.

Archibald Malmaison. Julian Hawthorne. LC 7-390117. (On cover: Standard library, no. 112). 1884. Funk & Wagnalls.

Archibald Malmaison. Julian Hawthorne. LC 99-5513. 1899. Funk & Wagnalls Company.

Archibald the Great. Clarence Budington Kelland. LC 43-100655. 1943. Harper & Brothers.

Archibishop's Pocket-Book. Herman Joseph Heuser. LC 28-125511. 1928. P. J. Kenedy & Sons.

Archie Lovell. Annie Edwards. (Seaside library. v. 29, no. 594). 1879. G. Munro.

Archie Lovell. Annie Edwards. (On cover: Seaside library Pocket ed. no. 843). 1886. G. Munro.

Archie Lovell: A Novel. Annie Edwards. 1867. W. C. & F. P. Church.

Archierey of Samara: A Semi-Historic Romance of Russian Life. Henry Iliowizi. LC 3-2082. 1903. H. T. Coates and Company.

Archipelago. R. A. Lafferty. (Lost Manuscript Ser.). 283p. 1979. 12.95 (ISBN 0-936414-03-0); signed & numbered 15.00x (ISBN 0-936414-02-2). Manuscript Pr.

Architect. Meyer Levin. LC 81-13622. 14.95 (ISBN 0-671-24892-8). Simon and Schuster.

Architects of the Self: George Eliot, D. H. Lawrence, and E. M. Forster. Calvin Bedient. LC 70-142056. 1972. 7.50 (ISBN 0-520-01873-7). University of California Press.

Architecture of the Arkansas Ozarks: A Novel. Donald Harington. LC 75-16492. (Illus.). 1975. (ISBN 0-316-34761-2). Little, Brown.

Archives of Haven. Julian Jay Savarin. LC 79-18307. (Gaskell, Jane, 1941-. The Atlan Ser.: No. 3). 1980. 10.95 (ISBN 0-312-04816-5). St. Martin's Press.

Archways. Chi Delta Phi. Alpha Gamma Chapter, Stephens College, Columbia, Mo. LC 33-15240. 1933. Stephens College.

Archy and Mehitabel. Don Marquis. LC 27-25597. 1927. Doubleday, Page & Company.

Archy Moore, the White Slave: Or, Memoirs of a Fugitive. Richard Hildreth. LC 69-18980. (Illus.). 1969. (ISBN 0-8371-1951-0). Negro Universities Press.

Archy Moore, the White Slave or Memoirs of a Fugitive. new ed. Richard Hildreth. LC 69-16309. (Illus.). Repr. of 1857 ed. lib. bdg. 22.50x (ISBN 0-678-00756-X). Kelley.

Archy Moore, the White Slave: Or, Memoirs of a Fugitive. With a New Introduction, Prepared for This Edition. Richard Hildreth. LC 7-4939. 1855. Miller, Orton & Mulligan.

Archy Moore, the White Slave; Or, Memoirs of a Fugitive. With a New Introduction, Prepared for This Edition. Richard Hildreth. LC 26-247013. 1857. Miller, Orton & Co.

Arctic Crusoe: A Tale of the Polar Sea; or, Arctic Adventures on the Sea of Ice. Percy Bolingbroke St. John. LC 8-3718. (Blue jacket series). 1875. Lee, Shepard and Dillingham.

Arctic Enemy. Linda Harrel. (Harlequin Romances Ser.). 192p. 1982. pap. 1.50 (ISBN 0-373-02459-2, Pub. by Harlequin). PB.

Arctic Nurse. Rose Dana, pseud. 1970. pap. 0.50 o.p. (50-505). Manor Bks.

Arctic Sheba: A Tale of the North Country. Arnold D Blythe. LC 49-13595. Burton Pub. Co.

Arctic SOS. Joseph Matheus Velter & Braithwaite, Rose Mary, Tr. LC 35-10588. 1935. Harper & Brothers.

Arctic Summer, and Other Fiction. Edward Morgan Forster. LC 80-26199. (Forster, Edward Morgan, 1879-1970. The Abinger Edition of E. M. Forster: Vol. 9). 1981. 35.00 (ISBN 0-8419-0670-X). Holmes & Meier.

Ardath, the Story of a Dead Self. Marie Corelli. LC 6-28749. Hurst & Company.

Ardath. The Story of a Dead Self. Marie Corelli. (On cover: Seaside library. Pocket ed, no. 2132). 1895. G. Munro's Sons.

Ardath: The Story of a Dead Self. Marie Corelli. LC 35-33407. Thompson & Thomas.

Arden. A Novel. Agnes Mary Frances Duclaux. LC 7-41413. (On cover: Lovell's library, v. 4, no. 134). 1883. J. W. Lovell Company.

Arden Acres. Jessica Nelson North MacDonald. LC 35-27102. Harcourt, Brace and Company.

Arden Court. Barbara Graham. LC 6-27649. (On cover: Seaside library. Pocket ed. no. 532). G. Munro.

Arden Massiter. William Francis Barry. LC 6578. 1900. The Century Co.

Ardent American. Anna Kneeland Crafts Codman. LC 11-12504. 1911. The Century Co.

Ardent Flame. Frances Vinciguerra Grebanier. LC 27-6051. The Century Co.

Ardent Flame. Frances Winwar. LC 27-6051. 1927. The Century Co.

Ardent Infidels. Maurice Druon. 1977. 1.95. Ace Books.

Ardent Protector. Bonnie Drake. (Candlelight Ecstasy Ser.: No. 42). (Orig.). 1982. pap. 1.75 (ISBN 0-440-10273-1). Dell.

Ardent Protector: Regency. Amanda Kent. (Second Chance at Love Ser.: No. 111). pap. 1.75 (ISBN 0-515-06899-3). Jove Pubns.

Ardent Suitor. Denice Greenlea. 1979. 1.75 (ISBN 0-449-23914-4). Fawcett Crest Books.

Ardent Years: A Novel. Janet Stevenson. LC 60-8512. 1960. Viking Press.

Ardiente suelo, fria Estacion. Pedro Juan Soto. 260p. 1980. pap. 5.25 (ISBN 0-940238-02-0). Ediciones Huracan.

Ardis Claverden. Frank Richard Stockton. LC 8-156698. Dodd, Mead and Company.

Ardis Claverden. Frank Richard Stockton. LC 8-156703. 1894. C. Scribner's Sons.

Ardistan and Djinnistan. Karl Friedrich May. LC 77-12605. (Collected works of Karl May; ser. 1, v. 1 & 2). 1977. 12.95 (ISBN 0-8164-9316-2). Seabury Press.

Ardistan and Djinnistan. Karl Friedrich May. 1980. 2.95 (ISBN 0-553-11842-0). Bantam Books.

Ardna Gashel: an Allegory. Olive Cook. LC 79-570631. (Illus.). 1970. 2.00 (ISBN 0-85262-004-7). Golden Head.

Ardor on Aros. Andrew J Offutt. 1973. (pbk.) 0.95. Dell.

Ardreys. Kay Vernon. (Illus.). 1979. pap. 1.95 (ISBN 0-89083-483-0). Zebra.

Are All Italians Lousy Lovers? Costanzo Costantini. LC 74-28697. 1975. 6.95 (ISBN 0-8184-0207-5). Lyle Stuart.

Are Daniels Needed Now? L. Amelia Gammell. LC 7-1524. 1895. Courier-Citizen Company.

Are Happier. James McLaughlin Neser. LC 58-8056. Dorrance.

Are Parents People? Alice Duer Miller. LC 24-4583. 1924. Dodd, Mead and Company.

Are the Fields Greener Beyond? Dominic Abraham Roina. LC 43-8180. 1943. D. A. Roina.

Are These Our Children? John Moynihan & Ruggles, Wesley. LC 31-31746. Grosset & Dunlap.

Are We There Yet? 1980. pap. 1.95 (ISBN 0-528-87766-6). Rand.

Are We There Yet? Diane Vreuls. LC 74-26905. 1975. 6.95 (ISBN 0-671-21952-9). Simon and Schuster.

Are We There Yet? Diane Vreuls. 1976. (pbk.) 1.25 (ISBN 0-380-00565-4). Avon.

Are You Decent? Wallace Smith. LC 75-140343. (Short story index reprint series). (Illus.). 1970. Books for Libraries Press.

Are You Decent! Wallace Smith. LC 27-182981. 1927. G. P. Putnam's Sons.

Are You Hungry, Are You Cold. 1st Ed. Ludwig Bemelmans. LC 60-114522. 1960. World Pub. Co.

Are You in the House Alone? Richard Peck. 1977. pap. 2.25 (ISBN 0-440-90227-4, LFL). Dell.

Are You Listening? A Novel. Joseph Patrick McEvoy. LC 32-21189. 1932. Houghton Mifflin Company.

Are You My Wife? Max Marcin. LC 10-26760. 1910. 1.25. Moffat, Yard and Company.

Are You My Wife? Kathleen O'Meara. 1876. The Catholic Publication Society.

Are You Sure You Love Me? Lois Wyse. LC 69-20040. 1969. 4.95 o.p. (ISBN 0-690-00332-3). T Y Crowell.

Are You with Me? A. Teplitsky & R. Hyman. 1976. pap. text ed. 3.92 (ISBN 0-13-045807-4). P-H.

Area of Darkness. Vidiadhar Surajprasad Naipaul. 1965. 5.95 o.p. (58827). Macmillan.

Area of Suspicion. John Dann MacDonald. LC 53-12669. (Dell first edition, 12). 1954. Dell Pub. Co.

Arena. Norman Bogner. LC 79-1286. 10.95 (ISBN 0-440-00190-0). Delacorte Press.

Arena. William Haggard. pap. 0.65 o.p. (ISBN 0-14-001879-4, 1879). Penguin.

Arena. Getulio E. Monteiro. 1970. 2.50 o.p. (ISBN 0-8059-1453-6). Dorrance.

Arena: A Novel. Maurice Ghnassia. LC 69-15659. 1969. 6.95. Viking Press.

Arena: By William Haggard Pseud. Richard Clayton. LC 61-141303. 1961. I. Washburn.

Arena of Antares. Alan Burt Akers. (Science Fiction Ser). (Orig.). 1974. pap. 1.25 o.p. (UY1145). DAW Bks.

Arena of Ants. James Schevill. LC 77-29531. (Illus.). 1977. pap. 7.50 (Pub. by Copper Beech). SBD.

Arena of Ants: A Novel. James Erwin Schevill. LC 77-151747. (Illus.). 7.50 (ISBN 0-914278-11-8). Copper Beech Press.

Arena of Love. Helene Eliat & Sakay, Yvette, Tr. LC 44-3529. 1944. Howell, Soskin.

Arena-Sports SF. Edward L Ferman & Barry N Malzberg. LC 75-11073. (Doubleday science fiction.). 1976. 5.95 (ISBN 0-385-06107-2). Doubleday.

Arena: Sports sf. Ed. by Edward L. Ferman. Barry N. Malzberg. LC 75-11073. 240p. 1976. 5.95 o.p. (ISBN 0-385-06107-2). Doubleday.

Arena Women. Richard E. Geis. 224p. 1972. pap. 1.95 o.p. (ISBN 0-87056-218-5, 6218). Brandon.

Aren't You Even Gonna Kiss Me Good-by. William Richert. LC 66-13788. bds., 4.50. McKay.

Aren't You Ever Gonna Kiss Me Goodbye? William Richert. 1972. pap. 0.95 o.p. (ISBN 0-515-02867-3, N2867). Pyramid Pubns.

Arethusa. Francis Marion Crawford. LC 7-33911. 1907. The Macmillan Company.

Arfao: Or, A. Rolend for an Oliver; the Romance of a Newspaper Personal. LC 6-46347. 1906. The Cosmos Publishing Club.

Arfive. Alfred Bertram Guthrie. LC 79-125648. 1971. 5.95. Houghton Mifflin.

Arfur: Teenage Pinball Queen: A Novel. Nik Cohn. LC 72-139618. 1971. 5.95 (ISBN 0-671-20818-7). Simon and Schuster.

Argal: Or, the Silver Devil, 2 vols. in one. George Hadley. Ed. by R. Reginald & Douglas Menville. LC 76-1461. (Supernatural & Occult Fiction Ser.). 1976. Repr. of 1793 ed. lib. bdg. 24.00x (ISBN 0-405-08420-X). Ayer Co.

Argal: Or, The Silver Devil, Being the Adventures of an Evil Spirit, Related by Himself. George Hadley. LC 76-1461. (Supernatural and Occult Fiction). 1976. 24.00 (ISBN 0-405-08420-X). Arno Press.

Argentine Deadline. Don Pendleton & Gar Wilson. (Phoenix Force Ser.). 192p. 1982. pap. 1.95 (ISBN 0-373-61301-6, Pub. by Worldwide). Harlequin Bks.

Argentine Interlude. Hermine Hallam-Hipwell Vivenot. LC 37-10348. The Penn Publishing Company.

Argonaut. Honore McCue Willsie Morrow. LC 33-25384. 1933. W. Morrow & Company.

Argonaut Gold. Charles Horace Snow. LC 36-7041. 1936. Macrae Smith Company.

Argonaut Stories ... LC 6-45361. 1906. Payot, Upham & Company.

Argonautica: Or, The Quest of Jason for the Golden Fleece, the Epic Poem First Set Down in the Ancient Greek Tongue by Apollonius of Rhodes in the Third Century B. C. Together with the Tr. into English Prose by Edward P. Coleridge. Pref. by Moses Hadas, Illus. by A. Tassos. Apollonius Rhodius. Tr. by Edward Philip Coleridge. LC 60-2154. 1961. bds., bxd. 6.00. Heritage Press Dist. Dial Press.

Argonauts. Eliza Orzeszkowa. Tr. by Curtin, Jeremiah. 1901. C. Scribner's Sons.

Argonauts. Yvonne Schoell. LC 72-4486. 1972. 8.95 (ISBN 0-13-045872-4). Prentice-Hall.

Argonauts. Yvonne Schoell. 1976. 1.95 (ISBN 0-553-08889-0). Bantam.

Argonauts of North Liberty. Bret Harte. LC 9-2510. 1888. Houghton, Mifflin and Company.

Argosy Book of Adventure Stories: Edited by Rogers Terrill. Argosy (New York) Ed. by Rogers Terrill. LC 52-8982. 1952. A. S. Barnes.

Argosy Book of Sea Stories. Ed. by Rogers Terrill. 1966. 2.95 o.p. (ISBN 0-498-08028-5). A S Barnes.

Argosy Book of Sea Stories: Edited by Rogers Terrill. Argosy (New York) Ed. by Rogers Terrill. LC 52-119221. 1953. A. S. Barnes.

Argosy Book of Sports Stories: Edited by Rogers Terrill. Argosy (New York) Ed. by Rogers Terrill. LC 52-11921. 1953. A. S. Barnes.

Argus Pheasant. John Charles Beecham. LC 18-12302. W. J. Watt & Company.

Argyle Case. Arthur Hornblow & Burns, William John, 1861- LC 13-187167. 1913. Harper & Brothers.

Aria. Brown Meggs. LC 77-5188. 1978. 10.95 (ISBN 0-689-10832-X). Atheneum.

Aria. Brown Meggs. 1979. 2.50 (ISBN 0-671-82024-9). Pocket Books.

Ariabella: The First. N. A Straight. LC 80-6024. 9.95 (ISBN 0-394-49346-X). Random House.

Ariadne. June Rachuy Brindel. LC 80-14013. 10.95 (ISBN 0-312-04911-0). St. Martin's Press.

Ariadne. Isadore Lhevinne. LC 28-24700. 1928. Globus Press.

Ariadne Clue. Carol Clemeau. LC 82-10359. 11.95 (ISBN 0-684-17764-1). Scribner.

Ariadne of Allan Water. Mary Fenollosa. LC 14-6239. 1914. 1.35. Little, Brown, and Company.

Ariadne Spinning. Eleanor Green. LC 41-201617. 1941. Doubleday, Doran and Company, Inc.

Ariadne. The Story of a Dream. Louise De La Ramee. LC 6-33375. 1877. J. B. Lippincott & Co.

Ariana Olisvos, Her Last Works and Days. David Dwyer. LC 76-8752. 1976. 7.00. (ISBN 0-87023-218-5) (ISBN 0-87023-219-3). University of Massachusetts Press.

Ariane. Jean Schopfer. Tr. by Chapman, Guy. 1927. A. A. Knopf.

Aricie Brun: Or, Les Vertus Bourgeoises... Emile Henriot & Rockwood, Robert Everett, Ed. (Contemporary France in literature, A. Morise, general editor). Ginn and Company.

Aricie Brun: Translated by Henry Longan Stuart. Emile Henriot & Stuart, Henry Longan, Tr. LC 26-3797. 1926. The Viking Press.

Arickaree Treasure: And Other Brief Tales of Adventurous Mountanians. Albert Gallatin Clarke. LC 1-31839. The Abbey Press.

Arid Heart. Carlo Cassola. LC 63-7354. 1964. Pantheon Books.

Ariel. Lawrence Block. 1982. pap. 2.75 (ISBN 0-425-05169-2). Berkley Pub.

Ariel: A Novel. Lawrence Block. LC 79-87835. 9.25 (ISBN 0-87795-234-5). Arbor House.

Ariel, and Other Writings. Wilbur Morris Stine. LC 6-20451. 1906. The Acorn Press.

Ariel Custer. Grace Livingston Hill. LC 61-49220. 1960. Grosset & Dunlap.

Ariel Custer. Grace Livingston Hill. LC 25-21261. 1925. J. B. Lippincott Company.

Aries I. John Grant. LC 80-464040. 14.00 (ISBN 0-7153-7777-9). David & Charles.

Aries Rising. Arthur Herzog. LC 80-12835. 12.95 (ISBN 0-399-90088-8). R. Marek.

Arigato. Richard Condon. LC 72-3618. 1972. 7.95. Dial Press.

Arilla Sundown. Virginia Hamilton. (YA) 1979. pap. 1.95 (ISBN 0-440-90165-0, LFL). Dell.

Arise from Sleep. Elizabeth Delehanty. LC 42-7493. 1942. The Viking Press.

Aristocracy. A Novel. LC 6-2042. (On cover: Appleton's town and country library, no. 12). 1888. D. Appleton and Company.

Aristocrat. Genevieve Greer. LC 46-505321. 1946. The Vanguard Press.

Aristocrat. Conrad Richter. LC 68-23945. 1968. 4.50. Knopf.

Aristocrat: A Memoir. Martin Boyd. LC 27-9859. The Bobbs-Merrill Company.

Aristocrat: An American Tale. Lloyd Wharton Bickley. LC 7-9734. 1833. Key & Biddle.

Aristocrat in America: Extracts from the Diary of the Right Honorable Lord William Henry Cavendish-Bentinck-Pelham-Clinton-St. Maur-Beauchamp-De Vere, K.G. Dickens, Charles, 1812-1870 & Nye, Edgar Wilson, 1839-1896. LC 6-2043. (On cover: American series, no. 71). M. J. Ivers & Co.

Aristocratic Miss Brewster. Joseph Crosby Lincoln. LC 27-19178. 1927. D. Appleton & Company.

Aristocratic Miss Bruster. Joseph Crosby Lincoln. (Illus.). 1929. A. L. Burt Company.

Aristocrats. Gertrude Franklin Horn Atherton. 1901. lib. bdg. 15.00 (ISBN 0-8414-3080-2). Folcroft.

Aristocrats. Gertrude Franklin Horn Atherton. LC 68-20003. (Americans in Fiction Ser.). lib. bdg. 14.00 (ISBN 0-8398-0062-2); pap. text ed. 4.95x (ISBN 0-89197-661-2). Irvington.

Aristocrats. Steven Barry. LC 70-187693. 1972. (ISBN 0-446-65514-7). Paperback Library.

Aristocrats. Gwen Davis. LC 76-57736. 8.95 (ISBN 0-87223-493-2). Playboy Press.

Aristocrats: Being the Impressions of the Lady Helen Pole During Her Sojourn in the Great North Woods As Spontaneously Recorded in Her Letters to Her Friend in North Britain, the Countess of Edge and Rose. Gertrude Franklin Horn Atherton. LC 68-20003. (Americans in Fic.). 1968. 10.00. Gregg Pr.

Aristocrats: Being the Impressions of the Lady Helen Pole During Her Sojourn in the Great North Woods As Spontaneously Recorded in Her Letters to Her Friend in North Britain, the Countess of Edge and Ross. 3d ed. Gertrude Franklin Horn Atherton. LC 1-31695. 1901. J. Lane.

Aristocrats. Translated from the French by Geoffrey. Sainsbury. 1st Ed. Michel De Saint-Pierre. LC 56-8274. 1956. Dutton.

Aristopia; a Romance History of the New World. Castello N Holford. LC 7-6128. 1895. Arena Publishing Company.

Aristotle Detective. Margaret Anne Doody. LC 79-1703. 1980. 10.95 (ISBN 0-06-011086-4). Harper & Row.

Arius the Libyan. Nathan Chapman Kouns. LC 22-2307. 1922. D. Appleton and Company.

Arius the Libyan: A Romance of the Primitive Church. Nathan Chapman Kouns. LC 14-22554. 1914. J. Howell.

Arius the Libyan. An Idyl of the Primitive Church. Nathan Chapman Kouns. LC 7-14162. 1884. D. Appleton and Company.

Arizona. Clarence Budington Kelland. 1939. Harper & Brothers.

Arizona: A Romance of the Great Southwest. Cyrus Townsend Brady & Thomas, Augustus. LC 14-16922. 1914. 1.25. Dodd, Mead and Company.

Arizona Ambush. abr. ed. Bruce Martin, pseud. Ed. by Alice Sachs. (Orig.). 1971. Repr. of 1967 ed. 3.95 o.p. Lenox Hill.

Arizona Ambush. Don Pendleton. (Executioner Ser.: No. 31). 1977. pap. 1.95 (ISBN 0-523-41095-6). Pinnacle Bks.

Arizona Ames. Zane Grey. LC 31-282993. 1932. Harper & Brothers.

Arizona Blood. Tom Curry. 1972. pap. 0.60 o.p. (06157). Curtis.

Arizona Clan. Zane Grey. (Keith Jennison large type ed.). 1965. 6.95, 4.95 lib. ed.,. Watts.

Arizona Clan. 1st Ed. Zane Grey. LC 58-8887. 1958. Harper.

Arizona Fancy Lady. Dirk Fletcher. (Spur Ser.: No. 2). 224p. (Orig.). 1982. pap. 2.25 (ISBN 0-8439-1125-5, Leisure Bks). Nordon Pubns.

Arizona Feud. Frank Ramsay Adams. LC 41-15430. 1941. Doubleday, Doran and Co., Inc.

Arizona Gold: A Western Story. Elwyn Whitman Chambers. LC 28-14411. 1927. Chelsea House.

Arizona Guns. William MacLeod Raine. 1975. (pbk.) 0.95. Popular Library.

Arizona Jim. Charles Alden Seltzer. LC 74-21533. 1974. (ISBN 0-88411-101-6). Aeonian Press.

Arizona Jim. Charles Alden Seltzer. LC 39-27699. 1939. Doubleday, Doran & Company, Inc.

Arizona Jim. Charles Alden Seltzer. LC 42-254424. 1942. The Sun Dial Press.

Arizona Justice. Gordon Donalds, pseud. LC 56-4655. 1956. Avalon Books.

Arizona Justice. Oscar Schisgall. LC 36-15686. Green Circle Books.

Arizona Justice. Gordon D Shirreffs. (Belmont Tower Book). 1977. 1.50 (ISBN 0-505-51195-9). Tower Pubns.

Arizona Nights. Stewart Edward White. LC 7-36101. 1907. The McClure Company.

Arizona Nights. Stewart Edward White. LC 37-39261. 1937. The Sun Dial Press, Inc.

Arizona Nights. Stewart Edward White & Wyeth, N.C., 1882- Illus. LC 18-12306. 1907. Grosset & Dunlap.

Arizona Ranch Murders & Other Stories. George Chew. 1976. 4.95 o.p. (ISBN 0-8059-2335-7). Dorrance.

Arizona Ranger Courage. A. Leslie. 1942. Gateway Books.

Arizona Rider. George Metcalf. LC 35-9494. E. J. Clode, Inc.

Arizona Roundup. William L Hopson. LC 48-3588. 1948. Phoenix Press.

Arizona Saddles. Lee Floren. 1954. Arcadia House.

Arizona Star. Faith Baldwin. 1976. Repr. of 1945 ed. lib. bdg. 16.60x (ISBN 0-88411-601-8). Amereon Ltd.

Arizona Star. Faith Baldwin Cuthrell. LC 73-86735. 1973. 5.95. Aeonian Press.

Arizona Star. Faith Baldwin Cuthrell. LC 45-2330. 1945. Farrar & Rinehart, Inc.

Arizona Star. Faith Baldwin Cuthrell. 1975. (pbk.) 1.50. Warner Paperback Library.

Arizonan. Jay Lucas. LC 37-287093. Green Circle Books.

Ark. Jarl Szydlow. 1978. pap. 1.50 (ISBN 0-532-15378-2). Woodhill.

Ark of Bones and Other Stories. Henry Dumas. LC 74-4143. 1974. 5.95 (ISBN 0-394-48971-3). Random House.

Ark of Bones, and Other Stories. Henry Dumas. LC 71-112386. 1971. 5.95 (ISBN 0-8093-0442-2). Southern Illinois University Press.

Ark of Bones: And Other Stories. Henry Dumas. Ed. by Eugene Redmond. LC 74-4143. 1974. pap. 2.95 o.p. (ISBN 0-394-70947-0). Random.

Ark of Doom. Richard Woodley. (Dell Book.). 1978. 1.50 (ISBN 0-440-15927-X). Dell Publishing Co.

Ark of the Covenant: A Romance of the Air and of Science. Victor MacClure. LC 24-7677. 1924. Harper & Brothers.

Ark of Venus. 1st Ed. Clyde B Clason. LC 55-895412. 1955. Knopf.

Arkansas Adios. Earl Mac Rauch. LC 71-154930. 1971. 3.50 (ISBN 0-394-47201-2). Knopf; Distributed by Random House.

Arkansas Guns. William MacLeod Raine. LC 54-5696. 1954. Houghton Mifflin.

Arkansas John the Baptist. Andy Powers & Lena Powers. LC 74-14136. 1975. 5.95 (ISBN 0-8283-1592-2). Branden Press.

Arkansas Planter. Opie Percival Read. LC 7-36625. Rand, McNally & Company.

Arkansas Planter. Opie Percival Read. LC 99-1352. (On cover: Oriental library, v. 1, no. 14). Rand, McNally & Company.

Arkansas Souvenir. Oliver Waldron Jennings. LC 15-25102. 1915. The Call Printing Co.

Arkham Collector, Vol. 1. Ed. by August William Derleth. 10.00 o.p. Arkham.

Arkinsaw Cousins: A Story of the Ozarks. John Breckenridge Ellis. LC 8-58783. 1908. H. Holt and Company.

Arlene Perry, Orthopedics Nurse see Arlene Perry, Special Nurse.

Arlene Perry, Special Nurse. Ruth MacLeod. Orig. Title: Arlene Perry, Orthopedics Nurse. pap. 0.50 o.p. (52-494). Paperback Lib.

Arlette. Nicolas Freeling. LC 80-8653. 10.95 (ISBN 0-394-51454-8). Pantheon Books.

Arlette & Her Friends. Jacques Federeaux. Bd. with Initiations of Suzon. 160p. pap. 1.95 o.p. (MP-104). Montmartre.

Arlie Gelston. Roger L Sergel. LC 24-3539. 1923. B. W. Huebsch, Inc.

Arlington: A Novel, 3 vols. in 2. Thomas Henry Lister. LC 79-8154. Date not set. Repr. of 1832 ed. Set. 84.50 (ISBN 0-404-61979-7); Vol. 1. (ISBN 0-404-61980-0); Vol. 2. (ISBN 0-404-61981-9). AMS Pr.

Arlo. Bertha Browning Barnes Cobb & Cobb, Ernest, 1877- Joint Author. LC 15-18830. 1915. 1.00. The Riverdale Press, Brookline.

Arlo. Bertha Browning Barnes Cobb & Cobb, Ernest, 1877- Joint Author. LC 18-2203. 1918. G. P. Putnam's Sons.

Arm. Clark Howard. (Orig.). 1970. pap. 0.75 o.p. (T2282, GM). Fawcett World.

Arm: A Novel. Clark Howard. LC 67-26929. 1967. Sherbourne Press.

Arm and the Darkness. Taylor Caldwell. LC 75-563. 1975. 11.95 (ISBN 0-88411-151-2). Aeonian Press.

Arm and the Darkness. Taylor Caldwell. LC 43-370906. 1943. C. Scribner's Sons.

Arm and the Darkness. Taylor Caldwell. (Crest Book, Q2006). 1973. (pbk) 1.50. Fawcett.

Arm-Chair at the Inn. Francis Hopkinson Smith. LC 12-19331. 1912. C. Scribner's Sons.

Arm of Flesh. 1st Ed. James Salter. LC 61-6205. 1961. Harper.

Arm of Gold. Charles William Gordon. LC 32-30782. 1932. Dodd, Mead & Company.

Arm of Mrs. Egan: And Other Strange Stories. 1st Ed. William Fryer Harvey. LC 52-5303. (Guilt edged mystery). 1952. Dutton.

Armada. Michael Jahn, pseud. 224p. (Orig.). 1981. pap. 2.25 (ISBN 0-449-14388-0, GM). Fawcett.

Armada of Antares. Alan Burt Aker. (Science Fiction Ser.). 1976. pap. 1.25 o.p. (UY1227). DAW Bks.

Armada of Antares. Alan Burt Akers. (Science Fiction Ser.). pap. 1.25 (ISBN 0-87997-227-0, UY1227). DAW Bks.

Armada of the Air. Norman Bentley. LC 37-3439. 1937. Lothrop, Lee and Shepard Company.

Armadale. Wilkie Collins. LC 70-107168. (works of Wilkie Collins, v. 8-9). (Illus.). 1972. (ISBN 0-403-00433-0). Scholarly Press.

Armadale. A Novel. Wilkie Collins. LC 3-27274. 1873. Harper & Brothers.

Armadale: A Novel. Wilkie Collins. LC 4-18947. 1902. Harper & Brothers.

Armadillo Book. Bill Bryant. 1983. pap. 3.95 (ISBN 0-88289-383-1). Pelican.

Armadillo in the Grass. Shelby Hearon. (Editors' Choice). 1973. 0.75. Curtis Books.

Armadillo in the Grass. Shelby Hearon. LC 68-23953. 1968. 4.50. Knopf.

Armageddon. Leon M. Uris. pap. 4.25 (ISBN 0-440-10290-1). Dell.

Armageddon. Stanley Waterloo. LC 76-9746. (Gregg Press science fiction series). 1976. 13.00 (ISBN 0-8398-2348-7). Gregg Press.

Armageddon: A Novel of Berlin. Leon M. Uris. LC 64-16837. 1964. Doubleday.

Armageddon: A Tale of Love, War, and Invention. Stanley Waterloo. LC 98-1279. Rand, McNally & Co.

Armageddon: A Tale of the Antichrist. Eleanor De Forest. LC 38-30228. 1938. Wm. B. Eredmans Publishing Company.

Armageddon Game. Mark Washburn. 1981. pap. 2.95 (ISBN 0-440-10089-5). Dell.

Armageddon Game: A Novel of Suspense. Mark Washburn. LC 76-58425. 7.95. Putnam.

Armageddon in the West. Jonathan Scofield, pseud. (Freedom Fighters Ser.: No. 12). (Orig.). 1982. pap. 2.95 (ISBN 0-440-00290-7, Bryans). Dell.

Armageddon Revisited. Ken Kemp. LC 78-65694. 1979. 8.95 (ISBN 0-533-04110-4). Vantage.

Armageddon Two Thousand Nineteen A.D. Buck Rogers. Francois Nowlan. (O.s.i.). 192p. 1978. pap. 2.25 (ISBN 0-441-02941-8). Ace Bks.

Armageddon 249 A.D. Philip Francis Nowlan. 1974. (pbk.) 1.25. Ace Books.

Armais and Others. Josephine White Bates. LC 6-9079. (On cover: The Ariel library, no. 21). 1892. F. J. Schulte & Company.

Armance. Marie Henri Beyle. Tr. by Charles Kenneth Scott-Moncrieff. LC 28-16170. (Half-title: The works of Stendhal). 1928. Boni & Liveright.

Armande. Edmond Louis Antoine Huot De Goncourt & Goncourt, Jules Alfred Huot De. Tr. by Haserick, Alfred E. LC 6-43735. ("World classics"). 1894. J. Knight Company.

Armchair Adventure for the Angler. Ed. by Charles Kunkel Fox. LC 78-88262. 1970. 6.95. A. S. Barnes.

Armchair Companion. 1st- Furman, Abraham Louis, 1902- LC 44-47307. Lantern Press, Inc. Etc.

Armchair in Hell. Henry Kane. LC 48-5116. (Inner Sanctum mystery). 1948. Simon and Schuster.

Armed Camps. Kit Reed, pseud. LC 79-113456. 1970. 4.95. Dutton.

Armed with a New Terror. Theodora DuBois. LC 36-17321. 1936. Houghton Mifflin Company.

Armed with Madness. Mary Butts. LC 28-11396. 1928. A. & C. Boni.

Armenian Maiden. Emma Sykes Richardson. LC 20-5195. Priv. Print.

Armenian Princess: A Tale of Anatolian Peasant-Life. Edgar James Banks. LC 14-10427. 1.25. The Gorham Press; Etc., Etc.

Armenian Romance. Marie Sarrafian Banker. LC 42-596. 1941. Wm. B. Eerdmans Publishing Company.

Armenians. A Tale of Constantinople. Charles MacFarlane. LC 7-3536. 1830. Carey and Lea.

Armes Miraculeuses. Aime Cesaire. (Coll. Poesie). pap. 4.50. French & Eur.

Armful of Warm Girl. William Mode Spackman. LC 77-21170. 1978. 6.95 (ISBN 0-394-50000-8). Knopf: Distributed by Random House.

Arminel of the West. Ernest George Henham. LC 9-7571. 1909. Moffat, Yard and Company.

Arminell. Sabine Baring-Gould. LC 6-7963. (On cover: Lovell's international series, no. 45). F. F. Lovell & Company.

Armistice, and Other Memories: Forming a Pendant to The Spanish Farm Trilogy. Ralph Hale Mottram. LC 79-160946. (Short story index reprint series). 1971. (ISBN 0-8369-3925-5). Books for Libraries Press.

Armistice, and Other Memories: Forming a Pendant to 'The Spanish Farm Trilogy' Ralph Hale Mottram. LC 29-4762. 1929. L. MacVeagh, The Dial Press.

Armor of Light. Tracy Dickinson Mygatt & Witherspoon, Frances. LC 30-8787. H. Holt and Company.

Armored Giants: A Novel of the Civil War. Francis Van Wyck Mason. LC 80-17751. 13.95 (ISBN 0-316-54922-3). Little, Brown.

Armored Giants: A Novel of the Civil War. F. Van Wyck Mason. 352p. 1980. 13.95 (ISBN 0-316-54922-3). Little.

Armorel of Lynoesse: A Romance of to-Day. Walter Besant. LC 6-12397. (On cover: Harper's Franklin square library, no. 674). 1890. Harper & Brothers.

Armorel of Lyonesse: A Romance of to-Day. Walter Besant. LC 41-34776. 1890. Harper & Brothers.

Armorel of Lyonesse: A Romance of to-Day. Walter Besant. LC 4-16295. 1900. Harper & Brothers.

Armorer of Tyre. Sylvanus Cobb. (On cover: The pastime series, no. 107). Laird & Lee.

Armorer of Tyre. Sylvanus Cobb. (arm chair library, no. 19). 1893. F. M. Lupton.

Armour Against Love. Barbara Cartland. 1975. pap. 1.25 o.p. (ISBN 0-515-03831-8, V3831). BJ Pub Group.

Armour Against Love. Barbara Cartland. 1974. (pbk.) 0.95 (ISBN 0-515-03294-8). Pyramid.

Armour: Or, What Are You Going to Do About It? C H Anderson. LC 6-3448. W. B. Smith & Co.

Armour Wherein He Trusted: A Novel and Some Stories. Mary Gladys Meredith Webb. LC 29-8254. E. P. Dutton & Company, Inc.C.

Armourer's Prentices. Charlotte Mary Yonge. (On cover: Seaside library. Pocket ed. no. 247). 1884. G. Munro.

Arms and the Girl. Marguerite Mooers Marshall. LC 42-211. 1942. Macrae-Smith-Company.

Arms and the Maid: Or, Anthony Wilding. Rafael Sabatini. LC 10-111332. 1910. G. P. Putnam's Sons.

Arms & the Woman. Hyacinthe Hill, pseud. 72p. Date not set. 3.50. New Orlando.

Arms and the Woman: A Romance. Harold MacGrath. LC 99-4673. 1899. Doubleday & McClure Co.

Arms Are Fair. Bradford Smith. LC 43-11948. 1943. The Bobbs-Merrill Company.

Arms for Adonis. Charlotte Jay. (Orig.). pap. 0.95 o.p. (02159). Macmillan.

Arms for Adonis: By Charlotte Jay. 1st Amer. Ed. Geraldine Jay. LC 60-15342. 1961. Harper.

Arms for Oblivion. Joseph Hedges. (Stark Ser.: No. 2). (Orig.). 1975. pap. 0.95 o.p. (ISBN 0-515-03563-7, N3563). Pyramid Pubns.

Arm's-Length. John Metcalfe. LC 30-8262. 1930. C. Scribner's Sons.

Arms of Venus. John Appleby. LC 51-9401. 1951. Coward-McCann.

Armstrong. Tom Stone. 1973. (pbk) 0.95. Warner.

Armstrong. Alan White. LC 76-42411. 1977. 6.95 (ISBN 0-385-12680-8). Published for the Crime Club by Doubleday.

Armstrong. Alec Whitney, pseud. LC 76-42411. (Crime Club Ser.). 1977. 6.95 o.p. (ISBN 0-385-12680-8). Doubleday.

Army Boys and Girls. Mary Greene Bonesteel. LC 6-10371. 1895. J. Murphy & Company.

Army Doctor. Jerome Darwin Engel. LC 42-10016. 1942. Gramercy Publishing Company.

Army Doctor. Elizabeth Seifert. LC 73-79139. 1973. 5.95. Aeonian Press.

Army Doctor. Elizabeth Seifert. LC 42-4615. 1942. Dodd, Mead & Company.

Army Doctor's Romance. Grant Allen. LC 6-66. (Breezy library, no. 3)). 1893. R. Tuck & Sons Co., Ltd.

Army Girls. Jerry Cole. LC 42-19683. 1942. J. Swift, Inc.

Army Mistress. William David, pseud. 1970. pap. 0.75 o.p. (75-303). Manor Bks.

Army Mule. Charles Miner Thompson. LC 10-116455. 1910. Houghton Mifflin Company.

Army of a Dream. Rudyard Kipling. LC 7-3085. 1904. Doubleday, Page & Company.

Army of Children: The Story of the Children's Crusade, A.D. 1212. Evan H Rhodes. LC 77-25749. 1978. 9.95 (ISBN 0-8037-0180-2). Dial Press.

Army of Chilren. Evan H Rhodes. 1979. 2.50 (ISBN 0-671-82538-0). Pocket Books.

Army of Darkness. Hugh Walker. 1979. 1.50 (ISBN 0-87997-438-9). DAW Books.

Army of Shadows. Joseph Kessel & Chevalier, Haakon Maurice, 1902- Tr. LC 44-5494. 1944. A. A. Knopf.

Army of the Undead. Rafe Bernard. Orig. Title: Invaders, No. (3). 1967. pap. 0.50 o.p. (R1711). Pyramid Pubns.

Army Post Murders. Mason Wright. LC 31-26886. Farrar & Rinehart Incorporated.

Army Society: Life in a Garrison Town; a Discursive Story. Henrietta Eliza Vaughan Stannard. LC 8-13874. (Harper's handy series. no. 78). 1886. Harper & Brothers.

Army Society: Or, Life in a Garrison Town, a Discursive Story. Henrietta Eliza Vaughan Stannard. LC 8-138733. (Lovell's Library). (On cover: Lovell's library. no. 1164: No. 1164). 1888. J. W. Lovell Company.

Army Surgeon. Genevieve May Fox. LC 44-249969. 1944. Little, Brown and Company.

Army Tramp. Doug Duperrault. 1969. pap. 0.75 o.p. (75-250). Manor Bks.

Army Widow. James Noble Gifford. LC 43-10302. 1943. Phoenix Press.

Army Wife. Charles King. LC 7-12226. 1896. F. T. Neely.

Army with Banners. Ruth Comfort Mitchell. LC 28-21974. 1928. D. Appleton & Company.

Army with Banners. J. N. Washburn. 3.50 o.p. Carlton.

Army Without Banners. John Beames. 1930. Little, Brown, and Company.

Arnaud's Masterpiece: A Romance of the Pyrenees. Walter Cranston Larned. LC 7-13843. 1897. C. Scribner's Sons.

Arncliffe Puzzle. Louis Tracy. LC 6-3003. 1906. E. J. Clode.

Arne. author's ed. Bjornstjerne Bjornson & Anderson, Rasmus Bjorn, 1846- Tr. LC 6-13120. 1881. Houghton, Mifflin and Company.

Arne. A Sketch of Norwegian Country Life. Bjornstjerne Bjornson. (On cover: Lovell's library, v. 1, no. 4). 1882. J. W. Lovell Company.

Arne: A Sketch of Norwegian Country Life. Bjornstjerne Bjornson & Plesner, Augusta, Tr. LC 6-13121. 1866. A. Strahan.

Arne: A Sketch of Norwegian Country Life. Bjornstjerne Bjornson & Plesner, Augusta, Tr. LC 6-13117. (On cover: Round table library). 1895. J. Knight Company.

Arne: And The Fisher Lassie. Bjornstjerne Bjornson & Low, Walter, Tr. LC 4-17556. (Half-title: Bohn's novelists' library. Bjornson's tales). 1894. G. Bell and Sons.

Arnold Bennett Omnibus Book: Containing Riceyman Steps, Elsie and the Child, Lord Raingo and Accident. Arnold Bennett. LC 74-5396. (collected works of Arnold Bennett). 1974. Books for Libraries Press.

Arnold Levenberg. David Pinsky & Goldberg, Isaac, 1887- Tr. LC 28-153828. 1928. Simon and Schuster.

Arnold Waterlow: A Life. May Sinclair. LC 24-215113. 1924. The Macmillan Company.

Arnold's Promise. Charlotte Mary Brame. (On cover: Lovell's library. no. 1043). J. W. Lovell Company.

Arnold's Promise. Bertha M. Clay. LC 44-11669. (On cover: Lovell's library, no. 1043). J. W. Lovell Company.

Arnold's Promise. Bertha M. Clay. LC 1-30005. (With Clay, Bertha M., pseud. Addie's husband. New York, 1900). 1900. Street & Smith.

Arnold's Tempter. Benjamin Freeman Comfort. LC 8-30704. 1908. The C. M. Clark Publishing Co.

Arnoul, the Englishman. Francis Aveling. LC 8-31820. 1908. B. Herder.

Aros of Atlantis. David L Manley. LC 72-185575. (Illus.). 1972. 4.95 (ISBN 0-8059-1662-8). Dorrance.

Around a Rusty God. Augusta Walker. LC 54-6001. (Illus.). 1954. Dial Press.

Around Bronton. Mary Ruth Baldwin. LC 6-6854. 1891. Hunt & Eaton.

Around Dark Corners. Hugh Pentecost. 1970. 3.75 o.p. (ISBN 0-396-06180-X). Dodd.

Around Dark Corners: A Collection of Mystery Stories. Judson Pentecost Philips. LC 71-111914. 1970. 3.75. Dodd, Mead.

Around Old Bethany: A Story of the Adventures ! of Robert and Mary Davis. Robert Lee Berry. LC 25-12520. Gospel Trumpet Company.

Around Old Chester. Margaret Wade Campbell Deland. LC 15-185660. 1915. Harper & Brothers.

Around Our House. Henry E. Giles & Janice Holt Giles. LC 76-151017. (Illus.). 1971. 7.95 (ISBN 0-395-12668-1). Houghton Mifflin.

Around the Camp-Fire. Charles George Douglas Roberts. T. Y. Crowell & Company.

Around the End. Ralph Henry Barbour. LC 13-203411. 1913. D. Appleton and Company.

Around the Golden Deep. A Romance of the Sierras. A P Reeder. LC 7-30945. 1888. Cupples and Hurd.

Around the Rugged Rock. Elizabeth Cadell. LC 54-5208. 1954. Morrow.

Around the World: A Sparkling Romance. George Weston. LC 29-22052. 1929. Dodd, Mead & Company.

Around the World in Eight Days. Jules Verne. LC 62-7926. (Golden illustrated classics). 1962. Golden Press.

Around the World in Eighty Days. Jules Verne. LC 56-2854. 1956. Grosset & Dunlap.

Around the World in Eighty Days! railroad ed. Jules Verne. LC 66-87099. 1876. Donnelley, Loyd.

Around the World in Eighty Days. Jules Verne. LC 64-4303. 1964. Junior Deluxe Editions.

Around the World in Eighty Days. Jules Verne. LC 62-5857. 1962. Heritage Press.

Around the World in Eighty Days. Jules Verne. Limited Editions Club, Inc., New York. LC 74-20475. (Illus.). 1962. Printed at the Plantin Press for the Members of the Limited Editions Club.

Around the World in Eighty Days. Jules Verne. LC 1-9857. (On cover: The sea and shore series no. 28). 1891. Street & Smith.

Around the World in Eighty Days. Jules Verne. LC 36-29341. 1906. C. Scribner's Sons.

Around the World in Eighty Days. Jules Verne & Gertrude Moderow. LC 52-1532.

Around the World in Eighty Days. Translated by Geo. M. Towle. With Biographical Illus. and Drawings Reporduced from Early Editions, Together with an Introd. and Captions by Anthony Boucher. Jules Verne. LC 56-14054. (Great illustrated classics). 1956. Dodd, Mead.

Around the World in Eighty Ways. Ed. by John W. Fitzgerald. pap. 2.95 o.p. (ISBN 0-87964-107-X). Academy-Parliament.

Around the World in Ninety-Nine Beds. Dorothy Miller. 1974. 3.95 o.s.i. Eden.

Around the World in 80 Days. Jules Verne & Didier Bardon. LC 79-3771. (Studio book). 1980. 8.95 (ISBN 0-670-13323-X). Viking Press.

Around the World in 80 Days. Complete and Unabridged. Jules Verne. LC 57-23336. (Avon, T-148). Avon Publications.

Around the World Is Not a Trip. Ted Mark. (man from O.R.G.Y.). 1973. (pbk.) 1.25. Dell.

Around the World with Auntie Mame: By Patrick Dennis Pseud. 1st Ed. Edward Everett Tanner. LC 58-8576. 1958. Harcourt, Brace.

Around the World with Josiah Allen's Wife. Marietta Holley. LC 5-26941. 1905. G. W. Dillingham Company.

Around the Yule Log. Willis Boyd Allen. LC 99-871. 1898. The Pilgrim Press.

Around Town Boys. Peter Joseph Oeland. LC 10-11872. 1910. Press of Walker, Evans & Cocswell ! Co.

Around Two Worlds: A Narrative of a World Cruise. Estelle Aubrey Brown. LC 40-7852. B. Humphries, Inc.

Arouse and Beware: A Novel. MacKinlay Kantor. LC 36-30938. Coward-McCann, Inc.

Arousers: A Novel. Merle Lynn Browne. LC 74-80702. 1974. 6.95 (ISBN 0-87795-064-4). Arbor House.

Arran: A Western Novel. Wayne Wallace. LC 76-46260. (Illus.). 3.95 (ISBN 0-913182-79-6). Grossmont Press.

Arranged Marriage. Flora Kidd. (Presents Ser.). 192p. (Orig.). 1980. pap. text ed. 1.50 (ISBN 0-373-10370-0, Pub. by Harlequin). PB.

Arranged Marriage. De Longgarde Longard. LC 7-15154. 1895. D. Appleton and Company.

Arranged Marriage. Inge Trachtenberg. LC 74-19148. 1975. 6.95 (ISBN 0-393-08705-0). Norton.

Arrangement. Elia Kazan. (W116). pap., 1.25. Avon.

Arrangement: A Novel. Elia Kazan. LC 67-10325. 1967. Stein and Day.

Arrangement for Life. Sheila Tagliavia. LC 79-3418. 9.95 (ISBN 0-06-014214-6). Harper & Row.

Arrangements. Harry Guest. 1968. 4.00 (Pub. by Anvil Pr); signed ed. 50 copies 12.50 ea.; pap. 2.50. SBD.

Arranmoor: A Novel. Loas Lucina Porter. LC 13-12597. 1.00. Roxburgh Publishing Co.

Arrant Rover. Berta Ruck. LC 21-17195. 1921. Dodd, Mead and Company.

Arranways Mystery... Edgar Wallace. LC 32-10114. Pub. for the Crime Club, Inc., by Doubleday, Doran & Company, Inc.

Arrest Sitting Bull. Douglas C Jones. LC 77-7645. 1977. 8.95 (ISBN 0-684-15183-9). Scribner.

Arrest Sitting Bull. Douglas C Jones. LC 77-19073. 1978. 12.95 (ISBN 0-8161-6555-6). G. K. Hall.

Arrest Sitting Bull. Douglas C Jones. 1978. (ISBN 0-446-81474-1). Warner Books Inc.

Arrested: A Novel. Amelie Claire Leroy. LC 3-22364. (Appleton's Town & Country Library). (Half-title: Appleton's town and country library, no. 209: No. 209). 1897. D. Appleton and Company.

Arrested Moment & Other Stories. Charles Caldwell Dobie. LC 27-22839. 1927. The John Day Company.

Arresting Delia. Sydney Fowler Wright. LC 33-16731. The Macaulay Company.

Arrival. Robert Nichols. LC 77-1362. (His Daily lives in Nghsi-Altai; book 1). 1977. 1.95 (ISBN 0-8112-0653-X). New Directions Pub. Corp.

Arrival and Departure. Arthur Koestler. LC 43-16520. 1943. The Macmillan Company.

Arrival and Departure. New Postscript by the Author. Danube Ed. Arthur Koestler. LC 67-15781. 1967. 5.95. Macmillan.

Arrival and Departure. Postscript by the Author. Danube Ed. Arthur Koestler. (NY4093). 1968. Bantam.

Arrival at Easterwine: The Autobiography of a Ktistec Machine. R. A Lafferty. 1973. 1.25 (ISBN 0-345-03164-4). Ballantine.

Arrival in Wycherly. Norman George Denny. LC 51-13049. 1951. Dodd, Mead.

Arrival: 12: 30: The Baltimore Plot Against Lincoln. Alan Hynd. LC 67-24667. (Illus.). 1967. Nelson.

Arrivals & Departures. Margaret A Robinson. LC 81-9032. 10.95 (ISBN 0-684-17161-9). Scribner.

Arrive at Easterwine: The Autobiography of a Ktistec Machine. R. A Lafferty. LC 74-143937. 1971. 4.95 (ISBN 0-684-12341-X). Scribner.

Arriving at the Nadir. Thomas Johnson. (Illus., Orig.). 1975. pap. 2.50 (ISBN 0-914278-06-1). Copper Beech.

Arriving Where We Started. Barbara Probst Solomon. LC 72-156552. 1972. 6.95 (ISBN 0-06-013944-7). Harper & Row.

Arrogance. Constance Leonie Caroline Borgstrom Aminoff. (Her Torchlight series of Napolonic romances. viii). E. P. Dutton & Company.

Arrogance: The Conquests of Xerxes. Louis Marie Anne Couperus. Tr. by Mariens, Frederick Herman. LC 30-7192. 1930. Farrar & Rhinehart, Inc.

Arrogant Alibi. Charles Daly King. LC 39-2605. 1939. D. Appleton-Century Company, Incorporated.

Arrogant Aristocrat. (Candlelight Regency Ser.: No. 695). (Orig.). 1982. pap. 1.75 (ISBN 0-440-10292-8). Dell.

Arrogant Beggar. Anzia Yezierska. LC 27-24899. 1927. Doubleday, Page & Co.

Arrogant Guns. Lewis B Patten. LC 65-13995. 3.50. Doubleday.

Arrogant History of White Ben. LC 30-30693. 1939. Doubleday, Doran & Company, Inc.

Arrow. Christopher Darlington Morley. LC 27-906526. 1927. Doubleday, Page & Company.

Arrow by Day. Cloyd Criswell. 1962. 3.00 (ISBN 0-8338-0020-5). M Jones.

Arrow in the Dust. Leonard London Foreman. LC 53-13262. (Dell first edition,11). 1954. Dell Pub. Co.

Arrow in the Heart. Denise Robins. 1973. pap. 0.75 o.p. (94333). Beagle Bks.

Arrow in the Hill: By Jefferson Cooper Pseud. Gardner F Fox. LC 55-620282. 1955. Dodd, Mead.

Arrow in the Moon: By Margaret and John Harris. Margaret Plumlee Harris & John Harris. LC 54-7102. 1954. Morrow.

Arrow in the Sun. Theodore V Olsen. LC 69-20087. 1969. 4.50. Doubleday.

Arrow in the Sun. Theodore V Olsen. (Western)). 1980. 1.95 (ISBN 0-671-83541-6). Pocket Books.

Arrow in the Sun. Theodore V. Olsen. 1980. pap. 1.95 (ISBN 0-671-83541-6). PB.

Arrow Lie Still: A Novel. Frank Cheavens. LC 51-1779. 1950. Story Book Press.

Arrow of Apollyon. Llew Devine. LC 74-155550. 1971. (ISBN 0-7700-0346-X). Ryerson Press.

Arrow of God. Chinua Achebe. LC 67-28702. 1967. John Day Co.

Arrow of Gold. Joseph Conrad. 1968. pap. 1.95 (ISBN 0-393-00458-9, Norton Lib). Norton.

Arrow of Gold: A Story Between Two Notes. Joseph Conrad. LC 19-632463. 1919. Doubleday, Page & Company.

Arrow of Gold: A Story Between Two Notes. Joseph Conrad. LC 22-106435. 1920. Doubleday, Page & Company.

Arrow of Love. Barbara Cartland. (Bantam Barbara Cartland Library 31). 1976. (pbk.) 1.25. Bantam Books.

Arrow of Love. Frederick Feikema Manfred. LC 61-109181. 1961. A Swallow.

Arrow of Terror. Jeanne Marie. 1973. (pbk.) 4.95 (ISBN 0-517-51419-2). Lenox Hill Press.

Arrow Pointing Nowhere. Elizabeth Daly. LC 43-178354. Farrar & Rinehart, Inc.

Arrow Points to Murder... Frederica De Laguna. LC 37-16072. Pub. for the Crime Club, Inc., by Doubleday, Doran & Company, Inc.

Arrowhead Rider. Lauran Paine. LC 56-8978. 1956. Arcadia House.

Arrowhead Territory. Jon Sharpe. (Trailsman Ser.: No. 14). 176p. 1983. pap. 2.50 (ISBN 0-451-12080-9, Sig). NAL.

Arrowmaker: A Story of Perry County, Pa. Roy F Chandler. LC 74-82451. (Illus.). 1975. Bacon and Freeman Publishers.

Arrows into the Sun. Jonreed Lauritzen. LC 42-50768. 1943. A. A. Knopf.

Arrows of Ambition: A Romance of the Thirty Years' War. Albert Frederick Hochwalt. LC 7-11591. 1907. Mayhew Publishing Company.

Arrows of Desire. Judith Clark. LC 30-7193. 1930. Minton, Balch & Company.

Arrows of Hercules. Lyon Sprague De Camp. LC 65-10595. 4.95. Doubleday.

Arrows of Hercules. Lyon Sprague De Camp. LC 65-10595. 1965. Doubleday.

Arrows of Love. Laura Daintrey. 1893. G. W. Dillingham.

Arrows of the Almighty. Owen McMahon Johnson. LC 1-31632. 1901. The Macmillan Company.

Arrowsmith. Sinclair Lewis. LC 66-1395. (Signet classic). New American Library.

Arrowsmith. Sinclair Lewis. LC 74-184472. (Harbrace modern classics). 1952. Harcourt, Brace & World.

Arrowsmith. Sinclair Lewis. LC 25-607849. Harcourt, Brace and Company.

Arrowsmith. Sinclair Lewis. LC 32-19537. 1932. Grosset & Dunlap.

Arrowsmith. Sinclair Lewis. LC 33-27092. (Half-title: The modern library of the world's best books). 1933. The Modern Library.

Arrowsmith. text ed. edited by barbara grace spayd. ed. Sinclair Lewis & Spayd, Barbara Grace, Ed. LC 45-5016. 1945. Harcourt, Brace and Company.

Arrowsmith. Text Edition. Sinclair Lewis & Spayd, Barbara Grace, Ed. LC 33-37019. 1933. Harcourt, Brace and Company.

Arroyo West. Kingsley West. 1976. (pbk.) 0.95 (ISBN 0-425-03041-5). Berkley Publishing Corp.

Arroz y Tartana see Tres Novelas Valencianas.

Arsareth; a Tale of the Luray Caverns. B. C Warren. LC 8-33690. A. Lovell & Co.

Arsenal for Skeptics. Richard W. Hinton, pseud. 1961. pap. 1.65 o.p. (ISBN 0-498-04019-4, Prpta). A S Barnes.

Arsene Lupin. Edgar Jepson & Leblanc, Maurice. LC 9-28119. 1909. Doubleday, Page & Company.

Arsene Lupin Intervenes. Maurice Leblanc. LC 29-3977. The Macaulay Company.

Arsene Lupin, Super-Sleuth. Maurice Leblanc. LC 27-13975. The Macaulay Company.

Arsene Lupin Versus Herlock Sholmes. Maurice Leblanc. Tr. by Morehead, George. LC 10-2659. (His The extraordinary adventures of Arsene Lupin v. 2). 0.25. M. A. Donohue & Co.

Arsene Lupin Versus Herlock Sholmes. Maurice Leblanc. Tr. by D'Apery, Helen (Burrell) LC 10-13390. (On back of cover: Railroad series, no. 59). 0.25. J. S. Ogilvie Publishing Company.

Arsenic and Gold, a Mystery-Adventure. Bertram Atkey. LC 39-258853. The Penn Publishing Company.

Arsenic for the Teacher. James H Mantinband. LC 51-9297. 1950. Phoenix Press.

Arslan. M. J Engh. 1976. (pbk.) 1.25. Warner Books.

Arson & Old Lace. Sylvia Amgus. 176p. 1974. pap. 1.25 (ISBN 0-532-12238-0). Woodhill.

Arson and Old Lace. Sylvia Angus. LC 72-84241. (Falcon's head mystery). 1972. 5.95 (ISBN 0-529-04828-0). World Publishing.

Arson and Old Lace. Sylvia Angus. 1974. (pbk.) 1.25. Manor Books.

Arson Job. Jack Moss. 1979. pap. 1.95 (ISBN 0-532-19228-1). Woodhill.

Art & Craft: A Novel. Olivier Bernier. LC 81-50314. 1981. 13.50 (ISBN 0-87223-719-2). Seaview Books.

Art Colony. Leland Cooley. 1975. (pbk.) 1.95 (ISBN 0-380-00464-X). Avon.

Art Colony. Clifton Cuthbert. LC 33-29639. 1933. W. Godwin, Inc.

Art Failure: A Story of the Latin Quarter As It Is. John William Harding. LC 7-1924. 1896. F. T. Neely.

Art of Disappearing. John Talbot Smith. 1902. W. H. Young and Company.

Art of Fiction. 3d ed. Ed. by Richard F. Dietrich. LC 77-13417. 6.95 (ISBN 0-03-039221-7). Holt, Rinehart and Winston.

Art of Fiction: A Handbook and Anthology. 2d ed. Ed. by Richard F. Dietrich. LC 73-10097. 1974. 6.25. Holt, Rinehart and Winston.

Art of Fiction: A Handbook and Anthology. Ed. by Richard F. Dietrich. LC 67-11742. 1967. Holt, Rinehart and Winston.

Art of Fiction: An Anthology. Richard F. Dietrich & R. H. Sundell. (gr. 11 up). 1967. pap. text ed. 5.75 o.p. (ISBN 0-03-062765-6, HoltC). HR&W.

Art of Huckleberry Finn: Text, Sources, Criticism. 2d ed. Samuel Langhorne Clemens. Ed. by Hamlin Lewis Hill & Walter Blair. LC 69-11252. (Illus.). 1969. Chandler Pub. Co.; Distributors: Science Research Associates, Chicago.

Art of Living. Ed. by Reader's Digest Editors. (Orig.). 1980. pap. 2.50 (ISBN 0-425-04549-8). Berkley Pub.

Art of Living, and Other Stories. John Champlin Gardner. LC 80-20988. 1981. 12.95 (ISBN 0-394-51674-5). Knopf: Distributed by Random House.

Art of Llewellyn Jones. Paul Hyde Bonner. LC 59-9702. 1959. Scribner.

Art of Mariano Azuela: Modernism in La Malhora, El Desquite, La Luciernaga. Eliud Martinez. LC 79-29682. 5.95 (ISBN 0-935480-02-1). Latin American Literary Review Press.

Art of Prose Fiction: Ed. by Ralph H. Singleton. Ed. by Ralph H Singleton. LC 67-136301. 1967. 1.50. World.

Art of Short Fiction. Ed. by Barbara Pannwitt. LC 64-3468. 1964. Ginn.

Art of the Mystery Story. Howard Haycraft. LC 75-28263. 1975. Repr. of 1946 ed. 16.00x (ISBN 0-8196-0289-2). Biblo.

Art of the Novella: Eight Short Novels. Ed. by Arnold B. Sklare. LC 65-11876. 1965. Macmillan.

Art of the Story: An Introduction by Robert Hollander, Sidney E. Lind. Robert Hollander & Sidney E Lind. 1968. pap., 5.20. Amer. Bk.

Art Studio Murders. Edward Sidney Aarons. 1975. pap. 1.25 (ISBN 0-532-12275-5). Woodhill.

Art Studio Murders. Edward Sidney Aarons. 1971. pap. 0.75 o.p. (75-429). Manor Bks.

Art Treasure Murders. John L Benton. LC 40-9136. 1940. Gateway Books.

Artapanos Comes Home. Mordecai Tsanin. LC 77-89647. 12.00 (ISBN 0-498-02165-3). A. S. Barnes.

Arte De Amar. new ed. Alvaro Sanchez. (Pimienta Collection Ser). (Illus.). 160p. (Span.). 1975. pap. 1.25 (ISBN 0-88473-238-X). Fiesta Pub.

Artemis, Fare Thee Well. Helena Carus. LC 35-1531. 1935. Little, Brown, and Company.

Artemis Sanction. Ashley Aasheim. 320p. (Orig.). 1981. pap. 2.95 (ISBN 0-440-10262-6). Dell.

Artemis Weds. Cicely Farmer. LC 32-17904. 1932. W. Merrow & Company.

Artery of Fire. Thomas N. Scortia. LC 72-79422. 1972. 4.95 (ISBN 0-385-08659-8). Doubleday.

Artful Anticks. Oliver Herford. LC 12-34091. 1894. The Century Co.

Artful Cousin. Victoria Heland. (Regency Romance Ser.). 192p. (Orig.). 1982. pap. 2.50 (ISBN 0-515-05707-X). Jove Pubns.

Artful Widow: A Novel... Richard Burleigh Kimball. LC 11-15059. 1881. G. W. Carleton & Co.; Etc., Etc.

Arthur. John Alexander Graham. LC 69-16088. 1969. 4.95. Harper & Row.

Arthur. A Novel. Eugene Sue & Christin, P. F., Tr. LC 8-17683. 1844. Harper & Brothers.

Arthur. A Novel. Eugene Sue & Christin, P. F., Tr. (Seaside library, v. 41, no. 835). 1880. G. Munro.

Arthur, Bear of Britain. Edward Frankland. (Arthuriana Ser.). (O.s.i.). 1977. Repr. of 1944 ed. 7.95 o.s.i. (ISBN 0-916988-09-0). Pendragon Hse.

Arthur Blane: Or, The Hundred Cuirassiers. James Grant. LC 42-26882. G. Routledge and Sons.

Arthur C. Clarke Trilogy, 3 bks. Arthur C. Clarke. (Reader's Request Ser.). 1980. Set. lib. bdg. 45.00 (ISBN 0-8161-3139-2, Large Print Bks). G K Hall.

Arthur De Gobineau and the Short Story. Rebecca M Valette. LC 77-628709. (North Carolina. University. Studies in the Romance Language and Literatures: No. 79). 1969. University of North Carolina Press.

Arthur Gordon Pym, Benito Cereno, and Related Writings. Ed. by John Seelye. Edgar Allan -. Narrative Of Arthur Gordon Pym Poe & Herman Melville. LC 67-15514. (Lippincott College English Ser.: P. 305-308). 1967. pap., 1.95. Lippincott.

Arthur Lee: A Tale of Clerical Life. Thomas Patrick Phelan. LC 35-248875. P. J. Kenedy & Son.

Arthur McCann and All His Women. Leslie Thomas. LC 73-14323. 1974. 6.95. Harper & Row.

Arthur McCann and All His Women. Leslie Thomas. 1975. (pbk.) 1.50. New American Library.

Arthur Merton: A Romance. David Dixon Porter. LC 7-37780. 1889. D. Appleton and Company.

Arthur Mervyn: Or, Memoirs of the Year 1793. Charles Brockden Brown. LC 63-24275. 1963. Kennikat Press.

Arthur Mervyn: Or, Memoirs of the Year 1793... Charles Brockden Brown. 1799. H. Maxwell.

Arthur Mervyn: Or, Memoirs of the Year 1793. Charles Brockden Brown. LC 41-34778. 1827. S. G. Goodrich.

Arthur Mervyn: Or, Memoirs of the Year 1793. Charles Brockden Brown. LC 6-19642. 1857. M. Polock.

Arthur Mervyn: Or, Memoirs of the Year 1793. Charles Brockden Brown. 1857. M. Polock.

Arthur Mervyn: Or, Memoirs of the Year 1793. Charles Brockden Brown. LC 17-13040. (Half-title: Charles Brockden Brown's novels, vols. ii, iii). 1887. D. McKay.

Arthur Mervyn, or Memoirs of the Year Seventeen Ninety-Three. Charles Brockden Brown. Ed. by Sydney J. Krause & S. W. Reid. LC 79-92808. (Novels & Related Works of Charles Brockden Brown Ser.: Vol. 3). 590p. 1980. 27.50x (ISBN 0-87338-241-2). Kent St U Pr.

Arthur Mervyn: Or, Memoirs of the Year 1793. Edited with an Introd. by Warner Berthoff. Charles Brockden Brown. (Rinehart editions, 112). 1962. Holt, Rinehart and Winston.

Arthur Norris: Or, A Modern Knight. Elizabeth Steward Phelps. LC 15-104895. 1915. 1.00. The Young Churchman Co.

Arthur of Albion: An Introduction to the Arthurian Literature & Legends of England. R. W. Barber. 1971. Repr. of 1961 ed. 8.75x o.p. (ISBN 0-06-490299-4). B&N.

Arthur O'Leary: His Wanderings and Ponderings in Many Lands. Charles James Lever & Cruikshank, George, 1792-1878, Illus. LC 24-11862. (On cover: Military novels). 1912. Little, Brown, and Company.

Arthur Pendragon of Britain: A Romantic Narrative by Sir Thomas Malory. Thomas Malory & Arthur, King (Romances, Etc.) LC 43-8223. 1943. G. P. Putnam's Sons.

Arthur Rex. Thomas Berger. 1979. pap. 5.95 (ISBN 0-440-50050-8, Delta). Dell.

Arthur Rex: A Legendary Novel. Thomas Berger. LC 78-7241. 10.95 (ISBN 0-440-00362-8). Delacorte Press/Seymour Lawrence.

Arthur St. Clair of Old Fort Recovery. S. A. D Whipple. LC 11-28363. Broadway Publishing Co.

Arthur Trent: Choosing a Career. Augustus William Trettien. LC 34-16167. The Stratford Company.

Arthur Woodleigh: A Romance of the Battle Field in Mexico. Robert F Greeley & Woodworth, Samuel. LC 6-45542. 1847. W. B. Smith & Co.

Arthurian Romances. Chretien De Troyes. Tr. by W. W. Comfort. 1976. 9.95x (ISBN 0-460-00698-3, Evman); pap. 2.50x (ISBN 0-460-01698-9, Evman). Biblio Dist.

Arthur's. 3d ed. Albert Michael Neil Lyons. LC 23-8961. 1915. John Lane.

Arthur's Faith. Anthony Kubek. Ed. by C. C. Clinkscales, III. LC 82-73312. 355p. (Orig.). 1982. 9.95 (ISBN 0-9605724-1-4); pap. 7.95 (ISBN 0-9605724-0-6). C & L Pub Co.

Artic Summer & Other Fiction. Edward Morgan Forster. (The Abinger Edition of E. M. Forster: Vol. 9). 342p. 1981. 44.75x (ISBN 0-8419-0670-X). Holmes & Meier.

Article Thirty-Two: A Novel. John Rathbone Oliver. LC 31-31119. 1931. The Macmillan Company.

Article 47. Adolphe Belot. (Seaside library, v. 55, no. 1111). G. Munro.

Article 47. A Romance. From the French of Adolphe Belot. Adolphe Belot. Tr. by Furbish, James. LC 11-7144. 1873. J. B. Lippincott & Co.

Articles of Faith. Ronald Harwood. LC 73-12857. 1974. 8.95 (ISBN 0-03-007706-0). Holt, Rinehart and Winston.

Artie. A Story of the Streets and Town. George Ade. LC 5-42618. 1896. H.S. Stone & Co.

Artie: A Story of the Streets and Town. George Ade & McCutcheon, John Tinney, 1870- Illus. LC 45-28257. 1899. H. S. Stone & Co.

Artie, and Pink Marsh: Two Novels. Drawings by John T. McCutcheon. Introd. by James T. Farrell. George Ade. LC 63-22584. (Chicago in fiction). 1963. University of Chicago Press.

Artifact. 1980. pap. write for info. (ISBN 0-88074-016-7). Metagam.

Artificial Fate. Clarence Miles Boutelle. LC 6-14919. (On cover: American series, no. 262)). 1891. M. J. Ivers & Co.

Artificial Kid. Bruce Sterling. LC 79-2661. (Harper Science Fiction Ser.). 224p. 1980. 10.95i (ISBN 0-06-014098-4, HarpT). Harper & Row.

Artificial Man. Leslie Purnell Davies. LC 67-10354. 1967. Published for the Crime Club by Doubleday.

Artificial Traveler. Warren Fine. LC 67-231423. 1968. 4.95. Coward.

Artillery & Ammunition of the Civil War. Warren Ripley. (Illus.). 1969. 22.50 o.p. Van Nos Reinhold.

Artillery of Time. Chard Powers Smith. LC 39-28950. 1939. C. Scribner's Sons.

Artist. Jan De Hartog. LC 63-7801. (I1). (YA) 1963. 5.00 o.p. (ISBN 0-689-00012-X). Atheneum.

Artist. Norman Garbo. LC 77-15027. 9.95. Norton.

Artist. Jan De Hartog. LC 63-7801. (Illus.). 1963. Atheneum.

Artist and Model (The Divorced Princess.) Leon Rene Delmas. (On cover: Globe library, no. 102). 1889. Rand, McNally & Company.

Artist Grows up in Mexico. With Illus. by Diego Rivera. Leah Brenner. LC 53-8029. 1953. Beechhurst Press.

Artist in Crime. Rodrigues Ottolengui. LC 7-30942. 1892. G. P. Putnam's Sons.

Artist in Love. Philip Lindsay. LC 54-10476. Roy Publishers.

Artist in the Family. Sarah Gertrude Liebson Millin. LC 28-7033. 1928. Boni and Liveright.

Artist Passes. Arndt Giusti. LC 29-154791. 1929. Dodd, Mead & Company.

Artist Sisters. A Story of Intrigue at the Nation's Capital. William H Mellen. (On cover: New York 10c library. no. 10). 1896. Katahdin Publishing Company.

Artist. Tr. from the French of Madame Jeanne Mairet Pseud. Marie Healy Bigot. Tr. by Page, Anna Dyer. LC 6-12740. Cassell Publishing Company.

Artist Type. Brian Glanville. LC 68-11871. 1968. Coward-McCann.

Artist-Wife: And Other Tales. Mary Botham Howitt. LC 17-7990. Stringer & Townsend.

Artiste. Maria M Grant. LC 6-44850. (Seaside library, v. 16, no. 312). G. Munro.

Artistic Temperament a Novel. Oliver Madox Hueffer. LC 7-21364. 1907. McClure, Phillips & Co.

Artist's Bride: Or, The Pawnbroker's Heir. Emerson Bennett. Garrett, Dick & Fitzgerald.

Artist's Daughter. Leslie O'Grady. LC 78-4000. 8.95 (ISBN 0-312-05507-2). St. Martin's Press.

Artist's Dream. Ellerton Vincent. LC 42-29485. 1868. G. W. Carleton & Co.

Artist's Honor. Octave Feuillet. (On cover: Dearborn series, no. 40). 1890. Donohue, Hennedberry & Co.

Artist's Honor. Octave Feuillet & Robins, E. P., Tr. LC 6-39528. Cassell Publishing Company.

Artists in Crime. Ngaio Marsh. LC 38-14592. 1938. L. Furman, Inc.

Artists in Crime. Ngaio Marsh. LC 79-21281. 1979-1980. 13.95 (ISBN 0-88411-471-6). Aeonian Press.

Artists in Rome. Translated from the Italian by William Weaver. Ugo Moretti. LC 58-12694. 1958.

Artist's Love. Emma Dorothy Eliza Nevitte Southworth & Baden, Mrs. Frances (Henshaw) D. 1911. LC 12-38894. T. B. Peterson & Brothers.

Artist's Married Life: Being That of Albert Durer. Leopold Schefer & Stodart, Mrs. John Riddle, Tr. LC 8-2027. 1861. J. Munroe and Company.

Artist's Model. Alan Dubois. LC 34-4859. 1934. W. Godwin, Inc.

Artist's Model. Clement Wood. LC 34-4859. 1934. W. Godwin, Inc.

Artists, Patrons & Lovemaking. Evan Burke. pap. 1.95 o.p. (ISBN 0-87682-263-4). Barclay Hse.

Artists' Wives. Alphonse Daudet. Tr. by Ensor, Laura. LC 6-33058. 1890. G. Routledge and Sons.

Artorius. John Heath-Stubbs. (Pap ed. 5.00 o.p.). 1974. 7.50 o.p. (Pub. by Enitharmon Pr). SBD.

Artorius Rex. John Gloag. LC 76-30653. (Illus.). 1977. 7.95 (ISBN 0-312-05548-X). St. Martin's Press.

Arts and Beyond: Visions of Man's Aesthetic Future. LC 76-50782. (Illus.). 1977. 7.95 (ISBN 0-385-12682-4). Doubleday.

Arts & Beyond: Visions of Man's Aesthetic Future. Thomas F. Monteleone. LC 76-50782. (Illus.). 1977. 7.95 o.p. (ISBN 0-385-12682-4). Doubleday.

Arts of Cheating, Swindling & Murder. Douglas Jerrold et al. Ed. by Jesse Lee Bennett. LC 74-10425. (Classics of Crime & Criminology Ser). (Illus.). 153p. 1975. Repr. of 1925 ed. 10.50 (ISBN 0-88355-192-6). Hyperion Conn.

Arturo's Island. Translated from the Italian by Isabel Quigly. 1st American Ed. Elsa Morante. LC 59-6225. 1959. Knopf.

Arundel. Edward Frederic Benson. LC 15-28513. 1.25. George H. Doran Company.

Arundel. Kenneth Roberts. 1976. pap. 2.95 (ISBN 0-449-24456-3, Crest). Fawcett.

Arundel: A Chronicle of the Province of Maine and of the Secret Expedition Led by Benedict Arnold Against Quebec. Kenneth Lewis Roberts. LC 33-19961. 1933. Doubleday, Doran & Company, Inc.

Arundel: A Chronicle of the Province of Maine and of the Secret Expedition Against Quebec. Kenneth Lewis Roberts. LC 38-7477. 1938. Doubleday, Doran & Company, Inc.

Arundel: Being the Recollections of Steven Nason of Arundel, in the Province of Maine, Attached to the Secret Expedition Led by Colonel Benedict Arnold Against Quebec and Later a Captain in the Continental Army Serving at Valcour Island Bemis Heights, and Yorktown. Kenneth Lewis Roberts. LC 30-3872. 1930. Doubleday, Doran & Company, Inc.

Arundel Motto. Mary Cecil Hay. (Seaside library, vo. 21, no. 407). 1878. G. Munro.

Arundel Motto. A Novel. Mary Cecil Hay. LC 7-3762. (On cover: Library of select novels, no. 472). 1877. Harper & Brothers.

Aryan Onslaught. Lionel Derrick, pseud. (Penetrator: No. 29). (Orig.). 1979. pap. 1.50 (ISBN 0-523-40269-4). Pinnacle Bks.

As a Cadger's Tale: Summer's Idyll of Scotland. Philip Harrower. Ed. by Millard, Bruce. LC 39-17475. Wetzel Publishing Co., Inc.

As a Driven Leaf. Milton Steinberg. LC 40-2698. The Bobbs-Merrill Company.

As a Jew Lives: A Novel. Abraham Simon Freedland. LC 36-7622. Alliance Press.
As-a-Land. Edie Boyer. 68p. 1982. pap. 6.95 (ISBN 0-932298-19-2). Copple Hse.
As a Man Falls. Howard Rigsby. LC 54-219110. (Gold medal books, 375). 1954. Fawcett Publications.
As a Man Grows Older. Ettore Schmitz. LC 77-10842. (Series: The Modern Readers' Series.). 1977. 18.50 (ISBN 0-8371-9819-4). Greenwood Press.
As a Man Grows Older. Ettore Schmitz. LC 49-11089. (Modern Readers Series). New Directions.
As a Man Lives: Or, The Mystery of the Yellow House. Edward Phillips Oppenheim. 1908. Little, Brown, and Company.
As a Man Sows, and Other Stories. Grace Denio Litchfield. LC 77-160940. (Short story index reprint series). 1971. (ISBN 0-8369-3919-0). Books for Libraries Press.
As a Man Sows: And Other Stories. Grace Denio Litchfield. LC 26-11634. 1926. G. P. Putnam's Sons.
As a Medicine. Founded on Fact. Lucius Manlius Sargent. (Temperance Tales). (On cover: Temperance tales, v. 6, no.13: Vol. 6, No. 13). 1839. Whipple & Damrell.
As a Soldier Would: An Army Novel. Abner Pickering. LC 11-26807. 1.50. Broadway Publishing Co.
As a Speckled Bird. Annabel Johnson. LC 57-569119. 1956. Crowell.
As a Thief in the Night. Richard Austin Freeman. LC 28-22667. 1928. Dodd, Mead & Company.
As a White Candle. 1st Ed. Margaret Mary Preston. LC 52-14519. 1952.
As a Woman Doeth. Flora J Robinson. LC 40-629. Carlyle House.
As a Woman Thinks. Corra May White Harris. LC 25-20051. 1925. Houghton Mifflin Company.
As Any Mountain of Its Snows. Joseph Davey. (American Fiction Ser.: Vol. 2). 96p. (Orig.). 1980. pap. 3.95 (ISBN 0-934040-15-X). Quality Ohio.
As Avon Flows. Henry Scott Vince. (On cover: The seaside library. Pocket ed. no. 347). 1885. G. Munro.
As Bad As I Am. William Ard. LC 59-5795. 1959. Rinehart.
As Battles Raged. Elizabeth Aspril. (Illus., Orig.). 1981. 12.95 (ISBN 0-9604750-1-X); pap. 7.95 (ISBN 0-9604750-0-1). E Keys.
As by Fire. Bertha B. Moore McCurry. LC 39-30064. 1939. William B. Eerdmans Publishing Co.
As by Fire. Bertha B Moore. LC 39-30064. 1939. William B. Eerdmans Publishing Co.
As Caesar's Wife: A Novel. Margarita Spalding Gerry. LC 12-21916. 1912. 1.30. Harper & Brothers.
As Common Mortals. A Novel. Anne Sheldon Coombs. LC 6-30193. 1886. Cassell & Co.
As Common Mortals: A Novel... Anne Sheldon Coombs. (On cover: Cassell's sunshine series. no. 6). 1888. Cassell & Company.
As Darker Grows the Night. Elizabeth Giles. (Orig.). 1972. pap. 0.95 o.s.i. (75-378). Lancer.
As Deep in the Mud. Maide O'Heeron Moyer. LC 41-817312. The Christopher Publishing House.
As Eagles Fly. Barbara Cartland. 1975. (pbk.) 1.25. Bantam Books.
As Empty As Hate. John Creasey. LC 77-185118. (Falcon's head mystery). 1972. 5.95 (ISBN 0-529-04486-2). World Pub.
As Empty As Hate. Kyle Hunt. 1972. 5.95 o.p. (ISBN 0-529-04486-2, A4312). World Pub.
As Far As Jane's Grandmother's. Edith Olivier. LC 29-26570. 1929. The Viking Press.
As Fate Would Have It. Evelyn Gray. (On cover: Munro's library, popular novels, v. 1, no. 105). N. L. Munro.
As for Me & My House. Louis A. Priolo. (Orig.). 1976. pap. 1.75 o.p. (ISBN 0-88368-077-7). Whitaker Hse.
As for Me and My House. Sinclair Ross. LC 78-16097. 10.95 (ISBN 0-8032-3850-9) (ISBN 0-8032-8900-6). University of Nebraska Press.
As for Me and My House: A Novel. Sinclair Ross. LC 41-3337. Reynal & Hitchcock.
As for the Woman. Anthony Berkeley Cox. LC 40-1222. 1939. Doubleday, Doran & Company, Inc.
As for the Woman. Francis Iles. LC 40-1222. 1939. Doubleday, Doran & Company, Inc.
As Gold in the Furnace" A College Story (Sequel to "Shadows Lifted". John Edwin Copus. LC 10-263793. 1910. Benziger Brothers.
As Good As a Comedy: Or, The Tennesseean's Story. William Gilmore Simms. LC 8-14237. 1852. A. Hart.
As Good As Dead. Thomas Blanchard Dewey. 1946. Jefferson House.
As Good As Gold. Edward Wymark. LC 67-29485. 1967. Coward-McCann.
As Good As Married. Peggy Gaddis, pseud. LC 45-3710. 1945. Phoenix Press.
As Good As Murdered. James D O'Hanlon. LC 40-6342. Random House.
As Having Nothing. Hester Caldwell Oakley. LC 7-33191. 1898. G. P. Putnam's Sons.
As High As the Sky. Norah Cordner James. LC 38-383301. The Macaulay Company.
As His Mother Saw Him. Charlotte Elvira Gray. LC 17-28850. 1.00. The Meridian Press.
As I Lay Dying. new ed. William Faulkner. LC 64-12609. 1964. Random House.
As I Lay Dying. William Faulkner. LC 67-1801. (Modern library of world's best books, 378). 1967. Modern Library.
As I Lay Dying. William Faulkner. LC 72-8023. 1973. (ISBN 0-394-70254-9). Vintage Books.
As I Lay Dying. William Faulkner. LC 30-276828. J. Cape, H. Smith.
As I Magic. Martin J. Rosenblum. LC 76-14330. (Orig.). 1976. pap. text ed. 7.00 (ISBN 0-89018-002-4); signed edn. 10.00 (ISBN 0-89018-003-2). Lionhead Pub.
As I Saw It. John Jackson McIntire. LC 72-8553. (Black Heritage Library Collection). 1972. (ISBN 0-8369-9189-3). Books for Libraries Press.
As I Saw It. John Jackson McIntire. LC 2-12484. 1902. Home Publishing Company.
As I Walked Out One Midsummer Morning. Laurie Lee. 1979. pap. 2.95 (ISBN 0-14-003318-1). Penguin.
As I Was Young and Easy. Drawings by Gloria Waerfield. 1st Ed. Clancy Carlile. LC 58-10961. 1958. Knopf.
As If. Kenneth Edgar. LC 73-7962. 1973. 7.95 (ISBN 0-13-049403-8). Prentice-Hall.
As If by Magic. Wilson, Angus. LC 72-9702. 1973. 8.95 (ISBN 0-670-13725-1). Viking Press.
As If It Will Matter. Jody Aliesan. LC 78-63399. 60p. (Orig.). 1978. 15.00 (ISBN 0-931188-04-0); pap. 4.00 (ISBN 0-931188-03-2). Seal Pr WA.
As in a Looking Glass. Francis Charles Philips. (On cover: Lovell's library, no. 1083). 1887. J. W. Lovell Company.
As in a Looking-Glass. Francis Charles Philips. (On cover: Seaside library. Pocket ed. no. 1018). 1887. G. Munro.
As It Fell Upon a Day.". Margaret Wolfe Hungerford & Walter Besant. (Seaside Library, Pocket Ed.). (On cover: The seaside library. Pocket ed., no. 541: No. 541). 1885. G. Gunro.
As It Happened. A. L Samms. LC 24-165692. 1924. Covici-McGee Co.
As It Happened: Being a Story in Three Books and Several Manners. Josephine Winfield Brake. LC 99-5590. 1899. The Neale Company.
As It Is... William Russell Smith. LC 8-9637. 1860. Munsell & Rowland.
As It May Be: A Story of the Future. Bessie Story Rogers. LC 6-7454. 1905. R. G. Badger.
As It May Happen. A Story of American Life and Character. Robert S. Davis. Porter & Coates.
As It Was! T. Lobsang Rampa, pseud. (Orig.). 1976. pap. 2.95 (ISBN 0-552-10087-0). Weiser.
As It Was in the Beginning. Philip Verrill Mighels. LC 12-12488. D. FitzGerald, Inc.
As It Was in the Beginning. Arthur Cheney Train. LC 21-2968. 1921. The Macmillan Company.
As It Was Written: A Jewish Musician's Story. Henry Harland. LC 7-1912. Cassell & Co.
As It Was Written: A Jewish Musician's Story. Henry Harland. (On cover: Cassell's rainbow series. v. no. 3). 1887. Cassell & Company, Limited.
As Lonely As the Damned. John Creasey. LC 73-185117. (Falcon's head mystery). 1972. 5.95 (ISBN 0-529-04485-4). World Pub.
As Lonely As the Damned. Kyle Hunt. 192p. 1972. 5.95 o.p. (ISBN 0-529-04485-4, A4311). World Pub.
As Long As I Live. Emilie Baker Loring. LC 37-359338. The Penn Publishing Company.
As Long As I Live. Ione Sandberg Shriber. LC 47-23977. 1947. Rinehart.
As Long As Love Shall Last. Violet Wolfinger Riebold. LC 53-2633. 1953. Vantage Press.
As Long As She Lived: A Novel. Frederick William Robinson. (seaside library, v. 70, no. 1420). 1882. G. Munro.
As Long As the Rivers Run. Sam J Slate. LC 72-76206. 1972. 6.95 (ISBN 0-385-08715-2). Doubleday.
As Long As Tomorrow. Bidwell Moore. LC 70-148959. 1971. 6.95. R. B. Luce.
As Love Knows How: By David and Alice Cheavens. David Cheavens & Alice Dawson Cheavens. LC 52-14261. 1952. Broadman Press.
As Merry As Hell. John Creasey. LC 73-90702. 1974. 6.95 (ISBN 0-8128-1662-5). Stein and Day.
As Merry As Hell. Kyle Hunt. 1974. 6.95 o.p. (ISBN 0-8128-1662-5). Stein & Day.
As Much As Twice. Dane Yorke. LC 35-3429. Minton, Balch & Company.
As Music and Splendour. Kate O'Brien. LC 57-821619. 1958. Harper.
As Night Follows Day. Suzanne Simmons. (Candlelight Ecstasy Ser.: No. 98). (Orig.). 1982. pap. 1.95 (ISBN 0-440-10220-0). Dell.
As No Woman Hath Loved. Laura Lou Brookman. LC 29-3972. Grosset & Dunlap.
As of a Trumphet. Aumra. 1968. 4.95. Cole-Outreach.
As of the Gods. Rollo Walter Brown. LC 37-1711. 1937. D. Appleton-Century Company, Incorporated.
As Old As Cain: A Novel of Suspense, by M. E. Chaber Pseud. 1st Ed. Kendell Foster Crossen. LC 54-105196. 1954. Holt.
As on a Darkling Plain. Benjamin Bova. LC 72-83756. 1972. 5.95 (ISBN 0-8027-5556-9). Walker.
As Once You Were. Arthur Stuart-Menteth Hutchinson. LC 38-27997. 1938. Little, Brown and Company.
As One. David Jaffin. 1975. 16.00 (Pub. by Elizabeth Pr); pap. 8.00. SBD.
As Other Men. Neill Phillipson. 199p. 1976. 3.95 (ISBN 0-85885-154-7). David & Charles.
As Other Men: A Novel. Neill Phillipson. LC 75-316387. 1974. 5.25 (ISBN 0-85885-154-7). Wren.
As Over the Highway I Came. Launah H. Myers. LC 79-129647. 1970. 3.95 o.p. (ISBN 0-8111-3692-2). Naylor.
As Queer As She Could Be: A Story. Jessie E Wright. LC 8-37212. 1895. Presbyterian Board of Publication and Sabbath-School Work.
As Runs the Glass. Evan John David. LC 43-159691. 1943. Harper & Brothers.
As Some Men Are. Marie Flaacke. LC 6-41124. 1890. The American News Company.
As Sounding Brass. Alan T Nolan. LC 64-17201. 1964. Houghton Mifflin.
As Strong As the Hills. Matalee T Lake. LC 21-10021. 1921. Terminal Press, Inc.
As Summers Die. Winston Groom. LC 80-17451. 12.95 (ISBN 0-671-40072-X). Summit Books.
As Tall As Pride. Sophie Kerr. LC 49-48131. 1949. Rinehart.
As the Clock Struck Twenty: By S. M. C. LC 53-5947. 1953. Ave Maria Press.
As the Curtain Falls. Robert Chilson. (Science Fiction Ser.). 1974. pap. 0.95 o.p. (UQ1105). DAW Bks.
As the Curtain Falls. Robert Chilson. 1974. (pbk.) 0.95. DAW Books.
As the Earth Turns. Gladys Hasty Carroll. LC 33-27115. 1933. The Macmillan Company.
As the Earth Turns. Gladys Hasty Carroll. LC 35-27142. (Half-Title: The Modern Reader's Series). 1935. The Macmillan Company.
As the Earth Turns. Gladys Hasty Carroll. LC 78-111471. 1978. 10.95 (ISBN 0-393-08830-8). Norton.
As the Earth Turns. Gladys Hasty Carroll. LC 80-11203. 1980. 10.95 (ISBN 0-89340-231-1). J. Curley.
As the Fates Decree. Venus G Booth. LC 16-15505. Fifth Ave. Publishing Co. Inc.
As the Gentle Rain... Isabel Constance Clarke. LC 31-33070. 1931. Longmans, Green and Co.
As the Gods Decree: A Novel of the Time of Augustus. Daniel Henry Morris. LC 10-31003. Broadway Publishing Co.
As the Green Star Rises. Lin Carter. 1975. (pbk.) 1.25. DAW Books.
As the Hart Panteth. Hallie Erminie Rives. LC 98-1763. 1898. G. W. Dillingham Co.
As the Kid Goes for Broke. G. B. Trudeau. 1979. pap. 1.75 (ISBN 0-553-14430-8). Bantam.
As the Light Led. James Newton Baskett. LC 3168. 1900. The Macmillan Company.
As the Morning Rising: A Novel. Sigrid Van Sweringen. LC 37-178. 1936. Benziger Brothers.
As the Pines Grow. Evelyn Voss Wise. LC 39-9395. 1939. D. Appleton-Century Company, Incorporated.
As the Seed Is Sown. Christine Whiting Parmenter. LC 40-32088. 1940. Thomas Y. Crowell Company.
As the Sparks Fly. A Novel. Margaret Eastvale. (Fawcett crest book). 1975. (pbk.) 1.25. Fawcett Publications.
As the Sparks Fly Upward. Cyrus Townsend Brady. LC 11-25433. 1911. 1.35. A. C. McClurg & Co.
As the Stars Forever. Joyce Berggren. LC 50-11714. 1950. Zondervan.
As the Twig Is Bent. Rachel Carter Goss. LC 51-30219. 1951. Dirigo Editions.
As the Twig Is Bent: A Story for Mothers and Teachers. Susan Chenery. LC 1-24578. 1901. Houghton, Mifflin and Company.
As the Twig Is Bent: And Other Stories. Emma C Street. (Catholic library, v. 17). 1898. C. Wilderman.
As the Wind Blows: A Novel. Eleanor Merron. LC 7-25878. Lovell, Coryell & Company.
As the Winds Blow. E Jay Shields. LC 50-8889. 1950. Exposition Press.
As the World Goes by. Elizabeth W Brooks. LC 5-11904. 1905. Little, Brown, and Company.
As They Did It: Or, The First Church of Warden a Story. Frederick Miron Coddington. LC 2-180. 1901. Jennings & Pye.
As They Reveled. Philip Wylie. LC 36-5638. Farrar & Rinehart, Incorporated.
As Thou Lovest: The Biography of a Benefaction. William Dudley Pelley. LC 55-56397. 1955. Soulcraft Chapels.
As Thyself!" A Novel. Sue W Hubard. LC 7-5664. 1881. J. B. Lippincott & Co.
As 'tis in Life: From the French. Albert Delpit. Tr. by Robins, E. P. LC 6-34176. 1890. Welch, Flacker Company.
As to Place. Peter Downsbrough. LC 78-65771. (Illus.). 1979. pap. 5.00 (ISBN 0-9602192-1-8). P Downsbrough.
As Told by the Typewriter Girl. Mabel Clare Ervin. LC 98-1500. E. R. Herrick and Company.
As Tough As They Come. William Charles Oursler. LC 51-3372. (Permabooks, 118). 1951. Permabooks.
As Towns with Fire. Anthony C. West. LC 78-79328. 1970. 7.95. Knopf.
As True As Sea Serpents. Richard Grover Conover. LC 29-3263. The Knickerbocker Press.
As We Are Now. May Sarton. 136p. 1973. 10.95 (ISBN 0-393-08372-1). Norton.
As We Are Now. May Sarton. 136p. 1982. pap. 3.95 (ISBN 0-393-30049-8). Norton.
As We Are Now: A Novel. May Sarton. LC 73-7555. 1973. 5.95 (ISBN 0-393-08372-1). Norton.
As We Are: Stories of Here and Now. Ed. by Walter Boughton Pitkin. LC 23-69503. Harcourt, Brace and Company.
As We Forgive. Frank Vandenberg. LC 46-225925. 1946. Wm. B. Eerdmans Publishing Company.
As We Forgive. 1st Ed. Frank S Pringle. LC 56-12195. 1957. Vantage Press.
As We See It. Robert Lewis Waring. LC 77-76122. 1969. McGrath Pub. Co.
As We See It. Robert Lewis Waring. LC 10-5053. 1910. Press of C. F. Sudwarth.
As We Went Marching on;" A Story of the War. George Washington Hosmer. LC 78-164567. (American fiction reprint series). 1971. (ISBN 0-8369-7044-6). Books for Libraries Press.
As We Went Marching on: A Story of the War. George Washington Hosmer. LC 6797. 1900. A. Wessels Company.
As We Went Marching on:" A Story of the War. George Washington Hosmer. LC 1-1206. 1885. Harper & Bros.
As Wide As the River. Dean Hughes. LC 80-14646. (Illus.). 1980. 6.95 (ISBN 0-87747-820-1). Deseret Book Co.
As Ye Have Sown. Dolf Wyllarde. LC 12-40177. 1907. John Lane Company.
As Ye Sow. A Romance of Cape Cod. by wm. a. brady and jos. r. grismer... ed. William A Brady & Snyder, John. LC 7-15549. (On cover: Play book series, no. 79). J. S. Ogilvie Publishing Company.
As Ye Sow: A Romance of Coosa Valley. Pattie Stone. LC 6-23161. 1906. The Neale Publishing Company.
As You Were, Bill!". Edward Streeter. LC 20-7517. Frederick A. Stokes Company.
Asa Holmes: Or, At the Cross-Roads. Annie Fellows Johnston. 1902. L. C. Page & Company.
Asa of Bethlehem and His Household. B. C. IV-A. D. Xxx. Mary Elizabeth Jennings. 1895. A. D. F. Randolph and Company.
Asahel: A Novel. Aharon Megged. LC 81-8822. 1982. 11.95 (ISBN 0-8008-0410-4). Taplinger Pub. Co.
Asaph: An Historical Novel. Alice Kingsbury Cooley. LC 6-28734. (American authors' series, no. 33). United States Book Company.
Asaph's Ten Thousand. Mary E. Bennett. LC 7-34097. Congregational Sunday-School and Publishing Society.
Asbein from the Life of a Virtuoso. Luis Kirschner. Tr. by Lathrop, Elise L. LC 21-21467. (On cover: Ross library. no. 2). 1890. Worthington Co.
Asbestos Diary. Casimir Dukahz. LC 65-28181. bds., 5.95. Oliver Layton Pr.
Asbestos Society of Sinners, Detailing the Diversions of Dives and Others on the Playground of Pluto: With Some Broken Threads of Drop-Stitch History, Picked up by a Newspaper Man in Hades and Woven into a Stygian Nights' Entertainment. Lawrence Daniel Fogg. LC 6-28456. Mayhew Publishing Company.
Ascanio. Alexandre Dumas & Meurice, Paul. (Half-title: The romances of Alexandre Dumas. Illustrated library ed. New series. vol. i-ii). 1895. Little, Brown, and Company.
Ascanio. ed. de medicis. ed. Alexandre Dumas & Paul Meurice. LC 4-18179. (On cover: Dumas' works). 1904. D. Estes & Company.

Ascendancies. David Guy Compton. LC 80-12386. 12.95 (ISBN 0-399-12484-5). Berkley Pub. Corp.: Distributed by Putnam.
Ascendancies. David Guy Compton. 12.95 o.p. (ISBN 0-399-12484-5). Putnam Pub Group.
Ascension. Charles L Grant. (Berkley Medallion Book.). 1977. 1.25 (ISBN 0-425-03412-7). Berkley Pub. Corp.
Ascent. Frances Rumsey. LC 22-16147. 1922. Boni and Liveright.
Ascent of D-Thirteen. Andrew Garve, pseud. (Joan Kahn Suspense Ser). 1969. 4.95 o.p. (ISBN 0-06-011449-5, HarpT). Har-Row.
Ascent of Mount Fuji. Chinquiz Aitmatov & K. Mukhamedzhanov. 1975. pap. 4.95 o.p. (ISBN 0-374-51215-9). FS&G.
Ascent of Rum Doodle. William Ernest Bowman. LC 57-7680. Vanguard Press.
Aschenbroedel. Kate Carrington. LC 6-242243. (No Name Series. 2d Series. V. 12). 1882. Roberts Brothers.
Ascutney Street: A Neighborhood Story. Adeline Dutton Train Whitney. LC 8-365499. 1890. Houghton, Mifflin and Company.
ASEAN Short Stories. Ed. by Robert Yeo. (Writing in Asia Ser.). xiv, 246p. (Orig.). pap. text ed. 7.50x (00257). Heinemann Ed.
Asenath of the Ford: A Romance of Red Earth Country. by "rita" pseud.... ed. Eliza M. J. Humphreys. (Broadway Ser.). (On cover: Broadway series, no. 15: No. 15). 1892. J. A. Taylor and Company.
Asendi: A West African Tale. George H. Strouse. LC 8-2610. The Chemical Publishing Co.
Aseptic Murders. Carter Brown, pseud. Bd. with Night Wheeler. 1979. pap. 2.50 (ISBN 0-451-11701-8, AE1701, Sig). NAL.
Aser, the Shepherd. Marion Ames Taggart. LC 8-255831. 1897. Benziger Brothers.
Asey Mayo Trio. Phoebe Atwood Taylor. 1970. Repr. 4.95 o.p. (ISBN 0-393-08596-1). Norton.
Asey Mayo Trio: Three Mystery Stories. Phoebe Atwood Taylor. LC 46-6177. 1946. J. Messner, Inc.
Ash. David Harry Walker. LC 76-4480. 1976. 8.95 (ISBN 0-395-24345-9). Houghton Mifflin.
Ash. David Harry Walker. LC 77-352519. 1976. 3.50 (ISBN 0-00-221042-8). Collins.
Ash Is the Candle's Wick. John Judson. 1979. pap. 4.50. Juniper Pr WI.
Ash on a Young Man's Sleeve. 2d ed. Dannie Abse. LC 69-14227. (Pergamon English Library). 1969. Pergamon Press.
Ash Road. Ivan Southall. LC 66-14636. (Illus.). 1966. St. Martin's Press.
Ashanti Doll. Francis Bebey. LC 76-58396. 1977. 6.50 (ISBN 0-88208-075-X). L. Hill.
Ashe of Rings. Mary Butts. LC 26-10199. 1926. A. & C. Boni.
Ashenden. Or; The British Agent. William Somerset Maugham. 1966. 4.95. Doubleday.
Ashenden: Or, The British Agent. William Somerset Maugham. LC 75-25348. (Maugham, William Somerset, 1874-1965. Works. 1976). 1977. 15.00 (ISBN 0-405-07805-6). Arno Press.
Ashenden: Or, The British Agent. William Somerset Maugham. LC 76-178451. (Short story index reprint series). 1971. (ISBN 0-8369-4052-0). Books for Libraries Press.
Ashenden: Or, The British Agent. William Somerset Maugham. LC 28-11055. 1928. Doubleday, Doran & Company, Inc.
Ashenden, or: The British Agent. William Somerset Maugham. LC 41-15448. 1941. Doubleday, Doran and Company, Inc.
Ashenden: Or, The British Agent. William Somerset Maugham. LC 44-8413. N.Y.
Asherwood Protegee. Mary A Garratt. LC 81-23199. 14.95 (ISBN 0-312-05610-9). St. Martin's Press.
Ashes. Charles Francis Coe. LC 52-7128. 1952. Random House.
Ashes... Stefan Zeromski & Zand, Helen Stankiewicz, Tr. LC 28-23664. 1928. A. A. Knopf.
Ashes. A Society Novel. Mary Johnson Holmes. LC 7-12590. 1890. Hurst & Co.
Ashes & Blood. Charles R. Pike, pseud. LC 80-70093. (Jubal Cade Westerns Ser.). 160p. 1981. pap. 2.95 (ISBN 0-87754-242-2). Chelsea Hse.
Ashes and Diamonds. Jerzy Andrzejewski. LC 80-466593. (Writers from the Other Europe). 1980. 3.95 (ISBN 0-14-005277-1). Penguin Books.
Ashes & Dust. George G. Gilman, pseud. (Edge Ser: No. 19). (Orig.). 1976. pap. 1.75 (ISBN 0-523-41297-5). Pinnacle Bks.
Ashes and Dust: /George G. Gilman. George G Gilman. (Edge series, 19) (ISBN 0-523-00894-5). Pinnacle Books.
Ashes and Stars. George Zebrowski. 1977. 1.50 (ISBN 0-441-87269-7). Ace Books.
Ashes, Ashes. Rene Barjavel. LC 67-15357. (Doubleday science fiction). 1967. Doubleday.
Ashes, Ashes, We All Fall Down: A Novel. Irene Schram. LC 72-75049. 1972. 5.95 (ISBN 0-671-21212-5). Simon and Schuster.
Ashes in an Urn. Jan Roffman. LC 66-24305. 1966. Published for the Crime Club by Doubleday.
Ashes in the Wilderness. William Greenough Schofield. LC 42-21305. 1942. Macrae-Smith-Company.
Ashes in the Wind: /Kathleen E. Woodwiss. Kathleen E Woodwiss. 4.95 (ISBN 0-380-46367-9). Avon Books.
Ashes of a God... Translated from the Original Manuscript by F. W. Bain... Francis William Bain. LC 11-827623. 1911. G. P. Putnam's Sons.
Ashes of Achievement. Frank A Russell. LC 22-7881. 1922. Brentano's.
Ashes of Conflict. Carl W Bordas. LC 58-3261. (milestone book). 1958. Comet Press Books.
Ashes of Desire. Winifred Mary Scott. LC 26-64782. The Macaulay Company.
Ashes of Empire: A Romance. Robert William Chambers. LC 98-138435. F. A. Stokes Company.
Ashes of Evidence. Eric Levison. LC 21-16532. The Bobbs-Merrill Company.
Ashes of Falconwyck. Angela Gray, pseud. pap. 0.95 o.s.i. (75-197). Lancer.
Ashes of Gold... Helen Virginia Botsford. LC 42-13382. 1942. Dodd, Mead & Company.
Ashes of Honor. Jo Calloway. 1978. pap. 2.25 (ISBN 0-532-22136-2). Woodhill.
Ashes of Loda. Andrew Garve. 1978. pap. 1.50i (ISBN 0-06-080430-0, P 430, PL). Har-Row.
Ashes of Loda. Andrew Garve. 1977. 9.95 o.p. (ISBN 0-86025-118-7). State Mutual Bk.
Ashes of Loda. large type ed. Paul Winterton. LC 68-1508. Harper & Row.
Ashes of Loda. Winterton, Paul. LC 64-25132. 1965. Harper & Row.
Ashes of Loda. large type ed. Paul Winterton. LC 68-1508. Harper & Row.
Ashes of Love. LC 47-30776. 1947. Phoenix Press.
Ashes of Love. Jessie Gooden. DeVorss & Co.
Ashes of My Heart. Edith Blinn. LC 16-6313. 1916. 1.35. Mark-Well Publishing Company Inc.
Ashes of Old Wishes and Other Darby O'Gill Tales. Herminie Templeton Kavanagh. LC 71-169556. (Short story index reprint series). 1971. (ISBN 0-8369-4018-0). Books for Libraries Press.
Ashes of Old Wishes, and Other Darby O'Gill Tales. Herminie Templeton Kavanagh. LC 26-17969. Jordan Publishing Company.
Ashes of Roses. Ezra Fairbanks Prist. LC 6-136. The Philosopher Press.
Ashes of Roses. Louise Knight Wheatley. LC 8-36056. Dodd, Mead & Company.
Ashes of Smyrna: A Novel of the Greco-Turkish War. Richard Reinhardt. LC 69-15284. 1971. 7.95 o.p. (ISBN 0-06-013541-7, HarpT). Har-Row.
Ashes of Tamar. Elizabeth Wade. 416p. (Orig.). 1978. pap. 2.50 (ISBN 0-89083-412-1). Zebra.
Ashes of Vengeance: A Romance of Old France. Ina Violet McComas. LC 23-16392. 1923. R. M. McBride & Company.
Ashes of Windrow. Juanita Tyree Osborne. 1976. 4.95. Avalon Books.
Ashes of Yesterday: A Historical Novel. Dan E L Patch. LC 42-212. Zondervan Publishing House.
Ashes Out of Hope: Fiction by Soviet-Yiddish Writers. Irving Howe & Eliezer Greenberg. LC 76-49731. 1977. 10.95 (ISBN 0-8052-3647-3). Schocken Books.
Ashes: The Story of a Man's Search for Class in a Classless Age. Orvel L. Trainer. LC 72-91954. 1972. (ISBN 0-87108-058-3). Pruett Pub. Co.
Ashes to Ashes. Emma Lathen, pseud. LC 77-139638. (Inner sanctum mystery). 1971. 5.95 (ISBN 0-671-20836-5). Simon and Schuster.
Ashes to Ashes. Isabel Egenton Ostrander. LC 19-18375. 1919. R. M. McBride & Co.
Ashes to the Wind. Robert John Graham. LC 64-23743. American Press Publication.
Ashes to the Wind. Charles Jerry Hannah. LC 78-58868. 1978. 1.95 (ISBN 0-380-39842-7). Avon Books.
Ashiel Mystery: A Detective Story. Charles Bryce. LC 15-21442. 1915. 1.25. John Lane.
Ashikari & the Story of Shunkin: Modern Japanese Novels. Junichiro Tanizaki. Repr. of 1936 ed. lib. bdg. 15.00x (ISBN 0-8371-3150-2, TAJN). Greenwood.
Ashleigh: A Tale of the Olden Time. Eliza Ann Dupuy. LC 6-35862. 1854. H. B. Pearson.
Ashley Hall. Susan Richard. 1970. pap. 0.60 o.p. (ISBN 0-446-63471-9, 63-471). Paperback Lib.
Ashley Landing. Spencer Dunmore. LC 76-40719. 8.95 (ISBN 0-688-03125-0). William Morrow.
Ashore at Maiden's Walk. Frasier Franklin Bingham. LC 14-230. 1.25. Broadway Publishing Company.
Ashton-Kirk, Criminologist. John Thomas McIntyre. LC 18-13906. 1918. The Penn Publishing Company.
Ashton-Kirk: Investigator. John Thomas McIntyre. LC 10-193799. 1910. The Penn Publishing Company.
Ashton-Kirk, Secret Agent. John Thomas McIntyre. LC 12-21145. 1912. 1.25. The Penn Publishing Company.
Ashton-Kirk, Special Detective. John Thomas McIntyre. LC 14-13257. 1914. 1.25. The Penn Publishing Company.
Ashurst: Or, "The Days That Are Not.". H. Hilton Broom. LC 6-19376. The News and Courier Book Presses.
Ashworth & Palmer. Thomas Hauser. LC 80-13086. 1980. 9.95 (ISBN 0-688-03700-3). W. Morrow.
Asia Pacific Stories. Murtagh Murphy. (Oxford Progressive English Readers Ser.). (Illus.). 1974. pap. text ed. 3.50x (ISBN 0-19-580718-9). Oxford U Pr.
Asian and Pacific Short Stories. Asian and Pacific Council. Cultural and Social Centre. LC 73-93869. 1974. 6.75 (ISBN 0-8048-1125-3). C. E. Tuttle Co.
Asian & Pacific Short Stories. Compiled by Cultural & Social Centre, Asian & Pacific Council. LC 73-93869. 1974. 6.75 (ISBN 0-8048-1125-3). C E Tuttle.
Asian Mantrap. Nick Carter. (Nick Carter Ser.). 256p. (Orig.). 1979. pap. 0.95 o.p. (ISBN 0-441-03180-3). Charter Bks.
Asiatics. Frederic Prokosch. LC 35-19872. 1935. Harper & Brothers.
Asiatics: A Novel. Frederic Prokosch. LC 70-138620. (Illus.). 1972. (ISBN 0-8371-5732-3). Greenwood Press.
Asiatics: A Novel by Frederic Prokosch. Frederic Prokosch. LC 41-20732. The Press of the Readers Club.
Asimov's Choice: Comets & Computers. Isaac Asimov & George H. Scithers. LC 78-51864. (Illus.). 1.75 (ISBN 0-89559-022-0). Dale Books.
Asimov's Mysteries. Isaac Asimov. (Fawcett Crest Book). 1.50 (ISBN 0-449-23223-9). Fawcett Pub.
Asimov's Mysteries. Isaac Asimov. LC 68-10573. 1968. Doubleday.
Ask a Policeman. E. C. Lorac. 1977. 8.00 o.p. State Mutual Bk.
Ask Adam. Watkins Eppes Wright. LC 42-24281. 1942. Arcadia House, Inc.
Ask Adam: A Shepherd and His Flock Face the Wolves Together. Barbara Bush. LC 78-8267. 6.95 (ISBN 0-8007-0942-X). F. H. Revell Co.
Ask Any Girl. Winifred Wolfe. LC 58-10314. 1958. Random House.
Ask at the Unicorn. Norman Thomas. LC 62-17273. 1963. New Directions.
Ask Connie. Suzanne Rand. 1982. pap. 1.95 (ISBN 0-553-11518-9). Bantam.
Ask for Linda see Love Kick.
Ask for Lois. John Barclay. 1969. pap. 0.75 o.p. (75-277). Manor Bks.
Ask for Love, & They Give You Rice Pudding. Angier Corcoran & Barbara Corcoran. (gr. 8 up). 1979. pap. 1.75 (ISBN 0-553-11947-8). Bantam.
Ask for May, Settle for June. G. B. Trudeau. 1982. 9.25 (ISBN 0-03-061532-1, Owl Bks); pap. 5.25 (ISBN 0-03-061522-4, Owl Bks). HR&W.
Ask for Me Tomorrow. Robert C Geiger. LC 64-14926. 1964. Atheneum.
Ask for Me Tomorrow. Margaret Millar. LC 76-10614. 6.95 (ISBN 0-394-40883-7). Random House.
Ask for Me Tomorrow. Margaret Millar. 1978. 1.50 (ISBN 0-380-01805-5). Avon Books.
Ask for Sally. William Arthur Neubauer. LC 44-9096. 1944. Phoenix Press.
Ask Her, Man! Ask Her: A Novel. Samuel Barton. LC 6-9100. 1888. G. W. Dillingham.
Ask Mamma; or, the Richest Commoner in England. Robert S. Surtees. LC 74-98877. x, 412p. Repr. of 1858 ed. lib. bdg. 19.25x (ISBN 0-8371-4035-8, SUAM). Greenwood.
Ask Mamma" Or, The Richest Commoner in England. Robert Smith Surtees. LC 74-98877. (Illus.). 1971. (ISBN 0-8371-4035-8). Greenwood Press.
Ask Me Another. Mullin. 1974. pap. 0.75 o.p. (ISBN 0-8024-0311-5). Moody.
Ask Me No Questions. Ursula Orange. LC 41-11501. 1914. W. Morrow & Company.
Ask Me Now. Al Young. LC 80-421. 10.95 (ISBN 0-07-072360-5). McGraw-Hill.
Ask Me Tomorrow. James Gould Cozzens. LC 40-111043. Harcourt, Brace and Company.
Ask Miss Mott. Edward Phillips Oppenheim. LC 79-128745. (Short story index reprint series). 1970. Books for Libraries Press.
Ask Miss Mott. Edward Phillips Oppenheim. LC 37-145802. 1937. Little, Brown and Company.
Ask My Brother. Constance Wagner. LC 58-12473. 1959. Harper.
Ask No Quarter. George Tracy Marsh. LC 45-239508. 1945. W. Morrow & Co.
Ask No Quarter. George Tracy Marsh. LC 46-3943. 1946. The Sun Dial Press.
Ask No Question. Mary Hocking. LC 67-19240. 1967. Morrow.
Ask No Questions. Beldon Duff. LC 30-7572. 1930. Pub. for The Crime Club, Inc., by Doubleday, Doran & Company, Inc.
Ask the Awakened: The Negative Way. Wei Wei-Wu. (Orig.). 1973. pap. 3.45 o.p. (ISBN 0-316-92810-0). Little.
Ask the Brave Soldier. Mary Nicholson. LC 36-18140. 1935. Longmans, Green and Co.
Ask the Cards a Question. Marcia Muller. LC 81-21554. 10.95 (ISBN 0-312-05653-2). St. Martin's Press.
Ask the Dust. John Fante. LC 79-22399. 1979. 14.00 (ISBN 0-87685-444-7) (ISBN 0-87685-443-9) (ISBN 0-87685-445-5). Black Sparrow Press.
Ask the Dust: A Novel. John Fante. LC 39-31197. Stackpole Sons.
Ask the Name of the Lion. 1st Ed. Ralph Allen. LC 62-11467. 1962. Doubleday.
Ask the Right Question. Michael Z Lewin. LC 78-160340. (Red mask mystery). 1971. 4.95. Putnam.
Ask the Right Question. Michael Z Lewin. (Berkley book). 1979. 1.75 (ISBN 0-425-04027-5). Berkley Pub. Corp.
Askaros Kassis, the Copt. A Romance of Modern Egypt. Edwin De Leon. LC 6-341959. 1870. J. B. Lippincott & Co.
Asking for It. Joan Taylor. LC 80-66701. 10.95 (ISBN 0-86553-005-X). Congdon & Lattes: Distributed by St. Martin's Press.
Asking for Trouble, by Joe Rayter Pseud. Mary F McChesney. LC 55-7108. (A Mill mystery). 1955. M.S. Mill Co., and W. Morrow.
Asking Price. Helen Rose Hull. LC 30-11285. 1930. Coward-McCann, Inc.
Asking Price: 1st Ed. Henry Cecil. LC 66-21715. 1966. 4.50. Harper.
Asleep and Awake. Lilian Blanche Fearing. LC 6-38769. 1893. C. H. Kerr and Company.
Asleep in the Afternoon. Ernest Charles Large. LC 77-84241. (Lost Race and Adult Fantasy Fiction). 1978. 22.00 (ISBN 0-405-10991-1). Arno Press.
Asleep in the Afternoon: A Novel. Ernest Charles Large. LC 39-21296. H. Holt and Company.
Asleep in the Sun. Adolfo Bioy-Casares. Tr. by Suzanne J. Levine from Sp. LC 77-91846. 1978. 8.95 (ISBN 0-89255-030-9). Persea Bks.
Asmendens: Or Legends of New York. Being a Complete Expense of the Mysteries, Vice and Doings, As Exhibited by the Fashionable Circles of New York... Harrison Gray Buchanan. 1848. Manson & Co.
Asmodeus: Or, The Devil on Two Sticks. Alain Rene Le Sage & John Alan Maxwell. LC 76-48436. (Classics of European Literature). (Hyperion library of world literature). 1977. 13.95. (ISBN 0-88355-568-9) (ISBN 0-88355-569-7). Hyperion Press.
Aspasia. C Holland. LC 7-6131. 1869. J. B. Lippincott & Co.
Aspasia. A Romance of Art and Live in Ancient Hellas. Robert Hamerling & Safford, Mary Joanna, Tr. LC 7-960. 1882. W. S. Gottsberger.
Aspasia: A Romance of Art and Love in Ancient Hellas, by Robert Hamerling. From the German by Mary J. Safford... Robert Hamerling & Safford, Mary Joanna, Tr. LC 7-959. 1893. Gottsberger Peck.
Aspects of Love. LC 72-78625. 1972. 0.95. Playboy Press.
Aspects of Love. 1st American Ed. David Garnett. LC 56-532777. 1956. Harcourt, Brace.
Aspen Incident. Tom Murphy. LC 78-4363. 1978. 8.95 (ISBN 0-312-05728-8). St. Martin's Press.
Aspen Shade: A Romance. Mabel Louise Fuller. LC 6-44571. 1889. De Wolfe, Fiske & Co.
Aspendale. Harriet Waters Preston. LC 7-30118. 1871. Roberts Brothers.
Aspern Papers. Henry James. Bd. with Turn of the Screw; Liar; Two Faces. LC 76-158791. (Novels & Tales of Henry James: Vol. 12). xxiii, 412p. Repr. of 1908 ed. 25.00x (ISBN 0-678-02811-7). Kelley.
Aspern Papers, and Other Stories. Henry James. LC 77-357165. (Penguin modern classics). 1976. 1.95 (ISBN 0-14-004101-X). Penguin.
Aspern Papers, Louisa Pallant, The Modern Warning. Henry James. LC 7-7559. 1888. Macmillan and Co.
Aspern Papers. The Europeans. Introd. by Joseph McG. Bottkol. Henry James. LC 50-8193. 1950. New Directions.
Aspern Papers. The Spoils of Poynton. With a General Introd. by R. P. Blackmur. Henry James. LC 59-1694. (Laurel Henry James, LC121). 1959. Dell Pub. Co.
Asphalt and Desire. Morton, Frederic. LC 52-6732. 1952. Harcourt, Brace.
Asphalt Jungle. William Riley Burnett. LC 49-10384. 1949. A. A. Knopf.
Asphodel. Mary Elizabeth Braddon Maxwell. (Seaside library, v. 46, no. 942). 1881. G. Munro.

Asphodel. Mary Elizabeth Braddon Maxwell. (On cover: Seaside library. Pocket ed. no. 560). 1885. G. Munro.

Asphodel. Mary Elizabeth Braddon Maxwell. (On cover: Lovell's library, no. 873). 1887. J. W. Lovell Company.

Asphodel. A Novel. Mary Elizabeth Braddon Maxwell. (Franklin square library, no. 161). 1881. Harper & Brothers.

Aspirations a Story. Helen Hays. LC 7-3749. 1886. T. Whittaker.

Aspirin Age. Tiah Devitt. LC 32-7611. Covici, Friede.

Assamese Short Stories: An Anthology. Ed. by Nirmalprbha Bardoloi. 1982. 40.00x (ISBN 0-7069-1590-9, Pub. by Garlandfold England). State Mutual Bk.

Assassin. James Anderson. LC 73-125771. (Inner sanctum mystery). 1970. 4.95 (ISBN 0-671-20774-1). Simon and Schuster.

Assassin. Evelyn Anthony. (YA) 1970. 5.95 o.p. (ISBN 0-698-10027-1). Coward.

Assassin. Selwyn Jepson. LC 56-8192. 1956. Lippincott.

Assassin. Robert Kearney. (Berkley Medallion Book). 1976. (pbk.) 1.50 (ISBN 0-425-03094-6). Berkley Publishing Corp.

Assassin. Uri Levi. LC 68-12159. 1968. Doubleday.

Assassin. Liam O'Flaherty. LC 28-20607. Harcourt, Brace and Company.

Assassin. John D. Revere. (Justin Perry Ser.: No. 1). 208p. 1983. pap. 2.25 (ISBN 0-523-41732-2). Pinnacle Bks.

Assassin. Leonard Wallace Robinson. LC 68-56138. (NAL book). 1968. 4.95. World Pub. Co.

Assassin. Paul Ross, pseud. (O.s.i.). 192p. (Orig.). 1974. pap. 1.25 o.s.i. (532-12200-125). Manor Bks.

Assassin. Eve Stephens, pseud. LC 72-104685. 1970. 5.95. Coward-McCann.

Assassin. Eve Stephens, pseud. (Berkley Book). 1978. 1.50 (ISBN 0-425-03678-2). Berkley Pub. Corp.

Assassin: Boston Bust-Out. Peter McCurtin. 1973. (pbk.) 0.95. Dell/Lorelei Book.

Assassin of Gor. John Norman. LC 76-30440. (His Chronicles of counter-earth, v. 5). 1970. 0.95 (ISBN 0-345-02094-4). Ballantine Books.

Assassin Who Gave up His Gun. E. V. Cunningham, pseud. 1969. 4.95 o.p. Morrow.

Assassin Who Gave up His Gun. Howard Melvin Fast. LC 75-84762. 1969. 4.95. Morrow.

Assassination. Ben Abro. 1963. 3.95 o.p. Morrow.

Assassination! LC 63-22293.

Assassination. Paul C. Metcalf. 16p. 1979. pap. 2.00 (ISBN 0-930794-13-3); ltd. signed ed. 10.00 (ISBN 0-930794-78-8). Station Hill Pr.

Assassination American Style. John Hurley. 209p. (Orig.). 1980. pap. 3.95 (ISBN 0-933990-03-0). Canterbury Pr.

Assassination Bureau, Ltd. Jack London & Robert L Fish. LC 77-13897. 1978. 1.95 (ISBN 0-14-004688-7). Penguin Books.

Assassination Bureau, Ltd. Completed by Robert L. Fish from Notes by Jack London. Jack London & Fish, Robert L. LC 63-20448. 1963. McGraw-Hill.

Assassination Day. Oliver Jacks, pseud. LC 75-35945. 1976. 7.95 (ISBN 0-8128-1887-3). Stein and Day.

Assassination Day. Oliver Jacks, pseud. LC 77-367423. 1976. 3.75 (ISBN 0-340-20724-8). Hodder and Stoughton.

Assassination Day. Ken Royce & Oliver Jacks. LC 75-35945. 224p. 1976. pap. write for info (ISBN 0-8128-7047-6). Stein & Day.

Assassination Day. Ken Royce & Oliver Jacks. LC 75-35945. 224p. 1976. 7.95 o.p. (ISBN 0-8128-1887-3). Stein & Day.

Assassination Factor. Lionel Derrick, pseud. (Penetrator Ser.: No. 40). 192p. (Orig.). 1981. pap. 1.75 (ISBN 0-523-41114-6). Pinnacle Bks.

Assassination Game. James Bellaugh. 192p. (Orig.). 1974. pap. 1.95 o.p. (ISBN 0-87056-365-3, 6365). Brandon.

Assassination Is Set for July 4. Lee Parker. (Donovan's Devils Ser). (O.s.i.). 192p. (Orig.). 1974. pap. 0.95 o.s.i. (AN1267, Award). Univ Pub & Dist.

Assassination of Federico Garcia Lorca. Ian Gibson. 268p. 1983. pap. 5.95 (ISBN 0-14-006473-7). Penguin.

Assassination of Mozart. David Weiss. 1970. 8.95 o.p. (ISBN 0-688-01078-4). Morrow.

Assassinator. David Vowell. 1975. (pbk.) 1.25. Bantam Books.

Assassins. Lee Falk & Carson Bingham. (Phantom,#14). 1975. (pbk.) 0.95 (ISBN 0-380-00298-1). Avon.

Assassins. Elia Kazan. (Crest Bk., A1795). 1973. 1.65. Fawcett.

Assassins. Elia Kazan. LC 70-164684. 1972. 7.95 (ISBN 0-8128-1427-4). Stein and Day.

Assassins. Frederic Mullally. LC 65-23572. (Walker mystery). 1965. bds., 3.50. Walker.

Assassins. Joyce Carol Oates. LC 75-25141. 576p. 1975. 12.95 (ISBN 0-8149-0767-9). Vanguard.

Assassins. Hildegarde Tolman Teilhet. LC 46-500189. 1946. Doubleday & Company, Inc.

Assassins: A Book of Hours. Joyce Carol Oates. LC 75-18424. 8.95 (ISBN 0-8149-0767-9). Vanguard Press.

Assassins: A Book of Hours. Joyce Carol Oates. 1976. 2.25 (ISBN 0-449-23000-7). Fawcett Crest.

Assassins: A Romance of the Crusades. Nevill Gauntlett Myers Meakin. 1902. H. Holt and Company.

Assassins and Victims. Campbell Black. LC 72-96014. 5.95. Harper's Magazine Press.

Assassins: By Hugh Pentecost Pseud. Judson Pentecost Philips. LC 55-7821. (Red badge detective). 1955. Dodd, Mead.

Assassin's Express. Axel Kilgore. (They Call Me the Mercenary Ser.: No. 8). (Orig.). 1982. pap. 2.50 (ISBN 0-89083-955-7). Zebra.

Assassins Have Starry Eyes. Donald Hamilton. Orig. Title: Assignment Murder. 1970. pap. 0.75 o.p. (T2304, GM). Fawcett World.

Assassins in White. 1st Ed. Robert Elmer Callahan. LC 56-5506. 1955. Vantage Press.

Assassins Play-off. Warren Murphy. (Destroyer Ser.: No. 20). 192p. (Orig.). 1975. pap. 1.95 (ISBN 0-523-41235-5). Pinnacle Bks.

Assassin's Road. Simon Harvester. 189p. 1983. pap. 2.95 (ISBN 0-8027-3014-0). Walker & Co.

Assassins Road. Simon Harvester. 1967. pap. 0.60 o.p. (60-303). Manor Bks.

Assassins Road: By Simon Harvester. Henry Gibbs. LC 65-23645. bds., 3.50. Walker.

Assassin's Shadow, No. 5. Randy Striker. (Macmorgan Ser.). (Orig.). 1981. pap. 1.95 (ISBN 0-451-11207-5, AE1207, Sig). NAL.

Assassins. 1st Amer. Ed. Nicholas Mosley. LC 67-15278. 1967. 4.95. Coward.

Assault. Michael Kelly. LC 68-12578. 1968. Harcourt, Brace & World.

Assault & Matrimony. James Anderson. LC 81-43249. (Crime Club Bks.). 192p. 1981. 10.95 (ISBN 0-385-17799-2). Doubleday.

Assault in Norway. Thomas Gallagher. 1975. Repr. lib. bdg. 11.95 o.p. (ISBN 0-8161-6289-1, Large Print Bks). G K Hall.

Assault on Aimata. Alan Caillou, pseud. 1975. (pbk.) 1.50 (ISBN 0-380-00432-1). Avon.

Assault on Bordeaux. 176p. (Orig.). pap. text ed. cancelled (ISBN 0-8439-1075-5, Pub. by Leisure Bks). Nordon Pubns.

Assault on Bordeaux. Bernhardt J. Hurwood. (Leisure Book.). 1978. 1.50 (ISBN 0-8439-0570-0). Nordon Pubns.

Assault on Childhood. Ron Goulart. 320p. 1969. 6.50 o.p. (ISBN 0-8202-0002-6). Sherbourne.

Assault on Eden. Eugenia Adams. LC 77-24656. 3.95 (ISBN 0-8028-1702-5). Eerdmans.

Assault on England. Nick Carter. (Nick Carter Ser). (O.s.i.). 176p. 1975. pap. 1.25 o.s.i. (AQ1490, Award). Univ Pub & Dist.

Assault on Mavis A. Norman Stahl. LC 78-57108. (Illus.). 8.95 (ISBN 0-394-50196-9). Random House.

Assault on the Gods. Stephen Goldin. LC 76-56498. 1977. 6.95 (ISBN 0-385-12269-1). Doubleday.

Assault with Intent. William X Kienzle. LC 82-1628. 9.95 (ISBN 0-8362-6117-8). Andrews and McMeel.

Assaults & Rituals. Sandy Boucher. 50p. pap. 2.50. Crossing Pr.

Assegai! Nickie McMenemy. LC 73-76490. 1973. 5.95 (ISBN 0-8415-0263-3). Saturday Review Press.

Assembly. John O'Hara. LC 61-12172. 1961. Random House.

Asses in Clove. Eimar O'Duffy. LC 33-22597. 1933. Putman.

Asses in Clover. Eimar O'Duffy. LC 33-22597. 1933. Putnam.

Assessor. Henry Henn. 1978. pap. 1.75 (ISBN 0-532-17196-9). Woodhill.

Assignation: And Other Tales. Edgar Allan Poe. (On cover: Lovell's library. v. 8. no. 438). 1884. J. W. Lovell Company.

Assignation in Algeria. John Lee. LC 72-152127. 1971. 5.95 (ISBN 0-8027-5228-4). Walker.

Assignation in Algiers. John Lee. 1971. 5.95 o.p. (ISBN 0-8027-5228-4). Walker & Co.

Assignment. Laurence Leamer. LC 80-20879. 1980. 9.95 (ISBN 0-8037-0266-3). Dial Press.

Assignment. Martin Myers. LC 73-122891. 1971. 7.95. Harper & Row.

Assignment. Per Wahloo. Tr. by J. Tate. 1966. 4.95 o.p. Knopf.

Assignment - Black Gold. Edward Sidney Aarons. (Sam Durell). (Fawcett gold medal book: Vol. 40). 1975. (pbk.) 1.25. Fawcett.

Assignment - Manchurian Doll. Edward Sidney Aarons. 1979. pap. 1.75 (ISBN 0-449-13449-0, GM). Fawcett.

Assignment - Sulu Sea. Edward Sidney Aarons. (Sam Durell Assignment Ser). 1971. pap. 0.75 o.p. (T2426, GM). Fawcett World.

Assignment--Afghan Dragon. Edward Sidney Aarons. (Assignment Ser.). 1978. pap. 1.95 (ISBN 0-449-14085-7, GM). Fawcett.

Assignment--Black Gold. Edward Sidney Aarons. 192p. (Orig.). 1975. pap. 1.95 (ISBN 0-449-13354-0, GM). Fawcett.

Assignment--Ceylon. Edward Sidney Aarons. 208p. 1981. pap. 1.95 (ISBN 0-449-13583-7, GM). Fawcett.

Assignment--Golden Girl. Edward Sidney Aarons. (Assignment Ser.). 1979. pap. 2.25 (ISBN 0-449-14140-3, GM). Fawcett.

Assignment--Lili Lamaris. Edward Sidney Aarons. 1978. pap. 1.50 (ISBN 0-449-13934-4, GM). Fawcett.

Assignment--Mara Tirana. Edward Sidney Aarons. (Assignment Ser). 1971. pap. 0.75 o.p. (T2378, GM). Fawcett World.

Assignment--Mermaid. Edward Sidney Aarons. 1979. pap. 1.75 (ISBN 0-449-14203-5, GM). Fawcett.

Assignment--Sulu Sea. Edward Sidney Aarons. 160p. 1981. pap. 1.95 (ISBN 0-449-13875-5, GM). Fawcett.

Assignment--the Girl in the Gondola. Edward Sidney Aarons. 1979. pap. 1.75 (ISBN 0-449-14165-9, GM). Fawcett.

Assignment--Zoraya. Edward Sidney Aarons. (Assignment Ser.). 1979. pap. 1.95 (ISBN 0-449-14184-5, GM). Fawcett.

Assignment Abacus. Leslie Purnell Davies. LC 74-33635. 1975. 5.95 (ISBN 0-385-01799-5). Published for the Crime Club by Doubleday.

Assignment-Amazon Queen. Edward Sidney Aarons. (Sam Durell). (Gold medal book: Vol. 37). 1974. (pbk.) 0.95. Fawcett Pubns.

Assignment: Angelina. Edward Sidney Aarons. 1970. pap. 0.75 o.p. (T2309, GM). Fawcett World.

Assignment: Assassination see Running Spy.

Assignment Basra. Francois Ponthier. LC 70-87779. 1969. 3.95. McKay.

Assignment: Black Viking. Edward Sidney Aarons. (Assignment Ser). 1970. pap. 0.75 o.p. (T2356, GM). Fawcett World.

Assignment: Burma. Lee O. Miller. (Orig.). 1980. pap. 1.75 o.s.i. (ISBN 0-505-51498-2). Tower Bks.

Assignment Ceylon. Edward Sidney Aarons. (Sam Durell). (Sam Durell Adventure, #36: Vol. 36). 1973. (pbk.) 0.95. Fawcett.

Assignment Devil's Playground. Patrick Barker. (Tac One Ser.: No. 2). 240p. 1975. pap. 1.25 o.p. (ISBN 0-532-12486-3). Woodhill.

Assignment Devil's Playground. Patrick Barker. (Tac One Ser.: No. 2). 240p. 1975. pap. 1.25 o.p. (ISBN 0-532-12486-3). Manor Bks.

Assignment for a Mercenary. Howard R. Simpson. LC 65-14664. 4.95. Harper.

Assignment: Girl in the Gondola. Edward Sidney Aarons. (Sam Durell Assignment Ser). (Orig.). 1969. pap. 0.60 o.p. (R2056, GM). Fawcett World.

Assignment in Andorra: A Novel. May Mackintosh. LC 73-7846. 1973. 6.95. Delacorte Press.

Assignment in Brittany. Helen MacInnes Highet. LC 42-179036. 1942. Little, Brown and Company.

Assignment in Brittany. Helen MacInnes. 1978. pap. 2.95 (ISBN 0-449-22958-0, Crest). Fawcett.

Assignment in Brittany. Helen MacInnes. LC 42-17993. 1971. 6.95 o.p. (ISBN 0-15-109620-1). HarBraceJ.

Assignment in Eternity, Four Long Science Fiction Stories. 1st Ed. Robert Anson Heinlein. LC 53-12678. 1953. Fantasy Press.

Assignment in Guiana. George Harmon Coxe. LC 42-5682. 1942. A. A. Knopf.

Assignment in Iraq. 1st Ed. Allan MacKinnon. LC 60-156597. 1960. Published for the Crime Club by Doubleday.

Assignment in Kashmir. Aamir Ali. (Orient Paperbacks Ser.). 200p. 1973. pap. 2.95 (ISBN 0-88253-246-4). Ind-US Inc.

Assignment in Tomorrow. Ed. by Frederik Pohl. 1972. pap. 1.25 o.p. (78-699). Lancer.

Assignment in Tomorrow: An Anthology. 1st Ed. Ed. by Frederik Pohl. LC 54-9852. 1954. Hanover House.

Assignment Intercept. Nick Carter. (Nick Carter Ser.). (O.s.i.). 176p. 1975. pap. 1.25 o.s.i. (AQ1512, Award). Univ Pub & Dist.

Assignment: Intercept. Nick Carter. (Nick Carter Killmaster series#AQ1512). 1976. (pbk.) 1.25. Award Books.

Assignment: Karachi. Edward Sidney Aarons. 1970. pap. 0.60 o.p. (R2231, GM). Fawcett World.

Assignment: Lili Lamaris. Edward Sidney Aarons. (Assignment Ser). 1970. pap. 0.60 o.p. (R2209, GM). Fawcett World.

Assignment: Lowlands. Edward Sidney Aarons. (Assignment Ser). (Orig.). 1968. pap. 0.60 o.p. (R2538, GM). Fawcett World.

Assignment: Manchurian Doll. Edward Sidney Aarons. (Assignment Ser). 1970. pap. 0.75 o.p. (T2301, GM). Fawcett World.

Assignment: Moon Girl. Edward Sidney Aarons. (Assignment Ser). (Orig.). 1968. pap. 0.60 o.p. (R2024, GM). Fawcett World.

Assignment: Murder. Donald Hamilton. LC 56-13164. (Dell first edition, A123). 1956. Dell Pub. Co.

Assignment Murder see Assassins Have Starry Eyes.

Assignment: North Africa. Joseph Decker. 192p. (Orig.). 1975. pap. 1.25 o.p. (ISBN 0-532-12256-9). Woodhill.

Assignment: North Africa. Joseph Decker. 192p. (Orig.). 1975. pap. 1.25 o.p. (ISBN 0-532-12256-9). Manor Bks.

Assignment: Nuclear Nude. Edward Sidney Aarons. 1970. pap. 0.75 o.p. (T2293, GM). Fawcett World.

Assignment Quayle Question. Edward Sidney Aarons. (Sam Durell). (Fawcett gold medal book: Vol. 39). 1975. (pbk.) 1.25. Fawcett.

Assignment Sheba. Will B Aarons. (Gold Medal) (ISBN 0-449-13696-5). Fawcett.

Assignment: Sorrento Siren. Edward Sidney Aarons. 1970. pap. 0.60 o.p. (R2254, GM). Fawcett World.

Assignment: Stella Marni. Edward Sidney Aarons. 1970. pap. 0.75 o.p. (T2308, GM). Fawcett World.

Assignment Stuffed Shirt. Rene MacColl. LC 52-5002. 1952. Little Brown.

Assignment: Suicide. Edward Sidney Aarons. (Assignment Ser). 1970. pap. 0.75 o.p. (T2313, GM). Fawcett World.

Assignment Suicide. Cover Painting by Barye Phillips. Edward Sidney Aarons. LC 57-1274. (Gold medal book, 621). 1956. Fawcett Publications.

Assignment: Suspense: A Three Novel Omnibus: Above Suspicion. Horizon. Assignment in Brittany. Helen MacInnes. LC 61-7253. 1961. Harcourt, Brace & World.

Assignment: The Cairo Dancers. Edward Sidney Aarons. (Assignment Ser). 1970. pap. 0.75 o.p. (T2352, GM). Fawcett World.

Assignment Tiger Devil. Will B Aarons. (Fawcett Gold Medal Book.). 1977. 1.50 (ISBN 0-449-13811-9). Fawcett Pubns.

Assignment to Disaster. Edward Sidney Aarons. LC 55-38191. (Gold medal books, 491). 1955. Fawcett Publications.

Assignment to Love: By Jennifer Ames Pseud. Maysie Greig. LC 53-12330. 1953. Avalon Books.

Assignment: Tokyo. Edward Sidney Aarons. (Assignment Ser). 1971. pap. 0.75 o.p. (T2733, GM). Fawcett World.

Assignment. Tr. from Swedish by Joan Tate. 1st Amer. Ed. Per Wahloo. LC 66-11346. (Borzoi bk.). 1966. bds., 4.95. Knopf.

Assignment: Treason. Edward Sidney Aarons. (Assignment Ser). 1970. pap. 0.75 o.p. (T2303, GM). Fawcett World.

Assignment Unicorn. Edward Sidney Aarons. (Gold Medal Book) (ISBN 0-449-13610-8). Fawcett.

Assignment Without Glory. Marcos Spinelli. LC 45-828. 1945. J. B. Lippincott Company.

Assistant. Bernard Malamud. 304p. 1980. pap. 2.95 (ISBN 0-380-51474-5, 56580). Avon.

Assistant. Bernard Malamud. 246p. 1957. 12.95 (ISBN 0-374-10644-4); pap. 4.95 (ISBN 0-374-50484-9). FS&G.

Assistant Angel: By Rebecca Marsh Pseud. William Arthur Neubauer. LC 54-5843. Arcadia House.

Assistant Wife. Josiah Pitts Woolfolk. LC 35-23306. Godwin.

Assize of the Dying. 2 Novelletes. Edith Pargeter. LC 58-13909. 1958. Published for the Crime Club by Doubleday.

Associate Hermits. Frank Richard Stockton. LC 98-1679. 1899. Harper & Brothers.

Associate Professor: A Novel. Robert Pease. LC 67-14965. 1967. 3.95. S.&S.

Associates: A Novel. John Jay Osborn. LC 78-25672. (Illus.). 1979. 9.95 (ISBN 0-395-27097-9). Houghton Mifflin.

Assorted Chocolates. Octavus Roy Cohen. LC 22-17937. 1922. 2.00. Dodd, Mead and Company.

Assualt on the Gods. Stephen Goldin. 192p. 1981. pap. 2.25 (ISBN 0-449-24455-5, Crest). Fawcett.

Assyrian: And Other Stories. William Saroyan. LC 50-5197. 1950. Harcourt, Brace.

Assyrian Bride. William Patrick Kelly. LC 25-3168. 1905. G. Routledge and Sons, Limited.

Astapovo, or What We Are to Do. Peter Whigham. 1970. 4.00 (Pub. by Anvil Pr); signed ed. 15.00; pap. 2.50. SBD.

Astarte. Alberto Readstone. 1973. (pbk) 1.25. Dell.

Astercote. Penelope Lively. LC 74-133112. 1971. 4.50 (ISBN 0-525-25975-9). Dutton.

Asterisk Destiny. Campbell Black. LC 78-13362. 1978. 9.95 (ISBN 0-688-03392-X). Morrow.

Aston Kings. Humphrey Pakington. LC 46-3950. 1946. W. W. Norton & Company, Inc.

Astonished Man: A Novel. Blaise Cendrars. LC 80-9056. 1982. 12.95 (ISBN 0-8128-2814-3). Stein and Day.

Astonishing Adventure of Jane Smith. Patricia Wentworth. LC 23-17476. Small, Maynard & Company.

Astonishing Adventure of Jane Smith. Patricia Wentworth. LC 23-12443. 1923. A. Melrose, Ltd.

Astonishing History of Troy Town. Arthur Thomas Quiller-Couch. (On cover: Cassell's "rainbow" series. v. 1, no. 29). 1888. Cassell & Company, Limited.

Astoria, 2 vols. Washington Irving. 200.00 (ISBN 0-87968-671-5). Gordon Pr.

Astounding Analog Reader, Vol. 1. Ed. by Harry Harrison & Brian W. Aldiss. LC 72-83145. (Science Fiction Ser). 504p. 1972. 7.95 o.p. (ISBN 0-385-02334-0). Doubleday.

Astounding Crime on Torrington Road: Being an Account of What Might Be Termed "The Pentecost Episode" in a Most Audacious Criminal Career. William Hooker Gillette. LC 27-12510. 1927. Harper & Brothers.

Astounding; John W. Campbell Memorial Anthology. John Wood Campbell. Ed. by Harry Harrison. LC 73-5058. 1973. 8.95. Random House.

Astounding: John W. Campbell Memorial Anthology of Science Fiction. Ed. by Harry Harrison. 1973. 7.95 o.p. (ISBN 0-394-48167-4). Random

Astounding Science Fiction Anthology. Astounding Science Fiction. Ed. by John Wood Campbell. LC 52-8065. 1952. Simon and Schuster.

Astounding Science Fiction Anthology. Selected and with an Introd. by John W. Campbell, Jr. Stories by Isaac Asimov and Others. Analog Science Fact & Science Fiction & Campbell, John Wood, 1910- Ed. LC 52-8065. 1952. Simon and Schuster.

Astounding Science Fiction, July 1939. John Wood Campbell & Martin Harry Greenberg. LC 81-122108. (Alternatives). (Illus.). 1980. 12.95 (ISBN 0-8093-0991-2). Southern Illinois University Press.

Astounding Science Fiction, July, 1939. Ed. by Martin Harry Greenberg. (Alternatives Ser.). 184p. 1981. Repr. of 1939 ed. 12.95 (ISBN 0-8093-0991-2). S Ill U Pr.

Astra. Grace Livingston Hill. LC 41-21281. J. B. Lippincott Company.

Astra and Flondrix. Seamus Cullen. LC 76-53815. 1977. 6.95 (ISBN 0-394-41254-0). Pantheon Books.

Astra and Flondrix. Seamus Cullen. 1979. 1.95 (ISBN 0-671-82256-X). Pocket Books.

Astragal. Albertine Sarrazin. LC 66-19862. 1967. Grove Press.

Astral Quest. John Rankine. (Space: 1999 series). (Illus.). 1976. (pbk.) 1.50 (ISBN 0-671-80392-1). Pocket Books.

Astrate: Or, Truant Loves. Alfred Delvau. Tr. by Davenport, Reuben Briggs. LC 6-34010. (On cover: Household library. v. 4, no. 4a). Belford, Clarke & Co.; Etc., Etc.

Astrid Cane. LC 82-84285. (Grove Press Victorian Library). 224p. 1983. pap. 3.95 (ISBN 0-394-62461-0, BC). Grove.

Astrid Factor. Douglas Orgill. LC 68-27385. 1968. 3.95. Walker.

Astrologer. John Cameron. 1973. (pbk.) 1.50. Warner Paperback Lib.

Astrologer. John Cameron. LC 75-159335. 1972. 5.95 (ISBN 0-394-46426-5). Random House.

Astrologer: A Satirical Novel. Edward S Hyams. LC 50-13209. 1950. Longmans, Green.

Astrologer of Chaldea: Or, The Life of Faith. William Peter Strickland. LC 8-16879. 1855. J. Ernst.

Astrologer's Day & Other Stories. R. K. Narayan. 229p. 1981. Repr. of 1964 ed. 4.95 (ISBN 0-88253-105-0). Ind-US Inc.

Astronaut. James Blumgarten. 1974. (pbk.) 1.25. Warner Paperback Library.

Astronauts & Androids. Intro. by Isaac Asimov. LC 77-81938. 1977. pap. 1.50 o.s.i. (ISBN 0-89559-005-0). Davis Pubns.

Astronauts & Androids. Intro. by Isaac Asimov. LC 77-81938. 1977. pap. 1.50 o.p. (ISBN 0-89559-005-0). Davis Pubns.

Astronomer, and Other Stories. Doris Betts. LC 65-20980. 1966. 5.95. Harper.

Astronomer at Large. A. G Thornton. LC 24-927310. 1924. A. Melrose, Ltd.

Astronomer at Large. A. G Thornton. LC 24-187693. 1924. G. P. Putnam's Sons.

Astronomy of Love. Jon Stallworthy. 1961. 2.50 o.p. (ISBN 0-19-211229-5). Oxford U Pr.

Astrophil and Stella. Philip Sidney. Ed. by Max Putzel. LC 67-21646. 1967. Anchor Books.

Astrotots. Constance Bannister. (O.s.i.). pap. 1.00 o.s.i. (ISBN 0-671-10358-X, Fireside). S&S.

Astrov Legacy. Constance Heaven. LC 73-14805. 1973. 10.95 (ISBN 0-8161-6157-7). G. K. Hall.

Astrov Legacy. Constance Heaven. 1974. (pbk.) 1.25. Dell.

Astyanax: An Epic Romance of Ilion, Atlantis & Amaraca. Joseph M Brown. LC 7-16747. 1907. Broadway Publishing Co.

Asutra. Jack Vance. 1974. (pbk.) 0.95. Dell.

Aswan! A Novel. Michael Heim. LC 76-178959. 1972. 6.95 (ISBN 0-394-47908-4). Knopf; Distributed by Random House.

Aswan Assignment. Andrew Sugar. (Israeli Commandos Ser.: No. 1). 192p. (Orig.). 1974. pap. 1.25 o.p. (ISBN 0-532-12208-9). Woodhill.

Aswan Assignment. Andrew Sugar. (Israeli commandos,#1). 1974. (pbk.) 1.25. Manor Books.

Aswan Solution. John Rowe. LC 78-14710. 1979. 8.95 (ISBN 0-385-14866-6). Doubleday.

Asylum. Aidan Higgins. 1980. 12.95 (ISBN 0-7145-0229-4); pap. 5.95 (ISBN 0-7145-0230-8). Riverrun NY.

Asylum. William Johnston. LC 72-8891. 1972. 0.95. Bantam Books.

Asylum & Circus. Michael D. Barrett. 1978. pap. 1.95 (ISBN 0-532-19172-2). Woodhill.

Asylum, and Other Stories. revised ed. Aidan Higgins. 1978. 5.95 (ISBN 0-7145-0230-8). J. Calder.

Asylum for the Queen. Mildred A. Jordan. LC 48-1018. 1948. A. A. Knopf.

Asylum Island: A Tale. Hilton Brown. LC 51-9466. 1951. Macmillan.

Asylum; or, Alonzo and Melissa. An American Tale, Founded on Fact. Daniel Jackson & Mitchell, Isaac. LC 10-22197. 1811. J. Nelson.

Asylum Piece. Helen Woods Edmonds. LC 46-6090. 1946. Doubleday & Company, Inc.

Asylum Piece. Anna Kavan. LC 79-28536. 1980. Repr. 11.95 o.p. (ISBN 0-935576-02-9). Orenda-Unity.

Asylum Piece and Other Stories. Helen Woods Edmonds. LC 79-28536. 1980. 11.95. M. Kesend Pub.

Asylum Piece & Other Stories. Anna Kavan. LC 79-28536. 1980. cloth 11.95 (ISBN 0-935576-02-9); pap. 6.95 (ISBN 0-935576-03-7). Kesend Pub Ltd.

Asylum World. John Jakes. 1969. pap. 0.60 o.p. (63-236). Paperback Lib.

Asymmetries 1-260. Jackson & Mac Low. 1981. pap. 19.95 (ISBN 0-914162-43-8); pap. 6.95. Knowles.

At a Dollar a Year: Ripples on the Edge of the Maelstrom. Robert Lovejoy Raymond. LC 76-157794. (Short story index reprint series). 1971. (ISBN 0-8369-3906-9). Books for Libraries Press.

At a Dollar a Year: Ripples on the Edge of the Maelstrom. Robert Lovejoy Raymond. LC 19-156706. 1919. Marshall Jones Company.

At a Girl's Mercy: Or, The Fortunes of War. Jean Kate Ludlum. LC 7-14724. (Street & Smith's select series, no. 40). 1890. Street & Smith.

At a Great Cost: A Novel. Effie Adelaide Maria Albanesi. (On Cover: The Choice Series, No. 124). 1895. R. Bonner's Sons.

At a High Price. author's ed. Elisabeth Burstenbinder. Tr. by Smith, Mary Stuart (Harrison) (On cover: Cobweb series of choice fiction). 1879. Estes and Lauriat.

At a High Price. Elisabeth Burstenbinder. Tr. by Tyrrell, Chtistina. (On cover: Seaside library. Pocket ed., no. 540). 1885. G. Munro.

At a Winter's Fire. Bernard Edward Joseph Capes. LC 78-101793. (Short story index reprint series). 1969. Books for Libraries Press.

At a Winter's Fire. Bernard Edward Joseph Capes. LC 99-2884. 1899. Doubleday & McClure Company.

At All Costs. Richard Aldington. 1930. 20.00 (ISBN 0-932062-01-6). Sharon Hill.

At an Old Chateau. Katharine Sarah Gadsden Macquoid. LC 7-16616. (On cover: Harper's Franklin square library. no. 678.). 1890. Harper & Brothers.

At Any Cost. Isabella Fyvie Mayo. (Seaside Library. Pocket Ed.). (On cover: The seaside library. Pocket ed. no. 352: No. 352). 1885. G. Munro.

At Any Price. Steve Radoycich. 1972. pap. 2.25 o.s.i. (01760-8). Review & Herald.

At Bay: A Novel. Annie French Hector. (On cover: Lovell's library, v 12, no. 664). 1885. J. W. Lovell Company.

At Bay. A Novel. Annie French Hector. (On cover: Seaside library. Pocket ed., no. 564). 1885. G. Munro.

At Bay: A Novel. Page Philips & Scarborough, George. LC 14-9284. 1914. 1.25. The Macaulay Company.

At Bay: A Novel Also Valerie's Fate. author's ed. Annie French Hector. (Leisure hour series, no. 172). 1885. H. Holt and Company.

At Bertram's Hotel. Agatha Miller Christie. 1973. (pbk.) 0.95 (ISBN 0-671-77702-5). Pocket Books.

At Bertram's Hotel. Agatha Miller Christie. LC 66-23217. 1966. Dodd, Mead.

At Break of Dawn. Fred John Meldau. LC 54-8393. 1954. Zondervan Pub. House.

At Brown's an Adirondack Story. Jean Kate Ludlum. LC 7-14725. 1890. Hunt & Eaton.

At Button's. Garry Wills. LC 78-27763. 8.95 (ISBN 0-8362-6108-9). Andrews & McMeel.

At Capri. A Story of Italian Life. Klara Bauer. Tr. by S., M. & MS. (On cover: International series of new approved novels). Porter and Coates.

At Christmas Time the World Grows Young. Amy Bruner Almy. LC 70-116926. (Short story index reprint series). (Illus.). 1970. Books for Libraries Press.

At Christmass Time: Being A Christmas Carol. Charles Dickens & Edgar, William Crowell. LC 25-11826. 1925. The Bellman Company.

At Close of Eve: An Anthology of New Curious Stories. Ed. by Jeremy Scott. LC 48-16375. 1947. Jarrolds.

At Close Range. Francis Hopkinson Smith. LC 75-37560. (Short story index reprint series). (Illus.). 1972. (ISBN 0-8369-4119-5). Books for Libraries Press.

At Close Range. Francis Hopkinson Smith. 1905. C. Scribner's Sons.

At Close Range. Francis Hopkinson Smith. LC 14-1810. 1906. C. Scribner's Sons.

At Cloudy Pass: A Tale of Love and Adventure in Idaho. Rufus Prentiss Hurlburt. LC 8-37061. 1908. The C. M. Clark Publishing Co.

At Dawn Set Free. Ann Maturin. LC 61-15960. 1961. Dorrance.

At Dawning: The Story of Blind Shamar. Sara Elizabeth Gosselink. LC 46-15682. 1946. Wm. B. Eerdmans Publishing Company.

At Dawson's Corners in the Gay Nineties. Edward Arthur Tuttle. LC 51-2168. 1951.

At Daybreak: A Novel. Annie Lydia Kimball. LC 7-12240. 1884. J. R. Osgood and Company.

At Eight Twenty-Five Evita Became Immortal. Mario Szichman. 220p. 1983. pap. 7.50. Ediciones Norte.

At Fame's Gateway: The Romance of a Pianiste. Jennie Irene Mix. LC 20-6128. 1920. H. Holt and Company.

At Fault. Kate O'Flaherty Chopin. 1890. 9.50 o.p. (ISBN 0-8398-0262-5, Lit Hse). Gregg.

At Fault. Hawley Smart. (Seaside library, v. 78, no. 1582). 1883. G. Munro.

At Fault. A Novel. Kate O'Flaherty Chopin. LC 6-20970. 1890. Nixon-Jones Printing Co.

At First Sight. Bill Boggs. LC 78-67235. 10.95 (ISBN 0-448-15778-0). Grosset & Dunlap.

At First Sight: A Novel. Walter John De La Mare. LC 28-25759. 1928. C. Gaige.

At Freddie's. Penelope Fitzgerald. LC 82-3143. 1982. 12.95 (ISBN 0-87923-439-3). D.R. Godine.

At God's Pleasure. Jean D' Ormesson. LC 77-75016. 1977. 10.95 (ISBN 0-394-49899-2). Knopf: Distributed by Random House.

At Good Old Siwash. George Helgeson Fitch. LC 11-24401. 1911. Little, Brown, and Company.

At Good Old Siwash. illustrated by g. c. widney. ed. George Helgeson Fitch. LC 26-14918. 1926. Little, Brown, and Company.

At Heart a Rake. Florence Marryat Church Lean. LC 7-13242. The Cassell Publishing Co.

At Heaven's Gate. Robert Penn Warren. LC 59-5736. 1959. Random House.

At Heaven's Gate. a special ed. Robert Penn Warren. LC 49-531090. (N.A.L. Signet books, 725). 1949. New American Library.

At Heaven's Gate. Robert Penn Warren. LC 43-131634. 1943. Harcourt, Brace and Company.

At High Risk. Palma Harcourt. LC 77-91361. 1978. 6.95 (ISBN 0-8027-5382-5). Walker.

At His Command. Stanley Baker. 192p. 1972. pap. 1.95 o.p. (ISBN 0-87977-148-8, DBB148). Dansk Blue Bk.

At His Gates. A Novel. Margaret Oliphant Wilson Oliphant. (On cover: Seaside library. Pocket ed., no. 528). 1890. G. Munro.

At Home. Naomi May. 1980. pap. 4.95 (ISBN 0-7145-0094-1). Riverrun NY.

At Home with the Jardines. Lilian Lida Bell. LC 4-22269. 1904. L. C. Page & Company.

At Lake Monona: An Episode of the Summer School. John Alphonsa Corry. LC 99-4431. 1899. D. H. McBride & Co.

At Large: A Novel. Ernest William Hornung. LC 2-5221. 1902. C. Scribner's Sons.

At Last. Maria Elise Turner Lauder. LC 7-13864. 1894. C. W. Moulton.

At Last. Olive Wadsley. LC 34-169012. 1934. Dodd. Mead & Company.

At Last. A Novel. Mary Virginia Terhune. LC 8-260482. 1870. Carleton; Etc., Etc.

At Last, Mr. Tolliver. William George Wiegand. LC 50-14210. 1950. Rinehart.

At Last the Island. Margaret Lane. LC 37-21533. 1937. Harper & Brothers.

At Last to Kiss Amanda. 1st Ed. Frank Callan Norris. LC 61-10469. 1961. McGraw-Hill.

At Love's Extremes. Maurice Thompson. LC 12-11053. 1885. Cassell & Company, Limited.

At Madame Bonnard's. Joseph Vogel. LC 35-18571. 1935. A. A. Knopf.

At Market Value. A Novel. Grant Allen. LC 1-30688. (Hawthorne library)). 1901. Hurst & Co.

At Mount Desert: A Summer's Sowing. Mildred Fairfax. LC 6-38430. Congregational Sunday-School and Publishing Society.

At Mrs. Lippincote's. Elizabeth Taylor. LC 46-3066. 1946. A. A. Knopf.

At Night All Cats Are Grey: And Other Stories. Patrick Boyle. LC 76-75804. 1969. 4.95. Grove Press.

At Nine Bells, Being the Odyssey of Henry Paxton. Samuel Emery. LC 32-121198. E. P. Dutton & Co., Inc.

At Odds. Jemima Montgomery Tautphoeus. LC 8-25556. 1863. J. B. Lippincott & Co.

At Odds. Jemima Montgomery Tautphoeus. 1879. G. Munro.

At Odds with the Regent: A Story of the Cellamare Conspiracy. Burton Egbert Stevenson. LC 1-29585. 1901. J. B. Lippincott Company.

At Odds with the Regent: A Story of the Cellamare Conspiracy. Burton Egbert Stevenson. 1905. J. B. Lippincott Company.

At One Fell Swoop. Oivian Collin Brooks. LC 64-7699. 1965. Roy Publishers.

At One Fell Swoop. Osmington Mills. LC 64-7699. 1965. bds., 2.95. Roy.

At One-Thirty: A Mystery. Isabel Egenton Ostrander. LC 15-5295. 1.30. W. J. Watt & Company.

At Paradise Gate: A Novel. Jane Smiley. LC 81-5706. 12.95 (ISBN 0-671-42598-6). Simon and Schuster.

At Passion's Tide. Pamela Windsor. 240p. (Orig.). 1980. pap. 2.25 (ISBN 0-515-05639-1). Jove Pubns.

At Play in the Fields of the Lord. Peter Matthiessen. 1976. (pbk.) 2.25. Bantam Books.

At Play in the Fields of the Lord. Peter Matthiessen. LC 65-21230. 1965. Random House.

At Random Sown. Margaret M. Sullivan. LC 45-2914. 1943. The Ave Maria Press.

At Sallygap: And Other Stories. Mary Lavin. LC 47-1334. 1947. Little, Brown and Company.

At Sea. Arthur Calder-Marshall. LC 34-354672. 1934. C. Scribner's Sons.

At Seneca Castle. William Walker Canfield. LC 12-16080. 1912. 1.25. E. P. Dutton & Company.

At Sight of Gold. Cynthia Lombardi. LC 22-15850. D. Appleton and Company.

At Some Forgotten Door. Doris Miles Disney. LC 66-16929. 4.50. Pub. for the Crime Club by Doubleday.

At Start and Finish. William Lindsey. 1899. Small, Maynard & Company.

At Sundown: The Tiger. Ethel Edith Mannin. LC 51-6673. 1951. New York, Jarrolds.

At Sundown the Tiger. Ethel Edith Mannin. LC 51-12480.

At Sundown with Merrylea. Kay Rusch. LC 67-31754. 1968.

At Sunrise, the Rough Music. Richard Llewellyn. LC 75-21334. 1976. 7.95 (ISBN 0-385-03375-3). Doubleday.

At Sunwich Port. William Wymark Jacobs. LC 2-13616. 1902. C. Scribner's Sons.

At Swim-Two-Birds. Flann O'Brien. 1976. pap. 5.95 (ISBN 0-452-25262-8, Z5262, Plume). NAL.

At Swim-Two-Birds. Flann O'Brien. 1967. pap. 2.25 o.p. (ISBN 0-670-00211-9, C211, Comp). Viking Pr.

At Swim-Two-Birds. Flann O'Brien. 1967. pap. 2.25 o.p. (ISBN 0-670-00211-9). Viking Pr.

At Swim-Two-Birds. Brian O'Nolan. LC 66-17221. 1966. Walker.

At Swim-Two-Birds. Brian O'Nolan. LC 51-1498. 1951. Pantheon.

At Swim-Two-Birds. Brian O'Nolan. LC 77-368310. 1976. 4.95 (ISBN 0-246-10890-8). Hart-Davis, MacGibbon.

At Swim-Two-Birds. Brian O'Nolan. LC 39-14807. 1939. Longmans, Green and Co.

At Swim-Two-Birds. By Flann O'Brien. Pseud. Brian Nolan, pseud. LC 66-172210. 4.95. Walker.

At Swords' Points. A Novel. Edward A Thomas. LC 8-27050. 1877. Claxton, Remsen & Haffelfinger.

At Swords' Points: By Andre Norton Pseud. 1st Ed. Alice Mary Norton. LC 54-8575. 1954. Harcourt, Brace.

At the Actors' Boarding House: And Other Stories. Helen Green. LC 6-45045. 1906. The Nevada Publishing Co.

At the Age of Eve. Kate Trimble Sharber. LC 11-27649. The Bobbs-Merrill Company.

At the Altar. Elisabeth Burstenbinder. Tr. by L. J. S. J. S. L. LC 6-19405. 1872. J. B. Lippincott & Co.

At the Bakery: By Lillian Colonius, Glenn W. Schroeder. New Ed., Rev. Lillian Colonius & Glenn W. Schroeder. LC 55-2199. 2.50. Melmont.

At the Bidding of the Heart. Mikhail Aleksandrovich Sholokhov. 265p. 1973. 4.45 (ISBN 0-8285-1079-2, Pub. by Progress Pubs USSR). Imported Pubns.

At the Blue Bell Inn. Joseph Smith Fletcher. LC 79-122697. (Short story index reprint series). 1970. Books for Libraries Press.

At the Blue Bell Inn. Joseph Smith Fletcher. LC 98-1216. Rand, McNally & Company.
At the Center. Norma Gangel Rosen. LC 81-7099. 1982. 12.95 (ISBN 0-395-31263-9). Houghton Mifflin.
At the Councillor's: Or, A Nameless History. Eugenie John. Tr. by Wister, Annis Lee (Furness) LC 7-9897. 1876. J. B. Lippincott & Co.
At the Councillor's: Or, A Nameless History. Eugenie John. Tr. by Wister, Annie Lee (Furness) LC 4-8708. 1904. J. B. Lippincott Company.
At the Court of Catherine the Great. Frederick J Whishaw. LC 99-1781. Frederick A. Stokes Company.
At the Court of Maharaja: A Story of Adventure. Louis Tracy. LC 7-25077. The American News Company, Publisher's Agents.
At the Court of the King: Being Romances of France. Ed. by George Hembert Westley. LC 3141. 1900. L. C. Page & Company (Incorporated).
At the Cross-Roads. Frances Frederica Montresor. LC 4-23568. 1897. D. Appleton and Company.
At the Crossing with Denis McShane. William Allen Knight. LC 12-237552. 1912. 0.60. The Pilgrim Press.
At the Crossroads. Sallie Lee Bell. LC 63-17744. 1963. Zondervan Pub. House.
At the Crossroads. Harriet Theresa Smith Comstock. LC 22-10863. 1922. Doubleday, Page & Company.
At the Crossroads. Evan S. Connell. LC 65-17106. bds., 5.50. S. & S.
At the Crossroads, and Other Stories and Sketches. 1st Ed. Marie S Grimson. LC 53-105419. 1953. Exposition Press.
At the Dawning: A Novel. S. S Morton. LC 7-32480. (Library of American fiction). 1890. Keystone Publishing Co.
At the Defense of Pittsburgh: Or, The Struggle to Save America's Fighting Steel" Supply. Harrie Irving Hancock. LC 16-22260. (His Conquest of the United States series. vol. III) $0.50). Henry Altemus Company.
At the Departure Gate with a Citizen of the Cosmos. Beredene Jocelyn. 1981. pap. 2.50 (ISBN 0-916786-61-7). St George Bk Serv.
At the Devil's Booth. 1st Ed. Erwin Christian Lessner. LC 52-5548. 1952. Doubleday.
At the Door of the Gate. Forrest Reid, pseud. LC 16-11969. 1916. Houghton Mifflin Company.
At the Earth's Core. Edgar Rice Burroughs. LC 62-17746. 1962. Canaveral Press.
At the Earth's Core. Edgar Rice Burroughs. LC 22-177274. 1922. A. C. McClurg & Co.
At the Earth's Core. Edgar Rice Burroughs. 1976. 1.75. Ace.
At the Earth's Core see Pellucidar Novels.
At the Earth's Core: Pellucidar, Tamar of Pelluicidar. Edgar Rice Burroughs. (Illus.). 9.00 (ISBN 0-8446-1778-4). Peter Smith.
At the Earth's Core; Pellucidar; Tanar of Pellucidar: Three Science Fiction Novels. Illus. by J. Allen St. John, Paul F. Berdanier. Edgar Rice Burroughs. (Dover bk. T1051 rebound). 1966. 4.00. P. Smith.
At the Earth's Core: Pellucidar; Tanar of Pellucidar; Three Science Fiction Novels. Edgar Rice Burroughs. LC 63-17927. (Illus.). 1963. Dover Publications.
At the Edge of the Shadow. 1st Ed. Elizabeth Mitchell Bacon Rodewald. LC 56-5860. Lippincott.
At the End of a Texas Rope. Caddo Cameron. LC 38-206465. 1938. Doubleday, Doran & Company, Inc.
At the End of a Texas Rope. Caddo Cameron. LC 39-16972. 1939. The Sun Dial Press, Inc.
At the End of the Rainbow. Julia A Sabine. LC 8-1365. 1892. T. Whittaker.
At the Eye of the Ocean. Hilbert Schenck. (Orig.). 1980. pap. 2.50 (ISBN 0-671-83265-4, Timescape). PB.
At the Foot of No-Man. Anna Elizabeth Scott Droke. LC 6-46254. Monfort & Company.
At the Foot of Sinai. Georges Eugene Benjamin Clemenceau & Ende, Mrs. Amelia (Kremper) Von, 1865- Tr. LC 22-24684. Bernart C. Richards Company.
At the Foot of the Rainbow. James Beardsley Hendryx. LC 24-213961. 1924. G. P. Putnam's Sons.
At the Foot of the Rainbow. Gene Stratton Porter. LC 76-46527. 1976. 7.95 (ISBN 0-89190-941-9). American Reprint Co.
At the Foot of the Rainbow. Gene Stratton Porter. LC 8-978. 1907. The Outing Publishing Company.
At the Foot of the Rainbow. Gene Stratton Porter. LC 16-8698. 1916. C. Scribner's Sons.
At the Foot of the Rainbow. Gene Stratton Porter. LC 21-8681. 1917. Doubleday, Page & Company.
At the Foot of the Rainbow. Gene Stratton Porter. LC 24-20478. 1919. Doubleday, Page & Company.
At the Foot of the Rainbow. Gene Stratton Porter. LC 21-214664. Grosset & Dunlap.
At the Foot of the Rainbow. Gene Stratton Porter. LC 43-13632. 1943. Triangle Books.
At the Foot of the Rainbow. Gene Stratton-Porter. 258p. 1981. Repr. of 1907 ed. lib. bdg. 30.00 (ISBN 0-89987-767-2). Darby Bks.
At the Foot of the Rainbow. Gene Stratton-Porter. 1974. Repr. of 1907 ed. lib. bdg. 25.00 (ISBN 0-8414-7974-7). Folcroft.
At the Foot of the Rockies. Abbe Carter Goodloe. LC 72-4424. (Short story index reprint series). 1972. 12.00 (ISBN 0-8369-4177-2). Books for Libraries Press.
At the Foot of the Rockies. Abbe Carter Goodloe. LC 5-14445. 1905. C. Scribner's Sons.
At the Gate of Samaria. William John Locke. LC 7-15540. 1907. J. Lane.
At the Gate of Samaria: A Novel. William John Locke. 1894. D. Appleton and Company.
At the Gate of the Fold, a Country Tale. Joseph Smith Fletcher. LC 6-41678. 1896. The Macmillian Company.
At the Ghost Hour. The Fair Abigail. Translated from the German of Paul Heyse. Paul Johann Ludwig Von Heyse. Tr. by Van Santford, Frances A. LC 7-6615. 1894. Dodd, Mead & Company.
At the Ghost Hour. The Forest Laugh. Tr. from the German of Paul Heyse. Paul Johann Von Heyse. Tr. by Van Santford, Frances A. LC 7-6614. 1894. Dodd, Mead & Company.
At the Ghost Hour. The House of the Unbelieving Thomas. Tr. from the German of Paul Heyse. Paul Johann Von Heyse. Tr. by Van Santford, Frances A. LC 7-6613. 1894. Dodd, Mead & Company.
At the Green Dragon. Also, An Idyll of London. Beatrice Harraden. (On cover: Happy thought library no. 31). Optimus Printing Company.
At the Green Dragon: and Other Stories. Beatrice Harraden. (On cover: Seaside library. Pocket ed., no. 2087). 1895. G. Munro's Sons.
At the Hands of Another. Arthur Lyons. LC 82-21315. (Rinehart Suspense Novel). 240p. 13.50 (ISBN 0-03-059616-5). HR&W.
At the Homeopath's. Margaret Chatterjee. (Writers Workshop Greenbird Ser.). 87p. 1975. 12.00 (ISBN 0-88253-504-8); pap. text ed. 5.00 (ISBN 0-88253-503-X). Ind-US Inc.
At the Homepath's and Other Stories. Margaret Chatterjee. (Writers Workshop greenbird book). 1975. (ISBN 0-88253-504-8). Writers Workshop.
At the House of Dree. Gordon Gardiner. 1928. Houghton Mifflin Company.
At the Inn of the Guardian Angel: Retold from the French of Madame la Comtesse De Segur. Sophie Rostopchine Segur & Pendleton, Amena. LC 31-305073. 1931. Houghton Mifflin Company.
At the Jerusalem. Paul Bailey. LC 67-14323. 1967. Atheneum.
At the King's Pleasure. Emma Downing Coolidge. LC 12-31657. 1.50. The C. M. Clark Publishing Co.
At the Last Moment. J. C. Layman. LC 78-63646. 1979. 6.95 o.p. (ISBN 0-533-03994-0). Vantage.
At the Manor When the British Held the Hudson. Mary Breck Sleight. LC 12-22591. 1.25. R. F. Fenno & Company.
At the Mercy of Fate: A Tale of TheShenandoah Valley. Olin Austin Palmer. LC 13-10501. Advance Press.
At the Mercy of the State. Bernie Smade Babcock. 1902. The New Voice Press.
At the Mercy of Tiberius. A Novel. Augusta Jane Evans Wilson. LC 8-37106. G. W. Dillingham Co.
At the Mercy of Tiberius: A Novel. Augusta Jane Evans Wilson. LC 40-130158. A. L. Burt Company.
At the Moon's Inn. Andrew Nelson Lytle. LC 41-23264. The Bobbs-Merrill Company.
At the Moorings. Rosa Nouchette Carey. LC 4-24512. 1904. J. B. Lippincott Company.
At the Mountains of Madness. Howard Phillips Lovecraft. 1964. 12.95 (ISBN 0-87054-027-0). Arkham.
At the Mountains of Madness: And Other Novels. LC 64-55401. 1964. Arkham House.
At the Mountains of Madness: And Other Novels. Howard Phillips Lovecraft. LC 64-55401. 1964. Arkham House.
At the Mountains of Madness & Other Tales of Terror. Howard Phillips Lovecraft. 192p. 1982. pap. 2.25 (ISBN 0-345-30232-X, Del Rey). Ballantine.
At the Mountains of Madness & Other Tales of Terror. Howard Phillips Lovecraft. 1971. pap. 0.95 o.p. (95041-095). Beagle Bks.
At the Narrow Passage. Richard C Meredith. LC 72-94264. 1973. 5.95 (ISBN 0-399-11100-X). Putnam.
At the North Pole. Jules Verne. 3.95 o.p. Assoc Bk.
At the North Pole: Or, The Advertures of Captain Hatteras. Jules Verne. LC 31-19510. Porter & Coates.
At the North Pole: The Adventures of Captain Hatteras. Jules Verne. (Illus.). 1976. Repr. of 1875 ed. lib. bdg. 15.45x (ISBN 0-88411-905-X). Amereon Ltd.
At the Point of a .38. Brett Halliday. (Mike Shayne mystery). 1974. (pbk.) 0.95. Dell.
At the Point of the Sword: A Romance of the Netherlands. Ellery P Ingham. 1962. The Abbey Press.
At the Queen's Mercy. Mabel Fuller Blodgett. LC 6-14215. 1897. Lamson, Wolffe and Company.
At the Red Glove: A Novel; Illustrated by C. S. Reinhart. Katharine Sarah Gadsden MacQuaid. LC 7-20290. 1885. Harper & Brothers.
At the Relton Arms. Evelyn Sharp. LC 8-4794. (On cover: Keynotes series, no. 13). 1895. Roberts Brothers; Etc., Etc.
At the Same Time Tomorrow. Maysie Greig. 1944. Doubleday, Doran and Co., Inc.
At the Shores. Thomas H. Rogers. LC 80-36839. 11.95 (ISBN 0-671-24969-X). Simon and Schuster.
At the Sign of Sagittarius. Richard Basil Ince. LC 79-163030. (Short story index reprint series). 1971. (ISBN 0-8369-3944-1). Books For Libraries Press.
At the Sign of the Blue Anchor: A Tale of 1776. Grace Rose Osgood. LC 9-24446. 1909. 1.50. The C. M. Clark Publishing Company.
At the Sign of the Blue Boar. A Story of the Reign of Charles Ii. Emma Leslie. LC 7-14487. 1885. Phillips & Hunt.
At the Sign of the Burning Bush. A Novel. M Little. LC 10-20745. 1910. H. Holt and Company.
At the Sign of the Cat and Racket: & Other Stories. Honore De Balzac. Tr. by Clara Courtenay Poynter Bell. LC 36-37161. (Half-title: Everyman's library, ed. by Ernest Rhys. Fiction. no. 3495d). 1930. J. M. Dent & Sons, Ltd.
At the Sign of the Dollar. Wallace Irwin. LC 5-33202. 1905. Fox, Duffield & Company.
At the Sign of the Fox: A Romance. Mabel Wright. LC 5-20914. 1905. The Macmillan Company.
At the Sign of the Goat and Compasses: A Novel. Martin Donisthorpe Armstrong. LC 25-157637. 1925. Harper & Brothers.
At the Sign of the Guillotine. Harold Spender. LC 8-14072. The Merriam Company.
At the Sign of the Jack O'Lantern. Myrtle Reed. LC 5-28186. 1905. G. P. Putnam's Sons.
At the Sign of the Lame Dog. Ralph Hale Mottram. LC 33-19083. 1933. Houghton Mifflin Company.
At the Sign of the Oldest House; a Modern Romance. Juliet Wilbor Tompkins. LC 17-30279. The Bobbs-Merrill Company.
At the Sign of the Queen Pedauque. Anatole France, pseud. LC 31-34098. Illustrated Editions Company.
At the Sign of the Queen Pedauque. Anatole France, pseud. Tr. by Jackson, Emillie. Boyd, Ernest Augustus. Limited Editions Club, Inc., New York. LC 34-2487. 1933. Printed for the Members of the Limited Editions Club by the Lakeside Press.
At the Sign of the Queen Pedauque. Anatole France, pseud. LC 32-7347. (Half-title: Universal library). Grosset & Dunlap.
At the Sign of the Red Swan. Ambrose Elwell. LC 19-190538. 1.60. Small, Maynard & Company.
At the Sign of the Reine Pedauque. Anatole France & Book League of America, Inc. LC 44-246238. 1931. The Book League of America.
At the Sign of the Silver Crescent. Helen Choate Pratt Prince. LC 7-30094. 1898. Houghton, Mifflin and Company.
At the Sign of the Silver Cup. Helen Atteridge. LC 27-59425. P. J. Kenedy & Sons.
At the Sign of the Silver Flagon. A Novel. Benjamin Leopold Farjeon. LC 43-31966. 1875. Harper & Brothers.
At the Sign of the Silver Ship. Stanley Hart Cauffman. LC 25-9691. 1925. The Penn Publishing Company.
At the Sign of the Sun: A Novel. Virginia MacFadyen. LC 25-20141. 1925. A. & C. Boni.
At the Sign of the White Swan: A Tale of Old Pennsylvania. Olivia Lovell Wilson. LC 8-37049. Estes and Lauriat.
At the South Gate. Grace Louise Smith Richmond. LC 28-25459. 1928. Doubleday, Doran & Company, Inc.
At the Still Point. Mary Benson. LC 78-91353. 1969. 5.95. Gambit.
At the Stone of Losses. T. Carmi & Grace Schulman. LC 82-17926. (Jewish Poetry Series). 1983. 13.95 (ISBN 0-8276-0218-9). Jewish Publication Society of America.
At the Threshold. Edmond Knowles. (Illus.). 1974. 4.50. E & E Enterprises.
At the Threshold. Nina Picton. LC 7-35911. ("unknown" library v. 20). Cassell Publishing Company.
At the Time Appointed. Anna Maynard Barour. LC 3-10933. 1903. J. B. Lippincott Company.
At the Villa Rose. Alfred Edward Woodley Mason. LC 10-19385. 1910. C. Scribner's Sons.
At the Water's Edge. J. H. Hammill, 3rd. 1972. pap. 4.00 (ISBN 0-9600652-1-0). J H Hammill.
At the Wind's Edge. Kathryn Davis. (Dakotas Ser.). 384p. (Orig.). 1983. pap. 3.25 (ISBN 0-523-41459-5). Pinnacle Bks.
At the World's Mercy. Florence Alice Price James. (On cover: Seaside library. Pocket ed., no. 182). 1884. G. Munro.
At the World's Mercy. Florence Alice Price James. (On cover: Lovell's library, v. 20, no. 980). 1887. J. W. Lovell Company.
At Top of Tobin. Stanley Olmsted. LC 26-926096. 1926. L. MacVeagh, The Dial Press.
At Tuxter's. George Brown Burgin. LC 6-18662. (On cover: The Hudson library, v. 10). 1895. G. P. Putnam's Sons.
At War As Children: A Novel. Kit Reed, pseud. LC 64-11455. 1964. Farrar, Straus.
At War with Herself. Charlotte Mary Brame. (On cover: Seaside library. Pocket ed. no. 923). G. Munro.
At War with Herself. Charlotte Mary Brame. LC 44-39932. (Seaside Library. Pocket Ed.). (On cover: Seaside library. Pocket ed. No. 287: No. 287). G. Munro.
At War with Herself. Charlotte Mary Brame. LC 4363. (Bertha M. Clay Library). (Bertha M. Clay library, no. 12: No. 12). 1900. Street & Smith.
At War with Passion. Benet Costa. LC 34-920717. Wetzel Publishing Co., Inc.
At Wit's End. Erma Bombeck. 1979. pap. 2.50 (ISBN 0-449-23784-2, Crest). Fawcett.
At You-All's House" A Missouri Nature Story. James Newton Baskett. 1898. The Macmilan Company.
At Your Age, Miss Russell? Lydia Heermann. LC 72-120031. 1970. 3.50. Zondervan Pub. House.
At Your Service. Albert Edward Ullman. LC 33-2070. The Macaulay Company.
Atague Diabolico. new ed. Joseph Rosenberger. Tr. by Margarita O. Castro from Eng. (Compadre Collection Ser., el Mercader De la Muerte: No. 5). Orig. Title: Satan Strike. 160p. (Span.). 1975. pap. 0.85 (ISBN 0-88473-505-2). Fiesta Pub.
Atahualpa, a Ta Wal Pa. Inca Chief, a Romance of Ancient Peru. June Cullison Otjen. LC 38-1580. Burton Publishing Company.
Atala. Francois Auguste Rene De Chateaubriand. Tr. by Harry, James Spence. LC 6-23437. Cassell & Company, Limited.
Atala and Rene. Francois August Rene de Chateaubriand. LC 63-24894. (Oxford library of French classics). 1963. Oxford University Press.
Atala & Rene. Francois-Rene De Chateaubriand. Tr. by Rayner Heppenstall. 1963. 2.50x o.p. (ISBN 0-19-255202-3). Oxford U Pr.
Atala: Or, The Love and Constancy of Two Savages in the Desert. Francois Auguste Rene De Chateaubriand. Tr. by Bingham, Caleb. Ed. by Schwartz, William Leonard. (Standford miscellany). Stanford University Press.
Atala. Rene. A New Translation by Irving Putter. Francois Auguste Rene De Chateaubriand. LC 52-1302. (MLA translation series). 1952. University of California Press.
Atalanta's Race: And Other Tales from The Earthly Paradise. William Morris & Adams, Oscar Fay, 1855-1919, Ed. LC 12-36886. 1888. Ticknor and Company.
Ataque En California. new ed. Don Pendleton. Tr. by O. J. Blanco from Eng. (Pimienta Collection Ser: El Verdugo Ser., No. 11). Orig. Title: California Hit. 160p. (Span.). 1974. pap. 0.75 (ISBN 0-88473-311-4). Fiesta Pub.
Atavar: A Craig Kennedy Novel. Arthur Benjamin Reeve. LC 24-11233. Harper & Brothers.
Athabasca. Alistair MacLean. LC 80-1067. 1980. 9.95 (ISBN 0-385-17204-4). Doubleday.
Athabasca. Alistair MacLean. LC 80-29312. 1981. 13.95 (ISBN 0-8161-3147-3). G. K. Hall.
Athaliah: A Novel. Joseph H Greene. LC 6-455600. 1869. Carleton; Etc., Etc.
Athalie. Robert William Chambers. LC 15-15607. 1915. 1.40. D. Appleton and Company.
Athalie. Robert William Chambers. LC 24-28535. 1917. A. L. Burt Company.
Athalie: Or, A Southern Villeggiatura: "A Winter's Tale.". Sarah Anne Dorsey. LC 6-33700. 1872. Claxton, Remsen, and Haffelfinger.
Athalinthia: Seven Stories Tr. from the Metrelingua Perme and Extended with Images & Diagrams. William Addison Dwiggins. LC 49-1801.
Atheist: A Novel. William Charles Oursler. LC 65-15776. 1965. P. S. Eriksson.

Atheist's Mass. Honore De Balzac. Tr. by Clara Courtenay Poynter Bell. LC 36-37114. (Half-title: Everyman's library, ed. by Ernest Rhys. Fiction. no. 229). 1929. J. M. Dent & Sons, Ltd.

Athelsons. Jocelyn Kettle. 1973. 1.50. Dell.

Athelsons. Jocelyn Kettle. LC 79-175265. 1972. 6.95. Putnam.

Athenian. Elbert L Harris. LC 57-3104.

Atherton: And Other Tales. Mary Russell Mitford. LC 7-19184. 1854. Ticknor and Fields.

Atherwood Terminal. Henry Henn. 1979. pap. 1.95 (ISBN 0-532-19227-3). Woodhill.

Athlete's Conquest: A Novel. Bernarr Adolphus Macfadden. LC 10-1609. (On cover: Brown library, no. 9). 1892. I. H. and C. W. Brown Publishing Co.

Athlete's Conquest: The Romance of an Athlete. Bernarr Adolphus Macfadden. LC 4-3589. The Physical Culture Pub. Co.

Athletic Sexperts. Jack Benjamin. (Orig.). 1969. pap. 1.95 o.p. (6060). Brandon.

Athmani. Robert Browne. LC 72-80763. 1972. 5.95 o.p. (ISBN 0-8128-1501-7). Stein & Day.

Athonia: Or, The Original Four Hundred. H. George Schuette. LC 10-8529. 1910. The Author.

Atla: A Story of the Lost Island. Ann Eliza Brainerd Smith. LC 8-8644. 1886. Harper & Brothers.

Atlan. Jane Gaskell. LC 77-77326. (Gaskell, Jane, 1941-. The Atlan Ser.: No. 3). 1977. 7.95 (ISBN 0-312-05940-X). St. Martin's Press.

Atlan in Danger. Kurt Brand. (Perry Rhodan, 82). 1975. (pbk.) 1.25. Ace Books.

Atlanta. Ralph Dennis. 1975. (pbk.) 1.50. Popular Library.

Atlanta. Milton Macklin. LC 78-65231. 1979. 2.50. Avon Books.

Atlanta Deathwatch. Ralph Dennis. (Hardman,#1). 1974. (pbk.) 0.95. Popular Library.

Atlanta in the South. A Romance. Maud Howe Elliott. LC 6-37785. 1886. Roberts Brothers.

Atlantean Document: A Novel. S. L. Smoke. LC 79-19737. 10.00 (ISBN 0-88280-077-9). ETC Publications.

Atlantean Nights' Entertainments. Edgar Pangborn. 1981. 17.95t (ISBN 0-930800-08-7). Pennyfarthing.

Atlanteans. David Hyatt. LC 79-11599. 1979. 4.95 (ISBN 0-915442-92-2). Donning Co.

Atlantic Avenue. Albert Halper. LC 56-8076. (Dell first edition, 94). 1956. Dell Pub. Co.

Atlantic City. Warren B. Murphy & Frank Stevens. 1979. pap. 2.50 (ISBN 0-523-40445-X). Pinnacle Bks.

Atlantic City Murder Mystery. Norman Goldsmith. LC 36-83833. The Macaulay Company.

Atlantic City Proof. Christopher Cook Gilmore. LC 78-14816. 8.95 (ISBN 0-671-24291-1). Simon and Schuster.

Atlantic Fury. Hammond Innes. 320p. Repr. of 1971 ed. lib. bdg. 13.30x (ISBN 0-88411-178-4). Amereon Ltd.

Atlantic Fury. Hammond Innes. 1962. 5.95 o.p. (ISBN 0-394-41575-2). Knopf.

Atlantic Harbors: Stories of People, Places, and Events on Vessels, in Harbors, and on Land, with the Historical and Geographical Backdrops of Storied Atlantic Provinces of Canada. Roland Harold Sherwood. LC 75-323107. 1972. Lancelot Press.

Atlantic Narratives: Modern Short Stories. The Atlantic Monthly. Ed. by Thomas, Charles Swain. LC 18-26401. The Atlantic Monthly Press.

Atlantic Narratives: Modern Short Stories. 2d series. ed. The Atlantic Monthly. Ed. by Thomas, Charles Swain. LC 18-22965. The Atlantic Monthly Press.

Atlantic Scramble. Don Pendleton & Gar Wilson. (Phoenix Force Ser.). 192p. 1982. pap. 1.95 (ISBN 0-373-61303-2, Pub. by Worldwide). Harlequin Bks.

Atlantic Tales. A Collection of Stories from the Atlantic Monthly. Edward Everett Hale et al. LC 6-3840. 1866. Ticknor and Fields.

Atlantic Tragedy. William Clark Russell. LC 8-1799. 1899. D. Biddle.

Atlantic Venture. John Groser. 1968. 6.00 o.p. De Graff.

Atlantis: A Novel. Gerhart Johann Robert Hauptmann & Seltzer, Mrs. Adele Szold, 1876- Tr. LC 12-29133. 1912. B. W. Huebech.

Atlantis Fire: A Novel. Gary Goshgarian. LC 79-23686. (Illus.). 8.95 (ISBN 0-8037-0337-6). Dial Press.

Atlantis: The Antediluvian World. Ignatius Donnelly. Ed. by E. F. Bleiler. LC 76-24138. 518p. 1976. pap. 5.00 (ISBN 0-486-23371-5). Dover.

Atlantis Times Two: A Science Fiction Tale Out of Time. R. C. Rapier. (O.s.i.). 1976. 5.00x o.s.i. R C Rapier.

Atlas of Fantasy. J. B. Post. (Illus.). 1979. pap. 8.95 (ISBN 0-345-27399-0). Ballantine.

Atlas Shrugged. Ayn Rand. LC 57-10033. 1957. Random House.

Atman: The Documents in a Strange Case. Francis Howard Williams. LC 8-36918. Cassell Publishing Company.

Atmosphere of Love. Andre Maurois. Tr. by Joseph Collins. LC 29-17386. 1929. D. Appleton & Company.

Atmosphere of Love: Tr. from French by Joseph Collins. Andre Maurois. 1965. 4.50, 1.75 pap.,. Ungar.

Atom at Spithead. Arthur Durham Divine. LC 53-1754. 1953. Macmillan.

Atom Clock. Lengyel. pap. 1.00. Fantasy Pub Co.

Atom Hell of Grautier. Kurt Mahr. (Perry Rhodan#71). (Illus.). 1975. (pbk.) 1.25. Ace Books.

Atom Station. Halldor Laxness, pseud. LC 81-85725. 208p. 1982. 16.95 (ISBN 0-933256-31-0, Dist. by Watts); pap. 8.95 (ISBN 0-531-07348-3). Second Chance.

Atomic Murder. Leonard Reginald Gribble. LC 47-31043. 1947. Ziff-Davis Pub. Co.

Atomic Phantasy: Krakatit, a Novel. Translated by Lawrence Hyde. Karel Capek. LC 51-13904. 1951. Arts.

Atomic Town. Nelson W Hope. LC 55-598. Comet Press Books.

Atomica. Steve Karpf & Elinor Karpf. (Orig.). 1981. pap. write for info. (ISBN 0-440-10384-3). Dell.

Atoms and Evil. Robert Bloch. LC 77-366878. 1976. 2.80 (ISBN 0-7091-5086-5). Hale.

Atoms of Empire. Charles John Cutcliffe Wright Hyne. LC 77-103519. (Short story index reprint series). 1969. Books for Libraries Press.

Atoms of Empire. Charles John Cutcliffe Wright Hyne. LC 4-31008. 1904. The Macmillan Company.

Atoms to Ashes. J. C. Garcia. 1965. 3.00 o.p. (ISBN 0-8059-0098-5). Dorrance.

Atomsk: A Novel of Suspense. by carmichael smith pseud. ed. Paul Myron Anthony Linebarger. LC 49-299974. 1949. Duell, Sloan and Pearce.

Atone with Evil. Jean Fiedler. 1976. (pbk.) 1.25. Bantam Books.

Atonement of Ashley Morden. Fred Bodsworth. LC 64-8222. 1964. Dodd, Mead.

Atonement of Leam Dundas. Elizabeth Lynn Linton. LC 41-41841. 1876. J. B. Lippincott & Co.

Atonement: Or, Fallen and Risen. Rudolph Leonhart. 1895. Roller Printing Co.

Atrip into Town. 1st Ed. Michael Rubin. LC 61-10249. 1961. Harper.

Atrocity. Ka-Tzetnik. 1963. 4.95 (ISBN 0-8184-0100-1). Lyle Stuart.

Atrocity: A Novel. Jackson Burgess. LC 61-5683. 1961. Putnam.

Atrocity Exhibition. J. G. Ballard. 4.95 o.p. (ISBN 0-525-05995-4). Dutton.

Atrocity Exhibition. J. G. Ballard. 1970. 4.95 o.p. Doubleday.

Atrocity Exhibition see Love & Napalm: Export U.S.A.

ATS Mystery. John Russell Warren. LC 44-1898. 1943. Hurst & Blackett, Ltd.

ATS Mystery. John Russell Warren. LC 44-4873. 1944. The Macmillan Company.

Atta: A Novel of a Most Extraordinary Adventure. Francis Rufus Bellamy. LC 53-9425. 1953. A. A. Wyn.

Atta: A Novel of a Most Extraordinary Adventure. Francis Rufus Bellamy. LC 55-16486. (Ace double novel books, D-79). Ace Books.

Atta: A Novel of a Most Extraordinary Adventure. Francis Rufus Bellamy. LC 53-9425. 1974. (pbk.) 0.95 (ISBN 0-671-77692-4). Pocket Books.

Attache. Thomas Chandler Haliburton. LC 3-21962. (With Herbert, H. W. Marmaduke Wyvil. New York, 1843). 1843. J. Winchester.

Attachments. Judith Rossner. LC 77-6421. 9.95 (ISBN 0-671-22591-X). Simon and Schuster.

Attachments. Judith Rossner. (Kangaroo Book). 1978. 2.50 (ISBN 0-671-81664-0). Pocket Books.

Attack. Collis Ehrlich. 160p. (Orig.). 1981. pap. 2.25 (ISBN 0-345-28476-3). Ballantine.

Attack! Leland Shattuck Jamieson. LC 40-10770. 1940. W. Morrow & Company.

Attack Alarm. Ralph Hammond-Innes. LC 42-3950. 1942. The Macmillan Company.

Attack Alarm. Hammond Innes. LC 42-3950. 1942. The Macmillan Company.

Attack at Fort Lookout: A Story of the Old Northwestern Frontier. Russell Potter Reeder. LC 59-5560. 1959. Duell, Sloan and Pearce.

Attack from Atlantis. pap. 0.75 o.p. (5306, Tempo). G&D.

Attack from Atlantis. Lester Del Rey. 176p. 1982. pap. 1.95 (ISBN 0-345-30501-9, Del Rey). Ballantine.

Attack from the Unseen. Darlton, Clark. (Perry Rhodan,#50). 1974. (pbk.) 0.95. Ace Books.

Attack in the Desert. Michael Home, pseud. LC 41-28080. 1942. W. Morrow & Co.

Attack In the Forest. Harold Calin. 288p. 1982. pap. 2.75 o.s.i. (ISBN 0-8439-1176-X, Leisure Bks). Nordon Pubns.

Attack on America. Ared White. LC 39-24438. 1939. Houghton Mifflin Company.

Attack on Vienna. Alan Nixon. LC 70-176064. 1972. 5.95. St. Martin's Press.

Attack the Lusitania! Raymond Hitchcock. LC 79-22387. 9.95. St. Martin's Press.

Attar's Revenge. Robert Graham. (Attar the Merman,#1). 1975. (pbk.) 0.95 (ISBN 0-671-77988-5). Pocket Books.

Attempt. John Hopkins. LC 67-13495. 1967. Viking Press.

Attempted Assassination of John F. Kennedy. Lucas Webb. LC 76-40282. 1976. 1.95 (ISBN 0-87877-204-9). Borgo Press.

Attendance List for a Funeral: Stories Tr. from German by Leila Vennewitz. 1st Ed. Alexander Kluge. LC 66-19464. 1966. 4.95. McGraw.

Attendant's Confession, the Fortune Teller, & Life. Joaquim M. Assis. Ed. & tr. by Isaac Goldberg. (International Pocket Library). pap. 3.00. Branden.

Attending Physician. R. B Dominic. LC 79-1702. 8.95 (ISBN 0-06-011084-8). Harper & Row.

Attention: Miss Wells. Sylvia Paul Jerman, pseud. LC 38-6965. Harcourt, Brace and Company.

Attic. Katherine Dunn. LC 77-95995. 1970. 4.95. Harper & Row.

Attic Guest: A Novel. Robert Edward Knowles. 1.20. F. H. Revell Company.

Attic Light. Allston James. LC 78-31541. 7.95 (ISBN 0-88496-094-3). Capra Press.

Attic Philosopher in Paris. Emile Souvestre. LC 99-3308. 1899. T. Y. Crowell & Company.

Attic Philosopher in Paris. Emile Souvestre. LC 4921. 1900. W. B. Conkey Co.

Attic Philosopher in Paris: Or, A Peep at the World from a Garret; Being the Journal of a Happy Man. From the French. Emile Souvestre. LC 51-54805. A. L. Burt Co.

Attic Philosopher in Paris: Or, A Peep at the World from a Garret. Emile Souvestre. LC 31-19508. (Appletons' new handy-volume series. 31). 1884. D. Appleton and Company.

Attic Philosopher in Paris: Or, A Peep at the World from a Garret, Being the Journal of a Happy Man. Emile Souvestre. LC 3-219423. 1895. D. Appleton and Company.

Attic Philosopher in Paris: Or, A Peep at the World from a Garret, Being the Journal of a Happy Man. Emile Souvestre. LC 4-21342. 1901. D. Appleton and Company.

Attic Philosopher in Paris. Or, A Peep at the World from a Garret. Being the Journal of a Happy Man. Emile Souvestre. LC 3-21940. 1854. D. Appleton & Company.

"Attic" Philosopher: Un Philosophe Sons les Toits. Emile Souvestre. LC 42-2247. 1910. Current Literature Publishing Company.

Attic Philospher in Paris: Or, A Peep at the World from a Garret, Being the Journal of a Happy Man. Emile Souvestre. LC 3-21943. 1892. D. Appleton and Company.

Attic Room. Katherine Wolffe. LC 42-25363. 1942. W. Morrow & Company.

Attic Rope. Dorothy Daniels. (Orig.). 1970. pap. 0.95 o.s.i. (75-228). Lancer.

Attic Tenant. Mary Dwinell Chellis. LC 6-23424. 1890. The National Temperance Society and Publication House.

Attila. A Romance. George Payne Rainsford James. LC 42-48367. 1837. Harper & Brothers.

Attila, a Romance of Old Aquileia. Paolo Ettore Santangelo & Dole, Nathan Haskell, 1852- Tr. LC 29-8394. Thomas Y. Crowell Company.

Attila and His Conquerors. A Story of the Days of St. Patrick and St. Leo the Great. Elizabeth Rundle Charles & Society for Promoting Christian Knowledge. Tract Committee. LC 1-223. 1894. Society for Promoting Christian Knowledge.

Attila the Hun: A Novel by the Great German Novelist. Felix Ludwig Sophus Dahn. LC 16-7016. 1891. The Minerva Publishing Company.

Attitude. Alan H. McDougall. 3.95 o.p. Vantage.

Attorney. Harold Q. Masur. LC 72-11641. 1973. 6.95 (ISBN 0-394-46517-2). Random House.

Attorney. Harold Q. Masur. 1974. (pbk.) 1.50. Bantam Books.

Attorney Conspiracy. C. Terry Cline. LC 82-72059. 15.50 (ISBN 0-87795-371-6). Arbor House.

Attorney: Or, The Correspondence of John Quod. John Treat Irving. LC 7-9707. 1853. R. M. De Witt.

Attorney: Or, The Correspondence of John Quod. new and rev. ed.... ed. John Treat Irving. LC 37-32810. 1853. S. Hueston.

Attorney: Or, The Correspondence of John Quod. John Treat Irving. LC 45-47536. 1842. R. M. De Witt.

Attorneys at Law, Forbes, Hathaway, Bryan Hathaway, Bryan & Dovore. James Reid Parker. LC 41-20731. 1941. Doubleday, Doran and Company, Inc.

Attraction of the Compass: A Romance of the North, Based Upon Facts of a Personal Experience. Howard Lewis Dodge. LC 12-14401. 1912. 1.25. Press of Dove & Courtney.

Attraction of the Compass: Or, The Blonde Eskimo; a Romance of the North, Based Upon Facts of a Personal Experience. 2d ed. Howard Lewis Dodge. LC 17-4709. 1916. Seaside Printing Co.

Au Pair Girls. Jackson Short. 1974. (pbk.) 1.50. Warner Paperback Library.

Aubade. Kenneth Martin. LC 58-13333. 1958. Citadel Press.

Aubrey Dene. Sylvia Denys Hooke. LC 30-525028. 1930. Longmans, Green and Co.

Auburn and Freckles. Marie Louise More Marsh. LC 13-19072. 1913. 1.00. F. G. Browne & Co.

Aucassin and Nicolete. Tr. by Lang, Andrew. LC 37-29182. 1936. Holiday House.

Aucassin & Nicolete: Being a Lovve Story. Tr. by Lang, Andrew. LC 3-1774. 1899. The Roycrofters.

Aucassin & Nicolete: Done into English. Tr. by Lang, Andrew. LC 1-26675. (Half-title: Old world series. no. 2). 1895. T. B. Mosher.

Aucassin & Nicolete: Done into English. Tr. by Lang, Andrew. LC 17-30427. (Half-title: Old world series. no. 2). 1898. T. B. Mosher.

Aucassin and Nicolette. Tr. by Moyer, Edward Francis. LC 38-16572. 1937. N. C., R. Linker.

Aucassin & Nicolette: An Old-French Love Story. 2d ed. the text collated afresh with the manuscript at paris, the translation revised & the introduction rewritten. ed. Tr. by Bourdillon, Francis William. LC 24-6293. 1897. Macmillan and Co., Limited.

Aucassin & Nicolette & Other Medieval Romances & Legends. Ed. by Eugene Mason. 1958. pap. 3.45 o.p. (ISBN 0-525-47019-0). Dutton.

Aucassin & Nicolette: Kritischer Text Mit Paradigmen & Glossar. Ed. by Hermann Suchier & Walther Suchier. LC 80-2239. Repr. of 1932 ed. 31.00 (ISBN 0-404-19035-9). AMS Pr.

Aucassin et Nicolette and Four Lais of Marie De France. Ed. by Williams, Edwin Bucher. LC 33-2896. 1938. F. S. Crofts & Co.

Auction. George Agnew Chamberlain. LC 33-6057. The Bobbs-Merrill Company.

Auction. A. Woodfin. LC 74-31240. (Flowering of the Novel). 1975. 25.00 (ISBN 0-8240-1153-8). Garland Pub.

Auction: A Modern Novel, 1760, 2 vols. in 1. A. Woodfin. Ed. by Michael F. Shugrue. (Flowering of the Novel, 1740-1775 Ser: Vol. 54). 1974. lib. bdg. 50.00x (ISBN 0-8240-1153-8). Garland Pub.

Auction Block: A Novel of New York Life. Rex Ellingwood Beach. LC 14-17991. 1914. 1.35. Harper & Brothers.

Auction Block: A Novel of New York Life. Rex Ellingwood Beach. LC 28-179145. A. L. Burt Company.

Auction Mart. Sybil Irene Eleanor Taylor Cookson. LC 15-13212. 1915. J. Lane.

Auction Mart. Sydney Tremayne. LC 15-13212. 1915. John Lane.

Auctioneer. Joan Samson. LC 75-23337. 1975. 7.95 (ISBN 0-671-22139-6). Simon and Schuster.

Auctioneer. Joan Samson. 1977. 1.95 (ISBN 0-380-00842-4). Avon.

Auctioning of Mary Angel. Coningsby William Dawson. LC 30-23441. 1930. Doubleday, Doran & Company, Inc.

Audacious Adventures of Miles McConaughy: An Epic of the Merchant Marine. Arthur Douglas Howden Smith. LC 18-11363. George H. Doran Company.

Audacious Adventuress. Barbara Cartland. 1972. pap. 1.25 o.p. (V2823). Pyramid Pubns.

Audacious Adventuress. Barbara Cartland. 1977. pap. 1.50 o.p. (ISBN 0-515-04345-1). BJ Pub Group.

Audacious Miss. Joan Vincent. (Candlelight Regency Ser.: No. 708). (Orig.). 1982. pap. 1.75 (ISBN 0-440-10228-6). Dell.

Audacity. Ben Ames Williams. LC 24-4705. E. P. Dutton & Company.

Auden Group. Ed. by Ronald Carter. 1981. pap. 30.00x (ISBN 0-333-29329-0, Pub. by Macmillan England). State Mutual Bk.

Audition. Karl Rockwood. pap. 1.95 o.p. (ISBN 0-87056-214-2, 6214). Brandon.

Audrey. Mary Johnston. LC 2-4948. 1902. Houghton, Mifflin and Company.

Audrey Craven. May Sinclair. 1906. H. Holt and Company.

Audrey-Gore Legacy. Edward Gorey. (Illus.). 64p. 1982. pap. 4.95 (ISBN 0-312-92032-6). Congdon & Weed.

Audrey Rose. Frank De Felitta. 1976. 1.95. Warner Books.

Audrey Rose: A Novel. Frank De Felitta. LC 75-24875. 1975. (ISBN 0-399-11606-0). Putnam.

Auerbach Will. Stephen Birmingham. 416p. 1983. 16.45 (ISBN 0-316-09646-6). Little.

Auf Wiedersehen, Captain Roman. K. Allan Kelley. LC 67-28337. 1968. Dorrance.

Auf Zwei Planeten see Two Planets.

August. Knut Hamsun & Gay-Tifft, Eugene, Tr. LC 31-29962. 1931. Coward-McCann, Inc.

August First. Mary Raymond Shipman Andrews & Murray, Roy Irving, Joint Author. LC 15-6337. 1915. C. Scribner's Sons.

August Folly. Angela Mackail Thirkell. LC 37-427729. 1937. A. A. Knopf.

August Heat. Richard Dokey. LC 81-23346. 1982. 10.50 (ISBN 0-931704-09-X) (ISBN 0-931704-08-1). Story Press.

August Incident. Amber Dean. LC 51-5561. 1951. Published for the Crime Club by Doubleday.

August Is a Wicked Month. Edna O'Brien. LC 65-17101. (Plume book). 1975. (pbk.) 2.95. New American Library.

August Is a Wicked Month, a Novel. Edna O'Brien. LC 65-17101. 1965. Simon and Schuster.

August Nineteen Fourteen. Aleksandr Isaevich Solzhenitsyn. 736p. 1974. pap. 2.50 (ISBN 0-553-02997-5). Bantam.

August Strangers. Mike Slosberg. LC 76-30811. 1977. 7.95 (ISBN 0-8037-0449-6). Dial Press.

August Strangers. Mike Slosberg. 1981. 2.50 (ISBN 0-425-04058-5). Berkley Books.

August 1914. Aleksandr Isaevich Solzhenitsyn. LC 75-318838. (Illus.). 1974. 0.75 (ISBN 0-14-003739-X). Penguin.

August 1914. Aleksandr Isaevich Solzhenitsyn. LC 78-178883. 10.00 (ISBN 0-374-10684-3). Farrar, Straus and Giroux.

August 22nd. Upton Beall Sinclair. LC 66-130. 1965. Award Books.

Augusta Played: A Novel. Kelly Cherry. LC 78-25666. 1979. 9.95 (ISBN 0-395-27573-3). Houghton Mifflin.

Augusta Played: A Novel. Kelly Cherry. 1980. 2.25 (ISBN 0-445-04561-2). Popular Library.

Augusta, the First. Katheryn Kimbrough. (Saga of the Phenwick women,#1). 1975. (pbk.) 1.25. Popular Library.

Augusta, the Second. Katheryn Kimbrough, pseud. (Saga of the Phenwick Women: No. 28). 1979. pap. 1.75 (ISBN 0-445-04472-1). Popular Lib.

Augustine; or, The Mysterious Beggar. From the French of Adrien Lemercier. Adrien Lemercier. 1873. D. & J. Sadlier & Co.

Augustus. Gunther Birkenfeld. Tr. by Ray, Winifred. LC 36-1850. Liveright Publishing Corp.

Augustus. Hermann Hesse. Ed. by Thomas E. Colby, 3rd. Bd. with Dichter; Mensch mit Namen Ziegler. (Ger.). 1958. pap. 1.95x (ISBN 0-393-09615-7, NortonC). Norton.

Augustus. John Edward Williams. (Laurel leaf edition, 1292). 1973. (pbk.) 1.50. Dell Books.

Augustus. John Edward Williams. LC 72-78984. (Illus.). 1972. 7.95 (ISBN 0-670-14112-7). Viking Press.

Augustus: A Novel. John Edward Williams. LC 79-10250. (Illus.). 1979. 2.95 (ISBN 0-14-005127-9). Penguin Books.

Augustus Carp, Esq. Augustus Carp. LC 24-26745. 1924. Houghton Mifflin Company.

Augustus Jones, Jr. The Little Brother and Other Stories. Fitz Hugh Ludlow. 1892. Lee and Shepard.

Auld Licht Idylls. James Matthew Barrie. 1895. R. F. Fenno & Company.

Auld Licht Idylls. cameo ed. James Matthew Barrie. 1897. C. Scribner's Sons.

Auld Licht Idylls. James Matthew Barrie. (On cover: Seaside library. Pocket ed. no. 2099). G. Munro's Sons.

Auld Licht Idylls & Better Dead. facsimile ed. James Matthew Barrie. LC 76-106246. (Short Story Index Reprint Ser.). 1896. 16.00 (ISBN 0-8369-3282-X). Ayer Co.

Auld Licht Idylls. Better Dead. James Matthew Barrie. LC 76-106246. (Short story index reprint series). (Illus.). 1970. Books for Libraries Press.

Auld Licht Idyls. James Matthew Barrie. LC 6-8644. Lovell, Coryell & Co.

Auld Licht Manse, and Other Sketches. James Matthew Barrie. LC 78-116936. (Short story index reprint series). 1970. Books for Libraries Press.

Auld Licht Manse and Other Sketches. James Matthew Barrie. LC 6-8646. 1893. J. Knox & Co.

Aunt Abby's Neighbors. Annie Trumbull Slosson. LC 2-20390. 1902. F. H. Revell Company.

Aunt Amity's Silver Wedding, and Other Stories. Ruth McEnery Stuart. LC 79-140344. (Short story index reprint series). (Illus.). 1970. Books for Libraries Press.

Aunt Amity's Silver Wedding: And Other Stories. Ruth McEnery Stuart. 1909. The Century Co.

Aunt Anne. Lucy Lane Clifford. LC 4-15291. 1892. Harper & Brothers.

Aunt Anne: A Novel. Lucy Lane Clifford. 1894. Harper & Brothers.

Aunt Beardie. Joseph Shearing. LC 40-7921. Harrison-Hilton Books.

Aunt Bel. Guy McCrone. LC 49-8319. 1949. Farrar, Straus.

Aunt Belindy's Points of View, and A Modern Mrs. Malaprop: Typical Character Sketches. Lydia Hoyt Farmer. The Merriam Company.

Aunt Billy: And Other Sketches. Eugenia Laura Morris. LC 7-10953. 1896. Lee and Shepard.

Aunt Crete's Emancipation. Grace Livingston Hill. LC 11-17627. The Golden Rule Company.

Aunt Diana. Rosa Nouchette Carey. LC 6-23109. (On cover: Seaside library. Pocket ed., no. 1135). G. Munro.

Aunt Diana. Rosa Nouchette Carey. LC 16-13112. 1909. J. B. Lippincott Company.

Aunt Dice: the Story of a Faithful Slave. Nina Hill Robinson. LC 72-2036. (Black Heritage Library Collection). 1972. 9.50 (ISBN 0-8369-9058-7). Books for Libraries Press.

Aunt Dice: The Story of a Faithful Slave. Nina Hill Robinson. LC 7-42176. 1897. Publishing House of the M. E. Church, South, Barbee & Smith, Agents.

Aunt Dinah's Pledge. Mary Dwinell Chellis. LC 6-23421. 1869. National Temperance Society and Publication House.

Aunt Dorothy: An Old Virginia Plantation Story. Margaret Junkin Preston. LC 72-1508. (Black Heritage Library Collection). (Illus.). 1972. 9.00 (ISBN 0-8369-9050-1). Books for Libraries Press.

Aunt Dorothy: An Old Virginia Plantation-Story. Margaret Junkin Preston. LC 7-30115. A. D. F. Randolph and Co.

Aunt Elsa. Edwin George Pinkham & Chappell, Warren, Illus. LC 41-51541. 1941. A. A. Knopf.

Aunt' Emily" Or, A Black Woman with a White Heart. Richard Welbourne Lewis. LC 32-5591. The Good Books Co.

Aunt Hepsy's Foundling. A Novel. Bertha Jane Grundy Laffan. LC 21-153631. (Seaside library, v. 44, no. 906). 1880. G. Munro.

Aunt Honor's Keepsake. A Chapter from Life. Mary Anne Madden Sadlier. LC 8-1644. (On cover: Parlor & cottage library). 1866. D. & J. Sadlier & Co.

Aunt Ivy Didditt: A Burlesque. Eleanor Green Gless. LC 49-140989. 1948. Chapman & Grimes.

Aunt Jane. Jennette Barbour Perry Lee. LC 15-186955. 1915. C. Scribner's Sons.

Aunt Jane McPhipps and Her Baby Blue Chips. Frances V Rummell. LC 60-13895. 1960. Prentice- Hall.

Aunt Jane of Kentucky. Eliza Caroline Calvert Obenchain. LC 30-12341. 1922. A. L. Burt Company.

Aunt Jane of Kentucky. Eliza Caroline Calvert Obenchain. 1907. Little, Brown, and Company.

Aunt Jessie. Isabella Holt. LC 42-5124. 1942. The Bobbs-Merril Company.

Aunt Jimmy's Will. Mabel Osgood Wright. 1903. The Macmillan Company.

Aunt Julia & the Scriptwriter. Mario Vargas Llosa. Tr. by Helen R. Lane from Span. 1982. 16.95 (ISBN 0-374-10691-6). FS&G.

Aunt Kipp. Louisa May Alcott. 1976. Repr. of 1868 ed. 25.00 o.p. (ISBN 0-403-05868-6, Regency). Scholarly.

Aunt Leanna: Or, Early Scenes in Kentucky. Elizabeth A. Roe. LC 9-3040. 1855. Pub. for the Author.

Aunt Liefy. Annie Trumbull Slosson. A. D. F. Randolph & Co.

Aunt Liza's "Praisin' Gate,". Effie Graham. LC 16-20108. 1916. 0.75. A. C. McClurg & Co.

Aunt Margot and Other Stories. Doris Peel. LC 35-1830. 1935. Houghton Mifflin Company.

Aunt Maud. Ernest James Oldmeadow. 1908. The McClure Company.

Aunt Minnie, the Pastor's Housekeeper. Auleen Bordeaux Eberhardt. LC 53-12821. 1953. Newman Press.

Aunt of England: An Account of the Bitter Fight Between Charlotte, Duchess of Hampshire on Her Eightieth Birthday in 1860 and Her Favourite and Lovely Granddaughter, Who, Imbued with the Fresh Ideas of Women's Freedom by Florence Nightingale, Revolted Against Traditions in the Vital Matter of Love. Cosmo Hamilton. LC 42-8905. 1942. Hutchinson & Company.

Aunt Olive in Bohemia: Or, The Intrusions of a Fairy Godmother. Leslie Moore. LC 13-8760. 1.25. Hodder & Stoughton, George H. Doran Company.

Aunt Parker. A Novel. Benjamin Leopold Farjeon. (Harper's Franklin square library. no. 513). 1886. Harper & Brothers.

Aunt Patty's Scrap-Bag. Caroline Lee Whiting Hentz. LC 7-4131. T. B. Peterson & Brothers.

Aunt Phillis's Cabin. Mary Henderson Eastman. LC 68-57524. (Muckrakers Ser.: Vol. 24). 1969. Repr. of 1852 ed. lib. bdg. 9.00x o.p. (ISBN 0-8398-0450-4). Gregg.

Aunt Phillis's Cabin: Or, Southern Life As It Is. Mary Henderson Eastman. LC 68-58054. (Illus.). 1968. Negro Universities Press.

Aunt Phillis's Cabin: Or, Southern Life As It Is. Mary Henderson Eastman. LC 6-37251. 1852. Lippincott, Grambo & Co.

Aunt Pleasantine. Ruth Doan MacDougall. LC 77-82658. 8.95 (ISBN 0-06-012853-4). Harper & Row.

Aunt Pleasantine. Ruth Doan MacDougall. 1979. 1.95 (ISBN 0-380-44628-6). Avon Books.

Aunt Pleasantine. Ruth Doan MacDougall. LC 78-12848. 1978. 7.95 (ISBN 0-89340-373-3). J. Curley.

Aunt Polly's Story of Mankind. Donald Ogden Stewart. 281p. 1981. Repr. of 1923 ed. lib. bdg. 15.00 (ISBN 0-89987-777-X). Darby Bks.

Aunt Quimby's Reminiscences of Georgia. L. R Fewell. LC 74-187382. 1972. (ISBN 0-87152-077-X). Reprint Co.

Aunt Rachel: A Rustic Sentimental Comedy. David Christie Murray. LC 7-25478. (Harper's handy series. no. 70). 1886. Harper & Brothers.

Aunt Rachel. A Rustic Sentimental Comedy. David Christie Murray. (On cover: Seaside library. Pocket ed., no. 737). 1886. G. Munro.

Aunt Rachel: A Rustic Sentimental Comedy. David Christie Murray. LC 43-42707. 1889. Macmillan and Co.

Aunt Sally's Boy Jack: A Novel. Nathaniel James Walter Le Cato. LC 7-12785. Belford, Clarke & Co.

Aunt Sarah: A Mother of New England. Agnes Louise Pratt. LC 6-37199. 1906. R. G. Badger.

Aunt Sarah & the War: A Tale of Transformations. Wilfrid Meynell. 1915. G. P. Putnam's Sons.

Aunt Sara's Wooden God. Mercedes Gilbert. LC 74-76108. 1969. McGrath Pub. Co.

Aunt Sara's Wooden God. Mercedes Gilbert. LC 76-144617. (Illus.). 1974. (ISBN 0-404-00161-0). AMS Press.

Aunt Sara's Wooden God. Mercedes Gilbert. LC 38-33205. The Christopher Publishing House.

Aunt Serena. Blanche Willis Howard Von Teuffel. LC 8-26778. 1881. J. R. Osgood and Company.

Aunt Serena. Blanche Willis Howard Von Teuffel. LC 4-16113. Houghton, Mifflin and Company.

Aunt Sophie's Diamonds. Joan Smith. (Regency Love Story). 1979. pap. 1.75 (ISBN 0-449-50015-2, Coventry). Fawcett.

Aunt Sunday Takes Command. Joseph Jefferson Farjeon. LC 40-33783. The Bobbs-Merrill Company.

Aunt Tirzah. Dora F Van Steinburg. LC 10-29748. Broadway Publishing Co.

Auntie Mame. Patrick Dennis, pseud. LC 54-11512. 1954. 11.00 (ISBN 0-8149-0085-2). Vanguard.

Auntie Mame: An Irreverent Escapade, by Patrick Dennis Pseud. Edward Everett Tanner. LC 56-32013. Vanguard Press.

Auntie Robbo. Ann Scott-Moncrieff. LC 41-135053. 1941. The Viking Press.

Aunts & Nephews. Warren. pap. 1.95 o.p. (ISBN 0-87682-185-9, 7185). Barclay Hse.

Aunt's Story. Patrick White. LC 48-510323. 1975. (pbk.) 1.95. Avon.

Aunt's Story. Patrick White. LC 48-5103. 1948. Viking Press.

Aunty High Over the Barley Mow. Dennis T. Patrick Sears. LC 78-302097. 12.50 (ISBN 0-7710-8026-3). McClelland and Stewart.

Aupres De Ma Blonde. Nicolas Freeling. LC 71-184382. 1972. 5.95 (ISBN 0-06-011351-0). Harper & Row.

Aupres De Ma Blonde. Nicolas Freeling. LC 79-10783. 1979. 1.95 (ISBN 0-394-74550-7). Vintage Books.

Aura. Carlos Fuentes. LC 75-2417. 1975. 7.95 (ISBN 0-374-10701-7) (ISBN 0-374-51171-3). Farrar, Straus and Giroux.

Aura of Love. Walter Rinder. LC 77-90026. (Illus.). 1978. pap. 4.95 (ISBN 0-89087-222-8). Celestial Arts.

Aura. Tr. from Spanish by Lysander Kemp. Carlos Fuentes. LC 65-23193. 3.95. Farrar.

Aurelia. R. A Lafferty. LC 82-5011. 5.95 (ISBN 0-89865-194-8). Donning Co.

Aurelia. R. A. Lafferty. Ed. by Hank Stine. LC 82-5011. (Illus., Orig.). 1982. pap. 5.95 (ISBN 0-89865-194-8, AACR2, Starblaze). Donning Co.

Aurelia. Gerard De Nerval. LC 77-10265. (Illus.). 1982. 23.50 (ISBN 0-404-16317-3). AMS Press.

Aurelia: Or, The Jews of Capena-Gate. Abel Quinton. Tr. by De Gournay, Paul F. 1870. Kelly, Piet & Co.

Aurelian: Or, Rome in the Third Century. Being Letters of Lucius M. Piso Pseud. from Rome, to Fausta, the Daughter of Gracchus, at Palmyra. William Ware. (On cover: Seaside library. Pocket ed. no. 760). 1886. G. Munro.

Aurelian: Or, Rome in the Third Century. In Letters of Lucius M. Piso Pseud. from Rome, to Fausta the Daughter of Gracchus, at Palmyra. William Ware. LC 8-37768. (Half-title: Francis & co.'s cabinet library of choice prose and poetry). 1848. C. S. Francis & Co.

Aurelian: Or, Rome in the Third Century, in Letters of Lucius M. Piso, from Rome, to Fausta, the Daughter of Gracchus, at Palmyra. 5th ed.... ed. William Ware. LC 24-28541. 1865. J. Miller.

Aurelian: Or, Rome in the Third Century, in Letters of Lucius M. Piso, from Rome to Fausta, the Daughter of Gracchus, at Palmyra. 5th ed. William Ware. 1866. T. R. Knox & Co.

Aurelien. Louis Aragon. Tr. by Wilkins, Eithne. LC 47-3903. 1947. Duell, Sloan and Pearce.

Aurelius Smith--Detective. Reginald Thomas Maitland Scott. LC 27-4640. E. P. Dutton & Company.

Aureola; or, The Black Sheep. A Story of German Social Life. Adelheid Mackenzie. LC 7-16285. 1871. Claxton, Remsen & Haffelfinger.

Aurette. Alice Marie Celeste Durand. LC 6-35701. (On cover: Idyiwild series, v. 1, no. 37). 1893. Morrill, Higgins & Co.

Aurielle. Annabel Erwin, pseud. 2.50 (ISBN 0-446-91126-7). Warner Books.

Aurifodina: Or, Adventures in the Gold Region: a Fantastical '49er Novel. George Washington Peck. LC 75-325677. (Book Club of California, San Francisco. Publication: No. 146). (Illus.). 1974. Book Club of California.

Aurilly, the Virgin Isle. Charles Walter Garrett. LC 23-13267. The Christopher Publishing House.

Auriol: Or, The Elixir of Life. William Harrison Ainsworth. LC 75-46248. (Supernatural and Occult Fiction). 1976. 16.00 (ISBN 0-405-08108-1). Arno Press.

Aurora. Jacob Boehm. Ed. by C. J. Barker & Henher. 1976. Repr. price not set o.p. Attic Pr.

Aurora. Joan Smith. LC 79-91752. 10.95 (ISBN 0-8027-0651-7). Walker.

Aurora. A Novel. Mary Agnes Tincker. LC 12-17301. 1886. J. B. Lippincott Company.

Aurora: Beyond Equality. Ed. by Susan Janice Anderson. (Fawcett Gold Medal Book). 1976. (pbk.) 1.25. Fawcett.

Aurora Carlyle. Alda Eaton. LC 68-22071. 1968. Dorrance.

Aurora Dawn. Herman Wouk. LC 56-13370. (Illus.). 1956. 11.95 (ISBN 0-385-04574-3). Doubleday.

Aurora Dawn. Herman Wouk. 1983. pap. 2.95. PB.

Aurora Dawn: Or, The True History of Andrew Reale Containing a Faithful Account of the Great Riot, Together with the Complete Texts of Michael Wilde's Oration and Father Stanfield's Sermon. Herman Wouk. LC 56-13370. (Illus.). 1973. 6.95. Doubleday.

Aurora Dawn: Or, The True History of Andrew Reale, Containing a Faithful Account of the Great Riot, Together with the Complete Texts of Michael Wilde's Oration and Father Stanfield's Sermon. Herman Wouk. LC 47-1680. 1947. Simon and Schuster.

Aurora Dawn: Or, The True History of Nadrew Reale, Containing a Faithful Account of the Great Riot. Herman Wouk. LC 56-13370. 1956. Doubleday.

Aurora Floyd. Mary Elizabeth Braddon Maxwell. LC 79-50468. (Maxwell, Mary Elizabeth Braddon, 1837-1915. The Fiction of Mary Elizabeth Braddon: 1). 1979. 96.00 (ISBN 0-8240-4350-2). Garland Pub.

Aurora Floyd. A Domestic Story. From "Temple Bar". Mary Elizabeth Braddon Maxwell. T. B. Peterson and Brothers.

Aurora Floyd. A Love Story. Mary Elizabeth Braddon Maxwell. (Seaside library. v. 2, no. 26). 1877. G. Munro.

Aurora Floyd. A Love Story. Mary Elizabeth Braddon Maxwell. (On cover: Seaside library. Pocket ed., no. 74.). 1883. G. Munro.

Aurora Floyd: A Novel. Mary Elizabeth Braddon Maxwell. (On cover: Lovell's library, no. 555). 1885. J. W. Lovell Company.

Aurora of Poverty Hill. Esmee Walton. LC 8-34811. Broadway Publishing Co.

Aurora the Magnificent. Gertrude Hall Brownell. LC 17-10200. 1917. The Century Co.

Auroraphone. A Romance. Cyrus Cole. LC 6-25416. 1890. C. H. Kerr & Company.

Aus Unseren Tagen. Heinrich Boll. Ed. by G. Stein. (Ger). 1960. pap. 2.70 o.p. (ISBN 0-03-016880-5). HR&W.

Aus Unserer Zeit: Dichter Des Zwanzigsten Jahrhunderts. Editied by Ian C. Loram and Leland R. Phelps. Ed. by Ian C. Loram & Leland R. Phelps. LC 56-11457. 1956. W. W. Norton.

Aussie Lawman. Glenn Holt. 1976. pap. 1.50 (ISBN 0-89041-111-5, 3111). Major Bks.

Austin Elliot. Henry Kingsley. (On cover: Lovell's library, v. 14, no. 726). 1886. J. W. Lovell Company.

Austin Elliot. Henry Kingsley. LC 4-17542. 1903. C. Scribner's Sons.

Austin Elliot. Henry Kingsley. LC 33-27135. (Half-title: The World's classics. 407). 1932. H. Milford, Oxford University Press.

TITLE INDEX AVALANCHE EXPRESS.

Austin Hall: Or, After Dinner Conversations Between a Father and His Children, on Subjects of Amusement and Instruction. LC 6-3860. 1834. A. Towar Etc.
Austral Globe. Milton Worth Ramsey. (On cover: Hiawatha library of fictio, v. 1, no. 1). 1892. M. W. Ramsey.
Australia. Nick Carter. (Nick Carter Ser.). (O.s.i.). (Orig.). 1970. pap. 0.60 o.s.i. (A598X, Award). Univ Pub & Dist.
Australia Felix. LC 30-4660. 1930. W. W. Norton & Co., Inc.
Australian Classics, 8 vols. Incl. For the Term of His Natural Life; Lawson's Best Stories; Bush Songs, Ballads & Other Verse; Such Is Life; Robbery Under Arms; Getting of Wisdom; Ralph Rashleigh; Fortunes of Richard Mahony. Set. deluxe ed. 29.95 incl. 45 rpm record o.s.i. Tri-Ocean.
Australian Short Stories: Second Series. Ed. by Brian James, pseud. LC 63-25172. (World's classics, 598). 1963. Oxford University Press.
Australian Stories of Today. Ed. by Charles Osborne. Repr. of 1914 ed. 6.50 o.p. Folcroft.
Austrian Connection. Frank Anvic, pseud. 1974. (pbk.) 1.95 (ISBN 0-87056-369-6). Brandon Books.
Authentic Death of Hendry Jones. Charles Neider. pap. 0.95 o.p. (ISBN 0-06-087017-6, HW). Har-Row.
Authentic Death of Hendry Jones: A Novel. 1st Ed. Charles Neider. LC 56-7227. 1956. Harper.
Authentic Shudder: True Tales of Haunted Houses & Assorted Specters. Warren Armstrong. 1967. 5.50 o.p. (ISBN 0-381-98004-9, A06600). John Day.
Authentic Touch. Jack Wodhams. (Orig.). 1971. pap. 0.75 o.p. (07142). Curtis.
Authentick Memoirs of the Life Intrigues and Adventures of the Celebrated Sally Salisbury. Charles Walker. LC 79-170557. (Foundations of the Novel). 1973. 22.00 (ISBN 0-8240-0553-8). Garland Pub.
Author, Author. P. G. Wodehouse. (O.S.I.). 1962. 4.50 o.s.i. (ISBN 0-671-06195-X). S&S.
Author Bites the Dust. Arthur William Upfield. 1967. 4.50 o.p. (ISBN 0-8277-0124-1). British Bk Ctr.
Author Bites the Dust. Arthur William Upfield. pap. 1.60 o.s.i. Tri-Ocean.
Author Bonnicastle: An American Novel. Josiah Gilbert Holland. LC 36-15506. 1873. Scribner, Armstrong & Co.
Author Bonnicastle: An American Novel. Josiah Gilbert Holland. LC 7-6133. 1882. C. Scribner's Sons.
Author Bonnicastle: An American Novel. Josiah Gilbert Holland. LC 4-4981. 1901. C. Scribner's Sons.
Author from a Savage People. Bette Pesetsky. LC 82-48731. 1983. 12.95 (ISBN 0-394-53033-0). Knopf.
Author of Beltraffio. Henry James. Bd. with Middle Years; Greville Fane; Broken Wings; Tree of Knowledge; Abastement of the Northmores; Great Good Place; Four Meetings; Paste; Europe; Miss Gunton of Poughkeepsie; Fordham Castle. LC 70-158795. (Novels & Tales of Henry James: Vol. 16). xi, 425p. Repr. of 1909 ed. 25.00x (ISBN 0-678-02816-8). Kelley.
Author of Beltraffio & Other Stories. Henry James. 1909. 7.50 o.p. Scribner.
Author of Beltraffio; Pandora; Georgina's Reasons; The Path of Duty; Four Meetings. Henry James. LC 10-4179. 1885. J. R. Osgood and Company.
Author Unknown. Winifred Ashton & Simpson, Helen, Joint Author. 1930. Cosmopolitan Book Corporation.
Authoritarians. Martin Ancel. Ed. by Edythe Martin. (Illus.). 1977. lib. bdg. 12.95x. Pleasure Trove.
Author's Choice; 40 Stories. MacKinlay Kantor. LC 44-8274. 1944. Coward-McCann, Inc.
Authors Digest: The World's Great Stories in Brief. Ed. by Rossiter Johnson. LC 70-12099. 1970. Mini-Print Corp.
Authors' Gold. Ed. by George Eaton. LC 48-825. 1947. Consolidated Book Publishers.
Authors in Paradise. Alan Griffiths. LC 39-32125. 1939. Frederick A. Stokes Company.
Author's Love: Being the Unpublished Letters of Prosper Merimec's 'Inconnue.' Elizabeth Balch & Prosper Merimee. LC 9-2701. 1889. Macmillan and Co.
Authorship: A Tale. John Neal. LC 7-23110. 1830. Gray and Bowen.
Auto Da Fe. Elias Canetti. LC 74-185790. (Penguin modern classics). 1973. 0.60 (ISBN 0-14-002287-2). Penguin.
Auto-Da-Fe. Elias Canetti. LC 78-24822. (Continuum book). 1979. 9.95 (ISBN 0-8164-9356-1). Seabury Press.
Auto-Da-Fe. Elias Canetti. LC 81-70794. 17.50 (ISBN 0-8264-0210-0) (ISBN 0-8264-0068-X). Continuum.
Auto-Orphan. John Stevenson Tarkington. LC 13-22754. R. G. Badger.
Autobiographical Novel. Kenneth Rexroth. LC 78-8823. 382p. 1978. pap. 6.95 (ISBN 0-915520-15-X). Ross-Erikson.
Autobiographical Novel. Kenneth Rexroth. LC 64-11754. 1969. pap. 2.95 o.p. (ISBN 0-8112-0175-9, NDP281). New Directions.
Autobiography. Gilbert Keith Chesterton. 1978. Repr. of 1936 ed. lib. bdg. 30.00 (ISBN 0-8495-0716-2). Arden Lib.
Autobiography and Deliverance. William Hale White. LC 70-8118. (Victorian Library). 1969-1970. 6.00. Humanities Press.
Autobiography of a Book. Walton Butterfield. LC 48-11040. 1947. R. W. Kelly Pub. Corp.
Autobiography of a Bottle. B F Hutchins. LC 7-9029. (On Cover: Fife and Drum Series, No. 8). National Temperance Society and Publication House.
Autobiography of a Boy. George Slythe Street. LC 76-19978. (Decadent Consciousness). 1977. 26.00 (ISBN 0-8240-2772-8). Garland Pub.
Autobiography of a Boy. 3d ed. George Slythe Street. LC 9-8357. 1894. J. Lane.
Autobiography of a Child. Hannah Lynch. LC 99-5680. 1899. Dodd, Mead & Company.
Autobiography of a Dakota Squatter: And Other Stories. Andrew Magnus Fleming. LC 34-627521. 1934. Meadow Publishing Company.
Autobiography of a Disembodied Soul. Monroe Guy Carleton. LC 10-15640. 1910. 1.50. Vreeland Publishing Company.
Autobiography of a Latin Reader. Samuel Syntax. LC 8-25586. 1859. A. D. F. Randolph.
Autobiography of a Married Woman. No Girlhood. LC 6-3856. 1859. S. A. Rollo & Co.
Autobiography of a New England Farm House: A Romance of the Cape Cod Lands. Nathan Henry Chamberlain. LC 6-23343. (Half-title: Collection of American authors... v. 2). 1888. Cupples and Hurd.
Autobiography of a New England Farm-House. A Book. Nathan Henry Chamberlain. LC 6-23345. 1865. Carleton.
Autobiography of a Pocket-Handkerchief. James Fenimore Cooper. Ed. by Brown, Walter Lee. LC 6-30186. 1897. The Golden-Book Press.
Autobiography of a Quack: And The Case of George Dedlow. Silas Weir Mitchell. LC 68-57542. (American novels of muckracking, propaganda, and social protest). (Illus.). 1968. Gregg Press.
Autobiography of a Quack: And The Case of George Dedlow. Silas Weir Mitchell. LC 1627. 1900. The Century Co.
Autobiography of a Quack & the Case of George Dedlow. Silas Weir Mitchell. LC 68-57542. (Muckrakers Ser.). (Illus.). Repr. of 1900 ed. lib. bdg. 14.00 (ISBN 0-8398-1264-7). Irvington.
Autobiography of a Race Horse. L. B Yates. LC 20-10769. George H. Doran Company.
Autobiography of a Runaway Slave. Ed. by Esteban Montejo & Miguel Barnet. pap. 1.95 o.s.i. (ISBN 0-394-71832-1, Vin). Random.
Autobiography of a Silver Dollar. Wallace LeGrande Henderson. LC 64-6011. (Reflection book). 1964. Carlton Press.
Autobiography of a Slander. Ada Ellen Bayly & Margaret Wolfe Hamilton Hungerford. (Seaside Library. Pocket Ed.). (On cover: Seaside library. Pocket ed., no. 1197.: No. 1197). 1889. G. Munro.
Autobiography of a Spy. Mary Bancroft. (Illus.). 320p. 1983. 15.95 (ISBN 0-688-02019-4). Morrow.
Autobiography of a Suicide: Anonymous ... LC 34-25915. Golden Galleon Press.
Autobiography of an Ex-Colored Man. James Weldon Johnson. LC 12-15155. 1912. Sherman, French & Company.
Autobiography of an Ex-Coloured Man. James Weldon Johnson. LC 49-34266. (Star book). 1927. Garden City Pub. Co.
Autobiography of an Ex-Coloured Man. James Weldon Johnson. LC 27-18249. (Half-title: Blue jade library). 1927. A. A. Knopf.
Autobiography of Arthur Ransome. Arthur Ransome. LC 76-380617. (Illus.). 1976. 5.95 (ISBN 0-224-01245-2). J. Cape.
Autobiography of Cassandra, Princess & Prophetess of Troy. Ursule Molinaro. LC 79-1410. 10.00 (ISBN 0-89097-013-0). Archer Editions Press.
Autobiography of Christopher Kirkland. Elizabeth Lynn Linton. LC 76-9634. (Victorian Fiction: Novels of Faith and Doubt; 80). 1976. 40.00 (ISBN 0-8240-1604-1). Garland Pub.
Autobiography of God. Herbert L. Beierle. 1979. 10.00 (ISBN 0-940480-05-0). U of Healing.
Autobiography of Mark Rutherford; Mark Rutherford's Deliverance. William Hale White. LC 75-1514. (Victorian Fiction: Novels of Faith and Doubt). 1976. 35.00 (ISBN 0-8240-1587-8). Garland Pub.
Autobiography of Mark Rutherford Pseud. Dissenting Minister. William Hale White. 1881. G. P. Putnam's Sons.
Autobiography of Mary Jane. Milton Henry Stine. LC 24-47004. The Christopher Publishing House.
Autobiography of Methuselah. John Kendrick Bangs. LC 9-27030. 1909. B. W. Dodge & Company.
Autobiography of Miss Jane Pittman. Ernest J. Gaines. LC 77-144380. (Illus.). 1971. 6.95. Dial Press.
Autobiography of Miss Jane Pittman. Ernest J. Gaines. LC 73-38101. 1971. 8.95 (ISBN 0-8161-6010-4). G. K. Hall.
Autobiography of My Mother. Rosellen Brown. LC 75-36581. 1976. 7.95 (ISBN 0-385-09896-0). Doubleday.
Autobiography of Ole Burt. Robert Jesse Gresham. 1944. Wolfer Printing & Engraving Co.
Autobiography of William Russell. Frederick William Thomas. LC 9-1479. 1852. Gobright, Thorne & Co.
Autocracy of Mr. Parham: His Remarkable Adventures in This Changing World. Herbert George Wells. LC 30-195083. 1930. Doubleday, Doran and Company, Inc.
Autocrat. Pearl Doles Bell. LC 23-7011. W. J. Watt & Company.
Autocrat. Pearl Doles Bell. 1924. A. L. Burt Company.
Autocrat of the Breakfast Table. Oliver Wendell Holmes. 1957. pap. 1.45 o.p. (ISBN 0-8090-0026-1, AmCen). Hill & Wang.
Autocrat of the Breakfast Table. Oliver Wendell Holmes. 2.50 o.p.; price not set repr.- o.p. HM.
Autocrat of the Breakfast Table. Oliver Wendell Holmes. 1960. 5.00x o.p. (ISBN 0-460-00066-7, Evman). Dutton.
Autocrats. Charles Keeler Lush. LC 1-10014. 1901. Doubleday, Page & Company.
Autograph Hound. John Lahr. LC 72-6776. 1973. 6.95 (ISBN 0-394-48093-7). Knopf; Distributed by Random House.
Automatic Capitalists. Will Payne. 1909. R. G. Badger.
Automatic Wife. A Novel of the New Code of Honor. In Three Parts. William Hosea Ballou. LC 6-6888. (On cover: The ideal series, no. 2). 1891. W. D. Rowland.
Automaton Ear: And Other Sketches. Florence McLandburgh. LC 7-19977. 1876. Jansen, McClurg & Co.
Autopsy & Other Short Stories. Ismail Ersevim. 96p. 1983. 6.50 (ISBN 0-682-49974-9). Exposition.
Autopsy for a Cosmonaut: A Novel. Jacob Hay & John M. Keshishian. LC 69-12634. 1969. 5.95. Little, Brown.
Autrefois: Tales of Old New Orleans and Elsewhere. James Albert Harrison. LC 7-2872. Cassell & Company, Limited.
Autrefois: Tales of Old New Orleans and Elsewhere. James Albert Harrison. LC 7-2873. (On cover: Cassell's sunshine series of choice fiction. v. 1. no. 16). Cassell & Company, Limited.
Autum Alley. Lena Kennedy. LC 79-19305. 1980. 10.95 (ISBN 0-448-22559-X). Paddington Press.
Autumn. Muriel Hine Coxon. LC 17-980983. 1917. 1.40. John Lane Company.
Autumn. A. G. Mojtabai. LC 81-23523. 1982. 9.95 (ISBN 0-395-32051-8). Houghton Mifflin.
Autumn. Robert Nathan. LC 21-17910. 1921. R. M. McBride & Company.
Autumn. Robert Nathan. 1935. R. M. McBride & Company.
Autumn Alley. Lena Kennedy. 384p. 1982. pap. 3.50 (ISBN 0-671-42559-5). PB.
Autumn Angels. Arthur B. Cover. (Orig.). 1975. pap. 1.25 o.p. (ISBN 0-515-03787-7). Pyramid Pubns.
Autumn Beginning. Kay Kirby. (Adventures in Love Ser.: No. 31). 1982. pap. 1.75 (ISBN 0-451-11785-9, AE1785, Sig). NAL.
Autumn Comes Early. Howard Breslin. LC 56-11118. Crowell.
Autumn Countess. Catherine Coulter. 1979. pap. 2.25 (ISBN 0-451-11445-0, AE1445, Sig). NAL.
Autumn Dream and Other Stories. Theodore Sarris. LC 35-25391. Center Clark Publishing Co.
Autumn Equinox. John Hearne. LC 61-5234. 1961. Vanguard Press.
Autumn Fires. Jackie Black. (Candlelight Ecstasy Ser.: No. 152). (Orig.). 1983. pap. 1.95 (ISBN 0-440-10272-3). Dell.
Autumn Glory. Elizabeth Carfrae, pseud. LC 42-182891. 1942. G. P. Putnam's Sons.
Autumn Gold. Norman McGlashan. LC 39-5401. Liveright Publishing Corporation.
Autumn Gold: A Novel. Charlotte Margaret Kreuger. LC 41-20050. Zondervan Publishing House.
Autumn Gold: A Novel by Charlotte M. Kruger... Charlotte Margaret Kruger Bryant. LC 41-20050. 1941. Zondervan Publishing House.
Autumn Heroes. Oliver Jacks, pseud. LC 77-4629. 1978. 8.95 (ISBN 0-312-06238-9). St. Martin's Press.
Autumn Heroes. Oliver Jacks, pseud. (Berkley book). 1979. 1.95 (ISBN 0-425-04037-2). Berkley Pub. Corp.
Autumn in Araby. Michael Butterworth. LC 82-45501. 1983. 14.95 (ISBN 0-385-17881-6). Doubleday.
Autumn in Araby. Carola Salisbury. LC 82-45501. 288p. 1983. 14.95 (ISBN 0-385-17881-6). Doubleday.
Autumn in the Spring & Other Stories. Ba Jin. 1981. pap. 2.50 (ISBN 0-8351-0865-1). China Bks.
Autumn Lace. Eileen Jackson. LC 76-13818. 8.95 (ISBN 0-8027-0538-3). Walker & Co.
Autumn Lace. Eileen Jackson. (Fawcett Crest Book). 1977. 1.50 (ISBN 0-449-23297-2). Fawcett Pubns.
Autumn Lace. Eileen Jackson. LC 78-31245. 1979. 12.50 (ISBN 0-8161-6675-7). G. K. Hall.
Autumn Leaves; Verse and Story. Mary Agnes Tincker. 1899. W. H. Young and Company.
Autumn Light: Illuminations of Age. Carson Smith McCullers & L. M Schulmann. LC 77-26582. 8.95 (ISBN 0-690-03885-2). Crowell.
Autumn Love & Spring. Geneva L. Jones. 4.50 o.p. Vantage.
Autumn Love and Spring. Geneva L Jones. 1974. 4.50. Vantage Press.
Autumn Madness. Francis Wallace. LC 37-40772. 1937. Macrae Smith Company.
Autumn Manaeuvres: Stories and Aketches from the French of Ludovic Halevy... Ludovic Halevy & Ford, Mary K., Tr. LC 6-46215. 1898. G. H. Richmond & Son.
Autumn Manoeuvres: Stories & Sketches. Ludovic Halevy. LC 77-121556. (Short Story Index Reprint Ser). 1897. 15.00 (ISBN 0-8369-3513-6). Ayer Co.
Autumn Manuvres: Stories and Sketches from the French of Ludovic Halevy. Ludovic Halevy. LC 77-121556. (Short story index reprint series). 1970. Books for Libraries Press.
Autumn of a Hunter. Pat Stadley. LC 71-102349. 1970. 4.95. Random House.
Autumn of a Hunter see Murder Hunt.
Autumn of the Fox. 1st Ed. Eric Rhodin. LC 62-11449. 1962. Doubleday.
Autumn of the Patriarch. Garcia Marquez, Gabriel. LC 75-30349. 10.00 (ISBN 0-06-011419-3). Harper & Row.
Autumn of the Patriarch. Garcia Marquez, Gabriel. Tr. by Gregory Rabassa. (Bard Book). 1977. 2.25 (ISBN 0-380-01774-1). Avon Books.
Autumn Rain. Frances Reinke. LC 75-5229. 1975. 2.95. Adams Press.
Autumn Rose. Fiona Hill. LC 78-7615. 8.95. Putnam.
Autumn Rose. Fiona Hill. 2.25 (ISBN 0-425-04224-3). Berkley Publishing Corp., C.
Autumn Saint. Maud Louise Hudnut Chapin. LC 26-172854. 1926. Duffield and Company.
Autumn Sowing. Edward Frederic Benson. 1.35. George H. Doran Company.
Autumn Sunset. Ralph Marcus. LC 49-8448. 1949. Free Press.
Autumn Testament. James K. Baxter. 54p. 1972. pap. 3.00x (ISBN 0-7055-0368-2). Intl Pubns Serv.
Autumn Thunder. Robert Wilder. LC 52-9850. 1952. Putnam.
Autumn Wind. Issa Kobayashi. Tr. by L. Mackenzie. (Wisdom of the East Ser). 2.50 o.p. (ISBN 0-7195-0871-1). Paragon.
Autumnal Face. Malcolm Muggeridge. LC 32-4566. 1931. Putnam.
Autumn's Bounty. George Pierre. LC 75-185837. 1972. 7.95 (ISBN 0-8111-0446-X). Naylor.
Autumn's Brightness. Daisy Newman. LC 55-673. 1955. Macmillan.
Autumn's Legacy. Alban Laureano. LC 82-6455. 77p. 1982. 18.95; pap. 10.95 (ISBN 0-8214-0696-5). Swallow.
Autumn's Torch... Cynthia Lombardi. LC 34-289678. 1934. D. Appleton-Century Company, Incorporated.
Avalanche. Gertrude Franklin Horn Atherton. 1919. lib. bdg. 17.50 (ISBN 0-8414-3081-0). Folcroft.
Avalanche! Steve Cohen. 1980. pap. 2.50 (ISBN 0-89083-672-8). Zebra.
Avalanche. Ernest Poole. LC 24-12277. 1924. The Macmillan Company.
Avalanche. John Wingate. LC 76-54635. (Illus.). 1977. 7.95. St. Martin's Press.
Avalanche: A Mystery Story. Gertrude Franklin Horn Atherton. LC 19-3497. Frederick A. Stokes Company.
Avalanche, a Novel. Kay Boyle. LC 43-181126. 1944. Simon and Schuster.
Avalanche Express. Colin Forbes, pseud. LC 77-6620. 1977. 8.95 o.p. (ISBN 0-525-06026-X). Dutton.
Avalanche Express. Colin Forbes, pseud. 1979. pap. 2.50 (ISBN 0-449-24252-8, Crest). Fawcett.

Avalanche Express. Raymond H. Sawkins. LC 77-6620. 8.95. Dutton.
Avalanche Hunters. Montgomery Meigs Atwater. LC 68-31147. (Illus.). 1968. 6.95 (ISBN 0-8255-1345-6). Macrae.
Avalanche of Time. Mary Mussel White De Noya. 1971. 4.95 o.p. (ISBN 0-8059-1538-9). Dorrance.
Avalanche of Time. Mary Musselwhite De Noya. LC 70-145528. 1971. 4.95 (ISBN 0-8059-1538-9). Dorrance.
Avalon. Anya Seton. LC 66-10215. 1965. Houghton Mifflin.
Avalovara. Osman Lins. LC 79-4214. 1980. 12.95 (ISBN 0-394-49851-8). Distributed by Randon House.
Avanti! A Tale of the Resurrection of Sicily 1860. James Meeker Ludlow. LC 13-313. Fleming H. Revell Company.
Avarice House. Julien Green. Tr. by Best, Marshall A. LC 27-22162. 1927. Harper & Brothers.
Avatar. Poul Anderson. LC 78-7875. 10.95 (ISBN 0-399-12228-1). Berkley Pub. Corp.: Distributed by Putnam.
Avatar in Vishnu Land: Concerning Chiefly Viroschand Gaeshkind, Merchant of India. Samuel Woods Hill. LC 28-25630. 1928. C. Scribner's Sons.
Avelaval. Lindsay Hill. 1974. 5.00 (Pub. by Oyez); pap. 2.00. SBD.
Avenelle: Or, The Lone Tree of Arlington. John Cranmer Baird. LC 9-11690. 1907. Mayhew Publishing Co.
Avenged on Society. H. Freeman Wood. LC 8-37557. J. W. Lovell Company.
Avenger. Samuel Gordon. LC 21-175442. The Macaulay Company.
Avenger. Sidney Floyd Gowing. LC 26-15959. 1926. G. P. Putnam's Sons.
Avenger. Edward Phillips Oppenheim. LC 8-13951. 1908. Little, Brown and Company.
Avenger. Howard Rigsby. LC 57-9243. 1957. Crowell.
Avenger. Charles Wesley Sanders. LC 26-9573. 1926. G. H. Watt.
Avenger. rev. ed. Edgar Wallace. 1970. 4.50 o.s.i. (ISBN 0-8277-0317-1). British Bk Ctr.
Avenger from Nowhere. William E Vance. (Ace Double Western). 1973. (pbk) 0.95. Ace Books.
Avenger of Antares. Alan Burt Akers. (Science Fiction Ser.). 1975. pap. 1.25 o.p. (JU1208). Daw Bks.
Avenger; Pictures of Death. Kenneth Robeson. 1973. (pbk.) 0.75. Warner Paperback Library.
Avenger Strikes. Walter S Masterman. LC 37-735. E. P. Dutton & Co., Inc.
Avengers. Charles Graves. LC 43-4735. Hutchinson & Co. Ltd.
Avengers: By Chad Merriman Pseud. Gifford Paul Cheshire. LC 58-13390. (Ballantine books, 289K). 1959. Ballantine Books.
Avengers of Carrig. John Brunner. (Science Fiction Ser.). 1980. pap. 1.75 o.p. (ISBN 0-87997-509-1, UE1509). DAW Bks.
Avenging Angel: A Gabe Wager Mystery. Rex Burns. LC 82-10862. 1983. 12.50 (ISBN 0-670-14317-0). Viking Press.
Avenging Angels. Linwood Carson. 1976. pap. 1.50 o.p. (ISBN 0-8439-0408-9, LB408, Leisure Bks). Nordon Pubns.
Avenging Angels. Linwood Carson. Leisure Books.
Avenging Bitch. Edgar Black. 192p. (Orig.). 1974. pap. 1.95 o.p. (ISBN 0-87682-386-X, 7386). Barclay Hse.
Avenging Brotherhood. Ivan Tattersall Hodgkinson. LC 29-522060. 1929. R. M. McBride & Company.
Avenging Gun. Johanas L. Bouma. 1978. pap. 1.50 o.s.i. (ISBN 0-505-51327-7). Tower Bks.
Avenging Hour. Harry Francis Prevost Battensky. LC 6-37929. 1906. Appleton and Company.
Avenging Ikon. Charles Bryson. LC 30-8175. E. P. Dutton & Co., Inc.
Avenging Liafail. Talbot Mundy. (Tros of Samothrace: No. 2). 1978. pap. 2.25 (ISBN 0-89083-378-8). Zebra.
Avenging Parrot. Anne Austin. LC 30-4654. Greenberg.
Avenging Ray... Austin J Small. LC 30-188682. 1930. Pub. for the Crime Club, Inc., by Doubleday, Doran & Company, Inc.
Avenging Saint. Leslie Charteris. LC 48-10520. (New Avon library, 147). 1948. Avon Book Co.
Avenging Saint... Leslie Charteris. LC 31-13710. Pub. for the Crime Club, Inc., by Doubleday, Doran & Company, Inc.
Aventine. Lee Killough. 160p. 1982. pap. 1.95 (Del Rey). Ballantine.
Aventuras De Amor Del Doctor Fonda (la Sombra De Helena) N. Puente-Duany. LC 78-73151. (Coleccion Caniqui). (Illus.). 1979. pap. 5.95 (ISBN 0-89729-215-4). Ediciones.
Aventuras De Don Quijote. Miguel de Cervantes de Saavedra. Ed. by H. Alpern & J. Martel. 1935. text ed. 3.40 o.p. (2-00960). HM.
Aventuras De Don Quijote. Miguel de Cervantes de Saavedra. Ed. by Hyman Alpern & Jose Martel. (Span). text ed. 2.55 s.p. o.p. HM.
Aventuras de Don Quijote: Relatos Ilustrados. Miguel de Cervantes de Saavedra. (Span.). 9.00 (ISBN 84-241-5412-6). E Torres & Sons.
Aventuras de Tom Sawyer. Mark Twain. (Span.). 9.00 (ISBN 84-241-5630-7). E Torres & Sons.
Aventures D'Arsene Lupin. Bruno Braunrot & Lester G. Crocker. LC 75-30883. 1975. pap. text ed. 8.95x (ISBN 0-684-14244-9, ScribC). Scribner.
Aventures Ou la Queste Del Saint Graal: La Mort le Roi Artus. Ed. by H. Oskar Sommer. (Vulgate Version of the Arthurian Romances: No. 6). Repr. of 1913 ed. 57.50 (ISBN 0-404-17636-4). AMS Pr.
Avenue. Ronald Frederick Delderfield. LC 69-14281. (O.s.i.). 1969. 9.95 o.s.i. (ISBN 0-671-20172-7). S&S.
Avenue of Stone. Pamela Hansford Johnson. LC 48-5814. 1948. MacMillan Co.
Avenue of Stone: A Novel. Pamela Hansford Johnson. LC 73-3966. 1973. 7.95 (ISBN 0-684-13442-X). Scribner.
Avenue of the Dead. Evelyn Anthony. LC 82-1519. 1982. 13.95 (ISBN 0-698-11124-9). Coward, McCann & Geoghegan.
Avenue of the Dead. large print ed. Evelyn Anthony. LC 82-19500. 12.95 (ISBN 0-89621-416-8). Thorndike Press.
Average Cabins: A Novel. Isabel Constance Clarke. LC 22-12021. 1922. Benziger Brothers.
Average Jones. Samuel Hopkins Adams. LC 75-32731. (Literature of Mystery and Detection). (Illus.). 1976. 19.00 (ISBN 0-405-07861-7). Arno Press.
Average Jones. Samuel Hopkins Adams. LC 11-26413. The Bobbs-Merrill Company.
Average Man. Robert Hugh Benson. LC 13-17957. 1913. Dodd, Mead and Company.
Average Man. Robert Grant. 1884. J. R. Osgood and Company.
Average Woman. LC 16-20588. George H. Doran Company.
Average Woman. Wolcott Balestier. LC 6-6329. United States Book Company.
Averages: A Story of New York. Eleanor Stuart Childs. LC 99-4327. 1899. D. Appleton and Company.
Averil. Rosa Nouchette Carey. LC 42-485917. (Library of famous books by famous authors.). 1899. H. M. Caldwell Company.
Averted Threat. Gershon Kranzler, pseud. saddle-stitched 3.00 (ISBN 0-87559-129-9). Shalom.
Avery. Elizabeth Stuart Phelps Ward. LC 2-24725. 1902. Houghton, Mifflin and Company.
Avery Glibun: Or, Between Two Fires. A Romance. Robert Henry Newell. LC 7-23135. 1867. G. W. Carleton & Co.; Etc., Etc.
Avery's Fortune. William M. Green. LC 72-187008. (Black Bat Mystery Ser.). 1972. 5.95 o.p. (ISBN 0-672-51682-9). Bobbs.
Avery's Fortune: A Novel of Suspense. William M. Green. LC 73-187008. (Black bat mystery). 1972. 5.95. Bobbs-Merrill.
Avery's Knot. Mary Cable. LC 81-8672. 11.95 (ISBN 0-399-12569-8). Putnam.
Avery's Mission. John Innes Mackintosh Stewart. LC 72-152675. 1971. 5.95 (ISBN 0-393-08650-X). Norton.
Aviator. Ernest Kellogg Gann. LC 81-6283. 1981. 11.95 (ISBN 0-8161-3257-7). G.K. Hall.
Aviator. Ernest Kellogg Gann. LC 80-68543. 10.95 (ISBN 0-87795-299-X). Arbor House.
Aviatrix. Richard H. Curtis. (Skymasters Ser.: No. 7). 320p. (Orig.). 1983. pap. 3.25 (ISBN 0-440-00333-4, Emerald). Dell.
Avila Gold. David Westheimer. LC 74-18568. 1974. 7.95 (ISBN 0-399-11466-1). Putnam.
Avima Affair. Ned Calmer. LC 72-76133. 1973. 6.95 (ISBN 0-385-02761-3). Doubleday.
Avion My Uncle Hew. C. Fisher. 1971. Repr. of 1946 ed. 3.95 o.p. Hawthorn.
Avis Benson: Or, Mine and Thine. With Other Sketches. Elizabeth Payson Prentiss. LC 41-41843. (On cover: Spare-hour series). A. D. F. Randolph & Company.
Avocado Is Not Your Color: And Other Scenes of Married Bliss. Edward Frascino. LC 82-16153. (Illus.). 112p. 1983. pap. 3.95 (ISBN 0-14-006364-1). Penguin.
Avon All-American Fiction Reader. LC 51-4767. (Avon double-size books, 1002). Avon Pub. Co.
Avon Annual ... 1944- LC 44-8265. Avon Book Company.
Avon Bedside Companion. LC 49-5928. (Avon, 182). 1949. Avon Pub. Co.
Avon Bedside Companion: A Treasury of Tales for the Sophisticated. LC 48-128724. (New Avon library, 109). 1947.
Avon Book of Modern Crime Stories. Cecil John Charles Street. LC 43-7360. (Avon Pocket-Size Bks.). (Avon pocket-size books). 1942. Avon Book Company.
Avon Fantasy Reader. No. 1- Ed. by Donald A. Wollheim. LC 50-554665. Avon Book Co.
Avon Ghost Reader ... LC 46-8580. (New Avon library No. 90). 1946. Avon Book Company.
Avon Mystery Storyteller. LC 48-12871. (New Avon library, 86). 1946.
Avon Story Teller. LC 46-155291. (New Avon library. 72). 1945.
Avraham's Good Week. G. Gyorgy Kardos. LC 72-186032. 1975. 7.95 (ISBN 0-385-04579-4). Doubleday.
Avram Davidson: Collected Fantasies. Avram Davidson & John Silbersack. (Orig.). 1982. pap. 2.50 (ISBN 0-425-05081-5). Berkley Pub.
Avrosimov. Bulat Shalvovich Okudzhava. Tr. by Leo Gruliow. 1970. 6.95 o.p. (ISBN 0-87777-015-8). R W Baron.
Aw Hell". Clarke Venable. LC 27-8664. The Reilly & Lee Co.
Awake and Rehearse. Louis Bromfield. LC 29-9726. Frederick A. Stokes Company.
Awake Deborah! Eden Phillpotts. LC 41-12721. 1941. The Macmillan Company.
Awake, Monique: Translated by Eva Johnson. 1st Ed. Astrid Van Royen. LC 57-11054. 1957. Duell, Sloan and Pearce.
Awake! My Heart. Gerrie Ollier Thielens. 1940. Harper & Brothers.
Awake to Darkness. Richard McMullen. LC 47-5252. 1947. Farrar, Straus.
Awake to Terror. Marilyn Ross. (Stewarts of Stormhaven-11). 1.75 (ISBN 0-445-04282-6). Popular Library.
Awakened. Zoe Oldenbourg. Tr. by Edward Hyams. 1976. (pbk.) 1.95 (ISBN 0-380-00713-4). Avon.
Awakened. Zoe Oldenbourg. LC 57-7167. 1957. Pantheon Books.
Awakened: A Novel. Margaret Abrams. LC 54-7435. 1954. Jewish Publication Society of America.
Awakened Eye. Frederick Franck. LC 79-2098. 1979. 12.95 (ISBN 0-394-50683-9); pap. 4.95 (ISBN 0-394-74021-1). Knopf.
Awakening. (On cover: American novelists' series, no. 27). 1890. F. F. Lovell & Company.
Awakening. Henry Bordeaux & Davis, Ruth Helen, Tr. LC 14-19165. E.P. Dutton & Company.
Awakening. Anna Gaskill Cartrette. LC 21-14622. Printed by Wilmington Printing Company.
Awakening. Kate O'Flaherty Chopin. LC 99-1948. 1899. H.S. Stone & Company.
Awakening. Kate O'Flaherty Chopin. LC 22-10839. 1906. Duffield & Company.
Awakening. Kate O'Flaherty Chopin & Margaret Culley. LC 76-55321. (Norton critical edition). 1977. 10.00 (ISBN 0-393-04434-3) (ISBN 0-393-09172-4). Norton.
Awakening. Mary Hornibrook Cummins. LC 13-21820. 1.00. Davis & Bond.
Awakening. Warwick Deeping. LC 32-175253. 1932. Grosset & Dunlap.
Awakening. Richard M Eyre. LC 81-67309. 6.95 (ISBN 0-88494-430-1). Bookcraft.
Awakening. Pierre Frondaie. LC 31-33064. Sears Publishing Company, Inc.
Awakening. Anne Hamilton Gordon. LC 15-3420. 1914. Marine Printing Bureau.
Awakening. Ira Hirschmann. LC 80-54447. (Illus.). 128p. 1981. 10.00 (ISBN 0-88400-073-7). Shengold.
Awakening. Richard C Meredith. LC 78-21361. 10.95 (ISBN 0-312-06260-5). St. Martin's Press.
Awakening. facsimile ed. Mary White Ovington. LC 70-39096. (Black Heritage Library Collection). Repr. of 1923 ed. 10.00 (ISBN 0-8369-9034-X). Ayer Co.
Awakening. Jean Baptiste Rossi. LC 51-11953. 1952. Harper.
Awakening: A Novel. Melvin Linwood Severy. LC 40-31344. Foster Hope Company, Inc.
Awakening: A Novel of Washington Life. Charles Wickliffe Yulee. LC 6-1262. 1905. The Neale Publishing Company.
Awakening: A Study in Possibilities. Katherine Helen Maud Marshall Diver. LC 11-16262. 1911. 1.30. John Lane Company.
Awakening: A Study in Possibilities. Katherine Helen Maud Marshall Diver. LC 24-20456. 1922. Dodd, Mead & Company.
Awakening: A Tale of English Life. Katharine Sarah Gadsden Macquoid. LC 7-20289. (Half-title: Harper's half-hour series, no. 99). 1879. Harper & Brothers.
Awakening, and Other Stories. Kate O'Flaherty Chopin. Ed. by Lewis Gaston Leary. LC 79-103399. (Rinehart editions, 142). 1970. Holt, Rinehart and Winston.
Awakening & Selected Short Stories. Kate O'Flaherty Chopin. (Bantam Classics Ser.). 224p. (Orig.). (gr. 9-12). 1981. pap. 1.95 (ISBN 0-553-21057-2). Bantam.
Awakening & Selected Stories. Kate O'Flaherty Chopin. Ed. by Nina Baym. 1981. pap. 3.95 (Mod LibC). Modern Lib.
Awakening, and Selected Stories of Kate Chopin. Kate O'Flaherty Chopin. LC 75-37380. (Signet classic). 1976. 1.50. New American Library.
Awakening & Selected Stories of Kate Chopin. Ed. by Barbara Solomon. (Orig.). 1976. pap. 2.95 (ISBN 0-451-51749-0, CE1749, Sig Classics). NAL.
Awakening & Short Tales. Kate Chapin. (Rinehart Editions). pap. price not set o.p. (HoltC). HR&W.
Awakening Dream. Kate Cameron, pseud. (Whispering hills gothic,#5). 1974. (pbk.) 0.95. Leisure Books.
Awakening Land. Conrad Richter. (YA) 1966. 19.95 (ISBN 0-394-41703-8). Knopf.
Awakening Land: I. The Trees; II The Fields: III. The Town. Conrad Richter. LC 66-213621. 1966. 7.95. Knopf.
Awakening of Helena Richie. Margaret Wade Campbell Deland. LC 78-96881. (Illus.). 1969. Literature House.
Awakening of Helena Richie. Margaret Wade Campbell Deland. LC 16-9366. 1906. Harper & Brothers.
Awakening of Hezekiah Jones: A Story Dealing with Some of the Problems Affecting the Political Rewards Due the Negro. John Edward Bruce. LC 16-10449. 0.50. P. H. Brown.
Awakening of Jenny. Lillian Colter. LC 50-4719. (Gold medal book, 109). 1950. Fawcett Publications.
Awakening of Jens Lyne. Peter Martin Peterson. LC 14-10522. 1914. 0.25. Standard Press.
Awakening of Lesterville: A Novel. Eugene Lester Small. LC 18-18952. 1918. Chicago, Englewood Print Shop.
Awakening of Lord Dalby. Margaret SeBastian, pseud. 1979. pap. 1.75 (ISBN 0-445-04447-0). Popular Lib.
Awakening of Mary Fenwick. Beatrice Whitby. (On cover: Seaside library. Pocket ed. no. 1264). 1889. G. Munro.
Awakening of Poccalito, a Tale of Telegraph Hill, and Other Tales. Eugenia Kellogg. LC 4-1340. 1908. The Unknown Publisher.
Awakening of the Duchess. Frances Asa Charles. 1903. Little, Brown, and Company.
Awakening of the Hartwells: A Tale of the San Francisco Earthquake. Emma S Allen. LC 14-153. American Tract Society.
Awakening of Zojas. Miriam Michelson. LC 10-7178. 1910. 1.00. Doubleday, Page & Company.
Awakening (The Resurrection) Lev Nikolaevich Tolstoi & Smith, William E., Tr. LC 1671. 1900. Street & Smith.
Awakening Thelma. Leo Freedman. LC 31-23469. 1931. Brentano's.
Award. Harriet Hinsdale. (Orig.). 1979. pap. 2.50 (ISBN 0-89083-537-3). Zebra.
Award of Justice: Or, Told in the Rockies. A Pen Picture of the West. Anna Maynard Barbour. Rand, McNally & Company.
Away All Boats. Kenneth Dodson. 480p. 1980. pap. 2.75 (ISBN 0-553-13573-2). Bantam.
Away All Boats: A Novel. 1st Ed. Kenneth Dodson. LC 54-512324. 1954. Little, Brown.
Away and Beyond. Alfred Elton Van Vogt. LC 52-9050. 1952. Pellegrini & Cudahy.
Away Boarders. Daniel V Gallery. 1973. (pbk) 0.95. Manor Books.
Away Boarders,". Daniel V Gallery. LC 79-116099. 1971. 5.95 (ISBN 0-393-03170-5). Norton.
Away from Home. Rona Jaffe. 1982. pap. 3.50 (ISBN 0-440-10401-7). Dell.
Away from Home: A Novel. Rona Jaffe. LC 60-6722. 1960. Simon and Schuster.
Away from It All. Mary Scott. LC 77-376303. 1977. 7.95 (ISBN 0-09-128980-7). Hurst & Blackett.
Away from Sin. Florenz Branch. LC 41-9388. Phoenix Press.
Away from Sin. Florence Stonebraker. LC 41-9388. 1941. Phoenix Press.
Away from the Here and Now: Stories in Pseudo-Science. Clare Winger Harris. LC 47-4642. 1947. Dorrance.
Away Went the Little Fish. Margot Bennett. LC 47-660. 1947-1946. Pub. for the Crime Club by Doubleday & Company, Inc.
Awdrey-Gore Legacy. Edward Gorey. LC 72-478. (Illus.). 64p. 1972. 4.95 o.p. (ISBN 0-396-06598-8). Dodd.
Awful Rainbow. Angela Morgan, pseud. LC 32-34579. 1932. The Harper Press.
Awkward Age. Henry James. LC 49-9455. (Novel library). 1949. Pantheon Books.
Awkward Age see Bodley Head Henry James.
Awkward Age: A Novel. Henry James. LC 99-1856. 1899. Harper & Brothers.
Awkward Lie. Michael Innes, pseud. (Crime Ser). 1974. pap. 2.95 (ISBN 0-14-003664-4). Penguin.
Awkward Lie. Michael Innes, pseud. (Red Badge Mystery Ser.). 1971. 4.95 o.p. (ISBN 0-396-06345-4). Dodd.
Awkward Lie. John Innes Mackintosh Stewart. LC 72-150165. (Red badge novel of suspense). 1971. 4.95 (ISBN 0-396-06345-4). Dodd, Mead.

Awkward Silence. W. D. Ehrhart. LC 79-92943. 1980. 13.50 (ISBN 0-89002-134-1); pap. 3.50 (ISBN 0-89002-133-3). Northwoods Pr.

AWOL, K-9 Commando. Bertrand Leslie Shurtleff. LC 44-129965. 1944. The Bobbs-Merrill Company.

Awol Musters Out. Bertrand Leslie Shurtleff & Thorne, Diana, 1895- Illus. LC 46-2768. 1946. The Bobbs-Merrill Company.

Ax. Ed McBain. 1964. 3.50 o.p. (ISBN 0-671-06283-2). S&S.

Ax: An 87th Precinct Inner Sanctum Mystery. Evan Hunter. LC 64-19938. 1964. Simon and Schuster.

Ax of Atlantis. Lee Grimes. (Chandra Smith adventure). 1975. (pbk.) 1.25 (ISBN 0-446-76704-2). Warner Paperback Library.

Axe. Sigrid Undset & Chater, Arthur G., Tr. LC 28-4666. 1928. A. A. Knopf.

Axe. Ludvik Vaculik. LC 73-4163. 1973. 6.95 (ISBN 0-06-014486-6). Harper & Row.

Axe Is Laid. John Mackworth. LC 25-608021. 1925. Longmans, Green and Co.

Axe of Wandsbek. Arnold Zweig & Sutton, Eric, Tr. LC 47-11321. 1947. Viking Press.

Axe-Thrower of the Tittabawassee. George Wallace Skinner. LC 35-2616. Printed by the Roe Printing Co.

Axe with Three Nicks. Eugene N Davis. LC 29-4755. The Christopher Publishing House.

Axel. Freda Lingstrom. LC 39-30072. 1939. Little, Brown and Company.

Axeman of the Hardwicks: A Novel. 1st Ed. Ralph McCroskey. LC 54-953717. 1954. Exposition Press.

Axis. Clive Irving. LC 79-55609. 1980. 12.95 (ISBN 0-689-11044-8). Atheneum.

Ayala's Angel. A Novel. Anthony Trollope. (seaside library. v. 51, no. 1047). 1881. G. Munro.

Ayala's Angle. Anthony Trollope. 10.95 o.p. (ISBN 0-19-250342-1). Oxford U Pr.

Ayes of Texas. Daniel Da Cruz. 256p. (Orig.). 1982. pap. 2.25 (ISBN 0-345-29602-8, Del Rey). Ballantine.

Ayesha: A Tale of the Times of Mohammed. Emma Leslie. LC 7-14761. (Church history stories, v. 4). Nelson & Phillips.

Ayesha: A Tale of the Times of Mohammed. Emma Leslie. LC 3-16069. (Church history stories, v. 4). Hunt & Eaton.

Ayesha of the Bosphorus: A Romance of Constantinople. Stanwood Cobb. LC 15-17762. 1915. 1.00. Murray and Emery Company.

Ayesha, the Return of She. Henry Rider Haggard. LC 5-32851. 1905. Doubleday, Page & Company.

Ayesha, the Return of She. Henry Rider Haggard. LC 18-5414. 1905. Grosset & Dunlap.

Ayesha: The Return of She. Henry Rider Haggard & Maurice Greiffenhagen. LC 77-95555. (Illus.). 1978. 3.00 (ISBN 0-486-23649-8). Dover Publications.

Ayesha: The Return of She. Illus. by Hookway Cowles. Henry Rider Haggard. LC 66-5438. 1966. bds., 2.95. Macdonald.

Ayisha. Helen Noga. 1973. (pbk) 1.25. Dell.

Ayisha. Helen Noga. LC 72-82179. 1972. 6.50 (ISBN 0-87795-048-2). Arbor House.

Aylwin. Theodore Watts-Dunton. LC 98-1169.

Aylwin. Theodore Watts-Dunton. 1899. Dodd, Mead and Company.

Aylwin: A Novel. Theodore Watts-Dunton. 1899. 18.50 o.p. (ISBN 0-404-06881-2). AMS Pr.

Aylwins. John Innes Mackintosh Stewart. LC 67-11094. 1967. Norton.

AZ 900. Martha Albrand. LC 73-16862. 1974. 6.95 (ISBN 0-03-012221-X). Holt, Rinehart and Winston.

Azadi. Chaman Lal Nahal. LC 75-4580. (Illus.). 1975. 8.95 (ISBN 0-395-19401-6). Houghton Mifflin.

Azalea's Silver Web. Elia Wilkinson Peattie. LC 16-2878. 0.75. The Reilly & Britton Co.

Azalim: A Romance of Old Judea. Mark Ashton. 1904. L. C. Page & Company.

Azanian Assignment. Iain Finlay. LC 78-1326. 1978. 10.95 (ISBN 0-06-011271-9). Harper & Row.

Azanian Assignment. Iain Finlay. LC 77-15929. 1978. 9.95 (ISBN 0-06-011271-9). Harper & Row.

Azarian: An Episode. Harriet Elizabeth Prescott Spofford. LC 8-14057. 1864. Ticknor and Fields.

Azef. Translated from the Russian by Mirra Ginsburg. Roman Borisovich Gul'. LC 61-12534. 1962. Doubleday.

Azemia: A Descriptive and Sentimental Novel. William Beckford. LC 74-8006. (Feminist Controversy in England, 1788-1810). 1974. 22.00 (ISBN 0-8240-0850-2). Garland Pub.

Azile: A Novel. Jane T. H. Cross. LC 1-5367. 1868. Pub. for the Author, by A. H. Redford.

Azilie of Bordeaux. Mary Dodgen Few. (Illus.). 286p. 1973. 7.95 (ISBN 0-914056-01-8). Carolina Edns.

Azilie of Bordeaux: A Novel. Mary Dodgen Few. LC 73-83755. (Illus.). 1973. 6.95 (ISBN 0-914056-01-8). Carolina Editions.

Azizona Ames. Zane Grey. 1973. (pbk.) 0.75 (ISBN 0-671-75777-6). Pocket Books.

Azor! Archie O'Neill, pseud. LC 76-28033. (Jeff Pride novel). 8.95. St. Martin's Press.

Aztec. Gary Jennings. LC 80-55608. 1980. 15.95 (ISBN 0-689-11045-6). Atheneum.

Aztec Gold. Chet Cunningham. (Jim Steele Ser.: No. 6). (Orig.). 1981. pap. 1.95 (ISBN 0-505-51690-X). Tower Bks.

Aztec Skull. Anthea Goddard. LC 76-56606. (O.s.i.). 1977. 5.95 o.s.i. (ISBN 0-8027-6285-9). Walker & Co.

Aztec Treasure House. Thomas Allibone Janvier. LC 77-104496. (Illus.). 1970. Literature House/Gregg Press.

Aztec Treasure-House: A Romance of Contemporaneous Atiquity. Thomas Allibone Janvier. LC 7-10526. 1890. Harper & Brothers.

Aztec Treasure-House: A Romance of Contemporaneous Antiquity. Thomas Allibone Janvier. LC 4-16480. (On cover: Harper quarterly, no. 1 extra). 1893. Harper & Brothers.

Aztec Treasure-House: A Romance of Contemporaneous Antiquity. Thomas Allibone Janvier. LC 20-7523. Harper & Brothers.

Aztec Treasure House for Boys. Thomas Allibone Janvier. LC 29-27454. 1929. Harper & Brothers.

Aztec Two-Step. Drawings by Marcelina. Stuart Sherman. LC 53-10915. 1953. Greenberg.

Azuela and the Mexican Underdogs. Stanley Linn Robe. LC 76-20031. (UCLA Latin American studies; v. 48). (Series: California. University. University at Los Angeles. Latin American Center.). (Latin American studies; v. 48.). (Illus.). 14.95 (ISBN 0-520-03293-4). University of California Press.

Azure Castle. Janette Radcliffe. (Candlelight Regency, 204). Dell.

Azure Cities. Romanov et al. LC 72-3284. (Short Story Index Reprint Ser.). 1972. Repr. of 1929 ed. 18.00 (ISBN 0-8369-4143-8). Ayer Co.

Azure Cities: Stories of a New Russia. Tr. by Robbins, J. J. Ed. by JX 4410. A85 1806. LC 29-4207. International Publishers.

Azure Cities; Stories of New Russia. LC 72-3284. (Short story index reprint series). 1972. (ISBN 0-8369-4143-8). Books for Libraries Press.

Azure Hand: A Novel. Samuel Rutherford Crockett. LC 17-22294. 1917. Hodder and Stoughton.

Azure Rose: A Novel. Reginald Wright Kauffman. LC 19-585120. 1919. 1.50. The Macaulay Company.

B

B As in Banshee. Lawrence Treat. LC 40-11567. Duell, Sloan and Pearce.

B C D: A Novel. David R. Slavitt. LC 72-77005. 1972. 6.95 (ISBN 0-385-03634-5). Doubleday.

B. F. Skinner's Walden Two: Introduction and Commentary by Daniel B. Stevick. Daniel B Stevick. (Religious dimensions in lit., RDL8). 1968. Seabury.

B for Murder... Jane Layhew. LC 46-61015. 1946. J. B. Lippincott Company.

B. F.'s Daughter. John Phillips Marquand. LC 46-7089. 1946. Little, Brown and Company.

B. M. Bower's Big Book of Western Stories: Four Rousing Novels of the West Complete in One Volume... Bertha Muzzy Sinclair. LC 33-28409. 1933. Grosset & Dunlap.

Baal. Brecht. 1969. pap. 3.25x o.s.i. (ISBN 0-536-00046-8). Xerox College.

Baal. mccammon. ed. Robert R McCammon. LC 78-58890. 1978. 2.25 (ISBN 0-380-36319-4). Avon Books.

Bab, a Sub-Deb. Mary Roberts Rinehart. LC 17-14952. 1917. George H. Doran Company.

Bab: a Sub-Deb. Mary Roberts Rinehart. 1918. A. L. Burt Company.

Babar a New York. Laurent De Brunhoff. LC 67-71943. (Grands albums Hachette). 1966. Hachette.

Babaru. B. Wongar. LC 82-4860. (Illinois Short Fiction Ser.). 112p. 1982. 11.95 (ISBN 0-252-00995-9); pap. 4.95 (ISBN 0-252-00996-7). U of Ill Pr.

Babaru: Stories. B Wongar. LC 82-4860. (Illinois Short Fiction). (Illus.). 11.95 (ISBN 0-252-00995-9) (ISBN 0-252-00996-7). University of Illinois Press.

Babbie: The Story of Babie Lee, and Some Further Doings of Peter Loomis and Daphne. Margaret Rebecca Piper Chalmers. LC 25-17585. L. C. Page & Company.

Babbitt. Sinclair Lewis. LC 22-14419. Harcourt, Brace and Company.

Babbitt. Sinclair Lewis. LC 31-19512. 1924. Grosset & Dunlap.

Babbitt. Sinclair Lewis. LC 42-360685. (Half-title: The Modern library of the world's best books 162). 1942. Modern Library.

Babble. Jonathan Baumbach. LC 76-2876. 117p. 1976. 8.95 (ISBN 0-914590-26-X); pap. 3.95 (ISBN 0-914590-27-8). Fiction Coll.

Babbling with Ecstasy. S. V. Baxter. (Orig.). 1970. pap. 1.95 o.s.i. (OPH-181, Ophelia). Olympia.

Babe. Joan Smith. LC 80-16923. 1980. 13.95 (ISBN 0-8161-3112-0). G. K. Hall.

Babe. Marianne Wiggins. (Equinox book). 1975. (pbk.) 2.95 (ISBN 0-380-00239-6). Avon.

Babe, B. A. Being the Uneventful History of a Young Gentleman at Cambridge University. Edward Frederic Benson. LC 6-11343. 1896. G. P. Putnam's Sons.

Babe, B. A. Being the Uneventful History of a Young Gentleman at Cambridge University. Edward Frederic Benson. LC 9-2675. (On cover: Bell's Indian & colonial library). 1897. G. P. Putnam's Sons.

Babe Evanson: A Novel. Catharine Brody. LC 28-21744. The Century Co.

Babe Gordon. Mae West. LC 30-29562. The Macaulay Company.

Babe in Arms. Peggy Gaddis, pseud. LC 43-3845. 1943. Phoenix Press.

Babe in the Wood. Roger Longrigg. LC 76-377982. 1976. 3.75 (ISBN 0-7181-1458-2). Joseph.

Babe Murphy. Patience Stapleton. LC 8-13450. 1890. Belford-Clarke Co.

Babe Ruth Caught in a Snowstorm. John Alexander Graham. LC 72-9072. 1973. 5.95 (ISBN 0-395-15923-7). Houghton Mifflin.

Babe Saunders: A Story of the Oklahoma Oil Fields. Marion Thomas Martin. LC 16-12751. Christian Union Herald Print.

Babe Unborn. Ernest James Oldmeadow. LC 11-11287. 1911. 1.20. The Century Co.

Babe with the Twistable Arm. Aaron Marc Stein. LC 62-17322. (Pan inner sanctum mystery?). 1962. Simon and Schuster.

Babe with the Twistable Arm. Hampton Stone, pseud. (Hampton Stone Mysteries Ser). 1971. pap. 0.75 o.p. (ISBN 0-446-64682-2, 64-682-2). Paperback Lib.

Babel. Alan Burns. pap. cancelled (ISBN 0-7145-0011-9). Riverrun NY.

Babel. John Cournos. LC 22-18399. Boni and Liveright.

Babel. Hugh MacNair Kahler. LC 21-3808. 1921. 2.00. G. P. Putnam's Sons.

Babel: A Novel. Alan Burns. LC 76-105561. 1970. 4.95. John Day Co.

Babel-Seventeen. Samuel R. Delany. (Science Fiction of Samuel R. Delany Ser.). 176p. 1976. Repr. of 1969 ed. lib. bdg. 9.95 o.p. (ISBN 0-8398-2328-2, Gregg). G K Hall.

Babel-17. Samuel R Delany. LC 76-10741. (Gregg Press science fiction series). 1976. 9.00 (ISBN 0-8398-2328-2). Gregg Press.

Babes and Sucklings. Philip Wylie. LC 29-9007. 1929. A. A. Knopf.

Babes in the Darkling Wood: A Novel. Herbert George Wells. LC 40-33030. Alliance Book Corporation.

Babes in the Wood: A Relaxation Intended for Those Who Are Always Travelling but Never Reaching a Destination. Michael Arlen. LC 30-32. 1929. Doubleday, Doran & Company, Inc.

Babes in the Wood: A Tragic Comedy. A Story of the Italian Revolution of 1848. James De Mille. 1875. W. F. Gill & Company, Successors to Shepard & Gill.

Babes in the Woods. Lillian O'Donnell. LC 65-15796. (Raven book). 1965. Abelard-Schuman.

Babette: A Novel. Frank Berkeley Smith. LC 16-6760. 1916. Doubleday, Page & Company.

Babette Bomberling's Bridegrooms. Alice Berend. Tr. by Nohowel, Margaret. LC 21-15329. Boni and Liveright.

Babi Yar: A Document in the Form of a Novel. Anatolii Vasilevich Kuznetsov. LC 70-125154. 1970. 10.00. Farrar, Straus and Giroux.

Babi Yar: A Documentary Novel. Anatolii Vasilevich Kuznetsov. LC 67-18091. (Illus.). 1967. Dial Press.

Babies. Gyo Fujikawa. LC 63-6965. (Illus.). 1963. McLoughlin Bros.

Babies Without Tails: Stories. Walter Duranty. LC 37-28667. (Modern age books. Blue seal books, no. 1). Modern Age Books, Inc.

Babiole, the Pretty Milliner. Fortune Du Boisgobey. (Seaside library, v. 95, nol 1925). 1884-85. G. Munro.

Babiole, the Pretty Milliner. Fortune Du Boisgobey. (On cover: Seaside library. Pocket ed. no. 328). 1884-85. G. Munro.

Babolain: A Novel; Translated from the French of Gustave Droz. Gustave Droz & MS, Tr. LC 6-34217. (Leisure hour ser. no. 18). 1873. Holt & Williams.

Baboon Rock. Robert W Krepps. LC 59-14043. 1959. Macmillan.

Babouk. S. Guy Endore. LC 34-286218. The Vanguard Press.

Babs the Impossible. Sarah Grand. 1900. Harper & Bros.

Baby. Robert Lieberman. LC 81-1491. 12.95 (ISBN 0-517-54488-1). Crown.

Baby. Genovieve Nolan. LC 31-108652. Brewer & Warren Inc.

Baby. Viva. 1975. 8.95 o.p. (ISBN 0-394-49198-X). Knopf.

Baby: A Novel. Kirsten Thorup. LC 80-17844. 9.95 (ISBN 0-8071-0772-7). Louisiana State University Press.

Baby: A Video Novel. Viva, pseud. LC 74-21332. (Illus.). 1975. 8.95 (ISBN 0-394-49198-X). Knopf: Distributed by Random House.

Baby, and One New Year's Eve. Margaret Wolfe Hungerford & Percy Greg. (Seaside Library. Pocket Ed.). (On cover: The seaside library. Pocket ed., no. 342: No. 342). 1885. G. Munro.

Baby, Baby. Paul Kropp. LC 82-12931. (Encounter Ser.). (Illus.). 96p. 1982. pap. text ed. 3.95 (ISBN 0-88436-962-5); wkbk. 1.20 (ISBN 0-88436-966-8). EMC.

Baby Bare. Sharri Templeton. pap. 1.95 o.p. (8013). Cameo.

Baby Blue Marine. Max Franklin. (Signet Book). 1976. (pbk.) 1.50. New American Library.

Baby Blue Rip-off. Max Collins. LC 82-50805. 11.95 (ISBN 0-8027-5475-9). Walker.

Baby Boy. Jess Gregg. LC 73-78624. 1973. 6.95 (ISBN 0-399-11158-1). Putnam.

Baby Bullet, the Bubble of Destiny. Lloyd Osbourne. LC 5-32702. 1905. D. Appleton and Company.

Baby Chocolate and Other Short Stories: Aspects of the Black Experience: an Original Collection. Clifton Bullock. LC 73-81865. 1975. 4.75. William-Frederick Press.

Baby Chocolate: Short Stories of the Modern Black Experience. Clifton Bullock. 1975. 4.75 (ISBN 0-87164-132-1). William-F.

Baby, Come on Inside. David Wagoner. LC 68-23743. 1968. Farrar, Straus and Giroux.

Baby Dear. Walter A. Runkle. 3.00 o.p. Carlton.

Baby Doctor. Florence Stonebraker. LC 43-557241. 1943. Phoenix Press.

Baby Doll. Tennessee Williams. LC 56-13347. 4.50 (ISBN 0-8112-0405-7). New Directions.

Baby Driver. Jan Kerouac. LC 81-8757. 1981. 12.95 (ISBN 0-312-06376-8). St. Martin's Press.

Baby Driver. Jan Kerouac. LC 82-15503. 1983. 4.95 (ISBN 0-03-062538-6). Holt, Rinehart, and Winston.

Baby Driver: A Story About Myself. Frances Casey Kerns. 1981. 11.95 (ISBN 0-312-06376-8). St Martin.

Baby Elton, Quarter-Back. Leslie W Quirk. LC 4-27672. 1904. The Century Co.

Baby Face. Dulcie Gray. LC 73-152723. 1972. 5.95 (ISBN 0-85617-902-7). White Lion.

Baby Grand. John Luther Long. LC 12-15146. 1.25. R. G. Badger.

Baby Grand: And Other Stories. Stacy Aumonier. LC 27-38113. H. Holt and Company.

Baby in the Ash Can. Harriette Ashbrook. LC 44-1298. 1944. Dodd, Mead & Company.

Baby in the Icebox: & Other Short Fiction. James Mallahan Cain. Ed. by Roy Hoopes. LC 80-28900. 320p. 1981. 14.95 (ISBN 0-03-058501-5). HR&W.

Baby in the Icebox and Other Short Fiction. James Mallahan Cain & Roy Hoopes. LC 80-28900. 14.95 (ISBN 0-03-058501-5). Holt, Rinehart & Winston.

Baby Island. Carol Ryrie Brink. (Collier Books, juvenile paperbacks). (Illus.). 1973. (pbk.) 0.95. Collier Books.

Baby, It's Cold Inside. Sidney J. Perelman. LC 70-116508. 1970. 6.50 o.s.i. (ISBN 0-671-20654-0). S&S.

Baby, I've Got Your Number. Cathy Guisewite. 128p. 1982. pap. 3.95 (ISBN 0-8362-1181-2). Andrews & McMeel.

Baby Killers, the Tragedy of Youth. William Jennings Jones. LC 31-29961. Printed by the Stratford Press, Inc.

Baby Lamb: A Novel. Jean Boley. 1948. E. P. Dutton.

Baby-Land. Almira L. Corey Frink. LC 12-1218.

Baby Love. Joyce Maynard. LC 80-2707. 1981. 11.95 (ISBN 0-394-51802-0). Knopf: Distributed by Random House.

Baby Love. Joyce Maynard. 1982. 2.95 (ISBN 0-380-59550-8). Avon Books.

Baby Love and Casey Blue. Darby Foote. LC 74-16597. 1975. 6.95 (ISBN 0-399-11436-X). Putnam.

Baby Love and Casey Blue. Darby Foote. 1976. 1.50 (ISBN 0-425-03158-6). Berkley Publishing Corp.

Baby Love: Too Young for Love But Not for Making Babies. Joyce Maynard. 224p. 1982. pap. 2.95 (ISBN 0-380-59550-8, 59550). Avon.

Baby Makes Three. Kim Savage. LC 53-8240. 1953. Vixen Press.

Baby Merchants. Lillian O'Donnell. LC 74-30573. (Red mask mystery). 1975. 5.95 (ISBN 0-399-11504-8). Putnam.

Baby Mine. Margaret Mayo. LC 11-27303. 1911. Dodd, Mead and Company.
Baby Perpetua, and Other Stories. Millicent Dillon. LC 78-133251. 1971. 5.95. Viking Press.
Baby Rue: Her Adventures and Misadventures, Her Friends and Her Enemies. Charlotte Clark. LC 6-25358. (No Name Ser.). (No name ser. 2d ser. v. 9: Second Ser., Vol. 9). 1881. Roberts Brothers.
Baby Sitters. John Salisbury. LC 77-88910. 1978. 9.95 (ISBN 0-689-10852-4). Atheneum.
Baby Sweet's. Raymond Andrews. LC 82-22181. (Illus.). 224p. 1983. 15.95 (ISBN 0-385-27426-2). Dial.
Babyburgers. Andrew G. Carrigan & Warren J. Hecht. LC 75-19940. (Illus.). 64p. (Orig.). 1975. pap. 2.45 o.p. (ISBN 0-914908-25-1). Street Fiction.
Babyhip. Patricia Welles. (Signet bk., Q3465). 1968. New Amer. Lib.
Babyhip. Patricia Welles. LC 67-20537. 1967. Dutton.
Babylon. Anthony Esler. LC 79-22333. 1980. 11.95 (ISBN 0-688-03561-2). Morrow.
Babylon. A Novel. Grant Allen. (On cover: Seaside library. Pocket ed., no. 610)). 1885. G. Monro.

Babylon Electrified: The History of an Expedition Undertaken to Restore Ancient Babylon by the Power of Electricity and How It Resulted. Albert Bleunard & Weitenkampf, Frank, 1866- Tr. 1889. Gebbie & Co.

Babylon on Hudson: Anonymous... LC 32-22967. 1932. Harper & Brothers.

Babylon Revisited, and Other Stories. Francis Scott Key Fitzgerald. LC 60-13027. (Scribner library, SL22). 1960. Scribner.

Babylonians. Nathaniel Norsen Weinreb. LC 53-5754. 1953. Doubleday.
Babyons: The Chronicle of a Family. Winnifred Ashton. LC 28-176408. 1928. Doubleday, Doran and Company, Inc.
Babyons: The Chronicle of a Family. Winnifred Ashton. LC 29-215568. 1929. Doubleday, Doran and Company, Inc.
Baby's First Years. Illus. by Ennie Di Majo. (Illus.). 64p. 1976. 5.95 (ISBN 0-8326-2209-5, 7479); pap. 2.50 (7503). Delair.
Baby's Grandmother. Lucy Bethia Colquhoun Walford. (On cover: Lovell's library. no. 1057). 1887. J. W. Lovell Company.
Baby's Grandmother. new impression. ed. Lucy Bethia Colquhoun Walford. LC 4-16586. 1901. Longmans, Green, and Co.
Baby's on the Toilet. Maurice Tripp. 2.75 o.p. Vantage.
Baby's Reward. Sarah Elizabeth Forbush G. S. Downs Downs. LC 6-45950. (On cover: The select series. no. 93). 1892. Street & Smith.
Babysitter. Robert Boyle. LC 75-32831. 1976. 7.95 (ISBN 0-8027-5335-3). Walker.
Babysitter. Andrew Coburn. 1980. 2.50 (ISBN 0-671-82864-9). Pocket Books.
Babysitter. John Fraser. LC 71-79712. 1969. 5.95. Putnam.
Babysitter. Gloria Russell. 192p. (Orig.). 1973. pap. 1.95 o.p. (ISBN 0-87977-194-1, DBB194). Dansk Blue Bk.
Babysitter. Norman Singer. LC 77-219469. 1968. 2.25. Ophelia Press.
Babysitter: A Novel. Andrew Coburn. LC 78-24150. 9.95 (ISBN 0-393-01189-5). Norton.
Babysitter Seducers. Donald A. Worth. 192p. (Orig.). 1973. pap. 1.95 o.p. (ISBN 0-87682-300-2, 7300). Barclay Hse.
Bac-Si My: In the Year of the Dog, Pt. 1. Richard O. Albert. 8.95 (ISBN 0-8062-0996-8). Carlton.
Baccarat. Julia Davis Frankau. LC 4-32318. 1904. J. B. Lippincott Company.
Baccarat Club. Jessie Louisa Moore Rickard. LC 29-112869. 1929. H. Liveright.
Baccarat; or, The Gambler's Career. Hector Henri Malot. LC 7-24364. (On cover: (Richard K. Fox's sensational series, no. 1). 1891. R. K. Fox.
Bacchante: The Story of a Brief Career. Robert Smythe Hichens. LC 27-17117. 1927. Cosmopolitan Book Corporation.
Bach and the Heavenly Choir. Translated from the German by Maurice Michael. 1st Ed. Johannes Ruber. LC 57-5888. World Pub. Co.
Bach Festival Murders. Blanche Bloch. LC 42-4711. 1942. Harper & Brothers.
Bachelor. Stella Gibbons. LC 44-8232. 1944. Dodd, Mead & Company.
Bachelor--of Arts. John Erskine. LC 34-140028. The Bobbs-Merrill Company.
Bachelor Apartment. Claire Kennedy. LC 38-22278. Pheonix Press.
Bachelor Ben. Ella Giles Ruddy. LC 6-44052. 1875. Atwood & Culver.
Bachelor Betty. Winifred Lewellin James. 1907. E. P. Dutton & Company.
Bachelor Buttons. Frank Chaffee. LC 6-23347. 1892. G. M. Allen Company.
Bachelor Dinner. Olive Mary Briggs. LC 12-9962. 1912. C. Scribner's Sons.
Bachelor Doctor. Elizabeth Seifert. LC 69-18474. 1969. 4.95. Dodd, Mead.
Bachelor Doctor. Marjorie Warby. 1971. pap. 0.75 o.p. (94103). Beagle Bks.
Bachelor Flat Mystery. Robert Alfred John Walling. LC 34-17652. 1934. W. Morrow & Co.
Bachelor Girl. A Novel of the 1400. William Hosea Ballou. LC 6-6092. (On cover: American novelists' series, no. 31). J. W. Lovell Company.
Bachelor Girl: From the French of "La Garconne". Victor Margueritte. Tr. by Burnaby, Hugh. LC 23-11514. 1923. A. A. Knopf.
Bachelor Husband. Ruby Mildred Ayres. LC 20-19580. W. J. Watt & Company.
Bachelor in Arcady. Halliwell Sutcliffe. 1904. T. Y. Crowell & Co.
Bachelor Maid. Constance Cary Harrison. LC 5-244449. 1894. The Century Co.
Bachelor of Arts. Dean Fales. LC 32-11457. 1932. L. MacVeagh, Dial Press, Inc.
Bachelor of Arts. R. K. Narayan. LC 80-16398. 1980. 13.00 (ISBN 0-226-56832-6) (ISBN 0-226-56833-4). University of Chicago Press.
Bachelor of Arts: A Novel. R. K. Narayan. LC 54-4796. 1954. Michigan State College Press.
Bachelor of Arts: A Novel. R. K. Narayan. LC 37-34173. 1937. T. Nelson and Sons, Limited.
Bachelor of Paris. John William Harding. (On cover: Neely's library of choice literature, no. 65). 1897. F. T. Neely.
Bachelor of Salamanca, 2 vols. in 1. Alain Rene Le Sage. Tr. by John Lockman. LC 80-2488. Repr. of 1767 ed. 98.50 (ISBN 0-404-19122-3). AMS Pr.
Bachelor of Salamanca: Translated from the French of M. Le Sage... Alain Rene Le Sage & Townsend, James, Tr. LC 44-23376. 1868. T. W. Hartley.
Bachelor of the Albany. Marmion W. Savage. LC 14-224582. 1848. Harper & Brothers.
Bachelor of the Albany. Marmion W. Savage. Ed. by Bonamy Dobree. LC 28-134995. (Rescue Ser.). 1928. Frederick A. Stokes Company.
Bachelor of the Albany. A Novel... Marmion W. Savage. (On cover: Seaside library. Pocket ed.). (On cover: Seaside library. Pocket ed., no. 443: No. 443). 1885. G. Munro.
Bachelor of the Barren Rim. Simon C Walburg. LC 35-38582. Zondervan Publishing House.
Bachelor of the Midway. St. George Rathborne. (On cover: Mascot library, no. 5). 1894. The Mascot Publishing Co.
Bachelor of the Midway. St. George Rathborne. LC 8-237. (On cover: Criterion series, no. 14). Street & Smith.
Bachelor Party. Hal Hickman. LC 77-4842. 7.95 (ISBN 0-397-01236-5). Lippincott.
Bachelor Seals. Martin Dibner. LC 48-504353. 1948. Doubleday.
Bachelor Vicar of Newforth: A Novel. J. Harcourt- Roe. LC 7-40252. (Harper's handy series, no. 44). 1885. Harper & Brothers.
Bachelor Vicar of Newforth. A Novel. J. Harcourt- Roe. (On cover: Seaside library. Pocket ed. no. 683). 1886. G. Munro.
Bachelors. Henry De Montherlant. LC 77-10926. 1977. 14.50 (ISBN 0-8371-9811-9). Greenwood Press.
Bachelors. Muriel Spark. LC 61-6333. 1961. Lippincott.
Bachelors: A Novel. William Dana Orcutt. LC 15-19863. 1915. 1.35. Harper & Brothers.
Bachelors and Butterflies. A Midsummer Diversion. Allis Arnold. (On cover: Satchel series, no. 40). W. B. Smith & Co.
Bachelors: And Other Tales, Founded on American Incidents and Character. Samuel Lorenzo Knapp. LC 49-32963. 1836. J. and W. Sandford.
Bachelors Anonymous. Pelham Grenville Wodehouse. LC 74-5030. 1974. 6.95 (ISBN 0-671-21741-0). Simon and Schuster.
Bachelors Anonymous. Pelham Grenville Wodehouse. LC 74-18275. 1974. (ISBN 0-8161-6247-6). G. K. Hall.
Bachelors Are Made. Eleanor Arnett Nash. LC 46-1250. 1946. D. Appleton-Century Company, Inc.
Bachelor's Baby. Coyne Fletcher. LC 6-39934. 1891. Clark & Zugalla.
Bachelor's Blunder. William Edward Norris. (On cover: Seaside library. Pocket ed. no. 871). 1886. G. Munro.
Bachelor's Bounty. Grace Louise Smith Richmond. LC 32-33983. 1932. Doubleday, Doran & Company, Inc.
Bachelor's Bounty. Grace Louise Smith Richmond. LC 41-4925. 1940. Triangle Books.
Bachelor's Bridges. Margaret Jane Prater. LC 50-8551. 1950. Humphries.
Bachelors' Buttons: The Candid Confessions of a Shy Bachelor. Edward Burke. LC 12-27596. 1912. 1.30. Moffat, Yard and Company.
Bachelor's Christmas. Robert Grant. LC 6-34976. 1906. C. Scribner's Sons.
Bachelor's Christmas: And Other Stories. Robert Grant. LC 4-151138. 1895. C. Scribner's Sons.
Bachelor's Christmas & Other Stories. Robert Grant. LC 70-94728. (Short Story Index Reprint Ser.). 1895. 19.00 (ISBN 0-8369-3107-6). Ayer Co.
Bachelor's Comedy. Annie Edith Foster Jameson. LC 12-14396. 1.25. Hodder & Stoughton, George H. Doran Company.
Bachelor's Daughter. Hubert Madere. LC 35-4417. Dorrance & Company, Inc.
Bachelor's Death. Arthur Shnitzler. (Arabic.). pap. 8.95x o.p. Intl Bk Ctr.
Bachelor's Establishment. Honore De Balzac. LC 52-9989. (Illustrated Novel Library). (Illus.). 1952. Farrar, Straus & Young.
Bachelor's Hall: A Novel. Reginald Underwood. LC 75-12353. (Homosexuality). 1975. 12.00 (ISBN 0-405-07391-7). Arno Press.
Bachelor's Heyday. Micheline Keating. LC 33-28730. A. H. King.
Bachelor's House. Translated by Frances Frenaye. Honore De Balzac. LC 56-9196. 1956. Juniper Press; Distributed by Criterion Books.
Bachelors. Les Celibataires. Henri de Montherlant. (1973). 1965. Penguin.
Bachelor's Plaything. Beverly Benson. LC 39-9941. 1939. Hill-Man-Curl, Inc.
Bachelor's Quarters: Stories from Two Worlds. Ed. by Norman Lockridge. LC 45-632143. 1944. Biltmore Publishing Company.
Bachelor's Story. Oliver Bell Bunce. LC 6-18679. 1859. Rudd & Carleton.
Bachelor's Story. Oliver Bell Bunce. LC 7-354869. 1860. W. A. Townsend and Company.
Bachelor's Wedding Trip. Charles Pomeroy Sherman. LC 8-51269. 1888. The Pen Publishing Company.
Bachelor's Widow: Translated by Alan French. Maurice Dekobra, pseud. LC 55-18985. (Ace books, S-85). 1954. Ace Books.
Bachelors' Wife. George A. Bagby, pseud. LC 32-2657. 1932. Covici, Friede.
Bachelor's Wife. Jessica Steele. 192p. 1982. pap. 1.50 (ISBN 0-373-02451-7, Pub. by Harlequin). PB.
Bachman's Law. Richard Thorman. LC 80-20504. 12.95 (ISBN 0-393-01443-6). Norton.
Back. Henry Green. 1967. pap., 2.45. Grosset.
Back. Henry Green. LC 50-9638. 1950. Viking Press.
Back. Henry Green. LC 81-721. 1981. 5.95 (ISBN 0-8112-0798-6). New Directions.
Back Again. Denis George Mackail. LC 36-20245. 1936. Doubleday, Doran & Company, Inc.
Back Bay. William Martin. LC 79-15706. (Illus.). 12.95 (ISBN 0-517-53602-1). Crown.
Back Bay Murders... Roger Scarlett. LC 30-23090. 1930. Pub. for the Crime Club, Inc., by Doubleday, Doran & Company, Inc.
Back Country. 1st Ed. William Hanscom Fuller. LC 53-13191. (First edition, 8). 1954. Dell Pub. Co.
Back Door Lovers. Angus Hertz. pap. 1.95 o.p. (ISBN 0-87682-216-2, 7216). Barclay Hse.
Back Door to Death: A Mr. Potter Mystery. Elinore Denniston. LC 63-9541. (Red badge detective). 1963. Dodd, Mead.
Back Door to Happiness. Ruth Cross. LC 37-14926. J. H. Hopkins & Sons. Inc.
Back Door Virgins. S. P. Blake. 192p. (Orig.). 1973. pap. 1.95 o.p. (ISBN 0-87682-351-7, 7351). Barclay Hse.
Back-Fence Story. Augusta Walker. LC 66-21363. (Illus.). 1967. Knopf.
Back Fire: A California Story. Lola Jean Simpson. LC 27-213440. 1927. The Macmillan Company.
Back from Goliad. George Whitfield Barrington & Duval, John Crittenden. Early Times in Texas. LC 35-13165. Southwest Press.
Back from the Dead: A Story of the Stage. Saqui Smith. LC 8-9628. ("unknown" library no. 12). Cassell Publishing Company.
Back from the Run: A Story of the Mountain Division of the S. & G. N. Perry Coler. LC 48-34216. 1934-1948. News.
Back Home. Peggy Gaddis, pseud. LC 50-8005. 1950. Arcadia House.
Back Home. Eugene Wood. LC 5-32329. 1905. McClure, Phillips & Co.
Back Home and Folks Back Home. Eugene Wood. LC 35-16783. 1935. Doubleday, Doran & Company, Inc.
Back Home: Being the Narrative of Judge Priest and His People. Irvin Shrewsbury Cobb. LC 12-250691. George H. Doran Company.
Back in Boston Again. Tom Clark. 1973. pap. 2.00 o.s.i. (ISBN 0-915890-33-X, Telegraph). Dynamic Learn Corp.
Back Numbers. Joseph Crosby Lincoln. LC 33-23916. Coward, McCann, Inc.
Back O' the Mountain. Margaret Flint. LC 40-316272. 1940. Dodd, Mead & Company.
Back of Beyond. James Watkins. LC 77-150946. 1971. 8.00. Cambrian Publications.
Back of Beyond. Stewart Edward White. LC 27-906861. 1927. Doubleday, Page & Company.
Back of Sunset. Jon Cleary. LC 59-739825. 1959. Morrow.
Back of the Book. Margaret Leech. LC 25-1249. Boni and Liveright.
Back of the Mountain: A Tale of Young China and the People's Party. Mary Brewster Hollister. LC 34-11657. Fleming H. Revell Company.
Back of Town. Maritta Martin Wolff. LC 52-5132. 1952. Random House.
Back-Office Girls. Rolf Kettering. 1974. (pbk.) 1.95 (ISBN 0-87056-371-8). Brandon Books.
Back Roads. Katharine Haviland Taylor. LC 30-13750. J. B. Lippincott Company.
Back Seat. Gladys Bronwyn Stern. LC 23-13188. 1923. A. A. Knopf.
Back-Seat Murder. Herman Landon. LC 31-1721. 1931. H. Liveright.

Back Stage: A Story of the Theater. Roland Oliver. LC 24-15188. 1924. The Macmillan Company.

Back Street. Fannie Hurst. LC 31-2908. 1931. Cosmopolitan Book Corporation.

Back Street. Fannie Hurst. LC 33-17504. 1932. A. L. Burt Company.

Back Then Tomorrow. Peter Blue Cloud. (Illus.). 1978. pap. 3.00 (ISBN 0-942396-27-8). Blackberry ME.

Back to Back. Edith Campion. (Orig.). Date not set. pap. 7.95 (ISBN 0-89407-041-X). Strawberry Hill.
Back to Back. A Story of to-Day. Edward Everett Hale. LC 7-3634. (On cover: Harper's half-hour series v. 48). 1878. Harper & Brothers.
Back-to-Backs. J C Grant. LC 30-24842. 1930. J. Cape & H. Smith.
Back to Battle. John Harris. LC 79-26232. 1980. 10.95 (ISBN 0-689-11042-1). Atheneum.
Back to Battle. Max Hennessy, pseud. LC 79-55585. 1980. 10.95 o.p. (ISBN 0-689-11042-1). Atheneum.
Back to Berlin: An Exile Returns. Verna B Carleton. LC 59-11893. 1959. Little, Brown.
Back to China: A Novel by Leslie A. Fiedler. Leslie A Fiedler. LC 65-14397. 1965. Stein and Day.
Back to Fire. James V Calire. LC 52-4484. 1952. Vantage Press.
Back to Fire Mountain. Richard Scowcroft. LC 72-8834. 1973. 7.50 (ISBN 0-316-77701-3). Little, Brown.
Back to God's Country: And Other Stories. James Oliver Curwood. LC 20-10308. Grosset & Dunlap.
Back to God's Country: And Other Stories. James Oliver Curwood. LC 30-123384. 1920. Grosset & Dunlap.
Back to Life. Thomas Wilkinson Speight. LC 8-15512. (On cover: Maydower library, no. 2). 1891. J. A. Taylor and Company.
Back to Nature. Robert William Alexander. LC 46-2252. S. Paul & Co. Ltd.
Back to School with Betsy. Carolyn Haywood. (Voyager Book). (Illus.). 1972. 1.15 (ISBN 0-15-610200-5). Harcourt.
Back to Stay. Jonathan Leonard. LC 28-9851. J. Leonard.
Back to Texas. Owen G. Irons. (YA) 1978. 6.95 (Avalon). Bouregy.
Back to the Barrios (Balikbario) Juan M. Flavier. 1979. pap. 4.75 (Pub. by New Day Pub). Cellar.
Back to the Old Home. Mary Cecil Hay. LC 7-3761. (On cover: Harper's half-hour series no. 73). 1878. Harper & Brothers.
Back to the Old Trail. Janet M Ingles. Evangelical Publishing House.
Back to the Soil: Or, From Tenement House to Farm Colony; a Circular Solution of an Angular Problem. Bradley Gilman. LC 1-18715. 1901. L. C. Page & Company.
Back to the Stone Age. Edgar Rice Burroughs. LC 63-21728. (Illus.). 1963. Canaveral Press.
Back to the Stone Age. Edgar Rice Burroughs. LC 37-39116. E. R. Burroughs, Inc.
Back to the Top of the World. (Kangaroo Book). (Illus.). 1977. 1.75. (ISBN 0-671-80929-6). Pocket Books.
Back to the Top of the World. (Kangaroo Book). (Illus.). 1977. 1.75. (ISBN 0-671-80929-6). Pocket Books.
Back to the Top of the World: A Novel. Hans Ruesch. LC 72-12172. 1973. 6.95 (ISBN 0-684-13308-3). Scribner.
Back to the Wall. Robert P Hansen. LC 57-13153. 1957. M. S. Mill Co. and W. Morrow.
Back to the Woods: The Story of a Fall from Grace. George Vere Hobart. 1903. G. W. Dillingham Co.
Back to the World. F Champol. Tr. by Leggatt, L. M. LC 12-4137. 1912. Benziger Brothers.

Back to the World, Translated from the French of Champol's "Les Revenantes,". Gaston Baselle De Lagreze & Leggatt, Lilian Marian (Phillips) Tr. LC 12-4137. 1912. Benziger Brothers.
Back to Treasure Island. Harold Augustin Calahan & Stevenson, Robert Louis. LC 35-24894. The Vanguard Press.
Back to Virtue, Betty. Margaret Widdemer. LC 34-185251. Farrar & Rinehart, Incorporated.
Back Tracking Bronco. Ernie Daniel. LC 68-55521. 1969. 2.50. Dorrance.
Back Trail to Danger: A Powder Valley Western. Peter Field. LC 51-12076. 1951. Jefferson House.
Back Trailers from the Middle Border see Collected Works.
Back Trails. Norman Daniels. 1962. Avalon Books.
Back-up Men. Ross Thomas. (Kangaroo Book). 1976. 1.75 (ISBN 0-671-81934-8). Pocket Books.
Backbone Two: New Fiction by Northwest Women. 154p. pap. 4.95 (ISBN 0-931188-07-5). Crossing Pr.
Backbone Two: New Fiction by Northwest Women. Ed. by Barbara Wilson & Da Silva. 160p. (Orig.). 1980. 4.95. Seal Pr WA.
Backfire. Daniel Chase. LC 31-20525. The Bobbs-Merrill Company.
Backfire. Clive Egleton. LC 79-63906. 1979. 8.95 (ISBN 0-689-10990-3). Atheneum.
Backfire. Edna Sherry. LC 56-6288. (Red badge detective). Dodd, Mead.
Backfire Is Hostile! James Barnett. LC 79-5164. 1979. 8.95 (ISBN 0-312-06481-0). St. Martin's Press.
Backflash. Laurence James. (Rack,#3). 1975. (pbk.) 1.25 (ISBN 0-523-00555-5). Pinnacle Books.
Backfurrow. Geoffrey Dell Eaton. LC 25-18177. 1925. G. P. Putnam's Sons.
Background for Caroline. Helen Ashton. LC 29-23244. Harcourt, Brace and Company.
Background for Venus. James Laver. LC 35-1173. 1935. A. A. Knopf.
Background to Danger. Eric Ambler. LC 37-17351. 1937. A.A. Knopf.
Background to Primula. Betty Evelyn Davies. LC 32-13786. 1932. L. MacVeagh, Dial Press, Inc.
Backhoe Gothic. Thomas Eugene DeWeese. LC 80-1670. 1981. 9.95 (ISBN 0-385-12099-0). Doubleday.
Backlash. Judson Pentecost Philips. LC 76-16005. (Red badge novel of suspense). 6.95. Dodd, Mead.
Backlash. James Radford Raisin. LC 49-135. 1949-1948. Simon and Schuster.
Backlash, a Novel. Morris L West. 1958. Morrow.
Backside. Marge Hazelton. (Illus.). 505p. 1979. pap. 2.95 (ISBN 0-930380-08-8). Quail Run.
Backside of Heaven: A Novel. 1st Ed. David Boyd. LC 57-7649. 1957. Exposition Press.
Backside: The Never-Before-Told Story of the Backside of the Racetrack and the People Who Train Racehorses. Marge Hazelton. LC 80-132071. (Illus.). 9.95 (ISBN 0-930380-07-X). Quail Run Publications.
Backslider. Max Crawford. LC 75-35706. 8.95 (ISBN 0-374-10800-5). Farrar, Straus and Giroux.
Backslider. Max Crawford. 1978. 1.75. Avon Books.
Backsliders. William Lindsey. LC 22-4675. 1922. 1.90. Houghton Mifflin Company.
Backstage. Melbert Brinckerhoff Cary. LC 38-357403. House of Field, Inc.
Backstage Mystery. Octavus Roy Cohen. LC 30-20632. 1930. D. Appleton and Company.
Backstage Nurse. Jane Rossiter, pseud. LC 63-6710. 1963. Avalon Books.
Backstage with Joe. Jack Charles Richard Aistrop. LC 47-157977. 1946. Roy Publishers.
Backstairs at the White House. Gwen Bagni & Paul Dubov. 1979. pap. 2.95 (ISBN 0-553-14067-1). Bantam.
Backstairs at the White House: A Novel. Gwen Bagni & Paul Dubov. LC 78-73717. (Illus.). 12.50. Prentice-Hall.
Backtrack. Joseph Hansen. LC 82-10315. 12.95 (ISBN 0-914378-96-1). Countryman Press.
Backtrack. Milton Lott. LC 65-22214. 4.95. Houghton.
Backtrack. Milton Lott. (Medallion bk., F1472). 1967.
Backup Men. Ross Thomas. LC 70-142412. 1971. 5.95. Morrow.
Backward Bride: A Sicilian Scherzo. Aubrey Menen. LC 50-8917. 1950. Scribner.
Backward Glances. Lois Greenhaw. (Orig.). 1980. pap. text ed. 2.25 o.s.i. (ISBN 0-505-51590-3). Tower Bks.
Backward in Time. Leo P. Kelley. LC 79-51079. (Space Police Bks.). 1979. pap. 4.24 (ISBN 0-8224-6380-6). Pitman Learning.
Backward Place. Ruth Prawer Jhabvala. LC 64-23879. 1965. Norton.
Backward Road. Edevain Park. LC 63-20505. 1963. Doubleday.
Backward Shadow. Lynne Reid Banks. LC 73-129876. 1970. 6.95 (ISBN 0-671-20671-0). Simon and Schuster.
Backward to the Front of the Day. James Robson. LC 69-10958. 1969. 4.50. Doubleday.
Backwash: A Death Valley Story of Love! Music! Gold! by edward henry holt. ed. Edward Henry Holt. LC 40-35092. Wetzel Publishing Co., Inc.
Backwater. Edd Winfield Parks. LC 57-290191. 1957. Twayne Publishers.
Backwater. Dorothy Miller Richardson. 286p. 1977. Repr. of 1916 ed. lib. bdg. 13.85x (ISBN 0-89966-154-8). Buccaneer Bks.
Backwater. Thomas Sigismund Stribling. LC 30-6730. 1930. Doubleday, Doran & Company, Inc.
Backwoods Bride see Lust Seekers.
Backwoods Girl. Joan Sherman. 1970. pap. 0.75 o.p. (75-309). Manor Bks.
Backwoods Princess. Hulbert Footner. LC 28-281060. George H. Doran Company.
Backwoods Teacher. Joseph Nelson. LC 49-105241. 1949. J. B. Lippincott Co.
Backwoodsman: Or, Life on the Indian Frontier. Frederick Charles Lascelles Wraxall. LC 8-37221. 1866. T. O. H. P. Burnham.
Backwoodsman: The Autobiography of a Continental on the New York Frontier During the Revolution. Hiram Alonzo Stanley. LC 1-23086. 1901. Doubleday, Page & Company.
Backwoodsmen. Charles George Douglas Roberts. LC 9-27965. 1909. 1.50. The Macmillan Company.
Backyard. Jean Femling. LC 74-15868. 1975. 6.95 (ISBN 0-06-011246-8). Harper & Row.
Backyard. Gloria Goddard. LC 26-19680. 1926. R. M. McBride & Company.
Bacon & Beans from a Gold Pan. Jesse Coffey & George Hoeper. (Comstock Editions). 1973. pap. 1.25 o.p. (ISBN 0-345-23231-3). Comstock Edns.
Bad-Ass Cell: A Novel. first ed. Raymond W. Jones. 1973. 8.50 (ISBN 0-682-47755-9). Exposition Press.
Bad Barons Daughter. Laura London. (Candlelight Regency Special). 1978. 1.25 (ISBN 0-440-10735-0). Dell.
Bad Blonde. Jack Webb. LC 56-9320. (Father Shanley-Sammy Golden mystery). 1956. Rinehart.
Bad Blood. Barbara Petty. 2.25 (ISBN 0-440-10438-6). Dell Publishing Co.
Bad Boy. Mario James Ghiselli. Ed. by McHugh, Harry T. LC 39-6471. Broadway Printers & Publishers Co.
Bad Boy. Edmund Schiddel. LC 81-17220. 283p. 1982. 12.95 (ISBN 0-02-607090-1). Macmillan.
Bad Boy and His Sister. John Roy Musick. LC 7-32296. (Fireside series, no. 34). 1887. J. S. Ogilvie & Company.
Bad Children's Book (a Decide for Yourself Book) Joel Wells. (Illus.). 1972. 1.95. Argus Communications.
Bad Communist. Max Crawford. LC 78-20637. 8.95. Harcourt Brace Jovanovich.
Bad Company. Liza Cody. LC 82-23145. 1982. 11.95 (ISBN 0-684-17760-9). Scribner.
Bad Company: By Gordon Semple Pseud. William Arthur Neubauer. LC 45-4661. 1945. Phoenix Press.
Bad Connections. Joyce Johnson. LC 77-16367. 8.95 (ISBN 0-399-12122-6). Putnam.
Bad Conscience. Jan Roffman. LC 77-171315. (Crime Club Ser.). 1972. 1.95 o.p. (ISBN 0-385-09170-2). Doubleday.
Bad Conscience. Margaret Summerton. (Ace gothic easy read large type). 1973. (pbk.) 0.95. Ace.
Bad Conscience. Margaret Summerton. LC 77-171315. 1972. 4.95. Published for the Crime Club by Doubleday.
Bad Day at Black Rock: By Michael Niall Pseud. Cover Painting by Barye Phillips. Howard Breslin. LC 55-22312. (Gold medal books, 451). 1954. Fawcett Publications.
Bad Debts. Geoffrey Wolff. LC 70-92198. 1969. 5.95. Simon and Schuster.
Bad Deeds. Kurt Newell. 256p. 1982. pap. write for info. (ISBN 0-523-41435-8). Pinnacle Bks.
Bad Die Young. Peter Chambers, pseud. 3.50 o.p. Roy.
Bad Die Young. Dennis John Andrew Phillips. LC 67-24917. 1967. Roy Publishers.
Bad Dream. Malcolm Gair. 1981. 18.95x (Pub. by Remploy England). State Mutual Bk.
Bad Dreams. Anthony Haden-Guest. 480p. 1983. pap. 3.95 (ISBN 0-345-30720-8). Ballantine.
Bad Dreams. Fedor Kuzmich Teternikov. LC 79-348580. (Illus.). 1978. 15.50 (ISBN 0-88233-128-0). Ardis.
Bad Example. Translated from the German by Leila Berg and Ruth Baer. 1st American Ed. Irmgard Keun. LC 55-10811. 1955. Harcourt, Brace.
Bad for Business. Rex Stout. 1973. pap. 0.95 o.p. (ISBN 0-515-02923-8, N2923). Pyramid Pubns.
Bad Girl. Vina Delmar. LC 28-111749. Harcourt, Brace and Company.
Bad Girl... Vina Delmar. LC 46-21776. 1946.
Bad Girl Leaves Town. Maysie Greig. LC 33-41630. 1933. Doubleday, Doran & Company, Inc.
Bad Girls. Ed. by John W. Fitzgerald. pap. 2.95 o.p. (ISBN 0-87964-104-5). Academy-Parliament.
Bad Guy. Nicholas Brady. (Belmont Tower Books). 1977. 1.50 (ISBN 0-505-51202-5). Tower Pubns.
Bad Guy. Rosalyn Drexler. LC 81-22138. 180p. 1982. 11.95 (ISBN 0-525-24107-8, 01160-350). Dutton.
Bad Hombre. William Wendell Flewelling. LC 31-12254. Meador Publishing Company.
Bad Investment. Louis Cassels. (Orig.). 1974. pap. 0.95 o.p. (ISBN 0-515-03445-2, N3445). Pyramid Pubns.
Bad Lands. Oakley M Hall. LC 77-15839. (Illus.). 1978. 10.95 (ISBN 0-689-10823-0). Atheneum.
Bad Lands: A Novel. Oakley M Hall. 2.25 (ISBN 0-449-23966-7). Fawcett Crest.
Bad Lot. A Novel. Emily Sharp H. Carmeron. LC 11-10530. 1894. J. B. Lippincott Company.
Bad Man. Stanley Elkin. LC 67-12719. 1967. 5.95. Random.
Bad Man: A Novel. Charles Hanson Towne & Browne, Porter Emerson, 1879- LC 21-1674. 1921. G. P. Putnam's Sons.
Bad Man's Return: A Three Mesquiteers Story. William Colt MacDonald. LC 47-11278. 1947. Doubleday.
Bad Man's Trail. Eli Colter. LC 31-30500. A. H. King.
Bad Men and Gold. David A Piatt. 1931. R. R. Rosamond.
Bad Men and Good: A Roundup of Western Stories by Members of the Western Writers of America; with a Foreword by Luke Short. Western Writers of America. LC 53-10257. 1953. Dodd, Mead.
Bad Moon. Dudley Bromley. LC 78-72330. (Pacemaker bestellers book). (Illus.). 3.32 (ISBN 0-8224-5362-2). Fearon Pitman Publishers.
Bad Moon Rising. Ed. by Thomas M. Disch. LC 72-9167. 1973. 6.95 (ISBN 0-06-011046-5). Harper & Row.
Bad Moon Rising: A Novel. Jonathan Kirsch. (Signet Book). 1978. 1.75 (ISBN 0-451-07877-2). New American Library.
Bad Moon Rising: An Anthology of Political Foreboding. Ed. by Thomas M. Disch. LC 72-9167. 314p. (YA) 1973. 6.95 o.p. (ISBN 0-06-011046-5, HarpT). Har-Row.
Bad Neighbor Murder. Charlotte Murray Russell, pseud. LC 46-8248. 1946. Pub. for the Crime Club by Doubleday & Company, Inc.
Bad News. Paul Spike. LC 70-138883. 1971. 5.95 (ISBN 0-03-085970-0). Holt, Rinehart and Winston.
Bad Night at Dry Creek. Cameron Judd. 1981. pap. 1.75 (ISBN 0-8439-0894-7, Leisure Bks). Nordon Pubns.
Bad One. John Farrow. LC 30-11609. A. L. Burt Company.
Bad Penny. Samuel Merwin. LC 33-22041. 1933. R. M. McBride & Company.
Bad Penny. John Tyler Wheelwright. LC 8-360471. (Half-title: Papyrus series). 1896. Lamson, Wolffe and Company.
Bad Ronald. John Holbrook Vance. 1973. (pbk.) 1.25 (ISBN 0-345-23477-4). Ballantine Books.
Bad Room. Christopher Cook Gilmore. 256p. 1983. pap. 2.95 (ISBN 0-380-82669-0, 82669-0). Avon.
Bad Samaritan. William Campbell Gault. (Raven House Mysteries Ser.). 224p. 1981. pap. 2.25 (ISBN 0-373-63018-2, Pub. by Worldwide). Harlequin Bks.
Bad Samaritan: A Novel. Justin Sturm. LC 26-154742. 1926. Harper & Brothers.
Bad Seed. William March. 1983. pap. 2.95 (ISBN 0-553-20820-9). Bantam.
Bad Seed: By William March Pseud. William Edward March Campbell. LC 54-5130. 1954. Rinehart.
Bad Sister. Emma Tennant. LC 78-17366. 1978. 8.95 (ISBN 0-698-10940-6). Coward, McCann & Geoghegan.
Bad Sister. Emma Tennant. 1980. 1.95 (ISBN 0-380-48280-0). Avon Books.
Bad Step. Mark Derby. LC 54-79828. 1954. Viking Press.
Bad Summer. John Appleby. LC 58-11500. (Chantecler novel of suspense). 1958. I. Washburn.
Bad Times Coming. Gil Martin. (Berkley medallion book). 1974. (pbk) 0.75. Berkley Pub Co.
Bad Times: A Novel. James Kirkwood. LC 68-25750. 1968. Simon and Schuster.
Bad to Beat. A Novel. Hawley Smart. 1886. Rand, McNally & Company.
Bad to Beat: A Novel. Hawley Smart. (On cover: Lovell's library, v. 16, no. 780). 1886. J. W. Lovell Company.
Bad to Beat. A Novel. Hawley Smart. (On cover: Seaside library. Pocket ed. no. 847). 1886. G. Munro.
Bad Trip. Kelley Roos. LC 75-158346. (Red badge novel of suspense). 1971. 4.95 (ISBN 0-396-06371-3). Dodd, Mead.
Bad Wife. Gladys Sloan. Phoenix Press.
Bad Wife. Leona Slottman. LC 40-13271. Phoenix Press.
Baddington Horror. Walter S Masterman. LC 34-19655. E. P. Dutton & Co., Inc.
Badenheim 1939. Aron Appelfeld. LC 80-66192. 1980. 10.00 (ISBN 0-87923-342-7). D. R. Godine.
Badenheim 1939. Aron. Appelfeld. LC 81-4910. 1981. 11.95 (ISBN 0-8161-3209-7). G.K. Hall.
Baders of Jacob Street. Karmel-Wolfe, Henia. LC 71-103598. 1970. 6.95. Lippincott.
Badge and a Gun. Victor George Charles Norwood. LC 75-2123. 1975. 4.95 (ISBN 0-517-52165-2). Lenox Hill Press.
Badge and Harry Cole. Clifton Adams. LC 72-157568. 1971. 4.95. Doubleday.
Badge for a Gunfighter. Clair Huffaker. 1975. (pbk.) 1.25 (ISBN 0-671-80056-6). Pocket Books.
Badge for Brazos see Aces Wild.
Badge in the Dust. George G. Gilman, pseud. (Steele Ser.: No. 9). 1977. pap. 1.50 (ISBN 0-523-40577-4). Pinnacle Bks.
Badge of Courage. Natalie King. 1973. pap. 0.75 o.s.i. (01-386). Lancer.
Badge of Evil. Whit Masterson, pseud. LC 56-574445. (Red badge detective). 1956. Dodd, Mead.
Badge of Honor. Dallas Barnes. 1974. (pbk.) 1.25. New American Library.
Badge of Honor. Dan Brennan. 1974. (pbk.) 0.95. Belmont Tower Books.
Badge of Infamy. Lester Del Rey. LC 77-375235. 1976. 2.95 (ISBN 0-234-77109-7). Dobson.
Badge of the Assassin. Robert Tanenbaum & Philip Rosenberg. 1982. pap. 2.95 (ISBN 0-449-24476-8, Crest). Fawcett.
Badge 373. Mike Roote. (O.s.i.). 160p. 1973. pap. 0.95 o.s.i. (AN1164, Award). Univ Pub & Dist.
Badger of Ghissi. Tra from German by Barrows Mussey. Wolf Von Niebelschutz. LC 65-6370. 1965. bds., 5.00. G. Allen & Unwin.
Badgers: A Novel. Leonid Maksimovich Leonov. LC 72-14053. 1973. 14.00 (ISBN 0-88355-008-3). Hyperion Press.
Badgers of Summercombe. Ewan Clarkson. LC 76-41219. 8.95. Dutton.
Badland Bill. Charles Horace Snow. LC 41-2707. Phoenix Press.
Badland Trail. George Brydges Rodney. LC 38-14883. Phoenix Press.
Badlanders. Jack Slade, pseud. (Lassiter Ser.). 1978. pap. 1.50 o.s.i. (ISBN 0-505-50597-5). Tower Bks.
Badlands. Bennett Foster. LC 88-8222. 1938. W. Morrow & Co.
Badlands Basin. William Frederick Bragg. LC 56-13445. 1956. Arcadia House.
Badlands Beyond. Norman A Fox. LC 57-7133. (Silver star westerns). 1957. Dodd, Mead.
Badlands Drifter. Dale Oldham. (Leisure book). 1.50 (ISBN 0-8439-0629-4). Nordon Pubns.
Badlands Justice. Dan Cushman. LC 51-9667. 1951. Macmillan.
Badlands Ranch. Lloyd Kevin. LC 53-11299. 1953. Arcadia House.
Badly Matched: Or, Woman Against Woman. Helen Corwin Pierce. (select series, no. 11). 1888. Street & Smith.
Badman of VX Ranch. Tevis Miller. LC 39-11569. Phoenix Press.
Badmen of Elk Head. Robert Claiborne Pitzer. LC 40-14083. Phoenix Press.
Badmen on Halfaday Creek. James Beardsley Hendryx. LC 50-7845. (Double-D western). 1950. Doubleday.
Badtime Stories. Berni Wrightson. LC 70-155308. (Illus.). 1972. Graphic Masters.
Baeu Wyndham. Georgette Heyer. LC 41-4921. 1941. Doubleday Doran and Co., Inc.
Baffled Conspirators: A Novel. William Edward Norris. LC 11-71473. (On cover: Lovell's international series, no. 93). J. W. Lovell Company.
Baffled Schemes. A Novel. LC 6-5013. 1867. Loring.
Baffling Quest. authorized ed. Richard Dowling. (Lovell's international ser. no. 150). United States Book Company, Successors to J. W. Lovell Company.
Bag. Sol Yurick. (Bard books.). 1974. (pbk.) 1.95 (ISBN 0-380-00162-4). Avon.
Bag. Sol Yurick. LC 68-18313. 1968. Trident Press.
Bag and Baggage: A Novel. Leon Sperry. LC 51-14515. 1951. Chapman & Grimes.
Bag O' Tales: 63 Famous Stories for Storytellers. Effie Power. (Illus.). 4.75 o.p. (ISBN 0-8446-4796-9). Peter Smith.
Bag of Diamonds. George Manville Fenn. (On cover: Lovell's library, no. 1060). 1887. J. W. Lovell Company.

Bag of Marbles. Joseph Joffo. LC 74-11132. 1974. 6.95 (ISBN 0-395-19392-3). Houghton Mifflin.

Bag of Marbles. Joseph Joffo. LC 74-32284. 1975. 11.95 (ISBN 0-8161-6262-X). G. K. Hall.

Bag of Saffron. Betsey Riddle Hutton Zum Stolzenberg. LC 18-3558. 1918. D. Appleton and Company.

Bagamoyo: Here I Leave My Heart. Leslie-Melville, Betty & Leslie-Melville, Jock. LC 82-14400. 1983. 14.95 (ISBN 0-688-00814-3). Morrow.

Bagatelle: A Novel. Maurice Denuziere. LC 78-655. 1978. 9.95 (ISBN 0-688-03316-4). Morrow.

Bagatelle and Some Other Diversions. George Preedy, pseud. LC 31-9002. 1931. Dodd, Mead & Company.

Bagdad Blues. Sam Greenlee. 1973. 6.95 o.p. (ISBN 0-87829-024-9). Emerson Hall.

Baghdad Defections. Beverly Keller. LC 72-89696. (Black bat mystery). 1973. 5.95 (ISBN 0-672-51810-4). Bobbs-Merrill.

Bagman. Frank McAuliffe. (Orig.). 1979. pap. 1.95 (ISBN 0-89083-468-7). Zebra.

Bagpipers. George Sand. LC 77-15563. 1977. 7.50. (ISBN 0-915864-46-0) (ISBN 0-915864-45-2). Cassandra Editions.

Bagpipers. George Sand & Wormeley, Katharine Prescott, 1830- Tr. LC 6-34621. 1890. Roberts Brothers.

Bagshot Mystery. Oscar Gray. LC 29-19689. 1929. The Macaulay Company.

Bagtime. Mike Holiday. 1977. 1.95 (ISBN 0-445-04057-2). Popular Library.

Bahadur Means Hero. Sheila Solomon Klass. LC 72-80059. 1969. 4.95. Gambit.

Bahama Bill: Mate of the Wrecking Sloop Sea-Horse. Thornton Jenkins Hains. LC 8-4909. 1908. L. C. Page & Company.

Bahama Rapture. Jolene P. Parker. (Orig.). 1982. pap. 3.50 (ISBN 0-8217-1018-4). Zebra.

Baileaus of Desert Home. D. B. Kapsian. 8.50 (ISBN 0-392-08474-0, SpS). Sportshelf.

Bailey's Daughters. John De Meyer. LC 35-9075. 1935. H. Smith and R. Haas.

Bailiff of Tewkesbury. Charles Edward Davis Phelps & Phelps, Elizabeth Steward. LC 7-360809. 1893. A. C. McClurg & Company.

Bailiff's Maid. Eugenie John. LC 7-9898. (On cover: Seaside library. Pocket ed. no. 1113). G. Munro.

Bailiff's Maid: A Romance from the German of E. Marlitt Pseud.... Eugenie John. Tr. by Wister, Annis Lee (Furness) LC 12-403881. (On cover: Marlitt's novels). 1881. J. B. Lippincott & Co.

Bailiff's Scheme. A Novel. Harriet Lewis. LC 7-14372. R. Bonner's Sons.

Bainbridge Murder. Cortland Fitzsimmons. LC 30-5405. 1930. R. M. McBride & Company.

Bainbridge Mystery: The Housekeeper's Story. Grace Tyler Pratt. LC 10-27739. 1911. 1.20. Sherman, French & Company.

Bait. Lionel Black. (Spy Thriller of Romantic Suspense). 1968. pap. 0.60 o.p. (53-626). Paperback Lib.

Bait. Dorothy Uhnak. LC 67-25377. (Inner sanctum mystery). 1968. 3.95. S. & S.

Bait. Dorothy Uhnak. LC 81-3110. 1981. 12.95 (ISBN 0-89340-347-4). J. Curley & Associates.

Bait and the Trap. George Challis. LC 51-9032. -, C.

Bait and the Trap: By George Challis Pseud. 1st Ed. Frederick Faust. LC 51-9032. Harper.

Bait for a Tiger. Bayard Veiller. LC 41-240803. Reynal & Hitchcock.

Bait for a Tiger. Bayard Veiller. LC 43-170407. (Black cat detective series. No. 2). 1943. Crestwood Publishing Co., Inc.

Bait for Murder. Kathleen Moore Knight. LC 48-8293. 1948. Pub. for the Crime Club by Doubleday.

Bait Money. Max Collins. 1973. pap. 0.75 o.p. (07265). Curtis.

Bait Money. Max Collins. 1973. 0.75. Curtis Books.

Bait of Perjury: A Novel of Suspense and Legal Intrigue. Wallace Savage. LC 71-123353. (Genesis Press book). 1970. 4.95. Droke House Publishers; Distributed by Grosset & Dunlap, New York.

Bait on the Hook: A Novel of Suspense. Frank Parrish. LC 83-1886. 1983. 10.95 (ISBN 0-396-08150-9). Dodd, Mead.

Baja. Jack Jones. 224p. 1982. pap. 2.50 (ISBN 0-449-14479-8, GM). Fawcett.

Baja Oklahoma. Dan Jenkins. LC 81-65996. 1981. 11.95 (ISBN 0-689-11173-8). Atheneum.

Baja People. Lee D. Willoughby. (Making of America Ser.: No. 32). 320p. 1983. pap. 3.25 (ISBN 0-440-00374-1, Bryans). Dell.

Baked Bean Supper Murders. Virginia Rich. 288p. 1983. 13.95 (ISBN 0-525-24185-X, 01354-410). Dutton.

Baked Bread: By the Author of "Boy of My Heart.". Boy of My Heart, Author of. LC 19-16369. 1919. Hodder and Stoughton.

Baked Head: And Other Tales ... LC 26-363891. (Putnam's library of choice stories). 1856. G. P. Putnam & Co.

Baked Meats of the Funeral. A Collection of Essays, Poems, Speeches, Histories, and Banquets. Charles Graham Halpine. LC 26-6573. 1866. Carleton.

Baker. Robert H. Adleman. 1973. pap. 0.75 o.p. (07276). Curtis.

Baker. Robert H Aldeman. 1973. 0.75. Curtis Books.

Baker, by Robert H. Adleman. Robert H. Adleman. 1973. 0.75. Curtis Books.

Baker Street By-Way (A Book About Sherlock Holmes) James E. Holroyd. 1978. Repr. of 1959 ed. lib. bdg. 25.00 o.s.i. (ISBN 0-89760-326-5, Telegraph). Dynamic Learn Corp.

Baker Street Irregulars. Anthony Boucher. 1962. pap. 0.95 o.p. (01751, Collier). Macmillan.

Baker's Cart: And Other Tales. Gerald William Bullett. LC 77-125208. (Short story index reprint series). 1970. Books for Libraries Press.

Baker's Cart, & Other Tales. facs. ed. Gerald William Bullett. LC 77-125208. (Short Story Index Reprint Ser.). 1926. 16.00 (ISBN 0-8369-3575-6). Ayer Co.

Baker's Daughter. Dorothy Emily Stevenson. LC 76-6109. 1976. 7.95 (ISBN 0-03-016856-2). Holt, Rinehart and Winston.

Baker's Daughter. Dorothy Emily Stevenson. LC 76-47548. 1976. 10.95 (ISBN 0-8161-6433-9). G. K. Hall.

Baker's Daughter. Dorothy Emily Stevenson. LC 38-27969. Farrar & Rinehart, Inc.

Baker's Daughter. Margaret Tabor. LC 78-25692. 1979. 8.95 (ISBN 0-698-10973-2). Coward, McCann & Geoghegan.

Bakers Dozen. Lydia Champlain Miller Letterman. LC 54-7401. 1954. Vantage Press.

Baker's Dozen. Kathleen Thompson Norris. LC 71-130068. (Short story index reprint series). 1970. Books for Libraries Press.

Baker's Dozen. Kathleen Thompson Norris. LC 38-37920. 1938. Doubleday, Doran & Company, Inc.

Baker's Hawk. Jack M Bickham. LC 73-79644. 1974. 6.95 (ISBN 0-385-05724-5) (ISBN 0-385-05724-5). Doubleday.

Balaam and His Master: And Other Sketches and Stories. Joel Chandler Harris. LC 73-94729. (Short story index reprint series). 1969. Books for Libraries Press.

Balaam and His Master: And Other Sketches and Stories. Joel Chandler Harris. LC 4-15116. 1891. Houghton, Mifflin and Company.

Balaam & His Master & Other Sketches & Stories. Joel Chandler Harris. LC 73-94729. (Short Story Index Reprint Ser.). 1891. 16.00 (ISBN 0-8369-3108-4). Ayer Co.

Balaam & His Master & Other Sketches & Stories. Joel Chandler Harris. 293p. 1981. Repr. of 1891 ed. lib. bdg. 35.00 (ISBN 0-89760-347-8). Telegraph Bks.

Balada de otro tiempo. Jose L. Gonzalez. 156p. 1980. pap. 5.95 (ISBN 0-940238-55-1). Ediciones Huracan.

Balance: A Novel. Francis Rufus Bellamy. LC 17-4706. 1917. 1.35. Doubleday, Page & Company.

Balance: A Novel of Today. William Dana Orcutt. LC 22-616264. Frederick A. Stokes Company.

Balance of Destiny. Martha Jane Garvin. LC 12-73010. The C. M. Clark Publishing Co.

Balance of Power. Brian M Stableford. 1979. 1.75 (ISBN 0-87997-437-0). DAW Books.

Balance of Power: A Novel. od ed. 12th thousand ed. Arthur Frederick Goodrich. LC 9-32304. 1906. The Outing Publishing Company.

Balance of Terror. Cynthia Van Hazinga. (Berkley Medallion) (ISBN 0-425-03204-3). Berkley.

Balance Wheel. Taylor Caldwell. LC 51-9053. 1951. Scribner.

Balance Wheel. Taylor Caldwell. LC 75-634. 1975. 9.95 (ISBN 0-88411-153-9). Aeonian Press.

Balancing Act. Paul R. Satran. (Finding Mr. Right Ser.). 1983. pap. 2.75 (ISBN 0-380-83659-9, 83659-9). Avon.

Balancing Acts. Lynne Sharon Schwartz. LC 80-8336. 9.95 (ISBN 0-06-013702-9). Harper & Row.

Balasaraswati. Narayana Menon. (Illus.). 29p. pap. 1.50 o.p. (ISBN 0-88253-060-7). InterCulture.

Balavariani (Barlaam & Josaphat): A Tale from the Christian East. Tr. by David M. Lang. (Near Eastern Center, UCLA). (Translated from the Old Georgian (O:BC)). 1966. 27.50x (ISBN 0-520-00697-6). U of Cal Pr.

Balck Beret: By Pete Fry Pseud. Clifford King. LC 59-13351. 1959. Roy Publishers.

Balcony. Dorothy Cameron Disney. LC 40-31178. Random House.

Balcony in the Forest. Julien Gracq. LC 59-12066. 1959. G. Braziller.

Balcony in the Forest: By Julien Gracq Pseud. Translated by Richard Howard. Louis Poirier. LC 59-12066. 1959. G. Braziller.

Balcony of Europe. Aidan Higgens. 450p. 1982. pap. 8.95 (ISBN 0-7145-3747-0). Riverrun NY.

Balcony of Europe. Aidan Higgins. LC 72-10772. 1973. 8.95 o.p. (ISBN 0-440-00654-6, Sey Lawr). Delacorte.

Balcony Stories. Grace Elizabeth King. LC 68-23722. (Illus.). 1968. Gregg Press.

Balcony Stories. Grace Elizabeth King. 1893. The Century Co.

Balcony Stories. Grace Elizabeth King. LC 25-19107. 1925. The Macmillan Company.

Bald-Knobbers: A Novel of the Ozarks. Clyde Edwin Tuck. LC 30-201609. Burton Publishing Co.

Bald Knobbers: A Romantic and Historical Novel. Clyde Edwin Tuck. LC 10-23131. 1910. B. F. Bowen & Company.

Baldine, and Other Tales. Karl Erdmann Edler & Lytton, Edward Robert Bulwer-Lytton, 1st Earl of, 1831-1891. LC 6-36800. 1887. Harper & Brothers.

Baldur's Gate. Eleanor Clark. LC 74-97226. 1970. 7.95. Pantheon Books.

Baldy's Point. Jeannette Ritchie Hadermann Walworth. LC 8-33254. Cassell & Company, Limited.

Baleful Beasts and Eerie Creatures. Rod Ruth. LC 76-20529. 5.95. (ISBN 0-528-82171-7) (ISBN 0-528-80211-9). Rand McNally.

Balfour Conspiracy. St. James, Ian. LC 80-69378. 1981. 10.95 (ISBN 0-689-11140-1). Atheneum.

Balisand... Joseph Hergesheimer. LC 24-22278. 1924. A. A. Knopf.

Balisand. Joseph Hergesheimer. LC 77-78311. 1982. 28.50 (ISBN 0-404-15119-1). AMS Press.

Balkan Assignment. Joe Poyer, pseud. LC 70-160889. 1971. 5.95. Doubleday.

Balkan Monastery: A Novel. Stephen Graham. LC 36-10523. 1936. Frederick A. Stokes Company.

Ball. Bartha Albrand. LC 61-6744. 1961. Atherneum.

Ball. Christine Lambert, pseud. 1961. 4.50 o.p. Atheneum.

Ball and Chain. Emma Start. LC 8-13444. 1884. Southern Methodist Publishing House.

Ball and the Cross. Gilbert Keith Chesterton. LC 9-29974. 1909. 1.00. J. Lane Company.

Ball Boys. David Edgar. 32p. (Orig.). 1981. pap 3.95 (ISBN 0-86104-202-6). Pluto Pr.

Ball Carrier. Keith Kerner. pap. 1.95 o.s.i. (OPH-159, Ophelia). Olympia.

Ball Four: By Inez and Loys Cowles. 1st Ed. Inez Cowles & Loys Cowles. LC 53-12636. 1953. Pageant Press.

Ball in the Family. Ellis Quick. 1973. pap. 1.95 o.s.i. (76-330). Lancer.

Ball, Jane (Eklund). LC 54-960515. 1955. Houghton Mifflin.

Ball Night: A Novel. Johan Carl Caristina Brosball. Tr. by Charles O. Due. (Minerva Ser.). (On cover: Minerva series, no. 38: No. 38). 1890. The Minerva Publishing Company.

Ball of Fire. George Randolph Chester & Chester, Lillian, Joint Author. LC 14-16916. 1914. 1.35. Hearst's International Library Co.

Ball-of-Tallow: And Short Stories. Guy De Maupassant. LC 10-7482. 1910. The Pearson Publishing Co.

Ball of Yarn; Its Unwinding. Robert Rudd Whiting. LC 7-31419. P. Elder & Company.

Ball Tournament Specialist. Gino A. Sky. (Illus.). 1973. pap. 1.00 (Pub. by Duende). SBD.

Ball. 1st Ed. Christine Lambert, pseud. LC 61-674497. 1961. Atheneum.

Balla: And Other Virgina Stories. James Poyntz Nelson. LC 14-18464. 1914. 1.00. The Bell Book and Stationery Co., Inc.

Ballad and the Source. Rosamond Lehmann. LC 74-17030. (Harvest book, HB 306). 1975. (pbk.) 3.95 (ISBN 0-15-610260-9). Harcourt Brace Jovanovich.

Ballad and the Source. Rosamond Lehmann. LC 46-4661. 1945. Reynal & Hitchcock.

Ballad of Artie Bremer. Stephen Vincent. 1974. 2.00x (ISBN 0-917672-02-X); signed ed. 15.00x. Momos.

Ballad of Beta Two. Samuel R. Delany. 144p. 1982. 2.50 (ISBN 0-553-20312-6). Bantam.

Ballad of Beta 2. Samuel R Delany. LC 77-13745. (Gregg Press science fiction series). 1977. 8.00 (ISBN 0-8398-2393-2). Gregg Press.

Ballad of Beta-2 and Empire Star. Samuel R Delany. 1975. (pbk.) 1.25. Ace Books.

Ballad of Castle Reef. Honor Lilbush Wingfield Tracy. LC 79-4785. 1980-1979. 8.95 (ISBN 0-394-50689-8). Random House.

Ballad of Cat Ballou. 1st Ed. Roy Chanslor. LC 56-5933. Little, Brown.

Ballad of Dingus Magee: Being the Immortal True Saga of the Most Notorious and Desperate Bad Man of the Olden Days, His Blood-Shedding, His Ruination of Poor Helpless Females, & Cetera. David Markson. LC 65-26504. 1966. bds., 4.00. Bobbs.

Ballad of Habit and Accident: A Novel. Rock Brynner. LC 80-19185. 1981. 10.95 (ISBN 0-671-41094-6). Wyndham Books.

Ballad of Joachim Murietta. Raymond F. Locke. (Orig.). 1980. pap. 2.00 (ISBN 0-87067-009-3, BH009). Holloway.

Ballad of Kintillo. Sally Rena. LC 74-21151. 1975. 7.95 (ISBN 0-672-52108-3). Bobbs-Merrill.

Ballad of Love. Frederic Prokosch. LC 60-12517. 1960. Farrar, Straus and Cudahy.

Ballad of Love. Frederic Prokosch. LC 74-178787. 1972. 12.75 (ISBN 0-8371-6287-4). Greenwood Press.

Ballad of Peckham Rye. Spark, Muriel. LC 60-8105. 1960. Lippincott.

Ballad of Peckham Rye. Muriel Spark. LC 82-5237. 1982. 5.95 (ISBN 0-399-50650-0). Perigee Books.

Ballad of T. Rantula: A Novel. Kit Reed, pseud. LC 78-20975. 8.95 (ISBN 0-316-73660-0). Little, Brown.

Ballad of T. Rantula: Kit Reed. Kit Reed, pseud. 1.95. Fawcett Juniper.

Ballad of the Flim-Flam Man. Guy Owen. LC 65-12854. 1965. Macmillan.

Ballad of the Hundred Days. Joseph Roth. Tr. by Rose, William. LC 36-18202. 1936. The Viking Press.

Ballad of the Sad Cafe see Collected Short Stories.

Ballad of the Sad Cafe & Other Stories. Carson Smith McCullers. (gr. 11 up). 1967. pap. 2.50 (ISBN 0-553-20453-X). Bantam.

Ballad of the Sad Cafe: The Novels and Stories of Carson McCullers. Carson Smith McCullers. LC 51-10969. 1951. Houghton Mifflin.

Ballad of the Stars. G Al Tov & V Zhuravleva. LC 82-17107. 15.75 (ISBN 0-02-501740-3). Macmillan.

Ballade. Helen Cohen. 1915. 27.50 o.p. Folcroft.

Ballade in G Minor. Ethel Mary Young Boileau. LC 38-5878. 1938. E. P. Dutton & Co., Inc.

Ballads, Blues & Swan Songs. William Wiser. LC 81-66032. 1982. 10.95 (ISBN 0-689-11188-6). Atheneum.

Ballads, Critical Reviews, Tales, Various Essays, Letters, Sketches, Etc. William Makepeace Thackeray & Stephen, Sir Leslie, 1832-1904. LC 12-31112. (Half-title: The biographical edition. The works of... Thackeray..: vol. XIII). 1899. Harper & Brothers.

Ballads of Peace in War. Michael Earls. LC 18-6934. 1917. Harrigan Press, Inc.

Ballads of the Big California Woman. Jeanie Keltner. 224p. (Orig.). 1982. pap. 4.95 (ISBN 0-380-79061-0, 79061). Avon.

Ballanger. Robert E. Trevathan. 192p. 1974. pap. 0.95 o.p. (532-95353-095). Manor Bks.

Ballanger. Robert E Trevathan. 1974. (pbk.) 0.95. Manor Books.

Ballantyne: A Novel. Helen Stuart Campbell. LC 1-31267. 1901. Little, Brown, and Company.

Ballenger. Robert E. Trevathan. 1978. pap. 1.15 (ISBN 0-532-12555-X). Woodhill.

Ballerina. LC 64-12005. (Illus.). 1964. Criterion Books.

Ballerina. Eleanor Furneaux Smith. LC 32-175099. The Bobbs-Merrill Company.

Ballerina. Edward Stewart. LC 78-52066. 1979. 10.95 (ISBN 0-385-13401-0). Doubleday.

Ballet! Tom Murphy. LC 77-90753. 2.25 (ISBN 0-451-08112-9). New American Library.

Ballet Dancer: And On Guard. Matilde Serao. LC 2-6299. 1901. Harper & Brothers.

Ballet Dancer's Husband. Ernest Aime Feydeau & Sherwood, Mrs. Mary (Neal) Tr. LC 6-39534. 1880. H. A. Sumner & Company.

Ballet for Three Masks. James Cleugh. LC 32-20225. 1932. L. MacVeagh, Dial Press, Inc.

Ballet of Brokers. John Kolyer. LC 75-36485. 1976. pap. 3.75 o.p. (ISBN 0-8283-1657-0). Branden.

Ballet of Comedians: A Novel Based on the Life of J. B. P. Moliere. Peter D Arnott. LC 71-155272. 1971. 7.95. Macmillan.

Ballet Poetique. Delina Margot-Parle. 1960. 2.75 o.p. (ISBN 0-8158-0143-2). Chris Mass.

Balling. Jacques Dorival. 160p. pap. 1.95 o.p. (MP-116). Montmartre.

Balliols. Alec Waugh. LC 34-22750. Farrar & Rinehart, Incorporated.

Ballonist. Macdonald Harris. LC 76-15679. 1976. 8.95 o.p. (ISBN 0-374-10874-9). FS&G.

Balloon. Henry Phelps Brown. LC 53-13470. 1953. Macmillan.

Balloon Affair: A Novel of Suspense. Marion Margery Layne. LC 81-4903. 8.95 (ISBN 0-396-07951-2). Dodd, Mead.

Balloon Girl. May Mackintosh. LC 76-16685. 1976. 7.95. St. Martin's Press.

Balloon Man. Charlotte Armstrong. (Berkley Medallion Book). 1976. (pbk.) 1.50 (ISBN 0-425-03117-9). Berkley Publishing Corp.

Balloon Man. Charlotte Armstrong. LC 68-17464. 1968. Coward-McCann.

Balloon Spies see TaleSpinners I.

Balloon Top: A Novel. Nobuko Albery. LC 77-17652. 8.95 (ISBN 0-394-50146-2). Pantheon Books.

Balloonist: A Novel. Donald W. Heiney. LC 76-15679. 8.95 (ISBN 0-374-10874-9). Farrar, Straus, Giroux.

Balloons. Elizabeth Asquith Bibescu. LC 22-23118. 2.00. George H. Doran Company.

Balloons Are Available. Jordan Crittenden. LC 67-13038. 1967. Atheneum.

Ballot. Robert Gaines. LC 79-84338. 1979. 9.95 (ISBN 0-312-06619-8). Hale.

Ballou's Pictorial Drawing-Room Companion: V. 1-17; May 3, 1851-Dec. 24, 1859. Ballou, Maturin Murray, 1820-1895, Ed. LC 3-3525. 1851. F. Gleason Etc.

Ballpark. Michael Schiffer. LC 81-14625. 4.50 (ISBN 0-671-41796-7). Simon and Schuster.

Ballplayer. Edward E Fitzgerald. LC 57-5737. 1957. A. S. Barnes.

Ballroom of Romance and Other Stories. William Trevor. LC 72-78200. 1972. 6.95 (ISBN 0-670-14681-1). Viking Press.

Ballroom of the Skies. John Dann MacDonald. LC 52-10870. (Science fiction). Greenberg.

Ballroom Repentance. Annie Edwards. (On cover: Seaside library. Pocket ed. no. 834). 1886. G. Munro.

Balls! Richard Rohmer. 352p. 1980. 12.95 (ISBN 0-8253-0003-7). Beaufort Bks NY.

Ballyhoo! Beth Brown. LC 27-20089. L. MacVeagh, The Dial Press.

Ballyshan Castle: A Tale Founded on Fact. Aaron Fletcher. LC 6-39936. 1857. N. Tibbals.

Balm in Gilead. Florence Morse Kingsley. LC 7-14255. 1907. Funk & Wagnalls Company.

Balm of Gilead. Agnes Edwards Rothery. LC 46-5162. 1946. Dodd, Mead & Company.

Balsam Boughs: Being Adirondack and Other Stories. Archibald Campbell Knowles. LC 7-14185. 1893. Porter & Coates.

Balsam Groves of the Grandfather Mountain: A Tale of the Western North Carolina Mountains. Together with Information Relating to the Section and Its Hotels Also a Table Showing the Height of Important Mountains, Etc. Shepherd Monroe Dugger. LC 6-34629. 1892. Printed by J. B. Lippincott Co., Philadelphia.

Balsam Groves of the Grandfather Mountain: A Tale of the Western North Carolina Mountains. Together with Information Relating to the Section and Its Hotels, Also a Table Showing the Height of Important Mountains, Etc. Shepherd Monroe Dugger. LC 15-12480. 1895. S. M. Dggger.

Balsam Groves of the Grandfather Mountain: A Tale of the Western North Carolina Mountains, Together with Information Relating to the Section and Its Hotels, Also a Vocabulary of Indian Names and a List of Altitudes of Important Mountains, Etc. Shepherd Monroe Dugger. LC 7-26341. 1907. S. M. Dugger.

Balsamo: Or, Memoirs of a Physician. Alexandre Dumas & Maquet, Auguste. (Seaside library, v. 10, no. 193). G. Munro.

Balshazzar: A Tale of the Fall of Babylon. William Stearns Davis. LC 2-17859. 1902. Doubleday, Page & Co.

Balthazar. Lawrence Durrell. 1961. pap. 2.50 o.p. (ISBN 0-525-47081-6). Dutton.

Balthazar: A Novel. Lawrence Durrell. LC 58-9583. 1958. Dutton.

Balthazar: Or, Science and Love. Honore De Balzac. Tr. by William Robson. LC 6-6313. 1859. Routledge, Warne, & Routledge.

Balthazar the Magus. Albert Van Der Naillen. LC 4-21728. 1904. R. F. Fenno & Company.

Baltic Emerald. Edmund Ward. LC 81-16530. 1982. 10.95 (ISBN 0-312-06626-0). St Martin's Press.

Baltimore Afro-American: Best Short Stories by Afro-American Writers 1925-50. Ed. by H. L. Faggett & Nick A. Ford. LC 50-12374. 1950. 18.00 (ISBN 0-527-04930-1). Kraus Repr.

Balzac: Fiction and Melodrama. Christopher Prendergast. LC 78-11267. 1978. 25.00 (ISBN 0-8419-0457-X). Holmes and Meier Publishers.

Balzac: Five Stories Edited with an Introd. by Edmund Fuller. Honore De Balzac. Ed. by Edmund Fuller. LC 61-989. (Laurel reader, LC156). 1960. Dell Pub. Co.

Balzac: Selected Short Stories. Honore De Balzac. Ed. & tr. by Sylvia Raphael. (Classics Ser). 1977. pap. 3.95 (ISBN 0-14-044325-8). Penguin.

Balzac's Le Message: The Text with Variants and Critical Comments Edited by George B. Raser. Honore De Balzac. Ed. by George Bernard Raser. LC 40-34787. 1940. Harvard University Press.

Balzac's Masterpieces: Ten Novels by Honore De Balzac, with an Introduction by James Gould Cozzens. Honore De Balzac. LC 31-28423. 1931. David McKay Company.

Balzac's Shorter Stories. Honore De Balzac. LC 9-2705. The Federal Book Company.

Balzac's Shorter Stories: English Versions by William Wilson and the Count Stenbock; with a Prefatory Notice. Honore De Balzac. Tr. by William Wilson. Stenbock, E., Tr. LC 13-20463. 1895. H. Altenus.

Balzan of the Cat People. Lyle Engel. 1975. pap. 1.25 o.p. (ISBN 0-515-03976-4). Pyramid Pubns.

Bambi. Marjorie Benton Cooke. LC 14-16478. 1914. Doubleday, Page & Company.

Bambi: A Life in the Woods. Felix Salten & Chambers, Whittaker, Tr. LC 28-17486. 1928. Simon and Schuster.

Bambi: By Felix Salten, Foreword. Felix Salten & Chambers, Whittaker, Tr. LC 29-523517. 1929. Simon and Schuster, Inc.

Bambi's Children: The Story of a Forest Family. Felix Salten & Fles, Barthold, Tr. LC 39-32485. The Bobbs-Merrill Company.

Bambolona. Alba De Cespedes. (O.s.i.). 1970. 6.50 o.s.i. (ISBN 0-671-20377-0). S&S.

Bamboo & the Heather. Nita Rosemeyer. (Orig.). 1980. pap. 2.75 (ISBN 0-345-28740-1). Ballantine.

Bamboo Bed. William Eastlake. LC 70-79630. 1969. 6.50. Simon and Schuster.

Bamboo Blonde. Dorothy Belle Flanagan Hughes. LC 41-5435. Duell, Sloan and Pearce.

Bamboo Bloodbath. Piers Anthony & Roberto Fuentes. (Berkley medallion book). 1974. (pbk.) 0.95 (ISBN 0-425-02716-3). Berkley Pub Co.

Bamboo Dancers. N. V. Gonzalez. LC 82-70134. 276p. 1961. 8.95 (ISBN 0-8040-0018-2). Swallow.

Bamboo Dancers. N. V. Gonzalez. 3.95 o.p. (ISBN 0-8040-0018-2). Swallow.

Bamboo Screen. Henry Gibbs. LC 68-29804. 1968. 3.95. Walker.

Bamboo Screen. Simon Harvester. 1970. pap. 0.75 o.p. (75-325). Manor Bks.

Bamboo Tales. Ira L Reeves. Hudson-Kimberly ! Publishing Co.

Bamboo: Tales of the Orient-Born. Lyon Sharman. LC 14-16472. P. Elder and Company.

Bamboo Terror: A Thrilling Tale of Vietnamese Espionage. William Ross. LC 69-13506. 1969. 3.25. C. E. Tuttle Co.

Bamboo Whistle: A Thrilling Story of International Intrigue Featuring Anthony Hamilton, America's Secret Agent Number One. Frederick Frost. 1937. Macrae-Smith Company.

Bamboo. 1st Ed. Robert O Bowen. LC 52-12200. 1953. Knopf.

Banana. Bonnie Charles Bluh. LC 75-28030. (Illus.). 8.95 (ISBN 0-02-511900-1). Macmillan.

Banana Bottom. Claude McKay. LC 73-147676. (Harvest book, HB 273). 1974. (ISBN 0-15-610650-7). Harcourt Brace Jovanovich.

Banana Bottom. Claude McKay. LC 78-129549. 1970. Chatham Bookseller.

Banana Bottom. Claude McKay. LC 33-7952. 1933. Harper & Brothers.

Banana Men. Max Catto. LC 67-20798. 1967. Simon and Schuster.

Banana Paradise. Frances Emery-Waterhouse. LC 47-1993. 1947. Stephen-Paul.

Banana Twist. Florence P. Heide. 112p. 1982. pap. 1.95 (ISBN 0-553-15159-2). Bantam.

Bananas Grow in Minsk. Serge A Alexander. LC 63-22696. T. Gaus' Sons.

Banbury Bog. Phoebe Atwood Taylor. 1978. Repr. of 1938 ed. lib. bdg. 9.00x (ISBN 0-89966-247-1). Buccaneer Bks.

Banbury Bog. Phoebe Atwood Taylor. 1970. pap. 0.60 o.p. (X2168). Pyramid Pubns.

Banbury Bog: An Asey Mayo Mystery. Phoebe Atwood Taylor. LC 38-34802. W. W. North & Co.

Banbury Tale. MacKeever, Maggie. (Fawcett Crest Book). 1977. 1.50 (ISBN 0-449-23174-7). Fawcett Pubns.

Banco: The Further Adventures of Papillon. Henri Charriere. Tr. by Patrick O'Brian from Fr. 228p. 1973. 7.95 o.p. (ISBN 0-688-00218-8). Morrow.

Bancock Murder Case. Albert Benjamin Cunningham. LC 42-21435. 1942. E. P. Dutton and Company, Inc.

Bancroft's Banco. Nelson Nye. 128p. (Orig.). 1976. pap. 2.25 (ISBN 0-441-04731-9). Ace Bks.

Bancroft's Banco. Nelson Nye. 126p. 1981. pap. 1.95 (ISBN 0-441-05074-3, Pub. by Charter Bks.). Ace Bks.

Band of Angels. Robert Penn Warren. LC 55-5814. 1955. Random House.

Band of Brothers. Ernest Kellogg Gann. LC 73-11828. 1973. 7.95 (ISBN 0-671-21630-9). Simon and Schuster.

Band of Brothers. Ernest Kellogg Gann. 1974. (pbk.) 1.50 (ISBN 0-345-24250-5). Ballantine Books.

Band Plays Dixie. Morris Markey. LC 27-5417. Harcourt, Brace & Company.

Band-Wagon: A Political Novel of Middle-America. Franklin Fowler Ellsworth. Dorrance and Company, Inc.

Band Will Not Play Dixie: A Novel of Suspense. 1st Ed. Theodore Browne. LC 55-11114. 1955. Exposition Press.

Bandaged Nude. Robert Finnegan. 1946. Simon and Schuster.

Bandaged Nude. Paul William Ryan. LC 47-1677. (Inner sanctum mystery). 1946-1947. Simon and Schuster.

Bandana Creek. Hilda Downer. (Red Clay Reader: Vol. 14., No. 1). 1979. pap. 3.95 (ISBN 0-911692-13-4). Red Clay.

Bandar-Log. Archibald William Smith. LC 30-29553. 1930. Little, Brown, and Company.

Bandbox. Louis Joseph Vance. LC 12-9512. 1912. Little, Brown, and Company.

Bandeet Maestro. Warren Edward Boyer. LC 35-15464. 1935. Webbooks Publishers.

Bandersnatch. Desmond Lowden. LC 69-16957. 1969. 5.95. Holt, Rinehart and Winston.

Bandicoot. Richard Condon. LC 77-17195. 7.95 (ISBN 0-8037-0447-X). Dial Press.

Bandido. Nelson Nye. 1977. 1.50 (ISBN 0-441-04739-4). Ace Books.

Bandido. Jack Slade, pseud. (Lassiter Ser.: No. 2). 192p. 1982. pap. 2.25 o.p. (ISBN 0-505-51845-7). Tower Bks.

Bandido. Jack Slade, pseud. (Lassiter Ser.: No. 2). 192p. 1983. pap. 2.25 (ISBN 0-8439-2005-X, Leisure Bks). Dorchester Pub Co.

Bandido. Jack Slade, pseud. 1972. pap. 0.75 o.p. (BT40132). Belmont-Tower.

Bandit. Blanche, August Teodor & Borg, Selma, Ed. and Tr. LC 6-13842. 1872. G. P. Putnam & Sons.

Bandit. Leslie Charteris. LC 30-549. 1930. Pub. for The Crime Club, Inc., by Doubleday, Doran & Company, Inc.

Bandit in Black. Paul Evan Lehman. 1979. pap. 1.25 o.s.i. (ISBN 0-505-51368-4). Tower Bks.

Bandit Justice. James Edward Hoskins. LC 64-25984. 1964. Arcadia House.

Bandit Love. Juanita Savage. LC 31-229065. 1931. L. MacVeagh, The Dial Press.

Bandit of Bloody Run. Nelson C Nye. LC 39-33089. Phoenix Press.

Bandit of Bloody Run. Nelson Coral Nye. LC 39-33089. Phoenix Press.

Bandit of Hell's Bend. Edgar Rice Burroughs. LC 25-10695. 1925. A. C. McClurg & Co.

Bandit of Hell's Bend. Edgar Rice Burroughs. LC 79-16673. (Series: Gregg Press Western Fiction Series.). (Illus.). 1979. 9.95 (ISBN 0-8398-2577-3). Gregg Press.

Bandit of Paloduro. Charles Horace Snow. LC 34-17976. 1934. W. Morrow and Company.

Bandit of Syracuse. A Novel. Sylvanus Cobb. (On cover: The choice series, no. 137). 1898. R. Bonner's Sons.

Bandit of the Black Hills. Max Brand. Repr. of 1976 ed. lib. bdg. 12.70x (ISBN 0-88411-512-7). Amereon Ltd.

Bandit of the Black Hills. Frederick Faust. LC 49-73113. (Silver star westerns). 1949. Dodd, Mead.

Bandit Prince. Sessue Kintaro Hayakawa. LC 26-133442. The Macaulay Company.

Bandit Trail. William MacLeod Raine. LC 49-4716. 1949. Houghton Mifflin Co.

Bandits. Panait Istrati. Tr. by William A. Drake from Fr. LC 72-116956. (Short Story Index Reprint Ser). 1929. 17.00 (ISBN 0-8369-3460-1). Ayer Co.

Bandits: Lea Haidoucs. Panait Istrati & Drake, William A., 1899. LC 29-114411. 1929. A. A. Knopf.

Bandits: Les Haidoucs). Panait Istrati. LC 72-116956. (Short story index reprint series). 1970. Books for Libraries Press.

Bandits of the Osage: A Western Romanace. Emerson Bennett. 1850. L. Stratton.

Bandits of the Osage. A Western Romance. Emerson Bennett. LC 7-34433. 1847. Robinson & Jones.

Bandit's Trail. Will Cook. LC 73-17593. 1974. 4.95 (ISBN 0-385-02780-X). Doubleday.

Bandit's Trail. Nelson Nye. 192p. 1975. pap. 0.95 o.p. Woodhill.

Bandit's Trail. Nelson Nye. 192p. 1975. pap. 0.95 o.p. Manor Bks.

Banditti of the Prairies. new ed. Bonney, Edward. LC 63-18077. (Western frontier library). University of Oklahoma Press.

Banditti of the Prairies: A Tale of the Mississippi Valley. Edward Bonney. LC 4-6070. Homewood Publishing Company.

Banditti of the Prairies. A Tale of the Mississippi Valley; an Authentic Narrative of Thrilling Adventures in the Early Settlement of the Western Country. 25th thousand. ed. Edward Bonney. LC 6-10343. 1856. D. B. Cooke & Co.

Banditti of the Prairies: Or, The Murder's Doom!!. A Tale of the Mississippi Valley. Edward Bonney. LC 6-26294. 1850. E. Bonney.

Banditti of the Prairies: Or, the Murderer's Doom. Edward Bonney. Repr. of 1850 ed. 11.00 o.s.i. Finch Pr.

Bandolero. John Benteen. (Belmont Tower Book). 1977. 1.25. Tower Pubns.

Bandolero. Paul Gwynne. LC 5-6936. 1905. Dodd, Mead & Company.

Bandolero. Ernest Slater. LC 4-22268. 1904. Dodd, Mead & Company.

Bandolier Crossing. Frank O'Rourke. Date not set. pap. 1.75 (ISBN 0-451-11137-0, AE 1137, Sig). NAL.

Banduk Jaldi Banduk! (Quick, My Rifle) Claude Perry Jones & Sykes, A. L. LC 42-267427. 1907. Cortlandt Publishing Co.

Banduk Jaldi Banduk! (Quick, My Rifle!) Claude Perry Jones & Sykes, A. L. LC 7-34172. 1907. Press of J. J. Little & Co.

Bandy Papers, Vol. 1: Three Cheers for Me. Donald Lamont Jack. LC 72-79396. 228p. 1973. 7.95 o.p. (ISBN 0-385-04882-3). Doubleday.

Bandy Papers, Vol. 2: That's Me in the Middle. Donald Lamont Jack. LC 72-79396. 312p. 1973. 7.95 o.p. (ISBN 0-385-04901-3). Doubleday.

Bane of Bendon: A Tale of New Hampshire in the Days of the Temperance Excitement. C. B Sparrow. LC 8-15519. 1885. Ogden Bros. & Co., Printers and Binders.

Bane of Lord Caladon. Craig Mills. 224p. (Orig.). 1982. pap. 2.50 (ISBN 0-345-28972-2, Del Rey). Ballantine.

Bane of the Black Sword. Michael Moorcock. 1977. 1.25 (ISBN 0-87997-316-1). D.A.W. Books.

Bane of the Black Sword: Elric Series, No. 5. rev. ed. Michael Moorcock. (Science Fiction Ser). 1977. pap. 2.25 (ISBN 0-87997-805-8, UE1805). DAW Bks.

Baneful Sorceries. Joan Sanders. 1971. pap. 0.95 o.p. (ISBN 0-447-75188-3). Lancer.

Baneful Sorceries: Or; The Countess Bewitched. Joan Sanders. LC 70-88366. 1969. 6.95. Houghton Mifflin.

Bang! Bang! A Collection of Stories Intended to Recall Memories of the Nickel Library Days When Boys Were Supermen and Murder a Fine Art. George Ade. LC 75-160929. (Short story index reprint series). (Illus.). 1971. (ISBN 0-8369-3908-5). Books for Libraries Press.

Bang Bang Birds. Adam Diment. LC 68-25770. 1968. 4.50. Dutton.

Bang Man. Phil Powers. pap. 1.95 o.p. (8018). Cameo.

Bang the Drum Slowly. Mark Harris. (Dell book). 1973. 1.25. Dell.

Bang the Drum Slowly: By Henry W. Wiggen Certain of His Enthusiams Restrained by Mark Harris. 1st Ed. Mark Harris. LC 56-5771. 1956. Knopf.

Banger. Ann Griffin. pap. 1.95 o.p. (8053). Cameo.

Banished. H. Dyke Walton. (Orig.). 1981. pap. 3.50 (ISBN 0-505-51668-3). Tower Bks.

Banished. J. N. Williamson. LC 81-80781. 256p. (Orig.). 1981. pap. 2.75 (ISBN 0-87216-920-0). Playboy Pbks.

Banished Son: And Other Stories of the Heart. Caroline Lee Whiting Hentz. LC 44-15600. T. B. Peterson.

Banishment. Alma Stone. LC 72-92246. 280p. 1973. 6.95 o.p. (ISBN 0-385-03899-2). Doubleday.

Banishment, and Three Stories. Alma Stone. LC 72-92246. 1973. 6.95 (ISBN 0-385-03899-2). Doubleday.

Banishment of Jessop Blythe: A Novel. Joseph Hatton. LC 7-2194. (Lippincott's series of select novels, no. 167). 1895. J. B. Lippincott Company.

Banjo. Jack Curtis. 1973. (pbk) 1.25. New American Library.

Banjo. Jack Curtis. LC 70-133561. 1971. 6.95. Macmillan.

Banjo. Claude McKay. LC 79-17798. 1970. pap. 5.95 (ISBN 0-15-610675-2, Harv). HarBraceJ.

Banjo. Frank Walker. LC 78-300990. (Illus.). 1977. 9.95 (ISBN 0-7181-1593-7). M. Joseph.

Banjo: A Story Without a Plot. Claude McKay. LC 79-17798. (Harvest book). 1970. Harcourt, Brace, Jovanovich.

Banjo: A Story Without a Plot. Claude McKay. LC 29-10435. 1929. Harper & Brothers.

Banjo on My Knee. Harry Hamilton. LC 36-4916. The Bobbs-Merrill Company.

Bank. Stephen Longstreet. 1978. pap. 1.95 (ISBN 0-425-03639-1, Medallion). Berkley Pub.

Bank: A Novel. Stephen Longstreet. LC 75-40494. 7.95 (ISBN 0-399-11658-3). Putnam.

Bank: A Novel. Stephen Longstreet. (Berkley Medallion Book). 1978. 1.95 (ISBN 0-425-03639-1). Berkley Pub. Corp.

Bank Job. Robert L. Pike, pseud. LC 73-83662. 216p. 1974. 5.95 o.p. (ISBN 0-385-07339-9). Doubleday.

Bank Job. Regan, Thomas B. LC 64-20649. (Torquil book). 1964. Distributed by Dodd, Mead.

Bank Job: A Lieutenant Reardon Novel. Robert L Fish. LC 73-83662. 1974. 5.95 (ISBN 0-385-07339-9). Doubleday.
Bank of America of Louisiana. Jim Morrison. LC 75-314318. 1975. (ISBN 0-915628-03-1). Zeppelin Pub. Corp.
Bank President. Lewis Graham. LC 33-14020. The Macaulay Company.
Bank Robber. Giles Tippette. LC 70-117966. 1970. 5.95. Macmillan.
Bank Robbers: Or, Fast and Loose. Arthur George Frederick Griffiths. (On cover: Calumet series, no. 18). 1894. G. Munroe's Sons.
Bank Shot. Donald E Westlake. 1973. 0.95 (ISBN 0-671-77643-6). Pocket Book.
Bank Shot. Donald E Westlake. LC 72-183763. 1972. 5.95 (ISBN 0-671-21180-3). Simon and Schuster.
Bank Tragedy: A Novel. Mary R. Platt Hatch. LC 7-2635. 1890. Welch, Fracker Company.
Bank Tragedy. A Novel. Mary R. Platt Hatch. (On cover: American series, no. 267). 1891. M. J. Ivers & Co.
Bank Vault Mystery. Louis F Booth. LC 33-5178. 1933. Dodd, Mead & Company.
Bank with the Bamboo Door. Dolores Birk Hitchens. LC 65-125937. (Inner sanctum mystery). 3.50. S. & S.
Bank with the Bamboo Door. Dolores Birk Hitchens. LC 65-12593. (Inner sanctum mystery). 1965. Simon and Schuster.
Banked Fires. Ethel Winifred Savi. LC 19-18604. 1919. G. P. Putnam's Sons.
Banker. Dick Francis. LC 82-18122. 14.95 (ISBN 0-399-12778-X). Putnam.
Banker. Leslie Waller. LC 63-12961. 1963. Doubleday.
Banker. Leslie Waller. 1973. (pbk.) 1.50. Dell.
Banker and the Bear: The Story of a Corner in Lard. Henry Kitchell Webster. LC 68-57559. (American novels of muckraking, propaganda, and social protest). 1968. Gregg Press.
Banker and the Bear: The Story of a Corner in Lard. Henry Kitchell Webster. LC 3593. 1900. The Macmillan Company.
Banker and the Typewriter. Navada McNeil. LC 6-6106. 1895. G. W. Dillingham.
Banker at the Boarding-House. Montgomery Rollins. LC 18-17245. 1918. Lothrop, Lee & Shepard Co.
Banker of Bankersville: A Novel. Maurice Thompson. LC 8-19968. Cassell & Company, Limited.
Banker of Bankersville: A Novel. Maurice Thompson. LC 2577. (On cover: Romance series, no. 5). Street & Smith.
Bankers. Martin Mayer. 608p. 1980. pap. text ed. 3.50 (ISBN 0-345-29569-2). Ballantine.
Banker's Bones. Margaret Scherf. LC 68-11757. 1968. Published for the Crime Club by Doubleday.
Banker's Daughter. Adapted from the Celebrated Play by Bronson Howard. Magdalen Barrett. (On cover: Library of American authors, no. 40). 1892. G. Munro.
Banking on Death. Emma Lathen, pseud. LC 61-147081. (Cock Robin mystery). 1961. Macmillan.
Banking on Death. Emma Lathen, pseud. LC 61-14708. 1975. (pbk.) 1.25 (ISBN 0-671-80108-2). Pocket Books.
Bankrupt Heart: A Novel. Florence Marryat Church Lean. LC 7-13241. 1894. C. B. Reed.
Bankrupt's Son: A Tale of the Panic of '73. C I Gordon. LC 6-27483. 1892. G. M. Collier, Printer.
Banks of Colne (the Nursery) Eden Phillpotts. LC 17-13955. 1917. 1.50. The Macmillan Company.
Banned and Blessed: After the German of E. Werner Pseud. Elisabeth Burstenbinder. Tr. by Wister, Annis Lee (Furness) LC 3-14800. 1884. J. B. Lippincott & Co.
Banned in Hollywood. Sybah Darrich. pap. 1.95 o.s.i. (OPH-240, Ophelia). Olympia.
Banner at Daybreak. Edwin Moultrie Lanham. LC 37-401008. 1937. Longmans, Green and Co.
Banner Bold and Beautiful. Ann Forman Barron. 1975. (pbk.) 1.75. Fawcett.
Banner by the Wayside. Samuel Hopkins Adams. LC 47-1795. 1947. Random House.
Banner for Pegasus. John Bonett & Emery Bonett. LC 81-47806. 240p. 1982. pap. 2.40i (ISBN 0-06-080554-4, P 554, PL). Har-Row.
Banner of Blue. Samuel Rutherford Crockett. LC 2-22664. 1902. McClure, Phillips & Co.
Banner of the Bull: Three Episodes in the Career of Cesare Borgia. Rafael Sabatini. LC 23-27442. 1923. Houghton Mifflin Company.
Banner of the Upright Seven & Ursula. Gottfried Keller. Tr. by Bayard Q. Morgan from Ger. LC 73-88032. 152p. 1974. 8.50 (ISBN 0-8044-2459-4); pap. 3.95 (ISBN 0-8044-6354-9). Ungar.
Banner Over Me: A Tale of the Norman Conquest. Margery Greenleaf. LC 68-25634. (Illus.). 1968. 4.95. Follett Pub. Co.
Banner with a Strange Device: A Novel. Arona McHugh. LC 63-12962. 1964. Doubleday.
Bannerman. Jay Flynn. 1976. pap. 1.25 o.p. (ISBN 0-8439-0389-9, LB389, Leisure Bks). Nordon Pubns.
Bannerman. Jay Flynn. 192p. 1982. pap. 2.25 o.s.i. (ISBN 0-8439-1119-0, Leisure Bks). Nordon Pubns.
Bannerman. Jay Flynn. 192p. 1983. pap. 2.25 (ISBN 0-8439-2030-0, Leisure Bks). Dorchester Pub Co.
Bannerman Border Incident. Jay Flynn. 1976. pap. 1.25 o.p. (ISBN 0-8439-0401-1, LB401, Leisure Bks). Nordon Pubns.
Bannerman Case. Jeremy Lord, pseud. LC 35-4798. 1935. Pub. for the Crime Club, Inc., by Doubleday, Doran & Company, Inc.
Banners Against the Wind. John Edward Jennings. LC 54-8291. 1954. Little, Brown.
Banners at Shenandoah. Bruce Catton. 254p. 1976. Repr. of 1955 ed. lib. bdg. 15.95x (ISBN 0-89244-019-8). Queens Hse.
Banners of Desire. Lorinda Hagen. 1978. pap. 2.25 o.s.i. (ISBN 0-8439-0598-0, Leisure Bks). Nordon Pubns.
Banners of Silk. Rosalind Laker. LC 80-1453. 480p. 1981. 13.95 (ISBN 0-385-15902-1). Doubleday.
Banners of Silk. Rosalind Laker. 1982. pap. 3.50 (ISBN 0-451-11545-7, AE1545, Sig). NAL.
Banners of Silk. Barbara Vstedal. LC 80-1453. 1981. 13.95 (ISBN 0-385-15902-1). Doubleday.
Banners of the Sa'yen. B. R. Stateham. (Science Fiction Ser.). 1981. pap. 2.25 o.p. (ISBN 0-87997-636-5, UE1636). DAW Bks.
Banners of War. Sacha Carnegie, pseud. LC 70-110623. 1970. 6.95. Dodd, Mead.
Banning and Blessing. Margaret Roberts. LC 44-27715. 1890. National Society's Depository.
Bannon's Law. Lauran Paine. LC 81-71396. 1982. 10.95 (ISBN 0-8027-4011-1). Walker and Co.
Banquet Before Dawn. Warren Adler. LC 75-31651. 7.95 (ISBN 0-399-11642-7). Putnam.
Banquet for Furies. Harold Weston. LC 35-2531. Coward, McCann, Inc.
Banquet: 5 Short Stories. Rosellen Brown et al. LC 78-56621. (Illus.). 1978. 12.00x (ISBN 0-915778-24-6); pap. 5.00 (ISBN 0-915778-25-4); deluxe ed. 175.00x deluxe ed (ISBN 0-915778-23-8). Penmaen Pr.
Banshee. Margaret Millar. LC 82-22848. 1983. 10.95 (ISBN 0-688-01897-1). Morrow.
Banshee Harvest. James Leo Phelan. LC 45-1814. 1945. The Viking Press.
Bantam Story. rev. ed. (Orig.). 1980. pap. cancelled (ISBN 0-553-13256-3). Bantam.
Bantan--God-Like Islander. Maurice B Gardner. LC 36-19444. 1936. Meador Publishing Company.
Bantan and the Island Goddess: Being the Further Adventures of "Bantan--God-Like Islander,". Maurice B Gardner. LC 42-21685. 1942. Meador Publishing Company.
Bantan and the Mermaids. Maurice B Gardner. LC 79-122445. (Illus.). 1970. 4.00. T. Gaus' Sons.
Bantan Defiant: Adventures of an Island Chieftain. 1st Ed. Maurice B Gardner. LC 55-7437. 1955. Greenwich Book Publishers.
Bantan Fearless. Maurice B Gardner. LC 63-24094. 1963. Forum Pub. Co.
Bantan of the Islands. New Rev. Ed. Maurice B Gardner. LC 57-14069. Meador Pub. Co.
Bantan Valiant. Maurice B Gardner. LC 57-14070. 1957. Meador Pub. Co.
Bantan's Quest. Maurice B Gardner. LC 74-17856. (Illus.). 1974. 4.00. T. Gaus' Sons.
Banyon. William Johnston & Ed Adamson. (Orig.). 1971. pap. 0.75 o.p. (ISBN 0-446-64669-5, 64-669). Paperback Lib.
Banyon's War. Terrell L. Bowers. 1982. 6.95 (Avalon). Bouregy.
Banzai! Ferdinand Heinrich Grautoff. LC 74-15975. (Science Fiction). (Illus.). 1975. (ISBN 0-405-06310-5). Arno Press.
Banzai! Ferdinand Heinrich Grautoff. LC 9-965. 1909. 1.50. T. Weicher.
Banzai (Hurrah!) John Paris, pseud. LC 26-10918. Boni and Liveright.
Banzai Noel! Garrett Graham. 1975. 2.00 o.p. (ISBN 0-8149-0539-0). Vanguard.
Baphomet's Meteor. Pierre Barbet, pseud. (Science Fiction Ser.). (Orig.). 1972. pap. 0.95 o.p. (UQ1035). DAW Bks.
Baptized with a Curse. Edith Stewart Drewry. (Lovell's library. no. 1351). 1889. J. W. Lovell Company.
Baptized with a Curse: A Romance. Edith Stewart Drewry. (Harper's handy ser. no. 94). 1886. Harper & Brothers.
Bar--20: Being a Record of Certain Happenings That Occured in the Otherwise Peaceful Lives of One Hopalong Cassidy and His Companions on the Range. Clarence Edward Mulford. LC 7-23640. 1907. The Outing Publishing Company.
Bar Belles. Trisha Stevens. 1976. (pbk.) 1.50. Pocket Books.
Bar D Boss. Charles Horace Snow. LC 43-2348. 1943. Phoenix Press.
Bar D Buckaroos. Earle E Perrenot. LC 49-48506. 1949. Phoenix Press.
Bar Five: A Roundup of Best Western Stories. facs. ed. Ed. by Scott Meredith. LC 79-75782. (Short Story Index Reprint Ser). 1956. 12.00 (ISBN 0-8369-3007-X). Ayer Co.
Bar-Fly Wives. Wright Williams. LC 44-7075. 1944. Phoenix Press.
Bar Harbor Days. Constance Cary Harrison. 1887. Harper & Brothers.
Bar K. Lawrence A Keating. LC 40-7015. Phoenix Press.
Bar-M Boss. T W Ford. LC 49-413020. 1949. Phoenix Press.
Bar-Maid at Battleton. Frederick William Robinson. (On cover: Harper's half-hour series v. 124). 1879. Harper & Brothers.
Bar Nothing Brand. Nelson Coral Nye. LC 39-5150. Phoenix Press.
Bar Nothing Ranch. Rosemary Drachman Taylor. LC 47-11686. 1947. Whittlesey House.
Bar of Song. Henry Elliot Harman. LC 14-22602. 1.50. The State Company.
Bar One: Roundup of Best Western Stories. facs. ed. Ed. by Scott Meredith. LC 79-75782. (Short Story Index Reprint Ser). 1952. 16.00 (ISBN 0-8369-3032-0). Ayer Co.
Bar-Rooms at Brantley: Or, The Great Hotel Speculation. Timothy Shay Arthur. LC 6-2462. Porter & Coates.
Bar Roundup of Best Western Stories. No. 1-1952- Ed. by Scott Meredith. LC 52-5305. (Dutton Diamond D western). Dutton.
Bar Sinister. Richard Harding Davis. LC 69-13877. (Illus.). 1969. Greenwood Press.
Bar Sinister. Richard Harding Davis. LC 76-8181. (Illus.). Scholarly Press.
Bar Sinister. Richard Harding Davis. LC 77-90081. (Illus.). 1969. AMS Press.
Bar Sinister. Holly Roth. LC 60-11375. 1960. Published for the Crime Club by Doubleday.
Bar-Sinister: A Social Study... Jeannette Ritchie Haderman Walworth. 1885. Cassell & Company, Limited.
Bar Sinister: A Tale of Love and Adventure. St. George Rathborne. LC 4499. (On cover: Eagle series. no. 173). 1900. Street & Smith.
Bar Sinister. 1st Ed. K. G. Ballard. LC 60-113759. 1960. Published for the Crime Club by Doubleday.
Bar Six: Roundup of Best Western Stories. facs. ed. Ed. by Scott Meredith. LC 79-75782. (Short Story Index Reprint Ser). 1957. 15.00 (ISBN 0-8369-3056-8). Ayer Co.
Bar Studs. Leonard Jordan. (Fawcett Gold Medal Book). 1976. (pbk.) 1.50. Fawcett.
Bar the Doors. Ed. by Alfred Hitchcock. LC 47-21952. (On cover: A Dell book. 143). 1946.
Bar Three: Roundup of Best Western Stories. facs. ed. Ed. by Scott Meredith. LC 79-75782. (Short Story Index Reprint Ser). 1954. 16.00 (ISBN 0-8369-3055-X). Ayer Co.
Bar Twenty. Clarence Edward Mulford. 382p. 1974. Repr. of 1906 ed. lib. bdg. 19.10x (ISBN 0-88411-213-6). Amereon Ltd.
Bar Twenty Days. Clarence Edward Mulford. 412p. 1974. Repr. of 1911 ed. lib. bdg. 19.95x (ISBN 0-88411-214-4). Amereon Ltd.
Bar Twenty Rides Again. Clarence Edward Mulford. 337p. 1974. Repr. of 1926 ed. lib. bdg. 17.70x (ISBN 0-88411-215-2). Amereon Ltd.
Bar Twenty Three. Clarence Edward Mulford. (Hopalong Cassidy Ser). 1976. Repr. of 1921 ed. lib. bdg. 17.95x (ISBN 0-88411-227-6). Amereon Ltd.
Bar Two: Roundup of Best Western Stories. facs. ed. Ed. by Scott Meredith. LC 79-75782. (Short Story Index Reprint Ser). 1952. 16.00 (ISBN 0-8369-3033-9). Ayer Co.
Bar X Golf Course. Ross Santee. LC 70-174996. (Illus.). 1971. 9.50 (ISBN 0-87358-085-0). Northland Press.
Bar X Golf Course. Ross Santee. LC 33-11788. Farrar & Rinehart, Inc.
Bar 2 Roundup of Best Western Stories: 1st Ed. Ed. by Scott Meredith. LC 52-13554. (Dutton Diamond D western). 1953. Dutton.
Bar-20: Being a Record of Certain Happenings That Occurred in the Otherwise Peaceful Lives of One Hopalong Cassidy and His Companions on the Range. Clarence Edward Mulford. LC 73-89632. (Illus.). 1974. 6.95. Aeonian Press.
Bar-20: Being a Record of Certain Happenings That Occurred in the Otherwise Peaceful Lives of One Hopalong Cassidy and His Companions on the Range. Clarence Edward Mulford. LC 27-7329. 1907. A. L. Burt Company.
Bar-20 Days. Clarence Edward Mulford. LC 73-89634. (Illus.). 1974. 6.95. Aeonian Press.
Bar-20 Days. Clarence Edward Mulford. LC 11-5995. 1911. 1.35. A. C. McClurg & Co.
Bar-20 Days. Clarence Edward Mulford. LC 27-7325. A. L. Burt Company.
Bar 20 Rides Again. Clarence Edward Mulford. LC 73-89635. 1974. 6.95. Aeonian Press.
Bar 20 Rides Again. Clarence Edward Mulford. LC 26-18390. 1926. Doubleday, Page & Company.
Bar 20 Rides Again. Clarence Edward Mulford. LC 45-45007. 1944. The Blakiston Company.
Bar-20 Three. Clarence Edward Mulford. LC 76-28249. 1976. 6.95 (ISBN 0-88411-227-6). Aeonian Press.
Bar-20 Three. Clarence Edward Mulford. LC 27-7330. 1921. A. L. Burt Company.
Bar-20 Three: Relating a Series of Startling and Strenuous Adventures, in the Cow-Town of Mesquite, of the Famous Bar-20 Trio--Hopalong Cassidy, Red Connors, and Johnny Nelson. Clarence Edward Mulford. LC 21-7329. 1921. 1.50. A. C. McClurg & Co.
Bar 3 Roundup of Best Western Stories. 1st Ed. Ed. by Scott Meredith. LC 54-5052. (Dutton Diamond D western). 1954. Dutton.
Bar 8 Buckaroos. Tony Adams. LC 40-85810. Phoenix Press.
Barabbas. Marie Corelli. LC 1-26213. 1901. J. B. Lippincott Co.
Barabbas. Marie Corelli. LC 33-17508. 1925. A. L. Burt Company.
Barabbas. Par Fabian Lagerkvist. LC 55-5728. (Modern library paperbacks, P13). 1955. Random House.
Barabbas. A Dream of the World's Tragedy. Marie Corelli. LC 6-27717. 1894. J. B. Lippincott Company.
Barabbas: A Novel of the Time of Jesus. Emery Bekessy & Hemberger, Andreas, D. 1946. LC 46-7817. 1946. Prentice-Hall, Inc.
Barb. William James McNally. LC 23-7830. 1923. G. P. Putnam's Sons.
Barb, Please Wake up! Roy B. Zuck. 128p. 1976. pap. 1.95 o.p. (ISBN 0-88207-653-1). Victor Bks.
Barb Wire. Walt Coburn. LC 31-22651. The Century Co.
Barb Wire. W. Ryerson Johnson. LC 47-18425. 1947. Arcadia House.
Barbara. Mary Andrews Denison. LC 6-34000. 1876. D. Lothrop & Co.
Barbara. Frank Newman, pseud. LC 78-9890. (Traveller's companion series, TC-433). 1968. 1.75. Traveller's Companion, Inc.
Barbara Blomberg: A Historical Romance. Georg Moritz Ebers. Tr. by Mary Joanne Stafford. LC 6-43723. 1897. D. Appleton and Company.
Barbara Greer. 1st Ed. Stephen Birmingham. LC 59-11103. 1959. Little, Brown.
Barbara Gwynne (Life) William Budd Trites. LC 13-6736. 1913. Duffield & Company.
Barbara Heathcote's Trial. Rosa Nouchette Carey. LC 6-23108. (On cover: Seaside library. Pocket ed., no. 551). G. Munro.
Barbara Heathcote's Trial, a Novel. Rosa Nouchette Carey. LC 16-937823. 1909. J. B. Lippincott Company.
Barbara Heck: A Tale of Early Methodism. William Henry Withrow. LC 8-37788. 1895. Cranston & Curts.
Barbara Justice: A Novel. Desemea Wilson. LC 22-11516. E. P. Dutton & Company.
Barbara Ladd. Charles George Douglas Roberts. LC 2-24321. 1902. L. C. Page & Company.
Barbara, Lady's Maid and Peeress. Annie French Hector. 1898. J. B. Lippincott Company.
Barbara Leybourne. A Story of Eighty Years Ago. Sarah Selina Hamer. Cranston and Stowe.
Barbara of Baltimore. Katharine Haviland Taylor. LC 19-14625. George H. Doran Company.
Barbara of the Snows. Harry Irving Greene. LC 11-5990. 1911. Moffat, Yard and Company.
Barbara on the Farm. Illustrated by Gwyneth Richardson. Mary Scott. LC 54-40032. 1953. A. H. & A. W. Reed.
Barbara; or, Splendid Misery. Mary Elizabeth Braddon Maxwell. (On cover: Lovell's library, no. 869). 1887. J. W. Lovell Company.
Barbara; or, Splendid Misery. A Novel. Mary Elizabeth Braddon Maxwell. (Seaside library. v. 34, no. 701). 1880. G. Munro.
Barbara; or, Splendid Misery. A Novel. Mary Elizabeth Braddon Maxwell. (On cover: Seaside library. Pocket ed., no. 234). 1884. G. Munro.
Barbara; or, Splendid Misery. A Novel. Mary Elizabeth Braddon Maxwell. (Franklin square library, no. 108). 1880. Harper & Brothers.
Barbara Owen, Girl Reporter. Adeline McElfresh. LC 56-3578. 1956. Avalon Books.
Barbara Owen: Girl Reporter by Jane Scott Pseud. Adeline McElfresh. LC 56-35789. 1956. Avalon Books.
Barbara Picks a Husband: A Comedy in Narrative. Hermann Hagedorn. LC 18-12616. 1918. 1.50. The Macmillan Company.
Barbara Selby. Nell 'Marry' Dean. LC 54-7497. 1954. Arcadia House.
Barbara Thayer, Her Glorious Career: A Novel. Annie Jenness Miller. LC 7-10208. 1884. Lee and Shepard.

Barbara, the Valiant. Katheryn Kimbrough, pseud. (Saga of the Phenwick Women: No. 16). 1977. pap. 1.75 (ISBN 0-445-03228-6). Popular Lib.
Barbara Winslow: Rebel. Elizabeth Ellis. LC 6-1372. 1906. Dodd, Mead & Company.
Barbarana. John Cleve, pseud. 176p. pap. 1.95 o.p. (6126). Brandon.
Barbara's History. Amelia Ann Blandford Edwards. (Seaside library. v. 1, no. 18). 1877. G. Munro.
Barbara's History. Amelia Ann Blandford Edwards. (On cover: Seaside library. Pocket ed. no. 99). 1883. G. Munro.
Barbara's Marriage and the Bishop. Esther Waggaman Neill. LC 25-4988. 1925. The Macmillan Company.
Barbara's Marriages: A Novel. Maude Lavinia Radford Warren. LC 15-711568. 1915. Harper & Brothers.
Barbara's Rival: Or, Only a Woman's Heart. Ernest A Young. (On cover: Lovell's library. v. 12, no. 666). 1885. J. W. Lovell Company.
Barbara's Triumphs: Or, The Fortunes of a Young Artist. Mary Andrews C. W. Denison Denison. LC 6-33999. (Munsey's popular ser. no. 4). 1887. F. A. Munsey.
Barbara's Vagaries. Mary Langdon Tidball. LC 11-7174. 1886. Harper & Brothers.
Barbarella: Tr. from French by Richard Seaver. Jean-Claude Forest. (Grove special, GS2). 1968. pap., 1.50. Grove.
Barbarian. Charles Wadsworth Camp. LC 25-7075. 1925. Doubleday, Page & Company.
Barbarian. John Jakes. (Brak Ser.: No. 1). 1981. pap. 2.25 (ISBN 0-505-51650-0). Tower Bks.
Barbarian. Naomi Haldane Mitchison. 1978. 2.25 (ISBN 0-445-04329-6). Popular Library.
Barbarian. Willard Price. LC 41-21406. The John Day Company.
Barbarian. Dickens Skinner. LC 29-644629. 1929. D. Appleton and Company.
Barbarian Lover. Margaret Bass Pedler. LC 23-15032. George H. Doran Company.
Barbarian Lover. Margaret Bass Pedler. LC 33-175060. 1925. Grosset & Dunlap.
Barbarian of World's End. Lin Carter. 1977. 1.50 (ISBN 0-87997-300-5). DAW Books.
Barbarian Princess. Laura Buchanan. (Berkley Medallion Book). 1978. 1.95 (ISBN 0-425-03701-0). Berkley Pub. Corp.
Barbarian Princess. Damion Hunter. LC 82-1658. (Centurions series; bk. 2). ((Series: Hunter, Damion.). (Centurions; bk. 2.). (Illus.). 1982. 3.50 (ISBN 0-345-29826-8). Ballantine Books.
Barbarian Princess. Florence King. 1978. pap. 1.95 (ISBN 0-425-03701-0, Medallion). Berkley Pub.
Barbarian Stories. Naomi Haldane Mitchison. LC 77-134970. (Short story index reprint series). 1970. Books for Libraries Press.
Barbarian Stories. Naomi Haldane Mitchison. LC 29-26897. 1929. Harcourt, Brace and Company.
Barbarian: The Corn King and Spring Queen. Naomi Haldane Mitchison. LC 61-66192. 1961. Cameron Associates.
Barbarians. Robert William Chambers. 1917. 1.40. D. Appleton and Company.
Barbarians. Virginia Faulkner. LC 35-4801. 1935. Simon and Schuster.
Barbarians. Francis Van Wyck Mason. LC 55-17927. (Pocket book, 1024). 1954. Pocket Books.
Barbarians and Black Magicians. Ed. by Lin Carter. (Flashing Swords). (Dell Book: 4). 1977. 1.50 (ISBN 0-440-12627-4). Dell Pub. Co.
Barbarians at the Gates: A Novel. Richard Bankowsky. LC 72-4886. 1972. 7.95. Little, Brown.
Barbarian's Country. Jean Hougron. Tr. by Geoffrey Sainsbury. 1961. 3.95 o.p. (ISBN 0-374-10840-4). FS&G.
Barbarians of Mars. Edward P. Bradbury, pseud. pap. 0.50 o.p. (ISBN 0-447-72127-5). Lancer.
Barbarossa: An Historical Novel of the Xii, Century. Josef Eduard Konrad Bischoff. LC 6-11716. 1867. E. Cummiskey.
Barbarous Coast. Kenneth Millar. LC 78-12829. 1979. 10.95 (ISBN 0-89340-169-2). J. Curley.
Barbarous Coast: By Ross Macdonald Pseud. 1st Ed. Kenneth Millar. LC 56-6507. 1956. Knopf.
Barbars, a Novel. 1st Ed. Wayne Robinson. LC 61-12572. 1962. Doubleday.
Barbary Bounty. Melissa Masters. 1980. pap. 2.50 (ISBN 0-440-10461-0). Dell.
Barbary Brew: A Romantic Novel. Zelda Stewart Charters. LC 37-21531. Stackpole Sons.
Barbary Coasters. Lee D. Willoughby. (Making of America Ser.: No. 36). (Orig.). 1983. pap. 3.25 (ISBN 0-440-00457-8). Dell.
Barbary Freight. Richard Burke. LC 43-6644. 1943. G. P. Putnam's Sons.
Barbary Hoard. John Appleby. LC 52-7311. 1952. Coward-McCann.
Barbary Sheep: A Novel. Robert Smythe Hichens. LC 7-24588. 1907. Harper & Brothers.
Barbary Shore. Norman Mailer. LC 51-10764. 1951. Rinehart.
Barbary Shore. Norman Mailer. LC 79-26233. 1980. 15.95 (ISBN 0-86527-218-2). H. Fertig.
Barbe of Grand Bayon. John Oxenham, pseud. LC 3-23483. 1903. Dodd, Mead & Company.
Barbed Wire. Elmer Kelton. LC 58-6913. (Ballantine books, 247). 1958. Ballantine Books.
Barbed Wire, and Other Stories. Robert Canzoneri. LC 70-101365. 1970. 4.95. Dial Press.
Barbed-Wire Empire. Harry Sinclair Drago. LC 37-122285. Green Circle Books.
Barbed Wire Entanglements. Paul Bernard Malone. LC 40-14426. Stackpole Sons.
Barbed Wire Kingdom. C. William Harrison. LC 55-1980. 1955. Jason Press.
Barbed Wire on the Isle of Man: The British Internment of Jews. Alexander Ramati. LC 79-3361. 9.95 (ISBN 0-15-110671-1). Harcourt Brace Jovanovich.
Barber of Seville & The Marriage of Figaro. Beaumarchais. Tr. by John Wood. (Classics Ser.). 224p. 1964. pap. 3.95 (ISBN 0-14-044133-6). Penguin.
Barber of Tubac. Nelson Coral Nye. LC 47-1901. 1947. The Macmillan Company.
Barberry Bush. Kathleen Thompson Norris. LC 27-18766. 1927. Doubleday Page & Company.
Barber's Clock: A Conversation Piece. Edward Verrall Lucas. LC 32-26246. 1932. J. B. Lippincott Company.
Barbie Murders & Other Stories. John Varley. 1980. pap. 2.25 (ISBN 0-425-04580-3). Berkley Pub.
Barboza Credentials. Peter Driscoll. LC 76-10483. 1976. 8.95 o.p. (ISBN 0-397-01145-8). Lippincott.
Barboza Credentials: A Novel. Peter Driscoll. LC 76-10483. 8.95 (ISBN 0-397-01145-8). Lippincott.
Barbry. Henry Milner Rideout. LC 23-14917. 1923. 2.00. Duffield and Company.
Barbury Witch: A Novel. Anthony Richardson. LC 27-19309. 1927. Dodd, Mead & Company.
Barca. Lou Cameron. (Berkley medallion book). 1974. (pbk.) 1.25. Berkley Pub. Co.
Barchester Pilgrimage. Ronald Arbuthnott Knox & Trollope, Anthony. LC 38-24915. 1936. Sheed & Ward, Inc.
Barchester Towers. Anthony Trollope. LC 58-4759. 1958.
Barchester Towers. Anthony Trollope. 1959. Heritage Press.
Barchester Towers. Anthony Trollope. (His The chronicles of Barsetshire, 2). 1962. Harcourt, Brace & World.
Barchester Towers. Anthony Trollope. LC 53-1190. 1953. Fine Editions Press.
Barchester Towers. Anthony Trollope. LC 49-40694. 1945. Garden City Pub. Co.
Barchester Towers. Anthony Trollope. LC 49-506899. (Rinehart editions, 21). 1949. Rinehart.
Barchester Towers. Anthony Trollope. (Half-title: Hand and pocket library. no. II-III). 1862. Dick & Fitzgerald.
Barchester Towers. Anthony Trollope. LC 27-136823. (Seaside library, v. 53, no. 1080). 1881. G. Munro.
Barchester Towers. Anthony Trollope. LC 2-29258. (English Comedie humaine.1st series, v. 12). 1902. The Century Co.
Barchester Towers. Anthony Trollope. LC 4-24963. (On cover: The chronicles of Barnetshire. 11). 1904. Dodd, Mead & Company.
Barchester Towers. Anthony Trollope. (Half-title: Everyman's library, ed. by Ernest Rhys. Fiction. no. 30). 1906. J. M. Dent & Co.
Barchester Towers. Anthony Trollope. LC 23-13651. (modern student's library). C. Scribner's Sons.
Barchester Towers. Anthony Trollope. LC 25-26587. (Half-title: The World's classics. cclxviii). 1925. H. Milford.
Barchester Towers. Anthony Trollope. LC 26-4940. (modern readers' series). 1926. The Macmillan Company.
Barchester Towers. Anthony Trollope. LC 29-30756. (Half-title: Everyman's library, edited by Ernest Rhys. Fiction. no. 30). 1929. J. M. Dent & Sons, Ltd.
Barchester Towers. Anthony Trollope. LC 36-37061. (Half-title: Everyman's library, ed. by Ernest Rhys. Fiction. no. 30). 1936. J. M. Dent & Sons, Ltd.
Barchester Towers. Anthony Trollope. LC 38-17093. (Half-title: Everyman's library, ed. by Ernest Rhys. Fiction. no. 30). 1936. J. M. Dent & Sons, Ltd.
Barchester Towers. Anthony Trollope & James R Kincaid. LC 79-42713. (World's classics). 1980. 4.95 (ISBN 0-19-281507-5). Oxford University Press.
Barchester Towers. Anthony Trollope & McKay, Donald 1895- Illus. LC 47-421788. Doubleday & Company, Inc.
Barchester Towers. Anthony Trollope & McKay, Donald, 1895- Illus. LC 45-9592. 1945. Doubleday, Doran & Company, Inc.
Barchester Towers. Anthony Trollope & Thorold, Algar Labouchere, 1866-1936, Ed. LC 12-394419. (new pocket library, vol. 5). 1902. John Lane.
Barchester Towers: And The Warden. Anthony Trollope. LC 50-11917. (Modern Library college editions, T37). 1950. Modern Library.
Barclay Place. Elinore Denniston. LC 75-29298. (Red badge novel of suspense). 5.95 (ISBN 0-396-07215-1). Dodd, Mead.
Barclay Place. Rae Foley, pseud. (Red Badge Novel of Suspence Ser.). 206p. 1975. 5.95 o.p. (ISBN 0-396-07215-1). Dodd.
Barclay's Daughter. Jean Kate Ludlum. LC 7-14726. 1893. The National Temperance Society and Publication House.
Barclays of Boston. Eliza Henderson Bordman Otis. LC 14-22462. 1854. Ticknor, Reed, and Fields.
Bard. Keith Taylor. (Orig.). 1982. pap. 2.50 (ISBN 0-441-05000-X). Ace Bks.
Bardell V. Pickwick: The Trial for Breach of Promise of Marriage Held at the Guildhall Sittings on April 1, 1828, Before Mr. Justice Stareleigh and a Special Jury of the City of London. Charles Dickens & Percy Hetherington Fitzgerald. LC 78-26151. 1978. 17.50 (ISBN 0-8414-4172-3). Folcroft Library Editions.
Bardel's Murder. Kenneth Giles. LC 73-90392. 1974. 5.95 (ISBN 0-8027-5293-4). Walker.
Bardel's Murder. Edmund McGirr. LC 73-90392. 160p. 1974. 5.95 o.p. (ISBN 0-8027-5293-4). Walker & Co.
Bardelys the Magnificent: Being an Account of the Strange Wooing Pursued by the Sieur Marcel De Saint-Pol, Marquis of Bardelys, and of the Things That in the Course of It Befell Him in Languedoc, in the Year of the Rebellion. Rafael Sabatini. 1924. Houghton Mifflin Company.
Bardelys the Magnificent: Being on ! Account of the Strange Wooing Pursued by the Sieur Marcel De Saint-Pol, Marquis of Bardelys, and of the Things That in the Course of It Befell Him in Languedoc, in the Year of the Rebellion. Rafael Sabatini. LC 30-123438. 1926. Grosset & Dunlap.
Bardiston--1775. Franklin Blackstone. LC 57-9836. 1957. Christopher Pub. House.
Bardmoor Murder: Including the Remarkable Deductions of Sir Henry Marquis of Scotland Yard. Melville Davisson Post. LC 29-5229. J. H. Sears & Company, Inc.
Bare Boobs in the World Book. Patricia Ryan. 1978. 5.95 o.p. (ISBN 0-533-03043-9). Vantage.
Bare Essence. Meredith Rich. 320p. (Orig.). 1981. pap. 2.95 (ISBN 0-449-14386-4, GM). Fawcett.
Bare Living. Elmer Holmes Davis & Holt, Guy. LC 33-30146. The Bobbs-Merrill Company.
Bare Nell. Leslie Thomas. LC 78-3960. 1978. 8.95 (ISBN 0-312-06641-4). St. Martin's Press.
Bare Trap: A Johnny. Liddell Mystery. Frank Kane. LC 52-11465. 1952. I. Washburn.
Baree, Son of Kazan. James Oliver Curwood. LC 17-25122. 1917. Doubleday, Page & Company.
Barefoot. Zaharia Stancu. LC 68-24278. 1971. Twayne Publishers.
Barefoot Boy with Cheek. Max Shulman. LC 43-6576. 1943. Doubleday, Doran and Company, Inc.
Barefoot Boy with Cheek. Max Shulman. LC 46-4507. The Blakiston Company.
Barefoot Boy with Cheek. Max Shulman. LC 76-11506. (Illus.). 1978. 15.00 (ISBN 0-404-15296-1). AMS Press.
Barefoot Bride. Dorothy Cork. (Harlequin Romances). 192p. 1981. pap. 1.25 (ISBN 0-373-02390-1, Pub. by Harlequin). PB.
Barefoot in the Head. Brian Wilson Aldiss. 224p. 1981. pap. 2.25 (ISBN 0-380-53561-0, 53561). Avon.
Barefoot in the Head: A European Fantasia. Brian Wilson Aldiss. LC 74-97644. 1970. 4.95. Doubleday.
Barefoot Mailman. Theodore Pratt. LC 43-118521. 1943. Duell, Sloan and Pearce.
Barefoot Mailman. Theodore Pratt. (Signet book). 1975. (pbk.) 1.25. New American Library.
Barefoot Man. Davis Grubb. LC 75-139624. 1971. 6.95 (ISBN 0-671-20821-7). Simon and Schuster.
Barefoot Spider. Anna B. Devlin. 1970. 2.95 o.p. Vantage.
Barefoot Trumpet Man. Dan T. Nolen. 3.00 o.p. Carlton.
Barent Creighton: A Romance. Donald Cameron Shafer. LC 20-11224. 1920. A. A. Knopf.
Baretta: Beyond the Law: A Novel. Andrew Patrick. (Berkley Medallion Book). 1977. 1.50 (ISBN 0-425-03515-8). Berkley Pub. Corp.
Baretta: Sweet Revenge: A Novel. Thom Racina. (Berkley Medallion Book). 1977. 1.50 (ISBN 0-425-03559-X). Berkley Pub. Corp.
Barford Cat Affair. P. H. H. Bryan. LC 58-6425. 1958. Abelard-Schuman.
Barforth Women. Brenda Jagger. LC 81-43054. 1982. 17.95 (ISBN 0-385-17623-6). Doubleday.
Bargain: A Historical Novel on the Defense of Londonderry. William Schoeler. LC 51-12160. 1951. Exposition Press.
Bargain Basement. Gloria Goddard. LC 34-4567. 1934. W. Godwin, Inc.
Bargain Basement. Cecil Roberts. LC 32-1753. 1932. D. Appleton and Company.
Bargain for Death. Robert Lee Martin. 1971. pap. 0.75 o.p. (07183). Curtis.
Bargain in Souls: An Impossible Story. Ernest De Lancey Pierson. LC 7-35897. (library of choice fiction no. 40). 1892. Laird & Lee.
Bargain True. Nalbro Isadorah Bartley. LC 19-424. Small, Maynard & Company.
Bargain with Death. Hugh Pentecost. LC 73-19081. 1974. 4.95 o.p. (ISBN 0-396-06919-3). Dodd.
Bargain with Death. Judson Pentecost Philips. LC 73-19081. (Red badge novel of suspense). 1974. 4.95 (ISBN 0-396-06919-3). Dodd, Mead.
Bargain with God. Thomas Savage. 1953. 3.00 o.p. (06700). S&S.
Bargain with the Devil. Jayne Castle. (Candlelight Ecstasy Ser.: No. 26). (Orig.). 1981. pap. 1.75 (ISBN 0-440-10423-8). Dell.
Barge of Haunted Lives. John Aubrey Tyson. LC 23-4980. 1923. The Macmillan Company.
Barham Downs. Robert Bage. LC 78-60850. (Novel, 1720-1805; 9). 1979. 56.00 (ISBN 0-8240-3658-1). Garland Pub.
Barham of Beltana. William Edward Norris. LC 4-36707. Longmans, Green and Co.,
Barington. Edward Tatum Wallace. LC 45-5730. 1945. Simon and Schuster.
Baritone. Lilian Lauferty. LC 48-7573. 1948. Doubleday.
Bark Tree. Raymond Queneau. Tr. by Barbara Wright from Fr. LC 75-145934. (Cloth ed. 9.50 o.p.). Orig. Title: Chiendent. 1971. pap. 3.95 (ISBN 0-8112-0167-8, NDP314). New Directions.
Barkeep of Blemont: Translated by Norman Denny. 1st Ed. Marcel Ayme. LC 50-7702. 1950. Harper.
Barkeep Stories. Frank Hutcheson. LC 7-9031. (On Cover: The Melbourne Series No. 48). 1896. E. A. Weeks & Company.
Barker: A Novel. Kenyon Nicholson. LC 27-23147. George H. Doran Company.
Barker's Luck: And Other Stories. Bret Harte. LC 70-113668. (Short story index reprint series). 1970. Books for Libraries Press.
Barker's Luck: And Other Stories. Bret Harte. LC 7-2869. 1896. Houghton, Miffin and Company.
Barker's Luck, & Other Stories. Bret Harte. LC 70-113668. (Short Story Index Reprint Ser). 1896. 16.00 (ISBN 0-8369-3397-4). Ayer Co.
Barkett's Lock. Margaret Greenway McClelland. (On cover: Cassell's sunshine series, v. 1, no. 22). 1889. Cassell & Company, Limited.
Barking Deer. Jonathan Rubin. LC 73-88042. 1974. 7.95 (ISBN 0-8076-0727-4). G. Braziller.
Barking Dog Murder Case. Evelyn Charles H Vivian. LC 38-303853. Hillman-Curl, Inc.
Barking of a Lonely Fox. Guido D'Agostino. LC 52-5344. 1952. McGraw-Hill.
Barks of a Nazi Dog. Lucy Bannard Van Sickle. LC 38-46502. The Tuttle Publishing Company, Inc.
Bar'l of Apples: A Gregory Clark Omnibus. Gregory Clark. LC 72-183911. 1971. (ISBN 0-07-092952-1). McGraw-Hill Ryerson.
Barlaams Ok Josaphats Saga. Ed. by R. Keyser & C. R. Unger. LC 80-1981. Repr. of 1851 ed. 38.50 (ISBN 0-404-18625-4). AMS Pr.
Barlasch of the Guard. Hugh Stowell Scott. LC 3-20061. 1903. McClure, Phillips & Co.
Barley. D. E. Briggs. 1978. 82.00x (ISBN 0-412-11870-X, NO.6043, Pub. by Chapman & Hall). Methuen Inc.
Barley Wood: Or, Building on the Road. Jane Marsh Parker. LC 7-34980. 1860. D. Dana, Jr.
Barley Wood: Or Building on the Rock. Jane Marsh Parker. (American Historical Novel Ser). 1860. 9.95 o.s.i. (ISBN 0-512-00867-1). Garrett Pr.
Barlow Comes to Judgment. Elwyn Jones. LC 75-40791. 148p. 1976. 7.95 o.p. (ISBN 0-312-06650-3). St Martin.
Barlow Exposed. Elwyn Jones. LC 76-28040. 7.95 (ISBN 0-312-06685-6). St. Martin's Press.
Barlow's Kingdom. Adam Kennedy. LC 69-13513. 1969. 4.50 (ISBN 0-671-27020-6). Trident Press.
Barlow's Kingdom. John Redgate. 1969. 4.50 o.s.i. (ISBN 0-671-27020-6). Trident.
Barly Fields: A Collection of Five Novels. Robert Nathan & Benet, Stephen Vincent. LC 38-27469. 1938. A. A. Knopf.
Barmecide's Feast. John Gore. LC 12-18728. 1912. John Lane.

Barmy in Wonderland. P. G. Wodehouse. 1958. 11.95 o.s.i. (ISBN 0-8277-0202-7). British Bk Ctr.

Barmy in Wonderland. P. G. Wodehouse. 1958. 11.95 o.s.i. (ISBN 0-8277-0202-7). British Bk Ctr.

Barn Blind. Jane Smiley. LC 79-3417. 1980. 9.95i (ISBN 0-06-014016-X, HarpT). Har-Row.

Barn Stormers: Being the Tragical Side of a Comedy. Alice Muriel Livingston Williamson. F. A. Stokes Company.

Barn-Yard Statesman: Or, Rum and Dynamite. Philip Henry Smith. 1886. P. H. Smith.

Barnabas Collins. Marilyn Ross. (Orig.). 1968. pap. 0.50 o.p. (62-001). Paperback Lib.

Barnabas Collins & Quentin's Demon. Marilyn Ross. (Orig.). 1970. pap. 0.60 o.p. (ISBN 0-446-63275-9, 63-275). Paperback Lib.

Barnabas Collins & the Gypsy Witch. Marilyn Ross. (Dark Shadows Ser). (Orig.). 1970. pap. 0.60 o.p. (ISBN 0-446-63296-1, 63-296). Paperback Lib.

Barnabas Collins & the Mysterious Ghost. Marilyn Ross. (Orig.). 1970. pap. 0.60 o.p. (ISBN 0-446-63258-9, 63-258). Paperback Lib.

Barnabas Collins Versus the Warlock. Marilyn Ross. (Dark Shadows, No. 11). (Orig.). 1969. pap. 0.50 o.p. (62-212). Paperback Lib.

Barnabas, Quentin & Dr. Jekyll's Son. Marilyn Ross. (Dark Shadows Ser). (Orig.). 1971. pap. 0.60 o.p. (ISBN 0-446-63554-5, 63-554). Paperback Lib.

Barnabas, Quentin, & the Avenging Ghost. Marilyn Ross. (Dark Shadows). (Orig.). 1970. pap. 0.60 o.p. (ISBN 0-446-63338-0, 63-338). Paperback Lib.

Barnabas, Quentin & the Body Snatchers. Marilyn Ross. (Dark Shadows Ser., No. 26). (Orig.). 1971. pap. 0.60 o.p. (ISBN 0-446-63534-0, 63-534). Paperback Lib.

Barnabas, Quentin & the Crystal Coffin. Marilyn Ross. (Dark Shadows, No. 19). (Orig.). 1970. pap. 0.60 o.p. (ISBN 0-446-63385-2, 63-385). Paperback Lib.

Barnabas, Quentin & the Frightened Bride. Marilyn Ross. (Dark Shadows). (Orig.). 1970. pap. 0.60 o.p. (ISBN 0-446-63446-8, 63-446). Paperback Lib.

Barnabas, Quentin & the Grave Robbers. Marilyn Ross. (Dark Shadows Ser). (Orig.). 1971. pap. 0.60 o.p. (ISBN 0-446-63585-5, 63-585). Paperback Lib.

Barnabas, Quentin & the Haunted Cave. Marilyn Ross. (Dark Shadows Ser). (Orig.). 1970. pap. 0.60 o.p. (ISBN 0-446-63427-1, 63-427). Paperback Lib.

Barnabas, Quentin & the Hidden Tomb. Marilyn Ross. (Dark Shadows Ser). (Orig.). 1971. pap. 0.75 o.p. (ISBN 0-446-64772-1, 64-772-8). Paperback Lib.

Barnabas, Quentin & the Mad Magician. Marilyn Ross. (Dark Shadows Ser). (Orig.). 1971. pap. 0.75 o.p. (ISBN 0-446-64714-4, 64-714-4). Paperback Lib.

Barnabas, Quentin & the Magic Potion. Marilyn Ross. (Dark Shadows Ser). (Orig.). 1971. pap. 0.60 o.p. (ISBN 0-446-63515-4, 63-515). Paperback Lib.

Barnabas, Quentin, & the Mummy's Curse. Marilyn Ross. (Dark Shadows Ser). (Orig.). 1970. pap. 0.60 o.p. (ISBN 0-446-63318-6, 63-318). Paperback Lib.

Barnabas, Quentin, & the Nightmare Assassin. Marilyn Ross. (Dark Shadows Ser). (Orig.). 1970. pap. 0.60 o.p. (ISBN 0-446-63363-1, 63-363). Paperback Lib.

Barnabas, Quentin & the Scorpio Curse. Marilyn Ross. (Dark Shadows). (Orig.). 1970. pap. 0.60 o.p. (ISBN 0-446-63468-9, 63-468). Paperback Lib.

Barnabas, Quentin & the Sea Ghost. Marilyn Ross. (Dark Shadows, No. 29). (Orig.). 1971. pap. 0.75 o.p. (64-663-6). Paperback Lib.

Barnabas, Quentin & the Serpent. Marilyn Ross. (Dark Shadows Ser). (Orig.). 1970. pap. 0.60 o.p. (ISBN 0-446-63491-3, 63-491). Paperback Lib.

Barnabas, Quentin & the Vampire Beauty. Marilyn Ross. (Orig.). 1972. pap. 0.75 o.p. (ISBN 0-446-64824-8). Paperback Lib.

Barnabas, Quentin & the Witch's Curse. pap. 0.60 o.p. (ISBN 0-446-63402-6, 63-402). Paperback Lib.

Barnabas: Restless Fighter. John Warren Steen. LC 75-155683. (Broadman inner circle book). 1971. (ISBN 0-8054-8702-6). Broadman Press.

Barnabe and His Whale. Rene Thevenin & Redman, Ben Ray, 1896- Tr. LC 23-13729. 1923. R. M. McBride & Company.

Barnabetta. Helen Reimensnyder Martin. LC 14-5311. 1914. The Century Co.

Barnaby Rudge. Charles Dickens. Ed. by Gordon William Spence. LC 74-177047. (Penguin English library). (Illus.). 1973-1974. (ISBN 0-14-043090-3). Penguin.

Barnaby Rudge. Charles Dickens. LC 26-24705. American Publishers Corporation.

Barnaby Rudge. Charles Dickens. (On cover: Lovell's library. v. 4, no. 150). 1883. J. W. Lovell Company.

Barnaby Rudge. Charles Dickens. Ed. by Vincent, Leon Henry. LC 20-1972. (Living literature series, R. Burton, PH. D., editor-in-chief). The Gregg Publishing Company.

Barnaby Rudge: A Tale of the Riots of 'eight. Charles Dickens. LC 31-28436. 1931. Dodd, Mead and Company.

Barnaby Rudge: A Tale of the Riots of '80. Charles Dickens. (Half-title: Everyman's library, edited by Ernest Rhys). 1906. J. M. Dent. & Co.

Barnaby Rudge: A Tale of the Riots of '80. Charles Dickens. LC 41-16889. The Heritage Press.

Barnaby Rudge: A Tale of the Riots of 'eighty. With the Original Illus. by Hablot K. Browne ("Phiz") and George Cattermole. Charles Dickens. LC 50-9747. (Macdonald illustrated classics, 9). 1950. Coward-McCann.

Barnaby Rudge: A Tale of the Riots of 'eighty. With the Original Illus. by Hablot K. Brown ('Phiz'), George Cattermole. Charles Dickens & Hablot Knight Browne. LC 66-5542. (Macdonald illus. classics, 9). 1966. 3.50. Macdonald.

Barnaby Rudge, and Hard Times. illustrated household ed. Charles Dickens. LC 6-36375. 1870. Fields, Osgood & Co.

Barnaby Rudge, and Hard Time. diamond ed. Charles Dickens. LC 6-36376. 1867. Ticknor and Fields.

Barnaby Rudge, and The Mystery of Edwin Drood. Charles Dickens. LC 9-819. Aldine Book Publishing Co.

Barnaby Rudge, by Charles Dickens: A Reprint of the First Edition, with the Illustrations, and an Introduction, Biographical and Bibliographical. Charles Dickens. Ed. by Dickens, Charles. LC 4-15297. 1892. Macmillan and Co.

Barnaby Rudge. Ed. by M. W. and G. Thomas. Illus. ByBrian Wildsmith. Charles Dickens. Ed. by Maurice Walton Thomas & Gladys - Thomas. LC 66-6592. (Shorter classics). 1966. bds., 2.50. Ginn.

Barnaby Rudge, Master Humphrey's Clock, and The Mystery of Edwin Drood. Charles Dickens. Ed. by Whipple, Edwin Percy. LC 15-23134. (Half-title: Works of Charles Dickens. New illustrated library ed. vol. viii-ix). Houghton Mifflin Company.

Barnaby Rudge. Sketches.--Part Ii... Charles Dickens. LC 15-203043. (Works of Charles Dickens. Globe ed.). 1871. Hurd and Houghton.

Barnaby Rudge. Sketches.--Pt. Ii... Charles Dickens. 1867. Hurd and Houghton.

Barnaby Rudge. Sketches.--Pt. Ii... Charles Dickens. LC 6-37044. 1867. Hurd and Houghton.

Barnaby Rudge. With Illus. by Darley, Gilbert, Cruikshank and "Phiz" and a Foreword by May Lamberton Becker. Charles Dickens. LC 49-4523. (Great Illustrated Classics). 1945. Dodd, Mead.

Barnards of Loseby. Sylvia Townsend Warner. 1977. 1.95 (ISBN 0-445-04049-1). Popular Library.

Barnard's Planet. Boyd Upchurch. LC 75-12873. 1975. 6.95. Berkeley Pub. Corp.: Distributed by Putnam.

Barnegat Ways. Alphyon Perry Richardson. LC 79-166564. (Short story index reprint series). (Illus.). 1971. (ISBN 0-8369-3994-8). Books for Libraries Press.

Barnegat Ways. Alphyon Perry Richardson. LC 31-24058. 2.00. The Century Co.

Barnegat Yarns: Tales of Jersey's Popular Barnegat Bay and Shore. F Alexander Lucas. LC 11-283626. 1.00. Broadway Publishing Co.

Barnett Frummer Is an Unbloomed Flower: And Other Adventures of Barnett Frummer, Rosalie Mondle, Roland Magruder, and Their Friends. Calvin Trillin. LC 72-91199. 1969. 4.50. Viking Press.

Barnett Frummer Is an Unbloomed Flower. Calvin Trillin. 1971. pap. 1.45 o.p. (ISBN 0-525-47292-4). Dutton.

Barney. Samuel Bertram Haworth Hurst. LC 23-8942. 1923. Harper & Brothers.

Barney. William Johnston. LC 70-117711. 1970. 6.95. Random House.

Barney's Gift. Linda H. Timberlake. (Illus.). 48p. (Orig.). (gr. 1-3). 1982. pap. 6.50 (ISBN 0-87397-244-9). Strode.

Barnham Rectory. Doreen Eileen Agnew Wallace, pseud. LC 35-1700. 1935. The Macmillan Company.

Barnstormer in Oz. Philip Jose Farmer. 1982. pap. 5.95 (ISBN 0-425-05641-4). Berkley Pub.

Barnstormers. Richard H. Curtis. (Skymasters Ser.). 1982. pap. 3.25 (ISBN 0-440-00375-X). Dell.

Barometer Rising. Hugh MacLennan. LC 41-20728. 1958. Duell, Sloan and Pearce.

Baron -- King Maker. Anthony Morton, pseud. LC 74-31910. 192p. 1975. 5.95 o.p. (ISBN 0-8027-5315-9). Walker & Co.

Baron & the Arrogant Artist. Anthony Morton, pseud. (Baron Ser). 192p. 1973. 5.95 o.p. (ISBN 0-8027-5283-7). Walker & Co.

Baron and the Arrogant Artist: The 44th Story of the Baron. John Creasey. LC 73-83310. 1973. 5.95 (ISBN 0-8027-5283-7). Walker.

Baron and the Beggar: By Anthony Morton Pseud. John Creasey. LC 50-6998. 1950. Duell, Sloan and Pearce.

Baron and the Chinese Puzzle: By John Creasey As Anthony Morton Pseud. John Creasey. LC 66-14523. 1966. 3.95. Scribners.

Baron and the Missing Old Masters. John Creasey. LC 69-15713. 1969. 4.50. Walker.

Baron and the Mogul Swords. John Creasey. (S348). 1968. Avon.

Baron and the Mogul Swords: By John Creasey As Anthony Morton. John Creasey. LC 66-22663. 1966. 3.95. Scribners.

Baron and the Stolen Legacy. John Creasey. (S 364). 1968. Avon.

Baron & the Stolen Legacy. Anthony Morton, pseud. 1967. 3.95 o.p. Scribner.

Baron and the Stolen Legacy: By John Creasey As Anthony Morton. John Creasey. LC 67-14168. 1967. 3.95. Scribners.

Baron and the Unfinished Portrait. John Creasey. LC 71-107144. 1970. 4.95. Walker.

Baron & the Unfinished Protrait. Anthony Morton, pseud. 1970. 4.95 o.p. (ISBN 0-8027-5215-2). Walker & Co.

Baron at Large. John Creasey. LC 75-24719. 1975. 6.95 (ISBN 0-8027-5337-X). Walker.

Baron Branches Out. John Creasey. LC 67-25563. 1967. Scribner.

Baron Goes a-Buying. John Creasey. LC 72-80533. 1972. 5.95 (ISBN 0-8027-5265-9). Walker.

Baron Goes a Buying. rev. ed. Anthony Morton, pseud. LC 72-80533. 192p. 1972. 5.95 o.p. (ISBN 0-8027-5265-9). Walker & Co.

Baron Goes Fast. John Creasey. 192p. 1975. pap. 1.25 (ISBN 0-532-12358-1). Woodhill.

Baron Goes Fast. Anthony Morton, pseud. 1972. 4.95 o.p. (ISBN 0-8027-5245-4). Walker & Co.

Baron in France. John Creasey. LC 76-24558. 1976. 6.95 (ISBN 0-8027-5355-8). Walker.

Baron in the Trees. Italo Calvino. LC 76-39704. (Harbrace paperbound library, 72). 1977. 2.95 (ISBN 0-15-610680-9). Harcourt Brace Jovanovich.

Baron in the Trees. Italo Calvino. LC 59-10800. 1959. Random House.

Baron Kinatas: A Tale of the Anti-Christ. Isaac Strange Dement. LC 6-34009. 1894. M. T. Need.

Baron, King-Maker. John Creasey. LC 74-31910. 1975. 5.95 (ISBN 0-8027-5315-9). Walker.

Baron Leo Von Oberg, M.D., a Story of Love Unspoken. From the German of A. Mels Pseud. Martin Cohn & Sigmund, Joseph A., Tr. LC 7-18728. (On cover: Loring's tales of the day). 1868. Loring.

Baron Montez of Panama and Paris: A Novel. Archibald Clavering Gunter. LC 6-456958. 1898. The Home Publishing Company.

Baron Munchausen & Other Tales from Germany. Raspe. 4.50 o.p. (ISBN 0-525-26230-X). Dutton.

Baron Munchausen's Miraculous Adventures on Land. Munchausen. English & Buerger, Gottfried August. Tr. by Steindorff, Ulrich L. LC 33-30274. U. S. Library Association, Inc.

Baron of Boot Hill: By Brad Ward Pseud. 1st Ed. Samuel Anthony Peeples. LC 54-8860. 1954. Dutton.

Baron of Diamond Tail. George Washington Ogden. LC 23-12437. 1923. A. C. McClurg & Co.

Baron of the Barrens. Will J Bloomfield. LC 23-605895. Dorrance.

Baron of the Colorados. William Atherton Du Puy. LC 40-951834. 1940. The Naylor Company.

Baron on Board. John Creasey. LC 68-27368. 1968. 3.95. Walker.

Baron Orgaz. Frank Lauria. 1974. (pbk.) 1.25. Bantam Books.

Baron Trigault's Vengeance: A Sequel to "The Count's Millions," Translated from the French of Emile Gaborian. Emile Gaboriau. LC 13-8287. 1913. C. Scribner's Sons.

Baroness. Henri Troyat. LC 61-16561. (His The light of the just). 1961. Simon and Schuster.

Baroness. Ernst Emil Wiechert & Blewitt, Mrs. Phyllis, Tr. LC 36-6806. W. W. Norton & Company, Inc.

Baroness: A Dutch Story. Frances Mary Peard. LC 7-33507. (On cover: Harper's Franklin square library, no. 716). 1892. Harper & Brothers.

Baroness Blank. A Novel of the New German Empire. August Niemann. LC 7-33194. (choice series, no. 20). 1890. R. Bonner's Sons.

Baroness of Bow Street. Gail Clark. LC 78-22609. 9.95 (ISBN 0-399-12334-2). Putnam.

Baronet in Corduroy. Albert Lee. LC 3-29280. 1903. D. Appleton and Company.

Baronet's Bride: Or, A Woman's Vengeance. May Agnes Early Fleming. LC 6-399151. (On cover: The library of American authors, no. 41). 1892. G. Munro.

Baronet's Bride: Or, A Woman's Vengeance. May Agnes Early Fleming. LC 6213. (On cover: Eagle series. no. 181). 1900. Street & Smith.

Baronet's Quest. Henry B Douglas. LC 38-162291. Dorrance and Company.

Baronet's Song. Rev. & abr. ed. George MacDonald. Ed. by Michael Phillips. 192p. 1983. pap. 4.95 (ISBN 0-87123-291-X). Bethany Hse.

Baroni. Alfred Harris. LC 75-25541. 1975. 7.95. Putnam.

Barons. Charles Wertenbaker. LC 50-9737. 1950. Random House.

Baron's Fancy. Gleb Botkin. LC 30-23092. 1930. Doubleday, Doran & Company, Inc.

Barons of Runnymede. Pamela Bennetts. LC 73-86656. 1974. 5.95. St. Martin's Press.

Baron's Sons: A Romance of the Hungarian Revolution of 1848. Mor Jokai. Tr. by Bicknell, Percy Favor. LC 3030. 1900. L. C. Page and Company.

Baron's Sons: A Romance of the Hungarian Revolution of 1848. Mor Jokai. Tr. by Bicknell, Percy Favor. LC 13-238. 1912. The Waltewr Scott Publishing Co., Ld.

Baron's Woman. Catherine Linden. 272p. 2.75 (ISBN 0-380-82982-7). Avon.

Baroque: A Mystery. Louis Joseph Vance. LC 23-9168. E. P. Dutton & Company.

Barossa. John Clive. LC 80-26429. 10.95 (ISBN 0-440-00433-0). Delacorte Press.

Barotique Mystery. George Harmon Coxe. LC 36-152644. 1936. A. A. Knopf.

Barozzi: Or, the Venetian Sorceress. Catherine Smith. Ed. by Devendra P. Varma. LC 77-2047. (Gothic Novels III). 1977. lib. bdg. 35.00x (ISBN 0-405-10145-7). Ayer Co.

Barque Future: Or, Life in the Far North. Jonas Lauritz Idemil Lie. Tr. by Bull, Sara Chapman (Thorp) LC 7-18774. 1879. S. C. Griggs and Company.

Barque Whisper. Alun Richards. LC 79-23069. 1980. 10.00 (ISBN 0-312-06707-0). St. Martin's Press.

Barquero. George Schenck & William Marks. (Orig.). 1970. pap. 0.60 o.p. (63-386). Paperback Lib.

Barraca see Tres Novelas Valencianas.

Barracoon. Harry Hervey. LC 50-6899. 1950. Putnam.

Barracuda. Irving A Greenfield. LC 77-90660. 8.95 (ISBN 0-87795-188-8). Arbor House.

Barracuda Gang. Malcolm J. Bosse. 192p. (YA) 1982. 9.95 (ISBN 0-525-66737-7, 0966-290). Lodestar Bks.

Barracudas. Keefe Brasselle. 1972. 6.95 o.p. Geis.

Barrancourt Destiny. Anne Worboys. LC 77-85331. 8.95 (ISBN 0-684-15293-2). Scribner.

Barrel Mystery. William James Flynn. LC 19-18224. 1919. The James A. McCann Company.

Barrel of Bastards. Ann Taylor. (Orig.). pap. 0.95 o.p. (1007). Brandon.

Barrel Organ Tune. Jane Oliver, pseud. LC 36-499024. 1936. Doubleday, Doran and Co., Inc.

Barren Beaches of Hell. Boyd Cochrell. LC 59-10468. 1959. Holt.

Barren Corn. Georgette Heyer. LC 31-10244. 1930. Longmans, Green and Co.

Barren Ground. Ellen Anderson Gholson Glasgow. LC 57-9766. (American century series, S-14). 1957. Sagamore Press.

Barren Ground. Ellen Anderson Gholson Glasgow. 1973. 4.25 (ISBN 0-8446-4019-0). Peter Smith.

Barren Ground. Ellen Anderson Gholson Glasgow. LC 25-879424. 1925. Doubleday, Page & Co.

Barren Ground. Ellen Anderson Gholson Glasgow. LC 39-824553. (Half-title: The modern library of the world's best books). 1936. The Modern Library.

Barren Ground. With a Pref. by the Author. Ellen Anderson Gholson Glasgow. LC 57-9766. (American century series, S-14). 1957. Sagamore Press.

Barren Harvest. Cholmondeley M Nelson. LC 49-4431. 1949. Pub. for the Crime Club by Doubleday.

Barren Heritage. Lavinia Riker Davis. LC 46-21563. 1946. Pub. for the Crime Club by Doubleday & Company, Inc.

Barren Land Murders see Barren Land Showdown.

Barren Land Murders: By Luke Short Pseud. Frederick Dilley Glidden. LC 51-27096. (Gold medal books 159). 1951. Fawcett Publications.

Barren Land Showdown. Luke Short. 1981. pap. 1.75 (ISBN 0-449-14138-1, GM). Fawcett.

Barren Land Showdown. Luke Short. Orig. Title: Barren Land Murders. pap. 0.60 o.p. (R2499, GM). Fawcett World.

Barren Lives. Graciliano Ramos. Tr. by Ralph E. Dimmick from Sp. LC 65-16468. (Texas Pan American Ser.). 165p. 1965. 10.95x (ISBN 0-292-73172-8); pap. 5.95x (ISBN 0-292-70133-0). U of Tex Pr.
Barren Lives: Vidas Secas) Tr. from Portuguese Introd. by Ralph Edward Dimmick. Illus. by Charles Umlauf. Graciliano Ramos. LC 65-16468. (Tex. Pan-Amer. ser.). 1965. 4.75. Unv. of Tex. Pr.
Barren Metal. Naomi Ellington Jacob. LC 36-17721. 1936. The Macmillan Company.
Barren Seed. Ruth Turk. 240p. (Orig.). 1981. pap. text ed. 2.25 (ISBN 0-553-20122-0). Bantam.
Barren Title: A Novel. Thomas Wilkinson Speight. LC 8-15511. (Harper's handy series, no. 38). 1885. Harper & Brothers.
Barricade. Oscar Jerome Friend. LC 50-19177. (Handi-book western, 113). 1950. Quinn Pub. Co.
Barricades. Philip Toynbee. LC 77-108401. 1970. (ISBN 0-8371-3824-8). Greenwood Press.
Barricades. Philip Toynbee. LC 44-7489. 1944. Doubleday, Doran and Company, Inc.
Barricades: A Novel. Albert Howard Hasbrook. LC 29-14759. Bryce, Gille & Co.
Barricades in Berlin. Klaus Neukrantz. LC 78-68131. 1979. 2.95 (ISBN 0-916650-07-3). Banner Press.
Barrie & Daughter. Rebecca Caudill & Williams, Berkeley, 1904- Illus. LC 43-130751. 1943. The Viking Press.
Barrier. Rex Ellingwood Beach. LC 31-237. 1918. A. L. Burt Company.
Barrier. Sallie Lee Bell. LC 58-183729. Zondervan Pub. House.
Barrier. Carmen Anthony Fiore. LC 65-332. 1964. Pageant Press.
Barrier. Dorothy Les Tina. LC 50-10333. 1950. Rinehart.
Barrier. Robin Maugham & John Betjeman. LC 73-164431. 1973. 2.00 (ISBN 0-491-00853-8). W. H. Allen.
Barrier. Hilda B. Powicke. 1964. pap. 0.75 o.p. (ISBN 0-377-80151-8). Friend Pr.
Barrier: A Novel. Rex Ellingwood Beach. LC 8-10616. 1908. Harper & Brothers.
Barrier: A Novel. Allen French. LC 4-12094. 1904. Doubleday, Page & Company.
Barrier: A Novel Containing Five Sonnets by John Betjeman Written in the Style of the Period. Robin Maugham & John Betjeman. LC 73-12733. 1973. 5.95 (ISBN 0-07-040970-6). McGraw-Hill.
Barrier (La Barriere) Rene Bazin & Frost, Mary D., Tr. LC 10-193886. 1910. C. Scribner's Sons.
Barrier Ranch. Hoffman Birney. LC 33-30453. The Penn Publishing Company.
Barrier Three Hundred and Forty-Six. Karl Zeigfreid, pseud. LC 66-9241. 1966. Arcadia House.
Barrier Unknown. A. J. Merak. LC 64-25985. 1964. Arcadia House.
Barrier World. Louis Charbonneau. 1970. pap. 0.75 o.p. (ISBN 0-447-74687-1). Lancer.
Barrier 346. Karl Ziegfreid. LC 66-9241. 1966. Arcadia House.
Barriers Between. Marcus Beresford. LC 49-7951. 1949. Dial Press.
Barriers Broken: Or, Right Makes Might. Jabez Burritt Smith. LC 8-8167. The Busy World Publishing Co.
Barriers Burned Away. Edward Payson Roe. LC 72-145270. 1970. Scholarly Press.
Barriers Burned Away. Edward Payson Roe. LC 70-129370. (Illus.). 1972. 12.00 (ISBN 0-404-05378-5). AMS Press.
Barriers Burned Away. Edward Payson Roe. LC 71-104552. (Illus.). 1970. (ISBN 0-8398-1762-2). Literature House.
Barriers Burned Away. Edward Payson Roe. 1872. Dodd & Mead.
Barriers Burned Away. new and rev. ed. Edward Payson Roe. LC 13-12935. 1885. Dodd, Mead and Company.
Barriers Burned Away. Edward Payson Roe. LC 7-40221. 1898. Dodd, Mead and Company.
Barriers to Eden: A Tale of the Social Blockade. Frank Charles Thompson. LC 39-25871. Fleming H. Revell Company.
Barriers We Create. Ned Sebastiano Strano. LC 53-10311. Vantage Press.
Barrington. Charles James Lever. LC 42-80876. (On cover: Lever's Novels). G. Routledge and Sons.
Barrington. Charles James Lever. (Seaside library, v. 29, no. 609). 1879. G. Munro.
Barrington. John Rowan Wilson. LC 72-150926. 1971. 6.95. Doubleday.
Barrington: Tales of the Trains. Charles James Lever. LC 16-7547. 1900. Little, Brown, and Company.
Barrington's Fate... Margaret Hunt. LC 4-35667. (No Name Ser.). (No name series 3d series, v. 15: Second Ser., Vol. 15). 1884. Roberts Brothers.
Barrio God. Tom Fitzpatrick. LC 81-85068. 127p. 1983. pap. 7.95 (ISBN 0-86666-038-0). GWP.
Barrister-at-Ease: By Henry C. Kessler, Jr. Henry C Kessler. LC 66-17330. 1966. Dorrance.
Barron Ixell: Crime Breaker. Oscar Schiegall. LC 29-18258. 1929. Longmans, Green and Co.
Barry and the Persuasions. Richard Walter (ISBN 0-446-78752-3). Warner Books.
Barry Bayne: Or, Who Was the Murderer; a Thrilling Detective Story. Allen Graves. (On cover: The Pinkerton detective series, no. 46). 1890. Laird & Lee.
Barry Gordon. William Farquhar Payson. 1908. The McClure Company.
Barry Leroy. Henry Christopher Bailey. LC 20-4707. E. P. Dutton & Company.
Barry Lyndon. William Makepeace Thackeray & Rhodes, Charles Elbert, Ed. LC 20-22160. (Living literature series; R. Burton, PH.D., editor-in-chief). The Gregg Publishing Company.
Barry Scott, M.D.... A Novel. Rhoda Truax. LC 35-183542. E. P. Dutton & Co., Inc.
Barry Wynn: Or, The Adventures of a Page Boy in the United States Congress. George Barton. LC 12-2684. 1.20. Small, Maynard and Company.
Bars and Threshold. Emma Miner. 1891. The Author.
Bars of Adamant: A Topical Novel, by Nathan Barrett. 1s ed. Nathan Noble Barrett. LC 66-16527. 1966. Fleet Pub. Corp.
Bars of Iron. Ethel May Dell. LC 16-4391. 1916. 1.35. G. P. Putnam's Sons.
Bars of Iron. Ethel May Dell. LC 21-136995. 1919. A. L. Burt Company.
Bars on Her Shoulders: A Story of a WAAC. Jean Stansbury. LC 43-9194. 1943. Dodd, Mead & Company.
Barseba of Rabenstein (Die Rabensteinerin) Ernst Von Wildenbruch & Appiano, Richard Von. LC 9-18557. Frederick Printing and Stationery Co.,
Barselma's Kiss: A Romance. Marion Beveridge Lee. LC 8-29733. 1908. The C. M. Clark Publishing Co.
Barsukov Triangle & the Two-Toned Blonde & Other Stories. Ed. by Carl R. Proffer & Ellendea Proffer. 330p. 1983. 25.00 (ISBN 0-88233-805-6); pap. 8.50 (ISBN 0-88233-806-4). Ardis Pubs.
Bart of Kane County: And Other Stories. Harrison R Merrill. LC 26-153620. Post Publishing Company.
Bart Ridgeley: A Story of Northern Ohio. Albert Gallatin Riddle. LC 7-41432. 1873. Nichols and Hall.
Bartenstein Mystery. Joseph Smith Fletcher. LC 27-19192. 1927. L. MacVeagh, The Dial Press.
Bartered Birthright. James Franklin Fitts. (On cover: Farm and fireside library, no. 65). Mast, Crowell & Kirkpartick.
Bartered Bride. Anne Hillary. (Candlelight Regency Specia). 1.50 (ISBN 0-440-10912-4). Dell Publishing.
Bartered Corn: A Novel. 1st Ed. Edward Albalos. LC 53-12639. 1953. Exposition Press.
Bartholf Street. James Edward Day. LC 47-3830. 1947. Dorrance & Company.
Bartleby the Scrivener. Herman Melville. (Illus.). 1977. ltd. ed. 250 hand-numbered copies 31.00,. Hunt Inst Botanical.
Bartlett Mystery. Louis Tracy. LC 19-12877. E. J. Clode.
Barton Experiment. John Habberton. LC 6-46686. 1877. G. P. Putnam's Sons.
Barton's Mills: A Saga of the Pioneers. Alpheus Hyatt Verrill. LC 32-126042. 1932. D. Appleton and Company.
Barzen Serpent. 1st Ed. Chesney Ramage. LC 55-5710. 1955. Vantage Press.
Bas' Theres: A Narrative-Drama of Tirol. Jean Porter Rudd. LC 8-957. 1897. The Bulletin Press.
Base Case. Julian Rathbone. LC 80-8651. 1981. 9.95 (ISBN 0-394-50911-0). Pantheon Books.
Baseball Classic. Merritt Clifton. 1978. pap. 2.50. Samisdat.
Baseball Joe at Yale: Or, Pitching for the College Championship, by Lester Chadwick... Lester Chadwick. LC 13-7522. (His The Baseball Joe series). 0.60. Cupples & Leon Company.
Baseball Round-up: An Anthology of Baseball Stories. Ed. by Leo Margulies. LC 48-8130. 1948. Cupples and Leon Co.
Baseless Fabric. Helen De Guerry Simpson. LC 26-125312. 1925. A. A. Knopf.
Basement. Sasha Newborn. LC 76-45983. (Illus.). 1978. 4.00 (ISBN 0-930012-06-2). Mudborn Press.
Bashful Woman. Kenneth O'Donnell Horan. LC 44-7325. 1944. Doubleday, Doran and Co., Inc.
Basic. rev. ed. W. Sharpe & N. Jacob. LC 70-143518. (O.s.i.). 1971. pap. text ed. 5.95 o.s.i. (ISBN 0-02-928520-8). Free Pr.
Basic Black with Pearls. Helen Weinzweig. LC 80-22304. 1981. 7.95 (ISBN 0-688-00397-4). W. Morrow.
Basic Kafka. (gr. 12). 1979. pap. 3.95 (ISBN 0-671-82561-5). PB.
Basil. Wilkie Collins. LC 80-66133. 1980. 4.50 (ISBN 0-486-24015-0). Dover Publications.
Basil. A Novel. Wilkie Collins. LC 3-27271. 1874. Harper & Brothers.
Basil and Annette. Benjamin Leopold Farjeon. LC 6-38646. (Lovell's international series, no. 133). 1890. United States Book Company.
Basil and Josephine Stories. Francis Scott Key Fitzgerald. LC 73-1120. 1973. 8.95 (ISBN 0-684-13398-9). Scribner.
Basil and Josephine Stories. by f. scott fitzgerald, edited with an introduction by jackson r. bryer and john kuehl. ed. Francis Scott Key Fitzgerald. 1976. 1.75. Popular Library.
Basil Everman. Elsie Singmaster. LC 20-54049. 1920. Houghton Mifflin Company.
Basil Seal Rides Again: Or, The Rake's Regress. Evelyn Waugh. LC 63-17422. 1963. Little, Brown.
Basildon. A Novel. Margaret Raine Hunt. LC 7-236538. (Franklin square library. no. 58). 1879. Harper & Brothers.
Basileus. Maurus E. Mallon. 3.95 o.p. Carlton.
Basilisk of St. James's: A Romance. Elizabeth Myers. 1979. Repr. of 1945 ed. lib. bdg. 20.00 o.s.i. (ISBN 0-89760-530-6, Telegraph). Dynamic Learn Corp.
Basilissa: A Tale of the Empress Theodora. John Masefield. LC 40-27654. 1940. The Macmillan Company.
Basket. Mary Hunter Austin. 1973. lib. bdg. 59.95 (ISBN 0-87968-710-X). Gordon Pr.
Basket of Chips. John Brougham. 1855. Bunce & Brother.
Basket Woman. Mary Hunter Austin. 1969. Repr. of 1904 ed. 14.00 (ISBN 0-404-00429-6). AMS Pr.
Basket Woman: A Book of Fanciful Tales for Children. Mary Hunter Austin. LC 4-27347. 1904. Houghton, Mifflin and Company.
Basket Woman: A Book of Indian Tales for Children. school ed. boston, houghton mifflin c1910 ed. Mary Hunter Austin. LC 70-7816. (Illus.). Scholarly Press.
Basket Woman: A Book of Indian Tales for Children. school ed. Mary Hunter Austin. LC 10-13392. Houghton Mifflin Company.
Basketball Diaries. Jim Carroll. (O.s.i.). 1978. pap. 4.00 o.s.i. (ISBN 0-939180-10-3). Tombouctou.
Basle Express. 1st Ed. Manning Coles, pseud. LC 56-543810. 1954. Published for the Crime Club by Doubleday.
Basque and the Boy. John Alton Croner. LC 80-15675. 1980. 19.95 (ISBN 0-87949-176-0). Ashley Books.
Basque People. Dorothea Frances Canfield Fisher. LC 31-24494. Harcourt, Brace and Company.
Basquerie. Eleanor Mercein Kelly. LC 27-22054. 1927. Harper & Brothers.
Bass Derby Murder. Kathleen Moore Knight. LC 49-11058. 1949. Pub. for the Crime Club by Doubleday.
Bass Saxophone. Josef Skvorecky & Polackova-Henley, Kaca. LC 78-7270. 1979. 7.95 (ISBN 0-394-50267-1). Knopf.
Basset: A Village Chronicle. Evelyn Beatrice Hall. LC 10-206103. 1910. Moffat, Yard and Company.
Bassett. Stella Gibbons. LC 34-8349. 1934. Longmans, Green and Co.
Bassett Claim. Henry Rutherford Elliot. (On cover: Knickerbocker novels v. 15). 1884. G. P. Putnam's Sons.
Bassington Murder. Charlotte Woodyatt Hough. LC 79-27324. 8.95 (ISBN 0-312-06917-0). St. Martin's Press.
Basso. Harold Flender. 224p. (Orig.). 1974. pap. 1.25 (ISBN 0-532-12226-7). Woodhill.
Basso. Harold Flender. 1974. (pbk.) 1.25. Manor Books.
Bastard. Erskine Caldwell. 1974. (pbk.) 1.25. Manor Books.
Bastard. Erskine Caldwell. Heron Press, Inc.
Bastard. book club ed.. ed. John W. Jakes. LC 78-105281. (Jakes, John W., 1932-. The American Bicentennial Ser.). (Kent chronicles; v. 1: Vol. 1). (Illus.). 1977. 13.99. N. Doubleday.
Bastard. John William Wainwright. LC 76-13430. 1976. 7.95. St. Martin's.
Bastard. John William Wainwright. LC 77-365914. 1976. 2.95 (ISBN 0-333-19699-6). Macmillan.
Bastard Angels: A Novel. George Borodin, pseud. LC 42-12605. 1942. Hutchinson & Co. Ltd.
Bastard Angels: A Novel by George Borodin Pseud. George Alexis Bankoff. LC 42-12605. 1942. Hutchinson.
Bastard Brigade. Peter Leslie. 1972. pap. 0.75 o.p. (T2682). Pyramid Pubns.
Bastard King. Eleanor Hibbert. LC 78-20970. (Illus.). 1979. 10.00 (ISBN 0-399-12322-9). Putnam.
Bastard King. Jean Plaidy. LC 78-20970. 1979. 10.00 (ISBN 0-399-12322-9). Putnam Pub Group.
Bastard. Translated by Mervyn Savill. Brigitte Von Tessin. 1959. D. McKay Co.
Bastard Verdict. Winifred Duke. LC 34-18685. 1934. A. A. Knopf.
Bastard's Name Was Bristow. Jack S Scott, pseud. LC 76-26275. 1977. 8.95 (ISBN 0-06-013856-4). Harper & Row.
Bastille Day Parade. Kenneth Church Lamott. LC 66-25563. 1967. D. McKay Co.
Bat. Mary Roberts Rinehart. 1.25. Dell.
Bat: A Novel from the Play. Mary Roberts Rinehart & Avery Hopwood. Grosset & Dunlap.
Bat: A Novel from the Play. Mary Roberts Rinehart & Avery Hopwood. LC 26-112534. George H. Doran Company.
Bat: A Novel from the Play. Mary Roberts Rinehart & Avery Hopwood. LC 42-50590. 1942. Triangle Books.
Bat: An Idyl of New York. Edward Marshall. LC 12-101376. 1.00. G. W. Dillingham Company.
Bat Flies Low... Arthur Sarsfield Ward. LC 35-30051. 1935. Pub. for the Crime Club, Inc., by Doubleday, Doran & Company, Inc.
Bat Out of Hell. Francis Durbridge. 1982. 18.00x (ISBN 0-86025-189-6, Pub. by Ian Henry Pubns England). State Mutual Bk.
Bat That Flits. 1st American Ed. Norman Collins. LC 52-9776. 1952. Duell, Sloan and Pearce.
Bat Wing. Arthur Sarsfield Ward. LC 21-10173. 1921. Doubleday, Page & Company.
Bat Wing Bowles. Dane Coolidge. LC 14-4587. 1914. 1.25. Frederick A. Stokes Company.
Bat Woman. Cromwell Gibbons. LC 38-18759. World Press.
Bataan Who. John J. Finan. 3.75 o.p. Vantage.
Batailles dans la Montagne see Oeuvres Romanesques.
Batalla del Caribe. new ed. Don Pendleton. Tr. by O. J. Blanco from Eng. (Compadre Collection Ser.: El Verdugo, No. 10). Orig. Title: Caribbean Kill. 160p. (Span.). 1974. pap. 0.75 (ISBN 0-88473-310-6). Fiesta Pub.
Batavia. Hendrik Conscience. LC 6-28069. 1885. J. Murphy & Co.
Batchelor-Keeper see Virgin Seducer.
Bates House. Clarence Edward Benadum. LC 51-9576. 1951. Greenberg.
Bath Assembly. Sheila Bishop. 1977. 1.75 (ISBN 0-441-04831-5). Ace Books.
Bath Comedy. Agnes Sweetman Castle & Castle, Egerton. LC 2066. Frederick A. Stokes Company.
Bath Tangle. Georgette Heyer. LC 55-10092. 1955. Putnam.
Bath Tangle. Georgette Heyer. LC 55-10092. (Berkley medallion book). 1975. (pbk.) 1.25 (ISBN 0-425-02742-2). Berkley Pub. Co.
Bath Tangle. 2d american ed. Georgette Heyer. LC 72-79524. 1972. 6.95 (ISBN 0-399-11030-5). Putnam.
Bathers. Robert Steiner. LC 79-23084. 45.00 (ISBN 0-8112-0752-8) (ISBN 0-8112-0753-6). New Directions Pub. Corp.
Bathing Girl. Ludovic Janvier. LC 76-376182. 1976. 4.95 (ISBN 0-7145-3519-2). J. Calder.
Bathing-Man. Agnes Gwynne. LC 16-19066. 1916. 1.25. John Lane.
Bathroom. new, enl ed. Alexander Kira. LC 75-19052. (Large Format Ser). (Illus.). 1976. pap. 7.95 o.p. (ISBN 0-14-004371-3). Penguin.
Bathsheba. Roberta K Dorr. LC 80-17334. 1980. 9.95 (ISBN 0-912376-51-1). Chosen Books Pub. Co.
Bathsheba's Letters to Her Cousin Deborah 1831-1861. Mary Jane Howland Taber. LC 13-169972. 1913. 1.50. The John C. Winston Company.
Bathtub Murder. Mabel Dana Lyon & Hughston, Josephine, Joint Author. LC 34-372. Williams Publishing Company.
Baton for the Conductor. 1st American Ed. Thomas Leslie Wallan Hubbard. LC 58-10193. 1958. Houghton Mifflin.
Baton Sinister. Carl J Spinatelli. LC 59-11097. 1959. Little, Brown.
Batouala. Rene Maran. LC 79-79304. 1969. Kennikat Press.
Batouala: A Novel by Rene Maran, Translated by Alvah C. Bessie and Illustrated by Miguel Covarrubias. Rene Maran. Tr. by Bessie, Alvah C. LC 32-32548. 1932. The Limited Editions Club.
Batouala: A True Black Novel. Rene Maran. Tr. by Barbara Beck & Alexandre Mboukou. LC 74-172330. (Illus.). 160p. 1972. 9.50 o.s.i. (ISBN 0-87953-000-6, BO). Inscape Corp.
Batouala, an African Love Story. Rene Maran. (New Perspectives Ser.). 160p. 1973. pap. 2.95 o.s.i. (ISBN 0-87953-300-5, BO). Inscape Corp.
Batovala: A True Black Novel. Rene Maran. LC 74-172330. (Fawcett Premier book). 1974. (pbk.) 1.25. Fawcett.
Bats. Richard Mandell. LC 80-83027. 1981. 4.50 (ISBN 0-9605008-0-4). Hermes House Press.
Bats Fly at Dusk. Erle Stanley Gardner. LC 42-22577. 1942. W. Morrow.

Bats Fly at Dusk. Erle Stanley Gardner. LC 47-292617. 1947. Triangle Books.
Bats Fly up for Inspector Ghote. Henry Reymond Fitzwalter Keating. LC 74-3527. 1974. 4.95 (ISBN 0-385-05859-4). Published for the Crime Club by Doubleday.
Bats in the Belfry. Norman Haghejm Matson & Smith, Thorne, 1893-1934. The Passionate Witch. LC 43-7354. 1943. Doubleday, Doran & Co., Inc.
Bats in the Belfry. Edith Caroline Rivett. LC 38-23776. 1937. The Macaulay Company.
Bats with Baby Faces: A Scenario for Caricatures. William Stanley Moss. LC 51-6672. 1951. T. V. Boardman.
Battalion Medics: A Novel of the Korean War. 1st Ed. Van B Philpot. LC 55-5723. 1955. Exposition Press.
Battalion of Saints: A Novel. Richard Edward Wormser. LC 60-13332. 1961. D. McKay Co.
Battalion 999. Heinz Gunther. LC 77-363463. 1976. 4.25 (ISBN 0-85628-033-X). A. Ellis.
Batter My Heart. Robb Murray. (Orion Ser.). 192p. 1980. pap. write for info. (ISBN 0-8127-0301-4). Review & Herald.
Batter up! A Story of American Legion Junior Baseball. Harold Morrow Sherman. LC 30-13112. Grosset & Dunlap.
Battered Bastards. Gordon French. (Leisure Book). 1.75 (ISBN 0-8439-0631-6). Nordon Publications.
Battery from Hellfire. Gordon Landsborough. 1978. pap. 1.50 (ISBN 0-532-15328-6). Woodhill.
Batting to Win: A Story of College Baseball. Lester Chadwick. LC 11-5377. 1.00. Cupples & Leon Company.
Battle. Alexander Kluge. LC 67-19149. 1967. McGraw-Hill.
Battle. Cleveland Moffett. LC 9-134303. G. W. Dillingham Company.
Battle. Stella Hamblen Tappmeyer. LC 29-16828. Meador Publishing Company.
Battle at Three-Cross. William Colt MacDonald. LC 41-4627. 1941. Doubleday, Doran and Company, Inc.
Battle-Ax of God. Davenport Steward. LC 58-9582. 1958. Dutton.
Battle Circle. Piers Anthony, pseud. LC 77-91015. 1978. 2.25. Avon Books.
Battle Cry. Charles Neville Buck. LC 14-12486. 1.25. W. J. Watt & Company.
Battle Cry. Leon M. Uris. LC 52-13645. 1953. Putnam.
Battle Done. S Leonard Rubinstein. LC 54-8434. 1954. Morrow.
Battle-Fields of Our Fathers. Virginia Frances Townsend. 1864. J. Bradburn (Late M. Doolady.
Battle for Inspector West. John Creasey. 1971. pap. 0.75 o.p. (ISBN 0-447-74749-5). Lancer.
Battle for Jerusalem. Motta Gur. 1978. pap. 2.50 (ISBN 0-445-04326-1). Popular Lib.
Battle for Moscow. Albert Seaton. (War Bks.). 336p. 1983. pap. 2.75 (ISBN 0-86721-158-X). Jove Pubns.
Battle for the Pacific: And Other Adventures at Sea. Stevens, Rowan. LC 8-12227. 1908. Harper & Brothers.
Battle for the Planet of the Apes. David Gerrold. (O.s.i.). 160p. 1975. pap. 0.95 o.s.i. (AN1139, Award). Univ Pub & Dist.
Battle for the Stars. Edmond Hamilton. LC 61-153004. (Torqull book). 1961. Distributed by Dodd, Mead.
Battle for the Sunlight. 2nd ed. Arvia MacKaye. 62p. Date not set. write for info. (ISBN 0-932776-07-8); pap. 4.00. Adonis Pr.
Battle for the Sunlight: A Modern Legend. Arvia MacKaye. LC 47-730. 1946. Adonis Press.
Battle Invisible: And Other Stories. Eleanor Caroline Reed. LC 71-125236. (Short story index reprint series). 1970. Books for Libraries Press.
Battle Invisible: And Other Stories. Eleanor Caroline Reed. LC 1-23664. 1901. A. C. McClurg & Co.
Battle Invisible, & Other Stories. Eleanor Caroline Reed. LC 71-125236. (Short Story Index Reprint Ser). 1901. 15.00 (ISBN 0-8369-3603-5). Ayer Co.
Battle Is Fought to Be Won: A Novel by Francis Clifford Pseud. Arthur Leonard Bell Thompson. LC 61-5432. 1961. Coward-McCann.
Battle Lost and Won. Olivia Manning. LC 78-21856. 1979. 8.95 (ISBN 0-689-10943-1). Atheneum.
Battle Mask. Don Pendleton. (Executioner Ser, No. 3). 1970. pap. 2.25 (ISBN 0-523-41699-7). Pinnacle Bks.
Battle Months of George Daurella. Beulah Marie Dix. LC 16-6723. 1916. 1.25. Duffield & Company.
Battle of Baguio City: Karpov-Korchnoi 1978. W. R. Hartston. (Illus.). 1979. pap. 4.95 (ISBN 0-09-134881-1, Pub. by Hutchinson). Merrimack Pub Cir.
Battle of Basinghall Street. Edward Phillips Oppenheim. LC 35-15037. 1935. Little, Brown, and Company.
Battle of Coney Island: Or, Free Trade Overthrown. A Scrap of History Written in 1900. William Elliott Smith Baker. LC 4-34776. 1883. J. A. Wagenseller.
Battle of Conscience. Joseph Kromolicki. LC 38-6759. 1938. Meador Publishing Company.
Battle of Disneyland. Thom Keyes. LC 74-195450. 1974. 2.15 (ISBN 0-491-01462-7). W. H. Allen.
Battle of el Alamain. C. Barnett. 1964. pap. 2.95 o.p. (70841). Macmillan.
Battle of Forever. Alfred Elton Van Vogt. LC 78-53319. (Illus.). 9.95 (ISBN 0-931150-01-9). Authors' Co-Op Pub. Co.
Battle of Leyte Gulf. Edwin P. Hoyt. (War Bks.). 368p. 1983. pap. 2.50 (ISBN 0-87216-629-5). Jove Pubns.
Battle of Life. A Love Story. Charles Dickens. LC 6-36373. (Half-title: Wiley & Putnam's library of choice reading no. 86). 1847. Wiley & Putnam.
Battle of Life. A Romance. rev. ed. John W Hatton. LC 7-2193. 1882. W. S. Bryan.
Battle of Love (La Lutte.) A Reaistic Novel. by alphonse daudet...tr. by henry llwellyn williams... ed. Alphonse Daudet. Tr. by Williams, Henry Llewellyn, Jr. LC 6-33057. (On cover: Optimus series. 19). 1892. Donohue, Henneberry & Co.
Battle of Pharsalus. Claude Simon. LC 72-138436. 1971. 5.95 (ISBN 0-8076-0579-4). G. Braziller.
Battle of Rich Mountain. Jack Zinn. 1978. pap. 3.50 (ISBN 0-87012-094-8). McClain.
Battle of the April Storm. Larry Forrester. LC 79-102261. 1970. 5.95. John Day Co.
Battle of the Bismarck Sea. Lawrence Cortesi, pseud. 1977. pap. 1.50 o.s.i. (ISBN 0-8439-0510-7, Leisure Bks). Nordon Pubns.
Battle of the Bismark Sea. Lawrence Cortesi, pseud. (Inflation Fighter Ser.). 192p. 1982. pap. cancelled (ISBN 0-8439-1109-3, Leisure Bks). Nordon Pubns.
Battle of the Books & Other Stories see Tale of a Tub.
Battle of the Horizons. Sylvia Thompson. LC 28-14825. 1928. Little, Brown, and Company.
Battle of the Monsters and Other Stories: An Anthology of American Science Fiction. David G Hartwell & L. W Currey. LC 76-15585. (Gregg Press science fiction series). 1976. 12.00. Gregg Press.
Battle of the Queens. Eleanor Hibbert. LC 80-24739. (Her The Plantagenet saga). 1981. 10.95 (ISBN 0-399-12604-X). Putnam.
Battle of the Queens. Jean Plaidy. 320p. 1981. 10.95 (ISBN 0-399-12604-X). Putnam Pub Group.
Battle of the Queens. Jean Plaidy. 384p. 1982. pap. 2.95 (ISBN 0-449-24565-9, Crest). Fawcett.
Battle of the Sexes. John Peere Miles. LC 29-521922. 1929. Art Cinema Corporation.
Battle of the Strong. Gilbert Parker. 1976. lib. bdg. 18.50x (ISBN 0-89968-078-X). Lightyear.
Battle of the Strong: A Romance of Two Kingdoms. Gilbert Parker. LC 7-349988. 1899. Houghton, Mifflin and Company.
Battle of the Villa Fiorita. Rumer Godden. 1975. (pbk.) 1.50 (ISBN 0-380-00310-4). Avon.
Battle of the Villa Fiorita. Rumer Godden. LC 63-14677. 1963. Viking Press.
Battle of the Weak: Or, Gossips Green. Alice Dudeney. LC 6-34645. 1906. G. W. Dillingham Company.
Battle of the Wild Turkey: And Other Tales. 1st Ed. Alvin Saunders Johnson. LC 61-127870. 1961. Atheneum.
Battle of Three-Cross. William Colt MacDonald. LC 42-24536. 1942. The Sun Dial Press.
Battle of Toulouse. Jose Cabanis. LC 68-11868. 1968. Coward-McCann.
Battle of Vallhome Dam. John Tedman & Alison Tedman. (New Oxford Supplementary Readers Ser). (Illus.). 128p. 1965. pap. text ed. 1.00x o.p. (ISBN 0-19-422466-X). Oxford U Pr.
Battle of Wills. Victoria Gordon. (Harlequin Romances Ser.). 192p. 1983. pap. 1.75 (ISBN 0-373-02540-8). Harlequin Bks.
Battle on Mercury. Jacket Design by Kenneth Fagg; Endpaper Design by Alex Schomburg. 1st Ed. Erik Van Lhin. LC 52-12900. (Science fiction novel). 1953. Winston.
Battle Pay. Peter McCurtin. (Soldier of Fortune Ser.: No. 9). 192p. 1982. pap. 2.25 o.p. (ISBN 0-505-51841-4). Tower Bks.
Battle Pay. Peter McCurtin. (Soldier of Fortune Ser.). 1978. pap. 1.50 o.s.i. (ISBN 0-505-51233-5). Tower Bks.
Battle Road. Henry Gibbs. LC 67-23109. 1967. Walker.
Battle Road. Simon Harvester. (Dorian Silk Ser). 1969. pap. 0.60 o.p. (60-391). Manor Bks.
Battle Royal. Frank O'Rourke. LC 56-6756. (Dell first edition, 89). Dell Pub. Co.
Battle Royal: A Western Drama in an Eastern Land. Willem De Veer. LC 14-19137. 1914. John Lane.
Battle Smoke. Adam Hardy. (Fox,#8). 1975. (pbk.) 1.25 (ISBN 0-523-00562-8). Pinnacle Books.
Battle Smoke: Or, The War Correspondent Among Guerrillas. A. Thrilling Tale of Perryville and Stone River. St. George Rathborne. (War library Pocket ed. v. 1, no. 2). 1883. Novelist Publishing Co.
Battle Stations! Wilfred Jay Holmes. LC 40-27152. 1940. The Macmillan Company.
Battle Summer. Donald Grant Mitchell. 1850. Repr. lib. bdg. 25.00 o.p. Folcroft.
Battle Surgeon. Frank Gill Slaughter. LC 75-40127. 1975. 9.95 (ISBN 0-89190-281-3). American Reprint Co.
Battle With Desire. Jocelyn Griffin. (Superromances). 384p. 1983. pap. 2.95 (ISBN 0-373-70069-5, Pub. by Worldwide). Harlequin Bks.
Battle with Fate: The Trials and Adventures of an Orphan Boy. A Demonstration of Caste, Rank and Society As Created by Riches and Position. Frank Wagner. Duncan Printing Co.
Battle Within: A Novel. Philip Hamilton Gibbs. 1944. Hutchinson & Co., Ltd.
Battle Within: A Novel. Philip Hamilton Gibbs. LC 45-1557. 1945. Doubleday, Doran and Company, Inc.
Battledores: Friendship. 0.90 (ISBN 0-87675-089-7). Horn Bk.
Battledores: The Horse. 0.90 (ISBN 0-87675-088-9). Horn Bk.
Battlefield Earth: A Saga of the Year 3000. L. Ron Hubbard. LC 82-5619. 1982. 24.00 (ISBN 0-312-06978-2). St. Martin's Press.
Battleground. Roy Gordon. (Orig.). 1978. pap. 1.75 (ISBN 0-87067-538-9, BH538). Holloway.
Battlement. Donald F. Drummond. 2.50 o.p. Swallow.
Battlement and Tower. Owen Vaughn. LC 7-30582. 1896. Longmans, Green and Co.
Battlers. Kylie Tennant. LC 41-11199. 1941. The Macmillan Company.
Battles at Thrush Green. LC 75-33794. (Illus.). 1976. (ISBN 0-395-24290-8). Houghton Mifflin.
Battles at Thrush Green. Miss Read. LC 76-6907. (Illus.). 1976. 10.95 (ISBN 0-8161-6370-7). G. K. Hall.
Battles of Boro. John Albert Comstock. 3.75 o.p. Vantage.
Battles Royal Down North. Norman Duncan. LC 70-125209. (Short story index reprint series). (Illus.). 1970. Books for Libraries Press.
Battles Royal Down North. Norman Duncan. LC 18-268231. Fleming. H. Revell Company.
Battleship. Wallace Louis Exum. LC 80-22891. 1980. 4.95 (ISBN 0-89865-093-3). Donning.
Battlestar Calactica. Glen A Larson & Thurston, Robert. (Berkley Medallion Book.). 1978. 1.95 (ISBN 0-425-03958-7). Berkley Pub. Corp.
Battlestar Galactica. Glen A Larson & Thurston, Robert. (Berkley Book.). 1978. 1.95 (ISBN 0-425-03958-7). MCA Publishing.
Battlestar Galactica: Flight to Kobal, No. 3. Glen A. Larson & Robert Thurston. 1979. pap. 2.25 (ISBN 0-425-04992-2). Berkley Pub.
Battlestar Galactica Four: the Young Warriors. Glen A. Larson & Robert Thurston. 288p. 1980. pap. 2.25 (ISBN 0-425-04997-3). Berkley Pub.
Battlestar Galactica, No. 6: The Living Legend. Glen A. Larson & Nicholas Yermakou. (Orig.). 1982. pap. 2.50 (ISBN 0-425-05249-4). Berkley Pub.
Battlestar Galactica, No. 7: War of the Gods. Glen A. Larson & Nicholas Yermakov. 192p. 1982. pap. 2.50 (ISBN 0-425-05660-0). Berkley Pub.
Battlestar Galactica 3: Battlestar Galactica Photo Novel. 1979. pap. 2.50 (ISBN 0-425-04139-5). Berkley Pub.
Battlewagon: Of the Nine Battleships at Pearl Harbor, One Got Underway. 1st. ed. Wallace Louis Exum. 1974. 5.95 (ISBN 0-533-01212-0). Vantage Press.
Battling Buckaroos. Galen C Colin. LC 40-10765. Phoenix Press.
Battling with Love and Fate. May V Allen. 1902. The Abbey Press.
Batu-Khan: A Tale of the 13th Century. Vasilii Grigorevich IAn & Sergei Vladimirovich Bakhrushin. LC 75-39019. (Early Soviet Literature in English Translation). 1978. 19.50 (ISBN 0-88355-420-8). Hyperion Press.
Batu-Khan: A Tale of 13th Century Asia. Vasilii G. Yan. Tr. by L. Britton. LC 75-39019. (Soviet Literature in English Translation Ser.). 320p. 1978. Repr. of 1945 ed. 19.50 (ISBN 0-88355-420-8). Hyperion-Conn.
Bauble: A Novel. Richard Hayes Barry. LC 11-29351. 1911. 1.25. Moffat, Yard and Company.
Bavarian Story. Ethel Edith Mannin. LC 50-3452. 1950. Appleton-Century-Crofts.
Bawd's Footman. Roger Bowdler. LC 74-178404. 1973. 2.50 (ISBN 0-491-01281-0). W. H. Allen.
Bawlerout. Forrest Halsey. LC 12-13488. D. Fitzgerald, Inc.
Baxter Bernstein: A Hero of Sorts. Stephen Seley. LC 49-9608. 1949. C. Scribner's Sons.
Baxter Letters. Dolores Birk Hitchens. LC 75-108012. (Red mask mystery). 1971. 4.95. Putnam.
Baxter's Second Death. Ian Greig. LC 33-19821. 1933. H. C. Kinsey & Company, Inc.
Bay. Leonard Alfred George Strong. LC 42-7504. 1942. J. P. Lippincott Company.
Bay City Blast. Warren Murphy. (Destroyer Ser.: No. 38). 1979. pap. 1.95 (ISBN 0-523-41253-3). Pinnacle Bks.
Bay Mild. Louis J Kintziger. LC 45-5091. 1945. The Bruce Publishing Company.
Bay of Lions: A Novel. Ned Calmer. LC 78-72924. 9.95 (ISBN 0-87795-214-0). Arbor House: Distributed by Dutton.
Bay of Noon. Shirley Hazzard. LC 81-47257. 256p. 1981. pap. 2.50 (ISBN 0-87216-901-4). Playboy Pbks.
Bay of Noon: A Novel. Shirley Hazzard. LC 70-103954. 1970. 5.95. Little, Brown.
Bay of Seals. James Wood. 1981. 18.95x (Pub. by Remploy England). State Mutual Bk.
Bay of Silence. Eduardo Mallea & Grummon, Stuart Edgar, Tr. 1944. A. A. Knopf.
Bay of Stars. Robyn Donald. (Harlequin Romances). 192p. 1981. pap. 1.25 (ISBN 0-373-02391-X, Pub. by Harlequin). PB.
Bay of the Dammed: A Novel. Warren Pendleton Carrier. LC 57-12024. 1957. J. Day Co.
Bay of the Damned: A Novel. Warren Pendleton Carrier. LC 57-12024. 1657. J. Day Co.
Bay of the Dancing Moonlight. Edward O Stotts. LC 34-37239. The Pocketbook Publishing Company.
Bay of Traitors. Garland Roark. LC 66-12181. 4.95. Doubleday.
Bay Path: A Tale of New England Colonial Life. Josiah Gilbert Holland. LC 7-6135. 1882. C. Scribner's Sons.
Bay Path: A Tale of New England Colonial Life. Josiah Gilbert Holland. 1885. C. Scribner's Sons.
Bay Path: A Tale of New England Colonial Life. Josiah Gilbert Holland. LC 4-15118. 1902. C. Scribner's Sons.
Bay Path: A Tale of New England Colonial Life. Josiah Gilbert Holland. LC 7-6134. 1857. G. P. Putnam & Co.
Bay Psalm Book Murder. Will Harriss. 192p. 1983. 12.95 (ISBN 0-8027-5494-5). Walker & Co.
Bayard from Bengal: Being Some Account of the... Career of Chunder Bindabun Bhosh... the whole ed. and rev. by f. anstey pseud.... with eight illustrations by bernard partridge. ed. Thomas Anstey Guthrie. LC 2-24329. 1902. D. Appleton and Company.
Bayard's Courier: A Story of Love and Adventure in the Cavalry Campaigns. Blackwood Ketcham Benson. LC 2-24245. 1902. The Macmillan Company.
Bayberry Lane. Sara Ware Bassett. LC 31-246552. The Penn Publishing Company.
Bayonets in No-Man's Land. Jonathan Scofield, pseud. (Freedom's Fighters Ser.: No. 11). (Orig.). 1982. pap. 2.95 (ISBN 0-440-00656-2, Bryans). Dell.
Bayonets in the Sun. William Moore. LC 77-76645. (Illus.). 1978. 7.95 (ISBN 0-312-74252-5). St. Martin's Press.
Bayou. Saliee O'Brien. 1979. pap. 2.25 (ISBN 0-553-12168-5). Bantam.
Bayou Boats. Alice Pauline Davis. LC 51-16689. 1950. New Voices Pub. Co.
Bayou Bride. Mary Edwards Bryan. (On cover: Seaside library. Pocket ed., no. 731). 1886. G. Munro.
Bayou Bride. Mary Edwards Bryan. (On cover: Library of American authors, no. 57). 1894. G. Munro's Sons.
Bayou Bride. large print ed. Patricia Maxwell. LC 81-16535. 1981. 9.95 (ISBN 0-89621-314-5). Thorndike Press.
Bayou Bride. Maxine Patrick. (Signet book). 1979. 1.75 (ISBN 0-451-08527-2). New American Library.
Bayou Folk. Kate O'Flaherty Chopin. LC 67-29262. (Americans in Fiction). 1967. Gregg Press.
Bayou Folk. Kate O'Flaherty Chopin. LC 70-96505. 1970. Garrett Press.
Bayou Folk. Kate O'Flaherty Chopin. 1894. Houghton, Mifflin and Company.
Bayou Guns. Jackson Cole. 1974. (pbk.) 0.75. Popular Library.
Bayou Nurse. Peggy Gaddis, pseud. LC 64-57498. 1964. Arcadia House.
Bayou Road. Mignon Good Eberhart. LC 78-11268. 8.95 (ISBN 0-394-50430-5). Random House.
Bayou Road. Mignon Good Eberhart. LC 79-13141. 10.95 (ISBN 0-89340-216-8). J. Curley.

Bayou Triste: A Story of Louisiana. Josephine Hamilton Nicholls. LC 72-1516. (Black Heritage Library Collection). (Illus.). 1972. 12.50 (ISBN 0-8369-9040-4). Books for Libraries Press.
Bayou Triste: A Story of Louisiana. Josephine Hamilton Nicholls. LC 2-26869. 1902. A. S. Barnes and Company.
Bazaar. Susan Wood. LC 80-14985. 64p. 1981. 10.95 (ISBN 0-03-057856-6, Owl Bk); pap. 5.95 (ISBN 0-03-057709-8). HR&W.
Bazaar: And Other Stories. Martin Donisthorpe Armstrong. LC 71-106242. (Short story index reprint series). 1970. Books for Libraries Press.
Bazaar & Other Stories. facsimile ed. Martin Donisthorpe Armstrong. LC 71-106242. (Short Story Index Reprint Ser.). 1924. 16.00 (ISBN 0-8369-3278-1). Ayer Co.
Bazaar of the Bizarre. Fritz Leiber. LC 79-103872. (Illus.). 1978. 20.00. D. M. Grant.
Bazalgettes: Or, Folly and Farewell. LC 35-8746. 1935. Harper & Brothers.
Bazzaris. Don Tracy. LC 65-26054. (Ravenna bks.). 4.95. Trident.
Bazzaris. Don Tracy. (75199). 1967. Pocket Bks.
B.C. Great Zot, I'm Beautiful. Johnny Hart. (B.C. Ser.). (Illus.). 1978. pap. 1.75 (ISBN 0-449-13614-0, GM). Fawcett.
Be a Good Boy. Joan Margaret Fleming. (Berkley medallion book). 1974. (pbk) 0.95 (ISBN 0-425-02488-1). Putnam.
Be a Good Boy. Joan Margaret Fleming. LC 76-46518. 1977. 8.95 (ISBN 0-89340-057-2). J. Curley.
Be a Good Boy. Joan Margaret Fleming. LC 74-175253. (Red mask mystery). 1971. 4.95. Putnam.
Be All and End All: A Novel. Evelyn Berckman. LC 77-364808. 1976. 3.50 (ISBN 0-241-89466-2). Hamilton.
Be Careful How You Live. 1st Ed. Ed Lacy. LC 58-12479. 1959. Harper.
Be Good, Gyps! Walter Mueller. LC 49-9897. 1949. Exposition Press.
Be Good, Sweet Maid. Alister McAllister. LC 24-21819. Boni and Liveright.
Be Happier, Be Healthier. Gayelord Hauser. 224p. 1981. pap. 2.50 (ISBN 0-449-24473-3, Crest). Fawcett.
Be Home by Eleven. Amber Dean. LC 72-97290. (Red mask mystery). 1973. 4.95 (ISBN 0-399-11142-5). Putnam.
Be My Guest! Gavin Ewart. 1975. 6.00 o.p. (Pub. by Trigram Pr); pap. 3.50 o.p. SBD.
Be My Love. Harriet Hinsdale. LC 50-9856. 1950. Creative Age Press.
Be My Love. Harriet Hinsdale. LC 52-2892. (Permabooks, P 170). 1952. Permabooks.
Be My Love. Daisy H. Thomson. 1974. pap. 0.95 o.p. (ISBN 0-515-03322-7, N3322). BJ Pub Group.
Be My Victim: By Robert Dietrich Pseud. Howard Hunt. LC 56-9450. (Dell first edition, 106). 1956. Dell Pub. Co.
Be Not Angry. 1st Ed. William Michelfelder. LC 60-11942. 1960. Atheneum.
Be Not Content. William J. Craddock. (Projections Ser). 1970. 6.95 o.p. (ISBN 0-385-03692-2); pap. 2.95 o.p. (ISBN 0-385-03694-9). Doubleday.
Be Not Content: A Subterranean Journal. William J Craddock. LC 70-89072. (Doubleday projections book). 1970. 6.95. Doubleday.
Be Quest. Cid Corman, pseud. (Cloth 7.00 o.p.). 1972. pap. 5.00 o.p. (Pub. by Elizabeth Pr). SBD.
Be Quick and Be Dead. A Parody. Frederick A Stearns. (On cover: American series, no. 109). M. J. Ivers & Co.
Be Ready with Bells & Drums. Elizabeth Kata. LC 61-13387. 1961. St. Martin's Press.
Be Rich. Warren W. Wiersbe. 176p. 1976. pap. 4.50 (ISBN 0-88207-730-9). Victor Bks.
Be Shot for Sixpence. 1st Ed. Michael Francis Gilbert. LC 57-6149. Harper.
Be Silent: Love, by Fan Nichols. Frances Nichols Hanna. LC 60-6102. (Inner sanctum mystery). 1960. Simon and Schuster.
Be Still, My Love. June Truesdell. LC 47-5297. 1947. Dodd, Mead.
Be Sure It's Love. Frances Nichols Hanna. LC 37-35648. 1937. Hillman-Curl, Inc.
Be Sure It's Love. Florence Stonebraker. LC 66-2953. 1966. Arcadia House.
Be Thou Pleased to Dwell with Me. William D Rodgers. LC 78-72869. 2.25 (ISBN 0-89636-007-5). Accent Books.
Be Thou Prepared, for Jesus Is Coming. Forrest Loman Oilar. LC 37-7990. 1937. Meador Publishing Company.
Be Thou the Bride. Christine Weston. LC 40-6344. 1940. C. Scribner's Sons.
Be Ye Begger or King. Mary Hampton Mills. LC 26-146. 1925. Advocate Publishing Co.
Be Young with Me: A Novel. Mary Nowell Frost. LC 42-13387. 1942. Coward-McCann, Inc.
Beach Boys' Mistress. Henry Matthews. 192p. (Orig.). 1972. pap. 1.95 o.p. (ISBN 0-87682-224-3, 7224). Barclay Hse.
Beach Brat. Ross Sloane. LC 36-181313. 1936. Godwin.
Beach Bums. Jack Owen. LC 59-7127. 1959. Coward-McCann.
Beach Cafe & The Voice. Mohammed Mrabet & Paul Frederic Bowles. LC 79-23691. (Illus.). 10.00 (ISBN 0-87685-406-4) (ISBN 0-87685-405-6) (ISBN 0-87685-407-2). Black Sparrow.
Beach Fires. Dolly Stearns Harman. LC 35-2726. The Christopher Publishing House.
Beach Generation. Daoma Winston. (Orig.). 1970. pap. 0.95 o.p. (ISBN 0-447-75134-4). Lancer.
Beach Haven and Other Stories. Harold B Allen. LC 82-174196. (Illus.). 4.95 (ISBN 0-941418-00-6). Long Beach Island Press.
Beach House. Stephen Longstreet. LC 52-6630. 1952. Holt.
Beach of Dreams: A Romance. Henry De Vere Stacpoole. LC 19-15016. 1919. John Lane Company.
Beach of Falsea. Robert Louis Stevenson. LC 57-23424. 1956. Printed by the Ward Ritchie Press for the Members of the Limited Editions Club.
Beach of Falsea. With an Introd. by J. C. Furnas and Illus. by Millard Sheets. Robert Louis Stevenson. LC 58-1480. 1958. Heritage Press.
Beach Patrol. Kerrk Rogers. LC 43-13079. 1943. M. S. Mill Co., Inc.
Beach Patrol: A Story of the Life-Saving Service. William Drysdale. LC 7-3334. (Half-title: Brain and brawn series). W. A. Wilde & Company.
Beach Queen Blowout. Patrick Morgan. (Hang Ten Ser). (Orig.). 1971. pap. 0.75 o.p. (532-75438-075). Manor Bks.
Beach Red: A Novel. Peter Bowman. LC 45-10493. 1945. Random House.
Beach Set. Fern Burke. (O.s.i.). 160p. 1974. pap. 0.95 o.s.i. (AN1299, Award). Univ Pub & Dist.
Beach Umbrella. Cyrus Colter. LC 72-122919. 1970. 5.00. University of Iowa Press.
Beachcomber. Patti Beckman. 192p. (Orig.). 1980. pap. 1.50 (ISBN 0-671-57037-4, Pub. by Silhouette Bks). S&S.
Beachcomber: A Novel. William McFee. LC 35-273206. 1935. Doubleday, Doran & Company, Inc.
Beached Keels. Henry Milner Rideout. LC 6-38551. 1906. Houghton, Mifflin and Company.
Beachhead in Bohemia: Stories. Willard Marsh. LC 71-86494. 1970. 5.95. Louisiana State University Press.
Beachhead on the Wind. Carl Jonas. LC 45-7651. 1945. Little, Brown and Company.
Beachheads in Space. Ed. by August William Derleth. LC 52-9049. 1952. Pellegrini & Cudahy.
Beacon. Susan Barrett. LC 81-14619. 10.95 (ISBN 0-312-07038-1). St. Martin's Press.
Beacon. Sara Ware Bassett. LC 46-493329. 1946. Doubleday & Company, Inc.
Beacon. Eden Phillpotts. LC 11-24975. 1911. 1.35. John Lane Company.
Beacon Hill. Henry Clement. (Illus.). 1975. (pbk.) 1.50. Popular Library.
Beacon Hill Murders. Roger Scarlett. LC 30-7561. 1930. Pub. for The Crime Club, Inc., by Doubleday, Doran & Company, Inc.
Beacon in the Night: 1st Ed.New York. 1958 ed. William Sanborn Ballinger. LC 58-12474. Harper.
Beacon Lights, 3. pap. 3.00 o.p. Kazi Pubns.
Beaded Banana. Margaret Scherf. LC 78-7767. 1978. 7.95 (ISBN 0-385-14536-5). Published for the Crime Club by Doubleday.
Beadle. Pauline Smith. LC 27-3818. George H. Doran Company.
Beads of Silence. Lillan Bamburg. LC 27-11721. E. P. Dutton & Company.
Beads of Tasmer. Amelia Edith Huddleston Barr. LC 6-7967. (On cover: Ledger library, no. 45). 1891. R. Bonner's Sons.
Beagle Has Landed. Charles M. Schulz. LC 78-53776. (New Peanuts Parade Ser). 1978. pap. 4.95 (ISBN 0-03-044781-X). HR&W.
Beagle Scented Murder... Frank Gruber. LC 47-255. 1946. Rinehart & Company, Inc.
Bealby: A Holiday. Herbert George Wells. LC 15-538074. 1915. The Macmillan Company.
Bealby: A Holiday. Herbert George Wells. LC 26-235640. 1922. The Macmillan Company.
Beam Ends. Errol Flynn. 1976. Repr. of 1937 ed. lib. bdg. 16.95 (ISBN 0-89966-092-4). Buccaneer Bks.
Beam of Black Light. Owen John. 1969. pap. 0.60 o.p. (63-085). Paperback Lib.
Beam of Malice. Alex Hamilton. 1967. 4.50 o.p. (ISBN 0-679-50105-3). McKay.
Beam of Malice: Fifteen Short, Dark Stories. 1st Amer. Ed. Hamilton, Alex. LC 67-165066. 1967. bds., 4.50. McKay.
Bean-Ball Bill and Other Stories. William Heyliger. LC 30-946951. Grosset & Dunlap.
Bean Nash: Or, Bath in the Eighteenth Century. William Harrison Ainsworth. LC 22-14555. G. Routledge and Sons.
Beanstalk. John Rackham, pseud. (Science Fiction Ser.). 1973. pap. 0.95 o.p. (UQ1080). DAW Bks.
Beanstalk. John Rackham. (Daw sf Books, no. 73). (Illus.). 1973. (pbk.) 0.95. Daw Books.
Beany-Eye. David Garnett. LC 35-23919. Harcourt, Braces and Company.
Beany, Gangleshanks, and the Tub: By Edward Streeter. Edward Streeter. LC 21-18471. 1921. G. P. Putnam's Sons.
Bear. Marian Engel. LC 76-15037. 1976. 6.95 (ISBN 0-689-10760-9). Atheneum.
Bear see Six Great Modern Short Novels.
Bear: A Novel. Marian Engel. LC 76-365957. 7.95 (ISBN 0-7710-3080-0). McClelland and Stewart.
Bear and the Lamb: A Tale of Ancient Barbarity Practised in Modern Times. Paul Howard Herman. LC 10-27187. 1910. 1.00. Cochrane Publishing Company.
Bear Claw Ranch. Freda Sellers. LC 56-112129. 1956. Vantage Press.
Bear Fell Free. Graham Greene. LC 77-3318. Repr. of 1935 ed. lib. bdg. 8.50 (ISBN 0-8414-4403-X). Folcroft.
Bear for the FBI. Melvin Van Peebles. LC 68-26709. 1968. 4.50. Trident Press.
Bear His Mild Yoke: The Story of Mary Dyer. a Quaker Martyr in Early New England. Ethel White. LC 66-21971. 1966. bds., 4.95. Abingdon.
Bear-Hunt, and Other Stories. Lev Nikolaevich Tolstoi. LC 24-27957. (Lettered on cover: Little leather library. no. 25). Little Leather Library Corporation.
Bear Island. Alistair MacLean. (Crest bk., P1766). 1972. 1.25. Fawcett.
Bear Island. Alistair MacLean. LC 70-38931. 1972. (ISBN 0-8161-6023-6). G. K. Hall.
Bear, Man, and God: Eight Approaches to William Faulkner's The Bear. 2d ed. Ed. by Francis Lee Utley. LC 78-140498. (Illus.). 1971. (ISBN 0-394-31546-4). Random House.
Bear, Man, & God: Seven Approaches to William Faulkner's The Bear. William Faulkner. Ed. by Francis Lee Utley. LC 63-8263. 1964. Random House.
Bear, Man, & God: Seven Approaches to William Faulkner's The Bear. Ed. by Francis Lee Utley. William Faulkner. LC 63-8263. (Illus.). 1964. Random House.
Bear Paw. Dane Coolidge. LC 41-7795. 1941. E. P. Dutton & Company, Inc.
Bear Paw Horses. Henry Wilson Allen. LC 72-13806. 1973. 5.95 (ISBN 0-397-00965-8). Lippincott.
Bear Paw Horses. Will Henry, pseud. 1973. 5.95 o.p. (ISBN 0-397-00965-8). Lippincott.
Bear Wallow Belles: A Love Story of the Civil War. Charles Robert Wilson. LC 3-26961. 1903. R. H. Carothers.
Bear Went Over the Mountain: Tall Tales of American Animals. Ed. by Robert Bingham Downs. LC 63-16101. Macmillan.
Bear Went Over the Mountain: Tall Tales of American Animals. Ed. by Robert Bingham Downs. LC 73-148835. (Illus.). 1971. Singing Tree Press.
Beard. Max Wilk. 1965. 4.95 o.p. (06880). S&S.
Beard. Max Wilk. 1965. 4.95 o.p. (06880). S&S.
Beard: A Novel. Max Wilk. LC 65-23246. 1965. Simon and Schuster.
Beard the Lion. William Raymond Manchester. LC 58-7582. 1958. M. S. Mill Co.
Bearded Mother. Anne Halley. LC 79-4020. 1979. lib. bdg. 8.00x (ISBN 0-87023-271-1); pap. 3.95 (ISBN 0-87023-282-7). U of Mass Pr.
Beardless Warriors. Richard Matheson. (A war novel). 1960. 5.95 o.p. (ISBN 0-316-55012-4). Little.
Beardless Warriors: A Novel. 1st Ed. Richard Matheson. LC 60-6534. 1960. Little, Brown.
Beard's Roman Women. Anthony Burgess, pseud. 1976. 8.95 (ISBN 0-07-008960-4, GB). McGraw.
Bearer Plot. Owen Sela. LC 72-11666. 1972. 5.95 (ISBN 0-394-48524-6). Pantheon Books.
Bearer Plot. Owen Sela. 1975. (pbk.) 1.25. Dell.
Bearing False Witness. Harriet Henry, pseud. LC 42-195663. 1942. Dodd, Mead & Company.
Bearing Gifts. Jascha Frederick Kessler. (Treacle Story Ser.: No. 9). (Illus.). 48p. 1979. signed ed. 8.00 (ISBN 0-914232-31-2); pap. 2.50 (ISBN 0-914232-30-4). McPherson & Co.
Bearknife Gold. Alan Marks. 1980. pap. 1.75 o.s.i. (ISBN 0-505-51453-2). Tower Bks.
Bear's Claws. Grace Sartwell Mason & John Northern Hilliard. LC 13-6731. 1913. A. C. McClurg & Co.
Bears of Blue River. Charles Major. LC 1-23050. 1901. Doubleday & McClure Co.
Bears on Hemlock Mountain. Alice Dalgliesh. LC 52-11023. 1981. pap. 2.95 (A-133, Pub. by Aladdin). Atheneum.
Beasley's Christmas Party. Booth Tarkington. LC 9-281113. 1909. Harper & Brothers.
Beast. Lacey Amy. LC 24-30659. Small, Maynard & Company.
Beast. Jonathan Fast. 1982. pap. 2.95 (ISBN 0-345-29896-9). Ballantine.
Beast. Hugh Fleetwood. LC 78-72979. 1979. 7.95 (ISBN 0-689-10956-3). Atheneum.
Beast. Walter J. Sheldon. (Orig.). 1980. pap. 1.95 (ISBN 0-449-14327-9, GM). Fawcett.
Beast. Robert Stallman. (Book of the Beast: Vol. 3). (Orig.). 1982. pap. 2.50 (ISBN 0-671-41383-X, Timescape). PB.
Beast. Alfred Elton Van Vogt. 160p. 1977. pap. 1.50 (ISBN 0-532-15265-4). Woodhill.
Beast. Alfred Elton Van Vogt. 160p. 1972. pap. 0.75 o.p. (532-00479-075). Manor Bks.
Beast: A Novel. Jonathan Fast. LC 80-6003. 12.95 (ISBN 0-394-51529-3). Random House.
Beast at the Door. Thomas H. Jones. 1963. 3.50 o.p. (ISBN 0-246-63517-7). Dufour.
Beast in Holger's Woods. August William Derleth. 1972. 5.95 o.s.i. Edco-Vis Assoc.
Beast in Man. Emile Zola. 1956. 13.95 o.p. (ISBN 0-236-31007-0, Pub. by Paul Elek). Merrimack Pub Cir.
Beast in the Cave. Pictures by Torson Gide. Mary Alice Philips. LC 59-5260. 1959. F. Watts.
Beast in the Jungle see Altar of the Dead.
Beast in View. Margaret Millar. 1955. Random House.
Beast in View. Margaret Millar. 1974. (pbk.) 1.25. Avon.
Beast in View. Margaret Millar. LC 80-10596. 1982. 11.50 (ISBN 0-89340-284-2). J. Curley.
Beast in View. Muriel Rukeyser. LC 44-6201. 1944. Doubleday, Doran and Company, Inc.
Beast Master. Andre Norton, pseud. 1977. 1.50. Ace Books.
Beast Master: By Andre Norton Pseud. 1st Ed. Alice Mary Norton. LC 59-895513. 1959. Harcourt, Brace.
Beast Must Die. Nicholas Blake. (Perennial Library). 1978. 1.95 (ISBN 0-06-080456-4). Harper & Row.
Beast Must Die. Lewis Cecil Day. LC 38-18282. 1938. Harper & Brothers.
Beast of Babylon. Archie Joscelyn. LC 63-16598. 1963. Augsburg Pub. House.
Beast of the City. Jack Lait & Burnett, William Riley. LC 32-5459. Grosset & Dunlap.
Beast of the Dove. Herbert Sherman Gorman. LC 50-6764. 1950. Rinehart.
Beast of the Haitian Hills. Philippe Thoby-Marcelin & Marcelin, Pierre, 1908- Joint Author. LC 46-8130. 1946. Rinehart & Company, Inc.
Beast with Five Fingers: And Other Tales. William Fryer Harvey. LC 29-7210. 1928. J. M. Dent and Sons Ltd.
Beast with Five Fingers: Twenty Tales of the Uncanny. William Fryer Harvey. LC 47-1580. 1947. E. P. Dutton & Company, Inc.
Beast Within. Edward Levy. LC 78-73871. 12.50 (ISBN 0-87795-225-6). Arbor House.
Beast Within. Edward Levy. 2.95 (ISBN 0-425-05222-2). Berkley Books.
Beastchild. Dean R. Koontz. 1970. pap. 0.75 o.p. (ISBN 0-447-74719-3). Lancer.
Beastly Beatitudes of Balthazar B. James Patrick Donleavy. (Laurel edition). 1974. (pbk.) 1.50. Dell.
Beastly Beatitudes of Balthazar B. James Patrick Donleavy. LC 68-8637. 1968. 6.95. Delacorte Press.
Beasts. John Crowley. LC 75-40719. (Doubleday science fiction.). 1976. 5.95 (ISBN 0-385-11260-2). Doubleday.
Beasts. Leslie Garrett. LC 66-22666. 1966. 3.95. Scribners.
Beasts. Leslie Garrett. (X-1659). 1967. Pyramid.
Beasts and Men. Pierre Gascar, pseud. LC 56-7052. 1956. Little, Brown.
Beasts & Saints. Helen Jane Waddell. (Illus.). 1960. Repr. of 1934 ed. 5.00x o.p. (ISBN 0-06-497275-5). B&N.
Beasts and Super-Beasts. Hector Hugh Munro. LC 14-17930. 1914. 1.25. John Lane.
Beasts & Super-Beasts. Hector Hugh Munro. LC 28-26462. (Half-title: The works of "Saki" (H. H. Munro). 1928. The Viking Press.
Beasts & Super-Beasts. Hector Hugh Munro. LC 77-91386. 1978. 17.50 (ISBN 0-8486-5003-4). Core Collection Books.
Beasts of Antares. Dray Prescot. (Science Fiction Ser.). 1980. pap. 1.95 (ISBN 0-87997-555-5, UJ1555). Daw Bks.
Beasts of Gor. John Norman. 1978. 1.95 (ISBN 0-87997-363-3). DAW Books.
Beasts of Hades. Graham Diamond. LC 80-84370. (Adventures of the Empire Princess Ser: No. 4). 256p. (Orig.). 1981. pap. 2.25 (ISBN 0-87216-821-2). Playboy Pbks.
Beasts of Tarzan. Edgar Rice Burroughs. LC 16-5897. 1916. 1.30. A. C. McClurg & Co.
Beasts of Tarzan. Edgar Rice Burroughs. LC 20-145596. 1917. A. L. Burt Company.
Beasts of the Southern Wild and Other Stories. Doris Betts. LC 73-4138. 1973. 6.95 (ISBN 0-06-010321-3). Harper & Row.
Beasts with Music. Dorothy Jeanne Williams. LC 67-20850. 1967. Meredith Press.

Beat a Distant Drum. Robert Emmett. (American Avenger Ser.: No. 1). (Orig.). 1982. pap. 2.25 (ISBN 0-451-11267-9, AE1267, Sig). NAL.
Beat Angels. Ed. by Arthur Knight & Kit Knight. (Illus.). 180p. 1982. pap. 9.00 (ISBN 0-934660-05-0). TUVOTI.
Beat Back the Tide. 1st Ed. Dolores Birk Hitchens. LC 54-55052. 1954. Published for the Crime Club by Doubleday.
Beat Generation, & the Angry Young Men. facsimile ed. Ed. by Gene Feldman & Max Gartenberg. LC 71-156639. (Essay Index Reprint Ser). Repr. of 1958 ed. 24.00 (ISBN 0-8369-2354-5). Ayer Co.
Beat It! George Vere Hobart. LC 7-6770. 1907. G. W. Dillingham Co.
Beat of Life. Barbara Probst Solomon. LC 60-13579. 1960. Lippincott.
Beat on a Damask Drum. Troy Kennedy Martin. LC 60-6072. 1960. Dutton.
Beat the Devil. By James Helvick Pseud. 1st Ed. Claud Cockburn. LC 51-10965. 1951. Lippincott.
Beat the Devil. 1st Ed. James Helvick, pseud. LC 51-10965. 1951. Lippincott.
Beat the Races. Thomas Flanagan. LC 72-650. 1973. pap. 1.45 o.p. (ISBN 0-668-02644-8). Arco.
Beat to Quarters. Cecil Scott Forester. LC 37-4609. 1937. Little, Brown and Company.
Beaten Path: A Novel of the Great Northwest. Joseph Burke Egan. LC 18-15262. 1918. The Gorham Press.
Beating Heart. Vivian Cory. LC 24-254111. Brentano's.
Beating Sea and Changeless Bar. Jacob Lazarre. LC 79-86149. (Short story index reprint series). 1969. Books for Libraries Press.
Beating Sea and Changeless Bar. Jacob Lazarre & Jewish Publication Society of America. LC 5-14448. 1905. The Jewish Publication Society of America.
Beating Wings. Robert William Chambers. LC 36-15261. 1936. D. Appleton-Century Company, Incorporated.
Beating Wings. Sara Lucile Jenkins. LC 54-8718. 1954. Crowell.
Beatitudes in Lincoln Square. John Helmer Olson. LC 31-32234. Augustana Book Concern.
Beaton's Bargain. Annie French Hector. (On cover: Seaside library. Pocket ed. no. 794). 1886. G. Munro.
Beaton's Bargain: A Novel. Annie French Hector. (On cover: Lovell's library, v. 14, no .746). 1886. J. W. Lovell Company.
Beatrice. Intro. by Patrick Henden. LC 81-48545. 208p. (Orig.). 1982. pap. 3.50 (ISBN 0-394-17973-0, B472, BC). Grove.
Beatrice. Julia Kavanagh. LC 7-11115. 1865. D. Appleton and Company.
Beatrice. Julia Kavanagh. (Seaside library, v. 12, no. 238). G. Munro.
Beatrice. Sonia Phillips. 1978. pap. 2.25 (ISBN 0-532-22142-7). Woodhill.
Beatrice. Arthur Schnitzler. Tr. by Agnes Jacques. LC 72-175440. Repr. of 1926 ed. 15.00 (ISBN 0-404-05612-1). AMS Pr.
Beatrice. Catherine Sinclair. LC 75-453. (Victorian Fiction: Novels of Faith and Doubt). 1975. 35.00 (ISBN 0-8240-1532-0). Garland Pub.
Beatrice, a Novel. Henry Rider Haggard. LC 6-45973. (On cover: Harper's Franklin square library. no. 671). 1890. Harper & Brothers.
Beatrice: A Novel. Arthur Schnitzler. Tr. by Jacques, Agnes. LC 26-9325. 1926. Simon and Schuster.
Beatrice and Benedick: A Romance of the Crimea. Hawley Smart. LC 8-9609. (On cover: Broadway series, no. 4). 1891. J. A. Taylor and Company.
Beatrice Ashleigh. Florence Ethel Mills Young. LC 18-17999. George H. Doran Company.
Beatrice Cenci. Francesco Domenico Guerrazzi. Tr. by Monti, Luigi. LC 7-3183. (Added t.-p.: The literature of Italy, 1265-1907. Ed. by Rossiter Johnsonand Dora Knowlton Ranous). The National Alumni.
Beatrice Cenci: A Historical Novel of the Sixteenth Century. Francesco Domenico Guerrazzi. LC 3-21958. 1859. Rudd & Carleton.
Beatrice Cenci: A Historical Novel of the Sixteenth Century. Francesco Domenico Guerrazzi & Monti, Luigi, 1830-1914, Tr. 1858. Rudd & Carleton.
Beatrice, Falling. Jane White. LC 69-14846. 1969. 4.95. Harcourt, Brace & World.
Beatrice of Bayou Teche. Alice Ilgenfritz D Jones. LC 7-12131. 1895. A. C. McClurg and Company.
Beatrice: Or, The Goldsmith's Daughter. Joseph Holt Ingraham. LC 44-53371. 1863. Dick & Fitzgerald.
Beatrice Sumpter. Carrie Vandiver Cheatham. 1908. The C. M. Clark Publishing Company.
Beatrice, the Goldsmith's Daughter. Story of the Region of the Last Charles. Joseph Holt Ingraham. LC 7-10519. 1847. Williams Brothers.
Beatrix. Honore De Balzac. LC 73-91778. (New library of French classics). 1970. 9.95. Prentice-Hall.
Beatrix. Balzac, Honore De. Tr. by Katharine Prescott Wormeley. LC 3-24480. (Half-title: The comedy of human life... Scenes from private life). 1895. Roberts Brothers.
Beatrix. Honore De Balzac. Tr. by George Burnham Ives. Moreau, Adrien, 1843-1906, Illus. LC 42-48870. (Half-title:... La Comedie humaine). The Neale Company.
Beatrix: Love in Duress. Tr. from French by Rosamond and Simon Harcourt-Smith. Honore De Balzac. LC 57-34231. 1965. bds., 3.95. Elek Bks.
Beatrix of Clare. John Reed Scott. LC 7-18101. 1907. J. B. Lippincott Company.
Beatrix Randolph: A Story. Julian Hawthorne. LC 7-3900. 1884. J. R. Osgood and Company.
Beatrix Rohan. A Novel. Harriet Lewis. (On cover: The choice series, no. 67). 1892. R. Bonner's Sons.
Beatty of the Yankees: A Novel. Hamilton Maule. LC 63-12149. 1963. D. McKay Co.
Beatuty Racket. Charles Stanley Strong. LC 36-19260. Phoenix Press.
Beau. Anita Blackmon Smith. LC 37-5032. 1937. Arcadia House.
Beau and the Bluestocking. Alice Chetwynd Ley. LC 77-13744. (Regency Romance). 1978. 8.95 (ISBN 0-89340-111-0). J. Curley.
Beau Barron's Lady. Helen Ashfield. LC 80-52655. 1981. 8.95 (ISBN 0-312-07057-8). St. Martin's Press.
Beau Blackstone. Richard Falkirk, pseud. LC 73-91847. 228p. 1974. 6.95 o.p. (ISBN 0-8128-1670-6). Stein & Day.
Beau Blackstone. Derek Lambert. LC 73-91847. 1974. 6.95 (ISBN 0-8128-1670-6). Stein & Day.
Beau Brocade. Emmuska Orezy. 357p. 1981. Repr. lib. bdg. 14.95 (ISBN 0-89968-228-6). Lightyear.
Beau Brocade: A Romance. Emmuska Orczy. LC 7-28961. 1907. J. B. Lippincott Company.
Beau Brummell. Virginia Stephen Woolf. 1979. 28.50. Porter.
Beau Brummell. Virginia Stephen Woolf. 1974. 12.50 o.p. (ISBN 0-911156-79-8). Porter.
Beau Clown. Translated by Diana Athill. Berthe Grimault. LC 57-5686. 1957. Rinehart.
Beau Geste. Percival Christopher Wren. LC 25-5548. 1925. Frederick A. Stokes Company.
Beau Geste. Percival Christopher Wren. LC 26-151883. Grosset & Dunlap.
Beau Ideal. Percival Christopher Wren. LC 28-18111. 1928. Frederick A. Stokes Company.
Beau John. Buddy Atkinson. 1980. 2.25 (ISBN 0-441-05240-1). Ace Books.
Beau Lover. Carman Dee Barnes. LC 30-20072. H. Liveright.
Beau Monde. Dotson Rader. LC 80-5293. 12.95 (ISBN 0-394-42593-6). Random House.
Beau Nash: Or, Bath in the Eighteenth Century. William Harrison Ainsworth. (Seaside library, v. 59. no 1200). G. Munro.
Beau" Rand. Charles Alden Seltzer. LC 21-18582. 1921. A. C. McClurg & Co.
Beau" Rand. Charles Alden Seltzer. LC 29-307515. 1923. Grosset & Dunlap.
Beau Sabreur. Percival Christopher Wren. LC 26-14103. 1926. Frederick A. Stokes Company.
Beau Sabreur... Percival Christopher Wren. LC 40-37800. 1939. Triangle Books.
Beau Tancrede. Alexandre Dumas & Maquet, Auguste. LC 6-42842. J. W. Lovell Company.
Beau Tancrede: Or, The Marriage Verdict. Alexandre Dumas & Maquet, Auguste. LC 6-42843. (On cover: Seaside library. Pocket ed. no. 717). G. Munro.
Beauacre: A Bread and Butter Fact Story. George Appleton. LC 12-84107. The C. M. Clark Publishing Co.
Beauchamp. Florence Bowes. LC 82-45142. 1983. 11.95 (ISBN 0-385-18076-4). Doubleday.
Beauchampe; or, The Kentucky Tragedy. William Gilmore Simms. 1974. Repr. of 1899 ed. lib. bdg. 30.00 (ISBN 0-8414-8074-5). Folcroft.
Beauchampe: Or, The Kentucky Tragedy. A Sequel to Charlemont. new and rev. ed. William Gilmore Simms. LC 68-54296. (Illus.). 1970. AMS Press.
Beauchampe: Or, The Kentucky Tragedy, a Sequel to Charlemont. new and rev. ed. William Gilmore Simms. LC 8-110223. 1882. A. C. Armstrong & Son.
Beauchampe: Or The Kentucky Tragedy. A Sequel to Charlemont. new and rev ed. William Gilmore Simms. (On cover:Lovell's library, v. 14, no. 705). 1886. J. W. Lovell Company.
Beauchampe: Or, The Kentucky Tragedy. A Tale of Passion. William Gilmore Simms. LC 29-25296. 1842. Lea and Blanchard.
Beauchamp's Career. rev. ed. George Meredith. LC 1-12787. 1897. C. Scribner's Sons.
Beaufort Now & Then. Ed McTeer. LC 79-184270. 4.95 o.p. Beaufort.
Beaufort Sisters. Jon Cleary. LC 78-71416. 1979. 10.95 (ISBN 0-688-03444-6). Morrow.
Beauforts: A Story of the Alleghanies. Cora Berkley. LC 9-2485. 1866. P. F. Cunningham.
Beaumarchais. An Historical Novel. Albert Emil Brachvogel. Tr. by Radford, Therese J. LC 6-15213. 1868. D. Appleton & Company.
Beaumont Tradition. Dorothy Daniels. (Orig.). 1971. pap. 0.75 o.p. (64-586). Paperback Lib.
Beauties and Furies. Christina Stead. LC 36-9347. 1936. D. Appleton-Century Company, Incorporated.
Beautiful. Rachel Billington. LC 74-79480. 1974. 6.95 (ISBN 0-698-10609-1). Coward, McCann & Geoghegan.
Beautiful Alien. Julia Magruder. LC 99-4094. 1900. R. G. Badger & Co.
Beautiful and Damned. Francis Scott Key Fitzgerald. LC 22-4437. 1922. C. Scribner's Sons.
Beautiful and Dead. Cover Painting by James Meese. Ross MacRoss. LC 54-24973. (Gold medal books, 386). 1954. Fawcett Publications.
Beautiful Bequest. 1st Ed. Eric Hatch. LC 50-5161. 1950. Little, Brown.
Beautiful Bird Without a Name: Or, A True Kentucky Girl. Belle Peterson. LC 7-361623. 1883. Courier-Journal Job Printing Company.
Beautiful Birthday Cake. Margaret Scherf. LC 72-139058. 1971. 4.50. Published for the Crime Club by Doubleday.
Beautiful Body. Watkins Eppes Wright. LC 48-20696. 1948. Phoenix Press.
Beautiful but Bad. Robert Colby. 1970. pap. 0.75 o.p. (75-326). Manor Bks.
Beautiful but Dangerous: Or, The Heir of Shadowdene. Thomas W Hanshew. (Street & Smith's select series, no. 86). 1891. Street & Smith.
Beautiful but Poor. John Russell Coryell. LC 44-116504. (Select Ser.). (Select series...No. 88: No. 88). 1890. Street & Smith.
Beautiful but Poor. Julia Edwards, pseud. (select ser. no. 38). 1890. Street & Smith.
Beautiful Butterfly. James Noble Gifford. LC 46-12922. 1946. Gramercy Pub. Co.
Beautiful Butterfly. Carol Holliston. LC 46-12922. 1946. Gramercy Publishing Co.
Beautiful Coquette: Or, The Love That Won Her... Laura Jean Libbey. LC 7-14367. 1892. N. L. Munro.
Beautiful Couple. William Woolfolk. LC 68-31467. 1968. 5.95 o.p. (HO268, NAL). Norton.
Beautiful Couple: A Novel. William Woolfolk. LC 68-31467. 1968. 5.95. World Pub. Co.
Beautiful Day. Dieter Wellershoff. LC 79-96005. 1971. 7.95 (ISBN 0-06-014547-1). Harper & Row.
Beautiful Days. Franz Innerhofer. LC 76-7341. 1976. 8.95. (ISBN 0-916354-10-5). Urizen Books.
Beautiful Dead. Hugh Pentecost. 184p. 1973. 4.95 o.p. (ISBN 0-396-06865-0). Dodd.
Beautiful Dead. Judson Pentecost Philips. LC 73-11551. (Red badge novel of suspense). 1973. 4.95 (ISBN 0-396-06865-0). Dodd, Mead.
Beautiful Derelict. Carolyn Wells. LC 35-7028. J. B. Lippincott Company.
Beautiful Dreamer. 1979. 3.95 (ISBN 0-8351-0661-6); pap. 1.50 (ISBN 0-8351-0592-X). China Bks.
Beautiful Dreamer. Cynthia Blair. (Love & Life Romance Ser.). 176p. (Orig.). 1983. pap. 1.75 (ISBN 0-345-30794-1). Ballantine.
Beautiful Feathers. Cyprian Ekwensi. (African Writers Ser.). 1971. pap. text ed. 3.00x (ISBN 0-435-90084-6). Heinemann Ed.
Beautiful Flagellants of New York. Lord Drialys. LC 79-155136. (Zebra books, Z-1069-T). 1971. 1.95. Grove Press.
Beautiful Frame. William Pearson. LC 53-2209. (inner sanctum mystery). 1953. Simon and Schuster.
Beautiful Fugitive: Or, Saved by a Detective... Harlan Page Halsey. LC 12-34576. (Old Sleuth's own. no. 113). 1898. The Parlor Car Publishing Co.
Beautiful Girl. Alice Boyd Adams. LC 78-54932. 1978. 8.95 o.s.i. (ISBN 0-394-42737-8). Knopf.
Beautiful Girl. Alice Boyd Adams. 240p. 1980. pap. 2.95 (ISBN 0-671-83218-2). WSP.
Beautiful Girl: Stories. Alice Boyd Adams. LC 77-20653. 8.95 (ISBN 0-394-42737-8). Knopf: Distributed by Random House.
Beautiful Girl: Stories. Alice Boyd Adams. LC 78-54932. 1979. 8.95 (ISBN 0-394-42737-8). Knopf: Distributed by Random House.
Beautiful Gold. Robert Bruce Thurber. LC 31-181778. Fleming H. Revell Company.
Beautiful Greed. David Madden. LC 61-106753. 1961. Random House.
Beautiful Hand of the Devil. Margaret Hobson. LC 1-30089. The Abbey Press.
Beautiful Humbug: By William H. Fielding Pseud. Cover Painting by Jack Floherty, Jr. Darwin Le Ora Teilhet. LC 54-43091. (Gold medal books, 430). 1954. Fawcett Publications.
Beautiful Ione's Lover. Laura Jean Libbey. (On cover: The library of American authors, no. 45). 1892. G. Munro.
Beautiful Jim of the Blankshire Regiment. Henrietta Eliza Vaughan Stannard. (Lovell's Library). (On cover: Lovell's library, no. 1165: No. 1165). 1888. J. W. Lovell Company.
Beautiful Kate. Newton Thornburg. LC 81-23677. 12.95 (ISBN 0-316-84394-6). Little, Brown.
Beautiful Lady. Mary Elizabeth Baldy. LC 50-12838. 1950. Christopher Pub. House.
Beautiful Lady. Henry Leyford Gates. LC 37-15192. 1937. Hillman-Curl, Inc.
Beautiful Lady. Booth Tarkington. LC 5-16519. 1905. McClure, Phillips & Co.
Beautiful Life: A Novel. Edwin Gilbert. LC 67-10954. 1966. Putnam.
Beautiful Lofty People. Helen Bevington. LC 73-15426. 1974. 7.95 o.p. (ISBN 0-15-111310-6). HarBraceJ.
Beautiful Losers. Leonard Cohen. LC 66-12635. 1966. Viking Press.
Beautiful Machine. Maggie Lettvin. (O.s.i.). (Illus.). 1972. 10.00 o.s.i. (ISBN 0-394-47468-6). Knopf.
Beautiful Miss Brooke. Louis Zangwill. LC 8-37868. 1897. D. Appleton and Company.
Beautiful Mrs. Davenant: A Novel of Love and Mystery. Violet Chambers Tweedale. LC 20-15067. Frederick A. Stokes Company.
Beautiful Mrs. Moulton. Nathaniel Wright Stephenson. LC 2-22481. 1902. John Lane.
Beautiful Ones Are Not Yet Born. Ayi Kwei Armah. 1969. pap. 1.95 o.p. (ISBN 0-02-048250-7, Collier). Macmillan.
Beautiful Rebel: A Romance of Upper Canada in Eighteen Hundred and Twelve. William Wilfred Campbell. LC 9-26141. Hodder & Stoughton.
Beautiful Rebel; a Romance of Upper Canada in Eighteen Hundred and Twelve. William Wilfred Campbell. LC 9-26141. 1909. Hodder & Stoughton.
Beautiful Rienzi: Or, The Secret Vendetta. J. M. Simpson. (Select Ser.). (On cover: The select series, no. 41: No. 41). 1890. Street & Smith.
Beautiful Rivals: Or, Life at Long Branch. Prentiss Ingraham. (On cover: Munro's library, popular novels. v. 1, no. 133). 1884. N. L. Munro.
Beautiful Side of Evil. Johanna Michaelsen. LC 82-82240. 224p. (Orig.). 1982. pap. 5.95 (ISBN 0-89081-322-1). Harvest Hse.
Beautiful Sinners. Paul Erikson. LC 82-81998. 384p. 1982. pap. 3.50 (ISBN 0-86721-185-7). Playboy Pbks.
Beautiful Soul. Florence Marryat Church Lean. LC 7-13243. ("unknown" library v. 37). The Cassell Publishing Co.
Beautiful Spy. An Exciting Story of Army and High Life in New York in 1776. Charles Burdett. LC 6-17387. J.E. Potter.
Beautiful Stairways. Effie E. Sanders. 1968. 3.00 o.p. (ISBN 0-682-46796-0). Exposition.
Beautiful Stranger. Bernice Carey. LC 51-11761. 1951. Published by the Crime Club by Doubleday.
Beautiful Stranger. Bernice Carey Martin. LC 51-11761. 1951. Published for the Crime Club by Doubleday.
Beautiful Target. Don Bartell. 1974. (pbk.) 1.95 (ISBN 0-87056-367-X). Brandon Books.
Beautiful Upon the Mountains. Murrell Edmunds. LC 66-12747. 4.50. Yoseloff.
Beautiful Vampire (La Morte Amoureuse) Theophile Gautier & Hookham, Paul, Tr. LC 28-28128. 1927. R. M. McBride & Company.
Beautiful Visit. Elizabeth Jane Howard. LC 50-9038. 1950. Random House.
Beautiful White Devil. Guy Newell Boothby. 1896. Ward, Lock & Bowden, Limited.
Beautiful White Devil. Guy Newell Boothby. (Half-title: Appletons' town and country library, no. 215). 1897. D. Appleton and Company.
Beautiful Widow. Timothy Shay Arthur. 1847. Carey and Hart.
Beautiful Woman. Sophie Kerr. LC 40-117540. Farrar & Rinehart, Incorporated.
Beautiful Woman on a Southern Plantation. Frances Best Simpson. LC 46-12925. 1946. Meador Publishing Company.
Beautiful Woman's Sin: Or, The Scarred Arm. Clara Augusta Jones. LC 7-12135. (select series. no. 51). 1890. Street & Smith.
Beautiful Wretch. William Black. LC 6-12942. (Harper's Franklin square library, no. 703). J. W. Lovell Company.
Beautiful Wretch: A Brighton Story. William Black. (Harper's Franklin square library. no. 195). 1881. Harper & Brothers.
Beautiful Years. Henry Williamson. LC 29-26899. E. P. Dutton & Co., Inc.
Beautifully Kept. Barbara Condos. LC 76-373333. 1976. 1.75 (ISBN 0-446-59762-7). Warner Books.
Beauty. Manoje Basu. Tr. by Sachindra L. Ghosh. Orig. Title: Rupavati. 103p. 1969. pap. 1.80 (ISBN 0-88253-011-9). Ind-US Inc.

Beauty. Faith Baldwin Cuthrell. LC 33-857973. Farrar & Rinehart, Incorporated.

Beauty. Rupert Hughes. LC 21-9366. Harper & Brothers.

Beauty. Nancy Mann Waddell Wilson Woodrow Woodrow. LC 10-7301. The Bobbs-Merrill Company.

Beauty and Mary Blair: A Novel. Ethel May Kelley. LC 21-5173. 1921. 2.00. Houghton Mifflin Company.

Beauty and Nick: A Novel of the Stage and the Home. Philip Hamilton Gibbs. LC 14-6801. The Devin-Adair Company.

Beauty and Sadness. Yasunari Kawabata. LC 74-21281. 1975. 7.95 (ISBN 0-394-46055-3). Knopf: Distributed by Random House.

Beauty and Sadness. Yasunari Kawabata. (Berkley Windhover Book). 1976. (pbk.) 2.45 (ISBN 0-425-03066-0). Berkley Publishing Corp.

Beauty and Sadness. Yasunari Kawabata. LC 80-39971. 1981. 4.95 (ISBN 0-399-50529-6). Perigee Books.

Beauty & the Beast. Chris Achilleos. (O.s.i.). 1978. 19.95 o.s.i. (ISBN 0-671-24297-0); pap. 7.95 o.s.i. (ISBN 0-671-24413-2). S&S.

Beauty and the Beast. Ed McBain. LC 82-11896. 13.50 (ISBN 0-03-062198-4). Holt, Rinehart, and Winston.

Beauty & the Beast. facs. ed. Bayard Taylor. LC 72-76930. (American Fiction Reprint Ser). 1872. 14.00 (ISBN 0-8369-7009-8). Ayer Co.

Beauty and the Beast. A Novel. Henrietta Keddie. LC 7-11134. (Harper's Franklin square library. no. 416). Harper & Brothers.

Beauty and the Beast: A Story of Old Russia and Tales of Home. Bayard Taylor. 1872. G. P. Putnam & Sons.

Beauty and the Beast, and Tales of Home. Bayard Taylor. LC 69-11921. (American short story series, v. 80). 1969. Garrett Press.

Beauty and the Beast, and Tales of Home. Bayard Taylor. LC 72-8194. (American short story series, v. 80). 1972. (ISBN 0-8422-8116-9). MSS Information Corp.

Beauty and the Bolshevist. Alice Duer Miller. LC 20-18254. Harper & Brothers.

Beauty and the Bug. Ted Mark. 1975. (pbk.) 1.25. Dell.

Beauty Beast: A Novel. MacKinlay Kantor. LC 68-12099. 1968. G. P. Putnam's Sons.

Beauty Contest Nurse. Diana Douglas. (Signet, T5576). 1973. (pbk.) 0.75. New American Lib.

Beauty Doctor. Harding Upton. LC 28-24471. 1928. G. H. Watt.

Beauty Doctor's Nurse. William Edward Daniel Ross. (Signet Book, T5669). 1973. (pbk.) 0.75. New American Library.

Beauty for Ashes. Grace Livingston Hill. 1962. New York, Grosset & Dunlap.

Beauty for Ashes. Grace Livingston Hill. LC 35-2965. J. B. Lippincott Company.

Beauty for Brutes. Frank Leonard. pap. 1.95 o.p. (ISBN 0-87977-160-7, DBB160). Dansk Blue Bk.

Beauty for Sale. Ethel Powelson Hueston. LC 34-22373. The Bobbs-Merrill Company.

Beauty for the Asking. Monica Ewer. LC 40-874431. 1940. Gateway Books.

Beauty? I Wonder. Dorothy Coursen. LC 29-14760. 1929. E. Holt.

Beauty in Being. Shirley Sealy. 171p. (gr. 7-12). 1980. 7.95 (ISBN 0-941254-01-1). Butterfly Pub.

Beauty Incorporated. Reita Lambert. LC 39-11265. 1939. Macrae Smith Company.

Beauty Is a Beast. 1st Ed. Kathleen Moore Knight. LC 59-7910. 1959. Published for the Crime Club by Doubleday.

Beauty Kill. Robert Hawkes. (Narc). (Signet book: Vol. 6). 1975. (pbk.) 1.25. New American Library.

Beauty Lies Beyond Hell! Howard W Roper. LC 32-16441. 1932. R. Long & R. R. Smith, Inc.

Beauty Makers: By Nedda Lamont Pseud. 1st Ed. Nedda Lemmon Barnitt. LC 58-7813. 1958. Dutton.

Beauty Market. Craig Winslow. LC 33-37029. 1933. A. L. Burt Company.

Beauty Married. Jane Dorset. LC 47-17761. 1947. Arcadia House, Inc.

Beauty Mask. Helen Mary Elizabeth Clamp. LC 28-27815. The Curtiss Press.

Beauty of Benburb. A Romance of the Days of Owen Roe O'Neill. Dennis O'Sullivan. (On cover: Munro's library, popular novels, v. 1, no. 419). N. L. Munro.

Beauty of Birds. Wayne Trimm. LC 73-88088. (Illus.). 48p. 1974. boxed 5.95 o.p. (ISBN 0-8378-1864-8). Gibson.

Beauty of Buttermere: Or a Maid Betrayed. Alasdair Brown. 1980. pap. text ed. 4.00x (ISBN 0-435-23135-9). Heinemann Ed.

Beauty of the Purple: A Romance of Imperial Constaninople Twelve Centuries Ago. William Stearns Davis. LC 24-22819. 1924. The Macmillan Company.

Beauty on Earth. Charles Ferdinand Ramuz. LC 29-16854. 1929. G. P. Putnam's Sons.

Beauty Parlor Girl. Lillie Trice Edwards. LC 52-6965. 1952. Vantage Press.

Beauty Prize. George Weston. LC 25-12850. 1925. Dodd, Mead and Company.

Beauty Queen. Patricia Nell Warren. LC 78-9172. 8.95 (ISBN 0-688-03350-4). Morrow.

Beauty Queen. Patricia Nell Warren. 2.50 (ISBN 0-553-12094-8).

Beauty Queen Killer. John Creasey. 1971. pap. 0.75 o.p. (ISBN 0-447-74757-6). Lancer.

Beauty Queen Killer. 1st American Ed. John Creasey. LC 55-11294. 1956. Harper.

Beauty Sleep. Ruth Darby. LC 42-10299. 1942. Published for the Crime Club by Doubleday, Doran & Co., Inc.

Beauty Sleep. Hildegarde Dolson. LC 76-58517. 7.95 (ISBN 0-397-01209-8). Lippincott.

Beauty-Spot. Alfred De Musset. LC 44-27719. Brentano's.

Beauty Spots. Rudyard Kipling. LC 32-317. 1931. Doubleday, Doran & Company, Inc.

Beauty to Burn. Peggy Gaddis, pseud. LC 37-541. 1937. Godwin.

Beauty Trap. Jeanne Rejaunier. LC 69-15568. 1969. Trident Press.

Beauty Unfoldment: A Spontaneous Soliloquy. Kenneth G. Mills. 1977. pap. 14.95 incl. cassette (ISBN 0-919842-51-8). Sun-Scape Pubns.

Beautyful Ones Are Not Yet Born: A Novel. Ayi Kwei Armah. LC 68-19987. 1968. Houghton Mifflin.

Beautyful Ones Are Not Yet Born: A Novel. Ayi Kwei Armah. LC 73-9992. (African/American library). 1969. (pbk) 1.50. Collier Books.

Beauty's Daughter. Mollie Hardwick. LC 76-28761. 1977. 8.95 (ISBN 0-698-10805-1). Coward, McCann & Geoghegan.

Beauty's Daughter. Mollie Hardwick. (Berkley Book). 1978. 1.95 (ISBN 0-425-03866-1). Coward McCann and Geoghegan.

Beauty's Daughter. Kathleen Thompson Norris. LC 35-8283. 1935. Doubleday, Doran & Company, Inc.

Beauty's Marriage. Charlotte Mary Brame. LC 44-39933. (On cover: Seaside library. Pocket ed. No. 1179). G. Munro.

Beauty's Marriage. Charlotte Mary Brame. LC 1-29445. (Bertha Clay Library). (Bertha Clay library, no. 46: No. 46). 1900. Street & Street.

Beauty's Peril: Or, The Girl from Macoupin; a Novel. Henry E Scott. LC 8-2921. (On cover: The pastime series, no. 128). Laird & Lee.

Beauvallet. Georgette Heyer. LC 68-12442. 1968. Dutton.

Beauvallet. Georgette Heyer. LC 30-82633. 1930. Longmans, Green and Co.

Bebbly: Or, The Victorious Preacher. Thomas Hamilton B Walker. LC 10-3294. Pepper Publishing and Printing Co.

Bebee: Or, Two Little Wooden Shoes. Louise De La Ramee. LC 6-33374. 1896. J. Knight Company.

Bebo's Girl. Translated from the Italian by Marguerite Waldman. Carlo Cassola. LC 62-11636. 1962. Pantheon Books.

Because I Love Women. Leslie Heron. (Signet book). 1974. (pbk.) 1.50. New American Library.

Because I Love You. Boone S. Salisbury. (Illus.). 80p. 1975. 4.00 o.p. (ISBN 0-8059-2164-8). Dorrance.

Because It Is Absurd. Pierre Boulle. LC 74-164984. 8.95 o.s.i. (ISBN 0-8149-0697-4). Vanguard.

Because It Is Absurd (on Earth As in Heaven) Pierre Boulle. LC 74-164984. 1971. 5.95 (ISBN 0-8149-0697-4). Vanguard Press.

Because of August. Joe E. Pierce. LC 81-81920. 200p. (Orig.). 1981. pap. 4.95 (ISBN 0-913244-54-6). Hapi Pr.

Because of Her Love for Him: Or, The Mystery of a Spell. Edna Winfield, pseud. LC 21741. (On cover: Holly library. no. 158). 1900. The Mershon Co.

Because of His Faith. Ernest Darwin Daniels. LC 37-18103. Manhattan Press.

Because of Jane. Annie Edith Foster Jameson. LC 13-9246. 1.25. Hodder & Stoughton, George H. Doran Company.

Because of My Love. Robert Paul Smith. LC 46-1513. 1946. H. Holt and Company.

Because of Rainbows. Lee Priestley. (Avalon Books). 4.95. Thomas Bouregy.

Because of Stephen. Grace Livingston Hill. LC 4-13290. 1904. The Golden Rule Co.

Because of the Cats. Nicolas Freeling. 1975. (pbk.) 1.25 (ISBN 0-14-002282-1). Penguin.

Because of the Lockwoods. Dorothy Whipple. LC 49-9918. 1949. Macmillan Co.

Because of the Zoo. L. P. Rich. 3.00 o.p. Carlton.

Because of You. Lewis R. Walton. 1975. pap. 1.25 (ISBN 0-8163-0215-4, 0208-0). Pacific Pr Pub Assn.

Because the Night Was Dark. Paul Chavchavadze. LC 79-176297. 1971. Durrell Publications.

Because You Are You. Kate Whiting Patch. LC 13-20825. 1913. 1.25. Dodd, Mead and Company.

Becca's Child. Willo Davis Roberts. pap. 0.95 o.s.i. (75-293). Lancer.

Bech: A Book. John Updike. LC 79-110813. 1970. 5.95. Knopf.

Bech: A Book. John Updike. LC 80-10775. 1980. 2.95 (ISBN 0-394-74509-4). Vintage Books.

Beckoning. Virginia Coffman. 1973. (pbk) 0.95. Ace Books.

Beckoning. Josh Webster. (Orig.). 1981. pap. 2.95 (ISBN 0-440-10943-4). Dell.

Beckoning Door. Mabel Seeley. LC 50-5542. 1950. Published for the Crime Club by Doubleday.

Beckoning Dream. Evelyn Berckman. LC 55-6196. (Red badge detective). 1955. Mead.

Beckoning Dream. Evelyn Berckman. LC 55-6196. 1974. (pbk.) 0.95. New American Library.

Beckoning from Moura. Virginia Coffman. 1977. 1.95. Ace Books.

Beckoning Glory. Mary Emery Hall. 1926. The Penn Publishing Company.

Beckoning Heights. Phoebe Fabian Leckey. LC 8-117093. 1908. The Neale Publishing Company.

Beckoning Hill. 1st Ed. James Playsted Wood. LC 54-7677. 1954. Longmans, Green.

Beckoning Ridge. Emerson Waldman. LC 40-35324. H. Holt and Company.

Beckoning Roads. Jeanne Judson. LC 19-3422. 1919. 1.50. Dodd, Mead and Company.

Beckoning Shadow. Denis Scott. LC 46-4285. 1948. The Bobbs-Merrill Company.

Beckoning Shore. E. V. Timms. 1975. pap. 1.25 o.p. (ISBN 0-515-03585-8, V3585). BJ Pub Group.

Beckoning Shore. E. V. Timms. 1967. Repr. pap. 1.80 o.s.i. Tri-Ocean.

Beckoning Star. William Neubauer. (Alouette Romance Ser.). 224p. (Orig.). 1981. pap. 2.25 (ISBN 0-89531-131-3, 0198-96). Sharon Pubns.

Beckoning Trails. Emilie Baker Loring. LC 76-29708. 1976. 6.95 (ISBN 0-88411-351-5). Aeonian Press.

Beckoning Trails. Emilie Baker Loring. LC 47-11507. 1947. Little, Brown.

Beckoning Waters. Robert Carse. LC 53-7597. 1953. Scribner.

Becky. Stephen Lister. LC 76-380235. 1976. 3.50 (ISBN 0-432-08717-6). P. Davies.

Becky. Rayner Seelig. LC 27-243493. Grosset & Dunlap.

Becky Bryan's Secret. Betty Baxter. LC 37-5828. The Goldsmith Publishing Company.

Becky: By Betty Blocklinger Pseud. Peggy O'More, pseud. LC 53-722940. 1953. Arcadia House.

Becky, Grandmother of New Hampshire: An Historical Novel, by Alice Clark Haubrich. Alice I. Clark Haubrich. LC 66-27863. 1966. 4.95.

Becky's Corset. Ellie Hill. LC 42-14395. 1942. House of Pettit.

Becky's Island. Elisabeth Ogilvie. Repr. lib. bdg. 12.05x (ISBN 0-88411-326-4). Amereon Ltd.

Becoming Coyote. Wayne Ude. (Orig.). 1979. pap. 4.00 (ISBN 0-89924-023-2). Lynx Hse.

Becoming of Oswald: Or, Wake up and Loaf. Emmanuel Horowitz. LC 40-627. Milestone Press.

Becoming of Ruth. Nancy McMurray. (Illus.). 64p. 1972. 4.95 o.p. (506556). Crown.

Becos. Bill Knott. LC 82-48897. 96p. 1983. pap. 5.95 (ISBN 0-394-71444-X, Vin). Random.

Bed & Board. large type ed. Robert Capon. 1969. Repr. of 1965 ed. 6.95 o.p. (20294). S&S.

Bed and Board. Virginia Bird Martin. LC 38-19253. Toronto, Farrar & Rinehart, Incorporated.

Bed and Bored. Illus. by Deborah Williams. Gordon Barry. LC 67-73310. 1966. bds., 6.50. Lansdowne.

Bed and Breakfast. Coralie Hobson. LC 27-18712. 1927. Boni & Liveright.

Bed and Breakfast. Wright Williams. LC 44-662. 1944. Phoenix Press.

Bed and Breakfast. Watkins Eppes Wright. LC 44-662. 1944. N. Y., Phoenix Press.

Bed in Hell. Elfrida Vipont Brown Foulds. LC 74-81465. 1975. 6.95. St. Martin's Press.

Bed in Hell. Elfrida Vipont, pseud. LC 74-81465. 224p. 1975. 7.95 o.p. (ISBN 0-312-07070-5). St Martin.

Bed Is Not for Sleeping. Gail Jordan. Orig. Title: Come Sin with Me. 1970. pap. 0.75 o.p. (75-337). Manor Bks.

Bed of Ashes see Last of the Mansions.

Bed of Fear. Doug Duperrault. 1969. pap. 0.75 o.p. (75-284). Manor Bks.

Bed of Lesbos. Paula Fontaine. (Orig.). pap. 1.25 o.p. (2060). Brandon.

Bed of Money. Gerrold Watkins. LC 75-28563. (Traveller's companion series, TC 474). 1.95. Traveller's Companion, Inc.

Bed of Roses. Walter Lionel George. LC 24-11837. (Half-title: The Modern library of the world's best books). Boni and Leveright, Inc.

Bed of Roses. Anne Weale. (Harlequin Romances Ser.). 192p. 1982. pap. 1.50 (ISBN 0-373-02484-3, Pub. by Harlequin). PB.

Bed of Roses. 1st American Ed. William Sansom. LC 54-6386. 1954. Harcourt, Brace.

Bed Pan Jungle. Victor McLeod. 2.75 o.p. Vantage.

Bed Rest. Rita Kashner. LC 81-3727. 10.95 (ISBN 0-02-560700-6). Macmillan.

Bed Rest: A Novel. Rita Kashner. 272p. 1981. 10.95 (ISBN 0-02-560700-6). Macmillan.

Bed Rock. Jack Bethea. LC 24-24689. 1924. Houghton Mifflin Company.

Bed Ruggs: Seventeen Twenty-Two to Eighteen Thirty-Three. William L. Warren. LC 72-88680. (Illus.). 1972. pap. 5.95x. Wadsworth Atheneum.

Bed She Made. Florence Stonebraker. LC 46-191138. 1946. Phoenix Press.

Bed She Made: A New Novel. Leslie Waller. LC 51-9688. 1951. Dial Press.

Bed Time Story. Jill Robinson. (Fawcett crest book). 1975. (pbk.) 1.75. Fawcett.

Bedelia. Vera Caspary. LC 52-299552. Blakiston Co.

Bedelia. Vera Caspary. LC 45-5841. 1945. Houghton Mifflin Company.

Bedelia. Vera Caspary. LC 47-20096. 1947. Triangle Books, the Blakiston Company.

Bedesman 4. Mary Jessie Hammond Tooke Skrine. LC 14-7569. 1914. The Century Co.

Bedeviled. Libbie Block. LC 47-3059. 1947. Pub. for the Crime Club by Doubleday & Company, Inc.

Bedeviled. Thomas Cullinan. LC 77-25418. 10.00. Putnam.

Bedfellow. Eliot Asinof. LC 68-11008. 1968. Simon and Schuster.

Bedfellows & Other Strangers. Stephen A. Jones. 160p. (Orig.). 1974. pap. 1.95 o.p. (ISBN 0-87682-397-5, 7397). Barclay Hse.

Bedford Incident. Mark Rascovich. LC 63-12784. 1963. Atheneum.

Bedford Row. Claire Rayner. LC 77-9360. (Her The performers; book 5). 8.95 (ISBN 0-399-11997-3). Putnam.

Bedford Village. Hervey Allen. LC 44-2461. Farrar & Rinehart, Inc.

Bedlam. John Domini. LC 81-71002. 135p. (Orig.). 1981. pap. 6.95 (ISBN 0-931362-03-2). Fiction Intl.

Bedlam. Andre Soubiran. LC 56-10247. 1957. Putnam.

Bedlam Planet. John Brunner. 1982. pap. 2.25 (ISBN 0-345-30678-3, Del Rey). Ballantine.

Bedlam. Translated by Oliver Coburn. 1st American Ed. Andre Soubiran. LC 56-102476. 1957. Putnam.

Bedmates. Herman Irving Bloom. LC 34-1230. 1934. W. Godwin, Inc.

Bedouin Girl. Sarah Jane Hatfield Higginson. LC 7-4772. J. S. Tait & Sons.

Bedouin Love. Arthur Edward Pearse Brome Weigall. George H. Doran Company.

Bedouin Lover. William Allen Knight. LC 13-23417. 1913. 0.50. The Pilgrim Press.

Bedrock: A Work of Fiction Composed of Fifteen Scenes from My Life. Peter Spielberg. LC 73-77321. 1973. 3.50 (ISBN 0-912278-39-0) (ISBN 0-912278-39-0). Crossing Press.

Bedroom Agent. Florenz Branch. LC 40-358834. Phoenix Press.

Bedroom Agent. Florence Stonebraker. LC 40-35883. 1940. Phoenix Press.

Bedroom and Bath. Gene Harvey. LC 39-5149. Phoenix Press.

Bedroom Blacklist. Richard E. Geis. (Orig.). pap. 0.95 o.p. (1010). Brandon.

Bedroom Coach. Lamar McMann. pap. 1.95 o.s.i. (TCP-003). Olympia.

Bedroom Eyes. Maurice Dekobra, pseud. Tr. by Terrell, Maverick. LC 35-8668. The Macaulay Company.

Bedroom in Berlin. Thomas Shire. pap. 1.95 o.p. (ISBN 0-87056-254-1). Brandon.

Bedroom Philosophers. Donatien Alphonse Francois Sade. 1969. pap. 1.25 o.p. (ISBN 0-447-78615-6). Lancer.

Bedroom Sex Doctors. H. D. Bartok. Orig. Title: Sex Doctors in the Bedroom. (Illus.). 168p. (Orig.). 1974. pap. 3.95 o.p. (ISBN 0-89040-102-0, ALP102). Alpha Lib Pr.

Bedrooms Have Windows. Erle Stanley Gardner. LC 48-9927. 1949. W. Morrow.

Beds. Wade Stevenson. 1970. 4.50 o.p. (ISBN 0-8415-0034-7). Sat Rev Pr.

Bedside Bonanza: Or, A Lodestone of Love and Laughter, Edited by Frank Owen. Ed. by Frank Owen. LC 45-278194. 1944. F. Fell.

Bedside Book of Famous American Stories. Ed. by John Angus Burrell. Cerf, Bennett Alfred, Joint Ed. LC 36-5255. Random House.

Bedside Book of Famous American Stories. Ed. by John Angus Burrell. Cerf, Bennett Alfred, Joint Ed. LC 39-3291. Random House.

Bedside Book of Famous American Stories. Ed. by John Angus Burrell. Cerf, Bennett Alfred, Joint Ed & Mott, Frank Luther, 1836- LC 40-34866. Random House, Inc.

Bedside Book of Famous British Stories. Ed. by Bennett Alfred Cerf & Moriarty, Henry Curran. LC 40-13734. Random House.
Bedside Book of Famous French Stories: Edited by Belle Becker and Robert N. Linscott. New Rev. Ed. Ed. by Belle Becker & Robert Newton Linacott. LC 56-10464. (Dell book. F57). Dell Pub. Co.
Bedside Book of Famous French Stories. Ed. by Belle Becker. Linscott, Robert Newton, 1886- Joint Ed. LC 45-10263. 1945. Random House.
Bedside Book of Great Detective Stories. Herbert Maurice Van Thal. LC 76-382231. 1976. 4.25 (ISBN 0-213-16577-5). Barker.
Bedside Manners. Isabel Glass. (Orig.). 1980. pap. 2.50 (ISBN 0-449-14310-4, GM). Fawcett.
Bedside Odyssey. Homer et al. pap. 1.25 o.s.i. (206, Travellers Comp). Olympia.
Bedside Thomas Hardy. Thomas Hardy & Edward Leeson. LC 79-64316. (Illus.). 1980. 15.00 (ISBN 0-312-07131-0). St. Martin's Press.
Bedside Treasury of Love; Supreme Stories of Romance, Rapture and Tragedy. Ed. by Thomas Everett Harre. LC 45-5906. 1945. Sheridan House.
Bedtime with Daddy. Keith Rockwell. 192p. (Orig.). 1972. pap. 1.95 o.p. (ISBN 0-87682-228-6, 7228). Barclay Hse.
Bedtimes. Leslie Thomas. LC 75-26198. 1976. 8.95. St. Martin's Press.
Bee and Butterfly: A Tale of Two Cousins. Lucy Foster Madison. LC 13-10665. M. A. Donohue & Co.
Bee and the Rose. Peter De Rosa. LC 75-7543. (Illus.). 1975. 1.95 (ISBN 0-913592-54-4). Argus Communications.
Bee-Hunter. A Tale. Gustave Aimard & St. John, Percy Bolingbroke, 1821-1889, Ed. LC 5-421970. (On cover: Lovell's library, no. 1104). J.W. Lovell Company.
Bee-Man of Orn: And Other Fanciful Tales. Frank Richard Stockton. LC 8-15667. 1887. C. Scribner's Sons.
Bee Sting Deal. George Beare. LC 72-184813. (Vic Stallard novel of suspense). 1974. (pbk.) 1.25. Warner Paperback Lib.
Beebo Brinker. 2nd ed. Ann Bannon. (Beebo Brinker Ser.). 208p. 1983. pap. 3.95 (ISBN 0-930044-38-X). Naiad Pr.
Beech Bluff: A Tale of the South. Fannie Warner. LC 8-33712. 1870. P. F. Cunningham.
Beech Haven. Dorothy Worley. LC 55-13571. 1955. Avalon Books.
Beechcroft. Charlotte Mary Yonge. LC 29-25300. 1871. D. Appleton and Company.
Beechcroft at Rockstone. Charlotte Mary Yonge. (On cover: Seaside library. Pocket ed. no. 1200). 1889. G. Munro.
Beecher. Dan McCall. 1979. 9.95 o.p. (ISBN 0-525-06215-7, Thomas Congdon Book). Dutton.
Beecher: A Novel. Dan McCall. LC 79-12358. 9.95 (ISBN 0-525-06215-7). Dutton.
Beechwood Tragedy. A Tale of the Chiokahcminy. Mary Jane Haw. LC 7-2617. 1889. J. W. Randolph & English.
Beechy: Or, The Lordship of Love. Betsey Riddle Hutton Zum Stolzenberg. LC 9-25818. 1909. 1.50. F. A. Stokes Company.
Beef, Iron, and Wine. Jack Lait. LC 78-116960. (Short story index reprint series). 1970. Books for Libraries Press.
Beef, Iron and Wine. Jack Lait. LC 16-19952. 1916. 1.25. Doubleday, Page & Company.
Beefy Jones, Novel. Eric Lawson Malpass. LC 57-274964. 1957. Longmans, Green.
Beelfontaine. Saliee O'Brien. (Kangaroo Book). 1978. 1.75 (ISBN 0-671-81877-5). Pocket Books.
Beelfontaine. Saliee O'Brien. (Berkley medallion book). 1974. (pbk.) 0.95 (ISBN 0-425-02640-X). Berkley Pub. Co.
Been Down So Long It Looks Like up to Me. Richard Farina. (0514). 1967. Dell.
Been Down So Long It Looks Like up to Me. Richard Farina. LC 66-12011. 1966. Random House.
Been There & Back. Frank L. Watson & Peggy Hoffmann. LC 76-49968. 1976. 10.00 (ISBN 0-910244-91-X); pap. 5.95 (ISBN 0-910244-92-8). Blair.
BEEP. George W Owen. 1973. 4.95 (ISBN 0-533-00546-9). Vantage.
Beer for Psyche. Dorothy Gardiner. LC 46-4935. 1946. Pub. for the Crime Club by Doubleday & Company, Inc.
Beer for the Kitten: A Heady Brew in Which to Toast the Pedagogues, Their Wives; in Which to Taste the Seductions of Higher Learning. Ladies and Gentlemen! The Faculty! Seen Through a Glass but Not Darkly. Hester Pine. LC 39-4385. Farrar & Rinehart, Incorporated.
Beer in the Snooker Club. Waguih Ghali. LC 64-12296. 1964. Knopf.
Bees: A Story of a Family. Elizabeth Boatwright Coker. LC 67-11389. 1968. Dutton.
Bees Have Stopped Working, and Other Stories. Bill Noughton. LC 76-373629. (Literature for life series). (Illus.). 1976. 0.80 (ISBN 0-08-020547-X). Wheaton.
Bees" The Story of the "B" Triplets and Their Aunt. M. Ellen Thonger. LC 11-27650. 1911. G. P. Putnam's Sons.
Beeseekers. Roger Elwood. 1974. 6.95 o.s.i. (ISBN 0-671-27113-X). Trident.
Beeswax and Gold: A Story of the Pacific, A.D. 1700. Thomas H Rogers. LC 29-13028. The J. K. Gill Company.
Beethoven: A Biographical Romance; Tr. Herbert Rau. Tr. by Randolph, S. E. LC 8-28635. O. Ditson Company.
Beethoven: A Biographical Romance. Tr. from the German of H. Rau... Herbert Rau. LC 8-593. O. Ditson & Company.
Beethoven, Master Musician. Madeleine Binkley Goss. LC 31-16671. 1931. Doubleday, Doran & Company, Inc.
Beethoven, Master Musician. Madeleine Binkley Goss. LC 46-8218. (Holt musical biography series). 1946. H. Holt and Company.
Beetle. Richard Marsh. LC 75-46291. (Supernatural & Occult Fiction). 1976. 19.00 (ISBN 0-405-08151-0). Arno Press.
Beetle. Richard Marsh. 1915. Brentano's.
Beetle. Richard Marsh. LC 17-3888. 1917. G. P. Putnam's Sons.
Beetle in the Anthill. Arkadii Natanovich Strugatskii & Boris Natanovich Strugatskii. LC 80-17172. (Macmillan's Best of Soviet Science Fiction). 9.95 (ISBN 0-02-615120-0). Macmillan.
Beetle in the Anthill. Arkadii Natanovich Strugatskii & Boris Natanovich Strugatskii. Tr. by Antonina W. Bouis. (Best of Soviet Science Fiction Ser.). 256p. 1980. 11.95 o.s.i. (ISBN 0-02-615120-0). Macmillan.
Beetle Leg. John Hawkes. LC 51-14554. 1967. pap., 1.50. New Directions.
Beetlecreek. William Demby. 223p. 1972. Repr. of 1950 ed. 7.50x (ISBN 0-911860-12-6). Chatham Bkseller.
Beetlecreek: A Novel. William Demby. LC 50-5374. 1950. Rinehart.
Beetlecreek: A Novel. William Demby. LC 77-187025. 1972. (ISBN 0-911860-12-6). Chatham Bookseller.
Before Adam. Jack London. LC 6-23159. 1906. The Macmillan Company.
Before Adam. Jack London. LC 7-71911. 1907. The Macmillan Company.
Before Adam. Biographical Introd. by Willy Ley; Epilogue by Loren Eiseley. Illustrated by Leonard Everett Fisher. Jack London. LC 62-17336. 1962. Macmillan.
Before and After Zachariah: A Family Story About a Different Kind of Courage. Fern Kupfer. LC 81-12510. 12.95 (ISBN 0-440-00507-8). Delacorte Press.
Before Dawn. Juliana Von Stockhausen & Johnson, Hilda C., Tr. LC 39-349294. 1939. E. P. Dutton & Co., Inc.
Before Ever the Earth: A Novel. Dorothy Park Clark. LC 46-738132. 1946. The Newell Post.
Before He Was Born: Or, The Scarlet Arm. Elias L. Macomb Bristol. LC 6-18247. 1891. M.J. Roth, Printer.
Before Honor. Gertrude Schweitzer. LC 73-83669. 1974. 6.95 (ISBN 0-385-06501-9). Doubleday.
Before Honor. Gertrude Schweitzer. LC 74-16019. 1974. (ISBN 0-8161-6238-7). G. K. Hall.
Before I Go Hence: Fantasia on a Novel. Frank Baker. LC 47-1532. 1947. Coward-McCann, Inc.
Before I Kill More. Lucy Freeman. (O.s.i.). 1966. pap. 0.75 o.s.i. (A170S, Award). Univ Pub & Dist.
Before I Wake. Hal Debrett, pseud. LC 49-8705. (Red badge mystery). 1949. Dodd, Mead.
Before I Wake. David Dury. 1971. pap. 0.95 o.p. (M2467, GM). Fawcett World.
Before I Wake. Margaret Echard. LC 43-18001. 1943. Pub. for the Crime Club by Doubleday, Doran and Co., Inc.
Before It's Too Late: A Mystery Novel. Jay Stewart. LC 50-6373. 1950. Mill.
Before Lunch. Angela Mackail Thirkell. LC 40-670919. 1940. A. A. Knopf.
Before Midnight. Elinor Mordaunt, pseud. LC 17-24101. 1917. Cassell & Company, Ltd.
Before Midnight. Rex Stout. 160p. 1981. pap. 2.25 (ISBN 0-553-14797-8). Bantam.
Before Midnight: A Nero Wolfe Novel. Rex Stout. LC 55-9642. 1955. Viking Press.
Before My Time. Maureen Howard. 1977. 1.50 (ISBN 0-445-03185-9). Popular Library.
Before My Time. Maureen Howard. LC 74-6212. 1975. (ISBN 0-316-37468-7). Little, Brown.
Before My Time. Maureen Howard. LC 80-10926. (Series: Penguin Contemporary American Fiction Series.). 1980. 3.95 (ISBN 0-14-005503-7). Penguin Books.
Before My Time. Niccolo Tucci. LC 61-12865. 1962. Simon and Schuster.
Before Noon: A Novel in Three Parts. Ramon Jose Sender. LC 57-145189. University of New Mexico Press.
Before the Ball Was Over. Alexandra Roudybush. LC 65-22580. 3.50. Pub. for the Crime Club by Doubleday.
Before the Bombardment. Osbert Sitwell. LC 26-20315. George H. Doran Company.
Before the Cock Crowed: Death Answered the Call of the Crowing Cock. William Edward Hayes. LC 37-17026. 1937. Pub. for the Crime Club, Inc., by Doubleday, Doran & Co., Inc.
Before the Conquerors: A Modern Adventure in the Land of the Incas. Alpheus Hyatt Verrill. LC 35-138157. 1935. Dodd, Mead and Company.
Before the Crisis. Frederick Blount Mott. LC 4-23769. 1904. J. Lane.
Before the Crossing. Margaret Storm Jameson. LC 47-1198. 1947. The Macmillan Company.
Before the Crying Ends. John L Hughes. LC 77-5014. 1977. 7.95 (ISBN 0-8076-0865-3). G. Braziller.
Before the Dawn. Joseph Alexander Altsheler. 1976. lib. bdg. 16.70x (ISBN 0-89968-000-3). Lightyear.
Before the Dawn. Eric Temple Bell. LC 74-16522. (Science Fiction). 1975. (ISBN 0-405-06314-8). Arno Press.
Before the Dawn. Eric Temple Bell. LC 34-167184. 1934. The Williams & Wilkins Company.
Before the Dawn. Toyohiko Kagawa. Tr. by Fukumoto, Ichiji. LC 24-24948. George H. Doran Company.
Before the Dawn: A Story of Paris and the Jacquerie. LC 7-30565. 1888. G. P. Putnam's Sons.
Before the Dawn: A Story of Russian Life. Lydia Lvovna Pimenoff Noble & Noble, Edmund. 1901. Houghton, Mifflin and Company.
Before the Dawn: A Story of the Fall of Richmond. Joseph Alexander Altsheler. LC 3-6141. 1903. Doubleday, Page & Company.
Before the Deluge. Mark Aleksandrovich Aldanov. Tr. by Routsky, Catherine. LC 47-6370. 1947. C. Scribner's Sons.
Before the Deluge. Mark Aleksandrovich Landau. Tr. by Catherine Routsky. LC 47-6370. 1947. C. Scribner's Sons.
Before the Fact. Anthony Berkeley Cox. LC 79-1143. (Series: Gregg Press Mystery Fiction Series.). (Illus.). 1979. 9.95 (ISBN 0-8398-2539-0). Gregg Press.
Before the Fact. Francis Iles. 1979. lib. bdg. 9.95 (ISBN 0-8398-2539-0, Gregg). G K Hall.
Before the Fact. Francis Iles. LC 80-7837. 352p. 1980. pap. 2.50i (ISBN 0-06-080517-X, P 517, PL). Har-Row.
Before the Fact. Francis Iles. 345p. 1981. Repr. lib. bdg. 14.95 (ISBN 0-89968-237-5). Lightyear.
Before the Fact: A Novel of Murder... Anthony Berkeley Cox. LC 32-33698. 1932. Doubleday, Doran & Company, Inc.
Before the Fact: A Novel of Murder... Francis Iles. LC 32-33698. 1932. Doubleday, Doran & Company, Inc.
Before the Glory Ended. Ursula Zilinsky. LC 67-14369. 1967. Lippincott.
Before the Golden Age. Isaac Asimov. LC 73-10965. 1008p. 1974. 19.95 (ISBN 0-385-02419-3). Doubleday.
Before the Golden Age, Vol. 1. Isaac Asimov. 1978. pap. 1.95 (ISBN 0-449-22913-0, Crest). Fawcett.
Before the Golden Age: A Science Fiction Anthology of the 1930's. Ed. by Isaac Asimov. (Fawcett crest book). 1975. (pbk.) 1.50 ea. Fawcett.
Before the Great Snow. Translated from the German by Robert Kee. 1st American Ed. Hans Wilhelm Pump. LC 58-10889. 1958. Harcourt, Brace.
Before the Gringo Came. Gertrude Franklin Horn Atherton. LC 6-4516. (On cover: Tait's Kenilworth series, no. 6). J. Selwin Tait & Sons.
Before the Gringo Came: "Resanov" and "The Doomswoman". Gertrude Franklin Horn Atherton. LC 15-3869. Frederick A. Stokes Company.
Before the Setting Sun: The Age Before Hambone. Saggittarus. LC 74-77416. 1974. 6.95. Nuclassics and Science Pub. Co.
Before the Storm. Marie Adelaide Belloc Lowndes. LC 41-788677. 1941. Longmans, Green and Co.
Before the Sun Goes Down. Elizabeth Metzger Howard. LC 46-250216. 1946. Doubleday & Company, Inc.
Before the Sun Goes Down. Elizabeth Metzger Howard. LC 47-23207. 1947. The Sun Dial Press.
Before the Violets Bloom. Sylvia McDaniel. LC 67-20527. 1967. Dorrance.
Before the War: Or, The Return of Hugh Crawford. Louise Edna Dearborn Keesing. LC 15-8710. 1915. 1.35. The Author.
Before the Wind. Janet Laing. LC 18-8317. E. P. Dutton & Company.
Before They Were Men. Charles Wertenbaker. LC 31-33679. 1931. H. Liveright, Inc.
Before William Penn. The Story of the First Settlers in Pennsylvania. Akseli Rauanheimo. LC 29-21553. Dorrance and Company.
Before You Go. Jerome Weidman. LC 60-12424. 1960. Random House.
Beg Pahdon." A Book Published to Fill a Long-Felt Want, a Want of the Author for Money... T. C McConnell. 1896. Press of L. Hardman.
Beg Pardon, Sir! Reginald Wright Kauffman. LC 29-88333. The Penn Publishing Company.
Beggar. Fereidoun M Esfandiary. LC 65-22601. 3.95. Obolensky.
Beggar. A. H Schulz. LC 73-84. 1973. 6.95 (ISBN 0-690-12917-3). Crowell.
Beggar in Evening Dress. George Elliott Fleming. LC 8-14764. 1908.
Beggar in Jerusalem. Eliezer Wiesel. (Kangaroo Book). 1978. 2.50 (ISBN 0-671-81253-X). Pocket Books.
Beggar in Jerusalem: A Novel. Eliezer Wiesel. LC 79-85614. 1970. 5.95. Random House.
Beggar in the Harem: Impudent Adventures in Old Bukhara. Leonid Vasilevich Solovev. LC 57-5538. 1957. Harcourt, Brace.
Beggar in the Heart. Martha Edith Rickert. 1909. Moffat, Yard and Company.
Beggar in the Street. Dorothea E. Hammond. 700p. (Orig.). 1983. pap. 14.95 (ISBN 0-942874-02-1). Hammond Records.
Beggar Maid. Alice Munro. 1982. pap. 2.95. Bantam.
Beggar Maid: Stories of Flo and Rose. Alice Munro. LC 79-63809. 1979. 8.95 (ISBN 0-394-50682-0). Knopf: Distributed by Random House.
Beggar My Neighbor. A Novel. Emily Gerard & Longard De Longgarde, Dorothea (Gerard) (Harper's Franklin square library, no. 235). 1882. Harper & Brothers.
Beggar of Nimes... By Alexandre Dumas, Author of Camille"... Alexandre Dumas. LC 6-42313. (On cover: The echo series, no. 36). 1888. Pollard & Moss.
Beggar on Horseback. George S. Kaufman & Marc Connelly. 3.00 o.p. Liveright.
Beggar on Horseback: Or, A County Family. James Payn. (Seaside library. v. 21. no. 401). 1878. G. Munro.
Beggarman. Jane Ludlow Drake Abbott. 1930. J. B. Lippincott Company.
Beggarman, Thief. Irwin Shaw. LC 77-24523. 9.95 (ISBN 0-440-00673-2). Delacorte Press.
Beggarman's Country. Jan Webster. LC 79-25426. 11.95 (ISBN 0-312-07161-2). St. Martin's Press.
Beggars All. Katharine Newlin Burt. LC 38-19082. 1938. Houghton Mifflin Company.
Beggars All: A Novel. new impression (1896) reissue. ed. Lily Dougall. LC 4-16518. 1903. Longmans, Green, and Co.
Beggars and Choosers. Cynthia King. LC 79-20184. 1980. 9.95 (ISBN 0-670-59758-9). Viking Press.
Beggars and Choosers. Thom Racina. LC 77-6126. 1.95 (ISBN 0-345-27241-2). Ballantine Books.
Beggars and Choosers: A Novel. Laura Kalpakian. LC 77-21267. 9.95 (ISBN 0-316-48235-8). Little, Brown.
Beggars and Sorners. Charlotte Stewart. LC 12-10821. 1912. 1.25. John Lane.
Beggar's Banquet. Gladys St. John-Loe. LC 24-4261. 1924. T. Seltzer.
Beggars Can Choose. Margaret Weymouth Jackson. LC 28-22666. The Bobbs--Merrill Company.
Beggar's Choice. George Axelrod. LC 47-30593. 1947. Howell, Soskin.
Beggar's Choice. Henry C Branson. LC 53-10043. (Inner sanctum mystery). 1953. Simon and Schuster.
Beggar's Choice. Patricia Wentworth. LC 31-8412. 1931. J. B. Lippincott Company.
Beggars' Christmas. John Aurelio. LC 79-65893. (Illus.). 96p. 1979. pap. 3.95 (ISBN 0-8091-2221-9). Paulist Pr.
Beggars' Gold. Ernest Poole. LC 21-18414. 1921. The Macmillan Company.
Beggar's Gulch. Cameron Judd. (Orig.). 1980. pap. 1.75 o.s.i. (ISBN 0-8439-0733-9, Leisure Bks). Nordon Pubns.
Beggars in the Sun. Paul Darcy Boles. LC 54-12506. 1954. Macmillan.
Beggar's King. Howard C Emmons. LC 53-17276. 1952. Van Kampen Press.
Beggars Might Ride. George Albert Glay. LC 51-4762. 1951. Appleton-Century-Crofts.
Beggars of Destiny: A Novel. George S Whittaker. LC 35-7527. 1935. Dorrance & Co., Inc.
Beggars of Life. Jane Nelson. LC 41-1980. Fortuny's Publishers, Inc.
Beggars of the Sea. Stephen Elmer Slocum. LC 28-26453. 1928. Minton, Balch & Company.
Beggars on Horseback. James Mossman. (75-192). 1968. Macfadden.

Beggars on Horseback: A Novel. James Mossman. LC 66-17209. bds., 5.95. Atlantic-Little.

Beggars on Horseback: A Novel. James Mossman. LC 66-17209. 1966. Little, Brown.

Beggar's Opera. Frank Kidson. 8.75 o.p. Blom.

Beggars' Revolt: A Historical Novel. Maurits Rudolph Joel Dekker. LC 38-6968. 1938. Doubleday, Doran.

Beggar's Story. Sue Froman Matthews. LC 7-24694. F.H. Revell Company.

Beggar's Tales: A Novel. Stephen Bronner. LC 78-60635. 1978. 5.95 (ISBN 0-918618-08-8). Pella Pub. Co.

Beggar's Virtue. Barbara Bennett. LC 78-24039. 1979. 8.95 (ISBN 0-312-07164-7). St. Martin's Press.

Beggars Would Ride. Harold Ohlson. LC 33-32874. Thomas Y. Crowell Company.

Begging the Dialect. Robin Skelton. 1960. 2.90 o.p. (ISBN 0-19-211223-6). Oxford U Pr.

Begin Again. Ursula Orange. G. P. Putnam's Sons.

Begin No Day. Wellington Roe. LC 38-12840. 1938. G. P. Putnam's Sons.

Begin Sweet World. John Pearson. LC 75-9228. 112p. 1976. Softbound 5.95 o.p. (ISBN 0-385-11065-0). Doubleday.

Beginner. Rhoda Broughton. LC 18-7776. (Macmillan's two shilling library. no. 18). 1899. Macmillan and Co., Limited.

Beginner: A Novel. Rhoda Broughton. LC 6-18957. (On cover: Appleton's town and country library, no. 138). 1894. D. Appleton and Company.

Beginners. Dan Jacobson. LC 66-14206. Macmillan.

Beginners. Maureen Strange. LC 78-7769. 1979. 8.95 (ISBN 0-385-14518-7). Doubleday.

Beginners; a Novel. Henry Kitchell Webster. LC 27-21013. The Bobbs-Merrill Company.

Beginners Luck. Emily Hahn. LC 31-214. Brewer, Warren & Putnam.

Beginner's Luck. 1st Ed. Paul Somers. LC 58-6175. 1958. Harper.

Beginning. George Snelling. (Illus.). 291p. 1981. pap. 3.95 (ISBN 0-934142-02-5). Vancento Pub.

Beginning: A Novel. David Peretsovich Markish. LC 76-371423. 1976. 4.50 (ISBN 0-340-18093-5). Hodder and Stoughton.

Beginning: A Novel. Patrick D. Smith. LC 67-6310. 1967. Exposition Press.

Beginning at Dusk: An Interlude. Thames Ross Williamson. LC 35-24888. 1935. Doubleday, Doran & Company, Inc.

Beginning Is the End: A Novel by Melinda Mayne Pseud. 1st Ed. Marie Mourer Blackmore. LC 53-6707. 1953. Exposition Press.

Beginning of a Crime. Dorris Roberts. LC 58-6878. 1958. Dorrance.

Beginning of Love. Daisy H. Thomson. 1975. pap. 0.95 o.p. (ISBN 0-515-03594-7, N3594). Pyramid Pubns.

Beginning of Love. Daisy H. Thomson. 1976. pap. 1.25 o.p. (ISBN 0-515-04182-3). BJ Pub Group.

Beginning of the End: And Other Stories (Designed for Film Adaptation. Tommy Valentine. LC 60-264. (Milestone book). 1959. Comet Press Book.

Beginning of Wisdom. Stephen Vincent Benet. LC 21-171938. 1921. 1.90. H. Holt and Company.

Beginning Place. Ursula K. Le Guin. LC 79-2653. 8.95 (ISBN 0-06-012573-X). Harper & Row.

Beginning Place. Ursula K. Le Guin. 192p. 1981. pap. 2.25 (ISBN 0-553-14259-3). Bantam.

Beginning to Feel the Magic. Linda Weltner. 160p. 1982. pap. 1.95 (ISBN 0-449-70022-4, Juniper). Fawcett.

Beginning with a Bash: A Leonidas Witherall Mystery. Alice Tilton, pseud. 1972. 5.95 o.p. (ISBN 0-393-08658-5). Norton.

Beginnings. Carol Lynn Pearson. LC 74-28894. 64p. 1975. 5.95 (ISBN 0-385-07904-4). Doubleday.

Beginnings of Rome for Beginners in Latin. Raymond F Haulenbeek. LC 29-4200. Harcourt, Brace and Company.

Begonia Bed. Agnes Mary Robertson Dunlop. LC 34-20017. The Bobbs-Merrill Company.

Beguiled. Thomas Cullinan. LC 66-16303. bds., 6.95. Horizon.

Begum's Daughter. f. t. merrill. ed. Edwin Lassetter Bynner. LC 6-16411. 1890. Little, Brown, and Company.

Begum's Fortune. Jules Verne. 1958. 3.00 o.p. Assoc Bk.

Begum's Fortune. Jules Verne. 3.00 o.p. Wehman.

Begun in Laughter. Martha Ellen Wright Shakespeare. LC 42-21560. 1942. Doubleday, Doran & Company, Inc.

Behemoth: A Legend of the Mound-Builders. Cornelius Mathews. LC 72-8315. 1972. (ISBN 0-8422-8138-X). MSS Information Corp.

Behemoth: A Legend of the Mound-Builders. Cornelius Mathews. LC 77-93643. (American Fiction Series). 1970. (ISBN 0-512-00515-X). Garrett Press.

Behemoth: a Legend of the Mound-Builders. Cornelius Mathews. LC 7-17931. 1839. J. & H. G. Langley.

Behind a Mask. A Novel. Louise Battles Cooper. (On cover: The pastime ser. no. 53). 1891. Laird & Lee.

Behind a Mask: Or, Numa Roumestan. Alphonse Daudet. Tr. by Lord, Grace Virginia. LC 98-2249. (On cover: Globe library. v. 2, no. 300). McNally & Company.

Behind a Mask: The Unknown Thrillers of Louisa May Alcott. Louisa May Alcott & Madeleine Bettina Stern. LC 74-31046. (Illus.). 1975. (ISBN 0-688-00338-9). Morrow.

Behind a Thousand Headlines. Bernard Herman Martin. LC 44-4333. 1944. The William-Frederick Press.

Behind Blue Glasses. Friedrich Wilhelm Hacklander & Robinson, Mary A., Tr. LC 7-3635. (On cover: Harper's half-hour series. v. 80). 1878. Harper & Brothers.

Behind Closed Doors. John Olin Knott. LC 27-28082. Authors & Publishers Corporation.

Behind Closed Doors. Anna Katharine Green Rohlfs. LC 7-40737. 1888. G. P. Putnam's Sons.

Behind Dark Glasses. Karen L. Hones. (Muchos Somos Ser: No. 2). Date not set. 1.00 o.s.i. (ISBN 0-914370-07-3). Mothers Hen.

Behind Hospital Walls. Ruth Dorset, pseud. Ed. by Alice Sachs. 1970. 3.95 o.p. Lenox Hill.

Behind Legs of the 'orse: And Other Stories. Ellis Parker Butler. LC 27-772611. 1927. Houghton Mifflin Company.

Behind Locked Doors: A Detective Story. Ernest M Poate. LC 24-630. Chelsea House.

Behind Locked Doors. 1st Ed. Rebecca Vera Bereslavsky. LC 57-591366. 1957. Pageant Press.

Behind Locked Shutters. 2nd ed. Dan Ross, pseud. 176p. 1975. pap. 0.95 o.p. (ISBN 0-532-95376-2). Woodhill.

Behind Locked Shutters. Dan Ross, pseud. 1970. Repr. pap. 0.60 o.p. (60-448). Manor Bks.

Behind Locked Shutters. 2nd ed. Dan Ross, pseud. 176p. 1975. pap. 0.95 o.p. (ISBN 0-532-95376-2). Manor Bks.

Behind Manhattan Gables: A Story of New Amsterdam, 1663-1664. Edward Augustus Rand. LC 8-218. 1896. T. Whittaker.

Behind Plastered Walls. A Novel. William W. M Cornish. LC 6-28732. 1896. G. W. Dillingham Co.

Behind Red Curtains. Mansfield Scott. LC 19-13368. 1.50. Small, Maynard & Company.

Behind That Curtain. Earl Derr Biggers. LC 28-125492. The Bobbs-Merrill Company.

Behind That Door Lies Your Fortune. Eva Thomas. 4.50 o.p. Vantage.

Behind That Mask: A Detective Novel. Harry Stephen Keeler. LC 38-144467. 1938. E. P. Dutton & Co., Inc.

Behind the Arras. A Novel. Constance Maude Neville. 1877. A. L. Bancroft and Company.

Behind the Bamboo Curtain: A Novel of the Air War Over Korea Skies. 1st Ed. Fred Skomra. LC 57-11644. 1957. Greenwich Book Publishers.

Behind the Banana Curtain. Hugh Lunn. 202p. (Orig.). 1980. pap. 9.95 (ISBN 0-7022-1499-X). U of Queensland Pr.

Behind the Baton. Charles Blackman. (Charos Bk.). 7.50 o.s.i. Fischer Inc.

Behind the Bead Curtain. Ralph Moreno. (Illus.). 1965. pap. 2.50x o.p. Hartmus Pr.

Behind the Blue Ridge. A Homely Narrative. Frances Courtenay Baylor Barnum. LC 6-8653. 1887. J. B. Lippincott Company.

Behind the Bolted Door? Arthur Emerson McFarlane. LC 16-6718. 1916. Dodd, Mead and Company.

Behind the Bronze Door. William Le Queux. LC 23-11826. The Macaulay Company.

Behind the Cloud. Emilie Baker Loring. Repr. lib. bdg. 11.50x (ISBN 0-88411-367-1). Amereon Ltd.

Behind the Cloud. Emilie Baker Loring. 208p. 1981. pap. 1.95 (ISBN 0-553-14295-X). Bantam.

Behind the Cloud. Emilie Baker Loring. 1959. 2.95 o.p. (ISBN 0-448-06303-4). G&D.

Behind the Cloud. 1st Ed. Emilie Baker Loring. LC 58-7850. 1958. Little, Brown.

Behind the Crimson Blind: Another Adventure of Sir Henry Merrivale by Carter Dickson Pseud. John Dickson Carr. LC 52-5055. 1952. Morrow.

Behind the Curtain. A Tale of Elville ... LC 6-9757. 1853. J. R. Trembly.

Behind the Devil Screen. Maud Keck & Orbison, Olive. LC 28-102961. 1928. I. Washburn.

Behind the Door. Giorgio Bassani. LC 75-29308. (Harbrace paperbound library; HPL 66). 1976. 2.25 (ISBN 0-15-611685-5). Harcourt Brace Jovanovich.

Behind the Door. Giorgio Bassani. LC 72-75413. 1972. (ISBN 0-15-111697-0). Harcourt Brace Jovanovich.

Behind the Door: A Novel. E. J Anders. LC 66-26969. 1966. Philosophical Library.

Behind the Evidence. Amelia Reynolds Long. LC 36-17716. 1936. Visionary Publishing Co.

Behind the Fog: A Tale of Adventure. Henry Howarth Bashford. LC 26-23687. 1927. Harper & Brothers.

Behind the Glass. Robert Merle. LC 72-81348. 1972. 7.95 (ISBN 0-671-21317-2). Simon and Schuster.

Behind the Hills. Hazel Danner Fretwell. LC 50-4413. 1949. Christopher.

Behind the Mirror: By Robin Maugham. 1st American Ed. Robert Cecil Romer Maugham. LC 55-532030. 1955. Harcourt, Brace.

Behind the Monocle: And Other Stories. Joseph Smith Fletcher. LC 72-122698. (Short story index reprint series). 1970. Books for Libraries Press.

Behind the Monocle: And Other Stories. Joseph Smith Fletcher. LC 30-18664. 1930. Doubleday, Doran & Company, Inc.

Behind the Monocle, & Other Stories. Joseph Smith Fletcher. LC 72-122698. (Short Story Index Reprint Ser). 1930. 15.00 (ISBN 0-8369-3531-4). Ayer Co.

Behind the Moon. Aryan Lewis Kelton. LC 46-18347.

Behind the Mountains. Oliver La Farge. LC 74-81915. xii, 180p. 1974. Repr. of 1956 ed. 15.00 (ISBN 0-88307-511-3); pap. 6.95 (ISBN 0-88307-527-X). Gannon.

Behind the Net Curtains. Allan Turpin. LC 76-383575. 1976. 3.50 (ISBN 0-241-89445-X). Hamilton.

Behind the Purple Mask. Josephine Chase. LC 33-2524. The Penn Publishing Company.

Behind the Purple Veil. Marilyn Ross. (Warner Paperback Library Gothic). 1973. (pbk.) 0.95. Warner Paperback Library.

Behind the Ranges. Anne Shannon Monroe. LC 25-9192. 1925. Doubleday, Page & Company.

Behind the Rising Sun. Sebastian Okechukwu Mezu. LC 73-167393. (African writers series, 113). 1972-1973. (ISBN 0-435-90113-3). Heinemann Educational.

Behind the Scarlet Door. Lou Cameron. (Orig.). 1971. pap. 0.75 o.p. (T2493, GM). Fawcett World.

Behind the Scarlet Mask. James T Upchurch. LC 24-12523. World Printers.

Behind the Scenes: A Story of the Stage. LC 8-37215. 1870. New England News Company.

Behind the Scenes of Destiny. James Semple Cahill. LC 24-124323. Dorrance & Company.

Behind the Screen: Hero, Robert Lansing; the Girl, Mary Brewster; the Villain, Jim Hazzard; with an Exceptionally Strong Company. William Almon Wolff. LC 16-10343. 1916. A. C. McClurg & Co.

Behind the Tattooed Face. Heretaunga Pat Baker. LC 76-354954. 1975. 10.50. Cape Catley.

Behind the Walls of Terra. Philip Jose Farmer. (World of Tiers; series 4). 1977. 1.50 (ISBN 0-441-05357-2). Ace Books.

Behind the Walls of Terra. Philip Jose Farmer. 1974. (pbk.) 1.25. Ace Books.

Behold a Cry. Alden Bland. LC 73-18554. 1974. (ISBN 0-404-11369-9). AMS Press.

Behold a Cry. Alden Bland. LC 47-2364. 1947. C. Scribner's Sons.

Behold a Door. Avin Harry Johnston. LC 69-11653. 1969. 2.95. Zondervan Pub. House.

Behold a Pale Horse: A Novel. Joe Musser. LC 71-121359. 1970. 3.50. Zondervan Pub. House.

Behold Goliath: A Collection of Stories. Alfred Chester. LC 64-10529. 1964. Random House.

Behold, Here's Poison. Georgette Heyer. LC 72-133578. 1971. 4.95 (ISBN 0-525-06265-3). Dutton.

Behold, Here's Poison! Georgette Heyer. LC 36-27458. 1936. Pub. for the Crime Club, Inc., by Doubleday, Doran & Company, Inc.

Behold That Star: A Christmas Anthology. Bruderhof Communities. LC 67-25968. (Illus.). 1967. Plough Pub. House.

Behold the Children. Mary Cranford. 1970. 3.95 o.p. Vantage.

Behold, the Druid Weeps. Marion Rippon. LC 76-123708. 1970. 4.95. Published for the Crime Club by Doubleday.

Behold the Fire: A Novel Based on Events That Took Place Between 1914 and 1918 in London, Cairo, Constantinople, Jerusalem, and Some of the Villages of Palestine. Michael Blankfort. LC 65-20637. (NAL-world book). 1965. New American Library.

Behold the Man. Dennis Kirkwood. LC 74-27759. 1975. 7.95 (ISBN 0-8059-2124-9). Dorrance.

Behold the Man. Dennis Kirkwook. 192p. 1975. 7.95 o.p. (ISBN 0-8059-2124-9). Dorrance.

Behold the Man. Michael Moorcock. 1978. pap. 1.50 (ISBN 0-380-00637-5, 39982). Avon.

Behold the Man: Being a Novel, Dealing with the Dual Personalities of the Peasants Who Appear in the Sacred Performance at Ober-Ammergau. Channing Pollock. 1901. The Neale Publishing Company.

Behold the Man: Being a Novel Dealing with the Dual Personalities of the Peasants Who Appear in the Sacred Performance at Ober-Ammergau. special author's autograph ed. Channing Pollock. LC 6-746. 1905. The Neale Publishing Company.

Behold the Mighty Dinosaur. David Jablonski. LC 80-25831. 9.95 (ISBN 0-525-66704-0). Elsevier/Nelson.

Behold the Woman! A Tale of Redemption. T Everett Harre. LC 16-9266. 1916. 1.35. J. B. Lippincott Company.

Behold the Woman! A Tale of Redemption. T Everett Harre. LC 24-22232. J. B. Lippincott Company.

Behold the Woman. Parable Sequel to Man Is Love. Bulah Brinton. LC 20-17779. 1886. Pub. for the Author by Bay View Herald Publishing Co.

Behold This Dreamer! Fulton Oursler. LC 29-30757. The Macaulay Company.

Behold This Hour. Ethel E Bangert. LC 52-14394. 1952. Arcadia House.

Behold This Woman. David Goodis. LC 47-11501. 1947. D. Appleton-Century Co.

Behold This Woman. Clarke Robinson. LC 38-36741. 1938. Godwin.

Behold Thy Daughter: A Novel. Neil Paterson. LC 50-5172. 1950. Random House.

Behold Trouble. Granville Hicks. LC 44-476072. 1944. The Macmillan Company.

Behold, We Live. Charles Dunscomb. LC 56-11116. 1956. Houghton Mifflin.

Behold Your King. Florence Anne Marvyne Bauer. 1945. The Bobbs-Merrill Company.

Beholden to None: The Decline and Fall of Gobble Government; a Novel. 1st. ed. Jean Dewees. 1974-1973. 6.50 (ISBN 0-682-47742-7). Exposition.

Beholder. Philip Freund. 1963. 4.95 o.p. British Bk Ctr.

Beholding As in a Glass." A Novel. Virginia Durant Young. LC 9-1196. 1895. Arena Publishing Company.

Beholding Runner. Owain Hughes. LC 67-11635. (Illus.). 1967. Morrow.

Being Busted. Leslie A. Fiedler. LC 69-17946. 1970. pap. 1.95 (ISBN 0-8128-1341-3). Stein & Day.

Being Met Together. William Vaughan Wilkins. LC 44-6481. 1944. The Macmillan Company.

Being Respectable. Grace C. Hodgson Flandrau. LC 23-3443. Harcourt, Brace and Company.

Being There. Jerzy N. Kosinski. LC 70-147229. 1971. 4.95 (ISBN 0-15-111700-4). Harcourt Brace Jovanovich.

Beirut Incident. Nick Carter. (Nick Carter Ser.). 192p. (Orig.). 1981. pap. 2.25 (ISBN 0-441-05381-5, Pub. by Charter Bks). Ace Bks.

Beirut Incident. Nick Carter. (Nick Carter Ser.). (O.s.i.). 208p. (Orig.). 1974. pap. 1.50 o.s.i. (AQ1333, Award). Univ Pub & Dist.

Beirut Pipeline. Ray Alan. 242p. 1980. 10.95 (ISBN 0-374-11018-2). FS&G.

Beirut Pipeline: A Novel. Ray Aan. LC 79-23972. 1980. 10.95 (ISBN 0-374-11018-2). Farrar Straus Giroux.

Bejeweled Boy. Miguel Angel Asturias. LC 79-160891. 1971. 4.95. Doubleday.

Bejewelled Death. Marian Babson. LC 81-71200. 1982. 10.95 (ISBN 0-8027-5467-8). Walker.

Beka Lamb. Zee Edgell. (Caribbean Writers Ser.: No. 26). 171p. (Orig.). 1982. pap. text ed. 4.50x (ISBN 0-435-98400-4). Heinemann Ed.

Bek's First Corner. Jennie Maria Drinkwater Conklin. LC 6-30392. 1883. R. Carter & Brothers.

Bel-Ami. Guy De Maupassant. LC 76-365370. (Penguin classics). 1975. 2.95 (ISBN 0-14-044315-0). Penguin.

Bel-Ami. Guy De Maupassant. Limited Editions Club, Inc., New York. LC 76-1602. (Illus.). 1968. Limited Editions Club.

Bel-Ami. Guy De Maupassant. LC 43-42357. Chicago Publishing Co.

Bel Ami. Guy De Maupassant. Tr. by Ernest Augustus Boyd. LC 47-21045. 1947. Avon Book Company.

Bel-Ami: A Novel. Guy De Maupassant. LC 7-25599. (On cover: The library of choice fiction, no. 22). 1891. Laird & Lee.

Bel-Ami: The History of a Heart. Guy De Maupassant. LC 10-732145. 1910. The Pearson Publishing Co.

Bel Ami. Tr. from French. Guy de Maupassant. (Living classics SP238). 1963. Popular Lib.

Bel-Ami. Tr., with Introd. by H.N.P. Sloman. Guy De Maupassant. Tr. by H. N. P. Soloman. Penguin Dist. New York, Atheneum.

Bel-Ami. Translated with an Introd. by H. N. P. Sloman. Guy De Maupassant. LC 61-66362. (Penguin classics, L115). 1961. Penguin Books.

Bel Lamington. Dorothy Emily Stevenson. LC 61-17246. 1961. Holt, Rinehart and Winston.

Bel Lamington. Dorothy Emily Stevenson. 1978. 1.95 (ISBN 0-441-05392-0). Ace Books.

Bel of Prairie Eden. A Romance of Mexico. George Lippard. 1848. Hotchkiss & Co.

Bel Ria. Sheila Every Burnford. LC 77-21082. 8.95 (ISBN 0-316-77139-2). Little, Brown.

Bel Ria. Sheila Every Burnford. LC 78-23869. 1979. 11.50 (ISBN 0-8161-6657-9). G. K. Hall.

Bel Rubio: A Novel. Frederick Whittaker. (On cover: The popular series, no. 12). 1891. R. Bonner's Sons.

Bel-Tane. 1st Ed. Stella Price McElrath. LC 56-5822. 1956. Vantage Press.

Bela Lugosi's White Christmas. Paul West. LC 73-181666. 1972. 6.95 (ISBN 0-06-014556-0). Harper & Row.

Belanger: Ou L'Histoire D'un Crime. Georges Crepeau. (Novels by Franco-Americans in New England 1850-1940 Ser.). 49p. (Orig., Fr.). (gr. 10 up). 1979. pap. 4.50 (ISBN 0-911409-14-9). Natl Mat Dev.

Belardo: A Novel of Old Spain. Durward Grinstead. LC 32-578. 1931. Covici, Friede.

Belarmino & Apolonio. Ramon P. De Ayala. Tr. by Murray Baumgarten & Gabriel Berns. 1983. pap. 5.95 (ISBN 0-520-04958-6, CAL 626). U of Cal Pr.

Belarmino and Apolonio. Perez De Ayala, Ramon. LC 79-126759. 1971. 6.95 (ISBN 0-520-01786-2). University of California Press.

Belated Reckoning. Phyllis Bottome. LC 27-20471. George H. Doran Company.

Belchamber. Howard Overing Sturgis. LC 76-15624. 1976. 14.00. H. Fertig.

Belchamber. Howard Overing Sturgis. LC 75-41266. 1976. 18.00 (ISBN 0-404-14613-9). AMS Press.

Belchamber. Howard Overing Sturgis. LC 5-12165. 1905. G. P. Putnam's Sons.

Belchamber. Howard Overing Sturgis. LC 35-27289. (Half-title: The world's classics. 429). 1935. H. Milford, Oxford University Press.

Belda in Blunderland. Lena B Ellingwood. LC 33-2810. 1937. Falmouth Book House.

Beleaguered: A Story of the Uplands of Baden in the Seventeenth Century. Herman Theodore Koerner. LC 7-14200. 1898. G. P. Putnam's Sons.

Beleaguered City. Margaret Oliphant Wilson Oliphant. Repr. of 1913 ed. lib. bdg. 15.00x (ISBN 0-8371-3137-5, OLBC). Greenwood.

Beleaguered City: Being a Narrative of Certain Recent Events in the City of Semur, in the Department of the Haute Bourgogne, a Story of the Seen and the Unseen. Margaret Oliphant Wilson Oliphant. LC 79-98862. 1970. Greenwood Press.

Beleaguered City: Being a Narrative of Certain Recent Events in the City of Semur, in the Department of the Haute Bourgogne; a Story of the Seen and the Unseen. Margaret Oliphant Wilson Oliphant. LC 4-16569. 1900. Macmillan and Co., Limited.

Beleaguered Forest. Elia Wilkinson Peattie. LC 1-15260. 1901. D. Appleton and Company.

Belfast Connection. Gerard De Villiers. (Malko series#12). 1976. (pbk.) 1.25 (ISBN 0-523-00844-9). Pinnacle Books.

Belford Regis: Or, Sketches of a Country Town. Mary Russell Mitford. LC 72-4457. (Short story index reprint series). 1972. (3 vols.) 38.50 (ISBN 0-8369-4185-3). Books for Libraries Press.

Belford Regis; or, Sketches of a Country Town, 3 vols, Vol. 1. Mary Russell Mitford. LC 72-4457. (Short Story Index Reprint Ser). Repr. of 1835 ed. 55.00 (ISBN 0-8369-4185-3). Ayer Co.

Belfriere. Kathleen Gooding. (Berkley Medallion Book). 1978. 1.50 (ISBN 0-425-03618-9). Berkley Pub. Corp.

Belfry. May Sinclair. LC 23-26513. (modern library of the world's best books). 0.95. Boni and Liveright, Inc.

Belfry. May Sinclair. LC 16-2958. 1916. The Macmillan Company.

Belgian Days. Kate Byam Martin. LC 7-25980. 1882. Jansen, McClurg & Company.

Belgrave Square: A Novel of Society. Rachel Summerson. LC 81-14516. 11.95 (ISBN 0-312-07427-1). St. Martin's Press.

Belgravia. David Linzee. LC 79-4882. 9.95 (ISBN 0-87223-561-0). Seaview Books.

Belhaven Tales: Crow's Nest; Una and King David. Constance Cary Harrison. LC 7-3005. 1892. The Century Co.

Believe! Richard M. Devos. 1976. pap. 1.75 o.p. WSP.

Believe. Richard M. Devos & Charles P. Conn. 1983. pap. 2.95 (ISBN 0-425-05637-6). Berkley Pub.

Believe in Me. Jean Carew. 1973. pap. 0.75 o.s.i. (01-370). Lancer.

Believe Me True. Alice Lent Covert. LC 47-12125. 1947. Arcadia House.

Believe My Love. Laurene Chambers Chinn. LC 62-20045. 1962. Crown Publishers.

Believe the Heart. Raymond Peckham Holden. LC 39-31689. H. Holt and Company.

Believe You Me! Nina Wilcox Putnam. LC 19-152266. 1.50. George H. Doran Company.

Believers. Janice Holt Giles. 1976. 1.75 (ISBN 0-380-00666-9). Avon Books.

Believers. Janice Holt Giles. LC 56-13222. 1957. Houghton Mifflin.

Believers. Janice Holt Giles. LC 79-28052. 1980. 15.95 (ISBN 0-8161-3052-3). G. K. Hall.

Believing in Giants. Claire Vincent. (Signet Book). 1978. 2.25 (ISBN 0-451-08289-3). New American Library.

Belinda. Katherine Blake, pseud. LC 67-10449. 1966. Reynal.

Belinda. Rhoda Broughton. (On cover: Seaside library. Pocket ed., no. 86). 1883. G. Munro.

Belinda. Rhoda Broughton. (On cover; Lovell's library, v. 5, no. 230). 1883. J. W. Lovell Company.

Belinda. Maria Edgeworth. (Half-title: The novels of Maria Edgeworth, vol. I, II). 1893. J. M. Dent & Co.

Belinda--and Some Others. Ethel Maude. LC 98-1996. (Half-title: Appleton's town and country library, no. 254). 1898. D. Appleton and Company.

Belinda: A Novel. Rhoda Broughton. LC 78-108463. 1970. Scholarly Press.

Belinda: A Novel. Rhoda Broughton. LC 18-77789. (Macmillan's two shilling library. no. 13). 1899. Macmillan and Co., Limited.

Belinda: A Tale of Affection in Youth and Age. Hilaire Belloc. LC 29-9485. 1929. Harper & Brothers.

Belinda Blue. Esther Wood & Kalab, Theresa, Illus. LC 40-313563. Longmans, Green and Co.

Belinda Grove. Helen Ashton. LC 33-5181. 1933. Doubleday, Doran and Company, Inc.

Belinda of the Red Cross. Robert W Hamilton, pseud. LC 17-24969. Sully and Kleinteich.

Belinda, or, the Rivals. A. S. Holmes. (Found Bks.: No. 2). 122p. (Orig.). 1975. pap. 3.95 (ISBN 0-88784-333-6, Pub. by Hse Anansi Pr Canada). U of Toronto Pr.

Belinda, the Impatient. Katheryn Kimbrough, pseud. (Saga of the Phenwick Women Ser.: No. 40). 224p. 1982. pap. 2.50 (ISBN 0-445-04731-3). Popular Lib.

Belisarius. Jean Francois Marmontel. LC 74-28092. (Flowering of the Novel). 1975. 25.00 (ISBN 0-8240-1180-5). Garland Pub.

Belisarius. Jean Francois Marmontel. LC 36-351316. 1796. Printed by William Barrett, for Thomas & Andrews, Boston.

Belisarius: A Historical Romance... From the French. Genlis, Stephanie Gelicite Ducrest De Saint Aubin. LC 8-30417. 1810. P. H. Nicklin & Co.

Bell, a Novel. Iris Murdoch. LC 58-12380. 1958. Viking Press.

Bell, Book & Candleflame. Isabel S. Way. (Orig.). 1971. pap. 0.75 o.p. (94056). Beagle Bks.

Bell Branch Rings. D. Hayes. 88p. 1972. 3.95 o.s.i. (ISBN 0-87233-028-1). Bauhan.

Bell Call. Sylvia Ashton-Warner. LC 64-21188. 1965. bds., 5.00. S. & S.

Bell Cow a Story. Bryant Elihu Sherman. LC 9-6. 1908. The C. M. Clark Publishing Company.

Bell for Adano. John Richard Hersey. LC 44-164. 1944. A. A. Knopf.

Bell for Adano. John Richard Hersey. LC 46-4509. (Half-title: The Modern library of the world's best books). 1946. The Modern Library.

Bell for Adano. New Foreword by the Author. John Richard Hersey. (Keith Jennison large type ed.). 1966. 6.95. Watts.

Bell Foundry. Victor Martin Otto Denk. LC 7-21531. 1907. Benziger Brothers.

Bell in the Fog... Dorothy Stockbridge Tillet. LC 36-35053. 1936. Pub. for the Crime Club, Inc., by Doubleday, Doran & Co., Inc.

Bell in the Fog: And Other Stories. Gertrude Franklin Horn Atherton. LC 68-55661. (American short story series, v. 1). 1968. Garrett Press.

Bell in the Fog. and Other Stories. Gertrude Franklin Horn Atherton. 1905. Harper & Brothers.

Bell Jar. Sylvia Plath. LC 76-149743. (Illus.). 1971. 6.95 (ISBN 0-06-013356-2). Harper & Row.

Bell Maker of Campania: And Other Stories. 1st Ed. Frances Stickney Nott. LC 56-6823. 1956. Greenwich Book Publishers.

Bell Maker of Campania, and Other Stories. 1st Ed. Frances Stickney Nott. LC 56-6823. 1956. Greenwich Book Publishers.

Bell of St. Paul's. Walter Besant. (On cover: Seaside library. Pocket ed., no. 1240). 1889. G. Munro.

Bell of St Paul's. Walter Besant. LC 6-123965. (On cover: Harper's Franklin square library, no. 660). 1889. Harper & Brothers.

Bell of Time. Charles Angoff. 1966. 4.00 (ISBN 0-87141-018-4). Manyland.

Bell on Lonely. Margaret Page Hood. LC 59-14883. 1959. Coward-McCann.

Bell or a Hook. Peter Fortunato. 1977. pap. 3.50 (ISBN 0-87886-087-8, Pub. by Ithaca Hse). SBD.

Bell-Ringer: An Old-Time Village Tale. Clara Endicott Sears. LC 18-18397. 1918. 1.35. Houghton Mifflin Company.

Bell Ringer & Other Stories. Abelardo S. Albis. 103p. (Orig.). 1982. pap. 4.75 (Pub. by New Day Philippines). Cellar.

Bell-Ringer of Angel's: And Other Stories. Bret Harte. LC 7-2868. 1894. Houghton, Mifflin and Company.

Bell-Ringer of Angel's, Etc. Bret Harte. LC 72-12500. (Short story index reprint series). 1973. (ISBN 0-8369-4236-1). Books for Libraries Press.

Bell Street Murders. Sydney Fowler Wright. LC 31-134851. The Macaulay Company.

Bell Timson: A Novel. Marguerite Steen. LC 46-587056. 1946. Doubleday & Company, Inc.

Bell Tower of Wyndspelle. Aola Vandergriff. 1975. (pbk.) 1.50. Warner Books.

Bell Witch at Adams. Gladys Hutchison Barr. LC 76-109386. (Famous witches and ghosts series). 1969. 4.50. D. Hutchison Pub. Co.

Bella. William Black. (Orig.). 1979. pap. 2.50 (ISBN 0-89083-498-9). Zebra.

Bella. Edward Charles Booth. LC 12-21280. 1912. 1.30. D. Appleton and Company.

Bella. Jilly Cooper. LC 77-353511. 1976. 2.75 (ISBN 0-85140-254-2). Arlington Books.

Bella. Jean Giraudoux. Tr. by Scanlan, J. F. LC 27-11716. 1927. A. A. Knopf.

Bella, Bella Kissed a Fella. Arthur Kober. LC 51-13316. 1951. Random House.

Bella-Demonia: A Dramatic Story by Selina Dolaro... Selina Stage Name Of Mme. Isaac Delaro Belasoo Dolaro. LC 11-10548. Belford, Clarke & Company; Etc., Etc.

Bella Donna: A Novel. 5th ed. Robert Smythe Hichens. LC 17-269923. 1909. A. L. Burt Company.

Bella Donna: A Novel. Robert Smythe Hichens. LC 9-28245. 1909. J. B. Lippincott Company.

Bella Figura. Trina Mascott. LC 76-28045. 8.95. St. Martin's Press.

Bella North: A Novel. Diana Julia Marr-Johnson. LC 55-769135. 1955. St. Martin's Press.

Bella: Or, The Cradle of Liberty. Martha Eugenia Berry. 1874. N. D. Berry.

Bellah: A Tale of Brittany. Octave Feuillet & Sherwood, Mrs. Mary (Neal) Tr. T. B. Peterson & Brothers.

Bellamy. Elinor Mordaunt, pseud. LC 14-16948. 1914. 1.35. John Lane Company.

Bellamy Case. James Hay. LC 25-756. 1925. Dodd, Mead and Company.

Bellamy Saga. john pearson. ed. John Pearson. 1.95 (ISBN 0-380-00813-0). Avon.

Bellamy Saga: A Novel. John Pearson. LC 75-36862. 1976. 8.95 (ISBN 0-275-22940-8). Praeger Publishers.

Bellamy Trial. Frances Noyes Hart. LC 28-183. 1927. Doubleday, Page & Company.

Bellamy Trial. Frances Noyes Hart. LC 29-25268. 1928. Doubleday, Doran & Company, Inc.

Bellamy Trial. Frances Noyes Hart. LC 40-14077. 1940. Triangle Books.

Bellamy Trial... Frances Noyes Hart. LC 46-17221. 1945.

Bell'Antonio. Vitaliano Brancati. LC 77-6960. 10.00. (ISBN 0-8044-2069-6) (ISBN 0-8044-6058-2). F. Ungar Pub. Co.

Bellarion the Fortunate: A Romance. Rafael Sabatini. LC 26-15182. 1926. Houghton Mifflin Company.

Bellary Bay. John Welcome, pseud. LC 79-51523. 1979. 10.95 (ISBN 0-689-11013-8). Atheneum.

Bella's Blessings. William Black. (Orig.). 1980. pap. 2.50 (ISBN 0-89083-562-4). Zebra.

Bellbird Eleven: Life in the Woods. Derek Robert. LC 66-46524. 1965. H. Hamilton.

Bellcroft Priory. W. Bourne Cooke. LC 11-5482. 1911. 1.50. John Lane.

Belle. Michael Stewart. LC 76-54312. 8.95 (ISBN 0-02-614670-3). Macmillan.

Belle Claudine. Patricia Muse. 1973. pap. 0.75 o.s.i. (01-369). Lancer.

Belle De Jour. Translated from the French by Geoffrey Wagner. Joseph Kessel. LC 62-111051. 1962. St. Martin's Press.

Belle Epoque. Raymond Rudorff. 1973. 10.00 o.p. (ISBN 0-8415-0225-0). Sat Rev Pr.

Belle Esperance. John Murray. LC 42-22691. 1942. The Ave Maria Press.

Belle from Catscratch. Richard Meade & Jay Rutledge. (Orig.). 1972. pap. 0.95 o.p. (M2605, GM). Fawcett World.

Belle Glen. Karen Kimpel-Johns. 1979. 1.95 (ISBN 0-515-04803-8). Jove /HBJ.

Belle Islers: A Novel. Franklin Kent Gifford. 1908. Lothrop, Lee & Shepard Co.

Belle Jones: A Story of Fulfilment. Allen Meacham. LC 16-21971. 0.50. E. P. Dutton & Company.

Belle-Mere. Kathleen Thompson Norris. LC 31-28035. Doubleday, Doran & Company, Inc.

Belle-Nivernaise. Ed. by George E. Wisewell. (gr. 9-10). 1938. pap. text ed. 2.04 o.p. (26963). Heath.

Belle O' Becket's Lane. An American Novel. John Beatty. LC 6-10264. 1883. J. B. Lippincott & Co.

Belle of Australia: Or, Who Am I? William Henry Thomes. LC 8-20098. 1883. De Wolfe, Fiske & Company.

Belle of Australia: Or, Who Am I? By William H. Thomes... William Henry Thomes. (On cover: The library of choice fiction, no. 33). 1891. Laird & Lee.

Belle of Bath. Lillian Shelley. LC 80-70557. 1981. 10.95 (ISBN 0-385-17585-X). Doubleday.

Belle of Bowling Green. Amelia Edith Huddleston Barr. LC 4-27350. 1904. Dodd, Mead & Company.

Belle of Brighton, No. 157. Georgina Grey, pseud. 224p. 1981. pap. 1.50 (ISBN 0-449-50230-9, Crest). Fawcett.

Belle of Fort Smith. Lee D. Willougby, pseud. (Women Who Won the West Ser.: No. 7). 288p. 1982. pap. 3.25 (ISBN 0-440-00575-2, Bryans). Dell.

Belle of Loveland River. Carrie Olivia Chesley Davis. LC 28-23872. The Grafton Press.

Belle of Lynn. Charlotte Mary Brame. (On cover: Lovell's library. v. 20 no. 986). J. W. Lovell Company.

Belle of Lynn: Or, The Miller's Daughter. Charlotte Mary Brame. (On cover: Seaside library. Pocket ed. no. 929). G. Munro.

Belle of Lynn: Or, The Miller's Daughter. Charlotte Mary Brame. LC 1-29652. (Bertha Clay library, no. 44: No. 44). 1900. Street & Smith.

Belle of Saratoga: Or, The Heart of the St. Severns. Lucy Randall Comfort. (On cover: The library of American authors. no. 25). 1890. G. Munro.

Belle of the Bluegrass Country. Studies in Black and White. Hannah Daviess Pittman. LC 6-28756. 1906. The C. M. Clark Publishing Co.

Belle of the Island City: Or, The Wreck of the Southern Star. A Romance of Galveston. Win C Livingstone. (On cover: New York 10 cent library, no. 6). 1896. Katahdin Publishing Company.

Belle of the Season: Or, The False Heir. Harriet Lewis. (On cover: Primrose edition no. 2). 1890. Street & Smith.

Belle of Washington. A True Story of the Affections. Nancy Polk Lasselle. LC 26-7514. 1858. T. B. Peterson and Brothers.

Belle of Wyandotte. James B Goode. (On cover: Goode's monthly stories. no. 2). 1894. The Kansas City Novel Publishing Co.

Belle-Plante and Cornelius. Claude Tillier & Tucker, Benjamin Ricketson, 1854- Tr. LC 8-27027. The Merriam Company.

Belle Rose: A Romance of the Cloak and Sword. Louis Amedee Eugene Archard & Hale, William, Tr. Howard, Ainslee & Co.

Belle-Rose. A Romance of the Cloak and Sword. Tr. by William Hale. Hale, William, Tr. LC 5-426003. (On cover: Paris series, no. 9). Street & Smith.

Belle Scott: Or, Liberty Overthrown! A Tale for the Crisis. John Jolliffe. LC 70-138332. (Black Heritage Library Collection). 1971. (ISBN 0-8369-8724-1). Books for Libraries Press.

Belle Scott: Or, Liberty Overthrown! A Tale for the Crisis... John Jolliffe. LC 7-11929. 1856. D. Anderson.

Belle Starr: A Novel. Speer Morgan. LC 78-10278. (Illus.). (ISBN 0-316-58296-4). Little, Brown.

Belle. Translated from the French by Louise Varese. Georges Simenon. LC 55-283055. (Signet books, 1124). 1954. New American Library.

Bellechasse: A Novella of French Canada. Stacey B. Day. LC 75-108343. (Orig.). 1970. pap. 1.95 o.s.i. (ISBN 0-87640-073-X, 1970A). Cultural Educ.

Bellefleur. Joyce Carol Oates. 1980. 13.95 (ISBN 0-525-06302-1, Henry Robbins Book). Dutton.

Bellefleur. Joyce Carol Oates. 688p. 1981. pap. 4.50 (ISBN 0-446-30732-7). Warner Bks.

Bellehelen Mine. Bertha Muzzy Sinclair. LC 24-19019. 1924. Little, Brown, and Company.

Bellehood and Bondage. Ann Sophia Winterbotham Stephens. LC 12-15061. T. B. Peterson & Brothers.

Bellemeade. Joanna Warren. (Conrad Chronicles Ser.: No. 1). (Orig.). 1978. pap. 2.50 (ISBN 0-89083-414-8). Zebra.

Bellerose Bargain. Robyn Carr. LC 82-145. 13.95 (ISBN 0-316-12973-9). Little, Brown.

Bellerue: Or, The Story of Rolf. Julia Louise Matilda Woodruff. LC 8-37537. 1891. E. P. Dutton & Company.

Belle's Castle. George Charles Appell. LC 59-10293. 1959. Macmillan.

Belles Images. Simone De Beauvoir, pseud. 1968. 4.95 o.p. (ISBN 0-399-10492-5). Putnam.

Belleview: A Story of the South from 1860 to 1865. John E Davis. LC 6-32867. J. B. Alden.

Belligerent Miss Boynton. Kasey Michaels. 224p. (Orig.). 1982. pap. 2.50 (ISBN 0-380-77073-3, 77073). Avon.

Belligerent Peter. David De Forest Burrell. (Green fund book, no. 24a). American Sunday-School Union.

Bellini Look. Carol Ryrie Brink. 1976. (pbk.) 1.25. Bantam Books.
Bellman and True. Desmond Lowden. LC 74-15490. 1975. 6.95 (ISBN 0-03-013756-X). Holt, Rinehart and Winston.
Bellman Book of Fiction... The Bellman. Ed. by Edgar, William Crowell. LC 21-21203. The Bellman Company.
Bellmeade: The Dreamers, No. 2. Joanna Warren. (Orig.). 1980. pap. 2.50 (ISBN 0-89083-586-1). Zebra.
Bellow's Herzog: Adventures of Augie March, and Other Works. Eugenie Harris. LC 66-27261. (Monarch notes & study gds., 810-2). pap., 1.00. Monarch Pr.
Bellringer. Lawrence Kamarck. LC 72-85631. 1969. 4.50. Random House.
Bells and Echoes from the White Temple. Walter Benwell Hinson. LC 14-12433. Printed by Brockmann Brothers.
Bells Are Ringing. Capwell Wyckoff. LC 51-31. 1950. Zondervan.
Bells Beneath the Sea. Willetta Balla. LC 78-59068. 1978. pap. 1.95 o.s.i. (ISBN 0-89559-068-9). Dale Books Inc.
Bells for the Dead: A Mystery Story. Kathleen Moore Knight. LC 42-25579. 1942. Published for the Crime Club by Doubleday, Doran and Co., Inc.
Bell's Landing. Gerald Warner Brace. 1955. 5.00 o.p. (ISBN 0-393-08432-9). Norton.
Bell's Landing: A Novel. Gerald Warner Brace. LC 55-14720. 1955. Norton.
Bells of Basel. Louis Aragon & Chevalier, Haakon M., Tr. LC 36-21002. Harcourt, Brace and Company.
Bells of Bicetre. Georges Simenon. LC 64-14642. 1964. Harcourt, Brace & World.
Bells of Helmus. Cobie De Lespinasse. LC 34-406701. 1934. The Metropolitan Press.
Bells of Love: By Norma Newcomb Pseud. William Arthur Neubauer. LC 53-13065. 1953. Arcadia House.
Bells of Old Bailey. Dorothy Bowers. LC 47-11835. 1947. Pub. for the Crime Club by Doubleday.
Bells of Rome. Goran Erik Stenius. LC 61-6857. 1961. P. J. Kenedy.
Bells of Saint Ivan's. Robert Spencer Carr. LC 44-4110. 1944. D. Appleton-Century Company, Incorporated.
Bells of St. John's. Grace Louise Smith Richmond. LC 21-1671. 1920. Doubleday, Page & Company.
Bells of St. Mary's. George Victor Martin & Dudley Nichols. LC 46-4245. (Grosset & Dunlap film classics library). 1946. Grosset & Dunlap.
Bells of Saint Mary's. Alice Lee Sharon. LC 31-19682. The John C. Winston Co.
Bells of St. Stephen's. Mary Esther MacGregor. LC 22-23904. George H. Doran Company.
Bells of San Filipo. Frederick Faust. (Kangaroo Book). 1977. 1.50 (ISBN 0-671-81236-X). Pocket Books.
Bells of San Juan. Jackson Gregory. LC 19-155613. 1919. C. Scribner's Sons.
Bells of Shoreditch. 1st American Ed. Kennaway, James. LC 64-11164. 1964. Atheneum.
Bells of the Blue Pagoda: The Strange Enchantment of a Chinese Doctor. Jean Carter Cochran. LC 22-13960. 1922. The Westminster Press.
Belltower. Kathleen A Shoesmith. (Ace gothic). 1974. (pbk.) 0.95. Ace Books.
Bellwood. Elisabeth Ogilvie. LC 69-12263. 1969. McGraw-Hill.
Belly Fulla Straw. David Cornel De Jong. LC 34-5409. 1934. A. A. Knopf.
Belmarch: A Legend of the First Crusade. Christopher Davis. LC 64-11224. 1964. Viking Press.
Belonging: A Nostalgic Look at Appalachia. Illus. by Emily Touraine. Martha Groves McKelvie. LC 65-262642. 1965. 3.95. Franklin Pub. Co.
Belonging: A Novel. Olive Wadsley. LC 20-8360. 1920. Cassell and Company, Ltd.
Belonging: A Novel. Olive Wadsley. LC 20-15700. 1920. Dodd, Mead and Company.
Beloved. P. C. Kuttykrishnan. Tr. by R. R. Menon from Malayalam. 194p. 1975. pap. 2.80 (ISBN 0-88253-696-6). Ind-US Inc.
Beloved. James Oppenheim. LC 15-9202. 1915. 1.25. B. W. Huebsch.
Beloved. Bertrice Small. 560p. (Orig.). 1983. pap. 6.95 (ISBN 0-345-29356-8). Ballantine.
Beloved Acres. John H Hamlin. LC 25-168185. The Century Co.
Beloved Ballerina. Roberta Leigh. (Presents Ser.). 1974. pap. 1.25 (ISBN 0-373-70564-6, 70564, Pub by Harlequin). PB.
Beloved Bondage. Elizabeth Yates. LC 48-8756. 1948. Coward-McCann.
Beloved Brat. James Noble Gifford. LC 46-1778. Arcadia House.
Beloved Brat. Warren Howard. LC 46-1778. 1946. Arcadia House, Inc.
Beloved Brute. Kenneth Perkins. LC 23-61448. The Macaulay Company.
Beloved Buff. Louise Platt Hauck. LC 40-7241. The Penn Publishing Company.
Beloved Captive. Florent D'Asherville. (Orig.). 1969. pap. 1.75 o.s.i. (OPH129, Ophelia). Olympia.
Beloved Captive. Catherine Dillon. (Signet Book). 2.25 (ISBN 0-451-08921-9). New American Library.
Beloved Diana. Alice Chetwynd Ley. LC 77-6144. 1977. 1.75 (ISBN 0-345-25612-3). Ballantine Books.
Beloved Enemy. Barbara Corcoran. 160p. (Orig.). 1981. pap. 1.95 (ISBN 0-345-28667-7). Ballantine.
Beloved Enemy. Amanda York, pseud. (Kangaroo Book). 1978. 1.95 (ISBN 0-671-81961-5). Pocket Books.
Beloved Exiles. Agnes Newton Keith. LC 72-175483. 1972. 7.95. Little, Brown.
Beloved Gypsy. Vera Murdock Stuart Jervis. LC 45-825. 1945. Arcadia House, Inc.
Beloved Intruder. Jocelyn Griffin. 1981. pap. 2.50 (ISBN 0-373-70008-3). Harlequin Bks.
Beloved Invader. Eugenia Price. (V2165). 1967. Avon.
Beloved Invader. Eugenia Price. LC 72-11644. 1973. 10.95 (ISBN 0-8161-6062-7). G. K. Hall.
Beloved Invader: A Novel. Eugenia Price. LC 65-20589. 1965. Lippincott.
Beloved Island: A Cuban Family's Fight for Freedom. Alida Sims Malkus. LC 67-21073. 1967. Chilton Book Co.
Beloved Jew. Donald Oscar Burling. LC 47-1157. 1946.
Beloved Lady. Barbara Jefferis. LC 55-9618. 1955. W. Sloane Associates.
Beloved! O Mon Goye. Drake, William A., 1899- Tr. LC 30-281779. 1930. Simon and Schuster.
Beloved Pawn. Harold Titue. LC 23-16043. 1923. Doubleday, Page & Company.
Beloved Pirate. Margie Michaels. LC 82-7387. (Second Chance at Love.). 1982. 11.95 (ISBN 0-89340-519-1). John Curley & Associates.
Beloved Prodigal: A Wheatland Romance. James French Dorrance. LC 29-11646. The Macaulay Company.
Beloved Rajah. A. Elsie Rundall Craig. LC 26-16336. 1926. Minton, Balch & Company.
Beloved Rake. Anne Hampson. (Presents Ser.). 1974. pap. 1.25 (ISBN 0-373-70559-X, 70559, Pub by Harlequin). PB.
Beloved Rebel. Chet Cunningham. 1978. 1.95 (ISBN 0-8439-0550-6). Nordon Pubns.
Beloved Rebel. Sylvia Thorpe. 1978. pap. 1.75 (ISBN 0-449-23607-2, Crest). Fawcett.
Beloved Returns. Lotte in Weimar, Translated from the German. Thomas Mann. Tr. by Helen Tracy Lowe. LC 40-27614. 1940. A. A. Knopf.
Beloved Scoundrel. Clarissa Ross, pseud. 1980. pap. 1.95 o.s.i. (ISBN 0-8439-0710-X, Leisure Bks). Nordon Pubns.
Beloved Sinner. Rachel Swete Macnamara. LC 19-4516. 1919. G. P. Putnam's Sons.
Beloved Sinner. Jessica Stirling. (Dell Book). 1978. 1.95 (ISBN 0-440-12116-7). Dell Pub. Co.
Beloved Son. Fanny Kemble Johnson. LC 16-19415. 1.35. Small, Maynard & Company.
Beloved Son. Cecil Maiden. LC 61-15929. 1961. Dodd, Mead.
Beloved Stranger. Jane Blackmore. 1973. (pbk) 0.95. Dell.
Beloved Stranger. Grace Livingston Hill. LC 33-29342. J. B. Lippincott Company.
Beloved Stranger. Grace Livingston Hill. 1976. (pbk.) 1.25. Bantam Books.
Beloved Stranger. Michelle Roland. (Second Chance at Love Ser.: No. 102). Date not set. pap. 1.75 (ISBN 0-515-06866-7). Jove Pubns.
Beloved Stranger. Dorothy Worley. LC 57-8737. 1957. Avalon Books.
Beloved Stranger: The Story of Carl and Anna. Leonhard Frank & Brooks, Cyrus Harry, 1890- Tr. LC 46-6984. 1946. L. B. Fischer.
Beloved Tales. Ed. by Byrna Ivens Untermeyer. (Golden treasury of childrens literature, v. 2). 1962. Golden Press.
Beloved Traitor. easy eye ed. Evelyn Bond, pseud. pap. 0.60 o.p. (ISBN 0-447-73673-6). Lancer.
Beloved Traitor. Frank Lucius Packard. LC 16-10838. 1915. George H. Doran Company.
Beloved Vagabond. Anne Hampson. (Harlequin Presents Ser.). 192p. 1981. pap. 1.75 (ISBN 0-373-10470-7). Harlequin Bks.
Beloved Vagabond. William John Locke. LC 6-37606. 1906. J. Lane Company; Etc., Etc.
Beloved Vagabond. William John Locke. 1907. J. Lane Company; Etc., Etc.
Beloved Vagabond. William John Locke. LC 9-8815. 1908. J. Lane Company; Etc., Etc.
Beloved Vagabond. William John Locke. 1928. A. L. Burt Company.
Beloved Was Bahamas: A Steer to Remember. Harriett E Weaver. LC 74-76442. (Illus.). 1974. 5.95 (ISBN 0-8149-0740-7). Vanguard Press.
Beloved Woman. Nancy Bruff, pseud. 1949. J. Messner.
Beloved Woman. Nancy Bruff Gardner. LC 49-8427. 1949. J. Messner.
Beloved Woman. Kathleen Thompson Norris. LC 21-155095. 1921. Doubleday, Page & Company.
Beloved Woman. Kathleen Thompson Norris. LC 34-37792. 1924. A. L. Burt Company.
Beloved. 1st Ed. Vina Delmar. LC 56-5336. Harcourt, Brace.
Below Grass Roots. Frank Waters. LC 38-528276. Liveright Publishing Corporation.
Below Houston Street. Kent Cooper. 1979. pap. 1.50 (ISBN 0-532-15365-0). Woodhill.
Below Stairs. Margaret Powell. LC 77-108042. 1970. 5.95 o.p. (ISBN 0-396-06076-5). Dodd.
Below Suspicion. John Dickson Carr. (O.s.i.). 1976. pap. 1.50 o.s.i. (Award). Univ Pub & Dist.
Below Suspicion: A Detective Novel. John Dickson Carr. LC 49-10186. 1949. Harper.
Below the Belt & Other Stories by Phil Andros. Phil Andros. LC 82-3141. 140p. (Orig.). 1982. pap. 6.50 (ISBN 0-912516-75-5). Grey Fox.
Below the Clock. John Victor Turner. LC 36-17323. (Tired business man's library of adventure, detective and mystery novels). 1936. D. Appleton-Century Company, Incorporated.
Below the Dead-Line. Frederick William Davis. LC 6-7721. 1906. G. W. Dillingham Company.
Below the Horizon. John Wingate. LC 74-21096. (Illus.). 1975. 7.95. St. Martin's Press.
Below the James: A Plantation Sketch. William Cabell Bruce. LC 18-216833. 1918. The Neale Publishing Company.
Below the James: A Plantation Sketch. William Cabell Bruce. LC 41-30724. 1927. Houghton Mifflin Company.
Below the Rio Grande. Roy Norton. LC 33-33460. E. J. Clode, Inc.
Below the Sahara. Ed. by Everett Franklin Bleiler. (Frank Reade Library: Vol. 9). 1980. lib. bdg. 44.00 (ISBN 0-8240-3547-X). Garland Pub.
Below the Salt. Thomas Bertram Costain. 1974. (pbk.) 1.50. Avon.
Below the Salt, a Novel. 1st Ed. Thomas Bertram Costain. LC 56-10757. 1957. Doubleday.
Below the Summit. Joseph V. Torres-Metzgar. LC 76-41036. 1976. pap. 5.00 (ISBN 0-89229-005-6). Tonatiuh-Quinto Sol Intl.
Below Third Street. Sigurd Jay Simonsen. LC 51-14. 1950. Vantage Press.
Below Zero: A Romance of the North Woods. Harold Titus. LC 32-7612. Macrae Smith Company.
Belshazzar. Henry Rider Haggard. LC 30-336106. 1930. Doubleday, Doran & Company, Inc.
Belshazzar: A Cat's Story for Humans. Chaim I. Bermant. 64p. 1982. pap. 2.95 (ISBN 0-380-58560-X, 58560, Bard). Avon.
Belshazzar: A Tale of the Fall of Babylon. William Stearns Davis. LC 26-26511. 1926. Th Macmillan Company.
Belshazzar: Prince of Babylon (a novel in four parts) Florence H. Anastassas. (Illus.). 304p. 1982. 15.00 (ISBN 0-682-49818-1, University). Exposition.
Belshazzar's Feast. Peter Way. LC 81-69150. 1982. 10.95 (ISBN 0-689-11261-0). Atheneum.
Beltane the Smith. Jeffery Farnol. LC 15-24858. 1915. 1.50. Little, Brown, and Company.
Beltane the Smith. Jeffery Farnol. LC 26-75123. 1924. Little, Brown, and Company.
Beltane the Smith: A Romance of the Greenwood. Jeffery Farnol. LC 35-285738. 1918. A. L. Burt Company.
Belted Seas. Arthur Willis Colton. LC 5-9062. 1905. H. Holt and Company.
Belteshazzar: A Romance of Babylon. Edward Reynolds Roe. LC 7-40247. 1890. Donohue, Henneberry & Co.
Belting Inheritance. Julian Symons. LC 65-14670. 3.95. Harper.
Belton Estate. Anthony Trollope. (Half-title: The world's classics. ccxi). 1923. H. Milford, Oxford University Press.
Belton Estate. A Novel. Anthony Trollope. LC 8-28904. 1866. Harper & Brothers.
Belvedare. Steve Welp. 18p. 1978. pap. 2.25 o.p. Hse of One Pub.
Belvedere. George Crenshaw. 256p. (Orig.). 1982. pap. 2.50 (ISBN 0-523-49004-6). Pinnacle Bks.
Belvedere. Ronald Pearsall. LC 77-352364. 3.50 (ISBN 0-297-77064-0). Weidenfeld and Nicolson.
Belvedere. Lawrence Perry Spingarn. (Illus.). 16p. 1982. pap. 15.00x (ISBN 0-930126-11-4). Typographeum.
Belvedere, No. 2. George Crenshaw. 256p. (Orig.). 1982. pap. 2.50 (ISBN 0-523-49020-8). Pinnacle Bks.
Belvedere: A Novel. Gwen Davenport. LC 47-3923. 1947. The Bobbs-Merrill Company.
Belvedere III. George Crenshaw. 256p. 1983. pap. 2.50 (ISBN 0-523-49027-5). Pinnacle Bks.
Bembo: A Tale of Italy. Bernard Edward Joseph Capes. LC 6-18582. 1906. E.P. Dutton & Company.
Ben. Gilbert A. Ralston. LC 72-3735. 1972. 0.75. Bantam Books.
Ben Abbott: A Temperance Story. Fanny Long. 1896. Curts & Jennings.
Ben-Beor: A Story of the Anti-Messiah, in Two Divisions. Pt. 1 Lumar Intaglios. The Man in the Moon, a Counterpart of Wallace's "Ben-Hur." Pt. 2. Historical Phantasmagoria. The Wandering Gentile, a Campanion Romance to Sue's "Wandering Jew". Herman M Bien. 1891. I. Friedenwald Co.
Ben Blair: The Story of a Plainsman. William Otis Lillibridge. LC 5-33981. 1905. A. C. McClurg & Co.
Ben Blunt: His Life and Story, Greatly Abridged and Truly Told with Much Thrilling and Ingenious Comment Thereon; an Historical Romance. Thomas Speed Mosby. LC 3-31938. 1903. Press of Commercial Printing Co.
Ben Brace: The Last of Nelson's Agamemnons. Frederick Chamier. LC 6-20161. 1836. Carey, Lea & Blanchard.
Ben Bryan: Morgan Rifleman. John Brick. LC 63-7415. 1963. Duell, Sloan and Pearce.
Ben Clough: a Lancashire Story. William Westall. LC 8-36231. J. W. Lovell Company.
Ben Comee: A Tale of Roger's Rangers, 1758-59. Michael Joseph Canavan. 1899. The Macmillan Company.
Ben Ezra: Or, The Midnight Cry. William L Beaumont. LC 30-32328. The Stratford Company.
Ben Green Tales, 4 vols. Ben K. Green. LC 73-85179. (Illus.). 272p. 1974. Set. deluxe ed. 50.00x o.p. (ISBN 0-87358-115-6). Northland.
Ben Hamed: Or, The Children of Fate. A Story of the Eastern World. Sylvanus Cobb. (On cover: Sea and shore series, no. 8). 1889. Street & Smith.
Ben-Hur. Lewis Wallace & Robin S Wright. LC 74-186807. (Illus.). 1972. 7.95 (ISBN 0-8212-0472-6). New York Graphic Society.
Ben-Hur: A Tale of the Christ. Lewis Wallace. LC 59-15325. 1959. Harper.
Ben-Hur: A Tale of the Christ. Lewis Wallace. LC 49-495450. (World's greatest literature). 1949. Fountain Press.
Ben-Hur: A Tale of the Christ. Lewis Wallace. LC 40-1457. Harper & Brothers.
Ben-Hur: A Tale of the Christ. the player's ed. Lewis Wallace. LC 1-31390. 1901. Harper & Brothers.
Ben-Hur: A Tale of the Christ. Lewis Wallace. LC 8-27803. Harper & Brothers.
Ben-Hur: A Tale of the Christ. Lewis Wallace. LC 42-26586. Grosset & Dunlap.
Ben-Hur: A Tale of the Christ. Lewis Wallace. LC 24-26089. Harper & Brothers.
Ben Hur: A Tale of the Christ. Lewis Wallace. LC 33-27476. (Half-title: The modern library of the world's best books. no. 139). 1933. The Modern Library.
Ben-Hur: A Tale of the Christ. Lewis Wallace. (Dolphin bk. C 175). 1961. Doubleday.
Ben-Hur: A Tale of the Christ. Lewis Wallace & Bessey, Mabel Abbot, 1884- Ed. LC 30-16248. (Harper's modern classics). Harper & Brothers.
Ben-Hur: A Tale of the Christ. the garfield ed.... ed. Lewis Wallace & Johnson, William Martin, 1862- Illus. 1892. Harper & Brothers.
Ben-Hur: A Tale of the Christ. Lewis Wallace & Johnson, William Martin, 1862- Illus. LC 99-5559. 1899. Harper & Brothers.
Ben-Hur: A Tale of the Christ. Abridged Ed. by I. O. Evans. Illus. by Gordon Nicoll. Lewis Wallace. LC 59-8059. 1959. F. Warne.
Ben-Hur, a Tale of the Christ. With an Introd. by Ben Ray Redman and Illus. by Joe Mugnaini. Lewis Wallace. LC 60-4241. 1960. Limited Editions Club.
Ben-Hur: Adapted by Glenn Holder. Lewis Wallace & Glenn Holder. LC 54-2764. 1954. Globe Book Co.
Ben-Hur: Eine Geschichte Aus der Zeit Des Herrn Jesu. Lewis Wallace & S., H. M., Tr. 1895. Harper & Brothers.
Ben-Hur: Istoriska Apysaka Is Jezaus Kristaus Laiku, Sulietuviro Jonas Montuila. Lewis Wallace & Montvila, Jonas, Tr. LC 42-26986. 1912. Turtu Ir Spauda "Kataliko,
Ben Juda: The Shepherd. William Schmidt. Tr. by Nesper, Paul W. LC 26-19345. The Book Concern.
Ben Nelson. Ted Linder. LC 81-7190. 1981. pap. 5.75 (ISBN 0-8309-0321-6). Herald Hse.
Ben Preserve Us. Chaim I. Bermant. (Illus.). 1966. 3.95 o.p. (ISBN 0-03-060185-1). HR&W.
Ben Preserve Us: By Chaim Bermant. 1st Ed. Chaim I Bermant. LC 66-21629. 1966. 3.95. Holt.
Ben Retallick. Ernest Victor Thompson. LC 80-27563. (Illus.). 1981. 19.95 (ISBN 0-312-07517-0). St. Martin's Press.

Ben Sees It Through. Joseph Jefferson Farjeon. LC 33-4504. 1933. L. MacVeagh, Dial Press, Inc.
Ben Slayton, T-Man, No. 1: A Clear & Present Danger. Buck Sanders. (Men of Action Ser.). 160p. (Orig.). 1981. pap. 1.95 (ISBN 0-446-30020-9). Warner Bks.
Ben Slayton, T-Man, No. 2: Star of Egypt. Buck Sanders. (Men of Action Ser.). 160p. (Orig.). 1981. pap. 1.95 (ISBN 0-446-30017-9). Warner Bks.
Ben Slayton, T-Man, No. 3: Trail of the Twisted Cross. Buck Sanders. (Men of Acton Ser.). 160p. (Orig.). 1982. pap. 1.95 (ISBN 0-446-30131-0). Warner Bks.
Ben Slayton, T-Man, No. 5: Bayou Brigade. Buck Sanders. (Men of Action Ser.). 176p. (Orig.). 1982. pap. 1.95 (ISBN 0-446-30200-7). Warner Bks.
Ben Stone at Oakdale. Morgan Scott. LC 11-36274. 0.60. Hurst & Company.
Ben Thorpe. Arthur Crabb. LC 21-15717. 1921. 2.00. The Century Co.
Ben Warman. Charles Edwin Winter. LC 26-75273. 1917. Printed by J. J. Little & Ives Company.
Benbow and Paradise. Francois Camoin. LC 75-14190. 1975. 8.95 (ISBN 0-525-06315-3). Dutton.
Bend in the Ganges. Manohar Malgonkar. 1975. (ISBN 0-88253-772-5). Orient Paperbacks.
Bend in the Ganges: A Novel. Manohar Malgonkar. bds., 5.95. Viking.
Bend in the River. Vidiadhar Surajprasad Naipaul. LC 78-21591. 1979. 10.00 (ISBN 0-394-50573-5). Knopf; Distributed by Random House.
Bend in the River. Vidiadhar Surajprasad Naipaul. LC 79-22317. 1980. 2.95 (ISBN 0-394-74314-8). Vintage Books.
Bend in the River. William Arthur Neubauer. LC 65-7581. 1965. Arcadia House.
Bend in the River... By Jan Valtin Pseud.... Richard Julius Herman Krebs. LC 42-8735. 1942. Alliance Book Corporation.
Bend in the Road. Margaret Thomsen Raymond. LC 34-27257. 1934. Longmans, Green and Co.
Bend of the Snake. Grover C Gulick. LC 50-8818. 1950. Houghton Mifflin.
Bend Sinister. Vladimir Vladimirovich Nabokov. LC 73-5990. 1973. 7.95 (ISBN 0-07-045738-7). McGraw-Hill.
Bend Sinister. Vladimir Vladimirovich Nabokov. LC 47-353432. 1947. H. Holt and Company.
Bend, the Lip, the Kid: Real Life Stories. Jaimy Gordon. LC 78-15579. 1978. pap. 4.00 (ISBN 0-915342-25-1). SUN.
Bend with the Wind. Elisabeth Sims Moore. LC 78-31664. 1979. 9.95 (ISBN 0-87949-142-6). Ashley Books.
Bend Your Heads All. Rowena Farrar. 1965. 5.95 o.p. (ISBN 0-03-053580-8). HR&W.
Bend Your Heads All: A Novel. Rowena Rutherford Farrar. LC 65-22452. 1965. Holt, Rinehart and Winston.
Bender. Paul Scott. LC 63-17692. 1963. Morrow.
Bendigo Shafter. Louis L'Amour. LC 80-21836. 1980. 15.95 (ISBN 0-8161-3144-9). G. K. Hall.
Bending of the Twig. Walter Bowman Russell. LC 3-27966. 1903. Dodd, Mead & Company.
Bending Reed. Elizabeth Dawson, pseud. (Harlequin Romances Ser.). (Orig.). 1980. pap. 1.25 (ISBN 0-373-02306-5, Pub. by Harlequin). PB.
Bending Sickle. Gerald William Bullett. LC 38-9509. 1938. A. A. Knopf.
Bending Sickle. Cicely Farmer. LC 31-216213. 1931. W. Morrow & Co.
Bendish: A Study in Prodigality. Maurice Henry Hewlett. LC 13-203448. 1913. C. Scribner's Sons.
Beneath a Spell. Effie Adelaide Maria Albanesi. LC 1-29114. (On Cover: Eagle Series. No. 186). 1900. Street & Smith.
Beneath an Opal Moon. Eric Van Lustbader. LC 79-7215. 1980. 9.95 (ISBN 0-385-14892-5). Doubleday.
Beneath an Opal Moon. Eric Van Lustbader. 1982. pap. 2.50 (ISBN 0-425-05080-7). Berkley Pub.
Beneath an Opal Moon. Eric Van Lustbader. (Double D Science Fiction Ser.). 1980. 10.95 (ISBN 0-385-14892-5). Doubleday.
Beneath Another Sun. Ernst Lothar & Mussey, June Barrows, 1910- Tr. LC 43-51017. 1943. Doubleday, Doran & Co., Inc.
Beneath Balmy Skies. Charles Smithline. LC 32-34282. 1932. Meador Publishing Company.
Beneath Shattered Moons. Bishop, Michael. 1977. 1.50 (ISBN 0-87997-305-6). DAW Books.
Beneath That Armor. Elizabeth Frayne. LC 38-30386. 1938. Arcadia House.
Beneath the Blue Mountain. Richard S Wheeler. LC 78-15842. 1979. 7.95 (ISBN 0-385-14748-1). Doubleday.
Beneath the Dome. Arnold Clark. LC 6-25363. 1894. The Schulte Publishing Company.
Beneath the Moors. Brian Lumley. LC 74-78130. 1974. 6.00 (ISBN 0-87054-066-1). Arkham House.
Beneath the Passion Flower. George Preedy, pseud. LC 32-137893. 1932. R. M. McBride & Company.
Beneath the Red Banner. Lao She. Tr. by Don J. Cohn from Chinese. (Panda Ser.). 215p. (Orig.). 1982. pap. 3.95 (ISBN 0-8351-1026-5). China Bks.
Beneath the Rising Mist. Dana Storrs Lamb. LC 79-11012. (Illus.). 15.00 (ISBN 0-913276-27-8). Stone Wall Press.
Beneath the Sea. A Story of the Cornish Coast. George Manville Fenn. LC 6-392586. T. Y. Crowell & Company.
Beneath the Stone. George Tabori. LC 45-76142. 1945. Houghton Mifflin Company.
Beneath the Stone; an Historical Romance. Jonathan Kellogg. LC 18-10174. 1918. 1.25. The Neale Publishing Company.
Beneath the Surface. Chris Illing. LC 81-80154. 224p. 1983. pap. 7.95 (ISBN 0-86666-005-4). GWP.
Beneath the Underdog. Charles Mingus. Ed. by Nel King. 1971. 6.95 o.p. (ISBN 0-394-43622-9). Knopf.
Beneath the Varnish. William Lloyd Griffin. LC 67-19552. 1967. Valley Publications.
Beneath the Visiting Moon: A Novel. Romilly Cavan. LC 41-21539. Coward-McCann, Inc.
Beneath the Wheel. Hermann Hesse. LC 68-23744. 1968. 4.95. Farrar, Straus, and Giroux.
Beneath These Trees. William Arthur Neubauer. LC 53-6222. 1953. Arcadia House.
Benedict Arnold Connection. Joseph DiMona. LC 77-7995. 1977. 8.95 (ISBN 0-688-03230-3). Morrow.
Benedict Arnold Slept Here: Jack Douglas' Honeymoon Mountain Inn. Jack Douglas. LC 74-16587. (YA) 1975. 7.95 o.p. (ISBN 0-399-11432-7). Putnam.
Benediction. Joseph Furek. (Orig.). 1979. pap. 2.50 (ISBN 0-89083-505-5). Zebra.
Benediction. Philomene De Laforest-Divonne. Tr. by Norton, Robert. LC 36-21647. 1936. D. Appleton-Century Company, Incorporated.
Benefactor. Susan Sontag. (Delta book). 1978. 4.95 (ISBN 0-440-50632-8). Dell Pub. Co.
Benefactor: By Marfa Flores Pseud. 1st Ed. Mary Foster Main. LC 60-6894. 1960. Doubleday.
Benefactress. Mary Annette Beauchamp Russell Russell. LC 1-256781. 1901. The Macmillan Company.
Benefit. Nick Mayo. LC 79-65106. 1979. 10.95 (ISBN 0-8128-2679-5). Stein and Day.
Benefit of the Doubt. Mary Clare Spenser. LC 8-14068. 1883. G. P. Putnam's Sons.
Benefit Performance. Richard Sale. LC 46-3161. 1946. Simon and Schuster.
Benefit Street. Jane Ludlow Drake Abbott. LC 30-103492. J. B. Lippincott Company.
Benefit Street. David Cornel De Jong. LC 42-24103. 1942. Harper & Brothers.
Benefits. Zoe Fairbairns. 224p. 1983. pap. 2.95 (ISBN 0-380-63164-4, Bard). Avon.
Benefits Forgot. Wolcott Balestier. LC 4-22072. 1894. D. Appleton and Company.
Benefits Forgot. A Novel. Wolcott Balestier. LC 6-6328. 1891. J. W. Lovell Company.
Benefits Forgot: A Story of Lincoln and Mother Love. Honore McCue Willsie Morrow. LC 17-24971. Frederick A. Stokes Company.
Benefits Received. Alice Grant Rosman. LC 32-26744. 1932. Minton, Balch & Company.
Benevant Treasure. 1st Ed. Patricia Wentworth. LC 54-874618. (Her A Miss Silver mystery). 1954. Lippincott.
Benevent Treasure. Patricia Wentworth. LC 76-47556. 1977. 5.95 (ISBN 0-88411-731-6). Aeonian Press.
Benevolent Bean. Margaret Keys & Ancel Keys. 192p. 1972. 5.95 o.p. (ISBN 0-374-11103-0); pap. 2.45 o.p. (ISBN 0-374-51009-1). FS&G.
Benevolent Man. Alexander Bicknell. LC 74-20621. (Flowering of the Novel). 1974. (ISBN 0-8240-1207-0). Garland Pub.
Benevolent Monster: A Novel. Charles Chauvet. LC 56-8626. 1956. Dorrance.
Bengal Peasant Life. Lal Behari Day. LC 76-44749. 1980. 34.50 (ISBN 0-404-15946-X). AMS Press.
Bengal Tiger: A Tale of India. Edison Marshall. LC 52-6357. 1952. Doubleday.
Bengali Inheritance. Owen Sela. LC 74-4757. 1975. 6.95 (ISBN 0-394-49410-5). Pantheon Books.
Bengali Women. Manisha Roy. LC 74-33521. 1979. pap. 4.95 (ISBN 0-226-73042-5, P847, Phoen). U of Chicago Pr.
Benghazi Breakout. Gordon Landsborough. 1977. pap. 1.50 (ISBN 0-532-15271-9). Woodhill.
Benia Krik: A Film-Novel. Isaak Emmanuilovich Babel. LC 72-90292. 1973. 7.50 (ISBN 0-88355-000-8). Hyperion Press.
Benign Reality. Harvey Jackins. (Orig.). 1981. 18.00 (ISBN 0-911214-77-1); pap. 15.00 (ISBN 0-911214-76-3). Rational Isl.
Benito Cereno. Herman Melville. LC 79-182154. (Illus.). 1972. (ISBN 0-87636-023-1). Imprint Society.
Benito Cereno see Seven Short Novel Masterpieces.
Benjamin Alexander Sheep: A Story. Bob Friedman. LC 73-83731. (Illus.). 1973. 1.25 (ISBN 0-8307-0264-4). G/L Regal Books.
Benjamin & Jon. Mary E. Heath. LC 79-84794. 1979. pap. 4.95 (ISBN 0-87123-024-0, 210024). Bethany Hse.
Benjamin & Jon. Mary E. Heath. LC 79-84794. (Orig.). 1979. pap. 2.95 (ISBN 0-89877-008-4). Jeremy Bks.
Benjamin Blake. Edison Marshall. LC 41-220839. Farrar & Rinehart, Incc.
Benjamin Bounces Back. Alan Baker. LC 78-59689. Lippincott.
Benjamin Disraeli. Richard A Levine. LC 68-17235. (Twayne's English authors series, 68). 1968. Twayne.
Benjamin Grabbed His Glicken and Ran: An Autobiography. Fred Gordon. LC 70-138785. 1971. 6.95 (ISBN 0-06-011583-1). Harper & Row.
Benjamin the Jew. Louis Pope Gratacap. LC 14-3562. 1913. 1.25. T. Benton.
Benjamin's Open Day. Jane White. 192p. 1979. 16.95 (ISBN 0-241-89978-8, Pub. by Hamish Hamilton England). David & Charles.
Benjamn Lawless. Ernest Kellogg Gann. LC 48-8793. 1948. W. Sloane Associates.
Benjy. George Stevenson. LC 20-5234. 1919. John Lane.
Benjy Boone: A Novel. Maurice Dolbier. LC 67-12661. (Illus.). 1967. Dial Press.
Bennett. Desmond Cory, pseud. LC 77-74296. 1977. 6.95 (ISBN 0-385-13136-4). Published for the Crime Club by Doubleday.
Bennett Cerf's Take Along Treasury. Ed. by Leonora Hornblow & Cerf, Bennett Alfred. LC 63-18206. 1963. Doubleday.
Bennett Malin. Elsie Singmaster. LC 22-12396. 1922. Houghton Mifflin Company.
Bennett, No. 5: Here Today, Dead Tomorrow. Elliott Lewis. 208p. (Orig.). 1982. pap. 2.25 (ISBN 0-523-41439-0). Pinnacle Bks.
Bennett, Number Three: People in Glass Houses. Elliott Lewis. 192p. (Orig.). 1981. pap. 1.95 (ISBN 0-523-41437-4). Pinnacle Bks.
Bennett Twins. Grace Marguerite Hurd. LC 5067. 1900. The Macmillan Company.
Bennett's Welcome. Inglis Clark Fletcher. LC 52-1027. 1951. Garden City Books.
Bennett's Welcome. Inglis Clark Fletcher. LC 78-5795. 1978. 13.50 (ISBN 0-89244-001-5). Queens House.
Bennie Ben Cree: Being the Story of His Adventure to Southward in the Year '62. Arthur Willis Colton. 1900. Doubleday & McClure Co.
Benoni. Knut Hamsun & Chater, Arthur G., Tr. LC 25-16055. 1925. A. A. Knopf.
Benoni & Rosa. Knut Hamsun & Chater, Arthur G., Tr. LC 32-272083. 1932. A. A. Knopf.
Bensley: a Story of to-Day. Oliver Bell Bunce. LC 6-186782. 1863. J. G. Gregory.
Benson Family. A Story for Old and Young. Alexander Streeter Arnold. LC 6-2065. 1869. E. L. Freeman.
Benson Murder Case. S. S. Van Dine, pseud. Repr. lib. bdg. 17.95x (ISBN 0-89190-511-1). Am Repr-Rivercity Pr.
Benson Murder Case. S. S. Van Dine, pseud. 1980. lib. bdg. 10.95 (ISBN 0-8398-2553-6, Gregg). G K Hall.
Benson Murder Case. Willard Huntington Wright. LC 79-22556. (Gregg Press Mystery Fiction Series). (Series: Philo Vance series.). (Illus.). 1980. 10.95 (ISBN 0-8398-2553-6). Gregg Press.
Benson Murder Case: A Philo Vance Story. Willard Huntington Wright. LC 26-22865. (Half-title: The Philo Vance series). 1926. C. Scribner's Sons.
Bent Copper. Jeremy Ashford. 1971. 4.95 o.p. (ISBN 0-8027-5232-2). Walker & Co.
Bent Copper. Roderic Jeffries. LC 70-161110. 1971. 4.95 (ISBN 0-8027-5232-2). Walker.
Bent Man. Arthur Maling. LC 74-15878. 1975. 6.95 (ISBN 0-06-012802-X). Harper & Row.
Bent Man. Arthur Maling. LC 75-26841. 1975. 11.95 (ISBN 0-8161-6225-5). G. K. Hall.
Bent Star. Patrick Andrews. 192p. (Orig.). 1982. pap. 2.25 o.p. (ISBN 0-505-51843-0). Tower Bks.
Bent to Evil. Kim Savage. LC 52-4486. 1952. Vixen Press.
Bent Twig. Dorothea Frances Canfield Fisher. LC 15-26659. 1915. H. Holt and Company.
Bent Twig. Dorothea Frances Canfield Fisher. LC 18-2279. 1916. H. Holt and Company.
Bent Twig. Dorothea Frances Canfield Fisher. 1917. Grosset & Dunlap.
Bent Twig. Dorothea Frances Canfield Fisher. LC 26-7447. H. Holt and Company.
Bentley. R. C. Jebb. 224p. 1980. Repr. of 1882 ed. lib. bdg. 17.50 (ISBN 0-89984-250-X). Century Bookbindery.
Bentley: Passion's Daughter. Marguerite Kloepfer. 1979. pap. 1.95 (ISBN 0-89041-234-0, 3234). Major Bks.
Benton of the Royal Mounted: A Tale of the Royal Northwest Mounted Police. Ralph Selwood Kendall. LC 18-20473. 1918. John Lane Company.
Benton's Row. Frank Yerby. LC 54-10533. 1954. Dial Press.
Benton's Row. Frank Yerby. 1974. (pbk.) 1.50. Dell.
Benton's Row. Frank Yerby. (Dell Book)). 1977. 1.75 (ISBN 0-440-10512-9). Dell Pub. Co.
Benvenuta: A Romance of the Hudson River. Adele Sarpy Morrison. LC 14-22591. 1914. The Thompson Company.
Beoni, the Sphinx. Ira L Jones. LC 7-11912.
Beowulf. Beowulf. Tr. by Green, Adwin Wigfall. LC 36-7135. B. Humphries, Inc.
Beowulf: A Novel. Winifred Bryher. LC 56-10411. 1956. Pantheon Books.
Beowulf: Guide Dog to the Blind. Ernest Blakeman Vesey. LC 36-13044. E. P. Dutton & Co., Inc.
Beowulf Is My Name. F. Rebsamen. LC 77-123680. (Rinehart Editions). 1971. pap. text ed. 2.95 o.p. (ISBN 0-03-084555-6, HoltC). HR&W.
Bequeath Them No Tumbled House. Yvonne MacManus. LC 76-16254. 1977. 5.95 (ISBN 0-385-12034-6). Doubleday.
Bequeathed: A Novel. Beatrice Whitby. LC 3142. 1900. Harper & Brothers.
Bequest (a Fictional First). Robert Elliot Wolff. LC 72-77489. (Illus.). (ISBN 0-913084-01-8). Parsindo Publishers.
Berber: Or The Mountaineer of the Atlas. William Starbuck Mayo. LC 7-25870. (Lovell's library. v. 2, no. 70). 1883. J. W. Lovell Company.
Berber: Or, The Mountaineer of the Atlas. A Tale of Morocco. William Starbuck Mayo. LC 7-18480. 1850. G. P. Putnam; Etc., Etc.
Berbora No. 1. Mike Sirota. 1978. pap. 1.95 (ISBN 0-532-19204-4). Woodhill.
Berbora No. 2. Mike Sirota. 1978. pap. 1.95 (ISBN 0-532-19213-3). Woodhill.
Berdoo. Eugene O'Donnell. LC 59-13735. 1959. Rinehart.
Bereaved Husband. Clell Edgar Bowman. 1976. 8.00 o.p. (ISBN 0-682-48519-5). Exposition.
Berenice. Ruth Jordan. LC 74-4794. (Illus.). 272p. 1974. text ed. 12.50x o.p. (ISBN 0-06-493402-0). B&N.
Berenice. Edward Phillips Oppenheim. LC 7-42461. Little, Brown, and Company.
Berenice. Edward Phillips Oppenheim. LC 11-1010. 1911. 1.25. Little, Brown, and Company.
Berenice: A Novel. Emily Pierpont De Lesdernier. LC 6-34180. 1856. Phillips, Sampson & Company.
Berenice. A Novel. E M Keplinger. LC 7-10949. 1878. Miss S. M. Haight.
Berenice: Princess of Judea. Leon Kolb. LC 59-14633. 1959. Twayne Publishers.
Berg. Ann Quin. LC 65-79991. 192p. 1979. pap. 6.95 (Pub. by M Boyars). Merrimack Pub Cir.
Berg: Novel. Ann Quin. LC 65-23985. (7061). 1965. 3.95, 1.65 pap.,. Scribners.
Bergkristall: (Rock Crystal) Adalbert Stifter. Tr. by J. R. Foster from Ger. (Harrap Bilingual Ser.). 114p. 1950. 5.00 (ISBN 0-911268-55-3). Rogers Bk.
Bergman's Trilogy. Ingmar Bergman. Tr. by Paul B. Austin. Incl. Through a Glass Darkly; The Communicants-Winter Light; The Silence. LC 67-21231. (Illus.). 144p. (O.s.i.). 1967. 5.95 o.s.i. (ISBN 0-670-15874-7, Orion Pr). Grossman.
Bergson and the Stream of Consciousness Novel. Shiv Kumar Kumar. LC 78-26162. 1979. 17.50 (ISBN 0-313-20806-9). Greenwood Press.
Beria Papers. Alan Williams. LC 73-8996. 1973. 7.95 (ISBN 0-671-21589-2). Simon and Schuster.
Bering's Potlatch. Lucile Saunders McDonald & Hogner, Nils, 1896- Illus. LC 44-1339. 1944. Oxford University Press.
Berkeley Street Mystery. Mary R. Platt Hatch. LC 28-25464. 1928. L. C. Page & Company.
Berkeley the Banker: Or, Bank Notes and Bullion. A Tale for the Times. Harriet Martineau. (On cover: Lovell's library, v. 7, no. 357). 1884. J. W. Lovell Company.
Berkeleys and Their Neighbors. Molly Elliot Seawell. LC 8-6427. The American News Company.
Berkeleys and Their Neighbors. rev. ed. Molly Elliot Seawell. LC 8-20161. (On cover: Appletons' town country library, no. 103). 1892. D. Appleton and Company.
Berkley Showcase, New Writings in Science Fiction & Fantasy. Ed. by Victoria Schochet & John Silbersack. 1981. pap. 2.25 (ISBN 0-425-04804-7). Berkley Pub.
Berkley Showcase: New Writings in Science Fiction, Vol. II. Ed. by Victoria Schochet & John Silbersack. (Orig.). 1980. pap. 2.25 (ISBN 0-425-04553-6). Berkley Pub.

Berkley Showcase: New Writings in Science Fiction and Fantasy. Ed. by Victoria Schochet. Silbersack, John. 1.95 (ISBN 0-425-04446-7). Berkley Books.

Berkley Showcase: Vol. 3. Victoria Schochet & Silbersack, John. 1981. 2.25 (ISBN 0-425-04697-4). Berkley Books.

Berkshire Mystery. George Douglas Howard Cole & Margaret Isabel Postgate Cole. LC 30-11858. 1930. Brewer & Warren Inc., Payson & Clarke Ltd.

Berl Make Tea. Chaim I. Bermant. 1977. 8.00 o.p. State Mutual Bk.

Berlin. Nick Carter. (Nick Carter Espionage Ser). (O.s.i.). (Orig.). 1970. pap. 0.60 o.s.i. (A455X, Award). Univ Pub & Dist.

Berlin. Nick Carter. (Nick Carter Ser.). (O.s.i.). 1976. pap. 1.25 o.s.i. (AQ1604, Award). Univ Pub & Dist.

Berlin. Theodor Plivier. LC 77-364504. 1976. 0.75 (ISBN 0-583-12516-6). Mayflower.

Berlin: A Novel. Tr. from German by Louis Hagen, Vivian Milroy. Theodor Plivier. LC 56-56383. 1966. bds., 4.50. Hammond, Hammond.

Berlin: A Novel. Translated by Louis Hagen and Vivian Milroy. 1st Ed. Theodor Plivier. LC 57-7071. 1957. Doubleday.

Berlin & Phenomena. Wolf Vostell. (Orig.). 1966. pap. 3.50 (ISBN 0-89366-074-4). Ultramarine Pub.

Berlin and Sans-Souci; or, Frederick the Great and His Friends. An Historical Romance. By L. Muhlbach Pseud.... Translated from the Germanby Mrs. Chapman Coleman and Her Daughters. Klara Muller Mundt. LC 7-24120. 1867. D. Appleton and Company.

Berlin and Sans-Souci: Or, Frederick the Great and His Friends. An Historical Novel. Klara Muller Mundt. Tr. by Coleman, Ann Mary Butler (Crittenden) LC 17-23006. (With her Frederick the Great and his court... New York, 1890). 1890. D. Appleton and Company.

Berlin and Sans-Souci: Tr. from the German by Mrs. Chapman Coleman and Her Daughters. Klara Muller Mundt. Tr. by Coleman, Ann Mary Butler (Crittenden) LC 16-1229. (historical romances of Louisa Muhlbach pseud.). D. Appleton and Company.

Berlin at Midnight. Robert Joseph. LC 48-6367. 1948. Greenberg.

Berlin Blind. Alan Scholefield. LC 80-13758. 1980. 8.95 (ISBN 0-688-03696-1). Morrow.

Berlin Connection. Johannes Mario Simmel. 1977. 1.95 (ISBN -0445-08607-6). Popular Library.

Berlin Ending. Howard Hunt. (Berkley medallion book). 1974. (pbk.) 1.25. Berkley Pub. Co.

Berlin Ending: A Novel of Discovery. Howard Hunt. LC 73-81028. 1973. 6.95 (ISBN 0-399-11223-5). Putnam.

Berlin Indictment. Erwin Fischer. LC 78-149418. 1971. 6.95. World Pub. Co.

Berlin Stories... Christopher Isherwood. LC 46-2158. 1946. J. Laughlin.

Berlin Stories. Christopher Isherwood. LC 79-17316. 1979. 12.50 (ISBN 0-8376-0449-4). R. Bentley.

Berlin Stories: The Last of Mr. Norris and Goodbye to Berlin. Christopher Isherwood. LC 55-2508. (New Directions book). 1954. J. Laughlin.

Berlin Tunnel, Twenty-One. Donald Lindquist. 1978. pap. 2.95 (ISBN 0-380-01843-8, 78394). Avon.

Berlin und Sans-Souci: Or, Frederick the Great and His Friends. An Historical Romance. Klara Muller Mundt. Tr. by Coleman, Ann Mary Butler (Crittenden) LC 7-24120. 1867. D. Appleton and Company.

Berlin Wall Affair. Troy Conway, pseud. (Coxeman Ser). (Orig.). 1967. pap. 0.60 o.p. (53-533). Paperback Lib.

Berlin Wall Affair see Don't Bite off More Than You Can Chew.

Berlinguer & the Professor. LC 75-35967. (Richard Seaver Book). 128p. 1976. 6.95 o.p. (ISBN 0-670-15882-8). Viking Pr.

Berlinguer and the Professor: Chronicles of the Next Italy. LC 75-35967. (Illus.). 1976. 6.95 (ISBN 0-670-15882-8). Viking Press.

Bermuda Burial. Charles Daly King. LC 41-426475. W. Funk, Inc.

Bermuda Calling. David Garth. LC 44-6126. 1944. G. P. Putnam's Sons.

Bermuda Lily. Virginia Wales Johnson. LC 12-25995. 1912. 1.25. The A. S. Barnes Company.

Bermuda Nurse. Rose Dana, pseud. (Orig.). 1969. pap. 0.50 o.p. (50-479). Manor Bks.

Bermuda Triangle. Adi-Kent T. Jeffrey. 96p. 1973. pap. 1.50 (ISBN 0-915460-02-5). New Hope.

Bermuda Triangle. Adi-Kent T. Jeffrey. (Illus.). 1975. pap. 1.95 (ISBN 0-446-90036-2). Warner Bks.

Bermuda Triangle & Other Mysteries of Nature. Edward F. Dolan, Jr. (Hi Lo Ser.). 96p. 1981. pap. 1.50 (ISBN 0-553-14824-9). Bantam.

Berna Boyle. Charlotte Eliza Lawson Cowan Riddell. (On cover: Seaside library. Pocket ed., no. 593). 1885. G. Munro.

Bernadette Black. Claire Gabriel. LC 73-82487. 1973. 5.95 (ISBN 0-517-50591-6). Crown Publishers.

Bernan Affair: A Novel. Translated from the French by Charles Lam Markmann. Joseph Kessel. LC 65-17309. 1965. St. Martin's Press.

Bernard Clare. James Thomas Farrell. LC 46-3585. 1946. The Vanguard Press.

Bernard Leslie: Or, A Tale of the Last Ten Years. William Gresley. LC 42-27481. 1843. J. A. Sparks.

Bernard Leslie: Or, A Tale of the Last Ten Years. 2d american ed. William Gresley. LC 6-44871. 1844. J. A. Sparks.

Bernard Lile: An Historical Romance, Embracing the Periods of the Texas Revolution, and the Mexican War. Jeremiah Clemens. LC 6-28764. 1856. J. B. Lippincott & Co.

Bernard Quesnay: A Novel. Andre Maurois. Tr. by Brian Westerdale Downs. LC 27-7186. 1927. D. Appleton & Company.

Bernardini Terrace. Suzanne Prou. LC 75-25096. 6.95 (ISBN 0-06-013445-3). Harper & Row.

Bernhard the Conqueror. Sam J. Lundwall. (Science Fiction Ser.). (Orig.). 1973. pap. 0.95 o.p. (UQ1058). DAW Bks.

Bernhard the Conqueror. Sam Jerrie Lundwall. 1973. (pbk.) 0.95. Daw Books.

Bernicia. Amelia Edith Huddleston Barr. 1985. Dodd, Mead and Company.

Bernstein, Aline. Mr. Feoelich, Herbert Wilson, Eugene. LC 34-96. 1933. Equinox Cooperative Press.

Bernthal: Or, The Son's Revenge. From the German of L. Muhlbach Pseud. Klara Muller Mundt. LC 7-25465. 1867. Harper & Brothers.

Berrigan: A Novel. Ginger Lox. LC 78-59620. (Illus.). 1978. 5.50 (ISBN 0-930044-09-6). Naiad Press.

Berris. Katharine Sarah Gadsden Macquoid. LC 1-29212. (On cover: Eagle series, no. 189). Street & Smith.

Berry and Co. Cecil William Mercer. LC 77-357783. (Illus.). 1976. 3.50 (ISBN 0-7063-1676-2). Ward Lock.

Berry and Co. Cecil William Mercer. LC 28-8131. 1928. Minton, Balch & Company.

Berry Scene. Cecil William Mercer. LC 48-1586. 1947. G. P. Putnam's Sons.

Berryhill. Barbara Bennett. (Orig.). 1979. pap. 1.95. Woodhill.

Berserker. Fred Saberhagen. 1978. 1.75 (ISBN 0-441-05404-8). Ace Books.

Berserker. Frank Spiering. 256p. 1981. pap. 2.75 (ISBN 0-515-05401-1). Jove Pubns.

Berserker Wars. Fred Saberhagen. 416p. 1981. pap. 2.95 (ISBN 0-523-48520-4). Pinnacle Bks.

Berserkers. Ed. by Roger Elwood. LC 73-82873. 1974. 6.95 (ISBN 0-671-27113-X). Trident Press.

Berserker's Planet. Fred Saberhagen. (Science Fiction Ser.). 1975. pap. 1.25 o.p. (UY1167). DAW Bks.

Berserker's Planet. Fred Saberhagen. 1975. (pbk.) 1.25. DAW Books.

Bert & I & Other Stories from Down East. Marshall Dodge & Robert Bryan. Intro. by Homer D. Babbidge. (Illus.). 140p. (Orig.). 1981. 11.95 (ISBN 0-9607546-0-1); pap. 7.95. Bert & I Bks.

Bertha: A Historical Romance of the Time of Henry Iv., Emperor of Germany. tr. by s. b. a. harper. ed. Josef Eduard Konrad Bischoff. LC 6-11716. 1876. D. & J. Sadlier & Co.

Bertha and Lily: Or, The Parsonage of Beech Glen. A Romance. Elizabeth Oakes Prince Smith. LC 8-8636. 1854. J. C. Derby.

Bertha Garlan. Arthur Schnitzler. LC 21-4141. (Half-title: The modern library of the world's best books no. 39). Boni and Liveright. Inc.

Bertha Laycourt. A Novel. Edgar C Blum. LC 6-14207. 1889. J. B. Lippincott Company.

Bertha: Or, The Consequences of a Fault. Louise Boyeldieu D'Auvigny. Tr. by Huntington, Mary. LC 6-15228. 1875. Benziger Brothers.

Bertha Percy: Or, L'esperance. Margaret Field. 1860. D. Appleton and Company.

Bertha the Beauty: A Story of the Southern Revolution. Sarah Johnson Cogswell Whittlesey. LC 8-36255. 1872. Claxton, Remsen & Haffelfinger.

Bertha Weiler, the Ballon Spy: Or the Flying Scout. The Secret O the German Victories Out at Last. A Thrilling Narrative of What Has Been Done by Means of a Flying Machine or Ballon, During the Present European War. C. W. Alexander.

Bertha's Christmas Vision: An Autumn Sheaf. Horatio Alger, Jr. (Illus.). 248p. 1978. Repr. of 1856 ed. 22.50. G K Westgard.

Bertha's Engagement. Ann Sophia Winterbotham Stephens. LC 12-150621. T. B. Peterson & Brothers.

Bertha's Secret. Fortune Du Boisgobey. (On cover: Lovell's library. no. 1172). J. W. Lovell Company.

Bertha's Secret. Fortune Du Boisgobey & Kendall, Laura E., Tr. LC 6-34435. (On cover: Seaside library. Pocket ed. no. 1080). G. Munro.

Bertha's Summer Boarders. Linne Sarah Harris. LC 7-2899. Congregational Sunday-School and Publsihing Society.

Bertie, Albert Edward, Prince of Wales: A Novel. Tyler-Whittle, Michael Sidney. LC 74-81462. (Illus.). 1974. 7.95. St. Martin's Press.

Bertie: Or, Life in the Old Field. A Humorous Novel. James Gregory. LC 6-44869. 1851. A. Hart.

Bertie Wooster Sees It Through. Pelham Grenville Wodehouse. LC 55-5948. 1955. Simon and Schuster.

Bertolt Brecht Short Stories, 1921-1946. Ed. by John Willett & Ralph Manheim. Tr. by Yvonne Knapp. 1983. 19.95 (ISBN 0-413-37050-X). Methuen Inc.

Bertram Cope's Year. Henry Blake Fuller. LC 78-63987. (Gay Experience Sev.). Repr. of 1919 ed. 26.00 (ISBN 0-404-61506-6). AMS Pr.

Bertram Cope's Year see Collected Works.

Bertram Cope's Year: A Novel. Henry Blake Fuller. LC 19-16363. 1919. R. F. Seymour.

Bertram Family. Elizabeth Charles. LC 42-357173. 1876. Dodd, Mead & Company.

Bertram Family. Elizabeth Rundle Charles. LC 75-494. (Victorian Fiction: Novels of Faith and Doubt; V. 46). 1975. 35.00 (ISBN 0-8240-1570-3). Garland Pub.

Bertram Noel: A Story for Youth. Edith J May. LC 52-50331. 1859. Appleton.

Bertrams. Anthony Trollope & Thorold, Algar Labouchere, Ed. LC 12-39442. (Half-title: The new pocket library. XX). 1905. John Lane.

Bertrams. A Novel. Anthony Trollope. LC 24-25004. 1859. Harper & Brothers.

Bertrams. A Novel. Anthony Trollope. (Franklin square library. no. 85). 1879. Harper & Brothers.

Bertrand De Ganges, Conte. Jules Romains. LC 44-8278. Editions De La'Maison Francaise, Inc.

Bertrand of Brittany. Warwick Deeping. LC 8-12223. 1908. Harper & Brothers.

Beryl's Husband: A Novel. Harriet Lewis. (On cover: The choice series, no. 34). 1891. R. Bonner's Sons.

Beside a Norman Tower. Mazo De La Roche. LC 34-42819. 1934. Little, Brown, and Company.

Beside a Southern Sea: A Novel. Elizabeth May Montague. LC 5-39868. 1905. The Neale Publishing Company.

Beside Still Waters. Arthur Christopher Benson. LC 7-15922. 1907. G. Putnam's Sons.

Beside the Bonnie Briar Bush. John Watson. LC 8-11269. 1895. Dodd, Mead and Company.

Beside the Bonnie Briar Bush. (authorized ed.) by rev. john watson... (ian maclaren) ed. John Watson. LC 99-5479. D. C. Cook Publishing Company.

Beside the Bonnie Brier Bush. John Watson. LC 47-35959. E. A. Weeks & Company.

Beside the Bonnie Brier Bush. John Watson. LC 4-15342. 1895. Dodd, Mead and Company.

Beside the Bonnie Brier Bush. John Watson. LC 28-179131. 1895. Dodd, Mead and Company.

Beside the Bonnie Brier Bush. John Watson. LC 8-34346. 1896. Dodd, Mead and Company.

Beside the Bonnie Brier Bush. John Watson. LC 4631. W. B. Conkey Company.

Beside the Fire. Obioma I. Eligwe. LC 74-1441. 1974. (pbk.) 1.75 (ISBN 0-914478-01-X). Three Continents Press.

Beside the Fire: A Collection of Irish Gaelic Folk Stories. Douglas Hyde. 203p. 1973. Repr. of 1910 ed. 12.50 o.s.i. (ISBN 0-87696-047-6). Lemma.

Beside the River. A Tale. Katharine Sarah Gadsden Macquoid. (Franklin square library, no. 182). 1881. Harper & Brothers.

Beside the River. A Tale. Katharine Sarah Gadsden Macquoid. (Seaside library, v. 49, no. 1006). 1881. G. Munro.

Beside the Tidewater: A Collection of Flotsam. Philip E Hubbard. LC 22-112881. 1922. The Cornhill Publishing Company.

Besides the Wench Is Dead. Margaret Erskine, pseud. LC 72-97090. (Crime Club Ser). 1973. 4.95 o.p. (ISBN 0-385-00435-4). Doubleday.

Besides, the Wench Is Dead. Robert Ullin. LC 35-7316. 1935. Doubleday, Doran & Company, Inc.

Besides the Wench Is Dead. Margaret Wetherby Williams. (Ace gothic). 1974. (pbk.) 0.95. Ace Books.

Besides the Wench Is Dead. Wetherby Williams. LC 72-97090. 1973. 4.95 (ISBN 0-385-00435-4). Published for the Crime Club by Doubleday.

Besieged. Thomas Cullinan. LC 75-114306. 1970. 6.95. Horizon Press.

Besieged: A Novel of Present-Day Family Life. Gerald Breckenridge. LC 37-487630. 1937. Doubleday, Doran & Company, Inc.

Besieger of Cities. Alfred Leo Duggan. LC 63-13698. 1963. Pantheon Books.

Besom of God! Oreon Marie Jackson McKee. LC 45-3444. 1945. House of Field-Doubleday, Inc.

Bespoken Mile: By March Cost Pseud. Peggy Morrison, pseud. LC 59-7770. 1959. Vanguard Press.

Bess." A Companion to "Jess.". John De Morgan. (Munro's library. no. 739). 1887. N. L. Munro.

Bess: A Companion to "Jess.". Andrew Lang & Walter Herries Pollock. LC 44-154907. (Munro's Library). (Munro's library. No. 739: No. 739). 1887. N. L. Munro.

Bess of Cobb's Hall: The Holy Maid of Kent. Enid Maud Dinnis. LC 40-13369. (Half-title: Science and culture series; Joseph Husslein... general editor). The Bruce Publishing Company.

Bess of the Woods. Warwick Deeping. LC 6-20454. 1906. Harper & Brothers.

Bess Streeter Aldrich Reader. Bess Streeter Aidrich. LC 50-7036. 1950. Appleton-CenturyCentury-Crofts.

Bess Streeter Aldrich Treasury. With an Introd. by Robert Streeter Aldrich. Bess Streeter Aldrich. LC 59-12539. 1959. Appleton-Century-Crofts.

Bessie. A Novel. Julia Kavanagh. (On cover: Library of choice novels. no. 43). 1872. D. Appleton and Company.

Bessie and Raymond: Or, Incidents Connected with the Civil War in the United States. Maria D. Weston. LC 8-34331. 1866. E. P. Weston.

Bessie Cotter. Wallace Smith. LC 34-6413. Covici-Friede.

Bessie of Bradenburg. John Marion Wolfe. LC 17-28607. 1917. The Roxburgh Publishing Company.

Bessie Wilmerton: Or, Money, and What Came of It. A Novel. Margaret Jane Cook Westcott. LC 8-36225. 1874. G. W. Carleton & Co.; Etc., Etc.

Bessie's House. P. Zdinak. 5.50 o.p. Carlton.

Bessy Rane. A Novel. Ellen Price Henry Wood Wood. LC 9-507. T. B. Peterson & Brothers.

Best American Humorous Short Stories. Ed. by Alexander Jessup. LC 20-12376. (Half-title: The modern library of the world's best books). 1920. Boni and Liveright.

Best American Humorous Short Stories: Edited with an Introductory Note. Ed. by Robert Newton Linscott. LC 45-10063. (Half-title: The Modern library of the world's best books). 1945. Random House.

Best American Love Stories of the Year: Selected and with an Introduction by Margaret Widdemer. Ed. by Margaret Widdemer. LC 32-268977. The John Day Company.

Best American Short Stories. Martha Foley. 1975-1976. Vol. 1. 10.00 o.p. (ISBN 0-395-20719-3); Vol. 2. 10.00 o.p. (ISBN 0-395-24770-5). HM.

Best American Short Stories: And the Yearbook of the American Short Story. Houghton Mifflin Co.

Best American Short Stories... And the Yearbook of the American Short Story... 1915- Ed. by Martha Foley. Foley, Martha, Ed & Yearbook Fo the American Short Story. LC 16-11387. Houghton Mifflin Company.

Best American Short Stories Nineteen Eighty. Ed. by Stanley Elkin & Shannon Ravenel. 496p. 1980. 12.95 (ISBN 0-395-29446-0). HM.

Best American Short Stories Nineteen Eighty-Two. John Gardner. 1982. 14.95 (ISBN 0-395-32207-3). HM.

Best American Short Stories of Nineteen Seventy-Nine. Joyce Carol Oates. Ed. by Shannon Ravenel. 1979. 11.95 (ISBN 0-395-27769-8). HM.

Best American Short Stories: The Yearbook of the American Short Story. Ed. by Martha Foley. 1973. 1.65. Ballantine.

Best American Short Stories (1961) . . . and the Yearbook of the American Story, Ed. by Martha Foley, David Burnett. 5.50. Houghton.

Best American Short Stories, 1961. Ed. by Martha Foley, David Burnett. (S572). Ballantine.

Best American Short Stories 1962 (The) And the Yearbook of the American Short Story. Ed. by Martha Foley, David Burnett. Ed. by Martha Foley & David Burnett. (S695). 1963. Ballantine.

Best American Short Stories, 1964. Ed. by Martha Foley & David Burnett. 5.95 o.p. (ISBN 0-395-07688-9). HM.

Best American Short Stories, 1965. Ed. by Martha Foley & David Burnett. 5.95 o.p. (ISBN 0-395-07689-7). HM.

Best American Short Stories 1965 (The) And the Yearbook of the American. Ed. by Martha Foley. Yearbook of the American Short Story. LC 16-11387. 5.95. Houghton.

Best American Short Stories, 1966. Ed. by Martha Foley & David Burnett. 6.95 o.p. (ISBN 0-395-07690-0). HM.

Best American Short Stories 1967. Ed. by Martha Foley & David Burnett. 1967. 6.00 o.p. (ISBN 0-395-07691-9). HM.

Best American Short Stories 1968. rev. ed. Ed. by Martha Foley & David Burnett. LC 16-11387. 1968. 6.50 o.p. (ISBN 0-395-07692-7). HM.

Best American Short Stories, 1969. Ed. by Martha Foley & David Burnett. LC 16-11387. 1969. 6.95 o.p. (ISBN 0-395-07693-5). HM.

Best American Short Stories, 1970. Ed. by Martha Foley & David Burnett. 1970. 6.95 o.p. (ISBN 0-395-10940-X). HM.

Best American Short Stories, 1971. Ed. by Martha Foley & David Burnett. 1971. 7.50 (ISBN 0-395-12709-2). HM.

Best American Short Stories 1972. Ed. by Martha Foley. 1972. 7.95 o.p. (ISBN 0-395-13950-3). HM.

Best American Short Stories 1973. Ed. by Martha Foley. 1973. 8.95 (ISBN 0-395-17119-9). HM.

Best American Short Stories 1974. Ed. by Martha Foley. LC 16-11387. 400p. 1974. 9.95 (ISBN 0-395-19415-6). HM.

Best American Short Stories, 1975. Martha Foley. LC 16-11387. (O.s.i.). 336p. 1975. 10.00 o.s.i. (ISBN 0-395-20719-3). HM.

Best American Short Stories 1977. Ed. by Martha Foley. 1977. 10.00 (ISBN 0-395-25701-8). HM.

Best American Short Stories 1978. Ed. by Theodore Solotaroff & Shannon Ravenel. 1978. 10.95 (ISBN 0-395-27104-5). HM.

Best American Short Stories, 1981. Ed. by Hortense Calisher & Shannon Ravenel. 1981. 12.95 (ISBN 0-395-31259-0). HM.

Best American Short Stories 1981. Ed. by Hortense Calisher & Shannon Ravenel. 365p. 1982. pap. 6.95 (ISBN 0-14-006135-5). Penguin.

Best American Stories: 1919-1924. Williams, Blanche Colton. LC 26-21115. 1926. Doubleday, Page & Company.

Best American Tales Chosen: With an Introduction. Ed. by William Peterfield Trent. Henneman, John Bell, 1864-1908, Joint Comp. LC 7-25511. (On cover: Handy volume classics). T. Y. Crowell & Co.

Best and the Last of Edwin O'Connor. Edwin O'Connor. Ed. by Arthur Meier Schlesinger. LC 74-99902. 1970. 10.00. Little, Brown.

Best and Worst of Times. Peter Sourian. LC 61-9202. 1961. Doubleday.

Best Army Short Stories: Winners of the U. S. Army Contest 1950- U. S. Army. Army Library Service. LC 50-103613. Rinehart.

Best Biker Fiction, No. 3. Ed. by Easyriders. (Paisano Bks.). 224p. (Orig.). 1983. pap. 2.95 (ISBN 0-440-01832-3). Dell.

Best Bird Stories I Know. Ed. by John Clair Minot. LC 30-32304. W. A. Wilde Company.

Best Black Magic Stories. John K. Cross. 1960. 3.50 o.p. Wehman.

Best Black Magic Stories. Ed. by John K. Cross. Repr. of 1960 ed. 20.00 (ISBN 0-89987-131-3). Darby Bks.

Best British Short Stories of. Ed. by O'Brien, Edward Joseph Harrington. Cournos, John, 1881- LC 22-23919. Houghton Mifflin Company.

Best Butter. Jean Dutourd. LC 76-90499. 1969. Greenwood Press.

Best Butter. Elinor Rice. LC 38-5359. 1938. W. Morrow & Co.

Best Butter. Translated Form the French by Robin Chancellor. Jean Dutourd. LC 54-5812. 1955. Simon and Schuster.

Best by Far. LC 66-12185. 1966. N.Y., Doubleday.

Best by Far. Roger Eddy. LC 66-12185. 1966. N.Y., Doubleday.

Best College Short Stories: 1917/18- Schnittkind, Henry Thomas, 1888- Ed. The Stratford Company.

Best College Stories I Know. Ed. by John Clair Minot. LC 31-28465. W. A. Wilde Company.

Best College Writing. 1961- Story (New York, 1931-) LC 62-8443. Random House.

Best Continental Short Stories of 1923-1927... Ed. by Eaton, Richard. LC 25-765. Dodd, Mead & Company.

Best Days. Julius Horwitz. LC 80-12649. (ISBN 0-03-057296-7). Holt, Rinehart, and Winston.

Best Detective Selections No. 1- 1942- LC 45-2333. Select Publications, Inc.,

Best Detective Stories of the Year. E.P. Dutton.

Best Detective Stories of the Year. Ed. by Anthony Boucher. LC 46-5872. (Annual Collection Ser, Vol. 22). 1968. 4.50 o.p. Dutton.

Best Detective Stories of the Year: Twenty-Seventh Annual Collection. Ed. by Allen J. Hubin. 1973. 6.95 o.p. (ISBN 0-525-06432-X). Dutton.

Best Detective Stories of the Year: 19th Annual Collection. Ed. by Anthony Boucher. Ed. by Anthony Boucher. LC 46-5872. 3.95. Dutton.

Best Detective Stories of the Year: 18th Annual Collection. Ed. by Anthony Boucher. Ed. by Anthony Boucher. LC 46-587227. 3.95. Dutton.

Best Detective Stories of the Year, 1976: Thirtieth Annual Collection. Ed. by Edward D. Hoch. 224p. 1976. 8.95 o.p. (ISBN 0-525-06435-4). Dutton.

Best Detective Stories of the Year, 1976: 13th Annual Collection. Ed. by Edward D. Hoch. 224p. 1976. 8.95 o.p. (ISBN 0-525-06435-4). Dutton.

Best Detective Stories of the Year, 1974: 28th Annual Collection. annual Ed. by Allen J. Hubin. LC 46-5872. 1974. 6.95 o.p. (ISBN 0-525-06433-8). Dutton.

Best Detective Stories of the Year, 1979: 33rd Annual Collection. Ed. by Edward D. Hoch. 1979. 9.95 o.p. (ISBN 0-525-06438-9). Dutton.

Best Detective Stories of the Year, 1977: 31st Annual Collection. Ed. by Edward D. Hoch. 1977. 8.95 o.p. (ISBN 0-525-06436-2). Dutton.

Best Detective Stories of the Year, 1980: 34th Annual Collection. Ed. by Edward D. Hoch. (F). 1980. 10.95 (ISBN 0-525-06439-7). Dutton.

Best Detective Stories of the Year, 1978: 32nd Annual Collection. Ed. by Edward D. Hoch. 1978. 8.95 o.p. (ISBN 0-525-06437-0). Dutton.

Best Detective Stories of the Year. 1945- Ed. by David Coxe Cooke. LC 46-5872. E. P. Dutton & Company, Inc.

Best Detective Stories of the Year: 24th Annual Collection. Ed. by Allen J. Hubin. LC 72-95478. 1970. 5.95 o.p. (ISBN 0-525-06429-X). Dutton.

Best Detective Stories of the Year: 25th Annual Collection. Ed. by Allen J. Hubin. 1971. 5.95 o.p. (ISBN 0-525-06430-3). Dutton.

Best Detective Stories of the Year: 26th Annual Collection. Ed. by Allen J. Hubin. 1972. 6.95 o.p. (ISBN 0-525-06431-1). Dutton.

Best Detective Stories of the Year: 21st Annual Collection. Ed. by Anthony Boucher. Ed. by Anthony Boucher. LC 46-5872. 4.50. Dutton.

Best Detective Stories of the Year: 22nd Annual Collection. Ed. by Anthony Boucher. Ed. by Anthony Boucher. LC 46-5872. 1967. 4.50. Dutton.

Best Dr. Poggioli Detective Stories. Thomas Sigismund Stribling. LC 75-21298. (Illus.). 1975. 3.00 (ISBN 0-486-23227-1). Dover Publications.

Best Dr. Thorndyke Detective Stories. Richard Austin Freeman. LC 72-78377. 1973. 3.00 (ISBN 0-486-20388-3). Dover Publications.

Best Encore. Peter Passell. 1978. pap. 1.95 (ISBN 0-345-27434-2). Ballantine.

Best English Detective Stories of. Ed. by Knox, Ronald Arbuthnott & Harrington, Henry. LC 29-208923. H. Liveright.

Best European Short Stories of. Ed. by Eaton, Richard. LC 29-7735. Dodd, Mead and Company.

Best Evidence. David Lifton. 1982. pap. 4.95 (ISBN 0-440-00586-8). Dell.

Best Fables of La Fontaine. Jean De La Fontaine. Tr. by Francis Duke. LC 65-27279. (Illus.). 1965. 7.50x o.p. (ISBN 0-8139-0161-8). U Pr of Va.

Best for Winter: A Selection from Twenty-Five Years of Winter's Tales. Alan Duart Maclean. LC 79-22851. 15.95 (ISBN 0-312-07708-4). St. Martin's Press.

Best Friend. Pat Feeley. LC 77-3678. 7.95. Dutton.

Best Friend: A Novel. Pat Feeley. 1979. 1.95 (ISBN 0-449-24154-8). Fawcett Crest.

Best Friends. Consuelo Baehr. (O.s.i.). 1980. 11.95 o.s.i. (ISBN 0-440-00841-7). Delacorte.

Best Friends. Consuelo Baehr. 432p. 1981. pap. 2.95 (ISBN 0-440-10510-2). Dell.

Best from Amazing. Ted White. LC 76-382971. (Hale SF). 1976. 2.90 (ISBN 0-7091-5127-6). Hale.

Best from Amazing Stories. Ed. by Ted White. 192p. (Orig.). 1973. pap. 0.95 o.p. (ISBN 0-532-95225-1). Woodhill.

Best from Amazing Stories. Ed. by Ted White. 192p. (Orig.). 1973. pap. 0.95 o.p. (ISBN 0-532-95225-1). Manor Bks.

Best from Fantastic. Ted White. LC 77-364053. (Hale SF). 1976. 3.10 (ISBN 0-7091-5128-4). Hale.

Best from Fantastic: Stories by Poul Anderson and Others. Edited by Ted White. Ed. by Ted White. 1973. (pbk.) 0.95. Manor Books.

Best from Fantasy & Science Fiction - Nineteenth Series. Edward L. Ferman. LC 77-150891. 1971. 5.95 o.p. (ISBN 0-385-04473-9). Doubleday.

Best From Fantasy & Science Fiction. 24th ed. Edward L. Ferman. 288p. 1982. 14.95 (ISBN 0-684-17490-1, ScribT). Scribner.

Best from Fantasy & Science Fiction. Ed. by Edward L. Ferman. 273p. 1981. pap. 2.50 (ISBN 0-441-05484-6). Ace Bks.

Best from Fantasy & Science Fiction. Ed. by Edward L. Ferman. LC 76-56287. (Science Fiction Ser.). 1977. 7.95 o.p. (ISBN 0-385-12451-1). Doubleday.

Best from Fantasy & Science Fiction. 24th ed. Ed. by Edward L. Ferman. 2.95 (ISBN 0-441-05485-4, Pub. by Ace Science Fiction). Ace Bks.

Best from Fantasy & Science Fiction. Ed. by Edward L. Ferman. LC 73-83589. 312p. 1973. 6.95 o.p. (ISBN 0-385-07816-1). Doubleday.

Best from Fantasy & Science Fiction. Ed. by Edward L. Ferman. LC 76-56287. (Science Fiction Ser.). 1977. 7.95 o.p. (ISBN 0-385-12451-1). Doubleday.

Best from Fantasy & Science Fiction. Ed. by Robert P. Mills. (Eleventh Ser.). 3.95 o.p. (ISBN 0-385-04473-9). Doubleday.

Best from Fantasy and Science Fiction. 1st. The Magazine of Fantasy and Science Fiction. Ed. by William Anthony Parker White. LC 52-5510. Little, Brown.

Best from Fantasy and Science Fiction: 16th Ser. Magazine of Fantasy & Science Fiction. Ed. by William Anthony Parker White & Avram Davidson. LC 52-5510. 4.50. Doubleday.

Best from Fantasy & Science Fiction, 18th Ser. Ed. by Edward L. Ferman. LC 52-5510. (Eighteenth Ser). 1969. 4.95 o.p. Doubleday.

Best from Fantasy & Science Fiction, 24th Series. Ed. by Edward L. Ferman. LC 82-696. 13.95 (ISBN 0-684-17490-1). Scribner.

Best from Fantasy & Science Fiction: Twenty-Third Series. Ed. by Edward L. Ferman. LC 79-7685. (Science Fiction Ser.). 1980. 10.95 o.p. (ISBN 0-385-15225-6). Doubleday.

Best from Fantasy and Science Fiction: 15th Ser. Ed. by Edward L. Ferman. Magazine of Fantasy and Science Fiction. Ed. by William Anthony Parker White. LC 52-5510. 1966. 4.50. Doubleday.

Best from Galaxy, Vol. 2. Galaxy Magazine Editors. (O.s.i.). 224p. (Orig.). 1974. pap. 1.25 o.s.i. (AQ1261, Award). Univ Pub & Dist.

Best from Galaxy, Vol. 4. Ed. by James Baen. (O.s.i.). (Orig.). 1976. pap. 1.75 o.s.i. (AR1599, Award). Univ Pub & Dist.

Best from Galaxy, Vol. 3. Galaxy Magazine Editors. (O.s.i.). 224p. (Orig.). 1975. pap. 1.50 o.s.i. (AD1506, Award). Univ Pub & Dist.

Best from IF. IF Magazine Editors. 224p. (Orig.). 1973. pap. 0.95 o.p. (AN1065, Award). Univ Pub & Dist.

Best from If. Ed. by If Magazine Editors. (O.s.i.). (Orig.). 1973. pap. 0.95 o.s.i. (AN1065, Award). Univ Pub & Dist.

Best from If, Vol. 2. If Magazine Editors. (O.s.i.). 224p. (Orig.). 1974. pap. 1.25 o.s.i. (AQ1360, Award). Univ Pub & Dist.

Best from If, Vol. 3. Ed. by James Baen. (O.s.i.). 224p. (Orig.). 1976. pap. 1.50 o.s.i. (AD1544, Award). Univ Pub & Dist.

Best from Startling Stories: Compiled by Samuel Mines; with an Introd. by Robert A. Heinlein. 1st Ed. Startling Stories. Ed. by Samuel Mines. LC 53-8980. 1953. Holt.

Best from the Rest of the World. Ed. by Donald A. Wollheim. (Science Fiction Ser). 1977. pap. 1.75 o.p. (ISBN 0-87997-343-9, UE1343). DAW Bks.

Best from the Rest of the World: European Science Fiction. Donald A Wollheim. LC 74-27594. 1976. 6.95 (ISBN 0-385-04550-6). Doubleday.

Best from the Rest of the World: European Science Fiction. Ed. by Donald A. Wollheim. 1977. 1.75 (ISBN 0-87997-343-9). DAW Books.

Best Ghost Stories. Algernon Blackwood. 7.50 (ISBN 0-8446-5006-4). Peter Smith.

Best Ghost Stories. Ed. by Joseph Lewis French. LC 19-25951. (Half-title: The modern library of the world's best books). 1919. Boni and Liveright, Inc.

Best Ghost Stories. Joseph Sheridan Le Fanu. Ed. by E. F. Bleiler. (Illus., Orig.). pap. 6.00 (ISBN 0-486-20415-4). Dover.

Best Ghost Stories. Joseph Sheridan Le Fanu. Ed. by Bleiler. 10.00 (ISBN 0-8446-2443-8). Peter Smith.

Best Ghost Stories. Ed. by John Gilbert Bohun Lynch. LC 24-14712. Small, Maynard & Company.

Best Ghost Stories. Anne Ridler. Repr. of 1945 ed. 20.00 (ISBN 0-89987-134-8). Darby Bks.

Best Ghost Stories. Ed., Introd. by E. F. Bleiler. Joseph Sheridan Le Fanu. (Dover bk. T415 rebound). 1965. 4.00. P. Smith.

Best Ghost Stories of Algernon Blackwood. Algernon Blackwood. Ed. by E. F. Bleiler. 396p. (Orig.). 1973. pap. 4.50 (ISBN 0-486-22977-7). Dover.

Best Ghost Stories of H. Russel Wakefield. Herbert Russel Wakefield. 232p. 1982. 14.95 (ISBN 0-89733-065-X); pap. 5.95 (ISBN 0-89733-066-8). Academy Chi Ltd.

Best Ghost Stories of J. S. LeFanu. Joseph Sheridan Le Fanu. LC 64-13463. (Illus.). 1964. Dover Publications.

Best Ghost Stories of M. R. James. Montague Rhodes James. LC 45-2056. 1944. The World Publishing Company.

Best Go First. Frank O'Rourke. LC 50-9964. 1950. Random House.

Best Horror Stories. John K. Cross. 1963. pap. 1.95 o.p. Wehman.

Best House in Stratford. Edward Fisher. LC 65-24778. 1965. Abelard-Schuman.

Best in Life. Muriel Hine Coxon. LC 18-4825. 1918. John Lane Company.

Best in the Green Wood. Josiah Carlton Titzell. LC 36-563933. 1936. Doubleday, Doran & Company, Inc.

Best Intentions. Firth Haring. LC 68-26435. 1968. 3.95. W. Morrow.

Best Irish Short Stories. David Marcus. LC 77-354925. 1976-1977. 7.95 (ISBN 0-236-40032-0). Elek.

Best Irish Short Stories Three. David Marcus. 1979. 9.95 (ISBN 0-236-40139-4, Pub. by Paul Elek). Merrimack Pub Cir.

Best Irish Short Stories Two. David Marcus. 1978. 9.95 (ISBN 0-236-40139-4, Pub. by Paul Elek). Merrimack Pub Cir.

Best Is Yet to Be. Bentz Plagemann. LC 66-16405. bds., 4.50. Morrow.

Best I've Read. Walter A. Weiss. 1973. text ed. 16.50x (ISBN 0-8422-5138-3); pap. text ed. 9.50x (ISBN 0-8422-0359-1). Irvington.

Best Kept Woman in the World. Cynthia Halstead. 1976. pap. 1.50 o.s.i. (ISBN 0-505-50998-9). Tower Bks.

Best Kind of Love. Jack Moffitt. LC 59-10563. 1959.

Best-Known Novels of George Eliot. George Eliot. (Modern Library Giants). 4.95 o.p. (G51). Modern Lib.

Best Known Works. facsimile ed. Nathaniel Hawthorne. Incl. Scarlet Letter; House of the Seven Gables; Best of Twice-Told Tales. LC 70-37548. (Short Story Index Reprint Ser.). Repr. of 1941 ed. 17.50 (ISBN 0-8369-4107-1). Ayer Co.

Best Known Works, Vol. 1. Anton Pavlovich Chekhov. LC 72-5899. (Short Story Index Reprint Ser). Repr. of 1929 ed. 37.75 (ISBN 0-8369-4198-5). Ayer Co.

Best Known Works of Gustave Flaubert. One Volume Edition. Gustave Flaubert. LC 33-34964. 1933. Blue Ribbon Books, Inc.

Best Known Works of Nathaniel Hawthorne: Including The Scarlet Letter, The House of the Seven Gables, the Best of the Twice-Told Tales. Nathaniel Hawthorne. LC 70-37548. (Short story index reprint series). 1972. (ISBN 0-8369-4107-1). Books for Libraries Press.

Best Known Works of Nathaniel Hawthorne: Including The Scarlet Letter, The House of the Seven Gables, the Best of the Twice-Told Tales. Nathaniel Hawthorne. LC 42-23861. 1941. Halcyon House.

Best Known Works of Robert Louis Stevenson: Including Treasure Island, Kidnapped, Dr. Jekyll and Mr. Hyde, New Arabian Nights. Robert Louis Stevenson. LC 42-23864. 1941. Halcyon House.

Best Known Works of Voltaire: The Complete Romances, Including Candide, The Philosophy of History, The Ignorant Philosopher, Dialogues and Philosophic Criticisms... Francois Marie Arouet De Voltaire. LC 31-334498. 1931. Blue Ribbon Books.

Best Laid Plans. Elaine R. Chase. (Finding Mr. Right Ser.). 224p. 1983. pap. 2.75 (ISBN 0-380-82743-3, 82743-3). Avon.

Best Laid Plans. Troy Conway, pseud. (Coxeman Ser). (Orig.). 1969. pap. 0.75 o.p. (64-623). Paperback Lib.

Best Laid Plans. Gail Parent. LC 80-15018. 10.95 (ISBN 0-399-12510-8). Putnam.

Best Laid Schemes. Larry Eisenberg. 1973. 1.25. Collier Books.

Best Laid Schemes. Larry Eisenberg. LC 71-142347. 1971. 4.95. Macmillan.

Best Laid Schemes. Meredith Nicholson. LC 22-859133. 1922. C. Scribner's Sons.

Best Laugh Last: A Novel. John B. Roseman. LC 81-12990. 10.95 (ISBN 0-914232-44-4). Treacle Press.

Best Little Boy in the World. John Reid. (YA) 1973. 7.95 o.p. Putnam.

Best Little Girl in the World. Steven Levenkron. LC 78-9063. 8.95 (ISBN 0-8092-7699-2). Contemporary Books.

Best Little Magazine Fiction, 1970. Ed. by Curt Johnson. LC 70-133024. 1970. 10.00x o.p. (ISBN 0-8147-4150-9); pap. 4.95 o.p. (ISBN 0-8147-4151-7). NYU Pr.

Best Little Magazine Fiction, 1971. Ed. by Curt Johnson & Alvin Greenberg. LC 70-133024. 1971. 10.00x o.p. (ISBN 0-8147-4152-5); pap. 4.95 o.p. (ISBN 0-8147-4153-3). NYU Pr.

Best Love Stories of... Ed. by Humphrey, Muriel Miller. LC 25-11154. Small, Maynard & Company.

Best Loved Classics, 10 vols. 1979. 36.00 o.p. Porter.

Best Loved Classics, 10 vols. 1979. 36.00 o.p. Porter.

Best-Loved Dog Stories. Albert Payson Terhune. 1954. Grosset & Dunlap.

Best Loved Short Stories of Jesse Stewart. Ed. by H. E. Richardson. 448p. 1982. 14.95 (ISBN 0-07-062305-8). McGraw.

Best-Loved Short Stories of Jesse Stuart. Jesse Stuart & H. Edward Richardson. LC 82-15264. 14.95 (ISBN 0-07-062305-8). McGraw-Hill.

Best Man. Grace Livingston Hill. LC 14-3289. 1914. J. B. Lippincott Company.

Best Man. Grace Livingston Hill. LC 22-16041. 1919. Grosset & Dunlap.

Best Man. William M. James, pseud. (Apache Ser.: No. 13). 1979. pap. 1.50 (ISBN 0-523-40356-9). Pinnacle Bks.

Best Man. Harold MacGrath. LC 7-30162. 1907. The Bobbs-Merrill Company.

Best Man No. 7. Grace Livingston Hill. 176p. 1981. pap. 1.95 (ISBN 0-553-14505-3). Bantam.

Best Man to Die. Ruth Rendell. LC 70-97683. (Ballantine mystery). 1975. (pbk.) 1.25 (ISBN 0-345-24421-4). Ballantine Books.

Best Man to Die. Ruth Rendell. LC 80-25306. (Series: Her Inspector Wexford Mystery.). 1981. 12.50 (ISBN 0-89340-317-2). J. Curley.

Best Martin Hewitt Detective Stories. Arthur Morrison. LC 76-2996. (Illus.). 3.00 (ISBN 0-486-23324-3). Dover Publications.

Best Max Carrados Detective Stories. Ernest Bramah, pseud. Ed. by E. F. Bleiler. LC 70-186096. 245p. 1972. pap. 3.50 (ISBN 0-486-20064-7). Dover.

Best Max Carrados Detective Stories. Ernest Bramah, pseud. 7.50 (ISBN 0-8446-4517-6). Peter Smith.

Best Max Carrados Detective Stories. Ernest Bramah Smith. LC 70-186096. 1972. (pbk) 3.00. Dover Publications.

Best Modern Short Stories from the Saturday Evening Post. Saturday Evening Post Editors. 5.95 o.p. (ISBN 0-385-04796-7). Doubleday.

Best Modern Short Stories: Selected from the Saturday Evening Post. LC 65-20463. 1965. Curtis Books; Distributed by Doubleday.

Best Mounted Police Stories. Dick Harrison. 268p. (Orig.). 1978. pap. 9.95 (ISBN 0-88864-054-4, Pub. by U Alberta Canada). Hydra Bk.

Best Must Die. Lewis Cecil Day. LC 44-3532. (Black Cat Detective Ser.). (Black cat detective series). 1943. Crestwood Publishing Co., Inc.

Best Not the Bones: By Charlotte Jay Pseud. 1st American Ed. Geraldine Jay. LC 52-11687. Harper.

Best Novellas of Medieval Germany. Tr. by J. W. Thomas from Ger. (Studies in German Literature, Linguistics, & Culture: Vol. 17). (Illus.). 160p. 1983. 15.00x (ISBN 0-938100-10-6). Camden Hse.

Best Novels and Stories. introd. by j. frank dobie. ed. Eugene Manlove Rhodes. LC 49-11703. Houghton Mifflin Co.,

Best of a Bad Job: A Hearty Tale of the Sea. Norman Duncan. LC 12-29132. 1.00. Fleming H. Revell Company.

Best of A. E. Van Vogt. Alfred Elton Van Vogt. LC 76-371363. 1976. 1.95 (ISBN 0-671-80546-0). Pocket Books.

Best of A. E. Van Vogt. Alfred Elton Van Vogt. 1976. 1.95 (ISBN 0-671-80546-0). Pocket Books.

Best of a Long Journey. Harriet L Nye. LC 68-22806. 1969. 3.50. Dorrance.

Best of All Possible Worlds. Peter De Rosa. LC 75-37086. (Illus.). 1.95 (ISBN 0-913592-55-2). Argus Communications.

Best of All Possible Worlds. Ed. by Spider Robinson. 1980. pap. 2.25 (ISBN 0-441-05483-8). Ace Bks.

Best of All Possible Worlds: Romances and Tales. Francois Marie Arouet De Voltaire. LC 72-3277. (Short story index reprint series). 1972. 14.75 (ISBN 0-8369-4165-9). Books for Libraries Press.

Best of Amazing. Ed. by Joseph Ross, pseud. 1975. pap. cancelled o.p. Belmont-Tower.

Best of Amazing. 1st Ed. Ed. by Joseph Ross, pseud. Amazing Stories. LC 67-15359. 1967. 4.50. Doubleday.

Best of Analog. Benjamin Bova. LC 79-112393. 1978. 5.95. (ISBN 0-89437-034-0). Baronet Pub. Co.

Best of Astounding. Benjamin Bova. (Illus.). 1977. pap. 5.95 (ISBN 0-89437-024-3). Baronet.

Best of Astounding. Tony Lewis & Clifford D. Simak. LC 79-114318. (Illus.). 1978. 5.95 (ISBN 0-89437-024-3). Baronet Pub. Co.

Best of Avram Davidson. Avram Davidson & Michael Kurland. LC 74-27579. 1979. 7.95 (ISBN 0-385-01384-1). Doubleday.

Best of Barbara Cartland. Barbara Cartland. LC 78-58107. 1979. 14.95 (ISBN 0-448-16248-2). Grosset & Dunlap.

Best of Barry N. Malzberg. Barry N Malzberg. 1976. (pbk.) 1.95 (ISBN 0-671-80256-9). Pocket Books.

Best of Beaumont. Charles Beaumont. 288p. 1982. pap. 2.95. Bantam.

Best of Both Worlds: An Anthology of Stories for All Ages. Designs by Paul Bacon. 1st Ed. Ed. by Georgess McHargue. LC 68-22466. 1968. 6.95. Doubleday.

Best of Buster. Ed. by Richard J. Anobile. (Illus.). 1976. 12.95 o.p. (ISBN 0-517-52801-0, Darien Hse Bk); pap. 5.95 o.p. (ISBN 0-517-52802-9). Crown.

Best of C. L. Moore. Ed. by Lester Del Rey. LC 77-5293. 1977. Repr. of 1976 ed. 9.95 (ISBN 0-8008-0722-7). Taplinger.

Best of C. L. Moore. Catherine L. Moore. LC 75-41450. 1976. 1.95 (ISBN 0-345-24752-3). Ballantine Books.

Best of C. L. Moore. Catherine L. Moore. LC 77-5293. 1977. 9.95 (ISBN 0-8008-0722-7). Taplinger Pub. Co.

Best of C. M. Kornbluth. Cyril M Kornbluth. LC 77-5294. 1977. 9.95 (ISBN 0-8008-0723-5). Taplinger Pub. Co.

Best of C. M. Kornbluth. Cyril M. Kornbluth & Frederick Pohl. LC 76-15620. 1976. 1.95 (ISBN 0-345-25461-9). Ballantine Books.

Best of C. M. Kornbluth. Ed. by Frederik Pohl. LC 77-5294. 1977. Repr. 9.95 (ISBN 0-8008-0723-5). Taplinger.

Best of Cordwainer Smith I.E. P. M. A. Linebarger. Paul Myron Anthony Linebarger. LC 75-19108. 1975. 1.95 (ISBN 0-345-24581-4). Nelson Doubleday.

Best of Crunch and Des. Philip Wylie. LC 54-9124. 1954. Rinehart.

Best of Damon Knight. Damon Knight (ISBN 0-671-80699-8). Pocket Books.

Best of Damon Knight. Damon Francis Knight. (gr. 10-12). 1980. pap. 2.50 (ISBN 0-671-83375-8, Timescape). PB.

Best of Damon Knight. Damon Francis Knight. LC 77-92176. 1978. Repr. of 1976 ed. 9.95 (ISBN 0-8008-0721-9). Taplinger.

Best of Damon Runyon. Damon Runyon. LC 66-22460. 1966. Hart Pub. Co.

Best of E. E. "Doc" Smith. E. E. Smith. (Family D'alembert Ser.). (Orig.). pap. 1.75 (ISBN 0-515-04245-5). Jove Pubns.

Best of Edmond Hamilton. Edmond Hamilton. LC 77-574. 1977. 1.95 (ISBN 0-345-25900-9). Ballantine Books.

Best of Edmond Hamilton. Edmond Hamilton & Leigh Brackett. LC 81-47372. (Best Science fiction). 1982. 19.95 (ISBN 0-8240-4209-3). Garland Pub.

Best of Eric Frank Russell. Eric Frank Russell. LC 78-61462. 1978. 1.95 (ISBN 0-345-27700-7). Ballantine Books.

Best of Eric Frank Russell. Eric Frank Russell & Alan Dean Foster. LC 81-47362. (Best science fiction). 1982. 19.95 (ISBN 0-8240-4211-5). Garland Pub.

Best of Everything. Rona Jaffe. 1976. (pbk.) 1.95 (ISBN 0-380-00581-6). Avon.

Best of Everything: A Novel. Rona Jaffe. LC 58-10357. 1958. Simon and Schuster.

Best of Families. Ellin Mackay Berlin. LC 72-111199. 1970. 5.95. Doubleday.

Best of Fiends. Ed. by Alfred Joseph Hitchcock. 1973. (pbk) 0.75. Dell.

Best of Frederik Pohl. Frederik Pohl. LC 77-5292. 1977. 9.95 (ISBN 0-8008-0724-3). Taplinger Pub. Co.

Best of Frederik Pohl. Frederik Pohl. 1975. (pbk.) 1.95 (ISBN 0-345-24507-5). Ballantine Books.

Best of Frederik Pohl; Introd. by Lester Del Rey; Afterword by Frederik Pohl. Frederik Pohl. LC 75-309858. 1975. N. Doubleday.

Best of Fredric Brown. Fredric Brown. LC 76-56422. 1977. 1.95. Ballantine Books.

Best of Fredric Brown. Fredric Brown. LC 77-365346. Nelson Doubleday.

Best of Friends. Mary Danby, pseud. LC 74-23090. 1975. 6.95 (ISBN 0-07-015284-5). McGraw-Hill.

Best of Friends: A Novel. Joy Fielding. LC 72-77937. 1972. 5.95 (ISBN 0-399-10979-X). Putnam.

Best of Fritz Leiber. Fritz Leiber. LC 74-195238. (Ballantine science fiction). 1974. 1.75 (ISBN 0-345-24256-4). Ballantine Books.

Best of Fritz Leiber. Fritz Leiber & Poul Anderson. LC 81-47370. (Best science fiction). 1982. 19.95 (ISBN 0-8240-4227-1). Garland.

Best of Glencannon: Twenty-Two Stories. Guy Gilpatric. LC 68-57199. 1968. 6.95. Dodd, Mead.

Best of H. E. Bates. Herbert Ernest Bates. LC 62-10532. 1963. Little, Brown.

Best of H. E. Bates. Herbert Ernest Bates. LC 76-167441. (Short story index reprint series). 1971. (ISBN 0-8369-3967-0). Books for Libraries Press.

Best of Harry Harrison. Harry Harrison. 1976. (pbk.) 1.95 (ISBN 0-671-80525-8). Pocket Books.

Best of Hawthorne: Edited with Introd. and Notes by Mark Van Doren. Nathaniel Hawthorne. LC 51-9259. 1951. Ronald Press Co.

Best of Henry Kuttner. Henry Kuttner. LC 75-308128. 1975. N. Doubleday.

Best of Henry Kuttner. Henry Kuttner. 1975. (pbk.) 1.95 (ISBN 0-345-24415-X). Ballantine Books.

Best of Henry Kuttner. Henry Kuttner & Ray Bradbury. LC 81-47371. (Best science fiction). 1982. 19.95 (ISBN 0-8240-4228-X). Garland.

Best of Hillbilly. Ed. by Otto Whittaker. 5.95 o.p. G&D.

Best of H.P. Lovecraft: Bloodcurdling Tales of Horror and the Macabre. Howard Phillips Lovecraft. LC 82-90468. (Illus.). 1982. 6.95 (ISBN 0-345-29468-8). Ballantine Books.

Best of Husbands. Alba De Cespedes. LC 52-13391. 1952. Macmillan.

Best of Intentions. Robert Molloy. LC 49-10919. 1949. J. B. Lippincott Co.

Best of Isaac Asimov. Isaac Asimov. LC 74-2863. (Doubleday science fiction). 1974. 6.95 (ISBN 0-385-05078-X). Doubleday.

Best of Issac Asimov. Isaac Asimov. (Fawcett Crest Book). 1976. (pbk.) 1.50. Fawcett.

Best of Jack Vance. Jack Vance. 1976. (pbk.) 1.95 (ISBN 0-671-80510-X). Pocket Books.

Best of Jack Vance. John Holbrook Vance. LC 78-56984. 1978. 9.95 (ISBN 0-8008-0726-X). Taplinger Pub. Co.

Best of Jack Williamson. Jack Williamson & Frederik Pohl. LC 81-47180. (Best science fiction). 1982. 19.95 (ISBN 0-8240-4214-X). Garland.

Best of James Blish. James Blish & Robert W Lowndes. LC 81-47361. (Best science fiction). 1982. 19.95 (ISBN 0-8240-4200-X). Garland Pub.

Best of John Collier. John Collier. 1975. (pbk.) 1.95 (ISBN 0-671-80076-0). Pocket Books.

Best of John Jakes. John Jakes. (Science Fiction Ser). 1977. pap. 1.75 o.p. (ISBN 0-87997-302-1, UE1302). DAW Bks.

Best of John Sladek. John Thomas Sladek. 1980. pap. 2.50 (ISBN 0-671-83131-3, Timescape). PB.

Best of John W. Campbell. John Wood Campbell. LC 76-7497. 1.95 (ISBN 0-345-24960-7). Nelson Doubleday.

Best of John W. Campbell. John Wood Campbell & Lester Del Rey. LC 81-47364. (Best science fiction). 1982. 19.95 (ISBN 0-8240-4204-2). Garland Pub.

Best of Judith Merril. Judith Merril. 1976. (pbk.) 1.25. Warner.

Best of Kathleen Norris. Kathleen Thompson Norris. LC 55-11334. Hanover House.

Best of Keith Laumer. rev. ed. Keith Laumer. 1980. pap. 2.25 (ISBN 0-671-83268-9, Timescape). PB.

Best of Keith Laumer. Keith Laumer. 1976. (pbk.) 1.75 (ISBN 0-671-80310-7). Pocket Books.

Best of Kipling. Rudyard Kipling. LC 68-622. (Illus.). 1968. N. Doubleday.

Best of L. Sprague De Camp. Lyon Sprague De Camp. LC 77-26949. 1978. 1.95 (ISBN 0-345-25474-0). Ballantine Books.

Best of L. Sprague De Camp. Lyon Sprague De Camp & Poul Anderson. LC 81-47374. (Best science fiction). 1982. 19.95 (ISBN 0-8240-4206-9). Garland Pub.

Best of Leigh Brackett. Leigh Brackett. LC 77-772. 1977. 1.95 (ISBN 0-345-25954-8). Ballantine Books.

Best of Leigh Brackett. Leigh Brackett & Edmond Hamilton. LC 81-47369. (Best science fiction). 1982. 19.95 (ISBN 0-8240-4202-6). Garland Pub.

Best of Lester Del Rey. Lester Del Rey. LC 78-62267. 1978. 1.95 (ISBN 0-345-27336-2). Ballantine Books.

Best of Lester Del Rey. Lester Del Rey & Frederik Pohl. LC 81-47366. (Best science fiction). 1982. 19.95 (ISBN 0-8240-4207-7). Garland Pub.

Best of Mack Reynolds. Mack Reynolds, pseud. LC 76-361138. 1976. 1.95. Pocket Books.

Best of Maupassant: Selected by J. I. Rodale. Guy De Maupassant. LC 50-11399. 1950. Story Classics.

Best of Mr. Fortune Stories. Henry Christopher Bailey. LC 43-3702. 1943. Pocket Books Inc.

Best of Murray Leinster. Murray Leinster & J. J Pierce. LC 81-47368. (Best science fiction). 1982. 19.95 (ISBN 0-8240-4210-7). Garland Pub.

Best of Nash Buckingham. Nash Buckingham. Ed. by George B. Evans. 1973. 15.95 (ISBN 0-87691-103-3). Winchester Pr.

Best of New Dimensions. Robert Silverberg. 1979. 2.50 (ISBN 0-671-82976-9). Pocket Books.

Best of O. Henry. O. Henry. LC 78-14841. 1978. lib. bdg. 12.90 (ISBN 0-89471-047-8); pap. 4.95 (ISBN 0-89471-046-X). Running Pr.

Best of O. Henry. William Sydney Porter. LC 78-14841. 9.80. (ISBN 0-89471-047-8) (ISBN 0-89471-046-X). Running Press.

Best of Our Time. William Stevens. LC 72-13926. 1973. 6.95 (ISBN 0-394-47977-7). Random House.

Best of Philip K. Dick. Philip K Dick. (Del Rey Book). 1977. 1.95 (ISBN 0-345-25359-0). Ballantine Books.

Best of Philip K. Dick. Philip K Dick & John Brunner. LC 81-47373. (Best science fiction). 1982. 19.95 (ISBN 0-8240-4208-5). Garland.

Best of Playguy Fantasies. Ed. by George Battle. 96p. 1980. pap. 3.95 o.p. (ISBN 0-89237-007-6). Modernismo.

Best of Poul Anderson. Poul Anderson. 1979. pap. 2.25 (ISBN 0-671-83140-2, Timescape). PB.

Best of Poul Anderson. Poul Anderson (ISBN 0-671-80671-8). Pocket Books.

Best of Raymond Z. Gallun. Raymond Z. Gallun & J. J Pierce. LC 81-47367. (Best science fiction). 1982. 19.95 (ISBN 0-8240-4226-3). Garland Pub.

Best of Rhys Davies. Rhys Davies. LC 79-310495. 1979. 13.95 (ISBN 0-7153-7756-6). David & Charles.

Best of Roald Dahl: Stories from Over to You, Someone Like You, Kiss Kiss, and Switch Bitch. Roald Dahl. LC 77-16579. 1978. 4.95 (ISBN 0-394-72549-2). Vintage Books.

Best of Robert Bloch. Robert Bloch. LC 77-3394. (Del Rey book). 1977. 1.95 (ISBN 0-345-25757-X). Ballantine Books.

Best of Robert Bloch. Robert Bloch & Lester Del Rey. LC 81-47363. (Best science fiction). 1982. 19.95 (ISBN 0-8240-4201-8). Garland Pub.

Best of Robert Heinlein. Robert Heinlein. Repr. lib. bdg. 15.15x (ISBN 0-88411-884-3). Amereon Ltd.

Best of Robert Silverberg. Robert Silverberg. LC 76-354019. 1976. 1.95 (ISBN 0-671-80282-8) (ISBN 0-671-80282-8). Pocket Books.

Best of Robert Silverberg. Robert Silverberg. LC 78-5575. (Gregg Press science fiction series). (Illus.). 13.00 (ISBN 0-8398-2445-9). Gregg Press.

Best of Rocky, the Complete Rocky II. Ed. by Fotonovel Publications Staff. (Illus., Orig.). 1979. pap. 2.95. Fotonovel.

Best of Runyon. Damon Runyon. Ed. by Bentley, Edmund Clerihew. LC 38-7468. 1938. Frederick A. Stokes Company.

Best of Runyon. Damon Runyon. Ed. by Bentley, Edmund Clerihew. LC 40-6011. 1940. Triangle Books.

Best of Saki (H. H. Munro) Hector Hugh Munro. LC 76-30598. 1977. 2.50 (ISBN 0-14-004484-1). Penguin Books.

Best of Saki (H. H. Munro) Hector Hugh Munro. Ed. by Graham Greene. LC 78-101367. (Viking compass book, C88). 1970. 1.25 (ISBN 0-670-00088-4). Viking Press.

Best of Saki (H. H. Munro) Selected and with an Introd. by Graham Greene. Hector Hugh Munro. LC 61-2191. (Compass books, C88). 1961. Viking Press.

Best of Science Fiction. Ed. by Groff Conklin. LC 46-55155. 1946. Crown Publishers.

Best of Shalom Aleichem. Shalom Rabinowitz & Irving Howe. LC 80-12492. 1980. 4.95 (ISBN 0-671-41092-X). Simon and Schuster.

Best of Sherlock Holmes. Arthur Conan Doyle. Grosset & Dunlap.

Best of Sherlock Holmes. Arthur Conan Doyle. 2.95 o.p. (ISBN 0-448-01007-0). G&D.

Best of Sholom Aleichem. Shalom Rabinowitz & Irving Howe. LC 79-9870. 1979. 12.50 (ISBN 0-915220-48-2). New Republic Books.

Best of Spidey Super Stories. 1978. 9.95 o.p. (ISBN 0-671-24220-2); pap. 3.95 o.p. (ISBN 0-671-22765-3). S&S.

Best of Stanley G. Weinbaum. Stanley G Weinbaum. 1974. (pbk.) 1.65 (ISBN 0-345-23890-7). Ballantine.

Best of Stanley G. Weinbaum. Stanley Grauman Weinbaum. LC 75-312981. 1974. 1.65 (ISBN 0-345-23890-7). Ballantine Books.

Best of Stillmeadow. Gladys Bagg Taber. (Spring Adult Ser.). 1977. lib. bdg. 12.95 o.p. (ISBN 0-8161-6449-5, Large Print Bks). G K Hall.

Best of Sydney J. Harris. Sydney J. Harris. 1976. pap. 5.95 (ISBN 0-395-24973-2). HM.

Best of the Best American Short Stories, 1915-1950. Edited by Martha Foley. The Best American Short Stories. Ed. by Martha Foley. LC 51-8996. 1952. Houghton Mifflin.

Best of the Best Detective Stories. Ed. by Allen J. Hubin. 1971. 7.95 o.p. (ISBN 0-525-06450-8). Dutton.

Best of the Best Detective Stories: 25th Anniversary Collection. Ed. by Allen J. Hubin. LC 70-158603. 1971. 7.95 (ISBN 0-525-06450-8). Dutton.

Best of the West: A Treasury of Western Adventure. LC 75-10496. (Illus.). 11.97. Reader's Digest Association.

Best of Thomas N. Scortia. Thomas N. Scortia & George Zebrowski. LC 80-2349. 1981. 11.95 (ISBN 0-385-14695-7). Doubleday.

Best of Thomas N. Scortia. George Zebrowski. LC 80-2349. (Science Fiction Ser.). 256p. 1981. 11.95 (ISBN 0-385-14695-7). Doubleday.

Best of Tish. Mary Roberts Rinehart. LC 54-934737. 1955. Rinehart.

Best of Trek, No. 4. Ed. by Walter Irwin & G. B. Love. (Illus., Orig.). 1981. pap. 2.75 (ISBN 0-451-12356-5, AE2356, Sig). NAL.

Best of Trek, No. 5. Ed. by Walter Irwin & G. B. Love. 1982. pap. 2.75 (ISBN 0-451-11751-4, AE1751, Sig). NAL.

Best of Trek: From the Magazine for Star Trek Fans, No. 2. Walter Irwin. (Illus., Orig.). 1980. pap. 2.50 (ISBN 0-451-09836-6, E9836, Sig). NAL.

Best of Trek No. 3. Ed. by Walter Irwin & G. B. Love. 1981. pap. 2.50 (ISBN 0-451-11807-3, AE1807, Sig). NAL.

Best of True Story. 1977. pap. 1.25 (ISBN 0-532-12506-1). Woodhill.

Best of Twice-Told Tales see Best Known Works.

Best of Walter M. Miller. Jr. Walter M. Miller, Jr. (Orig.). (gr. 10-12). 1980. pap. 2.95 (ISBN 0-671-83304-9, Timescape). PB.

Best of William Irish: Including Phantom Lady, After-Dinner Story and Deadline at Dawn. Cornell George Hopley-Woolrich. LC 60-16078. 1960. Lippincott.

Best of Wilson Tucker. Wilson Tucker. (Orig.). 1982. pap. 2.75 (ISBN 0-671-83243-3, Timescape). PB.

Best of Wodehouse: Selected and with an Introd. by Scott Meredith. Pelham Grenville Wodehouse. LC 49-52207. (Pocket book, 628). 1949. Pocket Books.

Best Offer. Robert Calder. 288p. (Orig.). 1981. pap. 2.95 (ISBN 0-515-04759-7). Jove Pubns.

Best People. Ruth Cranston. John Lane Company; Etc., Etc.

Best People. Helen Van Slyke. 1976. (pbk.) 1.75. Popular Library.

Best Place to Be. Helen Van Slyke. LC 75-40748. 1976. 8.95 (ISBN 0-385-01429-5). Doubleday.

Best Place to Be. 1st. ed. Helen Van Slyke. 1977. 2.25 (ISBN 0-445-04024-6). Popular Library.

Best Place to Be. large print ed. Helen Van Slyke. LC 82-19498. 1983. 13.95 (ISBN 0-89621-415-X). Thorndike Press.

Best Policy. Elliott Flower. LC 5-32327. The Bobbs-Merril Company.

Best Policy: A Novel. Richard Stiller. LC 65-24329. 1965. Crown Publishers.

Best Psychic Stories. Ed. by Joseph Lewis French. LC 20-11499. Boni & Liveright.

Best Religious Stories. Ed. by John Edward Lantz. LC 48-9219. 1948. Association Press.

Best Ride to New York: A Novel. Bob Levin. LC 78-2068. 9.95 (ISBN 0-06-012557-8). Harper & Row.

Best Russian Short Stories. Ed. by Thomas Seltzer. 2.95 o.p. (ISBN 0-394-60018-5, 18). Modern Lib.

Best Science Fiction for 1973. Ed. by Forrest J. Ackerman. LC 73-172833. 1973. 1.25. Ace Books.

Best Science Fiction, Nineteen Sixty-Eight. Ed. by Harry Harrison & Brian W. Aldiss. 1969. 4.95 o.p. Putnam.

Best Science Fiction of Arthur Conan Doyle. Arthur Conan Doyle & Charles Waugh. LC 81-8884. (Alternatives). 14.95 (ISBN 0-8093-1046-5). Southern Illinois University Press.

Best Science Fiction of Arthur Conan Doyle. Ed. by Charles G. Waugh & Martin H. Greenberg. LC 81-8884. (Alternatives Ser.). 209p. 1981. 14.95 (ISBN 0-8093-1046-5). S Ill U Pr.

Best Science Fiction of the Year, Number Two. Ed. by Terry Carr. 1973. (pbk) 1.25. Ballantine.

Best Science Fiction of the Year. Ed. by Terry Carr. LC 72-195467. 1972. 1.25 (ISBN 0-345-02671-3). Ballantine Books.

Best Science Fiction Stories. Ed. by Everett Franklin Bleiler & T. E. Dikty. 256p. 1980. Repr. lib. bdg. 20.00 (ISBN 0-8492-3582-0). R West.

Best Science Fiction Stories. Herbert George Wells. pap. 3.95 (ISBN 0-486-21531-8). Dover.

Best Science Fiction Stories. Herbert George Wells. 9.50 (ISBN 0-8446-3149-3). Peter Smith.

Best Science Fiction Stories of Clifford D. Simak. Clifford D. Simak. LC 70-131106. 1971. 4.95. Doubleday.

Best Science Fiction Stories of H. G. Wells. Herbert George Wells. (Dover bk. rebound). 1967. 3.75. P. Smith.

Best Science Fiction Stories of H. G. Wells. Herbert George Wells. LC 66-13832. 1966. Dover Publications.

Best Science Fiction Stories of the Year. Ed. by Lester Del Rey. 1973. (pbk.) 1.25. Ace.

Best Science Fiction Stories of the Year. Ed. by Lester Del Rey. LC 77-190700. 1972. 6.95 (ISBN 0-525-06490-7). E. P. Dutton.

Best Science Fiction Stories of the Year: Fifth Annual Collection. Ed. by Lester Del Rey. 224p. 1976. 8.95 o.p. (ISBN 0-525-06494-X). Dutton.

Best Science Fiction Stories of the Year: Sixth Annual Collection. Ed. by Gardner Dozois. 1978. 1.95 (ISBN 0-441-05482-X). Ace Books.

Best Science Fiction Stories of the Year, 1981: 10th Annual Collection. Ed. by Gardner Dozois. 256p. 1981. 12.50 (ISBN 0-525-06499-0, 01214-360). Dutton.

Best Science Fiction Stories of the Year, 1977: 6th Annual Collection. Ed. by Gardner Dozois. 1977. 8.95 o.p. (ISBN 0-525-06495-8). Dutton.

Best Science Fiction Stories of the Year, 1978: 7th Annual Collection. Ed. by Gardner Dozois. 1978. 8.95 o.p. (ISBN 0-525-06496-6). Dutton.

Best Science Fiction Stories of the Year, 1979: 8th Annual Collection. Gardner Dozois. 1979. 9.95 o.p. (ISBN 0-525-06497-4). Dutton.

Best Science Fiction Stories of the Year, 1980: 9th Annual Collection. Ed. by Gardner Dozois. (Sf). 1980. 11.95 o.p. (ISBN 0-525-06498-2). Dutton.

Best Science Fiction Stories: 1949- Editors: 1949-E. F. Bleiler, T. E. Dikty. Ed. by Bleiler, Everett Franklin. LC 49-104612. F. Fell.

Best Science Fiction Stories, 1973. Del Rey. 1973. 6.95 o.p. (ISBN 0-525-06491-5). Dutton.

Best Seller: The Story of a Young Man Who Came to New York to Write a Novel About a Young Man Who Came to New York to Write a Novel. Allen Clark Marple. LC 30-29564. The Bobbs-Merrill Company.

Best Seller. 1st Ed. William Murray. LC 57-529796. 1957. Harcourt, Brace.

Best Sellers. Stephen Lewis. 320p. 1981. pap. 2.50 (ISBN 0-8439-0960-9, Leisure Bks). Nordon Pubns.

Best Sellers. Stephen Lewis. (Fawcett Gold medal Book). 1976. 1.95. Fawcett.

Best Sellers from Reader's Digest Condensed Books. LC 73-172811. (Illus.). 1973. 8.98. Reader's Digest Association.

Best Sellers from Reader's Digest Condensed Books. LC 75-308848. (Illus.). 1975. Reader's Digest Association.

Best SF: 1967. Ed. by Harry Harrison. LC 68-5860. (Berkley medallion book). 1968. Berkley Pub. Corp.

Best SF: 1968. Ed. by Harry Harrison. LC 69-18178. 1969. 4.95. Putnam.

Best Shall Die: A Novel. Eric Roman. LC 61-12651. 1961. Prentice Hall.

Best Short Shorts of. Ed. by Anderson, Paul Ernest & White, Lionel. LC 32-32916. 1932. G. P. Putnam's Sons.

Best Short Stories. LC 59-10771. 1959. Dutton.

Best Short Stories. Fedor Mikhailovich Dostoevskii. LC 55-10655. (Modern library of the world's best books, 293). 1955. Modern Library.

Best Short Stories. Fedor Mikhailovich Dostoevskii. Tr. by David Magarshack. (YA) 1964. pap. 3.95x (ISBN 0-394-30966-9, T66, Mod LibC). Modern Lib.

Best Short Stories. Theodore Dreiser. 1956. 5.95 o.p. (1229). World Pub.

Best Short Stories. Theodore Dreiser. LC 56-5948. 1956. 7.50 o.p. (ISBN 0-690-00366-8). T Y Crowell.

Best Short Stories... Nathaniel Hawthorne. LC 7-15595. (nutshell library: ed. by S. Cody). The Old Greek Press.

Best Short Stories. Rudyard Kipling. Ed. by Randall Jarrell. LC 61-14717. 1961. 7.95 o.p. (ISBN 0-385-09812-X). Doubleday.

Best Short Stories. Guy de Maupassant. 2.95 o.p. (98). Modern Lib.

Best Short Stories. Frank Richard Stockton. LC 57-133921. 1957. Scribner.

Best Short Stories & Novels of Eugene Manlove Rhodes. Eugene Manlove Rhodes. Ed. by Frank Dearing. 6.95 o.p. (ISBN 0-395-08130-0). HM.

Best Short Stories... And the Yearbook of the American Short Story... Ed. by O'Brien, Edward Joseph Harrington. Yearbook of the American Short Story. LC 16-11387. Houghton Mifflin Company.

Best Short Stories by Afro-American Writers, 1925-1950. Ed. by Nick Aaron Ford & Harry Lee Faggett. LC 77-2570. 1977. 18.00. Kraus Reprint Co.

Best Short Stories: By Afro-American Writers, 1925-1950, Selected and Edited by Nick Aaron Ford and H. L. Faggett. Baltimore Afro-American. Ed. by Nick Aaron Ford & Harry Lee Faggett. LC 50-12374. 1950. Meador Pub. Co.

Best Short Stories by Negro Writers: An Anthology from 1899 to the Present. Ed. by Langston Hughes. LC 67-11221. 1967. Little, Brown.

Best Short Stories. Edited with an Introd. by Wayne Andrews. Edith Newbold Jones Wharton. LC 58-10825. 1958. Scribner.

Best Short Stories from the Southwest. Ed. by Hilton Ross Greer. LC 29-4426. The Southwest Press.

Best Short Stories. Introd. by William Styron. 1st Ed. The Paris Review. LC 59-10771. 1959. Dutton.

Best Short Stories of Bret Harte. Bret Harte & Linscott, Robert Newton, 1886- Ed. LC 47-30278. (Half-title: The Modern library of the world's best books. 250) "First Modern library edition, 1947."). 1947. The Modern Library.

Best Short Stories of Charles Dickens. Charles Dickens & Mitchell, Edwin Valentine, 1890-Comp. LC 47-12199. 1947. C. Scribner's Sons.

Best Short Stories of Dostoyevsky. Fedor Mikhailovich Dostoevskii. Tr. by David Magarshack. 6.95 (ISBN 0-394-60477-6). Modern Lib.

Best Short Stories of Frank R. Stockton. Frank Richard Stockton. LC 75-38759. 1975. Scholarly Press.

Best Short Stories of Fyoder Dostoyevsky. Fedor Mikhailovich Dostoevskii. Tr. by David Magarshack. 2.95 o.p. (293). Modern Lib.

Best Short Stories of Guy De Maupassant. Guy De Maupassant. (C1161). 1968. Airmont.

Best Short Stories of Guy De Maupassant. Guy De Maupassant. LC 45-1617. 1944. The World Publishing Company.

Best Short Stories of J. G. Ballard. J. G. Ballard. LC 77-28234. 11.95 (ISBN 0-03-042506-9). Holt, Rinehart and Winston.

Best Short Stories of Jack London. Jack London. LC 45-3930. 1945. The Sun Dial Press.

Best Short Stories of O. Henry. O. Henry. Ed. by Cerf & Cartmell. 6.95 (ISBN 0-394-60423-7). Modern Lib.

Best Short Stories of O. Henry: Pseud. Selected, and with an Introduction. William Sydney Porter. Compiled by Van H. Cartmell & Bennett Alfred Cerf. LC 45-351069. (Modern Library of the World's Best Books). (Modern library of the world's best books). 1945. The Modern Library.

Best Short Stories of Ring Lardner. Ring Wilmer Lardner. LC 57-13394. 1957. Scribner.

Best Short Stories of Rudyard Kipling. Rudyard Kipling. LC 61-14717. 1961. Hanover House.

Best Short Stories of the Modern Age. Ed. by Douglas Angus. LC 62-2250. (Premier book, d150). 1962. Fawcett Publications.

Best Short Stories of the War: An Anthology. Ed. by Minchin, Humphrey Cotton. LC 31-3841. 1931. Harper & Brothers.

Best Short Stories of the World. Konrad Bercovici. 25.00 (ISBN 0-89987-135-6). Darby Bks.

Best Short Stories of the World: Edited with an Introduction, by Konrad Bercovici. Ed. by Konrad Bercovici. 1925. The Stratford Company.

Best Short Stories of Theodore Dreiser. Theodore Dreiser & Fast, Howard Melvin, 1914- Ed. LC 47-3829. 1947. The World Publishing Company.

Best Short Stories of World War II: An American Anthology. Ed. by Charles A Fenton. LC 57-9489. 1957. Viking Press.

Best Short Stories. Selected, and with an Introd. by John Beecroft. 1st Modern Library Ed. William Somerset Maugham. (Modern library of the world's best books, 14). 1957. Modern Library.

Best Short Stories. With an Introd. by James T. Farrell. Theodore Deiser. LC 56-5948. World Pub. Co.

Best South Sea Stories. Ed. by Arthur Grove Day & Carl Stroven. LC 64-12430. 1964. Appleton-Century.

Best Sports Stories, 1973: A Panorama of the 1972 Sports World with the Year's Top Photographs. Ed. by Irving T. Marsh & Edward Ehre. (Illus.). 1973. 7.95 o.p. (ISBN 0-525-06619-5). Dutton.

Best Sports Stories: 27th Annual Edition - 1971. Ed. by Irving T. Marsh & Edward Ehre. (Illus.). 1971. 6.95 o.p. (ISBN 0-525-06617-9). Dutton.

Best Stories. Bret Harte. 2.95 o.p. (250). Modern Lib.

Best Stories, 2 vols. in 1. Sarah Orne Jewett. 10.00 (ISBN 0-8446-1248-0). Peter Smith.

Best Stories from New Writing. Ed. by John Lehmann. LC 51-141821. 1951. Harcourt, Brace.

Best Stories from Orbit, Volumes 1-10. Ed. by Damon Francis Knight. LC 74-16604. 1975. 7.95 (ISBN 0-399-11472-6). Berkley Pub. Co.: Distributed by Putnam.

Best Stories in the World. Thomas Lansing Masson. 258p. 1981. Repr. of 1923 ed. lib. bdg. 30.00 (ISBN 0-89760-575-6). Telegraph Bks.

Best Stories of Bert Vincent. Bert Vincent. LC 73-946. (Illus.). 1968. Printed by Brazos Press.

Best Stories of Guy De Maupassant. Guy De Maupassant. Compiled by Saxe Commins. LC 45-9767. (Half-title: The Modern library of the world's best books). 1945. Random House.

Best Stories of H. G. Wells. Herbert George Wells. (S414K). 1960. Ballantine Books.

Best Stories of Heroism I Know. Ed. by John Clair Minot. LC 72-10786. (Short story index reprint series). 1973. (ISBN 0-8369-4231-0). Books for Libraries Press.

Best Stories of Heroism I Know. Ed. by John Clair Minot. LC 35-2341. W. A. Wilde Company.

Best Stories of Mary E. Wilkins. Mary Eleanor Wilkins Freeman. LC 70-145023. 1971. (ISBN 0-403-00970-7). Scholarly Press.

Best Stories of Mary E. Wilkins. Mary Eleanor Wilkins Freeman. Ed. by Lanier, Henry Wysham. LC 27-5840. 1927. Harper & Brothers.

Best Stories of O. Henry. O. Henry. 1965. 10.95 (ISBN 0-385-00020-0). Doubleday.

Best Stories of O. Henry. by bennett cerf and van h. cartmell. ed. William Sydney Porter & Cerf, Bennett Alfred, 1898-Comp. LC 45-3611. 1945. The Sun Dial Press.

Best Stories of Paul Laurence Dunbar. Paul Laurence Dunbar. Ed. by Brawley, Benjamin Griffith. LC 38-5603. 1938. Dodd, Mead & Company.

Best Stories of the South Seas. Ed. by Philip Snow. 1973. pap. 2.95 o.p. Transatlantic.

Best Stories of Walter de la Mare. Walter De la Mare. 400p. (Orig.). Date not set. pap. 7.95 (ISBN 0-571-13076-3). Faber & Faber.

Best Stories of Wilbur Daniel Steele. Wilbur Daniel Steele. LC 75-36513. 1976. 25.00 (ISBN 0-8371-8637-4). Greenwood Press.

Best Stories of Wilbur Daniel Steele. Wilbur Daniel Steele. LC 46-557871. 1946. Doubleday & Company, Inc.

Best Summer Job. Patrick Skene Catling. LC 73-22783. (Illus.). 1974. 7.95 (ISBN 0-671-21753-4). Simon and Schuster.

Best Supernatural Stories of H. P. Lovecraft. Howard Phillips Lovecraft & August William Derleth. LC 45-4371. 1945. The World Publishing Company.

Best Supernatural Tales of Algernon Blackwood. Algernon Blackwood. LC 73-85121. 7.95 (ISBN 0-88356-020-8). Causeway Books.

Best Supernatural Tales of Arthur Conan Doyle. Arthur Conan Doyle & Everett Franklin Bleiler. LC 78-66710. 1979. 4.00 (ISBN 0-486-23725-7). Dover Publications.

Best Table. Richard Devon. 320p. (Orig.). 1981. pap. 2.95 (ISBN 0-515-05539-5). Jove Pubns.

Best Tales of Edgar Allan Poe. Edgar Allan Poe. Ed. by Cody, Sherwin. LC 3-28552. 1903. A. C. McClurg & Company.

Best Tales of Edgar Allan Poe. Edgar Allan Poe. Ed. by Cody, Sherwin. LC 25-26574. (Half-title: The modern library of the world's best books). 1924. Boni and Liveright.

Best Tales of Hoffmann. Ernst Theodor Amadeus Hoffmann. Ed. by Everett Franklin Bleiler. LC 67-18740. (Illus.). 1967. Dover Publications.

Best Tales of Hoffmann. E., Introd. by E. F. Bleiler. Ernst Theodor Amadeus Hoffmann. Ed. by Everett Franklin Bleiler. (Dover bk. rebound). 1968. 4.00. P. Smith.

Best Tales of Terror of Erckmann Chatrian. Ed. by Hugh Lamb. 1981. 35.00x (ISBN 0-86000-156-3, Pub. by Millington). State Mutual Bk.

Best Tales of the Yukon. Robert William Service. 208p. (Orig.). 1983. lib. bdg. 12.90 (ISBN 0-89471-202-0); pap. 4.95 (ISBN 0-89471-201-2). Running Pr.

Best That Ever Did It. Ed Lacy. LC 55-6585. 1955. Harper.

Best Thing That Ever Happened. Warren Leslie. LC 52-9454. 1952. McGraw-Hill.

Best "Thinking Machine" Dectective Stories. Jacques Futrelle. Ed. by E. F. Bleiler. 6.00 (ISBN 0-8446-5033-1). Peter Smith.

Best "Thinking Machine" Detective Stories. Jacques Futrelle. LC 73-85054. 1973. (pbk.) 3.00 (ISBN 0-486-20537-1). Dover Publications.

Best Time Ever: By Berta Ruck. Berta Ruck. LC 34-4676. 1934. Dodd, Mead & Company.

Best World Short Stories. 1947- Cournos, John, 1881- Ed. LC 47-7000. D. Appleton-Century Co.

Best World Short Stories. 1947- Editors: 1947-John Cournos and Sybil Norton. Ed. by Cournos, John. LC 47-7000. D. Appleton-Century Co.

Best Years. Pierre Gascar, pseud. LC 66-25398. 1967. G. Braziller.

Bestiaire Celeste. Henri De Montherlant. deluxe ed. 787.50. French & Eur.

Bestiaires. Henri De Montherlant. (Coll. Soleil). 1957. 13.95. French & Eur.

Bestseller. Toni Freedman. 1971. pap. 0.95 o.p. (ISBN 0-447-75160-3). Lancer.

Bestseller. Lila Ramsey. 1981. pap. 2.50 (ISBN 0-671-83277-8). PB.

Bet: And Other Stories. Anton Pavlovich Chekhov. Tr. by Kotellansky, Samuel, Solomonovitch. LC 16-6396. 1915. J. W. Luce & Co.

Beta Colony. Robert Enstrom. LC 78-22315. 1980. 8.95 (ISBN 0-385-14644-2). Doubleday.

Beth: A Sheepdog. Ernest Blakeman Vesey. LC 34-30043. E. P. Dutton & Co., Inc.

Beth Adams, Private Duty Nurse. Helene Chambers Schellenberg. 1964. Arcadia House.

Beth Book. Sarah Grand. LC 6-27659. 1897. D. Appleton and Company.

Beth Linden. Phyllis Yahnke. LC 53-856111. 1953. Arcadia House.

Beth Norvell: A Romance of the West. Randall Parrish. LC 7-30865. 1907. A. C. McClurg & Co.

Beth of Harbor House. 1st Ed. Evelyn Rhodes Collins. LC 53-119487. 1953. Pageant Press.

Beth Terry: Beauty Editor by Frances Dean Hancock Pseud. Jeanne Judson. LC 57-8724. 1957. Avalon Books.

Bethany. Anita Mason. LC 81-14606. 1981. 11.95 (ISBN 0-312-07720-3). St Martin's Press.

Bethany: A Story of the Old South. Thomas Edward Watson. LC 72-4596. (Black Heritage Library Collection). (Illus.). 1972. 16.75 (ISBN 0-8369-9131-1). Books for Libraries Press.

Bethany: A Story of the Old South. Thomas Edward Watson. LC 4-24504. 1904. D. Appleton and Company.

Bethany's Sin. Robert R. McCammon. 1980. pap. 2.50 (ISBN 0-380-47712-2, 47712). Avon.

Bethel. Eli Moffatt Millen. LC 29-27798. 1929. Doubleday, Doran & Company, Inc.

Bethel Merriday. Sinclair Lewis. LC 40-27224. 1940. Doubleday, Doran & Company, Inc.

Bethesda. Lenora B Halsted. LC 7-966. 1884. Macmillan & Co.

Bethesda: The Temperate Life. LC 23-133382. 1923. Moffat, Yard & Company.

Bethesda: The Temperate Life. LC 26-13560. 1926. The Stratford Company.

Bethia Wray's New Name. Amanda Minnie Douglas. LC 6-33491. 1893. Lee and Shepard.

Bething's Folly. Barbara Metzger. LC 80-54483. 1981. 12.95 (ISBN 0-8027-0677-0). Walker.

Bethlehem Inn, and Other Christmas Stories. Frederick M Meek. LC 72-2029. (Illus.). 1972. (ISBN 0-664-20943-2). Westminster Press.

Bethlehem: Or Border Lands of Faith. A Historical Novel. Henry Clay Badger. LC 6-5039. 1895.

Bethnal Inheritance. Martha Whitfield. (Orig.). 1981. pap. 2.95 (ISBN 0-89083-857-7). Zebra.

Bethrothed (I Promessi Sposi) By Alessandro Manzoni; with an Introduction by James, Cardinal Gibbons. Alessandro Manzoni. (Added t.-p.: The literature of Italy, 1265-1907. Ed. by Rossiter Johnson and Dora Knowlton Ranous). The National Alumni.

Beth's Promise. Anna Hanson McKenney Dorsey. 1887. J. Murphy & Co.

Bethsaida: A Story of the Time of Christ. Malcolm Dearborn. LC 3-22526. G. W. Dillingham Company.

Beti. Daphne Rooke. LC 59-6055. 1959. Houghton Mifflin Co.

Betrayal. Merritt Clifton. 1980. 2.50. Samisdat.

Betrayal. Finn Jensen. 1974. (pbk.) 0.95 (ISBN 0-671-77736-X). Pocket Books.

Betrayal. Charlotte Lamb, pseud. (Harlequin Presents Ser.). 192p. 1983. pap. 1.95 (ISBN 0-373-10585-1). Harlequin Bks.

Betrayal. Edward Phillips Oppenheim. 1904. Dood ? Mead and Company.

Betrayal. Ethel Erkkila Tigue. LC 59-12737. 1959. Dodd, Mead.

Betrayal. Alexia E Walter & Walter, H. C., Joint Author. LC 30-11717. E. P. Dutton & Co., Inc.

Betrayal: A Novel. Walter Neale & Hancock, Elizabeth Hazlewood. LC 10-11141. 1910. The Neale Publishing Company.

Betrayal in Eden. Philip Chase. Dell.

Betrayal in Tombstone. Ray Hogan. 1975. (pbk.) 0.95. Popular Library.

Betrayal into Darkness. Richard S. Hall. 3.50 o.p. Vantage.

Betrayal of Jean Whitney. Keith Leroy Brooks. LC 28-19455. The Biola Book Room.

Betrayal of John Fordham. Benjamin Leopold Farjeon. LC 6-38645. (On cover: Fenno's select series. no. 20). 1896. R. F. Fenno and Company.

Betrayed. Kenneth Bjorgum. LC 78-20057. 1979. 7.95 (ISBN 0-385-14751-1). Doubleday.

Betrayed. Marion Plunkett. Ed. by Sylvia Ashton. LC 74-76812. 1975. 7.95 (ISBN 0-87949-030-6). Ashley Bks.

Betrayed! Charles Stanley Strong. LC 35-5302. Phoenix Press.

Betrayed: A Northern Tale. In Seven Parts. John Dunbar Hylton. LC 1-15090. 1880.

Betrayed! A Novel. Charles Paul De Kock. LC 7-12801. (On cover: Mayfair series, no. 5). 1891. E. Brandus & Co.

Betrayed by Death. Peter Alding. 192p. 1982. 10.95 (ISBN 0-8027-5465-1). Walker & Co.

Betrayed by F. Scott Fitzgerald: A Novel. Ron Carlson. LC 77-3320. 7.95 (ISBN 0-393-08775-1). Norton.

Betrayed by Rita Hayworth. Manuel Puig. LC 72-122805. 1971. 6.95 (ISBN 0-525-06630-6). Dutton.

Betrayed by Rita Hayworth. Manuel Puig. LC 80-6123. 1981. 3.50 (ISBN 0-394-74659-7). Vintage Books.

Betrayed Skies: A Novel. Rudolf Braunburg. LC 79-7860. 1980. 12.95 (ISBN 0-385-15183-7). Doubleday.

Betrayed. Translated by Robert Kee. 1st American Ed. Michael Horbach. LC 59-5454. 1959. Coward-McCann.

Betrayed Trust: A Story of Our Own Times and Country, a Romance of the Middle West. Walter Tennant McClure. LC 3-32794. 1903. Publishing House of the M.E. Church, South, Smith & Lamar, Agents.

Betrayers. Ruth Chatterton. LC 53-7077. 1953. Houghton Mifflin.

Betrayers. Hamilton Drummond. LC 19-13644. E. P. Dutton & Company.

Betrayers. Donald Hamilton. 1978. pap. 2.25 (ISBN 0-449-14060-1, GM). Fawcett.

Betrayers. Peter Leslie. 1978. pap. 1.50 (ISBN 0-532-15310-3). Woodhill.

Betrayers. Ingram See. 1973. pap. 0.75 o.s.i. (01-388). Lancer.

Betraying Heart. Jessica Mandy. LC 57-11465. 1957. Arcadia House.

Betrothal of Elpholate: And Other Tales of the Pennsylvania Dutch. Helen Reimensnyder Martin. LC 7-30437. 1907. The Century Co.

Betrothal of Elypholate: And Other Tales of the Pennsylvania Dutch. Helen Reimensnyder Martin. LC 76-128739. (Short story index reprint series). (Illus.). 1970. Books for Libraries Press.

Betrothal of Elypholate, & Other Tales of the Pennsylvania Dutch. Helen Reimensnyder Martin. LC 76-128739. (Short Story Index Reprint Ser). (Illus.). 1907. 15.00 (ISBN 0-8369-3630-2). Ayer Co.

Betrothal of Felicity. Florence Drummond. LC 23-857980. 1923. Longmans, Green and Co.

Betrothed. Alessandro Manzoni. Tr. by Bruce Penman. LC 73-165908. (Penguin classics). 1972. 1.00 (ISBN 0-14-044274-X). Penguin.

Betrothed.--The Talisman. From the Last Rev. Ed., Containing the Author's Final Corrections, Notes, &C. parker's ed. Walter Scott. (Waverley novels: Library ed. v. 18).

Betrothed: A Tale of the Crusaders and The Chronicles of the Canongate. Walter Scott. (On cover: Lovell's library, no. 635). 1885. J. W. Lovell Company.

Betrothed: I Promessi Sposi. Alessandro Manzoni. LC 99-1580. (Half-title: The world's great books... Aldine ed.). 1898. D. Appleton and Company.

Betrothed: I Promessi Sposi. Alessandro Manzoni. LC 29-25280. (The International library). 1926. S. Paul & Co., Ltd.

Betrothed (I Promessi Sposi) A Milanese Story of the Seventeenth Century. Alessandro Manzoni. Tr. by Connor, Daniel J. LC 24-12438. 1924. The Macmillan Company.

Betrothed (I Promessi Sposi) a Tale of XVII Century Milan. Alessandro Manzoni. LC 51-7623. 1951. Dent.

Betrothed: "I Promessi Sposi," a Tale of XVII Century Milan. Alessandro Manzoni. LC 51-8225.

Betrothed, 'I Promessi Sposi' A Tale of XVII Century Milan. Translated with a Pref. by Archibald Colquhoun. Alessandro Manzoni. LC 56-2556. (Everyman's Library, 999. Fiction). 1956. Dent.

Betrothed, The Highland Widow: And Other Tales. Walter Scott. LC 36-36998. (Half-title: Everyman's library, ed. by Ernest Rhys. Fiction. no. 127). 1921. J. M. Dent & Sons, Ltd.

Betsey Jane on the New Woman. Herbert E Brown. LC 6-18966. 1897. C.H. Kerr & Company.

Betsey Jane on Wheels: A Tale of the Bicycle Craze. LC 6-18965. (On cover: White City series, v. 2, no. 11). 1895. W.B. Conkey Company.

Betsy. Harold Robbins. 1978. pap. 3.95 (ISBN 0-671-41708-8). PB.

Betsy. Harold Robbins. 1971. 7.95 o.s.i. (ISBN 0-671-27086-9). Trident.

Betsy. Harold Rubin. LC 74-169136. 1971. 7.95 (ISBN 0-671-27086-9). Trident Press.

Betsy Gaskins (Dimicrat) Wife of Jobe Gaskins (Republican) or, Uncle Tom's Cabin up to Date. William I. Hood & Schulte, Francis J. LC 7-5393. The Schulte Publishing Company.

Betsy Moran, R.N. Peggy Gaddis, pseud. LC 64-7369. 1964. Arcadia House.

Betsy Ross: A Romance of the Flag. Chauncey Crafts Hotchkiss. LC 1-30998. 1901. D. Appleton and Company.

Better a Dinner of Herbs. Byron Herbert Reece. LC 49-50367. 1950. Dutton.

Better Angels. Charles McCarry. LC 78-26968. 9.95 (ISBN 0-525-06631-4). Dutton.

Better Class: A Novel. Alice Colombo. LC 80-11536. (Illus.). 1980. 6.00 (ISBN 0-8037-0498-4). Dial Press.

Better Days: Or, A Millionaire of Tomorrow. new ed. rev... ed. Thomas Fitch & Fitch, Anna M., Joint Author. (On cover: The Ariel library, no. 11). F. J. Schulte & Company.

Better Dead. George Bagby, pseud. LC 77-89875. (Crime Club Ser.). 1978. 6.95 o.p. (ISBN 0-385-13456-8). Doubleday.

Better Dead. Aaron Marc Stein. LC 77-89875. 1978. 6.95 (ISBN 0-385-13456-8). Published for the Crime Club by Doubleday.

Better Dead. My Lady Nicotine. James Matthew Barrie. LC 3-28155. Lovell, Coryell & Company.

Better Dead Then Red. Stanley Reynolds. LC 65-3551. 1964. Elek Books.

Better Dream House. Joe Dunn. pap. 2.00. White Rabbit.

Better Man. Robert William Chambers. LC 78-157773. (Short story index reprint series). (Illus.). 1971. (ISBN 0-8369-3885-2). Books for Libraries Press.

Better Man. Robert William Chambers. LC 16-672087. 1916. 1.30. D. Appleton and Company.

Better Man: With Some Account of What He Struggled for and What He Won, by Cyrus Townsend Brady... Cyrus Townsend Brady. LC 10-22058. 1910. 1.50. Dodd, Mead and Company.

Better Mouse Trap. Emma Loomis Rose. LC 29-5964. R. G. Badger.

Better Occasions. Eliot Wagner. LC 73-22463. 1974. 6.95 (ISBN 0-690-00439-7). Crowell.

Better off Dead. R. M Laurenson & R. M. Laurenson. LC 55-140319. 1955. Arcadia House.

Better off Dead. Mary McMullen. LC 81-43396. 1982. 10.95 (ISBN 0-385-17943-X). Published for the Crime Club by Doubleday.

Better off Dead. Mary McMullen. LC 82-9172. 1982. 7.95 (ISBN 0-8161-3409-X). G.K. Hall.

Better Part. Kit Reed, pseud. LC 67-150062. 1967. 4.95. Farrar.

Better Part: A Story of Love and Service. Marietta Smith. 1918. Burbank Printing Co.

Better Part: A Tale from Real Life. Valentine Vattier & Murphy, Lady Blanche Elizabeth Mary Annunciata (Noel) 1850?-1881, Tr. (Catholic premium-book library, 1st series). Benziger Brothers.

Better Part of Valor: A Novel. Basil Heatter. LC 64-16216. 1964. Doubleday.

Better See George. Freeman Tilden. LC 41-5503. Harper & Brothers.

Better Sort. Henry James. LC 75-110201. (Short story index reprint series). 1970. Books for Libraries Press.

Better Sort. Henry James. LC 3-5531. 1903. C. Scribner's Sons.

Better Sunset. John E. Enck. 1973. 5.00 o.p. (ISBN 0-682-47839-3). Exposition.

Better Than a Dozen. Paul Arbose. pap. 2.50 o.p. William F.

Better Than Divorce. Thomas Jeffries Duvall. LC 14-62843. 1.50. Pentecostal Publishing Company.

Better Than Dying. Robert Faherty. LC 35-13543. 1935. Doubleday, Doran & Company, Inc.

Better Than Gold. Nugent Robinson. LC 20-23144. (Half-title: "Ave Maria" series, no. iii). 1885. "Ave Maria" Press.

Better Than Life. Charles Garvice. (On cover: Laurel library, no. 11). 1891. G. Munro's Sons.

Better Than Men. Rush Christopher Hawkins. LC 7-218919. 1896. J. W. Bouton.

Better Than New see TaleSpinners I.

Better Than One. Damon Francis Knight & Kate Wilhelm. LC 79-89652. 1980. 5.00 (ISBN 0-9603146-0-1). Nesfa Pr.

Better Think Twice About It, and Twelve Other Stories. Luigi Pirandello. LC 74-3429. (Short story index reprint series). 1974. 16.00 (ISBN 0-8369-4269-8). Books for Libraries Press.

Better Think Twice About It: And Twelve Other Stories. Luigi Pirandello & Mayne, Arthur, Tr. LC 34-42822. E. P. Dutton & Co., Inc.

Better Times Stories. Ellen Warner Olney Kirk. LC 7-12351. 1889. Ticknor and Company.

Better Times Than These. Winston Groom. 1982. pap. 2.95 (ISBN 0-425-05018-1). Berkley Pub.

Better Times Than These: A Novel. Winston Groom. LC 78-4182. (Illus.). 10.95 (ISBN 0-671-40007-X). Summit Books.

Better Times Than These: A Novel. Winston Groom. (Illus.). 1979. 2.75. Berkley Publishing Co.

Better to Burn. Gloria Goddard. LC 35-10048. Godwin.

Better to Eat You. Charlotte Armstrong. LC 54-5797. 1954. Coward-McCann.

Better Treasure. Mary Raymond Shipman Andrews. LC 8-30618. 1908. The Bobbs-Merrill Company.

Better Wed Than Dead. Henry Kane. Orig. Title: Unholy Trio. 1970. pap. 0.75 o.p. (76-647). Lancer.

Better World. E. B Southwick. LC 3-4387. The Truth Seeker Company.

Betterfly. Michael Rumaker. LC 62-963333. 1962. Scribner.

Bettina Colonna: Translated from the French by Michael Legat. 1st American Ed. Michel Durafour. LC 53-9863. 1953. Bobbs-Merrill.

Betting Man: And Other Stories. Brian Glanville. LC 73-79785. 1969. 5.95. Coward-McCann.

Betty. Faith Baldwin Cuthrell. LC 28-21892. E. J. Clode, Inc.

Betty. Georges Simenon. LC 74-22072. 1975. 6.95 (ISBN 0-15-111923-6). Harcourt Brace Jovanovich.

Betty: A Last Century Love Story. Anna Vernon Dorsey Williams. LC 6-33702. (On cover: American author's series, no. 10). 1889. J. W. Lovell Company.

Betty Alden, a Romance of Our Flag. Mary Polk Winn. LC 38-9838. The Christopher Publishing House.

Betty Alden: The First-Born Daughter of the Pilgrims. Jane Goodwin Austin. 1891. Houghton, Mifflin and Company.

Betty-All-Alone. Meg Villars. LC 14-22668. E. J. Clode.

Betty at Fort Blizzard. Molly Elliot Seawell. 1916. 1.25. J. B. Lippincott Company.

Betty Gaston the Seventh Girl: A Story. Marion Ames Taggart. LC 10-27860. (Six girls series) $1.50). 1910. W. A. Wilde Company.

Betty Grier. Joseph Laing Waugh. LC 16-26550. 1915. D. McKay.

Betty Leicester: A Story for Girls. Sarah Orne Jewett. LC 4-16142. 1890. Houghton, Mifflin and Company.

Betty Loring, Illustrator. Cateau De Leeuw. LC 48-904138. 1948. J. Messner.

Betty Marehand. Beatrice Barmby. LC 18-18340. George H. Forn Company.

Betty Moore's Journal. Mabel D Carry. LC 12-4141. 1912. 1.00. Rand McNally & Company.

Betty of New England. Laura Moorby Tooke. LC 31-8324. Fleming H. Revell Company.

Betty of the Rectory. Elizabeth Thomasina Meade Smith. LC 8-17993. Grosset & Dunlap.

Betty Page: Private Peeks. LC 78-50070. (Illus.). Vol. 2. pap. 6.50 (ISBN 0-914646-23-0); Vol. 3. pap. 6.50 (ISBN 0-914646-24-9). Belier Pr.

Betty Peach: A Tale of Colonial Days. Mary Devereux. LC 6-34598. 1896. M. H. Graves.

Betty Pembroke. Elizabeth Hazlewood Hancock. LC 7-415865. 1907. The Neale Publishing Company.

Betty Pritchard, Train Hostess. Elizabeth Beatty. 1963. Avalon Books.

Betty Standish: A Romance. Arthur James Anderson. LC 13-4986. 1913. 1.25. Dodd, Mead and Company.

Betty Starling: Private Secretary. Audrey Turner. LC 54-10749. 1955. Lantern Press.

Betty Tree. Kathryn Morgan Ryan. LC 72-76771. 1972. 7.95 (ISBN 0-671-27093-1). Trident Press.

Betty Zane. Zane Grey. LC 4-1342. 1903. C. Francis Press.

Betty Zane. Zane Grey. LC 21-13691. 1915. Grosset & Dunlap.

Betty Zane. Zane Grey. LC 33-185075. Grosset & Dunlap.

Betty Zane. Zane Grey. LC 42-11117. 1941. Triangle Books.

Betty Zane. Zane Grey. LC 80-14381. 1980. 12.60 (ISBN 0-89190-752-1). Aeonian Press.

Betty Zane. Zane Grey. 1978. pap. 1.75 (ISBN 0-89083-363-X). Zebra.

Betty Zane: An Abridged Edition of the Novel. Zane Grey. LC 40-11336. The Saalfield Publishing Company.

Bettyann. Kris Neville. 1970. pap. 0.75 o.p. (T-075-7). Tower.

Betty's Bright Idea. facsimile ed. Harriet Elizabeth Beecher Stowe. LC 72-37562. (Short Story Index Reprint Ser.). Repr. of 1875 ed. 12.00 (ISBN 0-8369-4121-7). Ayer Co.

Betty's Bright Idea. Also, Deacon Pitkin's Farm, and The First Christmas of New England. Harriet Elizabeth Beecher Stowe. LC 72-37562. (Short story index reprint series). (Illus.). 1972. 7.50 (ISBN 0-8369-4121-7). Books for Libraries Press.

Betty's Bright Idea. Also, Deacon Pitkin's Farm, and The First Christmas of New England. Harriet Elizabeth Beecher Stowe. LC 8-16281. 1876. J. B. Ford & Company.

Betty's Secret & Other Stories by Grandmother Lois. Mary M. Landis. 181p. 1972. 5.85. Rod & Staff.

Betty's Virginia Christmas. Molly Elliot Seawell. LC 14-18075. 1914. J. B. Lippincott Company.

Betty's Visions, and Mrs. Smith of Longmains. Rhoda Broughton. (On cover: Lovell's library, v. 16, no. 781). 1886. J. W. Lovell Company.

Between Battles: By James D. Houston. James D Houston. LC 69-29340. 1968. 4.95. Dial.

Between Cloris & Amy. John Colleton. 1976. pap. 2.75 (ISBN 0-451-11256-3, AE1256, Sig). NAL.

Between Cloris and Amy. John Colleton. (Signet Book). New American Library.

Between Crows and Indians. Roger Magini. LC 77-355264. Coach House Press.

Between Dances: Maggie Adams' Eighteenth Summer. Karen S. Dean. 176p. 1982. pap. 2.25 (ISBN 0-380-79285-0, 79285, Flare). Avon.
Between Dawn and Sunrise: Selections from the Writings of James Branch Cabell. James Branch Cabell. Ed. by Macy, John Albert. LC 30-30910. 1930. R. M. McBridge & Company.
Between Day and Dark. Charles Angoff. LC 58-12025. 1959. T. Yoseloff.
Between Fate and Akuas. Maud Kino-Ole Kinney. LC 25-19625. 1925. Dorrance and Company.
Between Friends. Robert William Chambers. LC 14-207802. 1914. 1.00. D. Appleton and Company.
Between Friends. Richard Aumerle Maher. 1909. Banziger Brothers.
Between Grief & Nothing. Laurence Vershel. 256p. 1973. 7.00 o.p. (ISBN 0-682-47715-X). Exposition.
Between Heaven & Earth. abr ed. Otto Ludwig. Tr. by Muriel Almon. LC 64-20047. 1964. 7.00 o.p. (ISBN 0-8044-2559-0); pap. 3.95 (ISBN 0-8044-6453-7). Ungar.
Between Heaven and Earth. With an Introd. by Paul Weigand. Translated and Condensed by Muriel Almon. Otto Ludwig. Ed. by Almon, Muriel. LC 64-20047. 1965. F. Ungar Pub. Co.
Between Language and Silence: The Novels of Virginia Woolf. Howard H Harper. LC 81-20779. 30.00 (ISBN 0-8071-0996-7) (ISBN 0-8071-1012-4). Lousiana State University Press.
Between Life and Death. Frank Barrett. LC 6-9066. (Lovell's international series, no. 125). United States Book Company.
Between Life and Death: A Novel. Nathalie Sarraute. LC 73-80820. 1969. 5.00. G. Braziller.
Between Me and Thee. Louise Dudley Cracraft. LC 6-28071. 1888. The Burrows Brothers Company.
Between Murders. Raymond Sherwood King. LC 35-5697. (Tired business man's library of adventure, detective and mystery novels). 1935. D. Appleton-Century Company, Incorporated.
Between My Legs. Chaim Sil. (Illus.). 1977. pap. 7.95. Right White Line.
Between Ourselves: And Other Short Stories. Blanche Aron. LC 17-44. Fifth Avenue Publishing Co., Inc.
Between Planets. Robert Anson Heinlein. (Illus.). 1951. Scribner.
Between Scarlet Thrones. Florence Willingham Pickard. LC 20-364. 1919. The Stratford Company.
Between the Acts. Virginia Stephen Woolf & Woolf, Leonard Sidney, 1880- Ed. LC 41-51933. Harcourt, Brace and Company.
Between the Covers. Frank Owen. LC 38-32353. The Macaulay Company.
Between the Crusts: Or, "Ticket 1939.". John A. Harrington. LC 7-2848. 1875. Collin & Small.
Between the Dark and the Daylight. Nancy Hale. LC 43-6813. 1943. C. Scribner's Sons.
Between the Dark and the Daylight: Romances. William Dean Howells. LC 7-34775. 1907. Harper & Brothers.
Between the Devil: A Novel. Murrell Edmunds. LC 39-209583. 1939. E. P. Dutton & Co., Inc.
Between the Hammer and the Anvil. Stefan Korbonski. LC 80-9065. 14.95 (ISBN 0-88254-585-X). Hippocrene Books.
Between the Hammer and the Anvil. Edwin Seaver. LC 37-2942. 1937. J. Messner, Inc.
Between the Hammer and the Anvil. Mildred Watt. LC 73-167992. 1972. 7.50 (ISBN 0-7256-0089-6). Hawthorn Press.
Between the Heather and the Northern Sea. A Novel. Mary Linskill. (Harper's Franklin square library. no. 402). 1884. Harper & Brothers.
Between the Heather and the Northern Sea. A Novel. Mary Linskill. (On cover: Seaside library. Pocket ed. no. 620). 1885. G. Munro.
Between the Hills and the Sea. K. B. Gilden, pseud. LC 72-144265. 1971. 7.95. Doubleday.
Between the Lines. Toni Freedman. 1973. pap. 1.25 o.s.i. (78-738). Lancer.
Between the Lines. Stephen McKenna. LC 29-18423. 1929. Dodd, Mead & Co.
Between the Lines: A Story of the War. Charles King. LC 16-7570. Harper & Brothers.
Between the Lines: A Story of the War. Charles King. LC 4-15132. 1889. Harper & Brothers.
Between the Star and the Cross. 1st Ed. William Lichtman. LC 57-90155. 1957. Citadel Press.
Between the Stirrup and the Ground: By Holmes Alexander. Holmes Moss Alexander. LC 67-29095. 1967. National Press.
Between the Thunder and the Sun. Alfred Coppel. LC 77-147228. 1971. 6.95 (ISBN 0-15-111950-3). Harcourt Brace Jovanovich.
Between Then and Now. Alba De Cespedes. LC 60-5219. 1960. Houghton Mifflin.
Between Then & Now. Alba De Cespedes. 1960. 3.00 o.p. HM.
Between Time & Timbuktu; or, Prometheus-5 a Space Fantasy. Kurt Vonnegut, Jr. 272p. 1974. pap. 4.95 (ISBN 0-440-50719-7, Delta). Dell.
Between Twelve and One. John George Haslette Vahey. LC 29-17656. 1929. W. Morrow & Company, Inc.
Between Two Autumns: A Novel. Percy Marks. LC 41-176156. Reynal & Hitchcock.
Between Two Fires & Other Stories. Morris Krichevsky. 1970. 3.95 o.p. Vantage.
Between Two Forces. A Record of a Theory and a Passion. Flora Helm. LC 7-4115. 1894. Arena Publishing Company.
Between Two Hearts. A Novel. Charlotte Mary Brame. (On cover: Street & Smith's select series, no. 113). Street & Smith.
Between Two Hearts. A Novel. Bertha M. Clay. LC 44-11668. (On cover: Street & Smith's select series, no. 113). Street & Smith.
Between Two Iron Curtains. Alexandar S. Petrovic. 320p. 1975. 8.00 o.p. (ISBN 0-682-48404-0). Exposition.
Between Two Loves. A Novel. Charlotte Mary Brame. (On cover: Seaside library. Pocket ed. no. 466). G. Munro.
Between Two Loves. A Novel. Charlotte Mary Brame. LC 44-38168. (Lovell's Library). (On cover: Lovell's library, v. 14, no. 720: Vol. 14, No. 720). J. W. Lovell Company.
Between Two Loves. A Novel. Charlotte Mary Brame. LC 44-381693. (Primrose Ser.). (Primrose series, no. 20: No. 20). 1891. Street & Smith.
Between Two Loves: A Tale of the West Riding. Amelia Edith Huddleston Barr. LC 6-8387. (Harper's handy series, no. 102). 1886. Harper & Brothers.
Between Two Masters. Gamaliel Bradford. 1906. Houghton, Mifflin and Company.
Between Two Midsummer Nights. Egils Kalme. LC 75-26147. 8.95 (ISBN 0-8283-1658-9). Branden Press.
Between Two Opinions: Or, The Question of the Hour. Elizabeth E Flagg. LC 6-41128. 1885. National Christian Association.
Between Two Rebellions. Asenath Carver Coolidge. LC 9-116. Hungeford-Holborook Co.
Between Two Sins. Charlotte Mary Brame. LC 44-11254. (Lovell's Library). (On cover: Lovell's library, v. 11, no. 593: Vol. 11, No. 593). John W. Lovell Company.
Between Two Sins. Charlotte Mary Brame. LC 44-38170. (On cover: Seaside library. Pocket ed. No. 476). 1885. G. Munro.
Between Two Sins. Charlotte Mary Brame. LC 44-31644. American Publishers Corporation.
Between Two Sins. Charlotte Mary Brame. LC 1-5264. (With her Beauty's marriage. New York 1900). 1900. Street & Smith.
Between Two Thieves. Clotilde Inez Mary Graves. LC 12-211476. 1912. Frederick A. Stokes Company.
Between Two Women. Peter Keyes. (Orig.). 1968. pap. 1.25 o.p. (2075). Brandon.
Between Two Worlds. Josephine H Blackfan. LC 563. F. T. Neely.
Between Two Worlds. Roman Pazderski. 3.95 o.p. Vantage.
Between Two Worlds... Anna Cyrene Porter Reifsnider. LC 7-41407. 1897. The A. C. Reifsnider Book Company.
Between Two Worlds. Upton Beall Sinclair. LC 41-437319. 1941. The Viking Press.
Between Two Worlds. Upton Beall Sinclair. ("Lanny Budd" ser., no. 2). 1973. 1.50. Curtis Bks.
Between Two Worlds. Eugenie C Smith. LC 67-23988. 1967. Dorrance.
Between Two Worlds: A Novel. Philip Everett Curtiss. LC 16-174939. 1.35. Harper & Brothers.
Between Two Worlds: A Novel. Schwarz-Bart, Simone. LC 81-47249. 15.75 (ISBN 0-06-039002-6). Harper & Row.
Between Two Worlds: True Ghost Stories of the British Isles. D. A. MacManus. 1977. text ed. 11.25x (ISBN 0-900675-83-7). Humanities.
Between Us and Evil. Charlotte Murray Russell, pseud. LC 50-9262. 1950. Published for the Crime Club by Doubleday.
Between Whiles. Helen Maria Fiske Hunt Jackson. LC 7-9473. 1887. Roberts Brothers.
Between Wind & Water. Brace. 1977. pap. 3.95 (ISBN 0-89272-029-8). Down East.
Betwixt My Love and Me. A Novel. Eleanor A. Towle. LC 6-2038. (Seaside Library. Pocket Ed.). (On cover: Seaside library. Pocket ed., no. 483: No. 483). G. Munro.
Beulah. Karl H Krause. LC 70-27464. (Illus.). 1970. Rook Press.
Beulah: A Novel. Augusta Jane Evans Wilson. LC 8-37104. 1887. G. W. Dillingham; Etc., Etc.
Beulah: A Novel. popular edition. ed. Augusta Jane Evans Wilson. LC 7-7469. 1899. G. W. Dillingham Co.
Beulah Bunny Tells All. Dorothy M Johnson. LC 42-21086. 1942. W. Morrow and Company.
Beulah Land. Lonnie Coleman. (Dell Book). 1977 (ISBN 0-440-11393-8). Dell Pub Co.
Beulah Land. William Laurence Coleman. LC 73-80011. 1973. 8.95 (ISBN 0-385-06244-3). Doubleday.
Beulah Land. Harold Lenoir Davis. LC 75-136062. (Illus.). 1971. (ISBN 0-8371-5212-7). Greenwood Press.
Beulah Land. Harold Lenoir Davis. LC 49-9058. 1949. W. Morrow.
Bevan Yorke: A Novel. William Babington Maxwell. LC 27-9368. 1927. Doubleday, Page & Company.
Beverly Family: Or, Home Influence of Religion... Joseph Ripley Chandler. 1875. P. F. Cunningham & Son.
Beverly of Graustark. George Barr McCutcheon. LC 4-24491. 1904. Dodd, Mead & Company.
Beverly of Graustark. George Barr McCutcheon. LC 9-32300. 1904. Grosset & Dunlap.
Beverly of Graustark. George Barr McCutcheon. LC 20-188303. 1920. Dodd, Mead & Company.
Beverly of Graustark. George Barr McCutcheon. LC 38-127680. 1926. Grosset & Dunlap.
Beverly: Or, The White Mask. A Novel. Mansfield Tracy Walworth. LC 8-33125. 1872. G. W. Carleton & Co. Etc.
Beverly: Or, The White Mask. A Novel. Mansfield Tracy Walworth. LC 2167. (On cover: Madison square series, no. 44). 1900. G. W. Dillingham Co.
Beverly Osgood: Or, When the Great City Is Awake. A Novel. Nellie J Meeker. 1900. G. W. Dillingham Co.
Bevis. Richard Jefferies. Ed. by Brian Jackson. 1974. pap. 1.50 o.p. (ISBN 0-14-030677-3, PS677, Puffin). Penguin.
Bevis: The Story of a Boy. Richard Jefferies. LC 67-91150. (Everyman's library, no 85p) 15/-). 1966. Dent.
Bevy of Beasts. Gerald Durrell. LC 72-87945. (O.s.i.). 1973. 8.95 o.s.i. (ISBN 0-671-21457-8). S&S.
Beware After Dark! The World's Most Stupendous Tales of Mystery, Horror, Thrills and Terror, Selected, and with an Introduction. Ed. by Thomas Everett Harre. LC 29-16668. The Macaulay Company.
Beware After Dark! The World's Most Stupendous Tales of Mystery, Horror, Thrills, and Terror. Ed. by Thomas Everett Harre. 1945. Emerson Books, Inc.
Beware, Beware the Bight of Benin. Philip McCutchan. LC 74-14153. 1975. 7.95. St. Martin's Press.
Beware More Beasts. Ed. by Vic Ghidalia & Roger Elwood. (Horror Anthology Ser). 1975. pap. 1.25 o.p. (ISBN 0-532-12276-3). Woodhill.
Beware More Beasts. Ed. by Vic Ghidalia & Roger Elwood. (Horror Anthology Ser). 1975. pap. 1.25 o.p. (ISBN 0-532-12276-3). Manor Bks.
Beware My Heart. Glenna Finley, pseud. (Signet Book). 1.50 (ISBN 0-451-08217-6). New American Library, C.
Beware My Love. Marilyn Ross. 1969. pap. 0.60 o.p. (63-154). Paperback Lib.
Beware of Caesar. Vincent Sheean. LC 65-11280. 4.95. Random.
Beware of Midnight. John Welcome, pseud. 1972. pap. 0.95 o.p. (ISBN 0-06-087026-5, HW). Har-Row.
Beware of Midnight: By John Welcome Pseud. 1st American Ed. John Brennan. LC 61-15044. 1961. Knopf.
Beware of Pity. Stefan Zweig. 1983. 14.95 (ISBN 0-517-54673-6, Harmony Bks). Crown.
Beware of Pity: A Novel, Translated from the German. Stefan Zweig & Blewitt, Mrs. Phyllis, Tr. LC 39-27216. 1939. The Viking Press.
Beware of Pity. Tr. by Phyllis and Trevor Blewitt. 3dHallam Ed. Stefan Zweig. LC 65-29943. 1965. 3.95. Cassell.
Beware of Romance. Peggy Gaddis, pseud. LC 48-177958. 1948. Gramercy Pub. Co.
Beware of the Bouquet. Joan Aiken. (Ace gothic). 1973. (pbk.) 0.95. Ace.
Beware of the Bouquet. Joan Aiken. LC 66-24307. 1974. (pbk.) 0.95 (ISBN 0-671-77731-9). Pocket Books.
Beware of the Bouquet. 1st Ed. Joan Aiken. LC 66-24307. 1966. 3.95. Pub. for the Crime Club by Doubleday.
Beware of the Cat, Stories of Feline Fantasy and Horror. Michel Parry. LC 72-75664. (Illus.). 1973. 6.50 (ISBN 0-8008-0730-8). Taplinger.
Beware of the Cat: Stories of Feline Fantasy & Horror. Michel Parry. LC 72-75664. (Illus.). 192p. 1972. 7.50 (ISBN 0-8008-0730-8). Taplinger.
Beware of the Dog! Charles North. LC 39-30371. 1939. W. Morrow and Company.
Beware of the Mouse. Leonard Patrick O'Connor Wibberley. LC 78-14993. 1978. 3.95 (ISBN 0-89370-226-9). Borgo Press.
Beware of the Mouse. Illus. by Ronald Wing. Leonard Patrick O'Connor Wibberley. LC 58-11003. 1958. Putnam.
Beware of the Trains. Edmund Crispin, pseud. 1981. pap. 2.95 (ISBN 0-14-005834-6). Penguin.
Beware of the Trains. Robert Bruce Montgomery. LC 80-28951. 1981. 2.95 (ISBN 0-14-005834-6). Penguin Books.
Beware, Sweet Maggie. Donald Olson. 1977. pap. 1.50 o.p. (ISBN 0-515-04166-1). BJ Pub Group.
Beware the Beasts. Ed. by Vic Ghidalia & Roger Elwood. 1970. pap. 0.95 o.p. (ISBN 0-532-95292-8). Woodhill.
Beware the Beasts. Ed. by Vic Ghidalia & Roger Elwood. 1970. pap. 0.95 o.p. (ISBN 0-532-95292-8). Manor Bks.
Beware the Beasts. Ed. by Vic Ghidalia & Roger Elwood. 1973. (pbk.) 0.95. Manor Books.
Beware the Bog. Myra Kingsbury. 1975. (pbk.) 0.95 (ISBN 0-345-26687-0). Ballantine Books.
Beware the Curves. Erle Stanley Gardner. LC 56-11951. 1956. Morrow.
Beware! the Hawks! A Novel. Kenneth Bradley. LC 34-1164. 1934. Frederick A. Stokes Company.
Beware the Hoot Owl. Nancy Rutledge. LC 44-3054. 1944. Farrar & Rinehart, Inc.
Beware the Kindly Stranger. Clarissa Ross, pseud. (Orig.). 1972. pap. 0.95 o.s.i. (75-353). Lancer.
Beware the Microbots. Kurt Mahr. (Perry Rhodan #35). 1973. (pbk) 0.75. Ace.
Beware the Pale Horse: A Mystery Story. Ben Benson. LC 51-12456. 1951. M. S. Mill Co. and W. Morrow.
Beware the Smiling Stranger. Mitchell Dana. LC 77-77878. 1977. 1.25 (ISBN 0-380-00830-0). Avon.
Beware the Young Stranger. Ellery Queen, pseud. LC 66-2861. 1965. Pocket Books.
Beware the Young Stranger. Ellery Queen, pseud. 1974. (pbk. 0.95. New American Library.
Beware Young Lovers. Hugh Pentecost. LC 82-15639. 1982. 7.95 (ISBN 0-8161-3458-8). G.K. Hall.
Beware Young Lovers. Judson Pentecost Philips. LC 79-24525. (Red badge novel of suspense). 7.95 (ISBN 0-396-07808-7). Dodd, Mead.
Bewildered Heart. Virginia Nielsen, pseud. LC 46-6098. 1946. Arcadia House, Inc.
Bewildering Widow. A Tale of Manhattan Beach. Julia E Dunn. LC 11-15091. (On cover: Satchel series, no. 30). W. B. Smith & Co.
Bewitched. Barbara Cartland. 1975. (pbk.) 1.25. Bantam Books.
Bewitched. Alice Muriel Livingston Williamson. LC 32-20306. 1932. H. C. Kinsey & Company, Inc.
Bewitched Fiddle: And Other Irish Tales. Seumas MacManus. 1900. Doubleday & McClure Co.
Bewitched Lands. Costa Du Rels, Adolfo & Grummon, Stuart Edgar, Tr. LC 45-8174. 1945. A. A. Knopf.
Bewitching Grace. Patricia Maxwell. 1974. (pbk.) 0.95. Popular Library.
Beyond. John Galsworthy. LC 17-22092. 1917. C. Scribner's Sons.
Beyond. I. A. Richards. LC 73-18249. 1974. 10.00 (ISBN 0-15-111985-6). HarBraceJ.
Beyond a Reasonable Doubt. Cornelius Warren Grafton. LC 75-44977. (Fifty Classics of Crime Fiction, 1900-1950; 22). 12.00 (ISBN 0-8240-2371-4). Garland Pub.,
Beyond a Reasonable Doubt: A Novel. Cornelius Warren Grafton. LC 50-6454. 1950. Rinehart.
Beyond All Love. Martin Walser. 1982. pap. 5.95 (ISBN 0-7145-3917-1). Riverrun NY.
Beyond All Passion. Don James. 1969. pap. 0.75 o.p. (75-244). Manor Bks.
Beyond All This Fiddle. A. Alvarez. LC 69-16460. 1969. 10.00 o.p. (ISBN 0-394-41674-0). Random.
Beyond Another Sun. Tom Godwin. (Orig.). 1971. pap. 0.75 o.p. (07129). Curtis.
Beyond Apollo. Barry N Malzberg. 1974. (pbk.) 0.95 (ISBN 0-671-77687-8). Pocket Books.
Beyond Apollo. Barry N Malzberg. LC 73-37427. 1972. 5.95 (ISBN 0-394-47923-8). Random House.
Beyond Bojador. Charles E Mercer. LC 65-14443. 1965. Holt, Rinehart and Winston.
Beyond Chance of Change. Sara Andrew Shafer. LC 5-6779. 1905. The Macmillan Company.
Beyond Control. Rex Ellingwood Beach. Farrar & Rinehart, Incorporated.
Beyond Control. Flora Kidd. (Harlequin Presents Ser.). 192p. 1981. pap. 1.50 (ISBN 0-373-10434-0, Pub. by Harlequin). PB.
Beyond Control. George Burr Leonard. LC 75-17505. 1975. 7.95 (ISBN 0-02-570350-1). MacMillan.
Beyond Control; Seven Stories of Science Fiction. Ed. by Robert Silverberg. LC 72-2897. 1972. 5.95 (ISBN 0-8407-6236-4). T. Nelson.
Beyond Control: Seven Stories of Science Fiction. Ed. by Robert Silverberg. LC 73-1896. 1973. 9.95 (ISBN 0-8161-6091-0). G. K. Hall.

Beyond Control: Seven Stories of Science Fiction. Ed. by Robert Silverberg. (Laurel leaf library). 1974. (pbk.) 0.95. Dell.
Beyond Courage. Clay Blair. (War Library). 208p. 1983. pap. 2.50 (ISBN 0-345-30824-7). Ballantine.
Beyond Defeat. Hans Werner Richter. LC 50-83881. 1950. Putnam.
Beyond Defeat: An Epilogue to an Era. Ellen Anderson Gholson Glasgow. Ed. by Luther Y. Gore. LC 66-28520. 1966. University of Virginia Press.
Beyond Desire. Sherwood Anderson. LC 32-25840. Liveright, Inc.
Beyond Desire: A Novel Based on the Life of Felix and Cecile Mendelssohn. Pierre La Mure. LC 55-8152.
Beyond Desire. With an Introd. by Walter B. Rideout. Black and Gold Ed. Sherwood Anderson. LC 61-18088. 1961. Liverright Pub. Corp.
Beyond Earth's Gates: By Lewis Padgett Pseud. and C. L. Moore. Henry Kuttner & Catherine L. Moore. LC 54-4384. (Ace double novel books, D--69). 1954. Ace Books.
Beyond Eden. David Duncan. LC 55-826944. 1955. Ballantine Books.
Beyond Forever. Morski, George. LC 52-6937. 1952. Vantage Press.
Beyond Heaven's River. Gregory Bear. 1980. pap. 1.95 (ISBN 0-440-10654-0). Dell.
Beyond Hell. Stephen McKenna. 1932. Dodd, Mead & Company.
Beyond Human Ken: Twenty-One Startling Stories of Science Fiction and Fantasy. Ed. by Judith Merril. LC 52-7134. 1962. Random House.
Beyond Human Power, Ten Years: A Novel. Boris Dimondstein. Ed. by Winburg, Lew Earl. LC 31-182130. 1930. Bee De Publishing Co., Inc.
Beyond Hypnotism: A Possible Story, or, an Impossible, As the Learned May Determine. David A Curtis. LC 6-31714. (On cover: Weird story library, no. 1). The Literary Casket Pub. Co.
Beyond Infinity. 1st Ed. Robert Spencer Carr. LC 51-5971. 1951. Fantasy Press.
Beyond Laughter: A Short Novel. Ashley Buck. LC 42-205. 1941. The Antioch Press.
Beyond Law. Frank Bird Linderman. LC 33-25688. The John Day Company.
Beyond Left & Right. Ed. by Richard Kostelanetz. LC 68-22431. 1978. pap. 10.00 o.p. (ISBN 0-932360-07-6). RK Edns.
Beyond Love. Laurence Hammond. LC 76-14542. 1976. pap. 3.50 o.p. (ISBN 0-88419-029-3). Creation Hse.
Beyond Love. George Stanley. 1968. pap. 2.00. White Rabbit.
Beyond Love and Other Stories. Shiv Kumar Kumar. LC 80-903658. (Vikas Library of Modern Indian Writing; 5). 1980. 13.50. Vikas.
Beyond Mars. Earl L Shaub. LC 59-40515. Space and Power Industries.
Beyond Midnight Chasm. James Denson Sayers. LC 36-14932. Godwin.
Beyond Midnight Chasm see Midnight Riders.
Beyond My Catnip Garden. Alice M. Swaim. 1970. 4.00 (ISBN 0-8233-0146-X). Golden Quill.
Beyond Our Measure. Mary L Spangler. LC 72-184133. 1972. 5.00 (ISBN 0-8059-1660-1). Dorrance.
Beyond Paradise. Charles Robert Mullong. LC 25-212. Dorrance & Company.
Beyond Pardon. A Novel. Charlotte Mary Brame. LC 11-10519. 1883. G. W. Carleton & Co.
Beyond Pardon. A Novel. Charlotte Mary Brame. (On cover: Lovell's library. v. 5. no. 287). 1883. J. W. Lovell Company.
Beyond Pardon. A Novel. Charlotte Mary Brame. (On cover: The primrose series, no. 11). 1890. Street & Smith.
Beyond Pardon. A Novel. Charlotte Mary Brame. LC 11-10519. 1883. G. W. Carleton & Co.
Beyond Pardon. A Novel. Charlotte Mary Brame. (On cover: Seaside library. Pocket ed. no. 308). G. Munro.
Beyond Reality: Eight Stories of Science Fiction. Ed. by Terry Carr. LC 79-1247. (Nelson Science Fiction Ser.). 1979. 8.95 o.p. (ISBN 0-525-66642-7). Lodestar Bks.
Beyond Reality: 8 Stories of Science Fiction. Ed. by Terry Carr. LC 79-1247. 7.95 (ISBN 0-525-66642-7). Elsevier/Nelson.
Beyond Reason. Margaret Trudeau. 1979. pap. 2.50 (ISBN 0-671-82778-2). PB.
Beyond Reasonable Doubt. Richard Henry Sampson. LC 41-3424. J. Messner, Inc.
Beyond Recall. Dorothy Fletcher. 1971. pap. 0.75 o.p. (ISBN 0-447-74725-8). Lancer.
Beyond Recall. A Novel. Adeline Sergeant. (On cover: Seaside library. Pocket ed. no. 257). 1884. G. Munro.
Beyond Rejection. Justin Leiber. 192p. (Orig.). 1980. pap. 2.25 (ISBN 0-345-29054-2, Del Rey). Ballantine.
Beyond Rope and Fence. David Grew. LC 22-190183. Boni and Liveright.
Beyond Surrender: A Novel. Marian McCamy Sims. LC 42-24435. 1942. J. B. Lippincott Company.
Beyond the Aegean: By Ilias Venezis Pseud. Translated from the Greek by E. D. Scott-Kilvert. Elias Mellos. LC 56-5032. 1956. Vanguard Press.
Beyond the Atlas. John Trench. LC 63-15699. 1963. Macmillan.
Beyond the Badlands. Stephen Payne. LC 37-5297. J. H. Hopkins & Son, Inc.
Beyond the Barrier. Damon Francis Knight. 1970. pap. 0.60 o.p. (60-444). Manor Bks.
Beyond the Barriers of Space and Time. With an Introd. by Theodore Sturgeon. Ed. by Judith Merril. LC 54-10743. 1954. Random House.
Beyond the Battle's Rim: A Story of the Confederate Refugees. Ida Withers Harrison. LC 18-21532. 1918. 1.50. The Neale Publishing Company.
Beyond the Bedroom Wall. L. Woiwode. 1970. price not set o.p. (ISBN 0-374-11237-1). FS&G.
Beyond the Bedroom Wall. Larry Woiwode. 1976. pap. 2.95 (ISBN 0-380-00684-7, 47670, Bard). Avon.
Beyond the Bedroom Wall: A Family Album. Larry Woiwode. LC 75-6922. 1975. 12.50 (ISBN 0-374-11237-1). Farrar, Straus, Giroux.
Beyond the Bedroom Wall: A Family Album. larry woiwode. ed. Larry Woiwode. 1.95 (ISBN 0-380-00684-7). Avon Books.
Beyond the Bend. Phyllis Primmer. (Orig.). 1966. pap. 0.95 o.p. (37-49, MG). Moody.
Beyond the Black Enigma. Bart Somers. 1968. pap. 0.60 o.p. (53-785). Paperback Lib.
Beyond the Black Hills. Betty Hart O'Rourke. LC 51-10753. 1951. Dorrance.
Beyond the Black Ocean: A Story of Social Revolution. Thomas McGrady. LC 75-154450. (Utopian Literature Ser). 1971. Repr. of 1901 ed. 17.00 (ISBN 0-405-03532-2). Ayer Co.
Beyond the Black Stump: A Novel, by Nevil Shute Pseud. Nevil Shute Norway. LC 56-69795. 1956. Morrow.
Beyond the Blue Event Horizon. Frederik Pohl. LC 79-21757. 1980. 9.95 (ISBN 0-345-28644-8). Ballantine Books.
Beyond the Blue-Grass: A Kentucky Novel. George Creswell Gill. LC 8-17785. 1908. The Neale Publishing Company.
Beyond the Blue Mountains. Eleanor Hibbert. LC 75-7951. 1975. 8.95 (ISBN 0-399-11599-4). Putnam.
Beyond the Blue Mountains. Eleanor Hibbert. (Fawcett Crest Book). 1976. (pbk.) 1.95. Fawcett.
Beyond the Blue Mountains. Eleanor Hibbert. LC 47-11599. 1947. D. Appleton-Century Co.
Beyond the Blue Mountains. Jean Plaidy. 480p. 1981. pap. 2.95 (ISBN 0-449-24451-2, Crest). Fawcett.
Beyond the Blue Mountains. Jean Plaidy. LC 75-7951. 464p. 1975. 8.95 (ISBN 0-399-11599-4). Putnam Pub Group.
Beyond the Blue Sierra. Honore McCue Willsie Morrow. LC 32-28882. 1932. W. Morrow & Company.
Beyond the Border... Walter Douglas Campbell. 1898. A. Constable and Co.
Beyond the Bourn: Reports of a Traveller Returned from "The Undiscovered Country," Submitted to the World. Amos Kidder Fiske. LC 6-41111. 1891. Fords, Howard, & Hulbert.
Beyond the Breakers. Sara Ware Bassett. LC 52-6360. 1952. Doubleday.
Beyond the Breakers. A Story of the Present Day. Robert Dale Owen. LC 7-23688. 1870. J. B. Lippincott & Co.
Beyond the Bridge. Jack Matthews. LC 70-78877. 1970. 4.95. Harcourt, Brace & World.
Beyond the Church. Frederick William Robinson. LC 75-1501. (Victorian Fiction: Novels of Faith and Doubt; 52). 1976. 40.00 (ISBN 0-8240-1576-2). Garland Pub.
Beyond the City. Arthur Conan Doyle. LC 9-25189. Rand, McNally & Company.
Beyond the City. Arthur Conan Doyle. LC 43-21299. Wm. L. Allison Company.
Beyond the City Gates: A Romance of Old New York. Augusta Campbell Watson. LC 8-34343. 1897. E. P. Dutton & Company.
Beyond the City: The Idyll of a Suburb. Arthur Conan Doyle. LC 80-67703. (Doyle, Arthur Conan, Sir, 1859-1930. Conan Doyle Centennial Ser.). (Illus.). 1982. 11.95 (ISBN 0-934468-44-3). Gaslight Publications.
Beyond the Cross & the Switchblade. Wilkerson. 1.75 o.p. (ISBN 0-8007-8236-4). Revell.
Beyond the Cross & the Switchblade. David Wilkerson. 1974. 5.95 o.p. (ISBN 0-912376-08-2). Chosen Bks Pub.
Beyond the Dark. Kieran Abbey. LC 44-272437. 1944. C. Scribner's Sons.
Beyond the Dark. Jennifer Hale. (Berkley Medallion Book). 1978. 1.75 (ISBN 0-425-03557-3). Berkley Pub. Corp.
Beyond the Dawn. Jo Ann Wendt. 480p. (Orig.). 1983. pap. 3.50 (ISBN 0-446-30566-9). Warner Bks.
Beyond the Desert. Eugene Manlove Rhodes. LC 34-30683. 1934. Houghton Mifflin Company.
Beyond the Desert: A Tale of Death Valley. Alfred Noyes. LC 20-18658. Frederick A. Stokes Company.
Beyond the Desert: By Eugene Manlove Rhodes. Eugene Manlove Rhodes. (Bison bk., BB363 rebound). 1968. Peter Smith.
Beyond the Desert: By Eugene Manlove Rhodes. Introd. by W. H. Hutchinson. Eugene Manlove Rhodes. (Bison bk., BB363). 1967. pap., 1.80. Univ. of Neb. Pr.
Beyond the Dreams of Avarice: A Novel. Walter Besant. LC 4-15283. 1895. Harper & Brothers.
Beyond the Edge of Adventure. Hassan Ghandhistani. 3.75 o.p. Carlton.
Beyond the End of Time. Ed. by Frederik Pohl. LC 52-19609. (Permabooks, 145). 1952. Permabooks.
Beyond the End. The Story of a Ghost's Year. Clarence Miles Boutelle. LC 6-14918. (On cover: Bijou series, no. 24)). 1892. The F. M. Lupton Publishing Company.
Beyond the Equator. Joseph A Loewinsohn. LC 40-34746. Fortuny's.
Beyond the Farthest Star. Edgar Rice Burroughs. 1982. pap. 2.25. Ace Bks.
Beyond the Flag. C Buonanno. 1.95 (ISBN 0-505-51616-0).
Beyond the Fog. Eliza A Goldie. LC 30-25884. 1930. Goldie Publishing Company.
Beyond the Frontier: A Romance of Early Days in the Middle West. Randall Parrish. LC 15-199742. 1915. A. C. McClurg & Co.
Beyond the Frozen Frontier. Harold McCracken. LC 37-1608. Robert Speiler Publishing Corporation.
Beyond the Galactic Lens. Gregory Kern. (DAW Science Fiction Books No. 176). 1975. (pbk.) 1.25. DAW Books.
Beyond the Garden Gate. Sophus Keith Winther. LC 47-582. 1946. The Macmillan Company.
Beyond the Gaslight: Science in Popular Fiction 1895-1905. Hilary Evans & Dik Evans. LC 77-352404. (Illus.). 1976. 4.95 (ISBN 0-584-31017-X). F. Muller.
Beyond the Gates. Dorothy Evelyn Smith. LC 56-8275. 1956. Dutton.
Beyond the Gates. Elizabeth Stuart Phelps H. D. Ward Ward. LC 8-33118. 1883. Houghton, Mifflin and Company.
Beyond the Gates of Dream. Lin Carter. (Inflation Fighters Ser.). 160p. 1982. pap. 1.50 (ISBN 0-8439-1082-8, Leisure Bks). Nordon Pubns.
Beyond the Gates of Dream. Lin Carter. (Orig.). 1969. pap. 0.60 o.p. (1032). Belmont-Tower.
Beyond the Gates of Dream. Lin Carter. (O.s.i.). 1972. pap. 0.75 o.s.i. (BT40145). Belmont-Tower.
Beyond the Glass. Antonia White. LC 55-13518. 1955. H. Regnery Co.
Beyond the Glass. Antonia White. LC 80-39826. (Virago Modern Classic). 1981. 5.95 (ISBN 0-8037-0670-7). Dial Press.
Beyond the Gold: A Trilogy of Utah Lore and the Lure of Gold Down Through the Ages. Mary Dawn. LC 57-664836. 1957. William-Frederick Press.
Beyond the Great South Wall. Frank Mackenzie Savile. LC 77-84265. (Lost Race and Adult Fantasy Fiction). (Illus.). 1978. 21.00 (ISBN 0-405-11006-5). Arno Press.
Beyond the Great South Wall: The Secret of the Antarctic. Frank Mackenzie Savile. LC 1-26954. 1901. New Amsterdam Book Company.
Beyond the Green World of Childhood: Reminiscenses. W. Kaufmann. pap. 2.50. Adler.
Beyond the Hills. Stephanie Marie Bridge. LC 51-8228. 1951. Christopher Pub. House.
Beyond the Himalayas. A Story of Travel and Adventure in the Wilds of Tibet. John Geddie. LC 42-489942. 1884. T. Nelson and Sons.
Beyond the Horizon. Frederick Nelson. LC 30-10985. 1930. The Author.
Beyond the Horizon: A Novel. Fred Brown Morrill. LC 18-21535. 1918. The Neale Publishing Company.
Beyond the Hungry Country. Louise A Stinetorf. LC 54-6110. 1954. Lippincott.
Beyond the Imperium. Keith Laumer. 384p. 1981. pap. 2.75 (ISBN 0-523-48513-1). Pinnacle Bks.
Beyond the Lagoon. Marjorie Lety. 192p. 1982. pap. 1.50 (ISBN 0-373-02450-9, Pub. by Harlequin). PB.
Beyond the Last Whisper. Helen Carrie Bowers. LC 71-182345. 1971. Adams Press.
Beyond the Law. Miriam Alexander. LC 19-5151. 1912. G. P. Putnam's Sons.
Beyond the Law. Andrew Patrick. 1977. pap. 1.50 (ISBN 0-425-03515-8, Medallion). Berkley Pub.
Beyond the Law: By Victor Barouh. Tr. by Elena Mladenova. Viktor Barukh. LC 66-723185. 1965. bds., 4.50. Foreign Languages Pr.
Beyond the Looking Glass: Extraordinary Works of Fairy Tale & Fantasy. Ed. by Jonathan Cott. LC 73-76410. (6 7/8 x 9 7/8. This is an extraordinary collection of quaint and curious Victoriana -- fantasy novels, stories, and poetry from the richest period of children's literature. Included are John Ruskin's "The King of the Golden River", George MacDonald's "The Golden Key" and Christina Rosetti's "Goblin Market." Illustrated with 200 black and white drawings and 8 in full color representing the work of Laurence Houseman, Walter Crane and Richard Doyle and others. Published by Stonehill Publishing Company in association with Bowker). (Illus.). 519p. 1974. 19.95 o.p. (ISBN 0-8352-0794-3, Pub by Stonehill Pr). Bowker.
Beyond the Menace. Harriett Graham Lewis. LC 23-9169. 1923. The Stratford Company.
Beyond the Mind. Sandra Gibson. (Orig.). 1981. pap. 2.50 (ISBN 0-505-51665-9). Tower Bks.
Beyond the Mountains. Alexander Ramati. LC 66-24427. 1966. bds., 4.95. New Amer. Lib.
Beyond the Night. Betty Swinford. 1964 (37-58). pap. 0.95 o.p. (37-58). Moody.
Beyond the Night: By Cornell Woolrich Pseud. Cornell George Hopley-Woolrich. LC 59-4777. (Avon, T -354). 1959. Avon Book Division, Hearst Corp.
Beyond the Outer Mirr. Julian Jay Savarin. LC 79-18308. (Savarin, Julian Jay. Lemmus). 1980. 10.95 (ISBN 0-312-07781-5). St. Martin's Press.
Beyond the Outpost. Peter Henry Morland. LC 25-219101. 1925. G. P. Putnam's Sons.
Beyond the Pale. A Novel. Bithia Mary Sheppard Croker. LC 13-7652. (On cover: The Fortnightly library. v. 15, no. 16). 1896. P. F. Collier.
Beyond the Pale, and Other Stories. William Trevor. LC 81-52221. 1982. 12.95 (ISBN 0-670-16115-2). Viking Press.
Beyond the Pass. Lee Leighton, pseud. 1982. pap. 1.95 (ISBN 0-345-29219-7). Ballantine.
Beyond the Pass: By Lee Leighton Pseud. Wayne D Overholser. LC 56-9443. 1956. Ballantine Books.
Beyond the Pass. 1st Ed. William Headen. LC 56-5507. 1956. Vantage Press.
Beyond the Pavement. Albert Drake. LC 80-53525. 9.95 (ISBN 0-917976-10-X). White Ewe Press.
Beyond the Planet Earth. Konstantin Eduardovich TSiolkovskii. LC 60-108383. 1960. Pergamon Press.
Beyond the Planet Earth. K. Tsiolkovsky. Tr. by Kenneth Syers. (Op). Pergamon.
Beyond the Plow. Edna Pinkerton Hirons. LC 55-8413. 1958. Bruce Humphries.
Beyond the Poseidon Adventure. Paul Gallico. LC 77-26905. 8.95 (ISBN 0-440-00453-5). Delacorte Press.
Beyond the Range. George Brydges Rodney. LC 34-4064. E. J. Clode, Inc.
Beyond the Ranges, Vineyard in a Valley, The Frost & the Fire. Gloria Bevan. (Harlequin Romances Ser.). 576p. 1982. pap. 3.50 (ISBN 0-373-20061-7). Harlequin Bks.
Beyond the Resurrection. Gordon Eklund. LC 72-84909. (Doubleday science fiction). 1973. 5.95 (ISBN 0-385-06737-2). Doubleday.
Beyond the Rim: A Tale of the Canadian Arctic. 1st Ed. Gordon Keith Lovelady. LC 58-11575. 1958. Greenwich Book Publishers.
Beyond the Rio Grande. William MacLeod Raine. LC 31-28158. 1931. Houghton Mifflin Company.
Beyond the Rio Grande. William MacLeod Raine. 1974. (pbk.) 0.75. Popular Library.
Beyond the River: A Novel. George Hamlin Ross. LC 38-216966. 1938. Meador Publishing Company.
Beyond the Rocks: A Love Story. Elinor Sutherland Glyn. 1906. Harper & Brothers.
Beyond the Rocks: A Love Story. Elinor Sutherland Glyn. LC 22-13776. 0.75. The Macaulay Company.
Beyond the Seas. William James Stamper. LC 35-6156. 1935.
Beyond the Shadows. Sallie Lee Bell. LC 60-513254. 1960. Zondervan Pub. House.
Beyond the Shadows. Eileen Mitson. pap. 1.50 o.p. Zondervan.
Beyond the Shining Mountains. Doris Shannon. LC 78-21358. 10.00 (ISBN 0-312-07782-3). St. Martin's Press.
Beyond the Shining River. Maryhelen Clague. LC 79-25749. 11.95 (ISBN 0-698-11021-8). Coward, McCann, & Geoghegan.
Beyond the Sound of Guns. Emilie Baker Loring. LC 45-9738. 1945. Little, Brown and Company.
Beyond the Sowdyhunk. Stanley Foss Bartlett. LC 36-6022. 1937. Falmouth Book House.
Beyond the Storm, & Other Stories. Phyllis B. Goody. 3.95 o.p. Vantage.

Beyond the Storm, and Other Stories. Phyllis B Goody. 1973. 3.95 (ISBN 0-533-00443-8). Vantage.

Beyond the Street. Edgar Calmer. LC 34-6714. Harcourt, Brace and Company.

Beyond the Sunrise. Observations by Two Travellers. LC 6-12944. (On cover: Lovell's library, no. 169). 1883. J. W. Lovell Company.

Beyond the Sunset. Virginia Langley. LC 54-32739. 1954. White Wing Pub. House & Press.

Beyond the Sunset. Arthur Douglas Howden Smith. LC 23-4009. Brentano's.

Beyond the Sunset: A Tale of Love and Pirate Gold. George Rothwell Brown. LC 19-14706. 1.75. Small, Maynard & Company.

Beyond the Tangled Mountain. Douglas Cecil Percy. LC 62-51774. 1962. Zondervan Pub. House.

Beyond the Threshold. Ronald Francis Patrick. LC 77-88368. (Illus.). 8.95 (ISBN 0-89343-008-0). Ermine Publishers.

Beyond the Veil... Giles Buckingham Willcox. A. D. F. Randolph & Company (Inc.

Beyond the Verge: Home of Ten Lost Tribes of Israel. De Witt C Chipman. LC 6-20974. 1896. J. H. Earle.

Beyond the Vicarage. Noel Streatfeild. LC 77-169824. 1972. 4.95 (ISBN 0-531-02018-5). Watts.

Beyond the Wall. Ann Boyle. 1975. 4.95. Avalon Books.

Beyond the Wall. John J. Maloney. 1973. perfect bdg. 2.95 (ISBN 0-912678-05-4). Greenfld Rev Pr.

Beyond the Wall. Norbert Weinberg. LC 78-60648. 6.95 (ISBN 0-8197-0462-8). Bloch Pub. Co.

Beyond the Wall of Sleep. Howard Phillips Lovecraft & August William Derleth. LC 43-18297. 1943. Arkham House.

Beyond the Wicked. 1st Ed. William H Bagbey. LC 55-7618. 1955. Pageant Press.

Beyond the Wild Missouri. Walt Coburn. LC 56-12457. 1956. Arcadia House.

Beyond These Voices: A Novel. Agnes Marie O'Leary. LC 9-22004. 1909. 1.25. Broadway Publisihing Co.

Beyond This Horizon. Robert Anson Heinlein. 1974. (pbk.) 0.95. New AmericanLibrary.

Beyond This Horizon. Robert Anson Heinlein. LC 48-7765. Fantasy Press,

Beyond This Horizon. Robert Anson Heinlein. LC 80-26888. (Series: Gregg Press Science Fiction Series.). 1981. 14.95 (ISBN 0-8398-2672-9). Gregg Press.

Beyond This Moment: A Novel. Shirley Sealy. LC 77-155900. 1977. Seventies Mission Bookstore.

Beyond This Night. Rachael Borne. LC 55-24555. 1955. Zondervan Pub. House.

Beyond This Place. Archibald Joseph Cronin. LC 53-7325. 1953. Little, Brown.

Beyond This Point Are Monsters. Margaret Millar. 1974. (pbk.) 0.95. Avon.

Beyond This Point Are Monsters. Margaret Millar. LC 70-117678. 1970. 4.95. Random House.

Beyond This Shore: A Novel. Virgilia Peterson Sapieha. LC 42-36074. 1942. J. B. Lippincott Company.

Beyond Time. Ed. by Sandra Ley (ISBN 0-671-80738-2). Pocket Books.

Beyond Time & Space. Ed. by August William Derleth. LC 50-7958. 1950. Pellegrini & Cudahy.

Beyond Tomorrow. Edna S. Arnold. 160p. 1978. 5.95 o.p. (ISBN 0-8059-2559-7). Dorrance.

Beyond Tomorrow. Ed. by Damon Francis Knight. 1969. pap. 0.75 o.p. (T2081, GM). Fawcett World.

Beyond Tomorrow. Lida Larrimore Thomas. LC 41-21547. Macrae Smith Company.

Beyond Tomorrow: An Anthology of Modern Science Fiction. LC 75-2915. 1976. 7.50 (ISBN 0-85885-169-5). David & Charles.

Beyond Tomorrow: An Anthology of Modern Science Fiction. Lee John Harding & World Science Fiction Convention. LC 77-361832. 1976. (ISBN 0-85885-169-5). Wren.

Beyond Tomorrow: Ten Science Fiction Adventures. Ed. by Damon Knight. Ed. by Damon Francis Knight. LC 65-20251. 4.50, 4.11 lib. ed.,. Harper.

Beyond Tomorrow: Ten Science Fiction Adventures. Edited by Damon Knight. 1st Ed. Ed. by Damon Francis Knight. LC 65-20251. 1965. Harper & Row.

Beyond Vengeance. Johanas L. Bouma. 1979. pap. 1.75 o.s.i. (ISBN 0-8439-0703-7, Leisure Bks). Nordon Pubns.

Beyond Wind River. 1s 1st Ed. Les Savage. LC 58-7798. (Double D western). 1958. Doubleday.

Beyond Woman: A Novel. Maurice Samuel. LC 34-34026. 1934. Coward-McCann, Inc.

Beyonders: By Manly Wade Wellman. new york warner books 1977 ed. Manly Wade Wellman. 1.50 (ISBN 0-446-88202-X).

Beyound the Rocks. 1st Ed. Peggy Ballard. LC 53-12633. 1953. Pageant Press.

Bezaleel. Marion Ames Taggart. LC 8-25582. 1897. Benziger Brothers.

Bezich. Peter D Zivkovic. LC 70-97217. 1969. Murray.

Bhowani Junction, a Novel. John Masters. LC 54-5226. 1954. Viking Press.

Bhunda Jewels. Anne Worboys. 224p. 1981. pap. 2.25 (ISBN 0-441-05901-5). Ace Bks.

Bianca. Mabel Cronquist. LC 56-5197. Putnam.

Bianca. A Tale of Erin and Italy. Edward Maturin. LC 7-17589. 1852. Harper & Brothers.

Bianca Capello: An Historical Tale. Rosina Doyle Wheeler Bulwer-Lytton Lytton. LC 42-439923. 1843. J. Winchester.

Bianca's Daughter: A Novel. Justus Miles Forman. 1910. Harper & Brothers.

Bibblings. Barbara Paul. 1979. pap. 1.75 (ISBN 0-451-08937-5, E8937, Sig). NAL.

Bible Salesman. Alma Stone. LC 62-11428. 1962. Doubleday.

Bible Stories: Co-Workers with God. Josie Cox. 1970. 3.00 o.p. Vantage.

Bibles, Bullets & Brides. J. D. Hardin. LC 82-60685. (J. D. Hardin Western Ser.). 224p. 1983. pap. 2.25 (ISBN 0-86721-241-1). Playboy Pbks.

Bibles, Bullets & Brides. J. D. Hardin. 224p. 1983. pap. 2.25 (ISBN 0-425-06001-2). Berkley Pub.

Biblical Prophecies: A Look into the Future. 1st Ed. Joseph Geraldi. LC 56-12189. 1957. Vantage Press.

Bicentennial Collection of Texas Short Stories. Ed. by James P. White. LC 74-81546. 1974. 5.95. Texas Center for Writers Press.

Bicentennial Man and Other Stories. Isaac Asimov. LC 76-2749. (Doubleday since fiction). 1976. 6.95 (ISBN 0-385-12198-9). Doubleday.

Bicentennial Man and Other Stories. Isaac Asimov. (Fawcett Crest Book). 1978. 1.75 (ISBN 0-449-23573-4). Fawcett Books.

Bichu, the Jaguar. Alan Caillou, pseud. LC 68-28117. (Illus.). 1969. 5.95 o.p. (HO245, NAL). Norton.

Bichu, the Jaguar. Lyle-Smythe, Alan. LC 68-28117. (Illus.). 1969. 4.95. World Pub. Co.

Bickerstaffiana, & Other Early Materials on Swift see Swiftiana.

Bickerton: Or, The Immigrant's Daughter. Elizabeth Strong Worthington. LC 6-12908. 1855. P. O'Shea.

Bickie's Thunder Egg. Bert Rhoads. 1980. pap. 2.95 (ISBN 0-8280-0043-3, 02362-2). Review & Herald.

Bicycle! John Canter. 91p. 1975. 5.00 o.p. (ISBN 0-682-48314-1). Exposition.

Bicycle of Cathay: A Novel. Frank Richard Stockton. 1900. Harper & Brothers.

Bicycle on the Beach. Peter Viertel. LC 71-156383. 1971. 7.95. Delacorte Press.

Bicycle Rider & Six Short Stories. Frederick L Keefe. LC 79-102805. ("A Seymour Lawrence book."). 1970. 5.95. Delacorte Press.

Bicycle Thieves: Translated by C. J. Richards. Luigi Bartolini. LC 50-105679. 1950. Macmillan.

Bicycle Tree. Robert Olver. LC 76-368157. 8.95 (ISBN 0-7710-6850-6). McClelland and Stewart.

Bid for Victory. B. Palmer. (Danny Orlis Ser.). pap. 0.95 o.p. Believers Bkshelf.

Bid Her Awake. Mary Grigs. LC 30-22208. 1930. Houghton Mifflin Company.

Bid Me to Live: A Madrigal. H. D, pseud. LC 83-2677. (Imagist Series). 1983. 20.00 (ISBN 0-933806-19-1). Black Swan Books.

Bid Time Return. Richard Matheson. LC 74-4550. 1975. 7.95 (ISBN 0-670-16232-9). Viking Press.

Bidden to the Feast. Jack Jones. 1981. 18.95x (Pub. by Remploy England). State Mutual Bk.

Bidders. John Baxter. LC 79-12325. 10.95 (ISBN 0-397-01365-5). Lippincott.

Bidders. John Baxter. (Berkley book). 1980. 2.75 (ISBN 0-425-04604-4). Berkley Pub. Corp.

Biddy Brogan's Boy. Jim Tully. LC 42-9125. 1942. C. Scribner's Sons.

Biddy Club: And How Its Members, Wise and Otherwise, Some Toughened and Some Tender-Footed in the Rugged Ways of Housekeeping, Grappled with the Troublous Servant Question to the Great Advantage of Themselves, and, As They Hope, of Many Others. 1888. A. C. McClurg and Company.

Biddy Finnigan's Botheration: Or, That Romp of a Girl. Mary Nolan. LC 7-33311. 1884. E. E. Carreras.

Biddy's Episodes. Adeline Dutton Train Whitney. 1904. Houghton, Mifflin and Company.

Bide Me Fair. J. Harvey Howells. LC 68-22969. 1968. 5.95. Simon and Schuster.

Bidou Inheritance, a Novel. 1st American Ed. Edith De Born. LC 52-6918. 1952. Norton.

Bienvenu, Bonvivant, A' Paris. Jacques Marin. (Illus.). 1978. pap. 6.00 o.p. (ISBN 0-682-48797-X). Exposition.

Bier for a Hussy. Allison Holt. LC 43-16442. 1943. Phoenix Press.

Biffen's Millions. Pelham Grenville Wodehouse. LC 64-17499. 1964. Simon and Schuster.

Big Abel and the Little Manhattan. Cornelius Mathews. LC 73-93642. (American Fiction Series). 1970. Garrett Press.

Big Abel and the Little Manhattan. Cornelius Mathews. LC 72-8144. 1972. (ISBN 0-8422-8093-6). MSS Information Corp.

Big Abel, and the Little Manhattan. Cornelius Mathews. (On cover: Wiley and Putnam's library of American books, no. 5). 1845. Wiley and Putnam.

Big Apple Circus. Peter A. Simon. (Large Format Ser.). (Illus.). 1978. pap. 5.95 o.p. (ISBN 0-14-004969-X). Penguin.

Big Apple Mysteries. Ed. by Carol-Lynn R. Waugh et al. 256p. 1982. pap. 2.75 (ISBN 0-380-80150-7, 80150). Avon.

Big As Life. E. L. Doctorow. LC 66-13845. 4.95. S. & S.

Big As Life. John Pleasant McCoy. LC 50-6679.

Big-Ball, a Novel. 1st Ed. Frank Earl Jones. LC 58-83017. 1958. Jones Publication.

Big Ball of Wax: A Story of Tomorrow's Happy World, a Novel. Shepherd Mead. LC 54-9809. 1954. Simon and Schuster.

Big Bang. Ron Goulart. 160p. 1982. pap. 2.25 (ISBN 0-87997-748-5, UE1748). DAW Bks.

Big Barbecue. Dorothy Belle Flanagan Hughes. LC 49-7422. 1949. Random House.

Big Barn. Walter Dumaux Edmonds. LC 30-23435. 1930. Little, Brown, and Company.

Big Bear, Little Bear. David Brierley. LC 81-9343. 1981. 10.95 (ISBN 0-684-17301-8). Scribner.

Big Bear of Arkansas, and Other Sketches, Illustrative of Characters and Incidents in the South and South-West. Ed. by William Trotter Porter. LC 75-144673. (Illus.). 1973. 8.50 (ISBN 0-404-05079-4). AMS Press.

Big Bear of Arkansas: And Other Sketches, Illustrative of Characters and Incidents in the South and Southwest. Ed. by William Trotter Porter. LC 7-37394. 1855. H. S. Getz.

Big Ben. Ruby Mildred Ayres. LC 39-11054. 1939. Doubleday, Doran & Company, Inc.

Big Ben: A Novel. Earl Schenck Miers. LC 42-86135. 1942. The Westminster Press.

Big Bend. Ben Haas. LC 68-22607. (Doubleday D western). 1968. 3.95. Doubleday.

Big Bend. Richard Meade, pseud. LC 68-22607. 1968. 3.95 o.p. Doubleday.

Big Bend: A Homesteader's Story. J. O. Langford & Fred Gipson. (Illus.). 191p. 1974. Repr. of 1952 ed. 8.95 o.p. (ISBN 0-292-70708-8). U of Tex Pr.

Big Beverage. William T Campbell. LC 52-12921. 1952. Tupper & Love.

Big Biazarro. Leonard Wise. LC 76-18374. 1977. 7.95 o.p. (ISBN 0-385-12063-X). Doubleday.

Big Biazarro: A Novel. Leonard Wise. LC 76-18374. 1977. 7.95 (ISBN 0-385-12063-X). Doubleday.

Big, Bigger, Biggest, by Edward W. Dolch and Marguerite P. Dolch. Illustrated by Fran Matera. Edward William Dolch & Marguerite Pierce Dolch. LC 63-22919. (Dolch first reading book). 1959. Garrard Pub. Co.

Big Bite. Gerry Travis, pseud. LC 57-13108. 1957. Mystery House.

Big Bite. Charles Williams. LC 56-114961. (Dell first edition, A114). 1956. Dell Pub. Co.

Big Bite. Charles Williams. 1973. (pbk) 0.95. Pocket Books.

Big Black Mark. A. Chandler. 1975. (pbk.) 1.25. DAW Books.

Big Black Mark. A. Bertram Chandler. (Science Fiction Ser). pap. 1.50 o.p. (ISBN 0-87997-726-4, UW1355). DAW Bks.

Big Black Mark. A. Bertram Chandler. (Science Fiction Ser). 1975. pap. 1.25 o.p. (UY1157). DAW Bks.

Big Blonde. Charles Edward Colahan. LC 35-25433. W. Godwin, Inc.

Big Blow. Theodore Pratt. LC 36-19091. 1936. Little, Brown, and Company.

Big Blue Soldier. Grace Livingston Hill. LC 75-46602. 1975. 9.95 (ISBN 0-89190-002-0). American Reprint Co.

Big Blue Soldier. Grace Livingston Hill. LC 23-5363. 1923. J. B. Lippincott Company.

Big Bob. Georges Simenon. LC 81-47557. 1981. 10.95 (ISBN 0-15-112075-7). Harcourt Brace Jovanovich.

Big Boodle. Robert Sylvester. 1954. Random House.

Big Book of Detective Stories. 1979. Repr. lib. bdg. 20.00 (ISBN 0-8495-0141-5). Arden Lib.

Big Book of Gleeb. Paul B. Lowney. (Illus.). 160p. 1975. 4.95 o.p. (ISBN 0-396-07223-2). Dodd.

Big Book of Great Short Stories. H. Douglas Thomson & C. Clark Ramsay. Repr. of 1935 ed. lib. bdg. 20.00 (ISBN 0-8495-5327-X). Arden Lib.

Big Book of Great Stories. H. Douglas Thomson. Ed. by C. Clark Ramsey. Repr. of 1935 ed. 20.00 (ISBN 0-8414-8455-4). Folcroft.

Big Book of Real Trains. George J. Zaffo & Elizabeth Cameron. LC 63-6923. (Illus.). Grosset & Dunlap.

Big Book of Science Fiction. Ed. by Groff Conklin. LC 50-9548. 1950. Crown Publishers.

Big Bow Mystery. Israel Zangwill. LC 8-37872. (On cover: Globe library, v. 1, no. 219). 1895. Rand, McNally & Company.

Big Boxcar: A Novel. Alfred Maund. LC 57-9979. 1957. Houghton Mifflin.

Big Boy: The Story of a Dog. Albert Pennington. 320p. 1971. 3.00; pap. 1.00. Pennington.

Big Boys: A Novel. Max Simon Ehrlich. LC 80-27399. 1981. 11.95 (ISBN 0-395-30525-X). Houghton Mifflin.

Big Bridge. Richard Martin Stern. LC 82-45149. 336p. 1982. 15.95 (ISBN 0-385-18018-7). Doubleday.

Big Broad Jump. Troy Conway, pseud. (Coxeman Ser). (Orig.). 1969. pap. 0.60 o.p. (ISBN 0-446-63240-6, 63-240). Paperback Lib.

Big Brother: And Other Stories. Rex Ellingwood Beach. LC 23-14204. Harper & Brothers.

Big Bruiser. Alfred Eichler. LC 41-16398. Phoenix Press.

Big Bubble: A Novel of the Florida Boom. Theodore Pratt. LC 51-10423. 1951. Duell, Sloan and Pearce.

Big Bug. Paul Rader. LC 32-34229. Fleming H. Revell Company.

Big Burn: Short Stories, Introd, by Norman Lindsay. Brian James, pseud. LC 66-81975. 1966. bds., 4.50. Angus & Robertson.

Big Business. Arthur Stuart-Menteth Hutchinson. LC 32-26873. 1932. Little, Brown, and Company.

Big Business Murder... George Douglas Howard Cole & Margaret Isabel Postgate Cole. LC 35-3930. 1935. Pub. for the Crime Club, Inc., by Doubleday, Doran & Company, Inc.

Big Cage. Robert James Collas Lowry. LC 49-11454. 1949. Doubleday.

Big Call. John Creasey. LC 74-15488. (Rinehart suspense novel). 1975. 5.95 (ISBN 0-03-013811-6). Holt, Rinehart and Winston.

Big Cat. Christopher Short. LC 65-22846. (Red badge detective). bds., 3.50. Dodd.

Big Cat. Christopher Short. LC 65-22846. (Red badge detective). 1965. Dodd, Mead.

Big Chance. B. Palmer. (Danny Orlis Ser.). pap. 0.95 o.p. Believers Bkshelf.

Big Cinch: A Society and Financial Novel. Leo A. Landau. LC 10-7174. The Franklin Co.

Big City Girl. Charles Williams. LC 51-6238. (Gold medal books, 165). 1951. Fawcett Publications.

Big City Nurse. Peggy Gaddis, pseud. 1971. pap. 0.60 o.p. (60-484). Manor Bks.

Big City Zulu. Translated from the Swedish by Margery Osberg. Gunnar Helander. LC 57-12013. 1957. Augustana Press.

Big Clock. Kenneth Fearing. LC 75-44971. (Fifty Classics of Crime Fiction, 1900-1950; 17). 1976. 12.00 (ISBN 0-8240-2366-8). Garland Pub.

Big Clock. Kenneth Fearing. LC 68-20832. (Seagull library of mystery and suspense). 1968. 4.95. Norton.

Big Clock. Kenneth Fearing. LC 46-6954. 1946. Harcourt, Brace and Company.

Big Company Look. 1st Ed. J. Harvey Howells. LC 58-10024. 1958. Doubleday.

Big Corral. Archie Joscelyn. LC 49-87024. (Silver Star Westerns). (Silver star westerns). 1949. Dodd, Mead.

Big Country. Donald Hamilton. 1980. pap. 1.50 (ISBN 0-440-10848-9). Dell.

Big Country. E. V. Timms. 1968. Repr. pap. 1.60 o.s.i. Tri-Ocean.

Big Cy. Gary Youree. LC 73-11800. 1974. 8.95 (ISBN 0-672-51880-5). Bobbs-Merrill.

Big Dallas Kill. Davis R. Baxter. 1980. 4.95 o.p. (ISBN 0-8062-1539-9). Carlton.

Big Day. Barry Unsworth. LC 77-363092. (Illus.). 1976. 3.95 (ISBN 0-7181-1551-1). Joseph.

Big Day: A Novel. Barry Unsworth. LC 77-22450. 1977. 7.95 (ISBN 0-88405-586-8). Mason/Charter.

Big Deal: A Novel. James A. Hall. LC 73-163268. 1972. 1.65 (ISBN 0-7260-0040-X). Gold Star Publications.

Big Deal in Veragua. Pablo Morales. 1979. pap. 1.50 o.s.i. (ISBN 0-8439-0632-4, Leisure Bks). Nordon Pubns.

Big Dick the King of the Negroes: Or, Virtue and Vice Contrasted. A Romance of High & Low Life in Boston. Justin Jones. LC 7-12248. 1846. "Star Spangled Banner" Office.

Big Die. Lee E Wells. LC 52-8733. 1952. Rinehart.

Big Dig. Slater McGurk, pseud. LC 68-19822. (Cock Robin mystery). 1968. Macmillan.

Big Doc & Little Doc. Harry R. Werner. 1979. pap. 8.00 (ISBN 0-87012-363-7). McClain.

Big Dream. Dean F. V Du Vall. LC 79-19159. 10.00. L. Stuart.

Big Dream. Stephen Gould Fisher. LC 77-89074. 1970. 5.95. Doubleday.

Big Dreams & Little Wheels. Wiggin. 1977. pap. 3.50 (ISBN 0-89272-025-5). Down East.

TITLE INDEX BIG SISTER.

Big Drive. Thorne Douglas. (Fawcet Gold Medal Book). 1973. (pbk.) 0.95. Fawcett.
Big Drum. Elizabeth Boatwright Coker. LC 56-8298. (Illus.). 1957. Dutton.
Big Dry: By George Garland Pseud. Garland Roark. LC 52-9586. 1953. Houghton Mifflin.
Big Ear & the Albino: Two Stories. Gil Fasier. LC 81-86420. 160p. 1983. pap. 5.95 (ISBN 0-86666-040-2). GWP.
Big Easy. James Conaway. LC 78-120831. 1970. 4.95. Houghton Mifflin.
Big Ember: A Novel. Edward Havill. LC 47-30420. 1947. Harper.
Big Enchilada. L. A. Morse. 224p. (Orig.). 1982. pap. 2.25 (ISBN 0-380-77602-2, 77602). Avon.
Big End of the Horn. Illus. by Bill Ballard. 1st Ed. Julia Canaday. LC 56-6842. 1956. Vantage Press.
Big Enough to Help. Mary Anne Forehand. LC 74-146431. (Foreign mission graded series, 1971). (Illus.). 1971. Convention Press.
Big Enough Wreath. William Garner. 256p. 1975. 7.95 o.p. (ISBN 0-399-11634-6). Putnam Pub Group.
Big Eye. Max Simon Ehrlich. LC 49-10563. (Doubleday science fiction). 1949. Doubleday.
Big Fall. Ralph Hayes. (Orig.). 1979. pap. 2.25 (ISBN 0-89083-487-3). Zebra.
Big Family. Vina Delmar. LC 61-6642. 1961. Harcourt, Brace.
Big Fella. Henry W. Clune. LC 56-7294. 1956. Macmillan.
Big Fellah. Ruby Mildred Ayres. LC 31-841611. Doubleday, Doran & Company, Inc.
Big Fellow. Frederick Palmer. 1908. Moffat, Yard and Company.
Big Fifty. Frank O'Rourke. LC 55-8349. (Dell first edition 59). 1955. Dell Pub. Co.
Big Firm. Amabel Williams-Ellis. LC 38-5289. 1938. Houghton-Mifflin Company.
Big Fish. Henry Brereton Marriott Watson. LC 12-8413. 1912. Little, Brown, and Company.
Big Fish: By Ronald Wills Pseud. Ronald Wills Thomas. LC 54-5638. (A Questing owl detective story). 1954. Roy Publishers.
Big Fisherman. Lloyd Cassel Douglas. LC 48-10352. 1948. Houghton Mifflin Co.
Big Fisherman: Illustrated by Dean Cornwell. Lloyd Cassel Douglas. LC 52-4265. 1952. Houghton Mifflin.
Big Fist. Clyde Byron Ragsdale. LC 50-8239. 1950. Putnam.
Big Fix. Albert Barker. (Orig.). 1973. pap. 0.95 o.p. Curtis.
Big Fix. Edward Jarvis. LC 70-96225. 1969. 3.95. Roy Publishers.
Big Fix. Ed Lacy. LC 60-29905. (Pyramid books, G484). 1960. Pyramid Books.
Big Fix. Roger Lichtenberg Simon. LC 72-88837. (Straight Arrow thriller). (Illus.). 1973. 3.00 (ISBN 0-87932-048-6). Straight Arrow Books.
Big Fix. Roger Lichtenberg Simon. (Moses Wine thriller, 77746). 1974. (pbk.) 0.95. Pocket Books.
Big Flat. Henry Oyen. LC 19-6412. George H. Doran Company.
Big Flight. Francis Drake & Drake, Mrs. Katharine (Zimmermann) Joint Author. LC 34-694. 1934. Little, Brown and Company.
Big Football Man. Harry Sylvester. LC 33-251943. Farrar & Rinehart, Incorporated.
Big Footprints. Hammond Innes. LC 76-43293. 1977. 8.95 (ISBN 0-394-41162-5). Knopf.
Big Foot's Range. Jack Slade, pseud. (Lassiter Ser.). 1979. pap. 1.75 o.s.i. (ISBN 0-505-51428-1). Tower Bks.
Big Four. Agatha Miller Christie. LC 27-17791. 1927. Dodd, Mead & Company.
Big Four. new ed. Dame Agatha Miller Christie. 1975. (pbk.) 1.25. Dell.
Big Frame: By the Gordons. 1st Ed. Mildred Gordon & Gordon Gordon. LC 57-5787. 1957. Published for the Crime Club by Doubleday.
Big Freak-Out. Troy Conway, pseud. pap. 0.75 o.p. (ISBN 0-446-64499-4, 64-499-4). Paperback Lib.
Big Friend, Little Friend. Richard E. Turner, pseud. 1972. pap. 0.75 o.p. (07216). Curtis.
Big Gamble. George Harmon Coxe. LC 58-10975. 1958. Knopf.
Big Gamble. Zeke Masters, pseud. 1980. pap. 1.95. PB.
Big Game. Max Brand. (O.S.I.). 192p. 1973. pap. 0.75 o.s.i. (ISBN 0-446-74046-2). Paperback Lib.
Big Game. Frederick Faust. (Paperback Lib., 74-045). 1973. 0.75. Warner Paperback Lib.
Big Game. Louis Lacy Stevenson. LC 24-6732. Brentano's.
Big Game. Francis Wallace. LC 36-5507. 1936. Little, Brown, and Company.
Big Game: A Story of the Girl of Today and the Game of Love. Vida Hurst. LC 28-28926. Grosset & Dunlap.
Big Game: And Other Stories. A. P Gaskell. LC 47-24987. 1947. The Caxton Press.
Big Gate. Elma Stuckey. LC 75-12115. 1975. 5.95 (ISBN 0-913750-11-5). Precedent Pub.
Big Girls. Nancy Holmes. LC 81-43290. 1982. 17.95 (ISBN 0-385-17293-1). Doubleday.
Big Gold Dream. Chester B. Himes. 160p. 1973. Repr. of 1960 ed. 7.95x (ISBN 0-911860-30-4). Chatham Bkseller.
Big Gold Dream. Chester B. Himes. (Coffin Ed Johnson and Grave Digger Jones,#4). 1975. (pbk.) 1.25. New American Library.
Big Golden Animal ABC. Garth Williams. LC 57-4312. 1957. Simon and Schuster.
Big Grab. John Trinian. 1973. (pbk) 0.95. Manor Books.
Big Gun. James Cavanaugh. LC 55-101956. 1955. Arcadia House.
Big H. Peter Bryan George. LC 63-11336. (Rinehart suspense novel). 1963. Holt, Rinehart and Winston.
Big Hamburger. 1st Ed. Harold Helfer. LC 56-10561. 1956. Vantage Press.
Big Heart: A Novel. Mulk Raj Anand. 1945. Hutchinson International Authors Ltd.
Big Heart: A Present-Day Adventure--Without a Moral. John Gordon Brandon. LC 23-126103. Brentano's.
Big Heat. William P McGivern. LC 52-14196. (Red badge detective). 1953. Dodd, Mead.
Big Hello. Morris Renek. 1970. pap. 0.75 o.p. (ISBN 0-446-64346-7, 64-346). Paperback Lib.
Big Hello: A Novel. Morris Renek. LC 61-10162. 1961. Dial Press.
Big Hit. James H. Readus. (Orig.). 1975. pap. 1.50 (ISBN 0-87067-476-5, BH476). Holloway.
Big Hitch. John Henry Reese. LC 76-180100. (Doubleday western). 1972. 4.95. Doubleday.
Big-Horn Treasure: A Tale of Rocky Mountain Adventure. John F Cargill. 1897. A. C. McClurg and Company.
Big Horse and Other Stories of Modern Macedonia. Ed. by Milne Holton. LC 73-93892. 1974. 9.50 (ISBN 0-8262-0162-8). University of Missouri Press.
Big House. Charles N. Aronson. LC 74-81876. (Illus.). 288p. 1974. 20.00 (ISBN 0-915736-04-7). C N Aronson.
Big House. Jack Lait & Marion, Frances. LC 30-166104. Grosset & Dunlap.
Big House. Mildred Wasson. LC 26-13914. 1926. Houghton Mifflin Company.
Big House of Inver. Edith Anna Œnone Somerville & Violet Florence Martin. LC 26-27551. 1925. Doubleday, Page & Company.
Big It. Alfred Bertram Guthrie, Jr. 1980. pap. 1.75 (ISBN 0-345-29195-6). Ballantine.
Big It, and Other Stories. Alfred Bertram Guthrie. LC 80-147207. (Gregg Press Western fiction series). 1980. 9.95 (ISBN 0-8398-2680-X). Gregg Press.
Big Ivy. James P. McCague. LC 55-10176. 1955. Crown Publishers.
Big Jake. Richard Deming et al. (Orig.). 1971. pap. 0.75 o.p. (64-676). Paperback Lib.
Big Jim Albright. Leslie Parker. LC 24-203844. 1924. C. F. Fraser Co.
Big Jim Turner. James Stevens. LC 75-7471. (Zia book). 1975. 2.95 (ISBN 0-8263-0380-3). University of New Mexico Press.
Big Jim Turner: A Novel. James Stevens. LC 48-8419. 1948. Doubleday.
Big Jock. O. R. Bassett. 192p. (Orig.). 1973. pap. 1.95 o.p. (ISBN 0-87056-314-9, 6314). Brandon.
Big John Baldwin: Extracts from the Journal of an Officer of Cromwell's Army Recording Some of His Experiences at the Court of Charles I and Subsequently at That of the Lord Protector and on the Fields of Love and War, and Finally in the Colony of Virginia. Wilson J Vance. LC 9-24322. 1909. H. Holt and Company.
Big Joke Game. Scott Corbett. (Dutton anytime book, AB-05). (Illus.). 1973. (pbk.) 0.95. E. P. Dutton.
Big Jump. Leigh Brackett. LC 55-33829. (Ace double novel books, D-103). 1955. Ace Books.
Big Jump. Leigh Brackett. 1976. Ace Books.
Big Kill. Frank Morrison Spillane. LC 51-11571. (Guilt edged mystery). 1951. Dutton.
Big Kiss-Off. Day Keene. 1969. pap. 0.60 o.p. (60-424). Manor Bks.
Big Kiss-off of 1944: A Jack Levine Mystery. Andrew Bergman. LC 73-9315. 1974. 6.95 (ISBN 0-03-011796-8). Holt, Rinehart and Winston.
Big Knives. Bruce Lancaster. LC 64-15047. 1964. Little, Brown.
Big Knockover. Dashiell Hammett. 1966. 5.95 o.p. (ISBN 0-394-41691-0). Random.
Big Knockover: Selected Stories and Short Novels. Dashiell Hammett. LC 72-1750. 1972. 1.25 (ISBN 0-394-71829-1). Vintage Books.
Big Knoockover: Selected Stories and Short Novels. Ed., Introd. by Lillian Hellman. Dashiell Hammett. LC 66-18326. 1966. 5.95. Random.
Big Land. Dwight Bennett. LC 75-186006. 192p. 1972. 4.95 o.p. (ISBN 0-385-02733-8). Doubleday.
Big Land. Zane Grey. Belmont Tower.
Big Land. Dwight Bennett Newton. 1974. (pbk.) 0.95. Dell.
Big Land. Dwight Bennett Newton. LC 75-186006. (Doubleday western). 1972. 4.95. Doubleday.
Big Laugh. John O'Hara. 1977. 1.95 (ISBN 0-445-04017-3). Popular Library.
Big Laugh: A Novel. John O'Hara. LC 62-127242. 1962. Random House.
Big Laurel. Frederick Orin Bartlett. LC 22-19552. 1922. 2.00. Houghton Mifflin Company.
Big League. Charles Emmett Van Loan. LC 75-152961. (Short story index reprint series). (Illus.). 1971. (ISBN 0-8369-3876-3). Books for Libraries Press.
Big League. Charles Emmett Van Loan. LC 11-189712. Small, Maynard & Company.
Big Lie. Howard Dodge. 6.95 o.p. Vantage.
Big Little Person: A Romance. Rebecca Lane Hooper Eastman. LC 17-24397. 1917. 1.40. Harper & Brothers.
Big Little World of Doc Pritham. Dorothy C. Wilson. 1982. pap. 7.95. Juniper Maine.
Big Lonely. Lou Cameron. 1978. pap. 2.25 (ISBN 0-445-04200-1). Popular Lib.
Big Lonesome. Will Bryant. 1973. 0.95. Popular Lib.
Big Lonesome. Will Bryant. LC 69-20069. 1971. 6.95. Doubleday.
Big Lonesome. Norford Scott. 1970. 3.95 o.p. Lenox Hill.
Big Loser. Elliot Kennedy. LC 72-3663. 1972. 3.95 (ISBN 0-87749-314-6). Drake Publishers.
Big Man. Jay Neugeboren. 1970. pap. 0.95 o.p. (B95-2030). Belmont-Tower.
Big Man. Henry Junior Taylor. LC 64-10358. 1964. Random House.
Big Man, a Fast Man. Benjamin Appel. LC 61-5631. 1961. Morrow.
Big Man: A Novel. Jay Neugeboren. LC 66-18108. 1966. Houghton Mifflin.
Big Man & Other Stories. Martha Kelley. LC 79-50388. 1979. 4.50 o.p. (ISBN 0-682-49308-2). Exposition.
Big Man in the Saddle. Mullin Garr. (Orig.). 1969. pap. 1.75 o.s.i. (OPH138, Ophelia). Olympia.
Big Matt: A Story. Brand Whitlock. LC 28-117041. 1928. D. Appleton and Company.
Big Men, Little Girls. Cynthia Boomis. 192p. pap. 1.95 o.p. (ISBN 0-87056-152-9, 6152). Brandon.
Big Midget Murders. Craig Rice. LC 42-15599. 1942. Simon and Schuster.
Big Mirror. Mohammed Mrabet & Paul Frederic Bowles. LC 77-5917. (Illus.). 1977. 10.00. (ISBN 0-87685-368-8) (ISBN 0-87685-369-6) (ISBN 0-87685-367-X). Black Sparrow Press.
Big Mogul. Joseph Crosby Lincoln. LC 26-15134. 1926. D. Appleton and Company.
Big Money. Hugh Atkinson. (Kangaroo Book). 1978. 1.95 (ISBN 0-671-81335-8). Pocket Books.
Big Money. John Dos Passos. LC 36-17476. Harcourt, Brace and Company.
Big Money. Harold Q Masur. LC 54-142896. (Inner sanctum mystery). 1954. Simon and Schuster.
Big Money. Pelham Grenville Wodehouse. LC 31-26366. 1931. Doubleday, Doran & Company, Inc.
Big Money. Pelham Grenville Wodehouse. LC 35-7868. 1932. A. L. Burt Company.
Big Morning Blues. Gordon Williams. (Leisure Book). 1977. 1.50. Nordon Publications.
Big Mouth: Confessions of a Porno Movie Star. Georgette Chalmers. (O.s.i.). (Orig.). 1975. pap. 1.50 o.s.i. (BT50837). Belmont-Tower.
Big Muskeg. Victor Rousseau Emanuel. LC 21-9369. Stewart Kidd Company.
Big Needle. Ken Follett. 1981. pap. 2.25 (ISBN 0-89083-787-2). Zebra.
Big Needle. Ken Follett. (Orig.). 1979. pap. 2.25 (ISBN 0-89083-512-8). Zebra.
Big Nick. Buranelli, Prosper. LC 31-31228. 1931. Doubleday, Doran and Company, Incorporated.
Big Nickel. Calder Willingham. LC 74-20583. 1975. 7.95. Dial Press.
Big Nickelodeon. Maritta Martin Wolff. LC 56-8810. 1956. Random House.
Big Night. Ian Andersen. LC 79-18569. 9.95 (ISBN 0-671-24826-X). Simon and Schuster.
Big Night. Ian Anderson. 1980. 10.00 o.p. (ISBN 0-671-24826-X). S&S.
Big Night at Mrs. Maria's. Barney Parrish. 1977. pap. 1.95 o.p. (ISBN 0-87216-365-2, E 16365). Playboy Pr Pbks.
Big Noise. Fielden Farrington. LC 46-17070. 1946. Crown Publishers.
Big O. Rosemary Saint. 208p. 1975. pap. 1.50 (ISBN 0-532-15153-4). Woodhill.
Big Old Sun. Robert Faherty. LC 41-4371. G. P. Putnam's Sons.
Big Ones Get Away! Philip Wylie. LC 40-7113. Farrar & Rinehart, Inc.
Big Out. Arnold Hano. LC 51-10434. (Barnes sports novel). 1951. Barnes.
Big Outfit: By Peter Dawson Pseud. Jonathan H Glidden. LC 55-619747. 1955. Dodd, Mead.
Big Ox. Don Tracy. 1976. 1.50 (ISBN 0-671-80773-0). Pocket Books.
Big Paddle. Robin Moore & Sid Levine. LC 77-90661. 9.95 (ISBN 0-87795-178-0). Arbor House.
Big Pasture. Allan Vaughan Elston. (Berkley Medallion Book). 1976. (pbk.) 1.25 (ISBN 0-425-03121-7). Berkley Publishing Corp.
Big Pasture: A Novel of New Lands and Old Emotions, the Forgotten Story of Montana's First Range War, by Clay Fisher Pseud. Henry Allen. LC 55-10021. 1955. Houghton Mifflin.
Big Pasture: A Novel of New Lands and Old Emotions, the Forgotten Story of Montana's First Range War. Clay Fisher, pseud. LC 55-10021. 1955. Houghton Mifflin.
Big Payoff. Janice Law, pseud. LC 75-20165. 1976. 7.95 (ISBN 0-395-21900-0). Houghton Mifflin.
Big Payoff. Robert Novak. (Joe Blaze#1). 1974. (pbk.) 0.95. Belmont Tower Books.
Big Peter. Archibald Marshall. LC 22-5603. 1922. 2.00. Dodd, Mead and Company.
Big Phil's Kid. M. M Parker. LC 69-16294. 1969. 4.95. Meredith Press.
Big Pick-up: A Novel of Dunkirk. Elleston Trevor. LC 55-149004. 1955. Macmillan.
Big Pink. Hugh MacNair Kahler. LC 32-16969. Farrar & Rinehart, Incorporated.
Big Planet. Jack Vance, pseud. LC 57-8746. 1957. Avalon Books.
Big Planet: By Jack Vance Pseud. Henry Kuttner. LC 57-8746. 1957. Avalon Books.
Big Rape. James Wakefield Burke. LC 52-11655. 1952. Farrar, Straus and Young.
Big Red. John Haase. LC 79-2648. 10.95 (ISBN 0-06-011809-1). Harper & Row.
Big Red One. Samuel Michael Fuller. 448p. (Orig.). 1980. pap. 2.50 (ISBN 0-553-14037-X). Bantam.
Big Red Pocketbook: A Novel. William Hawkins. LC 63-7417. 1963. Appleton-Century-Crofts.
Big Red Sun. Daniel Larany. LC 70-134203. 1972. (532-00140-125) 1.25. Manor Books.
Big Red Sun. Daniel Larnay. Tr. by R. Bullen & R. Letellier. 1971. 6.95 o.p. (ISBN 0-13-076166-4). P-H.
Big Red's Daughter. John McPartland. pap. 0.60 o.p. (60-342). Manor Bks.
Big Refit. Leonid Sergeevich Sobolev. 378p. 1978. 8.95 (ISBN 0-8285-1047-4, 181916, Pub. by Progress Pubs USSR). Imported Pubns.
Big Road. Ruth Cross. LC 31-28115. 1931. Longmans, Green and Co.
Big Rock Candy: A Novel by Annabel Johnson and Edgar Johnson. Annabel Johnson & Edgar Johnson. LC 58-536131. 1957. Crowell.
Big Rock Candy Mountain. Wallace Earle Stegner. LC 57-124391. (American century series, S-19). 1957. Sagamore Press.
Big Rock Candy Mountain. Wallace Earle Stegner. LC 43-512819. 1943. Duell, Sloan and Pearce.
Big Rock Candy Mountain. Wallace Earle Stegner. 1973. 8.95 (ISBN 0-385-07905-2). Doubleday.
Big Rock Candy Mountain. Wallace Earle Stegner. (Kangaroo Book.). 1977. 2.50 (ISBN 0-671-81094-4). Pocket Books.
Big Rumble: A Novel of Juvenile Delinquency. Wenzell Brown. LC 55-43684. (Popular library, 685). 1955. Popular Library.
Big Runaround. Darwin Le Ora Teilhet. LC 64-11631. 1964. Coward-McCann.
Big Runaround see Dangerous Encounter.
Big Saddle: A Novel of the Texas Panhandle, by West Jameson Pseud. Almus Day Jameson. LC 52-14249. 1952. Abelard Press.
Big Saturday. David Harper. LC 74-156862. 1971. 5.95 (ISBN 0-396-06362-4). Dodd, Mead.
Big Scalphunter: A Novel of the Old Southwest. A. Kinney Griffith. 1975. 6.00 (ISBN 0-87164-076-7). William-F.
Big Scalphunter: A Saga of the Great Southwest. Illustrated by the Author. A. Kinney Griffith. LC 60-7483. 1961. William-Frederick Press.
Big Score. Hugh Barron. (Orig.). 1969. pap. 0.95 o.p. (N1982). Pyramid Pubns.
Big Score. Clayton Matthews. 192p. (Orig.). 1973. pap. 1.95 o.p. (ISBN 0-87056-337-8, 6337). Brandon.
Big Score. Clayton Matthews. 1973. (pbk.) 1.95 (ISBN 0-87056-337-8). Brandon Books.
Big Shark. Helen Mary Greenwood Campbell Reynolds. LC 48-4221. 1948. T. Nelson.
Big Shot. Frank Lucius Packard. LC 29-21420. 1929. Pub. for the Crime Club, Inc., by Doubleday, Doran & Company, Inc.
Big Show. Charles Harris Cooke. LC 38-25097. 1938. Harper & Brothers.
Big Show. McCready Huston. LC 27-5018. 1927. C. Scribner's Sons.
Big Sin. Jack Webb. LC 52-5576. (Murray Hill mystery). 1952. Rinehard.
Big Sister. Degranamour. pap. 1.95 o.s.i. (Venus). Grove.

Big Sky. Alfred Bertram Guthrie. LC 47-3316. 1947. William Sloane Associates.
Big Sky: An Edition for Younger Readers. Illustrated by Jacob Landau. Rev. Ed. Alfred Bertram Guthrie. LC 50-5774. 1950. Sloane.
Big Sleep. Raymond Chandler. LC 76-11809. 1976. 1.95 (ISBN 0-394-72136-5). Vintage Books.
Big Sleep. Raymond Chandler. LC 39-3298. 1939. A. A. Knopf.
Big Sleep. Raymond Chandler. LC 44-7479. New Avon Library.
Big Sleep. Raymond Chandler. LC 44-8474. (Murder mystery monthly. No. 7). 1943. The Avon Book Company.
Big Smear. William R Reardon. LC 60-15385. 1960. Crown Publishers.
Big Snatch. Rod Gray. (The Lady from L.U.S.T. Ser.). (O.s.i.: No. 16). 1974. pap. 0.95 o.s.i. (BT50710). Belmont-Tower.
Big Snatch. Abdul Rahman. pap. 1.95 o.s.i. (OPH-218, Ophelia). Olympia.
Big Snow: Christmas at Jacoby's Corners. Herman Fetzer. LC 41-22668. 1941. Houghton Mifflin Company.
Big Spender. Ted Thorne. pap. 1.95 o.s.i. (OPA-231, Ophelia). Olympia.
Big Spread. Jessie Donaldson. LC 74-141687. 1971. 4.00 (ISBN 0-8059-1536-2). Dorrance.
Big Stash. Ron Peters. (Orig.). 1972. pap. 0.75 o.p. (07240). Curtis.
Big Steal. Evan A Beilke. LC 54-8377. 1954. Vantage Press.
Big Steal. 1st Ed. Earle Basinsky. LC 55-7127. (Dutton guilt edged mystery). 1955. Dutton.
Big Steel. Leslie J Swabacker. LC 3-20787. The Macaulay Company.
Big Still. Roderick Wilkinson. LC 67-13127. 1967. bds., 3.95. Walker.
Big Stony. Howard Talbot Walden. LC 40-12819. The Derrydale Press.
Big Stopper. Hal Kantor. 224p. 1982. pap. 2.50 (ISBN 0-445-04726-7). Popular Lib.
Big Store. Oscar Schisgall. LC 55-5857. 1955. Prentice-Hall.
Big Storm: A Factual Story of Wyoming's 'Operation Snowbound.' 1st Ed. Genevieve Christensen Gilfry. LC 53-16220. 1952. Pagenat Press.
Big Strike at Siwash. illustrated by frank crerie and may wilson preston. ed. George Helgeson Fitch. LC 9-28155. 1909. Doubleday, Page & Company.
Big Success. Ian Gordon, pseud. LC 56-10364. (Dell first edition, A111). 1956. Dell Pub. Co.
Big Sur. John Kerouac. LC 62-149570. 1962. Farrar, Straus and Cudahy.
Big Sur. John Kerouac. LC 81-8279. 1981. 5.95 (ISBN 0-07-034206-7). McGraw-Hill.
Big Swingers. Robert W Fenton. LC 66-24975. (Illus.). 1967. Prentice-Hall.
Big Switch. Kay Martin. 1969. pap. 0.75 o.p. (75-251). Manor Bks.
Big T Ramrod. Leslie Charles Ernenwein. LC 55-7937. 1955. Arcadia House.
Big Thicket: A Novel. Edmond E. Talbot. LC 73-82916. 1973. 5.95 (ISBN 0-913206-01-6). Little House Press.
Big Three. Timothy J Mahoney. LC 52-4577. 1952. Christopher Pub. House.
Big Thursday. Anne Z Sparklin. LC 66-26664. 1966. Dorrance.
Big Timber. Robert Ormond Case. LC 37-21535. 1937. Macrae Smith Company.
Big Timber: A Story of the Northwest. Bertrand William Sinclair. LC 16-162583. 1916. Little, Brown, and Company.
Big Time. Phil Berger. LC 81-14388. 31.95 (ISBN 0-671-24708-5). Summit Books.
Big Time. Fritz Leiber. LC 76-11734. (Gregg Press science fiction series). 1976. 7.50 (ISBN 0-684-14730-0). Gregg Press.
Big Town: How I and the Mrs. Go to New York to See Life and Get Katie a Husband, by Ring W. Lardner. Ring W Lardner. LC 21-18886. The Bobbs-Merrill Company.
Big Town: How I and the Mrs. Go to New York to See Life and Get Katie a Husband. Ring Wilmer Lardner. LC 25-10467. 1925. C. Scribner's Sons.
Big-Town Round-up. William MacLeod Raine. LC 20-19181. 1920. Houghton Mifflin Company.
Big-Town Round-up. William MacLeod Raine. 1974. (pbk.) 0.95. Popular Library.
Big Trail. Max Brand. 1976. Repr. of 1934 ed. lib. bdg. 14.40x (ISBN 0-88411-513-5). Amereon Ltd.
Big Trail. Max Brand. 1974. pap. 1.75 (ISBN 0-446-94333-9). Warner Bks.
Big Trail. Frederick Faust. LC 76-41324. 1976. 6.95 (ISBN 0-88411-513-5). Aeonian Press.
Big Trail. Frederick Faust. 1974. (pbk.) 0.95. Warner Paperback Library.
Big Tree Treaty; or, The Last Council on the Genesee. Thomas Kelly. LC 16-13315. 1916. 1.00. Pub. at Mt. Pleasant Farm.
Big Tremaine: A Novel. with frontispiece by w. b. king. ed. Marie Van Vorst. LC 14-307914. 1914. Little, Brown, and Company.
Big Trucker: A Magical Novel. Dennis Dunn. LC 79-51313. 5.00 (ISBN 0-931022-01-0). Dancing Rock Press.
Big V. William Pelfrey. LC 78-167289. (New Writers Ser.). 190p. 1972. 3.95 (ISBN 0-87140-548-2). Liveright.
Big War. Anton Myrer. LC 57-7795. 1957. Appleton-Century-Crofts.
Big Ward. Jacoba Van Velde. LC 60-8010. 1960. Simon and Schuster.
Big Water. Mark Derby. LC 53-5723. 1953. Viking Press.
Big Water: By Mark Derby Pseud. Harry Wilcox. LC 53-5723. 1953. Viking Press.
Big Wheel. John Nixon Brooks. 1973. 1.25. Manor Books.
Big Wheel. John Nixon Brooks. LC 71-89488. (Harper colophon books, CN 162). 1969. 1.60. Harper & Row.
Big Wheel. John Nixon Brooks. LC 49-5384. 1949. Harper.
Big White House: By Carol Holliston Pseud. James Noble Gifford. LC 53-11297. 1953. Arcadia House.
Big Win. Jimmy Miller. LC 70-79326. 1969. 5.95. Knopf.
Big Wind. Beatrice Coogan. LC 68-14173. 1969. 7.95. Doubleday.
Big Wind for Summer. Gavin Black. LC 75-25076. (Harper Novel of Suspense). 224p. 1976. 6.95 o.p. (ISBN 0-06-010366-3, HarpT). Har-Row.
Big Wind for Summer. Oswald Wynd. LC 75-25076. 7.95 (ISBN 0-06-010366-3). Harper & Row.
Big Woman. Mullin Garr. (Orig.). 1968. pap. 1.75 o.s.i. (109, Ophelia). Olympia.
Big Woods. William Faulkner. LC 55-8159. (Illus.). 1955. Random House.
Big X. Henry Hunt Searls. (Kangaroo Book.). 1977. 1.95. (ISBN 0-671-81164-9). Pocket Books.
Big X. 1st Ed. Henry Hunt Searls. LC 59-6333. 1959. Harper.
Bigamist. Florence Ethel Mills Young. LC 16-22142. 1916. John Lane Company.
Bigamist: A Novel. William Hegner. (Kangaroo Book). 1977. 1.95 (ISBN 0-671-80993-8). Pocket Books.
Bigamist's Daughter. Alice McDermott. 256p. 1983. pap. 3.50 (ISBN 0-449-20105-8, Crest). Fawcett.
Bigamist's Daughter: A Novel. Alice McDermott. LC 81-19232. 1982. 13.00 (ISBN 0-394-52202-8). Random House.
Bigamous Duchess: A Romantic Biography of Elizabeth Chudleigh, Duchess of Kingston. Muriel Elwood. 1975. (pbk.) 1.50. Manor Books.
Bigamous Dutchess. Muriel Elwood. 320p. 1975. pap. 1.50. Woodhill.
Bigamy Jones: Illustrated by Edwin Schmidt. 1st Ed. Frank X Tolbert. LC 54-5460. 1954. Holt.
Bigger and Blacker. Octavus Roy Cohen. LC 78-106268. (Short story index reprint series). 1970. Books for Libraries Press.
Bigger and Blacker. Octavus Roy Cohen. 1925. 2.00. Little, Brown, and Company.
Bigger Light. Austin Chesterfield Clarke. LC 74-17256. 1975. 7.95 (ISBN 0-316-14693-5). Little Brown.
Bigger Than Life. Defence Eakens. pap. 1.95 o.s.i. (TCP-002). Olympia.
Bigger They Come. A. A. Fair, pseud. LC 39-12733. 1939. W. Morrow and Company.
Bigger They Come. Erle Stanley Gardner. LC 39-12733. 1939. W. Morrow.
Biggs: The World's Most Wanted Man. Colin Mackenzie. 1975. 8.95 o.p. (ISBN 0-688-02959-0). Morrow.
Bijak of Kabir. Kabir. Ed. & tr. by Linda Hess. LC 82-73716. 208p. (Orig.). 1983. pap. 12.50 (ISBN 0-86547-114-2). N Point Pr.
Bijou. david madden. ed. David Madden. 1.95 (ISBN 0-380-00805-X). Avon Books.
Bijou: A Novel. David Madden. LC 72-96645. 1974. 8.95 (ISBN 0-517-50590-8). Crown Publishers.
Bijou Dream: A Novel. Jack Warner. LC 81-12609. 14.95 (ISBN 0-517-54333-8). Crown.
Bijou: The Founding of Nag's Head. Albert Plympton Southwick. LC 8-10805. 1889. The American News Company.
Bijou's Courtships, a Study in Pink. Sybille Gabrielle Marie Antoinette de Riquetti de Mirabeau Martel de Janville & Zerega, Katherine Berry Di. LC 7-243893. 1896. F. T. Neely.
Bike Freaks. Art Derfall. pap. 1.95 o.s.i. (OPH-233, Ophelia). Olympia.
Bike Riding in Los Angeles. Marc Norman. LC 72-82692. 1972. 4.50 (ISBN 0-525-06680-2). Dutton.
Bikka Road. 1st American Ed. Kathleen Sully. LC 56-7090. Coward-McCann.
Bilbao Looking Glass. Charlotte Macleod. LC 82-45500. (Crime Club Ser.). 192p. 1983. 11.95 (ISBN 0-385-18336-4). Doubleday.
Bildad Akers: His Book; the Notions and Experiences of a Quaint Rural Philosopher Who Thinks for Himself. Thomas Neal Ivey. LC 10-1353. Mutual Publishing Company.
Bildad Road. William Merriam Rouse. LC 40-32096. Orlin Tremaine Company.
Bildad, the Quill-Driver. William Caine. LC 16-2218. 1916. John Lane.
Bilgewater. Jane Gardam. LC 77-359303. 1976. 3.25 (ISBN 0-241-89398-4). Hamilton.
Bili the Axe. Robert Adams. 185p. 1983. pap. 2.50 (Sig). NAL.
Bili the Axe. Robert Adams. (Horseclans Ser.: No. 10). 192p. 1983. pap. 2.50 (ISBN 0-451-12021-3, Sig). NAL.
Bill--the Sheik. Alice Muriel Livingston Williamson. LC 27-9364. George H. Doran Company.
Bill Arp, So Called: Side Show of the Southern Side of the War. Bill Arp, pseud. LC 72-158277. (Illus.). Repr. of 1866 ed. 18.00 (ISBN 0-404-00213-7). AMS Pr.
Bill Arp's Peace Papers. Charles Henry Smith. LC 72-91093. (American humorists series). (Illus.). 1969. Literature House.
Bill Arp's Peace Papers. Charles Henry Smith. LC 79-158276. (Illus.). 1973. (ISBN 0-404-00405-9). AMS Press.
Bill Drock's Investment. Mary Dwinell Chellis. LC 6-23420. (Added t.-p: The standard series of temperance tales v. 1). H. A. Young & Co.
Bill Grimm's Progress. Harry Charles Witwer. LC 26-15957. 1926. G. P. Putnam's Sons.
Bill Had an Umbrella. Louise Platt Hauck. LC 34-1202. The Penn Publishing Company.
Bill Johnson, or The Outlaws of Arkansas. Friedrich Wilhelm Christian Gerstacker. Dick & Fitzgerald.
Bill Myron. Dean Fales. LC 27-643483. E. P. Dutton & Company.
Bill of Particulars. Ann Marbut. LC 55-13713. 1955. D. McKay Co.
Bill of Rites, a Bill of Wrongs, a Bill of Goods. Wright Morris. LC 80-389. x, 177p. 1980. 14.50x (ISBN 0-8032-3065-6); pap. 4.25 (ISBN 0-8032-8107-2, BB 738, Bison). U of Nebr Pr.
Bill Possum: His Book. Mary Brent Whiteside. LC 9-6575.
Bill S. Ballinger Triptych. Bill S. Ballinger. 640p. 1971. 7.50 o.p. (ISBN 0-8202-0097-2). Sherbourne.
Bill the Bachelor. Denis George Mackail. LC 23-26029. 1922. Houghton Mifflin Company.
Bill the Conqueror: His Invasion of England in the Springtime. Pelham Grenville Wodehouse. LC 25-5157. George H. Doran Company.
Bill, the Galactic Hero. Harry Harrison. LC 65-116228. 3.50. Doubleday.
Bill-Toppers. Andre Castaigne. LC 9-21870. The Bobbs-Merrill Company.
Bill Truetell: A Story of Theatrical Life. George Hugh Brennan. LC 9-6274. 1909. 1.50. A. C. McClurg & Co.
Bill Wannan Selects Stories from Old Australia. Bill Wannan, pseud. LC 77-358120. 1976. (ISBN 0-333-21067-0). Macmillan.
Billboard Madonna. Elleston Trevor. LC 61-7065. 1961. Morrow.
Billiards at Half-Past Nine. Heinrich Boll. LC 62-15141. 288p. 1973. pap. 4.95 (ISBN 0-07-006401-6, SP). McGraw.
Billiards at Half-Past Nine. Heinrich Boll. 1962. 4.95 o.p. (ISBN 0-07-006400-8); pap. 1.95 o.p. (ISBN 0-07-006401-6). McGraw.
Billie's Mother: A Novel. Mary Jessie Hammond Tooke Skrine. LC 15-3866. 1915. The Century Co.
Billikin Courier. T. C Lewellen. LC 68-14534. 1968. Random House.
Billingsgate Shoal. Rick Boyer. LC 81-7259. 1982. 11.95 (ISBN 0-395-32041-0). Houghton Mifflin.
Billion Barrel Oil Swindle. L. A. Sikabonyi. 240p. 1976. 8.50 o.p. (ISBN 0-682-48545-4, Banner). Exposition.
Billion-Dollar Body. Joseph Shallit. LC 47-11822. (Main line mysteries). 1947. J. B. Lippincott Co.
Billion Dollar Brain. Len Deighton. (Berkley Book). 1980. 2.25 (ISBN 0-425-04471-8). Berkley Publishing Corp.
Billion Dollar Brain: A Novel. Len Deighton. LC 66-10466. 1966. Putnam.
Billion Dollar Death. Joseph Nazel. (Iceman, #1). 1974. (pbk.) 1.50 (ISBN 0-87067-440-4). Holloway House.
Billion Dollar Sure Thing. Paul Emil Erdman. LC 72-11131. 1973. 6.95 (ISBN 0-684-13279-6). Scribner.
Billionaires. Aldo Lucchesi, pseud. 1973. pap. 1.25 o.s.i. (78-758). Lancer.
Billions. Ian Kennedy Martin, pseud. LC 79-55611. 1980. 8.95 (ISBN 0-689-11050-2). Atheneum.
Billow Prairie. Mary A Cragin. LC 6-31105. Congregational Sunday-School and Publishing Society.
Bill's Mistake: A Story of the California Redwoods. Robert Gale Barson. LC 21-104023. 1921. Harr Wagner Publishing Co.
Billtry. Mary Kyle Dallas. The Merriam Company.
Billy. Paul Methven. LC 11-168903. 1911. 1.50. John Lane Company.
Billy and Betty: A Novel. Twiggs Jameson. LC 68-22000. 1968. Grove Press.
Billy Baxter's Letters. William J Kountz. LC 3034. Duquesne Distributing Co.
Billy Bellew: A Novel. William Edward Norris. LC 7-33299. 1895. Harper & Brothers.
Billy-Boy: A Study in Responsibilities. John Luther Long. LC 6-34648. 1906. Dodd, Mead & Company.
Billy Budd. Herman Melville. Ed. by Frederic Barron Freeman. LC 48-9543. 1948. Harvard Univ. Press.
Billy Budd see Four Classic American Novels.
Billy Budd, and Other Stories. Herman Melville. LC 76-16646. (Riverside literature series). (Illus.). 1970. Houghton-Mifflin.
Billy Budd & Other Tales. Herman Melville. pap. 1.95 (ISBN 0-451-51714-8, CE1714, Sig Classics). NAL.
Billy Budd: Benito Cereno and The Enchanted Isles. Herman Melville. LC 42-222955. 1942. The Press of the Readers Club.
Billy Budd. Benito Cereno. Introd. by Maxwell Geismar. Paintings by Robert Shore. Herman Melville. LC 65-444553. 1966. 6.95. Heritage Dist. Dial.
Billy Budd, Foretopman see Six Great Modern Short Novels.
Billy Budd, Foretopman. Special Aids Prep. by Hart Day Leavitt. Herman Melville. Ed. by Hart Day Leavitt. LC 65-17433. (Bantam pathfinder eds., FP90). Bantam.
Billy Budd, Sailor. Herman Melville. Ed. by Harrision Hayford & Merton M. Sealts, Jr. LC 62-17135. (Orig.). 1962. pap. 4.95 (ISBN 0-226-32132-0, P99, Phoen). U of Chicago Pr.
Billy Budd, Sailor: An Inside Narrative. Herman Melville. Ed. by Milton R. Stern. LC 73-8967. (Library of literature, 43). (Illus.). 1975. 6.50 (ISBN 0-672-51466-4) (ISBN 0-672-51466-4). Bobbs-Merrill.
Billy Budd, Sailor: An Inside Narrative) Reading Text and Genetic Text. Herman Melville. Ed. by Harrison Hayford & Merton M. Sealts. LC 62-17135. (Illus.). 1962. University of Chicago Press.
Billy Budd, Sailor, and Other Stories. Herman Melville. LC 68-2041. (Penguin English library, EL29). 1967. Penguin Books.
Billy Budd, Sailor: And Other Stories. Herman Melville. LC 68-2041. (Penguin English library, EL29). (Illus.). 1967. Penguin Books.
Billy Fortune. William Rheem Lighton. LC 12-225162. 1912. 1.25. D. Appleton and Company.
Billy Hamilton: A Novel. Archibald Clavering Gunter. LC 6-46696. The Home Publishing Company.
Billy Liar on the Moon. Keith Waterhouse. LC 75-33571. 1976. 7.95 (ISBN 0-399-11682-6). Putnam.
Billy Lives. Gary Brandner. 1976. pap. 1.95 (ISBN 0-532-19120-X). Woodhill.
Billy Padley's Wife. Norman Venner. LC 27-815. George H. Doran Company.
Billy Phelan's Greatest Game. William Kennedy. LC 77-28374. 1978. 8.95 (ISBN 0-670-16667-7). Viking Press.
Billy Phelan's Greatest Game. William Kennedy. LC 82-13291. 1983. 4.95 (ISBN 0-14-006340-4). Penguin Books.
Billy Rags. Ted Lewis. LC 73-6315. 1973. 6.95 (ISBN 0-06-126315-X). Harper's Magazine Press.
Billy the Kid. Edwin Corle. LC 79-4930. (Zia book). 1979. 4.95 (ISBN 0-8263-0509-1). University of New Mexico Press.
Billy the Kid, Chicken Gizzards & Other Tales: Stories. James Ashbrook Perkins. LC 77-87775. (Illus.). 4.00. Dawn Valley Press.
Billy the Kid. 1st Ed. Edwin Corle. 1953. Duell, Sloan and Pearce.
Billy the Sil. Dorothy K. Lacey. 2.95 o.p. Vantage.
Billy To-Morrow's Chums. Sarah Pratt Carr. LC 13-24318. (Her "Billy To-morrow" series). 1913. 1.25. A. C. McClurg & Co.
Billyboy. William Wood. LC 75-1252. 1975. 5.95 o.p. (ISBN 0-688-02914-0). Morrow.
Billyboy. William Wood. LC 75-1252. 1975. 5.95 o.p. (ISBN 0-688-02914-0). Morrow.
Billyboy: A Novel. William Parker Wood. LC 75-1252. 1975. 5.95 (ISBN 0-688-02914-0). Morrow.
Billy's Army. Nicolas Babcock, pseud. LC 81-69129. (Illus.). 256p. 1982. 14.95 (ISBN 0-689-11242-4). Atheneum.
Billy's Mother.". A. Elmore. J. S. Ogilvie & Company.
Bilong Boi. Keith Pickard. LC 76-465036. 1969. 4.20. Jacaranda Press.

Bimal in Bog, 2 vols. Baldev K. Vaid. 1972. Set. 28.00 (ISBN 0-88253-818-7); Set. pap. text ed. 9.60 (ISBN 0-88253-819-5). Ind-US Inc.

Bimbashi Baruk of Egypt. Sax Rohmer, pseud. 1970. 6.50. Bookfinger.

Bimbashi Baruk of Egypt. Arthur Sarsfield Ward. LC 44-4734. 1944. R. M. McBride & Company.

Bimini Run. Howard Hunt. LC 49-10344. 1949. Farrar, Straus.

Binary. Michael Crichton. LC 72-178958. 1972. 5.95 (ISBN 0-394-47987-4). Knopf.

Binary. John Lange. (YA) 1972. 5.95 o.p. (ISBN 0-394-47987-4). Knopf.

Binary Divine. Jon Hartridge. LC 78-116211. 1970. 4.95. Doubleday.

Bind. Stanley Ellin. LC 77-102310. 1970. 5.95. Random House.

Bindaburra Outstation. Kerry Allyne. (Harlequin Presents Ser.). (Orig.). 1980. pap. text ed. 1.50 (ISBN 0-373-10361-1, Pub. by Harlequin). PB.

Binding of the Strong: A Love Story. Caroline Atwater Mason. LC 8-23544. F. H. Revell Company.

Binding with Briars. Paul V. Dallas. 1968. pap. 1.75 o.p. (0103). Essex Hse.

Bindle: The Story of a Cheerful Soul. Herbert George Jenkins. LC 16-22980. 1.35. Frederick A. Stokes Company.

Bindon Parvs. LC 25-17117. The Bobbs-Merrill Company.

Bindweed. Betty De Sherbinin. LC 42-7957. 1942. W. Morrow and Company.

Bindweed: A Romantic Novel Concerning the Late Queen of Servia. by nellie k. blissett... ed. Nellie K Blissett. LC 4-32397. 1904. The M Vynne Publishing Co.

Bingo Long Traveling All-Stars and Motor Kings. William Brashler. LC 72-121043. (Signet book). 1975. (pbk.) 1.50. New American Library.

Binny's Women. Gladys Knight. LC 31-7373. 2.00. The Century Co.

Binodini: A Novel. Rabindranath Tagore. Tr. by Krishna Kripalani. Orig. Title: Chokher Bali. 1965. 8.50 (ISBN 0-8248-0013-3, Eastwest Ctr). UH Pr.

Binodini: A Novel. Tr. by Krishna Kripalani; Sketches by Marilyn King. Rabindranath Tagore. LC 64-8251. 1965. 5.00. East-West Ctr. Pr.

Bio Factor. James Steel. LC 73-153243. 1972. 5.95. Heath Cote Pub. Co.

Bio-Futures: Science Fiction Stories About Biological Metamorphosis. Pamela Sargent. LC 75-39073. 1976. 1.95 (ISBN 0-394-71635-3). Vintage Books.

Biodroids Two Thousand Three Hundred. C. M. Alexander. (Orig.). 1979. pap. 1.95 (ISBN 0-532-23254-2). Woodhill.

Biographical Satire see Swiftiana.

Biographical Stories. Nathaniel Hawthorne. LC 7-3782. (On cover: Riverside literature series, no. 10). 1884. Houghton, Mifflin and Company.

Biographical Stories for Children. Benjamin West, Sir Isaac Newton, Samuel Johnson, Oliver Cromwell, Benjamin Franklin, Queen Christina. Nathaniel Hawthorne. LC 7-37812. 1842. Tappan and Dennet.

Biography see Swiftiana.

Biography of a Bottle. By a Friend of Temperance. LC 6-12729. 1835. Perkins, Marvin & Co.

Biography of a Boy. Josephine Dodge Daskam Bacon. LC 10-1778. 1910. Harper & Brothers.

Biography of a Million Dollars. George Kibbe Turner. LC 18-415818. 1918. Little, Brown, and Company.

Biography of G. Wash Carter, White: Life Story of a Mississippi Peckerwood, Whose Short Circuit Logic Kept Him Fantastically Embroiled. Ira Lunan Ferguson. LC 74-81532. 1969. 4.95. Lunan-Ferguson Library.

Biography of the Pumpkin Pullen Family. Les Pullen. LC 68-23122. (Illus.). 1968. 3.00. Dorrance.

Bipohl. Frederik Pohl. LC 81-22814. 1982. 2.75 (ISBN 0-345-30247-8). Ballantine.

Birch Coulie: A Novel of the Indian Uprising in Minnesota in 1862. 1st Ed. Bernard Francis Ederer. LC 56-11588. (Exposition-Lochinvar book). 1957. Exposition Press.

Birch Dene: A Novel. William Westall. (On cover: Harper's Franklin square library, no. 651). 1889. Harper & Brothers.

Birch in the Boudoir. LC 82-84058. (Grove Press Victorian Library). 208p. 1983. pap. 3.95 (ISBN 0-394-62448-3, B483, BC). Grove.

Birch Interval. Joanna Crawford. 1964. 3.95 o.p. HM.

Birchwood. John Banville. LC 73-1699. 1973. 5.95 (ISBN 0-393-08572-4). Norton.

Bird. Robert Easson. Bd. with Ghoul; In the Name of My Friends. 2.50 o.p. Vantage.

Bird. Liesel Moak Skorpen & Joan Sandin. (Illus.). 5.95 (ISBN 0-06-025693-1) (ISBN 0-06-025694-X). Harper & Row.

Bird Alone... Sean O'Faolain. LC 36-19450. 1936. The Viking Press.

Bird at My Window. Rosa Guy. LC 66-10347. 1966. Lippincott.

Bird Cage: A Theatrical Novel of Early Tombstone. Lynton Wright Brent. LC 45-6318. 1945. Dorrance & Company.

Bird Escaped. Jon Godden. LC 47-17968. 1947. Rinehart & Company, Inc.

Bird Fantasies: A Coloring Book. William Rowe. pap. 1.75 (ISBN 0-486-23655-2). Dover.

Bird House Man. Walter Prichard Eaton. LC 72-6078. (Short story index reprint series). (Illus.). 1972. (ISBN 0-8369-4215-9). Books for Libraries Press.

Bird House Man. Walter Prichard Eaton. LC 16-174161. 1916. 1.25. Doubleday, Page & Company.

Bird in a Box. Mary Milo. 335p. (Orig.). 1980. pap. 2.50 (ISBN 0-345-28673-1). Ballantine.

Bird in Last Year's Nest. Shaun Herron. LC 74-78360. 1974. 7.95 (ISBN 0-87131-162-3). M. Evans.

Bird in the Box. Mary Martha Mears. LC 10-263733. 1910. Frederick A. Stokes Company.

Bird in the Forest. Ethel E Bangert. LC 54-9909. 1954. Arcadia House.

Bird in the Hand. Lesley Rowlands. LC 66-453. 1966. bds., 4.50. U. Smith.

Bird in the Hand. Donald Wetzel. LC 72-88799. 1973. 5.50 (ISBN 0-15-112480-9). Harcourt Brace Jovanovich.

Bird in the House: Stories. Margaret Laurence. LC 70-98659. 1970. 5.95. Knopf.

Bird in the Mulberry. George Abbe. 2.50 o.p. (ISBN 0-8338-0001-9). M Jones.

Bird in the Tree. Elizabeth Goudge. LC 40-27487. Coward-McCann, Inc.

Bird of Bright Plumage. Desemea Wilson. LC 37-22962. E. P. Dutton & Co., Inc.

Bird of Dawning: Or, The Fortune of the Sea. John Masefield. LC 33-32011. 1933. The Macmillan Company.

Bird of Fire: A Tale of St. Francis of Assisi. Helen Constance White. LC 58-10473. 1958. Macmillan.

Bird of Freedom. Hugh Pendexter. LC 28-9654. The Bobbs-Merrill Company.

Bird of God: The Romance of El Greco. Virginia Davis Hersch. LC 29-19242. 1929. Harper & Brothers.

Bird of Night. Susan Hill. LC 72-88655. 1973. 5.95 (ISBN 0-8415-0223-4). Saturday Review Press.

Bird of Night. Susan Hill. LC 77-360414. 1976. 1.95 (ISBN 0-14-004072-2). Penguin.

Bird of Paradise. Winter Ames. (Second Chance at Love Ser.: No. 18). 192p. (Orig.). 1981. pap. 1.75 (ISBN 0-515-05977-3). Jove Pubns.

Bird of Paradise. Blanche Smith Ferguson. LC 39-9937. The Penn Publishing Company.

Bird of Paradise. Ada Leverson. LC 52-6916. 1952. W. W. Norton.

Bird of Paradise. Lily Powell. LC 70-123429. 1971. 6.95. Knopf.

Bird of Paradise. Elizabeth P. Wittermans. 3.95 o.p. Vantage.

Bird of Paradise: A Novel. 1979. 1.75 (ISBN 0-445-04468-3). Popular Library.

Bird of Passage. John Schoolcraft. LC 23-8245. 2.00. George H. Doran Company.

Bird of Passage. Grace Stair. LC 21-19771. R. G. Badger.

Bird of Passage. Mai Zetterling. LC 76-13050. 7.95. St. Martin's Press.

Bird of Passage. A Story. Joseph Sheridan Le Fanu. (Appletons' new handy-volume series no. 7). 1878. D. Appleton and Company.

Bird of Prey. Victor Canning. LC 51-9246. 1951. M. S. Mill Co. and W. Morrow.

Bird of Sorrow. John Romaniello. LC 56-8937. 1956. P. J. Kenedy.

Bird of the Wilderness. Vincent Sheean. LC 41-16491. Random House.

Bird of Time. Wallace West. LC 59-931556. Gnome Press.

Bird of Time: Being Conversations with Egeria. Nancy Mann Waddell Wilson Woodrow Woodrow. 1907. McClure, Phillips & Co.

Bird of Wonder. Una Taylor. LC 67-16096. 1967. bds., 5.25. Rigby.

Bird on a Burning Branch. Anne Huston Orr. LC 64-8773. 1965. Shorecrest.

Bird People. Kunigunde Duncan. 3.00 o.p. Branden.

Bird-Store Man: An Old-Fashioned Story. Norman Duncan. LC 14-15750. 0.75. Fleming H. Revell Company.

Bird Walking Weather: An Inspector Schmidt Story. George A Bagby, pseud. LC 39-23524. 1939. Pub. for the Crime Club, Inc., by Doubleday, Doran and Co., Inc.

Bird Walking Weather: An Inspector Schmidt Story. Aaron Marc Stein. LC 39-23524. 1939. Pub. for the Crime Club, Inc., by Doubleday, Doran and Co., Inc.

Bird Watcher. Joe Alex Morris. (60-2331). 1968. Popular Lib.

Bird Watcher. Joe Alex Morris. LC 66-24421. 1966. D. McKay Co.

Birdcage. Kenneth O'Hara. LC 70-85633. 1969. 4.50. Random House.

Birdcage: A Novel. John Bowen. LC 63-10609. Harper & Row.

Birdcage: A Novel. Victor Canning. LC 79-83541. 1979. 8.95 (ISBN 0-688-03453-5). W. Morrow.

Birds. Tarjei Vesaas. LC 75-81543. 1969. 5.00. Morrow.

Birds Around the Light. Jacob Paludan. LC 28-73334. 1928. G. P. Putnma's Sons.

Birds, Bees & Storks. Gerard Hoffnung. pap. 1.25 (ISBN 0-486-22760-X). Dover.

Birds Fall Down. Rebecca West. LC 67-10214. 1966. Viking Press.

Birds Fly South. Ethel Powelson Hueston. LC 30-67273. The Bobbs-Merrill Company.

Bird's Fountain. Betsey Riddle Hutton Zum Stolzenberg. LC 15-25698. 1915. 1.35. D. Appleton and Company.

Birds Got to Fly: A Novel in Six Parts by Ruth Blodgett. Ruth Blodgett. LC 29-179219. Harcourt, Brace and Company.

Birds in the Belfry. Laurence Payne. LC 67-20288. 1967. Lippincott.

Birds Make Music. Katharine Scott Graves Ayres. LC 45-950155. 1945. The Christopher Publishing House.

Bird's Nest. Shirley Jackson. LC 54-9352. 1954. Straus, and Young.

Birds of a Feather. Marcel Nadaud. Tr. by Converse, Florence. LC 19-6565. 1919. Doubleday, Page & Company.

Birds of America. Mary Therese McCarthy. LC 75-147230. 1971. 6.95 (ISBN 0-15-112770-0). Harcourt, Brace, Jovanovich.

Birds of Buna. John Kolyer. LC 75-36482. 1976. pap. 3.75 o.p. (ISBN 0-8283-1672-4). Branden.

Birds of Heaven, and Other Stories. Vladimir Galaktionovich Korolenko. LC 79-167458. (Short story index reprint series). 1971. (ISBN 0-8369-3984-0). Books for Libraries Press.

Birds of Heaven, and Other Stories. Vladimir Galaktionovich Korolenko. Tr. by Manning, Clarence Augustus. LC 19-15737. 1919. 1.50. Duffield & Company.

Birds of Ill Omen. Kathleen Moore Knight. LC 48-630274. 1948. Pub. for the Crime Club by Doubleday.

Birds of Paradise. Johanna Luchting. 1977. 10.00 o.p. (ISBN 0-682-48803-8). Exposition.

Birds of Paradise. Johanna Luchting. 1977. 10.00 o.p. (ISBN 0-682-48803-8). Exposition.

Birds of Paradise. Paul Scott. LC 62-14032. 1962. Morrow.

Birds of Passage. Bernice Rubens. LC 81-23209. 13.95 (ISBN 0-671-44798-X). Summit Books.

Birds of Passage: A Novel. Iven George Heilbut. Tr. by James Austin Galston. LC 43-14976. 1943. Doubleday, Doran and Company, Inc.

Birds of Prey. Mary Elizabeth Braddon Maxwell. LC 79-50471. (Maxwell, Mary Elizabeth Braddon, 1837-1915. The Fiction of Mary Elizabeth Braddon). 1980. 96.00 (ISBN 0-8240-4353-7). Garland Pub.

Birds of Prey. A Novel. Mary Elizabeth Braddon Maxwell. LC 7-17841. 1867. Harper & Brothers.

Birds of Prey: A Novel. Mary Elizabeth Braddon Maxwell. (On cover: Seaside library. Pocket ed., no. 553). 1885. G. Munro.

Birds of Prey: A Novel. Mary Elizabeth Braddon Maxwell. (On cover: Lovell's library, no. 881). 1887. J. W. Lovell Company.

Birds of Prey: Being Pages from the Book of Broadway. George Fitzalan Bronson Howard. LC 18-17606. W. J. Watt & Company.

Birds of Solomon, and Other Stoires. 1st Ed. Geoffrey Household. LC 58-7867. 1958. Little, Brown.

Birds of the Air. Alice Thomas Ellis. LC 81-65271. 1981. 10.95. Viking Press.

Birds of War. Richard H. Curtis. (Skymasters Ser.: No. 5). (Orig.). 1982. pap. 3.25 (ISBN 0-440-00377-6). Dell.

Birds of Winter. Theodore Vrettos. LC 80-11942. 1980. 9.95 (ISBN 0-395-29455-X). Houghton Mifflin.

Birds on the Trees. Nina Bawden. 192p. 1976. pap. 1.95 o.p. (ISBN 0-14-003430-7). Penguin.

Birds on the Trees. Nina Bawden. LC 73-138778. 1971. 5.95 o.p. (ISBN 0-06-010254-3, HarpT). Har-Row.

Birds. Pictures by Eloise Wilkin. Jane Werner Watson. LC 61-65992. (Big golden book, 544). Golden Press.

Birdsong. James P. White. LC 77-78818. 1978. pap. 6.50 o.s.i. (ISBN 0-914278-12-6). Tex Ctr Writers.

Birdsong: A Novel. James P White. LC 77-370539. 6.50 (ISBN 0-914278-12-6). Copper Beech Press.

Birdwatcher. Ethel Edison Gordon. LC 74-77147. 1974. 6.95 (ISBN 0-679-50446-X). McKay.

Birdwatcher's Quarry. Manning Coles, pseud. LC 56-11500. 1956. Published for the Crime Club by Doubleday.

Birdy. William Wharton. LC 77-28023. 1978. 9.95 (ISBN 0-394-42569-3). Knopf.

Birkwood: A Novel. Julia A. B Seiver. LC 8-6448. 1896. Arena Publishing Company.

Birmingham Counterfeit. LC 74-16027. (Flowering of the Novel). 1975. (ISBN 0-8240-1197-X). Garland Publishing.

Birth. Zona Gale. LC 18-20940. 1918. The Macmillan Company.

Birth. James Tucker. (Stone Ser.: No. 1). 1981. pap. 2.95 (ISBN 0-89083-760-0). Zebra.

Birth Clinic: A Novel. Karl Ashton. LC 34-3731. 1934. W. Godwin, Inc.

Birth of a Dark Soul. Brian Talbot Cleeve. LC 54-15024. 1953. Jarrolds.

Birth of a Grandfather. May Sarton. LC 57-9630. 1957. Rinehart.

Birth of a Hero: A Novel. Herbert Gold. LC 51-12089. 1951. Viking Press.

Birth of a Soul: A Psychological Study. Alfred Phillips. LC 7-36062. (On cover: Rialto series, no. 65). 1894. Rand, McNally & Company.

Birth of an Assassin. J. T. Missanelli. 3.50 o.p. Carlton.

Birth of an Island. Francois Clement. LC 74-19100. 1975. 8.95 (ISBN 0-671-21924-3). Simon and Schuster.

Birth of an Island. Francois Clement. 1977. 1.75. (ISBN 0-380-00952-8). Avon Books.

Birth of Fire. Jerry Pournelle. (Kangaroo Book). 1978. 1.75 (ISBN 0-671-82197-0). Pocket Books.

Birth of Freedom: A Socialist Novel. Henry Barnard Salisbury. LC 8-373861. (Half-title: The Twentieth century library no. 52). 1894. The Humboldt Publishing Co.

Birth of Humanity: A Novel (Sequel to "Tuned Higher Than the Race". Michael Reepmaker. LC 23-12781. 1923. Times-Mirror Press.

Birth of Liberty: A Story of Bacon's Rebellion. John Haden Lane. 1909. The Hermitage Press.

Birth of Logan Station. Bill Burchardt, pseud. LC 74-6795. 1974. 4.95 (ISBN 0-385-00519-9). Doubleday.

Birth of Logan Station. bill burchardt. ed. Bill Burchardt, pseud. 1976. 1.25. Belmont Tower.

Birth of Ludwig Kleinst. Silva-Coronel, Paul. LC 70-123985. 1971. 5.95 (ISBN 0-06-013872-6). Harper & Row.

Birth of Mischief. Rafael Sabatini. LC 45-6992. 1945. Houghton Mifflin Company.

Birth of Our Power. Victor Serge. Tr. by Richard Greeman from Fr. 288p. 1981. pap. 3.95 (ISBN 0-904613-49-6). Writers & Readers.

Birth of Our Power (Naissance De Notre Force) Victor Serge. LC 66-20960. 1967. Doubleday.

Birth of the Gods. Dmitrii Sergieevich Merezhkovskil. LC 26-10564. E. P. Dutton & Company.

Birth of the Martyr's Ghost: A Novel. W Warner Jackson. LC 57-7014. (Nobel book). 1957. Comet Press Books.

Birthday. Samuel Rogers. LC 32-3603. 1932. J. Cape & H. Smith.

Birthday Ball. Margaretta Brucker. LC 51-3129. 1951. Gramercy.

Birthday Boy. Al Hine. LC 59-6071. 1959. Scribner.

Birthday, Deathday. Hugh Pentecost. LC 71-38524. (Red Badge Suspense Novel Ser). 192p. 1972. 4.95 o.p. (ISBN 0-396-06523-6). Dodd.

Birthday, Deathday. Hugh Pentecost. 1973. pap. 0.75 o.p. (ISBN 0-515-03115-1, T3115). BJ Pub Group.

Birthday, Deathday. Judson Pentecost Philips. LC 71-38524. (Red badge novel of suspense). 1972. 4.95 (ISBN 0-396-06523-6). Dodd, Mead.

Birthday Gift. Ursula Reilly Curtiss. (Kangaroo Book). 1977. 1.50. Pocket Books.

Birthday Gift. Ursula Reilly Curtiss. (Kangaroo Book). 1977. 1.50 (ISBN 0-671-80923-7). Pocket Books.

Birthday Gift: A Novel. Thomas Shapcott. LC 82-6971. 221p. 1983. 16.50 (ISBN 0-7022-1861-8); pap. 8.95 (ISBN 0-7022-1871-5). U of Queensland Pr.

Birthday Gift: A Novel of Suspense. Ursula Reilly Curtiss. LC 76-5392. (ISBN 0-396-07302-6). Dodd, Mead.

Birthday King: A Romance. Alan Gabriel Barnsley. 1973. 0.95. Popular Library.

Birthday Murder. Jane Beynon. LC 75-44989. 1976. 12.00 (ISBN 0-8240-2381-1). Garland Pub.

Birthday Murder. Lange Lewis. LC 45-2942. 1945. The Bobbs-Merrill Company.

Birthday Murder. Kathleen Sproul. LC 32-5745. E. P. Dutton & Co., Inc.

Birthday of Waters. Rochelle Ratner. 1971. pap. 2.50 (Pub. by New Rivers Pr). SBD.

Birthday Party: And Other Stories. Alan Alexander Milne. LC 48-9270. 1948. E. P. Dutton.

Birthday Plan. Elizabeth Batt. 1971. pap. 1.50 (ISBN 0-87508-647-0). Chr Lit.

Birthday Present for Katheryn Kenyatta. C. A. Russell. 1970. text ed. 2.20 o.p. (ISBN 0-07-054341-0). McGraw.

Birthgrave. Tanith Lee. (Science Fiction Ser). 1975. pap. 3.50 (ISBN 0-87997-776-0, UE1776). DAW Bks.

Birthgrave. Tanith Lee. 1975. (pbk.) 1.50. DAW Books.
Birthmark of Fear. Marsha Alexander. LC 75-36122. 176p. (Orig.). 1975. pap. 1.25 (ISBN 0-89041-049-6, 3049). Major Bks.
Birthmarks. Carlo L Matraxia. LC 51-5018.
Birthplace. William S. Wilson. LC 81-83968. 256p. 1982. 15.00 (ISBN 0-86547-068-5). N Point Pr.
Birthplace see Altar of the Dead.
Birthpyre. Larry Brand. 288p. 1980. pap. 2.25 (ISBN 0-380-76539-X, 76539). Avon.
Birthright. Phillip Finch. LC 79-15047. 9.95 (ISBN 0-87223-528-9). Seaview Books: Trade Distribution by Simon and Schuster.
Birthright. Phillip Finch. 1981. 2.75 (ISBN 0-425-04590-0). Berkley Publishing Corporation.
Birthright. Lettie Hamlett Rogers. LC 57-5678. 1957. Simon and Schuster.
Birthright. Lettie Hamlett Rogers. LC 57-5678. 1957. Simon and Schuster.
Birthright: A Novel. Joseph Hocking. LC 7-4953. 1897. Dodd, Mead and Company.
Birthright: A Novel. Ezra James Poulsen. LC 50-3124. 1950. Granite Pub. Co.
Birthright: A Novel. Thomas Sigismund Stribling. LC 22-6160. 1922. The Century Co.
Birthright: The Book of Man. Mike Resnick. (Orig.). 1982. pap. 2.75 (ISBN 0-451-11358-6, AE1358, Sig). NAL.
Births, Deaths, and Marriages: A Novel. Theodore Edward Hook. LC 1-1719. 1839. Lea & Blanchard.
Bisbee 'seventeen. Robert Houston. LC 78-20285. 1979. 10.00 (ISBN 0-394-50081-4). Pantheon.
Biscuit-Shooter. Clifton Adams. LC 70-131062. 1973. (pbk.) 0.95. Manor Books.
Biscuits and Dried Beef. A Panacea. Linden Husted Morehouse. LC 7-26204. 1894. The Young Churchman Co.
Bishop. Bruce Marshall. LC 72-103767. 1970. Doubleday.
Bishop and Nannette. Frances Irene Burge Smith Griswold. LC 21-16369. 1874. T. Whittaker.
Bishop: And Other Stories. Anton Pavlovich Chekhov. Tr. by Garnett, Constance (Black) LC 19-14222. 1919. The Macmillan Company.
Bishop As Pawn: A Father Dowling Mystery. Ralph M McInerny. LC 78-54978. 7.95 (ISBN 0-8149-0806-3). Vanguard Press.
Bishop As Pawn: A Father Dowling Mystery. Ralph M McInerny. LC 79-1383. 10.95 (ISBN 0-89340-198-6). J. Curley.
Bishop Comes to Stow: A Fanciful Symposium. Cornish, Louis Craig, 1870- & American Unitarian Association. LC 33-34613. 1933. The Beacon Press, Inc.
Bishop Finds a Way. Michael Cunningham. LC 55-6682. 1955. Farrar, Straus and Young.
Bishop in Check. Adam Hall. (Hugo Bishop Mystery Ser). 1971. pap. 0.75 o.p. (T2538). Pyramid Pubns.
Bishop in Check. Elleston Trevor. LC 61-8794. 1961. M. S. Mill Co.
Bishop in Check: A Hugo Bishop Story by Simon Rattray Pseud. Elleston Trevor. LC 53-1771. 1953. T. V. Boardman.
Bishop in the Back Seat. Clarissa Watson. LC 79-2115. 1980. 8.95 (ISBN 0-689-11012-X). Atheneum.
Bishop Murder Case. S. S. Van Dine, pseud. Repr. lib. bdg. 17.95x (ISBN 0-89190-512-X). Am Repr-Rivercity Pr.
Bishop Murder Case. S. S. Van Dine, pseud. 1980. lib. bdg. 10.95 (ISBN 0-8398-2557-9, Gregg). G K Hall.
Bishop Murder Case. S. S. Van Dine, pseud. 1981. 18.95x (Pub. by Remploy England). State Mutual Bk.
Bishop Murder Case. Willard Huntington Wright. LC 79-23070. (Series: Philo Vance Series.). (Gregg Press mystery fiction series.). (Illus.). 1980. 10.95 (ISBN 0-8398-2557-9). Gregg Press.
Bishop Murder Case: A Philo Vance Story. Willard Huntington Wright. LC 29-6345. (The Philo Vance series). 1929. C. Scribner's Sons.
Bishop of Cottontown: A Story of the Southern Cotton Mills. John Trotwood Moore. LC 72-4610. (Black Heritage Library Collection). (Illus.). 1972. (ISBN 0-8369-9113-3). Books for Libraries Press.
Bishop of Cottontown: A Story of the Southern Cotton Mills. John Trotwood Moore. 1906. The J. C. Winston Company.
Bishop of Havana: The Romantic Story of a Bishop Who Tried to Swallow Life Whole. Pendleton Hogan. LC 33-287376. 1933. I. Washburn.
Bishop of the Ozarks. Milford W. Howard. LC 23-1207. 1923. Times-Mirror Press.
Bishop Pattern. Mary N Dolim. LC 63-12629. 1963. Morrow.
Bishop Pendle: Or, The Bishop's Secret. Fergus Hume. LC 2831. Rand, McNally & Company.
Bishop Sunbeams," And Other Stories of Service. Richard Lee Metcalfe. LC 9-26435. 1909. 1.00. The Woodruff-Collins Press.
Bishop's Apron. William Somerset Maugham. LC 75-30391. (Maugham, William Somerset, 1874-1965. Works. 1976). 1976. 15.00 (ISBN 0-405-07806-4). Arno Press.
Bishops' Bible: A Novel. authorized ed. David Christie Murray & Herman, Henry. LC 7-31830. (On cover: Lovell's international series, no. 89). 1890. J. W. Lovell Company.
Bishop's Candlesticks, from Les Miserables. Victor Marie Hugo. LC 66-23611. (Revell inspirational classic). 1966. F. H. Revell Co.
Bishop's Confession. Jim Bishop. 448p. 1981. 15.95 (ISBN 0-316-09669-5). Little.
Bishop's Conversion. Ellen Blackmar Maxwell. LC 7-172709. 1892. Hunt & Eaton.
Bishop's Crime. Henry Christopher Bailey. LC 41-301. 1941. Pub. for the Crime Club by Doubleday, Doran and Co., Inc.
Bishop's Daughter: A Novel. Ernest F MacDonald. LC 49-8181. 1949. W.B. Eerdmans Pub. Co.
Bishop's Emeralds. Houghton Townley. LC 8-206764. 1908. W. J. Watt & Company.
Bishop's Gambol. Roger Agile. LC 70-9359. (Traveller's companion series, TC-434). 1968. 1.75. Olympia Press.
Bishop's Granddaughter. Robert Grant. LC 25-5850. 1925. C. Scribner's Sons.
Bishop's Jaegers. Thorne Smith. LC 34-382942. 1933. Doubleday, Doran & Company, Inc.
Bishop's Jaegers. Thorne Smith. LC 36-8694. 1935. Doubleday, Doran & Company, Inc.
Bishop's Mantle. Agnes Sligh Turnbull. LC 47-31093. 1947. Macmillan Co.
Bishop's Nephew. Alice Duer Miller. LC 32-26290. 1932. Dodd, Mead and Company.
Bishop's Palace. Jan Alexander, pseud. 1973. 0.95. Popular Library.
Bishop's Pawn. Ritchie Perry. LC 79-1881. 8.95 (ISBN 0-394-50779-7). Pantheon Books.
Bishop's Progress: A Novel by D. Keith Mano. D. Keith Mano. LC 67-25888. 1968. 5.95. Houghton.
Bishop's Purse. Cleveland Moffett & Herford, Oliver, 1863- Joint Author. LC 13-5071. 1913. D. Appleton and Company.
Bishop's Room. Karl H. Meyer. 1978. pap. 1.25 (ISBN 0-532-12562-2). Woodhill.
Bishop's Scapegoat. Thomas Bailey Clegg. LC 8-14664. 1908. J. Lane Company; Etc., Etc.
Bishop's Son. A Novel. Alice Cary. LC 6-22802. 1867. G. W. Carlston & Co.; Etc., Etc.
Bishop's Wife. Robert Nathan. LC 28-21889. The Bobbs-Merrill Company.
Bismillah: A Story. Alec John Dawson. LC 1-5434. 1898. Macmillan and Co., Limited.
Bison of Clay. Max Begouen & Duffus, Robert Luther, Tr. LC 26-17608. 1926. Longmans, Green and Co.
Bistouri. Achille Melandri. LC 1-29763. 1900. Benziger Brothers.
Bit of a Shunt up the River. Desmond Cory, pseud. LC 73-10800. 1974. 4.95 (ISBN 0-385-01461-9). Published for the Crime Club by Doubleday.
Bit of Christmas Whimsy. David Edman. LC 74-6474. (Illus.). 160p. 1971. 6.95 (ISBN 0-570-03234-2, 15-2128). Concordia.
Bit of Christmas Whimsy: A Novella. David Edman. LC 74-6474. (Illus.). 1974. 4.95 (ISBN 0-570-03234-2). Concordia Pub. House.
Bit of Eden. Barbara Parker Robinson. LC 76-45759. 8.95. Dutton.
Bit of Finesse: A Story of Fifty Years Ago. Harriet Newell Lodge. LC 7-14798. 1894. The Bowen-Merrill Company.
Bit of Human Nature. David Christie Murray. (On cover: Seaside library. Pocket ed., no. 320). 1885. G. Munro.
Bit off the Map: And Other Stories. Angus Wilson. LC 57-12615. 1957. Viking Press.
Bit off the Map & Other Stories. Angus Wilson. 1978. pap. 3.95 (ISBN 0-14-002375-5). Penguin.
Bit O'silence. Helen Hill McWilliams. LC 12-10141. 1912. The McDowell Press.
Bit O'writin' and Other Tales. John Banim & Michael Banim. LC 78-32077. (Ireland, from the Act of Union, 1800, to the Dealth of Parnell, 1891; No. 24). 1979. 126.00 (ISBN 0-8240-3473-2). Garland Pub.
Bitch Goddess. Allan Nixon. (Orig.). 1969. pap. 0.95 o.p. (ISBN 0-446-65083-8, 65-083). Paperback Lib.
Bitch of Buchenwald. Joseph Como. pap. 1.95 o.s.i. (OPH-230, Ophelia). Olympia.
Bitch Witch. Roger Charlton. LC 74-180148. (Venus Library). 1971. 1.95. Grove Press.
Bitches & Sad Ladies: An Anthology of Fiction by and About Women. Ed. by Pat Rotter. LC 74-3902. 1975. 8.95 (ISBN 0-06-127515-8). Harper's Magazine Press.
Bitches & Sad Ladies: An Anthology of Short Fiction by & About Women. Ed. by Pat Rotter. LC 74-3902. 336p. 1974. 10.95 o.p. (ISBN 0-06-127515-8). Har-Row.
Bite. Eric Corder. 1975. (pbk.) 1.25. Dell.
Bite of an Apple. A Clew in a Thousand Pieces, The Man with an Extra Finger; Three Complete Stories of the Exploits of Nicholas Carter... John Russell Coryell. LC 99-5614. (On cover: Magnet detective library. no. 105). 1899. Street & Smith.
Bite of Benin: "Where Many Go in but Few Come Out,". Robert Simpson. LC 19-18639. 1919. The James A. McCann Company.
Bite of Eve's Apple: And Other Stories. Frances H. Mulliken. 1982. pap. 9.75 (ISBN 0-8309-0348-8). Herald Hse.
Bite of Hunger: A Novel of Africa. Hilda Kuper. LC 65-19063. 4.50. Harcourt.
Bite of Monsters. Dennis O'Neil. (Orig.). 1971. pap. 0.75 o.p. (B75-2134). Belmont-Tower.
Bite of the Apple. Molly Parkin. 220p. 1982. 14.95 (ISBN 0-86676-001-6). Riverrun NY.
Bite of the Ax. Francis Favill Bowman. LC 55-956. 1954. Comet Press Books.
Bite the Hand. 1st Ed. Ruth Fenisong. LC 56-10761. 1956. Published for the Crime Club by Doubleday.
Biter. Walter Samuel Cramp. LC 9-28694. 1909. 1.50. The C. M. Clark Publishing Company.
Bits & Pieces. David A. Wilson. 40p. 1969. pap. 1.50 o.p. (ISBN 0-934852-02-2). Lorien Hse.
Bits O' Border Breeze. Edward S Peterson. LC 17-11329. 1917. Kamman Art Ptg. Co.
Bits of Driftwood. Robert W. Barrow. 1970. 2.95 o.p. Vantage.
Bits of Driftwood. Paul Herbert Wesley. LC 36-15022. 1936. Walker, Evans & Cogswell Company.
Bits of Gossip. Rebecca Harding Davis. LC 72-78686. 1904. Repr. 20.00 o.p. (ISBN 0-403-08916-6). Somerset Pub.
Bits of Paradise. F. Scott Fitzgerald & Zelda Fitzgerald. LC 74-4648. 392p. 1974. 7.95 (ISBN 0-684-13902-2, ScribT). Scribner.
Bits of Paradise: 21 Uncollected Stories by F. Scott and Zelda Fitzgerald. Scottie Fitzgerald Smith & Matthew Joseph Bruccoli. LC 74-4648. 1974. 7.95. Scribner.
Bits of Paradise: 21 Uncollected Stories. Scottie Fitzgerald Smith. Francis Scott Key Fitzgerald & Zelda Sayre Fitzgerald. 1976. (pbk.) 1.95 (ISBN 0-671-80250-X). Pocket Books.
Bitter Almonds: A Novel. Paul Ludrug Hinkelman. LC 28-21371.
Bitter and Gay. Helen Bishop. J. Cape & H. Smith.
Bitter Atonement. Charlotte Mary Brame. LC 3414. (Bertha M. Clay Library). (Bertha M. Clay library, no. 1: No. 1). 1900. Street & Smith.
Bitter Atonement; a Novel. Charlotte Mary Brame. LC 49-40827. (Cornell series). A. L. Burt Co.
Bitter Atonement: A Novel. Charlotte Mary Brame. LC 26-23552. Syndicate Trading Co.
Bitter Atonement. A Novel. Charlotte Mary Brame. LC 44-122406. (Seaside library, v. 99, no. 1999). G. Munro.
Bitter Atonement: A Novel. Charlotte Mary Brame. LC 44-38090. (Lovell's Library). (On cover: Lovell's library, v. 14, no. 740: Vol. 14, No. 740). J. W. Lovell & Company.
Bitter Birthright: Or, Lady Gilmore's Temptation. authorized ed. Dora Russell. LC 8-1334. (On cover: Lovell's international series, no. 140 i. e. 144). 1890. United States Book Company.
Bitter Blood. Siegel, Scott. (Warhunter Ser.: No. 4). (Orig.). 1981. pap. 2.25 (ISBN 0-89083-905-0). Zebra.
Bitter Box. Eleanor Clark. LC 46-5407. 1946. Doubleday & Company, Inc.
Bitter Box. Eleanor Clark. LC 76-11510. 1979. 23.50 (ISBN 0-404-15279-1). AMS Press.
Bitter Bread. Nikolai Mikhailovich Gubskii. LC 34-9212. H. Holt and Company.
Bitter Bread: A Tale of Old Dunfermline. Allison Taylor. LC 29-3982. 1929. Longmans, Green and Co.
Bitter Breed. Martin Ryerson. 1977. pap. 1.50 (ISBN 0-89041-152-2, 3152). Major Bks.
Bitter Brew: A Novel. Mabel Setchell. LC 57-10772. 1957. Greenwich Book Publishers.
Bitter Conquest. 1st Ed. Norman Hendriksen. LC 56-127845. 1957. Vantage Press.
Bitter Country. Anita Pettibone. LC 25-42119. 1925. Doubleday, Page & Company.
Bitter Creek. James Boyd. LC 39-272329. 1939. C. Scribner's Sons.
Bitter Creek. Archie Joscelyn. LC 47-4929. 1947. Dodd, Mead.
Bitter Days of Finis McCanless. James Wyckoff. LC 80-2633. 1981. 10.95 (ISBN 0-385-15830-0). Doubleday.
Bitter Destiny: Translated from the Italian by Marianne Ceconi. Renato Cannavale. LC 53-9424. 1953. A. A. Wyn.
Bitter Enchantment. Yvonne Whittal. (Harlequin Romance Ser.). (Orig.). 1979. pap. 1.25 (ISBN 0-373-02304-9, Pub. by Harlequin). PB.
Bitter End. John Brophy. LC 28-19965. E. P. Dutton & Company.
Bitter Ending. Alexander Irving. LC 46-4462. 1946. Dodd, Mead & Company.
Bitter Finish. Linda J Barnes. LC 82-17040. 1983. 11.95 (ISBN 0-312-08236-3). St. Martin's Press.
Bitter Forfeit. Mabel Louise Robinson. LC 47-3875. 1947. The Bobbs-Merrill Company.
Bitter Fruit: A Novel by Mark Antony Pseud. 1st Ed. Anthony Marques. LC 59-7619. 1959. Greenwich Book Publishers.
Bitter Glass. Eilis Dillon. LC 59-13593. 1959. Appleton-Century-Crofts.
Bitter Gourd: Fang I-Chih and the the Impetus for Intellectual Change. I-Chih Fang & Willard J Peterson. LC 78-18491. 1979. 22.50 (ISBN 0-300-02208-5). Yale University Press.
Bitter Graces. Terrence Ross. 192p. 1980. pap. 2.25 (ISBN 0-380-76208-0, 76208). Avon.
Bitter Grass. Theodore V Olsen. (G-695). 1968. Ace.
Bitter Grass. Theodore V Olsen. 1975. (pbk.) 0.95. Ace Books.
Bitter Grass. Theodore V Olsen. LC 67-10357. (Double D western). 1967. Doubleday.
Bitter Grass. Theodore V. Olsen. 1980. pap. 1.75 (ISBN 0-671-83541-6). PB.
Bitter Ground. 1st Ed. William Riley Burnett. LC 57-10303. 1958. Knopf.
Bitter Harvest. Anne Hampson. 192p. 1982. pap. 1.75 (ISBN 0-373-10476-6). Harlequin Bks.
Bitter Harvest. L. A. Henderson. 4.50 o.p. Carlton.
Bitter Harvest. 1970 ed. John Steinbacher. pap. 2.00 (ISBN 0-913558-01-X). Educator Pubns.
Bitter Heritage. Margaret Bass Pedler. 1928. Doubleday, Doran & Company, Inc.
Bitter Heritage: A Modern Story of Love and Adventure. John Edward Bloundelle-Burton. (Half-title: Appletons' town and country library, no. 272). 1899. D. Appleton and Company.
Bitter Honey. Hermina Black. (Signet book). 1975. (pbk.) 0.95. New American Library.
Bitter Honey. Jan Cheux. pap. 1.95 o.p. (8025). Cameo.
Bitter Honey see Who Is Lucinda.
Bitter Honeycomb. June Meindl Scott. LC 70-181755. 1972. 4.00 (ISBN 0-8059-1646-6). Dorrance.
Bitter Honeymoon. Alberto Moravia. Tr. by Frances Frenaye et al. LC 56-6169. 224p. 1973. pap. 1.25 (ISBN 0-532-12168-6). Woodhill.
Bitter Honeymoon: And Other Stories, by Alberto Moravia Pseud. Alberto Pincherle. LC 56-6169. 1956. Farrar, Straus and Cudahy.
Bitter Iron. 1st Ed. Carter Travis Young. LC 64-11603. (Double D western). 1964. Doubleday.
Bitter Is the Fruit. Cornelius J Collins. (Berkley medallion book). 1974. (pbk.) 1.25. Berkley Pub. Co.
Bitter Is the Harvest. C. W. Thurlow Craig. LC 49-21354. 1949. Hutchinson.
Bitter Is the Harvest. Charles William Thurlow Craig. LC 49-21354. 1949. Hutchinson.
Bitter Justice. Sada Cowan. LC 43-6284. 1943. Pub. for the Crime Club by Doubleday, Doran & Co., Inc.
Bitter Lake. Lawrence Paul Bachmann. LC 78-99903. 1970. Little, Brown.
Bitter Lemons. Lawrence Durrell. (Illus.). 1959. pap. 5.75 (ISBN 0-525-47044-1, 0558-170). Dutton.
Bitter Lotus: A Novel. Louis Bromfield. LC 45-4532. 1945. The World Publishing Company.
Bitter Night. Wayne D Overholser. LC 61-6356. 1961. Macmillan.
Bitter Orange. Desmond Hamill. LC 80-14024. 1980. 10.95 (ISBN 0-688-03711-9). Morrow.
Bitter Orange Tree: A Novel. Panalt Istrati & Zoglin, Rosalind, Tr. LC 31-8640. 1931. The Vanguard Press.
Bitter Passion. James Noble Gifford. LC 45-121167. 1945. Phoenix Press.
Bitter Passion. John Wadleigh. LC 59-5814. 1959. Dutton.
Bitter Passion, Sweet Love. Patricia Ott. (Orig.). 1981. pap. 2.95 (ISBN 0-505-51718-3). Tower Bks.
Bitter Path of Death. Pierre Audemars. LC 82-60217. 1982. 11.95 (ISBN 0-8027-5484-8). Walker.
Bitter Path of Death. Pierre Audemars. 1983. 11.95 (ISBN 0-8027-5484-8). Walker & Co.
Bitter Pill. A. Bertram Chandler. LC 75-310960. 1974. (ISBN 0-85885-111-3). Wren.
Bitter Pill. Joe Weiss. 4.95 o.p. Brown Bk.
Bitter Promise. Ila D. Youngblood. 256p. 1982. pap. 2.50 (ISBN 0-380-79343-1, 79343). Avon.
Bitter Reckoning. James Payn. (On cover: Seaside library. Pocket ed. no. 430). 1885. G. Munro.
Bitter Revenge. Lilian Peake. (Harlequin Presents Ser.). 192p. 1982. pap. 1.75 (ISBN 0-373-10524-X). Harlequin Bks.
Bitter River Ranch. Stanley McShane. Phoenix Press.
Bitter Roots. Anne Krauel. LC 66-26661. 1966. Dorrance.
Bitter Roots. Norman Macleod. LC 41-9244. 1941. Smith & Durrell.

Bitter Sage. Frank Gruber. LC 54-5394. 1954. Rinehart.
Bitter Sage. Frank Gruber. LC 56-9321. (Signet Brand Western). 1973. (pbk) 0.75. New Amer. Lib.
Bitter Season. Robert Myron Coates. LC 46-6957. 1946. Harcourt, Brace and Company.
Bitter Seed. Henry Toledano. pap. 1.95 o.p. (0119). Essex Hse.
Bitter Shield. Dennis Adair & Janet Rosenstock. 288p. (Orig.). 1983. pap. 2.95 (ISBN 0-380-79053-X, 79053). Avon.
Bitter Spring. Charles Angoff. LC 60-11529. 1961. T. Yoseloff.
Bitter Sting: A Novel. 1st Ed. Jane Kent Plaginos. LC 57-8914. 1957. Greenwich Book Publishers.
Bitter-Sweet. Bertram J. Rochlus. 2.50 o.p. Vantage.
Bitter Tea. Gavin Black. LC 72-80373. (Novel of Suspense Ser.). 224p. 1972. 5.95 o.p. (ISBN 0-06-010371-X, HarpT). Har-Row.
Bitter Tea. Oswald Wynd. LC 72-80373. 1972. 5.95 (ISBN 0-06-010371-X). Harper & Row.
Bitter Tea of General Yen. Grace Zaring Stone. LC 30-248453. The Bobbs-Merrill Company.
Bitter Toast. Robert Allen Longworth. LC 44-47012. R. A. Longworth.
Bitter Trail. Elmer Kelton. 256p. 1981. pap. 2.25 (ISBN 0-441-06362-4). Ace Bks.
Bitter Victory. Rebecca Drury. (Women at War Ser.: No. 16). (Orig.). 1983. pap. 3.25 (ISBN 0-440-00648-1). Dell.
Bitter Victory: Amere Victire) Translated by Galway Kinnell. 1st Ed. Rene Hardy. LC 56-90575. 1956. Doubleday.
Bitter Victory (Amere Victoire) Translated by Galway Kinnell. 1st Ed. Rene Hardy. LC 56-90579. 1956. Doubleday.
Bitter Vines. Megan Lane. (Candlelight Ecstasy Ser.: No. 57). (Orig.). 1982. pap. 1.75 (ISBN 0-440-10825-X). Dell.
Bitter Water. Thomas Thompson. LC 60-5946. (Double D western). 1960. Doubleday.
Bitter Waters. Heinrich Hauser & Kirwan, Patrick, Tr. LC 29-29525. H. Liveright.
Bitter Winds. Joe E Pierce. LC 77-71932. 1977. 4.95 (ISBN 0-913244-12-0). HaPi Press.
Bitter Winds of Love. Barbara Cartland. 1976. pap. 1.25 o.p. (ISBN 0-515-03991-8). BJ Pub Group.
Bitter Wine. Albert Schonbar. LC 50-51138. 1949. Exposition Press.
Bittergreen. Anne Costello. 304p. (Orig.). 1980. pap. 2.25 (ISBN 0-345-28459-3). Ballantine.
Bittermeads Mystery. Ernest Robertson Punshon. LC 22-18857. 1922. A. A. Knopf.
Bittern Point. Virginia MacFadyen. LC 26-6474. 1926. A. & C. Boni.
Bitterroot Basin: By R. D. Whttinger Pseud. Marian Templeton Place. LC 55-10189. 1955. Arcadia House.
Bitterroot Trail. James William Johnson. LC 35-22395. 1935. The Caxton Printers, Ltd.
Bitters Wood. Ursula Nightingale. 1973. (pbk) 0.95. Popular Library.
Bittersweet. Ursula Bloom. 1978. pap. 1.95 (ISBN 0-89041-179-4, 3179). Major Bks.
Bittersweet. Dorothy Lester Chadwick. LC 37-2061. 1937. Arcadia House.
Bittersweet. Susan D Winkler. LC 54-9315. 1954. Avalon Books.
Bittersweet Love. Mary Ann Taylor. (Signet book). 1978. 1.50 (ISBN 0-451-08404-7). New American Library.
Bittersweet Revenge. Kelly Adams. (Second Chance at Love Ser.: No. 47). (Orig.). 1982. pap. 1.75 (ISBN 0-515-06423-8). Jove Pubns.
Bittersweet Temptation. John Donovan. (Orig.). 1979. pap. 2.50 (ISBN 0-89083-445-8). Zebra.
Bittersweet Waltz. Suzanne Roberts. (Candlelight Romance Ser.). (Orig.). Date not set. pap. 1.75 (ISBN 0-440-10589-7). Dell.
Bittersweet Winter. Pauline Wesley Wanderer. LC 63-23265. Bruce Pub. Co.
Bitterweed Path: A Novel. Thomas Hal Phillips. LC 50-8137. 1950. Rinehart.
Bitterwood. A Novel. Mason Arnold Green. LC 6-45551. 1878. G. W. Carleton & Co.
Bixby Girls. 1st Ed. Rosamond Van Der Zee Marshall. LC 57-10460. 1957. Doubleday.
Bixby of Boston: Being the Little Story of a Young Railway-Office Clerk. John Tornrose Fitzgerald. LC 6-42927. 1906. Broadway Publishing Co.
Bizarre Classix, Vol. 3. LC 76-41610. (Illus.). pap. 6.50 (ISBN 0-914646-21-4). Belier Pr.
Bizarre Classix, Vol. 4. LC 76-41640. (Illus.). 1980. pap. 7.00 (ISBN 0-914646-32-X). Belier Pr.
Bizarre Comix, Vol. 7. LC 77-84967. (Illus.). pap. 6.00 (ISBN 0-914646-11-7). Belier Pr.
Bizarre Comix, Vol. 9. LC 78-68098. (Illus.). pap. 6.50 (ISBN 0-914646-19-2). Belier Pr.
Bizarre Comix, Vol. 10. LC 78-68103. (Illus.). pap. 6.50 (ISBN 0-914646-20-6). Belier Pr.
Bizarre Comix, Vol. 11. (Illus.). 1980. pap. 7.00 (ISBN 0-914646-30-3). Belier Pr.
Bizarre Comix, Vol. 12. (Illus.). 1980. pap. 7.00 (ISBN 0-914646-31-1). Belier Pr.
Bizarre Fotos. LC 78-60517. (Illus.). Vol. 1. pap. 6.50 (ISBN 0-914646-17-6); Vol. 2. pap. 6.50 (ISBN 0-914646-25-7); Vol. 3. pap. 6.50 (ISBN 0-914646-26-5). Belier Pr.
Bizarre Happenings at Wellington Manor. Peter Walker. 1972. pap. 1.95 o.s.i. (V1102T, Venus). Grove.
Bizarre Katalogs. LC 79-55231. (Illus.). Vol. 1. pap. 8.00 (ISBN 0-914646-28-1); Vol. 2. pap. 8.00 (ISBN 0-914646-29-X). Belier Pr.
Bizarre Murders. Three Mysteries in One Volume, Complete and Unabridged: The Siamese Twin Mystery; The Chinese Orange Mystery; the Spanish Cape Mystery. Ellery Queen, pseud. LC 62-2376. 1962. Lippincott.
Bizarre Pain Seekers. Eugene Richards. 192p. (Orig.). 1973. pap. 1.95 o.p. (ISBN 0-87682-335-5, 7335). Barclay Hse.
Bizarre Sisters. Jay Walz & Audrey Walz. LC 50-6952. (Illus.). 1950. Duell, Sloan and Pearce.
Bizarre Voyage. Anthony Bell. 1972. pap. 1.95 o.s.i. (V1112T, Venus). Grove/
Bizzy-Quizzy the Great: Science-Detective-Fiction Adventures. William Rushton Bowker. LC 42-18294. 1942.
Black. Edgar Wallace. LC 30-5944. 1930. Pub. for The Crime Club, Inc., by Doubleday, Doran & Company, Inc.
Black Abbot. Edgar Wallace. LC 27-9366. 1927. Doubleday, Doran & Company.
Black Abyss. J L Powers. LC 66-5213. 1966. Arcadia House.
Black Ace. George Dilnot. LC 29-4532. 1929. Houghton Mifflin Company.
Black Ace: A Mystery Melodrama. C. Gordon Kurtz. LC 48-37516. (On cover: Playhouse plays). 1934. Fitzgerald Publishing Corporation.
Black Aces. Stephen Payne. LC 36-15379. J. H. Hopkins & Son, Inc.
Black Adonis. Linn Boyd Porter. LC 72-2028. (Black Heritage Library Collection). (Series: Dillingham's American authors library, no. 4). 1972. 14.50 (ISBN 0-8369-9060-9). Books for Libraries Press.
Black Adonis. Linn Boyd Porter. LC 7-37774. (Dillingham's American authors library, no. 4). 1895. G. W. Dillingham.
Black Against the Mob. Omar Fletcher. 1.75 (ISBN 0-87067-522-2). Holloway House Pub. Co.
Black Alibi. Cornell George Hopley-Woolrich. LC 42-10431. 1942. Simon and Schuster.
Black Alibi. Cornell Woolrich, pseud. LC 42-10431. 1942. Simon and Schuster.
Black Alibi: A Novel of Stalking Terror. Cornell George Hopley-Woolrich. LC 43-12150. (Handi-Book Mysteries). (Handi-book mysteries. No. 14: No. 14). 1943. Quinn Publishing Company, Inc.
Black Alice. Thom Demijohn. LC 68-22503. 1968. 4.95 o.p. Doubleday.
Black Alice: A Novel. Thomas M Disch & John Thomas Sladek. LC 68-22503. 1968. 4.95. Doubleday.
Black Amber. Phyllis A. Whitney. 224p. 1978. pap. 2.75 (ISBN 0-449-23943-8, Crest). Fawcett.
Black American. Florence Moss Blackwell. LC 19-4444. Phoenix Printing Company.
Black American Writer: Vol.1, Fiction. Ed. by C. W. Bigsby. 1971. pap. 2.95 o.p. (ISBN 0-14-021225-6, Pelican). Penguin.
Black and Blue. Octavus Roy Cohen. LC 71-106269. (Short story index reprint series). 1970. Books for Libraries Press.
Black and Blue. Octavus Roy Cohen. LC 26-2453. 1926. Little, Brown, and Company.
Black and Deadly. Charlie Avery Harris. 1.75 (ISBN 0-87067-524-9). Holloway House.
Black & Queer. Adrian Stanford. 1977. pap. 3.00 o.p. (ISBN 0-915480-11-5). Good Gay.
Black and the Red: A Homer Evans Mystery. Paul, Elliot Harold. 1956. Random House.
Black & the White. Ed. by J. Vernon Shea, Jr. Orig. Title: Strange Barriers. 1969. pap. 0.95 o.p. (N2090). Pyramid Pubns.
Black & White. Sarah Shears. 1978. 9.95 (ISBN 0-236-40128-9, Pub. by Paul Elek). Merrimack Pub Cir.
Black and White: A Novel. Elizabeth Avery Meriwether. LC 7-25964. 1883. E. J. Hale & Son.
Black and White Lion. Lyn Jank. LC 77-74607. (Illus.). 10.00 (ISBN 0-87706-100-9). Branch-Smith.
Black and White of It. Ann Allen Shockley. LC 80-80380. 1980. 5.95 (ISBN 0-930044-15-0). Naiad Press.
Black & White Stories in American Life. Ed. by Carol Anselment & Donald B. Gibson. (O.s.i.). (Orig.). 1971. pap. 0.95 o.s.i. (ISBN 0-671-47839-7). WSP.
Black & White Stories in American Life. Ed. by Carol Anselment & Donald B. Gibson. (O.s.i.). (Orig.). 1971. pap. 0.95 o.s.i. (ISBN 0-671-47839-7). WSP.
Black and White Tangled Threads. Zara Wright. LC 73-18566. (Illus.). 1975. 24.50 (ISBN 0-404-11378-8). AMS Press.
Black and White Tangled Threads. Zara Wright. LC 21-383. Barnard & Miller.
Black Angel. Cornell George Hopley-Woolrich. LC 43-2938. 1943. Pub. for the Crime Club by Doubleday, Doran and Company, Inc.
Black Angel... Cornell George Hopley-Woolrich. LC 45-16238. (Murder Mystery Monthly). (Murder mystery monthly. No. 27: No. 27).
Black Angel. Bettina Kingsley. (Ravenswood gothic). 1974. (pbk.). 0.95. Pocket Books.
Black Angel. Cornell Woolrich, pseud. 256p. 1982. pap. 2.25 (ISBN 0-345-30664-3). Ballantine.
Black Angels. Bruce Jay Friedman. (O.S.I.). 1966. 4.50 o.s.i. (09290). S&S.
Black Angels. Cicero T Ritchie. LC 59-100624. Abelard-Schuman.
Black Angels: A Novel. Maud Hart Lovelace. LC 26-183877. 1926. The John Day Company.
Black Angels: Stories. Bruce Jay Friedman. (75263). 1968. Pocket Bks.
Black Angus. Newton Thornburg. LC 78-7228. 8.95 (ISBN 0-316-84391-1). Little, Brown.
Black Angus. Newton Thornburg. 1980. 2.25 (ISBN 0-445-04524-8). Fawcett Popular Library.
Black April. Julia Mood Peterkin. LC 28-23054. 1928. Grosset & Dunlap.
Black April: A Novel. Julia Mood Peterkin. LC 73-163411. 1972. 9.95 (ISBN 0-910220-42-5). N. S. Berg.
Black April: A Novel. Julia Mood Peterkin. LC 27-5080. The Bobbs-Merrill Company.
Black Arrow. Robert Louis Stevenson. LC 62-21880. 1962. Collier Books.
Black Arrow. Robert Louis Stevenson. (golden books). D. McKay.
Black Arrow. Robert Louis Stevenson. Ed. by Holm, Dorothy Loomis. LC 27-4644. (Academy classics for junior high schools). Allyn and Bacon.
Black Arrow. Robert Louis Stevenson. LC 43-204479. (Newberry classics). 1939. David McKay Company.
Black Arrow. Robert Louis Stevenson & Davenport, Basil. LC 49-7624. (Great Illustrated Classics). 1949. Dodd, Mead.
Black Arrow. Robert Louis Stevenson & Johnson, Avery F., 1906- Illus. LC 47-6279. 1947. Grosset & Dunlap.
Black Arrow. Robert Louis Stevenson & Wallace, Lewis. LC 42-471751. (Prose and poetry individualized program The novel). 1942. The L. W. Singer Company.
Black Arrow: A Tale of the Two Roses. Robert Louis Stevenson. LC 58-835. (Children's illustrated classics). 1958. Dent.
Black Arrow: A Tale of the Two Roses. Robert Louis Stevenson. LC 51-20334. (Pocket book jr., J-57). 1950. Pocket Books.
Black Arrow: A Tale of the Two Roses. Robert Louis Stevenson. LC 50-41963. 1888. Cassell.
Black Arrow: A Tale of the Two Roses. Robert Louis Stevenson. LC 4-18331. 1888. C. Scribner's Sons.
Black Arrow: A Tale of the Two Roses. Robert Louis Stevenson. LC 5-24183. (Half-title: The biographical edition of the works of Robert Louis Stevenson). 1905. C. Scribner's Sons.
Black Arrow: A Tale of the Two Roses. Robert Louis Stevenson. LC 25-7163. (Half-title: The biographical edition of the works of Robert Louis Stevenson). 1914. C. Scribner's Sons.
Black Arrow: A Tale of the Two Roses. Robert Louis Stevenson. LC 10-21396. 1916. C. Scribner's Sons.
Black Arrow: A Tale of the Two Roses. Robert Louis Stevenson. LC 24-204873. (Half-title: The biographical edition of the works of Robert Louis Stevenson). 1922. C. Scribner's Sons.
Black Arrow: A Tale of the Two Roses. Robert Louis Stevenson. The Saalfield Publishing Company.
Black Arrow: A Tale of the Two Roses. Robert Louis Stevenson. Ed. by Wells, George Clair & Hadsell, Sardis Roy. LC 28-16168. (Western series of English and American classics). 1928. Harlow Publishing Co.
Black Arrow: A Tale of the Two Roses. Illustrated by Lawrence Beall Smith. Robert Louis Stevenson. LC 54-14558. 1954. Junior Deluxe Editions.
Black Arrows. Francis Beeding. LC 38-137920. 1938. Harper & Brothers.
Black As He Painted. Ngaio Marsh. 1976. Repr. of 1973 ed. lib. bdg. 13.25x (ISBN 0-88411-472-4). Amereon Ltd.
Black As He's Painted. Ngaio March. 1976. pap. 1.25 o.p. (ISBN 0-515-03613-7). BJ Pub Group.
Black As He's Painted. Ngaio Marsh. LC 73-22307. 1974. 6.95 (ISBN 0-316-54666-6). Little, Brown.
Black As He's Painted. Ngaio Marsh. LC 74-12183. 1974. (lib. bdg.) 11.95 (ISBN 0-8161-6232-8). G. K. Hall.
Black As He's Painted see Ngaio Marsh.
Black As Night. Daniel D Nern. LC 58-6247. 1958. Beacon Press.
Black Assassin. James H. Readus. 224p. (Orig.). 1975. pap. 1.95 (ISBN 0-87067-686-5, BH687). Holloway.
Black Assassin. James-Howard Readus. 1975. (pbk.) 1.50 (ISBN 0-87067-468-4). Holloway House.
Black August: A Novel. Dennis Yates Wheatley. LC 34-18835. E. P. Dutton & Co., Inc.
Black Aura. John Thomas Sladek. LC 79-88869. 1979. 8.95 (ISBN 0-8027-5413-9). Walker.
Black Autumn. Elaine Evans. 1973. pap. 1.25 o.s.i. (78-752). Lancer.
Black Avenger of the Spanish Main. A Thrilling Story of the Buccaneer Times. Edward Zane Carroll Judson. LC 7-114377. S. French.
Black Badges Are Bad Business-& Other Short Stories, Vol. 1. Hy Young & Mary Silberman. (American Short Story Ser.). 84p. 1979. pap. 3.50 (ISBN 0-934040-01-X). Quality Ohio.
Black Bag. Louis Joseph Vance. LC 8-980. The Bobbs-Merrill Company.
Black Bait. Leo Guild. 224p. (Orig.). 1975. pap. 1.95 (ISBN 0-87067-648-2, BH648). Holloway.
Black Ball: A Fantastic Romance. Ernest De Lancey Pierson. LC 7-35898. (On cover: The household library. v. 4, no. 28). Belford, Clarke & Company; Etc., Etc.
Black Ball: A Fantastic Romance... Ernest De Lancey Pierson. LC 1-29104. (On cover: Eagle series. no. 187). 1900. Street & Smith.
Black Baroness: A Novel. Dennis Yates Wheatley. LC 42-36267. 1942. The Macmillan Company.
Black Barque. facsimile ed. Thornton Jenkins Haines. LC 70-37304. (Black Heritage Library Collection). Repr. of 1905 ed. 18.75 (ISBN 0-8369-8941-4). Ayer Co.
Black Barque: A Tale of the Pirate Slave-Ship Gentle Hand on Her Last African Cruise. Thornton Jenkins Hains. LC 70-37304. (Black Heritage Library Collection). (Illus.). 1971. (ISBN 0-8369-8941-4). Books for Libraries Press.
Black Barque: A Tale of the Private Slave-Ship Gentle Hand on Her Last African Cruise. Thornton Jenkins Hains. LC 5-6783. 1905. L. C. Page & Company.
Black Bartlemy's Treasure. Jeffery Farnol. LC 20-20647. 1920. Little, Brown, and Company.
Black Bayou. Idwal Jones. LC 41-7863. Duell, Sloan and Pearce.
Black Beast. Nancy Springer. (Orig.). 1982. pap. 2.50 (ISBN 0-671-44117-5, Timescape). PB.
Black Beatitudes. George R. Ridge. 1964. 3.00 (ISBN 0-8233-0155-9). Golden Quill.
Black Beauty and the Runaway Horse. I. M Richardson. Anna Sewell. LC 82-7029. (Richardson, I. M. Anna Sewell's The Adventures of Black Beauty: Bk. 2). 1982. 6.89 (ISBN 0-89375-812-4) (ISBN 0-89375-813-2). Troll Assoicates.
Black Beauty Finds a Home. I. M Richardson. Anna Sewell. LC 82-7024. (Richardson, I. M. Anna Sewell's The Adventures of Black Beauty: Bk. 4). 1982. 6.89 (ISBN 0-89375-816-7) (ISBN 0-89375-817-5). Troll Associates.
Black Beauty Grows up. I. M Richardson. Anna Sewell. LC 82-7075. (Richardson, I. M. Anna Sewell's The Adventures of Black Beauty: Bk. 1). 8.79 (ISBN 0-89375-810-8) (ISBN 0-89375-811-6). Troll Associates.
Black Beauty: His Groom and Companions. Anna Sewell. LC 4-24555. 1902. L. C. Page & Company.
Black Beauty: The Autobiography of a Horse. Anna Sewell. LC 81-16038. 1982. 12.95 (ISBN 0-671-43789-5). Wanderer Books.
Black Belle Rides the Uplands. Vingie Eve Roe. LC 35-8289. 1935. Doubleday, Doran & Company, Inc.
Black Bethlehem. Lettice Ulpha Cooper. LC 47-11336. 1947. Macmillan Co.
Black Bird. Alexander Edwards. 1975. (pbk.) 1.25. Warner Books.
Black, Black Hearse. Frederic Freyer, pseud. LC 55-7298. 1955. St. Martin's Press.
Black, Black Rain. Urjit. 1966. 1.50 o.p. InterCulture.
Black Blood. Jon Hart. LC 80-71036. (Mercenaries Ser.). 128p. 1981. pap. 2.95 (ISBN 0-87754-227-9). Chelsea Hse.
Black Blood. A Peculiar Case. George Manville Fenn. LC 6-392576. (On cover: Lovell's library, no. 1208). 1888. J. W. Lovell Company.
Black Blood in Kentucky: By Stanley and Jeanette Bolton. 1st Ed. Stanley Bolton & Jeanette Bolton. LC 57-8401. 1957. Vantage Press.
Black Book. Lawrence Durrell. 1963. pap. 3.95 (ISBN 0-525-47115-4). Dutton.

Black Book: Being the Full Account of How the Book of the Betrayers Came into the Hands of Yorke Norroy, Secret Agent of the Department of State... George Fitzalan Bronson Howard. LC 20-14556. W. J. Watt & Company.
Black Boulder Ranch: By Brett Austin Pseud. Lee Floren. LC 50-8881. 1950. Phoenix Press.
Black Box. Edward Phillips Oppenheim. LC 15-13472. 0.50. Grosset & Dunlap.
Black Box. Robert George Sherrin. LC 77-366324. 5.95 (ISBN 0-88894-114-5). November House.
Black Box. Matthew Phipps Shiel. LC 31-3182. The Vanguard Press.
Black-Box Murder. authorized ed. Jozua Marius Willem Van Der Poorten Schwartz. LC 8-2903. (Lovell's international series, no. 123). United States Book Company, Successors to J. W. Lovell Company.
Black Boxer. Herbert Ernest Bates. LC 73-178437. (Short story index reprint series). 1971. (ISBN 0-8369-4037-7). Books for Libraries Press.
Black Boxer: Tales. facsimile ed. Herbert Ernest Bates. LC 73-178437. (Short Story Index Reprint Ser.). Repr. of 1932 ed. 16.00 (ISBN 0-8369-4037-7). Ayer Co.
Black Bread and Caviar. Maria Metlova. LC 58-337263. 1958. Vantage Press.
Black Bryony: With Five Woodcuts. Theodore Francis Powys. 1923. A. A. Knopf.
Black Buccaneer. Stephen Warren Meader. LC 20-16856. 1920. Harcourt, Brace and Howe.
Black Buck. Linton C. Hopkins. LC 31-602. 1931. Little, Brown, and Company.
Black Bull. Henry Bedford-Jones. LC 27-19117. 1927. G.P. Putnam's Sons.
Black Bulls. John Benteen. (Fargo Ser). (Orig.). 1971. pap. 0.75 o.p. (B75-2094). Belmont-Tower.
Black Bulls. John Benteen. (Fargo Ser.). (O.s.i.). 1972. pap. 0.75 o.s.i. (BT40129). Belmont-Tower.
Black Bulls see Toros Negros.
Black but Comely: Or, The Adventures of Jane Lee. new ed. George John Whyte-Melville. LC 42-350387. (On cover: Ward & Lock's library of select authors). Ward, Lock and Co.
Black Butterflies: A Story of Youth. Elizabeth Garver Jordan. LC 27-5947. 2.00. The Century Co.
Black Buttes. Clarence Edward Mulford. LC 73-89648. 1973. 6.95. Aeonian Press.
Black Buttes. Clarence Edward Mulford. LC 23-908096. 1923. Doubleday, Page & Company.
Black Buttes. Clarence Edward Mulford. LC 27-2862. 1925. A. L. Burt Company.
Black Cabin. Green Peyton Wertenbaker. LC 33-848. 1933. Little, Brown and Company.
Black Cabinet. Patricia Wentworth. Small, Maynard Company.
Black Caesar's Clan: A Florida Mystery Story. Albert Payson Terhune. LC 22-19051. George H. Doran Company.
Black Calla. John Kolyer. LC 75-36486. 1976. pap. 3.75 o.p. (ISBN 0-8283-1675-9). Branden.
Black Camel. Earl Derr Biggers. The Bobbs-Merrill Company.
Black Camel. Earl Derr Biggers. LC 30-16247. Grosset & Dunlop.
Black Camel. Earl Derr Biggers. (Charlie Chan,#5). 1975. (pbk.) 0.95. Bantam Books.
Black Camelot. Duncan Kyle. LC 78-3964. 8.95 (ISBN 0-312-08301-7). St. Martin's Press.
Black Camelot. Duncan Kyle. 1980. 2.25 (ISBN 0-425-04276-6). Berkley Publishing Corp.
Black Camels. Ronald Johnston. LC 78-6375. 1969. 4.95. Harcourt, Brace & World.
Black Canaan. Robert E. Howard. 1978. pap. 1.95 (ISBN 0-425-03711-8, Medallion). Berkley Pub.
Black Cap. Compiled by Cynthia Mary Evelyn Charteris Asquith. 318p. 1981. Repr. lib. bdg. 35.00 (ISBN 0-89987-008-2). Darby Bks.
Black Cap: New Stories of Murder and Mystery. Ed. by Cynthia Mary Evelyn Charteris Asquith. LC 29-12065. 1928. C. Scribner's Sons.
Black Cardinal; a Novel. John Talbot Smith. LC 14-130162. 1914. The Champlain Press.
Black Cargo. Harold Calin. (Orig.). 1969. pap. 0.95 o.p. (75-096). Lancer.
Black Cargo. John Phillips Marquand. LC 74-26118. (Labor Movement in Fiction and Non-Fiction). 1976. 16.50 (ISBN 0-404-58453-5). AMS Press.
Black Cargo. John Phillips Marquand. LC 25-5383. 1925. C. Scribner's Sons.
Black Cargo: And Other Stories. 1st Ed. John Morrison. LC 56-371595. 1955. Australasian Book Society.
Black Carnation: A Riddle. Fergus Hume. LC 7-5855. United States Book Company.
Black Carnation: A Riddle. Fergus Hume. LC 1-30594. (Magnet detective library, no. 169). 1901. Street & Smith.
Black Castle. Les Daniels. 1978. 8.95 o.p. (ISBN 0-684-15533-8). Scribner.
Black Castle: A Novel of the Macabre. Les Daniels. LC 77-28235. 8.95 (ISBN 0-684-15533-8). Scribner.
Black Cat. John Russo. (Orig.). 1982. pap. 2.50 (ISBN 0-671-41691-X). PB.
Black Cat. Louis Tracy. LC 25-208260. E. J. Clode, Inc.
Black Cats Are Lucky. Archibald E. Fielding. LC 38-6345. 1938. H. C. Kinsey & Company, Inc.
Black Chalice, Anonymous. John Antonio Moroso. LC 34-16180. The Macaulay Company.
Black Champion. Mary Turner, pseud. (Orig.). 1975. pap. 1.50 (ISBN 0-87067-474-9, BH474). Holloway.
Black Chanter: And Other Highland Stories. Nimmo Christie. LC 3-24300. 1903. The Macmillan Company.
Black Chapel File. L. Christian Balling. 1979. pap. 2.50 (ISBN 0-89041-266-9). Major Bks.
Black Charade. John Frederick Burke. 1977. 7.95 o.p. (ISBN 0-698-10847-7, Coward). Putnam Pub Group.
Black Chariots. Kenneth Robeson. (Avenger#30). 1974. (pbk.) 0.95. Warner Paperback Library.
Black Cherries. Grace Stone Coates. LC 31-57036. 1931. A. A. Knopf.
Black Chronicle. William Edward Hayes. LC 38-12957. 1938. Pub. for the Crime Club, Inc., by Doubleday, Doran & Company, Inc.
Black Circle. Mansfield Scott. LC 28-22058. E. J. Clode, Inc.
Black City. 1st American Ed. Malachy Francis Caulfield. LC 53-6062. 1953. Dutton.
Black Cliffs. Gunnar Gunnarsson. Tr. by Cecil Wood from Danish. (Nordic Translation Ser). 260p. 1967. 17.50 (ISBN 0-299-04471-8). U of Wis Pr.
Black Cliffs. Svartfugl. Gunnar Gunnarsson. LC 67-25943. (Nordic translation series). 1967. University of Wisconsin Press.
Black Cloth. Verne Dyson. LC 34-37771. 1925. Clandoin, Gale & Co.
Black Cloud. Fred Hoyle. LC 58-6160. Harper.
Black Cloud. Fred Hoyle. (Signet Science Fiction). 1973. (pbk) 0.75. New American Lib.
Black Cloud, White Cloud. Ellen Douglas, pseud. 1963. 4.95 o.p. (ISBN 0-395-07631-5). HM.
Black Coat. Constance Little & Gwenyth Little. LC 48-9093. 1948. Pub. for the Crime Club by Doubleday.
Black Cockade. Victor J. H Suthren. LC 82-16781. 1982. 10.95 (ISBN 0-312-08303-3). St. Martin's Press.
Black Cola. Frank Laric. 1978. pap. 1.75 (ISBN 0-532-17193-4). Woodhill.
Black Colossus. Robert E. Howard. 20.00 (ISBN 0-937986-03-8). D M Grant.
Black Company: A Mystery Story. William Blair Morton Ferguson. LC 24-85690. Chelsea House.
Black Conceit. John Leonard. LC 73-80732. 1973. 6.95 (ISBN 0-385-06776-3). Doubleday.
Black Connection. Randolph Harris. (Orig.). 1974. pap. 1.95 (ISBN 0-87067-671-7, BH671). Holloway.
Black Connection. Randolph Harris. 1974. (pbk.) 1.50 (ISBN 0-87067-458-7). Holloway House Pub. Co.
Black Cop. Dom Gober. (Black Cop Ser.: No. 1). (Orig.). 1974. pap. 1.95 (ISBN 0-87067-461-7). Holloway.
Black Corridor. Michael Moorcock. Bd. with Adventures of una Persson & Catherine Cornelius in the Twentieth Century. 52p. 1980. pap. 4.95 (ISBN 0-8037-1343-6). Dial.
Black Corridors. Constance Little & Little, Gwenyth. LC 40-314537. 1940. Pub. for the Crime Club by Doubleday, Doran & Co., Inc.
Black Council. Panteleimon Oleksandrovych Kulish. LC 72-97984. (Ukrainian Classics in Translation, No. 2). 1973. 7.50 (ISBN 0-87287-063-4). Ukrainian Academic Press.
Black Country. Bruce Beddow. LC 28-25. 1928. Doubleday, Doran and Company, Inc.
Black Creek Buckaroo. Anson Piper. LC 41-5695. 1941. W. Morrow and Company.
Black Crook, a Most Wonderful History. Now Being Performed with Immense Success in All the Principal Theatres Throughout the United States. LC 6-13835. Barclay & Co.
Black Cross. Olive Mary Briggs. LC 9-3877. 1909. Moffat, Yard and Company.
Black Cross Clove: A Story and a Study. James Patrick Kenyon Luby. LC 11-634. 1910. 1.20. B. W. Huebsch.
Black Crusoe. facsimile ed. Alfred Seguin. LC 73-38022. (Black Heritage Library Collection). Repr. 24.25 (ISBN 0-8369-8995-3). Ayer Co.
Black Curl: By Constance and Gwenyth Little. 1st Ed. Constance Little & Gwenyth Little. LC 53-9131. 1953. Published for the Crime Club by Doubleday.
Black Curtain... Cornell George Hopley-Woolrich. LC 41-9246. 1941. Simon and Schuster.
Black Curtain. Flora Haines Apponyi Loughead. 1898. Houghton, Mifflin & Co.
Black Curtain. Cornell Woolrich, pseud. 160p. 1982. pap. 2.25 (ISBN 0-345-30490-X). Ballantine.
Black Curtain... By Cornell Woolrich. Cornell Woolrich, pseud. LC 41-92461. 1941. Simon and Schuster.
Black Cypress. Frances Kirkwood Crane. LC 48-896932. 1948. Random House.
Black Daniel: The Love Story of a Great Man. Honore McCue Willsie Morrow. LC 31-24140. 1931. W. Morrow & Company.
Black Dawn. Shaw Desmond. LC 44-53035. 1944. Hutchinson & Co. Ltd.
Black Dawn. Theda Kenyon. LC 44-9628. 1944. J. Messner, Inc.
Black Dawn. Christopher Nicole. LC 77-76648. 10.95 (ISBN 0-312-08307-6). St. Martin's Press.
Black Dawn. Christopher Nicole. (Signet Book). 1978. 2.25. New American Library.
Black Day. Giles A Lutz. (Ace, 06575). 1974. (pbk.) 0.75. Ace Books.
Black Death. Nick Carter. (Nick Carter Ser.). (O.s.i.). 192p. 1972. pap. 1.25 o.s.i. (AQ1401, Award). Univ Pub & Dist.
Black Death. Gwyneth Cravens & Marr, John S. 1978. 2.50. Ballantine Books.
Black Death. Kenneth Robeson. (Avenger,#22). 1974. (pbk.) 0.95. Warner Paperback Lib.
Black Death: By Anthony Gilbert Pseud. Lucy Beatrice Malleson. 1953. Random House.
Black Debtor. Michael Peterson. LC 54-8344. 1954. Vantage Press.
Black Diamond. Jennie Gallant. 224p. (Orig.). 1981. pap. 2.25 (ISBN 0-449-24424-5, Crest). Fawcett.
Black Diamond. Francis Brett Young. LC 21-18416. E. P. Dutton & Company.
Black Diamonds. Jules Verne. 3.95 o.p. Assoc Bk.
Black Diamonds: A Novel; Tr. Mor Jokai. Tr. by Gerard, Frances A. LC 4-16923. 1896. Harper & Brothers.
Black Diamonds: Or, Humor, Satire, and Sentiment. William H. Levison. LC 7-14370. 1855. A. Ranney.
Black Doctor: And Other Tales of Terror and Mystery. Arthur Conan Doyle. LC 26-8495. 1925. George H. Doran Company.
Black Dog. Georgena Goff. (Orig.). 1971. pap. 0.75 o.p. (B75-2124). Belmont-Tower.
Black Dog. Georgena Goff. 1973. pap. 0.75 o.p. (BT50299). Belmont-Tower.
Black Dog: And Other Stories. Alfred Edgar Coppard. LC 24-26322. 1923. A. A. Knopf.
Black Dog & Other Stories. facsimile ed. Alfred Edgar Coppard. LC 74-106275. (Short Story Index Reprint Ser.). 1923. 16.00 (ISBN 0-8369-3312-5). Ayer Co.
Black Doll... William Edward Hayes. LC 36-34849. 1936. Pub. for the Crime Club Inc., by Doubleday, Doran & Company, Inc.
Black Door. Cleve Franklin Adams. LC 43-2267. (Handi-book mysteries). 1942. Quinn Publishing Co., Inc.
Black Door. Cleve Franklin Adams. LC 41-20720. 1941. E. P. Dutton & Co., Inc.
Black Door. Collin Wilcox. LC 67-12710. (Red badge mystery). 1967. Dodd, Mead.
Black Door: The Mystery of the Fate of Sir Anthony Veryan's Heirs in Kestrel's Eyrie Castle Near the Coast of Wales. Virgil Markham. LC 30-10243. 1930. A. A. Knopf.
Black Dougal. David Harry Walker. LC 73-14769. 1974. 6.95 (ISBN 0-395-17128-8). Houghton Mifflin.
Black Douglas. Samuel Rutherford Crockett. LC 99-1271. 1899. Doublesay & McClure Co.
Black Douglas. Donald Douglas. LC 27-19644. George H. Doran Company.
Black Drop. Alice Brown. LC 19-15577. 1919. The Macmillan Company.
Black Druid, and Other Stories. Frank Belknap Long. LC 76-356813. 1975. 0.50 (ISBN 0-586-04182-6). Panther.
Black Drums. Robert J. Scott. (Orig.). 1970. pap. 0.95 o.p. (ISBN 0-447-75124-7). Lancer.
Black Duchess: A Novel. Alanna Knight. LC 79-7668. (Illus.). 1980. 10.00 (ISBN 0-385-15326-0). Doubleday.
Black Dudley Murder. Margery Allingham. 176p. Repr. of 1929 ed. lib. bdg. 11.50x (ISBN 0-89190-188-4). Am Repr-Rivercity Pr.
Black Dudley Murder. Margery Allingham. 1976. pap. 1.25 (ISBN 0-532-12386-7). Woodhill.
Black Dudley Murder. Margery Allingham. 1966. pap. 0.60 o.p. (60-254). Manor Bks.
Black Dwarf. Walter Scott. (On cover: Lovell's library, no. 490). 1885. J. W. Lovell Company.
Black Dwarf: And A Legend of Montrose. Walter Scott. (On cover: Seaside library. Pocket ed. no. 353). 1885. G. Munro.
Black Dwarf: & A Legend of Montrose. Walter Scott. (Half-title: Everyman's library, ed. by Ernest Rhys. Fiction). 1907. J. M. Dent & Co.
Black Eagle. Anne Hampson. (Presents Ser.). 1975. pap. 1.25 (ISBN 0-373-70579-4, 70579, Pub by Harlequin). PB.
Black Eagle. Nico Heliopoulos & Millington, Frances, Joint Author. LC 47-117823. 1947. Ziff-Davis Pub. Co.
Black Eagle: Bertrand Du Gueslin, Sword of France. Marjorie Coyn. LC 34-3541. 1934. Funk & Wagnalls Company.
Black Eagle Mystery. Geraldine Bonner. LC 16-4388. 1916. 1.30. D. Appleton and Company.
Black Eagles Are Flying. Florence Vorpe Morse. LC 43-11853. 1943. Pub. for the Crime Club by Doubleday, Doran & Co.
Black Earl. Sharon Stephens. (Tapestry Romance Ser.). 1982. pap. 2.50. PB.
Black Earth. Hans Habe. LC 52-9834. 1952. Putnam.
Black Earth. Thomas Rowan. LC 35-15315. 1935. Hillman-Curl, Inc.
Black Earth: A Novel. Louis Cochran. LC 37-14275. B. Humphries, Inc.
Black Earth: By Hans Habe Pseud. Jean Bekessy, pseud. LC 52-9834. 1952. Putnam.
Black Easter. James Blish. 176p. 1982. pap. 2.50 (ISBN 0-380-59568-0, 59568). Avon.
Black Easter. James Blish. LC 68-18070. (Illus.). 1968. 3.95 o.p. Doubleday.
Black Easter. Arnold Kemp. 1973. pap. 1.25 o.p. (33-035). Lancer.
Black Easter; The Day After Judgment. James Blish. LC 80-17971. (Series: Gregg Press Science Fiction Series.). 1980. 16.95 (ISBN 0-8398-2644-3). Gregg Press.
Black Easter: Or, Faust Aleph-Null. James Blish. LC 68-18070. 1968. Doubleday.
Black Echo. Eugene Thomas. LC 33-2865. Pegasus Publishing Company.
Black Emperor. Stuart Jason, pseud. 1976. pap. 1.50 (ISBN 0-532-15213-1). Woodhill.
Black Emperor. Stuart Jason. 1971. pap. 0.95 o.p. (ISBN 0-447-75165-4). Lancer.
Black Envelope: Mr. Pinkerton Again! Zenith Jones Brown. LC 37-28703. Farrar & Rinehart, Inc.
Black Exchange. Patrick Kirwan. LC 34-17241. The Vanguard Press.
Black Exorcist. Joseph Nazel. (Orig.). 1974. pap. 1.50 (ISBN 0-87067-463-3, BH463). Holloway.
Black Experience in Children's Books. rev. ed. Augusta Baker. (Illus.). 1971. pap. 0.50 o.p. (ISBN 0-87104-226-6). NY Pub Lib.
Black Eye. Constance Little & Gwenyth Little. LC 45-9766. 1945. Pub. for the Crime Club by Doubleday, Doran and Company, Inc.
Black-Eyed Stranger. Charlotte Armstrong. LC 51-3718. 1951. Coward-McCann.
Black-Eyed Stranger. Charlotte Armstrong. (Berkley medallion book). 1974. (pbk.) 0.95 (ISBN 0-425-02650-7). Berkley Pub. Co.
Black-Eyed Susan. Megan Barker. 400p. 1982. pap. 2.95 (ISBN 0-446-90169-5). Warner Bks.
Black-Eyed Susans: Classic Stories by and About Black Women. Mary Helen Washington. LC 75-6169. 1975. 2.95 (ISBN 0-385-09043-9). Anchor Books.
Black Fan. Mary Boyle O'Reilly. LC 28-11819. The Reilly & Lee Co.
Black Fawn. Jim Kjelgaard, pseud. pap. 0.95 o.p. (ISBN 0-396-06265-2). Dodd.
Black Feather. Benge Atlee. LC 39-27915. 1939. C. Scribner's Sons.
Black Feather. Harold Titus. LC 36-173925. Macrea Smith Company.
Black Fire: A Story of Henri Christophe. Covelle Newcomb. LC 40-13267. 1940. Longmans, Green and Co.
Black Flame. Lynn Abbey. LC 80-123608. (Ace Science Fiction). (Illus.). 6.95 (ISBN 0-441-06583-X). Ace Books.
Black Flame. Stanley Grauman Weinbaum. LC 48-1786. 1948. Fantasy Press.
Black Flame; a Trilogy. William Edward Burghardt Du Bois. Incl. Bk. 1. Ordeal of Mansart. 15.00 (ISBN 0-527-25270-0); Bk. 2. Mansart Builds a School. 17.00 (ISBN 0-527-25271-9); Bk. 3. Worlds of Color. 17.00 (ISBN 0-527-25272-7). 1976. Repr. 49.00. Kraus Intl.
Black Flemings. Kathleen Thompson Norris. LC 26-734721. 1926. Doubleday, Page & Company.
Black Flemings see Gabrielle.
Black Flier. Edith Macvane. LC 9-14216. 1909. Moffat, Yard and Company.
Black Fog. Charles Judson Dutton. LC 34-9914. 1934. Dodd, Mead & Company.
Black Folder. David Brett, pseud. LC 76-365551. 1976. 3.25 (ISBN 0-245-52808-3). Harrap.
Black for a Bride. Jeanne Marie. 1973. 4.95. Lenox Hill Pr.
Black Forest. Meade Minnigerode. LC 37-24573. Farrar & Rinehart, Inc.
Black Forest Village Stories. Berthold Auerbach. LC 70-101791. (Short story index reprint series). (Illus.). 1969. Books for Libraries Press.
Black Forest Village Stories. Berthold Auerbach. Tr. by Goepp, Charles. LC 6-4501. (Leisure hour series. v. 36). 1874. H. Holt and Company.
Black Fortune. Eldred Kurtz Means. LC 72-4739. (Black Heritage Library Collection). 1972. 12.25 (ISBN 0-8369-9110-9). Books for Libraries Press.

Black Fortune. Eldred Kurtz Means. LC 31-20652. 1931. Brentano's.

Black Fountains. Oswald Wynd. LC 47-301793. 1947. Doubleday & Company, Inc.

Black Fox. Matthew Braun. 1979. pap. 1.95 (ISBN 0-671-44010-1). PB.

Black Fox: A Novel of the Seventies. Gerald Heard. LC 51-13533. 1951. Harper.

Black Friday. David Goodis. LC 54-145785. (Lion book, 224). 1954. Lion Books by Arrangement with Medalion Pub. Corp.

Black Friday. Frederic Stewart Isham. LC 4-262409. 1904. The Bobbs-Merrill Company.

Black Friday: A Story of Love and Speculation. Thomas Bernard Joseph Connery. LC 6-306833. (On cover: Once a week library, v. 10, no. 14). 1893. P.F. Collier.

Black Fugitive. Eddie Stone. 1977. 1.75 (ISBN 0-87067-512-5). Holloway House Pub. Co.

Black Fury. Michael A. Musmanno. 1972. pap. 0.95 o.p. (09110). Curtis.

Black Fury. Michael A. Musmanno. 5.95 o.s.i. Fountainhead.

Black Fury. Joseph Nazel. (Orig.). 1976. pap. 1.50 (ISBN 0-87067-497-8, BH058). Holloway.

Black Fury: By Michael A. Musmanno. Michael Angelo Musmanno. LC 66-14043. 1966. 5.95. Fountainhead.

Black Gale. Samuel Shellabarger. LC 29-19519. The Century Co.

Black Gambit: A Novel. Eric Clark. LC 77-88829. 1978. 8.95 (ISBN 0-688-03264-8). Morrow.

Black Gambit: A Novel. Eric Clark. 1979. 2.25 (ISBN 0-446-82810-6). Warner Books.

Black Gang. Herman Cyril McNeile. LC 22-23565. George H. Doran Company.

Black Gangster. Donald Goines. 288p. (Orig.). 1972. pap. 1.95 (ISBN 0-87067-629-6, BH028). Holloway.

Black Garden. Christine Arnothy. LC 69-16181. 1969. 4.95. Holt, Rinehart and Winston.

Black Gardenia: A Hollywood Murder Mystery. Elliot Harold Paul. LC 52-5135. 1952. Random House.

Black Gauntlet: A Tale of Plantation Life in South Carolina. Mary Howard Schoolcraft. LC 73-175581. 1973. 15.00 (ISBN 0-404-04625-8). AMS Press.

Black Gauntlet: A Tale of Plantation Life in South Carolina. Mary Howard Schoolcraft. LC 78-138345. (Black Heritage Library Collection). 1971. (ISBN 0-8369-8737-3). Books for Libraries Press.

Black Gauntlet: A Tale of Plantation Life in South Carolina. Mary Howard Schoolcraft. LC 8-2045. 1860. J. B. Lippincott & Co.

Black General. Audley Southcott. LC 70-94440. 1969. 5.95. Morrow.

Black Gestapo. Joseph Nazel. (Orig.). 1975. pap. 1.50 (ISBN 0-87067-477-3, BH477). Holloway.

Black Ghost. J. M. Walsh. LC 31-3866. 1931. Brewer & Warren Inc.

Black Ghost of the Highway. Gertrude Linnell. LC 31-4963. 1931. Longmans, Green and Co.

Black Girl Lost. Donald Goines. (Orig.). 1973. pap. 1.95 (ISBN 0-87067-656-3, BH042). Holloway.

Black Glass City: A Peter Styles Mystery. Judson Pentecost Philips. LC 65-11808. (Red badge detective). bds., 3.50. Dodd.

Black Glove. Geoffrey Miller. LC 80-54087. 1981. 12.95 (ISBN 0-670-17166-2). Viking Press.

Black Glove. Geraldine Gordon Salmon. LC 26-12591. George H. Doran Company.

Black Gloves. Constance Little & Little, Gwenyth. 1939. Pub. for the Crime Club, Inc., by Doubleday, Doran & Company, Inc.

Black Goatee. Constance Little & Gwenyth Little. LC 47-1626. 1947. Pub. for the Crime Club by Doubleday & Company, Inc.

Black God: A Story of the Congo. Doris Manners-Sutton. LC 34-14770. 1934. Longmans, Green and Co.

Black God: A Story of the Congo. Doris Manners-Sutton. LC 34-24487. 1934. Longmans, Green and Co.

Black Godfather. Omar Fletcher. 1.75 (ISBN 0-87067-525-7). Holloway House.

Black Gods, Green Islands. Geoffrey Holder & Tom Harshman. LC 71-98722. (Illus.). 1969. Negro Universities Press.

Black Gods: Green Islands, by Geoffrey Holder, with Tom Harshman. Drawings by Geoffrey Holder. 1st Ed. Geoffrey Holder. LC 59-12632. 1959. Doubleday.

Black God's Shadow. Catherine L. Moore. 15.00 o.p. D M Grant.

Black Gold. Jewel Gibson. LC 50-6307. 1950. Random House.

Black Gold. Lillian Elwyn Elliott Joyce. LC 20-19915. 1920. The Macmillan Company.

Black Gold. Paul Kenyon. (Baroness/8). 1975. (pbk.) 0.95 (ISBN 0-671-77962-1). Pocket Books.

Black Gold. Guy Eugene Morton. LC 24-17454. Small, Maynard & Company.

Black Gold. Albert Payson Terhune. LC 22-6320. George H. Doran Company.

Black Gold: A Romance. Robert McBlair. LC 29-644964. 1929. D. Appleton and Company.

Black Gold: A Story of the Texas Rangers. Jackson Cole, pseud. LC 38-5292. The William Carlson Company, Inc.

Black Gold: A Story of the Texas Rangers. Oscar Schiegall. The William Caslon Company, Inc.

Black Gold of Malaverde. Richard L Graves. LC 73-82144. (Illus.). 1973. 7.95 (ISBN 0-8128-1642-0). Stein and Day.

Black Gold of Malaverde. Richard L Graves. (Illus.). 1974. (pbk.) 1.50. Bantam Books.

Black Gold, Red Death. David Lindsey. 256p. 1983. pap. 2.75 (ISBN 0-449-12434-7, GM). Fawcett.

Black Gold Stampede. Edgar Moore. LC 40-31454. 1940. Doubleday, Doran and Co., Inc.

Black Gown. Ruth Hall. LC 5047. 1900. Houghton, Mifflin and Company.

Black Grape. Ruth Babcock. LC 50-6775. 1950. Coward-McCann.

Black Grapes. Livia De Stefani. LC 58-7781. 1958. Criterion Books.

Black Gulf. Konstantin Georgievich Paustovskii. LC 75-39008. (Early Soviet Literature). 1977. 12.75 (ISBN 0-88355-411-9). Hyperion Press.

Black Hand. Wilbert C Blakeman. LC 8-30938. Broadway Publishing Company.

Black Hand: And Other Stories About Schools. Charles William Bardeen. LC 14-22587. 1.00. C. W. Bardeen.

Black Harvest. Ida Alexa Ross Wylie. LC 26-8879. 1925. Cassell and Company, Ltd.

Black Harvest. Ida Alexa Ross Wylie. LC 26-2546. George H. Doran Company.

Black Hawthorn. Dorothy Stockbridge Tillet. LC 38-31655. 1933. Pub. for the Crime Club, Inc., by Doubleday, Doran & Company, Inc.

Black-Headed Pins. Constance Little & Little, Gwenyth. LC 39-27040. 1938. Pub. for the Crime Club, Inc., by Doubleday, Doran & Company, Inc.

Black Heart. Eric Van Lustbader. 544p. 1982. 16.95 (ISBN 0-87131-395-2). M Evans.

Black Hearts Murders. Ellery Queen, pseud. (Orig.). 1970. pap. 0.75 o.p. (ISBN 0-447-74640-5). Lancer.

Black Heat. Peter Turner. (Orig.). 1970. pap. 1.25 o.p. (B12-2027). Belmont-Tower.

Black Heather. Virginia Coffman. Bd. with Night at Sea Abbey. 1980. pap. 1.95 (ISBN 0-451-09468-9, J9468, Sig). NAL.

Black Heather. Virginia Coffman. (Signet Book). 1976. 1.25. New American Library.

Black Hell. Harold Calin. LC 75-100. (Orig.). 1970. pap. 0.95 o.p. (ISBN 0-447-75105-0). Lancer.

Black Hercules. Stuart Jason. 1969. pap. 0.95 o.p. (74-095). Lancer.

Black Heritage. Terry K Howel. LC 78-105882. 8.95 (ISBN 0-533-03171-0). Vantage Press.

Black Hills Duel. Owen Rountree. 160p. (Orig.). 1983. pap. 1.95 (ISBN 0-345-30758-5). Ballantine.

Black Hills Ghost Towns. Watson Parker & Hugh K. Lambert. LC 82-73468. (Illus.). 215p. 1974. 21.95 (ISBN 0-8040-0637-7, SB); pap. 11.95 (ISBN 0-8040-0638-5). Swallow.

Black Hit Woman. Laurie Mills et al. 224p. (Orig.). 1980. pap. 1.95 (ISBN 0-87067-681-4, BH681). Holloway.

Black Hole. Alan Dean Foster. LC 79-53894. (Illus., Orig.). 1979. pap. 1.95 (ISBN 0-345-28538-7). Ballantine.

Black Holes & Bug-Eyed-Monsters. Intro. by Isaac Asimov. LC 77-82629. 1977. pap. 1.50 o.s.i. (ISBN 0-89559-007-7). Davis Pubns.

Black Holes & Bug-Eyed-Monsters. Intro. by Isaac Asimov. LC 77-82629. 1977. pap. 1.50 o.p. (ISBN 0-89559-007-7). Davis Pubns.

Black Holocaust in Nineteen Eighty-Four. Greta Hawthorne. 1980. 6.95 o.p. (ISBN 0-8062-1289-6). Carlton.

Black Homer of Jimtown. Edward Harold Mott. LC 3-704. 1900. Grosset & Dunlap.

Black Honeymoon. Constance Little & Gwenyth Little. 1944. Pub. for the Crime Club by Doubleday, Doran and Co., Inc.

Black Hood. Thomas Dixon. LC 24-14019. 1924. D. Appleton and Company.

Black Horde. Richard Lewis. 1980. pap. 1.75 (ISBN 0-451-09454-9, E9454, Sig). NAL.

Black Horse Rider. Archie Joscelyn. LC 35-5307. Phoenix Press.

Black Horse Running. James Wood. LC 74-30874. 1977. 7.95 o.s.i. (ISBN 0-8149-0757-1). Vanguard.

Black Horse Tavern. Raymond Fraser. 188p. 1973. 7.00 o.s.i. (ISBN 0-919522-72-6); pap. 2.95 o.s.i. (ISBN 0-919522-73-4). Ingluvin Pubns.

Black Horse Troop. Thomas S. Byrd. 1970. 3.75 o.p. Vantage.

Black Horseman. Jack Scott. LC 32-14136. Grosset & Dunlap.

Black Hound. 1st Ed. Olive Mary Briggs. 1960. Vantage Press.

Black House. Roy Bridges. LC 21-5921. Hodder and Stoughton Limited.

Black House. Constance Little & Gwenyth Little. LC 50-5030. 1950. Published for the Crime Club by Doubleday.

Black House. Paul Theroux. LC 74-6135. 1974. 6.95 (ISBN 0-395-19400-8). Houghton Mifflin.

Black House in Harley Street. Joseph Smith Fletcher. LC 29-148086. 1928. Pub. for The Crime Club, Inc., by Doubleday, Doran & Company, Inc.

Black Humor. Ed. by Bruce Jay Friedman, pseud. LC 65-224851. Bantam.

Black Hunter. Eddie Stone. 1976. (pbk.) 1.50 (ISBN 0-87067-489-7). Holloway House Publishing Co.

Black Hunter: A Novel of Old Quebec. James Oliver Curwood. LC 26-13911. 1926. Cosmopolitan Book Corporation.

Black Ice. Albion Winegar Tourgee. LC 70-104581. 1970. Literature House.

Black Ice. Albion Winegar Tourgee. LC 8-29969. 1888. Fords, Howard, & Hulbert.

Black Imp: A Mystery Story with Intricate Race-Relations. Virgil S Powell. LC 64-14668. 1964. Greenwich Book Publishers.

Black in a White Paradise. Amos Brooke. (Orig.). 1978. pap. 1.75 (ISBN 0-87067-530-3, BH530). Holloway.

Black in Time. John Jakes. (Orig.). 1970. pap. 0.60 o.p. (ISBN 0-446-63426-3, 63-426). Paperback Lib.

Black Incense: Tales of Monte Carlo. Alice Muriel Livingston Williamson. LC 26-10803. George H. Doran Company.

Black Invader. Rebecca Stratton. 192p. 1982. pap. 1.50 (ISBN 0-373-02452-5). Harlequin Bks.

Black Is a Man. Harry Roskolenko. LC 54-5785. 1954. Padell.

Black Is Back. Joseph Nazel. (Black series). 1974. (pbk.) 0.95 (ISBN 0-523-00342-0). Pinnacle Books.

Black Is My Truelove's Hair. Elizabeth Madox Roberts. LC 76-51675. (Recovered Fiction by American Women). 1977. 22.00 (ISBN 0-405-10053-1). Arno Press.

Black Is My Truelove's Hair. Elizabeth Madox Roberts. LC 38-27966. 1938. The Viking Press.

Black Is the Color. John Brunner. (Orig.). 1969. pap. 0.60 o.p. (X1955). Pyramid Pubns.

Black Is the Colour of My True-Love's Heart: By Ellis Peters. Edith Pargeter. LC 67-211338. 1967. bds., 4.50. Morrow.

Black Is the Fashion for Dying. Jonathan Latimer. LC 58-989347. 1959. Random House.

Black Is White. George Barr McCutcheon. LC 14-527119. 1914. Dodd, Mead and Company.

Black Italian: A Crime Club Special Featuring Eve Gill. Selwyn Jepson. LC 54-10771. 1954. Published for the Crime Club by Doubleday.

Black Ivory. Polan Banks. LC 26-4583. 1926. Harper & Brothers.

Black Ivory. Saliee O'Brien. (Orig.). 1980. pap. 2.50 (ISBN 0-553-13021-8). Bantam.

Black Ivory: Being the Story of Ralph Rudd, His Early Adventures, Perils and Misfortunes on Land and Sea... Norman Collins. LC 48-8432. 1948. Duell, Sloan and Pearce.

Black Jack. Max Brand. 1970. 3.95 o.p. Dodd.

Black Jack. Max Brand. 1976. pap. 1.25 o.p. WSP.

Black Jack. Frederick Faust. LC 77-123498. 1970. 3.95. Dodd, Mead.

Black Jack Davy. John Milton Oskison. LC 26-15737. 1926. D. Appleton and Company.

Black Jade. Angeline Taylor. LC 47-121210. 1947. R. M. McBride.

Black John of Halfaday Creek. James Beardsley Hendryx. LC 39-20722. 1939. Doubleday, Doran & Company, Inc.

Black John of Halfaday Creek. James Beardsley Hendryx. LC 40-325602. 1940. The Sun Dial Press.

Black Joker. Isabel Egenton Ostrander. LC 25-23365. 1925. R. M. McBride & Company.

Black Key. Milton Scott Michel. LC 47-23585. (Hand-book mysteries. No. 61). 1947. Quinn Publishing Company, Inc.

Black Key: An Alexander Cornell Mystery. Milton Scott Michel. LC 47-17948. 1946. Mystery House.

Black Knight. Ethel May Dell. LC 27-2811. G. P. Putnam's Sons.

Black Knight. Lamarr McMann. 1972. pap. 1.95 o.s.i. (TCP-2129). Olympia.

Black Knight. Cecily Ullmann Sidgwick & Garstin, Crosbie, Joint Author. LC 20-14287. 1920. H. Holt and Company.

Black Lace. W H Griffey. LC 52-7486. Vantage Press.

Black Lady Luck. Joan Boren et al. (Orig.). 1979. pap. 1.95 (ISBN 0-87067-667-9, BH667). Holloway.

Black Lamb. Anna Robeson Brown Burr. LC 6-19369. 1896. J. B. Lippincott Company.

Black Land, White Land: A Reggie Fortune Novel. Henry Christopher Bailey. LC 37-3656. 1937. Pub. for the Crime Club, Inc., by Doubleday, Doran & Co., Inc.

Black Land, White Land: A Regie Fortune Novel. Henry Christopher Bailey. LC 38-9515. 1938. The Sun Dial Press, Inc.

Black Lazarus. Ben Frank Stoltzfus. Orig. Title: Lazarus. 1972. 5.95 o.s.i. (ISBN 0-87806-018-9); pap. 2.45 o.s.i. (ISBN 0-87806-019-7). Winter Hse.

Black Leather Barbarians. Pat Stadley. LC 60-7162. Bobbs-Merrill)

Black Leather Murders: By Douglas Rutherford. James Douglas Rutherford McConnell. LC 66-240759. 1966. bds., 3.50. Walker.

Black Leaves. Kenneth Rosen. LC 80-50370. (Illus.). 96p. 1980. pap. 3.00 (ISBN 0-89823-018-7). New Rivers Pr.

Black Letters: Love Letters from a Black Soldier in Viet Nam. Rita Southall & Saggittarus. LC 72-87414. 1972. 4.50. Nuclassics and Science Pub. Co.

Black Light. Drew Bonner. 1978. 6.95 (ISBN 0-533-02886-8). Vantage.

Black Light. rev. ed. Galway Kinnell. LC 80-16114. 128p. 1980. pap. 6.00 (ISBN 0-86547-016-2). N Point Pr.

Black Light. Talbot Mundy. LC 30-31029. The Bobbs-Merrill Company.

Black Light. Gertrude M. Robins Reynolds. LC 38-3724. 1938. Pub. for the Crime Club, Inc., by Doubleday, Doran & Company, Inc.

Black Light. Ed. by Talmadge Spratt. LC 72-82858. (Illus.). 64p. 1973. 3.00 o.p. (ISBN 0-87529-303-4). Hallmark.

Black Light: A Novel. Galway Kinnell. LC 66-10214. 3.95. Houghton.

Black Light: A Novel. Galway Kinnell. LC 80-16114. 1980. 5.00 (ISBN 0-86547-016-2). North Point Press.

Black Lion. P. A Fanthorpe & R. Lionel Fanthorpe. LC 80-19214. 1980. 8.95 (ISBN 0-906901-01-4). R. Reginald, Borgo Press.

Black Lion Inn. Alfred Henry Lewis. LC 3-122873. 1903. R. H. Russell.

Black List. Gifford Paul Cheshire. 1969. Repr. pap. 0.60 o.p. (0502-06053-060). Curtis.

Black List, Section H. Francis Stuart. LC 72-156788. (Crosscurrents-Modern Fiction Ser.). 1971. 10.00x o.p. (ISBN 0-8093-0527-5). S Ill U Pr.

Black List, Section H. With a Pref. and Postscript by Harry T. Moore. Francis Stuart. LC 72-156788. (Crosscurrents/modern fiction). 1971. 10.00 (ISBN 0-8093-0527-5). Southern Illinois University Press.

Black List. 1st American Ed. Ian Brook. LC 62-18249. 1962. Putnam.

Black List. 1st Ed. Gifford Paul Cheshire. LC 62-7612. (Double D western). 1962. Doubleday.

Black Look. Michael Butterworth. LC 76-180064. (Crime Club Ser). 168p. 1972. 4.95 o.p. (ISBN 0-385-02401-0). Doubleday.

Black Love. Stuart Jason. 1978. pap. 1.50 (ISBN 0-532-15200-X). Woodhill.

Black Love. Stuart Jason. 1976. pap. 1.50 o.p. (532-15200-150). Manor Bks.

Black Lust. Jean De Villiot & Eckar, Lawrence, Tr. LC 31-15556. Priv. Print. by the Panurge Press.

Black Lyon. Jude Deveraux, pseud. 1980. pap. 2.95 (ISBN 0-380-75911-X, 79749). Avon.

Black Macho & the Myth of the Superwoman. Michele Wallace. 1980. pap. 3.50 (ISBN 0-446-36234-4). Warner Bks.

Black Mafia. Peter Rabe. (Fawcett world library). 1974. (pbk.) 0.95. Fawcett.

Black Mafia. Arnett D Waters. 1973. 4.95 (ISBN 0-533-00630-9). Vantage.

Black Magic. R. T Larkin. 1974. (pbk.) 1.25. Dell.

Black Magic. Whitley Strieber. LC 81-16915. 1982. 13.50 (ISBN 0-688-01021-0). Morrow.

Black Magic Omnibus. Peter Haining. LC 75-28511. (Illus.). 1976. 10.95 (ISBN 0-8008-0809-6). Taplinger Pub. Co.

Black Magician: Another Adventure of "Secret Service Smith". Reginald Thomas Maitland Scott. LC 25-13519. E. P. Dutton & Company.

Black Man - White Witch. B. A. Molbert. 3.95 o.p. (ISBN 0-8062-0620-9). Carlton.

Black Mantle: A Novel. Fulton Colville. LC 11-319661. 1911. 1.50. The Cosmopolitan Press.

Black Marble. Joseph Wambaugh. LC 77-14262. 9.95 (ISBN 0-440-00523-X). Delacorte Press.

Black Marble. Joseph Wambaugh. (Dell book). 1979. 2.50 (ISBN 0-440-10647-8). Dell Pub. Co.

Black Market Soldiers. Anthony J. Levatino. (Orig.). 1983. pap. 3.25 (ISBN 0-440-10968-X). Dell.

Black Marsden. Wilson Harris. 1972. 4.95 o.p. (ISBN 0-571-10104-6). Faber & Faber.

Black Marshal. Bill Burchardt, pseud. LC 80-2951. 1981. 10.95 (ISBN 0-385-17553-1). Doubleday.

Black Mask: Or, Bonnie Orielle's Lovers. Lydia Annie Jocelyn Smith. LC 7-2762. (On cover: Smith-Tyler library). E. I. Tyler.

Black Mass. Petr Nikolaevich Krasnov. Tr. by Vitall, Olga. LC 31-25268. Duffield & Green.

Black Master. Stuart Jason. 1970. pap. 0.95 o.p. (ISBN 0-447-75146-8). Lancer.

Black Master: From the Shadow's Private Annals. Maxwell Grant. LC 74-10040. (Illus.). 1974. (pbk.) 0.95 (ISBN 0-515-03478-9). Pyramid Books.

Black Mesa. Zane Grey. 1956. 2.50 o.p. (ISBN 0-448-05154-0). G&D.

Black Mesa. Zane Grey. (Keith Jennison Large Type Bks). 8.95 o.p. (ISBN 0-531-00164-4). Watts.

Black Mesa. 1st Ed. Zane Grey. LC 55-8044. 1955. Harper.

Black Midas. 2nd ed. Jan Carew. 184p. 1981. cancelled o.s.i. (ISBN 0-89410-124-2); pap. 5.00x o.s.i. (ISBN 0-89410-125-0). Three Continents.

Black Minute. James H Artzner. LC 80-70729. 12.95 (ISBN 0-938936-00-X). Daring Press.

Black Mirror. Ben Benson. LC 57-5847. 1957. M. S. Mill Co. and W. Morrow.

Black Mischief. Evelyn Waugh. 1946. Little, Brown.

Black Mischief. Evelyn Waugh. LC 77-88226. (Illus.). 1977. 8.95 (ISBN 0-316-92613-2). Little, Brown.

Black Mischief: By Evelyn Waugh. Evelyn Waugh. LC 32-251715. Farrar & Rinehart, Incorporated.

Black Money. Ross Macdonald. 1966. 4.95 o.p. Knopf.

Black Money: By Ross Macdonald. Kenneth Millar. LC 66-10031. 1966. bds., 3.95. Knopf.

Black Monk, and Other Stories. Anton Pavlovich Chekhov. LC 79-121527. (Short story index reprint series). 1970. Books for Libraries Press.

Black Monk: And Other Stories. Anton Pavlovich Chekhov. Tr. by Long, Robert Edward Crozier. 1915. Frederick A. Stokes Company.

Black Moon. Winston Graham. LC 73-18086. (Illus.). 1974. 7.95 (ISBN 0-385-00111-8). Doubleday.

Black Moon. Clark McMeekin. LC 45-6106. 1945. D. Appleton-Century Company Incorporated.

Black Moon. Clements Ripley. LC 33-153894. Harcourt, Brace and Company.

Black Moon: Novel of Cornwall, 1794-1795. Winston Graham. LC 79-10062. 1979. 18.95 (ISBN 0-8161-6680-3). G. K. Hall.

Black Moth. Georgette Heyer. LC 68-12443. 1968. Dutton.

Black Moth: A Romance of the Xviii Century. Georgette Heyer. LC 22-3020. 1921. Houghton Mifflin Company.

Black Motor Car. John Burland Harris-Burland. LC 5-9278. 1905. G. W. Dillingham Company.

Black Mountain. Alan Hillgarth. LC 34-331. 1933. A. A. Knopf.

Black Mountain: A Nero Wolfe Novel. Rex Stout. LC 54-11617. 1954. Viking Press.

Black Mountain: A Novel. Robert Leasure. LC 75-17600. 1975. 8.95. Putnam.

Black Mountain Breakdown. Lee Smith. LC 80-17993. 10.95 (ISBN 0-399-12531-0). Putnam.

Black Muscle. Laurence Blaine. (Orig.). 1976. pap. 1.50 (ISBN 0-87067-499-4, BH499). Holloway.

Black Narc. Jeffrey Feinman. (Orig.). 1977. pap. 1.50 (ISBN 0-532-15249-2). Woodhill.

Black Narcissus. Rumer Godden. (Modern library of the world's best books). 1947. Modern Library.

Black Narcissus. Rumer Godden. LC 39-16410. 1939. Little, Brown and Company.

Black Nazi. Willus J. Arnold. LC 81-20526. 1983. 15.95 (ISBN 0-87949-198-1). Ashley Books.

Black Night Murders: A Fleming Stone Detective Novel. Carolyn Wells. J. B. Lippincott Company.

Black Night of the Iron Sphere. E. E. Smith & Gordon Eklund. (Lord Tedric Ser.). 1979. pap. 4.95 (ISBN 0-89437-069-3). Baronet.

Black No More. George Samuel Schuylar. 1971. pap. 1.50 (ISBN 0-02-053650-X, Collier). Macmillan.

Black No More. George Samuel Schuyler. LC 75-76119. 1969. Repr. of 1931 ed. 12.00x o.p. (ISBN 0-8434-0020-X). McGrath.

Black No More: Being an Account of the Strange and Wonderful Workings of Science in the Land of the Free, A.D. 1933-1940. George Samuel Schuyler. LC 71-75555. 1969. Negro Universities Press.

Black No More: Being an Account of the Strange and Wonderful Workings of Science in the Land of the Free, A.D. 1933-1940. George Samuel Schuyler. LC 75-76119. 1969. McGrath Pub. Co.

Black No More: Being an Account of the Strange and Wonderful Workings of Science in the Land of the Free, A.D. 1933-1940. George Samuel Schuyler. LC 79-134515. (American Library). 1971. 1.50. Collier Books.

Black No More: Being an Account of the Strange and Wonderful Workings of Science in the Land of the Free, A. D. 1933-1940. George Samuel Schuyler. LC 31-217416. The Macaulay Company.

Black Noon. Winston Graham. (Illus.). 1977. 1.95 (ISBN 0-345-26004-X). Ballantine Books.

Black Obelisk. Translated from the German by Denver Lindley. 1st Ed. Erich Maria Remarque. LC 57-884080. 1957. Harcourt, Brace.

Black on Black: Baby Sister and Selected Writings. Chester B. Himes. LC 72-76169. 1973. 6.95 (ISBN 0-385-02526-2). Doubleday.

Black on the Rainbow. 1st Ed. Dorothy Lee Dickens. LC 52-9713. 1952. Pageant Press.

Black Opal. LC 47-31443. 1947.

Black Opal. Mary Gleed Tuttiett. LC 18-20480. 1918. D. Appleton and Company.

Black Orchid. Nicholas Meyer & Barry Jay Kaplan. LC 77-10185. (Illus.). 8.95 (ISBN 0-8037-0630-8). Dial Press.

Black Orchids. Rex Stout. LC 82-927. 1982. 13.95 (ISBN 0-8161-3289-5). G.K. Hall.

Black Orchids: A Nero Wolfe Double Mystery. Rex Stout. LC 42-11451. 1942. Farrar & Rinehart, Inc.

Black Orpheus. Jean Paul Sartre. pap. 2.50 o.p. Univ Place.

Black Orpheus: An Anthology of New African and Afro-American Stories. Ed. by Ulli Beier. Ed. by Ulli Beier. LC 65-16755. 1965. 5.95, 1.95 pap.,. McGraw.

Black-Out in Gretley: A Story of and for Wartime. John Boynton Priestley. LC 43-454. 1942. Harper & Brothers.

Black Oxen. Gertrude Franklin Horn Atherton. LC 28-3136. Boni and Liveright.

Black Palace. Matthew Andrews. (O.s.i.). 1972. 5.95 o.s.i. (ISBN 0-440-00689-9, 0689-6). Delacorte.

Black Palace: A Novel. Matthew Andrews. LC 72-172796. (Illus.). 1972. 5.95. Delacorte Press.

Black Paradise: A Novel. Florenz H Hough. LC 52-13080. 1953. Dorrance.

Black Parrot: A Tale of the Golden Chersonese. Harry Hervey. LC 23-12965. 1923. The Century Co.

Black Path of Fear. Cornell George Hopley-Woolrich. LC 44-31051. 1944. Pub. for the Crime Club by Doubleday, Doran and Co., Inc.

Black Path of Fear. Cornell George Hopley-Woolrich. LC 47-20915. (On cover: New Avon library. 106). 1946.

Black Path of Fear. Cornell Woolrich, pseud. 160p. 1982. pap. 2.25 (ISBN 0-345-30488-8). Ballantine.

Black Paw. Constance Little & Little, Gwenyth. LC 41-2434. 1941. Pub. for the Crime Club by Doubleday, Doran and Co., Inc.

Black Pawl. Ben Ames Williams. LC 22-208802. E. P. Dutton & Company.

Black Pawn. Bruce Norman. LC 27-24669. 1927. L. MacVeagh, The Dial Press.

Black Pearl. Cynthia Harrod-Eagles. (Morland Dynasty Ser.: No. 5). (Orig.). 1983. pap. 3.95 (ISBN 0-440-10728-8). Dell.

Black Pearl. Scott O'Dell. 1967. Houghton Mifflin.

Black Pearl. Nancy Mann Waddell Wilson Woodrow Woodrow. LC 12-21277. 1912. D. Appleton and Company.

Black Pearl Murders. Madeleine Sharpe Buchanan. LC 31-6860. 1930. A. C. McClurg & Co.

Black Pearl of Passion. Anna Chandler Lindholm. LC 36-10013. The Galleon Press.

Black Pearl: Or Love Metamorphosis. Mildred A. McKee. (Illus.). 1982. 10.00 (ISBN 0-533-05131-2). Vantage.

Black Pearls. Robert William Alexander. LC 26-14218. 1926. D. Appleton and Company.

Black Pearls. Robert Kerr. LC 74-23423. 1975. 7.95 (ISBN 0-8128-1762-1). Stein and Day.

Black Pearls. Robert Kerr. 1976. 1.50 (ISBN 0-449-23036-8). Fawcett Crest.

Black Persian. Karl Friedrich May. 1979. 12.95 (ISBN 0-8264-0071-X). Continuum.

Black Persian: A Novel. Karl Friedrich May. LC 79-9382. (Collected works of Karl May; ser. 3, v. 5). (Continuum book). 1979. 12.95 (ISBN 0-8164-9363-4). Seabury Press.

Black Phallus & Phantasy. Charles Tucker. pap. 2.45 o.p. (4029). Cameo.

Black Phantom, or Woman's Endurance: A Narrative Connected with the Early History of Canada and the American Revolution. Charles Shrimpton. LC 8-7326. 1867. Crowen & Company.

Black Piano. Constance Little & Gwenyth Little. LC 48-556481. 1948. Pub. for the Crime Club by Doubleday.

Black Pigeon. Anne Austin. LC 29-8835. Greenberg.

Black Pirate. MacBurney Gates & Thomas, Elton. LC 26-14219. 1926. Grosset & Dunlap.

Black Pirate. Robert Tralins. (Orig.). 1970. pap. 0.95 o.p. (65-324). Paperback Lib.

Black Plumas. Margery Allingham. LC 40-27746. 1940. Pub. for the Crime Club by Doubleday, Doran & Co., Inc.

Black-Plumed Riflemen. A Tale of the Revolution. Newton Mallory Curtis. 1849. L. Willard.

Black Plumes. Margery Allingham. LC 76-2361. 1976. 6.95 (ISBN 0-89190-191-4). American Reprint Co.

Black Poodle: And Other Tales. Thomas Anstey Guthrie. (On cover: Lovell's library. no. 453). 1884. J. W. Lovell Company.

Black Pow-Wow. Ted Joans. 1969. pap. 1.95 o.p. (ISBN 0-8090-0093-8, AmCen). Hill & Wang.

Black Powder Empire. 1st Ed. Rutherford George Montgomery. LC 55-5536. Little, Brown.

Black Prince. Iris Murdoch. LC 72-91828. 1973. 7.95 (ISBN 0-670-17286-3). Viking Press.

Black Prince. Iris Murdoch. 1974. (pbk.) 1.75. Warner Paperback Library.

Black Prince, and Other Stories. Shirley Ann Grau. LC 55-5037. 1955. Knopf.

Black Prophet. William Carleton. 1972. Repr. of 1899 ed. 10.00x o.p. (Pub. by Irish Academic Pr Ireland). Biblio Dist.

Black Prophet. Joseph Nazel. (Orig.). 1976. pap. 1.50 (ISBN 0-87067-498-6, BH498). Holloway.

Black Prophet. Guy Fitch Phelps. LC 16-97790. 1916. 1.35. The Standard Publishing Company.

Black Prophet. 14th large ed. Guy Fitch Phelps. LC 38-10964. The Standard Publishing Company.

Black Prophet: A Tale of the Irish Famine. William Carleton. LC 79-4185. (Ireland, from the Act of Union, 1800, to the Death of Parnell, 1891). 1979. 42.00 (ISBN 0-8240-3490-2). Garland Pub.

Black Queen Stories. Barry Callaghan. 224p. 1982. 13.95 (ISBN 0-86538-017-1); pap. 7.95 (ISBN 0-86538-018-X). Ontario Rev NJ.

Black Rage. Butch Holmes. (Orig.). 1975. pap. 1.95 (ISBN 0-87067-650-4, BH053). Holloway.

Black Rain. Masuji Ibuse. Tr. by John Bester from Japanese. LC 69-16372. 1980. pap. 5.25 (ISBN 0-87011-364-X). Kodansha.

Black Rain: A Novel. Masuji Ibuse. LC 69-16372. 1969. 6.95 (ISBN 0-87011-077-2). Kodansha International Ltd.

Black Rain: A Novel. Georges Simenon & Sainsbury, Geoffrey, Tr. 1947. Reynal & Hitchcock.

Black Rainbow. Barbara Michaels. LC 82-7408. 13.95 (ISBN 0-86553-053-X). Congdon & Weed: Distributed by St. Martin's Press.

Black Ram of Dinwoody Creek: A Story of Rocky Mountain Bighorn Sheep. Nolie Mumey. LC 52-105. 1951. Range Press.

Black Ranger. Pete Jones. LC 40-29467. Phoenix Press.

Black Rapture of Love. Flora Caputo. 2.95 o.p. Vantage.

Black Renegade. Dana Faralla. LC 54-6103. 1954. Lippincott.

Black Renegades. James H. Readus. (Orig.). 1976. pap. 1.95 (ISBN 0-87067-672-5, BH672). Holloway.

Black Renegades. James-Howard Readus. 1976. (pbk.) 1.50 (ISBN 0-87067-490-0). Holloway House Publishing Corp.

Black Rhapsody. Translated from the Swedish by Margery Osberg. 1st American Ed. Gunnar Helander. LC 56-691513. 1956. Harper.

Black Rider. Burt Arthur, pseud. 1978. pap. 1.25 o.s.i. (ISBN 0-505-51258-0). Tower Bks.

Black Rider. Herbert Shappiro. LC 41-15455. 1941. Arcadia House.

Black Rider: A Mustang Marshall Western. Herbert Arthur, pseud. LC 41-15455. 1941. Arcadia House.

Black Riders. Al Cody, pseud. (Avalon Books). 4.95. Thomas Bouregy.

Black Rifle: A Novel of Perry County, Pa. Roy F Chandler. LC 76-3164. (Illus.). 1976. Bacon and Freeman Publishers.

Black Riumvirate: A Novel of Haiti. Benjamin H Levin. LC 74-186393. 1972. 6.95 (ISBN 0-8065-0268-1). Citadel Press.

Black River. Carleton Beals. LC 34-1683. 1934. J. B. Lippincott Company.

Black River Ranch. Archie Joscelyn. LC 48-3953. 1948. Phoenix Press.

Black Robe. Maurice Kenny. LC 81-85171. (Illus.). 1982. 14.95 (ISBN 0-940280-05-1); pap. 8.95 (ISBN 0-940280-06-X). No Country Comm Coll.

Black Robe. Guy Eugene Morton. LC 27-9860. 1927. Minton, Balch & Company.

Black Rock: A Tale of the Selkirks. Charles William Gordon. LC 41-40507. (On cover: Cornell series). A. L. Burt.

Black Rock: A Tale of the Selkirks. Charles William Gordon. (On cover: Alliance library. no. 18). 1900. Street & Smith.

Black Rock: A Tale of the Selkirks. Charles William Gordon. LC 6631. 1900. Fleming H. Revell Company.

Black Rock: A Tale of the Selkirks. Charles William Gordon. The Mershon Company.

Black Rock: A Tale of the Selkirks. Charles William Gordon. LC 32-335858. 1901. Fleming H. Revell Company.

Black Rock: A Tale of the Selkirks by Ralph Connor Pseud. Charles William Gordon. LC 8-31161. Fleming H. Revell Company.

Black Rococo. Ron Kurz. LC 75-16278. 1975. (ISBN 0-87131-196-8). M. Evans.

Black Room. Christopher Short. LC 66-8032. 1966. bds., 3.95. Dodd.

Black Room. Colin Wilson. 1975. pap. 1.50 o.p. (ISBN 0-515-03887-3). BJ Pub Group.

Black Rose. Thomas Bertram Costain. LC 48-318843. 1947. Sun Dial Pres.

Black Rose. Thomas Bertram Costain. LC 45-7847. 1945. Doubleday, Doran & Co., Inc.

Black Rose. Thomas Bertram Costain. LC 46-84623. 1946. Doubleday & Company, Inc.

Black Rose. Thomas Bertram Costain. LC 46-59883. 1946. Doubleday & Company, Inc., Garden City Publishing Co., Inc.

Black Rose: Illustrated by Herbert Ryman. 1st Illustrated Ed. Thomas Bertram Costain. LC 53-11082. 1953. Doubleday.

Black Rose Murder. Paul McGuire. LC 32-2659. 1932. Brentano's.

Black Roses. Francis Brett Young. LC 29-192522. 1929. Harper & Brothers.

Black Rustle. Constance Little & Gwenyth Little. LC 43-9807. 1943. Pub. for the Crime Club, Doubleday, Doran & Co., Inc.

Black Sabbat. J. B. Herman. 1979. pap. 2.25 (ISBN 0-89041-251-0, 3251). Major Bks.

Black Sabbath. Robert R Wilkens. 1974. (pbk.) 4.95 (ISBN 0-533-01116-7). Vantage Press.

Black Sadie. Thomas Bowyer Campbell. LC 28-24063. 1928. Houghton Mifflin Company.

Black Saga. Graham Montague Jeffries. LC 47-29234. 1947. Hutchinson.

Black Sage. Llewellyn Perry Holmes. LC 50-8311. (Double D western). 1950. Doubleday.

Black Sail: A Novel. Florence Mary Bennett Anderson. LC 48-5407. 1948. Crown Publishers.

Black Samurai. Marc Olden. (Black samurai,#1). 1974. (pbk.) 0.95. New American Library.

Black Sand & Gold. Ella Martinsen. LC 56-6862. (Cloth ed. 6.50 o.p.). (Illus.). 344p. 1974. pap. 6.95 (ISBN 0-8323-0189-2). Binford.

Black Sand, White Sand. Jean S. MacLeod. (Harlequin Romances Ser.). 192p. 1981. pap. 1.25 (ISBN 0-373-02414-2). Harlequin Bks.

Black Satin Jungle. Bart Frame. Orig. Title: Indiscretions of a French Model. 1967. pap. 0.50 o.p. (50-366). Manor Bks.

Black Sea Caper. Hugh McDonald & Robin Moore. LC 78-74945. 1978. pap. 2.25 o.s.i. (ISBN 0-89516-095-1). Condor Pub Co.

Black Secretary's Horror. Mary B. Bush. 1981. 8.95 (ISBN 0-533-04698-X). Vantage.

Black Seven. Carol Kendall. LC 46-15770. 1946. Harper & Brothers.

Black Shack Alley: La Rue Cases-Negres. Joseph Zobel. LC 78-13852. (Illus.). 14.00 (ISBN 0-914478-67-2). Three Continents Press.

Black Shadow. Frederick Annesley Michael Webster. LC 23-182169. 1923. Moffat, Yard & Company.

Black Sheep. Ruby Mildred Ayers. 1973. pap. 0.75 o.p. (345-26504-1-075). Beagle Bks.

Black Sheep. Honore de Balzac. Tr. by Donald Adamson. (Classics Ser.). 352p. 1976. pap. 4.95 (ISBN 0-14-044237-5). Penguin.

Black Sheep. Laura A. Bowser. 1964. 4.00 o.p. (ISBN 0-682-42085-9). Exposition.

Black Sheep. William Fitzgerald Jenkins. J. Messner, Inc.

Black Sheep. Evelyn La Selle. LC 7-13846. 1895. Edwards & Broughton.

Black Sheep. Jessie Payne. LC 30-10467. 1930. Macrae Smith Company.

Black Sheep. Joseph William Sharts. LC 9-244483. 1909. Duffield & Company.

Black Sheep. Edmund Hodgson Yates. (globe library of standard fiction, no. 1). 1877. Globe Publishing Company.

Black Sheep, and Other Fables. Augusto Monterroso. LC 70-144283. (Illus.). 1971. 3.95. Doubleday.

Black Sheep Chapel. Margaret Elsie Crowther Baillie-Saunders. LC 19-8073. George H. Doran Company.

Black Sheep: La Rabouilleuse) Honore De Balzac. LC 70-22484. (Penguin classics). 1970 (ISBN 0-14-044237-5). Penguin.

Black Sheep, Run. Bart Spicer. LC 51-13636. 1951. Dodd, Mead.

Black Sheep, White Lamb. Dorothy Salisbury Davis. LC 63-9462. 1963. Scribner.

Black Sheep. 1st Ed. Georgette Heyer. LC 67-11372. 1967. 4.95. Dutton.

Black Shilling: A Tale of Boston Towns. Amelia Edith Huddleston Barr. LC 3-24301. 1903. Dodd, Mead & Company.

Black Ship. Paul Mandel & Sheila Mandel. LC 67-12731. 1969. 5.95. Random House.

Black Ships. R. S Thomas. LC 27-5016. Brentano's.

Black Short Story Anthology. Ed. by Woodie King. LC 72-77398. (Signet book). 1972. 1.95. New American Library.

Black Short Story Anthology. Ed. by Woodie King. LC 72-6773. 1972. 12.50 (ISBN 0-231-03711-2). Columbia University Press.

Black Shrike. Alistair MacLean. 1978. pap. 2.50 (ISBN 0-449-14199-3, GM). Fawcett.

Black Shrike: By Ian Stuart Pseud. Alistair MacLean. LC 61-13361. 1961. Scribner.

Black Shrink. Phyllis James. (Orig.). 1975. pap. 1.50 (ISBN 0-87067-481-1, BH481). Holloway.

Black Shrink. James, Phyllis. 1975. (pbk.) 1.50 (ISBN 0-87067-481-1). Holloway House.

Black Shrouds. Constance Little & Little, Gwenyth. LC 41-20726. 1941. Pub. for the Crime Club by Doubleday, Doran & Company, Inc.

Black Sister. Vance Donovan. (Orig.). 1970. pap. 0.95 o.p. (ISBN 0-446-65429-9, 65-429). Paperback Lib.

Black Sister. Dagmar Ingeborg Jansson Edqvist. LC 63-12963. 1963. Published for the Crime Club by Doubleday.

Black Smith. Constance Little & Gwenyth Little. LC 50-10871. 1950. Published for the Crime Club by Doubleday.

Black Snow. Mikhail Bulgakov. (O.S.I.). 1968. 4.50 o.s.i. (09398). S&S.

Black Snow: A Theatrical Novel, by Mikhail Bulgakov. Tr. from Russian by Michael Glenny. Mikhail. Afanas'Evich Bulgakov. LC 68-19939. 1968. 4.50. S.&S.

Black Soil. Josephine Donovan. LC 30-188667. The Stratford Company.

Black Sombrero. William Colt MacDonald. LC 40-144252. 1940. Doubleday, Doran & Company, Inc.

Black Son: A Novel of the South. F. Edward Clay. 1977. 6.95 o.p. (ISBN 0-533-02912-0). Vantage.

Black Sorceress. A Tale of the Peassants' War. Alfred Guezenec. Tr. by H., A. D. LC 7-143. 1883. Rand, McNally & Co.

Black Spaniel, and Other Stories. Robert Smythe Hichens. LC 5-35301. 1905. F. A. Stokes Company.

Black Sparta: Greek Stories. Naomi Haldane Mitchison. LC 28-15627. Harcourt, Brace and Company.

Black Spectacles. John Dickson Carr. 1981. 18.95x (Pub. by Remploy England). State Mutual Bk.

Black Spice. Davenport Steward. LC 59-7795. 1959. Dutton.

Black Spider. Jeremias Gotthelf. Tr. by H. M. Waidson. 1980. pap. 5.95 (ISBN 0-7145-0126-3). Riverrun NY.

Black Spiders. John Creasey. 1975. (pbk.) 0.95. Popular Library.

Black Spirits & White: A Book of Ghost Stories. Ralph Adams Cram. LC 70-167445. (Short story index reprint series). 1971. (ISBN 0-8369-3971-9). Books for Libraries Press.

Black Spirits & White: A Book of Ghost Stories. Ralph Adams Cram. LC 6-30871. (Carnation series). 1895. Stone & Kimball.

Black Spirits and White. A Novel. Frances Eleanor Ternan Trollope. LC 37-327904. 1877. D. Appleton and Company.

Black Spot. Kenneth Robeson. (Doc Savage, no. 76). 1974. (pbk.) 0.75. Bantam Books.

Black Spring. Henry Miller. 1964. 5.00 o.p. (GP293). Grove.

Black Spring. Henry Miller. 1963. pap. 1.25 o.p. (Z1076Z, Zebra). Grove.

Black Spring: A Novel of Our Changing Times. Frederick William Oswad. LC 59-7893. 1959.

Black Stage. Lucy Beatrice Malleson. LC 47-298. 1946. A. S. Barnes and Company.

Black Stallion Mesa. Donald B. Hobart. (Orig.). 1973. pap. 0.60 o.p. (06139). Curtis.

Black Stallion Returns: Movie Storybook. Walter Farley. LC 82-3861. 1982. 9.95 (ISBN 0-394-85412-8). Random House.

Black Stamp. Will Scott. LC 26-6737. Macrae Smith Company.

Black Star. Lin Carter. 1973. (pbk) 0.95. Dell.

Black Star. Morton Cooper. LC 69-12360. 1969. 5.95. Bernard Geis Associates.

Black Star. Johnston McCulley. Repr. lib. bdg. 14.65x (ISBN 0-89190-995-8). Am Repr-Rivercity Pr.

Black Star: A Detective Story. Johnston McCulley. LC 22-63146. 1921. Chelsea House.

Black Star Passes. 1st Ed. John Wood Campbell. LC 53-126731. (FP science fiction). 1953. Fantasy Press.

Black Starlet. Bobbye B. Vance. (Orig.). 1975. pap. 1.50 (ISBN 0-87067-480-3, BH480). Holloway.

Black Star's Campaign. Johnston McCulley. Repr. lib. bdg. 14.65x (ISBN 0-89190-996-6). Am Repr-Rivercity Pr.

Black Star's Return. Johnston McCulley. Repr. lib. bdg. 14.40x (ISBN 0-89190-997-4). Am Repr-Rivercity Pr.

Black Steve: Or The Strange Warning. Martha Finley. LC 6-41222. Presbyterian Publication Committee.

Black Stocking. Constance Little & Gwenyth Little. LC 46-6292. 1946. Pub. for the Crime Club by Doubleday & Company, Inc.

Black Stone. George Fort Gibbs. LC 19-37013. 1919. D. Appleton and Company.

Black Stream. Nathalie Sedgwick Colby. LC 27-18964. Harcourt, Brace and Company.

Black Streets of Oakland. Kelly Eagle. 1.75 (ISBN 0-87067-520-6). Holloway House.

Black Sun. Edward Abbey. LC 80-27953. 1981. 5.95 (ISBN 0-88496-192-3). Capra Press.

Black Sun. Aben Kandel. LC 29-17390. 1929. Harper & Brothers.

Black Sun. Kyle Onstott & Lance Horner. 1978. pap. 2.50 (ISBN 0-449-14034-2, GM). Fawcett.

Black Sun. James Tarabilda. 1980. pap. 2.25 (ISBN 0-8439-0767-3). Nordon Pubns.

Black Sun: A Novel. Edward Abbey. LC 74-139613. 1971. 5.95 (ISBN 0-671-20896-9). Simon and Schuster.

Black Sun: A Novel. 1st Ed. Hugh Barnett Cave. LC 60-121721. 1960. Doubleday.

Black Sun & Other Stories. K. A. Abbas. 1963. pap. 1.50 o.p. (ISBN 0-88253-112-3). InterCulture.

Black Sunday. Thomas Harris. LC 74-16601. 1975. 7.95 (ISBN 0-399-11443-2). Putnam.

Black Sunlight. Dambudzo Marechera. LC 81-107346. (African Writers Series; 237). 1980. 8.50 (ISBN 0-435-90237-7). Heinemann.

Black Swan. Thomas Mann. LC 79-24136. (Harvest/HBJ book). 1980. 2.95 (ISBN 0-15-611865-3). Harcourt Brace Jovanovich.

Black Swan. Rachel Cosgrove Payes. (Berkley Large-Type Gothic). 1975. (pbk.) 0.95 (ISBN 0-425-03005-9). Berkley Pub. Co.

Black Swan. Rafael Sabatini. LC 32-13055. 1932. Houghton Mifflin Company.

Black Swan. Anne West Strawbridge. LC 35-16317. 1935. Coward-McCann.

Black Swan. Day Taylor, pseud. (Dell Book). 1978. 2.50 (ISBN 0-440-10611-7). Dell Pub. Co.

Black Swan: Translated from the German by Willard R. Trask. 1st American Ed. Thomas Mann. LC 54-719751. 1954. Knopf.

Black Symbol. Annabell Johnson & Edgar Johnson. LC 58-9780. 1959. Harper.

Black Symbol: By Annabel and Edgar Johnson. Annabel Johnson & Edgar Johnson. (Trophy). 1960. pap., 1.25. Harper.

Black Tarn. Philip Whitwell Wilson. LC 45-5130. 1945. Farrar & Rinehart, Inc.

Black Taurus & the Gemini. Robert MacLeod, pseud. (Orig.). 1970. pap. price not set o.p. (GM). Fawcett World.

Black Tent, and Other Stories. Robin Maugham. LC 74-162307. 1973. 2.25 (ISBN 0-491-01291-8). W. H. Allen.

Black Tents of Arabia. Carl Raswan. 240p. 1971. 6.95 (ISBN 0-374-11416-1). FS&G.

Black Terrace. Kathrya Kendall. LC 55-7935. 1955. Arcadia House.

Black Terror: A Romance of Russia. John Kirkwood Leys. LC 3043. 1900. L. C. Page & Company.

Black, the Gray, and the Gold. Norman Robert Ford. LC 61-9508. 1961. Doubleday.

Black Thorn Blooms. Cleon Marquis. LC 44-6379. 1944. B. Humphries, Inc.

Black Thumb. Constance Little & Gwenyth Little. LC 42-219599. 1942. Published for the Crime Club by Doubleday, Doran and Co., Inc.

Black Thunder. Arna Wendell Bontemps. LC 68-31383. 1968. 4.95. Beacon Press.

Black Thunder. Bertha Muzzy Sinclair. LC 47-20102. 1947. Triangle Books, the Blakiston Company.

Black Tickets. Jayne Anne Phillips. LC 79-12353. 1979. 8.95 (ISBN 0-440-00708-9) (ISBN 0-440-50777-4). Delacorte Press/S. Lawrence.

Black Tide. Hammond Innes. LC 82-45498. (Illus.). 384p. 1983. 16.95 (ISBN 0-385-18331-3). Doubleday.

Black Tiger: A Novel. Frederick Whittaker. (On cover: The popular series, no. 26). 1892. R. Bonner's Sons.

Black Tiger at Le Mans: By Patrick O'Connor Pseud. Leonard Patrick O'Connor Wibberley. LC 58-677687. 1958. Washburn.

Black to Nature. Octavus Roy Cohen. LC 35-3037. 1935. D. Appleton Century Company, Incorporated.

Black Tolts. William MacLeod Raine. LC 32-12124. 1932. Houghton Mifflin Company.

Black Top. 1st Ed. Bertha B. Moore McCurry. LC 56-14240. 1956. W. B. Eerdmans Pub. Co.

Black Tor. A Tale of the Reign of James I. George Manville Fenn. LC 6-39260. 1896. J. B. Lippincott Company.

Black Torrent. Leopold Buczkowski. LC 78-107998. 1969. 5.95. M.I.T. Press.

Black Tortoise, Being the Strange Story of Old Frick's Diamond. Christian Sparre & Braekstad, Gertrude Hughes, Tr. 1901. Doubleday, Page & Co.

Black Tower. P. D James. LC 75-15120. 6.95 (ISBN 0-684-14263-5). Scribner.

Black Tower. P. D James. 1976. 1.75 (ISBN 0-684-14263-5). Popular Library.

Black Tower. P. D James. LC 81-12421. 1981. 14.95 (ISBN 0-8161-6789-3). G.K. Hall.

Black Trail. Edith Macomber Mrs Hall. LC 12-453. 1911. Graves Publishing Company.

Black Treasure. Drawings by Lester Peterson. 1st Ed. Vinson Brown. LC 51-9319. 1951. Little, Brown.

Black Tulip. Alexandre Dumas. LC 4-22080. 1891. Little, Brown and Company.

Black Tulip. Alexandre Dumas. LC 6-42110. (On cover: Globe library, v. 1, no. 171). 1892. Rand, McNally & Company.

Black Tulip. Alexandre Dumas. LC 4-22089. 1893. Little, Brown, & Company.

Black Tulip. Alexandre Dumas. LC 6-42112. (Half-title: The romances of Alexandre Dumas. Illustrated library ed. vol. xxii). 1893. Little, Brown and Company.

Black Tulip. Alexandre Dumas. Tr. by O'Connor, A. J. Uzanne, Louis Octave. LC 15-6328. (Half-title: The French classical romances. v. 5). P. F. Collier & Son.

Black Tulip. Alexandre Dumas. Tr. by Frost, Mary D. LC 2-20826. 1902. T. Y. Crowell & Co.

Black Tulip. Alexandre Dumas. (The companion classics). W. J. Black, Inc.

Black Tulip. A Novel. Alexandre Dumas. LC 6-42109. (American series. no. 306). 1893. M. J. Ivers & Co.

Black Tulip. A Novel. Alexandre Dumas. LC 6-42111. (On cover: Seaside library. Pocket ed. no. 2111). G. Munro's Sons.

Black Tulip: A Romance. Alexandre Dumas. LC 26-23569. Rand, McNally & Company.

Black Tulip, a Romance. Translated by S. J. Adair Fitz-Gerald, with an Introd. by Ben Ray Redman. Alexandre Dumas. 1951. Printed for the Members of the Limited Editions Club by J. Enschede, Haarlem.

Black Tulip: Translated from the French of Alexandre Dumas, Pere. Alexandre Dumas. Tr. by O'Connor, A. J. LC 2-23744. (Half-title: A century of French romance. Parisian ed. vol. v.). D. Appleton & Co.

Black Turret. Patrick Wynnton. LC 25-14945. The Bobbs-Merrill Company.

Black Tux & Other Stories. Barbara Tymbios. 4.50 o.p. Vantage.

Black Ulysses. Jef Geeraerts. LC 78-58563. 1978. 12.95 (ISBN 0-670-17278-2). Viking Press.

Black Ulysses. Daniel Panger. LC 82-3517. (Illus.). 1982. 8.95 (ISBN 0-8214-0680-9). Ohio University Press.

Black Uprising. Joseph Nazel. (Orig.). 1976. pap. 1.50 (ISBN 0-87067-812-4, BH812). Holloway.

Black Valley. Raymond Melbourne Weaver. LC 26-5385. 1926. The Viking Press.

Black Valley: A Romance of the Argentine. Gustavo Adolfo Martinez Zuviria. Tr. by Ernest Herman Hespelt. Hespelt, Mrs. Miriam Hasbrouck (Van Dyck) Joint Tr. LC 28-6168. 1928. Longmans, Green and Co.

Black Valley: A Romance of the Argentine see Novels by Hugo Wast.

Black Valley: A Tale, from the German of Viet ! Weber Pseud.... Georg Philipp Ludwig Leonhard Wachter. LC 8-33097. 1801. Printed by S. Snowden & Co., for J. V. Thomas.

Black Velvet. Martha Bruce. 1974. 6.95 (ISBN 0-533-00813-1). Vantage Press.

Black Velvet. Joseph Chadwick. (Orig.). 1970. pap. 0.95 o.p. (65-262). Paperback Lib.

Black Velvet Girl. C. E. Poverman. LC 76-23408. 1976. 8.95. (ISBN 0-87745-068-4) (ISBN 0-87745-069-2). University of Iowa Press.

Black Vendetta. Matt Gattzden. 1970. pap. 0.95 o.p. (B95-2000). Belmont-Tower.

Black Vengeance. George G. Gilman, pseud. (Edge Ser.: No. 10). 1974. pap. 1.95 (ISBN 0-523-41771-3). Pinnacle Bks.

Black Vengeance. George G Gilman. (Edge,#10). 1974. (pbk.) 0.95 (ISBN 0-523-00333-1). Pinnacle Books.

Black Venus. Jef Geeraerts. Tr. by Jon Swan. 1973. 7.95 o.p. (ISBN 0-8184-0180-X). Grove.

Black Venus: A Novel. Rhys Davies. LC 46-18385. 1946. Howell, Soskin.

Black Venus. A Tale of the Dark Continent. Adolphe Belot. Tr. by Cox, George D. LC 6-11687. T. B. Peterson & Brothers.

Black Venus. Sequel to "The Thirst for the Unknown". Adolphe Belot. (Seasde library, v. 53, no. 1078). G. Munro.

Black Viking. Bill Downey. 320p. (Orig.). 1981. pap. 2.50 (ISBN 0-449-14393-7, GM). Fawcett.

Black Virgin, and Other Stories. Olga Petrova. LC 72-128746. (Short story index reprint series). 1970. Books for Libraries Press.

Black Virgin: And Other Stories. Olga Petrova. LC 27-12301. The Four Seas Company.

Black Vulmea's Vengeance. Robert E. Howard. 1979. pap. 1.95 (ISBN 0-425-04296-0). Berkley Pub.

Black Vulmea's Vengeance. Robert E. Howard. 15.00 (ISBN 0-937986-04-6). D M Grant.

Black Vulture. Gene Ashcroft. LC 41-215362. J. R. Burnett.

"Black Watch" Or, Forty-Second Highlanders. James Grant. LC 42-26883. 1892. G. Routledge and Sons.

Black Water. J. Simon Prager. 1978. pap. 1.95 (ISBN 0-532-19181-1). Woodhill.

Black Water O'Dee. James McKenzie Douglas. LC 23-3555. The Nelson E. Barton Publishing Co.

Black Weever: By Ronald Wills Pseud. Ronald Wills Thomas. LC 54-11004. Roy Publishers.

Black Wheel. Abraham Merritt & Bok, Hannes, 1914- LC 48-2474. 1947. New Collectors' Group.

Black, White, and Brindled. Eden Phillpotts. LC 77-142272. (Short story index reprint series). 1970. Books for Libraries Press.

Black, White and Brindled. Eden Phillpotts. LC 23-840513. 1923. The Macmillan Company.

Black, White, and Red: The Problem of Shawnee College. George Arthur Dunlap. LC 79-103341. 3.95 (ISBN 0-8059-2622-4). Dorrance.

Black Widow. Christina Crawford. LC 81-9671. 1982. 12.95 (ISBN 0-688-00773-2). Morrow.

Black Widower. Patricia Moyes. LC 74-15480. (Rinehart suspense novel). 1975. 5.95 (ISBN 0-03-013836-1). Holt, Rinehart and Winston.

Black Widower. Patricia Moyes. LC 78-301790. (Penguin crime fiction). 1977. 1.95 (ISBN 0-14-004334-9). Penguin Books.

Black Widower. Alan Riefe. (Cage,#3). 1975. (pbk.) 0.95. Popular Library.

Black William. Robert Neill. LC 55-5592. 1955. Doubleday.

Black Wind. Miriam Asher (ISBN 0-671-80722-6). Pocket Books.

Black Windmill. Clive Egleton. 224p. 1974. pap. 1.25 o.p. (P2230, Crest). Fawcett World.

Black Winds Blow. Frances Bainbridge Colby. LC 40-472709. 1940. Harrison-Hilton Books, Inc.

Black Wine. George Harold Bennett. LC 67-15360. 1968. Doubleday.

Black Wings Has My Angel. Elliott Chaze. LC 53-33929. (Gold medal books, 296). 1953. Fawcett Publications.

Black Wing's Rider. Cherry Wilson. LC 34-443. A. H. King.

Black Wolf. Galad Elflandsson & Randy Broecker. LC 80-114191. (Illus.). 1980. 12.00. D. M. Grant.

Black Wolf's Breed: A Story of France in the Old World and the New, Happening in the Reign of Louis Xiv. Harris Dickson. LC 99-5058. The Bowen-Merrill Company.

Black Work. Richard Frede. LC 76-940. 6.95 (ISBN 0-690-01104-0). Crowell.

Black Work. Richard Frede. (Signet Book). 1977. 1.75 (ISBN 0-451-07538-2). New American Library.

Black Work. Macdowell Frederics. 240p. 1976. 6.95 o.p. (ISBN 0-690-01104-0). T Y Crowell.

Black Yacht. John Baxter. 336p. 1982. pap. 2.95 (ISBN 0-515-06159-X). Jove Pubns.

Blackbeard: Or, The Pirate of the Roanoke. Benjamin Barker. LC 6-7211. 1847. F. Gleason.

Blackbeard's Bride. Jeramie Price. LC 59-9169. 1959. Crown Publishers.

Blackbeard's Ghost. Ben Stahl. LC 65-11022. (Illus.). 1965. Houghton Mifflin.

Blackberry Mountain. Mable A Wallace. LC 47-12300. 1947. Wartburg Press.

Blackberry Pickers. Evelyn S Leger Savile Randolph. LC 12-22519. 1912. 1.35. G. P. Putnam's Sons.

Blackberry Wilderness. Sylvia Berkman. LC 79-116939. (Short story index reprint series). 1970. Books for Libraries Press.

Blackberry Wilderness. 1st Ed. Sylvia Berkman. LC 59-6349. 1959. Doubleday.

Blackberry Winter. Evelyn Hanna. LC 38-28772. 1938. E. P. Dutton & Co., Inc.

Blackberry Winter. Louise Platt Hauck. LC 34-310800. The Penn Publishing Company.

Blackberry Winter. Margaret Mead. 1973. pap. 5.95 (ISBN 0-671-21642-2, Touchstone Bks). S&S.

Blackberry Winter. Robert Penn Warren. LC 47-23827. 1946. The Cummington Press.

Blackbird. Richard Stark. (Cock Robin Mystery Ser). 1969. 4.50 o.p. (61362). Macmillan.

Blackbird. Donald E Westlake. LC 71-75906. (Cock Robin mystery). 1969. Macmillan.

Blackbird: A Story of Mackinac Island. Edna Willa Troop. LC 8-32334. Citator Publishing Company.

Blackbird Days. Ken Chowder. 256p. 1981. pap. 2.75 (ISBN 0-523-41608-3). Pinnacle Bks.

Blackbird Days: A Novel. Ken Chowder. LC 79-1704. 9.95 (ISBN 0-06-011496-7). Harper & Row.
Blackbird Hill. A Novel. Esther Serle Kenneth. LC 7-10960. (On cover: The idle hour series. no. 15). The F. M. Lupton Publishing Company.
Blackbirder. Dorothy Belle Flanagan Hughes. LC 43-14286. 1943. Duell, Sloan and Pearce.
Blackbirder. Lionel Webb. (Berkley medallion book). 1974. (pbk.) 1.25 (ISBN 0-425-02563-2). Berkley Pub. Co.
Blackbirds on the Lawn: A Novel. Jane Morton. LC 44-40101. 1944. Coward-McCann, Inc.
Blackbirds on the Wing. Mitchel J Henderson. LC 43-51964. 1942. Dorrance and Company.
Blackboard. A Page from the Colonial History of Philadelphia ... 1835. Harper & Brothers.
Blackboard Bordello. Anne Saddens. 192p. (Orig.). 1973. pap. 1.95 o.p. (ISBN 0-87682-364-9, 7364). Barclay Hse.
Blackboard Cavalier. LC 66-16934. 4.50. Doubleday.
Blackboard Cavalier. John Morressy. (60-2185). 1967. Popular Lib.
Blackboard Cavalier. John Morressy. LC 66-16934. 1966. Doubleday.
Blackboard Jungle. Evan Hunter. 1.75 (ISBN 0-380-00859-9). Avon.
Blackboard Jungle: A Novel. Evan Hunter. LC 73-183139. 1971. (ISBN 0-8376-0404-4). R. Bentley.
Blackboard Jungle: A Novel. Evan Hunter. LC 54-8649. 1954. Simon and Schuster.
Blackbourne Hall. Elissa Grandower, pseud. LC 78-22771. (Romantic Suspense Ser.). 1979. 9.95 o.p. (ISBN 0-385-14472-5). Doubleday.
Blackbourne Hall. Hillary Waugh. LC 78-22771. 1979. 8.95 (ISBN 0-385-14472-5). Doubleday.
Blackcock's Feather. Maurice Walsh. 1974. (pbk.) 1.25. Bantam Books.
Blackcock's Feather: A Novel. Maurice Walsh. LC 32-15198. 1932. Frederick A. Stokes Company.
Blacker the Berry. Wallace Thurman. LC 69-18594. (American Negro, His History and Literature). (Afro-American culture series.). 1969. Arno Press.
Blacker the Berry... A Novel of Negro Life. Wallace Thurman. LC 78-102975. (American Library). 1970. 1.50. Collier Books.
Blacker the Berry: A Novel of Negro Life. Wallace Thurman. LC 74-177459. 1972. (ISBN 0-404-00217-X). AMS Press.
Blacker the Berry: A Novel of Negro Life. Wallace Thurman. LC 29-3978. 1929. The Macaulay Company.
Black'erchief Dick. Margery Allingham. LC 23-16270. 1923. Doubleday, Page & Company.
Blackfeet Tales of Glacier National Park. James Willard Schultz. Repr. of 1916 ed. 10.00 o.p. Folcroft.
Blackfire. Barbara Riefe. LC 80-82219. 368p. (Orig.). 1980. pap. 2.95 (ISBN 0-86721-123-7). Playboy Pbks.
Blackfoot Ambush. Catherine Weber. (American Indians Ser.: No. 2). 368p. (Orig.). 1981. pap. 2.75 (ISBN 0-440-00590-6, Banbury). Dell.
Blackgable Inn. Marie Eyre. (Kangaroo Book). 1977. 1.75 (ISBN 0-671-81690-X). Pocket Books.
Blackguard. Maxwell Bodenheim. LC 23-650013. 1923. Covici-McGee.
Blackhawk. Bill Rotsler. 176p. 1982. pap. 1.95 (ISBN 0-446-30498-0). Warner Bks.
Blackheath Poisoings: A Victorian Murder Mystery. Julian Symons. LC 79-24876. 1980. 2.50 (ISBN 0-14-005171-6). Penguin Books.
Blackheath Poisonings: A Victorian Murder Mystery. Julian Symons. LC 78-4745. 8.95 (ISBN 0-06-014211-1). Harper & Row.
Blacking Factory. Wilfrid Sheed. Bd. with Pennsylvania Gothic. 246p. 1968. 5.95 o.p. (ISBN 0-374-11428-5). FS&G.
Blacking Factory, & Pennsylvania Gothic: A Short Novel and a Long Story. Wilfrid Sheed. LC 68-13009. 1968. 5.50. Farrar.
Blacking Factory & Pennsylvania Gothic: A Short Novel and a Long Story. Wilfrid Sheed. LC 68-13009. 1975. (pbk.) 1.75 (ISBN 0-671-80035-3). Pocket Books.
Blackjack. Joseph E. Kelleam. LC 48-5832. 1948. W. Sloane Associates.
Blackjack Hijack. Charles Einstein. (Fawcett Crest Book). 1977. 1.50. Fawcett Pubns.
Blackjack Hijack. Charles Einstein. LC 75-35807. 6.95 (ISBN 0-394-49459-8). Random House.
Blackkerchief Dick. Margery Allingham. 320p. 1975. Repr. of 1923 ed. 6.50x o.p. Intl Pubns Serv.
Blackland. Harold Stern. LC 70-89075. 1970. 5.95. Doubleday.
Blacklash. John Brunner. Orig. Title: Plague on Both Your Causes. 1969. pap. 0.75 o.p. (T2107). Pyramid Pubns.
Blackleg: A Novel. Stacey William Hyde. LC 29-212930. 1930. Longmans, Green and Co.
Blackleg Bullets. Lee Floren. LC 54-113356. 1954. Arcadia House.
Blackleg Range. Bennett Foster. LC 39-33015. 1939. W. Morrow & Company.
Blackleg Range. Bennett Foster. 1941. The Sun Dial Press.
Blacklight. 1st Ed. Bill Knox. LC 67-14125. 1967. 3.95. Pub. for the Crime Club by Doubleday.
Blackmail. Penny Jordan. (Harlequin Presents Ser.). 192p. 1982. pap. 1.75 (ISBN 0-373-10517-7). Harlequin Bks.
Blackmail: An Episode in Finesse. William Timothy Call. LC 15-173180. 1915. 0.50. W. T. Call.
Blackmail Eighty-Seven. John Martin. LC 81-80164. 226p. 1983. pap. text ed. 7.95 (ISBN 0-86666-023-2). GWP.
Blackmailed Housewife. Roberts. price not set o.p. (ISBN 0-87977-125-9). Dansk Blue Bk.
Blackmailer. John Miles. LC 73-22660. 1974. 6.50 (ISBN 0-672-51934-8). Bobbs-Merrill.
Blackmailers. Henry Cecil. LC 69-15566. (Inner sanctum mystery). 1969. 4.50. Simon and Schuster.
Blackmoor. Julia Trevelyan. (Signet book). New American Library.
Blackout. Mark Andrews. (Leisure Book). 1.50 (ISBN 0-8439-0525-5). Nordon Pubns.
Blackout. Constance Little. LC 51-13255. 1951. Published for the Crime Club by Doubleday.
Blackout at Rehearsal. Marguerite Lucile Paine Rea. LC 43-14561. 1943. Pub. for the Crime Club by Doubleday, Doran & Co., Inc.
Blackrobe. Charles Corcoran. LC 38-94. The Bruce Publishing Company.
Blackrobe. Robert Emmet Wall. LC 81-670177. (Wall, Robert Emmett. The Canadians: Vol. 1). 16.95 (ISBN 0-920510-27-2). Personal Library.
Blackrobe: A Novel. Robert Emmet Wall. 1981. 16.95 o.p. Vanguard.
Blacksheep! Balcksheep! Meredith Nicholson. LC 20-7287. 1920. C. Scribner's Sons.
Blackshirt. Clarence Edward Benadum. LC 35-17485. Dorrance & Company, Inc.
Blackshirt. Graham Montague Jeffries. LC 25-12174. 1925. Dodd, Mead and Company.
Blackshirt: The Audacious. Graham Montague Jeffries. LC 35-22656. 1936. J. B. Lippincott Company.
Blacksmith & the Carpenter. Sun Li. Tr. by Sidney Shapiro & Gladys Yang. 311p. 1982. pap. 4.95 (ISBN 0-8351-1121-0). China Bks.
Blacksmith of Vilno: A Tale of Poland in the Year 1832. Eric Philbrook Kelly. LC 30-26899. 1930. The Macmillan Company.
Blacksmith of Voe: A Novel. Roland Alexander Wood-Seys. LC 9-1485. (On cover: Harper's Franklin square library, no. 720). 1892. Harper & Brothers.
Blacksmith's Daughter. A Novel. Virginia Rapp. LC 8-228. 1890. Commercial Herald.
Blacksmith's Hammer: Or, The Peasant Code. Eugene Sue & De Leon, Daniel, 1852-1914, Tr. LC 10-22413. 1910. New York Labor News Company.
Blacksnake Man. John Henry Reese. LC 75-36608. 1976. 5.95 (ISBN 0-385-11238-6). Doubleday.
Blacksnake Trail: A Powder Valley Western. Peter Field. LC 50-5302. 1950. Jefferson House.
Blackstock Affair. Franklin Bandy. 384p. (Orig.). 1980. pap. 2.50 (ISBN 0-441-06650-X, Pub. by Charter Bks). Ace Bks.
Blackstone. Richard Falkirk, pseud. LC 72-96476. 224p. 1973. 6.95 o.p. (ISBN 0-8128-1570-X). Stein & Day.
Blackstone. Derek Lambert. LC 72-96476. 1973. 6.95 (ISBN 0-8128-1570-X). Stein and Day.
Blackstone & the Scourge of Europe. Richard Falkirk, pseud. LC 74-78532. 192p. 1974. 6.95 o.p. (ISBN 0-8128-1726-5). Stein & Day.
Blackstone and the Scourge of Europe. Derek Lambert. LC 74-78532. 1974. 6.95 (ISBN 0-8128-1726-5). Stein and Day.
Blackstone's Fancy. Richard Falkirk, pseud. 1974. (pbk.) 1.25. Bantam Books.
Blackstone's Fancy. Derek Lambert. LC 73-80798. 1973. 6.95 (ISBN 0-8128-1604-8). Stein and Day.
Blackthorn. Dorothy Daniels. 1975. (pbk.) 1.25 (ISBN 0-671-80195-3). Pocket Books.
Blackthorn House. Cecil John Charles Street. LC 49-9684. (Red badge mystery). 1949. Dodd, Mead.
Blackthorn Winter. Phillippa Powys. LC 31-5763. 1930. R. R. Smith Inc.
Blackwater. Frank O'Rourke. LC 50-8114. 1950. Random House.
Blackwater Bayou. Marilyn Austin. (Orig.). 1979. pap. 1.75 (ISBN 0-532-17211-6). Woodhill.
Blackwater, I: The Flood. Michael McDowell. 1983. pap. 2.50 (ISBN 0-380-81489-7, 81489-7). Avon.
Blackwater, II: The Levee. Michael McDowell. 1983. pap. 2.50 (ISBN 0-380-82206-7, 82206-7). Avon.
Blackwater, III: The House. Michael McDowell. 176p. (Orig.). 1983. pap. 2.50 (ISBN 0-380-82594-5, 82594-5). Avon.
Blackwater, IV: The War. Michael McDowell. 192p. 1983. pap. 2.50 (ISBN 0-380-82776-X, 82776-X). Avon.
Blackwater: Rain. Michael McDowell. 1983. pap. 2.50 (ISBN 0-380-82792-1, 82792-1). Avon.
Blackwater Rivers. Alphonse Maria Grussi. LC 34-22030. The Christopher Publishing House.
Blackwater, V: The Fortune. Michael McDowell. 176p. 1983. pap. 2.50 (ISBN 0-380-82784-0, 8278-0). Avon.
Blackways of Kent. Hylan Lewis. 1955. pap. 3.45 (ISBN 0-8084-0064-9, B20). Coll & U Pr.
Blackwell's Ghost. Angela Gray, pseud. (Orig.). 1972. pap. 0.95 o.s.i. (75-377). Lancer.
Blackwood. Jocelyn Radcliffe. 1974. pap. 0.95 o.p. (09256). Curtis.
Blackwood Cult. T. A. Waters. 1970. pap. 0.75 o.p. (ISBN 0-447-74618-9). Lancer.
Blacky Finn of the Diamond D. Tevis Miller. LC 39-7773. Phoenix Press.
Blade Among the Boys. Onuora Nzekwu. (African Writers Ser.). 1972. pap. text ed. 5.00x (ISBN 0-435-90091-9). Heinemann Ed.
Blade for Sale: The Adventures of Monsieur De Mailly. David Lindsay. LC 27-4318. 1927. R. M. McBride & Company.
Blade, No. 13: The Golden Steed. Jeffrey Lord. 192p. 1975. pap. 1.75 (ISBN 0-523-40786-6). Pinnacle Bks.
Blade No. 22: The Forests of Gleor. Jeffrey Lord. (Blade Ser.). (Orig.). 1977. pap. 1.50 (ISBN 0-523-40457-3). Pinnacle Bks.
Blade No. 23: Empire of Blood. Jeffrey Lord. 1977. pap. 2.25 (ISBN 0-523-41723-3). Pinnacle Bks.
Blade No. 34: The Ruins of Kaldac. Jeffrey Lord. 192p. (Orig.). 1981. pap. 1.95 (ISBN 0-523-41208-8). Pinnacle Bks.
Blade of Castlemayne. Anthony Esler. LC 74-7271. 1974. 6.95 (ISBN 0-688-00317-6). Morrow.
Blade of Castlemayne. Anthony Esler. (Fawcett crest book). 1975. (pbk.) 1.50. Fawcett.
Blade of Fern. Edith L. Tiempo. (Writing in Asia Ser.). 1978. pap. text ed. 5.50x (00214). Heinemann Ed.
Blade of Honor. John J Pugh. LC 55-10749. 1955. Little, Brown.
Blade of Light. Don Carpenter. LC 68-12567. 1968. Harcourt, Brace & World.
Blade of Picardy. Fred McLaughlin. LC 28-9384. The Bobbs-Merrill Company.
Blade Runner. Philip K. Dick. 1982. pap. 2.75 (ISBN 0-345-30129-3, Del Rey). Ballantine.
Blade Runner. Les Martin. LC 81-48439. (Illus.). 1982. pap. 3.95 (ISBN 0-394-85303-2). Random.
Blade Runner: A Movie: Novel. William S. Burroughs. LC 78-21584. 1979. 8.95. (ISBN 0-912652-45-4) (ISBN 0-912652-46-2) (ISBN 0-912652-47-0). Blue Wind Press.
Bladed Barrier. Joseph Bushnell Ames. LC 29-17040. 2.00. The Century Co.
Bladed Barrier. Joseph Bushnell Ames. LC 77-84193. (Lost Race and Adult Fantasy Fiction). 1978. 24.00 (ISBN 0-405-10951-2). Arno Press.
Bladerunner. Alan E Norse. 1975. (pbk.) 1.50. Ballantine Books.
Blades. George Barr McCutcheon. LC 28-206053. 1928. Dodd, Mead & Company.
Blades of Passion. Claudette Williams. (Fawcett Crest Book.). 1.95 (ISBN 0-449-23481-9). Fawcett Crest.
Bladesman of Antares. Alan Burt Akers. (Science Fiction Ser). 1975. pap. 1.25 o.p. (UY1188). DAW Bks.
Bladys Stewponey. A Novel. Sabine Baring-Gould. LC 6-7962. Frederick A. Stokes Company.
Blaine's Law. Carter Travis Young. LC 73-9181. 1974. 4.95 (ISBN 0-385-01926-2). Doubleday.
Blaine's Law. Carter Travis Young. 1975. (pbk.) 0.95. Belmont Tower Books.
Blair Marriman: A Novel. Percy Marks. LC 49-7514. 1949. Doubleday.
Blair of the Bar XL. Clinton Dangerfield. LC 30-11278. 1930. G. H. Watt.
Blair's Attic. Joseph Crosby Lincoln & Lincoln, Freeman. LC 29-17926. 1929. Coward-McCann, Inc.
Blaize. Anne Melville, pseud. LC 79-8936. 1981. 10.00 (ISBN 0-385-14832-1). Doubleday.
Blake: Or, The Huts of America, a Novel. Martin Robison Delany. LC 79-119677. 1970. 8.50 (ISBN 0-8070-6418-1). Beacon Press.
Blakes and Flanagans: A Tale, Illustrative of Irish Life in the United States. 5th thousand. ed. Mary Anne Madden Sadlier. LC 8-1645. 1858. D. & J. Sadlier & Co.
Blake's Reach. Catherine Gaskin. 1971. pap. 1.25 o.p. (96062). Beagle Bks.
Blame the Baron: By Anthony Morton Pseud. John Creasey. LC 51-9601. 1951. Duell, Sloan and Pearce.
Blame the Dead. Gavin Lyall. LC 72-91827. 1973. 6.95 (ISBN 0-670-17343-6). Viking Press.
Blameless Woman. Henrietta Eliza Vaughan Stannard. LC 8-13871. The International News Company.
Blaming. Elizabeth Taylor. LC 76-41921. 1976. 7.95 (ISBN 0-670-17349-5). Viking Press.
Blampied Edition of Peter Pan: The Original Text of Peter & Wendy. James Matthew Barrie. LC 41-24260. 1940. C. Scribner's Sons.
Blanche Ellerslie's Ending. author's ed.... ed. George Alfred Lawrence. LC 11-15093. 1884. H. A. Sumner & Company.
Blanche Fury. Margaret Campbell. 1976. (pbk.) 1.50. New American Library.
Blanche, Lady Falaise: A Tale. Joseph Henry Shorthouse. LC 8-7335. 1891. Macmillan and Co.
Blanche of Brandywine: Or, September the Eleventh, 1777. A Romance, Combining the Poetry, Legend, and History of the Battle of Brandywine. George Lippard. LC 7-16590. 1846. G. B. Zicher & Co.
Blanche of Burgundy: A Novel. Sylvanus Cobb. LC 49-37124. (Choice Series. New York, No. 117). 1894. R. Bonner's Sons.
Blanche: Or, The Lost Diamond. A Tale of the Lights and Shades of London. LC 8-32284. (On cover: The Mercury stories). 1862. F. A. Brady.
Blanche; or, The Lost Diamond. A Tale of the Lights and Shades of London. Septimus R Urban. LC 8-32284. (On cover: The Mercury stories). F. A. Brady.
Blanche Talbot: Or, The Maiden's Hand. A Romance of the War of 1812. Also, Henry Temple: or, A Father's Crime. Joseph Holt Ingraham. 1847. Williams Brothers.
Blanco. Allen Wier. LC 78-9660. 9.95 (ISBN 0-8071-0473-6). Louisiana State University Press.
Blanco & Things About to Disappear. Allen Weir. 320p. 1980. pap. 3.50 (ISBN 0-380-49114-1, 49114, Bard). Avon.
Bland Beginning. Julian Symons. LC 49-11243. 1949. Harper.
Bland Beginning. Julian Symons. (Perennial library). 1979. 1.95 (ISBN 0-06-080469-6). Harper & Row.
Blandings Castle. Pelham Grenville Wodehouse. LC 35-27327. 1935. Doubleday, Doran & Company, Inc.
Blandings' Way. Eric Hodgins. LC 50-12058. 1950. Simon and Schuster.
Blank Book. Melinda Popham. LC 73-10703. 1974. 6.95 (ISBN 0-672-51844-9). Bobbs-Merrill.
Blank Page. K. C Constantine. LC 74-4013. 1974. 5.95 (ISBN 0-8415-0335-4). Saturday Review Press.
Blank Wall. Stacey William Hyde. 1929. Longmans, Green and Co.
Blank Wall: A Novel of Suspense. Elisabeth Sanxay Holding. LC 47-5834. 1947. Simon & Schuster.
Blanket: A Novel. A A Murray. LC 58-92462. Vanguard Press.
Blanket Boy. Cecil John Lanham Parker & Mopeli-Paulus, Attwell Sidwell. LC 53-5083. 1953. Crowell.
Blanket Boy, a Novel of South Africa. Peter Lanham & A. S. Mopeli-Paulus. 5.00 (ISBN 0-8446-0175-6). Peter Smith.
Blanket Boy: A Novel of South Africa. Peter Lanham & A. S. Mopeli-Paulus. 1971. pap. 2.45 o.p. (ISBN 0-8152-0284-9, A-284). Apollo Eds.
Blanket of the Dark. John Buchan. 1931. Houghton Mifflin Company.
Blanket Word. Honor Arundel. LC 73-1128. 137p. (YA) 1973. 5.95 o.p. (ISBN 0-8407-6306-9). Elsevier-Nelson.
Blarney Stone. John Henry Hewlett. LC 51-12681. 1951. Appleton-Century-Croft.
Blast of Trumpets. Gordon Ashe. LC 75-923. 192p. 1976. 6.95 o.p. (ISBN 0-03-014101-X). HR&W.
Blast of Trumpets. John Creasey. LC 75-923. (Rinehart suspense novel). 1975. 6.95 (ISBN 0-03-014101-X). Holt, Rinehart and Winston.
Blast of Trumpets. John Creasey. LC 76-27348. 1976. 9.95 (ISBN 0-8161-6402-9). G.K. Hall.
Blast-off at 0300. Hugh Walters, pseud. LC 58-5449. (Criterion book for young people.). 1958. Criterion Books.
Blaster No. 1: The Girl with the Dynamite Bangs. Lou Cameron. pap. 0.95 o.s.i. (75-462). Lancer.
Blatchford Bequest: And Other Stories. Frederick John Fargus. (On cover: The seaside library. Pocket ed. no. 302). 1884. G. Munro.
Blatchington Tangle. George Douglas Howard Cole & Margaret Isabel Postgate Cole. LC 26-19258. 1926. The Macmillan Company.
Blaxine, Halfbreed Girl. Margaret Smith Cobb. 1910. 1.50. The Neale Publishing Company.
Blayde, R.I.P. John William Wainwright. LC 81-21488. 10.95 (ISBN 0-312-08364-5). St Martin's Press.
Blaze. J. W. Baron. 192p. (Orig.). 1983. pap. 2.25 (ISBN 0-523-41745-4). Pinnacle Bks.

Blaze. Kenneth Roberts. (Orig.). 1969. pap. 0.95 o.p. (65-177). Paperback Lib.

Blaze Allan. Lillian Bos Ross. LC 44-823126. 1944. W. Morrow and Company.

Blaze Derringer. Eugene Percy Lyle. LC 10-141541. 1910. Doubleday, Page & Company.

Blaze McGee. Jay Lucas. LC 36-44708. 1935. The Macaulay Company.

Blaze of Autumn. Roe Richmond. 1980. pap. 1.95 (ISBN 0-8439-0841-6). Nordon Pubns.

Blaze of Noon. Ernest Kellogg Gann. LC 46-252617. 1946. H. Holt and Company.

Blaze of Noon. Rayner Heppenstall. LC 68-11311. 1968. Dufour.

Blaze of Noon. Rayner Heppenstall & Bowen, Elizabeth, 1899- LC 40-5395. Alliance Book Corporation.

Blaze of Passion. Stephanie Blake. LC 78-50087. 2.25 (ISBN 0-87216-462-4). Playboy Press.

Blaze of Roses. 1st American Ed. Elleston Trevor. LC 53-77514. Harper.

Blaze of the Sun. Translated from the French by Mervyn Savill. Jean Hougron. LC 54-937071. 1954. Farrar, Straus and Young.

Blaze Star. Paul Hutchens. LC 39-15713. 1939. Wm. B. Eerdmans Publishing Company.

Blazed Trail. Stewart Edward White. LC 68-57560. (American novels of muckraking, propaganda, and social protest). (Illus.). 1968. Gregg Press.

Blazed Trail. 21st impression ed. Stewart Edward White. LC 9-32286. Grosset & Dunlap.

Blazed Trail. Stewart Edward White. LC 2-7561. 1902. McClure, Philips & Co.

Blazed Trail. 15th impression ed. Stewart Edward White. LC 9-830. 1903. McClure, Phillips & Co.

Blazed Trail. Stewart Edward White. LC 20-193485. Grosset & Dunlap.

Blazed Trail. Stewart Edward White. LC 37-185. 1904. McClure, Phillips & Co.

Blazed Trail. Stewart Edward White. LC 37-22508. Grosset & Dunlap.

Blazed Trail Stories: And Stories of the Wild Life. Stewart Edward White. LC 68-55688. (American short story series, v. 28). (Illus.). 1969. Garrett Press.

Blazed Trail Stories, and Stories of the Wild Life. Stewart Edward White. LC 72-8145. (American short story series, v. 28). 1972. (ISBN 0-8422-8124-X). MSS Information Corp.

Blazed Trail Stories, and Stories of the Wild Life. Stewart Edward White. LC 4-25386. 1904. McClure, Philips & Co.

Blazed Trial. Stewart Edward White. LC 68-57560. (Muckrakers Ser.). (Illus.). Repr. of 1902 ed. lib. bdg. 14.00 (ISBN 0-8398-2162-X). Irvington.

Blazing Air. Oswald Wynd. LC 81-5671. 1981. 12.95 (ISBN 0-89919-047-2). Ticknor & Fields.

Blazing Border. Eugene E Halleran. LC 55-9226. 1955. Macrae Smith.

Blazing Dawn. James Wakefield Burke. 1975. pap. 1.75 o.p. (ISBN 0-515-03903-9). BJ Pub Group.

Blazing Frontier. Herman Edwin Mootz. LC 37-1122. 1936. Tardy Publishing Company.

Blazing Guns. Jake Logan. LC 81-82359. (Jake Logan Ser.). 224p. (Orig.). 1982. pap. 1.95 (ISBN 0-87216-990-1). Playboy Pbks.

Blazing Guns on the Chisholm Trail. Borden Chase. LC 48-5569. 1948. Random House.

Blazing Saddles. Tad Richards. (Illus.). 1974. (pbk.) 1.25. Warner Paperback Lib.

Blazing Star. Marcella Thum. 384p. (Orig.). 1983. pap. 2.95 (ISBN 0-449-20095-7, Crest). Fawcett.

Blazing Star: A Documentary Account of a Small Privateer During the American Revolution. C. Malcolm B Gilman. LC 72-5188. 1973. 6.95 (ISBN 0-498-01220-4). A. S. Barnes.

Blazing Sun. Clark Darlton. (Perry Rhodan#86). 1976. (pbk.) 1.25. Ace Books.

Blazing Trails. Francis W Hilton. LC 36-18152. 1936. H. C. Kinsey & Company, Inc.

Blazing Tumbleweed. Louise Platt Hauck. LC 31-7562. The Penn Publishing Company.

Blazon. Kenneth Bulmer, pseud. (Orig.). 1970. pap. 0.75 o.p. (0502-07099). Curtis.

Ble en Herbe. Sidonie Gabrielle Colette. Ed. by Pichois. (Coll. GF). pap. 3.95. French & Eur.

Bleak House. Charles Dickens. (English library). (Illus.). 1975. (pbk.) 3.95 (ISBN 0-14-043063-6). Penguin Books.

Bleak House. Charles Dickens. LC 77-350067. (Pan classic). 1976. 1.00 (ISBN 0-330-24472-8). Pan Books.

Bleak House. Charles Dickens. Ed. by Norman Page. LC 71-31227. (Penguin English library). (Illus.). 1971. 0.75 (ISBN 0-14-043063-6). Penguin.

Bleak House. Charles Dickens. LC 75-97848. (Rinehart editions, 141). 1970. Holt, Rinehart and Winston.

Bleak House. Charles Dickens. Ed. by Duane De Vries. LC 79-117439. (Crowell critical library). 1971. (ISBN 0-690-14691-4). Crowell.

Bleak House. Charles Dickens. LC 15-21854. 1853. Harper & Brothers.

Bleak House... Charles Dickens. LC 6-37042. 1867. Hurd and Houghton.

Bleak House... Charles Dickens. 1868. Hurd and Houghton.

Bleak House. Charles Dickens. LC 6-36368. 1870. Fields, Osgood & Co.

Bleak House. Charles Dickens. LC 6-36367. 1872. D. Appleton and Company.

Bleak House. Charles Dickens. LC 9-827. Aldine Book Publishing Co.

Bleak House. Charles Dickens. LC 6-36365. (Harper's Franklin square library, Duodecimo ed.). 1883. Harper & Brothers.

Bleak House. Charles Dickens. (On cover: Lovell's library, v. 5, no. 244). 1883. J. W. Lovell Company.

Bleak House. Charles Dickens. LC 41-31313. 1885. Hurst & Co.

Bleak House. Charles Dickens. Ed. by Whipple, Edwin Percy. LC 15-23137. (Half-title: works of Charles Dickens. New illustrated library ed. vol. xvi-xvii). Houghton, Mifflin and Company.

Bleak House. Charles Dickens. (Half-title: Everyman's library, ed. by Ernest Rhys. Fiction). 1907. J. M. Dent & Co.

Bleak House. Charles Dickens. (Half-title: The centenary ediution of the works of Charles Dickens in 36 volumes). 1911. Chapman & Hall, Ltd.

Bleak House. Charles Dickens. LC 36-37121. (Half-title: Everyman's library, ed. by Ernest Rhys. Fiction. no. 236). 1932. J. M. Dent & Sons, Ltd.

Bleak House. Charles Dickens. LC 49-750980. (New Oxford illustrated Dickens). 1948. Oxford Univ. Press.

Bleak House. Charles Dickens. Ed. by Dickens, Charles. LC 4-15298. 1895. Macmillan and Co.

Bleak House. Charles Dickens & Ball, Robert, 1890- Illus. LC 43-1889. 1942. The Heritage Press.

Bleak House: An Authoritative and Annotated Text, Genesis and Composition, Backgrounds, Criticism. Charles Dickens & George Harry Ford. LC 77-7783. (Norton critical edition). 17.50 (ISBN 0-393-04374-6). Norton.

Bleak House: Arr. for Modern Reading. Illustrated by Edward Gorey. Charles Dickens. LC 53-3464. 1953. International Collectors Library.

Bleak House. Arranged for Modern Reading, with an Introd. by Donald Friede, Illustrated by Edward Gorey. Centennial Ed. Charles Dickens. LC 53-10649. 1953. Doubleday.

Bleak House. Illus. by Phiz. Charles Dickens & Hablot Knight Browne. LC 66-5488. (Macdonald illus. classics, 32 cm.). 3.50. Macdonald.

Bleak House: With an Introd. by Morton Dauwen Zabel. Charles Dickens. LC 56-582965. (Riverside editions, B4). 1956. Houghton, Mifflin.

Bleak November. Rohan O'Grady, pseud. 1970. 5.95 o.p. Dial.

Bleak November. June O'Grady Skinner. LC 75-120466. 1970. 5.95. Dial Press.

Bleak Strand. George K Hohn. LC 73-181753. 1972. 4.50 (ISBN 0-8059-1649-0). Dorrance.

Bledding Sorrow. Marilyn Harris. LC 75-27418. 8.95 (ISBN 0-399-11657-5). Putnam.

Blednii Ogon' Vladimir Vladimirovich Nabokov. Tr. by Alexei Tsvetkov. (Rus.). 1982. 24.00 (ISBN 0-88233-602-9); pap. 15.00 (ISBN 0-88233-603-7). Ardis Pubs.

Bleeders Come First. Colin Douglas. LC 79-64156. 1979. 8.95 (ISBN 0-8008-0816-9). Taplinger Pub. Co.

Bleeding Heart. Marilyn French. 416p. 1981. pap. 3.50 (ISBN 0-345-28896-3). Ballantine.

Bleeding Heart. Marilyn French. LC 79-26346. 1980. 12.95 (ISBN 0-671-44784-X). Summit Bks.

Bleeding Hearts. Ed. by Alfred Joseph Hitchcock. 1974. (pbk.) 0.95. Dell.

Bleeding Land. Giles A Lutz. LC 65-106003. (Double D western). 3.50. Doubleday.

Bleeding Land. Giles A. Lutz. 1978. 1.50 (ISBN 0-671-82129-6). Pocket Books.

Bleeding Land: By Giles Lutz. 1st Ed. Giles A Lutz. LC 65-10600. (Double D western). 1965. Doubleday.

Bleeding Scissors. Bruno Fischer. LC 48-6346. (fingerprint mystery). 1948. Ziff-Davis Pub. Co.

Bleepers! Goes to High School. (Illus., Orig.). 1981. pap. 1.95 (ISBN 0-446-97867-1). Warner Bks.

Bleepers in Love. (Illus., Orig.). 1980. pap. 1.95 (ISBN 0-446-97568-0). Warner Bks.

Bleepers in Space. (Illus., Orig.). 1980. pap. 1.95 (ISBN 0-446-97569-9). Warner Bks.

Bleepers! Meets the Monsters. (Illus., Orig.). 1981. pap. 1.95 (ISBN 0-446-97865-5). Warner Bks.

Blemmertons: Or, Dottings by the Wayside. Joseph J Nicholson. LC 7-23128. 1856. Dana and Company; Etc., Etc.

Blencarrow: A Novel. Isabel Ecclestone Macpherson Mackay. LC 26-17801. 1926. Houghton Mifflin Company.

Blennerhasset: A Romance. Charles Felton Pidgin. 1901. lib. bdg. 17.95 o.s.i. (ISBN 0-512-00869-8). Garrett Pr.

Blennerhassett: Or, The Decrees of Fate; a Romance Founded Upon Events in American History. 4th ed. Charles Felton Pidgin. LC 7-35909. 1901. C. M. Clark Publishing Company.

Blennerhassett: Or, The Decrees of Fate; a Romance Founded Upon Events in American History. Charles Felton Pidgin. LC 41-31133. 1902. C. M. Clark Publishing Company.

Bless Me, Father. Neil Boyd. LC 77-9169. 1978. 8.95 (ISBN 0-312-08379-3). St. Martin's Press.

Bless Me, Father. Neil Boyd. 1978. 2.25 (ISBN 0-445-04364-4). Popular Library.

Bless Me Father. Eamon Kelly. LC 78-300457. 1.15 (ISBN 0-85342-489-6). Mercier Press.

Bless Me, Ultima. Rudolfo A. Anaya. LC 75-29996. 249p. 1976. pap. 8.00 (ISBN 0-89229-002-1). Tonatiuh-Quinto Sol Intl.

Bless Me, Ultima: A Novel. Rudolfo A Anaya. LC 72-192862. (Illus.). 1972. 3.75. Quinto Sol Publications.

Bless the Beasts and Children. Glendon Fred Swarthout. LC 79-94331. 1970. 5.95. Doubleday.

Bless This House. Norah Robinson Lofts. Repr. lib. bdg. 15.45x (ISBN 0-89190-225-2). Am Repr-Rivercity Pr.

Bless This House. Norah Robinson Lofts. 1977. Repr. of 1954 ed. lib. bdg. 15.95x (ISBN 0-89244-048-1). Queens Hse.

Bless This House. Norah Robinson Lofts. 352p. 1982. pap. 2.95 (ISBN 0-449-24471-7, Crest). Fawcett.

Bless This House. Norah Robinson Lofts. 1967. pap. 0.75 o.p. (T1702). Pyramid Pubns.

Bless This House. Norah Robinson Lofts. 1972. pap. 0.95 o.p. (N2680). Pyramid Pubns.

Bless This House. Norah Robinson Lofts. 1976. pap. 1.75 o.p. (ISBN 0-515-04039-8). BJ Pub Group.

Bless This House: American Palace No. 1. Evan H. Rhodes. (Orig.). 1982. pap. 3.25 (ISBN 0-425-05457-8). Berkley Pub.

Bless This House. 1st Ed. Norah Robinson Lofts. LC 54-5363. 1954. Doubleday.

Blessed Above Women. Pamela Hansford Johnson. LC 36-5933. Harcourt, Brace and Company.

Blessed Above Women: A Novel. Angus MacLeod. LC 66-24041. 1967. Roy Publishers.

Blessed Among Women. Arnold Michael. LC 48-9500. 1948. Willing Pub. Co.

Blessed Are the Booby Birds. first ed. Suzie Anne Robins. 1973. 6.00 (ISBN 0-682-47666-8). Exposition Press.

Blessed Are the Damned. Allan Nixon. 1968. pap. 0.75 o.p. (ISBN 0-446-54745-X, 54-745). Paperback Lib.

Blessed Are the Meek: A Novel About St. Francis of Assisi, by Zofia Kossak, Translated by Rulka Langer. Zofia Kossak-Szczucka. Tr. by Rulka Godlewska Langer. LC 44-3473. 1944. Roy.

Blessed Are They. Marjorie Shier Turner. LC 36-8944. 1936. The Caxton Printers, Ltd.

Blessed Are They: Eight Stories. Frank Baker. LC 52-6253. 1951. Newman Press.

Blessed Birthday. Florence Converse. LC 17-29642. E. P. Dutton & Company.

Blessed Is the Land. Louis Zara. LC 54-11173. 1954. Crown Publishers.

Blessed Is the Man. Louis Zara. LC 35-5377. 1935. The Bobbs-Merrill Company.

Blessed McGill. Edwin Shrake. LC 68-11761. 1968. Doubleday.

Blessed Ones. Ulla Isaksson. LC 74-87997. 1970. 6.95. R. B. Luce.

Blessed Peacemaker. The Convicts' Christmas. Two Stories. L. W Reilly. LC 7-30654. (Catholic library. v. 16). 1898. C. Wildermann.

Blessed Plot: A Novel. Evelyn Berckman. LC 76-375047. (Illus.). 1976. 3.25 (ISBN 0-241-89328-3). H. Hamilton.

Blessing. Nancy Mitford. LC 51-13267. 1951. Random House.

Blessing of Azar: A Tale of Dreams and Truth. Edith Virginia Gazella. LC 28-30775. The Christopher Publishing House.

Blessing of Business see Collected Works.

Blessing of Pan. Edward John Moreton Drax Plunkett Dunsany. LC 27-254273. G. P. Putnam's Sons.

Blessing of Pan. Edward John Moreton Drax Plunkett Dunsany. LC 28-317024. 1928. G. P. Putnam' Sons.

Blessing of the Heards. Alexandre Phillips. LC 52-7793. 1952. Dutton.

Blessing Papers. William Barnwell. 1980. pap. 2.50 (ISBN 0-671-83219-0, Timescape). PB.

Blessing Way. Tony Hillerman. LC 73-96009. 1970. 4.95. Harper & Row.

Blessing Way. Tony Hillerman. 1978. 1.75 (ISBN 0-380-39941-5). Avon Book.

Blessington Method: And Other Strange Tales. Stanley Ellin. LC 64-20021. 1964. Random House.

Bleston Mystery. Robert Milward Kennedy. LC 29-5962. 1929. Pub. for The Crime Club, Inc., by Doubleday, Doran & Company, Inc.

Blight. John Creasey. (Doctor Palfrey Ser). 1970. pap. 0.75 o.p. (ISBN 0-447-74623-5). Lancer.

Blight. Anne Rice. LC 28-11050. Payson & Clarke Ltd.

Blight. Mark Sonders. 320p. (Orig.). 1981. pap. 2.95 (ISBN 0-441-06709-3). Ace Bks.

Blight: A Novel. John Lang. LC 28-17820. The Peter Eckler Publishing Company.

Blight: A Story of Dr. Palfrey. John Creasey. LC 68-16370. (His The Dr. Palfrey series). 1968. 3.95. Walker.

Blighted Home: Or, The Pet of the Old Plantation. Adah M Howard & Hungerford, Mrs. Margaret Wolfe (Hamilton) 1855?-1897. (On cover: Munro's library, v. 1. no. 131). 1884. N. L. Munro.

Blighted Life. Annie A Gibbs. (On cover: American novelists' series, no. 52). 1890. J. W. Lovell Company.

Blighted Rose. Charlotte A. O'Loan. LC 2-14428. 1902. The Angelus Publishing Co.

Blighted Rose. Joseph F Wynne. LC 2-14428. 1902. The Angelus Publishing Co.

Blind: A Story of These Times. Ernest Poole. LC 20-18299. 1920. The Macmillan Company.

Blind Alley: A Novel. Georges Simenon & Gilbert, Stuart, Tr. LC 46-21572. 1946. Reynal & Hitchcock.

Blind Alley: Being the Picture of a Very Gallant Gentleman; the Adventures of His Spirit in War and Peace: the Tale of His Daughters, His Son, Their Friends; of Their Loves and Miseries: of the Way of the World Through the Great War into the Unexplored Regions of Peace. Walter Lionel George. LC 19-8071. 1919. Little, Brown, and Company.

Blind Alleys: A Novel of Nowadays. George Cary Eggleston. LC 6-24155. 1906. Lothrop, Lee & Shepard Co.

Blind Allies. Baynard Hardwick Kendrick. LC 54-6853. (His A Duncan Maclain mystery). 1954. Morrow.

Blind Ballots. Georg Mann. LC 62-8158. 1962. Macmillan.

Blind Barber. John Dickson Carr. LC 34-35308. 1934. Harper & Brothers.

Blind Bargain: A Novel. Robert Howe Fletcher. LC 6-41690. (On cover: The household library, v. 4, no. 48). 1889. Belford, Clarke & Col; Etc., Etc.

Blind Beauty. Boris Leonidovich Pasternak. LC 73-84870. (Helen & Kurt Wolff Bk). 1969. 3.95 o.p. HarBraceJ.

Blind Bend: The Chronicles of Invernevis. Lorn Macinnes Macintyre. LC 81-14604. 11.95 (ISBN 0-312-08388-2). St. Martin's Press.

Blind Bob: A Matter-of-Fact Romance. Frederick Robert Place. LC 7-38198. 1897. Union and Advertiser Co.

Blind Bow-Boy. Carl Van Vechten. LC 23-11805. 1923. A. A. Knopf.

Blind Bow-Boy. Carl Van Vechten. LC 28-19552. 1927. A. A. Knopf.

Blind Bow-Boy. Carl Van Vechten. LC 77-78305. 1982. 24.50 (ISBN 0-404-15125-6). AMS Press.

Blind Brothers. Tate W Peek. LC 23-14919. Dorrance.

Blind Bull. George Guion Williams. LC 52-9624. 1952. Abelard Press.

Blind Cartridges. 1st Ed. William Colt MacDonald. LC 51-10215. (Double D western). 1951. Doubleday.

Blind Cave. Leo Katcher. LC 66-15908. 4.50. Viking.

Blind Cave. Leo Katcher. (S359). 1968. Avon.

Blind Chance. Bettina Kingsley. 1974. (pbk.) 0.95. Dell.

Blind Circle. Maurice Renard & Jean, Albert. Tr. by Crewe-Jones, Florence. LC 28-22662. E. P. Dutton & Co., Inc.

Blind Clamour. James Wesley Ingles. LC 39-1208. Zondervan Publishing House.

Blind Corner. Cecil William Mercer. LC 27-18147. 1927. Minton, Balch & Company.

Blind Cupid. Josephine Dodge Daskam Bacon. LC 23-4901. 1923. D. Appleton and Company.

Blind Dan's Daughter. Florence Blackburn White Schoeffel. (On cover: The laurel library, no. 5). 1892. G. Munro.

Blind Date. Leigh Howard, pseud. LC 58-3632. (Inner sanctum mystery). 1958. Simon and Schuster.

Blind Date. Vida Hurst. LC 31-19094. Grosset & Dunlap.

Blind Date. Jerzy N. Kosinski. LC 77-21968. 1977. 8.95 (ISBN 0-395-25781-6). Houghton Mifflin.

Blind Date. Berta Ruck. 1953. Dodd, Mead.

Blind Date: A Novel. Leigh Howard, pseud. LC 56-1771. 1955. Longmans, Green.
Blind Drifts: A Theocritus Lucius Westborough Story. Clyde B Clason. LC 37-89580. 1937. Pub. for the Crime Club, Inc., by Doubleday, Doran & Company, Inc.
Blind Elsie's Crime. Mary Grace Halpine. LC 7-1212. (On cover: Munro's library, v. 1. no. 411). N. L. Munro.
Blind Fury. Sinclair Gluck. LC 30-24054. 1930. Dodd, Mead & Co.
Blind Gambit. James Reach. LC 54-579822. 1954. Coward-McCann.
Blind Girl of Wittenberg: A Life-Picture of the Times of Luther and the Reformation. Carl August Wildenhahn & Morris, John Gottlieb, 1863-1895, Tr. LC 9-2514. 1856. Lindsay & Blakiston.
Blind Girl's Buff: A Novel of Suspense. Evelyn Berckman. LC 62-16789. 1962. Dodd, Mead.
Blind Goddess. Arthur Cheney Train. LC 26-819421. 1926. C. Scribner's Sons.
Blind Goddess. Arthur Cheney Train. LC 41-12725. (His Criminal court series, v. 1). C. Scribner's Sons.
Blind Harper. Ed. by William Matheson. 1970. 15.00x (ISBN 0-7073-0007-X, Pub. by Scottish Academic Pr Scotland). Columbia U Pr.
Blind Heart. Margaret Storm Jameson. LC 64-12686. 1964. Harper & Row.
Blind Hypnotist. Marc Lovell, pseud. LC 75-36600. 1976. 5.95 (ISBN 0-385-11500-8). Published for the Crime Club by Doubleday.
Blind Journey. Bruce Lancaster. LC 53-7327. 1953. Little, Brown.
Blind Lead: Daring and Thrilling Adventures, Clever Detective Work. Emma Murdoch Van Eventer. LC 12-43561. Laird & Lee.
Blind Leaders of the Blind: The Romance of a Blind Lawyer. James R Cocke. LC 6-26755. 1896. Lee and Shepard.
Blind Love. Patrick Cauvin. LC 74-30192. 1975. 6.95 (ISBN 0-395-20508-5). Houghton Mifflin.
Blind Love. Patrick Cauvin. LC 75-17986. 1975. 10.95 (ISBN 0-8161-6302-2). G. K. Hall.
Blind Love: And Other Stories. Victor Sawdon Pritchett. LC 70-85570. 1970. 5.95. Random House.
Blind Loyalty. Margaret Bass Pedler. LC 40-539756. 1940. Doubleday, Doran & Company, Inc.
Blind Lust. Maurice Gauthier. pap. 1.75 o.p. (V1060K, Venus). Grove.
Blind Man. Walter Jens. LC 54-8660. 1954. Macmillan.
Blind Man. Reginald Wright Kauffman. LC 27-13796. 1927. Duffield & Company.
Blind Man with a Pistol. Chester B. Himes. LC 69-11692. 1969. 5.95. Morrow.
Blind Man's Bluff. Louis Hemon & Richmond, Arthur Cyril, 1879- LC 25-2968. 1925. The Macmillan Company.
Blind Man's Bluff. Baynard Hardwick Kendrick. LC 42-50914. 1943. Little, Brown and Company.
Blind Man's Buff. Francis Lynde. 1928. C. Scibner's Sons.
Blind Man's Buff. Florence Ryerson & Clements, Colin Campbell, 1894- Joint Author. LC 33-36073. R. Long & R. R. Smith, Inc.
Blind Man's Eyes. William Briggs MacHarg. LC 16-7232. 1916. Little, Brown, and Company.
Blind Man's House. Hugh Walpole. LC 41-13948. 1941. Doubleday, Doran and Company, Inc.
Blind Man's Mark. Bruce Palmer. LC 59-13129. 1959. Simon and Schuster.
Blind Man's Mark: A Novel. Martin Donisthorpe Armstrong. LC 31-450873. Harcourt, Brace and Company.
Blind Man's Year. Warwick Deeping. LC 37-9924. 1937. A. A. Knopf.
Blind Man's Year. Warwick Deeping. LC 39-475. 1938. The Sun Dial Press, Inc.
Blind Men and the Devil. John M. Hanifin. LC 7-36049. 1891. Lee and Shepard.
Blind Men & the Elephant. Russell M. Griffin. 336p. (Orig.). 1982. pap. 2.95 (ISBN 0-671-41101-2, Timescape). PB.
Blind Men Crossing a Bridge: A Novel. Ursula Wyllie Roberts. LC 35-2486. 1935. Frederick A. Stokes Company.
Blind Mice. Cyril Kay-Scott. LC 21-5476. George H. Doran Company.
Blind Miller. Catherine Cookson. 256p. 1974. pap. 1.50 (ISBN 0-451-06618-9, W6618, Sig). NAL.
Blind Mirror: Stories. Jan Benes. LC 75-143538. (Orion Press book). 1971. 7.95. Grossman Publishers.
Blind Musician. Vladimir Galaktionovich Korolenko. LC 69-13961. 1970. Greenwood Press.
Blind Musician. Vladimir Galaktionovich Korolenko. Tr. by Delano, Aline P. (Kuz'michova) LC 7-14114. 1890. Little Brown and Company.
Blind Musician. From the Russian of Korolenko. Vladimir Galaktionovich Korolenko. Tr. by Ethel Marryat & Westall, William. LC 7-141158. (On cover: Lovell's international series, no. 100). J. W. Lovell Company.
Blind Owl. Sadegh Hedayat. Tr. by D. P. Costello. 1958. pap. 1.95 (ISBN 0-394-17445-3, B205, BC). Grove.
Blind Owl. Sadegh Hedayat. 1957. 3.00 o.p. Fernhill.
Blind Owl. Translated by D. P. Costello. Sadegh Hedayat. LC 58-12114. (Evergreen original, E-100). Grove Press.
Blind Pig. Jon A Jackson. LC 78-57117. 7.95 (ISBN 0-394-42613-4). Random House.
Blind Plot. Ambrose Clancy. LC 80-10761. 1980. 10.95 (ISBN 0-688-03640-6). W. Morrow.
Blind Raftery and His Wife, Hilaria. Donn Byrne. LC 24-21810. The Century Co.
Blind Road. Hugh Gordon. LC 12-9853. 1912. 1.25. Moffat, Yard and Company.
Blind Ruth: Or, How Many I Do Good? Illustrating the Second Petition of the Lord's Prayer, "Thy Kingdom Come.". Presbyterian Board of Publication.
Blind Saw Murder. Howard C Huston. LC 54-10119. (Cock Robin mystery). 1954. Macmillan.
Blind Search. Lesley Egan, pseud. LC 76-23774. (Crime Club Ser.). 1977. 5.95 o.p. (ISBN 0-385-12356-6). Doubleday.
Blind Search. Elizabeth Linington. LC 76-23774. 1977. 5.95 (ISBN 0-385-12356-6). Published for the Crime Club by Doubleday.
Blind Ship. Jean Barreyre. LC 26-21491. 1926. L. MacVeagh. The Dial Press.
Blind Side. Arthur Leonard Bell Thompson. 1973. (pbk) 0.95. Pocket Books.
Blind Side. Arthur Leonard Bell Thompson. LC 78-150275. 1971. 6.95. Coward, McCann & Geoghegan.
Blind Side. Patricia Wentworth. LC 39-17423. J. B. Lippincott Company.
Blind Sight. B Y Benedialt. LC 15-16232. 1915. 1.35. Dodd, Mead and Company.
Blind Spot. John Creasey. LC 54-6011. 1954. Harper.
Blind Spot. Austin Hall & Homer Eon Flint. 1976. 1.75. Ace.
Blind Spot: A Lieutenant Kerrigan Mystery. Joseph Harrington. LC 66-18445. bds., 3.95. Lippincott.
Blind Spot: A Novel. Justus Miles Forman. LC 14-170935. 1914. Harper & Brothers.
Blind, the Story of the World Tragedy. William Henry McMasters. LC 34-497833. The Stratford Company.
Blind Tiger: A Novel by Robert Standish Pseud. 1st Ed. Digby George Gerahty. LC 56-11505. 1956. Doubleday.
Blind Trust Kills: A Novel of Suspense. James P Wohl. LC 78-55655. 1978. 8.95 (ISBN 0-672-52525-9). Bobbs-Merrill.
Blind Villain. Evelyn Berckman. LC 57-5871. (Red badge detective). 1957. Dodd, Mead.
Blind Voices. Tom Reamy. LC 78-3817. 7.95. Berkley Pub. Corp.: Distributed by Putnam.
Blind Voices. Tom Reamy. 1979. 1.95 (ISBN 0-425-04165-4). Berkley Pub. Coro.
Blind Who See. Marcia Rutledge Hale. LC 11-27454. 1911. The Century Co.
Blind Windows. Edwina Levin MacDonald. LC 27-165814. The Macaulay Company.
Blind Wisdom. Amanda Benjamin Hall. LC 20-17531. G. W. Jacobs & Company.
Blinde, Passagier. Max Von Eyth. Ed. by Bell, Clair Hayden. LC 32-188451. (Half-title: Oxford library of German texts). 1931. Oxford University Press.
Blinded by Love: A Romance of Life. Frederick William Wicker. LC 19-14704. Saulsbury Publishing Company.
Blinded Kings. J Kessel & Iswolsky, Helene, Joint Author. LC 27-10954. 1926. Doubleday, Page & Company.
Blindfold. Orrick Johns. LC 23-106923. 1923. Lieber & Lewis.
Blindfold. Florence Marryat Church Lean. (On cover: Lovell's international series. no. 85). 1890. J. W. Lovell Company.
Blindfold. Anthony Melville-Ross. LC 79-19436. 1980. 10.95 (ISBN 0-89340-226-5). John Curley & Associates.
Blindfold. Patricia Wentworth. LC 35-12785. 1935. J. B. Lippincott Company.
Blindfold: A Novel. Melville-Ross, Anthony. LC 78-2059. 1978. 9.95 (ISBN 0-06-012973-5). Harper & Row.
Blindfolded. Earle Ashley Walcott. LC 6-18590. 1906. The Bobbs-Merrill Company.
Blindman's World: And Other Stories. Edward Bellamy. LC 68-55664. (American short story series, v. 4). 1968. Garrett Press.
Blindman's World, and Other Stories. Edward Bellamy. LC 72-8154. (American short story series, v. 4). 1972. (ISBN 0-8422-8006-5). MSS Information Corp.
Blindman's World and Other Stories. Edward Bellamy & Howells, William Dean. LC 98-837. 1898. Houghton, Mifflin and Company.
Blindness. Henry Green. LC 26-18388. E. P. Dutton & Company.
Blindness. Henry Green. LC 78-57618. 1978. 8.95 (ISBN 0-670-17428-9). Viking Press.
Blindness: A Novel. Henry Green. LC 79-16423. 1979. 12.95 (ISBN 0-8161-6743-5). G. K. Hall.
Blindness of Dr. Gray: Or, The Final Law. Patrick Augustine Sheehan. 1909. Longmans, Green, and Co.
Blindness of Heart. Violet Colquhoun Bell. LC 24-3790. Harcourt, Brace and Company.
Blindness of Virtue. Cosmo Hamilton. LC 13-3315. George H. Doran Company.
Blindness of Virtue. Cosmo Hamilton. LC 33-17486. George H. Doran Company.
Blindpits. A Story of Scottish Life. Reprinted by Special Arrangement with the Edinburgh Publishers. LC 8-25661. 1869. G. P. Putnam & Son.
Blinds Down. Horace Annesley Vachell. LC 12-10140. Hodder & Stoughton, George H. Doran Company.
Blindside. Dave Klein. 320p. 1982. pap. 2.95 (ISBN 0-441-06736-0, Pub. by Charter Bks). Ace Bks.
Blinkards. Kobina Sekyi. (African Writers Ser: No. 136). 148p. (Orig.). 1974. pap. text ed. 2.25x (ISBN 0-435-90436-1). Humanities.
Blinkers: A Romance of the Preconceived Idea. Horace Annesley Vachell. LC 21-17813. George H. Doran Company.
Blinky: A Complete Dramatic Story of American Life, Condensed into Tabloid Form for the Convenience of Those Busy Readers Whose Imaginative Gifts Will Permit Them to Paint Their Own Scenes. William Nigh. LC 20-16162. Federal Printing Co.
Blinky Morgan: The Detective's Foe. John A Fraser. LC 6-43151. (Globe detective series. no. 5). 1888. The Eagle Publishing Co.
Bliss. Peter Carey. LC 81-47881. 13.41 (ISBN 0-06-014959-0). Harper & Row.
Bliss. Elizabeth Gundy. 1977. 11.95 (ISBN 0-670-17431-9). Viking Pr.
Bliss: A Novel. Elizabeth Gundy. LC 77-21721. 1977. 8.95 (ISBN 0-670-17431-9). Viking Press.
Bliss: A Novel. Elizabeth Gundy. (Jove/ HBJ edition). 1978. 1.95. Jove Books.
Bliss & Bluster. Janwillem Van De Wetering. (Illus.). 128p. (Orig.). 1982. pap. 7.95 (ISBN 0-395-31839-4). HM.
Bliss and Bluster, or, How to Crack a Nut. Janwillem Van De Wetering. LC 81-7275. (Illus.). 1982. 7.95 (ISBN 0-395-31839-4). Houghton Mifflin.
Bliss, and Other Short Stories. Katherine Mansfield. LC 72-11931. (Short story index reprint series). 1973. (ISBN 0-8369-4240-X). Books for Libraries Press.
Bliss, and Other Stories. Katherine Mansfield. LC 21-215541. 1921. A. A. Knopf.
Bliss: And Other Stories. Katherine Mansfield. LC 23-6756. 1922. A. A. Knopf.
Bliss: And Other Stories. Katherine Mansfield. LC 23-9577. 1923. A. A. Knopf.
Bliss Incorporated. Patrick Skene Catling. LC 76-380826. 1976. 3.65 (ISBN 0-297-77141-8). Weidenfeld and Nicolson.
Blister Jones. John Taintor Foote. LC 13-22759. The Bobbs-Merrill Company.
Blithe Baldwin. Ethel Powelson Hueston. LC 33-199670. The Bobbs-Merrill Company.
Blithedale Romance. Nathaniel Hawthorne. LC 7-3879. 1860. Ticknor and Fields.
Blithedale Romance. Nathaniel Hawthorne. LC 7-3878. 1870. Fields, Osgood, & Co.
Blithedale Romance. Nathaniel Hawthorne. LC 99-3546. T. Y. Crowell & Company.
Blithedale Romance. Nathaniel Hawthorne. LC 4579. W. B. Conkey Company.
Blithedale Romance. Nathaniel Hawthorne. (Half-title: Everyman's library, ed. by Ernest Rhys. Fiction no. 592). 1912. J. M. Dent & Sons, Ltd.
Blithedale Romance. Nathaniel Hawthorne. LC 36-37494. (Half-title: Everyman's library, ed. by Ernest Rhys. Fiction no. 592). 1926. J. M. Dent & Sons, Ltd.
Blithedale Romance: An Authoritative Text, Backgrounds and Sources, Essays in Criticism. Nathaniel Hawthorne & Seymour Lee Gross. LC 77-24887. (Norton critical edition). 1978. 12.95 (ISBN 0-393-04449-1). Norton.
Blithedale Romance & Fanshawe. Nathaniel Hawthorne. Ed. by William Charvat et al. (Centenary Edition of the Works of Nathaniel Hawthorne: Vol. 3). (Illus.). 1965. 15.00 (ISBN 0-8142-0061-3). Ohio St U Pr.
Blithedale Romance and Fanshawe: Fredson Bowers, Textual Ed. Nathaniel Hawthorne. Ed. by Fredson Thayer Bowers. LC 66-876. (His Centenary Ed. of the Works of Nathaniel Hawthorne, V.). 1966. 8.50. State Univ. Pr.
Blithedale Romance. Introd. by Arlin Turner. Nathaniel Hawthorne. LC 59-259320. (Norton library, N9). 1958. Norton.
Blithesome Jottings: A Diary of Humorous Days. Gertrude Sanborn. LC 18-21167. 1918. The Four Seas Company.
Blitz. David Fraser. LC 78-22758. 1979. 12.95 (ISBN 0-385-14318-4). Doubleday.
Blitzen the Conjurer. Frank Martin Bicknell. LC 6-32858. H. Altemus Company.
Blitzlicht Passage. Ivan Manson. 1976. pap. 1.50 o.p. (ISBN 0-515-04202-1). Pyramid Pubns.
Blix. Frank Norris. LC 74-95150. 1969. AMS Press.
Blix. Frank Norris. LC 99-4283. 1899. Doubleday & McClure Co.
Blix. Frank Norris. LC 17-5023. 1901. International Association of Newspapers and Authors.
Blix. Frank Norris. LC 25-23224. (The Lambskin library. no. 47). 1925. Doubleday, Page & Company.
Blix, Moran of the Lady Letty: A Story of Adventure off the California Coast. Frank Norris. LC 67-3228. (His Complete works, v. 3). 1967. Kennikat Press.
Blizzard. Robert Bahr. LC 80-14956. 1980. 9.95 o.p. (ISBN 0-13-077842-7). P-H.
Blizzard. Peter Dawson. 144p. 1982. pap. 1.95 (ISBN 0-553-22911-7). Bantam.
Blizzard. David James. (O.s.i.). (Orig.). 1975. pap. 1.50 o.s.i. (BT50845). Belmont-Tower.
Blizzard. David James. 1975. (pbk.) 1.50. Belmont Tower Books.
Blizzard. George Stone. 1979. 2.25 (ISBN 0-440-11080-7). Dell Pub. Co.
Blizzard: A Novel. George Stone. LC 76-559. 9.95 (ISBN 0-448-12250-2). Grosset & Dunlap.
Blizzard Herd. Alex Hawk, pseud. (Westerns Ser). (Orig.). 1971. pap. 0.60 o.p. (ISBN 0-446-63483-2, 63-483). Paperback Lib.
Blizzard of the Heart. Susan E. Kirby. 1982. 6.95 (Avalon). Bouregy.
Blizzard Pass. Theodore V. Olsen. 160p. 1982. pap. 2.25 (ISBN 0-449-12360-X, GM). Fawcett.
Blizzard. 1st Ed. Philip Duffield Stong. LC 55-7007. 1955. Doubleday.
Blobson's Dire Mishaps in a Barn Storming Company. This Story Deals with the Humorous As Well As the Serious Side of a Barn Storming Company on Its Travels... Mortimer M Shelley. LC 8-7677. M. M. Shelley.
Block Buster. Gerald Green. 1973. (pbk) 1.75. Warner Paperback Library.
Block Buster. Gerald Green. LC 73-171294. 1972. 7.95. Doubleday.
Block Busters. Lou Cameron. LC 64-18237. 1964. D. McKay Co.
Block Twenty Six: Sabotage at Buchenwald. Pierre Julitte. Tr. by Francis Price from Fr. (Illus.). 1971. 6.95 o.p. (ISBN 0-385-06359-8). Doubleday.
Block with the Oneholer: Stories and Adventures Concerning Bluey Jacks. Illus. by Paul Rigby. James Begley. LC 67-297818. 1968. 4.50. Rigby.
Blockade of Phalsburg: An Episode of the End of the Empire. Emile Erckmann & Chatrian, Alexandre, 1826-1890, Joint Author. LC 6-38411. 1871. C. Scribner & Co.
Blockade of Phalsburg: An Episode of the End of the Empire. Emile Erckmann & Chatrian, Alexandre, 1826-1890, Joint Author. LC 6-38410. (Half-title: Erckmann-Chatrian national novels). 1889. C. Scribner's Sons.
Blockade of Phalzburg: An Episode of the End of the Empire. Emile Erckmann & Chatrian, Alexander, 1826-1890, Joint Author. LC 98-1208. 1898. C. Scribner's Sons.
Blockade Runner. J. Perkins Tracy. (Added t.-p.: The flag series, no. 11). Street & Smith.
Blockade Runners in Verne, Jules, 1828-1905. Twenty Thousand Leagues Under the Sea... Jules Verne. LC 50-341426. 1950. Fountain Press.
Blockbuster. Stephen Barlay. LC 76-26909. (Illus.). 1977. 8.95 (ISBN 0-688-03127-7). Morrow.
Blockbuster. Stephen Barlay. 1978. 2.25 (ISBN 0-345-27443-1). New American Library.
Blocked Road. Hedwig Hermione Reinsch Purin. LC 41-7508. Chapman and Grimes.
Blocked Trail. Johnston McCulley. LC 33-1411. 1932. G. H. Watt.
Blockhouse. Translated from the French by Jonathan Griffin. Jean Paul Clebert. (T-379). Avon.
Blockhouse. Translated from the French by Jonathan Griffin. 1st American Ed. Jean Paul Clebert. LC 58-628460. 1958. Coward-McCann.
Blond Baboon. Janwillem Van De Wetering. 1978. 7.95 (ISBN 0-395-26307-7). HM.
Blond Baboon. Janwillem Van De Wetering. 1979. 1.95 (ISBN 0-671-82318-3). Pocket Books.
Blond Baboon: A Novel. Janwillem Van De Wetering. LC 78-24116. 1978. 12.50 (ISBN 0-8161-6646-3). G. K. Hall.

Blond Baboon: A Novel. Janwillem Van De Wetering. LC 77-17338. 1978. 6.95 (ISBN 0-395-26307-7). Houghton Mifflin.

Blond Beast. Robert Ames Bennet. LC 18-12615. 1.50. The Reilly & Britton Co.

Blond Trouble. Rob Eden. LC 33-8150. Grosset & Dunlap.

Blonde. Carter Brown, pseud. Bd. with Girl in a Shroud. 1979. pap. 2.50 (ISBN 0-451-11703-4, AE1703, Sig). NAL.

Blonde. Peggy Gaddis, pseud. LC 46-15974. 1946. Phoenix Press.

Blonde and Beaautiful. Peggy Gaddis, pseud. LC 48-15382. 1948. Phoenix Press.

Blonde and Beautiful: A Suspense Novel by Richard Foster Pseud. Kendell Foster Crossen. LC 55-328346. (Popular library, 667). 1955. Popular Library.

Blonde Baby. Wilson Collison. LC 31-7176. 1931. R. M. McBride & Company.

Blonde Corinthian. Illus. by Fritz Kredel; Introd. by Louis Bromlield. Herbert T Cobey. LC 51-8881. 1951. Farrar, Straus and Young.

Blonde Countess. Herbert Osborn Yardley. LC 34-112589. 1934. Longmans, Green and Co.

Blonde Creole. A Story of New Orleans. Alice Howard Hilton. LC 7-4681. (peerless series, no. 64). 1892. J. S. Ogilvie.

Blonde Cried Murder: By Brett Halliday Pseud. Davis Dresser. LC 56-13809. (Torquil book). 1956. Distributed by Dodd, Mead.

Blonde Died Dancing. Kelley Roos. LC 56-100605. (Red badge detective). 1956. Dodd, Mead.

Blonde Died First: A New Jim Steele Mystery. Albert Leffingwell. LC 41-511181. 1941. The Dial Press.

Blonde Dynamite. Jerome Darwin Engel. LC 41-13506. Phoenix Press.

Blonde Heathen, Northeast of Borneo: A Story of Intrigue, Murder and Espionage. Jim Allen Savage. LC 51-6445. 1951. Naylor.

Blonde Hurricane. P. Howard. 1965. pap. 1.00 o.p. (ISBN 0-8283-1106-4). Branden.

Blonde in Black: A Wade Paris Mystery. Ben Benson. LC 58-5916. 1958. M. S. Mill Co., and W. Morrow.

Blonde Interlude. Bourke Lee. LC 32-191892. 1932. Simon and Schuster.

Blonde Lady: Being a Record of the Duel of Wits Between Arsene Lupin and the English Detective. Maurice Leblanc. Tr. by Teixeira De Mattos, Alexander Louis. LC 10-2506. 1910. Doubleday, Page & Company.

Blonde on a Broomstick. Alan Geoffrey Yates. LC 66-3220. (Carter Brown mystery series). 1966. New American Library.

Blonde Peril. Bennie Caroline Hall. LC 47-12320. 1947. Phoenix Press.

Blonde Target, No. 2. Richard Reinsmith, pseud. (Bodyguard Ser.). (Orig.). 1980. pap. text ed. 1.95 o.s.i. (ISBN 0-505-51565-2). Tower Bks.

Blonde Trap: A Novel. Ernie Weatherall. LC 54-38450. 1954. Woodford Press.

Blonde Vampire. De Sacia Mooers. LC 20-22158. 1920. Moffat, Yard & Company.

Blonde Venus. William Arthur Neubauer. LC 45-2277. 1945. Phoenix Press.

Blonde Wore Black. Peter Chambers, pseud. 1968. 3.50 o.p. Roy.

Blonde Wore Black. Dennis John Andrew Phillips. LC 68-15897. 1968. Roy Publishers.

Blondes Don't Cry. Merlda Mace. LC 45-3041. 1945. J. Messner Inc.

Blondes Play Too Rough. Robert Neal Leath. LC 34-7030. 1934. W. Godwin, Inc.

Blondes Prefer Gentlemen: A Satire. The Ingenious Diary of an Amateur, by an Englishwoman. Nora K Strange & Johnson, Merle De Vers, 1874- LC 27-1101. J. S. Ogilvie Publishing Company.

Blondes' Requiem. Rene Ragmond. LC 46-168133. 1946. Crown Publishers.

Blondes' Requiem. Rene Raymond. LC 45-22130. 1945. Jarrolds Limited.

Blondie. Charles Edward Colahan. LC 38-17569. Godwin,

Blondie and Dagwood: A Novel of the Great American Family. Helga Lund & Young, Murat Bernard, 1901- LC 44-9890. 1944. Smith and Durell.

Blonds Die Young. Bill Peters. LC 52-12457. (Red badge detective). 1952. Dodd, Mead.

Blondy's Boy Friend: A Love Story. Leatrice Homesley. LC 30-12307. Chelsea House.

Blood. Allan Morgan. (Blood Ser.). (O.s.i.: No. 1). 192p. (Orig.). 1974. pap. 0.95 o.s.i. (AN1231, Award). Univ Pub & Dist.

Blood Alley. Albert Sidney Fleischman. LC 55-42186. 1955. Fawcett Publications.

Blood Alley. Cover Painting by Barye Phillips. Albert Sidney Fleishman. LC 53-42186. (Gold medal books, 499). 1955. Fawcett Publications.

Blood Amyot. Christopher Nicole. 1974. (pbk.) 1.25. Bantam Books.

Blood & Burning. Algis Budrys, pseud. 1978. 1.75 (ISBN 0-425-03861-0). Berkley Pub. Corp.

Blood and Celluloid. Heinrich Eduard Jacob. LC 30-292491. 1930. R. R. Smith, Inc.

Blood & Coal. Henry George. LC 50-8154. 1950. Dorrance.

Blood & Dreams. Leslie Waller. 1982. pap. 3.25 (ISBN 0-515-06426-2). Jove Pubns.

Blood & Dreams. Leslie Waller. 396p. 1980. 12.95 (ISBN 0-399-12564-7). Putnam Pub Group.

Blood and Flowers. 1st Ed. Elbert Epperson. LC 56-128058. 1957. Vantage Press.

Blood & Grits. Harry Crews. LC 78-54605. 1979. 11.49i (ISBN 0-06-010933-5, HarpT). Har-Row.

Blood & Guts in High School. Kathy Acker. (Illus.). 1979. 9.95 o.s.i. (ISBN 0-88373-095-2); pap. 5.95 o.s.i. (ISBN 0-88373-094-4). Stonehill Pub Co.

Blood and Guts Is Going Nuts. Christopher Leopold. LC 77-70903. (Illus.). 1977. 8.95 (ISBN 0-385-12980-7). Doubleday.

Blood and Guts Is Going Nuts". Christopher Leopold. LC 77-353353. (Illus.). 1976. 4.95 (ISBN 0-904291-06-5). Lemon Tree Press.

Blood and Guts Is Going Nuts. Christopher Leopold. (A Berkley Medallion Book.). 1978. 1.95 (ISBN 0-425-04062-3). Berkeley Pub. Corp.

Blood and Judgement. Michael Francis Gilbert. LC 80-20564. 1981. 12.50 (ISBN 0-89340-288-5). J. Curley & Associates.

Blood and Judgment. Michael Francis Gilbert. LC 59-6339. 1959. Harper.

Blood and Judgment. Michael Francis Gilbert. (Perennial Library). 1978. 1.95 (ISBN 0-06-080446-7). Harper & Row.

Blood & Money. Thomas Thompson. LC 75-36632. 480p. 1976. 10.95 (ISBN 0-385-09685-2). Doubleday.

Blood & Passion. Jeffrey Wallman. (Orig.). 1980. pap. 2.25 o.s.i. (ISBN 0-505-51514-8). Tower Bks.

Blood & Roses. Richard William Tregaskis. 1970. 6.95 o.p. M Evans.

Blood & Sand. Vicente Blasco Ibanez. Tr. by Frances Partridge. LC 62-12957. 11.00 (ISBN 0-8044-2051-3); pap. 4.95 (ISBN 0-8044-6046-9). Ungar.

Blood and Sand: A Novel. authorized american ed. Vicente Blasco Ibanez & Gillespie, Mrs. W. A., Tr. LC 19-5427. E. P. Dutton & Company.

Blood and Sand: A Novel. Vicente Blasco Ibanez & Gillespie, Mrs. W. A., Tr. LC 22-18406. E. P. Dutton & Company.

Blood and Sand, the Life and Loves of a Bullfighter: A New English Version of the Novel. Vicente Blasco Ibanez. LC 51-26058. (A Dell book, 500). 1951. Dell Pub. Co.

Blood and Tears. Balder Olden. LC 34-11035. 1934. D. Appleton-Century Company, Incorporated.

Blood and the Moon: Chronicles of Invernevis. Lorn Macinnes Macintyre. LC 76-360541. 1974. 0.90 (ISBN 0-902706-32-2) (ISBN 0-902706-31-4). Club Leabhar.

Blood and Thirsty. Audrey Walz. LC 49-4278. 1949. Duell, Sloan and Pearce.

Blood & Thunder. M. W. Disher. LC 73-21683. (English Literature Ser., No. 33). 1974. lib. bdg. 49.95x (ISBN 0-8383-1761-8). Haskell.

Blood and Water. Peter De Polnay. LC 75-40784. 7.95. St. Martin's Press.

Blood Bait. Bret Sanders. (Hawk Ser). (O.s.i.). 192p. (Orig.). 1974. pap. 0.95 o.s.i. (AN1327, Award). Univ Pub & Dist.

Blood Bargain: A Novel. Michael Bradley. (Adrano/for hire,#4). 1974. (pbk.) 1.25. Warner Paperback Library.

Blood Beast. Dean W. Ballenger. (Gannon Ser: No. 3). 192p. (Orig.). 1974. pap. 0.95 o.p. (ISBN 0-532-95343-6). Woodhill.

Blood Beast. Dean W. Ballenger. (Gannon Ser: No. 3). 192p. (Orig.). 1974. pap. 0.95 o.p. (ISBN 0-532-95343-6). Manor Bks.

Blood Bond. Emma Cave. LC 78-20200. 9.95 (ISBN 0-06-010627-1). Harper & Row.

Blood Brother. Elliott Arnold. LC 47-30174. 1947. Duell, Sloan and Pearce.

Blood Brother. Elliott Arnold. LC 78-26788. 16.95 (ISBN 0-8032-1003-5) (ISBN 0-8032-5901-8). University of Nebraska Press.

Blood Brother, Blood Brother. Niles N. Peebles. (Orig.). 1969. pap. 0.60 o.p. (X2042). Pyramid Pubns.

Blood Brother. Illustrated by Dale Nichols. Elliott Arnold. LC 50-13509. 1950. Duell, Sloan and Pearce.

Blood Brotherhood. Robert Barnard. LC 77-95195. 1978. 7.95 (ISBN 0-8027-5387-6). Walker.

Blood Brotherhood. Robert Barnard. LC 82-22255. 1983. 2.95 (ISBN 0-14-006552-0). Penguin Books.

Blood Brotherhood. John Van Der Zee. LC 79-95860. 1970. 5.95. Harcourt, Brace & World.

Blood Brothers. D. Anderson. LC 67-17800. (Illus.). 1969. 5.95 o.p. (ISBN 0-312-08400-5). St Martin.

Blood Brothers of Gor. John Norman. 1982. pap. 3.50 (ISBN 0-87997-777-9, UW1777). DAW Bks.

Blood Bullets. Ed Newsom. (Brannigan Ser.: No. 3). (Orig.). 1982. pap. 2.25 (ISBN 0-89083-920-4). Zebra.

Blood Carnelian. Jean Raynes. LC 79-7053. 1979. 7.95 (ISBN 0-385-15019-9). Doubleday.

Blood Countess. Kenneth Robeson. (Avenger,#33). 1975. (pbk.) 0.95 (ISBN 0-446-75783-7). Warner Paperback Library.

Blood County. Curt Selby. (Science Fiction Ser.). 1981. pap. 2.25 o.p. (ISBN 0-87997-622-5, UE1622). DAW Bks.

Blood Cult. David L. Robbins. 240p. (Orig.). 1981. pap. 2.25 (ISBN 0-8439-0950-1). Leisure Bks CT.

Blood Dance. William Oliver Turner. 176p. pap. 1.95 (ISBN 0-425-05338-5). Berkley Pub.

Blood Dance. William Oliver Turner. 1982. pap. 1.25 (ISBN 0-425-03569-7). Berkley Pub.

Blood Dance. William Oliver Turner. (Berkley medallion book). 1974. (pbk.) 0.95 (ISBN 0-425-02704-X). Berkley Pub. Co.

Blood Eagle, and Other Tales. ... 1st ed. Peter Henry Emerson. LC 25-25125. 1925. A. Melrose, Ltd.

Blood Emerald. Vanessa Blake. 1975. (pbk.) 0.95 (ISBN 0-671-77948-6). Pocket Books.

Blood Endures. Robert Inman. 1981. 16.95 (ISBN 0-671-41175-6, Wyndham Bks.). S&S.

Blood Endures: A Novel. Robert Inman. LC 81-11577. 13.95 (ISBN 0-671-61020-1). Wyndham Books.

Blood Feud. Edward Hannibal & Robert Boris. LC 78-11951. 1979. 10.00 (ISBN 0-345-28100-4). Ballantine Books.

Blood Feud. Giles A Lutz. (Fawcett Gold Medal). 1974. (pbk.) 0.75. Fawcett.

Blood Feud. Yusuf Sharouni. LC 82-50881. 130p. 1983. 12.00X (ISBN 0-89410-358-X); pap. 6.00X (ISBN 0-89410-350-4). Three Continents.

Blood Fix. Dean W. Ballenger. (Gannon Ser.: No. 2). 192p. (Orig.). 1974. pap. 0.95 o.p. (ISBN 0-532-95302-9). Woodhill.

Blood Fix. Dean W. Ballenger. (Gannon Ser.: No. 2). 192p. (Orig.). 1974. pap. 0.95 o.p. (ISBN 0-532-95302-9). Manor Bks.

Blood Fix. Dean W. Ballenger. (Mike Gannon series,#2). 1974. (pbk.) 0.95. Manor Books.

Blood Flies Upward. E. X Ferrars, pseud. LC 76-18343. 1977. 5.95 (ISBN 0-385-12121-0). Published for the Crime Club by Doubleday.

Blood for a Borgia. Richard Gaunt. LC 68-20995. 1968. Roy Publishers.

Blood for a Dirty Dollar. Joe Millard, pseud. 160p. 1980. pap. 1.95 (ISBN 0-441-06721-2, Pub. by Charter Bks). Ace Bks.

Blood for a Dirty Dollar. Joe Millard, pseud. (Dollar Western Ser.). (O.s.i.). 160p. 1973. pap. 0.95 o.s.i. (AN1418, Award). Univ Pub & Dist.

Blood for a Dirty Dollar. Joseph Millard. (Man with No Name Series). 1973. (pbk) 0.75. Award Books.

Blood for Breakfast. Dean W. Ballenger. (Gannon Ser.: No. 1). 192p. (Orig.). 1973. pap. 0.95 o.p. (ISBN 0-532-95276-6). Woodhill.

Blood for Breakfast. Dean W. Ballenger. (Gannon Ser.: No. 1). 192p. (Orig.). 1973. pap. 0.95 o.p. (ISBN 0-532-95276-6). Manor Bks.

Blood for Breakfast: A Novel. 1st Ed. R Cynewulf Robbins. LC 55-12417. Pageant Press.

Blood Fortunes. Tom Alibrandi. (Orig.). 1982. pap. 3.50 (ISBN 0-440-10741-5). Dell.

Blood from a Stone. Ruth Otis Sawtell Wallis. LC 45-349851. 1945. Dodd, Mead & Company.

Blood from the Sky. Piotr Rawicz. Tr. by Peter Wiles. (Helen & Kurt Wolff Book). 4.95 o.p. (ISBN 0-15-113215-1). HarBraceJ.

Blood Games. Chelsea Q. Yarbro. 1980. 11.95 o.p. (ISBN 0-312-08441-2). St Martin.

Blood Games: A Novel of Historical Horror, Third in the Count De Saint-Germain Series. Chelsea Quinn Yarbro. LC 79-22853. 11.95 (ISBN 0-312-08441-2). St. Martin's Press.

Blood Hunt. James Alphonsus Harvey. LC 76-27041. 1977. 5.95 (ISBN 0-385-12714-6). Doubleday.

Blood Hype. Alan Dean Foster. 1973. (pbk) 1.25 (ISBN 0-345-03163-6). Ballantine Books.

Blood in the Dust. Lewis Brant, pseud. LC 68-552. 1967. Arcadia House.

Blood in the Dust: A Novel of the Old West. 1st Ed. Helm Stephens. LC 53-8518. 1953. Exposition Press.

Blood in the Furrows: A Historical Novel. Ingrid Clairmont & Leonard Clairmont. (Illus.). 1979. 12.00 (ISBN 0-682-49504-2, Banner). Exposition.

Blood in the Sky. Dan Brennan. 1977. pap. 1.50 o.s.i. (ISBN 0-8439-0464-X, Leisure Bks). Nordon Pubns.

Blood in Your Eye: A Novel of Suspense. Robert Patrick Wilmot, pseud. LC 52-7467. 1952. Lippincott.

Blood Innocents. Thomas H Cook. LC 79-90929. 2.25 (ISBN 0-87216-632-5). Playboy Press Paperbacks.

Blood Is Not Enough: Stories of One Sq. Mile. Alex Blair. (Illus.). 172p. (Orig.). 1981. pap. 3.50 (ISBN 0-938918-00-1). Chong-Donnie.

Blood Is the Man. W. Lawton Lowth. LC 7-14500. 1890. The Bancroft Company.

Blood Kin. Harry T. Lawrence. 3.75 o.p. Vantage.

Blood Kin. Barbara Anne Pauley. 1973. (pbk) 0.95. Dell.

Blood Kin. Barbara Anne Pauley. LC 75-175394. 1972. 4.95. Published for the Crime Club by Doubleday.

Blood Kin. Buena Vista Stine. LC 42-17355. 1942. Wetzel Publishing Co., Inc.

Blood Knife. Jack Slade, pseud. (Leisure book). 1.75 (ISBN 0-8439-0626-X). Nordon Pubns.

Blood Knot. Bruce Algozin. (Orig.). 1982. pap. 2.95 (ISBN 0-8217-1073-7). Zebra.

Blood Knot. Burt Cole. LC 79-25427. 10.00 (ISBN 0-312-08445-5). St. Martin's Press.

Blood Knot. Burton Wohl. (Dell book). 1974. (pbk.) 1.50. Dell.

Blood Like New Wine. Toni Howard. LC 54-6212. 1954. Appleton-Century-Crofts.

Blood Line. William M James. (Apache series, 7) (ISBN 0-523-00913-5). Pinnacle Books.

Blood Lust. Tony Trelos, pseud. 192p. pap. 1.95 o.p. (6131). Brandon.

Blood Money. Max Collins. 1973. pap. 0.75 o.p. (07277). Curtis.

Blood Money. Max Collins. 1973. 0.75. Curtis Books.

Blood Money. Aaron Fletcher. (Leisure Books). 1977. 1.50 (ISBN 0-8439-0471-2). Nordon Pubns.

Blood Money. Sidney Floyd Gowing. 1932. Putnam.

Blood-Money. William C Morrow. LC 7-32483. 1882. F. J. Walker & Co.

Blood Money. Thomas B Reagan. LC 70-113163. 1970. 4.50. Putnam.

Blood Money: By Dan J. Stevens Pseud. Wayne D Overholser. LC 56-5639. (Perma books, M-3033. Western, 3). 1956. Permabooks.

Blood Moon. Jean Alexander. (Orig.). 1970. pap. 0.75 o.p. (ISBN 0-447-74648-0). Lancer.

Blood Moon see Shadows.

Blood-Moon: And Other Tales of Divorce. Irene Osgood. LC 11-25008. 1911. 1.50. Broadway Publishing Co.

Blood Mother. Allan Duane. LC 72-4732. 1972. (ISBN 0-393-08667-4). Norton.

Blood Oath. David Morrell. LC 82-5615. 11.95 (ISBN 0-312-08447-1). St. Martin's/Marek.

Blood of Adventure. Arnold R Logan. LC 51-14568. 1951. Vantage Press.

Blood of an Englishman. James McClure. LC 81-48255. (Pantheon International Crime). 1982. 2.95 (ISBN 0-394-71019-3). Pantheon Books.

Blood of Angels. Albert Barker. (Hawk Macrae Ser, No. 4). 1974. pap. 0.95 o.p. (09255). Curtis.

Blood of Gennaro. V T Calnan. LC 59-11001. 1960. Goward-McCann.

Blood of Her Ancestors. Lucy Agnes Hancock. LC 38-7573. The Penn Publishing Company.

Blood of Kings. Nelson Coral Nye. LC 46-240785. 1946. The Macmillan Company.

Blood of Kings: A Hopeful Romance. Reginald Wright Kauffman. LC 26-154255. 1926. Duffield & Company.

Blood of October. David Lippincott. (Signet Book). 1977. 1.95 (ISBN 0-451-07785-7). New American Library.

Blood of Others. Simone De Beauvoir. 1974. (pbk.) 1.75. Bantam Books.

Blood of Others. Simone de Beauvoir. Tr. by Senhouse, Roger. LC 48-7497. 1948. A. A. Knopf.

Blood of Paradise. Stephen Goodwin. LC 79-842. 8.95 (ISBN 0-525-06846-5). Dutton.

Blood of Strawberries. Henry Van Dyke. LC 69-11572. 1969. 5.50. Farrar, Straus and Giroux.

Blood of the Arena. Vicente Blasco Ibanez & Douglas, Frances, 1870- Tr. LC 11-288793. 1911. A. C. McClurg & Co.

Blood of the Bondmaster. Richard Tresillian. 1977. 2.25 (ISBN 0-446-82385-6). Warner Books.

Blood of the Breed. Theodore V Olsen. LC 81-43298. 1982. 10.95 (ISBN 0-385-17555-8). Doubleday.

Blood of the Conquerors. Harvey Fergusson. LC 76-1232. (Chicano Heritage). 1976. 11.00 (ISBN 0-405-09500-7). Arno Press.

Blood of the Conquerors. Harvey Fergusson. LC 21-18316. 1921. A. A. Knopf.

Blood of the Conquerors. Harvey Fergusson. LC 78-13369. (Gregg Press Western Fiction Series). 1978. 9.95 (ISBN 0-8398-2470-X). Gregg Press.

Blood of the Lamb. Charles Henry Baker. LC 46-202121. 1946. Rinehart & Company, Inc.

Blood of the Lamb. Peter De Vries. 1974. (pbk.) 1.25. Popular Library.

Blood of the Lamb. Peter De Vries. LC 82-7490. 1982. 4.95 (ISBN 0-14-006297-1). Penguin Books.

Blood of the Martyrs. Naomi Haldane Mitchison. 1973. Curtis Books.

Blood of the Martyrs. Naomi Haldane Mitchison. LC 48-8673. 1948. Whittlesey House.

Blood of the North. James Beardsley Hendryx. LC 39-25329. 1939. The Sun Dial Press, Inc.

Blood of the North. James Beardsley Hendryx. LC 42-25587. 1942. The Sun Dial Press.

Blood of the North: By James B. Hendryx. James Beardsley Hendryx. LC 38-19925. 1938. Doubleday, Doran & Company, Inc.

Blood of the Shark: A Romance of Early Hawaii. Beatrice Ayer Patton. LC 36-359891. Paradise of the Pacific Press.

Blood of the West. Paul Evan Lehman. LC 34-139962. The Macaulay Company.

Blood of Vintage... Thomas Kyd. LC 47-176974. 1947. J. B. Lippincott Company.

Blood on a Harvest Moon. David Anthony. LC 73-172626. 1972. 6.95. Coward, McCann & Geoghegan.

Blood on Biscayne Bay. Davis Dresser. LC 46-22596. 1946. Ziff-Davis Publishing Company.

Blood on Frisco Bay. Jay Flynn. 1976. pap. 1.25 o.p. (ISBN 0-8439-0360-0, LB36OZK, Leisure Bks). Nordon Pubns.

Blood on Her Shoe. Medora Field. LC 42-15422. 1942. The Macmillan Company.

Blood on Her Shoe. Medora Field Perkerson. LC 42-15422. 1942. The Macmillan Company.

Blood on Lake Louisa. Baynard Hardwick Kendrick. LC 35-36680. Greenberg.

Blood on Lake Louisa. Baynard Hardwick Kendrick. LC 43-6575. 1943. Triangle Books.

Blood on McAllister. Matt Chisholm, pseud. 1971. pap. 0.75 o.p. (94187). Beagle Bks.

Blood on My Rug. E Louise Cushing. LC 56-7013. 1956. Arcadia House.

Blood on My Sleeve. Ivon Baker. LC 79-5337. 1978. 7.95 (ISBN 0-312-08449-8). St. Martin's Press.

Blood on Nassau's Moon. Walbridge McCully. LC 45-2494. 1945. Pub. for the Crime Club by Doubleday, Doran & Co., Inc.

Blood on the Beach, a Miss Tessie Venable Mystery. Helen Holley. LC 47-13066. 1946. Mystery House.

Blood on the Black Market. Davis Dresser. LC 43-919396. 1943. Dodd, Mead & Company.

Blood on the Boards. William Campbell Gault. LC 53-10864. (Guilt edged mystery). 1953. Dutton.

Blood on the Bosom Devine. Alfred Harbage. LC 75-44988. (Fifty Classics of Crime Fiction, 1900-1950; 31). 1976. 12.00 (ISBN 0-8240-2380-3). Garland Pub.

Blood on the Bosom Devine. Thomas Kyd. LC 48-5271. (Main line mysteries). 1948. J. B. Lippincott Co.

Blood on the Cat. Nancy Rutledge. LC 44-418855. 1945. Farrar & Rinehart, Inc.

Blood on the Cat. Abridged Ed. Nancy Rutledge. LC 47-789. (Handi-book mysteries. 55). 1946. Quinn Publishing Co., Inc.

Blood on the Common... Anne Fuller. LC 33-162413. E. P. Dutton & Company, Inc.

Blood on the Curb. Joseph Thompson Shaw. LC 36-10011. Dodge Publishing Company.

Blood on the Desert: An Original Gold Medal Novel. Peter Rabe. LC 59-226. (Gold medal books, S825). 1958. Fawcett Publications.

Blood on the Dining-Room Floor. Gertrude Stein. LC 48-6835. 1948. Banyan Prss.

Blood on the Doves. Maude Phelps McVeigh Hutchins. LC 65-22967. bds., 3.95. Morrow.

Blood on the Doves by: Maud Hutchins. Maude Phelps McVeigh Hutchins. LC 65-22967. 1965. Morrow.

Blood on the Forge. William Attaway. 279p. 1969. Repr. of 1941 ed. 8.95x (ISBN 0-911860-00-2). Chatham Bkseller.

Blood on the Forge. William Attaway. Ed. by Charles R. Larson. (African-American Library). 1970. pap. 1.50 o.p. (04828, Collier). Macmillan.

Blood on the Forge: A Novel. William Attaway. LC 70-107046. (American Library). 1970. 1.50. Collier Books.

Blood on the Forge: A Novel. William Attaway. LC 77-96381. 1969. Chatham Bookseller.

Blood on the Forge: A Novel. William Attaway. LC 41-13929. 1941. Doubleday, Doran & Co., Inc.

Blood on the Heather... Stephen Chalmers. LC 32-184302. Pub. for the Crime Club, Inc., by Doubleday, Doran & Company, Inc.

Blood on the Heather. Alex A. Rattray. 4.50 o.p. Vantage.

Blood on the Ivy. Hal Ellson. (Orig.). 1970. pap. 0.75 o.p. (T2257). Pyramid Pubns.

Blood on the Knight. Lee Thayer. LC 52-8985. (Red badge detective). 1952. Dodd, Mead.

Blood on the Land. Frank Bonham. LC 52-14747. 1952. Ballantine Books.

Blood on the Land. Frank Bonham. (Berkley Book). 1978. 1.50 (ISBN 0-425-03759-2). Berkley Pub. Corp.

Blood on the Moon. Warren T. Longreee. (Ruff Justice Ser.: No. 3). (Orig.). 1981. pap. 2.50 (ISBN 0-451-11215-6, AE 1215, Sig). NAL.

Blood on the Moon. Jim Tully. LC 31-11734. 1931. Coward-McCann, Inc.

Blood on the Mountain. Arnold Rodin. Orig. Title: Woman Soldier. 1972. pap. 0.95 o.p. (532-00171-095). Manor Bks.

Blood on the Plains. Thomas Albert Curry. (Orig.). 1972. pap. 0.60 o.p. (06161). Curtis.

Blood on the Plains: A "Captain Mesquite" Novel. Thomas Albert Curry. LC 47-177635. 1947. Arcadia House, Inc.

Blood on the Prairie. John Benteen. (Sundance Ser: No. 18). 1978. pap. 1.50 o.s.i. (ISBN 0-8439-0577-8, Leisure Bks). Nordon Pubns.

Blood on the Prairie. John Benteen. (Sundance series). 1976. (pbk.) 1.25. Leisure Books.

Blood on the Range. Eli Colter. LC 39-70831. Dodge Publishing Company.

Blood on the Range. Owen G. Irons. 1980. pap. 1.95 (ISBN 0-89083-686-8). Zebra.

Blood on the Rhine. Hurk David. (Orig.). 1969. pap. 1.75 (ISBN 0-87067-171-5, BH171). Holloway.

Blood on the Sage. Louis E Legner. LC 37-23925. Greenberg.

Blood on the Shrine. Jay G. Brenter. (Orig.). pap. 0.95 o.p. (1111). Brandon.

Blood on the Snow: A Novel. John Elliott. LC 76-29859. 8.95 (ISBN 0-312-08452-8). St. Martin's Press.

Blood on the Stars. Aaron Marc Stein. LC 64-11307. 1964. Published for the Crime Club by Doubleday.

Blood on the Stars: A Michael Shayne Mystery. Davis Dresser. LC 48-7415. (Red badge detective). 1948. Dodd, Mead.

Blood on the Straw. Translated from the French by Lucienne Hill. Berthe Grimault. LC 59-8928. 3.50. Fleet Pub. Corp.

Blood on the Trail. Max Brand. 1982. pap. 1.95 (ISBN 0-671-44714-9). PB.

Blood on the Trail. Frederick Faust. LC 76-24875. 1976. 9.95 (ISBN 0-89340-034-3). J. Curley.

Blood on the Trail: By Max Brand Pseud. Frederick Faust. LC 57-11393. (Silver star westerns). 1957. Dodd, Mead.

Blood on the Yukon Trail: A Novel of Corporal Downey of the Mounted. James Beardsley Hendryx. LC 30-31186. 1930. Doubleday, Doran & Company, Inc.

Blood Oranges. John Hawkes. LC 74-152516. 1971. 6.95. New Directions.

Blood Order. Jack D Hunter. LC 78-20687. 19.95 (ISBN 0-8129-0820-1). Times Books.

Blood Orgy. Geoffrey Kyle. 160p. pap. 1.95 o.p. (6087). Brandon.

Blood Patrol see Patrulla Sangrienta.

Blood-Pearls of Sulu. first ed. Don Del Mar. 1972. 4.95 (ISBN 0-533-00455-1). Vantage.

Blood Rare. Mickey Phillips, pseud. LC 63-10151. 1963. Coward-McCann.

Blood Red Bangles. Ahmed M Akhtar. LC 77-900769. 1976. 6.00. P.K. Books.

Blood Red Dawn. Charles Caldwell Dobie. LC 20-10053. Harper & Brothers.

Blood-Red Death. Minna Bardon. LC 47-18599. 1947. Phoenix Press.

Blood-Red Dream. William Arden, pseud. LC 82-1362. 1982. 11.95 (ISBN 0-89340-396-2). J. Curley & Associates.

Blood-Red Dream. Michael Collins. (Red Badge Mystery Ser.). 1976. 6.95 o.p. (ISBN 0-396-07347-6). Dodd.

Blood Red Dream. Michael Collins, pseud. LC 80-83589. (Dan Fortune Detective Mystery Ser.). 192p. 1981. pap. 2.25 (ISBN 0-87216-812-3). Playboy Pbks.

Blood-Red Dream. Dennis Lynds. LC 76-21759. (Red badge novel of suspense). 6.95 (ISBN 0-396-07347-6). Dodd, Mead.

Blood Red Gold. Gary Blumberg. (Dell Book). 1977. 1.50 (ISBN 0-440-17051-6). Dell Pub. Co.

Blood Red Roses: A Romantic Novel of Hilton Head Island, South Carolina, During the War Between the States. Elizabeth Boatwright Coker. LC 77-1366. (Illus.). 9.95. Dutton.

Blood Red, Sister Rose. Thomas Keneally. LC 74-7840. (Illus.). 1974. (ISBN 0-670-17433-5). Viking Press.

Blood Red, Sister Rose: A Novel of the Maid of Orleans. Thomas Keneally. LC 74-7840. 384p. 1975. 8.95 o.p. (ISBN 0-670-17433-5). Viking Pr.

Blood Red Wine. Laurence Delaney. (Orig.). 1981. pap. 2.95 (ISBN 0-440-10714-8). Dell.

Blood Relations. Ellis Dillon. LC 77-24237. 9.95 (ISBN 0-671-22492-1). Simon and Schuster.

Blood Relations. Ellis Dil Lon. 1979. 2.25. Fawcett Crest Books.

Blood Relations. Philip Hamilton Gibbs. LC 35-27363. 1935. Doubleday, Doran & Company, Inc.

Blood Relations. Philip Hamilton Gibbs. LC 36-35620. The Sun Dial Press.

Blood Relations. Roberta Silman. LC 76-56749. 7.95 (ISBN 0-316-79108-3). Little, Brown.

Blood Relatives. Ed McBain. 1975. 6.95 o.p. (ISBN 0-394-48582-3). Random.

Blood Relatives. Ed McBain. 1982. pap. 2.50 (ISBN 0-451-11854-5, AE1854, Sig). NAL.

Blood Relatives: An 87th Precinct Mystery Novel. Evan Hunter. LC 75-10308. 1975. 6.95 (ISBN 0-394-48582-3). Random House.

Blood Remembers. Helen Hedrick. LC 41-24627. 1941. A. A. Knopf.

Blood Rising. William M. James, pseud. (Apache Ser.: No. 15). (Orig.). 1979. pap. 1.50 (ISBN 0-523-40592-8). Pinnacle Bks.

Blood Risk. Brian Coffey. LC 72-89691. (Black bat mystery). (Illus.). 1973. 5.95. Bobbs-Merrill.

Blood Rites. Barry Nazarian. (Orig.). 1980. pap. 2.25 (ISBN 0-451-09203-1, E9203, Sig). NAL.

Blood River. Jack Slade, pseud. (Lassiter Ser). (O.s.i.: No. 17). (Orig.). 1974. pap. 0.95 o.s.i. (BT50734). Belmont-Tower.

Blood River Gold. Swain Adams. (Orig.). 1981. pap. 1.95 o.s.i. (ISBN 0-505-51628-4). Tower Bks.

Blood Royal. Grant Allen. LC 6-68. 1892. Cassell Publishing Company.

Blood Royal. Cecil William Mercer. LC 30-237481. 1930. Minton, Balch & Company.

Blood Royal. Pierre Stephen Robert Payne. LC 52-9541. 1952. Prentice-Hall.

Blood Royal. Robert C. Sherman. 320p. (Orig.). 1982. pap. 3.25 (ISBN 0-505-51766-3). Tower Bks.

Blood Royal. Arden Winch. LC 81-65276. 1982. 12.95 (ISBN 0-670-17434-3). Viking Press.

Blood Rubies. Axel Young. (Orig.). 1982. pap. 2.95 (ISBN 0-380-79392-X, 79392). Avon.

Blood Runs Cold. Lois Christine Eby & Fleming, John Chester, 1906- Joint Author. LC 46-4806. 1946. E. P. Dutton & Company, Inc.

Blood Scenario. Peter Spain. LC 79-24536. 10.95 (ISBN 0-698-11029-3). Coward, McCann & Geoghegan.

Blood Secrets. Craig Jones. LC 78-4743. 8.95 (ISBN 0-06-012264-1). Harper & Row.

Blood Ship. Norman Springer. LC 22-27485. W. J. Watt & Company.

Blood Sisters: An Examination of Conscience. Valerie Miner. 224p. 1982. 11.95 (ISBN 0-312-08462-5); pap. 6.95 (ISBN 0-312-08461-7). St Martin.

Blood Snarl. Ivor Watkins. (Orig.). 1982. pap. 2.75 (ISBN 0-451-11270-9, AE1270, Sig). NAL.

Blood Sport. Dick Francis. LC 68-11821. 1975. (pbk.) 1.25 (ISBN 0-671-78913-9). Pocket Books.

Blood Sport. Dick Francis. LC 70-393675. 1968. (to members) 0.85. Readers Book Club in Association with the Companion Book Club, London.

Blood Sport. Robert F Jones. 1975. (pbk.) 1.50. Dell.

Blood Sport see Across the Board: Three Harper Novels of Suspense.

Blood Sport: A Journey up the Hassayampa. Robert F Jones. LC 73-18928. 1974. 7.95 (ISBN 0-671-21696-1). Simon and Schuster.

Blood Sport. 1st U. S. Ed. Dick Francis. LC 68-11821. 1968. bds., 4.95. Harper.

Blood Sports. Paul R. Rothweiler. (Orig.). 1980. write for info (ISBN 0-515-05410-0). Jove Pubns.

Blood Stones. Wallace Moore. (Balzan of the Cat People Ser.: No. 1). (Orig.). 1975. pap. 1.25 o.p. (ISBN 0-515-03628-5). BJ Pub Group.

Blood Summer. Don Asher. LC 77-7993. 8.95 (ISBN 0-399-12028-9). Putnam.

Blood Summer. Don Asher. (Berkley book). 1979. 1.95 (ISBN 0-425-03949-8). Berkley Pub. Corp.

Blood, Sweat & Gold. J. D. Hardin. LC 79-83969. (Pinkerton Ser.: No. 2). (Orig.). 1979. pap. 1.95 (ISBN 0-87216-840-9). Playboy Pbks.

Blood-Tax. Dorothea Gerard Longard De Longgarde. LC 2-20391. 1902. Dodd, Mead and Company.

Blood Tells. Toby Armour. 1973. (pbk) 0.75. Curtis Books.

Blood Tie. Mary Lee Settle. LC 77-8373. 1977. 10.95 (ISBN 0-395-25401-9). Houghton Mifflin.

Blood Ties. Warren Adler. LC 78-10738. 10.95 (ISBN 0-399-12309-1). Putnam.

Blood Ties. David Adams Richards. LC 76-368816. (ISBN 0-88750-188-5). Oberon Press.

Blood Ties. Alexandra Roudybush. LC 80-1852. 1981. 9.95 (ISBN 0-385-17339-3). Published for the Crime Club by Doubleday.

Blood Trail. Gardner F. Fox. 1979. pap. 1.50 o.s.i. (ISBN 0-505-51367-6). Tower Bks.

Blood Trail. Alex Hawk, pseud. (Orig.). 1970. pap. 0.60 o.p. (63-268). Paperback Lib.

Blood Trail to Bannack. Norman Daniels. 1973. pap. 0.75 o.s.i. (74-794). Lancer.

Blood Transfusion Murders. Milton Morris Propper. 1943. Harper & Brothers.

Blood Upon the Snow. Hilda Lawrence. LC 44-6837. 1944. Simon and Schuster.

Blood Vengeance. Stuart Jason. (Butcher,#13). 1975. (pbk.) 1.25 (ISBN 0-523-00539-3). Pinnacle Books.

Blood Wedding. Simeon Brooks. 1970. pap. 0.95 o.p. (B95-2010). Belmont-Tower.

Blood Wedding. Simeon Brooks. (O.s.i.). 1972. pap. 0.95 o.s.i. (BT50287). Belmont-Tower.

Blood Wedding. William M. James, pseud. (Apache Ser.: No. 21). 160p. (Orig.). 1981. pap. 1.75 (ISBN 0-523-41023-9). Pinnacle Bks.

Blood Will Have Blood. Linda J. Barnes. 192p. 1982. pap. 2.25 (ISBN 0-380-79368-7, 79368). Avon.

Blood Will Tell. Gary Cartwright. LC 78-22246. 1979. 10.95 (ISBN 0-15-169961-5). HarBraceJ.

Blood Will Tell. Gary Cartwright. 1980. pap. 3.25 (ISBN 0-671-42851-9). PB.

Blood Will Tell. Agatha Miller Christie. LC 54-30408. W.J.Black.

Blood Will Tell see Trio for Blunt Instruments: A Nero Woolfe Threesome.

Blood Will Tell: By George Bagby Pseud. Aaron Marc Stein. LC 50-8920. 1950. Published for the Crime Club by Doubleday.

Blood Will Tell: The Strange Story of a Son of Ham. Benjamin Rush Davenport. LC 78-38645. (Black Heritage Library Collection). (Illus.). 1972. (ISBN 0-8369-9003-X). Books for Libraries Press.

Blood Will Tell: The Strange Story of a Son of Ham. Benjamin Rush Davenport. LC 2-9135. 1902. Caxton Book Co.

Blood Wrath. Chester Krone. LC 80-82852. 272p. (Orig.). 1981. pap. 2.50 (ISBN 0-87216-778-X). Playboy Pbks.

Bloodbath. William Wingate. LC 79-21374. 1980. 9.95 (ISBN 0-312-08464-1). St. Martin's Press.

Bloodbath Hill. Pat Nobel. (Orig.). 1980. pap. 2.25 (ISBN 0-532-23187-2). Woodhill.

Bloodbird: A Novel. Thomas Burton, pseud. LC 41-3113. Smith & Durrell.

Bloodbird: A Novel. Stephen Longstreet. LC 41-3113. 1941. Smith & Durrell.

Bloodbrothers. Richard Price. LC 75-40369. 1976. 8.95 (ISBN 0-395-24303-3). Houghton Mifflin.

Bloodbrothers, Vol. 2. Robert Emmet Wall. (Canadians Ser.). (Orig.). 1981. pap. 2.95 (ISBN 0-553-20007-0). Bantam.

Bloodcurdling Tales of Horror & the Macabre: The Best of H. P. Lovecraft. Howard Phillips Lovecraft. 1982. pap. 6.95 (ISBN 0-345-29468-8). Ballantine.

Blooded on Arachne. Michael Bishop. LC 81-10830. (Illus.). 13.95 (ISBN 0-87054-093-9). Arkham House.

Bloodhounds Bay. Walter S Masterman. LC 36-20837. E. P. Dutton & Co., Inc.

Bloodhounds of Broadway and Other Stories. Damon Runyon. LC 81-4390. 1981. 12.95 (ISBN 0-688-00725-2) (ISBN 0-688-00625-6). Morrow.

Bloodhouse. Kenneth Cook. LC 74-81229. 1974. 6.50. St. Martin's Press.

Bloodhype. Alan Dean Foster. 1977. pap. 2.25 (ISBN 0-345-29476-9). Ballantine.

Bloodiest Bivouac. Karl H. Meyer. 1978. pap. 1.50 (ISBN 0-532-15332-4). Woodhill.

Blooding of the Guns. Alexander Fullerton. LC 76-383429. 1976. 3.75 (ISBN 0-7181-1448-5). Joseph.

Bloodline. Ernest J. Gaines. LC 75-42393. (Norton library; N798). 1976. 2.95. Norton.

Bloodline. Ernest J. Gaines. LC 68-14992. 1968. 4.95. Dial Press.

Bloodline. Sidney Sheldon. LC 77-21175. 1978. 9.95 (ISBN 0-688-03196-X). Morrow.

Bloodright. Peter Tremayne, pseud. 1980. pap. 2.25 (ISBN 0-440-10509-9). Dell.

Bloodright: A Memoir of Mircea, Son of Vlad Tepes, Prince of Wallachia, Also Known As Dracula... Born on This Earth in the Year of Christ 1431, Who Died in 1476 but Remained Undead... Peter Tremayne, pseud. LC 79-63160. 1979. 8.95 (ISBN 0-8027-0628-2). Walker.

Bloodroot. Thomas Mordane. 288p. 1982. pap. 2.95 (ISBN 0-440-10411-4). Dell.

Bloodroots in the Wake of Circumstance. Flora White. LC 42-23665. 1942. Burton Publishing Company.

Bloodroots Manor. Claudette Nicole. (Orig.). 1973. pap. 0.75 o.p. (T2731, GM). Fawcett World.

Bloodrush. Hugh Zachary. 1981. pap. 1.95 (ISBN 0-8439-0857-2, Leisure Bks). Nordon Pubns.

Bloods of the Equator. Alfred Lo Cascio. LC 39-24227. 1939. Meador Publishing Company.

Bloodshed and Three Novellas. Cynthia Ozick. LC 75-36790. 1976. 6.95 (ISBN 0-394-40126-3). Knopf.

Bloodsisters. John Russo. 1982. pap. 2.95 (ISBN 0-671-41692-8). PB.

Bloodskinners. Lee Floren. 1970. pap. 0.60 o.p. (ISBN 0-447-73203-X). Lancer.

Bloodsmoor Romance. Joyce Carol Oates. 640p. 1982. 16.95 (ISBN 0-525-24112-4, 01646-490). Dutton.

Bloodspoor. James McVean, pseud. LC 78-2653. 7.95 (ISBN 0-8037-0863-7). Dial Press/J. Wade.

Bloodsport. Don Pendleton. (Executioner Ser.). 192p. 1982. pap. 1.95 (ISBN 0-373-61046-7, Pub. by Worldwide). Harlequin Bks.

Bloodstain. 1st Ed. David Alexander. LC 61-8685. (His A Marty Land mystery). 1961. Lippincott.

Bloodstalk. Ron Goulart. (Vampirella#1). 1975. (pbk.) 1.25. Warner Books.

Bloodstar. Tom Topor. LC 78-18789. 9.95 (ISBN 0-393-08829-4). Norton.

Bloodstock, and Other Stories. 1st American Ed. Margaret Emma Faith Irwin. LC 54-9725. 1954. Harcourt, Brace.

Bloodstone. Lynn Benedict. (Orig.). 1973. pap. 0.95 o.p. (26543-2-095). Beagle Bks.

Bloodstone. Ken Eulo. 1981. pap. 2.95 (ISBN 0-671-43533-7). PB.

Bloodstone. Xavier Donald MacLeod. LC 7-16622. 1853. C. Scribner.

Bloodstone. Karl Edward Wagner. 304p. 1975. pap. 2.95 (ISBN 0-446-30629-0). Warner Bks.

Bloodstone. Karl Edward Wagner. 1975. (pbk.) 1.50 (ISBN 0-446-78711-6). Warner Paperback Library.

Bloodwater. John Crowe, pseud. 1977. pap. 1.25 (ISBN 0-532-12496-0). Woodhill.

Bloodwater. John Crowe, pseud. 1974. 4.95 o.p. (ISBN 0-396-06947-9). Dodd.

Bloodwater. Dennis Lynds. LC 74-101. (His A Buena Costa County mystery). 1974. 4.95 (ISBN 0-396-06947-9). Dodd, Mead.

Bloodwind. Charles L. Grant. 224p. 1982. pap. 2.50 (ISBN 0-445-04709-7). Popular Lib.

Bloodworth Orphans: A Novel. Leon Forrest. LC 76-14184. 10.00 (ISBN 0-394-49911-5). Random House.

Bloody Baron, the Story of Ungern-Sternberg. Vladimir Pozner. Tr. by Wells, Warre Bradley. LC 38-30222. Random House.

Bloody Bay. Sandra Riley. (Orig.). 1980. pap. text ed. 2.75 o.s.i. (ISBN 0-505-51576-8). Tower Bks.

Bloody Bokhara: 1st Ed. William Campbell Gault. LC 52-8241. (Guilt edged mystery). 1952. Dutton.

Bloody Boston. Lionel Derrick. (Penetrator#12). 1976. (pbk.) 1.25 (ISBN 0-523-00797-3). Pinnacle Books.

Bloody Bozeman. Dorothy M. Johnson. 384p. 1983. pap. 9.95 (ISBN 0-87842-152-1). Mountain Pr.

Bloody Brother: A Tragedy... facsimile ed. John Fletcher. (English Experience Ser.). 80p. Repr. of 1639 ed. 8.00 o.p. (179). Da Capo.

Bloody Bush. Gordon Davis, pseud. (Sergeant Ser.: No. 3). 288p. (Orig.). 1980. pap. 2.25 (ISBN 0-89083-647-7). Zebra.

Bloody Chamber. Angela Carter. LC 79-2645. 1980. 8.95 (ISBN 0-06-010708-1). Harper & Row.

Bloody Chasm. facsimile ed. John William De Forest. LC 72-38011. (Black Heritage Library Collection). Repr. of 1881 ed. 17.50 (ISBN 0-8369-8979-1). Ayer Co.

Bloody Chasm. John William De Forest. Ed. by Donald Pizer. LC 76-96520. (American Authors Ser). 1970. Repr. of 1881 ed. lib. bdg. 17.25 o.s.i. (ISBN 0-512-00138-3). Garrett Pr.

Bloody Chasm: A Novel. John William De Forest. LC 72-38011. (Black Heritage Library Collection). 1972. (ISBN 0-8369-8979-1). Books for Libraries Press.

Bloody Chasm. A Novel. John William De Forest. LC 6-33390. 1881. D. Appleton and Company.

Bloody Crossing. Robert J. Hogan. 1976. pap. 1.25. Woodhill.

Bloody Crossing. Robert J. Hogan. LC 73-863. Orig. Title: Apache Landing. 1969. Repr. of 1951 ed. pap. 0.60 o.p. Lancer.

Bloody Field. Edith Pargeter. LC 72-11061. 1973. 7.95 (ISBN 0-670-17435-1). Viking Press.

Bloody Forest. Alcuin Dornisch. LC 34-32565. 1934. Meador Publishing Company.

Bloody Gold. Chet Cunningham. 1980. pap. 1.75 o.s.i. (ISBN 0-505-51492-3). Tower Bks.

Bloody Gold. Chet Cunningham. 1975. (pbk.) 1.25. Pinnacle Books.

Bloody Gold: By Peter Dawson Pseud. Jonathan H Glidden. LC 63-14173. 1963. Bantam Books.

Bloody Grass. Hobe Gilmore. 1978. pap. 1.50 o.s.i. (ISBN 0-8439-0469-0, Leisure Bks). Nordon Pubns.

Bloody Ground. John F. Day. LC 79-57571. (Illus.). 352p. 1981. 19.50 (ISBN 0-8131-1454-3); pap. 8.00 (ISBN 0-8131-0148-4). U Pr of Ky.

Bloody Ground. Oscar J Friend. LC 28-8512. 1928. A. C. McClurg & Co.

Bloody Ground: A Cycle of the Southern Hills. Fiswoode Tarleton. LC 29-326427. 1929. L. MacVeagh, The Dial Press.

Bloody Hand. Matthew Braun. 1975. (pbk.) 1.25. Popular Library.

Bloody Head: By Dane Coolidge. Dane Coolidge. LC 40-12783. 1940. E. P. Dutton & Company, Inc.

Bloody Hills of Korea: A Boy's Initiation to War. Limited Ed. Edward Charles Polster. LC 54-28814. 1954. L. S. Simmons.

Bloody Junto: Or, The Escape of John Wilkes Booth. A Story Containing Many Interesting Particulars in Regard to the Trial and Execution of Mrs. Surratt and Other So-Called Conspirators. Robert Haskins Crozier. LC 6-31948. 1869. Woodruff & Blocher, Printers.

Bloody Kansas. Charles Morris Martin. 1969. Repr. pap. 0.60 o.p. (60-412). Manor Bks.

Bloody Kansas. Avon 1st Ed. Charles Morris Martin. LC 55-419949. (Avon, 654). 1955. Avon Publications.

Bloody Marvellous. Julian Rathbone. LC 75-9494. 1975. 7.95. St. Martin's Press.

Bloody Monday Conspiracy. Ralph Hayes. (Liquidator,#1). 1974. (pbk.) 0.95. Belmont Tower Books.

Bloody Moonlight. Fredric Brown. LC 49-119126. (Guilt edged mystery). 1949. E. P. Dutton.

Bloody Ohio of 1776. James Delmar Miller. LC 76-151274. 5.95 (ISBN 0-533-02505-2). Vantage Press.

Bloody Patch. Jack Colbaugh. 5.95 o.p. Vantage.

Bloody Poet: A Novel About Nero. Deszo Kosztolanyi. Tr. by Fadiman, Clifton P. LC 27-24004. 1927. Macy-Masius.

Bloody Saddles. Llewellyn Perry Holmes. LC 33-1033. Greenberg.

Bloody Sands. J. D. Hardin. LC 80-80989. (Pinkerton Ser.: No. 8). 208p. (Orig.). 1980. pap. 1.95 (ISBN 0-87216-842-5). Playboy Pbks.

Bloody September. C. A Haddad. LC 76-5541. 8.95 (ISBN 0-06-011709-5). Harper & Row.

Bloody Sevens: By Jefferson Cooper Pseud. Gardner F Fox. LC 57-516361. (Perma books, M-3064 4). Permabooks.

Bloody Spur. Charles Einstein. LC 53-10779. (Dell first edition, 5). 1953. Dell Pub. Co.

Bloody Summer. George G. Gilman, pseud. (Edge Ser.: No. 9). 192p. 1974. pap. 1.75 (ISBN 0-523-41287-8). Pinnacle Bks.

Bloody Summer. George G Gilman. (Edge series,#9). 1974. (pbk.) 0.95 (ISBN 0-523-00293-9). Pinnacle Books.

Bloody Sun. Marion Zimmer Bradley. 192p. (Orig.). 1975. pap. 2.75 (ISBN 0-441-06856-1). Ace Bks.

Bloody Sun. Marion Zimmer Bradley. 1979. lib. bdg. 12.00 (ISBN 0-8398-2513-7, Gregg). G K Hall.

Bloody Sun. Marion Zimmer Bradley. (Darkover Series). 1975. (pbk.) 1.25. Ace Books.

Bloody Sun and To Keep the Oath. Marion Zimmer Bradley. LC 79-9384. (Gregg Press science fiction series). (Illus.). 1979. 12.00 (ISBN 0-8398-2513-7). Gregg Press.

Bloody Sun at Noon. George Beare. LC 75-125647. (Midnight novel of suspense). 1971. 4.95. Houghton Mifflin Co.

Bloody Sunday. Aaron Fletcher. 192p. 1981. pap. 1.95 (ISBN 0-8439-1014-3, Leisure Bks). Nordon Pubns.

Bloody Sunday. Frank Scarpetta. (O.s.i.). (Orig.). 1976. pap. 1.25 o.s.i. (BT50909). Belmont-Tower.

Bloody Sunday. Frank Scarpetta. 1976. (pbk.) 1.25. Belmont Tower Books.

Bloody Sundown. Charles G. Muller. 1978. pap. 1.50 (ISBN 0-89041-192-1, 3192). Major Bks.

Bloody Sunrise: By Mickey Spillane. Frank Morrison Spillane. LC 65-116089. 3.50. Dutton.

Bloody Trail to Texas. Jake Logan. LC 76-1706. (Jake Logan Western Ser). 192p. 1982. pap. 1.95 (ISBN 0-86721-003-6). Playboy Pbks.

Bloody Trail to Texas. Jake Logan. LC 76-1706. (John Slocum Ser.: No. 7). 192p. 1976. pap. 1.75 (ISBN 0-87216-736-4). Playboy Pbks.

Bloody Vengeance. Jack Ehrlich. 1973. (pbk.) 0.95 (ISBN 0-671-77668-1). Pocket Books.

Bloody Wood. Michael Innes, pseud. (Red Badge Mystery Ser). 1966. 3.50 o.p. (ISBN 0-396-05295-9). Dodd.

Bloody Wood: By Michael Innes Pseud. John Innes Mackintosh Stewart. LC 66-14192. (Red badge detective). bds., 3.50. Dodd.

Bloody Ground, a Cycle of the Southern Hills. Fiswoode Tarleton. LC 71-152960. (Short story index reprint series). 1971. (ISBN 0-8369-3875-5). Books for Libraries Press.

Bloom and Brier: Or, As I Saw It, Long Ago. A Southern Romance. William Falconer. 1870. Claxton, Remsen & Haffelfinger.

Bloom High Way. Asa Elliot, pseud. LC 72-4253. (Illus.). 1973. 8.95. Delacorte Press.

Bloom of Cactus. Robert Ames Bennet. LC 20-7647. 1920. Doubleday, Page & Company.

Bloom of the Diamond Stone. Wison J. Hiare. (Orig.). 1981. pap. 4.95 (ISBN 0-86104-207-7). Pluto Pr.

Bloom of Youth. Dorothy Foster Gilman. LC 16-26318. 1.25. Small, Maynard & Company.

Bloom Where You Are Planted. Joyce Beaman. LC 75-34645. 1976. 7.95 (ISBN 0-87716-060-0, Pub. by Moore Pub Co). F Apple.

Blooming Angel. Wallace Irwin. LC 19-11941. George H. Doran Company.

Blooming of the Flame Tree. Roberta Kehle. 144p. 1983. pap. 3.95 (ISBN 0-89107-275-6, Crossway Bks). Good News.

Blossom and Fruit: Or, Madame's Ward. Charles Andrew. (On cover: The seaside library. Pocket ed. no. 968). 1887. G. Munro.

Blossom and the Fruit: A True Story of a Black Magician. Mabel Collins Cook. LC 6-28085. (On cover: Lovell's occult series, no. 1). 1889. J. W. Lovell Company.

Blossom-Bud and Her Genteel Friends. A Story. Julie P Smith. LC 8-8176. 1883. G. W. Carleton & Co.; Etc., Etc.

Blossom Hill. Peggy O'More, pseud. LC 51-2269. 1951. Arcadia House.

Blossom Like a Rose. Christopher Bray. LC 79-83226. 1969. 4.95. Viking Press.

Blossom Like the Rose. Norah Robinson Lofts. LC 39-28752. 1939. A. A. Knopf.

Blossom-Print. Louise Townsend Nicholl. LC 38-29970. 1938. E. P. Dutton & Company, Inc.

Blossom Shop: A Story of the South. Isla May Hawley Mullins. LC 13-119663. 1913. 1.00. L. C. Page & Company.

Blossom Valley. Peggy O'More, pseud. LC 46-16817. 1946. Grammercy Publishing Co.

Blossom Where You Are Planted. Ohla E. Nickerson. (Orig.). 1980. pap. 1.95 (ISBN 0-532-23200-3). Woodhill.

Blossoming Bough... Ethel Edith Mannin. LC 43-10907. 1942. Jarrolds Limited.

Blossoming of the Waste. Edith Nicholl Ellison. LC 8-17827. 1908. Calkins and Company.

Blossoming Rod. Mary Stewart Doubleday Cutting. LC 14-18804. 1914. 0.50. Doubleday, Page & Company.

Blossoming Year: A Novel. Bruce Carpenter. LC 52-10968. 1952. Lothrop, Lee & Shepard.

Blossoms in Darkness: A Novel. Krishna Sobti. Tr. by Kavita Nagpal from Hindi. 1979. 7.50x (ISBN 0-7069-0784-1, Pub. by Vikas India). Advent NY.

Blossoms in the Moon. Blanche Smith Ferguson. LC 34-32212. The Penn Publishing Company.

Blossoms of My Body. Else Lasker-Schuler. Tr. by Joan Wolf. LC 82-81351. 1983. 10.00 (ISBN 0-930100-13-1); pap. 4.00 (ISBN 0-930100-12-3). Holy Cow.

Blossomy Cottage. Montanye Perry. LC 16-664587. 0.50. The Abingdon Press.

Blot of Ink. Rene Bazin. Francke, Paul M., Tr. LC 6-10286. Cassell Publishing Company.

Blotted Brands. Charles Wesley Sanders. LC 33-23933. A. H. King.

Blotting Book. Edward Frederic Benson. LC 8-23104. 1908. Doubleday, Page & Company.

Bloudin Obeego Tsveta. Vladimir Maramzin. 1975. 9.00 o.p. (ISBN 0-88233-161-2). Ardis Pubs.

Blount's Anvil. Don Hendrie, Jr. (Orig.) 1979. 7.95 (ISBN 0-89924-025-9); pap. 4.98 (ISBN 0-89924-024-0). Lynx Hse.

Blow at the Heart. Bernard Glemser. LC 53-10671. 1953. Appleton-Century-Crofts.

Blow, Bugle, Blow. Ross Sloane. LC 43-4181. 1943. J. Swift, Incorporated.

Blow, Desert Winds! William Corcoran. LC 35-8034. 1935. D. Appleton-Century Company, Incorporated.

Blow-Down. Lawrence Goldtree Blochman. LC 39-8242. Harcourt, Brace and Company.

Blow-Dry. Nathan Butler. (Fawcett Gold Medal Book). 1976. (pbk.) 1.50. Fawcett.

Blow for a Landing. Ben Lucien Burman. LC 38-3830. 1938. Houghton Mifflin Company.

Blow for a Landing. Ben Lucien Burman. LC 46-4171. 1946. E. P. Dutton & Co., Inc.

Blow for a Landing. Ben Lucien Burman. (Mockingbird book). 1974. (pbk.) 1.50 (ISBN 0-345-24072-3). Ballantine Books.

Blow Hot, Blow Cold. Gerald Alfred Butler. LC 51-11602. 1951. Rinehart.

Blow Hot, Blow Cold. Ellery Queen, pseud. LC 64-5673. 1964. Pocket Books.

Blow Hot, Blow Cold. Ellery Queen, pseud. (Signet book). 1974. (pbk.) 0.95. New American Library.

Blow Hot, Blow Cold. Peggy Swenson, pseud. pap. 1.95 o.p. (ISBN 0-87682-238-3, 7238). Barclay Hse.

Blow My Mind. Rod Gray. 1970. pap. 0.95 o.p. (T095-3). Tower.

Blow My Mind. Rod Gray. (The Lady from L.U.S.T. Ser.). (O.s.i.). 1974. pap. 0.95 o.s.i. (BT50660). Belmont-Tower.

Blow Negative. Edward Carl Stephens. LC 62-8930. 1962. Doubleday.

Blow Out. William Harrison. 1981. pap. 2.50 (ISBN 0-553-20269-3). Bantam.

Blow the Man Down. Thomas William Broadhurst. LC 29-18559. 1929. L. MacVeagh. The Dial Press.

Blow the Man Down: A Romance of the Coast. Holman Francis Day. LC 16-14600. 1916. 1.35. Harper & Brothers.

Blow the Wind Southerly. Dorothy Emily Stevenson. LC 54-9862. 1954. Rinehart.

Blow to the Head. David J. Michael. LC 70-108689. 1970. 5.95. Houghton Mifflin.

Blow up a Storm. Garson Kanin. LC 59-7838. 1959. Random House.

Blow-up, and Other Stories. Julio Cortazar. LC 68-7668. 1968. 1.50. Collier Books.

Blow, Whistles, Blow! Sarah Henry Atherton. LC 80-7968. 1930. Brewer and Warren Inc., Payson and Clarke Ltd.

Blow Your Mind Job. Troy Conway, pseud. (Coxeman Ser). (Orig.). 1970. pap. 0.60 o.p. (63-280). Paperback Lib.

Blowback. Bill Pronzini. LC 76-53475. 6.95 (ISBN 0-394-40793-8). Random House.

Blower of Bubbles. Arthur Beverley Baxter. LC 20-169813. 1920. D. Appleton and Company.

Blowholers. John Henry Reese. LC 72-181793. 1974. 4.95 (ISBN 0-385-03428-8). Doubleday.

Blowing Clear. Joseph Crosby Lincoln. LC 30-23913. 1930. D. Appleton and Company.

Blowing Weather. John Thomas McIntyre. LC 23-4985. 1923. The Century Co.

Blowing Weather. John Thomas McIntyre. LC 28-21966. Frederick A. Stokes Company.

Blown Away: A Nonsensical Narrative Without Rhyme or Reason. Richard Mansfield. LC 31-32278. 1897. L. C. Page and Company.

Blown Away: A Novel. Hal Kantor. LC 79-27153. 1980. 10.95 (ISBN 0-688-03602-3). Morrow.

Blown Figures. Audrey Callahan Thomas. LC 75-8256. (Illus.). 1975. 7.95 (ISBN 0-394-49657-4). Knopf: Distributed by Random House.

Blown Seed. David Toulmin. LC 77-350081. 1976. 6.00 (ISBN 0-904505-06-5). P. Harris.

Blown to Hell. P. A Bechko. LC 75-32718. 1976. 5.95 (ISBN 0-385-11626-8). Doubleday.

Blowout. Robert De Maria. (Orig.). 1979. pap. 2.25 (ISBN 0-515-04527-6). Jove Pubns.

Blowtop: A Novel. Alvin Schwartz. LC 48-5153. 1948. Dial Press.

Blubber. Judy Blume. 1978. pap. 1.75 (ISBN 0-440-90707-1, LFL). Dell.

Blubber. Judy Blume. 160p. 1976. pap. 2.50 (ISBN 0-440-40707-9, YB). Dell.

Blue Adept. Piers Anthony, pseud. LC 80-21754. (Illus.). 1981. 10.95 (ISBN 0-345-29384-3). Ballantine Books.

Blue Aloes: Stories of South Africa. Cynthia Stockley. LC 19-261653. 1919. G. P. Putnam's Sons.

Blue Anchor Inn. Edwin Bateman Morris. LC 12-211411. 1912. The Penn Publishing Company.

Blue and Green Mat of Abdul Hassan: An Arabian Adventure. Constance Grenelle Wilcox. LC 25-5971. (Half title: Appleton short plays, no. 5). 1925. D. Appleton and Company.

Blue & the Gray. John Leekley. (Orig.). 1982. pap. 3.50 (ISBN 0-440-10631-1). Dell.

Blue Angel. Heinrich Mann. LC 75-31806. 1976. H. Fertig.

Blue Angel. combined ed. Heinrich Mann & Josef Von Sternberg. LC 78-20934. (Ungar film library). (Illus.). 12.50 (ISBN 0-8044-2591-4). F. Ungar Pub. Co.

Blue Arabian Nights: Tales of a London Decade. Wolf Mankowitz. (Illus.). 189p. 1973. 12.50x (ISBN 0-85303-165-7, Pub. by Vallentine Mitchell England). Biblio Dist.

Blue Arch. Alice Duer Miller. LC 10-23941. 1910. C. Scribner's Sons.

Blue Aspic. Edward St. John Gorey. LC 68-27839. (Illus.). 1969. 2.95. Meredith Press.

Blue Aura. Elizabeth York Miller. LC 17-24815. E. J. Clode.

Blue Barbarians. Stanton Arthur Coblentz. LC 58-9128. 1958. Avalon Books.

Blue Bed. Glyn Jones. LC 38-11890. 1938. E. P. Dutton & Co., Inc.

Blue Bell of Red-Neap: Or, Shingle Cord; a Christmas Story. Louisa Taylor Parr & Craik, Dinah Maria (Mulock) LC 7-34720. 1871. G. Routledge & Sons.

Blue Belle of the Forest: A Story of the Olden Time, in the Middle West. Matilda Downing Underwood. LC 21-861356. Journal-Republican Print.

Blue-Bird Weather. Robert William Chambers. LC 12-244853. 1912. 1.00. D. Appleton and Company.

Blue Blood: A Dramatic Interlude. Owen McMahon Johnson. LC 24-11021. 1924. Little, Brown, and Company.

Blue Blood and Red. Anna McClure Sholl. LC 15-5346. 1915. H. Holt and Company.

Blue Blood: Or, White May and Black June. Leon Dande. LC 72-37589. (Black Heritage Library Collection). (Illus.). 1972. (ISBN 0-8369-8965-1). Books for Libraries Press.

Blue Blood Will Out. Tim Heald. LC 73-92185. 1974. 5.95 (ISBN 0-8128-1688-9). Stein and Day.

Blue Bodice. Antoine Sorrel. LC 27-50177. 1927. The Writers Guild.

Blue Bone. Martin Woodhouse. LC 72-94119. 1973. 6.95 (ISBN 0-698-10513-3). Coward, McCann & Geoghegan.

Blue Bonnet. Augustus Muir. LC 26-16357. The Bobbs-Merrill Company.

Blue Boy. Jean Giono. LC 46-280215. 1946. The Viking Press.

Blue Boy. Jean Giono. LC 81-4371. 1981. 8.50 (ISBN 0-86547-037-5). North Point Press.
Blue Brotherhood. Ernest O. Zimmerman. 352p. (Orig.). 1981. pap. 2.75 (ISBN 0-8439-0986-2, Leisure Bks). Nordon Pubns.
Blue Bucket Mystery. Francis Durham Grierson. LC 30-27683. E. J. Clode, Inc.
Blue Buckle. William Hamilton Osborne. LC 14-4261. 1914. 1.25. McBride, Nast & Co.
Blue Calf: And Other Tales of Peter. Leroy Fairman. 1908. Griffith-Stillings Press.
Blue Camellia. Frances Parkinson Wheeler Keyes. LC 57-5083. 1975. (pbk.) 1.50 (ISBN 0-671-78756-X). Pocket Books.
Blue Camellia. Francis Parkinson Wheeler Keyes. LC 57-5083. 1957. J.Messner.
Blue Car Mystery. Natalie Sumner Lincoln. LC 26-681320. 1926. D. Appleton and Company.
Blue Castle: A Novel. Lucy Maud Montgomery. LC 26-15138. 1926. Frederick A. Stokes Company.
Blue Chair. Joyce Thompson. 256p. 1981. pap. 2.95 (ISBN 0-380-01656-7, 78386, Bard). Avon.
Blue Chair: A Novel. Joyce Thompson. LC 77-78140. 1977. 1.75 (ISBN 0-380-01656-7). Avon.
Blue Chip Haggerty: The Collected Stories. Ray Millholland. LC 56-9002. 1956. Morrow.
Blue Chip. 1st Ed. Ysabel Fisk Rennie. LC 53-11857. Harper.
Blue Chips: A Novel. Joseph Jay Deiss. LC 57-7310. 1957. Simon and Schuster.
Blue Circle: A Novel. Elizabeth Garver Jordan. LC 22-919359. 1922. 1.90. The Century Co.
Blue City. Kenneth Millar. LC 47-4527. 1947. A. A. Knopf.
Blue Climate: A Novel. Burt Cole. LC 75-30358. 10.95 (ISBN 0-06-121551-1). Harper & Row.
Blue Cloak. Temple Bailey. LC 41-4130. 1941. Houghton Mifflin Company.
Blue Cloak... Temple Bailey. LC 46-21817. (Bart house novel, 31). 1946.
Blue Clown. H. K. Rothrock. 192p. (Orig.). 1973. pap. 1.95 o.p. (ISBN 0-87056-331-9, 6331). Brandon.
Blue Cockade: A Story of the Confederacy... Flora McDonald Williams. LC 6-1023. 1905. The Neale Publishing Company.
Blue Comedian. John Ford. 1968. 7.00 o.s.i. (Pub. by Cowman). Tri-Ocean.
Blue Cup: And Other Stories. Beatrice Joy Chute. LC 57-8955. 1957. Dutton.
Blue Dahlia. Raymond Chandler. (Screenplay Ser.). (Illus.). 1979. pap. 2.50 (ISBN 0-445-04353-9). Popular Lib.
Blue Danube. Ludwig Bemelmans. LC 45-3158. 1945. The Viking Press.
Blue Danube. Ludwig Bemelmans. LC 46-22502. 1946. The Sun Dial Press.
Blue Day on Main Street. J. L Navarro. LC 73-88742. (Illus.). 1973. 2.25 (ISBN 0-88412-063-5). Quinto Sol Publications.
Blue Death. Michael Collins, pseud. (Dan Fortune Mystery Novel - Red Badge Mystery Ser.). 192p. 1974. 5.95 o.p. (ISBN 0-396-07000-0). Dodd.
Blue Death. Michael Collins, pseud. LC 79-84689. (Dan Fortune Detective Ser.). 176p. 1982. pap. 2.25 (ISBN 0-87216-991-X). Playboy Pbks.
Blue Death. Dennis Lynds. LC 74-23314. (Red badge novel of suspense). 1975. 5.95. (ISBN 0-396-07000-0). Dodd, Mead.
Blue Devil Suite. Dorothy Daniels. 1971. pap. 0.75 o.p. (B75-2175). Belmont-Tower.
Blue Devil Suite. Dorothy Daniels. (Belmont Tower Book). 1977. 1.25. Tower Publications.
Blue Devils All. Frank Lee Donoghue. (His State trooper adventure series. G riders in action). McLoughlin Bros., Inc.
Blue Diamond. Joan Smith. 224p. 1981. pap. 1.50 (ISBN 0-449-50213-9, Crest). Fawcett.
Blue Distance. Joan Sutherland. LC 33-6705. Farrar & Rinehart, Incorporated.
Blue Dog: And Other Fables for the French. Translated by Alice B. Toklas. Anne Bodart. 1956. Houghton Mifflin.
Blue Door. Rachel Mack. LC 36-70448. J. H. Hopkins & Son, Inc.
Blue Door & Other Stories. Lawrence Perry Spingarn. LC 77-73353. (Illus.). 60p. 1977. pap. 3.00 (ISBN 0-912288-10-8). Perivale Pr.
Blue Door: Murder--Mystery--Detection, in Ten Thrill Packed Novelettes. Vincent Starrett. LC 30-23189. 1930. Pub. for the Crime Club, Inc., by Doubleday, Doran & Company, Inc.
Blue Dragoons: A Novel by Curt Berg, Translated from the Swedish. Curt Berg. Tr. by Williamson, Eleanor Salberg. LC 38-6970. 1938. G. P. Putnam's Sons.
Blue Dreams. William Hanley. 1971. 6.95 o.p. (0723-6). Delacorte.
Blue Dreams: Or, The End of Romance and the Continued Pursuit of Happiness. William Hanley. LC 73-141625. 1971. 6.95. Delacorte Press.
Blue Dress. Dorothy Evelyn Smith. LC 62-7822. 1962. Dutton.
Blue Dwarfs. Kurt Mahr. (Perry Rhodan#54). (Illus.). 1974. (pbk.) 0.95. Ace Books.
Blue Envelope: A Novel. Sophie Kerr. LC 17-5983. 1917. Doubleday, Page & Company.
Blue Evening Gone. Jessica Stirling. LC 80-29291. 1981. 12.95 (ISBN 0-312-08717-9). St. Martin's Press.
Blue Eye: A Story of the People of the Plains. J. G. Mock. 1905. The Irwin-Hodson Company.
Blue-Eyed Boy: A Novel of Suspense. Christopher Short. LC 66-175926. bds., 3.75. Dodd.
Blue-Eyed Gypsy. Janette Ratcliffe. (Candlelight regency romance). 1974. (pbk.) 0.75. Dell.
Blue-Eyed Kid. Edward Beverly Mann. LC 32-661. 1932. W. Morrow & Company.
Blue-Eyed Manchu. Achmed Abdullah. LC 18-5647. R.J. Shores.
Blue-Eyed Satori: And Other Stories. Terrance R Lindall & Yuko Nii. LC 71-125027. 1970. T. Gaus Sons.
Blue-Eyed Shan. Stephen D. Becker. LC 81-48283. (Illus.). 13.50 (ISBN 0-394-50034-2). Random House.
Blue Eyed Six. Edna J Carmean. LC 74-191730. (Illus.). 1974. 7.50. S.N.
Blue Eyes. Jerome Charyn. LC 74-11142. 1975. 6.95 (ISBN 0-671-21856-5). Simon and Schuster.
Blue Eyes. Jerome Charyn. 1977. 1.75 (ISBN 0-380-00882-3). Avon.
Blue Eyes and Gray. Emmuska Orczy. LC 29-2734. 1929. Doubleday, Doran & Company, Inc.
Blue Falcon. Robyn Carr. LC 80-24878. 12.95 (ISBN 0-316-12972-0). Little, Brown.
Blue Feather. Zane Grey. 1972. 0.95. Manor Books.
Blue Feather: A Bit of Americana, Part Fact, Part Fiction. Cover Design by Alberta C. Dickerson. Alice Byington McKeand. LC 60-16403. (Creative legendary tales series, no. 1). 1960. Creative Press.
Blue Feather: A Story of Prehistoric Indian Life Based on a Navajo Lengend. Paul A Jones. LC 54-21571. Kan., Prairie Publishers.
Blue Feather: And Other Stories. Zane Grey. LC 62-5717. 1961. Grosset & Dunlap.
Blue Feather & Other Stories. Zane Grey. 2.95 o.p. G&D.
Blue Feather, and Other Stories. 1st Ed. Zane Grey. LC 61-136039. 1961. Harper.
Blue Fire. Phyllis A. White. LC 61-6489. (Fawcett crest book). 1975. (pbk.) 1.25. Fawcett.
Blue Fire. Phyllis A Whitney. LC 61-6489. 1961. Appleton-Century-Crofts.
Blue Flame. Joseph L Gilmore. LC 82-5163. 12.95 (ISBN 0-396-08087-1). Dodd, Mead.
Blue Flame. Doran Stewart. LC 41-18117. Fortuny's.
Blue Flower. Ed. by Hermann Kesten. LC 46-819146. 1946. Roy Publishers.
Blue Flower. Henry Van Dyke. LC 70-110221. (Short story index reprint series). (Illus.). 1970. Books for Libraries Press.
Blue Flower. Henry Van Dyke. LC 2-25606. 1902. C. Scribner's Sons.
Blue Flower. Henry Van Dyke. LC 16-6322. 1915. C. Scribner's Sons.
Blue-Flowered Tree. Jean-Louis Baghio'o. Tr. by Stephen Romer from Fr. 192p. 1983. Repr. of 1973 ed. text ed. 14.75x (ISBN 0-85635-470-8, Pub. by Carcanet New Pr England). Humanities.
Blue Flowers. Tr. from French by Barbara Wright. 1st Amer. Ed. Raymond Queneau. LC 67-14102. 1967. 5.00. Atheneum.
Blue Frogs. Jeffrey Helterman. (Orig.). 1980. pap. 1.95 (ISBN 0-532-23197-X). Woodhill.
Blue Geranium. Dolan Birkley. LC 41-1970. 1941. Simon and Schuster.
Blue Geranium: An Inner Sanctum Mystery. Dolores Birk Hitchens. LC 44-47610. (Bart house books. 8). 1944. Bartholomew House, Inc.
Blue Germ. Maurice Nicoll. LC 18-18099. George H. Doran Company.
Blue Ghost: Lafcadio Hearn's Work. J. Temple. LC 74-16485. (American Literature Ser., No. 49). 1974. lib. bdg. 49.95x (ISBN 0-8383-2027-9). Haskell.
Blue Gingham Folks. Dorothy Donnell Calhoun. LC 15-26848. 0.75. The Abingdon Press.
Blue Glory. Rebecca Drury. (Women at War Ser.: Bk. 6). 352p. 1982. pap. 3.25 (ISBN 0-440-00456-X, Emerald). Dell.
Blue God: An Epic of Mesa Verde. Louis Mertins. 1968. 7.50 o.p. (ISBN 0-378-07034-7). Ritchie.
Blue God Jazz. Donald Snow. LC 30-276882. E. J. Clode, Inc.
Blue Gold: A Romance of the Rockies. Agnes K Getty. LC 34-10327. 1934. The Caxton Printers, Ltd.
Blue Goose. Frank Lewis Nason. 1903. McClure, Phillips & Co.
Blue Goose Chase: A Camera-Hunting Adventure in Louisiana. Herbert Keightley Job. LC 11-8475. 1911. The Baker & Taylor Company.
Blue-Grass and Broadway. Maria Thompson Daviess. LC 19-8740. 1919. 1.50. The Century Co.
Blue-Grass Thoroughbred: A Novel. Tom Johnson. LC 6-459417. (On cover: The household library, v. 4, no. 14). Belford, Clarke & Co.; Etc., Etc.
Blue Guitar. Alex Austin. LC 64-17300. 1964. F. Fell.
Blue Hammer. Ross Macdonald. LC 75-36809. 1976. 7.95 (ISBN 0-394-40425-4). Knopf: Distributed by Random House.
Blue Hammer. Ross Macdonald. LC 76-45436. 1976. 12.95 (ISBN 0-8161-6431-2). G. K. Hall.
Blue Hand. Edgar Wallace. LC 28-7632. 1926. Small, Maynard & Company.
Blue Harpsichord. Francis Steegmuller. LC 49-7322. (Red badge mystery). 1919. Dodd, Mead.
Blue Hawk. Peter Dickinson. LC 76-1857. 8.95 (ISBN 0-316-18429-2). Little, Brown.
Blue Hawk. Peter Dickinson. (Del Rey Book). 1977. 1.95 (ISBN 0-345-25759-6). Ballantine Books.
Blue Hawk. Peter Dickinson. LC 76-382923. (Illus.). 1976. 2.95 (ISBN 0-575-02074-1). Gollancz.
Blue Heather, No. 54. Barbara Cartland. 1975. pap. 1.25 o.p. (ISBN 0-515-03792-3, V3792). BJ Pub Group.
Blue Heaven. Elizabeth Carfrae, pseud. LC 40-219228. G. P. Putnam's Sons.
Blue Heaven Bends All Over see Heart in the Highlands.
Blue Heaven Bends Over All. Jane Oliver, pseud. LC 70-173290. 1971. 6.95. Putnam.
Blue Hen's Chick. Alfred Bertram Guthrie. 1965. 5.95 o.p. (ISBN 0-07-025299-8). McGraw.
Blue Hill Avenue: A Novel. Mark Mirsky. LC 73-173205. 1972. 6.95. Bobbs-Merrill.
Blue Hills. Elizabeth Goudge. 288p. 1976. lib. bdg. 15.95x (ISBN 0-89966-100-9). Buccaneer Bks.
Blue Hills. Lee Washburn. LC 45-5128. 1945. Meador Publishing Company.
Blue Horizon. Faith Baldwin. 1976. Repr. of 1941 ed. lib. bdg. 15.45x (ISBN 0-88411-618-2). Amereon Ltd.
Blue Horizon. Mary Wolfe Thompson. LC 40-13053. 1940. Longmans, Green and Co.
Blue Horizons. Faith Baldwin Cuthrell. LC 76-40294. 1976. 6.95 (ISBN 0-88411-618-2). Aeonian Press.
Blue Horizons. Faith Baldwin Cuthrell. LC 42-14113. Farrar & Rinehart, Inc.
Blue Horizons. Faith Baldwin Cuthrell. LC 47-2712. 1947. Triangle Books, the Blakiston Company.
Blue Horse of Taxco. Kathleen Moore Knight. LC 47-4931. 1947. Pub. for the Crime Club by Doubleday.
Blue Horses: A Biographical Romance of the Civil War. Kathrn Bemis Wilson. LC 31-33067. Burton Publishing Company.
Blue Hotel. Joseph Katz. (Casebook Corbett Ser.). 1969. pap. text ed. 3.50x o.p. (ISBN 0-675-09444-5). Merrill.
Blue Hotel & Other Stories. Stephen Crane. Orig. Title: Maggie & Other Stories. 1982. pap. 3.95 (ISBN 0-671-46036-6). WSP.
Blue Hour. Morton Freedgood. LC 48-614285. Pub. for the Crime Club by Doubleday.
Blue House. And, The Fatal Duel. Hendrik Conscience. 1885. J. Murphy & Co.
Blue Hurricane. Francis Van Wyck Mason. (Berkley Medallion Book). 1976. 1.95 (ISBN 0-425-03182-9). Berkley.
Blue Hurricane. Francis Van Wyck Mason. LC 54-9417. (Illus.). 1954. Lippincott.
Blue Hussar: Translated from the French by Jacques Le Clercq. Roger Nimier. LC 53-10509. 1953. J. Messner.
Blue Ice. Ralph Hammond-Innes. LC 49-10191. 1948. Harper.
Blue in Chicago. Bette Howland. LC 76-26235. 8.95 (ISBN 0-06-011957-8). Harper & Row.
Blue Is the Grass: A Novel. Taomie Stanfield. LC 50-6207. 1949. Humphries.
Blue Is the Hero. Bill Berkson. 1976. 7.50 (Pub. by L Pubns); signed ed. 15.00; pap. 4.00. SBD.
Blue Jackets: Or, The Adventures of J. Thompson, A. B. Among "the Heathen Chinee." A Nautical Novel. Edward Greey. LC 6-44864. 1871. J. E. Tilton & Co.
Blue Jay. Max Brand. LC 27-718223. 1927. Dodd, Mead & Company.
Blue Jay. Max Brand. LC 81-4817. 1981. 12.95 (ISBN 0-8161-3241-0). G.K. Hall.
Blue Jay. Frederick Faust. LC 27-7182. 1927. Dodd, Mead & Company.
Blue Jay. Peggy Webling. LC 5-38487. P. R. Reynolds.
Blue Jay Summer. Elleston Trevor. (Dell Book). 1977. 1.75 (ISBN 0-440-10616-8). Dell Pub. Co.
Blue-Jay Yarn. Mark Twain. (Illus.). pap. 3.00. Turtles Quill.
Blue Jeans. Lorraine Levey Beim & Jerrold Bein. LC 41-3682. Harcourt, Brace and Company.
Blue John Diamond. Ernest Robertson Punshon. LC 29-8391. E. J. Clode, Inc.
Blue Key. Kathalyn Krause. 2.25 (ISBN 0-505-51536-9). Belmont Tower Books.
Blue Knight. Joseph Wambaugh. LC 72-4089. 1972. 11.95 (ISBN 0-8161-6037-6). G. K. Hall.
Blue Knight. Joseph Wambaugh. LC 79-175474. 1972. 7.95. Little, Brown.
Blue Knight. Joseph Wambaugh. (A dell book). 1979. 2.50 (ISBN 0-440-10607-9). Dell Pub. Co.
Blue Lacquer Box. George Frank Worts. LC 39-20723. 1939. H. C. Kinsey & Company, Inc.
Blue Ladies. Bettz Burr. LC 79-67608. 9.95 (ISBN 0-87223-585-8). Seaview Books.
Blue Ladies: Bettz Burr. Bettz Burr. LC 81-81977. 1981. 2.95 (ISBN 0-87216-944-8). Playboy Paperbacks.
Blue Lagoon: A Romance. 2d impression. ed. Henry De Vere Stacpoole. 1908. J. B. Lippincott Company Etc., Etc.
Blue Lagoon, a Romance. 2d impression ed. Henry De Vere Stacpoole. LC 9-1584. 1908. J. B. Lippincott Company; Etc., Etc.
Blue Lagoon Omnibus. Henry De Vere Stacpoole. 210p. (Orig.). 1981. Repr. of 1908 ed. 5.95x (ISBN 0-9605338-0-X). Blue Lagoon.
Blue Lamp. William Dudley Pelley. LC 31-294227. The Fiction League.
Blue Lantern. Sidonie Gabrielle Colette. LC 72-178781. 1972. 8.50 (ISBN 0-8371-6291-2). Greenwood Press.
Blue Lawn. Loretto Ellen Duffy Kolle. LC 10-17595. R. F. Fenno & Company.
Blue Leader. Walter H Wager. LC 78-67778. 9.95 (ISBN 0-87795-206-X). Arbor House: Distributed by Dutton.
Blue Leader. Walter H Wager. LC 79-19577. 1980. 10.95 (ISBN 0-89340-225-7). J. Curley & Associates.
Blue Lights. Frederic Arnold Kummer. LC 18-4809. 1.25. W. J. Watt & Company.
Blue Lights: Or, Hot Work in the Soudan. A Tale of Soldier Life in Several of Its Phases. Robert Michael Ballantyne. LC 8-7093. 1888. T. Nelson and Sons.
Blue Lily. Livius Beethoben & Gerri L. Herrick. LC 81-86318. (Orig.). 1982. write for info. (ISBN 0-942992-01-6). Peace on Earth.
Blue Locket. Elsie Frances Wilson Mack. LC 51-11471. 1951. Bouregy & Curl.
Blue Man: A Novel. Thomas Atkins. LC 77-77116. 1978. 7.95 (ISBN 0-385-12844-4). Doubleday.
Blue Marigolds. Helen Topping Miller. LC 34-227511. The Penn Publishing Company.
Blue Mask at Bay. John Creasey. LC 38-10325. 1938. J. B. Lippincott Co.
Blue Mask at Bay. Anthony Morton, pseud. LC 38-10325. J. B. Lippincott Company.
Blue Mask Strikes Again. John Creasey. LC 40-6703. 1940. J. B. Lippincott Co.
Blue Mask Strikes Again. Anthony Morton, pseud. LC 40-6703. J. B. Lippincott Company.
Blue Mask Victorios. John Creasey. LC 40-31184. 1940. J. B. Lippincott Co.
Blue Mask Victorious. Anthony Morton, pseud. LC 40-311844. J. B. Lippincott Company.
Blue Max. Jack D Hunter. (S2982). 1965. Bantam.
Blue Max. Jack D Hunter. LC 64-11083. 1964. Dutton.
Blue Meadow. Mary Longstreet Wallace. LC 74-20600. 1975. 8.95 (ISBN 0-688-02887-X). W. Morrow.
Blue Meadow. Mary Longstreet Wallace. 1976. 1.75 (ISBN 0-671-80536-3). Pocket Books.
Blue Meadows. May Stanley. 1933. Little, Brown, and Company.
Blue Mesa Trail. Tevis Miller. LC 39-25556. Phoenix Press.
Blue Mesa Trail. Joseph Reardon. LC 39-25556. Phoenix Press.
Blue Messiah. James David Horan. LC 70-168328. 1971. 7.95. Crown Publishers.
Blue Moon. Walter H. Wager. 1981. pap. 2.50 (ISBN 0-425-04929-9). Berkley Pub.
Blue Moon: A Novel. Walter H Wager. LC 79-87837. 9.95 (ISBN 0-87795-235-3). Arbor House.
Blue Moon: A Tale of the Flatwoods. David Wulf Anderson. LC 19-15542. The Bobbs-Merrill Company.
Blue Mountains of China. Rudy Henry Wiebe. LC 76-127628. 1970. 5.95. Eerdmans.
Blue Movie. Michael Perkins. pap. 1.75 o.p. (0101). Essex Hse.
Blue Movie. Terry Southern. LC 75-115799. 1970. 6.95. The World Pub. Co.
Blue Movie Murders. Ellery Queen, pseud. (Orig.). 1972. pap. 0.95 o.p. Lancer.
Blue Murder. Denise DeClue. LC 76-56156. 1977. 1.50 (ISBN 0-345-25456-2). Ballantine Books.
Blue Murder. Brett Halliday. (Mike Shayne Mystery). 1973. (pbk) 0.75. Dell.
Blue Murder. Harriet Rutland. LC 42-255802. 1942. Smith and Durrell Inc.

Blue Murder. Edmund Snell. LC 33-23775. 1933. J. B. Lippincott Company.

Blue Murder. Walter H. Wager. 1982. pap. 2.75 (ISBN 0-425-05444-6). Berkley Pub.

Blue Murder: A Novel. Walter H Wager. LC 80-67622. 11.95 (ISBN 0-87795-286-8). Arbor House.

Blue Mustang: A Novel Inspired by One of the Most Remarkable Rides in the History of the Southwest, by Clay Fisher Pseud. Henry Allen. LC 56-7136. 1956. Houghton Mifflin.

Blue Mustang: A Novel Inspired by One of the Most Remarkable Rides in the History of the Southwest. Clay Fisher. LC 56-713600. 1956. Houghton Mifflin.

Blue of Capricorn. Eugene Burdick. 1971. pap. 0.95 o.p. (N2591). Pyramid Pubns.

Blue of Capricorn. Eugene Burdick. pap. 1.95 o.p. (ISBN 0-515-04414-8). BJ Pub Group.

Blue of Heaven. (Stanyan Books Ser). 1970. 3.00 o.p. (ISBN 0-394-40462-9). Random.

Blue Pages. Eleanor Perry. 288p. 1980. pap. 2.72 (ISBN 0-553-13319-5). Bantam.

Blue Pages: A Novel. Eleanor Perry. LC 78-13503. 8.95 (ISBN 0-397-01254-3). Lippincott.

Blue Paroquet. Elizabeth York Miller. LC 29-239. 1928. Brentano's, Ltd.

Blue Parrakeet Murders. Robert Portner Koehler. 1948. Phoenix Press.

Blue Pastoral. Gilbert Sorrentino. LC 82-73720. 320p. 1983. 18.00 (ISBN 0-86547-095-2). N Point Pr.

Blue Pavilions. Arthur Thomas Quiller-Couch. LC 13-9385. Cassell Publishing Company.

Blue Pavilions. Arthur Thomas Quiller-Couch. LC 4-16507. 1898. C. Scribner's Sons.

Blue Pavillion. Williams James De L'Aigle Buchan. LC 66-19918. bds., 4.75. Morrow.

Blue Pete: Half Breed. Lacey Amy. LC 21-4717. The James A. McCann Company.

Blue Peter: Sea Yarns. Morley Roberts. LC 71-178458. (Short story index reprint series). 1971. (ISBN 0-8369-4059-8). Books for Libraries Press.

Blue Peter: Sea Yarns. Morley Roberts. LC 8-208618. 1908. L. C. Page & Company.

Blue Portfolio. Vera Marie Tracy. LC 33-37997. The Bruce Publishing Company.

Blue Print for Murder. Paul Winterton. LC 48-18748. 1948. Hutchinson.

Blue Prints. 2nd ed. D. Clarke. 1945. pap. 5.25x o.p. (ISBN 0-522-83789-1, Pub. by Melbourne U Pr). Intl Schol Bk Serv.

Blue Rags. David Meltzer. 1974. 5.00 (Pub. by Oyez); signed ed. 15.00; pap. 1.50. SBD.

Blue Rajah Murder... Harold MacGrath. LC 30-16609. 1930. Pub. for The Crime Club, Inc., by Doubleday, Doran & Company, Inc.

Blue Remembered Hills. Leone Mead. LC 47-361645. 1947. Coward-McCann, Inc.

Blue Ribbon. Cornell George Hopley-Woolrich. LC 49-7423. 1949. J. B. Lippincott Co.

Blue Ribbon. A Novel. Cornel George Hopley-Woolrich. LC 45-48719. 1874. Harper & Brothers.

Blue Ribbon. A Novel. Eliza Tabor Stephenson. (Seaside library, v. 42, no. 865). 1880. G. Munro.

Blue Ribbon for Marni. Dorothy Brenner Francis. (YA) 1973. 4.50 o.p. (Avalon). Bouregy.

Blue Ribbon for Marni. Dorothy Brenner Francis. (Avalon romances). 1973. 4.50. Avalon.

Blue Ribbons. Martha Lewis Beckwith Ewell Lewis. LC 6-38133. 1882. The Protective Publishing Company.

Blue Ridge Breezes. Joseph Medley Rowland. LC 27-8464. 1927. Printed for the Author, Publishing House M. E. Church, South.

Blue Ridge Mountain Boy. Charles T. Edwards. 1972. 3.50 o.p. (ISBN 0-682-47405-3). Exposition.

Blue Ridge Mystery: A Novel. Caroline Martin. LC 7-24379. R. L. Weed Company.

Blue Rise. Rebecca Hill. LC 82-14329. 1983. 12.95 (ISBN 0-688-01875-0). Morrow.

Blue River. Mary Frances Doner. LC 46-4734. 1946. Doubleday & Company, Inc.

Blue River Riders. Archie Joscelyn. LC 44-377. 1944. Phoenix Press.

Blue River: Stories. Betsy Hopkins Lochridge. LC 56-10627. 1956. Macmillan.

Blue Robe: The Story of Mary Magdalene. Sara Elizabeth Gosselink. LC 45-216876. 1945. Wm. B. Eerdmans Publishing Company.

Blue Rock Range. Ray Kelley, pseud. LC 77-16731. 1978. 7.95 o.p. (ISBN 0-312-08719-5); large type 9.95 o.p. (ISBN 0-312-08720-9). St Martin.

Blue Rock Range. Lauran Paine. LC 77-16731. 1978. 7.95. (ISBN 0-312-08719-5) (ISBN 0-312-08720-9). St. Martin's Press.

Blue Room. Cosmo Hamilton. LC 20-18662. 1920. Little, Brown and Company.

Blue Room. Georges Simenon. LC 78-7423. (Harvest/HBJ book). 1978. 2.25 (ISBN 0-15-613267-2). Harcourt Brace Jovanovich.

Blue Rose. Susan Lennox. LC 58-7594. 1958. Avalon Books.

Blue Roses: Or, Helen Malinofska's Marriage. Charlotte Louisa Hawkins Dempster. (Seaside library. v. 27, no. 564). 1879. G. Munro.

Blue Ruin. Grace Livingston Hill. LC 28-255462. 1928. J. B. Lippincott Company.

Blue Rum. Evelyn Scott. LC 39-9492. J. Cape & H. Smith.

Blue Russell. Will Bryant. LC 76-14170. 8.95 (ISBN 0-394-48759-1). Random House.

Blue Russell. Will Bryant. 1979. 1.95 (ISBN 0-449-23840-7). Fawcett Crest.

Blue Santo Murder Mystery. Margaret Neilson Armstrong. LC 41-220662. Random House.

Blue Sapphire. Dorothy Emily Stevenson. LC 63-17968. 1963. Holt, Rinehart and Winston.

Blue Sapphire. Dorothy Emily Stevenson. 1977. 1.50 (ISBN 0-441-06871-5). Ace Books.

Blue Sash, and Other Stories. Warren Beck. LC 41-12684. The Antioch Press.

Blue Scarab. David Graham Adee. (Library of choice fiction, no. 42). 1892. Laird & Lee.

Blue Scarab. Richard Austin Freeman. LC 24-1491. 1924. 2.00. Dodd, Mead and Company.

Blue Shovel. Robert Hershon. 1979. pap. 3.00 (ISBN 0-914610-14-7). Hanging Loose.

Blue Skies. Helen Hodgman. LC 77-354210. 1976. 2.95 (ISBN 0-7156-1177-1). Duckworth.

Blue Skies. Louise Harrison McCraw. LC 38-29541. Zondervan Publishing House.

Blue Skies: By Gay Rutherford Pseud. James Noble Gifford. LC 53-11303. 1953. Arcadia House.

Blue Skies, No Candy. Gael Greene. LC 76-17870. 1976. 7.95 (ISBN 0-688-03082-3). Morrow.

Blue Star. Fletcher Pratt. 1981. pap. 2.50 (ISBN 0-345-29852-7, Del Rey). Ballantine.

Blue Stocking. Annie Edwards. 1886. G. Munro.

Blue-Stocking Hall... William Pitt Scargill. LC 8-20233. 1828. Printed by J. & J. Harper, for Collings & Hannay; Etc., Etc.

Blue Streak. John Chesterfield Hines. LC 17-258607. 1.35. George H. Doran Company.

Blue String: And Other Sketches. Alma Newton. LC 19-57. 1918. Duffield & Company.

Blue Sunshine. Ken Johnson. LC 78-53424. 1978. pap. text ed. 1.75 o.s.i. (ISBN 0-89559-072-7). Dale Books Inc.

Blue System. K. H Scheer. (Perry Rhodan # 99). 1976. 1.25. Ace Books.

Blue Talisman: A Detective Story. Fergus Hume. LC 25-4855. E. J. Clode, Inc.

Blue Taper. Gimone Hall. (Orig.). 1970. pap. 0.60 o.p. (60-441). Manor Bks.

Blue Taper. Gimone Hall. (O.s.i.). 1971. pap. 0.75 o.s.i. (532-75437-075). Manor Bks.

Blue Train. Lawrence Clark Powell. LC 76-54947. 10.00 (ISBN 0-88496-073-0). Capra Press.

Blue Vehicle. Norman Solomon. LC 78-60314. 1978. pap. 2.00 (ISBN 0-912874-14-7). Out of the Ashes.

Blue Veil: Or, The Crime of the Tower. Fortune Du Boisgobey & Montaigu, A. De, Tr. LC 6-34434. (On cover: Lovell's library. no. 1080). J. W. Lovell Company.

Blue Vesuvius. Robert McNair Wilson. LC 31-841336. 1931. J. B. Lippincott Company.

Blue Voyage, by Conrad Aiken... Conrad Potter Aiken. LC 27-15974. 1927. C. Scribner's Sons.

Blue Wall. Richard Washburn Child. 1912. 1.25. Houghton Mifflin Company.

Blue Waters: An Indian Romance. Richard Izer Helm. LC 39-1205. Binfords & Mort.

Blue Wildfire. Faye Ashley. 320p. 1983. pap. 3.25 (ISBN 0-8439-2018-1, Leisure Bks). Dorchester Pub Co.

Blue Window. Temple Bailey. LC 28-17928. 1926. The Penn Publishing Company.

Blueback. Bill Knox. LC 70-84364. 1969. 4.50. Published for the Crime Club by Doubleday.

Bluebeard. Max Frisch. Tr. by Geoffrey Skelton. LC 82-21250. 120p. 1983. 10.50 (ISBN 0-15-113200-3). HarBraceJ.

Blueberry Pie and Other Stories. Thyra Samter Winslow. LC 82-47576. 1932. A. A. Knopf.

Blueberry Summer. Elisabeth Ogilvie. Repr. lib. bdg. 12.05x (ISBN 0-88411-327-2). Amereon Ltd.

Bluebird. Bernice N. Cross. 3.95 o.p. Carlton.

Bluebird Canyon. Dan McCall. LC 82-7402. 14.95 (ISBN 0-86553-032-7). Congdon & Weed: Distributed by St. Martin's Press.

Bluebird Canyon. Dan McCall. 384p. 1983. 14.95 (ISBN 0-312-92057-1). Congdon & Weed.

Bluebird Is at Home. Brooke Russell Astor. LC 65-14661. 1965. Harper & Row.

Bluebird Songs of Hope and Joy. William Lauriston Hill & Hill, Halbert Green, 1831-LC 16-22391. R. G. Badger.

Bluefeather. Laurence Walter Meynell. LC 28-21973. 1928. D. Appleton and Company.

Bluegrass. Borden Deal. LC 76-16249. 1976. 8.95 (ISBN 0-385-01821-5). Doubleday.

Bluegrass and Wattle: Or, The Man from Australia. Mary Addams Bayne. LC 9-28208. 1.25. The Standard Publishing Company.

Bluegrass Cavalier. Edwin Carlile Litsey. LC 22-6526. Dorrance.

Bluegrass Doctor: By Ethel Hamill Pseud. Jean Francis Webb. LC 53-9404. 1953. Bouregy & Curl.

Bluegrass Frontier. Dean Lipton. 368p. (Orig.). 1980. pap. 2.50 (ISBN 0-89083-667-1). Zebra.

Bluejacket Tales: "And See the World", Anchor Jones, It Happened in Shanghai. Bill Lang. LC 31-10357. 1931. Wetzel Publishing Co., Inc.

Blueprint. Philippe Van Rjndt. LC 77-2934. 8.95 (ISBN 0-399-12002-5). Putnam.

Blueprint. Philippe Van Rjndt. 1979. 2.25 (ISBN 0-425-03876-9). Berkley Pub. Corp.

Blueprint for Execution. Lee Parker. (Donovan's Devils Ser.). (O.s.i.). 208p. (Orig.). 1974. pap. 1.25 o.s.i. (AQ1338, Award). Univ Pub & Dist.

Blueprint for Terror. Bob Temmey. 1976. pap. 1.50 (ISBN 0-89041-119-0, 3119). Major Bks.

Blueprint for Yesterday. June Pat Wetherell. LC 71-161121. 1971. 5.95 (ISBN 0-8027-5545-3). Walker.

Blues Brother Private. Judith Jacklin. (Illus.). 128p. 1980. pap. 7.95 (ISBN 0-399-50476-1, Perige). Putnam Pub Group.

Blues Brothers: Private. Judith Jacklin. 1980. pap. 7.95 (Perigre). Putnam Pub Group.

Blues Cure: And Other Stories. Delia Lyman Porter. LC 7-377792. A. D. F. Randolph & Company (Incorporated.

Blues for a Black Sister. B. B. Johnson. (Superspade Ser, No. 6). (Orig.). 1971. pap. 0.75 o.p. (64-657). Paperback Lib.

Blues for a Dying Nation. Gerald Rosen. LC 70-163601. (Illus.). 1972. 7.95. Dial Press.

Blues for Mister Charlie. James B. Baldwin. 224p. 1964. 6.95 (ISBN 0-8037-0639-1). Dial.

Blues for the Prince. Bart Spicer. LC 50-7545. 1950. Dodd, Mead.

Blues I Can Whistle. A. E. Johnson. LC 78-81698. 1969. 4.95. Four Winds Press.

Blueschild Baby. George Cain. LC 72-137124. 1970. 6.95 (ISBN 0-07-009591-4). McGraw-Hill.

Bluesong. Sydney J. Van Scyoc. 272p. (Orig.). 1983. pap. 4.95 (ISBN 0-425-05881-6). Berkley Pub.

Bluest Eye: A Novel. Toni Morrison. LC 79-117270. 1970. 5.95. Holt, Rinehart and Winston.

Bluestocking in India: Her Medical Wards and Messages Home. Winifred Heston. LC 10-21636. Fleming H. Revell Company.

Bluethorne. Frances Y. McHugh. 1971. pap. 0.75 o.p. (532-75430-075). Manor Bks.

Bluewater. Warwick Deeping. LC 39-11412. 1939. A. A. Knopf.

Bluffer's Luck. Wilbur C Tuttle. LC 37-27368. 1937. Houghton, Mifflin Company.

Bluffton: A Story of to-Day. Minot Judson Savage. LC 8-1992. 1878. Lee and Shepard.

Bluffton: A Story of to-Day. 2d ed. Minot Judson Savage. LC 42-268162. 1887. G. H. Ellis.

Blufftown Tragedy: And Other Tales. Mary Moncure Parker. 1927. The Book Press, Inc.

Blume in Love: A Novelization. Josh Greenfeld & Paul Mazursky. 1973. (pbk.) 1.25. Warner Paperback Lib.

Blunderer. Patricia Highsmith. LC 54-6048. 1954. Coward-McCann.

Blunt Burt: The Fluke. Alpine Trotter Hinkle. LC 27-13371. The Author.

Blunt Instrument. Georgette Heyer. LC 75-44983. (Fifty Classics of Crime Fiction, 1900-1950; 26). 1976. 12.00 (ISBN 0-8240-2375-7). Garland Pub.

Blunt Instrument. Georgette Heyer. LC 70-122779. 1970. 4.95. Dutton.

Blunt Instrument. Georgette Heyer. LC 38-289082. 1938. Pub. for the Crime Club, Inc., by Doubleday, Doran & Co., Inc.

Blunt Instrument. Georgette Heyer. LC 39-32052. 1939. The Sun Dial Press, Inc.

Blunted Lance. John Harris. LC 81-66019. 1981. 10.95 (ISBN 0-689-11220-3). Atheneum.

Blush, and Other Stories. Elizabeth Taylor. LC 59-6737. 1959. Viking Press.

Blush Roses. A Novel. Clara Frances Morse. (On cover: Harper's library of American fiction, no. 7)). 1878. Harper & Brothers.

Blushing Monkey. Roman McDougald. LC 53-738832. (Inner sanctum mystery). 1953. Simon and Schuster.

Boar Hog Woman. Cleo Overstreet. LC 78-182841. 1972. 5.95. Doubleday.

Board Room. Clay Blair, Jr. 1969. 6.95 o.p. Dutton.

Board Room: A Novel. Clay Blair. LC 69-13342. 1969. 6.95. Dutton.

Board Stiff: By Robert James Pseud. 1st Ed. Iris Heitner. LC 51-14736. 1951. Published for the Crime Club by Doubleday.

Boarder up at Em's: A Story of New England Folks. Anice Morris Stockton Terhune. LC 25-8370. The Macaulay Company.

Boarders in the Rue Madame. Hallie Southgate Zeisel Burnett. 1966. 4.50 o.p. Morrow.

Boarders in the Rue Madame: Nine Gallic Tales, by Hallie Burnett. Hallie Southgate Burnett. LC 66-24964. 1966. bds., 4.50. Morrow.

Boarding House. Peter Delius. LC 35-538068. J. B. Lippincott Company.

Boarding House. Frank Haskell. 1969. pap. 0.60 o.p. (60-419). Manor Bks.

Boarding House. William Trevor. LC 65-16903. bds., 3.95. Viking.

Boarding House Blond. Joseph Calvitt Clarke. LC 36-8686. 1936. Godwin.

Boarding House Blues see Slum Street, U. S. A.

Boarding Round: Interesting Experiences of a Young Yankee Schoolmaster. John Otis Barrows. LC 15-9701. 1.25. The Roxburgh Publishing Company, Inc.

Boarding Schools: Setting for Seduction. Marsha Alexander. 1973. (pbk.) 1.95 (ISBN 0-87056-333-5). Brandon Books.

Boardman Family. Mary Stanbery Watts. LC 18-760016. 1918. The Macmillan Company.

Boardwalk. Robert Kotlowitz. LC 76-13727. 1977. 8.95 (ISBN 0-394-49226-9). Knopf.

Boardwalk. Margaret Widdemer. LC 20-773. 1920. Harcourt, Brace and Howe.

Boardwalk Is Burning. R. Michael Doane. 1979. pap. 2.95 (ISBN 0-89185-206-9). Anthelion Pr.

Boardwalk Love Letters of Hiram and Ella. George B Somerville. LC 15-5417. Boardwalk Publishing Company.

Boast. Miles Donald. LC 79-25430. 10.95 (ISBN 0-312-08722-5). St. Martin's Press.

Boat. Lothar Gunther Buchheim. LC 74-21314. 1975. 10.00 (ISBN 0-394-49105-X). Knopf: Distributed by Random House.

Boat. James Noble Gifford. LC 42-2568. 1941. Arcadia House.

Boat. Leslie Poles Hartley. LC 50-6428. 1950. Doubleday.

Boat. Warren Howard. LC 42-2568. 1941. Arcadia House, Inc.

Boat in the Evening. Tarjei Vesaas. LC 71-170216. 1972. 5.95. W. Morrow.

Boat Named Death. Jack M Bickham. LC 74-31512. 1975. 5.95 (ISBN 0-385-05161-1). Doubleday.

Boat of Fate: An Historical Novel. Keith Roberts. LC 73-20187. 1974. 6.95. Prentice-Hall.

Boat of Longing. Ole Edvart Rolvaag. LC 33-1840. 1933. Harper & Brothers.

Boat of Longing, a Novel. Ole Edvart Rolvaag. Tr. by Nora O. Solum. LC 73-11844. 304p. 1974. Repr. of 1933 ed. lib. bdg. 25.00x (ISBN 0-8371-7069-9, ROBL). Greenwood.

Boat Race. John William Rowdon. LC 61-14480. 1961. Appleton-Century-Crofts.

Boat to Nowhere. Maureen C. Wartski. 1981. pap. 1.50 (W9678, Sig). NAL.

Boat Who Wouldn't Float. Farley Mowat. 208p. 1981. pap. 2.50 (ISBN 0-553-14355-7). Bantam.

Boathouse Riddle. Alfred Walter Stewart. LC 31-15200. 1931. Little, Brown, and Company.

Boatload of Homefolk. Thea Astley. 1969. 6.50 o.s.i. Tri-Ocean.

Boats, Broads, Booze. Lea Black. 4.00 o.p. Carlton.

Boats of the "Glen Carrig" Being an Account of Their Adventures in the Strange Places of the Earth, After the Foundering of the Good Ship Glen Carrig Through Striking Upon a Hidden Rock in the Unknown Seas to the Southward, As Told by John Winterstraw, Gent., to His Son James Winterstraw, in the Year 1757, and by Him Committed Very Properly and Legibly to Manuscript. William Hope Hodgson. LC 75-28855. (Classics of science fiction; ser. 2). 1976. 12.50. (ISBN 0-88355-369-4) (ISBN 0-88355-454-2). Hyperion Press.

Bob and the Guides. Mary Raymond Shipman Andrews. LC 77-163019. (Short story index reprint series). (Illus.). 1971. (ISBN 0-8369-3933-6). Books for Libraries Press.

Bob and the Guides. Mary Raymond Shipman Andrews. LC 6-12555. 1906. C. Scribner's Sons.

Bob Carlton, American. Herbert Greyson Laing. LC 11-1851. 1910. 1.50. The C. M. Clark Publishing Company.

Bob Covington: A Novel. Archibald Clavering Gunter. LC 72-3165. (Black Heritage Library Collection). (Illus.). 1972. (ISBN 0-8369-9074-9). Books for Libraries Press.

Bob Dean: Or, "Our Other Boarder.". Emma Nelson Hood. LC 7-5398. 1882. E. Claxton & Company.

Bob Flame Among the Navajo. Dorr Graves Yeager. LC 47-362. 1946. Dodd, Mead & Company.

Bob Flame in Death Valley. Dorr Graves Yeager. LC 37-17364. 1937. Dodd, Mead & Company.

Bob Flame, Ranger. Dorr Graves Yeager. LC 34-10392. Sears Publishing Company, Inc.

Bob Flame, Rocky Mountain Ranger. Dorr Graves Yeager. LC 35-16583. 1935. Dodd, Mead & Company.

Bob Greenfellow's Sketches. John D Rullmann. LC 8-964. Johnson Bros. Ptg. Co. Printers.

Bob Hampton of Placer. Randall Parrish. 1906. A. C. McClurg & Co.

Bob Hardwick: The Story of His Life and Experiences. Henry Howard Harper. LC 11-26180. 1911. Issued Privately by the De Vinne Press and Printed Only on Advance Subscriptions from Members of the Bibliophile Society.
Bob Martin's Little Girl. David Christie Murray. LC 7-25477. (On cover: Broadway series, no. 17). 1892. J. A. Taylor and Company.
Bob Moran and the Fiery Claw. Henry Verne. LC 59-5659. 1960. Phoenix House.
Bob Rutherford and His Wife: An Historical Romance. Edwin F Moody. LC 7-17261. 1888. Printed for the Author, by J. P. Morton & Company.
Bob Ryalls, Clubman, Lover, Gambler: An Anglo-American Story. John Alexander Sheridan. LC 13-25940. Western Publishing Co.
Bob: Son of Battle. Alfred Ollivant. 1901. Doubleday & McClure Co.
Bob: Son of Battle. Alfred Ollivant. LC 24-27363. 1923. Doubleday, Page & Company.
Bob: Son of Battle. Alfred Ollivant. LC 39-16968. 1937. The Sun Dial Press, Inc.
Bob, Son of Battle. Alfred Ollivant. LC 4-15328. 1898. Doubleday & McClure Company.
Bob, Son of Battle. Alfred Ollivant. LC 32-21202. Garden City Publishing Co., Inc.
Bob Younger's Fate. Edwin S Deane. (On cover: Secret service series, no. 28). 1890. Street & Smith.
Bobbed Hair. Wells, Carolyn. LC 25-78291. 1925. G. P. Putnam's Sons.
Bobbed Tail Verses & One Long Tale. William F. Ward. 1968. 3.00 o.p. (ISBN 0-8059-0293-7). Dorrance.
Bobbed Wire V Bible. rev. ed. Jack Glover. ltd. ed. 20.00; pap. 7.95. Cow Puddle.
Bobbers with Tails. Dwight W. Emrick. LC 74-28318. (Illus.). 1974. (ISBN 0-915138-03-4). Pickwick Press.
Bobbie". Kate Lee Langley Bosher. LC 99-3475. 1899. Presses of B. F. Johnson Publishing Co.
Bobbie, General Manager: A Novel. Olive Higgins Prouty. LC 13-3300. 1913. 1.25. Frederick A. Stokes Company.
Bobbie McDuff. Clinton Ross. LC 8-666. 1898. L. C. Page and Company.
Bobbies, Baubles & Blood. J. D. Hardin. LC 82-82001. (J. D. Hardin Western Ser.). 224p. 1982. pap. 1.95 (ISBN 0-86721-226-8). Playboy Pbks.
Bobbo" and Other Fancies. Thomas Isaac Wharton. 1897. Harper & Brothers.
Bobbsey Twins at the Seashore. Laura Lee Hope. LC 29-3267. (Her The Bobbsey twins series). Grosset & Dunlap.
Bobby. John Joy Bell. LC 14-9768. 1.00. Hodder & Stoughton, George H. Doran Company.
Bobby Deerfield. Erich Maria Remarque. 1978. pap. 1.95 (ISBN 0-449-23367-7, Crest). Fawcett.
Bobby Jack Smith - You Dirty Coward. Max Evans. (O.s.i.). 1974. 6.95 o.s.i. (ISBN 0-8402-1342-5). Nash Pub.
Bobby Jack Smith, You Dirty Coward! A Novel. Max Evans. LC 73-92967. 1974. 6.95 (ISBN 0-8402-1342-5). Nash Pub.
Bobby Sherman Show, No. 1. Barry Kaplan. (Bobby Sherman Ser). 1971. pap. 0.75 o.p. (07137). Curtis.
Bobby Sherman Show, No. 2. C. Stratton. (Bobby Sherman Ser.). 1971. pap. 0.75 o.p. (07137). Curtis.
Bobby Stone: A Novel. Edna Shrieves. LC 47-6752. 1947. Exposition Press.
Bobcat of Hell's Gulch. Harry D Hubbard & Stellann Howeth. LC 68-23987. (Illus.). 1968. 4.00. Dorrance.
Bobcat of Jump Mountain. Elliott Whitney & Chesterman, Evan Rayland, 1870- LC 20-17173. (The boy's big game series). The Reilly & Lee Co.
Boca Grande. Loren Singer. LC 73-20531. 1974. 6.95 (ISBN 0-385-05521-8). Doubleday.
Boccaccio's Revenge. Cartier. 1977. pap. 18.50 (ISBN 90-247-1961-5, Pub. by Martinus Nijhoff Netherlands). Kluwer Boston.
Boccaccio's Revenge: A Literary Transposition of the Corbaccio (The Old Crow) Giovanni Boccaccio & Normand R Cartier. LC 77-558919. 1977. 7.50 (ISBN 9-02-471961-5). Nijhoff.
Bodbank. Richard Washburn Child. LC 16-19419. 1916. 1.35. Henry Holt and Company.
Bodelan Way. Louis Trimble. (Science Fiction Ser.). 1974. pap. 0.95 o.p. (UQ1090). DAW Bks.
Bodelan Way. Louis Trimble. 1974. (pbk.) 0.95. Daw Books.
Bodies and Shadows: Two Short Novels. Peter Weiss. LC 70-90906. (Illus.). 1970. 5.95. Delacorte Press.
Bodies & Soul. Al Young. 150p. 1981. pap. 6.95 (ISBN 0-916870-39-1). Creative Arts Bks.
Bodies and Souls. Maxence Van Der Meersch. Tr. by Eithne Wilkins. LC 48-5900. 1948. Pellegrini & Cudahy.
Bodies & Souls. Nancy Thayer. LC 82-45126. 384p. 1983. 15.95 (ISBN 0-385-18166-3). Doubleday.
Bodies & Souls. Maxence Ven Der Meersch. (O.s.i.). 1976. pap. 1.95 o.s.i. (AY1612, Award). Univ Pub & Dist.
Bodies and Souls: Edited by Dan Herr and Joel and Wells. 1st Ed. Ed. by Dan Herr & Joel Wells. LC 61-10346. 1961. Published for the Crime Club by Doubleday.
Bodies and Spirits. Ed. by Dan Herr. Wells, Joel. LC 64-21725. 1964. Published for the Crime Club by Doubleday.
Bodies Are Different. Herman Irving Bloom. LC 35-5261. Godwin.
Bodies Are Dust. P. J Wolfson. LC 31-19907. The Vanguard Press.
Bodies Are Where You Find Them: A Michael Shayne Story. Davis Dresser. LC 41-19307. H. Holt and Company.
Bodies Beautiful. John Hallowell. LC 72-3863. 1972. 1.25. Bantam Books.
Bodies in Bedlam. Richard S Prather. LC 51-23901. (Gold medal book, 147). 1951. Fawcett Publications.
Bodies in Motion. Zane Kotker. LC 76-181368. 1972. 5.95 (ISBN 0-394-47891-6). Knopf.
Bodies in Motion: A Novel. Zane Kotker. 1973. (pbk.) 0.75. Popular Lib.
Bodies in Revolt. Thomas L. Hanna. 1970. 6.95 o.p. (ISBN 0-03-085321-4). HR&W.
Bodily Harm. Margaret Eleanor Atwood. LC 81-18370. 13.95 (ISBN 0-671-44153-1). Simon and Schuster.
Bodkin. Barton Midwood. LC 67-14469. 1968. bds., 4.95. Random.
Bodley Head Henry James, 11 vols. Ed. by Leon Edel. Incl. Vol. 1. Europeans, Washington Square. 392p (ISBN 0-370-00616-X); Vol. 2. Awkward Age. 430p (ISBN 0-370-00617-8); Vol. 3. Bostonians. 448p (ISBN 0-370-00625-9); Vol. 4. Spoils of Poynton. 208p (ISBN 0-370-00626-7); Vol. 5. Portrait of a Lady. 626p (ISBN 0-370-00640-2); Vol. 6. What Maisie Knew. 284p (ISBN 0-370-00586-4); Vol. 7. Wings of the Dove. 540p (ISBN 0-370-01423-5); Vol. 8. Ambassadors. 468p (ISBN 0-370-01432-4); Vol. 9. Golden Bowl. 604p (ISBN 0-370-01456-1); Vol. 10. Princess Casamassima. 618p (ISBN 0-370-10237-1); Vol. 11. Daisy Miller, the Turn of the Screw. 198p (ISBN 0-370-10532-X). 1980. 12.95 ea. (Pub. by Chatto Bodley Jonathan); 130.00 set. Merrimack Pub Cir.
Bodley Head Henry James, 11 vols. Henry James. Incl. Vol. 1. The Europeans & Washington Square. 392p. 1967. 10.50x o.p. (ISBN 0-87471-341-2); Vol. 2. The Awkward Age. 432p. 1967. 14.50x o.p. (ISBN 0-87471-342-0); Vol. 3. The Bostonians. 448p. 1967. o.p. (ISBN 0-87471-343-9); Vol. 4. The Spoils of Poynton. 208p. 1967. 10.00x o.p. (ISBN 0-87471-344-7); Vol. 5. The Portrait of a Lady. 640p. 1968. 16.50x o.p. (ISBN 0-87471-345-5); Vol. 6. What Mazie Knew. 288p. 1969. 12.50x o.p. (ISBN 0-87471-346-3); Vol. 7. The Wings of the Dove. 544p. 1969. 11.00x o.p. (ISBN 0-87471-347-1); Vol. 8. The Ambassadors. 468p. 1970. 11.00x o.p. (ISBN 0-87471-348-X); Vol. 9. The Golden Bowl. 608p. 1971. 11.50x o.p. (ISBN 0-87471-349-8); Vol. 10. Princess Casamassima. 600p. 1972. 14.50x o.p. (ISBN 0-87471-350-1); Vol. 11. Daisy Miller & the Turn of the Screw. 208p. 1974. 10.00x o.p. (ISBN 0-87471-573-3). Rowman.
Bodley Head Jack London, 4 vols. Jack London. Ed. by Arthur Calder-Marshall. Incl. Vol. 1. Short Stories, Call of the Wild (ISBN 0-370-00550-3); Vol. 2. John Barley Corn, the Cruise of the Dazzler, the Road (ISBN 0-370-00573-2); Vol. 3. Martin Eden (ISBN 0-370-00585-6); Vol. 4. The Klondike Dream (ISBN 0-370-00613-5). 6.95 ea. o.p. Dufour.
Bodley Head Jack London: 3v. Ed., Introd. by Arthur Calder-Marshall. Jack London. Ed. by Arthur Calder-Marshall. LC 66-3327. 1966. 5.00 ea., Bodley Head.
Bodley Head Saki. Ed. by J. W. Lambert. 490p. 1978. 10.95 (ISBN 0-370-00551-1, Pub. by Chatto Bodley Jonathan). Merrimack Pub Cir.
Body. Carter Brown, pseud. LC 59-107. (Signet books, 1527). 1958. New American Library.
Body. William Sansom. LC 49-100968. 1949. Harcourt, Brace.
Body. Alan Geoffrey Yates. LC 59-107. (Signet books, 1527). 1958. New American Library.
Body a la Mode. Watkins Eppes Wright. LC 49-9916. 1949. Phoenix Press.
Body: A New Study, in Narrative, of the Anatomy of Society. Daniel Quilter. LC 31-10987. (Modern amatory classics. no. 3). 1931. W. Faro, Inc.
Body: A Novel. Richard Sapir. LC 82-45209. 1983. 16.95 (ISBN 0-385-18017-9). Doubleday.
Body: A Novel. Richard Sapir. LC 82-45193. 1983. 16.95 (ISBN 0-385-18017-9). Doubleday.
Body and Raiment. Eunice Hammond Tietjens. LC 19-156124. 1919. A. A. Knopf.
Body & Soul. Arnold Bennett. LC 74-5293. (Collected Works of Arnold Bennett: Vol. 6). 1976. Repr. of 1921 ed. 14.75 (ISBN 0-518-19087-0). Ayer Co.
Body and Soul... Gerald Foster. LC 34-32943. W. Godwin, Inc.
Body at Madmen's Bend. Arthur William Upfield. (Napoleon Bonaperte Mysteries). Repr. lib. bdg. 12.05x (ISBN 0-89190-552-9). Am Repr-Rivercity Pr.
Body Beautiful. 1st. ed. William Sanborn Ballinger. LC 49-5321. Harper.
Body Beautiful. Carl De Marco. 1970. pap. 0.75 o.p. (75-346). Manor Bks.
Body Beautiful Murder. Kin Platt. LC 75-42784. 6.95 (ISBN 0-394-49649-3). Random House.
Body Blow. Kenneth Hopkins. LC 65-14449. 1965. bds., 3.50. Holt.
Body Book. Julius Fast. (Orig.). 1981. pap. 2.25 (ISBN 0-505-51678-0). Tower Bks.
Body Brokers. Robert P. Eaton. 1970. 6.95 o.p. (ISBN 0-8402-1129-5). Nash Pub.
Body Brokers: A Novel. Robert P Eaton. LC 70-103880. 1970. 6.95. Nash Pub.
Body Came Back: Michael Shayne's 47th Case. Davis Dresser. LC 63-19720. Distributed by Dodd, Mead.
Body Count. William Turner Huggett. LC 72-97297. 1973. 7.95 (ISBN 0-399-11126-3). Putnam.
Body Count. William Turner Huggett. 1974. (pbk.) 1.75. Dell.
Body Count. Peter McCurtin. (Belmont Tower Book). 1977. 1.50 (ISBN 0-505-51172-X). Tower Pubns.
Body Count. Frank Scarpetta. (Marksman,#9). 1974. (pbk.) 0.95. Belmont Tower Books.
Body Count. Francie Schwartz. 1974. pap. 1.25 o.p. (ISBN 0-515-03332-4, V3332). Pyramid Pubns.
Body Dealer. Charles Richards. 192p. pap. 1.95 o.p. (6133). Brandon.
Body for a Buddy. Aaron Marc Stein. LC 80-2897. 1981. 9.95 (ISBN 0-385-17583-3). Published for the Crime Club by Doubleday.
Body for Bill. Ione Sandberg Shriber. LC 42-25808. 1942. Farrar & Rinehart, Inc.
Body for McHugh. Jay Flynn. 1970. pap. 0.75 o.p. (75-378). Manor Bks.
Body for Sale. James Noble Gifford. LC 49-13400. 1948. Phoenix Press.
Body for the Widow. George Warren. 192p. (Orig.). 1973. pap. 1.95 o.p. (ISBN 0-87056-346-7, 6346). Brandon.
Body Goes Round and Round. Theodora McCormick Du Bois. LC 42-9575. 1942. Houghton Mifflin Company.
Body Goes Round & Round. Theodora McCormick Du Bois. (Jeffrey McNeill Ser). (O.s.i.). 1971. pap. 0.75 o.s.i. (A800S, Award). Univ Pub & Dist.
Body in Bedford Square. Zenith Jones Brown. LC 36-179541. 1935. Longmans, Green and Co.
Body in the Barrage Balloon: Or, Who Killed the Corpse! Colin Curzon. LC 42-16502. 1942. The Macmillan Company.
Body in the Basement. Selected by Norman J. Muckerman. 192p. 1983. pap. 3.95 (ISBN 0-89243-177-6). Liguori Pubns.
Body in the Basket: By George Bagby Pseud. 1st Ed. Aaron Marc Stein. LC 54-9990. 1954. Published for the Crime Club by Doubleday.
Body in the Beck. Joanna Cannan, pseud. Ed. by J. Barzun & W. H. Taylor. LC 81-47393. (Crime Fiction 1950-1975 Ser.). 2097p. 1982. lib. bdg. 14.95 (ISBN 0-8240-4954-3). Garland Pub.
Body in the Bed. William Sanborn Ballinger. LC 48-7798. 1948. Harper.
Body in the Bed: A Gil Vine Investigation, by Stewart Sterling Pseud. 1st Ed. Prentice Winchell. LC 59-7779. (Main line mysteries). 1959. Lippincott.
Body in the Blue Room. Sidney Clark Williams. LC 22-369987. 1922. The Penn Publishing Company.
Body in the Bonfire. Christopher Bush. LC 36-202430. H. Holt and Company.
Body in the Bunker. Herbert Adams. LC 35-1321. London.
Body in the Library. Agatha Miller Christie. LC 42-36085. 1942. Dodd, Mead & Company.
Body in the Library. Agatha Miller Christie. 1973. (pbk) 0.95 (ISBN 0-671-77444-1). Pocket Books.
Body in the Library. Agatha Miller Christie & Fair, A. A. Double or Guits. LC 42-16021. 1942. Detective Book Club.
Body in the Road. Moray Dalton. LC 30-12379. 1930. Harper & Brothers.
Body in the Road. Moray Dalton. LC 44-443713. (Black cat detective series. No. 8). 1944. Crestwood Publishing Co., Inc.
Body in the Safe: A Detective Story. Cecil Freeman Gregg. LC 30-2370. 1930. L. MacVeagh, The Dial Press.
Body in the Silo. Ronald Arbuthnott Knox. LC 58-12438. (Murder revisited mystery novel, no. 22). 1958. Macmillan.
Body Is Faithful: And Other Stories. Alis De Sola. LC 47-1146. 1947. E.P. Dutton & Company, Inc.
Body Job. Will Henry, pseud. pap. 1.95 o.s.i. (Venus). Grove.
Body Lovers. Frank Morrison Spillane. LC 67-10068. 1967. Dutton.
Body-Master's Daughter. Alice Lee Moque. LC 7-26213. (Dillingham's American authors library, no. 31). 1897. G. W. Dillingham Co.
Body Missed the Boat. Jack Iams. LC 47-1337. 1947. W. Morrow and Company.
Body of a Girl. Michael Francis Gilbert. LC 80-20662. 1981. 12.50 (ISBN 0-89340-289-3). J. Curley.
Body of a Girl: Novel of Suspense. Michael Francis Gilbert. LC 76-175153. 288p. 1972. 5.95 o.p. (ISBN 0-06-011523-8, HarpT). Har-Row.
Body of a Young Man. Mildred Walker, pseud. LC 60-10922. 1960. Harcourt, Brace.
Body of Madman's Bend. Arthur William Upfield. LC 63-7845. 1963. Published for the Crime Club by Doubleday.
Body on Page One. Delano L Ames. LC 51-12433. (Murray Hill mystery). 1951. Rinehart.
Body on the Beach. Steve Brackeen. LC 57-13554. 1957. Mystery House.
Body on the Beach. Robert Wallace. LC 33-151. 1932. G. H. Watt.
Body on the Beam: A Detective Story. Lucy Beatrice Malleson. LC 32-10532. 1932. Dodd, Mead & Company.
Body on the Floor. Nancy Barr Mavity. LC 29-224293. 1929. Pub. for the Crime Club, Inc., by Doubleday, Doran & Company, Inc.
Body on the Pavement. Gordon Meyrick. LC 45-40481. 1945. Mystery House.
Body on the Sidewalk. Bernice Carey Martin. LC 50-7191. 1950. Published for the Crime Club by Doubleday.
Body on the Sidewalk. 1st Ed. Bernice Carey. LC 50-7191. 1950. Published for the Crime Club by Doubleday.
Body or Soul. Royal Peters. LC 35-443. Phoenix Press.
Body Politics. Julius Fast. (Orig.). 1980. pap. 2.25 (ISBN 0-505-51513-X). Tower Bks.
Body Rolled Downstairs. Inez Haynes Irwin. LC 38-23543. Random House.
Body Rub. Mark Andrews. 1976. pap. 1.50 o.p. (ISBN 0-8439-0419-4, LB419DK, Leisure Bks). Nordon Pubns.
Body Rub. Mark Andrews. Leisure Books.
Body Search. Aaron Marc Stein. LC 76-42400. 1977. 6.95 (ISBN 0-385-12756-1). Published for the Crime Club by Doubleday.
Body Snatcher. Robert Louis Stevenson. Ed. by Raymond Harris. (Jamestown Classics Ser.). (Illus.). 48p. (Orig.). 1982. pap. text ed. 2.00x (459); tchr's ed 3.00x (ISBN 0-89061-257-9, 461). Jamestown Pubs.
Body Snatchers. Jack Finney. LC 54-12494. (Dell first edition 42). 1955. Dell Pub. Co.
Body Snatchers. Jack Finney. LC 76-10717. (Gregg Press science fiction series). (Reprint of the ed. published by Dell Pub. Co., N.Y. in series: A Dell first edition.). (Illus.). 1976. 11.50 (ISBN 0-8398-2332-0). Gregg Press.
Body Talk. Maude Poiret. (O.s.i.). (Illus.). 1974. pap. 1.25 o.s.i. (AQ1595, Award). Univ Pub & Dist.
Body That Came by Post. George Worthing Yates. LC 37-186541. 1937. W. Morrow & Co.
Body That Came by Post. George Worthing Yates. LC 40-914318. 1940. Triangle Books.
Body That Wasn't Uncle. George Worthing Yates. LC 39-43828. 1939. W. Morrow & Company.
Body to Spare. Maurice Proctor. 1965. pap. 0.95 o.p. (02392, Collier). Macmillan.
Body to Spare. 1st Ed. Maurice Procter. LC 62-112251. 1962. Harper.
Body Unidentified. Cecil John Charles Street. LC 38-2429. 1938. Dodd, Mead & Company.
Body Vanishes. Yves Jacquemard & Jean Michel Senecal. LC 80-17077. 1980. 8.95 (ISBN 0-396-07884-2). Dodd, Mead.
Body Was Quite Cold: A New Tony Hunter Story. 1st Ed. Robert George Dean. LC 51-3178. (Guilt-edged mystery). 1951. Dutton.
Bodyguard. Adrian Mitchell. LC 76-143486. 1971. 5.95. Doubleday.
Body's Cage. Benjamin DeMott. LC 59-7630. 1959. Little, Brown.
Body's Guest: A Novel. Angus MacLeod. Roy Publishers.
Body's Rapture. Jules Romains & Rodker, John, 1894- Tr. LC 33-4376. Liveright, Inc.
Body's Rapture. Jules Romains & Rodker, John, 1894- Tr. LC 38-2498. 1937. Liveright Publishing Corporation.
Boer Boy of the Transvaal: From the German of AugustNiemann. August Niemann. Tr. by Rabb, Kate (Milner) LC 3531. 1900. The Penn Publishing Company.

Boeuf Clandestin. Marcel Ayme. (Illus.). deluxe ed. 61.25. French & Eur.
Bog: A Novel of the Irish Rebellion of Nineteen Sixteen and After. by patrick j. carroll, c. s. c. ed. Patrick Joseph Carroll. LC 35-12796. The Ave Maria Press.
Bog-Myrtle and Peat: Being Tales, Chiefly of Galloway, Gathered from the Years MDCCCLXXXIX-MDCCCXCV. Samuel Rutherford Crockett. LC 72-5909. (Short story index reprint series). 1972. (ISBN 0-8369-4206-X). Books for Libraries Press.
Bog-Myrtle and Peat: Being Tales, Chiefly of Galloway, Gathered from the Years Mdccclxxxix-Mdcccxcv. Samuel Rutherford Crockett. LC 6-31599. 1895. D. Appleton and Company.
Bog of Stars: And Other Stories and Sketches of Elizabethan Ireland. Standish O'Grady. LC 74-125234. (Short story index reprint series). 1970. Books for Libraries Press.
Boga. The Elephant. Dombrowski Zu Papros und Krusvic. LC 28-22383. 1928. The Macmillan Company.
Bogart Forty Eight. John Stanley & Kenn Davis. 1980. pap. 2.50 (ISBN 0-440-10853-5). Dell.
Bogey Beasts. Sidney Sime & Josef Holbrooke. (Illus.). 1975. pap. 5.00 (ISBN 0-9603300-0-3). Purple Mouth.
Bogeyman: A Novel. 1st Amer. Ed. Margaret Forster. LC 66-20272. 1966. 4.50. Putnam.
Boggs Boys: Or, Corralling the Kids of Kiddville. by a.w. conner. ed. Americus Wood Conner. LC 99-2218. (On cover: The boys' friend library, no. 1). 1899. The Boys' Friend Library.
Bogmail. Patrick McGinley. LC 80-26135. 1981. 9.95 (ISBN 0-89919-031-6). Ticknor & Fields.
Bogmail. Patrick McGinley. LC 82-375. 1982. 2.95 (ISBN 0-14-006195-9). Penguin.
Bogman. Walter Macken. LC 52-9517.
Bogue's Fortune. 1st American Ed. Julian Symons. LC 57-6155. 1957. Harper.
Boheme Combination. Robin Close. LC 74-82168. 1974. 5.95 (ISBN 0-8027-5306-X). Walker.
Bohemia Invaded: And Other Stories. James Lauren Ford. LC 6-41402. (The bijou series). F. A. Stokes Company.
Bohemian. A Tragedy of Modern Life. Charles De Kay. LC 6-33384. C. Scribner's Sons.
Bohemian Airs & Other Kefs. Robert Anbian. LC 81-90581. (Literature Ser.: No. 1). (Illus.). 74p. (Orig.). 1982. pap. 6.00 (ISBN 0-941842-00-2). Night Horn Books.
Bohemian Days: Three American Tales. George Alfred Townsend. LC 44-25794. H. Campbell & Co.
Bohemian Life. Ten Etchings. Henri Murger. Tr. by Ives, George Burnham. LC 6658. (Roman contemporain. Romancists. v. 1). 1899. Printed Only for Subscribers by G. Barrie & Son.
Bohemian Tragedy. Lily Curry. LC 6-31155. T. B. Peterson & Brothers.
Bohemians in the Fifteenth Century. Henri Guenot. Tr. by Sadlier, Mary Anne (Madde) LC 8-33273. (On cover: Parlor & cottage library). 1867. D. & J. Sadlier & Co.
Bohemians of the Latin Quarter: Scenes De la Vie De Boheme. Henri Murger. LC 76-50140. 1976. 15.00. H. Fertig.
Bohemians of the Latin Quarter: Scenes De la Vie De Boheme. art ed. Henri Murger. LC 99-3992. Laird & Lee.
Bohemians of the Latin Quarter: Scenes De la Vie De Boheme. Henri Murger. LC 5-32480. (Added t.-p.: Comedie d'amour series). 1905. Societe Des Beaux-Arts.
Boiled Front. William A Maertz. LC 51-35505. 1951.
Boiling Point. Richard Brooks. LC 48-5199. 1948. Harper.
Bois Bande: The Tree of Life. Ronald Beatson. 1979. 7.95 (ISBN 0-533-04180-5). Vantage.
Boka Lives. Henry Calvin, pseud. LC 69-17289. 1969. 4.95 o.p. (ISBN 0-06-010596-8, HarpT). Har-Row.
Boka Lives. Clifford Hanley. LC 69-17289. 1969. 4.95. Harper & Row.
Boken. George Shelley Hughs. LC 3-26154. 1903. The Author.
Bolanyo. Opie Percival Read. LC 2-5223. (Oriental library, no. 49). 1902. Rand, McNally & Co.
Bolanyo: A Novel. Opie Percival Read. LC 7-36624. 1897. Way & Williams.
Bold and the Lonely. Charles Little. LC 66-11349. bds., 4.95. McKay.
Bold Bendigo: A Romance of the Open Road. Paul Herring. LC 27-100484. 1927. J. B. Lippincott Company.
Bold Blades Flashing. Lorinda Hagen. 1979. pap. 2.25 o.s.i. (ISBN 0-8439-0689-8, Leisure Bks). Nordon Pubns.
Bold Blades of Donegal. Seumas MacManus. LC 35-145642. 1935. Frederick A. Stokes Company.
Bold Breathless Love. Valerie Sherwood. 576p. (Orig.). 1983. pap. 3.95 (ISBN 0-446-30849-8). Warner Bks.
Bold Encounter: A Novel Based on the Life of St. John of the Cross. Peter Thomas Rohrbach. LC 60-8292. 1960. Bruce Pub. Co.
Bold Galilean. Le Gette Blythe. LC 48-8146. 1948. Univ. of North Carolina Press.
Bold House Murders. Eugene Franklin, pseud. LC 72-96294. 1973. 5.95 (ISBN 0-8128-1567-X). Stein and Day.
Bold House Murders. Eugene Franklin, pseud. 1974. (pbk.) 0.95. Dell.
Bold Legend. Gordon D. Shirreffs. 320p. (Orig.). 1982. pap. 2.75 (ISBN 0-449-14488-7, GM). Fawcett.
Bold New Women: Ed., Introd. by Barbara Alson. Barbara Alson. (T1730). 1966. Fawcett.
Bold Ones. Gardner F. Fox. 1976. pap. 1.25 o.p. (LB398, Leisure Bks). Nordon Pubns.
Bold Ones: The Surrogate Womb. Bruce Cassiday. 1973. (pbk.) 0.95. Manor Books.
Bold Passage. Frank Bonham. LC 50-10965. (Essandess western). 1950. Simon and Schuster.
Bold Passage. Frank Bonham. (Berkley Book). (Illus.). 1978. 1.50 (ISBN 0-425-03753-3). Berkley Pub. Corp.
Bold Pursuit. Zabrina Faire, pseud. 192p. (Orig.). 1980. pap. 1.75 (ISBN 0-446-94464-5). Warner Bks.
Bold Rider. Luke Short. 1975. (pbk.) 0.95. Dell.
Bold Saboteurs. Chandler Brossard. LC 53-7085. 1953. Farrar, Straus and Young.
Bold Steer. Clell Edgar Bowman. LC 75-92508. 8.95 (ISBN 0-8283-1540-X). Branden Press.
Bold Water. Davida McCaslin. LC 54-7718. 1954. Comet Press Books.
Boldt. Ted Lewis. LC 76-382484. 1976. 3.95 (ISBN 0-7181-1460-4). Joseph.
Bolero: A Novel. Melanie L. Pflaum. LC 57-693195. 1957. St. Martin's Press.
Bolinvar. Marguerite Farlee Bayliss. LC 37-122411. 1937. The Derrydale Press.
Bolinvar. Marguerite Farlee Bayliss. LC 44-2722. 1944. H. Holt and Company.
Bolinvars. Marguerite Farlee Bayliss. LC 44-40371. 1944. H. Holt and Company.
Bolinvars. Marguerite Farlee Bayliss. LC 46-20992. 1945. The World Publishing Company.
Bolivar Brown. Bide Dudley. LC 21-16376. Harper & Brothers.
Bolivian Wedding. Gudrun Pausewang. LC 72-118717. 1971. 5.95. Knopf.
Bolo. Keith Laumer. (Orig.). 1982. pap. 2.25 (ISBN 0-425-05617-1). Berkley Pub.
Bolo. Keith Laumer. 1977. pap. 1.50 (ISBN 0-425-03450-X, Medallion). Berkley Pub.
Bolo: The Annals of the Dinochrome Brigade. Keith Laumer. LC 76-9769. 6.95 (ISBN 0-399-11794-6). Berkley Pub. Corp.: Distributed by Putnam.
Bolo: The Annals of the Dinochrome Brigade. Keith Laumer. (Berkley Medallion Book). 1977. 1.50 (ISBN 0-425-03450-X). Berkley Pub. Corp.
Bolt. Peter Redcliff Shore. LC 30-853. 1929. E. P. Dutton & Co., Inc.
Bolt, No. 10: Bawdy House Showdown. Cort Martin. 1983. pap. 2.25 (ISBN 0-8217-1176-8). Zebra.
Bolt, No. 1: First Blood. Cort Martin. (Orig.). 1981. pap. 2.25 (ISBN 0-89083-767-8). Zebra.
Bolt, No. 2: Dead Man's Bounty. Cort Martin. 1981. pap. 2.25 (ISBN 0-89083-783-X). Zebra.
Bolt, No. 3: Showdown at Black Mesa. Cort Martin. (Orig.). 1981. pap. 2.25 (ISBN 0-89083-812-7). Zebra.
Bolt, No. 4: The Guns of Taos. Cort Martin. (Orig.). 1981. pap. 2.25 (ISBN 0-89083-873-9). Zebra.
Bolt, No. 5: Shootout at Sante Fe. Cort Martin. (Orig.). 1982. pap. 2.25 (ISBN 0-89083-943-3). Zebra.
Bolt, No. 6: The Tombstone Honeypot. Cort Martin. 1982. pap. 2.25 (ISBN 0-8217-1009-5). Zebra.
Bolt, No. 7: Rawhide Woman. Cort Martin. (Orig.). 1982. pap. 2.25 (ISBN 0-8217-1057-5). Zebra.
Bolt, No. 8: Hard in the Saddle. Cort Martin. 1982. pap. 2.25 (ISBN 0-8217-1095-8). Zebra.
Bolt, No. 9: Badman's Bordello. Cort Martin. 1983. pap. 2.25 (ISBN 0-8217-1127-X). Zebra.
Bolted Door. George Fort Gibbs. LC 11-1452. 1911. 1.25. D. Appleton and Company.
Bom-Crioulo: The Black Man and the Cabin Boy. Adolfo Caminha. LC 82-11796. 20.00 (ISBN 0-917342-87-9) (ISBN 0-917342-88-7). Gay Sunshine Press.
Bomarzo: A Novel. Mujica Lainez, Manuel. LC 75-79634. 1969. 10.00. Simon and Schuster.
Bomb. Frank Harris. LC 9-49636. 1909. M. Kennerley.
Bomb: A Novel. Frank Harris. LC 63-22587. (Chicago in fiction). 1963. University of Chicago Press.
Bomb in the Attic. Jacob Hay. LC 61-15181. 1961. Macmillan.
Bomb Job. Henry Kane. (Orig.). 1970. pap. 0.75 o.p. (ISBN 0-447-74664-2). Lancer.
Bomb Run. Spencer Dunmore. LC 71-151904. 1971. 5.95. Morrow.
Bomb-Scare Mystery. Pauline Hannaford. LC 72-93415. (Illus.). 110p. 1973. pap. 4.75x (ISBN 0-87076-882-4). Stanwix.
Bomb Squad. Mark Andrews. (Leisure Books). 1977. 1.50 (ISBN 0-8439-0453-4). Nordon Pubns.
Bomb That Could Lip-Read. Donald Seaman. LC 73-92184. 1974. 7.95 (ISBN 0-8128-1687-0). Stein and Day.
Bomb That Failed. Ronald William Clark. LC 74-83691. 1969. 5.95. Morrow.
Bombardier. John W. Corrington. (YA) 1970. 5.95 o.p. (ISBN 0-399-10096-2). Putnam.
Bombardier. John W. Corrington. 1972. pap. 1.25 o.s.i. (78-691). Lancer.
Bombardier: A Novel. John William Corrington. LC 79-105586. 1970. 5.95. Putnam.
Bombay Mail. Lawrence Goldtree Blochman. LC 34-1682. 1934. Little, Brown, and Company.
Bombay Meeting: A Novel of Modern India. 1st Ed. Ira Victor Morris. LC 55-526795. 1955. Doubleday.
Bomber. Len Deighton. 1982. pap. 3.95 (ISBN 0-451-12029-9, AE2029, Sig). NAL.
Bomber. Len Deighton. LC 71-123980. 1970. 8.95 o.p. (ISBN 0-06-011014-7, HarpT). Har-Row.
Bomber: Events Relating to the Last Flight of an R.A.F. Bomber Over Germany on the Night of June 31, 1943. Len Deighton. LC 71-123980. 1970. 7.95. Harper & Row.
Bomber Raid. James Campbell. 1978. pap. 1.75 o.s.i. (ISBN 0-505-51272-6). Tower Bks.
Bombers: B-52. Steward Buettner. 1977. pap. 3.95x (ISBN 0-918258-00-6). New Earth.
Bombers in the Sky, by Arch Whitehouse. 1st Ed. Arthur George Joseph Whitehouse. LC 60-5446. 1960. Duell, Sloan and Pearce.
Bombing Officer. Jerome Doolittle. LC 82-5136. 12.95 (ISBN 0-525-24105-1). E.P. Dutton.
Bombing Run. Aaron Marc Stein. LC 82-45548. (Crime Club Ser.). 192p. 1983. 11.95 (ISBN 0-385-18381-X). Doubleday.
Bombs. Randee Russell. LC 82-9540. 5.00 (ISBN 0-932112-14-5). Carolina Wren Press.
Bombs Burst Once, a Novel of Adventure. Granville Church. LC 41-21998. M. S. Mill Co., Inc.
Bombshell. Richard Raine. 1969. 4.95 o.p. (ISBN 0-15-113436-7). HarBraceJ.
Bombshell. Raymond H. Sawkins. LC 69-14840. 1969. 4.95. Harcourt, Brace & World.
Bombshell see Lover.
Bombship. Bill Knox. LC 80-647. 1980. 8.95 (ISBN 0-385-17039-4). Published for the Crime Club by Doubleday.
Bon Repos. Gene Forrest. 192p. 1975. 7.50 o.p. (ISBN 0-682-48340-0, Banner). Exposition.
Bon Voyage. Noel Pierce Coward. LC 68-14174. 1968. Doubleday.
Bon Voyage! Marrijane Hayes & Joseph Arnold Hayes. LC 56-10951. 1957. Random House.
Bon Voyage for Kate. Margaret P. Drake. 1972. pap. 0.75 o.s.i. (01-360). Lancer.
Bon Voyage, My Darling. Mary Ann Taylor. (Signet Book). 1977. 1.50 (ISBN 0-451-07554-4). New American Library.
Bon Voyage, My Darling see Romance in the Headlines.
Bona Venture. May Cameron Quinby. LC 30-22222. 1929. The J. W. Burke Company.
Bonanza. William MacLeod Raine. 1976. Repr. of 1926 ed. lib. bdg. 18.55x (ISBN 0-88411-551-8). Amereon Ltd.
Bonanza: A Story of the Gold Trail. William MacLeod Raine. LC 26-967219. 1926. Doubleday, Page & Company.
Bonanza at Wishbone. Lee Floren. (Belmont Tower Books). 1977. 1.50 (ISBN 0-505-51183-5). Tower Pubns.
Bonanza at Wishborne. Lee Floren. LC 46-17776. 1946. Phoenix Press.
Bonanza Bible Class. Henry Frederick Cope. LC 4-13173. 1904. The Winona Publishing Company.
Bonanza Gulch: By Matt Stuart Pseud. 1st Ed. Llewellyn Perry Holmes. LC 50-10383. 1950. Lippincott.
Bonanza on the Big Muddy. William Heuman. LC 55-11870. 1955. Arcadia House.
Bonanza: One Man with Courage. Thomas Thompson. LC 66-29144. 1966. Media Books.
Bonanza Queen: A Novel of the Comstock Lode. Zola Helen Ross. LC 49-8076. 1949. Bobbs-Merrill Co.
Bonaparte and His Times: 1769. Theodore Iung. Tr. by Sherwood, Mary (Neal) (Seaside library. v. 66, no. 1332). 1882. G. Munro.
Bonaventure. George Washington Cable. LC 79-96876. 1969. Literature House.
Bonaventure see Collected Works.
Bonaventure: A Prose Pastoral of Acadian Louisiana. George Washington Cable. LC 72-84529. 1974. (lib. ed.) 12.95 (ISBN 0-403-02974-0). Scholarly Press.
Bonaventure: A Prose Pastoral of Acadian Louisiana. George Washington Cable. LC 4-15077. 1888. C. Scribner's Sons.
Bonaventure: A Prose Pastoral of Acadian Louisiana. George Washington Cable. LC 9-3846. 1901. International Association of Newspapers and Authors.
Bonaventure Des Periers's Novel Pastimes & Merry Tales. Bonaventure Des Periers. Ed. & tr. by Raymond C. La Charite. LC 70-109532. (Studies in Romance Languages: No. 6). 264p. 1972. 13.00x (ISBN 0-8131-1279-6). U Pr of Ky.
Bonchi: A Novel. Toyoko Yamasaki. Tr. by Harue Summersgill & Travis Summersgill. LC 81-23071. (Japanese.). 1982. 14.95 (ISBN 0-8248-0794-4). UH Pr.
Boncoeur Affair. Harvey Wickham. LC 23-7719. E. J. Clode.
Bond. Neith Boyce. LC 8-11083. 1908. Duffield & Company.
Bond and Free. Jean Connor. LC 13-22514. 1913. Benziger Brothers.
Bond & Free. facsimile ed. Grace Lintner. LC 79-38656. (Black Heritage Library Collection). Repr. of 1882 ed. 17.25 (ISBN 0-8369-9014-5). Ayer Co.
Bond and Free: A Tale of the South. Grace Lintner. LC 79-38656. (Black Heritage Library Collection). (Illus.). 1972. (ISBN 0-8369-9014-5). Books for Libraries Press.
Bond and Free: A True Tale of Slave Times. James H. W Howard. LC 70-76112. 1969. McGrath Pub. Co.
Bond and Free: A True Tale of Slave Times. James H. W Howard. LC 79-83908. 1969. Mnemosyne Pub. Co.
Bond and Free: A True Tale of Slave Times. James H. W Howard. LC 7-71502. 1886. E. K. Meyers, Printer.
Bond and the Free. Charles Dunscomb. LC 55-7952. 1955. Houghton Mifflin.
Bond Grayson Murdered! A Professor Wells Mystery. Norman Stanley Bortner. LC 36-20841. Macrae-Smith Company.
Bond-Master. Richard Tresillian. Warner Books.
Bond of Black. William Le Queux. LC 99-5858. 1899. G. W. Dillingham Co.
Bond of Blood. Roberta Gellis. LC 65-10601. 1965. Doubleday.
Bond of Blood. Roberta Gellis. 1976. (pbk.) 1.75 (ISBN 0-380-00714-2). Avon.
Bond of Evil. Melissa Cordell. 1977. pap. 1.75 (ISBN 0-532-17163-2). Woodhill.
Bond of Honor. Catherine Todd. LC 81-51638. 224p. 1982. 11.95 (ISBN 0-312-08763-2). St Martin.
Bond of Honour. Catherine Todd. LC 81-14618. 1981. 11.95 (ISBN 0-312-08763-2). St. Martin's Press.
Bond of the Flesh: A Novel. Rosamond Van Der Zee Marshall. LC 52-11619. 1952. Doubleday.
Bond Slave. Sallie Lee Bell. LC 58-21224. Zondervan Pub. House.
Bond. Tr., by Norman Denny. Jacques Borel. LC 67-11149. 1986. 6.95. Doubleday.
Bondage. Margaret Carruthers. LC 34-5092. Greenberg.
Bondage: Dervishes in Sudan.1st Ed. Milo Barry. LC 56-129599. United Service.
Bondage of Ballinger. Roswell Martin Field. LC 3-27218. 1903. F. H. Revell Company.
Bondage of Henri Stoddard. Lulu Meredith Stevens. LC 26-20525. Dorrance and Company.
Bondage Trash. Jon Horn. 1968. 3.95 o.s.i. (Ophelia); pap. 1.75 o.s.i. (101). Olympia.
Bondboy. George Washington Ogden. LC 22-209598. 1922. A. C. McClurg & Co.
Bonded Dead. M. E. Chaber, pseud. (Milo March Mystery Ser). 1971. pap. 0.75 o.p. (64-684). Paperback Lib.
Bonded Dead. M. E. Chaber, pseud. 1971. 4.50 o.p. (ISBN 0-03-085054-1). HR&W.
Bonded Dead. Kendell Foster Crossen. LC 75-117288. (Rinehart suspense novel). 1971. 4.50 (ISBN 0-03-085054-1). Holt, Rinehart, and Winston.
Bonded Fleming. Ian Fleming. 1965. 5.75 o.p. (ISBN 0-670-17825-X). Viking Pr.
Bonded Fleming: A James Bond Omnibus. Ian Fleming. LC 65-28952. 1965. bds., 5.75. Viking.
Bondman. new ed. Hall Caine. LC 16-6990. 1916. D. Appleton and Company.
Bondman. A New Saga. by hall caine... ed. Hall Caine. LC 7-29152. (On cover: Lovell's international series, no. 51). 1889. F. F. Lovell Company.
Bondman: A New Saga. Hall Caine. LC 41-28178. R. F. Fenno and Company.
Bondman: A New Saga. Hall Caine. LC 42-483639. (Alpha library). Rand, McNally & Company.
Bondman. A New Saga. Hall I. E. Thomas Henry Hall Caine. (On cover: Seaside library. Pocket ed. no. 1255). 1889. G. Munro.
Bondman. A Story of the Times of Wat Tyler. O'Neil. LC 7-15839. (Added t.-p.: The library of romance v.5). 1833. Carey, Lea and Blanchard.

Bondman Free: The Remarkable Adventures of a Gentleman Convict. John Oxenham, pseud. 1902. The Federal Book Company.
Bondmaster. Richard Tresillian. 448p. (Orig.). 1977. pap. 2.95 (ISBN 0-446-30225-2). Warner Bks.
Bondmaster Breed. Richard Tresillian. 2.50 (ISBN 0-446-81890-9). Warner Books.
Bonds in Common. George L Godfrey. LC 31-29306. F. J. Heer Prtg. Co.
Bonds of Enchantment. Marian Jones. (Superromances Ser.). 384p. 1983. pap. 2.95 (ISBN 0-373-70068-7, Pub. by Worldwide). Harlequin Bks.
Bonds of Eternity. Clark Darlton. (Perry Rhodan#69). (Illus.). 1975. (pbk.) 1.25. Ace Books.
Bonds of Liberty. Pauline Stiles. LC 37-388647. Farrar & Rhinehart, Inc.
Bonds of Love. Lisa Gregory, pseud. LC 78-58602. (Jove/ HJB Book.). 1978. 1.95. Jove Pubns.
Bondswoman. Caryl Ledner. 1978. 1.95 (ISBN 0-380-01781-4). Avon Books.
Bondswomen. Caryl Ledner. LC 76-62782. 7.95 (ISBN 0-312-08767-5). St. Martin's Press.
Bondwoman. Geoffrey Uther Ellis. LC 28-324. George H. Doran Company.
Bondwoman. Marah Ellis Martin Ryan. LC 99-4985. 1899. Rand, McNally & Company.
Bondy Jr. Lajos Hatvany & Waller, Hannah, Tr. LC 31-28141. 1931. A. A. Knopf.
Bone & a Hank of Hair. Leo Bruce, pseud. 1981. 18.95x (Pub. by Remploy England). State Mutual Bk.
Bone Is Pointed. Arthur William Upfield. LC 75-46003. (Fifty classics of crime fiction, 1900-1950). (Illus.). 1976. 12.00 (ISBN 0-8240-2395-1). Garland Pub.
Bone Is Pointed. Arthur William Upfield. LC 47-921. 1947. Pub. for the Crime Club by Doubleday & Company, Inc.
Bone of My Bones. Sylvia Wilkinson. LC 81-12053. 12.95 (ISBN 0-399-12628-7). Putnam.
Bonecrack. Dick Francis. 1978. 1.95 (ISBN 0-671-82159-8). Pocket Books.
Bonegrinder. John Lutz. LC 77-3312. 7.95 (ISBN 0-399-11990-6). Putnam.
Bones & Kim. Lynn Strongin. LC 80-53111. (Illus.). 5.50 (ISBN 0-933216-02-5). Spinsters, Ink.
Bones Don't Lie. Curtiss T Gardner. LC 46-21132. 1946. M. S. Mill Co., Inc.
Bones in the Barrow: By Josephine Bell Pseud. Doris Bell Collier Ball. LC 55-677. (Cock Robin mystery). 1955. Macmillan.
Bones in the Sand. Kenneth Royce. LC 67-104142. (Illus.). 1967. Cassell.
Bones of Contention. Nicholas Gage, pseud. LC 73-93728. 1974. 6.95 (ISBN 0-399-11308-8). Berkley Pub. Corp.: Distributed by Putnam.
Bones of Contention: And Other Stories. Frank O'Connor, pseud. LC 36-14280. 1936. The Macmillan Company.
Bones of Contention & Other Stories. Frank O'Connor, pseud. LC 77-91391. (Short Story Index in Reprint Ser.). 1978. Repr. of 1936 ed. 19.50x (ISBN 0-8486-5004-2). Core Collection.
Bones of Contention: And Other Stories. Michael O'Donovan. LC 36-14280. 1936. The Macmillan Company.
Bones of Contention, and Other Stories. Michael O'Donovan. LC 77-91391. (Short Story Index in Reprint). 1978. 19.50 (ISBN 0-8486-5004-2). Core Collection Books.
Bones of Contention: By Rae Foley Pseud. Elinore Denniston. LC 50-5156. (Red badge mystery). 1950. Dodd, Mead.
Bones of Napoleon. James Warner Bellah. LC 40-12030. 1940. D. Appleton-Century Company, Incorporated.
Bones of Plenty: A Novel. 1st Ed. Lois Phillips Hudson. LC 62-13911. 1962. Little, Brown.
Bones of the Buffalo. Lewis B Patten. LC 67-16899. (DD western). 1967. Doubleday.
Bone's Prayer. Shiv Kumar Kumar. 176p. 1980. pap. 3.25 (ISBN 0-86578-058-7). Ind-US Inc.
Boney's Hired Man. Alma Eloise Lewis James. LC 51-12059. 1951. Vantage Press.
Bonfield: Or, The Outlaw of the Bermudas. A Nautical Novel. Joseph Holt Ingraham. LC 7-10518. 1846. H. L. Williams; Etc., Etc.
Bonfire. Dorothea Frances Canfield Fisher. LC 33-29660. 1933. Harcourt, Brace and Company.
Bonfire (A Fogueira) Cecilio J. Carneiro. LC 75-139127. 1971. (ISBN 0-8371-5743-9). Greenwood Press.
Bonfire: A Fogueira. Cecilio J. Carneiro. Tr. by Dudley Poore from Port. LC 75-139127. 334p. 1972. Repr. of 1944 ed. lib. bdg. 17.00x (ISBN 0-8371-5743-9, CABF). Greenwood.
Bonfire (A Fogueira) Cecilio J. Carneiro & Poore, Dudley, Tr. LC 44-5212. 1944. Farrar & Rinehart, Inc.
Bonfire Murder. T. Arthur Plummer. LC 37-48383. The Macaulay Company.
Bongo. Arnold Ellis Grisman. LC 61-6204. 1961. Harper.
Bonheur au Passe. Joy St. Clair. (Harlequin Romantique Ser.). 192p. 1983. pap. 1.95 (ISBN 0-373-41182-0). Harlequin Bks.
Bonheur Fou: Roman. Jean Giono. 1957. 14.50. French & Eur.
Bonhomme; French-Canadian Stories and Sketches. Henry Cecil Walsh. LC 74-166493. (Toronto reprint library of Canadian prose and poetry). (ISBN 0-8020-7515-0). University of Toronto Press.
Bonin: A Novel by Robert Standish Pseud.... Digby George Gerahty. LC 44-787. 1944. The Macmillan Company.
Bonjour Tristesse. Francoise Quiorez. LC 55-5341. 1974. (pbk.) 0.95. Popular Library.
Bonjour Tristesse. Francoise Sagan, pseud. Ed. by David I. Grossvogel. (Integral Eds. Ser). 1965. pap. text ed. 1.75x o.p. Schoenhof.
Bonjour Tristesse. Francoise Sagan, pseud. 128p. 1983. pap. 4.95 (ISBN 0-525-48040-4, 0481-140). Dutton.
Bonjour Tristesse. Francoise Sagan, pseud. Tr. by Irene Ash. 1955. 4.50 o.p. (ISBN 0-525-06956-9, Evman). Dutton.
Bonnaire. Delphine Marlowe. 688p. (Orig.). 1980. pap. 2.75 (ISBN 0-515-04764-3). Jove Pubns.
Bonne-Marie. A Tale of Normandy and Paris. By Henry Greville Pseud.... Tr. from the French by Mary Neal Sherwood... Alice Marie Celeste Durand. Tr. by Sherwood, Mary (Neal) LC 6-35099. T. B. Peterson & Brothers.
Bonner Boys. Campbell Geeslin. 1981. 11.95 (ISBN 0-671-42430-0). S&S.
Bonner Deception. Dale Estey. LC 82-17053. 14.95 (ISBN 0-312-08780-2). St. Martin's Press.
Bonner's Stallion. Theodore V. Olsen. (Fawcett Gold Medal Book). 1.75 (ISBN 0-449-13925-5). Fawcett Books.
Bonnet Laird's Daughter. Barbara Annandale, pseud. 1977. 8.95 o.p. (ISBN 0-698-10781-0, Coward). Putnam Pub Group.
Bonnet Laird's Daughter. Jean Bowden. LC 76-25900. 8.95 (ISBN 0-698-10781-0). Coward, McCann & Geoghegan.
Bonnet Man. Gus Weill. LC 77-5648. 1978. 1.50 (ISBN 0-345-24097-9). Ballantine Books.
Bonnet Man. Gus Weill. LC 78-17288. 8.95 (ISBN 0-02-625540-5). Macmillan.
Bonney Family. Ruth Suckow. LC 28-3333. 1928. A. A. Knopf.
Bonney's Place. Leon Hale. LC 73-175380. 1972. 5.95. Doubleday.
Bonney's Place. Leon Hale. 1973. (pbk.) 0.95. Popular Lib.
Bonnie Belmont: A Historical Romance of the Days of Slavery and the Civil War. John Salisbury Cochran. LC 7-37710. Press of Wheeling News Lith. Co.
Bonnie Bess: Or, The Prettiest Girl in Fall River. David Druid. 1889. Goode & Adams.
Bonnie Kathleen. Peggy O'More. pap. 0.75 o.p. (532-75490-075). Manor Bks.
Bonnie Mackirby: An International Episode. Laura Dayton Fessenden. LC 6-38981. Rand, McNally & Company.
Bonnie May. Louis Dodge. LC 16-17070. 1916. 1.35. C. Scribner's Sons.
Bonnie Will. Cary Lyda. 3.50 o.p. Carlton.
Bonny Bride: By Gay Rutherford Pseud. James Noble Gifford. LC 57-771853. 1957. Arcadia House.
Bonny Jean, and A Severe Threat. Emma Augusta Sharkey. (Street & Smith's select series, no. 4). 1887. Street & Smith.
Bonny Kate. A Novel. Frances Christine Tiernan. (On cover: Appletons' library of American fiction no. 19). 1878. D. Appleton and Company.
Bonnybel Vane. Embracing the History of Henry St. John, Gentleman. John Esten Cooke. LC 6-28716. 1883. Harper & Brothers.
Bonnyborough. Adeline Dutton Train Whitney. LC 8-36548. 1886. Houghton, Mifflin and Company.
Bonnyclabber. George Chambers. LC 72-78523. (Illus.). 1972. pap. 4.00 o.p. (ISBN 0-913204-02-1). December Pr.
Bonstonofavitch! Thomas Carlisle. LC 74-78089. (Illus.). 176p. (Orig.). 1974. pap. 3.95 (ISBN 0-914580-00-0). Angst World.
Bonstonofavitch! A Novel of Madness. Thomas Carlisle. LC 74-78089. (Illus.). 1974. (ISBN 0-914580-00-0). Angst World Library.
Bontshe the Silent. Isaac Loeb Peretz. LC 77-178454. (Short story index reprint series). (Illus.). 1971. (ISBN 0-8369-4055-5). Books for Libraries Press.
Bonus Notches. Merle M. Funk. 1974. 4.95. Lenox Hill Press.
Bony and the Black Virgin. Arthur William Upfield. LC 65-3152. 1965. Collier.
Bony & the Kelley Gang. Arthur William Upfield. (Napoleon Bonaperte Mysteries). Repr. lib. bdg. 12.70x. Am Repr-Rivercity Pr.
Bony Buys a Woman. Arthur William Upfield. (Napoleon Bonaperte Mysteries). Repr. lib. bdg. 13.85x (ISBN 0-89190-555-3). Am Repr-Rivercity Pr.
Boo! A Parable for Children Over & Under 21. Jim Ballard. LC 75-25393. (Mandala Ser. in Education). 1975. pap. 2.50 (ISBN 0-916250-08-3). Irvington.
Booby Trap. Eliot Crawshay-Williams. LC 30-314880. Hale, Cushman & Flint.
Boogens. Charles E. Sellier, Jr. & Bob Weverka. 192p. 1981. pap. 2.50 (ISBN 0-553-20209-X). Bantam.
Boogeyman. Ronald Koertge. LC 79-16938. 9.95 (ISBN 0-393-01296-4). Norton.
Boojum. Charles Wertenbaker. LC 28-985067. 1928. Boni and Liveright.
Book. Nicole Brossard. LC 76-372735. Coach House Press.
Book About Little Brother: A Story of Married Life. Gustaf Af Geijerstam. Tr. by Bjorkman, Edwin August. LC 21-26984. (Half-title: Scandinavian classics, vol. xviii). 1921. The American-Scandinavian Foundation; Etc., Etc.
Book About Love & War & Death. Richard Carter Higgins. LC 71-14096. (Nova broadcast, 3). 1969. 1.25. Nova Broadcast Press.
Book Agent: His Book. Titus Keiber Smith. LC 4-16435. 1904. Thomson and Smith.
Book & a Love Affair. Helen Bevington. LC 68-20062. 1968. 4.75 o.p. (ISBN 0-15-113448-0). HarBraceJ.
Book and the Quest. Margit Strom Heppenstall. LC 66-19416. Review and Herald Pub. Association.
Book-Bills of Narcissus: An Account Rendered. Richard Le Gallienne. LC 7-12591. 1895. G.P. Putnam's Sons.
Book Concluding with As a Wife Has a Cow: A Love Story. Gertrude Stein. LC 72-90370. 1973. pap. 7.50 (ISBN 0-87110-092-4). Ultramarine Pub.
Book for the Hammock. William Clark Russell. (Harper's Franklin square library, no. 599). 1887. Harper & Brothers.
Book for the Times. Lucy Boston; or, Woman's Rights and Spiritualism: Illustrating the Follies and Delusions of the Nineteenth Century. Folio, Fred. LC 6-41424. 1855. Shepard, Clark & Co.
Book for the Winter-Evening Fireside. Stories and Poems. Wirt Sikes. LC 8-8989. 1858. Ingalls & Haddock.
Book O' Nine Tales. Arlo Bates. LC 6-90889. 1891. Roberts Brothers.
Book of Adventure: Edited by Nathan Haskell Dole. Ed. by Nathan Haskell Dole. LC 55-2138. (Young Folks Library 8). Auxiliary Educational League.
Book of Andre Norton. Andre Norton, pseud. (Science Fiction Ser.). 1975. pap. 2.25 (ISBN 0-87997-643-8, UE1643). DAW Bks.
Book of Ariel: A Novel. LC 42-16503. 1942. Doubleday, Doran and Company, Inc.
Book of Bebb. Frederick Buechner. LC 79-63795. 1979. 14.95 (ISBN 0-689-10986-5). Atheneum.
Book of Bette, Recording Further Experiences of the Family Urruty Among the Spains and Elsewhere. Eleanor Mercein Kelly. LC 29-10300. 1929. Harper & Brothers.
Book of Blanche. Dorothy Richardson. LC 24-6156. 1924. 2.00. Little, Brown, and Company.
Book of Brian Aldiss. Brian Wilson Aldiss. (Science Fiction Ser.). (Orig.). 1972. pap. 0.95 o.p. (UQ1029). DAW Bks.
Book of Bryn Mawr Stories. Ed. by Margaretta Morris. Congdon, Louise Buffum, Joint Ed. LC 1-319026. 1901. G. W. Jacobs and Company.
Book of Carlotta. Arnold Bennett. LC 11-1854. George H. Doran Company.
Book of Carlotta, Being a Revised Edition (with New Preface) of Sacred and Profane Love. rev. ed. Arnold Bennett. LC 74-6017. (Collected works of Arnold Bennett). 1974. (ISBN 0-518-19088-9). Books for Libraries Press.
Book of Change. Frederick Morgan. 1972. 7.95 o.p. (ISBN 0-684-12950-7). Scribner.
Book of Changes: A Novel. Richard H. W Dillard. LC 73-16619. 1974. 6.95 (ISBN 0-385-07157-4). Doubleday.
Book of Claudia: Containing the Two Novels; Claudia, Claudia and David. Rose Franken. LC 41-51923. 1941. Farrar & Rinehart, Inc.
Book of Common Prayer. Joan Didion. LC 76-50067. 8.95 (ISBN 0-671-22491-3). Simon and Schuster.
Book of Common Prayer. Joan Didion. (Kangaroo Book). 1978. 1.95 (ISBN 0-671-81785-X). Pocket Books.
Book of Contemporary Short Stories. Ed. by Dorothy Brewster. Gilkes, Lillian Barnard, 1902- LC 37-112. 1936. The Macmillan Company.
Book of Count Lucanor and Patronio: A Translation of Don Juan Manuel's El Conde Lucanor. Juan Manuel. LC 76-24342. (Studies in Romance Languages; 16). 15.00 (ISBN 0-8131-1350-4). University Press of Kentucky.
Book of Count Lucanor & Patronio: A Translation of Don Juan Manuel's "el Conde Lucanor". Ed. by John E. Keller & L. Clark Keating. Tr. by John E. Keller & L. Clark Keating. LC 76-24342. (Studies in Romance Languages: No. 16). 208p. 1977. 17.00x (ISBN 0-8131-1350-4). U Pr of Ky.
Book of Cowboy Stories. Will James. LC 51-10910. (Illus.). 1951. Scribner.
Book of Dan. Steele Rudd. (O.s.i.). (Illus.). 1970. pap. 2.25x o.s.i. (ISBN 0-7022-0619-9). U of Queensland Pr.
Book of Dan. Steele Rudd. (O.s.i.). (Illus.). 1970. pap. 2.25x o.s.i. (ISBN 0-7022-0619-9). U of Queensland Pr.
Book of Daniel: A Novel. E. L. Doctorow. LC 78-140700. 1971. 6.95 (ISBN 0-394-46271-8). Random House.
Book of Days. National Gallery. (Illus.). 160p. (Orig.). 1979. 8.95 (ISBN 0-03-052711-2). HR&W.
Book of Ebenezer Le Page. G. B Edwards. LC 80-2719. (Illus.). 1981. 13.95 (ISBN 0-394-51651-6). Knopf: Distributed by Random House.
Book of Eve. Beresford-Howe, Constance. LC 74-30242. 1975. 9.95 (ISBN 0-8161-6260-3). G. K. Hall.
Book of Eve: A Novel. Beresford-Howe, Constance. LC 74-5416. 1974. 5.95 (ISBN 0-316-09140-5). Little, Brown.
Book of Evelyn. Geraldine Bonner. LC 13-18475. 1.25. The Bobbs-Merrill Company.
Book of Fables and Folk Stories. new illustrated ed. Horace Elisha Scudder. LC 19-16216. Houghton Mifflin Company.
Book of Father Brown. Gilbert Keith Chesterton. Repr. lib. bdg. 16.60x (ISBN 0-89190-576-6). Am Repr-Rivercity Pr.
Book of Fire, Stories. Translated from the Yiddish by Joseph Leftwich. Isaac Loeb Peretz. LC 60-988137. 1960. T. Yoseloff.
Book of Flights: An Adventure Story. Jean Marie Gustave Le Clezio. LC 77-139315. 1972. 6.95. Atheneum.
Book of Folk Stories. Horace Elisha Scudder. LC 12-38499. 1887. Houghton, Mifflin and Company.
Book of Frank Herbert. Frank Herbert. (Orig.). 1980. pap. 2.25 (ISBN 0-425-04527-7). Berkley Pub.
Book of Frank Herbert. Frank Herbert. (Science Fiction Ser). pap. 1.50 (ISBN 0-87997-301-3, UW1301). DAW Bks.
Book of Frank Herbert. Frank Herbert. 1973. 0.95. DAW Books.
Book of Fritz Leiber. Fritz Leiber. 1974. (pbk.) 0.95. DAW Books.
Book of Fritz Leiber and The Second Book of Fritz Leiber. Fritz Leiber. LC 80-21422. (Gregg Press Science Fiction Series). 1980. 19.95 (ISBN 0-8398-2638-9). Gregg Press.
Book of Fu-Manchu. Arthur Sarsfield Ward. LC 29-7719. 1929. R. M. McBride & Company.
Book of George Adamski. George Adamski et al. (Illus.). 1967. pap. 3.95 o.p. Saucerian.
Book of Ghosts. Baring-Gould, Sabine. LC 71-81262. (Short story index reprint series). (Illus.). 1969. Books for Libraries Press.
Book of Ghosts. Sabine Baring-Gould. LC 5-8737. 1904. G. P. Putnam's Sons; Etc., Etc.
Book of Girls. Lilian Lida Bell. LC 3-24224. 1903. L. C. Page & Company.
Book of Gordon Dickson. Gordon R. Dickson. (Science Fiction Ser.). 1973. pap. 0.95 o.p. (UQ1055). DAW Bks.
Book of Imaginary Beings. Jorge Luis Borges. Tr. by Norman T. Di Giovanni. (Illus.). 1969. 7.95 o.p. (ISBN 0-525-06990-9). Dutton.
Book of Islands. Ed. by John Stewart Bowman. LC 76-131069. 1971. 5.95. Doubleday.
Book of Jamaica. Russell Banks. LC 79-25983. 1980. 10.95 (ISBN 0-395-29085-6). Houghton Mifflin.
Book of John Brunner. John Brunner. (DAW science fiction books, no. 177). 1976. (pbk.) 1.25. DAW Books.
Book of Kings: A Novel. Philip Freund. LC 38-15437. 1938. Pilgrim House.
Book of Kings and Queens. Manning-Sanders, Ruth & Robin Jacques. LC 77-16462. (Illus.). 1978. 7.95 (ISBN 0-525-26925-8). Dutton.
Book of Laughter and Forgetting. Milan Kundera. LC 80-7657. 1980. 9.95 (ISBN 0-394-50896-3). A. A. Knopf.
Book of Laughter and Forgetting. Milan. Kundera. LC 81-8533. (Writers from the Other Europe). 1981. 4.95 (ISBN 0-14-005924-5). Penguin Books.
Book of Lies. John Langdon Heaton. LC 7-5038. 1896. The Morse Company.
Book of Lights. Chaim Potok. LC 81-47505. 1981. 13.95 (ISBN 0-394-52031-9). Knopf: Distributed by Random House.
Book of Lights. large print ed. Chaim Potok. LC 82-3277. 1982. 13.95 (ISBN 0-89621-358-7). Thorndike Press.
Book of Long Stories. Ed. by Arthur Hobart Nethercot. LC 27-20666. 1927. The Macmillan Company.

TITLE INDEX BOON ISLAND.

Book of Longer Short Stories. Ed. by James Michie. LC 74-26613. 1975. 3.95 (ISBN 0-8128-1808-3). Stein and Day.
Book of Martyrs. Cornelia Atwood Pratt Comer. LC 77-94711. (Short story index reprint series). 1969. Books for Libraries Press.
Book of Martyrs. Cornelia Atwood Pratt Comer. LC 7-30292. (On cover: The ivory series). 1896. C. Scribner's Sons.
Book of Merlin: The Book of Sir Balin, from Malory's King Arthur, with Caxton's Preface. Thomas Malory & Child, Clarence Griffin, 1864- Ed. LC 4-6878. (Riverside literature series. no. 158). 1904. Houghton, Mifflin and Company.
Book of Merlyn. h. white; prologue by sylvia townsend warner; illustrations by trevor stubley. ed. T. H White. (Berkley Medallion Book). (Illus.). 1978. 2.25 (ISBN 0-425-03826-2). Berkley Publishing Corp.
Book of Merlyn: The Unpublished Conclusion to the Once and Future King. Terence Hanbury White. (Berkley Medallion Book). (Illus.). 1978. 2.25 (ISBN 0-425-03826-2). Berkley Pub. Corp.
Book of Merlyn: The Unpublished Conclusion to The Once and Future King. Terence Hanbury White & Terence Hanbury White. LC 77-3454. (Illus.). 9.95 (ISBN 0-292-70718-5). University of Texas Press.
Book of Merlyn: The Unpublished Conclusion to The Once and Future King. Terence Hanbury White & Terence Hanbury White. LC 77-19205. 1978. 9.95 (ISBN 0-8161-6557-2). G. K. Hall.
Book of Miracles. Ben Hecht. LC 39-14613. 1939. The Viking Press.
Book of Modern Ghosts. LC 53-6967. 1953. Scribner.
Book of Modern Short Stories. Ed. by Dorothy Brewster. LC 28-253466. 1928. The Macmillan Company.
Book of My Uncle Oswald. Roy Larcom McCardell. LC 31-6602. Farrar & Rinehart Incorporated.
Book of Narratives. Ed. by Oscar James Campbell. Rice, Richard Ashley, 1878- Joint Ed. LC 17-24246. 1917. D. C. Heath & Co.
Book of Narratives. Ed. by Oscar James Campbell & Richard Ashley Rice. LC 72-5901. (Short story index reprint series). 1972. (ISBN 0-8369-4196-9). Books for Libraries Press.
Book of Noodles: Stories of Simpletons. William A. Clouston. LC 67-24351. 1969. Repr. of 1888 ed. 30.00x (ISBN 0-8103-3519-0). Gale.
Book of Numbers. Robert Deane Pharr. LC 68-17809. 1969. 5.95. Doubleday.
Book of Paradise: The Wonderful Adventures of Shmuel-Aba Abervo. Illus. by Mendel Reif. Tr. from Yiddish by Leonard Wolf. Itzik Manger. LC 65-129442. bds., 5.00. Hill & Wang.
Book of Paradox. Louise Cooper. LC 73-6798. (Illus.). 1973. 5.95. Delacorte Press.
Book of Philip Jose Farmer. Philip Jose Farmer. (Science Fiction Ser.). 224p. (Orig.). 1973. pap. 0.95 o.p. (UQ1063). DAW Bks.
Book of Philip Jose Farmer: Or the Wares of Simple Simon's Custard Pie and Space Man. Philip Jose Farmer. 1973. (pbk) 0.95. DAW Books.
Book of Philip K. Dick. Philip K. Dick. (Orig.). 1973. pap. 0.95 o.p. (UQ1044). Daw Bks.
Book of Philip K. Dick. Philip K Dick. 1973. 0.95. DAW Books.
Book of Pity and Death. Louis Marie Julien Viaud & O'Connor, Thomas Power, 1848- Tr. LC 8-29998. 1892. Cassell Publishing Company.
Book of Poul Anderson. Poul Anderson. (Science Fiction Ser.). 1978. pap. 1.95 o.p. (ISBN 0-87997-347-1, UV1347). DAW Bks.
Book of Ptath. Alfred Elton Van Vogt. LC 75-438. (Garland Library of Science Fiction). (Illus.). 1975. 11.00 (ISBN 0-8240-1440-5). Garland Pub.
Book of Ptath see Two-Hundred Million A.D.
Book of Ptath: Illus. by A. J. Donnel. Alfred Elton Van Vogt. LC 48-448. 1947. Fantasy Press.
Book of Queer Stories & Stories Told on a Cellar Door. Edward Eggleston. Ed. by William P. Randel. LC 78-96526. (American Authors Ser). 1970. lib. bdg. 10.95 o.s.i. (ISBN 0-512-00157-X). Garrett Pr.
Book of Questions, Vol. 1. Edmond Jabes. Tr. by Rosmarie Waldrop from Fr. LC 75-34058. 1976. pap. 7.95 (ISBN 0-8195-6043-X, Pub. by Wesleyan U Pr). Columbia U Pr.
Book of Rack the Healer. Zach Hughes. (O.s.i.). 192p. (Orig.). 1973. pap. 0.95 o.s.i. (AN1149, Award). Univ Pub & Dist.
Book of Revelations. Rob Swigart. LC 81-3114. 13.50 (ISBN 0-525-03051-4). Dutton.
Book of Rook. Burt Cole. LC 76-116196. 1971. 6.95. Doubleday.
Book of Ruth. Syrell Rogovin Leahy. (Fawcett Crest Book). 1976. (pbk.) 1.95. Fawcett.
Book of Ruth. Syrell Rogovin Leahy. LC 74-13800. 1974. (ISBN 0-671-21894-8). Simon and Schuster.
Book of Ruth. A Novel. Patrick Leopold Gray. LC 6-45539. 1892. The Author.
Book of Saberhagen. Fred Saberhagen. (Science Fiction Ser). 1975. pap. 1.25 o.p. (ISBN 0-87997-153-3, UY1153). DAW Bks.
Book of Sand. Jorge Luis Borges. LC 77-8418. 1977. 7.95 (ISBN 0-525-06992-5). Dutton.
Book of Sansevero. Andrea Giovene. LC 70-108312. 6.95. Houghton Mifflin.
Book of Saucer News. James W. Moseley. 1967. pap. 5.95 o.p. Saucerian.
Book of Saucers. Gray Barker. (Illus.). 1966. 4.95 o.p.; pap. 3.95 o.p. Saucerian.
Book of Sherlock Holmes: Illustrated by Charlotte Ross. Introd. by May Lamberton Becker. Arthur Conan Doyle. LC 50-11366. (Rainbow classics). 1950. World Pub. Co.
Book of Short Stories. Maksim Gorkii. Ed. by Avrahm Yarmolinsky & Moura Budberg. LC 72-13528. 1973. 12.50 (ISBN 0-374-93216-6). Octagon Books.
Book of Short Stories. Maksim Gorkii. Ed. by Avrahm Yarmolinsky & Moura Budberg. LC 72-13528. x, 404p. 1972. Repr. lib. bdg. 24.00x (ISBN 0-374-93216-6). Octagon.
Book of Short Stories. Maksim Gorkii & Yarmolinsky, Avrahm, 1890- Ed. LC 39-11401. H. Holt and Company.
Book of Short Stories. Ed. by Sarah E. Laubacher. LC 76-8709. (Perspectives in literature). 1969. Harcourt, Brace & World.
Book of Short Stories. rev. ed. Ed. by Cynthia Ann Pugh. LC 41-150162. 1941. The Macmillan.
Book of Short Stories. Stuart Pratt Sherman. LC 74-169562. (Short story index reprint series). 1971. (ISBN 0-8369-4025-3). Books for Libraries Press.
Book of Short Stories. Ed. by Stuart Pratt Sherman. LC 15-400. (Half-title: English readings for schools. General editor: W. L. Cross). 1914. H. Holt and Company.
Book of Short Stories: A Collection for Use in High Schools. Ed. by Blanche Colton Williams. LC 18-19726. 1918. D. Appleton and Company.
Book of Short Stories: Edited, with Introduction, Biographies, and Bibliographies, by Cynthia Ann Pugh... Ed. by Cynthia Ann Pugh. LC 31-9622. 1931. The Macmillan Company.
Book of Short Stories, 1. Rosemary Cianciolo et al. (Perspectives in Literature Ser). (Orig.). (gr. 9). 1969. pap. text ed. 1.20 o.p.; price not set teachers' ed. o.p. HarBraceJ.
Book of Short Stories, 2. Rosemary Cianciolo et al. (Orig.). (gr. 9). 1969. pap. text ed. 1.20 o.p.; price not set teachers' ed. o.p. HarBraceJ.
Book of Skulls. Robert Silverberg. LC 72-162775. 1972. (ISBN 0-684-12590-0). Scribner.
Book of Skulls. Robert Silverberg. (Berkley book). 1979. 1.95 (ISBN 0-425-04042-9). Berkley Pub. Corp.
Book of Smith. Elsdon C. Smith. LC 79-10098. (Illus.). 1979. pap. 4.95 (ISBN 0-399-50393-5, Perige). Putnam Pub Group.
Book of Snobs. William Makepeace Thackeray. (Lovell's library. v. 5, no. 220). 1883. J. W. Lovell Company.
Book of Songs. Merritt Linn. LC 82-10493. 1982. 13.95 (ISBN 0-312-09013-7). St. Martin's Press.
Book of Spice. Wallace Irwin. LC 6-33536. 1906. J. W. Luce and Company.
Book of Stories. Ed. by Emily Hanson Obear. LC 28-5588. (Academy classics for junior high schools). Allyn and Bacon.
Book of Stories. Ed. by H Raphael. LC 61-2788. (Pageant of literature). Macmillan.
Book of Stories: Edited by Royal A. Gettmann and Bruce Harkness. Ed. by Royal Alfred Gettmann & Bruce Harkness. LC 55-10955. 1955. Rinehart.
Book of Strange Sins. Coulson Kernahan. 1894. Ward, Lock & Bowden.
Book of Strange Tales. George Brandon Saul. 1977. 12.50 o.p. Porter.
Book of Strangers. Ian Dallas. LC 72-184657. 1972. 4.95 (ISBN 0-394-47982-3). Pantheon Books.
Book of Strangers. Ian Dallas. (Quokka Book). 1978. 1.95 (ISBN 0-671-82082-6). Pocket Books.
Book of Suns. Nancy Springer. (Kangaroo Book.). 1977. 1.95 (ISBN 0-671-80920-2). Pocket Books.
Book of Susan: A Novel. Lee Wilson Dodd. LC 20-111477. E. P. Dutton & Company.
Book of the American Indian see Collected Works.
Book of the City of Ladies. Christine De Pisan. LC 82-331. 1982. 20.00 (ISBN 0-89255-061-9). Persea Books.
Book of the Crime. Elizabeth Daly. LC 51-9249. (Murray Hill mystery). 1951. Rinehart.
Book of the Damned. Charles Fort. Ed. by Lester Del Rey. LC 75-406. (Library of Science Fiction). 1975. lib. bdg. 17.50 (ISBN 0-8240-1411-1). Garland Pub.
Book of the Dead. Elizabeth Daly. LC 44-60272. 1944. Farrar & Rinehart, Inc.
Book of the Duke of True Lovers. Christine De Pisan. Ed. by Alice Kemp Welch. Laurence Binyon & Eric Robert Dalrymple Maclagan. LC 66-23313. (Medieval library). (Illus.). 1966. Cooper Square Publishers.
Book of the Dun Cow. Walter Wangerin, Jr. 1982. pap. 2.50 (ISBN 0-671-83217-4, Timescape). PB.
Book of the Epic: The World's Great Epics Told in Story. Helene A. Guerber. 1913. Repr. 14.00 o.p. Finch Pr.
Book of the Hackle. Frank Elder. 1979. 16.95 (ISBN 0-7073-0223-4, Pub. by Scottish Academic Pr Scotland). Columbia U Pr.
Book of the Serpent. Katharine Howard. LC 12-25806. 1912. Sherman, French & Company.
Book of the Short Story. new ed. Ed. by Henry S. Canby & Robeson Bailey. 1948. 7.95 o.p. (ISBN 0-13-079970-X). P-H.
Book of the Short Story. new and enl ed. Alexander Jessup. Ed. by Henry Seidel Canby. Balley, Robeson, 1906- Joint Ed. LC 48-743633. Appleton-Century-Crofts.
Book of the Short Story. Ed. by Alexander Jessup & Canby, Henry Seidel. LC 3-319489. 1903. D. Appleton and Company.
Book of the Short Story: Selected and Edited, with the History and Technique of the Short Story, Notes, and Bibliographies. Ethan Allen Cross. LC 34-389053. American Book Company.
Book of the Small Souls... By Louis Couperus; Translated by Alexander Teizeira De Mattos. Louis Marie Anne Couperus. Tr. by Teizeira De Mattos, Alexander Louis. LC 32-272584. 1932. Dodd, Mead & Company.
Book of Tish: Tish; More Tish; Tish Plays the Game; The Amazing Adventures of Letitia Carberry; Three Pirates of Penzance. Mary Roberts Rinehart. LC 31-27066. 1931. Farrar & Rinehart, Incorporated.
Book of True Lovers. Alice French. LC 78-94722. (Short story index reprint series). 1969. Books for Libraries Press.
Book of True Lovers. Alice French. LC 6-40028. 1897. Way and Williams.
Book of Uncles. Robert Peter Tristram Coffin. LC 42-22252. 1942. The Macmillan Company.
Book of Vagaries: Comprising the New Mirror for Travellers and Other Whim-Whams. James Kirke Paulding. Ed. by Paulding, William Irving. LC 7-34062. 1868. C. Scribner and Company.
Book of Vampires. D. Wright. 4.95 o.p. Wehman.
Book of van Vogt. Alfred Elton Van Vogt. (Science Fiction Ser.). (Orig.). 1972. pap. 0.95 o.p. (UQ1004). DAW Bks.
Book of Van Vogt see Lost: Fifty Sun.
Book of Voices. Brian Swann. 1980. write for info.; pap. write for info. Latitudes Pr.
Book of Witnesses. David Kossoff. 1973. 1.25. Warner Paperback Lib.
Book of Witnesses. David Kossoff. LC 72-185855. 1972. 4.95. St. Martin's Press.
Book of Wonder. Edward John Moreton Drax Plunkett Dunsany. LC 72-6079. (Short story index reprint series). 1972. (ISBN 0-8369-4213-2). Books for Libraries Press.
Book of Wonder. Edward John Moreton Drax Plunkett Dunsany. LC 34-6826. (Half-title: The modern library of the world's best books). The Modern Library.
Book of Wonder: A Chronicle of Little Adventures at the Edge of the World. Edward John Moreton Drax Plunkett Dunsany. LC 17-4465. J. W. Luce & Company.
Book of Yes. Janet Peterson. LC 76-20247. 1976. pap. 1.95 o.p. (ISBN 0-913592-76-5). Argus Comm.
Book Show: Spring, 1931. Hansen, Harry, 1884- LC 31-22064. 1931. The Book Show.
Book with the Orange Leaves: A Mystery Novel, with a Chapter Laid in London. Harry Stephen Keeler. LC 42-159757. 1942. E. P. Dutton & Company, Inc.
Book Without a Title: Or, Thrilling Events in the Life of Mira Dana. Martin W. Tyler. LC 5-2555. 1855. Printed for the Author.
Book 3. Andrew Carrigan et al. 1972. 7.50 (ISBN 0-912090-20-0); pap. 2.45 (ISBN 0-912090-19-7). Sumac Mich.
Bookful of Girls. Anna Fuller. LC 5-9059. 1905. G. P. Putnam's Sons.
Books Do Furnish a Room: A Novel. Anthony Dymoke Powell. LC 79-154967. (Music of time). 1971. 5.95. Little, Brown.
Books for the Baron: By Anthony Morton Pseud. 1st Ed. John Creasey. LC 51-10425. 1952. Duell, Sloan and Pearce.
Books of Rachel. Joel Gross. LC 79-4879. 10.95 (ISBN 0-87223-540-8). Seaview Books.
Books of the Emperor Wu Ti. Walter Meckauer. Tr. by Garner, J. J. Saville. LC 31-20746. 1931. Minton, Balch and Company.
Bookshop Mystery. James Saxon Childers. LC 30-3348. 1930. D. Appleton and Company.
Boom! Leland Gralapp. LC 65-162913. bds., 4.95. Dutton.
Boom in Paradise. Theyie H. Weigall. Repr. of 1932 ed. 15.00 o.s.i. Finch Pr.
Boom of a Western City. Ellen Hodges Cooley. LC 6-30198. (hearthstone series). 1897. Lee and Shepard.
Boom Town: A Novel of the Southwestern Silver Boom. Jack O'Connor, pseud. LC 38-5141. 1938. A. A. Knopf.
Boom Town Gals. Florenz Branch. LC 42-400129. 1942. Phoenix Press.
Boom Town Gals. Florence Stonebraker. LC 42-4601. 1942. Phoenix Press.
Boom Town Guns. William L. Hopson. (Orig.). 1971. pap. 0.60 o.p. Curtis.
Boomer: A Story of the Rails. Harry Bedwell. LC 42-23951. 1942. Farrar & Rinehart, Inc.
Boomer: By Clay Randall Pseud. Clifton Adams. LC 57-7786. (Permabooks, M-3077, Western, 7). 1957. Permabooks.
Boomerang. Mark Bartholomeusz. 1981. 7.50 (ISBN 0-8062-1792-8). Carlton.
Boomerang. William C Chambliss. LC 44-6704. 1944. Harcourt, Brace and Company.
Boomerang. 2d ed. William Hamilton Osborne. LC 15-21629. 1915. 1.35. R. M. McBride & Co.
Boomerang. Helen De Guerry Simpson. LC 32-760261. 1932. Doubleday, Doran & Company, Inc.
Boomerang: A Novel Based on the Play of the Same Name. David Gray. LC 18-184019. 1918. The Century Co.
Boomerang: An Australian Escapade. Andrew Garve. LC 70-96008. 1970. 5.95 o.p. (ISBN 0-06-011453-3, HarpT). Har-Row.
Boomerang: An Australian Escapade. Paul Winterton. LC 70-96008. 1970. 4.95. Harper & Row.
Boomerang Bride. Margaret Pargeter. (Harlequin Presents Ser.). 192p. 1981. pap. 1.75 (ISBN 0-373-10453-7, Pub. by Harlequin). PB.
Boomerang Clue. Agatha Miller Christie. 1975. (pbk.) 0.95. Dell.
Boomerang Clue. Agatha Miller Christie. LC 35-16314. 1935. Dodd, Mead & Company.
Boomerang Conspiracy. Michael Stanley. LC 77-88901. 1977. 1.95 (ISBN 0-380-01803-9). Avon Books.
Boomerang Jail. Frank Chester Robertson. LC 47-31384. 1947. E. P. Dutton.
Boomers. Joan Hurling. 1982. pap. 2.75 (ISBN 0-425-05484-5). Berkley Pub.
Boomers. Roy Norton. LC 14-7566. 1.25. W. J. Watt & Company.
Boomers: A Novel. Joan Hurling. LC 78-63640. 8.95 (ISBN 0-8149-0814-4). Vanguard Press.
Boomer's Gold. Jack Walker, pseud. 176p. 1982. pap. 2.95 (ISBN 0-380-60319-5, 60319-5). Avon.
Boomers' Gold: A Novel of Texas in the Twenties. Jack Walker, pseud. LC 77-16196. 1978. 10.00 (ISBN 0-914476-74-2). Thorp Springs Press.
Booming of Acre Hill: And Other Reminiscences of Urban and Suburban Life. John Kendrick Bangs. LC 79-98558. (Short story index reprint series). (Illus.). 1969. Books for Libraries Press.
Booming of Acre Hill: And Other Reminiscences of Urban and Suburban Life. John Kendrick Bangs. LC 2786. 1900. Harper & Brothers.
Booming of Acre Hill & Other Reminiscences of Urban & Suburban Life. facsimile ed. John Kendrick Bangs. LC 79-98558. (Short Story Index Reprint Ser.). 1900. 16.00 (ISBN 0-8369-3132-7). Ayer Co.
Boomkitchwatt: A Novel. first ed. Don Hendrie. LC 72-88011. 1972. 2.95 (ISBN 0-912528-04-4). John Muir Publications.
Boomtown. Larry D Names. LC 81-43055. 1981. 10.95 (ISBN 0-385-17429-2). Doubleday.
Boomtown Buccaneers. William Colt MacDonald. LC 42-18848. 1942. Doubleday, Doran and Company, Inc.
Boomtown Buccaneers. William Colt MacDonald. LC 43-18199. 1942. Sun Dial Press.
Boomtown Buccaneers. Abridged Ed. William Colt MacDonald. LC 54-31857. (Ace double novel books, D-52). 1954. Ace Books.
Boomtown Bustout. Zeke Masters, pseud. (Orig.). 1981. pap. 1.95 (ISBN 0-671-42620-6). PB.
Boomville. A Tale of Western Minnesota. M J Glennon. 1891. L. Kimball Printing Co.
Boon Island. Kenneth Roberts. LC 56-5443. 4.95 (ISBN 0-385-04044-X). Doubleday.
Boon Island. Kenneth Roberts. 192p. 1981. pap. 2.50 (ISBN 0-449-24408-3, Crest). Fawcett.
Boon Island. Presentation Ed. Kenneth Lewis Roberts. LC 56-5443. 1956. Doubleday.
Boon Island. Presentation Ed. Kenneth Lewis Roberts. LC 56-544354. 1956. Doubleday.

Boon: The Mind of the Race, The Wild Asses of the Devil, and The Last Trump; Being a First Selection from the Literary Remains of George Boon, Appropriate to the Times. Herbert George Wells. LC 15-16632. George H. Doran Company.

Boon, The Mind of the Race, The Wild Asses of the Devil, and The Last Trump: Being a First Selection from the Literary Remains of George Boon, Appropriate to the Times, Prepared for Publication by Reginal Bliss. Herbert George Wells & Bliss, Reginald. LC 15-16632. George H. Doran Company.

Boondocks. Desmond Lowden. LC 72-89907. 1973. 5.95 (ISBN 0-03-006496-1). Holt, Rinehart and Winston.

Boone Stop. Homer Croy. LC 18-14423. 1918. Harper & Brothers.

Boori. William Neville Scott. LC 79-320623. (Illus.). 1978. 7.95 (ISBN 0-19-550550-6). Oxford University Press.

Boosted Man. Tully Zetford. (Hook,#2). 1975. (pbk.) 1.25. Pinnacle Books.

Boosters. Mark Lee Luther. The Bobbs-Merrill Company.

Boot Camp. Henry Joseph Berkowitz. LC 48-10777. 1948. Jewish Publ. Society of America.

Boot-Heel Doctor: A Novel. Fannie Cook. LC 41-17611. 1941. Dodd,Mead & Company.

Boot Heel Range. Edwin Booth. LC 58-7595. 1958. Avalon Books.

Boot Hill: By Weston Clay Pseud. T. W. Ford. LC 50-13800. 1950. Phoenix Press.

Boot Hill Cowpoke. Katherine N. Mason. 1978. pap. 1.75 (ISBN 0-89041-216-2, 3216). Major Bks.

Boot Hill Gospel. Charles Morris Martin. LC 52-14854. 1952. Arcadia House.

Boot Hill Showdown. Walt Gordon. LC 75-36120. 160p. (Orig.). 1976. pap. 0.95 (ISBN 0-89041-044-5, 3044). Major Bks.

Booth and the Spirit of Lincoln: A Story of a Living Dead Man. Bernie Smade Babcock. LC 25-25281. 1925. J. B. Lippincott Company.

Boothill Court: By Lew Smith Pseud. Lee Floren. LC 54-748761. 1954. Arcadia House.

Boothill Riders. Lee Floren. 1978. pap. 1.25 (ISBN 0-532-12584-3). Woodhill.

Boothill Town. Leslie Scott. LC 58-368. 1958. Arcadia House.

Boothill Trail. C. William Harrison. LC 41-6944. Phoenix Press.

Bootleg Angel. Ed Mazzaro. 1978. pap. 1.75 o.s.i. (ISBN 0-89559-157-X). Dale Books Inc.

Bootleg Charlie. Brookes More. 1.00 (ISBN 0-8338-0047-7). M Jones.

Bootles' Children. Henrietta Eliza Vaughan Stannard. LC 8-13870. (On cover: Lovell's library, no. 1187). 1888. J. W. Lovell Company.

Bootles' Children. Henrietta Eliza Vaughan Stannard. (On cover: Seaside library. Pocket ed. no. 1121). 1888. G. Munro.

Boots Brevik Saga. Rodney Nelson. LC 78-11771. 8.95. (ISBN 0-914974-20-3) (ISBN 0-914974-19-X). Holmganers Press.

Boots of the Virgin. Earl Shorris. (0708). 1968. Dell.

Boots of the Virgin. Earl Shorris. LC 68-10324. 1968. Delacorte Press.

Booty. Isabel Egenton Ostrander. LC 19-8014. W. J. Watt & Company.

Booze: A Novel. Charles Richard Webb. LC 78-71503. 1978. 8.95 (ISBN 0-88373-087-1). Stonehill.

Booze Reader. George W. Bishop. 288p. 1965. 4.50 o.p. (ISBN 0-8202-0004-2). Sherbourne.

Borden Chantry. Louis L'Amour. (Orig.). 1977. pap. 2.25 (ISBN 0-553-14883-4, X12534-6). Bantam.

Border: A Missouri Saga. Dagmar Doneghy. LC 31-22900. 1931. W. Morrow & Company.

Border: A Novel. Anthony Delius. LC 77-352456. (Illus.). 1976. (ISBN 0-949968-68-4). D. Philip.

Border Ambush. Walker A. Tompkins. LC 50-11404. Macrae Smith.

Border: & A Young Man in the Know. Regis Debray. LC 68-29438. (Evergreen original, E-477). 1968. 1.45. Grove Press.

Border Bandit. Max Brand. (Illus.). 272p. 1982. pap. 2.50 (ISBN 0-441-07078-7, Pub. by Charter Bks). Ace Bks.

Border Bandit. Evan Evans, pseud. LC 47-2051. Harper & Brothers.

Border Bandit. Frederick Faust. LC 75-40384. 1975. 9.95 (ISBN 0-89190-201-5). American Reprint Co.

Border Beagles. George Simms. 1974. lib. bdg. 30.00 (ISBN 0-8414-8075-3). Folcroft.

Border Beagles: A Tale of Mississippi. new and rev. ed. 1st ams ed. William Gilmore Simms. LC 71-119151. (Illus.). 1970. AMS Press.

Border Beagles, a Tale of Mississippi. new and rev. ed. William Gilmore Simms. LC 8-11017. 1882. A. C. Armstrong & Son.

Border Beagles; a Tale of Mississippi. new and rev. ed. William Gilmore Simms. (On cover:Lovell's library, v. 13, no. 698). 1885. J. W. Lovell Company.

Border Beatitude. Erma E Black, pseud. LC 48-8472. 1948. Dorrance.

Border Bonanza. Walker A Tompkins. LC 43-6825. 1943. Phoenix Press.

Border Breed. William MacLeod Raine. LC 35-23330. 1935. Houghton Mifflin Company.

Border Breed. William MacLeod Raine. 1975. (pbk.) 0.95. Popular Library.

Border Buccaneers. Frank Castle. LC 55-42189. (Ace double novel books, D-112). 1955. Ace Books.

Border Canucks: Our Friendly Relations. A Novel. George Cameron Rankin. LC 13-338610. 1890. G. C. Rankin.

Border City. Hart Stilwell. LC 74-22818. (Labor Movement in Fiction and Non-Fiction). 1977. 17.00 (ISBN 0-404-58477-2). AMS Press.

Border City. Hart Stilwell. LC 45-35078. 1945. Doubleday, Doran and Company, Inc.

Border Crossings. Daniel Peters. LC 77-11545. 9.95 (ISBN 0-06-013307-4). Harper & Row.

Border Crossings: International Fiction in Translation. Ed. by Robert Bonazzi & Brian Swann. (New Departures in Fiction: Vol. 3). 1980. pap. write for info. Latitudes Pr.

Border Daring. Bradford Scott. (Orig.). 1973. pap. 0.75 o.p. (ISBN 0-515-02893-2, T2893). Pyramid Pubns.

Border Eagle. Walker A Tompkins. LC 39-127274. Phoenix Press.

Border Feud. Charles Horace Snow. LC 38-3236. 1938. Macrae Smith Company.

Border Fever. C. William Harrison. LC 56-5321. (Permabooks, M3030, Western). Permabooks.

Border Fever. William Jeffrey. 192p. (Orig.). pap. cancelled. Tower Bks.

Border Fever. William Jeffrey. 192p. 1983. pap. 2.25 (ISBN 0-8439-2017-3, Leisure Bks). Dorchester Pub Co.

Border Gold. Lee Floren. LC 54-13116. 1954. Arcadia House.

Border Graze. Dwight Bennett Newton. LC 52-10396. (Double D western). 1952. Doubleday.

Border Guns. Leigh Carder. LC 35-7574. Covici, Friede.

Border Guns. Frederick Faust. 1975. (pbk.) 1.25. Warner Paperback Library.

Border Jumper. Walt Coburn. 1970. pap. 0.60 o.p. (60-454). Manor Bks.

Border Jumpers. John Benteen. (Fargo Western Adventure Series). 1976. (pbk.) 1.25. Belmont Tower Books.

Border Jumpers: By Will C. Brown Pseud. 1st Ed. C. S. Boyles. LC 55-7128. (Dutton diamond D western). 1955. Dutton.

Border Justice. Amos Moore. LC 38-326307. I. Washburn. Inc.

Border Kid. Max Brand. LC 41-105028. 1941. Dodd, Mead & Company.

Border Kid. Frederick Faust. LC 41-1050. 1941. Dodd, Mead & Company.

Border Killing. William M. James, pseud. (Apache Ser.: No. 22). 208p. (Orig.). 1982. pap. 1.95 (ISBN 0-523-41024-7). Pinnacle Bks.

Border Leander. Howard Seely. LC 8-6441. 1893. D. Appleton and Company.

Border Legion. Zane Grey. LC 16-11386. 1916. Harper & Brothers.

Border Legion. Zane Grey. LC 21-13685. 1918. Grosset & Dunlap.

Border Line. Jackson Gregory. LC 42-4610. 1942. Dodd, Mead & Company.

Border Line. Walter S Masterman. LC 37-9926. 1937. E. P. Dutton & Co., Inc.

Border Lion. L. D. Henry. (Orig.). 1980. pap. 1.95 (ISBN 0-532-23207-0). Woodhill.

Border Lord. Jan Westcott. 1976. (pbk.) 1.50. Bantam Books.

Border Lord. Jan Vlachos Westcott. LC 46-730769. 1946. Crown Publishers.

Border of Darkness. John Latimer. LC 72-79404. 1972. 4.95 (ISBN 0-385-00539-3). Published for the Crime Club by Doubleday.

Border Outlaws. James W. Buel. Repr. of 1881 ed. 15.00 o.s.i. Finch Pr.

Border Queen. Nick Sumner. LC 53-631663. (Silver star westerns). 1953. Dodd, Mead.

Border Raider. William L Hopson. LC 50-5379. 1949. Phoenix Press.

Border Raider see Desert Maverick.

Border Raiders. A. Leslie. LC 45-11421. 1946. Arcadia House, Inc.

Border Range. Bruce Douglas. LC 42-569. 1942. Macrae-Smith Company.

Border Range. Theodore Wayland Douglas. LC 42-569. 1942. Macrae-Smith-Company.

Border Riders. Robert J. Steelman. 224p. (Orig.). Date not set. pap. cancelled o.p. (ISBN 0-505-51812-0). Tower Bks.

Border Rifles. A Narrative. Gustave Aimard & St. John, Percy Bolingbroke, 1821-1889, Ed. LC 5-42196. (On cover: Lovell's library, no. 1052). 1887. J.W. Lovell Company.

Border Shepherdess: A Romance of Eskdale. Amelia Edith Huddleston Barr. LC 6-838601. Dodd, Mead & Company.

Border Town. Carroll Graham. 1934. The Vanguard Press.

Border Town & Other Stories. Shen Congwen. 1981. pap. 2.50 (ISBN 0-8351-0852-X). China Bks.

Border Town Girl. John Dann MacDonald. 160p. 1982. pap. 2.50 (ISBN 0-449-13714-7, GM). Fawcett.

Border Town Girl. John Dann MacDonald. 1969. pap. 0.60 o.p. (R2512, GM). Fawcett World.

Border Town Girl: And Linda Two Compelling Novels. John Dann MacDonald. LC 56-498310. (Popular library, 750). 1956. Popular Library.

Border Town Girl and Linda: Two Compelling Novels. John Dann MacDonald. LC 56-4983. (Popular library, 750). 1956. Popular Library.

Border Trail. Harold Bindloss. LC 31-211872. 1931. Frederick A. Stokes Company.

Border Trumpet. Ernest Haycox. LC 39-169832. 1939. Little, Brown and Company.

Border Trumpet. Ernest Haycox. LC 40-33290. 1940. The Sundial Press.

Border Trumpet. Ernest Haycox. LC 78-14537. (Gregg Press Western Fiction Series). 1978. 8.95 (ISBN 0-8398-2474-2). Gregg Press.

Border Trumpet. Ernest Haycox. (Signet brand western). 1974. (pbk.) 0.95. New American Library.

Border Vengeance. Johanas L. Bouma. (Leisure Book). 1978. 1.25 (ISBN 0-8439-0605-7). Nordon Pub., Inc.

Border Vengeance. Bertha Muzzy Sinclair. LC 51-14015. 1951. Bouregy & Curl.

Border War. A. A Baker. 1976. 4.95. Avalon Books.

Border War. Bradford Scott. (Orig.). 1968. pap. 0.50 o.p. (R1878). Pyramid Pubns.

Border War: A Tale of Disunion. John Beauchamp Jones. LC 16-25030. 1859. Rudd & Carleton.

Border Watch. Joseph Alexander Altsheler. 1976. lib. bdg. 16.70x (ISBN 0-89968-001-1). Lightyear.

Border Wolf. Robert Ames Bennet. LC 32-16116. 1931. G. H. Watt.

Border Wolves, a Western: By Pete Danvers Pseud. James Maddock Henderson. LC 54-308818. 1954. Hammond, Hammond.

Borderers: Or, the Wept of Wish-Ton-Wish. James Fenimore Cooper. LC 74-162892. (Bentley's Standard Novels: No. 33). (Illus.). Repr. of 1833 ed. 15.50 (ISBN 0-404-54433-9). AMS Pr.

Borderland. neil claremon. ed. Neil Claremon. 1.75 (ISBN 0-380-00679-0). Avon Books.

Borderland. Robert Halifax. 1912. E. P. Dutton & Co.

Borderland: A Casebook of True Supernatural Stories. William Thomas Stead. LC 69-16361. 358p. 1970. 5.95 (ISBN 0-8216-0058-3). Univ Bks.

Borderland. A Country-Town Chronicle. Jessie Fothergill. LC 6-40011. (On cover: The seaside library. Pocket ed. no. 935). 1887. G. Munro.

Borderland: A Novel. Neil Claremon. LC 74-21331. 1975. 6.95 (ISBN 0-394-49619-1). Knopf.

Borderland Echoes: A West Virginia Story. Bruce Haymond. LC 22-12468. 1921. The Roxburgh Publishing Company.

Borderland of Society. Charles Belmont Davis. LC 79-140328. (Short story index reprint series). 1970. Books for Libraries Press.

Borderland of Society. Charles Belmont Davis. LC 98-1312. 1898. H. S. Stone & Co.

Borderline. Hanif Kureishi. 50p. 1982. pap. 5.95 (ISBN 0-413-49910-3, NO. 3642). Methuen Inc.

Borderline Case. Hugh McLeave. LC 78-11576. 8.95 (ISBN 0-684-15803-5). Scribner.

Borderline Case. Brad Williams. LC 60-7413. 1960. M. S. Mill Co.

Borderline Murder. Kathleen Moore Knight. LC 48-604. 1947. Pub. for the Crime Club by Doubleday.

Borderlines. Axel Madsen. LC 75-2366. (Illus.). 1975. 6.95 (ISBN 0-02-579180-X). Macmillan.

Borders to Cross. Parker Bonner. (Original Western Ser). (Orig.). 1969. pap. Paperback Lib.

Bordertown Blues. Allen Taylor. 1981. pap. 1.95 (ISBN 0-8439-0854-8, Leisure Bks). Nordon Pubns.

Bored Bridegroom. Barbara Cartland. LC 74-3488. 1974. Bantam Books.

Bored to Death. Michael Delving, pseud. 200p. 1975. 6.95 o.p. (ISBN 0-684-14210-4). Scribner.

Bored to Death. Jay Williams. LC 74-33137. 1975. 6.95 (ISBN 0-684-14210-4). Scribner.

Borges, a Reader: A Selection from the Writings of Jorge Luis Borges. Jorge Luis Borges & Rodriguez Monegal, Emir. LC 81-68076. 17.50 (ISBN 0-525-06998-4) (ISBN 0-525-47654-7). Dutton.

Borgia. Zona Gale. LC 29-21543. 1929. A. A. Knopf.

Borgia Blade. Gardner F Fox. LC 53-2320. (Gold medal books, 300). 1953. Fawcett Publications.

Borgia Blade. Florence Ryerson & Clements, Colin Campbell, 1894- Joint Author. LC 37-9859. 1937. D. Appleton-Century Company, Incorporated.

Borgia Cabinet. Joseph Smith Fletcher. LC 30-848192. 1930. A. A. Knopf.

Borgia Prince. Pamela Bennetts. LC 74-19857. 1975. 6.95 (ISBN 0-7091-0133-3). St. Martin's Press.

Borgia Testament. Nigel Balchin. LC 49-9687. 1949. Houghton Mifflin Co.

Borgias: Or, At the Feet of Venus. Vicente Blasco Ibanez & Livingston, Arthur, 1883- Tr. LC 30-25151. E. P. Dutton & Co., Inc.

Boris Godounov. Aleksandr Sergeevich Pushkin & Boris Vasil Evich Zvorykin. LC 82-70183. (Studio book). (Illus.). 1982. 19.95 (ISBN 0-670-18198-6). Viking Press.

Boris Karloff Presents: More Tales of the Frightened. Robert Lory. (Orig.). 1975. pap. 1.25 o.p. (ISBN 0-515-03716-8, V3716). BJ Pub Group.

Boris Karloff Presents More Tales of the Frightened. Robert Lory & Boris Karloff. LC 74-29421. 1975. 1.25 (ISBN 0-515-03716-8). Pyramid Books.

Boris Karloff Presents Tales of the Frightened. Ed. by Michael Avallone. 1973. pap. 1.25 o.p. (ISBN 0-515-03282-4, V3282). Pyramid Pubns.

Boris Story. Veronica Leigh. pap. cancelled o.s.i. Manor Bks.

Bormann Brief. Clive Egleton. LC 73-87786. 1974. 6.95 (ISBN 0-698-10572-9). Coward, McCann & Geoghegan.

Bormann Receipt. Madelaine Duke. LC 77-93993. 1978. 8.95 (ISBN 0-8128-2479-2). Stein and Day.

Born a Yankee. Grace Carstens. LC 53-13540. 1954. Macmillan.

Born Again. Allan Hartley. (Illus.). 1978. pap. 0.79 (ISBN 0-8007-8535-5, Spire Comics). Revell.

Born Again: Or, The Romance of a Dual Life. Daniel N Ford. LC 6-41405. 1893. Succanesset Press.

Born Aristocrat: A Story of the Stage. Matthew White. LC 8-36619. 1898. F. A. Munsey.

Born at Daybreak: An Historical Novel. Bertha M Peterson. LC 43-5571. Zondervan Publishing House.

Born at Sea: A Novel. Pamela Frankau. LC 22-7608. 1932. Doubleday, Doran & Company, Inc.

Born Coquette. A Novel. Margaret Wolfe Hungerford. LC 7-9367. (On cover: Lovell's international series, no. 80). 1890. J. W. Lovell Company.

Born Fool. John Walter Byrd. LC 19-129859. 1919. George H. Doran Company.

Born for Love. Ursula Bloom. 1978. pap. 1.95 (ISBN 0-89041-203-0, 3203). Major Bks.

Born for Malice. Bernard S. Smith. 1968. 3.95 o.p. Vantage.

Born Guilty: A Novel. Translated from the Spanish by Frank Gaynor. Manuel Rojas. LC 55-10310. 1955. Library Publishers.

Born in Captivity. 1st American Ed. John Barrington Wain. LC 53-9484. 1954. Knopf.

Born in Exile. George Robert Gissing. Ed. by Pierre Coustillas. (Society & the Victorians Ser.). 1978. text ed. 22.25x (ISBN 0-85527-872-2). Humanities.

Born in Exile: A Novel. George Robert Gissing. LC 68-54266. 1968. AMS Press.

Born in the Whirlwind. A Novel. William Adams. LC 5-42959. 1893. Arena Publishing Company.

Born in Wedlock: A Novel. Margaret Echard. LC 56-10760. 1956. Doubleday.

Born in 1921. Tr. from Czech by Alice Denesova. Karel Ptacnik. LC 65-29684. (Artia pocket bks.). pap., 2.00. Artia.

Born Innocent. Hurwood & Dipego. 1975. pap. 1.95 (ISBN 0-441-07122-8). Ace Bks.

Born Innocent. Bernhardt J Hurwood. 1975. (pbk.) 1.50. Ace Books.

Born Leader: By J. T. McIntosh Pseud. 1st Ed. James Murdoch Macgregor. LC 54-5173. 1954. Doubleday.

Born Losers. George MacBeth. 304p. 1982. pap. 2.95 (ISBN 0-446-90654-9). Warner Bks.

Born Nurse. Louise Lockhart. LC 50-39076. 1950. Printed by the J. W. Burke Co.

Born of Flame. A Rosicrucian Story. Margaret Bloodgood Peeke. LC 7-36468. 1892. J. B. Lippincott Company.

Born of Flame. A Rosicrucian Story. 3d ed. Margaret Bloodgood Peeke. LC 37-183157. 1896. Authors Publishing Co.

Born of Man and Woman: Tales of Science Fiction and Fantasy. Introd. by Robert Bloch. 1st Ed. Richard Matheson. LC 54-5703. 1954. Chamberlain Press.

Born of the Same Roots: Stories of Modern Chinese Women. Vivian Ling Hsu. LC 81-47009. (Chinese Literature in Translation). 27.50 (ISBN 0-253-19526-8) (ISBN 0-253-20270-1). Indiana University Press.

TITLE INDEX BOTH 1925.

Born of the Storm. Sidney B Carter. LC 49-7215. 1948. B. Humphries.
Born of the Storm. Nikolai Alekseevich Ostrovskii. Tr. by Louise Luke Hiler. LC 74-10089. 1974. 15.00 (ISBN 0-88355-175-6). Hyperion Press.
Born of the Storm. Nikolai Alekseevich Ostrovskii. Tr. by Hiler, Louise Luke. LC 41-24628. 1939. Critic's Group Press.
Born of the Sun. John H. Culp. 1978. pap. 1.95 (ISBN 0-441-07111-2). Ace Bks.
Born of Woman. Raymonde Vincent. LC 39-10237. 1939. W. Morrow and Company.
Born Player. Mary West. LC 8-36232. 1893. Macmillan and Co.
Born Rich. Hughes Cornell. LC 24-11879. G. W. Jacobs & Company.
Born Savage. William L. Hopson. 1970. pap. 0.60 o.p. (B60-1098). Belmont-Tower.
Born Savage. William L. Hopson. (O.s.i). 1974. pap. 0.95 o.s.i. (BT50694). Belmont-Tower.
Born Savage. William L. Hopson. (O.s.i.). 1976. pap. 1.25 o.s.i. (AQ1601, Award). Univ Pub & Dist.
Born Strangers: A Chronicle of Two Families. Helen Topping Miller. LC 49-5742. 1949. Bobbs-Merrill Co.
Born to Battle: Collection of Animal Stories. Squire Omar Barker. LC 51-12131. 1951. University of New Mexico Press.
Born to Be Bad. June Jennifer. LC 35-35380. Godwin.
Born to Be Hanged. M. E. Chaber, pseud. LC 72-93182. 192p. 1973. 4.95 o.p. (ISBN 0-03-085985-9). HR&W.
Born to Be Hanged. Kendell Foster Crossen. LC 72-93182. (Rinehart suspense novel). 1973. 4.95 (ISBN 0-03-085985-9). Holt, Rinehart and Winston.
Born to Be King. Constance Gluyas. LC 73-20459. 1974. 7.95 (ISBN 0-13-080259-X). Prentice-Hall.
Born to Be Murdered. Elinore Denniston. LC 45-4225. 1945. M. S. Mill Co., Inc.
Born to Betray: Or, A Game Well Played. Metta Victoria Fuller Victor. (select series. no. 63). 1890. Street & Smith.
Born to Command: Or, The Mistress of Hillmere. Clara Augusta Jones. (select series. no. 73). 1890. Street & Smith.
Born to Evil. Beverly Lippincott. 176p. (Orig.). 1976. pap. 1.25 (ISBN 0-89041-100-X, 3100). Major Bks.
Born to Exile. Phyllis Eisenstein. 1980. pap. 1.95 (ISBN 0-440-10854-3). Dell.
Born to Hang. Harley Hess. (Orig.). 1979. pap. 1.75 (ISBN 0-532-23228-3). Woodhill.
Born to Heal. Ruth Montgomery. 224p. 1976. pap. 2.50 (ISBN 0-445-08450-2). Popular Lib.
Born to Heal. Ruth Montgomery. (YA) 1973. 6.95 o.p. (ISBN 0-698-10493-5). Coward.
Born to Lose. Ed Morris. LC 74-12021. 216p. 1974. 7.95 o.p. (ISBN 0-88405-090-4). Mason Charter.
Born to Love. George Anthony. (Orig.). 1968. pap. 1.75 o.p. (3043). Brandon.
Born to Power: Manipulators II. Gloria V. Basile. (Orig.). 1979. pap. 3.50 (ISBN 0-523-41822-1). Pinnacle Bks.
Born to Serve a Story. Charles Monroe Sheldon. LC 1-29236. 1900. Advance Publishing Co.; Etc., Etc.
Born to Serve a Story. Charles Monroe Sheldon. 1901. Advance Publishing Co.
Born to Sin. Henry Leyford Gates. LC 34-389192. 1934. The Macaulay Company.
Born to the Purple: The Karma of Princess Minerva. Margarete Ward. LC 38-367409. Kellaway-Ide Company.
Born to the Saddle. Archie Joscelyn. LC 40-4091. Phoenix Press.
Born to Trouble. Nelson Nye. 1976. pap. 1.25 (ISBN 0-532-12389-1). Woodhill.
Born to Trouble. Nelson Coral Nye. pap. 0.50 o.p. (50-302). Manor Bks.
Born to Trouble. Joyce Stranger, pseud. LC 69-11722. 1968. 4.95. Viking Press.
Born to Win. Mike Roote. (Orig.). 1971. pap. 0.75 o.p. (A899S, Award). Univ Pub & Dist.
Born to Win. Mike Roote. (O.s.i.). (Orig.). pap. 0.75 o.s.i. (A899S, Award). Univ Pub & Dist.
Born Unwanted. Ross Edwin. LC 34-37887. The Maculay Company.
Born Victim. Hillary Waugh. LC 62-16786. 1962. Doubleday.
Born with a Golden Spoon. Gilbert Parker. LC 675. 1899. Doubleday & McClure Co.
Born with a Mask. Cleo M. Stephens. (YA) 1972. 4.50 o.p. (Avalon). Bouregy.
Born with the Century. William Kinsolving. LC 78-27078. 12.50 (ISBN 0-399-12270-2). Putnam.
Born with the Dead. Irina Kirk. LC 63-10657. 1963. Houghton Mifflin.
Born with the Dead. Robert Silverberg. 1979. pap. 1.95 (ISBN 0-425-04156-5). Berkley Pub.
Born with the Dead. Robert Silverberg. (O.s.i.). 1974. 5.95 o.s.i. (ISBN 0-394-48845-8). Random.
Born with the Dead: Three Novellas. Robert Silverberg. LC 73-20599. 1974. 5.95 (ISBN 0-394-48845-8). Random House.
Born with the Dead; Three Novellas. Robert Silverberg. LC 74-17406. 1975. (pbk.) 1.95 (ISBN 0-394-71447-4). Vintage Books.
Born with the Dead: Three Novellas About the Spirit of Man. Robert Silverberg. 1974. pap. 1.95 o.p. (ISBN 0-394-71447-4, Vin). Random.
Born Without Choice. M. B Nickolas. LC 71-143683. 1972. 5.00 (ISBN 0-8059-1532-X). Dorrance.
Born. 1st Ed. Gertrude Schweitzer. LC 60-10682. 1960. Doubleday.
Bornin' & the Dyin. Blossom Brown. 1970. 5.50 o.p. Carlton.
Bornless Keeper. P. B. Yuill. LC 74-31908. 1975. 5.95 (ISBN 0-8027-5314-0). Walker.
Borodino Mystery. Maria Longworth Storer. LC 16-174192. B. Herder.
Borough Treasurer. Joseph Smith Fletcher. LC 21-26728. 1921. A. A. Knopf.
Boroughmonger. Ralph Hale Mottram. LC 29-9003. 1929. Little, Brown, and Company.
Borovitsky Apartment. Frank Bourgholtzer. LC 65-18514. 1965. Morrow.
Borrasca. Octavus Roy Cohen. LC 53-12894. 1953. Macmillan.
Borrasca de Pasiones. new ed. Rogelio Jaimes. (Pimienta Collection Ser). 160p. 1974. pap. 1.00 o.p. (ISBN 0-88473-193-6). Fiesta Pub.
Borribles. Michael De Larrabeiti. LC 77-351885. (Illus.). 1976. 2.95 (ISBN 0-370-10898-1). Bodley Head.
Borribles Go for Broke. Michael De Lorrabeiti. 288p. 1982. pap. 2.50 (ISBN 0-441-07024-8). Ace Bks.
Borrow the Night. Helen Nielsen. LC 56-5142. 1956. Morrow.
Borrowdale Tragedy. William James Dawson. LC 20-199185. 1920. John Lane Company.
Borrowed Alibi: By Lesley Egan Pseud. 1st Ed. Elizabeth Linington. LC 62-112282. 1962. Harper.
Borrowed Crime, and Other Stories. Cornell George Hopley-Woolrich. LC 47-21439. (Murder mystery monthly. No. 42). 1946.
Borrowed Husband. Allene Soule Corliss. LC 43-4311. 1943. Farrar & Rinehart, Inc.
Borrowed Love. Florence Stonebraker. LC 49-9907. 1949. Phoenix Press.
Borrowed Lover: A Romance. Pauline Stiles. LC 32-8069. 1932. Doubleday, Doran and Company, Inc.
Borrowed Night. Aladar Farkas. LC 44-9915. 1944. Doubleday, Doran.
Borrowed Night. Oscar Ray & Szebenyei, Joseph, Tr. LC 44-9915. 1944. Doubleday, Doran and Co., Inc.
Borrowed Plumes. Elizabeth Ashton. (Harlequin Romances). 192p. 1981. pap. 1.25 (ISBN 0-373-02395-2, Pub. by Harlequin). PB.
Borrowed Plumes. Roseleen Milne. LC 77-5761. 1977. 7.95 (ISBN 0-698-10828-0). Coward, McCann & Geoghegan.
Borrowed Plumes. Mary Badger Wilson. LC 35-4590. The Penn Publishing Company.
Borrowed Reputations. Harry Sinclair Drago. LC 28-19010. The Macaulay Company.
Borrowed Shield: A Detective Story. Richard E Enright. LC 25-25116. 1925. G. H. Watt.
Borrowed Summer: And Other Stories. Elizabeth Enright. LC 46-5232. 1946. Rinehart & Company, Inc.
Borrower: An Alchemical Novel. Ursule Molinaro. LC 75-123981. 1970. 7.95. Harper & Row.
Borrower of the Night. Elizabeth Peters, pseud. LC 72-11252. 1973. 5.95 (ISBN 0-396-06769-7). Dodd, Mead.
Borrower of the Night. Elizabeth Peters, pseud. LC 73-13677. 1973. (lib. bdg.) 9.95 (ISBN 0-8161-6151-8). G. K. Hall.
Borrower of the Night. Elizabeth Peters. 1974. (pbk.) 0.95. Dell.
Borstal Boy. Brendan Behan. LC 81-81444. 384p. 1982. pap. 8.95 (ISBN 0-87923-415-6). Godine.
Borstal Boy. Brendan Behan. 1959. 6.95 o.p. (ISBN 0-394-41744-5). Knopf.
Borzoi Book of Short Fiction. David H. Richter. LC 82-18034. 1982. 11.95 (ISBN 0-394-32810-8). Knopf.
Boscobel. A Novel. Emma Newton. LC 6-15021. W. B. Smith & Co.
Bose. Larry D Names. LC 79-6283. 1980. 8.95 (ISBN 0-385-15014-8). Doubleday.
Bosman at His Best: A Choice of Stories and Sketches. Culled by Lionel Abrahams. Herman Charles Bosman. LC 66-32716. 1967. bds., 4.75. Human & Rousseau.
Bosnah. Myra Kelly. LC 8-32646. 1908. 1.50. D. Appleton and Company.
Bosnian Chronicale. Ivo Andric. LC 63-9138. 1963. Knopf.
Bosnian Story. Translated by Kenneth Johnstone. Ivo Andric. LC 60-453811. (Modern Yugoslav novels). 1959. Lincolns-Prager.
Bosom Friend. A Novel. Elizabeth Caroline Grey. LC 26-23565. (On cover: Library of select novels. no. 61). 1845. Harper & Brothers.
Bosom of the Family: A Novel on India. Evelyn Harter. 1978. 11.00x (ISBN 0-8364-0316-9). South Asia Bks.
Boss. Alfred Henry Lewis. LC 67-29272. (Americans in Fiction Ser.). lib. bdg. 16.00 (ISBN 0-8398-1157-8); pap. text ed. 4.95x (ISBN 0-89197-684-1). Irvington.
Boss. J. W McConaughy & Sheldon, Edward, Joint Author. LC 12-113039. The H. K. Fly Company.
Boss. Odette Tyler. LC 8-322975. 1896. The Transatlantic Publishing Company.
Boss. Odette Tyler. LC 8-32296. 1897. Continental Publishing Co.
Boss, and How He Came to Rule New York. Alfred Henry Lewis. LC 67-292721. (Americans in Fic.). 1967. Gregg Pr.
Boss, and How He Came to Rule New York. Alfred Henry Lewis. LC 3-268753. 1903. A. S. Barnes & Company.
Boss Bart, Politician. A Western Story of Love and Politics. Joseph Mitchell Chapple. LC 6-23118. (On cover: Neely's library of choice literature, no. 60). 1896. F. T. Neely.
Boss Came to Dinner & Other Stories. Bhisham Sahni. Tr. by Jai Ratan et al from Hindi. (Greenbird Bk.). 95p. 1975. 14.00 (ISBN 0-88253-264-2); pap. 6.75 (ISBN 0-88253-720-2). Ind-US Inc.
Boss Girl: A Christmas Story, and Other Sketches. James Whitcomb Riley. LC 76-160948. (Short story index reprint series). 1971. (ISBN 0-8369-3927-1). Books for Libraries Press.
Boss Girl, a Christmas Story: And Other Sketches. James Whitcomb Riley. LC 7-41648. 1886. The Bowen-Merrill Co.
Boss Lady. Ross Kenyon. 1974. (pbk.) 1.95 (ISBN 0-87056-390-4). Brandon Books.
Boss Man. Louis Cochran. LC 39-30682. 1939. The Caxton Printers, Ltd.
Boss Man. Roy Bernard Sparkia. LC 54-36461. (Lion book, 211). 1954. Lion Books by Arrangement with Cornell Pub. Corp.
Boss of Barbed Wire: By Barry Cord Pseud. Peter Germano. LC 55-118822. 1955. Arcadia House.
Boss of Broken Spur. Nick Sumner. LC 54-5580. (Silver star westerns). 1954. Dodd, Mead.
Boss of Eagle's Nest: A Western Story. William West Winter. LC 25-460405. Chelsea House.
Boss of Golden River. Strong, Charles Stanley. LC 52-7411. 1952. Arcadia House.
Boss of Little Arcady. Harry Leon Wilson. LC 5-23032. Lothrop Publishing Company.
Boss of Lonely Valley. Forrest Raymond Brown. LC 36-7483. Dodge Publishing Company.
Boss of Panamint. Leslie Charles Ernenwein. LC 43-205. 1942. Phoenix Press.
Boss of the Badlands. Claude Rister. LC 35-5817. E. J. Clode, Inc.
Boss of the Bic C. Tony Adams. LC 40-8130. Phoenix Press.
Boss of the Diamond A. Robert Ames Bennet. LC 26-8011. 1926. A. C. McClurg & Co.
Boss of the Far West. Herbert Arthur, pseud. LC 49-629. Phoenix Press.
Boss of the Lazy Y. Charles Alden Seltzer. 1915. A. C. McClurg & Co.
Boss of the Lazy Y. Charles Alden Seltzer. LC 29-307685. 1915. Grosset & Dunlap.
Boss of the Lazy 9. Peter Field. LC 48-104215. (Triple A western classic). 1948. Jefferson House.
Boss of the Lazy 9: By Peter Field. Peter Field. LC 36-7585. 1936. W. Morrow & Co.
Boss of the Northern Star. Archie Joscelyn. LC 44-30247. 1944. Phoenix Press.
Boss of the O K. Brett Rider. LC 40-32094. Phoenix Press.
Boss of the OK. Arthur Henry Godden. LC 40-32094. 1940. Phoenix Press.
Boss of the Plains. Harry Sinclair Drago. LC 40-826139. 1940. W. Morrow & Company.
Boss of the Plains: By Will Ermine Pseud. Harry Sinclair Drago. LC 52-5062. (Triple-A western classic). 1952. Jefferson House.
Boss of the Rafter C. Jay Lucas. LC 37-17500. Green Circle Books.
Boss of the Ragged O. Norma Bicknell Mansfield. LC 35-17491. Farrar and Rinehart, Incorporated.
Boss of the Tumbling H. Frank Chester Robertson. LC 27-1241. Barse & Hopkins.
Boss of the Ward: A Story of Municipal Politics. John S Vandiver. 1896. H. L. Collins Company.
Boss of Thunder Butte. W. D Hoffman. LC 30-288417. 1930. A. C. McClurg & Co.
Boss of Wind River. Arthur Murray Chisholm. LC 11-35750. 1911. 1.20. Doubleday, Page & Company.
Boss Tom, the Annals of an Anthracite Mining Villages. Matthew Stanley Kemp. LC 4-30143. 1904. The Saalfield Publishing Company.
Boss. Tr. from Italian by William Weaver. 1st Amer. Ed. Goffredo Parise. LC 66-193931. 1966. 4.95. Knopf.
Boston: A Documentary Novel of the Sacco-Vanzetti Case. Upton Beall Sinclair. LC 77-86279. (Illus.). 1978. 15.00 (ISBN 0-8376-0420-6). R. Bentley.
Boston: A Novel. Upton Beall Sinclair. LC 78-115273. 1970. Scholarly Press.
Boston, a Novel. Upton Beall Sinclair. LC 29-26043. 1928. A. & C. Boni.
Boston Adventure. Jean Stafford. LC 44-40176. 1944. Harcourt, Brace and Company.
Boston Bay Mysteries & Other Tales. Edward R. Snow. LC 77-10901. (Illus.). 1977. bds. 8.95 (ISBN 0-396-07505-3). Dodd.
Boston Blackie. Jack Boyle. LC 79-747. (Series: Gregg Press Mystery Fiction Series.). (Illus.). 1979. 9.95 (ISBN 0-8398-2536-6). Gregg Press.
Boston Common: Tale of Our Own Times. 2d ed. Farren. LC 6-38968. 1857. J. French & Company.
Boston Common: Tale of Our Own Times. Farren & Varnham, Mrs. R. G., Supposed Author. LC 42-47439. 1856. J. French & Company.
Boston Conspiracy: Or, The Royal Police. A Tale of 1773-75. John Hovey Robinson. LC 7-42155. 1847. Dow & Jackson.
Boston Girl: A Story of Boston, Bar Harbor, and Paris. Arthur Swazey. LC 8-25642. 1886. Belford, Clarke & Co.
Boston Girl's Ambitions. Virginia Frances Townsend. LC 8-29820. 1887. Lee and Shepard.
Boston Neighbours in Town and Out. Agnes Blake Poor. LC 7-39646. 1898. G. P. Putnam's Sons.
Boston Strangler. Gerold Frank. 1971. pap. 2.50 (ISBN 0-451-09553-7, E9553, Sig). NAL.
Bostonians. Henry James. LC 74-19093. (Library of literature). 1975. 5.95 (ISBN 0-672-61182-1). Bobbs-Merrill.
Bostonians. Henry James. LC 45-9737. 1945. Dial Press.
Bostonians see Bodley Head Henry James.
Bostonians: A Novel. Henry James. LC 73-16075. 1974. (pbk.). 4.95 (ISBN 0-8152-0347-0). Crowell.
Bostonians: A Novel. Henry James. LC 4-15126. 1886. Macmillan and Co.
Bostonians, a Novel. Introd. by Iriving Howe. Henry James. LC 56-5414. (Modern library of the world's best books 16). 1956. Modern Library.
Bostwick's Budget. Henry Payson Dowst. LC 20-18296. The Bobbs-Merrill Company.
Boswell. Stanley Elkin. 448p. 1980. pap. 2.75 (ISBN 0-446-95538-8). Warner Bks.
Boswell, a Modern Comedy. Stanley Elkin. LC 64-10531. 1964. Random House.
Boswell and Son. Donald McDougall. LC 77-17765. 1978. 8.95 (ISBN 0-312-09324-1). St. Martin's Press.
Botany Bay. Charles Bernard Nordhoff & James Norman Hall. LC 44-11969. 1944. The Sun Dial Press.
Botany Bay. Charles Bernard Nordhoff & Hall, James Norman. LC 41-22071. 1941. Little, Brown and Company.
Botchan. Soseki Natsume. LC 68-11974. 1967. C. E. Tuttle Co.
Botchan. Soseki Natsume. LC 71-174215. (Illus.). 1972. 5.95 (ISBN 0-87011-169-8). Kodansha International.
Botched Brand. Fred East. LC 49-942604. (Dutton Diamond D western). E. P. Dutton.
Both Banks of the River: A Novel. 1st Ed. Argye M Briggs. LC 54-123333.
Both Good and Evil. 1st Ed. Edna Hall Bothwell. LC 52-6254. 1951. Pageant Press.
Both Hands Screaming. Simon Perchik. (Pap. ed. 8.00 o.p.). 1975. 16.00 (Pub. by Elizabeth Pr). SBD.
Both in the Wrong. A Novel. Lilian Headland Spender. (Harper's Franklin square library. no. 544). 1886. Harper & Brothers.
Both One. Sidney Herschel Small. LC 25-198289. The Bobbs-Merrill Company.
Both Over Twenty-One. Samuel Hopkins Adams. LC 39-5592. Liveright Publishing Corp.
Both Sides of the Coin. Georgina Grey, pseud. (Regency Love Story Ser.). 224p. (Orig.). 1980. pap. 1.75 (ISBN 0-449-50043-8, Coventry). Fawcett.
Both Sides of the Law. Bertrand William Sinclair. LC 51-5731. (Western novel classic, 110). 1951. Novel Selections, Inc.
Both Sides of the Shield. Archibald Willingham Butler & Traft, William Howard. 1912. 1.00. J. B. Lippincott Company.
Both Were Mistaken. A Novel. Emma Boyden. LC 6-15231.
Both Were Young. Bennie Caroline Hall. LC 49-600. 1948. Arcadia House.
Both Your Houses, a Novel. Philip Hamilton Gibbs. 1949. Hutchinson.
Both 1925: A Novel of Youth. Vera Mary Brittain. LC 49-70723. 1949. Macmillan Co.

Botor Chaperon. Charles Norris Williamson & Alice Muriel Livingston Williamson. LC 7-25165. 1907. The McClure Company.

Botteghe Oscure Reader. Ed. by George Garrett. LC 73-15006. 496p. 1974. 17.50x (ISBN 0-8195-4071-4, Pub. by Wesleyan U Pr); pap. 7.95 (ISBN 0-8195-6033-2). Columbia U Pr.

Botticelli Madonna: A Novel. Richard Hubert Francis Cox. LC 78-25836. 9.95 (ISBN 0-07-013291-7). McGraw-Hill.

Bottle Factory Outing. Beryl Bainbridge. LC 74-25294. 1975. 7.95 (ISBN 0-8076-0781-9). G. Braziller.

Bottle Factory Outing. Beryl Bainbridge. (Signet book). 1976. 1.50. New American Library.

Bottle Fighters. George William Willis. LC 63-9357. 1963. Random House.

Bottle Gardens. Jack Kramer. 1973. pap. 1.95 o.s.i. (76-340). Lancer.

Bottle Imp. Robert Louis Stevenson. Ed. by Raymond Harris. (Jamestown Classics Ser.). (Illus.). 48p. (Orig.). 1982. pap. text ed. 2.00x (ISBN 0-89061-259-5, 463); tchr's ed 3.00x (ISBN 0-89061-260-9, 465). Jamestown Pubs.

Bottle in the Smoke. Louisa Cooke Don-Carlos. LC 7-31975. 1907. Mayhew Publishing Company.

Bottle in the Smoke. Louisa Cooke Don-Carlos. LC 8-167141. R. F. Fenno & Company.

Bottle with the Green Wax Seal. Harry Stephen Keeler. LC 42-51250. 1942. E. P. Dutton & Company, Inc.

Bottles in the Smoke. Clement Hankey. LC 30-33619. 1930. Longmans, Green and Co.

Bottom Deal. Zeke Masters, pseud. (Orig.). 1981. pap. 1.95 (ISBN 0-671-42618-4). PB.

Bottom Dogs. Edward Dahlberg. LC 74-22778. (Labor Movement in Fiction and Non-Fiction). 1976. 17.50 (ISBN 0-404-58418-7). AMS Press.

Bottom Dogs, From Flushing to Calvary, Those Who Perish, and Hitherto Unpublished and Uncollected Works. Edward Dahlberg. LC 75-25715. 10.00. (ISBN 0-690-01034-6) (ISBN 0-308-10230-4). Crowell.

Bottom Dogs: With an Introduction. Edward Dahlberg. LC 30-6431. 1930. Simon and Schuster.

Bottom Fishing: A Novella and Other Stories. W. F Lucas. LC 74-192039. 1974. 5.00. Carpetbag Press.

Bottom Line. Fletcher Knebel. LC 74-6990. 1974. 7.95 (ISBN 0-385-06135-8). Doubleday.

Bottom of the Barrel: Swiss Library. Plinio Martini. 260p. 1982. 16.95 (ISBN 0-7145-3935-X); pap. 7.95 (ISBN 0-7145-3943-0). Riverrun NY.

Bottom of the Matter: A Novel. Anna Robeson Brown Burr. LC 35-1085. 1935. D. Appleton-Century Company, Incorporated.

Bottom of the Well. Frederick Upham Adams. LC 6-15736. 1906. G. W. Dillingham Company.

Bottom of the Well. Doris Bell Collier Ball. LC 40-13036. 1940. Longmans, Green and Co.

Bottom of the Well. Josephine Bell. LC 40-13086. 1940. Longmans, Green and Co.

Bottom Rail. James Walter Daniel. LC 15-3419. 1.50. The Roxburgh Publishing Company Incorporated.

Bottom Rail on Top: A Novel of the Old South. Hamilton James Eckenrode. LC 35-5811. Greenberg.

Botts in War, Botts in Peace: Earthworms Can Take Anything. William Hazlett Upson. LC 44-6791. 1944. Farrar & Rinehart, Inc.

Boubou: The Blonde Gypsy. 1st Ed. A P Alexiades. LC 53-126463. 1953. Pageant Press.

Boucher's Choicest: A Collection Anthony Boucher's Favorites from Best Detective Stories of the Year. Anthony Boucher. Ed. by Jeanne Bernkapf. 5.95 o.p. (ISBN 0-525-07007-9). Dutton.

Boucher's Choicest: A Collection of Anthony Boucher's Favorites from Best Detective Stories of the Year. Ed. by Jeanne F. Bernkopf. William Anthony Parker White. LC 72-78383. 1969. 5.95. Dutton.

Boudapesti 3. Desmond Lowden. LC 78-13253. 7.95 (ISBN 0-03-044301-6). Holt, Rinehart and Winston.

Boudoir. 1971. pap. 1.95 o.p. (Z1064T, Zebra). Grove.

Boudoir: A Journal of Voluptuous Victorian Reading. LC 70-151439. 256p. (Orig.). 1980. pap. 3.50 o.p. (ISBN 0-394-17781-9, B 445, BC). Grove.

Boudoir Murder. Milton Morris Propper. LC 31-970824. 1931. Harper & Brothers.

Bougainville Breakout. (McLeane's Rangers Ser.: No. 1). (Orig.). 1983. pap. 2.50 (ISBN 0-8217-1207-1). Zebra.

Bough of Summer. Duane Carr. LC 75-39423. (Woodwind book). 4.00. Endeavors in Humanity Press.

Boughs Bend Over. Maida Parlow French. LC 44-954. Doubleday, Doran and Company Inc.

Boughs Bend Over. Maida Parlow French. LC 44-2706. 1944. Doubleday, Doran and Co., Inc.

Bought and Paid for: A Story of to-Day, from the Play of George Broadhurst. Arthur Hornblow. LC 12-4139. G. W. Dillingham Company.

Bought and Sold. Alberto Moravia. LC 72-96313. 1973. 6.95 (ISBN 0-374-11555-9). Farrar, Straus and Giroux.

Bought and Sold. Alberto Moravia. 1974. (pbk.) 1.50. Manor Books.

Bought for a Dollar & Other Exciting Stories of China. Elsie B. Ezzo. 1969. pap. 1.25 (ISBN 0-88243-505-1, 02-0505). Gospel Pub.

Bought with a Gun. new ed. Luke Short. 1979. 1.50 (ISBN 0-440-10744-X). Dell Book.

Bought with His Name. Penny Jordan. (Harlequin Presents Ser.). 192p. 1983. pap. 1.75 (ISBN 0-373-10562-2). Harlequin Bks.

Boulder Dam. Zane Grey. LC 64-21263. 1964. Grosset & Dunlap.

Boulder Dam. 1st Ed. Grey, Zane. LC 63-16524. 1963. Harper & Row.

Boulderstone: Or, New Men and Old Populations. A Novel. William Sime. (On cover: Seaside library. Pocket ed. no. 429). 1885. G. Munro.

Boule De Suif, and Other Stories. Guy De Maupassant. LC 76-157786. (Short story index reprint series). 1971. (ISBN 0-8369-3898-4). Books for Libraries Press.

Boule de Suif, & Other Stories: Collected Novels & Stories, Vol. 1. facsimile ed. Guy De Maupassant. Tr. by Ernest Boyd. LC 76-157786. (Short Story Index Reprint Ser.). Repr. of 1922 ed. 16.00 (ISBN 0-8369-3898-4). Ayer Co.

Boulevard. Katharine Haviland Taylor. LC 34-122671. J. B. Lippincott Company.

Boulevard Nights: A Novel /by Dewey Gram; from a Screenplay by Desmond Nakano. Dewey Gram. 1.95 (ISBN 0-446-90106-7). Warner Books Inc.

Boulevard. Translated by Lowell Bair. Robert Sabatier. LC 58-12252. 1958. D. McKay Co.

Boulevards All the Way - Maybe. James Montgomery Flagg. 1925. Repr. price not set o.s.i. Finch Pr.

Bounce. Steve Welp. 30p. 1978. pap. 2.25 o.p. Hse of One Pub.

Bounce Girl. Dean R. Koontz & Gerda Koontz. pap. 1.95 o.p. (8059). Cameo.

Bouncing Betsy. D. P. Lathrop. (O.s.i). 1964. 3.95 o.s.i. (ISBN 0-02-753150-3). Macmillan.

Bound by a Spell. Frederick John Fargus. (On cover: Lovell's library. v. 20. no. 968). 1887. J. W. Lovell Company.

Bound by His Vows: Or, At the Altar. A Romance. Elisabeth Burstenbinder & L., J. S., Tr. LC 6-19395. J. B. Lippincott & Co.

Bound by Love. Catherine Lanigan. 432p. 1981. pap. 2.95 (ISBN 0-380-79046-7, 79046). Avon.

Bound by the Law. Kate Thyson Marr. LC 98-2190. 1898. G. W. Dillingham Co.

Bound Down, or Life and Its Possibilities. Anna M Fitch. LC 6-41109. 1870. J. B. Lippincott & Co.

Bound for Bounty. Barry Cord. Ed. by Alice Sachs. 1969. lib. bdg. 3.50 o.p. Arcadia.

Bound for the Promised Land. Richard Marius. (Signet Book). 1977. 2.25 (ISBN 0-451-07459-9). New American Library.

Bound Girl. Everett Webber & Webber, Olga. LC 49-49798. 1949. E. P. Dutton.

Bound in Darkness. Olaf H Olseth. LC 56-7672. 1956. Comet Press Books.

Bound in Shallows (a Cape Cod Idyll) Marie Tello Phillips. LC 32-20152. Observer Press.

Bound in Shallows: A Novel. Eva Wilder McGlasson Brodhead. LC 6-17966. 1897. Harper & Brothers.

Bound in Shells. Richard Osborne. LC 79-67605. 9.95 (ISBN 0-87223-588-2). Seaview Books.

Bound in This Clay: A Story of the Ozarks. Royal Rosamond. LC 45-9582. 1945. The Gem Publishing Company.

Bound Man, and Other Stories. Ilse Aichinger. LC 72-144151. (Short story index reprint series). 1971. (ISBN 0-8369-3766-X). Books for Libraries Press.

Bound Man, and Other Stories. Translated from the German by Eric Mosbacher. Ilse Aichinger. LC 56-10354. 1956. Noonday Press.

Bound Not Blessed." A Novel. Annie Lyndsay MacGregor. LC 7-20002. 1892. G. W. Dillingham.

Bound to Die. William Price Turner. LC 67-23106. 1967. Walker.

Bound to Happen. Elswyth Thane. LC 30-29552. 1930. G. P. Putnam's Sons.

Bound to John Company: Or, Robert Ainsleigh. Mary Elizabeth Braddon Maxwell. (Seaside library. v. 32, no. 666). 1879. G. Munro.

Bound to Kill. John Blackburn. LC 63-17700. 1963. M. S. Mill Co., and W. Morrow.

Bound to Please. Charles Sackville. 1972. pap. 1.75 o.s.i. (V1117K, Venus). Grove.

Bound to the Wheel: A Novel. John Saunders. (Seaside library, v. 38, no. 782). 1880. G. Munro.

Bound to Violence. Yambo Ouologuem. LC 79-142093. 1971. (ISBN 0-15-113625-4). Harcourt Brace Jovanovich.

Boundaries. Roberta Silman. 272p. 1982. pap. 2.95 (ISBN 0-380-59501-X, 59501, Flare). Avon.

Boundaries: A Novel. Roberta Silman. LC 78-27089. 9.95 (ISBN 0-316-79109-1). Little, Brown.

Boundary Against Night. Edmund Gilligan. LC 38-320233. Toronto, Farrar & Rinehart, Incorporated.

Boundary Line. Denise Robins. LC 33-11793. 1932. G. H. Watt.

Bounder: A Vulgar Tale. Arthur Hodges. LC 19-7467. 1919. 1.60. Houghton Mifflin Company.

Boundless Quest: A Novel. Florence Shipple Simmons. LC 62-19090. 1962. Florshire.

Bountiful Hour. Marion Fox. LC 13-433631. 1912. John Lane.

Bounty Beware. Owen G. Irons. (Orig.). 1982. pap. 2.50 (ISBN 0-8217-1028-1). Zebra.

Bounty Guns. Luke Short. 0.95. Dell.

Bounty Hunter. Aaron Fletcher. (Leisure Books). 1977. 1.25 (ISBN 0-8439-0461-5). Nordon Pubns.

Bounty Hunter: A Killing Trade. William Boyles & Hank Nuwer. LC 81-81398. (Bounty Hunter Ser.). 224p. (Orig.). 1981. pap. 2.50 (ISBN 0-87216-902-2). Playboy Pbks.

Bounty Hunter: Blood Mountain. William Boyles & Hank Nuwer. LC 82-80020. (Bounty Hunter Ser.). 224p. (Orig.). 1982. pap. 2.50 (ISBN 0-86721-127-X). Playboy Pbks.

Bounty Hunter: Deadliest Profession. William Boyles & Hank Nuwer. LC 80-83561. 224p. (Orig.). 1981. pap. 2.50 (ISBN 0-87216-804-2). Playboy Pbks.

Bounty Hunter: The Wild Ride. William Boyles & Hank Nuwer. LC 81-82965. (Bounty Hunter Ser.). 224p. (Orig.). 1982. pap. 2.50 (ISBN 0-87216-996-0). Playboy Pbks.

Bounty Hunters. Elmore Leonard. LC 54-55630. 1954. Houghton Mifflin.

Bounty Hunter's Moon. Ray Hogan. (Shawn Starbuck Western). (Signet Book: Vol. 4). 1977. 1.25 (ISBN 0-451-07362-2). New American Library.

Bounty Killer. John Benteen. (Sundance Ser.: No. 15). 144p. 1981. pap. 1.75 (ISBN 0-8439-1050-X, Leisure Bks). Nordon Pubns.

Bounty Killer. John Benteen. (Sundance,#15). 1975. (pbk.) 0.95. Leisure Books.

Bounty Lands. William Donohue Ellis. LC 52-5196. 1952. World Pub. Co.

Bounty Man. John McGreevey. LC 55-44660. (Ace double novel books, D-120). 1955. Ace Books.

Bounty Man. Lewis B Patten. LC 73-14053. 1974. 4.95 (ISBN 0-385-09928-2). Doubleday.

Bounty Man Kildoon. Robert Eagle. LC 75-17079. 1978. pap. 1.50 (ISBN 0-89041-195-6, 3195). Major Bks.

Bounty Man's Target. Buck Adams. 176p. (Orig.). 1978. pap. 1.50 (ISBN 0-89041-196-4, 3196). Major Bks.

Bounty of Earth. Donald Culross Peattie & Peattie, Louise Redfield. LC 26-20524. 1926. D. Appleton and Company.

Bounty on Bannister. Dwight Bennett Newton. 1978. pap. 1.25 (ISBN 0-425-03736-3, Medallion). Berkley Pub.

Bounty on the Bannister. D. B Newton. 1975. (pbk.) 0.95 (ISBN 0-425-02925-5). Berkley Publishing Corp.

Bounty Road. Charles R. Pike, pseud. LC 80-70092. (Jubal Cade Westerns Ser.). 142p. 1981. pap. 2.95 (ISBN 0-87754-241-4). Chelsea Hse.

Bounty Trilogy: By Charles Nordhoff and James Norman Hall. A School Ed., by Florence Doerr Jones. Charles Bernard Nordhoff & James Norman Hall. LC 53-4194. 1953. Globe Book Co.

Bounty Trilogy: Comprising the Three Volumes, "Mutiny on the Bounty," "Men Against the Sea," and "Pitcairn's Island,". Charles Bernard Nordhoff & Hall, James Norman. LC 37-27024. 1936. Little, Brown, and Company.

Bounty Trilogy: Comprising the Three Volumes, "Mutiny on the Bounty," "Men Against the Sea," & "Pitcairn's Island,". Charles Bernard Nordhoff & Hall, James Norman. LC 40-32366. 1940. Little, Brown and Company.

Bounty War. A. A. Baker. (YA) 1972. 4.50 o.p. (Avalon). Bouregy.

Bouquet Boutique. Emily Brown. 10.00 o.s.i. Hearthside.

Bouquet of Barbed Wire. Andrea Newman. LC 70-101436. 1970. 5.95. Doubleday.

Bouquet of Brides. Rose Meadows. 1974. (pbk.) 0.95 (ISBN 0-671-77717-3). Pocket Books.

Bouquet of Eggs. Genevieve B Bowdoin. LC 68-55617. 1968. 3.75. Branden Press.

Bourbon Lilies. A Story of Artist Life. Elizabeth Williams Champney. LC 6-23326. (Wayside series). 1878. Lockwood, Brooks and Company.

Bourbon Lilies. A Story of Artist Life. Elizabeth Williams Champney. LC 6-23325. (On cover: Lovell's library, v. 3, no. 119). J. W. Lovell Company.

Bourdaloue and Louis Xiv. Or, The Preacher and the King. Laurence Louis Felix Bungener. LC 6-17242. D. Lothrop & Co.

Bourgeois Anonymous. Morris H. Philipson. LC 65-15428. 1965. bds., 4.95. Vanguard.

Bourlotas Fortune: A Novel. Nicholas Gage, pseud. LC 75-5456. 1975. (ISBN 0-03-015096-5). Holt, Rinehart and Winston.

Bourne Identity. Robert Ludlum. LC 79-23638. 12.95 (ISBN 0-399-90070-5). R. Merek Publishers.

Bourru, Soldier of France. new ed., with an introduction by coley taylor. ed. Jean Tabouréau & Wright, Ernest Hunter, 1882- Tr. LC 29-29101. E. P. Dutton & Co., Inc.

Bouvard and Pecuchet. Gustave Flaubert. LC 76-371814. (Penguin classics). 1976. 3.95 (ISBN 0-14-044320-7). Penguin.

Bouvard and Pecuchet. Gustave Flaubert. LC 78-12046. 1979. 20.50 (ISBN 0-313-21189-2). Greenwood Press.

Bouvard and Pecuchet: Translated by T. W. Earp and G. W. Stonier. With an Introd. by Lionel Trilling. Gustave Flaubert. LC 54-8413. 1954.

Bow and Arrows. Eugene Talmane. LC 74-196007. (Illus.). 1974. (ISBN 0-89023-000-5). Raven Print.

Bow Bells see Willis & His Friends Series.

Bow Down to Wood and Stone. Josephine Lawrence. LC 38-27101. 1938. Little, Brown and Company.

Bow-Legged Ghost: And Other Stories; a Book of Humorous Sketches, Verses, Dialogues, and Facetions Paragraphs. by leon mead... ed. Leon Mead. LC 99-5106. The Werner Company.

Bow of Orange Ribbon: A Romance of New York. Amelia Edith Huddleston Barr. LC 16-96872. Dodd, Mead and Company.

Bow of Orange Ribbon: A Romance of New York. Amelia Edith Huddleston Barr. LC 4-15066. 1893. Dodd, Mead & Company.

Bow Street Brangle. Margaret SeBastian, pseud. 1977. 1.50 (ISBN 0-445-04040-8). Popular Library.

Bow Street Gentleman. Margaret Sebastian, pseud. 1977. 1.50 (ISBN 0-445-03231-6). Popular Library.

Bow Street Terror. T. A. Waters. (Orig.). 1970. pap. 0.75 o.p. (ISBN 0-447-74629-4). Lancer.

Bow Strings. David MacGregor Cheney. LC 44-21020. B. Humphries, Inc.

Bow Without Arrow: By Cynthia Millburn Pseud. Anne Tedlock Brooks. LC 51-14519. 1951. Arcadia House.

Bowdrie. Louis L'Amour. 1983. pap. 2.95. Bantam.

Bowen's Ark. George Sakers. LC 82-828. 14.95 (ISBN 0-671-43635-X). Simon and Schuster.

Bowery Murder. Willard K Smith. LC 29-12533. 1929. Pub. for The Crime, Club, Inc., by Doubleday, Doran and Company, Inc.

Bowl of Baal. Robert Ames Bennet. 7.50 (ISBN 0-937986-06-2). D M Grant.

Bowl of Brass. Paul Iselin Wellman. LC 44-3156. 1944. J. B. Lippincott Company.

Bowl of Cherries. John Held. LC 32-33156. The Vanguard Press.

Bowl of Red. Frank X. Tolbert. LC 82-45368. 216p. 1983. pap. 6.95 (ISBN 0-385-18182-5, Dolp). Doubleday.

Bowleg Bill, the Sea-Going Cowboy. Josef Berger. LC 38-11789. 1938. The Viking Press.

Bowline Knot: A Novel. James D. Collins. 110p. 1972. 4.00 o.p. (ISBN 0-682-47439-8). Exposition.

Bowling Green Murders. Helen Rosen Woodward & Amherst, Frances, Joint Author. LC 40-30411. Random House.

Bowman Test. Albert J Elias. (Dell Book). 1977. 1.50 (ISBN 0-440-10787-3). Dell Pub. Co.

Bowman's Kid. Gordon D Shirreffs. (Gold medal book, T2738). 1973. (pbk.) 0.75. Fawcett.

Bowmanville Break. Sidney Shelley. LC 68-25136. 1968. 4.95. Delacorte Press.

Bows & Arrows. Eugene Talmane. (Illus.). 1974. 8.00 (ISBN 0-89023-000-5). Raven Print.

Bowsham Puzzle: A Novel. John Habberton. LC 6-466859. (On cover: Standard library. no. 110). 1884. Funk & Wagnalls.

Bowstring Murders. John Dickson Carr. LC 33-38222. 1933. W. Morrow & Company.

Box. Kendrew Lascelles. (O.s.i.). 1974. pap. 2.95 o.s.i. (ISBN 0-8402-8079-3). Nash Pub.

Box: A Conversation Piece. Allan Turpin. LC 66-106822. 1966. 4.95. Vanguard.

Box & Other Stories. Victor L. Kaplan. 72p. (Orig.). 1979. pap. 5.00 (ISBN 0-915306-18-2). Curbstone.

Box Car. Medford Lander. 1980. 8.50 o.p. (ISBN 0-8062-1137-7). Carlton.

Box Champ. Nord Southgate. pap. 1.95 o.p. (8056). Cameo.

Box from Japan... Harry Stephen Keeler. LC 32-33838. E. P. Dutton & Co., Inc.

Box Garden: A Novel. Carol Shields. LC 77-375961. 9.95 (ISBN 0-07-082547-5). McGraw-Hill Ryerson.

Box Hill Murder. Joseph Smith Fletcher. LC 29-20021. 1929. A. A. Knopf.

Box Man. Kobo Abe. LC 80-14709. (Illus.). 1980. 3.95 (ISBN 0-399-50485-0). Perigee Books.

Box Man. Doug Buck. (Orig.). 1968. pap. 1.25 o.p. (2063). Brandon.

Box of Matches. Joseph Hamblen Sears. LC 4-26861. 1904. Dodd, Mead & Company.

Box of Sandalwood. John Knoepfle. (WNU Ser.: No. 11). 1979. pap. 4.50. Juniper Pr WI.

Box of Spikenard. Ethel Mary Young Boileau. LC 23-7016. George H. Doran Company.

Box Office. Ed. by Marjorie Barrows. Eaton, George, Joint Comp. LC 43-17230. 1943. Ziff-Davis Publishing Company.

Box Office Murders. Freeman Wills Crofts. LC 75-44968. (Fifty Classics of Crime Fiction, 1900-1950; 14). 1976. 12.00 (ISBN 0-8240-2375-7). Garland Pub.

Box One Hundred. Frank Leonard. LC 70-175154. (Novel of Suspense). 192p. 1972. 6.95 o.p. (ISBN 0-06-012583-7, HarpT). Har-Row.

Box Star Buckaroo. Charles Morris Martin. LC 51-21215. 1951. Phoenix Press.

Box with Broken Seals. Edward Phillips Oppenheim. LC 19-15544. 1919. Little, Brown and Company.

Box 100. Frank Leonard. 1973. (pbk.) 0.95 (ISBN 0-671-77679-7). Pocket Books.

Box 100. Frank Leonard. LC 70-175154. 1972. 5.95 (ISBN 0-06-012583-7). Harper & Row.

Boxer Unit-OSS, No. 3: Operation Counter-Scorch. Ned Cort. (Men of Action Ser.). 192p. (Orig.). 1982. pap. 1.95 (ISBN 0-446-30128-0). Warner Bks.

Boxer Unit-OSS, No. 4: Target Norway. Ned Cort. (Men of Action Ser.). 160p. (Orig.). 1982. pap. 1.95 (ISBN 0-446-30121-3). Warner Bks.

Boxer Unit-OSS, No. 5: Partisan Demolition. Ned Cort. (Men of Action Ser.). 192p. 1982. pap. 1.95 (ISBN 0-446-30129-9). Warner Bks.

Boxwood. Blanche Smith Ferguson. LC 36-1429. The Penn Publishing Company.

Boxwood. Sylvia Townsend Warner. (Illus.). 1960. 4.50 o.p. (ISBN 0-7011-1191-7). Dufour.

Boxwood Maze. Bentz Plagemann. 1973. (pbk.) 0.95. Dell.

Boxwood Maze. Bentz Plagemann. LC 72-76753. 1972. 5.95 (ISBN 0-8415-0176-9). Saturday Review Press.

Boy. Luis Coloma. Ed. by Delly, Myron Bonham. LC 34-20387. (Half-title: Science and culture texts). The Bruce Publishing Company.

Boy. Christine De Rivoyre. Tr. by Eileen Ellenbogen from Fr. LC 74-79981. 288p. 1974. 6.95 (ISBN 0-87131-160-7). M Evans.

Boy! Ferdinand Oyono. LC 77-102972. (American Library). 1970. 1.25. Collier Books.

Boy: A Novel. James Hanley. LC 32-9371. 1932. A. A. Knopf.

Boy: A Sketch. Marie Corelli. 1900. J. B. Lippincott Company.

Boy Almighty. Frederick Feikema Manfred. LC 46-407. 1945. Itasca Press.

Boy Almighty: A Novel. Feike Feikema, pseud. LC 46-4073. 1945. The Itasca Press, a Division of the Webb Publishing Company.

Boy & the Gunfighter. Spencer Knight. (Orig.). 1979. pap. 1.50 (ISBN 0-532-15400-2). Woodhill.

Boy and the Outlaw: A Tale of John Brown's Raid on Harper's Ferry. Thomas J. Luke McManus. LC 4-27671. 1904. The Grafton Press.

Boy, and The Square Uncle. Nina Farewell, pseud. LC 67-17082. 1967. 4.50. Crown.

Boy, and The Square Uncle. Nina Farewell, pseud. (72011). 1968. Ballantine.

Boy & the Taniwha. R. L. Bacon. 1976. 4.55x o.p. (ISBN 0-8002-0767-X). Intl Pubns Serv.

Boy Apprenticed to an Enchanter. Padraic Colum. LC 20-21991. 1920. The Macmillan Company.

Boy at the Window. Owen Dodson. 212p. 1972. Repr. of 1951 ed. 7.50x (ISBN 0-911860-10-X). Chatham Bkseller.

Boy at the Window: A Novel. Owen Dodson. LC 51-9471. 1951. Farrar, Straus and Young.

Boy at the Window: A Novel. Owen Dodson. LC 74-182682. 1972. (ISBN 0-911860-10-X). Chatham Bookseller.

Boy Avengers. Karl Flinders. 224p. (Orig.). 1972. pap. 1.95 o.s.i. (T*C516). Olympia.

Boy Came Back. Charles H Knickerbocker. LC 51-13483. 1951. Wyn.

Boy Captive in Canada. Mary P. Smith. pap. 5.50. Pocumtuck Valley Mem.

Boy Captive in Old Deerfield. Mary P. Smith. (O.s.i.). 1967. 4.75 o.s.i. NH Pub Co.

Boy Captive of the Texas Mier Expedition. rev., reprinted and republished by the author; illustrations by bock. ed. Fanny Chambers Gooch Iglehart. LC 11-1761. Press of J. R. Wood Printing Co.

Boy Captive of the Texas Mier Expedition. Fanny Chambers Gooch Iglehart. LC 11-17613. Press of J. R. Wood Printing Co.

Boy Cat & the Light Mystery. Louise Wofford. 1983. pap. 5.95 (ISBN 0-932298-20-6). Copple Hse.

Boy Crazy. Grace Perkins Oursler. LC 31-29819. 1931. Covici, Friede.

Boy Crazy. Grace Perkins. 192p. 1982. pap. 2.95 (ISBN 0-441-07175-9). Ace Bks.

Boy Day. Robert Miller. LC 38-14006. 1938. Falmouth Book House.

Boy Detective: Or, The Chief of the Counterfeiters. Harlan Page Halsey. LC 7-1196. (On cover: The calumet series, no. 20). G. Munro's Sons.

Boy Emigrants. Noah Brooks. LC 4-17523. 1903. C. Scribner's Sons.

Boy from Beirut, and Other Stories. Robin Maugham & Peter G Burton. LC 82-11797. 20.00 (ISBN 0-917342-89-5) (ISBN 0-917342-90-9). Gay Sunshine Press.

Boy from Down Under. Christine Hunter, pseud. 1964. 1.50 o.p. (ISBN 0-87508-649-7). Chr Lit.

Boy from Hollow Hut: A Story of the Kentucky Mountains. Isla May Hawley Mullins. LC 11-26611. 1.60. Fleming H. Revell Company.

Boy from Ironbark & Other Tales. Herbert M. Barker. 2.95 o.p. Carlton.

Boy from Maine. Katharine Brush. LC 42-14626. 1942. Farrar & Rinehart, Inc.

Boy Gravely. Iris Dornfeld. LC 65-11101. bds., 4.95. Knopf.

Boy Grew Older. Heywood Campbell Broun. LC 22-201719. 1922. G. P. Putnam's Sons.

Boy Hungry. Kate Nickerson. 1969. pap. 0.75 o.p. (75-270). Manor Bks.

Boy Hunters. Thomas Mayne Reid. LC 68-23725. (Americans in Fiction Ser). 1968. Repr. of 1852 ed. lib. bdg. 9.00x o.p. (ISBN 0-8398-1750-9). Gregg.

Boy in Blue: A Novel. Monica Stirling. LC 55-10087. 1955. Coward-McCann.

Boy in Blue: A Novel of the Civil War. Royce Brier. 1937. D. Appleton-Century Company, Incorporated.

Boy in Darkness. Mervyn Laurence Peake. LC 76-371968. (Literature for life series). (Illus.). 1976. 0.60 (ISBN 0-08-019798-1). Wheaton.

Boy in the Bush. David Herbert Lawrence & Skinner, M. L. LC 24-23179. 1924. T. Seltzer.

Boy in the Bush. David Herbert Lawrence & Mary Louisa Skinner. LC 71-76193. (Crosscurrents: modern fiction). 1971. 10.00 (ISBN 0-8093-0456-2). Southern Illinois University Press.

Boy in the Bush. David Herbert Lawrence & Mary Louisa Skinner. LC 72-197184. (Viking compass book, C331). 1972. 2.95 (ISBN 0-670-00331-X). Viking Press.

Boy in the House, and Other Stories. 1st Ed. Mazo De La Roche. LC 52-10943. 1952. Little, Brown.

Boy in the Oil Belt. 1st Ed. Thomas Curtin. LC 52-2470. 1952. Pageant Press.

Boy in the Pool: A Novel. 1st Ed. Camilla R Bittle. LC 62-105360. 1962. Lippincott.

Boy in the Sun. Paul Rosenfeld. LC 28-23666. 1928. The Macaulay Company.

Boy King & the Witch. Dellanna Gordon. (Illus.). 124p. (Orig.). 1980. pap. 3.95 o.p. (ISBN 0-89260-180-9). Hwong Pub.

Boy Life in the United States Navy. Henry Howard Clark. LC 5-4152. 1885. Lothrop Publishing Co.

Boy Life on the Prairie. border ed. Hamlin Garland. LC 23-26596. 1923. Harper & Brothers.

Boy Life on the Prairie see Collected Works.

Boy Life on the Prairies. Hamlin Garland. LC 99-5834. 1899. The Macmillan Company.

Boy-Lollard: A Tale of the Readers of Tyndale's New Testament in the Times of Henry Vii. Frederic Alonzo Reed. LC 7-30952. Congregational Sunday-School and Publishing Society.

Boy Lost in the Wilderness. E. Slazas. 4.00 o.p. (ISBN 0-8062-0337-4). Carlton.

Boy-Loving Woman. Thomas Shire. 192p. (Orig.). 1973. pap. 1.95 o.p. (ISBN 0-87682-316-9, 7316). Barclay Hse.

Boy Madness. Douglas Duperrault. 1970. pap. 0.75 o.p. (75-301). Manor Bks.

Boy Next Door. Jean Katherine Baird. LC 10-207411. 1910. net 0.50. American Tract Society.

Boy of Sandalwood. John Kvoepple. (W.N.J. Ser.: No. 11). 1979. pap. 4.50. Juniper Pr WI.

Boy of the First Empire. Elbridge Streeter Brooks. LC 4-16454. 1895. The Century Co.

Boy of the Shoals. Christina M Welch. (Illus.). 1973. 5.95 (ISBN 0-533-00578-7). Vantage Press.

Boy Off the Farm. Irid Bjerk. 272p. pap. 11.95 (ISBN 0-931170-18-4). Ctr Western Studies.

Boy on the Block. Gene North. (Orig.). 1969. pap. 1.95 o.p. (7076). Barclay Hse.

Boy or Girl? Elizabeth Whelan. 1979. pap. 2.50 (ISBN 0-671-42283-9). PB.

Boy Scouts Patrol. Ralph Victor. LC 11-51910. A. L. Chatterton Co.

Boy Sexual. Thomas D'Alest. 160p. (Orig.). 1972. pap. 1.95 o.s.i. (TC 3318). Olympia.

Boy, the Deputies, the Jail: A Novel of Juvenile Deliquency. Frank James McSpaden. 1973. 5.50 (ISBN 0-87164-107-0). William-F.

Boy, the Deputies, the Jail: The Story of Joey. Frank James McSpaden. LC 79-94445. 1970. 4.40. William-Frederick Press.

Boy Who Followed Ripley. Patricia Highsmith. LC 79-29678. 11.50 (ISBN 0-690-01678-6) (ISBN 0-690-01911-4). Lippincott & Crowell.

Boy Who Invented the Bubble Gun. Paul Gallico. 1975. (pbk.) 1.50. Dell.

Boy Who Invented the Bubble Gun: An Odyssey of Innocence. Paul Gallico. LC 73-20287. 1974. 6.95 (ISBN 0-440-01789-0). Delacorte Press.

Boy Who Looked Like Shirley Temple. Bill Mahan. LC 79-25428. 10.95 (ISBN 0-312-09403-5). St. Martin's Press.

Boy Who Looked Like Shirley Temple. Bill Mahan. LC 80-29295. 1981. 14.95 (ISBN 0-8161-3155-4). G. K. Hall.

Boy Who Made Good: A Novel. Mary Deasy. LC 55-11225. 1955. Little, Brown.

Boy Who Saw Tomorrow: By Ian Niall Pseud. John McNeillie. LC 53-870228. 1953. Appleton-Century-Crofts.

Boy Who Set the Fire. Mohammed Mrabet. Tr. by Paul Bowles. 123p. (Orig.). 1978. 10.00 (ISBN 0-87685-175-8). Black Sparrow.

Boy Who Was Trained up to Be a Clergyman. 4th ed., rev., with an appendix. ed. John Nicholas Norton. LC 39-17501. 1857. H. Hooker.

Boy Who Would Not Listen. B. Palmer. (Danny Orlis Ser.). pap. 0.95 o.p. Believers Bkshelf.

Boy with a Gun. 1st Ed. James Dean Sanderson. LC 58-7648. 1958. Holt.

Boy with a Million: What He Did with It. Dozean Dreame. (On cover: University ser. no. 1). 1893. Rittenhouse & Company.

Boy with a Trumpet, and Other Selected Short Stories: With an Introd. by Bucklin Moon. 1st Ed. Rhys Davies. LC 51-1161. 1951. Doubleday.

Boy with Kite. Samantha Harvey. (Harlequin Romances Ser.). 192p. 1983. pap. 1.75 (ISBN 0-373-02541-6). Harlequin Bks.

Boy with the U.S. Census. Francis William Rolt-Wheeler. LC 11-31637. (His U.S. service series) $1.50). 1911. Lothrop, Lee & Shepard Co.

Boy with the U.S. Fisheries. Francis William Rolt-Wheeler. LC 12-25846. (His U.S. service series). 1912. Lothrop, Lee & Shepard Co.

Boy with Wings. Berta Ruck. LC 15-26844. 1915. 1.35. Dodd, Mead and Company.

Boy Woodburn: A Story of the Sussex Downs. Alfred Ollivant. LC 18-5502. 1918. Doubleday, Page & Company.

Boyar of the Terrible: A Romance of the Court of Ivan the Cruel, First Tsar of Russia. Frederick J Whishaw. 1896. Longmans, Green, and Co.

Boychick: A Novel. Leo Skir. LC 75-127424. 1971. 5.95 (ISBN 0-87806-010-3). Winter House.

Boyds of Black River. Walter Dumaux Edmonds. LC 53-5094. 1953. Dodd, Mead.

Boyhood Days on the Farm: A Story for Young and Old Boys. Charles Clark Munn. 1907. Lothrop. Lee & Shepard Co.

Boyhood of Diego Rivera. Leah Brenner. LC 64-16274. 1964. A. S. Barnes.

Boyhood of Grace Jones. Jane Langton. (Illus.). 1975. (pbk.) 1.50 (ISBN 0-06-440065-4). Harper & Row.

Boyne Water: A Tale. John Banim. LC 78-16349. (Ireland, from the Act of Union, 1800, to the Death of Parnell, 1891; No. 17). 1979. 96.00 (ISBN 0-8240-3466-X). Garland Pub.

Boyne Water: A Tale of the O'Hara Family, 3 vols. John Banim & Michael Banim. Ed. by Robert L. Wolff. (Ireland Nineteenth Century Fiction Ser. Two: Vol. 17). 1329p. 1979. Set. lib. bdg. 96.00 (ISBN 0-8240-3466-X). Garland Pub.

Boys. George Sumner Albee. LC 57-9142. 1958. Ballantine Books.

Boys' Adventure Library. Ed. by Katharine Isabel Bemis. LC 32-23881. Fleming H. Revell Company.

Boys and Ghouls Together. Ed. by Alfred Hitchcock. 1974. (pbk.) 0.95. Dell.

Boys and Girls Come Out to Play. Vera Randal. LC 74-16611. 1975. 6.95 (ISBN 0-399-11458-0). Putnam.

Boys & Girls Together. William Goldman. (N2981). 1965. Bantam.

Boys and Girls Together. William Goldman. LC 64-18889. 1964. Atheneum.

Boys and Girls Together. William Saroyan. LC 63-10597. 1963. Harcourt, Brace & World.

Boys and Men: A Story of Life at Yale. Richard Thayer Holbrook. 1900. C. Scribner's Sons.

Boy's Day & Other Stories. Richard A. Tool. 151p. 1975. 6.00 o.p. (ISBN 0-682-48275-7). Exposition.

Boys from Brazil. Ira Levin. LC 76-18852. 1976. 12.95 (ISBN 0-8161-6392-8). G. K. Hall.

Boys from Brazil. Ira Levin. (Dell Book). 1977. 2.25 (ISBN 0-440-10760-1). Dell Pub. Co.

Boys from Brazil: A Novel. Ira Levin. LC 75-33864. 8.95 (ISBN 0-394-40267-7). Random House.

Boys from Sharon. Louise Field Cooper. 1973. (pbk.) 1.25. Warner Paperback Lib.

Boys from Sharon. 1st Ed. Louise Field Cooper. LC 50-6640. 1950. Harper.

Boys in the Back Room. Jules Romains & Le Clercq, Jacques Georges Clemenceau, 1896- Tr. LC 37-5027. 1937. R. M. McBride & Company.

Boys in the Mail Room. Iris Rainer. 1981. 2.95 (ISBN 0-446-93676-6). Warner Books.

Boys in the Mail Room: A Novel. Iris Rainer. LC 79-20642. 1980. 9.95 (ISBN 0-688-03562-0). Morrow.

Boy's Novel. Barry Gifford. LC 72-92712. 1973. pap. 2.75 o.p. (ISBN 0-87922-014-7). Christopher's Bks.

Boys of Scrooby. Ruth Hall. LC 99-4210. 1899. Houghton, Mifflin and Company.

Boys of the Revolution. Everett Titsworth Tomlinson. LC 13-17000. (Stories of colony and nation.). Silver, Burdett and Company.

Boy's Own Story. Edmund White. LC 82-9536. 13.95 (ISBN 0-525-24128-0). Dutton.

Boy's Town. William Dean Howells. 1973. lib. bdg. 25.00 (ISBN 0-8414-5135-4). Folcroft.

Boy's Town. William Dean Howells. LC 75-131748. 247p. 1890. Repr. 10.00 (ISBN 0-403-00635-X). Scholarly.

Boy's Vision. Hervey White. The Maverick Press.

Boy's Way. August William Derleth. 4.95 (ISBN 0-88361-045-0). Stanton & Lee.

Boysi Himself. Glenn Allan. LC 46-2894. 1946. S. Curl Inc.

Bozambo's Revenge. Bertene Juminer. Tr. by Alexandre B. Warren from Fr. (Sun Lit Ser.). Orig. Title: Revanche De Bozambo. 117p. 1981. 10.00x (ISBN 0-89410-172-2); pap. 5.00x (ISBN 0-89410-173-0); orig. cased ed. 14.00 (ISBN 0-914478-09-5). Three Continents.

Bozambo's Revenge: Or, Colonialism Inside Out: a Novel. Bertene Juminer. LC 75-42512. 14.00. (ISBN 0-914478-09-5) (ISBN 0-914478-10-9). Three Continents Press.

Bozland: Dickens' Places & People. Percy Fitzgerald. LC 70-141754. 1971. Repr. of 1895 ed. 34.00 o.p. (ISBN 0-8103-3616-2). Gale.

Bra-Burners' Brigade. Mallory T. Knight. (Man from T. O. M. C. A. T. Ser). (Orig.). 1971. pap. 0.75 o.p. (A788S, Award). Univ Pub & Dist.

Bracebridge Hall. Washington Irving. LC 78-16387. (Illus.). Repr. of 1876 ed. 12.00 (ISBN 0-912882-35-2). Sleepy Hollow.

Bracebridge Hall: Or, The Humourists. A Medley. Washington Irving. (On cover: Lovell's library, v. 3, no. 281). 1883. J. W. Lovell Company.

Bracebridge Hall: Washington Irving. Ed. by Herbert F. Smith. (Critical Editions Program). 1977. lib. bdg. 25.00 (ISBN 0-8057-8506-X, Twayne). G K Hall.

Bracegirdle. Burris Atkins Jenkins. LC 22-602625. 1922. J. B. Lippincott Company.

Bracelet. Robert Smythe Hichens. LC 30-24349. 1930. Cosmopolitan Book Corporation.

Bracelet of Garnets, and Other Stories. Aleksandr Ivanovich Kuprin. Tr. by Pasvolsky, Leo. LC 17-13619. 1917. C. Scribner's Sons.

Bracelet of Wavia Lea: And Other Short Stories. Bessie Breuer. LC 47-11481. 1947. W. Sloane Associates.

Bracelet. 1st Ed. Beatrice Page. LC 52-13056. 1953. Bobbs-Merrill.

Bracero. Eugene Nelson. (Illus.). 309p. 1975. pap. 3.95 o.p. (ISBN 0-915238-00-4). Peace Pr.

Bracken: A Novel. Ernest George Henham. LC 13-1157. 1911. M. Kennerley.

Brackenford Story. Michael Home, pseud. LC 52-9007. 1952. Macmillan.

Brackenford Story: By Michael Home Pseud. Christopher Bush. LC 52-9007. 1952. Macmillan.

Brackenroyd Inheritance. Erica Lindley. (Signet Book). 1975. (pbk.) 1.50. New American Library.

Brackenroyd Inheritance. Eileen Quigley. (Orig.). 1975. pap. 1.50 (ISBN 0-451-06795-9, W6795, Sig). NAL.

Bracken's World. Daoma Winston. (Orig.). 1969. pap. 0.75 o.p. (64-237). Paperback Lib.

Bracken's World, No. 2# The High Country. Daoma Winston. (Bracken's World Ser). (Orig.). 1970. pap. 0.75 o.p. (64-279). Paperback Lib.

Bracken's World, No. 3# Sound Stage. Daoma Winston. (Orig.). 1970. pap. 0.75 o.p. (64-364). Paperback Lib.

Brackie, the Fool. Alfred Henschke & Herman George Schaeffauer. LC 27-8548. 1927. G. P. Putnam's Sons.

Bracknell's Law. Edmund Wallace Hildick. LC 76-373208. 1976. 3.50 (ISBN 0-241-89313-5). H. Hamilton.

Braddock: A Story of the French and Indian Wars. John Roy Musick. LC 7-32294. (On cover: Columbian historical novels. v. 8). 1893. Funk & Wagnalls Company.

Braddock's Gold: A Story of Adventure. Samuel Woods Shingleton. LC 80-81390. (Illus.). 1980. 3.50 (ISBN 0-87012-383-1). McClain Print. Co.

Bradford Horton: Man: A Novel. Richard Sill Holmes. LC 13-23201. 1.25. Fleming H. Revell Company.

Bradford Masters. Sherman Baker. LC 49-12586. 1949. E. P. Dutton.

Bradford Story. Amelia Elizabeth Walden. LC 56-857210. 1956. Appleton-Century-Crofts.

Brading Collection. Patricia Wentworth. 1969. pap. 0.75 o.p. (T2096). Pyramid Pubns.

Bradley Beach Rumba. David A Kaufelt. LC 74-79651. 1974. 6.95 (ISBN 0-399-11371-1). Putnam.

Bradmoor Murder. Melville Davisson Post. 297p. 1980. Repr. of 1929 ed. lib. bdg. 14.25x (ISBN 0-89968-197-2). Lightyear.

Bradshaws of Harniss. Joseph Crosby Lincoln. LC 43-15653. 1943. D. Appleton-Century Company, Incorporated.

Brady Bunch. William Johnston. 1969. pap. 0.60 o.p. (ISBN 0-447-73849-6). Lancer.

Braes of Yarrow. Charles Gibbon. (Franklin square library, no. 211). 1881. Harper & Brothers.

Braganza Pursuit. Sarah Neilan. LC 76-10033. 7.95 (ISBN 0-525-07047-8). Dutton.

Bragelonne, the Son of Athos: Or, Ten Year Later. Being the Conclusion of "The Three Guardsmen" and "Twenty Years After.". Alexandre Dumas & Maquet, Auguste. Tr. by Williams, Thoams. LC 6-42113. 1848. W. E. Dean.

Bragg, No. 3: Pieces of Death. Jack Lynch. 192p. 1982. pap. 2.50 (ISBN 0-449-14473-9, GM). Fawcett.

Brahmin Arrangement. Andrew Tully. LC 74-79686. 1974. 8.95 (ISBN 0-698-10623-7). Coward, McCann & Geoghegan.

Braid Circle. 1st Ed. Dee Burke Lopez. LC 56-11208. Vantage Press.

Braided Lives. Marge Piercy. 480p. 1982. 15.50 (ISBN 0-671-43834-4). Summit Bks.

Braided Lives. Marge Piercy. 576p. 1983. pap. 3.95 (ISBN 0-449-20018-3, Crest). Fawcett.

Brain. Robin Cook. LC 80-21361. 11.95 (ISBN 0-399-12563-9). Putman.

Brain. large print ed. Robin Cook. LC 81-14457. 11.95 (ISBN 0-89621-317-X). Thorndike Press.

Brain Drain. Warren Murphy. (Destroyer Ser.: No. 22). 192p. (Orig.). 1976. pap. 1.75 (ISBN 0-523-40898-6). Pinnacle Bks.

Brain Drain. Richard Sapir & Warren Murphy. 1976. (pbk.) 1.25 (ISBN 0-523-00805-8). Pinnacle Books.

Brain Guy. Benjamin Appel. LC 34-22374. 1934. A.A. Knopf.

Brain Machine. George Oliver Smith. LC 75-425. (Garland Library of Science Fiction). 1975. 11.00 (ISBN 0-8240-1430-8). Garland Pub.

Brain of the Planet. Mary M. Wright. LC 44-15712. (Science fiction series, no. 5). Stellar Publishing Corporation.

Brain Pickers. Hallie Southgate Burnett. LC 57-10508. 1957. J. Messner.

Brain Scavengers. Paul Edwards. 1973. (pbk) 0.95. Pyramid Books.

Brain-Stealers: By Murray Leinster Pseud. William Fitzgerald Jenkins. LC 55-164880. (Ace double novel books, D-79). 1954. Ace Books.

Brain Surgeon. Lawrence Shainberg. 320p. 1980. pap. 2.50 (ISBN 0-449-24308-7, Crest). Fawcett.

Brain Trust Murder. John Franklin Carter. LC 35-336480. 1935. Coward-McCann.

Brain Two Thousand. Ernest Kellogg Gann. LC 79-7048. 384p. 1980. 13.95 (ISBN 0-385-14393-1). Doubleday.

Brain Wave. Poul Anderson. LC 54-8910. (Ballantine books, 80). 1954. Ballantine Books.

Brain Wave. Poul Anderson. LC 69-14240. 1969. 4.50. Walker.

Brain-Waves and Death. Willard Rich. LC 40-831659. 1940. C. Scribner's Sons.

Brain World. Mack Reynolds, pseud. 1978. pap. 1.75 o.s.i. (ISBN 0-8439-0595-6, Leisure Bks). Nordon Pubns.

Brainchild. J. M. Johnston. (Orig.). 1979. pap. 1.95 (ISBN 0-532-23141-4). Woodhill.

Brainchild. Andrew Neiderman. (Orig.). 1981. pap. 2.75 (ISBN 0-671-42830-6). PB.

Brainfire. Campbell Black. LC 79-14594. 1979. 10.95 (ISBN 0-688-03524-8). Morrow.

Brainrack. Kit Pedler & Gerry Davis. 1975. (pbk.) 1.50 (ISBN 0-671-78943-0). Pocket Books.

Brains of the Family: A Side-Splitting Domestic Comedy. E. J Rath. LC 25-4767. 1925. G. H. Watt.

Brainstorms. Michael Brownstein. LC 71-142469. 1971. 5.00 o.p. (ISBN 0-672-51553-9); pap. 2.45 o.p. (ISBN 0-672-51554-7). Bobbs.

Braintree Mission: A Fictional Narrative of London and Boston, 1770-1771. Nicholas Elston Wyckoff. LC 57-6353. 1957. Macmillan.

Brainwash. John William Wainwright. LC 79-5057. 1979. 8.95 (ISBN 0-312-09440-X). St. Martin's Press.

Brainwashing. Edward Hunter. 1962. pap. 0.75 o.p. (T759). Pyramid Pubns.

Brak the Barbarian Versus the Mark of the Demons. John Jakes. (Brak the Barbarian Ser). (Orig.). 1969. pap. 0.60 o.p. (ISBN 0-446-63184-1, 63-184). Paperback Lib.

Brak the Barbarian Versus the Sorceress. John Jakes. (Orig.). 1969. pap. 0.60 o.p. (ISBN 0-446-63089-6, 63-089). Paperback Lib.

Brakespeare: Or, The Fortunes of a Free Lance. George Alfred Lawrence. LC 4-16438. 1904. F. M. Buckles & Company.

Bram. Charles Pelton Jacobs. LC 27-25921. E. J. Clode, Inc.

Bram of the Five Corners. Arnold Mulder. LC 15-7475. 1915. 1.25. A. C. McClurg & Co.

Bram Stoker Bedside Companion: Ten Stories by the Author of Dracula. Bram Stoker. Ed. by Charles Osborne. LC 72-7717. 1979. pap. 4.95 (ISBN 0-8008-0964-5). Taplinger.

Bram Stoker Bedside Companion: 10 Stories by the Author of Dracula. Ed. by Charles Osborne. LC 72-7717. 224p. 1973. 7.95 (ISBN 0-8008-0963-7). Taplinger.

Bram Stoker Bedside Companion: 10 Stories by the Author of Dracula. Bram Stoker. LC 72-7717. 1973. 6.50 (ISBN 0-8008-0963-7). Taplinger Pub. Co.

Bramble Bush. David Duncan. LC 48-7556. 1948. Macmillan Co.

Bramble Bush. Caroline Macomber Fuller. LC 11-6023. 1911. 1.25. D. Appleton and Company.

Bramble Bush. Charles Henry Mergendahl. LC 58-10754. 1958. Putnam.

Bramleighs of Bishop's Folly. By Charles Lever. With Illustrations by W. Cubitt Cooke, and E. J. Wheeler. Charles James Lever. LC 24-11855. (Half-title: The novels of Charles Lever. Library edition. Novels of foreign life). 1901. Little, Brown, and Company.

Brampton Sketches: Old-Time New England Life. Mary Bucklin Davenport Claflin. LC 6-25376. T.Y. Crowell & Co.

Bramton Wick. Elizabeth Fair. LC 54-6355. 1954. Funk & Wagnalls Co.

Branch-Bearers. Glen Petrie. LC 73-79227. 308p. 1973. 6.95 o.p. (ISBN 0-8128-1633-1). Stein & Day.

Branch Bearers. Glen Petrie. LC 73-79227. 1975. (pbk.) 1.50 (ISBN 0-671-78760-8). Pocket Books.

Branching Coral. James Arthur Stewart. LC 61-6091. 1961. Viking Press.

Brand. Orlando Rigoni. 1973. 4.95 (ISBN 0-517-51447-8). Lenox Hill Press.

Brand: A Tale of the Flathead Reservation. Therese Broderick. LC 9-31023. 1909. The Alice Harriman Company.

Brand Blotter: By Chuck Stanley. Charles Stanley Strong. LC 56-7020. Arcadia House.

Brand Blotters. Robert Ames Bennet. LC 39-27343. I. Washburn, Inc.

Brand Blotters. William MacLeod Raine. LC 12-21402. G. W. Dillingham Company.

Brand for the Burning. Don Lawson. LC 61-666212. 1961. Abelard-Schuman.

Brand Him Gunfighter. Alex Hawk, pseud. (Alex Hawk). (Orig.). 1970. pap. 0.60 o.p. (63-443). Paperback Lib.

Brand Inheritance. Dorothy Fletcher. (Orig.). 1973. pap. 0.95 o.s.i. (75-439). Lancer.

Brand New Doctor. Raymond Smith Devney. LC 8-34598. 1908. J. E. Hughes, Printer.

Brand New Life. James Thomas Farrell. LC 68-14217. (O.s.i.). 384p. 1973. pap. 1.50 o.s.i. (ISBN 0-532-15111-9). Woodhill.

Brand New Life. James Thomas Farrell. LC 68-14217. 1968. 5.95 o.p. Doubleday.

Brand New Life. James Thomas Farrell. LC 68-14217. (O.s.i.). 384p. 1973. pap. 1.50 o.s.i. (ISBN 0-532-15111-9). Manor Bks.

Brand New Parson. Sara Lucile Jenkins. LC 51-763. 1951. Crowell.

Brand New World. Ray Cummings. (Science Fiction From the Great Years Series). 1976. (pbk.) 1.25. Ace Books.

Brand of a Man. Thomas Thompson. LC 58-8110. 1958. Doubleday.

Brand of a Texan. Steven C. Lawrence, pseud. 1971. pap. 0.60 o.p. (R2397, GM). Fawcett World.

Brand of Cain: By Wade B. Cantrell Pseud. Robert J Hogan. LC 56-38208. (Pyramid books, 173). 1955. Pyramid Books.

Brand of Empire. Luke Short. (Dell Book). 1977. 1.25 (ISBN 0-440-10770-9). Dell Pub. Co.

Brand of Fear. Brad Lang. 1976. 1.25. Leisure Books.

Brand of Fury: A Western Novel by Jack Barton Pseud. Joseph Chadwick. LC 55-32831. (Popular library, 659). 1955. Popular Library.

Brand of Mirra Peena: An Outback Story. Edwin W. Barclay. 1982. 7.95 (ISBN 0-533-04864-8). Vantage.

Brand of Passion. Shirley Hart. (Candlelight Ecstacy Ser.: No. 107). (Orig.). 1983. pap. 1.95 (ISBN 0-440-10324-X). Dell.

Brand of Possession. Carole Mortimer. (Harlequin Presents Ser.). 192p. (Orig.). 1981. pap. 1.50 (ISBN 0-373-10406-5, Pub. by Harlequin). PB.

Brand of the Beast. Michael Arthur Lewis. LC 25-19434. 1925. L. Mac Veagh, The Dial Press.

Brand of the Damned. Jeffrey M. Wallmann. (Bronc: No. 1). 192p. 1982. pap. 1.95 o.s.i. (ISBN 0-8439-0983-8, Leisure Bks). Nordon Pubns.

Brand of the Outlaw. Paul Evan Lehman. LC 42-15556. (On cover: The Western novel of the month, no. 11). 1942. Hillman Periodicals, Inc.

Brand of the Outlaw. Al P. Nelson. 1970. pap. 0.75 o.p. (ISBN 0-447-74638-3). Lancer.

Brand of the Sea: Havet. Knud Andersen. Tr. by Colbron, Grace Isabel. LC 29-4756. The Century Co.

Brand of the Star. Theodore V. Olsen. 1970. pap. 0.60 o.p. (R2220, GM). Fawcett World.

Brand of Vengeance. Charles R. Pike, pseud. LC 80-70091. (Jubal Cade Westerns Ser.). 142p. 1981. pap. 2.95 (ISBN 0-87754-240-6). Chelsea Hse.

Brand of Yuma. Pete Stolpacker. (Orig.). 1979. pap. 1.95 (ISBN 0-532-23159-7). Woodhill.

Brand Rider. Ed La Vanway. (Silver star westerns). 1958. Dodd, Mead.

Brand Stealer. Charles Horace Snow. LC 42-7968. 1942. Macrae-Smith-Company.

Brand Whitlock's The Buckeyes: Politics and Abolitionism in an Ohio Town, 1836-1845. Brand Whitlock. LC 76-8306. (Illus.). 12.00. (ISBN 0-8214-0222-6). Ohio University Press.

Brand-X Anthology of Fiction: A Parody Anthology. Ed. by William Zaranka. (Illus.). 356p. 1983. 17.95 (ISBN 0-918222-41-9); prepub. 11.95 (ISBN 0-918222-42-7). Apple Wood.

Branded. Robert Ames Bennet. LC 24-27645. 1924. A. C. McClurg & Co.

Branded. Rosalie Cates. LC 79-19211. 1981. 12.95 (ISBN 0-87949-147-7). Ashley Bks.

Branded. Ray Conley. 192p. (Orig.). 1982. pap. 1.95 (ISBN 0-8439-0953-6). Leisure Bks CT.

Branded. Francis Lynde. LC 18-9077. 1918. C. Scribner's Sons.

Branded Bride. Carter A. Vaughan. (Hall of Fame Historical Novels). 1980. pap. 2.25 (ISBN 0-441-07810-9). Ace Bks.

Branded: By A. C. Abbott Pseud. 1st Ed. H A Meinzer. LC 53-6631. 1953. World Pub. Co.

Branded Lawman. William E Vance. LC 53-18611. (Ace double novel books, D-6). 1952. Ace Books.

Branded Man. Hal George Evarts. 1965. pap. 0.60 o.p. (R2496, GM). Fawcett World.

Branded Man. Luke Short. 1980. pap. 1.75 (ISBN 0-440-10785-7). Dell.

Branded Men. Frank Chester Robertson. LC 36-758941. Dodge Publishing Company.

Branded Men and Women: Story of a Western Town. William Francis Hooker. LC 22-4778. R. G. Badger.

Branded Spy Murders: A Captain North Mystery... Francis Van Wyck Mason. LC 32-82421. Pub. for the Crime Club, Inc., by Doubleday, Doran & Company, Inc.

Branded West: A Western Writers of America Anthology. Ed. by Don Ward. (Signet Brand Western). 1973. (pbk.) 0.75. New American Lib.

Branded West: A Western Writers of America Anthology. Western Writers of America. Ed. by Don Ward. LC 56-11846. 1956. Houghton Mifflin.

Branded West: An Anthology. Western Writers Of America. Ed. by Don Ward. LC 73-116967. (Short Story Index Reprint Ser). 1956. 16.00 (ISBN 0-8369-3471-7). Ayer Co.

Brandenburg Affair. Stanley White. LC 79-305000. 1979. 10.95 (ISBN 0-09-136330-6). Hutchinson.

Brandenburg Hotel. Pauline Glen Winslow. LC 75-26199. 8.95. St. Martin's Press.

Branding Bullets. Stetson Cody. LC 73-152515. 1972. 4.95 (ISBN 0-7075-0014-1). (Baker St., WM FA), Gold Lion Books Ltd.

Branding Iron. Katharine Newlin Burt. LC 19-13365. 1919. Houghton Mifflin Company.

Branding Iron. 1st Ed. John Burnis Allred. LC 55-7361. 1955. Pageant Press.

Branding Needle: Or, The Monastery of Charolles, a Tale of the First Communal Charter. Eugene Sue & De Leon, Daniel, 1852-1914, Tr. LC 8-19717. 1908. New York Labor News Company.

Brandon Affair. Charles Whited. (Signet Book). 1977. 1.75 (ISBN 0-451-07283-9). New American Library.

Brandon Case. Alfred Walter Stewart. LC 34-29567. 1934. Little, Brown, and Company.

Brandon Coyle's Wife: A Sequel to "A Skeleton in the Closet.". Emma Dorothy Eliza Nevitte Southworth. LC 8-14240. (On cover: The Ledger library, no. 93). 1893. R. Bonner's Sons.

Brandon Is Missing. Dennis Allan. LC 40-8380. 1940. M. S. Mill Co., Inc.

Brandon Is Missing. Elinore Denniston. LC 40-8380. 1940. M. S. Mill Co., Inc.

Brandon of the Engineers. Harold Bindloss. LC 16-242021. Frederick A. Stokes Cpmpany.

Brandon: Or, A Hundred Years Ago. A Tale of the American Colonies. Osmond Tiffany. LC 8-17690. 1858. Stanford & Delisser.

Brandons. Angela Mackail Thirkell. LC 39-27473. 1939. A. A. Knopf.

Brandon's Empire. Llewellyn Perry Holmes. 1979. 1.75 (ISBN 0-445-04370-9). Popular Library.

Brandon's Empire: By Dave Hardin Pseud. Llewellyn Perry Holmes. LC 53-13037. 1953. Ballantine Books.

Brands from the Burning. Ed. by Buford M Johnson. LC 52-34942. 1952. White Wing Pub. House & Press.

Brandy for a Hero. William O'Farrell. LC 48-5440. (A Bloodhound mystery). 1948. Duell, Slan and Pearce.

Brandy for the Parson. Raymond Foxall. LC 73-87401. 1974. 6.95. St. Martin's Press.

Brandy for the Parson. Raymond Foxall. 1976. 1.50 (ISBN 0-671-80737-4). Pocket Books.

Brandy in the Snow. Frederic Will. 1972. 5.00 (Pub. by New Rivers Pr); signed 10.00; pap. 2.50. SBD.

Brandy Kane. Constance Gluyas. 384p. 1983. pap. 3.50 (ISBN 0-451-12001-9, Sig). NAL.

Brandy's Awakening. Jean Woodard. 1982. 6.95 (Avalon). Bouregy.

Brandywine's War. Robert Vaughan & Monroe Lynch. (Crest Book, M1757). 1972. 0.95. Fawcett.

Brandywine's War. Robert Vaughan & Monroe Lynch. LC 77-155027. 1971. 5.95 (ISBN 0-87794-028-2). Bartholomew House.

Brann the Iconoclast: A Collection of the Writings of W. C. Brann... William Cowper Brann. LC 25-24428. 1911. Herz Brothers.

Brannigan. Ed Newsom. 208p. (Orig.). 1981. pap. 1.95 (ISBN 0-89083-713-9). Zebra.

Brannigan, No. 4: The Peacekeeper. Ed Newsom. 1983. pap. 2.25 (ISBN 0-8217-1163-6). Zebra.

Brannington's Leopard. Forrest Webb. LC 73-81453. 1974. 6.95 (ISBN 0-385-07371-2). Doubleday.

Bransford in Arcadia: Or, The Little Eohippus. new ed. Eugene Manlove Rhodes. LC 74-15905. (Western frontier library). 1975. 3.95 (ISBN 0-8061-1261-1). University of Oklahoma Press.

Bransford in Arcadia: Or, The Little Eohippus. Eugene Manlove Rhodes. LC 14-2899. 1914. H. Holt and Company.

Brant Adams: The Emperor of Detectives. Harlan Page Halsey. LC 7-1195. (Secret service series. no. 1). Street & Smith.

Brant's Bear. James A. Brody. 1978. 7.95 (ISBN 0-533-03680-1). Vantage.

Bras D'acier: Or, On the Gold-Path in '49. Alfred Guezenec. Tr. by Estociet, A. LC 7-141. Cassell Publishing Company.

Brashki: A Gypsy Fantasy. Barbara Housh. LC 79-18242. 8.95 (ISBN 0-8362-6109-7). Andrews and McMeel.

Brashtown Marshal. Charles O. Dorman. 1970. 2.95 o.p. Carlton.

Brass: A Novel of Marriage. Charles Gilman Norris. LC 21-16377. E. P. Dutton & Company.

Brass: A Novel of Marriage. Charles Gilman Norris. LC 23-6842. 1923. E. P. Dutton & Company.

Brass and the Blue: By James Keene Pseud. Will Cook. LC 56-8803. 1956. Random House.

Brass Bell: Or, The Chariot of Death, a Tale of Caesar's Gallic Invasion. Eugene Sue & De Leon, Solon, Tr. LC 7-39192. 1907. New York Labor News Company.

Brass Bottle. Thomas Anstey Guthrie. LC 5419. 1900. D. Appleton & Company.

Brass Bowl. Louis Joseph Vance. LC 7-12274. 1907. The Bobbs-Merrill Company.

Brass Butterfly. Gerald Jay Goldberg. 80p. 1969. pap. 4.95 (ISBN 0-571-09073-7). Faber & Faber.

Brass Buttons. Frank Leslie Hower. LC 41-6795. Dorrance and Company.

Brass Cannon. Charles Allen Smart. LC 33-4733. W. W. Norton & Company, Inc.

Brass Chills. Judson Pentecost Philips. LC 43-5355. 1943. Dodd, Mead & Company.

Brass Command: An Account of a Career Officer's Last Chance, and of the Base-Metal Rewards of Military Ambition in an Indian Territory Garrison of the Late 1870's, by Clay Fisher Pseud. Henry Allen. LC 55-6128. 1955. Houghton Mifflin.

Brass Commandments. Charles Alden Seltzer. LC 23-11810. 1923. The Century Co.

Brass Cupcake. John Dann MacDonald. LC 50-54781. (Gold medal book, 124). 1950. Fawcett Publications.

Brass Diamonds: A Novel. Berent Sandberg. LC 80-16977. 8.95 (ISBN 0-453-00383-4). New American Library.

Brass Dragon. Marion Zimmer Bradley. 1980. pap. 2.25 (ISBN 0-441-07180-5). Ace Bks.

Brass-Eagles. Sarah Henry Atherton. LC 35-14232. J. B. Lippincott Company.

Brass Go-Between. Oliver Bleeck. LC 82-48806. 224p. 1983. pap. 2.84i (ISBN 0-06-080645-1, P 645, PL). Har-Row.

Brass Go-Between. Oliver Bleeck. 1969. 5.95 o.p. Morrow.

Brass Go-Between. Ross Thomas. LC 76-81885. 1969. 5.95. Morrow.

Brass God. Richard Gibson Hubler. LC 52-11713. 1952. Coward-McCann.

Brass Gong Tree. James Warner Bellah. LC 36-190903. 1936. D. Appleton-Century Company, Incorporated.

Brass Halo. Jack Webb. LC 57-12551. (A Father Shanley -- Sammy Golden mystery). 1957. Rinehart.

Brass Kangaroo. Dusty Wolfe. LC 75-315179. 1973. 2.50 (ISBN 0-85887-016-9). Allara Publishing Co.

Brass Key. Francis Swann. LC 64-12510. (Inner sanctum mystery). 1964. Simon and Schuster.

Brass Knocker. Edward Rathbone. LC 34-20567. 1934. D. Appleton-Century Company, Incorporated.

Brass Knuckles: The Oliver Quade, Human Encyclopedia, Stories. Special Foreword: The Life and Times of the Pulp Story. Frank Gruber. LC 66-18299. 1966. bds., 5.95. Sherbourne.

Brass Rainbow. Michael Collins, pseud. LC 69-12468. (Red Badge Mystery Ser.). 1969. 3.95 o.p. (ISBN 0-396-05862-0). Dodd.

Brass Rainbow. Michael Collins, pseud. LC 79-57533. (Dan Fortune Detective Ser.). 192p. 1982. pap. 2.50 (ISBN 0-86721-016-8). Playboy Pbks.

Brass Rainbow. Michael Collins, pseud. LC 79-57533. (Dan Fortune Detective Mystery Ser.). 192p. 1980. pap. 1.95 (ISBN 0-87216-672-4). Playboy Pbks.

Brass Rainbow. Dennis Lynds. LC 69-12468. (Red badge mystery). 1969. 3.95. Dodd, Mead.

Brass Ring. Dorris M. Blough. (Illus.). 1975. (pbk.) 1.25 (ISBN 0-87178-105-0). Brethren Press.

Brass Ring. Henry Kuttner. LC 46-7706. 1946. Duell, Sloan and Pearce.

Brass Ring. Lapotko. 1971. pap. 1.95 (ISBN 0-87140-258-0). Liveright.

Brass Tacks. Homer Sherman. LC 18-15378. 1918. Miller Publishing Company.

Brass Target. Frederick W. Nolan. (Jove/HBJ book). 1978. 1.75 (ISBN 0-515-04849-6). Jove Pubns.

Brassbound. Mary Dupuy Bickel. LC 34-30546. 1934. Coward, McCann, Inc.

Brassbounder. David William Bone. LC 21-10400. E. P. Dutton & Company.

Brassington's Baby. William Kaye. Licari Press, Inc.

Brat. E. J. Rath. LC 27-13129. 1927. G. H. Watt.

Brat Farrar. Elizabeth Mackintosh. (Kangaroo Book). 1977. 1.75 (ISBN 0-671-80973-3). Pocket Books.

Brat Farrar. Elizabeth Mackintosh. LC 79-19666. 1981. 10.00 (ISBN 0-8376-0445-1). R. Bentley.

Brat Farrar. Josephine Tey. LC 79-19666. 1981. Repr. of 1949 ed. lib. bdg. 10.00x (ISBN 0-8376-0445-1). Bentley.

Brat Farrar. Josephine Tey. 1971. pap. 1.25 (ISBN 0-425-03031-8, Medallion). Berkley Pub.

Brat Farrar. large print ed. Josephine Tey. 1967. 6.95 o.p. (ISBN 0-02-489460-5). Macmillan.

Brat Farrar. Josephine Tey. 1982. pap. 2.95 (ISBN 0-671-44190-6). PB.

Brat Farrar: By Josephine Tey. Elizabeth Mackintosh. LC 67-7048. 1967. 6.95. Macmillan.

Bratsk Station & Other New Poems. Yevgeny Yevtushenko. Tr. by T. Tupikina-Glaessner et al. LC 67-10982. 1967. 4.95 o.p. Praeger.

Bravados. Frank O'Rourke. LC 57-6845. (Dell first edition, A131). 1957. Dell Pub. Co.

Brave African Huntress. Amos Tutuola. (Illus.). 1958. pap. 1.95 o.p. (ISBN 0-394-17325-2, E560, Ever). Grove.

Brave and the Blind. Michael Blankfort. LC 40-73960. The Bobbs-Merrill Company.

Brave and the Free. Leslie Waller. LC 78-27810. 10.95 (ISBN 0-440-06168-7). Delacorte Press.

Brave & the Lonely. Robert Vaughan. 1982. pap. 3.50 (ISBN 0-440-00649-X, Emerald). Dell.

Brave, Bad Girls. Thomas Blanchard Dewey. LC 56-14012. (Inner sanctum mystery). 1956. Simon and Schuster.

Brave Battle. Lucia E. F Kimball. D. Lothrop Company.

Brave Bulls: A Novel. Tom Lea. LC 49-75773. 1949. Little, Brown.

Brave Company. Guthrie Wilson. LC 50-12468. 1950. Putnam.

Brave Cowboy. Edward Abbey. 320p. 1982. pap. 2.75 (ISBN 0-380-58966-4, 58966). Avon.

Brave Cowboy: An Old Tale in a New Time. Edward Abbey. LC 76-57530. (Zia book). 1977. 3.45 (ISBN 0-8263-0448-6). University of New Mexico Press.

Brave Cowboy: An Old Tale in a New Time. Edward Abbey. LC 56-10061. 1956. Dodd, Mead.

Brave Die but Once. Grethe Grammer. (Orig.). 1977. pap. 6.50 (ISBN 0-89351-010-6). Western Her Texas.

Brave Enterprise. Dorothy Quentin. LC 43-8953. 1943. Arcadia House, Inc.

Brave Free Men. Jack Vance. (His Durdane, book 2). 1973. (pbk.) 0.95. Dell.

Brave General. Herbert Sherman Gorman. Farrar & Rinehart, Inc.

Brave Harvest: By Richard Cargoe Pseud. Pierre Stephen Robert Payne. LC 54-132953. 1954. Ballantine Books.

Brave Heart and True. A Novel. authorized ed. Florence Marryat Church Lean. LC 7-13587. (Lovell's international series, no. 135). 1890. United States Book Company.

Brave Heart. Illustrated by Harry Baerg. Lois M Parker. 1958. Review and Herald Pub. Association.

Brave Hearts. William Alexander Fraser. LC 76-103508. (Short story index reprint series). (Illus.). 1969. Books for Libraries Press.

Brave Hearts. William Alexander Fraser. LC 4-12775. 1904. C. Scribner's Sons.

Brave Hearts. An American Novel. Rossiter Worthington Raymond. LC 9-933. 1873. J. B. Ford and Company.

Brave Heritage. Peggy Gaddis, pseud. LC 42-814122. 1942. Arcadia House, Inc.

Brave in the Saddle. Harry Sinclair Drago. LC 43-11953. 1943. W. Morrow and Company.

Brave Island. Richard Lionel Spittel & Wilson, Christine Frances. 1966. Lake House Investments.

Brave Lads and Bonnie Lassies. Stories of Young Folks Who Have Helped to Make History. Frederick Myron Colby. LC 6-25421. 1893. Hunt & Eaton.

Brave Lady. Dinah Maria Mulock Craik. LC 41-31310. 1870. Harper & Brothers.

Brave Lady. Dinah Maria Mulock Craik. LC 4-165099. 1899. Harper & Brothers.

Brave Little Woman. A Novel. Mary Andrews Denison. (On cover: Idle hour series. no. 14). The F. M. Lupton Publishing Company.

Brave Mardi Gras: A New Orleans Novel of the '60s. Walter Adolphe Roberts. LC 46-1684. 1946. The Bobbs-Merrill Company.

Brave Men All. Noble P. Roth. 1981. pap. 2.95 (ISBN 0-89083-770-8). Zebra.

Brave New Baby. David M. Rorvik. LC 79-132510. 1971. 5.95 o.p. (ISBN 0-385-04000-8). Doubleday.

Brave New World. Aldous Leonard Huxley. LC 74-169246. (Illus.). 1974. Limited Editions Club.

Brave New World. Aldous Leonard Huxley. LC 50-6270. (Harper's modern classics). 1950. Harper.

Brave New World. Aldous Leonard Huxley. LC 46-21397. 1946. Harper & Brothers.

Brave New World: A Novel. Aldous Leonard Huxley. LC 32-3525. 1932. Doubleday, Doran & Company, Inc.

Brave New World: A Novel. Aldous Leonard Huxley. LC 33-11792. 1933. Garden City Publishing Company, Inc.

Brave New World: A Novel. Aldous Leonard Huxley. LC 37-815498. 1936. The Sun Dial Press.

Brave New World: & Brave New World Revisited. Aldous Leonard Huxley. LC 65-5333. (Harper torchbooks, TB3501. The university library). 1965. Harper & Row.

Brave New World & Brave New World Revisited. Aldous Leonard Huxley. LC 65-6532. 1965. Harper & Row.

Brave New World, and Brave New World Revisited. With a Foreword by the Author and an Introd. by Charles J. Rolo. Aldous Leonard Huxley. (Harper's modern classics). 1960. Harper.

Brave New World Revisited. Aldous Leonard Huxley. 1965. pap. 2.50i (ISBN 0-06-080023-2, P23, PL). Har-Row.

Brave New World. With a Special Foreword by the Author. Aldous Leonard Huxley. LC 56-8833. (Modern library of the world's best books 48). 1956. Modern Library.

Brave New Worlds. Aldous Leonard Huxley. 1982. Repr. lib. bdg. 15.95x (ISBN 0-89966-423-7). Buccaneer Bks.

Brave Paradise. Lillian Barker. LC 38-5306. The Dodge Publishing Company.

Brave Pursuit: A Novel. Marguerite Allis. LC 54-5475. (Illus.). 1954. Putnam.

Brave Rifles. Gordon D Shirreffs. (Leisure Books). 1977. 1.25 (ISBN 0-8439-0490-9). Nordon Pubns.

Brave Tears. Patricia Frane. LC 37-2060. 1937. Arcadia House.

Brave Tin Soldier. (Dean's Gold Medal Ser). pap. 1.95 o.p. Borden.

Brave Tin Soldier. Clifton Johnson. LC 20-6893. (Bedtime wonder tales). The Macaulay Company.

Brave Trail. Leigh Carder. LC 35-30566. Covici, Friede.

Brave Years: A Novel. William Heyliger. LC 37-9860. 1937. D. Appleton-Century Company, Incorporated.

Brave Young Hearts. Betty Lou Burris. LC 58-12372. 1958. Wilde.

Bravest of the Virginia Cavalry and Other Stories. Charles J Mullaly. LC 37-29387. Apostleship of Prayer.

Bravo. James Fenimore Cooper. Ed. by Donald A. Ringe. (Masterworks of Literature Ser.). 1963. 8.50x (ISBN 0-8084-0065-7); pap. 4.95x (ISBN 0-8084-0066-5, M14). Coll & U Pr.

Bravo: A Tale. James Fenimore Cooper. LC 6-30185. 1831. Carey & Lea.

Bravo. A Tale. James Fenimore Cooper. LC 26-24690. (Half-title: The choice works of Cooper. Revised and corrected series. v. 12). 1856. Stringer & Townsend.

Bravo: A Tale. James Fenimore Cooper. LC 22-198298. 1859. W. A. Townsend and Company.

Bravo: A Tale. people's ed. James Fenimore Cooper. LC 6-30183. 1859. Stringer & Townsend.

Bravo: A Tale. James Fenimore Cooper. (On cover: Lovell's library, no. 524). 1885. J. W. Lovell Company.

Bravo. A Tale. James Fenimore Cooper. (On cover: seaside library, Pocket ed. no. 394). 1885. J. Munro.

Bravo. A Tale. James Fenimore Cooper. LC 4-19571. 1886. D. Appleton and Company.

Bravo: a Tale. James Fenimore Cooper. LC 42-47064. 1833-36. Carey & Lea.

Bravo Jim. W. D Hoffman. LC 28-13167. 1928. A. C. McClurg & Co.

Bravo, My Monster. Oscar Tarcov. LC 53-8794. 1953. H. Regnery Co.

Bravo of Venice, A Romance. Matthew Gregory Lewis. LC 74-131327. (Gothic Novels Ser.). 1972. Repr. of 1805 ed. 35.00 (ISBN 0-405-00807-4). Ayer Co.

Bravo of Venice: A Romance. Heinrich Zschokke. Tr. by Matthew Gregory Lewis. LC 74-131327. (Gothic novels). 1972. (ISBN 0-405-00807-4). Arno Press.

Bravo Romeo: A Novel. Ralph Peters. LC 80-20872. 11.95 (ISBN 0-399-90097-7). R. Marek Publishers.

Bravo's Daughter: Or, The Tory of Carolina. A Romance Ot the American Revolution. Augustine Joseph Hickey Duganne. 1850. E. Winchester.

Bravo's Secret: Or, The Spy of the "Ten." A Venetian Tale. Founded on Incidents Which Occurred During the Latter Part of the Reign of Francesco Dandolo, Doge of Venice. Sylvanus Cobb & Kelly, Jonathan Falconbridge, 1818-1854. LC 7-12834. (With Judson, Edward Z. C. The black avenger of the Spanish Main. New York, c1847). 1851. F. Gleason.

Braw and the Bonny. J. Harvey Howells. LC 71-139631. 1971. 7.50 (ISBN 0-671-20831-4). Simon and Schuster.

Brawl. Gerard Bessette. LC 77-473823. (French writers of Canada series). 1976. 9.95. (ISBN 0-88772-227-X) (ISBN 0-88772-169-9). Harvest House.

Brawny-Man. James Stevens. LC 26-27441. 1926. A. A. Knopf.

Braxton's Bar. A Tale of Pioneer Years in California. Rollin M Daggett. LC 6-32224. 1882. G. W. Carleton & Co.; Etc., Etc.

Brazen. Carter Brown, pseud. LC 60-4488. (Signet book, S1836). 1960. New American Library of World Literature.

Brazen Calf. James Lauren Ford. LC 3-25205. 1903. Dodd, Mead and Company.

Brazen Ecstasy. Janelle Taylor. (Orig.). 1983. pap. 3.50 (ISBN 0-8217-1133-4). Zebra.

Brazen Gates: A True History of the Blossoms Which Grew in the Garden at Cragenfels. Fanny N. Smith & Smith, Julie P., D. 1883, Ed. LC 8-8985. 1872. G. W. Carleton & Co.; Etc., Etc.

Brazen Serpent. Poul Hoffmann. LC 63-19547. (Illus.). 1964. Fortress Press.

Brazenhead the Great. Maurice Henry Hewlett. LC 11-827598. 1911. C. Scribner's Sons.

Brazilian Short Stories. Monteoiro Lobato. 1977. lib. bdg. 59.95 (ISBN 0-8490-1550-2). Gordon Pr.

Brazilian Short Stories. Monteiro Lobato, Jose Bento. Ed. by Goldberg, Isaac. (Little blue book no. 733, ed. by E. Haldeman-Julius). Haldeman-Julius Company.

Brazilian Sleigh Ride: A Captain Jose Da Silva Novel. Robert L Fish. LC 65-26677. (Inner sanctum mystery). 1965. Simon and Schuster.

Brazilian Stardust. Marjorie McEvoy. LC 68-679. 1967. Arcadia House.

Brazilian Tales. Ed. by Isaac Goldberg et al. Machado De Assis, Joaguim Maria & Medeiros E Albuquerque, Jose Joaquim De Campos Da Costa. LC 22-2863. 1921. The Four Seas Company.

Brazilian Tales. Tr. from Portuguese. Introd. by Isaac Goldberg. Ed. by Isaac Goldberg. LC 64-220359. (IPL, 28). 1965. Intl. Pocket Lib.

Brazilian Tenement. Aluizio Azevedo. LC 75-44002. 1976. 14.00. H. Fertig.

Brazilian Tenement. Aluizio Azevedo. Tr. by Brown, Harry W. LC 26-10318. 1926. R. M. McBride and Company.

Brazos Crossing. Owen G Irons. (Avalon Books). 4.95. Thomas Bouregy.

Brea File. Louis Charbonneau. LC 80-698. 1983. 14.95 (ISBN 0-385-15508-5). Doubleday.

Breach. Prada Oropeza, Renato. LC 70-135716. 1971. 4.95. Doubleday.

Breach of Custom. A Novel. Reinhold Ortmann. Tr. by Lowrey, D. M. (On cover: The choice series, no. 32). 1891. R. Bonner's Sons.

Breach of Fate. John P. Evans & John B. Mannion. (Orig.). 1980. pap. 2.25 (ISBN 0-449-14325-2, GM). Fawcett.

Bread. Ed McBain. 1982. pap. 2.25 (ISBN 0-451-11279-2, AE1279, Sig). NAL.

Bread. Charles Gilman Norris. LC 23-12005. E. P. Dutton & Company.

Bread. Charles Gilman Norris. LC 32-19524. 1926. A. L. Burt Company.

Bread: An 87th Precinct Mystery Novel. Evan Hunter. LC 73-5648. 1974. 5.95 (ISBN 0-394-48580-7). Randon House.

Bread and a Stone. Alvah Cecil Bessie. LC 41-24401. Modern Age Books.

Bread and a Sword. Evelyn Scott. LC 37-612649. C. Scribner's Sons.

Bread and Beer. Mary Dwinell Chellis. LC 6-23419. (On cover: The Chellis library). 1881. National Temperance Society and Publication House.

Bread and Butter. Jack D Flam. LC 76-54940. 1977. 8.95 (ISBN 0-670-18803-4). Viking Press.

Bread & Butter Miss. George Paston. Date not set. lib. bdg. 9.95 (ISBN 0-915864-22-3); pap. 3.95 (ISBN 0-915864-21-5). Academy Chi Ltd.

Bread and Butter Miss. Emily Morse Symonds. LC 77-16313. 1977. 7.50. (ISBN 0-915864-19-3). Cassandra Editions.

Bread-and-Cheese and Kisses. Benjamin Leopold Farjeon. LC 6-38644. (On cover: Farm and fireside library. no. 6). 1881. Farm and Fireside Company.

Bread and Circuses. Christopher Sheridan. LC 49-981. 1947. J. Long.

Bread & Circuses. William E. Woodward. LC 25-22986. 1925. Harper & Brothers.

Bread and Fire: A Novel. Charles Rumford Walker. LC 27-107310. 1927. Houghton Mifflin Company.

Bread and Jam. Nalbro Isadorah Bartley. LC 25-19118. George H. Doran Company.

Bread and Love. Betty Ross. LC 30-8179. 1930. Modern Books.

Bread and Milk, and Other Stories. Eileen Gibbons Kump. LC 79-15754. 6.95 (ISBN 0-8425-1702-2). Brigham Young University Press.

Bread and Roses. Richard Gambino. LC 79-67598. 13.95 (ISBN 0-87223-651-X). Seaview Books.

Bread and Roses: Richard Gambino. Richard Gambino. 1982. 3.50 (ISBN 0-380-59014-X). Avon Books.

Bread and Wine. Ignazio Silone. LC 62-17288. 1962. Atheneum.

Bread and Wine: A Story of Graubunden. Maude Egerton Hine King. LC 2-13398. 1902. Houghton, Mifflin and Company.

Bread and Wine: Translated from the Italian. Ignazio Silone & David, Gwenda, Tr. LC 37-43784. 1937. Harper & Brothers.

Bread Eaten in Secret. John Antonio Moroso. LC 31-15684. The Macaulay Company.

Bread for the Hungry. Brenda Cannon. 1940. Bica Press.

Bread for the Hungry. Bertha B. Moore McCurry. LC 40-33698. 1940. Bica Press.

Bread for the Living. Mary Lasswell. 1948. Houghton Mifflin Co.

Bread from Heaven. Henrietta Buckmaster, pseud. LC 52-8811. 1952. Random House.

Bread from Heaven: By Henrietta Buckmaster Pseud. Henrietta Henkle. LC 52-8811. 1952. Random House.

Bread Givers: A Novel. Anzia Yezierska. LC 25-18697. Doubleday, Page & Company.

Bread Givers: A Novel: a Struggle Between a Father of the Old World and a Daughter of the New. Anzia Yezierska. LC 75-318683. 1975. 3.95 (ISBN 0-8076-0779-7). G. Braziller.

Bread Givers: A Struggle Between a Father of the Old World & a Daughter of the New World. Anzia Yezierska. LC 74-25319. 320p. 1975. 5.95 (ISBN 0-89255-014-7). Persea Bks.

Bread into Roses. Kathleen Thompson Norris. LC 37-271109. 1937. Doubleday, Doran & Company, Inc.

Bread Line: A Story of a Paper. Albert Bigelow Paine. LC 5515. 1900. The Century Co.

Bread of Heaven, and Husks of Swine: Or, The Curse of Jealousy. A Life History. M. E. Pinckard. LC 7-35808. 1874. Printed by J. Y. Slater.

Bread of Idleness: The Portrait of a Period--Circa 1932, U. S. A. 1st Ed. Mort E Shaw. LC 56-5505. Vantage Press.

Bread of Love: Karlekens Brod. Tr. from the Swedish by Richard B. Vowles. Peder Sjogren. LC 65-24189. (Nordic translation ser.) Bibl.). 1965. 4.00. Univ. of Wis. Pr.

Bread of Those Early Years. Heinrich Boll. LC 76-17547. 7.95 (ISBN 0-07-006427-X). McGraw-Hill.

Bread, Soul, and Acid. James Bryan. LC 75-24426. 1969. 1.75. Brandon House.

Bread to My Children. Ellen Key Blunt. LC 6-14199. 1856. J. P. Lippincott & Co.

Bread Upon the Waters. James W. Hall. 3.75 o.p. Vantage.

Bread Upon the Waters. Irwin Shaw. LC 81-3106. 14.95 (ISBN 0-440-00911-1). Delacorte Press.

Bread Upon the Waters. limited 1st ed. Irwin Shaw. LC 81-184498. (Illus.). 1981. 14.95. Franklin Library.

Bread Upon the Waters: The Spiritual Battle of Two G. I.'s in the Philippines in World War II. 1st Ed. Bernard N Bancroft. LC 59-1245. 1959. Exposition Press.

Bread-Winners. John Hay. LC 77-151978. (Masterworks of literature series, M-36). 1973. 2.95. College & University Press.

Bread-Winners. Susan D. Nickerson. LC 7-1511. 1871. Nichols and Hall.

Bread-Winners: A Social Study. John Hay. 1884. Harper & Brothers.

Breadfruit Lotteries: A Novel. Richard M Elman. LC 79-20725. 9.95. Methuen.

Break. Berkely Mather. LC 79-106540. 1970. 5.95. Scribner.

Break Away. Betty I. Lovelace. LC 81-510455. 329p. 1982. 11.95 (ISBN 0-533-05024-3). Vantage.

Break for the Border. Frank Bonham. (Orig.). 1982. pap. 1.95 (ISBN 0-425-05295-8). Berkley Pub.

Break in the Circle: A Novel. Philip Loraine. LC 51-13629. 1951. M. S. Mill Co. and W. Morrow.

Break in the Weather. Florence Jane Soman. LC 58-11004. 1959. Putnam.

Break in Training, and Other Athletic Stories. Arthur Brown Ruhl. LC 6-43781. 1906. The Outing Publishing Company.

Break o' Day. facs. ed. George Wharton Edwards. LC 74-90580. (Short Story Index Reprint Ser.). 1896. 13.00 (ISBN 0-8369-3063-0). Ayer Co.

Break O' Day. Con O'Leary. LC 27-15875. George H. Doran Company.

Break O' Day: And Other Stories. George Wharton Edwards. LC 6-36574. 1896. The Century Co.

Break O'day: And Other Stories. George Wharton Edwards. LC 74-90580. (Short story index repprint series). (Illus.). 1969. (ISBN 0-8369-3063-0). Books for Libraries Press.

Break of Dawn. Violet H. Curtis. 1970. 3.95 o.p. Vantage.

Break of Day. Sidonie Gabrielle Colette. Tr. by Enid McLeod. 143p. 1974. pap. 5.25 (ISBN 0-374-51221-3). FS&G.

Break of Day. Sidonie Gabrielle Colette. 128p. 1983. pap. 2.50 (ISBN 0-345-30858-1). Ballantine.

Break of Day. Clifford Green. LC 77-354287. 1976. Hodder and Stoughton.

Break of Day: A Novel. Basil King. LC 30-18558. 1930. Harper & Brothers.

Break of Day: A Novel. Tr. by Enid McLeod. Introd by Glenway Wescott. Sidonie Gabrielle Colette. LC 61-175024. bds., 3.75. Farrar.

Break of Day: Tr. by Enid McLeod; Introd. by Glenway Wescott; and The Blue Lantern, Tr. by Roger Senhouse. Sidonie Gabrielle Colette. LC 66-26523. 1966. bds., 5.95. Farrar.

Break-Out. Former Title: The Eagle and the Iron Cross. Glendon Fred Swarthout. (Signet bk., Q3351). 1968. New Amer. Lib.

Break the Toff. John Creasey. 1970. pap. 0.75 o.p. (ISBN 0-447-74626-X). Lancer.

Break the Young Land. Joshua Stark, pseud. LC 64-11507. (Double D western). 1964. Doubleday.

Break Thou My Heart. Vera Marie Tracy. LC 36-356. The Bruce Publishing Company.

Break-up. Esther Birdsall Darling. The Penn Publishing Company.

Break-up. Edmund Schiddel. LC 55-17021. 1954. Avon Publications.

Break up. Hagar Wilde. LC 31-12122. 1931. Little, Brown and Company.

Break-up of Our Camp, and Other Stories. Paul Goodman. LC 52-42171. (Direction, 14). 1949. New Directions.

Break-up of Our Camp, Stories 1932-1935: The Collected Stories, Vol. 1. Paul Goodman. Ed. by Taylor Stoehr. 300p. 1978. 14.00 (ISBN 0-87685-330-0); deluxe ed. 25.00 (ISBN 0-87685-331-9); pap. 7.50 (ISBN 0-87685-329-7). Black Sparrow.

Breakable Bird: A Novella. Erje Ayden. 46p. (Orig.). 1972. 8.00 (ISBN 0-89366-001-9). Ultramarine Pub.

Breakaway. Louise Field Cooper. LC 76-21125. 1977. 7.95 (ISBN 0-394-41044-0). Knopf: Distributed by Random House.

Breakaway. Louise Field Cooper. LC 77-14544. 1978. 8.95 (ISBN 0-89340-122-6). J. Curley.

Breakaway. Walter W Depew. LC 56-6106. 1956. W. Sloane Associates.

Breakaway. E. C. Tubb. (Space - 1999). 141p. 1975. lib. bdg. 5.95 (ISBN 0-88411-671-9). Amereon Ltd.

Breakdown. Louis Paul. LC 46-8060. 1946. Crown Publishers.

Breakdown. Victoria Wolf. 1973. (pbk) 0.75. Ace Books.

Breakdown and Bereavement: A Novel. Joseph Hayyim Brenner. LC 74-162545. (Illus.). 1971. 7.50 (ISBN 0-8014-0661-7). Cornell University Press.

Breakdown, by Patrick Marsh: Pseud. 1st American Ed. Leslie Hiscock. LC 56-6056. 1953. Longmans, Green.

Breaker. Kit Denton. 1982. pap. 3.50 (ISBN 0-671-44762-9). WSP.

Breaker of Laws. William Pett Ridge. LC 3554. 1900. The Macmillan Company.

Breaker: The Novel Behind Breaker Morant. Kit Denton. LC 81-5763. 11.95 (ISBN 0-312-09517-1). St. Martin's Press.

Breakers Ahead,by. Anna Maynard Barbour. LC 6-18843. 1906. J. B. Lippincott Company.

Breakfast at the Hermitage: A Novel of Nashville Rebuilding. Alfred Leland Crabb. LC 45-3049. 1945. The Bobbs-Merrill Company.

Breakfast at Tiffany's. Truman Capote. 1959. pap. 2.50 (ISBN 0-451-12042-6, AE2402, Sig). NAL.

Breakfast at Tiffany's. Truman Capote. 1958. 10.95 (ISBN 0-394-41770-4). Random.

Breakfast at Tiffany's: A Short Novel and Three Stories. Truman Capote. LC 58-10956. 1958. Random House.

Breakfast in Bed. Sylvia Thompson. LC 34-52893. 1934. Little, Brown, and Company.

Breakfast in the Ruins. Michael Moorcock. LC 73-18306. 1974. 5.95 (ISBN 0-394-49068-1). Random House.

Breakfast in the Ruins. Michael Moorcock. 1980. 1.95 (ISBN 0-380-49148-6). Avon Books.

Breakfast of Champions. Kurt Vonnegut, Jr. 320p. pap. 3.25 (ISBN 0-440-13148-0). Dell.

Breakfast of Champions. Kurt Vonnegut, Jr. 320p. 1974. pap. 2.65 (ISBN 0-440-53148-9, Delta). Dell.

Breakfast of Champions: Or, Goodbye Blue Monday! Kurt Vonnegut. LC 72-13086. (Illus.). 1973. 7.95. Delacorte Press.

Breakfast with a Stranger. Peter Kortner. LC 76-28043. 1977. 7.95 o.p. (ISBN 0-312-09520-1). St Martin.

Breakfast with the Nikolides. Rumer Godden. LC 42-2419. 1842. Little, Brown and Company.

Breakfast with the Nikolides. Rumer Godden. 1975. (pbk.) 1.50 (ISBN 0-380-00536-0). Avon.

Breakheart Pass. Alistair MacLean. LC 73-20824. (Illus.). 1974. 5.95. Doubleday.

Breakheart Pass. Alistair MacLean. LC 74-32367. (Illus.). 1975. 9.95 (ISBN 0-8161-6271-9). G. K. Hall.

Breakheart Pass. Alistair Maclean. (Fawcett crest book). 1975. (pbk.) 1.50. Fawcett.

Breaking a Butterfly: Or, Blanche Ellerslie's Ending. George Alfred Lawrence. LC 43-488836. (On cover: Library of select novels. no. 500). 1869. Harper & Brothers.

Breaking & Entering. Peter Makuck. LC 81-3406. (Illinois Short Fiction Ser.). 172p. 1981. 11.95 (ISBN 0-252-00898-7); pap. 4.95 (ISBN 0-252-00925-8). U of Ill Pr.

Breaking and Entering: Stories. Peter Makuck. LC 81-3406. (Illinois Short Fiction). 11.95 (ISBN 0-252-00898-7). University of Illinois Press.

Breaking Ground by Breaking Rules: Collected Stories. Donn A. Tenney. 80p. 1981. 5.95 (ISBN 0-533-04659-9). Vantage.

Breaking Hearts. James Magnuson. LC 81-43295. 1982. 14.95 (ISBN 0-385-17778-X). Doubleday.

Breaking in of a Yachtsman's Wife. Mary Marvin Heaton Vorse. LC 8-14521. 1906. Houghton, Mifflin and Company.

Breaking into Society: By George Ade... George Ade. LC 4-59196. 1904. Harper & Brothers.

Breaking of Bumbo. Andrew Sinclair. LC 59-11204. 1959. Simon and Schuster.

Breaking of Cassie. Lorimer White. 192p. 1973. pap. 1.95 o.p. (ISBN 0-87977-186-0, DBB186). Dansk Blue Bk.

Breaking of Northwall. Paul O Williams. 2.25 (ISBN 0-345-29259-6). Ballantine Books,, C.

Breaking of the Seals. Frances Ashton. Ed. by Hank Stine. LC 82-2386. (Illus.). 174p. 1982. pap. 6.95 (ISBN 0-89865-200-6). Donning Co.

Breaking Out. Derek Maitland. LC 78-19423. 10.00 (ISBN 0-312-09523-6). St. Martin's Press.

Breaking Point. James E. Gunn. LC 72-80728. 1972. 4.95 (ISBN 0-8027-5552-6). Walker.

Breaking Point. James E. Gunn. 1973. (pbk.) 0.95. DAW Books.

Breaking Point. new ed. Mary Roberts Rhinehart. 1975. (pbk.) 1.25. Dell.

Breaking Point. Mary Roberts Rinehart. LC 22-26762. George H. Doran Company.

Breaking Point. Denise Robins. 1975. (pbk.) 1.25. Bantam Books.

Breaking Point: A Novel. Annie Austin Flint. LC 16-79201. 1915. 1.50. Broadway Publishing Co.

Breaking-Point: A Novel. Fred Lewis Pattee. LC 12-2686. 1.25. Small, Maynard & Company.

Breaking Point. Translated by Barrows Mussey. 1st Ed. Jacob Presser. LC 58-675854. 1958. World Pub. Co.

Breaking Smith's Quarter Horse: By Paul St. Pierre. St. Pierre, Paul H. LC 68-14826. bds., 3.95. Follett.

Breaking Sod on the Prairies: A Story of Early Days in Dakota. Clarence Wilbur Taber. LC 24-5345. (Pioneer life series, ed.by H. R. Driggs). 1924. World Book Company.

Breaking Strain. John Masters. (0794). 1968. Dell.

Breaking Strain. John Masters. LC 67-11019. 1967. Delacorte Press.

Breaking String: The Plays of Anton Chekhov. 2nd ed.. ed. Maurice Jacques Valency. LC 82-3369. 1982. 20.00 (ISBN 0-8052-3809-3) (ISBN 0-8052-3809-3). Schocken Books.

Breaking the Shackles. Frank Barrett. 1900. L. C. Page & Company.

Breaking Up. Norma Klein. 176p. 1982. pap. 2.25 (ISBN 0-380-55830-0, 59972-4, Flare). Avon.

Breaking up: A Novel. William H Manville. LC 62-17324. 1962. Simon and Schuster.

Breaking up: Or, The Birth, Development and Death of the Earth and Its Satellite in Story. Lysander Salmon Richards. LC 7-41213. 1896. J. E. Farwell & Co., Printers.

Breaking Wave. Nevil Shute Norway. LC 80-20559. 1980. 16.95 (ISBN 0-933852-16-9). Nautical and Aviation Pub. Co. of America.

Breaking Wave. Nevil Shute. LC 80-83020. (Great War Stories Ser.). 310p. 1980. Repr. of 1955 ed. 16.95 (ISBN 0-933852-16-9). Nautical & Aviation.

Breaking Wave: By Nevil Shute Pseud. Nevil Shute Norway. LC 55-63695. 1955. Morrow.

Breakneck Brook. Margaret Flint. 1939. Dodd, Mead & Company.

Breakout. Kathryn Anger. LC 79-55871. (Feminist Novels Ser.). 128p. (Orig.). 1977. pap. 4.95 (ISBN 0-935772-01-4). Diotima Bks.

Breakout in Angola. Major DaSilva. (Mercenary Ser.). 1977. pap. 1.25 o.s.i. (ISBN 0-8439-0437-2, LB437, Leisure Bks). Nordon Pubns.

Breakpoint: A Novel. William Brinkley. LC 78-1773. 1978. 9.95 (ISBN 0-688-03288-5). Morrow.

Breakpoint: A Novel. William Brinkley. 1979. 2.50 (ISBN 0-345-28167-5). Ballantine Books.

Breaks. Richard Price. LC 82-16958. 16.50 (ISBN 0-671-45236-3). Simon and Schuster.

Breaks of the Game. David Halberstam. 480p. 1983. pap. 3.95 (ISBN 0-345-29625-7). Ballantine.

Breakthrough. Ken Grimwood. LC 75-32012. 1976. 7.95 (ISBN 0-385-11498-2). Doubleday.

Breakup Variations. Kathleen Spivack. 1983. pap. 5.95 (ISBN 0-918222-52-4). Apple Wood.

Breakwater: A Novel. Walter Alden Dyer. LC 27-90735. 1927. Doubleday, Page & Company.

Breakwater. 1st Ed. George Mandel. LC 60-10169. 1960. Holt, Rinehart and Winston.

Breast. Philip Roth. LC 72-84892. 1972. 4.95 (ISBN 0-03-003716-6). Holt, Rinehart and Winston.

Breath for Nothing. Hal Shows. pap. 3.00 o.s.i. Anhinga Pr.

Breath of Air. Rumer Godden. 1976. 1.50 (ISBN 0-380-00618-9). Avon Books.

Breath of Air. Rumer Godden. LC 51-9206. 1951. Viking Press.

Breath of Brimstone. Anthea Fraser. LC 76-54325. 6.95 (ISBN 0-396-07405-7). Dodd, Mead.

Breath of Brimstone. Anthea Fraser. LC 76-54325. 6.95 (ISBN 0-396-07405-7). Dodd, Mead.

Breath of French Air. 1st Ed. Herbert Ernest Bates. LC 59-11879. 1959. Little, Brown.

Breath of Kings. Gene Farrington. LC 81-43411. (Illus.). 1982. 19.95 (ISBN 0-385-15973-0). Doubleday.

Breath of Life. Faith Baldwin. 1976. Repr. of 1942 ed. lib. bdg. 15.45x (ISBN 0-88411-617-4). Amereon Ltd.

Breath of Life. Faith Baldwin Cuthrell. LC 76-41331. 1976. 6.95 (ISBN 0-88411-617-4). Aeonian Press.

Breath of Life. Faith Baldwin Cuthrell. LC 42-9790. 1942. Farrar & Rinehart, Inc.

Breath of Prairie, and Other Stories. William Otis Lillibridge. LC 11-7745. 1911. 1.20. A. C. McClurg & Co.

Breath of Rapture. Polly A. Hutchison. LC 77-22575. (Spire book). 1.50 (ISBN 0-8007-8286-0). F. H. Revell Co.

Breath of Scandal. Edwin Balmer. LC 22-15852. 1922. Little, Brown, and Company.

Breath of Snow. Joseph Cherwinski. (Orig.). 1969. pap. 1.95 o.p. (ISBN 0-8283-1039-4). Branden.

Breath of Suspicion. Morna Doris MacTaggart Brown. LC 78-186020. 1972. 4.95. Published for the Crime Club by Doubleday.

Breath of Suspicion. E. X Ferrars, pseud. LC 75-305680. (Penguin crime fiction). 1974. 1.25 (ISBN 0-14-003788-8). Penguin.

Breath of Suspicion: A Novel. Frances Isabel Currie. (On cover: Once-a-week library, v. 11, no. 1). 1893. P. F. Collier.

Breath of Suspicion: A Novel. Frances Isabel Currie. LC 6-31720. F. I. Webb.

Breath of the Desert. Charles Alden Seltzer. 302p. 1975. Repr. of 1932 ed. lib. bdg. 7.95x o.p. Aeonian Pr.

Breath of the Dragon. Abigail Hetzel Fitch. LC 24-20492. 1917. G. P. Putnam's Sons.

Breath of the Dragon. Abigail Hetzel Fitch. LC 16-21390. 1916. G. P. Putnam's Sons.

Breath of the Gods. Mary Fenollosa. LC 5-14826. 1905. Little, Brown, and Company.

Breath of the Hills: Tales of Country Life. Cornelia Boyden Pierce. LC 23-6915. Belisle Printing & Publishing Co.

Breath of the Jungle,". James Francis Dwyer. LC 15-7477. 1915. A. C. McClurg & Co.

Breath of the Runners: A Novel. Mary Martha Mears. LC 6-37599. 1906. F. A. Stokes Company.

Breathe No More. Marie Freid Rodell. LC 40-8822. H. Holt and Company.

Breathe No More, My Lady. Ruth Lenore Marting. LC 46-6841. 1946. Pub. for the Crime Club by Doubleday & Company, Inc.

Breathe the Air Again. Ward Moore. LC 42-3174. 1942. Harper & Brothers.

Breathe Upon These. Ludwig Lewisohn. LC 44-2500. 1944. The Bobbs-Merrill Company.

Breathe Upon These Slain. Evelyn Scott. LC 34-14543. 1934. H. Smith and R. Haas.

Breathing Driftwood. Margaret D Cloninger & Vogt, August, Joint Author. LC 25-133022. Reilly Publishing Company.

Breathing Space. John Bruce. LC 74-76302. (Anansi Fiction Ser.: No. 31). 120p. 1974. 10.95 (ISBN 0-88784-432-4, Pub. by Hse Anansi Pr Canada); pap. 5.95 (ISBN 0-88784-330-1). U of Toronto Pr.

Breathings. Philippe Jaccottet. Tr. by Cid Corman. (Illus.). 1974. pap. 5.95 (Pub. by Mushinsha Bks). SBD.

Breathless. Nalbro Isadorah Bartley. LC 33-153941. 1938. Farrar & Rinehart, Incorporated.

Breathless. Leonore Fleischer. 1983. pap. 2.95 (ISBN 0-440-10804-7). Dell.

Breathless Dawn. Susanna Collins. (Second Chance at Love Ser.: No. 94). 192p. 1983. pap. 1.75 (ISBN 0-515-06858-6). Jove Pubns.

Breathless Diversions. Anthony Delano. LC 73-14069. 1974. 6.95 (ISBN 0-06-011026-0). Harper & Row.

Breathless Moment. Muriel Hine Coxon. LC 20-13346. 1920. John Lane Company.

Breathless Passion. Catherine Creel. (Orig.). 1983. pap. 3.50 (ISBN 0-8217-1204-7). Zebra.

Breathless Summer. Kay Hooper. (Candlelight Ecstasy Ser.: No. 90). (Orig.). 1982. pap. 1.95 (ISBN 0-440-10574-9). Dell.

Brecon Castle. Caroline Farr. (Signet book). New American Library.

Bred in the Bone. Thomas Nelson Page. LC 77-86151. (Short story index reprint series). (Illus.). 1969. Books for Libraries Press.

Bred in the Bone. Thomas Nelson Page. LC 4-13282. 1904. C. Scribner's Sons.

Bred in the Bone. Eden Phillpotts. LC 32-34234. 1932. The Macmillan Company.

Bred in the Bone. Eden Phillpotts. LC 33-28332. 1933. The Macmillan Company.

Bred in the Bone, and Other Stories. Elsie Singmaster. LC 25-22111. 1925. Houghton Mifflin Company.

Bred of the Desert: A Horse and a Romance. Charles Marcus Horton. LC 15-7474. 1915. Harper & Brothers.

Bred to Kill. Lee Hoffman. 160p. 1981. pap. 1.75. Ballantine.

Brede's Tale from the Saga of Pliocene Exile. Julian. May. LC 82-5516. 1982. 85.00 (ISBN 0-916732-31-2) (ISBN 0-916732-32-0). Starmont House.

Bredon and Sons. Stephen Southwold. LC 34-5803. 1934. Little, Brown, and Company.

Breed of Basil. Thomas Bell. LC 30-10980. 1930. R. M. McBride & Company.

Breed of Giants. Joyce Stranger, pseud. (Illus.). 1967. 4.75 o.p. (ISBN 0-670-18886-7). Viking Pr.

Breed of Giants. Joyce Stranger, pseud. 1972. pap. 0.95 o.p. (95324). Beagle Bks.

Breed of Giants: A Novel. Illus. by David Rook. Joyce Stranger, pseud. LC 67-13497. 1967. 4.75. Viking.

Breed of Heroes. Alan Judd. LC 81-7760. 1981. 12.95 (ISBN 0-698-11087-0). Coward, McCann & Geoghegan.

Breed of the Chaparral. Nelson Coral Nye. LC 46-3693. 1946. R. M. McBride & Company.

Breed to Come. Alice Mary Norton. LC 71-183937. 1972. 4.95 (ISBN 0-670-18894-8). Viking Press.

Breed to Come. Alice Mary Norton. 1973. (pbk.) 1.25. Ace.

Breeze from Camelot. Vina Delmar. 3.95 o.p. (ISBN 0-15-113733-1). HarBraceJ.

Breeze of Morning. Charles Morgan. LC 51-13837. 1951. Macmillan.

Breeze Off the Ocean. Amii Loren. (Candlelight Ecstasy Ser.: No. 22). (Orig.). 1981. pap. 1.75 (ISBN 0-440-10817-9). Dell.

Brekneck Pass: A Powder Valley Western. Peter Field. LC 55-10226. 1955. Jefferson House.

Bremer's Works. Fredrika Bremer. Tr. by Mary Botham Howitt. LC 12-30915. (On cover; Bohn's libraries). 1892. G. Bell and Sons.

Brenda Maneuver. Stephen N. Rosenberg. LC 82-12601. 12.95 (ISBN 0-937858-12-9). Newmarket Press.

Brenda of the Flying U. Virginia Lee Moore. LC 49-987787. 1949. Wetzel Pub. Co.

Brenda Yorke. Mary Cecil Hay. (On cover: Lovell's library, no. 1029). 1887. J. W. Lovell Company.

Brenda Yorke: And Upon the Waters. Mary Cecil Hay. (On cover: Seaside library. Pocket ed., no. 987). 1887. G. Munro.

Brendan. Mary Longstreet Wallace. LC 66-19973. 4.95. Bruce.

Brenda's Murder. Stanton Forbes, pseud. LC 72-96264. 1973. 4.95 (ISBN 0-385-03808-9). Published for the Crime Club by Doubleday.

Brenda's Murder. Tobias Wells. LC 72-96264. 192p. 1973. 4.95 o.p. (ISBN 0-385-03808-9). Doubleday.

Brennan's Book: A Novel. Garrett Anderson. LC 72-86879. 1973. 7.95 (ISBN 0-399-11065-8). Putnam.

Brent. Cynthia McCarlie Jones. LC 53-388.

Brentons. Anna Chapin Ray. LC 12-1002. 1912. 1.25. Little, Brown, and Company.

Brentwood. Grace Livingston Hill. LC 37-20888. J. B. Lippincott Company.

Bressio. Richard Sapir. LC 75-10341. 6.95 (ISBN 0-394-49741-4). Random House.

Bret Harte's Stories of the Old West. Bret Harte. Ed. by Harper, Wilhelmina. LC 40-34192. 1940. Houghton Mifflin Company.

Brethren. Henry Rider Haggard. LC 4-26880. 1904. McClure, Phillips & Company.

Brethren. Illus. by Hookway Cowles. Henry Rider Haggard. LC 66-5441. 1966. bds., 2.95. Macdonald.

Brethren of the Axe. John Somers. LC 27-13762. E. P. Dutton & Company.

Brethren of the Beach. Henry De Clifford Couzens. LC 32-30637. L. C. Page & Company.

Breton Mills. A Romance. Charles Joseph Bellamy. LC 6-11702. 1879. G. P. Putnam's Sons.

Bretons of Elm Street. Henrietta Sperry Ripperger, pseud. LC 46-4004. 1946. G. P. Putnam's Sons.

Breughel Brothers. From the German of the Baron Von Sternberg. Ungern-Sternberg. LC 8-32290. 1854. Little, Brown, & Co.

Breughel Brothers. From the German of the Baron Von Sternberg. Ungern-Sternberg. LC 7-3056. 1873. J. R. Osgood and Company.

Brewers' Big Horses. Mildred Walker, pseud. LC 40-14429. Harcourt, Brace and Company.

Brewer's Fortune. Mary Dwinell Chellis. LC 6-23418. 1877. National Temperance Society and Publication House.

Brewsie and Willie. Gertrude Stein. LC 46-5457. 1946. Random House.

Brewster's Kingdom of God. Thurston Moore. LC 62-52767. 1962. Golden Bell Press.

Brewster's Millions. George Barr McCutcheon. LC 9-32298. Grosset & Dunlap.

Brewster's Millions. George Barr McCutcheon. Grosset & Dunlap.

Brewster's Millions. George Barr McCutcheon. LC 3-10197. 1903. H. S. Stone & Co.

Brewster's Millions. George Barr McCutcheon. 1904. H. S. Stone & Co.

Brewster's Millions. George Barr McCutcheon & David A Jasen. LC 80-17009. (Series: Continuum Classic of Humor.). 1980. 11.95 (ISBN 0-8264-0019-1). Continuum.

Brezhnev Memo. Morton Marcus. (Orig.). 1980. pap. 2.25 (ISBN 0-440-11034-3). Dell.

Brian Boru. Edward Henry Moeller. 1944. Foster & Stewart Publishing Corporation.

Briar and Palm: A Study of Circumstance and Influence. Annie S Swan Smith. LC 8-8194. 1890. Cranston and Stowe.

Briarcliff Manor. Sharon Anne Salvato. 1.50 (ISBN 0-440-10798-9). Dell.

Briarcliff Manor: A Novel. Sharon Anne Salvato. LC 73-90701. 1974. 6.95 (ISBN 0-8128-1661-7). Stein and Day.

Briarwood. Kay Ashby. 176p. (Orig.). 1976. pap. 1.25 (ISBN 0-89041-089-5, 3089). Major Bks.

Briarwood Summer. Kay Richardson. 1976. 4.95. Avalon Books.

Briary-Bush: A Novel. Floyd Dell. LC 21-20265. 1921. A. A. Knopf.

Bribed to Be Born: A Novel. Demetra Vaka Brown. LC 51-11601. 1951. Exposition Press.

Bric-a-Brac Dealer: Tr. from the French. E. Delauney de Melville. LC 6-34198. (On cover: The Catholic home library). 1892. Benziger Brothers.

Bric-a-Brac Man. Russell H Greenan. LC 76-7975. 7.95 (ISBN 0-394-40829-2). Random House.

Brick Alley. David Chacko. LC 80-28909. 10.95 (ISBN 0-440-00862-X). Delacorte Press.

Brick Foxhole. Richard Brooks. LC 45-453779. 1945. Harper & Brothers.

Brick Foxhole. Richard Brooks. LC 46-4404. 1946. The Sun Dial Press.

Brick Moon. Edward Everett Hale. LC 72-142575. 86p. 1971. Repr. of 1870 ed. 35.00 o.p. (ISBN 0-87636-012-6). Barre-Westover.

Brick Moon and Other Stories. Edward Everett Hale. LC 73-121555. (Short story index reprint series). (Illus.). 1970. Books for Libraries Press.

Brick Moon: From the Papers of Captain Frederic Ingham. Edward Everett Hale. LC 72-142575. (Illus.). 1971. (ISBN 0-87636-012-6). Printed at the Spiral Press for Members of the Imprint Society, Barre, Mass.

Brick Without Straw: A Story of Kentucky Mountain Life, by Lettie Saylor... Lettie Hoskins Saylor. LC 43-16526. 1943. The Hobson Press, Incorporated.

Bricks and Mortar: A Novel... Helen Ashton. LC 32-26063. 1932. Doubleday, Doran and Company, Inc.

Bricks Without Straw. Charles Gilman Norris. LC 38-253452. 1938. Doubleday, Doran & Co., Inc.

Bricks Without Straw. Albion Winegar Tourgee. LC 67-29282. (Americans in Fiction Ser.). Repr. of 1880 ed. lib. bdg. 16.00 (ISBN 0-8398-1963-3); pap. text ed. 4.50x (ISBN 0-89197-686-8). Irvington.

Bricks Without Straw. Albion Winegar Tourgee. Ed. by Otto H. Olsen. LC 74-80046. (Library of Southern Civilization). 1969. 35.00x (ISBN 0-8071-0906-1); pap. text ed. 8.95x (ISBN 0-8071-0211-3). La State U Pr.

Bricks Without Straw: A Novel. Albion Winegar Tourgee. LC 74-80046. (Library of Southern civilization). 1973. (pbk) 3.95 (ISBN 0-8071-0906-1). Louisiana State Univ. Pr.

Bricks Without Straw: A Novel. Albion Winegar Tourgee. LC 3-29968. Fords, Howard, & Hulbert; Etc., Etc.

Bricks Without Straw: A Novel, by Albion W. Tourgee. Albion Winegar Tourgee. LC 67-292821. (Americans in Fic). 1967. Gregg Pr.

Bridal Affair. Glenna Finley, pseud. 1972. pap. 1.95 (ISBN 0-451-11496-5, AJ1496, Sig). NAL.

Bridal Bed Murders. A. E. Martin. 1954. 2.50 o.p. (ISBN 0-671-10400-4). S&S.

Bridal Canopy. Samuel Joseph Agnon. Tr. by I. M. Lask from Hebrew. LC 67-19455. 300p. 1967. pap. 8.95 (ISBN 0-8052-0182-3). Schocken.

Bridal Canopy. Samuel Joseph Agnon & Lask, I. M., Tr. LC 37-271757. 1937. Doubleday, Doran & Company, Inc.

Bridal Canopy: By S. Y. Agnon. Tr. by I. M. Lask. Samuel Joseph. Agnon. LC 67-14955. (SB182). 1968. pap., 2.45. Schocken.

Bridal Eve: Or, Rose Elmer. Emma Dorothy Eliza Nevitte Southworth. LC 8-10810. 1881. T. B. Peterson & Brothers.

Bridal Gown: A Novel of Iceland. Kristmann Gudmundsson. Tr. by Theis, O. F. LC 31-28208. 1931. Cosmopolitan Book Corporation.

Bridal Journey. Dale Van Every. LC 50-6231. 1950. Mesner.

Bridal Journey. Dale Van Every. LC 50-6231. 1950. Messner.

Bridal March. Elizabeth Carfrae, pseud. LC 36-134594. G. P. Putnam's Sons.

Bridal March & Other Stories. facsimile ed. Bjornstjerne Bjornson. Tr. by Rasmos B. Anderson. LC 74-98562. (Short Story Index Reprint Ser.). 1882. 15.00 (ISBN 0-8369-3136-X). Ayer Co.

Bridal March: And Other Stories. author's ed. Bjornstjerne Bjornson & Anderson, Rasmus Bjorn, 1846- Tr. LC 6-11719. 1882. Houghton, Mifflin and Company.

Bridal of Anstace. Jessie Bedford. LC 6-19772. 1906. J. Lane.

Bridal Pond. Zona Gale. LC 30-27093. 1930. A. A. Knopf.

Bridal Trip in a Prairie Schooner: A Novel. Gilbert Guest. LC 21-9057. 1921. Burkley Printing Company.

Bridal Wreath: Tr. from the Norwegian of Sigrid Undset. Sigrid Undset. Tr. by Charles Archer. Scott, J. S., Joint Tr. LC 23-8081. 1923. A. A. Knopf.

Bride. Alex Austin. LC 64-11012. 1964. Holt, Rinehart and Winston.

Bride. Margaret Howe Freydberg. LC 52-8472. 1952. Harper.

Bride. Ladislav Grosman. LC 73-78666. 1970. 3.95. Doubleday.

Bride Adorned. David Leslie Murray. LC 29-7257. Harcourt, Brace and Company.

Bride & the Bachelors: The Heretical Courtship in Modern Art. Calvin Tomkins. (Illus.). 1965. 6.50 o.p. (ISBN 0-670-18919-7). Viking Pr.

Bride and the Pennant: The Greatest Story in the History of America's National Game... Frank Leroy Chance. LC 10-11301. 0.60. Laird & Lee.

Bride Dined Alone. Vera Kelsey. LC 43-13341. 1943. Pub. for the Crime Club by Doubleday, Doran and Co., Inc.

Bride Elect: Or, The Doom of the Double Roses. J. M. Simpson. (On cover: Street & Smith's select series, no. 13). 1888. Street & Smith.

Bride for a Captain. Flora Kidd. (Harlequin Presents Ser.). 192p. 1982. pap. 1.75 (ISBN 0-373-10485-5). Harlequin Bks.

Bride for a Night. Anne Hampson. (Harlequin Presents Ser.). 192p. 1981. pap. 1.75 (ISBN 0-373-10463-4). Harlequin Bks.

Bride for a Tiger. Jo Germany. 1975. (pbk.) 0.95 (ISBN 0-671-77992-3). Pocket Books.

Bride for Bedivere. Hilary Ford, pseud. LC 77-357175. 1976. 3.75 (ISBN 0-241-89499-9). Hamilton.

Bride for Hampton House. Hillary Waugh. LC 75-3645. 1975. 7.95 (ISBN 0-385-09741-7). Doubleday.

Bride for Narcissus: A Novel by Minnie H. Heim and Jane R. Preston. 1st Ed. Minnie H Heim & Jane R. Preston. LC 56-12280. 1957. Exposition Press.

Bride for New Orleans. 1st Ed. Edward Francis Murphy. LC 55-52754. Hanover House.

Bride for Sale. Jane Corrie. (Harlequin Romances Ser.). 192p. 1981. pap. 1.50 (ISBN 0-373-02431-2). Harlequin Bks.

Bride for the Sahib & Other Stories. Khushwant Singh. 168p. 1967. pap. 2.50 (ISBN 0-88253-087-9). Ind-US Inc.

Bride for Torment. Roberts. pap. 1.95 o.p. (ISBN 0-87977-133-X, DBB133). Dansk Blue Bk.

Bride from the Bush. Ernest William Hornung. (On cover: Arrow library, no. 93). Street & Smith.

Bride from the Desert. Grant Allen. LC 5-410353. 1896. R. F. Fenno & Company.

Bride Goes East. Romilly Brent. LC 47-1836. 1947. Arcadia House.

Bride in Black. Lillia Shaw Husted. LC 20-6866. 1920. The Four Seas Company.

Bride in the Parsonage. Illus. by Jim Padgett. Dorothy Lockwood Aitken. LC 66-3932. bds., 3.95. Southern Pub.

Bride Laughed Once. Marion K Sanders & Edelatein, Mortimer S., Joint Author. LC 43-10175. 1943. Farrar & Rinehart, Inc.

Bride of a Moment. Carolyn Wells. LC 16-16389. George H. Doran Company.

Bride of a Stranger. Patricia Maxwell. (Fawcett gold medal book). 1974. (pbk.) 0.95. Fawcett.

Bride of a Thousand Cedars. Bruce Lancaster. (Illus.). 344p. 1975. Repr. of 1939 ed. lib. bdg. 17.45x (ISBN 0-89190-883-8). Am Repr-Rivercity Pr.

Bride of a Thousand Cedars: A Novel of Bermuda. Bruce Lancaster. LC 75-33037. 1975. 9.95 (ISBN 0-89190-883-8). Rivercity Press.

Bride of a Thousand Cedars: A Novel of Bermuda. Bruce Lancaster & Brentano, Lowell. LC 39-28989. 1939. Frederick A. Stokes Company.

Bride of Alderburn. Marguerite Neilson, pseud. (Berkley Medallion Book). 1977. 1.50 (ISBN 0-425-03638-3). Berkley Pub. Corp.

Bride of Belvale. Harriet Rich. (Candlelight gothic). 1975. (pbk.) 0.75. Dell.

Bride of Bridal Hill. George Agnew Chamberlain. LC 42-252379. 1942. The Bobbs-Merrill Company.

Bride of Cairngore. Jean Francis Webb. LC 74-81605. 1974. 7.95 (ISBN 0-679-50514-8). McKay.

Bride of Donnybrook. Leslie Ames. pap. 0.75 o.s.i. (01-334). Lancer.

Bride of Donnybrook. William Edward Daniel Ross. LC 66-9243. 1966. Arcadia House.

Bride of Emersham. Leslie Lance. 1974. pap. cancelled o.p. (ISBN 0-515-03542-4). Pyramid Pubns.

Bride of Fortune: A Novel Based on the Life of Mrs. Jefferson Davis. Harnett Thomas Kane. LC 48-874637. 1948. Doubleday.

Bride of Frankenstein. Michael Egrement. 1976. 8.50. Bookfinger.

Bride of Fu Manchu. Sax Rohmer, pseud. 1976. Repr. of 1933 ed. lib. bdg. 12.05 (ISBN 0-89190-801-3). Am Repr-Rivercity Pr.

Bride of Fu Manchu. Sax Rohmer, pseud. 1969. pap. 0.60 o.p. (X2113). Pyramid Pubns.

Bride of Fu Manchu. Sax Rohmer, pseud. 1976. pap. 1.25 o.p. (ISBN 0-515-03940-3). BJ Pub Group.

Bride of Gaylord Hall. Saliee O'Brien. (Kangaroo Book). 1978. 1.50 (ISBN 0-671-81875-9). Pocket Books.

Bride of Glendearg: A Novel. Allan McIvor. 1904. W. J. Ritchie.

Bride of Glory: Being the Strange Story of Emy Lyon, a Blacksmith's Daughter, Who Married His Britannic Majesty's Envoy Extraordinary and Minister Plenipotentiary to the Court of Naples and Became Emma, Lady Hamilton, Companion of Royalty and the True Friend of Vice-Admiral Lord Nelson, K.B., Duke of Bronte. Bradda Field. LC 42-36110. 1942. The Greystone Press.

Bride of Infelice: A Novel. Laura Eugenia Newhall. LC 7-969. 1892. The Bancroft Company.

Bride of Invercoe. Charlotte Massey. LC 77-360351. (Troubadour). 1976. 3.50 (ISBN 0-356-08170-2). Macdonald and Jane's.

Bride of Israel, My Love. Richard Llewellyn. LC 74-186038. 1973. 6.95 (ISBN 0-385-05551-X). Doubleday.

Bride of Japan. William Carlton Lanyon Dawe. 1898. H. S. Stone & Company.

Bride of King Solomon. Florence McGehee. LC 58-109215. 1958. Macmillan.

Bride of Lammermoor. Walter Scott. (On cover: Lovell's library, no. 489). 1885. J. W. Lovell Company.

Bride of Lammermoor. Walter Scott. (On cover: Seaside library. Pocket ed. 362). 1885. G. Munro.

Bride of Lammermoor. Walter Scott. LC 36-37000. (Half-title: Everyman's library, ed. by Ernest Rhys. Fiction. no. 129). 1932. J. M. Dent & Sons, Ltd.

Bride of Landeck. George Payne Rainsford James. LC 7-7583. (On cover: Harper's half-hour series. no. 51). 1878. Harper & Brothers.

Bride of Lenore. Cynthia Kavanaugh. 1972. pap. 0.75 o.p. (T2742). Pyramid Pubns.

Bride of Lenore. Cynthia Kavanaugh. 1977. pap. 1.25 o.p. (ISBN 0-515-04237-4). BJ Pub Group.

Bride of Llewellyn. Emma Dorothy Eliza Nevitte Southworth. LC 12-38907. T. B. Peterson & Brothers.

Bride of Love: Or, The True Greatness of Female Heroism. Stopford James Ram. LC 8-29986. 1859. D. Rulison.

Bride of Lowther Fell: A Romance. Margaret Forster. LC 80-69370. 1981. 12.95 (ISBN 0-689-11129-0). Atheneum.

Bride of Menace. Ann Forman Barron. (Gold medal Book, M2896). 1973. (pbk) 0.95. Fawcett Pubns.

Bride of Misfortune. Vanessa Blake. (Ravenswood gothic). 1974. (pbk.) 0.95 (ISBN 0-671-77929-X). Pocket Books.

Bride of Mission San Jose: A Tale of Early California. John Augustine Cull. LC 21-108. The Abingdon Press.

Bride of Moat House. Norah Robinson Lofts. LC 59-6266. (Fawcett crest book). 1975. (pbk.) 1.50. Fawcett.

Bride of Monte Cristo. A Sequel to "The Count of Monte Cristo,". LC 6-26326. (On cover: Seaside library. Pocket ed. no 259). G. Munro.

Bride of Monte Cristo. A Sequel to "The Count of Monte Cristo.". (On cover: The library of American authors, no. 22). G. Munro.

Bride of Newgate. John Dickson Carr. 1972. pap. 0.95 o.p. (09140). Curtis.

Bride of Newgate. 1st Ed. John Dickson Carr. LC 50-6752. 1950. Harper.

Bride of Omberg. Emilia Smith Flygare Carlen. Tr. by Krause, Alex. L. & Perce, Elbert. LC 6-20149. 1853. C. Scribner.

Bride of Pendorric. Eleanor Hibbert. LC 63-12964. 1963. Doubleday.

Bride of Pendorric. Victoria Holt, pseud. 272p. 1981. pap. 2.50 (ISBN 0-449-23280-8, Crest). Fawcett.

Bride of Pontravon. Mair Unsworth. 1980. pap. 1.75 (ISBN 0-441-07307-7). Ace Bks.

Bride of Quietness. Alexander Knox. LC 33-20823. 1933. The Macmillan Company.

Bride of Raven Island. Ellen Orford. 1974. pap. 0.95 o.p. (09257). Curtis.

Bride of Revenge. Denise Robins. (Contemporary Romance Ser.). Orig. Title: Desire Is Blind. 1972. pap. 0.75 o.p. (T2736). Pyramid Pubns.

Bride of Revenge. Denise Robins. pap. 1.25 o.p. (ISBN 0-515-04299-4). BJ Pub Group.

Bride of Satan. Frank Anvic, pseud. 192p. 1974. pap. 1.95 o.p. (ISBN 0-87056-379-3, 6379). Brandon.

Bride of Sforza. Miranda Seymour, pseud. LC 74-23661. 1975. 7.95 (ISBN 0-395-20290-6). Houghton Mifflin.

Bride of Suleiman. Aileen Crawley. LC 81-14525. 1982. 10.95 (ISBN 0-312-09543-0). St. Martin's Press.

Bride of Terror. Evelyn Bond. 272p. 1975. pap. 1.25 (ISBN 0-532-12308-5). Woodhill.

Bride of Terror. Evelyn Bond. 1971. pap. 0.75 o.p. (ISBN 0-447-74912-9). Lancer.

Bride of the Beasts. Richard Christy. 192p. pap. 1.95 o.p. (ISBN 0-87056-170-7, 6170). Brandon.

Bride of the Conqueror: A Novel. Hartzell Spence. LC 54-937710. 1954. Random House.

Bride of the Delta Queen. Janet Dailey. (Harlequin Presents Ser.). 1979. pap. 1.25 (ISBN 0-373-70784-3, Pub. by Harlequin). PB.

Bride of the Desert: A Throbbing, Romantic Tale of Love and Adventure, Based on the Motion Picture Story. Arthur Hoerl. LC 30-15210. Jacobsen Publishing Company, Inc.

Bride of the Dullahan. Sharon Wagner. LC 76-3008. 1976. 5.95 (ISBN 0-385-11633-0). Doubleday.

Bride of the Innisfallen: And Other Stories. 1st Ed. Eudora Welty. LC 55-5248. 1955. Harcourt, Brace.

Bride of the Innisfallen & Other Stories. Eudora Welty. LC 55-5248. 1972. pap. 3.95 (ISBN 0-15-614075-6, Harv). HarBraceJ.

Bride of the MacHugh. Jan Cox Speas. 1978. 1.95 (ISBN 0-380-01825-X). Avon Books.

Bride of the MacHugh: A Novel. Jan Cox Speas. LC 54-9492. 1954. Bobbs-Merrill Co.

Bride of the Mistletoe. James Lane Allen. LC 9-16803. 1909. The Macmillan Company.

Bride of the Mistletoe. James Lane Allen. LC 45-32787. 1909. The Macmillan Company.

Bride of the Night. Louise Gerard. LC 30-5245. The Macaulay Company.

Bride of the Nile... Georg Moritz Ebers. Tr. by Bell, Clara Courtenay (Poynter) LC 16-15705. (historical romances of Georg Ebers. vol. viiii). 1915. D. Appleton and Company.

Bride of the Nile. Georg Moritz Ebers & Smith, Mrs. Mary Stuart (Harrison) 1834- Tr. (On cover: Seaside library. Pocket ed., no. 1056). 1887. G. Munro.

Bride of the Nile. A Romance. Georg Moritz Ebers. Tr. by Clara Courtenay Bell. (Harper's Franklin square library, no. 574). 1887. Harper & Brothers.

Bride of the Nile: A Romance by Georg Ebers... Georg Moritz Ebers. Tr. by Clara Courtenay Bell. 1887. W. S. Gottsberger.

Bride of the Northern Wilds. A Tale of 1743. rev., enl. and cor. ed. Newton Mallory Curtis. 1843. Burgess, Stringer & Co.

Bride of the Plains. Emmuska Orczy. LC 15-9698. 1.35. George H. Doran Company.

Bride of the Rain God: Princess of Chicken-Itza, the Sacred City of the Mayas; Being an Historical Romance of a Prince and Princess of Chichen- Itza in That Glamorous Land of the Ancient Mayas, Where Conflicting Human Passions Dominated the Lives of the Long-Dead Past As They Do Those of Today. Theodore Arthur Willard. LC 31-10523. The Burrows Bros. Co.

Bride of the Rif, the Girl at Eagles' Mount, Bird of Paradise. Margaret Rome. (Harlequin Romances Ser.). 576p. 1982. pap. 3.50 (ISBN 0-373-20063-3). Harlequin Bks.

Bride of the River. Laura B Harris. LC 56-11119. Crowell.

Bride of the Sabbath. Samuel Badisch Ornitz. LC 51-6975. 1951. Rinehart.

Bride of the Sun. Elizabeth Hunter. 192p. (Orig.). 1980. pap. 1.50 (ISBN 0-671-57051-X). S&S.

Bride of the Sun. Gaston Leroux. LC 77-84248. (Lost Race and Adult Fantasy Fiction). 1978. 18.00 (ISBN 0-405-10994-6). Arno Press.

Bride of the Tomb. Alexander McVeigh Miller. (On cover: Lovell's library, no. 1246). 1888. J. W. Lovell Company.

Bride of the Tomb: And Guy Kenmore's Wife. Alexander McVeigh Miller. (On cover: Clover series, no. 120). 1896. Street & Smith.

Bride of the Tomb: Or, Lancelot Darling's Betrothed. Alexander McVeigh Miller. (On cover: Munro's library, v. 1, no. 2). N. L. Munro.

Bride of the Unliving. Luanna Churchill. LC 74-31245. 1974-1975. 4.95 (ISBN 0-517-52116-4). Lenox Hill Press.

Bride of the Wilderness. Emerson Bennett. LC 7-344357. T. B. Peterson.

Bride of Thunder. Jeanne Williams. (Kangaroo Book). 1.95 (ISBN 0-671-81487-7). Pocket Books.

Bride Price: A Novel. Buchi Emecheta. LC 75-46608. 1976. 6.95 (ISBN 0-8076-0818-1). G. Braziller.

Bride Price: A Novel. Buchi Emecheta. LC 76-377899. 3.50 (ISBN 0-85031-165-9). Allison & Busby.

Bride Regrets. Marjorie Chalmers Carleton. LC 50-6260. 1950. Morrow.

Bride Saw Red. Robert Carson. LC 42-51120. G. P. Putnam's Sons.

Bride Stealer. Frank O'Rourke. LC 59-11703. 1960. W. Morrow.

Bride That Got Away. George Selmark, pseud. LC 67-24972. 1967. Published for the Crime Club by Doubleday.

Bride, the Story of Louise and Montrose: By Margaret Irwin. Margaret Emma Faith Irwin. LC 39-21664. 1939. bds., 3.95. Chatto & Windus.

Bride: The Story of Louise and Montrose. Margaret Emma Faith Irwin. LC 39-27804. Harcourt, Brace and Company.

Bride-to-Be. James Noble Gifford. LC 48-4479. 1948. Gramercy Pub. Co.

Bride to Be. Vida Hurst. LC 37-986131. M. S. Mill Co., Inc.

Bride to the King. Barbara Cartland. LC 79-14995. 8.95 (ISBN 0-525-07095-8). Dutton.

Bride Turned Gay. Wayne Wallace. (Orig.). pap. 0.95 o.p. (1148). Brandon.

Bride Was Beautiful. James Noble Gifford. LC 43-8697. 1943. Gramercy Pub. Co.

Bride Was Beautiful. Carol Holliston. LC 43-869775. 1943. Gramercy Publishing Co.

Bride Was Late. Myra Gay. LC 46-18419. 1946. Arcadia House, Inc.

Bride Wore Black. Cornell George Hopley-Woolrich. LC 48-12846. (Pocket book, 271). 1945. Pocket Books.

Bride Wore Black... Cornell Woolrich, pseud. LC 41-409246. 1940. Simon and Schuster.

Bride Wore Overalls. James Noble Gifford. LC 44-9903. 1944. Gramercy Pub. Co.

Bride Wore Overalls. Carol Holliston. LC 44-9903. 1944. Gramercy Publishing Company.

Bride Wore the Traditional Gold. Talbot Spivak. LC 70-171155. 1972. 5.95 (ISBN 0-394-47285-3). Knopf.

Bridegroom Cometh. Waldo David Frank. LC 39-13360. Doubleday, Doran & Company, Inc.

Bride's Boudoir. Miriam Ryon. LC 25-19527. 1925. Siebel Publishing Corporation.

Bride's Castle: A Mystery. Philip Whitwell Wilson. LC 44-6029. 1944. Farrar & Rinehart, Inc.

Bride's Confession & Other Indiscretions. James Holmes et al. 1972. pap. 1.75 o.s.i. (V1101K, Venus). Grove.

Bride's Fate. Emma Dorothy Eliza Nevitte Southworth. LC 65-78590. T. B. Peterson.

Bride's Hero. Alice Muriel Livingston Williamson. LC 12-22596. 1912. Frederick A. Stokes Company.

Bride's House. Dawn Powell. Brentano's.

Bride's Island: A Novel. Margaret Bell Houston. LC 51-12154. 1951. Crown Publishers.

Bride's Mirror: A Tale of Domestic Life in Delhi Forty Years Ago. Ahmad Nazir. Ed. by Ward, George Ernest. LC 44-16436. 1903. H. Frowde, Oxford University Press.

Brides of Bellenmore. Anne Maybury. 1976. 1.95. Ace.

Brides of Devil's Leap. Sandra Shulman. 1971. pap. 0.75 o.p. (64-693). Paperback Lib.

Brides of Lucifer. Miriam Lynch. 1976. pap. 1.25 (ISBN 0-532-12414-6). Woodhill.

Brides of Lucifer see Doomsday Bells.

Brides of Terror. John Slater. LC 70-397394. 1968. 0.55. Scripts.

Brides of the South Wind. Robinson Jeffers. 1974. 37.50 o.s.i. (ISBN 0-9600372-6-8). Cayucos Bks.

Brides of the Tiger. A Tale of Adventure When These Colonies Were New. William Henry Babcock. LC 6-503219. (On cover: Idylwild series, v. 1, no. 28). 1893. Morrill, Higgins & Co.

Bride's Progress. Harold Weston. LC 28-20922. 1928. W. Morrow and Company.

Bride's Return: Or, How Grand Avenue Church Came to Christ; a Story with a Supreme Purpose... Charles Augustus Jenkens. LC 11-14719. C. H. Robinson & Company.

Brideshead Revisited. Evelyn Waugh. 1982. 9.95 (ISBN 0-316-92627-2); pap. 4.95 (ISBN 0-316-92634-5). Little.

Brideshead Revisited. Evelyn Waugh. 1982. 20.00 (ISBN 0-316-92582-9). Little.

Brideshead Revisited: The Sacred and Profane Memories of Captain Charles Ryder: a Novel. Evelyn Waugh. LC 78-64588. 1979. 8.95 (ISBN 0-316-92627-2). Little, Brown.

Brideshead Revisited: The Sacred and Profane Memories of Captain Charles Ryder: a Novel. Evelyn Waugh. LC 82-9191. 1982. 15.95 (ISBN 0-8161-3400-6). G.K. Hall.

Brideshead Revisited: The Sacred and Profane Memories of of Captain Charles Ryder. Evelyn Waugh. LC 45-7846. 1945. Little, Brown and Company.

Bridge. Marguerite Allis. LC 49-107963. 1949. G. P. Putnam's Sons.

Bridge. Pamela Frankau. LC 56-11101. 1957. Harper.

Bridge. James Noble Gifford. LC 40-31629. 1940. Arcadia House.

Bridge. Warren Howard. LC 40-31629. 1940. Arcadia House, Inc.

Bridge. Franz Kafka. LC 83-2920. 1983. 5.95 (ISBN 0-8052-3856-5). Schocken Books.

Bridge. D. Keith Mano. LC 72-96248. 1973. 6.95 (ISBN 0-385-02870-9). Doubleday.

Bridge. D. Keith Mano. (Signet book). 1974. (pbk.) 1.25. New American Library.

Bridge. H. L Mountzoures. LC 76-37196. 1972. 8.95 (ISBN 0-684-12744-X). Scribner.

Bridge. Naomi Gwladys Royde-Smith. LC 33-2077. 1933. Doubleday, Doran & Company, Inc.

Bridge: A Story of the Great Lakes. Marjorie Lowry Christie Pickthall. LC 22-1721. 1922. The Century Co.

Bridge Across. Lizzie Allen Harker. LC 21-20438. 1921. C. Scribner's Sons.

Bridge Across Hell. Jessie Emerson Moffat. LC 42-21002. 1942. J. Swift, Incorporated.

Bridge & the Ballad. Margaret Forrest. (O.s.i.). 1975. pap. 1.95 o.s.i. (ISBN 0-912852-04-6). Echo Pubs.

Bridge at Arta and Other Stories. Michael Innes, pseud. LC 82-2228. 1982. 14.95 (ISBN 0-393-01590-4). Norton.

Bridge at Arta: And Other Stories. John Innes Mackintosh Stewart. 182p. 1982. 14.95 (ISBN 0-393-01590-4). Norton.

Bridge at Kilometer 575. Nolan J. Argyle. (Orig.). 1979. pap. 1.75 (ISBN 0-532-17244-2). Woodhill.

Bridge Builders. Anna Chapin Ray. LC 9-3333. 1909. 1.50. Little, Brown, and Company.

Bridge-Club Hostess. Sally Chayes. LC 34-34024. 1933. J. Collins, Inc.

Bridge for Passing. Pearl Sydenstricker Buck. 1962. 7.95 o.p. (ISBN 0-381-98019-7, A10200). John Day.

Bridge in the Jungle. B Traven. LC 38-17564. 1938. A. A. Knopf.

Bridge in the Jungle: By B. Traven. B Traven. LC 67-146508. 1967. 5.00. Hill & Wang.

Bridge of Ashes. Roger Zelazny. LC 78-26980. (Gregg Press Science Fiction Series). (Illus.). 1979. 10.00 (ISBN 0-8398-2466-1). Gregg Press.

Bridge of Ashes. Roger Zelazny. (Signet Book). 1976. 1.25. New American Library.

Bridge of Beyond. Simone Schwarz-Bart. (Illus.). 1974. 7.95 o.p. (ISBN 0-689-10589-4). Atheneum.

Bridge of Catzad-Dum and Other Stories. Mark E. Rogers. LC 80-116452. (Illus.). 1980. 6.00 (ISBN 0-937528-00-5). Burning Bush Press.

Bridge of Corvie. Jane Fraser. (cameo Romance#36). 1975. (pbk.) 0.95. Fawcett.

Bridge of Desire. Warwick Deeping. LC 31-7080. 1931. R. M. McBride & Company.

Bridge of Desire: A Story of Unrest. Warwick Deeping. LC 16-23362. (Illus.). 1916. R. M. McBride & Company.

Bridge of Fear. Dorothy Eden. 1976. pap. 1.95 (ISBN 0-441-07979-2). Ace Bks.

Bridge of Fortune. Harnett Thomas Kane. 1972. pap. 0.95 o.p. (09134). Curtis.

Bridge of Glass. A Novel. Frederick William Robinson. (seaside library. v. 81, no. 1632). 1883. G. Munro.

Bridge of Glass. A Novel. Frederick William Robinson. LC 43-27481. 1872. Harper & Brothers.

Bridge of Heaven. Murray Dyer. LC 51-11903. 1952. Harper.

Bridge of Heaven. Shih-I Hsiung. LC 43-106879. 1943. G. P. Putnam's Sons.

Bridge of Kisses. Berta Ruck. LC 20-17083. 1920. 2.00. Dodd, Mead and Company.

Bridge of Leaves. 1st Ed. Diana Cavallo. LC 61-12786. 1961. Atheneum.

Bridge of Light. Alpheus Hyatt Verrill. LC 50-8738. 1950. Fantasy Press.

Bridge of Lions. Henry Slesar. LC 63-16132. (Cock Robin mystery). 1963. Macmillan.

Bridge of Love. Charlotte Mary Brame. (On cover: Lovell's library. no. 1178). J. W. Lovell Company.

Bridge of Love. Leslie Caine. 192p. (Orig.). 1980. pap. 1.50 (ISBN 0-671-57010-2). S&S.

Bridge of Magpies. Geoffrey Jenkins. LC 74-28548. (Illus.). 1975. 7.95 (ISBN 0-399-11492-0). Putnam.

Bridge of Pilate. Esther Kellner. LC 59-10647. 1959. Appleton-Century-Crofts.

Bridge of San Luis Rey. Thornton Niven Wilder. 1976. (pbk.) 1.50 (ISBN 0-380-00589-1). Avon.

Bridge of San Luis Rey. Thornton Niven Wilder. LC 67-22516. 1967. Harper & Row.

Bridge of San Luis Rey. Thornton Niven Wilder. LC 27-23452. 1927. A. & C. Boni.

Bridge of San Luis Rey. Thornton Niven Wilder. LC 28-4669. 1928. A. & C. Boni.

Bridge of San Luis Rey. Thornton Niven Wilder & Kent, Rockwell, 1882- Illus. LC 29-21678. 1929. A. & C. Boni.

Bridge of San Luis Rey: By Thornton Wilder. Large Type Ed. Thornton Niven Wilder. LC 68-1657. 4.79. Harper.

Bridge of San Luis Rey. With an Introd. by Granville Hicks. Illustrated with Lithographs in Color by Jean Charlot. Thornton Niven Wilder. LC 62-524618. 1962. Heritage Press.

Bridge of San Luis Rey. With an Introd. by Granville Hicks. Illustrated with Lithographs in Color by Jean Charlot. Thornton Niven Wilder. 1962. Limited Editions Club.

Bridge of Sand. Frank Gruber. LC 63-18720. 1963. Dutton.

Bridge of Sighs. Jane Lane. LC 74-9360. 1975. (ISBN 0-381-98277-7). John Day Co.

Bridge of Strange Music. Jane Blackmore. 224p. (O.S.I). 1973. lib. bdg. 4.95 o.s.i. (ISBN 0-7075-0103-2). White Lion Pubs.

Bridge of Tears. Ruth Abbey. (Ace gothic). 1975. (pbk.) 0.95. Ace Books.

Bridge of the Gods. new ed. Frederic Homer Balch. LC 65-18447. (Illus.). 1965. 8.95 (ISBN 0-8323-0108-6). Binford.

Bridge of the Gods: A Romance of Indian Oregon. Frederic Homer Balch. LC 6-6860. 1890. A. C. McClurg and Company.

Bridge of the Gods: A Romance of Indian Oregon. 7th ed., with eight full-page illustrations by l. maynard dixon. ed. Frederic Homer Balch. LC 2-20268. 1902. A. C. McClurg & Co.

Bridge of Time. William Henry Warner. LC 9-19853. 1919. Scott & Seltzer.

Bridge of Unity. Renee Van Tuyll. 3.95 o.s.i. (ISBN 0-8181-0126-1). Pageant-Poseidon.

Bridge of Years. May Sarton. LC 46-3357. 1946. Doubleday & Company, Inc.

Bridge of Years: A Novel. May Sarton. LC 76-162709. 1971. 6.95 (ISBN 0-393-08652-6). Norton.

Bridge on Ice. Szymon Szechter. LC 77-366452. (Signature series; 26). 1977. 5.95 (ISBN 0-7145-2596-0). M. Boyars.

Bridge on the Drina. Ivo Andric. LC 77-368170. (Phoenix book; P746). 1977. 4.95 (ISBN 0-226-02045-2). University of Chicago Press.

Bridge on the Drina. Tr. from Serbo-Croat by Lovett F. Edwards. Afterword by John Simon. 1st Signet Classic Ed. Ivo Andric. LC 67-142187. (Signet classic ed.). (Signet classic). 1967. New Amer. Lib.

Bridge on the Drina. Translated from the Serbo-Croat by Lovett F. Edwards. Ivo Andric. LC 59-9676. 1959. Macmillan.

Bridge Over Dark Gods: An Occult Novel. Furze Morrish. LC 47-202269. Rider & Co.

Bridge Over Tano Gorge. Richard Martin Stern. LC 82-45149. 1982. 15.95 (ISBN 0-385-18018-7). Doubleday.

Bridge over the River Kwai. Pierre Boulle. LC 54-11508. 10.95 (ISBN 0-8149-0072-0). Vanguard.

Bridge Over the River Kwai. large type ed. Pierre Boulle. (Keith Jennison Bks). 7.95 o.p. (ISBN 0-531-00166-0). Watts.

Bridge Over the River Kwai: Translated by Xan Fielding. Pierre Boulle. LC 54-115081. 1954. Vanguard Press.

Bridge That Went Nowhere. Robert L. Fish. (Red Mask Mystery). (YA) 1968. 3.95 o.p. (ISBN 0-399-10099-7). Putnam.

Bridge That Went Nowhere: A Captain Jose Da Silva Novel. Robert L Fish. LC 68-19218. (Red mask mystery). 1968. Putnam.

Bridge to a Wedding. John Munonye. LC 79-307512. (African writers series; 195). (H.E.B. paperback). 1978. 3.95 (ISBN 0-435-90195-8). Heinemann Educational.

Bridge to Bonito Island. Burette Stinson Tillinghast. LC 78-6926. 6.95 (ISBN 0-8037-0612-X). Dial Press.

Bridge to Brooklyn. Albert Edward Idell. LC 44-9751. 1944. H. Holt and Company.

Bridge to Home: By Gay Rutherford Pseud. James Noble Gifford. LC 54-114651. 1954. Arcadia House.

Bridge to Israel. Harry Canelstein. LC 70-81634. 1969. 5.95. Pageant Press International.

Bridge to Paradise. Kathleen Rollins. LC 46-2675. 1946. Arcadia House, Inc.

Bridge to Paradise. Faith Shannon. LC 69-11657. 1969. 2.95. Zondervan Pub. House.

Bridge to the Other Side. Monika Kotowska. LC 75-116264. 1970. 4.50. Doubleday.

Bridge to Yesterday. Constance Gluyas. 1981. pap. 3.50 (ISBN 0-451-11013-7, AE1013, Sig). NAL.

Bridge Too Far. Cornelius Ryan. (O.s.i.). 1974. 14.95 o.s.i. (ISBN 0-671-21792-5). S&S.

Bridge. Tr. by Robert S. Rosen. Manfred Gregor. (T-532). 1961. Avon.

Bridge. Translated by Robert S. Rosen. Manfred Gregor. LC 60-12128. 1960. Random House.

Bridgeman of the Crossways. Justin Jr Heresford. LC 25-122488. Marshall Jones Company.

Bridgeport Bus. Maureen Howard. LC 65-19059. 4.95. Harcourt.

Bridgeport Bus. Maureen Howard. LC 80-13560. 1980. 4.50 (ISBN 0-14-005566-5). Penguin Books.

Bridges. Tarjei Vesaas. LC 78-121689. 1970. 5.00. Morrow.

Bridges & Bars. Rolf Schneider. Tr. by M. Bullock. 1967. 4.95 o.p. (ISBN 0-670-19019-5). Viking Pr.

Bridges and Bars. Tr. from German by Michael Bullock. Rolf Schneider. LC 67-11264. 1967. 4.95. Viking.

Bridges at Toko-Ri. James A Michener. LC 81-7009. 1981. 11.95 (ISBN 0-8161-3262-3). G.K. Hall.

Bridges at Toko-Ri. James Albert Michener. LC 52-7129. 1953. Random House.

Bridges at Toko-Ri: A School Edition by Richard L. Loughlin. James Albert Michener. 2.48. Globe Book Co.

Bridges of Price. Daniel Marcus Davin. LC 72-88402. 1973. 6.95 (ISBN 0-698-10510-9). Coward, McCann & Geoghegan.

Bridgestow: Some Chronicles of a Cornish Parish. Mark Guy Pearse. Jennings and Graham.

Bridget. Hermann Bosch. LC 8-11700. 1908. B. W. Dodge & Company.

Bridget Loves Bernie. Paul Fairman. 1972. 0.75. Lancer Books.

Bridget Malwyn. Martin Boyd. York.

Bridget: Or, What's in a Name? William Wilfrid Whalen. LC 6-22857. Mayhew Publishing Company.

Bridie Steen: With an Introd. by Lord Dunsany. Anne Crone. LC 48-8073. 1948. C. Scribner's Sons.

Bridle Paths. Isaac Rusling Pennypacker. LC 12-187. 1911. 1.00. Christopher Sower Company.

Bridle the Wind. Julia Davis. LC 53-8233. 1953. Rinehart.

Brief but Warm the Rain. Robert Merle Crowell. LC 74-196023. (Illus.). 1974. Windhover Press.

Brief Candle. Norman Venner. LC 28-21417. The Bobbs-Merrill Company.

Brief Candles. Aldous Leonard Huxley. LC 30-17438. 1930. The Fountain Press.

Brief Candles: Stories. Aldous Leonard Huxley. LC 30-20167. 1930. Doubleday, Doran & Company, Inc.

Brief Candles. 1st Ed. LC 54-6788. 1954. Doubleday.

Brief Case of Murder. Amelia Reynolds Long. LC 49-48487. 1949. Phoenix Press.

Brief Contacts. David Gibson. LC 32-292049. 1932. R. Long & R. R. Smith, Inc.

Brief Ecstasy. Denise Robins. 1976. pap. 1.25 (ISBN 0-345-25093-1). Ballantine.

Brief Ecstasy. Denise Robins. 1972. pap. 0.75 o.p. (94252). Beagle Bks.

Brief Flower. Dorothy Evelyn Smith. LC 66-11559. 1966. Dutton.

Brief Flower of Youth. Graham Heath. LC 37-16224. 1937. Longmans, Green and Co.

Brief Gaudy Hour. Margaret Campbell Barnes. 1981. pap. 2.75 (ISBN 0-441-08014-6). Ace Bks.

Brief Gaudy Hour. Margaret Campbell Barnes. 336p. 1972. 6.95 (ISBN 0-8255-1520-3). Macrae.

Brief Gaudy Hour: A Novel of Anne Boleyn. Margaret Campbell Barnes. 1949. Macrae-Smith-Co.

Brief Glory: A Novel. Rosamond Neal Du Jardin. LC 44-5841. 1944. Macrae-Smith-Company.

Brief Golden Time. Marjorie Vernon. pap. 0.50 o.p. (52-915). Paperback Lib.

Brief Honors: A Romance of the Great Dividable. Moses Lewis Scudder. LC 8-8390. 1877. Jansen, McClurg & Co.

Brief Hour of Francois Villon. John Erskine. LC 37-18661. The Bobbs-Merrill Company.

Brief Infinity: A Love Story in Haiku. Jayne May Murdock. LC 80-83998. 1981. 6.00 (ISBN 0-932916-06-6). May-Murdock Publications.

Brief Is the Glory. Constance Gluyas. LC 75-8567. 1975. 8.95 (ISBN 0-679-50560-1). D. McKay Co.

Brief Kingdom. Gerald Breckenridge. LC 36-29613. 1936. Doubleday, Doran & Company, Inc.

Brief Life. Juan Carlos Onetti. LC 75-28197. 1976. 10.00 (ISBN 0-670-19069-1). Grossman Publishers.

Brief Pleasure. Peggy Gaddis, pseud. LC 49-407953. 1949. Phoenix Press.

Brief Rapture. Polan Banks. LC 32-14440. 1932. H. Smith.

Brief Rapture. Anne Duffield. LC 40-959013. 1938. Arcadia House.

Brief Seduction of Eva, a Novel. Mathilde Eiker. LC 32-25591. 1932. Doubleday, Doran & Company, Inc.

Brief Tales from the Bench. Henry Cecil. LC 74-171605. (Inner Sanctum Mystery Ser.). (O.S.I.). 1972. 4.95 o.s.i. (ISBN 0-671-21145-5). S&S.

Brief Tales from the Bench: Eight Courtroom Vignettes. Henry Cecil & British Broadcasting Corporation. LC 74-171605. (Inner sanctum mystery special). 1972. 4.95 (ISBN 0-671-21145-5). Simon and Schuster.

Brief Year. Grace Jamison Breckling. LC 51-9318. 1951. Westminster Press.

Briefe on Milena. Franz Kafka. (Ger.). 1952. 14.50 (ISBN 0-8052-3022-X). Schocken.

Briefing for a Descent into Hell. Doris May Lessing. LC 71-136325. 1971. 6.95 (ISBN 0-394-42198-1). Knopf.

Briefing for a Descent into Hell. Doris May Lessing. LC 80-6142. 1981. 2.95 (ISBN 0-394-74662-7). Vintage Books.

Briefleigh: A Tale of the Times of Old John Brown. Robert S Bevier & Brown, John. LC 6-131273. (On cover: Minerva series, no. 2). 1889. Minerva Publishing Co.

Brierfield Tragedy. Rebecca Fergus Redd. (On cover: Lovell's library, v. 8, no. 408). 1884. J. W. Lovell Company.

Brigade. John Shirley. 256p. 1981. pap. 2.25 (ISBN 0-380-77156-X, 77156). Avon.

Brigade: By Hanoch Bartov. Tr. by David S. Segal. 1st Amer. Ed. Hanokh Bartov. LC 67-19049. (Romanized: Pits'e bagrut). 1968. 4.95. Holt.

Brigade of Terror. Hugh McDonald. LC 79-50898. pap. 2.25 o.s.i. (ISBN 0-89516-082-X). Condor Pub Co.

Brigadier & Other Stories. facsimile ed. Ivan Sergeevich Turgenev. Tr. by I. F. Hapgood from Rus. LC 71-178466. (Short Story Index Reprint Ser). Repr. of 1904 ed. 30.00 (ISBN 0-8369-4067-9). Ayer Co.

Brigadier, and Other Stories. On the Eve. Ivan Sergeevich Turgenev. Tr. by Isabel Florence Hapgood. LC 71-31495. (Short Story Index Reprint Ser. Works). 1971. (ISBN 0-8369-4067-9). Books for Libraries Press.

Brigadier and the Golf Widow. John Cheever. LC 64-20543. 1964. Harper & Row.

Brigadier Frederick and The Dean's Watch. Emile Erckmann & Chatrian, Alexandre, 1826-1890, Joint Author. LC 3-8444. (Half-title: A century of French romance, Parisian ed. vol. xi). D. Appleton & Co.

Brigand: A Romance of the Reign of Don Carlos. To Which Is Added Blanche De Beaulieu, a Story of the French Revolution. Alexandre Dumas. LC 6-43619. (romances of Alexandre Dumas. New series). 1897. Little, Brown and Company.

Brigand: Translated by Angus Davidson. Giuseppe Berto. LC 51-12418. 1951.

Brigand's Bride. Betty Hale Hyatt. (Candlelight Regency, 208). Dell.

Brigands of the Moon. Ray Cummings. LC 31-10362. 1931. A. C. McClurg & Co.

Bright Adventure. Geoffrey Rose. LC 75-13788. 1975. 7.95. St. Martin's Press.

Bright Angel. Samuel Andrew Wood. LC 33-18217. 1933. E. P. Dutton & Co., Inc.

Bright Angel Trail. Joseph Medley Rowland. LC 26-18631. 1926. Richmond Press, Inc.

Bright Arrows. Grace Livingston Hill. LC 75-31642. 1975. 9.95 (ISBN 0-89190-003-9). American Reprint Co.

Bright Arrows. Grace Livingston Hill. LC 46-250895. 1946. J. B. Lippincott Company.

Bright Avenues: A Novel. Josephine Bentham. LC 28-7331. 1928. R. D. Henkle Co. Inc.

Bright Banners. Elizabeth Seifert. LC 73-79142. 1973. 5.95. Aeonian Press.

Bright Banners. Elizabeth Seifert. LC 43-15654. 1943. Dodd, Mead & Company.

Bright Battalions. Howard Breslin. LC 52-13463. 1953. McGraw-Hill.

Bright Blue Death. Nick Carter. (Carter-Killmaster Ser). (O.s.i.). (Orig.). 1967. pap. 0.60 o.s.i. (A277X, Award). Univ Pub & Dist.

Bright Blue Sky. Max Hennessy, pseud. LC 82-73019. 250p. 1983. 10.95 (ISBN 0-689-11352-8). Atheneum.

Bright, Bright Water. William Richard Case. LC 51-12024. 1951. Appleton-Century-Crofts.

Bright Center of Heaven. William Maxwell. LC 34-28619. 1934. Harper & Brothers.

Bright Circle: A Novel. W Penn Kime. LC 51-768. 1951. Exposition Press.

Bright Clouds. Bettie Adams. LC 54-31828. 1954. White Wing Pub. House & Press.

Bright Coin. Elizabeth Seifert. LC 73-79154. 1973. 6.95. Aeonian Press.

Bright Coin. Elizabeth Seifert. LC 49-10986. 1949. Dodd, Mead.

Bright College Year. Edith Sherman. LC 50-9354. 1950. Doubleday.

Bright Companion. Edward Llewellyn. 1980. 1.75 (ISBN 0-87997-511-3). DAW Books.

Bright Concubine. Genevieve B. Wimsatt. (O.s.i.). 2.50 o.s.i. (ISBN 0-8283-1100-5). Branden.

Bright Concubine and Lesser Luminaries: Tales of Fair and Famous Ladies of China. Genevieve B Wimsatt. LC 29-7078. 1928. J. W. Luce and Company.

Bright Conquest. Ruth L. Hill, pseud. 253p. 1975. Repr. of 1951 ed. lib. bdg. 13.85 (ISBN 0-89190-251-1). Am Repr-Rivercity Pr.

Bright Conquest. Ruth L. Hill, pseud. 2.95 o.p. (ISBN 0-448-05210-5). G&D.

Bright Conquest. Ruth Livingston Hill Munce. LC 51-11203. 1951. Lippincott.

Bright Conquest. Ruth Livingston Hill Munce. LC 75-35721. 1975. 9.95 (ISBN 0-89190-251-1). American Reprint Co.

Bright Danger. Hugh MacNair Kahler. LC 42-50617. 1942. Triangle Books.

Bright Dawn. Francesca Greer, pseud. 400p. 1983. pap. 3.50 (ISBN 0-446-90942-4). Warner Bks.

Bright Day. John Boynton Priestley. LC 46-6988. 1946. Harper & Brothers.

Bright Day, Dark Runner: A Novel. George Cuomo. LC 64-15341. 1964. Doubleday.

Bright Days Are Done: A Novel of the Twenties. Rufus Colfax Phillips. LC 53-8776. 1954. William-Frederick Press.

Bright Days in the Old Plantation Time. Mary Ross Banks. 1882. Lee and Shepard.

Bright Destination. Darwin Le Ora Teilhet. LC 35-8480. 1935. Doubleday, Doran & Company, Inc.

Bright Destiny. Ruby Mildred Ayres. LC 52-9308. 1952. Arcadia House.

Bright Dreams, Dark Desires. Patricia Bird. (Orig.). 1980. pap. 2.75 (ISBN 0-8439-8005-2, Tiara Bks). Nordon Pubns.

Bright Enchantment. Cecile Gilmore. LC 43-2622. 1943. H. C. Kinsey & Company, Inc.

Bright Face, Dark Face: A Novel of Japan. Stuart Griffin. LC 58-10215. 1958. C. E. Tuttle Co.

Bright Face of Danger... Julius Fast. LC 46-6396. 1946. Rinehart & Company, Inc.

Bright Face of Danger: A Tale, Wherein Are Related the Adventures of Captain Francis Havenell, of Hookset Hundred in Henrico County, Virginia, During the Days of Bacon's Rebellion. Clifford MacClellan Sublette. LC 26-15604. 1926. Little, Brown, and Company.

Bright Face of Danger: Being an Account of Some Adventures of Henri De Launay, Son of the Sieur De la Tournoire. Freely Translated into Modern English. Robert Neilson Stephens. LC 4-10544. 1904. L. C. Page & Company.

Bright Feather: A Novel. Robert Wilder. LC 48-6793. G. P. Putnam's Sons.

Bright Feathers. John H Culp. LC 65-118568. 4.95. Holt.

Bright Flows the River. Taylor Caldwell. 1979. 2.95 (ISBN 0-449-24149-1). Fawcett Crest Books.

Bright Green Waistcoat. Pete Fry. 3.50 o.p. Roy.

Bright Green Waistcoat. Clifford King. 1967. Roy Publishers.

Bright Harvest. Dorothy Worley. LC 55-14332. 1955. Avalon Books.

Bright Harvest: A Christian Novel. Capwell Wyckoff. LC 44-32806. 1944. Wm. B. Eerdmans Publishing Company.

Bright Hill. Clarissa Fairchild Cushman. LC 36-4035. 1936. Little, Brown, and Company.

Bright Horizon. Dorothy Quentin. LC 47-139043. 1946. Arcadia House, Inc.

Bright Horizons. Horace G Joseph. LC 38-1038. 1937. The Caxton Printers, Ltd.

Bright Horizons. Helen Lowrie Marshall. 1954. 3.95 o.p. (ISBN 0-385-08266-5). Doubleday.

Bright Intervals. Eileen Helen Clements. LC 40-35459. 1941. E. P. Dutton & Co., Inc.

Bright Intervals. Nancy Hoyt. LC 29-17088. 1929. A. A. Knopf.

Bright Is the Morning. Robert Faucett Gibbons. LC 43-14969. 1943. A. A. Knopf.

Bright Is the Morning. Mona Goodwyn Williams. LC 34-32204. 1934. H. Smith and R. Haas.

Bright Is the Tide. Dorothy Lester Chadwick. LC 35-14577. Arcadia House.

Bright Island. Arnold Bennett. LC 74-5327. (Collected Works of Arnold Bennett: Vol. 9). 1976. Repr. of 1925 ed. 15.75 (ISBN 0-518-19090-0). Ayer Co.

Bright Island. Mabel Louise Robinson & War, Lynd Kendall, 1905- Illus. LC 37-274183. Random House.

Bright Journey. August William Derleth. LC 40-33102. 1940. C. Scribner's Sons.

Bright Lamp: By Cynthia Millburn Pseud. Anne Tedlock Brooks. LC 53-7035. 1953. Arcadia House.

Bright Land. Janet Ayer Fairbank. LC 33-852. 1932. Houghton Mifflin Company.

Bright Land. Janet Ayer Fairbank. 1973. (pbk.) 1.25. Popular Lib.

Bright Leaf. Foster Fitz-Simons. LC 48-4481. 1948. Rinehart.

Bright Lexicon. Donald Culross Peattie. LC 34-7411. G. P. Putnam's Sons.

Bright Lights. Isabel Egenton Ostrander. LC 24-5454. 1924. R. M. McBride & Company.

Bright Lights. Frank Arthur Swinnerton. LC 68-18073. 1968. 5.95. Doubleday.

Bright Lights, Dark Rooms. David Nemec. LC 79-7876. 1980. 10.00 (ISBN 0-385-15661-8). Doubleday.

Bright Lightu. John Wilson. 6.95 o.p. (ISBN 0-8062-1232-2). Carlton.

Bright Like Blood. Dick Rowden. (Orig.). 1969. pap. 0.75 o.p. (T2128). Pyramid Pubns.

Bright Messenger. Algernon Blackwood. LC 22-9189. E. P. Dutton & Company.

Bright Metal. Thomas Sigismund Stribling. LC 28-23105. 1928. Doubleday, Doran & Company, Inc.

Bright Midnight. Trumbull Reed. LC 56-52832. Westminster Press.

Bright Midnight. Trumbull Reed. LC 41-9501. The Westminster Press.

Bright Miracle. Vida Hurst. 1949. Gramercy Pub. Co.

Bright Mirror. Francine Findley. LC 34-37250. A. H. King.

Bright Mississippi. Dave Etter. 1979. 10.00; pap. 4.50. Juniper Pr WI.

Bright Moonlight. Betty Webb Lucas. LC 47-24201. 1947. Gramercy Pub. Co.

Bright Morning. Maria M Grant. (Seaside library, v. 19, no. 378). G. Munro.

Bright Morning. Jan Hathaway. (Contemporary Teens Ser.). 224p. (Orig.). 1981. pap. 2.25 (ISBN 0-89531-139-9, 0146-96). Sharon Pubns.

Bright Morning: A Novel. Frank O'Rourke. LC 62-14368. 1963. Morrow.

Bright Nemesis. John Gunther. LC 32-15760. The Bobbs-Merrill Company.

Bright Orange for the Shroud. John Dann MacDonald. LC 72-396. 1972. 4.95 (ISBN 0-397-00793-0). Lippincott.

Bright Pattern. Adelaide Humphries. LC 40-104449. 1940. Arcadia House, Inc.

Bright Pavilions. Hugh Walpole. 1972. pap. 1.25 o.p. (01038). Curtis.

Bright Pavilions. Sir Hugh Walpole. (His The Herries saga, no. 5). 1973. 1.25. Curtis Books.

Bright Pavilions: A Novel. Hugh Walpole. LC 40-33712. 1940. Doubleday, Doran and Co., Inc.

Bright Phoenix. Harold Mead. LC 56-9577. 1956. Ballantine Books.

Bright Prison. 1st American Ed. Penelope Mortimer. LC 57-5295. 1957. Harcourt, Brace.

Bright Procession. John Sedges, pseud. LC 52-7347. 1952. J. Day Co.

Bright Procession: By John Sedges Pseud. Pearl Sydenstricker Buck. LC 52-7347. 1952. J. Day Co.

Bright Promise. Richard Sherman. LC 47-4997. 1947. Little, Brown.

Bright Ramparts. Thelma Thompson. LC 43-16768. 1943. Arcadia House, Inc.

Bright Red Businessmen. Philip McCutchan. LC 75-85700. 1969. 4.50. John Day Co.

Bright Road to Fear. Richard Martin Stern. LC 57-14683. 1958. Ballantine Books.

Bright Sands. 1st Ed. Robert Lewis Taylor. LC 54-5504. 1954. Doubleday.

Bright Scalpel. Elizabeth Seifert. LC 73-79138. 1973. 5.95. Aeonian Press.

Bright Scalpel. Elizabeth Seifert. LC 41-21736. 1941. Dodd, Mead & Company.

Bright Serpent: A John and Suzy Marshall Mystery, by James M. Fox Pseud. 1st Ed. James M. W. Knipscheer. 1953. Little, Brown.

Bright Shawl. Joseph Hergesheimer. LC 22-19551. 1922. A. A. Knopf.

Bright Shawl. Joseph Hergesheimer. LC 77-78312. 1982. 20.00 (ISBN 0-404-15120-5). AMS Press.

Bright-Shining Place. Cheryl P. Blackwood & Kathryn Slattery. (Epiphany Ser.). 240p. 1983. pap. 2.75 (ISBN 0-345-30698-8). Ballantine.

Bright Side of Dark. Jeneth Murrey. (Harlequin Romances Ser.). 192p. 1982. pap. 1.50 (ISBN 0-373-02470-3). Harlequin Bks.

Bright Skies. Emilie Baker Loring. LC 76-41733. 1976. 6.95 (ISBN 0-88411-352-3). Aeonian Press.

Bright Skies. Emilie Baker Loring. LC 46-8106. 1946. Little, Brown and Company.

Bright Skies: 16. (Emilie Loring Ser.). 208p. 1981. pap. text ed. 1.95 (ISBN 0-553-14906-7). Bantam.

Bright Skin. Julia Mood Peterkin. LC 73-152499. 1973-1972. 9.95 (ISBN 0-910220-37-9). N. S. Berg.

Bright Skin. Julia Mood Peterkin. LC 32-263645. The Bobbs-Merrill Company.

Bright Spot in the Yard: Stories & Notes from a Prison Journal. Jerome Washington. 112p. 1981. 13.95 (ISBN 0-89594-063-9); pap. 5.95 (ISBN 0-89594-064-7). Crossing Pr.

Bright Star. Mary Schumann. LC 34-10755. 1934. Macrae Smith Company.

Bright Star of Danger. Elwyn Whitman Chambers. LC 40-5218. 1940. Doubleday, Doran & Co., Inc.

Bright Star of Life: A Novel. Benjamin Leopold Farjeon. LC 6-38643. (Harper's handy series. no. 104). 1886. Harper & Brothers.

Bright Star or Dark. Ruth Peabody Harnden. LC 45-9487. 1945. Whittlesey House, McGraw-Hill Book Company, Inc.

Bright Star-the Story of John Keats & Fanny Braione. J. Rees. 1968. 6.00 o.p. Verry.

Bright Stars. Norma Newcomb, pseud. (Alouette Romance Ser.). 224p. (Orig.). 1981. pap. 2.25 (ISBN 0-89531-128-3, 0198-96). Sharon Pubns.

Bright Stars of Wyoming. Norma Newcomb, pseud. 2.95. Arcadia House.

Bright Sun, Dark Moon. Frances Patton Statham. (Cameo Gothic Series#18). 1975. (pbk.) 0.95. Ace Books.

Bright Sunset. Jack Wilgus. LC 29-6863. The Avondale Press, Incorporated.

Bright Sword. Eleanor Spencer Stone Perenyi. LC 55-5303. 1955. Rinehart.

Bright Temptation. Austin Chesterfield Clarke. 1932. 8.50 o.p. Dufour.

Bright Temptation: A Romance. new ed. Austin Chesterfield Clarke. LC 64-25484. 1965. Dufour Editions.

Bright Temptation: A Romance. Austin Chesterfield Clarke. LC 32-34885. 1932. W. Morrow & Company.

Bright Thread. Cornelia Geer Le Boutillier. LC 29-11689. 1929. Doubleday, Doran and Company, Inc.

Bright Threshold. Janet Ramsay. LC 27-18557. 1927. Longmans, Green and Co.

Bright Tiger. Alice Glasgow. LC 30-6542. 1930. L. MacVeagh, The Dial Press.

Bright to the Wanderer. Bruce Lancaster. LC 75-33030. 1975. (ISBN 0-89190-885-4). Rivercity Press.

Bright to the Wanderer. Bruce Lancaster. LC 42-12031. 1942. Little, Brown and Company.

Bright Tomorrow. Dorothy Quentin. 1942. Arcadia House, Inc.

Bright Tomorrow. Lloyd Wendt. LC 45-3503. 1945. The Bobbs-Merrill Company.

Bright Tomorrow. Dorothy Worley. LC 51-1590. 1951. Macrae Smith.

Bright Torch. Gertrude Pahlow. LC 33-2527. The Penn Publishing Company.

Bright Valley. Nancy Olney. 192p. (OSI). 1972. 3.95 o.s.i. Lenox Hill.

Bright Was Their Destiny: A Novel. John De Meyer. W. Funk Inc.

Bright Web in the Darkness. Alexander Plaisted Saxton. 1958. St. Martin's Press.

Bright Windows. Mary Longstreet Wallace. LC 70-75813. 1969. Chilton Book Co.

Bright Yellow Gold. Horace Wilson Bennett. LC 35-4454. The J. C. Winston Company.

Bright Young Man. Mike Cohen. LC 66-11158. 1966. Lippincott.

Bright Young Things: By Amanda Vail Pseud. 1st Ed. Warren Miller. LC 58-12954. 1958. Little, Brown.

Brighten a Corner. Lucille Skoglund. (Illus.). 1975. pap. 2.95 o.p. (ISBN 0-8059-2227-X). Dorrance.

Brighten the Corner. Hollis Spurgeon Summers. LC 52-5542. 1952. Doubleday.

Brightener. Alice Muriel Livingston Williamson & Williamson, Charles Norris, 1859-1920. LC 21-17546. 1921. Doubleday, Page & Company.

Brightening Day: A Novel of Ireland. Michael McLaverty. LC 65-15176. 4.95. Macmillan.

Brightening Shadow. John Gay. LC 80-81852. (Illus., Orig.). 1980. pap. text ed. 6.95x (ISBN 0-933662-09-2). Intercult Pr.

Brighter Buccaneer: New Chapters in the Gay and Ruthless Career of Simon Templar. Leslie Charteris. LC 33-21274. 1933. Pub. for the Crime Club, Inc., by Doubleday, Doran & Company, Inc.

Brighter Flame, a Love Story. Eleanor Elliott Carroll. LC 35-2099. Chelsea House.

Brighter Side. new ed. Edith Brock. LC 77-92340. 1978. pap. 2.95 (ISBN 0-87148-109-X). Pathway Pr.

Brighter Sun. Samuel Selvon. 1972. pap. text ed. 2.95x o.p. (ISBN 0-582-78027-6). Longman.

Brighter Sun. Samuel Selvon. 215p. 1979. 10.00x o.s.i. (ISBN 0-89410-111-0); pap. 5.00 o.s.i. (ISBN 0-89410-110-2). Three Continents.

Brighter Sun: A Novel. Samuel Selvon. LC 52-124183. 1953. Viking Press.

Brighter Sun: An Historical Account of the Struggles of a Man to Free Himself and His Family from Human Bondage, by His Grandson. 1st Ed. 1954. Pageant Press.

Brightlight. Trevor Bernard. 1977. pap. 1.50 (ISBN 0-532-15278-6). Woodhill.

Brightness. Elizabeth Jenkins. (Cardinal ed., 50173). 1965. Pocket Bks.

Brighton Night. Margaret Lee. (On cover: Lovell's library. no. 600). J. W. Lovell Company.

Brighton Rock. Graham Greene. 1977. pap. 2.95 (ISBN 0-14-000442-4). Penguin.

Brighton Rock. Graham Greene. LC 38-15724. 316p. 1981. 14.95 (ISBN 0-670-19153-1). Viking Pr.

Brighton Rock. Graham Greene. 1956. pap. 3.50 o.p. (ISBN 0-670-00008-6). Penguin.

Brightwood Expedition. Kay L McDonald. LC 75-25793. 8.95 (ISBN 0-87140-605-5). Liveright.

Brigit: A Novel. Melesina Mary Blount. LC 30-31034. 1930. Benziger Brothers.

Brigitta. Berthold Auerbach. Ed. by Gore, James Howard. Tr. by McBrayer, James A. LC 2-232995. 1902. R. H. Carothers.

Brigitte and Other Stories. Niall. Quinn. LC 81-10171. 1981. 8.95 (ISBN 0-8076-1017-8). G. Braziller.

Brill Among the Ruins: A Novel. Vance Nye Bourjaily. LC 72-103436. 1970. 6.95. Dial Press.

Brilla. Anna Mooney Doling. LC 14-912687. 1913. 1.25. The Neale Publishing Company.

Brilliant Kids. Herbert H. Lieberman. (Kangaroo Book). 1978. 1.95 (ISBN 0-671-81411-7). Pocket Books.

Brilliant Kids: A Novel. Herbert H. Lieberman. LC 74-22127. 1975. 8.95. (ISBN 0-02-571810-X). Macmillan.

Brimming Cup. Hebe Elsna. 1971. pap. 0.95 o.p. (95076). Beagle Bks.

Brimming Cup. Dorothea Frances Canfield Fisher. LC 21-416853. 1921. Harcourt, Brace and Company.

Brimstone. Robert Lipscomb Duncan. LC 80-222. 1980. 10.95 (ISBN 0-688-03660-0). Morrow.

Brimstone Bed. Day Keene. pap. 0.60 o.p. (60-368). Manor Bks.

Brimstone Club. Francis Van Wyck Mason. LC 76-143707. (Illus.). 1971. 7.95. Little, Brown.

Brimstone in the Garden. Elizabeth Cadell. LC 50-8910. 1950. Morrow.

Bring Back the Spring: A Novel. Ruth Willock. LC 44-996. 1944. Macrae-Smith Company.

Bring Back the Summer. R. H Robinson. 1981. 2.50 (ISBN 0-505-51633-0). Tower Publications Inc.

Bring Down the Sun. Betty Lambert. LC 80-13757. 1980. 10.95 (ISBN 0-670-24857-6). Viking Press.

Bring 'em Back Dead. John Victor Turner. LC 36-173241. (Tired business man's library of adventure, detective and mystery novels). 1936. D. Appleton-Century Company, Incorporated.

Bring Forth the Body. Simon Raven. LC 75-31244. 1974. 12.50x (ISBN 0-85634-017-0). Intl Pubns Serv.

Bring Home the Bride. Gale Wilhelm. LC 40-12364. 1940. W. Morrow & Company.

Bring Larks and Heroes. Thomas Keneally. LC 68-22865. 1968. Viking Press.

Bring Me Another Corpse. Peter Rabe. LC 59-38115. (Gold medal books, 864). 1959. Fawcett Publications.

Bring Me Another Murder. Elwyn Whitman Chambers. LC 42-255144. 1942. E. P. Dutton & Company, Inc.

Bring Me Giants. John Hicks. 1978. pap. 1.95 (ISBN 0-532-19182-X). Woodhill.

Bring Me His Ears". Clarence Edward Mulford. LC 76-28255. 1976. 6.95 (ISBN 0-88411-228-4). Aeonian Press.

Bring Me His Ears". Clarence Edward Mulford. LC 22-20963. 1922. A. C. McClurg & Co.

Bring Me His Ears". Clarence Edward Mulford. LC 31-235. 1924. A. L. Burt Company.

Bring Me His Scalp. John Benteen. (Sundance Ser.: No. 8). 160p. 1981. pap. 1.75 (ISBN 0-8439-1047-X, Leisure Bks). Nordon Pubns.

Bring Me to the Banqueting House. Sol Biderman. LC 69-15657. 1969. 5.95. Viking Press.

Bring Me Wild Horses. Charles Morris Martin. LC 51-3127. 1951. Phoenix Press.

Bring My Sons from Far: A Novel of the Israeli War. Ralph Lynn Lowenstein. LC 66-184613. 4.95. World.

Bring the Bride a Shroud. Dolores Birk Hitchens. LC 45-982183. 1945. Pub. for the Crime Club by Doubleday, Doran & Company, Inc.

Bring the Jubilee. Ward Moore. LC 53-10417. 1953. Farrar, Straus and Young.

Bring the Wine Home & Twilight of a Firefly: A Thematic Novel in Two Parts, with Commentaries. Earl F Irey. LC 77-88538 (ISBN 0-9601492-1-X). Valkyrie Press.

Bring Your Own Thirst: A Novel. Jim Taylor. LC 52-130931. 1953. Dorrance.

Bringing Down the House. Richard P Brickner. LC 71-162756. 1971. 6.95 (ISBN 0-684-12575-7). Scribner.

Bringing It All Back Home. Ronald Friedland. (Berkley medallion book). 1974. (pbk.) 1.25. Berkley Pub. Co.

Bringing It All Back Home. Ronald Friedland. LC 75-134932. 1971. 6.95. Lippincott.

Bringing Out Barbara. Ethel Kissam Train. LC 17-10198. 1917. C. Scribner's Sons.

Brink. N. J Crisp. LC 81-69994. 1982. 14.95 (ISBN 0-670-19204-X). Viking Press.

Brink. N. J Crisp. LC 82-19786. 1982. 13.95 (ISBN 0-89340-553-1). J. Curley.

Brink. Daniel V Gallery. LC 68-24835. 1968. 4.95. Doubleday.

Brink. Rick Setlowe. LC 74-23660. 1975. (ISBN 0-525-63014-7). A. Fields Books.

Brink of Darkness. Yvor Winters. (Orig.). 1947. pap. 0.75 o.p. (ISBN 0-8040-0026-3, SP15). Swallow.

Brink of Disaster: By Guy Cullingford. Constance Lindsay Taylor. LC 66-22226. 1966. 3.25. Roy.

Brink of Silence: By Charlotte Jay Pseud. 1st American Ed. Geraldine Jay. LC 57-8210. 1957. Harper.

Brinkley Manor. P. G. Wodehouse. 1971. pap. 0.95 o.p. (95148). Beagle Bks.

Brinkley Manor: A Novel About Jeeves. Pelham Grenville Wodehouse. LC 34-28408. 1934. Little, Brown, and Company.

Brinkman. Ron Goulart. LC 78-18135. 9.95 (ISBN 0-385-13648-X). Doubleday.

Brinkman. Desmond Meiring, pseud. LC 65-10680. 1965. 5.95. Houghton Mifflin.

Brinkmanship of Galahad Threepwood. P. G. Wodehouse. 1964. 4.50 o.p. (ISBN 0-671-10550-7). S&S.

Brinkmanship of Galahad Threepwood: A Blandings Castle Novel. Pelham Grenville Wodehouse. LC 65-10386. 1965. 4.50. S. & S.

Brinktown. Sharon Ramirez. 160p. (Orig.). 1981. pap. 5.00 (ISBN 0-932112-12-9). Carolina Wren.

Brinton Eliot from Yale to Yorktown. James Eugene Farmer. LC 2-14433. 1902. The Macmillan Company.

Brion Gysin Let the Mice In. Brion Gysin. Ed. by Jan Herman. LC 72-96737. (Illus.). 74p. 1973. 15.00 (ISBN 0-87110-105-X). Ultramarine Pub.

Brionne. Louis L'Amour. 160p. (Orig.). 1981. pap. 2.25 (ISBN 0-553-14754-4). Bantam.

Brionne. Louis L'Amour. 1976. pap. 1.95 (ISBN 0-553-13606-2, Y13606-2). Bantam.

Briseis: A Novel. William Black. LC 6-12940. 1896. Harper & Brothers.

Bristling with Thorns. Oliver Thomas Beard. LC 6-11707. 1884. The Detroit News Company.

Bristling with Thorns: A Story of War and Reconstruction. Oliver Thomas Beard. LC 68-20006. (Americans in Fiction). (Illus.). 1968. Gregg Press.

Britannia Mews. Margery Sharp. 1946. Little, Brown and Company.

British Barbarians. Grant Allen. LC 76-20062. (Decadent Consciousness). 1977-1978. 26.00 (ISBN 0-8240-2751-5). Garland Pub.

British Barbarians: A Hill-Top Novel. Grant Allen. LC 74-15943. (Science Fiction). 1975. 12.00 (ISBN 0-405-06272-9). Arno Press.

British Barbarians. A Hill-Top Novel. Grant Allen. LC 6-70. 1895. G. P. Putnam's Sons.

British Museum Is Falling Down. David Lodge. LC 66-24081. 1967. Holt, Rinehart and Winston.

British Novel: Conrad to the Present. Compiled by Paul L. Wiley. LC 79-178291. (Goldentree Bibliographies in Language & Literature Ser). (Orig.). 1973. pap. 6.95x (ISBN 0-88295-530-6). Harlan Davidson.

British Partizan: a Tale of the Olden Time. Mary Elizabeth Moragne Davis. 1864. Burke, Boykin & Company.

British Short Stories: Classics and Criticism. Ed. by Leonard R. N. Ashley. LC 68-10190. (Prentice-Hall English literature series). 1968. Prentice-Hall.

Britt & Sex. Louis Du Valois. pap. 1.95 o.s.i. (Venus). Grove.

Britta. A Shetland Romance. Charles Joseph Galliari Rampini. LC 8-259664. (On cover: Seaside library. Pocket ed. no. 642). 1885. G. Munro.

Britta: A Shetland Romance. Charles Joseph Galliari Rampini. LC 8-25968. 1887. Harper & Brothers.

Brittany Stones. Lynna Cooper. (Beagle Book). 1974. (pbk.) 0.95 (ISBN 0-345-26614-5). Ballantine Books.

Brittle Glass. Vida Hurst. LC 33-307282. Grosset & Dunlap.

Brittle Glass. Norah Robinson Lofts. LC 43-51. 1943. A. A. Knopf.

Brittle Heaven. Babette Deutsch. LC 26-15576. Greenberg.

Brittle Soldier. Charles P. Monty. 4.95 o.p. Vantage.

Brittle Thread. Douglas Hall. LC 68-57430. 1973. 0.95. Zondervan.

Brittle Tree. 1st Ed. Sylvia Draper. LC 52-11478. 1952. Pageant Press.

Britton of the Seventh: A Romance of Custer and the Great Northwest. Cyrus Townsend Brady. LC 14-18114. 1914. 1.35. A. C. McClurg & Co.

Britz: Of Headquarters. Marcin Barber. LC 10-127823. 1910. 1.50. Moffat, Yard and Company.

Broad Aisle: A Realistic Tale of Early Ohio. Mary Stewart Daggett. (On cover: Neely's popular library no. 127). F. T. Neely.

Broad and Alien Is the World. Ciro Alegria. Tr. by Harriet De Onis. LC 41-223589. Farrar & Rinehart, Incorporated.

Broad Arrow. William MacLeod Raine. LC 33-6252. 1933. Houghton Mifflin Company.

Broad Back of the Angel. Leon Rooke. LC 77-70901. (Illus.). 9.95. (ISBN 0-914590-42-1) (ISBN 0-914590-43-X). Fiction Collective: Distributed by G. Braziller.

Broad Church. Charles Maurice Davies. LC 75-1505. (Victorian Fiction: Novels of Faith and Doubt; V. 55). 1975. 35.00 (ISBN 0-8240-1579-7). Garland Pub.

Broad Highway. Jeffery Farnol. LC 11-472. 1911. Little, Brown, and Company.

Broad Highway. Jeffery Farnol. LC 21-136968. 1920. A. L. Burt Company.

Broad Highway. Jeffery Farnol & Barbara Cartland. LC 81-100837. (Barbara Cartland's Library of love; 16). ((Series: Cartland, Barbara, 1902-). (Library of love; 16.). 1980. 12.95 (ISBN 0-7156-1476-2). Duckworth.

Broad Is the Way. Emerson Waldman. LC 39-23411. Farrar & Rinehart, Inc.

Broad Jump. Glen Chase, pseud. (Cherry Delight Ser., No. 11). 1974. pap. 1.25 o.p. (LB165ZK). Leisure Bks.

Broad Jump. Glen Chase, pseud. (Cherry Delight,#11). 1974. (pbk.) 1.25. Leisure Books.

Broad Players. Charlie Avery Harris. (Orig.). 1977. pap. 1.75 (ISBN 0-87067-521-4, BH521). Holloway.

Broadbelters. Maxine Schnall. LC 74-88698. 1970. 4.95. M. Evans; Distributed in Association with Lippincott.

Broadcast. John Dolben Mackworth. LC 25-200307. 1925. Longmans, Green, and Co.

Broadcast Murders. Fred Smith. LC 31-22242. The John Day Company.

Broadcast Stories. Eric Allen. 1947. Rich and Cowan.

Broadoaks. Margaret Greenway McClelland. LC 7-15265. The Price-McGill Company.

Broadsides: A Novel. Robert Welter Daly. LC 40-14807. 1940. The Macmillan Company.

Broadway: A Novel. Philip Dunning & Abbott, George. LC 27-152010. George H. Doran Company.

Broadway Bab. Johnston McCulley. LC 19-15733. W. J. Watt & Company.

Broadway Bride. Ethelda Bedford. LC 32-2124. Grosset & Dunlop.

Broadway Butterfly Murders. Tip Bliss. LC 30-247718. Greenberg.

Broadway Interlude. Abdullah, Achmed & Faith Cuthrell. LC 29-23491. 1929. Payson & Clarke Ltd.

Broadway Jones: From the Play of George M. Cohan. Edward Marshall & Cohan, George Michael. LC 13-182214. 1.25. G. W. Dillingham Company.

Broadway Melody. Jack Lait & Goulding, Edmund. LC 29-9795. Grosset & Dunlap.

Broadway Murders: A Night Club Mystery. Edward J Doherty. LC 29-16769. 1929. Pub for The Crime Club, Inc., by Doubleday, Doran & Company, Inc.

Broadway Virgin: A Novel. Lois Bull. LC 31-130932. The Macaulay Company.

Broadway Widow. Grant Williams. LC 34-42418. 1933. G. H. Watt.

Brocade. Jan Merlin. 400p. 1982. pap. 3.50 (ISBN 0-380-79939-1, 79939-1). Avon.

Broca's Brain. Carl Sagan. 384p. 1980. pap. 2.95 (ISBN 0-345-28823-8). Ballantine.

Brock & the Defectors. John Bingham. LC 82-45555. (Crime Club Ser.). 1982. 11.95 (ISBN 0-385-18360-7). Doubleday.

Brockely Moor. A Novel. J. W Lawson. 1874. D. Appleton and Company.

Brocklebank Riddle. Wales, Hubert. LC 14-21200. 1914. The Century Co.

Broderick: A Novel. William Heffernan. LC 79-24855. 11.95. Crown Publishers.

Brogan & Sons. David Batchelor. LC 76-362686. 1976. 3.50 (ISBN 0-436-03680-0). Secker and Warburg.

Broke Down Engine, and Other Troubles with Machines. Ron Goulart. LC 78-122292. 1971. MacMillan.

Broke of Covenden. (rewritten, 1914) ed. John Collis Snaith. LC 14-8238. 1914. Small, Maynard & Company.

Broken. Ruby Mildred Ayres. LC 28-20222. 1928. Doubleday, Doran & Company, Inc.

Broken Alibi. Thomas Curtis Hicks Jacobs. LC 57-9097. 1957. Roy Publishers.

Broken Angel. Floyd Mahannah. LC 57-12008. 1957. Macrae Smith.

Broken Arc. Mayette Bouchage Meyneng. LC 44-3317. 1944. Harper & Brothers.

Broken Arcs. Erika Zastrow. LC 32-3746. H. Holt and Comapny.

Broken Arrow. Robert Gessner. Farrar & Rinehart, Incorporated.

Broken Ashes. Lucille Wood Trost. LC 76-52076. 6.95 (ISBN 0-8283-1692-9). Branden Press.

Broken Ashes. Lucille Wood-Trost. 1977. pap. 6.95 o.p. (ISBN 0-8283-1692-9). Branden.

Broken Away. Beatrice Ethel Grimshaw. LC 7-290. 1897. J. Lane.

Broken Barriers. Barbara Cartland. 1976. pap. 1.25 o.p. (ISBN 0-515-03992-6). BJ Pub Group.
Broken Barriers. Meredith Nicholson. LC 22-187834. 1922. C. Scribner's Sons.
Broken Barriers. Orpha Winger. LC 74-131536. 1971. 3.95 (ISBN 0-8361-1630-5). Herald Press.
Broken Barriers. A Novel. Ardennes Jones-Foster. LC 6-40373. Belgravia Company (Limited.
Broken Bell. Marie Van Vorst. LC 12-108183. The Bobbs-Merrill Company.
Broken Bondage. Nancy Keen Brown. LC 11-21865. 1.50. The Roxburgh Publishing Company (Incorportated.
Broken Bonds: A Novel. William A H Stafford. LC 8-13885. 1885. A. F. Underhill & Co.
Broken Bow. Lizzie Allen Harker. LC 24-238071. 1924. C. Scribner's Sons.
Broken Bows and Arrows. J. H Beardsley. LC 45-8436. 1945. House of Field-Doubleday Inc.
Broken Boy. John Blackburn. 1982. 18.00x (ISBN 0-86025-207-8, Pub. by Ian Henry Pubns England). State Mutual Bk.
Broken Butterflies. Henry Walsworth Kinney. LC 24-353331. 1924. Little, Brown, and Company.
Broken Chain. Edouard Delpit. Tr. by Loranger, Alexina. LC 6-34171. (On cover: Optimus ser. no. 11). 1891. Donohue, Henneberry & Co.
Broken Chains. Elisabeth Burstenbinder. Tr. by Shaw, Frances A. LC 6-19396. 1875. J. R. Osgood and Company.
Broken Chalice. Myron S. Augsburger. LC 70-160721. 1971. 5.95 (ISBN 0-8361-1651-8). Herald Pr.
Broken Chords Crossed by the Echo of a False Note. Harriet Hare McClellan. LC 7-151821. 1893. J. B. Lippincott Company.
Broken Circle. Mark Saxton. LC 41-19650. Farrar & Rinehart, Inc.
Broken Citadel. Joyce B. Gregorian. 1983. pap. 3.95 (ISBN 0-441-08099-5, Pub. by Ace Science Fiction). Ace Bks.
Broken Colour. Harold Ohlson. LC 20-204302. 1920. John Lane.
Broken Commandment. Toson Shimazaki. LC 75-309384. (UNESCO Collection of Representative Works: Japanese Series). (Japan Foundation translation series). 12.00 (ISBN 0-86008-110-9). University of Tokyo Press.
Broken Commandments. Herman Alfred Kasen. LC 35-34. 1933. G. H. Watt.
Broken Creek. Lee Floren. 1981. pap. 1.95 (ISBN 0-8439-0939-0). Nordon Pubns.
Broken Creek: By Lee Thomas Pseud. Lee Floren. LC 52-13535. 1952. Arcadia House.
Broken Cycle. A. Bertram Chandler. (Science Fiction Ser.). 1979. pap. 1.75 o.p. (ISBN 0-87997-496-6, UE1496). Daw Bks.
Broken Doll. Jack Webb. LC 55-7731. (A Father Shanley-Sammy Golden mystery). 1955. Rinehart.
Broken Dolls. Von Amon. LC 81-14943. 1982. 13.95 (ISBN 0-87949-183-3). Ashley Books.
Broken Dream. Marcia Miller. (Starlight romance series). 1973. (pbk.) 0.75. Manor Books.
Broken Eggs: The Negro Novelette. George B Hoyt. LC 38-401. Quality Printing Company and Ament Printing Co.
Broken Engagement: Or, Speaking the Truth for a Day. Emma Dorothy Eliza Nevitte Southworth. LC 8-10811. 1862. T. B. Peterson and Brothers.
Broken Face Murders... Darwin L. Teilhet & Teilhet, Mrs. Hildegarde (Tolman) Joint Author. 1940. Pub. for the Crime Club by Doubleday, Doran & Company, Inc.
Broken Faith. Iza Duffus Hardy. (Seaside library, v. 32, no. 659). 1879. G. Munro.
Broken Family. Elizabeth Christman. LC 80-26430. 1981. 10.95 (ISBN 0-688-00473-3). Morrow.
Broken-Field Runner. Fred Segal. LC 67-16942. 1967. 4.50. New Amer. Lib.
Broken Flower. Franklin Bailey Janeway. LC 35-7526. 1935. The Keith Press.
Broken Gate. 1st ed. Charles Grayson. LC 48-6141. 1948. Doubleday.
Broken Gate: A Novel. Emerson Hough. LC 17-21973. 1917. D. Appleton and Company.
Broken Glass. Julia C Lieb. LC 38-6349. Dorrance and Company.
Broken Gun. Louis L'Amour. 1971. pap. 2.25 (ISBN 0-553-20468-8). Bantam.
Broken Halo. Florence Louisa Charlesworth Barclay. LC 13-21484. 1913. G. P. Putnam's Sons.
Broken Halo. Florence Louisa Charlesworth Barclay. 1913. G. P. Putnam's Sons.
Broken Heart. John Ford. Ed. by Brian Morris. 1966. 3.75 o.p. (ISBN 0-8090-3170-1, New Mermaid); pap. 1.25 o.p. (ISBN 0-8090-1102-6). Hill & Wang.
Broken Hearts and Lives. Lincoln Hulley. E. O. Painter Printing Co.
Broken Homes; and, Illegitimate, Two Novelettes. Evelyn Whitell. LC 61-8171. 1961. Pan Press.
Broken House. Ambrose South. LC 32-214253. 1932. H. Smith & R. Haas.
Broken Idols: "Jeems"; Two Stories. Adelaide Day Rollston. (On cover: Once a week library. v. 11, no. 11). 1893. P. F. Collier.
Broken Image. Virginia Ebert. LC 51-765. 1951. Morrow.
Broken Image. Gerald Stearn. 1972. 8.95 o.p. (ISBN 0-394-46876-7). Random.
Broken Jigsaw. 1st Ed. Paul Somers. LC 61-7595. 1961. Harper.
Broken Journey. Morley Callaghan. LC 32-23423. 1932. C. Scribner's Sons.
Broken Journey. Louisa Wilson. LC 35-10585. 1935. Harper & Brothers.
Broken Key. Mary Linn Roby. LC 72-7770. 1973. 5.95. Hawthorn Books.
Broken Lance. Frank Gruber. (Signet brand western). 1976. 1.25. New American Library.
Broken Lance. Frank Gruber. LC 49-7440. 1949. Rinehart.
Broken Lance. Herbert Quick. LC 7-32560. 1907. The Bobbs-Merrill Company.
Broken Laugh. Meg Villars. 1920. R. M. McBride & Co.
Broken Law. John Burland Harris-Burland. LC 8-33009. Cupples & Leon Company.
Broken Law, a Novel: The Story of the Love-Makers. Lorin Lynn Baker. LC 14-5509. 1.50. The Roxburgh Publishing Company Inc.
Broken Lights. Michael Aaronsohn. LC 47-15095. 1946. The Johnson & Hardin Company.
Broken Lights: A Novel. Narena Easterling. LC 29-14870. The Four Seas Company.
Broken Links. Job Taylor. LC 3-3674. 1908. The C. M. Clark Publishing Co.
Broken Links: A Love Story. Annie French Hector. The Cassell Publishing Co.
Broken Lives. Cyrus F McNutt. LC 7-20295. T. S. Denison.
Broken Lives. 2d Ed....with Appendix.) Circumstantial Evidence. A Short Story...Will Murder Out! by cyrus f. mcnutt. ed. Cyrus F McNutt. LC 7-20294. Moore & McNutt,
Broken Locket. Will A Garland. (Dillingham's American authors library, no. 54). 1899. G. W. Dillingham Co.
Broken Love Broken Dreams. Duncan Harper. LC 81-65704. (Illus.). 64p. (Orig.). 1981. pap. 4.95 o.s.i. (ISBN 0-939756-00-5). Essaye Pub.
Broken Marriage. Alan Sullivan. LC 29-89902. E. P. Dutton & Co., Inc.
Broken Melody. Ronald De Levington Kirkbride. LC 42-24437. 1942. Coward-McCann, Inc.
Broken Melody. Ellen J. MacLeod. 1970. 3.95 o.p. Lenox Hill.
Broken Melody. Ralph Michaels, pseud. LC 77-76599. (Spire books). 1977. 1.50. Revell.
Broken Moon. Sheridan Whipp. LC 32-35781. 1932. Hollycrofters, Inc., Ltd.
Broken Music. Morna McTaggart. LC 34-22749. 1934. E. P. Dutton & Co., Inc.
Broken Necks: And Other Stories. Ben Hecht. (Little blue book, no. 699, ed. by E. Haldeman-Julius)). Haldeman-Julius Company.
Broken Necks: Containing More "1001 Afternoons". Ben Hecht. LC 27-42. 1926. P. Covici.
Broken Nest (Nashtanir) Rabindranath Tagore. Tr. by Mary M. Lago & Supriya Sen. LC 73-137482. (Orig.). 1971. pap. 5.00 o.p. (ISBN 0-8262-0104-0). U of Mo Pr.
Broken O. Carolyn Wells. LC 33-153917. J. B. Lippincott Company.
Broken October: New Zealand 1985. Craig Harrison. 1977. 9.30 (ISBN 0-589-00966-4, Reed Books Australia). C E Tuttle.
Broken off. Gertrude M. Robins Reynolds. LC 7-380315. 1907. Brentano's.
Broken Paths. Grace Wallace Doonan. LC 23-12520. 1923. Extension Press.
Broken Penny. Julian Symons. LC 53-7747. 1980. pap. 1.95i (ISBN 0-06-080480-7, P 480, PL). Har-Row.
Broken Penny. Julian Symons. 1971. pap. 0.95 o.p. (95064). Beagle Bks.
Broken Penny. 1st American Ed. Julian Symons. LC 53-7747. 1953. Harper.
Broken Pinion. Emilie D Stonehill. LC 29-14871. The Torch Press.
Broken Pitcher. Naomi Gilpatrick. LC 45-35029. 1945. Dial Press.
Broken Place. Michael Shaara. LC 68-18254. 1968. New American Library.
Broken Place. Michael Shaara. LC 80-29351. 1981. 12.95 (ISBN 0-07-056377-2). McGraw-Hill.
Broken Places. Joseph Dionne. LC 75-181653. 1972. 6.95 (ISBN 0-06-011043-0). Harper & Row.
Broken Pledges. Philip Hamilton Gibbs. LC 40-7109. 1940. Doubleday, Doran and Company, Inc.
Broken Pledges. A Story of Noir et Blanc. Emma Dorothy Eliza Nevitte Southworth. LC 8-108128. 1891. T. B. Peterson & Brothers.
Broken Post in Every Fence. Mary Hansen. 203p. 1975. 8.50 o.p. (ISBN 0-682-48196-3). Exposition.
Broken Promise. Kent Hayes & Alex Lazzarino. LC 78-4832. 8.95. Putnam.
Broken Promise. Ellouise A. Rife. (Orig.). 1976. pap. 1.25 (ISBN 0-89041-106-9, 3106). Major Bks.
Broken Promises. Drusilla Campbell. (Hopewell Saga: No. 1). (Orig.). 1982. pap. 2.95 (ISBN 0-440-00837-9, Banbury). Dell.
Broken Promises: Four Chinese American Plays. David H. Hwang. 272p. 1983. pap. 3.95 (ISBN 0-380-81844-2, 81844-2, Bard). Avon.
Broken Rainbow Ranch. Samuel Anthony Peeples. LC 50-6870. (Dutton Diamond D western). 1950. Dutton.
Broken Rhapsody. Margaret Way. (Harlequin Presents Ser.). 1982. pap. 1.75 (ISBN 0-373-10549-5). Harlequin Bks.
Broken Rhythm. Dorothy Wagner. LC 38-33000. J. B. Lippincott Company.
Broken Ring: a Romance. Elizabeth Knight Tompkins. LC 8-25977. (The Hudson library, no. 15). 1896. G. P. Putnam's Sons.
Broken River. John Hawkins & Hawkins, Ward, Joint Author. LC 43-18844. 1944. Books, Inc., Distributed by E. P. Dutton and Company, Inc.
Broken Road. Alfred Edward Woodley Mason. LC 7-37552. 1907. C. Scribner's Sons.
Broken Root: Translated from the Spanish by Ilsa Barea. 1st American Ed. Arturo Barea. LC 51-1673. 1951. Harcourt, Brace.
Broken Rosary. Edward Henry Peple. LC 4-6741. 1904. J. Lane.
Broken Seal: A Novel. Dora Russell. (On cover: Lovell's library, v. 17, no. 816). 1886. J. W. Lovell Company.
Broken Shackles. John Gordon. LC 20-21004. Dorrance and Company, Inc.
Broken Shackles. John Oxenham, pseud. LC 15-23064. 1915. John Lane Company.
Broken Shaft: Tales in Mid-Ocean. Ed. by Henry Norman. Crawford, Francis Marion et al. 1886. D. Appleton and Company.
Broken Shield: A Ralph Lindsey Mystery. Ben Benson. LC 55-10234. 1955. M. S. Mill Co.
Broken Shore. Tr. from French by Alan Daventry. Armand Lanoux. LC 65-210662. bds., 4.50. Dutton.
Broken Sixpence. Brown Eyes or Blue? "What Will Ethel Say?". Henrietta Eliza Vaughan Stannard. (seaside library, v. 54, no. 1109). 1881. G. Munro.
Broken Snare. Ludwig Lewisohn. LC 8-28063. 1908. B. W. Dodge & Company.
Broken Soldier and the Maid of France. Henry Van Dyke. LC 19-14002. 1919. Harper & Brothers.
Broken Spoke. Edward Gorey. LC 76-13327. (Illus.). 1976. 6.95 o.p. (ISBN 0-396-07375-1). Dodd.
Broken Spoke. Edward Gorey. (Illus.). 64p. 1982. pap. 6.95 (ISBN 0-312-92066-0). Congdon & Weed.
Broken Spur. Dwight Bennett Newton. (Berkley Medallion Book). 1977. 1.25 (ISBN 0-425-03497-6). Berkely Pub Corp.
Broken Spur: By Dudley Dean Pseud. Cover Painting by Frank McCarthy. Dudley Dean McGaughy. LC 55-43672. (Gold medal books, 511). 1955. Fawcett Publications.
Broken Stowage. David William Bone. LC 22-186040. E. P. Dutton & Comapny.
Broken Sword. Poul Anderson. LC 54-10223. 1954. Abelard-Schuman.
Broken Sword. Poul Anderson. LC 74-20329. (Adult fantasy). 1971. 0.95 (ISBN 0-345-02107-X). Ballantine Books.
Broken Sword. Rhoda Edwards. LC 75-44522. (Illus.). 1976. 7.95 (ISBN 0-385-11581-4). Doubleday.
Broken Sword. T. Kassymbekov. 517p. 1980. 12.75 (ISBN 0-8285-1843-2, Pub. by Progress Pubs USSR). Imported Pubns.
Broken Sword: A Tale of the Civil War. Charles King. LC 5-204393. 1905. The Hobart Company.
Broken Sword: The Story of Fray Bartolome De las Casas. Decoration by Addison Burbank. Covelle Newcomb. LC 55-9348. 1955. Dodd, Mead.
Broken Tapestry. Rona Randall. 1973. (pbk) 0.75. Ace.
Broken Threads. Ethel Symonds Low. LC 49-3481. 1949. Zondervan Pub. House.
Broken Ties. Charles Elmo Robinson. LC 40-11561. Zondervan Publishing House.
Broken Ties, and Other Stories. Rabindranath Tagore. LC 76-37563. (Short story index reprint series). 1972. (ISBN 0-8369-4122-5). Books for Libraries Press.
Broken to Harness. A Story of English Domestic Life. Edmund Hodgson Yates. LC 10-2562. (On cover: Lovell's library. no. 724). 1886. J. W. Lovell Company.
Broken to the Plow: A Novel. Charles Caldwell Dobie. LC 21-14545. Harper & Brothers.
Broken Tower. Piero Sanavio. LC 68-29293. 1969. 6.95. Bobbs-Merrill Co.
Broken Tower. Tr. by Raymond Rosenthal. Piero Sanavio. LC 68-29293. 1968. 6.95. Bobbs.
Broken Trail. Harold Bindloss. LC 26-15962. 1926. Frederick A. Stokes Company.
Broken Treaty: A Story of the Osage Country. William Whites Graves. LC 35-37768. The Journal.
Broken Tryst. Anne M. Rensel. (YA) 1973. 4.50 o.p. (Avalon). Bouregy.
Broken Valley. Thomas Thompson. LC 49-501244. (double D western). 1949. Doubleday.
Broken Vase. Marie De S Canavarro. LC 33-1623. The Christopher Publishing House.
Broken Vase. Rex Stout. 1974. pap. 0.95 o.p. (ISBN 0-515-03454-1, N3454). Pyramid Pubns.
Broken Vase: A Tecumseh Fox Mystery. Rex Stout. LC 41-36. Farrar & Rinehart, Inc.
Broken Vows. Elizabeth Hewitt. 1982. pap. 2.25 (ISBN 0-451-11514-7, AE1514, Sig). NAL.
Broken Vows: A Novel of Betrayal. Robert J Charles. LC 80-25321. 10.95 (ISBN 0-934878-00-5). Dembner Books: Distributed by Norton.
Broken Wagon. Norman A Fox. LC 54-7148. 1954. Ballantine Books.
Broken Wall: Stories of the Mingling Folk. Edward Alfred Steiner. LC 73-152958. (Short story index reprint series). (Illus.). 1971. (ISBN 0-8369-3873-9). Books for Libraries Press.
Broken Waters. Frank Lucius Packard. LC 25-210679. George H. Doran Company.
Broken Wedding-Ring. Charlotte Mary Brame. (On cover: Seaside library. Pocket ed. no. 54). G. Munro.
Broken Wheel. Florence Land May. LC 10-9509. The C. M. Clark Publishing Company.
Broken Wheel Ranch. Wayne C Lee. LC 56-124529. 1956. Arcadia House.
Broken Wheels. Al Cody, pseud. 1976. pap. 1.25 (ISBN 0-532-12453-7). Woodhill.
Broken Wheels. Al Cody. 1973. 4.95 (ISBN 0-517-51392-7). Lenox Hill Press.
Broken-Winged Sparrow: A Novel. Frankie Lee. LC 62-21824. 1963. Exposition Press.
Broken Wings. Lula Kirschner. LC 7-12818. (On cover: Once a week library, v. 11, no. 13). P. F. Collier.
Broken Wings see Author of Beltraffio.
Broken Wings: One Voice for Peace. Max Tau. LC 82-11032. 14.95 (ISBN 0-88064-005-7). Fromm International.
Broken 3: A War Mystery of the A.E.F. Karl William Detzer. LC 29-17888. 1929. The Bobbs-Merrill Company.
Brokenburne: A Southern Auntie's War Tale. Virginia Frazer Boyle. LC 77-38642. (Black Heritage Library Collection). (Illus.). 1972. (ISBN 0-8369-9000-5). Books for Libraries Press.
Brokenburne: A Southern Auntie's War Tale. Virginia Frazer Boyle. LC 6-16082. 1897. E. R. Herrick & Company.
Broker. Max Collins. 1976. 1.25 (ISBN 0-425-03135-7). Berkley Publishing Corp.
Broker. Harold Q. Masur. LC 81-8756. 1981. 13.95 (ISBN 0-312-10589-4). St Martins Press.
Broker. Richard Stark. 208p. (Orig.). 1981. pap. 2.50. Bantam.
Brokers' End. Louis F Booth. LC 35-1977. 1935. Dodd, Mead & Company.
Broker's Wife. Max Collins. (Berkley Medallion). Berkley.
Bromas con Pimienta. new ed. Compiled by E. Caballero. (Pimienta Collection Ser). (Illus.). 160p. 1974. pap. 1.00 (ISBN 0-88473-218-5). Fiesta Pub.
Bromfield Galaxy: The Green Bay Tree, Early Autumn, A Good Woman. Louis Bromfield. LC 57-780266. 1957. Harper.
Bromius Phenomenon. John Rankine. (Ace science fiction). 1973. (pbk.) 0.95. Ace.
Bromley Neighborhood. Alice Brown. LC 17-18592. 1917. The Macmillan Company.
Bronc People. William Eastlake. LC 75-7572. (Zia book). 1975. 2.95 (ISBN 0-8263-0379-X). University of New Mexico Press.
Bronc Rider. William Crawford. LC 77-80453. 1977. Repr. of 1965 ed. 9.95 (ISBN 0-916546-04-7). Racz Pub.
Bronc Rider: A Novel. William Crawford. LC 65-10743. bds., 4.95. Putnam.
Bronc Stomper. Robert J McCaig. LC 56-741917. 1956. Dodd, Mead.
Bronc Twister. Arthur Hawthorne Carhart. LC 37-21966. 1937. Dodd, Mead & Company.
Broncbuster. Mike Clumpner. 220p. (Orig.). 1980. pap. 1.95 (ISBN 0-89083-671-X). Zebra.
Broncho Apache. Paul Iselin Wellman. 1971. pap. 0.75 o.p. (07165). Curtis.
Broncho Apache: A Novel. Paul Iselin Wellman. LC 36-15928. 1936. The Macmillan Company.
Bronco Blood. Lucien Waldo Emerson. LC 42-21232. 1942. Phoenix Press.
Bronco Trail. John Benteen. (Sundance Ser.: No. 6). 160p. 1981. pap. 1.75 (ISBN 0-8439-1045-3, Leisure Bks). Nordon Pubns.
Bronco Trail see En la Senda De los Renegados.
Bronson of the Rabble: A Novel. Albert Elmer Hancock. LC 9-25822. 1909. J. B. Lippincott Company.

Bronte Story. Margaret Lane. LC 75-108394. (Illus.). 1971. Repr. of 1953 ed. lib. bdg. 17.75x (ISBN 0-8371-3817-5, LABS). Greenwood.
Bronte Wilde: A Novel. Fanny Howe. LC 75-37448. (Equinox book). 1976. 2.95 (ISBN 0-380-00548-4). Avon Books.
Brontes and Their World. Phyllis Eleanor Bentley. LC 69-17972. (Studio book). (Illus.). 1969. 6.95. Viking Press.
Brontes Went to Woolworth's. Rachel Ferguson. LC 32-3492. E. P. Dutton & Co., Inc.
Bronze Angel. Elizabeth Ann Loring. LC 37-20748. Dodge Publishing Company.
Bronze Arrow Mystery. Leda A. Wadsworth. LC 44-53445. 1945. Farrar & Rinehart, Inc.
Bronze Axe. Jeffrey Lord. (Orig.). 1969. pap. 0.60 o.p. (60-376). Manor Bks.
Bronze Bell. Louis Joseph Vance. LC 24-22200. 1909. A. L. Burt Company.
Bronze Bell. Louis Joseph Vance. 1909. Dodd, Mead and Company.
Bronze Buddha: A Mystery. Cora Linn Morrison Daniels. LC 99-5617. 1899. Little, Brown and Company.
Bronze Bull. Charles Ellsworth Grapewin. LC 30-19628. The Christopher Publishing House.
Bronze Christ. Translated by Kenzoh Yada and Henry P. Ward. Yoshiro Nagaya. LC 57-111846. 1959. Taplinger Pub. Co.
Bronze Claws. Paul Kruger. LC 74-179583. (Inner Sanctum Mystery Ser.). (O.S.I.). 1972. 4.95 o.s.i. (ISBN 0-671-21155-2). S&S.
Bronze Collar: A Romance of Spanish California. John Frederick. LC 25-8123. 1925. G. P. Putnam's Sons.
Bronze Drums. Jean Larteguy. LC 67-18627. 1967. Knopf.
Bronze Drums. Jean Larteguy. LC 67-18627. 1967. Knopf.
Bronze Eagle: A Story of the Hundred Days. Emmuska Orczy. LC 15-24550. 1.35. George H. Doran Company.
Bronze God of Rhodes. Lyon Sprague De Camp. LC 82-23470. 12.95 (ISBN 0-89865-285-5) (ISBN 0-89865-284-7). Donning.
Bronze Hand: A Fleming Stone Story. Carolyn Wells. LC 26-701787. 1926. J. B. Lippincott Company.
Bronze Mermaid: A Mystery Novel. Paul Ernst. LC 52-9694. 1952. M. S. Mill Co. and W. Morrow.
Bronze Perseus. Stanley Bennett Hough. LC 81-47399. (Fifty Classics of Crime Fiction, 1950-1975). 1982. 14.95 (ISBN 0-8240-4967-5). Garland Pub.
Bronze Tempest. Davis White. 4.50 o.p. Vantage.
Brood of Ducklings. Frank Arthur Swinnerton. LC 28-29235. 1928. Doubleday, Doran & Company, Inc.
Brood of Eagles. Richard Martin Stern. LC 72-82159. (Illus.). 1969. 7.95. World Pub. Co.
Brood of Folly. Margaret Erskine, pseud. LC 70-157589. (Crime Club Ser). 1971. 1.95 o.p. (ISBN 0-385-03196-3). Doubleday.
Brood of Folly. Wetherby Williams. LC 70-157589. 1971. 4.95. Published for the Crime Club by Doubleday.
Brood of Fury; a Novel. 1st Ed. Jess Shelton. LC 59-9645. 1959. Chilton Co., Book Division.
Brood of Helios. Jack Bertin. LC 66-5427. 1966. Arcadia House.
Brood of the Witch-Queen. Arthur Sarsfield Ward. LC 24-27754. 1924. Doubleday, Page & Company.
Brooding House. Alice Brennan. 1973. pap. 0.95 o.s.i. (75-450). Lancer.
Brooding Lake. Dorothy Eden. 252p. 1981. pap. 2.25 (ISBN 0-441-08186-X). Ace Bks.
Brooding Mansion. Paulette Warren. 176p. 1973. pap. 0.95 o.s.i. (75-470). Lancer.
Brook Kerith. new ed. George Moore. LC 74-92700. 1969. 7.95 o.p. (ISBN 0-87140-507-5). Liveright.
Brook Kerith: A Syrian Story. George Moore. LC 74-92700. (Black & gold library). (Illus.). 1969. 5.95. Liveright Pub. Corp.
Brook Kerith: A Syrian Story. George Moore. LC 16-16521. 1916. The Macmillan Company.
Brook Kerith: A Syrian Story. new ed. with a preface. ed. George Moore. LC 24-22202. 1917. The Macmillan Company.
Brook Willow. Nelia Gardner White. 1944. The Macmillan Company.
Brooke's Daughter: By Adeline Sergeant... Adeline Sergeant. LC 5-6452. (On cover: Lovell's international series, no. 144). 1891. United States Book Company.
Brookes of Bridlemere. George John Whyte-Melville. LC 7-25849. 1899. Longmans, Green & Co.
Brookham Mystery. Ernest De Wil. LC 6-33397. 1893. The International Publishing Company, Ltd.
Brooklyn Bachelor: A Novel. Margaret Lee. LC 7-12624. (On cover: American novelists' series. no. 30). F. F. Lovell & Company.
Brooklyn Heights. William Cary Sanger. LC 30-315. 1929. American Printing Co.
Brooklyn Murders. George Douglas Howard Cole & Margaret Isabel Postgate Cole. LC 24-7111. 1924. T. Seltzer.
Brooks Evans. Susan Glaspell. LC 28-16619. 1928. Frederick A. Stokes Company.
Brooks Legend. William Donohue Ellis. LC 58-9717. 1958. Crowell.
Brooks Too Broad for Leaping: A Chronicle from Childhood. Flannery Lewis. LC 38-4885. 1938. The Macmillan Company.
Broom of the War God: A Novel. Henry Noel Brailsford. LC 6-17941. 1898. D. Appleton and Company.
Broom-Squire. Sabine Baring-Gould. LC 6-7961. Frederick A. Stokes Company.
Broom-Squire. Sabine Baring-Gould. LC 6-7960.
Broom Squires. Eden Phillpotts. LC 32-194957. 1932. The Macmillan Company.
Broome Stages. Winnifred Ashton, pseud. LC 31-233198. 1931. Doubleday, Doran & Company, Inc.
Broome Street Straws. Robert Cortes Holliday. LC 19-19590. George H. Doran Company.
Brooming to Paradise. Michael Corr. 1976. pap. 2.00 (ISBN 0-935388-03-6, Pub. by Workingmans Pr). SBD.
Broomstick in the Hall. Jane Blackmore. (Ace gothic). 1974. (pbk.) 0.95. Ace Books.
Broomsticks: And Other Tales. Walter John De La Mare. LC 25-24272. 1925. A. A. Knopf.
Broomtail Basin. Lee Floren. 1981. pap. 1.95 (ISBN 0-8439-0941-2). Nordon Pubns.
Broomtail Basin: By Brett Austin Pseud. Lee Floren. LC 52-2443. 1952. Areadia House.
Brothel. Chayym Zeldis. LC 78-13456. 1979. 12.50 (ISBN 0-399-12296-6). Putnam Pub Group.
Brothels of Nevada. rev., 2nd ed. Robert Engle. (Orig.). 1976. pap. 2.00 (ISBN 0-87067-608-3, BH608). Holloway.
Brother. Franklin D. Reeve. LC 77-143296. 1971. 6.95 (ISBN 0-374-11697-0). Farrar, Straus and Giroux.
Brother. Dorothy Clarke Wilson. LC 44-4715. 1944. The Westminster Press.
Brother, a Novel. Karlton Kelm. LC 36-22173. The Bobbs-Merrill Company.
Brother Against Brother: Or, The Tompkins Mystery. A Story of the Great American Rebellion. John Roy Musick. LC 7-33331. (Fireside series, no. 28). 1887. J. S. Ogilvie & Company.
Brother and Brother. Dorothy Graffe Van Doren. LC 28-215918. 1928. Doubleday, Doran and Company, Inc.
Brother and Sister. Jean Charruau. Tr. by Otten, S. T. LC 5-750. 1904. B. Herder.
Brother & Sister. Van Sterling. pap. 1.95 o.s.i. (Venus). Grove.
Brother & Sister: A Novel. Michael Nickolay. LC 79-16336. 10.00 (ISBN 0-397-01370-1). Lippincott.
Brother Angel. An Italian Romance. Founded on the Most Thrilling Incidents of Italian History in the Sixteenth Century. Tr. from the French ... LC 6-19370. 1845. H. G. Daggers.
Brother Assassin. Fred Saberhagen. 1978. 1.95 (ISBN 0-441-08215-7). Ace Books.
Brother Beloved. Francena Harriet Arnold. LC 57-585241. 1957. Moody Press.
Brother Cain. Simon Raven. LC 60-10979. 1960. Simon and Schuster.
Brother Carl. Susan Sontag. LC 72-82949. (Illus.). 192p. 1974. pap. 10.95 (ISBN 0-374-11700-4). FS&G.
Brother Copas. Arthur Thomas Quiller-Couch. LC 11-8277. 1911. C. Scribner's Sons.
Brother Death: A Novel. John Lodwick. LC 51-9532. 1951. Duell, Sloan and Pearce.
Brother Earth. Vaseleos Garson. LC 74-82576. Imagination Plus.
Brother Enemy. Speer Morgan. LC 81-11776. 13.95 (ISBN 0-316-58297-2). Little, Brown.
Brother Esau. Douglas Orgill & John R Gribbin. LC 82-48147. 13.95 (ISBN 0-06-039016-6). Harper & Row.
Brother Flo: An Imaginative Biography. George Nauman Shuster. LC 38-6971. 1938. The Macmillan Company.
Brother Gardner's Lime-Kiln Club. Charles Bertrand Lewis. LC 76-104513. (Illus.). 1970. (ISBN 0-8398-1159-4). Literature House.
Brother Gunsmoke. Lloyd Kevin. LC 56-8971. 1956. Arcadia House.
Brother Holyfield: A Novel. Jay Higginbotham. LC 72-81131. 1972. 5.95 (ISBN 0-913208-01-9). Thomas-Hull.
Brother Jacob.--The Lifted Veil. George Eliot. LC 6-40741. (On cover: Harper's half-hour series, v. 52). 1878. Harper & Brothers.
Brother John. Anton Fereva. LC 68-10623. 1968. 5.95 o.p. (ISBN 0-696-54230-7). Hawthorn.
Brother John: A Novel. Anton Fereva. LC 68-10623. 1968. Meredith Press.
Brother John: A Tale of the First Franciscans. Vida Dutton Scudder. LC 27-12369. 1927. Little, Brown, and Company.
Brother John: A Tale of the First Franciscans. Vida Dutton Scudder. LC 31-27239. 1931. E. P. Dutton & Co., Inc.
Brother Jonathan's Cottage: Or, A Friend to the Fallen. Henry H Tator. LC 8-25558. 1854. F. Hart.
Brother Joshua. Ada Brookfield. LC 41-25425. Dorrance and Company.
Brother Lover. Hardy Peters. 176p. pap. 1.95 o.p. (6103). Brandon.
Brother Luke. Elsie Rhea Smith. LC 9-32682. 1909. Johnston Company.
Brother Luther. Walter Molo. Tr. by Sutton, Eric. LC 30-5936. 1930. D. Appleton and Company.
Brother Man. Roger Mais. (Caribbean Writers Ser.). 1974. pap. text ed. 4.50x (ISBN 0-435-98585-X). Heinemann Ed.
Brother Mason, the Circuit Rider: Or, Ten Years a Methodist Preacher ... 1855. H. M. Rulison.
Brother Mason, the Circuit Rider: Or, Ten Years a Methodist Preacher ... LC 6-18963. 1864. J. R. Hawley & Co.
Brother of Christ: A Tale of Western Kentucky. Ingram Crockett. LC 5-37160. Broadway Publishing Company.
Brother of the Cheyennes. George Owen Baxter, pseud. LC 37-4771. The Macaulay Company.
Brother of the Cheyennes. Frederick Faust. LC 37-4771. 1936. The Macaulay Company.
Brother of the Kid. Paul Evan Lehman. LC 50-7692. (Dutton Diamond D western). 1950. Dutton.
Brother of the More Famous Jack. Barbara Trapido. LC 82-70236. 1982. 13.95 (ISBN 0-670-19246-5). Viking Press.
Brother of the Shadow: A Mystery of to-Day. Rosa Caroline Murray-Prior Praed. LC 75-46302. (Supernatural and Occult Fiction). 1976. 10.00 (ISBN 0-405-08162-6). Arno Press.
Brother of the Shadow: A Mystery of Today. Praed Campbell. Ed. by R. Reginald & Douglas Menville. LC 76-1539. (Supernatural & Occult Fiction Ser.). 1976. Repr. of 1886 ed. 10.00x (ISBN 0-405-08162-6). Ayer Co.
Brother of the Third Degree. William Lincoln Garver. LC 6-40710. 1894. Arena Publishing Company.
Brother Owl. Al Hine. LC 79-8966. 1980. 10.95 (ISBN 0-385-15818-1). Doubleday.
Brother Petroc's Return. C. S. M & S. M. C. LC 37-32422. 1937. Little, Brown and Company.
Brother Petroc's Return. Mary Catherine Sister of the English Dominican Congregation of Saint Catherine of Siena. LC 37-32422. 1937. Little, Brown and Company.
Brother Petroc's Return: By S. M. C. Mary Catherine. LC 55-14908. (Doubleday image book, D21). 1955. Image Books.
Brother Saul. Donn Byrne. LC 27-9613. The Century Co.
Brother Sinister. Charlotte Bramwell, pseud. (Orig.). 1973. pap. 0.75 o.p. (94323). Beagle Bks.
Brother-Sister Swappers. Ward Fulton. 192p. pap. 1.95 o.p. (7155). Barclay Hse.
Brother-Sister Swingers. Ward Fulton. pap. 1.95 o.p. (ISBN 0-87682-180-8). Barclay Hse.
Brother." Splendor and Woe. Isaac Broome. LC 6-19375. 1890. J. A. Craig.
Brother, Stranger. Bernard Cammarata. LC 79-19444. 1980. 10.00 (ISBN 0-448-22127-6). Paddington Press.
Brother, the Laugh Is Bitter. Lawrence Lipton. LC 42-12032. 1942. Harper & Brothers.
Brother to a Dragonfly. Will D. Campbell. 1980. pap. 5.95 (ISBN 0-8264-0032-9). Continuum.
Brother to Demons, Brother to Gods. Jack Williamson. LC 78-11210. 10.00 (ISBN 0-672-52140-7). Bobbs-Merrill.
Brother to Demons, Brother to Gods. Jack Williamson. 1981. 2.25 (ISBN 0-425-04529-3). Berkley Publishing Corporation.
Brother to Demons, Brother to Gods. Jack Willianson. 1981. pap. 2.25 (ISBN 0-425-04529-3). Berkley Pub.
Brother to Dragons. Amelie Rives Chanler Troubetzkoy. LC 78-113689. (Short story index reprint series). 1970. Books for Libraries Press.
Brother to Dragons. Robert Penn Warren. 1953. 10.95 (ISBN 0-394-40312-6). Random.
Brother to the Enemy. Bart Spicer. LC 58-13088. Dodd, Mead.
Brother, Which Drummer? 1st Ed. Robert Musser Brown. LC 60-7426. 1960. Harcourt, Brace.
Brother Will. Celia Larner. LC 75-9491. 205p. 1976. 7.95 o.p. (ISBN 0-312-10605-X). St Martin.
Brotherhood. Mary Cruger. LC 6-31179. D. Lothrop Company.
Brotherhood of Consolation. Honore De Balzac. Tr. by Katharine Prescott Wormeley. LC 3-231682. (Half-title: The comedy of human life... Scenes from political life). 1893. Roberts Brothers.
Brotherhood of Fear. Robert Ardrey. LC 52-5134. 1952. Random House.
Brotherhood of Mt. Shasta. Eugene Thomas. LC 48-15215. 1946. De Vorss.
Brotherhood of Satan. L. Q. Jones. (O.s.i.). (Orig.). 1971. pap. 1.25 o.s.i. (AQ1676, Award). Univ Pub & Dist.
Brotherhood of the Grape: A Novel. John Fante. LC 76-54684. 1977. 7.95. Houghton Mifflin.
Brotherhood of the Red Poppy. Henri Troyat. LC 61-7015. (His The light of the just). 1961. Simon and Schuster.
Brotherhood of War, Bk. I: The Lieutenants. W. E. Griffin. 432p. 1982. pap. 3.50 (ISBN 0-515-05643-X). Jove Pubns.
Brotherhood of War, Bk. II: The Captains. W. E. Griffin. 432p. 1982. pap. 3.50 (ISBN 0-515-05644-8). Jove Pubns.
Brotherhood of Wisdom. Frances J Armour. LC 9-17587. 1908. J. Lane Company.
Brotherkind. J. N. Williamson. 288p. (Orig.). 1982. pap. 3.25 (ISBN 0-8439-1025-9, Leisure Bks). Nordon Pubns.
Brotherly Faithfulness: Epistles from a Time of Persecution. Jakob Hutter. 1979. pap. 4.95 (ISBN 0-87486-191-8). Plough.
Brotherly House. Grace Louise Smith Richmond. LC 12-25323. 1912. Doubleday, Page & Co.
Brotherly Love. William D. Blankenship. LC 80-70212. 1981. 12.95 (ISBN 0-87795-301-5). Arbor Hse.
Brotherly Love: By Gabriel Fielding Pseud. Alan Gabriel Barnsley. LC 61-16539. 1961. Morrow.
Brotherly Love Unlimited. Ethel Powelson Hueston. LC 51-12228. 1951. Bobbs-Merrill.
Brothers. 2nd, rev., abr. ed. Judi Beckley. Ed. by Randall West. 85p. (Orig.). pap. 7.95x (ISBN 0-942478-00-2). Photopia Pr.
Brothers. Bobby Jack Nelson. (Signet book). 1976. 1.50. New American Library.
Brothers. Horace Annesley Vachell. LC 5-8378. 1905. Dodd, Mead and Company.
Brothers. Chayym Zeldis. LC 75-40555. 10.00 (ISBN 0-394-40331-2). Random House.
Brothers: A Novel. Bobby Jack Nelson. LC 74-30378. 1975. 7.95 (ISBN 0-02-588590-1). Macmillan.
Brothers: A Novel. Irving Reklaw. LC 17-14953. Broadway Publishing Company.
Brothers: A Novel. Leonard Alfred George Strong. LC 32-6310. 1932. A. A. Knopf.
Brothers: A Story. Herbert George Wells. LC 38-9619. 1938. The Viking Press.
Brothers. A Tale of the Fronde... Henry William Herbert. 1835. Harper & Brothers.
Brothers All: More Stories of Dutch Peasant Life by Maarten Maartens Pseud.... Jozua Marius Willem Van Der Poorten Schwartz. LC 9-21861. 1909. D. Appleton and Company.
Brothers & Enemies. Daniel Adams. 384p. 1982. pap. 3.50 (ISBN 0-515-05854-8). Jove Pubns.
Brothers and Lovers. Simpson John Frederick Norman Hampson. LC 34-23275. Farrar & Rinehart, Inc.
Brothers and Sisters. Ivy Compton-Burnett. LC 29-20650. Harcourt, Brace and Company.
Brothers & Sisters. Preston Harriman. pap. 1.95 o.p. (ISBN 0-87682-176-X). Barclay Hse.
Brothers and Sisters: A Novel. 1st American Ed. Ivy Compton-Burnett. LC 56-11330. 1956. Zero Press.
Brothers and Sisters. A Tale of Domestic Life. Fredrika Bremer. Tr. by Mary Botham Howitt. LC 6-17406. (On cover: Library of select novels, no. 115). 1848. Harper & Brothers.
Brothers and Sisters Have I None. Jack Usher. LC 58-11746. 1958. M. S. Mill Co.
Brothers and Sisters: Modern Stories by Black Americans. Ed. by Arnold Adoff. (Laurel-leaf library). 1975. (pbk.) 0.95. Dell.
Brothers and Sisters: Modern Stories by Black Americans. Ed. by Arnold Adoff. LC 76-102961. 1970. Macmillan.
Brothers and Strangers. Agnes Blake Poor. LC 7-38167. 1893. Roberts Brothers.
Brothers Ashkenazi. Israel Joshua Singer. LC 80-66017. 1980. 14.95 (ISBN 0-689-11102-9). Atheneum.
Brothers Ashkenazi. Israel Joshua Singer & Samuel, Maurice, 1895- LC 36-274446. 1936. A. A. Knopf.
Brothers Ashkenazi: By I. J. Singer; Tr. from Yiddish by Maurice Samuel. Israel Joshua Singer. Tr. by Maurice Samuel. (Universal lib., U.L211). 1967. pap., 2.95. Grosset.
Brothers Bellamy. 1st American Ed. Humphrey Pakington. LC 53-6016. 1953. Norton.
Brothers Divided: A Novel. 1st Ed. Edmund Fuller. LC 51-12910. 1951. Bobbs-Merrill.
Brothers in Arms. John Grant. LC 38-18532. 1938. David McKay Company.
Brothers in Arms. Hans Hellmut Kirst. LC 67-13696. 1967. Harper & Row.
Brothers in Blood. P. D. Ballard. 1972. pap. 0.75 o.p. (T2563, GM). Fawcett World.
Brothers in Blood. (Executioner Ser.). 192p. 1983. pap. 1.95 (Pub. by Worldwide). Harlequin Bks.

Brothers in Hand: The Tale of a Hectic Trip Over Kansas Roads. Raymond J Foster. LC 28-213783. Midland Publishing House.
Brothers in Kickapoo. Dan Cushman. LC 62-9985. 1962. McGraw-Hill.
Brothers in Law. 1st Ed. Henry Cecil. LC 55-106905. Harper.
Brothers in the West. Robert Raynolds. LC 31-21177. 1931. Harper & Brothers.
Brothers Karamazov. Fedor Mikhailovich Dostoevskii. LC 74-187562. (Modern library giant, G36). 1973. Random House.
Brothers Karamazov. Fedor Mikhailovich Dostoevskii. Tr. by Constance Black Garnett. LC 49-785. 1948. Macmillan.
Brothers Karamazov. Fedor Mikhailovich Dostoevskii. Tr. by Constance Black Garnett. LC 29-26372. (Half-title: The Modern library of the world's best books). 1929. The Modern Library.
Brothers Karamazov. Fedor Mikhailovich Dostoevskii. Tr. by Constance Black Garnett. Sharp, William, 1900- Illus. LC 43-51331. 1943. The Modern Library.
Brothers Karamazov. Fedor Mikhailovich Dostoevskii. Tr. by Andrew MacAndrew from Russian. (Classic Ser.). 936p. (gr. 9-12). 1981. pap. 2.75 (ISBN 0-553-21037-8). Bantam.
Brothers Karamazov. Fedor Mikhailovich Dostoevskii. Tr. by Constance Garnett. (YA) 1950. pap. 5.00x (ISBN 0-394-30912-X, T12, Mod LibC). Modern Lib.
Brothers Karamazov. Fedor Mikhailovich Dostoevskii. Ed. by Manuel Komroff-Hill. 1971. pap. 2.75 (ISBN 0-451-51464-5, CE1464, Sig Classics). NAL.
Brothers Karamazov, 2 Vols. Fedor Mikhailovich Dostoevskii. Tr. by David Magarshack. (Classics Ser.). (Orig.). 1958. Vol. 1. pap. 4.95 o.p. (ISBN 0-14-044078-X); Vol. 2. pap. 2.95 o.p. (ISBN 0-14-044079-8). Penguin.
Brothers Karamazov. Fedor Mikhailovich Dostoevskii. (Russian Library Ser). 1955. pap. 5.95 (ISBN 0-394-70722-2, V722, Vin). Random.
Brothers Karamazov. Fedor Mikhailovich Dostoevskii. Tr. by Constance Garnett. 8.95 (ISBN 0-394-60415-6). Modern Lib.
Brothers Karamazov. Fedor Mikhailovich Dostoevskii. 1956. 4.95 o.p. (ISBN 0-448-01011-9). G&D.
Brothers Karamazov. Fedor Mikhailovich Dostoevskii & Garnett, Mrs. Constance (Black) 1862- Tr. 1933. Random House.
Brothers Karamazov. Fedor Mikhailovich Dostoevskii & Garnett, Mrs. Constance (Black) 1862- Tr. LC 38-5761. (Half-title: The modern library of the world's best books). 1937. The Modern Library.
Brothers Karamazov. Fedor Mikhailovich Dostoevskii & Garnett, Constance (Black) 1862- Tr. LC 46-3856. 1945. The Illustrated Modern Library.
Brothers Karamazov. Fedor Mikhailovich Dostoevskii & Maugham, William Somerset, 1874- Ed. LC 49-10338. (Ten Greatest Novels of the World). 1949. J. C. Winston Co.
Brothers Karamazov, Vol. 2. Fedor Mikhailovich Dostoevskii. Tr. by Constance Garnett. 3.95x o.p. (ISBN 0-460-00803-X, Evman). Dutton.
Brothers Karamazov: A Novel in Four Parts and an Epilogue. Fedor Mikhailovich Dostoevskii. Tr. by Constance Black Garnett. LC 22-143544. (Half-title: The novels of Fyodor Dostoevsky. v. 1). 1919. The Macmillan Company.
Brothers Karamazov: A Novel in Four Parts and an Epilogue. Fedor Mikhailovich Dostoevskii. Tr. by Constance Black Garnett. LC 29-807. (Half-title: The novels of Fyodor Dostoevsky, v. 1). 1928. The Macmillan Company.
Brothers Karamazov in the Authoritative Modern Abridgment by Edmund Fuller. Translated by Constance Garnett. Fedor Mikhailovich Dostoevskii. (Dell book F55). 1956. Dell Pub. Co.
Brothers Karamazov: The Constance Garnett Translation Revised by Ralph E. Matlaw: Backgrounds and Sources, Essays in Criticism. Fedor Mikhailovich Dostoevskii & Constance Black Garnett. LC 75-37792. (Norton critical edition). 17.50 (ISBN 0-393-04426-2) (ISBN 0-393-09214-3). Norton.
Brothers Karamazov: Translated by Constance Garnett. Introd. by Marc Slonim. Fedor Mikhailovich Dostoevskii. LC 50-11913. (Modern Library college editions, T12). 1950. Modern Library.
Brothers Karamazov: Translation Rev. by Princess Alexandra Kropotkin. Illus. by Georgette De Lattre. Fedor Mikhailovich Dostoevskii. LC 53-27785. 1953. Literary Guild of America.
Brothers' Keepers. Frank Smith. LC 64-12477. 1964. Simon and Schuster.
Brothers Keepers. Donald E Westlake. 1976. 1.75 (ISBN 0-449-22962-9). Fawcett Crest.
Brothers Kresky: An Entertainment. Henry Bloomstein. LC 82-72590. 10.95 (ISBN 0-912650-04-4). Brookdale Press.
Brothers M. Tom Stacey. LC 61-10027. (Illus.). 1961. Pantheon Books.
Brothers of Earth. C. J. Cherryh. (Science Fiction Ser). 1976. pap. 1.95 o.p. (ISBN 0-87997-470-2, UJ1470). DAW Bks.
Brothers of Earth. C J Cherryh. Daw Books.
Brothers of No Kin, and Other Stories. Conrad Richter. LC 72-10812. (Short story index reprint series). 1973. (ISBN 0-8369-4225-6). Books for Libraries Press.
Brothers of No Kin: And Other Stories. Conrad Richter. LC 24-2251. Hinds, Hayden & Eldredge, Inc.
Brothers of Peril: A Story of Old Newfoundland. Roberts Theodore Goodridge. LC 5-18317. 1905. L. C. Page & Company.
Brothers of Silence. 1st Ed. Frank Gruber. LC 62-113222. 1962. Dutton.
Brothers of the Brand. Abel Shott. LC 47-30781. 1947. Phoenix Press.
Brothers of the Grape. Arnold Michael. LC 76-142525. 1971. 3.50. Scrivener.
Brothers of the Head. Brian Wilson Aldiss. (Illus.). 1977. pap. 7.95 o.p. (ISBN 0-8467-0386-6, Pub. by Two Continents). Hippocrene Bks.
Brothers of the Range. Budd Arthur & Burt Arthur. (Orig.). 1980. pap. text ed. 1.75 o.s.i. (ISBN 0-505-51550-4). Tower Bks.
Brothers of the Sea. D. R Sherman. (75257). 1968. Pocket Bks.
Brothers of the Sea: By D. R. Sherman. 1st Ed. D. R Sherman. LC 66-20806. 1966. bds., 4.95. Little.
Brothers of Uterica. Benjamin Capps. LC 67-26177. 1967. 5.95 o.p. (ISBN 0-696-54235-8). Hawthorn.
Brothers of Uterica: A Novel. Benjamin Capps. LC 67-26177. 1967. Meredith Press.
Brothers of Vengeance. Le Gette Blythe. LC 70-89013. (Illus.). 1969. 7.95. Morrow.
Brothers of Vengeance: A Novel Set in Rome & Palestine During the First Century A. D. Le Gette Blythe. 1969. 7.95 o.p. Morrow.
Brothers on the Trail. Max Brand. LC 34-37098. 1934. Dodd, Mead & Company.
Brothers on the Trail. Frederick Faust. LC 76-18870. 1976. 7.95 (ISBN 0-89340-031-9). J. Curley.
Brothers on the Trail. Frederick Faust. 1934. Dodd, Mead & Company.
Brothers: Or, Treachery Punish'd. LC 79-170581. (Foundations of the Novel). 1972. Garland Pub.
Brothers; or, Treachery Punish'd. Bd. with Memoirs of Capt. John Creichton. John Creichton; Perjur'd Citizen; or, Female Revenge. LC 79-170581. (Foundations of the Novel Ser.: Vol. 55). lib. bdg. 50.00 o.s.i. Garland Pub.
Brothers Sackville: By G. D. H. and M. Cole. George Douglas Howard Cole & Cole, Mrs. Margaret Isabel (Postgate) 1893- Joint Author. LC 37-925792. 1937. The Macmillan Company.
Brother's Sacrifice: Adapted from the Worrkd of A. Juengst. Antonie Jungst. Tr. by Eifel, Aloysius J. LC 10-122811. 0.50. Society of the Divine Word.
Brothers Three. John Milton Oskison. LC 35-153168. 1935. The Macmillan Company.
Brother's Touch. Owen Levy. 288p. (Orig.). 1982. pap. 2.75 (ISBN 0-523-41536-2). Pinnacle Bks.
Brothers' Wives. Tom Young. 192p. (Orig.). 1973. pap. 1.95 o.p. (ISBN 0-87682-314-2, 7314). Barclay Hse.
Brought Forward. Robert Bontine Cunninghame Graham. LC 77-169552. (Short story index reprint series). 1971. (ISBN 0-8369-4014-8). Books for Libraries Press.
Brought to Bay. John Russell Coryell. LC 1-30468. (On cover: Magnet detective library, no. 168). 1901. Street & Smith.
Brought to Bay: A Novel. Richard Henry Savage. (On cover: The welcome series, no. 56). 1900. The Home Publishing Co.
Brought to Cover: 15 Outdoor Tales of Action and Adventure. Paul Annixter, pseud. LC 51-12469. 1951. A. A. Wyn.
Brought to Cover: 15 Outdoor Tales of Action and Adventure, by Paul Annixter Pseud. Howard Allison Sturtzel. LC 51-12469. 1951.
Broughton House. Bliss Perry. LC 7-36177. 1890. C. Scribner's Sons.
Browmstone Angel: By Norma Newcomb Pseud. William Arthur Neubauer. LC 56-897365. 1956. Arcadia House.
Brown Ambassador. A Story of the Three Day's Moon. Mary Crawford Fraser. 1895. Macmillan and Co.
Brown Barriers: A South Sea Story. Glenn Robert Kershner. LC 39-30570. 1939. Press of Murray & Gee.
Brown Brethren. Patrick MacGill. LC 18-533. George H. Doran Company.
Brown Girl, Brownstones. Paule Marshall. LC 59-108049. 1959. Random House.
Brown Girl, Brownstones. Paule Marshall. LC 70-180041. 1972. (ISBN 0-911860-11-8). Chatham Bookseller.
Brown Girl, Brownstones: A Novel. Paule Marshall. 352p. 1981. pap. 6.95 (ISBN 0-912670-96-7). Feminist Pr.
Brown Honey. Lucy Agnes Hancock. LC 37-19746. The Penn Publishing Company.
Brown House at Duffield. A Story of Life Without and Within the Fold. Julia Amanda Sargent Wood. LC 8-37549. 1876. Kelly, Piet & Co.
Brown-Laurel Marriage. Landis Ayr. LC 6-3845. F. T. Neely.
Brown Lord of the Mountain. Walter Macken. 255p. 1970. pap. 2.95 (Pub. by Pan Bks England). Irish Bk Ctr.
Brown Maiden. Felicidad V Ocampo. LC 32-29195. 1932. Meador Publishing Company.
Brown Mare. Alfred Ollivant. LC 16-22756. 1916. 1.00. A. A. Knopf.
Brown Mask. Percy James Brebner. LC 11-273057. 1911. Cassell and Company, Limited.
Brown Moth. Oscar Graeve. LC 21-756. 1921. 2.00. Dodd, Mead and Company.
Brown Mouse. Herbert Quick. LC 15-16340. The Bobbs-Merrill Company.
Brown of Harvard. Rida Johnson Young & Gilbert Payson Coleman. LC 7-18595. 1907. G. P. Putnam's Sons.
Brown of Harvard. Rida Johnson Young & Gilbert Payson Coleman. LC 24-22207. 1908. G. P. Putnam's Sons.
Brown of Lost River: A Story of the West. Mary Etta Smith Stickney. (Half-title: Appletons' town and country library, no. 288). 1900. D. Appleton and Company.
Brown Princess. A Tale of the Death Canon. Metta Victoria Fuller Victor. (sea and shore series--no.3). 1888. Street & Smith.
Brown Skin Girl. Leo Horan. 3.50 o.p. Wehman.
Brown-Skin Girl: A Novel, by Leo Horan and Kate Gallaspy Horan. 1st Ed. Leo Horan & Kate Gallaspy Horan. LC 52-863271. 1952. Exposition Press.
Brown Smock: The Tale of a Tune. C. R Allen. LC 26-20327. Warne & Co., Ltd.
Brown Stone Boy: And Other Queer People. William Henry Bishop. LC 6-12717. Cassell & Company, Limited.
Brown Study. Grace Louise Smith Richmond. LC 17-117043. 1917. Doubleday, Page & Company.
Brown Study. Grace Louise Smith Richmond. LC 19-4855. A. L. Burt Company.
Brown Suede Jacket. Pete Fry. 1968. 3.50 o.p. Roy.
Brown Suede Jacket. Clifford King. LC 68-17213. 1968. 3.50. Roy.
Brown Sugar. Nancy Cato. LC 74-14874. 1975. 7.95. St. Martin's Press.
Brown, the Lawyer. A Novel. Albert Plympton Southwick. LC 8-10806. 1893. Franklin Publishing Company.
Brown, V. C. Annie French Hector. LC 99-930. 1899. R. F. Fenno & Company.
Brown Women and White. Andrew A Freeman. LC 32-790742. The John Day Company.
Brownie. George Robert Gissing. Ed. by Hastings, George Everett & Starrett, Vincent. LC 31-34811. 1931. Columbia University Press.
Brownie. Agnes Gordon Lennox. LC 16-167238. 1916. John Lane.
Brownie Makes the Headlines: Illustrated by Louis Ravielli. Ted Graham Wear. LC 53-10516. (Everyday adventure story). 1953. J. Messner.
Brownie of Bodsbeck. James Hogg. Ed. by Douglas S. Mack. 1976. 12.50x (ISBN 0-7073-0172-6, Pub. by Scottish Academic Pr Scotland). Columbia U Pr.
Brownie's Triumph. A Novel. Sarah Elizabeth Forbush G. S. Downs Downs. LC 6-45944. 1887. G. W. Dillingham; Etc., Etc.
Browning Touch. Donald Rohan. LC 79-1372. 8.95 (ISBN 0-8037-0967-6). Dial Press.
Browns. Annie Edith Foster Jameson. LC 12-24821. 1.25. Hodder & Stoughton, George H. Doran Company.
Browns at Mt. Hermon. Isabella Alden. LC 8-30010. 1908. Lothrop, Lee & Shepard Co.
Brown's Requiem. James Ellroy. 256p. (Orig.). 1981. pap. 2.50 (ISBN 0-380-78741-5, 78741). Avon.
Brown's Retreat, and Other Stories. Anna Eichberg Lane. LC 6-15450. 1893. Roberts Brothers.
Brownstone. Ken Eulo. (Orig.). 1981. pap. 2.95 (ISBN 0-671-43785-2). PB.
Brownstone: A Novel of New York. Arthur David Kahn. LC 53-12670. 1953. Independence Publishers.
Brownstone Cavalry. Howard Crook. 400p. 1983. pap. 3.50 (ISBN 0-425-05935-9). Berkley Pub.
Brownstone Cavalry: A Novel. Howard Crook. LC 81-5022. 13.95 (ISBN 0-671-44776-9). Summit Books.
Brownstone Front. Gilbert Wolf Gabriel. LC 24-20377. 2.00. The Century Co.
Brownstone Front. Guy Gilpatric. LC 75-37544. (Short story index reprint series). 1972. (ISBN 0-8369-4103-9). Books for Libraries Press.
Brownstone Front. Guy Gilpatric. LC 34-6049. Dodd, Mead & Company.
Brownstone Gothic. Elizabeth Shenkin. (Paperback Library Gothic). Orig. Title: Secret Heart. 1968. pap. 0.50 o.p. (52-637). Paperback Lib.
Brownstone House. Elinore Denniston. LC 74-3786. (Red badge novel of suspense). 1974. 5.95 (ISBN 0-396-06970-3). Dodd, Mead.
Brownstone House. Rae Foley. 192p. 1974. 5.95 o.p. (ISBN 0-396-06970-3). Dodd.
Brownstone Saga: Happenings of a New Yorker. Hanford Twitchell. LC 73-86551. 96p. 1973. 6.00 o.p. (ISBN 0-682-47811-3). Exposition.
Brownsville Murders. Burton Seely Keirstead & Campbell, Donald Frederick. LC 33-8143. 1933. The Macmillan Company.
Browse at Your Own Risk. George Price. (O.s.i.). (Illus.). 1977. 8.95 o.s.i. (ISBN 0-671-22816-1). S&S.
Browsing Goat: A Bucolic. Jack Kahane. LC 29-17257. 1929. Brentano's Ltd.
Brubaker. Harrison. 1980. pap. 2.25 (ISBN 0-345-29134-4). Ballantine.
Bruce Angelo: The City Detective. Harlan Page Halsey. (Secret service series, no. 2). 1887. Street & Smith.
Bruce Bartlett-Only Son. Thelma Harrison Lacey. LC 68-21565. 1968. Dorrance.
Bruce Douglas a Man of the People: A Novel. Robert Alexander Gunn. LC 10-745. 1909. 1.00. Mayhew Publishing Company.
Bruce Lee Lives? Max Caulfield. 1976. (pbk.) 1.50. Dell.
Bruce of the Circle A. Harold Titus. LC 18-949567. Small, Maynard & Company.
Brucknerstrasse: A Novel of Nazi Germany, 1944. Ilona Herisko. LC 64-15247. 1964. J. Messner.
Brueton's Bayou. John Habberton & Burnett, Mrs. Frances (Hodgson) 1849-1924. Miss Defarge. LC 42-264199. (On cover: American novels). 1888. J. B. Lippincott Company.
Bruise. John Cleve, pseud. LC 75-293912. (Brandon House library edition). (Brandon House book). 1.95. Brandon House.
Bruised Reeds and Other Stories. Alfred Henry Deutsch. LC 76-175129. (Illus.). 1971. Saint John's University Press.
Bruiser. Edward L McKenna. LC 29-23714. 1929. R. M. McBride & Company.
Bruiser. Jim Tully. LC 36-29308. Greenberg.
Brumaire. Mark Logan. LC 77-15864. 1978. 8.95 o.p. (ISBN 0-312-10677-7). St Martin.
Brumaire. Christopher Nicole. LC 77-15864. 1978. 8.95 (ISBN 0-312-10677-7). St. Martin's Press.
Brumby, the Wild White Stallion. Illustrated by Gerald McCann. Mary Elwyn Patchett. LC 59-9607. 1959. Bobbs-Merrill.
Brunel's Tower. Eden Phillpotts. 1915. The Macmillan Company.
Brunette and Blonde: Or, The Struggle for a Birthright. Alexander McVeigh Miller & Chappell, F. W. (On cover: Street & Smith's select series, no. 5). 1887. Street & Smith.
Brunhilda of Orr's Island. William Jasper Nicolls. LC 8-17253. 1908. G. W. Jacobs & Company.
Brunhilde: Or, The Last Act of Norma. Pedro Antonio De Alarcon & Darr, Lizzie (Townsend) "Mrs. Francis J. A. Darr", Tr. LC 5-42173. A. Lovell & Co.
Brunhilde's Paying Guest: A Story of the South to-Day. Caroline Macomber Fuller. LC 7-26461. 1907. The Century Co.
Bruno Lipshitz and the Disciples of Dogma. John Robert King. LC 76-376503. 1976. 3.50 (ISBN 0-575-02171-3). Gollancz.
Bruno Santini: La Costanza Della Ragione), a Novel. Tr. from Italian by Raymond Rosenthal. Vasco Pratolini. LC 65-10909. 1965. bds., 5.95. Atlantic-Little.
Bruno's Dream. Iris Murdoch. 1976. 1.95 (ISBN 0-14-003176-6). Penguin.
Bruno's Dream. Iris Murdoch. LC 69-11725. 1969. 5.75 (ISBN 0-670-19268-6). Viking Press.
Brush Coyotes. Sigurd Jay Simonsen. LC 74-30653. (American Farmers and the Rise of Agribusiness). 1975. 12.00 (ISBN 0-405-06829-8). Arno Press.
Brush Coyotes. Sigurd Jay Simonsen. LC 43-10911. 1943. Diana Press Publishing Co.
Brush with Hate. L. Kovnedhov. 310p. 1979. 7.45 (ISBN 0-8285-1566-2, Pub. by Progress Pubs USSR). Imported Pubns.
Brushes and Chisels: A Story. Teodoro Serrao. LC 8-6864. 1890. C. T. Dillingham.
Brushland Bill. Richard Huzarski. LC 43-6639. 1943. Thomas Y. Crowell Company.
Brushwood Boy. Rudyard Kipling. LC 508. 1899. Doubleday and McClure Company.
Brushwood Boy. Rudyard Kipling. LC 7-36228. 1907. Doubleday, Page & Company.

Brusilov's Breakthrough: A Novel of the First World War. Sergeev-TSenskii, Sergei Nikolaevich. LC 75-39014. (Early Soviet Literature in English Translation). 1978. 21.00 (ISBN 0-88355-416-X). Hyperion Press.
Brusilov's Breakthrough: A Novel of the First World War. Sergei Nikolaevich Sergeev-TSenskii & Altaschuler, Helen, Tr. LC 45-8919. 1945. Hutchinson & Co. Ltd.
Bruski: A Story of Peasant Life in Soviet Russia. Fedor Ivanovich Panferov. LC 75-37341. (Early Soviet Literature in English Translation). 1977. 19.00 (ISBN 0-88355-414-3). Hyperion Press.
Brusski: A Story of Peasant Life in Soviet Russia. Fedor Ivanovich Panferov. LC 70-9655. International Publishers.
Brusski: A Story of Peasant Life in Soviet Russia. Fedor Ivanovich Panferov & Mitrov, Z., Tr. LC 31-6871. 1930. International Publishers.
Brutal Bridegroom. Tracy Duncan. 192p. (Orig.). 1973. pap. 1.95 o.p. (ISBN 0-87977-187-9, DBB187). Dansk Blue Bk.
Brutal Question. Oliver Weld Bayer. LC 47-11091. 1947. Pub. for the Crime Club by Doubleday.
Brute. Frederic Arnold Kummer. LC 12-10134. 1.25. W. J. Watt & Company.
Brute. Millard Ward. LC 35-8033. 1935. D. Appleton Century Company, Incorporated.
Brute Brasada. Dean Owen. 1974. (pbk.) 0.75. Ace Books.
Brute: By W. Douglas Newton... Wilfrid Douglas Newton. LC 24-18675. 1924. D. Appleton and Company.
Brute Gods... Louis Umfreville Wilkinson. LC 19-14016. 1919. A. A. Knopf.
Brute: Translated by Michael Luke. Guy Des Cars. LC 52-5619. 1952. Greenberg.
Brutus Incident. Perry Tong. LC 73-86597. 1973. 7.95. Crescendo Pub. Co.
Brutus, or the Fall of Tarquin. John Howard Payne. 56p. 1818. Repr. 6.00 o.p. Somerset Pub.
Brutus Was an Honorable Man. Walter Marquiss. LC 46-3408. 1946. C. Scribner's Sons.
Bruvver Jim's Baby. Philip Verrill Mighels. LC 4-11538. 1904. Harper & Brothers.
Bryan Maurice: Or, The Seeker. Walter Mitchell. LC 7-31091. 1867. J. B. Lippincott & Co.
Bryan Maurice: Or, The Seeker. Walter Mitchell. 1888. T. Whittaker.
Bryan Tract: A Novel. Carey W Richmond. LC 60-2991. (Mileston book). 1960. Comet Press Book.
Bryercliffe: A Novel. Frances S Belote. LC 50-5042. Dorrance.
Brynhild: Or, The Show of Things. Herbert George Wells. LC 37-28561. 1937. C. Scribner's Sons.
Brysonia: A Story of the Newest South. Henry Taylor Noel. LC 7-334749. 1896. Arena Publishing Company.
BSOC: Big Stud on Campus. Jay Kaye. 192p. (Orig.). 1974. pap. 2.25 o.s.i. (ISBN 0-89053-104-8). Lambda Pr.
B.S.O.C. Big Stud on Campus. Jay Kaye. 1974. (pbk.) 2.25 (ISBN 0-89053-104-8). Lambda Press.
Buack Iris: By Constance and Gwenyth Little. 1st Ed. Constance Little. LC 52-13573. 1953. Published for the Crime Club by Doubleday.
Bub. C. R. Stanley. 1970. 3.95 o.p. Vantage.
Bubba & Me & Love Makes Three. Gertrude Cooper. 109p. 1972. 4.00 o.p. (ISBN 0-682-47435-5). Exposition.
Bubble. Lucy Bethia Colquhoun Walford. (On verse of half-title: The bijou series). F. A. Stokes Company.
Bubble Makers: A Novel. George J. W. Goodman. LC 55-8441. 1955. Viking Press.
Bubble Reputation. A Novel. Katharine King. (Franklin square library. no. 18). Harper & Brothers.
Bubbles. Fannie E Newberry. LC 7-17286. 1897. A. I. Bradley & Co.
Bubbles: A Novel. Maximilian Foster. LC 29-207890. 1929. J. B. Lippincott Company.
Bubbles of the Foam... Tr. from the Original Manuscript. Francis William Bain. LC 12-278518. 1912. 1.25. G. P. Putnam' Sons.
Bubble's Shadow: A Novel. Joel Gross. LC 73-127516. 1970. 4.95. Crown Publishers.
Bubbles We Buy: A Novel. Alice Jones. LC 3-129700. 1903. H. B. Turner & Co.
Bubbling Spring. Ross Santee. LC 49-505627. 1949. C. Scribner's Sons.
Bubblin's An' B'ilin's at the Center. Merle Dixon Graves. LC 75-122688. (Short story index reprint series). (Illus.). 1970. Books for Libraries Press.
Bubu of Montparnasse. Charles Louis Phillippe. LC 49-1792. (New Avon library 172). 1948. Avon Pub. Co.
Bubu of Montparnasse. Introd. by Alan Ross; with Illus. by Leonard Rosoman. Charles Louis Philippe. LC 53-9839. (Illustrated novel library). 1953. Roy Publishers.
Bubu of Montparnasse. With an Introd. by T. S. Eliot. Charles Louis Philippe. LC 57-48236. Shakespeare House.
Buccaneer. William S Furno. LC 52-10561. 1952. Dorrance.
Buccaneer. rev. ed. Anna Maria Fielding Hall. LC 74-162904. (Bentley's Standard Novels: No. 79). Repr. of 1840 ed. 17.00 (ISBN 0-404-54479-7). AMS Pr.
Buccaneer Chief. A Story. Gustave Aimard & St. John, Percy Bolingbroke, 1821-1889, Ed. LC 5-42976. (On cover: Lovell's library. no. 1115). 1888. J. W. Lovell Company.
Buccaneer Farmer. Harold Bindloss. LC 18-207802. Frederick A. Stokes Company.
Buccaneer Surgeon. Frank Gill Slaughter. 1976. Repr. of 1954 ed. lib. bdg. 16.30x (ISBN 0-89190-533-2). Am Repr-Rivercity Pr.
Buccaneer Surgeon: By C. V. Terry Pseud. 1st Ed. Frank Gill Slaughter. LC 54-9850. 1954. Hanover House.
Buccaneer (the Story of Jean Lafitte) Originally Published Under the Title: " Jean Lafitte, Gentleman Snuggler,". Mitchell Vaughn Charnley. Grosset & Dunlap.
Buccaneers. Edith Newbold Jones Wharton. LC 38-27761. 1938. D. Appleton-Century Company, Incorporated.
Buccaneers. A Historical Novel of the Times of William Iii. and Louis Xiv. Randolph Jones. 1878. The Authors' Publishing Company.
Buccaneers: A Romance of Our Own Country in Its Ancient Day; Illustrated with Divers Marvellous Histories, and Antique and Facetious Episodes; Gathered from the Most Authentic Chronicles & Affirmed Record Extant from the Settlement of the Nieuw Nederlandts, Until the Times of the Famous Richard Kid: Carefully Collated from the Laborious Researches, and Minute Investigations, of That Excellent Antiquary and Sub-Lime Philosopher, Yclept Terentius Phlogobombos Psued.... Samuel Benjamin Herbert Judah. LC 2-20896. 1827. Munroe & Francis.
Buccaneers: A Story of the Black Flag in Business. Henry Morrow Hyde. LC 4-35075. 1904. Funk & Wagnalls Company.
Buchanan Calls the Shots. Jonas Ward, pseud. (Buchanan Ser.). 144p. 1978. pap. 1.95 (ISBN 0-449-14210-8, GM). Fawcett.
Buchanan Calls the Shots. Jonas Ward. (Fawcett Gold Medal Book). 1975. (pbk.) 0.95. Fawcett.
Buchanan Gets Mad. Jonas Ward, pseud. (Buchanan Ser.). 1978. pap. 1.95 (ISBN 0-449-14209-4, GM). Fawcett.
Buchanan Gets Mad. Jonas Ward, pseud. (Orig.). 1968. pap. 0.50 o.p. (D2546, GM). Fawcett World.
Buchanan of "The Press" A Novel. Silas Bent. LC 32-29902. 1932. The Vanguard Press.
Buchanan on the Prod. Jonas Ward, pseud. (Buchanan Ser.). 144p. 1981. pap. 1.95 (ISBN 0-449-14107-1, GM). Fawcett.
Buchanan on the Run. Jonas Ward, pseud. (Buchanan Ser.). 1978. pap. 1.75 (ISBN 0-449-14208-6, GM). Fawcett.
Buchanan Says No. Jonas Ward, pseud. (Buchanan Ser.). 1979. pap. 1.95 (ISBN 0-449-14164-0, GM). Fawcett.
Buchanan Takes Over. Jonas Ward, pseud. 1978. pap. 1.95 (ISBN 0-449-14063-6, GM). Fawcett.
Buchanan Takes Over. Jonas Ward. (Fawcett gold medal). 1975. (pbk.) 0.95. Fawcett.
Buchanan's Big Showdown. Jonas Ward, pseud. 176p. 1978. pap. 1.95 (ISBN 0-449-14109-8, GM). Fawcett.
Buchanan's Big Showdown. Jonas Ward. 1976. 1.25. Fawcett Publications, Inc.
Buchanan's Gamble. Jonas Ward, pseud. 1979. pap. 1.95 (ISBN 0-449-14177-2, GM). Fawcett.
Buchanan's Gun. Jonas Ward, pseud. (Buchanan Ser.). 160p. 1982. pap. 1.95 (ISBN 0-449-14211-6, GM). Fawcett.
Buchanan's Manhunt. Jonas Ward, pseud. 1979. 1.75 (ISBN 0-449-14119-5). Fawcett Gold Medal Books.
Buchanan's Range War. Jonas Ward. 224p. 1980. pap. 1.75 (ISBN 0-449-14357-0, GM). Fawcett.
Buchanan's Revenge. Jonas Ward. 144p. 1982. pap. 2.25 (ISBN 0-449-12361-8, GM). Fawcett.
Buchanan's Siege. Jonas Ward. 160p. 1982. pap. 2.25 (ISBN 0-449-14086-5, GM). Fawcett.
Buchanan's Siege. Jonas Ward. 1973. (pbk) 0.75. Fawcett.
Buchanan's Stolen Railway. Jonas Ward. (Fawcett Gold Medal Book). 1978. 1.75 (ISBN 0-449-13977-8). Fawcett Books.
Buchanan's Texas Treasure. Jonas Ward. (Fawcett Gold Medal book). 1977. 1.25 (ISBN 0-449-13812-7). Fawcett Pubns.
Buchanan's War. Jonas Ward. (Orig.). 1981. pap. 1.95 (ISBN 0-449-14137-3, GM). Fawcett.
Buchanan's Wife: A Novel. Justus Miles Forman. 1906. Harper & Brothers.
Bucharest Ballerina Murders. Francis Van Wyck Mason. LC 40-34427. 1940. Frederick A. Stokes Company.
Buchwald Stops Here. Art Buchwald. 1979. pap. 2.75 (ISBN 0-425-04211-1). Berkley Pub.
Buck. Bill Burchardt, pseud. LC 78-1188. 1978. 7.95 (ISBN 0-385-13439-8). Doubleday.
Buck: Being Some Account of His Rise in the Great City of Chicago. Charles David Stewart. LC 19-2327. 1919. 1.60. Houghton Mifflin Company.
Buck Colter. Matthew Braun. 1979. pap. 1.95 (ISBN 0-671-44011-X). PB.
Buck Fever. James Lang. 3.75 o.p. Vantage.
Buck Holley of Cow Creek: A Novel of the West. 1st Ed. Leon Rovetta. LC 55-12470. Exposition Press.
Buck in the Snow see Second April.
Buck Parvin and the Movies. Charles Emmett Van Loan. LC 15-19474. George H. Doran Company.
Buck Parvin and the Movies: Stories of the Moving Picture Game. Charles Emmett Van Loan. LC 24-14943. Grosset & Dunlap.
Buck Passes Flynn. Gregory McDonald. LC 82-6057. 1982. 12.95 (ISBN 0-8161-3394-8). G.K. Hall.
Buck Peters, Ranchman. Clarence Edward Mulford. 1973. Repr. of 1912 ed. lib. bdg. 18.30x (ISBN 0-88411-202-0). Amereon Ltd.
Buck Peters, Ranchman: Being the Story of What Happened When Buck Peters, Hopalong Cassidy, and Their Bar-20 Associates Went to Montana. Clarence Edward Mulford & John Wood Clay. LC 73-89649. 1973. 6.95. Aeonian Press.
Buck Peters, Ranchman: Being the Story of What Happened When Buck Peters, Hopalong Cassidy, and Their Bar-20 Associates Went to Montana. Clarence Edward Mulford & Clay, John Wood. LC 12-7625. 1912. A. C. McClurg & Co.
Buck Peters, Ranchman: Being the Story of What Happened When Buck Peters, Hopalong Cassidy, and Their Bar-20 Associates Went to Montana. Clarence Edward Mulford & Clay, John Wood. LC 27-7338. A. L. Burt Company.
Buck Rogers in the Twenty-Fifth Century. Ed. by Fotonovel Publications Staff. (Illus., Orig.). 1979. pap. 2.75. Fotonovel.
Buck Rogers in the Twenty-Fifth Century. Gray Morrow & Jim Lawrence. (Illus.). 193p. 1981. pap. 12.95 (ISBN 0-8256-3221-8, Quick Fox). Putnam Pub Group.
Buck Rogers: That Man on Beta, No. 2. Addison E. Steele. 1979. pap. 1.95 (ISBN 0-440-10948-5). Dell.
Buckaroo. Herbert Arthur, pseud. LC 47-30652. 1947. Arcadia House.
Buckaroo. Herbert Shappiro. LC 47-30652. 1947. Arcadia House.
Buckaroo: A Tale of the Texas Rangers. Eugene Cunningham. LC 33-7187. 1933. Houghton Mifflin Company.
Buckaroo Clan of Montana. Clee Woods. LC 35-35381. The Macaulay Company.
Buckaroo's Code. Wayne D Overholser. LC 47-1305. 1947. The Macmillan Company.
Bucket of Money: A Novel of Life on a Louisiana Sugar Plantation in the Days of Huey Long. 1st Ed. Hubert Madere. LC 60-1709. Exposition Press.
Buckets & Leaves. Thomas Huntley. 5.95 o.p. Vantage.
Buckets of Water, a Novel. Mary Hayman. LC 60-524042. (Milestone book). 1960. Comet Press Books.
Buckeye Doctor: A Tale for Physicians and for Physicians' Patients. William Wesley Pennell. LC 3-12819. 1903. The Grafton Press.
Bucking the Tiger. Achmed Abdullah. LC 17-15283.
Buckingham Palace Connection. Ted Willis. LC 78-59728. 1978. 9.95 (ISBN 0-688-03371-7). Morrow.
Bucko. Cliff Farrell. LC 65-106031. (Double D western). 1965. 3.50. Doubleday.
Bucks County Idyll. Robert J Seidman. LC 79-23721. 10.95 (ISBN 0-671-24825-1). Simon and Schuster.
Buckskin and Smoke. Anna Hansen Hayes. LC 72-172674. 1971. 4.95 (ISBN 0-8111-0427-3). Naylor Co.
Buckskin Baronet. 1st Ed. Margaret Widdemer. LC 60-6919. 1960. Doubleday.
Buckskin Breeches. Philip Duffield Stong. Farrar & Rinehart, Incorporated,C.
Buckskin Brigades. La Fayette Ronald Hubbard. LC 37-20207. The Macaulay Company.
Buckskin Brigades. La Fayette Ronald Hubbard. LC 76-42914. 1977. 9.95 (ISBN 0-917972-01-5). Theta Pub. Co.
Buckskin Cavalier. John Clagett. LC 54-11170. 1954. Crown Publishers.
Buckskin Empire. Harry Sinclair Drago. LC 42-7028. 1942. Doubleday, Doran and Company, Inc.
Buckskin Girl. Gwen Moffat. 191p. 1982. 14.95 (ISBN 0-575-03049-6, Pub. by Gollancz England). David & Charles.
Buckskin Man. Thomas Wakefield Blackburn. 1980. pap. 1.50 (ISBN 0-440-10976-0). Dell.
Buckskin Man. Thomas Wakefield Blackburn. 1973. (pbk.) 0.75. Dell.
Buckskin Man Tales, 5 bks. Frederick Feikema Manfred. 1980. Set. lib. bdg. 70.00 (ISBN 0-8398-2734-2, Gregg). G K Hall.
Buckskin Marshal. Harry Sinclair Drago. LC 46-4461. 1945. Jefferson House.
Buckskin Mose: Or, Life from the Lakes to the Pacific, As Actor, Cirucs-Rider, Detective, Ranger, Gold-Digger, Indian Scout, and Guide. George W Perrie. Ed. by Rosenberg, C. G. LC 11-7141. 1873. H. L. Hinton.
Buckskin: Or, The Camp of the Besiegers. A Tale of the Revolution. 1847. W. H. Graham.
Buckskin Pards. Charles Stanley Strong. LC 49-1189. 1949. Phoenix Press.
Buckskin Rider. William Frederick Bragg. LC 56-10910. 1956. Arcadia House.
Buckskin Run. Louis L'Amour. LC 82-6047. 1982. 2.50 (ISBN 0-8161-3392-1). G.K. Hall.
Buckskin: The Story of a Western Horse. Thomas Clark Hinkle. LC 39-212993. 1939. W. Morrow & Co.
Buckstones: A Novel, by Paul I. Wellman. Paul Iselin Wellman. LC 67-15193. 1967. 5.95. Trident.
Bucky Follows a Cold Trail. William MacLeod Raine. LC 37-2946. 1937. Houghton Mifflin Company.
Bucky O'Connor: A Tale of the Unfenced Border. William MacLeod Raine. LC 10-17993. G. W. Dillingham Company.
Bucky O'Connor: A Tale of the Unfenced Border. William MacLeod Raine. LC 38-5611. Grosset & Dunlap.
Bud. Perry Davis Rich. LC 40-8388. The Pyramid Press.
Bud: A Novel. Neil Munro. LC 7-20870. 1907. Harper & Brothers.
Bud, a Story of the Church of the New Humanity. William Kennedy Marshall. LC 2-7577. 1901. Jennings & Pye.
Bud and Ella. C. A. Fox. LC 23-120396. C. A. Fox.
Bud, Blossom, Fruit. A Story. Julia R Parish. LC 7-35000. 1886. J. C. Chilton Publishing Company.
Bud of Promise. A Story for Ambitious Parents. Almira George Plympton. LC 7-38190. 1895. Roberts Brothers.
Budapest Parade Murders: Captain North's 8th Case. Francis Van Wyck Mason. LC 35-561. 1935. Pub. for the Crime Club, Inc., by Doubleday, Doran and Company, Inc.
Buddenbrooks. Thomas Mann. LC 63-16420. 1964. Knopf.
Buddenbrooks. Thomas Mann. Tr. by Helen Tracy Lowe. LC 37-17802. (Half-title: The modern library of the world's best books. 57). 1937. The Modern Library.
Buddenbrooks: Translated from the German. Thomas Mann. Tr. by Helen Tracy Lowe. LC 38-28071. 1938. A. A. Knopf.
Buddenbrooks: Translated from the German of Thomas Mann. Thomas Mann. Tr. by Helen Tracy Lowe. LC 24-4622. 1924. A. A. Knopf.
Buddha Tree. Fumio Niwa. LC 74-15259. 1971. pap. 6.25 (ISBN 0-8048-0995-X). C E Tuttle.
Buddha Tree. Fumio Niwa. Tr. by Kenneth Strong. 1966. 13.95 (ISBN 0-7206-1125-3). Dufour.
Buddha Tree: A Novel. Fumio Niwa. LC 74-157259. (Unesco Collection of Contemporary Works). (Tut books. L). 1971. 2.25 (ISBN 0-8048-0995-X). C. E. Tuttle Co.
Buddha's Return. Translated from the Russian by Nicholas Wreden. 1st Ed. Gaito Gazdanov. LC 51-12227. 1951. Dutton.
Buddhist Birth Stories; or Jataka Tales: The Oldest Collection of Folklore Extant. Rhys Davids. Tr. by Thomas Williams. Ed. by Richard M. Dorson. LC 77-70620. (International Folklore Ser.). 1977. Repr. of 1880 ed. lib. bdg. 27.00x (ISBN 0-405-10090-6). Ayer Co.
Buddhist Praying Wheel. William Simpson. 313p. 1970. 7.95 (ISBN 0-8216-0060-5). Univ Bks.
Buddhoe, the Man Who Shaped the History of St. Croix. Pat Gill. LC 76-53162. Wentworth Press.
Buddies: A Novel. James Whitfield Ellison. LC 82-19483. 17.95 (ISBN 0-399-31003-7). Seaview/Putnam.
Buddies of the Sea: A Story of Northern Latitudes. Dillon Wallace. LC 32-342311. Fleming H. Revell Company.
Buddwing: A Novel. Evan Hunter. (Cardinal ed., 7509). 1965. Pocket Bks.
Buddwing: A Novel. Evan Hunter. LC 64-14426. 1964. Simon and Schuster.
Buddy Boy: A Novel. Brian Thompson. LC 77-6109. 1978. 7.95 (ISBN 0-312-10684-X). St. Martin's Press.

Buddy System. Michael J. Hoffman. LC 77-138874. 1971. 4.95. Holt, Rinehart and Winston.

Buddy System. Michael J. Stewart. (Orig.). 1980. pap. text ed. 1.95 o.s.i. (ISBN 0-505-51593-8). Tower Bks.

Budge & Troddie: Or, Helen's Babies at Play; Being an Account of the Further Doings of Three Marvelously Precocious Children. John Habberton. LC 8-33785. Grosset and Dunlap.

Budget of Christmas Tales. Dickens, Charles et al. LC 6-37240. (Christmas Herald Library). (The Christmas herald library). The Christian Herald.

Budget of Short Stories... New York Tribune. LC 20-23166. (Library of tribune extras, v. 1, no. 9). 1889. The Tribune Association.

Buell Hampton. Willis George Emerson. LC 2-13617. 1902. Forbes & Company.

Buenavista: A Saga of Old Spain. Jack S. Bew. (Illus.). 168p. 1975. 5.95 o.p. (ISBN 0-8059-2138-9). Dorrance.

Buenos Aires Affair: A Detective Novel. Manuel Puig. LC 75-28198. 1976. 8.95. Dutton.

Buenos Aires Affair: A Detective Novel. Manuel. Puig. LC 80-11865. 1980. 3.45 (ISBN 0-394-74474-8). Vintage Books.

Buff and Blue: Or, The Privateers of the Revolution. A Tale of Long Island Sound. Charles F Sterling. LC 8-16308. 1847. W. H. Graham.

Buffalo, & Other Stories. Wayne Ude. 1975. pap. 3.00 (ISBN 0-89924-000-3). Lynx Hse.

Buffalo Bill. Edward Zane Carroll Judson. LC 18-5416. 1886. International Book Company.

Buffalo Bill and the Overland Trail: Being the Story of How Boy and Man Worked Hard and Played Hard to Blaze the White Trail, by Wagon, Train, Stage Coach and Pony Express, Across the Great Plains and the Mountains Beyond, That the American Republic Might Expand and Florish. Edwin Legrand Sabin. LC 14-17982. (On back: Trail blazers series). 1914. J. B. Lippincott Company.

Buffalo Bill's Best Shot. Edward Zane Carroll Judson. LC 7-11440. (sea and shore series--no. 23). 1890. Street & Smith.

Buffalo Bill's Last Victory: Or,S Dove Eye, the Lodge Queen. Edward Zane Carroll Judson. (sea and shore series--no. 24). 1890. Street & Smith.

Buffalo Box: A Simon Lash Mystery. Frank Gruber. LC 42-18155. 1942. Farrar & Reinhart, Inc.

Buffalo Brigade. Strong, Charles Stanley. LC 50-11862. 1950. Phoenix Press.

Buffalo Chips. Tom Stratton. (Illus.). 1979. pap. 1.95 (ISBN 0-930000-13-7). Mathom.

Buffalo Coat: A Novel. Carol Ryrie Brink. LC 44-94065. 1944. The Macmillan Company.

Buffalo Doctor. Toni A. M. LC 76-94254. 1970. 4.00. Dorrance.

Buffalo Gold. 1st Ed. R. G Choate, pseud. LC 58-139061. (Double D western). 1958. Doubleday.

Buffalo Grass: A Novel of Kansas. Frank Gruber. LC 56-9321. 1956. Rinehart.

Buffalo Hunt. Mel Marshall. 1975. (pbk.) 0.95 (ISBN 0-345-24453-2). Ballantine Books.

Buffalo Hunter. Zane Grey. 1979. pap. 1.75 o.s.i. (ISBN 0-505-51334-X). Tower Bks.

Buffalo Hunters. Thomas Albert Curry. LC 42-2564. 1941. Arcadia House.

Buffalo Hunters. Mari Sandoz. 1975. 10.95 (ISBN 0-8038-0717-1). Hastings.

Buffalo Man. Edward N. Todd. 1978. pap. 1.50 o.s.i. (ISBN 0-8439-0588-3, Leisure Bks). Nordon Pubns.

Buffalo Medicine. Don Coldsmith. LC 80-1690. 1981. 9.95 (ISBN 0-385-15970-6). Doubleday.

Buffalo People. Lee D. Wilby. (Making of America Ser.). (Orig.). 1981. pap. 2.75 (ISBN 0-440-00776-3). Dell.

Buffalo Roost. Frank Hobart Cheley. LC 13-8074. 1.25. Jennings and Graham.

Buffalo Run. Walt Coburn. pap. 0.60 o.p. (60-405). Manor Bks.

Buffalo Runners. Fred Grove. LC 68-27122. 1968. 4.50. Doubleday.

Buffalo Soldiers. 1st Ed. John Prebble. LC 59-10246. 1959. Harcourt, Brace.

Buffalo Spring. Fred Grove. LC 67-10363. 1967. Doubleday.

Buffalo Trace: Illustrated by Manning De V. Lee. Virginia Louise Snider Eifert. LC 55-5512. 1955. Dodd, Mead.

Buffalo Wagons. Elmer Kelton. LC 57-7623. (Ballantine books, 187). 1957. Ballantine Books.

Buffalo Wagons. Elmer Kelton. 1978. 1.75 (ISBN 0-441-08390-0). Ace Books.

Buffalo Wallow: A Prairie Boyhood. C. T. Jackson. 5.00 (ISBN 0-8446-2296-6). Peter Smith.

Buffalo War. Peter McCurtin. (Sundance Ser.: No. 39). 192p. (Orig.). 1981. pap. 1.95 (ISBN 0-8439-0990-0, Leisure Bks). Nordon Pubns.

Buffalo Woman. Dorothy M Johnson. LC 76-53436. 6.95 (ISBN 0-396-07423-5). Dodd, Mead.

Buffer: A Novel. Alice Caldwell Hegan Rice. LC 29-7503. The Century Co.

Buffoon. Louis Umfreville Wilkinson. LC 16-9542. 1916. A. A. Knopf.

Bug Eye. Alan Le May. LC 31-24659. Farrar & Rinehart, Incorporated.

Bug-Eyed Monsters. Bill Pronzini & Barry N Malzberg. LC 79-2771. (Harvest/HBJ original). (Illus.). 4.95 (ISBN 0-15-614789-0). Harcourt Brace Jovanovich.

Bug Jack Barron. Norman Spinrad. LC 69-16094. 1969. 5.95. Walker.

Bug Jack Barron. Norman Spinrad. LC 80-28939. (Gregg Press science fiction series). 1981. 15.95 (ISBN 0-8398-2617-6). Gregg Press.

Bug-Jargal: Or, A Tale of the Massacre in St. Domingo. 1791. Victor Marie Hugo. LC 7-5882. 1844. J. Mowatt and Co.

Bug-Jargal, The Last Day of a Condemned Man, and Claude Gueux. Victor Marie Hugo & Ward, Arabella, Tr. T. Y. Crowell & Company.

Bug-Jargal. To Which Are Added Claude Gueux, and The Last Days of a Condemned. library ed. Victor Marie Hugo. Tr. by George Burnham Ives. LC 7-6605. 1894. Little, Brown, and Company.

Bug off. Mabel A. Haverfield. 1976. 5.95 o.s.i.; pap. 3.95 o.s.i. Eden.

Bug Wars. Robert L. Asprin. LC 77-15339. (Illus.). 8.95 (ISBN 0-312-10761-7). St. Martin's Press.

Bugged! Donald F. Glut. 192p. 1974. pap. 1.25 o.p. (ISBN 0-532-12236-4, 532-12236-125). Woodhill.

Bugged! Donald F Glut. 1974. (pbk.) 1.25. Manor Books.

Bugged for Murder. Ed Lacy. LC 61-45335. (Avon original, T-538). 1961. Avon Book Division, Hearst Corp.

Bugle in the Wilderness. John Burress. LC 58-8071. (Illus.). 1958. Vanguard Press.

Bugler of Algiers. Perley Poore Sheehan & Davis, Robert Hobart, 1869- Joint Author. LC 17-391. George H. Doran Company.

Bugles and Brass. Garland Roark. LC 64-16217. (Double D western). 1964. Doubleday.

Bugles Are Silent: A Novel of the Texas Revolution. John R. Knaggs. LC 77-22775. 12.50 (ISBN 0-88319-030-3). Shoal Creek Publishers.

Bugles Blow No More. Clifford Dowdey. LC 57-5175. 1957. Rinehart.

Bugles Blow No More. Clifford Dowdey. LC 37-27301. 1937. Little, Brown and Company.

Bugles Blowing. Nicolas Freeling. LC 75-6366. 6.95 (ISBN 0-06-011354-5). Harper & Row.

Bugles Blowing. Nicolas Freeling. LC 79-23078. 1980. 1.95 (ISBN 0-394-74551-5). Vintage Books.

Bugles Going by. Joseph McCord. LC 33-304621. The Penn Publishing Company.

Bugles in Her Heart. Lida Larrimore Thomas. LC 44-871343. 1944. Macrae-Smith-Company.

Bugles in the Afternoon. Ernest Haycox. (Signet, Y5388). 1973. (pbk.) 1.25. New American Lib.

Bugles in the Afternoon. Ernest Haycox. LC 48-10595. 1948. Triangle Books.

Bugles in the Afternoon. Ernest Haycox. LC 44-2029. 1944. Little, Brown and Company.

Bugles in the Afternoon. Ernest Haycox. LC 78-14278. (Gregg Press Western Fiction Series). 1978. 8.95 (ISBN 0-8398-2473-4). Gregg Press.

Bugles in the Afternoon. Ernest Haycox. LC 80-29461. 1981. 15.95 (ISBN 0-8161-3152-X). G. K. Hall.

Bugles in the Night. Burt Arthur, pseud. (O.s.i.). 1976. pap. 0.95 o.s.i. Belmont-Tower.

Bugles in the Night. Barry Benefield. LC 27-59459. 2.00. The Century Company.

Bugles in the Night: An Historical Novel of the West, by Arthur Herbert Pseud. Herbert Arthur. LC 50-9308. 1950. Rinehart.

Bugles of Gettysburg. La Salle Corbell Pickett. LC 13-11967. 1913. F. G. Browne & Co.

Bugle's Wake. Curtis Kent Bishop. LC 51-14959. (Dutton Diamond D western). 1952. Dutton.

Bugles West. Frank Gruber. LC 54-792492. 1954. Rinehart.

Bugles West. Frank Gruber. LC 77-2259. 1977. 7.95 (ISBN 0-89340-075-0). J. Curley.

Bugs. Theodore Roszak. LC 80-2625. 1981. 14.95 (ISBN 0-385-17410-1). Doubleday.

Bugs in Your Ears. Betty Bates. (gr. 4-6). 1979. pap. 1.95 (ISBN 0-671-44144-2). Archway.

Bugs to Blizzards: Or, An Army Wife at Fort D. A. Russell. Martha Fleishman & Carol Joy Justice. LC 74-80793. (Illus.). 1974. Wigwam Pub. Co.

Build My Gallows High. Daniel Mainwaring. LC 46-289252. 1946. W. Morrow & Company.

Build Thee More Stately Mansions. 1st Ed. Harry E Dickson. LC 55-10849. Vantage Press.

Build-Up. William Carlos Williams. LC 52-5166. (Stecher Trilogy: Vol. 3). 1968. 6.50 (ISBN 0-8112-0425-1); pap. 2.35 (ISBN 0-8112-0227-5, NDP259). New Directions.

Build-up, a Novel. William Carlos Williams. LC 52-5166. 1952. Random House.

Build-up Boys. Jeremy Kirk, pseud. LC 51-246. 1951. Scribner.

Builder Also Grows. Elizabeth Rider Montgomery. LC 77-82653. 8.95 (ISBN 0-87949-099-3). Ashley Books.

Builder: By Norbert and Bessie Bergquist. Norbert Bergquist & Bessie Bergquist. LC 53-11178. 1953. Pageant Press.

Builder of Ships: The Story of Brander Cushing's Ambition. Charles Monroe Sheldon. LC 12-25076. Hodder & Stoughton, George H. Doran Company.

Builders. Willis George Emerson. LC 6-22317. 1906. Forbes & Company.

Builders. Ellen Anderson Gholson Glasgow. LC 19-27594. 1919. Doubleday, Page & Company.

Builders. William Woolfolk. LC 68-22609. 1969. 5.95. Doubleday.

Builder's Crown of Jewels. Evelyn Whitell. LC 25-13521. 1925. The Master Press.

Building of Jalna. whiteoak ed. Mazo De La Roche. LC 44-772819. 1944. Little, Brown, and Company.

Building of the City Beautiful. Joaquin Miller. 1893. Stone & Kimball.

Building of the City Beautiful. Joaquin Miller. LC 5-36818. 1905. A. Brandt.

Building of the Wall of China: A Novel. 1st Ed. Ida Allen Tomnovec. LC 53-11270. 1953. Exposition Press.

Building of Venus Four. Calder Willingham. 1977. pap. 2.25 (ISBN 0-532-22111-7). Woodhill.

Building to Win: Or, Fortunes and Misfortunes. Alexander Streeter Arnold. 1894. J. H. Earle.

Building up. Jane V. Barker & Sybil Downing. (Colorado Heritage Ser.: Bk. 7). (Illus.). 44p. (gr. 3-4). 1979. pap. text ed. 3.50x (ISBN 0-87108-228-4). Pruett.

Building. 1st Ed. Peter Martin. LC 60-5864. 1960. Little, Brown.

Built on the Rubble. Frances O'Brien. LC 75-25190. (O.s.i.). 136p. (Orig.). 1976. 6.95 o.s.i. (ISBN 0-89185-001-5); pap. 2.25 o.s.i. (ISBN 0-89185-000-7). Anthelion Pr.

Bukom. Bill Marshall. LC 79-313537. (Longman drumbeat). 1979. 4.00 (ISBN 0-582-64223-X). Longman.

Bulgarian Exclusive. Anthony Grey. LC 77-23198. (Illus.). 1977. 7.95 (ISBN 0-8037-0799-1). Dial Press/J. Wade Books.

Bulgarian Exclusive. Anthony Grey. LC 77-357077. 1976. 3.95 (ISBN 0-7181-1491-4). M. Joseph.

Bull & the Bear. Richard O'Brien. (Jazz Age Ser.: No. 4). 272p. (Orig.). 1983. pap. 3.25 (ISBN 0-440-00655-4, Emerald). Dell.

Bull by the Horns. Charles Bonner. LC 37-24832. 1937. Doubleday, Doran & Co., Inc.

Bull-Dog Drummond Double-Header: Including Third Round. The Final Count. Herman Cyril McNeile. LC 37-17354. 1937. The Sun Dial Press, Inc.

Bull-Dog Drummond: The Adventures of a Demobilized Officer Who Found Peace Dull. Herman Cyril McNeile. LC 20-18927. George H. Doran Company.

Bull-Dog Drummond's Third Round. Herman Cyril McNeile. LC 24-26490. George H. Doran Company.

Bull-Dog Drummond's Third Round. Herman Cyril McNeile. LC 45-9459. 1945. Triangle Books, the Blakiston Company.

Bull Fire. Donald W. Heiney. LC 72-8132. 1973. 6.95 (ISBN 0-394-48302-2). Random House.

Bull from the Sea. Mary Renault, pseud. (Modern lib., 386). 1968. 2.45. Random.

Bull from the Sea. Mary Renault, pseud. LC 74-20649. (Illus.). 1975. 2.45 (ISBN 0-394-71504-7). Vintage Books.

Bull from the Sea. Mary Renault, pseud. LC 62-8924. 1962. Pantheon Books.

Bull from the Sea. Mary Renault, pseud. LC 68-1653. (Modern library of the world's best books 386). (Illus.). 1968. Modern Library.

Bull Gallagher. Rothermel. 183p. 1975. 7.50 o.p. (ISBN 0-682-48260-9). Exposition.

Bull Hunter. Max Brand. LC 81-13213. 1981. 12.95 (ISBN 0-8161-3308-5). G.K. Hall.

Bull Hunter. Frederick Faust. LC 80-20858. (Silver star western.). 1981. 8.95 (ISBN 0-396-07916-4). Dodd, Mead.

Bull Hunter: A Western Story. David Manning, pseud. LC 25-469. Chelsea House.

Bull Hunter's Romance... A Western Story. David Manning, pseud. LC 25-468. Chelsea House.

Bull Moose. Ridgwell Cullum. LC 31-31124. 1931. J. B. Lippincott Company.

Bull on the Bench. Lowell Blake Mason. LC 67-26246. (Illus.). 1967. Arcturus Pub.

Bull Pen see KKK.

Bull Whip. Vera Murdock Stuart Jervis. LC 29-12910. 1929. Doubleday, Doran & Company, Inc.

Bullard of the Space Patrol: Edited by Andre Norton. 1st Ed. Malcolm Jameson. LC 51-12352. 1951. World Pub. Co.

Bulldog and Butterfly: And Julia and Her Romeo: a Chronicle of Castle Barfield. David Christie Murray & Black, William. (On cover: The seaside library. Pocket ed. no. 898). 1886. G. Munro.

Bulldog Carney. William Alexander Fraser. LC 19-146304. 1.50. George H. Doran Company.

Bulldog Drummond--and the Female of the Species. Herman Cyril McNeile. LC 43-4561. 1943. The Sun Dial Press.

Bulldog Drummond at Bay. Herman Cyril McNeile. LC 44-21954. 1944. Triangle Books.

Bulldog Drummond at Bay: By H. C. McNeile... Herman Cyril McNeile. LC 35-441827. 1935. Pub. for the Crime Club, Inc. by Doubleday, Doran & Company, Inc.

Bulldog Drummond Returns. Herman Cyril McNeile. LC 32-4110. Pub. for the Crime Club, Inc., by Doubleday, Doran & Company, Inc.

Bulldog Drummond Returns. Herman Cyril McNeile. LC 44-78434. 1944. Triangle Books.

Bulldog Drummond Strikes Back... Herman Cyril McNeile. LC 33-133319. 1933. Pub. for the Crime Club, Inc., by Doubleday, Doran & Company, Inc.

Bulldog Drummond Strikes Back... Herman Cyril McNeile. LC 43-18427. 1943. Triangle Books.

Bulldog Has the Key. Francis Woolsey Bronson. LC 49-105180. 1949. Farrar, Straus.

Bulldogger. Kim Knight. LC 39-21861. Dodge Publishing Company.

Bull'e Eye. Milward Rodon Kennedy Burge. LC 33-23672. 1933. H. C. Kinsey & Company, Inc.

Buller's Guns. Richard Alexander Hough. LC 80-28176. 1981. 10.95 (ISBN 0-688-00453-9). Morrow.

Bullet Ambush. William Macleod Raine. 1974. (pbk.) 0.75. Popular Library.

Bullet and Shell: A Soldier's Romance. George Forrester Williams. LC 34-38307. 1895. Fords, Howard, & Hulbert.

Bullet and Shell. War As the Soldier Saw It; Camp, March and Picket; Battlefield and Bivouac; Prison and Hospital. George Forrester Williams. LC 2-17772. 1883. Fords, Howard, & Hulbert.

Bullet Barricade. Leslie Charles Ernenwein. 1975. pap. 0.95 o.p. (LB312, Leisure Bks). Nordon Pubns.

Bullet Barricade. Leslie Charles Ernenwein. 1971. pap. 0.60 o.p. (R2475, GM). Fawcett World.

Bullet Barricade. Lessie Charles Ernenwein. 1975. (pbk.) 0.95. Leisure Books.

Bullet Brand. T. W. Ford. LC 47-203342. 1947. Phoenix Press.

Bullet Brand. Bradford Scott. 1973. pap. 0.75 o.p. (ISBN 0-515-03060-0, T3060). Pyramid Pubns.

Bullet Brand. Sumner, Nick. LC 55-9922. (Silver star westerns). 1955. Dodd, Mead.

Bullet-Brand Empire. William Hopson. 1976. (pbk.) 1.25. Award Books.

Bullet-Brand Empire. William L. Hopson. pap. 0.50 o.p. (50-462). Manor Bks.

Bullet Breed. Leslie Charles Ernenwein. LC 46-76659. 1946. R. M. McBride & Company.

Bullet Breed. Orlando Rigoni. Ed. by Alice Sachs. 1970. 3.95 o.p. B Franklin.

Bullet Crazy. Gene Tuttle. (YA) 1972. 4.50 o.p. (Avalon). Bouregy.

Bullet Eater. Oscar Jerome Friend. LC 25-18062. 1925. A. C. McClurg & Co.

Bullet for a Beast. Roger Simons. LC 65-25150. 1965. bds., 2.95. Roy.

Bullet for a Star. Stuart M Kaminsky. LC 76-62776. 6.95 (ISBN 0-312-10797-8). St. Martin's Press.

Bullet for Billy the Kid & Tough Company. Nelson Nye. 1978. pap. 1.95 (ISBN 0-89083-382-6). Zebra.

Bullet for Cinderella. John Dann MacDonald. LC 55-10720. (Dell first edition 62). 1955. Dell Pub. Co.

Bullet for Fidel. Nick Carter. (Nick Carter Ser). (O.s.i.). 160p. 1965. pap. 0.95 o.s.i. (AN1271, Award). Univ Pub & Dist.

Bullet for Georgie. Everett M Skehan. LC 78-27760. 1979. 9.95 (ISBN 0-395-27400-1) (ISBN 0-395-26294-1). Houghton Mifflin.

Bullet for Georgie. Everett M Skehan. 1980. 1.95 (ISBN 0-445-04535-3). Fawcett Popular Library.

Bullet for Mr Texas. Ray Hoga. Bd. with Marshall of Babylon. 1979. pap. 1.95 (ISBN 0-451-08563-9, J8563, Sig). NAL.

Bullet for My Love: A Novel. Octavus Roy Cohen. LC 50-5656. 1950. Macmillan.

Bullet for the Bride. Jon Messman. (Orig.). 1972. pap. 0.95 o.p. (ISBN 0-515-02792-8). Pyramid Pubns.

Bullet in His Cap. Robert Fleming. LC 43-2265. (Handi-book mysteries). 1942. Quinn Publishing Co., Inc.

Bullet in the Ballet. Doris Caroline Abrahams & Simon Jasha Skidelsky. LC 38-972710. 1938. Pub. for the Crime Club, Inc., by Doubleday, Doran & Co., Inc.

Bullet Justice. Bradford Scott. 1969. pap. 0.60 o.p. (X2092). Pyramid Pubns.

Bullet Law. Charles N Heckelmann. LC 57-1042. (Signet books, 1373). 1957. New American Library.

Bullet Law. Charles N Heckelmann. LC 55-10741. 1955. Little, Brown.

Bullet Park. John Cheever. 1969. 10.95 (ISBN 0-394-41819-0). Knopf.

Bullet Park: A Novel. John Cheever. LC 69-14730. 1969. 5.95. Knopf.

Bullet Proof. William Frederick Bragg. LC 55-14028. 1955. Arcadia House.

Bullet Proof. Frank Kane. LC 51-12798. 1951. Washburn.

Bullet-Proof Martyr. 1st Ed. James A Howard. LC 61-5512. 1961. Dutton.

Bullet Song. William Frederick Bragg. LC 53-11306. 1953. Arcadia House.

Bullet Trail. William Colt MacDonald. 1974. (pbk.) 0.95 (ISBN 0-380-00156-X). Avon.

Bullet Train. Joseph Rance & Arei Kato. LC 80-15550. (Illus.). 1980. 10.95 (ISBN 0-688-03702-X). Morrow.

Bulletproof Sheriff. John Earl Lewis. 1981. pap. 6.95 (Avalon). Bouregy.

Bullets at Dry Creek. Donald S Rowland. LC 65-7982. 1965. Arcadia House.

Bullets, Buzzards, Boxes of Pine. J. D. Hardin. LC 79-88844. (Pinkerton Ser.: No. 14). (Orig.). 1980. pap. 1.75 (ISBN 0-87216-591-4). Playboy Pbks.

Bullets Don't Bluff. Paul Evan Lehman. LC 54-342074. (Ace double novel books, D-64). 1954. Ace Books.

Bullets for Badwater. Al P. Nelson. 1970. pap. 0.60 o.p. (ISBN 0-447-73887-9). Lancer.

Bullets for Buckaroos. William Colt MacDonald. LC 36-16928. Covici, Friede.

Bullets for Macbeth. 192p. 1976. 8.95 o.p. (ISBN 0-8415-0424-5). Dutton.

Bullets for Macbeth. Marvin Kaye. LC 75-41317. 1976. 8.95 (ISBN 0-8415-0424-5). Saturday Review Press.

Bullets for the Blind. Steve Winsten. 1973. (pbk) 0.75. Curtis Books.

Bullets for the Bridegroom. David Dodge. 1944. The Macmillan Company.

Bullets on Bunchgrass. Louis Trimble. LC 54-10324. 1954. Avalon Books.

Bullets on the Border. Jonathan Scofield, pseud. (Freedom Fighters Ser.: No. 5). (Orig.). 1981. pap. 2.75 (ISBN 0-440-00668-6, Bryans). Dell.

Bullets on the Brazos. Lew Bishop. LC 57-366822. 1957. Arcadia House.

Bullets Over Broken Leg. Tom J Hopkins. LC 47-4702. 1947. Doubleday.

Bullets West. James D. Sayers. 1970. pap. 0.60 o.p. (ISBN 0-447-73893-3). Lancer.

Bullfighters. 1st Ed. Dorothy Eiland. LC 54-11226. 1954. Pageant Press.

Bullies: Stories. George Swift Trow. LC 79-28278. 9.95 (ISBN 0-316-85305-4). Little, Brown.

Bullion. Michael Woodman. 1971. pap. 0.95 o.p. (95141). Beagle Bks.

Bullion: A Novel by John Goldsmith, with Gordon Briggs and Don Bernard. John Goldsmith & Gordon Briggs. LC 83-2790. 1983. 13.95 (ISBN 0-89479-122-2). A & W Publishers.

Bullion Mystery: Or, Nick Carter's Case from Overseas. Nick Carter. LC 52-52920. (New magnet library, no. 852). 1914. Street & Smith.

Bullion on the Range. Tevis Miller. LC 38-4095. Phoenix Press.

Bulls and the Jonathans: Comprising John Bull and Brother Jonathan, and John Bull in America. James Kirke Paulding. LC 7-33784. 1867. C. Scribner and Company.

Bulls, Blood, and Passion: By David Williams Pseud. The Sinful Ones, by Fritz Leiber. Arnodl Scroog & Fritz Leiber. LC 53-20870. (Universal giant edition, no. 5). 1953. Universal.

Bull's Eye. Pia D'Alessandria. Tr. by J. R. Chanter. 1962. 3.50x o.p. Verry.

Bull's Eye. Tr. from Italian by J. R. Chanter. Pia D' Alessandria. LC 66-27772. 1966. 3.50. H. Hamilton.

Bulls of Parral. Marguerite Steen. 1969. 10.00x (ISBN 0-7182-0815-3). Intl Pubns Serv.

Bulls of Parral: 1st Ed. Marguerite Steen. 1954. Doubleday.

Bulls of Rome. Ludwig Huna & Pemberton, Madge, Tr. LC 30-89068. 1930. Brewer and Warren Inc., Payson and Clarke Ltd.

Bulls of Ronda. Eugene P. Benson. LC 75-39096. 200p. 1976. 8.95 o.p. (ISBN 0-8467-0159-6). Methuen Inc.

Bulls of San Isidro. Maurice Ivan Sicard. LC 54-7969. 1954. Farrar, Straus and Young.

Bulls of San Isidro: Adapted from the French by Herma Briffault. J Saint-Paulien. LC 54-7969. 1954. Farrar, Straus and Young.

Bullwhacker. James D. Nichols. (Orig.). 1981. pap. 1.95 (ISBN 0-505-51629-2). Tower Bks.

Bully. Jerome Alden. 1979. 7.95 (ISBN 0-517-53786-9). Crown.

Bulpington of Blue: Adventures, Poses, Stresses, Conflicts, and Disaster in a Contemporary Brain. Herbert George Wells. LC 33-27008. 1933. The Macmillan Company.

Bulwark: A Novel. Theodore Dreiser. LC 46-25076. 1946. Doubleday & Company Inc.

Bulwer's Lady of Lyons; Cardinal Richelieu; Calderon, the Courtier; and Money. Edward George Earle Lytton Bulwer-Lytton Lytton. LC 7-8337. (Franklin library. no. 4). 1887. Franklin News Co.

Bulwer's Novels, 30 Vols. Edward Bulwerlytton. Ed. by Knebworth. (Illus.). Set. 600.00 o.p.; Set. prepub. 500.00 o.p. Adler.

Bum Ticker: A Hearty Traveler's Tale. Gordon McShean. LC 76-13744. 1976. 9.95 (ISBN 0-917112-01-6); pap. 4.95 (ISBN 0-917112-62-8). Multinational Media.

Bumarap: The Story of a Male Virgin. Samuel Roth. LC 47-1740. 1947. Arrowhead Books.

Bumbler Strikes Again. William Johnston. 1970. pap. 0.60 o.p. (ISBN 0-447-73891-7). Lancer.

Bumerang. Igor Guberman. (Illus.). 128p. (Rus.). 1982. pap. 6.00 (ISBN 0-938920-15-4). Hermitage MI.

Bump and Grind Murders. Alan Geoffrey Yates. LC 64-57032. (Signet book). 1964. New American Library of World Literature.

Bump in the Night. Colin Watson. pap. 0.65 o.p. (ISBN 0-14-001966-9). Penguin.

Bump on Brannigan's Head. Myles Connolly. LC 50-6288. 1950. Macmillan.

Bumsby Papers (2d Series) Irish Echoes. By John Brougham... bumsby papers second series irish echoes. ed. John Brougham. LC 6-18959. 1856. Derby & Jackson.

Bumsider. C. C. MacApp. (Orig.). 1973. pap. 0.95 o.s.i. (75-421). Lancer.

Bunce. Michael De Larrabeiti. LC 81-43124. (Crime Club Ser.). 192p. 1981. 10.95 (ISBN 0-385-17753-4). Doubleday.

Bunch Grass: A Chronicle of Life on a Cattle Ranch. Horace Annesley Vachell. LC 75-178467. (Short story index reprint series). 1971. (ISBN 0-8369-4068-7). Books for Libraries Press.

Bunch Grass: By Joseph Wayne Pseud. 1st Ed. Wayne D Overholser. LC 54-5038. (Dutton Diamond D western). 1954. Dutton.

Bunch-Grass Stories. Josephine White Bates. LC 6-9078. 1895. J. B. Lippincott Company.

Bunch on McKellahan Street. Carol J Farley, pseud. LC 75-152736. 1971. 5.95 (ISBN 0-531-01992-6). F. Watts.

Buncha Crocs in Surch of Snac. Terry Galloway. LC 80-65065. 1980. 5.95 (ISBN 0-931604-04-4); pap. 2.95 (ISBN 0-931604-05-2). Curbstone Pub NY TX.

Bundarie Boy: National Gold Medal Winner, 1961. rev. ed. Sheik Sadeek. LC 77-365277. 1976. Sadeek.

Bundle for the Toff. John Creasey. LC 68-13571. 1968. Walker.

Bundle of Curves: By Jack Woodford Pseud. & Jeanne Renee Pseud. Josiah Pitts Woolfolk & Evis Joberg. LC 52-68109. 1952. Signature Press.

Bundle of Firewood. Nancy Dorer & Frances Dorer. (Orig.). 1979. pap. 1.95 (ISBN 0-532-23238-0). Woodhill.

Bundle of Letters. Henry James. LC 77-3718. 1977. 17.50 (ISBN 0-8414-5259-8). Folcroft Library Editions.

Bundle of Letters see Lady Barbarina.

Bundle of Life. Pearl Mary Teresa Richards Craigie. LC 12-243613. ("unknown" library v. 34). The Cassell Publishing Co.

Bundle of Life. Pearl Mary Teresa Richards Craigie. LC 6-31099. (On cover: The pseudonym library, no. 6). 1894. J. S. Tait and Sons.

Bundle of Straws. William Thomas Standen. LC 99-2850. 1899. T. D. Rich.

Bundle of the Living. Rene Aeschliman. 1970. 5.00 o.p. Vantage.

Bundle of Yarns. Fred Warner Shibley. 1899. H. Gregory.

Bunduki. John Thomas Edson. (Science Fiction Ser). 1976. pap. 1.50 o.p. (UW1243). DAW Bks.

Bunga-Bunga. Stephen King-Hall. LC 33-9687. W. W. Norton & Company, Inc.

Bungalow Harlot. James Merriam, Jr. 160p. 1974. pap. 1.95 o.p. (ISBN 0-87682-393-2, 7393). Barclay Hse.

Bungalow Nine. Norman Obee. 3.95 o.p. Walker & Co.

Bungalow Nine. Norman Ober. LC 62-12750. 1962. Walker.

Bungalow of Dead Birds. George Varney. LC 29-25040. 1929. T. Nelson & Sons, Ltd.

Bunk. William E. Woodward. LC 76-22715. (Prelude to depression). 1976. 22.50. Da Capo Press.

Bunk. William E. Woodward. Harper & Brothers.

Bunker Bean. Harry Leon Wilson. 1913. Doubleday, Page & Company.

Bunker Bean. Harry Leon Wilson. LC 24-204801. 1922. Doubleday, Page & Company.

Bunker Hill Failure: Or, A Failure That Was a Victory. Anna F Burnham. The Pilgrim Press.

Bunker Hill to Chicago. A Story. Eloise O. Randall Richberg. LC 7-412273. 1893. The Dibble Publishing Company.

Bunkhouse Logic. Benjamin Stein. 176p. (Orig.). 1981. pap. 2.75 (ISBN 0-380-78543-9, 78543). Avon.

Bunny Brown: And His Sister Sue on the Rolling Ocean. Laura Lee Hope. LC 25-9878. (Her Bunny Brown series). Grosset & Dunlap.

Bunny Lake Is Missing: By Evelyn Piper Pseud. 1st Ed. Merriam Modell. LC 57-615271. 1957. Harper.

Bunny's House: A Novel. E. M Walker. LC 22-3515. 1922. Benziger Brothers.

Bunny's Journal. bicentennial ed. Dwight Jarvis. LC 75-44754. W. R. Moore.

Burbank the Northerner. Jules Verne. 3.95. Assoc Bk.

Burbury Stoke. William John Hopkins. LC 14-3176. 1914. Houghton Mifflin Company.

Burden. Agatha Miller Christie. 1.25. Dell.

Burden. Jeffery Eardley Marston. LC 24-18764. 1924. T. Seltzer.

Burden. Catherine Amy Dawson Scott. LC 8-20714. P. R. Reynolds.

Burden. Mary Westmacott, pseud. LC 72-97687. 1973. 6.95 (ISBN 0-87795-057-1). Arbor Hse.

Burden: A Novel of Romance and Suspense. Agatha Miller Christie. LC 72-97687. 1973. 6.95 (ISBN 0-87795-057-1). Arbor House.

Burden: By Mary Westmacott Pseud. Agatha Miller Christie. LC 57-282999. 1956. W. Heinemann.

Burden Is Light. Eugenia Price. 192p. 1982. 11.95 (ISBN 0-385-27618-4). Dial.

Burden of Adrian Knowle. Alan Fry. LC 74-2716. 1974. 5.95 (ISBN 0-385-07464-6). Doubleday.

Burden of Christopher. Florence Converse. LC 2510. 1900. Houghton, Mifflin and Company.

Burden of Guilt. Ian Gordon, pseud. LC 51-10805. (Inner sanctum mystery). 1951. Simon and Schuster.

Burden of Honor. Christine Faber. LC 16-1108. 0.75. P. J. Kenedy & Sons.

Burden of Isabel. A Novel. James MacLaren Cobban. LC 6-26766. (On cover: Harper's Franklin square library, no. 740). 1893. Harper & Brothers.

Burden of Proof. Victor Canning. LC 56-511010. W. Sloane Associates.

Burden of Proof: A Novel. James Barlow. LC 68-25743. 1968. 4.95. Simon and Schuster.

Burden of Proof, by Jeffrey Ashford. 1st Ed. Roderic Jeffries. LC 63-10613. Harper & Row.

Burden of the Strong. Josephine Turck Baker. LC 19-18905. Correct English Publishing Company.

Bureaucracy: Or. A Civil Service Reformer. Honore De Balzac. Tr. by Katharine Prescott Wormeley. LC 3-23170. (Half-title: The comedy of human life... Scenes from Parisian life). 1889. Roberts Brothers.

Burg Neideck: Novelle. Wilhelm Heinrich Riehl. Ed. by Palmer, Arthur Hubbell. LC 12-38062. (Unterhaltungs-bibliothek). 1893. H. Holt & Company Etc.

Burger's Daughter. Nadine Gordimer. LC 78-20831. 1979. 10.00 (ISBN 0-670-19475-1). Viking Press.

Burger's Daughter. Nadine Gordimer. LC 80-23688. 1979. 4.95 (ISBN 0-14-005593-2). Penguin Books.

Burglar. Brigid Brophy. 1968. 4.50 o.p. (ISBN 0-03-069675-5). HR&W.

Burglar and the Blizzard: A Christmas Story. Alice Duer Miller. LC 14-193609. Hearst's International Library Co.

Burglar in the Closet. Lawrence Block. LC 78-57116. 6.95 (ISBN 0-394-42374-7). Random House.

Burglar Who Liked to Quote Kipling. Lawrence Block. LC 79-4788. 7.95 (ISBN 0-394-50417-8). Random House.

Burglar Who Moved Paradise. Herbert Dickinson Ward. LC 8-36032. 1897. Houghton, Mifflin and Company.

Burglar Who Studied Spinoza. Lawrence Block. LC 80-5288. 1981. 8.95 o.p. (ISBN 0-394-51065-8). Random.

Burglar Who Studied Spinoza. Lawrence Block. 1982. pap. 2.75. PB.

Burglar Who Studied Spinoza: A Bernie Rhodenbarr Mystery. Lawrence Black. LC 80-5288. 8.95 (ISBN 0-394-51065-8). Random House.

Burglars Can't Be Choosers. Lawrence Block. LC 77-5993. 6.95 (ISBN 0-394-41183-8). Random House.

Burglars' Club; a Romance in Twelve Chronicles. Henry Augustus Hering. LC 7-21178. 1906. B. W. Dodge and Company.

Burglars in Paradise. Elizabeth Stuart Phelps H. D. Ward Ward. (On cover: The Riverside paper series, no. 14). 1886. Houghton, Mifflin and Company.

Burglar's Life. Mark Jeffrey. 1968. 7.00 o.s.i. (Pub. by Cowman). Tri-Ocean.

Burgle the Baron. John Creasey. LC 74-80974. 1974. 5.95 (ISBN 0-8027-5312-4). Walker.

Burgle the Baron. Anthony Morton, pseud. LC 74-80974. 192p. 1974. 5.95 o.p. (ISBN 0-8027-5312-4). Walker & Co.

Burgomaster's Wife. Georg Moritz Ebers. Tr. by Safford, Mary Joanna. LC 16-15708. (historical romances of Georg Ebers. vol. xiii). 1915. D. Appleton and Company.

Burgomaster's Wife. Georg Moritz Ebers & Safford, Mary Joanne, Tr. LC 6-43719. 1882. W. S. Gottsberger.

Burgomaster's Wife. A Romance. Georg Moritz Ebers. (On cover: Seaside library. Pocket ed., no. 1097). 1888. G. Munro.

Burgomaster's Wife. A Romance. Georg Moritz Ebers & Ayer, Annie W., Tr. LC 6-43718. A. L. Burt.

Burgomaster's Wife; a Romance. Georg Moritz Ebers & Ayer, Annie W., Tr. LC 16-250535. (On cover: The home library). A. L. Burt Company.

Burgos Contract. Angus Ross. LC 79-88867. 1979. 7.95 (ISBN 0-8027-5407-4). Walker.

Burgraves. Victor Marie Hugo. (Fr). text ed. 1.75 o.p. Cambridge U Pr.

Burgundian: A Tale of Old France. Marion Polk Angellotti. LC 12-6582. 1912. The Century Co.

Burial in Portugal. Bill Knox. LC 73-10865. 1974. 4.95 (ISBN 0-385-00968-2). Published for the Crime Club by Doubleday.

Burial of the Fruit. David Dortort. LC 49-1755. ((New Avon library 183)). 1949. Avon Pub. Co.

Burial of the Fruit. David Dortort. LC 47-360. 1947. Crown Publishers.

Burial of the Guns. Thomas Nelson Page. LC 69-11914. (American short story series, v. 73). 1969. Garrett Press.

Burial of the Guns. Thomas Nelson Page. LC 72-8195. (American short story series, v. 73). 1972. (ISBN 0-8422-8103-7). MSS Information Corp.

Burial of the Guns. Thomas Nelson Page. LC 3-19538. 1894. C. Scribner's Sons.

Burial of the Sardine. Fernando Arrabal. 1980. pap. 4.95 (ISBN 0-7145-0146-8). Riverrun NY.

Buridan's Ass. G. De Bruyn. pap. 1.25 o.p. Adler.

Buried. Daniel Helfgott. 288p. 1981. pap. 2.50 (ISBN 0-380-77644-8, 77644). Avon.

Buried Alive. Arnold Bennett. LC 74-5395. (collected works of Arnold Bennett). 1974. (ISBN 0-518-19091-9). Books for Libraries Press.

Buried Alive. Arnold Bennett. LC 38-31832. 1938. The Sun Dial Press, Inc.

Buried Alive. Emile Zola. LC 28-1651. The Warren Press.

Buried Alive a Tale of These Days. Arnold Bennett. LC 58-104328. Doubleday.

Buried Alive: A Tale of These Days. Arnold Bennett. LC 13-26688. (On cover: The novels of Arnold Bennett). G. H. Doran Company Etc.

Buried Alive: A Tale of These Days. Arnold Bennett. LC 24-14925. (Murray Hill library). George H. Doran Company.

Buried Blossoms. Stephen Lewis. (Orig.). 1982. pap. 2.95 (ISBN 0-515-05153-5). Jove Pubns.

Buried Candelabrum. Stefan Zweig & Paul, Eden, 1865- Tr. LC 37-24268. 1937. The Viking Press.

Buried Diamonds. A Novel. Henrietta Keddie. (Harper's Franklin square library, no. 532). 1886. Harper & Brothers.

Buried for Pleasure. Edmund Crispin, pseud. 191p. Repr. of 1948 ed. lib. bdg. 12.50x (ISBN 0-89190-691-6). Am Repr-Rivercity Pr.

Buried for Pleasure. Edmund Crispin, pseud. LC 75-44967. (Crime Fiction Ser). (O.s.i.). 1976. Repr. of 1949 ed. lib. bdg. 17.50 o.s.i. (ISBN 0-8240-2362-5). Garland Pub.

Buried for Pleasure. Edmund Crispin, pseud. LC 49-8208. 1980. pap. 2.84i (ISBN 0-06-080506-4, P 506, PL). Har-Row.

Buried for Pleasure. Edmund Crispin, pseud. 1968. pap. 0.60 o.p. (X1937). Pyramid Pubns.

Buried for Pleasure. Robert Bruce Montgomery. LC 75-44967. (Fifty Classics of Crime Fiction, 1900-1950; 13). 1976. 12.00 (ISBN 0-8240-2362-5). Garland Pub.

Buried for Pleasure. Robert Bruce Montgomery. (Perennial Library edition). 1980. 1.95 (ISBN 0-06-080506-4). Harper & Row.

Buried for Pleasure: A Detective Story. Robert Bruce Montgomery. LC 49-820848. (Main line mysteries). 1949. J. B. Lippincott Co.

Buried in So Sweet a Place. Stanton Forbes, pseud. LC 73-83630. 1977. 6.95 (ISBN 0-385-07256-2). Published for the Crime Club by Doubleday.

Buried in the Past. Elizabeth Lemarchand. 1975. 7.95 o.p. (ISBN 0-8027-5327-2). Walker & Co.
Buried Land: A Novel. Madison Jones. LC 63-12357. 1963. Viking Press.
Buried Remembrance. Naomi Gladish Smith. (Ace Gothic no. 22). 1976. (pbk.) 0.95. Ace Books.
Buried Rose: Legends of Old Baltimore. Sidney Lauer Nyburg. LC 32-25851. 1932. A. A. Knopf.
Buried Rubies. Edgar Jepson. LC 26-13013. 1926. Siebel Publishing Corporation.
Buried Self: A Background to the Poems of Matthew Arnold, 1848-1851. Isobel MacDonald. LC 74-19408. 1974. (ISBN 0-8414-5910-X). Folcroft Library Editions.
Buried Stream. Ernest Brace. LC 46-3590. 1946. Harcourt, Brace and Company.
Buried Temple. Josephine Bell. LC 33-314173. The Federal Printing Company, Inc.
Buried Treasure. Elizabeth Madox Roberts. LC 31-28312. 1931. The Viking Press.
Burkburnett. Chauncey Logan. LC 73-7733. 1973. 7.95 (ISBN 0-8111-0479-6). Naylor Co.
Burkeses Amy,". Julie Mathilde Lippmann. LC 15-25348. 1915. 1.25. H. Holt and Company.
Burkett's Lock. Mary Greenway McClelland. LC 44-32108. (On cover: Cassell's sunshine series of choice fiction. Vol. I, no. 22). 1889. Cassell & Company, Limited.
Burl. Morrison Heady. LC 7-5046. 1884. Southern Methodist Publishing House.
Burlesque, from the Play. Dan Totheroh & Hopkins, Arthur Melancthon, 1878- LC 28-28104. 1928. Doubleday, Doran and Company, Inc.
Burlesque Girl. William Arthur Neubauer. 1948. Phoenix Press.
Burlesque Queen. Russell Higgins. LC 35-7021. Godwin.
Burlesque Queen. Albert Quandt. LC 35-7021. 1935. Godwin.
Burlesques. William Makepeace Thackeray. LC 12-378832. (Half-title: Illustrated library edition. The complete works of... Thackeray... vol. VI). 1889. Houghton, Mifflin and Company.
Burlesques: Novels by Eminent Hands... William Makepeace Thackeray & Doyle, Richard, 1824-1883, Illus. LC 31-264. Caxton Publishing Co.
Burlesques. Novels by Eminent Hands. Jeames's Diary. Adventures of Major Gahagan. A Legend of the Rhine. Rebecca and Rowena. The History of the Next French Revolution. Cox's Diary. William Makepeace Thackeray. LC 38-350561. 1869. Smith, Elder and Co.
Burlington Square. Laurence Walter Meynell. LC 74-25081. 1975. 7.95 (ISBN 0-698-10650-4). Coward, McCann & Geoghegan.
Burma Ruby. Joseph Smith Fletcher. LC 33-109816. 1933. L. MacVeagh, Dial Press, Inc.
Burmah Treasure: A Novel. Stephen Paul Sheffield. (On cover: Globe library, no. 139). 1890. Rand, McNally & Company.
Burmese Days: A Novel. new ed. Orwell, George. LC 50-3534. 1950. Harcourt, Brace.
Burmese Days: A Novel. George Orwell. LC 73-12947. (Harbrace paperbound library, HPL 62). 1974. (pbk.) 2.25 (ISBN 0-15-614850-1). Harcourt Brace Jovanovich.
Burmese Days: A Novel. George Orwell. LC 34-35694. 1934. Harper & Brothers.
Burn Bright Shadow. Susanne Richardson. LC 75-2117. 1975. 4.95 (ISBN 0-517-52166-0). Lenox Hill Press.
Burn, Candle, Burn. Harriet Henry, pseud. LC 36-17473. 1936. Harper & Brothers.
Burn Forever. Zenith Jones Brown. LC 35-17237. Farrar & Rinehart, Incorporated.
Burn, Red Lantern, Burn. Ralph Raymon Jump. 112p. 1975. 4.95 o.p. (ISBN 0-8059-2190-7). Dorrance.
Burn Then, Little Lamp. Margaret S Banister. LC 67-10924. 1967. Houghton Mifflin.
Burn Then. Little Lamp: By Margaret Banister. Margaret S Banister. LC 67-10924. 1967. 4.95. Houghton.
Burn This. Helen McCloy. LC 80-26053. 10.95 (ISBN 0-89621-261-0). Thorndike Press.
Burn This: A Novel of Suspense. Helen McCloy. LC 80-150. 7.95 (ISBN 0-396-07806-0). Dodd, Mead.
Burn, Witch, Burn! Abraham Merritt. LC 33-4497. Liveright, Inc.
Burn, Witch, Burn! Abraham Merritt. LC 43-12350. (Murder mystery monthly. No. 5). 1942. The Avon Book Company.
Burne-Jones Head and Other Sketches. Clara Harriot Sherwood Rollins. LC 7-40757. 1894. Lovell, Coryell & Company.
Burned Bridges. Bertrand William Sinclair. LC 19-135161. 1919. Little, Brown, and Company.
Burned Evidence. Nancy Mann Waddel Wilson Woodrow Woodrow. LC 25-8368. 1925. G. P. Putnam's Sons.
Burned Fingers. Kathleen Thompson Norris. LC 48-612. 1947. Triangle Books.
Burned Fingers. Kathleen Thompson Norris. LC 45-206094. 1945. Doubleday, Doran and Company, Inc.
Burned Fingers. Kathleen Thompson Norris. LC 46-6626. 1946. The Sun Dial Press.
Burned Man. Christopher Monig, pseud. 1971. pap. 0.75 o.p. (ISBN 0-446-64609-1, 64-609). Paperback Lib.
Burned Man. Bart Spicer. (S3530). 1967. Bantam.
Burned Man: By Christopher Monig Pseud. 1st Ed. Kendell Foster Crossen. LC 56-630834. (Guilt edged mystery). 1956. Dutton.
Burned Man. 1st Ed. Bart Spicer. LC 66-23575. 1966. 5.95. Atheneum.
Burnhams: Or, The Two Roads. A Novel. George Eliot Stewart. LC 8-15691. 1884. G. W. Carleton & Co.; Etc., Etc.
Burning. Jane Chambers. LC 77-91248. (Jove/HBJ Book). 1.50 (ISBN 0-515-04450-4). Jove Publications.
Burning. Jeff Fain. 1981. pap. 2.25 (ISBN 0-8439-0839-4, Leisure Bks). Nordon Pubns.
Burning. Diane Johnson. LC 78-153687. 1971. (ISBN 0-15-114979-8). Harcourt, Brace, Jovanovich.
Burning. Richard Snow. LC 80-2067. 1981. 12.95 (ISBN 0-385-17371-7). Doubleday.
Burning Air. Eugene Mirabelli. LC 59-5349. 1959. Houghton Mifflin.
Burning & Other Stories. Jack Cady. LC 72-76304. 1972. 5.95 (ISBN 0-87745-030-7). University of Iowa Press.
Burning Arrows. Elfrieda Hochbaum. 5.00 o.p. (ISBN 0-8283-1104-8). Branden.
Burning Beauty. Temple Bailey. LC 29-20969. The Penn Publishing Company.
Burning Bed. Faith McNulty. 288p. 1981. pap. 2.95. Bantam.
Burning Blue Death. Joseph Rosenberger. (Death Merchant Ser.: No. 38). 192p. (Orig.). 1980. pap. 1.95 (ISBN 0-523-41382-3). Pinnacle Bks.
Burning Bridge. J L Nusser. LC 60-117556. 1960. Appleton-Century-Crofts.
Burning Bright: A Play in Story Form. John Steinbeck. LC 50-10249. 1950. Viking Press.
Burning Bright: A Play in Story Form. John Steinbeck. LC 78-10732. 1979. 2.95 (ISBN 0-14-004999-1). Penguin Books.
Burning Bush. Poul Hoffmann. LC 61-6748. 1961. Muhlenberg Press.
Burning Bush. Sigrid Undset & Chater, Arthur G., Tr. LC 32-26891. 1932. A. A. Knopf.
Burning Bush and Other Stories. Robert Drake. LC 73-93410. 1975. 5.95 (ISBN 0-87695-171-X). Aurora Publishers.
Burning Cactus. Stephen Spender. LC 78-169563. (Short story index reprint series). 1971. (ISBN 0-8369-4026-1). Books for Libraries Press.
Burning Court. John Dickson Carr. LC 37-6686. 1937. Harper & Brothers.
Burning Dawn. Elspeth Sandys. (Orig.). 1981. pap. 2.95 (ISBN 0-440-10882-9). Dell.
Burning Daylight. Jack London. LC 69-12448. (Horizon edition of the works of Jack London). 1969. 4.95. Horizon Press.
Burning Daylight. Jack London. LC 10-22538. 1910. 1.50. The Macmillan Company.
Burning Daylight. Jack London. LC 20-18829. 1919. The Macmillan Company.
Burning Daylight. Jack London. LC 29-25270. Grosset & Dunlap.
Burning Desire. Peggy Gaddis, pseud. LC 47-199868. 1947. Phoenix Press.
Burning Desire. Margaret Mayo. (Harlequin Romances Ser.). 192p. (Orig.). 1981. pap. 1.25 (ISBN 0-373-02385-5, Pub. by Harlequin). PB.
Burning Eye. Victor Canning. LC 60-11160. 1960. W. Sloane Associates.
Burning Fires of Passion. Lucy Phillips. (Orig.). 1983. pap. 2.95 (ISBN 0-440-10850-0). Dell.
Burning Fountain. Eleanor Carroll Chilton. LC 29-8255. The John Day Company.
Burning Fuse. Jay Bernard, pseud. LC 69-12027. 1970. 5.95 o.p. (ISBN 0-15-114980-1). HarBraceJ.
Burning Fuse. Raymond H. Sawkins. LC 69-12027. 1970. 5.95. Harcourt, Brace & World.
Burning Fuse: A Wade Paris Mystery. Ben Benson. LC 54-10317. 1954. M. S. Mill Co.
Burning Glass. John Franklin Bardin. LC 50-8515. 1950. Scribner.
Burning Glass. Marjorie Bowen. LC 20-4785. 1920. E. P. Dutton & Company.
Burning Glass: A Novel. Samuel Nathaniel Behrman. LC 68-17266. 1968. Little, Brown.
Burning Gold. Robert Douglas Andrews, pseud. LC 45-7217. 1945. Doubleday, Doran and Company, Inc.
Burning Gold. Robert Douglas Andrews, pseud. LC 46-8552. 1946. The Sun Dial Press.
Burning Grass. Cyprian Ekwensi. (African Writers Ser.). 1962. pap. text ed. 2.50x (ISBN 0-435-90002-1). Heinemann Ed.
Burning Hills. Louis L'Amour. LC 56-9309. 1956. Jason Press.
Burning House: Short Stories. Ann Beattie. LC 82-5292. 12.50 (ISBN 0-394-52494-2). Random House.
Burning Jewel. Teresa Kay. LC 56-88829. 1956. Appleton-Century-Crofts.
Burning Lamp. Frances Murray, pseud. LC 73-77758. 1973. 6.50. St. Martin's.
Burning Mad. (Mad Ser.: No. 25). (Illus.). 1975. pap. 1.75 (ISBN 0-446-94360-6). Warner Bks.
Burning Man. Charles R. Pike, pseud. LC 80-69220. (Jubal Cade Westerns Ser.). 128p. 1980. pap. 2.95 (ISBN 0-87754-235-X). Chelsea Hse.
Burning Man: A Novel. Stephen Longstreet. LC 58-9886. 1958. Random House.
Burning Man: A Novel. Sarah Gertrude Liebson Millin. LC 52-9845. 1952. Putnam.
Burning Moon. Aron Spilken & Ed O'Leary. LC 78-18783. 8.95. Playboy Press.
Burning Mountain: A Novel of the Invasion of Japan. Alfred Coppel. LC 82-15444. 1983. 14.95 (ISBN 0-15-114978-X). Harcourt Brace Jovanovich.
Burning Mystery of Ana in Nineteen Fifty-One. Kenneth Koch. LC 78-21608. 1979. 8.95 o.p. (ISBN 0-394-50473-9); 4.95 (ISBN 0-394-73693-1). Random.
Burning Obsession. Carole Mortimer. (Harlequin Presents Ser.). 192p. pap. 1.75 (ISBN 0-373-10518-5). Harlequin Bks.
Burning of Billy Toober. Jonathan Ross. LC 75-42828. 184p. 1976. 6.95 o.p. (ISBN 0-8027-5347-7). Walker & Co.
Burning of Billy Toober. John Rossiter. LC 75-42828. 1976. 6.95 (ISBN 0-8027-5347-7). Walker.
Burning of los Angeles. Jack Hirschman. 17p. 1971. 3.00 o.p. Serendipity.
Burning of Rome: Or, A Story of the Days of Nero. Alfred John Church. LC 6-25402. 1891. Macmillan and Co.
Burning of Troy. Malcolm Gair. LC 58-13280. 1958. Published for the Crime Club by Doubleday.
Burning Perch. Louis McNeice. 1963. 3.75 o.p. (ISBN 0-19-519042-4). Oxford U Pr.
Burning Plain, and Other Stories. Juan Rulfo. LC 67-25698. (Texas pan-American series). 1967. University of Texas Press.
Burning Questions: A Novel. Alix Kates Shulman. LC 77-21534. 1978. 8.95 (ISBN 0-394-40021-6). Knopf: Distributed by Random House.
Burning Ring. Katharine Burdekin. LC 29-11972. 1929. W. Morrow & Company.
Burning Sands. Arthur Edward Pearse Brome Weigall. LC 21-155553. 1921. Dodd, Mead and Company.
Burning Season. B. Clarence Hall. LC 73-93731. 1974. 8.95 (ISBN 0-399-11299-5). Berkley Pub. Corp.: Distributed by Putnam.
Burning Secret. Stefan Zweig. LC 19-19850. 1919. Scott and Seltzer.
Burning Secrets. Susanna Good. 1979. 2.75 (ISBN 0-671-83216-6). Pocket Books.
Burning Sky. Ron Faust. LC 78-15806. 8.95 (ISBN 0-87223-509-2). Playboy Press.
Burning Sky. Arthur Moore. 1975. (pbk.) 1.25. Popular Library.
Burning Sky. James Hall Roberts. LC 66-12083. bds., 4.95. Morrow.
Burning Spear: Being Experiences of Mr. John Lavender in Time of War. John Galsworthy. LC 23-720133. 1923. C. Scribner's Sons.
Burning Spring. Fynette Rowe. LC 47-11418. 1947. Current Books.
Burning Springs & Other Tales of the Little Kanawha. Howard B. Lee. (Illus.). 1968. 8.00 (ISBN 0-87012-016-6). McClain.
Burning Valley. J. L Bouma. 1976. 0.95. Leisure Books.
Burning Valley. Johanas L. Bouma. 1976. pap. 0.95 o.p. (LB378NK, Leisure Bks). Nordon Pubns.
Burning Valley. Johanas L. Bouma. 160p. 1981. pap. 1.75 (ISBN 0-8439-0992-7, Leisure Bks). Nordon Pubns.
Burning Valley: A Novel. Phillip Bonosky. 1953. Masses & Mainstream.
Burning Water: A Novel. George Bowering. LC 80-21755. 1980. 12.95 (ISBN 0-8253-0005-3). Beaufort Books.
Burning Wheel. Slater Brown. LC 42-23590. 1942. The Bobbs-Merrill Company.
Burning Witches. Marie De Montalvo. LC 27-2316. J. H. Sears & Company, Inc.
Burning Woman. Margaret Ritter. LC 78-23850. 10.00 (ISBN 0-399-12310-5). Putnam.
Burning Woman. Margaret Ritter. 1981. 2.75 (ISBN 0-425-04463-7). Berkley Books.
Burning Wood. David Williams. (Anansi Fiction Ser.: No. 34). 204p. 1975. 12.95 (ISBN 0-88784-435-9, Pub. by Hse Anansi Pr Canada); pap. 6.95 (ISBN 0-88784-054-X). U of Toronto Pr.
Burnings. Barry N Malzberg. LC 74-16321. 1975. 6.95 (ISBN 0-8019-5955-1). Chilton Book Co.
Burnished Blade. Lawrence L Schoonover. LC 48-8377. 1948. Macmillan Co.
Burnished Sword. Jessie Hagart Maclehose. (Illus.). 1955. Philosophical Library.
Burnout. Tom Alibrandi. 288p. (Orig.). 1981. pap. 2.75 (ISBN 0-523-41057-3). Pinnacle Bks.
Burnt Child: A Novel. Translated from the Swedish by Alan Blair. Stig Halvard Dagerman. LC 50-14694. Morrow.
Burnt Million: A Novel. James Payn. LC 7-33779. (On cover: Harper's Franklin square library, no. 673). 1890. Harper & Brothers.
Burnt Million. A Novel. James Payn. LC 7-33778. (On cover: Lovell's international series, no. 81). 1890. J. W. Lovell Company.
Burnt Offereing. Edith Nicholl Bradley Ellison. LC 8-34601. Broadway Publishing Co.
Burnt Offering. Sara J. Duncan. (Toronto Reprint Library of Canadian Prose & Poetry). 1979. Repr. of 1909 ed. 35.00x (ISBN 0-8020-7535-5). U of Toronto Pr.
Burnt Offering: A Captain Heimrich Mystery, by Richard and Frances Lockridge. 1st Ed. Richard Lockridge & Frances Louise Davis Lockridge. LC 55-6311. (Main line mysteries). 1955. Lippincott.
Burnt Offering, a Novel. Daniel Spicehandler. LC 61-5384. 1961. Macmillan.
Burnt Offering: Introduction & Translation. Jeanne Galzy & Le Clercq, Jacques Georges Clemenceau, 1898- Tr. LC 30-25385. 1930. Brentano's.
Burnt Offering: Translated by Michael Hamburger. Albrecht Goes. LC 56-6015. 1956. Pantheon.
Burnt Offerings. Robert Marasco. LC 72-8888. 1973. 6.95. Delacorte Press.
Burnt Offerings. Robert Marasco. LC 73-8902. 1973. 9.95 (ISBN 0-8161-6122-4). G. K. Hall.
Burnt Offerings. Robert Marasco. 1974. (pbk.) 1.50. Dell.
Burnt Ones. Patrick White. LC 64-20679. 1964. Viking Press.
Burnt Orange Heresy: A Novel. Charles Ray Willeford. LC 77-167708. 1971. 5.95. Crown Publishers.
Burnt-Out Case. Graham Greene. LC 61-6090. 1961. Viking Press.
Burnt Powder: Or, The Young Army Detective. A Tale of the Slaughter at Spottsylvania. Anthony P Morris. (War library Pocket ed. v. 1, no. 7). 1883. Novelist Publishing Co.
Burnt Ranch. Walt Coburn. 1970. pap. 0.60 o.p. (60-465). Manor Bks.
Burnt Toast. Richard Roe. LC 79-87687. (Orig.). Date not set. pap. 3.95 (ISBN 0-9602100-2-4). R Hart.
Burnt Toast: A Novel. Peter Gould. LC 70-147880. (Illus.). 1971. 3.50 (ISBN 0-394-46948-8). Knopf.
Burnt Wagon Ranch. Lee Floren. Bd. with Thunder Valley. Burt Arthur. 1973. pap. 0.95 o.s.i. (532-95259-095). Manor Bks.
Burnt Wagon Ranch. Lee Floren & Burt Arthur. (Manor Books double Western). 1973. (pbk.) 0.95. Manor Books.
Burnt Wagon Ranch see Marauders.
Burnt Wagon Ranch: By Brett Austin Pseud. Lee Floren. LC 50-6860. 1950. Phoenix Press.
Burnt Water. Carlos Fuentes. Tr. by Margaret S. Peden from Span. 231p. 1980. 11.95 (ISBN 0-374-11741-1). FS&G.
Burntwood Men: A Novel of the Frontier West. LC 61-10340. 1961. Macmillan.
Burr. Gore Vidal. 576p. 1976. pap. 3.50 (ISBN 0-553-14373-5). Bantam.
Burr. Gore Vidal. 576p. 1982. pap. 3.95 (ISBN 0-345-30619-8). Ballantine.
Burr: A Novel. Gore Vidal. LC 73-3985. 1973. 14.95 (ISBN 0-394-48024-4). Random.
Burrill Coleman, Colored. A Tale of the Cotton Fields. Jeannette Downes Coltharp. LC 6-30671. 1896. The Editor Publishing Company.
Burritt Durand: A Romance of the Middle West. John McGovern. (On cover: Globe library, v. 1, no. 126). 1890. Rand, McNally & Company.
Burro Alley. Edwin Corle. LC 38-35987. Random House.
Burrowers Beneath. Brian Lumley. (Daw sf books, no. 91). (Illus.). 1974. (pbk.) 0.95. Daw Books.
Burrowing in, Digging Out. Rose Drachler. pap. 2.50. Tree Bks.
Bursting of a Boom. Frederick R Sanford. LC 8-1811. 1889. J. B. Lippincott Company.
Burt. Howard Buten. LC 80-11196. 5.95 (ISBN 0-03-056891-9). Holt, Rinehart, and Winston.
Burt Judson, Detective, and His Secret Agents: By George Barnaby Pseud. Kenneth Anderson. LC 49-50100. 1949. Van Kampen Press.
Burton and Speke. William Harrison. LC 82-5620. 1982. 17.95 (ISBN 0-312-10873-7). St. Martin's Press.
Burton Dane. Alfred E Charm. LC 12-28708. 1913. 1.35. The Alice Harriman Company.
Burton; or, The Sieges. A Romance. Joseph Holt Ingraham. LC 7-10359. 1838. Harper & Brothers.
Burton Street Folks. Anna Potter Wright. LC 13-22825. The Bible Institute Colportage Ass'n.
Burtons of Dunroe. Margaret W Brew. LC 79-263. (Ireland, from the Act of Union, 1800, to the Death of Parnell, 1891; No. 69). 1979. 96.00. Garland Pub.
Burts, Robert: A Nautical Romance. Robert Burts. LC 6-16691. 1851. A. Hart.

Burwyck's Wander. S. J. Treibich. 1972. pap. 0.95 o.s.i. (75-404). Lancer.
Bury Him Among Kings. Elleston Trevor. LC 70-111185. 1970. 6.95. Doubleday.
Bury Him Darkly. John Blackburn. LC 77-105599. (Red mask mystery). 1970. 4.50. Putnam.
Bury in Haste. Alfred Eichler. LC 57-9795. 1957. Arcadia House.
Bury Me Deep. Peter Lappin. LC 73-88180. (Illus.). 1974. (pbk.) 2.95 (ISBN 0-87973-865-0). Our Sunday Visitor.
Bury Me Deep. Harold Q Masur. LC 48-9816. (Pocket book 558). 1948. Pocket Books.
Bury Me Deep. Harold Q Masur. LC 47-6334. 1947. Simon and Schuster.
Bury Me in Gold Lame. Stanton Forbes, pseud. LC 73-22787. 1974. 4.95 (ISBN 0-385-07258-9). Published for the Crime Club by Doubleday.
Bury Me in Ravenna: A Novel of the Fifth Century Based on the Life of Galla Placidia, Gothic Queen and Roman Empress. Agnes Carr Vaughan. LC 62-15938. 1962. Doubleday.
Bury Me Not. Allan R Bosworth. LC 48-576946. (Double D western). 1948. Doubleday.
Bury Me Not. William Francis. LC 43-1014. 1943. W. Morrow & Company.
Bury Me Not. Harold Gauer. (Orig.). 1981. pap. 2.25 (ISBN 0-505-51605-5). Tower Bks.
Bury Me Not at Sea. Marie Eyre. 1974. (pbk.) 0.95. Popular Library.
Bury My Heart at Wounded Knee. Dee Alexander Brown. 512p. 1981. pap. 3.95 (ISBN 0-671-42029-1). WSP.
Bury the Hatchet. Manning Long. LC 44-7097. 1944. Duell, Sloan and Pearce.
Bury the Hatchet... Manning Long. LC 46-18355. (On cover: Bart house mystery. 26). 1946.
Bury the Past. Maysie Greig. LC 39-10380. 1939. Doubleday, Doran & Company, Inc.
Bury the Past. Maysie Greig. LC 40-9074. 1940. The Sun Dial Press.
Bury the Past. Richard Reinsmith. (Orig.). 1980. pap. 1.75 o.s.i. (ISBN 0-505-51558-X). Tower Bks.
Bury Their Dead: By Alex Fraser Pseud. Henry Brinton. LC 60-11366. 1960. Roy Publishers.
Burying of Kingsmith: A Novel. James Reichley. LC 57-8236. 1957. Houghton Mifflin.
Burying Road. Mary Wiltshire. LC 28-113953. 1928. Dodd, Mead & Company.
Bus Station Murders. Louise Revell. LC 47-3058. 1947. The Macmillan Company.
Bus That Vanished. Leon Groc. Tr. by Morris, Lawrence. LC 28-15795. The Macaulay Company.
Buscadero. Noel M. Loomis. LC 53-12516. 1953. Macmillan.
Bush Baby. Martin Woodhouse. 1968. 4.95 o.p. Coward.
Bush Baby: A Novel. Martin Woodhouse. LC 68-17571. 1968. Coward-McCann.
Bush Girl: A Tale of North Australia. Arthur Livingstone Brewer. LC 49-726653.
Bush Is Burning. A. Waskow. (O.s.i.). 1971. pap. 1.95 o.s.i. (ISBN 0-02-089710-3, Collier). Macmillan.
Bush-Rancher. Harold Bindloss. LC 23-5364. 1923. Frederick A. Stokes Company.
Bush Songs, Ballads & Other Verse see Australian Classics.
Bush Studies. Barbara Baynton & Gullett, H. B. LC 66-12764. 1965. Angus and Robertson.
Bush Studies. Memoir by H. B. Gullett, Foreword by A. A. Phillips. Barbara Baynton & H. B Gullett. LC 66-12764. 1966. 3.75. Angus & Robertson.
Bush That Burned. Marjorie Barkeley McClure. LC 25-19169. 1925. Minton, Balch & Company.
Bush Track. Fred Grove. LC 77-16847. 1978. 7.95 (ISBN 0-385-13158-5). Doubleday.
Bushido. Beresford Osbourne. 448p. 1981. pap. 2.95 (ISBN 0-441-08932-1, Pub. by Charter Bks). Ace Bks.
Bushido Code. Robert St. Louis. 256p. 1981. pap. 2.50 (ISBN 0-449-14438-0, GM). Fawcett.
Bushido Lawman. Patrick Lee. (Six-Gun Samurai Ser.: No. 6). 224p. (Orig.). 1982. pap. 1.95 (ISBN 0-523-41418-8). Pinnacle Bks.
Bushman Burke. Jean Crooks Devanny. LC 30-20585. The Macaulay Company.
Bushman Who Came Back. Arthur William Upfield. LC 57-7913. 1957. Published for the Crime Club by Doubleday.
Bushranger in the Skies. Arthur William Upfield. pap. 1.60 o.s.i. Tri-Ocean.
Bushrangers. A Yankee's Adventures During His Second Visit to Australia. William Henry Thomes. LC 8-20097. (Half-title: The gold-hunter's library). 1884. A. T. Loyd & Co.
Bushrangers. A Yankee's Adventures During His Second Visit to Australia. William Henry Thomes. (On cover: The detective and adventure library, no. 4). 1989. A. T. Loyd & Co.
Bushwack. Edwin Booth. 1974. (pbk.) 0.75. Ace Books.
Bushwack. Richard S Wheeler. LC 78-7772. 1978. 7.95 (ISBN 0-385-14281-1). Doubleday.
Bushwackers. Cliff Davis, pseud. 1979. pap. 1.75 (ISBN 0-89041-256-1). Major Bks.
Bushwackers. Cliff Davis, pseud. 1977. pap. 1.50 (ISBN 0-89041-176-X, 3176). Major Bks.
Bushwhack Basin. Fred East. LC 45-6219. 1945. E. P. Dutton & Company, Inc.
Bushwhack Bullets. Walker A Tompkins. LC 41-20053. Phoenix Press.
Bushwhack Range. Al Cody, pseud. (O.s.i.). 1973. pap. 0.75 o.s.i. (532-75493-075). Manor Bks.
Bushwhacked Piano. Thomas McGuane. 1973. 0.95. Warner Paperback Lib.
Bushwhacked Piano. Thomas McGuane. LC 72-139642. 1971. 5.95 (ISBN 0-671-20819-5). Simon and Schuster.
Bushwhackers. Lee Floren. (Orig.). 1980. pap. 1.75 o.s.i. (ISBN 0-505-51531-8). Tower Bks.
Bushwhackers. Frank Gruber. LC 59-5332. 1959. Rinehart.
Bushwhackers. Frank Gruber. LC 59-5332. (Signet book). 1975. (pbk.) 0.95. New American Library.
Bushwhackers & Other Stories. Mary Noailles Murfree. LC 73-90588. (Short story index reprint series). 1969. (ISBN 0-8369-3071-1). Books for Libraries Press.
Bushwhackers: And Others Stories. Mary Noailles Murfree. LC 99-2955. 1899. H. S. Stone & Co.
Business Adventures of Billy Thomas. Elmer Ellsworth Ferris. LC 15-7282. 1915. 1.25. The Macmillan Company.
Business As Usual. Jane Oliver & Stafford, Ann. LC 34-27025. 1934. Houghton Mifflin Company.
Business As Usual. Soliman Peters. LC 74-176084. (Venus library, V-1038-K). 1971. 1.75. Grove Press.
Business at Blanche Capel. 1st Ed. Brian Stanford Morgan. LC 53-7317. Little, Brown.
Business Career of Peter Flint. Harold Whitehead. LC 19-149174. 1919. The Page Company.
Business Convention. Tr. from Italian by Joseph Green 1st Amer. Ed. Libero Bigiaretti. LC 65-111096. bds., 3.95. Knopf.
Business Hours. Hugh Patrick McGraw. LC 34-329355. Coward-McCann.
Business House That Jack Built. J. W Warr. LC 8-33691. 1896. Plowman Publishing Company, Printers.
Business Is Business. Basil D Nicholson. LC 33-28407. 1933. A. A. Knopf.
Business Is Business: The Ruin of Materialism and the Hope of Idealism in the Interest of Justice. B. Harrison Harman. LC 22-107692. R. G. Badger.
Business Leader's Sweetpart, the Love Story of Wilbur and Elinor. Elinor Wolfsen. LC 34-33471. 1934. Meadow Publishing Company.
Business of a Gentleman. H. N Dickinson. LC 14-3976. 1914. 1.25. G. P. Putnam's Sons.
Business of Bodies. Stanton Forbes, pseud. LC 66-19749. 3.50. Pub. for the Crime Club by Doubleday.
Business of Bomfog. Madelaine Duke. LC 69-15202. 1969. 4.50 o.p. Doubleday.
Business of Life. Robert William Chambers. LC 13-20349. 1913. 1.40. D. Appleton and Company.
Business of Loving: A Novel. Godfrey Smith. LC 68-13355. 1968. Stein and Day.
Business Venture in Los Angeles: Or, A Christian Optimist. Louise Doissy. LC 99-5625. 1899. The R. Clake Company.
Busman's Holiday: A Comedy of the Open Road. Rowland Walker. LC 37-239272. The John C. Winston Company.
Busman's Honeymoon. Dorothy Leigh Sayers. 1968. pap. 2.95 (ISBN 0-380-01076-3, 62489-3). Avon.
Busman's Honeymoon. Dorothy Leigh Sayers. LC 60-9116. (O.s.i.). 1960. 12.95 o.p. (ISBN 0-06-013765-7, HarpT). Har-Row.
Busman's Honeymoon: A Love Story with Detective Interruptions. Dorothy Leigh Sayers. LC 37-27108. Harcourt, Brace and Company.
Busman's Honeymoon: A Love Story with Detective Interruptions. Dorothy Leigh Sayers. LC 81-6844. 1981. 16.95 (ISBN 0-8161-3041-8). G.K. Hall.
Bust of Lincoln. James Francis Dwyer. LC 12-239211. 1912. Doubleday, Page & Company.
Bust-Out King. rev. ed. Avery Corman. 224p. 1981. pap. 2.50 (ISBN 0-553-20233-2). Bantam.
Bust-up. Wallace Reyburn. LC 72-179624. (Illus.). 112p. 1972. pap. 2.45 o.p. (ISBN 0-13-108761-4). P-H.
Busted. Glen Chase, pseud. (Cherry Delight Ser: No. 16). 1974. pap. 1.25 o.p. (LB214ZK, Leisure Bks). Nordon Pubns.
Busted Range. Harry Sinclair Drago. LC 44-338195. 1944. Books Inc., Distributed by W. Morrow and Company.
Busted Range: By Will Ermine Pseud. Harry Sinclair Drago. LC 51-9347. (Triple-A western classic). 1951. Jefferson House.
Busted Wheeler. Carter Brown, pseud. 1979. pap. 1.50 o.s.i. (ISBN 0-505-51414-1). Tower Bks.
Buster. William Patterson White. LC 26-15371. 1926. Little, Brown, and Company.
Bustillo. Kenneth Royce. LC 76-26907. 1976. 8.95 (ISBN 0-698-10762-4). Coward, McCann & Geoghegan.
Busy Bodies. Ed Martin. LC 72-23987. (Traveller's companion series). Traveller's Companion.
Busy Body. Donald E Westlake. LC 66-13717. bds., 3.95. Random.
Busy, Busy People. Samuel Spewack. LC 48-9047. 1948. Houghton Mifflin Co.
Busy Moments of an Idle Woman... Sue Petigru Bowen. LC 6-16091. 1854. D. Appleton & Company.
But a Little Moment. 1st Ed. James Ballard. LC 50-6692. 1953. Dutton.
But a Philistine. Virginia Frances Townsend. LC 8-29821. 1884. Lee and Shepard.
But Beauty Vanishes: By Richard Blaker... Richard Blaker. LC 36-290975. The Bobbs-Merrill Company.
But Death Runs Faster. William P McGivern. LC 48-6368. (Red badge detective.). 1948. Dodd, Mead.
But Don't Go Alone. Katherine Court. LC 77-82172. 1978. pap. 1.50 o.p. (ISBN 0-87216-436-5, C16436). Playboy Pr Pbks.
But Even So. John Collis Snaith. LC 35-932266. 1935. D. Appleton-Century Company, Incorporated.
But Fetters I Cannot Wear. Olive Mary Briggs. LC 64-534. 1963. R. L. Kerridge.
But for Her Garden. Clarissa Fairchild Cushman. LC 35-27096. 1935. Little, Brown, and Company.
But for the Grace of God. John William Navin Sullivan. LC 32-20283. 1932. A. A. Knopf.
But for the Lovers: A Novel. Wilfrido D Nolledo. LC 74-95473. 1970. 7.95. Dutton.
But Gentlemen Marry Brunettes". Anita Loos. LC 23-14706. 1928. Boni & Liveright.
But Gently Day. Robert Nathan. LC 43-121458. 1943. A. A. Knopf.
But Half a Heart. Carrie L Brown. LC 6-19645. (On cover: V. I. F. series v. 7). D. Lothrop and Company.
But Half a Heart. Carrie L Brown. (On cover: The household library, no. 8). 1886. D. Lothrop and Company.
But Half the Universe. Edith M. Dean. LC 76-25555. 6.95 (ISBN 0-8111-0625-X). Naylor Co.
But I Wouldn't Want to Die There. Stanton Forbes, pseud. LC 71-185580. 1972. 4.95. Published for the Crime Club by Doubleday.
But I'm Ready to Go. Louise Alert. LC 76-9949. 6.95 (ISBN 0-87888-107-7). Bradbury Press.
But in Our Lives; a Novel. Francis Edward Younghusband. LC 26-12834. 1926. D. Appleton & Company.
But Know Not Why. Jessica Steele. (Harlequin Romances Ser.). 192p. 1982. pap. 1.50 (ISBN 0-373-02494-0). Harlequin Bks.
But Love Wants All: By Joan Garrison Pseud. William Arthur Neubauer. LC 55-14033. 1955. Arcadia House.
But Nellie Was So Nice. Mary McMullen. LC 78-22823. 1979. 7.95 (ISBN 0-385-15290-6). Published for the Crime Club by Doubleday.
But Nellie Was So Nice. Mary McMullen. LC 81-5336. 10.95. Thorndike Press.
But Never Be Denied. Fannie Kilbourne. LC 41-19192. G. P. Putnam's Sons.
But Not Farewell. Margaretta Brucker. LC 38-34538. Gramercy Publishing Co.
But Not for Love. Beatrice Kean Stapleton Seymour. LC 31-244325. 1931. A. A. Knopf.
But Not for Love. Edwin Shrake. LC 64-11405. 1964. Doubleday.
But Not for Love: A Novel. Elizabeth Savage. LC 71-108953. 1970. 5.95. Little, Brown.
But Not for Love: A Novel. May Natalie Tabak. LC 60-8163. 1960. Horizon Press.
But Not Forsaken. Helen Good Brenneman. LC 54-10827. 1954. Herald Press.
But Not My Heart. Garnett A. Schultz. 1969. 3.75 o.p. (ISBN 0-8059-1382-3). Dorrance.
But Not the End. Frederick Nebel. LC 34-5286. 1934. Little, Brown, and Company.
But Not to Keep. Roger Kahn. LC 80-80993. 336p. 1980. pap. 2.75 (ISBN 0-87216-691-0). Playboy Pbks.
But Not to Keep: A Novel. Roger Kahn. LC 75-6370. 9.95 (ISBN 0-06-012244-7). Harper & Row.
But Once a Year. Helen Partridge. 1941. Arcadia House, Inc.
But Once a Year. Christmas Stories. Eleanor Hallowell Abbott. LC 28-21967. 1928. D. Appleton & Company.
But She Meant Well. William Caine. LC 14-181155. 1914. 1.30. John Lane.
But Still a Man. Margaret Lizzie Knapp. LC 9-4954. 1909. 1.50. Little, Brown, and Company.
But That Was Yesterday. June Pat Wetherell. LC 42-51777. 1943. E. P. Dutton & Co., Inc.
But the Morning Will Come, Novel. Cid Ricketts Sumner. LC 49-80735. 1949. Bobbs-Merrill Co.
But the Patient Died. James William MacQueen. LC 48-8416. 1948. Pub. for the Crime Club by Doubleday.
But the Wolves'll Get You Here Too see Everything Else.
But We Are Exiles: A Novel. Robert Kroetsch. LC 65-24583. 1966. St. Martin's Press.
But We Didn't Get the Fox. Richard Llewellyn. LC 69-13644. 1969. 5.95. Doubleday.
But Where Is Love. Marguerite Kloepfer. 1980. pap. 2.25 (ISBN 0-380-46052-1, 46052). Avon.
But Who Wakes the Bugler? Peter De Vries. LC 40-14185. 1940. Houghton Mifflin Company.
But Yesterday-- Katherine Helen Maud Marshall Diver. LC 27-14953. 1927. Dodd, Mead and Company.
But Yet a Woman: A Novel. Arthur Sherburne Hardy. LC 70-164562. (American fiction reprint series). 1971. (ISBN 0-8369-7039-X). Books for Libraries Press.
But Yet a Woman: A Novel. Arthur Sherburne Hardy. LC 3-19539. Houghton, Mifflin and Company.
But Yet a Women: A Novel. 10th thousand. ed. Arthur Sherburne Hardy. LC 7-1929. 1883. Houghton, Mifflin and Company.
But You Are Young. Josephine Lawrence. LC 39-29459. 1940. Little, Brown and Company.
But You'll Be Back. Marguerite Steedman. LC 42-19437. 1942. Houghton Mifflin Company.
Butch Cassidy and the Sundance Kid. William Goldman. 1975. (pbk.) 1.25. Dell.
Butch Cassidy, the Sundance Kid & the Wild Bunch. David King. (Orig.). 1970. pap. 0.75 o.p. (64-351). Paperback Lib.
Butcher, Baker, Murder-Maker. Edited and with an Introd. by George Harmon Coxe. 1st Ed. Mystery Writers of America. LC 54-8768. 1954. Knopf.
Butcher, Baker, Nightmare Maker. Richard Natale & James Kahn. 1981. pap. 2.50 (ISBN 0-671-42935-3). PB.
Butcher Bird. Reuben Davis. LC 36-4195. 1936. Little, Brown, and Company.
Butcher Block. Mark Mandell. (Nazi Hunter Ser.: No. 4). 208p. 1983. pap. cancelled (ISBN 0-523-41447-1). Pinnacle Bks.
Butcher, No. Thirteen: Blood Vengeance. Stuart Jason. 192p. (Orig.). 1975. pap. 1.25 (ISBN 0-523-22539-3). Pinnacle Bks.
Butcher No. Twenty-Four: Venetian Vendetta. Stuart Jason. (The Butcher Series). (Orig.). 1977. pap. 1.25 (ISBN 0-523-40028-4). Pinnacle Bks.
Butcher, No. Twenty-Three: Appointment in Iran. Stuart Jason. (Butcher Ser). (Orig.). 1977. pap. 1.25 (ISBN 0-523-40007-1). Pinnacle Bks.
Butcher, No. 35: Gotham Gore. Stuart Jason. 208p. (Orig.). 1982. pap. 1.95 (ISBN 0-523-41666-0). Pinnacle Bks.
Butcher, Number Thirty: Coffin Corner. Stuart Jason. 192p. (Orig.). 1981. pap. 1.95 (ISBN 0-523-41260-6). Pinnacle Bks.
Butcher of Belgrade. Nick Carter. (Nick Carter Ser). (O.s.i.). 192p. 1973. pap. 1.25 o.s.i. (AQ1569, Award). Univ Pub & Dist.
Butcher Shop. Jean Crooks Devanny. LC 26-141055. The Macaulay Company.
Butcher, the Baker, the Candlestick Maker: Thirteen Stories. Cordero-Fernando. 1962. 5.75 o.p. Cellar.
Butcherknife Killings. Sterling Harkins. 1974. (pbk.) 1.95 (ISBN 0-87056-377-7). Brandon Books.
Butchers. Leonard Bishop. LC 56-8115. 1956. Dial Press.
Butcher's Boy. Thomas Perry. LC 82-653. 12.95 (ISBN 0-684-17455-3). Scribner's.
Butcher's Crossing. John Edward Williams. LC 78-14998. (Gregg Press Western Fiction Series). 1978. 9.95 (ISBN 0-8398-2451-3). Gregg Press.
Butcher's Moon. Donald E Westlake. LC 73-20600. 1974. 4.95 (ISBN 0-394-48343-X). Random House.
Butchers of Ghent: Or, El Maestro Del Campo. A Romance of the Reign of Philip Ii. From the French of Felix Borgaerts! Felix Guillanume Marie Bogaerts. Tr. by Weld, Horatio Hastings. LC 1-17358. (Brother Jonathan. Extra. v. 2, no. 4. July 9, 1842). 1842. Wilson & Company.
Butcher's Wife. Owen Cameron. LC 54-13183. (Inner sanctum mystery). 1954. Simon and Schuster.
Butler Did It. Pelham Grenville Wodehouse. LC 57-5676. 1957. Simon an Schuster.
Butler Died in Brooklyn. Ruth Fenisong. LC 43-51219. 1943. Pub. for the Crime Club by Doubleday, Doran & Co., Inc.

TITLE INDEX

BY NIGHT AT DINSMORE...

Butler's Story: Being the Reflections, Observations and Experiences of Mrs. Peter Ridges, of Wapping-on-Velly, Devon, Sometime in the Service of Samuel Carter, Esquire, of New York. Arthur Cheney Train. LC 9-7139. 1909. C. Scribner's Sons.
Butte Polka: A Novel. Donald McCaig. LC 79-9405. 8.95 (ISBN 0-8037-0933-1). Rawson, Wade.
Butte Was Like That: A Novel. Joseph H Duffy. LC 41-9494.
Buttercup. Russell Smith. pap. 1.95 o.s.i. (Venus). Grove.
Buttercup Chain. Janice Elliott. 1971. pap. 0.75 o.p. (T2246). Pyramid Pubns.
Buttercup Days. Ethel Cook Eliot. LC 24-16259. 1924. Doubleday, Page & Company.
Buttercup Spell. Henry Cecil. 1974. 6.95 o.s.i. (ISBN 0-8277-3345-3). British Bk Ctr.
Buttered Side Down. Edna Ferber. LC 12-7617. 1912. Frederick A. Stokes Company.
Buttered Side Down. 5th ed. Edna Ferber. LC 15-2004. 1912. Frederick A. Stokes Company.
Buttered Side Down; Stories. Edna Ferber. LC 74-169546. (Short story index reprint series). (Illus.). 1971. (ISBN 0-8369-4008-3). Books for Libraries Press.
Butterfield Eight. John O'Hara. LC 82-40030. 288p. 1982. pap. 3.95 (ISBN 0-394-71190-4). Random.
Butterfield 8. John O'Hara. LC 82-4850. 1982. 3.50 (ISBN 0-394-71190-4). Vintage Books.
Butterfield 8. John Henry O'Hara. 1976. (pbk.) 1.75. Popular Library.
Butterfield 8: A Novel. John O'Hara. LC 57-11400. (Modern library paperbacks, P32). 1957. Random House.
Butterfield 8: A Novel. John O'Hara. LC 35-19688. Harcourt, Brace and Company.
Butterfield 8: Complete & Unabridged. John O'Hara. LC 57-3877. (Avon T-183). 1957. Avon Publications.
Butterfingers Angel. William Gibson. 8.95 o.p. (ISBN 0-8091-0198-X); pap. 4.95 o.p. (ISBN 0-8091-1890-4). Paulist Pr.
Butterflies... If You Throw It: A Novel. R. C. Winslow. LC 77-83969. 1978. 9.95 (ISBN 0-916630-07-2). Press Pacifica.
Butterflies in Heat. Darwin Porter. (Orig.). 1976. pap. 1.95 (ISBN 0-532-19112-9). Woodhill.
Butterflies of the Province. Honor Lilbush Wingfield Tracy. LC 79-102340. 1970. 5.95. Random House.
Butterfly. James Mallahan Cain. LC 47-294. 1947. A. A. Knopf.
Butterfly. James Mallahan Cain. LC 79-10814. 1979. 1.95 (ISBN 0-394-74212-5). Vintage Books.
Butterfly. Kathleen Thompson Norris. LC 23-142016. 1923. Doubleday, Page & Company.
Butterfly. Michael Rumaker. LC 62-9633. 1962. Scribner.
Butterfly. Henry Kitchell Webster. LC 14-14181. 1914. D. Appleton and Company.
Butterfly & the Baron. Margaret Way. (Romances Ser.). 192p. (Orig.). 1980. pap. text ed. 1.25 (ISBN 0-373-02346-4). Harlequin Bks.
Butterfly: By Kathleen Norris... Kathleen Thompson Norris. LC 32-195031. 1925. A. L. Burt Company.
Butterfly Chase. Helen Cresswell. (puffin easy reader). (Illus.). 1975. (pbk.) 1.25 (ISBN 0-14-050139-8). Penguin Books.
Butterfly Flood. John Wyllie. LC 75-11364. 1975. 5.95 (ISBN 0-385-11154-1). Published for the Crime Club by Doubleday.
Butterfly Girl. Blossom Elfman. LC 79-26210. 1980. 7.95 (ISBN 0-395-28948-3). Houghton Mifflin.
Butterfly House. Mary Eleanor Wilkins Freeman. LC 12-3596. 1912. Dodd, Mead and Company.
Butterfly Hunter. Janwillem Van De Wetering. LC 82-7184. 1982. 12.50 (ISBN 0-395-32527-7). Houghton Mifflin.
Butterfly Hunter. Janwillem Van De Wetering. 1982. 12.95. HM.
Butterfly Kid. Chester Anderson. LC 77-4498. (Gregg Press science fiction series). 1977. 12.50 (ISBN 0-8398-2374-6). Gregg Press.
Butterfly Kid. Chester Anderson. 1980. 2.25. Pocket Books.
Butterfly Man. Lew Levenson. LC 34-28774. The Macaulay Company.
Butterfly Man. George Barr McCutcheon. LC 10-11143. 1910. Dodd, Mead & Company.
Butterfly Murder. Charlton Andrews. LC 32-24132. Sears Publishing Company.
Butterfly Net. Alethia Sheldon. LC 57-11137. 1957. Coward-McCann.
Butterfly on the Wheel: A Novel. Cyril Arthur Edward Ranger Gull & Hemmerde, Edward George, 1871- LC 12-14712. 1912. 1.25. W. Rickey & Company.
Butterfly Plague. Timothy Findley. LC 69-15658. 1969. 6.95. Viking Press.
Butterfly Revolution. William Butler. LC 67-10948. 1967. Putnam.
Butterfly Secret. Toni Tucci. (Orig.). 1978. pap. 2.50 (ISBN 0-89083-394-X). Zebra.
Butterfly Tree. 1st Ed. Robert E Bell. LC 59-710474. 1959. Lippincott.
Butterfly Ward. Margaret Gibson. LC 79-67815. 1980. 8.95 (ISBN 0-8149-0834-9). Vanguard Press.
Butterfly Ward. Margaret Gibson Gilboord. LC 76-368786. (ISBN 0-88750-186-9) (ISBN 0-88750-187-7). Oberon Press.
Butterfly's Dream & Other Chinese Tales. Shou-Kang Hsieh. LC 70-125561. (Illus.). 1970. 5.00 (ISBN 0-8048-0077-4). C. E. Tuttle Co.
Butterly Plague. Timothy Findley. 1969. 6.95 o.p. (ISBN 0-670-19798-X). Viking Pr.
Buttermilk: A Novel. Cora Greene Jenks. LC 39-337481. The Saravan House.
Buttermilk and Bran. Ora Pate Stewart. LC 64-19916. 1964. Naylor Co.
Buttermilk Road. Thomas Turner. LC 62-21577. 1963. McGraw-Hill.
Butternut. John Coder. LC 54-11878. Vantage Press.
Butternut Jones: A Lambkin of the West. Tilden Tilford. LC 3-28964. 1903. D. Appleton and Company.
Butternut Jones: A Lambkin of the West. Tilden Tilford. LC 25-7835. 1924. Lamar & Barton.
Butternut Tree. Bernice Dunn. LC 79-50897. pap. 2.25 o.s.i. (ISBN 0-89516-087-0). Condor Pub Co.
Butterscotch Prince. Richard Hall. LC 75-18500. 1975. 1.25 (ISBN 0-515-03750-8). Pyramid Books.
Buttes Landing. Jean Rikhoff. LC 72-4256. 1973. 8.95. Dial Press.
Button, Button. Marion Bramhall. LC 44-6031. 1944. Pub. for the Crime Club by Doubleday, Doran and Co., Inc.
Button, Button. Holly Roth. 1966. Harcourt, Brace & World.
Button, Button... a Mystery Story. William Lodewick Doty. LC 79-88030. (Illus.). 3.95 (ISBN 0-87973-528-7). Our Sunday Visitor.
Button Shoes. Esther Pence Garber. LC 76-350023. 1975. 1.50 (ISBN 0-87178-121-2). Brethren Press.
Buttons in the Back. With Illus. by David Levine. Elizabeth Kirtland. LC 58-9248. 1958. Vanguard Press.
Button's Inn. Albion Winegar Tourgee. LC 8-29835. 1887. Roberts Brothers.
Buttons: To Which Is Added, Bootles' Baby. Henrietta Eliza Vaughan Stannard. (On cover: Lovell's international series no. 43). 1889. F. F. Lovell & Company.
Buttonwood. Maritta Martin Wolff. LC 61-6241. 1962. Randon House.
Buttonwoods: Or, The Refugees of the Revolution. A Historical Sketch ... LC 10-4183. (On cover: Legends of the revolution, no. 1). 1849. M. E. Harmstead.
Buy Back the Dawn. Nicholas Garland. LC 80-13185. 1981. 2.75 (ISBN 0-425-05002-5). Berkley Publishing Co.
Buy It for a Song. John Dick Scott. LC 48-6623. 1948. Pellegrini & Cudahy.
Buy Jupiter, and Other Stories. Isaac Asimov. LC 74-33738. (Doubleday science fiction). 1975. 5.95 (ISBN 0-385-05077-1). Doubleday.
Buy Jupiter: And Other Stories. Isaac Asimov. 1977. 1.50 (ISBN 0-449-23062-7). Fawcett Crest.
Buy Yet a Woman: A Novel. Arthur Sherburne Hardy. 1883. Houghton, Mifflin and Company.
Buyer Beware. John Lutz. LC 76-14787. (Red mask mystery). 6.95 (ISBN 0-399-11811-X). Putnam.
Buyer of Dreams. Jeanne Judson. 1963. Avalon Books.
Buyer's Market: A Novel. Anthony Dymoke Powell. LC 53-65767. 1953. Scribner.
Buzz: New York in the Fifties. Sandy Darlington. LC 80-69533. 160p. (Orig.). 1981. pap. 3.50 (ISBN 0-9604152-1-1). Arrowhead Pr.
Buzzard & the Peacock. Ned O'Gorman, pseud. LC 64-11527. 1964. 4.50 o.p. (ISBN 0-15-115012-5). HarBraceJ.
Buzzard Bait. Jack Kane. 1975. 4.95. Avalon Books.
Buzzard Bait. Jory Sherman. 1978. pap. 1.50 (ISBN 0-89041-181-6, 3181). Major Bks.
Buzzard Barbara. Barbara Berne. 1978. pap. 1.75 (ISBN 0-532-17185-3). Woodhill.
Buzzard Is My Best Friend. Margaret Anne Barnes. LC 81-8170. 11.95 (ISBN 0-02-507260-9). Macmillan.
Buzzard Tracks. Tom J Hopkins. LC 48-723537. (Double D western). 1948. Doubleday.
Buzzards. Janet Burroway. LC 73-86615. 1969. 5.95. Little, Brown.
Buzzards of Bitter Creek. Galen C. Colin. LC 45-2204. 1945. Phoenix Press.
Buzzards Pick the Bones. Thomas Murray Ragg. LC 32-29198. Longmans, Green and Co.
Buzzard's Roost. William Frederick Bragg. LC 56-7014. 1956. Arcadia House.
Bwana Maswa. Christine Hunter, pseud. 1974. pap. 1.75 o.p. (ISBN 0-87508-240-8). Chr Lit.
BX Trail. Galen C. Colin. LC 46-20369. 1946. Phoenix Press.
By a Golden Cord. Dora Delmar. (On cover: Library of American authors. no. 67). 1896. G. Munro's Sons.
By a Hair's Breadth. Francis Edward Grainger. LC 6-27657. 1897. Dodd, Mead and Company.
By a Himalayan Lake. E M Cuttim. LC 6-322363. (On cover: Cassell's sunshine series. no. 105). Cassell Publishing Company.
By a Way She Knew Not. The Story of Allison Bair. Margaret Murray Robertson. LC 7-41957. A. D. F. Randolph & Company.
By a Way That They Knew Not. A. A Wellington. LC 8-367302. 1885. Rand, McNally & Co., Printers.
By a Woman Writt. Joan Goulianos. LC 72-80810. 1973. 14.95 o.p. (ISBN 0-672-51616-0). Bobbs.
By Advice of Counsel, Being Adventures of the Celebrated Firm of Tutt & Tutt, Attorneys & Counsellors at Law. Arthur Cheney Train. LC 21-4166. 1921. C. Scribner's Sons.
By Advice of Counsel: Being Adventures of the Celebrated Firm of Tutt & Tutt, Attorneys and Counsellors at Law. Arthur Cheney Train. LC 46-38955. 1928. C. Scribner's Sons.
By All of Promise. William P. Gleason. 3.75 o.p. (ISBN 0-8283-1276-1). Branden.
By an Unknown Disciple ... LC 19-253520. Hodder and Stoughton.
By an Unknown Disciple ... LC 19-2534. George H. Doran Company.
By and About Women: An Anthology of Short Fiction. Ed. by Beth Kline Schneiderman. LC 72-96987. 1973. 3.95 (ISBN 0-15-505665-4). Harcourt Brace Jovanovich.
By and by: An Historical Romance of the Future. Edward Maitland. LC 77-9582. (Gregg Press science fiction series). (Illus.). 1977. 20.00 (ISBN 0-8398-2379-7). Gregg Press.
By and by: An Historical Romance of the Future. Edward Maitland. LC 7-16598. 1873. G. P. Putnam's Sons; Etc., Etc.
By Appointment Only. Russell Boltar. LC 57-9289. (Dell first edition, B111). 1957. Dell Pub. Co.
By Appointment Only. Translated from the French by Waldemar Hansen. Lucie Heymann. LC 57-10978. 1957. Simon and Schuster.
By Berween Banks. Beynon Puddicombe. LC 99-1194. (Half-title: Appleton's town and country library no. 260). 1899. D. Appleton and Company.
By Berwen Banks: A Romance of Welsh Life. Beynon Puddincombe. LC 43-36298. A. L. Burt Company.
By Bolo and Krag. Chauncey M'Govern. LC 10-14586. The Escolta Press.
By Bread Alone. Will Creed. LC 41-977. James S. Nudi Publications.
By Bread Alone. Betty De Sherbinin. LC 45-267. 1945. W. Morrow & Company.
By Bread Alone. William Long. LC 41-977. J. S. Nudi Publications.
By Bread Alone. Edith Ann Ulmer. LC 40-37537. House of Field, Inc.
By Bread Alone: A Novel. Isaac Kahn Friedman. LC 1-25429. 1901. McClure, Phillips & Co.
By Candle-Light. Gertrude Knevels. LC 26-15734. 1926. D. Appleton and Company.
By Cecile. Tereska Torres. 1963. 3.95 o.p. (ISBN 0-671-11375-5). S&S.
By Celia's Arbour: A Tale of Portsmouth Town. library ed. Walter Besant & Rice, James. 1888. Dodd, Mead & Company.
By Command of the Viceroy. Duncan MacNeil. LC 75-9492. 224p. 1975. 8.95 o.p. (ISBN 0-312-11060-X). St Martin.
By Command of the Viceroy. Duncan MacNeil. (O.s.i.). 1977. pap. 1.50 o.s.i. (BT51119). Belmont-Tower.
By Command of the Viceroy: An 'Ogilvie' Novel. Philip McCutchan. LC 75-9492. 7.95. St. Martin's Press.
By Dawn's Early Light at One Hundred Twenty Miles Per Hour. Roger Aplon. Date not set. 10.00 (ISBN 0-931848-58-X); pap. 4.95 (ISBN 0-931848-57-1). Dryad Pr.
By Day and by Night. Johan Bojer & Bateson, Solvi, Tr. LC 37-273481. 1937. D. Appleton Century Company, Incorporated.
By Daybreak the Eagle. Nancy Dorer & Frances Dorer. (Orig.). 1979. pap. 1.95. Woodhill.
By Demons Possessed. Elizabeth Grayson. 1978. pap. 1.25 o.p. (ISBN 0-532-12542-8). Woodhill.
By Demons Possessed. Elizabeth Grayson. 1978. pap. 1.25 o.p. (ISBN 0-532-12542-8). Manor Bks.
By Demons Possessed. Elizabeth Grayson. 1973. (pbk) 0.95. Manor Books.
By Dim and Flaring Lamps. Alan Le May. LC 62-11479. 1962. Harper.
By Earthquake and Fire: Or, The Checkered Romance of Two Generations. Maria Louise Whaley. LC 14-21428. 1914. Brunt's.
By Executive Arrangement: A Novel. Taber McMordie. LC 78-26047. 9.95 (ISBN 0-07-045490-6). McGraw-HIll.
By Faith Alone. Doris Crofut. LC 72-77198. 1972. 5.95 (ISBN 0-912526-02-5). Library Research Associates.
By Faith Alone: A Novel of the Huguenot Settlement at New Paltz, New York. Doris Crofut. LC 72-77198. 147p. 1972. 5.95 (ISBN 0-912526-02-5). Lib Res.
By Flower and Dean Street, & the Love Apple. Patrice Chaplin. LC 77-352402. 1976. 3.25 (ISBN 0-7156-1113-5). Duckworth.
By Force of Circumstances. Louis Tracy. LC 9-7570. E. J. Clode.
By Foul Means. Patrick Leyton. LC 29-17395. International Fiction Library.
By Frequent Anguish. S. F. X Dean. LC 81-51977. 1982. 9.95 (ISBN 0-8027-5458-9). Walker and Co.
By Gaslight in Winter: A Victorian Family History Through the Magic Lantern. Colin Gordon. (Illus.). 128p. 1981. 27.50 (ISBN 0-241-10474-2, Pub. by Hamish Hamilton England). David & Charles.
By Grace of Love. Anne Jackson Fremantle. LC 57-10779. 1957. Macmillan.
By Grand Central Station I Sat Down and Wept: A Novel. Elizabeth Smart. 1975. (pbk.) 1.50. Popular Library.
By Gun and Spur. Wayne D Overholser. LC 52-5300. (Dutton diamond D western). 1952. Dutton.
By His Own Hand. Henry W. Clune. LC 52-14108. 1952. Macmillan.
By His Own Might. A Romance. Wilhelmine Birch Von Hillern. LC 7-4743. 1872. J. B. Lippincott & Co.
By Hook or by Crook. Emma Lathen, pseud. LC 74-23402. (Simon and Schuster novel of suspense). 1975. 6.95 (ISBN 0-671-21962-6). Simon and Schuster.
By Hook or by Crook. Emma Lathen, pseud. (Kangaroo Book). 1977. 1.50 (ISBN 0-671-81078-2). Pocket Books.
By Hook or by Crook: An Arthur Crook Mystery. Lucy Beatrice Malleson. LC 47-4139. 1947. A. S. Barnes & Company.
By Hook or Crook. Robert Alfred John Walling. LC 41-281876. 1941. W. Morrow & Company.
By Hudson's Banks; a Novel. Joanna McCornick. LC 7-15300. 1889. The Bancroft Company.
By Inheritance. Alice French. LC 10-8538. 1.50. The Bobbs-Merrill Company.
Last Good Kiss /by James Crumley. James Crumley. 1981. 2.75 (ISBN 0-671-82813-4). Pocket Books.
By Land and by Sea, a Tale by Casphagius. E. S. Cavanaugh, Narrator. Edmund S Cavanaugh. LC 51-11837. 1951. Exposition Press.
By Law of Might, of the Campaign in Sunset.. A Romance of the Real Wall Street. Newton I. E. Albert Newton Ridgely. LC 8-22562. 1908. H. A. Simmons & Co.
By Law Protected: A Novel. Alistair Keith Campsie. LC 77-353751. 1976. 3.50 (ISBN 0-903937-27-1). Canongate.
By-Line for Murder. pseud. 1st ed. Paul Winterton. LC 51-11706. 1951. Harper.
By Lions, Eaten Gladly. Miriam Merritt. LC 65-19064. 1965. Harcourt, Brace & World.
By Love Betrayed. Anne N. Reisser. (Candlelight Ecstasy Ser.: No. 81). (Orig.). 1982. pap. 1.95 (ISBN 0-440-14839-1). Dell.
By Love Betrayed. Daisy Thomson. 1974. (pbk.) 0.95 (ISBN 0-515-03292-1). Pyramid Books.
By Love Betrayed. Daisy H. Thomson. 1974. pap. 0.95 o.p. (ISBN 0-515-03292-1, V3292). BJ Pub Group.
By Love Bewitched. Dorothea J. Snow. (YA) 1981. 6.95 (Avalon). Bouregy.
By Love Divided. Rebecca Burton. (Leisure Book.). 1978. 1.95 (ISBN 0-8439-0558-1). Nordon Pubns.
By Love Fulfilled. Noreen Nash. 448p. (Orig.). 1980. pap. 2.50 (ISBN 0-446-91225-5). Warner Bks.
By Love Possessed. James Gould Cozzens. LC 57-10062. 1957. Harcourt, Brace.
By Lust Betrayed. Jerome Warr. 176p. pap. 1.95 o.p. (6109). Brandon.
By Mead and Stream. Charles Gibbon. (Harper's Franklin square library, no. 427). 1884. Harper & Brothers.
By Mead and Stream. Charles Gibbon. (On cover: Seaside library. Pocket ed., no. 317). 1885. G. Munro.
By Nature Free: A Novel. Hiram Collins Haydn. LC 43-4642. 1943. The Bobbs-Merrill Company.
By Neva's Waters: Being an Episode in the Secret History of Alexander the First, Czar of All the Russias. John R Carling. LC 7-21530. 1907. Little, Brown, and Company.
By Night. Robert Keating Clay. LC 27-18302. 1927. J. B. Lippincott Company.
By Night at Dinsmore... Samuel Shellabarger. LC 35-5969. 1935. Pub. for the Crime Club, Inc., by Doubleday, Doran & Company, Inc.

By Night the Strangers. Herbert E Stover. LC 54-11238. 1954. Dodd, Mead.
By Order of the Czar. A Novel. Joseph Hatton. LC 7-2195. (On cover: Lovell's international series, no. 78). 1890. J. W. Lovell Company.
By Order of the Magistrate. William Pett Ridge. LC 7-414417. 1898. Harper & Brothers.
By Order of the Prophet: A Tale of Utah. Alfred Hylas Henry. LC 2-20002. 1902. Fleming H. Revell Company.
By Our Beginnings. Jean Stubbs. LC 78-21408. 10.95 (ISBN 0-312-11114-2). St. Martin's Press.
By-Pass Control. Mickey Spillane, pseud. 1967. pap. 1.75 (ISBN 0-451-09226-0, E9226, Sig). NAL.
By-Pass Control: By Mickey Spillane. Frank Morrison Spillane. LC 66-12254. 3.95. Dutton.
By Passion Betrayed. John Scalzo. LC 78-56094. 1978. pap. text ed. 2.25 o.s.i. (ISBN 0-89559-074-3). Dale Books Inc.
By Passion Bound. Emma Bennett. (Candlelight Ecstasy Ser.: No. 135). (Orig.). 1983. pap. 1.95 (ISBN 0-440-10918-3). Dell.
By Passion Possessed. Ralph Hayes. (Belmont Tower Book). 1978. 1.95 (ISBN 0-505-51240-8). Tower Pubns.
By Paths They Know Not. David Taylor Robertson. LC 18-15377. 1918. 1.25. The Gorham Press.
By Pirate's Blood. Richard Silver. (Captain Shark,#1). 1975. (pbk.) 1.25 (ISBN 0-523-00631-4). Pinnacle Books.
By Proxy. A Novel. James Payn. (Seaside library. v. 15, no. 299).
By Reason of Insanity. Shane Stevens. LC 78-11395. 10.95 (ISBN 0-671-24058-7). Simon and Schuster.
By Reason of Strength. Gerald White Johnson. LC 31-262273. Minton, Balch & Company.
By Reef and Palm. Louis Becke. LC 75-116938. (Short story index reprint series). 1970. (ISBN 8-369-34407-0). Books for Libraries Press.
By Reef and Palm. Louis Becke. LC 5-41007. 1900. J. B. Lippincott Company.
By Reef and Palm and The Ebbing of the Tide. Louis Becke. LC 27-1855. 1924. J. B. Lippincott Company.
By Right Divine: By William Sage... with a Frontispiece by Ch. Grunwald. William Sage. 1907. Little, Brown, and Company.
By Right Not Law. Robert Harborough Sherard. LC 3-5122. Cassell Publishing Company.
By Right of Conquest: A Novel. Arthur Hornblow. LC 9-12277. G. W. Dillingham Company.
By Right of Purchase. Harold Bindloss. LC 8-7385. 1908. F. A. Stokes Company.
By Right of Purchase. Harold Bindloss. LC 8-24466. 1908. F. A. Stokes Company.
By Right of Sword. Arthur Williams Marchmont. LC 10-127782. 1897. Grosset & Dunlap.
By Rope and Lead. Ernest Haycox. LC 76-45860. 1976. 9.95 (ISBN 0-89190-972-9). Rivercity Press.
By Rope and Lead. 1st Ed. Ernest Haycox. LC 51-1322. 1951. Little, Brown.
By Royal Command. Cecil William Mercer. LC 31-26537. 1931. Minton, Balch & Company.
By Sanction of Law. Joshua Henry Jones. LC 70-76115. 1969. McGrath Pub. Co.
By Sanction of Law. Joshua Henry Jones. LC 73-144643. 1972. 14.50 (ISBN 0-404-00179-3). AMS Press.
By Sanction of Law. Joshua Henry Jones. LC 24-15984. 1924. B. J. Brimmer Company.
By Sanction of the Victim. Patte Wheat. LC 76-8655. (Illus.). 1.75 (ISBN 0-89041-077-1). Major Books.
By Scarlet Torch and Blade. Anthony Henderson Uewer. LC 23-14381. 1923. 2.00. G. P. Putnam's Sons.
By Sex Obsessed. Nell Collyer. (O.s.i.). (Orig.). pap. 0.75 o.s.i. (A321S, Award). Univ Pub & Dist.
By Shore and Sedge. Bret Harte. LC 72-121560. (Short story index reprint series). 1970. Books for Libraries Press.
By Shore and Sedge. Bret Harte. LC 7-2867. 1885. Houghton, Mifflin and Company.
By Snare of Love. Arthur Williams Marchmont. 1904. Frederick, A. Stokes Company.
By Soochow Waters. Louise Jordan Miln. LC 29-173936. 1929. Frederick A. Stockes Compnay.
By Starlight. Thomas Sancton. 1971. pap. 0.95 o.p. (09075). Curtis.
By Starlight: A Novel. 1st Ed. Thomas Sancton. LC 60-13555. 1960. Doubleday.
By Still Waters: A Story for Quiet Hours. Isabella Fyvie Mayo. LC 7-184853. 1874. Dodd & Mead.
By Strange Paths. Sallie Lee Bell. 192p. 1974. pap. 2.25 o.p. (ISBN 0-310-20992-7). Zondervan.
By Strange Paths: A Novel of Old Louisiana. Sallie Lee Bell. LC 53-172743. 1952. Zondervan Pub. House.
By Subtle Fragrance Held. Mary Fletcher Stevens. LC 8-160945. 1893. J. B. Lippincott Company.
By Sun and Candlelight: A Novel. Patricia Campbell. LC 55-652. 1955. Macmillan.
By That Sin Fell the Angels. Judith Ravel & Brentano, Lowell. The Macaulay Company.
By the Back Door. Joshua Kirby. LC 57-38386. Castle Books.
By the Beautiful Sea. William Miller Abrahams. LC 47-3615. 1947. The Dial Press.
By the Bend of the River: Tables of Connock Old and New. Charles Heber Clark. LC 14-17807. The John C. Winston Company.
By the Blue River: A Novel. Isabel Constance Clarke. LC 13-228141. 1913. 1.35. Benziger Brothers.
By the Body of the Earth: Or, The Sannayasin Sic: Unending History. Satprem. LC 76-9208. 6.95 (ISBN 0-06-013768-1). Harper & Row.
By the Clear: Cool Water, a Novel. 1st Ed. Vance Johnson. LC 57-6694. 1957. Greenwich Book Publishers.
By the Dim Lamps. Nathan Schachner. LC 41-4412. 1941. Frederick A. Stokes Company.
By the Eternal" A Novel. Opie Percival Read. LC 6-29777. Laird & Lee.
By the Gate of the Sea: A Novel. David Christie Murray. (Harper's Franklin square library. Duodecimo ed.). 1883. Harper & Brothers.
By the Gate of the Sea. A Novel. David Christie Murray. (On cover: Lovell's library, v. 4, no. 197). 1883. J. W. Lovell Company.
By the Gate of the Sea. A Novel. David Christie Murray. (On cover: Seaside library. Pocket ed., no. 58). 1883. G. Munro.
By the Good Sainte Ann: A Story of Modern Quebec. Anna Chapin Ray. LC 4-8581. 1904. Little, Brown, and Company.
By the Green of the Spring: A Novel. John Masters. LC 81-5981. (Masters, John, 1914-. Loss of Eden). (Illus.). 13.95 (ISBN 0-07-040783-5). McGraw-Hill.
By the Higher Law. Julia Helen Watts Twells. LC 1-281706. 1901. H. T. Coates and Co.
By the King's Command: A Novel. 1st Ed. Shirley Seifert. LC 62-18849. 1962. Lippincott.
By the King's Command: A Romance of Ferdinand De Soto. Mary Brabson Littleton. LC 28-255503. 1928. P. J. Kenedy & Sons.
By the Light of the Fire: A Collection of Short Stories. Benjamin Lease Crozer Griffith. LC 7-2935. 1896. The Penn Publishing Company.
By the Light of the Green Star. Lin Carter. (Green star saga,#3). 1974. (pbk.) 0.95. DAW Books.
By the Light of the Soul: A Novel. Mary Eleanor Wilkins Freeman. LC 6-31389. 1906. Harper & Brothers.
By the Light of the Soul: A Novel. Mary Eleanor Wilkins Freeman. LC 7-5069. 1907. Harper & Brothers.
By the Marshes of Minas. Charles George Douglas Roberts. LC 74-178456. (Short story index reprint series). (Illus.). 1971. (ISBN 0-8369-4057-1). Books for Libraries Press.
By the Marshes of Minas. Charles George Douglas Roberts. LC 1499. Silver, Burdett and Company.
By the North Door. Margaret Elizabeth Atkins. LC 74-15863. 1975. 6.95 (ISBN 0-06-010162-8). Harper & Row.
By the North Gate. Gwyn Griffin. LC 59-6177. 1959. Holt.
By the North Gate. Joyce Carol Oates. LC 63-13790. 1963. Vanguard Press.
By the Open Sea. August Strindberg. LC 72-3561. 1973. 12.95 (ISBN 0-8383-1547-X). Haskell House Publishers.
By the Pricking of My Thumbs. Agatha Miller Christie. 1983. pap. 2.95 (ISBN 0-671-46807-3). PB.
By the Pricking of My Thumbs. Agatha Miller Christie. LC 68-58446. 1968. 4.95 o.p. (ISBN 0-396-05840-X). Dodd.
By the Queen's Grace: A Novel. Virginia Stanton Sheard. LC 5-5069. 1905. F. A. Stokes Company.
By the Ramparts of Jezreel. Arnold Davenport. LC 3-1281. 1903. Longmans, Green, and Co.
By the Rivers of Babylon: A Novel. Nelson DeMille. LC 77-91474. 10.00 (ISBN 0-15-115278-0). Harcourt Brace Jovanovich.
By the Same Door: A Novel. Blanche Chenery Perrin. LC 51-10653. 1951. Macmillan.
By the Sea: By the Sea... A Novel. George Sumner Albee. LC 60-6732. 1960. Simon and Schuster.
By the Shores of Arcady. Isabel Graham Eaton. LC 9-2777. 1908. The Outing Publishing Company.
By the Silvery Moon. Barbara Corcoran. 1982. pap. 1.95 (ISBN 0-345-30259-1). Ballantine.
By the Sound. Edward Dorn. (Illus.). 200p. (Orig.). 1971. pap. 3.00. Frontier Press Calif.
By the Stage Door. Ada Patterson & Bateman, Victory. 1902. The Grafton Press.
By the Tiber. Mary Agnes Tincker. LC 8-27021. 1881. Roberts Brothers.
By the Watchman's Clock. Zenith Jones Brown. LC 32-137870. Farrar & Rinehart, Incorporated.
By the Waters of Babylon. Stephen Lister. LC 45-5125. 1945. Dodd, Mead & Company.
By the Waters of Babylon. Robert Neumann. LC 40-12659. 1940. Simon and Schuster.
By the Waters of Babylon: A Novel. Anna Farwell De Koven. LC 1-829591. 1901. H. S. Stone and Company.
By the Waters of Babylon: A Story of Ancient Israel. Louis Wallis. LC 31-627434. 1931. The Macmillan Company.
By the Waters of Manhattan. Charles Reznikoff. LC 30-17445. (Paper books). 1930. C. Boni.
By the Waters of Whitechapel. Bernard Kops. LC 75-103966. 1970. 5.95 (ISBN 0-393-08597-X). Norton.
By the Will of Apollo: Being the Strange Adventures of Cylon, a Spearman of Athens, with Doria of Apollo's Temple, As Related by Himself. Charles Kelsey Gaines. LC 76-3310. 7.95 (ISBN 0-8265-1204-6). Vanderbilt University.
By the Will of His Father. Guy Percy Benner. LC 27-175296. 1927. H. Vinal.
By the World Forgot. Ruby Mildred Ayres. LC 33-239323. 1933. Doubleday, Doran & Company, Inc.
By the World Forgot" A Double Romance of the East and the West. Cyrus Townsend Brady. LC 17-252435. 1917. A. C. McClurg & Co.
By Their Fruits. Edith M Nicholl Bowyer. LC 1-8312. The Abbey Press.
By Their Fruits. Anson Doner Eby. LC 26-4415. Conestoga Publishing Co., Inc.
By Their Fruits. Howard Manisch. LC 58-12869. 1958. Crown Publishers.
By Their Fruits: A Novel. Rosa Caroline Murray-Prior Praed. LC 8-37711. 1908. Cassell and Company, Limited.
By This Strange Fire. Edith Pargeter. LC 48-5971. 1948. Reynal and Hitchcock.
By Valour and Arms. James Howell Street. LC 49-5678. 1945. Sun Dial Press.
By Valour and Arms: By James Street. James Howell Street. LC 44-830844. 1944. Dial Press, Inc.
By Violence. Ernest George Henham. (Half title: International pocket library, ed. by E. R. Brown). The Four Seas Company.
By Way of Confession. Robert Gore-Browne. LC 30-5404. 1930. Pub. for The Crime Club, Inc., by Doubleday, Doran & Company, Inc.
By Way of People. Anne Marx. 1970. 4.00 o.p. (ISBN 0-8233-0147-8). Golden Quill.
By Way of the Silberthorns. Grace Livingston Hill. LC 41-34223. J. B. Lippincott Company.
By Way of the Silverthorns. Grace Livingston Hill. LC 75-31641. 1975. 9.95 (ISBN 0-89190-004-7). American Reprint Co.
By Way of the Wilderness. Isabella Alden & C. M. Livingston. LC 2191. 1899. Lothrop Publishing Company.
By Way of Wyoming. Curtis Kent Bishop. LC 46-8193. 1946. The Macmillan Company.
By-Ways of Braithe. Frances Powell Case. 1904. C. Scribner's Sons.
By What Authority? Edited, and with a Foreword, by Riley Hughes. Robert Hugh Benson. LC 57-100933. 1957. Kenedy.
By Whose Hand? Louise Guest Rice. LC 30-31596. The Macaulay Company.
By Whose Hand? Edith Sessions Tupper. 1889. W. Fracker & Company.
By Whose Hand? Edith Sessions Tupper. LC 3390. (On cover: Magnet detective library, no. 134). 1900. Street & Smith.
By Wild Waves Tossed: An Ocean Love Story. Jack Brand. LC 8-13949. 1908. The McClure Company.
By Wit of Woman. Arthur Williams Marchmont. LC 6-16736. 1906. F. A. Stokes Company.
By Woman's Wit. A Novel. Annie French Hector. (On cover: Seaside library. Pocket ed. no. 900). 1886. G. Munro.
By Woman's Wit: A Novel. Annie French Hector. (On cover: Lovell's library, v. 17, no 840). 1887. J. W. Lovell Company.
By Your Leave, Sir" The Story of a WAVE. Helen Hull Jacobs. LC 43-11945. 1943. Dodd, Mead & Company.
Bye, Baby Bunting. Day Keene. LC 63-11407. 1963. Holt, Rinehart and Winston.
Bye-Bye Blackbird. Anita Desai. 266p. 1971. pap. 3.50 (ISBN 0-88253-033-X). Ind-US Inc.
Bye-Bye Breeches. Peirson Ricks. LC 36-131931. Dorrance & Company.
Bye-Bye Lonesome Blues. William S. Doxey. 2.25 (ISBN 0-505-51652-7). Tower Publications, Inc.
Bye Bye Mista. Ongkar Narayan. LC 72-96111. 1973. 6.50 (ISBN 0-8022-2109-2). Philosophical Library.
Bye-Ways. Robert Smythe Hichens. LC 7-4758. 1897. Dodd, Mead and Company.
Bygones. Frank Cassedy Wilkinson. LC 80-27258. 12.95 (ISBN 0-399-12572-8). Putnam.
Bygones. Frank Williamson. 1982. pap. 3.75 (ISBN 0-8217-1030-3). Zebra.
Bylines. Bernard Weinraub. LC 80-3000. 1983. 17.95 (ISBN 0-385-17000-9). Doubleday.
Bylow Hill. George Washington Cable. LC 72-7806. (Illus.). Scholarly Press.
Bylow Hill. George Washington Cable. LC 75-80625. (Illus.). 1969. AMS Press.
Bylow Hill. George Washington Cable. LC 2-146843. 1902. C. Scribner's Sons.
Bylow Hill see Collected Works.
Byrd Flam in Town: Being a Collection of That Rising Young Author's Letters. Le Roy Armstrong. LC 6-2433. (Shadows library, v. 1, no. 1). 1894. J. Bearhope Company.
Byrd Songs. William Henry Bossence. LC 76-357615. 1975. 6.50 (ISBN 0-7256-0142-6). Hawthorn Press.
Byrdwhistle Option. Robert H Rimmer. LC 82-81709. 1982. 14.95 (ISBN 0-87975-184-3). Prometheus Books.
Byrnes of Glengoulah. A True Tale. Alice Nolan. LC 7-33182. 1870. P. O'Shea.
Byron, the Last Journey. Harold George Nicholson. 1973. Repr. of 1948 ed. 7.50 o.p. (ISBN 0-8274-0299-6). R West.
Bystander. Maksim Gorkii & Guerney, Bernard Guilbert, Tr. LC 30-9734. J. Cape and H. Smith.
Bystander. 1st Ed. Albert Joseph Guerard. LC 58-10070. 1958. Little, Brown.
Byway to Love. Margaret Sebastian, pseud. LC 82-7260. 1982. 10.95 (ISBN 0-89340-521-3). J. Curley.
Bywonner. Florence Ethel Mills Young. LC 16-11736. 1916. John Lane.
Byworlder. Poul Anderson. LC 78-727. (Gregg Press Science Fiction Series). (Worlds of Poul Anderson; 2). 1978. 8.50 (ISBN 0-8398-2432-7). Gregg Press.
Byzantine Honeymoon: A Tale of the Bosphorous. Philip Glazebrook. LC 78-72965. 1979. 8.95 (ISBN 0-689-10946-6). Atheneum.
Byzantine Saint. Sergei Hackel. 245p. 1982. lib. bdg. 22.95x (ISBN 0-89370-081-9); pap. text ed. 15.95x (ISBN 0-7044-0451-6). Borgo Pr.
Byzantine Wake: A Novel. Frank Aloi. LC 76-383241. 7.00 (ISBN 0-682-48524-1). E. Uhlan.

C

C. A. Stephens Looks at Norway. story-teller's ed. Charles Asbury Stephens. LC 73-12097. (Illus.). 1970. 4.75. C. A. Stephens Collection, Brown University.
C. A. T. No. 1: Tower of Blood. Spike Andrews. (Men of Action Ser.). 224p. (Orig.). 1982. pap. 1.95 (ISBN 0-446-30182-5). Warner Bks.
C. C. & Company. Mike Roote. (O.s.i.). (Orig.). 1970. pap. 0.75 o.s.i. (A721S, Award). Univ Pub & Dist.
C. I. D.". Talbot Mundy. LC 32-336949. 2.00. The Century Co.
C. J.'s Quest: Or, Last Winter I Visited Detroit. Cyril James Fox. LC 80-26887. 1980. 8.95 (ISBN 0-89962-024-8). Todd & Honeywell.
C. O. D. Natalie Sumner Lincoln. LC 15-4800. 1915. 1.30. D. Appleton and Company.
C. O. D. Natalie Sumner Lincoln. LC 20-18821. 1919. D. Appleton and Company.
C. W. Sanders' Big Book of Western Stories: Three Galloping Novels of the West Complete in One Volume... Charles Wesley Sanders. LC 34-1830. 1933. Grosset & Dunlap.
Ca Ira. A Novel. William Dugas Trammell. LC 8-29724. 1874. United States Publishing Company.
Ca Ira: A Novel. William Dugas Trammell. LC 76-42792. Repr. of 1874 ed. 26.00 (ISBN 0-404-60079-4). AMS Pr.
Cab at the Door. Victor Sawdon Pritchett. pap. 1.95 o.p. (ISBN 0-394-71232-3, V-232, Vin). Random.
Cab-Intersec. David Harry Walker. LC 67-28554. (Illus.). 1968. Houghton Mifflin.
Cab N Degres Forty-Four. Robert Frederick Foster. LC 10-2920. 1910. 1.25. Frederick A. Stokes Company.
Cabal. Norman Garbo. LC 78-17806. 10.95 (ISBN 0-393-08827-8). Norton.
Cabal, No. 2: The Black Moon. Philip Dunn. (Orig.). 1982. pap. 2.95 (ISBN 0-425-05194-3). Berkley Pub.
Cabal, No. 3: The Evangelist. Philip Dunn. 192p. 1982. pap. 2.25 (ISBN 0-425-05659-7). Berkley Pub.
Cabal. 1st Ed. Mark Lineman. LC 60-13591. 1960. Bobbs-Merrill.
Cabala. Thornton Niven Wilder. LC 26-9111. 1926. A. & C. Boni.
Cabala. Thornton Niven Wilder & Gorman, Herbert Sherman, 1893- LC 29-26504. (Half-title: The Modern library of the world's best books). The Modern Library.
Cabala: And The Woman of Andros. Thornton Niven Wilder & Wilder, Thornton Niven. LC 68-28228. 1968. 5.95. Harper & Row.
Caballero. Johnston McCulley. LC 47-11748. 1947. S. Curl.

Caballero, a Brother to "The Spaniard". Henry Leyford Gates. LC 35-3044. 1934. G. H. Watt.

Cabana Murders. Joseph Francis Delany. LC 37-17021. 1937. Pub. for the Crime Club, Inc., by Doubleday, Doran & Co., Inc.

Cabaret. Olive Wadsley. Dodd, Mead & Company.

Cabaret Love. Lillian Barker. LC 33-641243. Grosset & Dunlap.

Cabbage Holiday. Anthony Thorne. LC 40-27534. 1940. Random House.

Cabbages and Crime. Anne Nash. LC 45-6550. 1945. Pub. for the Crime Club by Doubleday, Doran & Co., Inc.

Cabbages and Harlequins, a Novel. Gene Gauntier. LC 29-24383. 1929. Coward-McCann, Inc.

Cabbages and Kings. William Sydney Porter. LC 18-7784. A. L. Burt Company.

Cabbages and Kings. William Sydney Porter. LC 4-327504. 1904. McClure, Phillips & Co.

Cabbages and Kings. William Sydney Porter. LC 42-26107. 1910. Doubleday, Page & Company.

Cabbages and Kings. William Sydney Porter. LC 15-17415. 1914. Doubleday, Page & Company.

Cabbages and Kings. William Sydney Porter. LC 17-793217. 1916. Doubleday, Page & Company.

Cabbages and Kings. William Sydney Porter. LC 19-135185. 1918. Doubleday, Page & Company.

Cabbages and Kings. William Sydney Porter. LC 22-16019. 1919. Doubleday, Page & Company, for Review of Reviews Co.

Cabbages and Kings. William Sydney Porter. LC 43-21542. 1908. The McClure Company.

Cabbages and Kings. William Sydney Porter. LC 47-18969. (On cover: Penguin books. 595). 1946. Penguin Books, Inc.

Cabby. Leonard Jordan. (Belmont Tower Book.). 1.95 (ISBN 0-505-51466-4). Tower Publications.

Cabildo on Jackson Square. rev. ed. Samuel Wilson, Jr. & Leonard V. Huber. LC 70-117643. 1973. pap. 4.95 (ISBN 0-911116-41-9). Pelican.

Cabin. Vicente Blasco Ibanez. LC 26-10854. (Borzoi pocket books). 1924. A. A. Knopf.

Cabin. Marquis William Childs. LC 44-1915. 1944. Harper & Brothers.

Cabin and Gondola. Charlotte Dunning Wood. LC 9-512. (Harper's handy series, no. 48). 1886. Harper & Brothers.

Cabin & Parlor. Charles Jacobs Peterson. 1852. 15.50 o.p. (ISBN 0-404-04618-5). AMS Pr.

Cabin and Parlor: Or, Slaves and Masters. Charles Jacobs Peterson. LC 77-149876. (Black Heritage Library Collection). (Illus.). 1971. (ISBN 0-8369-8756-X). Books for Libraries Press.

Cabin and Parlor: Or, Slaves and Masters. Charles Jacobs Peterson. T. B. Peterson.

Cabin at the Trail's End: A Story of Oregon. Sheba Hargreaves. LC 28-553735. 1928. Harper & Brothers.

Cabin Beyond. Albert Fernandes. LC 30-18313. 1930. Meador Publishing Company.

Cabin Book: Or, National Characteristics. Charles Sealsfield. Tr. by Powell, Sarah. LC 16-191441. 1871. St. John & Coffin.

Cabin Book: Or, Sketches of Life in Texas. Charles Sealsfield. Tr. by Mersch, Ch. Fr. LC 8-6425. (With his Life in the New world... New York c1884). 1844. J. Winchester.

Cabin Boy. Vincent J Dempsey. LC 56-7140. 1956. Coward-McCann.

Cabin Boy's Story. facs. ed. LC 70-83935. (Black Heritage Library Collection Ser). 1854. 18.75 (ISBN 0-8369-8527-3). Ayer Co.

Cabin Boy's Story: A Semi-Nautical Romance, Founded on Fact. James A. Maitland. LC 70-83935. (Illus.). 1969. Mnemosyne Pub. Co.

Cabin Fever: A Novel. Bertha Muzzy Sinclair. LC 18-138719. 1918. Little, Brown, and Company.

Cabin in the Cotton. Harry Harrison Kroll. LC 31-311272. 1931. R. Long & R. R. Smith, Inc.

Cabin in the Pines. Gertrude Pahlow. LC 35-7530. The Penn Publishing Company.

Cabin in the Redwoods. William Arthur Neubauer. LC 53-112968. 1953. Arcadia House.

Cabin: La Barraca. Blasco Ibanez, Vicente. LC 75-1109. 1975. 14.00. H. Fertig.

Cabin (La Barraca) Vicente Blasco Ibanez & Snow, Francis Haffkine, Tr. LC 18-574612. (On... of half-title: The Borzoi Spanish translations.). 1917. A. A. Knopf.

Cabin (La Barraca) Vicente Blasco Ibanez & Snow, Francis Haffkine, Tr. LC 19-3216. (On verse of half-title: The Borzoi Spanish translations. I=5d). 1919. A. A. Knopf.

Cabin (La Barraca) Vicente Blasco Ibanez & Snow, Francis Haffkine, Tr. LC 38-21699. 1938. A. A. Knopf.

Cabin of Dreams. James Noble Gifford. LC 39-31412. 1939. Gramercy Publishing Co.

Cabin of Dreams. Gay Rutherford. LC 39-314123. Gramercy Publishing Co.

Cabin Road. John Faulkner. LC 79-86496. 1969. 6.95. Louisiana State University Press.

Cabinda Affair. Matthew Head. LC 80-8715. 256p. 1981. pap. 2.25i (ISBN 0-06-080541-2, P541, PL). Har-Row.

Cabinda Affair: By Matthew Head Pseud. John Edwin Canaday. LC 49-804657. (inner sanetum mystery). Simon and Schuster.

Cabinet: A Collection of Romantic Tales; Embracing the Spirit of the English Magazines ... LC 15-12454. 1833. Kurst, Chance & Co.

Cabinet of Gems: Short Stories from the English Annuals. Ed. by Bradford Allen Booth. LC 38-14002. 1938. University of California Press.

Cabinet Secret. Guy Newell Boothby. LC 1-29443. 1901. J. B. Lippincott Company.

Cable: A Novel. Marion Ames Taggart. LC 23-7392. 1923. Benziger Brothers.

Cable Car. June Drummond. LC 67-10079. 1967. Holt, Rinehart and Winston.

Cable Car Murder. Elizabeth Atwood Taylor. LC 81-5809. 1981. 11.95 (ISBN 0-312-11311-0). St. Martin's Press.

Cable Car Murder. large print ed. Elizabeth Atwood Taylor. LC 82-5468. 1982. 11.95 (ISBN 0-89621-360-9). Thorndike Press.

Cable Harbor. Donald Bowie. 336p. 1982. pap. 3.50 (ISBN 0-380-59493-5, 59493, Flare). Avon.

Cable Harbor: A Novel. Donald Bowie. LC 81-2700. 11.95 (ISBN 0-87131-347-2). M. Evans.

Cables of Cobweb. Paul Jordan Smith, pseud. LC 23-82441. 1923. Lieber & Lewis.

Cables to Rage. Audre Lorde. (Heritage Ser). 1970. pap. 2.00x o.s.i. Broadside.

Cabot Wright Begins. James Purdy. LC 62-8754. 1964. Farrar, Straus & Giroux.

Cabriba, the Garden of the Gods. Mulla Hanaranda. LC 25-15122. 1925. American Library Service.

Cabu. John Robert Russell. (Science fiction). 1974. (pbk.) 0.95 (ISBN 0-671-77718-1). Pocket Books.

Cachalot. Alan Dean Foster. (Orig.). 1980. pap. 2.25 (ISBN 0-345-28066-0). Ballantine.

Cache. Leo Damore. LC 79-25351. 10.95 (ISBN 0-89340-252-4). J. Curley.

Cache. rev. ed. Philip Jose Farmer. 288p. 1981. pap. 2.75 (ISBN 0-523-48534-4). Pinnacle Bks.

Cache: A Novel of Suspense. Leo Damore. LC 78-73868. 8.95 (ISBN 0-87795-222-1). Arbor House: Distributed by Dutton.

Cache-Cache. Amy Louise Marsland. LC 79-6100. 1980. 8.95 (ISBN 0-385-17003-3). Published for the Crime Club by Doubleday.

Cache la Poudre: The Romance of a Tenderfoot in the Days of Custer. Herbert Myrick. LC 5-40407. 1905. Orange Judd Company; Etc., Etc.

Cache on the Rocks. Michael Sellers. LC 82-45606. (Crime Club Ser.). 192p. 1983. 11.95 (ISBN 0-385-18416-6). Doubleday.

Cachet: Or, The Secret Sorrow. A Novel. M. J. R Hamilton. 1873. G. W. Carleton & Co.; Etc., Etc.

Cactus. Charles Chadwick. LC 25-5851. Thomas Y. Crowell Company.

Cactus and Pine; Songs of the Southwest. 2d ed., rev. and enl. ed. Sharlot Mabridth Hall. LC 25-28. 1924. Arizona Republican Print Shop.

Cactus and Sagebrush. Ed. by Leo Margulies. LC 45-7928. 1945. The Hampton Publishing Company.

Cactus & the Crown. Catherine Gavin. 1970. pap. 1.25 o.p. (96009-125). Beagle Bks.

Cactus Cavalier. Norman A Fox. LC 47-5407. 1947. Dodd, Mead.

Cactus on the Range. Tex. Holt, pseud. LC 50-5763. 1950. Phoenix Press.

Cactus Pie: Ten Stories. Gerald Green. LC 78-23590. 1979. 9.95 (ISBN 0-395-27761-2). Houghton Mifflin.

Cactus Rose. Zandra Colt. (Second Chance at Love Ser.: No. 40). (Orig.). 1982. pap. 1.75 (ISBN 0-515-06400-9). Jove Pubns.

Cactus Rose. Margaret Dobson. (Candlelight Ecstasy Ser.: No. 145). (Orig.). 1983. pap. 1.95 (ISBN 0-440-11290-7). Dell.

Cactus Shroud, by Carolyn Thomas Pseud. 1st Ed. Actea Duncan. LC 57-8950. (Main line mysterles).

Cadastre. Aime Cesaire. Bd. with Soleil Cou Coupe; Corps Perdu. pap. 6.50. French & Eur.

Cadaver of Gideon Wyck. Alexander Kinnan Laing. LC 34-136636. 1934. Farrar & Rinehart, Inc.

Caddis. Marjorie Bartholomew Paradis. LC 29-221402. The Century Co.

Caddo: Or, Cupid in the Gas Belt. A Story from Real Life. James Charles. LC 8-323091. 1889. J. Charles.

Cade. Rene Raymond. 1973. 0.75 (ISBN 0-671-75736-9). Pocket Books.

Cade Curse. Willo Davis Roberts. (Black Pearl Series-II). 1978. 1.75 (ISBN 0-445-04266-4). Popular Library.

Cadenza: An Excursion. Ralph Cusack. LC 59-7617. 1959. Houghton Mifflin.

Cadet Days: A Story of West Point. Charles King. LC 4-35681. 1894. Harper & Brothers.

Cadet Days: A Story of West Point. Charles King. LC 16-7574. Harper & Brothers.

Cadet Days: A Story of West Point. Charles King. LC 4-18930. 1903. Harper & Brothers.

Cadet De Colobrieres. A Tale of the Old Convents of Paris. Henriette Etiennette Fanny Arnaud Reybaud. 1847. Carey and Hart.

Cadet Kit Carey: Or, The Young Soldier's Legacy. A Romance of a West Point Boy. Lionel Lounsberry. LC 99-1149. (Medal library, no. 2). 1899. Street & Smith.

Cadet Nurse. Peggy Gaddis, pseud. LC 45-13469. 1945. Arcadia House, Inc.

Cadet Stephen. Alice Pickford Evans. The Judson Press.

Cadet Widow. Virginia Nielsen, pseud. LC 42-255151. 1942. Doubleday, Doran and Company, Inc.

Cadets of Gascony: Two Stories of Old France. Burton Egbert Stevenson. 1904. J. B. Lippincott Company.

Cadillac Cowboys. Glendon Fred Swarthout. LC 75-29139. 1975. 3.95 (ISBN 0-89019-041-0). O'Sullivan Woodside & Co.

Cadillac Cowboys. Glendon Fred Swarthout. LC 64-10770. 1964. Random House.

Cadillac Jack: A Novel. Larry McMurtry. LC 82-5962. 15.95 (ISBN 0-671-45445-5). Simon and Schuster.

Cadwallader: A Diversion. Illustrated by N. M. Bodecker. 1st Ed. Russell Lynes. LC 59-6337. 1959. Harper.

Caesar. Ignatius Donnelly. LC 6-28454.

Caesar. Mirko Jelusich. Tr. by Miall, Bernard. LC 30-31597. 1930. R. R. Smith, Inc.

Caesar Cascabel. Jules Verne & Estoclet, A., Tr. LC 1-9787. Cassell Publishing Company.

Caesar Code. Johannes M. Simmel. 1976. pap. 2.95 (ISBN 0-445-08413-8). Popular Lib.

Caesar of the Narrow Seas. John Gloag. LC 72-163090. (Illus.). 1972. 6.95. St. Martin's Press.

Caesar or Nothing. Baroja y Nessi, Pio. LC 75-11674. 1976. 14.50. H. Fertig.

Caesar or Nothing. Pio Baroja y Nessi. Tr. by Louis How from Span. 337p. 1976. Repr. of 1919 ed. 21.50 (ISBN 0-86527-224-7). Fertig.

Caesar's Column: A Story of the Future. Ignatius Donnelly. LC 6-28454. Syndicate Publishing Company.

Caesar's Column. A Story of the Twentieth Century. Ignatius Donnelly. LC 6-36594. 1890. F. J. Schulte & Company.

Caesar's Column: A Story of the Twentieth Century. Ignatius Donnelly. (On cover: The classic library, no. 31, Jan. 10, 1901). Donohue Brothers.

Caesar's Column: A Story of the Twentieth Century. Ignatius Donnelly. LC 25-15522. M. A. Donohue & Company.

Caesar's Column: A Story of the Twentieth Century. Ignatius Donnelly. LC 76-42811. (Communal societies in America: an AMS reprint series). 1981. 36.00 (ISBN 0-404-60060-3). AMS Press.

Caesar's Gate. Robert Duncan. (Illus.). 1972. 8.50; pap. 3.75. Sand Dollar.

Caeur D'Alene. Mary Hallock Foote. 1894. Houghton, Mifflin and Company.

Cafe at St. Marks. Ed. by Van K. Brock & David Jordan. pap. 3.50. Anhinga Pr.

Cafe Celeste. Translated from the French by Herma Briffault. Francoise Mallet-Joris. LC 59-10754. 1959. Farrar, Straus and Cudahy.

Cafeteria Girl. Gerald Abner. LC 37-15599. The Macaulay Comapny.

Cage. Harold Begbie. LC 11-359643. 1911. Hodder & Stoughton, George H. Doran Company.

Cage. Susan Cheever. LC 82-9190. 1982. 11.95 (ISBN 0-395-32111-5). Houghton Mifflin.

Cage. Reg Gadney. LC 77-4924. 7.95 (ISBN 0-698-10833-7). Coward, McCann & Geoghegan.

Cage. Charlotte Teller Hirsch. LC 74-22788. (Labor Movement in Fiction and Non-Fiction). 1977. (2 vols.) 49.50 (ISBN 0-404-58442-X). AMS Press.

Cage. Peter McCurtin. (Sundance Ser.: No. 41). 208p. 1982. pap. 2.25 (ISBN 0-8439-1077-1, Leisure Bks). Nordon Pubns.

Cage. Andrea Newman. 1967. Dial Press.

Cage a Man. F. M Busby. LC 73-173432. 1973. Doubleday.

Cage Bird & Other Stories. Francis Brett Young. LC 33-105944. 1933. Harper & Brothers.

Cage: By Charlotte Teller. Charlotte Teller Hirsch. LC 7-9551. 1907. D. Appleton and Company.

Cage Door: And Other Stories. Aida Dawson. LC 68-76529. 1967. Stockwell.

Cage Five Is Going to Break. E. Richard Johnson. LC 78-96010. 1970. 4.95. Harper & Row.

Cage for Lovers. Dawn Powell. LC 57-9982. 1957. Houghton Mifflin.

Cage Me a Peacock. Noel Langley. LC 36-9696. 1936. W. Morrow & Co.

Cage of Ice. Duncan Kyle. LC 70-145433. 1971. 5.95. St. Martin's Press.

Cage of Light. Sonya Arcone. LC 67-11962. 1967. Harcourt, Brace & World.

Cage of Light. 1st Ed. Sonya Arcone. LC 67-11962. 1967. 5.95. Harcourt.

Cage of Love. Robert Carse. LC 59-7888. 1959. F. Fell.

Cage of Mirrors. Robert J Ray. LC 80-7867. 10.95 (ISBN 0-690-01938-6). Lippincott & Crowell.

Cage Until Tame. Laurence Henderson. LC 72-197738. 1972. (ISBN 0-245-50866-X). Harrap.

Caged. Terry Brykczynski. LC 79-21786. 10.00 (ISBN 0-517-53995-0). Crown.

Caged. Courtney Ryley Cooper. LC 30-10080. 1930. Little, Brown, and Company.

Caged Birds. 1st Ed. Le Roy Leatherman. LC 50-9491. 1950. Harcourt, Brace.

Caged Lion. Charlotte Mary Yonge. LC 4-168513. 1901. Macmillan and Co., Limited.

Caged Lion: A Story of James I. of Scotland. Charlotte Mary Yonge. (On cover: Seaside library. Pocket ed. no. 739). 1886. G. Munro.

Caged Tiger. Penny Jordan. (Harlequin Presents Ser.). 192p. pap. 1.75 (ISBN 0-373-10519-3, Harlequin). PB.

Cages. Paul Covert. LC 72-162428. (Liveright new writer). 1971. 3.95 (ISBN 0-87140-531-8). Liveright.

Caging the Raven. William Heffernan. LC 81-879. 13.95 (ISBN 0-671-61056-2). Wyndham Books.

Cahier d'un retour au Pays natal: Return to My Native Land. Aime Cesaire. (Livre-Poche Bilingue). pap. 4.50. French & Eur.

Cahill: U. S. Marshal. Joe Millard. 192p. (Orig.). 1979. pap. 1.75 o.p. (ISBN 0-441-09025-7). Charter Bks.

Cahill, United States Marshal. Joe Millard, pseud. (O.s.i.). 192p. (Orig.). 1973. pap. 0.95 o.s.i. (AN1145, Award). Univ Pub & Dist.

Cahill: United States Marshall. Joseph Millard. 1975. (pbk.) 0.95. Award Books.

Cahusac Mystery. Kate O'Brien Hesketh Prichard & Prichard, Hesketh Vernon Hesketh. LC 12-20791. 1912. 1.25. Sturgis & Walton Company.

Cain Basin: By Barry Cord Pseud. Peter Germano. LC 54-114685. 1954. Arcadia House.

Cain: By Rogier Van Aerde Pseud. Translated by I. and E. Graham-Wilson. Illustrated by Patricia K. Watters. Adolf Josef Hubert Frans Van Rijen. LC 54-7978. (Thomas More book to live). 1954. H. Regnery Co.

Cain Conspiracy. Johannes Mario Simmel. 1976. 1.95 (ISBN 0-445-08535-5). Popular Library.

Cain: Or, The Vagabond of Nod. Jesse B Thaxton. LC 6-4642. Broadway Publishing Company.

Cain Sixty-Seven. Johannes M. Simmel. 1972. 7.95 o.p. (ISBN 0-07-057385-9). McGraw.

Cain Times Three. James Mallahan Cain. 1969. 8.95 o.p. (ISBN 0-394-41828-X). Knopf.

Cain X 3: Three Novels. James Mallahan Cain. LC 69-11481. 1969. 6.95. Knopf.

Cain '67. Johannes Mario Simmel. LC 79-174627. 1971. (ISBN 0-07-057385-9). McGraw-Hill.

Caine Munity Court-Martial. Herman Wouk. 1974. pap. 1.95 o.p. (ISBN 0-671-77772-6). WSP.

Caine Mutiny. Herman Wouk. 1983. pap. 4.95 (ISBN 0-671-46017-X). PB.

Caine Mutiny: A Novel of World War II. Herman Wouk. LC 51-9977. 1951. Doubleday.

Caine Mutiny: A Novel of World War II. Herman Wouk. LC 52-4866. 1952. Doubleday.

Caine Mutiny: A Novel of World War II. Herman Wouk. LC 52-11615. 1952. Doubleday.

Caine Mutiny: A Novel of World War II. Herman Wouk. (Illus.). 1973. (pbk.) 1.95 (ISBN 0-671-78642-3). Pocket Books.

Caine Mutiny: A Novel of World War II. Herman Wouk. (Washington Square Press Enriched Classics). (Illus.). 1975. (pbk.) 1.95 (ISBN 0-671-48761-2). Pocket Books.

Caine Mutiny Court-Martial. Herman Wouk. LC 54-5354. 1954. 9.95 (ISBN 0-385-04054-7). Doubleday.

Cain's Book. Alexander Trocchi. LC 60-6344. 1960. Grove Press.

Cain's Daughters. Doris Shannon. LC 77-15323. 10.00 (ISBN 0-312-11390-0). St. Martin's Press.

Cairn. Thomas James Morrison. LC 35-15169. 1935. D. Appleton-Century Company, Incorporated.

Cairo. James Aldridge. LC 72-79364. (A biography of a city). (Illus.). 1969. 8.95 o.p. (ISBN 0-316-03118-6). Little.

Cairo Cabal. Alan Caillou, pseud. (Colonel Tobin War series). 1974. (pbk.) 1.25 (ISBN 0-523-00358-7). Pinnacle Books.

Cairo Concerto. John Rogers Shuman. LC 47-3526. 1947. Harcourt, Brace and Company.

Cairo Connection. Zola Levitt. LC 77-94046. 1978. pap. 1.95 o.p. (ISBN 0-89081-127-X, 127X). Harvest Hse.

Cairo Countdown. Robert Payne. (Able Team Ser.). 192p. 1983. pap. 1.95 (ISBN 0-373-61205-2, Pub. by Worldwide). Harlequin Bks.
Cairo Dawns: A Story Cycles with a Poem. James Leslie Mitchell. LC 31-246528. The Bobbs-Merrill Company.
Cairo Garter Murders. Francis Van Wyck Mason. LC 38-13191. 1938. Pub. for the Crime Club, Inc., by Doubleday, Doran & Company, Inc.
Cairo Mafia. Nick Carter. (Nick Carter Ser.). (O.s.i.). 160p. 1972. pap. 0.95 o.s.i. (AN1001, Award). Univ Pub & Dist.
Caisleain Oir Novel. new ed. Seamus O'Grianna. 1976. pap. 3.50 (ISBN 0-85342-461-6). Irish Bk Ctr.
Caitlin. August William Derleth. 4.00 o.p. Arkham.
Caitlyn McGregor. Kitt Brown. (Frontier Women Ser.: No. 1). 352p. (Orig.). 1981. pap. 2.95 (ISBN 0-449-14413-5, GM). Fawcett.
Cajun. Saliee O'Brien. 384p. 1982. pap. 3.50 (ISBN 0-553-20821-7). Bantam.
Cajun Odyssey: From Nova Scotia to Louisiana-with Love! Beryl Fangue Sauce Stiles. LC 82-158862. (Illus.). (pbk.) 8.99. Heritage Associates (Heritage Dr., Gautier): Order from the Author.
Cake Upon the Waters. Zoe Atkins. LC 19-13967. 1919. The Century Co.
Cake Without Icing. Maysie Greig. LC 32-12760. 1932. L. MacVeagh, Dial Press, Inc.
Cakes and Ale. William Somerset Maugham. LC 50-6793. (Modern library of the world's best books 270). 1950. Modern Library.
Cakes and Ale. William Somerset Maugham. LC 75-25349. (Maugham, William Somerset, 1874-1965. Works. 1976). 1976. 15.00 (ISBN 0-405-07807-2). Arno Press.
Cakes and Ale, and Other Favorites. William Somerset Maugham. LC 51-38089. (Cardinal edition, 19). 1951. Pocket Books.
Cakes and Ale at Woodbine: From Twelfth Night to New Year's Day. Robert Barry Coffin. LC 6-26747. 1868. Hurd and Houghton.
Cakes and Ale: Or The Skeleton in the Cupboard. William Somerset Maugham. LC 30-25744. 1930. Doubleday, Doran & Company, Inc.
Cakes and Ale: Or, The Skeleton in the Cupboard. William Somerset Maugham. LC 38-350582. 1931. Doubleday, Doran & Company, Inc.
Cakes and Ale: Or, The Skeleton in the Cupboard. William Somerset Maugham. LC 33-160712. 1933. Garden City Publishing Company, Inc.
Cakes and Ale: Or, The Skeleton in the Cupboard. William Somerset Maugham. LC 36-321175. The Sun Dial Press.
Cakes and Ale: Or, The Skeleton in the Cupboard. William Somerset Maugham. LC 44-7523. 1944. New Avon Library.
Cakes to Kill: A Mystery Novel. Henry Charlton Beck. LC 32-8910. E. P. Dutton & Co., Inc.
Cakewalk. Lee Smith. LC 81-8501. 12.95 (ISBN 0-399-12666-X). Putnam.
Calabash of Life: A Novel. Khadambi Asalache. LC 67-83364. 1967. pap., 1.50. Longmans.
Calabazas: Or, Amazing Recollections of an Arizona "City". James Cabell Brown. Valleau & Peterson.
Calabrian Summer. Marjorie McEvoy. LC 79-6540. 1980. 8.95 (ISBN 0-385-15939-0). Doubleday.
Calais. Kathleen Winsor. 672p. 1982. pap. 3.95 (ISBN 0-445-04703-8). Popular Lib.
Calais: A Novel. Kathleen Winsor. LC 78-14713. 1979. 12.95 (ISBN 0-385-14865-8). Doubleday.
Calamities of Jane. Alan McClyde. LC 73-163558. (Venus library). 1.75. Grove Press.
Calamity at Apache Wells. James R. Haning. 1972. 4.95. Lenox Hill Pr.
Calamity at Devil's Crossing. Denver Bardwell. (YA) 1973. 6.95 (Avalon). Bouregy.
Calamity at Devil's Crossing. James D. Sayers. LC 52-9205. 1952. Bouregy & Curl.
Calamity at Harwood. George Bellairs. LC 45-2833. 1945. The Macmillan Company.
Calamity Comes of Age. Gregory Baxter. LC 35-12784. The Macaulay Company.
Calamity Fair. Wade Miller, pseud. LC 50-7879. 1950. Farrar, Straus.
Calamity Jane: A Story of the Black Hills. William Loring Nunez Spencer. (On cover: Cassell's "rainbow" series of original novels. v, 1, no. 8). Cassell & Company, Limited.
Calamity Jane of Deadwood Gulch. Ethel Powelson Hueston. LC 37-21536. The Bobbs-Merrill Company.
Calamity Range. Paul Evan Lehman. LC 39-6266. The Macaulay Company.
Calamity Range: Valley of Hunted Men. Paul Evan Lehman. 1979. pap. 2.25 o.s.i. (ISBN 0-8439-0679-0). Nordon Pubns.
Calamity Row: Or, The Sunken Records. John Roy Musick. LC 7-33470. (On cover: Globe library. no. 37). 1887. Rand, McNally & Company.
Calamity Town see Dragon's Teeth.
Calamity Town: A Novel. Ellery Queen, pseud. LC 42-9585. 1942. Little, Brown and Company.
Calamity Town: A Novel. Ellery Queen, pseud. LC 47-19997. 1947. Triangle Books, the Blakiston Company.
Calamus: A Series of Letters Written During the Years 1868-1880. Walt Whitman & Bucke, Richard Maurice, 1837-1902, Ed. 1897. L. Maynard.
Calavar: Or, The Knight of the Conquest: a Romance of Mexico... Robert Montgomery Bird. LC 2-13125. 1834. Carey, Lea & Blanchard.
Calavar: Or, The Knight of the Conquest: a Romance of Mexico. By R. M. Bird... Robert Montgomery Bird. 1847. Lea and Blanchard.
Calavar; or The Knight of the Conquest: A Romance of Mexico, 2 vols. Robert Montgomery Bird. LC 78-64061. Repr. of 1834 ed. lib. bdg. 75.00 set (ISBN 0-404-17070-6). AMS Pr.
Calavar, Or, the Knight of the Conquest: A Romance of Mexico. Robert Montgomery Bird. Ed. by Curtis Dahl. (American Fiction Ser). 1970. Repr. of 1834 ed. lib. bdg. 22.50 o.s.i. Garrett Pr.
Calculated Risk. Elinore Denniston. LC 74-121984. (Red badge novel of suspense). 1970. 4.50. Dodd, Mead.
Calculated Risk. Rae Foley, pseud. (Red Badge Ser). 4.50 o.p. (ISBN 0-396-06193-1). Dodd.
Calculating. Joyce Hutton & Bill Hutton. 1975. pap. 1.95 (ISBN 0-09-910180-7, Pub. by Hutchinson). Merrimack Pub Cir.
Calculo. 4th ed. Louis Leithold. 1350p. (Span.). 1982. pap. text ed. 15.00 (ISBN 0-06-315013-1, Pub. by HarLA Mexico). Har-Row.
Calderon's Prisoner. Alice Duer Miller. LC 3-26169. 1903. C. Scribner's Sons.
Calderwood. Monica Heath. (Signet Book). 1975. (pbk.) 1.25. New American Library.
Caldo Largo. Earl Thompson. LC 76-22722. 8.95 (ISBN 0-399-11862-4). Putnam.
Caldwell Caravan: Novels and Stories. Erskine Caldwell. LC 46-4607. 1946. The World Publishing Company.
Caldwell Shadow. Dorothy Daniels. (Warner Paperback Lib. gothic). 1973. (pbk.) 0.95. Warner Paperback Lib.
Cale. Sylvia Wilkinson. 1970. 7.95 o.p. (ISBN 0-395-10958-2). HM.
Cale: A Novel. Sylvia Wilkinson. LC 76-120828. 1970. 7.95. Houghton Mifflin.
Caleb Abbott. Dexter Vinton Pierce. LC 5-39590. 1904. Farrington Printing Company.
Caleb Clickett: The Great Detective; or, Tracked by a Finger-Nail. Allen Graves. (On cover: The Pinkerton detective series, no. 45). 1890. Laird & Lee.
Caleb Conover, Railroader. complimentary ed. Albert Payson Terhune. LC 7-11205. 1907. The Authors and Newspapers Association.
Caleb Cutter, New Englander. Edwin Chapin Washburn. LC 30-3070. Washburn.
Caleb Field. A Tale of the Puritans... Margaret Oliphant Wilson Oliphant. LC 7-24127. 1851. Harper & Brother.
Caleb Field. A Tale of the Puritans. Margaret Oliphant Wilson Oliphant. (Seaside library, v. 29, no. 596). 1879. G. Munro.
Caleb Koons, a 'postle of Common Sense. Russell Kelso Carter. LC 11-1967. 1.50. The C. M. Clark Publishing Company.
Caleb Krinkle: A Story of American Life. Charles Carleton Coffin. LC 79-83924. 1969. Mnemosyne Pub. Co.
Caleb Krinkle. A Story of American Life. Charles Carleton Coffin. LC 6-26749. 1875. Lee and Shepard.
Caleb Matthews: An Idyl of the Maine Coast. Robert William McLaughlin. LC 13-148230. Eaton & Mains.
Caleb, My Son: A Novel. Lucy Daniels. LC 56-10817. 1956. Lippincott.
Caleb of the Hill Country. Charles Allen McConnell. LC 15-1051. 1914. Publishing House of the Pentecostal Church of the Nazarene.
Caleb Peaslee. Frank K Rich. LC 26-8592. Henry Altemus Company.
Caleb Pettengill, U.S.N. George Fielding Eliot. LC 56-11467. 1956. Messnor.
Caleb, the Irrepressible. Mary Moncure Paynter. LC 7-33763. (hammock series no. 6). 1883. H. A. Summer & Company.
Caleb Trench. Mary Imlay Taylor. LC 10-79343. 1910. Little, Brown, and Company.
Caleb West, Master Diver. Francis Hopkinson Smith. 1898. Houghton, Mifflin and Company.
Caleb West: Master Diver. Francis Hopkinson Smith. LC 4-15154. 1900. Houghton, Mifflin and Company.
Caleb West, Master Diver. Francis Hopkinson Smith. LC 46-30073. 1899. International Book and Publishing Company.
Caleb, Who Is Hotter Than a Two Dollar Pistol: An Historical Romance of Recent Days. Steven Ashley. LC 74-25718. 232p. 1975. 6.95 o.p. (ISBN 0-679-50536-9). McKay.
Caleb Williams. William Godwin & David McCracken. LC 77-22576. (Norton library). 3.95 (ISBN 0-393-00861-4). Norton.
Caleb Wright: A Story of the West. John Habberton. LC 1-25454. Lothrop Publishing Company.
Caleb's Bride. Norah Hess. LC 78-50088. 1978. 1.95 (ISBN 0-87216-459-4). Playboy Press.
Calendar. Edgar Wallace. LC 31-3409. Doubleday, Doran & Company, Inc.
Calendar Epic: A Novel of the Merchant Marine. James Kubeck. LC 56-102345. 1956. Putnam.
Calendar of Crime. Ellery Queen, pseud. LC 52-5000. 1952. Little, Brown.
Calendar of Love: A Novel. Clinch Calkins. LC 52-12496. 1952. Simon and Schuster.
Calendar of Love: And Other Stories. George Mackay Brown. LC 68-12582. 1968. Harcourt, Brace & World.
Calendar of Love & Other Stories. George Mackay Brown. 1968. 3.95 o.p. (ISBN 0-15-115370-1). HarBraceJ.
Calendar of Saints for Unbelievers. Glenway Wescott. LC 76-53923. (Illus.). 1977. pap. 8.95 (ISBN 0-918172-01-2). Leetes Isl.
Calendar of Sin: American Melodramas. Evelyn Scott. LC 31-28134. J. Cape & H. Smith.
Calendared Isles: A Romance of Casco Bay. Harrison Jewell Holt. LC 10-24902. 1910. 1.50. R. G. Badger.
Calentador De Fiestas. new ed. Fausto L. Corrales. (Pimienta Collection Ser). 160p. 1974. pap. 1.00 (ISBN 0-88473-219-3). Fiesta Pub.
Calf for Venus. Norah Robinson Lofts. LC 49-7634. 1949. Doubleday.
Calf for Venus see Letty.
Calf Love. Vernon Bartlett. LC 29-18547. J. B. Lippincott Company.
Calgaich the Swordsman. Gordon D. Shirreffs. LC 79-89959. 416p. (Orig.). 1980. pap. 2.50 (ISBN 0-87216-605-8). Playboy Pbks.
Calhoon. Thorne Douglas. 1978. pap. 1.75 (ISBN 0-449-13935-2, GM). Fawcett.
Calhoun Strout: Psychic. Josephine Park Holland. LC 9-14449. 1909. The Austin Publishing Company.
Caliban. Walter Lionel George. LC 20-15960. Harper & Brothers.
Caliban's Castle. Paulette Warren. (Berkley Medallion Book). 1976. (pbk.) 0.95. Berkley Publishing Corp.
Caliban's Castle, No. 1. large-type ed. Paulette Warren. 1976. pap. 0.95 (ISBN 0-425-03064-4, Medallion). Berkley Pub.
Caliban's Filibuster. Paul West. LC 78-116262. 1971. 5.95. Doubleday.
Calico Cat. Charles Miner Thompson. LC 8-30016. 1908. Houghton Mifflin Company.
Calico Palace. Gwen Bristow. 1973. pap. 2.50 (ISBN 0-671-81162-2). PB.
Calico Palace. Gwen Bristow. LC 72-106584. 1970. 12.45i (ISBN 0-690-16608-7). T Y Crowell.
Calico Shoes and Other Stories. James Thomas Farrell. LC 34-31643. The Vanguard Press.
Calif of Cordova: A Tale of Spain in the Thirteenth Century. Richard Dobson. LC 27-23865. The Christopher Publishing House.
Califfa. Alberto Bevilacqua. LC 69-15513. 1969. 5.95. Atheneum.
California. Dana Fuller Ross. 2.95 (ISBN 0-553-14260-7). Bantam Books.
California & Other States of Grace. Phyllis Theroux. 224p. 1981. pap. 2.50 (ISBN 0-449-24411-3, Crest). Fawcett.
California Bloodline. Terry McDonell. LC 79-25725. 8.95 (ISBN 0-02-583150-X). Macmillan.
California Bloodstock: A Novel. Terry McDonell. (Illus.). 1980. 8.95 o.s.i. (ISBN 0-02-583150-X). Macmillan.
California Cabellero. William Colt MacDonald. LC 36-7372. Covici-Friede.
California Coven Project. Bob Stickgold. 192p. 1981. pap. 2.25 (ISBN 0-345-28677-4, Del Rey). Ballantine.
California Dons. Ralph L. Milliken. 1967. 5.95 o.p. Valley Calif.
California Dreamers. Norman Bogner. 400p. 1982. pap. 3.50 (ISBN 0-345-30266-4). Ballantine.
California Dreamers: A Novel. Norman Bogner. LC 81-253. 14.95 (ISBN 0-671-42877-2). Wyndham Books.
California Dreaming. Roger Rapoport. 320p. (Orig.). 1982. pap. 9.95 (ISBN 0-917316-48-7). Nolo Pr.
California Experience: A Literary Odyssey. Warren A Beck, pseud. LC 76-10296. 1976. 5.95 (ISBN 0-87905-035-7). Peregrine Smith.
California Factor. Patricia Vernier. (Orig.). 1980. pap. 2.75 (ISBN 0-440-10989-2). Dell.
California Generation. Jacqueline Briskin. 1980. pap. 2.75 (ISBN 0-446-95146-3). Warner Bks.
California Generation: A Novel. Jacqueline Briskin. LC 75-103599. 1970. 7.95. Lippincott.
California Girl. (Teenage Romance Ser.). (Orig.). 1981. pap. 1.95. Bantam.
California Gold-Field Scenes: Selections from Quien Sabe's Gold-Field Manuscripts. Robert W Bigham. LC 6-13126. 1886. Southern Methodist Publishing House.
California Hit see Ataque En California.
California Kill. George G. Gilman, pseud. (Edge Ser., No. 7). 1974. pap. 1.75 (ISBN 0-523-41285-1). Pinnacle Bks.
California Ranger. Tex Holt, pseud. LC 46-20585. 1946. Arcadia House.
California Ranger. Claude Rister. LC 46-20585. 1946. Arcadia House, Inc.
California Rich. Stephen Birmingham. 1980. 16.95 (ISBN 0-671-24127-3). S&S.
California Split. Lou Cameron & Joseph Walsh. LC 74-186983. (Fawcett gold medal book). 1974. Fawcett Publications.
California Story Book. California. University, English Club. LC 10-404. 1909.
California Street. Niven Busch. (F101). 1960. Dell.
California Street: A Novel. Niven Busch. LC 59-6011. 1959. Simon and Schuster.
California Street No. 1. Elihu Blotnick. (Illus.). 1980. pap. 7.95 (ISBN 0-915090-21-X). Calif Street.
California Street, No. 2. Elihu Blotnick. (Illus.). 176p. (Orig.). 1981. pap. 6.95 (ISBN 0-915090-23-6). Calif Street.
California Three Hundred and Fifty Years Ago. Manuelo's Narrative, Tr. from the Portuguese, by a Pioneer. Cornelius Cole. 1888. S. Carson & Co.
California Thriller. Max Byrd. 224p. (Orig.). 1981. pap. 2.25 (ISBN 0-553-14508-8). Bantam.
California Time. Frederic Raphael. LC 75-5454. 1976. 7.95 (ISBN 0-03-014516-3). Holt, Rinehart and Winston.
California Trail. Henry Bedford-Jones. LC 48-2265. 1948. Phoenix Press.
Californian. Willis Todhunter Ballard. LC 75-157574. 1971. 6.95. Doubleday.
Californian: A Romance of the Last Frontier. Thomas Grant Springer. LC 36-7188. Greenberg.
Californians. Gertrude Franklin Horn Atherton. LC 68-23712. (Illus.). 1968. Gregg Press.
Californians. Gertrude Franklin Horn Atherton. LC 21-16854. (Half-title: Macmillan's standard library). 1908. Grosset & Dunlap.
Californians. new ed. Gertrude Franklin Horn Atherton. LC 8-7386. 1908. The Macmillan Company.
Californians. Louise Redfield Peattie. LC 40-4890. 1940. Doubleday, Doran & Company, Inc.
Californio. Robert MacLeod, pseud. 224p. 1981. pap. 1.75 (ISBN 0-449-14301-5). Fawcett.
Californios. Louis L'Amour. LC 73-19754. 1974. 5.95. Saturday Review Press.
Californios. Louis L'Amour. LC 74-9896. 1974. (lib. bdg.) 8.95 (ISBN 0-8161-6224-7). G. K. Hall.
Californios. Louis L'Amour. 1974. (pbk.) 0.95. Bantam Books.
Caligula. Albert Camus. Bd. with Malentendu. (Coll. Folio). pap. 3.95. French & Eur.
Calina. Lee Gardner. (Orig.). pap. 0.60 o.p. (A223X, Award). Univ Pub & Dist.
Caliph Intrigue. Robert Leigh James. LC 79-4215. 7.95 (ISBN 0-396-07673-4). Dodd, Mead.
Caliph of Bagdad: A Novel. Sylvanus Cobb. (On cover: The Popular series, no. 19). 1892. R. Bonner's Sons.
Caliph of Bagdad: A Novel. Sylvanus Cobb. LC 25-11394. 1925. George H. Doran Company.
Caliph of Cordova: Historical Romance of Moorish-Spain During the Golden Age of Abdul-Rahman III. Saul Saphire. LC 29-15566. 1929. Bloch Publishing Company.
Calix Stay. Niel Hancock. (Circle of light; 3). 1977. 1.95 (ISBN 0-445-04047-5). Popular Library.
Calked Boots & Other Northwest Writings. 3rd ed. Bert Russell. 1975. pap. 4.95 o.p. Lacon Pubs.
Calked Boots & Other Northwest Writings. 4th ed. Bert Russell. (Folklore). 1979. pap. 5.95 (ISBN 0-930344-00-6); 8.95 (ISBN 0-930344-03-0). Lacon Pubs.
Call. Cordelia Adelaide Camp Reed & Russell, Susan (Harrington) LC 25-3941. Hamilton Printing Co.
Call After Midnight. Mignon Good Eberhart. LC 64-22445. (Random House mystery). 1964. Random House.
Call After Midnight. Mignon Good Eberhart. LC 77-13549. 1978. 9.95 (ISBN 0-89340-101-3). J. Curley & Associates.
Call at Evening. Jessie Jane Ward. LC 21-1358. Herald Publishing House.
Call Back Love. Margaret Grant. LC 37-287126. Farrar & Rinehart, Inc.
Call Back the Years. Illus. by Richard Bobnick. Margarethe Erdahl Shank. LC 66-13055. 4.95. Augsburg.
Call Back Yesterday. James D. Forman. pap. 1.95 (ISBN 0-451-11851-0, AJ1851, Sig). NAL.

Call Back Yesterday. Natalie Shipman. 1945. Prentice-Hall, Inc.
Call Back Yesterday. Sara Woods, pseud. LC 82-17062. 1983. 10.95 (ISBN 0-312-11424-9). St. Martin's Press.
Call Collect. Lawrence Joers. Ed. by Juanita Tyson-Flyn. (Redwood Ser.). 96p. pap. 3.95 (ISBN 0-8163-0458-0). Pacific Pr Pub Assn.
Call Down the Storm. 1st Ed. Le Gette Blythe. LC 58-7637. 1958. Holt.
Call for a Chaperon. Sybil Bolitho. LC 36-22337. 1937. W. Morrow & Co.
Call for a Miracle. 1st Ed. Benedict Kiely. LC 51-11542. 1951. Dutton.
Call for an Exorcist. new ed. Jerome Bixby. Orig. Title: Devil's Scrapbook. 160p. 1974. pap. 1.50 o.p. (ISBN 0-87056-374-2, 6374). Brandon.
Call for Dr. Barton. Elizabeth Seifert. LC 56-109199. 1956. Dodd, Mead.
Call for Dr. Barton. Elizabeth Seifert. LC 73-791701. 1974. 6.95. Aeonian Press.
Call for Me? A New Look at Vocations. Martin W. Pable. LC 79-91056. 110p. (Orig.). 1980. pap. 2.50 (ISBN 0-87973-527-9, 527). Our Sunday Visitor.
Call for Michael Shayne. Davis Dresser. LC 49-10273. (Red badge mystery). Dodd, Mead.
Call for the Baron. rev. ed. John Creasey. LC 75-40756. 1976. 6.95 (ISBN 0-8027-5342-6). Walker.
Call for the Dead. David John Moore Cornwell. 1973. (pbk.) 0.95. Popular Lib.
Call for the Dead. John Le Carre. 1979. pap. 2.50 (ISBN 0-553-14856-7). Bantam.
Call for the Dead. John Le Carre. 1978. pap. 1.95 (ISBN 0-445-08416-2). Popular Lib.
Call for the Saint. Leslie Charteris. (Saint Ser.). 224p. 1981. pap. 2.25 (ISBN 0-441-09151-2, Pub. by Charter Bks). Ace Bks.
Call for the Saint. Leslie Charteris. 1967. pap. 0.60 o.p. (60-273). Manor Bks.
Call from Austria. Martha Albrand. LC 63-8341. 1963. Random House.
Call from Calle Moreno: By Maria Flores Pseud. 1st Ed. Mary Foster Main. LC 55-998927. 1955. Doubleday.
Call Girl. Charles Stanley Strong. LC 39-8020. Phoenix Press.
Call-Girls: A Tragi-Comedy. Arthur Koestler. LC 72-10283. 1973. 5.95 (ISBN 0-394-48435-5). Random House.
Call-Girls: A Tragic-Comedy. Arthur Koestler. 1974. (pbk.) 1.25. Dell.
Call Her Fannie. Helen Marion Edginton. LC 31-10174. 1931. The Penn Publishing Company.
Call Her Rosie: A Novel. Eva Bruce. LC 42-22825. 1942. I. Washburn.
Call Her Savage. Tiffany Thayer. LC 31-13802. 1931. C. Kendall.
Call Home the Heart. Elisabeth Ogilvie. LC 62-10599. McGraw-Hill.
Call Home the Heart: A Novel. Jessica Stirling. LC 76-28059. 1977. 8.95 (ISBN 0-312-11427-3). St. Martin's Press.
Call Home the Heart: A Novel of the Thirties. Tr. by Fielding Burke. 448p. 1983. pap. 8.95 (ISBN 0-935312-11-0). Feminist Pr.
Call House Madam,' The Story of the Career of Beverly Davis, As Told by Serge G. Wolsey Pseud. Gladys Adelina Lewis. LC 55-16607. 1954. M. Tudordale Corp.
Call House Madam," the Story of the Career of Beverly Davis, As Told by Serge G. Wolsey. Serge G Wolsey. LC 42-10818. 1942. Martin Tudordale Co.
Call If You Need Me. Mary Randall, pseud. LC 76-41683. 5.95 (ISBN 0-8007-0845-8). Revell.
Call in the Night. Susan Howatch. LC 73-79341. 1973. 6.95 (ISBN 0-8128-1602-1). Stein and Day.
Call It a Day! A Novel. Desemea Wilson. LC 28-4074. E. P. Dutton & Company.
Call It Accident. Rae Foley. ("Gothic"). 1975. (pbk.) 0.95. Dell.
Call It Accident: A Mr. Potter Mystery Novel. Elinore Denniston. LC 65-21421. (Red badge detective). 1965. Dodd, Mead.
Call It Freedom. Marian McCamy Sims. LC 37-630590. J. B. Lippincott Company.
Call It Love. Ginger Chambers. (Candlelight Ecstasy Ser.: No. 40). (Orig.). 1982. pap. 1.75 (ISBN 0-440-11128-5). Dell.
Call It Rhodesia. William Howard Baker, pseud. LC 68-15497. 1968. Putnam.
Call It Rhodesia. W. A. Ballinger, pseud. 1968. 6.95 o.p. (ISBN 0-399-10110-1). Putnam.
Call It Sleep. Henry Roth. (Equinox book). 1976. 4.95. Avon Books.
Call It Sleep. Henry Roth. LC 35-523. 1965. Cooper Square.
Call It Sleep. Henry Roth. LC 35-523. R. O. Ballou.
Call It Sleep: A Novel. Henry Roth. LC 60-13694. 1960. Pageant Books.
Call It Treason. George Locke Howe. LC 80-15043. 8.95 (ISBN 0-396-07870-2) (ISBN 0-396-07871-0). Dodd, Mead.
Call It Treason: A Novel. George Locke Howe. LC 49-10435. 1949. Viking Press.
Call McLean. George Goodchild. 320p. 1973. lib. bdg. 5.95 o.s.i. (ISBN 0-85617-671-0). White Lion Pubs.
Call Me Angie. Janet Dean. 1976. 5.50 o.p. (ISBN 0-682-48539-X). Exposition.
Call Me Angie. Janet Dean. 1976. 5.50 o.p. (ISBN 0-682-48539-X). Exposition.
Call Me Brandy. Brandon Jones. 1977. 3.95 o.p. Vantage.
Call Me Brick. Munroe Howard. LC 67-21211. (Black circle bk.). 1967. 5.00. Grove.
Call Me Captain. Paul Stanton. LC 59-5777. 1960. M. S. Mill Co. and W. Morrow.
Call Me Duke: By Harry Grey Pseud. Harry Goldberg. LC 55-723033. 1955. Crown Publishers.
Call Me Ishmael. Loyd Collins. LC 35-2814. 1935. Dodd, Mead & Company.
Call Me Ishtar. Rhoda Lerman. LC 72-92406. 1973. 6.95 (ISBN 0-385-07614-2). Doubleday.
Call Me Ishtar. Rhoda Lerman. LC 76-43495. 1977. 7.95 (ISBN 0-03-019916-6). Holt, Rinehart and Winston.
Call Me Killer. Harry Whittington. LC 51-28011. (Graphic mystery, 36). 1951. Graphic Publications.
Call Me Madam. Marianne Fournier. 1977. pap. 1.50 o.s.i. (ISBN 0-505-51136-3). Tower Bks.
Call Me Manneschewitz. Thomas John McMenamin. LC 70-143917. 1971. 5.95 (ISBN 0-684-10390-7). Scribner.
Call Me Margo. Judith St. George. Date not set. pap. 2.25 (ISBN 0-451-11850-2, AE1850, Sig). NAL.
Call Me Nate. Introd. by Elliot Paul, Illus. by Irma Selz. Wolfe Kaufman. LC 51-10483. (Banner book). 1951. Exposition Press.
Call Me Pandora. Amber Dean. LC 46-1628. 1946. Pub. for the Crime Club by Doubleday & Company, Inc.
Call Mr. Fortune. Henry Christopher Bailey. LC 21-3633. E. P. Dutton & Company.
Call My Brother Back, a Novel by Michael McLaverty. Michael McLaverty. 1939. Longmans, Green and Co.
Call of Empire. Clyde Walton Hill. LC 37-653. Tardy Publishing Company.
Call of Glengarron. Nancy Buckingham. 1980. pap. 1.95 (ISBN 0-441-09102-4). Ace Bks.
Call of Service. William Herbert Brown. LC 13-179749. The Standard Publishing Company.
Call of the Arctic. Robert J. Steelman. LC 60-12498. 1960. Coward-McCann.
Call of the Bells: A Novel. Edmund Mitchell. LC 16-24925. 1916. Menzies Publishing Company, Inc.
Call of the Blood. George Owen Baxter, pseud. LC 34-15637. The Macaulay Company.
Call of the Blood. Frederick Faust. LC 34-1563. 1934. The Macaulay Company.
Call of the Blood. Robert Smythe Hichens. LC 6-34641. 1906. Harper & Brothers.
Call of the Canyon. Zane Grey. LC 24-86787. 1924. Harper & Brothers.
Call of the Canyon. Zane Grey. LC 82-10448. 1982. 11.95 (ISBN 0-89621-386-2). Thorndike Press.
Call of the Canyon. Zane Grey. 1975. (pbk.) 0.95 (ISBN 0-671-77975-3). Pocket Books.
Call of the Cumberlands. Charles Neville Buck. LC 13-788285. 1.25. W. J. Watt & Company.
Call of the Deep: Being Further Adventures of Frank Brown. Frank Thomas Bullen. LC 8-30939. 1907. E. P. Dutton and Company.
Call of the Earth: A Novel. Averoff-Tossizza, Evangelos. LC 81-187348. 1981. 11.95. Caratzas Brothers.
Call of the East: A Romance of Far Formosa. Thurlow Fraser. LC 14-15749. 1.25. Fleming H. Revell Company.
Call of the East: Stories of Love and Adventure, by Mary and Robert Nyberg. 1st Ed. Mary Nyberg & Robert Nyberg. LC 55-113871. 1956. Exposition Press.
Call of the Farm,". Harry W Hillman. LC 11-2980. 1911. 1.50. Valley View Publishing Company.
Call of the Gun. Samuel Anthony Peeples. LC 55-44661. (Ace double novel books, D-120). 1955. Ace Books.
Call of the Heart. Barbara Cartland. (Barbara Cartland library, 23). 1975. (pbk.) 1.25. Bantam Books.
Call of the Heart. Barbara Corcoran. (Orig.). 1981. pap. 1.95 (ISBN 0-345-28668-5). Ballantine.
Call of the Heart. Wanda Dellamere. (Superromances Ser.). 384p. 1982. pap. 2.50 (ISBN 0-373-70024-5). Harlequin Bks.
Call of the Heart. L. N Way. G. W. Dillingham Company.
Call of the High Road. Vera Minshall. LC 66-25444. 1967. Zondervan Pub. House.
Call of the Hill Country. Rose B Johnston. LC 45-21686. 1945. The Wartburg Press.
Call of the Hills. Marshall Benjamin Van Leer. Jennings and Graham.
Call of the Hour. Lewis Albert Harding. LC 13-11288. 1913. The Sunflower Publishing Company.
Call of the House. Ruth Comfort Mitchell. LC 27-8551. D. Appleton & Company.
Call of the Land: A Novel of High Adventure in 4-H Club Work. Harold Morrow Sherman. LC 48-1845. 1948. M. A. Donohue.
Call of the Mate. Claud Francis Burton. LC 18-2600. 1917. Sherman, French & Company.
Call of the Mountain. Cornelia Lynde Meigs. LC 40-335916. 1940. Little, Brown and Company.
Call of the Mountains. Elizabeth Jones Boykin. Dorrance and Company.
Call of the North. Stewart Edward White. LC 41-16892. 1941. Triangle Books.
Call of the Offshore Wind. Ralph Delahaye Paine. LC 18-184001. 1918. Houghton Mifflin Company.
Call of the Owlhoot. Floyd Day. LC 52-13491. 1952. Arcadia House.
Call of the Phoenix. Dorothy Ada Feldhaus Thomas & Sleater, Charles E. I Am the Way. 1945. New Age Publishing Co.
Call of the Pines. Lucy Walker, pseud. LC 66-31657. 1966. Arcadia House.
Call of the Range. Arthur Henry Gooden. LC 51-11402. 1951. Macrae Smith.
Call of the Sea: Including: The Lost Sea, The Distant Shore, and A Sailor's Life. Jan De Hartog. LC 66-16893. 1966. 6.95. Atheneum.
Call of the Sea: Lost Sea, Distant Shore, & Sailor's Life. Jan De Hartog. LC 66-16893. (YA) 1966. 6.95 o.p. (ISBN 0-689-10063-9). Atheneum.
Call of the Soil: "L'appel Du Sol"--Prix Goncourt, 1916. Adrien Bertrand. Tr. by May, James Lewis. LC 19-15674. 1919. John Lane Company.
Call of the South. Louis Becke. LC 8-15152. 1908. J. Milne.
Call of the South. Robert Lee Durham. LC 8-9811.
Call of the Stars. Enki Bilal. Tr. by Thierry Nantier from Fr. (Illus.). 1979. pap. 2.45 (ISBN 0-918348-02-1). Flying Buttress.
Call of the Trail. Dollie Sullivan MacGregor. LC 27-6057. The Macaulay Company.
Call of the West. Rutherford George Montgomery. LC 33-638. Grosset & Dunlap.
Call of the West: By Paul Evan Pseud. Paul Evan Lehman. LC 55-14944. 1955. Avalon Books.
Call of the Western Prairie. Elizabeth Jane Leonard. LC 52-9626. 1952. Library Publishers.
Call of the Wild. John D'Amata. 3.00 o.p. Carlton.
Call of the Wild. Jack London. LC 61-1114. (Illus.). 1961. Heritage Press.
Call of the Wild. Jack London. LC 3-8560. 1903. The Macmillan Company.
Call of the Wild. Jack London. LC 9-32301. (Half-title: Macmillan's standard library). 1906. Grosset & Dunlap.
Call of the Wild. Jack London. LC 12-25072. 1912. 1.50. The Macmillan Co.
Call of the Wild. Jack London. LC 28-26458. (golden books). D. McKay.
Call of the Wild. Jack London. LC 21-4138. (On cover: Every boy's library. Boy scout edition). 1915. Grosset & Dunlap.
Call of the Wild. Jack London. LC 18-7607. 1916. The Macmillan Co.
Call of the Wild. Jack London. Ed. by Mitchill, Theodore Clarence. LC 17-31423. (Macmillan's pocket American and English classics). 1917. The Macmillan Company.
Call of the Wild. Jack London. LC 20-15623. 1919. The Macmillan Company.
Call of the Wild. Jack London. LC 24-20470. 1923. The Macmillan Company.
Call of the Wild. Mitsu Yamamoto & Jack London. LC 78-26979. (Stage 3 Newbury House reader). (Illus.). 1.25 (ISBN 0-88377-156-X). Newbury House Publishers.
Call of the Wild: And Other Stories. Jack London. Ed. by Mott, Frank Luther. LC 26-218951. (modern readers' series). 1926. The Macmillan Company.
Call of the Wild: And Other Stories. Jack London. Ed. by Mott, Frank Luther. LC 28-1744. (modern readers' series). 1927. The Macmillan Company.
Call of the Wild: And Other Stories. Jack London. Ed. by Mott, Frank Luther. LC 35-27143. (modern readers' series). 1935. The Macmillan Company.
Call of the Wild: And Other Stories. Illus. by Kyuzo Tsugami. Jack London. LC 65-21851. (Illus. jr. lib. 5927). 2.95, pap., 1.95, deluxe ed,, 3.95, bxd. Grosset.
Call of the Wild, and Other Stories. With Biographical Illus, and Pictures of Contemporary Scenes, Together with an Introd, and Captions by Louis B. Salomon. Jack London. LC 60-915417. (Great illustrated classics). 1960. Dodd. Mead.
Call of the Wild: And White Fang. Jack London. LC 68-56084. (Cambridge classics library). (Illus.). 1968. Cambridge Book Co.
Call of the Wild, and White Fang. With an Introd. by Abraham Rothberg. Jack London. LC 63-11278. (Bantam pathfinder editions. EP3). 1963. Bantam Books.
Call of the Wild. Edited by Mary Yost Sandrus. Designed by Marita Robinson. Illustrated by Leon Bishop. Jack London. LC 59-10842. 1959. Scott, Foresman.
Call of the Wild. Illustrated by Hamilton Greene. LC 63-18757. (Sunrise library). Hart Pub. Co.
Call of the Wild. Illustrated by Hamilton Greene. Jack London. LC 63-18757. (Sunrise library). Hart Pub. Co.
Call of the Wild. Illustrated by Karel Kezer. Jack London. LC 63-14831. (Macmillan classics, 12). 1963. Macmillan.
Call of the Wild. Illustrated by Lee Gregori. Jack London. LC 63-6895. (Companion library) "5458."). 1963. Grosset & Dunlap.
Call of the Wild: Illustrated by Robert Todd. Jack London. LC 56-2150. 1956. Macmillan.
Call of the Wild. Large Type Ed. Jack London. LC 66-31947. F. Watts.
Call of the Wild, The Cruise of the Dazzler, and Other Stories of Adventure: With the Author's Special Report: Gold Hunters of the North. Jack London. LC 60-12427. (Platt & Munk great writers collection). 1960. Platt & Munk.
Call of the Wild, White Fang, and Other Stories. Jack London & Andrew Sinclair. LC 80-19658. (Series: Penguin American Classics.). 1980. 3.95 (ISBN 0-14-039001-4). Penguin Books.
Call of the Wild. With an Introd. by Pierre Berton and Illus. by Henry Varnum Poor. Jack London. LC 60-24092. 1960. Printed for Members of the Limited Editions Club at the Ward Ritchie Press.
Call Out the Flying Squad, an Inspector Silver Mystery... Henry Holt. LC 33-16356. 1933. Pub. for the Crime Club, Inc., by Doubleday, Doran & Company, Inc.
Call Out the Malicia: Short Stories. John Anthony West. LC 62-14710. 1963. Dutton.
Call the Beast Thy Brother. William Oliver Turner. LC 73-83607. 1973. 5.95 (ISBN 0-385-05877-2). Doubleday.
Call the Darkness Light. N. L Zaroulis. LC 78-74714. 1979. 14.00 (ISBN 0-385-15219-1). Doubleday.
Call the Doctor. 1st Ed. Frederic Eugene Ayer. LC 54-116018. 1954. Pageant Press.
Call the Keeper. Nat Hentoff. (75276). 1968. Pocket Bks.
Call the Keeper: A Novel. Nat Hentoff. LC 66-20337. 1966. bds., 3.95. Viking.
Call the Lady Indiscreet. Paul Whelton. LC 46-150765. 1946. J. B. Lippincott Company.
Call the New World: A Novel. John Edward Jennings. LC 41-5490. 1941. The Macmillan Company.
Call the Next Witness. Phillip Mason. LC 46-25073. 1946. Harcourt, Brace and Company.
Call the Toff. John Creasey. LC 70-86396. 1969. 4.50. Walker.
Call the Turn. Zeke Masters, pseud. (Adult Western Ser.: No. 19). 1982. pap. 1.95 (ISBN 0-671-45178-2). PB.
Call the Witness. Edna Sherry. LC 60-16859. (Red badge detective). 1961. Dodd, Mead.
Call the Yard. Clevely, Hugh. LC 31-9256. Pub. for the Crime Club, Inc., by Doubleday, Doran & Company Inc.
Call to Battle: A Novel. Roderick Lull. LC 43-51005. 1943. Doubleday, Doran and Company, Inc.
Call to Geneva. Leon C. Ronce. 3.50 o.p. Carlton.
Call to Murralla. 1st Ed. George H McMurry. LC 59-133077. 1960. Harper.
Call Up the Morning. Clyde M. Brundy. 544p. 1983. 3.50 (ISBN 0-380-82339-X, 82339-X). Avon.
Call Up the Storm. Jane Donnelly. (Harlequin Romances Ser.). 192p. 1983. pap. 1.75 (ISBN 0-373-02552-1). Harlequin Bks.
Call Us Americans. Ed. by Dorothy A. Chernoff, pseud. LC 67-19095. (Illus.). 1968. Doubleday.
Call Within: A Novel. Boris Dimondstein. Ed. by Winburg, Lew Earl. LC 29-7084. 1929. Bee Dee Publishing Co., Inc.
Callaghen. Louis L'Amour. LC 78-27755. 1979. 10.95 (ISBN 0-8161-6686-2). G. K. Hall.
Callahan Goes South. Francis H Ames. LC 75-36577. 1976. 5.95 (ISBN 0-385-11262-9). Doubleday.
Callahan Goes South. Francis H Ames. LC 76-52462. 1977. 9.95 (ISBN 0-8161-6457-6). G. K. Hall.
Callahan Rides Alone. Lee Floren. 192p. 1981. pap. 1.95 (ISBN 0-505-51749-3). Tower Bks.
Callahans and the Murphys. Kathleen Thompson Norris. LC 24-8653. 1924. Doubleday, Page & Company.
Callahan's Crosstime Saloon. Spider Robinson. 1977. 1.50 (ISBN 0-441-09034-6). Ace Books.
Callahan's Crosstime Saloon. Spider Robinson. LC 78-8529. 1978. 7.95 (ISBN 0-89490-014-5). R. Enslow.

Callahans' Gamble. Francis H Ames. LC 76-89126. 1970. 5.95. Doubleday.

Callamura. Julia Pleasants. LC 7-38193. 1868. Claxton, Remsen & Haffelfinger.

Callander Square. Anne Perry. LC 79-22873. 1980. 10.00 (ISBN 0-312-11430-3). St. Martin's Press.

Callao Clue. Royce Howes. LC 36-7478. 1936. Pub. for the Crime Club, Inc., by Doubleday, Doran and Company, Inc.

Callaway Came Our Way. John C. Seabrook. 2.00 o.p. Carlton.

Callbacks. Margaret Wander Bonanno. LC 81-50315. 13.50 (ISBN 0-87223-718-4). Seaview Books.

Called and the Chosen: The Diary of Sister Ursula Auberon, Enclosed Nun at the Abbaye De la Sainte Croix, Framleghen. Monica Baldwin. LC 57-12161. 1957. Farrar, Straus and Cudahy.

Called Away. Perdita Buchan. LC 79-23689. 9.95 (ISBN 0-316-11407-3). Little, Brown.

Called Back. Frederick John Fargus. (On cover: Lovell's library. v. 8. no. 429). 1884. J. W. Lovell Company.

Called Back. Frederick John Fargus. LC 16-250513. 1915. Rand, McNally & Company.

Called Back. Philip Hamilton Gibbs. LC 53-103513. 1953. Roy.

Called Northwest. Samuel Alexander White. 1943. Phoenix Press.

Called to the Colors: And Other Stories. Caroline Atwater Mason. LC 15-22544. Christian Women's Peace Movement.

Called to the Field: A Story of Virginia in the Civil War. Lucy Meacham Kidd Thruston. 1906. Little, Brown, and Ocmpany.

Called to the Rescue. Anna Harriet Drury. LC 7-3752. 1880. G. Munro.

Callejon Sin Salida. new ed. W. B. Murphy. Tr. by Javier Lopez from Eng. (Compadre Collection Ser., Rivera y Razoni: No. 2). Orig. Title: Dead End Street. 160p. 1974. pap. 0.85 (ISBN 0-88473-609-1). Fiesta Pub.

Caller. Mary-Rose Hayes. 1979. pap. 2.25 (ISBN 0-523-40515-4). Pinnacle Bks.

Caller from Eternity. Kurt Brand. (Perry Rhodan, 106). (Illus.). Ace.

Caller of the Black. Brian Lumley. LC 70-169743. 1971. 5.00. Arkham House.

Callias. A Tale of the Fall of Athens... Alfred John Church. LC 6-25403. 1891. Flood and Vincent.

Callie Knight. Stephanie Blake. 432p. 1982. pap. 5.95 (ISBN 0-86721-075-3). Playboy Pbks.

Callie Knight. Jack Pearl, pseud. LC 73-17126. 1974. 8.95. Saturday Review Press.

Calling. Bob Randall. LC 81-8590. 12.95 (ISBN 0-671-42630-3). Simon and Schuster.

Calling Across Forever. Sam Hamill. (Orig.). 1976. pap. 4.00 (ISBN 0-914742-23-X). Copper Canyon.

Calling All Lovers. Gloria Goddard. LC 37-85646. 1937. Hillman-Curl, Inc.

Calling All Suspects. Carolyn Wells. LC 39-11996. J. B. Lippincott Company.

Calling Dr. Cardross. Hermina Black. 1972. pap. price not set o.p. (94207). Beagle Bks.

Calling Doctor Jane. Adeline McElfresh. 1957. Avalon Books.

Calling Dr. Kildare. Max Brand. LC 40-13549. 1940. Dodd, Mead & Company.

Calling Doctor Kildare. Max Brand. 1978. 15.00 (ISBN 0-86025-135-7). State Mutual Bk.

Calling Dr. Kildare. Frederick Faust. LC 40-13549. 1940. Dodd, Mead & Company.

Calling Doctor Kill. Andrew Sugar. (Enforcer Ser., No. 2). 1973. pap. 0.95 o.s.i. (75-461). Lancer.

Calling Doctor Kill! Andrew Sugar. (enforcer #2). 1973. (pbk) 0.95. Lancer Books.

Calling Doctor Merryman. Margaretta Brucker. LC 55-22308. 1954. Avalon Books.

Calling Dr. Patchwork. Ron Goulart. (Illus.). 1978. 1.50 (ISBN 0-87997-367-6). DAW Books.

Calling Nurse Blair. Lucy Agnes Hancock. LC 49-10210. 1949. Macrae-Smith-Co.

Calling of Bara. Sheila Sullivan. LC 75-32658. 1976. 7.95 (ISBN 0-525-07307-8). E. P. Dutton.

Calling of Bara. Sheila Sullivan. (Illus.). 1981. 2.50 (ISBN 0-380-53785-0). Avon Books.

Calling of Dan Matthews. Harold Bell Wright. 1909. The Book Supply Company.

Calling of Dan Matthews. Harold Bell Wright. LC 16-25023. 1909. A. L. Burt Company.

Calling of Elizabeth Courtland. Colleen L Reece. LC 81-18669. 3.95 (ISBN 0-8024-1145-2). Moody Press.

Calling of the Apostle. Zephine Humphrey. LC 1-30904. 1900. Bonnell, Silver & Co.

Calling of the Mercenaries. Arona McHugh. LC 72-84931. 1973. 8.95 (ISBN 0-385-02942-X). Doubleday.

Calling: Stories. Mary Gray Hughes. LC 80-20981. (Illinois short fiction). 10.00 (ISBN 0-252-00842-1) (ISBN 0-252-00843-X). University of Illinois Press.

Calling the Tune. Justin Huntly McCarthy. LC 13-106637. Hodder & Stoughton, George H. Doran Company.

Callingham's Girl. Arthur Somers Roche & Roche, Mrs. Ethel (Pettit) Joint Author. LC 37-1373. 1937. Dodd, Mead and Company.

Calliope Reef. Howard Rigsby. LC 65-12367. 1967. Doubleday.

Callirhoe. Maurice Sand & Da Ponte, Mrs. Sophie A., Tr. LC 7-1514. 1871. Claxton, Remsen, and Haffelfinger.

Callista: A Sketch of the Third Century. John Henry Newman. LC 22-17347. D. & J. Sadlier & Co.

Callista: A Sketch of the Third Century. John Henry Newman. LC 42-20566. (Catholic masterpiece tutorial series. Series i, no. 2). (Illus.). 1941. Sheed & Ward.

Callista: a Sketch of the Third Century. With an Introd. by Alfred Duggan. John Henry Newman. LC 62-52906. (Universe books). 1962. Newman Press.

Callista: A Tale of the Third Century. new impression. ed. John Henry Newman. LC 4-16568. 1901. Longmans, Green, and Co.

Calloused Eye... Ethel H Loban. LC 31-21435. Pub. for the Crime Club, Inc., by Doubleday, Doran & Company, Inc.

Calm Man. David Cort. LC 54-8034. (Dell first edition, 34). 1954. Dell Pub. Co.

Calm Yourself! Edward Hope Coffey. LC 34-289640. The Bobbs-Merrill Company.

Calmire. Henry Holt. LC 6-22258. 1892. Macmillan and Co.

Calmire; Man and Nature. 5th ed., rev. and enl. ed. Henry Holt. LC 5-15696. 1905. The Macmillan Company.

Calmire, Man and Nature. 6th ed., rev. ed. Henry Holt. 1906. Houghton, Mifflin and Company.

Calthorpe: Or, Fallen Fortunes. A Novel. Thomas Gaspey. LC 6-44468. 1821. T. Desilver.

Calum Tod. Norman Malcolm Macdonald. LC 77-353354. 1976. 3.50. (ISBN 0-902706-42-X) (ISBN 0-902706-39-X). Club Leabhar.

Calumet "K,". Samuel Merwin & Henry Kitchell Webster. LC 67-29813. (Illus.). 1967. NBI Press.

Calumet "K,". Samuel Merwin & Webster, Henry Kitchell. LC 1-24579. 1901. The Macmillan Company.

Calvary: A Novel. Octave Mirbeau & Rich, Louis, Tr. LC 22-710230. 1922. Lieber & Lewis.

Calvary Alley. Alice Caldwell Hegan Rice. LC 17-26784. 1917. The Century Co.

Calvert of Strathore. Abbe Carter Goodloe. LC 3-3871. 1903. C. Scribner's Sons.

Calvin Paxton's Patmos. James Henry McLaren. LC 99-1153. 1898. The Pilgrim Press.

Caly. Sharon Combes. 288p. (Orig.). 1980. pap. 2.50 (ISBN 0-89083-624-8). Zebra.

Calypso. Ed McBain. 208p. 1980. pap. 1.95 (ISBN 0-553-13399-3). Bantam.

Calypso: A Novel. Ed McBain. 1979. 10.95 (ISBN 0-670-20030-1). Viking Pr.

Calypso: An 87th Precinct Novel. Evan Hunter. LC 78-26874. 1979. 8.95 (ISBN 0-670-20030-1). Viking Press.

Cam. Nell H Scullen. LC 51-14898. 1951. Pageant Press.

Cam Clarke. John Henry Walsh. LC 16-6056. 1916. The Macmillan Company.

Cama-I Book. Ed. by Ann Vick. LC 82-45127. (Illus.). 416p. 1983. 19.95 (ISBN 0-385-15522-4, Anchor Pr); pap. 9.95 (ISBN 0-385-15212-4, Anch). Doubleday.

Camber of Culdi. Katherine Kurtz. LC 76-6977. 1.95 (ISBN 0-345-24590-3). Ballantine Books.

Camberwell Beauty. Louis Golding. LC 35-73830. Farrar & Rinehart, Inc.

Camberwell Beauty, and Other Stories. Victor Sawdon Pritchett. LC 74-5215. 1974. 6.95 (ISBN 0-394-49222-6). Random House.

Cambodia. Nick Carter. (Nick Carter Ser.). (O.s.i.). (Orig.). 1970. pap. 0.60 o.s.i. (A686X, Award). Univ Pub & Dist.

Cambodia File. Jack Anderson & Bill Pronzini. LC 80-5447. 1981. 3.95 (ISBN 0-385-14984-0). Doubleday.

Cambodian Quest. Robert Joseph Casey. LC 31-4178. The Bobbs-Merrill Company.

Cambric Mask: A Romance. Robert William Chambers. 1899. F. A. Stokes Company.

Cambridge Cavalcade. Victoria Amey. 1982. 6.95 (ISBN 0-533-04990-3). Vantage.

Camden; a Tale of the South... John Alexander McClung. LC 8-2120. 1830. Carey & Lea.

Camden Ruby Murder. Adam Bliss. LC 31-8999. Barse & Co.

Camden's Eyes. Austin McGiffert Wright. LC 69-15159. 1969. 5.95. Doubleday.

Came a Cavalier. Frances Parkinson Wheeler Keyes. 1974. (pbk.) 1.75 (ISBN 0-671-78699-7). Pocket Books.

Came a Cavalier. Frances Parkinson Wheeler Keyes. LC 49-3392. 1949. Sun Dial Press.

Came a Cavalier. Frances Parkinson Wheeler Keyes. LC 47-11106. 1947. J. Messner.

Came a Dark Rider. Edwina Taylor. 1974. (pbk.) 0.95 (ISBN 0-671-77787-4). Pocket Books.

Came a Gentleman: By Zas Fortmayer. 1st Ed. Aenida V Gonzalez Fortmayer. LC 56-5495. 1956. Vantage Press.

Came a Spider. Edward Levy. LC 78-57318. 8.95 (ISBN 0-87795-191-8). Arbor House.

Came a Stranger. Mair Unsworth. 1973. (pbk.) 0.75. Ace Books.

Came Back with the Wind: A Novel. Joseph M Kaufer. LC 52-11884. 1952. Vantage Press.

Came the Dawn. Daughters of St. Paul. (Encounter Ser.). (Illus.). 102p. 1982. 3.00 (ISBN 0-8198-1402-4, EN0045); pap. 2.00 (ISBN 0-8198-1403-2). Dghtrs St Paul.

Camel Gate. Mary Foot Griffing. LC 53-1961. Vantage Press.

Camel Trek. Rex Regan. LC 35-32779. R. Speller, Inc.

Camel Xiangzi. She Lao. LC 81-47584. 17.50 (ISBN 0-253-31296-5) (ISBN 0-253-20275-2). Indiana University Press.

Camelephamoose. Donald Hough. LC 46-6382. 1946. Duell, Sloan and Pearce.

Camelia-Lady: "La Dame Aux Camelias"). The True Original from Which Have Been Adapted for the Stage the Drama of "Camille" and the Opera of "La Traviata." Translated Literally from the French of Alexandre Dumas, the Younger... Alexandre Dumas. LC 6-42312. 1857. E. J. Hicken.

Camellia. Pearle Melville Garrett. LC 6-407138. 1897. News Printing Company.

Camelot see Idylls of the King: Selections.

Camelot Caper. Elizabeth Peters, pseud. LC 75-75694. 1969. 4.95. Meredith Press.

Camelot in Orbit. Arthur H. Landis. (Science Fiction Ser.). (Orig.). 1978. pap. 2.35 (ISBN 0-87997-782-5, UE1782). DAW Bks.

Cameo. Wendy Leeds. 320p. (Orig.). 1982. pap. 3.25 (ISBN 0-8439-1022-4, Leisure Bks). Nordon Pubns.

Cameo. Helen Topping Miller. LC 51-11039. 1951. Bobbs-Merrill.

Cameo Lady. Frances Allen Harris. LC 22-95719. Dorrance.

Cameo of the Empress. Sigmund Krausz. LC 12-20642. 1.25. Laird & Lee.

Cameos. Octavus Roy Cohen. LC 31-20076. 1931. D. Appleton and Company.

Cameos. Marie Corelli. LC 75-106278. (Short story index reprint series). 1970. Books for Libraries Press.

Cameos. Marie Corelli. LC 6-28746. 1896. J. B. Lippincott Company.

Cameos. Marie Corelli. LC 1-30966. (Perfection series). 1901. Street & Smith.

Camera, a Novel. Herbert D Kastle. LC 59-111960. 1959. Simon and Schuster.

Camera Always Lies. Hugh Hood. LC 67-19201. 1967. Harcourt, Brace & World.

Camera Chicks. Hector Lamar. pap. 1.95 o.p. (8057). Cameo.

Camera Clue. George Harmon Coxe. 1937. A. A. Knopf.

Camera Fiend. Ernest William Hornung. LC 11-5186. 1911. C. Scribner's Sons.

Cameron. William Shambough. LC 81-65661. (Double D Western Ser.). 192p. 1981. 10.95 (ISBN 0-385-17589-2). Doubleday.

Cameron Hall: A Story of the Civil War. Mary Anne Cruse. LC 6-31618. 1867. J. B. Lippincott & Co.

Cameron Hill. Mary Kay Simmons. 1979. 1.75 (ISBN 0-671-81026-X). Pocket Books.

Cameron Hill: The History of a Crime; a Novel. 1st Ed. Martin Flavin. LC 57-8204. 1957. Harper.

Cameron in the Gap. Philip McCutchan. LC 83-2895. 1983. 9.95 (ISBN 0-312-11448-6). St. Martin's Press.

Cameron Pride: Or, Purified by Suffering. A Novel. Mary Jane Hawes Holmes. LC 12-259531. G. W. Carleton & Co.

Cameron Pride; or, Purified by Suffering. A Novel. Mary Jane Hawes Holmes. 1891. G. W. Dillingham, Successor to G. W. Carleton & Co.

Cameron Pride; or, Purified by Suffering. A Nove. Mary Jane Hawes Holmes. (Madison square series, no. 38,). 1894. G. W. Dillingham.

Cameron Story. Morton Cooper. (Crest bk., P1767). 1972. 1.25. Fawcett.

Cameron Story: A Novel. Morton Cooper. LC 78-134216. 1971. 6.95. Bernard Geis Associates.

Cameronians. A Novel. James Grant. LC 6-27670. (Franklin square library, no. 206). Harper & Brothers.

Camerons. Robert Crichton. 1974. (pbk.) 1.95. Warner Paperback Library.

Camerons: A Novel. Robert Crichton. LC 72-2249. 1972. 7.95 (ISBN 0-394-46582-2). Knopf.

Cameron's Landing. Anne Stuart. LC 76-50792. 1977. 6.95 (ISBN 0-385-12077-X). Doubleday.

Camerton Slope: A Story of Mining Life. R. F Bishop. Cranston & Curtis.

Camilla. Fanny Burney. Ed. by Edward Bloom & Lillian D. Bloom. (Oxford English Novels Ser). 500p. 1972. 22.95x o.p. (ISBN 0-19-255327-5). Oxford U Pr.

Camilla. Madeleine L'Engle. LC 65-21416. 4.50. Crowell.

Camilla. Beatrice Marean. LC 22-19059. 1922. The Roxburgh Publishing Company, Inc.

Camilla. Elizabeth Robins. LC 18-18534. 1918. 1.60. Dodd, Mead and Company.

Camilla. A Novel. Richert Vogt Von Koch. LC 7-14194. T. Y. Crowell & Company.

Camilla: A Romance. Anne Stretton. LC 34-25175. 1934. W. Morrow & Company.

Camilla Dickinson: A Novel. Madeleine L'Engle. LC 51-3595. 1951. Simon and Schuster.

Camilla: or, A Picture of Youth. Frances D'Arblay, pseud. LC 1-5179. 1797. Printed by Manning & Loring, for S. Hall, W. Spotswood, J. White, Thomas & Andrews, D. West, E. Larkin, W. P. & Lemuel Blake, and J. West.

Camilla: Or, A Picture of Youth. Frances D'Arblay, pseud. LC 1-5180. 1797. S. Campbell.

Camilla: Or, A Picture of Youth. Frances Burney D'Arblay. LC 72-192391. (Oxford English novels). 1972. 6.50 (ISBN 0-19-255327-5). Oxford University Press.

Camille. Alexandre Dumas. LC 26-8619. (Half-title: The modern library of the world's best books). 1925. The Modern Library.

Camille. Alexandre Dumas. LC 27-877531. Grosset & Dunlap.

Camille. Alexander Dumas Fils. 2.95 o.p. (69); PLB 2.69g o.p. Modern Lib.

Camille: Illustrated by Bernard Lamotte. La Dame Aux Camelias, the Authorized Translation into English by Edmund Gosse, with an Introd. by Andre Maurois, a Prefatory Letter from the Author, and A Memoir of Marie Duplessis by Jules Janin. Alexandre Dumas. LC 55-13942. 1955. Limited Editions Club.

Camille: Or, The Camelia-Lady: ("La Dame Aux Camelias"). The Only True, Complete, and Original Translation. From Which Have Been Adapted for the Stage the Drama of "Camille" and the Oopera of "La Traviata." A Literal Translation from the French of Alexandre Dumas, the Younger. Alexandre Dumas. LC 6-42311. T. B. Peterson and Brothers.

Camille: Or, The Fate of a Coquette. Alexandre Dumas. LC 7-1507. (On cover: Lovell's library. no. 992). J. W. Lovell Company.

Camille Two Thousand. Sebastian Grant. (O.s.i.). (Orig.). 1969. pap. 0.75 o.s.i. (A457S, Award). Univ Pub & Dist.

Camino. Miguel Delibes, pseud. Ed. by Jose Amor Y Vasques & Ruth H. Kossoff. (Illus.). 1965. pap. text ed. 3.95 o.p. (ISBN 0-03-056605-3, HoltC). HR&W.

Camiola, a Girl with a Fortune. Justin McCarthy. (On cover: Seaside library. Pocket ed., no. 602). 1885. G. Munro.

Camomile: An Invention. Catherine MacFarlane Carswell. LC 22-9660. Harcourt, Brace and Company.

Camors. A Love Story. Octave Feuillet. T. B. Peterson & Brothers.

Camors: Or, Life Under the New Empire. From the French of Octave Feuillet... Octave Feuillet. LC 44-153317. 1868. Blelock & Company.

Camp. Alan Saperstein. LC 82-5811. 1982. 12.95 (ISBN 0-89919-094-4). Ticknor & Fields.

Camp. Jonathan Trask. (Belmont Tower Book). 1977. 1.50 (ISBN 0-505-51214-9). Tower Pubns.

Camp. Gordon M. Williams. LC 66-223446. bds., 5.95. Stein & Day.

Camp. Gordon M. Williams. (U6116). 1968. Ballantine.

Camp and Cabin: Sketches of Life and Travel in the West. Rossiter Worthington Raymond. 1880. Fords, Howard, & Hulbert.

Camp Brave Pine: A Camp Fire Girl Story. Harriet Theresa Smith Comstock. LC 13-18723. 1913. 1.25. Thomas Y. Crowell Company.

Camp Concentration. Thomas M Disch. LC 69-10960. (Doubleday science fiction). 1969. 4.95. Doubleday.

Camp Doctor. Florence Stonebraker. LC 43-8703. 1943. Phoenix Press.

Camp-Fire and Wigwam. By Edward S. Ellis... Edward Sylvester Ellis. LC 7-39305. ("Log cabin series."no. 2). The John C. Winston Co.

Camp-Fire Boys in African Jungles. Latharo Hoover. LC 30-10609. (His Camp-fire boy series). A. L. Burt Company.

Camp-Fire Boys: In Australiam Gold Fields, by Latharo Hoover... Latharo Hoover. LC 32-127249. (His Camp-fire boys series.). A. L. Burt Company.

Camp Fire Stories. A Series of Sketches of the Union Army in the Southwest. Edward Anderson. LC 6-21345. 1896. Star Publishing Company.

Camp Fires of the Red Men: Or, A Hundred Years Ago. Jason Rockwood Orton. 1855. J. C. Derby.

Camp Follower. LC 42-21231. 1942. Phoenix Press.

Camp Follower. LC 76-162236. (Confederate Imprints Collection Ser). 64p. 1973. Repr. of 1864 ed. 6.00 o.p. (ISBN 0-405-04341-4). Arno.

Camp Followers. Translated from the Italian by Archibald Calquhoun. 1st Ed. Ugo Pirro. LC 57-9001. 1958. Dutton.

Camp Girl. Frank Anvic, pseud. 192p. (Orig.). 1973. pap. 1.95 o.p. (ISBN 0-87977-191-7, DBB191). Dansk Blue Bk.

Camp Grant Massacre: A Novel. Elliott Arnold. LC 75-25995. 1976. 9.95 (ISBN 0-671-22193-0). Simon and Schuster.

Camp Jester; or, Amusement for the Mess. LC 76-162236. (Confederate Imprints Collection Ser.). 71p. 1973. Repr. of 1864 ed. 7.00 o.p. (ISBN 0-405-04342-2). Arno.

Camp-Meeting Murders. Vance Randolph & Clemens, Nancy. LC 36-18973. 1936. The Vanguard Press.

Camp-Meeting Murders. Vance Randolph & Clemens, Nancy, Pseud., Joint Author. LC 45-5018. (On cover: Prize mystery novels. No. 15). 1945.

Camp Nurse. Arlene Hale. 1975. (pbk.) 0.75. Ace Books.

Camp Nurse. Arlene Hale. 1976. 1.25. Ace.

Camp of All Saints. Translated by Norbert Guterman. Tadeusz Nowakowski. LC 61-13394. 1962. St. Martin's Press.

Camp of Refuge. Charles Macfarlane & Gomme, Sir George Laurence, 1853-1916, Ed. LC 24-25002. (Half-title: Library of historical novels and romances, ed. by G. L. Gomme). 1897. Longmans, Green, and Co; Etc., Etc.

Camp of the Saints. Jean Raspail. LC 74-34283. 1975. 8.95 (ISBN 0-684-14240-6). Scribner.

Camp of the Saints. Jean Raspail. 1977. 1.95 (ISBN 0-441-09120-2). Ace Books.

Campaign: A Political Novel. Fred Brown Morrill. LC 17-24972. 1917. The Neale Publishing Company.

Campaign Courtship. Paul Penniman. LC 15-11877. 0.50. The American Issue Publishing Company.

Campaign for Love. Jane Bliss. LC 46-21127. 1946. Gramercy Publishing Co.

Campaign of Chaos Seventeen Seventy-Six: In the Jaws of the Juggernaut an Eaglet Held the Stars. Peter Henderson. LC 75-9231. (Illus.). 1975. 16.00 (ISBN 0-915528-01-0). Archives Ink.

Campaign Trail Girls. Oliver Talbert. 192p. (Orig.). 1973. pap. 1.95 o.p. (ISBN 0-87056-354-8, 6354). Brandon.

Campaign Train. Mildred Gordon. LC 52-9063. 1952. Published for the Crime Club by Doubleday.

Campanile Murders. Elwyn Whitman Chambers. LC 33-23506. 1933. D. Appleton-Century Company, Incorporated.

Campbell's Kingdom: By Hammond Innes Pseud. 1st American Ed. Hammond-Innes, Ralph. LC 52-6405. 1952. Knopf.

Campbell's Kingdom. 1st American Ed. Hammond Innes. LC 52-6405. 1952. Knopf.

Campeon De Violencia. new ed. John Benteen. Tr. by Jacinto De Torres from Eng. (Compadre Collection Ser.: Fargo: No. 5). Orig. Title: Fargo Is His Name, Violence Is His Game. 160p. (Span.). 1975. pap. 0.85 (ISBN 0-88473-515-X). Fiesta Pub.

Campeonato De Sexo. Roberto Ramirez. (Pimienta Collection Ser). (Span.). 1977. pap. 1.00 (ISBN 0-88473-263-0). Fiesta Pub.

Camperlea Girls. Olivia Manning. LC 71-81002. 1969. 4.95. Coward-McCann.

Campfire Chillers. E. M. Freeman. LC 79-28318. 1980. 6.95 (ISBN 0-914788-23-X). East Woods Press.

Camphene Lamp: Or, Touch Not, Taste Not, Handle Not... Mary Hinckley. LC 13-17573. 1852. J. P. Walker.

Camping in Covenant Community. Geneva Giese. (Illus., Orig.). 1967. pap. 3.45 o.p. (ISBN 0-8042-9867-X). John Knox.

Camping on the Blue Ridge: Near the "Lick Log" Tunnel. E H Amis. LC 6-40. Presbyterian Committee of Publication.

Camping Together As Christians. John Ensign & Ruth S. Ensign. LC 58-6252. 1958. pap. 1.50 (ISBN 0-8042-1176-0). John Knox.

Campion Diamonds. Rebecca Sophia Clarke. LC 29-252992. (The hearthstone series.). 1897. Lee and Shepard Publishers.

Camps and Quarters. Archibald Forbes & Henty, George Alfred, 1832-1902. LC 13-177249. 1889. Ward, Lock and Co.

Campus Aflame. J. Edwin Orr. LC 71-185801. (Orig.). 1972. pap. text ed. 3.25 o.p. (ISBN 0-8307-0156-7, 5400406). Regal.

Campus Killings. Jessica Martin. 2.25 (ISBN 0-505-51609-8). Tower Publications.

Campus Memories. Lincoln Hulley. E. O. Painter Printing Co.

Campus Ministry. Ed. by George Earnshaw et al. 6.95 o.p. (ISBN 0-8170-0327-4). Judson.

Campus Murders. Ellery Queen, pseud. (Orig.). 1969. pap. 0.75 o.p. (ISBN 0-447-74527-1). Lancer.

Campus Nymph. Dan Gross. pap. 1.95 o.s.i. (Venus). Grove.

Campus on the River. William Van O'Connor. LC 60-6235. 1959. Crowell.

Campus Sleep-in. Leslie Adirondack. LC 72-28557. (Traveller's companion series, TC-497). 1.95. Traveller's Companion, Inc.

Campus Town. Hart Stilwell. 1950. Doubleday.

Can a Man Be True? Winifred Graham Cory. LC 15-5821. 1915. 1.00. M. Kennerley.

Can All This Grandeur Perish? and Other Stories. James Thomas Farrell. LC 37-7711. The Vanguard Press.

Can I Get There by Candlelight. Julius Horwitz. 1964. 4.50 o.p. Atheneum.

Can Love Sin? Mark Douglas. LC 6-35885. T. B. Peterson & Brothers.

Can She Atone? Abby Whitney Brown. LC 6-19372. 1880. J. B. Lippincott & Co.

Can Such Things Be? Ambrose Gwinnett Bierce. LC 73-153560. 1972. 5.95 (ISBN 0-85617-005-4). White Lion.

Can Such Things Be? Ambrose Gwinnett Bierce. LC 76-6978. 1976. 9.95 (ISBN 0-89190-185-X). American Reprint Co.

Can Such Things Be? Ambrose Gwinnett Bierce. LC 76-144152. (Short story index reprint series). 1971. (ISBN 0-8369-3767-8). Books for Libraries Press.

Can Such Things Be? Ambrose Gwinnett Bierce. LC 6-12103. The Cassell Publishing Co.

Can Such Things Be? Ambrose Gwinnett Bierce. LC 3-331. 1903. The Neale Publishing Company.

Can the Old Love? A Novel. Zadel Barnes Buddington. LC 6-19650. (On cover: Osgood's library of novels, no. 4). 1871. J. R. Osgood and Company.

Can This Be Love? Louisa Taylor Parr. LC 7-34719. 1893. Longmans, Green and Co.

Can This Be Wrong! Harriet Theresa Smith Comstock. LC 37-630623. 1937. Doubleday, Doran & Company, Inc.

Can We Know? Dale Rhoton & Elaine Rhoton. 1972. pap. 0.95 o.p. (ISBN 0-87508-465-6). Chr Lit.

Can Women Forget? Florence Riddell. LC 29-20109. 1929. J. B. Lippincott & Company.

Can You Feel Anything When I Do This? Robert Sheckley. 1974. (pbk.) 0.95. DAW Books.

Can You Feel Anything When I Do This? Robert Sheckley. LC 70-163095. (Doubleday science fiction). 1971. 4.95. Doubleday.

Can You Forgive Her? Anthony Trollope. LC 75-313883. (Palliser novels of Anthony Trollope). (Illus.). 1973. 3.00. (ISBN 0-19-254611-2) (ISBN 0-19-281143-6). Oxford University Press.

Can You Forgive Her? Anthony Trollope. LC 4-16585. (On cover: The parliamentary novels 1). 1903. Dodd, Mead & Company.

Can You Forgive Her? Anthony Trollope. LC 12-29443. (Half-title: The new pocket library). John Lane.

Can You Forgive Her? Anthony Trollope. LC 39-27169. (Half-title: The world's classics. 468-469). 1938. Oxford University Press, H. Milford.

Can You Tell Me How What You Are Doing Now Is to Do Something Philosophical? Peter H. Barnett. pap. 5.00. Assembling Pr.

Can You Trust Your Daughter? Madeleine Seymour. LC 32-30527. A. H. King.

Cana and Wine. Frances Casey Kerns. 1979. 2.50 (ISBN 0-446-82951-X). Warner Books.

Cana Cathedral: A Novel. Charles H Keller. LC 62-17318. 1962. Christopher Pub. House.

Cana Diversion. William Campbell Gault. (Raven House Mysteries Ser.). 224p. 1982. pap. 2.25 (ISBN 0-373-63029-8, Pub. by Worldwide). Harlequin Bks.

Canaan. Jose Pereira Da Graca Aranha. LC 75-44124. 1977. 34.95. H. Fertig.

Canaan. Jose Pereira Da Graca Aranha. Tr. by Lorente, Mariano Joaquin. LC 20-4216. 1920. The Four Seas Company.

Canaan. Jose Pereira De Graca Aranha. LC 75-44124. 1976. H. Fertig.

Canada Doctor: A Novel of to-Day. Clair Willard Perry & Pell, John Leggett Everitt. LC 33-33945. Hale, Cushman & Flint.

Canadian-American Pitchman. Ellis J. Brace. LC 73-76216. 1973. 5.95 (ISBN 0-8059-1847-7). Dorrance.

Canadian Bankclerk. John Preston Buschlen. LC 74-166663. (Toronto reprint library of Canadian prose and poetry). 1973. (ISBN 0-8020-7519-3). University of Toronto Press.

Canadian Ben. Steven L. Carson. LC 79-51132. (Illus.). 238p. 1979. 9.95 (ISBN 0-918628-25-3); pap. 5.95 (ISBN 0-918628-26-1). Bunkhouse.

Canadian Brothers: Or, The Prophecy Fulfilled: a Tale of the Late American War. John Richardson. LC 76-11733. (Literature of Canada, poetry and prose in reprint; 18). (Illus.). 18.50 (ISBN 0-8020-2179-4) (ISBN 0-8020-6264-4). University of Toronto Press.

Canadian Crisis. Don Pendleton. (Executioner Ser.: No. 24). 192p. 1975. pap. 1.75 (ISBN 0-523-40760-2). Pinnacle Bks.

Canadian Crisis. Don Pendleton. (executioner#24). 1975. (pbk.) 1.25 (ISBN 0-523-00779-5). Pinnacle Books.

Canadian Girl in London. Sara Jeannette Duncan Cotes. LC 8-14336. 1908. The Macmillan Company.

Canadian Gold. Kurt Mueller. 2.75 o.p. Carlton.

Canadian Healing Oil. Juan Antonio Butler. LC 75-310966. (Illus.). 8.95 (ISBN 0-88778-101-2). P. Martin Associates.

Canadian Kill. Joseph Nazel. (Iceman#6). 1974. (pbk.) 1.50 (ISBN 0-87067-462-5). Holloway House.

Canadian Nights. William Albert Hickman. LC 74-144157. (Short story index reprint series). (Illus.). 1971. (ISBN 0-8369-3772-4). Books for Libraries Press.

Canadian Nights. William Albert Hickman. LC 14-14363. 1914. 1.30. The Century Co.

Canadian Senator: A Novel. Christopher Oakes. LC 7-33273. (On cover: Lovell's Westminster series, no. 29). United States Book Company, Successors to J. W. Lovell Company.

Canadian Short Stories. Ed. by Raymond Knister. LC 79-160938. (Short story index reprint series). 1971. (ISBN 0-8369-3917-4). Books for Libraries Press.

Canadian Short Stories. Robert Leigh Weaver. pap. 7.50x (ISBN 0-19-540134-4). Oxford U Pr.

Canadian Short Stories: Selected and with an Introd. by Robert Weaver. Robert Leigh Weaver. LC 69-4671. (World's classics, 573). 1960. Oxford University Press.

Canadian Short Stories, Third Series. Robert Leigh Weaver. LC 79-313105. (Illus.). 1978. 6.50 (ISBN 0-19-540291-X). Oxford University Press.

Canadians. Lee D. Willoughby. (Making of America Ser.: No. 38). 256p. (Orig.). 1983. pap. 3.25 (ISBN 0-440-00978-2, Emerald). Dell.

Canadians of Old. Philippe Aubert De Gaspe & Roberts, Charles George Douglas, 1860- Tr. LC 6-44409. (On cover: Appletons' town and country library, no. 62). 1890. D. Appleton and Company.

Canal Boat Fracas. Louise Hale. LC 27-6049. H. Holt and Company.

Canal Town: A Novel. Samuel Hopkins Adams. LC 51-19147. (Forum books). 1945. World Pub. Co.

Canal Town: A Novel. Samuel Hopkins Adams. LC 44-40112. 1944. Random House.

Canal Water and Whiskey: Tall Tales from the Erie Canal Country. Illus. by Norman Truesdale. Marvin A Rapp. LC 65-22368. 3.95. Twayne.

Canalino. 1st Ed. Marianne Criswell. LC 54-6744. 1954. Pageant Press.

Canaris Legacy. Raymond Hitchcock. LC 80-23514. 1980. 10.95 (ISBN 0-312-11817-1). St. Martin's Press.

Canary. Tony Cohan. LC 80-2045. 1981. 13.95 (ISBN 0-385-17086-6). Doubleday.

"Canary" Murder Case. S. S. Van Dine, pseud. Repr. lib. bdg. 19.10x (ISBN 0-89190-513-8). Am Repr-Rivercity Pr.

Canary Murder Case. S. S. Van Dine, pseud. 1980. lib. bdg. 10.95 (ISBN 0-8398-2554-4, Gregg). G K Hall.

Canary Murder Case. S. S. Van Dine, pseud. 1979. pap. 2.25 (ISBN 0-684-16404-3, SL 900, ScribT). Scribner.

Canary Murder Case. S. S. Van Dine, pseud. 1981. 18.95x (Pub. by Remploy England). State Mutual Bk.

"Canary" Murder Case. Willard Huntington Wright. LC 79-22542. (Gregg Press Mystery Fiction Series). 1980. 2.25 (ISBN 0-8398-2554-4). Gregg Press.

"Canary" Murder Case: A Philo Vance Story. Willard Huntington Wright. LC 27-159726. (Half-title: The Philo Vance series). 1927. C. Scribner's Sons.

"Canary" Murder Case: A Philo Vance Story. Willard Huntington Wright. LC 29-5224. Grosset & Dunlap.

Canary Yellow. Elizabeth Cadell. LC 65-104436. 1965. 3.95. Morrow.

Canas y Barro see Tres Novelas Valencianas.

Cancel All Our Vows. John Dann MacDonald. LC 53-623014. 1953. Appleton-Century-Crofts.

Cancel All Our Vows. Elisabeth Bertram Margetson. 1945. Arcadia House, Inc.

Canceled Accounts. Harris Greene. LC 72-83143. 1972. 5.95 (ISBN 0-385-06345-8). Doubleday.

Canceled Accounts. Harris Greene. 1976. (pbk.) 1.50. Dell.

Cancelled in Red. Hugh Pentecost. LC 39-18884. 1939. Dodd, Mead & Company.

Cancelled in Red. Judson Pentecost Philips. LC 39-13884. 1939. Dodd, Mead & Company.

Cancelled Will. Eliza Ann Dupuy. LC 78-164559. (American fiction reprint series). 1971. (ISBN 0-8369-7035-7). Books for Libraries Press.

Cancelled Will. Eliza Ann Dupuy. LC 11-15079. T. B. Peterson & Brothers.

Cancer, Communism, and Christ: A Story of Christian Service and Victory. 1st Ed. Z Buford Randall. LC 58-59751. 1958. Greenwich Book Publishers.

Cancer in My Left Ball. John Giorno. LC 73-76849. (Illus.). 1973. 15.00 (ISBN 0-87110-100-9); pap. 6.00 (ISBN 0-87110-104-1). Ultramarine Pub.

Cancer Syndrome. Ralph W. Moss. LC 79-2300. 320p. 1982. pap. 4.95 (ISBN 0-394-17655-3, B-468, BC). Grove.

Cancer Ward. Aleksandr Isaevich Solzhenitsyn. LC 68-8813. 1969. 10.00. Farrar, Straus and Giroux.

Cancer Ward. Aleksandr Isaevich Solzhenitsyn. LC 68-58411. 1968. 8.50. Dial Press.

Cancerqueen, and Other Stories. Tommaso Landolfi. LC 75-150400. 1971. 7.95. Dial Press.

Candace & Other Stories. Alan Cheuse. 104p. 1980. 9.50 (ISBN 0-918222-18-4); pap. 4.50 (ISBN 0-918222-19-2). Apple-Wood.

Candaules' Wife, and Other Old Stories. Emily James Smith Putnam & Herodotus. LC 72-169559. (Short story index reprint series). 1971. (ISBN 0-8369-4022-9). Books for Libraries Press.

Candaules' Wife and Other Old Stories. Emily James Smith Putnam & Herodotus. LC 26-14725. 1926. G. P. Putnam's Sons.

Candelaria. The Guide. Hendrik Conscience. LC 6-28067. (Catholic library, v. 30). 1898. C. Wildermann.

Candid Adventurer. Anna Coleman Ladd. LC 13-4612. 1913. 1.25. Houghton Mifflin Company.

Candid Courtship. Madge Mears. LC 17-23340. 1917. John Lane.

Candid Impostor. George Harmon Coxe. LC 68-10381. 1968. Knopf.

Candida. George B. Shaw. (Plays Ser.). 1950. pap. 2.95 (ISBN 0-14-048103-6). Penguin.

Candida. Francois Marie Arouet De Voltaire. LC 78-110479. 1.75. Full Court Press.

Candidate. Luis Ricardo Alonso. LC 72-192514. 1972. 0.95 (ISBN 0-671-77619-3). Pocket Books.

Candidate: A Political Romance. Joseph Alexander Altsheler. 1905. Harper & Brothers.

Candidate for Hell. Deta Petersen Neeley. LC 39-16406. 1939. Meador Publishing Company.

Candidate for Lilies. Roger d'Este Burford. LC 34-179748. 1934. A. A. Knopf.

Candidate for Love. Maysie Greig. LC 47-31068. 1947. Random House.

Candidate for Murder. Charles C. Nelson. LC 73-84423. (Illus.). 1973. 6.95 (ISBN 0-8059-1900-7). Dorrance.

Candidate for Murder... Mortimer Post. LC 37-27083. 1936. Pub. for the Crime Club, Inc., by Doubleday, Doran & Co., Inc.

Candidate for Romance. Florence Stonebraker. LC 48-391787. 1948. Arcadia House.

Candidate for Truth. John Davys Beresford. LC 12-12866. 1912. 1.35. Little, Brown, and Company.

Candidate's Blood. Lionel Derrick, pseud. (Penetrator Ser.: No. 37). 192p. (Orig.). 1980. pap. 1.75 (ISBN 0-523-40674-6). Pinnacle Bks.

Candidate's Mistress. Tony Trelos, pseud. pap. 1.95 o.p. (ISBN 0-87056-216-9, 6216). Brandon.

Candidate's Wife. Burt Carrick. LC 76-22235. 1976. pap. 1.75 o.p. (ISBN 0-87216-342-3, K16342). Playboy Pr Pbks.

Candidate's Wife. Virginia Coffman. 1969. pap. 0.95 o.p. (ISBN 0-447-75093-3). Lancer.

Candide. Francios Marie Arouet De Voltaire. (Modern library of the world's best books).

Candide. illustrated by rockwell kent. translation by richard aldington. ed. Francois Marie Arouet De Voltaire. LC 59-11614. 1959. Hanover House.

Candide. Francois Marie Arouet De Voltaire. LC 62-19952. 1963. Barron's Educational Series.

Candide. Francois Marie Arouet De Voltaire. (Illus.). 1975. 15.00 (ISBN 0-394-49903-4). Random House.

Candide. Francois Marie Arouet De Voltaire. LC 18-14993. (Half-title: The modern library of the world's best books). Boni and Liveright, Inc.

Candide. Francois Marie Arouet De Voltaire. (On cover: World's great novels). Carlton House.

Candide. Francois Marie Arouet De Voltaire & Moreau, Adrien, Illus. LC 30-19719. 1930. Williams, Belasco and Meyers.

Candide. Francois Marie Arouet De Voltaire & Blaine, Mahlon, Illus. Williams, Belasco and Meyers.

Candide. Francois Marie Arouet De Voltaire & B., B. LC 38-24392. (Cameo classics). 1936. Grosset & Dunlap.

Candide. Francois Marie Arouet de Voltaire. Bd. with Zadig. (Classics Ser). pap. 1.25 (ISBN 0-8049-0117-1, CL-117). Airmont.

Candide. Francois Marie Arouet de Voltaire. LC 62-19952. 1963. pap. text ed. 2.95 (ISBN 0-8120-0038-2). Barron.

Candide. Francois Marie Arouet de Voltaire. Ed. by Norman L. Torrey. LC 47-15086. (Crofts Classics Ser.). 1946. pap. text ed. 2.95x (ISBN 0-88295-100-9). Harlan Davidson.

Candide. Francois Marie Arouet de Voltaire. Ed. by Robert M. Adams. (Critical Edition Ser). 1966. pap. 3.95x (ISBN 0-393-09649-1). Norton.

Candide. Francois Marie Arouet de Voltaire. Ed. by J. H. Brumfitt. 1968. pap. 10.95x (ISBN 0-19-832372-7). Oxford U Pr.

Candide. Francois Marie Arouet de Voltaire. Tr. by John Butt. (Classics Ser.). (Orig.). 1950. pap. 1.95 (ISBN 0-14-044004-6). Penguin.

Candide see Seven Short Novel Masterpieces.

Candide: And Other Philosophical Tales. Ed. by Morris Bishop. Francois Marie Arouet De Voltaire. 1962. pap., 1.50. Scribners.

Candide and Other Romances. Francois Marie Arouet De Voltaire & Aldington, Richard, 1892- Tr. LC 27-26616. (Half-title: Broadway translations). 1928. G. Routledge & Sons, Ltd.

Candide & Other Stories. Francois Marie Arouet De Voltaire. Ed. by J. Spencer. (World's Classics Ser). 5.95 o.p. (ISBN 0-19-250611-0). Oxford U Pr.

Candide & Other Stories. Francois Marie Arouet De Voltaire. Ed. by J. Spencer. (World's Classics Ser). 5.95 o.p. (ISBN 0-19-250611-0). Oxford U Pr.

Candide: And Other Stories by Voltaire; Tr. by Joan Spencer. Introd. by Theodore Besterman. Francois Marie Arouet Voltaire. LC 66-75409. (World's classics, no. 611). 1966. 3.00. Oxford Univ. Pr.

Candide, & Other Tales. Francois Marie Arouet De Voltaire. Ed. by J. C. Thorton. Tr. by Smollett. 1971. Repr. of 1937 ed. 9.95x (ISBN 0-460-00936-2, Evman). Biblio Dist.

Candide & Other Tales. Francois Marie Arouet De Voltaire. Tr. by Tobias Smollett. 1983. pap. text ed. 4.50x (ISBN 0-460-01936-8, Pub. by Evman England). Biblio Dist.

Candide and Other Writings. edited with an introd. by haskell m. block. ed. Francois Marie Arouet De Voltaire. LC 56-5416. 1956. Modern Library.

Candide: And Other Writings. Francois Marie Arouet De Voltaire. LC 56-5416. (Modern library of the world's best books 47). 1956. Modern Library.

Candide & Other Writings. Francois Marie Arouet de Voltaire. Ed. by Haskell M. Block. 2.95 o.p. (47). Modern Lib.

Candide, and the Critics. Francois Marie Arouet De Voltaire. Ed. by Milton Painter Foster. LC 62-19154. (Wadsworth guides to literary study). 1962. Wadsworth Pub. Co.

Candide & Zadig. Tr. from French by Tobias George Smollett. Ed., with Introd. by Lester G. Crocker. Francois Marie Arouet De Voltaire. Tr. by Tobias George Smollett. (W153). Washington Sq.

Candide: Bilingual Edition. Francois Marie Arouet De Voltaire. Ed. by Peter Gay. LC 63-10683. 300p. (Fr. & Eng.). 1969. pap. 8.95 (ISBN 0-312-85190-1). St Martin.

Candide. Introd. by Thomas Yoseloff. Francois Marie Arouet De Voltaire. LC 57-2696. 1957. Fine Editions Press.

Candide; or, All for the Best, 1759 see Prince of Abissinia: A Tale, 1759.

Candide: Or, Optimism. Francois Marie Arouet De Voltaire. Tr. by Richard Aldington. Limited Editions Club, Inc., New York. LC 73-164554. (Illus.). 1973. Arranged by R. Ellis for the Members of the Limited Editions Club.

Candide: Or, Optimism... Francois Marie Arouet De Voltaire & Torrey, Norman Lewis, 1894- Ed. LC 47-15086. (On cover: Crofts classics). 1946.

Candide: Or, Optimism. a limited ed. Francois Marie De Voltaire. LC 78-108882. (100 Greatest Books of All Time). (Illus.). 1978. 28.00. Franklin Library.

Candide; or, Optimism: A New Translation, Backgrounds, Criticism. Francois Marie Arouet De Voltaire. Ed. by Robert Martin Adams. LC 65-27469. (Norton critical edition). 1966. Norton.

Candide: Or Optimism. Ed. by Norman L. Torrey. Francois Marie Arouet De Voltaire. (New century classics). 1964. Appleton.

Candide: Ou, L'optimisme. Francois Marie Arouet De Voltaire & Havens, George Remington, 1890- Ed. LC 34-5316. H. Holt and Company.

Candide. Tr. by Tobias George Smollett. Ed., Introd. by Lester G. Crocker. Francois Marie Arouet Voltaire. (Collateral Classic, CC503). 1966. Washington Sq.

Candide. Tr. from French Illus. by Rockwell Kent. Introd. by W. H. Barber. Francois Marie Arouet De Voltaire & Rockwell Kent. LC 62-19952. pap., 1.25. Barron's.

Candide, Zadig & Selected Stories. Voltaire. Ed. by Donald M. Frame. 1960. 8.50 o.p. (ISBN 0-253-11040-8). Ind U Pr.

Candide; Zadig and Selected Stories. Francois Marie Arouet De Voltaire & Donald Murdoch - Frame. LC 60-89185. (Illus.). 1961. Indiana University Press.

Candide, Zadig & Selected Stories. Francois Marie Arouet de Voltaire. Tr. by Donald Frame. pap. 2.25 (ISBN 0-451-51609-5, CE1609, Sig Classics). NAL.

Candide, Zadig, and Selected Stories: Tr., Introd. by Donald M. Frame. Francois Marie Arouet De Voltaire. (Signet classic, CD35). 1961. New American Lib.

Candido; or, a Dream Dreamed in Sicily. Leonardo Sciascia. 168p. 1982. pap. text ed. 12.50x (ISBN 0-85635-404-X, Pub. by Carcanet Pr England). Humanities.

Candido: Or, A Dream Dreamed in Sicily. Leonardo Sciascia. LC 79-1842. 7.95 (ISBN 0-15-115380-9). Harcourt Brace Jovanovich.

Candle. Linton C. Hopkins. LC 37-59907. Green Circle Books.

Candle Against the Sun: A Novel by Sheridan Spearman Pseud. Elizabeth Fyre Spearman. LC 54-10069. 1954. Kenedy.

Candle and the Tower. Robert Donald Spector. (Warner gothic). 1974. (pbk.) 1.25. Warner Paperback Library.

Candle at Midnight. Frances Lynch. 1.25 (ISBN 0-440-19189-0). Dell.

Candle Flame. Starr Walklett. 3.50 o.p. Carlton.

Candle for a Corpse: A Marshal Pedley Mystery, by Stewart Sterling Pseud. 1st Ed. Prentice Winchell. LC 57-6828. (Main line mysteries). 1957. Lippincott.

Candle for a Star. Zoe Lund Schiller. LC 52-8369. 1952. Macmillan.

Candle for St. Jude. Rumer Godden. LC 48-7754. 1948. Viking Press.

Candle for the Dead. Hugh Marlowe. (O.s.i.). 160p. 1973. pap. 0.95 o.s.i. (AN1141, Award). Univ Pub & Dist.

Candle for the Dead see Rogan.

Candle for the Dead: By Hugh Marlowe Pseud. Henry Patterson. LC 66-101375. (Raven bk.). 3.50. Abelard.

Candle for the Dragon. Mary Craig. 1973. 0.75. Dell.

Candle for the Proud. Francis MacManus. LC 37-12731. 1937. Sheed & Ward.

Candle in Her Heart. Emilie Baker Loring. 1965. bds., 1.95. Grosset.

Candle in Her Heart. Emilie Baker Loring. LC 76-41734. 1976. 6.95 (ISBN 0-88411-353-1). Aeonian Press.

Candle in Her Room. Ruth M Arthur. LC 66-12854. (Illus.). 1966. Atheneum.

Candle in the Mist. Florence Crannell Means. (Orig.). (YA) (gr. 7-12). pap. 2.40x duraflex ed o.p. (2-48155, RRS, G5). HM.

Candle in the Morning. Helen Topping Miller. LC 47-2534. 1947. D. Appleton-Century Company, Inc.

Candle in the Night. Elizabeth Howard, pseud. LC 52-8041. Morrow.

Candle in the Night. Ruth Johnston. LC 45-6639. 1945. Wm. B. Eerdmans Publishing Company.

Candle in the Sun. Netta Muskett. LC 43-3872. 1943. Laveright Publishing Corporation.

Candle in the Sun. Edith Kneipple Roberts. LC 37-27366. The Bobbs-Merrill Company.

Candle in the Sun. Marguerite Steen. LC 64-11291. 1964. Doubleday.

Candle in the Wilderness: A Tale of the Beginning of New England. Irving Bacheller. LC 30-12987. The Bobbs-Merrill Company.

Candle in the Wind. Juan Arcocha. LC 66-16868. 1967. L. Stuart.

Candle in the Wind. Gene Lancour. (Carlisle Saga Ser.: No. 1). 368p. (Orig.). 1981. pap. 2.75 (ISBN 0-440-01180-9, Standish). Dell.

Candle in the Wind. Mozelle Richardson. LC 73-9562. 1973. 5.95 (ISBN 0-688-00195-5). W. Morrow.

Candle in the Wind. Mary Imlay Taylor. LC 19-13342. 1919. Moffat, Yard and Company.

Candle in the Wind. Sally Wentworth. (Presents Ser.). 192p. (Orig.). 1980. pap. text ed. 1.50 (ISBN 0-373-10372-7). Harlequin Bks.

Candle Indoors. Helen Rose Hull. LC 36-30937. 1936. Coward-McCann, Inc.

Candle Light. Ruby Mildred Ayres. LC 24-28338. 2.00. George H. Doran Company.

Candle-Lightin' Time. Paul Laurence Dunbar. LC 76-164797. (Illus.). Repr. of 1901 ed. 12.00 (ISBN 0-404-00030-4). AMS Pr.

Candle-Lightin' Time. facs. ed. Paul Laurence Dunbar. LC 73-78997. (Black Heritage Library Collection Ser). (Illus.). 1901. 10.00 o.p. (ISBN 0-8369-8554-0). Arno.

Candle of the Wicked. Thilo Andrej. (Orlando Ser). 180p. (Orig.). 1972. pap. price not set o.s.i. (0*R*L001). Olympia.

Candle of the Wicked. Elizabeth Brown. 3.95 o.p. (9780). Zondervan.

Candle of the Wicked. Manly Wade Wellman. LC 60-114363. 1960. Putnam.

Candle of the Wicked: A Mystery. Elizabeth Brown. LC 70-189576. 1972. 3.95. Zondervan Pub. House.

Candle of the Wicked: A Novel. Edwin Balmer. LC 6-7865. 1956. Longmans, Green.

Candle of Understanding. Vera Wheatley. LC 47-5957. 1947. S. Paul.

Candle of Understanding: A Novel. Elizabeth Bisland Wetmore. LC 3-23047. 1903. Harper & Brothers.

Candle Tales. Julia Cunningham. LC 64-11879. 1964. Pantheon Books.

Candle to Light the Sun. Patricia Jenkins Blondal. LC 76-371796. (New Canadian library; no. 125). 1976. 2.95 (ISBN 0-7710-9225-3). McClelland and Stewart.

Candleflame. Ruth Tracy Millard. LC 38-6012. The Penn Publishing Company.

Candleleer: A Modern Myth. William Wilson. 1973. 4.50 (ISBN 0-682-47691-9). Exposition Pr.

Candlelight Ecstasies. Anne Gisonny. Date not set. price not set. Dell.

Candlemas Bay. Ruth Moore. LC 50-10637. 1950. Morrow.

Candles for the Boardroom: A Novel of Subjective Values in American Business Life. Elliotte R Little. LC 68-15957. 1968. Kingsport Press.

Candles for the Dead. Harry Carmichael. 1976. 6.95 o.p. (ISBN 0-8415-0415-6). Dutton.

Candles for the Dead. Leopold Horace Ognall. LC 75-23948. 1976. 6.95 (ISBN 0-8415-0415-6). Saturday Review Press.

Candles for Therese. Ida Alexa Ross Wylie. LC 51-10099. 1951. Random House.

Candle's Glory. 1st Ed. Sylvia Thompson. LC 53-730595. 1953. Little, Brown.

Candles in Babylon. Denise Levertov. 144p. 1982. 12.95 (ISBN 0-8112-0830-3); pap. 5.95 (ISBN 0-8112-0831-1, NDP533). New Directions.

Candles in the Mud: A Novel. William Charles Lengel. LC 37-20608. I. Washburn.

Candles in the Night: Jewish Tales by Gentile Author. Ed. by Joseph Louis Baron. LC 40-12260. 1940. Farrar & Rinehart.

Candles in the Storm: A Novel. Robert Littell. LC 34-24860. 1934. Harper & Brothers.

Candles in the Sun: A Satire in Pastels. Dorothy Graham. LC 30-3072. 1930. Frederick A. Stokes Company.

Candles in the Wind. Katherine Helen Maud Marshall Diver. LC 9-27966. 1909. 1.50. John Lane Company.

Candles in the Wind. Katherine Helen Maud Marshall Diver. LC 24-149376. 1923. Dodd, Mead and Company.

Candles in the Wood. Alexandra Manners, pseud. LC 74-79657. 1974. 6.95 (ISBN 0-399-11371-1). Putnam.

Candles in the Wood. Alexandra Manners, pseud. (Berkley Medallion Book). 1976. (pbk.) 1.50 (ISBN 0-425-03050-4). Berkley Publishing Corp.

Candleshades: The Story of a Soul. Ursula Bloom. LC 28-134454. 1928. G. H. Watt.

Candleshine No More. J. Oliver. 1967. 5.95 o.p. (ISBN 0-399-10111-X). Putnam.

Candleshine No More: A Novel. Jane Oliver, pseud. LC 67-23134. (Illus.). 1967. Putnam.

Candleshoe. Michael Innes, pseud. 1978. pap. 2.95 (ISBN 0-14-004863-4). Penguin.

Candlestick & the Cross. Ruth Freeman Solomon. 416p. 1980. pap. 2.75 (ISBN 0-515-05249-3). Jove Pubns.

Candlestick Makers. Lucille Papin Borden. LC 23-136552. 1923. The Macmillan Company.

Candlesticks and the Cross. Ruth Freeman Solomon. (Signet bk., Q3439). 1968. New Amer. Lib.

Candlesticks and the Cross: A Novel. Ruth Freeman Solomon. 1974. (pbk.) 1.50 (ISBN 0-671-78667-9). Pocket Books.

Candlesticks and the Cross: A Novel. Ruth Freeman Solomon. LC 67-10962. 1967. Putnam.

Candy. Lillie McMakin Alexander & Kent, Rockwell, 1882- Illus. 1934. Dodd, Mead & Company.

Candy. Maxwell Kenton. 1965. pap. 0.75 o.p. (721). Brandon.

Candy. Maxwell Kenton. 1968. pap. 0.95 o.p. (ISBN 0-447-75043-7). Lancer.

Candy: A Novel. Terry Southern & Hoffenberg, Mason. LC 64-13030. 1964. Putnam.

Candy Butcher's Farewell. Lester Geran. LC 64-17906. 1964. McGraw-Hill.

Candy Factory. Sylvia Fraser. LC 75-650. 1975. 8.95. Little, Brown.

Candy for Breakfast: A Novel. Gwen Davenport. LC 50-10570. 1950. Doubleday.

Candy Kid. Dorothy Belle Flanagan Hughes. LC 50-10026. (A Bloodhound mystery). 1950. Duell, Sloan and Pearce.

Candy Killings. Gail Stockwell. LC 40-30184. The Graystone Press.

Candy Wagon. Sally Barry. 1980. 8.95 (ISBN 0-533-03960-6). Vantage.

Candywine Development. John Morris. 1974. (pbk.) 1.25. Dell.

Cane. Jean Toomer. LC 75-15630. 1975. 7.95 (ISBN 0-87140-611-X) (ISBN 0-87140-104-5). Liveright.

Cane. Jean Toomer. LC 79-855. (Perennial classic, P3087). 1969. 1.25. Harper & Row.

Cane. Jean Toomer. LC 67-9604. 1967. University Place Press.

Cane. Jean Toomer. LC 23-12749. Boni and Liveright.

Cane Juice, a Story of Southern Louisiana. John Earle Uhler. LC 31-24895. The Century Co.

Cane-Patch Mystery. Albert Benjamin Cunningham. LC 44-5939. 1944. E. P. Dutton & Company, Inc.

Canek: History and Legend of a Maya Hero. Abreu Gomez, Ermilo. LC 75-32674. 8.95 (ISBN 0-520-03148-2) (ISBN 0-520-03982-3). University of California Press.

Canfield Decision. 1st. ed. Spiro T. Agnew. LC 76-3475. 8.95 (ISBN 0-87223-452-5). Playbook Press.

Canfield Decision. Spiro T Agnew. (A Berkley Medallion Book). 1977. 1.95. (ISBN 0-425-03338-4). Berkley Pub. Corp.

Canis the Warrior. James Sinclair. 1980. pap. 2.50 (ISBN 0-425-04513-7). Berkley Pub.

Canis the Warrior. Reginald Thomas Staples. LC 78-19413. 12.50 (ISBN 0-312-90491-6) (ISBN 0-312-90492-4). St. Martin's Press.

Cannaway Concern. Graham Shelby. LC 78-22355. (Illus.). 1980. 10.95 (ISBN 0-385-14113-0). Doubleday.

Cannaways. Graham Shelby. LC 76-56335. 1978. 8.95 o.p. (ISBN 0-385-09424-8). Doubleday.

Cannaways. Graham Shelby. 1982. pap. 3.50 (ISBN 0-8217-1019-2). Zebra.

Cannaways. Graham Shelby. 1983. pap. 3.50 (ISBN 0-8217-1124-5). Zebra.

Cannery Anne. Morris Hull. LC 36-17124. 1936. Houghton Mifflin Company.

Cannery Boat. Takiji Kobayashi. LC 34-227613. 1933. International Publisher.

Cannery Boat: And Other Japanese Short Stories. Takiji Kobayashi. LC 68-30823. 1968. Greenwood Press.

Cannery Boat & Other Japanese Short Stories. Takiji Kobayashi. LC 70-122589. Repr. of 1933 ed. 12.50 (ISBN 0-404-03736-4). AMS Pr.

Cannery Boat & Other Japanese Short Stories. Takiji Kobayashi. LC 68-30823. (Illus.). 1968. Repr. of 1933 ed. lib. bdg. 15.00x (ISBN 0-8371-0133-6, KOCB). Greenwood.

Cannery Row. large type ed., complete and unabridged. ed. John Steinbeck. LC 68-2456. F. Watts.

Cannery Row. John Steinbeck. 1945. The Viking Press.

Cannery Row see Short Novels of John Steinbeck.

Cannibal. Nelson DeMille. (Keller Ser.: No. 2). 192p. 1975. pap. 1.25 o.p. (ISBN 0-532-12270-4). Woodhill.

Cannibal. Nelson DeMille. (Keller Ser.: No. 2). 192p. 1975. pap. 1.25 o.p. (ISBN 0-532-12270-4). Manor Bks.

Cannibal. Michael Harner & Alfred Meyer. LC 79-12939. (Illus.). 1979. 9.95 (ISBN 0-688-03499-3). Morrow.

Cannibal. John Hawkes. LC 63-4188. (New Directions paperbook, 123). 1962. New Directions.

Cannibal Heart. Margaret Millar. LC 49-103499. 1949. Random House.

Cannibal Isle: A Novel. William Stevens. LC 79-117029. 1970. 6.95. Little, Brown.

Cannibal Valley. Russell T. Hitt. (Illus.). pap. 2.95 o.p. (18085P). Zondervan.

Cannibal Who Overate. Hugh Pentecost. 1972. pap. 0.75 o.p. (T2655). Pyramid Pubns.

Cannibal Who Overate: By Hugh Pentecost Pseud. Judson Pentecost Philips. LC 62-100578. (Red badge detective). 1962. Dodd, Mead.

Cannibals. Keefe Brasselle. 6.95 o.p. Delacorte.

Cannibals: A Novel About Television's Savage Chieftains. Keefe Brasselle. LC 68-24230. 1968. 6.95. Bartholomew House.

Cannibals and Missionaries. Mary Therese McCarthy. LC 79-4869. 10.95 (ISBN 0-15-115387-6). Harcourt Brace Jovanovich.

Cannibals and Missionaries. Mary Therese McCarthy. 1980. 2.75 (ISBN 0-380-50690-4). Avon Books.

Cannon Hill. Mary Deasy. LC 49-938524. 1949. Little, Brown.

Cannon Law. Thomas Camborne Paynter. 1928. Longmans, Green, and Co., Ltd.

Cannon River. Trev Roberts, pseud. LC 66-31658. 1966. Arcadia House.

Cannonball Canyon. John Hunt. LC 78-2424. (Western Novel Ser.). 1978. 7.95 o.p. (ISBN 0-312-11849-X); large type 9.95 o.p. (ISBN 0-312-11850-3). St Martin.

Cannonball Canyon. Lauran Paine. LC 78-2414. 1978. 9.95 (ISBN 0-312-11849-X). St. Martin's Press.

Cannonball Run. Michael Avallone. 1981. pap. 2.50 (ISBN 0-8439-0993-5). Nordon Pubns.

Cannons & Roses. George Ogan & Margaret Ogan. 1979. pap. 2.50 (ISBN 0-440-01027-6). Dell.

Cannon's Law. Dennis Archer. LC 78-2410. (Western Novel Ser.). 1978. 7.95 o.p. (ISBN 0-312-11855-4); large type 9.95 o.p. (ISBN 0-312-11856-2). St Martin.

Cannon's Law. Lauran Paine. LC 78-2410. 1978. 7.95 (ISBN 0-312-11855-4) (ISBN 0-312-11856-2) (ISBN 0-312-11856-2) (ISBN 0-312-11856-2). St. Martin's Press.

Cannons of Lucknow. V. A Stuart. (Adventures of Alexander Sheridan,#4). (Illus.). 1974. (pbk.) 1.25 (ISBN 0-523-00340-4). Pinnacle Books.

Canny Mr. Glencannon: In Which Is Set Forth a True Account of Numerous Recent and Stirring Events in the Exemplary Life & Charitable Works of Colin St. Andrew MacThrockle Glencannon, Esq., Chief Engineer of the S. S. Inchcliffe Castle. Guy Gilpatric. LC 48-208753. 1948. E. P. Dutton.

Canol. Arthur T. Hixon. LC 46-17223. 1946. Dorrance & Company.

Canolles: The Fortunes of a Partisan of '81. John Esten Cooke. LC 6-27180. 1877. E. B. Smith & Company.

Canon Brett. Mary Badger Wilson. LC 42-7207. 1942. The Greystone Press.

Canon in Residence. Victor L Whitechurch. LC 11-11450. 1911. The Baker & Taylor Co.

Canon in Residence. Victor L Whitechurch. LC 11-18191. The Baker & Taylor Co.

Canon of Light. Kenneth Perkins. LC 32-6317. A. H. King.

Canon of Lost Waters. Hoffman Birney. LC 30-4488. The Penn Publishing Company.

Canon's Ward. A Novel. James Payn. (Harper's Franklin square library, no. 357). 1884. Harper & Brothers.

Canon's Ward. A Novel. James Payn. (Seaside library. v. 88, no. 1784). 1884. G. Munro.

Canopy of Time. Brian Wilson Aldiss. LC 75-12076. 1966. Faber and Faber.

Can't Get a Red Bird. Dorothy Scarborough. LC 74-26120. (Labor Movement in Fiction and Non-Fiction). (Illus.). 1977. 24.50 (ISBN 0-404-58468-3). AMS Press.

Can't Get a Red Bird. Dorothy Scarborough. LC 29-201121. 1929. Harper & Brothers.

Canterbury Tales. Geoffrey Chaucer. 1976. 12.95x (ISBN 0-460-10307-5, Evman); pap. 3.95x (ISBN 0-460-01307-6, Evman). Biblio Dist.

Canterbury Tales. Geoffrey Chaucer. Ed. by John Halverson. LC 79-153880. (Library of Literature Ser: No. 27). 1971. pap. text ed. 10.95 (ISBN 0-672-61006-X). Bobbs.

Canterbury Tales, 3 Vols. Geoffrey Chaucer. Ed. by Thomas Wright. Repr. of 1851 ed. 26.50 ea. (ISBN 0-384-08565-2). Johnson Repr.

Canterbury Tales. Geoffrey Chaucer. Ed. by Walter W. Skeat. (World's Classics Ser.). 15.95 o.p. (ISBN 0-19-250076-7). Oxford U Pr.

Canterbury Tales. Geoffrey Chaucer. Tr. by David Wright. (O.S.I.). 1965. 10.00 o.s.i. (ISBN 0-394-41837-9). Random.

Canterbury Tales. Harriet Lee. 1886. Houghton, Mifflin and Company.

Canterbury Tales. Harriet Lee & Lee, Sophia. LC 44-20547. 1886. Houghton Mifflin.

Canterbury Tales. Sophia Lee. LC 44-15357. 1886. Houghton, Mifflin and Company.

Canterbury Tales. Sophia Lee & Harriet Lee. LC 71-162886. (Illus.). 1978. 47.50 (ISBN 0-404-54550-5). AMS Press.

Canterbury Tales: A Selection. Geoffrey Chaucer. Ed. by Donald R. Howard & James M. Dean. 1969. pap. 2.95 (ISBN 0-451-51514-5, CE1514, Sig Classics). NAL.

Canterbury Tales: An Illustrated Selection. Geoffrey Chaucer. Tr. by Nevil Coghill. (Large Format Ser). (Illus.). 1977. pap. 12.95 (ISBN 0-14-004452-3). Penguin.

Canterbury Tales Printed by William Caxton. 2nd ed. Geoffrey Chaucer. 1976. text ed. 300.00x bd in calf o.s.i. (ISBN 0-8277-4528-1); pap. text ed. 75.00x bd in buckram o.s.i. (ISBN 0-8277-4545-1). British Bk Ctr.

Canterbury Tales: Selections. Geoffrey Chaucer. 1969. pap. 0.35 o.p. (LP68). Pyramid Pubns.

Canter's Chase. Margaret Archer. LC 46-591. 1945. Pub. for the Crime Book Society by Jarrolds, Limited.

Canterville Ghost. Oscar Wilde. pap. 2.00 (ISBN 0-8283-1442-X, 27, IPL). Branden.

Canterville Ghost: An Amusing Chronicle of the Tribulations of the Ghost of Canterville Chase When His Ancestral Halls Became the Home of the American Minister to the Court of St. James. Illus. by Wallace Goldsmith. Oscar Wilde. LC 64-22214. (IPL, 27). 1965. Intl. Pocket Lib.

Canticle for Leibowitz. Walter M. Miller. LC 75-5914. (Gregg Press science fiction series). 1975. 13.50 (ISBN 0-8398-2309-6). Gregg Press.

Cantina. Ornn Favelle Schee. LC 41-5676. Coward-McCann, Inc.

Canto for a Gypsy. Martin Cruz Smith. LC 72-79529. (Red mask mystery). 1972. 4.95 (ISBN 0-399-11024-0). Putnam.

Canto for a Gypsy. Martin Cruz Smith. 1975. (pbk.) 1.25. Dell.

Canton Barrier. Andrew Clare Geer. LC 56-6047. 1956. Harper.

Canuck. Camille Lessard-Bissonette. (Novels by Franco-Americans in New England 1850-1940 Ser.). 119p. (Fr.). (gr. 10 up). 1980. pap. 4.50x (ISBN 0-911409-19-X). Natl Mat Dev.

Canvas Coffin. William Campbell Gault. LC 52-129435. (Guilt edged mystery). 1953. Dutton.

Canvas Dagger. Helen Kieran Reilly. LC 56-882264. 1956. Random House.

Canvas Door. Mary Farley Sanborn Sanborn. LC 9-29777. 1909. B. W. Dodge & Company.

Canvas Falcons. Stephen Longstreet. (War Library). 416p. 1983. pap. 3.95 (ISBN 0-345-30891-3). Ballantine.

Canvas of Passion. Deidre Mardon. (Harlequin American Romance Ser.). 256p. 1983. pap. 2.25 (ISBN 0-373-16009-7). Harlequin Bks.

Canvas Prison. Gordon DeMarco. (Riley Kovachs, Detective Ser.). 250p. (Orig.). 1982. pap. 5.00 (ISBN 0-918064-06-6); cloth 10.95. Germinal Pr.

Canvas Sky. David Liebovitz. LC 46-251021. 1946. Harcourt, Brace and Company.

Canvassing: A Tale. John Banim & Michael Banim. LC 6-6114. 1835. Carey, Lea & Blanchard.

Canyon. Jack Warner Schaefer. LC 53-7076. 1953. Houghton Mifflin.

Canyon. Peter Viertel. LC 40-31346. Harcourt, Brace and Company.

Canyon Apache. Rene de Goscinny. (Lucky Luke Series). (French.). 1976. 5.95x (ISBN 2-205-00517-0). Intl Learn Syst.

Canyon Bunch. Jake Logan. LC 82-80215. (Jake Logan Western Ser.). 224p. 1982. pap. 1.95 (ISBN 0-86721-153-9). Playboy Pbks.

Canyon Country. Leonard Lupton. 1977. pap. 1.25 (ISBN 0-532-12515-0). Woodhill.

Canyon Country. Leonard Lupton. 1973. 4.95 (ISBN 0-517-51446-X). Lenox Hill Press.

Canyon Country. Samuel Anthony Peeples. LC 51-1167. (Dutton Diamond D western). 1951. Dutton.

Canyon Garden. Margaret Erwin. LC 23-812. 1922. A. M. Robertson.

Canyon Gold. Arthur Preston Hankins. LC 25-16896. The Masaplay Company.

Canyon Hide-Out. Peter Field. LC 51-3418. 1951. Jefferson House.

Canyon Kill. Jack Slade, pseud. (Leisure book). 1.75 (ISBN 0-8439-0618-9). Nordon Pubns.

Canyon of Death. Peter Field. (Tripie-A western classic). 1953. Jefferson House.

Canyon of Death. Peter Field. LC 38-34545. 1938. W. Morrow & Co.

Canyon of Gold. Roy Norton. LC 35-19148. The Macaulay Company.

Canyon of Golden Skulls. Harry Sinclair Drago. LC 37-12222. The Macaulay Company.

Canyon of No Return. W. D Hoffman. LC 32-249771. 1932. A. C. McClurg & Co.

Canyon of No Sunset. Annette Turngren. LC 42-5128. 1942. T. Nelson & Sons.

Canyon of Peril. Johnston McCulley. LC 35-381119. G. H. Watt.

Canyon of the Fools. Richard Matthews Hallet. LC 22-6937. Harper & Brothers.

Canyon of the Gun. Theodore V. Olsen. 1978. pap. 1.75 (ISBN 0-449-13943-3, GM). Fawcett.

Canyon of the Stars. Mae Van Norman Long. LC 27-1583. 1926. David Graham Fischer Company.

Canyon Passage. Ernest Haycox. LC 45-2268. 1945. Little, Brown and Company.

Canyon Passage. Ernest Haycox. LC 79-15832. (Gregg Press Western Fiction Series). 1979. 8.95 (ISBN 0-8398-2575-7). Gregg Press.

Canyon Passage. Ernest Haycox. (Signet brand western). 1974. (pbk.) 0.95. New American Library.

Canyon Rattlers. Eli Colter. LC 39-21176. Dodge Publishing Company.

Canyon Showdown. Peter Germano. LC 67-9388. 1967. Arcadia House.

Canyon Showdown. James Wesley. (YA) 1981. 6.95 (Avalon). Bouregy.

Canyon Trail. George Brydges Rodney. LC 33-163543. E. J. Clode, Inc.

Canyon War. Sam Bowie. 128p. (gr. 8 up). 1980. pap. 1.50 (ISBN 0-448-17224-0, G&D). Putnam Pub Group.

Canyons of Grace. Levi S. Peterson. LC 82-4720. (Illinois Short Fiction Ser.). 160p. 1982. 11.95 (ISBN 0-252-00997-5); pap. 4.95 (ISBN 0-252-00998-3). U of Ill Pr.

Cap and Bells. Selina B Avery. LC 37-4092. Burney Brothers Publishing Co.

Cap and Gown in Prose: Short Sketches Selected from Undergraduate Periodicals of Recent Years. Ed. by Frederic Lawrence Knowles. (On verso of half-title: The cap and gown series). 1900. L. C. Page & Company.

Cap for Corrine. Zillah Katherine Macdonald. LC 52-8391. (Romance for young moderns). 1952. J. Messner.

Cap of Youth. Naomi Ellington Jacob. LC 41-14757. 1941. The Macmillan Company.

Cap of Youth: Being the Love Romance of Robert Louis Stevenson. John Alexander Steuart. LC 27-22159. 1927. J. B. Lippincott Company.

Cap Sheaf: A Fresh Bundle. George Canning Hill. LC 7-4962. 1853. Redfield.

Capablanca Opening. David Thomas Chantler. LC 76-29858. 8.95. St. Martin's Press.

Capable of Honor. Allen Drury. LC 66-20961. 1966. 15.95 (ISBN 0-385-01028-1). Doubleday.

Capac Legacy: A Novel. Sal Giannetta. LC 75-6533. 1975. 6.95 (ISBN 0-671-22037-3). Simon and Schuster.

Capacitese Como Lider. LeRoy Ford. Tr. by Guillermo Blair. 64p. (Span.). 1982. pap. 3.75 (ISBN 0-311-17023-4, Edit Mundo). Casa Bautista.

Capacity and Extent of Human Understanding Exemplified in the Extraordinary Case of Automathes. John Kirkby. LC 74-23775. (Flowering of the Novel). 1974. (ISBN 0-8240-1114-7). Garland Pub.

Cape. Martin Caidin. LC 76-139008. 1971. 6.95. Doubleday.

Cape Breton Tales. with illustrations by oliver m. wiard. ed. Harry James Smith. LC 20-23022. The Atlantic Monthly Press.

Cape Cod and All Along Shore: Stories. Charles Nordhoff. LC 72-116964. (Short story index reprint series). (Illus.). 1970. Books for Libraries Press.

Cape Cod and All Along Shore: Stories. Charles Nordhoff. 1868. Harper & Brothers.

Cape Cod Caper. Margot Arnold, pseud. LC 81-17457. (Atlantic series). 1982. 11.95 (ISBN 0-89340-423-3). J. Curley & Associates.

Cape Cod Casket. Amerman, Lockhart. LC 64-17083. 1964. Harcourt, Brace & World.

Cape Cod Folks. 11th ed. Sarah Pratt McLean Greene. LC 6-35040. 1882. A. Williams & Company.

Cape Cod Folks. Sarah Pratt McLean Greene. 1904. De Wolfe, Fiske & Co.

Cape Cod Folks. Sarah Pratt McLean Greene. LC 4-15449. 1881. De Wolfe, Fiske & Co.

Cape Cod Folks: A Novel. Sarah Pratt McLean Green. LC 9-2679. 1881. A. Williams & Company.

Cape Cod Folks: A Novel. 2d ed. Sarah Pratt McLean Greene. 1881. A. Williams & Company.

Cape Cod Idyl. Faith Bickford. LC 48-20692. 1948.

Cape Cod Lighter: Stories. John O'Hara. LC 62-8455. 1962. Random House.

Cape Cod Lighter: Stories. John O'Hara. 1973. 1.25. Popular Lib.

Cape Cod Mystery. Phoebe Atwood Taylor. LC 31-200755. The Bobbs-Merrill Company.

Cape Cod Mystery: As Asey Mayo Mystery. Phoebe Atwood Taylor. 1971. 5.95 o.p. (ISBN 0-393-08651-8). Norton.

Cape Cod on the Subway: A Memoir of Pleasure Boating. Arthur McCaffery. LC 47-3663. 1947. The Dial Press.

Cape Cod Stories. Joseph Crosby Lincoln. 1976. Repr. of 1907 ed. lib. bdg. 15.70x (ISBN 0-88411-791-X). Amereon Ltd.

Cape Cod Stories. Joseph Crosby Lincoln. (Illus.). 1973. 5.95 (ISBN 0-87482-030-8). Wake-Brook.

Cape Cod Summer. Jeanne Judson. LC 56-942. Avalon Books.

Cape Cod Week. Annie Eliot Trumbull. LC 98-194. 1898. A. S. Barnes and Company.

Cape Cod Windsong. Russell G Moore. LC 76-9290. (Illus.). 2.95. Lower Cape Pub.

Cape Currey. Rene Juta. LC 20-13976. 1920. 1.75. H. Holt and Company.

Cape House. L. P Shepherd. 1974. (pbk.) 0.95. Dell.

Cape of Storms. John Gordon Davis. LC 79-157583. 1971. 7.95. Doubleday.

Cape of Storms. Percival Pollard. LC 44-17997. 1895. The Echo.

Cape of Storms: A Novel. Percival Pollard. 1900. R. G. Badger & Co.

Capella's Golden Eye. Christopher Evans. 256p. 1982. pap. 2.50 (Pub. by Ace Science Fiction). Ace Bks.

Caper. Lesley Andress. LC 79-17559. 10.95 (ISBN 0-399-12403-9). Putnam.

Caper. Lesley Andress. LC 80-16921. 1980. 14.95 (ISBN 0-8161-3117-1). G. K. Hall.

Caper. Lesley Andress. 1981. 2.95 (ISBN 0-671-83385-5). Pocket Books.

Caper. Thomas B Reagan. LC 69-12491. (Red mask mystery). 1969. 4.50. Putnam.

Caper of the Golden Bulls. William P McGivern. LC 66-134796. bds., 4.00. Dodd.

Caperberry Bush: A Novel. 1st Ed. Jack Guinn. LC 54-687796. 1954. Little, Brown.

Capillary Crime and Other Stories. Francis Davis Millet. LC 72-157793. (Short story index reprint series). (Illus.). 1971. (ISBN 0-8369-3905-0). Books for Libraries Press.

Capillary Crime and Other Stories. Francis Davis Millet. LC 7-31117. 1892. Harper & Brothers.

Capitaine De Quinze. Jules Verne. pap. 3.95. French & Eur.

Capital. Maureen Duffy. LC 75-42406. 222p. 1976. 6.95 (ISBN 0-8076-0817-3). Braziller.

Capital: A Fiction. Maureen Duffy. LC 75-42406. 1976. 6.95 (ISBN 0-8076-0821-1). G. Braziller.

Capital City. Mari Sandoz. LC 39-289619. 1939. Little, Brown and Company.

Capital City. Mari Sandoz. LC 81-14656. 1982. 20.00 (ISBN 0-8032-4130-5) (ISBN 0-8032-9126-4) (ISBN 0-8032-9126-4). University of Nebraska Press.

Capital City. Ruth Stewart. LC 33-31425. Sears Publishing Company, Inc.

Capital City Mystery. James Harold Wallis. LC 32-3605. E. P. Dutton & Co., Inc.

Capital Courtship. Alexander Black. LC 6-124241. 1897. C. Scribner's Sons.

Capital Crime. Alexandra Roudybush. LC 68-27136. 1969. 3.95. Published for the Crime Club by Doubleday.

Capital Crime. Alexandra Roudybusy. 1971. pap. 0.60 o.p. (06131). Curtis.

Capital of Pain. Paul Eluard. Tr. by Richard M. Weisman. (Illus.). 1973. pap. 4.95 o.p. (ISBN 0-670-20326-2, Grossman). Penguin.

Capital of Pain. Paul Eluard. Tr. by Richard Weisman. (O.s.i.). (Illus.). 1973. pap. 4.95 o.s.i. (ISBN 0-670-20326-2). Grossman.

Capital Stories. Samuel Langhorne Clemens et al. The Christian Herald.

Capitol. Orson Scott Card. (Analog Science Fiction Ser.). 1979. pap. 4.95 (ISBN 0-89437-072-3). Baronet.

Capitol Crime. Lawrence Meyer. LC 76-53795. 1977. 8.95 (ISBN 0-670-20336-X). Viking Press.

Capitol Crime. Lawrence Meyer. 1978. 1.95 (ISBN 0-380-01888-8). Avon Books.

Capitol Hell. Lionel Derrick. (Penetrator,#3). 1974. (pbk.) 0.95 (ISBN 0-523-00318-8). Pinnacle Books.

Capitol Hill: A Novel of Washington Life. Harvey Fergusson. LC 23-7732. 1923. A. A. Knopf.

Capitol Hill Affair. Leigh James. LC 68-28270. 1968. 5.50. Weybright and Talley.

Capitol Offense: An Entertainment, by Jocelyn Davey Pseud. 1st American Ed. Chaim Raphael. LC 56-7210. 1956. Knopf.

Capitol Offense: An Entertainment. 1st American Ed. Jocelyn Davey, pseud. LC 56-7210. 1956. Knopf.

Cap'n Abe: Storekeeper: a Story of Cape Cod. James A Cooper, pseud. LC 17-141901. Sully and Kleinteich.

Cap'n Alf's Log. Edith Austin Holton. LC 34-30880. Thomas Y. Crowell Company.

Cap'n Bailey and the Widder Dyer. Charles W Burton. LC 30-12383. Marshall Jones Company.

Cap'n Bodfish Takes Command. Edith Austin Holton. LC 35-114840. Thomas Y. Crowell Company.

Cap'n Dan's Daughter. Joseph Crosby Lincoln. LC 14-4302. 1914. D. Appleton and Company.

Cap'n Dan's Daughter. Joseph Crosby Lincoln. LC 26-551302. 1924. D. Appleton and Company.

Cap'n Eri. Joseph Crosby Lincoln. 1976. Repr. of 1907 ed. lib. bdg. 19.40x (ISBN 0-88411-792-8). Amereon Ltd.

Cap'n Eri, a Story of the Coast. Joseph Crosby Lincoln. 1904. A. S. Barnes & Company.

Cap'n Eri; a Story of the Coast. Joseph Crosby Lincoln. LC 16-3411. 1912. The A. S. Barnes Company.

Cap'n Fatso. Daniel V Gallery. LC 73-83751. 1969. 4.95. Norton.

Cap'n Gid. Elizabeth Lincoln Gould. LC 16-44252. 1916. 1.00. The Penn Publishing Company.

Cap'n Joe's Sister. Alice Louise Lee. LC 12-3377. 1912. Frederick A. Stokes Company.

Cap'n Jonah's Fortune: A Story of Cape Cod. James A Cooper, pseud. LC 19-7685. 1.50. G. Sully and Company.

Cap'n Simeon's Store. George Savary Wasson. LC 3-10625. 1903. Houghton, Mifflin and Company.

Cap'n Sue. Hulbert Footner. LC 28-7954. 1928 Doubleday, Doran & Company, Inc.

Cap'n Titus: Sketches of New England Country Folk. Clayton Mayo. LC 2-26349. 1902. Doubleday, Page & Company.

Cap'n Warren's Wards. Joseph Crosby Lincoln. LC 12-22163. 1912. D. Appleton and Company.

Cap'n Warren's Wards. Joseph Crosby Lincoln. LC 26-247041. 1913. A. L. Burt Company.
Cap'n Warren's Wards. Joseph Crosby Lincoln. LC 26-750941. 1926. D. Appleton and Company.
Caporetto. Agatha D. Anastasi. (Orig.). 1979. pap. 2.75 (ISBN 0-89083-543-8). Zebra.
Cappella. Israel Horovitz. LC 72-9097. 1973. 5.95 (ISBN 0-06-011962-4). Harper & Row.
Cappy Ricks Comes Back. Peter Bernard Kyne. LC 34-4861. 1934. H. C. Kinsey & Company, Inc.
Cappy Ricks: Or, The Subjugation of Matt Peasley. Peter Bernard Kyne. LC 16-11966. 1.35. The H. K. Fly Company.
Cappy Ricks: Or, The Subjugation of Matt Peasley. Peter Bernard Kyne. LC 21-136988. 1920. Grosset & Dunlap.
Cappy Ricks: Or, The Subjugation of Matt Peasley. Peter Bernard Kyne. LC 43-153296. 1943. Triangle Books.
Cappy Ricks Retires... Peter Bernard Kyne. LC 22-17149. 1922. Cosmopolitan Book Corporation.
Cappy Ricks Special. Peter Bernard Kyne. LC 35-127962. 1935. H. C. Kinsey & Company, Inc.
Cappy: Rollicking Rancher Atop Arizona's Mighty Rim. Vienna I. Curtiss. LC 79-84471. (Illus.). 1979. 12.00 (ISBN 0-9602742-0-0). Collectors Choice.
Capri Affair. David Hanna. (Orig.). 1980. pap. 1.95 o.s.i. (ISBN 0-505-51547-4). Tower Bks.
Capri Letters: A Novel Translated from the Italian by Archibald Colquhoun. 1st American Ed. Mario Soldati. LC 55-10584. 1956. Knopf.
Caprice. Sara Hylton. LC 80-51824. 1980. 11.95 (ISBN 0-312-11947-X). St. Martin's Press.
Caprice see Three More Novels.
Capricorn Games. Robert Silverberg. LC 74-29618. 5.95 (ISBN 0-394-49122-X). Random House.
Capricorn People. Aaron Fletcher. 512p. 1983. pap. 3.95 (ISBN 0-8439-2012-2, Leisure Bks). Dorchester Pub Co.
Capricorn Run. Denis J Cleary & Maher, Frank J. 1979. 1.50 (ISBN 0-87216-513-2). Playboy Press.
Capricorn Stone. Madeleine Brent. LC 78-22807. 10.00 (ISBN 0-385-14596-9). Doubleday.
Capricorn Stone. Madeleine Brent. LC 80-14238. 1980. 16.95 (ISBN 0-8186-3092-2). G. K. Hall.
Capricornia. Xavier Herbert. LC 43-5520. 1943. D. Appleton-Century Company, Incorporated.
Caprifoil. William P McGivern. LC 72-10358. 1972. 8.95 (ISBN 0-8161-6059-7). G. K. Hall.
Caprifoil. William P McGivern. LC 72-727. 1973. (pbk.) 1.50 (ISBN 0-515-03153-4). Pyramid Books.
Capsina; an Historical Novel. Edward Frederic Benson. LC 99-770. 1899. Harper & Brothers.
Capsize! A Story of Survival in the North Atlantic. Nicholas Angel. Tr. by Alan Wakeman from Fr. LC 81-389. (Illus.). 178p. 1981. 15.95 (ISBN 0-393-03264-7). Norton.
Captain. Jan De Hartog. LC 66-16358. 1966. 5.95 o.p. (ISBN 0-689-10064-7). Atheneum.
Captain. Jan De Hartog. (N183). 1968. Avon.
Captain. Jan De Hartog. LC 66-16358. (Illus.). 1966. Atheneum.
Captain. Seymour Shubin. LC 82-40011. 288p. 1982. 14.95 (ISBN 0-8128-2880-1). Stein & Day.
Captain. Francis Churchill Williams. LC 3-29490. 1903. Lothrop Publishing Company.
Captain, a Novel. Thacher, Russell. LC 51-10799. 1951. Macmillan.
Captain Adam. Donald Barr Chidsey. LC 53-5679. 1953. Crown Publishers.
Captain Antifer. Jules Verne. LC 1-9845. R. F. Fenno & Co.
Captain Antle, the Sailor's Friend. Charles Mortimer. LC 98-622. 1898. Damrell & Upham.
Captain Archer's Daughter. Margaret Wade Campbell Deland. LC 32-26340. 1932. Harper & Brothers.
Captain Barney. Jan Vlachos Westcott. 1977. Repr. of 1951 ed. lib. bdg. 15.95x (ISBN 0-89244-060-0). Queens Hse.
Captain Barney: A Novel. Jan Vlachos Westcott. LC 51-12010. 1951. Crown Publishers.
Captain Bashful. Donald Barr Chidsey. LC 55-7227. 1955. Crown Publishers.
Captain Black: A Romance of the Nameless Ship. Max Pemberton. LC 11-15859. 1.20. Hodder & Stoughton, George H. Doran Company.
Captain Blackman: A Novel. John Alfred Williams. 1974. (pbk.) 1.50. Bantam Books.
Captain Blackman: A Novel. John Alfred Williams. LC 75-171328. 1972. 6.95. Doubleday.
Captain Blake. Charles King. LC 42-303335. 1896. J. B. Lippincott Company.
Captain Blake. Charles King. 1902. J. B. Lippincott Company.
Captain Blood. Michael Blodgett. LC 81-20157. 1982. 5.95 (ISBN 0-517-54669-8). Harmony Books.
Captain Blood. new ed. Rafael Sabatini. LC 22-16175. (Illus.). 1977. Repr. of 1922 ed. 13.95 (ISBN 0-910220-87-5). Berg.
Captain Blood. Rafael Sabatini. 1.75 (ISBN 0-553-02725-5). Bantam.
Captain Blood: His Odyssey. Rafael Sabatini. LC 22-16175. 1922. Houghton Mifflin Company.
Captain Blood: His Odyssey. Rafael Sabatini. LC 26-7511. 1925. Grosset & Dunlap.
Captain Blood: His Odyssey. Rafael Sabatini. LC 36-896. Grosset & Dunlap.
Captain Blood, His Odyssey: By Rafael Sabatini... Rafael Sabatinia. LC 46-7688. 1946. Triangle Books, the Blakiston Company.
Captain Blood Returns. Rafael Sabatini. LC 31-10171. 1931. Houghton Mifflin Company.
Captain Blood Returns. Rafael Sabatini. LC 34-12179. 1933. Grosset & Dunlap.
Captain Bluitt: A Tale of Old Turley. Charles Heber Clark. LC 1-245960. 1901. H.T. Coates & Co.
Captain Bolton's Corpse. J. G Jeffreys, pseud. LC 81-71197. 1982. 10.95 (ISBN 0-8027-5470-8). Walker.
Captain Boycott. Philip Rooney & Charles Cunningham Boycott. 1966. pap., 1.25. Anvil Bks.
Captain Boycott: A Romantic Novel. Philip Rooney. LC 46-20584. 1946. D. Appleton-Century Company, Inc.
Captain Boycott & the Irish. Joyce Marlow. LC 73-78914. 1973. 8.95 o.p. (ISBN 0-8415-0271-4). Dutton.
Captain Brand, of the "Centipede". A Pirate of Eminence in the West Indies: His Loves and Exploits, Together with Some Account of the Singular Manner by Which He Departed This Life. Henry Augustus Wise. LC 24-11867. 1864. Harper & Brothers.
Captain Brand of the Schooner "Centipede," a Pirate of Eminence in the West Indies: His Loves and Exploits, Together with Some Account of the Singular Manner by Which He Departed This Life. Henry Augustus Wise. LC 9-2673. (On cover: Harper's Franklin square library. no. 756). 1894. Harper & Brothers.
Captain Bright: A Story of Missionary Heroism and Adventure in the Himalaya Country of Sikkim. Per Westerlund. LC 61-7247. 1961. Augustana Press.
Captain Cat. Robert O Holles. LC 60-12886. 1960. Macmillan.
Captain Caution. Kenneth Roberts. 14.95 (ISBN 0-385-04794-0). Doubleday.
Captain Caution. Kenneth Roberts. 224p. 1982. pap. 2.95 (ISBN 0-449-24509-8, Crest). Fawcett.
Captain Caution: A Chronicle of Arundel. Kenneth Lewis Roberts. LC 34-39946. 1934. Doubleday, Doran & Company, Inc.
Captain Caution: A Chronicle of Arundel. Kenneth Lewis Roberts. LC 37-21034. 1937. Doubleday, Doran & Company, Inc.
Captain Caution: A Chronicle of Arundel. Kenneth Lewis Roberts. LC 40-4093. 1938. Doubleday, Doran & Company, Inc.
Captain Cavalier. Jackson Gregory. LC 27-162322. 1927. C. Scribner's Sons.
Captain Close, and Sergeant Croesus: Two Novels. Charles King. LC 42-28976. 1895. J. B. Lippincott Company.
Captain Comes to Eden. Ethel Gardner. LC 52-13079. Dorrance.
Captain Conan. Roger Vercel & Wells, Warre Bradley, 1892- Tr. LC 35-13670. H. Holt and Company.
Captain Contanceau: Or, The Volunteers of 1792. From the French of Emile Gaboriau. Emile Gaboriau. (On cover: Seaside library. Pocket ed. no. 1167). 1889. G. Munro.
Captain Courageous. Rudyard Kipling. Repr. lib. bdg. 12.05x (ISBN 0-88411-818-5). Amereon Ltd.
Captain Courtesy. Edward Childs Carpenter. LC 6-34083. 1906. G. W. Jacobs & Co.
Captain Crossbones. Donald Barr Chidsey. (Illus.). 240p. Date not set. pap. 2.50 (ISBN 0-441-09131-8, Pub. by Charter Bks). Ace Bks.
Captain Cut-Throat. John Dickson Carr. 232p. 1980. pap. 1.95 (ISBN 0-441-09134-2, Pub. by Charter Bks). Ace Bks.
Captain Cut-Throat. John Dickson Carr. (O.s.i.). 1976. pap. 1.50 o.s.i. (AD1645, Award). Univ Pub & Dist.
Captain Cut-Throat. 1st Ed. John Dickson Carr. LC 55-6569. 1955. Harper.
Captain Cutlass. Gordon D Schirreffs. 1978. 1.95 (ISBN 0-449-14001-6). Fawcett Gold Medal Books.
Captain Dan Richards. Everett Titsworth Tomlinson. LC 14-6194. 1914. The Griffith & Rowland Press.
Captain D'Artagnan. Lucien Pemjean. Tr. by Boyd, Madeleine Elise (Reynier) LC 33-11075. 1933. Doubleday, Doran & Company, Inc.
Captain Desmond, V. C. Katherine Helen Maud Marshall Diver. LC 11-4101. 1910. John Lane Company.
Captain Desmond, V. C. rev ed., in large part rewritten... ed. Katherine Helen Maud Marshall Diver. LC 14-135811. 1914. G. P. Putnam's Sons.
Captain Dionysios: A Romance of Old Marseilles. Catherine Ann Drinker Janvier. LC 35-5195. Dorrance & Company, Inc.
Captain Dreams: And Other Stories. Ed. by Charles King. Sydenham, Alvin Humphrey, 1867-1893 et al. LC 7-12228. 1895. J. B. Lippincott Company.
Captain Dreams: And Other Stories. Ed. by Charles King. Sydenham, Alvin Humphrey, 1867-1893 et al. LC 18-20850. 1899. J. B. Lippincott Company.
Captain Ebony. Hamilton Cochran. LC 43-16343. 1943. The Bobbs-Merrill Company.
Captain Fantom. Reginald Hill. LC 80-13978. 1980. 10.00 (ISBN 0-312-11949-6). St. Martin's Press.
Captain Fly-by-Night. Johnston McCulley. LC 26-163326. 1926. G. H. Watt.
Captain for Elizabeth. Jan Vlachos Westcott. 1948. Crown Publishers.
Captain Fracasse. Theophile Gautier. LC 76-15300. 1976. 16.00. H. Fertig.
Captain Fracasse. Theophile Gautier. LC 12-24117. 1880. G. P. Putnam's Sons.
Captain Fracasse. Theophile Gautier. Tr. by Ellen Murray Beam. LC 4-16679. 1897. L. C. Page & Company, Incorporated.
Captain from Castile. Samuel Shellabarger. LC 48-17424. 1945. Little, Brown.
Captain from Castile. Samuel Shellabarger. LC 44-9241. 1945. Little, Brown and Company.
Captain from Castile. Samuel Shellabarger. (N2681). 1963. Bantam.
Captain from Castile. A School Ed., by Frederick Houk Law. Samuel Shellabarger. LC 55-30077. 1955. Globe Book Co.
Captain from Castile, & Prince of Foxes. Samuel Shellabarger. LC 65-18136. 1965. bds., 6.95. Little.
Captain from Connecticut. Cecil Scott Forester. (Pathfinder ed., FP77). 1965. Bantam.
Captain from Connecticut. Cecil Scott Forester. LC 41-51802. 1941. Little, Brown and Company.
Captain Gallant. Sylvia Thorpe. LC 79-25387. 1980. 10.95 (ISBN 0-89340-246-X). J. Curley.
Captain Gardiner of the International Police, by Robert Allen Pseud. Allen Robert Dodd. LC 16-7231. 1916. 1.35. Dodd, Mead and Company.
Captain Gault: Being the Exceedingly Private Log of a Sea Captain. William Hope Hodgson. LC 18-9292. 1918. 1.35. R. M. McBride & Co.
Captain General: An Historical Romance. John P. Stevenson, pseud. LC 56-9052. 1956. Doubleday.
Captain-General: Being the Story of the Attempt of the Dutch to Colonize New Holland. William John Gordon. 1888. F. Warne and Co.
Captain Gore's Courtship: His Narrative of the Affair of the Clipper "Conemaugh" and Loss of the "Countess of Warwick," As Set Down by His Friend and Counsel. Thornton Jenkins Hains. LC 6-46169. (On cover: The lotos library). 1896. J. B. Lippincott Company.
Captain Grant. Shirley Seifert. LC 46-3637. 1946. J. B. Lippincott Company.
Captain Gray's Company: Or, Crossing the Plains and Living in Oregon. Abigail Scott Duniway. LC 20-193369. 1859. S. J. McCormick.
Captain Grown-up: A Novel. Kit Reed, pseud. LC 75-25994. 1976. 8.95. Dutton.
Captain Had a Wife: Translated from the French. Oscar Paul Gilbert. Tr. by Wells, Warre, Bradley. LC 37-36931. 1937. Doubleday, Doran & Company, Inc.
Captain Haratio Hornblower: Edited by Ardis Edwards Burton Educational Ed. Cecil Scott Forester. LC 55-4192. 1955. Globe Book Co.
Captain Hates the Sea. Wallace Smith. LC 33-841764. 1933. Covici, Friede.
Captain Hollister. David Chandler. LC 72-90548. 228p. 1973. 5.95 o.s.i. (ISBN 0-02-523650-4). Macmillan.
Captain Hollister: A Novel. David Chandler. LC 72-90548. 1973. 5.95. Macmillan.
Captain Horatio Hornblower. Cecil Scott Forester. LC 74-184460. (Illus.). 1964. Little, Brown.
Captain Horatio Hornblower. Cecil Scott Forester. LC 39-273094. 1939. Little, Brown and Company.
Captain Horatio Hornblower. Cecil Scott Forester. LC 43-21291. 1939. Little, Brown and Company.
Captain in the Ranks: A Romance of Affairs. George Cary Eggleston. LC 4-28207. 1904. A. S. Barnes & Co.
Captain Ironhand. Rosamond Van Der Zee Marshall. LC 57-741857. 1957. Appleton-Century-Crofts.
Captain Jack: A Story of Vermont, Illustrating the Struggles of the Green Mountain Boys During the Most Romantic Period of Their History. Cyrus D Roys. LC 9-29431. 1909. The Lakeside Press.
Captain Jackman: Or, A Tale of Two Tunnels. William Clark Russell. LC 99-3203. 1899. F. M. Buckles.
Captain Jacobus. Leslie Cope Cornford. LC 6-28735. 1896. Stone & Kimball.
Captain Jan. Jan De Hartog & Carlos Peacock. LC 77-552152. 1976. 3.50. White Lion.
Captain Java. Lily Moresby Adams Beck. LC 26-23098. 1928. Doubleday, Doran & Company, Inc.
Captain Jinks, Hero. Ernest Howard Crosby. LC 68-57519. (American novels of muckraking, propaganda, and social protest). (Illus.). 1968. Gregg Press.
Captain Jinks, Hero. Ernest Howard Crosby. LC 2-7128. 1902. Funk & Wagnalls Co.
Captain Johnny Ford. Ernest. LC 38-15215. 1938. Printed by Burkert-Walton Company.
Captain Judas. Francis Van Wyck Mason. LC 55-10033. (Pocket book, 1076. Fiction, 6). 1955. Pocket Books.
Captain Justice. Anthony Forrest. LC 81-2808. 13.95 (ISBN 0-8090-3357-7). Hill and Wang.
Captain Justice: Secret Agent Against Napoleon. Anthony Forrest. LC 82-60691. 320p. 1983. pap. 3.25 (ISBN 0-86721-234-9). Playboy Pbks.
Captain Kidd: A Novelization of the Screen Play. Norman Reilly Raine & Lee, Robert Nelson, 1890- LC 46-3012. 1945. The World Publishing Company.
Captain Kiddle. Andrew Magnus Fleming. LC 6-399315. 1889. J. B. Alden.
Captain Kidd's Gold. The True Story of an Adventurous Sailor Boy. James Franklin Fitts. (On cover: Boys' home library, v. 1 no. 10). 1888. A. L. Burt.
Captain Kyd: Or, The Wizard of the Sea. A Romance. Joseph Holt Ingraham. 1839. Harper & Brothers.
Captain Kyd: Or, The Wizard of the Sea. A Romance. Joseph Holt Ingraham. LC 24-9051. De Witt & Davenport.
Captain Lightfoot. William Riley Burnett. 224p. Repr. of 1954 ed. lib. bdg. 13.25x (ISBN 0-89190-495-6). Am Repr-Rivercity Pr.
Captain Lightfoot. 1st Ed. William Riley Burnett. LC 54-5976. 1954. Knopf.
Captain Little Ax. James Howell Street. LC 56-11682. 1956. Lippincott.
Captain Love: The History of a Most Romantic Event in the Life of an English Gentleman During the Reign of His Majesty George the First. Containing Incidents of Courtship and Danger As Related in the Chronicles of the Period and Now Set Down in Print. Roberts Theodore Goodridge. LC 8-15150. 1908. L. C. Page & Company.
Captain Lucifer. Dora Barford. LC 32-124500. 1931. Houghton Mifflin Company.
Captain MacDonald's Daughter: A Novel. Anna Mary Macleod. LC 7-20436. 1887. Harper & Brothers.
Captain Macedoine's Daughter. William McFee. LC 20-26979. 1920. Doubleday, Page & Company.
Captain Macklin: His Memoirs. Richard Harding Davis. LC 2-22173. 1902. C. Scribner's Sons.
Captain Macklin: His Memoirs. Richard Harding Davis. 1910. C. Scribner's Sons.
Captain McRae: A Novel of the Northwest Frontier. William Heuman. LC 54-6382. 1954. Morrow.
Captain Madam. George H Walton. LC 73-17982. 1974. (pbk.) 1.25 (ISBN 0-515-03287-5). Pyramid Books.
Captain Mandeville: A Novel. John Robert McMahon. (Dillingham's American authors library. no. 6). 1895. G. W. Dillingham, Successor to G. W. Carleton & Co.
Captain Mansana: And Other Stories. author's ed. Bjornstjerne Bjornson. LC 79-103494. (Short story index reprint series). 1969. Books for Libraries Press.
Captain Mansana, and Other Stories. author's ed. Bjornstjerne Bjornson & Anderson, Rasmus Bjorn, 1846- Tr. LC 6-11718. 1882. Houghton, Mifflin and Company.
Captain Margaret: A Romance. John Masefield. LC 79-145166. 1972. (ISBN 0-403-01094-2). Scholarly Press.
Captain Marooner. Louis Bennett Davidson. LC 52-8851. 1952. Crowell.
Captain Marraday's Marriage. Thomas Cobb. LC 19-1776. 1918. 1.40. John Lane.
Captain Martha Mary. by avery abbott. ed. Avery Abbott. LC 12-357923. 1912. The Century Co.
Captain Millett's Island. Katharine Newlin Burt. LC 44-5241. 1944. Macrae-Smith-Company.
Captain Molly: A Love Story. Mary Andrews Denison. LC 6-33998. 1897. Lee and Shepard.

Captain Moonlight... Ethel Edith Mannin. LC 42-50909. 1942. Jarrolds Limited.

Captain Nancy. Peggy O'More, pseud. LC 41-19648. Gramercy Publishing Co.

Captain Nash and the Wroth Inheritance. Ragan Butler. LC 76-29856. 7.95 (ISBN 0-312-11970-4). St. Martin's Press.

Captain Needs a Mate. Eric Hatch. LC 38-213232. 1938. Lothrop, Lee & Shepard Company.

Captain Nelson: A Romance of Colonial Days. Samuel Adams Drake. (On cover: Harper's library of American Action. v. 12). 1879. Harper & Brothers.

Captain Nemesis. Francis Van Wyck Mason. LC 57-11173. (Pocket book, 1176. Fiction, 6). 1957. Pocket Books.

Captain Nemesis. Francis Van Wyck Mason. LC 31-1196. 1931. G. P. Putnam's Sons.

Captain Newman, M. D. 1st Ed. Leo Calvin Rosten. LC 61-122332. 1962. Harper.

Captain Newman, M.D. Leo Calvin Rosten. (YA) (gr. 7-12). 1968. pap. 0.75 o.p. (T1124, Crest). Fawcett World.

Captain Nice. William Johnston. LC 67-18859. (Tempo books, T-155). 1967. Grosset & Dunlap.

Captain Nicholas: A Modern Comedy. Hugh Walpole. LC 34-25933. 1934. Doubleday, Doran & Company, Inc.

Captain Nicholas: A Modern Comedy. Hugh Walpole. LC 37-1450. 1936. The Sun Dial Press, Inc.

Captain Norton's Diary: And A Moment of Madness. Florence Marryat Church Lean. LC 7-13588. (On cover: Lovell's library. v. 19. no. 938). 1887. J. W. Lovell Company.

Captain of Company K. Joseph Kirkland. LC 68-20016. (Americans in Fiction). (Illus.). 1968. Gregg Press.

Captain of Company K. Joseph Kirkland. LC 7-125159. 1891. Dibble Publishing Company.

Captain of Company K. see Collected Works.

Captain of His Soul. Henry James Forman. LC 14-19849. 1914. McBride, Nast & Company.

Captain of Industry. Enoch Johnson. LC 8-25744. 1908. The C. M. Clark Publishing Company.

Captain of Industry: Being the Story of a Civilized Man. Upton Beall Sinclair. LC 7-8534. 1906. The Appeal to Reason.

Captain of Industry, Being the Story of a Civilized Man... Upton Beall Sinclair. (Little blue book, no. 635, ed. by E. Haldeman-Julius). Haldeman-Julius Company.

Captain of Men. Enoch Anson More. LC 5-10446. 1905. L. C. Page & Company.

Captain of Raleigh's: A Romance. Roberts Theodore Goodridge. LC 11-3943. 1911. gfull name: george edward theodore roberts, surname after 1911 goodridge roberts 1.25. L. C. Page & Company.

Captain of St. Margaret's. Ferenc Molnar & Mussey, June Barrows, 1910- Tr. LC 44-51331. 1945. Duell, Sloan and Pearce.

Captain of the Amaryllis. Stoughton Cooley. LC 11-1926. 1.50. The C. M. Clark Publishing Company.

Captain of the Araby: The Story of a Voyage. Howard Pease. LC 53-52964. 1953. Doubleday.

Captain of the Avenger. Michael John Paris. LC 41-1476. The Falcon Press.

Captain of the Camp: Or, Ben the Young Boss. Edward Sylvester Ellis. LC 10-27194. (Half-title: Catamount camp series). 1.00. The John C. Winston Company.

Captain of the Gray-Horse Troop. Hamlin Garland. LC 73-104460. (Illus.). 1970. Literature House.

Captain of the Gray-Horse Troop: A Novel. special limited ed. new york, grosset & dunlap. ed. Hamlin Garland. LC 72-84706. 1974. 16.00 (ISBN 0-403-02966-X). Scholarly Press.

Captain of the Gray-Horse Troop: A Novel. Hamlin Garland. LC 20-16462. Harper & Brothers.

Captain of the Grayhorse Troop see Collected Works.

Captain of the Janizaries: A Story of the Times of Scanderbeg and the Fall of Constantinople. James Meeker Ludlow. LC 13-2071. 1886. Dodd, Mead & Company.

Captain of the Janizaries: A Story of the Times of Scanderbeg and the Fall of Constantinople. James Meeker Ludlow. 1890. Harper & Brothers.

Captain of the Janizaries: A Story of the Times of Scanderbeg and the Fall of Constinople. James Meeker Ludlow. LC 7-14743. (On cover: Harper's quarterly, no. 3). 1893. Harper & Brothers.

Captain of the Jehovah. Henry Burgess Drake. LC 36-23260. Greenberg.

Captain of the Kansas. Louis Tracy. LC 7-6181. 1907. E. J. Clode.

Captain of the King. Chester Leigh Saxby. LC 14-19280. 1914. Sherman, French & Company.

Captain of the Kittiewink. Herbert Dickinson Ward. LC 4-16478. 1892. Roberts Brothers.

Captain of the Medici. John J Pugh. LC 53-7310. 1953. Little, Brown.

Captain of the "Pole-Star," And Other Tales. Arthur Conan Doyle. (On cover: Seaside library. Pocket ed. no. 2077). 1894. G. Munro.

Captain of the Polestar: And Other Tales. Arthur Conan Doyle. LC 70-116950. (Short story index reprint series). (Illus.). 1970. Books for Libraries Press.

Captain of the Polestar: And Other Tales. Arthur Conan Doyle. LC 16-7554. 1913. Longmans, Green and Co.

Captain of the Polestar, & Other Tales. Arthur Conan Doyle. LC 70-116950. (Short Story Index Reprint Ser). 1894. 17.00 (ISBN 0-8369-3453-9). Ayer Co.

Captain of the Push. Kenneth Roberts. (Illus.). 8.50 o.p. (ABC). Soccer.

Captain of the Sands. Keith Dewhurst. LC 81-65268. 1981. 14.95 (ISBN 0-670-20351-3). Viking Press.

Captain of the Temple Guard: An Historical Tale from the Time of the Destruction of Jerusalem. Anton Ohorn. Tr. by Kjellstrand, August William. LC 29-5416. Augustana Book Concern.

Captain O'Sullivan: Or, Adventures, Civil, Military, and Matrimonial, of a Gentleman on Half Pay. William Hamilton Maxwell. LC 28-4873. 1846. Harper & Brothers.

Captain Pantoja and the Special Service. Vargas Llosa, Mario. LC 76-26280. 10.00 (ISBN 0-06-014494-7). Harper & Row.

Captain Paul. Edward Ellsberg. LC 41-7943. 1941. Dodd, Mead & Company.

Captain Pete in Alaska. James Cooper Wheeler. LC 10-18957. E. P. Dutton & Company.

Captain Pete of Cortesana. James Cooper Wheeler. LC 9-25823. E. P. Dutton & Company.

Captain Pete of Puget Sound. James Cooper Wheeler. E. P. Dutton & Company.

Captain Pott's Minister. Francis L Cooper. LC 22-17453. Lothrop, Lee & Shepard Co.

Captain Protheroe's Fortune: A Story of the Sea As Told to the Author by George Henry Grummet, Mate of the Schooner Effie Dean. Oswald Kendall. LC 13-20756. 1913. 1.25. A. C. McClurg & Co.

Captain Ravenshaw: Or, The Maid of Cheapside, a Romance of Elizabethan London. Robert Neilson Stephens. LC 1-20956. 1901. L. C. Page & Company.

Captain Rebel. Frank Yerby. LC 56-11248. 1956. Dial Press.

Captain Rebel. Frank Yerby. 1975. (pbk.) 1.75. Dell.

Captain Rediegs. Sabra Conner. LC 30-15100. The Reilly & Lee Co.

Captain Rougemont: Or, The Miraculous Conversion. And, The Disowned. Just Jean Etienne Roy. Tr. by Huntington, Mary. LC 8-95325. 1875. Benziger Brothers.

Captain Salt in Oz. Ruth P. Thompson. (Illus.). 1936. 3.50 o.p. Reilly & Lee.

Captain Salvation. Frederick William Wallace. LC 25-17060. 1925. Minton, Balch & Company.

Captain Sam's Daughter. Ella Booker Cook. LC 57-847212. 1957. Dorrance.

Captain Samson, A.B. Gavin Douglas. LC 37-19006. 1937. G. P. Putnam's Sons.

Captain Sazarac. Charles Tenney Jackson. LC 22-15472. The Bobbs-Merrill Company.

Captain Sazarac. Charles Tenney Jackson. LC 41-41839. 1922. Grosset & Dunlap.

Captain Sex. Cleo Conlon. 176p. pap. 1.95 o.p. (6112). Brandon.

Captain Shannon. Coulson Kernahan. LC 7-10818. 1896. Dodd, Mead and Company.

Captain Shapely: A Comedy of London Town and the Oxford Road in the Days of Queen Anne. Harold Brighouse. LC 24-81647. 1924. R. M. McBride & Company.

Captain Shays: A Populist of 1786. George Robert Russell Rivers. LC 7-410152. 1897. Little, Brown and Co.

Captain Sinbad. Graham Diamond. 250p. 1980. pap. 2.25 (ISBN 0-449-14341-4, GM). Fawcett.

Captain Singleton. Daniel Defoe. 1969. Repr. of 1906 ed. 8.95x (ISBN 0-460-00074-8, 74, Evman). Biblio Dist.

Captain Singleton. The King of Pirates. A New Voyage Around the World. Daniel Defoe. LC 36-737582. 1935. The Dial Press.

Captain Singleton: The Life, Adventures, & Pyracies of the Famous Captain Singleton. Daniel Defoe. Ed. & intro. by Shiv K. Kumar. (Oxford English Novels Ser). 312p. 1973. pap. 3.25x o.p. (ISBN 0-19-281139-8). Oxford U Pr.

Captain; Stories of the Black Border. Ambrose Elliott Gonzales. LC 78-37593. (Black Heritage Library Collection). (Illus.). 1972. (ISBN 0-8369-8969-4). Books for Libraries Press.

Captain Sutter's Gold. Jonreed Lauritzen. LC 64-11394. 1964. Doubleday.

Captain Ted. Mary Teresa Waggaman. LC 10-5878. 1910. Benziger Brothers.

Captain the Cure. Margaret Elsie Crowther Baillie-Saunders. LC 15-18106. 1915. Hodder and Stoughton.

Captain Tom. A Novel. St. George Rathborne. LC 8-238. (On cover: Primrose series, no 34). Street & Smith.

Captain. Tr. Aleksei Silych Novikou-Priboi. 1946. Hutchinson International Authors.

Captain Trafalgar: A Story of the Mexican Gulf. Paschal Groysset & Westall, William, 1835-1903, Ed and Tr. LC 44-14179. 1887. Cassell & Company, Limited.

Captain Wardlaw's Kitbags. Harold MacGrath. (On cover: Famous authors series, no. 36). 1923. Garden City Publishing Co., Inc.

Captain Waters: And Bill His Bo'son. A Tale of the Ocean and the Farm. Charles F Swain. LC 3-25647. 1877. J. P. Jewett.

Captain Whistler: A Historical Novel. Leon R Searles. LC 77-150114. 10.00 (ISBN 0-682-48701-5). Exposition Press.

Captain Whitecap. John Clagett. LC 55-10166. 1955. Crown Publishers.

Captain Wunder. Donald Serrell Thomas. LC 80-54088. 1981. 12.95 (ISBN 0-670-20355-6). Viking Press.

Captain Zillner: A Human Document. Rudolf Jeremias Kreutz. Tr. by Worster, W. J. Alexander. LC 20-9786. 1919. Hodder and Stoughton.

Captains All. William Wymark Jacobs. LC 71-86147. (Short story index reprint series). 1969. Books for Libraries Press.

Captains All. William Wymark Jacobs. LC 5-36927. 1905. C. Scribner's Sons.

Captains All. William Wymark Jacobs. LC 18-17615. 1917. C. Scribner's Sons.

Captains Alls. Albert Richard Wetjen. LC 24-15678. 1924. A. A. Knopf.

Captains and Kings. Taylor Caldwell. (Crest, X1819). 1973. (pbk.) 1.75. Fawcett.

Captains and the Kings. Taylor Caldwell. LC 74-178831. 1972. 8.95. Doubleday.

Captains and the Kings Depart: And Other Stories. Helen Eustis. LC 49-10968. 1949. Harper.

Captain's Beach. Sigrid De Lima. LC 50-5211. 1950. Scribner.

Captain's Bride: A Tale of the War. W. D. Herrington. LC 72-162219. (Confederate Imprints Collection Ser.). 22p. 1973. Repr. of 1864 ed. 6.00 o.p. (ISBN 0-405-04325-2). Arno.

Captain's Brigade. Alice Marie Dodge. 1973. pap. 0.75 o.s.i. (01-372). Lancer.

Captain's Chair: A Story of the North. Robert Joseph Flaherty. LC 38-29966. 1938. C. Scribner's Sons.

Captain's Compliments. B. E Mariner. 1974. 5.95 (ISBN 0-533-01043-8). Vantage Press.

Captains Courageous,". Rudyard Kipling. LC 28-1663. 1923. Doubleday, Page & Company.

Captains Courageous". Rudyard Kipling. 1924. Doubleday, Page & Company.

Captains Courageous". Rudyard Kipling. LC 39-174985. 1937. The Sun Dial Press, Inc.

Captains Courageous". Rudyard Kipling. 1937. The Sun Dial Press, Inc.

Captains Courageous. limited ed. Rudyard Kipling. LC 78-108871. (Collector's Library of the World's Best-Loved Books). (Illus.). 1978. 39.00. Franklin Library.

Captains Courageous: A Story of the Grand Banks. Large Type Ed. Complete, Unabridged. Rudyard Kipling. LC 66-4051. (Keith Jennison bk.). 1966. 6.95, 4.95 lib. ed.,. Watts.

Captains Courageous" A Story of the Grand Banks. Rudyard Kipling. 1897. The Century Co.

Captains Courageous" A Story of the Grand Banks. Rudyard Kipling. LC 20-123508. 1919. The Century Co.

Captains Courageous: Abridged Version Illustrated by Rafaello Busoni. Rudyard Kipling. LC 60-8671. (World-famous book, 211). 1960. Hart Pub. Co.

Captains Courageous and Other Stories: Including Rikkitikki-Tavi, and The Maltese Cat. With Biographical Illus. and Drawings Reproduced from Early Editions Together with an Introd. and Captions by DeLancey Ferguson. Rudyard Kipling. LC 59-13470. (Great illustrated classics). 1959. Dodd, Mead.

Captains Courageous. Illustrated by Lawrence Beall Smith. Rudyard Kipling. LC 57-3435. 1957. Junior Deluxe Editions.

Captain's Curio. Eden Phillpotts. LC 33-19690. 1933. The Macmillan Company.

Captain's Daughter. Elizabeth Jane Coatsworth. LC 50-7333. 1950. Macmillan.

Captain's Daughter. Aleksandr Sergeevich Pushkin. Tr. by Duddington, Natalia Aleksandrovna (Ertel') LC 29-175344. 1928. The Viking Press Inc.

Captain's Daughter & Other Great Stories. Aleksandr Sergeevich Pushkin. 6.50 o.p. (ISBN 0-8446-0228-0). Peter Smith.

Captain's Daughter: And Other Stories; Translated with an Introd. by Natalie Duddington. Aleksandr Sergeevich Pushkin. LC 61-199509. (Everyman's library, 898). 1961. Dent.

Captain's Daughter & Other Tales. Aleksandr Sergeevich Pushkin. Tr. by Natalie Duddington. 1978. 8.95x (ISBN 0-460-00898-6, Evman); pap. 2.95x (ISBN 0-460-01898-1, Evman). Biblio Dist.

Captain's Daughter. From the Russian of Pushkin... Aleksandr Sergeevich Pushkin. (On cover: Seaside library. Pocket ed. no. 149). 1883. G. Munro.

Captain's Doll: Three Novelettes. David Herbert Lawrence. LC 23-7638. 1923. T. Seltzer.

Captain's House. Mary Kay Simmons. 1980. 1.95 (ISBN 0-671-81021-9). Pocket Books.

Captain's Lady. Rachel Edwards. 240p. (Orig.). 1980. pap. 1.95 (ISBN 0-89083-640-X). Zebra.

Captain's Lady. Basil Heatter. LC 50-5300. 1950. Farrar, Straus.

Captain's Last Child: From the German of Ernst Von Wildenbruch. Ernst Wildenbruch & Wirtz, Margaret Curme, Tr. LC 13-569090. 1909. M. A. Donohue & Co.

Captain's Nurse. Ruth Burnett. (YA) 1980. 6.95 (Avalon). Bouregy.

Captains of Souls. Edgar Wallace. LC 22-18234. Small, Maynard and Company.

Captains of the World. Gwendolen Overton. LC 4-26875. 1904. The Macmillan Company.

Captain's Pleasure. Mary R. Myers. (Orig.). 1981. pap. 2.75 (ISBN 0-449-14399-6, GM). Fawcett.

Captain's Rangers. Elmer Kelton. 176p. 1981. pap. 1.95 (ISBN 0-553-14990-3). Bantam.

Captain's Romance: Or, Tales of the Backwoods. (Miss Madam. Opie Percival Read. (On cover: Neely's popular library, no. 54). F. T. Neely.

Captain's Room. A Novel. Walter Besant & Rice, James. (Harper's Franklin square library, no. 221). 1818. Harper & Brothers.

Captain's Rose. Bill Fewell. 1979. pap. 4.00 (ISBN 0-89502-030-0). FEB.

Captains Table. John Canning. 1981. 9.95 (ISBN 0-8062-1743-X). Carlton.

Captain's Table: A Transatlantic Log. Sisley Huddleston. LC 32-8691. 1932. J. B. Lippincott Company.

Captain's Table: By Richard Gordon Pseud. 1st American Ed. Gordon Ostlere. LC 55-5246. Harcourt, Brace.

Captains Three. Norman Way. LC 12-9566. E. J. Clode.

Captain's Tiger. Short Stories. Jerome Weidman. LC 47-30402. 1947. Reynal & Hitchcock.

Captain's Toll-Gate. Frank Richard Stockton. 1903. D. Appleton & Company.

Captain's Vixen. Wanda Owen. 400p. (Orig.). 1981. pap. 2.50 (ISBN 0-89083-709-0). Zebra.

Captain's Walk. Elisabeth Welles. 1976. (pbk.) 1.50 (ISBN 0-671-80439-1). Pocket Books.

Captain's Wife. Margaret Storm Jameson. LC 39-171000. 1939. The Macmillan Company.

Captain's Wife. Storm Jameson. (Berkley Medallion Book). 1975. (pbk.) 1.50. Berkley Pub. Co.

Captain's Wife. Eiluned Lewis. LC 43-513014. 1944. The Macmillan Company.

Captain's Wife. John Lloyd. LC 8-15725. M. Kennerley.

Captain's Woman. Saliee O'Brien. (Orig.). 1979. pap. 2.50 (ISBN 0-671-81287-4). PB.

Captain's Woman: A Novel of the French Revolution. Christopher Nicole. (Signet Book). 1977. 1.95 (ISBN 0-451-07488-2). New American Library.

Captian Dieppe. Anthony Hope Hawkins. LC 1545. 1900. Doubleday & McClure Co.

Captivating Mary Carstairs. Henry Sydnor Harrison. LC 11-5228. 1.30. Small, Maynard and Company.

Captivating Mary Carstairs. Henry Sydnor Harrison. LC 14-9529. 1914. 1.35. Small, Maynard and Company.

Captivator. Christopher Nicole. LC 73-82251. 1974. 4.95 (ISBN 0-385-08432-3). Published for the Crime Club by Doubleday.

Captivator. Andrew York. LC 73-82251. 192p. 1974. 4.95 o.p. (ISBN 0-385-08432-3). Doubleday.

Captive. John Barclett. pap. 1.75 o.s.i. (V1034K, Venus). Grove.

Captive. 1977. pap. 1.25 o.p. (ISBN 0-525-22370-3). Dutton.

Captive. Bettina Kingsley. 1974. (pbk.) 0.95. Dell.

Captive. Marcel Proust. LC 70-21444. (His Remembrance of things past). 1970. 1.95 (ISBN 0-394-70598-X). Vintage Books.

Captive. Marcel Proust. Tr. by Scott-Moncrieff, Charles Kenneth. LC 29-138269. (His Remembrance of things part. vi). 1929. A. & C. Boni.

Captive. Robert Stallman. (Book of the Beast: Vol. 2). (Orig.). 1981. pap. 2.50 (ISBN 0-671-41382-1, Timescape). PB.

Captive. Carter Travis Young. LC 72-96268. 1973. 4.95 (ISBN 0-385-02731-1). Doubleday.
Captive. Carter Travis Young. 1974. (pbk.) 0.95. Manor Books.
Captive & the Free. Joyce Cary. 369p. 1976. Repr. of 1959 ed. lib. bdg. 15.75x (ISBN 0-89244-071-6). Queens Hse.
Captive and the Free: A Novel. Joyce Cary. LC 78-3863. 1978. 11.75 (ISBN 0-89244-071-6). Queens House.
Captive and the Free: A Novel. Introd. by David Cecil; Editor's Note by Winifred Davin. 1st Ed. Joyce Cary. LC 58-888550. 1959. Harper.
Captive Audience. Jessica Mann. LC 75-27141. (M W suspense). 1975. 6.95 (ISBN 0-679-50557-1). McKay.
Captive Bride. Johanna Lindsey. LC 77-80560. 1977. 1.95 (ISBN 0-380-01697-4). Avon Books.
Captive Bride. Lucy P. Stewart. 1978. pap. 1.50 (ISBN 0-440-17768-5). Dell.
Captive by the Gordons. 1st Ed. Mildred Gordon & Gordon Gordon. LC 57-114207. 1957. Published for the Crime Club by Doubleday.
Captive City. John Appleby. LC 55-6995. 1955. W. Sloane Associates.
Captive City. Daniel Da Cruz. LC 76-8212. 1976. (ISBN 0-345-24769-8). Ballantine Books.
Captive Desire. Tate McKenna. (Candlelight Ecstasy Ser.: No. 74). (Orig.). 1982. pap. 1.95 (ISBN 0-440-11238-9). Dell.
Captive Desire. Kathleen Victor. 304p. 1982. pap. 2.95 (ISBN 0-86721-205-5). Playboy Pbks.
Captive Ecstasy. Elaine Barbieri. 1981. pap. 2.75 (ISBN 0-89083-738-4). Zebra.
Captive Flame. Patricia Phillips. 384p. (Orig.). 1980. pap. 2.50 (ISBN 0-515-05190-X). Jove Pubns.
Captive Goddess. Lois Bull. LC 35-22389. The Macaulay Compnay.
Captive Heart. Patti Beckman. 192p. (Orig.). 1980. pap. 1.50 (ISBN 0-671-57008-0, Pub. by Silhouette Bks). S&S.
Captive Heart. Barbara Cartland. 1973. pap. price not set o.p. (ISBN 0-515-03271-9). Pyramid Pubns.
Captive Heart see Royal Pledge.
Captive Herd. G Murray Atkin. LC 22-18553. Thomas Y. Crowell Company.
Captive in the Caucasus. Lev Nikolaevich Tolstoi. Tr. by Zlata Shoenberg & Jessie Domb. (Bilingual Ser.). (Illus.). 1945. 5.00 (ISBN 0-911268-45-6). Rogers Bk.
Captive in the Land. James Aldridge. LC 63-8742. 1963. Doubleday.
Captive in the Night. Donald Hubert Stokes. LC 51-12468. 1951. Coward-McCann.
Captive Innocence. Fern Michaels. 1981. pap. 2.95 (ISBN 0-345-27355-9). Ballantine.
Captive Island. August William Derleth. LC 60-13828. 5.95 (ISBN 0-88361-047-7). Stanton & Lee.
Captive Island. August William Derleth. 4.95 o.s.i. (ISBN 0-88451-032-8). Edco-Vis Assoc.
Captive Love. Anne N. Reisser. (Candlelight Ecstasy Ser.: No. 24). (Orig.). 1981. pap. 1.75 (ISBN 0-440-11059-9). Dell.
Captive Loving. Carole Mortimer. (Harlequin Presents Ser.). 192p. 1982. pap. 1.95 (ISBN 0-373-10603-3). Harlequin Bks.
Captive Mistress. Mark Revel. (Illus., Orig.). 1969. pap. 1.95 o.p. (6063). Brandon.
Captive of Desire. Alexandra Sellers. (Superromances Ser.). 384p. 1982. pap. 2.50 (ISBN 0-373-70013-X, Pub. by Worldwide). Harlequin Bks.
Captive of Kensington Palace. Eleanor Hibbert. LC 76-27122. (Queen Victoria series; 1). (Illus.). 1976. 8.95 (ISBN 0-399-11851-9). Putnam.
Captive of Kensington Palace. Eleanor Hibbert. (Queen Victoria Series; 1). (Illus.). 1.75 (ISBN 0-449-23413-4). Fawcett Crest Books.
Captive of Kensington Palace. Jean Plaidy. 1978. pap. 1.75 (ISBN 0-449-23413-4, Crest). Fawcett.
Captive of Kensington Palace. Jean Plaidy. LC 76-27122. 1976. 8.95 o.p. (ISBN 0-399-11851-9). Putnam Pub Group.
Captive of Love: Founded Upon Bakin's Japanese Romance Kumono Tayema Ama Yo No Tsuki (The Moon Shining Through a Cloud-Rift on a Rainy Night. Edward Greey & Takizawa, Bakin. LC 6-45441. 1886. Lee and Shepard.
Captive of the Heart. Kate Douglas. 1982. pap. 2.75 (ISBN 0-380-81125-1, 81125-1). Avon.
Captive of the Lust Master. Swenson. pap. 1.95 o.p. (ISBN 0-87977-141-0, DBB141). Dansk Blue Bk.
Captive of the Roman Eagles. Felix Ludwig Sophus Dahn. Tr. by Safford, Mary Joanna. 1902. A. C. McClurg & Co.
Captive of the Sahara. Edith Maude Hull. LC 31-19567. 1931. Dodd, Mead & Company.
Captive of the Studs. Ward Fulton. pap. 1.95 o.p. (ISBN 0-87977-130-5, DBB130). Dansk Blue Bk.
Captive Passions. Fern Michaels. LC 76-56142. 1977. pap. 2.50 (ISBN 0-345-29081-X). Ballantine.
Captive Princess: A Novel. Richard Henry Savage. (On cover: The welcome series, no. 34). 1898. The Home Publishing Company.
Captive Queen of Scots. Eleanor Hibbert. LC 72-105579. 1970. 6.95. Putnam.
Captive Queen of Scots. Jean Plaidy. (YA) 1970. 6.95 o.p. (ISBN 0-399-10116-0). Putnam.
Captive Rider. Anne Miller Downes. LC 56-6421. 1956. Lippincott.
Captive Scorpio. Alan Burt Akers. (Illus.). 1978. 1.50 (ISBN 0-87997-394-3). DAW Books.
Captive Splendors. Fern Michaels. 1980. pap. 2.50 (ISBN 0-394-28847-5). Ballantine.
Captive Universe. Harry Harrison. (Berkley Medallion Book). 1976. (pbk.) 1.25 (ISBN 0-425-03072-5). Berkley Publishing Corp.
Captive Universe. Harry Harrison. LC 69-11461. 1969. 4.50. Putnam.
Captive Wife. Warwick Deeping. 1933. Grosset & Dunlap.
Captive Witch. Dale Van Every. LC 51-12806. 1951. Messner.
Captive, Yet Conqueror: A Tale of the First Christian Century. Fanny Hooker. LC 7-5268. American Tract Society.
Captive Youths of Judah. Erasmus W Jones. 1856. J. C. Derby & Co.
Captives. Arthur Boardman. LC 75-12878. 1975. 8.95. Dutton.
Captives: A Novel in Four Parts. Hugh Walpole. LC 20-203219. (His The rising city: III). George H. Doran Company.
Captives in India, a Tale. metropolitan ed. Barbara Wreaks Hoole Hofland. LC 7-6592. 1835. D. Green.
Captives in Space. 2nd ed. Joseph Greene. (Griffon Ser). 1969. pap. 0.50 o.p. (Golden Pr). Western Pub.
Captives of Cupid: A Story of Old Detroit. Annetta Halliday Antona. LC 6-2053. 1896. J.F. Eby & Company.
Captives of the Desert. Zane Grey. LC 52-5441. 1952. Harper.
Captives of the Desert. Zane Grey. LC 81-6840. 1981. 13.95 (ISBN 0-8161-3240-2). G.K. Hall.
Captive's Return: The Story of Onesimus, the Runaway Servant. Sara Elizabeth Gosselink. LC 44-47311. 1944. Wm. B. Eerdmans Publishing Company.
Captivity. Margaret Pargeter. (Harlequin Romances Ser.). 192p. 1981. pap. 1.25 (ISBN 0-373-02422-3). Harlequin Bks.
Captivity of the Oatman Girls. R. B. Stratton. LC 76-104572. Repr. of 1857 ed. lib. bdg. 18.75 (ISBN 0-8398-1877-7). Irvington.
Capt'n Davy's Honeymoon: A Manx Yarn. Hall Caine. LC 6-21872. 1892. D. Appleton and Company.
Captors. John Farris. LC 79-80981. 1969. 5.95. Trident Press.
Capts. Speke's and Grant's Travels and Adventures in Africa. A Thrilling Narrative of the Perils and Hardships Experienced by Captains Speke and Grant, the Celebrated African Explorers. Who, After an Absence of Over Two Years, Have Just Returned from Central Africa... Felice Guzzoni. Barclay & Co.
Capture My Love. Mary Ann Taylor. (Signet Book). 1977. 1.50 (ISBN 0-451-07755-5). New American Library.
Capture of Crazy Dan. James Cogdell. 1979. 4.75 o.p. (ISBN 0-8062-1097-4). Carlton.
Capture of Jamaica: A Historical Novel. Taylor, Stanley Arthur Goodwin. LC 51-40024. (Pioneer Press series). 1951. Jamaica, Pioneer Press.
Capture of Paul Beck. Matthias McDonnell Bodkin. LC 11-14103. 1911. Little, Brown and Company.
Capture the Fleeting Moment. Eileen Finan & June Finan. 1970. 3.50 o.p. Vantage.
Captured! Ferdinand Huszti Horvath. LC 30-181952. 1930. Dodd, Mead & Company.
Captured By Love. Large Print ed. Jean Hager. LC 82-10667. 299p. 1982. 10.95 (ISBN 0-89621-389-7). Thorndike Pr.
Captured by the Navajos. Charles Albert Curtis. LC 4-9214. 1904. Harper & Brothers.
Captured Dream: And Other Stories. Alice French. LC 99-5639. (Little books by famous writers). 1899. Harper & Brothers.
Captured Heart. Glenna Finley, pseud. (Orig.). 1975. pap. 1.50 (ISBN 0-451-08310-5, W8310, Sig). NAL.
Captured Hearts. Mary Catherine Hanson. LC 81-43651. 1982. 10.95 (ISBN 0-385-17827-1). Doubleday.
Captured Hearts. Mary Catherine Hanson. LC 81-43651. 1982. 10.95 (ISBN 0-385-17827-1). Doubleday.
Captured: The Story of Sandy Ray. Charles King. LC 7-15592. R. F. Fenno & Company.
Captured Women. Photos by Jeff Dunas. (Illus.). 96p. pap. 12.95 (ISBN 0-394-62466-1). Grove.
Captures. John Galsworthy. LC 71-145026. 1970. Scholarly Press.
Captures. John Galsworthy. LC 23-12430. 1923. C. Scribner's Sons.
Capuchin. Othniel J Seiden. LC 81-85424. 12.95 (ISBN 0-917224-07-8). Gregory Publications.
Car: A Novel. Harry Crews. 1973. (pbk) 0.95 (ISBN 0-671-77630-4). Pocket Books.
Car: A Novel. Harry Crews. LC 76-166357. 1972. 5.95. Morrow.
Car and the Lady. Percy Freeman Megargel & Mason, Grace Sartwell. LC 8-22795. 1908. The Baker and Taylor Company.
Car Deal! Frank O'Rourke. LC 55-11308. 1955. Ballantine Books.
Car of Croesus. Ernest Poole. LC 30-860285. 1930. The Macmillan Company.
Car of Destiny. Charles Norris Williamson & Alice Muriel Livingston Williamson. LC 6-32362. 1906. McClure, Phillips & Co.
Car of Destiny. Charles Norris Williamson & Alice Muriel Livingston Williamson. LC 7-30841. 1907. The McClure Company.
Car Thief. Theodore Weesner. LC 75-140737. 1972. 6.95. Random House.
Car Thief. Theodore Weesner. 1973. (pbk) 1.50. Dell.
Car Trip to the City: A Juvenile. Betty Robinson. pap. 2.00 (ISBN 0-87164-083-X). William-F.
Cara Roma. Maria M Grant. (On cover: Seaside library. Pocket ed. no. 555). G. Munro.
Carabajal, the Jew. A Legend of Monterey, Mexico. Charles Kline Landis.
Caramour Woman. Charles Rigdon. 448p. 1983. pap. 2.95 (ISBN 0-446-90227-6). Warner Bks.
Cara's Masquerade. Jean Carew. (Alouette Romance Ser.). 128p. (Orig.). 1981. pap. 2.25 (ISBN 0-89531-135-6, 0198-96). Sharon Pubns.
Caravaggio: A Novel. Pierre Stephen Robert Payne. LC 68-17272. (Illus.). 1968. Little, Brown.
Caravan. John Galsworthy. LC 25-159823. 1925. C. Scribner's Sons.
Caravan. Eleanor Furneaux Smith. LC 43-13006. 1943. Doubleday, Doran and Company, Inc.
Caravan. Eleanor Furneaux Smith. LC 43-10419. 1943. Hutchinson & Co. Ltd.
Caravan for China: A Novel. Frank S Stuart. LC 41-532. 1941. Doubleday, Doran and Company, Inc.
Caravan from Ararat: A Novel. James P Terzian. LC 59-8793. 1959. Muhlenberg Press.
Caravan into Canaan. Grant Taylor. LC 34-4675. 1934. J. B. Lippincott Company.
Caravan Man. Ernest Goodwin. LC 18-18338. 1918. 1.50. Houghton Mifflin Company.
Caravan of Death. Karl May. 1979. 12.95 (ISBN 0-8264-0077-9). Continuum.
Caravan of Death: A Novel. Karl Friedrich May. LC 79-1248. (Collected works of Karl May; ser. 3, v. 2). 1979. 12.95 (ISBN 0-8164-9361-8). Seabury Press.
Caravan Passes. Tabori, George. LC 51-767. 1951. Appleton-Century-Crofts.
Caravan to Camul. John Clou. LC 54-6494. 1954. Bobbs-Merrill.
Caravan to Vaccares. Alistair MacLean. LC 77-124558. 1970. 5.95. Doubleday.
Caravan to Xanadu: A Novel of Marco Polo. Edison Marshall. LC 53-7572. 1953. Farrar, Straus and Young.
Caravaners. Mary Annette Beauchamp Russell Russell. LC 9-28154. 1909. Doubleday, Page & Company.
Caravans. Edward D Dunn. LC 38-29530. 1938. G. P. Putnam's Sons.
Caravans. James Michener. 1979. pap. 2.95 (ISBN 0-449-23959-4, Crest). Fawcett.
Caravans. James A. Michener. 1963. 14.95 (ISBN 0-394-41849-2). Random.
Caravans: A Novel. James A Michener. LC 81-7023. 1981. 16.95 (ISBN 0-8161-3261-5). G.K. Hall.
Caravans: A Novel. James Albert Michener. LC 63-16152. 1963. Random House.
Caravans: A Novel. James Albert Michener. LC 63-16152. (Fawcett Crest Book). 1973. (pbk.) 1.50. Fawcett.
Caravans by Night. by harry hervey. ed. Harry Hervey. LC 22-3894. 1922. 1.90. The Century Co.
Caravans to Santa Fe. Alida Sims Malkus. LC 28-231144. 1928. Harper & Brothers.
Caraways. George Looms. LC 25-8366. Doubleday, Page & Company.
Carbon Copies. Octavus Roy Cohen. LC 32-21685. 1932. D. Appleton and Company.
Carbon Gang. Roger Lewis, pseud. 64p. 1983. pap. 4.00x (ISBN 0-916156-64-8). Cherry Valley.
Carbonels: A Story. Charlotte Mary Yonge. LC 9-1219. 1895. T. Whitaker.
Carcase for Hounds. Meja Mwangi. (African Writers Ser.). 1974. pap. text ed. 3.00x (ISBN 0-435-90145-1). Heinemann Ed.
Carcase for Hounds. Meja Mwangi. (African Writers Ser.: No. 145). 1974. pap. 1.75x o.p. (ISBN 0-435-90145-1). Humanities.
Carcase for Hounds. Meja Mwangl. LC 75-300231. (African writers series; 145). 1974. 1.75 (ISBN 0-435-90145-1). Heinemann Educational.
Carcellini Emerald: With Other Tales. Constance Cary Harrison. LC 79-98574. (Short story index reprint series). (Illus.). 1969. Books for Libraries Press.
Carcellini Emerald: With Other Tales. Constance Cary Harrison. LC 99-2543. 1899. H. S. Stone and Comapny.
Card. John Kidgell. LC 74-18297. (Flowering of the novel). 1974. 25.00 (ISBN 0-8240-1142-2). Garland Pug.
Card Castle. Matty Simmons. LC 70-127727. 1970. 5.95. Putnam.
Card for the Players: A Novel. Roland S Jefferson. LC 78-58558. 10.00 (ISBN 0-931656-00-1). New Bedford Press.
Card from Morocco. Robert Shaw. LC 69-14843. 1969. Harcourt, Brace & World.
Card Game. Aaron Fletcher. 1980. pap. 1.75 o.s.i. (ISBN 0-505-51456-7). Tower Bks.
Card Index & Other Plays. Tadeusz Rozewicz. Tr. by Adam Czerniawski. Incl. Interrupted Act; Gone Out. 1970. pap. 1.95 o.p. (ISBN 0-394-17381-3, E338, Ever). Grove.
Card 13. Mark Lee Luther & Ford, Mrs. Lillian Cummings, 1881- Joint Author. The Bobbs-Merrill Company.
Cardboard Candidate. Edward B. Van Buren. 5.95 o.p. Carlton.
Cardboard Castle. Percival Christopher Wren. LC 38-8554. 1938. Houghton Mifflin Company.
Cardboard Crown. 1st American Ed. Martin Boyd. LC 52-12965. 1953. Dutton.
Carder's Paradise. Malcolm Levene. LC 76-86392. 1969. 4.95. Walker.
Cardiff Estate. A Story. Julia MacNair Wright. LC 9-920. American Tract Society.
Cardiff Giant. Kimball. LC 66-17037. 1966. 3.50 o.s.i. (ISBN 0-88361-020-5). Wisconsin Hse.
Cardigan. Robert William Chambers. LC 30-232003. Harper & Brothers.
Cardigan: A Novel. Robert William Chambers. LC 1-22992. 1901. Harper & Brothers.
Cardigan-Cowboy. Charles Horace Snow. LC 35-13548. 1935. Macrae Smith Company.
Cardigan Square. Alexandra Manners, pseud. 1978. pap. 1.95 (ISBN 0-425-03837-8, Medallion). Berkley Pub.
Cardigan Square. Anne Rundle. LC 76-57200. 8.95 (ISBN 0-399-11918-3). Putnam.
Cardillac. Robert Barr. LC 9-24961. 1909. 1.50. F. A. Stokes Company.
Cardinal. Henry Morton Robinson. LC 50-6669. 1950. Simon and Schuster.
Cardinal & the Queen. Evelyn Anthony. 1968. 5.95 o.p. (ISBN 0-698-10043-3). Coward.
Cardinal and the Queen. Eve Stephens, pseud. (Berkley Medallion Book). 1977. 1.50 (ISBN 0-425-03591-3). Berkley Pub. Corp.
Cardinal and the Queen. Eve Stephens, pseud. LC 68-23367. 1968. Coward-McCann.
Cardinal & the Secretary: Thomas Wolsey & Thomas Cromwell. Neville Williams. (O.s.i.). (Illus.). 288p. 1976. 9.95 o.s.i. (ISBN 0-02-629070-7). Macmillan.
Cardinal Family... Ludovic Halevy & Ives, George Burnham, 1856- Tr. LC 6-46665. (Added t.-p.: Roman contemporain. Realists. vol. iii). 1897. Printed Only for Subscribers by G. Barrie & Son.
Cardinal of the Medici: Being the Memoirs of the Nameless Mother of the Cardinal Ippolito De' Medici. Susan Emily Christian Hicks Beach. LC 37-9932. 1937. The University Press.
Cardinal of the Medici: Being the Memoirs of the Nameless Mother of the Cardinal Ippolito De' Medici. Susan Emily Christian Hicks Beach. LC 37-8400. 1937. The Macmillan Company.
Cardinal Richelieu. Taken from the Play. Lytton, Edward George Earle Lytton Bulwer-Lytton. LC 6-23112. (On cover: Lovell's library, v. 4, no. 152). J. W. Lovell Company.
Cardinal Sin. Eugene Sue & Donovan, Mrs. Alexina (Loranger) Tr. (On cover: Idylwild series, v. 1, no. 22). 1892. Morrill, Higgins & Co.
Cardinal Sin, a Novel. Frederick John Fargus. LC 6-384104. (On cover: Lovell's library. v. 14, no. 715). 1886. J. W. Lovell Company.
Cardinal Sins. Elizabeth Maury Coombs. LC 36-14276. Chapman & Grimes.
Cardinal Sins. Andrew M. Greeley. LC 80-25150. 12.95 (ISBN 0-446-51236-2). Warner Books.
Cardinalli Contract. E. Richard Johnson. (Orig.). 1975. pap. 1.25 o.p. (ISBN 0-515-03584-X, V3584). Pyramid Pubns.
Cardinal's Daughter. A Sequel to "Ferne Fleming.". Catherine Ann Ware Warfield. LC 8-34839. T. B. Peterson & Brothers.
Cardinal's Daughter: An Italian Historic Romance. LC 35-38585. 1935. Meador Publishing Company.
Cardinal's Mistress. Benito Mussolini. Tr. by Motherwell, Hiram. LC 28-19750. 1928. A. & C. Boni.

Cardinal's Musketeer. Mary Imlay Taylor. 1900. A. C. McClurg & Co.
Cardinal's Pawn. How Florence Set, How Venice Checked, and How the Game Fell Out. K. L. Montgomery, pseud. LC 12-18731. 1910. A. C. McClurg & Co.
Cardinal's Rose: A Novel. William Gilbert Van Tassel Sutphen. LC 1-3834. 1900. Harper & Brothers.
Cardinal's Rose: A Novel. William Gilbert Van Tassel Sutphen. LC 7-36485. 1901. Harper & Brothers.
Cardinal's Scar: The Story of a Matador. Christian Irby. LC 38-4882. 1938. Dodd, Mead & Company.
Cardinal's Snuff Box. Henry Harland. LC 2827. 1900. J. Lane.
Cardinal's Snuff-Box. Henry Harland. LC 3-25550. 1903. J. Lane.
Cardinal's Snuff-Box. Henry Harland. 1931. Dodd, Mead & Co.
Cardome: A Romance of Kentucky. Anna Catherine Minogue. LC 5-29451. P. F. Collier & Son.
Cardross Luck. Janet Louise Roberts. (Candlelight regency). 1974. (pbk.) 0.75. Dell.
Cards and Kings. Johannes Tralow & Chambers, Whitaker, Tr. LC 31-32984. 1931. R. Long & R. R. Smith, Inc.
Cards Never Lie. Laura A. Bowser. 1966. 4.00 o.p. (ISBN 0-682-44060-4). Exposition.
Cards of Identity. Nigel Forbes Dennis. 1955. Vanguard Press.
Cards on the Table. Agatha Miller Christie. 1974. (pbk.) 0.95. Dell.
Cards on the Table. Agatha Miller Christie. LC 68-6254. (Greenway edition 5). 1968. 3.95. Dodd, Mead.
Cards on the Table. Agatha Miller Christie. LC 37-27109. 1937. Dodd, Mead & Company.
Care of a Soul. Marie Healy Bigot. Tr. by Loranger, Alexina. LC 6-12739. (On cover: The optimus series, no. 14). 1891. Donohue, Henneberry & Co.
Care of American Embassy. David Coxe Cooke. 1967. 4.95 o.p. (ISBN 0-396-05494-3). Dodd.
Care of Devils. Sylvia Press. LC 58-6248. 1958. Beacon Press.
Care of Time. Eric Ambler. LC 81-7789. 60.00 (ISBN 0-374-11898-1) (ISBN 0-374-11897-3). Farrar Straus and Giroux.
Care of Time. Eric Ambler. LC 81-17260. 1982. 14.95 (ISBN 0-89340-382-2). J. Curley & Associates.
Careen. Virginia Coffman. (Dell Book). 1977. 1.50 (ISBN 0-440-18110-0). Dell Pub. Co.
Career. Dorothy Katherine Barclay Kennard. LC 23-6946. 1923. 1.90. The Century Co.
Career. Philip Duffield Stong. LC 36-27081. Harcourt, Brace and Company.
Career by Proxy. Faith Baldwin Cuthrell. 1974. (pbk.) 0.95. Warner Paperback Library.
Career by Proxy. Faith Baldwin Cuthrell. LC 39-11752. Farrar & Rinehart, Incorporated.
Career for Sale. Vida Hurst. LC 34-2144. Grosset & Dunlap.
Career for the Baron: By Anthony Morton Pseud. John Creasey. LC 50-10397. 1950. Duell, Sloan and Pearce.
Career in C Major. James Mallahan Cain. LC 48-15317. (New Avon library. 141). 1947. Avon Book Co.
Career Man. Nancy Hoyt. LC 33-116299. 1933. Doubleday, Doran & Company, Inc.
Career of a Beauty: A Novel. Henrietta Eliza Vaughan Stannard. LC 1-31061. 1901. J. B. Lippincott Company.
Career of a Nihilist: A Novel. Sergiei Mikhailovich Kravchinskii. LC 7-29003. 1889. Harper & Brothers.
Career of Beauty Darling. Dolf Wyllarde. LC 12-250672. 1912. John Lane Company.
Career of David Noble. Frances Parkinson Wheeler Keyes. LC 49-26247. 1949. Sun Dial Press.
Career of David Noble. Frances Parkinson Wheeler Keyes. LC 21-18092. Frederick A. Stokes Company.
Career of Dr. Weaver. Emma Henriette Schermeyer Backus. LC 13-6330. 1913. 1.25. L. C. Page & Company.
Career of Joy. Grace Eleanore Towndrow. LC 9-266688. 1909. The C. M. Clark Publishing Company.
Career of Katherine Bush. Elinor Sutherland Glyn. LC 16-22757. 1916. 1.30. D. Appleton and Company.
Career of Mrs. Osborne. Susan Carleton Jones & Milecete, Helen. 1903. The Smart Set Publishing Co.
Career of Philip Hazen. John Harriman. LC 41-223561. Howell, Soskin.
Career of Puffer Hopkins. Cornelius Mathews. LC 70-93644. (American fiction series). 1970. (ISBN 0-512-00516-8). Garrett Press.
Career of Puffer Hopkins. Cornelius Mathews. LC 72-8202. 1972. (ISBN 0-8422-8094-4). MSS Information Corp.
Career of Sin. Marvin Rhodes. 1970. pap. 0.75 o.p. (75-371). Manor Bks.
Career of the Stolen Boy: Charlie. Caroline Oakley & Fern, Willie, Joint Author. LC 7-33272. 1881. W. H. Briggs.
Career Triumphant. Henry Burnham Boone. LC 3-21295. 1903. D. Appleton and Company.
Career Wife see Tycoon for Ann.
Careers of Cynthia. Allena Champlin Best. LC 33-3087. Harcourt, Brace and Company.
Carefree Days Ideals. Ed. by James A. Kuse. (Illus.). 1979. pap. 2.95 (ISBN 0-89542-324-3). Ideals.
Careful, He Might Hear You. Sumner Locke Elliott. 1973. pap. 1.50 o.p. (02022). Curtis.
Careful, He Might Hear You. 1st Ed. Locke-Elliott, Sumner, pseud. LC 63-10611. 1963. Harper & Row.
Carefully Considered Rape of the World: A Novel About the Unspeakable. Shepherd Mead. LC 66-12964. 1966. bds., 4.95. S. & S.
Careless Caresses. Florence Stonebraker. 1946. Phoenix Press.
Careless Hangman: A Mrs. Pym Story. Nigel Morland. LC 41-1587. Farrar & Rinehart, Incorporated.
Careless Heart. Peggy O'More, pseud. LC 52-7407. 1952. Arcadia House.
Careless Hussy. Thomas Stone. LC 39-5399. Phoenix Press.
Careless Hussy. Florence Stonebraker. LC 39-5399. 1939. Phoenix Press.
Careless Love. Alice Boyd Adams. LC 66-15795. bds., 4.50. New Amer. Lib.
Careless Mrs. Christian. Charlotte Murray Russell, pseud. LC 49-7244. 1949. Pub. for the Crime Club by Doubleday.
Careless People, by Helen Fowler and Bernard Harris. Helen Marjorie Fowler & Bernard Harris. LC 55-9908. 1955. Morrow.
Careless Rapture. Louise Platt Hauck. LC 43-4377. 1943. Macrae-Smith-Company.
Caress and Farewell. Lionel Houser. LC 34-33270. J. Messner, Inc.
Caress Unseen. Roy McCoy. (Orig.). pap. 0.95 o.p. (1126). Brandon.
Caresses. Dorothy Fletcher. 1981. pap. 2.50 (ISBN 0-89083-831-3). Zebra.
Caretaker Wife. Barbara Whitehead. LC 76-51992. 1978. 7.95 (ISBN 0-385-12778-2). Doubleday.
Caretaker Wife. Barbara Whitehead. (Berkley book). 1979. 1.95 (ISBN 0-425-04038-0). Berkley Pub. Corp.
Caretakers. Dariel Telfer. LC 59-13142. 1959. Simon and Schuster.
Carey & Julie. George B Mettler. 1973. (pbk) 1.25. Dell.
Carey Brown. Marguerite Pearman McIntire. LC 42-33801. Farrar & Rinehart, Inc.
Carey Girl. Decorations by Georg Hartmann. Elizabeth Yates. LC 56-709116. Coward-McCann.
Carey Gun. Irving A Greenfield. (Dell western, 1858). 1974. (pbk.) 0.75. Dell.
Carfitt Crisis, and Two Other Stories. John Boynton Priestley. LC 75-34382. 1976. 7.95 (ISBN 0-8128-1890-3). Stein and Day.
Carfrae's Comedy. Gladys Parrish. LC 16-263253. 1916. G. P. Putnam's Sons.
Cargamento Mortifero. new ed. Richard Sapir & Warren Murphy. Tr. by Margarita O. Castro from Eng. (Compadre Collection Ser.: El Destructor, No. 4). Orig. Title: Mafia Fix. 160p. (Span.). 1974. pap. 0.75 (ISBN 0-88473-404-8). Fiesta Pub.
Cargo. A. B Poole. LC 81-21227. (Adult Readers Library). 2.25 (ISBN 0-673-24130-0). Scott, Foresman.
Cargo of Brides. 1st Ed. Helen Rucker. LC 56-9064. 1956. Little, Brown.
Cargo of Eagles. Margery Allingham. LC 68-12151. (Illus.). 1968. Morrow.
Cargo of Parrots. R. Hernekin Baptist. 1937. Little, Brown and Company.
Cargo Risk. Michael Kirk, pseud. LC 80-1123. (Crime Club Ser.). 1980. 10.95 o.p. (ISBN 0-385-17272-9). Doubleday.
Cargo Risk. Bill Knox. LC 80-1123. 1980. 8.95 (ISBN 0-385-17272-9). Published for the Crime Club by Doubleday.
Cargoes. William Wymark Jacobs. LC 64-22036. (ILP26). 1965. Pocket Lib.
Cargoes: Famous Stories of the Sea. William Wymark Jacobs. (Orig.). pap. 2.50 (ISBN 0-8283-1430-6, 26, IPL). Branden.
Carib Gold. Ellery Harding Clark. LC 26-4943. The Bobbs-Merrill Company.
Carib Queens. Charles Elmer Waterman. LC 32-33294. 1932. The Chapple Publishing Company, Ltd.
Caribbean Account. Alan Furst. LC 81-5505. 11.95 (ISBN 0-440-01393-3). Delacorte Press.
Caribbean Caper. Robin Moore, pseud. 1978. pap. 2.25 (ISBN 0-532-19138-2). Woodhill.
Caribbean Caper. Joseph Rosenberger. (Murder Master Ser.: No. 2). 192p. (Orig.). 1974. pap. 1.25 o.p. (ISBN 0-532-12202-X). Woodhill.
Caribbean Caper. Joseph Rosenberger. (Murder master,#2). 1974. (pbk.) 1.25. Manor Books.
Caribbean Cavalier. 1st Ed. Davenport Steward. LC 57-8954. 1957. Dutton.
Caribbean Cocktail. Jane Corrie. (Harlequin Romance Ser.). 1979. pap. 1.25 (ISBN 0-373-02285-9, Pub. by Harlequin). PB.
Caribbean Conspiracy. Brenda Conrad. LC 42-21688. 1942. C. Scribner's Sons.
Caribbean Fiction & Poetry. Ed. by Marjorie Engber. LC 75-147072. 1970. pap. 1.25 o.p. (ISBN 0-913456-81-0). Interbk Inc.
Caribbean Kill see Batalla del Caribe.
Caribbean Love Song. Marlene Perriche. (YA) 1980. 6.95 (Avalon). Bouregy.
Caribbean Mystery. Agatha Miller Christie. LC 65-20906. 1965. 4.50. Dodd.
Caribbean Mystery. Agatha Miller Christie. (50449). 1966. Pocket Bks.
Caribbean Mystery. Agatha Miller Christie. 1973. (pbk.) 0.95 (ISBN 0-671-77703-3). Pocket Books.
Caribbean Nurse. large-type ed. Diana Douglas. (Signet nurse bk., T5294). 1972. New American Lib.
Caribee. Christopher Nicole. LC 73-78130. 1974. 7.95. St. Martin's.
Caribee. Thelma Strabel. LC 57-6154. 1957. Harper.
Cariboo Runaway. Frances Duncan. LC 77-350189. (Illus.). (ISBN 0-88768-070-4). Burns & MacEachern.
Carillon in Bruges: By Susan Gillespie Pseud. Edith Constance Bradshaw Turton-Jones. LC 52-1853. 1952. Hutchinson.
Carillon of Scarpa. Flora Klickmann. LC 25-12173. 1925. G. P. Putnam's Sons.
Carina: A Novel. Isabel Constance Clarke. LC 23-2468. 1923. Benziger Brothers.
Caring for No Man: A Novel. Linn Boyd Porter. LC 7-37773. 1875. W. F. Gill & Company.
Carissima: A Modern Grotesque. Mary St. Leger Kingsley Harrison. LC 7-28751. 1896. H. S. Stone & Co.
Carita: A Cuban Romance. Louis Beauregard Pendleton. LC 7-36371. 1898. Lamson, Wolffe and Company.
Carita. A Novel. Margaret Oliphant Wilson Oliphant. (Seaside library, v. 50, no. 1017). 1881. G. Munro.
Carl. Alex Melancon. LC 44-9337. 1944. The Macmillan Company.
Carl and Anna. Leonhard Frank. Tr. by Brooks, Cyrus Harry. LC 31-18078. 1930. G. P. Putnam's Sons.
Carl and Violet. N. D Bagnell. LC 6-5025. 1890. Hunt & Eaton.
Carl Laemmle Presents Ken: Maynard. in "Gun Justice". Quigley, Robert. (On cover: The big little books). Whitman Publishing Company.
Carleton, a Tale of Seventeen Hundred and Seventy-Six. John R. Willis. LC 6-20990. 1841. Lea & Blanchard.
Carleton Case. Ellery Harding Clark. LC 10-8160. 1.50. The Bobbs-Merrill Company.
Carletons: A Novel. Robert Grant. LC 6-44746. (Choice series, no. 43). 1891. R. Bonner's Sons.
Carlino. Giovanni Domenico Ruffini. LC 8-962. 1870. J. B. Lippincott & Co.
Carlito's Way. Edwin Torres. LC 75-14349. 1976. 7.95. Saturday Review Press.
Carlito's Way. Edwin Torres. 1977. 1.75 (ISBN 0-446-59809-7). Warner Books.
Carlona Legacy. Orlando R Petrocelli. LC 81-2463. 12.95 (ISBN 0-89433-158-2). Caroline House.
Carlos Confessions. Martin A. Craven. 1978. pap. 2.25 (ISBN 0-532-22143-5). Woodhill.
Carlos Contract: A Novel of International Terrorism. David Atlee Phillips. LC 78-14378. 8.95 (ISBN 0-02-596110-1). Macmillan.
Carlos Must Die. Uri Dan & Mann, Peter. (leisure Book.). 1978. 1.95 (ISBN 0-8439-0543-3). Nordon Pubns.
Carlotta and the Scientist. 2d ed. Patricia Riley Lenthall. (Illus.). 2.00 (ISBN 0-914996-12-6). Lollipop Power.
Carlotta's Castle. Jane McCarthy. (Candlelight Castle). 1973. (pbk.) 0.75. Dell.
Carlotta's House. Carole Hinton. LC 81-21228. 2.75 (ISBN 0-673-24128-9). Scott, Foresman.
Carlotta's Intended: And Other Tales. Ruth McEnery Stuart. LC 71-101822. (Short story index reprint series). (Illus.). 1969. Books for Libraries Press.
Carlotta's Intended: And Other Tales. Ruth McEnery Stuart. LC 8-16871. 1894. Harper & Brothers.
Carlovingian Coins: Or, The Daughters of Charlemagne; a Tale of the Ninth Century. Eugene Sue & De Leon, Daniel, 1852-1914, Tr. LC 9-8423. 1908. New York Labor News Company.
Carlyles. Stewart Collis. 1973. 6.95 o.p. (ISBN 0-396-06637-2). Dodd.
Carlyles: A Story of the Fall of the Confederacy. Constance Cary Harrison. LC 5-34474. 1905. D. Appleton and Company.
Carmela. Paul Gillette. LC 72-82178. 1973. (pbk.) 1.75. Warner Paperback.
Carmela. Frances Christine Tiernan. (On cover: Catholic library). H. L. Kilner & Co.
Carmela. Rowland Winn. LC 55-7510. 1955. W. Sloane.
Carmelite: A Novel. Elgin Earl Groseclose. LC 55-14640. 1955. Macmillan.
Carmen. John Benton. 1974. (pbk.) 1.25. Bantam Books.
Carmen. John Benton. LC 74-112463. 1970. 4.50. Revell.
Carmen. Prosper Merimee. Ed. by Walter Frank Charles Ade. LC 75-22471. 1976. 1.50 (ISBN 0-8120-0427-2). Barron's Educational Series, Inc.
Carmen. Prosper Merimee. Ed. by De Vries, Louis & Towne, Laura. LC 30-4008. 1930. Prentice-Hall, Inc.
Carmen. Prosper Merimee. Tr. by Garrett, Edmund Henry. Guiney, Louise Imogen. LC 4-16887. 1896. Little, Brown and Company.
Carmen. Prosper Merimee. Tr. by Johnson, Alfred Edwin. LC 18-19725. 1915. Hearst's International Library Co.
Carmen. Prosper Merimee. Tr. by Sterner, Albert. William Farquhar Payson.
Carmen. Prosper Merimee. Tr. by Lloyd, Mary. Limited Editions Club, Inc., New York. LC 41-10289. 1941. The Limited Edition Club.
Carmen and Colomba. Prosper Merimee. LC 66-1927. (Penquin classics, L168). 1965. Penguin Books.
Carmen and Mr. Dryasdust. Humfrey Robertson Jordan. LC 14-4586. 1914. 1.35. G. P. Putnam's Sons.
Carmen: And Other Stories. Prosper Merimee. Ed. by Manley, Edward. LC 7-21263. (International modern language series). Ginn & Company.
Carmen: And Other Stories. Prosper Merimee. Ed. by Manley, Edward. LC 19-8168. (International modern language series). Ginn and Company.
Carmen Ariza. Charles Francis Stocking. LC 16-723. 1916. The Maestro Co.
Carmen Ariza. Charles Francis Stocking. LC 31-241. 1927. The Maestro Co.
Carmen, Baby. Sebastian Grant. (Orig.). 1968. pap. 0.75 o.p. (A327S, Award). Univ Pub & Dist.
Carmen, Colomba, and Selected Stories. Prosper Merimee. LC 64-95. (Signet classic). 1963. New American Library.
Carmen, Colomba: And Selected Stories. New Tr. from French by Walter J. Cobb. Foreword by George Steiner. Prosper Merimee. (Signet classic, CP180). New Amer. Lib.
Carmen et Autres Nouvelles. Prosper Merimee. Ed. by Blondheim, David Simon. LC 30-32531. (Heath's modern language series). D. C. Heath and Company.
Carmen: La Venus d'Ille. Prosper Merimee. (Nouveaux Classiques Larousse). (Fr). pap. 2.95 (180). Larousse.
Carmen Miranda Memorial Flagpole. Gerald Rosen. LC 77-73554. 1977. 8.95 (ISBN 0-89141-032-5); pap. 3.95 (ISBN 0-89141-033-3). Presidio Pr.
Carmen Miranda Memorial Flagpole: A Novel. Gerald Rosen. LC 77-73554. 1977. 8.95. (ISBN 0-89141-032-5) (ISBN 0-89141-033-3). Presidio Press.
Carmen Miranda Memorial Flagpole: A Novel. Gerald Rosen. 1979. 3.95 (ISBN 0-380-43109-2). Avon Books.
Carmen of the Rancho. Frank Hamilton Spearman. LC 37-28770. 1937. Doubleday, Doran & Co., Inc.
Carmen of the Rancho. Frank Hamilton Spearman. LC 40-11461. 1940. The Sun Dial Press.
Carmen Sheila. Robert Keating Clay. LC 29-7071. 1929. J. B. Lippincott Company.
Carmen's Inheritance. Frances Christine Tiernan. LC 3-19820. (On cover: "To-day" series of standard novels, no. 1). 1873. To-Day Printing and Publishing Company.
Carmen's Messenger. Harold Bindloss. LC 17-13719. Frederick A. Stokes Company.
Carmichael. Anison North. LC 7-12002. 1907. Doubleday, Page & Company.
Carmilla & the Haunted Baronet. Joseph Sheridan Le Fanu. 1970. pap. 0.75 o.p. (ISBN 0-446-64323-8, 64-323). Paperback Lib.
Carnaby Curse. Daoma Winston. 1976. (pbk.) 1.50. Ace Books.
Carnaby Rex. Roderick MacLeish. LC 76-382506. 1976. 3.75 (ISBN 0-297-77146-9). Weidenfeld and Nicolson.
Carnacki: The Ghost-Finder. William Hope Hodgson. LC 48-5230. 1947. Mycroft and Moran.
Carnacki the Ghost-Finder. William Hope Hodgson. 3.00 o.p. Arkham.
Carnacki, the Ghost Finder, and a Poem. William Hope Hodgson. LC 10-26039. 0.25. P. R. Reynolds.
Carnac's Folly. Gilbert Parker. LC 24-25016. 1922. J. B. Lippincott Company.
Carnady Feud. Dean Owen. 192p. (Orig.). 1974. pap. 0.95 o.p. (ISBN 0-532-12473-1). Woodhill.

Carnady Feud. Dean Owen. 192p. (Orig.). 1974. pap. 0.95 o.p. (ISBN 0-532-12473-1). Manor Bks.
Carnage in Mexico. John A. Wilson. 1977. pap. 1.95 (ISBN 0-532-19161-7). Woodhill.
Carnage of the Realm. Charles A Goodrum. LC 78-27374. 8.95 (ISBN 0-517-53504-1). Crown Publishers.
Carnage of the Realm. Charles A Goodrum. LC 80-10633. 9.95 (ISBN 0-89340-265-6). J. Curley.
Carnal Cargo. Barry Devlin. LC 52-33577. 1952. Vixen Press.
Carnal Countess. Louis Du Valois. 1972. pap. 2.25 o.s.i. (V1115R, Venus). Grove.
Carnal Cruise. 1972. pap. 1.75 o.s.i. (V1114K, Venus). Grove.
Carnal Days of Helen Seferis. rev. ed. Alexander Trocchi. pap. 1.25 o.p. (2034). Brandon.
Carnal Kiss. Hudson Carr. pap. 1.95 o.p. (ISBN 0-87056-233-9, 6233). Brandon.
Carnal Knowledge. James Kerstetter. pap. 1.95 o.s.i. (OPH-215, Ophelia). Olympia.
Carnal Savage. Ted Hudson. 192p. (Orig.). 1974. pap. 1.95 o.p. (ISBN 0-87682-383-5, 7383). Barclay Hse.
Carnation Petals. Lois Fox. LC 16-6426. 2.00. The Schilling Press, Inc.
Carnavaron's Castle. Jean Francis Webb. LC 70-91864. 1969. 4.95. Meredith Press.
Carnelian Cube. Lyon Sprague De Camp & Fletcher Pratt. 1970. pap. 0.75 o.p. (ISBN 0-447-74676-6). Lancer.
Carnelian Cube: A Humorous Fantasy. Lyon Sprague De Camp & Pratt, Fletcher. LC 48-281722. 1948. Gnome Press.
Carnelian Throne. Janet E. Morris. 256p. (Orig.). 1981. pap. 2.50 (ISBN 0-553-14924-5). Bantam.
Carnellian Circle. Hendrix John. LC 75-10981. 1975. 8.95 (ISBN 0-689-10683-1). Atheneum.
Carnie Girls. Stan O'Dair. 192p. (Orig.). 1973. pap. 1.95 o.p. (ISBN 0-87682-376-2, 7376). Barclay Hse.
Carnival. Compton Mackenzie. LC 12-6560. 1912. 1.30. D. Appleton and Company.
Carnival. Compton Mackenzie. LC 25-23765. 1921. D. Appleton and Company.
Carnival! Julian Rathbone. LC 76-27622. 1976. 7.95. St. Martin's Press.
Carnival! Julian Rathbone. LC 77-359677. 1976. 3.95 (ISBN 0-7181-1505-8). Joseph.
Carnival by the Sea. Sigrid De Lima. LC 54-591595. 1954. Scribner.
Carnival Colors. Maude Lavinia Radford Warren. LC 25-5963. The Bobbs-Merrill Company.
Carnival: Entertainments and Posthumous Tales. Karen Blixen. LC 77-5666. 1977. 10.00 (ISBN 0-226-15303-7). University of Chicago Press.
Carnival: Entertainments & Posthumous Tales. Isak Dinesen, pseud. LC 77-5666. 1979. pap. 4.95 (ISBN 0-226-15304-5, P851). U of Chicago Pr.
Carnival: Entertainments & Posthumous Tales. Isak Dinesen, pseud. Tr. by Mitchell & Paden. LC 77-5666. 1977. 10.00 (ISBN 0-226-15303-7). U of Chicago Pr.
Carnival for Killing. Nick Carter. (Nick Carter Ser). (O.s.i.). (Orig.). 1969. pap. 0.75 o.s.i. (A938S, Award). Univ Pub & Dist.
Carnival Girl. Jane Littell. LC 31-7409. 1931. L. MacVeagh, The Dial Press.
Carnival Girl: A Novel. Richard Glendinning. LC 56-26165. (Popular library, 718). 1956. Popular Library.
Carnival Is for Lovers. Barry Caldwell. LC 36-20247. 1936. Godwin.
Carnival Murder. John Victor Turner. LC 33-23353. H. Holt and Company.
Carnival Night. Marta Teodonno. LC 46-50. 1945. The Christopher Publishing House.
Carnival of Destiny. Vance Thompson. LC 72-4415. (Short story index reprint series). 1972. 11.25 (ISBN 0-8369-4191-8). Books for Libraries Press.
Carnival of Destiny. Vance Thompson. LC 16-881046. 1916. Moffat, Yard & Company.
Carnival of Sadists. Mason George. pap. 1.95 o.s.i. (Venus). Grove.
Carnival of Swappers. Rex Weldon, pseud. 176p. pap. 1.95 o.p. (6102). Brandon.
Carnival on Quicksand. Valerie Dade Savage. LC 37-15349. 1937. Doubleday, Doran and Company, Inc.
Carnival. 1st Ed. Berry Fleming. 1953. Lippincott.
Caro. Bernard Packer. 1.95 (ISBN 0-380-00841-6). Avon.
Caro: A Novel. Bernard Packer. LC 75-11858. 1975. 8.95 (ISBN 0-525-07650-6). Dutton.
Carol, the Pursued. Katheryn Kimbrough, pseud. (Saga of the Phenwick Women: No. 29). (Orig.). 1979. pap. 1.75 (ISBN 0-445-04505-1). Popular Lib.
Carol Trent: Air Stewardess. Jeanne Judson. LC 56-3372. 1956. Avalon Books.
Carola: A Novel. Paul Myron Anthony Linebarger. LC 48-5102. Duell, Sloan and Pearce.
Carolina. Leonora Blythe. 224p. 1981. pap. 1.95 (ISBN 0-449-50205-8, Crest). Fawcett.
Carolina. James Noble Gifford. 1949. Arcadia House.
Carolina Cavalier: A Romance of the American Revolution. George Cary Eggleston. LC 1-31170. Lothrop Publishing Company.
Carolina Chansons: Legends of the Low Country. Du Bose Heyward & Allen, Hervey. LC 22-24847. 1922. The Macmillan Company.
Carolina Corsair. Don Tracy. LC 55-544462. 1955. Dial Press.
Carolina Ghost Tales. Nell S. Graydon. 3.95 o.p. Beaufort.
Carolina in the Morning. Mabel C Merritt. LC 77-153416. 1971. 5.00 (ISBN 0-8059-1529-X). Dorrance.
Carolina Jewel. Mary Dodgen Few. (Illus.). 225p. 1973. Repr. of 1970 ed. 6.95 (ISBN 0-914056-02-6). Carolina Edns.
Carolina Jewel. Mary Dodgen Few. LC 73-117160. 1970. 4.95 o.p. (ISBN 0-87667-058-3). Droke-Hallux.
Carolina Jewel: A Novel. Mary Dodgen Few. LC 73-117160. (Illus.). 1970. 4.95. Hallux.
Carolina Lee. Lilian Lida Bell. LC 6-772424. 1906. L. C. Page & Company.
Carolina Love Song. Peggy Gaddis, pseud. (O.s.i.). 176p. 1976. Repr. of 1966 ed. pap. 1.25 o.s.i. (AQ1571, Award). Univ Pub & Dist.
Carolina Love Story. Peggy Gaddis. 1976. (pbk.) 1.25. Award Books.
Caroline. Mollie Chappell. (Cameo Romance). (Fawcett gold medal book). 1975. (pbk.) 0.95. Fawcett.
Caroline. Jane Morgan. 1976. (ISBN 0-425-03145-4). Berkley Publishing Corp.
Caroline. Andre Norton, pseud. 320p. (Orig.). 1983. pap. 2.95 (ISBN 0-523-48059-8). Pinnacle Bks.
Caroline. Cynthia Wright. LC 77-6200. 1977. 1.95 (ISBN 0-345-27323-0). Ballantine Books.
Caroline, No. 152. Barbara Hazard. 224p. 1981. pap. 1.50 (ISBN 0-449-50225-2). Fawcett.
Caroline Affair. Gibbs-Smith, Charles Harvard. LC 54-6423. 1954. Viking Press.
Caroline and Julia. Clare Darcy. LC 81-51969. 1982. 9.95 (ISBN 0-8027-0694-0). Walker.
Caroline and Julia. Clare Darcy. LC 82-3085. 1982. 12.95 (ISBN 0-8161-3307-7). G.K. Hall.
Caroline, Caroline. Margaret Ritter. LC 75-40000. 1976. 6.95 (ISBN 0-684-14590-1). Scribner.
Caroline Cherie: By Cecil Saint-Laurent Pseud. Laurent-Cely, Jacques. LC 52-1578. 1952. Prentice-Hall.
Caroline Cherie, by Cecil Saint-Laurent Pseud. Translated from the French by Lawrence G. Blochman. 1st American Ed. Jacques Laurent. LC 52-1578. 1952. Prentice-Hall.
Caroline Coquette by Cecil Saint-Laurent Pseud. Translated from the French by Lawrence G. Blochman. Jacques Laurent. LC 53-5734. 1953. Fiction Library.
Caroline England: A Novel. Noel Streatfeild. Reynal & Hitchcock.
Caroline Hicks. Walter Karig. LC 51-427. 1951. Rinehart.
Caroline Minuscule. Andrew Taylor. LC 82-23443. 1983. 10.95 (ISBN 0-396-08149-5). Dodd, Mead.
Caroline of Courtlandt Street. Weymer Jay Mills. 1905. Harper & Brothers.
Caroline Ormesby's Crime. Herbert Adams. LC 29-6668. 1929. J. B. Lippincott Company.
Caroline R. Tim Heald. LC 80-66765. 1980. 11.95 (ISBN 0-87795-285-X). Arbor Hse.
Caroline's Waterloo. Betty Neels. (Harlequin Romances Ser.). 192p. 1981. pap. 1.25 (ISBN 0-373-02393-6, Pub. by Harlequin). PB.
Caroline's Way. Peter De Polnay. LC 73-174999. 1972. 1.80 (ISBN 0-491-00901-1). W. H. Allen.
Caroling Dusk. Countee Cullen. 1927. 8.00x o.p. (ISBN 0-06-101423-0, J & J Harper). Har-Row.
Carolinian. Rafael Sabatini. LC 25-5390. 1925. Houghton Mifflin Company.
Carolinian. Rafael Sabatini & Hahn, Barbara M., Ed. LC 26-21002. (Riverside literature series). Houghton Mifflin Company.
Carolinians: An Old-Fashioned Love Story of Stirring Times in the Early Colony of Carolina. Annie Lee Sloan. LC 5-2440. 1904. The Neale Publishing Company.
Carolinians. 1st Ed. Jane Barry. LC 59-8255. 1959. Doubleday.
Carolyn Had a Dream & Other Tales. Hassie C. Dunnegan. 3.00 o.p. Carlton.
Carolyn of the Corners. Ruth Belmore Endicott. LC 18-29063. 1918. 1.35. Dodd, Mead and Company.
Carolyn of the Sunny Heart. Ruth Belmore Endicott. LC 19-3421. 1919. 1.50. Dodd, Mead and Company.
Carousel. Rosamunde Pilcher. LC 82-5629. 1982. 9.95 (ISBN 0-312-12255-1). St. Martin's Press.
Carousel. Rosamunde Pilcher. LC 82-23322. 1983. 7.95 (ISBN 0-8161-3488-X). G.K. Hall.
Carp Among Minnows. Katharine Oliver Stanley-Brown. LC 61-16623. 1961. Dorrance.
Carpaccio Caper. Bill Strutton. LC 73-78749. 1973. 5.95 (ISBN 0-698-10550-8). Coward, McCann & Geoghegan.
Carpathian Caper. Jacques Sandulescu & Annie Gottlieb. LC 74-30584. 1975. 8.95 o.p. (ISBN 0-399-11511-0). Putnam Pub Group.
Carpathian Caper: A Novel. Jacques Sandulescu & Annie Gottlieb. LC 74-30589. 1975. 8.95 (ISBN 0-399-11511-0). Putnam.
Carpathian Castle. Jules Verne. 3.95. Assoc Bk.
Carpenter, Detective. Hamilton T. Caine. 256p. 1981. pap. 2.50 (ISBN 0-441-09162-8). Ace Bks.
Carpenter Years: A Novel. Arthur Allen Cohen. LC 67-11790. 1967. New American Library.
Carpentered Hen. John Updike. 1958. 6.95 o.p. (ISBN 0-06-014475-0, HarpT). Har-Row.
Carpenter's Son. Rosemary Haughton. LC 67-400. (Illus.). 1967. Macmillan.
Carpenter's Wife. B. A. Tompkins. 1977. pap. 1.00 o.p. (ISBN 0-931832-05-5). No Dead Lines.
Carpet-Baggery: A Novel by Clifford Lanier... 1871. Clifford Anderson Lanier. LC 39-24449. The Paragon Press.
Carpet from Bagdad. Harold MacGrath. LC 11-22327. The Bobbs-Merrill Company.
Carpet Knight: A Novel. Harriet Hare McClellan. LC 7-196572. 1885. Houghton, Mifflin and Company.
Carpet-Slipper Murder. Allan Campbell McLean. LC 57-11039. 1957. Washburn.
Carpetbagger: A Novel. Opie Percival Read & Frank Pixley. LC 72-2070. (Black Heritage Library Collection). (Illus.). 1972. 15.75 (ISBN 0-8369-9056-0). Books for Libraries Press.
Carpetbagger: A Novel. Opie Percival Read & Pixley, Frank. LC 99-4105. Laird & Lee.
Carpetbaggers. Harold Robbins. 1977. pap. 3.95 (ISBN 0-671-41709-6). PB.
Carpetbaggers. Harold Robbins. 1961. 7.95 o.s.i. (ISBN 0-671-12495-1). Trident.
Carpetbaggers. Harold Rubin. LC 61-12290. 1961. Simon and Schuster.
Carpets from Baghdad. Gershon Kranzler, pseud. saddle-stitched 3.00 (ISBN 0-87559-127-2). Shalom.
Carr. Phyllis Eleanor Bentley. LC 33-17285. 1933. The Macmillan Company.
Carradine Affair. Paula Allardyce, pseud. 1.95 (ISBN 0-671-80690-4). Pocket Books.
Carrefours Des Ivresses see Crossroads of Ectasy.
Carreta. B Traven. LC 72-88014. 1970. 5.95. Hill and Wang.
Carriage Entrance. Polan Banks. LC 47-2393. 1947. G. P. Putnam's Sons.
Carriage Seven, Seat Fifteen. Claude Aveline. 1969. 4.50 o.p. Doubleday.
Carriage Trade. Robert Thomsen. (Signet, W5564). 1973. (pbk.) 1.50. New American Lib.
Carriage Trade: A Novel. Robert Thomsen. LC 74-189746. 1972. 7.95 (ISBN 0-671-21161-7). Simon and Schuster.
Carriage 7, Seat 15. Claude Aveline. LC 70-78668. 1969. 4.50. Doubleday.
Carribbeans. Lee D. Willoughby. (Making of America Ser.: No. 42). 320p. (Orig.). 1983. pap. 3.25 (ISBN 0-440-01081-0, Bryans). Dell.
Carricks. Brooke Miller. (American Dynasty Ser.: Vol. 2). 352p. 1982. pap. 3.75 (ISBN 0-440-01413-1, Emerald). Dell.
Carrie. Stephen King. LC 73-9037. 216p. 1974. 12.95 (ISBN 0-385-08695-4). Doubleday.
Carrie: A Novel of a Girl with a Frightening Power. Stephen King. LC 73-9037. 1974. 5.95 (ISBN 0-385-08695-4). Doubleday.
Carrie Dumain. Harris Downey. LC 66-15153. 4.95. Regnery.
Carrie Emerson; or, Life at Cliftonville. 2d ed. Caroline A Hayden. 1856. J. French and Company.
Carrie: Movie Edition. Stephen King. 1976. pap. 2.95 (ISBN 0-451-11963-0, AE1963, Sig). NAL.
Carried by Storm: As Published in the New York Weekly, Vol. 34, No. 4. A Novel. May Agnes Early Fleming. LC 7-28446. G. W. Dillingham Co.
Carrie's War: T.V. Ed. Nina Bawden. (Illus.). 1980. pap. 2.95 (ISBN 0-14-005581-9). Penguin.
Carrington: A Novel of the West. Michael Whitney Straight. LC 59-15494. 1960. Knopf.
Carrington Incident. Niven Busch. LC 41-2707. 1941. W. Morrow and Co.
Carringtons of High Hill: An Old Virginia Chronicle. Mary Virginia Terhune. LC 19-14197. 1919. C. Schribner's Sons.
Carrion Eaters. William Howard Baker, pseud. LC 73-149335. 1971. 6.95. Putnam.
Carrion Eaters. Evan H Rhodes. LC 73-90694. 1974. 7.95 (ISBN 0-8128-1652-8). Stein and Day.
Carriston's Gift. Frederick John Fargus. LC 6-38440. (On cover: Lovell's library v. 12. no. 612). 1885. J. W. Lovell Company.
Carriston's Gift: And Other Tales. Frederick John Fargus. LC 6-38418. (Leisure hour series.--no. 166). 1885. H. Holt and Company.
Carroll Dare. Mary Teresa Waggaman. LC 3-28967. 1903. Benziger Brothers.
Carroll O'Donoghue: A Tale of the Irish Struggles of 1866, and of Recent Times. Christine Faber. LC 6-37859. 1881. P. J. Kennedy.
Carrol's Conversion: A Story of Life. Helen Van Metre Van-Anderson Gordon. LC 4-37049. The New York Magazine of Mysteries.
Carrots, As We All Know, Do Not Cast Shadows. Gregory W. Bitz. Ed. by George F. Bedell & Charles Fowler. (Illus.). 1977. pap. 7.95 (ISBN 0-916320-04-9). Red Studio.
Carrousel in the Congo. Jack V Wright. LC 74-129781. 1971. 4.50 (ISBN 0-8059-1491-9). Dorrance.
Carry Me Back. Shirley Brander. LC 35-310283. R. Speller, Inc.
Carry Me Back. Ed. by Mary MacArthur. (Orig.). 1978. pap. 4.95 (ISBN 0-916300-13-7). Gallimaufry.
Carry My Coffin Slowly. Lee Herrington. LC 51-4764. (Inner sanctum mystery). 1951. Simon and Schuster.
Carry on, Jeeves! Pelham Grenville Wodehouse. LC 27-23957. George H. Doran Company.
Carry on, Jeeves! Pelham Grenville Wodehouse. LC 30-123235. 1929. A. L. Burt Company.
Carry-Over. Ruth Suckow. LC 36-146251. Farrar & Rinehart, Incorporated.
Carry the Wind. Terry Johnston. 1982. 13.95 (ISBN 0-89803-106-0). Green Hill.
Carrying Signals". Frank R Robinson. LC 32-322. F. R. Robinson.
Carry's Confession. A Novel. Frederick William Robinson. (seaside library, v. 67, no. 1366). 1882. G. Munro.
Carson of Red River. Harold Bindloss. LC 24-219161. 1924. Frederick A. Stokes Company.
Carson of Venus. Edgar Rice Burroughs. LC 63-21729. (Illus.). 1963. Canaveral Press.
Carson of Venus. Edgar Rice Burroughs. LC 39-8614. E. R. Burroughs, Inc.
Carson of Venus. Edgar Rice Burroughs. 1973. (pbk) 0.95. Ace Books.
Cart: A Novel. Jacques Ferron. LC 81-189500. 1981. 7.95 (ISBN 0-920428-38-X). Exile Editions: Thornhill, Ont.: Distributed in Canada and the United States by Firefly Books.
Cartagena: Or, The Lost Brigade; a Story of Heroism in the British War with Spain, 1740-1742. Charles Winslow Hall & Cartagena, Colombia--Siege, 1741--Fiction. LC 98-1532. 1898. Lamson, Wolffe and Company.
Cartaret Affair. St. George Rathborne. LC 8-239. (On cover: The library of choice fiction, no. 13). 1891. Laird & Lee.
Cartas Boca Abajo see En la Ardiente Obscuridad.
Cartel. Edward Jay Epstein. LC 78-7490. 8.95 (ISBN 0-399-12086-6). Putnam.
Cartel. Edward Jay Epstein. 1980. 2.50 (ISBN 0-425-04480-7). Berkley Publishing Corp.
Carter, and Other People. Don Marquis. LC 75-142269. (Short story index reprint series). 1970. (ISBN 0-8369-3753-8). Books for Libraries Press.
Carter and Other People. Don Marquis. LC 21-14288. 1921. D. Appleton and Company.
Carter of Fear. Patrick Moore. LC 62-16751. Harvey House.
Carter Quarterman. A Novel. William Mumford Baker. LC 11-10554. 1876. Harper & Brothers.
Carteret's Cure. Clifford James Kosken. LC 26-22416. 1926. Houghton Mifflin Company.
Cartoon Crimes. Kenneth Robeson. (Avenger, no. 31). 1974. (pbk.) 0.95. Warner Paperback Library.
Cartoon Sexhibit. Ed. by Harold Straubing. (Illus., Orig.). 1969. pap. 1.95 o.p. (6049). Brandon.
Cartoon Sexhibit. Ed. by Harold Straubing. 192p. 1974. pap. 1.25 o.p. (ISBN 0-87056-395-5, 6395). Brandon.
Cartouche. Frances Mary Peard. (Seaside library. v. 31, no. 642). 1879. G. Munro.
Cartridge Carnival. William Colt MacDonald. LC 45-2949. 1945. Doubleday, Doran & Co., Inc.
Cartridge Creek. Ben Haas. LC 73-79695. 1973. 4.95 (ISBN 0-385-01020-6). Doubleday.
Cartridge Creek. Richard Meade, pseud. 192p. 1975. pap. 0.95 o.p. (ISBN 0-532-95389-4). Woodhill.
Cartridge Creek. Richard Meade, pseud. LC 73-79695. (Double D Western Ser.). 192p. 1973. 4.95 o.p. (ISBN 0-385-01020-6). Doubleday.
Cartridge Creek. Richard Meade, pseud. 192p. 1975. pap. 0.95 o.p. (ISBN 0-532-95389-4). Manor Bks.
Cartwheels. Roger Burlingame. LC 35-4875. 1935. Doubleday, Doran & Company, Inc.
Cartwright Gardens Murder. Joseph Smith Fletcher. LC 26-122430. 1926. A. A. Knopf.

Cartwright Is Dead, Sir! Hugh Baker. LC 34-139981. 1934. Houghton Mifflin Company.
Carty. Gardner F Fox. LC 77-76238. 1977. 8.95 (ISBN 0-385-12866-5). Doubleday.
Caruthers Affair. William Nathaniel Harben. LC 98-1534. (Neely's universal library. v. 42). 1898. F. T. Neely.
Caruthers Affair. William Nathaniel Harben. LC 2525. (On cover: Magnet detective library. no. 128). 1900. Street & Smith.
Carved in Findruine: Tales Out of Irish Tradition. George Brandon Saul. LC 77-27876. Walton Press.
Carver. Patrick Barker. 1973. (pbk.) 0.95. Popular Lib.
Carvers of the Twelve Oaks. Louise Justice. 4.95 o.p. Vantage.
Cary Fordyce. Louise Platt Hauck. LC 43-10500. 1943. Dodd, Mead & Company.
Casa Braccio. Francis Marion Crawford. 1894. Macmillan and Co.
Casa con dos Puertas Mala Es de Guardar see Magico Prodigioso.
Casa Dorada. Janet Louise Roberts. (Candlelight Regency). 1973. (pbk) 0.75. Dell.
Casa Grande. Jude Deveraux. 304p. 1982. pap. 3.50 (ISBN 0-380-80192-2, 80192-2). Avon.
Casa Grande. Tomas Rivera. LC 76-15026. 1976. pap. 4.25 o.p. (ISBN 0-915808-40-4). Editorial Justa.
Casa Grande: A California Pastoral. Charles Duff Stuart. LC 6-34370. 1906. H. Holt and Company.
Casa Madrone. Mignon Good Eberhart. LC 79-5545. 8.95 (ISBN 0-394-50955-2). Random House.
Casablack. Christopher Leopold. LC 78-20238. 1979. 10.00 (ISBN 0-385-14388-5). Doubleday.
Casanova Embrace. Warren Adler. LC 77-18423. 9.95 (ISBN 0-399-12107-2). Putnam.
Casanova, M. D. Albert Quandt. LC 39-24924. 1939. Phoenix Press.
Casanova, M.D. Charles Thornton. LC 39-24924. Phoenix Press.
Casanova the Courier. David Skaats Foster. LC 6-40371. (On cover: Sunnyside series. no. 55). 1892. J. S. Ogilvie.
Casanova's Chinese Restaurant. 1st Ed. Anthony Dymoke Powell. LC 60-11639. 1960. Little, Brown.
Casanova's Homecoming. Arthur Schnitzler. LC 74-175576. 1971. 9.00 (ISBN 0-404-05619-9). AMS Press.
Casanova's Homecoming. Arthur Schnitzler. LC 48-10518. (New Avon Library, 160). 1948. Avon Book Co.
Casanova's Homecoming. Arthur Schnitzler. Tr. by Paul, Eden. LC 22-11593. 1921. Priv. Print. for Subscribers Only.
Casanova's Homecoming. Arthur Schnitzler. Tr. by Paul, Eden. Paul, Cedar. LC 22-25369. 1922. T. Seltzer.
Casanova's Homecoming. Arthur Schnitzler. Tr. by Paul, Eden. LC 30-317988. 1930. Simon and Schuster.
Casanova's Homecoming. A Novel. Arthur Schnitzler & Kent, Rockwell, 1882- Illus. LC 47-29042. 1947. Priv. Print. for the Sylvan Press.
Casanova's Women: Eleven Moments of a Year. John Erskine. LC 41-4406. 1941. Frederick A. Stokes Company.
Casbah Killers. Nick Carter. (Nick Carter Ser.). (O.s.i.). (Orig.). 1969. pap. 0.60 o.s.i. (A560X, Award). Univ Pub & Dist.
Casca: God of Death. Barry Sadler. 1982. pap. 2.50 (ISBN 0-441-29532-0). Ace Bks.
Casca, No. 6: The Persian. Barry Sadler. 224p. (Orig.). 1982. pap. 2.50 (ISBN 0-441-09219-5, Pub. by Charter Bks). Ace Bks.
Casca: Panzer Soldier. Barry Sadler. 1982. pap. 2.50. Ace Bks.
Casca: The Barbarian. Barry Sadler. (Casca Ser.). 208p. (Orig.). 1981. pap. 2.50 (Pub. by Charter Bks). Ace Bks.
Casca: The Eternal Mercenary. Barry Sadler. (Casca Ser.). 256p. (Orig.). 1979. pap. 2.50 (ISBN 0-441-21772-9, Pub. by Charter Bks). Ace Bks.
Casca: The Panzer Soldier. Barry Salder. (Casca Ser.). 224p. (Orig.). 1980. pap. 2.50 (ISBN 0-441-09222-5, Pub. by Charter Bks). Ace Bks.
Casca: The War Lord. Barry Sadler. (Casca Ser.). 196p. (Orig.). 1980. pap. 2.50 (ISBN 0-441-09221-7, Pub. by Charter Bks). Ace Bks.
Cascade Ghost. Lou Cameron. 1978. 1.50 (ISBN 0-445-04237-0). Popular Library.
Case Against Butterfly. Gregory Tree, pseud. LC 51-9733. 1951. Scribner.
Case Against Colonel Sutton: A Novel. Bruce Cameron. LC 61-12705. 1961. Coward-McCann.
Case Against Love. Tr. from French by Helen Weaver. Didier Decoin. LC 67-142234. 1967. 4.50. New Amer. Lib.
Case Against Myself. Gregory Tree, pseud. LC 50-8736. 1950. Scribner.
Case Against Org. Mark Dintenfass. 1970. 5.95 o.p. (ISBN 0-316-18601-5). Little.
Case Against Org: A Novel. Mark Dintenfass. LC 76-121431. 1970. 5.95. Little, Brown.
Case Against Satan. Ray Russell. 1962. 7.95 (ISBN 0-8392-1008-6). Astor-Honor.
Case Against Satan. Ray Russell. (O.s.i.). 192p. 1972. pap. 1.25 o.s.i. (AQ1326, Award). Univ Pub & Dist.
Case Against Satan: A Melodramatic Novel. Ray Russell. LC 62-10803. 1962. I. Obolensky.
Case and Exceptions: Stories of Counsel and Clients. Frederick Trevor Hill. LC 5738. Frederick A. Stokes Company.
Case and the Dreamer. Edward Hamilton Waldo, pseud. LC 74-166250. 1974. 4.95. N. Doubleday.
Case and the Dreamer: And Other Stories. Theodore Sturgeon. (Signet book). 1974. (pbk.) 0.95. New American Library.
Case and the Girl. Randall Parrish. LC 22-26240. 1922. A. A. Knopf.
Case Book of Jimmie Lavender. Vincent Starrett. LC 44-5857. 1944. Gold Label Books, Inc.
Case Book of Mr. Campion. Margery Allingham & Queen, Ellery, Pseud., Ed. LC 47-4655. (Mercury mysteries, 112). 1947. The American Mercury.
Case Book of Sherlock Holmes. Arthur Conan Doyle. LC 27-13974. George H. Doran Company.
Case Closed. June Thomson. LC 76-19623. 1977. 5.95 (ISBN 0-385-12267-5). Published for the Crime Club by Doubleday.
Case File: FBI, by the Gordons. 1st Ed. Mildred Gordon & Gordon Gordon. LC 53-6941. 1953. Published for the Crime Club by Doubleday.
Case File: The Best of the "Nameless Dectective" Stories. Bill Pronzini. 256p. 1983. 13.95 (ISBN 0-312-12338-8). St Martin.
Case for Appeal: By Lesley Egan Pseud. 1st Ed. Elizabeth Linington. LC 61-620982. 1961. Harper.
Case for Equity. Katharine Hill. LC 45-8331. 1945. E. P. Dutton & Company, Inc.
Case for Mr. Crook. Lucy Beatrice Malleson. LC 52-7153. 1952. Random House.
Case for Mr. Fortune... Henry Christopher Bailey. LC 32-26636. Pub. for the Crime Club, Inc., by Doubleday, Doran & Company, Inc.
Case for Mr. Paul Savoy. Jackson Gregory. LC 33-15009. 1933. C. Scribner's Sons.
Case for Nurse Marian. Adelaide Humphries. LC 57-8747. 1957. Avalon Books.
Case for Passion: By Jack Woodford Pseud. & James Matthews. Josiah Pitts Woolfolk & James Matthews. LC 53-25378. 1953. Signature Press.
Case for Sargeant Beef. Leo Bruce, pseud. 1977. 5.50 o.p. (ISBN 0-86025-017-2). State Mutual Bk.
Case for Sergeant Beef. Leo Bruce, pseud. 198p. 1980. 14.95 (ISBN 0-89733-037-4); pap. 4.50 (ISBN 0-89733-036-6). Academy Chi Ltd.
Case for Sergeant Beef. Leo Bruce, pseud. 198p. 1975. Repr. of 1951 ed. 7.95 o.p. (ISBN 0-86025-017-2, Pub. by Ian Henry Pubns England). Academy Chi Ltd.
Case for Sergeant Beef. Leo Bruce, pseud. 1979. 11.00x o.p. (ISBN 0-86025-017-2, Pub. by Ian Henry Pubns England). State Mutual Bk.
Case for Sergeant Beef. Croft-Cooke, Rupert. LC 80-20038. 1980. 9.95 (ISBN 0-89733-037-4) (ISBN 0-89733-036-6). Academy Chicago.
Case for the Angels. Gavin Lambert. LC 68-18640. 1968. Dial Press.
Case for the Baron. John Creasey. LC 49-48770. 1949. Duell, Sloan and Pearce.
Case for the Defendant. Hans Aufricht-Ruda. Tr. by Miall, Bernard. Wassermann, Jakob. LC 29-7072. 1929. Little, Brown, and Company.
Case for the Sea Serpent. Rupert T. Gould. LC 72-75791. 1969. Repr. of 1930 ed. 30.00x (ISBN 0-8103-3833-5). Gale.
Case for Three Detectives. Leo Bruce, pseud. LC 37-5301. 1937. Frederick A. Stokes Company.
Case History. Heinz Liepmann. LC 50-11135. 1950. Beechhurst Press.
Case History. Benjamin Siegel. LC 74-149090. 1971. 5.95. McKay.
Case History of Comrade V. A Novel. James Park Sloan. LC 71-184114. 1972. 4.95 (ISBN 0-395-13526-5). Houghton Mifflin.
Case in Camera. Oliver Onions. LC 21-3414. 1921. The Macmillan Company.
Case in Madrid. Edmund Naughton. 1973. pap. 0.75 o.p. (07285). Curtis.
Case in Nullity. Evelyn Berckman. LC 68-11768. 1968. Doubleday.
Case Is Altered. William Charles Franklyn Plomer. LC 32-22211. Farrar & Rinehart, Inc.
Case Is Altered. Sara Woods, pseud. LC 67-28827. 1967. Harper & Row.
Case Is Closed: A Romantic Mystery Novel. Patricia Wentworth. LC 37-2024. J. B. Lippincott Company.
Case Load-Maximum. E. Richard Johnson. LC 72-160659. 1971. 5.95 (ISBN 0-06-012213-7). Harper & Row.
Case of Anne Bickerton. Sydney Fowler Wright. LC 30-251581. 1930. A. & C. Boni.
Case of Bottled Murder. Elaine Wagner. LC 72-92249. 1973. 4.95 (ISBN 0-385-00318-8). Published for the Crime Club by Doubleday.
Case of Caroline Animus. Albert Leffingwell. LC 46-7099. 1946. The Dial Press.
Case of Charles Dexter Ward. Howard Phillips Lovecraft. 1982. pap. 1.95 (ISBN 0-345-30234-6, Del Rey). Ballantine.
Case of Charles Dexter Ward. Howard Phillips Lovecraft. (Boxer Ser). 1971. pap. 0.95 o.p. (95123). Beagle Bks.
Case of Charles Dexter Ward. Howard Phillips Lovecraft. LC 60-1069. 1969. Repr. pap. 0.60 o.p. (B60-1069). Belmont-Tower.
Case of Comrade Tulayev. Victor Serge. LC 70-362883. (Penguin modern classics). 1968. Penguin.
Case of Comrade Tulayev: A Novel. Victor Serge. LC 63-11248. (Doubleday anchor book). 1963. Anchor Books.
Case of Comrade Tulayev, a Novel. Victor Serge. LC 50-9058. 1950. Doubleday.
Case of Conscience. James Blish. LC 58-85690. (Ballantine books, BB256). 1958. Ballantine Books.
Case of Conscience. James Blish. LC 69-13673. 1969. 4.50. Walker.
Case of Conscience. Isabel Constance Clarke. LC 27-12296. 1927. Benziger Brothers.
Case of Conscience: Science Fiction Ser. James Blish. 1981. lib. bdg. cancelled o.s.i. (ISBN 0-8398-2673-7, Gregg). G K Hall.
Case of Constable Shields. Richard Greaves. LC 40-84744. Dorrance & Co., Inc.
Case of Constable Shields. Peter Simonds. LC 40-34744. Dorrance & Co., Inc.
Case of Doctor Horace: A Study of the Importance of Conscience in the Detection of Crime. John Harcourt Prentis. LC 7-12637. 1907. The Baker and Taylor Company.
Case of General Ople and Lady Camper. George Meredith. LC 26-23581. (On cover: Lovell's Westminister series. no. 3). 1890. J. W. Lovell Company.
Case of Jennie Brice. Mary Roberts Rinehart. LC 13-3809. 1.00. The Bobbs-Merrill Company.
Case of Jennie Brice. Mary Roberts Rinehart. LC 78-24222. 1978. 10.95 (ISBN 0-8161-6642-0). Hall.
Case of Jennie Brice. new ed. Mary Roberts Rinehart. 1975. (pbk.) 0.95. Dell.
Case of Jenny Brice. Mary Roberts Rinehart. 1976. lib. bdg. 12.95x (ISBN 0-89968-182-4). Lightyear.
Case of Jezebel: A Novel of the Biblical Queen of Evil. Frank Gill Slaughter. (A Kangaroo Book). 1977. 1.95 (ISBN 0-671-80921-0). Pocket Books.
Case of Joshua Locke: A New Tony Hunter Story. 1st Ed. Robert George Dean. LC 51-12812. (Guilt-edged mystery). 1951. Dutton.
Case of Kitty Ogilvie. Jean Stubbs. 1971. 5.95 o.p. (ISBN 0-8027-0356-9). Walker & Co.
Case of Kitty Ogilvie: A Novel. Jean Stubbs. (Bantam Gothic). 1974. (pbk.) 1.25. Bantam Books.
Case of Kitty Ogilvie: A Novel. Jean Stubbs. LC 74-161103. 1971. 5.95 (ISBN 0-8027-0356-9). Walker.
Case of Lady Broadstone. Arthur Williams Marchmont. LC 8-266806. 1908. Empire Book Company.
Case of Lucy Bending. Lawrence Sanders. 480p. 1982. 14.95 (ISBN 0-399-12724-0). Putnam Pub Group.
Case of Lucy Bending. Lawrence Sanders. 1983. pap. 3.95 (ISBN 0-425-06077-2). Berkley Pub.
Case of Marie Corwin: A Swivel Chair Solution. Jacob D. Posner. LC 33-23179. Covici, Friede.
Case of Mary Fielding. Margaret Erskine, pseud. (Ace gothic.). 1974. (pbk.) 0.95. Ace Books.
Case of Mary Fielding. Wetherby Williams. LC 73-103743. 1970. 4.50. Published for the Crime Club by Doubleday.
Case of Mary Sherman: A Novel. Jasper Ewing Brady. LC 17-20178. Britton Publishing Company.
Case of Matthew Crake. Adam Gordon MacLeod. LC 33-1958. 1933. L. MacVeagh, Dial Press, Inc.
Case of Mr. Cassidy: A Murder Mystery About a Chicago Book Collector. William Targ & Herman, Lewis, 1905- Joint Author. LC 39-314147. Phoenix Press.
Case of Mr. Crump. Ludwig Lewisohn. LC 65-9110. 1965. Farrar, Straus & Giroux.
Case of Mr. Crump. Ludwig Lewisohn. LC 47-2396. 1947. Farrar, Straus and Company.
Case of Mister Crump. rev. ed. Ludwig Lewisohn. 1965. pap. 2.25 o.p. (ISBN 0-374-50448-2, N284, Noonday). FS&G.
Case of Mr. Lucraft, and Other Tales: By Walter Besant and James Rice. Walter Besant & Rice, James. 1888. Dodd, Mead & Company.
Case of Mohammed Benani: A Story of to-Day. Ion Pericaris. LC 7-363591. 1888. D. Appleton and Company.
Case of Mrs. Wingate. Oscar Micheaux. LC 73-18593. (Illus.). 1975. 26.00 (ISBN 0-404-11404-0). AMS Press.
Case of Mrs. Wingate. Oscar Micheaux. LC 46-2765. 1944. Book Supply Company.
Case of Naomi Clynes: Inspector Richardson's Third Case. Basil Home Thomson. LC 34-35470. 1934. Pub. for the Crime Club, Inc., by Doubleday, Doran & Company, Inc.
Case of Need. Jeffery Hudson. (Signet Book, Q3924). 1973. (pbk.) 0.95. New American Lib.
Case of Need. Jeffery Hudson. LC 68-23845. 1974. (pbk.) 1.25. New American Library.
Case of Need: A Novel. Jeffery Hudson. LC 68-238454. 1968. 5.95. World.
Case of Paul Breen. Anthony Tudor. LC 11-18563. 1911. L. C. Page & Company.
Case of Reuben Malachi. Henry Sutherland Edwards. LC 6-36578. 1886. Rand, McNally & Co.
Case of Reuben Malachi. Henry Sutherland Edwards. (On cover: Seaside library. Pocket ed. no. 917). 1887. G. Munro.
Case of Richard Meynell. Mary Augusta Arnold Humphry Ward Ward. LC 11-27651. 1911. Doubleday, Page & Company.
Case of Robert Quarry. Andrew Garve. LC 72-181671. (Novel of Suspense). 208p. 1972. 5.95 o.p. (ISBN 0-06-011454-1, HarpT). Har-Row.
Case of Robert Quarry. Paul Winterton. LC 72-181671. 1972. 5.95 (ISBN 0-06-011454-1). Harper & Row.
Case of Robert Robertson. Sven Elvestad & Platt, Agnes, Tr. LC 30-16616. 1930. A. A. Knopf.
Case of Sardines: A Story of the Maine Coast. Charles Poole Cleaves. LC 4-136608. 1904. The Pilgrim Press.
Case of Sergeant Grischa. Arnold Zweig. LC 69-16144. (Great Novels and Memoirs of World War I, 5). (Giniger book.). 1970. 6.95. Stackpole Books.
Case of Sergeant Grischa. Arnold Zweig & Sutton, Eric, Tr. LC 28-30156. 1928. The Viking Press.
Case of Silent Partner. Erle Stanley Gardner. LC 40-325583. 1940. W. Morrow and Company.
Case of Sir Edward Talbot. Valentine Francis Taubman-Goldie. LC 22-14353. E. P. Dutton & Company.
Case of Sonia Wayward. John Innes Mackintosh Stewart. LC 60-11933. (Red badge detective). 1960. Dodd, Mead.
Case of Spirits. Peter Lovesey. LC 75-17758. (Red badge novel of suspense). 1975. 5.95 (ISBN 0-396-07218-6). Dodd, Mead.
Case of Spirits. Peter Lovesey. LC 77-4188. 1977. 8.95 (ISBN 0-89340-064-5). J. Curley.
Case of Spirits. Peter Lovesey. LC 78-302258. (Penguin crime fiction). 1977. 1.95 (ISBN 0-14-004333-0). Penguin Books.
Case of Summerfield. William Henry Rhodes. LC 7-29687. (Half-title: Western classics, no. 2). P. Elder & Company.
Case of Susan Dare. Mignon Good Eberhart. 303p. 1975. Repr. of 1934 ed. lib. bdg. 16.60x (ISBN 0-88411-751-0). Amereon Ltd.
Case of the Absent-Minded Professor. Aaron Marc Stein. LC 43-3873. 1943. Pub. for the Crime Club by Doubleday, Doran & Company, Inc.
Case of the Advertised Murder. Minna Bardon. LC 39-2606. 1939. Hillman-Curl, Inc.
Case of the Amateur Actor. Christopher Bush. LC 56-10960. (Cock Robin mystery). 1956. Macmillan.
Case of the Amorous Aunt. Gardner, Erle Stanley. LC 63-8803. 1963. Morrow.
Case of the Angry Mourner. Erle Stanley Gardner. LC 51-13232. 1951. Morrow.
Case of the April Fools. Christopher Bush. LC 33-7683. 1933. W. Morrow and Company.
Case of the Backward Mule. Erle Stanley Gardner. LC 46-188173. 1946. W. Morrow and Company.
Case of the Baited Hook. Erle Stanley Gardner. LC 40-27296. 1940. W. Morrow and Company.
Case of the Baited Hook. Erle Stanley Gardner. LC 78-3519. 1979. 10.95 (ISBN 0-89340-141-2). J. Curley.
Case of the Baker Street Irregulars. Anthony Boucher. 1980. lib. bdg. 11.95 (ISBN 0-8398-2655-9, Gregg). G K Hall.
Case of the Baker Street Irregulars. William Anthony Parker White. LC 40-85454. 1940. Simon and Schuster.
Case of the Baker Street Irregulars. William Anthony Parker White. LC 80-17973. (Gregg Press Mystery Fiction Series). 1980. 11.95 (ISBN 0-8398-2655-9). Gregg Press.
Case of the Barking Clock. Harry Stephen Keeler. LC 47-23768. 1947. Phoenix Press.
Case of the Beautiful Beggar. Erle Stanley Gardner. LC 65-18511. 1965. W. Morrow.
Case of the Beautiful Beggar. Erle Stanley Gardner. LC 76-47645. 1977. 8.95 (ISBN 0-89340-027-0). J. Curley.
Case of the Beautiful Beggar. Erle Stanley Gardner. (Perry Mason Mystery.). 1981. 1.95 (ISBN 0-345-29497-1). Pocket Books.
Case of the Benevolent Bookie. Christopher Bush. LC 56-261. (Cock Robin mystery). 1956. Macmillan.

Case of the Bigamous Spouse. Erle Stanley Gardner. 1961. 4.50 o.p. Morrow.
Case of the Black-Eyed Blonde. Erle Stanley Gardner. LC 44-8970. 1944. W. Morrow and Company.
Case of the Black Sheep: By Scott Finley Pseud. Winifred Clark. LC 50-6014. 1950. Phoenix Press.
Case of the Black Twenty-Two. Brian Flynn. LC 29-1804. 1929. Macrae Smith Company.
Case of the Blank Cartridge. Louis Trimble. LC 49-6579. 1949. Phoenix Press.
Case of the Blind Mouse. Martin Joseph Freeman. LC 35-821787. E. P. Dutton & Co., Inc.
Case of the Blonde Bonanza. Erle Stanley Gardner. 1962. 4.50 o.p. Morrow.
Case of the Borrowed Brunette. Erle Stanley Gardner. 1946. W. Morrow and Company.
Case of the Borrowed Brunette: And The Case of the Careless Cupid. Erle Stanley Gardner. (Perry Mason 2 in 1). 1976. (pbk.) 1.95 (ISBN 0-671-80470-7). Pocket Books.
Case of the Buried Clock. Erle Stanley Gardner. LC 43-6286. 1943. W. Morrow and Company.
Case of the Burnt Bohemian. Christopher Bush. LC 53-13507. 1954. Macmillan.
Case of the Canny Killer. Harry Stephen Keeler. LC 46-17778. 1946. Phoenix Press.
Case of the Careless Cupid. Erle Stanley Gardner. LC 76-55720. 1977. 9.95 (ISBN 0-8161-6447-9). G. K. Hall.
Case of the Careless Cupid. Erle Stanley Gardner. LC 68-18770. 1968. Morrow.
Case of the Careless Kitten. Erle Stanley Gardner. LC 42-199394. 1942. W. Morrow and Company.
Case of the Careless Kitten: A. New Perry Mason Story. Erle Stanley Gardner. LC 48-10594. 1948. Triangle Books.
Case of the Caretaker's Cat. Erle Stanley Gardner. LC 35-16584. 1935. W. Morrow and Company.
Case of the Cautious Coquette. Erle Stanley Gardner. LC 49-880943. 1949. W. Morrow.
Case of the Cheating Bride. Milton Morris Propper. LC 38-32407. 1938. Harper & Brothers.
Case of the Cheating Bride. Milton Morris Propper. LC 43-18841. (Black cat detective series. No. 5). 1943. Crestwood Publishing Co., Inc.
Case of the Chinese Gong. Christopher Bush. LC 35-21564. H. Holt and Company.
Case of the Chinese Gong. Christopher Bush. LC 41-4913. 1940. Triangle Books.
Case of the Cold Murderer. Ellen Godfrey. LC 76-367063. 1976. 4.95 (ISBN 0-7737-0023-4). Musson Book.
Case of the Constant God: Lieutenant Valcour's Most Exciting Case. Rufus King. LC 36-19978. 1936. Pub. for the Crime Club, Inc., by Doubleday, Doran & Company, Inc.
Case of the Constant God: Lieutenant Valcour's Most Exciting Case. Rufus King. LC 37-30673. 1937. The Sun Dial Press, Inc.
Case of the Constant Suicides. John Dickson Carr. LC 41-106775. Harper & Brothers.
Case of the Copy-Hook Killing. Royce Howes. LC 45-5843. 1945. E. P. Dutton & Company, Inc.
Case of the Corner Cottage. Christopher Bush. LC 52-3554. 1952. Macmillan.
Case of the Counterfeit Coin. George Wyatt. 1969. pap. 0.50 o.p. (Golden Pr). Western Pub.
Case of the Counterfeit Colonel. Christopher Bush. LC 53-11157. 1953. Macmillan.
Case of the Counterfeit Eye. Erle Stanley Gardner. LC 76-28465. 1976. 6.95 (ISBN 0-88411-406-6). Aeonian Press.
Case of the Counterfeit Eye. Erle Stanley Gardner. LC 35-6653. 1935. W. Morrow and Company.
Case of the Counterfeit Eye. Erle Stanley Gardner. LC 47-1742. 1947. Blakiston Co.
Case of the Crawling Cockroach. Harlan Reed. LC 37-13860. 1937. E. P. Dutton & Co., Inc.
Case of the Crimson Kiss. Erle Stanley Gardner. 1971. 7.95 (ISBN 0-688-01275-2). Morrow.
Case of the Crimson Kiss: A Perry Mason Novelette, and Other Stories. Erle Stanley Gardner. LC 70-142395. 1971. 4.95. W. Morrow.
Case of the Crooked Candle. Erle Stanley Gardner. LC 75-44974. (Fifty Classics of Crime Fiction, 1900-1950; 19). 1976. 12.00 (ISBN 0-8240-2368-4). Garland Pub.
Case of the Crooked Candle. Erle Stanley Gardner. LC 44-4331. 1944. W. Morrow and Company.
Case of the Crumpled Knave. William Anthony Parker White. LC 39-10129. 1939. Simon and Schuster.
Case of the Crumpled Knave. William Anthony Parker White. LC 41-6946. 1940. Mystery Book of the Month, Inc.
Case of the Crying Swallow. Erle Stanley Gardner. 1971. 7.95 (ISBN 0-688-01274-4). Morrow.
Case of the Crying Swallow: A Perry Mason Novelette and Other Stories. Erle Stanley Gardner. LC 79-151914. 1971. 4.95. W. Morrow.
Case of the Curious Bride. Erle Stanley Gardner. LC 34-381846. 1934. W. Morrow and Company.
Case of the Curious Bride. Erle Stanley Gardner. LC 43-5936. 1935. Grosset & Dunlap.
Case of the Curious Bride. Erle Stanley Gardner. LC 46-22505. 1946. Triangle Books, the Blakiston Company.
Case of the Curious Bride. Erle Stanley Gardner. 1973. (pbk.) 0.95 (ISBN 0-671-77890-0). Pocket Books.
Case of the Curious Chair: A Mystery Novel... Richard Pitts Powell. LC 45-15787. (Handi-book mysteries. 31).
Case of the Curious Client. Christopher Bush. LC 48-755721. 1948. Macmillan Co.
Case of the Dangerous Dowager. Erle Stanley Gardner. LC 76-41236. 1976. 6.95 (ISBN 0-88411-410-4). Aeonian Press.
Case of the Dangerous Dowager. Erle Stanley Gardner. LC 37-66873. 1937. W. Morrow and Company.
Case of the Daring Decoy. Erle Stanley Gardner. LC 57-10931. 1957. W. Morrow.
Case of the Daring Divorcee. Erle Stanley Gardner. LC 64-10510. 1964. Morrow.
Case of the Daring Divorcee. Erle Stanley Gardner. 1973. (pbk.) 0.95 (ISBN 0-671-77887-0). Pocket Books.
Case of the Daring Divorcee. Erle Stanley Gardner. LC 81-9857. (Perry Mason Mystery). 1982. 11.95 (ISBN 0-89340-361-X). J. Curley.
Case of the Dark Hero. Peter Cheyney. LC 48-161308. (New Avon library, 123). 1947. Avon Book Co.
Case of the Dead Cadet. Robert Portner Koehler. LC 39-20475. Phoenix Press.
Case of the Dead Diplomat: Inspector Richardson's Fourth Case. Basil Home Thomson. LC 35-18572. 1935. Pub. for the Crime Club, Inc., by Doubleday, Doran & Company, Inc.
Case of the Dead Grandmother. Minna Bardon. LC 37-25339. Phoenix Press.
Case of the Deadly Diamonds. Christopher Bush. LC 69-10609. (Cock Robin mystery). 1969. Macmillan.
Case of the Deadly Diary. William Edward Burghardt Du Bois. LC 40-2006. 1940. Little, Brown and Company.
Case of the Deadly Drops. Gerald Benedict. LC 41-2803. Phoenix Press.
Case of the Deadly Toy. Erle Stanley Gardner. LC 80-27287. 1980. 10.00 (ISBN 0-8376-0397-8). R. Bentley.
Case of the Deadly Triangle. Ronald Ayers. (Leonard Robinson mystery). 1975. (pbk.) 1.50 (ISBN 0-87067-466-8). Holloway House.
Case of the Demure Defendant. Erle Stanley Gardner. LC 56-5052. 1956. Morrow.
Case of the Dowager's Etchings. Rufus King. LC 44-4923. 1944. Pub. for the Crime Club by Doubleday, Doran and Co., Inc.
Case of the Drowning Duck. Erle Stanley Gardner. LC 76-46331. 1976. 6.95 (ISBN 0-88411-421-X). Aeonian Press.
Case of the Drowning Duck. Erle Stanley Gardner. LC 42-140857. 1942. W. Morrow and Company.
Case of the Drowning Duck: And the Case of the Crooked Candle. Stanley Erle Gardner. (Perry Mason 2 in 1). 1976. (pbk.) 1.95 (ISBN 0-671-80281-X). Pocket Books.
Case of the Drowsy Mosquito. Erle Stanley Gardner. LC 43-13073. 1943. W. Morrow and Company.
Case of the Drowsy Mosquito: And The Case of the Empty Tin. Erle Stanley Gardner. (Perry Mason 2 in 1). 1976. (pbk.) 1.95 (ISBN 0-671-80390-5). Pocket Books.
Case of the Dubious Bridegroom. Erle Stanley Gardner. 224p. 1983. pap. 2.25 (ISBN 0-345-30881-6). Ballantine.
Case of the Dubious Bridegroom. Erle Stanley Gardner. LC 49-8017. 1949. W. Morrow.
Case of the Duplicate Daughter. Erle Stanley Gardner. LC 80-12488. 1980. 9.95 (ISBN 0-89340-262-1). J. Curley.
Case of the Ebony Queen. Cleo Adkins. LC 55-8981. 1955. Arcadia House.
Case of the Eight Brothers. Mary Violet Heberden. LC 48-8294. 1948. Pub. for the Crime Club by Doubleday.
Case of the Eighteenth Ostrich. Colin Curzon. LC 43-18235. 1943. Hurst & Blackett Ltd.
Case of the Eighteenth Ostrich. Colin Curzon. LC 44-873. 1944. The Macmillan Company.
Case of the Empty Tin. Gardner, Erle Stanley. LC 41-193065. 1941. W. Morrow and Company.
Case of the Empty Tin. Erle Stanley Gardner & Christie, Agatha (Miller) Evil Under the Sun. LC 42-20996. 1942. Detective Book Club.
Case of the Extra Man. Christopher Bush. LC 57-842056. (Cock Robin mystery). 1957. Macmillan.
Case of the Fabulous Fake. Erle Stanley Gardner. LC 76-47648. 1977. 7.95 (ISBN 0-89340-024-6). J. Curley.
Case of the Fabulous Fake. Erle Stanley Gardner. LC 70-90761. 1969. 4.95. Morrow.
Case of the Famished Parson. George Bellairs. LC 49-9295. 1949. Macmillan Co.
Case of the Fan-Dancer's Horse. Erle Stanley Gardner. LC 47-3657. 1947. W. Morrow & Company.
Case of the Fenced-in Woman. Erle Stanley Gardner. LC 72-13892. 1973. 8.95 (ISBN 0-8161-6083-X). G. K. Hall.
Case of the Fenced-in Woman. Erle Stanley Gardner. 1973. (pbk.) 0.95 (ISBN 0-671-77884-6). Pocket Books.
Case of the Fenced-in Woman. Erle Stanley Gardner. LC 77-188554. (Illus.). 1972. 5.95. Morrow.
Case of the Fiery Fingers. Erle Stanley Gardner. 1981. pap. 1.95 (ISBN 0-345-29494-7). Ballantine.
Case of the Fifth Key: A Swivel Chair Solution. Jacob D. Posner. LC 34-702679. Covici-Friede.
Case of the Five Orange Pips. Arthur Conan Doyle. Ed. by Walter Pauk & Raymond Harris. (Jamestown Classics Ser.). (Illus.). 41p. (gr. 5). 1976. pap. text ed. 2.00x (ISBN 0-89061-062-2, 545); tchrs. ed. 3.00 (ISBN 0-89061-063-0, 547). Jamestown Pubs.
Case of the Flery Fingers. Erle Stanley Gardner. LC 51-10604. 1951. Morrow.
Case of the Flowery Corpse. Christopher Bush. LC 57-119445. 1957. Macmillan.
Case of the Foot-Loose Doll. Erle Stanley Gardner. 1958. 4.50 o.p. Morrow.
Case of the Forty Thieves: By John Rhode Pseud. Cecil John Charles Street. LC 54-5627. (Red badge detective). 1954. Dodd, Mead.
Case of the Foster Father. Virginia Perdue. LC 42-19353. 1942. Published for the Crime Club by Doudleday, Doran & Company, Inc.
Case of the Friendly Corpse. L. Ron Hubbard. 1979. 11.00 (ISBN 0-917972-03-1). Theta Bks.
Case of the Frightened Fish. William Edward Burghardt Du Bois. LC 40-13043. 1940. Little, Brown and Company.
Case of the Frightened Mannequin. Christopher Bush. LC 51-11317. 1951. Macmillan.
Case of the Frozen Scream. Thomas Brace Haughey. LC 79-50829. (Series: Baker Street Mystery.). 1.95 (ISBN 0-87123-045-3). Bethany Fellowship.
Case of the Fugitive Nurse. Erle Stanley Gardner. LC 54-5300. 1954. Morrow.
Case of the Fugitive Nurse. Erle Stanley Gardner. LC 57-1044. (Pocket book, 1138. Mystery, 8). 1957. Pocket Books.
Case of the Fugitive Nurse. Erle Stanley Gardner. LC 81-12619. (Perry Mason Mystery). 1982. 12.95 (ISBN 0-89340-363-6). J. Curley.
Case of the Giant Killer. Henry C Branson. LC 44-208528. 1944. Simon and Schuster.
Case of the Gilded Fly. Edmund Crispin, pseud. 1980. pap. 2.50 (ISBN 0-380-50187-2, 63552-6). Avon.
Case of the Gilded Fly. Edmund Crispin, pseud. 1970. 4.95 o.s.i. (ISBN 0-8277-0339-2). British Bk Ctr.
Case of the Gilded Fly. Edmund Crispin, pseud. (General Ser.). 1980. lib. bdg. 13.95 (ISBN 0-8161-3018-3, Large Print Bks). G K Hall.
Case of the Gilded Fly. Edmund Crispin, pseud. LC 79-52173. (Walker Mystery Ser.). (O.s.i.). 223p. 1979. Repr. 8.95 o.s.i. (ISBN 0-8027-5410-4). Walker & Co.
Case of the Gilded Fly. Edmund Crispin, pseud. 1970. 4.95 o.s.i. (ISBN 0-8277-0339-2). British Bk Ctr.
Case of the Gilded Fly. Robert Bruce Montgomery. LC 76-109536. 1970. 4.95. London House & Maxwell.
Case of the Gilded Fly. Robert Bruce Montgomery. LC 79-52173. (Illus.). 1979. 8.95 (ISBN 0-8027-5410-4). Walker.
Case of the Gilded Fly. Robert Bruce Montgomery. LC 79-24673. 1980. 13.95 (ISBN 0-8161-3018-3). G. K. Hall.
Case of the Gilded Lily. Erle Stanley Gardner. LC 56-9456. (His A Perry Mason mystery). ((A Morrow mystery). 1956. Morrow.
Case of the Gilded Lily. Erle Stanley Gardner. LC 80-27291. 1980. 10.00 (ISBN 0-8376-0396-X). R. Bentley.
Case of the Glamorous Ghost. Erle Stanley Gardner. LC 55-5941. Morrow.
Case of the Golddigger's Purse. Erle Stanley Gardner. LC 45-4046. 1945. W. Morrow and Company.
Case of the Good Employer. Christopher Bush. LC 67-135879. (Cock robin mystery). bds., 3.95. Macmillan.
Case of the Grand Alliance: 1st Amer. Ed. Christopher Bush. LC 65-20198. (Cock Robin mystery). 1965. bds., 3.95. Macmillan.
Case of the Green-Eyed Sister. Erle Stanley Gardner. LC 53-11063. 1953. Morrow.
Case of the Green-Eyed Sister. Erle Stanley Gardner. LC 78-3520. 1979. 10.95 (ISBN 0-89340-140-4). J. Curley.
Case of the Green Felt Hat: A Ludovic Travers Story. Christopher Bush. LC 39-4286. H. Holt and Company.
Case of the Grieving Monkey. Virginia Perdue. LC 41-11797. 1941. Pub. for the Crime Club by Douleday, Doran & Company, Incorporated.
Case of the Grinning Gorilla. Erle Stanley Gardner. LC 52-10782. 1952. Morrow.
Case of the Grinning Gorilla. Erle Stanley Gardner. 1973. (pbk.) 0.95 (ISBN 0-671-77889-7). Pocket Books.
Case of the Half-Wakened Wife... Erle Stanley Gardner. LC 45-8181. 1945. The M. S. Mill Company, Inc.
Case of the Hanging Lady. Nard Jones. LC 38-487894. 1938. Dodd, Mead & Company.
Case of the Happy Medium. Christopher Bush. LC 52-3695. 1952. Macmillan.
Case of the Haunted Brides. William Edward Burghardt Du Bois. LC 40-29873. 1941. Little, Brown and Company.
Case of the Haunted Husband. Erle Stanley Gardner. LC 68-86714. 1941. W. Morrow.
Case of the Haunted Husband. Erle Stanley Gardner. LC 41-437273. 1941. W. Morrow and Company.
Case of the Hesitant Hostess. Erle Stanley Gardner. LC 53-533606. 1953. Morrow.
Case of the Hijacked Moon. Thomas B. Haughey. LC 81-67134. (Baker Street Mystery Ser.). 176p. 1981. pap. 2.95 (ISBN 0-87123-143-3, 200143). Bethany Hse.
Case of the Hook-Billed Kites. J. S Borthwick. LC 82-5617. (Illus.). 12.95 (ISBN 0-312-12335-3). St. Martin's Press.
Case of the Horrified Heirs. Erle Stanley Gardner. LC 64-23582. 1964. Morrow.
Case of the Horrified Heirs. Erle Stanley Gardner. LC 76-47558. 1977. 7.95 (ISBN 0-89340-029-7). J. Curley & Associates.
Case of the Housekeeper's Hair. Christopher Bush. LC 49-10332. 1949. Macmillan Co.
Case of the Howling Dog. Erle Stanley Gardner. LC 34-176491. 1934. W. Morrow and Company.
Case of the Hypnotized Virgin: Based on 'Corpse on the Town.' John Roeburt. LC 56-46419. (Avon, 730). 1956. Avon Publications.
Case of the Ice-Cold Hands. Erle Stanley Gardner. LC 80-22816. 1980. 11.95 (ISBN 0-8161-3174-0). G. K. Hall.
Case of the Innocent Victims. John Creasey. LC 66-13258. 1966. 3.95. Scribners.
Case of the Invisible Thief. Thomas Brace Haughey. LC 78-68424. (Baker Street Mystery Ser.). 1978. pap. 2.95 (ISBN 0-87123-086-0, 200086). Bethany Hse.
Case of the Irate Witness. Erle Stanley Gardner. 1972. 7.95 (ISBN 0-688-00102-5). Morrow.
Case of the Irate Witness: A Perry Mason Mystery and Other Stories. Erle Stanley Gardner. 1973. (pbk.) 0.95. Pocket Books.
Case of the Irate Witness: A Perry Mason Mystery and Other Stories. Erle Stanley Gardner. LC 75-170217. 1972. 4.95. Morrow.
Case of the Ivory Arrow. Harry Stephen Keeler. LC 45-233160. 1945. Phoenix Press.
Case of the Jeweled Ragpicker. Harry Stephen Keeler. LC 48-1129. 1948. Phoenix Press.
Case of the Journeying Boy. John Innes Mackintosh Stewart. LC 49-8751. (Red badge mystery). Dodd, Mead.
Case of the Jumbo Sandwich. Christopher Bush. LC 66-15372. (Cock Robin mystery). 1966. bds., 3.95. Macmillan.
Case of the Kidnapped Angel. E. V. Cunningham, pseud. (Nightingale Ser.). 1983. pap. 7.95 (ISBN 0-8161-3471-5, Large Print Bks). G K Hall.
Case of the Kidnapped Angel. Howard Melvin Fast. LC 82-23336. 1983. 7.95 (ISBN 0-8161-3471-5). G.K. Hall.
Case of the Kidnapped Angel: A Masao Masuto Mystery. E. V. Cunningham, pseud. 192p. 1982. 12.95 (ISBN 0-440-01103-5). Delacorte.
Case of the Kidnapped Angel: A Masao Masuto Mystery. Howard Melvin Fast. LC 82-7386. 12.95 (ISBN 0-440-01103-5). Delacorte Press.
Case of the Kidnapped Shadow. Thomas B. Haughey. LC 80-65945. (Baker Street Mysteries Ser.). (Orig.). 1980. pap. 2.95 (ISBN 0-87123-112-3, 200112). Bethany Hse.
Case of the Kippered Corpse. Margaret Scherf. LC 41-122783. G. P. Putnam's Sons.
Case of the Lame Canary. Erle Stanley Gardner. LC 48-773. Triangle Books.
Case of the Lame Canary. Erle Stanley Gardner. LC 37-222174. 1937. W. Morrow and Company.
Case of the Lame Canary. Erle Stanley Gardner. LC 78-2655. 1979. 9.95 (ISBN 0-89340-139-0). J. Curley.
Case of the Lavender Gripsack. Harry Stephen Keeler. 1944. Phoenix Press.
Case of the Lazy Lover. Erle Stanley Gardner. LC 47-11142. 1947. W. Morrow.

Case of the Lazy Lover. large print ed. Erle Stanley Gardner. LC 81-15266. (Perry Mason Mystery). 1982. 12.95 (ISBN 0-89340-362-8). John Curley.

Case of the Little Green Men. Mack Reynolds. LC 51-12283. 1951. Phoenix Press.

Case of the Lombard Street Murder. Bud Long. 1978. pap. 2.50 o.s.i. (ISBN 0-930524-03-9). Gluxlit Pr.

Case of the Lonely Heiress. Erle Stanley Gardner. 1973. (pbk.) 0.95 (ISBN 0-671-77886-2). Pocket Books.

Case of the Lonely Heiress. Erle Stanley Gardner. LC 48-578680. (His A Perry Mason mystery). 1948. W. Morrow.

Case of the Lonely Lovers. Will Daemer. LC 51-28875. (Suspense novel no. 2). 1951. Farrell Pub. Corp.

Case of the Long-Legged Models. Erle Stanley Gardner. 1958. 3.95 o.p. Morrow.

Case of the Los Angeles Chamelean. Bud Long. 1978. pap. 2.50 o.s.i. (ISBN 0-930524-02-0). Gluxlit Pr.

Case of the Lucky Legs. Erle Stanley Gardner. LC 34-2223. 1934. W. Morrow and Company.

Case of the Lucky Legs. Erle Stanley Gardner. 1973. (pbk.) 0.95 (ISBN 0-671-77891-9). Pocket Books.

Case of the Lucky Loser. Erle Stanley Gardner. 1957. 4.50 o.p. Morrow.

Case of the Malevolent Twin. Lois Christine Eby & Fleming, John Chester, 1906- Joint Author. LC 46-403. 1946. E. P. Dutton & Co.

Case of the Maltese Treasure. Thomas B. Haughey. LC 79-54939. (Baker Street Mysteries). 1979. pap. 2.95 (ISBN 0-87123-048-8, 200048). Bethany Hse.

Case of the Marsden Rubies. Leonard Reginald Gribble. LC 30-141904. 1930. Pub. for The Crime Club, Inc., by Doubleday, Doran & Company, Inc.

Case of the Mischievous Doll. Erle Stanley Gardner. LC 62-17600. 1963. Morrow.

Case of the Mischievous Doll. Erle Stanley Gardner. LC 80-29296. 1981. 11.95 (ISBN 0-8161-3215-1). G. K. Hall.

Case of the Missing Bronte: A Perry Trethowan Mystery. Robert Barnard. 192p. 1983. 11.95 (ISBN 0-684-17910-5, ScribT). Scribner.

Case of the Missing Cincinnatian. Bud Long. 1977. pap. 1.00 o.s.i. (ISBN 0-930524-01-2). Gluxlit Pr.

Case of the Missing Corpse. Joan Sanger. LC 36-208641. Green Circle Books.

Case of the Missing Diary. Archibald E. Fielding. LC 36-6318. 1936. H. C. Kinsey & Company, Inc.

Case of the Missing Gardener: By Harry Walker Pseud. Hillary Waugh. LC 54-7486. 1954. Arcadia House.

Case of the Missing Lovers: By Lee Roberts Pseud. Robert Lee Martin. LC 57-5866. (Red badge detective). 1957. Dodd, Mead.

Case of the Missing Men. Christopher Bush. LC 47-22234. 1947. The Macmillan Company.

Case of the Missing Photographs. Charles Edward Eaton. LC 77-89652. 19.95 (ISBN 0-498-02174-2). A. S. Barnes.

Case of the Missing Sandals: A Peter Piper Detective Story... Nancy Barr Mavity. LC 30-31489. 1930. Pub. for the Crime Club, Inc., by Doubleday, Doran & Company, Inc.

Case of the Moth-Eaten Mink. Erle Stanley Gardner. LC 52-5788. 1952. Morrow.

Case of the Muckrakers. Wilfred McNeilly. 1967. pap. 0.50 o.p. (50-369). Manor Bks.

Case of the Murdered Madame. An Avon 1st Ed. Henry Kane. LC 55-43392. (Avon, 646). 1955. Avon Publications.

Case of the Murderer's Bride. Erle Stanley Gardner. Intro. by Ellery Queen. LC 77-81936. 1977. pap. 1.50 o.s.i. (ISBN 0-89559-003-4). Davis Pubns.

Case of the Murderer's Bride and Other Stories. Erle Stanley Gardner. Ed. by Ellery Queen. LC 74-175913. (Ellery Queen presents, no. 5). 1974. (pbk.). 1.35. Davis Publications.

Case of the Murderer's Bride and Other Stories. Erle Stanley Gardner. Ed. by Ellery Queen. LC 78-22210. (Ellery Queen presents, no. 1). 1969. 1.00. Davis Publications.

Case of the Musical Cow. Erle Stanley Gardner. LC 50-7856. 1950. Morrow.

Case of the Mysterious Moll. Harry Stephen Keeler. LC 45-776524. 1945. Phoenix Press.

Case of the Mythical Monkeys. Erle Stanley Gardner. LC 80-27190. 1980. 10.00 (ISBN 0-8376-0398-6). R. Bentley.

Case of the Mythical Monkeys. Erle Stanley Gardner. LC 82-6041. 1982. 12.95 (ISBN 0-8161-3384-0). G.K. Hall.

Case of the Nameless Corpse. 1st Ed. Clarence Budington Kelland. LC 57-615009. Harper.

Case of the Negligent Nymph. Erle Stanley Gardner. LC 49-50387. 1950. Morrow.

Case of the Negligent Nymph. Erle Stanley Gardner. 1973. (pbk.) 0.95 (ISBN 0-671-77892-7). Pocket Books.

Case of the Nervous Accomplice. Erle Stanley Gardner. LC 55-10261. (His A Perry Mason mystery). 1955. Morrow.

Case of the One-Eyed Witness. Erle Stanley Gardner. LC 50-10518. 1950. Morrow.

Case of the One Penny Orange. E. V. Cunningham, pseud. LC 77-71362. 1977. 6.95 (ISBN 0-03-021361-4). HR&W.

Case of the One-Penny Orange. E. V. Cunningham, pseud. LC 81-80704. (Masao Masuto Mystery Ser.). 176p. (Orig.). 1982. pap. 3.50 (ISBN 0-03-059858-3, Owl Bks). HR&W.

Case of the One-Penny Orange. Howard Melvin Fast. LC 81-20119. 1982. 11.95 (ISBN 0-8161-3334-4). G.K. Hall.

Case of the One Penny Orange: A Masao Masuto Mystery. Howard Melvin Fast. LC 77-71362. (Rinehart suspense novel). 6.95 (ISBN 0-03-021361-4). Holt, Rinehart and Winston.

Case of the Perfumed Mouse. Theodora McCormick Du Bois. LC 44-679255. 1944. Pub. for the Crime Club by Doubleday, Doran & Co., Inc.

Case of the Perjured Parrot. Erle Stanley Gardner. LC 39-271503. 1939. W. Morrow and Company.

Case of the Perjured Parrot: A Perry Mason Mystery. Erle Stanley Gardner. LC 80-12217. 1980. 9.95 (ISBN 0-89340-263-X). J. Curley.

Case of the Phantom Fingerprints. Ken Crossen. LC 45-221278. 1945. Vulcan Publications, Inc.

Case of the Phantom Fortune. Erle Stanley Gardner. LC 64-12524. 1964. Morrow.

Case of the Philosophers' Ring by Dr. John H. Watson. Randall Collins. LC 78-12689. (Illus.). 7.95 (ISBN 0-517-53530-0). Crown Publishers.

Case of the Platinum Blonde. Christopher Bush. LC 49-8003. 1949. Macmillan Co.

Case of the Poisoned Eclairs. E. V. Cunningham, pseud. 1980. pap. 2.25 (ISBN 0-440-11256-7). Dell.

Case of the Poisoned Eclairs. E. V. Cunningham, pseud. LC 78-14164. 1979. 6.95 (ISBN 0-03-044721-6). HR&W.

Case of the Poisoned Eclairs. E. V. Cunningham, pseud. (Nightingale Ser.). 1982. pap. 7.95 (ISBN 0-8161-3333-6, Large Print Bks). G K Hall.

Case of the Poisoned Eclairs. Howard Melvin Fast. LC 82-11916. (Nightingale Series). 1982. 7.95 (ISBN 0-8161-3333-6). G.K. Hall.

Case of the Poisoned Eclairs: A Masao Masuto Mystery. Howard Melvin Fast. LC 78-14164. (Rinehart suspense novel). 7.95 (ISBN 0-03-044721-6). Holt, Rinehart and Winston.

Case of the Postponed Murder. Erle Stanley Gardner. LC 72-1344. 1973. 5.95. Morrow.

Case of the Postponed Murder. Erle Stanley Gardner. 1974. (pbk.) 0.95 (ISBN 0-671-77894-3). Pocket Books.

Case of the Postponed Murder. Erle Stanley Gardner. LC 73-2627. 1973. (ISBN 0-8161-6090-2). G. K. Hall.

Case of the Presidents' Heads. Manning Lee Stokes. LC 56-89825. 1956. Arcadia House.

Case of the Prodigal Daughter. Christopher Bush. LC 73-75901. (Cock Robin mystery). 1969. Macmillan.

Case of the Purloined Picture. Christopher Bush. LC 51-9024. 1951. Macmillan.

Case of the Queenly Contestant. Erle Stanley Gardner. LC 76-47646. 1977. 8.95 (ISBN 0-89340-025-4). J. Curley.

Case of the Queenly Contestant. Erle Stanley Gardner. LC 67-19246. 1967. Morrow.

Case of the Red Brunette. Christopher Bush. LC 54-147716. (Cock Robin mystery). 1955. Macmillan.

Case of the Redoubled-Cross. Rufus King. LC 49-7926. 1949. Pub. for the Crime Club by Doubleday.

Case of the Reluctant Model. Erle Stanley Gardner. 1962. 4.50 o.p. Morrow.

Case of the Restless Redhead. Erle Stanley Gardner. LC 54-7103. 1954. Morrow.

Case of the Restless Redhead. Erle Stanley Gardner. LC 80-12079. 1980. 10.95 (ISBN 0-89340-261-3). J. Curley.

Case of the Rolling Bones. Erle Stanley Gardner. LC 39-232942. 1939. W. Morrow and Company.

Case of the Rolling Bones. Erle Stanley Gardner. LC 43-5935. 1940. Grosset & Dunlap.

Case of the Runaway Corpse. Erle Stanley Gardner. LC 54-92553. 1954. Morrow.

Case of the Running Man. Christopher Bush. LC 59-9303. (Cock Robin mystery). 1959. Macmillan.

Case of the Russian Cross: A Ludovic Travers Mystery Novel. Christopher Bush. LC 58-6729. (Cock Robin mystery). 1958. Macmillan.

Case of the Russian Diplomat. E. V. Cunningham, pseud. 1978. 6.95 (ISBN 0-03-022456-X). HR&W.

Case of the Russian Diplomat. E. V. Cunningham, pseud. LC 81-80705. (Masao Masuto Mystery Ser.). 176p. 1982. pap. 3.50 (ISBN 0-03-059857-5, Owl Bks). HR&W.

Case of the Russian Diplomat: A Masao Masuto Mystery. Howard Melvin Fast. LC 77-15210. (Rinehart suspense novel). 6.95 (ISBN 0-03-022456-X). Holt, Rinehart, and Winston.

Case of the Sapphire Brooch. Christopher Bush. LC 61-635725. (Cock Robin mystery). 1961. Macmillan.

Case of the Screaming Woman. Erle Stanley Gardner. LC 57-514526. (His A Perry Mason mystery). (Morrow mystery). 1957. Morrow.

Case of the Second Chance: A Ludovic Travers Mystery Novel. Christopher Bush. LC 47-12181. 1947. Macmillan Co.

Case of the Seven Bells. Christopher Bush. LC 50-6191. 1950. Macmillan.

Case of the Seven of Calvary. Anthony Boucher. pap. 0.95 o.p. (01759, Collier). Macmillan.

Case of the Seven of Calvary. William Anthony Parker White. LC 37-21033. 1937. Simon and Schuster.

Case of the Seven of Calvary: By Anthony Boucher Pseud.54. William Anthony Parker White. LC 54-489409. (Murder revisited mystery novel, no. 8). 1954. Macmillan.

Case of the Seven of Calvary: By Anthony Bucher Pseud. William Anthony Parker White. LC 61-18126. (Collier books mystery, AS97). 1961. Collier Books.

Case of the Seven Sneezes. William Anthony Parker White. LC 42-15268. 1942. Sinon and Schuster.

Case of the Seven Whistlers. George Bellairs. LC 48-786795. 1948. Macmillan Co.

Case of the Severed Skull. Stephen Longstreet. LC 41-7080. 1940. Mystery Book of the Month, Inc.

Case of the Severed Skull. Henri Weiner, pseud. LC 41-708043. 1940. Mystery Book of the Month, Inc.

Case of the Shapely Shadow. Erle Stanley Gardner. 1981. 1.95. Ballantine Books.

Case of the Shivering Chorus Girls. James Atlee Phillips. LC 42-166144. 1942. Coward-McCann, Inc.

Case of the Shoplifter's Shoe. Erle Stanley Gardner. LC 38-27745. 1938. W. Morrow and Company.

Case of the Shoplifter's Shoe. Erle Stanley Gardner. 1973. (pbk.) 0.95. Pocket Books.

Case of the Shoplifter's Shoes. Erle Stanley Gardner. LC 43-5934. 1939. Grosset & Dunlap.

Case of the Silent Partner. Erle Stanley Gardner. LC 43-59334. 1941. Grosset & Dunlap.

Case of The Silken Petticoat. Christopher Bush. LC 54-111921. (Cock Robin mystery). 1954. Macmillan.

Case of the Singing Skirt. Erle Stanley Gardner. LC 80-27263. 1980. 10.00 (ISBN 0-8376-0399-4). R. Bentley.

Case of the Six Bullets. R M Laurenson. LC 49-2152. 1949. Phoenix Press.

Case of the Six Napoleons. Arthur Conan Doyle. Ed. by Walter Pauk & Raymond Harris. (Jamestown Classics Ser.). (Illus.). 45p. (gr. 5). 1976. pap. text ed. 2.00x (ISBN 0-89061-058-4, 537); tchrs. ed. 3.00 (ISBN 0-89061-059-2, 539). Jamestown Pubs.

Case of the Sleepwalker's Niece. Erle Stanley Gardner. 1973. (pbk.) 0.95. Pocket Books.

Case of the Sleepwalker's Niece. Erle Stanley Gardner. LC 36-6810. 1936. W. Morrow and Company.

Case of the Sleepwalker's Niece. Erle Stanley Gardner. LC 42-173873. 1942. Triangle Books.

Case of the Sleepwalker's Niece... Erle Stanley Gardner. LC 45-16800. 1944.

Case of the Sliding Pool. E. V. Cunningham, pseud. (O.s.i.). 1981. 10.95 o.s.i. (ISBN 0-440-01114-0). Delacorte.

Case of the Sliding Pool. E. V. Cunningham, pseud. 1983. pap. 2.95 (ISBN 0-440-12092-6). Dell.

Case of the Sliding Pool: A Masao Masuto Mystery. Howard Melvin Fast. LC 81-3221. 10.95 (ISBN 0-440-01114-0). Delacorte Press.

Case of the Sliding Pool: A Masao Masuto Mystery. Howard Melvin Fast. LC 82-2863. (Nightingale Series). 1982. 7.95 (ISBN 0-8161-3348-4). G.K. Hall.

Case of the Smoking Chimney... Erle Stanley Gardner. LC 42-51968. 1943. W. Morrow and Company.

Case of the Snowbound Spy. E. W. Hildick. (McGurk Mystery: No. 9). (Illus.). (gr. 3-5). 1981. pap. 1.75 (ISBN 0-671-41869-6). Archway.

Case of the Solid Key. William Anthony Parker White. 1941. Simon and Schuster.

Case of the Spurious Spinster. Erle Stanley Gardner. LC 82-2845. 1982. 8.95 (ISBN 0-8161-3393-X). G.K. Hall.

Case of the Stepdaughter's Secret. Erle Stanley Gardner. LC 63-14889. 1963. Morrow.

Case of the Stepdaughter's Secret. Erle Stanley Gardner. LC 66-29733. (Sightsaver series). 1966. Largeprint Publications.

Case of the Stuttering Bishop. Erle Stanley Gardner. LC 76-41234. 1976. 6.95 (ISBN 0-88411-409-0). Aeonain Press.

Case of the Stuttering Bishop. Erle Stanley Gardner. LC 36-19455. 1936. W. Morrow and Company.

Case of the Substitute Face. Erle Stanley Gardner. LC 38-27316. 1938. W. Morrow and Company.

Case of the Substitute Face. Erle Stanley Gardner. LC 47-641971. 1947. Triangle Books.

Case of the Sulky Girl. Erle Stanley Gardner. LC 76-2373. 1976. 7.95. Aeonian Press.

Case of the Sulky Girl. Erle Stanley Gardner. LC 33-239804. 1933. W. Morrow and Company.

Case of the Sulky Girl... Erle Stanley Gardner. LC 45-3543. 1944. Triangle Books, the Blakiston Company.

Case of the Sun Bather's Diary. Erle Stanley Gardner. LC 55-6972. 1955. Morrow.

Case of the Talking Bug. Mildred Gordon & Gordon Gordon. LC 55-6480. 1955. Published for the Crime Club by Doubleday.

Case of the Terrified Typist. Erle Stanley Gardner. LC 56-6201. (His A Perry Mason mystery). Morrow.

Case of the Three Lost Letters. Christopher Bush. LC 55-14866. (Cock Robin mystery). 1955. Macmillan.

Case of the Topaz Flower. Charlotte Murray Russell, pseud. LC 39-466068. 1939. Pub. for the Crime Club, Inc., by Doubleday, Doran & Co., Inc.

Case of the Transposed Legs. Harry Stephen Keeler & Goodwin, Hazel. 1948. Phoenix Press.

Case of the Triple Twist. Christopher Bush. LC 58-124990. (Cock Robin mystery). 1958. Macmillan.

Case of the Troubled Trustee. Erle Stanley Gardner. LC 65-11487. bds., 3.50. Morrow.

Case of the Troubled Trustee. Erle Stanley Gardner. LC 76-48271. 1977. 8.95 (ISBN 0-89340-028-9). J. Curley.

Case of the Tudor Queen. Christopher Bush. LC 38-6006. H. Holt and Company.

Case of the Turning Tide. Erle Stanley Gardner. LC 41-11978. 1941. W. Morrow and Company.

Case of the Twisted Scarf see Scarf.

Case of the Two Pearl Necklaces. Archibald E. Fielding. LC 36-939019. Pub. for the Crime Club by Collins.

Case of the Two Pearl Necklaces. Archibald E. Fielding. LC 36-181465. 1936. H. C. Kinsey & Company, Inc.

Case of the Two Strange Ladies. Harry Stephen Keeler. LC 43-119620. 1943. Phoenix Press.

Case of the Unconquered Sisters. Todd Downing. LC 36-18265. 1936. Pub. for the Crime Club, Inc., by Doubleday, Doran & Company, Inc.

Case of the Vagabond Virgin. Erle Stanley Gardner. 1973. (pbk.) 0.95 (ISBN 0-671-77885-4). Pocket Books.

Case of the Vagabond Virgin. Erle Stanley Gardner. LC 48-770968. (His A Perry Mason story). 1948. W. Morrow.

Case of the Vanishing Beauty. Richard S Prather. LC 51-15117. (Gold medal book, 127). 1950. Fawcett Publications.

Case of the Vanishing Beauty. Cover Painting by Barye Phillips. Richard S Prather. LC 56-116747. (Gold medal book 425). 1956. Fawcett Publications.

Case of the Vanishing Boy. Alexander Key. (Archway Paperback). 1979. 1.75 (ISBN 0-671-56006-9). Pocket Books.

Case of the Vanishing Women. Robert Archer. LC 42-18849. 1942. Howell, Soskin, Publishers, Inc.

Case of the Vanishing Women: A Mystery Novel. Robert Archer. LC 43-771045. (Handi-book mysteries. 10). 1943. Quinn Publishing Co., Inc.

Case of the Velvet Claws. Erle Stanley Gardner. LC 76-2372. 1976. 7.95. Aeonian Press.

Case of the Velvet Claws. Erle Stanley Gardner. 1933. W. Morrow and Company.

Case of the Walking Corpse: A Michael Shayne Mystery. Davis Dresser. LC 43-13333. (Handi-book mysteries. 15). 1943. Quinn Publishing Co., Inc.

Case of the Waylaid Wolf & the Case of the Shapely Shadow. Eric Gardner. (O.s.i.). 1976. pap. 1.95 o.s.i. WSP.

Case of the Weird Sisters. Charlotte Armstrong. LC 43-1891. 1943. Coward-McCann, Inc.

Case of the Well-Dressed Corpse: By Greer Gay Pseud. 1st Ed. Hazel Belle Saulisberry Payne. LC 53-13373. 1953. Pageant Press.

Case of the Worried Waitress. Erle Stanley Gardner. LC 66-199212. bds., 3.50. Morrow.

Case of the Worried Waitress. Erle Stanley Gardner. LC 76-47644. 1977. 7.95 (ISBN 0-89340-026-2). J. Curley.

Case of the 16 Beans. Harry Stephen Keeler. LC 44-803077. 1944. Phoenix Press.

Case of Torches. Clark Smith. LC 64-3238. (Penguin crime). 1963. Penguin Books.

Case of William Smith: A Miss Silver Mystery. Patricia Wentworth. LC 48-7958. (Main line mysteries). 1948. J. B. Lippincott Co.

Case on Cloud Nine. Lucy Freeman. LC 74-18155. 1975. 6.95 (ISBN 0-87795-103-9). Arbor House.

Case Pending: By Dell Shannon Pseud. 1st Ed. Elizabeth Linington. 1960. Harper.

Case with Four Clowns. Leo Bruce, pseud. LC 40-16997. 1939. Frederick A. Stokes Company.

Case with Nine Solutions. Alfred Walter Stewart. LC 29-923. 1929. Little, Brown, and Company.

Case with Ropes & Rings. Leo Bruce, pseud. 192p. 1980. 14.95 (ISBN 0-89733-034-X); pap. 4.50 (ISBN 0-89733-035-8). Academy Chi Ltd.

Case with Ropes & Rings. Leo Bruce, pseud. 192p. 1975. Repr. of 1949 ed. 7.95 o.p. (ISBN 0-86025-028-8, Pub. by Ian Henry Pubns England). Academy Chi Ltd.

Case with Ropes & Rings. Leo Bruce, pseud. 1977. 7.50 o.p. State Mutual Bk.

Case with Ropes and Rings. Croft-Cooke, Rupert. LC 80-36840. 1980. 9.95 (ISBN 0-89733-034-X). Academy Chicago Limited.

Case with Three Husbands. Margaret Erskine. (Ace gothic). 1974. (pbk.) 0.95. Ace Books.

Case with Three Husbands. Wetherby Williams. LC 67-11155. 1967. Published for the Crime Club by Doubleday.

Case Without a Clue. Nigel Morland. LC 38-19408. Farrar & Rinehart, Incorporated.

Case Without a Corpes. Leo Bruce, pseud. LC 37-18100. 1937. Frederick A. Stokes Company.

Case Without a Corpse. Leo Bruce, pseud. (Sgt. Beef Mysteries). 284p. 1982. Repr. of 1937 ed. 14.95 (ISBN 0-89733-052-8); pap. 4.50 (ISBN 0-89733-051-X). Academy Chi Ltd.

Case Worker. Gyorgy Konrad. LC 73-16408. 1974. 6.95 (ISBN 0-15-115790-1). Harcourt Brace Jovanovich.

Case Worker. Gyorgy Konrad. LC 78-6633. (Harvest/HBJ book). 1978. 2.95 (ISBN 0-15-615412-9). Harcourt Brace Jovanovich.

Casebook of Jimmy Lavender. Vincent Starrett. 1973. 6.50. Bookfinger.

Casebook of Lucius Leffing. Joseph Payne Brennan. LC 73-163901. (Illus.). 1973. 5.00. Macabre House.

Casebook of Solar Pons. Foreword by Vincent Starrett. Monograph by Michael Harrison. August William Deleth. LC 65-4398. 5.00. Mycroft & Moran Dist. Arkham.

Casebook of the Black Widowers. Isaac Asimov. LC 79-7812. 1980. 7.95 (ISBN 0-385-15704-5). Published for the Crime Club by Doubleday.

Casebook: Sex, Seduction & Jealousy. Helen Gaultson. pap. 2.45 o.p. (4012). Cameo.

Casebook: The Incest Lovers. James L. Brown. pap. 2.45 o.p. (4017). Cameo.

Casement: A Diversion. Swinnerton, Frank Arthur. LC 27-278032. 1927. Goerge H. Doran Company.

Cases of Susan Dare. Mignon Good Eberhart. LC 75-29119. 1975. 7.95. Aeonian Press.

Cases of Susan Dare. Mignon Good Eberhart. LC 34-41048. 1934. Pub. for the Crime Club, Inc., by Doubleday, Doran & Company, Inc.

Cases of Susan Dare. Mignon Good Eberhart. LC 42-50908. 1942. The Sun Dial Press.

Casey. Charles Rodrigues. 1979. pap. write for info. (ISBN 0-671-79096-X, Wallaby). PB.

Casey. Ramona Stewart. LC 68-11528. 1968. Little, Brown.

Casey Agonistes, and Other Science Fiction and Fantasy Stories. Richard McKenna. LC 69-15281. 1973. 5.95 (ISBN 0-06-012911-5). Harper & Row.

Casey Grant Caper No. 1: The Ring-A-Ding Girl. Don Rico. (Orig.). 1969. pap. 0.75 o.p. (64-004). Paperback Lib.

Casey Grant Caper No. 2: The Swinging Virgin. Don Rico. (Casey Grant Ser). (Orig.). 1969. pap. 0.75 o.p. (64-158). Paperback Lib.

Casey Grant Caper: No. 3, So Sweet, So Deadly. Don Rico. (Orig.). 1970. pap. 0.75 o.p. (64-428). Paperback Lib.

Casey Ryan. Bertha Muzzy Sinclair. LC 21-13416. 1921. Little, Brown, and Company.

Cash Intrigue: A Fantastic Melodrama of Modern Finance. George Randolph Chester. LC 9-27745. 1.50. The Bobbs-Merrill Company.

Cash Item. Catharine Brody. LC 33-287336. 1933. Longmans, Green and Co.

Cash McCall. Cameron Hawley. 1977. Repr. of 1955 ed. lib. bdg. 15.50x (ISBN 0-89244-038-4). Queens Hse.

Cash McCall. Cameron Hawley. 1970. pap. 1.25 o.p. (P1389, Crest). Fawcett World.

Cash McCall: A Novel. Cameron Hawley. LC 55-9966. 1955. Houghton Mifflin.

Cash on Delivery. Rubis Sur L'ongle. Fortune Du Boisgobey. LC 6-34433. (On cover: Seaside library. Pocket ed. no. 942). G. Munro.

Cashel Byron's Profession. George Bernard Shaw. LC 68-25565. (Crosscurrents: modern fiction). 1968. 6.95. Southern Illinois Univeristy Press.

Cashel Byron's Profession. George Bernard Shaw. LC 12-18725. 1909. Brentano's.

Cashel Byron's Profession. George Bernard Shaw & Dan H Laurence. LC 79-314876. 1979. 2.95 (ISBN 0-14-004886-3). Penguin Books.

Cashel Byron's Profession: A Novel. George Bernard Shaw. LC 8-4806. (Harper's handy series, no. 109). 1886. Harper & Brothers.

Cashel Byron's Profession. A Novel. George Bernard Shaw. (On cover: Seaside library. Pocket ed. no. 967). 1887. G. Munro.

Cashelmara. Susan Howatch. LC 73-22333. 1974. 9.95 (ISBN 0-671-21736-4). Simon and Schuster.

Cashew-Nut Girl & Other Stories of India. Bryn Gunnell. 1974. 9.95 (ISBN 0-236-17623-4, Pub. by Paul Elek). Merrimack Pub Cir.

Cashier. Translated by Harry Binsee. 1st Ed. Gabrielle Carbotte Roy. LC 54-63973. 1955. Harcourt, Brace.

Cashing in. Antonia Gowar. LC 81-23960. 1982. 14.95 (ISBN 0-395-32112-3). Houghton Mifflin.

Cashmere. Nicola Thorne, pseud. LC 81-43622. 1982. 18.50 (ISBN 0-385-17644-9). Doubleday.

Cashmir of the R. C. A. F. 1st Ed. Stan Obodiac. LC 55-120156. 1955. Pageant Press.

Casimir Maremma. Arthur Helps. LC 8-26640. 1870. Roberts Brothers.

Casine. Arelo Sederbert. 1977. 1.75 (ISBN 0-440-18038-4). Dell Pub. Co.

Casino: A Novel of Las Vegas. Robert R. Kirsch. LC 79-10936. 10.00 (ISBN 0-8184-0275-X). L. Stuart.

Casino: A Novel of Las Vegas. Robert R. Kirsch. 1980. 2.75 (ISBN 0-671-82931-9). Pocket Books.

Casino Girl in London. Curtis Dunham. LC 6-35867. 1898. R. F. Fenno & Company.

Casino Greystone. large print ed. Louisa Bronte, pseud. LC 76-20653. (Greystone Tavern series). 1976. 9.95 (ISBN 0-89340-003-3). J. Curley.

Casino Greystone. Louisa Bronte. LC 76-6926. 1976. 1.50 (ISBN 0-345-24962-3). Ballantine Books.

Casino Murder Case: A Philo Vance Story. Willard Huntington Wright. LC 34-32210. 1934. C. Scribner's Sons.

Casino Nurse. Diana Douglas. 1974. (pbk.) 0.75. New American Library.

Casino Royale. Ian Fleming. LC 54-1306. 1954. Macmillan.

Casino Royale: Reissue. Ian Fleming. LC 66-62. 1966. bds., 3.95. Macmillan.

Cask. Freeman Wills Crofts. LC 76-46040. 1977. 3.50 (ISBN 0-486-23457-6). Dover Publications.

Cask. Freeman Wills Crofts. LC 24-24340. 1924. T. Seltzer.

Cask. Freeman Wills Crofts. LC 28-244871. (S. S. Van Dine detective library). 1928. C. Scribner's Sons.

Cask. Introd. by James Nelson. Freeman Wills Crofts. LC 67-18687. (Seagull lib. of mystery and suspense). 1967. 4.50. Norton.

Casket Crew. Arthur George Joseph Whitehouse. LC 79-150925. 1971. 5.95. Doubleday.

Caspar Hauser. Jakob Wassermann. Tr. by Caroline Newton. LC 28-223553. 1928. H. Liveright.

Caspar Hauser, the Enigma of a Century. Jakob Wassermann. LC 76-159504. (Steinerbooks, 1722). (Illus.). 1973. (pbk.) 2.95. Rudolf Steiner Publications.

Caspian Circle: A Novel. Donne Raffat. LC 77-20803. 1978. 10.00 (ISBN 0-395-25933-9). Houghton Mifflin.

Casque' Lark: Or, Victoria, the Mother of the Camps, a Tale of the Frankish Invasion of Gaul. Eugene Sue & De Leon, Daniel, 1852-1914, Tr. LC 9-28392. 1909. New York Labor News Company.

Cass Timberlane. Sinclair Lewis. 400p. 1974. pap. 1.95 (ISBN 0-532-19103-X). Woodhill.

Cass Timberlane. Sinclair Lewis. 1982. Repr. lib. bdg. 18.95x (ISBN 0-89966-401-6). Buccaneer Bks.

Cass Timberlane: A Novel of Husbands and Wives. Sinclair Lewis. LC 45-4918. 1945. Random House.

Cass Timberlane: A Novel of Husbands and Wives. 1st Modern Library Ed. Sinclair Lewis. LC 57-11171. (Modern library of the world's best books 221). 1957. Random House.

Cassady. Jefferson Sutton. LC 79-16517. 1979. 8.95 (ISBN 0-312-12343-4). St. Martin's Press.

Cassandra. Frances Clippinger. LC 56-7482. 1956. Rinehart.

Cassandra. Elizabeth Lodge. (Orig.). 1980. pap. 2.25 (ISBN 0-8439-8009-5, Tiara Bks). Nordon Pubns.

Cassandra. Claudette Williams. 1979. 2.25 (ISBN 0-449-23895-4). Fawcet Crest Books.

Cassandra, a Pillar of Salt. Catherine Vincent. LC 75-38766. 8.95 (ISBN 0-914042-06-8) (ISBN 0-914042-05-X). Coral Reef Publications.

Cassandra at the Wedding. Dorothy Dodds Baker. LC 62-811546. 1962. Houghton Mifflin.

Cassandra Rising. Alice Laurance. LC 77-92218. 1978. 7.95 (ISBN 0-385-12857-6). Doubleday.

Cassandra Singing: A Novel. David Madden. LC 75-89872. 1969. 5.95. Crown Publishers.

Cassandra Speaking. Judy Hogan. LC 77-3471. (Orig.). 1977. pap. 3.50x (ISBN 0-914476-62-9). Thorp Springs.

Cassanova in Khaki. LC 46-21102. 1946. Vickers and Company.

Casse-Noisette (Nutcracker) Translated by Jeanine B. Sebastian. Illustrated by Jose Correas. Jean Lee Latham. LC 61-14967. Bobbs-Merrill.

Cassette Piece. Gerald Kaminski. LC 77-4995. 2.95 (ISBN 0-914974-14-9). Holmgangers Press.

Cassidy. Lee Leighton, pseud. 1980. pap. 2.25 (ISBN 0-345-29530-7). Ballantine.

Cassie. Sandra Berkley. 1973. 0.95 (ISBN 0-515-02914-9). Pyramid Bks.

Cassilda: Or, The Moorish Princess of Toledo. A Legend of Spain. Tr. by Monroe, Mary C. LC 6-231104. 1875. Benziger Brothers.

Cassilee. Susan Coon. 1980. pap. 2.25 (ISBN 0-380-75887-3, 75887). Avon.

Cassio & the Life Divine. David George Rubin. LC 65-176468. bds., 4.95. Farrar.

Cassio and the Life Divine. David George Rubin. LC 66-76394. 1966. Macmillan.

Cassiodore Case. A. Richard Martin. LC 28-5559. 1928. R. M. McBride & Company.

Cassiopeia Affair. Chloe Zerwick & Harrison Scott Brown. LC 68-10575. 1968. Doubleday.

Cassis... Resort to Vengeance. Mark Walker. LC 78-68542. 8.95 (ISBN 0-8027-5405-8). Walker.

Cassock of the Pines: And Other Stories. Joseph Gordian Daley. LC 1-27703. 1901. W. H. Young and Company.

Cassowary: What Chanced in the Cleft Mountains. Stanley Waterloo. LC 7-20621. Monarch Book Company.

Cassy. Elizabeth Lyle. LC 81-8723. 1981. 10.95 (ISBN 0-312-12352-3). St. Martin's Press.

Cassy Scandal: A Novel. Zola Helen Ross. LC 54-6499. 1954. Bobbs-Merrill.

Cast a Cold Eye. Mary Therese McCarthy. LC 50-9761. 1950. Harcourt, Brace.

Cast a Green Shadow. Mary V. Hunt. 1973. pap. 0.75 o.s.i. (01-395). Lancer.

Cast a Long Shadow. Dorothy Phoebe Ansle. LC 78-52329. 1978. 6.95 (ISBN 0-525-07790-1). Dutton.

Cast a Long Shadow. Frank Bonham. (Berkley Book)). 1980. (ISBN 0-425-04465-3). Berkley Publishing Corp.

Cast a Long Shadow. Laura Conway. 1978. 6.95 o.p. (ISBN 0-525-07790-1). Dutton.

Cast a Long Shadow. Wayne D Overholser. LC 55-3772. 1955. Macmillan.

Cast a Long Shadow. Wayne D Overholser. 1974. (pbk.) 0.95. Dell.

Cast a Long Shadow. Mary Emily Pearce. LC 83-2953. 11.95 (ISBN 0-312-12353-1). St. Martin's Press.

Cast a Tender Shadow. Isabel Dix. (Harlequin Presents Ser.). 192p. 1982. pap. 1.50 (ISBN 0-373-02491-6). Harlequin Bks.

Cast a Wistful Eye. Martha Stephens. LC 76-40910. 6.95 (ISBN 0-02-614110-8). Macmillan.

Cast a Yellow Shadow. Ross. Thomas. (S367). 1968. Avon.

Cast a Yellow Shadow. Ross Thomas. LC 67-25321. 1967. Morrow.

Cast Adrift. Timothy Shay Arthur. LC 6-2464. 1873. J. M. Stoddart & Co.

Cast-Away. William Cowper. Ed. by Charles Ryskamp. (Illus.). 1963. 2.00 o.p. (ISBN 0-87811-007-0). Princeton Lib.

Cast Away at the Pole. William Wallace Cook. LC 77-84215. (Lost Race and Adult Fantasy Fiction). 1978. 20.00 (ISBN 0-405-10970-9). Arno Press.

Cast Down the Laurel. Arnold Gingrich. LC 35-233565. 1935. A. A. Knopf.

Cast for Death. Margaret Yorke. LC 76-13823. 1976. 6.95 (ISBN 0-8027-5353-1). Walker.

Cast, in Order of Disappearance: A Crime Novel. Simon Brett. LC 76-12134. 6.95 (ISBN 0-684-14707-6). Scribner.

Cast in Order of Disappearance: A Crime Novel. Simon Brett. (Berkley book). 1979. 1.75 (ISBN 0-425-04134-4). Berkley Pub. Corp.

Cast-Iron Duke. Stephen McKenna. LC 31-1202. 1931. Dodd, Mead & Company.

Cast No Stone. Daisy Ashley. LC 54-8326. 1954. VantagePress.

Cast of Characters: A Novel. 1st Ed. Albert Morgan. LC 57-8967. 1957. Dutton.

Cast of Characters: Stories of Broadway and Hollywood. Garson Kanin. LC 69-15509. 1969. 8.95. Atheneum.

Cast of Stars. Allan Prior. LC 82-1029. (William Abrahams Bk.). 444p. 1983. 16.95 (ISBN 0-03-061943-2). HR&W.

Cast of Thousands: A Novel. Philip Oakes. LC 76-381824. 1976. 4.40 (ISBN 0-575-02130-6). Gollancz.

Cast on a Certain Island. Charles Roger Tennant. LC 75-89107. 1970. 5.95. Doubleday.

Cast the First Stone. Chester B. Himes. 346p. 1973. Repr. of 1952 ed. 8.95x (ISBN 0-911860-31-2). Chatham Bkseller.

Cast the First Stone: A Novel. Chester B Himes. LC 52-11709. 1952. Coward-McCann.

Cast to Death. Nigel Orde-Powlett. LC 32-33842. 1932. Houghton Mifflin Company.

Cast up by the Sea. Samuel White Baker. LC 6-6874. (Franklin square library, no. 137). 1880. Harper & Brothers.

Cast up by the Sea. Samuel White Baker. LC 6-687328. (On cover: Farm and fireside library. no. 14). 1882. Farm and Fireside Company.

Cast up by the Sea. Samuel White Baker. LC 6-6872. (Lovell's library, v. 5, no. 206). 1883. J. W. Lovell Company.

Cast up by the Sea. Samuel White Baker. LC 16-14094. 1916. Harper & Brothers.

Cast Upon His Care. A Novel. Dora Delmar. (On cover: Library of American authors. no. 53). 1894. G. Munro's Sons.

Cast Upon the Breakers. Horatio Alger. LC 73-9003. 1974. 6.95 (ISBN 0-385-08386-6). Doubleday.

Castanets. Carlos Reyles & Le Clercq, Jacques Georges Clemenceau, 1898- Tr. LC 29-18266. 1929. Longmans, Green and Co.

Castang's City. Nicolas Freeling. LC 80-7699. 8.95 (ISBN 0-394-50895-5). Pantheon Books.

Castang's City. Nicolas Freeling. LC 81-40075. 1981. 2.95 (ISBN 0-394-74747-X). Vintage Books.

Castang's City. Nicolas Freeling. LC 81-126684. 1980. 9.95 (ISBN 0-434-27185-3). Heinemann.

Castara. W. Habington. Ed. by E. Arber. Repr. of 1868 ed. 6.00x o.p. (ISBN 0-87556-118-7). Saifer.

Castaway. James Gould Cozzens. LC 67-1907. 1967. 3.50. Harcourt.

Castaway. James Gould Cozzens. LC 67-192078. (Harvest bk., HB 134). 1968. pap., 1.15. Harcourt.

Castaway. James Gould Cozzens. LC 34-374283. 1934. Random House.

Castaway. James Gould Cozzens. LC 34-36239. 1934. Longmans, Green and Co.

Castaway. Austin C. King. 1978. 5.95 o.p. (ISBN 0-533-02914-7). Vantage.

Castaway. Frances Murray. LC 78-12653. 7.95 (ISBN 0-684-16064-1). Scribner.

Castaway: A Story for the Young. Elizabeth Maria Beskow. LC 18-17355. Augustana Book Concern.

Castaway: Three Great Men Ruined in One Year--a King, a Cad and a Castway-- Hallie Erminie Rives. LC 4-31678. The Bobbs-Merrill Company.

Castaway: Three Great Men Ruined in One Year--a King, a Cad and a Castaway. Hallie Erminie Rives. LC 26-3671. Grosset & Dunlap.

Castaways. Jamie Lee Cooper. LC 79-98278. 1970. 5.50. Bobbs-Merrill.

Castaways. William Wymark Jacobs. LC 17-2478. 1917. C. Scribner's Sons.

Castaways in Time. Robert Adams & Polly Freas. LC 79-11600. (Starblaze editions). 1980. 4.95 (ISBN 0-915442-96-5). Donning.

Castaways of Tanagar. Brian M. Stableford. (Science Fiction Ser.). 1981. pap. 2.50 o.p. (ISBN 0-87997-609-8, UE1609). DAW Bks.

Castaways of the Flag: The Final Adventures of the Swiss Family Robinson. Jules Verne & Metcalfe, Cranstoun, Tr. LC 24-196629. 1924. G. H. Watt.

Castaways of the Yuken. Ella M Rea. LC 36-10521. 1936. Meador Publishing Company.

Caste. William Alexander Fraser. LC 22-25227. 2.00. George H. Doran Company.

Caste. Cosmo Hamilton. LC 27-18714. 1927. G. P. Putnam's Sons.

Caste: A Novel. I. L Hauser. LC 8-27106. 1908. I. L. Hauser & Co.

Caste: a Story of Republican Equality. Mary Hayden Green Pike. LC 73-152931. (Black Heritage Library Collection). 1971. (ISBN 0-8369-8776-4). Books for Libraries Press.

Caste for Comedy. Audrey Curling. 1973. (pbk.) 0.75. Ace.

Caste of Heroes. Lona B Kenney. LC 66-15768. 4.50. Dodd.

Castel Del Monte: A Romance of the Fall of the Hohenstaufen Dynasty in Italy. Nathan Gallizier. LC 5-6947. 1905. L. C. Page & Company.

Castilian Caper. Vincent A. Paradis. 1978. pap. 1.95 (ISBN 0-532-12232-1). Woodhill.

TITLE INDEX CASTLE RACKRENT AND THE

Casting Away of Mrs. Lecks and Mrs. Aleshine. Frank Richard Stockton. LC 61-1253. 1961. Dover Publications.

Casting Away: Of Mrs. Lecks and Mrs. Aleshine. Stockton, Frank Richard. LC 4-16110. 1898. The Century Co.

Casting Away of Mrs. Lecks and Mrs. Aleshine: The Vizier of the Two-Horned Alexander. Frank Richard Stockton. LC 13-14965. (novels and stories of Frank R. Stockton. xiii). 1900. C. Scribner's Sons.

Casting Away of Mrs. Lecks and Mrs. Aleshine: With Its Sequel, The Dussantes. Frank Richard Stockton. LC 33-17942. D. Appleton-Century Company, Incorporated.

Casting of Nets. Richard Bagot. LC 1-17684. 1901. John Lane.

Castle. definitive ed. Franz Kafka. LC 73-14772. 1974. (pbk.) 2.45 (ISBN 0-394-71991-3). Vintage Books.

Castle. definitive ed. Franz Kafka. LC 73-90729. 1974. (pbk.) 2.45 (ISBN 0-8052-0415-6). Schocken Books.

Castle. definitive ed. Franz Kafka. LC 72-3630. (Modern library books, 388). 1969. 2.45. Modern Library.

Castle. definitive ed. Franz Kafka. LC 54-59793. 1954. Knopf.

Castle. Franz Kafka. Tr. by Muir, Edwin. LC 30-24952. 1930. A. A. Knopf.

Castle. Franz Kafka. Tr. by Muir, Edwin. LC 41-305262. 1941. A. A. Knopf.

Castle. Franz Kafka & Willa Muir. LC 75-325793. (Penguin modern classics). 1974. 0.75 (ISBN 0-14-001235-4). Penguin.

Castle and the Ring. Cyril Charlie Martindale. LC 55-9612. 1955. Kenedy.

Castle at Glencarris. Jean Vicary. 1977. pap. 1.25 o.s.i. (ISBN 0-8439-0449-6, LB449, Leisure Bks). Nordon Pubns.

Castle Barebane. Joan Aiken. LC 76-3467. 1976. 7.95 (ISBN 0-670-20628-8). Viking Press.

Castle Barebane. Joan Aiken. (Kangaroo Book). 1977. 1.95 (ISBN 0-671-81140-1). Pocket Books.

Castle Black. Catherine Morland. 1972. pap. 0.75 o.p. (94272). Beagle Bks.

Castle Blair: A Story of Youthful Days. Flora Louisa Shaw Lugard. LC 8-4782. 1881. Roberts Brothers.

Castle Blair: A Story of Youthful Days. Flora Louisa Shaw Lugard. 1903. Little, Brown, and Company.

Castle Builder. Etta Merrick Graves. LC 16-23585. 1916. 1.25. Sherman, French & Company.

Castle Builder: A Missionary Story of the Northland. 2d ed., rev. ed. Nephi Anderson. LC 53-18608. 1952. Deseret News Press.

Castle Builders. Charles Clark Munn. LC 10-834003. 1910. 1.50. Lothrop, Lee & Shepard Co.

Castle by the Sea. Henry Brereton Marriott Watson. 1909. Little, Brown, and Company.

Castle Clodha. Alanna Knight. (Belmont Tower Book). 1977. 1.25 (ISBN 0-505-51118-5). Tower Pubns.

Castle Cloud. Joan Grant. (Ace Gothic). 1973. (pbk.) 0.95. Ace Books.

Castle Cloud. Elizabeth Norman. 1977. pap. 2.50 (ISBN 0-380-00889-0, 50062). Avon.

Castle Comedy. Thompson Buchanan. LC 4-23716. 1904. Harper & Brothers.

Castle Conquer. Padraic Colum. LC 23-9942. 1923. The Macmillan Company.

Castle Corner. Joyce Cary. LC 63-20302. 1963. Harper & Row.

Castle Craggs. Virginia H. Maas. (Orig.). 1979. pap. 1.95 (ISBN 0-532-19253-2). Woodhill.

Castle Craneycrow. George Barr McCutcheon. LC 2-20393. 1902. H. S. Stone and Company.

Castle Daly. Annie Keary. LC 79-9474. (Ireland, from the Act of Union, 1800, to the Death of Parnell, 1891; 65). 1979. 42.00 (ISBN 0-8240-3514-3). Garland Pub.

Castle Daly: the Story of an Irish Home Thirty Years Ago. Annie Keary. (Seaside library, v. 39, no. 793). G. Munro.

Castle Daly: The Story of an Irish Home Thirty Years Ago. Annie Keary. LC 4-16535. H. T. Coates & Co.

Castle Danger. Theodore V. Olsen. 1973. (pbk.) 0.95. Manor Books.

Castle Danger. Walter O'Meara. 224p. 1977. pap. 1.25 (ISBN 0-532-12493-6). Woodhill.

Castle Dangerous. Walter Scott. (On cover: Lovell's library, no. 492). 1885. J. W. Lovell Company.

Castle Dangerous. Walter Scott. (On cover: Seaside library. Pocket ed. no. 364). 1885. G. Munro.

Castle Dangerous. Kate Ward. 1973. (pbk) 0.95. Ace Books.

Castle Dangerous: & The Surgeon' Daughter. Walter Scott. (Half-title: Everyman's library, ed. by Ernest Rhys. Fiction). 1907. J. M. Dent & Co.

Castle Dangerous: And The Surgeon's Daughter. Walter Scott. LC 36-37001. (Half-title: Everyman's library, ed. by Ernest Rhys. Fiction. no. 130). 1920. J. M. Dent & Sons, Ltd.

Castle Doom. Marjorie McEvoy. (Orig.). 1973. pap. 0.75 o.p. (94346). Beagle Bks.

Castle Dor. Arthur Thomas Quiller-Couch & Daphne DuMaurier. 1974. (pbk.) 1.25 (ISBN 0-380-00157-8). Avon.

Castle Dubrava. Yuri Kapralov. LC 82-5100. 13.54. Dutton.

Castle Foam: Or, The Heir of Meerschaum. A Russian Story. Henry Willard French. LC 6-40031. 1880. Lee and Shepard.

Castle for Sale. Mona Naomi Anne Hocking Messer. LC 30-25907. 1930. L. MacVeagh, The Dial Press.

Castle Garac. Nicholas Monsarrat. LC 55-10129. 1955. Knopf.

Castle Garac. Nicholas Monserrat. 1976. pap. 1.25 o.p. (ISBN 0-515-04120-3). Pyramid Pubns.

Castle Gay. John Buchan. LC 30-21167. 1930. Houghton Mifflin Company.

Castle Gregory: A Story of the Western Reserve Woods in the Olden Times. Albert Gallatin Riddle. LC 3-26200. 1884. Leader Printing Company.

Castle Heritage. Elisabeth Barr. LC 77-77645. 1978. 6.95 (ISBN 0-385-12997-1). Doubleday.

Castle Heritage. Elisabeth Barr. 1979. Playboy Press.

Castle Hohenwald: A Romance After the German of Adolph Streckfuss... Adolf Streckfuss & Wister, Mrs. Annie Lee (Furness) 1830-1908, Tr. LC 6-39728. 1906. J. B. Lippincott Company.

Castle in Andalusia. Elizabeth Sprigge. LC 35-411103. 1935. The Macmillan Company.

Castle in Bavaria. Prince Thibaut & Princess Marion d'Orleans. LC 76-51207. (O.s.i.). 1977. 8.95 o.s.i. (ISBN 0-671-22575-8). S&S.

Castle in Bavaria: A Novel. Thibaut Orleans & Marion Orleans. LC 76-51207. 8.95 (ISBN 0-671-22575-8). Simon and Schuster.

Castle in Carinthia. Johan Wigmore Fabricius. Tr. by Renier, Gustaaf Johann. LC 40-980618. 1940. Random House.

Castle in Spain. Caroline Farr. Bd. with So Near & Yet... 1978. pap. 2.50 (ISBN 0-451-11694-1, AE1694, Sig). NAL.

Castle in Spain. Margaret Rome. (Harlequin Romances Ser.). 192p. 1982. pap. 1.50 (ISBN 0-373-02464-9, Pub. by Harlequin). PB.

Castle in Spain. Benjamin Tammuz. LC 72-88270. 304p. 1973. 7.95 o.p. (ISBN 0-672-51823-6). Bobbs.

Castle in Spain. Benjamin Tamuz. LC 72-88270. 1973. 7.95. Bobbs-Merrill.

Castle in Spain: A Novel. James De Mille. (On cover: Library of select novels, no. 615). Harper & Brothers.

Castle in the Air. Hugh Boyle Ewing. LC 20-16491. (Leisure hour series no. 214). 1888. H. Holt and Company.

Castle in the Air. Donald E Westlake. LC 79-27514. 9.95 (ISBN 0-87131-322-7). M. Evans.

Castle in the Mist. Maureen E. Wakefield. Ed. by Alice Sachs. 1970. 3.95 o.p. B Franklin.

Castle in the Moonlight. Anne Stewart. LC 38-15227. Gramercy Publishing Company.

Castle in the Rock. Eileen Jackson. LC 78-73361. 1979. 8.95 (ISBN 0-8027-0623-1). Walter.

Castle in the Sand. Richard Julius Herman Krebs. LC 47-11731. 1947. Beechhurst Press.

Castle in the Sea. Translated by Charlotte Haldane. Michelle Lorraine. LC 57-9086. 1957. Beacon Press.

Castle in the Swamp: A Tale of Old Carolina. Edison Marshall. LC 48-8887. 1948. Farrar, Straus.

Castle in the Trees. Rachel Lindsay. (Presents Ser.). 1974. pap. 1.25 (ISBN 0-373-70560-3, 70560, Pub by Harlequin). PB.

Castle Inn. Stanley John Weyman. LC 545. 1898. Longmans, Green, and Co.

Castle Island. Ralph Hale Mottram. LC 31-17599. 1931. Harper & Brothers.

Castle Island Case. Francis Van Wyck Mason. LC 37-232408. Reynal & Hitchcock.

Castle Keep. William Eastlake. LC 65-11975. bds., 5.95. S. & S.

Castle Keep. William Eastlake. 1973. (pbk.) 1.25. Ballantine.

Castle, Knight & Troubadour: In an Apology and Three Tableaux. Elia Wilkinson Peattie. LC 3-31943. 1903. The Blue Sky Press.

Castle Made for Love. Barbara Cartland. LC 77-17359. 6.95 (ISBN 0-87272-031-4). Duron Books.

Castle Malandine. Hilary Ford. (Adult Ser.). 1975. Repr. lib. bdg. 12.95 o.p. (ISBN 0-8161-6331-6, Large Print Bks). G K Hall.

Castle Malindine. Hilary Ford, pseud. LC 74-25033. 1975. 7.95 (ISBN 0-06-011314-6). Harper & Row.

Castle Malindine. Hilary Ford, pseud. LC 75-30978. 1975. 12.95 (ISBN 0-8161-6331-6). G. K. Hall.

Castle Midnight. Archie Joscelyn. 1966. Arcadia House.

Castle Mirage. Alice Brennan. 1976. pap. 1.25 o.p. (LB392, Leisure Bks). Nordon Pubns.

Castle Mirage. Alice Brennan. (Orig., Osi). 1971. pap. 0.75 o.s.i. (B75-2133). Belmont-Tower.

Castle Mirage. Alice Brennan. 1976. 1.25. Leisure Books.

Castle Nowhere: Lake Country Sketches. Constance Fenimore Woolson. LC 69-11927. (American short story series, v. 86). 1969. Garrett Press.

Castle Nowhere: Lake-Country Sketches. Constance Fenimore Woolson. LC 79-137308. 1971. (ISBN 0-404-07035-3). AMS Press.

Castle Nowhere: Lake-Country Sketches. Constance Fenimore Woolson. LC 8-37232. 1875. J. R. Osgood and Company.

Castle of Argol. Julien Gracq. LC 51-14938. (Direction series, 22). J. Laughlin, ?

Castle of Argol. Louis Poirier. LC 51-14938. (Direction series, 22). J. Laughlin.

Castle of Crossed Destinies. Italo Calvino. LC 76-27423. (Illus.). 10.00 (ISBN 0-15-115998-X). Harcourt Brace Jovanovich.

Castle of Crossed Destinies. Italo Calvino. LC 78-23588. (Harvest/HBJ book). 1979. 3.95 (ISBN 0-15-615455-2). Harcourt Brace Jovanovich.

Castle of Dawn. Harold Morton Kramer. LC 8-10278. 1908. Lothrop, Lee & Shepard Co.

Castle of Deception. Ed. Fitch. Ed. by Carl L. Weschke. LC 83-80166. (Llewellyn's Magical Fantasy Ser.). (Illus.). 250p. (Orig.). 1983. pap. 6.95 (ISBN 0-87542-231-4, L 231). Llewellyn Pubns.

Castle of Doubt. John Harvey Whitson. LC 7-16940. 1907. Little, Brown, and Company.

Castle of Dreams. William Arthur Neubauer. LC 48-117731. 1948. Arcadia House.

Castle of Dreams. Paulette Warren. (Berkley Medallion Book). 1977. 1.25 (ISBN 0-425-03390-2). Berkley Pub. Corp.

Castle of Eagles. Constance Heaven. LC 73-87784. 1974. 6.95 (ISBN 0-698-10574-5). Coward, McCann & Geoghegan.

Castle of Ehrenstein: Its Lords, Temporal and Spiritual; Its Inhabitants,Earthly and Unearthly. George Payne Rainsford James. LC 7-7581. (On cover: Library of select novels, no. 97). 1847. Harper & Brothers.

Castle of Ehrenstein: Its Lords, Temporal and Spiritual; Its Inhabitants, Earthly and Unearthly. George Payne Rainsford James. (Seaside library, v. 29, no. 599). 1879. G. Munro.

Castle of Fear. Sandra Abbott. 1974. (pbk.) 0.95. Avon.

Castle of Fear. Barbara Cartland. (Barbara Cartland Library,#11)). 1974. (pbk.) 1.25. Bantam Books.

Castle of Foxes. Alanna Knight. LC 80-952. 1981. 11.95 (ISBN 0-385-15327-9). Doubleday.

Castle of Foxes. Alanna Knight. LC 81-6279. 1981. 16.95 (ISBN 0-8161-3258-5). G.K. Hall.

Castle of Fratta. Ippolito Nievo. LC 74-10017. 1974. (ISBN 0-8371-7660-3). Greenwood Press.

Castle of Fratta. Translated by Lovett F. Edwards. Ippolito Nievo. 1957. Oxford University Press.

Castle of Fratta. Translated by Lovett F. Edwards. Ippolito Nievo. LC 57-13458. 1958. Houghton Mifflin.

Castle of Hape. Shirley R. Murphy. LC 79-22764. 1980. 8.95 (ISBN 0-689-30753-5, Argo). Atheneum.

Castle of Hape. Shirley R. Murphy. 160p. 1981. pap. 1.95 (ISBN 0-380-54783-X, 54783). Avon.

Castle of Kudora. Betty Hale Hyatt. (Candlelight regency romance). 1974. (pbk.) 0.75. Dell.

Castle of Lies. Arthur Henry Vesey. LC 6-12139. 1906. D. Appleton and Company.

Castle of Love: 1549? San Pedro, Diego De, Fl & John Bourchier Berners. LC 51-634. 1950. Scholars' Facsimiles & Reprints.

Castle of Lugas: A Romantic Detective Story. Alfonso Fernandez. LC 27-128239. 1972. Jamaica Publishing Co.

Castle of Many Mirrors and Their Sequel. Ella Heustis Dunn. LC 7-3083. M. A. Donohue & Company.

Castle of Otranto. Horace Walpole. (On cover: Seaside library. Pocket ed. no. 770). 1886. G. Munro.

Castle of Otranto. Horace Walpole & George Gordon Noel Byron Byron. Ed. by Everett Franklin Bleiler. LC 64-16338. 1966. Dover Publications.

Castle of Otranto. Horace Walpole & Scott, Sir Walter, Bart., 1771-1832. (Half-title: The Kings classics under the general editorship of... I Gallancz... no. 38). 1907. Chatto and Windus.

Castle of Otranto see Three Gothic Novels.

Castle of Otranto: A Gothic Story. new ed. reprinted with additional notes. ed. Horace Walpole. Ed. by Wilmarth Sheldon Lewis. Joseph W Reed. LC 70-454902. (Oxford English novels). (Illus.). 1969. Oxford U. P.

Castle of Otranto: A Gothic Story. Horace Walpole. LC 7-30682. 1854. H. C. Baird.

Castle of Otranto: A Gothic Story. Horace Walpole & W. S Lewis. LC 82-3604. (World's classics). 1982. 3.95 (ISBN 0-19-281606-3). Oxford University Press.

Castle of Otranto: A Gothic Story, Ed., Introd. by W. S. Lewis. Horace Walpole. Ed. by Wilmarth Sheldon Lewis. LC 64-56281. (Oxford English novels) Bibl.). 1965. Oxford.

Castle of Otranto: By Horace Walpole. The Mysteries of Udolpho, by Ann Radcliffe (Abridged) Northanger Abbey, by Jane Austen. Ed., Introd. by Andrew Wright. Horace Walpole & Ann Ward Radcliffe. Ed. by Andrew H. Wright. (Rinehart editions, 121 rebound) Bibl.). 1965. 4.00. P. Smith.

Castle of Otranto: By Horace Walpole. Vathek, by William Beckford. The Vampyre, by John Polidori. Three Gothic Novels, and a Fragment of a Novel, by Lord Byron, Ed. by E. F. Bleiler. Horace Walpole et al. Ed. by Everett Franklin Bleiler. (Dover Book: T1232). 1966. 4.00. P. Smith.

Castle of Otranto (Three Gothic Novels) 2nd ed. Horace Walpole. Ed. by E. F. Bleiler. Bd. with Vathek. William Beckford. Ed. by E. F. Bleiler. Tr. by Samuel Henley; Vampyre. John Polidori. Ed. by E. F. Bleiler; Fragment of a Novel. Lord Byron. pap. 4.50 (ISBN 0-486-21232-7). Dover.

Castle of San Salvo: A Novel. Isabel Constance Clarke. LC 26-214982. 1926. Benziger Brothers.

Castle of the Demon. Patrick Ruell. LC 72-14092. 1973. 5.95. Hawthorn Books.

Castle of the Fountains. Margaret Rome. (Harlequin Presents Ser.). 192p. 1982. pap. 1.75 (ISBN 0-373-10532-0). Harlequin Bks.

Castle of the Otter. Gene Wolfe. LC 82-70013. 1982. 16.95 (ISBN 0-917488-10-5); limited ed. o.p. 26.95 (ISBN 0-917488-11-3). Ziesing Bros.

Castle of the Sea. Burt Dean. LC 54-8355. 1954. Vantage Press.

Castle of the Shadows: By Mrs. C. N. Williamson... Alice Muriel Livingston Williamson. LC 10-3291. 1909. The Hudson Press.

Castle of the Whip. A. De Granamore. 1972. pap. 1.95 o.s.i. (V1111T, Venus). Grove.

Castle of Twilight. Margaret Horton Potter. 1903. A. C. McClurg & Co.

Castle of Wolfenbach: By Eliza Parsons. Eliza Phelp Parsons. LC 68-98583. (Northanger Set of Jane Austen Horrid Novels). 1968. Folio Pr.

Castle Omeragh. Frank Frankfort Moore. LC 3-12519. 1903. D. Appleton and Company.

Castle on the Coast. Anne Tedlock Brooks. LC 54-11463. 1954. Arcadia House.

Castle on the Hill. Elizabeth Goudge. LC 42-36216. 1942. Coward-McCann, Inc.

Castle on the Loch. Caroline Fair. 1979. pap. 1.75 (ISBN 0-451-08830-1, L8830, Sig). NAL.

Castle on the Prairie. Sonja Wilson. LC 72-86313. 200p. 1973. 5.95 o.p. (ISBN 0-8283-1481-0). Branden.

Castle on the River. Charles Mercer. 1975. (pbk.) 1.25. Popular Library.

Castle Rackrent. Maria Edgeworth. LC 64-561706. (Norton Lib. N288). 1965. Norton.

Castle Rackrent. Maria Edgeworth. LC 64-66320. (Miami, University of, Coral Gables, Fla. Critical Studies: No. 4). 1964. University of Miami Press.

Castle Rackrent. Maria Edgeworth. LC 12-19569. (Half-title: The English Comedie humaine). 1904. The Century Co.

Castle Rackrent. Maria Edgeworth. LC 6-397589. (Half-title: The English Comedie humaine). 1905. The Century Co.

Castle Rackrent. Maria Edgeworth. LC 12-19570. (Half-title: The English Comedie humane). 1906. The Century Co.

Castle Rackrent. Maria Edgeworth. LC 78-17959. (Ireland, from the Act of Union, 1800, to the Death of Parnell, 1891). 1979. 32.00 (ISBN 0-8240-3450-3). Garland Pub.

Castle Rackrent. Maria Edgeworth & George Watson. LC 80-49865. (World's classics). 1980. 43.50 (ISBN 0-19-281539-3). Oxford University Press.

Castle Rackrent, and The Absentee. Maria Edgeworth. (Half-title: Everyman's library, ed. by Ernest Rhys. Fiction (no. 410). 1909. J. M. Dent & Sons, Ltd.

Castle Rackrent and The Absentee. Maria Edgeworth. LC 36-37185. (Half-title: Everyman's library, ed. by Ernest Rhys. Fiction no. 410). J. M. Dent & Sons, Ltd.

Castle Rackrent and The Absentee. Maria Edgeworth. LC 79-19220. (Series: Irish Heritage Series (Wilmington, Del.). 1980. 25.00 (ISBN 0-934204-02-0). M. P. Browne.

Castle Rackrent and The Absentee. Maria Edgeworth & Ritchie, Anne Isabella (Thackeray) Lady, 1837-1919, Ed. LC 4-15309. 1895. Macmillan and Co.
Castle Richmond. Anthony Trollope. (seaside library. v. 73, no. 1473). 1883. G. Munro.
Castle Richmond. Anthony Trollope & Thorold, Algar Labouchere, Ed. LC 12-39444. (Half-title: The new pocket library. xxxiv). 1906. John Lane.
Castle Rock Mystery. George Fort Gibbs. LC 27-18263. 1927. London, D. Appleton and Company.
Castle Roogna. Piers Anthony, pseud. 1979. pap. 2.50 (ISBN 0-345-29421-1, Del Rey Bks). Ballantine.
Castle Skull. John Dickson Carr. LC 31-25564. 1931. Harper & Brothers.
Castle Stories. Atwood, Anne. LC 8-23919. 1908. Van Tassell-Odell Press.
Castle That Whispered. Mona Farnsworth. (O.s.i.). 192p. 1976. pap. 1.25 o.s.i. (AQ1558, Award). Univ Pub & Dist.
Castle That Whispered. Mona Farnsworth. 1976. (pbk.) 1.25. Award Books.
Castle Three. Gertrude Margaret Shields. LC 18-11823. 1918. The Century Co.
Castle to Castle. Louis-Ferdinand Celine. Tr. by Ralph Manheim. 1976. pap. 2.95 o.p. (ISBN 0-14-004341-1). Penguin.
Castle to Castle. Louis Ferdinand Destouches. LC 76-46529. 1976. 2.95 (ISBN 0-14-004341-1). Penguin Books.
Castle to Let. Gertrude M. Robins Reynolds. LC 17-23550. 1917. George H. Doran Company.
Castle Ugly. Mary Ellin Barrett. 4.95 o.p. Dutton.
Castle Ugly. 1st Ed. Mary Ellin Barrett. LC 65-11407. 1966. 4.95. Dutton.
Castle Wafer: Or, The Plain Gold Ring. Ellen Price Henry Wood Wood. LC 9-506. 1868. Dick & Fitzgerald.
Castle Warlock: A Homely Romance. George Macdonald. (Seaside library. v. 68, no. 1375). 1882. G. Munro.
Castlecliffe. Sandra Shulman. 1971. pap. 0.60 o.p. (ISBN 0-446-63535-9, 63-535). Paperback Lib.
Castlecourt Diamond Case: Being a Compilation of the Statements Made by the Various Participants in This Curious Case Now, for the First Time, Given to the Public. Geraldine Bonner. LC 6-10195. 1906. Funk & Wagnalls Company.
Castledoom see Torre Siniestra.
Castledown: A Haunting Tale of Magic & Nature. Joyce B. Gregorian. 1983. pap. 2.95 (ISBN 0-441-09240-3, Pub. by Ace Science Fiction). Ace Bks.
Castleford Conundrum. Alfred Walter Stewart. LC 32-253229. 1932. Little, Brown, and Company.
Castlemore. Charles Roy MacKinnon. LC 73-3498. 1973. 8.95. Delacorte Press.
Castlemore. Charles Roy MacKinnon. 1974. (pbk.) 1.50. Dell.
Castler Crosier. A Romance. James F. Brice. LC 6-18266. 1827. Printed by W. M. M'Neir.
Castlereagh. Monica Heath. (Signet Book). 1978. 1.50 (ISBN 0-451-08056-4). New American Library.
Castlereagh. Janet Louise Roberts. 1975. (pbk.) 1.25 (ISBN 0-671-78932-5). Pocket Books.
Castles. Neal Travis. 304p. 1982. pap. 3.50 (ISBN 0-380-79913-8, 79913). Avon.
Castles: An Enduring Fantasy. Naomi R. Kline. (Illus.). 224p. 1983. 30.00 (ISBN 0-89241-374-3). Caratzas Pub Co.
Castles Burning. Arthur Lyons. LC 79-1935. (Rinehart suspense novel). 8.95 (ISBN 0-03-047621-6). Holt, Rinehart, and Winston.
Castles Burning. Arthur Lyons. LC 82-6210. (Jacob Asch mystery). ((Series: Lyons, Arthur.). (Jacob Asch mystery.). 1982. 3.95 (ISBN 0-03-062417-7). Holt, Rinehart, and Winston.
Castles in Kenya. Florence Riddell. LC 29-898909. 1929. J. B. Lippincott Company.
Castles in Spain. Orvill E. Ault. 1976. 7.50 o.p. (ISBN 0-682-48496-2). Exposition.
Castles in Spain. Orvill E. Ault. 1976. 7.50 o.p. (ISBN 0-682-48496-2). Exposition.
Castles in Spain. Nakley Risk. 1970. 2.95 o.p. Vantage.
Castles in the Air. Patricia Gallagher. 1976. pap. 2.50 (ISBN 0-380-00570-0, 75143). Avon.
Castles in the Air. Hervey Smith McCowan. LC 30-150982. The Character Building Company.
Castles in the Air, and Other Phantasies. Robert Barry Coffin. LC 6-26746. 1871. Hurd and Houghton.
Castles in the Air: Being the Adventures of M. Hector Ratichon. Emmuska Orczy. LC 22-7884. 1.75. George H. Doran Company.
Castles in the Sand. Joseph Calvitt Clarke. LC 35-8041. 1935. Arcadia House.
Castles in the Sand. William Standish Stone. LC 55-6373. 1955. Morrow.
Castles of Athlin and Dunbayne: A Highland Story. Ann Ward Radcliffe. LC 78-131336. (Gothic novels). 1972. (ISBN 0-405-00808-2). Arno Press.
Castles of Athlin and Dunbayne: A Highland Story. Ann Ward Radcliffe. LC 70-136973. (Belles lettres in English). 1970. Johnson Reprint Corp.
Castles of Clay. 1st Ed. Richard Charles Kuhnen. LC 56-8087. 1956. Vantage Press.
Castles of Sand. Anne Mather. (Harlequin Presents Ser.). 192p. 1981. pap. 1.50 (ISBN 0-373-10449-9). Harlequin Bks.
Castrati. Sven Delblanc. Tr. by C. W. Williams from Swedish. LC 79-88924. 151p. 1979. 7.95 (ISBN 0-89720-020-9). Karoma.
Castrato: A Novel. Lawrence L. Goldman. LC 72-12077. 1973. 7.95 (ISBN 0-381-98232-7). John Day Co.
Castrators see Night Games.
Castro File. Joseph Rosenberger. (Death Merchant,#7). 1974. (pbk.) 0.95 (ISBN 0-523-00264-5). Pinnacle Books.
Casual Company. Claude Francis Koch. LC 65-20902. 4.95. Chilton.
Casual Murderer: More Cases from Madame Storey's File. Hulbert Footner. LC 38-2674. 1937. J. B. Lippincott Company.
Casual Observer. Elizabeth Whitson. LC 73-85108. (Illus.). 1973. 3.95 (ISBN 0-8378-8001-7). C. R. Gibson Co.
Casual Slaughters. Virginia Hanson. LC 39-25148. 1939. Pub. for the Crime Club, Inc., by Doubleday, Doran & Co., Inc.
Casuals of the Sea. William McFee. LC 31-28460. (Half-title: The modern library of the world's best books). 1931. The Modern Library.
Casuals of the Sea: The Voyage of a Soul. William McFee. LC 17-702. 1916. Doubleday, Page & Co.
Casualties. Katherine Carlson. LC 82-61652. (Minnesota Voices Project Ser.: No. 9). (Illus.). 124p. 1982. pap. 5.00. New Rivers Pr.
Casualties of Peace. Edna O'Brien. LC 76-414592. 1968. Penguin.
Casualties of Peace. Edna O'Brien. LC 67-12920. 1967. Simon and Schuster.
Casualties of War. D. Lang. 1969. pap. 1.50 (ISBN 0-07-036235-1, SP). McGraw.
Casualty. Robert James Collas Lowry. LC 78-138160. 1971. (ISBN 0-8371-5617-3). Greenwood Press.
Casualty. Robert James Collas Lowry. LC 46-7271. 1946. New Directions.
Casuarina Tree. William Somerset Maugham. LC 75-26128. (Maugham, William Somerset, 1874-1965. Works. 1976). 1977. 15.00 (ISBN 0-405-07851-X). Arno Press.
Casuarina Tree: Six Stories. William Somerset Maugham. LC 26-161433. George H. Doran Company.
Casusoes of Sunday Island. 1st Ed. Elsie Katherine Morton. LC 58-11108. 1958. Norton.
Cat. Helen Chetin. 1977. pap. 1.00 o.p. (ISBN 0-931832-06-3). No Dead Lines.
Cat. Sidonie Gabrielle Colette. 1974. (pbk.) 0.95. Popular Library.
Cat. Sidonie Gabrielle Colette. Tr. by Bentinck, Morris. LC 36-17719. Farrar & Rinehart, Incorporated.
Cat. Val Henry Gielgud. LC 57-5365. 1957. Random House.
Cat. Theodore Isaac Rubin. LC 67-598. 1966. Ballantine Books.
Cat. Georges Simenon. LC 76-18871. (Harbrace paperbound library; HPL 71). 1976. (ISBN 0-15-615549-4). Harcourt Brace Jovanovich.
Cat. Georges Simenon. LC 67-25070. 1967. Harcourt, Brace & World.
Cat Across the Path. Ruth Feiner & Alexander, Norman, Tr. J. B. Lippincott Company.
Cat Alley: A Long Short Novel. Richard Carter Higgins. LC 77-353035. 1976. 2.00. Tuumba Press.
Cat Among the Pidgeons. Agatha Miller Christie. 1980. pap. 2.50 (ISBN 0-671-41888-2). PB.
Cat Among the Pigeons. Agatha Miller Christie. 1973. (pbk.) 0.95 (ISBN 0-671-77704-1). Pocket Books.
Cat and a King. Diana Forbes-Robertson. Random House.
Cat and Candle: A Lively Tale. Palls Adam Vilhelm Rosenkrantz. Tr. by Guiterman, M. LC 26-26616. 1926. Doubleday, Page & Company.
Cat and Capricorn: By D. B. Olsen. 1st Ed. Dolores Birk Hitchens. LC 51-14221. 1951. Published for the Crime Club by Doubleday.
Cat and Fiddle Murders. E B Ronald. LC 54-8258. 1954. Rinehart.
Cat & Mouse. Christianna Brand, pseud. 1982. 18.00x (ISBN 0-86025-210-8, Pub. by Ian Henry Pubns England). State Mutual Bk.
Cat and Mouse. Eaton K Goldthwaite. LC 46-819277. 1946. Duell, Sloan and Pearce.
Cat and Mouse. Gunter Grass. LC 66-73243. (B 66-10144). 1966. Penguin Books in Association with Secker & Warburg.
Cat and Mouse. Gunter Grass. LC 63-13499. 1963. Harcourt, Brace & World.
Cat & Mouse. Rodney Peppe. 1980. pap. 2.50 (ISBN 0-14-050297-1, Puffiner.). Penguin.
Cat and Shakespeare: A Tale of India. Rao Raja. LC 65-11572. 3.95. Macmillan.
Cat and Shakespeare: A Tale of Modern India. Raja Rao. 1975. (ISBN 0-88253-775-X). Orient.
Cat and the Canary. Margaret H. C. Cameron. LC 8-5576. 1908. Harper & Brothers.
Cat & the Canary. Gerry Kingsley. 1978. pap. text ed. 1.95 o.s.i. (ISBN 0-89559-121-9). Dale Books Inc.
Cat and the Cherub: And Other Stories. Chester Bailey Fernald. LC 70-113660. (Short story index reprint series). (Illus.). 1970. Books for Libraries Press.
Cat and the Cherub: And Other Stories. Chester Bailey Fernald. LC 4-15102. 1896. The Century Co.
Cat & the Cherub & Other Stories. Chester Bailey Fernald. LC 70-113660. (Short Story Index Reprint Ser). 1896. 16.00 (ISBN 0-8369-3389-3). Ayer Co.
Cat and the Clock. Charles Gordon Booth. LC 36-209. 1935. Pub. for the Crime Club, Inc., by Doubleday, Doran & Company, Inc.
Cat and the Curate: A Phenomenal Experience. by charles gilson. ed. Charles James Louis Gilson. LC 34-28965. 1934. Frederick A. Stokes Company.
Cat and the King. Louis Auchincloss. LC 80-20884. 1981. 10.00 (ISBN 0-395-30225-0). Houghton Mifflin Co.
Cat Ate My Gymsuit. Paula Danziger. 128p. 1975. pap. 1.95 (ISBN 0-440-91612-7, LFL). Dell.
Cat Cay Warrant. Allan Morgan. (Blood Ser.). (O.s.i.). 208p. (Orig.). 1974. pap. 1.25 o.s.i. (AQ1395, Award). Univ Pub & Dist.
Cat Chaser. Elmore Leonard. LC 81-71687. 1982. 13.95 (ISBN 0-87795-398-8). Arbor Hse.
Cat Climbs. C. A Tarrant. LC 37-127270. J. B. Lippincott Company.
Cat Country: A Satirical Novel of China in the 1930's. Lao She. Tr. by William A. Lyell, Jr. LC 78-83144. 1970. 8.00 (ISBN 0-8142-0013-3). Ohio St U Pr.
Cat Five. Robert P Davis. LC 77-9446. 1977. 8.95 (ISBN 0-688-03223-0). Morrow.
Cat Five. Robert P Davis. (Kangaroo Book). 1978. 1.95 (ISBN 0-671-82069-9). Pocket Books.
Cat from Outer Space. Ted Key, pseud. 1978. 1.50 (ISBN 0-671-81740-X). Pocket Books.
Cat Got Your Tongue? Carleton Carpenter. 1973. 0.75. Curtis Books.
Cat in the Convoy. William Greenough Schofield. LC 46-4398. 1946. Macrae-Smith-Company.
Cat in the Ghetto, Four Novelettes. Translated from the Original Yiddish by S. Morris Engel. With an Introd. by Sol. Liptzin and Pref. by Irving Howe. Rachmil Bryks. LC 59-10482. 1959. Bloch Pub. Co.
Cat in the Mirror. Mary Slattery Stolz. 1978. pap. 1.95 (ISBN 0-440-91123-0, LFL). Dell.
Cat Man. Edward Hoagland. LC 55-8877. 1956. Houghton Mifflin.
Cat Man. Edward Hoagland. 1973. 1.25. Ballantine Books.
Cat Must Come Down. Imre Panda. LC 77-359671. 1976. (ISBN 0-85553-003-0). Alpha Books.
Cat-Nappers. P. G. Wodehouse. (O.s.i.). 192p. 1975. 7.95 o.s.i. (ISBN 0-671-21972-3). S&S.
Cat-Nappers. P. G. Wodehouse. (Adult Ser.). 1975. Repr. lib. bdg. 8.95 o.p. (ISBN 0-8161-6313-8, Large Print Bks). G K Hall.
Cat-Nappers: A Jeeves and Bertie Story. Pelham Grenville Wodehouse. LC 74-23181. 1975. 6.95 (ISBN 0-671-21972-3). Simon and Schuster.
Cat-Nappers: A Jeeves and Bertie Story. Pelham Grenville Wodehouse. LC 75-20490. 1975. 8.95 (ISBN 0-8161-6313-8). G. K. Hall.
Cat Nips. Ray Shaw. (O.s.i.). pap. 1.00 o.s.i. (ISBN 0-671-10526-4, Fireside). S&S.
C.A.T. No. Three: Cult of the Damned. Spike Andrews. 224p. (Orig.). 1983. pap. 2.25 (ISBN 0-446-30183-3). Warner Bks.
C.A.T., No. Two: Kidnap Hotel. Spike Andrews. (Men of Action Ser.). 224p. 1983. pap. 1.95 (ISBN 0-446-30185-X). Warner Bks.
Cat O' Mountain. Arthur O Friel. LC 23-99404. 1923. The Penn Publishing Company.
Cat of Many Tails. Ellery Queen, pseud. LC 65-23042. (World's great novels of detection). 1965. Bantam Books.
Cat of Many Tails. Ellery Queen, pseud. LC 49-10982. 1949. Little H Brown.
Cat of Many Tails. Ellery Queen, pseud. LC 79-19435. (Ellery Queen Mystery). 1980. 10.95 (ISBN 0-89340-234-6). J. Curley & Associates.
Cat of Many Tails. Ellery Queen. 1975. (pbk.) 1.50. Ballantine Books.
Cat of Nine Tales. Veronica Leigh. 1976. pap. 1.25 (ISBN 0-532-12430-8). Woodhill.
Cat of Silvery Hue: Horseclaus IV. Robert Adams. (Orig.). 1979. pap. 2.25 (ISBN 0-451-11579-1, AE1579, Sig). NAL.
Cat on a Leash. Elizabeth Gundy. LC 77-27248. 1978. 8.95 (ISBN 0-670-20654-7). Viking Press.
Cat O'Nine Tails. Paul Gillette. (O.s.i.). (Orig.). 1971. pap. 0.75 o.s.i. (A870S, Award). Univ Pub & Dist.
Cat Saw Murder. Dolores Birk Hitchens. LC 39-17652. 1939. Pub. for the Crime Club, Inc., by Doubleday, Doran & Co., Inc.
Cat Saw Murder. Dolores Birk Olsen. LC 39-17652. 1939. Pub. for the Crime Club, Inc., by Doubleday, Doran & Co., Inc.
Cat Screams. Todd Downing. LC 34-25150. 1934. Pub. for the Crime Club, Inc., by Coubleday, Doran & Company, Inc.
Cat-Tails: And Other Tales. Mary H Howliston. LC 99-5429. 1899. A. Flanagan.
Cat Tales. Richard Watherwax. (Illus.). (gr. 7-10). 1979. pap. 3.95 (ISBN 0-671-79078-1, Wallaby). PB.
Cat Walk, by D. B. Olsen. 1st Ed. Dolores Birk Hitchens. LC 53-6521. 1953. Published for the Crime Club by Doubleday.
Cat Wears a Mask. Dolores Birk Hitchens. LC 49-7928. 1949. Pub. for the Crime Club by Doubleday.
Cat Wears a Noose. Dolores Birk Hitchens. LC 44-3967. 1944. Pub. for the Crime Club by Doubleday, Doran and Co., Inc.
Cat Who Ate Danish Modern. Lilian Jackson Braun. LC 67-11390. 1967. Dutton.
Cat Who Could Read Backwards. Lilian Jackson Braun. LC 66-11535. 3.95. Dutton.
Cat Who Saw God. Anna Gordon Keown. LC 32-32570. 1932. W. Morrow & Co.
Cat Who Tasted Cinnamon Toast. Ann Spencer. LC 68-13644. (Illus.). 1968. 4.95. Knopf.
Cat Who Turned on and off. Lilian Jackson Braun. LC 68-25791. 1968. 4.50. Dutton.
Cat Without Substance. Sylva Norman. LC 31-113794. W. W. Norton & Co., Inc.
Catacomb Years. Michael Bishop. LC 78-18438. 10.95. Berkley Pub. Co.: Distributed by Putnam.
Catacombs. Jay Bennett. LC 59-57907. (An Abelard-Schuman mystery). 1959. Abelard-Schuman.
Catacombs. William Demby. LC 64-18343. bds., 4.95. Pantheon.
Catacombs. John Farris. LC 81-3259. 12.95 (ISBN 0-440-01120-5). Delacorte Press.
Catacombs of Paris. Elie Bertrand Berthet. Tr. by Helmore, M. C. LC 29-30766. 1900. A. Constable and Co. Ltd.
Catador De Mujeres. new ed. Ernesto Del Valle. (Pimienta Collection Ser.). 160p. (Span.). 1975. pap. 1.00 o.p. (ISBN 0-88473-225-8). Fiesta Pub.
Catalans. 1st Ed. Patrick O'Brian. LC 53-784439. 1953. Harcourt, Brace.
Catalina: A Romance. William Somerset Maugham. LC 75-25350. (Maugham, William Somerset, 1874-1965. Works. 1976). 1976. 15.00 (ISBN 0-405-07808-0). Arno Press.
Catalina: A Romance. William Somerset Maugham. LC 48-88182. 1948. Doubleday.
Catalog of Crime. Jacques Barzun & Wendell Hertig Taylor. LC 73-20705. (Illus.). 864p. 1974. 25.00 o.p. (ISBN 0-06-010266-7, HarpT). Har-Row.
Catalogue. Patrick Skene Catling. LC 75-140055. 1971. 6.50 (ISBN 0-671-20806-3). Simon and Schuster.
Catalogue: A Novel. George Milburn. LC 36-19976. Harcourt, Brace and Company.
Catalyst. Doris Bell Collier Ball. LC 67-22398. 1967. Macmillan.
Catalyst. William Daniel. LC 70-465064. 1969. 3.75. Cassell Australia.
Catalyst. Charles L Harness. 1980. 1.95. Pocket Books.
Catalyst. Trumbull Reed. LC 42-18728. 1942. The Westminster Press.
Catalyst: By Kenneth Lowe Pseud. 1st Ed. Elma K Lobaugh. LC 58-5948. 1958. Published for the Crime Club by Doubleday.
Catalyst Club: A Murder Mystery. George Dyer. LC 36-7826. 1936. C. Scribner's Sons.
Catamount Camp. Edward Sylvester Ellis. LC 10-27193. (Half-title: Catamount camp series). 1.00. The John C. Winston Company.
Catastrophe. Dino Buzzati. 200p. 1982. pap. 9.95 (ISBN 0-7145-3914-7). Riverrun NY.
Catastrophe at Cliff Haven. Theodore Kenyon Cook. LC 40-140730. Dorrance and Company.
Catastrophe in Bohemia: And Other Stories. Henry S Brooks. LC 6-19385. 1893. C. L. Webster & Company.
Catastrophe: Strange Stories of Dino Buzzati. Dino Buzzati. 1965. 6.00 o.p. Fernhill.
Catastrophes. Ed. by Isaac Asimov et al. 416p. (Orig.). 1981. pap. 2.50 (ISBN 0-449-24425-3, Crest). Fawcett.
Catch. John Boland. LC 66-10287. (Rinehart suspense novel). 1966. bds., 3.50. Holt.
Catch a Brass Canary. Donna Hill. LC 64-22179. 1965. Lippincott.
Catch a Falling Clown. Stuart M. Kaminsky. 160p. 1982. 10.95 (ISBN 0-312-12377-9). St Martin.
Catch a Falling Clown: A Toby Peters Mystery. Stuart M Kaminsky. LC 81-14607. 1982. 9.95 (ISBN 0-312-12377-9). St Martin's Press.

Catch a Falling Spy. Nathaniel Benchley. LC 62-21801. 1963. McGraw-Hill.

Catch a Falling Spy. Len Deighton. (Kangaroo Book). 1977. 1.95 (ISBN 0-671-81685-3). Pocket Books.

Catch a Falling Spy: Originally Published in England Under the Title Twinkle Twinkle Little Spy. Len Deighton. LC 76-18248. 7.95. Harcourt Brace Jovanovich.

Catch a Falling Star. John Brunner. 224p. 1982. pap. 2.75 (ISBN 0-345-30681-3, Del Rey). Ballantine.

Catch a Falling Star. Frederick Franklyn Van De Water. LC 49-7427. 1949. Duell, Sloan and Pearce.

Catch a Killer. Robert Lee Martin. LC 56-9753. (Red badge detective). 1956. Dodd, Mead.

Catch a Rising Star. Danielle Branton. (Gold Medal Book) (ISBN 0-449-13636-1). Fawcett.

Catch a Star. Alexandra Scott. (Harlequin Romances Ser.). 192p. 1983. pap. 1.75 (ISBN 0-373-02554-8). Harlequin Bks.

Catch a Tiger. Owen Cameron. LC 52-12460. (Inner sanctum mystery). 1952. Simon and Schuster.

Catch & Other Stories. Kenzaburo Oe et al. Tr. by John Bester et al. LC 80-84420. 156p. 1981. pap. 4.95 (ISBN 0-87011-457-3). Kodansha.

Catch and Other War Stories. Kenzaburo Oe & Shoichi Saeki. LC 80-84420. (Illus.). 1981. 4.95 (ISBN 0-87011-457-3). Kodansha International.

Catch and Saddle. Llewellyn Perry Holmes. LC 59-14714. (Silver star westerns). 1959. Dodd, Mead.

Catch and Saddle. Llewellyn Perry Holmes. 1979. 1.75 (ISBN 0-445-04400-4). Popular Library.

Catch and Squeeze. Craig Cooper. LC 68-8327. 1968. 3.95. Roy Publishers.

Catch As Catch Can: By Frances and Richard Lockridge. 1st Ed. Frances Louise Davis Lockridge & Richard Lockridge. LC 57-13213. (Main line mysteries). 1958. Lippincott.

Catch in the Breath: A Novel by Gene Horowitz. 1st Ed. Eugene Horowitz. LC 68-10879. 1968. bds., 4.95. Norton.

Catch Kid Curry. W. R Garwood. LC 81-71394. (Diamond Back Westerns). 13.95 (ISBN 0-937618-02-0). Bath Street Press.

Catch Me -- If You Can. Belton Cobb. LC 77-548673. 1970 (ISBN 0-491-00455-9). W. H. Allen.

Catch Me a Colobus. Gerald Durrell. 1977. pap. 1.95 o.p. (ISBN 0-14-004337-3). Penguin.

Catch Me a Phoenix! Alan Geoffrey Yates. LC 65-3275. (Signet book, D2637). 1965. New American Library of World Literature.

Catch Me a Spy. George Marton & Tibor Meray. LC 69-17291. 1969. 4.95. Harper & Row.

Catch Me If You Can. Frank W. Abagnale, Jr. 1982. pap. 2.95 (ISBN 0-671-43145-5). PB.

Catch Me If You Can. Patricia McGerr. LC 48-9217. 1948. Pub. for the Crime Club by Doubleday.

Catch Me: Kill Me. William H. Hallahan. 1978. pap. 1.95 (ISBN 0-380-37986-4, 37986). Avon.

Catch Me, Kill Me: A Novel. William H Hallahan. LC 76-46697. 1977. 7.95 (ISBN 0-672-52311-6). Bobbs-Merrill.

Catch Me Killer. Bob Erler & John C. Souter. 1981. 3.50 (ISBN 0-8423-0214-X). Tyndale.

Catch Me Only with Love: A Novel of Southern Illinois, 1920's-1940's. Frank W. Hamilton. 1973. 3.95 o.p. (ISBN 0-911938-03-6). Walden Pr.

Catch My Breath - a Lally Reader. Michael Lally. LC 75-40539. (Lucky Heart Bks.). 85p. 1975. pap. 2.95 o.p. (ISBN 0-913198-04-8). Salt Lick.

Catch My Breath - a Lally Reader. Michael Lally. LC 75-40539. (Nelson Heart Bks.). 85p. 1975. pap. 2.95 o.p. (ISBN 0-913198-04-8). Salt Lick.

Catch Rides. Sara McAulay. LC 74-21330. 1975. (ISBN 0-394-49553-5). Knopf: Distributed by Random House.

Catch Rides. Sara McAuley. 1975. 7.95 o.p. (ISBN 0-394-49553-5). Knopf.

Catch the Brass Ring: By Stephen Marlowe Pseud. Milton Lesser. LC 55-19317. (Ace double novel books, D-77). 1954. Ace Books.

Catch the Gentle Dawn. Cynthia Freeman, pseud. LC 82-72075. 356p. 1983. 15.50 (ISBN 0-87795-440-2). Arbor Hse.

Catch the Gold Ring: By John Stephen Strange Pseud. 1st Ed. Dorothy Stockbridge Tillett. LC 55-5251. 1955. Doubleday.

Catch the Saint. Fleming Lee & Leslie Charteris. LC 74-25098. (Saint series). 1975. 5.95 (ISBN 0-385-09936-3). Published for the Crime Club by Doubleday.

Catch the Star Winds. easy eye ed. A. Bertram Chandler. (Orig.). 1969. pap. 0.75 o.p. (74-533). Lancer.

Catch the Wind. James Grady. LC 80-14149. (Illus.). 1980. 12.95 (ISBN 0-698-11043-9). Coward, McCann & Geoghegan.

Catch Trap. Marion Zimmer Bradley. LC 78-19623. 12.50 (ISBN 0-345-28090-3). Ballantine Books.

Catch Twenty-Two. Joseph Heller. 1961. 13.95 (ISBN 0-671-12805-1). S&S.

Catch Twenty Two. large type ed. Joseph Heller. 1969. Repr. of 1961 ed. 10.95 o.p. (20296). S&S.

Catch Twenty-Two: A Dramatization. Joseph Heller. 1973. 6.95 o.p. (ISBN 0-440-01098-5). Delacorte.

Catch-22: A Novel. Joseph Heller. (Dell book). 1973. 1.25. Dell.

Catch-22: A Novel. Joseph Heller. LC 61-12846. 1961. Simon and Schuster.

Catcher: And The Manager; Two Baseball Fables. Frank O'Rourke. LC 53-830419. (Barnes sports novel series). 1953. A. S. Barnes.

Catcher in the Rye. J. D. Salinger. LC 58-114716. (Modern library of the world's best books 90). Modern Library.

Catcher in the Rye. J. D. Salinger. LC 51-4713. 1951. Little, Brown.

Catcher in the Rye: J. D. Salinger. Richard Lettis. LC 63-171684. (Barron's studies in Amer. lit.). 1964. Barron's.

Catching Fire. Kay Nolte Smith. LC 81-22175. 13.95 (ISBN 0-698-11134-6). Coward, McCann & Geoghegan.

Catching Fire. Wyatt Wyatt. LC 76-50572. 8.95 (ISBN 0-394-40764-4). Random House.

Catching Saradove. Bertha Harris. LC 69-18132. 1969. Harcourt, Brace & World.

Catchworld. Chris Boyce. 1978. 1.75 (ISBN 0-449-23635-8). Fawcett Crest.

Category. Edward Gorey. Repr. of 1973 ed. 8.50 (ISBN 0-910664-29-3). Gotham.

Cater Street Hangman. Anne Perry. LC 78-19435. 1979. 8.95 (ISBN 0-312-12385-X). St. Martin's Press.

Caterfly. Don De Paul. LC 76-39691. (Quest book). (Illus.). 6.50 (ISBN 0-8356-0490-X). Theosophical Pub. House.

Caterina. Eveline Amstutz. LC 72-126114. 1970. 5.95 (ISBN 0-8027-0327-5). Walker.

Caterina. Bridget Boland. (O.s.i.). 331p. 1976. 8.95 o.s.i. (ISBN 0-312-12390-6). St Martin.

Caterina: A Novel. Bridget Boland. LC 75-26174. (Illus.). 8.95. St. Martin's Press.

Caterina Soave. From the Italian. Gemma Ferruggia. LC 6-38980. (Dillingham's globe library, no. 9). 1866. G. W. Dillingham.

Caterpillar Cop. James McClure. LC 72-9769. 1973. 5.95 (ISBN 0-06-012897-6). Harper & Row.

Caterpillar Cop. James McClure. LC 82-8622. 1982. 2.95 (ISBN 0-394-71058-4). Pantheon Books.

Catfish. Charles Marriott. LC 13-7849. 1.35. The Bobbs-Merrill Company.

Catfish Man: A Conjured Life. Jerome Charyn. LC 79-54007. 10.00 (ISBN 0-87795-249-3). Arbor House: Distributed by Dutton.

Cathara Clyde: A Novel. Inconnu. LC 7-8836. 1860. C. Scribner.

Catharine. 7th ed. Nehemiah Adams. LC 5-42972. 1869. Gould and Lincoln.

Catharine Furze. William Hale White & Shapcott, Reuben, Ed. LC 8-36560. 1893. Macmillan Co.

Catharine Furze. William Hale White & Shapcott, Reuben, Ed. LC 38-108546. 1936. Oxford University Press, H. Milford.

Catharine Furze; Clara Hopgood. William Hale White. LC 75-1516. (Victorian Fiction: Novels of Faith and Doubt). 1976. 35.00 (ISBN 0-8240-1589-4). Garland Pub.

Catharine; with Portrait of Author. Jules Sandeau. LC 8-3757. J. G. Cupples Company.

Cathay. Helene Thornton. 320p. 1982. pap. 2.95 (ISBN 0-449-14471-2, GM). Fawcett.

Cathedral. Nelson DeMille. 1982. pap. 3.95 (ISBN 0-440-11620-1). Dell.

Cathedral. Joris Karl Huysmans. LC 77-10270. 1981. 32.50 (ISBN 0-404-16322-X). AMS Press.

Cathedral. Hugh Walpole. 1922. 7.50 o.p. (ISBN 0-312-12425-2). St Martin.

Cathedral: A Novel. Nelson DeMille. LC 80-29126. 13.95 (ISBN 0-440-01140-X). Delacorte Press.

Cathedral: A Novel. Hugh Walpole. LC 22-26984. George H. Doran Company.

Cathedral: A Novel. Hugh Walpole. LC 34-11264. George H. Doran Company.

Cathedral Close. Margaret Matthews. LC 37-27460. 1937. C. Scribner's Sons.

Cathedral Courtship. Kate Douglas Smith Wiggin. LC 1-26204. 1901. Houghton, Mifflin and Company.

Cathedral Courtship, and Penelope's English Experiences. Kate Douglas Smith Wiggin. LC 1-13907. 1893. Houghton, Mifflin and Company.

Cathedral Folk. Nikolai Semenovich Leskov. LC 76-23885. (Classics of Russian literature). (Hyperion library of world literature). 1977. 5.95 (ISBN 0-88355-488-7). Hyperion Press.

Cathedral Folk. Nikolai Semenovich Leskov. LC 75-110855. 1971. (ISBN 0-8371-4522-8). Greenwood Press.

Cathedral Folk: Translated from the Russian of Nicolai Lyeskov. Nikolai Semenovich Leskov. LC 24-2326. 1924. A. A. Knopf.

Cathedral Glorious: The Story of the Man Who Lost God. Strickland, Arthur Barsalou. LC 52-25164. 1951. House-Warven.

Cathedral in the Sun. Anne Benson Fisher. LC 40-27265. 1940. Carlyle House.

Cathedral of Ice. James Schevill. Ed. by Peter Kaplan. LC 75-33465. 1975. 3.00x (ISBN 0-915176-10-6). Pourboire.

Cathedral of the Pines. Myron David Orr. LC 38-37575. 1938. Capper Harmon Slocum, Inc.

Cathedral Option. Ron Montana. (Orig.). 1978. pap. 2.25 (ISBN 0-89083-404-0). Zebra.

Cathedral Ringing. Violette Newton. 1976. 5.95 (ISBN 0-89015-150-4). Eakin Pubns.

Cathedral Singer. James Lane Allen. LC 16-6440. 1916. The Century Co.

Cathedral Street. Ann Michael. LC 31-64921. Printed by the Haddon Craftsmen, Inc.

Catherine. Nehemiah Adams. LC 5-42970. 1859. J. E. Tilton and Company.

Catherine. rev. ed. Nehemiah Adams. LC 5-42971. 1863. Ticknor and Fields.

Catherine--Paris. Marthe Lucie Lahovary Bibesco. Tr. by Cowley, Malcolm. LC 28-13444. Harcourt, Brace & Company.

Catherine: A Novel. Frances Mary Peard. LC 7-33504. 1893. Harper & Brothers.

Catherine. A Story. William Makepeace Thackeray. (On cover: Lovell's library, v. 4, no. 148). 1883. J. W. Lovell Company.

Catherine Carmier. Ernest J Gaines. LC 64-22101. 1964. Atheneum.

Catherine Carmier. Ernest J. Gaines. LC 72-86778. 1972. 7.50 (ISBN 0-911860-24-X). Chatham Bookseller.

Catherine Carmier: A Novel. Ernest J. Gaines. LC 80-27402. 1981. 6.50 (ISBN 0-86547-022-7). North Point Press.

Catherine Carter. Pamela Hansford Johnson. LC 51-13229. 1952. Knopf.

Catherine Chailey: A Novel. Humphrey Pakington. LC 60-9807. 1960. Norton.

Catherine De Gardeville. Bertha Radford Sutton. LC 30-15339. 1930. The Macmillan Company.

Catherine De' Medici: A Historical Novel. Honore De Balzac. Tr. by Clara Courtenay Poynter Bell. LC 45-40841. (Balzac's masterpieces). Laird & Lee.

Catherine De'Medici. Honore De Balzac. Tr. by Katharine Prescott Wormeley. LC 3-23189. (Half-title: The comedy of human life... Philosophical studies). 1894. Roberts Brothers.

Catherine Duval: Sketches of Paris Life. Ludovic Halevy. Tr. by Mary K. Ford from Fr. LC 70-125214. (Short Story Index Reprint Ser). 1899. 12.00 (ISBN 0-8369-3581-0). Ayer Co.

Catherine Duval: Sketches of Paris Life, from the French of Ludovic Halevy. Ludovic Halevy. LC 70-125214. (Short story index reprint series). (Illus.). 1970. Books for Libraries Press.

Catherine Duval: Sketches of Paris Life, from the French of Ludovic Halevy... Ludovic Halevy & Ford, Mary K., Tr. LC 99-3542. (On cover: Round table library). 1899. L. C. Page and Company (Incorporated.

Catherine Foster. Herbert Ernest Bates. LC 29-189448. 1929. The Viking Press.

Catherine Furze, 1893. William H. White. Ed. by Robert L. Wolff. Bd. with Clara Hopgood, 1896. LC 75-1516. (Victorian Fiction Ser.). 1975. lib. bdg. 66.00 (ISBN 0-8240-1589-4). Garland Pub.

Catherine, Her Book. John Wheatcroft. LC 81-66295. 14.95. Cornwall Bks.

Catherine of Calais. Elizabeth Bonham De La Pasture. LC 7-38454. 1907. E. P. Dutton & Company.

Catherine Sidney. Francis Deming Hoyt. LC 12-221254. 1912. Longmans, Green, and Co.

Catherine Wheel. Jean Stafford. 1974. (pbk.) 1.25. Manor Books.

Catherine Wheel. Jean Stafford. LC 81-2065. 1981. 7.95 (ISBN 0-912946-87-3). Ecco Press.

Catherine-Wheel. Patricia Wentworth. LC 49-101978. (Her A Miss Silver mystery). 1949. J. B. Lippincott Co.

Catherine Wheel: A Novel. Jean Stafford. LC 52-6161. 1952. Harcourt, Brace.

Catherine: 1st Amer. Ed. Hilda Winifred Lewis. LC 66-165809. 1966. 5.95. Putnam.

Catherine's Child. Elizabeth Bonham De La Pasture. 1908. E. P. Dutton & Company.

Catherine's Coquetries: A Tale of French Country Life, by Camille Debans; Tr. Camille I. E. Jean Baptiste Camille Debans. Tr. by Mead, Leon. LC 6-32897. (On cover: The rose library, no. 1). 1890. Worthington Co.

Catherine's Twins. Larry Raygor. (Orig.). 1979. pap. 1.95 (ISBN 0-532-23107-4). Woodhill.

Catherwood Mystery: A Novel. Albert Plympton Southwick. (On cover: Broadway series, no. 10). 1892. J. A. Taylor and Company.

Cathie Remembers. Grace W. Haight. 0.75 o.p. (ISBN 0-87213-290-0). Loizeaux.

Cathleen in Houlihan. William Butler Yeats. 59.95 (ISBN 0-87968-816-5). Gordon Pr.

Catholic: A Tale of Contemporary Society. LC 2-12214. 1902. J. Lane.

Catholic Crusoe: Adventures of Owen Evans, Esq., Surgeon's Mate, Set Ashore with Five Companions on a Desolate Island in the Caribbean Seas, 1739. Given from the Original Mass. William Henry Anderson. P. J. Kenedy.

Catholic Education: A Novel. Robert Benard. LC 82-1041. 15.50 (ISBN 0-03-061123-7). Holt, Rinehart, and Winston.

Catholic Man: A Study. Francese Hubbard Litchfield Turnbull. LC 8-32671. D. Lothrop Company.

Catholics: A Novel. Brian Moore. LC 72-91557. 1973. 4.95. Holt, Rinehart and Winston.

Cathouse Showdown. Dallas Todd. 224p. (Orig.). 1982. pap. 2.25 (ISBN 0-8439-1029-1, Leisure Bks). Nordon Pubns.

Cathra Mystery. Adam Gordon MacLeod. LC 26-24560. 1926. L. MacVeagh, The Dial Press.

Cathy Chronicles. Cathy Guisewite. LC 78-70403. (Treasury Ser.). (Illus.). 1978. 12.95 o.p.; pap. 7.95 (ISBN 0-8362-1116-2). Andrews & McMeel.

Cathy Come Home. Jeremy Sandford. LC 76-381157. (Open forum). 1976. 4.95. (ISBN 0-7145-2515-4) (ISBN 0-7145-2516-2). M. Boyars.

Cathy Rossiter. Jessie Louise Richard. LC 20-1974. 1919. Hodder and Stoughton.

Cathy Rossiter. Jessie Louisa Moore Rickard. LC 20-1974. 1919. Hodder and Stoughton.

Cathy Rossiter. Jessie Louisa Moore Rickard. LC 20-772. G. H. Doran Co.

Cathy Rossiter. Jessie Louisa Moore Rickard. LC 20-772. George H. Doran Company.

Cathy's Choice. Vivian Donald, pseud. (Signet Book). 1978. 1.50. (ISBN 0-451-08033-5). New American Library.

Catlin. Don Higgins. LC 79-23241. 10.00 (ISBN 0-312-12471-6). St. Martin's Press.

Catlow. Louis L'Amour. LC 63-14180. (Bantam western, J2579). 1963. Bantam Books.

Catmur's Cave. Richard Dowling. LC 6-34402. (On cover: Premier ser. no. 6). 1892. National Book Company.

Catmur's Cave. Richard Dowling. LC 1-30050. (On cover: Medal library. no. 86). Street & Smith.

Catnapped! The Further Adventures of Undercover Cat. Mildred Gordon & Gordon Gordon. LC 74-5915. 1974. 5.95 (ISBN 0-385-08901-5). Doubleday.

Catofy the Clever. Cynthia Jameson. (Illus.). 1972. PLB 4.69 o.p. (ISBN 0-698-30038-6, Coward). Putnam Pub Group.

Cato's War: A Novel of the American Revolution. Guy Wheeler. 1980. 13.95 o.s.i. (ISBN 0-02-626190-1). Macmillan.

Cats. Nick Sharman. 1979. pap. 1.95 (ISBN 0-451-08654-6, J8654, Sig). NAL.

Cats-a-Plenty. Bessie Kenney. 3.95 o.p. Vantage.

Cats' Bridge: Tr. from the German. With a Biographical Sketch. Hermann Sudermann. LC 48-36690. P. F. Collier.

Cat's Claw. Dolores Birk Hitchens. LC 43-14562. 1943. Pub. for the Crime Club by Doubleday, Doran and Co., Inc.

Cat's Company. Michael Joseph. 1973. pap. 0.95 o.p. (09172). Curtis.

Cats' Convention. Eunice Gibbs Allyn. LC 9-32372. 1909. Cochrane Publishing Company.

Cat's Cradle. Maurice Baring. LC 26-26530. 1926. Doubleday, Page & Company.

Cat's Cradle. Pat Flower. LC 77-15008. 1978. 7.95 (ISBN 0-8128-2416-4). Stein and Day.

Cat's Cradle. Kurt Vonnegut. LC 63-10930. 1963. Holt, Rinehart and Winston.

Cat's Cradle-Book. Sylvia Townsend Warner. LC 40-32371. 1940. The Viking Press.

Cats Don't Care for Money. Tr. from French by Helen Eustis. Christiane Rochefort. LC 65-14002. 1965. 3.95. Doubleday.

Cats Don't Need Coffins. Dolores Birk Hitchens. LC 46-5573. 1946. Pub. for The Crime Club by Doubleday & Company, Inc.

Cats Don't Smile. Dolores Birk Hitchens. LC 45-3440. 1945. Pub. for the Crime Club by Doubleday, Doran and Company, Inc.

Cat's-Eye. Claude Aveline. LC 73-175356. 1973. 5.95 (ISBN 0-385-00571-7). Doubleday.

Cat's Eye. Richard Austin Freeman. LC 27-27693. 1927. Dodd, Mead and Company.

Cat's Eye. Harold Will. LC 37-127631. B. Mussey.

Cat's Eye: A Novel. Monica Furlong. LC 76-372630. 3.25 (ISBN 0-297-77054-3). Weidenfeld and Nicolson.

Cat's-Eye Ring: A Secret of Paris Life. Fortune Du Boisgobey. Tr. by Henry Llewellyn Williams. LC 6-34432. 1888. G. Routledge and Sons.

Cat's Eyes. Lee Jordan. LC 81-22460. 11.95 (ISBN 0-453-00416-4). New American Library.

Cat's Eyes. Anthony Taber. (Illus.). 1980. pap. 6.95 (ISBN 0-525-03162-6, Thomas Congdon Book). Dutton.
Cat's Got Our Tongue. Claire Necker. 1973. 10.00 o.p. (ISBN 0-8108-0545-6). Scarecrow.
Cats Have Tall Shadows. Dolores Birk Hitchens. LC 48-1375. (Fingerprint mystery).
Cats in the Isle of Man. Daisy Fellowes. LC 29-20022. 1929. L. MacVeagh, The Dial Press.
Cats of Benares. Geraldine Halls. LC 67-22515. 1967. Harper & Row.
Cats of Ulthar. Howard Phillips Lovecraft. 2.50 o.p. Necronomicon.
Cats of Venice. Hal Porter. LC 66-2985. 1966. 3.75. Angus & Robertson.
Cat's Pajamas. Leonore Fleischer. LC 82-47907. (Illus.). 192p. 1982. pap. 6.68i (ISBN 0-06-090974-9, CN 974, CN). Har-Row.
Cat's Pajamas & Witch's Milk; Two Novels. Peter De Vries. LC 68-30874. 1975. (pbk.) 1.50. Popular Library.
Cat's Pajamas & Witch's Milk: Two Novels. 1st Ed. LC 68-30874. 1968. bds., 5.95. Little, Brown.
Cat's-Paw. Clarence Budington Kelland. LC 34-12333. 1934. Harper & Brothers.
Cat's Paw. Natalie Sumner Lincoln. LC 22-18095. 1922. D. Appleton and Company.
Cat's Paw... Roger Scarlett. LC 31-33332. Pub. for the Crime Club, Inc., by Doubleday, Doran & Company, Inc.
Cat's-Pay. Marion Armour Salter. LC 52-6617. (Murray Hill mystery). 1952. Rinehart.
Cat's Pilgrimage: A Fable. James Anthony Froude. LC 50-13834. 1949. East Rock Press.
Cat's Prey. Dorothy Eden. 1975. (pbk.) 1.50. Ace Books.
Cats Prowl at Night. Erle Stanley Gardner. LC 43-11952. 1943. W. Morrow.
Cats Prowl at Night. Erle Stanley Gardner. 1975. (pbk.) 0.95. Dell.
Cat's Revenge. Philip Lief. 1981. pap. 3.95 o.s.i. S&S.
Cats Tale. Mai Zetterling & David Hughs. 3.50 o.p. (ISBN 0-87556-422-4). Saifer.
Cats to Come. Geoffrey Household. (Greenwich Ed.). 1975. 5.95 o.p. (ISBN 0-7181-1347-0, Pub. by Michael Joseph). Merrimack Pub Cir.
Cat's Whisker: A Reggie Fortune Novel. Henry Christopher Bailey. LC 44-47149. 1944. Pub. for the Crime Club by Doubleday, Doran & Co., Inc.
Catseye. Andre Norton, pseud. LC 79-24271. (Gregg Press science fiction series). 1980. 9.95 (ISBN 0-8398-2637-0). Gregg Press.
Catseye: By Andre Norton Pseud. 1st Ed. Alice Mary Norton. LC 61-117503. 1961. Harcourt, Brace & World.
Catskill Witch & Other Tales of the Hudson Valley. James McMurry. (Illus.). 160p. 1974. 6.95 (ISBN 0-8156-0105-0). Syracuse U Pr.
Catspaw. William Hamilton Osborne. LC 11-5185. 1911. Dodd, Mead and Company.
Catspaw. Robert Terry Shannon. LC 29-7065. E. J. Clode, Inc.
Catspaw for Murder. Dolores Birk Hitchens. LC 43-589538. 1943. Pub. for the Crime Club by Doubleday, Doran and Company, Inc.
Catspaw Ordeal: By Edward Ronns Pseud. Edward Sidney Aarons. LC 51-16237. (Gold medal book, 133). 1950. Fawcett Publications.
Catspaw. 1st American Ed. Mary Borden. LC 50-9458. 1950. Longmans, Green.
Cattle. Winnifred Eaton Babcock. LC 24-7942. C.
Cattle Annie and Little Britches. Robert Ward. LC 77-24131. 1978. 7.95 (ISBN 0-688-03252-4). Morrow.
Cattle Baron. Robert Ames Bennet. LC 25-171521. 1925. A. C. McClurg & Co.
Cattle Baron. Jack Slade, pseud. (Belmont Tower Book). 1.25 (ISBN 0-505-51163-0). Tower Pubns.
Cattle Barons. Jesse Edward Grinstead. LC 39-17109. Phoenix Press.
Cattle-Baron's Daughter. Harold Bindloss. LC 6-34082. 1906. F. A. Stokes Company.
Cattle Boat Mygghavet. Andrew Swanson. LC 54-9555. 1954. Comet Press Books.
Cattle Brands: A Collection of Western Camp-Fire Stories. Andy Adams. LC 70-150534. (Short story index reprint series). 1971. (ISBN 0-8369-3831-3). Books for Libraries Press.
Cattle Brands: A Collection of Western Camp-Fire Stories, by Andy Adams. Andy Adams. LC 6-9625. 1906. Houghton, Mifflin and Company.
Cattle Camp: By Chuck Stanley Pseud. Charles Stanley Strong. LC 57-7721. 1957. Arcadia House.
Cattle Car Express: A Prisoner of War in Siberia. Emil Lengyel. LC 31-7633. 1931. Ralph Beaver Strassburger Foundation.
Cattle Country. Wes Harding. Ed. by Alice Sachs. 1969. lib. bdg. 3.50 o.p. Arcadia.
Cattle Country Adventure. H. Elwyn Blake. 5.95 o.p. Vantage.
Cattle King. Ion L. Idriess. 1968. Repr. pap. 1.60 o.s.i. Tri-Ocean.
Cattle King. Edward F. Treadwell. (Illus.). 7.95 o.p. (ISBN 0-913548-00-6). Valley Calif.
Cattle King: By Chuck Stanley Pseud. Charles Stanley Strong. LC 54-11336. 1954. Arcadia House.
Cattle Kingdom. Alan Le May. LC 33-12236. Farrar & Rinehart, Inc.
Cattle Mutilators. John J. Dalton. (Orig.). 1980. pap. 1.95 (ISBN 0-532-23117-1). Woodhill.
Cattlemen. Mari Sandoz. 1975. Repr. 12.95 (ISBN 0-8038-1087-3). Hastings.
Catwalk: A Novel. Richard B Erno. LC 64-238064. 1964. 3.95. Crown.
Caught. Henry Green. LC 70-83158. Repr. of 1950 ed. lib. bdg. 12.50x (ISBN 0-678-03157-6). Kelley.
Caught: A Novel. Homer Croy. LC 28-151562. 1928. Harper & Brothers.
Caught: A Novel. Henry Green. LC 50-11006. 1950. Viking Press.
Caught. A Romance of Three Days. George Douglas Tallman. LC 8-25565. 1895. G. W. Dillingham, Successor to G. W. Carleton & Co.
Caught, and Dreams and Compound Interest. Emanuel Haldeman-Julius & Haldeman-Julius, Mrs. Anna Marcet (Haldeman) 1888- Joint Author. (Five cent pocket series, no. 334, ed. by E. Haldeman-Julius). Haldeman-Julius Company.
Caught in Mid-Ocean. A Thrilling Tale Founded on the Greatest Murder Mystery of the Century - the Famous Crippen Case - in Which, for the First Time, the Wireless Telegraph Was Used for the Capture of a Criminal. Helen Burrell D'Apery. LC 12-32996. (On back of cover: Play book series. no. 155). J. S. Ogilvie Publishing Company.
Caught in That Music. Seymour Epstein. LC 67-25920. 1967. Viking Press.
Caught in the Act. John Lee. LC 68-14807. 1968. W. Morrow.
Caught in the Crossfire: The Trials and Triumphs of African Believers Through an Age of Tribulation. Levi O Keidel. LC 79-10910. 1979. 5.95 (ISBN 0-8361-1888-X). Herald Press.
Caught in the Net. Emile Gaboriau. LC 6-44565. (secret service series. no. 42). 1891. Street & Smith.
Caught in the Net: Tr. from the French of Emile Caboriau. Emile Gaboriau. LC 13-82851. 1913. C. Scribner's Sons.
Caught in the Rain. Shirley Hart. (Candlelight Ecstasy Ser.: No. 116). (Orig.). 1983. pap. 1.95 (ISBN 0-440-10999-X). Dell.
Caught in the Whirl. Hazle Hancock. LC 38-34132. The Christopher Publishing House.
Caught in the Wild. Robert Ames Bennet. LC 32-30521. 1932. I. Washburn.
Caul. Edwina Lindsay Travers. 1976. 5.00 o.p. (ISBN 0-682-48395-8). Exposition.
Caulder's Badge. Will C Knott. 1977. 1.50 (ISBN 0-441-09272-1). Ace Books.
Cauldron. Zeno. (1150). 1968. Dell.
Cauldron. Zeno. LC 67-14095. (Illus.). 1967. Stein and Day.
Cauldron of Hell. Nick Carter. (Nick Carter Ser.). 224p. (Orig.). 1981. pap. 2.50 (ISBN 0-441-09274-8). Ace Bks.
Cauldron of Witches: The Story of Witchcraft. Clifford Lindsey Alderman. (O.s.i.). pap. 1.25 o.s.i. (ISBN 0-671-29558-6). Archway.
Cauldron of Witches: The Story of Witchcraft. Clifford Lindsey Alderman. (O.s.i.). pap. 1.25 o.s.i. (ISBN 0-671-29558-6). Archway.
Cauliflower Heart. Marian Mira Grosberg Champagne. LC 44-2955. 1944. Dial Press.
Cause. Barbara Griffin & Bett Pbhnka. 164p. 1976. 5.95x o.p. (ISBN 0-89185-003-1); pap. 2.25x o.p. (ISBN 0-89185-002-3). Anthelion Pr.
Cause and Effect. Ellinor Meirion. LC 7-25857. 1895. G. P. Putnam's Sons.
Cause for a Killing. John William Wainwright. LC 75-301116. 1974. 1.95 (ISBN 0-333-16647-7). Macmillan.
Cause for Alarm. Eric Ambler. LC 29-2716. 1939. A.A. Knopf.
Cause for Alarm. Eric Ambler. 1974. (pbk.) 1.25. Bantam.
Cause for Wonder. Wright Morris. LC 77-14594. 1978. 12.50 (ISBN 0-8032-0966-5) (ISBN 0-8032-5885-2). University of Nebraska Press.
Causeway. Philip Maitland Hubbard. LC 77-352234. 1976. 2.95 (ISBN 0-333-19634-1). Macmillan.
Causeway. Philip Maitland Hubbard. LC 77-7013. 1978. 6.95 (ISBN 0-385-13404-5). Published for the Crime Club by Doubleday.
Causeway. Winifred Lear Heap. LC 48-8423. 1948. Macmillan Co.
Causeway to the Past. William O'Farrell. LC 50-5858. 1950. Duell, Sloan and Pearce.
Caution! Inflammable! Thomas N. Scortia. LC 74-18831. (Doubleday science fiction). 1975. 5.95 (ISBN 0-385-02819-9). Doubleday.
Cautionary Tales. Chelsea Quinn Yarbro. LC 78-3265. 1978. 7.95 (ISBN 0-385-13145-3). Doubleday.
Cautionary Tales. Chelsea Quinn Yarbro. 1.95 (ISBN 0-446-90162-8)., C.
Cautious Amorist. Norman Lindsay. LC 32-32261. Farrar & Rinehart, Incorporated.
Cautious Heart. Philippa Heywood. (Second Chance at Love Ser.: No. 9). 192p. (Orig.). 1981. pap. 1.75 (ISBN 0-515-05801-7). Jove Pubns.
Cautious Heart. William Sansom. LC 58-12944. 1958. Reynal.
Cautious Husband. New York: Coward-McCann. Virginia Evans. LC 49-9060.
Cautious Maiden. Jacques Laurent. LC 55-7231. 1955. Crown Publishers.
Cautious Overshoes. 1st Ed. Margaret Scherf. LC 56-6537. 1956. Published for the Crime Club by Doubleday.
Cautiva Gozadora. Jacinto Lopez. (Pimienta Collection Ser). 1977. pap. 1.00 o.p. (ISBN 0-88473-265-7). Fiesta Pub.
Cautley Mystery. Archibald E. Fielding. LC 34-7413. (Illus.). 1934. H. C. Kinsey & Company, Inc.
Cavalcade to California. Richard Aldrich Summers. LC 41-5225. Oxford University Press.
Cavalier. julia marlowe ed. new york, scribner, 1903. ed. George Washington Cable. LC 72-84534. (Illus.). 1974. 34.00 (ISBN 0-403-02956-2). Scholarly Press.
Cavalier. George Washington Cable. 1901. C. Scribner's Sons.
Cavalier. julia marlowe ed. George Washington Cable. LC 3-8341. 1903. C. Scribner's Sons.
Cavalier see Collected Works.
Cavalier. An Historical Novel. George Payne Rainsford James. LC 7-7575. T. B. Peterson and Brothers.
Cavalier Blanc. Rene de Goscinny. (Lucky Luke Series). (French.). 1976. 5.95x (ISBN 2-205-00867-6). Intl Learn Syst.
Cavalier Infidele. Casey Douglas. (Harlequin Seduction Ser.). 332p. 1983. pap. 3.25 (ISBN 0-373-45020-6, Pub. by Worldwide). Harlequin Bks.
Cavalier Maid. Emilie Benson Knipe & Knipe, Alden Arthur. LC 19-155728. 1919. The Macmillan Company.
Cavalier of Navarre: A Tale of Pikemen and Musketeers. Charles B Stilson. 1925. G. H. Watt.
Cavalier of Tennessee. Meredith Nicholson. LC 28-176433. The Bobbs-Merrill Company.
Cavalier of Virginia: A Romance. Roberts Theodore Goodridge. LC 10-9076. 1910. 1.50. L. C. Page & Company.
Cavalier's Corpse. Theodora McCormick Du Bois. 1969. pap. 0.75 o.p. (74-584). Lancer.
Cavalier's Corpse. 1st Ed. Theodora McCormick Du Bois. LC 52-10044. 1952. Published for the Crime Club by Doubleday.
Cavalier's Cup: Another Adventure of Sir Henry Merrivale. John Dickson Carr. LC 53-5333. 1953. Morrow.
Cavaliers of Death. Rosita Torr Forbes. LC 30-17942. The Macaulay Company.
Cavaliers of England: Or The Times of the Revolutions of 1642 and 1688. Henry William Herbert. LC 7-4283. 1852. Redfield.
Cavaliers of Virginia, Or, the Recluse of Jamestown. William Alexander Caruthers. Ed. by Curtis C. Davis. LC 77-93600. (American Fiction Ser). 1970. Repr. of 1935 ed. lib. bdg. 21.95 o.s.i. (ISBN 0-512-00087-5). Garrett Pr.
Cavaliers of Virginia, or, The Recluse of Jamestown. An Historical Romance of the Old Dominion. William Alexander Caruthers. LC 41-82194. 1834-35. Harper & Brothers.
Cavalier's Woman. Joan Hunter. (Kangaroo Book.). 1977. 1.95 (ISBN 0-671-81085-5). Pocket Books.
Cavalleria Rusticana: And Other Narratives. Giovanni Verya. LC 50-11400. 1950. Story Classics.
Cavalleria Rusticana, and Other Stories. Giovanni Verga. LC 75-9590. 1975. 14.75 (ISBN 0-8371-8105-4). Greenwood Press.
Cavalleria Rusticana: And Other Stories. Giovanni Verga. Tr. by David Herbert Lawrence. LC 28-20569. 1928. L. MacVeagh, the Dial Press.
Cavalry Girl. Elizabeth Harman. F. T. Neely.
Cavalry Life: Or, Sketches and Stories in Barracks and Out. Henrietta Eliza Vaughan Stannard. LC 8-13876. (Harper's handy series. no. 59). 1886. Harper & Brothers.
Cavalry Life: Or, Sketches and Stories in Barracks and Out. Henrietta Eliza Vaughan Stannard. (On cover: Lovell's library. no. 1168). 1888. J. W. Lovell Company.
Cavalry Raid. Sidney Edgerton Whitman. LC 56-117645. 1956. Houghton Mifflin.
Cavalry Raid. Sidney Edgerton Whitman. (Ballantine books, 188). 1957. Ballantine Books.
Cavalry Scout. Dee Alexander Brown. LC 57-10536. (Permabooks, M-3101. Western 1). Permabooks.
Cavalryman. Harold Sinclair. LC 57-8213. 1958. Harper.
Cavalryman: A Novel of Peace-Time Army Life with Background of the United States Cavalry School at Fort Riley, Kansas. Topliffe Sawyer. LC 39-4481. The Penn Publishing Company.
Cavanagh, Forest Ranger. sunset edition. new york, harper. ed. Hamlin Garland. LC 72-84716. (Illus.). 1974. (lib. ed.) 12.50 (ISBN 0-403-02985-6). Scholarly Press.
Cavanagh, Forest Ranger see Collected Works.
Cavanaugh, Forest Ranger: A Romance of the Mountain West. Hamlin Garland. LC 20-164638. 1910. Harper & Brothers.
Cavanaugh Keep. Miriam Leslie. 1973. pap. 0.95 o.s.i. (75-471). Lancer.
Cavanaugh Quest. Thomas Gifford. LC 75-37083. 8.95 (ISBN 0-399-11631-1). Putnam.
Cave. Joan Dunham. 3.50 o.p. Vantage.
Cave. Robert Penn Warren. LC 59-5719. 1959. Random House.
Cave and the Rock. Raoul Cohen Faure. LC 53-5335. 1953. Morrow.
Cave by the Beech Fork: A Story of Kentucky--1815. Henry Stanislaus Spalding. 1901. Benziger Brothers.
Cave Girl. Edgar Rice Burroughs. LC 62-21541. 1962. Canaveral Press.
Cave Girl. Edgar Rice Burroughs. LC 25-7076. 1925. A. C. McClurg & Co.
Cave Girl. Edgar Rice Burroughs. 1978. 1.95 (ISBN 0-441-09285-3). Ace Books.
Cave-in. Wal Watkins. LC 73-163334. 1972. 1.65 (ISBN 0-7260-0049-3). Gold Star Publications.
Cave Man. John Corbin. LC 7-14254. 1907. D. Appleton and Company.
Cave of Bats: By Robert MacLeod. Pseud. Bill Knox. LC 66-13103. (Rinehart suspense novel). 1966. bds., 3.95. Holt.
Cave of Hegobar: Or, The Fiend of 1878. A Story. Robert Haskins Crozier. LC 6-319479. 1885. Presbyterian Publishing Co.
Cave of Ice. 1st American Ed. Penelope Mortimer. LC 59-6425. 1959. Harcourt, Brace.
Cave of the Ancients. Rampa T. Lobsang. LC 65-190799. 1965. Ballantine.
Cave of the Ancients. T. Rampa. pap. 2.95. Weiser.
Cave of the Chinese Skeletons. Jack Seward. LC 64-19686. 1964. Rutland, Vt., C. E. Tuttle Co.
Cave of the Moaning Wind. Gene DeWeese. LC 76-45210. (Zodiac gothic: Virgo). 1977. 8.95 (ISBN 0-89340-014-9). J. Curley & Associates.
Cave of the Moaning Wind: An Astrological Gothic Novel: Virgo. Gene DeWeese. LC 76-11817. 1976. 1.25 (ISBN 0-345-25160-1). Ballantine Books.
Cave of the Nymphs. Porphyry & Robert Lamberton. LC 82-16969. 1983. 10.00 (ISBN 0-930794-71-0) (ISBN 0-930794-72-9). Station Hill Press.
Cave Woman. Norval Richardson. LC 22-18094. 1922. C. Scribner's Sons.
Cave-Woman: A Novel of to-Day. Viola Burhans. LC 10-143661. 1910. 1.50. H. Holt and Company.
Cavenaugh's Revenge. Brian O'Neill. 192p. (Orig.). 1982. pap. 2.25 (ISBN 0-523-41637-7). Pinnacle Bks.
Cavender's Balkan Quest. Elliot Tokson. (Fawcett Gold Medal Book). 1.75 (ISBN 0-449-13917-4). Fawcett Books.
Cavendish: Or, The Patrician at Sea. new ed. William Johnson Neale. LC 41-313324. 1854. D. Appleton & Co.
Cavendish Pride. Kathryn Ewing. LC 76-56440. 1977. 1.50 (ISBN 0-345-25386-8). Ballantine Books.
Cavendish Square. Kathryn Ewing. LC 75-45079. 1.50 (ISBN 0-345-24910-0). Ballantine Books.
Cavern of Death, a Moral Tale. Printed and Sold by Bonsal & Niles, 173, Market-Street. LC 6-22279.
Cavern of Death: Or, The Counterfeiters' Victims; a Story of a Great Detective Triumph. Allen Graves. (On cover: The Pinkerton detective series, no. 44). 1890. Laird & Lee.
Cavern of Destiny. Ben Aronin. LC 43-10718. 1943. Behrman's Jewish Book House.
Cavern of Silver. Jordan Allen. LC 82-60152. 1982. 11.95 (ISBN 0-8027-4014-6). Walker.
Caverns of Crail: A Novel. Thomas Sawyer Spivey. LC 12-21767. 1912. The Cosmopolitan Press.
Caverns of Dawn. James Paxton Voorhees. LC 10-14153. 1910. The Raidabaugh-Voorhees Company.
Caverns of Sunset: Being the Story of Patricia Percy's Quest in the Pays En Haute. Paul Leland Haworth. LC 30-5931. The Boobs-Merrill Company.
Caverns: The Journeys of McGill Feighan, Bk. I. Kevin O'Donnell, Jr. (Orig.). 1981. pap. 2.25 (ISBN 0-425-04730-X). Berkley Pub.
Caves. Norman T. Vane & R. Rude. 1979. pap. 1.75 (ISBN 0-89041-243-X, 3243). Major Bks.
Caves Du Vatican. Andre Paul Guillaume Gide. 1956. 18.95. French & Eur.

Caves of Drach. Hugh Walters, pseud. LC 79-670249. 1977. 6.95 (ISBN 0-571-11037-1). Faber.

Caves of Guernica. Samuel Edwards, pseud. LC 74-11920. 400p. 1975. 8.95 o.p. (ISBN 0-275-05170-6). Praeger.

Caves of Guernica. Noel Bertram Gerson. LC 74-11920. 1975. 8.95 (ISBN 0-275-05170-6). Praeger.

Caves of Night. John Christopher. LC 58-6277. 1958. Simon and Schuster.

Caves of Reglathium. Mike Sirota. 1978. pap. 2.25 (ISBN 0-532-22129-X). Woodhill.

Caves of Steel. Isaac Asimov. LC 54-5418. 1954. Doubleday.

Caves of the Druufs. Kurt Mahr. (Perry Rhodan#72). (Illus.). 1975. (pbk.) 1.25. Ace Books.

Caviar: By Theodore Sturgeon Pseud. Edward Hamilton Waldo, pseud. LC 55-12088. 1955. Ballantine Books.

Caviar Cruise. Forrest-Webb, Robert. LC 74-27592. 1977. 6.95 (ISBN 0-385-02086-4). Doubleday.

Caviar Cruise. Forrest Webb. 1978. 1.75 (ISBN 0-380-01880-2). Avon Books.

Caviar for Breakfast. James Noble Gifford. LC 51-15416. 1931. Sears Publishing Company.

Caviar for Breakfast. Inez Lopez. LC 40-335814. 1940. D. Appleton-Century Company, Incorporated.

Caviare. Grant Richards. LC 12-22860. 1912. Houghton, Mifflin Company.

Caviare. Godfrey Smith. LC 76-25854. 1976. 8.95 (ISBN 0-698-10800-0). Coward, McCann & Geoghegan.

Cawthorn Journals. Stephen Marlowe. LC 74-31079. 276p. 1975. 7.95 o.p. (ISBN 0-13-121335-0). P-H.

Cawthorn Journals: A Novel. Stephen Marlowe. LC 74-31079. 1975. 7.95 (ISBN 0-13-121335-0). Prentice-Hall.

Caxtons, a Family Picture. Edward George Earle Lytton Bulwer-Lytton Lytton. LC 75-145149. (Illus.). 1971. (ISBN 0-403-00763-1). Scholarly Press.

Caxtons: A Family Picture. lord lytton ed. Edward George Earle Lytton Bulwer-Lytton Lytton. LC 49-329599. 1878. J.B. Lippincott.

Caxtons: A Family Picture. Edward George Earle Lytton Bulwer-Lytton Lytton. (Library of Famous Novels). G. P. Putnam's Sons.

Caxtons; a Family Picture. new ed. Edward George Earle Lytton Bulwer-Lytton Lytton. LC 7-83601. 1855. G. Routledge & Co.

Caxtons, a Family Picture. library ed.... ed. Edward George Earle Lytton Bulwer-Lytton Lytton. LC 7-8359. (Half-title: Novels of Sir Edward Bulwer Lytton. Library ed. The Caxton novels, vol. I-II). 1860. J. B. Lippincott & Co.

Caxtons, a Family Picture. Edward George Earle Lytton Bulwer-Lytton Lytton. LC 8-11034. G. Routledge and Sons.

Caxtons. A Family Picture. Edward George Earle Lytton Bulwer-Lytton Lytton. LC 7-8358. (On cover: Lovell's library. v. 5, no. 250). 1883. J. W. Lovell Company.

Caxtons. A Family Picture. Edward George Earle Lytton Bulwer-Lytton Lytton. (Half-title: Novels of Sir Edward Bulwer Lytton. Library ed. The Caxton novels, vol. I-II). 1892. Little, Brown, and Company.

Caxton's Book. William Henry Rhodes. LC 73-13263. (Classics of Science Fiction Ser.). 308p. 1974. 12.50 (ISBN 0-88355-117-9); pap. 3.75 (ISBN 0-88355-146-2). Hyperion Conn.

Caxtons, Zicci. The Haunted and the Haunters: Or, The House and the Brain. Edward George Earle Lytton Bulwer-Lytton Lytton. LC 31-32281. (The novels and romances of Edward Bulwer Lytton. v.1). Aldine Book Publishing Co.

Caybigan. James Hopper. LC 6-33591. 1906. McClure, Phillips & Co.

Cayuse Courier. Strong, Charles Stanley. LC 50-13802. 1950. Phoenix Press.

CB Angel. Lary Adcock. 1977. 1.75 (ISBN 0-445-04088-2). Popular Library.

CB Baby. Clark Whelton. LC 76-43530 (ISBN 0-380-00814-9). Avon.

C.B. Greenfield: No Lady in the House. Lucille Kallen. LC 82-4903. 10.95 (ISBN 0-89621-365-X). Thorndike Press.

CB Jockey. Gary Paulsen. 1977. pap. 1.75 (ISBN 0-89041-141-7, 3141). Major Bks.

Ce qui Etait Perdu: Nouvelles. Francois Mauriac. pap. 7.95. French & Eur.

Ceasar Dies. new ed. Talbot Mundy. (Time-Lost Ser.). Orig. Title: Falling Star. 160p. 1973. pap. 1.25 o.p. (ISBN 0-87818-009-5). Centaur.

Cease Firing. Mary Johnston. LC 12-25843. 1912. Houghton Mifflin Company.

Cease Upon the Midnight: By Simon Troy Pseud. 1st Amer. Ed. Thurman Warriner. LC 65-201674. (Cock Robin mystery). 1965. bds., 3.95. Macmillan.

Cebe's Tablet. new ed. Cebes. Ed. & intro. by Sandra Sider. (Renaissance Text Ser.: No. 6). (Illus.). 1979. 9.95 (ISBN 0-9602696-2-2). Renaissance Soc Am.

Cecil, a Peer, 3 vols. in 2. Catherine Grace Frances Moody Gore. LC 79-8274. Repr. of 1841 ed. Set. 84.50 (ISBN 0-404-61879-0). Vol. 1 (ISBN 0-404-61880-4). Vol. 2 (ISBN 0-404-61881-2). AMS Pr.

Cecil Castlemaine's Gage, Lady Marabout's Troubles: And Other Stories. Louise De La Ramee. LC 75-121534. (Short story index reprint series). 1970. Books for Libraries Press.

Cecil Castlemaine's Gage: Lady Marabout's Trouble, and Other Stories. author's ed. Louise De La Ramee. 1877. J. B. Lippincott & Co.

Cecil Castlemaine's Gage, Lady Marabout's Troubles & Other Stories. Louise De La Ramee. LC 75-121534. (Short Story Index Reprint Ser). 1867. 19.50 (ISBN 0-8369-3490-3). Ayer Co.

Cecil Dreeme. Theodore Winthrop & Curtis, George William, 1824-1892. LC 3-4375. 1861. Ticknor and Fields.

Cecil Dreeme. Theodore Winthrop & Curtis, George William, 1824-1892. 1862. Ticknor and Fields.

Cecil Dreeme. 15th ed. Theodore Winthrop & Curtis, George William, 1824-1892. 1863. Ticknor and Fields.

Cecil Dreeme. Theodore Winthrop & Curtis, George William, 1834-1892. 1871. J. R. Osgood and Company.

Cecil Dreeme. Theodore Winthrop & Curtis, George William, 1824-1892. LC 3-4390. (Leisure hour series. no. 61). 1876. H. Holt and Company.

Cecil; or the Adventures of a Coxcomb, 3 vols. in 2. Catherine Grace Frances Moody Gore. LC 79-8273. Repr. of 1841 ed. Set. 84.50 (ISBN 0-404-61875-8). Vol. 1 (ISBN 0-404-61876-6). Vol. 2 (ISBN 0-404-61877-4). AMS Pr.

Cecil Rosse: A Sequel to Edith Trevor's Secret. A Novel. Harriet Lewis. (On cover: The choice series, no. 60). 1892. R. Bonner's Sons.

Cecile. Frank Laurence Lucas. LC 30-27767. H. Holt and Company.

Cecile's Marriage: Or, The Heiress of Earnseliff. Lucy Randall Comfort. (Street & Smith's select series, no. 35). 1890. Street & Smith.

Cecilia. Vivian Connolly. 224p. 1981. pap. 1.95 (ISBN 0-449-50211-2, Crest). Fawcett.

Cecilia: A Story of Modern Rome. Francis Marion Crawford. LC 2-25439. Etc.

Cecilia De Noel. Mary Elizabeth Hawker. LC 4-316739. 1891. Macmillan and Co.

Cecilia Howard: Or, The Young Lady Who Had Finished Her Education. Timothy Shay Arthur. LC 45-43209. 1844. J. Allen.

Cecilia of Rome. Lawrence James Babin. LC 77-86697. 4.00. Pyquag Books.

Cecilia of the Pink Roses. Katharine Haviland Taylor. LC 17-13951. George H. Doran Company.

Cecilia: Or Memoirs of an Heiress. Frances D'Arblay, pseud. LC 6-2067. 1793-94. By William Greenough, for Ebenezer Larkin, Jun., Bookseller & Stationer, No., Cornhill.

Cecilia: The Story of a Girl and Some Circumstances. Stanley Victor Makower. 1897. J. Lane.

Cecilia Valdes, or, Angel's Hill: A Novel of Cuban Customs. Cirolo Villaverde. LC 63-461. Vantage Press.

Cecilia's Lovers. Amelia Edith Huddleston Barr. LC 5-29991. 1905. Dodd, Mead & Company.

Cecilie and the Oil King. William Henry Irwin. LC 23-14123. 1928. Etc. Brentano's, Ltd.

Cecil's Crown. Jennie M Stratton. LC 8-17651. 1891. The Williams Publishing Company.

Cecily. Clare Darcy. LC 77-14014. (Regency Romance). 1978. 9.95 (ISBN 0-89340-114-5). J. Curley.

Cecily: A Novel. Isabelle Holland. LC 67-11307. 1967. Lippincott.

Cecily: A Tale of the English Reformation. Emma Leslie. LC 7-14488. (Church history stories, 2d ser., v. 3). 1879. Phillips & Hunt.

Cecily and the Wide World: A Novel of American Life Today. Elizabeth Frances Corbett. LC 16-185643. 1916. 1.40. H. Holt and Company.

Cecily: Or, A Young Lady of Quality. Clare Darcy. LC 74-186184. 1972. 5.95 (ISBN 0-8027-0381-X). Walker.

Cecily or a Young Lady of Quality. Clare Darcy. 1973. (pbk) 1.25. Dell.

Cedar Acres. Loretta Smith. 160p. 1983. 8.95 (ISBN 0-89962-287-9). Todd & Honeywell.

Cedar and the Star. Yoram Hamizrachi. LC 80-36777. 9.95 (ISBN 0-525-66680-X). Elsevier/Nelson Books.

Cedar Grove. Francis E. Lundstedt, 2nd. 1970. 3.95 o.p. Vantage.

Cedar Hill. Katie West. LC 82-81126. 180p. (Orig.). 1982. 12.95 (ISBN 0-88100-002-7); pap. 6.95 (ISBN 0-88100-001-9). Ranch House Pr.

Cedar of Lebanon. John Cosgrove. LC 52-14375. 1952. McMullen Books.

Cedar Star. Mary E. Rackham Mann. LC 7-20458. R. F. Fenno & Company; Etc., Etc.

Cedarhaven. Patricia Campbell. LC 65-13593. (queen-size gothic). 1974. (pbk.) 0.95. Popular Library.

Cedarhaven: A Novel of the Early Northwest. Patricia Campbell. LC 65-13593. 5.95. Macmillan.

Cedarhurst Alley. Denison Hatch. LC 76-131243. 1970. 6.95. P. S. Eriksson.

Ceiling of Amber. Elisabeth Ogilvie. Repr. text ed. 11.50x (ISBN 0-88411-329-9). Amereon Ltd.

Ceiling Zero. Sidney Davidson & Wead, Frank. Ceiling Zero. LC 36-4036. Lynn Publishing Co., Inc.

Celebrant: A Novel. Eric Rolfe Greenberg. LC 82-9236. 13.95 (ISBN 0-89696-171-0). Everest House.

Celebrate Joy! Velma S. Daniels. 1982. pap. 2.50 (ISBN 0-451-11945-2, AE1945, Sig). NAL.

Celebrate the Sun. James Joseph Kavanaugh. LC 72-95238. (Illus.). 1973. 4.95 (ISBN 0-8402-1308-5). Nash Pub.

Celebrate the Temporary. Clyde Reid. LC 73-160643. 1974. pap. 4.95i (ISBN 0-06-066816-4, RD81, HarpR). Har-Row.

Celebrate the Unicorn. Jack Voelpel. 161p. 1981. 13.95 (ISBN 0-940534-00-2); pap. 7.95 (ISBN 0-940534-01-0). Beekman Hill.

Celebrated Cases of Charlie Chan... Earl Derr Biggers. LC 33-27076. 1933. The Bobbs-Merrill Company.

Celebrated Cases of Dick Tracy, Nineteen Thirty-One to Nineteen Fifty-One. abr. ed. Chester Gould. Ed. by Herb Galewitz. LC 70-127010. (Illus.). 290p. 1981. pap. 12.50 (ISBN 0-87754-220-1). Chelsea Hse.

Celebrated Cases of Judge Dee Dee Goong an: An Authentic Eighteenth-Century Chinese Detective Novel. unabridged, slightly corr. version. ed. Robert Hans Van Gulik, pseud. LC 76-5059. (Illus.). 1976. 3.50 (ISBN 0-486-23337-5). Dover Publications.

Celebrated Jumping Frog of Calaveras County. Samuel Langhorne Clemens. LC 75-91075. (American Humorist Ser.). Repr. of 1867 ed. lib. bdg. 18.75 (ISBN 0-8398-0267-6). Irvington.

Celebrated Jumping Frog of Calaveras County. Mark Twain. LC 65-29784. (Wild & Woolly West Ser., No. 2). (Illus.). 1965. 7.00 (ISBN 0-910584-63-X); pap. 1.50 (ISBN 0-910584-02-8). Filter.

Celebrated Jumping Frog of Calaveras County: And The Man That Corrupted Hadleyburg. Samuel Langhorne Clemens. LC 68-10281. (Illus.). 1968. F. Watts.

Celebrated "Moon Story" Its Origin and Incidents; with a Memoir of the Author, and an Appendix, Containing, I. An Authentic Description of the Moon; Ii. A New Theory of the Lunar Surface in Relation to That of the Earth. Richard Adams Locke & Griggs, William N. LC 7-14295. 1852. Bunnell and Price.

Celebration. Ivan Angelo. LC 81-66489. 2.95 (ISBN 0-380-78808-X). Avon Books.

Celebration. Mary Deasy. LC 63-13553. 1963. Random House.

Celebration: A Novel. Harvey Swados. LC 74-23733. 1975. 8.95 (ISBN 0-671-21951-0). Simon and Schuster.

Celebration for Murder. Ruth Wissman. LC 78-22806. (Romantic Suspense Ser.). 1979. 7.95 o.p. (ISBN 0-385-12830-4). Doubleday.

Celebration for Murder. Ruth H Wissmann. LC 78-22806. 1979. 7.95 (ISBN 0-385-12830-4). Doubleday.

Celebration of the Flesh. Benjamin Grimm. LC 71-9875. (Traveller's companion series, TC-435). 1968. 1.75. Traveller's Companion, Inc.

Celebrations. Alan Burns. 1980. pap. cancelled (ISBN 0-7145-0072-0). Riverrun NY.

Celebrations. Virginia Huntington. 1971. 4.00 (ISBN 0-8233-0153-2). Golden Quill.

Celebrations: A Novel. Alan Burns. LC 67-107942. 1967. 4.50. Calder & Boyars.

Celebrisi's Journey. David Rounds. 176p. (Orig.). 1976. pap. 4.00 (ISBN 0-917512-14-6). Buddhist Text.

Celebrisi's Journey. David Rounds. LC 81-50011. 216p. (Orig.). 1982. pap. 6.95 (ISBN 0-87477-202-8). J P Tarcher.

Celebrisi's Journey: A Novel. David Rounds. LC 76-28912. 1976. 3.25 (ISBN 0-917512-14-6). Ten Thousand Buddhas Press.

Celebrisi's Journey: A Novel. David Rounds. LC 81-50011. 6.95 (ISBN 0-87477-202-8). J.P. Tarcher.

Celebrity. Thomas Thompson. LC 81-43387. 1982. 17.95 (ISBN 0-385-15969-2). Doubleday.

Celebrity: A Novel. Laura Keane Zametkin Hobson. LC 51-12714. 1951. Simon and Schuster.

Celebrity: An Episode. Winston Churchill. LC 21-4152. (People's library, no. 7). 1901. The American News Company.

Celebrity: An Episode. Winston Churchill. LC 11-7161. (Half-title: Macmillan). 1908. Grosset & Dunlap.

Celebrity: An Episode. Winston Churchill. LC 41-30727. 1913. Grosset & Dunlap.

Celebrity: An Episode. Winston Churchill. LC 16-6995. 1914. The Macmillan Company.

Celebrity: An Episode. Winston Churchill. LC 20-18832. 1919. The Macmillan Company.

Celebrity: An Episode. Winston Churchill. LC 6-25394. 1898. The Macmillan Co.

Celebrity Nurse. Ann Gilmer. 1974. 4.50. Avalon Books.

Celebrity's Daughter. Violet Hunt. LC 42-26363. 1914. Brentano's.

Celesetial Navigation. Anne Tyler. 256p. 1983. pap. 3.50 (ISBN 0-446-31169-3). Warner Bks.

Celeste. Rosamond Van Der Zee Marshall. LC 49-2445. 1949. Prentice-Hall.

Celeste. A Novel. Elizabeth M Sutton. 1895. G. W. Dillingham, Successor to G. W. Carleton & Co.

Celeste & Other Stories. Minnie Merochnik. LC 51-1929. 1950. Storm Publishers.

Celeste: The Pirate's Daughter. A Tale of the Southwest. Eliza Ann Dupuy. LC 6-35861. 1849. Stratton & Barnard.

Celestia. D Lull. 1907. Press of the Reliance Trading Company.

Celestial Chess. Thomas J Bontly. LC 78-2058. 9.95 (ISBN 0-06-010433-3). Harper & Row.

Celestial City. Emmuska Orczy. LC 26-14101. George H. Doran Company.

Celestial Escapade. Stella Kirby. LC 50-11089. 1951. Viking Press.

Celestial Escapade: By Stella Kirby Pseud. Virginia Arnhold. LC 50-11089. 1951. Viking Press.

Celestial Navigation. Anne Tyler. LC 73-18189. 1974. 6.95 (ISBN 0-394-49038-X). Knopf.

Celestial Navigation: Anne Tyler. Anne Tyler. 1980. 2.50 (ISBN 0-445-04513-2). Popular Library.

Celestial Omnibus and Other Stories. Edward Morgan Forster. LC 76-10586. 1976. 2.45 (ISBN 0-394-72176-4). Vintage Books.

Celestial Pilgrimage. Robert Lee Berry. LC 28-29234. Gospel Trumpet Company.

Celestial Railroad, and Other Stories. Nathaniel Hawthorne. LC 66-1223. (Signet classics). 1963. New American Library.

Celestial Telegraph. R. A. Ferguson. 3.95 o.p. Carlton.

Celestial Twelve. John F. Hubickey. 1975. 3.95 o.p. (ISBN 0-8059-2212-1). Dorrance.

Celestina. Fernando De Rojas. (Illus.). 1970. Repr. of 1909 ed. 7.50 (ISBN 0-87535-001-1). Hispanic Soc.

Celestina. Fernando De Rojas. lea. bdg. 3.50 o.s.i.; pap. 1.95 o.s.i.; pap. 1.50 o.s.i.; pap. 1.25 o.s.i. French & Eur.

Celestina: A Novel in Dialogue. Tr. by Lesley B. Simpson. LC 55-7961. (£0.95). 1955. pap. 2.95 (ISBN 0-520-01177-5, CAL26). U of Cal Pr.

Celestine: Being the Diary of a Chambermaid. Octave Mirbeau & Durst, Alan, Tr. LC 31-82152. (Modern amatory classics. no. 2). 1930. W. Faro, Inc.

Celia. Emily Hilda Young. LC 38-271479. Harcourt, Brace and Company.

Celia Amberley. Victoria Lincoln. LC 49-10974. 1949. Rinehart.

Celia Garth. Gwen Bristow. LC 59-10435. 1959. Crowell.

Celia Scarfe. Barbara Willard, pseud. LC 51-3334. 1951. Appleton-Century-Crofts.

Celia's House. Dorothy Emily Stevenson. LC 76-29915. 1977. 7.95 (ISBN 0-03-020441-0). Holt, Rinehart and Winston.

Celia's House. Dorothy Emily Stevenson. LC 43-25175. 1943. Farrar & Rinehart, Inc.

Celia's House. Dorothy Emily Stevenson. (Ace Book). 1978. 1.95 (ISBN 0-441-09799-5). Ace Books.

Celibacy: A Novel. Leon Ralph Jacobs. LC 11-185591. 1.50. Broadway Publishing Co.

Celibataires. Henri De Montherlant. 1958. 7.95. French & Eur.

Celibate at Twilight, and Other Stories. John Chapin Mosher & Petty, Mary, Illus. LC 40-10776. Ramdom House.

Celibate Father. William Wilfrid Whalen. LC 27-28080. 1927. B. Herder Book Co.

Celibates. George Moore. LC 7-25300. 1895. Macmillan and Co.

Celibates. George Moore. LC 18-21681. 1915. Brentano's.

Celibates, Bachelor's Establishment & Other Stories. Honore De Balzac. Repr. of 1899 ed. 14.00 o.s.i. Finch Pr.

Celibates' Club: Being the United Stories of The Bachelors' Club and The Old Maids' Club, by I. Zangwill... Israel Zangwill. LC 5-87103. 1905. The Macmillan Company.

Celine. Patrick McCarthy. LC 75-45212. 1976. 10.00. Viking Press.

Celio: Or, New York Above Ground and Under-Ground. George G Foster. LC 6-403697. Dewitt & Davenport.
Cell. Horst Bienek. LC 74-134739. (Illus.). 1972. 5.95. Unicorn.
Cell Car 54. James M. Fox. 1977. pap. 1.75 (ISBN 0-89041-165-4, 3165). Major Bks.
Cell Murder Mystery. Donald Bayne Hobart. LC 31-6786. 1931. The Fiction League.
Cell Number Thirty One. Zijadin Qira. 1970. 4.50 o.p. Vantage.
Cell: Three Tales of Horror. David Case. LC 69-16829. 1969. 5.00. Hill and Wang.
Cell 13." A Nihilist Episode in the Secret History of New York and St. Petersburg; Culminating in the Assassination of Alexander II. Edwin H Trafton. (Fireside series, no. 39). 1888. J. S. Ogilvie & Company.
Cell 13" A Nihilist Episode in the Secret History of New York and St. Petersburg; Culminating in the Assassination of Alexander II. Edwin H Trafton. (On cover: Columbia library, no. 23). Street & Smith.
Cellar. Richard Laymon. 1980. 2.25 (ISBN 0-446-92246-3). Warner Books.
Cellar at No.5: By Shelley Smith Pseud. Nancy Bodington. LC 55-804856. Harper.
Cellar Club see Vinnie.
Cellars. John Shirley. 304p. 1982. pap. 2.75 (ISBN 0-380-79871-9, 79871). Avon.
Cellini Plaque. Harold MacGrath. LC 25-217649. 1925. Doubleday, Page & Company.
Cellini Smith, Detective. Robert Reeves. LC 43-6455. 1943. Houghton Mifflin Company.
Celluloid Asylum. Sidney Alexander. LC 51-14072. 1951. Bobbs-Merrill.
Celt and Saxon. George Meredith. LC 10-16008. 1910. C. Scribner's Sons.
Celtic Heart. Eileen Sherman. LC 80-50889. 328p. 1980. 12.95 (ISBN 0-9604382-0-3); pap. 4.00 (ISBN 0-9604382-1-1). Resolute Pr.
Celtic Queen. Brian Dyer, pseud. 192p. 1976. pap. 1.25 (ISBN 0-532-12372-7). Woodhill.
Celtic Queen: A Novel. Brian Dyer, pseud. LC 74-13207. 1974. 7.95 (ISBN 0-88405-089-0). Mason & Lipscomb Publishers.
Cement. Fedor Vasilevich Gladkov. Tr. by Arthur, A. S. LC 30-156234. 1929. International Publishers.
Cement: A Novel. Fedor Vasilevich Gladkov. Tr. by A. S. Arthur & C. Ashleigh. LC 60-13978. 10.00 (ISBN 0-8044-2234-6); pap. 5.95 (ISBN 0-8044-6178-3). Ungar.
Cement Garden. Ian McEwan. LC 78-19099. (ISBN 0-671-24288-1). Simon and Schuster.
Cement Garden. Ian McEwan. 1979. 3.25 (ISBN 0-425-04496-3). Berkley Publishing Corp.
Cemeteries Are for Dying. William L. Story. LC 82-45078. (Crime Club Ser.). 192p. 1982. 10.95 (ISBN 0-385-18190-6). Doubleday.
Cemetery World. Clifford D. Simak. LC 72-83333. 1973. 5.95 (ISBN 0-399-11071-2). Putnam.
Cemtery World. Clifford D. Simak. (Berkley medallion book). 1974. (pbk.) 0.95 (ISBN 0-425-02626-4). Berkley Pub. Co.
Cenotaph Road. Robert E. Vardeman. LC 82-81387. 224p. 1982. pap. 2.75 (ISBN 0-86721-203-9); No. 2. pap. 2.75 (ISBN 0-86721-222-5). Playboy Pbks.
Cenotaph Road. Robert E. Vardeman. 1983. pap. 2.75 (ISBN 0-441-09845-2, Pub. by Ace Science Fiction). Ace Bks.
Cension. A Sketch from Paso Del Norte. Maude Mason Austin. (On cover: Harper's little novels). 1896. Harper & Brothers.
Censor Twain. Northwind. 1972. 4.00 o.p. (ISBN 0-682-47404-5). Exposition.
Censoria Lictoria of Facts and Folks, from the Notes and Minutes of Miss Betsey Trotwood's Official Tour Under the Frank Pierce Dynasty. 8th ed., rev. and enl. ed. Louise Elemjay. LC 6-39362. (With her Rising young men, and other tales. 4th ed. New York, 1859). 1859. J. F. Trow, Printer.
Centaur. Algernon Blackwood. LC 75-46254. (Supernatural & Occult Fiction). 1976. 20.00 (ISBN 0-405-08113-8). Arno Press.
Centaur. John Updike. LC 63-7873. 1963. Knopf.
Centaur Isle. Piers Anthony, pseud. 304p. (Orig.). 1982. pap. 2.75 (ISBN 0-345-29770-9, Del Rey). Ballantine.
Centaur Letters. David Herbert Lawrence. LC 75-110977. 1970. Humanities Research Center, University of Texas.
Centauri Device. Mike John Harrison. LC 73-83635. 1974. 4.95 (ISBN 0-385-01839-8). Doubleday.
Centaurians: A Novel. L D Biagi. LC 11-290843. 1.50. Broadway Publishing Co.
Centenarian: Or, The Two Beringhelds. Honore De Balzac. LC 75-46250. (Supernatural and Occult Fiction). 1976. 23.00 (ISBN 0-405-08110-3). Arno Press.
Centenarian: Or, the Two Beringhelds. Ed. by R. Reginald & Douglas Alver Menville. Tr. by George E. Slusser. LC 75-46250. (Supernatural & Occult Fiction Ser.). (Illus.). 1976. lib. bdg. 23.00x (ISBN 0-405-08110-3). Ayer Co.
Centenary at Jalna. Mazo De La Roche. 1978. pap. 1.75 (ISBN 0-449-23691-9, Crest). Fawcett.
Centenary at Old First. Harvey Reeves Calkins. LC 19-10147. The Methodist Book Concern.
Centenary Corbiere. bi-lingual ed. Tristan Corbiere. Tr. by Val Warner from Fr. (Translation Ser.). 1980. 12.95 o.p. (ISBN 0-85635-060-5, Pub. by Carcanet New Pr England). Humanities.
Centennial. James Albert Michener. LC 74-5164. (Illus.). 1974. 10.00 (ISBN 0-394-47970-X) (ISBN 0-394-47970-X). Random House.
Centennial. James Albert Michener. 1975. (pbk.) 2.75. Fawcett.
Centennial Ball. Lee S. Teller. (Historical Romance). 368p. (Orig.). 1981. pap. 2.75 (ISBN 0-515-05864-5). Jove Pubns.
Centennial Summer. Cathryn Ladd. (Adventures in Love Ser.: No. 23). 1982. pap. 1.75 (ISBN 0-451-11524-4, Sig). NAL.
Centeola: And Other Tales. Daniel Pierce Thompson. LC 3-28177. 1864. Carleton.
Center Aisle. Claudia Holland. LC 49-9052. 1949. Rinehart.
Center Court. Helen Hull Jacobs. LC 50-6110. (Barnes sport novel). 1950. Barnee.
Center Door Fancy. Joan Blondell. 1973. (pbk.) 1.50. Dell.
Center Door Fancy. Joan Blondell. LC 72-6077. 1972. 7.95. Delacorte Press.
Center-Fire Smith. Nelson Coral Nye. LC 39-25443. Phoenix Press.
Center of Harley Street: Being Some Familiar Correspondence of Peter Harding, M.D. Pseud. 3d impression. ed. Henry Howarth Bashford. LC 11-35696. 1911. Houghton Mifflin Company.
Center of the Action. Jerome Weidman. LC 68-28559. 1969. 6.95. Random House.
Center of the Stage, a Novel. Gerald Sykes. LC 52-12286. 1952. Farrar, Straus and Young.
Center of the Web. Katharine Roberts. LC 42-150373. 1942. Published for the Crime Club by Doubleday, Doran & Company, Inc.
Centerville, U. S. A. Charles Merz. LC 24-203825. 2.00. The Century Co.
Centerville, U.S.A. Charles Merz. LC 78-160943. (Short story index reprint series). 1971. (ISBN 0-8369-3922-0). Books for Libraries Press.
Central Park Murder. Beldon Duff. LC 29-8651. 1929. Pub. for The Crime Club, Inc., by Doubleday, Doran & Company, Inc.
Central Passage. Lawrence L Schoonover. LC 62-9298. 1962. W. Sloane Associates.
Central Standard Time. Harlan Henthorne Hatcher. LC 37-3592. Farrar & Rinehart, Incorporated.
Centralia Dead March. Thomas Churchill. LC 79-9146. 1979. 7.50 (ISBN 0-915306-17-4). Curbstone Press.
Centuries Apart. Edward Tracy Bouve. LC 6-14915. 1894. Little, Brown, and Company.
Centurion. Leonard Patrick O'Connor Wibberley. LC 66-24963. 1966. Morrow.
Centurion: A Romance of the Time of the Messiah... Adolphe Basile Routhier. Tr. by Borden, Lucille Papin. LC 10-233221. 1910. 1.50. B. Herder.
Centurions. Damion Hunter. 384p. (Orig.). 1981. 6.95 (ISBN 0-345-29809-8); pap. 2.95 (ISBN 0-345-29691-5). Ballantine.
Centurions II. Damion Hunter. 1982. pap. 3.50 (ISBN 0-345-29826-8). Ballantine.
Century. Fred Mustard Stewart. LC 80-22417. 576p. 1981. 13.95 (ISBN 0-688-00398-2). Morrow.
Century. Fred Mustard Stewart. 1982. pap. 3.95 (ISBN 0-451-11407-8, AE1407, Sig). NAL.
Century: A Novel. Fred Mustard Stewart. LC 80-22417. 1981. 13.95 (ISBN 0-688-03763-1). Morrow.
Century God Slept. David Chagall. LC 63-1569. 1963. T. Yoseloff.
Century God Slept see Like Now.
Century Hence: Or, A Romance of 1941. George Fox Tucker. LC 76-41223. 1977. 9.75 (ISBN 0-8139-0668-7). University Press of Virginia.
Century in Scarlet. Lajos Zilahy. LC 64-794575. bds., 6.95. McGraw.
Century List. Mervin S. Baker. 1977. pap. 3.95 (ISBN 0-916608-04-2). Quill Pubns.
Century of a Lifetime. Illustrated by the Author. A T Johnston. LC 56-3200. 1956. Macmillan.
Century of Australian Short Stories. Ed. by C. Hadgraft & R. Wilson. 1964. pap. text ed. 4.50x o.p. Heinemann Ed.
Century of Creepy Stories. LC 74-37261. (Short story index reprint series). 1971. (ISBN 0-8369-4072-5). Books for Libraries Press.
Century of Creepy Stories. facsimile ed. LC 74-37261. (Short Story Index Reprint Ser.). Repr. of 1934 ed. 40.25 (ISBN 0-8369-4072-5). Ayer Co.
Century of Detective Stories. Intro. by G. K. Chesterton. 1979. Repr. lib. bdg. 35.00 (ISBN 0-8495-0947-5). Arden Lib.
Century of Fiction by American Negroes: 1853-1952. Maxwell Whiteman. 1969. Repr. 10.00x (ISBN 0-87556-409-7). Saifer.
Century of French Romance. LC 12-19964. D. Appleton & Co.
Century of Gossip: Or, The Real and the Seeming. Willard Glover Nash. LC 7-25796. 1876. W. B. Keen, Cooke & Co.
Century of Great Science Fiction Novels. Ed. by Damon Francis Knight. 1965. Dell.
Century of Horror Stories. Ed. by Dennis Wheatley. LC 71-160952. (Short story index reprint series). 1971. (ISBN 0-8369-3931-X). Books for Libraries Press.
Century of Nature Stories, Vol. 1. Intro. by J. Robertson Scott. LC 72-5951. (Short Story Index Reprint Ser). Repr. of 1937 ed. 48.00 (ISBN 0-8369-4197-7). Ayer Co.
Century of Science Fiction. Ed. by Damon Francis Knight. LC 62-12409. 1962. Simon and Schuster.
Century of Sea Stories. Rafael Sabatini. 40.00 (ISBN 0-89987-139-9). Darby Bks.
Century of the Manikin. E. C. Tubb. (Science Fiction Ser.). 144p. 1972. pap. 0.95 o.p. (UQ1018). DAW Bks.
Century of Thrillers ... LC 37-16380. President Press.
Century of Western Stories. George Goodchild. Repr. lib. bdg. 20.00 o.p. Folcroft.
Century Readings in the American Short Story. Ed. by Fred Lewis Pattee. LC 27-196375. The Century Co.
Century Too Soon: A Story of Bacon's Rebellion. John Roy Musick. LC 7-33332. (On cover: Columbian historical novels. v. 6). 1893. Funk & Wagnalls Company.
Century Was Young. Louis Aragon & Josephson, Hannah, Tr. LC 41-24634. Duell, Sloan and Pearce.
Century's Ebb: The Thirteenth Chronicle. Dos Passos, John. LC 75-920. 1975. 9.95 (ISBN 0-87645-089-3). Gambit.
Century's End. Russell M. Griffin. 272p. (Orig.). 1981. pap. 2.25 (ISBN 0-553-14525-8). Bantam.
Cepherine: Or, The Secret Cabal. John Hovey Robinson. LC 7-42156. F. A. Brady.
Cerberus: A Wolf in the Fold. Jack L. Chalker. (Four Lords of the Diamond Ser.: Bk. 2). 240p. 1982. pap. 2.50 (ISBN 0-345-29371-1, Del Rey). Ballantine.
Cerberus Murders. Rodney Quest. LC 73-122150. 1970. 4.95. McCall.
Ceremonia Secreta y Otros Cuentos. Marco Denevi & Donald A. Yates. LC 65-14958. (Macmillan modern Spanish American literature series). 1965. Macmillan.
Ceremonial, Stories 1936-1940: The Collected Stories of Paul Goodman, Vol. 2. Paul Goodman. Ed. by Taylor Stoehr. 273p. 1978. 14.00 (ISBN 0-87685-354-8); deluxe ed. 25.00 (ISBN 0-87685-355-6); pap. 7.50 (ISBN 0-87685-353-X). Black Sparrow.
Ceremonies. Josh Webster. 304p. (Orig.). 1982. pap. 2.95 (ISBN 0-425-05466-7). Berkley Pub.
Ceremonies of Love. Deneen Peckinpah. pap. 1.95 o.s.i. (OPS-9). Olympia.
Ceremonies: So Long As You Both Shall Live. Ed McBain. 1976. 6.95 o.p. (ISBN 0-394-48583-1). Random.
Ceremony. Robert B. Parker. 1983. pap. 2.95 (ISBN 0-440-10993-0). Dell.
Ceremony. Leslie Marmon Silko. LC 76-46936. 1977. 10.00 (ISBN 0-670-20986-4). Viking Press.
Ceremony. Leslie Marmon Silko. (Signet Book.). 1978. 1.95 (ISBN 0-451-08017-3). New American Library.
Ceremony: A Spenser Novel. Robert B. Parker. LC 81-15106. 12.95. Delacorte Press /S. Lawrence.
Ceremony in Lone Tree. Wright Morris. LC 60-7775. viii, 304p. 1973. pap. 6.95 (ISBN 0-8032-5782-1, BB 560, Bison). U of Nebr Pr.
Ceremony in Lone Tree. Morris Wright. (Bison bk.). 1973. 2.25 (ISBN 0-8032-5782-1). Univ. of Nebraska Pr.
Ceremony in Lone Tree. 1st Ed. Wright Morris. LC 60-7775. 1960. Atheneum.
Ceremony in the Lincoln Tunnel: A Novel. Richard Cunningham. LC 78-14995. 9.95 (ISBN 0-8362-6105-4). Sheed, Andrews, and McMeel.
Ceremony of Innocence. Robert Wool. LC 68-28118. (NAL book). 1968. 5.95. World Publishers.
Ceremony of Innocence. Novel. Elizabeth Charlotte Webster. LC 49-7413. 1949. Harcourt Brace.
Ceremony of Love. 1st Ed. Thomas Williams. LC 55-7635. 1955. Bobbs-Merrill.
Ceremony of the Innocent. Taylor Caldwell. LC 75-36582. 1976. 10.95 (ISBN 0-385-07042-X). Doubleday.
Ceremony of the Innocent. Taylor Caldwell. (Fawcett Crest Book). 1977. 2.25 (ISBN 0-449-23338-3). Fawcett Books.
Cerissa. Jessica St. Claire. (Leisure Book). 2.25 (ISBN 0-8439-0681-2). Nordon Publications.
Cerro Lobo. Tevis Miller. LC 41-19649. Phoenix Press.
Cerro Lobo. Joseph Reardon. LC 41-196495. Phoenix Press.
Certain Blindness. Roy Lewis. LC 80-29324. 1980. 9.95 (ISBN 0-312-12782-0). St. Martin's Press.
Certain Crossroad. Emilie Baker Loring. LC 25-6387. 1925. The Penn Publishing Company.
Certain Desire. Jean Gautiere. 160p. pap. 1.95 o.p. (MP-112). Montmartre.
Certain Doctor French. Elizabeth Seifert. LC 73-79141. 1973. 5.95. Aeonian Press.
Certain Doctor French. Elizabeth Seifert. LC 43-3410. 1943. Dodd, Mead & Company.
Certain Dr. Thorndike. Richard Austin Freeman. LC 28-586819. 1928. Dodd, Mead and Company.
Certain Evil: By David Kraslow, Robert S. Boyd. David Kraslow & Robert S. Boyd. LC 65-10898. 5.95. Little.
Certain Harvest: A Novel of the Time of Peter Cooper. 1st Ed. Ruth Adams Yingling Knight. LC 60-5935. 1960. Doubleday.
Certain Hour: Dizain Des Poetes. James Branch Cabell. LC 16-22262. 1916. R. M. McBride & Company.
Certain Hour: Dizain Des Poetes. James Branch Cabell. LC 24-20489. 1920. R. M. McBride & Company.
Certain Island. Robert William Murphy. LC 67-10833. (Illus.). 1967. Published by M. Evans and Distributed in Association with Lippincott, Philadelphia.
Certain Man. Zane Kotker. LC 76-26162. 1976. 8.95 (ISBN 0-394-40262-6). Knopf.
Certain Men..... Bryan T Holland. LC 24-76781. Small, Maynard & Company.
Certain People. Edith Newbold Jones Wharton. LC 30-28849. 1930. D. Appleton and Company.
Certain People of Importance. Kathleen Thompson Norris. LC 22-16601. 1922. Doubleday Page & Company.
Certain Protocol. Lawrence Robbins. LC 74-15890. 1975. 8.95 (ISBN 0-06-013566-2). Harper & Row.
Certain Radiance. Grace F Watkins. LC 66-29827. 1966. Zondervan Pub. House.
Certain Rich Girls. Ann Pinchot. LC 77-79537. 9.95 (ISBN 0-87795-174-8). Arbor House.
Certain Rich Man. Vincent Sheean. LC 47-11066. 1947. Random House.
Certain Rich Man. William Allen White. LC 71-107850. (Series in American studies). 1970. Johnson Reprint Corp.
Certain Rich Man. William Allen White. LC 79-104763. (Novel as American social history). 1970. 6.50. University Press of Kentucky.
Certain Rich Man. William Allen White. LC 9-18720. 1909. The Macmillan Company.
Certain Rich Man. William Allen White & Flagg, Mildred Buchanan, Ed. (Half-title: Modern readers' series). 1923. The Macmillan Company.
Certain Rich Man. William Allen White & Flagg, Mrs. Mildred Buchanan, 1886- Ed. LC 34-8653. (Half-title: Modern readers' series). 1925. The Macmillan Company.
Certain Riches. Emma Lee Hohstadt. LC 47-30555. 1947. Christopher Pub. House.
Certain Slant of Light. Margaret Wander Bonanno. LC 78-31373. 9.95 (ISBN 0-87223-532-7). Seaview Books: Trade Distribution by Simon and Schuster.
Certain Slant of Light. Frances Rickett. LC 68-15520. 1968. Putnam.
Certain Sleep. Helen Kieran Reilly. LC 61-12153. (Random House mystery). 1961. Random House.
Certain Smile. Francoise Quiorez. LC 56-8276. 1974. (pbk.) 0.95. Popular Library.
Certain Smile. Francoise Sagan, pseud. Tr. by Anne Greene. 1956. 3.95 o.p. (ISBN 0-525-07840-1). Dutton.
Certain Smile: By Francoise Sagan Pseud. Translated from the French by Anne Green. 1st American Ed. Francoise Quiorez. LC 56-8276. 1956. Dutton.
Certain Star: A Novel. Corolin Malcolm. LC 47-637243. 1946. B. Humphries.
Certain Summer. Tom Clarkson. LC 66-10120. bds., 3.75. Abelard.
Certain Widow: A Novel. Joseph Dever. LC 51-4039. 1951. Bruce.
Certain Woman: The Story of Mary Magdalene. Victor MacClure. LC 51-11823. 1951. Pellegrini & Cudahy.
Certain Women. Erskine Caldwell. LC 57-93198. 1957. Little, Brown.
Certainty of a Future Life in Mars: Being the Posthumous Papers of Bradford Torrey Dodd. Louis Pope Gratacap & Schiaparelli, Giovanni Virginio, 1835-1910. LC 3-10193. 1903. Irving Press.
Certainty of Love. Alfred Coppel. LC 66-19485. 4.50. Harcourt.
Certainty of Love. Alfred Coppel. (S352). 1968. Avon.
Cesar and Augusta. Ronald Harwood. LC 80-80123. 1979. 10.95 (ISBN 0-316-34991-7). Little, Brown.

Cesar Biroteau. Honore De Balzac. (Coll. Prestige). 1950. 12.95 o.p. French & Eur.
Cesar Birotteau. Honore De Balzac. Tr. by Katharine Prescott Wormeley. LC 3-23178. (Half-title: The comedy of human life... Scenes from Parisian life). 1886. Roberts Brothers.
Cesar Birotteau. Honore De Balzac. Tr. by Katharine Prescott Wormeley. LC 9-2703. (Half-title: The comedy of human life... Scenes from Parisian life). 1887. Roberts Brothers.
Cesar Birotteau. Honore De Balzac. Tr. by Katharine Prescott Wormeley. LC 3-23179. (Half-title: The comedy of human life... Scenes from Parisian life). 1888. Roberts Brothers.
Cesar Birotteau. A Novel. Translated from the French of. Honore De Balzac. LC 6-6310. (choice series, no. 19). 1890. R. Bonner's Sons.
Cesar Birotteau. Translated by Frances Frenaye. Honore De Balzac. LC 55-779121. (His The human comedy).
Cesarine Dietrich. George Sand & Stanwood, Edward, 1841-1923, Tr. LC 6-34620. 1871. J. R. Osgood and Company.
C'est la Guerre! The Best Stories of the World War. Ed. by James Gerald Dunton. LC 27-24664. 1927. The Stratford Company.
Cest Oaucasi & De Nicolete. Ed. by F. W. Bourdillon & Francis William Bourdillon. LC 80-2241. (Illus.). Repr. of 1896 ed. 17.50 (ISBN 0-404-19036-7). AMS Pr.
Ceylon. Margaret Rebecca Lay. LC 47-1015. 1947. Rinehart & Company, Inc.
Chad Hanna. Walter Dumaux Edmonds. 1940. Little, Brown and Company.
Chadbourne Luck. Lucia Curzon, pseud. (Second Chance at Love, Regency Ser.: No. 3). 192p. (Orig.). 1981. pap. 1.75 (ISBN 0-515-05624-3). Jove Pubns.
Chadwick Ring. Julia Jeffries. (Orig.). 1982. pap. 2.25 (ISBN 0-451-11346-2, AE1346, Sig). NAL.
Chaff Before the Wind. Sigurd Wesley Christiansen. LC 73-22750. 1974. 13.75 (ISBN 0-8371-7349-3). Greenwood Press.
Chaff Before the Wind. Sigurd Wesley Christiansen & Anderson, Isaac, 1868- Tr. LC 34-35473. Liveright Publishing Corporation.
Chaffee of Roaring Horse. Ernest Haycox. LC 30-7788. 1930. Doubleday, Doran & Company, Inc.
Chain. Jack McLaren. LC 27-17794. The Curtiss Press.
Chain. Paul Iselin Wellman. 1971. pap. 0.95 o.p. (09096). Curtis.
Chain: A Novel. Charles Hanson Towne. LC 22-17773. 1922. G. P. Putnam's Sons.
Chain: A Novel. Paul Iselin Wellman. LC 49-832291. 1949. Doubleday.
Chain & Ball. Herbert El Toro. (Orig.). 1969. pap. 1.95 o.p. (OPH-172, Ophelia). Olympia.
Chain and the Link. David Micah Miller. LC 51-3333. 1951. World Pub. Co.
Chain Hearings. Aaron Fogel. 1976. pap. 2.50 o.p. (ISBN 0-8180-1530-6). Horizon.
Chain Hearings. Aaron Fogel. 1976. pap. 2.50 o.p. (ISBN 0-8180-1530-6). Horizon.
Chain in the Heart. Hubert Creekmore. LC 52-7130. 1953. Random House.
Chain Invisible. Anonymous... Herman Alfred Kasen. LC 41-34805. G. H. Watt.
Chain of Chance. Stanislaw Lem. LC 78-5828. 7.95. Harcourt Brace Jovanovich.
Chain of Death. 1st Ed. Nancy McLarty. LC 62-8955. 1962. Published for the Crime Club by Doubleday.
Chain of Evidence. Carolyn Wells. LC 12-9955. 1912. J. B. Lippincott Company.
Chain of His Sins. Ethel Almaz Stout. LC 29-2733. 1928. G. P. Putnam's Sons.
Chain of Love. Martha McClymonds. 288p. (Orig.). 1981. pap. 2.75 (ISBN 0-8439-1002-X, Leisure Bks). Nordon Pubns.
Chain of Voices. Andre Philippus Brink. LC 82-80315. 1982. 15.50 (ISBN 0-688-01131-4). Morrow.
Chain of Voices. Andre Philippus Brink. LC 82-18566. 1983. 5.95 (ISBN 0-14-006538-5). Penguin Books.
Chain Reaction. Nicholas Guild. 384p. 1983. 13.95 (ISBN 0-312-12785-5). St Martin.
Chain Reaction. Hodder-Williams, Christopher. LC 59-8266. 1959. Doubleday.
Chain Reaction. Gordon Pape & Tony Aspler. LC 78-3528. 1978. 9.95 (ISBN 0-670-21102-8). Viking Press.
Chain Reaction. Gilbert Ralston. (Dakota Series#5). 1975. (pbk.) 1.25 (ISBN 0-523-00730-2). Pinnacle Books.
Chainbearer: Or, The Littlepage Manuscripts. James Fenimore Cooper. LC 70-37651. 1973. 12.50 (ISBN 0-404-01704-5). AMS Press.
Chainbearer: Or, The Littlepage Manuscripts. James Fenimore Cooper. LC 78-7896. 1968. Scholarly Press.
Chainbearer: Or, The Littlepage Manuscripts. James Fenimore Cooper. (On cover: Lovell's library, no. 576). 1885. J. W. Lovell Company.
Chainbearer: Or, The Littlepage Manuscripts. James Fenimore Cooper. (On cover: Seaside library. Pocket ed. no. 419). 1885. G. Munro.
Chainbearers: Or, The Littlepage Manuscripts. James Fenimore Cooper. LC 4-195696. 1888. D. Appleton and Company.
Chainbreakers. Richard James Talbot. LC 14-13575. The Roxburgh Publishing Company, Inc.
Chaindearer: Or. The Littlepage Manuscripts. James Fenimore Cooper. LC 6-32149. 1845. Burges, Stringer & Co.
Chained Reaction. Warren Murphy. (Destroyer Ser.: No. 34). 1978. pap. 1.95 (ISBN 0-523-41249-5). Pinnacle Bks.
Chaining the Lady. Piers Anthony, pseud. LC 77-95091. 1978. 1.75 (ISBN 0-380-01779-2). Avon.
Chains. Justin Adams. (Dell Book). 1977. 1.95 (ISBN 0-440-13993-7). Dell Pub. Co.
Chains. Henri Barbusse & Guest, Stephen Haden, Tr. LC 25-207101. 1925. International Publishers.
Chains. Joseph Delmont. Tr. by Paterson, Huntley. LC 29-20023. 1929. L. MacVeagh, The Dial Press.
Chains. Gerald Green. LC 79-4885. 10.95 (ISBN 0-87223-567-X). Seaview Books.
Chains of Command. Thomas Goethals. LC 54-7818. 1955. Random House.
Chains of Fear. Translated from the Russian by Christopher Bird. Nikolai Narokov. LC 58-7216. 1958. Regnery.
Chains of Gold. Yvonne Whittal. (Harlequin Presents Ser.). 192p. 1983. pap. 1.95 (ISBN 0-373-10590-8). Harlequin Bks.
Chains of Lightning. John Calvin Mellett. LC 29-569849. The Bobbs-Merrill Company.
Chains of Love. Zoe Oldenbourg. 1976. 1.95 (ISBN 0-380-00620-0). Avon Books.
Chains of Love. Translated from the French by Michael Bullock. Zoe Oldenbourg. LC 59-8582. 1959. Pantheon.
Chains of Shadows: A Romance of Judas Iscariot. Jack Howard Sanders. LC 43-9804. 1943. Fleming H. Revell Company.
Chains of Silk. Barry Devlin. LC 54-194687. 1954. Vixen Press.
Chains of the Sea: Three Original Novellas of Science Fiction. George Alec Effinger. LC 73-6444. 1973. 6.50 (ISBN 0-8407-6314-X). T. Nelson.
Chains That Bind. Gus Stevens. (Orig.). 1969. pap. 1.25 o.p. (2084). Brandon.
Chair: A Historical Novel. Joel Lieber. LC 69-15923. 1969. 4.50. McKay.
Chair for Martin Rome. Henry Edward Helseth. LC 47-2397. 1947. Dodd, Mead & Company.
Chair on the Boulevard. Leonard Merrick. LC 21-137062. (Half-title: The works of Leonard Merrick). E. P. Dutton & Company.
Chairman. William Flanagan. (Orig.). 1981. pap. 2.50 (ISBN 0-440-11546-9). Dell.
Chairman. Jay Richard Kennedy. LC 74-99089. 1970. 6.95. World Pub. Co.
Chairman, Lady Vibrat. Jeffery Farnol. LC 32-32770. 1932. Little, Brown, and Company.
Chairman of the Board. Hank Messick, pseud. 1971. 5.95 o.p. Putnam.
Chairman of the Bored. Edward Streeter. LC 61-6468. 1961. Harper.
Chaka. Thomas Mofolo. Tr. by Daniel Kunene. (African Writers Ser.: No. 229). (Orig.). 1981. pap. text ed. 6.50x (ISBN 0-435-90229-6). Heinemann Ed.
Chakidji the Popular Bandit. Novel. James Avzar. A. Martin.
Chakra. Jayawant Dalvi. Tr. by Gauri Deshpande from Marathi. LC 75-901575. 1974. lib. bdg. 4.00 (ISBN 0-8364-0484-X, Orient Longman). South Asia Bks.
Chaldean Magician: An Adventure in Rome, in the Reign of the Emperor Diocletian. Ernst Eckstein & Safford, Mary Joanna, D. 1916, Tr. LC 1-18024. 1886. W. S. Gottsberger.
Chalice: A Novel. Mary Frances Doner. LC 40-8547. The Penn Publishing Company.
Chalice of Courage: A Romance of Colorado. Cyrus Townsend Brady. LC 12-3597. 1912. 1.30. Dodd, Mead and Company.
Chalice of Eminent Desire. 1st Ed. Auralee S Shreve. LC 56-5540. 1956. Vantage Press.
Chalk Face. Waldo David Frank. LC 24-23480. Boni and Liveright.
Chalk Giants. Keith Roberts. LC 75-10687. 1975. 6.95 (ISBN 0-399-11559-5). Putnam.
Chalk Giants. Keith Roberts. (Berkley Medallion Book). 1976. (pbk.) 1.25 (ISBN 0-425-03115-2). Berkley Publishing Corp.
Chalk Line. Ruth Cranston. LC 15-4802. 1915. 1.30. John Lane Company.
Chalk Line. Jerry Greenfield, pseud. LC 63-12082. 1963. Chilton Books.
Chalkdust. Myra B. Cook. 1969. 3.00 o.p. (ISBN 0-8059-1366-1). Dorrance.
Chalky. Matthew Vaughan. LC 74-26906. 1975. 7.95 (ISBN 0-316-89809-0). Little, Brown.
Challenge. Kerry Allyne. (Harlequin Romances). 192p. 1981. pap. 1.25 (ISBN 0-373-02389-8, Pub. by Harlequin). PB.
Challenge. Harold Begbie. LC 11-283686. Hodder and Stoughton.
Challenge. Harold Begbie. LC 11-311292. Hodder & Stoughton, George H. Doran Company.
Challenge. Warren Cheney. LC 6-7396. 1906. The Bobbs-Merrill Company.
Challenge. Victoria Mary Sackville-West. LC 23-262423. 1923. George H. Doran Company.
Challenge. Victoria Mary Sackville-West. 1975. (pbk.) 1.50 (ISBN 0-380-00359-7). Avon.
Challenge. Joan Sutherland. LC 26-727270. 1925. Cassell and Company, Ltd.
Challenge. Joan Sutherland. LC 26-6143. 1926. Harper & Brothers.
Challenge. E. V. Timms. 1975. pap. 1.25 o.p. (V3704). BJ Pub Group.
Challenge: A Bulldog Drummond Novel. Herman Cyril McNeile. LC 38-23773. 1938. The Sun Dial Press, Inc.
Challenge: A Romance Based on Jesus' Mission. Harry Lee Williams. LC 40-32140. Dorrance and Company.
Challenge: A Story of Conspiracy and the Coming Crash. Eustace Dudley. LC 28-208390. 1928. Longmans, Green and Co.
Challenge at Changsha. Paul Hughes. LC 45-10159. 1945. The Macmillan Company.
Challenge Blue Mask. John Creasey. LC 39-23039. 1939. J. B. Lippincott Co.
Challenge Blue Mask! Anthony Morton, pseud. LC 39-23039. J. B. Lippincott Company.
Challenge for Dr. Jane. Adeline McElfresh. LC 63-6701. Avalon Books.
Challenge for Dr. Mays. Elizabeth Seifert. LC 55-972399. 1955. Dodd, Mead.
Challenge for Dr. Mays. Elizabeth Seifert. LC 73-79168. 1974. 6.95. Aeonian Press.
Challenge for Doctor Mays. Elizabeth Seifert. 1973. Repr. of 1955 ed. lib. bdg. 15.45x (ISBN 0-88411-033-8). Amereon Ltd.
Challenge for Three. David Garth. LC 38-194071. 1938. H. C. Kinsey & Company, Inc.
Challenge from Beyond. Catherine L. Moore et al. (Illus.). 1978. pap. 5.95 o.p. Necronomicon.
Challenge of Love. Warwick Deeping. LC 32-6322. 1932. R. M. McBride & Company.
Challenge of Smoke Wade. Robert J Hogan. LC 51-11031. (Silver star westerns). 1951. Dodd, Mead.
Challenge of Spring. Iris Bromige. 1972. pap. 0.75 o.p. (94261). Beagle Bks.
Challenge of the Barons. Lekan Are. 1977. 6.50 (ISBN 0-533-02680-6). Vantage.
Challenge of the Bush. Courtney Ryley Cooper. LC 29-16853. 1929. Little, Brown, and Company.
Challenge of the North. William Byron Mowery. LC 34-740967. 1934. Little, Brown, and Company.
Challenge of the Unknown. Clark Darlton. (Perry Rhodan, 32). 1973. (pbk.) 0.75. Ace Books.
Challenge: Plan of Action for a Better Tomorrow. A Major Novel of the Near Future, by Arthur C. Mangels and Albert F. Byers. Arthur C Mangels & Albert F. Byers. LC 61-9045. 1961. Rolley & Reynolds.
Challenge That Changed the World. Ensign B Stebbins. LC 32-9430. Dorrance & Company, Inc.
Challenge the Hellmaker. Walt Richmond & Leigh Richmond. (Ace Science Fiction Special#6). 1976. (pbk.) 1.25. Ace Books.
Challenge the Wind: A Novel. John Tomerlin. LC 66-11562. 1966. Dutton.
Challenge to Adventure. Alice Turner Curtis. LC 19-15227. 1919. Marshall Jones Company.
Challenge to Anne. Dorothy Quentin. LC 44-598695. 1944. Arcadia House, Inc.
Challenge to Caesar: A Historical Romance. Saul Saphire. LC 38-154890. Covici, Friede.
Challenge to Candia. Phyllis Waite. LC 40-8659. 1939. Arcadia House.
Challenge to Danger. William MacLeod Raine. LC 32-391. 1952. Houghton, Mifflin.
Challenge to Happiness. Maysie Greig. LC 37-652430. 1937. Doubleday, Doran and Co., Inc.
Challenge to Happiness. Maysie Greig. LC 38-12697. 1938. The Sun Dial Press, Inc.
Challenge to Love. Ethel Hamill, pseud. LC 46-6022. 1946. Arcadia House, Inc.
Challenge to Love. Jean Francis Webb. LC 46-6022. 1946. Arcadia House.
Challenge to Sirius. Sheila Kaye-Smith. LC 19-6143. 1918. E. P. Dutton & Company.
Challenge to Venus. Charles Morgan. LC 57-711484. 1957. Macmillan.
Challenged. Caroline Atwater Mason. LC 32-3188. Fleming H. Revell Company.
Challenged: A Novel. Helen Reimensnyder Martin. LC 25-2963. 1925. Dodd, Mead and Company.
Challenged: A Novel. Helen Reimensnyder Martin. LC 31-195232. 1926. Grosset & Dunlap.
Challenged Land. Betty De Sherbinin. LC 45-11150. 1946. W. Morrow & Company.
Challenger. Giles A Lutz. 1974. (pbk.) 0.95. Ace Books.
Challengers. Blue Love. 1982. 8.95 (ISBN 0-533-05446-X). Vantage.
Challengers. Grace Livingston Hill. LC 32-9029. 1932. J. B. Lippincott Company.
Challengers for the Unknown. Ron Goulart. (Dell Book). 1977. 1.50 (ISBN 0-440-11337-7). Dell Pub. Co.
Challoners. Edward Frederic Benson. LC 4-17216. 1904. J. B. Lippincott Company.
Challoners of Bristol. Leal Hayes. 1977. pap. 1.25 o.p. (LB441, Leisure Bks). Nordon Pubns.
Challoners of Bristol. Leal Hayes. (O.s.i.). 1976. pap. 1.75 o.s.i. Belmont-Tower.
Chalmers Comes Back. William James Dawson. LC 19-149159. 1919. John Lane Company.
Chalmette: The History of the Adventures & Love Affairs of Captain Robe Before & During the Battle of New Orleans: Written by Himself. Clinton Ross. LC 8-667. 1898. J. B. Lippincott Company.
Chamaco. Ralph J Erwin. LC 78-57627. (Illus.). 6.95. Erwin.
Chamber Music. Doris Grumbach. LC 78-13033. 8.95 (ISBN 0-525-07920-3). Dutton.
Chamber of Horrors: An Anthology of the Macabre in Words and Pictures 1st Amer. Ed. Ed. by John Hadfield. LC 65-15240. bds., 7.95. Little.
Chamber of Love: A Selection of the Complete Works, Edited by Wolfgang Kraus. Translated by Gertrude Flor. Giovanni Boccaccio. 1958. Philosophical Library.
Chamber Over the Gate. Margret Holmes Ernsperger Bates. LC 6-20958. 1886. C. A. Bates.
Chambered Tomb. Charlotte Hunt. (Ace gothic). 1975. (pbk.) 1.25. Ace Books.
Chambermaid's Diary. Octave Mirbeau & Tucker, Benjamin Ricketson, 1854- Tr. 1900. B. R. Tucker.
Chambre D'Hotel. Sidonie Gabrielle Colette. 1964. pap. 3.95 (1312). French & Eur.
Chambre Rouge. Francoise Mallet-Joris. 1968. pap. 1.10 o.s.i. Paris Pubns.
Chameleon. William Diehl. LC 81-40228. 13.95 (ISBN 0-394-51961-2). Random House.
Chameleon. Gathorne-Hardy, Jonathan. LC 67-23642. 1967. Walker.
Chameleon. James Weber Linn. LC 3-5783. 1903. McClure, Phillips & Co.
Chameleon. Edward L. Meyerson. 4.00 o.p. (ISBN 0-8283-1277-X). Branden.
Chameleon: A Mystery-Adventure Novel. Harry Stephen Keeler. LC 39-271719. 1939. E. P. Dutton & Co., Inc.
Chameleon Corps & Other Shape Changers. Ron Goulart. LC 73-183861. 1972. Macmillan.
Chameleon Course. Donald Seaman. LC 75-31796. 1976. 8.95 (ISBN 0-698-10722-5). Coward, McCann & Geoghegan.
Chameleon File. Leigh James. LC 67-20362. 1967. Weybright and Talley.
Chameleon: Or, The Mysterious Cruiser! Ingraham, Joseph Holt. 1848. Smith, Adams & Smith.
Chameleon Three: Garde Save the World. Jerry La Plante. (Orig.). 1980. pap. 1.95 (ISBN 0-89083-564-0). Zebra.
Chameleon Variant. Carol K Mack & David Ehrenfeld. LC 79-24886. 8.95 (ISBN 0-8037-1748-2). Dial Press.
Chameleons. John Broderick. 1961. 7.95 (ISBN 0-8392-1010-8). Astor-Honor.
Chameleons. David Levy. LC 64-19929. 1964. Dodd, Mead.
Chameleons: A Novel. John Broderick. LC 61-131799. I. Obolensky.
Chamiel. Edward Pearson. 1974. (pbk.) 0.95 (ISBN 0-671-77790-4). Pocket Books.
Champ. Ed. by Fotonovel Publications Staff. (Illus., Orig.). 1979. pap. 2.75. Fotonovel.
Champ: Novelized. Harry Sinclair Drago. LC 32-1642. A. L. Burt Company.
Champagne and a Gardener: A Little Maine Murder. Betty Jane Morison. LC 82-16787. 10.95 (ISBN 0-89621-069-3). Thorndike Press.
Champagne & Red Roses. Sheila Paulos. (Candlelight Ecstasy Ser.: No. 75). (Orig.). 1982. pap. 1.95 (ISBN 0-440-11262-1). Dell.
Champagne and Roses. Nancy Bacon. LC 81-22864. (Love & Life; 1). 1982. 1.75 (ISBN 0-345-29758-X). Ballantine Books.
Champagne Blues. Nan Lyons & Ivan Lyons. LC 78-31303. 9.95 (ISBN 0-671-24764-6). Simon and Schuster.
Champagne Charlie. John Franklin Carter. LC 50-8845. 1950. Duell, Sloan and Pearce.
Champagne for One. Rex Stout. 160p. 1980. pap. 1.95 (ISBN 0-553-13657-7). Bantam.
Champagne for One; a Nero Wolfe Mystery. Rex Stout. LC 58-13992. 1958. Viking Press.
Champagne in Sunshine. Elizabeth Frayne. LC 40-8419. 1939. Arcadia House Publictions.
Champagne Killer. Judson Pentecost Philips. LC 72-2342. (Red badge novel of suspense). 1972. 4.95 (ISBN 0-396-06611-9). Dodd, Mead.
Champagne Killer: A Julian Quist Mystery Novel. Hugh Pentecost. 194p. 1972. 4.95 o.p. (ISBN 0-396-06611-9). Dodd.
Champagne Secretary. Millicent Kent. LC 35-3810. W. Godwin.

Champavert: Seven Bitter Tales, by Petrus Borel, the Lycanthrope. Translated from the French by Tom Moran. Petrus Pierre Joseph Borel D'Hauterive Borel. LC 60-359. 3.00. Indigo Press W. North Ave.

Champdoce Mystery. Emile Gaboriau. (secret service series. no. 43). 1891. Street & Smith.

Champdoce Mystery: Tr. from the French of Emile Gaboriau. Emile Gaboriau. LC 13-8318. 1913. 1.50. C. Scribner's Sons.

Champion. John Colin Dane. LC 7-15596. 1907. G. W. Dillingham Company.

Champion. Mary Noailles Murfree. LC 2-16924. 1902. Houghton, Mifflin and Company.

Champion from Far Away. Ben Hecht. LC 31-33894. 1931. Covici, Friede.

Champion in the Seventies. Edith A Barnett. LC 6-7203. 1898. H. S. Stone & Co.

Champion of Liberty: The Story of Roger Williams. Norman Eugene Nygaard. LC 63-17750. 1964. Zondervan Pub. House.

Champion of Sourwood Mountain. Billy C. Clark. (Illus.). (YA) 1966. 4.95 o.p. Putnam.

Champion Road. Tilsley, Frank. LC 50-9977. 1950. Messner.

Champions & the All Americans. Jerry L. Preas. (Illus.). 1979. pap. 4.95x. Texan-Am Pub.

Champions of Freedom, or: The Mysterious Chief, a Romance of the Nineteenth Century, Founded on the Events of the War, Between the United States and Great Britain. by samuel woodworth... ed. Samuel Woodworth. LC 8-37792. 1816. Printed and Published by Charles N. Baldwin, Bookseller, No. Division-Street.

Champions of Freedom; or, the Mysterious Chief, 2 vols. Samuel Woodworth. LC 78-64108. Repr. of 1816 ed. 75.00 set (ISBN 0-404-17450-7). AMS Pr.

Champions of Love. Victor D'Andorra. 1970. pap. 1.50 o.p. (ISBN 0-87067-403-X, 88-403). Holloway.

Champlain Monster. Jeff Danziger. (Illus.). 64p. 1981. pap. 3.95 (ISBN 0-9603900-7-3). Lanser Pr.

Champlain Road. Franklin Davey McDowell. The Bruce Publishing Company.

Chan Osborne's Wife. Louise Platt Hauck. LC 38-128468. The Penn Publishing Company.

Chance. Joseph Conrad. LC 57-338819. (Doubleday anchor books, A113). 1957. N. Y., Doubleday.

Chance. Joseph Conrad. LC 29-307621. 1914. Doubleday, Page & Company.

Chance. Sara McAulay. LC 81-15664. 1982. 12.50 (ISBN 0-394-51869-1). Knopf.

Chance. Carol L. Symms. 1970. 3.50 o.p. Vantage.

Chance--and the Woman: A Romance. Ellis Middleton. LC 24-30781. 1924. Frederick A. Stokes Company.

Chance: A Tale in Two Parts. Joseph Conrad. LC 75-320055. (Penguin modern classics). 1974. 0.60 (ISBN 0-14-003821-3). Penguin.

Chance: A Tale in Two Parts. Joseph Conrad. LC 18-21354. 1913. Doubleday, Page & Company.

Chance: A Tale in Two Parts. Joseph Conrad. LC 22-106442. 1921. Doubleday, Page & Company.

Chance Acquaintance. William Dean Howells. LC 71-98765. 1970. Greenwood Press.

Chance Acquaintance. William Dean Howells. LC 76-92320. (Selected edition of W. D. Howells, v. 6). (Illus.). 1971. 8.50 (ISBN 0-253-31335-X). Indiana University Press.

Chance Acquaintance. William Dean Howells. LC 76-104493. 1970. Literature House.

Chance Acquaintance. William Dean Howells. LC 79-131749. (Illus.). 1970. Scholarly Press.

Chance Acquaintance. William Dean Howells. LC 1-1655. 1873. J. R. Osgood & Co.

Chance Acquaintance. William Dean Howells. LC 4-154566. Houghton, Mifflin and Company.

Chance Acquaintance. William Dean Howells. LC 43-36859. 1886. Houghton, Mifflin and Company.

Chance Awakening. George Markstein. LC 78-17501. 1978. 7.95 (ISBN 0-345-27717-1). Ballantine Books.

Chance Child: Comrades, Hendrex and Margotte, and Persephone. Marah Ellis Martin Ryan. LC 8-1353. 1896. Rand, McNally & Company.

Chance Discovery: Or, A Woman's Desperate Dilemma. John Russell Coryell. (On cover: Shield series, no. 35). Street & Smith.

Chance Encounters. Maxwell Struthers Burt. LC 21-167942. 1921. C. Scribner's Sons.

Chance for Glory. 1st Ed. Constance Wright. LC 57-6197. 1957. Holt.

Chance for Love. Iris Bromige. (Beagle romance#36). 1975. (pbk.) 0.95 (ISBN 0-345-26712-5). Ballantine Books.

Chance Fortune. Bill Starr. 352p. (Orig.). 1981. pap. 2.75 (ISBN 0-523-41141-3). Pinnacle Bks.

Chance Has a Whip. Raymond Peckham Holden. LC 35-185669. 1935. C. Scribner's Sons.

Chance in Chains: A Story of Monte Carlo. Cyril Arthur Ranger Gull. LC 14-4933. 1914. 1.00. Sturgis & Walton Company.

Chance McGraw. Mary L. Manning, pseud. (Orig.). 1980. pap. 2.75 (ISBN 0-440-11523-X). Dell.

Chance Marriage. From the French of Emile Gaboriau. Emile Gaboriau. Tr. by Calfa, Vincenzo. 1878. Printed for the Translator.

Chance Medley of Light Matter. Thomas Colley Grattan. LC 6-45434. (On cover: Library of select novels, no. 59). 1845. Harper & Brothers.

Chance Meeting. Kay Thorpe. (Harlequin Romance Ser.). 192p. 1980. pap. 1.50 (ISBN 0-373-10378-6, Pub. by Harlequin). PB.

Chance of a Lifetime. Grace Livingston Hill. LC 75-33029. 1975. 9.95 (ISBN 0-89190-005-5). American Reprint Co.

Chance of a Lifetime. Grace Livingston Hill. LC 31-27217. 1931. J. B. Lippincott Company.

Chance of Morning. John Jeffords. (Orig.). 1979. pap. 2.50 (ISBN 0-89083-530-6). Zebra.

Chance the Winds of Fortune. Laurie McBain. 416p. 1980. pap. 3.95 (ISBN 0-380-75796-6, 82545-7). Avon.

Chance to Kill. Elizabeth Linington. LC 67-19247. 1967. Morrow.

Chance to Kill. Dell Shannon. 1971. pap. 0.75 o.p. (T2388). Pyramid Pubns.

Chance to Live. Bess A. Balcob. 1978. 4.95 (ISBN 0-533-01828-5). Vantage.

Chance to Live. Zoe Beckley. LC 18-21376. 1918. The Macmillan Company.

Chance to Sit Down. Meredith Daneman. (Signet Book, Y5464). 1973. 1.25. New American Lib.

Chance to Sit Down. Meredith Daneman. LC 76-175362. 1972. 5.95. Doubleday.

Chance to Sit Down. Meredith Daneman. 1981. 2.25 (ISBN 0-380-54163-7). Avon Books.

Chance Tomorrow. Dixie Browning. 192p. 1981. pap. 1.50 (ISBN 0-671-57053-6). S&S.

Chancellor. Jules Verne. 3.95. Assoc Bk.

Chancellor Manuscript. Robert Ludlum. LC 76-57768. 1977. 8.95 (ISBN 0-8037-1274-X). Dial Press.

Chancellor of Mars: A Novel. Jay Moon. LC 78-107201. 8.00 (ISBN 0-682-49075-X). Exposition Press.

Chancellor. 1st Ed. Lawrence L Schoonover. LC 60-11648. 1961. Little, Brown.

Chances. Jackie Collins. (Orig.). 1982. 14.95 (ISBN 0-446-51237-0); pap. 3.95 (ISBN 0-446-30268-6). Warner Bks.

Chances. Arthur Hamilton Gibbs. LC 30-15406. 1930. Little, Brown, and Company.

Chances and Changes. Charles Burdett. LC 79-76921. (American fiction reprint series). 1969. Books for Libraries Press.

Chances We Take. Richard Goldhurst. LC 79-108971. 1970. 5.95. R. W. Baron Pub. Co.

Chancy. Louis L'Amour. 176p. (Orig.). 1973. pap. 1.95 (ISBN 0-553-14126-0). Bantam.

Chandler. William Denbow. (Belmont Tower Book). 1977. 1.50 (ISBN 0-505-51169-X). Tower Pubns.

Chandler Heritage. Ben Haas. LC 74-156148. 1973. (671-78256-8) 1.25. Pocket Books.

Chandler Policy. Doris Miles Disney. LC 75-156881. (Red mask mystery). 1971. 4.95. Putnam.

Chandos. Louise De La Ramee. LC 4-656. (seaside library, v. 3, no. 59). 1877. G. Munro.

Chandos... Louise De La Ramee. LC 6-33372. (Lovell's library, no. 1228). 1888. J. W. Lovell Company.

Chandos: A Novel. Louise De La Ramee. LC 4-875. 1875. J. B. Lippincott & Co.

Chandos. A Novel. Louise De La Ramee. (On cover: Seaside library. Pocket ed. no. 1003). 1887. G. Munro.

Chane) 0ge of Climiate. Stanley Kauffmann. LC 54-8253. 1954. Rinehart.

Chaney's Stratagem. Hannah Courtney Pinnix. LC 9-28952. 1909. The C. M. Clark Publishing Company.

Chaneysville Incident. David Bradley. LC 80-8225. 480p. 1981. 12.95i (ISBN 0-06-010491-0, HarpT). Har-Row.

Chaneysville Incident. David Bradley. 456p. 1982. pap. 3.50 (ISBN 0-380-58586-3, 58586). Avon.

Change, and Other Short Stories About Contemporary Alaska. Charles J Keim. LC 77-150138. (Illus.). 10.00. Alaska Methodist University Press.

Change for the Better. uniform ed. Susan Hill. LC 76-381834. 1976. 3.50 (ISBN 0-241-89410-7). Hamilton.

Change for the Worse. Elizabeth Lemarchand. LC 80-52079. (Illus.). 1981. 9.95 (ISBN 0-8027-5429-5). Walker.

Change Here for Happiness. Berta Ruck. LC 33-16064. 1933. Dodd, Mead & Company.

Change in the Wind. Leslie Waller. LC 79-96281. 1969. 5.95. Bernard Geis Associates.

Change of Air. Katharine Fullerton Gerould. LC 17-25861. 1917. 1.25. C. Scribner's Sons.

Change of Air. Anthony Hope Hawkins. LC 7-2620. 1894. H. Holt and Company.

Change of Air. Anthony Hope Hawkins. (On cover: Seaside library. Pocket ed., no. 2097). 1895. G. Munro's Sons.

Change of Face. Aaron Binder. 1974. (pbk.) 1.50 (ISBN 0-523-00350-1). Pinnacle Books.

Change of Gods. 1st Ed. Neal Oxenhandler. LC 62-167278. 1962. Harcourt, Brace & World.

Change of Heart. Faith Baldwin. 1974. Repr. of 1944 ed. lib. bdg. 15.45x (ISBN 0-88411-606-9). Amereon Ltd.

Change of Heart. Faith Baldwin. 1980. pap. 2.95 (ISBN 0-671-41762-2). PB.

Change of Heart. Ursula Bloom. 1979. pap. 2.25 (ISBN 0-89041-252-9, 3252). Major Bks.

Change of Heart. Michel Butor. 260p. pap. 6.95 (ISBN 0-941324-04-4). Van Vactor & Goodheart.

Change of Heart. LC 72-7642. (Red badge novel of suspense). 1973. 4.95 (ISBN 0-396-06716-6). Dodd, Mead.

Change of Heart. Laura Chapman. LC 75-33358. 7.95 (ISBN 0-525-07938-6). Dutton.

Change of Heart. Laura Chapman. 1977. 1.50 (ISBN 0-380-00977-3). Avon.

Change of Heart. Leona Collier. (Orig.). 1981. pap. 1.75 (ISBN 0-8439-8028-1, Tiara Bks). Nordon Pubns.

Change of Heart. Faith Baldwin Cuthrell. LC 74-82145. 1974. Aeonian Press.

Change of Heart. Faith Baldwin Cuthrell. LC 44-7189. 1944. Farrar & Rinehart, Inc.

Change of Heart. Faith Baldwin Cuthrell. LC 46-3481. 1944. Grosset & Dunlap.

Change of Heart. Harold Adam Ehrensperger. LC 54-6189. 1954. Friendship Press.

Change of Heart. Grace M Hendron. LC 72-5231. (Red rose romance, 130). 1972. 0.75. Bantam Books.

Change of Heart. Adelaide Humphries. LC 49-2291. 1949. Arcadia House.

Change of Heart. Ed. by Earl Jones. LC 81-80157. 128p. text ed. 9.95 (ISBN 0-86666-014-3). GWP.

Change of Heart. Helen McCloy. 194p. 1973. 4.95 o.p. (ISBN 0-396-06716-6). Dodd.

Change of Heart. Helen McCloy. 1974. (pbk.) 0.75. Dell.

Change of Heart. Sally Mandel. LC 79-24693. 9.95 (ISBN 0-440-01475-1). Delacorte Press.

Change of Heart. Sally Mandel. 1981. pap. 2.95 (ISBN 0-440-11355-5). Dell.

Change of Heart see Passing Time.

Change of Heart: Six Love Stories. Margaret Sutton Briscoe Hopkins. LC 3-21298. 1903. Harper & Brothers.

Change of Heart. Translated from the French by Jean Stewart. Michel Butor. LC 59-7261. 1959. Simon and Schuster.

Change of Hearts. Elizabeth Frayne. LC 38-1584. 1937. Arcadia House.

Change of Heir. Michael Innes, pseud. (Red Badge Mystery Ser). 1966. 3.50 o.p. (ISBN 0-396-05396-3). Dodd.

Change of Heir: By Michael Innes. John Innes Mackintosh Stewart. LC 66-22907. (Red badge mystery). 1966. bds., 3.50. Dodd.

Change of Idols. John Taintor Foote. LC 35-127667. 1935. D. Appleton-Century Company, Incorporated.

Change of Light and Other Stories. Julio Cortazar. LC 80-7656. 1980. 10.95 (ISBN 0-394-50721-5). Knopf.

Change of Love. Vivienne Koch. LC 60-9043. 1960. McDowell, Obolensky.

Change of Mind. Chris Stratton. (Orig.). 1969. pap. 0.75 o.p. (T2084). Pyramid Pubns.

Change of Opinion. John Rupert Farrell. LC 20-3711. R. G. Badger.

Change of Plea. Camilla R Bittle. LC 63-20383. 1964. Lippincott.

Change of Scene. Elizabeth Cullinan. LC 81-18875. 10.95 (ISBN 0-393-01568-8). Norton.

Change of Season. Ilya Ehrenburg. 1962. 5.95 o.p. Knopf.

Change of Skin. Carlos Fuentes. LC 67-15015. 1968. Farrer, Straus & Giroux.

Change Partners. Peggy Smith Shane. LC 34-1467. 1934. R. Long & R. R. Smith.

Change Partners: A Vagabondage. Horace Annesley Vachell. LC 23-700413. George H. Doran Company.

Change Song. Lee Hoffman. LC 78-171298. (Doubleday science fiction). 1972. 4.95. Doubleday.

Change the Sky and Other Stories. Margaret St. Clair. (Ace science fiction). 1974. (pbk.) 0.95. Ace Books.

Change War. Fritz Leiber. LC 78-21479. (Gregg Press Science Fiction Series). 1978. 15.00 (ISBN 0-8398-2493-9). Gregg Press.

Change with the Seasons: A Novel. Duncan Cumming. LC 6-31941. 1897. The Dunsmuir Publishing Co.

Changed Brides. Emma Dorothy Eliza Nevitte Southworth. LC 4-22054. 1869. T. B. Peterson & Brothers.

Changed Brides; or, Winning Her Way. Emma Dorothy Eliza Nevitte Southworth. LC 4-8636. 1884. T. B. Peterson.

Changed M? N. Jody Ayers. LC 72-94208. (Pic epic). (Illus.). 1973. (pbk.) 1.95 (ISBN 0-913562-00-9). Rocking Chair Press.

Changed Man. Jody Ayers & Lynn H. Rogers. LC 72-94208. (Pic Epic Ser.). 172p. 1973. pap. 1.95 (ISBN 0-913562-00-9). Rocking Chair Pr.

Changed Man: The Waiting Supper, and Other Tales, Concluding with The Romantic Adventures of a Milkmaid. Thomas Hardy. LC 13-22815. 1913. Harper & Brothers.

Changed Man: The Waiting Supper, and Other Tales, Concluding with The Romantic Adventures of a Milkmaid. Thomas Hardy. LC 24-24991. Harper & Brothers.

Changed Man: Waiting Supper & Other Tales. Thomas Hardy. 1913. 8.25 o.p. (ISBN 0-312-12915-7). St Martin.

Changeling. Margaret Higgins. (Ace gothic read easy large type). 1973. (pbk.) 0.95. Ace Books.

Changeling. Alfred Elton Van Vogt. 1976. pap. 0.95 o.p. Woodhill.

Changeling. Alfred Elton Van Vogt. 1979. pap. 1.25 (ISBN 0-532-12589-4). Woodhill.

Changeling. Alfred Elton Van Vogt. 1976. pap. 0.95 o.p. Manor Bks.

Changeling. 3rd ed. Alfred Elton Van Vogt. (O.s.i.). 96p. 1974. pap. 0.75 o.s.i. (532-75521-075). Manor Bks.

Changeling. Joy Williams. LC 76-507871. 1978. 7.95 (ISBN 0-385-08154-5). Doubleday.

Changeling. Joy Williams. LC 78-11336. 1978. 7.95 (ISBN 0-385-08154-5). Doubleday.

Changeling. Mary Wilson. 1975. (pbk.) 0.95. Dell.

Changeling. Roger Zelazny. 272p. (Orig.). 1981. pap. 2.50 (ISBN 0-441-10257-3). Ace Bks.

Changeling: A Novel. Walter Besant. LC 12-31391. F. A. Stokes Company.

Changeling, and Other Stories. Donn Bryne. LC 23-13454. The Century Co.

Changeling Conspiracy: A Novel of Suspense. Helen McCloy. LC 76-25862. (Red badge novel of suspense). 6.95 (ISBN 0-396-07370-0). Dodd, Mead.

Changeling Earth. Fred Saberhagen. (Orig.). 1973. pap. 0.95 o.p. (UQ1041). Daw Bks.

Changelings: By Jo Sinclair Pseud. Ruth Seid. LC 55-955354. 1955. McGraw-Hill.

Changes. Ed. by Michael Bishop & Ian Watson. 320p. (Orig.). pap. 2.75 (ISBN 0-441-10260-3). Ace Bks.

Changes. Richard Perry. LC 73-13224. 1974. 6.95 (ISBN 0-672-51850-3). Bobbs-Merrill.

Changes: A Psycho-Visual Novel. Matt Howarth. LC 78-14397. 9.80. (ISBN 0-89471-051-6) (ISBN 0-89471-050-8). Running Press.

Changes of Venue: Fourteen Stories and Sketches of and from Sundry Places. James Everhart Whinnery. LC 21-8169. 1919. The Author, J. E. Whinnery.

Changing All Those Changes. James P. Girard. Ed. by Al Young. LC 76-11428. 1976. pap. 3.95 (ISBN 0-918412-01-3). Yardbird Wing.

Changing Land. Roger Zelany. 224p. 1981. pap. 2.50 (ISBN 0-345-25389-2, Del Rey). Ballantine.

Changing Light at Sandover. James Merrill. LC 81-70062. (Illus.). 512p. 1982. 25.00 (ISBN 0-689-11282-3); pap. 12.95 (ISBN 0-689-11283-1). Atheneum.

Changing of the Guard. John Ehle. 1.75 (ISBN 0-380-00858-0). Avon.

Changing of the Guard: A Novel. John Ehle. LC 74-9083. 1974. (ISBN 0-394-49499-7). Random House.

Changing of the Guard: A Novel. John Scholl. LC 63-16028. 1963. Simon and Schuster.

Changing Partners. Vicky Martin, pseud. 288p. 1981. pap. 2.75 (ISBN 0-445-04675-9). Popular Lib.

Changing Partners. Vicky Matin. LC 79-26743. 10.95 (ISBN 0-312-12965-3). St. Martin's Press.

Changing Patterns: A Novel... William Dana Orcutt. LC 33-298026. 1933. Dodd, Mead & Company.

Changing Pilots. Ruby Mildred Ayres. LC 22-22212. 1932. Doubleday, Doran & Company, Inc.

Changing Places. David Lodge. (Orig.). 1979. pap. 3.95 (ISBN 0-14-004656-9). Penguin.

Changing Pulse of Madame Touraine. Archibald Clavering Gunter. LC 6-6259. The Home Publishing Company.

Changing Road. Harold MacGrath. LC 28-7949. 1928. Doubleday, Doran & Company, Inc.

Changing Seasons. Maurice Barker. LC 65-27565. 1965. Dorrance.

Changing States. Barbara Rogan. LC 80-2061. 1981. 10.95. Doubleday.

Changing the Past. Laurie Taylor. LC 81-83881. (Minnesota Voices Project Ser.: No. 6). (Illus.). 72p. 1981. pap. 3.00 (ISBN 0-89823-029-2). New Rivers Pr.

Changing Tide. Sebastian B. Gilleto. (Fictional Ser.). 246p. 1981. Leatherette cover 4.00. Intl Print.

Changing Tide. large print ed. Sylvia Thorpe. LC 83-1954. 1983. 11.95 (ISBN 0-89340-600-7). J. Curley.

Changing Tide. Sylvia Thorpe. 1978. pap. 1.75 (ISBN 0-449-23418-5, Crest). Fawcett.

Changing Winds: A Novel. St. John Greer Ervine. LC 17-9813. 1917. The Macmillan Company.

Changing Winds: A Novel. St. John Greer Ervine. LC 42-290213. 1920. The Macmillan Company.

Changing World of Anthony Trollope. Robert M Polhemus. LC 68-16111. 1968. University of California Press.

Changing World of Charles Dickens. Robert Giddings. LC 83-3769. (Critical studies). 1983. 26.50 (ISBN 0-389-20372-6). Barnes & Noble Books.

Changing Years. Denise Robins. 224p. 1974. pap. 0.95 o.p. (26601-3-095). Beagle Bks.

Changing Years. Denise Robins. (Beagle romance, 28). 1974. (pbk.) 0.95 (ISBN 0-345-26601-3). Beagle Books.

Channay Syndicate. Edward Phillips Oppenheim. LC 27-1237. 1927. Little, Brown, and Company.

Channel Assault. Kenneth Royce. LC 82-7132. 1982. 13.95 (ISBN 0-07-054172-8). McGraw-Hill.

Channel Fever. Barney Goldberg. LC 66-28190. 1967. 4.95. Jonah.

Channel Shore. Charles Bruce. LC 55-5225. 1955. St. Martin's Press.

Channel X Short-Short Stories. Ed. by Laclan P. MacDonald. 1982. pap. 5.95 (ISBN 0-914598-52-X). Padre Prods.

Channel's Destiny. Jean Lorrah & Jacqueline Lichtenberg. LC 80-2421. (Gen Series). 1982. 10.95 (ISBN 0-385-17028-9). Doubleday.

Channing Comes Through. Charles Alden Seltzer. LC 25-19168. The Century Co.

Channings. Ellen Price Wood. LC 68-12385. (Doughty library, no. 5). 1968. Stein and Day.

Channings. Ellen Price Henry Wood Wood. (Seaside library, v. 15, no. 288). 1878. G. Munro.

Channings. Ellen Price Henry Wood Wood. (Half-title: Everyman's library, ed. by Ernest Rhys. Fiction). 1906. J. M. Dent & Co.

Channings. Ellen Price Henry Wood Wood. LC 36-37094. (Half-title: Everyman's library, ed. by Ernest Rhys. Fiction. (no. 84). 1924. J. M. Dent & Sons, Ltd.

Channings of Everleigh. Margaret Maitland, pseud. (Belmont Tower Books). 1977. 1.95 (ISBN 0-505-51199-1). Tower Pubns.

Chan's Wife: A Story. Jessie Anderson Chase. LC 19-15220. 1919. Marshall Jones Company.

Chant d'Amour see Oeuvres Completes.

Chant de la Montagne see Oeuvres Romanesques.

Chant of Jimmie Blacksmith. Thomas Keneally. 1973. (pbk.) 1.25 (ISBN 0-345-23558-4). Ballantine.

Chant of Jimmie Blacksmith. Thomas Keneally. LC 70-186732. 1972. 6.50 (ISBN 0-670-21165-6). Viking Press.

Chant of the Hawk: By John & Margaret Harris. John Harris & Margaret Plumlee Harris. LC 59-5718. 1959. Random House.

Chant of the Night: An Indian Mission Story. Cornelius Kuipers. LC 36-7004. 1934. Zondervan Publishing House.

Chantal. Claire Lorimer. 480p. (Orig.). 1981. pap. 2.95 (ISBN 0-553-13992-4). Bantam.

Chantemesle: By Robin Fedden. Henry Romilly Fedden. LC 66-15543. 1966. 4.00. Braziller.

Chanters Chase. Jill Tattersall. 1979. pap. 1.95 (ISBN 0-449-23839-3, Crest). Fawcett.

Chanters Chase: A Novel. Jill Tattersall. LC 77-10910. 1978. 7.95 (ISBN 0-688-03262-1). Morrow.

Chantey of the Keys. Lydia P De Bechevet. LC 36-8972. 1936. The Caxton Printers, Ltd.

Chantic Bird. David Ireland. LC 68-17331. 1968. Scribner.

Chanticleer: A Pastoral Romance. illustrated by w. granville smith. ed. Violette Hall. 1902. Lothrop Publishing Company.

Chanticleer: A Thanksgiving Story of the Peabody Family. 2d ed. Cornelius Mathews. LC 7-17926. 1850. B. B. Mussey & Co.

Chanticleer: a Thanksgiving Story of the Peabody Family. Cornelius Mathews. LC 7-17925. (On cover: Loomis' illuminated classics, v. 1). Brown, Loomis & Co.

Chanticleer: a Thanksgiving Story of the Peabody Family. Cornelius Mathews. LC 7-17927. The American News Company.

Chanticleer's Muffled Crow. Amber Dean. 1945. Pub. for the Crime Club by Doubleday, Doran & Co., Inc.

Chantilly. Betty Hale Hyatt. (Candlelight Regency). 1973. 0.75. Dell.

Chanting of Children. Margaret Sand. LC 77-10104. 8.95 (ISBN 0-698-10859-0). Coward, McCann & Geoghegan.

Chanting Wheels: A Novel. Hubbard Hutchinson. LC 22-589474. 1922. 1.75. G. P. Putnam's Sons.

Chantry House. Charlotte Mary Yonge. (On cover: Seaside library. Pocket ed. no. 788). 1886. G. Munro.

Chantry Priest of Barnet: A Tale of the Two Roses. Alfred John Church. Dodd, Mead and Company.

Chaos & Night. Henri De Montherlant. 1964. 4.95 o.p. (53084). Macmillan.

Chaos & Night. Henry De Montherlant, pseud. 1968. pap. 2.45 o.p. (ISBN 0-448-00218-3, UL). G&D.

Chaos and Night: A Novel. Henry De Montherlant. LC 64-21757. 1964. Macmillan.

Chaos Below Heaven. Eugene Vale. LC 64-19235. 1966. Doubeday.

Chaos et la Nuit. Henri De Montherlant. (Coll. Soleil). 1963. 13.25. French & Eur.

Chaos Fighters. Robert Moore Williams. LC 55-22310. (Ace books, S-90). 1955. Ace Books.

Chaos Is Come Again. Claude Houghton Oldfield. LC 32-260701. 1932. Doubleday, Doran & Company, Inc.

Chaos Weapon. Colin Kapp. LC 77-3393. (Del Rey book). 1977. 1.50 (ISBN 0-345-27115-7). Ballantine Books.

Chaparral and Oranges. Joe Clay Wilson. LC 38-35015. 1938. The Naylor Company.

Chaparral Marauders. Thomas Albert Curry. 1970. pap. 0.60 o.p. (06093). Curtis.

Chaparral Trail. Lauran Paine. LC 68-17. 1967. Arcadia House.

Chapayeca. G. C Edmondson. LC 71-150887. (Doubleday science fiction). 1971. 4.95. Doubleday.

Chapayev. Dmitrii Andreevich Furmanov. LC 72-90294. 1973. (ISBN 0-88355-004-0). Hyperion Press.

Chapel Lyrics of Faith, Hope and Love. Lincoln Hulley. LC 25-16158. E. O. Painter Printing Co.

Chapel of Saint-Christophe: A Novel. Boris Sokoloff. LC 62-6491. 1962. Vantage Press.

Chapel of St. Mary. Clara M Thompson. LC 6-38137. 1861. J. E. Tilton and Company.

Chapel Road. Louis Paul Boon. LC 72-153455. (Library of Netherlandic literature, v. 1). 1972. Twayne Publishers.

Chapel, the Story of a Welsh Family. Miles Lewis. LC 16-17185. 1916. George H. Doran Company.

Chaperon. Charles Norris Williamson & Alice Muriel Livingston Williamson. LC 12-15955. 1912. A. L. Burt Company.

Chaperone. Ethel Edison Gordon. LC 72-87590. 1972. 6.95 (ISBN 0-698-10492-7). Coward, McCann & Geoghegan.

Chaperone. Ethel Edison Gordon. 1974. (pbk.) 1.25. Dell.

Chaperone. William Hegner. 1975. (pbk.) 1.50 (ISBN 0-671-80153-8). Pocket Books.

Chaperoned; a Brief Page from a Summer Romance. Albert Ulmann. LC 8-32293. (On cover: The "unknown" library no. 32). The Cassell Publishing Co.

Chaperoning Adrienne: A Tale of the Yellowstone National Park. Alice Harriman Browne. LC 7-24787. Metropolitan Press.

Chapin Sisters. Fynette Rowe. LC 45-9779. 1945. Current Books, Inc., A. A. Wyn.

Chaplain of the Chaplain of the Fleet. A Novel. Walter Besant & Rice, James. (Seaside library, v. 54, no. 1104). 1881. G. Munro.

Chaplain of the Fleet. library ed. Walter Besant & Rice, James. LC 3-28169. 1888. Dodd, Mead & Company.

Chaplain of the Fleet. A Novel. Walter Besant & Rice, James. (Franklin square library, no. 185). 1881. Harper & Brothers.

Chaplain on Bourbon St. Bob Harrington & Walter Wagner. 1971. pap. 1.25 o.p. (V2535). Pyramid Pubns.

Chaplain's Craze: Being the Mystery of Findon Friars. George Manville Fenn. LC 6-39261. (Harper's handy series, no. 101). 1886. Harper & Brothers.

Chaplain's Daughter. Misunderstood and Jascha. Bertha Behrens. Tr. by Kate Dykers. LC 6-3765. (On cover: The Marguerite series. 19). E. A. Weeks & Company.

Chaplains Raid. Richards L Hardman. LC 65-13272. 1965. Coward-McCann.

Chaplains Raid: By Ric Hardman. Richards L Hardman. (H3141). 1966. Bantam.

Chaplet of Grace. Basil Partridge. LC 56-570464. 1956. Westminster Press.

Chaplet of Pearls. Charlotte Mary Yonge. LC 4-16852. 1903. Macmillan and Co., Limited.

Chaplet of Pearls: Or, The White and Black Ribaumont. Charlotte Mary Yonge. 1869. D. Appleton and Company.

Chaplet of Pearls: Or, The White and Black Ribaumont. Charlotte Mary Yonge. Ed. by R. D. Chamberlin. LC 26-141009. L. C. Page & Company.

Chaplet of Pearls: Or, The White and Black Ribaumont a Romance of French History, 1572. Charlotte Mary Yonge. (On cover: Seaside library. Pocket ed. no. 790). 1886. G. Munro.

Chapman. Havelock Ellis. 1934. 20.00 (ISBN 0-8274-2024-2). R West.

Chapman Report. Irving Wallace. LC 60-11476. 1960. Simon and Schuster.

Chapman's Homer: the Iliad, the Odyssey: And the Lesser Homerica. Edited, with Introductions, Textual Notes, Commentaries, and Glossaries, by Allardyce Nicoll. Homerus. Tr. by George Chapman. LC 55-10027. (Bollingen Series, 41). 1956. Pantheon Books.

Chappie and Me: An Autobiographical Novel. John Craig. LC 79-664. 8.95 (ISBN 0-396-07660-2). Dodd, Mead.

Chaps and Chukkers. Joseph Bushnell Ames. LC 26-556237. 1928. The Century Co.

Chapter Seven: From The Hour of the Bell: a Novel Concerning the Greek War of Independence. Harry Mark Petrakis. LC 77-358626. (Illus.). Perishable Press.

Chapter the Last. Knut Hamsun & Chater, Arthur G., Tr. LC 29-18548. 1929. A. A. Knopf.

Chapters for the Orthodox. Don Marquis. LC 74-130066. (Short story index reprint series). 1970. Books for Libraries Press.

Chapters in the History of Actors and Acting in Ancient Greece. Together with a Prosopographia Histrionum Graecorum. John Bartholomew O'Connor. LC 65-21095. 1966. Haskell House.

Chapters on Wives. Sarah Stickney Ellis. LC 6-37850. 1860. Harper & Brother.

Character. Samuel Smiles. (Harper's Franklin square library, no. 612). 1887. Harper & Brothers.

Character: A Novel of Father & Son. Ferdinand Bordewijk. Tr. by E. M. Price. 1966. 12.95 (ISBN 0-7206-1611-5). Dufour.

Character and Situation: Six Short Stories. Christopher Sykes. LC 50-9929. 1950. Knopf.

Character Assassins: The Story of a Branded Schoolgirl and of a Long, Agonizing Legal Struggle to Rehabilitate Her Reputation. Ezra Josephs. LC 66-28358. 1966. Reportorial Press.

Character Readings from "George Eliot," Selected and Arranged. George Eliot & Sheppard, Nathan, 1834-1898. LC 7-3108. (Harper's Franklin square library, no. 293). 1883. Harper & Brothers.

Character Sketches: The Tremendous Adventures of Major Gehagan; and History of the French Revolution. William Makepeace Thackeray. LC 8-28248. (On cover: Lovell's library, v. 6, no. 303). 1883. J. W. Lovell Company.

Characteristics: A Novel. Silas Weir Mitchell. LC 4-15133. 1892. The Century Co.

Characters in Order of Appearance: A Novel. Romilly Cavan. LC 38-16582. 1938. The Macmillan Company.

Characters of Steel and Steel... George W Grice. LC 38-24559.

Characters of Steel and Steel. George W Grice. LC 40-7417. The Christopher Publishing House.

Charade. Edita Morris. LC 48-4570. 1948. Viking Press.

Charade. Rebecca Stratton. (Harlequin Romances Ser.). 192p. 1982. pap. 1.50 (ISBN 0-373-02508-4). Harlequin Bks.

Charade for Happiness: A Novel of Ballet Life, by Daniel Arensky and Arthur Cummings. Drawings by Tricia Davis. 1st Ed. Daniel Arensky & Arthur J. Cummings. LC 57-7648. 1957. Exposition Press.

Charades. Jane Austen. 1977. 16.50. Porter.

Charbonneau, Man of Two Dreams: A Novel. Winfred Blevins. LC 74-83043. 1975. 8.95 (ISBN 0-8402-1358-1). Nash Pub.

Charca (The Pond) Manuel Zeno-Gandia. Tr. by Kal Wagenheim from Span. 250p. 1983. 18.95 (ISBN 0-943862-03-5); pap. 10.00 (ISBN 0-943862-04-3). Waterfront NJ.

Charco Harbour: A Novel of Unknown Seas and a Fabled Shore Passaged with Coral Reefs and Magnetical Islands, of Shipwreck and a Lonely Haven; the True Story of the Last of the Great Navigators, His Bark, and the Men in Her. Godfrey Blunden. LC 68-8083. (Illus.). 1968. 6.95 (ISBN 0-8149-0001-1). Vanguard Press.

Charcoal Horse: A Novel. Edward Loomis. LC 59-8210. 1959. A. Swallow.

Charcoal Sketches: Or, Scenes in a Metropolis. Joseph Clay Neal. LC 6-15469. 1838. E. L. Carey and A. Hart.

Charcoal Sketches: Or, Scenes in a Metropolis. 6th ed. Joseph Clay Neal. LC 7-23106. 1841. E. L. Carey and A. Hart.

Charcoal Sketches; Stories of the Present-Day Southern Negro. Katharine Scott Graves Ayres. LC 72-6512. (Black Heritage Library Collection). 1972. (ISBN 0-8369-9156-7). Books for Libraries Press.

Charcoal Sketches: Stories of the Present-Day Southern Negro. Katharine Scott Graves Ayres. LC 26-4242. 1927. The J. W. Burke Company.

Charcoal's World. Hugh A. Dempsey. LC 79-14920. (Illus.). x, 178p. 1979. 11.95 (ISBN 0-8032-1651-3); pap. 3.95 (ISBN 0-8032-6552-2, BB 717, Bison). U of Nebr Pr.

Charette: A Tale "of Lovers' Sorrows and Their Tangled Sin"... Robert F. Sage. LC 8-3398. 1875. G. W. Carleton & Co.; Etc., Etc.

Charge...! Bill Amidon. LC 74-142475. 1971. 9.95. Bobbs-Merrill.

Charge for France, and Other Stories. John Heard. LC 7-5048. (On cover: Harper's Franklin square library, no. 72). 1892. Harper & Brothers.

Charge It" Or, Keeping up with Harry; a Story of Fashionable Extravagance and of the Successful Efforts to Restrain It Made by the Honorable Socrates Potter, the Genial Friend of Lizzie. Irving Bacheller. LC 12-20561. 1912. Harper & Brothers.

Charge Nurse. Patricia Rae. 368p. (Orig.). 1980. pap. 2.50 (ISBN 0-89083-663-9). Zebra.

Charge Nurse. Patricia Rae. (Orig.). 1982. pap. 2.95 (ISBN 0-8217-1044-3). Zebra.

Charge of Cowardice. Philip McCutchan. LC 78-4365. 1978. 8.95 (ISBN 0-312-13006-6). St. Martin's Press.

Charge of Cowardice. Duncan MacNeil. LC 78-4365. 1978. 8.95 o.p. (ISBN 0-312-13006-6). St Martin.

Charge of the Model T's. Lee Somerville. LC 72-7460. 1972. 7.95 (ISBN 0-8111-0467-2). Naylor Co.

Charged with Inspiration and Power. Katherine Thompson. LC 75-30777. 6.95 (ISBN 0-8111-0589-X). Naylor Co.

Charing Cross. Claire Rayner. LC 79-13844. (Her The performers; 7). 1979. 10.00 (ISBN 0-399-12368-7). Putnam.

Charing Cross Mystery. Joseph Smith Fletcher. LC 23-4005. 1923. G. P. Putnam's Sons.

Chariot of Fire. Edward Elton Young Hales. LC 76-18349. 1977. 6.95 (ISBN 0-385-12399-X). Doubleday.

Chariot of Fire. Edward Elton Young Hales. 1978. 1.75 (ISBN 0-380-01853-5). Avon Books.

Chariot of Fire: An American Novel. Bernard De Voto. LC 26-18161. 1926. The Macmillan Company.

Chariot of Israel: A Tale of Elijah. James S Sangster. LC 64-750. Exposition Press.

Chariot of the Flesh. Hedley Peek. 1897. Longmans, Green and Co.

Chariot of Wrath: A Novel. Leonid Maksimovich Leonov & Guterman, Norbert, 1900- Tr. LC 46-6951. 1946. L. B. Fischer.

Chariot-Race from Ben-Hur. Lewis Wallace. LC 8-30247. 1908. Harper & Brothers.

Chariot Wheels. Sylvia Thompson. LC 29-20978. 1929. Little, Brown, and Company.

Charioteer. Mary Renault, pseud. 1974. (pbk.) 1.75. Bantam Books.

Charioteer. Mary Renault, pseud. LC 59-8583. 1959. Pantheon.

Charioteer. Gladys Skelton. LC 30-19507. 1930. D. Appleton and Company.

Charioteer: A Story of Old Egypt in the Days of Joseph. Gertrude Eberle. LC 46-20993. 1946. Wm. B. Eerdmans Publishing Company.

Charioteers. Mary Tappan Wright. LC 12-11707. 1912. D. Appleton and Company.

Chariots of Fire. Michel Parry. 1.50 (ISBN 0-445-03175-1). Popular Library.

Chariots of Fire. W. J. Wetherby. 1982. pap. 2.75 (ISBN 0-440-01149-3). Dell.

Charis Sees It Through. Margaret Widdemer. LC 24-21401. Harcourt, Brace and Company.

Charisma Campaigns. Jack Matthews. LC 71-174511. 1972. (ISBN 0-15-116800-8). Harcourt Brace Jovanovich.

Charitable End. Jessica Mann. LC 75-159824. 1971. 4.95. McKay.

Chariton. Gareth L Schmeling. LC 73-14672. (Twayne's world authors series, TWAS 295. Greece). 1974. 5.95 (ISBN 0-8057-2207-6). Twayne Publishers.

Chariton Drive. Etta Althece Lowry. LC 45-10694. 1945. F. A. Wagenfuehr.

Charity. Sarah Nichols. (Wyndham Saga;). 1979. 1.75 (ISBN 0-445-04373-3). Popular Library.

Charity Ball. Jessie Scott. LC 46-3696. 1946. The Macmillan Company.

Charity Ball. Translated from the Czech by Philip H. Smith, Jr. Egon Hostovsky. LC 58-5944. 1958. Doubleday.

Charity Chance a Novel. Walter Raymond. LC 7-36635. 1896. Dodd, Mead and Company.

Charity Corner. Andrew Soutar. LC 15-3644. 1915. Cassell and Company, Ltd.

Charity Ends at Home. Colin Watson. LC 68-25467. (Red mask mystery). 1968. 4.50. Putnam.

Charity Girl. Daniel Ahearn. LC 36-36430. The Macaulay Company.

Charity Girl. Effie Adelaide Maria Albanesi. LC 956. (On cover: Eagle library, no. 143). 1900. Street & Smith.

Charity Girl. Georgette Heyer. LC 74-122799. 1970. 5.95. E. P. Dutton.

Charity Green: Or The Varieties of Love. Theodore Hartmann. LC 7-3660. 1859. J. W. Norton.

Charity Patient. Henry Lieferant & Sylvia Saltzberg Lieferant. LC 39-8476. 1939. E. P. Dutton & Co., Inc.
Charity Strong. Marguerite Allis. 1945. G. P. Putnam's Sons.
Charity, Sweet Charity. Rose Porter. LC 7-37751. A. D. F. Randolph & Company.
Charity's Chosen. Ruby Mildred Ayres. LC 26-15266. George H. Doran Company.
Charka Memorial. Wallace Ware, pseud. LC 54-12015. 1954. Published for the Crime Club by Doubleday.
Charlatan. Robert Williams Buchanan & Murray, Henry. LC 6-19885. (The Hawthorne library). F. T. Neely.
Charlatan. Robert Williams Buchanan & Murray, Henry. LC 1-30703. (Hawthorne library). 1901. Hurst & Company.
Charlatan. Noel Bertram Gerson. LC 59-12653. 1959. Doubleday.
Charlatan. Sydney Horler. LC 35-4879. 1934. Little, Brown, and Company.
Charlatan. Translated by Antonia White. Christine Arnothy. LC 59-5819. 1959. Dutton.
Charlatan. 1st Ed. Carter A Vaughan, pseud. LC 59-12653. 1959. Doubleday.
Charlatans. Bert Leston Taylor. LC 6-309265. 1906. The Bobbs-Merrill Company.
Charlatan's Prophecy. Georgiana Holmes. LC 15-186259. R. G. Badger.
Charlemagne: Or, The Church Delivered. An Epic Poem, in Twenty-Four Books. Lucien Bonaparte & Butler, Samuel, Bp. of Lichfield and Coventry, 1774-1839, Tr. LC 12-20933. 1815. J. Conrad and Co.
Charlemont; or, the Pride of the Village: A Tale of Kentucky. rev. ed. Gilmore Simms. LC 78-119150. Repr. of 1866 ed. 10.00 (ISBN 0-404-06008-0). AMS Pr.
Charlemont: Or, The Pride of the Village, a Tale of Kentucky. William Gilmore Simms. LC 78-119150. 1970. AMS Press.
Charlemont; or, The Pride of the Village, a Tale of Kentucky. William Gilmore Simms. (With his Border becyles. New York 1882). 1882. A. C. Armstrong & Son.
Charlemont; or, The Pride of the Village. A Tale of Kentucky. new and rev. ed. William Gilmore Simms. (On cover: Lovell's library, v. 14, no. 702). 1886. J. W. Lovell Company.
Charlemont; or, the Pride of the Village. William Gilmore Simms. 1974. Repr. of 1890 ed. lib. bdg. 30.00 (ISBN 0-8414-8073-7). Folcroft.
Charles, a Novel. 1st Ed. Victoria Lincoln. LC 61-138932. 1962. Little, Brown.
Charles and Elizabeth: A Novel. William John Burley. LC 81-51973. 1981. 9.95 (ISBN 0-8027-5447-3). Walker.
Charles Auchester. Elizabeth Sara Sheppard. (Half-title: Everyman's library: ed. by Ernest Rhys. Fiction). 1911. J. M. Dent & Sons, Ltd.
Charles Auchester. Elizabeth Sara Sheppard. LC 36-37327. (Half-title: Everyman's library, ed. by Ernest Rhys. Fiction. no. 505). 1928. J. M. Dent & Sons, Ltd.
Charles Auchester. Elizabeth Sara Sheppard & Upton, George Putnam, 1834-1919, Ed. LC 4-153340. 1891. A. C. McClurg and Company.
Charles Auchester. A Memorial. Elizabeth Sara Sheppard. (Seaside library. v. 58, no. 1178). 1882. G. Munro.
Charles Auchester: A Memorial. Elizabeth Sara Sheppard. (On cover: Lovell's library, no. 901). 1887. J. W. Lovell Company.
Charles Dickens. Charles Dickens & Richard Burton. LC 78-3884. (Illus.). 1978. 30.00 (ISBN 0-8414-1718-0). Folcroft Library Editions.
Charles Dickens' A Tale of Two Cities. Charles Dickens. Ed. by Roe, Frederick William. LC 10-14672. (Half-title: Longman's English classics...). 1910. Longmans, Green, and Co.
Charles Dickens' A Tale of Two Cities: An Adaptation. Helen Strickler & Dickens, Charles, 1812-1870. A Tale of Two Cities. LC 35-8186.
Charles Dickens: Bleak House. Ed. by A. E. Dyson. 1981. pap. 20.00x (ISBN 0-333-05425-3, Pub. by Macmillan England). State Mutual Bk.
Charles Dickens Christmas. Charles Dickens. LC 76-382082. (Illus.). 1976. 14.95. Oxford University Press.
Charles Dickens Christmas: A Christmas Carol, The Chimes, The Cricket on the Hearth. Charles Dickens. (Illus.). 1976. 17.95 (ISBN 0-19-519899-9). Oxford U Pr.
Charles Dickens: David Copperfield. W. Keith Kraus. LC 66-28278. (Barnes & Noble book series, 805). 1966. Barnes & Noble.
Charles Dickens Originals. Edwin William Pugh. LC 71-148288. 1975. 18.00 (ISBN 0-404-08895-3). AMS Press.
Charles Dickens, 1812-1870: An Anthology. Charles Dickens. Ed. by Lola L. Szladits. LC 77-127001. (Illus.). 1970. New York Public Library.
Charles Dickens's New Christmas Story. Mrs. Lirriper's Lodgings... Charles Dickens. 1864. Printed at the Office of the Daily Advertiser and Register.
Charles Dickens's Stories from the Christmas Numbers of "Household Words" and "All the Year Round," 1852-1867; Ed. Charles Dickens. Ed. by Dickens, Charles. LC 6-37061. 1896. Macmillan and Co.
Charles Fort Never Mentioned Wombats. Gene DeWeese & Robert Coulson. LC 76-23756. (Doubleday science fiction). 1977. 6.95 (ISBN 0-385-12111-3). Doubleday.
Charles Hopewell: Or, Society As It Is, and As It Should Be. John Patterson. 1853. Longley & Brother.
Charles Killbuck: An Indian's Story of the Border Wars of the American Revolution. Francis Christian Huebner. LC 2-24928. 1902. The Herbert Publishing Comapny.
Charles Lever; or, the Man of the Nineteenth Century, 1841 see Portrait of an English Churchman, 1838.
Charles Men. Verner Von Heidenstam. Tr. by Charles Wharton Stork. LC 72-122718. (Short story index reprint series). 1970. Books for Libraries Press.
Charles Men. Verner Von Heidenstam & Stork, Charles Wharton, 1881- Tr. LC 21-16931. (Half title: Scandinavian classics, vol. xv--xvi). 1920. The American--Scandinavian Foundation; Etc., Etc.
Charles Morgan, Christian Rich Man. Jerry Clevenger. LC 44-7026. 1944. Brown-White-Lowell Press.
Charles O'Malley: The Irish Dragoon. Charles James Lever. 1841. Carey and Hart.
Charles O'Malley: The Irish Dragoon. Charles James Lever. LC 1-19334. 1841-42. Carey and Hart.
Charles O'Malley: The Irish Dragoon... Charles James Lever. LC 1-19336. 1862. T. B. Peterson & Brothers.
Charles O'Malley: The Irish Dragoon. new ed. with autobiographical introduction. ed. Charles James Lever. LC 8-7706. G. Routledge and Sons.
Charles O'Malley: The Irish Dragoon. Charles James Lever. (Seaside library, v. 8, no. 146). 1877. G. Munro.
Charles O'Malley: The Irish Dragoon. Charles James Lever. LC 42-15606. 1884. G. Routledge and Sons.
Charles O'Malley: The Irish Dragoon... Charles James Lever. (On cover: Lovell's library, v. 16, no. 789). 1886. J. W. Lovell Company.
Charles O'Malley: The Irish Dragoon. Charles James Lever. LC 9-3438. (Half-title: The military novels of Charles Lever). 1896. Little, Brown, and Company.
Charles O'Malley: The Irish Dragoon. Charles James Lever. LC 26-268972. (home library). 1926. A. L. Burt Company.
Charles Rex. Ethel May Dell. LC 22-17941. 1922. 2.00. G. P. Putnam's Sons.
Charles Rex. Ethel May Dell & Barbara Cartland. LC 81-100878. (Barbara Cartland's Library of Love; 18). 1980. 12.95 (ISBN 0-7156-1478-9). Duckworth.
Charles Ryder's Schooldays and Other Stories. Evelyn Waugh. LC 82-214221. 5.95 (ISBN 0-316-92639-6). Little, Brown.
Charles Scribner's Sons Present Ring W. Lardner: In The Golden Honeymoon and Haircut, American Booksellers Association, St. Louis May 13, 1926. Ring W Lardner. LC 26-113153.
Charles the Chauffeur. Samuel Ellsworth Kiser. LC 5-13958. 1905. F. A. Stokes Company.
Charles the King. Evelyn Anthony. 1971. pap. 0.95 o.p. (09079). Curtis.
Charles, the King. Eve Stephens, pseud. LC 61-12586. 1961. Doubleday.
Charles Tyrrell: Or, The Bitter Blood. George Payne Rainsford James. LC 43-45739. 1839. Harper & Brothers.
Charles Vavasseur: Or, The Outcast Heir. John Frederick Smith. LC 21-15374. (Seaside library, v. 73, no. 1489). 1883. G. Munro.
Charles Vincent: Or, The Two Clerks. A Tale of Commercial Life... W. N. Willet. LC 8-36923. 1839. Harper & Brothers.
Charles Williams Novels, 7 vols. Charles Williams. Set. pap. 32.95. Eerdmans.
Charleston. Ralph Hayes. (Orig.). 1982. pap. 3.50 (ISBN 0-89083-937-9). Zebra.
Charleston. Alexandra Ripley. LC 79-8568. 1981. 14.95 (ISBN 0-385-14572-1). Doubleday.
Charleston & Other Stories. Jose Donoso. LC 76-19449. 1977. (ISBN 0-87923-197-1). D. R. Godine.
Charleston Edition of Porgy: A Novel. Du Bose Heyward. LC 28-30266. 1928. Doubleday, Doran & Company, Inc.
Charleston Knife's Back in Town. Ralph Dennis. (Hardman,#2). 1974. (pbk.) 0.95. Popular Library.
Charley: A Village Story. Susy Denson Gallaudet. LC 6-44488. 1893. G. P. Putnam's Sons.
Charley Is My Darling. Joyce Cary. LC 59-13306. 1960. Harper.
Charley Manning. Elizabeth Frances Corbett. LC 39-23757. 1939. D. Appleton-Century Company, Incorporated.
Charley Moon. Reginald Arkell. LC 53-5652. 1953. Harcourt, Brace.
Charley's World. Dancey R. Smith. 1970. 3.50 o.p. Carlton.
Charlie: A Novel. George Mikes. LC 77-356889. 1976. 2.95 (ISBN 0-233-96842-3). Deutsch.
Charlie and the Ice Man. John Eller. LC 81-5761. 1981. 9.95 (ISBN 0-312-13065-1). St. Martin's Press.
Charlie Boy. Peter S. Feibleman. LC 79-24524. 12.95 (ISBN 0-316-27700-2). Little, Brown.
Charlie Chan--Great Stories from the Saturday Evening Post. Earl Derr Biggers. LC 77-90936. 320p. 1977. 5.95 o.p. (ISBN 0-89387-015-3, Co-Pub by Sat Eve Post). Curtis Pub Co.
Charlie Chan Carries on. Earl Derr Biggers. LC 30-248401. The Bobbs-Merrill Company.
Charlie Chan Carries on. Earl Derr Biggers. (Charlie Chan,#6). 1975. (pbk.) 1.25. Bantam Books.
Charlie Chan, Five Complete Novels. avenel 1981 ed. Earl Derr Biggers. LC 81-3570. 6.98 (ISBN 0-517-34707-5). Avenel Books: Distributed by Crown Books.
Charlie Chan Omnibus: The House Without a Key, Behind That Curtain, Keeper of the Keys. Earl Derr Biggers. 1936. Grosset & Dunlap.
Charlie Chan Returns. Dennis Lynds. (Charlie Chan mystery series.). 1974. 0.95. Bantam Books.
Charlie Chan, The House Without a Key: From the Saturday Evening Post. Earl Derr Biggers. LC 77-90936. 1977. 5.95 (ISBN 0-89387-015-3). Curtis Pub. Co.
Charlie, Come Home. Ronald Frederick Delderfield. LC 76-10600. 1976. 8.95 (ISBN 0-671-22325-9). Simon and Schuster.
Charlie, Come Home. Ronald Frederick Delderfield. LC 77-4999. 1977. 16.95 (ISBN 0-8161-6448-7). G. K. Hall.
Charlie, Come Home. Ronald Frederick Delderfield. (Kangaroo Book). 1977. 1.95 (ISBN 0-671-80847-8). Pocket Books.
Charlie Dell: By Anderson Wayne Pseud. Davis Dresser. LC 52-8022. 1952. Coward-McCann.
Charlie Eagletooth's War. John J Templeton. LC 69-14481. 1969. 5.95. Morrow.
Charlie Flowers & the Melody Gardens. Fred Steven Howard. LC 72-78409. 1972. 6.95 (ISBN 0-87140-555-5). Liveright.
Charlie Gallagher, My Love. Simon Kent. pap. 0.95 o.p. (02191, Collier). Macmillan.
Charlie Galligher, My Love. Maxwell Jeffrey Catto. (Signet book). 1976. 1.50. New American Library.
Charlie, Horses, Et Al. James L. Henry. 3.95 o.p. Vantage.
Charlie in the House of Rue. Robert Coover. Ed. by Michael Peich. (Fiction Ser.: No. 1). (Illus.). 1980. 12.00 o.p. (ISBN 0-915778-30-0); ltd. signed ed. 50.00x (ISBN 0-915778-31-9). Penmaen Pr.
Charlie Is My Darling. Mollie Hardwick. LC 77-22839. 1977. 8.95 (ISBN 0-698-10867-1). Coward, McCann & Geoghegan.
Charlie M. Brian Freemantle. LC 77-75383. 1977. 7.95 (ISBN 0-385-13021-X). Doubleday.
Charlie Muffin. Brian Freemantle. LC 77-368329. 1977. 3.50 (ISBN 0-224-01312-2). Cape.
Charlie Muffin, U.S.A. Brian Freemantle. LC 79-8019. 1980. 10.95 (ISBN 0-385-14392-3). Doubleday.
Charlie Pocock and the Princess. George Beardmore, pseud. LC 67-260810. 1967. 4.95. Viking.
Charlie Romo's Flying Field. Donald M. Griffith. 256p. 1980. 10.00 (ISBN 0-931980-03-8); pap. 6.00 (ISBN 0-931980-04-6). Iroquois Hse.
Charlie Sent Me! Alan Geoffrey Yates. LC 64-3065. (Signet book, G2394). 1963. New American Library of World Literature.
Charlie Simpson's Apocalypse. Joe Eszterhas. LC 73-5036. 1973. 7.95 o.p. (ISBN 0-394-48424-X). Random.
Charlie's Angels Number Two: The Killing Kind: Based on The Killing Kind by Rick Husky, a Spelling-Goldberg Production. Richard Deming. LC 76-56165. 1.50 (ISBN 0-345-25707-3). Ballantine Books.
Charlie's Back in Town. Jacqueline Park. 1975. (pbk.) 0.95. Popular Library.
Charlie's Daughter. Susan Child. 1982. pap. 2.50 (ISBN 0-451-11409-4, AE1409, Sig). NAL.
Charlie's Daughter: A Novel. Susan Child. LC 81-9498. 12.95 (ISBN 0-453-00405-9). New American Library.
Charlie's Monument: An Allegory of Love. Blaine M. Yorgason. LC 76-42164. (Illus.). 1976. 2.95. Ricks College Press: Distributed by Yorgason Enterprises.
Charlie's Monument: An Allegory of Love. Blaine M. Yorgason. LC 77-83143. (Illus.). 3.50 (ISBN 0-88494-324-0). Bookcraft.
Charlie's Monument: An Allegory of Love. 2d ed. Blaine M. Yorgason. LC 79-56176. (Illus.). 3.95 (ISBN 0-88494-389-5). Bookcraft.
Charlotte. Amanda Hart Douglass. 1978. 1.95 (ISBN 0-505-51271-8). Tower Publications.
Charlotte and Dr. James. Guy McCrone. LC 56-615740. 1956. Farrar, Straus & Cudahy.
Charlotte and Lucy Temple. Susanna Haswell Rowson. LC 18-4345. 1864. J. B. Lippincott & Co.
Charlotte Armstrong Festival. Charlotte Armstrong. LC 75-10480. 9.95 (ISBN 0-698-10696-2). Coward, McCann & Geoghegan.
Charlotte Armstrong Reader. Charlotte Armstrong. LC 74-113531. 1970. 7.95. Coward-McCann.
Charlotte Armstrong Reader: The Turret Room, a Dram of Poison, the Unsuspected. Charlotte Armstrong. (YA) 1970. 7.95 o.p. (ISBN 0-698-10049-2). Coward.
Charlotte Armstrong Treasury. Charlotte Armstrong. LC 73-166234. 1972. 8.95. Coward, McCann & Geoghegan.
Charlotte Bronte: Jane Eyre & Villette. Ed. by Miriam Allott. 1981. pap. 20.00x (ISBN 0-333-13657-8, Pub. by Macmillan England). State Mutual Bk.
Charlotte Bronte's Jane Eyre: Chapter Notes and Criticism. Text by Bronson Dudley, Patricia Truelsen. Bronson Dudley & Patricia Truelse. (Study master pubn., 203). 1966. pap., 1.00. Amer. R. D. M.
Charlotte Lowenskold. Selma Ottiliana Lovisa Lagerlof. Tr. by Howard, Velma (Swanston) LC 27-249531. 1927. N. Y., Doubleday, Page & Company.
Charlotte Morel. Maria Lodi. (YA) 1969. 5.95 o.p. (ISBN 0-399-10131-4). Putnam.
Charlotte Morel: The Dream. Maria Lodi. (YA) 1970. 5.95 o.p. (ISBN 0-399-10224-8). Putnam.
Charlotte Morel: The Siege. Maria Lodi. (YA) 1970. 5.95 o.p. (ISBN 0-399-10728-2). Putnam.
Charlotte Perkins Gilman Reader: The Yellow Wallpaper, and Other Fiction. Charlotte Perkins Stetson Gilman & Ann J. Lane. LC 80-7711. 1980. 10.95 (ISBN 0-394-51085-2) (ISBN 0-394-73933-7). Pantheon Books.
Charlotte Perkis Gilman Reader: "The Yellow Wallpaper" & Other Fiction. Ed. by Ann Lane. 1980. 10.95 (ISBN 0-394-51085-2); pap. 5.95 (ISBN 0-394-73933-7). Pantheon.
Charlotte Temple. Susanna Haswell Rowson. LC 36-29651. American Publishers Corporation.
Charlotte Temple. Susanna Haswell Rowson. (On cover: Lovell's library, v. 4, no. 159). 1883. J. W. Lovell Company.
Charlotte Temple, a Tale of Truth. Susanna Haswell Rowson. LC 64-14446. (Twayne's United States classics series). 1964. Twayne Publisher.
Charlotte Temple. A Tale of Truth. 3d american ed. Susanna Haswell Rowson. LC 1-15061. Printed for Mathew Carey, by Stephen C. Ustick.
Charlotte Temple. A Tale of Truth. 5th american ed. Susanna Haswell Rowson. LC 1-15062. 1802. Printed for Mathew Carey of Philadelphia by John Wyeth.
Charlotte Temple: A Tale of Truth. Susanna Haswell Rowson. LC 16-13095. 1815. P. Merrifield.
Charlotte Temple: A Tale of Truth. Susanna Haswell Rowson & Halsey, Francis Whiting. LC 5-39587. 1905. Funk & Wagnalls Company.
Charlotte Wade. Adeline McElfresh. LC 52-14403. 1952. Arcadia House.
Charlotte's Daughter: or, The Three Orphans. A Sequel to Charlotte Temple. to which is prefixed, a memoir of the author. ed. Susanna Haswell Rowson. LC 8-942. 1828. Richardson & Lord.
Charlotte's Daughter: Or the Three Orphans. Susanna Haswell Rowson. LC 72-78812. 1828. Repr. 29.00 (ISBN 0-403-01983-4). Somerset Pub.
Charlotte's Inheritance. Mary Elizabeth Braddon Maxwell. (On cover: Lovell's library, no. 882). 1887. J. W. Lovell Company.
Charlotte's Inheritance. Mary Elizabeth Braddon Maxwell. (Seaside library. v. 13, no. 260). 1878. G. Munro.
Charlotte's Inheritance. Mary Elizabeth Braddon Maxwell. (On cover: Seaside library. Pocket ed., no. 554). 1885. G. Munro.
Charlotte's Row. Herbert Ernest Bates. LC 32-260446. 1931. J. Cape.
Charlotte's Temple, a Tale of Truth. Susanna Haswell Rowson. LC 72-78814. 1794. Repr. 19.00 (ISBN 0-403-01984-2). Somerset Pub.
Charlston Stories: L4. Jerry Messec. Ed. by Jean McConochie. (Regents Readers Ser.). (gr. 7-12). pap. text ed. 1.95 (ISBN 0-88345-455-6, 20951). Regents Pub.
Charly. Jack Weyland. LC 80-11216. (Illus.). 1980. 5.95 (ISBN 0-87747-814-7). Deseret Books Co.

Charm. Alice Robinson Perrin. LC 12-5559. 1916. D. Fitzgerald, Inc.
Charm Broken. From the French of Leon De Tinseau. Leon De Tinseau & Miller, Hettie F., Tr. (On cover: Dearborn series, no. 52). 1891. Donohue, Henneberry & Co.
"Charm" Girl. Edward L Delaney. LC 35-16448. Liveright Publishing Corporation.
Charm of Hours: A Novel. Peter Skelton. LC 54-7099. 1954. Morrow.
Charm School. Alice Duer Miller. LC 19-140064. Harper & Brothers.
Charmaine. Lynn Lowry. 432p. (Orig.). 1981. pap. 2.75 (ISBN 0-553-14150-3). Bantam.
Charmed Circle. Peggy Lamson. LC 50-5421. 1950. Lippincott.
Charmed Circle: A Comedy. Edward Alden Jewell. LC 21-16930. 1921. A. A. Knopf.
Charmed Circle. 1st Ed. Susan Ertz. LC 55-10708. 1956. Harper.
Charmed Life. Diana W. Jones. (gr. 8-12). 1980. pap. 2.25 (ISBN 0-671-83281-6, Timescape). PB.
Charmed Life. Mary Therese McCarthy. (Plume book). 1974. (pbk) 3.95. New American Library.
Charmed Life of Miss Austin. Samuel Merwin. LC 14-15744. 1914. 1.35. The Century Co.
Charmed Life. 1st Ed. Mary Therese McCarthy. LC 55-101537. 1955. Harcourt, Brace.
Charmed Sea: Or, Polanders in Siberia. Harriet Martineau. (On cover: Lovell's library, v. 7, no. 379). 1884. J. W. Lovell Company.
Charmeuse. Ernest Temple Thurston. LC 24-289627. 1924. Cassell and Company, Ltd.
Charmeuse. Ernest Temple Thurston. LC 25-546024. 1925. G. P. Putnam's Sons.
Charming Cheat. Clara Sharpe Hough. LC 32-154367. Grosset & Dunlap.
Charming Children of Dickens' Stories... Containing the Beautiful Life Stories of the Twenty Child Heroes and Heroines of... Charles Dickens, Retold by His Granddaughter and Others... Charles Dickens. LC 6-37919. Hertel, Jenkins & Company.
Charming Humbug. Imogen Clark. LC 9-17657. 1909. 1.20. E. P. Dutton & Company.
Charming Murder. Frank Shay. LC 30-23194. The Macaulay Company.
Charming Sally: A Novel. Maud Hart Lovelace. LC 32-22550. The John Day Company.
Charming to Her Latest Day: A Novel. Alan Muir. (On cover: Harper's Franklin square library, no. 725). 1892. Harper & Brothers.
Charming Young Man. Florence Stonebraker. LC 49-6165. 1949. Arcadia House.
Charms. Jonathan Cott. LC 80-28181. 1980. 4.00 (ISBN 0-915124-48-3). Toothpaste Press.
Charmstone. Eleanor Hoffman. pap. 4.00 (ISBN 0-87461-037-0). McNally.
Charnel House. Graham Masterton. (Orig.). 1978. pap. 2.95 (ISBN 0-523-48072-5). Pinnacle Bks.
Charon: A Dragon at the Gate, Bk. 3. Jack L. Chalker. (Orig.). 1982. pap. 2.95 (ISBN 0-345-29370-3, Del Rey). Ballantine.
Charred Witness. George Harmon Coxe. LC 42-18660. 1942. A. A. Knopf.
Charred Wood. Francis Clement Kelley. LC 17-30273. The Reilly & Britton Co.
Charro! Harry Whittington. 1981. pap. 1.75 (ISBN 0-449-14189-6, GM). Fawcett.
Charter House of Parma: By Stendhal Pseud. Tr. Introd., by Margaret R. B. Shaw. Marie Henri Beyle. LC 58-3631. (Penguin classics, L61). 1967. pap., 1.95. Penguin Books.
Chartered Libertine. Ralph Allen. LC 54-31282. 1954. Macmillan.
Chartered Libertine. Ralph Allen. LC 55-141505. 1955. St. Martin's Press.
Charterhouse of Parma. Marie Henri Beyle. Tr. by Scott-Moncrieff. Charles Kenneth. LC 37-27114. (Half-title: The modern library of the world's best books. 150). 1937. The Modern Library.
Charterhouse of Parma. Stendhal. 634p. 1980. 13.95 (ISBN 0-7011-1248-4, Pub. by Chatto Bodley Jonathan). Merrimack Pub Cir.
Charterhouse of Parma. Stendhal. Tr. by C. K. Scott-Moncrieff. (Orig.). pap. 3.95 (ISBN 0-451-51731-8, C1731, Sig Classics). NAL.
Charterhouse of Parma. Stendhal. Tr. by M. R. Shaw. (Classics Ser.). (Orig.). 1958. pap. 4.95 (ISBN 0-14-044061-5). Penguin.
Charterhouse of Parma. By Marie-Henri Beyle (Stendhal) Translated from the French by C. K. Scott Moncrieff. Marie Henri Beyle. LC 53-35249. (Doubleday anchor books. A1). 1953. Doubleday.
Charterhouse of Parma: By Marie-Henri Beyle (Stendhal) The Translation by Lady Mary Loyd, Rev. by Robert Cantwell. The Pref. by Honore De Balxac and Illus. by Rafaello Busoni. Marie Henri Beyle. LC 56-110738. 1955. Limited Editions Club.
Charterhouse of Parma: By Stendahl (Marie-Henri Beyle) Tr. from the French by Lowell Bair. With an Introd. by Harry Levin. Marie Henri Beyle. (Bantam Classic SC67). Bantam Books.
Charterhouse of Parma: Translated from the French by C. K. Scott Moncrieff... Marie Henri Beyle. Tr. by Scott-Moncrieff, Charles Kenneth. LC 25-23227. (Half-title: The works of Stendhal, i-ii). Boni & Liveright.
Charteris. A Romance. Mary Miller Meline. LC 7-25853. 1874. J. B. Lippincott & Co.
Charteris Mystery: A Pointer Problem. Archibald E. Fielding. LC 25-21208. 1925. A. A. Knopf.
Charteuse of Parma. Marie Henri Beyle. Tr. by Loyd, Lady Mary Sophia (Hely-Hutchinson) LC 2-23745. (Half-title: A century of French romance. Parisian ed. vol. 1). D. Appleton & Co.
Charting by the Stars. Linsey Abrams. LC 79-16760. 9.95 (ISBN 0-517-53898-9). Harmony Books.
Chartreuse of Parma. Marie Henri Beyle. Tr. by Loyd, Mary Sophia Hely-Hutchinson. Hewlett, Maurice Henry. LC 24-25023. (Half-title: Crown gems of France, edited by Edmund Gosse). The St. Hubert Guild.
Chartreuse of Parma. Marie Henri Beyle. Tr. by Loyd, Mary Sophia Hely-Hutchinson. Hewlett, Maurice Henry. LC 9-32288. (Half-title: The French classical romances... editor-in-chief, Edmund Gosse...). P. F. Collier & Son.
Charwoman's Daughter. James Stephens. 128p. 1972. pap. 2.25 (ISBN 0-7171-0633-0). Irish Bk Ctr.
Charwoman's Shadow. Edward John Moreton Drax Plunkett Dunsany. LC 26-13667. 1926. G.P. Putnam's Sons.
Charwoman's Shadow. Edward John Moreton Drax Plunkett Dunsany. LC 26-13667. 1926. G. P. Putnam's Sons.
Charwoman's Shadow. Edward John Moreton Drax Plunkett Dunsany. (Ballantine adult fantasy series). 1973. 1.25 (ISBN 0-345-03085-0). Ballantine.
Chase. Norman Daniels. (Berkley medallion book). 1974. (pbk) 0.95 (ISBN 0-425-02553-5). Berkley Pub. Co.
Chase. K. R. Dwyer. LC 72-2745. (O.S.I.). 1973. 5.95 o.s.i. (ISBN 0-394-47990-4). Random.
Chase. Richard Gibson Hubler. LC 52-8021. 1952. Coward-McCann.
Chase. Dean Koontz. LC 72-2745. 1972. 5.95 (ISBN 0-394-47990-4). Random House.
Chase. Gerald Locklin. LC 76-5706. (Illus.). 1976. pap. 3.00 (ISBN 0-916918-00-9). Duck Down.
Chase. Mollie Panter-Downes. LC 25-8318. 1925. G. P. Putnam's Sons.
Chase. Richard Unekis. LC 62-19517. Walker.
Chase a Green Shadow. Anne Mather. (Presents Ser.). 1974. pap. 1.25 (ISBN 0-373-70561-1, 70561, Pub by Harlequin). PB.
Chase: A Novel. Horton Foote. LC 55-110165. 1956. Rinehart.
Chase a Rainbow. abr. ed. Hettie Grimstead. Ed. by Alice Sachs. 1970. Repr. of 1968 ed. 3.95 o.p. Lenox Hill.
Chase: A Tale of the Southern States. Jules Hippolyte Lermina & Sergeant, Adeline, 1851-1904, Tr. (On cover: Lovell's library, no. 469). 1884. J. W. Lovell Company.
Chase a Tall Shadow. John Ell. (Orig.). 1981. pap. 1.95 o.s.i. (ISBN 0-505-51655-1). Tower Bks.
Chase into Mexico. Terrell L. Bowers. 1982. pap. 6.95 (Avalon). Bouregy.
Chase of an Heiress. Frances Christine Tiernan. 1898. G. P. Putnam's Sons.
Chase of Saint-Castin and Other Stories of the French in the New World. Mary Hartwell Catherwood. LC 77-128723. (Short story index reprint series). 1970. Books for Libraries Press.
Chase of Saint-Castin: And Other Stories of the French in the New World. Mary Hartwell Catherwood. LC 4-22070. 1894. Houghton, Mifflin and Company.
Chase of the Golden Plate. Jacques Futrelle. LC 6-39731. 1906. Dodd, Mead & Company.
Chase of the Meteor: And Other Stories. Edwin Lassetter Brynner. LC 79-81264. (Short story index reprint series). (Illus.). 1969. Books For Libraries Press.
Chase of the Meteor, and Other Stories. Edwin Lassetter Bynner. LC 6-164103. 1891. Little, Brown, and Company.
Chase Round the World: Or, A Detective by Chance. Mariposa Weir. (secret service series--no. 31). 1890. Street & Smith.
Chase Royal: A Novel. Donald Seaman. LC 81-14515. 14.95 (ISBN 0-312-13134-8). St. Martin's Press.
Chase the Wind. Ernest Victor Thompson. LC 77-1844. 1977. 9.95 (ISBN 0-698-10822-1). Coward, McCann & Geoghegan.
Chasing a Dream. Susan E. Kirby. 1982. 6.95 (Avalon). Bouregy.
Chasing Dad. Candace Flynt. LC 79-28214. 8.95 (ISBN 0-8037-1392-4). Dial Press.
Chasing Hairy. Michael L Fleisher. LC 78-21198. 9.95 (ISBN 0-312-13139-9). St. Martin's Press.
Chasing Rainbows. Esther Sager. 352p. (Orig.). 1981. pap. 2.95 (ISBN 0-515-05849-1). Jove Pubns.
Chasing the Wind. Kenneth R. Van Der Spuy. (Illus.). 1966. 8.00 o.s.i. Tri-Ocean.
Chasm. Victor Canning. LC 47-11444. 1947. M. S. Mill Co.
Chasm: A Novel. Reginald Wright Kauffman & Carpenter, Edward Childs. LC 3-27965. 1903. D. Appleton and Company.
Chasm: A Novel by George Cram Cook... George Cram Cook. LC 11-185539. 1911. Frederick A. Stokes Company.
Chasseur De Primes. Rene de Goscinny. (Lucky Luke Series). (French.). 1976. 5.95x (ISBN 2-205-00604-5). Intl Learn Syst.
Chaste... June Jennifer. LC 35-2184. W. Godwin, Inc.
Chaste Diana: A Romance of "The Beggar's Opera,". Lily Moresby Adams Beck. LC 28-7992. 1923. Dodd, Mead and Company.
Chaste Man... Louis Umfreville Wilkinson. LC 17-239769. 1917. A. A. Knopf.
Chaste Wife. Frank Arthur Swinnerton. LC 17-357344. George H. Doran Company.
Chastity: A Drama of the East. Joan Conquest. LC 29-11017. 1929. The Macaulay Company.
Chastity Belt. Laura Fredericks. 3.95 (ISBN 0-8315-0071-9). Speller.
Chastity of Gloria Boyd. Donald Henderson Clarke. LC 32-880491. 1932. The Vanguard Press.
Chastity of Gloria Boyd. Donald Henderson Clarke. LC 47-19984. 1946. Triangle Books, The Blakiston Company.
Chastity's Prize. Darrell Husted. LC 81-12530. 1980. 11.95 (ISBN 0-89340-371-7). J. Curley.
Chata and Chinita: A Novel. Louise Palmer Heaven. 1889. Roberts Brothers.
Chateau. Stephen Coulter. LC 73-20756. 1974. 9.95 (ISBN 0-671-21730-5). Simon and Schuster.
Chateau Bon Vivant. Frankie Richmond O'Rear & John O'Rear. LC 67-23485. (Illus.). 1967. Macmillan.
Chateau De la Rage: The Chateau of the Mad Dog. Leopold Louis Stapleaux & Cooke, H. O., Tr. (On cover: Idylwild series, v. 2, no. 43). 1893. Morrill, Higgins & Co.
Chateau D'or. Norah, and Kitty Craig. Mary Jane Hawes Holmes. LC 12-25954. 1880. G. W. Carleton & Co.
Chateau D'Or; Norah and Kitty Craig: As Published in the New York Weekly, Vol. 31, No. 19. Mary Jane Hawes Holmes. LC 8-27360. G.W. Dillingham Company.
Chateau in the Palms. Anne Hampson. (Harlequin Presents Ser.). 192p. 1982. pap. 1.75 (ISBN 0-373-10535-5). Harlequin Bks.
Chateau Laurens. Esther L. Neely. (Orig.). 1980. pap. 1.95 o.s.i. (ISBN 0-505-51515-6). Tower Bks.
Chateau Merville: Or, Life in Touraine. From the French. Reed, Emily. LC 6-23440. (Half-title: The Morville series). 1872. Claxton, Remsen & Haffelfinger.
Chateau of Dreams. (Harlequin Romances Ser.). 192p. 1982. pap. 1.50 (ISBN 0-373-02465-7). Harlequin Bks.
Chateau of Montplaisir. Molly Elliot Seawell. LC 6-12136. 1906. D. Appleton and Company.
Chateau of St. Avrell. Violet Winspear. (Presents Ser.). 1974. pap. 1.25 (ISBN 0-373-70570-0, 70570, Pub by Harlequin). PB.
Chateau of Shadows. Monica Heath. Bd. with Legeng of Crown Point. 1977. pap. 2.50 (ISBN 0-451-11692-5, AE1692, Sig). NAL.
Chateau of Shadows. Monica Heath. (Signet Book). 1973. (pbk) 0.95. New American Lib.
Chateau of Shadows and The Legend of Crownpoint. Monica Heath. (Signet Book). 1977. 1.95 (ISBN 0-451-07754-7). New American Library.
Chateau Saxony. Susan Richard. 1971. pap. 0.60 o.p. (ISBN 0-446-63565-0, 63-565). Paperback Lib.
Chateau Venus. Jim Dobbs. (Orig.). 1968. pap. 1.75 o.s.i. (103, Ophelia). Olympia.
Chateau. 1st Ed. William Maxwell. LC 61-712526. 1961. Knopf.
Chateaubriand. Tr. from German by Violet M. Macdonald. Friedrich Sieburg. LC 62-82715. 1962. 5.95. St. Martin's.
Chatelaine. Claire Lorrimer. LC 81-20525. 1982. 3.95 (ISBN 0-345-29884-5). Ballantine Books.
Chatelaine of La Trinite. Henry Blake Fuller. LC 6-44582. 1892. The Century Co.
Chatelaine of La Trinite see Collected Works.
Chatham Killing. Jack Ehrlich, pseud. 1976. pap. 1.25 o.p. WSP.
Chato's Land. Joe Millard, pseud. (O.s.i.). 160p. (Orig.). 1972. pap. 0.75 o.s.i. (AS1034, Award). Univ Pub & Dist.
Chattanooga... John Jolliffe. LC 9-2710. 1858. Wrightson & Company, Printers.
Chattanooga... John Jolliffe. LC 7-119309. 1858. Anderson, Gates & Wright.
Chattanooga: A Romance of the American Civil War. 3d ed. Frederick Augustus Mitchel. LC 7-17260. The American News Company.
Chatte. Sidonie Gabrielle Colette. 1955. pap. 3.95. French & Eur.
Chatte. Sidonie Gabrielle Colette. 1955. 5.95 o.p.; pocket ed. 0.95 o.p. French & Eur.
Chattering Gods. Rayburn Crawley. LC 31-117270. 1931. Harper & Brothers.
Chattooga Griffin: A Heart Story of the Blue Ridge Mountains. Victor Louis Norman. LC 24-14374. 1924. The Stratford Company.
Chaturanga: A Novel. Rabindranath Tagore. Tr. by Asok Mitre. (Sahitya Akademi Publications Series). 1967. 3.00 o.p. Verry.
Chaturanga: A Novel. Tr. from Bengali by Asok Mitra. 1st Ed. Rabindranath Tagore. 1967. bds., 2.50. Sahitya Akademi.
Chaucer's Canterbury Tales: The Prologue and Four Tales, with the Book of the Duchess & Six Lyrics in Modern Verse. Tr. by F. E. Hill. pap. 2.95 o.p. (ISBN 0-679-14003-4, Tartan). McKay.
Chaucer's Troylus & Crysede. Geoffrey Chaucer. LC 76-23188. 1976. Repr. of 1873 ed. lib. bdg. 50.00 (ISBN 0-8414-7338-2). Folcroft.
Chauffeur and the Chaperon. Charles Norris Williamson & Alice Muriel Livingston Williamson. LC 8-16473. 1908. The McClure Company.
Chauncey and Kitty: Also Bob's Dilemma. Lincoln Hulley. LC 25-16156. E. O. Painter Printing Co.
Chautauqua: A Novel, by Day Keene and Dwight Vincent. From a Story by Mauri Grashin. Day Keene & Dwight Vincent. LC 60-527389. 1960. Putnam.
Chautauquans, a Novel. John Habberton. (Ledger library, no. 51). 1891. R. Bonner's Sons.
Chauvinist & Other Stories. Toshio Mori. Ed. by Russell C. Leong. LC 79-52265. 1979. pap. 5.00x (ISBN 0-934052-01-8). Asian Am Stud UCLA.
Chauvinisto. Sam Merwin, Jr. 176p. (Orig.). 1976. pap. 1.25 (ISBN 0-89041-085-2, 3085). Major Bks.
Cheap Jack Zita. Sabine Baring-Gould. LC 6-7959. 1894. J. S. Tait & Sons.
Cheap Thrills. Ron Goulart. (O.s.i.). 280p. 1972. 7.95 o.s.i. (ISBN 0-87000-172-8). Arlington Hse.
Cheapest Nights. Yusef Idris. Tr. by Wadida Wassef from Arabic. LC 78-72967. 1978. 10.00 (ISBN 0-89410-040-8); pap. 5.00 (ISBN 0-89410-041-6). Three Continents.
Cheapjack: Being the True History of a Young Man's Adventures As a Fortune-Teller, Grafter, Knocker-Worker, and Mounted Pitcher on the Market-Places and Fair-Grounds of a Modern but Still Romantic England. Philip Allingham. LC 34-295413. 1934. Frederick A. Stokes Company.
Cheat. based upon the story by hector turnbull. pola negri ed, illustrated with scenes from the paramount picture. ed. Russell Holman & Turnbull, Hector. LC 23-12068. Grosset & Dunlap.
Cheat: By Robert Dietrich Pseud. Howard Hunt. LC 55-20533. (Pyramid books, 135). 1954. Pyramid Books.
Cheat Grass. Cheryl Van Dyke. (Copperhead Chapbook Ser.). 24p. (Orig.). 1975. pap. 5.00. Copper Canyon.
Cheat-the-Boys: A Story of the Devonshire Orchards. Eden Phillpotts. LC 24-2250. 1924. The Macmillan Company.
Cheat the Hangman. Morna Doris MacTaggart Brown. LC 46-4357. 1946. Published for the Crime Club by Doubleday.
Cheat the Hangman: By E. X. Ferrars. E. X. Ferrars, pseud. LC 46-4357. 1946. Pub. for the Crime Club by Doubleday & Company, Inc.
Cheaters' Clubs. James Montague Clark. LC 83-487. 1932. W. Godwin, Inc.
Cheating Butcher. Aaron Marc Stein. LC 79-55372. 1980. 8.95 (ISBN 0-385-15861-0). Published for the Crime Club by Doubleday.
Cheating the Devil. Juanita Cassil Burbridge. LC 25-9140. 1925. N.L. Brown.
Chechahco and Sourdough: A Story of Alaska. Scott Cardelle Bone. LC 26-7446. Printed by Western Publishers, Inc.
Check Force. Ralph Hayes. (Clouds of War: No. 2). 192p. (Orig.). 1975. pap. 1.25 o.p. (ISBN 0-532-12291-7). Woodhill.
Check Force. Ralph Hayes. (Clouds of War: No. 2). 192p. (Orig.). 1975. pap. 1.25 o.p. (ISBN 0-532-12291-7). Manor Bks.
Check Force: Fires of Hell. Ralph Hayes. (Action Novel Ser.: No. 6). 1976. pap. 1.25 o.p. (ISBN 0-532-12445-6). Woodhill.
Check Force: Fires of Hell. Ralph Hayes. (Action Novel Ser.: No. 6). 1976. pap. 1.25 o.p. (ISBN 0-532-12445-6). Manor Bks.
Check Force: The Peking Plot. Ralph Hayes. (Action Novel Ser.: No.4). 192p. (Orig.). 1975. pap. 1.25 o.p. (ISBN 0-532-12348-4). Woodhill.
Check Force: The Peking Plot. Ralph Hayes. (Action Novel Ser.: No.4). 192p. (Orig.). 1975. pap. 1.25 o.p. (ISBN 0-532-12348-4). Manor Bks.

Check No. 777: Or, Tracking the Same Man Twice. John Russell Coryell. LC 98-63. (On cover: Magnet detective library, no. 46). Street & Smith.

Check to the Queen. Renato Ghiotto. LC 68-25432. 1969. 6.95. Putnam.

Check to Your King. Robin Hyde. 1977. 8.50 o.p. (ISBN 0-85558-448-3). Transatlantic.

Checked Love Affair: And "The Cortelyon Feud". Paul Leicester Ford. LC 3-25879. 1903. Dodd, Mead and Company.

Checked Through, Missing Trunk No. 17580: A Story of New York City Life. Richard Henry Savage. LC 8-1995. (On cover: Rialto series, no. 73). 1896. Rand, McNally & Company.

Checkerboard Caper. John Morris. LC 74-29549. 1975. 7.95 (ISBN 0-8065-0469-2). Citadel Press.

Checkerboard Corridor. Rixie Hunter. LC 67-30724. 1968. J. F. Blair.

Checkered Flag. John Mersereau. LC 25-110031. Small, Maynard & Company.

Checkered Lights: A Novel. Fulton Gardner. 1887. Laird & Lee.

Checkers: A Hard-Luck Story. Henry Martyn Blossom. LC 6-14209. 1896. H. S. Stone & Company.

Checkers: A Hard-Luck Story. Henry Martyn Blossom. LC 16-13103. 1896. Grosset & Dunlap.

Checkers, a Hard-Luck Story. Henry Martyn Blossom. LC 45-31649. 1896. H. S. Stone & Company.

Checklist. Walter De La Mare. Ed. by D. Cecil. 1956. lib. bdg. 8.50 (ISBN 0-8414-2457-8). Folcroft.

Checkmate. Dorothy Dunnett. LC 75-5837. (Illus.). 1975. 9.95. Putnam.

Checkmate. Dorothy Dunnett. 1976. 1.95. Popular Library.

Checkmate. Joseph Sheridan Le Fanu. LC 76-4184. (Le Fanu, Joseph Sheridan, 1814-1873. Works. 1976). 1976. (3vols.) 62.00 (ISBN 0-405-09194-X). Arno Press.

Checkmate. Joseph Sheridan Le Fanu. LC 42-27126. 1871. Evans, Stoddart & Co.

Checkmate. Norah Robinson Lofts. 1978. pap. 1.75 (ISBN 0-449-23488-6, Crest). Fawcett.

Checkmate and Deathmate. Martin Ashley. 1973. 5.95 (ISBN 0-533-00425-X). Vantage.

Checkmate by the Colonel: By George Griswold Pseud. 1st Ed. Robert George Dean. LC 52-12970. (Gullt edged mystery). 1953. Dutton.

Checkmate in Rio. Nick Carter. (Nick Carter Ser.). (O.s.i.). (Orig.). pap. 0.60 o.s.i. (A639X, Award). Univ Pub & Dist.

Checkmate to Murder. Edith Caroline Rivett. LC 44-6989. 1944. Arcadia House, Inc.

Checkmate: Universe. Kurt Mahr. (Perry Rhodan#74). (Illus.). 1975. (pbk.) 1.25. Ace Books.

Checkpoint, a Novel. Charles Wheeler Thayer. LC 63-20306. 1964. Harper & Row.

Checkpoint Charlie. Brian Wynne Garfield. LC 81-208891. 1981. 10.00 (ISBN 0-89296-054-X) (ISBN 0-89296-055-8). Mysterious Press.

Checkpoint Charlie. Gerard De Villiers. (Malko,#9). 1975. (pbk.) 1.25. Pinnacle Books.

Chedayne of Kotono. A Story of the Early Days of the Republic. Towner, Ausburn. LC 8-29832. Dodd, Mead & Company.

Chedworth. Robert Cedric Sherriff. LC 44-8653. 1944. The Macmillan Company.

Cheer for the Dead: A Pat Campbell Detective Story. Eli Colter. LC 47-16955. 1947. M. S. Mill Co., Inc.

Cheer Me On! Judith Enderle. (Caprice Romance Ser.). 192p. 1982. pap. 1.95 (ISBN 0-441-06980-0, Pub. by Tempo). Ace Bks.

Cheerful. Edna Ferber. LC 18-17641. 1918. Doubleday, Page & Company.

Cheerful Americans. Charles Battell Loomis. LC 73-86150. (Short story index reprint series). (Illus.). 1969. Books for Libraries Press.

Cheerful Americans. Charles Battell Loomis. LC 3-17013. 1903. H. Holt and Company.

Cheerful Blackguard. Roger S. Pocock. LC 15-55970. 1.35. The Bobbs-Merrill Company.

Cheerful, by Request. Edna Ferber. LC 78-169547. (Short story index reprint series). 1971. (ISBN 0-8369-4009-1). Books for Libraries Press.

Cheerful Captive: Or, The Nine Days' Astonishment. Illustrated by Paul Galdone. 1st Ed. Louise Field Cooper. LC 54-9719. 1954. Harcourt, Brace.

Cheerful Fraud. Kenneth Robert Gordon Browne. LC 25-16603. 1925. G. P. Putnam's Sons.

Cheerful Moments; Short Humorous Stories. Jacob Adler & London, Abraham, Tr. LC 40-34188. 1940. Bloch Publishing Company.

Cheerful Smugglers. Ellis Parker Butler. LC 8-11086. 1908. The Century Co.

Cheerful Weather for the Wedding. Julia Strachey. LC 33-3292. 1933. The Viking Press.

Cheerfulness Breaks in, No. 3. Angela Mackail Thirkell. (Bersetshire Romance Ser, No. 3). 1972. pap. 0.95 o.p. (N2686). Pyramid Pubns.

Cheerfulness Breaks in: A Barsetshire War Survey. Angela Mackail Thirkell. LC 41-1947. 1941. A. A. Knopf.

Cheerios Kid. Douglas Terry. LC 79-6624. 1982. 14.95 (ISBN 0-385-15373-2). Doubleday.

Cheerleader. Ruth Doan MacDougall. LC 72-87621. 1973. 6.95 (ISBN 0-399-11085-2). Putnam.

Cheerleader. Ruth Doan MacDougall. 1974. (pbk.) 1.50. Bantam Books.

Cheers, Major Barlow: A Novel. William Fain. LC 58-8319. 1958. Crown Publishers.

Cheese & the Worms. Carlo Ginzburg. Tr. by John Tedeschi & Anne Tedeschi. (Illus.). 1982. pap. 6.95 (ISBN 0-14-006046-4). Penguin.

Cheetahs. Alan Caillou, pseud. 1970. 6.95 o.p. (A3352). World Pub.

Cheetahs: A Novel. Lyle-Smythe, Alan. LC 79-128481. 1970. 6.95. World Pub. Co.

Chekhov Proposal. Constance Caray. LC 75-7983. 1975. 8.95 (ISBN 0-399-11530-7). Putnam.

Chekhov Proposal. Constance Carey. LC 75-7983. 320p. 1975. 8.95 o.p. (ISBN 0-399-11530-7). Putnam.

Chekhov Proposal. 1976. pap. 1.75 o.p. (ISBN 0-515-04086-X). BJ Pub Group.

Chekhov: Selected Stories. Anton Pavlovich Chekhov. Tr. by Ann Dunnigan. pap. 2.50 (ISBN 0-451-51527-7, CE1527, Sig Classics). NAL.

Chekhov: Seven Stories. Anton Pavlovich Chekhov. Ed. by Ronald Hingley. 1974. (pbk.) 3.95 (ISBN 0-19-281159-2). Oxford University Press.

Chekhov: The Early Stories 1883-88. Anton Pavlovich Chekhov. Tr. by Patrick Miles & Harvey Pitcher. (Illus.). 224p. 1983. 13.95 (ISBN 0-02-524620-8). Macmillan.

Chekov's Enterprise. Walter Koenig. (Orig.). (gr. 8-10). 1980. pap. 2.25 (ISBN 0-671-83286-7). PB.

Chel; a Story of the Swiss Mountains. Johanna Heusser Spyri & Boll, Helene H., Tr. LC 13-7884. Eaton & Mains.

Chela & the Path. El Morya. Ed. by Elizabeth C. Prophet. LC 76-7634. (Illus.). 128p. (Orig.). 1976. pap. 2.95 (ISBN 0-916766-12-8). Summit Univ.

Chelbury Abbey. Denis George Mackail. LC 34-5591. 1934. Doubleday, Doran & Company, Inc.

Chelsea. Nancy Fitzgerald. LC 78-60290. 1979. 8.95 (ISBN 0-385-12686-7). Doubleday.

Chelsea. Nancy Fitzgerald. LC 79-28646. 1980. 13.95 (ISBN 0-8161-3059-0). G. K. Hall.

Chelsea Murders. Lionel Davidson. (Crime Monthly Ser.). 1980. pap. 2.95 (ISBN 0-14-005136-8). Penguin.

Chelsea Way: Or, Marcel in England, a Proustian Parody. Andre Maurois. LC 67-11676. (Illus.). 1967. J. H. Heineman.

Chelynne. Robyn Carr. LC 79-23759. 9.95 (ISBN 0-316-12971-2). Little, Brown.

Chemin de L'Inca. Laura Benjamin. (Collection Colombine). 192p. 1983. pap. 1.95 (ISBN 0-373-48060-1). Harlequin Bks.

Chemmeen. Thakazhi S. Pillai. Tr. by Narayana Menon. (Writing in Asia Ser.). 1978. pap. text ed. 5.50 (00216). Heinemann Ed.

Chemmeen: A Novel. Sivasankara Pillai, Thakazhi. LC 62-9921. (UNESCO collection of representative works: Indian series). 1962. Harper.

Chemmeen: A Novel. Sivasankara Pillai, Thakazhi. LC 78-12828. (Series: UNESCO Collection of Representative Works: Indian Series.). 1979. 18.00 (ISBN 0-313-21213-9). Greenwood Press.

Chenango Pass. Herbert Shappiro. LC 42-7967. 1942. Arcadia House, Inc.

Chenango Pass: A Mustag Marshall Western. Herbert Arthur, pseud. LC 42-7967. 1942. Arcadia House.

Chendru: The Boy and the Tiger. English Version Translated from the French by William Sanson. Photos. by Arne Sucksdorff. All Photographs in This Book Were Taken by Astrid Bergman Sucksdorff. Bergman Sucksdorff, Astrid. LC 60-2381. 1960. half cloth 3.25. Harcourt, Brace.

Chengtu Strain. Kenneth Kay & Marshall Goldberg. 1976. (pbk.) 1.50 (ISBN 0-523-00819-8). Pinnacle Books.

Cheque for Three Thousand. Arthur Henry Veysey. LC 8-30000. 1897. G. W. Dillingham Co.

Chequer-Board. Robert Keating Clay. LC 26-20631. 1927. J. B. Lippincott Company.

Chequer-Board. Sybil Grant. LC 12-252074. 6.00. Hodder and Stoughton.

Chequer-Board. Sybil Grant. Hodder & Stoughton, George H. Doran Company.

Chequer Board. Nevil Shute Norway. LC 47-30177. 1947. W. Morrow & Company.

Chequer Board. Nevil Shute. (Keith Jennison Books). 8.95 o.p. (ISBN 0-531-00174-1). Watts.

Cher Papa. Frederick Kohner. LC 59-14388. 1960. Putnam.

Cheri. Sidonie Gabrielle Colette. Tr. by Flanner, Janet. LC 29-22047. 1929. A. & C. Boni.

Cheri, and the Last of Cheri. Sidonie Gabrielle Colette. 1974. (pbk.) 1.50 (ISBN 0-14-001020-3). Penguin Books.

Cheri, and The Last of Cheri. Translated by Roger Senhouse. Sidonie Gabrielle Colette. LC 53-10039. 1953. Farrar, Straus & Young.

Cherish: A Love Story. Collen L. Reece. (Orig.). 1983. pap. 3.95 (ISBN 0-8024-0172-4). Moody.

Cherish the Dream. Holly A. Mascott. (Orig.). 1983. pap. 3.95 (ISBN 0-440-11614-7). Dell.

Cherished Destiny. Irene Robinson. (Superromances Ser.). 384p. 1982. pap. 2.50 (ISBN 0-373-70015-6, Pub. by Worldwide). Harlequin Bks.

Cherished Heart. Nancy Macdougall Kennedy. 1970. pap. 0.60 o.p. (ISBN 0-447-73899-2). Lancer.

Cherokee. Muriel Naomi Evans. LC 55-9494. 1955. Little, Brown.

Cherokee. Don Tracy. LC 56-9546. 1957. Dial Press.

Cherokee Diamondback. John Henry Reese. LC 77-80956. 1977. 6.95 (ISBN 0-385-13095-3). Doubleday.

Cherokee Fowler. Charles Stanley Strong. LC 45-9224. 1945. Phoenix Press.

Cherokee Love Story of a Trail of Tears. Jayne Bremyer. (Orig.). 1979. pap. 1.95 (ISBN 0-532-23283-6). Woodhill.

Cherokee Mission. Karl Meyer. (American Indians Ser.: No. 7). 352p. 1982. pap. 2.95 (ISBN 0-440-01183-3, Banbury). Dell.

Cherokee Outlet: By Dwight Bennett Pseud. 1st Ed. Dwight Bennett Newton. LC 61-9540. (Double D western). 1961. Doubleday.

Cherokee Rustlers: By Eli Chiappe. Eli Albert Chappe. LC 43-18234. 1943. Phoenix Press.

Cherokee Strip. Marquis James. (Orig.). 1965. pap. 1.65 o.p. (ISBN 0-670-00178-3). Penguin.

Cherokee Trail. Louis L'Amour. LC 82-23215. 1983. 12.95 (ISBN 0-8161-3464-2). G.K. Hall.

Cherokee Trail. Louis L'Amour. 1982. 12.95 (ISBN 0-553-05029-X); pap. 2.95 (ISBN 0-553-20846-2). Bantam.

Cherokee Trail. Louis L'Amour. (General Ser.). 1983. lib. bdg. 12.95 (ISBN 0-8161-3464-2, Large Print Bks). G K Hall.

Cherokee Trails. George Washington Ogden. LC 28-5867. 1928. Dodd, Mead & Company.

Cherokee Woman. Francis M Daves. LC 72-81196. 1973. 8.95 (ISBN 0-8283-1474-8). Branden Press.

Cherron. Sharon Combes. 336p. (Orig.). 1981. pap. 2.75 (ISBN 0-89083-700-7). Zebra.

Cherry... Sophy Beckett. (On cover: The seaside library. Pocket edition, no. 506). 1885. G. Munro.

Cherry. Booth Tarkington. LC 3-25882. 1903. Harper & Brothers.

Cherry. Alvin Winston. LC 35-1831. Phoenix Press.

Cherry Ames: The Mystery of Rogue's Cave. Helen Wells. 1982. pap. 1.95 (ISBN 0-448-16866-9, Pub. by Tempo). Ace Bks.

Cherry, and Beasley's Christmas Party. Booth Tarkington. LC 26-3002. 1925. Harper & Brothers.

Cherry Bed: A Novel. Karlton Kelm. LC 36-7719. The Bobbs-Merrill Company.

Cherry Delight up Your Ante. Glen Chase, pseud. 1976. pap. 1.25 o.p. (LB407, Leisure Bks). Nordon Pubns.

Cherry Girl. Marcus Van Heller, pseud. (Orig.). 1968. pap. 1.95 o.s.i. (220, Ophelia). Olympia.

Cherry Harvest. Eileen Helen Clements. LC 44-3415. 1944. J. Messner, Inc.

Cherry in the Martini. Rona Jaffe. (O.S.I.). 1966. 4.50 o.s.i. (ISBN 0-671-13360-8). S&S.

Cherry Isle. Evelyne Close. LC 20-20001. 1.90. G. W. Jacobs & Company.

Cherry Pickers. Kent Roland. 192p. (Orig.). 1973. pap. 1.95 o.p. (ISBN 0-87682-359-2, 7359). Barclay Hse.

Cherry Pit. Donald Harington. LC 65-11272. 1965. Random House.

Cherry Pit. Donald Harington. 1975. (pbk.) 1.50 (ISBN 0-515-03769-9). Pyramid Books.

Cherry Pool. M. Aleveyev. 327p. 1978. pap. 6.45 (ISBN 0-8285-0938-7, Pub. by Progress Pubs USSR). Imported Pubns.

Cherry Square: A Neighbourly Novel. Grace Louise Smith Richmond. LC 27-1343. 1926. Doubleday, Page & Co.

Cherry Tree. Adrian Bell. LC 32-22549. 1932. Dodd, Mead & Company.

Cherryfield Hall. An Episode in the Career of an Adventuress. Frederic Henry Balfour. LC 6-6883. (The Hudson library, no. 11). 1895. G. P. Putnam's Sons.

Cherub Devine: A Novel. Sewell Ford. LC 9-10791. M. Kennerley.

Chesapeake. James Albert Michener. LC 78-2892. 12.95 (ISBN 0-394-50079-2). Random House.

Chesapeake Autumn. Stephanie Richards. (Rapture Romance Ser.: No. 5). 192p. 1983. pap. 1.95 (ISBN 0-451-12064-7). NAL.

Chesapeake Cavalier. Don Tracy. LC 49-10837. 1949. Dial Press.

Chesapeake Duke. Gilbert Byron. LC 75-40037. (Illus.). 168p. 1975. pap. 5.00 (ISBN 0-87033-210-4, Pub. by Tidewater). Cornell Maritime.

Cheshire Cat's Eye: A Sharon McCone Mystery. Marcia Muller. LC 82-16919. 1983. 10.95 (ISBN 0-312-13175-5). St. Martin's Press.

Chess Murders. Means Davis. LC 37-15191. Random House.

Chess Players. Frances Parkinson Wheeler Keyes. LC 60-14365. (Illus.). 1960. Farrar, Straus and Cudahy.

Chess Players & Other Stories. Premchand. 174p. 1967. pap. 1.75 o.p. (ISBN 0-88253-068-2). InterCulture.

Chessboard Queen. Sharan Newman. LC 82-16905. 1983. 13.95 (ISBN 0-312-13176-3). St. Martin's Press.

Chessboard Spies. Geoffrey Davison. LC 70-80987. 1969. 3.95. Roy Publishers.

Chessman of Mars. Edgar Rice Burroughs. 1973. pap. 1.95 (ISBN 0-345-27838-0). Ballantine.

Chessmaster. Nick Carter. (Nick Carter Ser.). 224p. (Orig.). 1982. pap. 2.50 (ISBN 0-441-10351-0, Pub. by Charter Bks). Ace Bks.

Chessmen of Mars. Edgar Rice Burroughs. LC 22-23905. 1922. A. C. McClurg & Co.

Chessmen of Mars. Edgar Rice Burroughs. LC 22-350671. 1922. Grosset & Dunlap.

Chessmen of Mars see Three Martian Novels.

Chester Family: Or, The Curse of the Drunkard's Appetite. Julia M Friend. LC 6-44725. 1869. W. White and Company.

Chester Himes. James Lundquist. LC 75-42864. (Modern literature monographs). 7.00 (ISBN 0-8044-2561-2). Ungar.

Chestermarke Instinct. Joseph Smith Fletcher. LC 21-6796. 1921. A. A. Knopf.

Chester's Paradise. Harry Deuel. LC 70-92576. (Illus.). 1971. 2.00. Total Graphics, Inc.

Chestnut Tree. Evelyn Page. 1964. 4.50 o.p. (ISBN 0-8149-0177-8). Vanguard.

Chevalier Casse-Cou. Fortune Du Boisgobey & Merighi, Mrs. Caroline A., Tr. LC 21-13963. (Seaside library, v. 89, no. 1793). 1884. G. Munro.

Chevalier Casse-Cou... Fortune Du Boisgobey & Picton, Thomas, Tr. LC 6-34431. 1875. R. M. De Witt.

Chevalier D'Auriac. Sidney Kilner Levett-Yeats. LC 9-12255. 1897. Longmans, Green and Co.

Chevalier De Maison-Rouge. Alexandre Dumas & Maquet, Auguste. LC 6-42105. (Half-title: The Marie Antoinette romances. v. 5). 1890. Little, Brown and Company.

Chevalier De Maison Rouge: A Tale of the Reign of Terror: a Sequel to "The Countess De Charny,". Alexandre Dumas & Maquet, Auguste. LC 3-27817. G. Routledge and Sons, Limited.

Chevalier De Maison Rouge. A Tale of the Reign of Terror. Alexandre Dumas & Maquet, Auguste. LC 6-42103. (On cover: Seaside library. Pocket ed. no. 2124). G. Munro's Sons.

Chevalier De Maison Rouge: A Tale of the Reign of Terror. Alexandre Dumas & Maquet, Auguste. LC 6-42106. (American series. no. 324). M. J. Ivers & Co.

Chevalier De St. Denis. Alice Ilgenfritz D Jones. LC 66554. 1900. A. C. McClurg and Company.

Chevalier D'Harmental: Or, The Conspirators. Alexandre Dumas & Maquet, Auguste. LC 6-42846. (On cover: Seaside library. Pocket ed. no. 2113). G. Munro's Sons.

Chevalier of Dixie. Samuel Jackson Shields. LC 7-26338. 1907. The Neale Publishing Company.

Chevalier of Pensieri-Vani. Henry Blake Fuller. LC 72-84585. (Illus.). 1974. (lib. ed.) 6.95 (ISBN 0-403-02963-5). Scholarly Press.

Chevalier of Pensieri-Vani. Henry Blake Fuller. LC 71-104457. 1970. Literature House.

Chevalier of Pensieri-Vani. 4th ed., rev. ed. Henry Blake Fuller. 1892. The Century Co.

Chevalier of Pensieri-Vani see Collected Works.

Chevalier of Pensieri-Vani: Together with Frequent References to the Prorege of Arcopia. Henry Blake Fuller. LC 6-44581. J. G. Cupples Co.

Chevalier's Lady. Betty Hale Hyatt. 1979. 1.50 (ISBN 0-440-11015-7). Dell Pub. Co.

Chevaliers of France, from the Crusaders to the Marechals of Louis Xiv. Henry William Herbert. 1853. Redfield.

Chevengur. Andrei Platonovich Platonov. LC 78-57177. 16.95 (ISBN 0-88233-309-7). Ardis.

Chevrons. Leonard Hastings Nason. LC 26-17804. George H. Doran Company.

Chewsday. Dan Greenburg. 1969. pap. 0.75 o.p. (T2026). Pyramid Pubns.

Chewsday: A Sex Novel. Dan Greenburg. LC 68-29279. 1968. Stein and Day.

Cheyenne Autumn. Mari Sandoz. 1975. Repr. 12.95 (ISBN 0-8038-1094-6). Hastings.

Cheyenne Captives. Lewis B Patten. LC 77-78513. 1978. 6.95 (ISBN 0-385-13258-1). Doubleday.

Cheyenne Country. Al Cody, pseud. (YA) 1974. 4.95 o.p. (Avalon). Bouregy.

Cheyenne Country. Al Cody. (Avalon westerns). 1974. 4.50. Avalon Books.

Cheyenne Encounter. Dwight Bennett. LC 75-28736. 1976. 5.95. Doubleday.

Cheyenne Gold. Max Brand. LC 74-180925. 256p. 1972. 4.95 o.p. (ISBN 0-396-06476-0). Dodd.

Cheyenne Gold. Max Brand. LC 74-180925. 1975. (pbk.) 1.25. Warner Books.

Cheyenne Gold. Frederick Faust. LC 76-17612. 1976. 7.95 (ISBN 0-89340-030-0). J. Curley.

Cheyenne Lance. John Legg. (Orig.). 1980. pap. text ed. 1.95 o.s.i. (ISBN 0-505-51584-9). Tower Bks.

Cheyenne Manhunt. Lester Wayne Merha. (Orig.). 1980. pap. 1.75 o.s.i. (ISBN 0-8439-0742-8, Leisure Bks). Nordon Pubns.

Cheyenne Payoff. Chet Cunningham. 368p. (Orig.). 1981. pap. 2.25 (ISBN 0-440-01269-4). Dell.

Cheyenne Pool. Lewis B Patten. (Signet brand Western, T5667). 1973. (pbk.) 0.75. New American Library.

Cheyenne Pool. Lewis B Patten. LC 72-79415. (DD western). 1972. 4.95 (ISBN 0-385-02262-X). Doubleday.

Cheyenne Pool. Lewis B Patten. LC 82-3084. 1982. 11.95. G.K. Hall.

Cheyenne Raiders. Jim O'Reilly. (American Indian Ser.: No. 6). (Orig.). 1982. pap. 2.95 (ISBN 0-440-01179-5, Bryans). Dell.

Cheyenne River Wild Track. Steve Katz. LC 73-91968. 4.95 (ISBN 0-87886-033-9) (ISBN 0-87886-033-9). Ithaca House.

Cheyenne River Wild Track. Steve Katz. LC 73-91968. 2.95 (ISBN 0-87886-033-9) (ISBN 0-87886-034-7). Ithaca House.

Cheyenne Saddle. James R. Laird. LC 82-50497. (Illus.). 100p. (Orig.). 1982. pap. 9.95 (ISBN 0-9609648-0-0). Cheyenne Cor.

Cheyenne, the White Wolf Home. Allen R. Densmore. 3.75 o.p. Carlton.

Cheyenne Vengeance. Jackson Flynn, pseud. (Gunsmoke Ser). (O.s.i.). 160p. (Orig.). 1975. pap. 0.95 o.s.i. (AN1403, Award). Univ Pub & Dist.

Cheyenne Vengeance. Robert J. Steelman. LC 73-10974. 1974. 4.95 (ISBN 0-385-05252-9). Doubleday.

Cheyenne Vengeance. Robert J Steelman. 1975. (pbk.) 0.95. Belmont Tower Books.

Cheyenne's Woman. Robert E. Mills. (Kansan Ser.: No. 9). 208p. (Orig.). 1982. pap. 2.25 o.s.i. (ISBN 0-8439-1171-9, Leisure Bks). Nordon Pubns.

Cheyenne's Woman. Robert E. Mills. (Kansan Ser.: No. 9). 208p. 1983. pap. 2.50 (ISBN 0-8439-2015-7, Leisure Bks). Dorchester Pub Co.

Cheyne Mystery. Freeman Willis Crofts. (Crime Ser). 1978. pap. 2.95 (ISBN 0-14-000917-5). Penguin.

Cheyne Mystery: An Inspector French Story. Freeman Wills Crofts. LC 26-17966. 1926. A. & C. Boni.

Cheyne of the Rocking K. George Brydges Rodney. LC 43-13634. 1943. Phoenix Press.

Cheyney, Peter. LC 53-11135. (Red badge detective). 1953. Dodd, Mead.

Chez Charlotte & Emily. Jonathan Baumbach. LC 79-52033. 1979. 9.95 (ISBN 0-914590-56-1); pap. 4.95 (ISBN 0-914590-57-X). Fiction Coll.

Chez Cordelia. Kitty Burns Florey. LC 80-5194. 10.95 (ISBN 0-87223-623-4). Seaview Books.

Chez Krull. Georges Simenon. LC 75-328654. 1974. 2.10 (ISBN 0-85617-206-5). White Lion Publishers.

Chianti Flask. Marie Adelaide Belloc Lowndes. LC 34-360662. 1934. Longmans, Green and Co.

Chicago. Charles Carroll (ISBN 0-671-80740-4). Pocket Books.

Chicago Deadline. Ed Mazzaro. 1979. pap. text ed. 1.75 o.s.i. (ISBN 0-89559-152-9). Dale Books Inc.

Chicago Girl. Tony Kenrick. LC 76-20651. 7.95 (ISBN 0-399-11810-1). Putnam.

Chicago Girl. Tony Kenrick. (Berkley Medallion Book). 1978. 1.75 (ISBN 0-425-03652-9). Berkley Pub. Corp.

Chicago Hustle. Odie Hawkins. (Orig.). 1977. pap. 1.95 (ISBN 0-87067-640-7, BH640). Holloway.

Chicago Princess. Robert Barr. LC 4-16433. 1904. F. A. Stokes Company.

Chicago Princess. Robert Barr. LC 4-25388. 1904. F. A. Stokes Company.

Chicago Slaughter. Mike Barry. (Lone Wolf). (Berkley medallion book: Vol.). 1974. (pbk.) 0.95 (ISBN 0-425-02555-1). Berkley Pub. Co.

Chicago Story: A Novel. Ira Victor Morris. LC 52-5531. 1952. Doubleday.

Chicano. Richard Vasquez. LC 79-78670. 1970. 6.95. Doubleday.

Chicano: from Caricature to Self-Portrait. Ed. by Edward Simmen. LC 77-27048. (Mentor book, MY 1069). 1971. 1.25. New American Library.

Chicano Kid. Sebastian Morales. 1973. pap. 0.75 o.p. (07264). Curtis.

Chicano Kid. Sebastian Morales. 1973. (pbk) 0.75. Curtis Books.

Chichester Intrigue. Thomas Cobb. LC 8-6033. 1908. J. Lane Company; Etc., Etc.

Chichi. Rachel Grant. LC 35-3039. Thomas Y. Crowell Company.

Chichikov's Journeys: Or, Home Life in Old Russia. Nikolai Vasilevich Gogol & Guerney, Bernard Guilbert, Tr. LC 42-21081. 1942. The Readers Club.

Chicho. Sue Lindberg & William Lindberg. LC 81-940. 352p. 1982. 11.95 (ISBN 0-86666-031-3). GWP.

Chickadee. L. D. Henry. 1979. pap. 1.25 (ISBN 0-532-12591-6). Woodhill.

Chickamauga: A Romance of the American Civil War. Frederick Augustus Mitchel. LC 7-17250. The Star Book Comapny.

Chicken Chronicles. Paul Diamond. (Dell Book). 1977. 1.50 (ISBN 0-440-11121-8). Dell Pub Co.

Chicken Every Sunday: My Life with Mother's Boarders. Rosemary Taylor. LC 43-3406. 1943. Whittlesey House, McGraw-Hill Book Company, Inc.

Chicken Executive. Butch McCue. 1970. 3.95 o.p. Vantage.

Chicken Prince & Other Old Tales of Cabala. Ed. by Wayne Wright. (O.s.i.). 1978. pap. write for info o.s.i. (ISBN 0-931376-00-9). Rhinoceros Pr.

Chicken-Wagon Family. Barry Benefield. LC 25-171188. The Century Co.

Chicken-Wagon Family. Barry Benefield. 1942. Triangle Books.

Chickens Come Home to Roost. Dorothy Walworth. LC 27-15973. 1927. Harper & Brothers.

Chickens Come Home to Roost: A Novel. Frances S Belote. LC 51-14645. 1951. Dorrance.

Chickens Come Home to Roost. A Novel. Lewis Baker Hilles. LC 99-4221. F. T. Neely.

Chickens Don't Have Chairs. Copi. Tr. by Richard Seaver. 1969. pap. 1.50 o.p. (GS5). Grove.

Chickens in the Airshaft. Steve Franklin, pseud. LC 75-186022. 1972. 4.95. Published for the Crime Club by Doubleday.

Chickie" A Hidden, Tragic Chapter from the Life of a Girl of This Strange "Today". Elenore Meherin. LC 25-11318. Grosset & Dunlap.

Chickie" A Sequel. Elenore Merherin. LC 25-24273. Grosset & Dunlap.

Chickie's Daughter. Elenore Meherin. LC 34-259353. Grosset & Dunlap.

Chicot the Jester. Alexandre Dumas & Maquet, Auguste. LC 36-37190. (Half-title: Everyman's library, ed. by Ernest Rhys. Fiction. no. 421). 1933. J. M. Dent & Sons, Ltd.

Chicot, the Jester. A Historical Romance. Alexandre Dumas & Maquet, Auguste. LC 6-42114. (Seaside library, v. 33, no. 688). G. Munro.

Chicot, the Jester: A Sequel to "Marguerite De Valis,". Alexandre Dumas & Maquet, Auguste. LC 3-27809. G. Routledge and Sons, Limited.

Chicot the Jester: Being a Continuation of "Marguerite De Valois". Alexandre Dumas & Maquet, Auguste. LC 6-42115. (American series, no. 329). M. J. Ivers & Co.

Chicot the Jester: By Alexandre Dumas. Alexandre Dumas. (Half-title: Everyman's library ed. by Ernest Rhys. Fiction). 1910. J. M. Dent & Sons, Ltd.

Chief. Frank Bonham. (Laurel-leaf library). 1973. (pbk.) 0.95. Dell.

Chief Counsel, by A. L. Furman... Abraham Loew Furman. LC 34-373. 1934. The Macaulay Commpany.

Chief Factor: A Tale of the Hudsonhs Bay Company, Being the History of Master Andrew Venlaw, Chief Factor, Mistress Jean Fordie, and Others. Gilbert Parker. LC 7-34997. Trow Directory Company.

Chief Hi Hawk-Thunder Butte Genesis. Georgia Aydelotte-Holden. LC 74-158979. (Illus.). 1973. Printed by Fleetwood Art Studios.

Chief Inspector's Daughter. Sheila Radley. (Murder Ink Mystery Ser.: No. 31). 1981. pap. 2.25 (ISBN 0-440-11193-5). Dell.

Chief Inspector's Daughter. Sheila Radley. 256p. 1981. 8.95 (ISBN 0-684-16730-1, ScribT). Scribner.

Chief Inspector's Daughter. Sheila Radley. (Nightingale Ser.). 1982. pap. 9.95 (ISBN 0-8161-3413-8, Large Print Bks). G K Hall.

Chief Inspector's Daughter. Hester Rowan. LC 80-53221. 8.95 (ISBN 0-684-16730-1). Scribner.

Chief Inspector's Daughter. Hester Rowan. LC 82-11917. 1982. 9.95 (ISBN 0-8161-3413-8). G.K. Hall.

Chief Joseph's Alps. Dallas W. Green. 1972. 5.95x (ISBN 0-87315-003-1). Golden Bell.

Chief Justice. Karl Emil Franzos. LC 6-43160. (Lovell's foreign literature series, no. 5). J. W. Lovell Company.

Chief Legatee. Anna Katharine Green Rohlfs. LC 6-45694. McLeod & Allen.

Chief Legatee. Anna Katharine Green Rohlfs. LC 16-20445. 1916. Dodd, Mead & Company.

Chief Mitigomish. Alphonse Maria Grussi. LC 36-103440. The Christopher Publishing House.

Chief of Police. Being the Continuation of "Rose-De-Noel". Alexandre Dumas & Sherwood, Mary Neal, Tr. LC 3661. (On cover: Seaside library. Pocket ed., no. 2046). 1900. G. Munro's Sons.

Chief of the Ranges: A Tale of the Yukon. Hiram Alfred Cody. LC 13-222857. 1.25. Hodder & Stoughton, George H. Doran Company.

Chief the Honourable Minister. R. MofOlorynso Aluko. (African Writers Ser.). 1970. pap. text ed. 4.50x (ISBN 0-435-90070-6). Heinemann Ed.

Chiefs. Stuart Woods. LC 80-27350. 15.95 (ISBN 0-03-901461-4). Norton.

Chiefs: A Novel. Stuart Woods. 1981. 14.95 (ISBN 0-393-01461-4). Norton.

Chieftain: A Story of the Nez Perce People by Robert Payne. Pierre Stephen Robert Payne. LC 53-6363. 1953. Prentice-Hall.

Chieftain of Andor. Andrew J Offutt. 1976. Dell.

Chieftain of Churubusco: Or, The Spectre of the Cathedral. A Romance of the Mexican War. Harry Halyard. 1848. F. Gleason.

Chieftain Without a Heart. Barbara Cartland. LC 77-28876. 6.95. Dutton.

Chieko and Other Poems of Takamura Kotaro. Kotaro Takamura. LC 80-10792. 10.95 (ISBN 0-8248-0689-1). University Press of Hawaii.

Chien Blanc. Romain Gary, pseud. (Coll. Soleil). 11.50. French & Eur.

Chien D'or. The Golden Dog; a Legend of Quebec. William Kirby. LC 7-13211. 1878. R. Worthington.

Chien Negre: A Tale of the Vaudoux. Nemours Henry Nunez. LC 72-4645. (Black Heritage Library Collection). 1972. 12.25 (ISBN 0-8369-9116-8). Books for Libraries Press.

Chien Negre: A Tale of the Vaudoux. Nemours Henry Nunez. LC 38-12959. Burney Brothers Puplishing Co.

Chiendent see Bark Tree.

Chiffon Scarf. Mignon Good Eberhart. LC 75-29117. 1975. 6.95. Aeonian Press.

Chiffon Scarf. Mignon Good Eberhart. LC 48-11218. 1939. Book League of America.

Chiffon Scarf. Mignon Good Eberhart. LC 30-27747. 1939. Doubleday, Doran & Co., Inc.

Chiffon Scarf. Mignon Good Eberhart. 1940. The Sun Dial Press.

Chiffon Scarf. Mignon Good Eberhart. LC 42-21557. 1942. Triangle Books.

Chiffon's Marriage. Sibylle Gabrielle Marie Antoinette De Riquetti De Mirabeau Martel De Janville. F. A. Stokes Company.

Chiffon's Marriage. Sibylle Gabrielle Marie Antoinette De Riquetti De Mirabeau Martel De Janville. Tr. by Teller, Nora. LC 7-24386. (On cover: The enterprise series, no.63). E. A. Weeks & Company.

Chiffon's Marriage. Sybille Gabrielle Marie Antoinette De Riquetti De Mirabeau Martel De Janville. Tr. by Robins, E. P. (On cover: Globe library, v. 1, no. 216). Rand, McNally & Company.

Chiffon's Marriage. Sybille Gabrielle Marie Antoinette De Riquetti De Mirabeau Martel De Janville. Tr. by Coffey, Edward Lees. 1895. Hurst & Company.

Chiffon's Marriage Le Mariage De Chiffon. Sybille Gabrielle Marie Antoinette De Riquetti De Mirabeau Martel De Janville. Tr. by Jones, Myrta Leonora. LC 42-27297. 1895. Lovell, Coryell & Company.

Chihuahua Trail, 1868: A Novel. Rudolph Mellard. LC 74-170454. (Illus.). 1973. Anson Jones Press.

Chihuahua 1916. Otis Carney. LC 80-15076. 9.95 (ISBN 0-13-130286-8). Prentice-Hall.

Chilblains of the Heart. James Sunwall. 1983. pap. 2.95 (ISBN 0-939736-38-1). Wings ME.

Chilcotes: Or, Two Widows. A Novel. Grace L Keith Johnston. (Harper's Franklin square library, no. 537). 1886. Harper & Brothers.

Child and the Serpent. Sy Cook. LC 80-5197. 9.95 (ISBN 0-87223-616-1). Seaview Books.

Child and Woman. Clementine Helm Beyrich. Tr. by Cocke, Zitella. LC 7-4668. 1878. J. A. Moore.

Child Buyer. John Richard Hersey. 240p. 1982. pap. 2.95 (ISBN 0-553-20937-X). Bantam.

Child Buyer: A Novel in the Form of Hearings Before the Standing Committee on Education, Welfare, & Public Morality of a Certain State Senate, Investigating the Conspiracy of Mr. Wissey Jones, with Others, to Purchase a Male Child. John Richard Hersey. LC 60-13850. 1960. Knopf.

Child Characters from Dickens: Re-Told by L. L. Weedon; with 6 Colour Plates & 70 Half-Tone, Illustrations by Arthur A. Dixon. Charles Dickens & Weedon, Lucy L. LC 8-12226. 1905. E. Nister.

Child Christopher and Goldilind the Fair. William Morris. LC 80-19163. 1980. 10.95 (ISBN 0-87877-511-0). Borgo Press.

Child Divided. Henry Cecil. LC 66-10642. 3.95. Harper.

Child Ellen. Frank Trippett. LC 74-30088. (Illus.). 1975. (ISBN 0-13-130757-6). Prentice-Hall.

Child from the Sea. Elizabeth Goudge. LC 79-113527. 1970. 8.95. Coward-McCann.

Child Healers. Murray Kappelman. (Dell 1215). 1973. 1.25. Dell.

Child Healers. Murray Kappelman. LC 76-165088. 1971. 5.95. D. McKay Co.

Child-Hunters. Charles Wheeler Denison. LC 11-10510. 1877. Claxton, Remsen & Haffelfinger.

Child-Hunters. Charles Wheeler Denison. (On cover: Lovell's library. no. 483). 1885. J. W. Lovell Company.

Child in Her Arms. Louise Redfield Peattie. LC 38-6753. 1938. G. P. Putnam's Sons.

Child in the Dark: Three Novelettes. Rosemary Timperley. LC 56-10603. 1956. Crowell.

Child in the Temple: A Novel. Frank James Mathew. 1897. J. Lane.

Child in the Vatican. Violet Paget. LC 2-24055. (The brocade series, XXIV). 1900. T. B. Mosher.

Child in White Fog. J. D. Jansen. 5.95 o.p. Vantage.

Child Is Born. Mary McDougal Axelson. LC 39-21675. 1939. The Caxton Printers,Ltd.

Child Is Born. Charles Yale Harrison. LC 31-6792. J. Cape & H. Smith.

Child Is Born: A Romance. Raymonde Machard & Boyd, Madeleine, Tr. LC 26-15788. 1926. Cosmopolitan Book Corporation.

Child Is Missing. Charlotte Paul. LC 77-24469. 8.95 (ISBN 0-399-12072-6). Putnam.

Child Is Missing. Charlotte Paul. (Bernard Geis Associates Book). 1978. 1.95 (ISBN 0-425-03833-5). Berkley Pub. Corp.

Child Killer. Edson T. Hamill. (Ryker#5). 1975. (pbk.) 1.25. Leisure Books.

Child Love. Phyllis Norroy. 1971. pap. 1.75 o.p. (Z1065K, Zebra). Grove.

Child Lovers. Lisa Balson. 224p. pap. 1.95 o.p. (6148). Brandon.

Child Manuela. Christa Winsloe. LC 75-12360. (Homosexuality). 1975. 12.00 (ISBN 0-405-07377-1). Arno Press.

Child Manuela, the Novel of "Maedchen in Uniform". Christa Winsloe & Scott, Agnes Neill, Tr. LC 39-27424. Farrar & Rinehart, Incorporated.

Child Mind. Ralph Harold Bretherton. LC 3-7171. 1903. J. Lane.

Child of Circumstance. Lillian Lawrence Nelson. LC 37-4082. B. Humphries, Inc.

Child of Conflict: A Love Story. Mary Frances Doner. LC 36-409. Chelsea House.

Child of Darkness. Dorothy Daniels. LC 77-3649. 1977. 7.95 (ISBN 0-89340-081-5). J. Curley & Associates.

Child of Darkness. Dorothy Daniels. 1974. (pbk.) 0.95 (ISBN 0-671-77755-6). Pocket Books.

Child of Divorce: A Startling Story of an Amazing Modern Evil--Its Insidious Warfare Upon All That Is High and Holy in Marriage and Its Blasting Influence Upon Innocent Lives. Marie Le Nart. LC 22-226568. The Standard Publishing Company.

Child of Evil. Octavus Roy Cohen. LC 36-8771. 1936. D. Appleton Century Company, Incorporated.

Child of Flame. Ruth Stull. LC 55-32182. 1955. Van Kampen Press.

Child of Fortune. Yuko Tsushima. LC 82-48168. 1982. 14.95 (ISBN 0-87011-532-4). Kodansha International.

Child of Genius. A Sketch Book for Winter Evenings, and Summer Afternoons. Jerome James Wood. LC 32-521555. Wood's Bookstore.

Child of Gentle Courage. Sarah Shears. 1974. 8.95 o.p. (ISBN 0-236-31065-8, Pub. by Paul Elek). Merrimack Pub Cir.

Child of God. Cormac McCarthy. LC 73-3986. 1974. 5.95 (ISBN 0-394-48771-0). Random House.

Child of Hell. William Dobson. 1982. pap. 2.95 (ISBN 0-451-11768-9, AE1768, Sig). NAL.

Child of Israel. A Novel. Edouard I. E. Victor Edouard Cadol. Tr. by Kendall, Laura E. LC 11-10532. T. B. Peterson & Brothers.

Child of Light. Viola Taylor Garvin. LC 37-14400. 1937. Longmans, Green and Co.

Child of Light. Mary Lockwood. LC 63-17689. 1963. Morrow.

Child of Love. Lela Burger. 288p. 1976. 8.95 (ISBN 0-87881-045-5); pap. 3.95 (ISBN 0-87881-046-3). Mojave Bks.

Child of Love: A Startling Story of the Struggles of a Girl Born Out of Wedlock Against the Sins and Perversions of to-Day. John Russell Coryell. LC 4-37020. 1904. Physical Culture Publishing Co.
Child of Love: A Startling Story of the Struggles of a Girl Born Out of Wedlock Against the Sins and Preversions of to-Day. Margaret Grant. LC 4-37020. 1904. Physical Culture Publishing Co.
Child of Nature. Claude Adrien Helvetius. LC 74-16205. (Flowering of the Novel). 1974. (ISBN 0-8240-1204-6). Garland Pub.
Child of Nature a Novel. Abner Thorp. LC 8-19949. 1896. Curts & Jennings.
Child of Nature. A Romance. Robert Williams Buchanan. (Franklin square library, no. 189). 1881. Harper & Brothers.
Child of Night. Anne Edwards. LC 75-9565. 1975. 6.95 (ISBN 0-394-49087-8). Random House.
Child of Our Time. Michel Del Castillo. LC 58-10964. 1958. Knopf.
Child of Our Time: A Novel. Odon Horvath. LC 39-303323. 1939. The Dial Press.
Child of Our Time: Translated from the French by Peter Green. (D319). 1959. Dell.
Child of Pity, the Little Prince Rides Away. Ekaterina Rzewuska Radziwill & Catherwood, Grace Adele. Sears Publishing Company, Inc.
Child of Pleasure. Gabriele D' Annunzio & Harding, Georgina, Tr. LC 25-26571. (Half-title: The modern library of the world's best books). Boni and Liveright.
Child of Pleasure. Gabriele D'Annunzio & Harding, Georgina, Tr. (His The romances of the rose). 1898. G. H. Richmond & Son.
Child of Rage. Jim Thompson. (Orig.). 1972. pap. 0.95 o.s.i. (75-342). Lancer.
Child of Satan. Melissa Napier. 1973. (pbk) 0.95. Pocket Books.
Child of Satan House. Ruby Jean Jensen. 1978. pap. 1.75 (ISBN 0-532-17176-4). Woodhill.
Child of Sorrow. Lillian Sincere Ahrens. LC 13-24399. Broadway Publishing Company.
Child of Storm. with a frontispiece in color and two illustrations by a. c. michael. ed. Henry Rider Haggard. LC 13-257259. 1913. 1.35. Longmans, Green, and Co.
Child of Storm. Illus. by Hookway Cowles. Henry Rider Haggard. LC 66-5442. 1966. bds., 2.95. Macdonald.
Child of the Age. Francis William Lauderdale Adams. LC 76-20045. (Decadent Consciousness). (Series: The Keynotes series; v. 4.). 1977. 26.00 (ISBN 0-8240-2750-7). Garland Pub.
Child of the Age. Francis William Lauderdale Adams. LC 5-42956. 1894. Roberts Bros.; Etc, Etc.
Child of the Alps. Margaret Symonds. LC 21-15550. 1921. Frederick A.Stokes Company.
Child of the Amazons: And Other Poems. Max Eastman. LC 13-10637. 1913. 1.00. M. Kennerley.
Child of the Ball. Pedro Antonio De Alarcon & Serrano, Mrs. Mary Jane (Christie) D. 1923, Tr. LC 5-42174. (On Cover: Cassell's Sunshine Series, No. 124). Cassell Publishing Company.
Child of the Bay: Or, The Old Sailor's Protege. A Tale of England, India, and the Ocean. Sylvanus Cobb. LC 6-20723. 1852. F. Gleason.
Child of the Century. John Tyler Wheelwright. 1887. C. Scribner's Sons.
Child of the Covenant. Virginia Carter Castleman. 1894. The Young Churchman Co.
Child of the Islands: Or, The Shipwrecked Gold Seekers. Robert F Greeley. LC 6-45543. 1850. Stringer & Townsend.
Child of the Jago. Arthur Morrison. LC 7-32487. 1896. H. S. Stone & Co.
Child of the Morning. Pauline Gedge. LC 77-4385. 1977. 8.95 (ISBN 0-8037-1462-9). Dial Press.
Child of the Morning. Pauline Gedge. 1978. 2.25 (ISBN 0-445-04227-3). Popular Library.
Child of the Night. Cornelia Tree. 1983. pap. 2.95 (ISBN 0-553-23054-9). Bantam.
Child of the North. Ridgwell Cullum. LC 26-12287. George H. Doran Company.
Child of the Orient. Demetra Vaka Brown. 1914. Houghton Mifflin Company.
Child of the Parish. A Novel. Ebner Von Eschenbach, Marie & Robinson, Mary A., Tr. (choice ser. no. 81). 1893. R. Bonner's Sons.
Child of the Parish. A Novel. Ebner Von Eschenbach, Marie & Robinson, Mary A., Tr. (Ledger library. no. 81). 1893. R. Bonner's Sons.
Child of the Plains. Wayne Groves Barrows. LC 12-6583. 1910. 1.50. The C. M. Clark Publishing Co.
Child of the Pogrom. Louis Volat. LC 35-6538. The Saverg Press.
Child of the Revolution. Emmuska Orczy. LC 32-5029. 1932. Doubleday, Doran & Company, Inc.
Child of the Revolution: A Novel. Margaret Roberts. (Harper's handy series, no. 111). 1887. Harper & Brothers.
Child of the Revolution. A Novel. Margaret Roberts. (On cover: Seaside library. Pocket ed. no. 920). 1887. G. Munro.
Child of the Snapping Turtle, Mike Fink: A Novel. Julian Lee Rayford. LC 51-12374. 1951. Abelard Press.
Child of the Sun. Kyle Onstott & Lance Horner. 352p. 1982. pap. 2.95 (ISBN 0-449-13775-9, GM). Fawcett.
Child of the Wild: A Story of Alaska. Edison Marshall. LC 26-801252. 1926. Cosmopolitan Book Corporation.
Child of the Wind. Ethel E Bangert. LC 57-980299.
Child of Thirty-Six Fathers: A Serious, Comic and Moral Romance. Translated from the French. 1809. Issac Riley.
Child of Two Worlds. Mugo Gatheru. (African Writers Ser.: No. 20). 230p. 1966. pap. text ed. 4.50 (ISBN 0-435-90020-X). Heinemann Ed.
Child of Unknown Parents: And Other Stories. Joseph S Salzburg. LC 54-12006. 1954. Vantage Press.
Child Possessed: A Novel. Ray Coryton Hutchinson. LC 64-251284. 1965. 4.95. Harper.
Child Possessed by Chess. James A. Howard. 1978. 4.00 o.p. (ISBN 0-682-48587-X). Exposition.
Child: Prologue to an Earthquake. John Symonds. LC 76-368434. 1976. 3.45 (ISBN 0-7156-0962-9). Duckworth.
Child Sellers. Wendy Leeds. 1981. pap. 2.25 (ISBN 0-8439-0889-0, Leisure Bks). Nordon Pubns.
Child-Sketches from George Eliot: Glimpses at the Boys and Girls in the Romances of the Great Novelist. George Eliot & Magruder, Julia, 1854-1907, Ed. LC 6-40740. 1895. Lothrop Publishing Company.
Child Stealers. Fred Grove. LC 72-89311. (Doubleday western). 1973. 4.95 (ISBN 0-385-02596-3). Doubleday.
Child Swappers. Richard E. Stanton. 192p. (Orig.). 1973. pap. 1.95 o.p. (ISBN 0-87682-341-X, 7341). Barclay Hse.
Child Wife: Or, Married at School. Adah M Howard. (On cover: Munro's library. v. 1. no. 132)). N. L. Munro.
Child with a Flower: Translated by C. J. Richards. Elda Bossi. LC 54-877178. 1954. Macmillan.
Child Witness. Helen Norwood Halsey. LC 98-1819. F. T. Neely.
Child You Used to Be. Leonora Pease. LC 9-25394. 1909. 1.50. A. C. McClurg & Co.
Childermass. Wyndham Lewis. LC 28-22138. Covici, Friede.
Childermass. Part 1. Wyndham Lewis. LC 76-145141. 1971. (ISBN 0-403-01072-1). Scholarly Press.
Childgrave. Ken Greenhall. 304p. (Orig.). 1982. pap. 2.95 (ISBN 0-671-42161-1). PB.
Childhood. Teo Savory. LC 78-8912. 10.00. (ISBN 0-87775-123-4) (ISBN 0-87775-124-2). Unicorn Press.
Childhood. Teo Savory. LC 80-104. 1980. 8.95 (ISBN 0-8161-3065-5). G. K. Hall.
Childhood: A Memoir. Jona Oberski. LC 81-43731. 1983. 11.95 (ISBN 0-385-17768-2). Doubleday.
Childhood and Other Neighborhoods. Stuart Dybek. LC 79-21609. 1980. 9.95 (ISBN 0-670-21618-6). Viking Press.
Childhood, Boyhood & Youth. Lev Nikolaevich Tolstoi. LC 64-21015. 1965. McGraw-Hill.
Childhood, Boyhood and Youth. Lev Nikolaevich Tolstoi. LC 49-11209. 1949. Lear.
Childhood, Boyhood, Youth. Lev Nikolaevich Tolstoi. Tr. by Leo Wiener. Limited Editions Club, Inc., New York. LC 72-172719. (Illus.). 1972. Printed for the Limited Editions Club, New York at the Press of A. Colish.
Childhood, Boyhood, Youth. Lev Nikolaevich Tolstoi & Hapgood, Isabel Florence, 1850-1928, Tr. T. Y. Crowell & Co.
Childhood, Boyhood, Youth. Lev Nikolaevich Tolstoi & Hapgood, Isabel Florence, 1850-1928, Tr. LC 16-19161. T. Y. Crowell & Co.
Childhood Days. Bess Hughes Burns. LC 41-420821. The Story Book Press.
Childhood Fancies. Henry White. The Maverick Press.
Childhood Is Not Forever. James Thomas Farrell. LC 72-78734. 1969. 5.95. Doubleday.
Childhood of David Copperfield. Charles Dickens. Ed. by Hale, Edward Everett. LC 98-1952. (Standard literature series. double no. 36). University Publishing Company.
Childhood of the Magician. Nancy Willard. LC 73-82429. (Liveright new writer). 1973. 5.95. Liveright.
Childhood's End. Arthur Charles Clarke. LC 63-2407. 1963. Harcourt, Brace & World.
Childhood's End. Arthur Charles Clarke. LC 53-10419. 1953. Ballantine Books.
Childkeeper. Sol Stein. LC 75-15823. 1975. (ISBN 0-15-117233-1). Harcourt Brace Jovanovich.
Childless Women. Sewell Peaslee Wright. LC 37-20199. Phoenix Press.
Childlike Life of the Black Tarantula. rev. ed. Kathy Acker. LC 78-58942. (Viper's Tongue Bks.). (Orig.). 1978. pap. 4.00 (ISBN 0-931106-20-6). TVRT.
Childlike Life of the Black Tarantula. Kathy Acker. (Viper's Tongue Books Ser.). 1975. 3.65 o.p. TVRT.
Childlike Life of the Black Tarantula by the Black Tarantula. Kathy Acker. LC 78-58943. 1978. pap. text ed. 4.00 (ISBN 0-931106-20-6). Printed Matter.
Childmare. A. G. Scott. (Orig.). 1981. pap. 2.50 (ISBN 0-451-09807-2, E9807, Sig). NAL.
Children. Howard Melvin Fast. 1947. Duell, Sloan & Pearce.
Children. Antonina Fedorovna Riasonovsky. LC 42-6835. 1942. Little, Brown and Company.
Children. Charles Robertson. 384p. 1982. pap. 3.50 (ISBN 0-553-20920-5). Bantam.
Children. Edith Newbold Jones Wharton. LC 28-20466. 1928. D. Appleton and Company.
Children: A Comedy for Grownups. 1st Ed. Babette Rosmond. LC 56-9931. 1956. Harcourt, Brace.
Children & Fools. Thomas Mann. Tr. by Herman George Scheffauer. LC 71-142268. (Short story index reprint series). 1970. (ISBN 0-8369-3752-X). Books for Libraries Press.
Children & Fools: Translated from the German. Thomas Mann & Scheffauer, Herman George, 1878-1927, Tr. LC 28-10625. 1928. A. A. Knopf.
Children & Lovers: Fifteen Stories. Helga Sandburg. LC 75-42207. 8.50 (ISBN 0-15-117250-1). Harcourt Brace Jovanovich.
Children and Older People. Ruth Suckow. LC 31-21755. 1931. A. A. Knopf.
Children and Others. James Gould Cozzens. LC 64-22665. 1964. Harcourt, Brace & World.
Children & Their Pets. Hal Edwards. 192p. pap. 1.95 o.p. (7146). Barclay Hse.
Children Are Bored on Sunday. 1st Ed. Jean Stafford. LC 52-13766. 1953. Harcourt, Brace.
Children Are Civilians Too. Heinrich Boll. LC 77-365298. 1976. 0.60 (ISBN 0-14-004125-7). Penguin.
Children Are Gone: A Novel. Arthur Cavanaugh. LC 66-11956. 1966. Simon and Schuster.
Children at Sherburne House. Amanda Minnie Douglas. LC 6-33490. (Sherburne series). 1897. Dodd, Mead & Company.
Children at the Gate. Edward Lewis Wallant. LC 64-11543. 1964. Harcourt, Brace & World.
Children at the Gate. Edward Lewis Wallant. LC 79-24169. (Harvest/HBJ book). 1980. 3.50 (ISBN 0-15-616861-8). Harcourt Brace Jovanovich.
Children at the Gate: A Novel. Lynne Reid Banks. LC 68-14832. 1968. Simon and Schuster.
Children. Centennial Ed. Edith Newbold Jones Wharton. LC 62-580. 1962. Appleton-Century-Crofts.
Children in the Mist. George Madden Martin. LC 20-11222. 1920. D. Appleton & Company.
Children Is All. James Purdy. LC 62-16923. 1971. pap. 2.25 o.p. (ISBN 0-8112-0166-X, NDP327). New Directions.
Children of a Lesser God. Mark Medoff. LC 80-24379. xxii, 91p. 1980. 8.95 (ISBN 0-88371-032-3); pap. 4.95 (ISBN 0-88371-034-X). J T White.
Children of Abraham. Sholem Asch. (Short Story Index Reprint Ser.). 433p. 1982. Repr. of 1942 ed. lib. bdg. 24.00 (ISBN 0-8290-0827-6). Irvington.
Children of Abraham: The Short Stories of Sholem Asch. Shalom Asch. LC 74-152934. (Short story index reprint series). 1971. (ISBN 0-8369-3792-9). Books for Libraries Press.
Children of Abraham: The Short Stories of Sholem Asch. Shalom Asch. Tr. by Samuel, Maurice. LC 42-11242. 1942. G. P. Putnam's Sons.
Children of All. Silas Jones. LC 78-68069. 1978. pap. 3.95 (ISBN 0-932442-00-5). Funkshunal.
Children of Alsace. Rene Bazin. (The Lotus library). 1915. Brentano's.
Children of Alsace (Les Oberles) Rene Bazin. LC 12-13195. 1912. John Lane Company.
Children of Banishment. Francis William Sullivan. 1914. G. P. Putnam's Sons.
Children of Blindness. Trish Sheppard. LC 77-375227. 1976. (ISBN 0-7254-0304-7). U. Smith.
Children of Capricorn. William Miller Abrahams. LC 63-7638. 1963. Random House.
Children of Chance. Gladys Alexandra Milton. LC 23-6497. 1923. Houghton Mifflin Company.
Children of Circumstance. Kathleen Mannington Hunt Caffyn. LC 6-218819. 1894. D. Appleton and Company.
Children of Darkness. Viacheslav IAkovlevich Shishkov. LC 72-90313. 1973. 13.00 (ISBN 0-88355-023-7). Hyperion Press.
Children of Destiny. Molly Elliot Seawell. LC 8-64283. (On cover: Appletons' town and country library, no. 113). 1893. D. Appleton and Company.
Children of Destiny. Molly Elliot Seawell. LC 3-8337. 1903. The Bobbs-Merrill Company.
Children of Divorce. Owen McMahon Johnson. LC 27-56065. 1927. Little, Brown, and Company.
Children of Dune. Frank Herbert. LC 75-43670. 8.95 (ISBN 0-399-11697-4). Berkley Pub. Corp.: Distributed by Putnam.
Children of Dune. Frank Herbert. (Berkley Medallion Book). 1977. 1.95 (ISBN 0-425-03310-4). Berkley Pub.Corp.
Children of Dynmouth. William Trevor. LC 76-53741. 1977. 7.95 (ISBN 0-670-21665-8). Viking Press.
Children of Eve. Isabel Constance Clarke. LC 18-18953. 1918. Benziger Brothers.
Children of Fate. Marice Rutledge Hale. LC 17-9707. Frederick A. Stokes Company.
Children of Fate: A Story of Passion. Adolphe Danziger De Castro. LC 5-33315. 1905. Brentano's.
Children of Gabelawi. Najib Mahfuz. Tr. by Philip Stewart from Arabic. (Arab Writers Series). ix, 355p. (Orig.). 1981. pap. 7.00x (ISBN 0-89410-213-3). Three Continents.
Children of Gibeon. A Novel. Walter Besant. (Harper's Franklin square library, no. 551). 1886. Harper & Brothers.
Children of Gibeon. A Novel. Walter Besant. (On cover: Harper's Franklin square library, no. 681). 1890. Harper & Brothers.
Children of Gibeon: A Novel. Walter Besant. LC 4-15284. Harper & Brothers.
Children of God. Vardis Fisher. 1977. 12.95 (ISBN 0-918522-50-1). O L Holmes.
Children of God. Shanta Rameshwar Rao. (Orig.). 1976. 4.50x (ISBN 0-88386-928-4, Orient Longman); pap. text ed. 2.50x (Orient Longman). South Asia Bks.
Children of God: An American Epic. Vardis Fisher. LC 39-27649. 1939. Harper & Brothers.
Children of God: An American Epic. Vardis Fisher. LC 49-8464. Vanguard Press.
Children of Guernica: A Novel. Hermann Kesten & Dunlop, Geoffrey, 1894- Tr. LC 39-10125. Alliance Book Corporation, Longmans, Green and Co.
Children of Heaven. Christiane Rochefort. LC 62-15776. 1962. D. McKay Co.
Children of Hollywood. Phyllis Gordon Demarest. LC 29-1196. The Macaulay Company.
Children of Hope: A Novel. Stephen French Whitman. LC 16-9958. 1916. The Century Co.
Children of Iroko. Tanure Ojaide. 1973. perfect bdg. 2.25 (ISBN 0-912678-09-7). Greenfld Rev Pr.
Children of Issachar. 1 Chronicles, Xii: 32.) A Story of Wrongs and Remedies... Willis Brewer. LC 6-161063. 1884. G. P. Putnam's Sons.
Children of Kaywana. Edgar Mittelholzer. 1976. (pbk.) 1.95 (ISBN 0-553-02775-1). Bantam Books.
Children of Kaywana. new ed. Edgar Mittelholzer. LC 77-350498. (Illus.). 1976. 0.75 (ISBN 0-552-10000-5). Corgi.
Children of Kaywana: A Novel. Edgar Mittelholzer. LC 52-9609. 1952. J. Day Co.
Children of Light. Gerald Sykes. LC 55-6681. 1955. Farrar, Straus & Young.
Children of Light: A Theme for the Time. Caroline Chesebro' LC 6-24218. 1853. Redfield.
Children of Lir: Stories from Ireland. Desmond Hogan. LC 81-3820. 1981. 8.95 (ISBN 0-8076-1015-1). G. Braziller.
Children of Llyr. Evangeline Walton. LC 77-28096. (Adult fantasy). 1971. 0.95 (ISBN 0-345-02332-3). Ballantine Books.
Children of Loneliness: Stories of Immigrant Life in America. Anzia Yezierska. LC 23-16037. 1923. Funk & Wagnalls Company.
Children of Lucifer: A Novel. Dana Faralla. LC 63-17675. 1963. Lippincott.
Children of Men. Rudolph Edgar Block. LC 76-103496. (Short story index reprint series). (Illus.). 1969. Books for Libraries Press.
Children of Men. Rudolph Edgar Block. LC 3-24299. 1903. McClure, Phillips & Co.
Children of Men. Eden Phillpotts. LC 23-728620. 1923. The Macmillan Company.
Children of Mount Ida, and Other Stories. Lydia Maria Francis Child. LC 42-482946. 1871. C. S. Francis.
Children of Noah: Glimpses of Unknown America. Ben Lucien Burman. LC 51-12087. (Illus.). 1951. Messner.
Children of Passage. Frederick Watson. LC 17-31649. E. P. Dutton & Company.
Children of Passion. Elizabeth Bright. (Orig.). 1982. pap. cancelled (Gallen). PB.

Children of Pleasure. Larry Barretto. LC 32-923600. Farrar & Rinehart, Incorporated.
Children of Power. Susan Richards Shreve. LC 78-26828. 9.95 (ISBN 0-02-610510-1). Macmillan.
Children of Ruth. Marvin Sutton. LC 34-509617. Greenberg.
Children of Shiny Mountain. David Dvorkin. 288p. 1981. pap. 2.50 (ISBN 0-671-43121-8, Timescape). PB.
Children of Shiny Mountain. David Dvorkin. (Kangaroo Book). 1977. 1.75 (ISBN 0-671-80954-7). Pocket Books.
Children of Sisyphus see Dinah.
Children of Sisyphus: A Novel 1st Amer. Ed. Horace Orlando Patterson. LC 65-10682. 1965. 4.00. Houghton.
Children of Storm. Ida Alexa Ross Wylie. LC 20-18388. 1920. John Lane Company.
Children of Strangers. Lyle Saxon. LC 64-9538. 1948. R. L. Crager.
Children of Strangers. Lyle Saxon. LC 37-14577. 1937. Houghton Mifflin Company.
Children of the Abbey. A Tale. Regina Maria Dalton Roche. LC 7-25594. 1816. R. Scott.
Children of the Abbey. A Tale... Regina Maria Dalton Roche. LC 7-39648. 1827. J. J. Woodward.
Children of the Age. Knut Hamsun & Scott, J. S., Tr. LC 24-4588. 1924. A. A. Knopf.
Children of the Albatross. Nin, Anais. LC 66-6826. A. Swallow.
Children of the Albatross. Anais Nin. LC 47-11456. 1947. E. P. Dutton.
Children of the Archbishop. 1st American Ed. Norman Collins. LC 51-10883. 1951. Duell, Sloan and Pearce.
Children of the Ash-Covered Loam & Other Stories. N. V. Gonzalez. 212p. 1979. pap. 5.00x o.p. (Pub. by Bookmark Philippines). Cellar.
Children of the Atom. Wilmar H. Shiras. LC 78-62473. 1978. 14.95 (ISBN 0-930800-01-X); pap. 5.95 (ISBN 0-930800-02-8). Pennyfarthing.
Children of the Atom. 1st Ed. Wilmar H Shiras. LC 53-10534. 1953. Gnome Press.
Children of the Black-Haired People. Robert Spencer Ward. LC 55-5309. (Illus.). 1955. Rinehart.
Children of the Chapel: A Tale. Disney Leith & Algernon Charles Swinburne. LC 82-6436. 1982. 18.95 (ISBN 0-8214-0631-0). Ohio University Press.
Children of the Covenant. Richard Scowcroft. LC 45-7202. 1945. Houghton Mifflin Company.
Children of the Dark. Charles Veley. LC 78-55858. 1979. 10.00 (ISBN 0-385-14160-2). Doubleday.
Children of the Dark. 1st Ed. Irving Shulman. Holt.
Children of the Dear Cotswolds. Lizzie Allen Harker. 1.50. C. Scribner's Sons.
Children of the Desert. Louis Dodge. LC 17-7927. 1917. 1.35. C. Scribner's Sons.
Children of the Dragon. Frank S. Robinson. 1977. pap. 1.95 (ISBN 0-380-01819-5, 35774). Avon.
Children of the Dragon: Frank S. Robinson. Frank S Robinson. 1978. 1.95 (ISBN 0-380-01819-5). Avon Books.
Children of the Earth. Annie Robertson Macfarlane. LC 7-20097. (On cover: Leisure hour series no. 192). 1886. H. Holt and Company.
Children of the Earth. Ethel Edith Mannin. LC 30-12992. 1930. Doubleday, Doran and Company, Inc.
Children of the Fog: A Novel of Southwark. Carmel Goldsmid Guest. LC 27-21466. 1927. G. P. Putnam's Sons.
Children of the Forest. LC 27-13675. (American tract society. Tracts. no. 245). American Tract Society.
Children of the Forest: A Story of Indian Love. Egerton Ryerson Young. LC 4-22671. 1904. F. H. Revell Company.
Children of the Frost. Jack London. LC 13-12909. 1902. The Macmillan Company.
Children of the Frost. Jack London. LC 2-23409. 1902. The Macmillan Company.
Children of the Ghetto. Israel Zangwill. LC 73-153007. 1972. 6.95 (ISBN 0-85617-840-3). (Baker St., WM FA), White Lion Publishers.
Children of the Ghetto: A Study of a Peculiar People. Israel Zangwill. LC 77-355325. (Victorian library). (Illus.). 1977. 12.50 (ISBN 0-7185-5028-5). Leicester University Press.
Children of the Ghetto: A Study of a Peculiar People. Israel Zangwill. 1895. Macmillan and Co.
Children of the Ghetto: A Study of a Peculiar People. Israel Zangwill. LC 41-33257. 1899. The Macmillan Company.
Children of the Ghetto: A Study of a Peculiar People. Israel Zangwill. LC 19-5140. 1916. The Jewish Publication Society of America.
Children of the Ghetto. Being Pictures of a Peculiar People. Israel Zangwill. LC 9-2205. 1892. The Jewish Publication Society.
Children of the Griffin. Elizabeth Giles. 1971. pap. 0.75 o.p. (ISBN 0-447-74755-X). Lancer.
Children of the Heart & Other Stories. Victoria Bellett. 2.50 o.p. Vantage.
Children of the Holocaust: The Collected Stories of Arnost Lustig. Arnost Lustig. LC 76-41229. vol.) 8.95(ea. Inscape.
Children of the King: A Tale of Southern Italy. Francis Marion Crawford. LC 4-15087. 1893. Macmillan and Co.
Children of the Lens: Illustrated by Ric Binkley. 1st Ed. Edward Elmer Smith. LC 54-5692. 1954. Fantasy Press.
Children of the Lion. Peter Danielson. 480p. (Orig.). 1980. pap. 2.95 (ISBN 0-553-14249-6). Bantam.
Children of the Market Place. Edgar Lee Masters. LC 22-4211. 1922. The Macmillan Company.
Children of the Marshes. Translated from the French by Gerard Hopkins; Illustrated by Richard Kennedy. Michel Aime Baudouy. LC 59-8589. 2.95. Pantheon.
Children of the Mist. Eden Phillpotts. LC 7-361869. 1899. G. P. Putnam's Sons.
Children of the Morning. Walter Lionel George. 1927. G. P. Putnam's Sons.
Children of the Night. John Blackburn. LC 76-83366. (Red mask mystery). 1969. 4.50. Putnam.
Children of the Night. Michael Kring. (Space Mavericks Ser.: No. 2). 192p. (Orig.). 1981. pap. 1.95 (ISBN 0-8439-1016-X, Leisure Bks). Nordon Pubns.
Children of the Night. Richard Lortz. 1974. (pbk.) 1.25. Dell.
Children of the Night. Mary Hulbert Rogers. LC 11-24361. 1911. Duffield & Company.
Children of the Outlaw: A Story of the Middle Ages. Rudolph Leonhart. LC 7-13164. 1879. Stevenson, Foster & Co.
Children of the Pool and Other Stories. Arthur Machen. LC 76-1366. (Supernatural and Occult Fiction). 1976. 14.00 (ISBN 0-405-08424-2). Arno Press.
Children of the Poor. LC 34-25173. The Vanguard Press.
Children of the Rainbow. Bryan MacMahon. LC 52-5297. 1952. Dutton.
Children of the Ritz. Cornell Woolrich, pseud. LC 27-22472. 1927. Boni and Liveright.
Children of the River. William Lavendar. 448p. (Orig.). 1980. pap. 2.50 (ISBN 0-515-05388-0). Jove Pubns.
Children of the River: A Romance of Old New Orleans. Harris Dickson. LC 28-23940. J. H. Sears & Company, Inc.
Children of the Saints: An Early Christian Romance. Normand Smith Boardman. LC 11-8951. 1911. Cochrane Publishing Company.
Children of the Sea. James R. Nichols. LC 77-20046. 9.95 (ISBN 0-89587-001-0). J. F. Blair.
Children of the Sea. Henry De Vere Stacpoole. LC 13-254386. 1913. 1.25. Duffield & Company.
Children of the Sea: A Tale of the Forecastle. Joseph Conrad. LC 6-30679. 1897. Dodd, Mead and Company.
Children of the Shadow: A Novel. Isabel Constance Clarke. LC 24-304488. 1924. Benziger Brothers.
Children of the Soil. Henryk Sienkiewicz. Tr. by Jeremiah Curtin. LC 10-4195. 1895. Little, Brown and Company.
Children of the Soviet Arctic. Tikhon Semushkin. 1944. Hutchinson & Co., Ltd.
Children of the Stars. Laura Kinkel. 4.95 o.p. Vantage.
Children of the Stars: Bk. 1, Tomorrow's Heritage. Juanita Coulson. 384p. 1981. pap. 2.75 (ISBN 0-345-28178-0, Del Rey). Ballantine.
Children of the Stars: Bk. 2 Outward Bound. Juanita Coulson. (Orig.). 1982. pap. 2.95 (ISBN 0-345-28179-9, Del Rey). Ballantine.
Children of the Stone Lions. Paul Hackett. LC 55-5918. Putnam.
Children of the Storm. Deanna Dwyer. (Orig.). 1972. pap. 0.95 o.s.i. (75-365). Lancer.
Children of the Street. Viacheslan Iakoulevich Shishkou. LC 78-65005. 14.00 (ISBN 0-931554-12-8). Strathcona Pub. Co.
Children of the Sun. Oakley M Hall. LC 82-73039. 1983. 14.95 (ISBN 0-689-11348-X). Atheneum.
Children of the Tenements. Jacob August Riis. LC 75-122732. (Short story index reprint series). (Illus.). 1970. Books for Libraries Press.
Children of the Tenements. Jacob August Riis. LC 3-28289. 1903. The Macmillan Company.
Children of the Void. William Dexter. pap. 0.50 o.p. (52-357). Paperback Lib.
Children of the Way. Anne Crosby Emery Allinson. LC 74-103490. (Short story index reprint series). 1969. Books for Libraries Press.
Children of the Way. Anne Crosby Emery Allinson. LC 23-12871. Harcourt, Brace and Company.
Children of the Whirlwind. Leroy Scott. LC 21-127034. 1921. 2.00. Houghton Mifflin Company.
Children of the Wild. Charles George Douglas Roberts. LC 13-203464. 1913. 1.35. The Macmillan Company.
Children of the Wind. Burgess Drake. 1954. Lippincott.
Children of the Wind. Matthew Phipps Shiel. LC 23-11807. 1923. A. A. Knopf.
Children of the Wind: A Novel. Doris Peel. LC 27-196348. 1927. Houghton Mifflin Company.
Children of the Wolf. Alfred Leo Duggan. LC 59-12491. 1959. Coward-McCann.
Children of the World. new ed., rev. ed. Paul Johann Ludwig Von Heyse. LC 7-25670. 1894. H. Holt and Company.
Children of the World. A Novel. Paul Johann Von Heyse. (Seaside library, v. 78, mo. 1577). G. Munro.
Children of Their Time: A Novel. Franz Carl Weiskopf. Tr. by Norden, Heinz. LC 48-8448. 1948. A. A. Knopf.
Children of This Earth. Bruce Marshall. LC 31-25765. 1930. The Macaulay Company.
Children of to-Morrow. Clara Elizabeth Laughlin. LC 11-22132. 1911. 1.30. C. Scribner's Sons.
Children of to-Morrow: A Romance. William Sharp. LC 13-93849. (On cover: Lovell's international series, no. 70). F. F. Lovell & Company.
Children of Tomorrow. Alfred Elton Van Vogt. 1975. (pbk.) 1.25. Ace Books.
Children of Transgression. Georgie Vere Tyler. LC 22-6316. 1922. H. Holt and Company.
Children of Union. Albert A Small. LC 25-10304. The Union Publishing Co.
Children of Vienna: A Novel. Robert Neumann. LC 47-30128. 1947. E. P. Dutton & Co., Inc.
Children of Violence: 2v. in1. Doris May Lessing. LC 64-22409. bds., 6.95. S. & S.
Children of Wonder: 21 Remarkable and Fantastic Tales, Edited and with an Introd. by William Tenn Pseud. Written by Poul Anderson and Others. Ed. by Philip Klass. LC 53-8490. 1953. Simon and Schuster.
Children Reap. Henry Burgess Drake. LC 29-796223. 1929. Macy Masius, The Vanguard Press.
Children Robbers. Phillip C. Snyder. LC 80-66622. 261p. (Orig.). 1980. pap. 3.75 (ISBN 0-940560-00-3). Custom Hse.
Children Sing. Mackinlay Kantor. 1977. pap. 1.75 o.s.i. (ISBN 0-505-51108-8). Tower Bks.
Children Sing: A Novel. MacKinlay Kantor. LC 73-2607. 1973. 7.95. Hawthorn Books.
Children Sing: A Novel. MacKinlay Kantor. (Belmont Tower Book). 1.75. C.
Children with Emerald Eyes. Mira Rothenberg. 1978. pap. 2.75 (ISBN 0-671-81966-6). PB.
Children, You Are Very Little. Betsy Drake Grant. LC 70-165207. 1971. 6.95. Atheneum.
Children's Book of Animal Stories. Amelia Gonzalez. (Illus.). 1973. 3.50 (ISBN 0-533-00441-1). Vantage Press.
Children's Carpenter, an Easter Fable. Katherine L. West. (Illus., Orig.). pap. 5.00. Amata Graphics.
Children's Children. Dorothea Maria Pauline Alice Sibylle Pietzsch Moholy-Nagy. LC 45-8868. 1945. H. Bittner and Company.
Children's Inferno: Stories of the Great Famine in Greece. Lilika Nakos & Macdougall, Allan Ross, 1893- Tr. LC 46-8869. 1946. Gateway Books.
Children's Inferno: Stories of the Great Famine in Greece. by lilika nakos. translated from the french by allan ross macdougall, with an introduction by bessie breuer. ed. Lilika Nakou. LC 46-8669. 1946. Gateway Books.
Children's Party. Arthur H. Lewis. LC 72-76770. 1972. 5.95 (ISBN 0-671-27090-7). Trident Press.
Children's Party. Arthur H. Lewis. 1973. (pbk) 0.95 (ISBN 0-671-77646-0). Pocket Books.
Children's Poems That Never Grow Old: For Little Folks from Six to Twelve Years Old. Ed. by Chement F Benoff. LC 22-135549. The Reilly & Lee Co.
Children's War. David Bellin. LC 79-54050. 1980. 10.95 (ISBN 0-935210-00-8); pap. 4.95 (ISBN 0-935210-01-6). Dundee Pub.
Children's Ward. Howard L Weiner. LC 80-16365. 10.95 (ISBN 0-399-12509-4). Putnam.
Child's Eye View of the World. Marc Simont. 96p. 1972. 4.95 o.p. Delacorte.
Child's Garden of Death. Richard Forrest. (Kangaroo Book.) 1977 (ISBN 0-671-80924-5). Pocket Books.
Child's Garden of Death: A Novel of Suspense. Richard Forrest. LC 75-6387. 1975. 7.95 (ISBN 0-672-52151-2). Bobbs-Merrill.
Child's Play. Kate Christie. LC 69-12030. 1969. Harcourt, Brace & World.
Child's Play. Warren Murphy. (Destroyer No. 23). 192p. 1976. pap. 2.25 (ISBN 0-523-41884-1). Pinnacle Bks.
Child's Play. Richard Sapir & Warren Murphy. (Destroyer Series#23). 1976. (pbk.) 1.25 (ISBN 0-523-00842-2). Pinnacle Books.
Child's Play. David R. Slavitt. LC 72-79338. 1972. 4.95 (ISBN 0-8071-0238-5). Louisiana State University Press.
Child's Romance. authorized ed., rev. and cor. in the united states. ed. Julien Viaud. Tr. by Bell, Mrs. Clara Courtenay (Poynter) LC 9-3454. 1891. W. S. Gottsberger & Co.
Childsong. Barbara Wood. LC 80-1821. 1981. 12.95 (ISBN 0-385-15560-3). Doubleday.
Childsplay. Eda Lord. LC 61-5840. 1961. Simon and Schuster.
Childwold. Joyce Carol Oates. LC 76-42086. 8.95 (ISBN 0-8149-0777-6). Vanguard Press.
Chilean Spring Discoveries. Fernando Alegria. Ed. by Yvette Miller. Tr. by Stephen Fredman from Span. 160p. (Orig.). 1980. pap. 7.95 (ISBN 0-935480-00-5). Lat Am Lit Rev Pr.
Chill. Ross Macdonald. 1964. 4.95 o.p. Knopf.
Chill. Kenneth Millar. LC 63-20837. 1964. Knopf.
Chill and the Kill. Joan Margaret Fleming. LC 64-23491. 1964. Washburn.
Chill Factor. Richard Falkirk, pseud. LC 75-150888. 1971. 5.95 o.p. (ISBN 0-385-08153-7). Doubleday.
Chill Factor. Richard Falkirk, pseud. 1973. pap. 1.25 o.p. (ISBN 0-515-03072-4, V3072). Pyramid Pubns.
Chill Factor. Derek Lambert. LC 75-150888. 1971. 5.95. Doubleday.
Chill Factor. Aaron Marc Stein. LC 77-11754. 1978. 6.95. Published for the Crime Club by Doubleday.
Chill Hours. Helen Gansevoort Edwards Mackay. LC 77-178446. (Short story index reprint series). 1971. (ISBN 0-8369-4047-4). Books for Libraries Press.
Chill Hours. Helen Gansevoort Edwards Mackay. LC 20-3265. 1920. Duffield and Company.
Chill of Dusk. Stephen Minot. LC 64-19236. 1964. Doubleday.
Chill Winds of Ravenhall. Mary Bishop. 1981. pap. 1.95 (ISBN 0-89083-757-0). Zebra.
Chilling and Killing. Joan Kahn. LC 77-20093. 1978. 11.95 (ISBN 0-395-26287-9). Houghton Mifflin.
Chillon: A Tale of the Great Reformation of the Sixteenth Century. Jane Louisa Willyams. LC 9-3423. 1845. George & Wayne.
Chilly Scenes of Winter. Ann Beattie. LC 75-44519. 1976. 7.95 (ISBN 0-385-11658-6). Doubleday.
Chilly Scenes of Winter. Ann Beattie. 1978. 1.95 (ISBN 0-445-04261-3). Popular Library.
Chim: His Washington Winter: By Madeleine Vinton Dahlgren. Madeleine Vinton Dahlgren. LC 6-32183. 1892. C. L. Webster & Co.
Chime of Wedding Bells. Ethlyn P. Cooke Sturgess. LC 6-42431. The Bell Publishing Company.
Chimera. John Barth. LC 72-3389. 1972. 6.95. Random House.
Chimera. Stephen Gallagher. LC 82-5786. 1982. 12.95 (ISBN 0-312-13387-1). St. Martin's Press.
Chimera. Ebba Maria Rankin & Beamish, Ellenora. LC 34-904. J. H. Hopkins & Son.
Chimes. Charles Dickens. LC 8-31690. 1908. 2.00. The Baker & Taylor Company.
Chimes. Charles Dickens. LC 11-28776. 1911. 1.75. G. P. Putnam's Sons.
Chimes. Charles Dickens & Wagenknecht, Edward Charles. 1931. Printed by G. W. Jones for the Members of the Limited Editions Club.
Chimes. Robert Herrick. LC 73-145080. 1976. (ISBN 0-403-03194-X). Scholarly Press.
Chimes. Robert Herrick. LC 26-9569. 1926. The Macmillan Company.
Chimes see Collected Works.
Chimes from a Jester's Bells: Stories and Sketches. Robert Jones Burdette. LC 6-18666. 1897. The Bowen-Merrill Company.
Chimes of Freedom. Mary Putnam Denny. LC 13-26610. 0.75. R. G. Badger.
Chimmie Fadden and Mr. Paul. Edward Waterman Townsend. LC 2-13638. 1902. Printed by the Century Co.
Chimmie Fadden Explains; Major Max Expounds. Edward Waterman Townsend. (On cover: Belgravia series, no. 5). 1895. United States Book Company.
Chimmie Fadden," Major Max, and Other Stories. Edward Waterman Townsend. LC 69-11923. (American short story series, v. 82). (Illus.). 1969. (ISBN 0-512-00703-9). Garrett Press.
Chimmie Fadden," Major Max, and Other Stories. Edward Waterman Townsend. LC 72-8193. (American short story series, v. 82). 1972. (ISBN 0-8422-8117-7). MSS Information Corp.
Chimmie Fadden"; Major Max; and Other Stories. Edward Waterman Townsend. LC 8-29829. Lovell, Coryell & Company.
Chimmie Fadden Out West: A Sequel to Chimmie Fadden. William A Phelon. (On cover: The enterprise series. no. 68). 1896. E. A. Weeks & Company.
Chimney-Corner. Harriet Elizabeth Beecher Stowe. LC 8-16278. 1896. Houghton, Mifflin and Company.

Chimney Murder. Ethel Mary Channon. LC 30-12582. 1930. Little, Brown, and Company.

Chimneys of Summer. Maria Fagyas. 1970. 5.95 o.p. Putnam.

Chimps Are Coming: Harassment at Mendel Gorilla High School. Celia Uhrman. LC 74-20305. 1975. 4.95 (ISBN 0-8059-2104-4). Dorrance.

Chimps Are Coming: (Harrassment at Mendel Gorilla High School) Celia Uhrman. 96p. 1975. 4.95 o.p. (ISBN 0-8059-2104-4). Dorrance.

Chin Ping Mei: The Adventurous History of Hsi Men and His Six Wives. Introd. by Arthur Waley. LC 66-4000. 1959. bds., 6.50. Bodley Head.

Chin Ping Mei: The Adventurous History of Hsi Men and His Six Wives; with an Introduction by Arthur Waley; Translated by Bernard Miall. Hsiao-Hsiao-Sheng & Bernard Miall. LC 82-5261. 1982. 10.95 (ISBN 0-399-50657-8). Perigee Books.

China Alley. Henry Henn. 1979. pap. 1.95 (ISBN 0-532-19226-5). Woodhill.

China Bomb. Richard William Tregaskis. (N179). 1968. Avon.

China Bomb. Richard William Tregaskis. LC 67-18206. 1967. Washburn.

China Boy. Idwal Jones. LC 70-163033. (Short story index reprint series). 1971. (ISBN 0-8369-3947-6). Books for Libraries Press.

China Boy. Idwal Jones. LC 36-25549. The Primavera Press.

China Card. Donald Freed. LC 80-66506. 1980. 12.95 (ISBN 0-87795-281-7). Arbor Hse.

China Coaster: A Novel of Suspense. 1st Ed. Don Smith. LC 52-13075. 1953. Holt.

China Doll. Nick Carter. (O.s.i.). (Orig.). pap. 0.60 o.s.i. (A638X, Award). Univ Pub & Dist.

China Expert. Michael Delving, pseud. 1977. 7.95 o.p. (ISBN 0-684-14737-8). Scribner.

China Expert. Jay Williams. LC 76-23316. 1977. 6.95 (ISBN 0-684-14737-8). Scribner.

China Flight. Pearl Sydenstricker Buck. LC 45-2945. 1945. Triangle Books the Blakiston Company.

China Governess. Margery Allingham. LC 75-35634. 1975. 9.95. American Reprint Co.

China Governess: A Novel of Suspense. 1st Ed. Margery Allingham. LC 62-17700. 1962. Doubleday.

China Hand. Bruno Skoggard. LC 79-522. 8.95 (ISBN 0-396-07662-9). Dodd, Mead.

China Heart. Helen Ingham. LC 76-124484. 1970. 4.00. Dorrance.

China House. Vince Lardo. 180p. (Orig.). 1983. pap. 4.95 (ISBN 0-932870-33-X). Alyson Pubns.

China Journey. Milton Caniff. Ed. by Bill Chadbourne. LC 77-75667. (Milton Caniff's Terry & the Pirates Ser.: Vol. 1). (Illus.). 1977. pap. 6.95. Nostalgia Pr.

China Option. Nancy Milton. LC 82-47879. 13.95 (ISBN 0-394-52721-6). Pantheon Books.

China Princess. Hebe Elsna. 1971. pap. 0.95 o.p. (95075). Beagle Bks.

China Red (a Novel)... Hsi-Tseng Chiang. LC 31-81130. The Author.

China Run: A Book of Stories. Neil Paterson. LC 51-9270. 1951. Random House.

China Seas: A Novel of the East. Crosbie Garstin. LC 31-1201. 1931. Frederick A. Stokes Company.

China Shadow. Clarissa Ross. 1974. (pbk.) 1.75 (ISBN 0-380-00189-6). Avon.

China Shepherdess. Translated from the French by David Hughes and Marie-Jacqueline Mason. Felicien Marceau. LC 57-5569. 1957. Abelard-Schuman.

China Shop. Gladys Bronwyn Stern. LC 21-201146. 1921. A. A. Knopf.

China Shop. Gladys Bronwyn Stern. LC 26-14384. (Borzoi pocket books). 1926. A. A. Knopf.

China Sky. Pearl Sydenstricker Buck. LC 42-51181. 1942. Triangle Books.

China Song. Elizabeth Lane. (China Ser.: No. 1). (Orig.). 1983. pap. 3.50 (ISBN 0-440-01493-X). Dell.

China Spy. George Watt. 1979. pap. 2.00 (ISBN 0-88264-027-5). Diane Bks.

China Station. Donald R Morris. LC 51-10297. 1951. Farrar, Straus, and Young.

China: The Land of Contradictions. Arthur D Hall. LC 522986. (On cover: Historical series, no. 16). 1900. Street & Smith.

China Trader. Cornelia Spencer, pseud. LC 40-320997. The John Day Company.

China Trader. Grace Yaukey. 1940. The John Day Company.

China Venture: A Novel. Dorothy Graham. LC 29-1805. 1929. Frederick A. Stokes Company.

Chinaberry. William Lavender. (Orig.). 1976. pap. 2.95 (ISBN 0-515-05838-6). Jove Pubns.

Chinaberry. William Lavender. 1976. (pbk.) 1.95. Pyramid Books.

Chinaberry Tree. Jessie Redmon Faust. LC 70-95405. Repr. of 1931 ed. 17.00 (ISBN 0-404-00256-0). AMS Pr.

Chinaberry Tree. Jessie Redmon Faust. LC 70-76107. 1969. Repr. of 1931 ed. 17.00x o.p. (ISBN 0-8434-0008-0). Consortium Pr.

Chinaberry Tree: A Novel of American Life. Jessie Redmon Fauset. LC 70-76107. 1969. McGrath Pub. Co.

Chinaberry Tree: A Novel of American Life. Jessie Redmon Fauset. LC 70-95405. 1969. AMS Press.

Chinaberry Tree: A Novel of American Life. Jessie Redmon Fauset. LC 74-89033. 1969. (ISBN 0-8371-1919-7). Negro Universities Press.

Chinaberry Tree: A Novel of American Life. Jessie Redmon Fauset. LC 31-286929. 1931. Frederick A. Stokes Company.

Chinaman's Chance. Ross Thomas. 1979. pap. 2.25 (ISBN 0-380-41517-8, 41517). Avon.

Chinaman's Chance. Ross Thomas. (O.s.i.). 1978. 9.95 o.s.i. (ISBN 0-671-24070-6). S&S.

Chinaman's Chance: A Novel. Ross Thomas. LC 77-25326. 9.95 (ISBN 0-671-24070-6). Simon and Schuster.

China's Crucifixion. Bertram Lenox Simpson. LC 28-139141. 1928. The Macmillan Company.

China's Magic Brush. L. E Preston. LC 72-7659. 1973. (lib. bdg.) 4.50 (ISBN 0-87614-037-1). Carolrhoda Books.

Chinatown Family. Lin Yutang. 307p. 1980. 6.95x (ISBN 0-89955-169-6, Pub. by Mei Ya China); pap. 4.95x (ISBN 0-89955-198-X). Intl Schol Bk Serv.

Chinatown Family: A Novel. Lin Yutang. LC 48-8761. 1948. J. Day Co.

Chindera. Nancy Cato. 1976. 1.75. Dell Publishing Co.

Chindi. Brad Steiger. (Orig.). 1980. pap. 2.75 (ISBN 0-440-11119-6). Dell.

Chinese Agenda. Joe Poyer. 1974. (pbk.) 1.50 (ISBN 0-515-03382-0). Pyramid Books.

Chinese Agenda. Joe Poyer, pseud. LC 72-79418. 1972. 6.95 (ISBN 0-385-04493-3). Doubleday.

Chinese Agent. Michael Moorcock. LC 79-96746. (Cock Robin mystery). 1970. Macmillan Co.

Chinese Assassin. Anthony Grey. LC 78-14163. 1979. 8.95 (ISBN 0-03-046786-1). Holt, Rinehart, and Winston.

Chinese Bandit. Stephen D. Becker. LC 75-10255. (Illus.). 1975. 7.95 (ISBN 0-394-48561-0). Random House.

Chinese Bandit. Stephen D. Becker. (Berkley Medallion Book). (Illus.). 1977. 1.95 (ISBN 0-425-03403-8). Berkley Pub. Corp.

Chinese Bell Murders. Robert Van Gulik. LC 77-80378. 1977. pap. 3.25 (ISBN 0-226-84862-0). U of Chicago Pr.

Chinese Bell Murders: Three Cases Solved by Judge Dee. A Chinese Detective Story Suggested by Three Original Chinese Plots. With 15 Plates Drawn by the Author in Chinese Style. 1st American Ed. Robert Hans Van Gulik, pseud. LC 59-6343. (Judge Dee mystery). 1959. Harper.

Chinese Box. Marjorie McEvoy. 1973. 4.95. Lenox Hill Pr.

Chinese Chop. Sheridan, Juanita. LC 49-501229. Publisher for the Crime Club by Doubleday.

Chinese City. Frederick Anthony Edwards. LC 48-537. 1946. T.V. Boardman.

Chinese Coat. Jennette Barbour Perry Lee. LC 20-14288. 1920. C. Scribner's Sons.

Chinese Coffin. Joseph Hedges. (Stark Ser.: No. 3). (Orig.). 1975. pap. 0.95 o.p. (ISBN 0-515-03591-2, N3591). Pyramid Pubns.

Chinese Connection. Pai Ye Loh. LC 78-16880. Revell.

Chinese Doll... Wilson Tucker. LC 46-855342. 1946. Rinehart & Company, Inc.

Chinese Donavan. Carter Brown, pseud. (Signet book). New American Library.

Chinese Door. Virginia Coffman. (Signet book). 1.25. New American Library.

Chinese Door see Of Love & Intrigue.

Chinese Earth: Stories. morningside ed. Tsung-Wen Shen. LC 81-18150. 1982. 25.00 (ISBN 0-231-05484-X) (ISBN 0-231-05485-8). Columbia University Press.

Chinese Fire Drill. Michael Wolfe, pseud. LC 75-6380. 6.95 (ISBN 0-06-014716-4). Harper & Row.

Chinese Fish. Jean Bommart & Waldman, Milton, 1895- Tr. LC 35-16902. 1935. Longmans, Green and Co.

Chinese Game. Charles Larson. LC 69-11308. 1969. 4.95. Lippincott.

Chinese Godfather. Paul Gillette. 416p. (Orig.). 1980. pap. 2.75 (ISBN 0-449-14344-9, GM). Fawcett.

Chinese Gold Murders. Robert Hans Van Gulik, pseud. LC 79-1536. 1979. 2.95 (ISBN 0-226-84864-7). University of Chicago Press.

Chinese Gold Murders. Robert Van Gulik. LC 79-1536. 1979. pap. 2.95 (ISBN 0-226-84864-7). U of Chicago Pr.

Chinese Hammer. Simon Harvester. 1969. pap. 0.60 o.p. (60-415). Manor Bks.

Chinese Keyhole. Richard Himmel. LC 51-20414. (Gold medal book, 143). 1951. Fawcett Publications.

Chinese Kiss. J. J. Montague. (Black Swan). 192p. 1974. pap. 1.50 o.p. (ISBN 0-89014-101-0, CB-101). Canyon Bks.

Chinese Kiss. J. J Montague. (Black swan, #1). 1974. (pbk.) 1.50 (ISBN 0-89014-101-0). Canyon Books.

Chinese Label. James Francis Davis. LC 20-642930. 1920. Little, Brown, and Company.

Chinese Lake Murders. Robert Hans Van Gulik, pseud. LC 79-1537. 2.95 (ISBN 0-226-84865-5). University of Chicago Press.

Chinese Lake Murders. Robert Van Gulik. LC 79-1537. 1979. pap. 2.95 (ISBN 0-226-84865-5). U of Chicago Pr.

Chinese Letter. large & easy to read type. ed. Nicole, Claudette. (Queen Size Gothic). 1973. (pbk) 0.95. Popular Library.

Chinese Literature: An Anthology from the Earliest Times to the Present Day. Ed. by William McNaughton. LC 73-75284. 1974. pap. 11.75 (ISBN 0-8048-0882-1). C E Tuttle.

Chinese Literature: Popular Fiction & Drama. Ed. by H. C. Chang. 466p. 1982. pap. 10.00 (ISBN 0-231-05367-3). Columbia U Pr.

Chinese Love Stories from "Ching-Shih". Meng-Lung Feng & Hua-Yuan Li Mowry. LC 82-6859. 1982. 29.50 (ISBN 0-208-01920-0). Archon Books.

Chinese Love Stories from Ch'ing-shih. Hua-yuan L. Mowry. 1983. 29.50 (ISBN 0-208-01920-0, Archon). Shoe String.

Chinese Love Tales: Translated from the Original of George Soulie Sic De Morant. Ed. by Charles Georges Soulie. LC 50-4234. Halcyon House.

Chinese Lovesong... Frederick Anthony Edwards. LC 33-23175. 1933. Doubleday, Doran & Company, Inc.

Chinese Mask. William Sanborn Ballinger. LC 65-6058. (Signet thriller D2715). 1965. New American Library.

Chinese Maze Murders. Robert Van Gulik. 379p. 1981. Repr. lib. bdg. 14.95 (ISBN 0-89968-231-6). Lightyear.

Chinese Nail Murders. Robert Van Gulik. LC 77-80379. 1977. pap. 3.25 (ISBN 0-226-84863-9). U of Chicago Pr.

Chinese Nights Entertainment: Stories of Old China. Brian Brown. lib. bdg. 59.95 (ISBN 0-87968-491-7). Krishna Pr.

Chinese Nights Entertainment: Stories of Old China. Brian Brown. Repr. of 1922 ed. 12.00 o.s.i. Finch Pr.

Chinese Novels (1822) a facsim. reproduction / with an introd. by ben harris mcclary. ed. John Francis Davis. LC 76-43332. 1976. 22.00 (ISBN 0-8201-1278-X). Scholars' Facsimiles & Reprints.

Chinese Nursery Rhymes. Ed. by Isaac T. Headland. (Inspirational Classics Ser). 1967. 1.95 o.p. (ISBN 0-8007-1004-5). Revell.

Chinese Orange Mystery. Ellery Queen. 300p. 1976. lib. bdg. 15.75x (ISBN 0-89966-153-X). Buccaneer Bks.

Chinese Orange Mystery. Ellery Queen, pseud. LC 46-391029. 1945. Triangle Books, the Blakiston Company.

Chinese Orange Mystery: A Problem in Deduction. Ellery Queen, pseud. LC 34-27176. 1934. Frederick A. Stokes Company.

Chinese Parrot. Earl Derr Biggers. pap. 0.75 o.p. (T1970). Pyramid Pubns.

Chinese Parrot: A Novel. Earl Derr Biggers. LC 26-15964. The Bobbs-Merrill Company.

Chinese Parrot: A Novel. Earl Derr Biggers. LC 29-808. 1927. Grosset & Dunlap.

Chinese Paymaster. Nick Carter. (Nick Carter Ser.). (O.s.i.). 1976. pap. 1.25 o.s.i. (AQ1592, Award). Univ Pub & Dist.

Chinese Puzzle. Marian Bower & Lion, Leon M., Joint Author. LC 19-12981. 1919. H. Holt and Company.

Chinese Puzzle. Warren Murphy. (Destroyer Ser.: No. 3). 192p. (Orig.). 1982. pap. 2.25 (ISBN 0-523-41811-6). Pinnacle Bks.

Chinese Quaker: An Unfictitious Novel. Nellie Blessing Eyster. LC 2-21404. Fleming H. Revell Company.

Chinese Red. Richard Burke. LC 42-182889. (On cover: A Quincy Hite mystery). 1942. G. P. Putnam's Sons.

Chinese River. Frederick Anthony Edwards. LC 37-23083. 1937. Lothrop, Lee & Shepard Company.

Chinese Roulette. (Butler: No. 4). 1979. pap. 1.75 o.s.i. (ISBN 0-8439-0691-X, Leisure Bks). Nordon Pubns.

Chinese Shawl. Patricia Wentworth. 1973. pap. 0.95 o.p. (ISBN 0-515-03052-X). Pyramid Pubns.

Chinese Shawl: A Miss Silver Mystery. Patricia Wentworth. LC 43-464403. 1943. J. B. Lippincott Company.

Chinese Slave-Girl: A Story of Woman's Life in China. John A Davis. LC 6-32484. Presbyterian Board of Publication.

Chinese Stories from Taiwan, 1960-1970. Joseph S. M. Lau & Timothy A Ross. LC 75-43971. 1976. 20.00 (ISBN 0-231-04007-5) (ISBN 0-231-04008-3). Columbia University Press.

Chinese Straight. J. J Lamb. LC 75-45246. 1976. 1.50 (ISBN 0-345-25014-1). Ballantine Books.

Chinese Torture Garden. Octave Mirbeau. (O.s.i.). Orig. Title: Garden of Tortures. 1969. pap. 0.95 o.s.i. (A490N, Award). Univ Pub & Dist.

Chinese Ultimatum. Edward McGhee & Robin Moore (ISBN 0-523-00974-7). Pinnacle Books.

Chinese Visitor. James Eastwood. (1264). 1967. Dell.

Chinese Visitor: A Novel of Espionage 1st Amer. Ed. James Eastwood. LC 65-25505. 4.50. Coward.

Chinese White: A Novel. by david calder wilson. ed. David Calder Wilson. LC 27-157101. J. H. Sears & Company, Inc.

Chinese Word for Horse: And Other Stories. John Lewis. LC 79-25679. (Illus.). 96p. (Orig.). 1980. 9.95x o.p. (ISBN 0-8052-3736-4); pap. 5.95 o.p. (ISBN 0-8052-0640-X). Schocken.

Chink in the Armour. Marie Adelaide Belloc Lowndes. LC 12-5154. 1912. 1.30. C. Scribner's Sons.

Chink in the Armour. Marie Adelaide Belloc Lowndes. LC 37-27119. 1937. Longmans, Green and Co.

Chinks in the Curtain. Joyce Porter. LC 68-12493. 1968. Scribner.

Chinook Winter. Maureen Temple. (Orig.). 1979. pap. 1.95 (ISBN 0-532-23277-1). Woodhill.

Chinua Achebe. David Carroll. LC 76-120477. (Twayne's world authors series, TWAS, 101). 1970. Twayne Publishers.

Chiodo 2: The Decoy Man. Robert Baker Elder. LC 74-27574. 1975. pap. 1.75 o.p. (ISBN 0-87216-272-9, K16272). Playboy Pr Pbks.

Chion of Heraclea: A Novel in Letters. Ingemar During. LC 78-24389. (Greek Texts and Commentaries). (Series: Gothenburg, Sweden. Universitetet.). 1979. 12.00. Arno Press.

Chip. Florence Ethel Mills Young. LC 10-35851. 1909. John Lane Company.

Chip and the Block. Edmee Elizabeth Monica De La Pasture. LC 26-5625. Harper & Brothers.

Chip-Chip Gatherers. Shiva Naipaul. LC 72-11045. 1973. 6.95 (ISBN 0-394-48345-6). Knopf; Distributed by Random House.

Chip Harrison Scores Again. Chip Harrison. (Orig.). 1971. pap. 0.75 o.p. (T2421, GM). Fawcett World.

Chip, of the Flying U. B. M. Bower. 1975. lib. bdg. 13.35x (ISBN 0-89966-012-6). Buccaneer Bks.

Chip, of the Flying U. Bertha Muzzy Sinclair. LC 6-13689. 1906. G. W. Dillingham Company.

Chip, of the Flying U. Bertha Muzzy Sinclair. Grosset & Dunlap.

Chip on My Shoulder: By Eric North Pseud. Bernard Cronin. LC 56-8465. Roy Publishers.

Chippendales. Robert Grant. LC 9-9472. 1909. C. Scribner's Sons.

Chippewa Daughter. Jane Toombs. (American Indian Ser.: No. 4). (Orig.). 1982. pap. 2.75 (ISBN 0-440-01270-8, Standish). Dell.

Chippinge Borough. Stanley John Weyman. LC 6-37198. 1906. McClure, Phillips & Co.

Chips and Splinters. George W Wear. LC 34-2275. 1934. Meador Publishing Company.

Chips Are Down: Les Jeux Sont Faite. Jean Paul Sartre. LC 48-10358. 1948. Lear.

Chips from My Chisel. Grace H. Turnbull. (Illus.). 1953. 5.00 o.s.i. (ISBN 0-87233-860-6). Bauhan.

Chips from the Granite. A Collection of Whimsical Bits... Which Still Symbolize the Old Down East Illustrated by Gillette French. Walt Wandell. LC 53-7071. 1953. Falmouth Pub. House.

Chipstead of the Lone Hand. Sydney Horler. LC 29-2243. H. Holt and Company.

Chiricahua. Henry Wilson Allen. LC 72-5326. 1972. 10.95 (ISBN 0-8161-6042-2). G. K. Hall.

Chiricahua. Henry Wilson Allen. LC 78-38941. 1972. 5.95 (ISBN 0-397-00887-2). Lippincott.

Chiricahua. Will Henry, pseud. LC 78-38941. (YA) 1972. 10.53i (ISBN 0-397-00887-2). Har-Row.

Chiricahua. Will Henry, pseud. (Adult Ser.). 490p. 1972. Repr. 10.95 o.p. (ISBN 0-8161-6042-2, Large Print Bks). G K Hall.

Chiricuhua. Will Henry, pseud. 256p. 1982. pap. 2.50 (ISBN 0-553-20718-0). Bantam.

Chiropractic Procedure Procedure and Practice. Otto C Reinert. LC 62-5041. 1962.

Chirundu. Mphahlele Es'Kia. 168p. cancelled (ISBN 0-88208-121-7); pap. 7.95 (ISBN 0-88208-122-5). Lawrence Hill.

Chirundu. Ezekiel Mphahlele. LC 81-7253. 1981. 12.00 (ISBN 0-88208-122-5). Lawrence Hill.

Chisholms: A Novel of the Journey West. Evan Hunter. LC 75-25086. 8.95 (ISBN 0-06-012013-4). Harper & Row.

Chit of Sixteen: And Other Stories. Miriam Coles Harris. 1892. G. W. Dillingham, Successor to G. W. Carleton & Co.

Chita: a Memory of Last Island. Lafcadio Hearn. LC 74-131737. 1970. Scholarly Press.

Chita: a Memory of Last Island. Lafcadio Hearn. LC 75-95145. 1969. AMS Press.

Chita; a Memory of Last Island. Lafcadio Hearn. LC 78-77315. (Southern literary classics series). 1969. 7.50. University of North Carolina Press.

Chita: A Memory of Last Island. by lafcadio hearn... ed. Lafcadio Hearn. LC 7-5049. 1889. Harper & Brothers.

Chita: a Memory of Last Island. Introd. by Van Wyck Brooks. Lafcadio Hearn. LC 61-65995. (Premier classic of American realism, d135).

Chitralekha. Bhagwati C. Verma. Tr. by Chandra B. Karki. 1966. pap. 2.50 (ISBN 0-88253-198-0). Ind-US Inc.

Chitty Chitty Bang Bang: The Magical Car. Ian Fleming. LC 64-21282. (Illus.). 1964. Random House.

Chivalrous Deed: And What Came of It. Christine Faber. LC 6-37858. 1891. P. J. Kenedy.

Chivalry. James Branch Cabell. LC 71-140326. (Short story index reprint series). 1970. Books for Libraries Press.

Chivalry. Rafael Sabatini. LC 35-22965. 1935. Houghton Mifflin Company.

Chivalry and the Gibbet (Rope Law) George Curtis & Curtis, Josephine Denver. LC 27-10734. 2.00. The Devin-Adair Company.

Chivalry: Dizain Des Reines. rev. and enl. ed. James Branch Cabell. LC 21-20441. 1921. R. M. McBride & Company.

Chivalry: Dizain Des Reines. rev. and enl. ed. James Branch Cabell. LC 28-27595. 1926. R. M. McBride & Company.

Chivalry of Keith Leicester: A Romance of British Columbia. Robert Allison Hood. LC 18-18001. 1.50. George H. Doran Company.

Chivalry of Mr. Channing. Ellis Middleton. LC 26-16146. 1926. L. MacVeagh, The Dial Press.

Chivalry Peak. Irvin Shrewsbury Cobb. LC 27-19116. 1927. Cosmopolitan Book Corporation.

Chiy-une. Susan Coon. 320p. (Orig.). 1982. pap. 2.75 (ISBN 0-380-79301-6, 79301). Avon.

Chloe Again. Bonnie Golightly. (O.s.i.). 1967. pap. 0.75 o.s.i. (A252S, Award). Univ Pub & Dist.

Chloe Dusts Her Mantel: A Pioneer Woman's Idyl. Frances Gill. LC 36-8381. 1935. The Press of the Pioneers, Incorporated.

Chloe Malone. Fannie Heaslip Lea. LC 16-17422. 1916. 1.35. Little, Brown, and Company.

Chloe Marr. Alan Alexander Milne. LC 46-5051. 1946. E. P. Dutton and Company, Inc.

Chloride Mines & Murals. Ed. by Stanley W. Paher. (Illus.). 1978. pap. 1.95 (ISBN 0-913814-15-6). Nevada Pubns.

Chloris of the Island: A Novel. Henry Brereton Marriott Watson. LC 5853. 1900. Harper & Brothers.

Cho-Fur: Is a True Automobile Love Story Where the Chauffeur Gets Engaged to His Own Sister and Eventually Marries Her... Harry Morris Gordon. LC 7-22820. H. M. Gordon.

Chocky. John Beynon Harris. LC 78-106363. (Athena books). 1970. Pergamon Press.

Chocolate: A Novel. Tarasov-Rodionov, Aleksandr Ignatevich. LC 72-90315. 1973. 13.50 (ISBN 0-88355-025-3). Hyperion Press.

Chocolate: A Novel. Aleksandr Ignat'Evich Tarasov-Rodionov & Malamuth, Charles, Tr. LC 32-10534. 1932. Doubleday, Doran & Company, Inc.

Chocolate Charlie. Tom Fitzgerald. Ed. by Billie Young. LC 72-91129. 1973. 11.95 o.p. (ISBN 0-87949-006-3). Ashley Bks.

Chocolate Charlie: A Novel. Tom Fitzgerald. LC 72-91129. 1973. 6.95. Ashley Books.

Chocolate Cobweb. Charlotte Armstrong. 1948. Coward-McCann.

Chocolate Crucifix. John Rowe. LC 73-167360. 1972. 4.95 (ISBN 0-85885-025-7). Wren Publishing.

Chocolate Days, Popsicle Weeks. Edward Hannibal. LC 70-108307. 1970. 6.95. Houghton Mifflin.

Chocolate Deal: By Haim Gouri. Tr. by Seymour Simckes. 1st Ed. Haim Guri. LC 68-11827. 1968. 4.50. Holt.

Chocolate or Vanilla: And Other Stories. Fannie Ferber Fox. LC 35-15162. 1935. A. A. Knopf.

Chocolate Sauce. David Chaloner. 1973. pap. 3.00 (Pub. by Ferry Pr). SBD.

Chocolate Spy. David M Alexander. LC 78-3579. 8.95 (ISBN 0-698-10909-0). Coward, McCann & Geoghegan.

Chocolate Spy. David M Alexander. 1980. 1.95 (ISBN 0-87216-759-3). Playboy Paperbacks.

Chocolates for Breakfast. Pamela Moore. LC 56-9814. 1956. Rinehart.

Choctaw County War. Peter McCurtin. (Sundance Ser.: No. 42). 208p. 1982. pap. 2.25 (ISBN 0-8439-1101-8, Leisure Bks). Nordon Pubns.

Chog, a Gothic Fable. Quentin Crisp. LC 79-15617. (Illus.). 5.95 (ISBN 0-416-00131-9). Methuen.

Choh Lin, the Chinese Boy Who Become a Preacher. John A Davis. LC 6-32482. Presbyterian Board of Publication.

Choice. Charles Guernon. LC 25-77505. 1925. J. B. Lippincott Company.

Choice. Ivan J. Laszlo. LC 71-146468. 1971. 5.00. Libra Publishers.

Choice. Arthur M Litoff. (Illus.). 1973. (pbk.) 1.50. Caleb-Keturah.

Choice. Michael McLaverty. LC 58-8907. 1958. Macmillan.

Choice. Charles Mills. LC 43-5034. 1943. The Macmillan Company.

Choice. Harold Lawrence Myra. 1980. 7.95 (ISBN 0-8423-0248-4). Tyndale.

Choice. Maurice Weyl. LC 19-11435. 1919. M. Kennerley.

Choice. Samuel Youd. LC 61-12851. 1961. Simon and Schuster.

Choice & Other Stories. Ed. by Winifred Roderman. (Read on! Write on! Ser.). (Illus.). 64p. (gr. 7 up). 1980. pap. 3.10 (ISBN 0-915510-41-3). Janus Bks.

Choice: By Mare Brandel Pseud. Marcus Beresford. LC 50-10013. 1950. Dial Press.

Choice Cuts. Ellery Queen, pseud. LC 79-118216. (Masterpieces of mystery). (Illus.). 1.25. Davis Publications.

Choice Cuts: By Pierre Boileau, Thomas Narcejac. Tr. from French by Brian Rawson. Pierre Boileau. (S3578). 1968. Bantam.

Choice Cuts: By Thomas I.E. Pierre Boileau, Pierre I.E. Thomas Narcejac. Tr. from French by Brian Rawson. 1st Amer. Ed. Pierre Boileau & Thomas Narcejac. LC 66-251289. 1966. bds., 3.95. Dutton.

Choice Humorous and Satirical Works. Quevedo y Villegas, Francisco Gomez De. LC 76-48454. (Classics of European Literature). (Hyperion library of world literature). 1977. 14.50. (ISBN 0-88355-602-2) (ISBN 0-88355-603-0). Hyperion Press.

Choice in the Gathering: Or, Sowing and Waiting. Sarah Maria Burnham. LC 1-24974. A. I. Bradley & Company.

Choice of Angels. Adele Louise De Leeuw. 1973. (pbk.) 0.75. Ace.

Choice of Assassins. William P. McGivern. 1974. pap. 1.25 o.p. (ISBN 0-515-03386-3, V3386). Pyramid Pubns.

Choice of Catastrophes. Isaac Asimov. 384p. 1981. pap. 6.95 (ISBN 0-449-90048-7, Columbine). Fawcett.

Choice of Cousins. April Kihlstrom. (Orig.). 1982. pap. 2.25 (ISBN 0-451-11347-0, AE1347, Sig). NAL.

Choice of Crimes. Lesley Egan, pseud. LC 80-1121. (Crime Club Ser.). 1980. 8.95 o.p. (ISBN 0-385-17269-9). Doubleday.

Choice of Crimes. Elizabeth Linington. LC 80-1121. 1980. 8.95 (ISBN 0-385-17269-9). Published for the Crime Club by Doubleday.

Choice of Don Luis: A Great First Novel. Robert Earl Brough. LC 46-205484. 1946. The Southern Authors Literary Guild.

Choice of Enemies. Ted Allbeury. LC 72-79501. 1972. 6.50. St. Martin's Press.

Choice of Flowers. Tr. by Jan Knappert from Swahili. (African Writers Ser.). (Orig.). 1981. pap. text ed. 5.50x (ISBN 0-435-90093-5). Heinemann Ed.

Choice of Gods. Clifford D. Simak. (Berkley Medallion Book). 1977. 1.25 (ISBN 0-425-03415-1). Berkley Pub. Corp.

Choice of Gods. Clifford D. Simak. LC 78-171472. 1971. 4.95. Putnam.

Choice of Heaven. 1st Ed. James Maurice Scott. LC 60-5976. 1960. Dutton.

Choice of Life. Georgette Leblanc. LC 14-16445. 1914. Dodd, Mead and Company.

Choice of Masks. Oscar Pinkus. LC 70-84451. 1970. 6.95. Prentice-Hall.

Choice of Murders: 23 Stories by Members of the Mystery Writers of America. Edited by Dorothy Salisbury Davis. 1st Ed. Mystery Writers of America. Ed. by Dorothy Salisbury Davis. LC 58-11648. 1958. Scribner.

Choice of Paris: A Romance of the Troad. Samuel Greene Wheeler Benjamin. LC 7-34440. 1870. Hurd and Houghton.

Choice of Straws. Edward Ricardo Braithwaite. LC 66-29451. 1967. Bobbs-Merrill.

Choice of Violence: By Hugh Pentecost Pseud. Judson Pentecost Philips. LC 61-144261. (Red badge detective). 1961. Dodd, Mead.

Choice Readings. enl. & rev. ed. Ed. by Robert L. Fulton & Thomas C. Trueblood. LC 72-5590. (Granger Index Reprint Ser.). 1972. Repr. of 1884 ed. 36.00 (ISBN 0-8369-6383-0). Ayer Co.

Choices. Corinne Gerson. (Orig.). 1980. pap. 1.75 o.s.i. (ISBN 0-505-51476-1). Tower Bks.

Choices. Marcia Kamien & Rose Novak. 384p. (Orig.). 1982. pap. 2.95 (ISBN 0-345-29151-4). Ballantine.

Choices. Marcia Rose, pseud. LC 82-6669. 1982. 2.95 (ISBN 0-345-29151-4). Ballantine Books.

Choices. Katherine Stapleton. 1981. pap. 2.50 (ISBN 0-89083-802-X). Zebra.

Choices. Nancy Toder. LC 80-20836. 6.00 (ISBN 0-930436-05-9). Persephone Press.

Choices of an Etonian,a Novel: By Horace Buckley. Horace Buckley. LC 19-1589. 1918. 1.40. John Lanef.

Choices of Fiction. Ed. by Donald E. Morse. LC 73-13522. 1974. (pbk.) 5.25 (ISBN 0-87626-126-8). Winthrop Publishers.

Choir Invisible. James Lane Allen. LC 73-86169. 1969. AMS Press.

Choir Invisible. James Lane Allen. LC 76-7882. Scholarly Press.

Choir Invisible. James Lane Allen. 1897. The Macmillan Co.

Choir Invisible. James Lane Allen. LC 1-17994. 1898. The Macmillan Company.

Choir Invisible. James Lane Allen. LC 1-17995. 1898. The Macmillan Co.

Choir Invisible. James Lane Allen. 1899. The American News Company.

Choir Invisible. James Lane Allen. LC 33-17496. 1899. The Macmillan Company.

Choir Invisible. James Lane Allen. LC 41-30712. 1905. The Macmillan Company.

Choir Invisible. James Lane Allen. 1974. (pbk.) 0.95. Avon.

Choir Invisible. Marianne Hauser. 1958. 8.95 (ISBN 0-8392-1014-0). Astor-Honor.

Choir Invisible: A Novel. Marianne Hauser. LC 58-6504. 1958. McDowell, Obolensky.

Choirboys. Joseph Wambaugh. LC 75-17969. 1975. 8.95 (ISBN 0-440-05363-3). Delacorte Press.

Choirboys. Joseph Wambaugh. (Dell book). 1979. 2.50 (ISBN 0-440-11188-9). Dell Pub. Co.

Choisy. A Novel. James P Story. LC 8-16288. (On cover: Osgood's library of novels, no. 20). 1872. J. R. Osgood and Company.

Choix De Contes. Francios Marie Arouet De Voltaire. LC 51-137161. 1951. University Press.

Choix De Contes. Francois Marie Arouet de Voltaire. Ed. by F. C. Green. (Fr). text ed. 3.50 o.p. Cambridge U Pr.

Choix De Simenon. Georges Simenon. Ed. by Frank W. Lindsay & Anthony M. Nazzaro. (Illus., Fr.). 1972. pap. 8.95x o.p. (ISBN 0-13-133033-0). P-H.

Chokecherry Tree. Frederick Feikema Manfred. LC 75-7470. (Zia book). 1975. 2.95 (ISBN 0-8263-0378-1). University of New Mexico Press.

Chokecherry Tree. Frederick Feikema Manfred. LC 48-6300. 1948. Doubleday.

Chokecherry Tree. Rev. Ed. Frederick Feikema Manfred. LC 61-4753. (Swallow paperbooks). 1961. A. Swallow.

Chokher Bali see Binodini: A Novel.

Cholla Kid. Oscar Schisgall. LC 35-3812. G. H. Watt.

Cholla Kid: By Jackson Cole... Jackson Cole, pseud. LC 35-3812. G. H. Watt.

Cholly's Homespun Rhymes. Charles V. De Bevoise. 1968. 2.50 o.p. Vantage.

Cholo. Robert Houston. 176p. 1981. pap. 2.25 (ISBN 0-380-77891-2, 77891). Avon.

Chombo: Novela. Carlos G. Wilson. LC 81-65413. (Coleccion Caniqui Ser.). (Illus.). 100p. (Orig., Span.). 1981. pap. 7.95 (ISBN 0-89729-287-1). Ediciones.

Choose a Bright Morning. Hillel Bernstein. LC 36-13191. 1936. Frederick A. Stokes Company.

Choose from the Stars: A Romantic Novel. Winifred Mary Scott. LC 38-33737. 1938. Doubleday, Doran & Company, Inc.

Choose This Day. Jean Nielsen. LC 59-8810. 1959. Funk & Wagnalls.

Choose This Day. Stanley J. Rowland. 1964. pap. 0.75 o.p. (ISBN 0-377-80141-0). Friend Pr.

Chopin Express. Howard S Kaplan. LC 78-5567. 8.95. Dutton.

Chopin Nocturne, and Other Sketches. Fannie Kimball Reed. LC 1-29558. 1900. Privately Printed for the Author.

Chorale. Barry N Malzberg. LC 77-82765. 1978. 7.95 (ISBN 0-385-13138-0). Doubleday.

Chord from a Violin. Winifred Agnes Haldane. LC 6-46163. Laird & Lee.

Chord in Crimson. Gale Gallagher, pseud. LC 49-722863. (Gargoyle mystery). 1949. Coward-McCann.

Chords and Discords. Walter Everette Hawkins. LC 9-23838. 1909. 1.20. The Murray Brothers Press.

Chords and Discords. Walter Everette Hawkins. LC 20-1241. R. G. Badger.

Chorus: A Tale of Love and Folly. Sylvia Dryhurst Lynd. LC 20-5196. 1916. E. P. Dutton & Company.

Chorus Girl: And Other Stories. Anton Pavlovich Chekhov. Tr. by Garnett, Constance (Black) LC 20-3884. (Half-title: The tales of Chekhov, vol. viii). 1920. The Macmillan Company.

Chorus Girl's Luck in New York. A Thrilling Story Founded Upon the Play of the Same Name. Grace Miller White & Woods, Albert Herman. LC 33-28359. (On cover: Play book series. no. 111). 1907. J. S. Ogilvie Publishing Company.

Chorus Lady. James Forbes. LC 8-10283. 1908. G. W. Dillingham Company.

Chosen. Edward J Edwards. LC 49-104871. 1949. Longmans, Green.

Chosen. Chaim Potok. 1978. pap. 2.95 (ISBN 0-449-24200-5, Crest). Fawcett.

Chosen. large type ed. Chaim Potok. 1969. Repr. of 1967 ed. 7.95 o.p. (20302). S&S.

Chosen: A Novel. Chaim Potok. LC 67-13026. 1967. Simon and Schuster.

Chosen Country. John Dos Passos. LC 51-7856. 1951. Houghton Mifflin.

Chosen Few. Hari Rhodes. LC 78-10960. 1965. 0.60. Bantam Books.

Chosen Few. facs. ed. Frank Richard Stockton. LC 75-90591. (Short Story Index Reprint Ser.). 1895. 15.00 (ISBN 0-8369-3074-6). Ayer Co.

Chosen Few: Short Stories. Frank Richard Stockton. LC 75-90591. (Short story index reprint series). (Illus.). 1969. Books for Libraries Press.

Chosen Few: Short Stories. cameo ed. Frank Richard Stockton. LC 8-15666. 1895. C. Scribner's Sons.

Chosen Few: Short Stories. cameo ed. Frank Richard Stockton. LC 4-16111. 1903. C. Scribner's Sons.

Chosen Man: Or, The Mystery of the Secret Service. Harlan Page Halsey. LC 7-119396. (Secret service series. no. 7). 1888. Street & Smith.

Chosen One. Harry Simonhoff. LC 63-18239. 1964. T. Yoseloff.

Chosen One: And Other Stories. Rhys Davies. LC 67-21518. 1967. Dodd, Mead.

Chosen People. Bennett Michelson. 256p. (Orig.). 1982. pap. 2.50 (ISBN 0-505-51772-8). Tower Bks.

Chosen People. Sidney Lauer Nyburg. LC 74-29512. (Modern Jewish Experience). 1975. 22.00 (ISBN 0-405-06738-0). Arno Press.

Chosen People. 3d ed. Sidney Lauer Nyburg. LC 17-26391. 1917. J. B. Lippincott Company.

Chosen People. Bernice Rubens. LC 74-75955. 1969. 5.95. Atheneum.

Chosen Place, the Timeless People. Paule Marshall. 1976. (pbk.) 1.95 (ISBN 0-380-00661-8). Avon.

Chosen Place, the Timeless People. Paule Marshall. LC 72-78880. 1969. 8.95. Harcourt, Brace & World.

Chosen Prey. William Brashler. LC 80-8226. 10.12 (ISBN 0-06-014863-2). Harper & Row.

Chosen Race. Edgar Albion Lyons. LC 38-2495. 1936. The Cavalier Publishing Co.

Chosen Races. Margaret Sothern & Ward, Maisie, 1889- Tr. LC 39-10867. 1939. Sheed & Ward.

Chosen Sparrow. Vera Caspary. LC 64-13028. 1964. Putnam.

Chosen Valley. Mary Hallock Foote. 1892. Houghton, Mifflin and Company.

Chouans. Honore De Balzac. LC 72-187000. (Penguin classics, L260). (Illus.). 1972. (0.50, 2.45 u.s.) (ISBN 0-14-044260-X). Penguin.

Chouans. A Passion in the Desert. Illustrated by G. Bourgain. Honore De Balzac. Tr. by Katharine Prescott Wormeley. LC 26-269787. (Half-title: The works of Balzac. Custumary ed. vol. xx). Little, Brown, and Company.

Chouans. Brittany in 1799. Honore De Balzac. Tr. by Katharine Prescott Wormeley. LC 3-23190. (Half-title: The comedy of human life... Scenes from military life). 1893. Roberts Brothers.

Chouans (Les Chouans) Honore De Balzac. Tr. by Ellen Marriage. LC 4-21346. (Half-title:... Comedie humaine...). 1896. J. M. Dent and Co.

Choy Susan: And Other Stories. William Henry Bishop. LC 6-12716. 1885. Houghton, Mifflin and Company.

Chris. William Edward Norris. LC 41-274324. 1888. Macmillan and Co.

Chris. William Edward Norris. (On cover: Lovell's library, no. 1181). 1888. J. W. Lovell Company.

Chris. William Edward Norris. (On cover: Seaside library. Pocket ed. no. 1084). 1888. G. Munro.

Chris and Ortho: The Pansies and Orange-Blossoms They Found in Roaring River and Rosenbloom. A Sequel to Widow Goldsmith's Daughter... Julie P. Smith. LC 8-8177. 1871. Carleton; Etc., Etc.

Chris and Otho: the Pansies and Orange-Blossoms They Found in Roaring River and Rosenbloom. A Sequel to "Widow Goldsmith's Daughter.". Julie P. Smith. G. W. Dillingham Co.

Chris Gascoyne: An Experiment in Solitude, from the Diaries of John Trevor. Arthur Christopher Benson. LC 24-27431. 1924. E. P. Dutton and Company.

Chrisna: The Queen of the Danube; A Story of Montenegro. Joseph Xavier Santine & Wood, Mrs. Anne Toppan (Wilbur) 1817-1864, Tr. LC 8-3729. (On cover: Tales of the Living age). 1859. Delisser & Procter.

Christ and MacGregor in the Plan That Changed the World. Alexander Fyfe. LC 39-11572. 1939. A. Fyfe.

Christ and the Third Wise Man. John Oxenham, pseud. LC 34-20212. 1934. Longmans, Green and Co.

Christ Before Pilate: An American Story, by Waldemar Ager. Waldemar Theodor Ager. LC 24-24953. Augsburg Publishing House.
Christ Child in Flanders. Felix Timmermans. 1960. 3.95 o.p. (ISBN 0-8092-9526-1). Regnery.
Christ Child in Flanders. Translated by Elinor C. Briefs. Felix Timmermans. 1960. Regnery Co.
Christ Commission. Og Mandino. LC 79-25828. 9.95 (ISBN 0-690-01914-9). Lippincott & Crowell.
Christ in Bohemia: A Novel. Pauline Eleanore Stephens. LC 36-781. 1935. The Alexander Press.
Christ in Concrete: A Novel. Pietro Di Donato. LC 39-10762. The Bobbs-Merrill Company.
Christ in Flanders: And Other Stories. Honore De Balzac. Tr. by Clara Courtenay Poynter Bell. LC 36-37137. (Half-title: Everyman's library, ed. by Ernest Rhys. Fiction. no. 284). 1931. J. M. Dent & Sons, Ltd.
Christ in Italy; Being the Adventures of a Maverick Among Masterpieces. By Mary Austin... Mary Hunter Austin. LC 12-8983. 1912. 1.00. Duffield & Company.
Christ of Coorabeen. Assumpta O'Hanlon. LC 55-7867. 1955. Bruce Pub. Co.
Christ of the Red Planet. Eleanor Maria Easterbrook Ames. LC 9-28702. The Publishers' Printing Company.
Christ or Barabbas: A Psychic Novel. Benjamin Fish Austin. LC 21-14290. Austin Publishing Co.
Christ Revenge. A Tale of Intemperance and Impurity. Nathan Hoyt Sheppard. LC 8-5120. 1897. N. H. Sheppard.
Christ: The Socialist, by the Author of Philip Meyer's Scheme... 1894. Arena Publishing Company.
Christabel. Amanda Hart Douglass. 1978. pap. 2.25 o.s.i. (ISBN 0-505-51310-2). Tower Bks.
Christabel's Room. Abigail Clements. (Fawcett gold medal book). 1974. (pbk.) 0.95. Fawcett.
Christening Party. Francis Steegmuller. LC 60-14364. 1960. Farrar, Straus & Cudahy.
Christian. 6th ed. Hall Caine. LC 6-218710. 1897. D. Appleton and Company.
Christian but a Roman. Mor Jokai. LC 2837. 1900. Doubleday & McClure Co.
Christian College in the Twentieth Century. Bernard Ramm. 1963. 3.00 o.p. (ISBN 0-8028-3214-8). Eerdmans.
Christian Endeavor Stories. Grace Livingston Hill. Repr. lib. bdg. 37.05x (ISBN 0-89190-036-5). Am Repr-Rivercity Pr.
Christian Herald: New York, 1878-) Days of Grass. Ed. by Rachel Hartmann. LC 65-24853. bds., 5.95. Channel Dist. Meredith.
Christian Hero. Richard Steele. Ed. by Rae Blanchard. 1978. Repr. of 1932 ed. lib. bdg. 13.00x (ISBN 0-374-97608-2). Octagon.
Christian Hymns. Lincoln Hulley. LC 25-5354. E. O. Painter Printing Co.
Christian Indian: Or, Times of the First Settlers ... The First of a Series of American Tales. LC 6-209653. 1825. Collins & Hannay Etc.
Christian Rosenkreutz Anthology. Paul M. Allen. LC 68-13130. (O.s.i.). (Illus.). 1969. pap. 20.00 o.s.i. (ISBN 0-8334-0708-2, Steinerbooks). Multimedia.
Christian Thal: A Novel. Mary E. Sweetman Blundell. LC 3-962363. London Etc.
Christian Vellacott, the Journalist: Or, The Slave of the Lamp; a Story of Jesuitism, Royalism, and Republicanism. Hugh Stowell Scott. (On cover: Fortnightly series, no. 15). American Publishers Corporation.
Christian Woman. Pardo Bazan, Emilia. Tr. by Springer, Mary. LC 7-35769. Cassell Publishing Company.
Christiana. Michel Fattah. LC 80-53458. (Illus.). 12.95. Alpha Communications.
Christian's Mistake. Dinah Maria Mulock Craik. LC 4-16510. 1901. Harper & Brothers.
Christian's Mistake. Dinah Maria Mulock Craik. LC 42-43710. 1866. Harper & Brothers.
Christie Bell of Goldenrod Valley: A Tale of Southern Indiana and of Cincinnati in the Olden Time. Henry Thew Stephenson. LC 18-7925. 1918. Federal Publishing Company.
Christie Classics: The Murder of Roger Ackroyd, And Then There Were None, The Witness for the Prosecution, PhilmoelCottage and Three Blind Mice. Agatha Miller Christie. LC 57-7694. Dodd, Mead.
Christie Johnstone. A Novel. Charles Reade. LC 8-28089. 1855. Ticknor and Fields.
Christie Malry's Own Double-Entry. Bryan Stanley Johnson. LC 73-4172. (Illus.). 1973. 5.95 (ISBN 0-670-22013-2). Viking Press.
Christie, the King's Servant: A Sequel to "Christie's Old Organ,". Octavius Frank Walton. LC 98-199. F. H. Revell Company.
Christie's Rapture. Veronica Sattler. (Orig.). 1982. pap. 3.50 (ISBN 0-8217-1074-5). Zebra.
Christina. Caroline Arnett. (Coventry Romance Ser.: No. 65). 224p. 1980. pap. 1.75 (ISBN 0-449-50096-9, Coventry). Fawcett.
Christina. Claude Houghton Oldfield. LC 36-666326. 1936. Doubleday, Doran and Company, Inc.
Christina. Dee Stewart. 1977. pap. 1.25 o.p. (ISBN 0-515-04270-6). BJ Pub Group.
Christina Alberta's Father. Herbert George Wells. LC 25-17932. 1925. The Macmillan Company.
Christina Chard. Rosa Caroline Murray-Prior Praed. LC 7-30303. 1893. D. Appleton and Company.
Christina Enchanted. Blakely St. James. LC 79-88836. (Christina Ser.). 256p. (Orig.). 1980. pap. 2.50 (ISBN 0-87216-826-3). Playboy Pbks.
Christina in Love. Blakely St. James. LC 81-81147. (Christina Van Bell Ser.). 256p. (Orig.). 1981. pap. 2.75 (ISBN 0-87216-925-1). Playboy Pbks.
Christina Stead Reader. Christina Stead & Jean B Read. LC 78-57134. 12.95 (ISBN 0-394-50095-4). Random House.
Christina's Awakening. Blakely St. James. 256p. (Orig.). 1983. pap. 2.95 (ISBN 0-425-05997-9). Berkley Pub.
Christina's Bliss. Blakely St. James. LC 81-47268. (Christina Van Bell Ser.). 256p. (Orig.). 1981. pap. 2.75 (ISBN 0-87216-898-0). Playboy Pbks.
Christina's Conquest. Blakely St. James. LC 82-81386. (Christina Van Bell Ser.). 256p. 1982. pap. 2.95 (ISBN 0-86721-202-0). Playboy Pbks.
Christina's Delight. Blakely St. James. LC 81-84147. (Christina Van Bell Ser.). 256p. (Orig.). 1982. pap. 2.95 (ISBN 0-86721-065-6). Playboy Pbks.
Christina's Desire. Blakely St. James. LC 77-88263. (Christina Van Bell Ser.). 1978. pap. 2.50 (ISBN 0-87216-888-3). Playboy Pbks.
Christina's Ecstasy. Blakely St. James. LC 80-82855. (Christina Ser.). 256p. (Orig.). 1981. pap. 2.75 (ISBN 0-86721-018-4). Playboy Pbks.
Christina's Escape. Blakely St. James. LC 80-85110. (Christina Van Bell Ser.). 256p. (Orig.). 1981. pap. 2.50 (ISBN 0-87216-820-4). Playboy Pbks.
Christina's Fantasy. Blakely St. James. 256p. (Orig.). 1983. pap. 2.95 (ISBN 0-425-06131-0). Berkley Pub.
Christina's Hunger. Blakely St. James LC 77-73824. 1.95. Playboy Press.
Christina's Island. Blakely St. James. LC 81-83264. 256p. (Orig.). 1982. pap. 2.95 (ISBN 0-86721-011-7). Playboy Pbks.
Christina's Need. Blakely St. James. 256p. (Orig.). 1983. pap. 2.95 (ISBN 0-425-06134-5). Berkley Pub.
Christina's Nights. Blakely St. James. LC 77-72969. (Christina Van Bell Ser.: No. 6). (Orig.). 1977. pap. 2.75 (ISBN 0-87216-980-4). Playboy Pbks.
Christina's Obsession. Blakely St. James. LC 81-80095. (Christina Van Bell Ser.). 256p. (Orig.). 1981. pap. 2.75 (ISBN 0-87216-853-0). Playboy Pbks.
Christina's Passion. Blakely St. James. LC 75-40708. (Christina Van Bell Ser.: No. 2). 1976. pap. 2.50 (ISBN 0-87216-884-0). Playboy Pbks.
Christina's Pleasure. Blakely St. James. LC 79-92147. (Christina Van Bell Ser.). 240p. (Orig.). 1980. pap. 2.95 (ISBN 0-87216-653-8). Playboy Pbks.
Christina's Promise. Blakely St. James. LC 80-82220. (Christina Van Bell Ser.). 256p. 1980. pap. 2.75 (ISBN 0-86721-047-8). Playboy Pbks.
Christina's Quest. Blakely St. James. LC 75-40707. (Christina van Bell Ser.: No 1). 288p. 1976. pap. 2.50. Playboy Pbks.
Christina's Quest: A Sensual Odyssey of Love. St. James, Blakely. LC 75-40707. Playboy Press.
Christina's Rapture. Blakely St. James. LC 78-60269. (Christina Van Bell Ser.). 272p. 1978. pap. 2.95 (ISBN 0-86721-157-1). Playboy Pbks.
Christina's Search. Blakely St. James. LC 78-51094. (Christina Van Bell Ser.: No. 8). 256p. 1978. pap. 2.50 (ISBN 0-87216-886-7). Playboy Pbks.
Christina's Sins. Blakely St. James. LC 80-81522. (Christina Van Bell Ser.). 256p. 1980. pap. 2.50 (ISBN 0-87216-953-7). Playboy Pbks.
Christina's Surrender. St. James, Blakely. LC 78-78150. 1979. 1.95 (ISBN 0-87216-520-5). Playboy Press.
Christina's Temptation. Blakely St. James. LC 82-80288. (Christina Van Bell Ser.). 256p. (Orig.). 1982. pap. 2.95 (ISBN 0-86721-146-6). Playboy Pbks.
Christina's Torment. Blakely St. James. LC 79-83963. (Christina Van Bell Ser.). 256p. (Orig.). 1979. pap. 2.75 (ISBN 0-86721-045-1). Playboy Pbks.
Christina's Touch. Blakely St. James. LC 81-85827. (Christina Van Bell Ser.). 256p. (Orig.). 1982. pap. 2.95 (ISBN 0-86721-110-5). Playboy Pbks.
Christina's Treasure. Blakely St. James. LC 80-81004. (Christina Van Bell Ser.). 256p. (Orig.). 1980. pap. 2.50 (ISBN 0-87216-916-2). Playboy Pbks.
Christina's Virtue. Blakely St. James. LC 76-49401. (Christina Van Bell Ser.: No. 4). 272p. 1977. pap. 2.50 (ISBN 0-87216-887-5). Playboy Pbks.
Christina's World. Blakely St. James. LC 80-82662. (Christina Van Bell Ser.). 256p. (Orig.). 1981. pap. 2.95 (ISBN 0-86721-124-5). Playboy Pbks.
Christine. Alice Cholmondeley. LC 17-21644. 1917. The Macmillan Company.
Christine. Stephen King. LC 82-20105. 1983. 16.95 (ISBN 0-670-22026-4). Viking Press.
Christine. Thiel, Derek W. LC 52-19613. 1951. House-Warven.
Christine, a Fife Fisher Girl. Amelia Edith Huddleston Barr. LC 17-222932. 1917. London. D. Appleton and Company.
Christine: A Novel. Adeline Sergeant. LC 8-6454. (On cover: Holyrood series no. 4). Tait, Sons & Company.
Christine. A Tale of the Revolution. John H Mancur. LC 24-11869. (Tales of the revolution, no. 1). 1843. W. H. Colyer.
Christine and Other Stories. Julien Green. Tr. by Bruerton, Courtney. LC 30-8169. 1930. Harper & Brothers.
Christine Diamond. Marie Adelaide Belloc Lowndes. LC 40-8747. 1940. Longmans, Green and Co.
Christine of the Hills. Max Pemberton. LC 7-36382. 1897. Dodd, Mead and Company.
Christine of the Young Heart: A Novel. Louise Marks Clancy. LC 20-17176. Small, Maynard & Company.
Christine Roux: A Novel. Thames Ross Williamson. LC 45-9930. 1945. Current Books, Inc., A. A. Wyn.
Christine, the Model: Or Studies of Love... Emile Zola. LC 12-37826. T. B. Peterson & Brothers.
Christine's Career: A Story for Girls. Pauline King. LC 7-127943. 1896. D. Appleton and Company.
Christman. Dwight Edwards Marvin. LC 8-12765. Broadway Publishing Company.
Christmas: A Story. Zona Gale. LC 12-25068. 1912. 1.30. The Macmillan Company.
Christmas Accident: And Other Stories. Annie Eliot Trumbull. LC 75-98601. (Short story index reprint series). 1969. Books for Libraries Press.
Christmas Accident: And Other Stories. Annie Eliot Trumbull. LC 8-284792. 1897. A. S. Barnes and Company.
Christmas: An American Annual of Christmas Literature & Art, Vol. 39. Ed. by Randolph E. Haugan. (Illus.). 1970. 3.50 o.p.; pap. 1.75 o.p. Augsburg.
Christmas Angel. Abbie Farwell Brown. LC 10-24182. 1920. Houghton Mifflin Company.
Christmas Angel. Benjamin Leopold Farjeon. LC 6-386423. (Harper's handy series. no. 42). 1885. Harper & Brothers.
Christmas at Big Moose Falls. Charles Seely Wood. LC 11-26614. C.
Christmas at Candleshoe: By Michael Innes Pseud. John Innes Mackintosh Stewart. LC 53-10557. 1953. Dodd, Mead.
Christmas at Cold Comfort Farm and Other Stories. Stella Gibbons. LC 41-332949. 1940. Longmans, Green and Co.
Christmas at Dingley Dell: From the Posthumous Papers of the Pickwick Club. Charles Dickens & Edgar, William Crowell. LC 26-21003. 1926. The Bellman Company.
Christmas at Fontaine's. William Kotzwinkle. LC 82-5355. 11.95 (ISBN 0-399-12737-2). Putnam.
Christmas at Monticello with Thomas Jefferson. 1st Ed. Helen Topping Miller. LC 59-11264. 1959. Longmans, Green.
Christmas at Mount Vernon with George and Martha Washington. 1st Ed. Helen Topping Miller. LC 57-13214. 1957. Longmans, Green.
Christmas at Old Court: A Fireside Book. Charles Benjamin Tayler. LC 8-201290. 1852. W. P. Hazard.
Christmas at Sagamore Hill with Theodore Roosevelt. 1st Ed. Helen Topping Miller. LC 60-53227. 1960. Longmans, Green.
Christmas at Sea. Ed. by Edward Shippen. LC 8-7840. 1892. L. R.Hamersly & Co.
Christmas at Sea. Ed. by Edward Shippen. LC 8-7341. 1882. L. R. Hamersly & Co.
Christmas at the Desert's Edge: And Other Stories. Edna G Cornell. LC 34-686. 1933. Meador Publishing Company.
Christmas at Thompson Hall. Anthony Trollope. LC 8-28902. (On cover: Harper's half hour series v. 4). 1877. Harper & Brothers.
Christmas at Thompson Hall: A Mid-Victorian Christmas Tale. Anthony Trollope. LC 78-68078. (Harting Grange library series). (Illus.). 6.95 (ISBN 0-932282-07-5) (ISBN 0-932282-09-1). Caledonia Press.
Christmas at Thompson Hall: A Tale. Anthony Trollope. LC 8-28901. ("Cozy corner series"). 1894. J. Knight Company.
Christmas Bishop. Winifred Margaretta Kirkland. LC 13-249788. 1.00. Small, Maynard and Company.
Christmas Book. Elizabeth Goudge. LC 67-29484. 1967. Coward-McCann.
Christmas Books. Charles Dickens. LC 72-188448. (Penguin English library). (Illus.). 1971. (v. 1) 0.30 (ISBN 0-14-043068-7) (ISBN 0-14-043069-5). Penguin.
Christmas Books. Charles Dickens. LC 54-13472. (New Oxford illustrated Dickens). (Illus.). 1954. Oxford University Press.
Christmas Books... Charles Dickens. LC 6-37055. 1867. Hurd and Houghton.
Christmas Books. Charles Dickens. (Half-title: Everyman's library, ed. by Ernest Rhys. Fiction). 1907. J. M. Dent & Co.
Christmas Books. Charles Dickens. (Centenary Edition of the Works of Charles Dickens in Thirty-Six Volumes). (Half-title: The centenary edition of the works of Charles Dickens in 36 volumes). 1910. Chapman & Hall, Ltd.
Christmas Books. Charles Dickens. LC 36-37124. (Half-title: Everyman's library, ed. by Ernest Rhys. Fiction. no. 239). 1934. J. M. Dent & Sons, Ltd.
Christmas Books. William Makepeace Thackeray. (Half-title: Everyman's library, ed. by Ernest Rhys. Fiction). 1909. J. M. Dent & Co.
Christmas Books. William Makepeace Thackeray. LC 36-37170. (Half-title: Everyman's library, ed. by Ernest Rhys. Fiction. no. 359). J. M. Dent & Sons, Ltd.
Christmas Books: And Sketches by Boz, Illustrative of Everyday Life and Every-Day People. Charles Dickens. LC 34-377660.
Christmas Books: Christmas Carol, Chimes, Cricket on the Hearth, Battle of Life, Haunted Man, & Ghost's Bargain. Charles Dickens. (Illus.). 1892. 4.25 o.p. St Martin.
Christmas Books of Mr. M. A. Titmarsh. Mrs. Perkins' Ball. Our Street. Dr. Birch. The Kickleburgs on the Rhine. The Rose and the Ring. The Book of Snobs, and Ballads. William Makepeace Thackeray. LC 31-352291. Caxton Publishing Co.
Christmas Books of Mr. M. A. Titmarsh. Mrs. Perkins's Ball. Our Street. Dr. Birch. The Kickleburys on the Rhine. William Makepeace Thackeray. LC 8-28247. (On cover: Lovell's library, v. 6, no. 304). 1883. J. W. Lovell Company.
Christmas Books of Mr. M. A. Titmarsh, Etc.... William Makepeace Thackeray & Doyle, Richard, 1824-1883, Illus. LC 4-16319. (Half-title: The biographical edition. The works of... Thackeray... vol. IX). 1899. Harper & Brothers.
Christmas Bower. Polly Redford. LC 67-20136. (Illus.). 1967. Dutton.
Christmas Bride. Grace Livingston Hill. LC 34-32944. J. B. Lippincott Company.
Christmas Candles. Caroline Hardee Godfrey. LC 34-244908. 1933. R. D. Henkle.
Christmas Card. Paul Theroux & John Lawrence. LC 78-16973. 1978. 6.95 (ISBN 0-395-27204-1). Houghton Mifflin.
Christmas Card Murderers. Earl Schenck Miers. LC 51-11101. 1951. Knopf.
Christmas Carol. large type ed. complete and unabridged ed. Charles Dickens. LC 69-15377. 1968. F. Watts.
Christmas Carol. Charles Dickens. LC 71-3942. (Illus.). 1969. F. Watts.
Christmas Carol. Charles Dickens. LC 73-172707. (Illus.). 1964. Lippincott Co.
Christmas Carol. new amplified ed. Charles Dickens. Ed. by Henry E. Vittum. LC 66-28554. (Bantam pathfinder editions, EP137). 1966. Bantam Books.
Christmas Carol. Charles Dickens. LC 6615. 1900. G. P. Putnam's Sons.
Christmas Carol. Charles Dickens. LC 1-23632. H. M. Caldwell Co.
Christmas Carol. Charles Dickens. LC 14-3104. (cosy corner series). 1913. 0.50. L. C. Page & Company.
Christmas Carol. Charles Dickens. LC 14-13406. D. McKay.
Christmas Carol. Charles Dickens. 1915. J. B. Lippincott Co.
Christmas Carol. Charles Dickens. LC 24-7480. Thomas Y. Crowell Company.
Christmas Carol. Charles Dickens. LC 29-16852. The Saalfield Publishing Company.
Christmas Carol. Charles Dickens. LC 36-27035. 1935. Dodd, Mead & Company.
Christmas Carol. Charles Dickens. LC 39-29836. Grosset & Dunlap.
Christmas Carol. Charles Dickens. LC 40-3029. 1939. Pocket Books, Inc.

Christmas Carol. Ed. by Lynne Goldsmith. pap. 0.75 o.p. (9167, Starline). Schol Bk Serv.

Christmas Carol: A Facsim. of the Manuscript in the Pierpont Morgan Library. Charles Dickens & Pierpont Morgan Library, New York. LC 67-11683. (Illus.). 1967. J. H. Heineman.

Christmas Carol: A Ghost Story of Christmas. Charles Dickens. LC 31-33675. Hall & McCreary Company.

Christmas Carol & Other Christmas Books. Charles Dickens. 2.75x o.p. (239). Dutton.

Christmas Carol, and The Chimes. Charles Dickens. LC 65-9592. (Perennial classic). 1965. Harper & Row.

Christmas Carol and The Chimes. Charles Dickens. LC 1-428. (On cover: Lovell's library. v. 5, no. 274). 1883. J. W. Lovell Company.

Christmas Carol: And The Chimes. Charles Dickens. 1978. 9.95x (ISBN 0-460-00239-2, Evman); pap. 1.95x (ISBN 0-460-01239-8, Evman). Biblio Dist.

Christmas Carol, and The Chimes. Introd. by Walter Allen. Charles Dickens. (Perennial classic, HP6045V) Bibl.). 1.50, .50 pap.,. Harper.

Christmas Carol and The Cricket on the Hearth. Charles Dickens. LC 5-33313. The Baker & Taylor Company.

Christmas Carol and The Cricket on the Hearth. Charles Dickens. Ed. by Sawin, James M. & Thomas, Ida M. LC 5-8072. (Macmillan's pocket American and English classics). 1905. The Macmillan Company.

Christmas Carol and The Cricket on the Hearth Charles Dickens. Ed. by Wannamaker, Olin Dantzier. LC 15-26850. (Eclectic English classics). American Book Company.

Christmas Carol. Being a Ghost Story of Christmas. Abridged. Charles Dickens. Ed. by Bistadell, Albert Franklin. LC 1-4278. (On cover: English classics, no. 33). Clark & Maynard.

Christmas Carol: Being a Ghost Story of Christmas. Charles Dickens. LC 8-16471. (Crane classics. no. 39). 1908. Crane & Company.

Christmas Carol. Illus. by John Leech. A Facsim. of the 1st Ed., with an Introd. and a Bibliographical Note by Edgar Johnson. Charles Dickens. LC 56-13446. 1956. Columbia University Press.

Christmas Carol. Illus. by John Leech. Facsim. of the 1st Ed. 1843 Introd. and a Bibliographical Note by Edgar Johnson. Charles Dickens. LC 67-24329. 1967. 8.95. Univ. Microfilms.

Christmas Carol. Illustrated by Arthur Rackham. Charles Dickens. LC 52-133309. 1952. Lippincott.

Christmas Carol: In Prose, Being a Ghost Story for Christmas. The Cricket on the Hearth; a Tale of Home. Charles Dickens. LC 63-25493. (Children's illustrated classics no. 59). 1963. Dutton.

Christmas Carol: In Prose, Being A Ghost Story of Christmas. Charles Dickens. LC 63-14837. (Macmillan classics, 22). 1963. Macmillan.

Christmas Carol: In Prose; Being a Ghost Story of Christmas. 2d ed. Charles Dickens. LC 65-8628. 1965. J. G. Ferguson Pub. Co.; Distributed by Doubleday, New York.

Christmas Carol in Prose: Being a Ghost Story of Christmas. Charles Dickens. LC 50-12201. (New children's classics). (Illus.). 1950. Macmillan.

Christmas Carol. In Prose. Being a Ghost Story of Christmas. Charles Dickens. LC 42-31847. 1843. G. Routledge and Sons, Limited Pref.

Christmas Carol in Prose. Being a Ghost Story of Christmas. Charles Dickens. LC 1-425. 1869. Ticknor and Fields.

Christmas Carol in Prose: Being a Ghost Story of Christmas... Charles Dickens. LC 1-431. (Riverside literature series no. 57). 1893. Houghton, Mifflin and Company.

Christmas Carol in Prose: Being a Ghost Story of Christmas. Charles Dickens. LC 99-1673. (On cover: Ten cent classics, v. 1, no. 10). 1898. Educational Publishing Company.

Christmas Carol in Prose: Being a Ghost Story of Christmas. Charles Dickens. LC 2-16198. (The young of heart series, 31). 1902. Estes & Company.

Christmas Carol in Prose: Being a Ghost Story of Christmas. Charles Dickens. LC 9-27259. 1909. Duffield & Company.

Christmas Carol, in Prose: Being a Ghost Story of Christmas. Charles Dickens. Ed. by West, Katherine Gill. LC 12-18554. (Half-title: The Canterbury classics...). Rand, McNally & Company.

Christmas Carol in Prose: Being a Ghost Story of Christmas. Charles Dickens. Ed. by Demarest, Abraham Jay. LC 12-6228. (Classics in the grades). 0.35. Christopher Sower Company.

Christmas Carol, in Prose: Being a Ghost Story of Christmas. Charles Dickens. LC 21-21948. The Atlantic Monthly Press.

Christmas Carol (in Prose) Being: A Ghost Story of Christmas. Charles Dickens. LC 32-17296. 1932. Cheshire House.

Christmas Carol in Prose: Being a Ghost Story of Christmas. Charles Dickens. Barrymore, Lionel. LC 39-255. 1938. The John C. Winston Company.

Christmas Carol (in Prose) Being a Ghost Story of Christmas. Charles Dickens. LC 39-22343. Whitman Publishing Company.

Christmas Carol in Prose: Being a Ghost Story of Christmas. Charles Dickens. LC 41-608. Printed by the Monastery Hill Press for Holiday House.

Christmas Carol: In Prose, Being a Ghost Story of Christmas. Charles Dickens & Peter Fluck. LC 79-65390. (Illus.). 1979. 9.95 (ISBN 0-312-13403-7). St. Martin's Press.

Christmas Carol, in Prose: Being a Ghost Story of Christmas. Charles Dickens & Leacock, Stephen Butler. LC 32-846019. 1934. Printed for the Members of the Limited Editions Club at the Merrymount Press.

Christmas Carol, in Prose: Being a Ghost Story of Christmas. Charles Dickens & John Leech. LC 76-383518. (Illus.). 1976. 9.95 (ISBN 0-385-12816-9). J. G. Ferguson Pub. Co.

Christmas Carol, in Prose: Being a Ghost Story of Christmas. Illus. by John Leech. 2d Ed. Charles Dickens & John Leech. LC 65-862877. 1965. 3.95. Chapman & Hall, J. G. Ferguson Pub. Co.

Christmas Carol in Prose: Being a Ghost Story of Yule-Tide. Charles Dickens. LC 23-9413. 1902. The Roycroft Shop.

Christmas Carol. Prepared by Van B. Hooper; Illus. by Charles Rapp. Charles Dickens. 1962. bds., 1.50. Ideals.

Christmas Carol: The Charles Dickens Story Retold for Children. Charles Dickens. LC 40-320774. McLoughlin Bros., Inc.

Christmas Carol, The Chimes, The Cricket on the Hearth. Charles Dickens. LC 33-484. (companion classics). W. J. Black, Inc.

Christmas Carol: the Original Manuscript. Charles Dickens. Pierpont Morgan Library, New York. LC 77-177891. (Illus.). 1971. 3.00 (ISBN 0-486-20980-6). Dover.

Christmas Carol: The Original Manuscript. Charles Dickens. 1971. pap. 5.00 (ISBN 0-486-20980-6). Dover.

Christmas Carol: The Original Manuscript. Charles Dickens. 10.50 (ISBN 0-8446-0078-4). Peter Smith.

Christmas Carol: The Public Reading Version. Charles Dickens. LC 75-163360. 1971. (ISBN 0-87104-228-2). New York Public Library.

Christmas Carol. The Wreck of the Golden Mary, Richard Doubledick. The Cricket on the Hearth. Charles Dickens. Ed. by Broadus, Edmund Kemper. LC 6-37920. (Lake English classics). 1906. Scott, Foresman and Company.

Christmas Carol: The Wreck of the Golden Mary, Richard Doubledick, The Cricket on the Hearth, by Charles Dickens; Ed. for School Use by Edmund Kemper Broadus... Charles Dickens. Ed. by Broadus, Edmund Kemper. LC 20-5575. (Lake English classics). Scott, Foresman and Company.

Christmas Carol: With Numerous Original Illustrations by George T. Tobin. Charles Dickens. LC 99-4902. (Collection of "masterpieces"). Frederick A. Stokes Company.

Christmas Carp. Vicki Baum. LC 41-231672. 1941. Doubleday, Doran and Company Inc.

Christmas Child. Melvyn Bragg & Hugo Van Der Goes. LC 77-354825. (Illus.). 1976. 1.95 (ISBN 0-436-06713-7). Secker and Warburg.

Christmas Child. Hesba Stretton. LC 9-25181. 1909. T. Y. Crowell & Co.

Christmas Days. Joseph Crosby Lincoln. LC 38-28967. 1938. Coward-McCann, Inc.

Christmas Egg. Mary Kelly. LC 66-13101. (Rinehart suspense novel). 1966. bds., 3.95. Holt.

Christmas Eve & Christmas Day. Edward Everett Hale. LC 71-101814. (Short Story Index Reprint Ser.). 1873. 16.00 (ISBN 0-8369-3202-1). Ayer Co.

Christmas Eve and Christmas Day: Ten Christmas Stories. Edward Everett Hale. LC 71-101814. (Short story index reprint series). (Illus.). 1969. Books for Libraries Press.

Christmas Eve and Christmas Day. Ten Christmas Stories. Edward Everett Hale. LC 6-46166. 1873. Roberts Brothers.

Christmas Eve and Christmas Day. Ten Christmas Stories. Edward Everett Hale. LC 1-29717. 1894. Roberts Brothers.

Christmas Eve at Rancho los Alamitos. Katharine Hotchkis. pap. 1.75 (ISBN 0-910312-03-6). Calif Hist.

Christmas Eve at Swamp's End. Norman Duncan. LC 15-233698. 0.25. Fleming H. Revell Company.

Christmas Eve: Illustrated by Marc Simont. 1st Ed. Alistair Cooke. LC 52-12942. 1952. Knopf.

Christmas-Eve in a Light-House: Or, A Batch of Old Stories Re-Told. Henry S Hicks. LC 7-4763. The American News Company.

Christmas Eve on Lonesome: And Other Stories. John Fox. LC 4-268719. 1904. C. Scribner's Sons.

Christmas Eve on Lonesome, & Other Stories. John Fox. LC 70-121546. (Short Story Index Reprint Ser). (Illus.). 1904. 17.00 (ISBN 0-8369-3502-0). Ayer Co.

Christmas Eve on Lonesome: "Hell-Fer-Sartain", and Other Stories. John Fox. LC 9-139169. 1909. C. Scribner's Sons.

Christmas Eve: 13 Stories. Maeve Brennan. LC 73-1117. 1974. 7.95 (ISBN 0-684-13643-0). Scribner.

Christmas Evergreens. Rose Porter. LC 7-37750. A. D. F. Randolph & Company.

Christmas Flower. Joseph Henry Jackson. LC 51-13796. (Illus.). 1951. Harcourt, Brace.

Christmas Ghosts: An Anthology. Seon Manley & Gogo Lewis. LC 77-26517. 6.95. (ISBN 0-385-14032-0) (ISBN 0-385-14033-9). Doubleday.

Christmas Gift. Lucy Agnes Hancock. LC 38-33393. The Penn Publishing Company.

Christmas Gift. 1st Ed. Margaret Cousins. LC 52-11012. 1952. Doubleday.

Christmas Greeting. Marie Corelli. 1901. Dodd, Mead and Company.

Christmas Guest. A Collection of Stories. Emma Dorothy Eliza Nevitte Southworth & Frances Henshaw Baden. 1870. T. B. Peterson & Brothers.

Christmas Heretic: And Other Stories. John Edgar Park. LC 26-23680. The Pilgrim Press.

Christmas Hill. Peggy Gaddis, pseud. LC 47-1724. 1946. Arcadia House, Inc.

Christmas Hirelings: A Novel. Mary Elizabeth Braddon Maxwell. LC 7-25590. 1894. Harper & Brothers.

Christmas Holiday. William Somerset Maugham. LC 75-25351. (Maugham, William Somerset, 1874-1965. Works. 1976). 1977. 15.00 (ISBN 0-405-07809-9). Arno Press.

Christmas Holiday. William Somerset Maugham. LC 76-397744. 1967. Penguin in Association with Heinemann.

Christmas Holiday. William Somerset Maugham. LC 39-279244. 1939. Doubleday, Doran & Company, Inc.

Christmas Honeymoon. Frances Aymar Mathews. LC 12-23206. 1912. 1.00. Moffat, Yard and Company.

Christmas Horse. Glenn Balch. (Illus.). 4.00 o.p. (ISBN 0-8446-0019-9). Peter Smith.

Christmas in August: The Story of a Prostitute. Anne Estock. LC 62-14155. (Black cat book). 1962. Grove Press.

Christmas in Maine. Robert Peter Tristram Coffin. LC 42-268744. 1941. Doubleday, Doran and Company, Inc.

Christmas in Matabeleland. Stuart Cloete. LC 42-25510. 1942. Doubleday, Doran and Co., Inc.

Christmas in Modern Story: An Anthology for Adults. Ed. by Maud Van Buren. Bemis, Katharine Isabel, Joint Ed. LC 27-20754. The Century Co.

Christmas in Narragansett. Edward Everett Hale. LC 6-46167. (On cover: Standard library. no. 130). 1884. Funk & Wagnalls.

Christmas in the Mountains: La Navidad En las Montanas) Translated, with Introd. and Notes, by Harvey L. Johnson. Ignacio Manuel Altamirano. LC 61-641671. (Latin American monograph series). 1961. University of Florida Press.

Christmas Is Everywhere, Including Asia Minor. Morton Fineman. LC 66-20831. 1966. Norton.

Christmas Is Everywhere: Including Asia Minor. 1st Ed. Morton Fineman. LC 66-20831. 1966. bds., 3.50. Norton.

Christmas Legend. Robert L. Merriam. (Illus.). 9p. (Orig.). 1970. pap. 1.25. R L Merriam.

Christmas Memory. Truman Capote. LC 66-21461. 1966. Random House.

Christmas Mouse. LC 73-9686. (Illus.). 1973. 4.95 (ISBN 0-395-17703-0). Houghton, Mifflin.

Christmas Mouse. Miss Read. (O.s.i.). (Illus.). 1973. 4.95 o.s.i. (ISBN 0-395-17703-0). HM.

Christmas Mystery: The Story of Three Wise Men. William John Locke. LC 10-23938. 1910. John Lane Company.

Christmas of the Purple Pugassus. Garven Dalglish. (Illus.). 1972. 1.95. Argus Communications.

Christmas Outside of Eden. Coningsby William Dawson. LC 22-20050. 1922. 1.00. Dodd, Mead and Company.

Christmas Party. Adrienne Adams. LC 78-16230. 1982p. 1982. pap. 2.95 (ISBN 0-689-70747-9, A-123, Aladdin). Atheneum.

Christmas Pony. Dorothy Crader & Helen McCully. LC 67-22225. 1967. 5.00 o.p. Bobbs.

Christmas Pudding. Nancy Mitford. 1974. pap. 0.94 o.p. (09262). Curtis.

Christmas Readings for the L. D. S. Family. Ed. by George Bickerstaff. LC 67-30387. 1967. 1.50. Bookcraft.

Christmas Rising. David Serafin. LC 82-17056. 1983. 10.95 (ISBN 0-312-13414-2). St. Martin's Press.

Christmas Rose: A Blossom in Seven Petals. Robert Edward Francillon. LC 6-43269. (On cover: Harper's Franklin square library, no. 632). 1888. Harper & Brothers.

Christmas Roses: And Other Stories. Anne Douglas Sedgwick. LC 70-152957. (Short story index reprint series). 1971. (ISBN 0-8369-3872-0). Books for Libraries Press.

Christmas Roses, and Other Stories. Anne Douglas Sedgwick. LC 20-21186. 1920. Houghton Mifflin Company.

Christmas Secret. William Allen Knight. LC 46-225934. 1946. W. A. Wilde Company.

Christmas Spy. John Howlett. LC 75-20164. 1975. 6.95 (ISBN 0-15-117879-8). Harcourt Brace Jovanovich.

Christmas Spy. John Howlett. 1977. 1.75 (ISBN 0-380-01783-0). Avon Books.

Christmas Stories. Ed. by Betty J. Breyer. LC 79-15520. (Anthony Trollope; The Complete Short Stories Ser.: Vol. I). 1979. 17.50 (ISBN 0-912646-56-X). Tex Christian.

Christmas Stories. Charles Dickens. LC 57-8076. (New Oxford illustrated Dickens). (Illus.). 1956. Oxford University Press.

Christmas Stories. Charles Dickens. LC 6-37054. 1868. D. Appleton and Company.

Christmas Stories. Charles Dickens. LC 6-37050. (Standard literature series, no. 5). 1896. University Publishing Company.

Christmas Stories. Charles Dickens. LC 13-210623. 1913. Frederick A. Stokes Company.

Christmas Stories. Charles Dickens. Ed. by Lane, Martha Allen (Luther) LC 27-20825. Ginn and Company.

Christmas Stories. Jacob August Riis. LC 23-17186. 1923. The Macmillan Company.

Christmas Stories. Charles Nicholas Trivess. LC 13-20395. 1913. Printed by Wm. H. Pool Printing and Binding Co.

Christmas Stories. Anthony Trollope & Betty Jane Breyer. LC 79-15520. 9.95 (ISBN 0-912646-56-X). Texas Christian University Press.

Christmas Stories: A Christmas Carol. The Chimes. The Cricket on the Hearth. Charles Dickens. LC 46-18416. (Rainbow classics). 1946. World Pub. Co.

Christmas Stories. A Christmas Carol. The Chimes. The Cricket on the Hearth. Charles Dickens & Simon, Howard, 1902- Illus. LC 46-18416. (Half-title: Rainbow classics). 1946. The World Publishing Company.

Christmas Stories from French and Spanish Writers. Tr. by Ogden, Antoinette. LC 13-42928. 1892. A. C. McClurg and Company.

Christmas Stories from "Household Words" and "All the Year Round". Charles Dickens. Ed. by Lang, Andrew. LC 32-17202. (Half-title: Gadshill edition. The works of Charles Dickens... vol. xxxi-xxxii). 1898. Chapman & Hall, Ld.

Christmas Stories from "Household Words" & "All the Year Round. Charles Dickens. (Half-title: Everyman's library, ed. by Ernest Rhys. Fiction. no. 414). 1909. J. M. Dent & Co.

Christmas Stories from "Household Words" and "All the Year Round,". Charles Dickens. (Half-title: The centenary edition of the works of Charles Dickens in 36 volumes). 1911. Chapman & Hall, Ltd.

Christmas Stories from Many Lands. Ed. by Herbert Henry Wernecke. LC 61-9871. 1961. Westminster Press.

Christmas Stories. Illustrated by Walter Seaton. Charles Dickens. LC 56-60. 1955. Junior Deluxe Editions.

Christmas Stories of George MacDonald. George MacDonald. LC 81-68187. (Chariot classics). (Illus.). 11.95 (ISBN 0-89191-491-9). David C. Cook Pub. Co.

Christmas Story. B.J.H., Jr & J.H.B., Jr. LC 33-9592. 1932.

Christmas Story. Samuel Ward Francis. LC 6-43166. 1867. G. H. Mathews.

Christmas Story. Henry Louis Mencken. LC 46-20990. 1946. A. A. Knopf.

Christmas Story. Katherine Anne Porter. (O.s.i.). 1967. 4.95 o.s.i. (ISBN 0-440-01284-8, Sey Lawr). Delacorte.

Christmas Story and Its Easter Sequel. William Allen Knight. LC 55-9055. 1955. W. A. Wilde Co.

Christmas Story from David Harum. wm. h. crane ed. Edward Noyes Westcott. 1900. D. Appleton and Company.

Christmas Tales. Charles Dickens. LC 34-28484. 1934. Dodd, Mead & Company.

Christmas Tales. Charles Dickens. LC 47-11849. (Great Illustrated Classics). 1947. Dodd, Mead.

Christmas Tales. Being Reprinted Pieces from All the Year Round, Household Words, Etc. Charles Dickens. LC 43-431099. W. L. Allison.

Christmas Through the Years. Gladys Hasty Carroll. LC 68-25904. 1968. 6.95. Little, Brown.

Christmas-Tide in Story. Ed. by Henry Fitz Randolph. Irving, Washington et al. LC 7-41012. A. D. F. Randolph and Company (Incorporated.

Christmas Treasury. Jack Newcombe. LC 81-50583. 1982. 19.95 (ISBN 0-670-22110-4). Viking Press.

Christmas Tree. Michel Bataille. LC 73-98097. 1969. 5.95. Morrow.

Christmas Tree. Jennifer Johnston. LC 81-18972. 1982. 10.50 (ISBN 0-688-01133-0). W. Morrow.

Christmas Tree. Mary Britton Miller. LC 49-7858. 1949. C. Scribner's Sons.

Christmas Tree. Eleanor Furneaux Smith. LC 33-34148. The Bobbs-Merrill Company.

Christmas-Tree: A Story of German Domestic Life. Henrietta Skelton. LC 12-38826. 1883. Walden & Stowe.

Christmas Tree Murders: A Sergeant Cass Harty Detective Story. Joseph Francis Delany. LC 38-33400. 1938. Pub. for the Crime Club, Inc., by Doubleday, Doran & Company, Inc.

Christmas Turkey or Prairie Vulture? David R. Harvey. (Illus.). 119p. 1980. pap. text ed. 10.95x (ISBN 0-920380-66-2, Pub. by Inst Res Pub Canada). Renouf.

Christmas When the West Was Young. Cyrus Townsend Brady. LC 13-20747. 0.50. A. C. McClurg & Company.

Christmas with Mr. Pickwick: Being Chapters from The Pickwick Papers. Illustrated by Fritz Kredel. Charles Dickens. LC 51-6596. Peter Pauper Press.

Christmas Without Johnny. Gladys Hasty Carroll. LC 50-10362. 1950. Macmillan.

Christobel. Mary Linn Roby. 1976. 1.50 (ISBN 0-425-03141-1). Berkley Publishing Corp.

Christophe: A Tragedy in Prose of Imperial Haiti. William Edgar Easton. LC 31-375. Press Grafton Publishing Company.

Christopher. Geoffrey Drayton. (Caribbean Writers Ser.). 1972. pap. text ed. 4.00x (ISBN 0-435-98235-4). Heinemann Ed.

Christopher. Richard Pryce. LC 11-319670. 1911. Houghton Mifflin Company.

Christopher and Columbus. Mary Annette Beauchamp Russell Russell. LC 19-6409. 1919. Doubleday, Page & Company.

Christopher and Cressida. Montgomery Carmichael. 1924. The Macmillan Company.

Christopher and His Father. 1st Amer. Ed. Hans Habe. LC 67-15285. 1967. 6.95. Coward.

Christopher: And Other Stories. Amelia Edith Huddleston Barr. LC 6-8384. 1888. Phillips & Hunt.

Christopher, & Other Stories. facsimile ed. Amelia Edith Huddleston Barr. LC 72-167440. (Short Story Index Reprint Ser.). Repr. of 1888 ed. 18.00 (ISBN 0-8369-3966-2). Ayer Co.

Christopher Brand: Looking Forward. Cuthbert Yerex. LC 36-7368. Wetzel Publishing Co., Inc.

Christopher Columbus. Johannes Vilhelm Jensen. Tr. by Chater, Arthur G. LC 24-6736. (His The long journey. v). 1924. A. A. Knopf.

Christopher Comes Across. Hawthorne Hurst. LC 32-349538. A. H. King.

Christopher Durang Explains It All for You. Christopher Durang. 240p. 1983. pap. 3.95 (ISBN 0-380-82636-4, Bard). Avon.

Christopher Hibbault, Roadmaker. Marguerite Bryant. LC 9-35333. 1909. Duffield & Company.

Christopher Holt. Mary Dallas Street. LC 46-381115. 1946. M. S. Mill Co., Inc.

Christopher Homm. Charles Hubert Sisson. 1975. (ISBN 0-85635-103-2). Carcanet Press.

Christopher Homm: A Novel. Charles Hubert Sisson. (Prose Ser.). 1980. 7.95 o.p. (ISBN 0-85635-103-2, Pub. by Carcanet New Pr England). Humanities.

Christopher Humble. Charles Burnet Judah. LC 56-655920. 1956. Morrow.

Christopher Isherwood. Carolyn G. Heilbrun. LC 73-126543. (Columbia Essays on Modern Writers, 53). 1970. 1.00 (ISBN 0-231-03257-9). Columbia University Press.

Christopher Isherwood. Claude J Summers. LC 80-5335. 9.95 (ISBN 0-8044-2846-8). Ungar.

Christopher Isherwood. Alan Wilde. LC 75-120013. (Twayne's United States authors seris, 173). 1971. Twayne Publishers.

Christopher Kenrick: His Life and Adventures. Joseph Hatton. LC 7-2196. G. P. Putnam & Son,

Christopher Laird. Mary Fenollosa. LC 19-149406. 1919. Dodd, Mead and Company.

Christopher Lee's New Chamber of Horrors. Ed. by Peter Haining. (Illus.). 1977. 9.50 (ISBN 0-285-62152-1, Pub. by Souvenir Pr). Intl Schol Bk Serv.

Christopher Lee's "X" Certificate. Christopher Lee & Michel Parry. LC 76-382248. 1976. 2.75 (ISBN 0-491-01925-4). W. H. Allen.

Christopher Quarles: College Professor and Master Detective. Percy James Brebner. LC 14-16921. 1.35. E. P. Dutton & Company.

Christopher Strange: A Novel. Ruth Eleanor McKee. LC 41-10773. 1941. Doubleday, Doran & Co., Inc.

Christopher Street Reader. Ed. by Michael Denneny et al. 416p. 1983. 18.95 (ISBN 0-698-11103-6, Coward). Putnam Pub Group.

Christopher Strong: A Romance. Gilbert Frankau. LC 32-200429. E. P. Dutton & Co., Inc.

Christopher Superstud. Clif David. 1972. pap. price not set o.s.i. (OPH-267, Ophelia). Olympia.

Christopher Syn. Arthur Russell Thorndike & Buck, William Ray. LC 60-7504. 1960. Abelard-Schuman.

Christopher und Peregrin und Was Weiter Geschah. H. C. Artmann & Barbara Wehr. (Insel Taschenbucher Fur Kinder: It 488). 44p. (Orig., Ger.). 1980. pap. text ed. 3.90 (ISBN 3-458-32188-8, Pub. by Suhrkamp Verlag Germany). Suhrkamp.

Christopher's Wife. Renee Shann. LC 46-639322. 1946. Random House.

Christo's Running Fence. Anthony Haden-Guest. (Illus.). pap. cancelled o.s.i. (ISBN 0-525-47470-6). Dutton.

Christov's Testament: A Bizarre Account of a Young Russian Officer's Entanglement in the Most Macabre Set of Circumstances Ever Recorded in Literature. Yuri Diakonov. LC 76-369673. (Illus.). 1.95. Tsar Pub. Co.

Christowell. A Dartmoor Tale. Blackmore, Richard Doddridge. (Harper's Franklin square library. no. 213). Harper & Brothers.

Christowell. A Dartmoor Tale. Richard Doddridge Blackmore. LC 6-13867. 1882. S. Low, Marston, Searle & Rivington.

Christowell. A Dartmoor Tale. Richard Doddridge Blackmore. LC 7-2906. (On cover: Seaside library. Pocket ed. no. 631). G. Munro.

Christus Judex. A Traveller's Tale. Edward Roth. LC 8-684. 1864. F. Leypoldt.

Christy. Catherine Wood Marshall. LC 67-24957. (Illus.). 1967. McGraw-Hill.

Christy: By Catherine Marshall. Catherine Wood Marshall. 1968. pap., 1.25. Avon.

Christy Carew. A Novel. May Laffan Hartley. (Seaside library, v. 36, no. 739). 1880. G. Munro.

Christy King Is Kidnapped. Polan Banks. (Orig.). 1970. pap. 0.75 o.p. (75-357). Manor Bks.

Christy of Rathglin: An Entertaining and Exciting Story of the Life of an Irish Lad. James Riley. LC 7-19041. 1907. The C. M. Clark Publishing Co.

Chrome. George Nader. LC 77-17370. 8.95 (ISBN 0-399-12125-0). Putnam.

Chrome. George Nader. 1979. 1.75 (ISBN 0-515-04846-1). Jove Publications.

Chrome Yellow see Krom Zheltyi.

Chronic Loafer. Nelson McAllister Lloyd. LC 2110. 1900. J. F. Taylor & Company.

Chronicle. Joel Zoss. (Orig.). 1980. pap. 1.95 (ISBN 0-671-41458-5, Timescape). PB.

Chronicle of a Camera," By Paul Ingelow Pseud.... J. B. Drake. (On cover: American author's ser. no. 2). 1892. Melbourne Publishing Company.

Chronicle of a Death Foretold. Garcia Marquez, Gabriel. LC 81-47248. 12.50 (ISBN 0-06-014841-1). Harper & Row.

Chronicle of Aaron Kane. Frederick Stallknecht Wight. LC 36-32111. Farrar & Rinehart, Inc.

Chronicle of an Infamous Woman. David Liebovitz. LC 33-34145. The Macaulay Company.

Chronicle of an Old Town: A Novel. Albert Benjamin Cunningham. LC 19-15318. The Abingdon Press.

Chronicle of Caroline Quellen, Centenarian. Seton Peacey. LC 34-6052. 1934. H. Smith and R. Haas.

Chronicle of Conquest. Frances Campbell Sparhawk. LC 8-12382. D. Lothrop Company.

Chronicle of Dawn. Ramon Jose Sender & Trask, Willard Ropes, 1900- Tr. LC 44-2957. 1944. Doubleday, Doran & Company, Inc.

Chronicle of Louisiana: Being an Account of One of the Wars of Don Diego Ross, Called He, of the Iron Arm, the Last Catholic Governor of That Province. Prado, Pedro, Pseud. LC 6-25405. 1838. Linen & Fennell.

Chronicle of Small Beer. John Reid. LC 8-33276. The Anglo-American Publishing Co.

Chronicle of the Calypso, Clipper: A Novel of the Golden Days of the California Trade, of the Great Ocean Race Around Cape Horn, of the Clipper Ships, and of the Men-and Women-Who Sailed in Them. John Edward Jennings. LC 55-10742. (Illus.). 1955. Little, Brown.

Chronicle of the Reign of Charles IX. Prosper Merimee. LC 75-4910. (Illus.). 1975. 14.00. H. Fertig.

Chronicle of the Reign of Charles Ix. Prosper Merimee. Tr. by Saintsbury, George Edward Bateman. LC 7-18494. 1890. Cassell Publishing Company.

Chroniclers. Keith Wheeler. (Old West Ser.). (Illus.). 1976. 14.95 (ISBN 0-8094-1529-1). Time-Life.

Chronicles of a Comer, and Other Religious Science Fiction Stories. Ed. by Roger Elwood. LC 73-16910. 1974. (pbk.). 2.95 (ISBN 0-8042-1933-8). John Knox Press.

Chronicles of a Country School Teacher. Barbara Tucker Pugh. LC 19-163648. Saulsbury Publishing Company.

Chronicles of a Farm House. Winfield Scott Sly. LC 23-17644. 1923. Cere Root Specialty Company.

Chronicles of a Gigolo. Arthur Applin. LC 29-16426. 1929. H. Liveright.

Chronicles of a Great Prince. Marguerite Bryant & McAnnally, George H. LC 24-23374. 1924. Duffield and Company.

Chronicles of a Kentucky Settlement. William Courtney Watts. 1897. G. P. Putnam's Sons.

Chronicles of a School Rooms. Anna Maria Fielding Hall. LC 7-546697. 1830. Cottons and Bernard.

Chronicles of a Texas Pioneer. Marie Love. LC 78-12718. (National History Series, USA). 1978. 9.95 (ISBN 0-89482-038-9) (ISBN 0-89482-039-7). Stevenson Press.

Chronicles of Aunt Minervy Ann. Joel Chandler Harris. LC 68-55680. (American short story series, v. 21). (Illus.). 1969. Garrett Press.

Chronicles of Aunt Minervy Ann. Joel Chandler Harris. LC 72-8086. (American short story series, v. 21). 1972. (ISBN 0-8422-8070-7). MSS Information Corp.

Chronicles of Aunt Minervy Ann. Joel Chandler Harris. LC 99-4922. 1899. C. Scribner's Sons.

Chronicles of Aunt Minervy Ann. Joel Chandler Harris. LC 13-110362. 1912. C. Scribner's Sons.

Chronicles of Avonlea: In Which Anne Shirley of Green Gables and Avonlea Plays Some Part... Lucy Maud Montgomery. LC 12-13191. 1912. L. C. Page & Company.

Chronicles of Break O' Day. Edward Everett Howe. LC 7-7122. 1894. Arena Publishing Company.

Chronicles of Budgepore. 2nd ed. Iltudus Pritchard. 1972. 7.50x o.p. South Asia Bks.

Chronicles of Bustos Domeco. Jorge Luis Borges & Adolfo Bioy-Casares. 1976. 7.95 o.p. (ISBN 0-525-08047-3). Dutton.

Chronicles of Carlingford: A Novel. Margaret Oliphant Wilson Oliphant. LC 52-46780. 1863. Harper.

Chronicles of Castle Brass. Michael Moorcock. LC 73-175152. (Mayflower science fantasy). (v. 1) 0.30 (ISBN 0-583-12198-5). Mayflower.

Chronicles of Castle Cloyne. Margaret W Brew. LC 79-10388. (Ireland, from the Act of Union, 1800, to the Death of Parnell, 1891). 1979. 96.00 (ISBN 0-8240-3519-4). Garland Pub.

Chronicles of Clovis. Hector Hugh Munro. LC 12-37017. 1912. John Lane.

Chronicles of Corum. Michael Moorcock. 400p. 1983. pap. 2.75 (ISBN 0-425-05849-2). Berkley Pub.

Chronicles of Count Antonio. Anthony Hope Hawkins. LC 7-2621. 1895. D. Appleton and Company.

Chronicles of Count Antonio. Anthony Hope Hawkins. LC 3-24944. (Half title: Author's edition. Works of Anthony Hope...). D. Appleton and Company.

Chronicles of Don Q. Kate O'Brien Hesketh Prichard & Prichard, Hesketh Vernon Hesketh. 1904. J. B. Lippincott Company.

Chronicles of Elkinstown. Grace Dwight Gibb. LC 34-37100. Dorrance & Company, Inc.

Chronicles of Fairacre, Comprising Village School, Village Diary, and Storm in the Village. Miss Read. LC 76-53543. (Illus.). 1977. 10.95 (ISBN 0-395-25181-8). Houghton Mifflin.

Chronicles of Golden Friars. Joseph Sheridan Le Fanu. LC 76-4178. (Le Fanu, Joseph Sheridan, 1814-1873. Works. 1976). 1976. (3 vols.) 60.00 (ISBN 0-405-09198-2). Arno Press.

Chronicles of Kedaram. Krishnaswami Nagarajan. LC 61-19513. Asia Pub. House.

Chronicles of Lucius Leffing. Joseph Payne Brennan. LC 77-154081. (Illus.). 1977. 7.00. D. M. Grant.

Chronicles of Mansoul: A John Bunyan Classic. 3d ed. Ethel Barrett. LC 80-119375. 1980. 5.95 (ISBN 0-8307-0736-0). GL Regal Books.

Chronicles of Mansoul: John Bunyan's Classic Fantasy As Told by Ethel Barrett. rev. ed. Ethel Barrett. LC 75-100980. 224p. 1980. pap. 5.95 (ISBN 0-8307-0736-0, 5413907). Regal.

Chronicles of Manuel Alanus: A True Story of Old San Francisco. Leopold Ernest Wyneken. LC 9-14. 1908. Cochrane Publishing Co.

Chronicles of Martin Hewitt. Arthur Morrison. LC 74-144165. (Short story index reprint series). 1971. (ISBN 0-8369-3780-5). Books for Libraries Press.

Chronicles of Martin Hewitt. Arthur Morrison. LC 9-8356. 1896. D. Appleton and Company.

Chronicles of Martin Hewitt, Detective. New Illustrated Ed. Arthur Morrison. 1907. L. C. Page & Company.

Chronicles of Mount Benedict. A Tale of the Urauline Convent. LC 6-25404. 1837. Printed for the Publisher.

Chronicles of Old Riverby. Jane Felton Sampson. LC 13-265581. 1913. Sherman, French & Company.

Chronicles of Oldfields. Thomas Newton Allen. LC 9-30633. 1909. The Alice Harriman Company.

Chronicles of Pineville: Embracing Sketches of Georgia Scenes, Incidents, and Characters. William Tappan Thompson. 1852. Getz & Buck.

Chronicles of Quincy Adams Sawyer: Dectective. Charles Felton Pidgin & John M. Taylor. LC 12-23924. 1912. L. C. Page & Company.

Chronicles of Quincy Adams Sawyer, Detective. Charles Felton Pidgin & John M. Taylor. LC 75-32774. (Literature of Mystery and Detection). (Illus.). 1976. 19.00 (ISBN 0-405-07893-5). Arno Press.

Chronicles of Rhoda. Florence Tinsley Cox. 1.25. Small, Maynard & Company.

Chronicles of St. Tid. Eden Phillpotts. LC 78-132124. (Short story index reprint series). 1970. Books for Libraries Press.

Chronicles of St. Tid. Eden Phillpotts. LC 18-4544. 1918. The Macmillan Company.

Chronicles of Solar Pons. August William Derleth. LC 73-169744. 1973. 6.00. Mycroft & Moran.

Chronicles of Solar Pons. August William Derleth. LC 73-169744. 1973. 6.00. Mycroft & Moran.

Chronicles of Tarrytown & Sleepy Hollow. Edgar M. Bacon. Repr. 20.00 (ISBN 0-8274-2060-9). R West.

Chronicles of the Bastile... Louis Alexis Chamerovzow. LC 6-20170. 1859. Stanford & Delisser.

Chronicles of the Canongate: The Highland Widow and The Two Drovers. Walter Scott. (On cover: Lovell's library, no. 607). 1885. J. W. Lovell Company.

Chronicles of the Canongate: The Highland Widow and The Two Drovers. Walter Scott. (On cover: Seaside library. Pocket ed. no. 507). 1885. G. Munro.

Chronicles of the City of Gotham: From the Papers of a Retired Common Councilman. Containing: The Azure Hose. The Politician. The Dumb Girl. James Kirke Paulding. LC 4-35649. 1830. G. & C. & H. Carvill.

Chronicles of "the Little Sisters,". Mary Ellen Mannix. LC 1307. The Ave Maria.

Chronicles of the Marvilou Company: "Just Girls,". Marian Evans Gillespie. LC 14-232. 1.20. H. N. Halsey.

Chronicles of the Schonberg-Cotta Family: A Tale of the Reformation. Elizabeth Rundle Charles. (On cover: The home library). A. L. Burt Company.

Chronicles of the Schonberg-Cotta Family. Elizabeth Charles. LC 44-15362. 1887. T. Nelson and Sons.

Chronicles of the Schonberg-Cotta Family. Elizabeth Rundle Charles. LC 4-16505. 1864. M. W. Dodd.

Chronicles of the Schonberg-Cotta Family. Elizabeth Rundle Charles. LC 15-23117. (On back of cover: Nelson's family library). 1864. T. Nelson and Sons.

Chronicles of the Schonberg-Cotta Family. Elizabeth Rundle Charles. LC 41-32197. Dodd, Mead & Company.

Chronicles of the Schonberg-Cotta Family. Elizabeth Rundle Charles. LC 34-37763. 1870. T. Nelson and Sons.

Chronicles of the Schonberg-Cotta Family. Elizabeth Rundle Charles. LC 33-7891. 1888. J. B. Alden.

Chronicles of the Schonberg-Cotta Family. Elizabeth Rundle Charles. LC 42-43997. (On cover: Vassar series). Wm. L. Allison Company.

Chronicles of Thomas Convenant, 3 vols. Stephen R. Donaldson. 1982. pap. 8.85 (ISBN 0-345-30072-6, Del Rey). Ballantine.

Chronicles of Thomas Covenant: The Unbeliever, 3 vols. Stephen R. Donaldson. LC 77-73868. 1977. 10.00 ea.; Vol. 1. Vol. 2. (ISBN 0-03-022776-3); Vol. 3. (ISBN 0-03-022781-X). HR&W.

Chronicles of Turkeytown: Or, The Works of Jeremy Peters Pseud. 1st Ser. Containing the History of a Dreadful Catastrophe, the Amours of Dr. Post and Mrs. Peweetle, and the History of a Tatterdemalion... Thomas L Smith. LC 8-9632. 1829. R. H. Small.

Chronique Du Regne De Charles Ix. Prosper Merimee. Ed. by Desages, P. (Heath's modern language series). D. C. Heath & Co.

Chronolysis. Michel Jeury. LC 80-18271. 10.95 (ISBN 0-02-559220-3). Macmillan.

Chronopolis. J. G. Ballard. 1979. pap. 2.25 (ISBN 0-425-04191-3). Berkley Pub.
Chronopolis: And Other Stories. J. G. Ballard. LC 74-163404. 1971. 6.95. Putnam.
Chronopolis: The Great Science Fiction or J.G. Ballard. J. G Ballard. 1979. 2.25 (ISBN 0-425-04191-3). Berkley Pub. Corp.
Chrysal. Charles Johnstone & Malcolm J. Bosse. LC 78-60839. (Series: Novel, 1720-1805; 5.). 1979. 112.00 (ISBN 0-8240-3654-9). Garland Pub.
Chrysal: Or, the Adventures of a Guinea. Montague Rhodes James. Ed. by R. Reginald & Douglas Menville. LC 75-46283. (Supernatural & Occult Fiction Ser.). (Illus.). 1976. Repr. of 1764 ed. lib. bdg. 34.00x (ISBN 0-405-08142-1). Ayer Co.
Chrysal: Or, The Adventures of a Guinea. Charles Johnstone. Ed. by Baker, Ernest Albert. (On verse of half-title: Library of early novelists, ed. by E. A. Baker. v. 23). 1907. G. Routledge & Sons, Ltd.
Chrysal, or the Adventures of a Guinea, 4 vols. Charles Johnstone. Ed. by Ronald Paulson. LC 78-60839. (Novel 1720-1805 Ser.: Vol. 5). 1979. Set. lib. bdg. 124.00 (ISBN 0-8240-3654-9). Garland Pub.
Chrysal: Or, The Adventures of a Guinea. Charles Johnstone & An Adept. LC 75-46283. (Supernatural and Occult Fiction). 1976. (2 vols. in one) 34.00 (ISBN 0-405-08142-1). Arno Press.
Chrysalis. Joyce Ellen Davis. LC 80-84927. 6.95. Olympus Pub. Co.: Utah Arts Council.
Chrysalis. Zephine Humphrey. LC 29-2252. E. P. Dutton & Company, Inc.
Chrysalis. Harold Morton Kramer. LC 9-7042. 1909. Lothrop, Lee & Shepard Co.
Chrysalis: A Novel. Louise H Howell. LC 51-9086. Exposition Press.
Chrysalis Eight. Ed. by Roy Thorgeson. LC 80-649. (Double D Science Fiction Ser.). 192p. 1980. 10.95 (ISBN 0-385-17040-8). Doubleday.
Chrysalis Eight. Ed. by Roy Torgeson. 1982. pap. 2.50 (ISBN 0-89083-959-X). Zebra.
Chrysalis Five. Ed. by Roy Torgeson. (Orig.). 1979. pap. 1.95 (ISBN 0-89083-518-7). Zebra.
Chrysalis I. Ed. by Roy Torgeson. 288p. (Orig.). 1980. pap. 1.95 (ISBN 0-89083-629-9). Zebra.
Chrysalis II. Ed. by Roy Torgeson. (Orig.). 1978. pap. 1.95 (ISBN 0-89083-381-8). Zebra.
Chrysalis IV. Ed. by Roy Torgeson. (Orig.). 1979. pap. 1.95 (ISBN 0-89083-449-0). Zebra.
Chrysalis Nine. Ed. by Roy Thorgeson. LC 81-640147. (Science Fiction Ser.). 192p. 1981. 10.95 (ISBN 0-385-17251-6). Doubleday.
Chrysalis of Death. Eleanor Robinson. 1976. (pbk.) 1.50 (ISBN 0-671-80516-9). Pocket Books.
Chrysalis Seven. Ed. by Roy Torgeson. (Orig.). 1980. pap. 1.95 (ISBN 0-89083-575-6). Zebra.
Chrysalis Six. Ed. by Roy Torgeson. (Orig.). 1980. pap. 1.95 (ISBN 0-89083-567-5). Zebra.
Chrysalis Ten. Ed. by Roy Torgeson. LC 81-640147. (Science Fiction Ser.). 192p. 1983. 11.95 (ISBN 0-385-17598-1). Doubleday.
Chrysanthemum Chain. James Melville. LC 82-5546. 1982. 9.95 (ISBN 0-312-13463-0). St. Martin's Press.
Chrysanthemum Garden. Joseph Cowley. LC 80-28313. 11.95 (ISBN 0-671-41632-4). Simon and Schuster.
Chrysolyte: Or The Journey to Light. Emma Pow Smith. LC 8-8982. 1891. Brunt & Co.
Chthon. Piers Anthony, pseud. (Orig.). 1982. pap. 2.75 (ISBN 0-425-06260-0). Berkley Pub.
Chthon. Piers Anthony, pseud. (Berkley medallion book). 1975. (pbk.) 1.25. Berkley.
Chuck. Carl Sterland. LC 72-77343. 1969. 4.95. Doubleday.
Chuck Blue of Sterling. George B Chadwick. LC 27-207564. 1.75. The Century Co.
Chuck You Farley! see Sexo, Dinero y Balas.
Chuckle and a Laugh: A Tale of the C. A. Stephens Collection. Louise Harris. LC 67-4789. (Illus.). 1967. C. A. Stephens Collection, Brown University.
Chucklebait; Funny Stories for Everyone. Margaret Clara Scoggin. LC 45-5276. 1945. A. A. Knopf.
Chuckling Fingers. Mabel Seeley. LC 48-41353. 1943. Grosset & Dunlap.
Chuckling Fingers. Mabel Seeley. LC 41-18053. 1941. Pub. for the Crime Club by Doubleday, Doran & Company, Inc.
Chudesnaia Zhizn' Iosifa Bal'Zamo, Grafa Kaliostro. Mikhail A. Kuzmin. 250p. (Rus.). 1982. pap. 9.95 (ISBN 0-89830-037-1). Russica Pubs.
Chums. A Satirical Sketch. Howard MacSherry. LC 7-20278. C. S. Clarke, Jr.
Chums: Or, An Experiment in Ecomonics. Danna Riets Bramhall Cole & Tubby, Gertrude Ogden, Ed. LC 9-162. G. O. Tubby.
Chun Ti-Kung: His Life and Adventures. Claude A Rees. LC 3-14821. 1897. Dodd, Mead and Company.
Chunda: A Story of the Navajos. Horatio Oliver Ladd. LC 6-37926. Eaton & Mains.
Church Amusements." The Church Dramatic and Terpsichorean Association, (Limited,) Promotors of Novity. A Satire, by James Francis Conover. James Francis Conover. 1895. Raynor & Taylor.
Church and Chapel. Frederick William Robinson. LC 75-1500. (Victorian Fiction: Novels of Faith and Doubt; V. 51). 1975. 35.00 (ISBN 0-8240-1575-4). Garland Pub.
Church & State: A Novel of Politics and Power. Russell B Shaw. LC 79-88084. 9.95 (ISBN 0-87973-669-0) (ISBN 0-87973-649-6). Our Sunday Visitor.
Church & the Children. Ed. by Jesse P. Sewell & Henry E. Speck. 1935. 1.50 (ISBN 0-88027-104-3). Firm Foun Pub.
Church & the S'ngle Person. Frances Bontrager. (Family Life Ser). (Orig.). 1969. pap. 0.50 (ISBN 0-8361-1575-9). Herald Pr.
Church at Libertyville: As Seen by Thomas Bradley. John Wesley Conley. LC 7-6769. 1907. The Griffith and Rowland Press.
Church Chatter. Elizabeth Granderson. LC 65-291836. 1966. 3.00. Pageant.
Church Clavering; or, the Schoolmaster, 1843 see Portrait of an English Churchman, 1838.
Church Dogmatics. Karl Barth. text ed. 3.95x o.p. British Bk Ctr.
Church in the Markets. Benjamin Ifor Evans. LC 49-502445. 1949. Macmillan.
Church Moths. Ella Compton Hoy. LC 19-9655. Saulsbury Publishing Company.
Church of Brotherly Love. James Mark Darby. LC 33-3165. 1937. City Printing Company.
Church on Quintuple Mountain: A Story of Pennsylvania Oil Country Life, Possibly a Trifle Exaggerated in Spots. Bion H. Butler. LC 12-16335. 1912. 1.25. Foss, Stradley & Butler.
Church on the Avenue: A Novel. Helen Reimensnyder Martin. LC 23-1447. 1923. 2.00. Dodd, Mead and Company.
Church Republic: A Romance of Methodism. Zerelda F. Pierce. LC 7-35905. 1892. W. B. Ketcham.
Church Street: Stories of American Village Life. Jean Carter Cochran. LC 23-8757. 1922. The Westminster Press.
Church Yard Story. Beverly Carradine. LC 14-4497. 1904. The Christian Witness Co.
Churchill Commando. Ted Willis. LC 77-7935. 7.95 (ISBN 0-688-03240-0). Morrow.
Churchill Street. Mildred Wasson. LC 28-278113. 1928. Coward-McCann, Inc.
Churchill's Gold. James Follett. LC 80-27177. 1981. 9.95 (ISBN 0-395-30526-8). Houghton Mifflin.
Churchmanship of Saint Cyprian. G. S. Walker. LC 69-12121. (Ecumenical Studies in History, No. 9). (Orig.). 1969. pap. 1.95 o.p. (ISBN 0-8042-3742-5). John Knox.
Church's Growing Edge: Single Adults. Ed. by Russell Claussen. 1981. pap. 4.95 (ISBN 0-8298-0429-3). Pilgrim NY.
Chute. Albert Halper. LC 37-32423. 1937. The Viking Press.
CIA: Mission to Burundi. John M. Bernier. (Orig.). 1979. pap. 1.95. Woodhill.
Cian of the Chariots: A Romance of the Days of Arthur, Emperor of Britain, and His Knights of the Round Table; How They Delivered London and Overthrew the Saxons After the Downfall of Roman Britain. William Henry Babcock. LC 6-6891. Lothrop Publishing Company.
Ciascuno Il Suo. Iole F. S. Magri. LC 75-29713. 1976. pap. text ed. 9.50 (ISBN 0-395-13398-X). HM.
Cicely: A Tale of the Georgia March. Sara Beaumont Cannon Kennedy. LC 11-264148. 1911. 1.20. Doubleday, Page & Company.
Cid Campeador: A Historical Romance by D. Antonio De Trueba y la Quintana. Trueba y la Quintana, Antonio, Manuel Maria De & Gill, Henry Joseph, 1836-1908, Tr. LC 1-11830. 1895. Longmans, Green and Co.
C.I.D. of Dexter Drake. Elsa Barker. LC 29-220533. J. H. Sears & Company, Inc.
Cider from Eden. Nancy Bruff, pseud. LC 47-182865. 1947. E. P. Dutton & Co., Inc.
Cider from Eden. Nancy Bruff Gardner. LC 47-1828. 1947. Dutton.
Ciderville Folks As Seen by Silas Ganderfoot. Elijah P Brown. LC 9-1842. The Date Publishing Company.
Ciganka. Paul Gallik. LC 36-418. The Christopher Publishing House.
Cigarette-Maker's Romance. Francis Marion Crawford. LC 8-7681. 1890. Macmillan and Co.
Cigarette-Maker's Romance and Khaled. Francis Marion Crawford. LC 4-15441. 1901. The Macmillan Company.
Cigarette-Maker's Romance: And Khaled. Francis Marion Crawford. LC 16-19152. (Lettered on cover: Works of F. Marion Crawford). 1912. The Macmillan Company.
Cigarette Smuggler. Ed Edell. 1978. 15.00 (ISBN 0-89002-110-4); pap. 5.00 (ISBN 0-89002-109-0). Northwoods Pr.
Cikanka: Or, A Rose of Romany. Vera Kralik Proksa. LC 29-6448. Dorrance and Company.
Cimarron. Edna Ferber. 1961. Grosset & Dunlap.
Cimarron. Edna Ferber. LC 43-4733. 1943. Triangle Books.
Cimarron. Edna Ferber. LC 47-240906. (On cover: Penguin books, 605). 1946. Penguin Books, Inc.
Cimarron. Edna Ferber. LC 81-2086. 1981. 16.95 (ISBN 0-8161-3195-3). G.K. Hall.
Cimarron. A School Ed. by Frederick Houk Law. Edna Ferber. LC 54-1357. 1954. Globe Book Co.
Cimarron & the Manging Judge. Leo P. Kelley. (Cimarron Ser.: No. 1). 192p. 1983. pap. 2.50 (ISBN 0-451-12058-2, Sig). NAL.
Cimarron Bend. Lucien Waldo Emerson. LC 36-32329. The Macaulay Company.
Cimarron Crossing: By Michael Carder Pseud. Vernon L Fluharty. LC 51-13079. 1951. Macrae Smith.
Cimarron Jordan. Matthew Braun. (Fawcett gold medal book). 1975. (pbk.) 1.25. Fawcett.
Cimarron Jordon. Matthew Braun. 1978. pap. 2.25 (ISBN 0-671-44012-8). PB.
Cimarron Rides the Outlaw Trail. Leo P. Kelley. (Cimarron Ser.: No. 2). 192p. 1983. pap. 2.50 (ISBN 0-451-12059-0, Sig). NAL.
Cimarron Thunder. Eugene E. Halleran. 1981. pap. 1.75 (ISBN 0-345-29492-0). Ballantine.
Cimarron Trace: An Original Western, by James Norman Pseud. James Norman Schmidt. LC 56-11902. (Dell first edition, A119). 1956. Dell Pub. Co.
Cimbrians. Johannes Vilhelm Jensen. Tr. by Chater, Arthur G. LC 23-14110. (His The long journey. iii-iv). 1923. A. A. Knopf.
Cimmarron. Edna Ferber. LC 30-8609. 1930. Doubleday, Doran and Company, Inc.
Cinch: And Other Stories; Tales of Tennessee. William Allen Dromgoole. LC 96-721. 1898. D. Estes & Company.
Cincinnati Kid. Richard Jessup. (1279). 1965. Dell.
Cincinnati Kid: A Novel. Richard Jessup. LC 63-10157. 1963. Little, Brown.
Cinder. Rick De Marinis. LC 78-6739. 1978. 7.95 (ISBN 0-374-12364-0). Farrar, Straus, Giroux.
Cinder. Rick De Marinis. 1980. 1.95 (ISBN 0-380-48298-3). Avon Books.
Cinder Buggy: A Fable in Iron and Steel. Garet Garrett. LC 23-139466. E. P. Dutton & Company.
Cinder Path. Catherine Cookson. 304p. Date not set. pap. 2.95 (ISBN 0-553-12694-6). Bantam.
Cinder Path: A Novel. Catherine Cookson. LC 78-54993. 1978. 9.95 (ISBN 0-688-03339-3). Morrow.
Cinder-Path Tales. William Lindsey. LC 7-190113. 1896. Copeland and Day.
Cinder Pond. Carroll Watson Rankin. LC 15-18624. 1915. 1.25. H. Holt and Company.
Cinderella. Samuel Rutherford Crockett. LC 1-13969. 1901. Dodd, Mead and Company.
Cinderella? William Springer. 1979. pap. 1.50. Eldridge Pub.
Cinderella After Midnight. Fred Zackel. LC 79-9445. 9.95 (ISBN 0-698-10990-2). Coward, McCann & Geoghegan.
Cinderella, and Other Stories. Richard Harding Davis. LC 70-90579. (Short story index reprint series). 1969. Books for Libraries Press.
Cinderella for Short. Peggy O'More, pseud. LC 54-11338. 1954. Arcadia House.
Cinderella Girl. William Arthur Neubauer. LC 45-1216. 1945. Grammercy Publishing Co.
Cinderella Had Two Sisters. Tempest, Jan. LC 50-8409. 1950. Arcadia House.
Cinderella Jane. Marjorie Benton Cooke. LC 17-11703. 1917. Doubleday, Page & Company.
Cinderella Liberty. Darryl Ponicsan. 1974. (pbk.) 1.25. Bantam Books.
Cinderella Liberty: A Novel. Darryl Ponicsan. LC 72-9767. 1973. 5.95 (ISBN 0-06-013402-X). Harper & Row.
Cinderella Man: A Romance of Youth. Helen Knipe Carpenter & Carpenter, Edward Childs. LC 16-220481. 1.35. The H. K. Fly Company.
Cinderella Married: Or, How They Lived Happily Ever After, a Divertissement. Sherry Mangan. LC 32-943524. 1932. A. & C. Boni.
Cinderella Nurse. Dorothy Worley. 1973. pap. 0.75 o.s.i. (01-373). Lancer.
Cinderella's Cousin: A Story for Girls. Mildred Travers Anderson. LC 38-32416. Dorrance and Company.
Cinderella's Housework Dialectics. 1st ed. Lela Meinhardt & Paul Meinhardt. LC 77-89885. (Illus.). 1977. pap. 5.00 o.s.i. (ISBN 0-930226-00-3). Incunabula.
Cindy. John Benton. LC 78-372. (Spire books). 1.50 (ISBN 0-8007-8319-0). Revell.
Cindy: A Romance of the Ozarks. Rose Wilder Lane. LC 28-19243. 1928. Harper & Brothers.
Cindy on Fire. Burt Hirschfeld. 1971. pap. 2.50 (ISBN 0-380-00267-1, 49270). Avon.
Cinema City. Cyril Arthur Edward Ranger Gull. LC 23-5950. Harcourt, Brace and Company.
Cinema Murder. Edward Phillips Oppenheim. LC 21-13718. 1920. A. L. Burt Company.
Cinema Murder: A Novel. Edward Phillips Oppenheim. LC 17-15545. 1917. Little, Brown and Company.
Cing-Mars: Or, A Conspiracy Under Louis XIII. Alfred Victor Vigny & Hazlitt, William, 1811-1898, Tr. LC 8-32707. 1889. Little, Brown, and Company.
Cinnabar. Edward Bryant. LC 75-20160. 1976. 7.95 (ISBN 0-02-518000-2). Macmillan.
Cinnamon Gardens. Jeanette Rebuth. (Orig.). 1980. pap. 2.25 (ISBN 0-553-12958-9). Bantam.
Cinnamon Murder. Frances Kirkwood Crane. LC 46-6328. 1946. Random House.
Cinnamon Seed. Hamilton Basso. LC 34-714829. 1934. C. Scribner's Sons.
Cinnamon Skin. John MacDonald. 1983. pap. 3.50 (ISBN 0-449-12505-X, GM). Fawcett.
Cinnamon Skin. John Dann MacDonald. (General Ser.). 1983. lib. bdg. 14.95 (ISBN 0-8161-3504-5, Large Print Bks). G K Hall.
Cinnamon Skin: The Twentieth Adventure of Travis McGee. John Dann MacDonald. LC 81-48159. (MacDonald, John Dann, 1916-. The Travis McGee Ser.). 13.41 (ISBN 0-06-014990-6). Harper & Row.
Cinq-Mars see Oeuvres Completes.
Cinq-Mars: Or, A Conspiracy Under Louis XIII. Alfred Victor Vigny. LC 75-1382. 1975. 17.50. H. Fertig.
Cinq Nouvelles. Ed. by Raymond Federman. LC 70-115011. (Illus., Orig., Fr.). 1970. pap. text ed. 6.95x (ISBN 0-89197-079-7). Irvington.
Cinq Semaines En Ballon. Jules Verne. pap. 4.95. French & Eur.
Cipher: A Romance... Jane Goodwin Austin. LC 6-38091. 1869. Sheldon & Company.
Cipher of Death. Franklin Long Gregory. LC 34-12274. 1934. Harper & Brothers.
Ciphered. Scott Keech. LC 79-2737. 10.00 (ISBN 0-06-012294-3). Harper & Row.
Ciphers. Ellen Warner Olney Kirk. LC 7-12352. 1891. Houghton, Mifflin and Company.
Circe Complex. Desmond Cory, pseud. LC 74-9480. (Crime Club). 1975. 6.95 (ISBN 0-385-09735-2). Published for the Crime Club by Doubleday.
Circe Factor. Barry Nazarian. LC 80-52407. 11.95 (ISBN 0-87223-664-1). Seaview Books.
Circe's Daughter. Teignmouth Shore. LC 13-12496. 1913. Duffield & Company.
Circle. Francine Di Natale. LC 74-9901. (Traveller's companion series, TC-444). 1969. 1.75. Olympia Press.
Circle. Lois E. McCormack. (Orig.). 1978. pap. 1.95 (ISBN 0-89083-402-4). Zebra.
Circle. Beatrissia Marye. LC 27-8666. 1927. The Austin Publishing Co.
Circle. Steve Shagan. LC 82-2248. 448p. 1982. 14.95 (ISBN 0-688-01115-2). Morrow.
Circle. Steve Shagan. 1983. pap. 3.95. Bantam.
Circle. Katherine Cecil Thurston. 1903. Dodd, Mead & Co.
Circle C Moves in: A Western Novel. Brett Rider. LC 44-3689. 1944. Macrae-Smith-Company.
Circle C Moves in: A Western Novel by Brett Rider Pseud. Arthur Henry Gooden. LC 44-3689. 1944. Macrae-Smith-Co.
Circle, Crescent, Star. Ansen Dibell, pseud. (Science Fiction Ser.). 1981. pap. 2.25 o.p. (ISBN 0-87997-603-9, UE1603). Daw Bks.
Circle-Dot: A True Story of Cowboy Life Forty Years Ago. Milford Hill Donoho. LC 8-270. 1907. Monotyped and Printed by Crane & Company.
Circle F Cowboy. Charles Morris Martin. LC 52-6499. 1952. Arcadia House.
Circle Game. Joel Lieber. LC 77-130482. 1970. 6.95. Simon and Schuster.
Circle Home. Edward Hoagland. LC 60-11534. 1960. Crowell.
Circle Home. Edward Hoagland. 1977. 1.75 (ISBN 0-380-01680-X). Avon.
Circle in the Sand. Kate F. M. Vermilye. Jordan. 1898. Lamson, Wolffe and Company.
Circle in the Water. James McKimmey. LC 65-15334. 4.95. Morrow.
Circle in the Water. James McKimmey. (S257). 1967. Avon.
Circle in the Water: By Helen Hull. Helen Rose Hull. LC 42-36435. 1943. Coward-McCann, Inc.
Circle K: Or, Fighting for the Flock. Edwin Legrand Sabin. LC 11-20817. Thomas Y. Crowell Company.

Circle M Triggers: By Brett Austin Pseud. Lee Floren. LC 54-584203. Arcadia House.

Circle of a Century. Constance Cary Harrison. LC 99-5412. 1899. The Century Co.

Circle of Death. Charles Judson Dutton. LC 33-393045. 1933. Dodd, Mead & Company.

Circle of Death. Maggie Rennert. LC 74-534. (Illus.). 1974. 6.95. Prentice-Hall.

Circle of Evil. Sharon Wagner. 1971. pap. 0.75 o.p. (ISBN 0-447-74769-X). Lancer.

Circle of Fire. Mark Sadler, pseud. LC 72-10822. 1973. 4.95 (ISBN 0-394-47974-2). Random House.

Circle of Friends. Lou D'Angelo, pseud. LC 75-36583. 1977. 7.95 (ISBN 0-385-05492-0). Doubleday.

Circle of Friends. 1st Amer. Ed. Julian Mitchell. LC 67-144626. 1967. bds., 4.95. McGraw.

Circle of Guilt. Dorotthy Daniels. 1976. 1.50 (ISBN 0-671-80617-3). Pocket Books.

Circle of Light, No. 1: Greyfax Grimwald. Niel Hancock. 1982. pap. 2.95 (ISBN 0-446-31093-X). Warner Bks.

Circle of Light, No. 2: Faragon Fairingay. Niel Hancock. 1982. pap. 2.95 (ISBN 0-446-31095-6). Warner Bks.

Circle of Light, No. 3: Calix Stay. Niel Hancock. 1982. pap. 2.95 (ISBN 0-446-31097-2). Warner Bks.

Circle of Light, No. 4: Squaring the Circle. Niel Hancock. 1982. pap. 2.95 (ISBN 0-446-31099-9). Warner Bks.

Circle of Love. Syrell Rogovin Leahy. LC 79-25439. 10.95 (ISBN 0-399-12475-6). G. P. Putnam.

Circle of Love. Roderick Thorp. LC 73-87212. 1974. 7.95 (ISBN 0-399-11273-1). Berkley Pub. Corp.: Distributed by Putnam.

Circle of Lust. Nikki Marshall. pap. 1.95 o.s.i. (Venus). Grove.

Circle of Revenge. Mike Mwaura. LC 76-980034. (Illus.). 1976. East African Pub. House.

Circle of Sand. Richard Karlan. LC 66-160263. bds., 5.00. Bobbs.

Circle of Sand. Richard Karlan. (75-188). 1968. Macfadden.

Circle of Sin. 3rd ed. Ted Mark, pseud. 1968. pap. 1.25 o.p. (78-633). Lancer.

Circle of Squares. William Price Turner. LC 78-86966. 1969. 4.50. Walker.

Circle of the Day: A Novel. Helen Huntington Howe. LC 50-4882. 1950. Simon and Schuster.

Circle of the Minotaur. Stuart Clink Hood. LC 50-14209. 1950. Viking Press.

Circle of the Stars. Joan Sutherland. 1925. Doubleday, Page & Company.

Circle of Trees. Dana Faralla. LC 55-6719. 1955. Lippincott.

Circle of Vengeance. Nora Jorgenson & Jorgenson, George E. LC 30-4725. 1930. D. Appleton & Company.

Circle of Witches: An Anthology of Victorian Witchcraft Stories. Ed. by Peter Haining. LC 79-126286. (Illus.). 1971. 5.95 (ISBN 0-8008-1590-4). Taplinger Pub. Co.

Circle of Women. Drury L Pifer. LC 74-97679. 1970. Doubleday.

Circle on the Plain. James Baxter. LC 61-933396. 1961. Dorrance.

Circle R. Range. Stack Sutton. 2.95. Arcadia.

Circle W. Lee Floren. LC 45-6675. 1945. Phoenix Press.

Circle W. Lee Thomas. LC 45-6675. 1945. Phoenix Press.

Circled by Fire. A True Story. Julia MacNair Wright. LC 9-91921. 1879. National Temperance Society and Publication House.

Circles: A Washington Story. Abigail Quigley McCarthy. LC 76-42345. 1977. 7.95 (ISBN 0-385-08321-1). Doubleday.

Circles: A Washington Story. Abigail Quigley McCarthy. 1978. 1.95 (ISBN 0-380-39305-0). Avon Books.

Circles of Time. Phillip Rock. LC 80-54514. 13.95 (ISBN 0-87223-691-9). Seaview Books.

Circling Byzantium. Gordon Weaver. LC 80-13628. 1980. 14.95 (ISBN 0-8071-0694-1). Louisiana State University Press.

Circling Prairie. Yetive H Dean. LC 63-17747. Zondervan Pub. House.

Circling the World in Suspense. Ralph Charles Carter, pseud. LC 65-28064. 1965.

Circuit. Ralph M Demers. LC 76-11833. 1976. (ISBN 0-670-22268-2). Viking Press.

Circuit Rider. Edward Eggleston. Ed. by William Randel. (Masterworks of Literature Ser). 1966. 6.50x (ISBN 0-8084-0077-0); pap. 3.95x (ISBN 0-8084-0078-9, M17). Coll & U Pr.

Circuit Rider. Edward Eggleston. 1901. lib. bdg. 15.00 (ISBN 0-8414-3887-0). Folcroft.

Circuit Rider. Edward Eggleston. Ed. by Donald Pizer. LC 73-96530. (American Authors Ser). 1970. lib. bdg. 18.95 o.s.i. (ISBN 0-512-00161-8). Garrett Pr.

Circuit Rider: A Tale of the Heroic Age. Edward Eggleston. LC 65-29509. 1965. 4.00. P. Smith.

Circuit Rider: A Tale of the Heroic Age. Edward Eggleston. LC 66-24153. (Masterworks of literature series). College & University Press.

Circuit Rider: A Tale of the Heroic Age. Edward Eggleston. LC 72-84566. 1974. (lib. ed.) 13.50 (ISBN 0-403-02989-9). Scholarly Press.

Circuit Rider: A Tale of the Heroic Age. Edward Eggleston. LC 77-104768. (Novel as American social history). (Illus.). 1970. University Press of Kentucky.

Circuit Rider: A Tale of the Heroic Age. Edward Eggleston. LC 6-37566. 1874. J. R. Ford & Company.

Circuit Rider: A Tale of the Heroic Age. Edward Eggleston. LC 12-19573. C. Scribner's Sons.

Circuit Rider: A Tale of the Heroic Age. Edward Eggleston. 1892. C. Scribner's Sons.

Circuit Rider: A Tale of the Heroic Age. Edward Eggleston. LC 2-11134. 1902. C. Scribner's Sons.

Circuit Rider: Or, Suffering for Christ's Sake. Sumpter Lee Flowers. LC 12-12482. 1.00. The Flowers Publishing Company.

Circuit Rider's Widow. Corra May White Harris. LC 16-189135. 1916. 1.50. Doubleday, Page & Company.

Circuit Rider's Wife. Corra May White Harris. LC 33-27295. 1933. Houghton Mifflin Company.

Circular Seesaw. Saul Finkel. LC 76-1779. 7.95. (ISBN 0-912282-05-3) (ISBN 0-912282-06-1). PULSE-Finger Press.

Circular Staircase. Mary Roberts Rinehart. LC 8-23102. 1908. The Bobbs-Merrill Company.

Circular Staircase. Mary Roberts Rinehart. LC 24-12441. Grosset & Dunlap.

Circular Staircase. Mary Roberts Rinehart. LC 22-235024. Grosset & Dunlap.

Circular Staircase. Mary Roberts Rinehart. LC 76-50687. (Mystery Library; 3). (Illus.). 1977. 6.95 (ISBN 0-89163-027-9). University Extension, University of California, San Diego.

Circular Staircase. Mary Roberts Rinehart. LC 78-24292. 1979. 11.95 (ISBN 0-8161-6641-2). G. K. Hall.

Circular Staircase. Mary Roberts Rinehart. (Dell bk., 1278). 1972. Dell.

Circular Study. Anna Katherine Green. LC 75-44978. (Crime Fiction Ser). 1976. Repr. of 1900 ed. lib. bdg. 17.50 (ISBN 0-8240-2372-2). Garland Pub.

Circular Study. Anna Katharine Green Rohlfs. LC 75-44978. (Fifty Classics of Crime Fiction, 1900-1950; No. 23). 1976. 12.00 (ISBN 0-8240-2372-2). Garland Pub.

Circular Study. Anna Katharine Green Rohlfs. LC 4394. 1900. McClure, Phillips & Co.

Circumspections from an Equestrian Statue. Jaimy Gordon. (Burning Deck Fiction Ser.). (Illus.). 1979. 15.00 (ISBN 0-930900-77-4); pap. 4.00 (ISBN 0-930900-78-2). Burning Deck.

Circumstance. William Mestrezat John. LC 35-22658. 1935. The Macmillan Company.

Circumstance. Silas Weir Mitchell. 1901. The Century Co.

Circumstantial Affection: A Realistic Romance of the New York Ghetto. Nathaniel Isaiah Gillman. F. T. Neely Co.

Circumstantial Evidence. Alice Irving Abbott. LC 5-42191. W.B. Smith & Co.

Circumstantial Evidence. Bessie A. Turner. (On cover: Munro's library, popular novels, V. 1, no. 122). N. L. Munro.

Circumstantial Evidence: A Legal Novel. Uriah Barnes & Barnes, Lena Belle (Los) "Mrs. Uriah Barnes," 1880- Joint Author. LC 21-7407. 1930. L. H. Brietenbach.

Circus. Juanita Casey. LC 78-55227. 1978. 8.95 (ISBN 0-917712-04-8). Longship Press.

Circus. Netta Gillespie. Ed. by Robert Bensen. (Chapbook: No. 6). 1980. pap. 3.50 (ISBN 0-932884-05-9). Red Herring.

Circus. Alistair MacLean. LC 74-33988. (Illus.). 1975. 6.95 (ISBN 0-385-11003-0). Doubleday.

Circus. Alistair MacLean. LC 75-30980. 1975. 10.95 (ISBN 0-8161-6332-4). G. K. Hall.

Circus Buffoon. Danny Chapman. 238p. (Orig.). 1983. pap. 6.00. S K Chapman.

Circus Couronne. R. Wright Campbell. LC 77-22232. 7.95. Putnam.

Circus Couronne. R. Wright Campbell. LC 78-7852. 1978. 12.95 (ISBN 0-8161-6594-7). G. K. Hall.

Circus Couronne. R. Wright Campbell. 1979. 2.25 (ISBN 0-671-82110-5). Pocket Books.

Circus Day, Akron, Ohio. George Ade. 1976. Repr. of 1903 ed. 25.00 o.p. (ISBN 0-403-05794-9, Regency). Scholarly.

Circus Girl. Nell Marr Dean. LC 56-129364. 1956. Arcadia House.

Circus in the Attic, and Other Stories. Robert Penn Warren. LC 68-6530. (Harbrace paperbound library). 1968. Harcourt, Brace & World.

Circus in the Attic: And Other Stories. Robert Penn Warren. LC 48-5123. 1947. Harcourt, Brace.

Circus Nurse. Ruth McCarthy Sears. Ed. by Alice Sachs. 192p. (OSI). 1972. 3.95 o.s.i. Lenox Hill.

Circus of Dr. Lao. Charles Grandison Finney. LC 61-2237. (Compass books, C82). (Illus.). 1961. Viking Press.

Circus of Dr. Lao. Charles Grandison Finney. 1974. (pbk.) 1.25 (ISBN 0-380-00007-5). Avon.

Circus of Dr. Lao: And Other Improbable Stories. Ed. by Ray Bradbury. LC 56-10486. (Bantam giant, A 1519 9). 1956. Bantam Books.

Circus of Hells. Poul Anderson. LC 79-12731. (Gregg Press science fiction seres). (Illus.). 1979. 12.50 (ISBN 0-8398-2524-2). Gregg Press.

Circus Parade. Jim Tully. LC 27-173572. 1927. A. & C. Boni.

Circus Parade. Jim Tully. LC 30-9495. 1929. Garden City Publishing Co., Inc.

Circus-Rider's Daughter. Ferdinande Brackel. Tr. by Mitchell, Mrs. Mary A. 1896. Benziger Brothers.

Circus World. Barry B. Longyear. 192p. 1981. pap. 2.25 (ISBN 0-425-04709-1). Berkley Pub.

Circut Rider's Wife. Corra May White Harris. LC 10-156362. Henry Altemus Company.

Cirillo: A Story. Putnam, Effie Douglass. LC 3-19440. 1903. Life Publishing Company.

Cirque: A Novel of the Far Future. Ed. by Terry Carr. LC 76-47113. 1977. 8.95 (ISBN 0-672-52014-1). Bobbs-Merrill.

Cirque: A Novel of the Far Future. Ed. by Terry Carr. (Fawcett Crest Book). 1978. 1.75 (ISBN 0-449-23556-4). Fawcett Crest Books.

Cis Martin: Or,The Furriners in the Tennessee Mountains. Louise Regina Baker. LC 98-1372. 1898. Eaton & Mains; Cincinnati, Curts, Jennings.

Ciske the Rat. Translated by Celina Wieniewska and Peter Janson-Smith. 1st Ed. Piet Bakker. 1958. Doubleday.

Cissie - Sweet Child of Grace. Anita Morse. 4.50 o.p. Vantage.

Cistern and the Fountain. Jean Matheson. LC 51-11742. 1951. Scribner.

Citadel. Archibald Joseph Cronin. LC 37-27496. 1937. Little, Brown, and Company.

Citadel. Archibald Joseph Cronin. LC 38-13110. 1938. Little, Brown and Company.

Citadel: A Novel. Joseph Husband. LC 24-22678. 1924. Houghton Mifflin Company.

Citadel: A Romance of Unrest. Samuel Merwin. LC 12-13899. 1912. 1.25. The Century Co.

Citadel. A School Ed. by Frederick Houk Law. Archibald Joseph Cronin. LC 53-20876. 1953. Globe Book Co.

Citadel Is Yours. 1st American Ed. Brigid Knight. LC 57-7070. 1957. Doubleday.

Citadel of Fear. Francis Stevens. 1970. pap. 0.95 o.p. (ISBN 0-446-65401-9, 65-401). Paperback Lib.

Citadel of the Autarch. Gene Wolfe. LC 82-5964. (His Book of the new Sun; v. 4). ((Series: Wolfe, Gene.). (Book of the new Sun; v. 4.). 14.95 (ISBN 0-671-45251-7). Timescape Books: Distributed by Simon and Schuster.

Citadel of the Autarch. Gene Wolfe. (Book of the New Sun Ser.: Vol. 4). 1983. 14.95 (ISBN 0-671-45251-7, Timescape). PB.

Citadel of the Lakes. Orr, Myron David. LC 52-6501. 1952. Dodd, Mead.

Citadel of the Mighty: An Allegorical Narrative. 1st Ed. Florence E Miller. LC 57-14568. Greenwich Book Publishers.

Cities. Robert Kelly. 65p. (Orig.). 1971. pap. 1.00. Frontier Press Calif.

Cities and Years: A Novel. Konstantin Aleksandrovich Fedin. LC 75-2695. 1975. 19.50 (ISBN 0-8371-8029-5). Greenwood Press.

Cities Burning. Dudley Randall. 1966. 1.00 o.p. (ISBN 0-910296-10-3); tape 5.00 o.p. Broadside.

Cities in Flight. James Blish. 608p. 1982. pap. 3.50 (ISBN 0-380-00998-6, 58602). Avon.

Cities of Gold. Levine. (Illus.). 100p. 1981. pap. 4.95 (ISBN 0-937050-19-9). Stonehenge.

Cities of Refuge: A Novel. Philip Hamilton Gibbs. LC 38-17014. 1937. Doubleday, Doran and Company, Inc.

Cities of the Deep. Edward Lyons. LC 49-4936. 1949. Appleton-Century-Crofts.

Cities of the Flesh; or, The Story of Roger De Montbrun. Zoe Oldenbourg. LC 63-13696. 1963. Pantheon Books.

Cities of the Flesh: Or, The Story of Roger De Montbrun. Zoe Oldenbourg. 1976. (pbk.) 1.95. Avon.

Cities of the Flesh. Or. The Story of Roger De Montbrun. Tr. from French by Anne Carter. Zoe Oldenbourg. (U7032). 1966. Ballantine.

Cities of the Interior. Anais Nin. LC 74-21884. (Illus.). 1974. 15.00. (ISBN 0-8040-0665-2) (ISBN 0-8040-0666-0). Swallow Press.

Cities of the Plain. Marcel Proust. LC 78-22052. (His Remembrance of things past). 1970. 1.95 (ISBN 0-394-70597-1). Vintage Books.

Cities of the Plain. Marcel Proust. Tr. by Scott-Moncrieff, Charles Kenneth. LC 28-397720. (His Remembrance of things past, v). 1927. A. & C. Boni.

Cities of the Plain. Marcel Proust. Tr. by Scott-Moncrieff, Charles Kenneth. LC 34-37446. (His Remembrance of things past, v). 1930. A. & C. Boni.

Cities of the Plain. Marcel Proust. Tr. by Scott-Moncrieff, Charles Kenneth. LC 38-27952. (Half-title: The modern library of the world's best books). 1938. The Modern Library.

Cities of the Plain, Volume Two. translated by c. k. scott moncrieff ed. Marcel Proust. Tr. by Scott-Moncrieff, Charles Kenneth. LC 37-12449. (His Remembrance of things past. v-vi in this 4-volume edition. vol. iii). 1934. Random House.

Cities of the Red Night. William S. Burroughs. LC 80-13637. 14.95 (ISBN 0-03-053976-5). Holt, Rinehart, and Winston.

Cities of the Sun. Elizabeth Rachel Cannon Porter. LC 11-314. 1910. The Desert News.

Cities of the Sun: Stories of Ancient America Founded on Historical Incidents in the Book of Mormon. Elizabeth Rachel Cannon. LC 11-314. 1910. 0.35. The Deseret News.

Cities of Wonder. Ed. by Damon Francis Knight. LC 66-11767. 4.50. Doubleday.

Citizen from Lebanon. 1st Ed. Philip Louis Gabriel. LC 57-117677. 1957. Citadel Press.

Citizen in Space: Stories. Robert Sheckley. LC 56-665219. Ballantine Books.

Citizen "M" Speaks, Vol. 1. Karl E. Matthias. LC 82-74183. (Illus.). 120p. 1983. pap. 6.95 (ISBN 0-9609110-0-6). Creative Lit.

Citizen of the Galaxy. Robert Anson Heinlein. 1975. (pbk.) 1.25. Ace Books.

Citizen of the Galaxy. Robert Anson Heinlein. LC 57-10008. 1957. Scribners.

Citizen of the World & the Bee. Oliver Goldsmith. 1970. Repr. of 1934 ed. 7.95x (ISBN 0-460-00902-8, Pub. by Evman England). Biblio Dist.

Citizen Tom Paine. Howard Melvin Fast. LC 43-51139. 1943. Duell, Sloan and Pearce.

Citizen Tom Paine. Howard Melvin Fast. LC 46-860337. (Half-title: The Living library). 1946. The World Publishing Company.

Citizen U. S. A. 1st Ed. Rubynn M English. LC 57-8284. 1957. Pagent Press.

Citizen Vampire. Les Daniels. LC 80-29452. 1981. 9.95 (ISBN 0-684-16827-8). Scribner.

Citizens: A Novel. Meyer Levin. LC 40-724617. 1940. The Viking Press.

Citizen's Arrest. H. C. Nash. 1977. 7.95; pap. 3.95. Latitudes Pr.

Citizens Band: Novelization. Eric M. Corder. (Kangaroo Book). 1977. 1.75 (ISBN 0-671-81180-0). Pocket Books.

Citizen's Novel. Ernst Herhaus. LC 76-156561. 1971. 7.95 (ISBN 0-06-011828-8). Harper & Row.

Citizens of Mist. Roger McDonald. 1968. 10.00x o.s.i. (ISBN 0-7022-0650-4). U of Queensland Pr.

Citoyenne Jacqueline: A Woman's Lot in the Great French Revolution. Henrietta Keddie. LC 7-11136. 1865. A. Strahan.

Citronaloes. A Novel. Walter Marion Raymond. LC 7-36629. 1888. J. W. Randolph & English.

City. Jane Gaskell. LC 77-23530. (Gaskell, Jane, 1941-. The Atlan Ser.). 1978. 8.95 (ISBN 0-312-13982-9). St. Martin's Press.

City. Jane Gaskell. (Her The Atlan series;). 1979. 1.95 (ISBN 0-671-82052-4). Pocket Books.

City. Frans Masereel. Orig. Title: Die Stadt. (Illus.). 1970. pap. 2.00 o.p. (ISBN 0-486-22448-1). Dover.

City, Clifford D Simak. 1976. 1.75. Ace Books.

City and Country Life: Or, Moderate Better Than Rapid Gains. Mary Idle Torrey. LC 42-27377. 1853. Tappan & Whittemore.

City and Suburban. Florence Alice Price James. LC 7-7421. (On cover: Lovell's Westminister series, no. 10). 1890. J. W. Lovell Company.

City and the Dream. Ernest Raymond. LC 75-6810. 1975. 8.95 (ISBN 0-8415-0384-2). Saturday Review Press.

City and the Lion's Den. Marat Kaufman. LC 69-10829. 1968. 5.95. Morrow.

City & the Mountains. Tr. from Portuguese by Roy Campbell. Jose Maria de. Eca de Queiros. LC 67-17895. 1967. 4.50. Ohio Univ. Pr.

City and the Pillar Revised: Including an Essay: Sex and the Law, and An Afterword. Rev. Ed. Gore Vidal. LC 65-18637. 1965. 4.95. Dutton.

City & the Stars. Arthur C. Clarke. pap. 0.95 o.p. (ISBN 0-15-618022-7, HPL1, HPL). HarBraceJ.

City & the Stars. Arthur C. Clarke. LC 56-5328. 1966. 7.50 o.p. (ISBN 0-15-118023-7). HarBraceJ.

City and the Stars. 1st Ed. Arthur Charles Clarke. LC 56-5328. Harcourt, Brace.

City and the Wave. Jon Godden. LC 54-539523. 1954. Rinehart.

City and the World: And Other Stories. Francis Clement Kelley. LC 78-130059. (Short story index reprint series). (Illus.). 1970. Books for Libraries Press.

TITLE INDEX CIVIL PRISONERS.

City and the World, and Other Stories. Francis Clement Kelley. LC 13-20696. 1913. Extension Magazine.
City at Bay. David Thoreau. LC 79-87838. 1979. 9.95 (ISBN 0-87795-231-0). Arbor Hse.
City at World's End. Edmond Hamilton. LC 51-10074. (Fell's science-fiction library). 1951. F. Fell.
City Below the Hill. H. B. Ames. LC 78-163831. (Social History of Canada Ser.). 112p. 1972. pap. 5.00 o.p. (ISBN 0-8020-6142-7). U of Toronto Pr.
City Beneath the Bermuda Triangle. David G. Jungclaus. LC 81-86421. 80p. 1983. pap. 5.95 (ISBN 0-86666-047-X). GWP.
City Beyond Devil's Gate. Lillian Janet. LC 50-10479. 1950. Random House.
City Beyond. 1st Ed. Lucille Emerick. LC 52-7813. 1952. Holt.
City Block. Waldo David Frank. LC 75-112789. 1970. AMS Press.
City Block. Waldo David Frank. LC 22-20427. 1922. W. Frank.
City Block. Waldo David Frank. 1932. C. Scribner's Sons.
City Boy. Herman Wouk. 1980. pap. 4.95 (ISBN 0-671-41511-5). PB.
City Boy: A Novel. Herman Wouk. LC 52-6369. 1952. Doubleday.
City Boy: The Adventures of Herbie Bookbinder and His Cousin Cliff, a Novel. Herman Wouk. LC 48-3810. 1948. Simon and Schuster.
City Boy: The Adventures of Herbie Bookbinder. twentieth anniversary edition. ed. Herman Wouk. 1974. (pbk.) 1.25. Pocket Books.
City Boy: The Adventures of Herbie Bookbinder. 20th anniversary ed. Herman Wouk. LC 69-10961. 1969. 5.95. Doubleday.
City Cool: A Ritual of Belonging. James De Jongh & Carles Cleveland. LC 77-15637. 8.95 (ISBN 0-394-42470-0). Random House.
City Cousin & Other Stories. 124p. 1973. 1.95 o.p. (ISBN 0-8351-0043-X). China Bks.
City Cousin & Other Stories. 124p. 1973. 1.50 o.p. (ISBN 0-8351-0043-X). China Bks.
City Destroyer. Grant Stockbridge. (Spider # 3). 1975. (pbk.) 0.95 (ISBN 0-671-77943-5). Pocket Books.
City Doctor. Florence Stonebraker. LC 43-150663. 1943. Phoenix Press.
City Dogs: A Novel. William Brashler. LC 75-9350. 8.95 (ISBN 0-06-010448-1). Harper & Row.
City for Conquest. Aben Kandel. LC 36-5634. Covici, Friede.
City for St. Francis. Evelyn Wells. LC 67-13783. 1967. Doubleday.
City for Sale. Jon Messman. (Revenger). (Signet book: Vol. 5). 1975. (pbk.) 1.25. New American Library.
City Girl. Eunice Chapin. LC 32-1754. 1932. Brewer, Warren & Putnam.
City Girl: A New Novel. Ben Smith. LC 52-11259. 1952. Arco Pub. Co.
City Girl: A New Novel. Robert W. Tracy. LC 52-11259. 1952. Arco Pub. Co.
City Girl in the Country: And Other Stories. Norma Lee Browning. LC 55-7737. 1955. H. Regnery Co.
City Grew on the Sod: A Novel of Western Pioneers. 1st Ed. George O Criswell. LC 52-7650. 1952. Exposition Press.
City Harvest. Margaret Cheney Dawson. LC 34-2557. 1934. The Macmillan Company.
City Hotel. Jane Manning. 1970. pap. 0.75 o.p. (75-302). Manor Bks.
City in Heat see Ciudad al Rojo Vivo.
City in the American Novel, 1789-1900. George A. Dunlap. LC 65-17889. 1965. Repr. of 1934 ed. 10.00 o.p. (ISBN 0-8462-0576-9). Russell.
City in the Clouds. Cyril Arthur Edward Ranger Gull. LC 22-396223. Harcourt, Brace and Company.
City in the Dawn. Hervey Allen. LC 50-14381. 1950. Rinehart.
City in the Foreground: A Novel of Youth. Gerard Hopkins. LC 22-4829. 1921. E. P. Dutton and Company.
City in the Glacier. Robert E. Vardeman & Milan, Victor. LC 80-82200. 1980. 2.25 (ISBN 0-87216-754-2). Playboy Paperbacks.
City in the North. Marta Randall. 1976. (pbk.) 1.50 (ISBN 0-446-88117-1). Warner Books.
City in the Sahara. Jules Verne. 1960. 3.95. Assoc Bk.
City in the Sea. Henry De Vere Stacpoole. LC 27-26386. 1925. George H. Doran Company.
City in the Sea. Wilson Tucker. LC 51-13119. 1951. Rinehart.
City in the Sky. Curt Siodmak. LC 73-93745. 1974. 5.95 (ISBN 0-399-11333-9). Putnam.
City in the Sun. Karon Kehoe. LC 46-118614. 1946. Dodd, Mead & Company.
City Jungle. Felix Salten & Chambers, Whittaker, Tr. LC 32-14434. 1932. Simon and Schuster, Inc.
City Kid. Mary MacCracken. 1982. pap. 2.95 (ISBN 0-451-11336-5, AE1336, Sig). NAL.
City Lies Four-Square: A Novel. Edith Pargeter. LC 39-27065. Reynal & Hitchcock.
City Life. Donald Barthelme. 1976. 1.95 (ISBN 0-671-80770-6). Pocket Books.
City Life. Donald Barthelme. LC 74-113775. (Illus.). 1970. 5.95. Farrar, Straus & Giroux.
City Life, City Love. Beverly Sommers. (Harlequin American Romance (Canada) Ser.). 256p. 1983. pap. 2.25 (ISBN 0-373-16011-9). Harlequin Bks.
City Limit. Hollis Spurgeon Summers. LC 48-7902. 1948. Houghton Mifflin Co.
City Limits. Josiah Pitts Woolfolk. LC 32-13778. 1932. W. Godwin, Inc.
City Lover. Andrea Newman. LC 69-15162. 1969. 4.95. Doubleday.
City Man. Rachel Rivers-Coffey. LC 77-97. 7.95 (ISBN 0-06-013576-X). Harper & Row.
City Nurse. Peggy Gaddis, pseud. LC 56-11699. 1956. Arcadia House.
City of a Hundred Gates. Isobel Stone. LC 42-15419. 1942. B. Humphries, Inc.
City of Angels. Rupert Hughes. LC 41-3907. 1941. C. Scribner's Sons.
City of Angels. Steve Shagan. LC 74-16618. 1975. 6.95 (ISBN 0-399-11478-5). Putnam.
City of Anger. William Raymond Manchester. LC 53-6975. (Furiously paced novel about the struggle for power in a great American city). 1967. 8.95 (ISBN 0-316-54488-4). Little.
City of Anger: A Novel. William Raymond Manchester. LC 53-6975. 1953. Ballantine Book.
City of Anger: A Political Novel. William Raymond Manchester. LC 67-9755. 1967. Little, Brown.
City of Baraboo. Barry B Longyear. LC 79-17674. 10.95 (ISBN 0-399-12477-2). Berkley Pub. Corp.: Distributed by Putnam.
City of Baraboo. Barry B Longyear. 1981. 2.25 (ISBN 0-425-04940-X). Berkley Publishing Corp.
City of Beautiful Nonsense. Ernest Temple Thurston. LC 9-28691. 1909. Dodd, Mead & Company.
City of Beautiful Nonsense. Ernest Temple Thurston. LC 28-4840. 1926. D. Appleton and Company.
City of Bells. Elizabeth Goudge. LC 36-246762. Coward-McCann, Inc.
City of Bread. Alexander Neverov, pseud. LC 72-90302. (Soviet Literature in English Translation Ser). (Illus.). 242p. 1973. Repr. of 1927 ed. 18.50 (ISBN 0-88355-013-X). Hyperion Conn.
City of Bread. Aleksandr Sergeevich Skobelev. LC 72-90302. (Illus.). 1973. (ISBN 0-88355-013-X). Hyperion Press.
City of Bread. Aleksandr Sergeevich Skobelev. LC 27-24576. George H. Doran Company.
City of Broken Promises. Austin Coates. LC 68-23439. 1968. John Day Co.
City of Cain. Kate Wilheim. 1982. pap. 2.75 (ISBN 0-671-44705-X, Timescape). PB.
City of Cain. Kate Wilhelm. LC 73-15818. 1974. 6.95 (ISBN 0-316-94076-3). Little, Brown.
City of Cain. Kate Wilhelm. (Kangaroo Book). 1978. 1.75 (ISBN 0-671-81342-0). Pocket Books.
City of Comrades. Basil King. LC 19-5044. 1919. Harper & Brothers.
City of Darkness. Benjamin Bova. 176p. 1982. pap. 2.50 (ISBN 0-425-05774-7). Berkley Pub.
City of Delight: A Love Drama of the Siege and Fall of Jerusalem. Elizabeth Jane Miller. LC 8-9528. 1908. The Bobbs-Merrill Company.
City of Desire. Juanita Savage. LC 30-4240. 1930. L. MacVeagh, The Dial Press.
City of Encounters. Horace Hazeltine. LC 8-28636. M. Kenzerley.
City of Encounters. Charles Stokes Wayne. LC 8-28636. 1908. M. Kennerley.
City of Encounters: A London Divertissement. Thomas Burke. LC 32-26953. 1932. Little, Brown, and Company.
City of Endeavor: A Religious Novel Devoted to the Interests of Good Citizenship in the City of Brooklyn, N. Y. Harold McGill Davis. LC 6-32488. 1895. Collins & Day.
City of Endless Night. Milo Hastings. LC 73-13257. (Classics of science fiction). 1974. 9.95 (ISBN 0-88355-112-8) (ISBN 0-88355-112-8). Hyperion Press.
City of Endless Night. Milo Hastings. LC 20-15704. 1920. 1.75. Dodd, Mead and Company.
City of Fingerless Men: By Marsh Morrison Pseud. Morris Marsh. LC 51-8660. 1951. Vantage Press.
City of Fire. Grace Livingston Hill. LC 76-40909. 1976. 8.95 (ISBN 0-89190-019-5). American Reprint Co.
City of Fire. Grace Livingston Hill. LC 22-26490. 1922. J. B. Lippincott Company.
City of Fools: A Novel. Michel Bataille. LC 68-20457. 1968. Crown Publishers.
City of Friends. Elias Tobenkin. LC 34-362367. Minton, Balch & Company.
City of Frozen Fire. William Vaughan Wilkins. LC 51-320. 1951. Macmillan.
City of God. Cecelia Holland. 1981. 2.50 (ISBN 0-394-41277-X). Warner Books.
City of God: A Novel of the Borgias. Cecelia Holland. LC 78-7622. 1979. 9.95 (ISBN 0-394-41277-X). Knopf; Distributed by Random House.
City of Gold. William Arthur Neubauer. LC 51-3126. 1951. Arcadia House.
City of Gold. Francis Brett Young. LC 39-27839. Reynal & Hitchcock.
City of Gold and Lead. John Christopher. LC 67-21245. 1967. Macmillan.
City of Gold and Shadows. Edith Pargeter. LC 74-153421. (Illus.). 1974. 5.95. W. Morrow.
City of Gold & Shadows. Ellis Peters. 224p. 1974. 5.95 o.p. (ISBN 0-688-00226-9). Morrow.
City of Gold & Shadows. Ellis Peters. 1975. pap. 1.25 o.p. (ISBN 0-515-03590-4, V3590). BJ Pub Group.
City of Golden Cages. Jon Rosenberg. LC 78-3967. 7.95 (ISBN 0-312-14115-7). St. Martin's Press.
City of Hermits. Gina Covina. LC 82-74335. 232p. (Orig.). 1983. 11.95 (ISBN 0-9609626-2-X); pap. 6.95 (ISBN 0-9609626-1-1). Barn Owl Bks.
City of Illusion. Vardis Fisher. (Illus.). 400p. 1982. pap. 3.25 (ISBN 0-441-10707-9, Pub. by Charter Bks). Ace Bks.
City of Illusion: A Novel. Vardis Fisher. LC 49-846588. 1949. Vanguard Press.
City of Illusions. Ursula K. Le Guin. LC 75-417. (Garland Library of Science Fiction). 1975. 11.00 (ISBN 0-8240-1422-7). Garland Pub.
City of Illusions. Ursula K. Le Guin. LC 77-11783. 1978. 8.95 (ISBN 0-06-012569-1). Harper & Row.
City of Illusions. Ursula K. Le Guin. Ed. by Lester Del Rey. LC 75-417. (Library of Science Fiction). 1975. lib. bdg. 17.50 (ISBN 0-8240-1422-7). Garland Pub.
City of Illusions. Ursula K. Le Guin. 1974. (pbk.) 1.25. Ace Books.
City of Illustion: A Novel. Vardis Fisher. LC 41-5220. Harper & Brothers.
City of Joy. Arthur Wentworth Hewitt. LC 26-21666. 1926. The Tuttle Company.
City of Libertines. William George Hardy. LC 57-12735. 1957. Appleton-Century-Crofts.
City of Light. Alison Macleod. LC 69-15022. 1969. 4.95. Houghton Mifflin.
City of Lilies. Agnes Russell Weekes & Weekes, Rose Kirkpatrick, 1874- Joint Author. LC 23-11517. 1923. R. M. McBridge & Company.
City of Love: Stories of the Gaiety, the Excitement, the Spirit of Paris. Ed. by Daniel Talbot. LC 54-13202. (Dell first edition 45). 1955. Dell Pub. Co.
City of Many Days. Shulamith Hareven. LC 76-24044. 1977. 7.95 (ISBN 0-385-12250-0). Doubleday.
City of Many Days. Shulamith Hareven. 1978. 1.95 (ISBN 0-445-04251-6). Popular Library.
City of Masks. George Barr McCutcheon. LC 18-17912. 1918. Dodd, Mead and Company.
City of Masques. Alan Brennert. LC 77-93131. 1.75 (ISBN 0-87216-456-X). Playboy Press.
City of Night. John Rechy. LC 61-11775. 1963. Grove Press.
City of Numbered Days. Francis Lynde. LC 14-148071. 1914. C. Scribner's Sons.
City of Oil: A Novel. Ruben Chudlarian. LC 53-11080. 1953. William-Frederick Press.
City of Peril. Arthur John Arbuthnott Stringer. LC 23-2811. 1923. A. A. Knopf.
City of Pleasure. Arnold Bennett. LC 74-5394. (Collected Works of Arnold Bennett: Vol. 11). 1976. Repr. of 1907 ed. 20.75 (ISBN 0-518-19092-7). Ayer Co.
City of Purple Dreams: Frontispiece by M. Wilson Craig. Edwin Baird. LC 13-19327. 1913. 1.30. F. G. Browne & Co.
City of Refuge: A Novel. Walter Besant. LC 6-12394. F. A. Stokes Company.
City of Refuge: A Novel, by Sir Walter Besant... Walter Besant. LC 6-12395. F. A. Stokes Company.
City of Revelation. John Michell. LC 72-88116. 176p. 1972. 5.95 o.p. McKay.
City of St. Anna: The Story of the Man Child. Edward A Merrit. LC 9-4488.
City of Sin: A Novel. Hattie Lee Johnston. LC 7-10798. 1896. Gospel Advocate Publishing Company.
City of Six. Chauncey De Leon Canfield. LC 10-8159. 1910. 1.50. A. C. McClurg & Co.
City of Spades. Colin MacInnes. LC 58-12524. 1958. Macmillan.
City of Splendid Night. John William Harding. LC 9-4958. G. W. Dillingham Company.
City of Splintered Gods. Gyorgy Faludy. LC 66-12608. 1966. W. Morrow.
City of the Beast. Michael Moorcock. (Science Fiction Ser.). 1979. pap. 1.50 o.p. (ISBN 0-87997-436-2, UW1436). DAW Bks.
City of the Beast. Michael Moorcock. 1970. pap. 0.75 o.p. (ISBN 0-447-74668-5). Lancer.
City of the Chasch. Jack Vance, pseud. (Science Fiction Ser.). 1979. pap. 1.75 (ISBN 0-87997-461-3, UE1461). DAW Bks.
City of the Dead. Herbert H. Lieberman. LC 76-4969. 8.95 (ISBN 0-671-22272-4). Simon and Schuster.
City of the Dead. Herbert H. Lieberman. (Kangaroo Book). 1977. 1.95 (ISBN 0-671-80877-X). Pocket Books.
City of the Discreet. Baroja y Nessi, Pio. Tr. by Fassett, Jocob Sioat. LC 18-261732. (On verso of half-title: The Borzol Spanish translations, ii). 1917. A. A. Knopf.
City of the Flags. Clark McMeekin. LC 50-10336. 1950. Appleton-Century-Crofts.
City of the Living, and Other Stories. Wallace Earle Stegner. LC 56-120883. 1956. Houghton, Mifflin.
City of the Living: And Other Stories. Wallace Earle Stegner. LC 73-81276. (Short story index reprint series). 1969. Books for Libraries Press.
City of the Living Dead. Jeffrey Lord. (Blade Ser.: No. 26). 1978. pap. 1.50 (ISBN 0-523-40193-0). Pinnacle Bks.
City of the Singing Flame. Clark A. Smith. pap. 2.95 (ISBN 0-671-83415-0, Timescape). PB.
City of the Sun. Edwin Legrand Sabin. LC 24-34010. G. W. Jacobs & Company.
City of the Sun. Brian M Stableford. 1978. 1.50 (ISBN 0-87997-377-3). DAW Books.
City of the Yellow Devil. Maksim Gorkii. 138p. 1972. 4.45 (ISBN 0-8285-0977-8, Pub. by Progress Pubs USSR). Imported Pubns.
City of Trembling Leaves. Walter Van Tilburg Clark. LC 45-35081. 1945. Random House.
City of Trembling Leaves. Walter Van Tilburg Clark. LC 46-7655. 1946. The Sun Dial Press.
City of Whispering Stone. George C Chesbro. LC 77-28481. 8.95 (ISBN 0-671-24003-X). Simon and Schuster.
City of White Night. Nikolai Mikhailovich Gubskii. LC 31-181825. 1931. W. W. Norton & Company, Inc.
City of Wonder. Evelyn Charles H. Vivian. (Time-Lost Set.). 184p. 1973. pap. 1.25 o.p. (ISBN 0-87818-010-9). Centaur.
City on a Hill. George V. Higgins. LC 74-21308. 1975. 7.95 (ISBN 0-394-49540-3). Knopf: Distributed by Random House.
City on the Hill: A Novel. Marian McCamy Sims. LC 40-32625. J. B. Lippincott Company.
City on the Moon by Murray Leinster Pseud. William Fitzgerald Jenkins. LC 57-87349. 1957. Avalon Books.
City on the River. Roderick MacLeish. LC 72-82703. 1973. 10.00 (ISBN 0-525-08166-6). Dutton.
City Out of the Sea. Alfred Boller Stanford. LC 24-122788. 1924. D. Appleton and Company.
City Outside the World. Lin Carter. (Berkley Medallion Book). 1977. 1.50 (ISBN 0-425-03549-2). Berkley Pub. Corp.
City Primeval: High Noon in Detroit. Elmore Leonard. LC 80-66762. 10.95 (ISBN 0-87795-282-5). Arbor House.
City Sparrow. William Arthur Neubauer. 1955. Arcadia House.
City Square. Benjamin S Burkett. LC 45-753464. 1945. Dorrance & Company.
City Streets see Violated One.
City, the Family, & the Sexual Web. Andrew MacInnes. pap. 1.95 o.p. (ISBN 0-87056-235-5, 6235). Brandon.
City Under Ground. Suzanne Chouinard Martel. LC 64-229689. (Illus.). 1964. Viking Press.
City Walls. Kirby Congdon & Paul Mariah. 1975. pap. 3.00 o.p. (ISBN 0-916266-01-X). A Bifrost.
City Wise. Micheline Keating. LC 32-942928. 1932. R. Long & R. R. Smith, Inc.
City Within. Elisabeth Newbold. LC 72-93322. 1973. 6.95 (ISBN 0-8184-0226-1). M. Girodias Associates.
City Without a Heart. LC 22-756420. 1933. Houghton Mifflin Company.
City Without Jews: A Novel of Our Time. Hugo. Bettauer. Tr. by Brainin, Salomea Neumark. LC 26-23683. 1926. Bloch Publishing Company.
City. 1st Ed. Julius Horwitz. LC 53-6632. 1953. World Pub. Co.
City, 2000 A.D. Urban Life Through Science Fiction. Ralph S. Clem & Martin Harry Greenberg. LC 76-8814. (Fawcett Crest book). 1976. 1.95 (ISBN 0-449-22892-4). Fawcett Publications.
Ciudad al Rojo Vivo. new ed. W. B. Murphy. Tr. by Gomez Kemp from Eng. (Compadre Collection: Rivera & Rozoni Ser., No. 1). Orig. Title: City in Heat. 160p. (Span.). 1974. pap. 0.75 (ISBN 0-88473-608-3). Fiesta Pub.
Civil Actions. Steven Phillips. LC 82-45365. 1983. 16.95 (ISBN 0-385-15988-9). Doubleday.
Civil Contract. Georgette Heyer. (Berkley medallion book). 1974. (pbk.) 1.25 (ISBN 0-425-02578-0). Berkley Pub. Co.
Civil Contract. 2d american ed. Georgette Heyer. LC 72-22194. 1971. 5.95. Putnam.
Civil Prisoners. Meriol Trevor. LC 77-77919. (Illus.). 1977. 8.95 (ISBN 0-525-08175-5). Dutton.

Civil Prisoners. Meriol Trevor. (Regency Romance). 1978. 1.50 (ISBN 0-449-23580-7). Fawcett Books.
Civilian Attache: A Story of a Frontier Army Post. Helen Dawes Brown. LC 99-2074. (ivory series). 1899. C. Scribner's Sons.
Civilization: Tales of the Orient. Ellen Newbold La Motte. LC 76-122727. (Short story index reprint series). 1970. Books for Libraries Press.
Civilization: Tales of the Orient. Ellen Newbold La Motte. LC 19-6867. 1.50. George H. Doran Company.
Civilization, 1914-1917. George Duhamel. Tr. by Brooks, E. S. LC 19-4853. 1919. The Century Co.
Civilization's Last Hurrah. 208p. 1975. pap. 1.95 o.p. (ISBN 0-8024-1568-7). Moody.
Civilization's Last Hurrah. Gary G Cohen. LC 73-15086. 1974. 4.95 (ISBN 0-8024-1567-9). Moody Press.
Civilizing Cricket: A Story for Girls. Forrestine Cooper Hooker. LC 38-23551. (Young moderns bookshelf). 1938. The Sun Dial Press, Inc.
Clabe's Daughter. Nel Sweeten Cooper. LC 73-88550. 1974. 6.95. Cooper Pub. Co.
Clad in Doublet and Hose: And Other Stories of Colonial Times. May Kelsey Champion. LC 35-19417. 1935. The Bingham Press.
Clad in Purple Mist. Catherine Isabel Dodd. LC 27-264456. 1927. George H. Doran Company.
Claim Jumper. Doyle Trent. 1981. pap. 1.95 (ISBN 0-8439-0938-2). Nordon Pubns.
Claim Jumpers. Stewart Edward White. lib. bdg. 15.70x (ISBN 0-88411-828-2). Amereon Ltd.
Claim Jumpers: A Romance. Stewart Edward White. LC 1-31397. (Half-title: Appletons' town and country library. no. 297). 1901. D. Appleton and Company.
Claim Number One. George Washington Ogden. LC 22-11289. 1922. A. C. McClurg & Co.
Claim of Forty Mile Creek. Jules Verne. 3.95. Assoc Bk.
Claim of the Flashless Corpes. George Bruce. LC 37-19455. Dodge Publishing Company.
Claimant. Hollis Alpert. LC 68-10829. 1968. Dial Press.
Claimants. Archibald Marshall. LC 34-5825. 1934. Houghton Mifflin Company.
Claiming of Sleeping Beauty. A. N. Roquelaure. 288p. 1983. pap. 6.95 (ISBN 0-525-48054-4, 0869-260). Dutton.
Claims and Counterclaims. Maud Wilder Goodwin. LC 5-26852. 1905. Doubleday. Page & Company.
Claims Game. Vladimir P. Chernik. (O.s.i.). 208p. 1969. 5.95 o.s.i. (ISBN 0-8202-0008-5). Sherbourne.
Clair De Lune. Agnes Russell Weekes. LC 22-19907. 1922. Dodd, Mead and Company.
Claire. Leslie Burton Blades. LC 19-5198. 1919. George H. Doran Company.
Claire. Dorothea Malm. LC 55-10094. Putnam.
Claire: A Portrait in Motion. Erin Samson. LC 45-5905. 1945. Harper & Brothers.
Claire Ambler. Booth Tarkington. LC 28-3166. 1928. Doubleday, Doran & Company, Inc.
Claire and the Forge-Master. Georges Ohnet. Tr. by Valentine, Ferdinand C. (On cover: Munro's library, popular novel, v. 1, no. 206). N. L. Munro.
Claire Serrat: A Novel. Ida Alexa Ross Wylie. LC 59-6094. 1959. Putnam.
Claire's Love-Life. A Tale of English Society. Lucy Randall Comfort. LC 6-30665. (On cover: The Laurel library, no. 10). 1892. G. Munro.
Clairon SF. Ed. by Kate Wilhelm. (Berkley Medallion Book). 1977. 1.25 (ISBN 0-425-03293-0). Berkley Pub. Corp.
Clairvoyant. Hans Holzer. (Orig.). 1980. pap. text ed. 2.25 o.s.i. (ISBN 0-505-51573-3). Tower Bks.
Clairvoyant. Ernst Lothar. Tr. by Ryan, Beatrice. LC 32-26202. 1932. H. C. Kinsey & Company, Inc.
Clairvoyant Countess. Dorothy Gilman Butters. LC 74-33642. 1975. 6.95 (ISBN 0-385-08922-8). Doubleday.
Clairvoyant Countess. Dorothy Gilman Butters. LC 76-20549. 1976. 10.95 (ISBN 0-8161-6396-0). G. K. Hall.
Clairvoyant Countess. Dorothy Gilman. 224p. 1978. pap. 1.95 (ISBN 0-449-23561-0, Crest). Fawcett.
Clam Shell. Mary Lee Settle. LC 78-175648. 1972. 6.95. Delacorte Press.
Clammer. William John Hopkins. LC 79-116955. (Short story index reprint series). 1970. Books for Libraries Press.
Clammer. William John Hopkins. LC 6-831277. 1906. Houghton, Mifflin & Company.
Clammer and the Submarine. William John Hopkins. 1917. 1.25. Houghton Mifflin Company.
Clamoring Self. Leonhard Frank. Tr. by Brooks, Cyrus Harry. LC 30-28635. 1930. G. P. Putnam's Sons.
Clan Call. Hapsburg Liebe. LC 20-19762. 1920. Doubleday, Page & Company.
Clan McGuire. Ila Cornelius Mangold. LC 50-6701. 1950. Rinehart.
Clan of the Cave Bear. Jean M. Auel. 512p. 1981. pap. 3.75 (ISBN 0-553-14800-1). Bantam.
Clan of the Cave Bear. Jean M. Auel. 480p. 1980. 12.95 (ISBN 0-517-54202-1). Crown.
Clan of the Cave Bear: A Novel. Jean M Auel. LC 80-14581. (Author's Earth's Children; 1). 12.95 (ISBN 0-517-54202-1). Crown.
Clancy. Frederic Mullally. LC 77-183357. 1972. 7.95. Morrow.
Clandara. Evelyn Anthony. 1971. pap. 0.95 o.p. (09065). Curtis.
Clandestine. James Ellroy. 352p. 1982. pap. 2.75 (ISBN 0-380-81141-3, 81141-3). Avon.
Clandestine Affair. Sally James. (Coventry Romance Ser.: No. 64). 224p. 1980. pap. 1.75 (ISBN 0-449-50095-0, Coventry). Fawcett.
Clandestine Betrothal. Alice Chetwynd Ley. LC 77-14008. (Regency Romance). 1978. 8.95 (ISBN 0-89340-115-3). J. Curley.
Clandestine Marriage. Eliza Ann Dupuy. T. B. Peterson & Brothers.
Clang Birds: A Novel. John L'Heureux. LC 72-77652. 1972. 5.95. Macmillan.
Clangor in the Bell Tower. Mab Graff. LC 77-91493. 2.95 (ISBN 0-916406-89-X). Accent Books.
Clanking of Chains: A Story of Sinn Fein. Brinsley MacNamara. LC 19-17481. Brentano's.
Clanking of Chains: A Story of Sinn Fein. A. E. Weldon. LC 19-17481. Brentano's.
Clanking of Chains: By Brinsley MacNamara. A. E. Weldon. LC 66-7476. pap., 1.25. Anvil Bks.
Clans of Darkness: Scottish Stories of Fantasy and Horror. Ed. by Peter Haining. LC 78-162964. 1971. 5.95 (ISBN 0-8008-1621-8). Taplinger Pub. Co.
Clans of the Alphane Moon. Philip K Dick. LC 79-17744. (Gregg Press science fiction series). (Illus.). 1979. 12.95 (ISBN 0-8398-2598-6). Gregg Press.
Clansman. Thomas Dixon. LC 41-13227. 1941. Triangle Books.
Clansman: An Historical Romance of the Ku Kux Klan. Thomas Dixon. LC 5-1488. 1905. Doubleday, Page & Company.
Clansman: An Historical Romance of the Ku Klux Klan. Thomas Dixon. LC 75-3881. 1975. 35.00 (ISBN 0-87968-194-2). Gordon Press.
Clansman: An Historical Romance of the Ku Klux Klan. Thomas Dixon. LC 71-104761. (Novel as American social history). 1970. University Press of Kentucky.
Clansman: An Historical Romance of the Ku Klux Klan. Thomas Dixon. LC 24-25008. 1906. Doubleday, Page & Company.
Clansman: An Historical Romance of the Ku Klux Klan. Thomas Dixon. 1914. Doubleday, Page & Company.
Clansman: An Historical Romance of the Ku Klux Klan. Thomas Dixon. LC 21-86048. Grosset & Dunlap.
Clansman: An Historical Romance of the Ku Klux Klan. Illus. by Arthur I. Keller. Thomas Dixon. LC 67-292646. (Americans in Fic.). 1967. Gregg Pr.
Clansmen. Ethel Mary Young Boileau. LC 36-10946. 1936. E. P. Dutton & Co., Inc.
Clap Your Hands. Glynn Compton Harper. LC 81-3643. 1983. 16.95 (ISBN 0-87949-205-8). Ashley.
Clara. William Laurence Coleman. LC 51-14964. 1952. Dutton.
Clara Alice. Julia A Norton. LC 31-6861. 1931. Julia A. Norton.
Clara Barron. Harvey Jerrold O'Higgins. LC 26-5626. 1926. Harper & Brothers.
Clara Hopgood. William Hale White & Shapcott, Reuben, Ed. LC 8-36559. 1896. Dodd, Mead and Company.
Clara Hopgood. William Hale White & Shapcott, Reuben, Ed. 1836. Oxford University Press, H. Milford.
Clara Hopgood, 1896 see Catherine Furze, 1893.
Clara Howard: Or, The Enthusiasm of Love. Charles Brockden Brown. LC 41-34780. (With his Ormond; or, The secret witness. Boston, 1827). 1827. S. G. Goodrich.
Clara Howard: Or, The Enthusiasm of Love. Charles Brockden Brown. (With his Ormond. Philadelphia, 1857). 1857. M. Polock.
Clara Moreland: Or, Adventures in the South-West. Emerson Bennett. LC 7-34436. T. B. Peterson.
Clara, or, Slave Life in Europe. with a preface by the late sir archibald alison... ed. Hacklander, Friedrich Wilhelm. LC 6-45968. (Harper's Franklin square library. Duodecimo ed.). 1883. Harper & Brothers.
Clara Reeve. Leonie Hargrave. LC 74-25267. 1975. 8.95 (ISBN 0-394-48490-8). Knopf: Distributed by Random House.
Clara, Some Scattered Chapters in the Life of a Hussy. Albert Michael Neil Lyons. 1912. John Lane Company.
Clara: Thirteen Short Stories and a Novel. Luisa Valenzuela. LC 75-42311. Harcourt Brace Jovanovich.
Clara Vaughan. Richard Doddridge Blackmore. (On cover: Lovell's library, no. 1037). J. W. Lovell Company.
Clara Vaughan. A Novel. Richard Doddridge Blackmore. (Harper's Franklin square library, no. 120). 1880. Harper & Brothers.
Clara Vaughan. A Novel. Richard Doddridge Blackmore. LC 6-13866. (On cover: Seaside library. Pocket ed., no. 632). G. Munro.
Clare: A Light in the Garden. Murray Bodo. (Orig.). 1979. pap. 2.75 (ISBN 0-912228-54-7). St Anthony Mess Pr.
Clare and Bebe. A Novel. Ellen Warner Olney Kirk. LC 7-12353. 1879. J. B. Lippincott & Co.
Clare Darcy Trilogy. Clare Darcy. 1979. 14.95 (ISBN 0-8027-0627-4). Walker & Co.
Clare Duval: A Novel. Henry Leavitt Goodwin. G. W. Dillingham Company.
Clare Lincoln. A Novel. Decius S Wade, pseud. LC 8-33098. 1876. Printed at the Riverside Press.
Clare of Claresmede. Charles Gibbon. (Harper's Franklin square library, no. 546). 1886. Harper & Brothers.
Clarel, 2 vols. Herman Melville. 250.00 (ISBN 0-87968-875-0). Gordon Pr.
Claremont: Or, The Undivided Household. LC 6-2537. 1857. Parry and McMillan.
Clarence. Bret I. E. Francis Bret Harte. LC 11-349. 1895. Houghton, Mifflin and Company.
Clarence Milton, the Heroic Fireman. A Tale of Love and Romance Founded on Facts. Abraham Lincoln MacKenzie. 1900. United Printing Co.
Clarence; or, A Tale of Our Own Times. Catharine Maria Sedgwick. LC 10-224844. 1830. Carey & Les.
Clarence: Or, A Tale of Our Own Times. author's rev. ed.... ed. Catharine Maria Sedgwick. LC 8-11240. 1849. G. P. Putnam; Etc., Etc.
Clarence: or, A Tale of Our Own Times. author's rev. ed.... ed. Catharine Maria Sedgwick. LC 42-29641. 1854. J. C. Derby; Boston, Phillips, Sampson and Company; Etc., Etc.
Clarence Rhett: Or, The Cruise of a Privateer. An American Sea Story. Edward Zane Carroll Judson. LC 7-11442. F. A. Brady.
Clarentine: A Novel. Sarah Harriet Burney. LC 6-19871. 1818. Published by M. Cary & Son, No., Chestnut Street.
Claret, Sandwiches, and Sin. Madelaine Duke. LC 66-24308. (Doubleday science fiction). 1966. Doubleday.
Claribel's Love Story. Charlotte Mary Brame. (On cover: Lovell's library. v. 19. no. 926). J. W. Lovell Company.
Clarimonde. Theophile Gautier & Hearn, Lafcadio, 1850-1904, Tr. LC 99-4202. Brentano's.
Clarion. Samuel Hopkins Adams. LC 14-17921. 1914. Houghton Mifflin Company.
Clarion II: An Anthology of Speculative Fiction and Criticism. Ed. by Robin Scott Wilson. LC 72-193218. 1972. 0.95. New American Library.
Clarion III: An Anthology of Speculative Fiction and Criticism. Ed. by Robin Scott Wilson. (Signet Book). 1973. (pbk.) 0.95. New American Lib.
Clarion People. Audrey Lee. LC 68-13883. 1968. McGraw-Hill.
Clarissa. Caroline Arnett, pseud. LC 79-1447. (Regency romance). 1979. 10.95 (ISBN 0-89340-195-1). J. Curley.
Clarissa. Caroline Arnett, pseud (ISBN 0-449-22893-2). Fawcett Crest.
Clarissa. Richardson. LC 70-139506. (Rinehart Editions). 1971. pap. text ed. 2.95 o.p. (ISBN 0-03-084014-7, HoltC). HR&W.
Clarissa. Samuel Richardson. Ed. by George Sherburn. LC 62-52256. (YA) (gr. 9 up). 1962. pap. 5.50 (ISBN 0-395-05164-9, B69, RivEd, 3-47703). HM.
Clarissa Furiosa: A Novel. William Edward Norris. LC 7-33298. 1896. Harper & Brothers.
Clarissa Harlowe. new and abridged ed. by mrs. ward. ed. Samuel Richardson. LC 26-26892. G. Routledge & Sons, Limited.
Clarissa: Or, The History of a Young Lady. Samuel Richardson. LC 50-11853. (Modern library of the world's best books 10). 1950. Modern Library.
Clarissa: Or, The History of a Young Lady. Samuel Richardson. Ed. by Philip Stevick. LC 70-139506. (Rinehart editions, 128). 1971. (ISBN 0-03-084014-7). Rinehart Press.
Clarissa: Or, The History of a Young Lady. Samuel Richardson & Jones, C. H., Ed. (Leisure hour series. v. 39). 1874. H. Holt and Company.
Clarissa: Or The History of a Young Lady. Comprehending the Most Important Concerns of Private Life. Samuel Richardson. LC 7-32447. By H. & O. Farnsworth, for Oliver D. & I. Cooke, Booksellers, Hartford.
Clarissa Putman of Tribes Hill: A Romantic History of Sir William Johnson, His Family and Mohawk Valley Neighbors Through the Flaming Years 1767-1780. John J Vrooman. LC 51-1139. (On lining paper) 24 cm.). 1950. Baronet Litho Co.
Clarissa's Ordeal... Sophy Beckett. LC 6-9773. (On cover: Seaside library. Pocket edition, no. 1040). 1887. G. Munro.
Clark Gifford's Body. Kenneth Fearing. LC 42-17798. 1942. Random House.
Clark Inheritance. Sophia Yarnall. LC 80-54812. 1981. 11.95 (ISBN 0-8027-0679-7). Walker.
Clark Inheritance. Sophia Yarnall. LC 81-16569. 11.95 (ISBN 0-89621-328-5). Thorndike Press.
Clark's Field. Robert Herrick. LC 71-104481. 1970. Literature House.
Clark's Field. Robert Herrick. LC 14-11043. 1914. 1.40. Houghton Mifflin Company.
Clark's Field see Collected Works.
Clarkton: A Novel. Howard Melvin Fast. LC 47-31432. 1947. Duell, Sloan and Pearce.
Clarus Saga. Ed. by G. Cederschiold. LC 80-1979. Repr. of 1879 ed. 32.00 (ISBN 0-404-18630-0). AMS Pr.
Clash. Margaret Storm Jameson. LC 22-16332. 1922. 1.90. Little, Brown, and Company.
Clash by Night: By Susan Gillespie Pseud. Edith Constance Bradshaw Turton-Jones. LC 50-13903. 1950. Hutchinson.
Clash of Angels. Jonathan Daniels. LC 30-8165. 1930. Brewer and Warren Inc., Payson and Clarke Ltd.
Clash of Arms: A Romance. John Edward Bloundelle-Burton. LC 6-16699. (Half-title: Appletons' town and country library, no. 227). 1897. D. Appleton and Company.
Clash of Arms: Stories of Chivalry by Famous Writers. Ed. by John R. Colter. LC 31-29495. 1931. Dodd, Mead and Company.
Clash of Distant Thunder. Alfred Coppel. LC 68-12585. 1968. Harcourt, Brace & World.
Clash of Distant Thunder. A. C. Marin, pseud. 1968. 3.95 o.p. (ISBN 0-15-118120-9). HarBraceJ.
Clash of Distant Thunder: By A. C. Marin. 1st Ed. A. C Marin. LC 68-12585. 1968. 3.95. Harcourt.
Clash of Hawks. Robert Charles, pseud. 1975. (pbk.) 1.25 (ISBN 0-523-00686-1). Pinnacle Books.
Clash of Shadows. 1st. ed. Howard Rigsby. LC 59-13078. 1959. Lippincott.
Clash of the Titans. Alan Dean Foster. 1981. pap. 3.25 (ISBN 0-446-96675-4). Warner Bks.
Class: A Novel. Brutus, pseud. 1973. 6.95 o.p. (ISBN 0-316-11320-4). Little.
Class: A Novel. John D Spooner. LC 72-10991. 1973. 6.95 (ISBN 0-316-11320-4). Little, Brown.
Class Act. Terry Fisher. 1976. 1.75 (ISBN 0-446-84242-7). Warner Books.
Class G-Zero. Walter B. Hendrickson, Jr. (Orig.). 1976. pap. 1.25 (ISBN 0-89041-110-7, 3110). Major Bks.
Class Notes. Kate Stimpson. LC 78-58172. 1979. 8.95 (ISBN 0-8129-0794-9). Times Books.
Class Notes: A Novel. Kate Stimpson. LC 78-58172. 1979. 8.95 o.p. (ISBN 0-8129-0794-9). Times Bks.
Class of 1902. Ernst Glaeser. Tr. by Muir, Wills. LC 29-20116. 1929. The Viking Press.
Class of '44. Madeleine Shaner & Herman Raucher. LC 73-160577. 1973. (pbk.) 1.25 (ISBN 0-446-76308-X). Warner Paperback Library.
Class Prophecy: Murder. Dean F. Du Vall. LC 80-65177. (Derek Dax Adventure Ser.: No. 2). 228p. 1982. pap. 6.95 (ISBN 0-931232-25-2). Du Vall Financial.
Class Report: A Novel. John Francis Purcell. LC 47-12105. 1947. Vanguard Press.
Class Reunion. Franz V. Werfel. Tr. by Whittaker Chambers. LC 29-129174. 1929. Simon and Schuster, Inc.
Class Reunion: A Novel. Rona Jaffe. LC 78-25838. 2.75 (ISBN 0-440-01408-5). Delacorte Press.
Class Warfare: Selected Fiction. 2d ed. Donald Murray Fraser. LC 77-354297. 8.95. (ISBN 0-88978-012-9) (ISBN 0-88978-010-2). Pulp Press.
Classic American Short Novels. Martha H. Cox. 528p. 1969. pap. text ed. 6.75x o.p. Chandler Pub.
Classic American Short Stories. rev. ed. Ed. by Vincent F. Hopper. LC 63-23444. (Orig.). 1984. text ed. 5.95 o.p.; pap. text ed. 2.95 (ISBN 0-8120-2334-X). Barron.
Classic Australian Short Stories. Judah L Waten & Murray-Smith, Stephen. LC 75-307748. 1974. 6.25. (ISBN 0-85885-037-0) (ISBN 0-85885-075-3). Wren.
Classic Book of Science Fiction. 1982 ed. Conklin Groff. LC 81-12232. 6.98 (ISBN 0-517-35726-7). Bonanza Books: Distributed by Crown.

Classic Crime Stories: The Criminal in Literature. Ed. by Arthur Liebman. LC 74-30432. (Masterworks of mystery series). 1975. 7.97 (ISBN 0-8239-0310-9). R. Rosen Press.
Classic European Short Stories. Ed. by Robert Beum. 276p. (Orig.). 1982. pap. 6.95 (ISBN 0-89385-025-X). Sugden.
Classic Ghost Stories. Charles Dickens. LC 74-12599. 1975. 3.50 (ISBN 0-486-20735-8). Dover Publications.
Classic Hassidic Tales. Meyer Levin. 378p. 1975. pap. 3.95 (ISBN 0-14-004042-0). Penguin.
Classic of Tea. Lu Yu. Tr. by Francis R. Carpenter from Chinese. LC 74-5312. (Illus.). 192p. 1974. 8.50 o.p. (ISBN 0-316-53450-1). Little.
Classic Science Fiction: The First Golden Age. Ed. by Terry Carr. LC 74-1798. 9.95 (ISBN 0-06-010634-4). Harper & Row.
Classic Short Fiction: An International Collection: Twenty-Five Short Stories, Five Novellas, Readings and Criticism. Ed. by James K. Bowen. LC 70-183111. 1972. Bobbs-Merrill.
Classic Short Stories. LC 80-54129. (Silver Classic). 2.95 (ISBN 0-382-03444-9). Silver Burdett Co.
Classic Short Stories of Crime & Detection. J. D. Carr et al. Tr. by J. Barzun & W. H. Taylor. LC 81-47406. (Crime Fiction 1950-1975 Ser.). 290p. 1982. lib. bdg. 14.95 (ISBN 0-8240-4975-6). Garland Pub.
Classic Short Story. Ed. by Ira Konigsberg. LC 71-144238. (Illus.). 1971. (ISBN 0-06-043748-0). Harper & Row.
Classic Stories of Crime and Detection. Jacques Barzun & Wendell Hertig Taylor. LC 75-44953. (Fifty Classics of Crime Fiction, 1900-1950; No. 1). 1976. 10.00 (ISBN 0-8240-2350-1). Garland Pub.
Classic Stories of Crime & Detection. LC 75-44953. (Crime Ficion Ser). 1976. lib. bdg. 17.50 (ISBN 0-8240-2350-1). Garland Pub.
Classic Tales from Modern Spain. Ed. by William Edward Colford. LC 63-23445. 1964. Barron's Educational Series.
Classic Tales from Spanish America. Ed. by William Edward Colford. LC 61-18356. (Barron's library of literary masterpieces). Barron's Educational Series.
Classic Tales of Horror. Stephanie Dowrick. LC 77-353078. (Illus.). 1976. Constable.
Classical Education. Robert Woods Kennedy. LC 73-9752. 1973. 6.50 (ISBN 0-393-08370-5). Norton.
Classical Storybook. Ed. by Morris Bishop. 256p. 1970. 14.50 o.p. (ISBN 0-8014-0577-7). Cornell U Pr.
Classics for Modern Fiction: Ten Short Novels. 2d ed. Ed. by Irving Howe. LC 72-80430. 1972. 5.95 (ISBN 0-15-507645-0). Harcourt Brace Jovanovich.
Classics in Slang. Harry Charles Witwer. LC 27-285135. 1927. G. P. Putnam's Sons.
Classics of Humour. Michael O'Mara. LC 77-356281. (Illus.). 1976. 3.75 (ISBN 0-09-461440-7). Constable.
Classics of Modern Fiction: Eight Short Novels. Ed. by Irving Howe. Ed. by Irving Howe. LC 68-14380. 1968. pap., 4.50. Harcourt.
Classics of Modern Fiction: Ten Short Novels. 3d ed. Ed. by Irving Howe. LC 79-91647. 10.95 (ISBN 0-15-507645-0). Harcourt Brace Jovanovich.
Classics Set, 10 bks. Incl. Adventures of Huckleberry Finn; Alice's Adventures in Wonderland & Through the Looking Glass; Pride & Prejudice; Red Badge of Courage; Scarlet Pimpernel; Scarlet Letter; Tale of Two Cities; Vicar of Wakefield; Washington Square; Wuthering Heights. (General Ser.). 1980. Set. lib. bdg. 110.00 (Large Print Bks). G K Hall.
Classified Death. Claire Taschdjian. (Raven House Mysteries Ser.). 224p. 1982. pap. 2.25 (ISBN 0-373-63028-X, Pub. by Worldwide). Harlequin Bks.
Classmates: A Story of West Point. Walter F Eberhardt & De Mille, William Churchill, 1878- LC 25-235037. Grosset & Dunlap.
Clattering Hoofs. William Macleod Raine. LC 46-6293. 1946. Houghton Mifflin Company.
Clattering Hoofs. William MacLeod Raine. (Signet Brand Western, T5575). 1973. (pbk.) 0.75. New American Lib.
Clauberg Trigger. Clive Egleton. LC 78-12455. 1979. 8.95 (ISBN 0-689-10938-5). Atheneum.
Clauberg Trigger. John Tarrant. (Orig.). 1980. pap. 1.95 o.s.i. (ISBN 0-505-51523-7). Tower Bks.
Claude. Genevieve Alice Marie Fauconnier. Tr. by Ford, Lauren. LC 37-19004. The Macmillan Company.
Claude Duval of Ninety Five. Fergus Hume. (Dillingham's globe library, no. 29). 1897. G. W. Dillingham Co.
Claude Melnotte As a Detective, and Other Stories. Allan Pinkerton. LC 7-39636. 1875. W. B. Keen, Cooke & Co.
Claudea's Island. Amelie Claire Leroy. (On cover: Neely's popular library, no. 37). 1895. F. T. Neely.
Claudelle Inglish. Erskine Caldwell. LC 58-106891. 1959. bds., 3.75. Little, Brown.
Claude's Confession. Emile Zola. LC 79-16664. 1979. 15.75. H. Fertig.
Claude's Confession. Emile Zola & Cox, George D., Tr. LC 12-40350. T. B. Peterson & Brothers.
Claudia. new ed. Rose Franken. 224p. Repr. 5.95 o.s.i. White Lion Pubs.
Claudia, Vol. 2. Rose Franken. 1968. pap. 1.25 o.p. (78-603). Lancer.
Claudia, Vol. 3. Rose Franken. pap. 1.25 o.p. (78-604). Lancer.
Claudia: A Novel. Arnold Zweig & Sutton, Eric, Tr. 1930. The Viking Press.
Claudia and David. Rose Franken. LC 40-333618. Farrar & Rinehart, Inc.
Claudia and David. Rose Franken. LC 46-7721. (Triangle books). 1946. The Blakiston Company.
Claudia Hyde: A Novel. Frances Courtenay Baylor Barnum. LC 3-22875. 1894. Houghton, Mifflin and Company.
Claudia: The Story of a Marriage. Rose Franken. Farrar & Rinehart, Inc.
Claudia, the Story of a Marriage. 1st Ed. Rose Franken. LC 51-11595. 1951. Doubleday.
Claudian: With an English Translation. Claudius Claudianus & Platnauer, Maurice, Tr. LC 23-3396. (Half-title: The Loeb classical library). 1922. W. Heinemann.
Claudie's Kinfolks. 1st. Ed. Dillon Anderson. LC 54-111240. 1954. Little, Brown.
Claudine. Charlotte Ruth Miller. 1976. (pbk.) 1.50 (ISBN 0-380-00564-6). Avon.
Claudine a L'Ecole. Sidonie Gabrielle Colette. 1956. pap. 3.95. French & Eur.
Claudine at School. Sidonie Gabrielle Colette & Henry Gauthier-Villars. LC 30-29633. 1930. A. & C. Boni.
Claudine at School. Translated by Antonia White. Sidonie Gabrielle Colette. LC 57-5310. 1957. Farrar, Straus and Cudahy.
Claudine in Paris. Sidonie Gabrielle Colette. 192p. 1982. pap. 2.50 (ISBN 0-345-30708-9). Ballantine.
Claudine Married. Translated from the French by Antonia White. Sidonie Gabrielle Colette. LC 61-512611. 3.50. Farrar, Straus and Cudahy.
Claudine's Black Stud. Ken Kessler. 192p. pap. 1.95 o.p. (2042). Intimate Lib.
Claudine's Daughter. Rosalind Laker. LC 78-19328. 1979. 10.00 o.p. (ISBN 0-385-14759-7). Doubleday.
Claudine's Daughter. Rosalind Laker. 1980. pap. 2.25 (ISBN 0-451-09159-0, E9159, Sig). NAL.
Claudine's Daughter. Barbara Vstedal. LC 78-19328. 1979. 10.00 (ISBN 0-385-14759-7). Doubleday.
Claudio and Anita: A Historical Romance of San Gabriell's Early Mission Days. Maria Sacramenta Lopez De Cummings. LC 21-16001. 1921. J. F. Rowny Press.
Claudius Bombarnac. Jules Verne. LC 1-9795. Lovell, Coryell & Co.
Claudius, the Cowboy of Ramapo Valley. A Story of Revolutionary Times in Southern New York. P. Demarest Johnson. 1894. Slauson & Boyd, Press Steam Print.
Claudius: The Goal of His Wife Messalina... Robert Graves. 1935. H. Smith and R. Haas.
Claudius the God. Robert Graves. 592p. 8.95 (ISBN 0-394-60812-7). Modern Lib.
Claverings. Anthony Trollope. LC 76-46037. (Illus.). 1977. (5.00, 5.75 can) (ISBN 0-486-23464-9). Dover Publications.
Claverings. Anthony Trollope. LC 25-2849. (Half-title: The world's classics. cclii). 1924. H. Milford.
Claverleigh Curse. Sandra DuBay. (Orig.). 1982. pap. 2.50 (ISBN 0-89083-958-1). Zebra.
Claverse Affair: A Novel of Suspense. Janet Gregory Vermandel. LC 73-21162. 1974. 5.95 (ISBN 0-396-06924-X). Dodd, Mead.
Claverton Affair. Cecil John Charles Street. LC 33-22821. 1933. Dodd, Mead & Company.
C.L.A.W. Richard L Graves. LC 76-13620. 1976. 8.95. Stein and Day.
Claw. Norah Robinson Lofts. LC 81-43635. 1982. 12.95 (ISBN 0-385-17582-5). Doubleday.
Claw. Katherine Elspeth Oliver. LC 15-2642. 1914. 1.50. Out West Magazine.
Claw. Cynthia Stockley. LC 11-10639. 1911. G. P. Putnam's Sons.
Claw. Jack Younger. 224p. (Orig.). 1976. pap. 1.50 (ISBN 0-532-15177-1). Woodhill.
Claw of the Conciliator. Gene Wolfe. LC 80-20569. (Wolfe, Gene. Book of the Sun: Vol. 2). 11.95 (ISBN 0-671-41370-8). Timescape Books.
Clawhammer Ranch. Frank Chester Robertson. LC 30-5691. Barse & Co.
Claws. D. Gunther Wilde, pseud. 1978. pap. 1.50 o.s.i. (ISBN 0-8439-0579-4, Leisure Bks). Nordon Pubns.
Claws Are Showing. Richard Stour. LC 76-28060. 8.95. St. Martin's Press.
Claws of Death. Carlo Bove. 304p. 1978. 10.00 o.p. (ISBN 0-682-48433-4). Exposition.
Claws of the Crow. Ruth Wissmann. 160p. 1974. pap. 0.95 o.s.i. (ISBN 0-446-75529-X). Paperback Lib.
Claws of the Crow. Ruth Wissmann. 1974. (pbk.) 0.95. Warner Paperback Lib.
Claws of the Eagle. Ernest V. Correale. (Orig.). 1982. pap. 2.95 (ISBN 0-89083-957-3). Zebra.
Claws of the Hawk: The Incredible Life of Wahker the Ute by Paul Bailey. Paul Dayton Bailey. LC 66-28685. 1966. bds., 5.95. Westernlore Pr.
Claws of the Hawk: The Incredible Life of Wahker the Ute. Paul Dayton Bailey. LC 66-28685. 1966. Westernlore.
Clay Acres: A Novel, by Pauline Benedict Fischer. Pauline Benedict Fischer. LC 38-33399. The Penn Publishing Company.
Clay and Rainbows: A Novel. Dion Clayton Calthrop. LC 14-15369. 1.25. Frederick A. Stokes Company.
Clay Grew Tall. Eamonn McGrath. LC 72-176369. 1972. 6.95 (ISBN 0-665-00004-9). Herder and Herder.
Clay Hand. Dorothy Salisbury Davis. LC 49-50432. 1950. Scribner.
Clay in the Sand. 1st Ed. Katherine Neuhaus Haffner. LC 53-12318. 1953. Pageant Press.
Clay Oscar. William Fadiman. 1977. pap. 1.95 (ISBN 0-89041-162-X, 3162). Major Bks.
Clayborne Concept. Marion Clayborne. 64p. 1973. 3.50 o.p. (ISBN 0-682-47792-3). Exposition.
Claybornes: A Romance of the Civil War, by William Sage... William Sage. LC 2-10718. 1902. Houghton, Mifflin and Co.
Claybrooks. Edwin Glenn Huddleston. LC 51-11289. 1951. Macmillan.
Clayhanger. Arnold Bennett. LC 74-5390. (Collected works of Arnold Bennett). 1974. (ISBN 0-518-19093-5). Books for Libraries Press.
Clayhanger. Arnold Bennett. LC 10-21748. E. P. Dutton & Company.
Clayhanger. Arnold Bennett. LC 24-118712. George H. Doran Company.
Clayhanger Family. Arnold Bennett. LC 75-144874. 1971. (ISBN 0-403-00861-1). Scholarly Press.
Claymore Estate: A Sequel to "The Oregon Quartette.". May Anderson Hawkins. Presbyterian Committee of Publication.
Clayton Clan. Mary Heathfield. J. H. Hopkins, Inc.
Clayton's Rangers: Or, The Quaker Partisians. A Story of the American Revolution. (On cover: Lovell's library, no. 340). 1884. J. W. Lovell Company.
Clayton's Rangers: Or, The Quaker Partisans. A Story of the American Revolution... Edward H. Williamson. LC 8-34351. 1876. J. B. Lippincott & Co.
Cle des Champs. Andre Breton. 15.95. French & Eur.
Clea. Lawrence Durrell. 1961. pap. 4.95 (ISBN 0-525-47083-2, 0481-140). Dutton.
Clea: A Novel. Lawrence Durrell. LC 60-5969. 1960. Dutton.
Clean Break. 1st Ed. Lionel White. LC 55-5394. (Dutton guilt edged mystery). 1955. Dutton.
Clean Decision. Robert L. Grant & Carl Gardner. 1972. price not set o.p. Lippincott.
Clean Heart. Arthur Stuart-Menteth Hutchinson. LC 14-16208. 1914. Little, Brown, and Company.
Clean Heart. Arthur Stuart-Menteth Hutchinson. LC 22-2104. 1921. Little, Brown, and Company.
Clean Sweep. Jeffrey M Wallmann. LC 77-357992. 1976. 3.25 (ISBN 0-214-20245-3). Barrie and Jenkins.
Clean-up. Joe Barry Lake. LC 47-1838. 1947. Arcadia House.
Clean up. Mark Lee Luther. LC 26-19109. The Bobbs-Merrill Company.
Clean-up on Deadman. Frank Chester Robertson. LC 27-7332. (On cover: A pocket copyright, no. 75). 1926. Garden City Publishing Co., Inc.
Cleaner Breed. Nicholas J Corea. 1974. (pbk.) 1.25 (ISBN 0-380-00167-5). Avon.
Cleaning House. Nancy Hayfield. LC 80-19029. 10.95 (ISBN 0-374-12483-3). Farrar, Straus, Giroux.
Clear and Present Danger. 1st Ed. Baynard Hardwick Kendrick. LC 58-6644. (His A Duncan Mystery). 1958. Published for the Crime Club by Doubleday.
Clear As the Sun. Muriel Hine Coxon. LC 38-8563. 1938. D. Appleton-Century Company, Incorporated.
Clear Before 'leven. Edith Austin Holton. The Penn Publishing Company.
Clear Call. Walter E Butts. LC 32-23570. Augustana Book Concern.
Clear Case of Suicide. Michael Underwood. LC 79-25389. 8.95 (ISBN 0-312-14326-5). St. Martin's Press.
Clear for Action! Noel Bertram Gerson. LC 75-123693. 1970. 5.95. Doubleday.
Clear for Action! Simon White. LC 77-11765. 1978. 7.95 (ISBN 0-312-14334-6). St. Martin's Press.
Clear for Action: A Novel About John Paul Jones. Clements Ripley. LC 40-13553. 1940. D. Appleton-Century Company, Incorporated.
Clear Light of Day. Anita Desai. LC 81-23422. 1982. 4.95 (ISBN 0-14-005860-5). Penguin Books.
Clear Light of Day. Anita Desai. LC 81-110221. 1980. 11.95 (ISBN 0-06-010984-X). Heinemann.
Clear Road to Archangel: A Story of Escape in 1917. Geoffrey Rose. LC 75-9497. 1976. 7.95. St. Martin's Press.
Clear Shining After Rain. Annie Barclay Kerr. LC 41-13502. The Womans Press.
Clear Shining After Rain, and Other Stories. Stella Breyfogle McDonald. LC 7-41583. 1907. Calkins and Company.
Clear Spring. Clyde Burke Millspaugh. LC 41-11499. House of Field, Inc.
Clear the Decks! A Tale of the American Navy to-Day. Commander. LC 18-233477. 1918. J. B. Lippincott Company.
Clear the Fast Lane. James Douglas Rutherford McConnell. LC 72-78093. 1972. 5.95 (ISBN 0-03-001326-7). Holt, Rinehart and Winston.
Clear the Track!" Freie Bahn) A Story of to-Day. Elisabeth Burstenbinder. Tr. by Smith, Mary Stuart (Harrison) LC 6-19397. (On cover: The author's library, no. 2). 1893. The International News Company.
Clear the Trail. Charles Alden Seltzer. LC 76-28475. 1976. 6.95 (ISBN 0-88411-120-2). Aeonian Press.
Clear the Trail. Charles Alden Seltzer. LC 33-233513. 1933. Doubleday, Doran & Company, Inc.
Clear to Land. Gertrude Ethel Mallette. LC 50-9715. 1950. Doubleday.
Cleared for Action: A Story of the Spanish-American War of 1898; a Sequel to "Navy Blue". Willis Boyd Allen. LC 99-2062. 1899. E. P. Dutton & Company.
Clearer Voice. Nettie Turnipseed Ault. LC 41-16484. The Caxton Printers, Ltd.
Clearing. Gary Clark. (Norwegian Trilolgy Ser.). 200p. (Orig.). 1981. write for info. (ISBN 0-913124-45-1). Nordland Pub.
Clearing. Mary Elsie Robertson. LC 81-69164. 1982. 12.95 (ISBN 0-689-11275-0). Atheneum.
Clearing. Therese De Saint Phalle. 1978 (ISBN 0-445-04234-6). Popular Library.
Clearing & Beyond. May Halsey Miller. LC 73-93070. 1974. 7.50 (ISBN 0-910350-08-6). Charioteer.
Clearing in the Fog. Daria Macomber, pseud. LC 77-119470. 1970. 5.95. World Pub. Co.
Clearing of the Mist. Richard Fleck. (American Dust Ser.: No. 10). 1979. 7.95 (ISBN 0-913218-86-3); pap. 2.95 (ISBN 0-913218-85-5). Dustbooks.
Cleek of Scotland Yard: Being the Record of the Further Life and Adventures of That Remarkable Detective Genius, "the Man of the Forty Faces," Once Know to the Police As "the Vanishing Cracksman.". Thomas W Hanshew. LC 14-4584. 1914. Doubleday, Page & Company.
Cleek, the Man of the Forty Faces. Thomas W Hanshew. LC 18-2503. 1913. Cassell & Company.
Cleek, the Man of the Forty Faces. Thomas W Hanshew. LC 21-8678. A.L. Burt Company.
Cleek, the Master Detective. Thomas W Hanshew. LC 18-4548. 1918. Doubleday, Page & Company.
Cleek's Government Cases. Thomas W Hanshew. LC 17-5982. 1917. Doubleday, Page & Company.
Cleft. Paul Tabori. (Orig.). 1969. pap. 0.60 o.p. (X-1940). Pyramid Pubns.
Cleft in the Rock. Frieda Kenyon Franklin, pseud. LC 55-7326. 1955. Crowell.
Cleft Mooring. Lillian Buck Saminsky. LC 38-117831. 1938. Margent Press.
Cleft of Stars. Geoffrey Jenkins. LC 73-87194. 1973. 6.95 (ISBN 0-399-11259-6). Putnam.
Cleft Rock: A Novel. Alice Tisdale Nourse Hobert. LC 48-7817. 1948. Bobbs-Merrill Co.
Cleft Roots. Philip Jerome Simon. LC 75-7152. 1975. 7.50. Priam Press.
Cleft Stick: Or, "Its the Same the World Over". Walter Greenwood. LC 38-10123. 1938. Frederick A. Stokes Company.
Cleg Kelly: Arab of the City, His Progress and Adventures. Samuel Rutherford Crockett. LC 6-31598. 1896. D. Appleton and Company.
Clem. Edna Kenton. LC 8-11008. 1907. The Century Co.
Clem Anderson. Robert Verlin Cassill. 1961. 5.95 o.p. (13930). S&S.
Clemenceau Case. Alexandre Dumas. Tr. by Fleron, William. LC 6-42309. (On cover: Eytings series. no. 3). 1890. The American News Company.

Clemenceau Case. Alexandre Dumas. Tr. by Lyster, Frederic. LC 6-42310. (On cover: Pollard's popular publications. no. 3). Pollard Publishing Company.
Clemencia. Ignacio Manuel Altamirano. LC 48-9028. (Spanish American Series). 1948. D. C. Heath.
Clemencia's Crisis. Edith Ogden Harrison. LC 15-21420. 1915. 1.25. A. C. McClug & Co.
Clemens of the Call: Mark Twain in San Francisco. Mark Twain. Ed. by Edgar M. Branch. LC 69-15084. (£4.75). (Illus.). 1969. 14.50x o.p. (ISBN 0-520-01385-9). U of Cal Pr.
Clement: A Suburban Romance. D. B. Hutley. LC 76-381819. 1976. (ISBN 0-7254-0280-6). Ure Smith.
Clement Falconer: Or, The Memoirs Fo a Young Whig... William Price. LC 7-13306. 1838. N. Hickman.
Clement Lorimer: Or, The Book with the Iron Clasps. A Romance. Angus Bethune Reach. LC 6-35182. 1856. G. Routledge & Co.
Clementina. Alfred Edward Woodley Mason. LC 7-25581. F. A. Stokes Company.
Clementina's Highwayman: A Romance. Robert Neilson Stephens & Westley, George Hembert. LC 7-27613. 1907. L. C. Page & Company.
Clementine. Peggy Goodin. LC 46-4252. 1946. E. P. Dutton & Company, Inc.
Clemmie. John Dann MacDonald. 240p. 1982. pap. 2.50 (ISBN 0-449-12359-6, GM). Fawcett.
Clenched Fist. Alice M Brooks & Kuppler. Willietta E. LC 49-7121. 1948. Dorrance.
Cleng Peerson. Alfred Hauge. LC 75-9740. (Library of Scandinavian Literature; V. 28-29). 1975. 25.00 (ISBN 0-8057-8153-6). Twayne Publishers.
Cleo. Mary Lutyens. LC 73-90695. 1974. 6.95. Stein and Day.
Cleo the Magnificent: Or, The Muse of the Real; a Novel. Louis Zangwill. LC 8-37867. 1898. G. W. Dillingham Co.; Etc., Etc.
Cleomenes. Edith S. Billings. LC 17-139229. 1917. 1.40. John Lane Company.
Cleopatra. Alice Marie Celeste Durand. LC 6-35700. 1886. Ticknor and Company.
Cleopatra. Jack Lindsay. 1971. Repr. 8.95 o.p. (ISBN 0-698-10059-X). Coward.
Cleopatra: A Romance. Georg Moritz Ebers & Safford, Mary Joanne, Tr. LC 4-16858. 1894. D. Appleton and Company.
Cleopatra: Being an Account of the Fall and Vengeance of Harmachis (the Royal Egyptian), As Set Forth by His Own Hand. Henry Rider Haggard. LC 19-729. Hurst & Co.
Cleopatra Boy. Eric Lawson Malpass. LC 74-76713. 1974-1975. 6.95. St. Martin's Press.
Cleopatra. Illus. by Hookway Cowles. Henry Rider Haggard. LC 66-5443. 1966. bds., 2.95. Macdonald.
Cleopatra Jones. Ron Goulart. 1973. (pbk) 1.25. Warner.
Cleopatra's Carpet. Sarah Carlisle. (Regency Love Story). 1979. pap. 1.75 (ISBN 0-449-50009-8, Coventry). Fawcett.
Cleopatra's Daughter. Romance of a Branch of Roses. William Armstrong. 1889. De Wolfe, Fiske & Co.
Cleopatra's Private Diary. Henry Thomas Schnittkind. LC 27-6807. 1927. The Stratford Co.
Cleopatra's Tears: A Mystery Novel. Harry Stephen Keeler. LC 40-33065. 1940. E. P. Dutton & Company, Inc.
Clerambault; the Story of an Independent Spirit During the War: By Romain Rolland; Tr. by Katherine Miller. Romain Rolland & Miller, Katherine, Tr. LC 21-12084. 1921. H. Holt and Company.
Clergyman's Daughter. Julia Jeffries. 224p. 1983. pap. 2.25 (ISBN 0-451-12009-4, Sig). NAL.
Clergyman's Daughter. George Orwell. LC 60-10943. 1969. pap. 3.95 (ISBN 0-15-618065-0, Harv). HarBraceJ.
Clergyman's Son and Daughter. William Josephus Robinson. LC 22-5176. 1922. The Critic and Guide Company.
Clergyman's Wife, and Other Sketches. A Collecttion of Pen Portraits and Painting. Anna Cora Ogden Mowatt Ritchie. LC 7-41654. 1867. G. W. Carlton & Co.; Etc., Etc.
Clerical Error. Colwyn Edward Vulliamy. LC 32-14951. 1932. Little, Brown, and Company.
Cleric's Secret. Warwick Deeping. LC 44-375447. 1944. Dial Press.
Clerk Barton's Crime: Or, The Mysteries of a Night. Steele Penn. LC 49-561414. (Library of choice romance, fiction and adventure). Hurst.
Clermont: A Tale, by Regina Maria Roche. Regina Maria Dalton Roche. LC 68-985819. (Northanger Set of Jane Austen Horrid Novels). 1968. 65.00 set.,. Folio Pr.
Clerycastle & Return to Clerycastle. Monica Heath. 1978. pap. 2.50 (ISBN 0-451-11693-3, AE1693, Sig). NAL.
Clevalier De Maison-Rugue. Alexandre Dumas & Maquet, Auguste. LC 6-42107. (Half-title: The romances of Alexandre Dumas. Illustrated library ed. vol. xxxviii). 1894. Little, Brown and Company.
Clevedon Case. Marguerite Aspinwall & Oakley, John, Joint Author. LC 24-29999. 1924. J. B. Lippincott Company.
Cleveland Pipeline. Don Pendleton. (Executioner Ser: No. 30). 1977. pap. 1.95 (ISBN 0-523-41094-8). Pinnacle Bks.
Clevelanders. Archie Bell. Broadway Publishing Co.
Clever Betsy: A Novel. Clara Louise Root Burnham. LC 10-21603. 1910. Houghton Mifflin Company.
Clever Business Sketches. Albert Stoll & Business Man's Publishing Co., Ltd., Detroit, Pub. LC 9-13966. 1909. The Business Man's Publishing Co., Ltd.
Clever Claudia: A Scientific Quest for a Mate. Hugo Frederick Herfurth. LC 32-68983. 1932. National Capital Press, Inc.
Clever-Lazy: The Girl Who Invented Herself. Joan Bodger. LC 79-10484. 1979. 8.95 (ISBN 0-689-30674-1, Argo). Atheneum.
Clever One. Edgar Wallace. LC 28-23108. 1928. Pub. for the Crime Club, Inc., by Doubleday, Doran & Company, Inc.
Clever Ones. Jesse Edgar Middleton. LC 38-175. 1936. T. Nelson & Sons, Ltd.
Clever Sister. Margaret Culkin Banning. LC 47-187939. 1947. Harper & Brothers.
Clever Tales. Ed. by Charlotte Endymion Porter. Helen Archibald Clarke. LC 2831. 1897. Copeland and Day.
Clever Turtle. A. K Roche, pseud. LC 69-14809. (Illus.). 1969. 4.50. Prentice-Hall.
Clever Wife: A Novel. William Pett Ridge. LC 7-41440. 1896. Harper & Brothers.
Clever Woman of the Family. Charlotte Mary Yonge. LC 75-1523. (Victorian Fiction: Novels of Faith and Doubt). 1975. 35.00 (ISBN 0-8240-1595-9). Garland Pub.
Clever Woman of the Family. Charlotte Mary Yonge. LC 9-1218. 1865. D. Appleton and Company.
Cleverdale Mystery: Or, The Machine and Its Wheels. A Story of American Life. W. A Wilkins. LC 8-37018. 1882. Fords, Howard, & Hubert.
Cleverings. Kelsey Ballou Sweatt. LC 28-11815. The Robinson Press.
Clew of the Forgotten Murder. Erle Stanley Gardner. LC 35-2260. 1935. W. Morrow.
Clew of the Forgotten Murder. Carleton Kendrake, pseud. LC 35-2260. 1935. W. Morrow & Co.
Clewiston Test. Kate Wilhelm. LC 75-31683. 1976. 8.95 (ISBN 0-374-12500-7). Farrar Straus Giroux.
Clewiston Test. Kate Wilhelm. (Kangaroo Book). 1977. 1.75 (ISBN 0-671-80888-5). Pocket Books.
Cliche. Viola Streimikes Omang. LC 72-81633. 1972. 5.00 (ISBN 0-8059-1726-8). Dorrance.
Click of the Gate. Alice Ormond Campbell. LC 31-29964. Farrar & Rinehart, Incorporated.
Click of Triangle T, by Oscar J. Friend... Oscar J Friend. LC 25-8790. 1925. A. C. Mc Clurg & Co.
Click Song. John Alfred Williams. LC 81-13166. 1982. 14.95 (ISBN 0-395-31841-6). Houghton Mifflin.
Clicking of Cuthbert. P. G. Wodehouse. 1956. 11.95 o.s.i. (ISBN 0-8277-0205-1). British Bk Ctr.
Clickster Clackxter. Anthony Who. LC 78-52185. (Illus.). 2.95 (ISBN 0-87714-061-8). Denlinger's Publishers.
Clickwhistle. William Jon Watkins. LC 73-83608. (Doubleday science fiction). 1973. 4.95 (ISBN 0-385-05212-X). Doubleday.
Client Is Canceled: A Captain Heimrich Mystery. Richard Lockridge. LC 51-11206. (Main line mysteries). 1951. Lippincott.
Cliff-Dwellers. Henry Blake Fuller. LC 72-82587. (Rinehart editions, 155). 1973. 2.95 (ISBN 0-03-085873-9). Holt, Rinehart and Winston.
Cliff Dwellers see Collected Works.
Cliff-Dwellers: A Novel. Henry Blake Fuller. LC 68-23721. (Americans in fiction). (Illus.). 1968. Gregg Press.
Cliff-Dwellers: A Novel. Henry Blake Fuller. LC 75-45065. 1976. Scholarly Press.
Cliff-Dwellers: A Novel. Henry Blake Fuller. LC 43-39956. Harper & Brothers.
Cliff-Dwellers: A Novel. Henry Blake Fuller. LC 80-22261. 1980. 8.95 (ISBN 0-8290-0413-0) (ISBN 0-89197-699-X). Irvington Publishers.
Cliff Dweller's Daughter: Or, How He Loved Her. An Indian Romance of Prehistoric Times. Charles T Abbott. LC 99-2485. (On cover: Neely's imperial library, no. 36). 1899. F.T. Neely.
Cliff Hangers: A Novel. 1st Ed. Janet O'Daniel. LC 61-8684. 1961. Lippincott.
Cliffhaven. Dan Ross, pseud. 1971. pap. 0.60 o.p. (60-468). Manor Bks.
Clifford Affair. Archibald E. Fielding. LC 27-238679. 1927. A. A. Knopf.
Clifford Troup: A Georgia Story. Maria Elizabeth Jourdan Westmoreland. 1873. G. W. Carleton & Co.; Etc., Etc.
Cliffords: Or, "Almost Persuaded.". Orpheus Everts. 1898. The R. Clarke Company.
Cliff's Edge, and Other Stories. Masaaki Tachihara & Clark Malcolm. LC 79-92855. 1980. 11.95 (ISBN 0-936208-00-7). Midwest Publishers, International.
Cliffs of Death. Claude Nicole. (O.s.i.). 1976. pap. 1.25 o.s.i. (BT50941). Belmont-Tower.
Cliffs of Dread. Virginia Coffman. (Signet book). 1978. 1.75 (ISBN 0-451-08301-6). New American Library.
Cliffs of Fall. Shirley Hazzard. LC 81-47258. 208p. (Orig.). 1981. pap. 2.50 (ISBN 0-87216-913-8). Playboy Pbks.
Cliffs of Fall, & Other Stories. Shirley Hazzard. 1963. 4.95 o.p. (ISBN 0-394-41953-7). Knopf.
Cliffs of Night. Beatrice Brandon, pseud. LC 73-14041. 1974. 6.95 (ISBN 0-385-09628-3). Doubleday.
Cliffside Castle. easy eye ed. Dorothy Daniels. (Orig.). pap. 0.75 o.p. (75-234). Lancer.
Clifton Contract. Nelson Nye. 1974. (pbk.) 0.95. Ace Books.
Clifton Picture: A Novel. George James Atkinson Coulson. LC 6-289961. (The "Odd trump" series of novels). 1878. J. B. Lippincott & Co.
Climate of Hell. Herbert H. Lieberman. LC 78-17094. 9.95 (ISBN 0-671-24363-2). Simon and Schuster.
Climate of Hell. John Roeburt. 1975. (pbk.) 1.25. Belmont Tower Books.
Climate of Hell a Novel of Suspense. John Roeburt. LC 58-6756. 1958. Abelard-Schuman.
Climate of Passion: By Marsh Morrison Pseud. Morris Marsh. LC 59-6491. 1959. F. Fell.
Climate of Violence. Russell O'Neil. LC 61-133377. 1961. Appleton Century Crofts.
Climax. Louise Platt Hauck. LC 38-6017. The Penn Publishing Company.
Climax. George C Jenks & Locke, Edward. LC 9-30112. The H. K. Fly Company.
Climax: From the Screen Play by Curt Siodmak and Lynn Starling of the Universal Motion Picture Produced and Directed by George Waggner... Florence Jay Lewis & Siodmak, Kurt, 1902- LC 45-17333. (Midnite mysteries). 1944. Books, Inc.
Climax: Or, What Might Have Been; a Romance of the Great Republic. Charles Felton Pidgin. LC 2-208130. 1902. C. M. Clark Publishing Company.
Climb Back. Frank Lanzendorfer. (Illus.). 144p. 1983. 9.95 (ISBN 0-89962-313-1). Todd & Honeywell.
Climb the Dark Mountain. Julie Wellsley. (Orig.). 1970. pap. 0.60 o.p. (ISBN 0-447-73882-8). Lancer.
Climb the Wall: By Michael Cronin Pseud. Brendan Leo Cronin. LC 56-12825. (Chantecler novel of suspense). 1957. Washburn.
Climber. Edward Frederic Benson. LC 9-3204. 1909. Doubleday, Page & Company.
Climber. Amy D'Arcy Wetmore. LC 14-18466. The Norman, Remington Co.
Climbers: A Story of Sun-Kissed Sweethearts. Yorke Jones. LC 12-27203. 0.50. Glad Tidings Publishing Co.
Climbie. Bernard Binlin Dadie. LC 77-161231. 1971. (ISBN 0-8419-0089-2). Africana Pub. Corp.
Climbing Courvatels. Edward Waterman Townsend. LC 9-4192. 1909. F. A. Stokes Company.
Climbing Doom. Laurence Ditto Young. LC 9-8995. G. W. Dillingham Company.
Climbing Path. Louis Claude Whiton & Markey, Mrs. Corinne (Harris) Joint Author. LC 31-9825. A. H. King.
Climbing Road. Donald C. Lane. 3.00 o.p. Carlton.
Climbing the Heights. Martha Ellen Hale. LC 2-175487. 1902. Scroll Publishing Company.
Climbing up to Nature... By Florence J. Lewis. Florence Jane Lewis. LC 8-16467. 1908. The C. M. Clark Publishing Company.
Climbing Willie's Ladder. Alan Lebowitz. LC 71-86084. 1969. 5.95. D. McKay Co.
Cinemark's Tale. Robert W Burda. LC 79-51199. 1980. 10.95 (ISBN 0-89696-066-8). Everest House.
Cling of the Clay. Milton Hayes. LC 25-18874. 1925. Adelphi Company.
Clinging. Ernest T. Jahn. 336p. (Orig.). 1981. pap. 2.50 cancelled (ISBN 0-89083-705-8). Zebra.
Clinging Vine. Peggy O'More, pseud. LC 47-177597. 1947. Grammercy Publishing Co.
Clinic. George Harry. 1976. 7.50 o.p. (ISBN 0-682-48394-X). Exposition.
Clinic: A Novel. James Kerr. LC 68-13322. 1968. Coward-McCann.
Clinic Nurse. Carol Morris. LC 47-1389. 1946. Arcadia House, Inc.
Clinic of Dr. Aicadre. Muriel Harris. LC 32-18615. Harper & Brothers.
Clinta: Or, The Inside of Life. Mary Magdalene Shipe. LC 99-4015. 1899. W. J. C. Dulany Company.
Clinton Bradshaw: Or, The Adventures of a Lawyer... Frederick William Thomas. LC 10-3742. 1835. Carey, Lea & Blanchard Griggs & Co., Printers.
Clinton Bradshaw: Or, The Adventures of a Lawyer. Frederick William Thomas. LC 35-285701. 1847. Robinson and Jones.
Clinton Is Assigned. Malcolm McConnell. (Kangaroo Book). (Illus.). 1.95 (ISBN 0-671-81195-9). Pocket Books.
Clinton Street, and Other Stories. Gershon Einbinder. LC 75-323366. YKUF Publishers.
Clinton Twins and Other Stories. Archibald Marshall. LC 70-130062. (Short story index reprint series). 1970. (ISBN 0-8369-3661-2). Books for Libraries Press.
Clinton Twins: And Other Stories. Archibald Marshall. LC 23-6953. 1923. Dodd, Mead and Company.
Clintons, and Others. Archibald Marshall. LC 73-130063. (Short story index reprint series). 1970. Books for Libraries Press.
Clintons: And Others. Archibald Marshall. LC 19-7465. 1919. Dodd, Mead and Company.
Clio. Anatole France, pseud. Tr. by Winifred Stephens Whale. LC 70-122704. (Short story index reprint series). 1970. Books for Libraries Press.
Clio. Anatole France, pseud. Tr. by Whale, Winifred (Stephen) LC 22-18712. (Half-title: The works of Anatole France in an English translation, ed. by James Lewis May and Bernard Miall. v. 31). 1922. John Lane.
Clio. Leopold Hamilton Myers. LC 77-131786. 1971. (ISBN 0-403-00673-2). Scholarly Press.
Clio. Leopold Hamilton Myers. LC 25-22987. 1925. G. P. Putnam's Sons, Ltd.
Clio. Leopold Hamilton Myers. LC 25-23221. 1925. C. Scribner's Sons.
Clio: a Child of Fate. Ella May Powell. LC 74-137730. (American fiction reprint series). 1970. Books for Libraries Press.
Clio: A Child of Fate. Ella May Powell. LC 7-303133. 1889. J. P. Harrison & Co., Printers.
Clipped Wings. Adah Glasener Harris. LC 43-13041. 1943. Dorrance and Company.
Clipped Wings: A Novel. Rupert Hughes. LC 24-285344. 1918. A. L. Burt Company.
Clipped Wings: Published As "the Barge of Dreams"; a Novel. Rupert Hughes. LC 16-1399. 1916. Harper & Brothers.
Clipper of the Clouds. Jules Verne. 3.95. Assoc Bk.
Clique. Nicholas Yermakov. 1982. pap. 2.50 (ISBN 0-425-05500-0). Berkley Pub.
Clique of Gold. Emile Gaboriau. LC 6-44562. (On cover: The secret service series. no. 50). 1891. Street & Smith.
Clique of Gold: Tr. from the French of Emile Gaboriau. Emile Gaboriau. LC 13-8284. 1913. C. Scribner's Sons.
Cliquot. A Racing Story of Ideal Beauty. Kate Lee Ferguson. LC 6-38982. (Peterson's 25 cent series). T. B. Peterson & Brothers.
Cliveden. Frances Louis Howland. LC 3-5785. 1903. Lothrop Publishing Company.
Clives of Burcot. A Novel. Hesba Stretton. LC 8-16885. 1867. G. Routledge and Sons.
Cloak and Doctor. 1st. ed. Frank Gibson. 1974. 7.00 (ISBN 0-682-47980-2). Exposition Press.
Cloak of Aesir. John Wood Campbell. LC 75-10664. (Classics of Science Fiction Ser.). 255p. 1976. 12.50 (ISBN 0-88355-359-7); pap. 3.95 (ISBN 0-88355-449-6). Hyperion-Conn.
Cloak of Aesir. John Wood Campbell. 1972. pap. 0.95 o.p. (75-333). Lancer.
Cloak of Darkness. Helen MacInnes. LC 82-47667. 13.95 (ISBN 0-15-118171-3). Harcourt, Brace, Jovanovich.
Cloak of Folly. Burke Boyce. pap. 0.75 o.p. (74-886). Lancer.
Cloak of Folly: A Novel. Burke Boyce. LC 49-110934. 1949. Harper.
Cloak of Illusion. Stanislaw Dygat. Tr. by David Welsh. 1970. 17.50x (ISBN 0-262-04029-8). MIT Pr.
Cloak of Laughter. May Mellinger. LC 50-6455. 1950. Putnam.
Cloak of Monkey Fur. Julian Duguid. LC 36-182019. 1936. D. Appleton-Century Company, Incorporated.
Cloak Room Thief: And Other Stories About Schools. Charles William Bardeen. LC 8-118288. 1906. C. W. Bardeen.
Clochemerle-les-Bains. Tr. from French by Xan Fielding. Gabriel Chevallier. LC 65-15031. 1965. 5.95. S. & S.
Clock. Aleksei Mikhailovich Remizov. LC 76-23894. (Classics of Russian literature). (Hyperion library of world literature). 1977. 10.50. (ISBN 0-88355-509-3) (ISBN 0-88355-510-7). Hyperion Press.
Clock & Bell. Susan Claudia. LC 74-5525. (Crime Club Ser.). 192p. 1974. 4.95 o.p. (ISBN 0-385-03777-5). Doubleday.

Clock and Bell. William Johnston. LC 74-5525. 1974. (ISBN 0-385-03777-5). Published for the Crime Club by Doubleday.

Clock at Ravenswood. Jon A. Teta. 1973. pap. 0.95 o.p. (ISBN 0-515-03166-6, N3166). Pyramid Pubns.

Clock at 8: 16. Edwin Moultrie Lanham. LC 72-111172. 1970. 5.95. Doubleday.

Clock in the Hatbox. Anthony Gilbert, pseud. 256p. Date not set. Repr. of 1943 ed. 5.95 o.s.i. (ISBN 0-85617-271-5). White Lion Pubs.

Clock Strikes. Marie Troubetzkoy. LC 43-13013. 1943. Rich & Cowan.

Clock Strikes Thirteen. Herbert Brean. LC 52-10781. (A Morrow mystery). 1952. Morrow.

Clock Strikes Twelve. Herbert Russell Wakefield. LC 46-8110. 1946. Arkham House.

Clock Strikes Twelve. Patricia Wentworth. LC 44-3245. 1944. J. B. Lippincott Company.

Clock Strikes Two. Henry Kitchell Webster. LC 28-4240. The Bobbs-Merrill Company.

Clock Struck One. Todd Decker. 4.50 o.p. Vantage.

Clock That Wouldn't Stop: By E. X. Ferrars Pseud. Morna Doris MacTaggart Brown. LC 52-5962. 1952. Published for the Crime Club by Doubleday.

Clock Ticks on. Valentine Williams. LC 33-12648. 1933. Houghton Mifflin Company.

Clock Winder. Anne Tyler. 1977. 1.95 (ISBN 0-445-04050-5). Popular Library.

Clock Winder. Anne Tyler. LC 70-178960. 1972. 6.95 (ISBN 0-394-47898-3). Knopf.

Clock Winder. Anne Tyler. LC 81-4810. 1981. 13.95 (ISBN 0-89340-321-0). J. Curley.

Clock Without Hands. Carson Smith McCullers. LC 61-10351. 1961. Houghton Mifflin.

Clock Without Hands. Betty C. Mowery. 1982. pap. 6.95 (Avalon). Bouregy.

Clockmaker. Thomas Chandler Haliburton. LC 74-91080. (American Humorists Ser.). 1979. Repr. of 1838 ed. lib. bdg. 18.75 (ISBN 0-8398-0754-6). Irvington.

Clockmaker. Georges Simenon. LC 77-4646. (Harvest/HBJ book). 1977. 2.95 (ISBN 0-15-618170-3). Harcourt Brace Jovanovich.

Clockmaker: Or, The Sayings and Doings of Samuel Slick, of Slickville... 2d ed. Thomas Chandler Haliburton. LC 20-16080. 1837. Carey, Lea, and Blanchard.

Clockmaker: Or, The Sayings and Doings of Samuel Slick, of Slickville... 3d ser. ed. Thomas Chandler Haliburton. LC 21-20589. 1840. Lea and Blanchard.

Clockmaker: Or, The Sayings and Doings of Samuel Slick of Slickville. Thomas Chandler Haliburton & Baker, Ray Palmer, 1883- LC 27-18266. 1927. The Leviathan Press.

Clockmaker: Sayings and Doings of Samuel Slick of Slickville. Thomas Chandler Haliburton. (On cover: Riverside classics). 1872. Hurd and Houghton.

Clocks. Agatha Miller Christie. 1980. pap. 2.50 (ISBN 0-671-42879-9). PB.

Clocks of Iraz. L. Sprague de Camp. (Orig.). 1971. pap. 0.75 o.p. (T2584). Pyramid Pubns.

Clocktower. Gordon McDonell. LC 51-3691. 1951. Little, Brown.

Clockwork Orange. Anthony Burgess, pseud. 1963. 9.95 o.s.i. (ISBN 0-393-08519-8); pap. 3.95 (ISBN 0-393-00224-1). Norton.

Clockwork Orange. Anthony Burgess. Bd. with Honey for the Bears. 448p. 1968. Repr. of 1963 ed. 2.95 o.p. (191). Modern Lib.

Clockwork Orange. John Anthony Burgess Wilson. LC 63-7983. 1963. W. W. Norton.

Clockwork Testament or Enderby's End. Anthony Burgess. (O.s.i.). 1975. 6.95 o.s.i. (ISBN 0-394-48438-X). Knopf.

Clockwork Testament: Or, Enderby's End. John Anthony Burgess Wilson. LC 74-7754. (Illus.). 1975. 5.95 (ISBN 0-394-48438-X). Knopf; Distributed by Random House.

Clockwork Testament: Or, Enderby's End. John Anthony Burgess Wilson. 1976. (pbk.) 1.75. Bantam.

Clockwork Traitor. E. E. Smith & Stephen Goldin. (Family d'Alembert Ser.). 160p. 1982. pap. 2.25 (ISBN 0-425-05661-9). Berkley Pub.

Clodhopper. Sigurd Jay Simonsen. LC 40-13807. Fortuny's.

Clodia. Robert De Maria. LC 65-11800. bds., 5.95. St Martin's.

Clods' Letters to Mad. Al Jaffee & Jerry Defuccio. (Illus.). 1974. pap. 1.75 (ISBN 0-446-94282-0). Warner Bks.

Cloisonne Vase. Edwina Noone, pseud. (Orig.). 1972. pap. 0.95 o.p. (09150). Curtis.

Cloister and the Hearth. Charles Reade. (Seaside library, v. 11, no. 203). 1878. G. Munro.

Cloister and the Hearth. Charles Reade. Ed. by Hart, Olive Ely. LC 20-19508. (On verso of half-title: Macmillan's pocket American and English classics). 1920. The Macmillan Company.

Cloister and the Hearth. Charles Reade. LC 36-37060. (Half-title: Everyman's library, ed. by Ernest Rhys. Fiction. no. 29). 1933. J. M. Dent & Sons, Ltd.

Cloister and the Hearth. Charles Reade & Keene, Charles Samuel, 1823-1891, Illus. LC 44-5771. (On cover: Great illustrated classics). 1944. Dodd, Mead & Company.

Cloister and the Hearth. Charles Reade & West, Michael Phillip. (On cover: New method readers... Second supplementary reader 4). 1931. Longmans, Green and Co.

Cloister & the Hearth: A Tale of the Middle Ages. Charles Reade. (Half-title: Everyman's library, ed. by Ernest Rhys. Fiction. no. 29). 1907. J. M. Dent & Co.

Cloister and the Hearth: A Tale of the Middle Ages. Charles Reade. Ed. by De Mille, Alban Bertram. LC 17-15287. (Lake English classics). 0.50. Scott, Foresman and Company.

Cloister and the Hearth: A Tale of the Middle Ages. Charles Reade. Ed. by De Mille, Alban Bertram. LC 20-7520. (Half-title: The Lake English classics. General editor, L. T. Damon). Scott, Foresman and Company.

Cloister and the Hearth: A Tale of the Middle Ages. Charles Reade. LC 37-27407. (Half-title: The modern library of the world's best books). 1937. The Modern Library.

Cloister & the Hearth: Or, Maid, Wife, and Widow; a Matter-of-Fact Romance. Charles Reade. LC 12-37998. 1894. Harper & Brothers.

Cloister and the Hearth: Or, Maid, Wife, and Widow; a Matter-of-Fact Romance. Charles Reade. LC 24-1980. 1922. Thomas Y. Crowell Company.

Cloister and the Hearth. With an Introd. by Morris Gall. New Ed. Charles Reade. LC 60-51194. (A). 1960. Washington Square Press.

Cloister to Court: Scenes from the Life of Charlotte of Bourbon, Abbess of Jouarre, Princess of Orange. Frances M Cotton Walker. 1909. Longmans, Green, and Co.

Cloistered Romance. Florence Olmstead. LC 15-773624. 1915. 1.25. C. Scribner's Sons.

Cloistering of Ursula: Being Certain Chapters from the Memorial of Andrea, Marquis of Uccelli, and Count of Castelpulchio. Clinton Scollard. LC 2-4950. 1902. L. C. Page & Co.

Clone. Richard Cowper, pseud. 1979. 1.75 (ISBN 0-671-82543-7). Pocket Books.

Clone. Colin Murry. LC 73-79657. (Doubleday Science fiction). 1973. 5.95 (ISBN 0-385-03691-4). Doubleday.

Clone Rebellion. Lief, Evelyn. 2.25 (ISBN 0-671-83156-9). Pocket Books.

Cloning. David Shear. LC 72-83119. 1972. 5.95 (ISBN 0-8027-5555-0). Walker.

Clorecrest. Irving A. Greenfield. (Orig.). 1969. pap. 0.60 o.p. (1036). Belmont-Tower.

Clorinda: Or, The Rise and Reign of His Excellency Eugene Rougon. The Man of Progress. Three Times Minister. Emile Zola & Sherwood, Mrs. Mary (Neal) Tr. LC 12-37861. (Rougon-Macquart series, v. 6). T. B. Peterson & Brothers.

Close and Quiet Love. Faith Cutherell Baldwin. 1974. (pbk.) 0.95. Warner Paperback Library.

Close Associates. Catherine Linden. 1980. pap. 1.95 (ISBN 0-380-75473-8, 75473). Avon.

Close Brush with Reality. Bart Parker. LC 81-51478. (Artist Book Ser.). (Illus.). 56p. (Orig.). 1981. pap. 12.95 (ISBN 0-89822-018-1). Visual Studies.

Close Call. John Louis Berry. LC 6-10379. (red cover series, no. 26). 1888. J. S. Ogilvie.

Close Call. Eden Phillpotts. LC 36-13879. 1936. The Macmillan Company.

Close Call: Or, Detective Meade's Dilemma, a Striking Detective Story. Harlan Page Halsey. LC 12-34578. (Old Sleuth's own, no. 98). 1897. The Parlor Car Publishing Co.

Close Encounters of the Deaf Kind. Kenneth Keith. 1979. pap. cancelled o.s.i. Gluxlit Pr.

Close Encounters of the Third Kind. Steven Spielberg. 1977. pap. 2.50 (ISBN 0-440-11332-6). Dell.

Close Encounters of the Third Kind: A Novel. Steven Spielberg. LC 77-12922. 8.95 (ISBN 0-440-01373-9). Delacorte Press.

Close Her Pale Blue Eyes. Helen Rose Hull. LC 63-14374. (Red badge detective). 1963. Dodd, Mead.

Close of Play. Nina Warner Hooke. LC 36-4027. 1936. E. P. Dutton & Co., Inc.

Close of Play. Simon Raven. 1981. 18.95x (Pub. by Remploy England). State Mutual Bk.

Close of the Day. Frank Hamilton Spearman. LC 4-9459. 1904. D. Appleton and Company.

Close Pursuit. Katharine Newlin Burt. LC 47-30062. 1947. C. Scribner's Sons.

Close Quarters. Larry Heinemann. LC 77-2245. 1977. 8.95 (ISBN 0-374-12523-6). Farrar, Straus, Giroux.

Close Quarters. Angela Mackail Thirkell. LC 58-10968. 1958. Knopf.

Close Relations. Susan Isaacs. LC 80-7858. 10.95 (ISBN 0-690-01940-8). Lippincott & Crowell.

Close Shave at Pozo. Orlando Rigoni & Alice Sachs. 1970. 3.95 o.p. Crown.

Close the Door on Murder. John Creasey. LC 72-87141. (His Superintendent Folly of Scotland Yard books). 1973. 4.95. D. McKay Co.

Close to Critical. Hal Clement. 192p. (Orig.). 1975. pap. 1.95 (ISBN 0-345-29168-9). Ballantine.

Close to Death. John Crowe, pseud. LC 79-1213. (Bueno Costa County Mystery-Red Badge Novel of Suspence Ser.). 1979. 7.95 o.p. (ISBN 0-396-07675-0). Dodd.

Close to Death. Dennis Lynds. LC 79-1213. (His A Buena Costa County mystery). 7.95 (ISBN 0-396-07675-0). Dodd, Mead.

Close to Home. Erskine Caldwell. LC 62-115279. 1962. Farrar, Straus and Cudahy.

Close to My Heart. Margaret Gorman Nichols. LC 46-2186. (At head of title: Margaret Nichols.). 1946. Macrae-Smith-Company.

Close to My Heart. Margaret Gorman Nichols. LC 47-6425. 1947. Triangle Books.

Close to the Heart. Helen Lowrie Marshall. 1958. 2.50 o.p. (ISBN 0-385-08261-4). Doubleday.

Close to the Heart. Rebecca Stratton. (Harlequin Romance Ser.). (Orig.). 1979. pap. 1.25 (ISBN 0-373-02303-0, Pub. by Harlequin). PB.

Close to the Sun Again: A New Novel. Morley Callaghan. LC 78-54697. 8.95 (ISBN 0-312-14483-0). St. Martin's Press.

Close to the Wind. John Harris. LC 56-969959. 1956. W. Sloane Associates.

Close-up. Len Deighton. (Signet Book, W5656). 1973. (pbk.) 1.50. New American Library.

Close-up. Len Deighton. LC 77-190404. 1972. 7.95. Atheneum.

Close-up. Robert Maxwell. 4.95 o.p. (9186, Pyramid Hse). BJ Pub Group.

Close-up. Margaret Turnbull. LC 18-20326. 1918. Harper & Brothers.

Close Within My Own Circle. Prudence Andrew. LC 79-28148. 1980. 6.95 (ISBN 0-525-66650-8). Elsevier/Nelson Books.

Closed All Night. Paul Morand. LC 78-130067. (Short story index reprint series). 1970. Books for Libraries Press.

Closed All Night. Paul Morand. Tr. by C., G. P. LC 25-219117. 1925. T. Seltzer.

Closed Book: Concerning the Secret of the Borgias. William Le Queux. LC 4-27870. 1904. The Smart Set Publishing Company.

Closed Circle. Barney Parrish. LC 76-22224. 1976. pap. 1.75 o.p. (ISBN 0-87216-343-1, K16343). Playboy Pr Pbks.

Closed Circuit. William Haggard. (Crime Ser). 1970. pap. 0.65 o.p. (ISBN 0-14-001755-0, 1755). Penguin.

Closed Circuit: By William Haggard Pseud. Richard Clayton. LC 60-133253. (Chantecler mystery novel). 1960. Washburn.

Closed Door. Ronald MacDonald Douglas. LC 41-3116. Modern Age Books.

Closed Door. Hannah Julia Price. LC 13-202029. 1913. 1.00. Knoxville Lithographing Co.

Closed Door. Agnes Louise Provost. LC 33-57720. 1933. Macrae Smith Company.

Closed Door. By F. Du Boisgobey... Fortune Du Boisgobey. LC 6-34430. (On cover: Seaside library. Pocket ed. no. 782). G. Munro.

Closed Doors. Roberta Watson. 1968. 3.50 o.p. (ISBN 0-682-46780-4). Exposition.

Closed Doors: Studies of Deaf and Blind Children. Margaret Prescott Montague. LC 15-19069. 1915. Houghton Mifflin Company.

Closed Doors: Studies of Deaf and Blind Children. new and enl. ed. Margaret Prescott Montague. LC 34-5968. 1934. Houghton Mifflin Company.

Closed Garden. Julien Green & Stuart, Henry Longman. LC 28-11925. 1928. Harper & Brothers.

Closed Harbor. 1st American Ed. James Hanley. LC 53-3912. 1953. Horizon Press.

Closed Lips. George Vane. LC 17-233391. 1917. John Lane.

Closed Range. Harry Sinclair Drago. LC 36-9394. The Macaulay Company.

Closed Road. Rosena A Giles. LC 23-85303. 1923. The Cornhill Publishing Company.

Closed Wall. Leslie William Vedrenne. LC 25-9196.

Closely Watched Trains. Bohumil Hrabal. LC 80-28160. (Writers from the Other Europe). 1981. 4.95 (ISBN 0-14-005808-7). Penguin Books.

Closeout. Donald Conger. 1980. pap. 1.75 o.s.i. (ISBN 0-8439-0722-3, Leisure Bks). Nordon Pubns.

Closer to Saturday. Theo Brandow. LC 74-136453. 1971. 4.00 (ISBN 0-87426-025-6). Whitmore Pub. Co.

Closest Kin There Is. Clara Winston. LC 52-6456. 1952. Harcourt, Brace.

Closet Bones. Thomas Bunn. LC 76-49788. 1977. 8.95 o.p. (ISBN 0-399-11874-8). Putnam Pub Group.

Closet Bones. Thomas Bunn. LC 76-49788. 1977. 8.95 o.p. (ISBN 0-399-11874-8). Putnam.

Closet Bones: A Novel. Thomas Bunn. LC 76-49788. 8.95 (ISBN 0-399-11874-8). Putnam.

Closet Full of Clients. Lynn Paul. LC 73-91537. 1974. 10.95 (ISBN 0-8059-1977-5). Dorrance.

Closing Ceremonies. Harold King. LC 79-10582. 10.95 (ISBN 0-698-10950-3). Coward, McCann & Geoghegan.

Closing Ceremonies. Harold King. 1980. 2.50 (ISBN 0-671-83396-0). Pocket Books.

Closing Circle. Lou Cameron. (Berkley medallion book). 1974. (pbk.) 1.50 (ISBN 0-425-02707-4). Berkley Pub. Co.

Closing Hour... Norah Hoult. LC 30-5537. 1930. Harper & Brothers.

Closing Net. Henry Cottrell Rowland. LC 12-24248. 1912. 1.25. Dodd, Mead and Company.

Closing Net. Henry Cottrell Rowland. LC 22-24760. 1920. Dodd, Mead and Company.

Closing Time. Norman Oliver Brown. LC 73-4820. 1973. 5.95 (ISBN 0-394-48567-X). Random House.

Closing Time. Norman Oliver Brown. LC 74-4226. 1974. (pbk.) 1.95 (ISBN 0-394-71161-0). Vintage Books.

Closing Times. Daniel Marcus Davin. 1975. 15.00x (ISBN 0-19-212197-9). Oxford U Pr.

Closing Web. Marjorie Harte, pseud. 1977. pap. 1.25 (ISBN 0-532-12503-7). Woodhill.

Closing Web. Marjorie Harte. 1973. 4.95. Lenox Hill Pr.

Clotel. William Wells Brown. LC 75-75852. (American Negro, His History and Literature). (Afro-American culture series.). (Illus.). 1969. 8.00. Arno Press.

Clotel: A Narrative of Slave Life. William Wells Brown. Repr. of 1853 ed. lib. bdg. 10.50x o.p. (ISBN 0-8398-0176-9). Gregg.

Clotel, Or, the President's Daughter. William Wells Brown. (African American Library). 1970. pap. 1.25 (ISBN 0-02-049130-1, Collier). Macmillan.

Clotel; or, The President's Daughter: A Narrative of Slave Life in the United States. William Wells Brown. LC 73-101722. (American Library). 1970. 1.25. Collier Books.

Clotel: Or, The President's Daughter: a Narrative of Slave Life in the United States. William Wells Brown. LC 76-78569. (Illus.). 1969. Gregg Press.

Clotel; or, The President's Daughter: A Narrative of Slave Life in the United States. William Wells Brown. LC 77-90396. (Illus.). 1969. 6.95. Citadel Press.

Clotelle: a Tale of the Southern States. William Wells Brown. (On cover: Redpath's books for the camp area, no. 2). J. Redpath.

Clotelle: A Tale of the Southern States. The 1st American Ed. Reproduced in Facsim. with a Biographical Introd. by Maxwell Whiteman. William Wells Brown. 1955. A. Saifer.

Clotelle: Or, the Colored Heroine. William Wells Brown. pap. 1.95 (N247P). Mnemosyne.

Cloth: An Electric Novel. Aram Saroyan. LC 76-158199. 1971. 4.95 (ISBN 0-695-80259-3) (ISBN 0-695-80258-5). Big Table Pub. Co.

Cloth of Gold. Elswyth Thane. 1976. Repr. of 1929 ed. lib. bdg. 15.95x (ISBN 0-88411-965-3). Amereon Ltd.

Cloth of Gold: A Novel. Elswyth Thane. LC 29-4417. 1929. Frederick A. Stokes Company.

Cloth of Silver. Lenore Glen Offord. LC 39-5007. 1939. Macrae Smith Company.

Cloth of the Tempest. Kenneth Patchen. 3.00. Assoc Bk.

Clothes for a Summer Hotel. Tennessee Williams. 96p. 1983. 12.00 (ISBN 0-8112-0870-2, NDP556); pap. 4.75 (ISBN 0-8112-0871-0). New Directions.

Clothes Make the Pirate. Holman Francis Day. LC 25-5619. 1925. Harper & Brothers.

Clotilde: By Cecil Saint Laurent Pseud. Translated by Humphrey Hare. Jacques Laurent. LC 59-552852. 1959. Morrow.

Clotilde: Or, The Secret of Three Generations. From the French of Alexandre De Pontmartin. Alexandre De Pontmartin. Tr. by Barton, Kate C. LC 11-7169. 1871. J. M. Stoddart & Co.

Cloud Across the Sun. George Franklin Allee. LC 48-152059. 1947. Zondervan Pub. House.

Cloud by Day. Pauline Stiles. LC 29-5965. 1929. Doubleday, Doran & Company, Inc.

Cloud Catchers. Ursula Holden. LC 79-13064. 9.95 (ISBN 0-416-00011-8). Methuen.

Cloud Chamber. Dexter Masters. LC 70-135436. (Illus.). 1971. 6.95. Little, Brown.

Cloud Cuckoo Land. Peter De Rosa. LC 75-21682. 1975. pap. 1.95 o.p. (ISBN 0-913592-56-0). Argus Comm.

Cloud Cuckoo Land. Naomi Haldane Mitchison. LC 26-3569. Harcourt, Brace and Company.

Cloud Eight. Miles Donis. 1975. (pbk.) 1.25 (ISBN 0-446-76757-3). Warner Paperback Library.

Cloud Forest. Peter Matthiessen. 1966. pap. 0.75 o.p. (T1470). Pyramid Pubns.

Cloud Howe. J. Leslie Mitchell. LC 34-1168. 1934. Doubleday, Doran & Company, Inc.

Cloud Nine. James Mallahan Cain. LC 77-81173. 1977. cancelled o.s.i. (ISBN 0-88373-070-7). Stonehill Pub Co.

Cloud of Arrows. Mary Frances Doner. LC 50-8305. 1950. Doubleday.

Cloud on the Land. Julia Davis. LC 51-12036. 1951. Rinehart.

Cloud Over Calderwood. Kathleen A Shoesmith. (Ace gothic read easy large type). 1973. (pbk.) 0.95. Ace.
Cloud Over Catawba. Chalmers Gaston Davidson. LC 49-4493. 1949. Pub. Under the Sponsorship of the Mecklenburg Historical Society.
Cloud Over Paradise. Abra Taylor. (Superromances Ser.). 384p. 1981. pap. 2.50 (ISBN 0-373-70005-9, Pub. by Worldwide). Harlequin Bks.
Cloud Over the Sun. Renee Shann. 1971. pap. 0.75 o.p. (94133). Beagle Bks.
Cloud-Pictures. 1. The Exile of Von Adelstein's Soul. 2. Topankalon. 3. Herr Regenbogen's Concert. 4. A Great-Organ Prelude. Francis Henry Underwood. LC 8-32285. 1872. Lee and Shepard.
Cloud-Walking. Marie Campbell. LC 71-146878. (Illus.). 1971. 7.50 (ISBN 0-253-31385-6). Indiana University Press.
Cloud-Walking. Marie Campbell & Spelman, John Adams, 1912- Illus. LC 42-22724. 1942. Farrar & Rinehart, Inc.
Cloud with a Golden Border. Helen Hazlett. LC 7-3668. 1861. T. E. Zell.
Cloud with the Silver Lining: By the Author of "A Trap to Catch a Sunbeam", "Only"... Matilda Anne Planche Mackarness. LC 7-16442. 1853. J. Munroe and Company.
Cloudcry. Sydney J Van Scyoc. LC 76-49828. Berkley Pub. Corp.: Distributed by Putnam.
Clouded Amber. Jeannette Garr Washburn Kelsey. LC 15-25347. 1.35. R. G. Badger.
Clouded Fountain. 1st Ed. McCready Huston. LC 59-7783. 1959. Lippincott.
Clouded Happiness. A Novel. Harriet Anne Frances Gardiner Orsay. (On cover: Library of select novels, no. 184). 1853. Harper & Brothers.
Clouded Mirror. Evelyn Bond. 288p. 1975. pap. 1.25 (ISBN 0-532-12297-6). Woodhill.
Clouded Mirror. easy eye ed. Evelyn Bond. pap. 0.75 o.p. Lancer.
Clouded Mirror. E. Kirker Kranz. Ed. by Alice Sachs. (OSI). 1971. 3.95 o.s.i. (L#). Lenox Hill.
Clouded Moon. Mary Howard, pseud. LC 48-10016. 1948. Arcadia House.
Clouded Moon. Max Saltmarsh. LC 38-51354. 1938. A. A. Knopf.
Clouded Pearl: A Novel. Berta Ruck. LC 24-23921. 1924. 2.00. Dodd, Mead and Company.
Clouded Rapture. Margaret Pargeter. (Harlequin Presents Ser.). 192p. 1983. pap. 1.95 (ISBN 0-373-10588-6). Harlequin Bks.
Clouded Sky. John Iggulden. LC 64-19671. 1964. Macmillan.
Clouded Star. Anne Parrish. LC 48-8288. 1948. Harper.
Cloudesley: A Tale, 3 vols. in 1. William Godwin. LC 79-8270. Repr. of 1830 ed. 44.50 (ISBN 0-404-61863-4). AMS Pr.
Cloudgap. Helen La Penta. LC 51-10530. 1951. Harper.
Cloudless May. Margaret Storm Jameson. LC 44-2956. 1944. The Macmillan Company.
Clouds & Dust. Nunzio I. LaSpina. 96p. 1975. 4.95 o.s.i. (ISBN 0-8181-0348-5). Pageant-Poseidon.
Clouds & Sunshine. facsimile ed. Sarah Lee Brown Fleming. LC 70-173606. (Black Heritage Library Collection). Repr. of 1920 ed. 8.75 (ISBN 0-8369-8916-3). Ayer Co.
Clouds and Sunshine. Margaret Harper. LC 7-2858. 1890. Printed by J. B. Lippincott Company.
Clouds and Sunshine. And Art: a Dramatic Tale. Charles Reade. 1855. Ticknor and Fields.
Clouds in the Wind. Frederick Lawrence Green. LC 51-10266. 1951. Coward-McCann.
Clouds of Destiny. Lou Ellen Davis. LC 77-15567. 9.95 (ISBN 0-399-12055-6). Putnam.
Clouds of the Abyss. Edwin R. Papin. 5.95 o.p. Vantage.
Clouds of Witness. Dorothy Leigh Sayers. Harper.
Clouds of Witness. Dorothy Leigh Sayers. LC 79-10577. 1979. 14.95 (ISBN 0-8161-6721-4). G. K. Hall.
Clouds of Witness. Dorothy Leigh Sayers & Eustace, Robert, Joint Author. LC 38-27556. 1938. Harcourt, Brace and Company.
Clouds of Witnesses. Dorothy Leigh Sayers. LC 27-6433. 1927. L. MacVeagh, The Dial Press.
Clouds Over Destiny. 1st Ed. Charles Raymond Stumbo. LC 56-12872. 1957. Vantage Press.
Clouds Over the Valley: A Novel. Bonner Semple Marquis. LC 51-12923. 1951. Exposition Press.
Clouds Over Vellanti. Elsie Lee. (Dell book). 1979. 1.50 (ISBN 0-440-11133-1). Dell Pub. Co.
Cloudy in the West. William Patterson White. LC 28-5566. 1928. Little, Brown, and Company.
Cloudy Jewel. Grace Livingston Hill. LC 20-206482. 1920. J. B. Lippincott Company.
Cloudy Sky: Or, the Unfortunate Children; a True Tale. Narcissa Smith Springer. LC 12-14352. 1882.
Cloudy Summits. Isabel Constance Clarke. LC 40-7589. 1939. Longmans, Green & Co.
Cloudy Trophies. Anne Goodwin Winslow. LC 46-4513. 1946. A. A. Knopf.
Cloudy Trophy: The Romance of Victor Hugo. Leon Daudet & Whitall, James. LC 38-39430. 1938. W. Morrow & Company.
Cloudy Weather: A Romance of Fenian Days. Elizabeth Angela Henry. LC 21-21943. Printed by the Union and Times Press.
Clout. Don Gibbons. 1974. (pbk.) 1.50 (ISBN 0-380-00005-9). Avon.
Clovecrest. Alicia Grace. 1978. pap. 1.25 (ISBN 0-532-12534-7). Woodhill.
Cloven Foot. Mary Elizabeth Braddon Maxwell. (Seaside library, v. 25, no. 482). 1879. G. Munro.
Cloven Foot. Mary Elizabeth Braddon Maxwell. (On cover: Seaside library. Pocket ed., no. 499). 1885. G. Munro.
Cloven Foot. Mary Elizabeth Braddon Maxwell. (On cover: Lovell's library. no, 894). 1887. J. W. Lovell Company.
Cloven Foot. A Novel. Mary Elizabeth Braddon Maxwell. (Franklin square library, no. 49). 1879. Harper & Brothers.
Cloven Foot: Being an Adaptation of the English Novel "The Mystery of Edwin Drood". Robert Henry Newell & Dickens, Charles, 1812-1870. 1870. Carleton: Etc., Etc.
Cloven-Footed Angel. Maurice Dekobra, pseud. Tr. by Sloan, Samuel. LC 32-19820. The Macaulay Company.
Clover: A Love Story. Otto Friedrich. 1979. 12.95 o.p. (ISBN 0-671-22509-X). S&S.
Clover and Blue Grass. Elizabeth Caroline Obenchain. LC 16-26774. 1916. Little, Brown, & Company.
Cloverdale Skeleton. Cyrus Lauron Hooper. LC 7-5265. 1889. J. B. Alden.
Cloverly. Mary R Higham. LC 7-4775. A. D. F. Randolph & Company.
Clovernook Children. Alice Cary. LC 6-22800. 1855. Ticknor and Fields.
Clovernook: Or, Recollections of Our Neighbourhood in the West. 1st- 2d series. by alice carey ! ed. Alice Cary. LC 6-22801. 1852. Redfield.
Clovis. Michael Fessier. LC 48-6143. 1948. Dial Press.
Clovis. Michael Fessier. LC 50-290443. 1949. Wingate.
Clovis. Walter Harris. LC 79-93752. 1969. 5.95. Putnam.
Clown. Heinrich Boll. Tr. by Leila Vennewitz from Ger. LC 64-7935. (Cloth ed. 6.95 o.p.). 1971. pap. 5.95 (ISBN 0-07-006420-2, SP). McGraw.
Clown. Heinrich Boll. Tr. by Leila Vennewitz. 1965. 5.00 o.p. (ISBN 0-07-006402-4). McGraw.
Clown. Alan Geoffrey Yates. LC 73-153999. (Signet mystery). 1972. 0.75. New American Library.
Clown in the Moonlight. James Howard Kunstler. LC 80-29382. 10.95 (ISBN 0-312-14495-4). St. Martin's Press.
Clown of Bombay: A Novel. Aaron Judah. LC 68-18638. 1968. Dial Press.
Clown of the Gods: By Agatha Young Pseud. Agnes Brooks Young. LC 54-5967. 1954. Random House.
Clown of the Hemlock: A Novel. 1st Ed. Richard Ashby. LC 59-11047. 1959. Chilton Co.
Clown on Fire. Aaron Judah. LC 67-10703. 1967. Dial Press.
Clown Prince. Maurice Dekobra, pseud. Tr. by Wainwright, Neal. LC 28-25636. 1928. Payson & Clarke Ltd.
Clown: Translated by Gerard Hopkins. Alfred Kern. LC 59-11953. 1960. Pantheon Books.
Clown. Translated from the German by Leila Vennewitz. Boll, Heinrich. LC 64-7935. McGraw-Hill.
Clowns and Criminals: The Oppenheim Omnibus. Edward Phillips Oppenheim. 1931. Little, Brown, and Company.
Clowns Courage: Undergraduate Rubrics in Part from the Magazine of the University of Being the Scarlet Fairy Book for Wise Children, Sick People and the Half-Grown. A Breviary of Rising Inflections for the Disillusioned, for the Compleat Sinner a Whimseymissal and a Petty Psalter for the Wee Small Voice. LC 15-15465. 1915. R. G. Badger; Etc,, Etc.
Clown's Nose. Bernard Wiseman. 1981. Garrard Pub. Co.
Clowns of God. Morris L. West. 1981. pap. 3.95. Bantam.
Clowns of God: A Novel. Morris L. West. LC 80-27153. 1981. 14.95 (ISBN 0-688-00449-0). Morrow.
Club. Steven Gaines & Robert Jon Cohen. LC 79-25831. 1980. 10.95 (ISBN 0-688-03592-2). W. Morrow.
Club. Andrew Graham. LC 57-8325. (Illus.). 1957. Reynal.
Club. Stephen Lewis. 2.25 (ISBN 0-440-11410-1). Dell Publishing Co.
Club-Book: Being Original Tales. Ed. by Andrew Picken. James, George Payne Rainsford et al. LC 21-4131. 1836. Harper and Brothers.
Club Car Mystery. Grace Isabel Colbron. LC 28-5804. The Macaulay Company.
Club Caribe. Michael French. ()A Fawcett Gold Medal Book.). (Illus.). 1.75. (ISBN 0-449-13772-4). Fawcett Publications.
Club Exotica. Charles Fritch. (Orig.). pap. 0.95 o.p. (1125). Brandon.
Club; Novel. Earl Conrad. LC 73-80070. 1974. 6.95 (ISBN 0-913984-01-9). West-Lewis Pub. Co.
Club of Masks. Allen Upward. LC 26-17769. 1926. J. B. Lippincott Company.
Club of Queer Trades. Gilbert Keith Chesterton. LC 5-10540. 1905. Harper & Brothers.
Club Paradise. Raynald Jennings. (Orig.). 1971. pap. 0.95 o.p. (B95-2128). Belmont-Tower.
Club Stories: Washington State Federation of Women's Clubs. Washington State Federation of Women's Clubs. LC 15-27937. 1915. 1.00. Lowman & Hanford Co.
Club Tropicale. Susanne Jaffe. (Berkley medallion book). 1974. (pbk.) 1.75 (ISBN 0-425-02679-5). Berkley Pub. Co.
Clubfoot the Avenger: Being Some Further Adventures of Desmond Okewood, of the Secret Service. Valentine Williams. LC 24-113313. 1924. Houghton Mifflin Company.
Cluck Abroad. Tiffany Thayer. LC 35-3665. 1935. Doubleday, Doran & Company, Inc.
Clue. Carolyn Wells. LC 9-25642. 1909. J. B. Lippincott Company.
Clue. Carolyn Wells. LC 20-15605. 1918. A. L. Burt Company.
Clue for Mr. Fortune; Reggie at His Best. Henry Christopher Bailey. LC 36-198366. 1936. Pub. for the Crime Club, Inc., by Doubleday, Doran & Company Inc.
Clue for Murder. Ronald Ernest Barker. LC 62-10816. 1962. Abelard-Schuman.
Clue from the Stars. Eden Phillpotts. LC 32-662. 1932. The Macmillan Company.
Clue in the Air: A Detective Story. Isabel Egenton Ostrander. LC 17-298644. 1.35. W. J. Watt & Company.
Clue in the Air: A Detective Story. Isabel Egenton Ostrander. LC 20-9482. Grosset & Dunlap.
Clue in the Clay. Dolores Birk Hitchens. LC 39-25874. Phoenix Press.
Clue in the Clay. Dolores Birk Hitchens. LC 47-133043. (On cover: A Bart house mystery, 35). 1946. Bartholomew House, Inc.
Clue in the Clay. Dolores Birk Olsen. LC 39-258741. Phoenix Press.
Clue in the Mirror. Nigel Morland. LC 38-65798. Farrar & Rinehart, Incorporated.
Clue in Two Flats. R. L. F McCombs. LC 40-31341. 1940. Mystery House.
Clue of the Artificial Eye. Joseph Smith Fletcher. LC 39-15961. 1939. Hillman-Curl, Inc.
Clue of the Bricklayer's Aunt. Nigel Morland. LC 38-1973. 1937. Farrar & Rinehart, Incorporated.
Clue of the Clock. Marion Harvey. LC 29-24372. E. J. Clode, Inc.
Clue of the Clot. Charles Bryson. LC 29-5705. E. P. Dutton & Company, Inc.
Clue of the Dead Goldfish. Victor MacClure. LC 34-24358. J. B. Lippincott Company.
Clue of the Eyelash: A Fleming Stone Detective Story. Carolyn Wells. LC 33-4392. J. B. Lippincott Company.
Clue of the Fourteen Keys. Miles Burton. LC 37-18249. 1937. Pub. for the Crime Club, Inc., by Doubleday, Doran & Co., Inc.
Clue of the Hungry Corpse. Inigo Jones. LC 40-46621. 1939. Arcadia House, Inc.
Clue of the Judas Tree. Zenith Jones Brown. LC 33-21132. Farrar & Rinehart, Incorporated.
Clue of the Leather Noose. Donald Bayne Hobart. LC 30-7422. Whitman Publishing Co.
Clue of the Naked Eye: A Jane Amanda Edwards Story, by Charlotte Murray Russell. Charlotte Murray Russell, pseud. LC 39-30322. Pub. for the Crime Club, Inc.
Clue of the New Pin. Edgar Wallace. LC 28-6952. Small, Maynard and Company.
Clue of the Poor Man's Shilling. Kathleen Moore Knight. LC 36-4912. 1936. Pub. for the Crime Club, Inc., by Doubleday, Doran & Company Inc.
Clue of the Primrose Petal. Harvey Wickham. LC 21-26736. E. J. Clode.
Clue of the Rising Moon. Valentine Williams. 1935. Houghton Mifflin Company.
Clue of the Second Murder. Dorothy Stockbridge Tillet. LC 29-256046. 1929. Pub. for The Crime Club, Inc., by Doubleday, Doran & Company, Inc.
Clue of the Silver Brush... Miles Burton. LC 36-8018. (Pub. for the Crime club by Collins) has title: The milk-churn murder.). 1936. Pub. for the Crime Club, Inc., by Doubleday, Doran & Co., Inc.
Clue of the Silver Cellar. Miles Burton. 1937. Pub. for the Crime Club, Inc., by Doubleday, Doran & Company, Inc.
Clue of the Stone Lantern. Margaret Sutton. (Judy Bolton Mysteries). 1976. Repr. of 1950 ed. lib. bdg. 12.95x (ISBN 0-88411-712-X). Amereon Ltd.
Clue of the Twisted Candle. Edgar Wallace. LC 16-22900. Small, Maynard & Company.
Clue to Romance. Florence Faulkner. 1976. 4.95. Avalon Books.
Clues for Dr. Coffee. Lawrence Goldtree Blochman. 1964. 3.95 o.p. (ISBN 0-397-00317-X). Lippincott.
Clues for Dr. Coffee: A Second Casebook. Lawrence Goldtree Blochman. LC 64-22177. (Main line mysteries). 1964. Lippincott.
Clues of the Caribbees: Being Certain Criminal Investigations of Henry Poggioli, PH.D. Thomas Sigismund Stribling. LC 29-243761. 1929. Doubleday, Doran & Company,Inc.
Clues of the Caribbees: Being Certain Criminal Investigations of Henry Poggioli, Ph.D. Thomas Sigismund Stribling. LC 76-56999. (Illus.). 1977. 3.50 (ISBN 0-486-23486-X). Dover Publications.
Clues to Burn. Lenore Glen Offord. LC 42-16613. 1942. Duell, Sloan and Pearce.
Clues to Christabel. Mary Fitt. LC 44-7254. 1944. Pub. for the Crime Club by Doubleday, Doran and Company, Inc.
Clues to Christabel. Kathleen Freeman. LC 44-7254. 1944. Published for the Crime Club by Doubleday, Doran.
Clumsy Partners. Geoffrey Clark. 1974. 6.95 o.p. (ISBN 0-87777-047-6). R W Baron.
Clung. Max Brand. 1982. 18.00x (ISBN 0-86025-205-1, Pub. by Ian Henry Pubns England). State Mutual Bk.
Clung. Max Brand. 1969. 3.95 o.p. (ISBN 0-396-06004-8). Dodd.
Clung. Frederick Faust. LC 77-88069. (Silver star westerns). 1969. Dodd, Mead.
Cluny Brown. Margery Sharp. LC 44-7101. 1944. Little, Brown and Company.
Cluny Brown. Margery Sharp. LC 46-492716. 1946. Triangle Books, The Blakiston Company.
Cluny MacPherson. A Tale of Brotherly Love. Amelia Edith Huddleston Barr. LC 6-7996. American Tract Society.
Cluny Problem. Archibald E. Fielding. LC 29-9000. 1929. A. A. Knopf.
Cluster. Piers Anthony, pseud. pap. 2.95 (ISBN 0-380-01755-5, 813645). Avon.
Cluster of Separate Sparks. Joan Aiken. 1973 (ISBN 0-671-77624-X). Pocket Bks.
Cluster of Separate Sparks. Joan Aiken. LC 79-175352. 1972. 5.95. Doubleday.
Clutch and Differential. George Anthony Weller. LC 79-130078. (Short story index reprint series). 1970. Books for Libraries Press.
Clutch and Differential. George Anthony Weller. LC 36-29602. 1936. Random House.
Clutch of Circumstance. James Barnes. LC 8-12555. 1908. D. Appleton and Company.
Clutch of Circumstance. Arthur Lemuel Hardy. LC 9-28033. 1909. Mayhew Publishing Co.
Clutch of Circumstance. Leighton Graves Osmun. LC 14-9166. 1914. 1.25. Suly and Kleinteich.
Clutch of Constables. Ngaio Marsh. LC 69-15063. 1969. 4.95. Little, Brown.
Clutch of Coppers. Gordon Ashe. LC 69-11807. (Rinehart Suspense Novel Ser). 1969. 3.95 o.p. (ISBN 0-03-076380-0). HR&W.
Clutch of Coppers. John Creasey. LC 69-11807. (Rinehart suspense novel). 1969. 3.95. Holt, Rinehart and Winston.
Clutch of Fables. Teo Savory & Emil Antonucci. LC 77-355241. (Illus.). 1976. 10.00. Unicorn Press.
Clutch of the Corsican: A Tale of the Days of the Downfall of the Great Napoleon. Alfred Hoyt Bill. LC 25-8052. The Atlantic Monthly Press.
Clutch of the Marriage Tie: Or, Jilbett, a Story of the Second Glass. Laura Jean Libbey. LC 20-7296. Brooklyn Eagle Press.
Clutch of Vipers. Jack S Scott, pseud. LC 78-22451. 8.95 (ISBN 0-06-014008-9). Harper & Row.
Clutches of Circumstances. 1st Ed. Thomas Playfair Ward. LC 54-11458. 1954. Pageant Press.
Clutching Hand. Charles Judson Dutton. LC 28-813245. 1928. Dodd, Mead and Company.
Clutching Hand: A Craig Kennedy Novel. Arthur Benjamin Reeve. LC 34-8976. The Reilly & Lee Co.
Clutha Plays a Hunch. Hugh Munro. LC 59-12252. (Chantecler mystery novel). 1959. Washburn.
Clutterkill. Gary Paulsen. (Raven House Mysteries Ser.). 224p. 1982. pap. 2.25 (ISBN 0-373-63040-9, Pub. by Worldwide). Harlequin Bks.
Clyde, the Resolute Detective: Or, His Own Mystery. Harlan Page Halsey. LC 12-34575. (Old Sleuth's own; no. 101). 1897. The Parlor Car Publishing Co.
Clyde Wardleigh's Promise. Mary Dummett Nauman Robinson. LC 7-23113. 1873. Claxton, Remsen & Haffelfinger.

Clyffords of Clyffe. James Payn. (Seaside library, v. 51, no. 1045). 1881. G. Munro.
Clym. Mary V Hillmann. LC 31-347769. The Devin-Adair Company.
Clytia: A Romance of the Sixteenth Century. by george taylor pseud.... from the german by mary j. safford. ed. Adolf Hausratin & Safford, Mary Joanna, Tr. LC 7-2604. 1884. W. S. Gottsberger.
Clytie. A Novel of Modern Life. Joseph Hatton. (On cover: Lovell's library, v. 1, no. 7). 1882. J. W. Lovell Company.
Co.". Jean Richard Bloch & Scott-Moncrieff, Charles Kenneth, 1880-1930, Tr. LC 30-3347. 1929. Simon and Schuster.
Co-Citizens. Corra May White Harris. LC 15-190683. 1915. 1.00. Doubleday, Page & Company.
Co-Ed. Olive Deane Hormel. LC 26-141531. 1926. C. Scribner's Sons.
Co-Ge-We-a, the Half-Blood: A Depiction of the Great Montana Cattle Range. Hom-Ishu-Ma & Sho-Pow-Tan. LC 28-13788. The Four Seas Company.
Co-Ge-We-a, the Half-Blood: A Depiction of the Great Montana Cattle Range, by Hum-Ishu-Ma, "Mourning Dove"... Given Through Sho-Pow-Tan. Mourning Dove & Sho-Pow-Tan. LC 28-13788. The Four Seas Company.
Co-Op; a Novel of Living Together. Upton Beall Sinclair. LC 36-20848. Farrar & Rinehart, Incorporated.
Co-Opolitan: A Story of the Co-Operative Commonwealth of Idaho. Zebina Forbush. LC 13-33846. (On verso of t.-p.: Library of progress. no. 26). 1898. C. H. Kerr & Company.
Co-Ordinator. Christopher Nicole. LC 67-24011. 1967. Lippincott.
Co-Ordinator. Andrew York. pap. 0.75 o.p. Lancer.
Co-Ordinator. Andrew York. 1967. 4.50 o.p. Lippincott.
Co-Respondent. Nell Ashley. LC 33-198201. 1932. G. H. Watt.
Co-Stars: Cecil Spooner & Oscar Wilde: A Mere Little Comedy About More or Less Legitimate Actors on Two Sunday Mornings and One Sunday Night. William Wilfrid Whalen. LC 30-146685. White Squaw Press.
Coach from the City. Alan O'Toole. 1967. pap. 1.20 o.s.i. Tri-Ocean.
Coach from the City: A Story About Australian Rules Football. Illus. by Paul Rigby. Alan O'Toole. LC 67-21196. 1967. bds., 4.95. Rigby.
Coach North. Philip McCutchan. LC 75-12187. 1975. 6.95 (ISBN 0-8027-5330-2). Walker.
Coach Phyllis. Lynn Beckwith. 1982. 10.00 (ISBN 0-533-05487-7). Vantage.
Coachman's Love: Or, The Heiress of a Million. Herbert Bernard. LC 6-11328. (On cover: Munro's library. v. l, no. 125). N. L. Munroe.
Coal. J. Jason Grant. 1978. 1.95 (ISBN 0-87067-615-6). Holloway House Pub. Co.
Coal. Tom Hillstrom. LC 80-12069. 512p. 1980. 13.95 (ISBN 0-688-03658-9). Morrow.
Coal Camp Girl. Lois Lenski. LC 59-12356. (Illus.). 1959. Lippincott.
Coal County. Tom Hillstrom. 1981. pap. 2.95 (ISBN 0-440-11616-3). Dell.
Coal Mine No. 7. Robert Louis Nathan. LC 80-23521. 1981. 12.95 (ISBN 0-312-14499-7). St. Martin's Press.
Coal War. Upton Beall Sinclair. Ed. & intro. by John Graham. LC 75-40885. 335p. 1976. text ed. 17.50x (ISBN 0-87081-067-7). Colo Assoc.
Coal War: A Sequel to "King Coal". Upton Beall Sinclair & John N Graham. LC 75-40885. 12.50 (ISBN 0-87081-067-7). Colorado Associated University Press.
Coalitions. David Rounds. LC 76-126584. 1970. 5.95. Outerbridge & Dienstfrey, Distributed by Dutton.
Coals from Newcastle. Bruce Beddow. LC 29-19783. 1929. Doubleday, Doran and Company, Inc.
Coals of Fire. Mary Frances Hanford Delanoy. LC 1-31610. The Abbey Press.
Coals of Fire, and Other Stories. By David Christie Murray... David Christie Murray. (Seaside library, v. 76, no. 1541). 1883. G. Munro.
Coals of Fire: Illustrated by Allan Eitzen. Elizabeth Hershberger Bauman. LC 53-12197. 1954. Herald Press.
Coarse Gold. Edwin Corle. LC 52-9779. 1952. Duell, Sloan & Pearce.
Coarse Gold. Edwin Corle. LC 42-197546. 1942. E. P. Dutton and Company, Inc.
Coast Guard Girl. Georgia Craig. LC 45-6725. 1945. Arcadia House, Inc.
Coast Guard Girl. Peggy Gaddis, pseud. LC 45-6725. 1945. Arcadia House.
Coast of Adventures. Harold Bindloss. LC 15-194104. Frederick A. Stokes Company.
Coast of Bohemia. biographical ed. William Dean Howells. LC 99-5418. 1899. Harper & Brothers.
Coast of Bohemia: A Novel. William Dean Howells. LC 7-5781. 1893. Harper & Brothers.
Coast of Chance. Esther Chamberlain & Chamberlain, Lucia. LC 8-13722. 1908. The Bobbs-Merrill Company.
Coast of Eden. Robert Luther Duffus. LC 23-2976. 1923. The Macmillan Company.
Coast of Enchantment. Burton Egbert Stevenson. LC 26-19108. 1926. Dodd, Mead and Company.
Coast of Fear. K. G. Ballard. 1969. pap. 0.60 o.p. (0502-06039-060). Curtis.
Coast of Fear. Caroline Crane. LC 80-26819. 224p. 1981. 8.95 (ISBN 0-396-07950-4). Dodd.
Coast of Fear. Caroline Crane. 1982. pap. 2.50 (ISBN 0-451-11456-6, AE1456, Sig). NAL.
Coast of Fear. Holly Roth. LC 57-6703. 1957. Published for the Crime Club by Doubleday.
Coast of Fear. Leslie Waller. LC 73-20536. 1974. 6.95 (ISBN 0-385-09660-7). Doubleday.
Coast of Fear. Leslie Waller. 1975. (pbk.) 1.50. Bantam.
Coast of Fear: A Novel of Suspense. Caroline Crane. LC 80-26819. 8.95 (ISBN 0-396-07950-4). Dodd, Mead.
Coast of Fear. 1st Ed. K. G. Ballard. LC 57-6703. 1957. Published for the Crime Club by Doubleday.
Coast of Folly. Coningsby William Dawson. LC 24-629. 1924. Cosmopolitan Book Corporation.
Coast of Freedom: A Romance of the Adventurous Times of the First Self-Made American. Adele Marie Shaw & Shaw, Albert Judson, Joint Author. LC 2-11736. 1902. Doubleday, Page & Co.
Coast of Intrigue. Elwyn Whitman Chambers. LC 28-25958. Rae D. Henkle Co., Inc.
Coast of Opportunity. Page Philips. LC 17-8468. 1917. 1.35. The Macaulay Company.
Coast Rangers. J. Ross Browne. (Illus.). Repr. of 1862 ed. 7.50. Acoma Bks.
Coast to Coast: A Novel About Corruption in High Places. Walter Ross. LC 62-7557. 1962. Simon and Schuster.
Coast to Coast Wife. Elsa Welsh. LC 40-21980. The Saravan House.
Coasts of Folly. John Edward Jennings. LC 42-3176. 1942. Reynal & Hitchcock.
Coasts of Folly. Joel Williams, pseud. LC 42-3176. 1942. Reynal & Hitchcock.
Coasts of the Earth. Harold Livingston. LC 54-5701. 1954. Houghton Mifflin.
Coat. Hugo Charteris. LC 74-100499. 1970. 5.50. Harcourt, Brace & World.
Coat for the Tsar. Richard M. Elman. (Illus.). 1958. 2.50 o.p. (ISBN 0-292-73193-0). U of Tex Pr.
Coat I Wore. Lucile Finlay. LC 47-2343. 1947. C. Scribner's Sons.
Coat of Blackmail. James Murdoch Macgregor. LC 76-131093. 1971. 4.50. Published for the Crime Club by Doubleday.
Coat of Blackmail. J. T. McIntosh. (Crime Club Ser). 1971. 4.50 o.p. (ISBN 0-385-06481-0). Doubleday.
Coat of Many Colors. 1969. 4.95 (ISBN 0-87645-012-5). Gambit.
Coat of Many Colors. Hulda Peterson Putzke. LC 50-8622. 1950. Dorrance.
Coat of Many Colors. Edwin Samuel. LC 60-7210. 1960. Abelard-Schuman.
Coat of Many Colors: A Rural Romance of the Eighteenineties. St. John, Robert Porter. LC 43-8273. 1943. Dorrance and Company.
Coat of Varnish. Charles Percy Snow. LC 79-16221. 10.45 (ISBN 0-684-16315-2). Scribner.
Coat Without Seam. Maurice Baring. LC 29-11281. 1929. A. A. Knopf.
Cobalt. Nathan Aldyne. LC 81-21540. 9.95 (ISBN 0-312-14515-2). St. Martin's Press.
Cobalt 60. Richard L Graves. LC 74-28006. 1975. 7.95 (ISBN 0-8128-1779-6). Stein and Day.
Cobble Stone Gardens. William S. Burroughs. LC 76-40473. 1976. 3.00 (ISBN 0-916156-14-1). Cherry Valley Editions.
Cobbler. William Benson Richter. LC 51-2018. 1951. Christopher Pub. House.
Cobbler. Elma Allen Travis. LC 8-17997. 1908. The Outing Publishing Company.
Cobbler of Canterbury: Frederic Ouvry's Edition of 1862. Frederic Ouvry & H. Neville Davies. LC 78-309233. (Illus.). 1977. 12.50 (ISBN 0-85991-018-0). D. S. Brewer.
Cobbler of Nimes. Mary Imlay Taylor. LC 6475. 1900. A. C. McClurg & Co.
Cobbler's Dream. Monica Dickens. LC 63-12276. 1963. Coward-McCann.
Cobbler's Dream. Monica Dickens. LC 72-184127. (Peacock books). 1971. 0.25 (ISBN 0-14-047072-7). Penguin.
Coble Hill. Edwin Joseph Becker. LC 47-382238. 1947. R. M. McBride and Company.
Cobra. Martin Brown & Holman, Russell, Joint Author. LC 25-17580. Grosset & Dunlap.
Cobra. Severo Sarduy. LC 74-7041. 1975. 6.95. Dutton.
Cobra Candlestick. Elsa Barker. LC 29-1199. J. H. Sears & Company, Inc.
Cobra Kill. Nick Carter. (Nick Carter Series). (O.s.i.). Date not set. pap. 1.50 o.s.i. (AD1675, Award). Univ Pub & Dist.
Cobra Team. Robin Moore & Edward E. Mayer. LC 78-68626. 1979. pap. 2.50 o.s.i. (ISBN 0-89516-064-1). Condor Pub Co.
Cobras with False Faces. Richard S. White. 5.95 o.p. Vantage.
Cobweb. George Agnew Chamberlain. LC 21-16430. Harper & Brothers.
Cobweb. Pat Flower. LC 77-18073. 1978. 7.95 (ISBN 0-8128-2414-8). Stein and Day.
Cobweb. William Gibson. LC 54-5977. 1954. Knopf.
Cobweb. Margaretta Muhlenberg Perkins Tuttle. LC 25-8315. 1925. Little, Brown, and Company.
Cobweb Castle. Joseph Smith Fletcher. LC 28-15158. 1928. A. A. Knopf.
Cobweb Cloak. Helen Gansevoort Edwards Mackay. LC 12-16853. 1912. 1.25. Duffield & Company.
Cobweb House. Elizabeth Hughes Holloway. LC 31-6080. 1931. E. P. Dutton & Co. Inc.
Cobweb Palace. Rosamund Nugent. LC 25-394328. 1925. D. Appleton and Company.
Cobwebs and Clues. Ernestine Malan & Ledig, Alma K., Joint Author. LC 44-41888. 1944. Dorrance & Company.
Cocaine and Blue Eyes. Fred Zackel. LC 78-5379. 1978. 8.95 (ISBN 0-698-10934-1). Coward, McCann & Geoghegan.
Cocaine and Blue Eyes. Fred Zackel (ISBN 0-698-10934-1). Berkley Publishing Corp., C.
Cocaine Blues. Walter Satterthwait. (Orig.). 1980. pap. 2.25 (ISBN 0-440-11055-6). Dell.
Cocaine Blues Mission. Lyle Coxe. (Orig.). 1979. pap. 1.95 (ISBN 0-532-23316-6). Woodhill.
Cocaine Caper. Vincent A. Paradis. 1978. pap. 1.75 (ISBN 0-532-17186-1). Woodhill.
Cocaine Connection. R. L. Brent. (Liquidator Ser.). 192p. (Orig.). 1980. pap. 1.95 o.p. (ISBN 0-441-11300-1). Charter Bks.
Cocaine Connection. R. L. Brent. (Liquidator Ser.). (O.s.i.: No. 3). 160p. 1974. pap. 1.25 o.s.i. (AQ1361, Award). Univ Pub & Dist.
Cochise. Peter Wild. LC 73-79725. 98p. 1973. Softbound 2.50 o.p. (ISBN 0-385-05792-X). Doubleday.
Cochrane, the Unconquerable. Archibald Douglas Turnbull & Van der Veer, Norman Reeve, 1884- Joint Author. LC 29-4536. The Century Co.
Cock-a-Doodle-Dew. Joe Brandon. 1973. (pbk) 1.25. Manor Books.
Cock-A-Doodle-Dew. Bob Davis. (Orig.). 1973. pap. 1.25 (ISBN 0-532-12165-1, 532-12165-125). Woodhill.
Cock and Anchor. Joseph Sheridan Le Fanu. LC 79-19270. (Ireland, from the Act of Union, 1800, to the Death of Parnell, 1891). 1979. 42.00 (ISBN 0-8240-3508-9). Garland Pub.
Cock and Anchor, Being a Chronicle of Old Dublin City. Joseph Sheridan Le Fanu. LC 76-4606. (Le Fanu, Joseph Sheridan, 1814-1873. Works. 1976). 1976. (3vols.) 62.00 (ISBN 0-405-09202-4). Arno Press.
Cock for Esclepius. C. W. Calhoun. 4.50 o.p. Vantage.
Cock Jarvis. Joyce Cary. LC 75-2471. 1975. 8.95. St. Martin's Press.
Cock O' the North. Talbot Mundy. LC 29-256072. The Bobbs-Merrill Company.
Cock Pit. James Gould Cozzens. LC 28-21891. 1928. W. Morrow & Company.
Cock-Pit of Roses. James Fraser, pseud. 1970. 4.75 o.p. (ISBN 0-15-118262-0); 4.75 o.p. HarBraceJ.
Cock-Pit of Roses. Alan White. LC 70-95866. 1970. Harcourt, Brace & World.
Cock Still Crows. Induk Pahk. 1977. 6.95 o.p. (ISBN 0-533-02656-3). Vantage.
Cock-the-Roach. K. Chukovsky. 22p. 1981. pap. 1.60 (ISBN 0-8285-2217-0, Pub. by Progress Pubs USSR). Imported Pubns.
Cockades: A Romance. Meade Minnigerode. LC 27-7506. 1927. G. P. Putnam's Sons.
Cockatoos. Patrick White. 288p. 1983. pap. 4.95 (ISBN 0-14-004463-9). Penguin.
Cockatoos: New Stories. Patrick White. LC 74-3792. 312p. 1975. 12.95 (ISBN 0-670-22648-3). Viking Pr.
Cockcrow at Night, the Heroic Journey, & 18 Other Stories. Lawrence Lee. (Illus.). 250p. (Orig.). 1973. 6.00 o.p. (ISBN 0-910286-35-3); pap. 4.50 o.p. (ISBN 0-910286-30-2). Boxwood.
Cockeyed Boom Shack Cat and Other Stories. Florence Morrison. 1974. 5.00 (ISBN 0-87881-009-9). Mojave Books.
Cockeyed Corpse. Richard S. Prather. (Shell Scott). 1970. pap. 0.60 o.p. (R2302, GM). Fawcett World.
Cockeyed Cuties. Troy Conway, pseud. (Coxeman Ser., No. 31). 1972. pap. 0.75 o.p. (ISBN 0-446-64834-5). Paperback Lib.
Cockfighter: A Novel. Charles Ray Willeford. LC 79-185077. 1972. 5.95. Crown Publishers.
Cockle in the Wheat. J. J. Fretz. 4.00 o.p. Carlton.
Cockleburr. Hugh C Rae. LC 75-112904. (Red mask mystery). 1970. 4.50. Putnam.
Cockney's Farming Experiences. Virginia Stephen Woolf. LC 74-166282. 1972. State University Press.
Cockpit. Jerzy N. Kosinski. 288p. 1976. pap. 2.75 (ISBN 0-553-14952-0). Bantam.
Cockpit: A Novel. Jerzy N. Kosinski. LC 75-4619. 1975. 8.95 (ISBN 0-395-20671-5). Houghton Mifflin.
Cockpit of Santiago Key. David Solon Greenberg. LC 20-775. (His The open road series). Boni and Liveright.
Cockroach. Norman Solomon. LC 74-84718. (Illus.). 130p. (Orig.). 1974. pap. 1.00 (ISBN 0-912874-08-2). Out of the Ashes.
Cock's Feather: A Novel. Katharine Newlin Burt. LC 28-22358. 1928. Houghton Mifflin Company.
Cock's Funeral. Ben Field. LC 37-17236. International Publishers.
Cock's Tail Murder. Hugh Austin. LC 38-38328. 1938. Pub. for the Crime Club, Inc., by Doubleday, Doran & Co., Inc.
Cocksure: A Novel. Mordecai Richler. LC 68-14845. 1968. Simon and Schuster.
Cocktail Time. Pelham Grenville Wodehouse. LC 58-10351. 1958. Simon and Schuster.
Cocoa Blades: A Novel. Paul Marttin. LC 71-37657. 1972. 6.95. Delacorte Press.
Cocoanut Suite: Stories of the West Indies. Corinne Dean. LC 44-3683. 1944. Meador Publishing Company.
Coconut Killings. Patricia Moyes. LC 76-29910. (Rinehart suspense novel). 6.95 (ISBN 0-03-018481-9). Holt, Rinehart and Winston.
Coconut Planter. Doris Egerton Jones. LC 17-10985. 1916. Cassell and Company, Ltd.
Coconut Wireless. Ray Franklin Kauffman. LC 48-255314. 1948. Macmillan Co.
Cocoon. Cheryl Ann Baxter. LC 80-131779. 1980. 4.95 (ISBN 0-87747-830-9). Deseret Book Co.
Cocoon: A Rest-Cure Comedy. Ruth McEnery Stuart. Hearst's International Library Co.
Cocos Island Venture. Marie Briggs. 3.00 (ISBN 0-87505-120-0). Borden.
Cocos Island Venture. 1st Ed. Marie Briggs. LC 51-16795. 1950. Borden Pub. Co.
Cocotte. Theodore Pratt. LC 51-25335. (Gold medal book, 153). 1951. Fawcett Publications.
Cocotte (Boule De Suif) and Three Other Stories. Guy De Maupassant. LC 72-181271. (Illus.). 1971. 1.00 (ISBN 0-85166-154-8). Franklin Watts Ltd.
Cod Cod Molly. John Broad. LC 53-10286.
Coda Alliance. Michael Brady. (Orig.). 1981. pap. 2.50 (ISBN 0-440-11415-2). Dell.
Code. Nick Carter. (Nick Carter Ser). (O.s.i.). 192p. (Orig.). 1973. pap. 0.95 o.s.i. (AN1146, Award). Univ Pub & Dist.
Code Conquistador. William Kennedy. (Orig.). 1982. pap. 2.95 (ISBN 0-671-83686-2). PB.
Code Five. Frank Gill Slaughter. LC 76-150919. 1971. 5.95. Doubleday.
Code-Letter Mystery. David Sharp. LC 32-26575. 1932. Houghton Mifflin Company.
Code Name Hangman. Paul Geddes. 1979. 1.95 (ISBN 0-14-004769-7). Penguin.
Code Name: Icy. Lucien Agniel. (Orig.). 1970. pap. 0.60 o.p. (63-310). Paperback Lib.
Code Name Nimrod. James Leasor. LC 81-83492. 272p. 1982. pap. 2.95 (ISBN 0-86721-030-3). Playboy Pbks.
Code Name, Sebastian. 1st Ed. James Johnson. LC 67-143686. 1967. bds., 4.50. Lippincott.
Code Name: Werewolf. Nick Carter. (Nick Carter Ser.). (Illus.). 176p. pap. cancelled (ISBN 0-441-11365-6, Pub. by Charter Bks). Ace Bks.
Code Name Werewolf. Nick Carter. (Nick Carter Ser.). (O.s.i.). 192p. 1973. pap. 1.25 o.s.i. (AQ1329, Award). Univ Pub & Dist.
Code Name: Werewolf. Nick Carter. (Nick Carter/Killmaster Series). 1973. (pbk) 0.95. Award Books.
Code of a Champion. Frederic Nelson Litten. LC 50-10334. 1950. Westminster Press.
Code of Arms. Lawrence Block & Harold King. LC 80-26811. 12.95 (ISBN 0-399-90029-2). Coward, McCann, and Geoghegan/Richard Marek Publishers.
Code of Arms. Lawrence Block & Harold King. 1982. 2.95. Berkley Books.
Code of Conduct: A Novel. Elliott Arnold. LC 76-106526. 1970. 5.95. Scribner.
Code of Men: A Western Story. Homer King Gordon. LC 26-12835. Thomas Y. Crowell Company.
Code of the Karstens. Henry Walsworth Kinney. LC 23-130135. 1923. Little, Brown, and Company.
Code of the Lifemaker. James P Hogan. LC 82-22676. 1983. 13.95 (ISBN 0-345-30925-1). Ballantine Books.
Code of the Mountains. Charles Neville Buck. LC 15-11004. W. J. Watt & Company.
Code of the North. Harold Titus. LC 33-5770. Macrae Smith Company.
Code of the Northwest. Samuel Alexander White. LC 40-2388. Phoenix Press.

Code of the West. Zane Grey. LC 24-218358. 1934. Harper & Brothers.

Code of the West. Zane Grey. LC 78-2658. (Zane Grey western). 1979. 10.95 (ISBN 0-89340-138-2). J. Curley.

Code of the Woosters. Pelham Grenville Wodehouse. LC 75-13376. 1975. 1.95 (ISBN 0-394-72028-8). Vintage Books.

Code of the Woosters. Pelham Grenville Wodehouse. LC 76-4718. (P. G. Wodehouse classic). 1969. 4.95. Simon and Schuster.

Code of the Woosters. Pelham Grenville Wodehouse. LC 38-27897. 1938. Doubleday, Doran & Co., Inc.

Code of the Woosters. Pelham Grenville Wodehouse. LC 39-317877. 1939. The Sun Dial Press, Inc.

Code of Victor Jallot: A Romance of Old New Orleans. Edward Childs Carpenter. LC 7-314212. 1907. G. W. Jacobs & Company.

Code Seven. Lou Cameron. (Berkley Medallion Book). 1977. 1.25 (ISBN 0-425-03296-5). Berkley Pub. Corp.

Code Three: A Science Fiction Novel. Rick Raphael. 1966. 3.95. S & S.

Code Three: By James M. Fox Pseud. 1st Ed. James M. W. Knipscheer. LC 53-7328. 1953. Little, Brown.

Code Z. Joel Swerdlow. LC 78-17969. 8.95. Putnam.

Code 1013: Assassin. Leslie Trevor. (Police Woman,#2). 1975. (pbk.) 1.25. Award Books.

Codebreakers. David Kahn. (RL 7). 1973. pap. 2.50 (ISBN 0-451-08967-7, E8967, Sig). NAL.

Codex Frisianus. Ed. by C. R. Unger. LC 80-1968. Repr. of 1871 ed. 70.00 (ISBN 0-404-18666-1). AMS Pr.

Codfish Watch. Edward R. Knowlton. Ed. by Alice Sachs. 1970. 3.95 o.p. Lenox Hill.

Codicil: A Novel. Henry Howard Harper. LC 15-8938. 1915. 5.00. Issued Privately by the Vail-Ballon Company and Printed Only on Advance Subscriptions from Members of the Bibliophile Society.

Codline's Child: The Autobiography of Wilbert Snow. Wilbert Snow. LC 73-15008. (Illus.). 1974. 14.95 (ISBN 0-8195-4069-2). Wesleyan University Press.

Coed & the Lady. Wallace Greer. 1972. pap. 1.95 o.s.i. (V1088T, Venus). Grove.

Coeds. Alison Lord. (Orig.). 1970. pap. 0.75 o.p. (T2160). Pyramid Pubns.

Coeds. Gretchen Wade. 1974. (pbk.) 1.25. Ace Books.

Coeds: Part II. Olivia Harmston. 1975. (pbk.) 1.25. Ace Books.

Coeds Three. Carlton Joyce. 1970. pap. 0.75 o.p. (75-294). Manor Bks.

Coelebs in Search of a Wife. Hannah More. LC 22-17344. 1857. Derby & Jackson.

Coelebs in Search of a Wife. Hannah More. (seaside library. v. 64, no. 1303). 1882. G. Munro.

Coelebs in Search of a Wife. Comprehending Observations on Domestic Habits and Manners, Religion and Morals... Hannah More. 1810. Printed by Thomas & William Bradford.

Coelebs: The Love Story of a Bachelor. Florence Ethel Mills Young. LC 18-6309. 1917. John Lane.

Coeur D'Alene. Mary Hallock Foote. LC 74-22783. (Labor Movement in Fiction and Non-Fiction). 1976. 16.00 (ISBN 0-404-58430-6). AMS Press.

Coeur-Menteur. Paule Jeanin. (Collection Colombine Ser.). 192p. 1983. pap. 1.95 (ISBN 0-373-48059-8). Harlequin Bks.

Coffee. Suzanne T. Moore. 144p. 1974. pap. 4.95 (ISBN 0-938758-00-4). MTM Pub Co.

Coffee and a Love Affair: An American Girl's Romance on a Coffee Plantation. Mary Boardman Sheldon. LC 8-21616. 1908. F. A. Stokes Company.

Coffee and Conspiracy. Thomas Grant Springer. LC 26-22410. 1926. H. Vinal.

Coffee & Repartee. John Kendrick Bangs. Repr. of 1893 ed. lib. bdg. 20.00 (ISBN 0-8414-1664-8). Folcroft.

Coffee and Repartee and The Idiott. new ed., from new plates... ed. John Kendrick Bangs. LC 7286. 1900. Harper & Brothers.

Coffee at Charlie's. Bettina Bird. LC 68-16545. (Trend books). (Illus.). 1968. 0.90. Cheshire.

Coffee Cream. Carolyn Overstreet. LC 42-21900. 1942. E. P. Dutton & Co., Inc.

Coffee Tea or Me: Girls' Around-The-World Diary. Trudy Baker & Rachel Jones. 1970. 5.95 o.p. (0820). G&D.

Coffee, Tea or Me Girls Get Away from It All. Trudy Baker & Rachel Jones. LC 73-15125. 240p. 1974. 6.95 o.p. (ISBN 0-448-11560-3). G&D.

Coffee, Three A.M. Brenda Hillman. 1982. signed 35.00x; pap. 17.50x. Penumbra Press.

Coffee Train. Margarethe Erdahl Shank. LC 53-9129. (Illus.). 1968. 5.50 o.p. (ISBN 0-8066-0821-8, 10-1451). Augsburg.

Coffer Dams: A Novel. Kamala Markandaya, pseud. LC 71-75598. 1969. 5.95. John Day Co.

Coffin Break. Ed. by Alfred Joseph Hitchcock. 1974. (pbk.) 0.95. Dell.

Coffin Corner. Ed. by Alfred Joseph Hitchcock. 1975. (pbk.) 0.95. Dell.

Coffin Corner. Dell Shannon. 1970. pap. 0.75 o.p. (T2295). Pyramid Pubns.

Coffin Corner: By Dell Shannon. Elizabeth Linington. LC 66-2076. 1966. W. Morrow.

Coffin Country. Aaron Marc Stein. LC 79-36613. 1976. 5.95 (ISBN 0-385-11588-1). Published for the Crime Club by Doubleday.

Coffin for Baby. Gwendoline Butler. LC 63-20275. 1963. Walker.

Coffin for Christopher: A Jane and Dagobert Brown Mystery. Delano L Ames. LC 54-12500. 1954. I. Washburn.

Coffin for Dimitrios. Eric Ambler. 214p. Repr. of 1937 ed. lib. bdg. 12.95x (ISBN 0-89190-461-1). Am Repr-Rivercity Pr.

Coffin for Dimitrios. Eric Ambler. LC 75-50689. (Mystery Library: Vol. 6). 1977. Repr. 10.95 o.p. (ISBN 0-89163-029-5). Pubs Inc.

Coffin for Dimitrois. Eric Ambler. LC 39-27993. 1939. A.A. Knopf.

Coffin for McCullough. John M. Murray. Ed. by Alice Sachs. 1971. 3.95 o.p. Lenox Hill.

Coffin for One. Francis Beeding. LC 44-7480. New Avon Library.

Coffin for Pandora. Gwendoline Butler. 1973. price not set o.p. St Martin.

Coffin from the Past. Gwendoline Butler. (Scene of the Crime Ser.: No. 54). 1982. pap. 2.50 (ISBN 0-440-11590-6). Dell.

Coffin Full of Dollars. Joe Millard, pseud. (Dollar Western Ser.). (O.s.i.). 160p. 1975. pap. 1.25 o.s.i. (AQ1470, Award). Univ Pub & Dist.

Coffin Full of Dreams. Frisco Hitt. 1977. 11.95 (ISBN 0-285-62157-2, Pub. by Souvenir Pr). Intl Schol Bk Serv.

Coffin Full of Dreams. Frisco Hitt. 1976. (pbk.) 1.95. Bantam Books.

Coffin Hollow & Other Ghost Tales. Ruth A. Musick. LC 76-51157. (Illus.). 216p. 1977. 14.00 o.p. (ISBN 0-8131-1346-6); pap. 6.50 (ISBN 0-8131-1416-0). U Pr of Ky.

Coffin in Malta. Gwendoline Butler. LC 65-232645. 1967. bds., 3.50. Walker.

Coffin Nails: The Story of Jane McGregor. Rosetta Butler Hastings. LC 8-28312. The Dispatch Publishing Company.

Coffin, Scarcely Used. Colin Watson. LC 63-1946. 1962. Penguin Books.

Coffin, Scarely Used. Colin Watson. LC 67-28438. 1967. Putnam.

Coffin Things. Michael Avallone. 1970. Repr. of 1968 ed. pap. 0.75 o.p. (ISBN 0-447-74636-7). Lancer.

Coffin Things. easy eye ed. Michael Avallone. (Orig.). 1968. pap. 0.75 o.p. (74-942). Lancer.

Coffin Waiting. Gwendoline Butler. LC 65-15420. 1965. 3.50. Walker.

Coffins for Three. Frederick Clyde Davis. LC 38-216953. 1938. Pub. for the Crime Club, Inc., by Doubleday, Doran & Co., Inc.

Coffins for Two. Vincent Starrett. LC 24-3917. 1924. Covici-McGee Co.

Coffy. Paul Fairman. 1973. pap. 0.95 o.s.i. (75-487). Lancer.

Cogan's Trade. George V. Higgins. LC 73-20438. 1974. 5.95 (ISBN 0-394-49057-6). Knopf.

Coggin. Ernest James Oldmeadow. LC 20-818. 1920. 1.75. The Century Co.

Cognac Hill. Charles Divine. LC 27-17813. Payson & Clarke Ltd.

Cohens and Kellys: A Story of East-Side West-Side New York, Based on the Play "Two Blocks Away". Aaron Hoffman. LC 26-13137. (On cover: Popular plays and screen library). Jacobsen-Hodgkinson Corporation.

Coign of Vantage. John Seymour Wood. LC 8-37550. Dodd, Mead & Company.

Coil of Carne. John Oxenham, pseud. LC 11-25054. 1911. John Lane Company.

Coil of Serpents. Anne Stevenson. LC 76-53832. 8.95 (ISBN 0-399-11930-2). Putnam.

Coil of the Serpent: A Novel. Dexter Allen. LC 55-10075. Coward-McCann.

Coils. Clayton Eshleman. 150p. (Orig.). 1973. pap. 4.00 (ISBN 0-87685-153-7). Black Sparrow.

Coils. Fred Saberhagen & Roger Zelazny. 288p. 1983. pap. 2.95 (ISBN 0-523-48539-5). Pinnacle Bks.

Coin in Nine Hands. Marguerite Yourcenar. LC 82-9324. 1982. 12.95 (ISBN 0-374-12522-8). Farrar, Straus, and Giroux.

Coin of Carthage. Winifred Bryher. LC 63-13687. (Harvest Bk., HB90). 1965. pap., 1.35. Harcourt.

Coin of Contraband. Garland Roark. 1970. pap. 0.95 o.p. (0502-09037). Curtis.

Coin of Edward VII. A Detective Story. Fergus Hume. LC 3-3564. 1903. G. W. Dillingham Company.

Coin of Love. Barbara Cartland. (Historical Romance Ser. No. 3). 1972. pap. 0.95 o.p. (N2735). Pyramid Pubns.

Coin of Love. Barbara Cartland. 1974. pap. 1.25 o.p. (ISBN 0-515-03491-6, V3491). BJ Pub Group.

Coin Pin. Grace Carstens. LC 61-7055. 1961. Macmillan.

Coins in the Fountain. John H. Secondari. LC 52-8785. 1952. Lippincott.

Cokurburn: By Kirkland Brown Pseud. Marian Kirkland Brown. LC 64-8882. bds., 4.95. Riverbend Pr., Box.

Col. Judson of Alabama: A Southerner's Experience at the North. Fannie Bean. LC 6-10272. (On cover: The Waldorf series, no. 3). 1893. Saalfield & Fitch.

Col. Judson of Alabama: Or, A. Southerner's Experience at the North. Fannie Bean. United States Book Company.

Colas Breugnon. Romain Rolland & Miller, Katherine, Tr. LC 19-15969. 1919. H. Holt and Company.

Colby Stories: As Told by Colby Men of the Classes 1832 to 1902. Ed. by Herbert Carlyle Libby. 1900. The Rumford Press.

Colchicine Factor. Robert Bryce. 1978. pap. 1.95 (ISBN 0-89041-225-1, 3225). Major Bks.

Colcorton. Edith Pope. LC 44-2813. 1944. C. Scribner's Sons.

Cold Bed in the Clay. Ruth Otis Sawtell Wallis. LC 47-1633. 1947. Dodd, Mead & Company.

Cold Blood. Leo Bruce, pseud. 205p. 1980. Repr. of 1952 ed. 14.95 (ISBN 0-89733-039-0). Academy Chi Ltd.

Cold Blood. Leo Bruce, pseud. 205p. 1976. Repr. of 1952 ed. 7.95 o.p. (ISBN 0-86025-024-5, Pub. by Ian Henry Pubns England). Academy Chi Ltd.

Cold Blood. Leo Bruce, pseud. 1979. 11.00x o.p. (ISBN 0-86025-024-5, Pub by Ian Henry Pubns England). State Mutual Bk.

Cold Blood. Leo Bruce, pseud. 1977. 6.50 o.p. State Mutual Bk.

Cold Blood. Croft-Cooke, Rupert. LC 80-24027. 1980. 3.95 (ISBN 0-89733-038-2). Academy Chicago.

Cold-Blooded Murder: An Inspector French Mystery. Freeman Wills Crofts. LC 48-16132. (New Avon library, 126). 1947. Avon Book Co.

Cold Blue Death. Ken Stanton. 1978. pap. 1.25 o.p. (ISBN 0-532-12533-9). Woodhill.

Cold Blue Death. Ken Stanton. (Aquanauts Ser). 1970. pap. 0.75 o.p. (532-75333-075). Manor Bks.

Cold Blue Death. Ken Stanton. 1978. pap. 1.25 o.p. (ISBN 0-532-12533-9). Manor Bks.

Cold Blue Moon: Black Ulysses Afar off. Howard Washington Odum. LC 31-8823. The Bobbs-Merrill Company.

Cold Cash War. Robert L. Asprin. LC 76-62747. 7.95 (ISBN 0-312-14717-1). St. Martin's Press.

Cold Chills. Robert Bloch. LC 76-24039. 1977. 5.95 (ISBN 0-385-12421-X). Doubleday.

Cold Comforf Farm. Stella Gibbons. 4.50 o.p. (13311). Delacorte.

Cold Comfort. Hal Z. Bennett. 1979. pap. 4.95 o.p. (ISBN 0-517-53594-7, C N Potter Bks). Crown.

Cold Comfort: A Novel. David R. Slavitt. LC 79-24475. 10.95 (ISBN 0-416-00621-3). Methuen.

Cold Comfort Farm. Stella Gibbons. LC 32-29206. 1932. Longmans, Green and Co.

Cold Comfort Farm. Stella Gibbons. LC 38-388323. (Half-title: The Longman stories of laughter, 1). 1936. Longmans, Green and Co.

Cold Coming. Mary Kelly. LC 68-26790. 1968. 3.95. Walker.

Cold Companion: A Novel. Jack Sher. LC 48-3499. 1948. Rinehart.

Cold Dark Night. Sarah Gainham. (O.s.i.). pap. 0.75 o.s.i. (A246S, Award). Univ Pub & Dist.

Cold Day in Hell. Rick Horrington & Sharron Horrington. 1982. pap. cancelled (ISBN 0-913024-13-9). Tandem Pr.

Cold Days of Summer. Carsbie C. Adams. 1970. 4.00 o.p. (ISBN 0-8233-0145-1). Golden Quill.

Cold Embers: A Romance of Old California. Corinne King Wright. LC 32-5030. 1931. Wetzel Publishing Co., Inc.

Cold Fear: New Tales of Terror. Ed. by Hugh Lamb. LC 77-86367. 1978. 8.95 (ISBN 0-8008-1686-2). Taplinger.

Cold Fire Burning. Nathan C Heard. LC 73-20548. 1974. 5.95 (ISBN 0-671-27120-2). Simon and Schuster.

Cold Flame. James Recves. 1969. 3.95 o.p. Hawthorn.

Cold Front. Bridget Everitt. LC 72-95764. 1973. 4.95 (ISBN 0-8027-5271-3). Walker.

Cold Ground Was My Bed Last Night. George Palmer Garrett. LC 64-12987. 1964. University of Missouri Press.

Cold Hand in Mine. Robert Aickman. 1979. pap. 1.95 (ISBN 0-425-04109-3). Berkley Pub.

Cold Hand in Mine: Strange Stories. Robert Aickman. LC 77-3042. 1977. 7.95 (ISBN 0-684-15132-4). Scribner.

Cold Hand in Mine: Strange Stories. Robert Aickman. (Berkley book). 1979. 1.95 (ISBN 0-425-04109-3). Berkley Pub. Corp.

Cold Hands. Joseph Pintauro. LC 79-13715. 10.95 (ISBN 0-671-24726-3). Simon and Schuster.

Cold Hands. Joseph Pintauro. (Signet Book.). 1980. New American Library.

Cold Harbors. C. W. Truesdale. 1973. 4.50. Latitudes Pr.

Cold Harbour. Francis Brett Young. LC 68-10893. (Seagull library of mystery and suspense). 1968. Norton.

Cold Harbour. Francis Brett Young. LC 25-19110. 1925. A. A. Knopf.

Cold Hazard. Richard Armstrong. (Orig.). (YA) (gr. 7-12). pap. 2.40x duraflex ed o.p. (2-48153, RRS, G3). HM.

Cold-Hearted Lady. J. D. Hardin. LC 81-80086. (J. D. Hardin Ser.). 224p. (Orig.). 1981. pap. 1.95 (ISBN 0-87216-877-8). Playboy Pbks.

Cold Heaven. Doris Murphy. LC 48-5624. 1948. Doubleday.

Cold in the Sea. Edward Latimer Beach. LC 77-18841. 9.95 (ISBN 0-03-013916-3). Holt, Rinehart and Winston.

Cold Iron. Robert Stone Pryor. LC 74-104944. 1970. 5.50. McCall Pub. Co.

Cold Journey. Grace Zaring Stone. LC 34-27281. 1934. W. Morrow & Co.

Cold Journey. Grace Zaring Stone. LC 43-51186. 1943. The Press of the Readers Club.

Cold Jungle. Gavin Black. LC 69-17288. 1969. 4.95 o.p. (ISBN 0-06-010374-4, HarpT). Harper & Row.

Cold Jungle. Oswald Wynd. LC 69-17288. 1969. 4.95. Harper & Row.

Cold Moon Over Babylon. Michael McDowell. LC 79-56235. 2.50 (ISBN 0-380-48660-1). Avon Books.

Cold Nights: A Novel. Fei-Kan Li. LC 78-21758. (Illus.). 1979. 8.95. Chinese University Press.

Cold Nights: A Novel. Pa Chin. Tr. by Nathan K. Mao & Liu Ts'un-yan. LC 78-21758. (Illus.). 202p. 1979. 10.95 (ISBN 0-295-95639-9). U of Wash Pr.

Cold Night's Death. Barbara Harrison. (O.s.i.). 160p. (Orig.). 1973. pap. 0.95 o.s.i. (AN1163, Award). Univ Pub & Dist.

Cold Ones. R. E Sebenthall. LC 72-80192. (Inner sanctum mystery). 1972. 5.95 (ISBN 0-671-21291-5). Simon and Schuster.

Cold Ones: An Inner Sanctum Mystery. Paul Kruger. (O.s.i.). 1972. 5.95 o.s.i. (ISBN 0-671-21291-5). S&S.

Cold Pogrom. Max Ludwig Berges. Tr. by Epstein, Benjamin R. LC 39-33521. 1939. The Jewish Publication Society of America.

Cold Poison: A Hildegarde Withers Mystery. Stuart Palmer. LC 54-6453. 1954. M. S. Mill Co., and W. Morrow.

Cold River: A Novel. William Judson, pseud. LC 74-19497. 1975. 7.95 (ISBN 0-88405-095-5). Mason & Lipscomb.

Cold Room. Jeffrey Caine. LC 76-22721. 1977. 7.95 (ISBN 0-394-40903-5). Knopf: Distributed by Random House.

Cold Snows of Carbonate. Lena M. Urquhart. (Illus.). 1967. pap. 1.00x (ISBN 0-87315-004-X). Golden Bell.

Cold Spring in Russia. Olga C. Andreyev. Tr. by Michael Carlisle from Russian. 1978. 15.00 (ISBN 0-88233-303-8); pap. 7.50 o.p. (ISBN 0-88233-306-2). Ardis Pubs.

Cold Steal. Alice Tilton, pseud. (Foul Play Press Bks.). 1981. pap. 4.95 (ISBN 0-914378-54-6). Countryman.

Cold Steal. Alice Tilton, pseud. 1968. 4.95 o.p. (ISBN 0-393-08500-7). Norton.

Cold Steal: A Leonidas Witherall Mystery, by Alice Tilton Pseud. Phoebe Atwood Taylor. 1968. bds., 4.95. Norton.

Cold Steel. Matthew Phipps Shiel. LC 29-10223. 1929. The Vanguard Press.

Cold Terror. R. Chetwynd-Hayes. 1975. pap. 1.25 o.p. (ISBN 0-515-03633-1, V3633). Pyramid Pubns.

Cold Trail. Paul Evan Lehman. 1970. pap. 0.50 o.p. (50-305). Manor Bks.

Cold Trail. Elizabeth Linington. LC 77-17350. 1978. 7.95 (ISBN 0-688-03287-7). Morrow.

Cold Trail. Dell Shannon. LC 77-17350. 1978. 7.95 o.p. (ISBN 0-688-03287-7). Morrow.

Cold Turkey. Timothy Childs. LC 78-22441. 8.95 (ISBN 0-06-010758-8). Harper & Row.

Cold Victory. Poul Anderson. (Psychotechnic League Ser.). 284p. (Orig.). 1982. pap. 2.75 (ISBN 0-523-48527-1). Pinnacle Bks.

Cold War in a Country Garden. Lindsay Gutteridge. 1973 (ISBN 0-671-77623-1). Pocket Bks.

Cold War in a Country Garden. Lindsay Gutteridge. LC 72-161534. 1971. 5.95. Putnam.

Cold War in Hell. Harry Blamires. LC 56-395222. 1955. Longmans, Green.

Cold War of Kitty Pentecost. Alexander Blackburn. 1979. 8.95 o.p.; pap. 4.50 o.p. Writers West.

Cold War of Kitty Pentecost: A Novel. Alexander Blackburn. LC 78-58533. 8.95. Writers West Books.

TITLE INDEX COLLECTED WORKS.

Cold War Swap. Ross Thomas. LC 66-245616. bds., 3.95. Morrow.
Cold War Swap. Ross Thomas. 1976. 1.50 (ISBN 0-671-80540-1). Pocket Books.
Cold Waters. Philip Maitland Hubbard. LC 69-18794. 1969. 4.95. Atheneum.
Cold, Wild Wind. Frances Casey Kerns. LC 73-16099. 1974. 7.95 (ISBN 0-690-00160-6). Crowell.
Cold Wind from Orion. Scott Asnin. 288p. (Orig.). 1980. pap. 2.25 (ISBN 0-345-28498-4). Ballantine.
Cold Wind River. Kent Nelson. LC 80-20013. 233p. 1981. 8.95 (ISBN 0-396-07835-4). Dodd.
Coldest Place on Earth. Robert B. Thomson. (Illus.). 1969. 7.50 o.p. Intl Pubns Serv.
Coldest Winter in Peking: A Novel from Inside China. Chih-Yen Hsia. LC 77-26522. (Illus.). 1978. 10.00 (ISBN 0-385-13402-9). Doubleday.
Coldstone. Patricia Wentworth. LC 30-231882. 1930. J. B. Lippincott Company.
Cole of Spyglass Mountain. Arthur Preston Hankins. LC 23-5621. 1928. Dodd, Mead and Company.
Cole of the Broken Spur. Lewis C Merrill. LC 43-6903. 1943. Phoenix Press.
Colegialas Libertinas. Jose Pantoja. (Pimienta Collection Ser). (Span.). 1977. pap. 1.00 (ISBN 0-88473-260-6). Fiesta Pub.
Colette. Elaine Marks. LC 60-9694. 1960. Rutgers University Press.
Colfax Book-Plate: A Mystery Story. Agnes Miller. LC 26-15714. The Century Co.
Colin. Edward Frederic Benson. LC 23-12674. George H. Doran Company.
Colin Ii. Edward Frederic Benson. LC 25-16490. George H. Doran Company.
Colin Lowrie. Norah Robinson Lofts. LC 38-29023. 1939. A. A. Knopf.
Colin of the Ninth Concession: A Tale of Scottish Pioneer Life in Eastern Ontario. R. L Richardson. LC 74-169295. (Toronto reprint library of Canadian prose and poetry). 1973. (ISBN 0-8020-7526-6). University of Toronto Press.
Coliseum. Barney Cohen. 1975. (pbk.) 1.25. Dell.
Coll Doll, and Other Stories. Walter Macken. LC 70-239545. 1969. Gill & Macmillan.
Collaborator. S. L Stebel. LC 68-14536. 1968. Random House.
Collages. Anais Nin. LC 82-70308. 122p. 1964. 3.95 (ISBN 0-8040-0045-X). Swallow.
Collages, a Novel. Anais Nin. LC 64-25338. 1964. Swallow Press.
Collapse of Homo Sapiens. Peter Anderson Graham. LC 23-12223. 1923. G. P. Putnam's Sons.
Collapsible Man. Laurie Clancy, pseud. LC 77-76630. 1977. 7.95 (ISBN 0-312-14725-2). St. Martin's Press.
Collapsing Cosmoses. Howard Phillips Lovecraft & Robert H. Barlow. (F & SF Fragments Ser.: No. 1). 1977. pap. 1.00 o.p. Necronomicon.
Collapsing Cosmoses. Howard Phillips Lovecraft & Robert H. Barlow. (F & SF Fragments Ser.: No. 1). 1977. pap. 1.00 o.p. Necronomicon.
Collect. Lois Bull. LC 31-33897. The Macaulay Company.
Collected Fantasies. Avram Davidson. 1982. pap. 2.50. Berkley Pub.
Collected Fiction of Isaac Asimov. Isaac Asimov. LC 78-112842. (v. 1) 12.95 (ISBN 0-385-13269-7). Doubleday.
Collected Ghost Stories. Mary Eleanor Wilkins Freeman. LC 73-88393. 1974. 6.00. Arkham House.
Collected Ghost Stories. Montague R. James. 1931. 5.95 o.p. St Martin.
Collected Ghost Stories. Ed. by Oliver Onions. 6.50 o.p. (ISBN 0-8446-0222-1). Peter Smith.
Collected Ghost Stories. Mary E. Wilkins-Freeman. 1974. 7.95 (ISBN 0-87054-065-3). Arkham.
Collected Ghost Stories of Mrs. J. H. Riddell. Charlotte Eliza Lawson Cowan Riddell. LC 76-10907. (Illus.). 5.00 (ISBN 0-486-23430-4). Dover Publications.
Collected Ghost Stories of Oliver Onions. Oliver Onions. LC 75-172183. 1971. 4.00 (ISBN 0-486-20726-9). Dover Publications.
Collected Novels. H. Babcock. 1970. 6.95 o.p. (ISBN 0-03-081838-9). HR&W.
Collected Novels: Blue Voyage, Great Circle, King Coffin, a Heart for the Gods of Mexico and Conversation. Introd. by R. P. Blackmur. Conrad Potter Aiken. LC 63-20431. 1964. Holt, Rinehart and Winston.
Collected Novels of Conrad Aiken. Conrad Potter Aiken. 1964. 7.95 o.p. (ISBN 0-03-042985-4). HR&W.
Collected Poems of Babette Deutsch. Babette Deutsch. LC 68-22508. (Illus.). 1969. 5.95 o.p. Doubleday.
Collected Prose. Dylan Thomas. Incl. Adventures in the Skin Trade; Portrait of the Artist As a Young Dog; Quite Early One Morning. 1969. pap. 4.90 slipcased o.p. New Directions.
Collected Prose of Elinor Wylie. Elinor Hoyt Wylie. LC 33-27444. 1933. A. A. Knopf.
Collected Short Fiction, 1892-1912. rev. ed. Willa Sibert Cather. LC 73-126046. 1970. 9.50 (ISBN 0-8032-0770-0). University of Nebraska Press.
Collected Short Prose. Boris Leonidovich Pasternak & Christopher J Barnes. LC 73-189901. 1977. 12.95 (ISBN 0-275-50390-9). Praeger.
Collected Short Prose of James Agee. James Agee. Ed. by Robert Fitzgerald. LC 68-29549. 1968. 5.95. Houghton Mifflin.
Collected Short Stories. Conrad Potter Aiken. LC 60-10537. 1960. World Pub. Co.
Collected Short Stories. Sinai C. Hamada. 1975. wrps. 7.50x o.p. Cellar.
Collected Short Stories. Aldous Leonard Huxley. LC 57-11799. Harper.
Collected Short Stories. Carson McCullers. Bd. with Ballad of the Sad Cafe. 9.95 (ISBN 0-395-07982-9). HM.
Collected Short Stories. Anthony Trollope. LC 80-1909. (Trollope, Anthony, 1815-1882. Selections. 1981). 1981. 30.00 (ISBN 0-405-14117-3). Arno Press.
Collected Short Stories, Vol. 1. William Somerset Maugham. 1977. pap. 3.95 (ISBN 0-14-001871-9). Penguin.
Collected Short Stories, Vol. 2. William Somerset Maugham. 1977. pap. 3.95 (ISBN 0-14-001872-7). Penguin.
Collected Short Stories, Vol. 4. William Somerset Maugham. 1978. pap. 2.95 (ISBN 0-14-001874-3). Penguin.
Collected Short Stories of Conrad Aiken. Conrad Potter Aiken. LC 81-84243. 1982. 10.95 (ISBN 0-8052-0690-6). Schocken Books.
Collected Short Stories of Edith Wharton. Edith Newbold Jones Wharton. Ed. by Richard Warrington Baldwin Lewis. LC 67-24055. 1968. 12.50. Scribner.
Collected Short Stories of Julia Peterkin. Julia Mood Peterkin. LC 70-120576. 1970. 10.00 (ISBN 0-87249-184-6). University of South Carolina Press.
Collected Short Stories of Mary Johnston. Mary Johnston & Annie Woodbridge. LC 80-54204. (Illus.). 1982. 25.00 (ISBN 0-87875-204-8). Whitston Pub.
Collected Short Stories of Mary Johnston. Ed. by Annie Woodbridge & Hensley C. Woodbridge. LC 80-54204. 1982. 25.00x (ISBN 0-87875-204-8). Whitston Pub.
Collected Short Stories of Ring Lardner. Ring Wilmer Lardner. LC 41-51967. (Half-title: The Modern library of the world's best books 211). 1941. The Modern Library.
Collected Short Tales. Lino Leitao. 3.95 o.p. Carlton.
Collected Stories. Isaak Emmanuilovich Babel. Ed. & tr. by Walter Morison. pap. 7.95 (ISBN 0-452-00594-9, F594, Mer). NAL.
Collected Stories. J. Busch. 3.00 o.p. Carlton.
Collected Stories. William Faulkner. LC 50-9187. 1950. Random House.
Collected Stories. Ellen Anderson Gholson Glasgow. Ed. by Richard Kilburn Meeker. LC 63-13240. 1963. Louisiana State University Press.
Collected Stories. Graham Greene. 1973. 16.95 (ISBN 0-670-22911-3). Viking Pr.
Collected Stories. Mary Lavin. LC 73-132790. 1971. 8.95 (ISBN 0-395-12099-3). Houghton Mifflin.
Collected Stories. Amado Muro. 1979. 10.00 (ISBN 0-914476-82-3); pap. 5.00 (ISBN 0-914476-83-1). Thorp Springs.
Collected Stories. Fitz James O'Brien. LC 72-3371. (Short story index reprint series). 1972. (ISBN 0-8369-4157-8). Books for Libraries Press.
Collected Stories. Fitz James O'Brien. Ed. by O'Brien, Edward Joseph Harrington. LC 25-20972. (The American library. V. 17). 1925. A. & C. Boni.
Collected Stories. Fitz James O'Brien & O'Brien, Edward Joseph Harrington, 1890- Ed. LC 25-20972. (The American library. V. 17). 1925. A. & C. Boni.
Collected Stories. Frank O'Connor, pseud. LC 81-1253. 1981. 17.50 (ISBN 0-394-51602-8). Knopf.
Collected Stories. Frank O'Connor, pseud. LC 82-40039. 1982. 8.95 (ISBN 0-394-75296-1). Vintage Books.
Collected Stories. Katherine Anne Porter. LC 65-14706. 1965. Harcourt, Brace & World.
Collected Stories. Victor Sawdon Pritchett. LC 81-48279. 20.00 (ISBN 0-394-52417-9). Random House.
Collected Stories. Osbert Sitwell. LC 53-11861. 1953. Harper.
Collected Stories. Jean Stafford. 463p. 1969. 17.50 (ISBN 0-374-12632-1); pap. 8.95 (ISBN 0-374-51540-9). FS&G.
Collected Stories. Peter Taylor. 544p. 1969. 17.50 (ISBN 0-374-12548-1); pap. 9.95 (ISBN 0-374-51542-5). FS&G.
Collected Stories. Mark Van Doren. LC 62-15221. Hill and Wang.
Collected Stories: Edited and Translated by Walter Morison. With an Introd. by Lionel Trilling. Isaak Emmanuilovich Babel. LC 55-7842. 1955. Criterion Books.
Collected Stories. Edited and Translated by Walter Morison. With an Introd. by Lionel Trilling. Isaak Emmanuilovich Babel. LC 60-6743. (Meridian fiction. MF3). 1960. Meridian Fiction.
Collected Stories, Including May We Borrow Your Husband? A Sense of Reality, Twenty-One Stories. Graham Greene. LC 73-2334. 1973. 10.00 (ISBN 0-670-22911-3). Viking Press.
Collected Stories. Introd. by Winfield Townley Scott. Jack Warner Schaefer. LC 66-22612. 1966. 6.00. Houghton.
Collected Stories of Amado Muro. Amado Muro. LC 78-18406. 8.00. (ISBN 0-914476-82-3) (ISBN 0-914476-83-1). Thorp Springs Press.
Collected Stories of Andre Maurois. Andre Maurois. LC 67-17359. 1967. Washington Square Press.
Collected Stories of Ben Hecht. Ben Hecht. LC 45-5017. 1945. Crown Publishers.
Collected Stories of Bertrand Russell. Ed. by Barry Feinberg. LC 72-90594. 1973. 9.95 o.p. (ISBN 0-671-21489-6). S&S.
Collected Stories of Bertrand Russell. Bertrand Russell Russell. LC 72-90594. (Illus.). 1973. 9.95 (ISBN 0-671-21489-6). Simon and Schuster.
Collected Stories of Betrand Russell. Betrand Russell. Ed. by Barry Feinberg. 1974. pap. 5.95 o.p. (ISBN 0-671-21673-2, Touchstone Bks). S&S.
Collected Stories of Caroline Gordon; with an Introd. by Robert Penn Warren. Caroline Gordon. LC 80-28675. 15.00 (ISBN 0-374-12630-5). Farrar, Straus, Giroux.
Collected Stories of Dorothy Parker. Dorothy Rothschild Parker. LC 42-86281. (Half-title: The Modern library of the world's best books). 1942. The Modern Library.
Collected Stories of Elizabeth Bowen. Elizabeth Bowen. LC 80-8729. (Illus.). 1981. 20.00 (ISBN 0-394-51666-4). Knopf.
Collected Stories of Elizabeth Bowen. Elizabeth Bowen. LC 81-52874. (Illus.). 1982. 8.95 (ISBN 0-394-75296-1). Vintage Books.
Collected Stories of Eudora Welty. Eudora Welty. LC 80-15160. 1980. 14.95 (ISBN 0-15-118994-3). Harcourt Brace Jovanovich.
Collected Stories of Eudora Welty. Eudora Welty. LC 80-7947. 14.95 (ISBN 0-15-118994-3). Harcourt Brace Jovanovich.
Collected Stories of Hortense Calisher. Hortense Calisher. LC 75-11148. 15.00 (ISBN 0-87795-115-2). Arbor House Pub. Co.
Collected Stories of Hortense Calisher. Hortense Calisher. (Illus.). 1977. 6.95 (ISBN 0-87795-166-7). Arbor House Pub. Co.
Collected Stories of Jean Stafford. Jean Stafford. LC 68-29471. 1969. 10.00. Farrar, Straus, and Giroux.
Collected Stories of Katherine Anne Porter. a limited ed. Katherine Anne Porter. LC 77-367313. (Illus.). 1976. Franklin Library.
Collected Stories of Katherine Anne Porter. Katherine Anne Porter. LC 79-10398. (Harvest/HBJ book). 1979. 5.95 (ISBN 0-15-618876-7). Harcourt Brace Jovanovich.
Collected Stories of L. P. Hartley. Leslie Poles Hartley. LC 72-92713. 1969. 7.95 o.p. (ISBN 0-8180-0606-4). Horizon.
Collected Stories of O. Henry. William Sydney Porter. Ed. by Paul J. Horowitz. LC 79-20162. (Illus.). 1979. 6.98 (ISBN 0-517-29455-9). Avenel Books: Distributed by Crown Publishers.
Collected Stories of Paul Bowles. Paul Frederic Bowles. 419p. 1981. 14.00 (ISBN 0-87685-397-1); pap. 9.00 (ISBN 0-87685-396-3). Black Sparrow.
Collected Stories of Peter Taylor. Peter Hillsman Taylor. LC 71-87215. 1969. 10.00. Farrar, Straus and Giroux.
Collected Stories of William Faulkner. William Faulkner. LC 76-40938. 1977. 5.95 (ISBN 0-394-72257-4). Vintage Books.
Collected Stories of William Goyen. William Goyen. LC 75-6157. 1975. 7.95 (ISBN 0-385-00734-5). Doubleday.
Collected Stories. 1st Amer. Ed. Muriel Spark. LC 68-21519. 1968. v. 1, 6.95. Knopf.
Collected Stories, 1893-1897. Hubert Montague Crackanthorpe. LC 74-75379. (Illus.). 1969. Scholars' Facsimiles & Reprints.
Collected Tales... Barry Eric Odell Pain. LC 16-8699. 1916. F. A. Stokes Company.
Collected Tales and Stories. Mary Wollstonecraft Godwin Shelley. LC 75-36931. (Illus.). 15.00 (ISBN 0-8018-1706-4). Johns Hopkins University Press.
Collected Tales: Chosen, and with an Introd. Walter John De La Mare. LC 50-5738. 1950. Knopf.
Collected Tales of A. E. Coppard. Alfred Edgar Coppard. LC 75-46260. (Supernatural and Occult Fiction). 1976. 30.00 (ISBN 0-405-08119-7). Arno Press.
Collected Tales of A. E. Coppard. Alfred Edgar Coppard. LC 48-530219. 1948. A. A. Knopf.
Collected Tales of E. M. Forster. Edward Morgan Forster. LC 68-2040. (Modern library of the world's best books ML385). 1968. Modern Library.
Collected Tales of E. M. Forster. Edward Morgan Forster. LC 47-4482. 1947. A. A. Knopf.
Collected Tales of Pierre Louys. Pierre Louys. LC 70-160941. (Short story index reprint series). (Illus.). 1971. (ISBN 0-8369-3920-4). Books for Libraries Press.
Collected Tales of Pierre Louys. Pierre Louys. LC 30-1692. 1930. Argus Books.
Collected Works, 19 vols. George W. Cable. Incl. Old Creole Days. 1879. Repr. 19.00 (ISBN 0-403-03056-0); Grandissimes. 1880. Repr. 18.00 (ISBN 0-403-02979-1); Madame Delphine. 1881. Repr. 13.00 (ISBN 0-403-02287-8); Creoles of Louisiana. 1884. Repr. 23.00 (ISBN 0-403-04550-9); Doctor Sevier. 1885. Repr. 19.00 (ISBN 0-403-02953-8); Silent South. 1885. Repr. 15.00 (ISBN 0-403-04551-7); Bonaventure. 1888. Repr. 15.00 (ISBN 0-403-02974-0); Strange True Stories of Louisiana. 1889. Repr. 18.00 (ISBN 0-403-02952-X); Negro Question. 1890. Repr. 18.00 (ISBN 0-403-04553-3); John March, Southerner. 1894. Repr. 21.00 (ISBN 0-403-04554-1); Strong Hearts. 1899. Repr. 16.00 (ISBN 0-403-02990-2); Cavalier. 1901. Repr. 16.00 (ISBN 0-403-02956-2); Bylow Hill. 1902. Repr. 18.00 (ISBN 0-403-02297-5); Kinkaid's Battery. 1908. Repr. 31.00 (ISBN 0-403-04555-X); Posson Jone & Pere Raphael. 1909. Repr. 15.00 (ISBN 0-403-02950-3); Gideon's Band: A Tale of the Mississippi. 1914. Repr. 36.00 (ISBN 0-403-02959-7); Amateur Garden. 1914. Repr. 29.00; Flower of the Chapdelaines. 1918. Repr. 23.00 (ISBN 0-403-02991-0); Lovers of Louisiana. 1918. Repr. 22.00 (ISBN 0-403-04557-6). Set. 695.00. Somerset Pub.
Collected Works, 19 vols. special limited ed. Ivy Compton-Burnett. Incl. Vol. 1. Pastors & Masters. 96p. 1925; Vol. 2. Brothers & Sisters. 231p. 1929; Vol. 3. Men & Wives. 231p. 1931; Vol. 4. More Women Than Men. 231p. 1933; Vol. 5. A House & Its Heads. 276p. 1935; Vol. 6. Daughters & Sons. 288p. 1937; Vol. 7. A Family & a Fortune. 292p. 1939; Vol. 8. Parents & Children. 318p. 1941; Vol. 9. Elders & Betters. 304p. 1944; Vol. 10. Manservant & Maidservant. 301p. 1947; Vol. 11. Two Worlds & Their Ways. 310p. 1949; Vol. 12. Darkness & Day. 254p. 1951; Vol. 13. The Present & the Past. 192p. 1953; Vol. 14. Mother & Son. 208p. 1955; Vol. 15. A Father & His Fate. 214p. 1957; Vol. 16. A Heritage & Its History. 190p. 1959; Vol. 17. The Mighty & Their Fall. 184p. 1961; Vol. 18. A God & His Gifts. 173p. 1963; Vol. 19. The Last and the First. 139p. 1971. 1972. boxed set 120.00x o.p. (ISBN 0-575-01570-5). Intl Pubns Serv.
Collected Works, 14 vols. Harold Frederic. Incl. Seth's Brother's Wife. 1887. Repr. 13.00; Lawton Girl. 1890. Repr. 40.00; In the Valley. 1890. Repr. 36.00; Young Emperor: William the Second of Germany. 1891. Repr. 19.00; Return of O'Mahony. 1892. Repr. 27.00; New Exodus. 1892. Repr. 25.00; Copperhead. 1893. Repr. 20.00; Marsena & Other Stories of the Wartime. 1894. Repr. 18.00; Mrs. Albert Grundy. 1896. Repr. 21.00; Damnation of Theron Ware. 1896. Repr. 41.00; March Hares. 1896. Repr. 23.00; Deserter & Other Stories. 1898. Repr. 33.00; Gloria Mundi. 1898. Repr. 47.00; Market Place. 1899. Repr. 33.00. Set. 300.00. Somerset Pub.
Collected Works. Freeman-Ishill, Rose. LC 65-50081. 1962. Oriole Press.

Collected Works, 15 vols. Henry Blake Fuller. Incl. Chevalier of Pensieri-Vani. 1890. Repr. 18.00 o.p. (ISBN 0-403-04583-5); Chatelaine of La Trinite. 1892. Repr. 18.00 o.p. (ISBN 0-403-04584-3); Cliff Dwellers. 1893. Repr. 30.00 o.p. (ISBN 0-403-03199-0); With the Procession. 1895. Repr. 27.00 o.p. (ISBN 0-403-04585-1); Puppet Booth. 1896. Repr. 18.00 o.p. (ISBN 0-403-04586-X); From the Other Side. 1898. Repr. 19.00 o.p. (ISBN 0-403-04587-8); New Flag. 1899. Repr. 18.00 o.p. (ISBN 0-403-04588-6); Last Refuge. 1900. Repr. 23.00 o.p. (ISBN 0-403-04589-4); Under the Skylights. 1901. Repr. 20.00 o.p. (ISBN 0-403-04590-8); Waldo Trench. 1908. Repr. 28.00 o.p. (ISBN 0-403-04591-6); Lines Long & Short. 1917. Repr. 18.00 o.p. (ISBN 0-403-04592-4); On the Stairs. 1918. Repr. 22.00 o.p. (ISBN 0-403-04593-2); Bertram Cope's Year. 1919. Repr. 25.00 o.p. (ISBN 0-403-04594-0); Gardens of the World. 1929. Repr. 19.00 o.p. (ISBN 0-403-02964-3); Not on the Screen. 1930. Repr. 23.00 o.p. (ISBN 0-403-04595-9). Set. 290.00 o.p. (ISBN 0-403-03458-2). Somerset Pub.

Collected Works. Hamlin Garland. Incl. Boy Life on the Prairie. 1899. Repr. 35.00 (ISBN 0-403-04596-7); Her Mountain Lover. 1901. Repr. 32.00 (ISBN 0-403-04597-5); Captain of the Grayhorse Troop. 1902. Repr. 34.00 (ISBN 0-403-02966-X); Hesper. 1903. Repr. 36.00 (ISBN 0-403-02951-1); Light of the Star. 1904. Repr. 23.00 (ISBN 0-403-02980-5); Tyranny of the Dark. 1905. Repr. 29.00 (ISBN 0-403-02283-5); With's Gold. 1906. Repr. 21.00; Long Trail. 1907. Repr. 23.00; Money Magic. 1907. Repr. 31.00 (ISBN 0-403-02988-0); Shadow World. 1908. Repr. 24.00 (ISBN 0-403-04600-9); Moccasin Ranch. 1909. Repr. 18.00 (ISBN 0-403-02282-7); Cavanaugh, Forest Ranger. 1910. Repr. 25.00 (ISBN 0-403-02985-6); Other Main Travelled Roads. 1910. Repr. 29.00 (ISBN 0-403-02975-9); Victor Ollnee's Disciple. 1911. Repr. 25.00 (ISBN 0-403-02970-8); Forester's Daughter. 1914. Repr. 24.00 (ISBN 0-403-04601-7). Somerset Pub.

Collected Works. Hamlin Garland. Incl. They of the High Trails. 1916. Repr. 31.00 (ISBN 0-403-04614-9); Son of the Middle Border. 1917. Repr. 41.00 (ISBN 0-403-02998-8); Daughter of the Middle Border. 1921. Repr. 34.00 (ISBN 0-403-02968-6); Pioneer Mother. 1922. Repr. 18.00 (ISBN 0-403-04615-7); Book of the American Indian. 1923. Repr. 23.00 (ISBN 0-403-04616-5); Trail Markers of the Middle Border. 1926. Repr. 34.00 (ISBN 0-403-00984-7); Westward March of American Settlement. 1927. Repr. 18.00 (ISBN 0-403-04617-3); Back Trailers from the Middle Border. 1928. Repr. 31.00 (ISBN 0-403-02986-4); Roadside Meetings. 1930. Repr. 39.00 (ISBN 0-403-02982-1); Companions of the Trail. 1931. Repr. 44.00 (ISBN 0-403-02978-3); My Friendly Contemporaries. 1932. Repr. 45.00 (ISBN 0-403-00982-0); Afternoon Neighbors. 1934. Repr. 49.00 (ISBN 0-403-04618-1); Iowa, O Iowa. Repr. 18.00 (ISBN 0-403-04619-X); Forty Years of Psychic Research. 1936. Repr. 32.00 (ISBN 0-403-04620-3); Mystery of the Buried Crosses. 1939. Repr. 28.00 (ISBN 0-403-04621-1). Somerset Pub.

Collected Works, 25 vols. Robert Herrick. Incl. Man Who Wins. 1897. Repr. 18.00 (ISBN 0-403-04625-4); Literary Love Letters & Other Stories. 1897. Repr. 20.00 (ISBN 0-403-04626-2); Gospel of Freedom. 1898. Repr. 23.00 (ISBN 0-403-04627-0); Love's Dilemmas. 1898. Repr. 18.00 (ISBN 0-403-04628-9); Web of Life. 1900. Repr. 29.00 (ISBN 0-403-04629-7); Real World. 1901. Repr. 29.00 (ISBN 0-403-04630-0); Their Child. 1903. Repr. 18.00 (ISBN 0-403-04631-9); Common Lot. 1904. Repr. 35.00 (ISBN 0-403-04632-7); Memoirs of an American Citizen. 1905. Repr. 29.00 (ISBN 0-403-02969-4); The Master of the Inn. 1908. Repr. 18.00 (ISBN 0-403-03055-2); Together. 1908. Repr. 48.00 (ISBN 0-403-03198-2); Life for a Life. 1910. Repr. 35.00 (ISBN 0-403-03197-4); Healer. 1911. Repr. 37.00 (ISBN 0-403-03193-1); His Great Adventure. 1913. Repr. 33.00 (ISBN 0-403-04633-5); One Woman's Life. 1913. Repr. 33.00 (ISBN 0-403-04634-3); Clark's Field. 1914. Repr. 39.00 (ISBN 0-403-04635-1); Conscript's Mother. 1916. Repr. 18.00 (ISBN 0-403-04636-X); World Decision. 1916. Repr. 29.00 (ISBN 0-403-03074-9); Homely Lilla. 1923. Repr. 23.00 (ISBN 0-403-03050-1); Waste. 1924. Repr. 36.00; Wanderings. 1925. Repr. 26.00 (ISBN 0-403-04637-8); Chimes. 1926. Repr. 25.00 (ISBN 0-403-03194-X); Little Black Dog. 1931. Repr. 18.00 (ISBN 0-403-04638-6); End of Desire. 1932. Repr. 30.00 (ISBN 0-403-03195-8); Sometime. 1933. Repr. 28.00. Set. 620.00 (ISBN 0-403-03460-4). Somerset Pub.

Collected Works, 15 vols. Edgar Watson Howe. Incl. Story of a Country Town. 1884. Repr. 34.00 (ISBN 0-403-03053-6); Mystery of the Locks. 1885. Repr. 24.00 (ISBN 0-403-04641-6); Moonlight Boy. 1886. Repr. 27.00 (ISBN 0-403-04642-4); Man Story. 1889. Repr. 31.00 (ISBN 0-403-02961-9); Ante-Mortem Statement. 1891. Repr. 18.00 (ISBN 0-403-04643-2); Daily Notes on a Trip Around the World. 1907. Repr. 37.00 (ISBN 0-403-02284-3); Trip to the West Indies. 1910. Repr. 29.00 (ISBN 0-403-04644-0); Country Town Sayings. 1911. Repr. 24.00; Travel Letters from New Zealand, Australia & Africa. 1913. Repr. 38.00 (ISBN 0-403-04646-7); Success Easier Than Failure. 1917. Repr. 18.00 (ISBN 0-403-04647-5); Blessing of Business. 1918. Repr. 18.00 (ISBN 0-403-04648-3); Ventures in Common Sense. 1919. Repr. 22.00 (ISBN 0-403-04649-1); Anthology of Another Town. 1920. Repr. 18.00 (ISBN 0-403-03192-3); Plain People. 1929. Repr. 26.00 (ISBN 0-403-02963-5); Indignations of E.W. Howe. 1933. Repr. 18.00 (ISBN 0-403-04624-6). Set. 340.00 (ISBN 0-403-03460-4). Somerset Pub.

Collected Works, 14 vols. Sarah Orne Jewett. Incl. Deephaven. 1877. Repr. 20.00 (ISBN 0-403-03190-7); Old Friends & New. 1879. Repr. 13.00 (ISBN 0-403-03182-6); Country by-Ways. 1881. Repr. 13.00 (ISBN 0-403-03183-4); Mate of the Daylight & Friends Ashore. 1884. Repr. 20.00 (ISBN 0-403-03185-0); Country Doctor. 1884. Repr. 15.00 (ISBN 0-403-03191-5); Marsh Island. 1885. Repr. 24.00 (ISBN 0-403-03186-9); White Heron & Other Stories. 1886. Repr. 16.00 (ISBN 0-403-03187-7); King of Folly Island & Other People. 1888. Repr. 20.00 (ISBN 0-403-03188-5); Strangers & Wayfarers. 1890. Repr. 14.00 (ISBN 0-403-03184-2); Native of Winby & Other Tales. 1893. Repr. 14.00 (ISBN 0-403-03189-3); Life of Nancy. 1895. Repr. 14.00 (ISBN 0-403-03181-8); Country of the Pointed Firs. 1896. Repr. 20.00 (ISBN 0-403-03174-5); Queen's Twin & Other Stories. 1899. Repr. 14.00 (ISBN 0-403-03180-X); Tory Lover. 1901. Repr. 26.00 (ISBN 0-403-02994-5). Set. 395.00 (ISBN 0-403-03462-0). Somerset Pub.

Collected Works, 3 vols. Joseph Kirkland. Incl. Zury, the Meanest Man in Spring County. 1887. Repr; McVeys. 1888. Repr; Captain of Company K. 1890. Repr. 36.00 ea.; Set. 95.00. Somerset Pub.

Collected Works. Andrei Platonovich Platonov. LC 78-110678. 1978. (ISBN 0-88233-134-5). Ardis.

Collected Works. Introd. by Truman Capote. 1st Amer. Print. Jane Auer Bowles. LC 66-225924. 1966. 6.95. Farrar.

Collected Works of Billy the Kid. Michael Ondaatje. LC 74-10727. (Redtail Reprint Ser). (Illus.). 1978. pap. 3.50 (ISBN 0-914728-26-1). Wingbow Pr.

Collected Works of David Graham Phillips, 26 Vols. David Graham Phillips. (American Authors Ser). 1970. lib. bdg. 484.95 o.s.i. (ISBN 0-512-00542-7). Garrett Pr.

Collected Works of Karl May. Karl Friedrich May. LC 77-12604. Seabury Press.

Collected Works of Mrs. Peter Willoughby. Mary Elizabeth Plummer. LC 44-179816. 1944. Little, Brown and Company.

Collected Works of Nathanael West. Nathanael West. LC 76-350764. 1975. 0.65 (ISBN 0-14-003907-4). Penguin.

Collected Works of Pierre Louys... Pierre Louys. LC 33-1083. (The black and gold library). Liveright, Inc.

Collected Works of Rudyard Kipling... Rudyard Kipling. LC 42-8935. 1941. Doubleday, Doran & Company, Inc.

Collected Writings. D. R. Scott. Ed. by Kvam & Bauer. text ed. 3.95 o.p. (ISBN 0-87543-040-6). Lucas.

Collected Writings of Ambrose Bierce. Ambrose Gwinnett Bierce. Ed. by Clifton Fadiman. LC 72-13283. (Biography index reprint series). 1973. (ISBN 0-8369-8141-3). Books for Libraries Press.

Collection Litteraire, 6 vols. A. Lagarde & L. Michard. Incl. Vol. 1. Moyen Age. 11.75; Vol. 2. Seizieme Siecle. 11.75; Vol. 3. Dix-Septieme Siecle. 13.95; Vol. 4. Dix-Huitieme Siecle. 13.95; Vol. 5. Dix-Neuvieme Siecle. 16.25; Vol. 6. Vingtieme Siecle. 17.50. (Fr.). Schoenhof.

Collection Litteraire Lagarde & Michard: Les Grand Auteurs Francais Du Programme, 6 Vols. 37.00 o.p. French & Eur.

Collection of American Short Stories. Ed. by Irene Pettit McKeehan. LC 28-212191. (western series of English and American classics). 1928. Harlow Publishing Company.

Collection of French Stories: Ed. by Edmond A. Meras, Fernand Vial. Ed. by Edmond Albert Meras & Fernand Vial. LC 61-6275. 1966. pap., 2.50. Harper.

Collection of Hearts: Short Stories. William Blannie Hight. LC 56-43537. 1956.

Collection of Short-Stories. Ed. by Lemuel Arthur Pittenger. LC 13-24785. (Macmillan's pocket American and English classics). 1913. The Macmillan Company.

Collection of Short-Stories. Ed. by Lemuel Arthur Pittenger. LC 41-34147. (Macmillan's pocket American and English classics). 1919. The Macmillan Company.

Collection of Short Stories. Ursula. 1982. 6.95 (ISBN 0-533-05201-7). Vantage.

Collection of Strangers. Dolores Birk Hitchens. LC 75-81657. 1969. 5.95. Putnam.

Collection of Tales from Uji. D. E. Mills. LC 72-114604. (Cambridge Oriental Publications: No. 15). (Illus.). 1970. 49.50 (ISBN 0-521-07754-0). Cambridge U Pr.

Collection of Unusual Tales. Edward A. Altman. 2.75 o.p. Carlton.

Collective Works of Cigar-Box Nellie & Melody Artside. Karen Korell & Judy Levy. (Illus.). 1977. pap. text ed. 3.00. Oil Bks.

Collector. John Fowles. LC 63-13451. 1963. Little, Brown.

Collectors: Being Cases Mostly Under the Tenth Commandment. Frank Jewett Mather. LC 36-23. H. Holt and Company.

Collector's Choice. Peter Marks, pseud. LC 79-37064. 1972. 5.95 (ISBN 0-394-47426-0). Random House.

Collectors' Item. 1st Ed. Amber Dean. LC 53-5044. 1953. Published for the Crime Club by Doubleday.

Colleen. Michael Mannion. 1978. 1.75 (ISBN 0-505-51274-2). Tower Pubns.

Colleen Bawn: Or, The Collegians. A Tale of Garryowne. Gerald Griffin. (Seaside library. v. 47, no. 968). 1881. G. Muro.

College Book of Modern Fiction: Edited by Walter B. Rideout and James K. Robinson. Ed. by Walter Bates Rideout & James K. Robinson. LC 61-10906. 1961. Row, Peterson.

College-Bred Ruth: A Romance of the Living. Elton Burroughs. 1895. New York Recorder Linotype Print.

College Chaps. John Weymouth. LC 7-190394. 1902. The Mutual Book Company.

College Days. Stella Parker Peterson. LC 36-10827. Review and Herald Pub. Assn.

College Days in Earthquake County. Herbert Wilner & Leo Litwak. 1972. 7.95 o.p. (ISBN 0-394-47228-4). Random.

College Days: Or, Harry's Career at Yale. John Seymour Wood. LC 8-37793. 1894. The Outing Company, Limited.

College Girls. Abbe Carter Goodloe. LC 4-23575. 1895. C. Scribner's Sons.

College Greeks: The Saga of One Fraternity Year in Nine Episodes and an Aftermath, the Tenth. Frank Fletcher Catron. LC 32-16966. The Riverview Press.

College Housemother. Helen Reich. LC 68-21256. 1968. pap. text ed. 3.50x (ISBN 0-8134-0157-7, 157). Interstate.

College Love: A Throbbing Romance of Love and Adventure Based on the Motion Picture Story. Leonard Fields. Jacobean Publishing Company, Inc.

College Nurse. Florence Stonebraker. LC 65-7993. 1965. Arcadia House.

College of One. Sheilah Graham. LC 67-10218. (Illus.). 1967. Viking Press.

College Readings in the Modern Short Story: Edited with a Review of the Technique of the Modern Short Story. Ed. by George Rupert MacMinn. Eagleson, Harvey, Joint Ed. LC 31-15409. Ginn and Company.

College Short Story Reader. Ed. by Harry Worthington Hastings. LC 48-2409. 1948. Odyssey Press.

College Square: A Novel. Margaret Matthews. LC 38-27218. 1938. C. Scribner's Sons.

College Widow: A Novel. Frank Howard Howe. LC 7-66269. (On cover: Belford American novel series, no. 4). 1890. Belford, Clarke and Company.

College Widow: An Improbable Story. Charles W Seymour. LC 8-6878. 1881. G. W. Carleton & Co.; Etc., Etc.

College Years. Ralph Delahaye Paine. 1909. 1.50. C. Scribner's Sons.

College Years. Ralph Delahaye Paine. LC 32-7132. 1931. C. Scribner's Sons.

Collegians... Gerald Griffin. LC 6-45423. 1829. Printed by J. & J. Harper.

Collegians. Gerald Griffin. LC 78-12000. (Ireland, from the Act of Union, 1800, to the Death of Parnell, 1891). 1979. 42.00 (ISBN 0-8240-3477-5). Garland Pub.

Collegians. A Tale of Garryowen. Gerald Griffin. LC 7-3514. 1857. G. Routledge & Co.

Collegians: A Tale of Garryowen. Gerald Griffin & Gibbons, James, Cardinal. LC 98-877. (Half-title: The world's great books... Aldine ed.). 1898. D. Appleton and Company.

Collegians: Or The Colleen Bawn: a Tale of Garryowen. Gerald Griffin. LC 79-19267. (Series: Irish Heritage Series (Wilmington, Del.). (Irish heritage series). 1980. 42.00 (ISBN 0-934204-01-2). M. P. Browne.

Collegians: Or, The Colleen Bawn, a Tale of Garryowen. Gerald Griffin. LC 6-11551. (Half-title: The English Comedie humaine. 2d series). 1906. The Century Co.

Collier's Best: A Selection of Short Stories from the Magazine with an Introd. and Notes by Knox Burger. 1st Ed. Collier's, The National Weekly. Ed. by Knox Burger. LC 51-10596. 1951. Harper.

Colliers Row. Jan Webster. LC 77-3961. 8.95 (ISBN 0-397-01228-4). Lippincott.

Colliery Jim: The Autobiography of a Mine Mule. Nora Jane I. E. Elnora Jane Finch. LC 4-22854. A. Flanagan Company.

Collin. Stefan Heym. LC 80-19286. 12.95 (ISBN 0-8184-0300-4). L. Stuart.

Colline see Oeuvres Romanesques.

Colline: Roman. Jean Giono. (Coll. Soleil). 1960. 11.50. French and Eur.

Collision. Spencer Dunmore. LC 74-17488. 1975. 7.95 (ISBN 0-688-02886-1). W. Morrow.

Collision. James Gordon. LC 47-882. 1917. Farrar, Straus and Company.

Collision! James Broom Lynne. LC 72-96247. 1973. 6.95 (ISBN 0-385-07926-5). Doubleday.

Collision. Jack Pulman. LC 78-11450. 1979. 9.95 (ISBN 0-689-10941-5). Atheneum.

Collision Ahead. Ronald Johnston. LC 65-11054. 1965. 4.50. Doubleday.

Collision Course. Barrington J. Bayley. (Science Fiction Ser.). (Orig.). 1973. pap. 0.95 o.p. (UQ1043). DAW Bks.

Collision Course. Robert Silverberg. 1977. 1.50. Ace Books.

Collision Course. E. C. Tubb. (Space - 1999). 159p. 1975. lib. bdg. 5.95 (ISBN 0-88411-674-3). Amereon Ltd.

Collision Course. E C Tubb. (Space: 1999,#4). (Illus.). 1976. (pbk.) 1.50. Pocket Books.

Collision: Short Stories. Grace A Lamacchia. LC 73-86312. (Illus.). 1974. Washington Irving Pub.

Collison Course. Robert Silverberg. 192p. 1982. pap. 2.25 (ISBN 0-441-11511-X). Ace Bks.

Collusion. Theodore D Irwin. LC 32-320199. 1932. W. Godwin, Inc.

Colomba. Prosper Merimee. Ed. by Fontaine, Joseph A. LC 12-28359. (Heath's modern language series). 1891. D. C. Heath and Co.

Colomba. Prosper Merimee. Ed. by Cameron, Arnold Guyot. LC 12-36672. 1894. H. Holt and Company Etc.

Colomba. Prosper Merimee. Ed. by Schinz, Albert. LC 3-880. (International modern language series). 1903. Ginn & Company.

Colomba. Prosper Merimee. Ed. by Williamson, Hiram Parker. LC 3-29812. 1903. American Book Company.

Colomba. rev. ed. Prosper Merimee. Ed. by Fontaine, Joseph A. LC 6-6925. (Heath's modern language series). 1906. D. Heath and Co.

Colomba. Prosper Merimee. Ed. by Barney, Winfield Supply. LC 16-16943. Allyn and Bacon.

Colomba. Prosper Merimee. Ed. by Lamb, William W. LC 17-12022. (Lake French series. General editor, C. Gauss). Scott, Foresman and Company.

Colomba. Prosper Merimee. Ed. by Francois, Victor Emmanuel. LC 19-6966. (Half-title: Macmillan French series). 1919. The Macmillan Company.

Colomba. Prosper Merimee. Ed. by Schinz, Albert. LC 20-5141. (International modern language series). Ginn and Company.

Colomba. Prosper Merimee. Ed. by Young, Charles Edmund. LC 22-11036. (Merrill's French texts). Charles E. Merrill Company.

Colomba. Prosper Merimee. Ed. by Fougeray, G. P. LC 24-25324. The Iroquois Publishing Company Inc.

Colomba. Prosper Merimee. Ed. by Ford, Harry Egerton & Hicks, Rivers Keith. LC 31-251793. (Direct reading in French, vol. ii). H. Holt and Company.

Colomba. Prosper Merimee. Tr. by Sherman, Rose. T. Y. Crowell & Company.

Colomba: And Carmen. Prosper Merimee. Tr. by Loyd, Mary Sophia (Hely-Hutchinson) LC 2-23742. (Half-title: A century of French romance. Parisian ed. vol. vi.). D. Appleton & Co.

Colombian Connection. Robert Silverman. 1977. pap. 1.50 (ISBN 0-532-15273-5). Woodhill.

Colombian Gold: A Novel of Power and Corruption. Jaime Manrique. LC 83-3978. 12.95 (ISBN 0-517-54649-3). C.N. Potter: Distributed by Crown Publishers.

Colombo. Prosper Merimee. Ed. by Hawkins, Richmond Laurin. LC 20-19660. H. Holt and Company.

Colonel. Laisdell Mitchell. LC 72-1512. (Black Heritage Library Collection). (Illus.). 1972. (ISBN 0-8369-9037-4). Books for Libraries Press.

Colonel: A Novel. Laisdell Mitchell. LC 7-31098. 1896. A. J. Rowlands.

Colonel and the Quaker. Francis Von Albede Cabeen. 1906. Goodman's Sons & Co.

Colonel Berry's Challenge: A Novel. George Ernest Miller. LC 15-23638. G. E. Miller.
Colonel Blessington. Pamela Frankau & Diana Raymond. LC 69-11674. 1969. 4.50. Delacorte Press.
Colonel Bob and a Double Love: A Story from the Civil Side Behind the Southern Lines. Charles William Buck. The Standard Press.
Colonel Brooks, Roman. Gerhard Henschel. LC 53-36549. 1953. Deutsche Hausbucherie.
Colonel Butler's Wolf. Anthony Price. LC 72-95132. 1973. 4.95 (ISBN 0-385-02646-3). Published for the Crime Club by Doubleday.
Colonel by Brevet: A Novel. St. George Rathborne. (On cover: Idle moments series, no. 15). 1892. The Price-McGill Company.
Colonel by Brevet. A Novel. St. George Rathborne. LC 8-5789. (On cover: Criterion series, no. 9). 1894. Street & Smith.
Colonel Carter of Cartersville. Francis Hopkinson Smith. LC 73-104566. (Illus.). 1970. Literature House.
Colonel Carter of Cartersville. Francis Hopkinson Smith. LC 3-26190. 1892. Houghton, Mifflin and Company.
Colonel Carter of Cartersville. Francis Hopkinson Smith. LC 7-39301. 1901. Houghton, Mifflin and Co.
Colonel Carter of Cartersville. Francis Hopkinson Smith. LC 20-156009. Houghton Mifflin Company.
Colonel Carter's Christmas. Francis Hopkinson Smith. LC 3-25210. 1903. C. Scribner's Sons.
Colonel Carter's Christmas & the Romance of an Old-Fashioned Gentleman. Francis Hopkinson Smith. (Illus.). 206p. 1981. pap. write for info. (ISBN 0-86649-033-7). Twentieth Century.
Colonel Crockett's Co-Operative Christmas. Rupert Hughes. 1906. G. W. Jacobs and Company.
Colonel De Surville. A Tale of the Empire--1810. Eugene Sue & Pooley, Thomas, Tr. LC 8-17682. J. Winchester.
Colonel Dunwoddie: Millionaire. William Mumford Baker. (On cover: Harper's library of American fiction, no. 5). 1878. Harper & Brothers.
Colonel Enderby's Wife. A Novel. Mary St. Leger Kingsley Harrison. (On cover: Seaside library. Pocket ed. no. 493). 1885. G. Munro.
Colonel Enderby's Wife: A Novel, by Lucas Malet Pseud. Mary St. Leger Kingsley Harrison. LC 56-51687. (On cover: Seaside library, Pocket ed. no.496). 1885. G. Munro.
Colonel from Wyoming. John Alexander Hugh Cameron. LC 7-31206. 1907. Christian Press Association Publishing Company.
Colonel Gore's Second Case. Alister McAllister. LC 26-6265. Harper & Brothers.
Colonel Grant's to-Morrow. Graham Seton Hutchison. LC 32-2660. Farrar & Rinehart, Incorporated.
Colonel Greatheart. Henry Christopher Bailey. 1908. The Bobbs-Merrill Company.
Colonel Hungerford's Daughter. Story of an American Girl. James Alonzo Adams. LC 5-42958. 1896. C. H. Kerr & Company.
Colonel Johnson of Johnson's Corners. Joanis Orlando Harris. LC 1-17660. C. A. Hewitt.
Colonel Julian: And Other Stories. 1st American Ed. Herbert Ernest Bates. LC 52-5505. 1952. Little, Brown.
Colonel Markesan: And Less Pleasant People, by August Derleth, Mark Schorer. August William Derleth & Mark Schorer. LC 66-8627. 1966. 5.00. Arkham.
Colonel Markesan & Others. August William Derleth & Mark Schorer. 1966. 5.00 o.p. (ISBN 0-87054-045-9). Arkham.
Colonel Markeson & Less Pleasant People. August William Derleth & Mark Schorer. 1966. 5.00 o.p. Arkham.
Colonel Mint: A Novel. Paul West. LC 71-188330. 1972. 6.95 (ISBN 0-525-08268-9). E. P. Dutton.
Colonel Norton: A Novel. Florence Montgomery. LC 7-31806. 1895. Longmans, Green, and Co.
Colonel of the Red Huzzards. John Reed Scott. 1906. J. B. Lippincott Company.
Colonel of the 10th Cavalry. A Story of the War. O. P Clarke. LC 13-2080. 1891. L. C. Childs & Son.
Colonel Quaritch, V.C. Henry Rider Haggard. LC 6-45976. (On cover: Lovell's library. no. 1306). 1888. J. W. Lovell Company.
Colonel Starbottle's Client, and Some Other People. Bret Harte. LC 70-110196. (Short story index reprint series). 1970. Books for Libraries Press.
Colonel Starbottle's Client: And Some Other People. Bret Harte. LC 4-15117. 1892. Houghton, Mifflin and Company.
Colonel Starbottle's Client and Some Other People. Bret Harte. LC 40-37526. 1892. Houghton Mifflin Company.
Colonel Sun: James Bond Adventure. Robert Markham. LC 68-15976. 1968. 5.95 o.p. (ISBN 0-06-012763-5, HarpT). Har-Row.
Colonel Thorpe's Scenes in Arkansaw... Ed. by William Trotter Porter. Thorpe, Thomas Bangs & Field, Joseph M. LC 28-17921. (On cover: Petersons illustrated uniform edition of humorous American works). 1858. T. B. Peterson & Brothers.
Colonel Timothy Bigelow: A Historical Novel. Louise Bigelow. LC 41-15198. 1941. Meador Publishing Company.
Colonel Todhunter of Missouri. Ripley Dunlap Saunders. LC 11-1759. The Bobbs-Merrill Company.
Colonel's Christmas Dinner. Ed. by Charles King. LC 7-12229. 1890. L. R. Hamersly & Co.
Colonel's Christmas Dinner and Other Stories. Ed. by Charles King. LC 75-98581. (Short story index reprint series). 1969. Books for Libraries Press.
Colonel's Christmas Dinner: And Other Stories. Ed. by Charles King. LC 12-232661. 1892. J, B. Lippincott Company.
Colonel's Christmas Dinner: And Other Stories. Ed. by Charles King. LC 3-27803. 1896. J. B. Lippincott Company.
Colonel's Christmas Morning: And Other Stories. Robert Cornelius V Meyers. LC 2727. 1900. Franklin Book Co.
Colonel's Daughter. Charles King. LC 81-592. (Gregg Press Western fiction series). 1981. 14.95 (ISBN 0-8398-2699-0). Gregg Press.
Colonel's Daughter: A Novel. Richard Aldington. LC 31-23197. 1931. Doubleday, Doran & Company, Inc.
Colonel's Daughter: Or, Winning His Spurs. Charles King. LC 12-23269. 1883. J. B. Lippincott & Co.
Colonel's Daughter: Or Winning His Spurs. Charles King. LC 3-27795. 1892. J. B. Lippincott Company.
Colonel's Dream. Charles Waddell Chesnutt. LC 68-57517. 1968. Gregg Press.
Colonel's Dream. Charles Waddell Chesnutt. LC 73-83928. 1969. Mnemosyne Pub. Co.
Colonel's Dream. Charles Waddell Chesnutt. LC 77-100261. 1970. Negro Universities Press.
Colonel's Dream. Charles Waddell Chesnutt. LC 5-23066. 1905. Doubleday, Page & Company.
Colonel's Experiment. Edith Barnard Delano. LC 13-214809. 1913. 1.00. D. Appleton and Company.
Colonel's Ladies: A Novel. Eric Hatch. LC 68-19992. 1968. Crown Publishers.
Colonel's Money. Lucy Cecil White Lillie. LC 11-714330. 1888. Harper & Brothers.
Colonel's Nieces. Guy De Maupassant. LC 78-21840. 1970. 1.50 (ISBN 0-87067-407-2). Holloway House Pub. Co.; Distributed by All America Distributors Corp.
Colonel's Nieces. Guy de Maupassant. 1970. pap. 1.50 o.p. (ISBN 0-87067-407-2). Holloway.
Colonel's Nieces. Guy de Maupassant. pap. 1.95 o.p. (ISBN 0-87056-256-8, 6256). Brandon.
Colonel's Opera Cloak. Christine Chaplin Brush. LC 78-137723. (American fiction reprint series). (No name series.). 1970. (ISBN 0-8369-7022-5). Books for Libraries Press.
Colonel's Opera Cloak. Christine Chaplin Brush. LC 3-32164. 1904. Little, Brown, and Company.
Colonel's Opera Cloak. Christine Chaplin Brush. LC 7-20624. (Half-title: No name series). 1905. Little, Brown, and Company.
Colonel's Photograph. Eugene Ionesco. LC 67-20347. 1969. 4.95. Grove Press.
Colonel's Photograph & Other Stories. Eugene Ionesco. Tr. by Jean Stewart & John Russell. 1969. pap. 1.95 o.p. (ISBN 0-394-17300-7, E415, Ever). Grove.
Colonel's Story. Sara Agnes Rice Pryor. LC 11-540632. 1911. The Macmillan Company.
Colonel's Thunder. Joe Morris. LC 30-5934. 1929. Printed at the State School for the Deaf.
Colonel's Wife. Warren Edwards. (On cover: Flag ser. no. 6). Street & Smith.
Coloney Effingham's Raid. Berry Fleming. LC 43-51062. 1943. Duell, Sloan and Pearce.
Colonial Boy: Or, The Treasures of an Old Link Closet. Nellie Blessing Eyster. LC 6-38130. D. Lothrop Company.
Colonial Dame: A Pen-Picture of Colonial Days and Ways. Laura Dayton Fessenden. LC 6-39516. Rand, McNally & Company.
Colonial Days: A Tale of Rhode Island and Providence Plantations. Maria Frances Hill Anderson. LC 8-34325. 1886. American Baptist Publ. Society.
Colonial Free-Lance. Chauncey Crafts Hotchkiss. LC 7-7152. (Appleton's town and country library, no. 222). 1897. D. Appleton and Company.
Colonial Maid of Old Virginia. Lucy Foster Madison. LC 2-19731. 1902. The Penn Publishing Company.
Colonial Reformer. Thomas Alexander Browne. LC 42-26571. 1890. Macmillan and Co.
Colonial Stories: Being Legends of the Province House. Nathaniel Hawthorne. LC 7-4965. 1897. J. Knight Company.
Colonial Survey: By Murray Leinster Pseud. 1st Ed. William Fitzgerald Jenkins. LC 57-7110. 1957. Gnome Press.
Colonial Witch: Being a Study of the Black Art in the Colony of Connecticut. Frank Samuel Child. LC 6-20984. 1897. The Baker & Taylor Co.
Colonial Wooing. Charles Conrad Abbott. LC 5-42998. 1895. J.B. Lippincott Company.
Colonial. 1st American Ed. John Sykes. LC 63-8945. 1963. Coward McCann.
Colonials: Being a Narrative of Events Chiefly Connected with the Siege and Evacuation of the Town of Boston in New England. Allen French. LC 2-3926. 1902. Doubleday Page and Co.
Colony. Benjamin Bova. (Kangaroo Book). 1.95 (ISBN 0-671-81916-X). Pocket Books.
Colony. Ray Russell. LC 75-4348. 1969. 6.50. Sherbourne Press.
Colony. Mary Vigliante, pseud. (Orig.). 1979. pap. 1.75 (ISBN 0-532-17213-2). Woodhill.
Colony of Girls: A Novel. Kate Linvingston Willard. LC 8-37011. 1892. Dodd, Mead & Co.
Color-Blind. Catherine Cookson. (Signet Book). 1977. 1.75 (ISBN 0-451-07394-0). New American Library.
Color from a Light Within: A Novel Based on the Life of El Greco. Donald Braider. LC 66-20265. 1967. Putnam.
Color Her Adulteress. Stephan Gregory, pseud. (Orig.). pap. 0.95 o.p. (1144). Brandon.
Color Me Princess. Mary Simons. (Illus.). 1982. pap. 2.95 (ISBN 0-440-51634-X, Dell Trade Pbks). Dell.
Color of Darkness. James Purdy. LC 74-26739. 175p. 1975. Repr. lib. bdg. 19.25x (ISBN 0-8371-7874-6, PUCD). Greenwood.
Color of Darkness: Eleven Stories and a Novella. James Purdy. LC 57-12947. 1957. New Directions.
Color of Darkness: Eleven Stories and a Novella. James Purdy. LC 74-26739. 1975. 10.75 (ISBN 0-8371-7874-6). Greenwood Press.
Color of Evening. 1st Ed. Robert Nathan. LC 60-8104. 1960. Knopf.
Color of Green. 1st Ed. Lenard Kaufman. LC 56-10513. 1956. Holt.
Color of Loneliness. Mary Ross. LC 58-9496. 1958. Dorrance.
Color of Murder. Julian Symons. LC 58-6177. 1957. Harper.
Color of Murder. Julian Symons. (Perennial Library). 1978. 1.95. Harper & Row.
Color of Ripening. Matthea Thorseth. LC 49-5954. 1949. Superior Pub. Co.
Color of the East. John Russell. LC 30-27118. 1929. W. W. Norton & Co., Inc.
Color Purple. Alice Walker. 204p. 1982. 11.95 (ISBN 0-15-119153-0). HarbraceJ.
Color Right On. Afua Adoma. 1976. pap. 1.50 o.p. (ISBN 0-913358-09-6). Shabazz Pr.
Color Studies. Thomas Allibone Janvier. LC 69-11904. (American short story series, v. 63). 1969. Garrett Press.
Color Studies. Thomas Allibone Janvier. LC 72-8169. (American short story series, v. 63). 1972. (ISBN 0-8422-8080-4). MSS Information Corp.
Color Studies. Thomas Allibone Janvier. LC 7-10382. 1885. C. Scribner's Sons.
Color Studies and A Mexican Campaign. Thomas Allibone Janvier. LC 7-10333. 1891. C. Scribner's Sons.
Colorado. Louis Bromfield. LC 47-11221. 1947. Harper.
Colorado. William MacLeod Raine. LC 76-40936. 1976. 6.95 (ISBN 0-88411-557-7). Aeonian Press.
Colorado. William MacLeod Raine. LC 28-3167. 1928. Doubleday, Doran & Company, Inc.
Colorado Colonel, and Other Sketches. William Carey Campbell. LC 2-3. 1901. Crane & Co.
Colorado Crossing. Gene Curry. (Jim Saddler Ser.: No. 3). 1979. pap. 1.75 o.s.i. (ISBN 0-505-51418-4). Tower Bks.
Colorado Gold: Novel By Chad Merriman Pseud. & Lee Leighton Pseud. Gifford Paul Cheshire & Wayne D. Overholser. LC 58-13389. (Ballantine books, 282K). 1958. Ballantine Books.
Colorado Gun. W. Edwin Booth. (Orig.). 1981. pap. 1.75 (ISBN 0-505-51614-4). Tower Bks.
Colorado Jim". George Goodchild. LC 23-700808. W. J. Watt & Company.
Colorado Kill. Robert L. Trimnell. (Loner Ser.: No. 1). 192p. 1974. pap. 0.95 o.p. (ISBN 0-532-95358-4). Woodhill.
Colorado Kill. Robert L. Trimnell. (Loner Ser.: No. 1). 192p. 1974. pap. 0.95 o.p. (ISBN 0-532-95358-4). Manor Bks.
Colorado Kill Zone. Don Pendleton. (Executioner Ser.: No. 25). 192p. (Orig.). 1976. pap. 1.95 (ISBN 0-523-41089-1). Pinnacle Bks.
Colorado Kill-Zone. Don Pendleton. (Executioner Series#25). 1976. (pbk.) 1.25 (ISBN 0-523-00824-4). Pinnacle Books.
Colorado Manhunt. Dick Taylor. 208p. (Orig.). 1982. pap. 2.25 o.s.i. (ISBN 0-8439-1181-6, Leisure Bks). Nordon Pubns.
Colorado Woman. Patricia Greenlaw. (Orig.). 1980. pap. text ed. 2.50 o.s.i. (ISBN 0-505-51589-X). Tower Bks.
Colorblind. Esther Taylor. LC 79-19755. 1980. 9.95 (ISBN 0-87949-136-1). Ashley Books.
Colored Gentleman, a Product of Modern Civilization. Dennis I Imbert. LC 73-18581. (Illus.). 1975. (ISBN 0-404-11392-3). AMS Press.
Colored Gentleman: A Product of Modern Civilization by D. I. Imbert. Dennis I Imbert. LC 31-13090. 1931. Williams Printing Service.
Colored Soldiers. William Irwin MacIntyre. LC 23-11928. 1923. The J. W. Burke Company.
Colored Water: A Novel. Jim Yount. LC 68-1928. Gonine Associates.
Colors from the Zohar. Jerry Winston. LC 75-45790. 1977. pap. 3.95. Barah.
Colors of Life: Poems and Songs and Sonnets. Max Eastman. LC 18-18779. 1918. A. A. Knopf.
Colors of Space. Rev. ed. Marion Zimmer Bradley. Ed. by Hank Stine. LC 82-5008. (Illus.). 146p. 1983. pap. 5.95 (ISBN 0-89865-191-3, AACR2, Starblaze). Donning Co.
Colors of the Day: A Novel; Translated from the French by Stephen Becker. Romain Gary, pseud. LC 53-121704. 1953. Simon and Schuster.
Colors of Vaud. Winifred Bryher. LC 77-95857. 1969. Harcourt, Brace & World.
Colors of War. Matthew Cohen. LC 77-29135. 10.00 (ISBN 0-458-93250-7). Methuen.
Colors Roar By. Alexander Reck. (Orig.). 1969. pap. 1.95 o.s.i. (TC456, Travellers Comp). Olympia.
Colossus. Dennis Feltham Jones. LC 67-10957. 1967. Putnam.
Colossus. Harold Everett Porter. LC 30-21638. Sears Publishing Company, Inc.
Colossus... Edgar Wallace. LC 32-16971. Pub. for the Crime Club, Inc., by Doubleday, Doran & Company, Inc.
Colossus: A Novel About Goya and a World Gone Mad. Stephen Marlowe. LC 72-762821. 1973. (pbk.) 1.50. Popular Library.
Colossus a Story. Opie Percival Read. LC 7-36623. (On cover: The Ariel library, no. 26). F. J. Schulte & Company.
Colossus: A Story of to-Day. Morley Roberts. LC 99-5322. 1899. Harper & Brothers.
Colossus and the Crab. D. F Jones. (Berkley Medallion Book). 1.50 (ISBN 0-425-03467-4). Berkley Pub. Corp.,
Colossus of Arcadia. Edward Phillips Oppenheim. LC 38-14593. 1938. Little, Brown and Company.
Colossus of Arcadia. Edward Phillips Oppenheim. LC 39-32056. 1939. Triangle Books.
Colour Blind. Catherine Marchant, pseud. 1971. pap. 1.25 o.p. (96114). Beagle Bks.
Colour of Canada. 2nd rev ed. Hugh MacLennan. 1972. 6.95 o.p. (ISBN 0-316-54252-0). Little.
Colour of the Glass. Rose Thurburn. LC 53-5339. 1953. Morrow.
Colour of Violence. Jeffrey Ashford, pseud. (o.s.i.). 185p. 1974. 5.95 o.s.i. (ISBN 0-8027-5305-1). Walker & Co.
Colour of Youth. V H Friedlaender. LC 24-24342. 1924. 2.00. G. P. Putnam's Sons.
Colour Out of Space. 3rd ed. Howard Phillips Lovecraft. 1969. pap. 0.75 o.p. (75-248). Lancer.
Colour Scheme. Ngaio Marsh. LC 43-10321. 1943. Little, Brown and Company.
Colour Schemes. Ngaio Marsh. (Ngaio Marsh Mystery Ser.). 288p. 1982. pap. 2.50 (ISBN 0-515-06014-3). Jove Pubns.
Coloured Dome. Francis Stuart. LC 33-1249. 1933. The Macmillan Company.
Colours of the Day. Romain Gary, pseud. LC 77-366437. 1976. 3.75 (ISBN 0-85617-882-9). White Lion Publishers.
Colours of War. Matthew Cohen. LC 77-379162. 10.00 (ISBN 0-7710-2175-5). McClelland and Stewart.
Colt Comrades. Harry Sinclair Drago. LC 39-4902. 1939. Doubleday, Doran and Co., Inc.
Colt Fever. Stetson Cody. LC 73-152518. 1972. 4.95 (ISBN 0-7075-0011-7). Gold Lion Books.
Colt Law. Norman Daniels. LC 56-59227. 1956. Avalon Books.
Colt Law. J W Pelkie. LC 51-2275. 1951. Phoenix Press.
Colt Legacy. Ellsworth S. Grant. LC 81-85196. (Illus.). 234p. 1982. 30.00; pap. 17.00. MowBray Co.
Colt Lightin' Harry Sinclair Drago. LC 38-16091. The Macaulay Company.
Colt Master. T. W. Ford. LC 49-9889. 1949. Phoenix Press.
Colt of the Alcan Road. Bertrand Leslie Shurtleff. 1951. Bobbs-Merrill.
Colt-Packin' Parson. Edwin Booth. 1975. 4.95. Avalon Books.
Colt That Carried a King. Agnes Sligh Turnbull. Fleming H. Revell Company.

Colter's Hell, a Story of the Yellowstone. Grace Johnson. LC 38-16090. Maple Publishers.

Colt's Castle. Garth Davis. LC 56-8983. 1956. Arcadia House.

Colum of Derry. Eona K Macnicol. LC 55-286428. 1954. Sheed and Ward.

Columbanus, the Celt: A Tale of the Sixth Century. Walter Thomas Leahy. LC 13-189832. H. L. Kilner & Co.

Columbella. Phyllis A. Whitney. LC 66-13193. 4.95. Doubleday.

Columbella. Phyllis A. Whitney. LC 66-131931. (Crest bk., t1037). 1967. Fawcett.

Columbia Stories. Albert Payson Terhune. (Dillingham's metropolitan library, no. 28). 1897. G. W. Dillingham Co.

Columbine. Raymond A Kennedy. LC 80-16133. 12.95 (ISBN 0-374-12643-7). Farrar Straus Giroux.

Columbine. Raymond A Kennedy. LC 80-29380. 1981. 12.95 (ISBN 0-14-005882-6). Penguin Books.

Columbine. Viola Meynell. LC 15-248920. 1915. G. P. Putnam's Sons.

Columbine Cabin Murders. Philip Mechem. LC 32-21681. 1932. C. Scribner's Sons.

Columbine Time. William Henry Irwin. LC 21-19770. The Stratford Company.

Columbus: A Romance. Rafael Sabatini. LC 42-574. 1942. Houghton Mifflin Company.

Columbus Affair. K. H Scheer. (Perry Rhodan,#80). 1975. (pbk.) 1.25. Ace Books.

Columbus Cannon. Herbert Best. LC 54-4134. 1954. Viking Press.

Columbus Dancer. Barry Reidel. (Orig.). 1968. pap. 1.75 o.s.i. (105, Ophelia). Olympia.

Columbus of Space. Garrett Putman Serviss. LC 73-13265. (Classics of science fiction). (Illus.). 1974. 9.50 (ISBN 0-88355-119-5) (ISBN 0-88355-119-5). Hyperion Press.

Columbus of Space. Garrett Putman Serviss. LC 11-238389. 1911. D. Appleton and Company.

Columbus Tree. Peter S. Feibleman. LC 72-90511. 1973. 8.95. Atheneum.

Columbus Tree. Peter S. Feibleman. (Signet Book, J5784). 1974. (pbk.) 1.95. New American Library.

Column: A Novel. Charles Marriott. LC 1-31202. 1901. J. Lane.

Columnist Murder. Lawrence Saunders. LC 31-162402. Farrar & Rinehart, Incorporated.

Coma: A Novel. Robin Cook. LC 76-52951. 8.95 (ISBN 0-316-15510-1). Little, Brown.

Comanch'. Cliff Farrell. LC 66-17432. 3.50. Doubleday.

Comanch'. Cliff Farrell. LC 66-17432. (Signet brand western). 1974. (pbk.) 0.95. New American Library.

Comanch: Ride the Wild Trail. Cliff Farrell. 1982. pap. 2.50 (ISBN 0-451-11565-1, AE1565, Sig). NAL.

Comanche Belle. Charles Thomas. LC 63-7720. (Double D western). 1963. Doubleday.

Comanche Chaser. Dane Coolidge. LC 38-5865. 1938. E. P. Dutton & Co., Inc.

Comanche Kid. Edward Beverly Mann. LC 37-124316. 1937. W. Morrow & Company.

Comanche Moon: A Novel of the West. William Robert Cox. LC 59-14443. 1959. McGraw-Hill.

Comanche Revenge. Jeanne Sommers. (American Indians Ser.: No. 1). 368p. (Orig.). 1981. pap. 2.75 (ISBN 0-440-01525-1, Standish). Dell.

Comanche Scalp. William C. MacDonald. 224p. 1982. pap. 2.25 (ISBN 0-8439-1062-3, Leisure Bks). Nordon Pubns.

Comanche Scalp: A Gregory Quist Story. 1st Ed. William Colt MacDonald. LC 55-10465. 1955. Lippincott.

Comanche Stallion. Tom Millstead. LC 58-9126. 1958. Avalon Books.

Comanche Vengeance. Richard Jessup. 1977. pap. 1.75 (ISBN 0-449-13910-7, GM). Fawcett.

Comanchero Blood. Paul Ledd. (Shelter Ser.: No. 13). (Orig.). 1983. pap. 2.25 (ISBN 0-8217-1208-X). Zebra.

Comanchero Kill. W. L. Fieldhouse. (Gun Lust Ser.: No. 2). 224p. 1982. pap. cancelled (ISBN 0-505-51820-1). Tower Bks.

Comanchero Kill. William Fieldhouse. (Gun Lust Ser.: No. 2). 224p. 1983. pap. 2.50 (ISBN 0-8439-2027-0, Leisure Bks). Dorchester Pub Co.

Comancheros. new ed. Jack Slade, pseud. Tr. by E. Caballero from Eng. (Compadre Collection Ser., Sundance: No. 4). 160p. (Span.). 1975. pap. 0.85 (ISBN 0-88473-534-6). Fiesta Pub.

Comancheros. Jack Slade, pseud. (Sundance Ser.: No. 11). 160p. 1981. pap. 1.75 (ISBN 0-8439-1049-6, Leisure Bks). Nordon Pubns.

Comancheros. Paul Iselin Wellman. LC 52-11616. 1952. Doubleday.

Comancheros and Renegade. Jack Slade, pseud. (Leisure book). 1978. 2.25 (ISBN 0-8439-0569-7). Nordon Pubns.

Comanche's Woman. Jake Logan. LC 75-36298. (Jake Logan Western Ser.: No. 5). 192p. (Orig.). 1976. pap. 1.95 (ISBN 0-86721-041-9, B16301). Playboy Pbks.

Comatose Kids. Seymour Simckes. LC 75-10747. (Illus.). 8.95. (ISBN 0-914590-18-9) (ISBN 0-914590-19-7). Fiction Collective: Distributed by G. Braziller.

Combat. Kole Omotoso. (African Writers Ser.). 1972. pap. text ed. 4.00x (ISBN 0-435-90122-2). Heinemann Ed.

Combat Command. Frederick C. Sherman. 400p. 1982. pap. 2.95 (ISBN 0-553-22917-6). Bantam.

Combat in the Sky: By Arch Whitehouse. 1st Ed. Arthur George Joseph Whitehouse. LC 61-6911. Duell, Sloan and Pearce.

Combat Journal for Place D'Armes: A Personal Narrative. Scott Symons. LC 78-316550. (Illus.). 1978. 5.95 (ISBN 0-7710-9811-1). McClelland & Stewart.

Combat of Shadows. Manohar Malgonkar. 292p. 1968. pap. 2.50 (ISBN 0-88253-056-9). Ind-US Inc.

Combat Pay. Robin Moore, pseud. 1977. pap. 1.95 (ISBN 0-532-19130-7). Woodhill.

Combat SF. Gordon R Dickson. LC 74-24486. (Doubleday science fiction). 1975. 6.95 (ISBN 0-385-04575-1). Doubleday.

Combat Stories of World War Ii and Kores. William Chamberlain. LC 62-15131. 1962. John Day Co.

Combination. Andrew York. LC 82-45615. (Crime Club Ser.). 192p. 1983. 11.95 (ISBN 0-385-18434-4). Doubleday.

Combined Maze. May Sinclair. LC 13-3068. 1913. Harper & Brothers.

Combray. Edited with an Introd. and Notes by Germaine Bree and Carlos Lynes. Marcel Proust. Ed. by Germaine Bree & Carlos Lynes. LC 52-10627. Appleton-Century-Crofts.

Comdey in Spasms. Kathleen Mannington Hunt Caffyn. LC 6-21879. (On cover: West end series). F. A. Stokes Company.

Come. Carroll Arnett. (Pap ed. 8.00 o.p.). 1973. 16.00 (Pub. by Elizabeth Pr). SBD.

Come. Sheila Solomon Klass. LC 60-1174.

Come, Now, Let Us Reason Together. M. J. Orth. 1970. 3.95 o.p. Vantage.

Come a Long Journal: A Novel. Alan Fry. LC 74-103746. 1972. (532-00140-125) 1.25. Manor Books.

Come a Long Journey. Alan Fry. LC 74-103746. 1971. 5.95 o.p. (ISBN 0-385-02986-1). Doubleday.

Come a-Smokiin'. Nelson Coral Nye. LC 53-10214. (Silver star westerns). 1953. Dodd, Mead.

Come A-Smokin' Nelson Nye. 240p. (Orig.). 1980. pap. 1.95 (ISBN 0-89083-626-4). Zebra.

Come Again. Lee Digby. (Orig.). 1970. pap. 1.95 o.s.i. (OPH-180, Ophelia). Olympia.

Come Again, Hugh Pecker. Marc Clinton. 1973. pap. 1.95 o.s.i. (76-344). Lancer.

Come Again in Spring. Francis Ebejer. 1979. 7.50 (ISBN 0-533-04091-4). Vantage.

Come Alone. Nancy Mann Waddel Wilson Woodrow Woodrow. LC 29-138252. The Macaulay Company.

Come Along with Me: Part of a Novel, Sixteen Stories, and Three Lectures. Shirley Jackson. Ed. by Stanley Edgar Hyman. LC 68-22864. 1968. (ISBN 0-670-23158-4). Viking Press.

Come Alongside. Archibald Bruce Campbell. 1946. S. Paul & Co., Ltd.

Come & Be Killed. Nancy Bodington. LC 47-3821. 1947. Harper.

Come and Be Killed! Shelley Smith. LC 47-3821. 1947. Harper & Brothers.

Come and Find Me. Elizabeth Robins. LC 8-5885. 1908. The Century Co.

Come and Get It. Edna Ferber. LC 35-27049. 1935. Doubleday, Doran & Company, Inc.

Come and Get Me: A Realistic Novel by Johnny Laredo Pseud. Gene Caesar. LC 56-26167. (Popular library, 720). 1956. Popular Library.

Come and Get Me, a Realistic Novel: By Johny Larede Pseud. Gene Caesar. LC 56-26167. (Popular library, 720). 1956. Popular Library.

Come and See My Shining Palace. Nicholas Samstag. LC 66-12197. 4.95. Doubleday.

Come As You Are. John Clifford Mortimer. 1971. pap. 6.95 o.p. (ISBN 0-416-63280-7, NO.3006). Methuen Inc.

Come Away. Margaret Cabell Self. LC 48-6374. 1948. A. S. Barnes.

Come-Back. Morris De Camp Crawford. LC 25-554482. 1925. Minton, Balch & Company.

Come Back. Carolyn Wells. LC 21-951519. George H. Doran Company.

Come Back, Africa! Short Stories from South Africa, by Phyllis Altman Others Ed. by Herbert L. Shore, Megchelina Shore-Bos. Ed. by Herbert L Shore. LC 68-637739. (New world paperbacks, NW-S-3). 1968. pap., 1.25. Intl. Pubs.

Come Back, Dr. Caligari. Donald Barthelme. 1971. pap. 3.95 (ISBN 0-316-08254-6). Little.

Come Back, Doctor Caligari. Donald Barthelme. pap. 1.25 o.p. (A470, Anch). Doubleday.

Come Back, Doctor Caligari. Donald Barthelme. 1964. 4.95 o.p. (Pub. by Atlantic Monthly Pr). Little.

Come Back, Geordie. David Harry Walker. LC 66-11219. 4.95. Houghton.

Come Back If It Doesn't Get Better. Penelope Gilliatt. LC 69-16422. 1969. 5.95. Random House.

Come Back, Lolly Ray. Beverly Lowry. LC 76-22895. 1977. 7.95. Doubleday.

Come Back, Miranda. Anne Duffield. (Berkley medallion book). 1974. (pbk.) 0.95 (ISBN 0-425-02518-7). Berkley Pub. Co.

Come Back, My Love. Edward Sidney Aarons. 1970. pap. 0.60 o.p. (R2239, GM). Fawcett World.

Come Back to Erin. Sean O'Faolain. LC 72-170602. 398p. 1972. Repr. of 1940 ed. lib. bdg. 25.50 (ISBN 0-8371-6255-6, OFCB). Greenwood.

Come Back to Erin: A Novel. Sean O'Faolain. LC 40-141892. 1940. The Viking Press.

Come Back to Love. Joyce Dingwell. (Harlequin Romances). 192p. 1981. pap. 1.25 (ISBN 0-373-02402-9, Pub. by Harlequin). PB.

Come Back to Me, Beloved. Kathleen Thompson Norris. LC 76-903. 1976. 9.95 (ISBN 0-89190-302-X). American Reprint Co.

Come Back to Me, Beloved. Kathleen Thompson Norris. LC 42-23636. 1942. The Sun Dial Press.

Come Back to Sorrento. Joseph Petracca. LC 52-9781. 1952. Little, Brown.

Come Back to the Farm. Jesse Stuart. LC 71-152010. 1971. 6.95 (ISBN 0-07-062239-6). McGraw-Hill.

Come Be My Guest. Elizabeth Cadell. 1964. 4.95 o.p. Morrow.

Come Be My Love. Diana Brown. LC 81-5737. 1981. 13.95 (ISBN 0-312-15090-3). St Martin's Press.

Come Be My Love. Lavinia Riker Davis. LC 49-102175. 1949. Doubleday.

Come Be with Me. Leonard Nimoy. (Illus., Orig.). 1978. pap. 4.95 (ISBN 0-88396-033-8). Blue Mtn Pr CO.

Come Before Winter. Carroll Voss. LC 53-9658. 1953. Muhlenberg Press.

Come Blonde, Came Murder. Peter George. LC 52-4353. (Boardman bloodhound, no. 42). 1952. T. V. Boardman.

Come Clean, My Love. Rosemary Drachman Taylor. LC 49-9249. 1949. T. Y. Crowell Co.

Come Climb, My Hill. autographed gift ed. 4.95 (ISBN 0-918114-03-9). Inspiration Conn.

Come Dream with Me. Betty Jane Kamensky. LC 66-27485. 1967. Dorrance.

Come Easy-Go Easy. James Hadley Chase. 1974. (pbk.) 0.95 (ISBN 0-671-77927-3). Pocket Books.

Come Easy, Go Easy. Arthur Mason. LC 33-241082. The John Day Company.

Come Faith, Come Fire. Vanessa Royall. 1979. 2.50 (ISBN 0-440-12170-1). Dell Pub. Co.

Come, Fill the Cup. Harlan Ware. LC 52-5133. 1952. Random House.

Come Fill the Cup: A Novel. Rosalind Wade. LC 56-10412. 1956. Pantheon.

Come for Cocktails, Stay for Supper. M. Burros & L. Levine. 1971. pap. 2.95 (ISBN 0-02-009260-1, Collier). Macmillan.

Come Forth. Elizabeth Stuart Phelps H. D. Ward Ward & Ward, Herbert Dickinson, 1861- Joint Author. LC 8-33116. 1891. Houghton, Mifflin and Company.

Come Gentle Spring. Evelyn Bolster. LC 42-12643. 1942. The Vanguard Press.

Come, Gentle Spring. Jesse Stuart. LC 75-76825. 1969. McGraw-Hill.

Come Go with Me: High Rock and Spring Bank. Mary Drummond. LC 73-81340. 1973. 4.95 (ISBN 0-8059-1885-X). Dorrance.

Come Hell or High Water. 1st Ed. Marvin L York. LC 54-68050. 1954. Pageant Press.

Come Here. Richard Kostelanetz. 1975. 2.50, signed & lettered A-Z 25.00 ea. Assembling Pr.

Come Here & Die see Death of a Stranger.

Come Home: A Romance of the Louisiana Rice-Lands. Stella George Stern Perry. LC 28-18008. 1923. Frederick A. Stokes Company.

Come Home and Be Killed. Jennie Melville, pseud. LC 64-8018. (A London House mystery). 1964. House & Maxwell.

Come Home at Even. Le Grand Cannon. LC 51-9708. 1951. Holt.

Come Home Early Child. Owen Dodson. 1977. 1.75 (ISBN 0-445-08549-5). Popular Library.

Come Home Holly Lowman. Georgia Craig. (Alouette Romance Ser.). 128p. (Orig.). 1981. pap. 2.25 (ISBN 0-89531-130-5, 0198-96). Sharon Pubns.

Come Home, My Love: A Novel. 1st Ed. Suzan Zollicoffer White. LC 61-183832. Greenwich Book Publishers.

Come Home, Nurse Jenny. Colleen L. Reece. (YA) 1978. 6.95 (Avalon). Bouregy.

Come Home to Love. Paula Roberts. (Orig.). 1980. pap. 2.25 o.s.i. (ISBN 0-505-51484-2). Tower Bks.

Come Home, Traveller. Claude Kinnoull. LC 47-1303. 1947. Doubleday & Company, Inc.

Come in & Get Lost. Joshua H. Garrett. 64p. 1975. pap. 2.75 o.p. (ISBN 0-913182-57-5). Grossmont Pr.

Come in Number One, Your Time Is up. Derek Jewell. 1973. (pbk.) 1.25 (ISBN 0-345-23412-X). Ballantine.

Come in Number One, Your Time Is up. Derek Jewell. LC 70-152791. 1971. 6.95. Doubleday.

Come in Spinner! By Dymphna Cusack and Florence James. Ellen Dymphna Cusack & Florence James. LC 51-9342. 1951. Morrow.

Come into My Heart. Peggy Gaddis, pseud. LC 50-12676. 1950. Arcadia House.

Come into My Parlor. Josiah Pitts Woolfolk. LC 36-14929. 1936. Godwin.

Come into My Parlour, a Novel. Dennis Yates Wheatley. LC 47-18542. 1946. Hutchinson & Co., Ltd.

Come Jericho. George J. Bellak. 384p. 1983. pap. 2.95 (ISBN 0-425-05508-6). Berkley Pub.

Come Jericho: A Novel. George J Bellak. LC 81-4858. 1981. 12.95 (ISBN 0-688-00125-4). Morrow.

Come Kill with Me. Henry Kane. (Peter Chambers Ser.). (Orig.). 1972. pap. 0.95 o.s.i. (75-410). Lancer.

Come Kill with Me: A Novel of Suspense. Fred Kassak. LC 76-11624. 1976. 8.95. Bobbs-Merrill.

Come Like Shadows. LC 73-163618. (Alms for Oblivion Ser.: No. 8). 1972. 8.50x (ISBN 0-85634-003-0). Intl Pubns Serv.

Come Live My Life. Robert H. Rimmere. (Orig.). 1977. pap. 2.25 (ISBN 0-451-07421-1, E7421, Sig). NAL.

Come Live with Me. Kate Kellogg. Ed. by Alice Sachs. 1970. 3.95 o.p. Lenox Hill.

Come Live with Me. Lois Wyse. (Little Volumes of Love Ser). 1.95 o.p. (ISBN 0-529-01364-9, A4224). World Pub.

Come, Live with Me, and Be My Love. Robert Williams Buchanan. LC 6-19884. J. W. Lovell Company.

Come Live with Me, and Be My Love;" An English Pastoral. Robert Williams Buchanan. LC 6-19883. Lovell, Coryell & Company.

Come Love, Call My Name. Anne N. Reisser. (Candlelight Ecstasy Ser.: No. 76). (Orig.). 1982. pap. 1.95 (ISBN 0-440-11321-0). Dell.

Come Love, Come Hope. Iris Bromige. 1972. pap. 0.75 o.p. (94301). Beagle Bks.

Come Meet Abraham, God's Friend. Anna Griffiths. (Come Meet Ser.). pap. 1.95 o.p. (ISBN 0-310-25201-6). Zondervan.

Come Meet Abraham the Pioneer. Anna Griffiths. (Come Meet Ser.). pap. 1.95 o.p. (ISBN 0-310-25191-5). Zondervan.

Come Meet Jacob, God's Prince. Anna Griffiths. (Come Meet Ser.). pap. 1.95 o.p. (ISBN 0-310-25281-4). Zondervan.

Come Meet Jacob, the Grabbing Twin. Anna Griffiths. (Come Meet Ser.). pap. 1.95 o.p. (ISBN 0-310-25271-7). Zondervan.

Come Meet Jesus, the Baby. Anna Griffiths. (Come Meet Ser.). pap. 1.95 o.p. (ISBN 0-310-25241-5). Zondervan.

Come Meet Jesus, the Boy. Anna Griffiths. (Come Meet Ser.). pap. 1.95 o.p. (ISBN 0-310-25251-2). Zondervan.

Come Meet Joseph, God's Dreamer. Anna Griffiths. (Come Meet Ser.). pap. 1.95 o.p. (ISBN 0-310-25221-0). Zondervan.

Come Meet Joseph the Grand Vizier. Anna Griffiths. (Come Meet Ser.). pap. 1.95 o.p. (ISBN 0-310-25231-8). Zondervan.

Come, Meet My Friend. Allan Hartley. (Spire Books). 1977. pap. 0.95 o.p. (ISBN 0-8007-9001-4). Revell.

Come Meet Noah. Anna Griffiths. (Come Meet Ser.). pap. 1.95 o.p. (ISBN 0-310-25181-8). Zondervan.

Come Meet, Ruth. Anna Griffiths. (Come Meet Ser.). pap. 1.95 o.p. (ISBN 0-310-25261-X). Zondervan.

Come Monday Mornin'. Chris Loken. LC 73-87702. 1974. 7.95 (ISBN 0-87131-137-2). M. Evans.

Come Monday Mornin'. Chris Loken. 1976. (pbk.) 1.95 (ISBN 0-671-80436-7). Pocket Books.

Come Murder Me. James Kieran. LC 51-22485. (Gold medal book, 150). 1951. Gold Medal Books.

Come, My Beloved. Pearl Sydenstricker Buck. LC 53-9556. 1953. J. Day Co.

Come, My Coach! Marjorie Muir Worthington. LC 35-581663. 1935. A. A. Knopf.

Come Near. Alexander Hamilton Leighton. LC 73-116104. 1971. 6.95 (ISBN 0-393-08617-8). Norton.

Come Nineveh, Come Tyre. Allen Drury. 1974. (pbk.) 1.75. Avon.

Come Nineveh, Come Tyre: The Presidency of Edward M. Jason. Allen Drury. LC 73-9347. 1973. 8.95 (ISBN 0-385-04392-9). Doubleday.

Come-on. Margaret Yorke. LC 78-69513. 8.95 (ISBN 0-06-014774-1). Harper & Row.

Come on Buck". Opie Percival Read. LC 26-5826. 1926. The Blackhawk Press, Inc.

TITLE INDEX COMING OF THE LAW.

Come-on Girl. Jerome Darwin Engel. LC 40-13270. Phoenix Press.
Come on Out, Daddy. Bernard Wolfe. LC 63-17240. 1963. 10.95. Boulevard.
Come on Out, Daddy. Bernard Wolfe. LC 63-17240. 1963. 8.95 o.p. (ISBN 0-910278-02-4). Boulevard.
Come on Out, Daddy: A Novel. Bernard Wolfe. LC 63-17240. 1963. Scribner.
Come One, Come All. Troy Conway, pseud. (Coxeman Ser). (Orig.). 1968. pap. 0.60 o.p. (ISBN 0-446-53735-7, 53-735). Paperback Lib.
Come Out and Fight! A Double D Western. Allan Vaughan Elston. LC 41-5492. 1941. Doubleday, Doran and Company, Inc.
Come Out, Come Out. George Malcolm-Smith. LC 65-185275. 3.50. Pub. for the Crime Club by Doubleday.
Come Out, Come Out Whoever You Are! Geraldine Richelson. (Illus.). 32p. 1980. pap. 2.95 (ISBN 0-8252-1113-1); pap. text ed. 5.95 (ISBN 0-8252-1112-3). Quist.
Come Out of the Kitchen! A Romance. Alice Duer Miller. LC 16-10120. 1916. The Century Co.
Come Out of the Kitchen! A Romance. Alice Duer Miller. LC 26-223146. 1917. The Century Co.
Come Out of the Pantry. Alice Duer Miller. 1934. Dodd, Mead & Company.
Come Out to Play. Alexander Comfort. LC 75-2008. 1975. 7.95 (ISBN 0-517-52147-4). Crown Publishers.
Come Over, Red Rover: A Novel of Suspense, by Stephen Marlowe. Milton Lesser. LC 68-12933. 1968. 4.95. Macmillan.
Come Over, Red Rover: A Novel of Suspense. Stephen Marlowe. LC 68-12933. 1968. Macmillan.
Come Pour the Wine. Cynthia Freeman, pseud. LC 80-66501. 1980. 12.95 (ISBN 0-87795-276-0). Arbor Hse.
Come Pour the Wine. Cynthia Freeman, pseud. 368p. 1981. pap. 3.95 (ISBN 0-553-20026-7). Bantam.
Come Pour the Wine: A Novel. Cynthia Freeman, pseud. LC 81-5095. 1981. 15.95 (ISBN 0-8161-3201-1). G.K. Hall.
Come Rack, Come Rope. Robert Hugh Benson. LC 12-29473. 1912. Dodd, Mead and Company.
Come Rack! Come Rope! Edited, and with a Foreword by Philip Caraman. Robert Hugh Benson. LC 57-637860. Kenedy.
Come Seven. Octavus Roy Cohen. LC 20-16928. 1920. 1.75. Dodd, Mead and Company.
Come Seven, Come Death. Ed. by Henry Morrison. LC 65-3746. 1965. Pocket Books.
Come Sin with Me see Bed Is Not for Sleeping.
Come Slowly, Eden. Charlene Keel. 1978. pap. 1.75 o.s.i. (ISBN 0-505-51322-6). Tower Bks.
Come Slowly, Eden: A Novel About Emily Dickinson. Laura Benet. LC 42-21082. 1942. Dodd, Mead & Company.
Come Soon, Tomorrow. Gladys Swarthout. LC 43-182043. 1943. The Blakiston Company; Distributed by Dodd, Mead & Company.
Come Spring. Ben Ames Williams. LC 40-27248. 1940. Houghton Mifflin Company.
Come Spring: An Autobiographical Novel. Maria Lewitt. LC 82-5575. 10.95 (ISBN 0-312-15099-7). St. Martin's Press.
Come Summer, Come Love. Isabel Cabot. (Avalon Books). 4.95. Thomas Bouregy.
Come Sunday: A Religious Novel. 1st Ed. George Shepard Southworth. 1954. Exposition Press.
Come, Take My Hand. Luli Kollsman. LC 49-110597. 1949. Duell, Sloan and Pearce.
Come, Take My Hand. Kay Munson. 192p. (YA) 1974. 4.95 o.p. (Avalon). Bouregy.
Come, Take My Hand. Kay Munson. (Avalon romances). 1974. 4.50. Avalon Books.
Come Tell Me How You Live. Agatha Miller Christie. 1980. pap. 2.50 (ISBN 0-671-43282-6). PB.
Come, the Restorer: A Novel. William Goyen. LC 74-2829. 1974. 4.95 (ISBN 0-385-00767-1). Doubleday.
Come to Dust. Anne Jackson Fremantle. LC 41-9495. G. P. Putnam's Sons.
Come to Dust. Emma Lathen, pseud. LC 68-25751. (Inner sanctum mystery). 1968. 4.95. Simon and Schuster.
Come to Greenleaves. Kay Richardson. (Avalon Books). 4.95. Thomas Bouregy.
Come to Grief. Helen Foley. LC 77-366994. 1976. 3.50 (ISBN 0-340-20477-X). Hodder and Stoughton.
Come to My Arms. Eva Pearl Murphy Keating. LC 34-32566. The Macaulay Company.
Come to My House. John McIntosh. LC 68-20071. 1968. Harcourt, Brace & World.
Come to My House. Arthur Somers Roche. LC 27-19629. The Century Co.
Come to My Wedding. Ruby Mildred Ayres. LC 33-316562. 1933. Doubleday, Doran & Company, Inc.
Come to the Bower: A Novel. Jack Yeaman Bryan. LC 63-10934. 1963. Viking Press.
Come to the War. Leslie Thomas. 1970. 4.95 o.p. (ISBN 0-684-10601-9). Scribner.
Come to the War. Leslie Thomas. 1969. 5.95 o.p. Coward.
Come Walk Among the Stars. LC 66-29141. autographed gift ed 4.95 (ISBN 0-918114-00-4). Inspiration Conn.
Come Winter. Evan Hunter. LC 72-89317. 1973. 5.95 (ISBN 0-385-01605-0). Doubleday.
Come with Me: A Novel. 1st Ed. Ethel June Drost. LC 55-9400. 1955. Exposition Press.
Come with Me Home. Gladys H. Carroll. (A novel). 1960. 5.95 o.p. (ISBN 0-316-12991-7). Little.
Come with Me into Babylon: A Story of the Fall of Nineveh. Josiah Mason Ward. 1902. F. A. Stokes Company.
Come with Me to Macedonia. Leonard Drohan. LC 57-8911. 1957. Knopf.
Come Yo Te Amo. Rafael Crespo. (Romance Real Ser.). 192p. (Span.). 1981. pap. 1.50 (ISBN 0-88025-003-8). Roca Pub.
Come Young, Come Old. S. C. Carew, pseud. 192p. pap. 1.95 o.p. (6143). Brandon.
Comeback. Edgar Franklin Stearns. LC 28-13448. 1928. G. H. Watt.
Comeback. John Tomerlin. (Orig.). 1969. pap. 0.60 o.p. (63-142). Paperback Lib.
Comeback for Stark. Hamish Reade, pseud. LC 68-25452. 1968. 4.95. Putnam.
Comedian: And Other Stories. Ernest Lehman. LC 58-26500. (Signet book, 1446). 1957. New American Library.
Comedian Dies. Simon Brett. (Berkley Book). 1980. 2.25 (ISBN 0-425-04702-4). Berkley Publishing Corp.
Comedian Dies: A Crime Novel. Simon Brett. LC 79-13712. 1979. 7.95 (ISBN 0-684-16168-0). Scribner.
Comedians. Graham Greene. LC 66-12636. 1966. Viking Press.
Comedians. Tedd Thomey & Norman Wilner. 1970. pap. 0.75 o.p. (T2264). Pyramid Pubns.
Comedians: A Story of Ancient Rome. Louis Marie Anne Couperus. LC 26-18630. (Half-title: The novels of Louis Couperus). George H. Doran Company.
Comedienne. Wladyslaw Stanislaw Reymont & Obecny, Edmund, Tr. LC 20-20943. 1920. G. P. Putnam's Sons.
Comedies and Errors. Henry Harland. LC 74-169554. (Short story index reprint series). 1971. (ISBN 0-8369-4016-4). Books for Libraries Press.
Comedies & Errors. Henry Harland. LC 4-889. 1898. J. Lane.
Comedies of Courtship. Anthony Hope Hawkins. LC 7-2622. 1896. C. Scribner's Sons.
Comedy. Barr, Robert et al. LC 1-25677. (Stories from Mc Clure's). (Half-title: Stories from McClure's). 1901. McClure, Phillips & Co.
Comedy, American Style. Jessie Redmon Fauset. LC 76-95401. 1969. AMS Press.
Comedy American Style. Jessie Redmon Fauset. LC 77-76106. 1969. McGrath Pub. Co.
Comedy, American Style. Jessie Redmon Fauset. LC 79-90131. 1969. Negro Universities Press.
Comedy, American Style. Jessie Redmon Fauset. LC 33-32766. 1933. Frederick A. Stokes Company.
Comedy in Faeto. Nicholas Pavia. LC 28-25473. The Stratford Company.
Comedy in Spasms. Kathleen Mannington HuntMrs Caffyn. LC 6-21880. F. A. Stokes Company.
Comedy Man. Douglas Hayes. LC 60-13626. 1961. Abelard-Schuman.
Comedy of a Country House. A Novel. Julian Sturgis. (On cover: Lovell's international series, no. 29). 1889. F. F. Lovell & Company.
Comedy of Circumstance. Emma Gavf. LC 11-9232. 1911. Doubleday, Page & Company.
Comedy of Conscience. Silas Weir Mitchell. LC 3-765933. 1903. The Century Co.
Comedy of Counterplots. Edgar Fawcett et al. LC 6-39542. (Outing Library). (Outing library. v. 1. no. 2): Vol. 1, No. 2). 1894. Outing Publishing Company.
Comedy of Elopement. Frances Christine Tiernan. LC 8-19817. (On cover: Appletons' town and country library, no. 108). 1893. D. Appleton and Company.
Comedy of Mammon. Ina Garvey. LC 8-14956. D. Estes & Co.; Etc., Etc.
Comedy of Masks. Ernest Christopher Dowson & Arthur Collin Moore. LC 76-20066. (Decadent Consciousness). 1977. 26.00. Garland Pub.
Comedy of Masks: A Novel. Ernest Christopher Dowson & Moore, Arthur, Joint Author. LC 6-34244. (On cover: Appletons' town and country library. no. 124). 1893. D. Appleton and Company.
Comedy of Petty Conflicts. Ida Blanche Ford Wall. Broadway Publishing Co.
Comedy of Senator Kopenhauser. A. P. Feretra. LC 73-87792. 90p. 1974. pap. 5.00 o.p. (ISBN 0-8283-1531-0). Branden.
Comedy of Senator Kopenhouser. A. P. Faretra. LC 73-87792. 1974. (pbk.) 5.95 (ISBN 0-8283-1531-0). Branden Press.
Comedy of Sentiment: A Novel. authorized ed. Max Simon Nordau. LC 7-33473. F. T. Neely.
Comedy of Terrors. James De Mille. (On cover: Osgood's library of novels. no. 25). 1872. J. R. Osgood and Company, Late Ticknor & Fields, and Fields, Osgood, & Co.
Comedy of Terrors. John James Mackintosh Stewart. LC 40-10804. 1940. Dodd, Mead & Company.
Comedy of Terrors see Appleby Intervenes.
Comedy of Women. John North. Small, Maynard & Company.
Comer Girl. Jason Dobbins. pap. 1.95 o.p. (8077). Cameo.
Comes an Echo on the Breeze. Edward James Ryan. LC 49-2629. 1949. Exposition Press.
Comes the Blind Fury. Raymond Escholier. LC 27-18268. 1925. John Lane.
Comes the Blind Fury. John Saul. (Orig.). 1980. pap. 3.50 (ISBN 0-440-11428-4). Dell.
Comet: A Novel. Jane White. LC 75-30357. 7.95 (ISBN 0-06-014608-7). Harper & Row.
Comet Is Coming: The Ferverish Legacy of Mr. Halley. Nigel Calder. (Illus.). 1982. pap. 6.95 (ISBN 0-14-006069-3). Penguin.
Comet of a Season. A Novel. Justin McCarthy. (Franklin square library, no. 214). 1881. Harper & Brothers.
Cometeers. Jack Williamson. LC 50-11000. 1950. Fantasy Press.
Cometh up As a Flower. Rhoda Broughton. (Seaside library, v. 15 no. 285). 1878. G. Munro.
Cometh up As a Flower. Rhoda Broughton. (On cover: Lovell's library, no. 1024). 1887. J. W. Lovell Company.
Cometh up As a Flower. A Novel. Rhoda Broughton. LC 9-5704. (On cover: Seaside library. Pocket Ed. 769). 1886. G. Munro.
Cometh up As a Flower: An Autobiography... Rhoda Broughton. LC 9-15520. 1899. Macmillan and Co., Limited.
Comets Have Long Tails. Madeleine Johnston. LC 38-108488. 1938. Pub. for the Crime Club, Inc., by Doubleday, Doran & Co., Inc.
Comfort Letter: A Novel. Arthur R. G Solmssen. LC 74-34029. 1975. 7.95 (ISBN 0-316-80368-5). Little, Brown.
Comfort Me with Apples. Peter De Vries. 1977. 1.95 (ISBN 0-445-04048-3). Popular Library.
Comfort Me with Apples. Peter De Vries. 1968. 5.75 o.p. (ISBN 0-316-18174-9). Little.
Comfort Me with Apples. 1st Ed. Peter De Vries. LC 56-6765. 1956. Little, Brown.
Comfort of Strangers. Ian McEwan. LC 81-1746. 9.95 (ISBN 0-671-42850-0). Simon and Schuster.
Comfortable Coffin: A Gold Medal Anthology. Richard S. Prather. LC 63-3634. (Gold medal books, k1297). 1963. Fawcett Publications.
Comfortable Corner. Vincent Virga. 1982. pap. 3.50 (ISBN 0-380-80895-1, 80895-1). Avon.
Comforters. Muriel Spark. LC 57-1149. 1957. Macmillan.
Comforters. Muriel Spark. LC 57-918549. 1957. Lippincott.
Comic. Brian Glanville. LC 74-26616. 1975. 7.95 (ISBN 0-8128-1787-7). Stein and Day.
Comic Journey to Washington... Charles Edwards.
Comical Romance. Paul Scarron. LC 67-12469. (Illus.). 1968. B. Blom.
Comin' Round Right. Sidney M. Jourard. Date not set. cancelled o.p. (ISBN 0-913592-41-2); pap. cancelled o.p. (ISBN 0-913592-44-7). Argus Comm.
Comin' Thro' the Rye. Helen Buckingham Mathers Reeves. LC 7-30682. (On cover: Lovell's library, no. 1046). 1887. J. W. Lovell Company.
Coming. John Collis Snaith. LC 17-24695. 1917. 1.50. D. Appleton and Company.
Coming: A Novel. Garet W Earle. LC 72-154653. 1972. 5.95 (ISBN 0-8375-6767-X). Droke House/Hallux.
Coming Apart. Milton M. Ginsberg. pap. 1.25 o.p. Lancer.
Coming Apart. Jean Renvoize. LC 80-6202. 1981. 12.95 (ISBN 0-8128-2780-5). Stein and Day.
Coming Attraction. Fannie Flagg. 1982. pap. text ed. 2.95 (ISBN 0-451-11507-4, AE1507, Sig). NAL.
Coming Attractions. Sandra Berkley. LC 78-122801. 1971. 5.95. Dutton.
Coming Attractions: A Wonderful Novel. Fannie Flagg. LC 80-29451. 1981. 12.95 (ISBN 0-688-00472-5). Morrow.
Coming Attractions: A Wonderful Novel. Fannie Flagg. LC 81-6776. 14.95 (ISBN 0-8161-3294-1). G.K. Hall.
Coming Back Alive. Dennis J. Reader. 256p. 1983. pap. 2.25 (ISBN 0-380-61416-2, Flare). Avon.
Coming Back of Laurence Averil. Maurice Drake. 1.25. E.J. Clode.
Coming Back with the Spitball: A Pitcher's Romance. James Marie Hopper. LC 14-406577. 1914. 0.50. Harper & Brothers.
Coming Close. Bernard Harper Friedman. 224p. 1982. 11.95 (ISBN 0-914590-70-7); pap. 5.95 (ISBN 0-914590-71-5). Fiction Coll.
Coming Close: A Novella and Three Stories As Alternative Autobiographies. Bernard Harper Friedman. LC 81-71643. 11.95 (ISBN 0-914590-70-7) (ISBN 0-914590-71-5). Fiction Collective: Order from Flatiron Book Distributors.
Coming Conquest of England. August Niemann. Tr. by Freese, John Henry. LC 5-11899. 1904. G. P. Putnam's Sons.
Coming Dark Age. Roberto Vacca. LC 73-81118. pap. 2.50 (ISBN 0-385-00497-4, Anch). Doubleday.
Coming Dawn. Charles Egerton. LC 6-35450. 1906. J. Lane Company; Etc., Etc.
Coming-Down Time. Joan L Oppenheimer. LC 70-39249. 1972. 4.95. Hawthorn Books.
Coming Event. E. C. Tubb. 1982. pap. 2.25 (ISBN 0-87997-725-6, UW1725). DAW Bks.
Coming from the Fair. Norah Hoult. LC 38-154941. Covici, Friede.
Coming from the Mind. J. Smith. 4.00 o.p. (ISBN 0-8062-1014-1). Carlton.
Coming Harvest (Le Ble Qui Leve) Rene Bazin. Tr. by Edna K. Hoyt. LC 8-25122. 1908. C. Scribner's Sons.
Coming Hell. Walter E. Adams. 376p. (Orig.). 1981. pap. 4.95 (ISBN 0-937408-06-9). Gospel Pubns FL.
Coming Home. Lester Cohen. LC 45-4134. 1945. The Viking Press.
Coming Home. George Davis. LC 78-140699. 1975. (pbk.) 1.25. Dell.
Coming Home. George Davis. LC 78-140699. 1972. 5.95 (ISBN 0-394-46223-8). Random House.
Coming Home from the War, an Idyll. James Kruss. LC 77-116227. 1970. 3.95. Doubleday.
Coming of a God. Jerry Fonarrow. (Orig.). 1969. pap. 0.95 (ISBN 0-87067-201-0, BH201). Holloway.
Coming of Age. new ed. Lisa Courtney. LC 78-54786. (Illus.). 1978. 8.95 (ISBN 0-932464-01-7). TREK-CIR.
Coming of Age of Francois Cocteau. Aime Von Rod. 1972. pap. 1.75 o.s.i. (V1079K, Venus). Grove.
Coming of Amos. William John Locke. LC 24-20558. 1924. 2.00. Dodd, Mead and Company.
Coming of Bill. P. G. Wodehouse. 1967. 4.95 o.p. (ISBN 0-8277-0233-7). British Bk Ctr.
Coming of Billy. Margaret Westrup. 1905. Harper & Brothers.
Coming of Cassidy. Clarence Edward Mulford. 438p. 1974. Repr. of 1908 ed. lib. bdg. 21.30x (ISBN 0-88411-216-0). Amereon Ltd.
Coming of Cassidy--and the Others: By Clarence E. Mulford... Clarence Edward Mulford. LC 13-22509. 1913. A. C. McClurg & Co.
Coming of Cassidy-and the Others. Clarence Edward Mulford. LC 73-89637. (Illus.). 1974. 6.95. Aeonian Press.
Coming of Cassidy and the Others. Clarence Edward Mulford. LC 27-7328. 1913. A. L. Burt Company.
Coming of Chloe. Margaret Wolfe Hamilton Hungerford. LC 7-9366. 1897. J. B. Lippincott Company.
Coming of Conan. 1st Ed. Robert E. Howard. LC 53-12602. (His Hyborian Age). 1953. Gnome Press.
Coming of Cosgrove. Laurie York Erskine. LC 26-326872. 1926. D. Appleton and Company.
Coming of Fabrizze. Raymond De Capite. LC 60-9630. 1960. D. McKay Co.
Coming of Rain. Richard Marius. LC 69-11787. 1969. 6.95. Knopf.
Coming of the Amazons: A Satiristic Speculation on the Scientific Future of Civilization. Owen McMahon Johnson. LC 31-30596. 1931. Longmans, Green and Co.
Coming of the Dawn. Jane Susanna Anderson Pierson. LC 17-25123. The Standard Publishing Company.
Coming of the Demons. Gwenyth Hood. LC 81-11263. 1982. 10.95 (ISBN 0-688-00794-5). Morrow.
Coming of the Dry Season. Charles Mungoshi. LC 72-983357. (New Fiction from Africa Series). 1972. 6.50. Oxford University Press.
Coming of the Gunman. Al Cody, pseud. 1973. pap. 0.95 o.p. (ISBN 0-532-95338-X). Woodhill.
Coming of the Gunman. Al Cody, pseud. 1973. pap. 0.95 o.p. (ISBN 0-532-95338-X). Manor Bks.
Coming of the Gunman. Al Cody. 1973. (pbk) 0.75. Manor Books.
Coming of the Horseclans. Robert Adams. (Illus.). 1975. (pbk.) 1.25 (ISBN 0-523-00662-4). Pinnacle Books.
Coming of the King. Bernie Smade Babcock. LC 21-6264. The Bobbs-Merrill Company.
Coming of the Law. Charles Alden Seltzer. LC 12-239183. 1912. Outing Publishing Company.
Coming of the Law. Charles Alden Seltzer. LC 24-285229. 1914. A. L. Burt Company.

Coming of the Lord. Sarah Gertrude Liebson Millin. LC 28-22141. H. Liveright.

Coming of the New Man. Ted Spivey. 1970. 4.95 o.p. Vantage.

Coming of the Preachers: A Tale of the Rise of Methodism, 1901 see Minder: The Story of the Courtship, Call & Conflicts of John Ledger, Minder & Minister, 1900.

Coming of the Robots. Ed. by Samuel Moskowitz. LC 63-10945. 1963. Collier Books.

Coming of the Strangers. John Lymington, pseud. 1978. pap. 1.50 (ISBN 0-532-15322-7). Woodhill.

Coming of the Strangers. John Lymington, pseud. (O.s.i.). 1971. pap. 0.75 o.s.i. (532-75423-075). Manor Bks.

Coming of the Terrans. Leigh Brackett. 1976. 1.50. Ace.

Coming of the Tide. Margaret Pollock Sherwood. 1905. Houghton, Mifflin and Company.

Coming of the Voidal. Adrian Cole. Ed. by Hank Stine. (Voidal Trilogy Ser.). (Illus.). 198p. (Orig.). 1983. pap. 5.95 (ISBN 0-89865-287-1). Donning Co.

Coming of Theodora: A Novel. Eliza Orne White. LC 8-36622. 1895. Houghton, Mifflin and Company.

Coming of Toni's Black Brothers. Clarke Hammond. pap. 1.95 o.p. (ISBN 0-87056-205-3, 6205). Brandon.

Coming on Strong. Norman Singer. pap. 1.95 o.s.i. (OPH-229, Ophelia). Olympia.

Coming Out. Wallace Hamilton. (Orig.). 1977. pap. 2.50 (ISBN 0-451-09972-9, E9972, Sig). NAL.

Coming Out. Theodore Isaac Rubin. (75260). 1968. Pocket Bks.

Coming Out. Theodore Isaac Rubin. LC 67-16404. 1967. Trident Press.

Coming Out: By Wallace Hamilton. Wallace Hamilton. (Signet Book.). 1.75 (ISBN 0-451-07425-4). New American Library.

Coming Out Party. John Caffey. 224p. (Orig.). 1982. pap. 2.50 (ISBN 0-523-41707-1). Pinnacle Bks.

Coming-Out Party. Richard Frede. LC 77-85599. 1969. 5.95. Random House.

Coming Out Stories. Ed. by Julia P. Stanley & Susan J. Wolfe. LC 79-27073. 286p. (Orig.). 1980. pap. text ed. 6.95 (ISBN 0-930436-03-2). Persephone.

Coming Race: And The Haunted and the Haunters. Edward George Earle Lytton Bulwer-Lytton Lytton & Darton, Frederick Joseph Harvey. LC 29-14112. (Half-title: The World's classics. CCCXXVII). 1928. Oxford University Press.

Coming Race, Falkland, Zicci and Pausanias the Spartan. Edward George Earle Lytton Bulwer-Lytton Lytton, Edward Robert Bulwer-Lytton, 1st Earl of, 1831-1891, Ed. LC 8-11035. G. Routledge and Sons.

Coming Revolution. Marcus Van Heller, pseud. 1972. pap. 1.95 o.s.i. (OPH-266, Ophelia). Olympia.

Coming Round the Mountain. Barbara Webb. LC 36-55120. 1936. Doubleday, Doran & Company, Inc.

Coming Round the Mountain by Barbara Webb. Barbara Webb. LC 36-32341. 1936. The Sun Dial Press.

Coming Self-Destruction of the United States of America. Alan Seymour. LC 73-116171. 1971. 6.95. Grove Press.

Coming Storm. Francis Deming Hoyt. 1913. P. J. Kenedy & Sons.

Coming Through. John H. Irsfeld. LC 74-14348. (YA) 1975. 7.95 o.p. (ISBN 0-399-11557-9). Putnam.

Coming Through: A Novel. John H. Irsfeld. LC 75-14348. 1975. 7.95 (ISBN 0-399-11557-9). Putnam.

Coming Through Slaughter. Michael Ondaatje. LC 77-23225. (Illus.). 7.95 (ISBN 0-393-08765-4). Norton.

Coming Through Slaughter. Michael Ondaatje. 1979. 2.25 (ISBN 0-380-42911-X). Avon Books.

Coming Through the Rye. Grace Livingston Hill. LC 26-178032. 1926. J. B. Lippincott Company.

Coming to. Alan Brody. LC 74-16576. 1975. 8.95 (ISBN 0-399-11479-3). Berkley Pub. Corp.: Distributed by Putnam.

Coming to. Alan Brody. (Berkley Medallion Book). 1976. (pbk.) 1.75 (ISBN 0-425-03046-6). Berkley Publishing Corp.

Coming to Life. Norma Klein. LC 74-13608. 1974. 7.95 (ISBN 0-671-21857-3). Simon and Schuster.

Coming to Life. Norma Klein. 1976. (pbk.) 1.50. New American Library.

Coming to Terms with the Short Story. Susan Lohafer. LC 82-20366. 18.95 (ISBN 0-8071-1086-8). Louisiana State University Press.

Coming Together. Alice Denham. 1970. pap. 0.95 o.p. (ISBN 0-447-75144-1). Lancer.

Coming Together: Modern Stories by Black & White Americans. Adam A. Casmier & Sally Souder. LC 77-157746. 1972. pap. text ed. 6.95 o.p. (ISBN 0-8221-0002-9). Dickenson.

Coming up for Air. Orwell, George. LC 50-5002. 1950. Harcourt, Brace.

Coming up of Mr. Rattus: A Fable. Everett Hoffman. LC 68-30752. (Illus.). 1968. 2.95. Adams Press.

Coming World Earthquake. Joe Musser. 1982. pap. 2.95 (ISBN 0-8423-0405-3). Tyndale.

Comings of Cousin Ann. Emma Speed Sampson. LC 23-12160. Reilly & Lee Co.

Command. William McFee. LC 22-26977. 1922. Doubleday, Page & Company.

Command a King's Ship. Alexander Kent. LC 73-87196. 1974. 6.95 (ISBN 0-399-11278-2). Putnam.

Command and I Will Obey You. Alberto Moravia. LC 78-82628. 1969. 5.50. Farrar, Straus & Giroux.

Command and I Will Obey You: And Other Stories. Alberto Pincherle. 1973. (pbk) 0.95. Manor Books.

Command at Sea. 1981. pap. text ed. write for info. (ISBN 0-88074-252-6). Metagam.

Command Decision. William Wister Haines. LC 47-300448. 1947. Little, Brown and Company.

Command Decision. William Wister Haines. LC 80-15034. 8.95 (ISBN 0-396-07872-9) (ISBN 0-396-07873-7). Dodd, Mead.

Command Decision. William Wister Haines. LC 81-9774. 1981. 12.95 (ISBN 0-89340-360-1). J. Curley.

Command Strike. Don Pendleton. (The Executioner Ser.: No. 29). 1977. pap. 1.95 (ISBN 0-523-41093-X). Pinnacle Bks.

Command the Morning, a Novel. Pearl Sydenstricker Buck. LC 59-7169. 1959. J. Day Co.

Commandant: A Novel of an Early Australian Penal Station. Jessica Anderson. LC 76-5366. 1976. 8.95 o.p. (ISBN 0-312-15155-1). St Martin.

Commander Amanda. George Revelli. 1969. 4.95 o.p. (GP501). Grove.

Commander Amanda Nightingale. George Revelli. LC 68-29443. 1968. Grove Press.

Commander: An Autobiographical Novel of 1940-1941. Robert David Quixano Henriques. LC 68-13247. 1968. Viking Press.

Commander Mendoza. Valera y Alcala Galiano, Juan. Tr. by Mary Jane Serrano. LC 8-30869. (On cover: Appletons' town and country library, no. 111). 1893. D. Appleton and Company.

Commander of Malta. Eugene Sue. (Seaside library, v. 50, no. 1030). 1881. G. Munro.

Commander of the Mists. David Leslie Murray. LC 38-9832. 1938. A. A. Knopf.

Commander Prince, USN. James Bassett. 1977. pap. 1.95 (ISBN 0-532-19148-X). Woodhill.

Commander Prince, U.S.N. James Bassett. LC 77-154089. 1974. (pbk.) 1.50. Manor Books.

Commander-1. Peter Bryan George. LC 64-24932. 4.95. Delacorte Dist. Dial.

Commandment of Moses. Stephen McKenna. LC 23-171640. George H. Doran Company.

Commandments of Men: And Other Short Stories. Sivert Erdahl. LC 43-17632. 1942. Shaw Publishing Company.

Commandments of Men: ByEunice Pollard Williams Pseud. 1st Ed. Osgood, Eunice S. LC 51-13166. 1951. Dutton.

Commando Attack! Alan Marks. 256p. (Orig.). 1982. pap. 2.50 (ISBN 0-505-51784-1). Tower Bks.

Commando Force, No. 133. Bill Strutton. 224p. 1981. pap. 2.50 (ISBN 0-553-13581-3). Bantam.

Commando of the Clouds. Steuart Mackie Emery. LC 43-18837. 1943. Cupples & Leon Company.

Commandos. Elliott Arnold. 304p. 1982. pap. 2.75 o.p. (ISBN 0-505-51859-7). Tower Bks.

Commandos. Elliott Arnold. 304p. pap. 2.75 (ISBN 0-8439-2009-2, Kable Bks). Dorchester Pub Co.

Commandos: A Novel. Elliott Arnold. 1942. Duell, Sloan and Pearce.

Commemorations. Hans Herlin. LC 75-9485. 1975. 8.95. St. Martin's Press.

Commemorative: A Work of Fiction. 1st Ed. Ingeborg Iversen Duffy. LC 56-10617. 1956. Pageant Press.

Commencement. Ernest Brace. LC 24-195303. 1924. Harper & Brothers.

Commencement Day Murders. Louise McKnight Floyd. LC 54-8347. 1954. Vantage Press.

Commencement Days: A Novel. Virginia Church. LC 10-10509. 1910. L. C. Page & Company.

Commend the Devil. Howard Coxe. LC 41-654683. Duell, Sloan and Pearce.

Commentaries of the Great Alfonso Dalboquerque, Second Viceroy of India, 4 Vols. Alfonso D'Albuquerque. Ed. & tr. by Walter D. Birch. LC 74-134712. (Hakluyt Society Ser). 1970. Repr. of 1883 ed. Set. lib. bdg. 118.00 (ISBN 0-8337-0289-0). B Franklin.

Commentary. John Galsworthy. LC 77-134962. (Short story index reprint series). 1970. Books for Libraries Press.

Commissar: A Novel of Stalinist Russia. Grigory Vinokur, pseud. LC 65-18221. 5.95. Twayne.

Commissar Krilenko. Anna M Kluchansky. LC 39-103793. Liveright Publishing Corporation.

Commissar of the Gold Express: An Episode in the Civil War. Vladimir Pavlovich Matveev. LC 74-10088. (Illus.). 1975. (ISBN 0-88355-174-8). Hyperion Press.

Commissar of the Gold Express: An Episode in the Civil War. Vladimir Pavlovich Matveev. LC 34-19032. 1933. International Publishers.

Commission. Richard Barrett. LC 82-72373. (Illus.). 438p. 1982. 25.00 (ISBN 0-9609396-0-1). Barrett.

Commission Man. Thomas H Hilton. (Original Brandon Book). 1973. (pbk.) 1.95 (ISBN 0-87056-338-6). Brandon Books.

Commissioner Hume: A Story of New York Schools. Charles William Bardeen. (On cover: Standard teachers' library). 1899. C. W. Bardeen.

Commitment. Cynthia Blair. (Love & Life Romance Ser.). 176p. (Orig.). 1983. pap. 1.75 (ISBN 0-345-30795-X). Ballantine.

Committal Chamber. Russell Braddon. LC 67-12432. 1967. Norton.

Committed Men. Mike John Harrison. LC 70-157597. (Doubleday science fiction). 1971. 4.95. Doubleday.

Committee. Hank Braxton. (Orig.). 1979. pap. 2.25 (ISBN 0-89083-484-9). Zebra.

Committee. Donald Seaman. LC 77-12358. 1978. 6.95 (ISBN 0-689-10838-9). Atheneum.

Commodity Character. Paul Rutkovsky. LC 82-51222. (Artists' Bk.). 72p. (Orig.). 1982. pap. 7.50 (ISBN 0-89822-030-0). Visual Studies.

Commodity of Dreams & Other Stories. Howard Nemerov. LC 59-601519. 1959. Simon and Schuster.

Commodore. Mary Howard Hoopes. LC 14-17287. 1914. 1.25. Lothrop, Lee & Shepard Co.

Commodore Hornblower. Cecil Scott Forester. (Hornblower Saga,#8). 1975. (pbk.) 1.50 (ISBN 0-523-00388-9). Pinnacle Books.

Commodore Hornblower. Cecil Scott Forester. LC 45-3524. 1945. Little, Brown and Company.

Commodore Hornblower see Indomitable Hornblower.

Commodore Junk. George Manville Fenn. LC 6-39263. (On cover: Seaside library--Pocket ed. no. 1169). 1889. G. Munro.

Common Cause: A Novel of the War in America. Samuel Hopkins Adams. LC 19-2326. 1919. Houghton Mifflin Company.

Common Cheat. Sophia Cleugh. LC 28-21189. 1928. The Macmillan Company.

Common Chord: A Story of the Ninth Ward. Henry Rutherford Elliot. LC 6-372619. Cassell & Company, Limited.

Common Chord: Stories and Tales by Frank O'Connor Pseud. Michael O'Donovan. LC 48-53763. 1948. A. A. Knopf.

Common Clay: A Novelization of Cleves Kinkead's Drama. D. Torbert. LC 16-6477. E. J. Clode.

Common Enemy. John Davys Beresford. LC 42-247392. 1942. Hutchinson & Co. Ltd.

Common Feelings. Carson E. Bench & Maryann Carpenter. Ed. by Kathy Galchutt. (Illus.). 56p. 1982. pap. 3.95 (ISBN 0-9608146-0-4). Western Sun Pubns.

Common Garden. Martha Moffett. 1977. 1.50 (ISBN 0-425-03365-1). Berkley Pub. Corp.

Common Heart. Paul Horgan. LC 42-25235. 1942. Harper & Brothers.

Common Law. Robert William Chambers. LC 11-21861. 1911. D. Appleton and Company.

Common Law. Robert William Chambers. LC 16-6727. 1912. D. Appleton and Company.

Common Lot. Robert Herrick. LC 71-110148. (Series in American Studies). 1970. Johnson Reprint Corp.

Common Lot. Robert Herrick. LC 68-57529. (American novels of muckraking, propaganda, and social protest). 1968. Gregg Press.

Common Lot. Robert Herrick. LC 4-24576. 1904. The Macmillan Company.

Common Lot see Collected Works.

Common Man. Lewis Vital Bogy. LC 6-14186. (On cover: Once a week library, v. 11, no. 9). 1893. P. F. Collier.

Common Mistake. Jeanne M Howell. LC 7-6621. The Merriam Company.

Common Mistake. Jeanne M Howell. LC 7-6622. (On cover: The golden library, no. 3). 1892. The Price-McGill Company.

Common of Angels. Dorothy A Beckett Terrell. LC 26-9570. 1926. D. Appleton and Company.

Common Passion. James Noble Gifford. LC 47-299. 1946. Phoenix Press.

Common Pasture. Hilary Masters. LC 67-17210. 1967. 4.95. Macmillan.

Common Problem. Sara Lindsay Coleman. LC 29-17530. 1929. Doubleday, Doran & Company, Inc.

Common Sense. A Novel. Emma Newby. LC 7-261197. (On cover: Turners' select novels, no. 3). Turner Brothers & Co.

Common Sense Deserted. Alvin A Bullock. LC 43-201. 1949. Dorrance and Company.

Common Story. Ivan Aleksandrovich Goncharov. Tr. by Garnett, Constance (Black) LC 6-44068. (On cover: Once-a-week library). 1894. P. F. Collier.

Common Story: A Novel. Ivan Aleksandrovich Goncharov. LC 76-23878. (Hyperion library of world literature). (Classics of Russian literature). 1977. 11.50. (ISBN 0-88355-485-2) (ISBN 0-88355-486-0). Hyperion Press.

Common Thread: A Book of Stories. Michael Seide. LC 74-29523. (Modern Jewish Experience). 1975. 13.00 (ISBN 0-405-06748-8). Arno Press.

Common Thread: A Book of Stories. Michael Seide. LC 44-295454. 1944. Harcourt, Brace and Comapny.

Common Touch. Terence A Keenleyside. LC 76-50775. 1977. 7.95 (ISBN 0-385-12275-6). Doubleday.

Common Wilderness. Michael Seide. LC 81-71646. 600p. 1983. 16.95 (ISBN 0-914590-74-X). Fiction Coll.

Commonplace. A Tale of to-Day; and Other Stories.. Christina Georgina Rossetti. LC 8-682. 1870. Roberts Brothers.

Commonplace Book of Thoughts, Memories, and Fancies, Original and Selected... Anna Brownell Murphy Jameson. LC 25-24446. 1855. D. Appleton & Company.

Commonwealth Short Stories. Ed. by Anna Rutherford & Donald Hannah. 245p. 1980. text ed. 19.50x (ISBN 0-8419-5075-X); pap. text ed. 9.50x. Holmes & Meier.

Commune 2000 A.D. Mack Reynolds. (Bantam science fiction). 1974. (pbk.) 0.95. Bantam Books.

Commune's Child. Sparky Ascani. (Orig.). 1981. pap. 2.25 (ISBN 0-505-51681-0). Tower Bks.

Communicating Door. Stella Allan. 224p. 1981. pap. 2.25 (ISBN 0-380-78451-3, 78451). Avon.

Communicating Door. Charles Wadsworth Camp. LC 23-9229. 1923. Doubleday, Page & Company.

Communipath Worlds. Suzette Haden Elgin. (Orig.). 1980. pap. 2.75 (ISBN 0-671-83392-8, Timescape). PB.

Communist's Corpse. Richard Edward Wormser. LC 35-8979. 1935. H. Smith and R. Haas.

Communities of Honor and Love in Henry James. Manfred Mackenzie. LC 75-17756. 1976. 11.00 (ISBN 0-674-15160-7). Harvard University Press.

Community Nurse. Lucy Agnes Hancock. LC 44-7720. 1944. Macrae-Smith-Company.

Community of Men. John Kiddell. LC 79-97960. 1969. Chilton Book Co.

Commuters: a Novel. James Broom Lynne. LC 73-164736. 1973. 2.10 (ISBN 0-491-00863-5). W. H. Allen.

Commuters: The Story of a Little Hearth and Garden. Albert Bigelow Paine. LC 4-7538. 1904. J. F. Taylor & Company.

Comp Box. Kytle. 1972. pap. 5.95 o.s.i. (ISBN 0-536-00923-6). Xerox College.

Compact Edition of Rudyard Kipling... Rudyard Kipling. LC 37-3788. C. Scribner's Sons.

Compact Homer. abridged. with summaries of the omitted books, notes and an introd. by mildred e. marcett. ed. Homerus & Mildred Elizabeth Marcett. LC 70-159670. (Illus.). 1971. per vol. 0.95 (ISBN 0-8120-0422-1) (ISBN 0-8120-0423-X). Barron's Educational Series.

Compact Homer: The Iliad and the Odyssey. In the Tr. of S. H. Butcher Others Abridged, Summaries of the Omitted Books, Notes, Introd. by Mildred E. Marcett. Illus. with Reproductions of Greek Vase Paintings. Ed. by Mildred Elizabeth Marcett. LC 62-18312. pap., 1.95. Barron S.

Compact Homer: The Iliad and the Odyssey. Ed. by Marcett, Mildred Elizabeth. LC 62-18312. 1963. Barron's Educational Series.

Compact: The Story of an Unrecorded Conspiracy in South Africa. Ridgwell Cullum. LC 9-31026. 1909. Hodder & Stoughton.

Compadres. Dan Price. 224p. (Orig.). 1981. pap. 1.95 (ISBN 0-440-11416-0). Dell.

Companion of the Tour of France. George Sand. Tr. by F. G. Shaw from Fr. LC 76-7364. x, 396p. 1976. Repr. of 1847 ed. 20.00 o.p. (ISBN 0-86527-230-1). Fertig.

Companion to Danger. Jacquelyn Aeby. (Candlelight romance). 1975. (pbk.) 0.75. Dell.

Companionate Separation. J Walter Redfern. LC 29-23879. R. G. Badger.

Companions. Thomas Dixon. LC 31-11729. 1931. Otis Publishing Corporation.

Companions Along the Way. Ruth Montgomery. 256p. 1976. pap. 2.50 (ISBN 0-445-08452-9). Popular Lib.

Companions of Jehu. Alexandre Dumas. LC 8-7676. 1894. Little, Brown, and Company.

Companions of Jehu. Alexandre Dumas. LC 6-43616. (Half-title: The romances of Alexandre Duman, Illustrated library ed. vol. xxxix-xl). 1894. Little, Brown and Company.

Companions of the Day & Night. Wilson Harris. 1975. 6.95 o.p. (ISBN 0-571-10663-3). Faber & Faber.

Companions of the Holiday. Donald Richie. LC 70-121065. 208p. 1968. 4.95 o.p. (ISBN 0-8348-0030-6). Weatherhill.

Companions of the Holiday: A Novel. Donald Richie. LC 76-43409. 1977. 3.75 (ISBN 0-8048-1218-7). Charles E. Tuttle.

Companions of the Holiday: A Novel. Donald Richie. LC 68-28770. 1968. 4.95. Walker/Weatherhill.

Companions of the Left Hand. George Tabori. LC 46-25201. 1946. Houghton Mifflin Company.

Companions of the Left Hand. George Tabori. LC 46-42553. 1946. T. V. Boardman and Company Limited.

Companions of the Trail see Collected Works.

Companions of the Unseen. Paul Tabori. (O.s.i.). pap. 0.75 o.s.i. (A664S, Award). Univ Pub & Dist.

Companions on the Trail. Hamlin Garland. Ed. by Donald Pizer. LC 74-96605. (American Authors Ser., Collected Works of Hamlin Garland, 45 Vols). 1969. Repr. of 1931 ed. lib. bdg. 26.75 o.s.i. (ISBN 0-512-00268-1). Garrett Pr.

Company. John Ehrlichman. (O.s.i.). 320p. 1976. 8.95 o.s.i. (ISBN 0-671-22273-2). S&S.

Company. Edwin Seaver. LC 30-7962. 1930. The Macmillan Company.

Company: A Novel. John Ehrlichman. LC 76-2508. 8.95 (ISBN 0-671-22273-2). Simon and Schuster.

Company: A Novel /by John Ehrlichman. John Ehrlichman. (Kangaroo Book). 1977. 1.95 (ISBN 0-671-80878-8). Pocket Books.

Company Doctor: An American Story. Henry Edward Rood. LC 7-40762. The Merriam Company.

Company K. William March. 1957. pap. 4.95 o.p. (ISBN 0-8090-0009-1, AmCen). Hill & Wang.

Company K: By William March Pseud. William Edward March Campbell. (American century series, S-9). 1957. Sagamore Press.

Company Man. John G Burnett. LC 56-8776. 1956. Harper.

Company Man. Joe Maggio. 1974. (pbk.) 1.25 (ISBN 0-523-00326-9). Pinnacle Books.

Company Man: A Novel. Joe Maggio. LC 76-175267. 1972. 6.95 (ISBN 0-399-10929-3). Putnam.

Company Nurse. Charles Stanley Strong. LC 40-11565. Phoneix Press.

Company of Cowards. Jack Warner Schaefer. LC 57-10781. 1957. Houghton Mifflin.

Company of Friends. John Crosby. LC 76-45639. 1977. 8.95 o.s.i. (ISBN 0-8128-2155-6). Stein & Day.

Company of Friends: A Novel. John Crosby. LC 76-45639. 1977. 8.95. Stein and Day.

Company of Friends: A Novel. John Crosby. 1978. 2.25 (ISBN 0-446-82424-0). Warner Books.

Company of Glory. Edgar Pangborn. LC 74-10048. (Pyramid Science fiction). 1975. 1.25 (ISBN 0-515-03568-8). Pyramid Books.

Company of Jehu... Alexandre Dumas. Tr. by Wormeley, Katherine Prescott. LC 6-43615. 1894. Estes and Lauriat.

Company of Jehu... Alexandre Dumas. LC 6-43618. (On cover: Dumas' romances. 19). 1894. Estes and Lauriat.

Company of Men, a Novel: Translated from the French by Joseph Barnes. Romain Gary, pseud. LC 50-7120. 1950. Simon and Schuster.

Company of Players. Victor Chapin. LC 59-5371. 1959. Houghton Mifflin.

Company of Shadows. J. M. Walsh. LC 31-180643. 1931. Brewer & Warren, Inc.

Company of Women. Mary Gordon. 304p. 1982. pap. 2.95 (ISBN 0-345-29861-6). Ballantine.

Company of Women. Mary Gordon. LC 80-5284. 293p. 1981. 12.95 (ISBN 0-394-50508-5). Random.

Company Owns the Tools. Henry Gregor Felsen. LC 42-23595. 1942. The Westminster Press.

Company Owns the Tools. Henry Vicar, pseud. LC 42-23595. 1942. The Westminster Press.

Company Parade. Margaret Storm Jameson. LC 34-12268. 1934. A. A. Knopf.

Company Parade. Storm Jameson. 1976. 1.95. Berkley Publishing Corp.

Company Q. Richard O'Connor. LC 57-579315. 1957. Doubleday.

Company She Keeps. Mary McArthy. 224p. 1981. pap. 3.50 (ISBN 0-380-55509-3, 55509, Bard). Avon.

Company She Keeps. 2nd ed.. ed. Mary Therese McCarthy. LC 76-350644. 1975. 0.50 (ISBN 0-14-002327-5). Penguin.

Company She Keeps. Mary Therese McCarthy. LC 42-13269. 1942. Simon and Schuster.

Company She Kept. Doris Grumbach. LC 66-26531. (Illus.). 1967. Coward-McCann.

Comparative Short Stories - Present & Past. Ed. by David Lougee & Nathan Halpern. (Noble's Comparative Classics Ser). (YA) (gr. 9 up). 1967. text ed. 3.96, s.p. 2.97 o.p. Noble.

Compare These Dead! Margaret Lucile Paine Rea. LC 42-1113. 1941. Pub. for the Crime Club by Doubleday, Doran & Company, Inc.

Comparisons: A Short Story Anthology. Ed. by Nicolaus Mills. LC 70-170867. 1972. (ISBN 0-07-042370-9). McGraw-Hill.

Compartamos Mi Esposa. new ed. Juan Castellanos. (Pimienta Collection Ser). (Illus.). 160p. (Span.). 1975. pap. 1.25 (ISBN 0-88473-237-1). Fiesta Pub.

Compartment East: Love and Adventure on the Orient Express. Pierre Jean Remy, pseud. LC 80-23875. 1980. 11.95 (ISBN 0-688-03739-9). Morrow.

Compartment K. Helen Kieran Reilly. LC 55-8172. 1955. Random House.

Compartments. David E. Fisher. LC 73-162548. 1972. 1.95 (ISBN 0-491-00602-0). W. H. Allen.

Compass Error. Sybille Bedford. LC 69-11477. 1969. 5.95. Knopf.

Compass of Destiny. 1st Ed. Jeannette Osburn. LC 53-16402. 1952. De Vorss.

Compass Rose. Ursula K. Le Guin. LC 81-48158. 224p. 1982. 14.37i (ISBN 0-06-014988-4, HarpT). Har-Row.

Compass Rose. Ursula K. Le Guin. (Illus.). 292p. 1982. PLB 40.00x (ISBN 0-934438-60-9). Underwood-Miller.

Compass Rose: Short Stories. Ursula K. Le Guin. LC 81-48158. 14.37 (ISBN 0-06-014988-4). Harper & Row.

Compassion. a modern translation with notes by joan maclean. introd. by lgen willbern, ed. Benito Perez Galdos. LC 66-28723. (Study master publication, T-42). 1966. American R. D. M. Corp.

Compassion: A Novel. authorized ed. Benito Perez Galdos. LC 62-18092. 1962. F. Ungar Pub. Co.

Compassion: By Galdos. A Modern Tr. with Notes by Joan MacLean. Introd. by Glen Willbern. Benito Perez Galdos. LC 66-287231. (Study master pubn., T-42). pap., 1.95. Amer. R. D. M. Corp.

Compassionate Deathmakers. Denk Bobkins. (Orig.). 1980. pap. 2.25 (ISBN 0-532-23209-7). Woodhill.

Compelled Hero. Richard Heron Ward. LC 31-24776. J. Cape & H. Smith.

Compelled to Kill. Leonard Gribble. 1977. 8.95 (ISBN 0-09-129010-4, Pub. by Hutchinson). Merrimack Pub Cir.

Compensation. Ruth Cranston. LC 11-29762. 1911. John Lane Company.

Compensation. A Tale of Temperance. Mary Evalin Warren. LC 8-33687. The National Temperance Society and Publication House.

Compensation: Or, Always a Future. 2d ed. Ann Maria Hampton Brewster. 1870. J.B. Lippincott & Co.

Competing Artists. Sara Currie Palmer. LC 18-20783. The Bible Institute Colportage Ass'n.

Competitive Nephew. Montague Marsden Glass. LC 15-8002. 1915. 1.20. Doubleday, Page & Company.

Competitor. Thomas J Bontly. LC 66-13335. 3.95. Scribners.

Competitor. Thomas J Bontly. (75218). 1968. Pocket Bks.

Complacent Wife. Barbara Cartland. (Barbara Cartland Ser.: No. 9). 272p. 1981. pap. 1.75 (ISBN 0-515-05568-9). Jove Pubns.

Complacent Wife, No. 53. Barbara Cartland. 1975. pap. 1.25 o.p. (ISBN 0-515-03828-8, V3828). BJ Pub Group.

Complaining Millions of Men: A Novel. Edward Fuller. LC 6-44586. 1893. Harper & Brothers.

Complaisant Lover. Graham Greene. 1961. 3.00 o.p. (ISBN 0-670-23373-0). Viking Pr.

Compleat Bachelor: A Novel. Oliver Onions. LC 1-11793. F. A. Stokes Company.

Compleat Enchanter: The Magical Misadventures of Harold Shea. Lyon Sprague De Camp & Fletcher Pratt. 432p. (Orig.). 1980. pap. 2.50 (ISBN 0-345-28929-3, Del Rey Bks.). Ballantine.

Compleat Enchanter: The Magical Misadventures of Harold Shea. Lyon Sprague De Camp & Fletcher Pratt. 1976. (pbk.) 1.95. Ballantine.

Compleat English Gentleman. Daniel Defoe. LC 74-2440. 1974. 30.00. Folcroft Library Editions.

Compleat Frisbee. Stancil E. Johnson. LC 72-89319. 192p. 1973. 3.00 o.p. (ISBN 0-385-01764-2). Doubleday.

Compleat OAK Leaves. David A. Kraft. LC 80-23937. 192p. 1980. Repr. of 1979 ed. lib. bdg. 16.95x (ISBN 0-89370-092-4). Borgo Pr.

Compleat OAK Leaves: Volume One of the Official Journal of Otis Adelbert Kline and His Works. Otis Adelbert Kline & David Anthony Kraft. LC 80-23937. 1980. 16.95. Borgo Press.

Compleat Werewolf. Anthony Boucher. (O.s.i.). 1969. 6.95 o.s.i. (ISBN 0-671-20382-7). S&S.

Compleat Werewolf, and Other Stories of Fantasy and Science Fiction. William Anthony Parker White. LC 71-92185. 1969. 6.50. Simon and Schuster.

Complete Adventures & Memoirs of Sherlock Holmes. Arthur Conan Doyle. (Illus.). 336p. 1976. pap. 3.95 o.p. (ISBN 0-517-52512-7, C N Potter Bks). Crown.

Complete Adventures and Memoirs of Sherlock Holmes: A Facsimile of the Original Strand Magazine Stories, 1891-1893. Arthur Conan Doyle & Sidney Paget. LC 75-29741. (Illus.). 3.95 (ISBN 0-517-52512-7). C. N. Potter: Distributed by Crown.

Complete Adventures of Tom Sawyer and Huckleberry Finn. centennial ed., 1st ed. Samuel Langhorne Clemens. LC 78-55538. (Illus.). 1978. 17.50 (ISBN 0-06-014461-0). Harper & Row.

Complete Adventures of Tom Sawyer & Huckleberry Finn. Mark Twain. LC 78-55538. (Illus.). 1979. deluxe ed. 14.95i (ISBN 0-06-014461-0, HarpT). Har-Row.

Complete Book of Claudia. Rose Franken. 1968. pap. 1.25 o.p. (78-602). Lancer.

Complete Claudine. Sidonie Gabrielle Colette. LC 76-21070. 10.00. Farrar, Straus, and Giroux.

Complete Critical Outline of Don Quixote by Miguel De Cervantes: Prepared by Paul B. Bass. Miguel de Cervantes de Saavedra & Bass, Paul B. LC 56-38559. (Hymarx outline series). Student Outlines Co.

Complete Darkover Series. Marion Zimmer Bradley. (Science Fiction Ser.). 1979. 120.00 o.p. (Gregg). G K Hall.

Complete Dashiell Hammett... Dashiell Hammett. LC 42-20563. 1942. A. A. Knopf.

Complete Edgar Allan Poe. avenel 1981 ed. Edgar Allan Poe. LC 80-29540. 1981. 6.98 (ISBN 0-517-33634-0). Avenel Books: Distributed by Crown Publishers.

Complete Fairy Stories of Oscar Wilde. 6th ed. Oscar Wilde. (Illus.). 203p. 1971. 7.00 (ISBN 0-7156-0550-X, Pub. by Duckworth England). Biblio Dist.

Complete Fairy Tales. Mary De Morgan. LC 63-7489.

Complete Fairy Tales. Oscar Wilde. LC 60-167604. (Illus.). 1961. F. Watts.

Complete Fairy Tales. Introd. by Roger Lancelyn Green. Original Illus. by William De Morgan, Walter Crane, Olive Cockerell. Mary De Morgan. LC 63-7489. 4.95. Watts.

Complete Fritz the Cat. R. Crumb. LC 78-60512. (Illus.). pap. 6.00 o.s.i. (ISBN 0-914646-16-8). Belier Pr.

Complete Gentleman. John Gilbert Bohun Lynch. LC 16-11965. George H. Doran Company.

Complete Ghost Stories of Charles Dickens. Charles Dickens. Ed. by Peter Haining. LC 82-13481. (Illus.). 342p. 1983. 15.95 (ISBN 0-531-09885-0). Watts.

Complete Ghost Stories of Charles Dickens. Charles Dickens & Peter Haining. LC 82-13481. (Illus.). 1983. 15.95 (ISBN 0-531-09885-0). F. Watts.

Complete in Him. Elizabeth Cary Kratzer. LC 13-25374. 1.25. G. A. Kratzer.

Complete L'Amour, 9 bks. Louis L'Amour. Incl. To Tame a Land; Heller With a Gun; Tall Stranger; Last Stand at Papago Wells; Hondo; Kilkenny; Showdown at Yellow Butte; Utah Blaine; Crossfire Trail. (Western Fiction Ser.). 1981. Repr. of 1978 ed. Set. lib. bdg. 74.50 (ISBN 0-8398-2662-1, Gregg). G K Hall.

Complete Maigret Short Stories. Georges Simenon. LC 77-367938. (v. 1) 4.95 (ISBN 0-241-89513-8). Hamilton.

Complete Murder Sampler. Ed. by James Nelson. 1946. Pub. for the Crime Club by Doubleday & Company, Inc.

Complete Mystery of Edwin Drood. Charles Dickens & John Cuming Walters. LC 74-31327. 1974. 30.00 (ISBN 0-8414-9371-5). Folcroft Library Editions.

Complete Mystery of Edwin Drood. Charles Dickens & John Cuming Walters. LC 74-31327. 1974. 30.00 (ISBN 0-8414-9371-5). Folcroft Library Editions.

Complete Mystery of Edwin Drood. J. Cuming Walters. LC 74-31327. Repr. of 1912 ed. lib. bdg. 30.00 (ISBN 0-8414-9371-5). Folcroft.

Complete Narrative Prose of Conrad Ferdinand Meyer. Conrad Ferdinand Meyer. LC 76-168824. 1975. 22.50 (ISBN 0-8387-1547-8). Bucknell University Press.

Complete Novels. Stephen Crane. Ed. by Thomas A. Gullason. LC 67-10369. 1967. Doubleday.

Complete Novels, 3 Vols. Victor Marie Hugo. (O.s.i.). (Fr). 35.00x o.s.i. Colton Bk.

Complete Novels & Selected Tales. Nathaniel Hawthorne. (Modern Library Giants). 1960. 5.95 o.p. (ISBN 0-394-60737-6, G37). Modern Lib.

Complete Novels and Selected Tales of Nathaniel Hawthorne. Nathaniel Hawthorne & Pearson, Norman Holmes, Ed. LC 37-28752. (Half-title: The modern library of the world's best books). 1937. The Modern Library.

Complete Novels. Introd. by Amy Loveman; Illustrated by Warren Chappell. Jane Austen. LC 50-11331. 1950. Random House.

Complete Novels of Charlotte & Emily Bronte. avenel 1981 ed. LC 81-10808. 7.98 (ISBN 0-517-34800-4). Avenel : Distributed by Crown Publishers.

Complete Novels of Guy De Maupassant. one volume ed. Guy De Maupassant. LC 36-13067. 1932. Blue Ribbon Books.

Complete Novels of Guy De Maupassant. Guy de Maupassant. 756p. 1980. Repr. of 1928 ed. lib. bdg. 35.00 (ISBN 0-89987-564-5). Darby Bks.

Complete Novels of Jane Austen. Jane Austen. LC 75-28070. 3.95 (ISBN 0-394-72053-9). Vintage Books.

Complete Novels of Jane Austen. Jane Austen. LC 33-27127. (Half-title: The modern library of the world's best books). 1933. The Modern Library.

Complete Novels of Jane Austen. Jane Austen. LC 38-8345. 1937. Carlton House.

Complete Novels of Jane Austen. de luxe ed. Jane Austen. LC 38-35081. 1938. Garden City Publishing Co., Inc.

Complete Novels of Jane Austen. Jane Austen. LC 80-107435. 7.95 (ISBN 0-394-60436-9). Modern Library.

Complete Novels of Mark Twain. Samuel Langhorne Clemens. Ed. by Charles Neider. LC 64-19239. 1964. Doubleday.

Complete Novels of Stephen Crane. Stephen Crane. Ed. by Thomas A. Gullason. 5.95 o.p. Doubleday.

Complete Novels of Stephen Crane. Ed. by Thomas A. Gullason. LC 67-10369. 5.95 o.p. (ISBN 0-385-04182-9). Doubleday.

Complete Poems: Biographical Introduction. George Eliot & Wood, Esther. LC 1-31172. (Her Works. Personal edition). 1901. Doubleday, Page & Co.

Complete Poetry. Miklos Radnoti & Emery Edward George. LC 80-123526. (Illus.). 17.50 (ISBN 0-88233-514-6). Ardis.

Complete Poetry of John Reed. John Reed. LC 73-80931. Pine Hill Press.

Complete Professor Challenger Stories. Arthur Conan Doyle. LC 77-351884. 1976-1977. 12.50 (ISBN 0-7195-0360-4). J. Murray.

Complete Professor Challenger Stories. Arthur Conan Doyle. 1952. 20.00 (ISBN 0-7195-0360-4). Transatlantic.

Complete Prose Tales of Alexander Sergeyevitch Pushkin. Tr. from Russsian by Gillon R. Aitken. Aleksandr Sergeevich Pushkin. Tr. by Gillon R Aitken. (Norton lib., N465). 1968. pap., 2.95. Norton.

Complete Prose Tales of Alexandr Sergeyevitch Pushkin. Tr. from Russian by Gillon R. Aitken. Aleksandr Sergeevich Pushkin. Tr. by Gillon R. Aitken. LC 67-17685. 1966-1967. 6.95. Norton.

Complete Robot. Isaac Asimov. LC 81-43134. 9.95 (ISBN 0-385-14707-4) (ISBN 0-385-17724-0). Doubleday.

Complete Ronald Firbank. Pref. by Anthony Powell. Arthur Annesley Ronald Firbank. LC 61-162056. 7.75. Dist. New Directions, New York.

Complete Sherlock Holmes. Arthur Conan Doyle. LC 65-6074. Doubleday.

Complete Sherlock Holmes. the a. conan coyle memorial edition, with preface by christopher morley... ed. Arthur Conan Doyle. Ed. by Arthur Conan Doyle. LC 35-21958. 1933. Doubleday, Doran & Company, Inc.

Complete Sherlock Holmes. Arthur Conan Doyle & Morley, Christopher Darlington, 1890- LC 36-334185. 1936. Doubleday, Doran & Company, Inc.

Complete Sherlock Holmes. deluxe ed. Arthur Conan Doyle & Morley, Christopher Darlington, 1890- LC 38-27775. 1938. Garden City Publishing Company, Inc.

Complete Sherlock Holmes: The A. Conan Doyle Memorial Edition. Arthur Conan Doyle & Morley, Christopher Darlington, 1800- LC 30-23546. 1930. Doubleday, Doran & Company, Inc.

Complete Sherlock Holmes. With a Pref. by Christopher Morley. Arthur Conan Doyle. LC 52-4772. Garden City Books.

Complete Sherlock Holmes: With a Pref. by Christopher Morley and an Introd. by John Dickson Carr. Arthur Conan Doyle. LC 53-1290. 1953. Doubleday.

Complete Short Stories. Andrei Bely, pseud. Ed. by Ronald Peterson. 1979. 14.00 (ISBN 0-88233-466-2); pap. 5.00 o.p. Ardis Pubs.

Complete Short Stories. Valery Briusov. Tr. by Gail Gilbert & Pierre Hart. 200p. 1983. 20.00 (ISBN 0-88233-790-4); pap. 5.00 (ISBN 0-88233-791-2). Ardis Pubs.

Complete Short Stories. Boris Nikolaevich Bugaev. LC 79-51640. (Illus.). 15.00 (ISBN 0-88233-466-2) (ISBN 0-88233-468-9). Ardis.

Complete Short Stories. Nathaniel Hawthorne. LC 59-10561. (Illus.). 1959. Hanover House.

Complete Short Stories. Jean Kerr. (Illus.). 1957. 3.50 o.p. Doubleday.

Complete Short Stories. David Herbert Lawrence. LC 77-23233. 1.95 (ISBN 0-14-004383-7). Penguin Books.

Complete Short Stories. William Somerset Maugham. LC 52-11626. 1952. Doubleday.

Complete Short Stories. Guy De Maupassant. LC 55-9990. 1955. Hanover House.

Complete Short Stories. Mark Twain. Ed. by Charles Neider. (gr. 8 up). pap. 2.95 (ISBN 0-553-14112-0). Bantam.

Complete Short Stories. Herbert George Wells. LC 79-145813. 1971. 14.95 o.p. (ISBN 0-312-15855-6, C4000). St Martin.

Complete Short Stories. Herbert George Wells. 12.50 o.p. Wehman.

Complete Short Stories & Sketches. Stephen Crane. Ed. by Thomas A. Gullason. LC 63-20507. 1963. Doubleday.

Complete Short Stories of Ambrose Bierce. Ambrose Gwinnett Bierce. LC 79-103758. 1970. 7.95. Doubleday.

Complete Short Stories of Ambrose Bierce. Ed. by Ernest J. Hopkins. LC 79-103758. (Illus.). 1970. 7.95 o.p. (ISBN 0-385-03946-8). Doubleday.

Complete Short Stories of D. H. Lawrence. David Herbert Lawrence. LC 71-101368. (Viking compass book, C96). (v. 2) 1.45 (ISBN 0-670-00096-5). Viking Press.

Complete Short Stories of De Maupassant. Guy De Maupassant. LC 47-7216. 1947. Halcyon House.

Complete Short Stories of Edgar Allan Poe. Edgar Allan Poe. Ed. by Killis Campbell. LC 43-6175. 1943. The Sun Dial Press.

Complete Short Stories of Guy De Maupassant... Guy De Maupassant. LC 34-41607. 1934. Blue Ribbon Books, Inc.

Complete Short Stories of Guy De Maupassant. Guy de Maupassant. 8.95 o.p. Doubleday.

Complete Short Stories of Mark Twain. Ed. by Charles Neider. (Bantam Classics Ser.). 704p. 1981. pap. 2.95 (ISBN 0-553-21053-X). Bantam.

Complete Short Stories of Mark Twain. Mark Twain. LC 57-5536. 1957. 12.95 (ISBN 0-385-01502-X). Doubleday.

Complete Short Stories of Mark Twain: Pseud. Now Collected for the First Time. Edited with an Introd. by Charles Neider. Samuel Langhorne Clemens. LC 57-553662. 1957. Hanover House.

Complete Short Stories of Mark Twain Pseud. Now Collected for the First Time. Samuel Langhorne Clemens. LC 57-5536. 1957. Hanover House.

Complete Short Stories of Nathaniel Hawthorne. Nathaniel Hawthorne. LC 59-15337. 1959. 12.95 (ISBN 0-385-01560-7). Doubleday.

Complete Short Stories of Robert Louis Stevenson: With a Selection of the Best Short Novels. Robert Louis Stevenson. Ed. by Charles Neider. LC 75-91111. 1969. 10.00. Doubleday.

Complete Short Stories of Saki H. H. Munro: With an Introduction by Christopher Morley. Hector Hugh Munro & Munro, Ethel M. LC 39-16969. 1939. Halcyon House.

Complete Short Stories of W. Somerset Maugham, 4 bks. William Somerset Maugham. Incl. Bk. 1. Rain & Other Stories (W936); Bk. 2. The Letter & Other Stories. pap. o.p. (W937); Bk. 3. The Book Bag & Other Stories (W938); Bk. 4. The Human Element & Other Stories (W939). pap. 0.75 ea o.p. WSP.

Complete Shorter Fiction of Oscar Wilde. Oscar Wilde & Isobel Murray. LC 79-41100. (World's classics). 1979. 14.95 (ISBN 0-19-251001-0) (ISBN 0-19-281500-8). Oxford University Press.

Complete Stalky & Co. Rudyard Kipling. LC 48-9818. 1946. Doubleday.

Complete Stalky & Co. Rudyard Kipling. LC 30-22025. 1930. Doubleday, Doran & Company, Inc.

Complete State of Death. John E Gardner. LC 76-83228. 1969. 4.95. Viking Press.

Complete Stories. Franz Kafka. Ed. by Nahum Norbert Glatzer. LC 75-161559. 1971. 12.50 (ISBN 0-8052-3419-5). Schocken Books.

Complete Stories. Flannery O'Connor. LC 72-171492. 1971. 10.00 (ISBN 0-374-12752-2). Farrar, Straus and Giroux.

Complete Stories of Erskine Caldwell. Erskine Caldwell. 1953. 8.95 o.p. (ISBN 0-316-12421-4). Little.

Complete Stories of Herman Melville. Herman Melville. Ed. by Jay Leyda. LC 49-8911. 1949. Random House.

Complete Stories of Lu Xun. Hsun Lu. LC 81-47585. 17.50 (ISBN 0-253-31396-1) (ISBN 0-253-20274-4). Indiana University Press.

Complete Stories. 1st Ed. Erskine Caldwell. LC 53-10243. 1953. Duell, Sloan and Pearce.

Complete Stranger. Van Siller. 1969. pap. 0.60 o.p. (0502-06066-060). Curtis.

Complete Stranger: By Van Siller. Hilda Van Siller. LC 65-23785. 3.50. Pub. for the Crime Club by Doubleday.

Complete Surrender. Sidney Grant. LC 39-15714. 1939. Godwin.

Complete Tales and Poems of Edgar Allan Poe. Edgar Allan Poe. LC 38-272791. (Half-title: The modern library of the world's best books). 1938. The Modern Library.

Complete Tales from Shakespeare: All Those Told by Charles & Mary Lamb, with 12 Others Newly Told by J. C. Trewin. Charles Lamb & Mary Ann Lamb. LC 64-23192. (Nonesuch cygnet). 1965. 7.95. Watts.

Complete Tales of Henry James. Henry James & Leon Joseph Edel. LC 62-11335. 1962. Lippincott.

Complete Tales of Washington Irving. Washington Irving & Charles Neider. LC 74-12702. 1975. 8.95 (ISBN 0-385-08945-7). Doubleday.

Complete Uncle Abner. Melville Davisson Post. LC 76-50688. (Mystery Library; 4). (Illus.). 6.95 (ISBN 0-89163-028-7). University Extension, University of California.

Complete Venus Equilateral. George Oliver Smith. LC 76-15588. 1976. 1.95 (ISBN 0-345-25551-8). Ballantine Books.

Complete White Oxen: Collected Short Fiction. Kenneth Burke. LC 68-17629. (£3.40; pap. £1.20). (Clothe ed. 7.50 o.p.). 1968. pap. 2.45 (ISBN 0-520-00155-9). U of Cal Pr.

Complete Wild Body. Wyndham Lewis & Bernard Lafourcade. LC 82-4498. (Illus.). 1982. 20.00 (ISBN 0-87685-552-4) (ISBN 0-87685-551-6) (ISBN 0-87685-553-2). Black Sparrow Press.

Complete Works. Charles Lutwidge Dodgson. LC 75-28505. 1976. 5.95 (ISBN 0-394-72054-7). Vintage Books.

Complete Works. Nathanael West. LC 57-625949. 1957. Farrar, Straus and Cudahy.

Complete Works of Charles Dickens... Ed. with Annotations, Bibliography and Topography by Frederic G. Kitton. Autograph Ed. Charles Dickens. Ed. by Kitton, Frederic George. LC 3-554. G. D. Sproul.

Complete Works of Gustave Flaubert: Embracing Romances, Travels, Comedies, Sketches and Correspondence; with a Critical Introduction by Ferdinand Bruentiere... and a Biographical Preface by Robert Arnot, M.A. Brunetiere Ed. Gustave Flaubert & Brunetiere, Ferdinand, 1849-1906. LC 4-21641. 1904. Printed Only for Subscribers by M. W. Dunne.

Complete Works of Guy De Maupassant... Translations and Critical Interpretive Essays. Guy De Maupassant. Tr. by Sumichrast, Frederick Caesar John Martin Samuel Roussy De et al. LC 10-6737. The C. T. Brainard Publishing Co.

Complete Works of Kate Chopin. Kate O'Flaherty Chopin. Ed. by Per Seyersted. LC 73-80043. (Southern Literary Studies). (Illus.). 1970. 20.00. Louisiana State University Press.

Complete Works of Lewis Carrol Pseud. Charles Lutwidge Dodgson. LC 36-27494. (Half-title: The modern library of the world's best books). 1936. The Modern Library.

Complete Works of Lewis Carroll Pseud. Charles Lutwidge Dodgson. 1937. Random House.

Complete Works of Lewis Carroll Pseud. Charles Lutwidge Dodgson. LC 40-34498. 1939. The Nonesuch Press.

Complete Works of Michael Fairless: Pseud. with a Biographical Note by M. E. Dowson. Margaret Fairless Barber & Dowson, Mary Emily, 1848- LC 32-32271. E. P. Dutton & Co., Inc.

Complete Works of Nathanael West. Nathanael West. LC 77-26787. 1978. 20.00 (ISBN 0-374-98358-5). Octagon Books.

Complete Works of O. Henry. O. Henry. LC 53-6098. 1953. 19.95 (ISBN 0-385-00961-5). Doubleday.

Complete Works of O. Henry Pseud. authentic ed. William Sydney Porter. LC 37-5369. 1937. Garden City Publishing Co., Inc.

Complete Works of William Makepeace Thackeray. bedford ed.... ed. William Makepeace Thackeray. LC 4-19861. 1904-09. G. D. Sproul.

Complete Works of William Makepeace Thackeray. William Makepeace Thackeray & Trent, William Peterfield. LC 4-32381. T. Y. Crowell & Co.

Complete Works of William Makepeace Thackeray: With Illustrations by the Author, and with Introductory Notes Setting Forth the History of the Several Works in Twenty-Two Volumes... William Makepeace Thackeray & Scudder, Horace Elisha, 1838-1902, Ed. LC 12-39377. Houghton, Mifflin and Company.

Complex Counterpart: A Novel. 1st Ed. Marie J Yager. LC 56-125068. Pageant Press.

Complex Man. Marie C Farca. LC 72-92206. (Doubleday science fiction). 1973. 5.95 (ISBN 0-385-06620-1). Doubleday.

Complex Mother. Rick Luas. LC 55-43687. 1955. Vixen Press.

Complex Vision: A Collection of Short Stories. Ed. by Ray Kytle. LC 70-187854. (Illus.). 1972. (ISBN 0-15-512615-6). Harcourt Brace Jovanovich.

Complex Vision of Philo St. John. R. Martin Helick. LC 75-27035. 10.00 (ISBN 0-912710-07-1). Regent Graphic Services.

Complication in Hearts: A Novel. Edmund Pendleton. LC 7-363671. 1893. The Home Publishing Company.

Compliments of a Fiend. 1st Ed. Fredric Brown. LC 50-6242. (Guilt edged mystery). 1950. Dutton.

Complot del Psicotron. new ed. Joseph Rosenberger. Tr. by Margarita O. Castro from Eng. (Compadre Collection: El/Mercader De la Muerte Ser.). Orig. Title: Psychotron Plot. 160p. (Span.). 1974. pap. 0.75 (ISBN 0-88473-503-6). Fiesta Pub.

Compose Yourself: The Music Nothingbook. (Nothing Book Ser.). 1979. pap. 4.95 (ISBN 0-517-53891-1, Harmony). Crown.

Composer. Agnes Sweetman Castle & Castle, Egerton. LC 11-26606. 1911. Doubleday, Page & Company.

Compost: A Cosmic View with Practical Suggestions. Jeanne Baumgarten & Caroline Goldsmith. 1973. pap. 1.95 o.p. (ISBN 0-06-090330-9, CN330, CN). Har-Row.

Compost Heap. Christopher Fahy. LC 79-126582. 1970. 5.95. Outerbridge & Dienstfrey; Distributed by Dutton.

Compound for Death. Doris Miles Disney. LC 43-18203. 1943. Pub. for the Crime Club by Doubleday, Doran and Co., Inc.

Compression Tested: A Novel. Margie Summerfield. LC 79-663. 8.95 (ISBN 0-07-062573-5). McGraw-Hill.

Compromise. Ruby Mildred Ayres. LC 36-89941. 1936. Doubleday, Doran & Company, Inc.

Compromise. Ruby Mildred Ayres. LC 37-38613. 1937. The Sun Dial Press, Inc.

Compromise. Royal Wilbur France. LC 36-9936. Dorrance and Company.

Compromise: A Novel. Sergei Dovlatov. LC 83-47854. 1983. 11.95 (ISBN 0-394-52855-7). A.A. Knopf.

Compromise: A Novel. Jay Gelzer. LC 23-13727. 1923. R. M. McBride & Company.

Compromises. Agnes Repplier. LC 78-98626. Repr. of 1904 ed. 9.50 (ISBN 0-404-05259-2). AMS Pr.

Compromising Positions. Susan Isaacs. LC 77-13896. 8.95 (ISBN 0-8129-0736-1). Times Books.

Compromising Positions. Susan Isaacs. (Jove/HBJ book). 1979. 2.25 (ISBN 0-515-04701-5). Jove Pubns.

Compulsion. Lyn Barrow. 1969. pap. 2.95 o.s.i. Tri-Ocean.

Compulsion. Charlotte Lamb, pseud. (Harlequin Presents Ser.). 192p. 1981. pap. 1.50 (ISBN 0-373-10422-7, Pub. by Harlequin). PB.

Compulsion. Meyer Levin. 1956. Simon and Schuster.

Compulsion & Other Tales. Howard R. Myers, Jr. 2.00 o.p. Carlton.

Computer Connection. Alfred Bester. LC 74-30544. 1975. 6.95 (ISBN 0-399-11481-5). Berkley Pub. Corp.: Distributed by Putnam.

Computer Connection. Alfred Bester. (Berkley Medallion Book). 1976. (pbk.) 1.50 (ISBN 0-425-03039-3). Berkley Publishing Corp.

Computer Dating Game. Gerald Summers. 192p. (Orig.). 1974. pap. 1.95 o.p. (ISBN 0-87056-384-X, 6384). Brandon.

Computer Kill. Lionel Derrick, pseud. (Penetrator Ser.: No. 30). 1979. pap. 1.50 (ISBN 0-523-40270-8). Pinnacle Bks.

Computer Sweetheart. Florence Stonebraker. LC 66-31660. 1966. Arcadia House.

Comrad Don Camillo. Giovanni Guareschi. LC 64-13881. 1964. Farrar, Straus.

Comrade Forest. Michael Leigh. LC 47-3062. 1947. Whittlesey House, McGraw-Hill Book Company, Inc.

Comrade in White. William Harvey Leathem. LC 16-14279. Fleming H. Revell Company.

Comrade Jill. Herbert Adams. LC 27-38262. 1927. J. B. Lippincott Company.

Comrade John. Samuel Merwin & Webster, Henry Kitchell. LC 7-33593. 1907. The Macmillan Company.

Comrade Loves of the Samurai. Saikaku Ihara. Ed. by Edward Powys Mathers. LC 70-184817. (Illus.). 1972. 2.50 (ISBN 0-8048-1024-9). Tuttle.

Comrade O Comrade: Or, Low-Down on the Left. Ethel Edith Mannin. LC 47-22614. 1947. Jarrolds (London) Ltd.

Comrade of Navarre: A Tale of the Huguenots. Harriet Malone Hobson. LC 15-157. 1914. The Griffith & Rowland Press.

Comrade Spy: A New Spy Novel. Lev Sergeevich Ovalov. LC 66-1620. 1965. Award Books.

Comrade, the Love Life of a Girl Communist. George Boyle. LC 34-37394. Author's Publications, Inc.

Comrade Venka: A Novel. Translated from the Russian by Joseph Barnes. Pavel F Nilin. LC 59-6014. 1959. Simon and Schuster.

Comrade Yetta. Arthur Bullard. LC 68-57516. (American novels of muckraking, propaganda, and social protest). 1968. Gregg Press.

Comrade Yetta. Arthur Bullard. LC 13-376037. 1913. 1.35. The Macmillan Company.

Comrades. Mary C Johnson Dillon. LC 18-2414. 1918. The Century Co.

Comrades. Alan Siegler. LC 75-10000. 8.95. St. Martin's Press.

Comrades: A Story of Social Adventure in California. Thomas Dixon. LC 9-20403. 1909. 1.50. Doubleday, Page & Company.

Comrades at Arms: The Further Adventures of D'Artagnan and Cyrano. Paul Feval. Tr. by Cleveland Bruce Chase. LC 30-26897. 1930. Longmans, Green and Co.

Comrades in Arms: A Novel. Alan Boatman. LC 73-4139. 1974. 7.95 (ISBN 0-06-010403-1). Harper & Row.

Comrades in Arms: A Tale of Two Hemispheres. Charles King. LC 4-28952. 1904. The Hobart Company.

Comrades of Kiowa Valley. Harlan C Thomas. LC 36-486. E. J. Clode, Inc.

Comrades of Peril. Randall Parrish. LC 19-156783. 1919. 1.50. A. C. McClurg & Co.

Comrades of the Colt. John Keith Bassett. LC 96-226172. Greenberg.

Comrades of the Lone Star. Will Henry Spindler. LC 21-7720. The Roxburgh Publishing Company.

Comrades of the Storm. Peter Bernard Kyne. LC 33-28590. 1933. H. C. Kinsey & Company, Inc.

Comrades True. Annie Hall Thomas Cudlip. LC 3842. 1900. F. M. Buckles & Company; Etc., Etc.

Comstock Club. Charles Carroll Goodwin. LC 6-27479. 1891. Tribune Printing Company.

Comstock Lode. Thomas Albert Curry. LC 42-79565. 1941. Arcadia House, Inc.

Comstock Lode. Louis L'Amour. LC 80-70357. 1981. 6.95 (ISBN 0-553-01307-6). Bantam Books.

Comte De Monte-Cristo, 2 tomes. Alexandre Dumas, Sr. (Coll. Prestige). 1963-64. Set. 25.95 o.p. French & Eur.

Con. Peter Shaw. LC 78-1834. 94p. 1976. pap. 9.95 (ISBN 0-89713-010-3). Richboro Pr.

Con. M. E White. LC 77-181667. 1972. 6.95 (ISBN 0-06-014610-9). Harper & Row.

Con Artist of the Sunset Strip. Caesar S. Kersten. LC 78-52390. 1978. pap. 2.95 o.p. (ISBN 0-89260-122-1). Hwong Pub.

Con Game. 1st Ed. Hillary Waugh. LC 67-22448. 1968. 3.95. Pub. for the Crime Club by Doubleday.

Con Man. Charlie Avery Harris. (Orig.). 1978. pap. 1.75 (ISBN 0-87067-542-7, BH542). Holloway.

Con Man. F. C. A McBain. LC 57-6060. (Permabooks, M-3055. Mystery, 5). 1957. Permabooks.

Con O'Regan: Or, Emigrant Life in the New World. Mary Anne Madden Sadlier. LC 8-1646. (On cover: Cottage and parlor library). D. & J. Sadlier & Co.

Con Teaser. Eddie Francis. pap. 1.95 o.p. (8048). Cameo.

Conagher. Louis L'Amour. 1977. pap. 1.95 (ISBN 0-553-13602-X, Y13602-X). Bantam.

Conagher. Louis L'Amour. Date not set. pap. 2.50 (ISBN 0-553-22843-9). Bantam.

Conan. Robert E. Howard et al. (Conan Ser.: No. 1). 1982. pap. 2.25 (ISBN 0-441-11630-2, Pub. by Ace Science Fiction). Ace Bks.

Conan. Robert E. Howard et al. 1970. pap. 1.25 o.s.i. (78-744). Lancer.

Conan & the Spider God, No. 6. L. Sprague de Camp. 192p. (Orig.). 1980. pap. 2.25 (ISBN 0-553-13837-5). Bantam.

Conan Doyle Historical Romances. Arthur Conan Doyle. 9.75 o.p. Transatlantic.

Conan Doyle Stories. Arthur Conan Doyle. 9.75 o.p. Transatlantic.

Conan of Aquilonia. Robert E. Howard. (Conan Ser.: No. 11). 192p. 1982. pap. 2.25 (ISBN 0-441-11640-X, Pub. by Ace Science Fiction). Ace Bks.

Conan of Cimmeria. Robert E. Howard et al. (Conan Ser.: No. 2). 192p. 1982. pap. 2.25 (ISBN 0-441-11631-0, Pub. by Ace Science Fiction). Ace Bks.

Conan of Cimmeria. Robert E. Howard et al. 1970. pap. 1.25 o.s.i. (78-742). Lancer.

Conan of the Isles. Robert E. Howard. (Conan Ser.: No. 12). 192p. 1982. pap. 2.25 (ISBN 0-441-11641-8, Pub. by Ace Science Fiction). Ace Bks.

Conan of the Isles. Robert E. Howard. 1970. pap. 1.25 o.s.i. (78-745). Lancer.

Conan Reader. Lyon Sprague De Camp. LC 70-14082. (Voyager series). (Illus.). 1968. 4.00. Mirage.

Conan the Adventurer. Robert E. Howard. (Orig.). 1968. pap. 1.25 o.s.i. (78-743). Lancer.
Conan, the Adventurer. Robert E. Howard & L. Sprague de Camp. (Conan Ser.: No. 5). 192p. 1982. pap. 2.25 (ISBN 0-441-11634-5, Pub. by Ace Science Fiction). Ace Bks.
Conan, the Avenger. Robert E. Howard. (Conan Ser.: No. 10). 192p. 1982. pap. 2.25 (ISBN 0-441-11639-6, Pub. by Ace Science Fiction). Ace Bks.
Conan the Avenger. Robert E. Howard. (Conan Ser. No. 6). (Orig.). 1968. pap. 1.25 o.s.i. (78-747). Lancer.
Conan the Barbarian. Lyon Sprague De Camp & Lin Carter. 1982. pap. 2.50. Bantam.
Conan the Barbarian. 1st Ed. Robert E. Howard. LC 54-12146. Gnome Press.
Conan the Buccaneer. Lyon Sprague De Camp & Lin Carter. 1971. pap. 0.95 o.s.i. (75-181). Lancer.
Conan, the Buccaneer. L. Sprague de Camp & Lin Carter. (Conan Ser.: No. 6). 192p. 1982. pap. 2.25 (ISBN 0-441-11635-3). Ace Bks.
Conan, the Conquerer. Robert E. Howard. (Conan Ser.: No. 9). 192p. 1982. pap. 2.25 (ISBN 0-441-11638-8, Pub. by Ace Science Fiction). Ace Bks.
Conan the Conqueror. Robert E. Howard. LC 51-2043. (His The Hyborean Age). 1950. Gnome Press.
Conan the Defender. Robert Jordan. 288p. 1982. pap. 5.95 (ISBN 0-523-48063-6). Pinnacle Bks.
Conan: The Devil in Iron. Robert E. Howard. 6.95 o.p. (ISBN 0-448-14580-4, G&D). Putnam Pub Group.
Conan! The Flame Knife. Robert E. Howard. (Conan Ser.). 160p. (Orig.). 1981. pap. 2.50 (ISBN 0-441-11666-3). Ace Bks.
Conan the Freebooter. Robert E. Howard & L. Sprague De Camp. pap. 0.95 o.s.i. (75-119). Lancer.
Conan, the Freebooter. Robert E. Howard & L. Sprague De Camp. (Conan Ser.: No. 3). 192p. 1977. pap. 2.25 (ISBN 0-441-11632-9, Pub. by Ace Science Fiction). Ace Bks.
Conan, the Freebooter. Robert E. Howard et al. (Conan Ser.: No. 3). 192p. 1982. pap. 2.50 (ISBN 0-441-11596-9, Pub. by Ace Science Fiction). Ace Bks.
Conan: The Invincible. Robert Jordan. 288p. (Orig.). 1982. pap. 2.95 (ISBN 0-523-48050-4). Pinnacle Bks.
Conan the Liberator, No. 2. Lyon Sprague De Camp & Lin Carter. 1979. pap. 1.95 (ISBN 0-553-12706-3). Bantam.
Conan, the Mercenary. Andrew J. Offutt. (Conan Ser.). 192p. (Orig.). 1981. pap. 2.50 (ISBN 0-441-11659-0). Ace Bks.
Conan: The People of the Black Circle. authorized ed. Robert E. Howard & Karl Edward Wagner. LC 78-20392. (Illus.). 9.95 (ISBN 0-399-12147-1). Berkley Pub. Corp.: Distributed by Putnam.
Conan the Rebel, No. 5. Poul Anderson. 224p. (Orig.). 1980. pap. 2.25 (ISBN 0-553-13831-6). Bantam.
Conan the Swordsman, No. 1. Lyon Sprague De Camp & Lin Carter. 1978. pap. 1.95 (ISBN 0-553-12018-2). Bantam.
Conan: The Tower of the Elephant. Robert E. Howard. LC 78-59788. (Illus.). 1978. (6.95, 7.95 can) (ISBN 0-448-16238-5). Grosset & Dunlap.
Conan the Unconquered. Robert Jordan. (Tor Conan Ser.: Bk. 3). 288p. (Orig.). 1983. pap. 2.95 (ISBN 0-523-48053-9). Pinnacle Bks.
Conan, the Ursurper. Lyon Sprague De Camp & Robert E. Howard. (Conan Ser.: No. 8). 192p. 1983. pap. 2.50 (ISBN 0-441-11602-7, Pub. by Ace Science Fiction). Ace Bks.
Conan the Usurper. Robert E. Howard. (Orig.). 1968. pap. 0.95 o.s.i. (75-103). Lancer.
Conan, the Wanderer. Robert E. Howard et al. (Conan Ser.: No. 4). 192p. 1983. pap. 2.50 (Pub. by Ace Science Fiction). Ace Bks.
Conan the Wanderer. Robert E. Howard et al. (Orig.). 1970. pap. 1.25 o.s.i. (78-741). Lancer.
Conan, the Warrior. Robert E. Howard. Ed. by L. Sprague De Camp. (Conan Ser.: No. 7). 192p. 1982. pap. 2.50 (ISBN 0-441-11636-1, Pub. by Ace Science Fiction). Ace Bks.
Conan the Warrior. Robert E. Howard. (Orig.). 1968. pap. 1.25 o.s.i. (78-746). Lancer.
Concannon. Clifton Adams. 1973. (pbk.) 0.75. Manor Books.
Concannon. Clifton Adams. LC 72-76112. 1972. 4.95. Doubleday.
Concannon. Frank O'Rourke. LC 52-14046. 1953. Ballantine Books.
Concave Mirror. William Babington Maxwell. LC 31-21436. 1931. Dodd, Mead & Company.
Conceal and Disguise. Henry Kane. LC 66-21158. (Cock robin mystery). bds., 3.95. Macmillan.
Concealed Turnings. Winifred Mary Scott. LC 27-18470. The Macaulay Company.
Conceived in Liberty: A Novel of Valley Forge. Howard Melvin Fast. LC 39-27589. 1939. Simon and Schuster.
Concentrations of Bee. Lilian Lida Bell. 1909. 1.50. L. C. Page & Company.
Conception of the Beast. Benjamin Grimm. LC 72-9906. 1969. 1.75. Ophelia Press.
Concerning Belinda. Eleanor Hoyt Brainerd. LC 78-86138. (Short story index reprint series). (Illus.). 1969. (ISBN 0-8369-3042-8). Books for Libraries Press.
Concerning Him. LC 25-237284. George H. Doran Company.
Concerning Himself: The Story of an Ordinary Man. Victor L Whitechurch. LC 11-35807. 1911. The Baker & Taylor Company.
Concerning Isabel Carnaby. Ellen Thorneycroft Fowler. LC 6-43284. 1899. D. Appleton and Company.
Concerning Martha: A Novel. Charlotte L White. LC 26-15736. 1926. The Stratford Company.
Concerning Paul and Fiammetta. Lizzie Allen Harker. LC 6-106426. 1906. C. Scribner's Sons.
Concerning Sally. William John Hopkins. LC 12-21770. 1912. 1.35. Houghton Mifflin Company.
Concerning the Death of Charlie Bowman. Michael Hammonds. LC 70-139028. 1971. 4.50. Doubleday.
Concerning the Eccentricities of Cardinal Pirelli. Arthur Annesley Ronald Firbank. LC 78-308645. 1977. 4.95 (ISBN 0-7156-1099-6). Duckworth.
Concert Pitch. Theodora Benson. LC 34-345903. 1934. The Macmillan Company.
Concert Pitch. Julia Davis Frankau. LC 13-2501. 1913. 1.35. The Macmillan Company.
Concert Pitch. Elliot Harold Paul. LC 38-7320. Random House.
Concerto for Hell. 1st Ed. Nicholas Tymkin. LC 53-209393. 1952. Pageant Press.
Concerto for Ten Broken Fingers. Gerry Max. 162p. 1978. pap. 4.95 (101). William of Orange.
Concerto for Two Voices: A Prose-Poem in Three Movements. 1st Ed. Shirley Seigfred. LC 57-9222. 1957. Exposition Press.
Concerto in the Key of Death. Barbara Fried. (Orig.). 1980. pap. 1.75 o.s.i. (ISBN 0-505-51508-3). Tower Bks.
Concerto: The Study of a Great Soul. Elsie Pain. LC 27-22758. 1927. Adelaide Ambrose, Inc.
Concession. large print ed. Ann Ashton, pseud. LC 81-8852. 10.95 (ISBN 0-89621-290-4). Thorndike Press.
Concession. John M. Kimbro. LC 79-7484. 1981. 12.95 (ISBN 0-385-13210-7). Doubleday.
Concessions. Stephen Hudson. LC 14-5274. 1913. John Lane.
Conch Eaters. Leo Rost. LC 73-82726. 1973. 6.95 (ISBN 0-88381-005-0). Wollstonecraft.
Concha: "My Dancing Saint.". Rebecca Lawrence Lee. LC 67-3487. 1966.
Concierto de Primavero. Antonio B. Rey. (Romance Real Ser.). 180p. 1981. pap. 1.50 (ISBN 0-88025-001-1). Roca Pub.
Conclave: A Novel. Lawrence D Klausner. LC 81-5960. 12.95 (ISBN 0-07-035028-0). McGraw-Hill.
Concluding: A Novel. Henry Green. LC 73-122055. (Viking reprint editions). 1970. A. M. Kelley.
Concomitant Soldier: Woman & War. Sonya Jason. LC 73-92563. (O.s.i.). 376p. 1974. pap. 3.00 o.s.i. (ISBN 0-915082-25-X, Gemini Pr). Proj Pub & Des.
Concord Bridge. Robert Payne. LC 52-8310. 1952. Bobbs-Merrill.
Concord in Jeopardy. Doris Oppenheim Leslie, pseud. LC 38-13179. 1938. The Macmillan Company.
Concorde: Airport 79. Kerry Stewart, pseud. (Orig.). pap. 2.25 (ISBN 0-515-05348-1). Jove Pubns.
Concordia. Frances Fleetwood. 1978. 1.955 (ISBN 0-441-11653-1). Ace Books.
Concordia Errant. Frances Fleetwood. (Ace Book). 1978. 1.95 (ISBN 0-441-11685-X). Ace Books.
Concordia Errant: The Story of Francesca Da Rimini's Daughter. Frances Fleetwood. LC 73-163465. (Illus.). 1973. 2.75 (ISBN 0-491-00514-8). W.H. Allen.
Concordia: The Story of Francesca Da Rimini. Frances Fleetwood. LC 72-94046. 1973. 6.50. St. Martin's Press.
Concrete Boot. Kenneth Royce. LC 70-165089. (MW suspense). 1971. 4.95. McKay.
Concrete Cage. Robert Novak. (Joe Blaze,#3). 1974. (pbk.) 0.95. Belmont Tower Books.
Concrete Castle Murders. Francis Gerard. LC 36-82112. H. Holt and Company.
Concrete Island. J. G. Ballard. LC 73-87699. 1974. 6.95 (ISBN 0-374-12807-3). Farrar Straus and Giroux.
Concrete Judasbird. F. X Mathews. LC 68-18777. 1968. Houghton Mifflin.
Concrete Kimono. John Paddy Carstairs. LC 65-234221. bds., 3.50. Walker.
Concrete Strip. Roy Bernard Sparkia. 192p. (Orig.). 1975. pap. 1.25 (ISBN 0-532-12261-5). Woodhill.
Concrete Wilderness. Jack Couffer. LC 67-20852. (Illus.). 1967. 4.95 o.p. (ISBN 0-696-56495-5). Hawthorn.
Concretions. Drawings by Milton Avery. Arlene Zekowski. LC 62-7480. (Archives of modern literature series). 1962. G. Wittenborn.
Concubine. Elechi Amadi. (African Writers Ser.: No. 25). (Orig.). 1966. pap. text ed. 2.50x o.p. (ISBN 0-435-90325-X). Humanities.
Concubine. Elechi Emmanuel Amadi. (African Writers Ser.). 1966. pap. text ed. 3.00x (ISBN 0-435-90025-0). Heinemann Ed.
Condamne a Mort see Oeuvres Completes.
Condemned. Paul Kuttner. LC 83-1872. 1983. 10.95 (ISBN 0-911025-02-2). Dawnwood Press.
Condemned. Jo Pagano. LC 47-31379. 1947. Prentice-Hall.
Condemned Door: Porte Close) or, The Secret of Trigabon Castle. Fortune Du Boisgobey. LC 6-344294. (On cover: Lovell's library. no. 1013). J. W. Lovell Company.
Condemned to Live: A Novel. Johann Rabener. Tr. by Dunlop, Geoffery. LC 35-6352. 1935. Doubleday, Doran & Company, Inc.
Condensed Books Anthology. The Reader's Digest. LC 56-58521. 1956. Reader's Digest Association.
Condensed Novels. Bret Harte. LC 71-122715. (Short story index reprint series). (Illus.). 1970. Books for Libraries Press.
Condensed Novels. Bret Harte. LC 34-305736. 1871. J. R. Osgood and Company.
Condensed Novels. Bret Harte. LC 4-15398. 1899. Houghton,Mifflin and Company.
Condensed Novels. Bret Harte. LC 99-2108. 1899. Houghton, Mifflin and Company.
Condensed Novels. And Other Papers. Bret Harte. LC 7-3638. 1867. G. W. Carleton & Company; Etc., Etc.
Condensed Novels. And Other Papers. Bret I. E. Francis Bret Harte. LC 7-3638. 1867. G. W. Carleton & Company; Etc., Etc.
Condensed Novels and Stories. Bret Harte. LC 75-122716. (Short story index reprint series). 1970. Books for Libraries Press.
Condensed Novels and Stories. Bret Harte. LC 12-27748. (Half-title: The works of Bret Harte. Riverside edition. v. 5). 1882. Houghton, Mifflin and Company.
Condensed Novels of Bret Harte. Bret Harte. LC 78-91081. (American humorists series). (Illus.). 1969. Literature House.
Condensed Novels, Second Series; New Burlesques. Bret Harte. LC 74-110197. (Short story index reprint series). 1970. Books for Libraries Press.
Condensed Novels. Second Series. New Burlesques. Bret Harte. LC 2-23598. 1902. Houghton, Mifflin and Company.
Condition Green. Neil Goble. 1966. 2.95. Tuttle.
Condition Humaine. Andre Malraux. (Coll. Soleil). 1933. 17.50. French & Eur.
Condition Is Red: A Biographical Novel. A B Edelmann. LC 57-59034. 1957. Pageant Press.
Condition of Muzak. Michael Moorcock. LC 77-27425. (Gregg Press science fiction series). (Illus.). 1978. 13.50 (ISBN 0-8398-2434-3). Gregg Press.
Condition Pink. Leland Frederick Cooley. LC 67-11735. 1967. Doubleday.
Condition Three: A Novel. 1st Ed. Peter Bowman. LC 62-114230. 1962. Doubleday.
Conditional Sentence. Hugh Fleetwood. 1979. 1.95 (ISBN 0-671-81789-2). Pocket Books.
Condominium. John Dann MacDonald. 1978. pap. 2.75 (ISBN 0-449-23525-4, Crest). Fawcett.
Condominium: A Novel. John Dann MacDonald. LC 76-30593. 10.00 (ISBN 0-397-01203-9). Lippincott.
Condominium Trap. Hugo Paul, pseud. LC 79-65558. 1983. 7.50 (ISBN 0-916620-36-0). Portals Pr.
Condor. Glenn Pierce. (Orig.). 1980. pap. 1.95 o.s.i. (ISBN 0-505-51520-2). Tower Bks.
Condor Conspiracy. Charlotte Yarborough. (Orig.). 1980. pap. 1.75 o.s.i. (ISBN 0-8439-0739-8, Leisure Bks). Nordon Pubns.
Condor Passes. Shirley Ann Grau. LC 71-159831. 1971. 7.95 (ISBN 0-394-47249-7). Knopf.
Condottiere. Jan Vlachos Westcott. LC 62-8468. 1962. Random House.
Conduct of Major Maxim. Gavin Lyall. LC 82-10887. 1983. 14.95 (ISBN 0-670-23711-6). Viking Press.
Conduct Unbecoming. Rupert Croft Cooke. 1975. (pbk.) 1.50 (ISBN 0-671-80097-3). Pocket Books.
Conduct Unbecoming. Charles Fenton. LC 54-8035. (Dell first edition, 19). 1954. Dell Pub. Co.
Conducted Tour. Gil Meynier. LC 31-20401. 1931. Thomas S. Rockwell Company.
Conducting Bodies. Claude Simon. LC 73-17681. 1974. 7.95 (ISBN 0-670-23712-4). Viking Press.
Cone Cut Corners: The Experiences of a Conservative Family in Fanatical Times; Involving Some Account of a Connecticut Village, the People Who Live in It, and Those Who Come There from the City. Benjamin Vaugham Abbott & Abbott, Austin, 1831-1896, Joint Author. LC 5-42004. Mason Brothers.
Cone Cut Corners; the Experiences of a Conservative Family in Fanatical Times: Involving Some Account of a Connecticut Village, the People Who Live in It, and Those Who Come There from the City. Benauly. LC 5-42604. Mason Brothers.
Cone Gatherers: A Novel. Robin Jenkins. LC 80-25757. 1981. 9.95 (ISBN 0-8008-1808-3). Taplinger Pub. Co.
Cone of Silence. David Beaty. LC 58-10566. 1959. Morrow.
Cone of Silence. Archibald Fleming MacLiesh. LC 44-6699. 1944. Houghton Mifflin Company.
Conehead. Gardner F Fox. 1973. (pbk.) 0.95. Ace Books.
Cones for the Camp Fire. William Henry Harrison Murray. LC 7-32494. De Wolfe, Fiske & Co.
Conestoga Cowboy. Roe Richmond. LC 49-48414. 1949. Phoenix Press.
Conexion Italiana. new ed. Glen Chase, pseud. Tr. by Miguel Sarria from Eng. (Pimienta Collection: Cereza Delicias Ser., No. 1). Orig. Title: Italian Connection. 160p. (Span.). 1974. pap. 1.00 o.p. (ISBN 0-88473-204-5). Fiesta Pub.
Coney Island. Homer Croy. LC 29-190221. 1929. Harper & Brothers.
Coney Island Quickstep: A Novel. George Gipe. LC 76-56764. 8.95 (ISBN 0-690-01197-0). Crowell.
Confait Confessions. Christopher Price & Jonathan Caplan. LC 78-303941. 144p. 1979. 10.95 (ISBN 0-7145-2564-2, Pub. by M Boyars); pap. 6.95 (ISBN 0-7145-2565-0). Merrimack Pub Cir.
Confederacy of Dunces. John Kennedy Toole. LC 79-20190. 1980. 15.95 (ISBN 0-8071-0657-7). Louisiana State University Press.
Confederacy of Dunces. John Kennedy Toole. LC 81-85394. 1982. 3.95 (ISBN 0-394-17969-2). Grove Press.
Confederate Chieftains: A Tale of the Irish Rebellion of 1641. Mary Anne Madden Sadlier. LC 8-1647. 1868. D. & J. Sadlier & Co.
Confederate General from Big Sur. Richard Brautigan. LC 64-24078. 1965. 3.95. Grove.
Confederate General from Big Sur. Richard Brautigan. LC 79-17234. 1979. 8.95 (ISBN 0-440-01692-4). Delacorte Press/S. Lawrence.
Confederate Raider. Showell Styles. LC 67-12611. 1967. I. Washburn.
Confederate Spy: A Story of the War of 1861. Robert Haskins Crozier. LC 8-26632. 1866. R. B. Harmon.
Confederate Spy: Or, Startling Incidents of the War Between the States. A Novel. 5th ed. Robert Haskins Crozier. LC 4-19005. 1885. Printed by J. P. Morton & Company.
Confederates. Thomas Keneally. LC 80-7606. 12.95 (ISBN 0-06-012299-4). Harper & Row.
Confederation Matador. Jesse Franklin Bone. LC 78-2196. (Illus.). 1978. 4.95 (ISBN 0-915442-53-1). Starblaze Editions.
Confed'ric Gol' Anne Fluker & Fluker, Winifred, Joint Author. LC 27-12826. 1926. The J. W. Burke Company.
Conference of the Birds: A Sufi Fable. Farid Ud-Din Attar. Tr. by C. S. Nott. (Clear Light Ser). (Illus., Orig.). 1971. pap. 5.50 (ISBN 0-394-73001-1). Shambhala Pubns.
Conference of Victims. 1st Ed. Gina Berriault. LC 62-11688. 1962. Atheneum.
Confess, Fletch. Gregory McDonald. LC 76-43536. 1.75 (ISBN 0-380-00814-9). Avon Books.
Confession. Maksim Gorkii & Strunsky, Rose, Tr. LC 16-8813. Frederick A. Stokes Company.
Confession. Mario Soldati. LC 58-5822. 1958. Knopf.
Confession: A Novel. Cosmo Hamilton. LC 26-245572. 1926. Doubleday, Page & Company.
Confession and Letters of Terence Quinn McManus. Miles Goodyear Hyde. LC 12-10815. 1.00. R. G. Badger.
Confession D'un Enfant Du Siecle. Alfred De Musset. Ed. by Allem. (Coll. Class. Garnier). 1962. pap. 10.95. French & Eur.
Confession from the Malaga Madhouse: A Christmas Diary. Charlotte Painter. LC 76-163600. (Illus.). 1971. 5.95. Dial Press.
Confession of a Child of the Century. Alfred De Musset. LC 76-48445. (Classics of European Literature). (Series: Library of classical romantic realism.). (Hyperion library of world literature). 1977. 12.95. (ISBN 0-88355-586-7) (ISBN 0-88355-587-5). Hyperion Press.

Confession of a Child of the Century. Alfred De Musset. Tr. by Warren, Kendall. LC 7-32291. (On cover: The medallion series). C. H. Sergel and Company.

Confession of a Child of the Century. Thomas H. Rogers. (Signet Book). 1973. (pbk.) 1.50. New American Lib.

Confession of a Child of the Century. Ten Etchings. Alfred De Musset. Tr. by Rogerson, T. F. LC 1633. (Half-title:... Roman contemporain. Romancisis. v. 2). Printed by G. Barrie & Son.

Confession of a Child of the Century by Samuel Heather: A Novel. Thomas H. Rogers. LC 72-189740. 1972. 7.95 (ISBN 0-671-21266-4). Simon and Schuster.

Confession of a Child of the Century: Confession D'un Enfant Du Siecle. Musset, Alfred De. LC 76-50122. 1976. 13.50. H. Fertig.

Confession of a Fool. August Strindberg. Tr. by Ellie Schleussner. LC 79-39042. 1972. 11.95 (ISBN 0-8383-1397-3). Haskell House.

Confession of a Fool. August Strindberg & Schleussner, Ellie, Tr. LC 25-207073. 1925. The Viking Press.

Confession of a Lover. Mulk Raj Anand. 404p. 1976. pap. 5.75 (ISBN 0-86578-073-0). Ind-US Inc.

Confession of a Lover: A Novel. Mulk Raj Anand. LC 76-900795. 1976. 50.00. Arnold-Heinemann Publishers (India)

Confession of Andrew Clare: A Novel. David Robinson. LC 68-18470. 1968. D. McKay Co.

Confession of Lorraine Herschel: A Story of Mystery. E. O. Tilburn. (On cover: The pastime series, no. 33 175). 1896. Laird & Lee.

Confession of Seymour Vane. Ellen Snow. LC 9-114. R. F. Fenno & Company.

Confession of Stephen Whapshare. Emma Frances Brooke. LC 6-19393. 1898. G. P. Putnam's Sons.

Confession: Or, The Blind Heart. A Domestic Story. new and rev. ed. William Gilmore Simms. LC 79-116013. 1970. AMS Press.

Confession; or, the Blind Heart, a Domestic Story. new and rev. ed. William Gilmore Simms. LC 3-110218. (With his Beauchampe. New York, 1882). 1882. A. C. Armstrong & Son.

Confession; or, The Blind Heart. A Domestic Story. new and rev. ed. William Gilmore Simms. (On cover: Lovell's library, v 13, no. 680). 1885. J. W. Lovell Company.

Confessional. Georges Simenon. LC 68-18962. 1968. Harcourt, Brace & World.

Confessions. Enid Dame. Ed. by Stanley H. Barkan. (Cross-Cultural Review Chapbook 12: American Poetry 6). 16p. 1980. pap. 2.00 (ISBN 0-89304-811-9). Cross Cult.

Confessions of a Bank Burglar. LC 23-7997. (True story series. no. 3). 1923. Macfadden Publications, Inc.

Confessions of a Business Man's Wife Who Made Her Husband a Success. LC 31-32951. Sears Publishing Company, Inc.

Confessions of a Clarionet Player: A Novel. Emile Erckmann & Adam, Graeme Mercer, 1839- Ed. LC 3-7663. (The Manhattan library of new copyright fiction). 1903. A. L. Burt Company.

Confessions of a Con Man. William Henry Irwin. 1909. B. W. Huebsch.

Confessions of a Convict. LC 6-30385. 1893. R. C. Hartranft.

Confessions of a Crap Artist. Philip K. Dick. 272p. 1982. pap. 2.95 (ISBN 0-671-44213-9, Timescape). PB.

Confessions of a Crap Artist-Jack Isidore (of Seville, Calif.) A Chronicle of Verified Scientific Fact, 1945-1959: a Novel. Philip K Dick. LC 78-105009. 1978. 3.95 (ISBN 0-9601428-2-7). Entwhistle Books.

Confessions of a Daddy. Ellis Parker Butler. LC 7-18096. 1907. The Century Co.

Confessions of a Dancer. Bobbie Tremaine. LC 23-7731. (True story series. no. 4). 1923. Macfadden Publications, Inc.

Confessions of a Debutante: With Illustrations by R. M. Crosby. Roger Livingston Scaife. LC 13-24111. 1913. Houghton Mifflin Company.

Confessions of a Detective. Alfred Henry Lewis. LC 14-1811. 1906. A. S. Barnes & Company.

Confessions of a Detective. Alfred Henry Lewis. LC 7-6652. 1907. A. S. Barnes & Company.

Confessions of a Disloyal European. Jan Myrdal. 1969. pap. 1.65 o.p. (ISBN 0-394-70490-8, V490, Vin). Random.

Confessions of a Frivolous Girl: A Story of Fashionable Life. Robert Grant. LC 17-497. 1880. Houghton Mifflin Company.

Confessions of a Frivolous Girl. A Story of Fashionable Life. Robert Grant. LC 6-447447. 1880. A. Williams and Co.

Confessions of a Grass Widow: A Novel. Kate Thyson Marr. LC 1-29938. F. Tennyson Neely Co.

Confessions of a Homing Pigeon. Nicholas Meyer. 384p. 1981. 14.95 (ISBN 0-385-27198-0). Dial.

Confessions of a Homing Pigeon: A Novel. Nicholas Meyer. LC 81-3154. 14.95 (ISBN 0-385-27198-0). Dial Press.

Confessions of a Ladykiller. George Stade. LC 79-16351. 10.95 (ISBN 0-393-08837-5). Norton.

Confessions of a Macedonian Bandit. Albert Sonnichsen. LC 9-24946. 1909. Duffield & Company.

Confessions of a Mask. Yukio Mishima, pseud. LC 58-12637. 1958. New Directions.

Confessions of a Minister. Being Leaves from the Diary of the Rev. Josephus Leonhardt, D.D.... Josephus Leonhardt. LC 7-13163. 1874. H. Peterson & Co.

Confessions of a Modern Midas. Theodore Williamson Nevin. LC 6-43784. 1906.

Confessions of a Monopolist. Frederic C. Howe. LC 78-57533. (Muckrakers Ser.). 1979. Repr. of 1906 ed. lib. bdg. 15.00 (ISBN 0-8398-0793-7). Irvington.

Confessions of a Murderer, Rapist, Fascist, Bomber, Thief; or, A Year in the Journal of an Ordinary American: A Superfiction. Arias-Misson, Alain. LC 74-81095. (Illus.). 12.50. (ISBN 0-914090-05-4). Chicago Review Press.

Confessions of a Negro Preacher. LC 73-18597. 1974. (ISBN 0-404-11408-3). AMS Press.

Confessions of a Nowaday Child: A Novel. Erje Ayden. LC 66-17319. 1966. 4.95. New Wave Pubns.

Confessions of a Pimp. 1970. pap. 1.25 o.p. (B12-1076). Belmont-Tower.

Confessions of a Poet... Laughton Osborn. LC 7-3036. 1835. Carey, Lea & Blanchard.

Confessions of a Princess. LC 8-19575. C. H. Doscher & Co. C.

Confessions of a Publisher: Being the Autobiography of Abel Drinkwater. Henrietta Eliza Vaughan Stannard. LC 8-13867. (world library, no. 17). 1892. The Waverly Company.

Confessions of a Racy Receptionist. Graham Masterton. 1976. (pbk.) 1.50 (ISBN 0-523-00849-X). Pinnacle Books.

Confessions of a Rake. (Orig.). 1969. pap. 1.25 o.p. (B12-1007). Belmont-Tower.

Confessions of a Rum-Runner. James Barbican. LC 28-7036. 1928. I. Washburn.

Confessions of a Sex Researcher. Bernhardt J. Hurwood. 1976. pap. 1.95 o.p. WSP.

Confessions of a Social Secretary. Corinne Martin Lowe. LC 17-5813. 1917. 1.25. Harper & Brothers.

Confessions of a Society Man. Samuel Williams Cooper. LC 11-10559. 1887. Belford, Clarke & Co.

Confessions of a Specialist. William Joby. pap. 1.95 o.p. (6003). Brandon.

Confessions of a Spent Youth: A Novel. Vance Nye Bourjaily. LC 60-14690. 1960. Dial Press.

Confessions of a Story Writer. Paul Gallico. LC 46-6952. 1946. A. A. Knopf.

Confessions of a Teen-Age Hooker. Francie. (Orig.). 1969. pap. 1.75 o.p. (3059). Brandon.

Confessions of a Teenage Baboon. Paul Zindel. (gr. 9 up). 1978. pap. 2.25 (ISBN 0-553-20170-0). Bantam.

Confessions of a Thug. Meadows Taylor. LC 68-12384. (Doughty library, no. 6). 1968. Stein and Day.

Confessions of a Well-Meaning Woman. Stephen McKenna. LC 22-164728. 1922. Cassell and Company, Ltd.

Confessions of a Well-Meaning Woman. Stephen McKenna. LC 22-235663. 2.00. George H. Doran Company.

Confessions of a Wife. Elizabeth Stuart Ward. LC 2-23848. 1902. The Century Co.

Confessions of a Woman. Mabel Collins Cook. LC 6-28084. (On cover: Lovell's international series, no. 111). J. W. Lovell Company.

Confessions of a Young Exile. Mark Ivor Satin. LC 77-372319. (ISBN 0-7715-9954-4). Gage Pub.

Confessions of a Young Man. George Moore. LC 2-20395. 1901. Brentano's.

Confessions of a Young Man. George Moore. LC 41-6979. (On cover: Penguin books. 185). 1939. Penguin Books Limited.

Confessions of an American Citizen. Clayton Lemars. LC 42-34047. 1898. The Schulte Publishing Company.

Confessions of an Apostate. Mary Anne Madden Sadlier. LC 8-1648. (On cover: Parlor & cottage library). 1868. D. & J. Sadlier & Co.

Confessions of an Apostate. Mary Anne Madden Sadlier. LC 77-11308. (American Catholic Tradition). (Illus.). 1978. 15.00 (ISBN 0-405-10850-8). Arno Press.

Confessions of an Author. Tr. by Paul Anhalt. (Orig.). pap. 1.75 o.p. (3014). Brandon.

Confessions of an English Maid. Jessie. 1972. pap. 2.25 o.s.i. (V1062R, Venus). Grove.

Confessions of an English Maid. Intro. by Geoffrey Lowndes. pap. 1.75 o.p. (3022). Brandon.

Confessions of an English Opium-Eater. Thomas De Quincey. 300p. 1983. pap. text ed. 4.95 o.p. (ISBN 0-460-01223-1, Evman). Biblio Dist.

Confessions of an English Opium-Eater. Thomas De Quincey. 1960. pap. 1.50 o.p. (ISBN 0-460-01223-1, Evman). Dutton.

Confessions of an Imp. A Narrative. Harlan Page Halsey. J. E. Rhodes & Co.

Confessions of an Inconstant Man. LC 14-6155. 1914. D. Appleton and Company.

Confessions of an Innocent Widow. Sara E Worts. LC 12-22810. 1912. Broadway Publishing Co.

Confessions of Arsene Lupin. Maurice Leblanc. LC 67-23098. 1967. Walker.

Confessions of Arsene Lupin. Maurice Leblanc. Tr. by Teixeira De Mattos, Alexander Louis. LC 13-20128. 1913. 1.25. Doubleday, Page & Company.

Confessions of Artemas Quibble: Being the Ingenuous and Unvarnished History of Artemas Quibble, Esquire, One-Time Practitioner in the New York Criminal Courts, Together with an Account of the Divers Wiles, Tricks, Sophistries, Technicalities, and Sundry Artifices of Himself and Others of the Fraternity, Commonly Yclept "Shysters" or "Shyster Lawyers", As Edited by Arthur Train... Arthur Cheney Train. LC 11-25091. 1911. C. Scribner's Sons.

Confessions of Cherubino. Bertha Harris. LC 77-95003. 1978. pap. 5.00 (ISBN 0-913780-23-5). Daughters.

Confessions of Cherubino. Bertha Harris. LC 73-174509. 1972. 5.95 o.p. (ISBN 0-15-121855-2). HarBraceJ.

Confessions of Christine. Pierre Chevalier. pap. 1.95 o.p. (6021). Brandon.

Confessions of Claude: A Romance. Edgar Fawcett. LC 6-38955. 1887. Ticknor and Company.

Confessions of Con Cregan. The Irish Gil Blas. Charles James Lever. (Seaside library, v. 9, no. 168). 1877. G. Munro.

Confessions of Con Cregan: The Irish Gil Blas. Charles James Lever. LC 7-14382. 1895. Little, Brown, and Company.

Confessions of Elisabeth Von S. The Story of a Young Woman's Rise and Fall in Nazi Society. Gillian Freeman. LC 78-60670. 1978. 8.95 (ISBN 0-525-08453-3). Dutton.

Confessions of Elizabeth Von S. Gillian Freeman. 316p. 1982. pap. 2.95 (ISBN 0-441-11702-3). Ace Bks.

Confessions of Emilia Harrington. Lambert A. Wilmer. LC 9-1828. 1835. L. A. Wilmer.

Confessions of Felix Krull, Confidence Man. Thomas Mann. 1955. 12.50 (ISBN 0-394-42012-8). Knopf.

Confessions of Felix Krull, Confidence Man: The Early Years. Thomas Mann. LC 65-6704. (Mod. lib. of the world's best bks. 360). 1965. 2.45. Random.

Confessions of Felix Krull, Confidence Man: The Early Years. Thomas Mann. LC 55-9263. 1955. Knopf.

Confessions of Georgina. Julian Robinson. pap. 1.95 o.p. (ISBN 0-87056-237-1, 6237). Brandon.

Confessions of Gerald Estcourt. Florence Marryat Church Lean. (On cover: Seaside library. Pocket ed. no. 1013). 1887. G. Munro.

Confessions of Harry Lorrequer... 3d american ed. Charles James Lever. LC 41-35141. 1842. Carey and Hart.

Confessions of Harry Lorrequer. Charles James Lever. LC 6-39756. (Half-title: The English Comedie humaine). 1905. The Century Co.

Confessions of Josef Baisz. Dan Jacobson. LC 78-2063. 10.00 (ISBN 0-06-012203-X). Harper & Row.

Confessions of Nat Turner. William Styron. (Signet bk. Y3596). 1968. pap., 1.25. New Amer. Lib.

Confessions of Nat Turner. William Styron. LC 77-364850. (Illus.). 1976. Franklin Library.

Confessions of Nat Turner. William Styron. LC 67-12732. 1967. Random House.

Confessions of Phoebe Tyler. Ruth Warrick & Don Preston. 1982. pap. 2.95 (ISBN 0-425-05202-8). Berkley Pub.

Confessions of Sir Henry Longueville. A Novel... Robert Pearse Gillies. 1814. Longman, Hurst, Rees, Orme, and Brown.

Confessions of Some Lonely Housewives. Earl Vendryes Campbell. LC 72-97518. 1973. 4.95. Dade Variety Press.

Confessions of Summer. Phillip Lopate. LC 78-19715. 330p. 1979. 6.00 (ISBN 0-385-12619-0). SUN.

Confessions of Summer: A Novel. Phillip Lopate. LC 77-12877. 1979. 9.95 (ISBN 0-385-12619-0). Doubleday.

Confessions of That Little English Girl: Or, So Inexperienced. Elsie M Cawthorne. LC 6-222781. The Fagan Publishing Company.

Confessions of the Nun of St. Omer: A Tale. Charlotte Dacre. LC 76-131314. (Gothic novels). 1972. 35.00 (ISBN 0-405-00803-1). Arno Press.

Confessions of Two. A Novel. Marianne Gaillard Spratley & Willisson, Elizabeth Octavia, Joint Author. LC 8-140460. 1886. G. W. Dillingham; Etc., Etc.

Confessions of Two Brothers: John Cowper Powys and Llewelyn Powys. John Cowper Powys & Powys, Llewelyn. LC 16-5332. 1916. The Manas Press.

Confessions of Westchester County. Barry N. Malzberg. pap. 1.95 o.s.i. (OPS-29). Olympia.

Confessions of Zeno. Ettore Schmitz. LC 70-137074. 1973. 15.25 (ISBN 0-8371-5537-1). Greenwood Press.

Confessions of Zeno. Italo Svevo. pap. 3.95 (ISBN 0-394-70063-5, V-63, Vin). Random.

Confessions to a Heathen Idol. Anna Botsford Comstock. 1906. Doubleday, Page & Company.

Confessions to a Heathen Idol. Anna Botsford Comstock. LC 41-42331. 1908. Doubleday, Page & Company.

Confessor. Jackson Donahue. LC 63-10989. 1963. World Pub. Co.

Confessors of Connaught: Or, The Tenants of a Lord Bishop. A Tale of Our Own Times. LC 7-18508. 1865. P. F. Cunningham.

Confessors of the Name: A Novel. Gladys Schmitt. LC 52-5946. 1952. Dial Press.

Confetti: A Book of Short Stories. Sophie Kerr. LC 27-13976. George H. Doran Company.

Confetti for Gino. Lawrence Madalena. LC 59-10679. 1959. Doubleday.

Confetti Man. Bonnie Jones Reynolds. LC 74-79421. 1975. 8.95 (ISBN 0-8128-1740-0). Stein and Day.

Confidence. Henry James. LC 10-13531. 1880. Houghton, Osgood and Company, The Riverside Press, Cambridge.

Confidence, Eighteen Eighty. Henry James. Ed. by Herbert Ruhm. LC 76-39775. 1977. Repr. of 1962 ed. lib. bdg. 20.00x (ISBN 0-8371-9296-X, JACO). Greenwood.

Confidence in Magic. Ramona Stewart. LC 65-17250. 1965. Doubleday.

Confidence Man. Laurie York Erskine. 1925. D. Appleton and Company.

Confidence Man. Herman Melville. Ed. by Elizabeth S. Foster. (Complete Works of Herman Melville Ser.). 1979. 13.00 (ISBN 0-87532-009-0). Hendricks House.

Confidence Man. Herman Melville. pap. 3.50 (ISBN 0-451-51698-2, CE1698, Sig Classics). NAL.

Confidence-Man. Herman Melville. 1978. Repr. of 1948 ed. lib. bdg. 17.50 o.p. (ISBN 0-8482-1714-4). Norwood Edns.

Confidence-Man. Herman Melville. Ed. by Harrison Hayford. 375p. 1982. 7.95 (ISBN 0-8101-0325-7). Northwestern U Pr.

Confidence-Man see Writings of Herman Melville.

Confidence-Man: His Masquerade. Herman Melville. LC 64-12514. (Rinehart editions, 126). 1964. Holt, Rinehart and Winston.

Confidence-Man: His Masquerade. Herman Melville. LC 68-10819. (Chandler facsimile editions in American literature). (Illus.). 1968. Chandler Pub. Co.; Science Research Associates, Distributors, Chicago.

Confidence-Man: His Masquerade. Herman Melville. 1949. Grove Press.

Confidence Man: His Masquerade. Herman Melville. 1857. Dix, Edwards & Co.

Confidence-Man: His Masquerade: An Authoritative Text, Backgrounds and Sources, Reviews, Criticism and an Annotated Bibliography. Herman Melville. LC 71-141591. (Norton critical edition). 1971. 2.25 (ISBN 0-393-04345-2) (ISBN 0-393-09968-7). Norton.

Confidence-Man: His Masquerade. Ed., Introd., Annotation, by H. Bruce Franklin. Herman Melville. Ed. by Howard Bruce Franklin. LC 66-304456. (Lib. of lit., 13). 1967. 6.50. Bobbs.

Confidence Man: His Masquerade. Ed., Introd. by Hennig Cohen. Herman Melville. (Rinehart eds., 126 rebound) Bibl.). 1965. 3.50. P. Smith.

Confidence-Man: His Masquerade: Edited by Elizabeth S. Foster. Herman Melville. Ed. by Elizabeth Sophia Foster. LC 55-188. 1954. Hendricks House.

Confidence, 1880. Now First Edited from the Manuscript. With Notes, Introd., and Bibliography by Herbert Ruhm. With Contemporary Reviews, and Excerpts from the Note-Books. 1st Ed. Henry James. LC 62-52943. (Universal library, UL146). 1962. Grosset & Dunlap.

Confidences. Edith Cecilia O'Hara & Ely, Mary S. LC 12-28707. 1.35. Press of Louisiana Printing Company, Limited.

Confident Morning. Val Henry Gielgud. LC 77-357096. 1976. 2.95 (ISBN 0-85617-489-0). White Lion Publishers.

Confident Morning: A Novel. Arthur Stanwood Pier. LC 25-12733. 1925. Houghton Mifflin Company.

Confident Tomorrow: A Novel of New York. Brander Matthews. LC 99-529383. 1900. Harper & Brothers.

Confidential. Donald Henderson Clarke. LC 36-20639. The Vanguard Press.

Confidential Agent. Graham Greene. 208p. 1981. pap. 2.95 (ISBN 0-14-001895-6). Penguin.

Confidential Agent. Graham Greene. 256p. 17.95 (ISBN 0-670-23725-6). Viking Pr.

Confidential Agent. Graham Greene. 1975. (pbk.) 1.50. Pocket Books.

Confidential Agent see Three by Graham Greene.

Confidential Agent. A Novel. James Payn. (Franklin square library, no. 152). 1880. Harper & Brothers.

Confidential Agent. A Novel. James Payn. (Seaside library. v. 44, no. 892). 1880. G. Munro.

Confidential Agent: An Entertainment. Graham Greene. LC 39-23873. 1939. The Viking Press.

Confidential Memoranda: The Tortured Island. Noel Jackson. 1973. 5.95 (ISBN 0-533-00562-0). Vantage.

Confirmed Bachelor. Roberta Leigh. (Harlequin Presents Ser.). 192p. 1981. pap. 1.75 (ISBN 0-373-10461-8). Harlequin Bks.

Conflict. Anne Constance Smedley Maxwell Armfield Armfield. LC 7-9556. 1907. Moffat, Yard & Company.

Conflict. Richard Bowler. LC 40-1423. William Byrd Press, Inc.

Conflict. Clarence Budington Kelland. LC 22-5896. Harper & Brothers.

Conflict. David Graham Phillips. 1911. lib. bdg. 19.25 o.s.i. (ISBN 0-512-00885-X). Garrett Pr.

Conflict. Olive Higgins Prouty. 1975. (pbk.) 1.50. Popular Library.

Conflict: A Narrative Based on the Fundamentalist Movement. Elizabeth Knauss. LC 23-106942. Bible Institute of Los Angeles.

Conflict: A Novel. David Graham Phillips. LC 72-84646. 1974. (lib. ed.) 19.25 (ISBN 0-403-02965-1). Scholarly Press.

Conflict: A Novel. David Graham Phillips. LC 11-23841. 1911. 1.30. D. Appleton and Company.

Conflict: A Novel. David Graham Phillips. LC 16-9363. 1912. D. Appleton and Company.

Conflict: A Novel. Olive Higgins Prouty. LC 27-229504. 1927. Houghton Mifflin Company.

Conflict and Conquest. The Experience of Father Flynn. George Carter Needham. LC 7-25791. American Baptist Publication Society.

Conflict: By Viola Burhans; Illustrations & Cover by Wm. L. Hudson. Viola Burhans. LC 7-13953. Broadway Publishing Co.

Conflict Center: Naator. Clark Darlton. (Perry Rhodan#77). (Illus.). 1975. (pbk.) 1.25. Ace Books.

Conflict of Desire. Joseph Calvitt Clarke. LC 34-12180. 1934. W. Godwin, Inc.

Conflict of Evidence. Rodrigues Ottolengui. G. P. Putnam's Sons.

Conflict of Interest. Jayne Castle. (Candlelight Ecstasy Ser.: No. 130). (Orig.). 1983. pap. 1.95 (ISBN 0-440-10927-2). Dell.

Conflict of Interest. Larston D. Farrar. 1970. 5.95 o.p. Bartholomew.

Conflict of Interest. Larston D. Farrar. 1971. pap. 1.25 o.p. (B12-2090). Belmont-Tower.

Conflict of Interest. Larston D. Farrar. (O.s.i.). 1976. pap. 1.50 o.s.i. (BT50917). Belmont-Tower.

Conflict of Interest. Leslie H. Whitten. LC 75-30461. (Concept book). 1976. 8.95 (ISBN 0-385-11169-X). Doubleday.

Conflict of Interest. Brad Williams & J. W. Ehrlich. (Sam Benedict Mystery). 1974. (pbk.) 0.95. Popular Library.

Conflict of Interest. Brad Williams & Jacob W. Ehrlich. LC 78-138869. (Rinehart suspense novel). 1971. 4.95 (ISBN 0-03-086020-2). Holt, Rinehart and Winston.

Conflict of Interest: A Novel. Larston D Farrar. LC 79-110742. 1970. 5.95. Bartholomew House.

Conflict of Women. Emma Darby. 1973. 0.75. New American Library.

Conflict of Women. Emma Darby. LC 70-183292. 1972. 4.95. St. Martin's Press.

Conflicting Eye. Eseoghene. (Heritage Ser). 1973. pap. 2.50x. Broadside.

Conflicts: Three Tales. Stefan Zweig & Paul-Eden, 1865- LC 27-19639. 1927. The Viking Press.

Conformist. Alberto Moravia. LC 75-29294. 1975-1976. 19.00 (ISBN 0-8371-8391-X). Greenwood Press.

Conformist. Alberto Pincherle. LC 51-13615. 1951. Farrar, Straus and Young.

Confounding of Camelia. Anne Douglas Sedgwick. LC 99-1480. 1899. C. Scribner's Sons.

Confounding of Camelia. Anne Douglas Sedgwick. LC 2-13637. 1902. The Century Co.

Confrontation. Jozsef Lengyel. Tr. by Anna Novotny from Hung. 256p. 1973. 6.95 (ISBN 0-8065-0367-X). Citadel Pr.

Confrontation, and Other Stories. Lenore Guinzburg Marshall. LC 72-3796. 1972. (ISBN 0-393-08448-5). Norton.

Confrontation: By Norman Garbo, Howard Goodkind. Norman Garbo. (N160). 1967. Avon.

Confrontation: By Norman Garbo, Howard Goodkind. Norman Garbo & Howard Goodkind. LC 66-106436. 6.95. Harper.

Confucius Comes to Broadway. Francis Page. LC 41-7612. 1940. Wisdom House.

Confucius Enigma. Margaret Jones. LC 80-29602. 1981. 10.95 (ISBN 0-312-16238-3). St. Martin's Press.

Confusion: A Novel. James Gould Cozzens. LC 24-15988. 1924. B. J. Brimmer Company.

Cong Kiss. J. J. Montague. (Black Swan Ser: No. 2). 192p. (Orig.). 1974. pap. 1.50 o.p. (ISBN 0-89014-106-1, CB-106). Canyon Bks.

Cong Kiss. J. J Montague. (Black Swan,#2). 1974. (pbk.) 1.50 (ISBN 0-89014-106-1). Canyon Books.

Congai. Harry Hervey. LC 27-3815. 1927. Cosmopolitan Book Corporation.

Congaree Sketches: Scenes from Negro Life in the Swamps of the Congaree and Tales by Tad and Scip of Heaven and Hell with Other Miscellany. Edward Clarkson Leverett Adams. LC 27-13768. 1927. The University of North Carolina Press.

Conger's Woman. Ray Hogan. LC 72-83146. (DD western). 1973. 4.95 (ISBN 0-385-07274-0). Doubleday.

Conger's Woman. Ray Hogan. (Signet brand western). 1974. (pbk.) 0.95. New American Library.

Congo. Michael Crichton. LC 80-7972. 1980. 10.95 (ISBN 0-394-51392-4). Knopf: Distributed by Random House.

Congo. Michael Crichton. LC 81-186586. 1981. 10.95. Knopf.

Congo Diary and Other Uncollected Pieces. Joseph Conrad & Zdzislaw Najder. LC 72-89333. 7.95 (ISBN 0-385-00771-X). Doubleday.

Congo Doctor. Stephen Van Nuys. LC 44-6679. 1944. Phoenix Press.

Congo Gods. Otto Lutken. 1929. Coward-McCann, Inc.

Congo Landing. Wilson Collison. LC 34-110339. 1934. R. M. McBride & Company.

Congo Song. Stuart Cloete. LC 43-3611. 1943. Houghton Mifflin Company.

Congo Song. Stuart Cloete. LC 44-6598. 1944. The Sun Dial Press.

Congo Song. Stuart Cloete. LC 46-396725. 1946. Triangle Books, the Blakiston Company.

Congo Venus. John Edwin Canaday. LC 75-44982. (Fifty Classics of Crime Fiction, 1900-1950; 25). 1976. 12.00 (ISBN 0-8240-2374-9). Garland Pub.

Congo Venus. John Edwin Canaday. LC 50-12059. (Inner sanctum mystery). 1950. Simon and Schuster.

Congo Venus. Matthew Head. LC 75-44982. (Crime Fiction Ser). 1976. Repr. of 1950 ed. lib. bdg. 17.50 (ISBN 0-8240-2374-9). Garland Pub.

Congo Venus. Matthew Head. LC 82-47561. 224p. 1982. pap. 2.84i (ISBN 0-06-080597-8, P 597, PL). Har-Row.

Congress. Jorge Luis Borges. Tr. by Jorge L. Borges & Norman T. Di Giovanni. 1973. ltd. ed. 8.50 o.p. Enitharmon Pr.

Congress at Aix. Solange Fasquelle. Tr. by N. Ryan. 1961. 3.50x o.p. Verry.

Congress at Aix. Tr. from French by Nigel Ryan. Solange Fasquelle. LC 66-3070. 1966. bds., 3.00. H. Hamilton.

Congress-The Drum Corps Science Fiction. Larry R. Kirk & Phylys E. Kirk. LC 82-70928. (In Congress & Prelude to Congress Ser.: No. 1). (Illus.). 332p. (Orig.). 1982. pap. 8.00 (ISBN 0-9608212-0-1). Ebaesy.

Congressman Hardie, a Born Democrat. Courtney Wellington. LC 3140. G. W. Dillingham Co.

Congressman John and His Wife's Satisfaction: A Novel. Emma W MacCarthy. 1891. G. W. Dillingham.

Congressman John L. A History of His Trials and Triumphs in Washington. Wellington Yale. 1892. The St. James Publishing House.

Congressman Pumphrey: The People's Friend. John Tinney McCutcheon. LC 7-12275. 1907. The Bobbs-Merrill Company.

Congressman Swanson. Charles Cyrel Post. LC 7-30321. (On cover: Sergel's international library. v. 1, no. 16). C. H. Sergel & Company.

Congressman Who Loved Flaubert, and Other Washington Stories. Ward S Just. LC 73-3189. 1973. 5.95. Little, Brown.

Congressman's Christmas Dream, and the Lobby Member's Happy New Year: A Holiday Sketch. Abraham Oakey Hall. LC 7-549. 1870-71. Scribner, Welford & Co.

Congressman's Wife: A Story of American Politics. John Daniel Barry. LC 3-23053. 1903. The Smart Set Publishing Co.

Congresswoman. Isabel Gordon Curtis. LC 14-6798. 1914. 1.35. Browne & Howell Company.

Congreve: Incognita, and The Way of the World. William Congreve. LC 78-116471. (English library). 1970. 2.25 (ISBN 0-87249-156-0). University of South Carolina Press.

Coniackers" Or, The Driggs-Guyon Gang of Notorious Counterfeiters. Ronald Rivers. (On cover: The Pinkerton's detective series, v. 29). 1889. Laird & Lee.

Coningsby. Benjamin Disraeli Beaconsfield. LC 36-37342. (Half-title: Everyman's library, ed. by Ernest Rhys. Fiction. no. 535). 1933. J. M. Dent & Sons, Ltd.

Coningsby. Benjamin Disraeli Beaconsfield. (Half-title: Everyman's library, ed. by Ernest Rhys. Fiction. no. 585). 1911. J. M. Dent & Sons, Ltd.

Coningsby. Benjamin Disraeli. 1979. lib. bdg. 69.95 (ISBN 0-87700-296-7). Revisionist Pr.

Coningsby. Benjamin Disraeli. 1983. pap. 5.95 (ISBN 0-14-043192-6). Penguin.

Coningsby. Benjamin Disraeli. 5.00x o.p. (ISBN 0-460-00535-9, E535, Evman). Dutton.

Coningsby: Or, The New Generation. Benjamin Disraeli Beaconsfield. LC 73-22022. 1974. 19.50 (ISBN 0-403-00459-4). Scholarly Press.

Coningsby: Or, The New Generation. Benjamin Disraeli Beaconsfield. LC 6-28845. 1844. W. H. Coyler.

Coningsby: Or, The New Generation. new ed. Benjamin Disraeli Beaconsfield. LC 6-28843. G. Routledge and Sone.

Coningsby: Or, The New Generation. Benjamin Disraeli Beaconsfield. (English Comedie humaine. 1st series, v. 7). 1902. The Century Co.

Coningsby: Or, The New Generation. Benjamin Disraeli Beaconsfield. LC 32-261588. (Half-title: The world's classics. CCCLXXXI). 1931. H. Milford, Oxford University Press.

Coningsby: Or, The New Generation. Benjamin Disraeli Beaconsfield. LC 43-43110. (On cover: Library of choice novels. No. 23). 1870. D. Appleton and Company.

Coningsby: Or, The New Generation. Benjamin Disraeli Beaconsfield. (In his The Bradenham edition of the novels and tales. New York, 1934? vol. VIII). Alfred A. Knopf.

Coningsby: Or, The New Generation. With an Introd. and Notes by Bernard N. Langdon-Davies. Benjamin Disraeli Beaconsfield. LC 61-65863. (Capricorn book, CAP59). 1961. Capricorn Books.

Coniston. Winston Churchill. LC 72-96877. (Illus.). 1969. Literature House.

Coniston. Winston Churchill. 1906. The Macmillan Company.

Coniston. Winston Churchill. LC 41-80728. 1925. The Macmillan Company.

Conjugal Love. Alberto Moravia. 1973. (pbk) 1.25. Manor Books.

Conjugal Love. Alberto Pincherle. LC 51-9840. 1951. Farrar, Straus and Young.

Conjuration De Fiesque. Jean De Retz. Ed. by D. A. Watts. 1967. 6.10x o.p. (ISBN 0-19-815372-4). Oxford U Pr.

Conjure-Man Dies. Rudolph Fisher. LC 78-140605. 320p. Repr. of 1932 ed. 9.00 (ISBN 0-405-02800-8). Ayer Co.

Conjure-Man Dies: A Mystery Tale of Dark Harlem. Rudolph Fisher. LC 78-140605. 1971. 5.95. Arno Press.

Conjure Man Dies: A Mystery Tale of Dark Harlem. Rudolph Fisher. LC 32-194973. Covici, Friede.

Conjure Wife. Fritz Leiber. LC 77-5756. (Gregg Press science fiction series). (Illus.). 1977. 9.50 (ISBN 0-8398-2377-0). Gregg Press.

Conjure Wife. Fritz Leiber. 1977. 1.95 (ISBN 0-441-11686-8). Ace Books.

Conjure Woman. Charles Waddell Chesnutt. LC 68-20007. (Americans in Fiction). 1968. Gregg Press.

Conjure Woman. Charles Waddell Chesnutt. LC 70-8946. (Ann Arbor paperbacks). 1969. 2.45. University of Michigan Press.

Conjure Woman. Charles Waddell Chesnutt. LC 4-15426. 1899. Houghton Mifflin and Company.

Conjure Woman. Charles Waddell Chesnutt. 1899. Riverside Press.

Conjurer Dick: Or, The Adventure of a Young Wizard. Angelo John Lewis. LC 37-32786. 1886. G. Warne and Co.

Conjurers. Marilyn Harris. LC 74-8370. 1974. 6.95 (ISBN 0-394-49097-5). Random House.

Conjurers. Marilyn Harris. 1976. (pbk.) 1.75. Dell.

Conjurer's Coffin. Constance Lindsay Taylor. LC 54-942551. (Mainline mysteries). 1954. Lippincott.

Conjuror of Phantoms. John William Harding. LC 98-1826. F. T. Neely.

Conjuror's House: A Romance of the Free Forest. Stewart Edward White. LC 3-71697. 1903. McClure, Phillips & Co.

Conjuror's Journal: Excerpts from the Journal of Joshua Medley, Conjuror, Juggler, Ventriloquist, and Sometime Balloonist: a Novel. Frances Shine. LC 78-17869. 8.95 (ISBN 0-396-07598-3). Dodd, Mead.

Conn of the Coral Seas. Beatrice Ethel Grimshaw. LC 22-929. 1922. The Macmillan Company.

Connecticut Circle: A Novel. Edwin Gilbert. LC 72-80352. 1972. 6.95 (ISBN 0-399-11030-5). Putnam.

Connecticut Yankee see Prince & the Pauper.

Connecticut Yankee at King Arthur's Court. Samuel Langhorne Clemens. LC 72-181285. (Penguin English library, EL 64). (Illus.). 1971. (u.s.) 2.75. Penguin Books.

Connecticut Yankee at King Arthur's Court. Mark Twain. Ed. by Justin Kaplan. (English Library Ser.). 1972. pap. 2.75 o.p. (ISBN 0-14-043064-4, EL64). Penguin.

Connecticut Yankee in King Arthur's Court: By Mark Twain Pseud. Introd. by Charles Neider. Samuel Langhorne Clemens. LC 60-105169. (American century series, AC30). 1960. Hill and Wang.

Connecticut Yankee in King Arthur's Court: By Mark Twain Pseud. with a Foreword by John T. Winterich and Illustrations by Warren Chappell. Samuel Langhorne Clemens & Chappell, Warren, Illus. LC 42-16020. 1942. The Heritage Press.

Connecticut Yankee in King Arthur's Court: By Mark Twainc3pseud. With an Introd. by William M. Gibson. Samuel Langhorne Clemens. LC 60-9440. (Harper's modern classics). 1960. Harper.

Connecticut Yankee in King Arthur's Court. Illus. by Henry Pitz. Samuel Langhorne Clemens. 1966. lib. ed., 3.79. Harper.

Connecticut Yankee in King Arthur's Court. Samuel Langhorne Clemens. Ed. by Hamlin Lewis Hill. LC 63-9890. 1963. Chandler Pub. Co.

Connecticut Yankee in King Arthur's Court. Samuel Langhorne Clemens. LC 65-6523. (Perennial classic). 1965. Harper & Row.

Connecticut Yankee in King Arthur's Court. Samuel Langhorne Clemens. LC 67-351. (Legacy library facsimile). (Illus.). 1966. University Microfilms.

Connecticut Yankee in King Arthur's Court. Samuel Langhorne Clemens. LC 49-9037. (Modern library of the world's best books). 1949. Modern Library.

Connecticut Yankee in King Arthur's Court. Samuel Langhorne Clemens. LC 3-19531. 1889. C. L. Webster & Company.

Connecticut Yankee in King Arthur's Court. Samuel Langhorne Clemens. LC 15-28118. Harper and Brothers.

Connecticut Yankee in King Arthur's Court. Samuel Langhorne Clemens. 1891. C. L. Webster & Company.

Connecticut Yankee in King Arthur's Court. Samuel Langhorne Clemens. LC 26-37463. Harper & Brothers.

Connecticut Yankee in King Arthur's Court. Samuel Langhorne Clemens & King, Ruth Thompson. LC 48-194159. 1948. Globe Book Co.

Connecticut Yankee in King Arthur's Court. Samuel Langhorne Clemens & Otto, William Nalll. Ed. LC 30-18659. (Harper's modern classics). Harper & Brothers.

Connecticut Yankee in King Arthur's Court. Mark Twain. (Literature Ser). (gr. 7-12). 1970. pap. text ed. 4.42 (ISBN 0-87720-723-2). AMSCO Sch.

Connecticut Yankee in King Arthur's Court. Mark Twain. 274p. (gr. 9-12). 1981. pap. 1.75 (ISBN 0-553-21003-3). Bantam.

Connecticut Yankee in King Arthur's Court. Mark Twain. LC 15-23118. (Holiday Editions). (Illus.). Repr. of 1889 ed. 7.95 o.p. (ISBN 0-06-014445-9, HarpT). Har-Row.

Connecticut Yankee in King Arthur's Court. Mark Twain. pap. 1.75 (ISBN 0-451-51460-2, CE1460, Sig Classics). NAL.

Connecticut Yankee in King Arthur's Court. Mark Twain. (English Library Ser.). 1972. pap. 2.95 (ISBN 0-14-043064-4). Penguin.

Connecticut Yankee in King Arthur's Court. Mark Twain. (Regents Illustrated Classics Ser.). 62p. 1982. pap. text ed. 2.25. Regents Pub.

Connecticut Yankee in King Arthur's Court. Mark Twain. 368p. pap. 2.50 (ISBN 0-671-41017-2). WSP.

Connecticut Yankee in King Arthur's Court. Mark Twain. 1982. Repr. lib. bdg. 19.95 (ISBN 0-89966-381-8). Buccaneer Bks.

Connecticut Yankee in King Arthur's Court. Mark Twain. Ed. by Ralph B. Church. (Classics Lib). (Illus.). (gr. 7-12). 1968. pap. text ed. 1.00 o.p.; teacher's guide free, with 25 o.p. Cambridge Bk.

Connecticut Yankee in King Arthur's Court. Mark Twain. (Harper Modern Classics Ser). (gr. 9-12). 1960. text ed. 2.52, s.p. 1.89 o.p. (ISBN 0-06-534068-X). Har-Row.

Connecticut Yankee in King Arthur's Court. Mark Twain. Ed. by Harry Shefter et al. (YA) pap. 0.75 o.p. (301, RE). WSP.

Connecticut Yankee in King Arthur's Court. Mark Twain. (Illus.). 1889. 10.00 o.p. (ISBN 0-06-014370-3, HarpT); holiday ed. 7.95 o.p. (ISBN 0-06-014445-9). Har-Row.

Connecticut Yankee in King Arthur's Court. Mark Twain. (Facsimile Series in American Literature). 607p. 1968. pap. 3.75x o.p. (ISBN 0-8102-0063-5). Chandler Pub.
Connecticut Yankee in King Arthur's Court. Mark Twain. (Illus.). 288p. cancelled 3-piece bdg with decorated paper sides o.p. (ISBN 0-89050-227-7). Heritage Conn.
Connecticut Yankee in King Arthur's Court. Mark Twain. 1960. pap. 1.95 o.p. (ISBN 0-8090-0030-X, AmCen). Hill & Wang.
Connecticut Yankee in King Arthur's Court. Mark Twain. LC 15-23118. (Holiday Editions). (Illus.). Repr. of 1889 ed. 7.95 o.p. (ISBN 0-06-014445-9, HarpT). Har-Row.
Connecticut Yankee in King Arthur's Court. With Photos. of Mark Twain and His Environment As Well As Drawings from Early Editions of the Book, Together with an Introd. by E. Hudson Long. Samuel Langhorne Clemens. LC 60-11017. (Great illustrated classics). 1960. Dodd, Mead.
Connecting Door. Rayner Heppenstall. LC 68-12795. 1968. 3.50. Dufour.
Connecting Rooms. Hugh Williams. (O.s.i.). 1969. pap. 0.75 o.s.i. (A538S, Award). Univ Pub & Dist.
Connector. Tony Williamson. LC 75-34348. 1976. 7.95 (ISBN 0-8128-1930-6). Stein and Day.
Connector. Tony Williamson. LC 76-374691. 1976. 3.50 (ISBN 0-00-222010-5). Collins.
Connie Morgan in the Cattle Country. James Beardsley Hendryx. LC 23-144884. 1923. G. P. Putnam's Sons.
Connie's Short Stories. C. M. Benson. 3.00 o.p. Carlton.
Connie's Short Stories, Vol. 2. C. M. Benson. 3.50 o.p. Carlton.
Connoisseur. Evan S. Connell. LC 74-7216. 1974. 6.95 (ISBN 0-394-49203-X). Knopf.
Connoisseur. Evan S Connell. 1977. Avon Books.
Connoisseur: And Other Stories. Walter John De La Mare. LC 26-11209. 1926. A. A. Knopf.
Connoisseur's Science Fiction. Ed. by Tom Boardman. 240p. 1976. pap. 1.50 o.p. (ISBN 0-14-002223-6). Penguin.
Connoisseur's Science Fiction: An Anthology. Thomas Volney Boardman. LC 65-4269. (Penguin sci. fic.). 1965. Penguin.
Connolly's Life. Ralph M McInerny. LC 82-73021. 1983. 12.95 (ISBN 0-689-11356-0). Atheneum.
Connor D'Arcy's Struggles. W M Bertholds. LC 6-10373. 1893. Benziger Brothes.
Connubial Bliss Passages in the Lives of Alice and Arthur... Carrie L. Shove. LC 8-7329. (Humorous books, Rhodes & McClure series. no. 4). 1882. Rhodes & McClure.
Conquer: A Tale of the Nika Rebellion in Byzantium. John Masefield. LC 41-21171. 1941. The Macmillan Company.
Conquered. Naomi Haldane Mitchison. 1968. Repr. of 1954 ed. 14.95 (ISBN 0-224-60496-1). Dufour.
Conquered: A New Novel by Token West Pseud. Adelaide Humphries. LC 51-518. 1950. Woodford Press.
Conquered. A Novel... Elizabeth P. Strong. LC 8-16878. 1878. G. W. Carleton & Co.; Etc., Etc.
Conquered by Love. Ida May Linkins Broughton. LC 36-10607. Chapman & Grimes.
Conquered City: A Novel. Victor Serge. LC 76-6027. 1975. 7.95 (ISBN 0-385-05748-2). Doubleday.
Conquered Place. Robert Shafer. LC 54-7865. 1954. Putnam.
Conquering Corps Badge: And Other Stories of the Philippines. Charles King. LC 72-122726. (Short story index reprint series). (Illus.). 1970. Books for Libraries Press.
Conquering Corps Badge: And Other Stories of the Philippines. Charles King. 1902. L. A. Rhoades & Company.
Conquering Family. Thomas Bertram Costain. (Plantagenets Ser: No. 1). 1976. pap. 3.50 (ISBN 0-445-08511-8). Popular Lib.
Conquering Hero. John Murray Gibbon. LC 20-16160. 1920. John Lane Company.
Conquering Horse. Frederick Feikema Manfred. LC 80-17156. (Series: Gregg Press Western Fiction Series.). 1980. 15.95 (ISBN 0-8398-2590-0). Gregg Press.
Conquering Horse: A Novel. Frederick Feikema Manfred. LC 59-9886. 1959. McDowell, Obolensky.
Conquering Kitty: A Romance of the Sassafras River, by Gertrude Crownfield. Gertrude Crownfield. LC 35-196745. J. B. Lippincott Company.
Conquering Lover. Winifred Mary Scott. LC 29-383019. 1929. Doubleday, Doran & Company, Inc.
Conquering of Kate. Andrew Carpenter Wheeler. LC 3-10031. 1903. Doubleday, Page & Company.
Conquering Seas. L Luard. LC 35-18149. 1935. Longmans, Green and Co.
Conqueror. Georgette Heyer. LC 65-199679. 1966. 4.95. Dutton.
Conqueror. Georgette Heyer. (S3823). 1968. Bantam.
Conqueror,". Louise Lanier. LC 14-20500. 1.00. J. A. La Hattie Printing House.
Conqueror: A Dramatized Biography of Alexander Hamilton. Gertrude Franklin Horn Atherton. LC 62-3606. Lippincott.
Conqueror: A Dramatized Biography of Alexander Hamilton. Gertrude Franklin Horn Atherton. LC 16-1397. Frederick A. Stokes Company.
Conqueror: A Dramatized Biography of Alexander Hamilton. Gertrude Franklin Horn Atherton. LC 18-13115. Frederick A. Stokes Company.
Conqueror: A Dramatized Biography of Alexander Hamilton. Gertrude Franklin Horn Atherton. LC 32-195131. Frederick A. Stokes Company.
Conqueror: A Novel. Tebbel, John William. LC 51-9844. 1951. Dutton.
Conqueror: Being the True and Romantic Story of Alexander Hamilton. Gertrude Franklin Horn Atherton. LC 2-8117. 1902. The Macmillan Company.
Conqueror Inn. Ernest Robertson Punshon. LC 44-4438. 1944. The Macmillan Company.
Conqueror of the Clouds. William F Hallstead. LC 80-12383. 7.95 (ISBN 0-525-66681-8). Elsevier/Nelson Books.
Conqueror or Conquered, or, The Sex Challenge Answered: A Revelation of Scientific Facts from Highest Medical Authorities, Based Upon the Relations of Sex Life to the Mental, Moral and Physical Welfare of Both Sexes--Young and Old. A Dramatic Story of Real Life Written in a Fascinating and Entertaining Style, Describing the Tragic Results of Ignorance Surrounding the Mysteries of Sex, Together with Scientific Instruction for Fathers, Mothers, Husbands, Wives, Young Men and Young Women, and a Thrilling Appeal for the Promotion of Happiness, Success and Honor for the Boys and Girls of the Present Generation and the Unborn Millions, Depicting the Impending Disaster to Health and Character from Lack of Knowledge Essential to Safety. Belle Kearney. LC 21-2819. (personal help library, v. 1). The S. A. Mullikin Company.
Conqueror Passes. Larry Barretto. LC 24-1142. 1924. Little, Brown, and Company.
Conqueror: The Story of Cortes and Montezuma and the Slave Girl, Malinal. Arthur Douglas Howden Smith. LC 33-23359. J. B. Lippincott Company.
Conqueror. 1st Ed. Edison Marshall. LC 62-17017. 1962. Doubleday.
Conquerors. Allan W. Eckert. (Winning of America Ser.). 1971. 17.50 (ISBN 0-316-20865-5). Little.
Conquerors. Andre Malraux. LC 72-91594. 10.00 (ISBN 0-03-007716-8). Holt, Rinehart and Winston.
Conquerors, Vol. 3. Allan W. Echert. 928p. 1981. pap. text ed. 3.95 (ISBN 0-553-13384-5). Bantam.
Conquerors All, Based on Facts. Francena Hill Higgins. LC 18-269. 1917. The Gnostic Press.
Conqueror's Lady, Ines Suarez. Stella Burke May. LC 30-283994. Farrar & Rinehart, Incorporated.
Conqueror's Stone. Berry Fleming. LC 27-9854. 1927. The John Day Company.
Conquerors: Translated by Winifred Stephens Whale. With a New Postface Translated by Jacques Le Clercq. Andre Malraux. LC 56-11538. (Beacon paperback, BP30). 1956. Beacon Press.
Conqueror's Wife. 1st Ed. Noel Bertram Gerson. LC 57-8142. 1957. Doubleday.
Conquest. Daisy Fitzhugh Ayres. LC 7-8214. 1907. The Neale Publishing Company.
Conquest. Henry Bedford-Jones. LC 14-216259. David C. Cook Publishing Company.
Conquest. James McKinley Bryant. LC 72-96550. 1972. 2.00. Rocket Pub. Co.
Conquest. Mark A. Calde. LC 79-26731. 1980. 12.95 (ISBN 0-312-16257-X). St. Martin's Press.
Conquest. Sidney Lauer Nyburg. LC 16-5618. 1916. 1.25. J. B. Lippincott Company.
Conquest. Gerald O'Donovan. LC 21-14132. 1921. G. P. Putnam's Sons.
Conquest. Gerald O'Donovan. LC 21-14132. 1921. 2.00. G. P. Putnam's Sons.
Conquest. Oliver Payne. (Northwest Territory Ser.: Bk. 2). 416p. 1982. pap. 3.50 (ISBN 0-425-05532-9). Berkley Pub.
Conquest: A Novel of the Old Southwest. Jack O'Connor, pseud. LC 30-24051. 1930. Harper & Brothers.
Conquest After Battle. Dan Gilbert. LC 42-209. Zondervan Publishing House.
Conquest and Self-Conquest. Maria Jane McIntosh. LC 74-76928. (American fiction reprint series). 1969. Books for Libraries Press.
Conquest Before Autumn. Matthew Eden. LC 72-12780. 1973. 6.95 (ISBN 0-200-04009-X). Abelard-Schuman.
Conquest of America: A Romance of Disaster and Victory: U.S.A., 1921 A.D., Based on Extracts from the Diary of James E. Langston, War Correspondent of the "London Times,". Cleveland Moffett. LC 16-10122. George H. Doran Company.
Conquest of California: A Dramatic Romance of an Unknown Hero. William Benjamin Gross. LC 30-31027. The Stratford Company.
Conquest of Canaan. Booth Tarkington. LC 73-104574. 1970. Literature House.
Conquest of Canaan. Booth Tarkington. LC 20-15608. A. L. Burt Company.
Conquest of Canaan: A Novel. Booth Tarkington. LC 5-35295. 1903. Harper & Brothers.
Conquest of Canaan: A Novel. Booth Tarkington. LC 35-25355. 1935. Harper & Brothers.
Conquest of Charlotte. David Storrar Meldrum. LC 2-21982. 1902. Dodd, Mead & Company.
Conquest of Death. John Middleton Murry. LC 53-859486. 1951. P. Nevill.
Conquest of Don Pedro. Harvey Fergusson. 1954. Morrow.
Conquest of Don Pedro. Harvey Fergusson. LC 74-84231. (Zia book). 1974. 2.95 (ISBN 0-8263-0359-5). University of New Mexico Press.
Conquest of Earth. Manly Miles Banister. LC 57-8752. (Science fiction). 1957. Avalon Books.
Conquest of Ines Ripley. Thomas F McCue. LC 13-813. The Roxburgh Publishing Company, Incorporated.
Conquest of London. Dorothea Gerard Longard De Longgarde. 1900. F. M. Buckles & Company; Etc., Etc.
Conquest of Paris. Camille I. E. Jean Baptiste Camille Debans. (brookside library, no. 399). 1884. F. Tousey.
Conquest of Plassans: Or, The Priest in the House; a Realistic Novel. Emile Zola & Chalmers, Edward Wharton, Ed. LC 9-1333. (On cover: The pastime series. no. 67). 1891. Laird & Lee.
Conquest of Rome. Matilde Serao. LC 3-713. 1902. Harper & Brothers.
Conquest of Rome: La Conquista Di Roma. Matilde Serao & Ranous, Mrs. Dora Knowlton Thompson, 1859-1916, Tr. LC 7-3181. (Added t.-p.: The literature of Italy, 1265-1907. Ed. by Rossiter Johnson and Dora Knowlton Ranous). The National Alumni.
Conquest of the Moon: A Story of the Bayouda. Paschal Grousset. LC 74-16504. (Science Fiction). (Illus.). 1975. 19.00 (ISBN 0-405-06302-4). Arno Press.
Conquest of the Planet of the Apes. John Jakes. (O.s.i.). (Orig.). 1974. pap. 0.95 o.s.i. (AN1241, Award). Univ Pub & Dist.
Conquest: The True Story of Lewis and Clark. Eva Emery Dye. LC 2-27733. 1902. A. C. McClurg & Company.
Conquest: The True Story of Lewis and Clark. Eva Emery Dye. 1922. Doubleday, Page & Company.
Conquest: The True Story of Lewis and Clark. Eva Emery Dye. LC 38-4101. 1936. Wilson-Erickson, Inc.
Conquistador. Loraine Burdick. LC 64-8950. 3.95. Amer. Southern.
Conquistador. Loraine Burdick. LC 64-8950. 1965. American Southern.
Conquistador. Katharine Fullerton Gerould. LC 23-7200. 1923. C. Scribner's Sons.
Conrad: A Tale of Wiclif and Bohemia. Emma Leslie. LC 7-14489. (Church history stories, 2d ser., v. 1). 1879. Phillips & Hunt.
Conrad De Valgeneuse. Being the Continuation of "Salvtor". Alexandre Dumas. Tr. by Sherwood, Mary (Neal) LC 2965. (On cover: Seaside library. Pocket ed. no. 2044). G. Munro's Sons.
Conrad Hagen's Mistake. A Novel. Frolm the German of Otto Roquette. Otto Roquette. Tr. by Crozer, S. A. 1881. J. B. Lippincott & Co.
Conrad in Quest of His Youth. Leonard Merrick. LC 18-232281. (Half-title: The works of Leonard Merrick). 1918. Hodder & Stoughton.
Conrad in Quest of His Youth: An Extravagance of Temperament. Leonard Merrick. LC 17-13502. 1911. M. Kennerley.
Conrado De Beltran: Or, The Buccaneer of the Gulf. A Romantic Story of the Sea and Shore. Julius Warren Lewis. LC 7-14317. 1851. F. Gleason.
Conrad's Manifesto: Preface to a Career: The History of the Preface to The Nigger of the "Narcissus," with Facsimiles of the Manuscripts. Joseph Conrad. Ed. by David Rodman Smith. LC 66-30146. (Illus.). 1966. Philip H. and A. S. W. Rosenbach Foundation.
Conrad's Short Fiction. Lawrence Graver. LC 69-14302. 1969. 7.50. University of California Press.
Cons & Lovers. Leo Guild. (Orig.). 1977. pap. 1.75 (ISBN 0-87067-514-1, BH514). Holloway.
Conscience. Hector Henri Malot & Rice, Lita Angelica, Tr. LC 7-243635. (On cover: Worthington's international library. no. 24). 1892. Worthington Company.
Conscience Interplanetary. Joseph Green. LC 72-96240. (Doubleday science fiction). 1973. 5.95 (ISBN 0-385-01086-9). Doubleday.
Conscience Interplanetary. Joseph Green. 1974. (pbk.) 1.25. Daw Books.
Conscience of Coralie. Frank Frankfort Moore. LC 6820. 1900. H. S. Stone & Company.
Conscience of Love. Marcel Ayme. 1962. 4.50 o.p. Atheneum.
Conscience of Sarah Platt. Alice Gerstenberg. LC 15-6335. 1915. 1.25. A. C. McClurg & Co.
Conscience of the King. Alfred Leo Duggan. LC 52-7789. Coward-McCann.
Conscience of the Rich. Charles Percy Snow. LC 58-5808. (His Strangers and brothers 7). 1958. Scribner.
Conscience of the World: A Novel. Jackson M Bowling. LC 59-44065. 1959. Big Mountain Press.
Conscience on Ice. A Story of the Stage. Alfred J. Cohen. LC 6-26740. N.C. Smith Publishing Company.
Conscience: Or, The Shattered Bust. Henry Bernstein. LC 28-18561. Fox Film Corporation.
Conscientious Objector. Yitka R. Kozak. 80p. 1972. 3.50 o.p. (ISBN 0-682-47507-6). Exposition.
Conscientious Objector. first ed. Yitka R Kozak. 1973. 3.50 (ISBN 0-682-47507-6). Exposition Press.
Consciousness: The End of Authority. Frank R. Wallace. 1980. pap. 2.00 (ISBN 0-911752-32-3). I & O Pub.
Conscript: A Story of the French War of 1813. Emile Erckmann & Chatrian, Alexandre. (Half-title: Erckmann-Chatrian national novels). 1889. C. Scribner's Sons.
Conscript: A Story of the French War of 1813. Emile Erckmann & Chatrian, Alexandre. LC 98-1209. 1898. C. Scribner's Sons.
Conscript: A Tale of War. Alexandre Dumas. LC 6-42829. T. B. Peterson & Brothers.
Conscript. An Historical Novel of the Days of the First Napoleon. Alexandre Dumas. LC 6-42830. T. B. Peterson & Brotghers.
Conscript, and Blind Rosa. Two Tales. Hendrik Conscience. LC 42-35083. 1864. Murphy & Co.
Conscript Mother. Robert Herrick. LC 72-84662. (Illus.). 1974. (lib. ed.) 3.95 (ISBN 0-403-02993-7). Scholarly Press.
Conscript Mother. Robert Herrick. LC 16-11230. 1916. C. Scribner's Sons.
Conscript's Mother see Collected Works.
Conscripts of Conscience. Caroline Atwater Mason. LC 20-2641. Fleming H. Revell Company.
Consecrated Anew: A Story of Christian Endeavor Work. Belle V Chisholm. Presbyterian Board of Publication.
Consenting Adult. Laura Keane Zametkin Hobson. LC 74-18808. 1975. 7.95 (ISBN 0-385-03498-9). Doubleday.
Consenting Adult. Laura Keane Zametkin Hobson. 1976. (pbk.) 1.95. Warner Books.
Consenting Adults: Or, The Duchess Will Be Furious: a Novel. Peter De Vries. LC 80-14054. 9.95 (ISBN 0-316-18184-6). Little, Brown.
Consenting Adults, or, The Duchess Will Be Furious. Peter De Vries. LC 81-2472. 1981. 3.95 (ISBN 0-14-005833-8). Penguin Books.
Consenting Adults, or, the Duchess Will Be Furious. Peter De Vries. 244p. 1980. 10.95 (ISBN 0-316-18184-6). Little.
Consenting Adults, or the Duchess Will Be Furious. Peter De Vries. 1981. pap. 3.95 (ISBN 0-14-005833-8). Penguin.
Consequence of Crime. Elizabeth Linington. LC 80-710. 1980. 8.95 (ISBN 0-385-17074-2). Published for the Crime Club by Doubleday.
Consequences. Sheila Bishop. 224p. 1981. pap. 1.95 (ISBN 0-449-50208-2, Coventry). Fawcett.
Consequences. Edmee Elizabeth Monica De La Pasture. LC 19-11438. 1919. Hodder and Stoughton.
Consequences. Edmee Elizabeth Monica De La Pasture. LC 19-11563. 1919. A. A. Knopf.
Consequences. Julia Ellsworth Ford. LC 29-27935. 1929. E. P. Dutton & Co., Inc.
Consequences. Concordia Merrel. LC 31-312313. 1931. Doubleday, Doran & Company, Inc.
Consequences. Kelly Stearn. LC 80-51823. 1980. 11.95 (ISBN 0-312-16269-3). St. Martin's Press.
Consequences: A Complete Story in the Manner of the Old Parlour Game in Nine Chapters. LC 33-21392. 1933. Houghton Mifflin Company.
Consequences: A Novel. Egerton Castle. LC 592179. 1900. Frederick A. Stokes Company.
Consequences: Or, A Bowl of Punch and What Came of It. Annie Ketchum Dunning. LC 6-35865. Presbyterian Board of Publication.
Conservation of Strangeness. Dennis Ross. LC 80-22044. 1980. pap. 3.95 (ISBN 0-914974-18-1). Holmgangers.

Conservationist. Nadine Gordimer. LC 74-7768. 1975. 7.95 (ISBN 0-670-23883-X). Viking Press.

Conservationist. Nadine Gordimer. LC 76-23435. 1976. 9.95 (ISBN 0-07-023781-6). McGraw-Hill.

Conservative Crime: A View of the Political and Social Scene of Our Time. Clinton Thomas Post. LC 67-30511. 1968. Exposition Press.

Conservatory. Phyllis Hastings. 1974. (pbk.) 0.95 (ISBN 0-671-77739-4). Pocket Books.

Consider Miss Lily. Alyene Porter. LC 62-9385. 1962. Abingdon Press.

Consider My Servant: A Novel Based Upon the Life of Jonathan Edwards. 1st Ed. Jack Duncan Coombe. LC 57-10657. 1957. Expisition Press.

Consider Sappho Burning. Nicholas Delbanco. LC 68-59599. 1969. 5.95. W. Morrow.

Consider the Daisies. Gertrude Carrick. LC 41-20886. J. B. Lippincott Company.

Consider the Evidence. Roderic Jeffries. LC 66-23929. bds., 3.50. Walker.

Consider the Evidence: Stories of Mystery and Suspense. Ed. by Phyllis Reid Fenner. LC 73-792. (Illus.). 1973. 4.95 (ISBN 0-688-20080-X) (ISBN 0-688-20080-X). W. Morrow.

Consider the Lilies. Crichton Smith, Iain. LC 70-106361. (Pergamon English Library). (Athena books.). 1970. Pergamon Press.

Consider the Lilies. Auberon Waugh. LC 69-11336. 1969. 4.95. Little, Brown.

Consider the Lilies of the Field: A Novel. Erico Verissimo. LC 71-88988. 1969. Greenwood Press.

Consider the Lilies of the Field: A Novel. Erico Verissimo & Karnoff, Jean Neel, Tr. LC 47-239476. 1947. The Macmillan Company.

Consider the Lilies of the Field. Erico Verissimo. Tr. by Jean N. Karnoff. Repr. of 1947 ed. lib. bdg. 15.75x (ISBN 0-8371-2320-8, VELF). Greenwood.

Consider the Season. Reuben R Merliss. LC 68-22610. 1968. 5.95. Doubleday.

Consider the Verdict: A Novel of Crime and Punishment. Anders Bodelsen. LC 75-25077. 8.95 (ISBN 0-06-010408-2). Harper & Row.

Consider Yourself Lucky. Lyn Mandelbaum. LC 79-91629. (Illus.). 52p. (Orig.). 1979. pap. 6.00 (ISBN 0-935694-00-5); pap. 12.00 signed. St Edns.

Considering Her Condition. Margaret Gibson. LC 81-19661. 1981. 18.95 (ISBN 0-8149-0855-1). Vanguard Press.

Consolidator: Or, Memoirs of Sundry Transactions from the World in the Moon. Daniel Defoe. LC 75-170513. (Foundations of the Novel). 1972. (ISBN 0-8240-0521-X). Garland Pub.

Consolidator or Memoirs of Sundry Transactions from the World in the Moon. Daniel De Foe. LC 75-170513. (Foundations of the Novel Ser.: Vol. 9). lib. bdg. 50.00 (ISBN 0-8240-0521-X). Garland Pub.

Consort: A Romantic Fantasy. Heckstall-Smith, Anthony. LC 65-23857. 1965. Grove Press.

Consort for Victoria. William Vaughan Wilkins. LC 59-637822. 1959. Doubleday.

Consorts & Castles. Alison Nicholas. 1970. 4.95 o.p. Vantage.

Conspiracion China. Joseph Rosenberger. Tr. by Margarita O. Castro from Eng. (Compadre Collection: Mercader De la Muerte Ser., No. 4). 160p. (Span.). 1974. pap. 0.75 (ISBN 0-88473-504-4). Fiesta Pub.

Conspiracy. Robert Melville Baker & Emerson, John. LC 13-9718. 1913. 1.25. Duffield & Company.

Conspiracy. Arthur Somers Roche. LC 34-799. Sears Publishing Company, Inc.

Conspiracy: A Cuban Romance. Adam Badeau. LC 6-50153. 1885. R. Worthington.

Conspiracy: A Cuban Romance. Adam Badeau. (On cover: Lovell's library, v. 15, no. 756). 1886. J. W. Lovell Company.

Conspiracy: A Novel. John Richard Hersey. LC 75-173775. 1972. 6.95 (ISBN 0-394-47929-7). Knopf.

Conspiracy Novel: Structure and Metaphor in Balzac's Comedie Humaine. James W Mileham. LC 81-68004. (French Forum Monographs; 31). (Illus.). 9.50 (ISBN 0-917058-30-5). French Forum.

Conspiracy of Poisons. J. G Jeffreys, pseud. LC 76-57848. 1977. 6.95 (ISBN 0-8027-5359-0). Walker.

Conspiracy of Silence. Marie Blizard. LC 54-5851. 1954. M. S. Mill Co. and W. Morrow.

Conspiracy of Silence. Mel Silverstein & Karen Silverstein. LC 78-22357. 1980. 10.00 (ISBN 0-385-14431-8). Doubleday.

Conspiracy of the Absent: A Novel. Translated from the Polish by Maurice Michael and Harry Stevens. Maria Szczepanska Kuncewiczowa. LC 50-98207. Roy.

Conspiracy of the Carbonari. Klara Muller Mundt. Tr. by Safford, Mary Joanna. LC 7-31819. 1896. F. T. Neely.

Conspiracy of Women. Aubrey Menen. LC 65-11259. bds., 4.95. Random.

Conspiracy of Yesterday. P. J. Moroney. LC 1-29769. The Abbey Press.

Conspirator. Eliza Ann Dupuy. 1850. D. Appleton & Company.

Conspirator: A Novel. Humphrey Slater. LC 48-6314. 1948. Harcourt, Brace.

Conspirator of Cordova. A Novel. Sylvanus Cobb. (On cover: The popular series, no. 8). 1891. R. Bonner's Sons.

Conspirator of Cordova. A Novel. Sylvanus Cobb. (On cover: The choice series, no. 132). 1896. R. Bonner's Sons.

Conspirator Who Saved the Romanovs. Gary Null. (Illus.). 1972. 6.95 o.p. P-H.

Conspirators. Richard Clayton. LC 68-13441. 1968. Walker.

Conspirators. Frederic Prokosch. LC 43-1142. 1943. Harper & Brothers.

Conspirators. Alan Riefe. (Cage,#2). 1975. (pbk.) 0.95. Popular Library.

Conspirators: A Romance. Robert William Chambers. 1898. Harper & Brothers.

Conspirators: A Romance. Robert William Chambers. LC 12-22661. Harper & Brothers.

Conspirators: A Romance. Robert William Chambers. LC 96-29338. 1900. Harper & Brothers.

Conspirators: Or, The Chevalier D'Harmental. Alexandre Dumas & Maquet, Auguste. LC 3-278102. G. Routledge and Sons, Limited.

Conspirators: Or, The Chevalier D'Harmental. Alexandre Dumas & Maquet, Auguste. LC 6-436172. (NAmerican series. no. 36). M. J. Ivers & Co.

Constable Around the Village. Nicholas Rhea, pseud. LC 82-197659. 10.95 (ISBN 0-312-16441-6). St. Martin's Press.

Constable De Bourbon. William Harrison Ainsworth. (Seaside library, v. 68, no 1383). G. Munro.

Constable in the Making. Cecil Worthington. LC 40-9906. House of Field, Inc.

Constable on the Hill. Nicholas Rhea, pseud. LC 79-83824. 8.95 (ISBN 0-312-16439-4). St. Martin's Press.

Constables Don't Count: By Alex Fraser Pseud. Henry Brinton. LC 59-14101. Roy Publishers.

Constable's Tower: Or, The Times of Magna Charta. Charlotte Mary Yonge. LC 9-3433. 1891. T. Whittaker.

Constance. Lawrence Durrell. LC 81-69998. 365p. 1982. 15.95 (ISBN 0-670-23909-7). Viking Pr.

Constance. Francis Charles Philips. LC 7-360753. (On cover: Broadway series, no. 13). J. A. Taylor and Company.

Constance: A Novel. Herve-Bazin, Jean Pierre Marie. LC 54-11174. 1955. Crown Publishers.

Constance: A Novel. Translated from the French by Herma Briffault. Herve Bazin. LC 54-11174. Crown Publishers.

Constance, and Calbot's Rival: Tales. Julian Hawthorne. LC 7-389913. (On cover: Appletons' town and country library, no. 23). 1889. D. Appleton and Company.

Constance Aylmar. A Story of the Seventeenth Century. Helen Eliza Fitch Parker. 1869. C. Scribner & Company.

Constance Aylmer: A Tale of the Times of Peter Stuyvesant. Helen Eliza Fitch Parker. LC 7-34702. 1889. J. B. Alden.

Constance Beverly: A Tale of Southern Life in 1850. C A Fraser. 1879. Sunday Times Publishing House.

Constance D'Brolie. Florence White Ruger. LC 2-20465. 1902. The Abbey Press.

Constance Dunlap: Woman Detective. Arthur Benjamin Reeve. LC 16-6818. 1916. Hearst's International Library Co.

Constance of Acadia. A Novel. Edward Payson Tenney. LC 8-26044. 1886. Roberts Brothers.

Constance Trescot: A Novel. Silas Weir Mitchell. 1905. The Century Co.

Constance Vallerie. Anne Arrington Tyson. LC 36-6811. B. Humphries, Inc.

Constance Winter's Choice. Anna Louise Beckwith. LC 6-976796. (On cover: Globe library, v. 1, no. 144). 1891. Rand, McNally & Company.

Constance's Fate: A Story of Denzil Place. Mary Montgomery Lamb Singleton Currie. LC 41-38050. 1876. G. W. Carleton & Co.

Constancia Herself. Margaret Widdemer. LC 44-27231. 1944. Farrar & Rinehart, Inc.

Constancia Herself. Margaret Widdemer. LC 45-23931. 1945. Farrar & Rinehart, Inc.

Constant Companion. Marion Chesney. 224p. 1980. pap. 1.75 (ISBN 0-449-50114-0, Coventry). Fawcett.

Constant De Rebecque, Henri Benjamin: 1767-1830. Adolphe in Murry, John Middleton, 1889- The Conquest of Death. LC 53-859435. 1951. P. Nevill.

Constant Heart. Ruby Mildred Ayres. LC 42-20801. 1942. The Sun Dial Press.

Constant Nymph. Margaret Kennedy. LC 25-6197. 1925. Doubleday, Page & Company.

Constant Rebel. INew York: Comet Press Books. Kengi Hamada. LC 55-850194.

Constant Sex. Elizabeth Frances Corbett. LC 35-13552. Reynal & Hitchcock.

Constant Simp. Nell Columbia Boyer Martin. LC 27-14345. 1927. Rae D. Henkle Co., Inc.

Constant Travellers. Gordon Allen Basichis. LC 77-17432. 9.95. Putnam.

Constantia De Valmont. A Novel. Harriet Lee. LC 7-12622. 1799. M. Carey.

Constantine. Ramsay MacMullen. (O.s.i.). (Illus.). 1969. 7.95 o.s.i. (ISBN 0-8037-1486-6). Dial.

Constantine Cay. Catherine Dillon. 1976. (pbk.) 1.50. New American Library.

Constantine: The Miracle of the Flaming Cross. Frank Gill Slaughter. (Pathway of faith ser.). 5.95. Doubleday.

Constantine: The Miracle of the Flaming Cross. Frank Gill Slaughter. LC 65-19873. (The Pathway of faith series). 1965. Doubleday.

Constantine's Triumph: A Tale of the Era of the Martyrs. W. H. Spears. LC 63-19710. 1964. Adams Press.

Constanza. Willis Vernon Cole. LC 28-3691. 1927. The Writers Guild.

Constellation of Heroes. David Cort. LC 73-144067. 1971. 5.95 (ISBN 0-448-00676-6). Grosset & Dunlap.

Constitution of el Salvador, Nineteen Sixty-Two. 1974. pap. 1.00 o.p. OAS.

Construction Camp Nurse. Dana. pap. 0.75 o.s.i. (01-329). Lancer.

Consuela Bright. Sussman, Cornelia (Silver) LC 62-15275. 1962. Sheed and Ward.

Consuelo. Pedro Lopez De Ayala. (Span). pap. 2.25 o.s.i.; pap. 1.75 o.s.i. French & Eur.

Consuelo. George Sand. LC 21-214626. (Manhattan library. vol. 1, no. 15). 1891. A. L. Burt.

Consuelo. George Sand & Potter, Frank Hunter, Tr. 1889. Dodd, Mead & Company.

Consuelo. George Sand & Shaw, Francis George, 1809-1882, Tr. LC 13-12907. 1846. W. D. Ticknor and Company.

Consuelo. 4th ed. George Sand & Shaw, Francis George, 1809-1882, Tr. 1850. Dewitt and Davenport.

Consuelo. A Novel. George Sand & Robinson, Fayette, D. 1859, Tr. LC 6-34617. T. B. Peterson & Brothers.

Consuelo. A Novel. By George Sand... Tr. from the French, by Fayette Robinson... George Sand & Robinson, Fayette, D. 1859, Tr. 1882. T. B. Peterson & Brothers.

Consuelo: A Romance of Venice. George Sand. LC 4-17502. A. L. Burt Company.

Consuelo: A Romance of Venice. George Sand. LC 79-15632. 1979. 8.95 (ISBN 0-306-80102-7). Da Capo Press.

Consuelo: Translated by Fayette Robinson. George Sand. LC 61-3990. (Premier world classic, t125). 1961. Fawcett Publications.

Consul. Richard Harding Davis. LC 11-10953. 1911. C. Scribner's Sons.

Consul at Sunset. Gerald Hanley. LC 51-6203. 1951. Macmillan.

Consul to China. Elizabeth W P Lomax. LC 10-985226. F. T. Neely.

Consul's File. Paul Theroux. LC 77-6431. 1977. 8.95 (ISBN 0-395-25399-3). Houghton Mifflin.

Consul's Wife. 1st Ed. William Lawrence Shirer. LC 56-6761. Little, Brown.

Consultant: A Novel of Computer Crime. John McNeil. LC 77-27034. 8.95 (ISBN 0-698-10907-4). Coward, McCann & Geoghegan.

Consulting Specialist. Abraham Loew Furman. LC 37-1120. The Macaulay Company.

Contact. Eva Tucker. LC 66-707315. 1966. bds., 4.50. Calder & Bovars.

Contact: A Romance of the Air. Elliott White Springs. LC 30-10083. Sears Publishing Company, Inc.

Contact: And Other Stories. Frances Noyes Hart. LC 23-9537. 1923. Doubleday, Page & Company.

Contact and Other Stories. Frances Noyes Hart. LC 30-7673. 1930. Doubleday, Doran & Company, Inc.

Contact Lost. David Craig. LC 76-104635. 1970. 4.95 o.p. (ISBN 0-8128-1286-7). Stein & Day.

Contact Lost. Leif Hamre. LC 67-18866. 1967. Harcourt, Brace & World.

Contact Lost. Allan James Tucker. LC 76-104635. 1970. 4.95. Stein and Day.

Contact Mercury. Leonard Hastings Nason. LC 46-2154. 1946. Doubleday & Company, Inc.

Contaminant. Leonard Reiffel. LC 78-4744. 8.95 (ISBN 0-06-013519-0). Harper & Row.

Contance Dunlap, Vol. 2. Arthur Benjamin Reeve. (Graig Kennedy Ser.). 342p. 1981. pap. write for info. (ISBN 0-86649-003-5). Twentieth Century.

Contarini Fleming: A Psychological Romance. Benjamin Disraeli Beaconsfield. LC 76-12449. (Works of Benjamin Disraeli, Earl of Beaconsfield; v. 5-6). 1976. (ISBN 0-404-08800-7). AMS Press.

Contarini Fleming: A Psychological Romance. Benjamin Disraeli Beaconsfield. (In his The Bradenham edition of the novels and tales. New York, 1934? vol. IV). Alfred A. Knopf.

Contarini Fleming; a Psychological Romance. The Rise of Iskander. new ed. Benjamin Disraeli Beaconsfield. G. Routledge and Sons.

Contemplative Man. Herbert Lawrence. LC 74-17278. (Flowering of the Novel). 1974. (ISBN 0-8240-1195-3). Garland.

Contemporary American Short Stories. Ed. by Douglas Angus. LC 67-28680. (Fawcett premier book, m359). 1967. Fawcett Publications.

Contemporary Chinese Novels & Short Stories, 1949-1972: An Annotated Bibliography. Meishi Tsai. (East Asian Monographs: No. 78). 1979. text ed. 30.00x (ISBN 0-674-16681-7). Harvard U Pr.

Contemporary Chinese Stories. Tr. by Wang Chi-Chen. LC 69-14137. 1969. Repr. of 1944 ed. lib. bdg. 20.50x (ISBN 0-8371-0738-5, WACS); pap. 4.95 (ISBN 0-8371-8943-8, WAC). Greenwood.

Contemporary Danish Prose: An Anthology. Elias Bredsdorff. LC 74-41. 1974. 15.25 (ISBN 0-8371-7358-2). Greenwood Press.

Contemporary German Novel. Ernst E. Noth. 1961. pap. 1.95 o.p. (ISBN 0-87462-422-3). Marquette.

Contemporary Hindi Short Stories. Tr. by Jai Ratan. (Writers Workshop Saffronbird Ser.). 180p. 1975. 12.00 (ISBN 0-88253-518-8); pap. text ed. 4.80 (ISBN 0-88253-517-X). Ind-US Inc.

Contemporary Indian Short Stories. Ed. by Ka N. Subramanyam. 1982. o. p. 12.50x (ISBN 0-7069-0684-5, Pub. by Vikas India); pap. 3.95 (ISBN 0-7069-1624-7). Advent NY.

Contemporary Indian Short Stories Series 1 & 2. 1966. 3.50 ea. o.p. Verry.

Contemporary Italian Short Stories. Ed. by Howard Rosario Marraro. LC 28-30832. H. Holt and Company.

Contemporary Japanese Fiction, 1926-1968. Mitsuo Nakamura. (Illus.). pap. 3.75 o.p. (ISBN 0-87040-015-0). Japan Pubns.

Contemporary Japanese Literature: An Anthology of Fiction, Film, & Other Writing Since 1945. Howard Hibbett. LC 77-4762. 1977. 15.00 o.s.i. (ISBN 0-394-49141-6); pap. 10.95 (ISBN 0-394-73362-2). Knopf.

Contemporary Jewish Fiction. Bernard Berenson. 1976. lib. bdg. 59.95 (ISBN 0-87968-939-0). Gordon Pr.

Contemporary Northwest Writing: A Collection of Poetry & Fiction. Ed. by Roy Carlson. 1979. text ed. 12.50 (ISBN 0-87071-324-8); pap. text ed. 6.00x (ISBN 0-87071-323-X). Oreg St U Pr.

Contemporary Portraits & Other Stories. Murray Bail. (Paperback Prose). 1975. 14.95x (ISBN 0-7022-0979-1); pap. 7.95x (ISBN 0-7022-0978-3). U of Queensland Pr.

Contemporary Potraits. Robert W. Meals. LC 82-80003. 166p. 1983. pap. 5.95 (ISBN 0-86666-075-5). GWP.

Contemporary Short Stories. Ed. by Gordon Hall Gerould, Jr. & Charles Bayly. LC 28-24155. 1927. Harper and Brothers.

Contemporary Short Stories, Vol. 3. Ed. by Maurice Baudin, Jr. 1954. 1.45 o.p. (AHS14). Bobbs.

Contemporary Short Stories & Representive Selections, Vol. 2. Ed. by Maurice Baudin, Jr. 1954. pap. 4.35 o.p. (ISBN 0-672-60017-X, AHS13). Bobbs.

Contemporary Short Stories & Representive Selections, Vol. 2. Ed. by Maurice Baudin, Jr. 1954. pap. 4.35 o.p. (ISBN 0-672-60017-X, AHS13). Bobbs.

Contemporary Short Stories: Representative Selections. Ed. by Maurice Baudin, Jr. LC 54-732. (American heritage series, no. 12). Liberal Arts Press.

Contemporary Short Stories: Selected by Kenneth Allan Robinson... Ed. by Kenneth Allan Robinson. LC 24-244598. Houghton Mifflin Company.

Contemporary Supernatural Tales of the Baltimore Area: 20 Tales, by Karl B. Knust, Jr. 1st Ed. Karl B Knust. LC 64-66088. 1964.

Contemporary Turkish Short Stories: An Intermediate Reader. Ed. by Richard L. Chambers & Gunay Kut. LC 76-21045. (Middle Eastern Languages & Linguistics, 3). 1977. 12.50x (ISBN 0-88297-013-5). Bibliotheca.

Contemporary Types of the Short Story. Ed. by Gordon Hall Gerould, Jr. & Charles Bayly. LC 27-4643. 1927. Harper & Brothers.

Contemporary Writers. Virginia Stephen Woolf. LC 66-19489. 1966. Harcourt, Brace & World.

Contempt Power. Ronald L. Goldfarb. 1971. pap. 1.95 o.p. (ISBN 0-385-01953-X, Anch). Doubleday.

Contend with Horses. Grace Lillian Irwin. LC 68-54100. 1968. 4.95. W. B. Eerdmans Pub. Co.

Contender. Ibrahim Kamil Haddad. LC 35-31443. Printed by R. E. Simpson & Son, Inc.

Contenders: A Novel. John Barrington Wain. LC 58-8593. 1958. St. Martin's Press.

Contending Forces: A Novel. Pauline Elizabeth Hopkins. LC 77-18724. (Lost American Fiction Ser.). (Illus.). 414p. 1978. Repr. of 1900 ed. 9.95 (ISBN 0-8093-0874-6). S Ill U Pr.

Contending Forces: A Romance Illustrative of Negro Life North and South. Pauline Elizabeth Hopkins. LC 72-83909. (Illus.). 1969. Mnemosyne Pub. Co.

Contending Forces: A Romance Illustrative of Negro Life North and South. Pauline Elizabeth Hopkins. LC 78-144639. (Illus.). 1971. (ISBN 0-404-00173-4). AMS Press.

Contending Forces: A Romance Illustrative of Negro Life North and South. Pauline Elizabeth Hopkins. LC 1-29735. 1900. The Colored Co-Operative Publishing Co.

Contending Forces: A Romance Illustrative of Negro Life North and South. Pauline Elizabeth Hopkins. LC 77-18724. (Lost American fiction). (Illus.). 1978. 9.95 (ISBN 0-8093-0874-6). Southern Illinois University Press.

Content Assignment. Holly Roth. LC 53-10808. (Inner sanctum mystery). 1954. Simon and Schuster.

Contents for Sale. Becky L. Weyrich. 1978. pap. 1.50 (ISBN 0-532-15370-7). Woodhill.

Contes. Francois Marie Arouet de Voltaire. Ed. by H. W. Preston. 1912. 1.30 o.p. Oxford U Pr.

Contes albanais. A. Dozon. LC 78-20111. (Collection de contes et de chansons populaires: Vol. 3). Repr. of 1881 ed. 21.50 (ISBN 0-404-60353-X). AMS Pr.

Contes Choises. Guy de Maupassant. Ed. by Herbert F. Collins. 1967. 3.50x o.p. St Martin.

Contes Choisis. Alphonse Daudet. 1962. 3.50 o.p. French & Eur.

Contes Choisis. Guy de Maupassant. 1965. pap. 4.95 o.p. French & Eur.

Contes de Jacques Tournebroche, Histoire Contemporaine see Romans et Contes.

Contes de l'Inattendu. Ed. by Richard Parker. 1959. text ed. 3.95x o.p. (ISBN 0-669-28357-6); pap. text ed. 2.95x o.p. (ISBN 0-669-28381-9). Heath.

Contes D'Hier et D'aujourd'hui. Clifford Stetson Parker. (Rinehart Editions). 1958. 6.25 o.p. (ISBN 0-03-016070-7, HoltC). HR&W.

Contes et Nouvelles Du Temps Present. Ed. by Maurice Edgar Coindreau. Loy, J. Robert, Joint Ed. LC 41-121713. Reynal & Hitchcock.

Contes Francais et Legendes Canadiennes. S. Cooper et al. (Illus., Fr.). (gr. 10-12). 1968. text ed. 2.40 o.p. St Martin.

Contes Populaires. Edmond Albert Meras & Andre Celieres. (Fr). 1966. text ed. 3.36 o.p. (2-37425). HM.

Contes populaires du Soudan Egyptien. Y. Artin. LC 78-20143. (Collection de contes et de chansons populaires: Vol. 34). Repr. of 1909 ed. 21.50 (ISBN 0-404-60384-X). AMS Pr.

Contes romans de l'Egypte chretienne, 2 vols. D. Amelineau. LC 78-20122. (Collection de contes et de chansons populaires: Vols. 13-14). Repr. of 1888 ed. Set. 43.00 (ISBN 0-404-60396-3). AMS Pr.

Contessa. Helene Thornton. LC 81-43536. 1982. 18.95 (ISBN 0-385-17300-8). Doubleday.

Contessa's Sister: A Novel. Gardner Callahan Teall. LC 11-72613. 1911. Houghton Mifflin Company.

Contest. Mort Weisinger. LC 72-128482. 1970. World Pub. Co.

Contest of Ladies. William Sansom. LC 56-8053. 1956. Reynal.

Continent Makers: And Other Tales of the Viagens. Lyon Sprague De Camp. LC 53-6455. 1953. Twayne Publishers.

Continental Cavalier: The Record of Some Incidents Pertaining to the Chevalier De Marc, Brevet Major in the Army of the Colonies, Aid-De-Camp to General, the Marquis Lafayette. Frank Kimball Scribner. LC 2327. The Abbey Press.

Continental Dragoon: A Love Story of Philipse Manor-House in 1778. Robert Neilson Stephens. LC 8-34327. 1898. L. C. Page and Company.

Continental Drift. James D Houston. LC 78-306. 1978. 8.95 (ISBN 0-394-50124-1). Knopf: Distributed by Random House.

Continental Op. Dashiell Hammett. LC 74-9050. 1974. 7.95 (ISBN 0-394-48704-4). Random House.

Continental Op. Dashiell Hammett. LC 75-11735. 1975. Vintage Books.

Continental Op. Dashiell Hammett. LC 45-8056. (On cover: Bestseller mystery. B62). 1945. L. E. Spivak.

Continental Tales of Henry Wadsworth Longfellow: Selected by J. I. Rodale With Drawings by Richard Lindner. Henry Wadsworth Longfellow & Rodale, Jerome Irving, 1896- Comp. LC 48-7174. 1948. Story Classics.

Continental Tales of Longfellow. Henry Wadsworth Longfellow. pap. 1.25 o.p. (ISBN 0-498-04018-6, Prpta). A S Barnes.

Continental Touch. Josef Wechsberg. LC 48-5119. 1948. Houghton Mifflin Co.

Continent's Edge. Niven Busch. LC 79-21784. 11.95 (ISBN 0-671-24235-0). Simon and Schuster.

Continual Interest in the Sun & Sea & Inland Missing the Sea. Keith Gunderson. (Illus.). 154p. 1977. pap. 3.95. Nodin Pr.

Continuing City. Elizabeth Frances Corbett. 1973. pap. 0.95 o.p. (95331). Beagle Bks.

Continuing City: A Novel. Elizabeth Frances Corbett. LC 65-12608. 4.95. Appleton-Century Dist. Meredith.

Continuous Katherine Mortenhoe. David Guy Compton. LC 79-16337. (Gregg Press science fiction series). (Illus.). 1980. 15.00 (ISBN 0-8398-2567-6). Gregg Press.

Continuous Struggle, Bk. 1. J. W. Comer. LC 73-81488. 160p. 1973. text ed. 2.95 (ISBN 0-88429-900-7). Collegiate Pub.

Continuum. Ed. by Roger Elwood. LC 73-87184. (v. 1) 5.95. Putnam.

Continuum 4. Ed. by Roger Elwood. (Berkley Medallion Book). 1976. (pbk.) 0.95 (ISBN 0-425-03077-6). Berkley Publishing Corp.

Contours of Darkness. Marco Vassi. 1976. pap. 2.25 (ISBN 0-532-22103-6). Woodhill.

Contours of Darkness. Marco Vassi. 288p. (Orig.). 1971. pap. 2.25 o.s.i. (OPS6180). Olympia.

Contraband. Clarence Budington Kelland. LC 23-535933. Harper & Brothers.

Contraband. Henry Barnard Safford. LC 36-7720. The Penn Publishing Company.

Contraband" A Romance of the North Atlantic. Randall Parrish. LC 16-219391. 1916. A. C. McClurg & Co.

Contraband, A Romance of the North Atlantic. Randall Parrish. 1976. lib. bdg. 18.25x (ISBN 0-89968-085-2). Lightyear.

Contraband of War: A Tale of the Hispano-American Struggle. Matthew Phipps Shiel. LC 68-23727. (Illus.). 1968. Gregg Press.

Contraband Rocket: By Lee Correy Pseud. George Harry Stine. LC 56-26716. (Ace double novel books, D-146). 1956. Ace Books.

Contraband. 1st Ed. Cleve Franklin Adams. LC 50-32364. 1950. Knopf.

Contrabando. Karl William Detzer. LC 36-175358. The Bobbs-Merrill Company.

Contract. Henry C. Carlisle. LC 68-27629. 1968. 5.95. Bobbs-Merrill.

Contract. Joe Poyer, pseud. LC 78-55610. 1978. 10.95 (ISBN 0-689-10907-5). Atheneum.

Contract. Allan Prior. LC 78-133093. 1971. 7.95 (ISBN 0-671-20807-1). Simon and Schuster.

Contract. Gerald Seymour. LC 80-26198. 1981. 13.95 (ISBN 0-03-059132-5). Holt, Rinehart and Winston.

Contract for a Killing. R. L. Brent. (Liquidator Ser.). (O.s.i.: No. 2). 192p. (Orig.). 1974. pap. 0.95 o.s.i. (AN1275, Award). Univ Pub & Dist.

Contract for Marriage. Megan Alexander. (Superromances Ser.). 384p. 1982. pap. 2.50 (ISBN 0-373-70017-2, Pub. by Worldwide). Harlequin Bks.

Contract on Cherry Street. Rosenberg, Philip. 1976. (pbk.) 1.75 (ISBN 0-380-00591-3). Avon.

Contract on Cherry Street: A Novel. Philip Rosenberg. LC 74-23295. 1975. 8.95 (ISBN 0-690-00718-3). Crowell.

Contract on Stone. D. R. Addleman. 1976. pap. 1.50 (ISBN 0-89041-123-9, 3123). Major Bks.

Contract on the President. John Crosby. 1973. (pbk.) 1.25. Dell.

Contract Surgeon. Robert T Crowley. LC 68-24834. 1969. 5.95. Doubleday.

Contract with God. Will Eisner. (Illus.). 1978. 10.00 (ISBN 0-89437-035-9); pap. 4.95 (ISBN 0-89437-045-6). Baronet.

Contract with Love. Lois Coleman Nelson. 1975. 4.95. Avalon Books.

Contract with the World. Jane Rule. LC 80-7939. 12.95 (ISBN 0-15-122578-8). Harcourt Brace Jovanovich.

Contracting Circle. Elliot Lovegood Grant Watson. LC 25-170632. 1925. Boni & Liveright.

Contractor. David Storey. (O.S.I.). 1971. 4.95 o.s.i. (ISBN 0-394-47002-8). Random.

Contradance: A Puritan's Progress in New Orleans. Willson Whitman. LC 30-293391. The Bobbs-Merrill Company.

Contralto. Charles Raymond Maloy. LC 12-18553. R. G. Badger.

Contrary Cousins. Judith Harkness. 1981. pap. 2.25 (ISBN 0-451-11022-6, AE1022, Sig). NAL.

Contrary Mary. Temple Bailey. LC 15-1639. 1914. The Penn Publishing Company.

Contrary Pleasure. John Dann MacDonald. LC 54-992523. 1954. Appleton-Century-Crofts.

Contrary Winds. Edith Snyder Pedersen. LC 51-11558. 1951. Zondervan.

Contrary Winds. Irma Peixotto Sellars. LC 48-6152. 1948. Doubleday.

Contrast: A Tale of Facts. Designed to Show the Advantages of a Religious Over an Irreligious Education in the Family. Darnall Dowden. LC 6-34405. 1880. A.C. Caperton & Co.

Contrast; or, Modes of Education. A Novel. Hannah Farnham Sawyer Lee. LC 7-12614. 1837. Whipple and Damrell.

Contrast: Paul Placid. LC 75-7069. (Garland Library of Narratives of North American Indian Captivities ; V. 47). 1977. 25.00. Garland Pub.

Contrasts: A Story. M. R Grendel. LC 6-44872. 1881. G. P. Putnam's Sons.

Contributions to "Punch" Etc. William Makepeace Thackeray & Punch, London. LC 12-31082. (Half-title: The biographical edition. The works of... Thackeray... vol. VI). 1898. Harper & Brothers.

Contrite Hearts. Herman Bernstein. LC 5-36815. A. Wessels Company.

Control. William Goldman. LC 81-17334. 14.95 (ISBN 0-440-01471-9). Delacorte Press.

Control of Surface Quality. 11th ed. James A. Broadston & Donald A. Broadston. LC 77-73765. (Illus.). 1977. pap. 24.00 (ISBN 0-911464-02-6). Surf-Chek.

Control Tower. Robert P Davis. LC 79-12567. 9.95 (ISBN 0-399-12175-7). Putnam.

Controlling Interest: A Novel. Peter H Engel. LC 80-23185. 13.95 (ISBN 0-312-16919-1). St. Martin's Press.

Convalescents. Charles Frederic Nirdinger. LC 23-9233. 1923. 1.75. The Century Co.

Convenant with the Dead. A Novel. Clara Lemore Roberts. LC 7-41031. (On cover; Lippincott's series of selected novels, no. 132). 1892. J. B. Lippincott Company.

Convenient Bride. Betty Henrichs. (Candlelight Regency Ser.: No. 699). (Orig.). 1982. pap. 1.75 (ISBN 0-440-11472-1). Dell.

Convenient Coward. 1st Ed. Shiflet, Kenneth E. LC 61-14912. 1961. Stackpole Co.

Convenient Marriage. Georgette Heyer. (SB4017). 1967. Bantam.

Convenient Marriage. Georgette Heyer. LC 66-25130. 1966. Dutton.

Convenient Season. David Joseph Manners. LC 41-11686. 1941. E. P. Dutton & Co., Inc.

Convent. Angelica. pap. 1.75 o.p. (V1024K, Venus). Grove.

Convent and the Manse. Jane Dunbar Chaplin. LC 6-23122. 1853. J. P. Jewett & Company.

Convent Girl. Helene Mullins. LC 29-168583. 1929. Harper & Brothers.

Convention: By Fletcher Knebel and Charles W. Bailey, II. 1st Ed. Fletcher Knebel & Bailey, Charles Waldo. LC 64-12687. 1964. Harper & Row.

Convention. By Fletcher Knebel, Charles W. Bailey, II. Fletcher Knebel & Charles Waldo Bailey. (N2943). 1965. Bantam.

Convention Girl. William Arthur Neubauer. 1945. Phoenix Press.

Convention Girls. Ellen Evans, pseud. 224p. 1982. pap. 2.50 o.p. (ISBN 0-505-51850-3). Tower Bks.

Convention Girls. Ellen Evans, pseud. 224p. 1983. pap. 2.50 (ISBN 0-8439-2021-1, Leisure Bks). Dorchester Pub Co.

Convention Hotel. Howard Raven. 192p. (Orig.). 1972. pap. 1.95 o.p. (ISBN 0-87056-277-0, 6277). Brandon.

Convention, M. D. Frank Gill Slaughter. LC 73-186043. 408p. 1972. 6.95 o.p. (ISBN 0-385-00848-5). Doubleday.

Convention, M.D. A Novel of Medical in-Fighting. Frank Gill Slaughter. LC 73-186043. 1972. 6.95 (ISBN 0-385-00848-5). Doubleday.

Convention, M.D. A Novel of Medical Infighting. Frank Gill Slaughter. 1973. (pbk.) 1.25. Pocket Books.

Conventional Bohemian. 2d ed. Edmund Pendleton. LC 29-30777. 1886. D. Appleton and Company.

Conventional Wisdom. John Bart Gerald. LC 74-186097. 1972. 5.95 (ISBN 0-374-12892-8). Farrar, Straus & Giroux.

Conventionalists. Robert Hugh Benson. 1908. B. Herder.

Convergence. Jack Fuller. LC 81-43483. 1982. 16.95 (ISBN 0-385-18023-3). Doubleday.

Convergent Series. Larry Niven. 1979. pap. 2.25 (ISBN 0-345-29566-8, Del Rey Bks). Ballantine.

Conversation in Sicili. Tr. from Italian by Wilfrid David. Introd. by Ernest Hemingway. Elio Vittorini. (1651). 1961. Penguin Bks. Dist. Boston, Houghton.

Conversation in The Cathedral. Vargas Llosa, Mario. LC 74-1892. 1975. 12.50 (ISBN 0-06-014502-1). Harper & Row.

Conversation: Or, Pilgrims' Progress. Conrad Potter Aiken. LC 40-6292. Duell, Sloan & Pearce.

Conversations: A Kind of Fiction. James Kern Feibleman. 360p. 1982. 15.95 (ISBN 0-8180-1134-3). Horizon.

Conversations with a Corpse. Robert C Dennis. LC 73-11807. (Black bat mystery). 1974. 5.95 (ISBN 0-672-51901-1). Bobbs-Merrill.

Conversations with a Pocket Gopher, and Other Outspoken Neighbors. Jack Warner Schaefer & Irene Brady. LC 78-23541. 1978. 4.50 (ISBN 0-88496-088-9). Capra Press.

Conversations with Rabbi Small. Harry Kemelman. LC 81-1131. 1981. 11.95 (ISBN 0-688-00627-2). Morrow.

Conversion. Kelly Cherry. (Story Ser.: No. 8). (Illus.). 52p. 1979. signed 8.00 (ISBN 0-914232-29-0); pap. 2.50 (ISBN 0-914232-28-2). McPherson & Co.

Conversion. Victor Perera. LC 72-108948. 1970. 5.95. Little, Brown.

Conversion of Brian O'Dillon. Mattie M Boteler. LC 6-15019. The Standard Publishing Co.

Conversion of Chaplain Cohen: A Novel. Herbert Tarr. LC 63-9443. 1963. B. Geis Associates; Distributed by Random House.

Conversion of John Stoneman. Alfred Havermyer. LC 11-1644. Berea Printing Company.

Conversions. Harry Mathews. LC 62-8437. (Illus.). 1962. Random House.

Convert. Oresets A. Brownson. 1885. 30.00 o.p. Folcroft.

Convert. Charles Buckner Hudgins. LC 8-3676. 1908. The Neale Publishing Company.

Convert. Elizabeth Robins. LC 7-35623. 1907. The Macmillan Company.

Convert. 1st Ed. Margaret Culkin Banning. LC 57-8199. 1957. Harper.

Convertible Hearse. William Campbell Gault. LC 57-10044. 1957. Random House.

Converts: A Historical Novel. Rex Warner. LC 67-14454. 1967. Little Brown.

Conveyor. James Steele. LC 74-22817. (Labor Movement in Fiction & Non-Fiction). Repr. of 1935 ed. 18.50 (ISBN 0-404-58476-4). AMS Pr.

Conveyor: A Novel. James Steele. LC 74-22817. (Labor Movement in Fiction and Non-Fiction). 1976. 15.00 (ISBN 0-404-58476-4). AMS Press.

Conveyor: A Novel. James Steele. LC 36-125460. International Publishers.

Convict B 14: A Novel. Rose Kirkpatrick Weekes. LC 20-21967. Brentano's.

Convict Colonel. Fortune Du Boisgobey. LC 6-34428. (On cover: Secret service series, no. 48). Street & Smith.

Convict Guns. James Harvey. (Belmont Tower Book). 1.50 (ISBN 0-505-51366-8). Tower Publications.

Convict: Or, The Hypocrite Unmasked. A Tale. George Payne Rainsford James. LC 7-7579. (On cover: Library of select novels, no. 107). 1847. Harper & Brothers.

Convict 72. (On cover: Globe detective series, no. 8). 1888. The Eagle Publishing Co.

Convict 999. A Thrilling Story Founded Upon the Play of the Same Name. Grace Miller White & Woods, Albert Herman. LC 33-28361. (On cover: Play book series, no. 114). 1907. J. S. Ogilvie Publishing Company.

Convictions of Christopher Sterling: A Novel. Harold Begbie. 1919. R. M. McBride & Company.

Convicts and Their Children. Berthold Auerbach. Tr. by Brooks, Charles Timothy. LC 6-4502. (Leisure hour series, v. 74). 1877. H. Holt and Company.

Convoy Through the Dream. Scott Graham Williamson. LC 48-10566. 1948. Macmillan Co.

Cony-Catching. Kirby Farrell. LC 75-135570. 1971. 8.95. Atheneum.

Coo-Aush-Akee Country. Charles Everett Johnson. LC 77-357236. (Illus.). 8.95. S.N.

Cook. Harry Kressing. LC 64-20032. bds., 4.95. Random.

Cook and the Captain Bold. Arthur Mason. LC 70-128740. (Short story index reprint series). (Illus.). 1970. Books for Libraries Press.

Cook and the Captain Bold. Arthur Mason. LC 24-7948. The Atlantic Monthly Press.

Cook and the Captive: Or, Attalus the Hostage. Charlotte Mary Yonge. LC 9-2224. 1894. T. Whittaker.

Cook and the Carpenter. June Arnold. LC 73-86277. 1973. 3.00. Daughters, Inc.

Cook General: An Account of the Barnes Mystery of 1879. John Cashman, pseud. LC 74-1879. 1974. (ISBN 0-06-010658-1). Harper & Row.

Cook up a Crime. Charlotte Murray Russell, pseud. LC 51-12482. 1951. Published for the Crime Club by Doubleday.

Cooke, John Estes. A Summer Comedy. Publishers, The Tamawaca Press, U. S. A.

Cooking School Murders. Virginia Rich. LC 81-22162. 11.50 (ISBN 0-525-24110-8). Dutton.

Cookout Conspiracy. James Kamins. LC 73-83917. 7.95 (ISBN 0-87949-020-9). Ashley Books.

TITLE INDEX CORDELIA.

Cook's Wedding: And Other Stories. Anton Pavlovich Chekhov. Tr. by Garnett, Constance (Black) LC 22-5609. (Half-title: The tales of Chekhov. vol. xii). 1922. The Macmillan Company.
Cool Approach. Thomas Mario & Playboy Editors. LC 74-21119. 1975. pap. 1.50 o.p. (ISBN 0-87216-268-0, C16268). Playboy Pr Pbks.
Cool Cottontail. John Dudley Ball. (F3487). 1967. Bantam.
Cool Cottontail. John Dudley Ball. LC 66-20754. 1966. Harper & Row.
Cool Day for Killing. Richard Clayton. LC 68-27388. 1968. 3.95. Walker.
Cool Day for Killing. William Haggard. 192p. Date not set. pap. 2.95 (ISBN 0-8027-3010-8). Walker & Co.
Cool Entertaining. Irma Rhode. LC 75-41420. 1976. 8.95 (ISBN 0-689-10710-2). Atheneum.
Cool Generation. Mitchell Masters. 157p. 1975. 6.50 o.p. (ISBN 0-682-48086-X). Exposition.
Cool Generation:: a Novel. 1st. ed. Mitchell Masters. 1975. 6.50 (ISBN 0-682-48086-X). Exposition Press.
Cool Hand Luke. Donald Pearce. LC 65-218789. 4.95. Scribners.
Cool Hand Luke. By Donn Pearce.Reenwich, Conn. 1967, c. 1965 ed. Donald Pearce. (Gold medal bk., d1858).
Cool Man. William Riley Burnett. LC 76-7945. (Fawcett gold medal book). 1968. 0.50. Fawcett Publications.
Cool Meridian. Sarah Kilpatrick. LC 65-10220. 1965. bds., 3.95. Abelard.
Cool Million see Dream Life of Balso Snell & A Cool Million.
Cool Million: the Dismantling of Lemuel Pitkin. Nathanael West. LC 34-18190. Covici, Friede.
Cool Repentance: A Jemima Shore Mystery. Antonia Fraser. 1983. 12.95 (ISBN 0-393-01625-0). Norton.
Cool Sleeps Balaban. Donald MacKenzie. 1964. 3.75 o.p. (ISBN 0-395-07940-3). Hm.
Cool War. Frederik Pohl. LC 80-23589. 288p. 1981. 10.95 (ISBN 0-345-29383-5, Del Rey). Ballantine.
Cool War. Frederik Pohl. 288p. 1982. pap. 2.75 (ISBN 0-345-30137-4, Del Rey). Ballantine.
Cool World: A Novel. Warren Miller. LC 59-9106. 1959. Little, Brown.
Cooleemee: A Tale of Southern Life. Annie E Johns. LC 7-99154. 1882. Leaksville "Gazette" Print.
Cooler. George Markstein. LC 73-10811. 1974. 6.95 (ISBN 0-385-02534-3). Doubleday.
Coolie. Mulk Raj Anand. LC 52-68107. 1952. Liberty Press.
Coolie. Mulk Raj Anand. LC 47-4062. (Penguin books. 474). 1945. Peguin Books.
Coolie. Madelon Lulofs & Renier, Gustaaf Johnson, 1893- Tr. LC 36-272563. 1936. The Viking Press.
Coolie. Mulk Raj Anand. 320p. (gr. 10-12). 1981. pap. 4.00 (ISBN 0-86578-005-6). Ind US Inc.
Coombe St. Mary's. Katherine Helen Maud Marshall Diver. LC 25-22116. 1925. Houghton Mifflin Company.
Coomer Ali. Samuel Bertram Haworth Hurst. LC 22-318932. 1922. Harper & Brothers.
Coonardoo. Katharine Susannah Prichard. LC 30-259109. W. W. Norton & Company, Inc.
Coopers: Or, Getting Under Way. Alice Bradley Haven. LC 7-2864. 1858. D. Appleton and Company.
Cooper's The Last of the Mohicans. James Fenimore Cooper. (Silver series of English and American clasics). 1901. Silver, Burdett and Co.
Cooper's The Last of the Mohicans. James Fenimore Cooper. Ed. by Crowther, Clifford T. LC 32-7906. (Golden key series). D. C. Heath and Company.
Cooper's The Last of the Mohicans: A Narrative of 1757. James Fenimore Cooper. Ed. by Dunbar, John Brown. LC 98-2245. (On cover: Standard English classics). 1898. Ginn & Company.
Cooper's The Last of the Mohicans: A Narrative of 1757. James Fenimore Cooper. Ed. by Dunbar, John Brown. LC 24-6691. Ginn and Company.
Coorinna: A Novel of the Tasmanian Uplands. Erle Wilson. LC 53-9197. 1954. Random House.
Cop. Jack Karney. LC 51-12788. 1951. Holt.
Cop & the Preacher. Leo Lewis. LC 78-63047. 1979. 10.95 (ISBN 0-533-03943-6). Vantage.
Cop Cade. John Dudley Ball. LC 78-7750. 1978. 7.95 (ISBN 0-385-14374-5). Published for the Crime Club by Doubleday.
Cop Hater. Ed McBain. 1973. (pbk) 0.95. New American Library.
Cop Hater. F. C. A McBain. LC 56-6722. (Permabooks, M-3037. Mystery, 7). 1956. Permabooks.
Cop Hater: By Ed McBain Pseud. Evan Hunter. LC 56-6722. (Permabooks, M-3037. Mystery, 7). 1956. Permabooks.
Cop in a Tight Frame. Neill Graham. 1978. 4.95 (ISBN 0-09-114180-X, Pub. by Hutchinson). Merrimack Pub Cir.
Cop-Kill. William Crawford. (Stryker,#2). 1974. (pbk.) 0.95 (ISBN 0-523-00308-0). Pinnacle Books.
Cop Killer: By George Bagby Pseud. 1st Ed. Aaron Marc Stein. LC 56-10755. 1956. Published for the Crime Club by Doubleday.
Cop Killer: The Story of a Crime. Maj Sjowall & Per Wahloo. LC 74-26197. 1975. 7.95 (ISBN 0-394-48531-9). Pantheon Books.
Cop Killer: The Story of a Crime. Maj Sjowall & Per Wahloo. LC 77-16363. (Their A Martin Beck Policy Mystery; 9). 1978. 1.75 (ISBN 0-394-72444-5). Vintage Books.
Cop Killers. Max Rabinowitz. (Hunter Group Ser.: No. 1). (Orig.). 1979. pap. 1.95 (ISBN 0-89083-450-4). Zebra.
Cop Killers. Steve Scott, pseud. 1972. pap. 1.25 o.p. (ISBN 0-532-12125-2). Woodhill.
Cop Killers. Steve Scott, pseud. 1972. pap. 1.25 o.p. (ISBN 0-532-12125-2). Manor Bks.
Cop Out. Ellery Queen. Bd. with Last Woman in His Life. 1982. pap. 2.50 (ISBN 0-451-11562-7, AE1562, Sig). NAL.
Cop Out. H. L Lasher. (Belmont Tower Books). 1978. 1.75 (ISBN 0-505-51284-X). Tower Pubns.
Cop Out. Ellery Queen, pseud. LC 69-12876. 1969. 5.95 o.p. (HO302, NAL). Norton.
Cop Out: A Novel. Ellery Queen, pseud. LC 69-12876. 1969. 4.95. World Pub. Co.
Copeland Bride. Justine Cole. (Orig.). 1983. pap. 3.50 (ISBN 0-440-11235-4). Dell.
Copenhagen Connection. Elizabeth Peters, pseud. LC 82-1385. 12.95 (ISBN 0-86553-041-6) (ISBN 0-312-92105-5). Congdon & Lattes: Distributed by St. Martin's Press.
Copenhagen Connection. Elizabeth Peters, pseud. LC 82-15749. 1982. 13.95 (ISBN 0-8161-3467-7). G.K. Hall.
Copernican Revolution. Paul Goodman. Repr. of 1947 ed. 4.50 (ISBN 0-910664-37-4). Gotham.
Copito: The Christmas Chihuahua. Jean N. Erichsen. (Illus.). 80p. 12.95x (ISBN 0-943864-08-9); pap. 2.95x (ISBN 0-943864-07-0). MD Bks.
Coppa Hamba: By Blanche Ashley Amborse; with "The Wimp and the Woodle." by Helen Von Kolnitz Hyer, and "The Doll Who Was Too Sharp". by Muriel Smith; All Illustrated by Willy Pogany. Blanche Ashley Ambrose & Smith, Muriel. LC 37-15336. 1936. Suttonhouse, Ltd.
Copper: A Novel. Tom McGrath. LC 41-8079. B. Humphries, Inc.
Copper Beeches. Arthur H. Lewis. LC 72-154803. 1971. 6.95 (ISBN 0-671-27083-4). Trident Press.
Copper Bottle. Edward J. Millward. LC 29-20968. E. P. Dutton & Co., Inc.
Copper Box. Joseph Smith Fletcher. LC 24-118595. 1923. Hodder and Stoughton, Ltd.
Copper Box. Joseph Smith Fletcher. LC 23-9235. 1923. George H. Doran Company.
Copper Canyon. Edward N Todd. LC 74-7637. 1974. 4.95 (ISBN 0-385-09898-7). Doubleday.
Copper' Children - the Rise & Fall of a Mexican Mining Camp. Inez Horton. LC 68-24874. 1968. 5.50 o.p. (ISBN 0-682-46818-5). Exposition.
Copper Clew: A Mythical Novel of the Legendary Minotaur of Ancient Crete. Ann Maturin. LC 73-85545. 1973. 5.95 (ISBN 0-8059-1914-7). Dorrance.
Copper Country. Mary Synon. LC 31-31930. P. J. Kenedy & Sons.
Copper Disc... Robert James Campbell Stead. LC 31-7180. Pub. for the Crime Club, Inc., by Doubleday, Doran & Company, Inc.
Copper Frame. Ellery Queen, pseud. LC 66-6217. Pocket Books.
Copper Frame. Ellery Queen, pseud. LC 66-6217. 1975. (pbk.) 0.95. New American Library.
Copper Gold. Pauline Glen Winslow. LC 77-15324. 8.95 (ISBN 0-312-16966-3). St. Martin's Press.
Copper, Gold & Treasure. David Williams. LC 81-23178. 210p. 1982. 9.95 (ISBN 0-312-16967-1). St Martin.
Copper Highway. E. Curtis Smith. LC 70-187338. 1972. 5.95 (ISBN 0-8059-1678-4). Dorrance.
Copper House: A Detective Story. Julius Regis. LC 23-14118. 1923. H. Holt and Company.
Copper Kings. Lee D. Willoughby. (Making of America Ser.: No. 41). 320p. (Orig.). 1983. pap. 3.25 (ISBN 0-440-01076-4, Bryans). Dell.
Copper King's Daughter. Dorothy L. McCall. LC 74-188836. (Illus.). 200p. 1972. pap. 5.95 (ISBN 0-8323-0203-1). Binford.
Copper Lady. Hugh Lawrence Nelson. LC 47-243104. 1947. Rinehart.
Copper Lake. Kay Thorpe. (Harlequin Presents Ser.). 192p. 1981. pap. 1.75 (ISBN 0-373-10455-3, Pub. by Harlequin). PB.
Copper Mask, and Other Stories. Hugh Wiley. LC 32-4759. 1932. A. A. Knopf.
Copper Moon. Edwin Bateman Morris. LC 28-8708. 1928. The Penn Publishing Company.
Copper Moon. Margaret Way. (Presents Ser.). 1975. pap. 1.25 (ISBN 0-373-70582-4, 70582, Pub by Harlequin). PB.
Copper Pot. Oliver La Farge. LC 42-15420. 1942. Houghton Mifflin Company.
Copper Scrolls. Nathaniel Norsen Weinreb. LC 58-8064. 1958. Putnam.
Copper Streak Trail. Eugene Manlove Rhodes. LC 77-111551. (Western frontier library, v. 44). (Illus.). 1970. 2.95. University of Oklahoma Press.
Copper Streak Trail. Eugene Manlove Rhodes. LC 22-108624. 1922. Houghton Mifflin Company.
Copperbelt. Nigel Sligh. LC 49-48115. 1949. G. P. Putnam's Sons.
Copperhead. Harold Frederic. LC 69-11893. (American short story series, v. 51). 1969. Garrett Press.
Copperhead. Harold Frederic. LC 6-431384. 1893. C. Scribner's Sons.
Copperhead. James Henderson. LC 79-136335. 1971. 5.95 (ISBN 0-394-46921-6). Knopf.
Copperhead see Collected Works.
Copperhead and Other Stories of the North During the American War. Harold Frederic. LC 70-144610. 1972. 10.00 (ISBN 0-404-02571-4). AMS Press.
Copperhead Colonel. James R. Dowler. 192p. (OSI). 1972. 4.95 o.p. Lenox Hill.
Copperhead Moon. Herbert E Stover. LC 52-10918. 1952. Dodd, Mead.
Copperheads. William James Blech. 1941. The Dial Press.
Coppers and Gold. Henry Brinton. LC 58-5798. (Cock Robin mystery). 1958. Macmillan.
Coppers Girl. Rosalie Henaghan. (Harlequin Romances Ser.). 192p. 1982. pap. 1.50 (ISBN 0-373-02462-2, Pub. by Harlequin). PB.
Coppersmith. Robert J. Griffin. 1969. pap. 0.75 o.p. (T1919). Pyramid Pubns.
Coppersmith's Dolls. Robert J. Griffin. (Orig.). 1969. pap. 0.95 o.p. (N2072). Pyramid Pubns.
Coprolites. Albert Goldbarth. (Signed ed. 10.00 o.p.). 1973. 5.00 (Pub. by New Rivers Pr); pap. 2.50. SBD.
Cops and Robbers. Donald E Westlake. (Signet book, Y5462). 1973. (pbk.) 1.25. New American Library.
Cops and Robbers. Donald E Westlake. LC 72-83735. 1972. 5.95. M. Evans; Distributed in Association with Lippincott, Philadelphia.
Cops & Women. Micki Siegel. (Orig.). 1980. pap. 2.25 o.s.i. (ISBN 0-505-51524-5). Tower Bks.
Copsi Castle. y ed. Juliet Astley, pseud. LC 78-484. (Fic). 1978. 9.95 o.p. (ISBN 0-698-10913-9, Coward). Putnam Pub Group.
Copsi Castle. Juliet Astley, pseud. (General Ser.). 1979. lib. bdg. 16.95 (ISBN 0-8161-6669-2, Large Print Bks). G K Hall.
Copsi Castle. Norah Robinson Lofts. LC 78-484. 1978. 8.95 (ISBN 0-698-10913-9). Coward, McCann & Geoghegan.
Copsi Castle. Norah Robinson Lofts. LC 79-10639. 1979. 16.95 (ISBN 0-8161-6669-2). G. K. Hall.
Cops'n Robbers. John Russell. LC 31-26392. 1930. W. W. Norton & Company, Inc.
Copulation Explosion. Rod Gray. (The Lady from L.U.S.T. Ser.). (O.s.i.). 1974. pap. 0.95 o.s.i. (BT50678). Belmont-Tower.
Copy-Cat: & Other Stories. Mary Eleanor Wilkins Freeman. LC 71-122707. (Short story index reprint series). (Illus.). 1970. Books for Libraries Press.
Copy-Cat: & Other Stories. Mary Eleanor Wilkins Freeman. LC 14-16474. 1914. Harper & Brothers.
Copy-Cat, & Other Stories. Mary Eleanor Wilkins Freeman. LC 71-122707. (Short Story Index Reprint Ser). 1914. 17.00 (ISBN 0-8369-3540-3). Ayer Co.
Copy for Crime. Edith Caroline Rivett. LC 51-13658. 1951. Published for the Crime Club by Doubleday.
Copy for Mother. Jeannette Clarke Phillips Gibbs. 1934. Little, Brown, and Company.
Copy-Maker. William Farquhar Payson. LC 7-33757. New Amsterdam Book Company.
Copy Shop. Edward Hungerford. LC 25-5772. 1925. G. P. Putnam's Sons.
Copycat. Barbara Samuels. 64p. (Orig.). 1982. pap. 3.95 (ISBN 0-380-57018-1, 57018). Avon.
Coquette. Hannah Webster Foster. 1797. 10.50 o.p. (ISBN 0-8398-0561-6, Lit Hse). Gregg.
Coquette. Hannah Webster Foster. Ed. by J. V. Ridgely. LC 73-93618. (American Fiction Ser). 1970. lib. bdg. 14.50 o.s.i. (ISBN 0-512-00183-9). Garrett Pr.
Coquette. Frederic Mansel Reynolds. LC 9-2687. 1835. E. L. Carey & A. Hart.
Coquette. Frank Arthur Swinnerton. LC 21-15558. George H. Doran Company.
Coquette: A Novel. Frederic Mansel Reynolds. LC 7-4427. T. B. Peterson.
Coquette: Or, The History of Eliza Wharton; a Novel; Founded on Fact. Hannah Webster Foster. LC 37-10723l. 1797. Printed by Samuel Etheridge, for E. Lerkin, No., Cornhill.
Coquette: Or, The History of Eliza Wharton. A Novel: Founded on Fact. 3d ed.... ed. Hannah Webster Foster. LC 37-10722. 1811. Published by Thomas & Whipple, Proprietors of the Copy-Right. Sold at Their Book-Store, No., State-Street-and by Henry Whipple, Salem, Mass.
Coquette: Or, The History of Eliza Wharton, by Hannah Webster Foster. Reproduced from the Original Edition of 1797. Hannah Webster Foster. LC 39-6806. (Half-title: The Facsimile text society. Publication no. 46). 1939. Pub. for the Facsimile Text Society by Columbia University Press.
Coquette's Conquest. A Novel. Richard Ashe King. (Harper's Franklin square library. no. 484). 1885. Harper & Brothers.
Coquette's Conquest. A Novel. Richard Ashe King. (On cover: Seaside library. Pocket ed., no. 547). 1885. G. Munro.
Cora. Ruth Suckow. LC 29-20015. 1929. A. A. Knopf.
Cora: A Novel. Daphne Athas. LC 78-15426. 1978. 10.95 (ISBN 0-670-24116-4). Viking Press.
Cora: A Tale of Right and Wrong. A Novel of to-Day... A. E. Welton. LC 8-36244. J. S. Olgilvie.
Cora Fry. Rosellen Brown. 1977. 9.95 (ISBN 0-393-04455-6); pap. 2.95 o.p. (ISBN 0-393-04461-0). Norton.
Cora Lee: Gone from the Valley. John Vergara. (Orig.). 1979. pap. 2.25 (ISBN 0-532-23247-X). Woodhill.
Cora Lynn. A Novel. John M Hartley. LC 7-3656. 1879. R. J. Hayward & Co.
Cora O'Kane; or, The Doom of the Rebel Guard. A Story of the Great Rebellion. Containing Incidents of the Campaign in Missouri Under Generals Fremont and Sigel, and the Thrilling Exploits of the Unionists Under Major Zagonyi. James Winston. LC 8-37776. 1868. Pub. by an Association of Disabled Soldiers.
Cora Potts: A Pilgrim's Progress. Ward Greene. LC 29-17526. J. Cape and H. Smith.
Coral: A Sequel to "Carnival". Compton Mackenzie. LC 25-10812. 1925. Cassell and Company, Ltd.
Coral: A Sequel to "Carnival". Compton Mackenzie. LC 25-164842. George H. Doran Company.
Coral Cay. Kerry Allyne. (Harlequin Presents Ser.). 192p. 1982. pap. 1.75 (ISBN 0-373-10513-4). Harlequin Bks.
Coral Island. Robert Michael Ballantyne. LC 36-37129. (Half-title: Everyman's library, ed. by Ernest Rhys. For young people. (no. 245). 1933. J. M. Dent & Sons, Ltd.
Coral Lady: Or, The Bronzed Beauty of Paris... Emma Dorothy Eliza Nevitte Southworth. LC 21-20591. C. W. Alexander.
Coral Lips Smiling at You. Van Cardui, pseud. LC 70-28499. (Traveller's companion series, TC-480). 1.95. Traveller's Companion.
Coral Pin. Fortune Du Boisgobey & Merighi, Mrs. Carolina A., Tr. (Seaside library. v. 86. no. 1742). G. Munro.
Coral Princess Murders. Frances Kirkwood Crane. LC 54-7451. 1954. Random House.
Coral Tower. William Standish Stone. LC 60-1667. 1959. T. Bouregy.
Coralie's Son. Albert Delpit. Tr. by Page, Anna Dyer. LC 6-34175. (primrose ser. no. 21). 1891. Street & Smith.
Coranna: A Novel. Ella Harding Davis. 1890. Nixon-Jones Printing Co.
Corbaccio. Giovanni Boccaccio. LC 75-9844. 1975. 7.95 (ISBN 0-252-00479-5). University of Illinois Press.
Corbells at War. Ralph Hale Mottram. LC 43-105044. 1943. Hutchinson & Co.
Corbie. Robert Newman. LC 66-123738. 5.95. Harcourt.
Corbie. Newman, Robert. LC 66-12373. 1966. Harcourt, Brace & World.
Corbin Necklace. Henry Kitchell Webster. LC 26-14756. The Bobbs-Merrill Company.
Corcho Bliss. Austin Olsen. LC 72-830911. 1973. (pbk) 1.25. Warner.
Corcorans. Mark Lee Luther & Ford, Mrs. Lillian Cummings, 1881- Joint Author. LC 31-23361. The Bobbs-Merrill Company.
Cord. Owen Rowntree. LC 81-22838. 1982. 1.95 (ISBN 0-345-29589-7). Ballantine.
Cord and Creese: A Novel. James De Mille. LC 6-34006. (On cover: Harper's Franklin square library, no. 746). 1894. Harper & Brothers.
Cord and Creese: A Novel. James De Mille. LC 6-34007. (On cover: Harper's Franklin square library. no. 746.). Harper & Brothers.
Cord: The Nevada War. Owen Rountree. 160p. (Orig.). 1982. pap. 1.95 (ISBN 0-345-29590-0). Ballantine.
Cordelia? Garson Kanin. LC 82-194893. 13.95 (ISBN 0-87795-397-X). Arbor House.
Cordelia: A Novel. Winston Graham. LC 50-5377. 1950. Doubleday.
Cordelia: A Story for the Homemaker and the Bread-Winner. Leander M. Zimmerman. LC 15-4590. Meyer & Thalheimer, Printers.

Cordelia: & Other Stories by Francoise Mallet-Joris. Tr. from French by Peter Green. Francoise Mallet-Joris. LC 65-20101. bds., 4.95. Farrar.
Cordelia Blossom: By George Randolph Chester... Illustrated by Henry Raleigh. George Randolph Chester. LC 14-7689. 1914. 1.35. Hearst's International Library Co.
Cordelia Chantrell: A Romance. Meade Minnigerode. 1926. G. P. Putnam's Sons.
Cordelia the Magnificent. Leroy Scott. LC 23-8185. 1923. H. Holt and Company.
Corder Index. Raymond H. Sawkins. LC 67-20316. (Illus.). 1967. Harcourt, Brace & World.
Cords of Love. Clarence W. Duff. 1980. pap. 7.50 (ISBN 0-87552-248-3). Presby & Reformed.
Cords of Vanity. James Branch Cabell. LC 9-4297. 1909. Doubleday, Page & Company.
Cords of Vanity: A Comedy of Shirking. James Branch Cabell. LC 20-21191. 1920. R. M. McBride & Co.
Corduroy. Adrian Bell. 1974. 4.95 (ISBN 0-09-120480-1, Pub. by Hutchinson). Merrimack Pub Cir.
Corduroy. Ruth Comfort Mitchell. LC 23-5518. 1923. D. Appleton and Company.
Corduroy Prince. Hoke Smith Drake. LC 21-6362. Muse-Whitlock Co.
Corduroy Road: A Tale of Pioneer Life in the Middle West in the Early 40's. Anna Cross I. E Dunham. LC 9-28076. 1.25. The Werner Company.
Corentyne Thunder. Edgar Mittelholzer. (Caribbean Writers Ser.). 1970. pap. text ed. 4.50x (ISBN 0-435-98593-0). Heinemann Ed.
Corey Lane. Norman Zollinger. LC 81-5670. 1981. 13.95 (ISBN 0-89919-048-0). Ticknor & Fields.
Corey's Revenge. Harley Hess. (Orig.). 1980. pap. 1.75 (ISBN 0-532-23231-3). Woodhill.
Corianton: A Nephite Story. Brigham Henry Roberts. LC 2-22302. 1902.
Corinna." A Study. Eliza M. J. Humphreys. (On cover: Seaside library. Pocket ed., no. 598). 1885. G. Munro.
Corinne: Or, Italy... Anne Louise Germaine Necker Stael-Holstein. Tr. by Isabel Hill. Landon, Letitia Elizabeth, 1802-1838, Tr. LC 41-42511. 1857. Derby & Jackson.
Corinne: Or, Italy... Anne Louise Germaine Necker Stael-Holstein & Hill, Isabel, 1800-1842, Tr. LC 4-8798. W. I. Pooley & Co.
Corinne: Or, Italy... Anne Louise Germaine Necker Stael-Holstein & Hill, Isabel, Tr. LC 8-13455. 1873. Mason, Baker & Pratt.
Corinne's Vow. Mary Teresa Waggaman. LC 2-3958. 1902. Benziger Brothers.
Corinthian. Georgette Heyer. LC 66-12255. 1966. 3.95. Dutton.
Corinthian. Georgette Heyer. 1974. (pbk.) 1.25. Bantam Books.
Corinthians: A Novel. Nicholas Elston Wyckoff. LC 60-13809. 1960. Macmillan.
Coriolanos, the Chariot! Alan Yates. (Illus.). 1978. 1.75 (ISBN 0-441-11739-2). Ace Books.
Corioli Affair. Mary Deasy. LC 54-5131. 1954. Little, Brown.
Cork in Bottle. Macdonald Hastings. LC 54-15013. 1953. M. Joseph.
Cork in Bottle. 1st American Ed. Macdonald Hastings. LC 54-5264. 1954. Knopf.
Cork in the Doghouse. 1st American Ed. Macdonald Hastings. LC 58-65321. 1958. Knopf.
Cork on Location. Macdonald Hastings. LC 67-23108. 1967. Walker.
Cork on the Telly. Macdonald Hastings. 1981. 18.95x (Pub. by Remploy England). State Mutual Bk.
Cork on the Water. Macdonald Hastings. LC 51-13324. 1951. Random House.
Cork Street: Next to the Hatter's, a Novel in Bad Taste. Pamela Hansford Johnson. LC 65-22876. 1965. Scribner.
Corker's Freedom. John Berger. 288p. 1981. 9.95 (ISBN 0-906495-08-3); pap. 4.95 (ISBN 0-904613-40-2). Writers & Readers.
Corky's Brother. Jay Neugeboren. LC 78-87214. 1969. 5.95. Farrar, Straus and Giroux.
Corleone: A Tale of Sicily. Francis Marion Crawford. LC 4-15088. 1896. Macmillan and Co.
Corm. Frank Cebulski. 1974. 5.00 (Pub. by Oyez); pap. 2.50. SBD.
Cormac Legend. Dorothy Daniels. 1979. pap. 2.25 (ISBN 0-451-11555-4, AE1555, Sig). NAL.
Cormorant Crag. A Tale of the Smuggling Days. George Manville Fenn. LC 6-39262. 1895. Dodd, Mead and Company.
Cormorant's Brood. Inglis Clark Fletcher. 1975. (pbk.) 1.50. Bantam Books.
Cormorant's Brood. Inglis Clark Fletcher. LC 78-5779. 1978. 10.95 (ISBN 0-89244-002-3). Queens House.
Cormorants Isle. 1st Ed. Allan MacKinnon. LC 62-114605. 1962. Published for the Crime Club by Doubleday.
Corn for the Oxen. Kate Randall Blackwell. LC 50-13901. 1950. Story Book Press.
Corn in Egypt. Warwick Deeping. LC 42-1188. 1942. A. A. Knopf.
Corn in Egypt. Carl Eric Bechhofer Roberts. LC 29-20434. The Bobbs-Merrill Company.
Corn King and the Spring Queen. Naomi Haldane Mitchison. LC 73-145186. (Illus.). 1972. (ISBN 0-403-01111-6). Scholarly Press.
Cornbread and Milk: A Family Gathering. Gordon H Soles. LC 59-6373. 1959. Doubleday.
Cornbread Aristocrat. Claud Garner. LC 50-9433. 1950. Creative Age Press.
Cornbread Earl and Me. Ronald L Fair. 1975. (pbk.) 1.25. Bantam Books.
Cornelia: A Novel. LC 18-20782. S. D., Sessions Printing Co.
Cornelia, a Novel. Rene Leilani Kuhn. LC 48-6758. 1948. Random House.
Cornelius. Frank W Zern. The Christopher Publishing House.
Cornelius Chronicles. Michael Moorcock. LC 77-78116. (Illus.). 1977. 2.95 (ISBN 0-380-00878-5). Avon.
Cornelius of Beaufort. Ruth Saffold De Treville. LC 70-17636. (Illus.). 1969. 4.95. Printed by R. L. Bryan Co.
Cornell Scribblings. Charles Loomis Funnell & Royce, Knibloe Perry. LC 16-6015. 0.50. Andrus & Church.
Cornell Stories. James Gardner Sanderson. LC 8-4775. 1898. C. Scribner's Sons.
Corner Back: A Novel of Professional Football. Hamilton Maule. LC 67-22395. 1967.
Corner Box. Herbert Simmons. pap. 0.75 o.p. (75-198). Manor Bks.
Corner Boy. Herbert Simmons. 1971. pap. 0.95 o.p. (532-00174-095). Manor Bks.
Corner Boy: A Novel. Herbert Simmons. LC 57-12108. 1957. Houghton Mifflin.
Corner House. Dorothy Black. LC 37-35184. Green Circle Books.
Corner House. Fred Merrick White. LC 7-10618. R. F. Fenno & Company.
Corner in Coffee. Cyrus Townsend Brady. LC 4-3587. 1904. G. W. Dillingham Company.
Corner in Crime. Norman Lucas. LC 57-6614. 1957. Roy Publishers.
Corner in Diamonds. John Jessop Teague. LC 16-19067. 1916. Hodder and Stoughton.
Corner in William. Fannie Kilbourne. LC 22-17945. 1922. Dodd, Mead and Company.
Corner of Heaven. Kathleen Thompson Norris. LC 43-15964. 1943. Doubleday, Doran and Co., Inc.
Corner of Paradise. Leonard Holton, pseud. LC 76-28036. 1977. 7.95 o.p. (ISBN 0-312-16975-2). St Martin.
Corner of Paradise. Leonard Patrick O'Connor Wibberley. LC 76-28036. 7.95 (ISBN 0-312-16975-2). St. Martin's Press.
Corner of the Moon. Shirley Barker. LC 61-10301. 1961. Crown Publishers.
Corner Shop. Elizabeth Cadell. LC 66-27952. 1967. Morrow.
Corner Shop. Philip Keeley. LC 34-16711. 1934. The Macmillan Company.
Corner Stone. Margaret Hill McCarter. LC 15-19476. 1915. A. C. McClurg & Co.
Corner Store, a Novel. 1st Ed. Albert Edward Idell. LC 53-5755. 1953. Doubleday.
Corner Work: Or, "Look up and Liftt up.". Myra Goodwin Plantz. LC 7-38196. 1892. Cranston & Curts.
Cornered at Six: A Novel of Suspense. Thomas Patrick McMahon & Brian Patrick McMahon. LC 72-83903. 1972. 6.95 (ISBN 0-671-21367-9). Simon and Schuster.
Cornermen. John E Gardner. LC 75-150896. 1976. 7.95 (ISBN 0-385-00525-3). Doubleday.
Cornerstone to Riot Rocks. Walter F. King. 1970. 3.75 o.p. Vantage.
Cornerstone: Translated by Edward Hyams. Zoe Oldenbourg. LC 55-5062. Pantheon.
Cornet Strong of Ireton's Horse: An Episode of the Ironsides. Dora Greenwell McChesney. LC 3-11330. 1903. J. Lane.
Cornish Camp Mystery. H. P. Benney. 1970. 1.50 o.p. (ISBN 0-87508-657-8). Chr Lit.
Cornish Heiress. Roberta Gellis. (Heiress Ser.: No. 2). (Orig.). 1981. pap. 3.50 (ISBN 0-440-11515-9). Dell.
Cornish Penny. Coulson T Cade. LC 22-4036. 1922. Frederick A. Stokes Company.
Cornish Stories. Alfred Leslie Rowse. LC 67-82362. 1967. Melbourne Etc. Macmillan.
Cornish Tales. Charles Lee. LC 42-14083. 1942. E. P. Dutton and Co., Inc.
Cornishman's Gold. Anthony Mawes. LC 35-44460. 1934. T. Nelson and Sons, Ltd.
Cornstalk Grew. Agnes O'Neill. LC 44-6939. 1944. Murray & Gee.
Corobite Mines. Peter Roberts. 1978. pap. 1.50 (ISBN 0-532-15352-9). Woodhill.
Coromandel! A Novel. John Masters. LC 54-11618. (Illus.). 1955. Viking Press.
Corona Affair. Eve Simson. (Mark Malone Dossier Mystery Ser.). (Illus.). 165p. 1983. pap. 15.95 (ISBN 0-89651-101-4). Icarus.
Corona of the Nantahalas: A Romance. Louis Beauregard Pendleton. LC 7-363721. The Merriam Company.
Coronado Trail. George Brydges Rodney. LC 32-831163. E. J. Clode, Inc.
Coronary Event. Michael Halberstam & Stephan Lesher. 1978. pap. 1.95 (ISBN 0-445-04213-3). Popular Lib.
Coronation for Cinderella... Lois Bull. LC 37-23530. 1937. Hillman-Curl, Inc.
Coronation for Cinderella. Bennie Caroline Hall. LC 53-8566. 1953. Arcadia House.
Coronation Summer. Angela Mackail Thirkell. LC 37-27267. 1937. Oxford University Press.
Coronation Summer: A Novel of 1838. Angela Mackail Thirkell. LC 53-686644. 1953. Knopf.
Coronation. Tr. from Spanish by Jocasta Goodwin 1st Amer.Ed. Jose Donoso. LC 64-11416. bds., 4.95. Knopf.
Coroner Creek. Luke Short. LC 76-48108. 1977. 8.95 (ISBN 0-89340-036-X). J. Curley.
Coroner Presides: A Novel. Seldon Truss, pseud. LC 32-242769. 1932. Minton, Balch & Company.
Coroners Creek. large print ed. Luke Short. 1981. 18.00x o.p. (ISBN 0-89340-036-X, Pub. by Curley Assoc England). State Mutual Bk.
Coroner's Pidgin. Margery Allingham. LC 74-168475. 1973. 0.35 (ISBN 0-14-000736-9). Penguin.
Coroner's Verdict: Accident... Clifford James Wheeler Hosken. LC 45-4660. 1945. David McKay Company.
Coronet. Manuel Komroff. LC 29-299702. 1929. Coward-McCann, Inc.
Coronet. Manuel Komroff. LC 37-18301. 1930. The Literary Guild of America.
Coronet Among the Weeds. Charlotte Bingham. LC 63-11617. 1963. Random House.
Coronet of Shame. Charles Garvice. (On cover: Laurel library, no. 30). 1897. G. Munro's Sons.
Coronets and Buckskin. Raven Barratt. LC 57-10792. (Illus.). 1957. Houghton Mifflin.
Coronica Del Muy Esforcado: Y Inuencible Cauallero et Cid Ruy Diaz Campeador Delas Espanes Colophon: Aqui Fenesce el Breue Tratado Delos Nobles Hechos y Batallas Que el Buen Canallero Cid Ruy Diaz Vencio Con Fauvor y Ayuda D'nuestro Senor. El Quai Se Acabo a Ij. Dias Del Mes De Julio: Por Miguel De Eguis: Enla Muy Noble y Leal Ciudad De Toledo. Enel Ano De Nuestro Redemptor y Salvador Jesu Christo De Mil y Quinientos y Veynte y Seys Anos. LC 4-36818. 10.00. De Vinne Press.
Corporal Cameron of the North West Mounted Police: A Tale the Macleod Trail, by Ralph Connor Pseud.... Charles William Gordon. LC 12-25203. Hodder & Stoughton, George H. Doran Company.
Corporal Cat: The Story of a German Parachute Soldier. Martin Flavin. LC 41-21168. Harper & Brothers.
Corporal Downey Takes the Trail. James Beardsley Hendryx. LC 31-29490. Doubleday, Doran & Company, Inc.
Corporal Glass's Island: The Story of Tristan Da Cunha. Nancy Hosegood. LC 66-126960. 1966. 4.95. Farrar.
Corporal Glory: A Novel. 1st Ed. S Robert Tralins. LC 53-8519. 1953. Exposition Press.
Corporal Once. Leonard Hastings Nason. LC 30-25290. 1930. Doubleday, Doran & Company, Inc.
Corporal Punishment. Gerda Mundinger. 1971. pap. 1.95 o.p. (V1020, Venus). Grove.
Corporal Si Klegg and His "Pard." How They Lived and Talked, and What They Did and Suffered While Fighting for the Flag. Wilbur F Hinman. LC 7-25992. 1887. The Williams Publishing Company.
Corporal, the Sergeant, and the Major. 1st Ed. Julius V Szabo. LC 53-111841. 1953. Pageant Press.
Corporal Tune. Leonard Alfred George Strong. LC 34-22754. 1934. A. A. Knopf.
Corporate Affair. Mike Dolinsky, pseud. (Orig.). 1981. pap. 2.95 (ISBN 0-440-11435-7). Dell.
Corporate Hooker, Inc. Manning Lee Stokes. 1975. (pbk.) 1.50 (ISBN 0-671-78724-1). Pocket Books.
Corporate Oligarch. David Finn. LC 69-14282. (O.s.i.). 1969. 6.95 o.s.i. (ISBN 0-671-20173-5). S&S.
Corps Perdu see Cadastre.
Corps That Knew Everybody. Cedric Worth. LC 41-11688. 1941. E. P. Dutton and Company, Inc.
Corpse and Robbers. Douglas Stapleton. LC 54-13115. 1954. Arcadia House.
Corpse and the Three Ex-Husbands. Sue MacVeigh. LC 41-21734. 1941. Houghton Mifflin Company.
Corpse and the Three Ex-Husbands. Elizabeth Nearing. LC 41-21734. 1941. Houghton Mifflin Company.
Corpse and the Three Ex-Husbands. Elizabeth Nearing. LC 45-275. 1944.
Corpse at Casablanca: A Cheviot Burmann Mystery. Belton Cobb. LC 56-103529. Abelard-Schuman.
Corpse at the Carnival. George Bellairs. pap. 0.65 o.p. (ISBN 0-14-002077-2). Penguin.
Corpse at the Quill Club. Amelia Reynolds Long. LC 40-33787. Phoenix Press.
Corpse Awaits. Oscar Jerome Friend. LC 46-174257. 1946. Mystery House.
Corpse Awaits. Abridged Ed.... Oscar Jerome Friend. LC 47-21041. (Handi-book mysteries. 58). 1947.
Corpse by Any Other Name. Robert Alfred John Walling. LC 43-3842. 1943. W. Morrow & Company.
Corpse by the River: By Helen Arre Pseud. Zola Helen Ross. LC 53-11292. 1953. Arcadia House.
Corpse Came Back. Amelia Reynolds Long. LC 49-862220. 1949. Phoenix Press.
Corpse Came Calling. George Clinton Bestor. LC 41-9887. Phoenix Press.
Corpse Came Calling. Davis Dresser. LC 42-18361. 1942. Dodd, Mead & Company.
Corpse Came C.O.D. Jimmy Starr. LC 44-3883. 1944. Murray & Gee, Inc.
Corpse Candle: By George Bagby. 1st Ed. Aaron Marc Stein. LC 67-20916. 1967. 3.95. Pub. for the Crime Club by Doubleday.
Corpse Comes Ashore. John Mersereau. LC 41-12275. J. B. Lippincott Company.
Corpse De Ballet. Lucy Michaella Cores. LC 44-401308. 1944. Duell, Sloan and Pearce.
Corpse Died Twice. Barbara Frost. LC 52-6119. (Gargoyle mystery). Coward-McCann.
Corpse Diplomatique. Delano L Ames. LC 51-9243. (A Murray Hill mystery). 1951. Rinehart.
Corpse Diplomatique. Delano L. Ames. LC 82-48239. (Perennial library; P637). 1983. 2.95 (ISBN 0-06-080637-0). Harper & Row.
Corpse for a Candidate. Michael Geller. (Bud Dugan Ser.: No. 2). 1980. pap. text ed. 1.75 o.s.i. (ISBN 0-505-51478-8). Tower Bks.
Corpse for Breakfast. Max Murray. LC 57-13514. 1957. Washburn.
Corpse for Christmas. Alan Geoffrey Yates. LC 65-4805. (Carter Brown mystery series). 1965. New American Library of World Literature.
Corpse for Christmas see Dance of Death.
Corpse for Christmas. 1st Ed. Henry Kane. LC 51-11787. (Main line mysteries). 1951. Lippincott.
Corpse Grows a Beard. Margaret Scherf. LC 40-135562. G. P. Putnam's Sons.
Corpse Guards Parade. Milward Rodon Kennedy Burge. LC 30-2696. 1930. Pub. for the Crime Club, Inc., by Doubleday, Doran & Company, Inc.
Corpse Hangs High. Edward Sidney Aarons. LC 39-11749. Phoenix Press.
Corpse Hangs High. Edward Ronns, pseud. LC 39-11749. Phoenix Press.
Corpse in Cold Storage. Milward Rodon Kennedy Burge. LC 34-25152. 1934. H. C. Kinsey & Company, Inc.
Corpse in Company K. Robert Avery. LC 42-6129. 1942. J. Swift, Inc.
Corpse in Diplomacy. Miriam Borgenicht. LC 49-8476. 1949. M. S. Mill Co. Distributed by W. Morrow.
Corpse in My Bed. Original Title: Most Men Don't Kill. David Alexander. LC 54-31289. (Ace double novel books, D-59). 1954. Ace Books.
Corpse in the Car. Cecil John Charles Street. LC 35-12793. 1935. Dodd, Mead & Company.
Corpse in the Castle. Ed Friend. 1970. pap. 0.60 o.p. (ISBN 0-447-73200-5). Lancer.
Corpse in the Constable's Garden. George Douglas Howard Cole & Margaret Isabel Postgate Cole. LC 31-7174. 1931. W. Morrow & Company.
Corpse in the Coppice. Robert Alfred John Walling. LC 35-9704. 1935. W. Morrow & Company.
Corpse in the Corner Saloon. Aaron Marc Stein. LC 48-10157. (Inner sanctum mystery). 1948. Simon and Schuster.
Corpse in the Corner Saloon. Hampton Stone, pseud. (Hampton Stone Mysteries Ser). (O.S.I.). 1971. pap. 0.75 o.s.i. (64-629-6). Paperback Lib.
Corpse in the Cove: By Evalina Mack Pseud. Lena Brooke McNamara. LC 55-7929. 1955. Arcadia House.
Corpse in the Crimson Slippers. Robert Alfred John Walling. LC 36-47881. 1936. W. Morrow & Co.
Corpse in the Derby Hat. Howard Swiggett. LC 37-109237. 1937. Little, Brown and Company.
Corpse in the Elevator. M. M. Mannon. LC 56-8970. 1956. Arcadia House.
Corpse in the Flannel Nightgown. Margaret Scherf. LC 65-13996. 1965. Published for the Crime Club by Doubleday.
Corpse in the Green Pyjamas. Robert Alfred John Walling. LC 35-225947. 1935. W. Morrow & Co.

Corpse in the Guest Room: A Skelton Keyne Mystery. Clement Wood. 1945. Arcadia House, Inc.

Corpse in the Snowman. Nicholas Blake. 1977. pap. 1.95i (ISBN 0-06-080427-0, P427, PL). Har-Row.

Corpse in the Snowman. Cecil Day-Lewis. LC 41-21277. Harper & Brothers.

Corpse in the Waxworks. John Dickson Carr. LC 32-8075. 1932. Harper & Brothers.

Corpse in the Wind. Robert Portner Koehler. LC 44-9091. 1944. Phoenix Press.

Corpse Is Indignant. Douglas Stapleton & Carey, Helen A., Joint Author. LC 46-18349. (On cover: Five star mystery. 44). 1946. Five-Star Mysteries, Inc.

Corpse-Maker. David Wilson. (McCloud Ser.). (O.s.i.). 160p. 1974. pap. 0.95 o.s.i. (AN1365, Award). Univ Pub & Dist.

Corpse Moved Upstairs. Frank Gruber. (Johnny Fletcher Ser.). (O.s.i.). 1973. pap. 0.95 o.s.i. (BT50293). Belmont-Tower.

Corpse on Ice. Joseph Hedges. (Stark Ser.: No. 6). 1975. pap. 1.25 o.p. (ISBN 0-515-03812-1). BJ Pub Group.

Corpse on the Bridge. Charles Bryson. LC 28-25552. E. P. Dutton & Co., Inc.

Corpse on the Dike. Janwillem Van De Wetering. 1976. 6.95 (ISBN 0-395-24675-X). HM.

Corpse on the Dike. Janwillem Van De Wetering. 1981. pap. 2.95 (ISBN 0-671-43527-2). PB.

Corpse on the Dike. Wetering, Janwillem Van De. LC 76-18086. 1976. 6.95 (ISBN 0-395-24675-X). Houghton Mifflin.

Corpse on the Dike: Janwillem Van De Wetering. Janwillem van de Wetering. (Kangaroo Book). 1978. 1.95. Pocket Books.

Corpse on the Flying Trapeze: A Mrs. Pym Mystery. Nigel Morland. LC 41-11500. Farrar & Rinehart, Inc.

Corpse on the Hearth. Harry Lang. LC 46-3215. 1946. Macrae-Smith Company.

Corpse on the Town. John Roeburt. LC 59-38634. (Graphic mystery, 27). 1950. Graphic Publications.

Corpse on the White House Lawn. John Franklin Carter. LC 32-33050. Covici, Friede.

Corpse Said No. Barbara Frost. LC 49-9867. (Gargoyle mystery). 1949. Coward-McCann.

Corpse Steps Out. Craig Rice. LC 40-6206. 1940. Simon and Schuster.

Corpse That Came Back: By Peter Piper Pseud. Theo Lang. LC 54-9031. 1954. Random House.

Corpse That Never Was: Michael Shayne's 46th Case. Davis Dresser. LC 63-14313. 1963. Distributed by Dodd, Mead.

Corpse That Refused to Stay Dead. Aaron Marc Stein. LC 52-2158. (Inner sanctum mystery). 1952. Simon & Schuster.

Corpse That Refused to Stay Dead. Hampton Stone, pseud. (Hampton Stone Mystery Ser). 1971. pap. 0.75 o.p. (ISBN 0-446-64567-2, 64-567). Paperback Lib.

Corpse That Spoke. Robert H Leitfred. LC 36-11954. Green Circle Books.

Corpse That Traveled. Arthur John Rees. LC 38-175624. 1938. Dodd, Mead & Company.

Corpse That Walked. Octavus Roy Cohen. LC 51-17384. (Gold medal book, 138). 1950. Fawcett Publications.

Corpse That Walked. Roy Winsor. (Fawcett gold medal book). 1974. (pbk.) 0.95. Fawcett.

Corpse Was No Bargain at All. Aaron Marc Stein. LC 68-28919. (Inner sanctum mystery). 1968. 4.50. Simon and Schuster.

Corpse Was No Bargain at All. Hampton Stone, pseud. LC 68-28919. (O.s.i.). 1968. 4.50 o.s.i. (ISBN 0-671-20095-X). S&S.

Corpse Was No Bargain at All. Hampton Stone, pseud. (Hampton Stone Mystery Ser). 1971. pap. 0.75 o.p. (ISBN 0-446-64505-2, 64-505). Paperback Lib.

Corpse Who Had Too Many Friends. Hampton Stone, pseud. (Hampton Stone Mysteries Ser). 1971. pap. 0.75 o.p. (ISBN 0-446-64588-5, 64-588). Paperback Lib.

Corpse Who Had Too Many Friends: By Hampton Stone Pseud. Aaron Marc Stein. LC 53-1215. (Inner sanctum mystery). 1953. Simon and Schuster.

Corpse Who Wouldn't Die. Edward Joseph Doherty. LC 45-6099. 1945. Mystery House.

Corpse with Knee Action. B. J Maylon. LC 40-30104. Phoenix Press.

Corpse with Sticky Fingers. Aaron Marc Stein. 1973. 0.95. Warner Paperback Lib.

Corpse with Sticky Fingers: By George Bagby Pseud. Aaron Marc Stein. LC 52-10399. 1952. Published for the Crime Club by Doubleday.

Corpse with the Blistered Hand. Robert Alfred John Walling. LC 39-2164. 1939. W. Morrow & Co.

Corpse with the Blistered Hand. Robert Alfred John Walling. LC 40-914221. 1940. Triangle Books.

Corpse with the Blue Cravat. Robert Alfred John Walling. LC 38-122951. 1938. W. Morrow & Co.

Corpse with the Blue Cravat. Robert Alfred John Walling. LC 40-3482. 1939. Triangle Books.

Corpse with the Dirty Face. Robert Alfred John Walling. LC 36-13691. 1936. W. Morrow & Co.

Corpse with the Eerie Eye. Robert Alfred John Walling. LC 42-12645. 1942. W. Morrow & Company.

Corpse with the Floating Foot. Robert Alfred John Walling. LC 36-315733. 1936. W. Morrow & Company.

Corpse with the Grimy Glove. Robert Alfred John Walling. LC 38-32994. 1938. W. Morrow & Co.

Corpse with the Listening Ear. Laurence Dwight Smith. LC 40-315312. 1940. Mystery House.

Corpse with the Missing Watch. Robert Alfred John Walling. LC 49-10757. 1949. W. Morrow.

Corpse with the Purple Thighs. George A Bagby. LC 40-306635. 1939. Pub. for the Crime Club by Doubleday, Doran and Company, Inc.

Corpse with the Purple Thighs. Aaron Marc Stein. LC 40-3026. 1939. Pub. for the Crime Club by Doubleday, Doran and Company, Inc.

Corpse with the Red-Headed Friend. Robert Alfred John Walling. LC 39-27875. 1939. W. Morrow & Company.

Corpse with the Sunburned Face. Christopher St. John Sprigg. LC 35-202970. 1935. Pub. for the Crime Club, Inc., by Doubleday. Doran & Company, Inc.

Corpse Without a Clue. Robert Alfred John Walling. LC 44-5989. 1944. W. Morrow & Company.

Corpse Wore a Wig. George A Bagby, pseud. LC 40-301764. 1940. Pub. for the Crime Club by Doubleday, Doran and Co., Inc.

Corpse Wore a Wig. Aaron Marc Stein. LC 40-30176. 1940. Pub. for the Crime Club by Doubleday, Doran and Co., Inc.

Corpses at Indian Stones. Philip Wylie. LC 43-2518. 1943. Farrar & Rinehart, Inc.

Corpses in Corsica. Shirley Deane. LC 77-79778. 1969. 5.95. Vanguard Press.

Corpus of Joe Bailey: A Novel. Oakley M Hall. LC 52-14032. 1953. Viking Press.

Corral of Death. Malcolm Wheeler-Nicholson. LC 29-19254. 1929. Houghton Mifflin Company.

Correction. Thomas Bernhard. LC 78-15184. 1979. 10.00 (ISBN 0-394-41141-2). Knopf.

Corrector of Destinies: Being Tales of Randolph Mason As Related by His Private Secretary, Courtlandt Parks. Melville Davisson Post. LC 8-251209. E. J. Clode.

Corrector of Destinies: Vol. 3 of Randolph Mason Stories. facsimile ed. Melville Davisson Post. LC 72-150559. (Short Story Index Reprint Ser.). Repr. of 1908 ed. 16.00 (ISBN 0-8369-3856-9). Ayer Co.

Corrector: Or, Independent American. no. 1-2; 1815-16. ed. LC 14-5696. 1815-16.

Corregidor. James H. Belote & William M. Belote. LC 80-80981. (World War II Ser.). (Illus.). 288p. 1982. pap. 2.95 (ISBN 0-86721-103-2). Playboy Pbks.

Corregidora. Gayl Jones. LC 74-8476. 1975. 6.95 (ISBN 0-394-49323-0). Random House.

Correspondance see Oeuvres Completes.

Correspondence of Prince Talleyrand and King Louis Xviii. During the Congress of Vienna (Hitherto Unpublished.) From the Manuscripts Preserved in the Archives of the Ministry of Foreign Affairs at Paris. Charles Maurice De Talleyrand-Perigord & Louis XVIII, King of France, 1755-1824. (Seaside library. v. 50, no 1015.). 1881. G. Munro.

Correspondence of Theodosius and Constantia, Before and After Her Taking the Veil... To Which Is Added the Country Justice... John Langhorne. LC 31-25881. 1802. Printed by James Oram, No., Water-Street.

Correspondences. James L. Weil. 1968. 5.00 o.p. Elizabeth Pr.

Correspondent. Ruth Shimer. (Queen-size gothic). 1974. (pbk.) 0.95. Popular Library.

Corrida at San Feliu. Paul Scott. LC 64-23577. 1964. W. Morrow.

Corrido De California. Fausto Avendano. LC 79-89. 1979. pap. 3.75 (ISBN 0-915808-35-8). Editorial Justa.

Corridor of Whispers. Edwina Noone. (Ace Gothic). 1973. (pbk.) 0.95. Ace Books.

Corridors: A Novel. Edith Milton. LC 67-11848. 1967. Delacorte Press.

Corridors of Death. Ruth Dudley Edwards. LC 81-21461. 10.95 (ISBN 0-312-17012-2). St Martin's Press.

Corridors of Power. Charles Percy Snow. LC 64-23106. (His Strangers and brothers 9). 1964. Scribner.

Corridors of Time. Poul Anderson. LC 65-214232. 3.95. Doubleday.

Corridors of Time: Poul Anderson. Poul Anderson. (Berkley Medallion Book). 1978. 1.50 (ISBN 0-425-03659-6). Berkley Pub. Corp.

Corrie. Lorinda Hagen. 1978. pap. 1.95 o.s.i. (ISBN 0-505-51289-0). Tower Bks.

Corrie Who? Maximilian Foster. LC 8-309372. 1908. Small, Maynard and Company.

Corrigan. Cameron Judd. 1980. pap. 1.75 (ISBN 0-8439-0853-X). Nordon Pubns.

Corroboree. Kenneth Gangemi. LC 76-27241. 96p. 1977. pap. 2.95. Assembling Pr.

Corrupt and Ensnare. Francis M Nevins. LC 78-1755. 7.95 (ISBN 0-399-12203-6). Putnam.

Corrupters. Clayton Moore. (Berkley medallion book). 1974. (pbk.) 1.25. Berkley Pub. Co.

Corrupters. Dariel Telfer. LC 64-17496. 1964. Simon and Schuster.

Corruption. Richard Curle. LC 33-5177. The Bobbs-Merrill Company.

Corruption: A Novel. Percy White. LC 8-36617. 1895. D. Appleton and Company.

Corruption: A Novel. 1st American Ed. Nicholas Mosley. LC 58-565411. (Atlantic monthly press book). Little, Brown.

Corruption of Harold Hoskins: A Novel. John Williams Malone. LC 72-92638. 1973. 5.95. Charterhouse.

Corruption of Linda. Tony Trelos, pseud. (Orig.). 1968. pap. 1.75 o.p. (3047). Brandon.

Corruptors. Gerald G. Griffin. LC 77-76528. 1977. pap. 1.95 o.s.i. (ISBN 0-89516-001-3). Condor Pub Co.

Corsair. Walton Atwater Green. LC 31-1720. Doubleday, Doran & Company, Inc.

Corsair. Geraldine Gordon Salmon. LC 52-1332. 1951. Hutchinson.

Corsair: A Biographical Novel of Jean Lafitte, Hero of the Battle of New Orleans. 1st Ed. Madeleine Kent. LC 55-9758. 1955. Doubleday.

Corsican. William Sanborn Ballinger. LC 73-19085. 1974. 7.95 (ISBN 0-396-06918-5). Dodd, Mead.

Corsican Brothers. from the french by gerardus van dam... ed. Alexandre Dumas. Tr. by Van Dam, Gerardus. LC 6-42828. (On cover: Seaside library, Pocket ed. no. 2128). G. Munro's Sons.

Corsican Brothers. Alexandre Dumas. LC 6-42827. T. B. Peterson & Brothers.

Corsican Cross. Michael Bradley. (Adrano/For Hire#1). 1974. (pbk.) 1.25. Warner Paperback Lib.

Corsican Death. Robert Hawkes. (Narc). (Signet book: Vol. 7). 1975. (pbk.) 1.25. New American Library.

Corsican Justice. Geraldine Gordon Salmon. LC 27-3370. George H. Doran Company.

Corsican Lovers: A Story of the Vendetta. Charles Felton Pidgin. LC 6-6745. 1906. B. W. Dodge & Company.

Corsican Takeover. Don Smith. 192p. (Orig.). 1974. pap. 0.95 o.p. (449-02914-95, GM). Fawcett World.

Corsican Takeover. Don Smith. (Tim Parnell Action Suspense Novel). (Gold medal book, M2914: Vol. 4). 1974. (pbk.) 0.95. Fawcett Publications.

Corsicana! Henry Barsha. LC 59-13183. 1959. L. C. Page.

Corson of the J C. Clarence Edward Mulford. LC 27-4062. 1927. Doubleday, Page & Company.

Corson of the JC. Clarence Edward Mulford. LC 73-89650. 1973. 6.95. Aeonian Press.

Cortenay Treasure. Percival Christopher Wren. LC 36-8016. 1936. Houghton Mifflin Company.

Cortes the Conqueror: His Romance with Donna Marina. Elizabeth Rachel Cannon Porter. LC 44-54639. 1944. Dorrance & Company.

Cortlandt Laster, Capitalist. Harley Deen. (On cover: Laird & Lee's prize novels, no. 1). 1892. Laird & Lee.

Cortlandts of Washington Square. Janet Ayer Fairbank. LC 22-18892. The Bobbs-Merrill Company.

Corydon. Andre Paul Guillaume Gide. 1978. lib. bdg. 17.50x (ISBN 0-374-93051-1). Octagon.

Coryston Family: A Novel. Mary Augusta Arnold Humphry Ward Ward. LC 13-217398. 1913. Harper & Brothers.

Cosa Nostra. Peter McCurtin. (Orig.). 1971. pap. 0.95 o.p. (B95-2158). Belmont-Tower.

Cosas Que Se Cuentan: Stories to Tell. (Span). pap. 0.75 o.p. (ISBN 0-8024-1320-X). Moody.

Cosette. Katharine Sarah Gadsden Macquoid. (On cover: Lovell's international series, no. 61). F. F. Lovell & Company.

Cosette: Episode Tire De 'Les Miserables.' Adapted and Edited by Marc Ceppi. Victor Marie Hugo & Marc Ceppi. LC 62-1110. (Junior French series). 1954. Clarendon Press.

Cosgrove Report. George O'Toole. 1981. pap. 2.95 (ISBN 0-440-11594-9). Dell.

Cosgrove Report: Being the Private Inquiry of a Pinkerton's Detective into the Death of President Lincoln by Nicholas Cosgrove: Edited and Verified by Michael Croft, Col., U.S. Army (Ret.): an Annotated Novel. George O'Toole. LC 78-64794. 10.95 (ISBN 0-89256-091-6). Rawson, Wade.

Cosimo's Wife. Akbar Del Piombo. (TC-202). 1967. pap., 1.25. Traveller's Companion.

Cosimo's Wife of the Vengeance of a Duke. Akbar Del Piombo. pap. 1.95 o.s.i. (OPS40, Travellers Comp). Olympia.

Cosmas, or, The Love of God. Pierre De Calan. LC 80-508. 1980. 9.95 (ISBN 0-385-17059-9). Doubleday.

Cosmic Carousel. David S Garnett. LC 76-381297. (Hale SF). 1976. 2.90 (ISBN 0-7091-5003-2). Hale.

Cosmic Crusaders. Pierre Barbet, pseud. (Science Fiction Ser.). 1980. pap. 2.25 o.p. (ISBN 0-87997-583-0, UE1583). DAW Bks.

Cosmic Encounter. Alfred Elton Van Vogt. LC 79-7570. (Doubleday science fiction). 1980. 7.95 (ISBN 0-385-11277-7). Doubleday.

Cosmic Engineers. Clifford D. Simak. 1970. pap. 0.60 o.p. (63-432). Paperback Lib.

Cosmic Engineers, an Interplanetary Novel. Clifford D Simak. LC 51-9901. 1950. Gnome Press.

Cosmic Eye. Mack Reynolds. (Leisure book). 1979. 1.25 (ISBN 0-8439-0610-3). Nordon Pubns.

Cosmic Eye. Mack Reynolds. 1975. (pbk.) 0.95. Belmont Tower Books.

Cosmic Gash. Ray Kainen. LC 74-9881. (Traveller's companion series, TC-447). 1969. 1.75. Olympia Press.

Cosmic Geoids. Taine. 5.00; pap. 2.00. Fantasy Pub Co.

Cosmic Geoids: And One Other. Eric Temple Bell. LC 49-16335. 1949. Fantasy Pub. Co.

Cosmic Giggle: A Novel. Robert C. French. 1979. pap. 5.95 o.p. (ISBN 0-87613-076-7). New Age.

Cosmic Harp. Corinne Heline. pap. 5.95 (ISBN 0-87613-058-9). New Age.

Cosmic Kaleidoscope. Bob Shaw. LC 76-56334. 1977. 6.95 (ISBN 0-385-12996-3). Doubleday.

Cosmic Kaleidoscope. Bob Shaw. (Dell book). 1979. 1.75 (ISBN 0-440-11079-3). Dell Pub. Co.

Cosmic Manhunt. Lyon Sprague De Camp. LC 54-332696. (Ace double novel books, D-61). 1954. Ace Books.

Cosmic Rape. Sturgeon, Theodore. (Kangaroo Book). 1977. 1.50 (ISBN 0-671-81414-1). Pocket Books.

Cosmic Rape and "To Marry Medusa". Theodore Sturgeon. LC 77-5762. (Gregg Press science fiction series). 1977. 9.50 (ISBN 0-8398-2362-2). Gregg Press.

Cosmic Reality Kill. Joseph Rosenberger. (Death Merchant Ser.: No. 36). (Orig.). 1979. pap. 1.95 (ISBN 0-523-41380-7). Pinnacle Bks.

Cosmic-The La Raza Sketchbook. Ruben Dario Salaz. 1975. pap. 6.95 (ISBN 0-932482-00-7). Blue Feather.

Cosmic Traitor. Kurt Brand. (Perry Rhodan, 26). 1973. (pbk.) 0.75. Ace.

Cosmicomics. Italo Calvino. LC 76-14795. (Harbrace paperbound library; HPL 69). 1976. 2.25 (ISBN 0-15-622600-6). Harcourt Brace Jovanovich.

Cosmicomics. Italo Calvino. LC 76-15133. 1970. Collier Books.

Cosmicomics. Tr., from Italian by William Weaver. 1st Ed. Italo Calvino. LC 68-24386. 1968. 3.95. Harcourt.

Cosmo Report. Linda Wolfe. 368p. 1982. pap. 3.95 (ISBN 0-553-22685-1). Bantam.

Cosmographical Lobster: A Poetic Novel. Henry Chopin. LC 76-361204. 1976. (ISBN 0-85247-111-4) (ISBN 0-85247-112-2). Gaberbocchus.

Cosmopolis. authorized ed. Paul Charles Joseph Bourget. Tr. by Hettie E. Miller. LC 6-15006. (On cover: Sergel's international library, v. 1, no. 19). 1893. C. H. Sergel and Company.

Cosmopolis. Rupert Croft-Cooke. LC 33-10596. 1933. L. MacVeagh, Dial Press, Inc.

Cosmopolis: A Novel. Paul Charles Joseph Bourget. Tr. by Cleveland Moffett. LC 6-15008. (On cover: Forget-me-not series, no. 1). 1893. M. J. Ivers & Co.

Cosmopolis: A Novel. authorized ed. Paul Charles Joseph Bourget. LC 6-15007. (On cover: Holyrood series no. 5). 1893. Tait, Sons & Company.

Cosmopolis: A Novel. new york herald ed., ed. Paul Charles Joseph Bourget. Tr. by Cleveland Moffett. LC 6-15005. (On cover: World library, no. 22)). 1893. The Waverly Company.

Cosmopolitan Comedy. Anna Robeson Brown Burr. (Half-title: Appletons' town and country library, no. 266). 1899. D. Appleton and Company.

Cosmopolitan Crimes: Foreign Rivals of Sherlock Holmes. Ed. by Hugh Greene. LC 73-162550. 1971. 6.95 (ISBN 0-394-47340-X). Pantheon Books.

Cosmopolitan Girl. Rosalyn Drexler. 1976. (pbk.) 1.75 (ISBN 0-446-59057-6). Warner Books.

Cosmopolitans. William Somerset Maugham. LC 75-26129. (Maugham, William Somerset, 1874-1965. Works. 1976). 1977. 15.00 (ISBN 0-405-07852-8). Arno Press.

Cosmopolitans. William Somerset Maugham. LC 36-5632. 1936. Doubleday, Doran and Company, Inc.

Cosmopolitans. William Somerset Maugham. LC 38-31839. 1938. The Sun Dial Press, Inc.
Cosmopolitans: Twenty-Nine Short Stories. William Somerset Maugham. LC 44-11970. (On cover: Avon modern short story monthly. No. 1). N.Y.
Cosmos. John Wood Campbell et al. Ed. by Richard A. Lupoff. 1980. Repr. of 1934 ed. 17.95t (ISBN 0-930800-03-6). Pennyfarthing.
Cosmos. Witold Gombrowicz. Tr. by Eric Mosbacher. LC 68-22003. 1969. pap. 2.95 o.p. (ISBN 0-394-17323-6, E557, Ever). Grove.
Cosmos, and Other Blooms. Flora Huling. LC 18-23638.
Cossack Lover. Martha Gilbert Dickinson Bianchi. LC 11-1132. 1911. 1.30. Duffield & Company.
Cossacks: a Tale of the Caucasus in 1852. Lev Nikolaevich Tolstoi & Schuyler, Eugene, 1840-1890, Tr. LC 12-39625. 1878. C. Scribner's Sons.
Cossacks; a Tale of the Caucasus in 1852. Lev Nikolaevich Tolstoi & Schuyler, Eugene, 1840-1890, Tr. LC 8-26749. 1887. W. S. Gottsberger.
Cossacks; a Tale of the Caucasus Inthe Year 1852. Lev Nikolaevich Tolstoi & Dole, Nathan Haskell, 1852- Tr. LC 8-26748. T. Y. Crowell & Co.
Cossacks, a Throbbing Romance of Love and Adventure, Based on the Motion Picture Story. Lev Nikolaevich Tolstoi. LC 28-15792. Jacobsen-Hodgkinson-Corporations.
Cossacks & the Raid. Lev Nikolaevich Tolstoi. 1961. pap. 2.25 (ISBN 0-451-51494-7, CE1494, Sig Classics). NAL.
Cossacks and The Raid. Tolstoi, Lev Nikolaevich, Graf. LC 61-4507. (Signet classic, CD56). 1961. New American Library.
Cossacks. By Count Lyof Tolstoi. Lev Nikolaevich Tolstoi & Kendall, Mrs. Laura E., Tr. (On cover: Seaside library. Pocket ed., no. 1090). 1888. G. Munro.
Cossacks: Sevastopol, The Invaders, and Other Stories. Lev Nikolaevich Tolstoi. LC 70-113687. (Short story index reprint series). 1970. Books for Libraries Press.
Cossacks, Sevastopol, the Invaders & Other Stories. Lev Nikolaevich Tolstoi. (Short Story Index Reprint Ser.). 1899. 29.00 (ISBN 0-8369-3416-4). Ayer Co.
Cossacks: The Death of Ivan Hyich; Happy Ever After. Lev Nikolaevich Tolstoi. LC 61-606. (Penguin classics, L109). 1960. Penguin Books.
Cossier Captain: A Tale of the Boston Waterfront. James Brendan Connolly. LC 27-17361. 1927. Macy-Masius.
Cost. David Graham Phillips. LC 72-84623. (Illus.). 1974. 16.00 (ISBN 0-403-02955-4). Scholarly Press.
Cost. David Graham Phillips. LC 76-80427. (Series in American Studies). (Illus.). 1969. Johnson Reprint Corp.
Cost. David Graham Phillips. 1904. The Bobbs-Merrill Company.
Cost. David Graham Phillips. LC 9-32291. Grosset & Dunlap.
Cost of a Promise: A Novel in Three Parts. Gertrude M. Robins Reynolds. LC 14-15174. Geroge H. Doran Company.
Cost of Her Pride. Annie French Hector. LC 96-1027. J. B. Lippincott Company.
Cost of It. Elinor Mordaunt, pseud. LC 12-15815. 1912. 1.35. Sturgis & Walton Company.
Cost of Living. Ruth Doan MacDougall. 1973. (pbk.) 1.25 (ISBN 0-671-78359-9). Pocket Books.
Cost of Living. Ruth Doan MacDougall. LC 71-132614. 1971. 5.95. Putnam.
Cost of Living Like This. James Kennaway. LC 72-86541. 1969. 5.95. Atheneum.
Cost of Seriousness. Peter Porter. 1978. pap. 6.50x (ISBN 0-19-211880-3). Oxford U Pr.
Cost of Silence. Margaret Yorke. LC 77-79964. 1977. 6.95 (ISBN 0-8027-5379-5). Walker.
Cost of Things. Francis Ryck. Date not set. price not set o.p. Stein & Day.
Cost of Wings: And Other Stories. Clotilde Inez Mary Graves. LC 14-7729. 1914. 1.25. Frederick A. Stokes Company.
Costals & the Hippogriff. Henry De Montherlant. Tr. by Rodker, John. LC 40-14407. 1940. A. A. Knopf.
Costigan's Funeral and Other Stories. William F. Short. LC 99-214. 1898. Henderson & Depew.
Costigan's Needle. Jerry Sohl. LC 53-77194. 1953. Rinehart.
Costly Freak. Mary Gleed Tuttiett. LC 8-323173. (On cover: Appleton's town and country library, no. 137). 1894. D. Appleton and Company.
Costly Heritage. A Novel. Alice O'Hanlon. (Franklin square library, no. 193). 1881. Harper & Brothers.
Costumes by Eros. Conrad Potter Aiken. LC 28-21485. 1928. C. Scribner's Sons.
Cotillion. Georgette Heyer. LC 52-136419. 1953. Putnam.
Cotillion for Mandy. Claudette Williams. (Regency Romance Ser.). 1978. pap. 1.75 (ISBN 0-449-23664-1, Crest). Fawcett.
Cotillion for Maudy. Claudette Williams. 1978. 1.75 (ISBN 0-449-23664-1). Fawcett Crest Books.
Cotillion: Or, One Good Bull Is Half the Herd. John Oliver Killens. LC 70-101243. 1971. 6.50. Trident Press.
Cotswold Case. Robert McNair Wilson. LC 33-3858. J. B. Lippincott Company.
Cottage. Gretchen Travis. LC 72-87631. 1973. 5.95 (ISBN 0-399-11068-2). Putnam.
Cottage. Gretchen Travis. 1974. (pbk.) 1.50. Dell.
Cottage at Barron Ridge. Juanita Tyree Osborne. 192p. (YA) 1975. 4.95 o.p. (Avalon). Bouregy.
Cottage at Barron Ridge. Juanita Tyree Osborne. 1975. 4.95. Avalon Books.
Cottage at Chapelyard: A Novel of Romantic Suspense. Frances Keinzley. LC 74-21152. 224p. 1975. 7.95 o.p. Bobbs.
Cottage by the Lake. Rosa Petzel. Tr. by Schively, Rebecca H. LC 12-31416. 1869. Lutheran Board of Publication.
Cottage by the Sea. James Carey Coale. LC 6-20725. 1896. J. Murphy & Company.
Cottage Colony. Peggy Gaddis, pseud. LC 25-18237. Arcadia House.
Cottage in Galilee: Stories. Edwin Samuel. LC 58-5158. 1958. Abelard-Schuman.
Cottage Murder. Ernest Robertson Punshon. LC 32-214431. 1932. Houghton Mifflin Company.
Cottage of Delight: A Novel. William Nathaniel Harben. LC 19-14005. Harper & Brothers.
Cottage Pety Exemplified. LC 6-29018. 1869. J. B. Lippincott & Co.
Cottage Pie, a Country Spread. Albert Michael Neil Lyons. LC 11-4106. 1911. John Lane.
Cottage Sinister. Q. Patrick. LC 32-58037. 1931. Roland Swain Company.
Cottagers of Glenburnie: A Tale for the Farmer's Ingle-Nook. Elizabeth Hamilton. LC 73-22147. (Feminist Controversy in England, 1788-1810). 1974. 22.00 (ISBN 0-8240-0864-2). Garland Pub.
Cotter's Son (Husmandsgutten) Hans Andersen Foss. LC 63-3633. 1963. Park Region Pub. Co.
Cotton: A Novel. Jack Bethea. LC 26-10296. 1928. Houghton Mifflin Company.
Cotton Cavalier. The Campus Prize Novel--1932. John Thomas Goodrich. LC 33-2523. Farrar & Rinehart, Incorporated.
Cotton Comes to Harlem. Chester B Himes. LC 64-25572. 1965. Putnam.
Cotton in My Ears. Frances Warfield. LC 48-6249. 1948. Viking Press.
Cotton King. A Story of Love and Duty. Sutton Vane. (On cover: Drama series, no. 9). Street & Smith.
Cotton Kingdom. Frederich L. Olmsted. 1981. pap. 6.95 (Mod LibC). Modern Lib.
Cotton-Pickers. B Traven. LC 68-30762. 1969. 5.00. Hill and Wang.
Cotton Picker's Dreams, and Other Stories. Stephen G Prokopoff. LC 64-15613. 1964. Christopher Pub. House.
Cotton Road. Frank Feuille. LC 54-10303. 1954. W. Morrow.
Cotton Stealing. A Novel. Chamberlain, J. E. LC 6-31151. 1866. J. R. Walsh & Co.
Cotton Web. Barbara Hunt. LC 60-600257. 1960. Dutton.
Cottonmouth. Julian Lee Rayford. LC 41-3538. 1941. C. Scribner's Sons.
Cottonwood Canyon. Archie Joscelyn. LC 40-12265. Phoenix Press.
Cottonwood Gulch. Clarence Edward Mulford. LC 73-89651. 1973. 5.95. Aeonian Press.
Cottonwood Gulch. Clarence Edward Mulford. LC 25-384789. 1925. Doubleday, Page & Company.
Cottonwood Pards. Lee Floren. LC 45-265648. 1944. Phoenix Press.
Cottonwood Spring. pap. 2.95 o.s.i. (ISBN 0-910040-11-7). Allan Pubns.
Cottonwoods Grow Tall. Margaret Bell Houston. LC 58-12866. 1958. Crown Publishers.
Cottonwood's Story. Margaret Hill McCarter. LC 3-32589. 1903. Crane & Company, Printers.
Couch. Robert Bloch. LC 62-4785. (Gold medical books, S1192). 1962. Fawcett Publications.
Couch Trip. Ken Kolb. LC 77-117677. 1970. 5.95. Random House.
Coucou. Evelyn Pember. LC 29-23246. 1929. Houghton Mifflin Company.
Cougar Basin: By Wade Hamilton Pseud. Lee Floren. LC 53-129214. 1953. Arcdda House.
Cougar Basin War. Philip Ketchum. 160p. 1981. pap. 1.95 (ISBN 0-441-11786-4). Ace Bks.
Cougar Canyon: A Powder Valley Western. Peter Field. LC 62-11902. 1976. (pbk.) 1.25 (ISBN 0-671-80263-1). Pocket Books.
Cougar Kid. Johnston McCulley. LC 45-8333. 1945. Arcadia House, Inc.
Cougar of Canyon Caballo. Paul Evan Lehman. LC 36-3133. 1936. Green Circle Books.
Cougar-Tamer & Other Stories of Adventure. Franklin Welles Calkins. LC 79-153541. (Short story index reprint series). (Illus.). 1971. (ISBN 0-8369-3795-3). Books for Libraries Press.
Cougar-Tamer & Other Stories of Adventure. Franklin Welles Calkins. LC 99-1403. 1899. H. S. Stone & Company.
Could I Forget. Denise Robins. 1.25 (ISBN 0-380-00723-1). Avon.
Couldn't Say No. John Habberton. LC 6-46681. (On cover: Household library. v. 4, no. 43). Belford Company.
Couldn't Say No. John Habberton. LC 3341. (On cover: Eagle library, no. 164). 1900. Street & Smith.
Coulter's Woman. Catherine Weber. (Orig.). 1980. pap. 1.95 (ISBN 0-532-23199-6). Woodhill.
Council of Egypt. Tr. from Italian by Adrienne Foulke 1st Amer. Ed. Leonardo Sciascia. LC 66-107509. 1966. bds., 4.95. Knopf.
Council of Seven. John Collis Snaith. LC 21-19925. 1921. D. Appleton and Company.
Council of Ten. Sylvanus Cobb. (On cover: Fireside series, no. 98). J. S. Ogilvie.
Council of Ten. Sylvanus Cobb. (On cover: Columbia library, vol. II, no. 24). 1900. Street & Smith.
Councils of Croesus. Mary Knight Potter. LC 2-21105. (Added t.-p.; Page's commonwealth series, no. 6). 1903. L. C. Page & Company.
Counsel for the Defense. Jeffrey Ashford, pseud. (01636). 1965. Collier.
Counsel for the Defense. Roderic Jeffries. LC 61-10250. 1961. Harper.
Counsel for the Defense. Leroy Scott. LC 12-5551. 1912. 1.20. Doubleday, Page & Company.
Counsel of Perfection. Mary St. Leger Kingsley Harrison. LC 7-2876. 1888. D. Appleton and Company.
Counsel of the Ungodly. Charles Brackett. LC 20-13703. 1920. D. Appleton and Company.
Counsellor. Alfred Walter Stewart. LC 39-16965. 1939. Little, Brown and Company.
Counsellor. Goland Ziran. LC 82-72058. 1982. 14.95 (ISBN 0-87795-420-8). Arbor Hse.
Counsellor Heart. Pauline Glen Winslow. LC 79-25350. 1980. 8.95 (ISBN 0-312-17014-9). St. Martin's Press.
Counselor Ayres' Memorial. Machado De Assis, Joaquim Maria. LC 72-187876. 1972. 7.50 (ISBN 0-520-02227-0). University of California Press.
Counselors-at-Law: A Novel. Jerome Weidman. LC 78-14712. 1980. 12.95 (ISBN 0-385-12880-0). Doubleday.
Count a Lonely Cadence: A Novel. Gordon Weaver. LC 68-18277. 1968. H. Regnery Co.
Count and the Congressman. Constance Cary Harrison. LC 8-15151. Cupples & Leon Company.
Count at Harvard: Being an Account of the Adventures of a Young Gentleman of Fashion at Harvard University. Rupert Sargent Holland. LC 6-11305. 1906. L. C. Page & Company.
Count Backwards to Zero. Brett Halliday. (Mike Shayne mystery). 1975. (pbk.) 0.95. Dell.
Count Belisarius. Robert Graves. LC 38-35991. Random House.
Count Bohemond. Alfred Leo Duggan. LC 65-10007. 1965. Pantheon Books.
Count Bohemond. Pref. by Evelyn Waugh. Alfred Leo Duggan. (Image bk., D223). 1967. N.Y. Doubleday.
Count Brass. Michael Moorcock. 1976. 1.25. Dell Books.
Count Brass. Michael Moorocock. LC 73-175159. (Mayflower science fantasy). ((His). (Chronicles of Castle Brass, v.). 1973. 0.30 (ISBN 0-583-12198-5). Mayflower.
Count Brugs. Ben Hecht. LC 40-37528. 1926. Boni & Liveright.
Count Bunker: Being a Bald Yet Veracious Chronicle Containing Some Further Particulars of Two Gentlemen Whose Previous Careers Were Touched Upon in a Tone Entitled "The Lunatic at Large,". Joseph Storer Clouston. LC 7-13950. 1907. Brentano's.
Count De Camors. The Man of the Second Empire. Octave Feuillet. LC 6-39525. T. B. Peterson & Brothers.
Count De Latour: A Tale of Mystery... William Henry Watson. 1898. American Publishing Company.
Count De Mornay: Or, Back from the Dead. A Novel. Samuel Watson Wheeler. LC 8-36052. 1894.
Count D'Orgel. Translated from the French, by Violet Schiff Pref. by Jean Cocteau. Raymond Radiguet. LC 53-1963. 1953. Grove Press.
Count-Down to Black Genocide. Saggittarus. LC 73-78108. 1973. 5.95. Nuclassics and Science Pub. Co.
Count Erbach: A Story of the Reformation. Hermann Otto Nietschmann. Tr. by Helm, James I. LC 8-28112. A. D. F. Randolph & Company.
Count Falcon of the Eyrie: A Narrative Wherein Are Set Forth the Adventures of Guido Orrabelli Dei Falchi During a Certain Autumn of His Career. Clinton Scollard. LC 3-23050. 1903. J. Pott & Company.
Count Hannibal. Stanley John Weyman. 326p. 1977. Repr. lib. bdg. 14.95x (ISBN 0-89966-278-1). Buccaneer Bks.
Count Hannibal: A Romance of the Court of France. Stanley John Weyman. 1901. Longmans, Green, and Co.
Count Julian. Juan Goytisolo. LC 73-3506. (Illus.). 1974. 7.95 (ISBN 0-670-24407-4). Viking Press.
Count Julian. Juan Goytisolo. LC 74-23147. (Viking compass book). 1975. 2.95 (ISBN 0-670-00586-X). Viking Press.
Count Kostia: A Novel. Victor Cherbuliez & Ashley, O. D., Tr. LC 6-27169. (Leisure hour series. v. 13). 1873. Holt & Williams.
Count Lucanor: Or, The Fifty Pleasant Tales of Patronio. Juan Manuel. LC 76-48427. (Classics of European Literature). (Hyperion library of world literature). 1977. 12.95. (ISBN 0-88355-550-6) (ISBN 0-88355-551-4). Hyperion Press.
Count Lucanor: Or, the Fifty Pleasant Tales of Patronio. Juan Manuel, Infante De Castile. Tr. by James York from Span. LC 76-48427. (Library of World Literature Ser.). (o.s.i.). (Illus.). 1978. Repr. of 1924 ed. 19.50 (ISBN 0-88355-550-6). Hyperion Conn.
Count Luna: Two Tales of the Real and Theunreal: Baron Bagge Translated by Richard & Clara Winston and Count Luna Translated by Jane B. Greene Introd. by Robert Pick. Alexander Maria Lernet-Holenia. 1956. Criterion Books.
Count Manfred. Miranda Seymour, pseud. LC 76-26896. 1977. 8.95 (ISBN 0-698-10796-9). Coward, McCann & Geoghegan.
Count Me Among the Living. Ethol Sexton. LC 46-3858. 1946. Harper & Brothers.
Count Me In. Fan Nichols. pap. 0.60 o.p. (60-377). Manor Bks.
Count Mirabeau. An Historical Novel. Theodor Mundt. Tr. by Radford, Therese J. LC 7-36658. 1868. D. Appleton and Company.
Count of Monte Christo. Alexandre Dumas et al. LC 41-19668. 1941. The Limited Editions Club.
Count of Monte-Cristo. Alexandre Dumas. 1961. Grosset & Dunlap.
Count of Monte Cristo. Alexandre Dumas. (Rittenhouse classics). 1922. G. W. Jacobs & Company.
Count of Monte Cristo. Alexandre Dumas & Holmes, Mabel Dodge, 1883- LC 46-804. Globe Book Company.
Count of Monte-Cristo. Alexandre Dumas & Maquet, Auguste. 1888. G. Routledge and Sons.
Count of Monte Cristo. Alexandre Dumas & Maquet, Auguste. LC 6-42821. 1889. Little, Brown and Company.
Count of Monte-Cristo. Alexandre Dumas & Maquet, Auguste. LC 12-19572. T. Y. Crowell & Company.
Count of Monte-Cristo... Alexandre Dumas & Maquet, Auguste. LC 16-9385. (Half-title: The romances of Alexandre Dumas. Handy library edition). Little Brown and Company.
Count of Monte-Cristo. Alexandre Dumas & Maquet, Auguste. LC 6-42825. (Half-title: The romances of Alexande Dumas. Illustrated library ed. vol. xliii-xlvi). 1894. Little Brown, and Company.
Count of Monte Cristo. Alexandre Dumas & Maquet, Auguste. LC 3-27792. 1897. Little Brown, and Company.
Count of Monte Cristo. Alexandre Dumas & Maquet, Auguste. LC 1-23009. (Added t.-p.: The works of Alexandre Dumas. v. 1-2). 1901. T. Y. Crowell & Co.
Count of Monte Cristo... Alexandre Dumas & Maquet, Auguste. (Half-title: Everyman's library, ed. by Ernest Rhys, Fiction no. 303-394). 1909. J. M. Dent & Sons, Ltd.
Count of Monte Cristo. Alexandre Dumas & Maquet, Auguste. LC 28-24066. Dodd, Mead & Company.
Count of Monte Cristo. Alexandre Dumas & Maquet, Auguste. LC 31-26980. (golden books). 1931. D. McKay.
Count of Monte Cristo... Alexandre Dumas & Maquet, Auguste. LC 36-87183. (Half-title: Everyman's library, ed. by Ernest Rhys. Fiction. no. 393-394). 1934. J. M. Dent & Sons, Ltd.
Count of Monte-Cristo. Alexandre Dumas & Auguste Maquet. LC 46-22836. 1946. Whittlesey House, McGraw-Hill Book Company Inc.
Count of Monte Cristo. Introd. by Raymond C. Canon. Alexandre Dumas. (Classics ser., CL154). 1967. Airmont.

Count of Monte-Cristo: Or, The Adventures of Enmond Dantes. Alexandre Dumas. LC 3-27816. G. Routledge and Sons, Limited.

Count of Monte-Cristo: Or, The Adventures of Edmond Dantes. Alexandre Dumas & Auguste Maquet. LC 3-27816. G. Routledge and Sons, Limited.

Count of Monte Cristo: Or, The Revenge of Edmond Dantes. Alexandre Dumas & Maquet, Auguste. Tr. by Thiese, William. LC 6-42823. (American series no. 289). 1892. M. J. Ivers & Co.

Count of Monte Cristo: Or, The Revenge of Edmond Dantes. Alexandre Dumas & Maquet, Auguste. Tr. by Williams, Henry Llewlyn, Jr. LC 6-42824. (On cover: The souvenir series, no. 36). The F. M. Lupton Publishing Company.

Count of Monte Cristo. Translated by Lowell Bair. Alexandre Dumas. LC 56-10489. (Bantam fifty, F1520 9). 1956. Bantam Books.

Count of the Saxon Shore: Or, The Villa in Vectic. by the rev. alfred j. church... with the collaboration of ruth putnam... ed. Alfred John Church & Putnam, Ruth, D. 1931, Joint Author. LC 6-25401. 1887. G. P. Putnam's Sons.

Count on Two Days. Mannix Walker. LC 43-14968. 1943. Dodd, Mead & Company.

Count Raven. Agnes Sweetman Castle & Castle, Egerton. LC 17-545389. 1916. Cassell and Company, Ltd.

Count Robert of Paris. Walter Scott. LC 26-24720. (Seaside libary. v. 53, no. 1082). 1881. G. Munro.

Count Robert of Paris. Walter Scott. (On cover: Lovell's library, no. 557). 1885. J. W. Lovell Company.

Count Robert of Paris. Walter Scott. (Half-title: Everyman's library, ed. by Ernest Rhys. Fiction). 1907. J. M. Dent & Co.

Count Robert of Paris. Walter Scott. LC 36-37092. (Half-title: Everyman's library, ed. by Ernest Rhys. Fiction. no. 131). 1929. J. M. Dent & Sons, Ltd.

Count Robert of Paris. Walter Scott. (His Waverley novels). De Wolfe, Fiske, & Co.

Count Roderic's Castle: Or, Gothic Times, a Tale ... LC 5-41061. Printed by Samuel Sower. For Keating's Book-Store.

Count Roller Skates. 1st Ed. Thomas Sancton. LC 56-7533. 1956. Doubleday.

Count St. Blancard: Or, The Prejudiced Judge: a Novel. Mary Meeke. LC 77-2044. (Gothic Novels III). 60.00 (ISBN 0-405-10142-2). Arno Press.

Count Ten. Mildred Evans Gilman. LC 27-18713. 1927. Boni and Liveright.

Count Ten. Hans Otto Storm. LC 40-32626. 1940. Longmans, Green and Co.

Count the Cost: By E. X. Ferrars Pseud. 1st Ed. Morna Doris MacTaggart Brown. LC 57-10452. 1957. Published for the Crime Club by Doubleday.

Count the Stars. Barbara Cartland. (Barbara Cartland Ser.: No. 10). 192p. (Orig.). 1981. pap. 1.75 (ISBN 0-515-05860-2). Jove Pubns.

Count the Ways. Doris Miles Disney. LC 49-114471. 1949. Published for the Crime Club by Doubleday.

Count Tolstoi's Gospel Stories. Lev Nikolaevich Tolstoi & Dole, Nathan Haskell, 1852- Tr. 1890. T. Y. Crowell & Co.

Count up to Blast-Down. William Johnston. (Brady Bunch Ser., No. 3). (Orig.). 1970. pap. 0.60 o.p. (ISBN 0-447-73872-0). Lancer.

Count Vronsky's Daughter. Michael Butterworth. LC 80-2065. 1981. 12.95 (ISBN 0-385-15918-8). Doubleday.

Count Vronsky's Daughter. Carola Salisbury. LC 80-2065. 312p. 1981. 12.95 (ISBN 0-385-15918-8). Doubleday.

Count Without Castles. Jeanne Humphreys. LC 56-9594. 1956. Duell, Sloan and Pearce.

Count Your Blessings. Rhys Davies. LC 32-11569. 1932. Putnam.

Count Your Dead. John Rowe. 1969. 7.00 o.s.i. Tri-Ocean.

Countdown. Frank Gill Slaughter. LC 76-103776. 1970. 6.95. Doubleday.

Countdown at Eighty: An American Perspective. Henry Chapin. LC 77-4360. (Illus.). 1977. pap. 4.95 (ISBN 0-87233-041-9). Bauhan.

Countdown on an Empty Streetcar. Hugh Fox. (Orig.). 1969. pap. 3.75 o.s.i. (ISBN 0-911856-02-1). Abyss.

Countdown to Action: An Anthology of General Fiction. Ed. by Robert Hoskins. (Griffon Ser). (Orig.). 1969. pap. 0.50 o.p. (Golden Pr). Western Pub.

Countdown to China. Steven Thompson. 304p. 1982. pap. 2.95 (ISBN 0-446-90647-6). Warner Bks.

Countdown to Rapture. Salem Kirban. (Illus.). 1977. pap. 2.95 (ISBN 0-912582-26-X). Kirban.

Countdown to Terror. Lionel Derrick. (Penetrator, 18). 1.25 (ISBN 0-523-00995-X). Pinnacle Books.

Countdown to Terror. Lionel Derrick. (Penetrator, 18). 1.25 (ISBN 0-523-00995-X). Pinnacle Books.

Countdown Zero. T. H. Saffer & O. Kelly. 1983. pap. 5.95 (ISBN 0-14-006724-8). Penguin.

Counted Worthy. Isabel Anderson. LC 64-56720. (T.E.A.M. bk.). 1964. 2.95. Moody.

Countees Sarah. (La Comtesse Sarah) Georges Ohnet. Tr. by S. B. (On cover: The world library, no. 7). 1890. The Waverly Company.

Counter-Clock World. Philip K Dick. LC 79-4211. (Gregg science fiction series). (Reprint of the ed. published by Berkeley Pub. Corp., New York, in series, A Berkeley medallion book.). 1979. 11.95 (ISBN 0-8398-2485-8). Gregg Press.

Counter-Clock World. Philip K Dick. (Berkley medallion book). 1974. (pbk.) 0.95 (ISBN 0-425-02568-3). Berkley Pub. Co.

Counter-Clockwise. John M. Lee. LC 73-18591. 1975. 9.50 (ISBN 0-404-11402-4). AMS Press.

Counter-Clockwise. John M Lee. LC 40-33588. 1940. W. Malliet and Company.

Counter Currents. Elsie Janis & Aspinwall, Marguerite. LC 26-3001. 1926. G. P. Putnam's Sons.

Counter Force. Dan Streib. 192p. (Orig.). 1983. pap. 2.50 (ISBN 0-449-12387-1, GM). Fawcett.

Counter Paradise. Nichol Fleming. LC 68-57007. 1968. 4.50. Coward-McCann.

Counter Play. Anne Snyder. (Orig.). 1981. pap. 2.25 (ISBN 0-451-11898-7, AE1898, Sig). NAL.

Counter Spy Murders. Peter Cheyney. LC 44-7717. (Murder mystery monthly. No. 21). 1944. Avon Book Company.

Counterattack. Frank Scarpetta. (Marksman,#11). 1974. (pbk.) 0.95. Belmont Tower Books.

Counterclockwise. Mary Jane Ward. LC 70-88852. 1969. 5.95. H. Regnery.

Countercommandment. John Wood Campbell. Orig. Title: Analog Five. 1970. pap. 0.75 o.p. (0502-07067). Curtis.

Counterfeit. Lee Thayer. LC 33-22046. Sears Publishing Company.

Counterfeit. William H Wheeler. LC 78-72326. (Pacemaker bestellers book). (Illus.). 3.32 (ISBN 0-8224-5363-0). Fearon Pitman Publishers.

Counterfeit Agent. Nick Carter. (Nick Carter Ser.). (O.s.i.). 176p. 1975. pap. 1.25 o.s.i. (AQ1439, Award). Univ Pub & Dist.

Counterfeit Agent. Nick Carter. (Killmaster spy chiller). 1975. (pbk.) 1.25. Award Books.

Counterfeit Bride. Vivian Connolly. (Coventry Romance Ser.: No. 68). 224p. 1980. pap. 1.75 (ISBN 0-449-50099-3, Coventry). Fawcett.

Counterfeit Bride. Sara Craven. (Harlequin Presents Ser.). 192p. 1983. pap. 1.75 (ISBN 0-373-10561-4). Harlequin Bks.

Counterfeit Bridegroom. 1st Ed. Lowell Mason Borden. LC 56-10560. 1956. Vantage Press.

Counterfeit Citizen. Sam Scudder. LC 8-19724. Broadway Publishing Company.

Counterfeit Corpse. Nii Akrampahene Vanderpuije. LC 56-12338. Comet Press Books.

Counterfeit Courtship. Prudence Martin. (Candlelight Regency Ser.: No. 710). (Orig.). 1982. pap. 1.95 (ISBN 0-440-11314-8). Dell.

Counterfeit Honeymoon. Julia Anders. (Orig.). 1980. pap. 1.50 (ISBN 0-440-11138-2). Dell.

Counterfeit Husband. Elizabeth Mansfield, pseud. 224p. 1982. pap. 2.25 (ISBN 0-425-05336-9). Berkley Pub.

Counterfeit Kill. Howard Hunt. 1975. (pbk.) 1.25 (ISBN 0-523-00589-X). Pinnacle Books.

Counterfeit Lady Unveiled: And Other Criminal Fiction of Seventeenth-Century England. 1st Ed. Ed. by Spiro Peterson. LC 61-6791. (Anchor books, A232). 1961. Doubleday.

Counterfeit Life. Inna Varlamova. Tr. by David Lowe from Rus. 107p. 1983. lib. bdg. 15.00 (ISBN 0-88233-823-4); pap. price not set (ISBN 0-88233-824-2). Ardis Pubs.

Counterfeit Love. Jacquelyn Aeby. (Candlelight romance). 1975. (pbk.) 0.75. Dell.

Counterfeit Marriage. Joan Wolf. LC 81-17518. 1982. 12.95 (ISBN 0-89340-387-3). J. Curley & Associates.

Counterfeit Murder. William Bannister. (Orig.). pap. 0.60 o.p. (73-710). Lancer.

Counterfeit Venus. Norma Gilbert. (Orig.). pap. 0.95 o.p. (1120). Brandon.

Counterfeit Virgin. Roy McCoy. 1968. pap. 1.25 o.p. (2072). Brandon.

Counterfeit Wife. Davis Dresser. LC 47-3422. 1947. Ziff-Davis Publishing Company.

Counterfeit Wife. Richard Kent. LC 36-7193. Phoenix Press.

Counterfeiter, and Other Stories. Yasushi Inoue. LC 65-20614. (Series: UNESCO Collection of Representative Works: Japanese Series). (Library of Japanese literature). 1965. C. E. Tuttle Co.

Counterfeiter: And Other Stories. Tr. from Japanese Introd. by Leon Picon. Yasushim Inoue. LC 65-20614. (Lib. of Japanese lit.). (Title: (Series: UNESCO collection of representative works: Japanese series). 3.50. Tuttle.

Counterfeiters. Andre Paul Guillaume Gide. 1951. 4.95 o.s.i. (ISBN 0-394-60327-3, M327). Modern Lib.

Counterfeiters: Les Faux-Monnayeurs. Andre Paul Guillaume Gide. Tr. by Bussy, Dorothy (Strachey) LC 27-191824. 1927. A. A. Knopf.

Counterfeiters: Les Faux-Monnayeurs. Andre Paul Guillaume Gide. Tr. by Raymond Melbourne Weaver. LC 31-27009. (Half-title: The modern library of the world's best books). The Modern Library.

Counterfeiters: Les Faux-Monnayeurs. Andre Paul Guillaume Gide. Tr. by Dorothy Strachey Bussy. Weaver, Raymond Melbourne, 1888- LC 44-22836. (Half-title: The Modern library of the world's best books). The Modern Library.

Counterfeiters; with Journal of The Counterfeiters. Andre Paul Guillaume Gide. LC 72-8064. 1973. (pbk.) 2.45 (ISBN 0-394-71842-9). Vintage Books.

Counterfeiters: With Journal of The Counterfeiters. Andre Paul Guillaume Gide. LC 51-2384. 1951. Knopf.

Counterfeits. Marjorie Colville Strachey. LC 27-7672. 1927. Longmans, Green and Co.

Counterflood. Kit Thackeray. LC 79-89486. 1979. 8.95 (ISBN 0-688-03579-5). Morrow.

Counterpane Fairy. Katharine Pyle. LC 4-161509. 1898. E. P. Dutton & Co.

Counterpart. Joseph Harmor Coates. LC 9-25629. 1909. 1.00. The Macaulay Company.

Counterparts. Dean S. Flower. LC 75-149164. (Fawcett premier book, P510). 1971. 1.25. Fawcett Publications.

Counterparts: A Novel. Tom Baum. LC 74-120471. 1970. 4.95. Dial Press.

Counterparts: Classic & Contemporary American Short Stories. Ed. by Dean S. Flower. (Orig.). 1971. pap. 1.25 o.p. (P624, Prem). Fawcett World.

Counterparts: Or, The Cross of Love. Elizabeth Sara Sheppard & Upton, George Putnam, 1834-1919, Ed. 1893. A. C. McClurg and Company.

Counterplot. Hope Mirrlees. 1925. A. A. Knopf.

Counterpoint. Isabelle Holland. LC 79-91330. 9.95 (ISBN 0-89256-121-1). Rawson, Wade Publishers.

Counterpoint. Isabelle Holland. LC 80-27954. 11.95 (ISBN 0-89621-262-9). Thorndike Press.

Counterpoint Murder. George Douglas Howard Cole & Margaret Isabel Postgate Cole. LC 41-5218. 1941. The Macmillan Company.

Counterpol. John Boland. LC 65-15552. 1965. Walker.

Counterpol in Paris. John Boland. LC 65-18630. 1965. bds., 3.50. Walker.

Countersign: A Story of Tibet. Claude Perry Jones. LC 9-29779. 1909. 1.50. R. G. Badger.

Counterspy. Brian Talbot Cleeve. Orig. Title: Vote X for Treason. pap. 0.60 o.p. (73-520). Lancer.

Counterspy Express. Albert Sidney Fleischman. LC 54-31247. (Ace double novel books, D-57). 1954. Ace Books.

Counterstroke. Andrew Garve. (Crime Monthly Ser). 1979. pap. 1.95 o.p. (ISBN 0-14-005270-4). Penguin.

Counterstroke. Andrew Garve. LC 78-378. 1978. 11.49i (ISBN 0-690-01748-0, TYC-T). T Y Crowell.

Counterstroke. Patrick Wayland. LC 64-17030. 1964. Published for the Crime Club by Doubleday.

Counterstroke. Paul Winterton. LC 78-378. 8.95 (ISBN 0-690-01749-9). Crowell.

Counterstroke. Paul Winterton. LC 79-15290. (Penguin crime fiction). 1979. 1.95 (ISBN 0-14-005270-4). Penguin Boks.

Counterweight. 1st Ed. Daniel Broun. LC 62-149150. (Rinehart suspense novel). 1962. Holt, Rinehart and Winston.

Countess. Eddie Constantine. (Orig.). 1980. pap. 2.50 (ISBN 0-440-11501-9). Dell.

Countess. March Cost, pseud. LC 63-13789. (O.s.i.). 1963. 6.95 o.s.i. (ISBN 0-8149-0076-3). Vanguard.

Countess. Josephine Edgar, pseud. LC 77-18457. 1978. 8.95 (ISBN 0-312-17027-0). St Martin.

Countess. Mary Howard, pseud. LC 77-18457. 8.95 (ISBN 0-312-17027-0). St. Martin's Press.

Countess. Peggy Morrison, pseud. LC 63-13789. 1963. Vanguard Press.

Countess Angelique. Anne Golon. 1968. Putnam.

Countess at War. Jane Lane. 1971. pap. 0.95 o.p. (95129). Beagle Bks.

Countess Below Stairs. Eva Ibbotson. 288p. 1982. pap. 2.95 (ISBN 0-380-61374-3, 61374-3). Avon.

Countess Bettina: The History of an Innocent Acandal... Clinton Ross. LC 8-669. (On cover: The Hudson library, no. 5). 1895. G. P. Putnam's Sons.

Countess: By Hans Habe Pseud. Translated from the German by Catherine Hutter. Hans Habe. LC 63-17770. 1963. Harcourt, Brace & World.

Countess Carrots. Molly Costain Haycraft. LC 72-11773. 1973. 4.95 (ISBN 0-397-00963-1). Lippincott.

Countess Daphne. Eliza M. J. Humphreys. LC 41-42128. (On cover: Lovell's library, no. 1155). 1888. J. W. Lovell Company.

Countess De Charny: A Sequel to "Taking the Bastile,". Alexandre Dumas. LC 3-276185. G. Routledge and Sons, Limited.

Countess De Charny. An Historical Romance. Alexandre Dumas. (Seaside library, v. 10, no. 184). G. Munro.

Countess De Charny. An Historical Romance. Alexandre Dumas. LC 6-42833. (American series, no. 317). M. J. Ivers & Co.

Countess De Charny: An Historical Romance. Alexandre Dumas. LC 6-42831. (On cover: Seaside library. Pocket ed. no. 2122). G. Munro's Sons.

Countess De Greenpoint-Brooklyn: A Novelistic Extravaganza. Witold D Sokolinski. LC 54-24183. 1954. Ignis Co.

Countess Diane. Henry Cottrell Rowland. LC 8-22243. 1908. Dodd, Mead & Company.

Countess Dracula. Michel Parry. 1971. pap. 0.75 o.p. (94081). Beagle Bks.

Countess Dynar: Or, Polish Blood. A Novel. From the German of Natally Von Eschstruth. with illustrations by james fagan. ed. Nataly Von Eschstruth & Turner, Cora Louise, Tr. LC 6-38159. (choice ser. no. 102). 1894. R. Bonner's Sons.

Countess Erika's Apprenticeship. Lula Kirschner. Tr. by Wister, Annia Lee (Furness) LC 7-12816. 1891. J. B. Lippincott Company.

Countess Eve. Joseph Henry Shorthouse. LC 34-377949. 1888. Macmillan and Co.

Countess Eve. Joseph Henry Shorthouse. LC 8-7334. (On cover: Harper's Franklin square library, no. 633). 1888. Harper & Brothers.

Countess Eve. Joseph Henry Shorthouse. LC 10-1171. (On cover: Lovell's library. no. 1305). 1888. J. W. Lovell Company.

Countess Eve. Joseph Henry Shorthouse. (On cover: Seaside library. Pocket ed. no. 1148). 1888. G. Munro.

Countess Gisela. Eugenie John. LC 7-9899. (On cover: Seaside library. Pocket ed. no. 1115). G. Munro.

Countess Gisela: From the German of E. Marlitt Pseud.... Eugenie John. Tr. by Wister, Annis Lee (Furness) LC 4-31665. 1879. J. B. Lippincott & Co.

Countess Gisela, from the German of E. Marlitt Pseud.... Eugenie John. Tr. by Wister, Annis Lee (Furness) LC 13-12925. 1897. J. B. Lippincott Company.

Countess Helena: A Novel, by Gertrude Hague. Gertrude Hague. LC 3682. 1900. G. W. Dillingham Company.

Countess Ida. A Tale of Berlin. Theodore Sedgwick Fay. LC 6-38774. 1840. Harper & Brothers.

Countess Janina: An Historical Novel from Russian Life. Gustav Genrychowitch Taube. LC 9-2225. 1894. G. W. Dillingham.

Countess Loreley: A Novel; Tr. from the German of Rudolf Menger. Rudolf Menger. Tr. by Dandridge, Miss. LC 7-25842. (On cover: Appletons' town and country library. no. 43). 1889. D. Appleton and Company.

Countess Margo. Scott Stone. LC 55-2509. 1955. Vixen Press.

Countess Obernau. A Novel. Ida Marie Louise Sophie Friedericke Gustava Hann-Hahn & Cruger, Julie Grinnell (Storrow) "Mrs. Van Rensselaer Cruger," Tr. LC 6-46157. (choice series. no. 106). 1894. R. Bonner's Sons.

Countess of Lowndes Square: And Other Stories. Edward Frederic Benson. LC 22-15674. 1920. Cassell and Company, Ltd.

Countess of Monte Cristo... A Sequel to The Count of Monte Cristo, by Alexander Drumas. Jean Charles Du Boys. LC 6-34634. (On cover: Lovell's library. no. 891). J. W. Lovell Company.

Countess of Pembroke's Arcadia. Philip Sidney & Bellings, Richard, D. 1677. (On cover: Early novelists; ed. by E. A. Baker). 1907. G. Routledge and Sons, Ltd.

Countess of Pembroke's Arcadia. Philip Sidney & Maurice Evans. LC 78-301565. (Penguin English library). 1977. 4.95 (ISBN 0-14-043111-X). Penguin.

Countess of Pembroke's Arcadia. Philip Sidney & Stirling, William Alexander, 1st Earl of, 1567?-1640. LC 24-11849. (Library of early novelists, ed. by E. A. Baker. v. 12). 1921. G. Routledge and Sons, Ltd.

Countess of Pembroke's Arcadia (the Old Arcadia). Philip Sidney. Ed. by Jean Robertson. LC 73-163390. (Illus.). 1973. Clarendon Press.

Countess of Rudolstadt, a Sequel to Consuelo. George Sand. LC 12-23264. A. L. Burt Company.

Countess of Rudolstadt. A Sequel to "Consuelo". George Sand & Robinson, Fayette, D. 1859, Tr. LC 6-34615. T. B. Peterson & Brothers.

Countess of Sedgwick. Marie Duell. LC 79-9471. 1980. 12.95 (ISBN 0-07-017976-X). McGraw-Hill.

Countess Pharamond: A Sequel to "Sheba". Eliza M. J. Humphreys. LC 7-5788. United States Book Company.

Countess Radna: A Novel. William Edward Norris. LC 7-33297. Lovell, Coryell & Company.

Countess Rudolstadt: Being a Sequel to "Consuelo.". George Sand & Potter, Frank Hunter, Tr. LC 6-34613. 1891. Dodd, Mead & Company.

Countess to Boot. Jack Iams. LC 41-1828. 1941. W. Morrow & Company.

Countess Vera. Alexander McVeigh Miller. (Lovell's library, no. 1252). 1888. J. W. Lovell Company.

Countess Vera: Or, The Oath of Vengeance. Alexander McVeigh Miller. (On cover: Munro's library, v. 1, no. 8). N. L. Munro.

Countess Yalta: Or, The Nihilist Spy. Fortune Du Boisgobey & Lee, S., Tr. LC 6-34427. (On cover: Echo series. no. 88). 1889. Pollard & Moss.

Counting My Buttons. Esther Pence Garber. LC 79-544. 1.95 (ISBN 0-87178-157-3). Brethren Press.

Counting the Cost: Or, A Summer at Chautauqua. Cornelia Adele Teal. LC 8-26034. 1889. Hunt & Eaton.

Counting the Days. James Sterling Tippett & Wolcott, Elizabeth Tyler, 1803- Illus. LC 40-32647. Harper & Brothers.

Counting the Eons. Isaac Asimov. LC 82-45068. 192p. 1983. 13.95 (ISBN 0-385-17976-6). Doubleday.

Country. David Plante. LC 81-66002. 1981. 9.95 (ISBN 0-689-11189-4). Atheneum.

Country & Fatal. George Bagby, pseud. LC 79-6097. (Crime Club Ser.). 192p. 1980. 8.95 o.p. (ISBN 0-385-17004-1). Doubleday.

Country and Fatal. Aaron Marc Stein. LC 79-6097. 1980. 8.95 (ISBN 0-385-17004-1). Published for the Crime Club by Doubleday.

Country Band. Henry Augustus Shute. LC 9-112. 1909. R. G. Badger.

Country Beyond. James Oliver Curwood. LC 44-219539. 1943. Triangle Books.

Country Beyond: A Romance of the Wilderness. James Oliver Curwood. LC 22-15205. 1922. Cosmopolitan Book Corporation.

Country Beyond: A Romance of the Wilderness. James Oliver Curwood. LC 30-123429. 1925. Grosset & Dunlap.

Country Born. Theodore R. Connely. 1974. 8.95 o.s.i. (ISBN 0-8181-0329-9). Pageant-Poseidon.

Country Boy. Forrest Crissey. LC 3-28136. 1903. F. H. Revell Company.

Country Boy. Charles Sarver & Selwyn, Edgar. LC 12-1132. The H. K. Fly Company.

Country Bunch. Read. 256p. 1963. 9.95 o.p. (ISBN 0-7181-0069-7, Pub. by Michael Joseph). Merrimack Pub Cir.

Country Bunny and the Little Gold Shoes: As Told to Jennifer. Du Bose Hayward. (Sandpiper book). 1974. (pbk.) 1.25 (ISBN 0-395-18557-2). Houghton, Mifflin.

Country by-Ways. Sarah Orne Jewett. LC 76-94735. (Short story index reprint series). 1969. Books for Libraries Press.

Country by-Ways. 8th ed. Sarah Orne Jewett. LC 3-26183. 1892. Houghton, Mifflin and Company.

Country by-Ways see Collected Works.

Country Child. Alison Uttley. LC 32-1165. 1931. The Macmillan Company.

Country Child. Illus. by C. F. Tunnicliffe. Alison Uttley. (Peacock bk. PK9). 1963. pap., 1.25. Penguin.

Country Chronicle. Grant Showerman. LC 16-22047. 1916. The Century Co.

Country Chronicle. Gladys Bagg Taber. (Adult Ser.). 318p. 1974. Repr. lib. bdg. 8.95 o.p. (ISBN 0-8161-6212-3, Large Print Bks). G K Hall.

Country Club. Nancy Bruff, pseud. 1969. 6.95 o.p. Bartholomew.

Country Club. Nancy Bruff Gardner. LC 79-96135. 1969. 6.95. Bartholomew House.

Country Club. Russell O'Neil. 2.50 (ISBN 0-671-81288-2). Pocket Books.

Country Club Caper. Grover C Gulick. LC 76-125528. 1971. 5.95. Doubleday.

Country Club People. Margaret Culkin Banning. LC 23-8187. George H. Doran Company.

Country Cooking & Other Stories. Harry Mathews. (Burning Deck Fiction Ser.). (Illus.). 90p. 1980. 15.00 (ISBN 0-930900-81-2); pap. 4.00 (ISBN 0-930900-82-0). Burning Deck.

Country Cousin. Louis Auchincloss. LC 78-7233. 1978. 8.95 (ISBN 0-395-26687-4). Houghton Mifflin.

Country Cousin. Louis Auchincloss. LC 79-21560. 1980. 2.25 (ISBN 0-89340-243-5). J. Curley.

Country Cousin. Douglas C. Gallery. 3.95 o.p. Vantage.

Country Cousin: A Novel. Frances Mary Peard. (On cover: Harper's Franklin Square library, no. 643). 1889. Harper & Brothers.

Country Cousins. Michael Brownstein. LC 74-79059. 256p. 1974. 7.95 (ISBN 0-8076-0749-5, Venture Bks.). Braziller.

Country Dance. Margiad Evans. 1980. 11.50 (ISBN 0-7145-3593-1); pap. 4.95 (ISBN 0-7145-3728-4). Riverrun NY.

Country Dance. Katharine Morris. LC 53-6063. 1953. Dutton.

Country Doctor. Honore De Balzac. Tr. by Katharine Prescott Wormeley. LC 3-23174. (Half-title: The comedy of human life... Scenes from country life). 1887. Roberts Brothers.

Country Doctor. Honore De Balzac. Tr. by Katharine Prescott Wormeley. LC 3-23173. (Half-title: The comedy of human life... Scenes from country life). 1889. Roberts Brothers.

Country Doctor. Honore De Balzac. Tr. by Katharine Prescott Wormeley. LC 26-26979. (Half-title: The works of Balzac. Centenary ed. vol. xxiv). 1904. Little, Brown, and Company.

Country Doctor. Honore De Balzac. (Half-title: Everyman's library, ed. by Ernest Rhys. Fiction. no. 530). 1911. J. M. Dent & Sons, Ltd.

Country Doctor. Honore De Balzac. Tr. by Ellen Marriage. LC 36-37337. (Half-title: Everyman's library, ed. by E. Rhys. Fiction. no. 530). 1923. J. M. Dent & Sons, Ltd.

Country Doctor. Honore De Balzac. Tr. by E. Marriage. 3.95x o.p. (ISBN 0-460-00530-8, E530, Evman). Dutton.

Country Doctor. Sarah Orne Jewett. LC 70-104497. 1970. Literature House.

Country Doctor. Sarah Orne Jewett. LC 4-23597. 1884. Houghton, Mifflin and Company.

Country Doctor see Collected Works.

Country Doctor's Notebook. Mikhail Afanasevich Bulgakou. 1975. (pbk.) 1.50. Bantam Books.

Country Dying: A Novel. Robert C. Down. LC 75-31686. 224p. 1976. 7.95 o.p. (ISBN 0-672-52193-8). Bobbs.

Country Dying: A Novel. Robert C S Downs. LC 75-31686. 7.95 (ISBN 0-672-52193-8). Bobbs-Merrill.

Country Editor. Grace Edgington Jordan. LC 76-40707. 1976. 9.00. Syms-York.

Country Editor's Boy see High, Wide & Lonesome.

Country Folk. Peter H. Ditchfield. 256p. 1974. Repr. of 1923 ed. text ed. 19.00x o.s.i. (ISBN 0-8277-3239-2). British Bk Ctr.

Country for Old Men and Other Stories. E. R Zietlow. LC 76-58238. 4.95. (ISBN 0-917624-05-X) (ISBN 0-917624-02-5). Lame Johnny Press.

Country Full of Guns. E. R. Slade. (Orig.). 1979. pap. 1.50 (ISBN 0-532-15402-9). Woodhill.

Country Gentleman. Margaret Oliphant Wilson Oliphant. (On cover: Lovell's library, v. 14. no. 717). 1886. J. W. Lovell Company.

Country Gentleman. A Novel. Margaret Oliphant Wilson Oliphant. (Harper's Franklin square library, no. 507). 1886. Harper & Brothers.

Country Gentleman. A Novel. Margaret Oliphant Wilson Oliphant. (On cover: Seaside library. Pocket ed., no. 687). 1886. G. Munro.

Country Girl. Margaretta Brucker. LC 42-733645. 1942. Gramercy Publishing Co.

Country Girl. Lillian Cornell. LC 6-28736. The Irving Company.

Country Girl. Darrell Husted. LC 79-19640. 1980. 9.95 (ISBN 0-89340-240-0). J. Curley.

Country Girl in Town. Brighton. pap. 1.95 o.p. (ISBN 0-87977-140-2, DBB140). Dansk Blue Bk.

Country Girls. Edna O'Brien. 1975. pap. 1.95 o.p. (ISBN 0-14-001851-4). Penguin.

Country Girls. 1st Ed. Edna O'Brien. LC 60-7490. 1960. Knopf.

Country Growth. August William Derleth. LC 40-11748. 1940. C. Scribner's Sons.

Country-Harbor-Quite-Act-Around (Selected Prose) Larry Eigner, pseud. Ed. by Barrett Watten. (Orig.). 1978. 10.00 (Pub by This Pr); pap. 4.00; signed ltd. ed. 15.00. SBD.

Country Heart. Isabel Dick. LC 46-2359. 1946. Thomas Y. Crowell Company.

Country Holiday. Frances Woodhouse. LC 35-14723. 1935. G. P. Putnam's Sons.

Country Home: Or, Events of a Season. Maria Hildreth Parker. LC 7-34983. 1894. Citizen Newspaper Co., Printers.

Country House. Desmond Greig. LC 69-11691. 1969. 4.95. Viking Press.

Country House: A Novel. John Galsworthy. LC 7-15919. 1907. G. P. Putnam's Sons.

Country-House Burglar. Michael Francis Gilbert. LC 55-8043. 1955. Harper.

Country in the Boy. William Thomas. LC 75-14049. 1975. (ISBN 0-8407-6435-9). T. Nelson.

Country Interlude: A Novelette. Hildegarde Hawthorne. LC 4-394919. 1904. Houghton, Mifflin and Company.

Country Judge: A Novel of Chile. Pedro Prado. LC 68-10396. 1968-1967. University of California Press.

Country Killing. Max F. Harris. 1980. pap. 1.95 (ISBN 0-8439-0836-X). Nordon Pubns.

Country Kind of Death. Mary McMullen. LC 74-31516. 1975. 5.95 (ISBN 0-385-07733-5). Published for the Crime Club by Doubleday.

Country Lanes and City Pavements: A Realistic Story of Metropolitan Life. Maurice Meyer Minton. LC 1317. (On cover: Eagle library, no. 145). 1900. Street & Smith.

Country Lass: By Regina and Roy D'Ariano. Regina D'Ariano & Roy D'Ariano. LC 53-6470. Vantage Press.

Country Lawyer. Henry Augustus Shute. LC 11-27806. 1911. Houghton Mifflin Company.

Country Love and Poison Rain. Peter Tate. LC 72-89352. (Doubleday science fiction). 1973. 5.95 (ISBN 0-385-06695-3). Doubleday.

Country Luck. John Habberton. LC 6-466791. 1887. J. B. Lippincott Company.

Country Man. Charles Kennon Henderson. LC 7-255049. 1907. The Neals Publishing Company.

Country Music. Nancy Bacon. (Love & Life Romance Ser.). 160p. (Orig.). 1982. pap. 1.75 (ISBN 0-345-29759-8). Ballantine.

Country Music. Charles William Smith. LC 75-8952. 1975. 8.95 (ISBN 0-374-13030-2). Farrar, Straus and Giroux.

Country Neighborhood. Eliza Ann Dupuy. LC 6-35859. 1855. Harper & Brothers.

Country Neighbors. Alice Brown. LC 10-9516. 1910. 1.20. Houghton Mifflin Company.

Country Neighbors: A Long Island Pastoral. Susan Taber. LC 12-3791. 1912. 1.20. Duffield & Company.

Country of Again. Philip Maitland Hubbard. LC 67-29715. 1968. Atheneum.

Country of Love. 1st Ed. Malissa Redfield, pseud. LC 66-209796. 1966. 3.95. Doubleday.

Country of Marriage: A Novel. Jon Cleary. LC 62-140085. 1962. Morrow.

Country of Old Men. Paul Olsen. 1966. 4.95 o.p. (ISBN 0-03-057175-8). HR&W.

Country of Old Men: A Novel. Paul Olsen. LC 66-13105. 4.95. Holt.

Country of Our Consciousness, Selected Poems. Theodore Enslin. 1971. signed ed. fifty copies o.p. 15.00 ea.; pap. 3.50. Sand Dollar.

Country of Strangers. Conrad Richter. 1975. (pbk.) 1.25. Bantam Books.

Country of Strangers. Conrad Richter. LC 66-14921. (Illus.). 1966. Knopf.

Country of Strangers. Conrad Richter. LC 81-16548. 1982. 5.95 (ISBN 0-8052-0695-7). Schocken Books.

Country of the Blind, & Other Stories. facsimile ed. Herbert George Wells. LC 78-144174. (Short Story Index Reprint Ser.). Repr. of 1913 ed. 25.00 (ISBN 0-8369-3789-9). Ayer Co.

Country of the Pointed Firs. Sarah Orne Jewett. LC 72-84612. (Series: Riverside Library.). (Illus.). 1974. 12.50 (ISBN 0-403-03092-7). Scholarly Press.

Country of the Pointed Firs. Sarah Orne Jewett. LC 7-9931. 1896. Houghton, Mifflin and Company.

Country of the Pointed Firs. 13th thousand ed. Sarah Orne Jewett. LC 4-15463. Houghton, Mifflin and Company.

Country of the Pointed Firs. Sarah Orne Jewett. LC 10-23633. Houghton, Mifflin Company.

Country of the Pointed Firs see Collected Works.

Country of the Pointed Firs, and Other Stories. Sarah Orne Jewett. LC 54-359416. (Doubleday anchor books, A 26). 1954. Doubleday.

Country of the Pointed Firs: And Other Stories. Sarah Orne Jewett. Ed. by Mary Ellen Chase. LC 68-22719. (Illus.). 1968. 5.79. Norton.

Country of the Pointed Firs, and Other Stories. Sarah Orne Jewett & Mary Ellen Chase. LC 81-16796. 1982. 5.95 (ISBN 0-393-00048-6). W.W. Norton.

Country of the Strangers. Frances Shelley Wees. LC 60-6917. 1960. Published for the Crime Club of Doubleday.

Country of the Wolf. Sharon Wagner. 1970. pap. 0.75 o.p. (ISBN 0-447-74681-2). Lancer.

Country of the Wolf see Curse of Still Valley.

Country of the Young. Catherine Lindsay. LC 46-6842. 1946. Reynal & Hitchcock.

Country of the Young: A Novel. Marvin Schiller. LC 65-24330. 4.95. Crown.

Country Parson. Honore De Balzac. LC 37-30950. (Everyman's library, ed. by Ernest Rhys. Fiction. no. 686). 1930. J. M. Dent & Sons, Ltd.

Country People. Ruth Suckow. LC 76-51678. (Recovered Fiction by American Women). 1977. 17.00 (ISBN 0-405-10056-6). Arno Press.

Country People. Ruth Suckow. LC 24-122819. 1924. A. A. Knopf.

Country Place. Ann Lane Petry. LC 71-151616. 1971. (ISBN 0-911860-04-5). Chatham Bookseller.

Country Place. Ann Lane Petry. LC 47-11040. 1947. Houghton Mifflin Co.

Country Romance. P. V. Collins & Case, J. I., Threshing Machine Co., Racine, Wis. LC 6-26960. 1896. J. H. Yewdale & Sons Co.

Country Salt: A Historical Novel. Howard Babcock Drake. LC 51-11414. 1951. Dorrance.

Country Scene Digest. Ed. by James A. Kuse. (Illus.). 1979. pap. 6.95 (ISBN 0-89542-353-7). Ideals.

Country Sketches. M I Pollock. LC 10-8935. 1910. Cochrane Publishing Company.

Country Stories. Mary Russell Mitford. LC 70-110208. (Short story index reprint series). (Illus.). 1970. (ISBN 0-8369-3359-1). Books for Libraries Press.

Country Style Romance. Marzee King Tew. (YA) 1979. 6.95 (Avalon). Bouregy.

Country Sweetheart. Dora Russell. (On cover: Globe library, v. l., no. 199). 1895. Rand, McNally & Company.

Country Team. Robert Lowell Moore. LC 66-26198. 1967. Crown Publishers.

Country to Serve. Edythe Watson Jakoubek. LC 56-12361. 1956. Pageant Press.

Country Town Sayings see Collected Works.

Country Waif: Francois le Champi. George Sand. LC 76-14125. 10.95 (ISBN 0-8032-0888-X) (ISBN 0-8032-5850-X). University of Nebraska Press.

Country Wedding. Berry Fleming. 128p. 1983. 8.95 (ISBN 0-932298-29-X). Copple Hse.

Country Window. Mabel Goode Frantz. LC 38-5871. Fleming H. Revell Company.

Countryside Ideals. Ed. by James A. Kuse & Ralph D. Luedke. 1978. pap. 2.50 o.p. (ISBN 0-89542-315-4). Ideals.

Countrywoman: A Novel. Paul Smith. LC 61-13360. 1961. Scribner.

Count's Ball. Raymond Radiguet. Tr. by Cowley, Malcolm. LC 29-23796. W. W. Norton & Company, Inc.

Count's Millions... Emile Gaboriau. LC 6-44561. (On cover: Lovell's library. no. 1123). 1888. J. W. Lovell Company.

Count's Millions: Tr. from the French of Emile Gaboriau. Emile Gaboriau. LC 13-8286. 1913. C. Scribner's Sons.

Count's Secret. From the French of Emile Gaboriau... Emile Gaboriau. LC 6-44558. Estes and Lauriat.

Count's Snuff-Box: A Romance of Washington and Buzzard's Bay During the War of 1812. George Robert Russell Rivers. LC 98-1073. 1898. Little, Brown, and Company.

County: A Story of Social Life. LC 6-28994. (On cover: Harper's Franklin square library, no. 654). 1889. Harper & Brothers.

County Agent Meets a Home Demon: A Novel. 1st Ed. Olga Inez Ross. Pageant Press.

County Chronicle. Thirkell, Angela (Mackail) LC 50-9976. 1950. Knopf.

County Court. Roy Catesby Flannagan. LC 37-33112. 1937. Doubleday, Doran & Company, Inc.

County Court. Roy Catesby Flannagan. LC 40-2692. (A Mercury book. no. 22). The American Mercury, Inc.

County Doctor. Peggy Gaddis, pseud. LC 45-9831. 1945. Arcadia House, Inc.

County Fair: A Comedy in Four Acts. Charles Barnard & Burgess, Neil. LC 6-7209. (Street & Smith's select series, no. 23). 1890. S. French; Street & Smith.

County Lines: Stories and Songs of the West. Lincoln Fitzell. LC 47-11925. 1947. Swallow Press.

County Nurse. Maud McCurdy Welch. LC 56-13509. Avalon Books.

County Nurse: By Peggy Dern. Peggy Gaddis, pseud. LC 56-7017. 1956. Arcadia House.

County of Talavera: From the Dutch of J. Van Lennep, by A. Arnold Pseud. Jakob Van Lennep & Salomons, Alfred, Tr. LC 8-30864. (Modern foreign library). 1884. J.W. Lovell Company.

County Road. Alice Brown. LC 68-23713. 1968. Gregg Press.

County Road. Alice Brown. 1906. Houghton, Mifflin and Company.

County Seat. Paul Corey. LC 41-14431. The Bobbs-Merrill Company.

County Woman. Joan Williams. LC 81-18571. 13.95 (ISBN 0-316-94237-5). Little, Brown.

Coup. John Updike. 1980. 2.95 (ISBN 0-449-24259-5). Fawcett Crest Books.

Coup: A Novel. John Updike. LC 78-55399. 1978. 8.95 (ISBN 0-394-50268-X). Knopf.

Coup De Grace: Translated from the French by Grace Frick in Collaboration with the Author. Marguerite Yourcenar. LC 57-10687. 1957. Farrar, Straus and Cudahy.

Coup D'etat. Jacque Lloyd Morgan. LC 13-6076. R. F. Fenno & Company.

Couple Called Moebius: Eleven Sensual Stories. Carol Berge. LC 72-80797. 1972. 6.50. Bobbs-Merrill.
Couple of Comedians: A Novel. Don Carpenter. LC 79-18103. 9.95 (ISBN 0-671-22839-0). Simon and Schuster.
Couple of Quick Ones. Eric Hatch. LC 28-27593. 1928. R. M. McBride & Company.
Coupled. John U. Pike. Orig. Title: Matinees. 1969. pap. 0.95 o.p. (1029). Belmont-Tower.
Coupled. Gil Porter. pap. 1.95 o.p. (0110). Essex Hse.
Coupled. Gil Porter. pap. 1.95 o.p. (ISBN 0-87056-250-9, 6250). Brandon.
Couples. John Updike. 1978. pap. 2.95 (ISBN 0-449-24023-1, Crest). Fawcett.
Couples. John Updike. LC 68-12996. 1968. 12.50 (ISBN 0-394-42066-7). Knopf.
Couples: A Short Story. John Updike. LC 76-23525. 1976. (ISBN 0-912604-10-7). Halty Ferguson.
Couples, Loving Couples. Marco Vassi. LC 77-2264. 1977. 7.95 (ISBN 0-8128-2273-0). Stein and Day.
Coupling Game. Peter Kanto. LC 74-9995. (Traveller's companion series, TC-452). 1969. 1.95. Traveller's Companion, Inc.
Couplings: A Book of Stories. Richard Walter Hall. LC 80-26609. 12.00 (ISBN 0-912516-57-7) (ISBN 0-912516-58-5). Grey Fox Press.
Coupon Bonds: And Other Stories. John Townsend Trowbridge. LC 69-11924. (American short story series, v. 83). 1969. (ISBN 0-512-00704-7). Garrett Press.
Coupon Bonds, and Other Stories. John Townsend Trowbridge. LC 72-8313. (American short story series, v. 83). 1972. (ISBN 0-8422-8119-3). MSS Information Corp.
Coupon Bonds: And Other Stories. John Townsend Trowbridge. LC 5-26929. Lee and Shepard.
Courage. John H Shannon. LC 74-23961. (Illus.). 1975. 6.95 (ISBN 0-393-08711-5). Norton.
Courage Covenant. Blaine M. Yorgason. LC 82-165010. 1982. 6.95 (ISBN 0-88494-455-7). Bookcraft.
Courage Has Eyes. Trumbull Reed. LC 48-3510. 1945. Westminister Press.
Courage in Crisis: Dramatic Tales of Heroism in the Face of Danger. Vincent H. Gaddis. 192p. 1973. 6.95 o.p. (ISBN 0-8015-1782-6). Hawthorn.
Courage in Darkness. Sarah Shears. 1974. 8.95 (ISBN 0-236-31066-6, Pub. by Paul Elek). Merrimack Pub Cir.
Courage in Her Pocket. Janice Longley. LC 34-35701. 1934. Macrae-Smith Company.
Courage in Korea: Stories of the Korean War. 1st Ed. Ed. by Albert B Tibbets. LC 62-12384. 1962. Little, Brown.
Courage in Parting. Sarah Shears. LC 77-374408. 1977. 7.95 (ISBN 0-236-40098-3). P. Elek.
Courage in War. Sarah Shears. LC 77-361825. 1976. 7.95 (ISBN 0-236-40064-9). Elek.
Courage Is Not Given. Katherine Drayton Mayrant Simons. LC 52-11822. 1952. Appleton-Century-Crofts.
Courage of Black Beauty. I. M Richardson. Anna Sewell. LC 82-7090. (Richardson, I. M. Anna Sewell's The Adventures of Black Beauty: Bk. 3). 8.79 (ISBN 0-89375-814-0) (ISBN 0-89375-815-9). Troll Associates.
Courage of Blackburn Blair. Eleanor Talbot Kinkead. LC 7-34180. 1907. Moffat, Yard & Company.
Courage of Captain Plum. James Oliver Curwood. LC 71-144593. (Illus.). 1972. 10.00 (ISBN 0-404-01895-5). AMS Press.
Courage of Captain Plum. James Oliver Curwood. 1908. The Bobbs-Merrill Company.
Courage of Captain Plum. James Oliver Curwood. LC 24-27980. Grosset & Dunlap.
Courage of Conviction: A Novel. Thomas Russell Sullivan. LC 2-148542. 1902. C. Scribner's Sons.
Courage of Marge O'Doone. James Oliver Curwood. LC 18-454730. 1918. Doubleday, Page & Company.
Courage of Paula. Jean Noel. LC 13-17099. 1913. 1.00. Broadway Publishing Co.
Courage of the Commonplace. Mary Raymond Shipman Andrews. LC 11-24404. 1911. C. Scribner's Sons.
Courage of the North. James Beardsley Hendryx. LC 46-7882. 1946. Doubleday & Company, Inc.
Courage of Turtles. Edward Hoagland. 1970. 7.95 o.p. (ISBN 0-394-42064-0). Random.
Courage Stout. William MacLeod Raine. LC 44-401284. 1944. Houghton Mifflin Company.
Courage, the Adventuress & The False Messiah. Hans Jacob Grimmelshausen & Grimmelshausen, Hans Jacob Christoffel Von. LC 63-23415. 1964. Princeton University Press.
Courage to Serve. Sarah Shears. 1975. 7.95 (ISBN 0-236-31067-4, Pub. by Paul Elek). Merrimack Pub Cir.
Courageous Beauty. Justine Sommers. (Ace Book). 1.75. Grosset & Dunlap.
Courageous Houstons: Saga of an American Family. Gertrude Dixon Enfield. LC 51-13810. 1951. Vantage Press.
Courageous Marriage. Marguerite Bryant. LC 21-5171. 1921. Duffield and Company.
Courier. Clement R Hoopes. LC 73-77537. (Illus.). 1973. 6.95 (ISBN 0-8059-1854-X). Dorrance.
Courier. Charles Fish Howell. LC 36-21199. Greenberg.
Courier to Marrakesh: A Clubfoot Story. Valentine Williams. LC 46-1075. 1946. Houghton Mifflin Company.
Courier to Peking. G. June Goodfield. LC 72-78378. 1973. 6.95. Dutton.
Courier to Peking. G. June Goodfield. 1974. (pbk.) 1.25 (ISBN 0-671-78354-8). Pocket Books.
Courier's Fist. Harvey A Eysman. LC 80-27338. 12.95 (ISBN 0-8253-0034-7). Beaufort Books.
Courrier. Georges Bernanos. 5.95. French & Eur.
Course of Empire. Ruth Bowlen. LC 56-14505. 1956. Moody Press.
Court & City Vagaries, or Intrigues, of Both Sexes. Bd. with Tell-Tale or the Invisible Witness; Entertainments of Gallantry or Remedies of Love. LC 70-170525. (Foundations of the Novel Ser.: Vol. 18). lib. bdg. 50.00 (ISBN 0-8240-0530-9). Garland Pub.
Court and City Vagaries. The Tell-Tale. Entertainments of Gallantry. LC 70-170525. (Foundations of the Novel). 1973. 22.00 (ISBN 0-8240-0530-9). Garland Pub.
Court House Square. Phil LaMar Anderson. LC 34-6046. Augsburg Publishing House.
Court-House Square. Hamilton Basso. LC 36-29599. 1936. C. Scribner's Sons.
Court Intrigue. Basil Thompson. LC 8-199731. (Half-title: Appletons' town and country library, no. 201). 1896. D. Appleton and Company.
Court-Martial. Robin Moore & Henry B. Rothblatt. LC 75-139048. 1971. 6.95. Doubleday.
Court-Martial of Daniel Boone. Allan W Eckert. LC 73-11159. 1973. 7.95 (ISBN 0-316-20870-1). Little, Brown.
Court-Martial of George Armstrong Custer. Douglas C Jones. LC 76-12606. 1976. 8.95 (ISBN 0-684-14738-6). Scribner.
Court-Martial of George Armstrong Custer. Douglas C Jones. 1977. 2.25 (ISBN 0-446-82333-3). Warner Books.
Court Netherleigh. Ellen Price Henry Wood Wood. (Seaside library, v. 57, no. 1166). 1881. G. Munro.
Court of Atalantis. LC 76-170532. (Foundations of the novel). 1973. (ISBN 0-8240-0533-3). Garland.
Court of Belshazzar: A Romance of the Great Captivity. Earl Willoughby Williams. LC 18-145338. The Bobbs-Merrill Company.
Court of Boyville. William Allen White. LC 77-116968. (Short Story Index Reprint Ser). 1899. 20.00 (ISBN 0-8369-3472-5). Ayer Co.
Court of Charles Iv. A Romance of the Escorial. Benito Perez Galdos. Tr. by Bell, Clare Courtenay (Poynter) 1888. W. S. Gottsberger.
Court of Crows. 1st Ed. Robert Almy Knowlton. LC 61-645904. 1961. Harper.
Court of Domestic Revelation. Charles De Spelder. 1976. 7.50 o.p. (ISBN 0-682-48464-4). Exposition.
Court of Domestic Revelation. Charles De Spelder. 1976. 7.50 o.p. (ISBN 0-682-48464-4). Exposition.
Court of Dusty Feet. Geraldine Gordon Salmon. LC 42-22177. 1942. Hutchinson & Co. Ltd.
Court of Fair Maidens. Wilhelm Speyer & Blewitt, Phyllis, Tr. LC 36-20846. 1936. Simon and Schuster.
Court of Foxes. Mary Christianna Milne Lewis. LC 76-30787. 1977. 6.95 (ISBN 0-912588-25-X). Brooke House.
Court of Honor. Maria Fagyas. LC 77-27114. 9.95 (ISBN 0-671-22498-0). Simon and Schuster.
Court of Honor. Maria Fagyas. 1979. 1.95 (ISBN 0-445-04362-8). Popular Library.
Court of Honor. Geoff Taylor. LC 66-11954. 1966. Simon and Schuster.
Court of Human Relations: 10 True Stories Used in the Radio Trials. True Story Magazine & True Story Publishing Corporation, New York. LC 35-17490. 1935. True Story Publishing Corporation.
Court of Inquiry. Grace Louise Smith Richmond. LC 9-24945. 1909. Doubleday, Page & Company.
Court of Inquiry. Grace Louise Smith Richmond. A. L. Burt Company.
Court of Love. Alice Brown. LC 6-15111. 1906. Houghton, Mifflin and Company.
Court of Lucifer: A Tale of the Renaissance. Nathan Gallizier. LC 10-23744. 1910. 1.50. L. C. Page & Company.
Court of Nideck. Emile Erckmann & Chatrian, Alexandre, 1826-1890, Joint Author. LC 7-3331. 1897. L. C. Page & Company, Incorporated.
Court of Pilate: A Story of Jerusalem in the Days of Christ. Roe Raymond Hobbs. LC 6-34676. R. F. Fenno & Company.
Court of Sacharissa, a Midsummer Idyll, Compiled Out of the Traditions of the Irresponsible Club. Hugh Sheringham & Meakin, Nevill Myers, Joint Author. LC 4-9458. 1904. The Macmillan Company.
Court of St. Simon. Edward Phillips Oppenheim. LC 12-21762. 1912. 1.25. Little, Brown, and Company.
Court of Shadows. Albert Leffingwell. LC 43-5353. 1943. The Dial Press.
Court of Silver Shadows. Beatrice Brandon, pseud. LC 75-40713. 1980. 10.00 (ISBN 0-385-09629-1). Doubleday.
Court of Silver Shadows. Robert W. Krepps. LC 75-40713. 1980. 8.95 (ISBN 0-385-09629-1). Doubleday.
Court of the Flowering Peach. Janette Radcliffe. (Orig.). 1981. pap. 3.50 (ISBN 0-440-11497-7). Dell.
Court of the Last Resort. Erle Stanley Gardner. 1952. 5.00 (ISBN 0-688-01379-1, Sloane Assocs). Morrow.
Court of Thorntree. Patricia Maxwell. (Queen-size gothic). 1974. (pbk.) 0.95. Popular Library.
Court of Three Sisters. 1st Ed. Clarence McNamee. LC 56-10620. 1956. Pageant Press.
Court Royal. A Story of Cross Currents... Sabine Baring-Gould. LC 9-815. (On cover: The seaside library. Pocket ed., no. 787). G. Munro.
Court Royal: A Story of Cross Currents. Sabine Baring-Gould. LC 42-36155. 1888. J. B. Lippincott Company.
Courtesan. Peggy Gaddis, pseud. LC 36-194492. 1936. Godwin.
Courtesan's Caresses. Anne Zorine. Tr. by L. E. LaBan. pap. 1.95 o.p. (6020). Brandon.
Courtesan's Jewel Box. 1981. 12.50 (ISBN 0-8351-0877-5). China Bks.
Courtesy Dame: A Novel. Robert Murray Gilchrist. LC 5040. 1900. Dodd, Mead and Company.
Courtesy of Death. Geoffrey Household. 1982. 15.00x (ISBN 0-86025-150-0, Pub. by Ian Henry Pubns England). State Mutual Bk.
Courtesy of Death: A Novel. Geoffrey Household. LC 67-11218. 1967. Little, Brown.
Courthouse. John Nicholas Iannuzzi. LC 74-9454. 1975. 7.95 (ISBN 0-385-01148-2). Doubleday.
Courthouse. Glen M. Stadler. LC 81-86351. 300p. 1983. pap. 8.95 (ISBN 0-86666-066-6). GWP.
Courtin' Christina. John Joy Bell. LC 13-12593. 1.00. Hodder & Stoughton, George H. Doran Company.
Courting. Darrell Husted. LC 81-15089. (Regency romances). 1982. 11.95 (ISBN 0-89340-377-6). J. Curley.
Courting and Farming: Or, Which Is the Gentleman? Julie P Smith. LC 8-8178. 1876. G. W. Carleton & Co.; Etc., Etc.
Courting Danger. Deborah Knaff. (Illus.). 12p. 1975. pap. 0.50 o.p. Samisdat.
Courting of Dinah Shadd. Rudyard Kipling. LC 9-3018. F. F. Lovell Company.
Courting of Dinah Shadd. Rudyard Kipling. LC 99-4246. 1899. Doubleday and McClure Company.
Courting of Dinah Shadd, & Other Stories. facsimile ed. Rudyard Kipling. LC 78-144158. (Short Story Index Reprint Ser.). Repr. of 1890 ed. 12.50 (ISBN 0-8369-3773-2). Ayer Co.
Courting of Dinah Shadd: And Other Stories. Rudyard Kipling & Andrew Lang. LC 78-144158. (Short story index reprint series). (Illus.). 1971. (ISBN 0-8369-3773-2). Books for Libraries Press.
Courting of Dinah Shadd: And Other Stories. Rudyard Kipling & Andrew Lang. (On cover: Harper's Franklin square library, no. 680). 1890. Harper & Brothers.
Courting of Mary Smith. A Novel. Frederick William Robinson. (Harper's Franklin square library, no. 491). 1885. Harper & Brothers.
Courting of Mary Smith. A Novel. Frederick William Robinson. (On cover: The seaside library. Pocket ed. no. 590). 1885. G. Munro.
Courting of Susie Brown. Erskine Caldwell. 1965. pap. 0.50 o.p. (50-237). Manor Bks.
Courting of Susie Brown. 1st Ed. Erskine Caldwell. LC 51-10889. 1952. Duell, Sloan and Pearce.
Courting Stick. Clarence C Johnson. LC 48-21613. 1948. Christopher Pub. House.
Courtney Entry. John Harris. LC 74-116210. 1970. 6.95. Doubleday.
Courts of Chaos. Roger Zelazny. LC 78-3263. 1978. 9.95 o.p. (ISBN 0-385-13685-4). Doubleday.
Courts of Love: A Romance of Medieval France by Peter Bourne Pseud. Graham Montague Jeffries. LC 58-9712. 1958. Putnam.
Courts of Memory: A Novel. Frank Rooney. LC 54-6989. 1954. Vanguard Press.
Courts of the Lion. Robert W Krepps. LC 49-49741. 1950. Rinehart.
Courts of the Morning. John Buchan. LC 29-168234. 1929. Houghton Mifflin Company.
Courtship and Marriage: Or, The Joys and Sorrows of American Life. Caroline Lee Whiting Hentz. LC 7-4133. T. B. Peterson.
Courtship by Command: A Story of Napoleon at Play. M. M Blake. LC 6-13846. 1895. D. Appleton and Company.
Courtship of a Careful Man: And a Few Other Courtships. Edward Sandford Martin. LC 77-125232. (Short story index reprint series). (Illus.). 1970. Books for Libraries Press.
Courtship of a Careful Man, and a Few Other Courtships. Edward Sandford Martin. LC 5-10919. 1905. Harper & Brothers.
Courtship of Colonel Crowne. Margaret SeBastian, pseud. 1.75 (ISBN 0-445-04351-2). Popular Library.
Courtship of Eddie's Father. Mark Toby. LC 61-7832. 1961. B. Geis Associates; Distributed by Random House.
Courtship of Miles Standish: And Other Poems. Henry Wadsworth Longfellow. LC 22-10917. 1859. Ticknor and Fields.
Courtship of Morrice Buckler, a Romance: Being a Record of the Growth of an English Gentleman During the Years 1685-1687, Under Strange and Difficult Circumstances, Written Some While Afterwards in His Own Hand, and Now. Alfred Edward Woodley Mason. LC 4-16566. 1903. Macmillan and Co., Limited.
Courtship of Nurse Genie Hayes. Peggy Gaddis, pseud. pap. 0.50 o.p. (50-383). Manor Bks.
Courtship of Sweet Anne Page. Ellen V Talbot. (hour-glass series, 1). 1902. Funk & Wagnalls Co.
Courtships in the Air: Or, The Strange Adventures of Hurry Harry. Charles Lorensen. LC 14-120755. 1914. 1.50. Broadway Publishing Company.
Cousin Beatie: A Memory of Beatrix Potter. Ulla Hyde Parker & Beatrix Potter. LC 81-215632. (Illus.). 1981. 8.95 (ISBN 0-7232-2793-4). F. Warne.
Cousin Beryl. John Collis Snaith. LC 29-175526. 1929. D. Appleton & Company.
Cousin Bette. Honore De Balzac. LC 58-11475. (Modern library of the world's best books 299). 1958. Modern Library.
Cousin Bette. Honore De Balzac. Tr. by Katharine Prescott Wormeley. LC 3-24481. (Half-title: The comedy of human life... Scenes from Parisian life). 1888. Roberts Brothers.
Cousin Bette. Honore De Balzac. Tr. by Katharine Prescott Wormeley. LC 3-24482. (Half-title: The comedy of human life... Scenes from Parisian life). 1890. Roberts Brothers.
Cousin Bette. Honore De Balzac. Tr. by Katharine Prescott Wormeley. LC 39-17470. 1928. Little, Brown, and Company.
Cousin Bette. Honore De Balzac. 2.95 o.p. (299). Modern Lib.
Cousin Bette: Part One of Poor Relations. Tr. from French by Marion Ayton Crawford. Honore De Balzac. LC 65-580164. (Penguin classics, L160). pap., 1.45. Penguin.
Cousin Bette. Translated by Anthony Bonner. With an Introd. by Wallace Fowlie. Honore De Balzac. LC 61-5102. (Bantam classic, SC81). 1961. Bantam Books.
Cousin Bette. Translated from the French by Kathleen Raine. Honore De Balzac. LC 58-11475. (Modern library of the world's best books 299). 1958. Modern Library.
Cousin Betty, Cousin Pons, and Other Stories. saintsbury ed. Honore De Balzac. LC 8-7692. 1899. Gebbie Pub. Co.
Cousin Betty: Cousin Pons, and Other Stories. saintsbury ed. Honore De Balzac. Tr. by James Waring. Marriage, Ellen, Joint Tr. LC 8-7002. 1899. The Gebbie Publishing Co., Ltd.
Cousin Caroline. Lillie Gilliland McDowell. LC 45-3015. 1945. Wm. B. Eerdmans Publishing Co.
Cousin Cinderella. Sara Jeannette Duncan Cotes. LC 8-24455. 1908. The Macmillan Company.
Cousin Drewey and the Holy Twister: A Novel. John L. Sinclair. LC 80-17753. 1980. 14.95 (ISBN 0-914366-18-1). Columbia Pub. Co.
Cousin Elva: With Illus. by the Author. Stuart Trueman. LC 56-17833. 1955. McCleland & Stewart.
Cousin Franck's Household: Or, Scenes in the Old Dominion. Emily Clemens Pearson. LC 72-1517. (Black Heritage Library Collection). (Illus.). 1972. 14.50 (ISBN 0-8369-9041-2). Books for Libraries Press.
Cousin Franck's Household: Or, Scenes in the Old Dominion. 2d ed. Emily Clemens Pearson. LC 7-33498. 1853. Upham, Ford and Olmstead.
Cousin from Fiji: By Norman Lindsay. Norman Lindsay. LC 46-2494. 1946. Random House.

Cousin Harriet. Susan Charlotte Grosvenor Buchan Tweedsmuir. LC 61-19051. 1961. Penguin Books.

Cousin Harriet: By Susan Tweedsmuir. Susan Grosvenor Buchan. LC 61-19051. (Penguin books, 1569). 1961. Penguin Books.

Cousin Henrietta. Emma Cave. LC 81-21412. 10.95 (ISBN 0-312-17049-1). St Martin's Press.

Cousin Henry. reprint ed. / introduction by j. hillis miller. ed. Anthony Trollope. LC 80-1898. (Trollope, Anthony, 1815-1882. Selections. 1981). 1981. 50.00 (ISBN 0-405-14172-6). Arno Press.

Cousin Honore. Margaret Storm Jameson. LC 41-515291. 1941. The Macmillan Company.

Cousin in Terror. Charlotte Bramwell, pseud. (Orig.). 1972. pap. 0.75 o.p. (94253). Beagle Bks.

Cousin Jane. Harry Leon Wilson. LC 25-21775. 1925. Cosmopolitan Book Corporation.

Cousin Julia. Grace C. Hodgson Flandrau. LC 17-22295. 1917. D. Appleton and Company.

Cousin Kate. Georgette Heyer. (Fawcett Crest Book). 1976. (pbk.) 1.50. Fawcett.

Cousin Kate. Georgette Heyer. LC 68-25792. 1969. 4.95. E. P. Dutton.

Cousin Mercedes & the White Russian. A. G. Heinsohn, Jr. LC 74-18736. 1974. 7.00 (ISBN 0-88279-231-8). Western Islands.

Cousin Mona: A Story for Girls. Rosa Nouchette Carey. LC 6-23107. 1896. J. B. Lippincott Company.

Cousin Phillis & Other Tales. Elizabeth Cleghorn Stevenson Gaskell. (Half-title: Everyman's library, ed. by Ernest Rhys. Fiction. no. 615). J. M. Dent & Sons, Ltd.

Cousin Phillis and Other Tales, Etc. Elizabeth Cleghorn Stevenson Gaskell. (Half-title: The novels and tales of Mrs. Gaskell.--vii.). H. Frowde, Oxford University Press.

Cousin Phillis: To Which Are Added Lois the Witch--The Crooked Branch--Curious If True--Right at Last--The Grey Woman--Six Weeks at Heppenheim--A Dark Night's Work--The Shah's English Gardener--French Life--Crowley Castle--Two Fragments of Ghost Stories. Elizabeth Cleghorn Stevenson Gaskell. Ed. by Adolphus William Ward. LC 7-5066. (Half-title: The works of Mrs. Gaskell... Knutsford ed. v. 7). 1906. G. P. Putnam's Sons; Etc., Etc.

Cousin Phillis. To Which Are Added: Lois the Witch, The Crooked Branch, Curious If True, Right at Last, The Grey Woman, Six Weeks at Heppenheim, A Dark Night's Work, The Shah's English Gardener, French Life, Crowley Castle, Two Fragments of Ghost Stories. knutsford ed. 1st ams ed. new york, putnam, 1906. ed. Elizabeth Cleghorn Stevenson Gaskell. LC 72-186538. (works of Mrs. Gaskell, v. 2). (Illus.). 1972. 24.00 (ISBN 0-404-07257-7). AMS Press.

Cousin Polly's Gold Mine: A Novel. Lydia Ann Emerson Porter. LC 7-37757. (On cover: Harper's library of American fiction. no. 10). 1878. Harper & Brothers.

Cousin Pons. Honore De Balzac. Tr. by Katharine Prescott Wormeley. LC 3-23172. (Half-title: The comedy of human life... Scenes from Parisian life). 1886. Roberts Brothers.

Cousin Pons. Honore De Balzac. Tr. by Katharine Prescott Wormeley. LC 3-23171. (Half-title: The comedy of human life... Scenes from Parisian life). 1888. Roberts Brothers.

Cousin Pons. Honore De Balzac. Tr. by Philip Kent. (On cover: Seaside library. Pocket ed., no. 1128). 1888. G. Munro.

Cousin Pons. Honore De Balzac. Tr. by Ellen Marriage. LC 36-37319. (Half-title: Everyman's library, ed. by Ernest Rhys. Fiction. no. 463). 1933. J. M. Dent & Sons, Ltd.

Cousin Pons. Honore De Balzac. Ed. by Allem. (Coll. Prestige). 27.95. French & Eur.

Cousin Pons. A Novel, Tr. from the French of. Honore De Balzac. (choice series, no. 27) PZ3.B22Cup5). 1890. R. Bonner's Sons.

Cousin Pons. Illustrated by Lucias Rossi. Honore De Balzac. Tr. by Katharine Prescott Wormeley. LC 26-26980. (Half-title: The works of Balzac. Centenary ed. vol. xix). Little, Brown, and Company.

Cousin Pons: Le Cousin Pons. Honore De Balzac. Tr. by Ellen Marriage. LC 4-21345. (Half-title:... Comedie humaine...). 1897. J. M. Dent and Co.

Cousin Pons: Part Two of Poor Relations. Honore De Balzac. Tr. by Herbert James Hunt. LC 79-1059. (Penguin classics, L205). 1968. 1.45. Penguin Books.

Cousin Sadie. Daisy Anderton. LC 20-13144. 1920. The Stratford Co.

Cousin Stud. Thomas H. Hilton. pap. 1.95 o.p. (ISBN 0-87056-206-1, 6206). Brandon.

Cousin Suzanne. Myrna Blyth. LC 75-15642. 1975. 7.95 (ISBN 0-88405-113-7). Mason/Charter.

Cousin Suzanne. Myrna Blyth. 1976. 1.75 (ISBN 0-380-00668-5). Avon.

Cousin to Human. 1st Ed. Jane Mayhall. LC 60-543218. 1960. Harcourt, Brace.

Cousin Wilhelmina. Anna Theresa Sadlier. LC 7-40798. 1907. B. Herder.

Cousin William: Or, The Fatal Attachment. Theodore Edward Hook. LC 41-311069. G. Routledge and Sons.

Cousine Bette. Honore De Balzac. Ed. by Allem. (Coll. Prestige). 27.95. French & Eur.

Cousinhood. Chaim I. Bermant. (O.s.i.). 1972. 10.95 o.s.i. (ISBN 0-02-510080-7). Macmillan.

Cousins, 2 Vols. Coutesse De Courer-Brulant. Tr. by Henrik Van Breda. pap. 1.95 ea. o.p. (6035). Brandon.

Cousins. Emily Nonnen. LC 39-3404. Augustana Book Concern.

Cousins. Lucy Bethia Colquhoun Walford. (On cover: Lovell's library. no. 1059). 1887. J. W. Lovell Company.

Cousins: An Israeli War - Love Story. Shabetai B. Gormezano. Tr. by Keith S. Gormezano from Hebrew. LC 81-69807. (Foreign Artists, Poets & Authors Ser.: No. 2). 50p. 1981. pap. 4.95 (ISBN 0-935954-10-4). Beacon Presse IA.

Cove in Darkness. Sharon Wagner. 1973. pap. 1.50 o.s.i. (71-360). Lancer.

Cove in Darkness. Sharon Wagner & Bernard L. Casey. (Lancer gothic). 1973. (pbk.) 1.50. Lancer Books.

Cove of Fear. Virginia K. Smiley. 192p. (YA) 1974. 4.95 o.p. (Avalon). Bouregy.

Cove of the Silver Fish. Thelma Peters. LC 59-13161. 1959. Lothrop, Lee & Shepard.

Coven. Carter Brown, pseud. Bd. with Creative Murders. 1978. pap. 2.50 (ISBN 0-451-11697-6, AE1697, Sig). NAL.

Coven. E. Howard Hunt. LC 75-186562. (Fawcett Crest Book). 1973. (pbk) 0.95. Fawcett.

Coven. David St. John, pseud. LC 75-186562. 160p. 1972. 4.94 o.p. (ISBN 0-679-50183-5). McKay.

Covenant. Brigid Knight. LC 43-13938. 1943. Crowell.

Covenant. James Albert Michener. LC 80-5315. 15.95 (ISBN 0-394-50505-0). Random House.

Covenant. Paige Mitchell, pseud. LC 72-92615. 1973. 7.95. Atheneum.

Covenant. Paige Mitchell, pseud. 1976. (pbk.) 1.95. Popular Library.

Covenant. Kathleen Henrietta Nash-Webber Sinclair. LC 43-13938. 1943. Thomas Y. Crowell Company.

Covenant: A Novel of the Life of Abraham the Prophet. Translated by H. C. Stevens. Kossak-Szczucka, Zofia. LC 51-113551. 1951. Roy Publishers.

Covenant of Despair. Omar Eby. LC 72-4651. 1973. 5.95 (ISBN 0-8361-1691-7). Herald Press.

Covenant of Dispair. Omar Eby. LC 72-4651. 308p. 1973. 5.95 o.p. (ISBN 0-8361-1691-7). Herald Pr.

Covenant of Grace. Jane Gilmore Rushing. LC 81-43307. 1982. 16.95 (ISBN 0-385-17702-X). Doubleday.

Covenant of the Crown. Howard Weinstein. 192p. (Orig.). Date not set. pap. 2.50 (ISBN 0-671-83307-3, Timescape). PB.

Covenant with Death. Stephen D. Becker. LC 64-14929. 1965. bds., 4.50. Atheneum.

Covenant with Death. John Harris. LC 61-135441. 1961. W. Sloane Associates.

Covent Garden. Claire Rayner. LC 78-18439. (Her The performers; 6). 1978. 9.95 (ISBN 0-399-12205-2). Putnam.

Coventry Option. Anthony Burton. LC 76-10607. 7.95. Putnam.

Cover Charge. Cornell Woolrich, pseud. LC 26-7343. 1926. Boni & Liveright.

Cover Girl. (Sweet Dreams: No. 9). 1982. pap. write for info. Bantam.

Cover Girls. Paul W. Fairman. 1969. pap. 0.75 o.p. (75-286). Manor Bks.

Cover Her Face. P. D James. LC 66-22525. 1966. 3.95. Scribners.

Cover Her Face. P. D James. LC 79-16503. 1979. 12.95 (ISBN 0-8161-6793-1). G. K. Hall.

Cover Her Face. P. D James. LC 81-47380. (Fifty Classics of Crime Fiction, 1950-1975). 1982. 14.95 (ISBN 0-8240-4893-7). Garland.

Cover Her with Roses. Rex Anderson. LC 69-14277. (Inner sanctum mystery). 1969. 4.50. Simon and Schuster.

Cover His Face. Neil Bell. 1943. 20.00 (ISBN 0-8274-2108-7). R West.

Cover His Face. Thomas Pseud Kyd. LC 49-93061. (Main line mysteries). 1949. J. B. Lippincott Co.

Cover My Rear. Mack Leonard. 5.00 o.p. Vantage.

Cover Stories. Robert J. Rosenblum. 1980. pap. 2.75 (ISBN 0-440-11522-1). Dell.

Cover Stories: A Navel. Robert J Rosenblum. LC 79-15376. 9.95 (ISBN 0-440-01531-6). Delacrote Press.

Cover the Embers. Andrew Blummer Burris. LC 41-197161. 1949. Mathis, Van Nort & Company.

Cover-Up at Mojave Green. Jo-Bradley Jackson. 1980. pap. 2.25 (ISBN 0-8439-0816-5). Nordon Pubns.

Covered Bridge. Herman Petersen. LC 50-12307. 1950. Crowell.

Covered Wagon. Emerson Hough. LC 22-11082. 1922. D. Appleton and Company.

Covered Wagon. Emerson Hough. LC 24-24985. 1923. Grosset & Dunlap.

Covered Wagon. Emerson Hough & Stratton, Clarence, 1880- Ed. LC 27-87551. (Half-title: Appleton modern literature series). D. Appleton and Company.

Covering Two Years. Ira Victor Morris. LC 34-203. Rey & Hitchcock, Inc.

Covert-Side Courtship. Katharine Roosevelt Reeve. LC 10-741. 1909. Printed by J. B. Lippincott Company.

Coverts. 1st Ed. Rebecca Sonnenberg Brown. LC 53-10078. 1953. Pageant Press.

Coveted Inheritance". Bruce Hughes. LC 7-35621. 1907. Central Printing & Publishing House.

Covey of Peacocks. Harris J. Nadley. LC 68-56169. 1969. 5.95. Whitmore Pub. Co.

Covici, Friede Presents Two Maids Go to Market: A Novel of the Theatre. Laurence Schwab. LC 32-33158. Covici, Friedo.

Covington Inheritance. Barbara Hazard. (Coventry Romance Ser.: No. 166). 224p. 1982. pap. 1.50 (ISBN 0-449-50267-8, Coventry). Fawcett.

Covntesse of Pembrokes Arcadia. Philip Sidney. LC 78-85106. (Kent English reprints. The Renaissance). (pbk) 4.75 (ISBN 0-87338-044-4). Kent State University Press.

Cow-Country. Bertha Muzzy Sinclair. LC 21-491. 1921. Little, Brown, and Company.

Cow Country. Bertha Muzzy Sinclair. LC 44-21222. 1944. Triangle Books.

Cow Country: Stories. Will James. (Bison Book). (Illus.). 1973. 1.95 (ISBN 0-8032-5774-0). Univ. of Nebraska Pr.

Cow Is Too Much Trouble in Los Angeles. 1st Ed. Joseph O'Kane Foster. LC 52-9082. 1952. Duell, Sloan and Pearce.

Cow Jerry. George Washington Ogden. LC 25-2965. 1925. Dodd, Mead & Company.

Cow Killers' With the Aftosa Commission in Mexico. Drawings by Bill Leftwich. Frederick Benjamin Gipson. LC 56-11771. 1956. University of Texas Press.

Cow Kingdom. Paul Evan Lehman. LC 45-949022. 1945. S. Curl, Inc.

Cow of the Barricades and Other Stories. Rao Raja. LC 48-19915. (Champak library). 1947. Oxford University Press.

Cow Puncher. Robert James Campbell Stead. LC 18-22164. 1918. Harper & Brothers.

Cow Thief Empire. William L Hopson. LC 53-855942. 1953. Arcadia House.

Cow Thief Trail. Bennett Foster. LC 37-28669. 1937. W. Morrow & Company.

Cow Women: A Western Story. George Gilbert. LC 24-138593. Chelsea House.

Coward. Robert Hugh Benson. LC 12-813947. 1911. 1.50. B. Herder.

Coward. Tom Tiede. LC 68-18311. 1968. Trident Press.

Coward. Neal Wainwright. LC 28-9837. Payson & Clarke Ltd.

Coward. A Novel of Society and the Field in 1863. Henry Morford. T. B. Peterson & Brothers.

Coward & Other Stories. William Drews. 2.50 o.p. Carlton.

Coward & Other Stories. Imre Sarkadi. 4.00x o.p. Vanous.

Coward Conscience. A Novel. Frederick William Robinson. LC 7-41961. (Franklin square library. no. 48). 1879. Harper & Brothers.

Coward Heart. Anna Reiner & Blewitt, Trevor Eaton, 1900- Tr. LC 41-11687. 1941. A. A. Knopf.

Coward of Thermopylae. Caroline Dale Parke Snedeker. LC 11-9233. 1911. 1.20. Doubleday, Page & Company.

Cowardice Before Courage. Richard Pape. LC 78-549038. 1970 (ISBN 0-491-00425-7). W. H. Allen.

Cowardice Court. George Barr McCutcheon. 1906. Dodd, Mead & Company.

Cowardice Court. George Barr McCutcheon & Fisher, Harrison, 1875- Illus. LC 18-20843. 1907. Dodd, Mead & Company.

Cowards. Josef Skvorecky. Tr. by Jeanne Nemcova from Czech. LC 80-13087. (Neglected Books of the 20th Century). 416p. 1980. pap. 8.95 (ISBN 0-912946-75-X). Ecco Pr.

Cowards. Josef Skvorecky. Tr. by Jeanne Nemuova. 1971. pap. 1.95 o.p. (Z1079, Zebra). Grove.

Coward's Paradise. Valerie Elliston. LC 74-15867. (Signet Book). 1975. (pbk.) 1.50. New American Library.

Cowboy. Aaron Fletcher. 224p. 1982. pap. 2.25 (ISBN 0-8439-1107-7, Leisure Bks). Nordon Pubns.

Cowboy. Aaron Fletcher. (Orig.). 1977. pap. 1.50 o.s.i. (ISBN 0-505-51152-5, BT51152). Tower Bks.

Cowboy. Clair Huffaker. 1975. (pbk.) 1.25 (ISBN 0-671-80128-7). Pocket Books.

Cowboy. Frank Roderus. LC 80-1866. 1981. 9.95 (ISBN 0-385-17120-X). Doubleday.

Cowboy. Frank Roderus. LC 82-7295. 1982. 12.95 (ISBN 0-89340-508-6). J. Curley & Associates.

Cowboy. Ross Santee. LC 64-56556. 1964. Hastings House.

Cowboy. Ross Santee. LC 77-7271. (Illus.). 1977. 11.95 (ISBN 0-8032-0931-2). University of Nebraska Press.

Cowboy and the Cossack. Clair Huffaker. LC 72-96817. (Illus.). 1973. 7.95 (ISBN 0-671-27100-8). Trident Press.

Cowboy and the Cossack. Clair Huffaker. LC 82-10540. 1982. 11.95 (ISBN 0-89621-385-4). Thorndike Press.

Cowboy and the Duchess. Alden Arthur Knipe. LC 32-15763. 1932. Dodd, Mead and Company.

Cowboy Cavalier... Harriet Clara Morse. 1908. The C. M. Clark Publishing Company.

Cowboy Comes a-Fightin' Frank Chester Robertson. LC 40-6805. 1940. E. P. Dutton & Co., Inc.

Cowboy Detective. Charles A. Siringo. 1912. Repr. 15.00 o.s.i. Finch Pr.

Cowboy from Alamos. Charles Horace Snow. LC 33-31658. 1933. Macrae Smith Company.

Cowboy Heaven. Ron Goulart. LC 77-27672. (Doubleday science fiction). 1979. 7.95 (ISBN 0-385-12784-7). Doubleday.

Cowboy Life on the Sidetrack: Being an Extremely Humorous and Sarcastic Story of the Trials and Tribulations Endured by a Party of Stockmen Making a Shipment from the West to the East. Frank Benton. LC 3-28959. 1903. The Western Stories Syndicate.

Cowboy Love Song. Marie Lussi. LC 35-5194. Lilly Printing Company.

Cowboy Luck. Charlton Lawrence Edholm. LC 38-22277. Phoenix Press.

Cowboy on a Wooden Horse: A Novel. Yuri Suhl. LC 53-12775. 1953. Macmillan.

Cowboy, Say Your Prayers! Harry Sinclair Drago. LC 39-27573. 1939. W. Morrow & Company.

Cowboy, Say Your Prayers! By Will Ermine Pseud. Harry Sinclair Drago. LC 51-13200. (Triple-A western classic). 1951. Jefferson House.

Cowboys. William Dale Jennings. LC 76-164683. (Illus.). 1971. 5.95 (ISBN 0-8128-1428-2). Stein and Day.

Cowboy's Courtship and Other Courtships. Fanny Williams Gresham. LC 4-3588. 1904. The Neale Publishing Company.

Cowboys Don't Cry. Lawrence J Davis. LC 69-18795. 1969. 5.75. Viking Press.

Cowboys in Alaska, & Other Stories. English Language Services. (English Readers Ser). pap. 1.40 (ISBN 0-02-971370-6). Macmillan.

Cowgirl Kate. Decorations by Frank McCarthy. Enid Johnson. LC 50-7340. 1950. Messner.

Cowhand for the Heiress. Robert F. Slatzer. 192p. 1972. pap. 1.95 o.p. (ISBN 0-87977-146-1, DBB146). Dansk Blue Bk.

Cowhands of Crystal Creek. Tevis Miller. LC 40-2311. Phoenix Press.

Cowhide Trunk. Eleanor Weakley Nolen. LC 41-5302. Oxford University Press.

Cowled Menace. Willard E. Hawkins. LC 30-7295. Sears Publishing Company, Inc.

Cowman's Jack-Pot. Frank Chester Robertson. LC 42-14392. 1942. E. P. Dutton & Co., Inc.

Cowman's Wife. Mary Rak. 1934. Repr. 14.00 o.s.i. Finch Pr.

Cowpoke Justice. William L Hopson. LC 41-1975. Phoenix Press.

Cowpokes of Bitter Creek. George C Henderson. LC 89-52186. Phoenix Press.

Cowpuncher. Bradford Scott. LC 42-24286. 1942. Gateway Books.

Cowpuncher. Charles Horace Snow. LC 34-3087. 1934. W. Morrow and Company.

Cowpunchers of Badwater. Al P Nelson. LC 39-33007. Phoenix Press.

Coxon Fund see Lesson of the Master.

Cox's Diary: The Bedford-Row Conspiracy; A Little Dinner at Timmins's. William Makepeace Thackeray. LC 8-28246. (On cover: Lovell's library, v. 5, no. 286). 1883. J. W. Lovell Company.

Coxswain. Robert H. Sheldon. pap. 1.95 o.p. (8033). Cameo.

Coxswain Drake of the Seascouts. Isabel Katherine Hornibrook. LC 20-18607. 1920. Little, Brown, and Company.

Coykendall Webb: And Other Stories About Schools. Charles William Bardeen. LC 19-17884. 1.00. C.W. Bardeen.

Coyote Currency. Georges Brydges Rodney. LC 35-366743. E. J. Clode, Inc.

Coyote Gulch. Peter Field. LC 51-2039. (Triple-A western classic). 1951. Jefferson House.

TITLE INDEX

CRAVINGS OF DESIRE.

Coyote Gulch. Peter Field. LC 36-22613. 1936. W. Morrow & Co.
Coyote Hunter. A Double D Western. James Denson Sayers. LC 40-5181. 1940. Doubleday, Doran & Co., Inc.
Coyote Song. Clem Colt, pseud. 1978. pap. 1.50 (ISBN 0-505-51317-X). Tower Bks.
Coyote Song. Nelson Coral Nye. LC 47-242972. 1947. S. Curl.
Coyote Space. Gene Anderson. (Kestrel Ser.: No. 6). 28p. 1983. pap. 3.00 (ISBN 0-914974-38-6). Holmgangers.
Coyote Valley. George Brydges Rodney. LC 33-220116. Phoenix Press.
Coyote Winter. Dorothy Jeanne Williams. LC 65-18038. 1965. Norton.
Coyotes of Willow Brook: By Brett Austin Pseud. Lee Floren. LC 52-12720. 1952. Arcadia House.
Coyotes of Willowbrook. Lee Floren. 224p. (Orig.). 1981. pap. 1.95 (ISBN 0-8439-0951-X). Leisure Bks CT.
CQ" Or, In the Wireless House. Arthur Cheney Train. LC 12-19325. 1912. The Century Co.
Crab Apple Jelly: Stories and Tales by Frank O'Connor Pseud. Michael O'Donovan. LC 44-9575. 1944. A. A. Knopf.
Crab Canon. John Keeble. LC 79-114942. 1971. 8.95. Grossman Publishers.
Crabtree Affair. John Innes Mackintosh Stewart. LC 62-14891. (Red badge detective). 1962. Dodd, Mead.
Crack in Space. Philip K Dick. 1974. (pbk.) 0.95. Ace Books.
Crack in the Bell. Peter Clark Macfarlane. LC 18-18889. 1918. Doubleday, Page & Company.
Crack in the Column: A Novel. George Anthony Weller. LC 49-10328. 1949. Random House.
Crack in the Sidewalk. Ruth Wolff. LC 65-23039. (John Day Bk.). (YA) 1965. 6.95 o.p. (ISBN 0-381-98201-7, A16460, TYC-T). T Y Crowell.
Crack in the Teacup. Michael Francis Gilbert. LC 66-114734. bds., 4.50. Harper.
Crack in the Wall. Karl H. Meyer. 1978. pap. 1.50 (ISBN 0-532-15347-2). Woodhill.
Crack in Time. Lauran Paine. LC 73-173682. 1972. 4.95. Roy Publishers.
Crack of Doom. Hugh Edwards. LC 34-28970. The Bobbs-Merrill Company.
Crack of Doom. Willi Heinrich. 320p. 1981. pap. 2.75 (ISBN 0-553-14925-3). Bantam.
Crack of Doom. A Novel. William Minto. LC 7-25449. (Harper's Franklin square library, no. 530). Harper & Brothers.
Crack of Doom. Translated from the German by Oliver Coburn. Willi Heinrich. LC 58-783812. 1958. Farrar, Straus and Cudahy.
Crack Shot. Glen Chase, pseud. 1976. pap. 1.25 o.p. (LB400ZK, Leisure Bks). Nordon Pubns.
Crack Shot see Tiradora Infalible.
Cracked Looking Glass; Stories of Other Realities. Ed. by L. M. Schulman. LC 78-138302. 1971. 4.95. Macmillan.
Cracker Box School. Elizabeth Miller Lutton. LC 17-108621. The Reilly & Britton Co.
Cracker Factory. Rebeta-Burditt, Joyce. LC 76-48898. 8.95 (ISBN 0-02-601250-2) (ISBN 0-02-023840-1). Macmillan.
Cracker Joe. LC 6-31147. (No name series. v. 23). 1887. Roberts Brothers.
Cracker Tales. Albert Wadsworth Harris. LC 13-251. Priv. Print. by the Caslon Press.
Crackerjack Marines. Ben Masselink. LC 59-11105. 1959. Little, Brown.
Crackers. Roy Blount, Jr. 1982. pap. 2.95 (ISBN 0-345-29805-5). Ballantine.
Cracking of Spines. Roy Harley Lewis. LC 81-14526. 1982. 10.95 (ISBN 0-312-17073-4). St. Martin's Press.
Crackpot. Ron Goulart. LC 76-23764. 1977. 5.95 (ISBN 0-385-11640-3). Doubleday.
Cracks in the Image: Stories by Gay Men. Ed. by Richard Dipple. 136p. 1981. pap. 5.50 (ISBN 0-907040-08-X). Gay Mens Pr.
Cracksman on Velvet. Francis Selwyn. LC 74-78535. 1974. 7.95 (ISBN 0-8128-1729-X). Stein and Day.
Cradle and Spade. William Sime. (On cover: Seaside library. Pocket ed. No. 649). 1885. G. Munro.
Cradle and Spade. A Novel. William Sime. (Harper's Franklin square library, no. 500). 1885. Harper & Brothers.
Cradle and the Grave. Aaron Marc Stein. LC 48-7576. 1948. Pub. for the Crime Club by Doubleday.
Cradle Builder. Walter Schoenstedt. LC 40-2314. Farrar & Rinehart, Inc.
Cradle of a Poet. Jessie Bedford. LC 11-4103. 1910. John Lane.
Cradle of Life: The Story of One Man's Beginnings. Louis Adamic. LC 36-21009. 1936. Harper & Brothers.
Cradle of Neptune: A Novel. John Lodwick. LC 55-5921. 1955. Roy Publishers.
Cradle of the Deep. Joan Lowell. LC 29-7122. 1929. Simon and Schuster.
Cradle of the Deep: An Account of the Adventures of Eleanor Channing and John Starbuck. Sabine W. Wood. LC 12-22130. 1912. L. C. Page & Company.
Cradle of the Rose. Marguerite De Godart Cunliffe-Owen. LC 8-30708. 1908. Harper & Brothers.
Cradle of the Sun. John Clagett. LC 52-10771. 1952. Crown Publishers.
Cradle Valley: A Novel. Lettie Hoskins Saylor. LC 46-20583. 1946. The Hobson Book Press.
Cradle Will Fall. Mary Higgins Clark. LC 80-121. 10.95 (ISBN 0-671-25268-2). Simon and Schuster.
Cradle Will Fall. Mary Higgins Clark. LC 80-19281. 1980. 13.95 (ISBN 0-8161-3121-X). G. K. Hall.
Cradle Will Fall. Stephen Seley. LC 45-4230. 1945. Harcourt, Brace and Company.
Cradled in Murder. Rudd Fleming. LC 38-9730. 1938. Simon and Schuster.
Cradled in Thunder. Matthea Thorseth. LC 46-22550. 1946. Superior Publishing Company.
Cradock Nowell... Richard Doddridge Blackmore. LC 6-13864. (On cover: Lovell's library, v. 19, no. 955). J. W. Lovell Company.
Cradock Nowell. A Tale of the New Forest. Richard Doddridge Blackmore. (On cover: Seaside library. Pocket ed. no. 630). G. Munro.
Craft and Vision: The Best Fiction from the Sewanee Review. Ed. by Andrew Nelson Lytle. LC 78-164847. 1971. 12.50. Delacorte Press.
Crafty Coyote. Mildred J. Baker. 1970. 3.50 o.p. Carlton.
Crag-Nest. A Romance of the Days of Sheridan's Ride. Thomas Cooper De Leon. LC 6-341929. 1897. The Gossip Printing Co.
Crag-Nest. A Romance of the Days of Sheridan's Ride. Thomas Cooper De Leon. LC 10-7027. 1.25. G. W. Dillingham Company.
Cragg's Roost: Or, Life Among the Cow-Boys on the Frontier. N. H Miles. LC 13-38. American Tract Society.
Craghold Creatures. Edwina Noone, pseud. (Orig.). 1972. pap. 0.75 o.p. (94209). Beagle Bks.
Craghold Crypt. Edwina Noone, pseud. 1973. pap. 0.95 o.p. (09165). Curtis.
Craghold Curse. Edwina Noone, pseud. (Orig.). 1972. pap. 0.75 o.p. (94126). Beagle Bks.
Craghold Curse. Edwinna Noone, pseud. 1977. pap. 1.25 o.s.i. (ISBN 0-505-51156-8). Tower Bks.
Craghold Curse, Sixty-One Dollars. Edwina Noone, pseud. (Belmont Tower Books). 1977. 1.25 (ISBN 0-505-51156-8). Tower Pubns.
Craghold Legacy. Edwina Noone, pseud. (Orig.). 1971. pap. 0.75 o.p. (94105). Beagle Bks.
Cragsmoor. Jennette Dowling Letton. LC 66-26496. 1966. Macrae Smith.
Cragsmore. Jennette Dowling Letton. 1978. pap. 1.25 (ISBN 0-532-12546-0). Woodhill.
Craig and the Jaguar. Kenneth Benton. LC 73-90393. 1974. 5.95 (ISBN 0-8027-5294-2). Walker.
Craig and the Midas Touch. Kenneth Benton. LC 75-36549. (Illus.). 1976. 7.95 (ISBN 0-8027-5340-X). Walker.
Craig and the Tunisian Tangle. Kenneth Benton. LC 74-82529. 1975. 5.95 (ISBN 0-8027-5304-3). Walker.
Craig Kennedy Listens in: Adventures of Craig Kennedy, Scientific Detective. Arthur Benjamin Reeve. LC 23-142000. Harper & Brothers.
Craig Kennedy on the Farm. Arthur Benjamin Reeve. LC 25-17274. 1925. Harper & Brothers.
Craig of the Circle J. H Ralph Goller. LC 48-1234. 1947. Phoenix Press.
Craig Poisoning Mystery. Archibald E. Fielding. LC 30-34416. 1930. Cosmopolitan Book Corporation.
Craigie. Agnes Bowes Hall. LC 14-15183. The Roxburgh Publishing Company, Inc.
Craig's Spur. E. S. Madden. (O.s.i.). 1962. 3.95 o.s.i. (ISBN 0-8149-0152-2). Vanguard.
Craigshaw Curse: A Novel. Jean Francis Webb. LC 68-28716. 1968. 4.95. Meredith Press.
Craine's First Case: The Murder of Katherine Doherty. Eugene P Healy. LC 38-25881. H. Holt and Company.
Crainquebille. Anatole France, pseud. Tr. by Winifred Stephens Whale. LC 74-122705. (Short story index reprint series). 1970. Books for Libraries Press.
Crainquebille: L'affaire Crainquebille. Anatole France & Lamotte, Bernard. LC 49-49007. 1949. Limited Editions Club.
Crainquebille: L'affaire Crainquebille. Anatole France & Lamotte, Bernard, 1903-Illus. Heritage Press.
Crainquebille, Putois, Riquet: And Other Profitable Tales. Anatole France, pseud. Tr. by Whale, Winifred (Stephens) LC 26-6028. (Half-title: The works of Anatole France in an English translation, edited by Frederic Chapman). 1924. John Lane.
Cranberry Cove Stories. Mary Chapin Smith. LC 15-6343. R. G. Badger; Etc., Etc.
Cranberry Red. Edward Garside. LC 38-30379. 1938. Little, Brown and Company.
Cranes of Ibycus. Mary Craig. 1974. 6.95 o.p. (ISBN 0-8015-1800-8). Hawthorn.
Cranes of Ibycus. Mary Francis Shura, pseud. LC 73-10646. 1974. 6.95. Hawthorn Books.
Cranford. Elizabeth Cleghorn Stevenson Gaskell. Ed. by Elizabeth Porges Watson. LC 72-190763. (Oxford English novels). 1972. 2.00 (ISBN 0-19-255351-8). Oxford University Press.
Cranford. Elizabeth Cleghorn Stevenson Gaskell. Ed. by Elizabeth Porges Watson. LC 75-36070. (Illus.). 3.95 (ISBN 0-8055-1169-5) (ISBN 0-8055-0250-5). Hart Pub. Co.
Cranford. Elizabeth Cleghorn Stevenson Gaskell. Tr. by Elizabeth Porges Watson. LC 48-35763. 1902. Macmillan.
Cranford. Elizabeth Cleghorn Stevenson Gaskell. Ed. by Elizabeth Porges Watson. LC 6-15465. (Harper's handy series, no. 116). 1887. Harper & Brothers.
Cranford. Elizabeth Cleghorn Stevenson Gaskell. LC 42-43615. Home Book Company.
Cranford. Elizabeth Cleghorn Stevenson Gaskell. Ed. by Anne Isabella Thackeray Ritchie. LC 6-15466. 1892. T. Y. Crowell & Co.
Cranford. Elizabeth Cleghorn Stevenson Gaskell. LC 6-15464. (On cover: Handy volume classics). 1892. T. Y. Crowell & Co.
Cranford. Elizabeth Cleghorn Stevenson Gaskell. Ed. by Herford Brooke. LC 11-161578. 1892. Nims and Knight.
Cranford. Elizabeth Cleghorn Stevenson Gaskell. Ed. by Anne Isabella Thackeray Ritchie. Thomson, Hugh, 1860-1920, Illus. LC 16-25027. 1896. Macmillan and Co., Limited.
Cranford. Elizabeth Cleghorn Stevenson Gaskell. LC 99-4201. T. Y. Crowell & Company.
Cranford. Elizabeth Cleghorn Stevenson Gaskell. LC 4852. W. B. Conkey Company.
Cranford. Elizabeth Cleghorn Stevenson Gaskell. LC 4-16526. 1903. Macmillan and Co., Limited.
Cranford. Elizabeth Cleghorn Stevenson Gaskell. Ed. by Martin Wright Sampson. LC 5-347003. (Macmillan's pocket American and English classics). 1905. The Macmillan Company.
Cranford. Elizabeth Cleghorn Stevenson Gaskell. Ed. by William Edward Simonds. LC 6-17875. (Standard English classics). Ginn & Company.
Cranford. Elizabeth Cleghorn Stevenson Gaskell. Ed. by Charles Elbert Rhodes. LC 7-9840. (Half-title: The gateway series of English texts. General editor: H. Van Dyke). American Book Company.
Cranford. Elizabeth Cleghorn Stevenson Gaskell. (Half-title: Everman's library, ed. by Ernest Rhys. Fiction). 1908. E. P. Dutton & Co.
Cranford. Elizabeth Cleghorn Stevenson Gaskell. Ed. by Margaret Abbott Eaton Whiting. LC 9-18436. Educational Publishing Company.
Cranford. Elizabeth Cleghorn Stevenson Gaskell. Ed. by Harry Evan Coblentz. LC 10-7952. (Riverside literature series) $0.40.). Houghton, Mifflin Company.
Cranford. Elizabeth Cleghorn Stevenson Gaskell. Ed. by Albert Elmer Hancock. LC 10-23321. (Half-title: The Lake English classics, ed. by L. T. Damon...). Scott, Foreman and Company.
Cranford. Elizabeth Cleghorn Stevenson Gaskell. Ed. by Helen Elizabeth Davis. LC 14-5511. (Merrill's English texts) $0.40.). Charles E. Merrill Company.
Cranford. Elizabeth Cleghorn Stevenson Gaskell. Ed. by Albert Elmer Hancock. LC 21-116355. (Lake English classics). Scott, Foreman and Company.
Cranford. Elizabeth Cleghorn Stevenson Gaskell. LC 24-470. (Half-title: The Bedside series). 1923. J. M. Dent & Sons Ltd.
Cranford. Elizabeth Cleghorn Stevenson Gaskell. LC 27-280843. (Half-title: The series of English idylls). 1926. E. P. Dutton & Company.
Cranford. Elizabeth Cleghorn Stevenson Gaskell. LC 6-33575. (Half-title: The works of Mrs. Gaskell... Knutsford ed. v. 2). 1906. G. P. Putnam's Sons; Etc., Etc.
Cranford. Elizabeth Cleghorn Stevenson Gaskell. Ed. by Elizabeth Porges Watson. LC 79-40907. (World's classics). 1980. 2.95 (ISBN 0-19-281531-8). Oxford University Press.
Cranford; and, Cousin Phillis. Elizabeth Cleghorn Stevenson Gaskell. LC 77-357254. (Penguin English library). 1976. 2.95 (ISBN 0-14-043104-7). Penguin.
Cranford: A Tale. Elizabeth Cleghorn Stevenson Gaskell. LC 36-37093. (Half-title: Everyman's library, ed. by Ernest Rhys. Fiction. no. 83). 1928. J. M. Dent & Sons, Ltd.
Cranford, and Other Tales. knutsford ed. 1st ams ed. london, j. murray. ed. Elizabeth Cleghorn Stevenson Gaskell. Ed. by J. Murray. LC 72-186539. (works of Mrs. Gaskell, v. 2). (Illus.). 1972. 24.00 (ISBN 0-404-07252-6). AMS Press.
Cranford: Ed., with Introductions and Notes. Elizabeth Cleghorn Stevenson Gaskell. Ed. by Katherine E. Forster. LC 10-9823. (Half-title: The Scribner English classics, ed. by F. H. Sykes) $0.25.). 1910. C. Scribner's Sons.
Cranford, The Cage at Cranford, The Moorland Cottage. Elizabeth Cleghorn Stevenson Gaskell. LC 33-34496. (Half-title: The novels and tales of Mrs. Gaskell--iii). H. Milford, Oxford University Press.
Cranford: The Cage at Cranford, The Moorland Cottage. Elizabeth Cleghorn Stevenson Gaskell. (World's Classics Ser: No. 110). 5.25 o.p. (ISBN 0-19-250110-0). Oxford U Pr.
Cranford. With an Introd. by Angela Thirkell. Elizabeth Cleghorn Stevenson Gaskell. LC 51-14134. (Novel library 40). Hamilton.
Crank in the Corner. Christopher Bush. LC 33-29637. 1933. W. Morrow & Co.
Crankadom. Maud Daws. LC 6-32255. 1895. J. North & Co., Printers.
Cranmer. Steve Knickmeyer. LC 77-90267. 6.95 (ISBN 0-394-41153-6). Random House.
Cranmer Paul. Rolf Bennett. LC 28-11170. Harcourt, Brace and Company.
Craque O' Doom. Mary Hartwell Catherwood. LC 2-18934. 1902. Street & Smith.
Craque-O'-Doom. A Story. Mary Hartwell Catherwood. LC 6-22285. 1881. J. B. Lippincott & Co.
Crash. J. G. Ballard. LC 73-84112. 1973. 6.95 (ISBN 0-374-13072-8). Farrar, Straus and Giroux.
Crash! Scott Lisetor & Scott Shirley. (Perspective I Novel Ser.). 48p. 1982. 2.50 (ISBN 0-87879-297-X). Acad Therapy.
Crash. Denise Robins. 1972. pap. 0.75 o.p. (94304). Beagle Bks.
Crash. Noah A Stewart & John Reed Crawford. LC 73-97030. 1969. 5.95. Gladiator Production.
Crash & the Cannibals. Theodore Clifford, pseud. 1973. pap. 1.25 o.s.i. (78-748). Lancer.
Crash and the Cannibals. Theodore Clifford. 1973. (pbk.) 1.25. Lancer.
Crash Course: A Novel. Stephen Barlay. LC 79-1696. 1979. 10.95 (ISBN 0-06-010326-4). Harper & Row.
Crash of Seventy-Nine. Paul Emil Erman. 1977. pap. 3.95 (ISBN 0-671-81249-1). PB.
Crash of Twenty Eighty-Six. Morris Hershman. 176p. 1976. pap. 1.25 (ISBN 0-89041-090-9, 3090). Major Bks.
Crash of '79. Paul Emil Erdman. LC 76-22150. 8.95 (ISBN 0-671-22365-8). Simon and Schuster.
Crash of '79. Paul Emil Erdman. (Kangaroo Book). 1977. 2.50 (ISBN 0-671-81249-1). Pocket Books.
Crashing. Enid Harlow. LC 79-25420. 10.95 (ISBN 0-312-17099-8). St. Martin's Press.
Crater. Robert Gore-Browne. LC 26-10843. George H. Doran Company.
Crater. Richard Slotkin. LC 80-65988. 1980. 17.95 (ISBN 0-689-11107-X). Atheneum.
Crater and the Krater. Kathleen Maxwell. LC 78-152848. 1971. 4.95 (ISBN 0-8111-0406-0). Naylor Co.
Crater: Or, Vulcan's Peak. James Fenimore Cooper. (His Works. Mohawk ed.). 1896. G. P. Putnam's Sons.
Crater: Or, Vulcan's Peak. James Fenimore Cooper. LC 76-42723. (Communal Societies in America). (Works of James Fenimore Cooper). ((Series: Cooper, James Fenimore, 1789-1851.). (Works. 1979.). (Illus.). 1979. 37.50 (ISBN 0-404-60058-1). AMS Press.
Crater: Or, Vulcan's Peak. A Tale of the Pacific. James Fenimore Cooper. Ed. by Cooper, Susan Fenimore. LC 6-30182. 1847. Burgees, Stringer & Co.
Crater: Or, Vulcan's Peak. A Tale of the Pacific. new ed. James Fenimore Cooper. LC 6-30181. 1859. Stringer and Townsend.
Crater: Or, Vulcan's Peak, a Tale of the Pacific. James Fenimore Cooper. (On cover: Lovell's library, no. 559). 1885. J. W. Lovell Company.
Crater: Or, Vulcan's Peak. A Tale of the Pacific. James Fenimore Cooper. LC 4-19570. 1889. D. Appleton and Company.
Crater: Or, Vulcan's Peak; a Tale of the Pacific. James Fenimore Cooper. (On cover: The works of J. Fenimore Cooper. Household ed.). 1880. Houghton, Mifflin and Company.
Crater: Or, Vulcan's Peak, a Tale of the Pacific. household ed. James Fenimore Cooper. Ed. by Cooper, Susan Fenimore. LC 11-105721. Houghton, Mifflin and Company.
Crater's Edge. Stephen Bagnall. LC 46-5572. 1946. W. Morrow and Company.
Crater's Gold: A Novel. Philip Everett Curtiss. LC 19-59940. 1919. Harper & Brothers.
Craven House. Patrick Hamilton. LC 27-5081. 1927. Houghton Mifflin Company.
Craving. Emily Arnold. 256p. 1982. pap. 2.95 (ISBN 0-380-79442-X, 79442, Bard). Avon.
Craving. Arthur Herzog. (Orig.). 1982. pap. 3.25 (ISBN 0-440-11014-9). Dell.
Cravings of Desire. Woodland Kahler. LC 60-10148. 1960. Liveright Pub. Corp.

Crawlspace. Herbert H. Lieberman. LC 78-155255. 1971. 6.95. McKay.
Crayfish Dinner. Carlton Keith, pseud. Ed. by J. Barzun & W. H. Taylor. LC 81-47336. (Crime Fiction 1950-1975 Ser.). 181p. 1982. lib. bdg. 14.95 (ISBN 0-8240-4984-5). Garland Pub.
Crayfish Dinner. Keith Robertson. LC 66-25984. 1966. Published for the Crime Club by Doubleday.
Crayfish Dinner. Keith Robertson. LC 81-47336. (Fifty Classics of Crime Fiction, 1950-1975). 1982. 14.95 (ISBN 0-8240-4984-5). Garland Pub.
Crayfishing with Grandmother: Illustrated by Barbara Strathdee. Maori Text by Hapi Potae. Jill Bagnall. (Illus.). 1974. Collins.
Crayon Clue. Minnie Josephine Reynolds. LC 15-8936. 1915. M. Kennerley.
Craze of Christian Engelhart. Henry Faulkner Darnell. LC 6-330659. (On cover: Appleton's town and country library, no. 50). 1890. D. Appleton and Company.
Crazy Americans. Arthur Talmage Abernethy. Glenn Printing Co.
Crazy Angel. Annette Lucile Noble & Collin, Grace Lathrop. LC 1-24892. 1901. G. P. Putnam's Sons.
Crazy Doctor: Translated from the Dutch by Alfred Van Ameyden Van Duym. Arie Van Der Lugt. LC 54-7797. 1954. Random House.
Crazy February. Carter Wilson. LC 66-10259. 1966. bds., 4.95. Lippincott.
Crazy February. Carter Wilson. LC 66-10259. C.
Crazy Fool. Donald Ogden Stewart. LC 25-11319. 1925. A. & C. Boni.
Crazy Fox Remembers. Don Preston & Sue Preston. LC 81-1590. 10.95 (ISBN 0-13-188896-X). Prentice-Hall.
Crazy from the Sane. Peter Roger Breggin. LC 76-150726. 1971. 7.95. L. Stuart.
Crazy Glasspecker. David Dodge. (Illus.). 1949. 2.75 o.p. Random.
Crazy Glasspecker: Or, High Life in the Andes. David Dodge. LC 49-11553. 1949. Random House.
Crazy Green of Second Avenue & from Hauptbahnhof I Took a Train: Two Novels. Erje Ayden. 307p. 1971. pap. 8.00 (ISBN 0-89366-002-7). Ultramarine Pub.
Crazy Horse. Mari Sandoz. 1975. Repr. 12.95 (ISBN 0-8038-1119-5). Hastings.
Crazy Hunter: Three Short Novels. Kay Boyle. LC 40-6737. Harcourt, Brace and Company.
Crazy in Berlin. Thomas Berger. LC 58-11644. 1958. Scribner.
Crazy in Berlin: A Novel. Thomas Berger. LC 82-5148. 1982. 8.95. Delcorte Press/S. Lawrence.
Crazy in Berlin: An Novel. Thomas Berger. LC 82-9997. 1982. 8.95 (ISBN 0-440-51085-6). Delta Books/S. Lawrence.
Crazy Joe: A Novel. Mike Barone. 1974. (pbk.) 1.25. Bantam Books.
Crazy Kid. Grace Perkins Oursler. LC 38-21852. Farrar & Rinehart, Inc.
Crazy Kill. Chester B. Himes. (Coffin Ed Johnson and Grave Digger Jones series, no. 3). (Signet book). 1975. (pbk.) 1.25. New American Library.
Crazy Ladies. Joyce Elbert. LC 69-15077. 1974. (pbk.) 1.50. New American Library.
Crazy Lovers. Joyce Elbert. LC 78-64804. 9.95 (ISBN 0-89256-079-7). Rawson, Wade.
Crazy Lovers. Joyce Elbert. (SignetBook). 1979. 2.75 (ISBN 0-451-08917-0). New American Library.
Crazy Man. Maxwell Bodenheim. LC 24-37913. Harcourt, Brace and Company.
Crazy Mary. John Benton. LC 77-9028. (Spire books). 1.50. F. H. Revell Co.
Crazy Pavements, by Beverley Nichols. Beverley Nichols. LC 27-7176. George H. Doran Company.
Crazy Quilt Murders. H. W Sandberg. Phoenix Press.
Crazy Snake and the Smoked Meat Rebellion. Mel Hallin Bolster. LC 75-32880. (Illus.). 8.95 (ISBN 0-8283-1649-X). Branden Press.
Crazy Sundays: F. Scott Fitzgerald in Hollywood. Aaron Latham. LC 70-132860. 1971. 7.95 (ISBN 0-670-24550-X). Viking Press.
Crazy to Kill. Jean Powley. LC 44-7590. (Black cat detective series. No. 10). 1944. Crestwood Publishing Co., Inc.
Crazy to Kill. Jean Markins Powley. LC 42-2912. 1941. Mystery House.
Crazy Weather. Charles Longstreth McNichols. LC 44-2654. 1944. The Macmillan Company.
Crazy Weather: By Charles L. McNichols. Charles Longstreth McNichols. (Bison bk., BB354). 1967. pap., 1.65. Univ. of Neb. Pr.
Crazy Wild. Jett Sage. LC 75-9892. (Traveller's companion series, TC-2228). 1.25. Traveller's Companion, Inc.
Crazy Wild Breaks Loose. Jett Sage. LC 79-9893. (Traveller's companion series, TC-429). 1968. 1.25. Traveller's Companion, Inc.
Crazy Woman Blues. Jackson F. Burke. 1978. 7.95 o.p. (ISBN 0-525-08700-1). Dutton.
Crazy Woman Blues: A Novel. J. F. Burke. LC 78-7491. 7.95. Dutton.
Creaking Gate. Victor Bridges. 1981. 18.95x (Pub. by Remploy England). State Mutual Bk.
Cream of the Crime: The 15th Mystery Writers of America Anthology. With a Foreword by Hugh Pentecost. 1st Ed. Mystery Writers of America. LC 62-18759. 1962. Holt, Rinehart and Winston.
Cream of the Jest. James Branch Cabell. LC 35-285573. (Half-title: The modern library of the world's best books). The Modern Library.
Cream of the Jest: A Comedy of Evasions. James Branch Cabell. LC 22-535. 1921. R. M. McBride & Company.
Cream of the Jug: An Anthology of Humorous Stories. Ed. by Grant Martin Overton. LC 27-20252. 1927. Harper & Brothers.
Creamy and Delicious: Eat My Words (in Other Words. Steve Katz. LC 72-85560. (Illus.). 1970. 5.95. Random House.
Created Legend. Fyodor Sologub. Tr. by J. Cournos from Rus. LC 75-1093. 318p. 1975. Repr. of 1916 ed. 13.50x (ISBN 0-86527-232-8). Fertig.
Created Legend. Fyodor Sologub. Tr. by John Cournos from Russian. LC 76-23899. (Classics of Russian Literature). 1977. pap. 4.95 (ISBN 0-88355-518-2). Hyperion Conn.
Created Legend. Fedor Kuzmich Teternikov. LC 75-1093. 1975. 13.75. H. Fertig.
Created Legend. Fedor Kuzmich Teternikov. LC 74-11994. 1975. 15.25 (ISBN 0-8371-7714-6). Greenwood Press.
Created Legend. Fedor Kuzmich Teternikov. LC 76-23899. (Classics of Russian literature). (Hyperion library of world literature). 1977. 4.95 (ISBN 0-88355-518-2). Hyperion Press.
Created Legend. Fedor Kuzmich Teternikov. LC 79-121547. v. 2 17.00 (ISBN 0-88233-142-6). Ardis.
Created Legend. Fedor Kuznich Teternikov & Cournos, John, Tr. LC 17-24700. 1916. Frederick A. Stokes Company.
Created, the Destroyer. Warren Murphy. (Destroyer Ser.: No. 1). 1976. pap. 2.25 (ISBN 0-523-41756-X). Pinnacle Bks.
Creative Murders see Coven.
Creative Writing: The Story Form. Mabel Louise Robinson & Hull, Helen Rose, Joint Author. LC 32-182614. American Book Company.
Creator. William Hegner. (Kangaroo Book). 1978. 1.95 (ISBN 0-671-80994-6). Pocket Books.
Creator. Jeremy Leven. LC 79-17932. 11.95 (ISBN 0-698-11012-9). Coward, McCann & Geoghegan.
Creators: A Comedy. May Sinclair. LC 10-24179. 1910. The Century Co.
Creature! A Chrestomathy of "Monstery". Bill Pronzini. LC 80-70221. 304p. 1981. 12.95 (ISBN 0-87795-310-4); pap. 5.95 (ISBN 0-87795-321-X). Arbor Hse.
Creature from the Black Lagoon. Carl Dreadstone & Zimm, Maurice. (Berkley Medallion Book). (Illus.). 1977. 1.25 (ISBN 0-425-03464-X). Berkley Pub. Corp.
Creature of the Night: An Italian Enigma. Fergus Hume. LC 7-5795. J. W. Lovell Company.
Creature of the Twilight: His Memorials. Being Some Account of Episodes in the Career of His Excellency Manfred Arcane, Minister Without Portfolio to the Hereditary President of the Commonwealth of Hamnegri, and De Facto Field Commander of the Armies of That August Prince. Russell Kirk. LC 66-16524. 5.95. Fleet.
Creature Was Stirring. Stanton Forbes, pseud. LC 76-50800. 1977. 5.95 (ISBN 0-385-07331-3). Published for the Crime Club by Doubleday.
Creature Was Stirring. Tobias Wells. LC 76-50800. 1977. 6.95 o.p. (ISBN 0-385-07331-3). Doubleday.
Creature Was Stirring: And Other Stories. Jess Carr. LC 70-108094. 1970. 3.95. Commonwealth Press.
Creature Was Stirring & Other Stories. Jess Carr. 128p. 1970. 3.95 (ISBN 0-89227-022-5). Commonwealth Pr.
Creatures from Beyond: Nine Stories of Science Fiction and Fantasy. Ed. by Terry Carr. LC 75-16244. 1975. 6.95 (ISBN 0-8407-6459-6). T. Nelson.
Creatures Great & Small. Sidonie Gabrielle Colette. Tr. by Enid McLeod from Fr. 292p. 1978. 10.00 (ISBN 0-374-13102-3); pap. 3.95 (ISBN 0-374-51467-4). FS&G.
Creatures in an Alphabet. Djuna Barnes. 64p. 1982. signed limited ed. 35.00 (ISBN 0-385-27806-3); 10.95 (ISBN 0-385-27797-0). Dial.
Creatures of Circumstance. William Somerset Maugham. LC 75-26130. (Maugham, William Somerset, 1874-1965. Works. 1976). 1976. 15.00 (ISBN 0-405-07853-6). Arno Press.
Creatures of Circumstances. William Somerset Maugham. LC 47-5077. 1947. Doubleday.
Creatures of Light and Darkness. Roger Zelazny. LC 70-78673. (Doubleday science fiction). 1969. 4.50. Doubleday.
Creatures That Once Were Men. Maksim Gorkii & Shirazi, J. K. M., Tr. LC 28-7825. (Half-title: The Modern library of the world's best books). Boni and Liveright, Inc.
Crecy. Edith Lawrence Bailey. LC 4-14893. 1904. F. M. Buckles & Company.
Credit for a Murder: By Spencer Dean Pseud. 1st Ed. Prentice Winchell. LC 61-9206. 1961. Published for the Crime Club by Doubleday.
Credit of the County: A Novel. William Edward Norris. (Appletons' town and country library, no. 313). 1902. D. Appleton and Company.
Credo: A Utopian Novel. Bernardino Dell'Osso. 1978. 10.95 (ISBN 0-87164-037-6). William-F.
Creed Country. Jenny Overton. LC 78-89590. 1970. Macmillan.
Creed of Her Father: A Novel. Van Zandt Wheeler. LC 19-14623. Britton Publishing Co.
Creed of the Range. George Brydges Rodney. LC 32-330567. E. J. Clode, Inc.
Creeds to Love & Live by. Ed. by Sandpiper Studios. LC 77-93902. (Illus.). 1978. pap. 4.95 (ISBN 0-88396-027-3). Blue Mtn Pr CO.
Creek Called Wounded Knee. Douglas C Jones. LC 78-16660. (Illus.). 8.95 (ISBN 0-684-15822-1). Scribner.
Creek Called Wounded Knee. Douglas C Jones. 1979. 2.50 (ISBN 0-446-91121-6). Warner Books, Inc.
Creek Mary's Blood. Dee Alexander Brown. 496p. 1981. pap. 3.50 (ISBN 0-671-42028-3). PB.
Creek Mary's Blood: A Novel. Dee Alexander Brown. LC 79-9060. (Illus.). 12.95 (ISBN 0-03-044281-8). Holt, Rinehart and Winston.
Creek Rifles. David Moltke-Hansen. (American Indian Ser.: No. 5). (Orig.). 1982. pap. 2.75 (ISBN 0-440-01215-5). Dell.
Creek Street. 3rd ed. Mary G. Balcom. (Illus.). 1979. pap. 3.25 o.p. Balcom.
Creek Street. 3rd ed. Mary G. Balcom. (Illus.). 1979. pap. 3.25 o.p. Balcom.
Creel of Irish Stories. Jane Barlow. LC 70-116934. (Short story index reprint series). 1970. Books for Libraries Press.
Creel of Irish Stories. Jane Barlow. LC 9-3335. 1899. Dodd, Mead and Company.
Creep: A Novel. Jeffrey Frank. LC 68-10645. 1968. Farrar, Straus and Giroux.
Creep into Thy Narrow Bed. Leonard Bishop. LC 54-712455. 1954. Dial Press.
Creep, Shadow!... Abraham Merritt. LC 34-39747. 1934. Pub. for the Crime Club, Inc., by Doubleday, Doran & Company, Inc.
Creep, Shadow!... Abraham Merritt. LC 38-32641. 1938. The Sun Dial Press, in.
Creep, Shadow, Creep! Abraham Merritt. LC 48-171355. (New Avon library, 117). 1947. Avon Book Co.
Creep, Shadow, Creep! Abraham Merritt. LC 44-8911. (Murder mystery monthly. No. 11). Avon Book Company.
Creepers. Robert Craig. 1982. pap. 2.95 (ISBN 0-451-11823-5, AE1823, Sig). NAL.
Creepers. John Creasey. 1970. pap. 0.75 o.p. (ISBN 0-447-74712-6). Lancer.
Creepers. easy eye ed. John Creasey. 1968. pap. 0.75 o.p. (74-933). Lancer.
Creepers. 1st Ed. John Creasey. LC 52-116819. 1952. Harper.
Creeping Death. Maxwell Grant, pseud. (Shadow Ser.: No. 14). 1977. pap. 1.25 o.p. (ISBN 0-515-04206-4). BJ Pub Group.
Creeping Flesh. James Douglas Rutherford McConnell. LC 65-15424. 1965. 3.50. Walker.
Creeping Hours: A John Jericho Mystery Novel. Judson Pentecost Philips. LC 66-27939. (Red badge mystery). 1966. Dodd, Mead.
Creeping Jenny, and Other New England Stories. Kate Douglas Smith Wiggin. LC 24-22460. 1924. Houghton Mifflin Company.
Creeping Peril Mystery. Gertrude Ethel Mallette. LC 52-5761. 1952. Doubleday.
Creeping Siamese: A Dashiell Hammett Detective. Short Stories Collected and Edited with Introd. by Ellery Queen Pseud. Dashiell Hammett. LC 50-14987. (Jonathan Press mystery, J48). 1950. L. E. Spivak.
Creeping Tides: A Romance of an Old Neighborhood. Kate F. M. Vermilye. Jordan. LC 13-35388. 1913. 1.30. Little, Brown, and Company.
Creeping Vicar. Ian Hamilton. LC 67-14366. 1967. bds., 4.50. Lippincott.
Creeps: Being a Full Statement About the Crimes at Buzzards Bay, a Thatcher Colt Detective Mystery. Fulton Oursler. Farrar & Rinehart, Incorporated.
Creeps by Night: Chills and Thrills. Ed. by Dashiell Hammett. LC 31-28327. The John Day Company.
Creezy. Felicien Marceau, pseud. LC 71-94092. 1970. 5.95. Orion Press.
Creighton's Castle. Miriam Lynch. LC 75-22241. 1975. 1.25 (ISBN 0-345-24616-0). Ballantine Books.
Creole. Ray La Scola. LC 61-5535. 1961. Morrow.
Creole Dusk: A New Orleans Novel of the '80s. Walter Adolphe Roberts. LC 48-8337. 1948. Bobbs-Merrill Co.
Creole Folk Tales: A Stories of the Louisiana Marsh Country. Hewitt Leonard Ballowe. LC 48-8088. 1948. Louisiana State Univ. Press.
Creole: Or, Siege of New Orleans. An Historical Romance. Founded on the Events of 1814-15. Joseph Beckham Cobb. LC 6-21342. 1850. A. Hart.
Creole Orphans: Or, Lights and Shadows of Southern Life. A Tale of Louisiana. James S Peacocke. 1856. Derby & Jackson.
Creole Slave's Revenge. A Melodrama of the South. Helen Burrell D'Apery & Lawerence, Walter. LC 33-28364. (On cover: Play book series. no. 129). 1908. J. S. Ogilvie Publishing Company.
Creole Stories. George Washington Cable & Cable, George Washington, 1844-1925. LC 36-510079. Pelican Publishing Company.
Creole Stories: By George W. Cable; Briefly Retold by His Niece, Kinne Cable Oechsner. With Pen and Ink Sketches by Wiley Churchill. Kinne Cable Oechsner & George Washington Cable. LC 55-20869. 1954. Harmanson.
Creole Surgeon. Mitchell Caine, pseud. 1977. 1.95 (ISBN 0-449-13924-7). Fawcett Books.
Creoles and Cajuns; Stories of Old Louisiana. Edited by Arlin Turner. 1st Ed. George Washington Cable. LC 59-913396. (Doubleday anchor books, A179). 1959. Doubleday.
Creoles and Cajuns: Stories of Old Louisiana. George Washington Cable. LC 59-9133. 1965. P. Smith.
Creoles of Louisiana see Collected Works.
Crepuscule des Vieux: Essai. Georges Bernanos. 5.95. French & Eur.
Cresap Pension: The Story of a Peculiar ! Pension Fraud. Emma Upton Vaughn. LC 16-373. 1915. Burton Publishing Company.
Crescendo. Henry Bellamann. LC 28-21982. Hacourt, Brace & Company.
Crescendo. Phyllis Eleanor Bentley. LC 58-12922. 1958. Macmillan.
Crescendo. Charlotte Lamb, pseud. (Harlequin Presents Ser.). 192p. 1981. pap. 1.75 (ISBN 0-373-10451-0, Pub. by Harlequin). PB.
Crescendo. Harriet Buren McKeever. 3.75 o.p. (ISBN 0-8062-0700-0). Carlton.
Crescendo. J. J Savage. LC 77-6400. 1968. 1.75. Ophelia Press.
Crescendo: Being the Dark Odyssey of Gilbert Stroud. Ethel Edith Mannin. LC 29-12913. 1929. Doubleday, Doran and Company, Inc.
Crescent and the Cross. A Story of the Siege of Malta. Sarah Towne Martyn. LC 29-30778. (Lettered on cover: Life illustrated). 1869. The American Tract Society.
Crescent Brotherhood: Or, Nick Carter's Chicago Double. John Russell Coryell. LC 99-2892. (On cover: Magnet detective library. no. 83). 1899. Street & Smith.
Crescent Carnival. Frances Parkinson Wheeler Keyes. LC 42-24673. 1942. J. Messner, Inc.
Crescent Carnival. Frances Parkinson Wheeler Keyes. 1974. (pbk.) 1.75 (ISBN 0-671-78729-2). Pocket Books.
Crescent City: A Novel. William Edward Wilson. LC 47-6381. 1947. Simon and Schuster.
Crescent Moon. Eileen Shaw. LC 49-8011. 1949. W. Morrow.
Crescent Moon. Francis Brett Young. LC 19-919. E. P. Dutton & Company.
Cress. Clara Hiemenz. Nixon-Jones Ptg. Co.
Cress Delahanty. Jessamyn West. LC 66-1430. (Reader's enrichment series). 1965. Washington Square Press.
Cress Delahanty. Jessamyn West. LC 53-5654. (Illus.). 1953. Harcourt, Brace.
Cresselly Inheritance. Jane Blackmore. (Ace Gothic, 12170). 1974. (pbk.) 0.95. Ace Books.
Cressey & Poictiers: The Story of the Black Prince's Page. John George Edgar. (Half-title: Everyman's library, edited by Ernest Rhys. Fiction. (no. 17). J. M. Dent & Co.
Cressida. Claire Darcy. (Signet Book). 1978. 1.75 (ISBN 0-451-08287-7). New American Library.
Cressida. Clare Darcy. LC 77-73662. 1977. 8.95 (ISBN 0-8027-0575-8). Walker.
Cressida. Clare Darcy. LC 78-14302. 1978. 9.95 (ISBN 0-8161-6606-4). G. K. Hall.
Cressida. Joyce Wilson, pseud. (Orig.). 1980. pap. 1.95 (ISBN 0-445-04547-7). Popular Lib.
Cressida: No Mystery. Marie Adelaide Belloc Lowndes. LC 30-16619. 1930. A. A. Knopf.
Cressida's First Lover: A Tale of Ancient Greece. Jack Lindsay. LC 32-16444. 1932. R. Long & R. R. Smith, Inc.
Cressy. Bret Harte. LC 7-3639. 1889. Houghton, Mifflin and Company.
Cressy, a Maid of Japan: A Story of the Conversion of a High Class Girl to Christianity, Setting Forth Religious and Social Conditions, in Japan. Frederick Albertus Perry. LC 10-199585. 1910. The Hammond Publishing Company.

Crest of the Broken Wave: A Novel of the Life and Loves of Robert Burns. James Barke. LC 53-12082. (His Immortal memory v.4). 1953. Macmillan.
Crest of the Little Wolf: A Tale of "the Young Lovell" and the Wars of the Roses. Thomas Daniel Rhodes. LC 4-27350. 1904. The Robert Clarke Company.
Crested Sea. James Brendan Connolly. LC 7-30867. 1907. C. Scribner's Sons.
Cresten, Queen of the Toltus: Or, Under the Auroras. W. J Shaw. Excelsior Publishing House.
Cresting Wave. Edwin Bateman Morris. LC 20-4440. 1920. The Penn Publishing Company.
Crestlands: A Centennial Story of Cane Ridge. Mary Addams Bayne. LC 7-36246. The Standard Publishing Company.
Creston Meadows: A Story of Love and Daring. Sheridan Franzell Wood. Dorrance and Company.
Creston, the Detective: Or, Following a Light Clue. Harlan Page Halsey. LC 7-11913. (Old Sleuth's own. no. 96). 1897. Parlor Car Publishing Co.
Crevice. William John Burns & Ostrander, Isabel Egenton 1883- Joint Author. LC 15-17132. W. J. Watt & Company.
Crew of the "Sam Weller,". John Habberton. LC 6-466803. 1878. G. P. Putnam's Sons.
Crewe Train. Rose Macaulay. LC 26-27438. 1926. Boni & Liveright.
Crezz. Sean Hignett. LC 77-363624. 1976. 3.75 (ISBN 0-213-16623-2). Barker.
Crib. Hal Friedman. 288p. (Orig.). 1982. pap. 2.75 (ISBN 0-671-43115-3). PB.
Crick Crack, Monkey. Merle Hodge. LC 81-143132. (Caribbean Writers Series; 24). 1981. 4.95 (ISBN 0-435-98401-2). Heinemann.
Crick in the Neck. Henry Herbert Erhardt. LC 66-16642. 1966. Dorrance.
Cricket. Marjorie Benton Cooke. LC 19-6411. 1919. Doubleday, Page & Company.
Cricket. Nathaniel Lande. 1981. 12.95 (ISBN 0-453-00392-3, H392). NAL.
Cricket Beneath the Waterfall: And Other Stories. Miroslav Krleza. LC 72-83354. 1973. 7.95 (ISBN 0-8149-0699-0). Vanguard Press.
Cricket Cage. Ruth H Shimer. LC 75-6376. 1975. 7.95 (ISBN 0-06-013851-3). Harper & Row.
Cricket Cage. Ruth H Shimer. LC 76-18951. 1976. 13.95 (ISBN 0-8161-6393-6). G. K. Hall.
Cricket in the Road. Michael Anthony. (Caribbean Writers Ser.). 1973. pap. text ed. 4.00x (ISBN 0-435-98032-7). Heinemann Ed.
Cricket on the Hearth". Gilmor Brown & Dickens, Charles. The Cricket on the Hearth. S. French, Inc.
Cricket on the Hearth. Charles Dickens. LC 6616. 1900. G. P. Putnam's Sons.
Cricket on the Hearth. Charles Dickens. (wayfarer's library). 1914. J. M. Dent & Sons Ltd.
Cricket on the Hearth. A Fairy Tale of Home. Charles Dickens. LC 15-4346. (Half-title: Wiley & Putnam's library of choice reading. no. lv). 1846. Wiley & Putnam.
Cricket on the Hearth. A Fairy Tale of Home. Charles Dickens. LC 1-437. (On cover: Lovell's library, v. 4, no. 140). 1883. John W. Lovell Company.
Cricket on the Hearth. A Fairy Tale of Home. Charles Dickens. (English classic series. no. 86). 1890. E. Maynard & Co.
Cricket on the Hearth: A Fairy Tale of Home. Charles Dickens. Ed. by Alton, George Briggs. LC 2-20987. (Canterbury classics). Rand, McNally & Company.
Cricket on the Hearth: A Fairy Tale of Home. Charles Dickens. LC 28-26083. 1927. Harper & Brothers.
Cricket on the Hearth, and Doctor Marigold. Charles Dickens. LC 1-436. (On cover: Seaside library. Pocket ed., no. 108). 1883. G. Munro.
Cricket Sings: A Novel of Pre-Columbian Cahokia. Kathleen King. LC 82-8046. 1983. 15.95 (ISBN 0-8214-0704-X) (ISBN 0-8214-0705-8). Ohio University Press.
Cricket Sings: A Novel of Pre-Columbian Cahokia. Kathleen King. LC 82-8046. 172p. 1983. 15.95 (ISBN 0-8214-0704-X, 82-84747); pap. 8.95 (ISBN 0-8214-0705-8, 82-84754). Ohio U Pr.
Cricket Smith. 1st Ed. Monte Linkletter. LC 58-12470. 1959. Harper.
Cricket Voices. Hazel Bowers. 1970. 4.00 (ISBN 0-8233-0152-4). Golden Quill.
Crickets All Look Alike: By Bill Davidson. Illus. by Bob Bugg. William Davidson. LC 65-20425. 4.95. Harper.
Criers and Kibitzers, Kibitzers and Criers. Stanley Elkin. LC 65-21228. 1966. bds., 4.95. Random.
Criers and Kibitzers, Kibitzers and Criers. Stanley Elkin. (Plume Book, Z5077). 1973. (pbk.) 3.95. New American Library.
Cries in the Night. James Harold Wallis. LC 33-170010. E. P. Dutton & Company, Inc.
Crime. Georges Bernanos. Tr. by Green, Anne. LC 36-98613. E. P. Dutton & Co., Inc.
Crime: A Novel. Stephen Longstreet. LC 59-13146. 1959. Simon and Schuster.
Crime Across the Way. Frances Millington. LC 38-10696. Phoenix Press.
Crime & Co. Sydney Fowler Wright. LC 31-340032. The Macaulay Company.
Crime & Compromise. William Shawcross. LC 73-15503. 1974. 10.00 o.p. (ISBN 0-525-08735-4). Dutton.
Crime and Detection. Ed. by Edward Murray Wrong. LC 27-17362. (Half-title: The World's classics, CCCI). 1926. Oxford University Press, H. Milford.
Crime & Miss Olivia: By Joan Sargent Pseud. Sara Lucile Jenkins. LC 52-14739. 1952. Bouregy & Curl.
Crime and Mr. Campion. 1st Ed. Margery Allingham. LC 59-11579. 1959. Published for the Crime Club by Doubleday.
Crime and Punishment. Fedor Mikhailovich Dostoevskii. Tr. by Sidney Monas. LC 67-27378. (Signet classic, CT362). 1968. New American Library.
Crime and Punishment. Fedor Mikhailovich Dostoevskii. LC 63-20470. (Great illustrated classics: Titan editions). 1963. Dodd, Mead.
Crime and Punishment. Fedor Mikhailovich Dostoevskii. LC 63-23753. 1963. Washington Square Press.
Crime and Punishment. rev. ed. Fedor Mikhailovich Dostoevskii. Tr. by Jessie Senior Coulson. Ed. by George Gibian. LC 74-16325. (Norton critical edition). 1975. 15.00 (ISBN 0-393-05534-5) (ISBN 0-393-05534-5) (ISBN 0-393-05534-5). Norton.
Crime and Punishment. Fedor Mikhailovich Dostoevskii. LC 64-10893. (Norton critical editions, N310). 1964. W. W. Norton.
Crime and Punishment. a limited ed. Fedor Mikhailovich Dostoevskii. LC 75-327280. (Illus.). 1975. Franklin Library.
Crime and Punishment. Fedor Mikhailovich Dostoevskii. Tr. by Constance Black Garnett. LC 17-17426. (Harvard classics shelf of fiction, selected by C. W. Eliot. 18). P. F. Collier & Son.
Crime and Punishment. Fedor Mikhailovich Dostoevskii. Tr. by Constance Black Garnett. Brewster, Dorothy, 1883- LC 27-6050. (modern readers' series). 1927. The Macmillan Company.
Crime and Punishment. Fedor Mikhailovich Dostoevskii. Tr. by Constance Black Garnett. Reisman, Philip, 1904- Illus. LC 44-40199. (Illustrated modern library). 1944. A. S. Barnes & Co. Inc.
Crime and Punishment. Fedor Mikhailovich Dostoevskii. Tr. by Constance Black Garnett. Reisman, Philip, 1904- Illus. LC 46-177422. (Illustrated modern library). 1945. A. S. Barnes & Co., Inc.
Crime and Punishment. Fedor Mikhailovich Dostoevskii. Tr. by Constance Black Garnett. LC 47-426517. (Half-title: The Living library). 1947. The World Publishing Company.
Crime & Punishment. Fedor Mikhailovich Dostoevskii. (Literature Ser). (gr. 9-12). 1969. pap. text ed. 4.58 (ISBN 0-87720-705-4). AMSCO Sch.
Crime & Punishment. Fedor Mikhailovich Dostoevskii. Tr. by Constance Garnett from Russian. (Bantam Classics Ser.). 472p. (gr. 10-12). 1981. pap. 2.50 (ISBN 0-553-21038-6). Bantam.
Crime & Punishment. Fedor Mikhailovich Dostoevskii. Tr. by Constance Garnett. 1977. Repr. of 1955 ed. 9.95x (ISBN 0-460-00501-4, Evman); pap. 3.75x (ISBN 0-460-01501-X). Biblio Dist.
Crime & Punishment. Fedor Mikhailovich Dostoevskii. Tr. by Constance Garnett. 1959. 6.95 (ISBN 0-394-60450-4). Modern Lib.
Crime & Punishment. Fedor Mikhailovich Dostoevskii. Tr. by Constance Garnett. (YA) 1950. pap. 4.00 (ISBN 0-394-30911-1, T11, Mod LibC). Modern Lib.
Crime & Punishment. Fedor Mikhailovich Dostoevskii. Tr. by Sidney Monas. pap. 2.25 (ISBN 0-451-51745-8, CE1745, Sig Classics). NAL.
Crime & Punishment. rev. ed. Fedor Mikhailovich Dostoevskii. Ed. by George Gibian. (Critical Editions Ser). (gr. 9-12). pap. text ed. 2.95x, 1964 o.s.i. (ISBN 0-393-09633-5, 9633, NortonC); pap. 6.95x, 1975 (ISBN 0-393-09292-5). Norton.
Crime & Punishment. Fedor Mikhailovich Dostoevskii. Tr. by Jessie Coulson from Rus. (World's Classics Paperback Ser.). 1981. pap. 5.95 (ISBN 0-19-281549-0). Oxford U Pr.
Crime & Punishment. Fedor Mikhailovich Dostoevskii. (Now Age Illustrated V Ser.). (Illus.). 64p. (gr. 4-12). 1979. text ed. 5.00; pap. text ed. 1.95 (ISBN 0-88301-386-X); student activity bk. 1.25 (ISBN 0-88301-410-6). Pendulum Pr.
Crime & Punishment. Fedor Mikhailovich Dostoevskii. Tr. by David Magarshack. (Classics Ser.). (Orig.). 1952. pap. 3.95 (ISBN 0-14-044023-2). Penguin.
Crime & Punishment. Fedor Mikhailovich Dostoevskii. 1982. Repr. lib. bdg. 29.95 (ISBN 0-89966-397-4). Buccaneer Bks.
Crime & Punishment. Fedor Mikhailovich Dostoevskii. 1982. pap. 10.00x (ISBN 0-330-25853-2, Pub. by Pan Bks). State Mutual Bk.
Crime and Punishment. Fedor Mikhailovich Dostoevskii & Ten Eyck, Alice. LC 49-53113. (N.A.L. Signet books, 733). 1949. New American Library.
Crime and Punishment. Fedor Mikhailovich Dostoevskii & Whishaw, Frederick J., Tr. (Half-title: Everyman's library, ed. by Ernest Rhys. Fiction no. 501). 1911. J. M. Dent & Sons, Ltd.
Crime & Punishment: A Novel in Six Parts and an Epilogue. Translated by Jessie Coulson. Fedor Mikhailovich Dostoevskii. LC 53-12884. 1953. Oxford University Press.
Crime & Punishment: A Novel in Six Parts and an Epilogue. Fedor Mikhailovich Dostoevskii. Tr. by Constance Black Garnett. LC 14-19364. (Half-title: The novels of Fyodor Dostoevsky. vol. IV). 1914. The Macmillan Co.
Crime & Punishment: A Novel in Six Parts and an Epilogue. Fedor Mikhailovich Dostoevskii & Garnett, Mrs. Constance (Black) 1862- Tr. LC 24-222046. (Half-title: The novels of Fyodor Dostoevsky. vol. IV). 1922. The Macmillan Company.
Crime & Punishment: A Novel in 6 Pts. & Epilogue. Fedor Mikhailovich Dostoevskii. Tr. by Jessie Coulson. (World Classics Ser). Set. 9.95 o.p. (ISBN 0-19-250619-6). Oxford U Pr.
Crime and Punishment: A Russian Realistic Novel. Fedor Mikhailovich Dostoevskii. LC 3-28158. T. Y. Crowell & Co.
Crime and Punishment: By Fyodor Dostoyevsky; Translated by Constance Garnett... Fedor Mikhailovich Dostoevskii & Garnett, Mrs. Constance (Black) 1862- Tr. LC 32-26051. (Half-title: The modern library of the world's best books). 1932. The Modern Library.
Crime and Punishment. Rev. Translation by Princess Alexandra Kropotkin; Arr. for Modern Reading. Illus. by Marian Larer. Fedor Mikhailovich Dostoevskii. LC 53-7344. 1953. International Collectors Library.
Crime and Punishment: Tr., Afterword, by Sidney Monas. Fedor Mikhailovich Dostoevskii. Tr. by Sidney Monas. LC 67-27368. (Signet classic, CT362). 1968. New Amer. Lib.
Crime and Punishment. Translated from the Russian by Constance Garnett. Introd. by Clifton Fadiman; Illus. by Benjamin Kopman. Fedor Mikhailovich Dostoevskii. LC 56-141841. 1956. Random House.
Crime and Punishment. Translated from the Russian by Constance Garnett. Fedor Mikhailovich Dostoevskii. LC 50-2467. 1950. Macmillan.
Crime and Punishment. Translated from the Russian by Constance Garnett; with an Introd. by Ernest J. Simmons. Fedor Mikhailovich Dostoevskii. LC 50-137141. (Modern Library college editions, T11). 1950. Modern Library.
Crime and Punishment: Translated from the Russian by Constance Garnett; with an Introd. by Avrahm Yarmolinsky. Fedor Mikhailovich Dostoevskii. LC 51-6231. (Harper's modern classics). 1951. Harper.
Crime & Punishment with Reader's Guide. Fedor Mikhailovich Dostoevskii. (Amsco Literature Program). (gr. 10-12). 1970. pap. text ed. 5.42 (ISBN 0-87720-805-0); tchr's ed. 3.45 (ISBN 0-87720-905-7). AMSCO Sch.
Crime & Puzzlement: Twenty-Four Solve-Them-Yourself Picture Mysteries. Lawrence Treat. LC 81-47331. (Illus.). 80p. (Orig.). 1981. pap. 4.95 (ISBN 0-87923-419-9). Godine.
Crime and the Criminal. Richard Marsh. LC 3-26178. Ward, Lock & Co. Ltd.
Crime Apart. Michael Underwood. 1979. 15.00x (ISBN 0-86025-067-9, Pub. by Ian Henry Pubns England). State Mutual Bk.
Crime Apart. Michael Underwood. 1977. 8.00 o.p. State Mutual Bk.
Crime at Black Dudley. Margery Allingham. 1950. pap. 2.50 o.p. (ISBN 0-14-000770-9). Penguin.
Crime at Black Dudley see Margery Allingham Omnibus.
Crime at Christmas. Clifford Henry Benn Kitchin. LC 35-1691. Harcourt, Brace and Company.
Crime at Cobb's House. Herbert Corey. LC 34-21300. (Tired business man's library of adventre. detcetive, and mysyery novels). 1934. D. Appleton-Century Company, Incorporated.
Crime at Diana's Pool. Victor Lorenzo Whitechurch. LC 27-3515. 1927. Duffield and Company.
Crime at Guildford. Freeman Wills Crofts. LC 65-4560. (Penguin crime). 1965. Penquin Books.
Crime at Nornes: An Inspector French Detective Story. Freeman Wills Crofts. LC 35-10046. 1935. Dodd, Mead & Company.
Crime at Red Towers. Chester K Steele. LC 27-23276. E. J. Clode, Inc.
Crime at the Conquistador. Sloane Callaway. Phoenix Press.
Crime at the Crossways. Brian Flynn. LC 32-10115. 1932. Macrae Smith Company.
Crime at Vanderlynden's. Ralph Hale Mottram. LC 26-589159. 1926. L. MacVeagh, The Dial Press.
Crime by Chance. Elizabeth Linington. LC 72-12517. 1973. 5.95 (ISBN 0-397-00959-3). Lippincott.
Crime by Computer. Donn B. Parker. LC 76-1836. 1978. pap. 7.95 (ISBN 0-684-15576-1, ScribT). Scribner.
Crime Club. William Edward Bradden Holt-White. LC 10-8417. (Illus.). 1910. 1.50. The Macaulay Company.
Crime Club Encore: Chosen and with a Foreword. Ed. by Howard Haycraft. Postgate, Raymond William, 1896- Verdict of Twelve et al. LC 42-25189. 1942. Doubleday, Doran & Co., Inc.
Crime Club Golden Book of Best Detective Stories. LC 33-14026. 1933. Pub. for the Crime Club, Inc., by Doubleday, Doran & Company, Inc.
Crime Coast: A Murder Mystery of the French Riviera... Elizabeth Gill. LC 31-60810. Pub. for the Crime Club, Inc., by Doubleday, Doran & Company, Inc.
Crime Code. William Le Queux. LC 28-5872. The Macaulay Company.
Crime Conductor, an Adventure of Colonel Anthony Gethryn. Philip MacDonald. LC 31-214324. Pub. for the Crime Club, Inc., by Doubleday, Doran & Company, Inc.
Crime Cult. Maxwell Grant, pseud. (Shadow Ser.: No. 6). 1975. pap. 0.95 o.p. (ISBN 0-515-03699-4). BJ Pub Group.
Crime De Luxe. Elizabeth Gill. LC 33-23921. 1933. Pub. for the Crime Club. Inc., by Doubleday, Doran & Company, Inc.
Crime de Sylvestre Bonnard see Romans et Contes.
Crime Doctor. Ernest William Hornung. LC 14-13374. The Bobbs-Merrill Company.
Crime File. Elizabeth Linington. LC 74-7374. 1974. 5.95 (ISBN 0-688-00268-4). Morrow.
Crime File. Dell Shannon. 256p. 1974. 5.95 o.p. (ISBN 0-688-00268-4). Morrow.
Crime for Two: By Members of the Mystery Writers of America. Edited by Frances and Richard Lockridge. 1st Ed. Mystery Writers of America. Ed. by Frances Louise Davis Lockridge. LC 55-10460. 1955. Lippincott.
Crime Hound: A Mystery Novel. Mary Semple Scott. LC 40-32567. 1940. C. Scribner's Sons.
Crime in Car 13. Stephen Chalmers. LC 30-2053. 1930. Pub. for the Crime Club, Inc., by Doubleday, Doran & Company, Inc.
Crime in Corn-Weather. Mary Melgs Atwater. LC 35-5966. 1935. Houghton Mifflin Company.
Crime in Crystal. Harriette Russell Campbell. LC 46-813. 1946. Harper & Brothers.
Crime in Quarantine. Rosa Lambert & Lambert, Dudley. LC 39-428174. 1938. T. Nelson and Sons, Ltd.
Crime in Reverse. John De Navarre Kennedy. LC 40-107718. 1939. T. Nelson and Sons Ltd.
Crime in the Crypt: A Fleming Stone Story. Carolyn Wells. LC 28-6755. 1928. J. B. Lippincott Company.
Crime in the Crystal. Robert Hare. LC 33-975. 1933. Longmans, Green and Co.
Crime in the Dutch Garden. Herbert Adams. LC 30-27750. 1930. J. B. Lippincott Company.
Crime in the Schools: A Novel, by Stephen and Sylvia Wright Pseuds. 1st Ed. Stephen W Andurer & Sylvia H. Andurer. LC 60-14130. 1959. Contemporary Research Library.
Crime, Inc. John S Endicott. LC 32-31615. The Fiction League.
Crime Incarnate. Carolyn Wells. LC 40-30579. J. B. Lippincott Company.
Crime Is Murder. Helen Nielsen. LC 56-10605. 1956. Morrow.
Crime Is of the Essence. Joe Csida. LC 46-21406. (On cover: Five star mystery, 43). 1946. Five-Star Mysteries.
Crime Is of the Essence. Joe Csida. LC 47-23204. 1947. Arcadia House.
Crime of a Countess: Or, The American Detective and the Russian Nihilist. John Russell Coryell. (On cover: Secret service series, no. 54). 1892. Street & Smith.
Crime of Christmas-Day. A Tale of the Latin Quarter. Peter Hay Hunter. (On cover: The seaside library. Pocket ed., no. 376). 1885. G. Munro.
Crime of Colin Wise. John Michael Evelyn. LC 64-11605. 1964. Published for the Crime Club by Doubleday.
Crime of Colin Wise. Michael Underwood. 1982. 15.00x (ISBN 0-86025-151-9, Pub. by Ian Henry Pubns England). State Mutual Bk.

Crime of Dr. Garine. Boris Fedorovih Sokoloff & Dreiser, Theodore. LC 29-133680. 1928. Covici-Friede.
Crime of Dorothy Sheridan. Leo Damore. LC 77-93047. 1978. 9.95 (ISBN 0-87795-189-6). Arbor Hse.
Crime of Giovanni Venturi. Howard Shaw. LC 59-10865. 1959. Holt.
Crime of Henry Vane: A Study with a Moral. Frederic Jesup Stimson. LC 8-156805. 1884. C. Scribner's Sons.
Crime of Innocence. Nicholas Garland. 288p. 1982. pap. 2.95 (ISBN 0-425-05657-0). Berkley Pub.
Crime of Inspector Maigret. Georges Simenon. LC 32-35927. Covici, Friede.
Crime of Laura Sarelle. Joseph Shearing. LC 41-80813. Smith & Durrell.
Crime of Maltaverne. A Drama of the Orient. Charles Buet. ("Vatican library". no. 15). 1883. Hickey & Co.
Crime of One's Own. Edward Grierson. LC 67-23139. (Red mask mystery). 1967. Putnam.
Crime of Passion. Steven Schrader. 1976. pap. 2.50 o.p. (ISBN 0-8180-0621-8). Horizon.
Crime of Philip Guthrie. Lulah Ragsdale. LC 8-202. (On cover: The midland series, v. 4 no. 33). 1892. Morrill, Higgins & Co.
Crime of Sylvestre Bonnard. Anatole France, pseud. Tr. by Hearn, Lafcadio. LC 33-7855. 1931. John Lane.
Crime of Sylvestre Bonnard: Member of the Institute. Anatole France, pseud. Tr. by Hearn, Lafcadio. LC 3-26201. (On cover: Harper's Franklin square library. no. 665). 1890. Harper & Brothers.
Crime of Sylvestre Bonnard: Member of the Institute). Anatole France, pseud. Tr. by Ward, Arabella. LC 3-26202. 1897. T. Y. Crowell & Company.
Crime of Sylvestre Bonnard: Member of the Institute. Anatole France, pseud. Tr. by Hearn, Lafcadio. Limited Editions Club, Inc., New York. LC 38-3924. 1937. The Limited Editions Club.
Crime of the Boulevard. Jules Claretie. LC 75-32739. (Literature of Mystery and Detection). 1976. 14.00 (ISBN 0-405-07867-6). Arno Press.
Crime of the Boulevard. Jules Claretie & Kingsbury, Mrs. Carlton A., Tr. LC 6-25367. 1897. R. F. Fenno & Co.
Crime of the Century. Rodrigues Ottolengui. LC 9-2495. (On cover: Hudson library. v. 12). 1896. G. P. Putnam's Sons.
Crime of the Century & Other Misdemeanors. Morton Freedgood. LC 73-78638. 1973. 6.95 (ISBN 0-399-11226-X). Putnam.
Crime of the Century & Other Misdemeanors. John Godey. 192p. (YA) 1973. 6.95 o.p. (ISBN 0-399-11226-X). Putnam.
Crime of the Chromium Bowl. Elizabeth Best Black. LC 34-308852. Loring & Mussey.
Crime of the French Cafe: Nick Carter's Ghost Story; The Mystery of St. Agnes' Hospital; Three Complete Stories of the Exploits of Nicholas Carter, America's Greatest Detective. John Russell Coryell. LC 3640. (On cover: Magnet detective library. no. 135). 1900. Street & Smith.
Crime of the Just. Andre Chamson. Tr. by Brooks, Van Wyck. LC 30-8259. 1930. C. Scribner's Sons.
Crime of the Opera House. Le Crime De L'opera. Fortune Du Boisgobey. (Seaside library, v. 55, no. 1123). G. Munro.
Crime of Violence. Rufus King. LC 37-15786. 1937. Pub. for the Crime Club, Inc., by Doubleday, Doran & Co., Inc.
Crime of Violence. Rufus King. LC 38-32640. 1938. The Sun Dial Press, Inc.
Crime on Canvas. Fred Merrick White. LC 9-65743. R. F. Fenno & Company.
Crime on Her Mind: Fifteen Stories of Female Sleuths from the Victorian Era to the Forties. Ed. by Michele B. Slung. LC 74-26201. 1975. 10.00 (ISBN 0-394-49573-X). Pantheon Books.
Crime on My Hands. George Sanders. LC 44-8332. 1944. Simon and Schuster.
Crime on the Cuff. Stephen Longstreet. LC 36-22614. 1936. W. Morrow & Co.
Crime on the Cuff. Henri Weiner, pseud. LC 36-22614. 1936. W. Morrow & Co.
Crime on the Limited: Or, Nat Ridley in the Follies. Nat Jr Ridley. LC 26-13046. (His Nat Ridley series--4). 1926. Garden City Publishing Co., Inc.
Crime on the Solent: An Inspector French Mystery. Freeman Wills Crofts. LC 34-30038. 1934. Dodd, Mead & Company.
Crime on Their Hands. Elizabeth Linington. LC 76-85407. 1969. 5.95. Morrow.
Crime on Their Hands. Dell Shannon. 1971. pap. 0.75 o.p. (T2467). Pyramid Pubns.
Crime on Their Hands. Dell Shannon. LC 76-85407. 1969. 5.95 o.p. Morrow.
Crime Out of Mind. Delano L Ames. LC 56-59228. 1956. I. Washburn.
Crime Over Casco & The Mother Goose Murders. Walter Brown Gibson. LC 78-73188. 1979. 7.95 (ISBN 0-385-15061-X). Published for the Crime Club by Doubleday.
Crime Partners. Al C Clark. 1974. (pbk.) 1.50 (ISBN 0-87067-445-5). Holloway House.
Crime Partners. Donald Goines. (Orig.). 1974. pap. 1.95 (ISBN 0-87067-625-3, BH029). Holloway.
Crime Prevention in the 30th Century. Ed. by Hans Stefan Santesson. LC 70-86393. 1969. 5.95. Walker.
Crime Story. Jay Robert Nash. 1981. 10.95 (ISBN 0-440-01534-0). Delacorte.
Crime Story. Jay Robert Nash. 1982. pap. 3.50 (ISBN 0-440-11386-5). Dell.
Crime Tears on. Carolyn Wells. LC 39-202414. J. B. Lippincott Company.
Crime, the Place, and the Girl. Douglas Stapleton. LC 55-11874. 1955. Arcadia House.
Crime Times Three. P. D. James. 1979. 12.95 o.p. (ISBN 0-684-16065-X, ScribT); encore ed. 4.95 (ISBN 0-684-17701-3). Scribner.
Crime Times Three: Three Complete Novels Featuring Adam Dalgliesh of Scotland Yard. P. D James. LC 78-12790. 15.00 (ISBN 0-684-16065-X). Scribner.
Crime to Music. Eric Elrington Addis. LC 39-4903. 1939. D. Appleton-Century Co.
Crime Unlimited. John Victor Turner. LC 33-304503. 1933. R. M. McBride & Company.
Crime Upon Crime. Michael Underwood. LC 80-51822. 9.95 (ISBN 0-312-17204-4). St. Martin's Press.
Crime Wave at Blandings. Pelham Grenville Wodehouse. LC 37-151898. 1937. Doubleday, Doran & Company, Inc.
Crime Wave at Blandings. Pelham Grenville Wodehouse. LC 38-31833. 1938. The Sun Dial Press, Inc.
Crime Wind. Marion Holbrook. LC 45-350135. 1945. Dodd, Mead & Company.
Crime Within Crime. Eric Elrington Addis. LC 38-6756. 1938. D. Appleton-Century Co.
Crime Within Crime. Peter Drax. LC 38-6756. 1938. D. Appleton-Century Company, Incorporated.
Crime Without Murder: An Anthology of Stories. Ed. by Dorothy Salisbury Davis. Mystery Writers of America. LC 78-123833. 1970. 5.95. Scribner.
Crimefile Number 1: File on Bolitho Blane... Dennis Yates Wheatley. LC 36-21692. W. Morrow & Company.
Crimefile Number 2... File on Rufus Ray. Helen Kieran Reilly. LC 37-10493. W. Morrow & Company.
Crimefile Number 3... File on Fenton & Farr. Q. Patrick, pseud. LC 37-39535. W. Morrow & Company, Inc.
Crimefile Number 4, File on Claudia Cragge. Q. Patrick, pseud. LC 38-33944. W. Morrow & Co.
Crimes Across the Sea: The 19th Annual Anthology of the Mystery Writers of America. Ed. by John Creasey. LC 64-18074. 1964. Harper & Row.
Crimes & Misfortunes, Vol. 1. Ed. by J. Francis McComas. 1971. pap. 0.95 o.p. (95069). Beagle Bks.
Crimes and Misfortunes: The Anthony Boucher Memorial Anthology of Mysteries. Ed. by J. Francis McComas. William Anthony Parker White. LC 72-102341. 1970. 7.95. Random House.
Crimes & Misfortunes Vol. 2. Ed. by J. Francis McComas. 1971. pap. 0.95 o.p. (95083). Beagle Bks.
Crimes of Love: Three Novellas. Donatien Alphonse Francois Sade. LC 64-17889. 1964. Bantam Books.
Crimes of Passion. David Patridge. Repr. of 1947 ed. 25.00 o.p. (ISBN 0-89987-145-3). Darby Bks.
Crimes of Passion. Donatien Alphonse Francois Sade. Ed. by Wade Baskin. LC 65-23491. 1965. Castle Books.
Crimes Past. Mary Challis. (Raven House Mysteries). 224p. 1982. pap. 2.25 (ISBN 0-373-63021-2, Pub. by Worldwide). Harlequin Bks.
Crimes Without Punishment & Other Tales. Culver Sherrill. 1977. 6.00 o.p. (ISBN 0-682-48931-X). Exposition.
Crimes Without Punishment & Other Tales. Culver Sherrill. 1977. 6.00 o.p. (ISBN 0-682-48931-X). Exposition.
Crimet Oracle & the Teeth of the Dragon: Two Adventures of the Shadow. Maxwell Grant, pseud. 1975. pap. 2.50 o.p. (ISBN 0-486-23116-X). Dover.
Criminal. Havelock Ellis. 1914. Repr. 17.00 o.s.i. Finch Pr.
Criminal. James Myers Thompson. LC 54-27801. (Lion book, 184). 1954. Lion Books.
Criminal C. O. D. An Asey Mayo Mystery Reissue. Phoebe Atwood Taylor. LC 40-27297. 1965. bds., 3.50. Norton.
Criminal Code. Martin Flavin. 1956. 4.95 o.p. (ISBN 0-87140-797-3). Liveright.
Criminal Conservation. Nicolas Freeling. LC 80-6127. (Inspector Van der Valk Suspense Novel Ser.). 213p. 1981. pap. 2.50 (ISBN 0-394-74692-9, V-692, Vin). Random.
Criminal Conversation. Nicolas Freeling. LC 66-13936. 1966. Harper & Row.
Criminal Justice Through Science Fiction. Joseph D Olander & Martin Harry Greenberg. LC 77-8557. 1977. 15.00 (ISBN 0-531-05392-X). New Viewpoints.
Criminal Mischief. Paul Chevigny. LC 76-62704. 1977. 7.95 o.p. (ISBN 0-394-41139-0). Pantheon.
Criminal Mischief: A Novel. Paul Chevigny. LC 76-62704. 7.95 (ISBN 0-394-41139-0). Pantheon Books.
Criminology in Literature. Paul E Dow. LC 79-21758. (Longman English and Humanities Series). 9.95 (ISBN 0-582-28164-4). Longman.
Crimora: Or, Love's Cross. George Leighton Ditson. LC 6-33874. 1852. G. L. Ditson.
Crimshaw Memorandum. Lionel White. LC 66-21319. 1967. Dutton.
Crimson Alibi. Octavus Roy Cohen. LC 19-2014. 1919. 1.50. Dodd, Mead and Company.
Crimson Alibi. Octavus Roy Cohen & Broadhurst, George H., 1866. LC 20-4538. Grosset & Dunlap.
Crimson Altars: Or A Minister's Sin. James Thomas Franklin. LC 10-4184. 1895. Great South Press.
Crimson Azaleas: A Novel. Henry De Vere Stacpoole. LC 10-7477. 1910. Duffield & Co.
Crimson Blind. Fred Merrick White. LC 5-12705. 1905. R. F. Fenno & Company.
Crimson Blotter. Isabel Egenton Ostrander. LC 21-8029. 1921. R. M. McBride & Company.
Crimson Brand. George Brydges Rodney. 1932. G. H. Watt.
Crimson Capsule see Animal People.
Crimson Chalice. Victor Canning. LC 76-371408. (Illus.). 1976. 3.10 (ISBN 0-434-10789-1). Heinemann.
Crimson Chalice. Victor Canning. LC 78-7510. (Illus.). 1978. 10.95 (ISBN 0-688-03340-7). Morrow.
Crimson Circle. Edgar Wallace. LC 74-168913. 1973. 1.70 (ISBN 0-85617-165-4). White Lion Publishers.
Crimson Circle. Edgar Wallace. LC 29-25030. 1929. Pub. for The Crime Club, Inc., by Doubleday, Doran & Company, Inc.
Crimson City: A Glowing Romance on the China Coast, Based on the Motion Picture Story. Anthony Coldeway. LC 28-9845. Jacobsen-Hodgkinson-Corporation.
Crimson Clue. 1st Ed. George Harmon Coxe. LC 52-12201. 1953. Knopf.
Crimson Coach. Gyula Krudy. Tr. by Paul Tabori. 4.00x o.p. (H345). Vanous.
Crimson Conquest: A Romance of Pizarro and Peru. Charles Bradford Hudson. LC 7-32156. 1907. A. C. McClurg & Co.
Crimson Cross. Charles Edmonds Walk & Lynch, Millard, Joint Author. LC 13-673438. 1913. A. C. McClurg & Co.
Crimson Dawn. Norton S Parker. LC 30-7096. 1930. L. MacVeagh, The Dial Press.
Crimson Desire. Katherine Kincaid. (Orig.). 1983. pap. 3.75 (ISBN 0-8217-1190-3). Zebra.
Crimson Falcon. Sara Hylton. 272p. 1983. 11.95 (ISBN 0-312-17214-1). St Martin.
Crimson Feather. Sara Elizabeth Mason. LC 45-5728. 1945. Pub. for the Crime Club by Doubleday, Doran and Co., Inc.
Crimson Friday. Dorothy Cameron Disney. LC 43-8946. 1943. Random House.
Crimson Gardenia. Rex Ellingwood Beach. 1975. lib. bdg. 16.70x (ISBN 0-89966-015-0). Buccaneer Bks.
Crimson Gardenia: And Other Tales of Adventure. Rex Ellingwood Beach. LC 16-86912. 1916. Harper & Brothers.
Crimson Gate. Henry Gibbs. LC 63-11478. 1963. Walker.
Crimson Glory. Theresa Conway. 2.25 (ISBN 0-449-14112-8). Fawcett Gold Medal.
Crimson Goddess. Elaine Sterne Carrington. LC 36-18130. 1936. D. Appleton-Century Company, Incorporated.
Crimson Gondola: A Tale of Venice and Constantinople at the Beginning of the Thirteenth Century. Nathan Gallizier. LC 15-19076. 1915. 1.35. The Page Company.
Crimson Hair Murders. Darwin L. Teilhet & Teilhet, Mrs. Hildegarde (Tolman) Joint Author. LC 36-309338. 1936. Pub. for the Crime Club, Inc., by Doubleday, Doran & Company, Inc.
Crimson Hair Murders. Darwin L. Teilhet & Teilhet, Mrs. Hildegarde (Tolman) Joint Author. LC 38-3737. 1937. The Sun Dial Press, Inc.
Crimson Hairs. 2nd ed. LC 75-116169. 128p. (Orig.). 1983. pap. 3.25 (ISBN 0-394-62462-9, B487, BC). Grove.
Crimson Hairs. Whidden Graham. pap. 1.25 o.p. (Z10492, Zebra). Grove.
Crimson Handkerchief: And Other Stories. Joseph Arthur Gobineau. Tr. by Stuart, Henry Longan. Ed. by Boyd, Ernest Augustus. LC 27-203442. 1927. Harper & Brothers.
Crimson Horseshoe. Peter Dawson. 192p. (Orig.). 1980. pap. 1.75 (ISBN 0-553-14184-8). Bantam.
Crimson Horseshoe. Jonathan H. Glidden. LC 41-1943. 1941. Dodd, Mead & Company.
Crimson Ice: A Hockey Mystery. Cortland Fitzsimmons. LC 35-7885. 1935. Frederick A. Stokes Company.
Crimson in the Purple. Holly Roth. LC 56-13928. (Inner Sanctum Mystery). 1956. Simon and Schuster.
Crimson Is the Eastern Shore. Don Tracy. LC 53-512646. 1953. Dial Press.
Crimson Kisses. Asa Drake. 304p. 1981. pap. 2.50 (ISBN 0-380-77131-4, 77131). Avon.
Crimson Kisses (Melinite) Adolphe Belot. Tr. by Le Rodeur, -- LC 6-455297. 1892. N. C. Smith Publ. Co.
Crimson Madness of Little Doom. Mark McShane. LC 66-19750. 3.50. Pub. for the Crime Club by Doubleday.
Crimson Memories, Golden Days and Other Short Stories. John Forney. LC 81-52624. 8.95 (ISBN 0-87397-225-2). Strode Publishers.
Crimson Morning. Jackie Black. (Candlelight Ecstasy Ser.: No. 92). (Orig.). 1982. pap. 1.95 (ISBN 0-440-11141-2). Dell.
Crimson Mountain. Grace Livingston Hill. LC 75-31599. 1975. 9.95 (ISBN 0-89190-006-3). American Reprint Co.
Crimson Mountain. Grace Livingston Hill. LC 42-159742. 1942. J. B. Lippincott Company.
Crimson Pall: A Novel. Francis Warrington Dawson & Conrad, Joseph. LC 27-17814. The Bernard Publishing Company.
Crimson Patch. Phoebe Atwood Taylor. 1971. pap. 0.75 o.p. (T2491). Pyramid Pubns.
Crimson Patch: An Asey Mayo Mystery of Cape Cod. Phoebe Atwood Taylor. LC 36-986272. W. W. Norton & Company, Inc.
Crimson Patch: An Asey Mayo Mystery Reissue. Phoebe Atwood Taylor. LC 64-57254. 1965. bds., 3.50. Norton.
Crimson Phillipine Jungle. Howard Granville Sharpe. LC 43-15775. 1943. Wetzel Publishing Co., Inc.
Crimson Quest. Dennis Barr. LC 28-21961. J. H. Sears & Company, Inc.
Crimson Quirt. William Colt MacDonald. LC 45-13281. 1942. The Sun Dial Press.
Crimson Quirt: A Double D Western. William Colt MacDonald. LC 42-50441. 1942. Doubleday, Doran & Company, Inc.
Crimson Ramblers of the World, Farewell. Jessamyn West. LC 72-117578. 1970. Harcourt Brace Jovanovich.
Crimson Roses. Grace Livingston Hill. 1928. J. B. Lippincott Company.
Crimson Roses. Grace Livingston Hill. LC 78-12352. 1979. 10.95 (ISBN 0-89340-162-5). J. Curley.
Crimson Roundup. Raymond A Berry. LC 38-7470. Greenberg.
Crimson Serpent. Kenneth Robeson. (Doc Savage series,#78). 1974. (pbk.) 0.75. Bantam Books.
Crimson Stain. Annie Bradshaw. (On cover: Lovell's library. v. 14. no. 716). J. W. Lovell Company.
Crimson Stain. Annie Bradshaw. (On cover: Seaside library. Pocket ed., no. 706). G. Munro.
Crimson Stain. Annie Bradshaw. LC 6-15193. (On cover: Cassell's "rainbow" series, no. 20). Cassell & Company, Limited.
Crimson Thread. Lilian Lauferty. LC 42-290835. 1942. Simon and Schuster.
Crimson Tide: A Novel. Robert William Chambers. LC 19-18840. 1919. D. Appleton and Company.
Crimson Trail. Charles Wesley Sanders. LC 27-11966. 1927. G. H. Watt.
Crimson Trail of Josquin Murieta. Ernest Klette. LC 28-20228. Wetzel Publishing Company.
Crimson Universe. K. H Scheer. (Perry Rhodan#67). (Illus.). 1975. (pbk.) 1.25. Ace Books.
Crimson Weed. Christabel Marshall. 1901. H. Holt and Company.
Crimson Weed. St. John, Christopher Marie. LC 1-30533. 1901. H. Holt.
Crimson Wing. Hobart Chatfield Chatfield-Taylor. LC 2-7629. 1902. H. S. Stone & Co.
Crimson Witch. Dean R. Koontz. 1971. pap. 0.75 o.p. (07156). Curtis.
Crimsoned Millions. John Willoughby. LC 27-153913. E. J. Clode, Inc.
Crinkled Crown. William Le Queux. LC 29-22139. The Macaulay Company.
Crinoline to Calico. Nan Heacock. LC 76-30665. 1977. 7.95 (ISBN 0-8138-0065-X). Iowa State University Press.
Cripple Mah & the New Order. C. Y. Lee. 1961. 3.95 o.p. (ISBN 0-374-13164-3). FS&G.
Cripple Mah and the New Order: A Novel. Chin-Yang Li. LC 61-15030. 1961. Farrar, Straus and Cudahy.

Cripple of Nuremberg. Felicia Buttz Clark. LC 4-29456. 1900. Jennings & Pye.
Crippled Muse. Hugh Callingham Wheeler. LC 52-5557. 1952. Rinehart.
Crippled Splendour: A Novel. Evan John Simpson. LC 38-27688. 1938. E. P. Dutton & Co., Inc.
Cripps, the Carrier. Richard Doddridge Blackmore. LC 6-13862. (On cover: Seaside library. Pocket ed., no. 629). 1885. G. Munro.
Cripps the Carrier. Richard Doddridge Blackmore. (On cover: Lovell's library, no. 1038). 1887. J. W. Lovell Co.
Criquette. Ludovic Halevy & Cooney.. LC 6-46174. (brookside library. No. 390). 1884. F. Tousey.
Criquette. Ludovic Halevy & Hall, Arthur D., Tr. LC 6-46666. (On cover: Rialte series, no. 32). 1891. Rand, McNally & Company.
Crisis. Winston Churchill. 1901. The Macmillan Company.
Crisis. Winston Churchill. 1902. The Macmillan Company.
Crisis. Winston Churchill & Barnes, Walter, 1880- LC 21-1177. (Macmillan's pocket American and English classics). 1921. The Macmillan Company.
Crisis. Winston Churchill & Barnes, Walter, 1880- Ed. (Half-title: New pocket classics). The Macmillan Company.
Crisis. Winston Churchill & Christy, Howard Chandler, 1873- Illus. LC 23-16044. 1905. Grosset & Dunlap.
Crisis. Winston Churchill & Christy, Howard Chandler, 1873- Illus. LC 16-648144. 1914. The Macmillan Company.
Crisis. David E. Fisher. LC 75-131074. 1971. 5.95. Doubleday.
Crisis. Claude Houghton Oldfield. LC 29-5952. 1929. Harper & Brothers.
Crisis at Cornerstone: A Nevada Jim Western. Marshall McCoy. LC 70-399411. 1968. australian cents 0.40. Bantam Books in Association with Horwitz.
Crisis at Harrison High. John Farris. 1974. (pbk.) 0.95 (ISBN 0-671-77725-4). Pocket Books.
Crisis Corporation. first ed. Walter Cameron Childs. 1972. 4.95. Vantage.
Crisis in Morningdale: Keeping Faith When God Seems Against Us. William Allen Knight. LC 47-11118. 1947. W. A. Wilde Co.
Crisis Inn the Catskills. Mary Bogardus. 1976. 6.95. Hope Farm.
Crisis Makers. Keith Edwin Davis. LC 74-17558. 1975. 6.95 (ISBN 0-8059-2098-6). Dorrance.
Crispan Magicker. Mark M Lowenthal. LC 78-67748. 1979. 1.95 (ISBN 0-380-42333-2). Avon.
Crispus Attucks-the First to Die. Edmund F Curley. LC 73-85340. 1973. 6.95 (ISBN 0-8059-1909-0). Dorrance.
Criss-Cross. Grace Denio Litchfield. LC 7-19002. 1885. G. P. Putnam's Sons.
Criss-Cross. Don Tracy. LC 48-18946. 1948. Triangle Books.
Criss-Cross. Don Tracy. LC 35-427. 1934. The Vanguard Press.
Criss-Cross. Don Tracy. LC 38-157297. (A Mercury book, no. 9). The American Mercury, Inc.
Crisscross. Pat Flower. LC 77-15652. 1977. 7.95 (ISBN 0-8128-2415-6). Stein and Day.
Crisscross. Harmon Henkin. LC 76-2505. 7.95 (ISBN 0-399-11747-4). Putnam.
Cristina and I. Arthur John Arbuthnott Stringer. LC 29-18938. The Bobbs-Merrill Company.
Cristina's Fantasy. Ivy Valdes. (Signet Bk., P5302: Rainbow romance #56). 1972. New American Lib.
Cristowell. Richard Doddridge Blackmore. (On cover:Lovell's library, no. 1306). 1887. J. W. Lovell Company.
Critical Edition of Tirso De Molina's Marta la Piadosa. Elvira F. Garcia. (Salzburg Studies in English Literature: Elizabethan & Renaissance Studies: No. 78). 1978. pap. text ed. 25.00x (ISBN 0-391-01380-7). Humanities.
Critical Threshold. Brian M Stableford. 1977. 1.25 (ISBN 0-87997-282-3). DAW Books.
Crittenden: A Kentucky Story of Love and War. John Fox. LC 1-29187. 1900. C. Scribner's Sons.
Crittenden: A Kentucky Story of Love and War. John Fox. 1920. C. Scribner's Sons.
Critter Chronicles: Tales for Here & Now. John Barnetson. LC 80-66262. (Illus.). 96p. 1982. cancelled o.p. (ISBN 0-89742-037-3, Dawne-Leigh). Celestial Arts.
Croaker. Gordon Ashe. (Rinehart Suspense Novel Ser.). 1973. 4.95 o.p. (ISBN 0-03-001361-5). HR&W.
Croaker. John Creasey. LC 72-78129. (Rinehart suspense novel). 1972. 4.95 (ISBN 0-03-001361-5). Holt, Rinehart and Winston.
Croatan. Mary Johnston. LC 23-15821. 1923. Little, Brown, and Company.
CROC. David James. (O.s.i.). 1976. pap. 1.50 o.s.i. (BT50959). Belmont-Tower.
Croc. David James. Belmont Tower.
Crocer Greatheart: A Tropical Romance. Arthur Henyr Adams. LC 15-8088. 1915. John Lane.
Crochet Woman. Ruth Manning-Sanders. LC 30-25741. 1930. Coward-McCann, Inc.
Crock. Bill Rechin et al. 1978. pap. 1.25 (ISBN 0-449-13868-2, GM). Fawcett.
Crock of Gold. James Stephens. LC 12-27198. Small, Maynard and Company.
Crock of Gold. James Stephens. 1922. The Macmillan Company.
Crock of Gold. James Stephens. LC 27-260890. 1926. The Macmillan Company.
Crock of Gold. With Decorative Headings and Tailpieces by Thomas Mackenzie. James Stephens. (Macmillan paperback 13). 1960. Macmillan.
Crock-Your're All Heart. Bill Rechin & Don Wilder. 128p. 1981. pap. 1.75 (ISBN 0-449-14434-8). Fawcett.
Crockett: Brand of Fear. Brad Lang. 1976. pap. 1.25 o.p. (LB367ZK, Leisure Bks). Nordon Pubns.
Crockett on the Loose. Brad Lang. (Crockett Ser). (Orig.). 1975. pap. 1.25 o.p. (LB283ZK, Leisure Bks). Nordon Pubns.
Crockett's Woman. Eric Hatch. LC 51-35746. (Gold medal books, 176). 1951. Fawcett Publications.
Crockford's: Or, Life in the West. -- Deale. LC 6-32901. 1828. Printed by J. & J. Harper.
Crocodile. Vincent Eri. LC 73-168690. (Pacific writers series, v. 1). 1972. (ISBN 0-7016-8125-X). Jacaranda Press.
Crocodile on the Sandbank. Elizabeth Peters, pseud. LC 74-31490. 1975. 7.95 (ISBN 0-396-07080-9). Dodd, Mead.
Crocodile on the Sandbank. Elizabeth Peters, pseud. LC 75-9976. 1975. 13.95 (ISBN 0-8161-6301-4). G. K. Hall.
Crocodile on the Sandbank. Elizabeth Peters, pseud. (Fawcett Crest Book). 1976. (pbk.) 1.50. Fawcett.
Crocus: A Novel. Stephen Southwold. LC 37-4276. 1937. Doubleday, Doran & Company, Inc.
Croesus Conspiracy. Benjamin Stein. LC 78-1401. 8.95 (ISBN 0-671-22870-6). Simon and Schuster.
Croesus's Widow. Dora Russell. (Seaside library, v. 67, no. 1370). 1882. G. Munro.
Crofton Boys. new ed. Harriet Martineau. LC 7-17825. 1865. G. Routledge and Sons.
Crofton Boys. Harriet Martineau. LC 1-30345. (On cover: Heath's home and school classics. The young reader's series). 1900. D. C. Heath & Co.
Cromaboo Mail Carrier: A Canadian Love Story. James T. Jones. (Toronto Reprint Library of Canadian Prose & Poetry). 1973. Repr. of 1878 ed. 22.50x o.p. (ISBN 0-8020-7512-6). U of Toronto Pr.
Cromaboo Mail Carrier: A Canadian Love Story. Mary Leslie. LC 74-168357. (Toronto reprint library of canadian prose and poetry). (ISBN 0-8020-7512-6). University of Toronto Press.
Crome Yellow. Aldous Leonard Huxley. LC 22-6512. George H. Doran Company.
Crompton Divided. Robert Sheckley. LC 78-4694. 1978. 7.95 (ISBN 0-03-043996-5). Holt, Rinehart and Winston.
Cromptons. Mary Jane Hawes Holmes. LC 14-1827. (On cover; The works of Mary J. Holmes). G. W. Dillingham Company.
Cromwell. An Historical Novel. Henry William Herbert. LC 7-42853. 1838. Harper & Brothers.
Cromwell of Virginia: A Story of Bacon's Rebellion. Edward Sylvester Ellis. LC 4-33124. (His Colonial series, no. 2). 1904. H.T. Coates & Co.
Cromwell's Own: A Story of the Great Civil War. Arthur Henry Paterson. 1899. Harper & Brothers.
Cronica Del Alba: 2v. in Spanish Ed. Definitiva. LC 63-4792. 1964. 14.00 set,. Las Americas.
Cronin Mystery. A Complete History of the Murder, and the Quarrel in the Brotherhood. John A Fraser. LC 6-43150. (Globe detective series no. 18). 1889. The Eagle Publishing Co.
Cronopios and Famas. Julio Cortazar. LC 69-15477. (Illus.). 1969. 4.95. Pantheon Books.
Crook. Jonathan Starr. LC 30-4844. J. Cape & H. Smith.
Crook in the Lot. Thomas Boston. (O.s.i.). 1971. pap. 1.00 o.s.i. (ISBN 0-8254-2223-X, RBDH). Kregel.
Crook of the Bough. Menie Muriel Dowie. LC 7-33309. 1898. C. Scribner's Sons.
Crooked. Maximilian Foster. LC 28-8367. 1928. J. B. Lippincott Company.
Crooked Adam. Dorothy Emily Stevenson. LC 70-80365. 1970. 5.95. Holt, Rinehart and Winston.
Crooked Adam. Dorothy Emily Stevenson. LC 42-22720. 1942. Farrar & Rinehart, Inc.
Crooked Alley. Irene Alexander. LC 33-756733. The Penn Publishing Company.
Crooked City. Robert Kyle, pseud. LC 54-7349. (Dell first edition, 17). 1954. Dell Pub. Co.
Crooked Computer. William G. Shingler, Jr. (Orig.). 1979. pap. 1.95 (ISBN 0-532-19232-X). Woodhill.
Crooked Cop. Bob Parker. 1976. pap. 1.25 (ISBN 0-532-12189-9). Woodhill.
Crooked Cop. Bob Parker. 192p. (Orig.). 1973. pap. 1.25 o.p. (532-12189-125). Manor Bks.
Crooked Coronet: And Other Misrepresentations of the Real Facts of Life. Michael Arlen. LC 38-1966. 1937. Doubleday, Doran & Co., Inc.
Crooked Cross. Charles Judson Dutton. LC 26-281424. 1926. Dodd, Mead and Company.
Crooked Cross. Brendan Kennelly. 1963. 3.50 o.p. (ISBN 0-900372-78-8). Irish Bk Ctr.
Crooked Cross. Barth J. Sussman. (Orig.). 1982. pap. 2.95 (ISBN 0-451-11203-2, AE1203, Sig). NAL.
Crooked Eye. Katharine Virden. LC 30-12990. 1930. Pub. for The Crime Club, Inc., by Doubleday, Doran & Company, Inc.
Crooked Frame. William P McGivern. LC 52-8707. (Red badge detective). 1952. Dodd, Mead.
Crooked Furrow. Jeffery Farnol. LC 38-7465. 1938. Doubleday, Doran & Company, Inc.
Crooked Furrow. Jeffery Farnol. LC 39-22933. 1939. The Sun Dial Press, Inc.
Crooked Hinge. John Dickson Carr. LC 76-56880. (Mystery Library; 2). (Illus.). 1976. (ISBN 0-89163-026-0). University Extension, University of California, San Diego.
Crooked Hinge. John Dickson Carr. LC 38-30227. 1938. Harper & Brothers.
Crooked House. Agatha Miller Christie. LC 49-8190. (Red badge detective). 1949. Dodd, Mead.
Crooked House. Brandon Fleming. LC 21-1277. E. J. Clode.
Crooked House see Nursery Rhyme Murders: An Anthology.
Crooked Lane... Frances Noyes Hart. LC 34-27220. 1934. Doubleday, Doran & Company, Inc.
Crooked Lanes. Rupert Sargent Holland. LC 23-14568. G. W. Jacobs & Company.
Crooked Letter. Linda DuBreuil. (Belmont Tower books). 1.75 (ISBN 0-505-51385-4). Tower Pubns.
Crooked Man: By Shelley Smith Pseud. 1st American Ed. Nancy Bodington. LC 52-7297. 1952. Harper.
Crooked Mile. Bernard Augustine De Voto. LC 24-22274. 1924. Minton, Balch & Company.
Crooked Mile. Oliver Onions. LC 14-13579. 1.25. George H. Doran Company, Publishers in America for Hodder & Stoughton.
Crooked Path. Annie French Hector. (On cover: Seaside library. Pocket ed., no. 1189). 1889. G. Munro.
Crooked Path. Annie French Hector. LC 43-40126. Hurst & Co.
Crooked River Canyon. Dwight Bennett Newton. LC 66-20962. (Double D western). 1966. Doubleday.
Crooked River Canyon: By Dwight Bennett. Dwight Bennett Newton. (Medallion bk., F1471). 1967. Berkeley.
Crooked Road. Morris L. West. LC 57-10589. 1975. (pbk.) 1.50 (ISBN 0-671-78820-5). Pocket Books.
Crooked Road: A Novel. Morris L West. LC 57-105890. 1957. W. Morrow.
Crooked Rows. Mary E Sullivan. LC 55-14257. 1955. Christopher Pub. House.
Crooked Shadow. Rudolf Kagey. LC 39-30066. 1939. Little, Brown and Company.
Crooked Shadows. John Crowe, pseud. LC 75-9542. (Red Badge Novel of Suspense Ser.). 212p. 1975. 5.95 o.p. (ISBN 0-396-07135-X). Dodd.
Crooked Shadows. Dennis Lynds. LC 75-9542. (Buena Costa County mystery). 1975. (ISBN 0-396-07136-8). Dodd, Mead.
Crooked Shadows. Gordon Ray Young. LC 24-7482. (Famous authors series, no. 44). 1924. Garden City Publishing Co., Inc.
Crooked Shamrock. C. B Gilford. LC 74-85925. 1969. 5.95. Doubleday.
Crooked Spur. Jack Hazard, pseud. LC 60-2456. 1960. Arcadia House.
Crooked Stick. Pauline Stiles. LC 27-15672. George H. Doran Company.
Crooked Stick: Or, Pollie's Probation. Thomas Alexander Browne. 1895. Macmillan and Co.
Crooked Trail. Fred Donaldson. 208p. (Orig.). 1982. pap. 2.25 o.s.i. (ISBN 0-8439-1134-4, Leisure Bks). Nordon Pubns.
Crooked Trail. Fred Donaldson. 208p. 1983. pap. 2.25 (ISBN 0-8439-2008-4, Leisure Bks). Dorchester Pub Co.
Crooked Trail: The Story of a Thousand-Mile Saddle Trip up and Down the Texas Frontier in Pursuit of a Runaway Ox, with Adventures by the Way. Lewis Bennett Miller. LC 8-9818. (On cover: Stockman series, no. 1). The Axtell-Rush Publishing Company.
Crooked Trail: The Story of a Thousand-Mile Saddle Trip up and Down the Texas Frontier in Pursuit of a Runaway Ox. Lewis Bennett Miller. LC 11-20546. D. Estes & Company.
Crooked Trails. Frederic Remington. LC 72-104547. (Illus.). 1970. Literature House.
Crooked Trails. Frederic Remington. LC 74-101820. (Short story index reprint series). (Illus.). 1969. Books for Libraries Press.
Crooked Trails. Frederic Remington. LC 98-93539. 1898. Harper & Brothers.
Crooked Trails. Frederic Remington. LC 23-13376. Harper & Brothers.
Crooked Trails and Straight. William MacLeod Raine. LC 13-54125. G. W. Dillingham Company.
Crooked Tree. Robert Charles Wilson. LC 79-23321. 10.95 (ISBN 0-399-12488-8). Putnam.
Crooked Wood. Michael Underwood. LC 77-14662. 1978. 7.95 (ISBN 0-312-17653-8). St. Martin's Press.
Crooked Wreath. Mary Christina Lewis. LC 47-218. 1946. Dodd, Mead & Company.
Crooking Finger. Cleve Franklin Adams. LC 44-41823. Reynal & Hitchcock.
Crooking Finger. A Rex McBride Murder Mystery. Cleve Franklin Adams. LC 47-6142. (Dell book, 104).
Crook's Castle. George Dilnot. LC 35-4606. 1934. Houghton Mifflin Company.
Crooks' Game. George Dilnot. LC 27-161460. 1927. Houghton Mifflin Company.
Crook's Hill. San Antonio. Tr. by Barry Jaggers. (San Antonio Ser). 1970. pap. 0.60 o.p. (ISBN 0-446-63342-9, 63-342). Paperback Lib.
Crooks in the Sunshine. Edward Phillips Oppenheim. LC 32-30641. 1933. Little, Brown, and Company.
Crook's Shadow. Joseph Jefferson Farjeon. LC 27-595029. 1927. L. MacVeagh, The Dial Press.
Crooks' Shepherd. Seldon Truss, pseud. LC 36-185663. 1936. Lothrop, Lee and Shepard Company.
Crooks' Tour: By Members of the Mystery Writers of America; Edited by Bruno Fischer. Mystery Writers of America. Ed. by Bruno Fischer. LC 53-9600. 1953. Dodd, Mead.
Crookshaven Murder. Alexander Morrison. LC 27-16971. 1927. Houghton Mifflin Company.
Crooner. Rian James. LC 32-149479. A. H. King.
Croppy. A Tale. John Banim & Michael Banim. LC 6-6112. 1839. E. L. Carey & A. Hart.
Croppy: A Tale of 1798. Michael Banim & John Banim. LC 78-14040. (Ireland, from the Act of Union, 1800, to the Death of Parnell, 1891). 1978. 42.00 (ISBN 0-8240-3468-6). Garland Pub.
Croquet Player. Herbert George Wells. LC 37-2458. 1937. The Viking Press.
Cross Above the Crescent. A Romance of Constantinople... Horatio Southgate. LC 8-108043. 1878. J. B. Lippincott & Co.
Cross and the Arrow. Albert Maltz. LC 44-7663. 1944. Little, Brown and Company.
Cross and the Blatnoi. Lewis Segesvary. LC 64-15395. 1965. Caxton Printers.
Cross & the Chameleon. Paul H. LaFlamme. 3.75 o.p. Vantage.
Cross and the Eagle: A Novel Based on the Life of St. Paul. Julius Berstl. LC 55-14747. 1955. Muhlenberg Press.
Cross and the Hammer: A Tale of the Days of the Vikings. Henry Bedford-Jones. LC 12-253831. David C. Cook Publishing Co.
Cross & the Needle. Bob Bennett. LC 72-92042. (Redwood Ser.). 190p. 1972. pap. 2.95 o.p. (ISBN 0-8163-0051-8, 03652-5). Pacific Pr Pub Assn.
Cross and the Shamrock. Hugh Quigley. LC 79-104546. 1970. Literature House.
Cross & the Shamrock: An Irish-American Tale. Hugh Quigley. LC 79-104546. Repr. of 1853 ed. lib. bdg. 15.50 (ISBN 0-8398-1650-2). Irvington.
Cross & the Shamrock: An Irish-American Tale of Real Life. Hugh Quigley. LC 79-104546. 1970. Repr. of 1853 ed. lib. bdg. 10.50x o.p. (ISBN 0-8398-1650-2). Gregg.
Cross & the Switchblade. David Wilkerson. (YA) 1963. 4.95 o.p. (ISBN 0-87035-005-6). Geis.
Cross & the Switchblade. David Wilkerson et al. pap. 1.95 (ISBN 0-8007-8009-4, Spire Bks); pap. 1.95 o.p. movie edition (ISBN 0-8007-8054-X, Spire Bks). Revell.
Cross and the Sword. Jonreed Lauritzen. LC 65-12368. 1965. 4.95. Doubleday.
Cross and the Sword. Evangeline Walton. LC 56-13320. Bouregy & Curl.
Cross Bearers. Alexander Moriz Frey. LC 30-276810. 1930. The Viking Press.
Cross-Country. Herbert D Kastle. LC 74-13066. 1975. 7.95 (ISBN 0-440-03383-7). Delacorte Press.
Cross Country Trick. Eugene Squire. 1969. pap. 1.25 o.p. (88-606). Lancer.
Cross Creek. Marjorie Kinnan Rawlings. LC 42-36118. 1942. C. Scribner's Sons.
Cross Creek: By Marjorie Kinnan Rawlings; Decorations by Edward Shenton. Marjorie Kinnan Rawlings. (SL 65). 1962. pap., 1.65. Scribners.
Cross Current. C. Terry Cline. LC 78-14652. 1979. 8.95 (ISBN 0-385-14503-9). Doubleday.

Cross Currents. Sara Ware Bassett. LC 41-9275. 1941. Doubleday, Doran & Company, Inc.
Cross Currents. Kate Mayhew Speake Penney. LC 40-3859. B. Humphries, Inc.
Cross Currents. Katharine Haviland Taylor. LC 22-9190. 1922. G. W. Jacobs & Company.
Cross-Cut. Courtney Ryley Cooper. LC 21-740938. 1921. 1.90. Little, Brown, and Company.
Cross-Eyed Bear. Dorothy Belle Flanagan Hughes. LC 40-359934. Duell, Sloan and Pearce.
Cross-Fire. Cliff Farrell. LC 65-198749. (Double D western). 3.50. Doubleday.
Cross-Fire. Cliff Farrell. LC 65-19874. (Signet Brand Western). 1975. (pbk.) 1.25. New American Library.
Cross Fire. William Lloyd Griffin. LC 75-11472. 1975. 4.95 (ISBN 0-911562-04-4) (ISBN 0-911562-05-2). Valley Publications.
Cross Fire. Dennis Lynds. 1975. (pbk.) 1.25 (ISBN 0-671-80241-0). Pocket Books.
Cross Hangs Low. 1st Ed. John Geddie Macdonald. LC 53-5921. 1952. Pageant Press.
Cross in the Caribbean: A Novel. Albert Edward Idell. LC 41-154434. 1941. H. Holt and Company.
Cross Knife Ranch. Arthur Henry Gooden. LC 40-2383. Phoenix Press.
Cross My Heart. 1st Ed. Naomi John Sellers, pseud. LC 53-7977. 1953. Doubleday.
Cross of Ares: And Other Sketches. Lawrence Perkins. LC 20-186106. 1920. Brentano's.
Cross of Berny; or, Irene's Lovers. A Novel. Delphine Gay Girardin et al. Tr. by Fendall, Florence. LC 6-43991. Porter and Coates.
Cross of Canyon Crest. George Melvin Hayes. LC 34-36235. 1934. Concordia Publishing House.
Cross of Carl. Walter Owen. LC 31-22140. 1931. Little, Brown, and Company.
Cross of Fire. Barry N. Malzberg. 224p. (Orig.). 1982. pap. 2.50 (ISBN 0-441-12266-3). Ace Bks.
Cross of Fire: A Romance of Love and War to-Day. Robert Gordon Anderson. LC 18-216821. 1918. 1.50. Houghton Mifflin Company.
Cross of Frankenstein. Robert John Myers. 1976. 1.75 (ISBN 0-671-80542-8). Pocket Books.
Cross of Heart's Desire. Gertrude Pahlow. LC 16-17073. 1916. 1.30. Duffield and Company.
Cross of Iron. Translated from the German by Richard and Clara Winston. Willi Heinrich. LC 56-7605. 1956. Bobbs-Merrill.
Cross of Lassitude: Portraits of Five Delinquents. Joan Colebrook. LC 67-11120. 1967. Knopf.
Cross of Lazzaro. John Harris. LC 65-22977. bds., 4.95. Morrow.
Cross of Peace. Philip Hamilton Gibbs. LC 34-905. 1934. Doubleday, Doran & Company, Inc.
Cross on the Drum. Hugh Barnett Cave. LC 59-7901. 1959. Doubleday.
Cross on the Moon. John Henry Hewlett. LC 46-6302. 1946. Whittlesey House, McGraw-Hill Book Company, Inc.
Cross Over Nine. Walter C Butler. LC 36-1531. The Macaulay Company.
Cross Providences. J. Williams Hopkins. LC 13-15523. 1.25. The Roxburgh Publishing Company, Incorporated.
Cross Pull. Hal George Evarts. LC 20-42696. 1920. A. A. Knopf.
Cross Purposes. Henry Cecil. LC 76-363922. 1976. 3.75 (ISBN 0-7181-1442-6). Joseph.
Cross Purposes. Jim Thomas, pseud. LC 78-139543. (A McCall suspense novel). 1971. 4.95 (ISBN 0-8415-0091-6). McCall Pub. Co.
Cross Purposes. A Christmas Experience in Seven Stages. Thomas Cooper De Leon. LC 6-34189. 1871. J. B. Lippincott & Co.
Cross-Roads. Ina L. Brown. 1970. 4.00 (ISBN 0-8233-0154-0). Golden Quill.
Cross Roads. Edgar T. Chrisemer. 3.75 o.p. (ISBN 0-8283-1149-8). Branden.
Cross Roads. Ovid Pullen. (Hearthstone bk.). 3.75. Carlton.
Cross-Section: Anthology of Short Stories of the PEN Centre, German Democratic Republic. Ed. by W. Herzfelde & G. Cwojdrak. pap. 2.95 o.p. Adler.
Cross-Sections. Julian Leonard Street. LC 23-131895. 1923. Doubleday, Page & Company.
Cross, Sword, and Arrow. Gladys Hutchison Barr. LC 55-5559. 1955. Abingdon Press.
Cross the Border-Close the Gap. Leslie A. Fiedler. LC 72-81822. pap. 2.95 (ISBN 0-8128-1479-7). Stein & Day.
Cross the Great Desert. Michael Ross. 1977. 16.95 (ISBN 0-86033-026-5). Gordon-Cremonesi.
Cross Timbers. Elizabeth Kitchell. 5.95 o.p. Vantage.
Cross Trails. Harold Bindloss. LC 25-4861. 1925. Frederick A. Stokes Company.
Cross Trails. Victor Waite. 1898. L. C. Page and Company (Incorporated.
Cross Trails: The Story of One Woman in the North Woods. Herman Whitaker. LC 14-11358. 1914. Harper & Brothers.
Cross: Translated from the Norwegian of Sigrid Undset. Sigrid Undset. Tr. by Charles Archer. LC 27-4320. 1927. A. A. Knopf.
Cross Triumphant. Florence Morse Kingsley. LC 99-186225. 1899. H. Altemus.
Cross Winds. Elinor Mordaunt, pseud. LC 32-7344. The John Day Company.
Crossbreed. Allan W Eckert. LC 68-11524. (Illus.). 1968. Little, Brown.
Crosscuts", a Story of the Pacific Northwest: A Picturesque Tide of Life, Moving in and Out of Vancouver, British Columbia. Jessie Garden Smith. LC 33-22045. 1933. Printed by the Metropolitan Press.
Crossed Trails. Robert Ames Bennet. LC 37-20432. I. Washburn, Inc.
Crossed Wires: Or, A Tangle of Crime. John Russell Coryell. LC 9650. (On cover: Magnet detective library. no. 138). 1900. Street & Smith.
Crosses at Zarin. Jean Bell Mosley. LC 67-22030. 1967. Broadman Press.
Crosses: Now First Completely Done into English from the Original Lithuanian of Vincas Ramonas by Milton Stark. 1st English Ed. Vincas Ramonas. LC 54-35676. 1954. Lithuanian Days Publishers.
Crossexion. Clell Edgar Bowman. 1976. 8.00 o.p. (ISBN 0-682-48518-7). Exposition.
Crossfire. Edwin Booth. 1977. 1.50 (ISBN 0-441-12269-8). Ace Books.
Crossfire. Alex Hawk, pseud. (Orig.). 1968. pap. 0.50 o.p. (62-007). Paperback Lib.
Crossfire. Nigel Slater. LC 77-15543. 1978. 6.95 (ISBN 0-689-10844-3). Atheneum.
Crossfire. Louis Trimble. LC 53-127965. 1953. Avalon Books.
Crossfire at Barbed M and Sidewinder Showdown. Tom West. (Ace double western). 1975. (pbk.) 0.95. Ace Books.
Crossfire Creek. Heuman, William. LC 64-7362. 1964. Arcadia House.
Crossfire Trail. Louis L'Amour. LC 54-31862. (Ace double novel books, D-52). 1954. Ace Books.
Crossfire Trail. Louis L'Amour. LC 79-28248. (Gregg Press Western Fiction Series). (Illus.). 1980. 9.95 (ISBN 0-8398-2691-5). Gregg Press.
Crossfire Trail. Louis L'Amour. (Fawcett gold medal book). 1974. (pbk.) 0.95. Fawcett.
Crossfire Trail see Complete L'Amour.
Crossin' Over. Effie Williams Leland. LC 37-21831. The State Company.
Crossing. Alain Albert. LC 64-12397. 1964. G. Braziller.
Crossing. Winston Churchill. LC 76-96878. (Illus.). 1969. Literature House.
Crossing. Winston Churchill. LC 16-6482. 1912. The Macmillan Comapny.
Crossing. Clay Fisher. 288p. (Orig.). 1980. pap. 1.75 (ISBN 0-553-14178-3). Bantam.
Crossing. Clay Fisher. 1974. (pbk.) 0.95. Bantam.
Crossing. Christopher Keane. LC 77-93004. 8.95 (ISBN 0-87795-187-X). Arbor House.
Crossing. Christopher Keane. 1979. 2.25. (ISBN 0-440-11412-8). Dell Publishing Co.
Crossing. Brian Rothery. LC 70-129674. 1971. 5.95. Lippincott.
Crossing. Jan Yoors. LC 78-156165. (O.s.i.). 1971. 6.95 o.s.i. (ISBN 0-671-20988-4). S&S.
Crossing see War Party.
Crossing: A Novel. Translated by Edward Hyams. Jean Reverzy. LC 56-104103. 1956. Pantheon.
Crossing America. Leo Connellan. LC 77-152049. Penmaen Press.
Crossing: By Clay Fisher Pseud. Henry Allen. LC 58-12364. 1958. Houghton Mifflin.
Crossing in Berlin. Fletcher Knebel. LC 80-2748. 1981. 14.95 (ISBN 0-385-17290-7). Doubleday.
Crossing Over, and Other Tales. Richard M Elman. LC 72-1191. 1973. 6.95 (ISBN 0-684-13021-1). Scribner.
Crossing Point. Gerda Charles. 1961. 4.50 o.p. Knopf.
Crossing the Border. Joyce Carol Oates. 1978. 2.50 (ISBN 0-449-23751-6). Fawcett Crest.
Crossing the Border: Fifteen Tales. Joyce Carol Oates. LC 76-7148. 8.95 (ISBN 0-8149-0774-1). Vanguard Pr.
Crossing the Border: Fifteen Tales. Joyce Carol Oates. 1979. 2.50. Fawcett Crest Books.
Crossing the Plains. Edith Starbuck. LC 27-8149. Southern Publishing Association.
Crossings. Hua Chuang. LC 68-29341. 1968. 3.95. Dial Press.
Crossings. Chuang Hua. 1969. 3.95 o.p. Dial.
Crossings. Alice Massie. LC 31-299683. The Century Co.
Crossings. Earl H Rovit. LC 73-9960. 1973. 7.95 (ISBN 0-15-123150-8). Harcourt Brace Jovanovich.
Crossings. Danielle Steel. LC 82-2485. 15.95 (ISBN 0-440-01130-2). Delacorte.
Crossings: A Novel. Betty Lambert. LC 80-481494. 11.95 (ISBN 0-88978-068-4) (ISBN 0-88978-070-6). Pulp Press.
Crossings; Stories. Stephen Minot. LC 74-14915. (Illinois short fiction). 1975. (pbk.) 2.95 (ISBN 0-252-00472-8). University of Illinois Press.
Crossover. Ida L. Brinckley. 5.95 o.p. Carlton.
Crossover. Wilfred Greatorex. LC 76-383417. 1976. 3.95 (ISBN 0-297-77161-2). Weidenfeld and Nicolson.
Crossroad Murders. Georges Simenon. LC 33-262684. Covici, Friede.
Crossroads. Elizabeth Frances Corbett. LC 65-23022. 4.95. Appleton-Century Dist. Meredith.
Crossroads. John Dann MacDonald. LC 59-13136. (Inner sanctum mystery). 1959. Simon and Schuster.
Crossroads. Mary Morris. LC 82-15468. 1983. 13.95 (ISBN 0-395-33104-8). Houghton Mifflin.
Crossroads. Erico Verissimo. LC 75-88989. 1969. Greenwood Press.
Crossroads. Erico Verissimo & Kaplan, Lewis C., 1911- Tr. LC 43-1549. 1943. The Macmillan Company.
Crossroads, a Novel. Jacket and Map by the Author. Claude Gentry. LC 54-21763. 1954. Magnolia Publishers.
Crossroads: A Novel of the Twentieth Century South. John Owen Beaty. LC 56-44726. 1956. Wilkinson Pub. Co.
Crossroads: An Autobiographical Novel 1st Ed. James McConkey. LC 67-20558. 1968. 3.95. Dutton.
Crossroads for Nurse Cathy. Arlene Hale. (Ace nurse novel). 1974. (pbk.) 0.75. Ace Books.
Crossroads for Nurse Cathy. Arlene Hale. (Arlene Hale Nurse Romance). 1976. (pbk.) 0.95. Ace Books.
Crossroads (Fortune Carree) Joseph Kessel & Walff, William Almon, 1885- Tr. LC 32-23417. 1932. G. P. Putnam's Sons.
Crossroads of Destiny. John P Ritter. G. W. Dillingham Company.
Crossroads of Destiny. Eric H Wilkinson. LC 29-12130. The Macaulay Company.
Crossroads of Ectasy. Tr. by L. E. LaBan. Orig. Title: Carrefours Des Ivresses. (Orig.). Date not set. pap. 1.95 o.p. (6014). Brandon.
Crossroads of Time. Andre Norton, pseud. LC 77-25531. (Norton, Andre. The Space Adventure Novels of Andre Norton). 1978. 7.95 (ISBN 0-8398-2418-1). Gregg Press.
Crossroads of Time. Andre Norton. (Ace science fiction). 1974. (pbk.) 1.25. Ace Books.
Crosstalk. Dennis Bloodworth. LC 77-20044. 8.95 (ISBN 0-698-10872-8). Coward, McCann and Geohegan.
Crosstown. John Held. LC 33-31312. 1933. The Vanguard Press.
Crossways. Helen Reimensnyder Martin. LC 16-66515. 1912. The Century Co.
Crossways, by Helen Reimensnyder Martin... Helen Reimensnyder Martin. LC 10-5305. 1910. The Century Co.
Crosswind. Robert Henry, pseud. 1961. 4.95 o.p. (ISBN 0-670-24865-7). Viking Pr.
Crosswind: A Novel by Robert Henry Pseud. Robert Henry Schmeizer. LC 61-15701. 1961. Viking Press.
Crosswinds. Martha Louise Cheavens. LC 48-8413. 1948. Houghton Mifflin Co.
Crossword Murder. Ernest Robertson Punshon. LC 34-365463. 1934. A. A. Knopf.
Crossword Mystery. Robert B. Gillespie. (Raven House Mysteries). 224p. 1981. pap. 2.25 (ISBN 0-373-63019-0, Pub. by Worldwide). Harlequin Bks.
Crouchback. Carola Mary Anima Oman Lenanton, pseud. LC 29-17551. H. Holt and Company.
Crouching Beast, a Clubfoot Story. Valentine Williams. LC 28-24947. 1928. Houghton Mifflin Company.
Crow; a Novel. Donald Stewart. LC 59-6374. 1959. Doubleday,
Crow and the Cat. Peter De Polnay. LC 75-16206. 1975. 6.95. St. Martin's Press.
Crow Eaters. Bapsi Sidhwa. LC 81-14498. 10.95 (ISBN 0-312-17717-8). St. Martin's Press.
Crow Field. Margaret Currier Boylen. LC 47-2418. 1947. Doubleday & Company, Inc.
Crow Flies Crooked. Jack Kisling. LC 66-14499. bds., 4.95. McKay.
Crow Goddess. Patricia Finney. LC 79-1322. (Illus.). 11.95 (ISBN 0-399-12315-6). Putnam.
Crow Hollow. Dorothy Eden. 1977. pap. 1.95 (ISBN 0-441-12356-2). Ace Bks.
Crow on the Spruce. Chenoweth Hall. LC 46-1515. 1946. Houghton Mifflin Company.
Crow Speaks. Ezeekiel Zorrian Zinderman. LC 72-77029. (Illus.). 1972. 4.95. Hickoryville Publications.
Crow-Step. Georgia Fraser. LC 10-22983. 1910. 1.50. Witter and Kintner.
Crow Warriors. Bill Hotchkiss. (Indian Ser.: No. 3). (Orig.). 1981. pap. 2.75 (ISBN 0-440-01588-X, Banbury). Dell.
Crowd, Based on the Motion Picture Story: A King Vidor Production, Novelized. Allie Lowe Miles. LC 28-14116. Grosset & Dunlap.
Crowd in the Bedroom. Garth Brandtson. 192p. (Orig.). 1974. pap. 1.95 o.p. (ISBN 0-87056-366-1, 6366). Brandon.
Crowd Is Not Company. Robert Kee. LC 47-11266. 1947. Doubleday.
Crowd of Voices: A Novel of a Family in Conflict. 1st Ed. Richard Lortz. LC 58-12907. 1958. Bobbs-Merrill.
Crowd Pleasers. Rosemary Rogers. LC 78-57656. 3.95. Avon Books.
Crowd Your Luck on Death. Harry Kapustin. LC 75-160937. (Short story index reprint series). 1971. (ISBN 0-8369-3916-6). Books for Libraries Press.
Crowd Your Luck on Death. Harry Kapustin. LC 30-6152. Harcourt, Brace and Company.
Crowded Bed. Henry Sackerman, pseud. 256p. 1967. 4.95 o.p. (ISBN 0-8202-0015-8). Sherbourne.
Crowded Bed: A Novel. Henry Sackerman, pseud. LC 67-26928. 1967. 4.95. Sherbourne.
Crowded Hill. Le Roy MacLeod. LC 34-39744. Reynal & Hitchcock.
Crowded House. Katharine Ball Ripley. LC 36-18545. 1936. Doubleday Doran & Company, Inc.
Crowded Loneliness. Max Weatherly. Orig. Title: Mantis & the Moth. 1973. pap. 1.25 o.p. (ISBN 0-515-03110-0, V3110). Pyramid Pubns.
Crowded Sky. Henry Hunt Searls. (Kangaroo Book). 1977. 1.95 (ISBN 0-671-81163-0). Pocket Books.
Crowded Sky. 1st Ed. Henry Hunt Searls. LC 60-7551. 1960. Harper.
Crowded Solitude. Benjamin Kittredge. LC 30-12148. 1930. Coward-McCann, Inc.
Crowded Street. Winifred Holtby. LC 76-380629. 1976. 0.65 (ISBN 0-552-10121-4). Corgi.
Crowder Household: The Rationalization of a Mystery; a Novel. 1st. ed. Stella M Stroecker. (Illus.). 1974. 3.50 (ISBN 0-682-47917-9). Exposition.
Crowder Tales. Nixon Smiley. LC 73-80589. (Illus.). 1973. 5.95 (ISBN 0-912458-22-4). E. A. Seemann Pub.
Crowds and the Veiled Woman. Marian Metcalf Cox. LC 10-10321. 1910. 1.50. Funk & Wagnalls Company.
Crowing Hen... Reginald Davis. LC 36-18150. 1936. Pub. for the Crime Club, Inc., by Doubleday, Doran & Co., Inc.
Crown. Elisabeth Bergstrand-Poulsen & Williamson, Eleanor Salberg, Tr. LC 39-13364. 1939. Coward-McCann, Inc.
Crown. Archie Joscelyn. LC 60-529520. 1960. Augustana Press.
Crown. Francis Pollini. (N3735). 1968. Bantam.
Crown. Francis Pollini. LC 67-15116. 1967. Putnam.
Crown. Robert F Truesdell. LC 56-323629. 1956. Christopher Pub. House.
Crown & the Loin Cloth: A Novel. Chaman Lal Nahal. 400p. 1982. 40.00x (ISBN 0-7069-1285-3, Pub. by Garlandfold England). State Mutual Bk.
Crown & the Loincloth: A Novel. Chaman Lal. 432p. 1981. 25.00x (ISBN 0-7069-1285-3, Pub. by Vikas India). Advent NY.
Crown and the Loincloth: A Novel. Chaman Lal Nahal. LC 81-900404. (Vikas Library of Modern Indian Writing; 10). 25.00 (ISBN 0-7069-1285-3). Vikas.
Crown and the Shadow: The Story of Francoise D'Aubigne, Marquise De Maintenon. Pamela Hill. LC 55-5667. 1955. Putnam.
Crown Court. James Follett. LC 77-24773. 1978. 7.95. St. Martin's Press.
Crown Estate. Evelyn Berckman. LC 75-25437. 1976. 6.95 (ISBN 0-385-11533-4). Doubleday.
Crown Estate. Evelyn Berckman. 1978. 1.75 (ISBN 0-380-38422-1). Avon Books.
Crown for Ashes. Teresa Kay. LC 52-14135. 1952. Bruce Pub. Co.
Crown for Carlotte. Daniel MacIntyre Henderson. LC 29-18165. 1929. Frederick A. Stokes Company.
Crown for Thomas Peters. Hennessy, Maurice N & Sauter, Edwin. LC 64-13800. I. Washburn.
Crown from the Spear. Cecilia Viets Dakin Jamison. LC 7-10323. 1872. J. R. Osgood and Company.
Crown in Candlelight. Rosemary Hawley Jarman. LC 78-654. (Illus.). 9.95 (ISBN 0-316-45782-5). Little, Brown.
Crown in Darkness. Margaret Mullally. LC 74-24836. 1975. 8.95 o.p. (ISBN 0-312-17745-3). St Martin.
Crown in Darkness: A Novel About Lady Jane Grey. Margaret Mullally. LC 74-24836. (Troubadour). 8.95. St. Martin's Press.
Crown of Aloes. Norah Robinson Lofts. LC 73-79689. 1974. 6.95 (ISBN 0-385-03220-X). Doubleday.
Crown of Aloes. Norah Robinson Lofts. LC 74-5019. 1974. 13.95 (ISBN 0-8161-6207-7). G. K. Hall.

TITLE INDEX CRUSOE TEST.

Crown of Desire. Marjorie DeBoer. 704p. (Orig.). 1983. pap. 3.95 (ISBN 0-8439-1166-2, Leisure Bks). Dorchester Pub Co.

Crown of Feathers. Isaac Bashevis Singer. 1979. pap. 2.95 (ISBN 0-449-23465-7, Crest). Fawcett.

Crown of Feathers and Other Stories. Isaac Bashevis Singer. LC 73-81055. 1973. 8.95 (ISBN 0-374-13217-8). Farrar, Straus and Giroux.

Crown of Flowers. Joel Kurtzman. LC 79-108892. 1970. 5.50. Dutton.

Crown of Gold. Lauretta J. Ngcobo. (Sun-Lit Ser.). 250p. (Orig.). 1981. 10.00x o.s.i. (ISBN 0-89410-170-6); pap. 6.00x o.s.i. (ISBN 0-89410-171-4). Three Continents.

Crown of Grass. Charles Andrew Brady. LC 64-15770. 1964. Doubleday.

Crown of Life. George Robert Gissing. LC 72-80635. 1969. AMS Press.

Crown of Life. George Robert Gissing. LC 99-4915. 1899. F. A. Stokes Company.

Crown of Life. Gordon Arthur Smith. LC 15-19189. 1915. C. Scribner's Sons.

Crown of Night. 1st American Ed. Pierre Audemars. LC 62-201268. 1962. Harper & Row.

Crown of Passion. Jocelyn Carew, pseud. 416p. 1980. pap. 2.75 (ISBN 0-380-76414-8, 76414). Avon.

Crown of Shame. Oscar F G Day. (On cover: Idylwild series, v. 2, no. 41). 1893. Morrill, Higgins & Co.

Crown of Shame. Florence Marryat Church Lean. (On cover: Seaside library. Pocket ed. no. 1184). 1889. G. Munro.

Crown of Straw. Allen Upward. LC 10-9918. 1896. Dodd, Mead and Company.

Crown of Terror. Kenneth W Bush. LC 71-90026. 1970. 4.50. Dorrance.

Crown of Terror. Kenneth Wayne. 1969. 4.50 o.p. (ISBN 0-8059-1391-2). Dorrance.

Crown of the Sword God. Manning Norvil. (Odan Ser., Science Fiction Ser.). 1980. pap. 1.75 (ISBN 0-87997-542-3, UE1542). DAW Bks.

Crown of Thorns. Richard Capp. Ed. by Billie Young. LC 77-78802. 1979. 12.95 (ISBN 0-87949-096-9). Ashley Bks.

Crown of Wild Myrtle. Herbert Ernest Bates. 1963. 3.95 o.p. FS&G.

Crown Princess & Other Stories. Brigid Brophy. LC 53-277894. 1953. Viking Press.

Crown Rides High. 1st Ed. Tom J Hopkins. LC 53-106481. (Double D western). 1953. Doubleday.

Crown Tree. Le Gette Blythe. LC 57-6101. 1957. John Knox Press.

Crown Valley. Kay Ashley. 1973. (pbk.) 0.75. Dell.

Crown Without Sceptre. William Vaughan Wilkins. LC 52-9375. 1952. Macmillan.

Crownbird. Kit Thackeray. LC 77-350039. 1976. 3.50 (ISBN 0-432-16512-6). P. Davies.

Crowned at Elim. Stella Eugenie Asling Riis. LC 3-28965. 1903. Smith & Wilkins.

Crowned Heads. Thomas Tryon. LC 75-36813. 1976. 8.95 (ISBN 0-394-40468-8). Knopf.

Crowning an Indeal: A Story of the World War. Annie Bunker. LC 20-8861. 1.00. Christopher Publishing House.

Crowning Event: And Other Stories. Virginia T Mankin. LC 53-12271. 1953. Dorrance.

Crowning of a King. Arnold Zweig & Sutton, Eric, Tr. LC 38-27455. 1938. The Viking Press.

Crowning of Candace. Katharine Pearson Woods. LC 8-37535. (On cover: The feather library). 1896. Dodd, Mead and Company.

Crows Are Black Everywhere. Herbert Osborn Yardley & Grabo, Carl Henry, 1881- Joint Author. 1945. G. P. Putnam's Sons.

Crows Can't Count. Erle Stanley Gardner. LC 46-2891. 1946. W. Morrow.

Crows in a Green Tree. W. H Canaway. LC 65-17251. 1965. Doubleday.

Crow's Inn Tragedy. Annie Haynes. LC 27-10051. 1927. Dodd, Mead and Company.

Crow's-Nest. Sara Jeannette Duncan Cotes. LC 1-31608. 1901. Dodd, Mead and Company.

Crows of Edwina Hill: A Novel. 1st Ed. Allan R Bosworth. LC 61-6201. 1961. Harper.

Crows of Mephistopheles & Other Stories. George Fitzmaurice. Ed. by Robert Hogan. 1971. 7.50 o.p. Dufour.

Crowthers of Bankdam. Thomas Armstrong. LC 41-4403. 1941. The Macmillan Company.

Croxley Master: A Great Tale of the Prize Ring. Arthur Conan Doyle. LC 7-12635. 1907. McClure, Phillips & Co.

Croxley Master: And Other Tales of the Ring and Camp. Arthur Conan Doyle. LC 26-8496. 1925. George H. Doran Company.

Croyd: A Downtime Fantasy. Ian Wallace. LC 67-23599. 1967. 3.95. Putnam.

Cruachan & the Killane. Cristabel, pseud. (Orig.). 1970. pap. 0.75 o.p. (0502-07093). Curtis.

Crucial Conversations. May Sarton. 156p. 1975. 12.95 (ISBN 0-393-08725-5). Norton.

Crucial Conversations: A Novel. May Sarton. LC 74-32232. 1975. 5.95 (ISBN 0-393-08725-5). Norton.

Crucial Instances. Edith Newbold Jones Wharton. LC 75-8801. 1969. Scholarly Press.

Crucial Instances. Edith Newbold Jones Wharton. LC 76-86376. 1969. AMS Press.

Crucial Instances. Edith Newbold Jones Wharton. LC 1-31395. 1901. C. Scribner's Sons.

Crucial Instances. Edith Newbold Jones Wharton. LC 25-15508. 1909. C. Scribner's Sons.

Crucial Test. May Elizabeth Costello Firestone. LC 99-5505. The A. Lincoln Firestone Co.

Crucible. Mark Lee Luther. 1907. The Macmillan Company.

Crucible. Arthur Miller. (gr. 6 up). pap. 2.25 (ISBN 0-553-13902-9, B13902-9). Bantam.

Crucible Island: A Romance, an Adventure and an Experiment. Conde Benoist Pallen. LC 19-11567. The Manhattanville Press.

Crucifixion of Pete McCabe. Jack Pearl, pseud. (75277). 1968. Pocket Bks.

Crucifixion of Pete McCabe. Jack Pearl, pseud. LC 66-16180. 1966. Trident Press.

Crucifixion of Philip Strong. Charles Monroe Sheldon. LC 8-5091. 1894. A. C. McClurg and Company.

Crucifixion of Philip Strong. Charles Monroe Sheldon. LC 99-5888. (On cover: Alliance library, no. 3). 1899. Street & Smith.

Crucifixion of Phillip Strong. Charles Monroe Sheldon. 1898. The Advance Publishing Co.

Crucify Her! A Story of Now. Ramsay Morris. LC 7-20133. The Eclectic Publishing Co.

Crude. Robert Hyde. LC 27-21140. Payson & Clarke Ltd.

Cruel As a Cat. Kyle Hunt, pseud. 1970. pap. 0.95 o.p. (95017). Beagle Bks.

Cruel As the Grave. Emma Dorothy Eliza Nevitte Southworth. LC 13-2060. T. B. Peterson & Brothers.

Cruel but Courageous. 1st Ed. Peggy Ballard. LC 53-12634. 1953. Pageant Press.

Cruel City: After the Russian of Dimitry Grigorovitch, with a Sketch of the Author. Dmitrii Vasil'Evich Grigorovich. Ed. by Pierson, Ernest De Lancey. LC 7-291. Cassell Publishing Company.

Cruel Coast: By William Gage. William H Gage, pseud. LC 66-26047. (Signet bk., T3287). 1967. New Amer. Lib.

Cruel Cocks. Garland Roark. 1970. pap. 0.75 o.p. (0502-07089). Curtis.

Cruel Cocks. 1st Ed. Garland Roark. LC 57-6712. 1957. Doubleday.

Cruel Count. Barbara Cartland. (Barbara Cartland Library#28). 1975. (pbk.) 1.25. Bantam Books.

Cruel Easter. Michael Sandys. LC 58-8264. 1958. Pantheon Books.

Cruel Fellowship. Cyril Hume. LC 25-10305. George H. Doran Company.

Cruel Flame. Charlotte Lamb, pseud. (Harlequin Presents Ser.). 192p. 1980. pap. 1.50 (ISBN 0-373-10387-5, Pub. by Harlequin). PB.

Cruel in the Shadow. Lorn Macinnes Macintyre. LC 80-51294. 1980. 11.95 (ISBN 0-312-17765-8). St. Martin's Press.

Cruel Legacy. Laura H. Hudson. pap. 0.60 o.p. Lancer.

Cruel Lips. rev. ed. Marcus Van Heller, pseud. pap. 1.75 o.p. (2040). Brandon.

Cruel Lips. Marcus Van Heller, pseud. pap. 1.95 o.p. (V1039T, Venus). Grove.

Cruel Lips. Marcus Van Heller, pseud. 192p. 1971. pap. 1.95 o.s.i. (O*P*H254, Ophelia). Olympia.

Cruel London. A Novel. Joseph Hatton. (On cover: Lovell's library, v. 3, no. 137). 1883. J. W. Lovell Company.

Cruel Month. Osbert Sitwell. 4.95 (ISBN 0-7043-3155-1, Pub. by Quartet England). Charles River Bks.

Cruel Sea. Nicholas Monsarrat. LC 51-11056. 1951. Knopf.

Cruel Sea. Edited for School Use by Joseph Gallant. Nicholas Monsarrat. LC 57-4131. (Modern literature series). 1957. Oxford Book Co.

Cruel Secret. A Novel ... LC 6-31943. 1883. G. W. Carleton & Co.; Etc., Etc.

Cruel Tales. Villiers de l'Isle-Adam. LC 63-24947. (Oxford library of French classics). 1963. Oxford University Press.

Cruel Tower. William B Hartley. LC 55-9433. 1955. Appleton-Century-Crofts.

Cruel Trail. William M. James, pseud. (Apache Ser.: No. 11). 1978. pap. 1.50 (ISBN 0-523-40560-X). Pinnacle Bks.

Cruel Way to Live. Jon F. Langione. 1973. 5.00 o.p. (ISBN 0-682-47846-6). Exposition.

Cruel Woman. Annie A Gibbs. (Lovell's library, no. 1396). J. W. Lovell Company.

Cruicble. Ben Ames Williams. LC 37-272091. 1937. Houghton Mifflin Company.

Cruise. Peter Gorton Baker. LC 68-12094. 1968. Putnam.

Cruise. Paula Christian. LC 82-60183. 224p. (Orig.). 1982. pap. 8.95 (ISBN 0-931328-09-8). Timely Bks.

Cruise into Chaos. Lionel Derrick, pseud. (Penetrator Ser.: No. 39). 192p. (Orig.). 1980. pap. 1.75 (ISBN 0-523-40924-9). Pinnacle Bks.

Cruise of a Woman Hater. William Parker Greenough. (On cover: Ticknor's paper series, no. 3). 1887. Ticknor and Company.

Cruise of the Albatross; or, When Was Wednesday the Tenth. Grant Allen. Repr. of 1898 ed. lib. bdg. 20.00 (ISBN 0-8414-3053-5). Folcroft.

Cruise of the Albatross: Or, When Was Wednesday the Tenth? A Story of the South Pacific. Grant Allen. LC 6-71. 1898. Lothrop Publishing Company.

Cruise of the "Black Prince," Privateer. Verney Lovett Cameron. (On cover: Lovell's library. v. 17, no. 817). J. W. Lovell Company.

Cruise of the Breadwinner... Herbert Ernest Bates. LC 47-30203. 1947. Little, Brown and Company.

Cruise of the Cachalot. Frank Thomas Bullen. LC 62-69866. 1962. Dover Publications.

Cruise of the Cachalot. Frank Thomas Bullen. LC 25-913703. 1925. D. Appleton and Company.

Cruise of the Cachalot. Frank Thomas Bullen. LC 25-27481. (Fairmount classics). 1925. Macrae Smith Company.

Cruise of the Cachalot. Frank Thomas Bullen. Ed. by Schweikert, Harry Christian. LC 26-238890. (Half-title: Appleton modern literature series). D. Appleton and Company.

Cruise of the Cachalot. Frank Thomas Bullen. LC 27-21620. (father and son library). J. H. Sears & Company, Inc.

Cruise of the Cachalot. Frank Thomas Bullen. LC 28-26457. (golden books). 1927. D. McKay.

Cruise of the Cachalot Around the World After Sperm Whales. Frank Thomas Bullen. LC 1-25398. 1899. D. Appleton and Company.

Cruise of the Cachalot Round the World After Sperm Whales. Frank Thomas Bullen. LC 20-220387. 1920. D. Appleton and Company.

Cruise of the Cachalot Round the World After Sperm Whales. Illus. by Schaeffer, Mead. LC 26-27488. 1926. Dodd, Mead & Company.

Cruise of the Colleen Bawn: An Adventure Story. Frank Carruthers. LC 26-19024. Chelsea House.

Cruise of the Conqueror: Being the Further Adventures of the Motor Pirate. George Sidney Paternoster. LC 6-10653. 1906. L. C. Page & Company.

Cruise of the Coral Queen. Mary Collins Dunne. 192p. (YA) 1975. 4.95 o.p. (Avalon). Bouregy.

Cruise of the Dazzler. Jack London. LC 2-22486. (St. Nicholas books). 1902. The Century Co.

Cruise of the Dazzler. Jack London. LC 18-17316. (St. Nicholas books). 1916. The Century Co.

Cruise of the Dry Dock. Thomas Sigismund Stribling. LC 17-21794. 1917. The Reilly & Britton Co.

Cruise of the Frolic. A Sea Story. William Henry Giles Kingston. LC 22-24768. 1866. J. E. Tilton and Company.

Cruise of the "Ghost,". William Livingston Alden. LC 10-29132. Harper & Brothers.

Cruise of the Jasper B. Don Marquis. LC 16-10724. 1916. 1.30. D. Appleton and Company.

Cruise of the Jasper B. Don Marquis. LC 23-642047. 1923. D. Appleton and Company.

Cruise of the Make-Believes. Tom Gallon. LC 7-32034. 1907. Little, Brown, and Company.

Cruise of the Midge. Michael Scott. LC 8-3034. (Seaside library, v. 68, no. 1387). 1882. G. Munro.

Cruise of the Midge. Michael Scott. LC 4-16578. (Half-title: Sea stories of Michael Scott). 1894. Gibbings & Co., Ld.

Cruise of the Mystery in McAll Mission Work. Louise Seymour Houghton. LC 7-7138. The American Tract Society.

Cruise of the "Odin". John Coleman. LC 23-14203. 1923. The Cornhill Publishing Company.

Cruise of the Petrel: A Story of 1812. Thornton Jenkins Hains. LC 1-31871. 1901. McClure, Phillips & Co.

Cruise of the Pnyx. Robert Kelly. LC 79-64918. 50p. 1979. ltd. signed ed. 30.00 (ISBN 0-930794-09-5); pap. 4.50 (ISBN 0-930794-08-7). Station Hill Pr.

Cruise of the Pretty Polly: A Voyage of Incident. William Clark Russell. LC 4304. 1901. J. B. Lippincott Company.

Cruise of the Raider "Wolf". Roy Alexander. Repr. of 1939 ed. 12.00 o.s.i. Finch Pr.

Cruise of the Rolling Junk. Francis Scott Key Fitzgerald. 1976. 25.00 (ISBN 0-89723-008-6). Bruccoli.

Cruise of the "Scandal" And Other Stories. Victor Bridges. LC 23-1100. 1920. G. P. Putnam's Sons.

Cruise of the Shining Light. Norman Duncan. LC 7-15117. 1907. Harper & Brothers.

Cruise of the Snap Dragon. Ruth P Barbour. LC 76-40443. 8.95 (ISBN 0-910244-88-X). J. F. Blair.

Cruise of the Violetta. Arthur Willis Colton. LC 6-376045. 1906. H. Holt and Company.

Cruise Ship M.D. Susanne Jaffe. 1975. (pbk.) 1.50. Ace Books.

Cruise Ship Nurse. Rose Dana, pseud. 1970. pap. 0.60 o.p. (ISBN 0-447-73885-2). Lancer.

Cruise Ship Nurse. Michelle Josephs. (Orig.). 1969. pap. 0.50 o.p. (1028). Belmont-Tower.

Cruise Under Six Flags. Olaf Abraham Ericsson. LC 6-38162. 1883. J. B. Lippincott & Co.

Cruise with Death. F. Draco, pseud. LC 52-7157. (Murray Hill mystery). 1952. Rinehart.

Cruiser. Warren Tute. 1981. pap. 2.75 (ISBN 0-345-29573-0). Ballantine.

Cruiser: A Novel. Tute, Warren. LC 56-11226. 1956. Ballantine Books.

Cruiser: A Romance of the Idaho Timber Land Frauds. James Orville Adams. LC 10-2923. 1909. J. O. Adams.

Cruiser Dreams. Janet Morris. 1982. pap. 2.75 (ISBN 0-425-05382-2). Berkley Pub.

Cruisin for a Bruisin. Winifred Rosen. (Laurel-Leaf Library). 1977. 1.25 (ISBN 0-440-91608-9). Dell Pub. Co.

Cruisin for a Bruisin. Rosen Winifred. (YA) 1977. pap. 1.95 (ISBN 0-440-91608-9, LFL). Dell.

Cruising. Gerald Walker. LC 73-122422. 1970. 5.95. Stein and Day.

Cruising and Blockading. William Henry Winslow. LC 41-40530. 1885. J. R. Weldin & Co.

Cruising for the Cross. Charles Abbott Schneider Dwight. LC 4-25105. American Tract Society.

Cruisings: Afloat and Ashore. 2d. ed. Edward Zane Carroll Judson. LC 7-11443. 1848. R. Craighead, Printer.

Crum Elbow Folks. Percy Raymond Barnes. LC 38-27837. 1938. J.B. Lippincott Company.

Crumbling Pedestal. Mark Jasen. 4.50 o.p. Carlton.

Crumbling Walls. Joan Conquest. LC 27-166695. The Macaulay Company.

Crumbs and His Times. Mary Schell Hoke Bacon. LC 6-297811. 1906. Doubleday, Page & Company.

Crunch and Des: Stories of Florida Fishing. Philip Wylie. LC 48-9263. 1948. Rinehart.

Crusade. Royce Brier. LC 31-738019. 1931. D. Appleton and Company.

Crusade. Donn Bryne. LC 28-73717. 1928. Little, Brown, and Company.

Crusade of the Excelsior. Bret Harte. LC 7-3640. 1887. Houghton, Mifflin and Company.

Crusade of the Excelsior: And Other Tales. Bret Harte. LC 12-277750. (Half-title: Standard library edition. The writings of Bret Harte... vol. vi). Houghton, Mifflin and Company; Etc., Etc.

Crusader. Frank X. Hurley. LC 74-16811. 1975. 4.95 (ISBN 0-8059-2087-0). Dorrance.

Crusader: A Novel on the Life of Margaret Sanger. Noel Bertram Gerson. LC 78-105358. 1970. 6.95. Little, Brown.

Crusader: Books 3 & 4, The Accursed Tower & The Passionate Princess. John Cleve, pseud. LC 80-1000. 384p. (Orig.). 1981. pap. 4.95 (ISBN 0-394-17736-3, B-441, BC). Grove.

Crusader No. 1: The Accursed Tower. John Cleve, pseud. 1974. pap. 1.50 o.p. (D3444, Dist. by Dell). Grove.

Crusader No. 2: The Passionate Princess. John Cleve, pseud. 1974. pap. 1.50 o.p. (D6039, Dist. by Dell). Grove.

Crusader No. 3: Julanar the Lioness. John Cleve, pseud. 1975. pap. 1.50 o.p. (D4731, Dist. by Dell). Grove.

Crusader No. 4: My Lady Queen. John Cleve, pseud. 1975. pap. 1.50 o.p. (D5749, Dist. by Dell). Grove.

Crusader: The Accursed Tower. John Cleve. (Dell-Grove book). 1974. (pbk.) 1.50. Dell.

Crusaders. Stefan Heym. LC 48-7318. 1948. Little Brown.

Crusader's Tomb. Archibald Joseph Cronin. 1981. 20.00x (ISBN 0-575-00242-5, Pub. by Gollancz England). State Mutual Bk.

Crusading for Kronk: A Novel. Stanley Price. LC 60-11417. 1960. Putnam.

Crushed Flower: And Other Stories. Leonid Nikolaevich Andreev & Bernstein, Herman, 1876-1935, Tr. LC 16-217119. 1916. A. A. Knopf.

Crushed Roses. Hugh Joseph Morley. LC 67-28991. 1968. Dorrance.

Crusher. Shelly Gross. 1973. pap. 0.75 o.p. (07268). Curtis.

Crushing. Ronald Cecil Hamlyn McKie. LC 78-21981. 1979. 8.95 (ISBN 0-684-15919-8). Scribner.

Crusoe in New York, and Other Tales. Edward Everett Hale. LC 68-55678. (American short story series, v. 19). 1969. Garrett Press.

Crusoe in New York: And Other Tales. Edward Everett Hale. 1880. Roberts Brothers.

Crusoe in New York: And Other Tales. 3d ed. Edward Everett Hale. LC 8-20133. 1887. Roberts Brothers.

Crusoe Test. Mark Nelson. LC 76-7282. 1976. 7.95. St. Martin's Press.

Crusoe Test. Mark Nelson. 1977. 1.75 (ISBN 0-380-01748-2). Avon Books.

Crusoe Warburton. Victor Wallace Germains. LC 53-5301. 1954. Coward-McCann.
Crusty Crossed. Dorris Heffron. LC 77-362015. 1976. 2.95 (ISBN 0-333-19735-6). Macmillan.
Crutches for Sale. An Osteopathic Novel. John Roy Musick & Smith, William Mrs. Crutches for Sale. (On cover: Neely's universal library. no. 72). F. T. Neely.
Cruz Stories. Henry H Roth. LC 74-169206. (Lillabulero prose pamphlet no. 2). 2.00. Lillabulero Press.
Cry Above the Winds: A Novel of Old California. Jenniebelle Bartlett. LC 51-9063. 1951. Morrow.
Cry and the Covenant. Morton Thompson. LC 49-11171. 1949. Doubleday.
Cry, Coyote. Steve Frazee. LC 55-580. 1955. Macmillan.
Cry Dance: A Novel of the American Indian. Coe Smith Hayne. LC 39-9059. 1939. Harper & Brothers.
Cry Down the Lonely Night. Cover Painting by Barye Phillips. Milton White. LC 54-42473. (Gold medal books, 427). 1954. Fawcett Publications.
Cry for a Shadow. Chrys Paul Fletcher. LC 68-15505. 1968. Putnam.
Cry for Fools. Johannes Egbers. 1975. 5.50 (ISBN 0-682-48130-0). Exposition Press.
Cry for Happy. George Campbell. LC 58-5474. 1958. Harcourt, Brace.
Cry for Help. Doris Miles Disney. LC 74-14377. 1975. 5.95 (ISBN 0-385-03441-5). Published for the Crime Club by Doubleday.
Cry for Love. Ann Lorraine Thompson. 1974. (pbk.) 1.25. Avon.
Cry for Peace. Jean Springer. 200p. (Orig.). 1982. pap. 4.95 (ISBN 0-934998-07-8). Bethel Pub.
Cry for the Baron. John Creasey. LC 76-109004. 1970. 4.50. Walker.
Cry for the Baron. Anthony Morris, pseud. LC 76-109004. (Mystery Ser). 1970. 4.50 o.p. (ISBN 0-8027-5045-1). Walker & Co.
Cry for the Demon. Julia Grice. 400p. (Orig.). 1980. pap. 2.75 (ISBN 0-446-95497-7). Warner Bks.
Cry for the Lost. Gina Dessart. LC 59-10619. 1959. Harper.
Cry for the Strangers. John Saul. 1979. pap. 3.50 (ISBN 0-440-11870-0). Dell.
Cry Geronimo. Forrest Carter. 1980. pap. 2.25 (ISBN 0-440-11039-4). Dell.
Cry Guilty. Sara Woods, pseud. LC 80-29319. 1981. 9.95 (ISBN 0-312-17802-6). St. Martin's Press.
Cry Hard: Cry Fast. John Dann MacDonald. LC 55-42203. (Popular library, 675).
Cry Hard, Cry Fast. John Dann MacDonald. 160p. 1981. pap. 1.95 (ISBN 0-449-13969-7, GM). Fawcett.
Cry Havoc. Richard Martin Stern. LC 63-14033. 1963. Scribner.
Cry Heard. Ella Perry Price. LC 99-147230. Curts & Jennings.
Cry Hunger: A Novel. Sidney Bliss. LC 54-12633. 1955. Vantage Press.
Cry in the Night. Kat Brosnan. 1978. pap. 1.50 o.s.i. (ISBN 0-8439-0518-2, Leisure Bks). Nordon Pubns.
Cry in the Night. Mary Higgins Clark. LC 82-10289. 13.95 (ISBN 0-671-41701-0). Simon and Schuster.
Cry in the Night. Mary Higgins Clark. 1982. 13.95 (ISBN 0-671-43128-5). S&S.
Cry in the Night. Mary Higgins Clark. (General Ser.). 1983. lib. bdg. 15.95 (ISBN 0-8161-3482-0, Large Print Bks). G K Hall.
Cry in the Night. Dorothy Quick. LC 57-11461. 1957. Arcadia House.
Cry in the Night. Kelley Pseud. Roos. LC 66-14191. (Red badge mystery). bds., 3.50. Dodd.
Cry in the Wilderness. Mary Ella Waller. LC 12-24560. 1912. Little, Brown, and Company.
Cry Love Aloud. Margaret Tsuda. (Illus.). 96p. 1972. 4.95 (ISBN 0-913976-02-4). Discovery Bks.
Cry Macho: A Novel. N. Richard Nash. LC 74-32233. 1975. 7.95 (ISBN 0-440-04996-2). Delacorte Press.
Cry Murder. Edith Howie. LC 44-47772. (On cover: Circle Mill mysteries). 1944. M. S. Mill Co., Inc.
Cry Murder. William MacLeod Raine. LC 47-31383. 1947. Phoenix Press.
Cry Murder. Nancy Rutledge. LC 54-10915. (Dutton guilt edged mystery). 1954. Dutton.
Cry of a Bastard: A Novel of TheSouthland. 1st Ed. C B Woltz. LC 60-16832. Greenwich Book Publishers.
Cry of a Man Running. Ward McNally. 1968. 6.50 o.s.i. (Pub. by Cowman). Tri-Ocean.
Cry of Absence: A Novel. Madison Jones. LC 72-147338. 1971. 5.95. Crown Publishers.
Cry of Angels. Jeff Fields. LC 73-91623. 1974. 8.95 (ISBN 0-689-10593-2). Atheneum.
Cry of Angry Thunder. G. Clifton Wisler, pseud. LC 79-7885. 1980. 8.95 (ISBN 0-385-15657-X). Doubleday.
Cry of Bees. Melissa Hardy. LC 78-104133. 1970. 5.95. Viking Press.
Cry of Blood. Fortune Du Boisgobey & Kendall, Laura E., Tr. LC 6-34426. (On cover: Seaside library. Pocket ed. no. 851). G. Munro.
Cry of Children. 1st Ed. John Horne Burns. LC 52-9547. 1952. Harper.
Cry of Crickets. Brian Glanville. LC 75-104683. 1970. 5.95. Coward-McCann.
Cry of Dolores. Herbert Sherman Gorman. LC 47-7053. 1947. Rinehart.
Cry of Neptune. Anne-Marie Bretonne. (Berkley Medallion Book). 1977. 1.50. (ISBN 0-425-03314-7). Berkley Pub. Corp.
Cry of Peacocks. Dayton Rommel. LC 63-8713. 5.95. Dodd.
Cry of the Cat. Sharon Wagner. (O.s.i.). (Orig.). 1973. pap. 0.75 o.s.i. (BT50600). Belmont-Tower.
Cry of the Condor. Richard H. Curtis. (Skymasters Ser.: No. 10). (Orig.). 1983. pap. 3.25 (ISBN 0-440-01510-3). Dell.
Cry of the Daughter. Kit Reed, pseud. LC 70-133580. (Fawcett crest book, M1777). 1973. (449-01777-095) 0.95. Fawcett Publications.
Cry of the Flesh. Cover Painting by Jack Floherty. Richard Himmel. LC 55-35942. (Gold medal books, 488). 1955. Fawcett Publications.
Cry of the Halidon. Robert Ludlum. LC 74-1108. 1974. 8.95 (ISBN 0-440-02120-0). Delacorte Press.
Cry of the Hawk. Hy Steirman. (Orig.). 1970. pap. 0.95 o.p. (65-297). Paperback Lib.
Cry of the Kestel. James Wood. 1981. 18.95x (Pub. by Remploy England). State Mutual Bk.
Cry of the Kite. 1st Ed. Maarten Schiemer. LC 56-760815. 1956. Bobbs-Merrill.
Cry of the Night Hawk. Nancy Dorer & Frances Dorer. 1979. pap. 1.50 (ISBN 0-532-15389-8). Woodhill.
Cry of the Owl. Patricia Highsmith. 1970. pap. 0.75 o.p. (532-75334-075). Manor Bks.
Cry of the Owl. Margaret Mayhew. LC 76-50781. 1977. 7.95 (ISBN 0-385-12892-4). Doubleday.
Cry of the Owl. Margaret Mayhew. 1979. 1.95. Popular Library.
Cry of the Owl. 1st Ed. Patricia Highsmith. LC 62-15730. 1962. Harper & Row.
Cry of the Soul: A Romance of 1862. Anne Christena Isaacson Newbigging. LC 17-30728. 1917. Sherman, French & Company.
Cry of the Street. A Novel. Mabel Adelaide Farnum. LC 13-254022. 1.00. Angel Guardian Press.
Cry of the Whippoorwill. Juanita Tyree Osborne. 1981. pap. 6.95 (Avalon). Bouregy.
Cry of the Wild Goose: By Joan Garrison Pseud. William Arthur Neubauer. LC 55-8985. 1955. Arcadia House.
Cry of Utah. Samuel O Sisco. LC 56-13099. (Pan Press fiction library book). 1956. Pan Press.
Cry of Whiteness. Thomas J Fleming. LC 67-7498. 1967. Morrow.
Cry of Youth. Cynthia Lombardi. LC 20-5773. 1920. D. Appleton and Company.
Cry Out of the Depths: Translated from the French by E. F. Bozman. 1st American Ed. Georges Duhamel. LC 54-51172. 1954. Little, Brown.
Cry Passion. Richard Jessup. LC 56-10363. (Dell first edition, 109). 1956. Dell Pub. Co.
Cry Revenge! Al C Clark. 1974. (pbk.) 1.50 (ISBN 0-87067-456-0). Holloway House.
Cry Revenge! Donald Goines. (Orig.). 1974. pap. 1.95 (ISBN 0-87067-660-1, BH660). Holloway.
Cry Scandal. William Ard. LC 56-9815. 1956. Rinehart.
Cry Silver Bells. Thomas Burnett Swann. (Science Fiction Ser). (Illus., Orig.). 1977. pap. 1.50 o.p. (ISBN 0-87997-345-5, UW1345). DAW Bks.
Cry, the Beloved Country. Alan Paton. (Lib. Rep. Ed.). (YA) 1961. 17.50x (ISBN 0-684-15559-1, ScribT); pap. 4.95 (ISBN 0-684-71863-4, SL7, ScribT); pap. text ed. 6.95 (ISBN 0-684-51544-X, SSP7, ScribC). Scribner.
Cry, the Beloved Country. Alan Paton. 304p. 1982. pap. 3.50 (ISBN 0-684-17473-1, ScribT). Scribner.
Cry, the Beloved Country: A Critical Commentary. Text by Gilliam McMichael. Including Paton's Beloved Country and the Morality of Geography by Sheridan Baker. Gillian McMichael & Sheridan Baker. (Study master pubn., 473). pap., 1.00. Amer. R.D.M.
Cry, the Beloved Country: The Novel, the Critics, the Setting. Ed. by Sheridan Baker. Alan Paton. Ed. by Sheridan Warner Baker. LC 68-14024. (Scribner res. anthologies). 1968. 2.56, pap., 1.92 text ed.,. Scribners.
Cry, the Beloved Country. With an Introd. by Lewis Gannett. Alan Paton. LC 61-4669. (Modern standard authors). 1960. Scribner.
Cry the Peacock. Anita Desai. (Orient Paperbacks Ser.). 218p. 1980. pap. 4.50 (ISBN 0-86578-083-8). Ind-US Inc.
Cry the Soft Rain. Dwyer-Joyce, Alice. LC 74-3055. 1974. 8.95 (ISBN 0-8161-6195-X). G. K. Hall.
Cry the Soft Rain. Dwyer-Joyce, Alice. LC 73-84333. 1973-1974. 6.95. St. Martin's Press.
Cry Tiger? Michael Storm. LC 58-9139. 1958. Mystery House.
Cry to Heaven. Anne Rice. LC 81-19368. 1982. 15.95 (ISBN 0-394-52351-2). Knopf: Distributed by Random House.
Cry to the Hills: By Clarence Lewis with Esther Kellber. Clarence Lewis. LC 66-11736. 4.95. Doubleday.
Cry to the Wind. Esther Loewen Vogt. LC 64-8850. bds., 2.50. Zondervan.
Cry Tough? A Novel. Irving Shulman. LC 49-7948. 1949. Dial Press.
Cry Vengeance. Ludovic Peters. LC 61-5405. (Raven book). 1961. Abelard-Schuman.
Cry Viva! William L Hopson. LC 53-123335. 1953. Bouregy & Curl.
Cry Witch. Naomi A Hintze. LC 74-19063. 1975. 6.95 (ISBN 0-394-49548-9). Random House.
Cry Wolf. Marjorie Chalmers Carleton. LC 45-36982. 1945. W. Morrow and Company.
Cry Wolf. Marjorie Chalmers Carleton. 1946. The Sundial Press.
Cry Wolf. Wilbur A Smith. LC 76-50791. 1977. 9.95 (ISBN 0-385-12449-X). Doubleday.
Cry Wolf. Wilbur A Smith. (Dell book). 1978. 2.25 (ISBN 0-440-11495-0). Dell Pub. Co.
Cry Wolf see Demarest Inheritance.
Crybaby of the Western World: A Novel of Petit Guignol in Long Beach, California. John Leonard. LC 69-11565. 1969. 4.95. Doubleday.
Cryder. George Clifford Shedd. LC 22-20683. 1922. Doubleday, Page & Company.
Crying at the Lock: A Novel. Adeline Rumsey. LC 44-5768. 1944. Simon and Schuster.
Crying Child. Barbara Mertz. LC 79-165670. 1971. 5.95 (ISBN 0-396-06392-6). Dodd, Mead.
Crying Child. Barbara Michaels. 1971. 5.95 o.p. (ISBN 0-396-06392-6). Dodd.
Crying Game. John Braine. LC 68-9195. 1968. 5.95. Houghton Mifflin.
Crying Heart. Clara Bernice Miller. LC 62-716022. 1962. Herald Press.
Crying Heart Tattoo. David Lozell Martin. LC 81-6956. 13.95. Holt, Rinehart, and Winston.
Crying in the Wilderness. Floydene Partain. (Caribbean Chronicles: Bk. 1). 432p. (Orig.). 1982. pap. 3.50 (ISBN 0-380-82271-7, 82271-7). Avon.
Crying of Lot Forty-Nine. Thomas Pynchon. pap. 2.75 (ISBN 0-553-13888-X, A13888-X). Bantam.
Crying of Lot Forty-Nine. Thomas Pynchon. LC 66-12340. 1966. 5.95 o.p. (ISBN 0-397-00418-4). Lippincott.
Crying of Lot 49. Thomas Pynchon. (S3384). 1967. Bantam.
Crying of Lot 49. Thomas Pynchon. LC 66-12340. 1966. Lippincott.
Crying Out Loud: A Novel. Jacky Gillott. LC 77-368311. 1976. 4.25 (ISBN 0-340-21127-X). Hodder and Stoughton.
"Crying Pig" Murder. Victor MacClure. LC 30-3951. 1930. W. Morrow & Co.
Crying Shame. William W. Johnstone. 1983. pap. 2.95 (ISBN 0-8217-1171-7). Zebra.
Crying Sisters. Mabel Seeley. LC 45-47537. Grosset & Dunlap.
Crying Sisters. Mabel Seeley. LC 45-13289. 1944. Triange Books.
Crying Sisters: A Mystery Story. Mabel Seeley. LC 39-27931. 1939. Pub. for The Crime Club, Inc., by Doubleday, Doran & Company, Inc.
Crying Wind. LC 80-3843. 192p. 1981. pap. 2.95 (ISBN 0-89081-263-2). Harvest Hse.
Crying Winds. J. H. Rhodes. (YA) 1980. 6.95 (Avalon). Bouregy.
Cryogenic Nightmare. Lionel Derrick, pseud. (Penetrator Ser.: No. 24). 1978. pap. 1.50 (ISBN 0-523-40177-9). Pinnacle Bks.
Cryptogram. James De Mille. (Toronto Reprint Library of Canadian Prose & Poetry). 1973. Repr. of 1871 ed. 20.00x (ISBN 0-8020-7516-9). U of Toronto Pr.
Cryptogram: A Novel. James De Mille. LC 74-169313. (Toronto reprint library of Canadian prose and poetry). (Illus.). 18.50. Toronto University Press.
Cryptozoic! Brian Wilson Aldiss. LC 68-10576. (Doubleday science fiction). 1968. Doubleday.
Crystal, Bk. VII. Helen Luster. 1980. pap. 5.00. Man-Root.
Crystal. William Wingate. LC 82-5660. 1982. 13.95 (ISBN 0-312-17819-0). St. Martin's Press.
Crystal Age. William Henry Hudson. LC 50-6045. 1950. Doric Books.
Crystal Age. William Henry Hudson. LC 72-181651. (collected works of W. H. Hudson.). 1968. AMS Press.
Crystal Age. William Henry Hudson. 1916. E. P. Dutton and Company.
Crystal Age. William Henry Hudson. LC 23-15896. (Half-title: The collected works of W. H. Hudson). 1922. J. M. Dent & Sons, Ltd.
Crystal Ball. Dorothy Spicer. 1975. (pbk.) 0.95 (ISBN 0-345-26696-X). Ballantine Books.
Crystal Ball. Terje Stigen. Tr. by Amanda Langemo. 1971. 4.50 o.p. Exposition.
Crystal Ball: Short Stories. Terje Stigen. LC 70-23188. 1971. 4.50 (ISBN 0-682-47217-4). Exposition Press.
Crystal Boat: A Novel. Dorothy Erskine. LC 46-3406. 1946. L. B. Fischer.
Crystal Button. Chauncey Thomas. (Science Fiction Ser). 368p. 1975. Repr. of 1891 ed. lib. bdg. 15.00 o.p. (ISBN 0-8398-2314-2). Gregg.
Crystal Cave. Mary Stewart. LC 75-120616. (Illus.). 1970. 7.95. Morrow.
Crystal Cave. Mary Stewart. LC 82-11928. 1982. 19.95 (ISBN 0-8161-3338-7). G.K. Hall.
Crystal Chandelier. Anne Kaple. (O.s.i.). 1976. pap. 1.95 o.s.i. (ISBN 0-912852-15-1). Echo Pubs.
Crystal City. Paschal Grousset. Tr. by Smith, L. A. LC 7-15450. Estes and Lauriat.
Crystal Claw. William Le Queux. LC 24-1953. The Macaulay Company.
Crystal Clear. Elizabeth Cadell. LC 52-8038. 1953. Morrow.
Crystal Clear. Eugenia Sheppard & Earl Blackwell. LC 77-82445. 1978. 10.00 (ISBN 0-385-13527-0). Doubleday.
Crystal Clear. Richard F. West. 256p. 1981. pap. 2.50 (ISBN 0-445-04670-8). Popular Lib.
Crystal Clear Case. Lee Head. LC 77-8431. 7.95. Putnam.
Crystal Crow. Joan Aiken. (Ace Gothic). 1973. (pbk.) 0.95. Ace Books.
Crystal Crow. Joan Aiken. LC 68-10587. 1975. (pbk.) 1.50 (ISBN 0-671-78956-2). Pocket Books.
Crystal Crow. 1st Ed. Joan Aiken. LC 68-10587. 1968. 4.95. Doubleday.
Crystal Crown. Cynthia Harrod-Eagles. (Morland Dynasty Ser.: No. 4). (Orig.). 1983. pap. 3.50 (ISBN 0-440-11568-X). Dell.
Crystal Cup. Gertrude Franklin Horn Atherton. LC 25-17967. 1925. Boni & Liveright.
Crystal Eye. William R Randall. LC 37-815. Regent House.
Crystal Fortress. Paul Petersen. (Smuggler no. 5). 1975. (pbk.) 0.95 (ISBN 0-671-77942-7). Pocket Books.
Crystal Garden. Elaine Feinstein. LC 73-16792. 1974. 6.95. E. P. Dutton.
Crystal Garden. Elaine Feinstein. 1977. 1.50 (ISBN 0-380-00976-5). Avon Books.
Crystal Gardens. Phillip A. Harrell. 40p. 1971. pap. 1.50 (ISBN 0-934852-50-2). Lorien Hse.
Crystal Gryphon. Alice Mary Norton. 1973. (pbk) 0.95. DAW Books.
Crystal Gryphon. Alice Mary Norton. LC 70-190559. 1972. 5.50. Atheneum.
Crystal Heart. Phyllis Bottome. LC 21-170843. 1921. The Century Co.
Crystal Heart. Lisa Gregory, pseud. 288p. (Orig.). 1982. pap. 2.95. Jove Pubns.
Crystal Icicle. Katherine Keith. LC 30-3538. Harcourt, Brace and Company.
Crystal Man: Landmark Science Fiction. Edward Page Mitchell. LC 73-79697. 1973. 7.95 (ISBN 0-385-03139-4). Doubleday.
Crystal Mirror, Vol. IV. Tarthang Tulku. (Illus.). 300p. 1975. pap. 9.95 (ISBN 0-913546-11-9). Dharma Pub.
Crystal Mountain. Peter Whigham. (Illus.). 1970. pap. 2.25 o.p. Sand Dollar.
Crystal Mouse. Babs H Deal. LC 72-84903. 1973. 5.95 (ISBN 0-385-05875-6). Doubleday.
Crystal Mouse. Babs H Deal. 1973. 0.95. Popular Library.
Crystal Nights. Michele Murray. 272p. 1975. pap. 1.25 (ISBN 0-440-93355-2, LFL). Dell.
Crystal Nights: A Novel. Michele Murray. LC 72-93807. 1973. 6.95 (ISBN 0-8164-3098-5). Seabury Press.
Crystal Pagoda. Helen R Bamberger. LC 30-23890. 1930. L. MacVeagh, The Dial Press.
Crystal Palace. Maye Barrett. (Berkley Medallion Book). 1.95 (ISBN 0-425-03677-4). Berkley Pub. Corp.
Crystal Phoenix. Michael Berlyn. 224p. (Orig.). 1980. pap. 1.95 (ISBN 0-553-13468-X). Bantam.
Crystal Rood. Viola Kathrine Clemmous Gould. LC 15-2640. 1.25. John Lane Company.
Crystal Sceptre: A Story of Adventure. Philip Verrill Mighels. 1906. Harper & Brothers.
Crystal Sea. Louise Harrison McCraw. LC 47-667. 1946. Fleming H. Revell Company.
Crystal Seas. Jeffrey Lord. (Blade Series#16). 1975. (pbk.) 1.25 (ISBN 0-523-00780-9). Pinnacle Books.
Crystal Ship: Three Original Novellas of Science Fiction. Vonda N McIntyre & Marta Randall. Ed. by Robert Silverberg. (Kangaroo Book). 1977. 1.50. Pocket Books.
Crystal Ship: Three Original Novellas of Science Fiction. Robert Silverberg. LC 76-26902. 1976. 6.95 (ISBN 0-8407-6527-4). T. Nelson.
Crystal Singer. Anne McCaffrey. 320p. (Orig.). 1982. pap. 2.95 (ISBN 0-345-28598-0, Del Rey). Ballantine.
Crystal Sky. Mary Ann Taylor. (Candlelight Romance Ser.). (Orig.). Date not set. pap. 1.75 (ISBN 0-440-11453-5). Dell.

Crystal Star. Ellen Argo. LC 78-13325. 8.95 (ISBN 0-399-12253-2). Putnam.
Crystal Stopper. Maurice Leblanc. Tr. by Teixeira De Mattos, Alexander Louis. LC 13-4421. 1913. Doubleday, Page & Company.
Crystal Tree. Louise Platt Hauck. LC 35-10318. The Penn Publishing Company.
Crystal Tree. Jean Temple. LC 30-11279. J. Cape and H. Smith.
Crystal Villa. abr. ed. Mary Howard, pseud. Ed. by Alice Sachs. 1970. Repr. of 1960 ed. 3.95 o.p. Crown.
Crystal Vision. Gilbert Sorrentino. LC 81-2628. 1981. 14.50 (ISBN 0-86547-041-3). North Point Press.
Crystal Vision: A Novel. Gilbert Sorrentino. LC 82-12280. 1982. 6.95 (ISBN 0-14-006320-X). Penguin Books.
Crystal World. J. G. Ballard. LC 66-11685. bds., 4.50. Farrar.
Crystalline: Or, The Heiress of Fall Down Castle. A Romance. Frederick William Shelton. LC 33-7803. 1854. C. Scribner.
Crystallised Carbon Pig: By John Wainwright. John William Wainwright. LC 67-13248. 1967. 3.95. Walker.
Crystals of Mida. Sharon Green. 352p. 1982. pap. 2.95 (ISBN 0-87997-735-3, UE1735). DAW Bks.
Crystal's Secret. James H Connelly. LC 6-30690. (On cover: Once a week library, v. 9, no. 9). 1892. P.F. Collier.
Csardas. Diane Pearson. LC 75-5880. 1975. 10.00 (ISBN 0-397-01085-0). Lippincott.
CTZ Paradigm. Yves Regis Francois. LC 74-17769. 1975. 5.50 (ISBN 0-385-07745-9). Doubleday.
Cuando Llora un Guerrillero. Luis A. Maldonado. 89p. 1981. pap. 1.95 (ISBN 0-311-37014-4). Casa Bautista.
Cuatro Novelas Modernas De la America Hispana. Ed. by H. Alpern, D. DeGuzman Illus. by Martha Zelt. Ed. by Hyman Alpern. (Chilton 906). 3.50. Chilton.
Cub Reporter. Edward Mott Woolley. LC 13-189571. 1913. Frederick A. Stokes Company.
Cuba Libre: A Story. MacKinlay Kantor. LC 40-272229. Coward-McCann, Inc.
Cuba Libre: A Story of the Hispano-American War. John Roy Musick. LC 3724. (Columbian historical novels. v. 13). 1900. Funk & Wagnalls Company.
Cuban Amazon. Virginia Lyndall Dunbar. LC 6-35870. 1897. The Editor Publishing Company.
Cuban Death Lift. (Dusky MacMorgan Ser.: No. 3). (Orig.). 1981. pap. 1.95 (ISBN 0-451-09768-8, J9768, Sig). NAL.
Cuban Heel: An Antic Debauch. Paul Jefferson. LC 69-16491. 1969. Macmillan.
Cuban Heiress. A Novel. Mary Kyle Dallas. (On cover: Idle hour series. no. 6). The F. M. Lupton Publishing Co.
Cuban Inferno. Sam Victor, pseud. 192p. (Orig.). 1981. pap. 2.25 (ISBN 0-441-12476-3). Ace Bks.
Cuban Liberated: Or, Saved by the Sword. Robert Rexdale. LC 7-30932. (On cover: The Belmore series, no. 42). 1896. American Publishers Corporations.
Cuban Passage. Norman Lewis. LC 81-48229. 13.50 (ISBN 0-394-52069-6). Pantheon Books.
Cubano..., Go Home! Angel Castro. 1972. pap. 3.00. E Torres & Sons.
Cubans. Manuel Douglas. LC 79-67603. (Illus.). 13.95 (ISBN 0-87223-678-1). Seaview Books.
Cube Root of Uncertainty. Robert Silverberg. LC 70-107051. 1970. Macmillan.
Cubical City. Janet Flanner. LC 26-179930. 1926. G. P. Putnam's Sons.
Cubical City: A Novel. Janet Flanner. LC 74-8655. (Lost American Fiction Ser). 440p. 1974. Repr. of 1926 ed. 13.95 (ISBN 0-8093-0700-6). S Ill U Pr.
Cubs and Other Stories. Vargas Llosa, Mario. LC 78-20217. 10.00 (ISBN 0-06-014491-2). Harper & Row.
Cubwood. Lewis Walter Reginald Sunderland. LC 26-8882. 1926. A. & C. Boni.
Cuckold. Louis Copman. LC 74-76811. 7.95 (ISBN 0-87949-031-4). Ashley Books.
Cuckoo. Katherine Blake. LC 68-11271. 1968. Reynal.
Cuckoo. Margaret Morrison. LC 52-7340. Roy.
Cuckoo: A Comedy of Adjustments. Douglas Goldring. LC 26-7647. 1926. R. M. McBride & Company.
Cuckoo Clock. Milton K Ozaki. LC 47-6110. 1946. Ziff-Davis Publishing Company.
Cuckoo in Spring. Elizabeth Cadell. LC 54-6124. 1954. W. Morrow.
Cuckoo in Spring. Elizabeth Cadell. LC 77-8857. 1977. 8.50 (ISBN 0-89244-067-8). Queens House.
Cuckoo in the Nest. Margaret Oliphant Wilson Oliphant. LC 7-32508. United States Book Company.
Cuckoo in the Nest. Ben Travers. LC 26-1386. 1925. Doubleday, Page & Company.
Cuckoo in the Nest. Ben Travers. LC 41-6551. (On cover: Penguin books. 44). 1939. Penguin Books Limited.
Cuckoo Line Affair. Andrew Garve. 1978. pap. 1.95i (ISBN 0-06-080451-3, P 451, PL). Har-Row.
Cuckoo Line Affair. Paul Winterton. (Perennial Library). 1978. 1.95 (ISBN 0-06-080451-3). Harper & Row.
Cuckoo Line Affair: By Andrew Garve Pseud. 1st American Ed. Paul Winterton. LC 53-11866. 1953. Harper.
Cuckoo Time. Ralph Temple. LC 45-2790. 1945. G. P. Putnam's Sons.
Cuckoo's Nest. Martha Gilbert Dickinson Bianchi. 1909. Duffield and Company.
Cuckoo's Nest. Chrishne Jope-Slade. LC 23-3783. 1922. Houghton Mifflin Company.
Cuckoo's Progress. Steve Dahlstrom. 304p. (Orig.). 1972. pap. 2.25 o.s.i. (O*P*S50). Olympia.
Cucumber King: And Other Stories. Edwin Samuel. LC 65-15795. 5.00. Abelard.
Cucumber Sandwiches & Other Stories. John Innes Mackintosh Stewart. 1970. 5.95 o.p. (ISBN 0-393-08600-3). Norton.
Cuddy, and Other Stories. 4th ed. Margaret Hill McCarter. LC 9-84389. 1908. Crane & Company.
Cuddy of the White Tops. Earl Chapin May. LC 24-14017. 1924. D. Appleton and Company.
Cuddy Yarborough's Daughter. Una Lucy Silberrad. LC 14-5194. George H. Doran Company, Publishers in America for Hodder & Stoughton.
Cuddy's Baby. Margaret Hill McCarter. LC 17-25985. 1917. A. C. McClurg & Co.
Cuddy's Baby: A Story of Kansas Folks. Margaret Hill McCarter. LC 7-40795. 1907. Crane & Company.
Cudgel. Thomas Polsky. LC 50-8599. (Guilt edged mystery). 1950. Dutton.
Cue for Murder. Matt Bryant. LC 54-11511. Vanguard Press.
Cue for Murder. Helen McCloy. LC 42-22690. 1942. W. Morrow & Co.
Cue for Passion. William Arthur Neubauer. LC 45-21683. 1945. Phoenix Press.
Cuentistas de Hoy. Mario B. Rodriguez. LC 52-14409. (Span). 1952. pap. text ed. 10.50 (ISBN 0-395-05317-X). HM.
Cuentistas Hispanoamericanos del Siglo Veinte. Louis Leal. 256p. 1972. pap. text ed. 9.00 (ISBN 0-394-31669-X, RanC). Random.
Cuento de la mujer del mar. Manuel Ramos. 120p. 1979. pap. 4.00 (ISBN 0-940238-12-8). Ediciones Huracan.
Cuento del coqui valiente. Kalman Barsy. LC 81-68705. (Illus.). 75p. 1982. pap. text ed. cancelled (ISBN 0-940238-53-5). Ediciones Huracan.
Cuento Mexicano Index. Compiled by Herbert H. Hoffman. LC 79-127156. (Humanitas Books). 600p. 1978. 22.00x (ISBN 0-89537-007-7). Headway Pubns.
Cuentos. Jorge Luis Borges. (Monticello College edition, v. 4). Monticello College Press.
Cuentos. Felix Pita Rodriguez. LC 61-13161. (Monticello College edition, v.6). Monticello College Press.
Cuentos Americanos. 3rd ed. Ed. by Donald Walsh & L. B. Kiddle. (Illus., Span.). 1970. pap. 6.95x (ISBN 0-393-09907-5, NortonC). Norton.
Cuentos: An Anthology of Short Stories from Puerto Rico. Kal Wagenheim. LC 78-54399. 1978. 9.50. (ISBN 0-8052-3698-8) (ISBN 0-8052-0608-6). Schocken Books.
Cuentos Contemporaneos. Ed. by Doris K. Arjona & Edith F. Helman. (O.s.i.). (Orig., Span.). 1935. pap. 6.95x o.s.i. (ISBN 0-393-09432-4, NortonC). Norton.
Cuentos Costenos: Una Version Literaria Del Caracter De la Costa Atlantica. Antonio Escribano Belmonte. LC 63-33360. 1962.
Cuentos De Aca y De Alla. 2nd ed. C. M. Batchelor. (Span). 1962. pap. text ed. 3.50x o.p. (3-03175). HM.
Cuentos De Espana y De America. Sterling Aubrey Stoudemire. 1942. 4.00 o.p. (ISBN 0-03-016410-9). HR&W.
Cuentos De la Abeja Encinta. 1. ed. Marigloria Palma. LC 76-6153. (Coleccion Uprex; 48: Serie Ficcion). 1976. 2.00 (ISBN 0-8477-0048-8). Editorial Universitaria, Universidad De Puerto Rico.
Cuentos Del Mundo Hispanico. Ed. by Robert E. Osborne. (Orig.). 1957. pap. text ed. 3.95x o.p. (ISBN 0-442-25376-1). Van Nos Reinhold.
Cuentos Escogidos. Ed. by Jean Franco. 1st Ed. Horacio Quiroga. Ed. by Jean Franco. LC 68-18894. (Pergamon Latin Amer. ser.). 1968. 5.00, 3.00 pap., Pergamon.
Cuentos Espanoles. Albert Brent & R. Kirsner. (Fr). 1950. 3.95 o.p. (ISBN 0-03-015015-9). HR&W.
Cuentos Fantasticos. Estudio Preliminar De Antonio Pages Larraya. Eduardo Ladislao Holmberg. Ed. by Antonio Pages Larrays. LC 57-43185. (Colecion 'El Pasado argentino'). 1957. Aires, Libreia Hachette.
Cuentos Hispanicos. John A. Crow. (Rinehart Editions). (Sp). 1939. 4.60 o.p. (ISBN 0-03-015130-9, HoltC). HR&W.
Cuentos Misteriosos. Ed. by Ruth Stanton Lamb & Sonia Misuraca. LC 63-9289. 1963. Ronald Press Co.
Cuentos Nuevos Del Sur: Argentina, Chile, Paraguay, Uruguay. Ed. by Hugo Rodriguez-Alcala & Sally Rodriguez-Alcala. (Orig., Span.,.). 1967. pap. text ed. 4.95 o.p. (ISBN 0-13-195115-7). P-H.
Cuentos Ticos: Short Stories of Costa Rica. 3d ed. Fernandez Guardia, Ricardo. LC 78-121540. (Short story index reprint series). (Illus.). 1970. Books for Libraries Press.
Cuentos y Patranas. Juan Antonio De Zunzunegui. Ed. by Rex E. Ballinger. LC 66-15549. (Span.). 1966. pap. text ed. 3.95x (ISBN 0-89197-120-3). Irvington.
Cuentos y Patranas: Ed. by Rex Edward Ballinger. Juan Antonio De Zunzunegui. Ed. by Rex Edward Ballinger. LC 66-15549. pap., 2.45. Appleton.
Cuernavaca Question. Lydia Kirk. LC 73-11711. 1974. 4.95 (ISBN 0-385-06775-5). Doubleday.
Cues for Church Camping, for Counselors of Juniors & Junior Highs. pap. 1.00 o.p. (ISBN 0-664-24274-X, Pub. by Geneva). Westminster.
Cuirass of Diamonds. Edgar Jepson. LC 29-8267. 1929. Macy-Masius, The Vanguard Press.
Cujo. Stephen King. LC 81-50265. 1981. 13.95 (ISBN 0-670-45193-2). Viking Press.
Cullum. Eileen Arbuthnot Robertson. LC 28-21181. H. Holt and Company.
Culminations: A Novel. Aella Greene. LC 6-45553. 1892. C. W. Bryan & Co., Printers.
Cult. Max Simon Ehrlich. LC 77-18188. 9.95 (ISBN 0-671-24053-6). Simon and Schuster.
Cult Breakers. Andrew Sugar. 1979. pap. 1.75 (ISBN 0-532-17205-1). Woodhill.
Cult of Flesh. Hugh Knox. (Orig.). 1970. pap. 0.95 (ISBN 0-87067-202-9, BH202). Holloway.
Cult of Killers. Donald Macivers. 1976. pap. 1.50 o.p. (LB364DK, Leisure Bks). Nordon Pubns.
Cult of Pain. Edmond Dumoulin. Tr. by Paul Anhalt. pap. 1.75 o.p. (3020). Brandon.
Cult of the Atom. Daniel Ford. 1982. 13.95 (ISBN 0-671-25301-8). S&S.
Cult Sunday. William D Rodgers. LC 79-54713. 4.95 (ISBN 0-89636-041-5). Accent Books.
Culture: A Modern Method. Elkiott Emerson Furney. LC 6-44568. 1891. I. H. Brown & Company; Etc., Etc.
Cumberer of the Ground: A Novel. Constance Isabella Stuart Smith. LC 8-8631. (On cover: Harper's Franklin square library, no. 752). 1894. Harper & Brothers.
Cumberland Decision. Robert Silverman. 1977. pap. 1.50 (ISBN 0-532-15283-2). Woodhill.
Cumberland Rifles. 1st Ed. Noel Bertram Gerson. LC 52-6367. 1952. Doubleday.
Cumberland Vendetta: A Novel. John Fox. LC 2702. 1900. Harper & Brothers.
Cumberland Vendetta: And Other Stories. John Fox. LC 7-7533. 1896. Harper & Brothers.
Cumberland Vendetta, & Other Stories. John Fox. LC 73-121547. (Short Story Index Reprint Ser). 1895. 15.00 (ISBN 0-8369-3503-9). Ayer Co.
Cumboto. Diaz Sanchez, Ramon. LC 73-79541. (Texas pan American series). (Illus.). 1969. 6.50. University of Texas Press.
Cummer's Son: And Other South Sea Folk. Gilbert Parker. LC 10-9257. 1910. 1.50. Harper & Brothers.
Cumulative Analytical Index to the Dickensian, 1905-1974. Frank T Dunn. LC 76-368162. 1976. 25.00 (ISBN 0-85527-049-7). Dickens Fellowship.
Cunning. Robert Bloch. 1981. pap. 2.50 (ISBN 0-89083-825-9). Zebra.
Cunning and the Haunted. Cover Painting by Ray Johnson. Richard Jessup. LC 55-18991. (Gold medal books, S 440). 1954. Fawcett Publications.
Cunning As a Fox. John Creasey. 1971. pap. 0.95 o.p. (95046-095). Beagle Bks.
Cunning As a Fox: By Kyle Hunt Pseud. John Creasey. LC 65-11567. (Cock Robin mystery). 1965. 3.95. Macmillan.
Cunning Culprit: Or, A "Novel" Novel; a Composite Romance by Twenty Different Popular Writers. LC 6-31734. 1895. The Hobart Publishing Company.
Cunning Murrell. Arthur Morrison. LC 6022. 1900. Doubleday, Page & Company.
Cunning of the Dove. Alfred Leo Duggan. (Image bk., D208). 1966. Doubleday.
Cunning of the Dove. Alfred Leo Duggan. LC 60-6791. (Illus.). 1960. Pantheon Books.
Cunninghams. David Watt Ballantyne. LC 48-9412. 1948. Vanguard Press.
Cunningham's Revenge: A 'James Ogilvie' Novel. Duncan MacNeil. LC 81-131630. 1980. 24.50 (ISBN 0-340-25216-2). Hodder and Stoughton.
Cup and the Lip. E. X Ferrars, pseud. LC 75-36592. 1976. 5.95 (ISBN 0-385-11335-8). Published for the Crime Club by Doubleday.
Cup and the Sword. Alice Tisdale Nourse Hobart. LC 42-19567. 1942. The Bobbs-Merrill Company.
Cup: Chief-of-Police Dogs. Reginald M Cleveland. LC 28-28050. 1928. Milton Bradley Company.
Cup for Janet. Emily Thorne. LC 57-8736. 1957. Avalon Books.
Cup of Bitterness & Other Stories. Antranig Antreassian. Tr. by Jack Antreassian from Armenian. LC 79-21572. 1979. 8.95 (ISBN 0-935102-00-0); pap. 4.95 (ISBN 0-935102-01-9). Ashod Pr.
Cup of Cold Water. Paul Hutchens. LC 41-18110. 1941. Wm. B. Eerdmans Publishing Co.
Cup of Elijah. Harry Zankel. 3.50 o.p. Vantage.
Cup of Fury. Henry Gregor Felsen. LC 54-5384. 1954. Random House.
Cup of Fury. Adam Gillon. 1962. 4.50 o.p. Twayne.
Cup of Fury: A Novel. Adam Gillon. LC 62-19778. 1962. Astra Books.
Cup of Fury: A Novel of Cities and Shipyards. Rupert Hughes. LC 19-8070. 1919. Harper & Brothers.
Cup of Gold. John Steinbeck. 1976. pap. 3.95 (ISBN 0-14-004234-2). Penguin.
Cup of Gold. John Steinbeck. 1929. 2.50 o.p. (ISBN 0-670-25116-X). Viking Pr.
Cup of Gold: A Life of Henry Morgan, Buccaneer, with Occasional Reference to History. John Steinbeck. LC 29-17823. 1929. R. M. McBride & Company.
Cup of Gold: A Life of Sir Henry Morgan, Buccanner, with Occasional Reference to History... John Steinbeck. LC 76-22716. 1976. 1.95 (ISBN 0-14-004234-2). Penguin Books.
Cup of Gold: A Life of Sir Henry Morgan, Buccaneer, with Occasional Reference to History. John Steinbeck. LC 39-8918. Covici, Friede.
Cup of Gold: The Amazing Career of Sir Henry Morgan, Buccaneer, with Occasional References to History. John Steinbeck. LC 39-25037. (A Mercury book. no. 20). The American Mercury, Inc.
Cup of Honor. Judie M. Coffman. 1965. 2.75 o.p. (ISBN 0-8059-0063-2). Dorrance.
Cup of Silence. Arthur John Rees. LC 25-755756. 1925. Dodd, Mead and Company.
Cup of Stars. Addie M. Hedrick. LC 69-19405. 1969. 4.00 o.p. (ISBN 0-8233-0128-1). Golden Quill.
Cup of Strength. Charlotte Paul. LC 58-767395. 1958. Random House.
Cup of Tea for Mr. Thorgill. Margaret Storm Jameson. LC 57-11800. 1957. Harper.
Cup of the Sun. Octavia Waldo. LC 61-11909. 1961. Harcourt, Brace & World.
Cup of Trembling: And Other Stories. Mary Hallock Foote. LC 74-110189. (Short story index reprint series). 1970. Books for Libraries Press.
Cup of Trembling, and Other Stories. Mary Hallock Foote. LC 6-41412. 1895. Houghton, Mifflin and Company.
Cup of Trembling. 1st Ed. Karl Brown. LC 53-6454. 1953. Duell, Sloan and Pearce.
Cupboard. Rose Tremain. LC 81-21410. 14.50 (ISBN 0-312-17910-3). St Martin's Press.
Cupboard Love. Nancy Hoyt. LC 31-15090. 1931. Doubleday, Doran & Company, Inc.
Cupboard Love. Roberta Leigh. (Alpha Books). 1979. pap. text ed. 2.95x (ISBN 0-19-424165-3). Oxford U Pr.
Cupid & Commonsense. Arnold Bennett. LC 74-6015. (Collected Works of Arnold Bennett: Vol. 13). 1976. Repr. of 1910 ed. 16.25 (ISBN 0-518-19094-3). Ayer Co.
Cupid and Mr. Pepys: A Romance of the Days of the Great Diarist. Netta Syrett. LC 23-12119. 1923. Frederick A. Stokes Company.
Cupid and Psyche. Apuleius Madaurensis & Walter Horatio Pater. LC 78-305282. (Illus.). 1977-1978. 6.95 (ISBN 0-571-11115-7). Faber.
Cupid & Psyche: A Short Story. Joyce Carol Oates. LC 79-23994. (Albondocani Press publication, no. 10). 1970. Albondocani Press.
Cupid and the Sphinx. Harriet Hare McClellan. LC 7-15183. 1878. G. P. Putnam's Sons.
Cupid En Route. Ralph Henry Barbour. LC 12-21768. 1.00. R. Q. Badger.
Cupid in Hell. Clara Eleanor Wagner. LC 10-28637. 1910. Nitschke Brothers.
Cupid in Oilskins. John Joy Bell. LC 17-84. 1.00. Fleming H. Revell Company.
Cupid Intelligent. Julia Anna Nenninger Balbach. LC 10-9518. 1910. Press of J. J. Little & Ives Co.,
Cupid, M.D. A Story. Augustus M. Swift, pseud. LC 8-25639. 1882. C. Scribner's Sons.
Cupid Misbehaves. Frances Nichols Hanna. LC 40-10296. 1939. Arcadia House, Inc.

Cupid Napoleon. Slater La Master. LC 52-46782. Humphries.
Cupid on Crutches: Or, One Summer at Narragansett Pier. Augustus B. Wood. LC 9-517. 1879. G. W. Carleton & Co.; Etc., Etc.
Cupid on the Stairs: A Romance in Rococo. Howard Rollin Patch. LC 42-51182. 1942. Sheed & Ward.
Cupid Rides Pillion see Secret Heart.
Cupid: The Cow-Punch. Eleanor Gates. LC 7-37708. 1907. The McClure Company.
Cupid the Devil's Stoker: Or, Heaven's Gate to Hell; a Romance of Heredity in Argentine and Old Spain. Nellie Bingham Van Slingerland. LC 5-27079. 1905. Fifth Avenue Publishing Co.
Cupidevil. Hubert Monteilhet. LC 70-117931. 1970. 5.95. Simon and Schuster.
Cupidevil. Hubert Montheihet. (O.S.I.). 1970. 5.95 o.s.i. (ISBN 0-671-20214-6). S&S.
Cupid's Album. Archie Argyle. 1866. M. Doolady.
Cupid's Executioners. Hubert Monteilhet. LC 67-16721. (Inner sanctum mystery). 1967. Simon and Schuster.
Cupid's Game with Hearts: A Tale As Told by Documents. James Frederick Mason. LC 9-1827. Dodge Book and Stationery Co.
Cupid's Middleman. Edward Burcham Lent. LC 6-34812. Cupples and Leon.
Cupid's Understudy. Edward Salisbury Field. LC 9-28464. 1909. W. J. Watt & Company.
CUPPI. Sandy Johnson. LC 79-11595. 8.95 (ISBN 0-440-01190-6). Delacorte Press/E. Friede.
Cups of Illusion. Henry Bellamann. 59.95 (ISBN 0-87968-976-5). Gordon Pr.
Cups, Wands & Swords. Helen De Guerry Simpson. LC 28-2670. 1928. A. A. Knopf.
Cur and the Coyote. Edward Henry Peple. LC 13-19079. 1913. 0.50. Moffat, Yard & Company.
Curate of Linwood: Or, The Real Strength of the Christian Ministry. C. G. Hamilton. LC 7-1221. Protestant Episcopal Society for the Promotion of Evangelical Knowledge.
Curate of Orsieres. Otto Roquette. Tr. by Robinson, Mary A. LC 8-1797. (Added t.-p.: Harper's half-hour series, no. 71). Harper & Brothers.
Curate's Crime. Sybl Alexandra Erickson. LC 45-10702. 1945. Pub. for the Crime Book Society by Hurst & Blackett Ltd.
Curate's Crime. Sibyl Alexandra Erikson. LC 49-44454. 1946. Mystery House.
Curate's Egg: A Volume of Stories. Betsey Riddle Hutton Zum Stolzenberg. LC 78-150476. (Short story index reprint series). 1971. Books for Libraries Press.
Curate's Wife. Emily Hilda Young. LC 34-34587. Harcourt, Brace and Company.
Curb of Honor. Matilda Barbara Bertram Edwards. Anglo-American Publishing Company.
Cure. Paul Ferris. (O.s.i.). 352p. 1974. 7.95 o.s.i. (ISBN 0-8037-1806-3). Dial.
Cure. Len Goldberg. 1982. pap. 2.50 (ISBN 0-451-11509-0, AE1509, Sig). NAL.
Cure. Morris Hershman. (Berkley medallion book). 1974. (pbk.) 1.25 (ISBN 0-425-02510-1). Berkley Pub. Co.
Cure: A Novel. Paul Ferris. LC 74-9958. 1974. 7.95 (ISBN 0-8037-1806-3). Dial Press.
Cure: A Novel. Paul Ferris. 1978. 1.75. Avon.
Cure: A Novel for Speed Readers. Gerald Locklin. LC 78-69789. 1979. pap. 2.75 (ISBN 0-930090-04-7). Applezaba.
Cure for the Blues. Samuel Langhorne Clemens & Samuel Watson Royston. LC 64-16074. 1964. C. E. Tuttle Co.
Cure for the Blues. Jonathan Jinks. 1878. Solheimer & Moore, Printers.
Cure It with Honey. Thurston Scott. LC 51-13890. 1951. Harper.
Cure of Flesh. James Gould Cozzens. LC 36-3542. (Half-title: The Longman novels. 13). 1934. Longmans, Green and Co.
Cure of Souls. May Sinclair. LC 24-2249. 1924. The Macmillan Company.
Cure, the Story of an Alcoholic. Prepared in the Form of a Novel with the Collaboration of James Loring. Carsbie C Adams. LC 50-14494. 1950. Exposition Press.
Curfew & a Full Moon. Ediriwira Sarachchandra. (Writing in Asia Ser.). 1978. pap. text ed. 5.50x (00217). Heinemann Ed.
Curing Christopher. Horace Tremlett. LC 15-134732. 1914. John Lane.
Curiosities of the Search-Room. Julia Byrne. LC 70-78117. 1969. Repr. of 1880 ed. 34.00x (ISBN 0-8103-3573-5). Gale.
Curiosity Didn't Kill the Cat. M. K Wren, pseud. LC 73-83609. 1973. 4.95 (ISBN 0-385-06478-0). Published for the Crime Club by Doubleday.
Curiosity Killed a Cat. Anne Von Melborn Rowe. LC 41-76573. 1941. W. Morrow and Company.
Curiosity of Mr. Treadgold. Valentine Williams. LC 76-37571. (Short story index reprint series). 1972. (ISBN 0-8369-4130-6). Books for Libraries Press.
Curiosity of Mr. Treadgold. Valentine Williams. LC 37-211412. 1937. Houghton Mifflin Company.
Curious Adventure of Major Fosdick. Ethel Edith Mannin. 1972. 4.95 (ISBN 0-09-109850-5, Pub. by Hutchinson). Merrimack Pub Cir.
Curious Affair of the Third Dog. Patricia Moyes. LC 73-3068. (Rinehart suspense novel). 1973. 4.95 (ISBN 0-03-010401-7). Holt, Rinehart and Winston.
Curious Career of Roderick Campbell. Jean Newton McIlwraith. LC 1-31019. 1901. Houghton, Mifflin and Company.
Curious Case of Gen. Delaney Smythe. William Henry Gardner. LC 1-30070. The Abbey Press.
Curious Case of Kenelm Digby. Christopher Darlington Morley. LC 76-358645. (Illus.). 1975. Universal Coterie of Pipe Smokers.
Curious Case of Marie Dupont. Adele Luehrmann. LC 16-16390. 1916. The Century Co.
Curious Courtship of Kate Poins: A Romance of the Regency. Louis Evan Shipman. 1901. D. Appleton and Co.
Curious Crime. A. E. Martin. LC 52-11009. 1952. Published for the Crime Club by Doubleday.
Curious Custard Pie. Margaret Scherf. LC 50-8315. 1950. Published for the Crime Club by Doubleday.
Curious Diversity. 118p. 1982. 30.00x (Pub. by U of Glasgow Pr Scotland). State Mutual Bk.
Curious Facts Preceding My Execution: And Other Fictions. Donald E Westlake. 1973. (pbk) 0.95. Ballantine Books.
Curious Facts Preceding My Execution: And Other Fictions. Donald E Westlake. LC 68-14538. 1968. Random House.
Curious Fragments: Jack London's Tales of Fantasy Fiction. Jack London & Dale L Walker. LC 75-29450. (National university publications). 1975. 12.95 (ISBN 0-8046-9114-2). Kennikat Press.
Curious George Takes a Job. H. A Roy. (Sandpiper book). (Illus.). 1974. (pbk.) 0.95 (ISBN 0-395-18649-8). Houghton, Mifflin.
Curious Happenings to the Rooke Legatees. Edward Phillips Oppenheim. LC 38-6761. 1938. Little, Brown and Company.
Curious Happenings to the Rooke Legatees. Edward Phillips Oppenheim. LC 40-377825. 1939. Triangle Books.
Curious Landlord. Pauline D. Geisse. LC 3459. 1900. D. Biddle.
Curious Life for a Lady. Pat Barr. 1972. pap. 1.25 o.p. (ISBN 0-345-02650-0). Comstock.
Curious Locket. Leanore Traugot. 176p. (Orig.). 1978. pap. 1.50 (ISBN 0-89041-201-4, 3201). Major Bks.
Curious Mr. Tarrant. Charles Daly King. LC 77-78591. 1977. 3.50 (ISBN 0-486-23540-8). Dover Publications.
Curious Moog. Milton Bloch. 1978. pap. 3.95 (ISBN 0-911692-12-6). Red Clay.
Curious Proposal. Freda Michel. 224p. 1980. pap. 1.75 (ISBN 0-449-50071-3, Coventry). Fawcett.
Curious Quest. Edward Phillips Oppenheim. LC 19-771778. 1919. 1.50. Little, Brown, and Company.
Curious Quest. Edward Phillips Oppenheim. LC 24-20461. 1921. A. L. Burt Company.
Curious Relations. William D'Arfey & Plomer, William Charles Franklyn, 1903- Ed. LC 47-30219. 1947. William Sloane Associates, Inc.
Curious Republic of Gondour. Samuel Langhorne Clemens. LC 74-10998. Repr. of 1919 ed. lib. bdg. 21.00 (ISBN 0-8414-3603-7). Folcroft.
Curious Sofa. Edward Gorey. LC 61-12368. 64p. 1980. 5.95 o.p. (ISBN 0-396-07861-3). Dodd.
Curious Sofa. Edward Gorey. (Illus.). 64p. 1982. pap. 5.95 (ISBN 0-312-92112-8). Congdon & Weed.
Curious Sofa, Ogdred Weary. Edward Gorey. (Illus.). 1961. pap. 4.75 (ISBN 0-8392-1020-5). Astor-Honor.
Curious What You Might Find When You Go Out to Look for Elephants. Mary Macur. LC 48-29. pap. 5.00. First Amend.
Curious Wine. Bianca Bradbury. LC 48-9475. 1948. Beechhurst Press.
Curious Wine. Mena Webb. LC 78-77149. 1969. 8.95 (ISBN 0-87716-006-6, Pub. by Moore Pub Co). F Apple.
Curious Wine: A Novel. Mena Webb. LC 78-77149. 1969. 4.95. Moore Pub. Co.
Curlew's Cry. 1st Ed. Mildred Walker, pseud. LC 55-524380. Harcourt, Brace.
Curling: A Novel. Robert Boles. LC 68-12778. 1968. Houghton Mifflin.
Curly: A Tale of the Arizona Desert. Roger S. Pocock. LC 5-13965. 1905. Little, Brown, and Company.
Curly: an Actor's Story. John Coleman & Smythies, Harriet Maria (Gordon) (On cover: Seaside library. Pocket ed., no. 504). 1885. G. Munro.
Curly, and Others: Stories and Sketches for the Christmas-Tide. Winifred M Reynolds. LC 13-15524. The Rumford Press.
Curly and the Aztec Gold. Joseph Bushnell Ames. LC 20-14291. 1920. 1.75. The Century Co.
Curly Graham, Cowpuncher. Joseph Bushnell Ames. LC 24-20381. The Century Co.
Curly Wolf. Frank Gruber. LC 77-2376. 1977. 9.95 (ISBN 0-89340-077-7). J. Curley.
Currency of Love. Mary Ellen Clouse. LC 38-2816. 1937. Meador Publishing Company.
Currents: A Novel. Paul E. McCoy. LC 79-10293. 1979. 8.95 (ISBN 0-87949-155-8). Ashley Books.
Currents in Fiction. rev. ed. Ed. by Virginia Alwin. LC 68-2687. (Macmillan literary heritage). 1968. Macmillan.
Currents of Space. Isaac Asimov. 1978. pap. 2.25 (ISBN 0-449-23829-6, Crest). Fawcett.
Currents of Space. Isaac Asimov. pap. 0.60 o.p. (73-703). Lancer.
Currents of Space. 1st Ed. Isaac Asimov. LC 52-10054. 1952. Doubleday.
Currer Lyle: Or, The Stage in Romance, and the Stage in Reality. Louise Reeder. 1856. E. D. Long.
Currita: Countess of Albornoz; a Novel of Madrid Society. Luis Coloma. Tr. by Attwell, Estelle Huyck. LC 2801. 1900. Little, Brown, and Company.
Curse. Charles L. Grant. 1977. pap. 1.95 (ISBN 0-89041-150-6, 3150). Major Bks.
Curse: A Novel. Ethel Arnold Smith Dorrance. LC 54-13120. 1955. Bittner; Distributors: Address-Mail Book Service.
Curse and the Cup. Julia MacNair Wright. LC 9-918. 1879. The National Temperance Society and Publication House.
Curse at the Door. Clara Morris Diggs. LC 22-23120. 1922. The Cornhill Publishing Company.
Curse Entailed. Harriet Hamline Bigelow. LC 6-12743. 1857. Wentworth and Company.
Curse in the Colophon. Edgar Johnson Goodspeed. LC 36-862720. 1935. Willett, Clark & Company.
Curse of Anubis. Jack Younger. 1976. pap. 1.50 (ISBN 0-532-15204-2). Woodhill.
Curse of Bigness. Louis D. Brandeis. Ed. by O. K. Fraenkel. 1934. 11.00 o.p. (ISBN 0-8046-0041-4). Kennikat.
Curse of Black Charlie. Marilyn Ross. 1976. 1.25. Popular Library.
Curse of Cain... Duane W Rimel. LC 46-1346. David McKay Company.
Curse of Carne's Hold. A Tale of Adventure. George Alfred Henty. LC 31-352249. (Lettered on cover: Lovell's international series. no. 32). F. F. Lovell & Company.
Curse of Carranca, by Elsie Lee. Elsie Lee Sheridan. (Dell Book). 1973. (pbk) 0.95. Dell Pub. Co.
Curse of Casa Del Monte. Eleanor Elford Cameron, pseud. 1975. (pbk.) 0.95. Dell.
Curse of Caste. Nathaniel James Walter Le Cato. LC 75-39092. (Black Heritage Library Collection). 1972. (ISBN 0-8369-9030-7). Books for Libraries Press.
Curse of Caste... Nathaniel James Walter Le Cato. 1903. Walker-Ellerson Publishing Co.
Curse of Castle Eagle. Katharine Tynan Hinkson, pseud. LC 15-6760. 1915. 1.25. Duffield & Company.
Curse of Clifton. Emma Dorothy Eliza Nevitte Southworth. LC 74-124769. 1970. AMS Press.
Curse of Clifton: Or, The Widowed Bride. Emma Dorothy Eliza Nevitte Southworth. LC 24-20468. T. B. Peterson & Brothers.
Curse of Collinwood. Marilyn Ross. (Orig.). 1968. pap. 0.60 o.p. (63-368). Paperback Lib.
Curse of Crawfish Reef: A Novel of High Adventure. Howard L Sutton. LC 62-12463. Greenwich Book Publishers.
Curse of Dangerfield: Or, The Test of a Hundred Years. Elsie Snow. LC 8-10206. (On cover: Munro's library, v. 1, no. 56). 1883. N. L. Munro.
Curse of Dead Man's Gold. Bradford Scott. 1973. pap. 0.75 o.p. (ISBN 0-515-03061-9, T3061). Pyramid Pubns.
Curse of Deepwater. Christine Randell. (Warner paperback library gothic). 1974. (pbk.) 0.95. Warner Paperback Lib.
Curse of Doone. Sydney Horler. LC 30-19504. 1930. The Mystery League, Inc.
Curse of Gold. Ann Sophia Winterbotham Stephens. T. B. Peterson & Brothers.
Curse of Ham. J W Aker. LC 9-10491. Broadway Publishing Co.
Curse of Jezebel: A Novel of the Biblical Queen of Evil. Frank Gill Slaughter. LC 61-12582. 1961. Doubleday.
Curse of Life. Joe E. Pierce. 190p. (Orig.). 1980. pap. 4.95 (ISBN 0-913244-24-4). Hapi Pr.
Curse of Magira: A Novel of German East Africa and Tanganyika. Drawings by Joan Markham. David Bee. LC 65-20979. 1965. 4.95. Harper.
Curse of Mallory Hall. Dorothy Daniels. (Orig.). 1970. pap. 0.60 o.p. (R2555, GM). Fawcett World.
Curse of Malvern. Henry Edmister. LC 6-36799. 1892. W. G. Hubbard & Co.
Curse of Marriage: A True Story of Domestic Life. Walter Hubbell. 1888. The American News Company.
Curse of Nightwind. Regina Hubbard. (queen-size gothic). 1975. (pbk.) 1.25. Popular Library.
Curse of Rathlaw. Peter Saxon. (Orig.). 1968. pap. 0.60 o.p. (73-750). Lancer.
Curse of Ravenwood. Sarah MacIvers. (Ravenwood,#1). 1974. (pbk.) 0.95. Belmont Tower Books.
Curse of Still Valley. Sharon Wagner. Bd. with Country of the Wolf; Maridu. 1972. pap. 1.65 o.s.i. (70-407). Lancer.
Curse of the Bronze Lamp. John Dickson Carr. LC 45-5064. 1945. W. Morrow & Company.
Curse of the Clans. Barbara Cartland. 1977. 6.95 (ISBN 0-87272-070-5, Duron Bks). Brodart.
Curse of the Clodaghs. Frances Cowen. (Ace gothic). 1974. (pbk.) 0.95. Ace Books.
Curse of the Concullens. Florence Stevenson. LC 77-124278. 1970. 6.95. World Pub. Co.
Curse of the Crystal Ball: A Mystery Play in Three Acts. St. Clair, Robert. LC 39-64451. (On cover: Eldridge royalty plays). Eldridge Entertainment House, Incorporated.
Curse of the Fleers. Basil Copper. LC 76-46671. 1977. 7.95 (ISBN 0-312-17972-3). St. Martin's Press.
Curse of the Golden Skull. Josephine Kains, pseud. (Mystery Puzzlers Ser.: No. 7). (Illus., Orig.). 1978. pap. 1.95 (ISBN 0-89083-410-5). Zebra.
Curse of the Island Pool. Virginia Coffman. Bd. with High Terrace. 1980. pap. 1.95 (ISBN 0-451-09126-4, J9126, Sig). NAL.
Curse of the Island Pool. easy eye ed. Virginia Coffman. (Orig.). pap. 0.75 o.p. (74-908). Lancer.
Curse of the Island Pool. Virginia Coffman. 1975. (pbk.) 0.95. New American Library.
Curse of the Killer. James P Olsen. LC 41-23968. Dodge Publishing Company.
Curse of the Kings. Eleanor Hibbert. LC 72-96242. 1973. 6.95 (ISBN 0-385-01153-9). Doubleday.
Curse of the Kings. Eleanor Hibbert. LC 73-13973. 1973. 11.95 (ISBN 0-8161-6156-9). G. K. Hall.
Curse of the Kings. Victoria Holt, pseud. LC 72-96242. 336p. 1973. 13.95 (ISBN 0-385-01153-9). Doubleday.
Curse of the Kings. Victoria Holt, pseud. 1978. pap. 2.50 (ISBN 0-449-23284-0, Crest). Fawcett.
Curse of the Kings. Victoria Holt, pseud. (Adult Ser.). 1973. Repr. lib. bdg. 11.95 o.p. (ISBN 0-8161-6156-9, Large Print Bks). G K Hall.
Curse of the Kings. Victoria Holt. (Fawcett crest book). 1974. (pbk.) 1.50. Fawcett.
Curse of the Moors. Florence Hurd. 256p. (Orig.). 1975. pap. 1.25 (ISBN 0-532-12283-6). Woodhill.
Curse of the Pharaohs. Elizabeth Peters, pseud. LC 80-27945. 9.95 (ISBN 0-396-07963-6). Dodd, Mead.
Curse of the Pharaohs. Elizabeth Peters, pseud. LC 81-6853. 1981. 14.95 (ISBN 0-8161-3274-7). G.K. Hall.
Curse of the Pharaohs. Jack Younger. (O.s.i.). 1976. pap. 1.50 o.s.i. (532-15204-150). Manor Bks.
Curse of the Rebellars. Georgia M. Shewmake. 192p. (YA) 1975. 6.95 (Avalon). Bouregy.
Curse of the Reckaviles. Walter S Masterman. LC 27-1760. E. P. Dutton & Company.
Curse of the Ring: An Archetypal Translation of Richard Wagner's The Rhinegold. Melvin Ezell Gorham & Richard Wagner. LC 75-309115. (Illus.). 1975. 1.50 (ISBN 0-914752-06-5). Sovereign Press.
Curse of the Tarniffs. Eduard Heinrich Nikolaus Graf Von Keyserling & Ashton, Arthur Jacob, 1855- Tr. LC 28-2231. 1928. The Macaulay Company.
Curse of the Trawler Charon. Ewart Brookes. LC 57-12123. 1957. Dodd, Mead.
Curse of the Two-Headed Bull. Lee Falk. (story of the Phantom,#15). 1975. (pbk.) 0.95 (ISBN 0-380-00381-3). Avon.
Curse of the Undead. M. L. Carter. (Orig.). 1970. pap. 0.75 o.p. (T2276, GM). Fawcett World.
Curse of the Vampire. Karl Alexander. 320p. (Orig.). 1983. pap. 2.95 (ISBN 0-523-41874-4). Pinnacle Bks.
Curse of the White Panther: A Story of the Days of the Toledo War. Chapter Head Drawings by Jane Penfold. Merritt Greene. LC 60-16585. 1960. Hillsdale School Supply.
Curse of the Wise Woman. Edward John Moreton Drax Plunkett Dunsany. LC 33-31153. 1933. Longmans, Green and Co.

TITLE INDEX

CZAR'S GIFT.

Curse of the Witch-Queen. Paula Volsky. 384p. (Orig.). 1982. pap. 2.95 (ISBN 0-345-29520-X, Del Rey). Ballantine.
Curse of Valkyrie House. Cathy Cunningham, pseud. 176p. 1981. pap. 1.95 (ISBN 0-8439-0970-6, Leisure Bks). Nordon Pubns.
Curse Upon Mitre Square: A.D. 1530-1888. John Francis Brewer. (On cover- Lovell's library no. 1379). 1889. J.W. Lovell Company.
Cursed. George Allan England. LC 19-13297. Small, Maynard, & Company.
Cursed & the Raped. Sam Aldock. (Orig.). 1969. pap. 1.25 o.p. (2086). Brandon.
Cursed Be the Treasure. Henry Burgess Drake. LC 28-3435. 1928. Macy Masius.
Cursed Before Birth. A Few Straight Tips Regarding Our Social Condition. John H Tilden. LC 8-27028. The Author.
Cursed Heiress. June Harris. (Orig.). 1982. pap. 2.95 (ISBN 0-89083-973-5). Zebra.
Cursed Inheritance. (Orig.). 1981. pap. 2.50 (ISBN 0-89083-875-5). Zebra.
Curtain. Agatha Miller Christie. LC 75-16368. 1975. 7.95 (ISBN 0-396-07191-0). Dodd, Mead.
Curtain: An Anecdote. Alexander Macfarlan. LC 21-3811. 1921. Dodd, Mead and Company.
Curtain Between. Hilda Van Siller. LC 47-2033. 1947. Pub. for the Crime Club by Doubleday & Company, Inc.
Curtain Call for a Corpse. Doris Bell Collier Ball. LC 65-15588. (Cock Robin mystery). 1965. bds., 3.95. Macmillan.
Curtain Call. 1st Ed. Russell Janney. LC 57-757539. 1957. Duell, Sloan and Pearce.
Curtain Falls: A Modern Trilogy. Translated from the French by Humphrey Hare. Maurice Druon. LC 59-11661. 1960. 5.95. Scribner.
Curtain for a Jester. Frances Louise Davis Lockridge & Richard Lockridge. 222p. 1975. Repr. of 1953 ed. lib. bdg. 13.25x (ISBN 0-89190-904-4). Am Repr-Rivercity Pr.
Curtain for a Jester: A Mr. and Mrs. North Mystery. Frances Louise Davis Lockridge & Richard Lockridge. LC 53-12291. (Main Line mysteries). 1953. Lippincott.
Curtain for a Jester: A Mr. and Mrs. North Mystery. Frances Louise Davis Lockridge & Richard Lockridge. LC 75-45284. 1976. (ISBN 0-89190-904-4). Rivercity Press.
Curtain for Crime. Margaret Lucile Paine Rea. LC 41-5880. 1941. Pub. for the Crime Club by Doubleday, Doran & Company, Inc.
Curtain Going up. Sophie Kerr. LC 40-4092. Farrar & Rinehart, Inc.
Curtain Never Falls. Joey Adams. LC 49-11067. F. Fell.
Curtain of Flesh. Norman Singer. LC 70-8935. (Traveller's companion series, TC-3303). 1.75. Traveller's Companion, Inc.
Curtain of Green. Eudora Welty. LC 41-52028. 1941. Doubleday, Doran and Company, Inc.
Curtain of Green, and Other Stories. Eudora Welty. LC 79-10389. (Harvest/HBJ book). 1979. 4.50 (ISBN 0-15-623492-0). Harcourt Brace Jovanovich.
Curtain of Life. John Preston Buschlen & Lasky, Jesse Lenard, 1910- Joint Author. LC 34-30684. The Macaulay Company.
Curtain of Night. David Petri. (Orig.). 1983. pap. 3.25 (ISBN 0-440-11135-8). Dell.
Curtain of Storm. Joseph Gollomb. LC 33-30145. 1933. The Macmillan Company.
Curtain Rises. Hilda Vaughan. LC 35-15163. 1935. C. Scribner's Sons.
Curtain Rises: And Other Stories. Enid Maud Dinnis. LC 39-1752. 1937. B. Herder Book Co.
Curtaine-Drawer of the World. William Parkes. LC 79-84130. (English Experience, Its Record in Early Printed Books Published in Facsimile: No. 948). 1979. 9.00 (ISBN 90-221-0948-8). Theatrum Orbis Terrarum.
Curtained Sleep. Archie E Roy. LC 75-148412. (Falcon's head suspense novel). (Illus.). 1971. 5.95. World Pub. Co.
Curtains. Gloria Gonzalez. 1976. pap. 1.65x. Dramatists Play.
Curtains for the Copper. Thomas Polsky. LC 41-4717. 1941. E. P. Dutton & Co. Inc.
Curtains for the Editor. Thomas Polsky. LC 39-8722. E. P. Dutton & Company, Inc.
Curtains for the Judge. Thomas Polsky. LC 39-33091. 1939. E. P. Dutton and Company, Inc.
Curtains for Three. Rex Stout. 192p. 1980. pap. 1.95 (ISBN 0-553-13548-1). Bantam.
Curtains for Three: A Nero Wolfe Threesome. Rex Stout. LC 51-938. 1951. Viking Press.
Curtis Wives. Marsha Alexander. 1979. pap. 1.75 (ISBN 0-89041-245-6, 3245). Major Bks.
Curve & the Tusk. Stuart Cloete. 1971. pap. 0.95 o.p. (95-144). Manor Bks.
Curve and the Tusk: A Novel of Change Among Elephants and Men. Stuart Cloete. LC 52-8272. 1952. Houghton Mifflin.
Curve of the Sigmord. William Barnwell. (Blessing Trilogy Ser.: Vol. III). 1981. pap. 2.75 (ISBN 0-671-83451-7, Timescape). PB.
Curve of the Snow of Lake. 1st Ed. William Grey Walter. LC 56-100936. 1956. W. W. Norton.
Curved Blades. Carolyn Wells. LC 16-5580. 1916. J. B. Lippincott Company.
Curving Road. John Stewart. LC 75-2286. (Short Fiction Ser.). 130p. 1975. pap. 4.95 (ISBN 0-252-00532-5). U of Ill Pr.
Curving Road: Stories. John Stewart. LC 75-2286. (Illinois short fiction). 1975. 6.95. (ISBN 0-252-00517-1) (ISBN 0-252-00532-5). University of Illinois Press.
Cushing of Boston: A Candid Portrait. Joseph Dever. 15.00 (ISBN 0-8283-1382-2). Branden.
Custard Boys. John Rae. 1961. 3.95 o.p. FS&G.
Custard Cup. Florence Bingham Livingston. LC 21-68970. George H. Doran Company.
Custodian. Archibald Eyre. LC 4-28947. 1904. H. Holt and Company.
Custodians, and Other Stories. Colin Murry. LC 76-381393. 1976. 3.40 (ISBN 0-575-02096-2). Gollancz.
Custody. Tom Alibrandi. (Orig.). 1979. pap. 2.95 (ISBN 0-523-41871-X). Pinnacle Bks.
Custody Children. Everett Young, pseud. LC 26-17297. H. Holt and Company.
Custom-House of Desire: A Half-Century of Surrealist Stories. J. H Matthews. LC 74-16712. (Illus.). 12.95 (ISBN 0-520-02865-1). University of California Press.
Custom of the Country. Edith Newbold Jones Wharton. LC 13-222075. 1913. C. Scribner's Sons.
Custom of the Country: Tales of New Japan. Mary Crawford Fraser. LC 70-101811. (Short story index reprint series). 1969. Books for Libraries Press.
Custom of the Country: Tales of New Japan. Mary Crawford Fraser. LC 99-3022. The Macmillan Company; London.
Custom of the Country; With an Introd. by Blake Nevius. Edith Newbold Jones Wharton. LC 56-585206. (Modern standard authors). 1956. Scribner.
Customer Is Always. Lewis Meyer. LC 65-13095. 3.95. Doubleday.
Customer Is Always Right. Anne Pence Davis. LC 40-27314. 1940. The Macmillan Company.
Customers' Man. Boyden Sparkes. LC 31-13487. 1931. Frederick A. Stokes Company.
Customer's Man: A Novel. Rory Harrity. LC 69-12972. 1969. 5.95. Prentice-Hall.
Customs. Lisa Zeidner. LC 80-21478. 1981. 11.95 (ISBN 0-394-51475-0). Knopf: Distributed by Random House.
Cut and a Kiss. Anthony Hope Hawkins. LC 77-86143. (Short story index reprint series). 1969. Books for Libraries Press.
Cut and a Kiss. Anthony Hope Hawkins. LC 99-2544. 1899. Brown and Company.
Cut by the Country: Or, Grace Darnel. Mary Elizabeth Braddon Maxwell. (On cover: Seaside library. Pocket ed., no. 544). 1885. G. Munro.
Cut by the County: A Novel. Mary Elizabeth Braddon Maxwell. (Harper's handy series, no. 19). 1885. Harper & Brothers.
Cut Direct. Alice Tilton, pseud. (Foul Play Press Bks.). 1979. pap. 4.50 (ISBN 0-914378-49-X). Countryman.
Cut Direct. Alice Tilton, pseud. 1968. 4.95 o.p. (ISBN 0-393-08552-X). Norton.
Cut Direct: A Leonidas Witherall Mystery, by Phoebe Atwood Taylor Writing As Alice Tilton. Phoebe Atwood Taylor. 1968. bds., 4.95. Norton.
Cut for Partners. Eaton K Goldthwaite. LC 51-10402. 1951. Duell, Sloan and Pearce.
Cut-Hand, the Mountain Man. Joseph Millard. LC 64-22772. 1964. Chilton Books.
Cut Me in. Hunt Collins, pseud. LC 54-10222. 1954. Abelard-Schuman.
Cut Me in: By Hunt Collins Pseud. Evan Hunter. LC 54-10222. 1954. AbelardSchuman.
Cut 'n' Run. Frank Deford. LC 72-79003. 1973. 6.95 (ISBN 0-670-25184-4). Viking Press.
Cut 'n' Run. Frank Deford. 1973. (pbk.) 1.25 (ISBN 0-345-23404-9). Ballantine.
Cut of Her Jib. Illus. by Gordon Grant and Walker Cain. Clara Nickerson Boden. LC 53-125604. 1953. Cotuit Library Association.
Cut of the Ax. Delmar Jackson. LC 53-9220. 1953. Harcourt, Brace.
Cut off. William Davidson. 1974. (pbk.) 1.50 (ISBN 0-515-03377-4). Pyramid Books.
Cut-Out: A Novel. Colin Smith. LC 80-25176. 1981. 10.95 (ISBN 0-670-25192-5). Viking Press.
Cut the Tree Down: A Novel. Winfred B Senior. LC 52-6098. 1952. Exposition Press.
Cut Thin to Win. A. A. Fair, pseud. 1965. 4.50 o.p. (ISBN 0-688-01403-8). Morrow.
Cut Thin to Win: By A. A. Fair (Erle Stanley Gardner. Erle Stanley Gardner. LC 65-18515. bds., 3.50. Morrow.
Cut Throat. Christopher Bush. LC 32-191883. 1932. W. Morrow & Company.
Cut with His Own Diamond: A Novel. Roland Alexander Wood-Seys. LC 9-148345. (On cover: Harper's Franklin square library, no. 714). 1891. Harper & Brothers.
Cute & Deadly Surf Twins. Patrick Morgan. (Operation Hang Ten Ser). 1970. pap. 0.75 o.p. (532-75315-075). Manor Bks.
Cute Kid. Jerome Darwin Engel. LC 42-24974. 1942. Phoenix Press.
Cutlass Empire. Francis Van Wyck Mason. LC 49-1719. 1949. Doubleday.
Cutler No. 4: Yellowstone. H. V. Elkin. (Orig.). 1980. pap. 1.75 o.s.i. (ISBN 0-505-51512-1). Tower Bks.
Cutter and Bone. Newton Thornburg. LC 76-17622. 8.95 (ISBN 0-316-84390-3). Little, Brown.
Cutter and Bone: A Novel. Newton Thornburg. 1977. 1.95 (ISBN 0-445-04029-7). Popular Library.
Cutters. Bess Streeter Aldrich. LC 75-29206. 1975. 6.95. Aeonian Press.
Cutters. Bess Streeter Aldrich. LC 26-14221. 1926. D. Appleton and Company.
Cutters. Bess Streeter Aldrich. LC 44-7848. 1944. Triangle Books.
Cutting Edge. Penelope Gilliatt. LC 78-13161. 1979. 8.95 (ISBN 0-698-10948-1). Coward, McCann & Geoghegan.
Cutting Edge. Ken Jackson. LC 70-101878. (Inner sanctum mystery). 1970. 4.95. Simon and Schuster.
Cutting Edge. Joni L. Scalia. 240p. 1983. pap. 2.95 (ISBN 0-425-05598-1). Berkley Pub.
Cutting Edges; Young American Fiction for the '70s. Ed. by Jack Hicks. LC 72-86412. 1973. 2.95 (ISBN 0-03-088517-5). Holt, Rinehart and Winston.
Cutting It! Gisella Heinemann. LC 78-27838. 8.95 (ISBN 0-8037-1586-2). Dial Press.
Cutting-Room. Harry Guest. 1970. 4.00 (Pub. by Anvil Pr); signed ed. 50 copies 15.00 ea.; pap. 2.50. SBD.
Cutting Through: A Novel. Keith Maillard. LC 82-12955. 16.95 (ISBN 0-8253-0120-3). Beaufort Books.
C.V.C. Murders. Kirby Williams. LC 29-910124. 1929. Pub. for the Crime Club, Inc., by Doubleday, Doran & Company, Inc.
Cy Ross.". Mellen Cole. (On cover: Sunnyside series, no. 27). 1891. J. S. Ogilvie.
Cy Whittaker's Place. Joseph Crosby Lincoln. LC 8-27807. 1903. D. Appleton and Company.
Cy Whittaker's Place. Joseph Crosby Lincoln. LC 13-9364. 1910. D. Appleton and Company.
Cyanide with Compliments. Elizabeth Lemarchand. LC 72-95787. 1973. 4.95 (ISBN 0-8027-5275-6). Walker.
Cybele. Joyce Carol Oates. LC 79-20305. 1979. 14.00 (ISBN 0-87685-425-0) (ISBN 0-87685-426-9) (ISBN 0-87685-424-2). Black Sparrow Press.
Cyberiad; Fables for the Cybernetic Age. Stanislaw Lem. LC 73-6420. (Continuum book). (Illus.). 1974. 9.50 (ISBN 0-8164-9164-X). Seabury Press.
Cyberiad: Fables for the Cybernetic Age. Stanislaw Lem. 240p. 1976. pap. 2.50 (ISBN 0-380-00517-4, 51557, Bard). Avon.
Cybernetic Brains. Raymond F. Jones. 1969. pap. 0.60 o.p. (63-063). Paperback Lib.
Cyborg. Martin Caidin. LC 73-183758. 1972. 7.95 (ISBN 0-87795-025-3, A4159). Arbor Hse.
Cyborg. Martin Caidin. LC 73-183758. 1972. pap. 1.25 o.p. (ISBN 0-446-66986-5). Paperback Lib.
Cyborg: A Novel. Martin Caidon. 1973. 1.25. Warner Paperback Lib.
Cyborg & the Sorcerers. Lawrence Watt-Evans. 1982. pap. 2.75 (ISBN 0-345-30441-1, Del Rey). Ballantine.
Cyborg Four. Martin Caidin. LC 74-80703. 1975. 7.95 (ISBN 0-87795-085-7). Arbor Hse.
Cyborg IV. Martin Caidin. (Six Million Dollar Man#6). 1976. (pbk.) 1.50. Warner Books.
Cycle. Edward Dorn. (Illus.). 32p. (Orig.). 1971. pap. 2.00. Frontier Press Calif.
Cycle: A Novel. Carl Colony. LC 32-13243. Dorrance & Company, Inc.
Cycle of Existence: By 5marion H. Duncan. Marion Herbert Duncan. LC 66-74130. 1966. 3.00. Mitre Pr.
Cycle of Fire. Hal Clement. 192p. 1981. pap. 2.25 (ISBN 0-345-29172-7, Del Rey). Ballantine.
Cycle of Fire: By Hal Clement. Harry C Stubbs. LC 57-14440. (Ballantine books, 200). 1957. Ballantine Brooks.
Cycle of Sonnets. Edith Lenore Willis Linn. LC 18-3206. 1918. J. T. White & Co.
Cycles. Richard G Nilges. LC 80-12889. 1980. 10.95 (ISBN 0-87949-182-5). Ashley Books.
Cyclone Jim... Edward Earl Repp. LC 35-233041. Godwin.
Cyclone of Silence. Benedict Freedman & Nancy Mars Freedman. LC 69-16055. 1969. 5.95. Trident Press.
Cyclone of the Sage Brush. James Lyon Rubel. LC 37-38601. Phoenix Press.
Cylon Death Machine. Robert Thurston. 1979. pap. 1.95 (ISBN 0-425-04080-1). Berkley Pub.
Cynic Fortune: A Tale of a Man with a Conscience. David Christie Murray. LC 7-254762. (Harper's handy series, no. 81). 1886. Harper & Brothers.
Cynics: A Novel. Anatolii Borisovich Mariengof. LC 72-90301. 1973. 12.00 (ISBN 0-88355-012-1). Hyperion Press.
Cynics: A Novel. Anatolii Borisovich Mariengof. Tr. by Bell, Valdemar D. LC 30-25817. 1930. A. & C. Boni.
Cynic's Sacrifice: A Novel. Lewis Vital Bogy. LC 6-14185. 1893. G. W. Dillingham.
Cynthia. E. V. Cunningham, pseud. 1968. 4.50 o.p. Morrow.
Cynthia. Allen Eppes. LC 39-7779. Gramercy Publishing Co.
Cynthia. Leonard Merrick. LC 19-9658. (Half-title: The works of Leonard Merrick). E. P. Dutton and Company.
Cynthia. Leonard Merrick. LC 20-5622. (Half-title: The works of Leonard Merrick). 1919. E. P. Dutton and Company.
Cynthia. Watkins Eppes Wright. LC 39-7779. 1939. Gramercy Pub. Co.
Cynthia: A Daughter of the Philistines. Leonard Merrick. LC 13-8055. 1912. D. FitzGerald, Inc.
Cynthia: A Novel. Howard Melvin Fast. LC 68-31904. 1968. W. Morrow.
Cynthia Codentry. Ernest Pascal. LC 26-5443. Brentano's.
Cynthia Freeman: A World Full of Strangers, the Days of Winter, Portraits, & Come Pour the Wine. Cynthia Freeman. 1981. boxed set 50.00 (ISBN 0-87795-353-8). Arbor Hse.
Cynthia in the Wilderness. Hubert Wales. LC 8-18723. 1908. The Stuyvesant Press.
Cynthia in the Wilderness. Hubert Wales. LC 15-174013. 1909. The Stuyvesant Press.
Cynthia-of-the-Minute: A Romance. Louis Joseph Vance. LC 11-6444. 1911. Dodd, Mead and Company.
Cynthia Stands Fast. Florence Nye Whitwell. LC 28-19550. The Biola Book Room.
Cynthia Wakeham's Money. Anna Katharine Green Rohlfs. LC 7-40738. 1892. G. P. Putnam's Sons.
Cynthia's Chauffeur. Louis Tracy. LC 10-14585. E. J. Clode.
Cynthia's Chauffeur. Louis Tracy. LC 22-24776. 1912. Grosset & Dunlap.
Cynthia's Rebellion. Albert Ellsworth Thomas. 1904. C. Scribner's Sons.
Cynthia's Sons. A Commonplace Story. Julia MacNair Wright. LC 9-9173. The National Temperance Society and Publication House.
Cynthia's Way. Cecily Ullmann Sidgwick. LC 1-25433. 1901. Longmans, Green, and Co.
Cyparissus: A Romance of the Isles of Greece. Ernst Eckstein & Stafford, Mary Joanna, Tr. LC 6-26322. 1897. G. G. Peck.
Cypress Chest. Innokentii Fedorovich Annenskii. LC 80-20923. 1980. 7.50 (ISBN 0-88233-474-3). Ardis.
Cypress Man. Jane Beynon. LC 44-20858. 1944. The Bobbs-Merrill Company.
Cypresses Believe in God. Jose Maria Gironella. LC 54-7195. 1955. Knopf.
Cyprus Love Affair. Denise Robins. 1974. pap. 0.75 o.p. (26568-075). Beagle Bks.
Cyr Myrddin, the Coming of Age of Merlin. Michael De Angelo. LC 79-54369. 1980. 12.95. Gododdin Pub.
Cyrano. Henry Bedford-Jones. LC 30-7596. 1930. G.P. Putnam's Sons.
Cyrilla: Or, The Mysterious Engagement. A Charming Story. Jemima Montgomery Tautphoeus. 1870. Turner & Co.
Cyrion. Tanith Lee. 304p. 1982. pap. 2.95 o.p. (ISBN 0-87997-765-5). DAW Bks.
Cyrus, the Magician: A Story of Magic in the Worship of Diana, and the Gospel in Asia. David Beaton. The Pilgrim Press.
Cyrus the Persian. Sherman A Nagel. LC 41-6176. 1941. Wm. B. Eerdmans Publishing Co.
Cytherea. Joseph Hergesheimer. LC 22-1720. 1922. A. A. Knopf.
Cytherea. Joseph Hergesheimer. LC 82-6819. 1982. 28.50 (ISBN 0-404-15121-3). AMS Press.
Cytherea's Breath. Sarah Aldridge. 1976. 5.00. The Naiad Press: Distributed by The Ladder.
Czar. Thomas Wiseman. LC 66-16154. 1966. bds., 6.50. S. & S.
Czar. A Tale of the Time of the First Napoleon. Deborah Alcock. LC 44-22016. 1888. T. Nelson and Sons.
Czar of Halfday Creek. James Beardsley Hendryx. LC 40-8134. 1940. Doubleday, Doran & Company, Inc.
Czar of Halfday Creek. James Beardsley Hendryx. LC 42-50082. 1942. Triangle Books.
Czardas: A Story of Budapest. Jeno Heltai. Houghton Mifflin Company.
Czar's Gift. William Ordway Partridge. LC 6-23702. 1906. Funk & Wagnalls Company.

Czar's Spy: The Mystery of a Silent Love. William Le Queux. (red novels). 1905. The Smart Set Publishing Co.

Czechoslovak Stories. Tr. by Sarka B. Hrbkova. LC 79-149662. (Interpreters' series). 1971. (ISBN 0-404-03371-7). AMS Press.

D

D. A. Breaks a Seal. Erle Stanley Gardner. LC 46-25070. 1946. W. Morrow and Company.

D. A. Breaks an Egg. Erle Stanley Gardner. LC 49-10309. (A Morrow mystery). 1949. W. Morrow.

D. A. Calls a Turn. Erle Stanley Gardner. LC 44-380. 1944. Books Inc., Distributed by W. Morrow and Company.

D. A. Calls It Murder. Erle Stanley Gardner. LC 37-271513. 1937. W. Morrow and Company.

D. A. Calls It Murder. Erle Stanley Gardner. LC 42-912017. 1941. Triangle Books.

D. A. Calls It Murder... Erle Stanley Gardner. LC 45-13592. 1944.

D. A. Cooks a Goose. Erle Stanley Gardner. LC 41-27717. 1942. W. Morrow and Company.

D. A. Cooks a Goose. Erle Stanley Gardner. LC 47-20168. 1946. Triangle Books, the Blakiston Company.

D. A. Draws a Circle. Erle Stanley Gardner. LC 39-32381. 1939. W. Morrow and Company.

D. A. Draws a Circle... Erle Stanley Gardner. LC 46-170694. 1946.

D. A. Goes to Trial. Erle Stanley Gardner. LC 40-10769. 1940. W. Morrow and Company.

D. A. Holds a Candle. Erle Stanley Gardner. LC 38-28978. 1938. W. Morrow and Company.

D. A. Holds a Candle. Erle Stanley Gardner. LC 42-21558. 1942. Triangle Books.

D. A. Takes a Chance. Erle Stanley Gardner. LC 48-9072. (A Morrow mystery). 1948. W. Morrow.

D As in Dead. Treat, Lawrence. LC 41-24079. 1941. Duell, Sloan and Pearce.

D-Day Seers Speak. Michael X. 1969. pap. 6.95. G Barker Bks.

D. Dinkelspiel, His Gonversationings. George Vere Hobart. LC 1945. 1900. New Amsterdam Book Company.

D. H. Lawrence: Artist & Rebel; a Study of Lawrence's Fiction. Ernest Warnock Tedlock. 5.00. Univ. of N. M. Pr.

D. H. Lawrence: Sons & Lovers. Ed. by Gamini Salgado. 1981. pap. 20.00x (ISBN 0-333-02367-6, Pub. by Macmillan England). State Mutual Bk.

D Is for Dutch: A Last Regional Novel. Thames Ross Williamson. LC 34-31294. Harcourt, Brace and Company.

D. W. Owen's Rock Mysteries: Death Group. D. W. Owen. LC 78-71377. (Rock Mysteries Ser.). (Illus.). pap. cancelled (ISBN 0-89169-545-1). Reed Bks.

Da Capo: A Story. Anne Isabella Thackeray Ritchie. LC 7-41959. (On cover: Harper's half-hour series, no. 50). 1878. Harper & Brothers.

Da Silva Da Silva's Cultivated Wilderness: And, Genesis of the Clowns. Wilson Harris. LC 77-367264. (Illus.). 1977-1978. 9.95 (ISBN 0-571-10819-9). Faber.

Da Silva's Widow: And Other Stories. Mary St. Leger Kingsley Harrison. LC 22-12971. 1922. Dodd, Mead and Company.

Da Vinci Legacy. Lewis Purdue. 400p. (Orig.). 1983. pap. 3.50 (ISBN 0-523-41762-4). Pinnacle Bks.

Da Vinci Machine. Earl Conrad. 1970. pap. 0.75 o.p. (0502-07105). Curtis.

Da Vinci Machine: Tales of the Population Explosion. Earl Conrad. LC 66-25986. 1969. 7.95 (ISBN 0-8303-0067-8). Fleet.

Da Vinci Machines: Tales of the Population Explosion. Earl Conrad. LC 66-25986. 1969. 5.95. Fleet Press Corp.

Da Vinci Rose. Archie O'Neill. 1973. (pbk.) 0.95. Bantam.

Da Vinci's Bicycle: Ten Stories. Guy Davenport. LC 78-20513. 12.95 (ISBN 0-8018-2208-4) (ISBN 0-8018-2220-3). Johns Hopkins University Press.

Da Vinci's Bicycle: Ten Stories by Guy Davenport. Guy Davenport. LC 78-22513. 1979. 12.95 o.p. (ISBN 0-8018-2208-4); pap. 5.95 (ISBN 0-8018-2220-3). Johns Hopkins.

Dabney Todd. Frank Noyes Westcott. LC 17-2483. The H. K. Fly Company.

Dabney Will. Lois H.Bacheller. LC 4157. 1900. Warner & Brownell.

Dacey Hamilton. Dorothy Graffe Van Doren. LC 42-216920. 1942. Harper & Brothers.

Dachau Treasure. Anthony DeStefano. 1977. pap. 1.50 (ISBN 0-532-15294-8). Woodhill.

Dacobra. Harris Burland. 1979. 8.50 o.p. Bookfinger.

Dacolard. A Sequel to "The Parricide.". Adolphe Belot & Dautin, Jules. (Seaside library, v. 46, no. 934). G. Munro.

Dad. Albert Payson Terhune. LC 14-19620. W. J. Watt & Company.

Dad. William Wharton. 432p. 1982. pap. 3.50 (ISBN 0-380-58594-4, 58594). Avon.

Dad: A Novel. William Wharton. LC 80-2725. 1981. 12.95 (ISBN 0-394-51097-6). Knopf: Distributed by Random House.

Dad" A Treasure Story of the Caribbean Sea. Edgar William Croft. LC 28-5401. 1928. Consolidated Book Publishers, Inc.

Dad and I. Eva Little McElevey. LC 30-182951. 1930. E. P. Dutton & Co., Inc.

Dad in Politics, & Other Stories. Steele Rudd. (O.s.i.). (Illus.). 1968. pap. 2.25x o.s.i. (ISBN 0-7022-0652-0). U of Queensland Pr.

Dada Caper. Ross H Spencer. 1978. 1.75 (ISBN 0-380-01839-X). Avon.

Dada Dog. Larry Couch. Ed. by Bradley R. Strahan. (Black Buzzard Illustrated Poetry Chapbook Ser.). (Illus.). 24p. 1983. pap. text ed. 2.50 (ISBN 0-938872-04-4). Black Buzzard.

Daddy. Nancy Winters. LC 79-20165. 1979. 8.95 o.p. (ISBN 0-399-90055-1, Marek). Putnam Pub Group.

Daddy: A Novel. Nancy Winters. LC 79-20165. 8.95 (ISBN 0-399-90055-1). R. Marek.

Daddy and I: A Chronicle of Small-Town Life and Youth, As Seen Through the Eyes of an Ultra-Modern Young Lady of Fifteen. Elizabeth Garver Jordan. LC 35-5116. 1935. D. Appleton-Century Company, Incorporated.

Daddy & Me. 192p. (Orig.). 1972. pap. 1.95 o.p. (ISBN 0-87977-170-4, DBB170). Dansk Blue Bk.

Daddy Cool. Donald Goines. (Orig.). 1974. pap. 1.95 (ISBN 0-87067-649-0, BH041). Holloway.

Daddy Damm's Kin-Folks... Good for Grouch. Minda A. McLintock. LC 15-20986.

Daddy Darwin's Dovecot: A Country Tale. Juliana Horatia Gatty Ewing. LC 36-15511. 1886. Roberts Brothers.

Daddy Dave. Fanny Witherspoon Mason. LC 7-25603. 1886. Funk & Wagnalls.

Daddy Davy; or, David Brauer, Master. George William Marque Maier. LC 30-30778. The Christopher Publishing House.

Daddy Dearest. Lara Stanford. (Orig.). 1979. pap. 2.25 (ISBN 0-89083-511-X). Zebra.

Daddy Jake, the Runaway: And Short Stories Told After Dark by Uncle Remus. facsimile ed. Joel Chandler Harris. LC 79-37545. (Short Story Index Reprint Ser.). Repr. of 1889 ed. 16.00 (ISBN 0-8369-4104-7). Ayer Co.

Daddy-Long-Legs. Jean Webster. LC 12-225148. 1912. The Century Co.

Daddy-Long-Legs. Jean Webster. LC 42-27134. 1912. Grosset & Dunlap.

Daddy-Long-Legs. Jean Webster. LC 14-10516. 1913. The Century Co.

Daddy-Long-Legs. Jean Webster & Carter, Ray Cecil, Ed. LC 37-6521. (Half-title: Appleton modern literature series). D. Appleton-Century Company, Incorporated.

Daddy-Long-Legs: By Jean Webster, with Illustrations by the Author. daddylonglegs ed. Jean Webster. LC 15-15243. 1915. The Century Co.

Daddy-Long-Legs. With New Illus. by Edward Ardizzone. Jean Webster. LC 67-30959. (Illus.). 1967. Meredith Press.

Daddy Pig. Mel Arrighi. LC 73-11792. 1974. 7.50 (ISBN 0-672-51911-9). Bobbs-Merrill.

Daddy Was a Number Runner. Louise Meriwether. LC 71-98887. 1970. 5.95. Prentice-Hall.

Daddy Was a Numbers Runner. Louise Meriwether. 1976. pap. 2.25 (ISBN 0-515-06342-8). Jove Pubns.

Daddy, What Did You Do to Me? Theobald-Neal, Vickie. LC 82-6822. 1983. 12.95 (ISBN 0-87949-221-X). Ashley Books.

Daddy's Girl. Charlotte Vale Allen. 1982. pap. 2.95 (ISBN 0-425-05172-2). Berkley Pub.

Daddy's Girl. Beverly Lowry. LC 81-50517. 1981. 12.95 (ISBN 0-670-25393-6). Viking Press.

Daddy's Girl, a Novel. Thomas Savage. LC 76-121423. 1970. 5.95. Little, Brown.

Daddy's Goodnight Kiss. Carter Sprague. 192p. (Orig.). 1972. pap. 1.95 o.p. (ISBN 0-87682-274-X, 7274). Barclay Hse.

Daddy's Little Sinners. Geoffrey Kyle. pap. 1.95 o.p. (ISBN 0-87056-207-X). Brandon.

Daddy's Loving Daughters. Thomas Shire. pap. 1.95 o.p. (ISBN 0-87056-184-7). Brandon.

Daddy's Sword. Amy Le Feuvre. LC 15-12990. 1915. Hodder and Stoughton.

Daddy's Widow: A Long Island Story. Margaret Barnes Price. LC 16-6643. 1916. 1.50. Broadway Publishing Co.

Dad's Girl: The Story of a Girl Who Deserved to Win. Edna Robb Webster. LC 33-7086. Grosset & Dunlap.

Dadsie Dan. John Wagley Hill. LC 14-21586. 1914. W. D. Poessnecker.

Daemon Posessed. Faith Monroe. 4.95 o.p. (ISBN 0-8062-1049-4). Carlton.

Daffodil Affair. Michael Innes, pseud. LC 75-44986. (Crime Fiction Ser). 1976. Repr. of 1942 ed. lib. bdg. 17.50 (ISBN 0-8240-2378-1). Garland Pub.

Daffodil Affair. John Innes Mackintosh Stewart. LC 75-44986. (Fifty Classics of Crime Fiction, 1900-1950; 29). 1976. 12.00 (ISBN 0-8240-2378-1). Garland Pub.

Daffodil Affair. John Innes Mackintosh Stewart. LC 42-22452. 1942. Dodd, Mead & Company.

Daffodil Blonde. Frances Kirkwood Crane. LC 50-5540. 1950. Random House.

Daffodil Murder. Edgar Wallace. LC 21-1520. Small, Maynard & Company.

Daffodil Sky. Herbert Ernest Bates. LC 56-10650. 1956. Little, Brown.

Daffodils, or, The Death of Love: Short Fiction. Corinne Demas Bliss. LC 82-11048. (Breakthrough Book; No. 39). 1983. 6.95 (ISBN 0-8262-0385-X). University of Missouri Press.

Daft Davie: And Other Sketches of Scottish Life and Character. 3d ed. Sarah R. Whitehead. LC 8-36556. 1895. A. D. F. Randolph & Co.

Dafydd. Haydn Stephens. LC 78-5377. (Illus.). 7.95 (ISBN 0-517-53299-9). Crown Publishers.

Dagda's Harp. Sharan Newman. LC 76-10559. 7.50. St. Martin's Press.

Dagger. Mary Dahlberg. LC 30-10703. 1930. Duffield and Company.

Dagger. Robert McNair Wilson. LC 29-748785. 1929. J. B. Lippincott Company.

Dagger and Jewels: The Gorgeous Adventures of Benvenuto Cellini, a Romantic Novel. William Dana Orcutt. LC 31-24892. 1931. Dodd, Mead and Company.

Dagger and the Cup. Myna Lockwood. LC 47-2542. 1947. The Bobbs-Merrill Company.

Dagger in the Dark. Walter F Eberhardt. LC 32-16106. 1932. W. Morrow & Company.

Dagger in the Heart. Mario Lazo. 1969. pap. 1.45 o.s.i. Fidelis.

Dagger of the Mind. Kenneth Fearing. LC 41-2089. Random House.

Daggerman. Richard H. Francis. LC 79-5344. 1980. 8.95 (ISBN 0-394-50990-0). Pantheon Books.

Daggers Drawn. Alan Ernest Wentworth Thomas. LC 30-24947. 1930. Brewer & Warren Inc.

Dagmar of Green Hills. 1st Ed. Joe Smith. LC 57-8306. 1957. Pageant Press.

Dagny. Louise Redfield Peattie. LC 28-12653. 1928. Doubleday, Doran & Company, Inc.

Dago Red. John Fante. LC 40-31624. 1940. The Viking Press.

Dagon. Fred Chappell. LC 67-20307. 1968. 4.75 o.p. (ISBN 0-15-123740-9). HarBraceJ.

Dagon: And Other Macabre Tales. Selected, Introd. by August Derleth. Howard Phillips Lovecraft. LC 65-5859. 6.50. Arkham.

Dagon & Others. Howard Phillips Lovecraft. 1965. 12.95 (ISBN 0-87054-028-9). Arkham.

Dagon. 1st Ed. Fred Chappell. LC 67-20307. 1968. 4.75. Harcourt.

Daguerreotypes, and Other Essays. Karen Blixen. LC 78-27543. 1979. 12.95 (ISBN 0-226-15305-3). University of Chicago Press.

Dahomean: An Historical Novel. Frank Yerby. (Dell Book). 1977. 1.95 (ISBN 0-440-11725-9). Dell Pub. Co.

Dahomean: An Historical Novel. Frank Yerby. LC 72-144387. 1971. 7.95. Dial Press.

Dai-San. Eric Van Lustbader. LC 77-26520. 1978. 7.95 (ISBN 0-385-12987-4). Doubleday.

Dai-San. Eric Van Lustbader. 272p. 1981. pap. 2.50 (ISBN 0-425-04454-8). Berkley Pub.

Dai-San. Eric Van Lustbader. LC 77-26520. 1978. 9.95 o.p. (ISBN 0-385-12987-4). Doubleday.

Dai-Sho. Marc Olden. 480p. 1983. 15.95 (ISBN 0-87795-501-8). Arbor Hse.

Daily and Sunday. Richard Pitts Powell. LC 65-10483. 1965. 4.95. Scribners.

Daily Bread. Ralph Maloney. LC 60-130032. 1960. Houghton Mifflin.

Daily Notes on a Trip Around the World see Collected Works.

Daily Rate.". Grace Livingston Hill. LC 3882. The Union Press.

Daily Rate. Grace Livingston Hill. LC 81-19941. (Hill, Grace Livingston, 1865-1947. Classic Ser.: 4). 4.95 (ISBN 0-8007-1296-X). F.H. Revell Co.

Dain Curse. Dashiell Hammett. LC 72-1755. 1972. 1.25 (ISBN 0-394-71827-5). Vintage Books.

Dain Curse. Dashiell Hammett. LC 29-152869. 1929. A. A. Knopf.

Dain Curse. Dashiell Hammett. LC 36-29818. 1930. Grosset & Dunlap.

Dain Curse... Dashiell Hammett. LC 45-8055. 1945.

Dainty Devils: A Novel. Helen Beekman. LC 3-12001. 1903. W. H. Young & Co. Etc., Etc.

Dainty Inquity. A Novel. Granville, Margaret. (Dillingham's metropolitan library, no. 10). 1896. G. W. Dillingham.

Daireen. A Novel. Frank Frankfort Moore. LC 7-26214. (Franklin square library. no. 115). 1880. Harper & Brothers.

Daireen: A Novel. Frank Frankfort Moore. LC 7-25309. R. F. Fenno & Company.

Dairy Maid. Watkins Eppes Wright. LC 40-35813. 1940. Gramercy Pub. Co.

Dairyman's Daughter. Leigh Richmond. pap. 1.50 o.p. (ISBN 0-8254-3611-7, RBDH). Kregel.

Daishi-San: A Novel. Robert Lund. LC 61-82820. 1961. John Day Co.

Daisies and Buttercups. A Novel. Charlotte Eliza Lawson Cowan Riddell. (Harper's Franklin square library, no. 279). 1882. Harper & Brothers.

Daisies and Buttercups. A Novel. Charlotte Eliza Lawson Cowan Riddell. LC 28-4877. (Seaside library. v. 72, no. 1451). G. Munro.

Daisy. (Orig.). 1980. pap. 1.50 (ISBN 0-440-11683-X). Dell.

Daisy. Susan Warner. LC 8-33710. 1894. J. B. Lippincott Company.

Daisy Adrift: By Linda Walsh and Katherine Bartels. 1st Ed. Linda Walsh & Katherine Bartels. LC 53-12705. 1953. Pageant Press.

Daisy & Daphne. Rose Macaulay. LC 28-946321. 1928. Boni & Liveright.

Daisy Ashford; Her Book: A Collection of the Remaining Novels by the Author of "The Young Visiters," Together with "The Jealous Governes,". Daisy Ashford. LC 20-9783. George H. Doran Company.

Daisy Brooks: Or, A Perilous Love. Laura Jean Libbey. (On cover: The library of American authors, no. 4). 1889. G. Munro.

Daisy Burns: A Tale. 9th ed. Julia Kavanagh. LC 7-11118. 1866. Appletons.

Daisy Canfield. Ben Haas. LC 72-90795. 1973. 6.95 (ISBN 0-671-21484-5). Simon and Schuster.

Daisy Chain for Satan. 1st American Ed. Joan Fleming. LC 50-11086. 1950. Published for the Crime Club by Doubleday.

Daisy Chain; or, Aspirations. A Family Chronicle. Charlotte Mary Yonge. LC 41-425168. 1875. D. Appleton and Company.

Daisy Chain; or, Aspirations. A Family Chronicle. Charlotte Mary Yonge. LC 4-16595. 1904. Macmillan and Co., Limited.

Daisy. Continued from "Melbourne House.". Susan Warner. LC 8-33711. 1868-69. Lippincott & Company.

Daisy Darrell. Laura C Ford. LC 6-41399. (On cover: Munro's library. v. 1, no. 307). 1885. N. L. Munro.

Daisy Dilemma. Don Rico. (Orig.). pap. 0.60 o.p. (73-639). Lancer.

Daisy Gordon's Folly: Or, The World Lost for Love's Sake. Laura Jean Libbey. LC 7-14368. 1892. N. L. Munro.

Daisy Kenyon. Elizabeth Janeway. LC 45-9584. 1945. Doubleday, Doran & Co., Inc.

Daisy Miller. Henry James. 1974. (pbk.) 1.25. Warner Paperback Library.

Daisy Miller. Henry James. LC 6-32114. 1906. Harper & Brothers.

Daisy Miller. Henry James. LC 17-230105. 1916. Harper & Brothers.

Daisy Miller. Henry James & McVickar, Harry Whitney. LC 4-15461. 1901. Harper & Brothers.

Daisy Miller see Four Selected Novels of Henry James.

Daisy Miller: A Study. Henry James. LC 7-7558. (On cover: Harper's half-hour series no. 82). 1879. Harper & Brothers.

Daisy Miller: A Study; and Other Stories. Henry James. (Harper's Franklin square library. no. 803). 1883. Harper & Brothers.

Daisy Miller: And An International Episode. Henry James. LC 49-39800. Harpers.

Daisy Miller & An International Episode. Henry James. LC 7-7557. 1892. Harper & Brothers.

Daisy Miller and An International Episode. Henry James. Ed. by Sampson, Martin Wright. LC 27-11491. (modern readers' series). 1927. The Macmillan Company.

Daisy Miller & Other Stories. Henry James. 1983. pap. price not set (ISBN 0-14-006721-3). Penguin.

Daisy Miller & Other Stories. Henry James. 1964. 7.50 o.p. Scribner.

Daisy Miller, Pandora, The Patagonia: And Other Tales. Henry James. LC 78-158797. (Scribner reprint editions). 1971. (ISBN 0-678-02818-4). A. M. Kelley.

Daisy Miller, the Turn of the Screw see Bodley Head Henry James.

Daisy Nichol. A Novel. Mary McDowell Duffus Hardy. (Seaside library, v. 13, no. 243). 1878. G. Munro.

Daisy: Or. A Flower of the Tenements of Little Old New York by Gilbert Guest. Gilbert Guest. LC 21-2969. 1921. Burkley Printing Company.

Daisy Plains. Susan Warner. LC 8-33709. R. Carter & Brothers.

Daisy Seymour. LC 6-381273. (Added t.-p.: New $300 prize ser.). 1871. D. Lothrop & Co.

Daisy Summerfields Style. M. B. Goffstein. 1979. pap. 1.25 (ISBN 0-440-91744-1). Dell.

Daisy Thornton and Jessie Graham. Mary Jane Hawes Holmes. LC 11-16152. G. W. Carleton & Co.

Daisy's Dilemma. Emily Sharp H. Carmeron. LC 6-21857. (On cover: Seaside library. Pocket ed., no. 1025). G. Munro.

Daisy's Fanny. Katharine Sherman. LC 51-3860. 1951. Vantage Press.

Daisy's Necklace: And What Came of It. (A Literary Episode. Thomas Bailey Aldrich. LC 8-11009. 1857. Derby & Jackson.

Dakota Badlands. John Benteen. (Belmont Tower Book). 1.50 (ISBN 0-505-51173-8). Tower Pubns.

Dakota Deal. Riley Ryan. LC 54-37755. (Lion book, 187). 1954. Lion Books.

Dakota Deathtrap. Lauran Paine. 1979. pap. 1.50 o.s.i. (ISBN 0-505-51421-4). Tower Bks.

Dakota Dreamin' Janet Dailey. (Harlequin Presents Ser.). 192p. 1981. pap. 1.50 (ISBN 0-373-10445-6). Harlequin Bks.

Dakota Gold. Tim Champlin. LC 82-6666. 1982. 2.25 (ISBN 0-345-30529-9). Ballantine Books.

Dakota in the Morning. William Harlowe Briggs. LC 42-18490. 1942. Farrar & Rinehart, Inc.

Dakota Land: Or, The Beauty of St. Paul. An Original Illustrated Historic and Romantic Work on Minnesota, and the Great North-West. 2d ed. C Hankins. LC 7-2164. 1869. Hankins & Son.

Dakota Love Story. Donald Beard. LC 76-2297. 6.95 (ISBN 0-87949-058-6). Ashley Books.

Dakota Marshal. Archie Joscelyn. LC 38-6960. Phoenix Press.

Dakota Project. Jack Beeching. LC 73-87533. 1968. 4.95. Delacorte Press.

Dakota Rifle. Frank O'Rourke. LC 54-9937. (Dell first edition, 41). 1955. Dell Pub. Co.

Dakota Territory. John Benteen. (Sundance: No. 3). 1979. pap. 1.75 o.s.i. (ISBN 0-8439-0708-8, Leisure Bks). Nordon Pubns.

Dakota Territory. Robert J. Steelman. LC 74-10633. 1974. (pbk.). 0.95. Ballantine Books.

Dakota Wild. Jon Sharpe. (Trailsman Ser.: No. 6). (Orig.). 1981. pap. 2.50 (ISBN 0-451-11988-6, AE1988, Sig). NAL.

Dalam Pencarian. Noorjaya. (Karyawan Malaysia). (Malay.). 1979. pap. text ed. 4.25x o.p. (00351). Heinemann Ed.

Dale King, the Apostle of Sunshine. Gus Ward. LC 25-18066.

Dale Loves Sophie to Death. Robb Forman Dew. LC 80-28737. 11.95 (ISBN 0-374-13450-2). Farrar, Straus, Giroux.

Dale Loves Sophie to Death. Robb Forman Dew. LC 81-21021. 1982. 4.95 (ISBN 0-14-006183-5). Penguin Books.

Dalehouse Murder. Francis William Stokes. LC 27-19191. The Bobbs-Merrilll Company.

Dalesacres. Florence Jeannette Baier Ward. LC 39-25870. E. P. Dutton & Co., Inc.

Daleth Effect. Harry Harrison. 1977. pap. 1.50 (ISBN 0-425-03649-9, Medallion). Berkley Pub.

Daleth Effect: A Science Fiction Novel. Harry Harrison. LC 79-102647. 1970. 4.95. Putnam.

Daley Twins. Joseph W. Tluczek. 3.75 o.p. Carlton.

Dalkey Archive. Brian O'Nolan. LC 77-6678. 1977. 1.95 (ISBN 0-14-004516-3). Penguin Books.

Dalkey Archive: A Novel. Flann O'Brien. 1977. pap. 3.50 (ISBN 0-14-004516-3). Penguin.

Dalkey Archive: By Flann O'Brien Pseud. Brian O'Nolan. LC 65-124872. 1965. 4.95. Macmillan.

Dalla the Lion-Cub: A Story of South Africa. Cynthia Stockley. LC 24-21312. 1924. G. P. Putnam's Sons.

Dallas. Archie Joscelyn. (YA) 1974. 4.95 o.p. (Avalon). Bouregy.

Dallas. Clayton Matthews. (O.s.i.). 1976. pap. 1.75 o.s.i. (ISBN 0-671-80799-4). WSP.

Dallas. Clayton Matthews (ISBN 0-671-80799-4). Pocket Books.

Dallas. Lee Raintree. 1980. pap. 2.50 (ISBN 0-440-11752-6). Dell.

Dallas Blue. L. V. Davis. 240p. (Orig.). 1982. pap. 2.50 (ISBN 0-505-51785-X). Tower Bks.

Dallas: From the Warner Bros. Motion Picture Written by John Twist. William Fitzgerald Jenkins & Dallas (Motion Picture) LC 51-15118. (Gold medal book, 126). 1950. Fawcett Publications.

Dalleszona and the Seventh Treasure. Allen Kendrick Wright. LC 23-115. (Taw-no-ker series). The Roxburgh Publishing Co., Inc.

Dally. Maria Louise Pool. LC 7-38181. 1891. Harper & Brothers.

Dally. Maria Louise Pool. LC 7-38180. (On cover: Harper's quarterly, no. 2). 1893. Harper & Brothers.

Dalmatian Tapes. Don Smith. (Secret Mission Ser.). (O.s.i.). (Orig.). 1976. pap. 1.25 o.s.i. (AQ1598, Award). Univ Pub & Dist.

Dalrymple: A Romance of the British Prison Ship, the Jersey. Mary Cornelia Francis. LC 4-12976. 1904. J. Pott & Company.

Dalton Brothers and Their Astounding Career of Crime. Edgar De Valcourt-Vermont. (On cover: The Pinkerton detective series, no. 6). 1892. Laird & Lee.

Dalton Brothers and Their Astounding Career of Crime: By an Eye Witness. Introd. by Burton Rascoe. Edgar De Valcourt-Vermont. LC 54-144646. 1954. F. Fell.

Dalton City. Rene de Goscinny. (Lucky Luke Ser.). (French.). 1976. 5.95x (ISBN 2-205-00340-2). Intl Learn Syst.

Daltons: Or, Three Roads in Life. Charles James Lever. LC 7-3532. (On cover: Library of select novels. no. 170). 1852. Harper & Brothers.

Daltons: Or, Three Roads in Life. Charles James Lever. LC 24-11865. (Lettered on cover: Novels of foreign life). 1904. Little, Brown, and Company.

Dalys of Dalystown. Dillon O'Brien. 1866. Pioneer Printing Company.

Dam. Robert Byrne. LC 80-22109. (Illus.). 1981. 12.95 (ISBN 0-689-11123-1). Atheneum.

Dam. Angus MacLeod. LC 71-79826. 1969. 3.95. Roy Publishers.

Dam, a Novel. Earl Jerome Ellison. LC 41-51776. Random House.

Dam & the River. Harold W. Burke. (Orig.). 1979. pap. 1.95 (ISBN 0-532-23164-3). Woodhill.

Dam for Nothing. Leslie Stephan. LC 65-11936. 1966. Viking Press.

Dam-Mania! Another Glowing Chapter of a Dark Era in the Long Creative Epic of America. Harry E Sever. LC 54-10247. 1955. Vantage Press.

Dama en Calor. new ed. Rod Gray. Tr. by Silvia Orejuela from Eng. (Ninfa De G.O.C.E Set: No. 2). Orig. Title: Lady in Heat. 160p. (Span.). 1975. pap. 1.00 o.p. (ISBN 0-88473-224-X). Fiesta Pub.

Damage Within the Community. Edward Mycue. (Illus.). 1973. pap. 4.00 (ISBN 0-915572-11-7). Panjandrum.

Damaged Goods: The Great Play "Les Avaries" of Brieux, Novelized with the Approval of the Author. Upton Beall Sinclair & Brieux, Eugene, 1858- Les Avaries. The John C. Winston Company.

Damaged Reputation. Harold Bindloss. LC 8-29868. R. F. Fenno & Company.

Damaged Wives. Carlotta Baker. LC 40-4189. Phoenix Press.

Damaged Wives. pseud. ed. Leona Slottman. LC 40-4189. 1940. Phoenix Press.

Damaris. Jane Sheridan. 1980. pap. 2.75 (ISBN 0-425-04482-3). Berkley Pub.

Damaris. Pauline Glen Winslow. LC 78-4383. 1978. 10.95 (ISBN 0-312-18210-4). St. Martin's Press.

Damaris: A Novel. Mary St. Leger Kingsley Harrison. LC 16-19458. 1916. 1.40. Dodd, Mead and Company.

Damascus Cover. Howard S Kaplan. LC 76-40311. 8.95 (ISBN 0-525-08850-4). Dutton.

Damascus Cover. Howard S. Kaplan. (Fawcett Crest Book). 1978. 1.75 (ISBN 0-449-23412-6). Fawcett Books.

Damascus Gate. Ernest Raymond. LC 23-11971. 1923. Cassell and Company, Ltd.

Damascus Gate. Ernest Raymond. LC 23-178443. 2.00. George H. Doran Company.

Damascus Road. Leon De Tinseau & Gilmour, Florence Belknap, Tr. LC 8-267703. 1894. G. H. Richmond & Co.

Damask Girl: And Other Stories. Morrison Isaac Swift. LC 6-17874. 1906. The M. I. Swift Press.

Dame. Carter Brown, pseud. LC 59-498148. (Signet books, 1738). 1959. New American Library of World Literature.

Dame. Richard Stark. LC 69-10611. 1969. 4.50 o.p. (ISBN 0-02-613610-4). Macmillan.

Dame. Donald E Westlake. LC 69-10611. (Cock Robin mystery). 1969. Macmillan.

Dame America. Robert B. Sweet. LC 76-47637. 1977. 8.95 (ISBN 0-87929-064-1). Barlenmir House.

Dame Care. Hermann Sudermann. LC 8-16317. 1891. Harper & Brothers.

Dame Care. Hermann Sudermann & Overbeck, Bertha, Tr. LC 4-17555. 1902. Harper & Brothers.

Dame Care. Hermann Sudermann & Overbeck, Bertha, Tr. LC 35-8297. (Half title: The modern library of the world's best books). 1918. The Modern Library.

Dame Durden: A Novel. Eliza M. J. Humphreys. (On cover: Lovell's library, v. 11, no. 556). 1885. J. W. Lovell Company.

Dame Durden. A Novel. Eliza M. J. Humphreys. (On cover: Seaside library. Pocket ed., no. 446). 1885. G. Munro.

Dame Durden's Daughter. Joan Smith. LC 78-56288. 1978. 8.95 (ISBN 0-8027-0603-7). Walker.

Dame Durden's Daughter. Joan Smith. 1979. 1.75 (ISBN 0-449-23968-3). Fawcett Crest.

Dame Durden's Daughter. Joan Smith. LC 80-12487. (Regency romance). 1980. 9.95 (ISBN 0-89340-267-2). J. Curley.

Dame Fortune Smiled. The Doctor's Story. Willis Barnes. LC 6-7206. 1896. Arena Publishing Company.

Dame in Distress. Craig Cooper. LC 68-20997. 1968. Roy Publishers.

Dame Orange. Roman Von Hans Wachenhusen... Hans Wachenhusen. LC 17-789538. (Die deutsche library, bd. 2, no. 54). 1881. G. Munro.

Damen's Ghost... Edwin Lassetter Bynner. LC 6-16409. (Round-robin series). 1881. J. R. Osgood and Company.

Dames. Elizabeth North. LC 80-29607. 1981. 11.95 (ISBN 0-394-51968-X). Knopf: Distributed by Random House.

Dames of High Estate. Henriette Guizot Witt & Yonge, Charlotte Mary, 1823-1901, Ed. LC 9-3430. 1872. F. Warne and Co.

Damiano: The Story of a Poor Family. ed. de luxe ed. Giulio Carcano. Tr. by Walsh, William Shepard. (Added t.-p.: The literature of Italy, 1265-1907. Ed. by Rossiter Johnson and Dora Knowing Ranous). The National Alumni.

Damion's Daughter. 1sted. ed. Edwin Gilbert. LC 49-102443. 1949. Doubleday.

Damnation Alley. Roger Zelazny. (Berkley Medallion Book). (Illus.). 1977. 1.75 (ISBN 0-425-03641-3). Berkley Pub. Corp.

Damnation Alley. Roger Zelazny. LC 77-95238. 1969. 4.95. Putnam.

Damnation Alley. Roger Zelazny. LC 79-3895. (Gregg Press science fiction series). (Illus.). 1979. 10.00 (ISBN 0-8398-2505-6). Gregg Press.

Damnation of Theron Ware. Harold Frederic. LC 6-43137. 1896. Stone & Kimball.

Damnation of Theron Ware. Harold Frederic. LC 24-28528. 1915. Duffield & Company.

Damnation of Theron Ware. Harold Frederic. LC 25-460837. 1924. A. & C. Boni.

Damnation of Theron Ware see Collected Works.

Damnation of Theron Ware. Introd by John Henry Raleigh. Harold Frederic. (Rinehart editions, 108 rebound). 1965. 3.25. P. Smith.

Damnation of Theron Ware: Or, Illumination. Harold Frederic. LC 72-84580. 1974. 20.50 (ISBN 0-403-03054-4). Scholarly Press.

Damnation of Theron Ware: Or, Illumination. Harold Frederic. LC 32-33613. 1896. Stone & Kimball.

Damnation of Theron Ware: Or, Illumination. Harold Frederic. LC 37-32813. 1900. H. S. Stone & Company.

Damnation Reef. Jill Tattersall. LC 79-10530. 1979. 8.95 (ISBN 0-688-03475-6). Morrow.

Damnation Reef. Jill Tattersall. LC 80-14125. 11.95 (ISBN 0-89340-270-2). J. Curley.

Damned. John Dann MacDonald. 1978. pap. 2.25 (ISBN 0-449-13997-2, GM). Fawcett.

Damned Don't Cry. Harry Hervey. LC 39-6265. The Greystone Press.

Damned Don't Drown. A. V Sellwood. 1975. (pbk.) 1.25 (ISBN 0-523-00550-4). Pinnacle Books.

Damned If They Do. Helena Huntington Smith. 1933. W. Morrow & Company.

Damned Little Fool: A Tragic Comedy. Cosmo Hamilton. LC 31-5702. Brewer and Warren Inc.

Damned Lovely. Jack Webb. LC 54-825419. (A Father Shanley-Sammy Golden story). 1954. Rinehart.

Damned Lover. Frank Owen. LC 33-78001. The Macaulay Company.

Damned Spot. Barry Cuff, pseud. 1969. pap. 1.75 (ISBN 0-87067-172-3, BH172). Holloway.

Damned: The Intimate Story of a Girl. LC 23-6148. The Macaulay Company.

Damned to Desire. J. De La Beuque. pap. 1.95 o.s.i. (Venus). Grove.

Damned to Success. Hans Hellmut Kirst. LC 72-94118. 1973. 6.95 (ISBN 0-698-10522-2). Coward, McCann & Geoghegan.

Damned to Success. Hans Helmut Kirst. (Berkley medallion book). 1975. (pbk.) 1.50. Berkley.

Damned Wear Wings. 1st Ed. David M Camerer. LC 58-5932. 1958. Doubleday.

Damning Trifles. Maurice C Johnson. LC 32-943812. 1932. A. A. Knopf.

Damocles Sword. Elleston Trevor. 384p. 1982. pap. 3.50 (ISBN 0-87216-932-4). Playboy Pbks.

Damon. C. Terry Cline. LC 74-16585. 1975. 7.95 (ISBN 0-399-11429-7). Putnam.

Damon and Pythias: A Story of Old Syracuse. P. C Kibbe. LC 30-5540. 1930. Independent Publishing Co.

Damon Runyan Omnibus. Damon Runyan. 1976. Repr. of 1944 ed. lib. bdg. 18.75x (ISBN 0-89190-441-7). Am Repr-Rivercity Pr.

Damon Runyon Favorites. Damon Runyon. Repr. lib. bdg. 13.85x (ISBN 0-89190-440-9). Am Repr-Rivercity Pr.

Damon Runyon Omnibus. Damon Runyon. LC 75-32557. 1975. 9.95 (ISBN 0-89190-441-7). American Reprint Co.

Damon Runyon Omnibus... Damon Runyon. LC 39-106. 1939. Blue Ribbon Books.

Damon Runyon Omnibus... Damon Runyon. LC 45-1951. 1944. The Sun Dial Press.

Damon Runyon's Blue Plate Special. Damon Runyon. LC 34-22757. 1934. Frederick A. Stokes Company.

Damphool in the Kentucky Legislature. Henry Clinton Kennedy. LC 9-16800. 1.25. W. B. Conkey Company.

Dams Can Break: A Novel. Emeline Fate Christian. LC 51-14467. 1951. Storm Publishers.

Damsel. Richard Stark. LC 67-14419. 1967. Macmillan.

Damsel. Donald E Westlake. LC 67-14419. 1967. Macmillan.

Damsel and the Sage: A Woman's Whimsies. Elinor Sutherland Glyn. LC 3-25401. 1963. Harper & Brother.

Damsel Debonaire: A Simple Love Story. Maurice Walsh. LC 48-6787. 1948. J. B. Lippincott Co.

Damsel in Distress. Pelham Grenville Wodehouse. LC 19-15566. George H. Doran Company.

Damsel in Distress. Pelham Grenville Wodehouse. LC 29-8992. 1922. A. L. Burt Company.

Damsel of the Eighteenth Century: Or, Cicely's Choice. Mary Harriott Norris. 1889. Phillips & Hunt.

Damyank. William MacLeod Raine. LC 42-362834. 1942. Houghton, Mifflin Company.

Dan: An Allegory in Three Parts in Which the Subjects of Birth, Life and Death Are Represented in the Story of Dan Mannering. F. Lewis Starbuck. LC 17-470899. Pantagraph Printing and Stationary Co.

Dan Barry's Daughter. Max Brand. LC 24-1971. 1924. 1.90. G. P. Putnam's Sons.

Dan Barry's Daughter. Max Brand. LC 82-5179. 1982. 14.95 (ISBN 0-89340-503-5). J. Curley.

Dan Barry's Daughter. Frederick Faust. LC 76-41325. 1976. 6.95 (ISBN 0-88411-516-X). Aeonian Press.

Dan Barry's Daughter. Frederick Faust. 1976. (pbk.) 1.25. Warner Books.

Dan Black, Editor and Proprietor: A Story. Seymour Eaton. LC 43-26888. The Library Publishing Company.

Dan England and the Noonday Devil. Myles Connolly. LC 51-13207. 1951. Bruce.

Dan McLean's Adventures. Frederick Walworth Brown. LC 11-5224. 1.50. The Baker & Taylor Company.

Dan Merrithew. Lawrence Perry. LC 10-730254. 1910. 1.50. A. C. McClurg & Co.

Dan Minturn. Marion Hawthorne Hedges. LC 27-28081. Vanguard Press.

Dan of Millbrook. A Story of American Life. Charles Carleton Coffin. LC 6-26748. 1894. Estes and Lauriat.

Dan Owen and the Angel Joe: A Novel. Ronald Elwy Mitchell. LC 48-5700. 1948. Harper.

Dan Russel the Fox: An Episode in the Life of Miss Rowan. Edith Anna CEnone Somerville & Violet Florence Martin. LC 12-252101. 1912. Methuen & Co., Ltd.

Dana, the Irrelevant Man: A Novel. Douglass Cater. LC 72-124136. 1970. 6.95. McGraw-Hill.

Danae. Marianne Gauss. LC 25-19523. 1925. Harper & Brothers.

Dana's Dream: A Novel. Katherine E Mack. LC 55-161439. American Book Institute.

Danbury Curve: A Novel, by Ruth and Gregory Mason. Ruth Fitch Mason & Gregory Mason. LC 62-13676. 1962. Whittier Books.

Danbury Fair. Peter E Osborn. LC 7-231982. 1894. The Danbury Medical Printing Co.

Danbury Rodd: Aviator. Frederick Palmer. LC 10-11136. 1910. C. Scribner's Sons.

Dance a White Horse to Sleep: And Other Stories. Antonio Enriquez. (Asian & Pacific Writings Ser). 1977. 16.95x (ISBN 0-7022-1471-X); pap. 8.50x (ISBN 0-7022-1472-8). U of Queensland Pr.

Dance and Skylark: A Novel. John Cecil Moore. LC 52-11199. 1952. Macmillan.

Dance As They Desire. Elizabeth Carden Brown. LC 36-192634. 1936. Godwin.

Dance Back the Buffalo. Milton Lott. LC 58-906858. 1959. Houghton Mifflin.

Dance Card. John R Feegel. LC 80-24011. 9.95 (ISBN 0-8037-1593-5). Dial Press.

Dance for a Lady. Eileen Jackson. 224p. 1981. pap. 1.95 (ISBN 0-449-50201-5, GM). Fawcett.

Dance Goes on. Louis Golding. LC 37-10646. Farrar & Rinehart, Inc.

Dance Hall Lady. Joan Clayton. LC 37-992819. 1937. Godwin.

Dance Hall of the Dead. Tony Hillerman. LC 73-4150. 1973. 5.95 (ISBN 0-06-011898-9). Harper & Row.

Dance in Darkness. easy eye ed. Dorothy Daniels. (Orig.). pap. 0.75 o.p. (74-982). Lancer.

Dance in the Dust. Denise Robins. LC 78-58889. (Avon Book.). 1978. 1.75. Avon Books.

Dance in the Sun. Dan Jacobson. LC 56-533429. 1956. Harcourt, Brace.

Dance, Little Gentleman! Gilbert Frankau. LC 30-2371. 1930. Harper & Brothers.

Dance Magic. Clarence Budington Kelland. LC 27-265520. 1927. Harper & Brothers.

Dance Night. Dawn Powell. LC 80-277685. 1930. Farrar & Rine Hart Incorporated.

Dance of Death. Carter Brown, pseud. Bd. with Corpse for Christmas. 1982. pap. 2.75 (ISBN 0-451-11926-6, AE1926, Sig). NAL.

Dance of Death. Helen McCloy. LC 38-5024. 1938. W. Morrow and Company.

Dance of Death. Jeremy Potter. LC 69-15725. 1969. 4.50. Walker.

Dance of Death. Alan Geoffrey Yates. LC 64-3807. (Signet book). 1964. New American Library of World Literature.

Dance of Death. And Other Stories. Minnette Slayback- Carper. 1894. Buxton & Skinner.

Dance of Death, and Other Tales. Algernon Blackwood. LC 28-20620. (Half-title: The fireside library). 1928. L. MacVeagh, The Dial Press.

Dance of Desire. Barbara Bonham. LC 78-54991. 416p. (Orig.). 1978. pap. 1.95 (ISBN 0-87216-470-5). Playboy Pbks.

Dance of Desire. Lisa Lenore. (Superromances Ser.). 384p. 1982. pap. 2.50 (ISBN 0-373-70018-0, Pub. by Worldwide). Harlequin Bks.

Dance of Genghis Cohn. Romain Gary, pseud. LC 68-28113. 1968. World Pub. Co.

Dance of Genghis Cohn. Romain Gary, pseud. LC 81-16531. 1982. 6.95 (ISBN 0-8052-0693-0). Schocken Books.

Dance of Love. Terry Bowers. 1981. pap. 6.95 (Avalon). Bouregy.

Dance of Love. Dion Clayton Calthrop. LC 7-31413. 1907. H. Holt and Company.

Dance of Love. Daniel B Dodson. (Fawcett Crest Book.). 1977. 1.75 (ISBN 0-449-23110-0). Fawcett Publications.

Dance of Love. Jocelyn Saal. 1982. pap. 1.95 (ISBN 0-553-20790-3). Bantam.

Dance of Sycamore Street. Julie L'Enfant. 384p. 1983. 17.95 (ISBN 0-312-18212-0). St Martin.

Dance of the Assassins. Maria Fagyas. LC 72-97291. 1973. 7.95 (ISBN 0-399-11118-2). Putnam.

Dance of the Assassins. Maria Fagyas. 1975. (pbk.) 1.50. Dell.

Dance of the Dwarfs. Geoffrey Household. LC 68-30871. 1968. 5.95. Little, Brown.

Dance of the Dwarfs. Geoffrey Household. LC 79-12942. 1979. 1.95 (ISBN 0-14-005227-5). Penguin Books.

Dance of the Glass Ladies. Robert Neal Leath. LC 34-364043. W. Godwin, Incorp.

Dance of the Golden Calf. Eugene Endrey & Bestercey, Ilona, Tr. LC 35-176833. 1935. The New Men Publishing Co.

Dance of the Happy Shades and Other Stories. Alice Munro. LC 73-4443. 1973. (ISBN 0-07-044048-4). McGraw-Hill.

Dance of the Snake. Yvonne Whittal. (Harlequin Presents Ser.). 192p. 1982. pap. 1.75 (ISBN 0-373-10550-9). Harlequin Bks.

Dance of the Tiger. Bjorn Kurten. 288p. 1981. pap. 2.95 (ISBN 0-425-05184-6). Berkley Pub.

Dance of the Tiger: A Novel of the Ice Age. Bjorn Kurten. LC 80-7724. (Illus.). 1980. 10.95 (ISBN 0-394-51267-7). Pantheon Books.

Dance of the Tiger: A Novel of the Ice Age. Bjorn Kurten. (Illus.). 1981. 2.95 (ISBN 0-425-05184-6). Berkley Publishing Corp.

Dance of the Wild Mouse. Daniel Panger. LC 79-51409. 9.95 (ISBN 0-9601428-4-3). Entwhistle Books.

Dance of Youth. Hermann Sudermann. Tr. by Eden Paul. Paul, Cedar, Joint Tr. LC 30-238943. 1930. H. Liveright.

Dance on My Heart. Barbara Cartland. 1977. pap. 1.25 o.p. (ISBN 0-515-03986-1). BJ Pub Group.

Dance on the Tortoise. Marion Patton. LC 31-1388. 1930. L. Mac Veagh, The Dial Press.

Dance on the Volcano. Translated from the French by Salvator Attanasio. Marie Chauvet. LC 59-5507. 1959. W. Sloan Associates.

Dance on, Tzigane. Caryl Bergman. LC 45-907. Dorrance & Company.

Dance Out the Answer. David McCloud. LC 32-30516. 1932. Longmans, Green and Co.

Dance Over Fire and Water. Elie Faure. Tr. by Fletcher, John Gould. LC 26-6378. 1926. Harper & Brothers.

Dance-Partner. Berta Ruck. LC 31-21891. 1931. Dodd, Mead and Company.

Dance Studio. Charles Stanley Strong. LC 40-84008. Phoenix Press.

Dance Studio Hucksters. Robert Sinclair. 192p. (Orig.). 1973. pap. 1.95 o.p. (ISBN 0-87056-300-9, 6300). Brandon.

Dance Team. Sarah Addington. LC 31-18422. D. Appleton and Company,

Dance the Eagle to Sleep. Marge Piercy. LC 75-124560. 1970. 5.95. Doubleday.

Dance Time. Jablons, Beverly. 1981. 2.25 (ISBN 0-425-04797-0). Berkley Books.

Dance Time: A Novel. Beverly Jablons. LC 79-15755. 1979. 9.95 (ISBN 0-688-03517-5). Morrow.

Dance to the Music of Time: First Movement. Anthony Powell. Incl. A Question of Upbringing; A Buyer's Market; The Acceptance World. 1963. 12.50 (ISBN 0-316-71535-2). Little.

Dance to the Music of Time: Fourth Movement, Incl. Books Do Furnish a Room, Temporary Kings, Hearing Secret Harmonies. Anthony Dymoke Powell. 1976. 12.50 (ISBN 0-316-71548-4). Little.

Dance to the Music of Time: Second Movement. Anthony Powell. Incl. At Lady Molly's; Casanova's Chinese Restaurant; The Kindly Ones. 1964. 12.50 (ISBN 0-316-71536-0). Little.

Dance to the Music of Time: Third Movement. Anthony Dymoke Powell. LC 70-161417. (His The music of time). 1971. 8.95. Little, Brown.

Dance to the Music of Time: Vol. 1 Spring. Anthony Dymoke Powell. 1976. (pbk.) 2.50. Popular Library.

Dance to the Music of Time: Vol. 2 Summer. Anthony Dymoke Powell. 1976. (pbk.) 2.50. Popular Library.

Dance to the Music of Time: Vol. 3 Autumn. Anthony Dymoke Powell. 1976. (pbk.) 2.50. Popular Library.

Dance with a Ghost. large-type ed. Kate Ostrander. 1976. pap. 1.25 (ISBN 0-425-03062-8, Medallion). Berkley Pub.

Dance with a Ghost. Kate Ostrander. (Berkley Medallion Book). 1976. (pbk.) 1.25 (ISBN 0-425-03062-8). Berkley Publishing Corp.

Dance with a Stranger. Elizabeth Van Steenwyk. (Caprice Romances Ser.). (Illus.). 192p. 1982. pap. 1.95 (ISBN 0-448-16983-5, Pub. by Tempo). Ace Bks.

Dance with the Dead. Richard S. Prather. 1971. pap. 0.75 o.p. (T2424, GM). Fawcett World.

Dance with the Devil. D. Dwyer. pap. 0.95 o.s.i. (75-309). Lancer.

Dance With the Devil. Aleece Jacques. 320p. (Orig.). 1981. pap. 2.50 (ISBN 0-8439-0981-1, Leisure Bks). Nordon Pubns.

Dance Without Music. Peter Cheyney. LC 48-6150. (Red badge detective). 1948. Dodd, Mead.

Dancehall. Bernard F Conners. LC 82-17793. 1983. 14.95 (ISBN 0-672-52757-X). Bobbs-Merrill.

Dancer. Leland Frederick Cooley. LC 77-81040. 1978. 9.95 (ISBN 0-8128-2319-2). Stein and Day.

Dancer and the Friar: A Ballad in Prose. Eugene Paul Metour. LC 26-16194. George H. Doran Company.

Dancer Disappears. Andre Sax. (Illus.). 192p. 1982. pap. 2.25 (ISBN 0-441-13595-1, Pub. by Charter Bks). Ace Bks.

Dancer from Atlantis. Poul Anderson. LC 74-28256. 1971. N. Doubleday.

Dancer from the Dance. Andrew Holleran. 1979. pap. 2.95 (ISBN 0-553-12323-8). Bantam.

Dancer from the Dance: A Novel. Janet Burroway. LC 68-11523. 1968. Little, Brown.

Dancer from the Dance: A Novel. Andrew Holleran. LC 78-6600. 1978. 9.95 (ISBN 0-688-03357-1). Morrow.

Dancer in Darkness. David Stacton. LC 62-14265. 1962. Pantheon Books.

Dancer in the Shadows. Linda Wisdom. 192p. (Orig.). 1980. pap. 1.50 (ISBN 0-671-57049-8, Pub. by Silhouette Bks). S&S.

Dancer in Yellow. William Edward Norris. LC 7-33296. (Half-title: Appletons' town and country library, no. 190). 1896. D. Appleton and Company.

Dancer in Yellow. Elisabeth Ogilvie. LC 78-23852. 10.95 (ISBN 0-07-047600-4). McGraw-Hill.

Dancer of El Touran. Olive Lethbridge. LC 32-24058. 1932. L. MacVeagh, Dial Press, Inc.

Dancer of Fortune. John Munonye. (Africa Writers Series; 153). 1975. (ISBN 0-435-90153-2). Heinemann.

Dancer of Fortune. John Munoyne. (African Writers Ser.: No. 153). 256p. 1975. pap. text ed. 2.50 o.p. (ISBN 0-435-90153-2). Humanities.

Dancer of Tuluum. Marah Ellis Martin Ryan. LC 25-1016. 1924. A. C. McClurg & Co.

Dancer with One Leg: A Novel. Stephen Dobyns. 228p. 1983. 13.95 (ISBN 0-525-24169-8, 01354-410). Dutton.

Dancers. Hubert Parsons. LC 23-16387. 1923. A. A. Knopf.

Dancers & Lovers, a Novel. Robert Wolfson. 1974. (pbk.) 1.50. Warner Paperback Library.

Dancers at the End of Time. Michael Moorcock. LC 76-354798. Harper & Row.

Dancer's Cat. Celia Anna Nicholson. LC 26-663733. The Bobbs-Merrill Company.

Dancer's Death. Phil Davis. 176p. 1981. pap. 2.25 (ISBN 0-380-76612-4, 76612). Avon.

Dancers in Mourning. Margery Allingham. LC 75-44954. (Fifty Classics of Crime Fiction, 1900-1950; 2). 1976. 12.00. Garland Pub.

Dancers in Mourning. Margery Allingham. LC 37-20887. 1937. Doubleday, Doran & Company, Inc.

Dancers in Mourning. Margery Allingham. LC 39-257. 1938. The Sun Dial Press, Inc.

Dancers in Mourning. Margery Allingham. LC 42-17383. 1942. Triangle Books.

Dancers in the Afterglow. Jack L. Chalker. 1982. pap. 2.50 (ISBN 0-345-30493-4, Del Rey). Ballantine.

Dancers in the Dark. Dorothy Speare. LC 22-8045. George H. Doran Company.

Dancers in the Scalp House. William Eastlake. LC 75-16135. 1975. 10.00 (ISBN 0-670-25467-3). Viking Press.

Dancers in the Wind. Allan Eugene Updegraff. LC 25-20825. 1925. Boni & Liveright.

Dancers of Arum. Elizabeth A Lynn. (Berkley book). (Illus.). 1980. 1.95 (ISBN 0-425-04565-X). Berkley Pub Corp.

Dancers of Arun. Elizabeth A Lynn. LC 78-31536. (Illus.). 10.95. Berkley Pub. Corp.: Distributed by Putnam.

Dancers of Noyo. Margaret St. Clair. (Ace S-F). 1973. (pbk.) 0.95. Ace.

Dancers on the Shore. William Melvin Kelley. LC 72-95318. 1973. 7.50 (ISBN 0-911860-25-8). Chatham Bookseller.

Dances of Death: Short Stories on a Theme. Gillian Tindall. LC 72-96501. 1973. 6.95 (ISBN 0-8027-0426-3). Walker.

Dancing Aztecs. Donald E Westlake. (Fawcett Crest Book). 1977. 1.95 (ISBN 0-449-23395-2). Fawcett Books.

Dancing Bear. James Crumley. 256p. 1983. 12.95. Random.

Dancing Beggars. Eric Brett Young. LC 29-265731. 1929. J. B. Lippincott Company.

Dancing Dead. Eugene T omas. LC 33-967933. Sears Publishing Company.

Dancing Death... Christopher Bush. LC 31-246609. Pub. for the Crime Club, Inc., by Doubleday, Doran & Company, Inc.

Dancing Desire. Petronilla Clayton. LC 31-4176. International Fiction Library.

Dancing Detective. Cornell George Hopley-Woolrich. LC 46-4753. 1946. J. B. Lippincott Company.

Dancing Dodo. John E Gardner. LC 77-80888. 1978. 8.95 (ISBN 0-385-12462-7). Doubleday.

Dancing Doll. Frank Condon & Edholm, Charlton Lawrence, Joint Author. LC 27-1581. Barse & Hopkins.

Dancing Dollars. Ruth Hammitt Kauffman. LC 31-6864. The Penn Publishing Company.

Dancing Fakir, and Other Stories. John Seymour Eyton. LC 77-101810. (Short story index reprint series). (Illus.). 1969. Books for Libraries Press.

Dancing Fakir: And Other Stories. John Seymour Eyton. LC 22-14190. 1922. Longmans, Green and Co.

Dancing Feather: And Its Sequel Moris Graeme: or, The Cruise of the Sea-Slipper. Joseph Holt Ingraham. LC 7-10358. Williams Brother; Etc., Etc.

Dancing Feet. Rob Eden. LC 31-31664. Grosset & Dunlap.

Dancing Floor. John Buchan. LC 26-16356. 1926. Houghton Mifflin Company.

Dancing Floor. Michael M. McNamara. LC 77-20654. 7.95 (ISBN 0-517-53249-2). Crown Pubishers.

Dancing for Men. Robley Wilson, Jr. LC 82-2602. (Drue Heinz Literaure Prize Winner Ser.). vi, 154p. 1982. 12.95 (ISBN 0-8229-3466-3). U of Pittsburgh Pr.

Dancing Girl. Gladys Malvern. LC 59-132579. Macrae Smith.

Dancing Girl of Gilead. Annette Joelson. LC 30-547. 1930. Doubleday, Doran and Company, Inc.

Dancing Girl of Shamakha: And Other Asiatic Tales. Joseph Arthur Gobineau. Ed. by Fox, Helen Morgenthau. LC 26-7657. Harcourt, Brace and Company.

Dancing Girls and Other Stories. Margaret Eleanor Atwood. LC 82-10308. 14.50 (ISBN 0-671-24249-0). Simon and Schuster.

Dancing Hill. Sheila Holland. LC 78-55739. 1978. 1.50 (ISBN 0-87216-479-9). Playboy Press.

Dancing Horses. Helen Griffiths. LC 81-6762. 1982. 9.95 (ISBN 0-8234-0437-4). Holiday House.

Dancing Hours. Harold Ohlson. LC 17-2486. 1916. 1.25. John Lane.

Dancing in the Dark. Janet Hobhouse. LC 82-18620. 225p. 1983. 12.95 (ISBN 0-394-52940-5). Random.

Dancing in the Shadows. Anne Saunders. Ed. by Gene DeRoin. (Aston Hall Presents Ser.). (Orig.). 1980. pap. 1.50 (ISBN 0-89936-018-1). Aston Hall.

Dancing Lady. James Warner Bellah. LC 32-16962. Farrar & Rinehart, Incorporated.

Dancing Man. Edward Hannibal. LC 73-8226. 1973. 6.95 (ISBN 0-671-21595-7). Simon and Schuster.

Dancing Man. Philip Maitland Hubbard. LC 76-145630. 1971. 5.95. Atheneum.

Dancing-Master. Lillian Trimble Bradley. LC 14-9764. 1914. 0.75. Minden-Burkert Printing Co.

Dancing Mermaid. Jean Francis Webb. LC 52-8064. 1952. Bouregy & Curl.

Dancing Saints. Leslie Georgiana Cameron. LC 43-51203. 1943. Doubleday, Doran and Company, Inc.

Dancing Season. Carla Neggers. (Finding Mr. Right Ser.). 208p. 1983. pap. 2.75 (ISBN 0-380-82602-X, 82602X). Avon.

Dancing Star: A Novel. Berta Ruck. LC 23-13573. 1923. 2.00. Dodd, Mead and Company.

Dancing Tales. D. Allen. (Shorey Historical Ser.). 95p. Repr. of 1951 ed. pap. 3.95 (ISBN 0-8466-0287-3, SJS287). Shorey.

Dancing Waters. 1st Ed. Leontine A Schidlof-Fair. LC 56-123015. 1957. Vantage Press.

Dancing with a Tiger. Susan Morrow. LC 68-11773. 1968. Published for the Crime Club by Doubleday.

Dancing Years. Clarissa Ross, pseud. 288p. (Orig.). 1982. pap. 2.95 (ISBN 0-523-41183-9). Pinnacle Bks.

Danda. Nkem Nwankwo. (African Writers Ser.). 1970. pap. text ed. 5.50x (ISBN 0-435-90067-6). Heinemann Ed.

Dandelion Days. Henry Williamson. LC 30-10257. E. P. Dutton & Co., Inc.

Dandelion: Or, Out of the Shadows. Mary Evelyn Wood Lovejoy. LC 1552. F. T. Neely.

Dandelion Wine. Ray Bradbury. 1975. 10.95 (ISBN 0-394-49605-1). Knopf.

Dandelion Wine: A Novel. Ray Bradbury. LC 74-21285. 1975. 7.95 (ISBN 0-394-49605-1). Knopf: Distributed by Random House.

Dandelion Wine: A Novel. Ray Bradbury. LC 57-7824. 1957. Doubleday.

Dandelions. Coulson T Cade. LC 17-195073. 1917. A. A. Knopf.

Dandil: Stories from Iranian Life. Gholam-Hossein Sa'edi. Tr. by Robert Campbell et al from Farsi. LC 80-6042. 223p. 1981. 11.95 (ISBN 0-394-50511-5). Random.

Dandil: Stories from Iranian Life. Ghulam Husayn Saidi. LC 80-6042. 11.95 (ISBN 0-394-50511-5). Random House.

Dando and the Summer Palace. William Clive. LC 72-79518. 1975. (pbk.) 1.25 (ISBN 0-671-78822-1). Pocket Books.

Dando on Delhi Ridge. William Clive. LC 75-163407. (Illus.). 1971. 5.95. Putnam.

Dando Shaft! Donald Gilmore Calhoun. LC 65-22273. bds., 4.95. Stein & Day.

Dandruff in My Eyebrows. Robert B. Challenger. 3.00 o.p. Carlton.

Dandy. Peter Gethers. LC 77-15638. 8.95 (ISBN 0-525-08852-0). Dutton.

Dandy Hart. Cuthbert Hamilton Ellis. LC 48-6347. 1948. Macmillan Co.

Dandy in Aspic. 1st Amer. Ed. Derek Marlowe. LC 66-23814. 4.95. Putnam.

Dane Walraven. (A Tale of Old Boston) Luman Allen. LC 6-45. 1892. Donohue, Henneberry & Co.

Daneclere. Pamela Hill. LC 78-3969. 1978. 8.95 (ISBN 0-312-18215-5). St. Martin's Press.

Danesbury House. Ellen Price Wood. LC 52-50334. 1860. Harper.

Danesbury House. Ellen Price Henry Wood Wood. 1890. G. Munro.

Danesbury House. Ellen Price Henry Wood Wood. (On cover: Rialto series, no. 50). 1893. Rand, McNally & Company.

Danewood Legacy. Jasmine Cresswell. (Coventry Romance Ser.: No. 188). 224p. 1982. pap. 1.50 (ISBN 0-449-50290-2, Coventry). Fawcett.

Danger. LC 12-13898. 1.25. R. G. Badger.

Danger. Ernest Poole. LC 23-8358. 1923. The Macmillan Company.

Danger. Evans Wall. LC 33-2630. The Macaulay Company.

Danger Ahead. Joseph Thompson Shaw. LC 32-34676. The Mohawk Press.

Danger! And Other Stories. Arthur Conan Doyle. LC 19-1585. George H. Doran Company.

Danger at Black Dyke. Winifred Finlay. LC 68-31174. 1968. S. G. Phillips.

Danger at Bravo Key. 1st Amer. Ed. Ronald Johnston. LC 65-172523. 3.95. N. Y.

Danger at Cliff House: A Tale of Inspector Higgins. Cecil Freeman Gregg. LC 36-20145. The Dial Press.

Danger at Dahlkari. T. E Huff. LC 75-24850. 1975. 7.95 (ISBN 0-399-11607-9). Berkley Pub. Corp.: Distributed by Putnam.

Danger at Dahlkari. T. E Huff. (Berkley Medallion Book). 1977. 1.95 (ISBN 0-425-03448-8). Berkley Pub. Corp.

Danger at Hand. Anne-Marie Cox. LC 77-361274. (Aerial books: Intermediate level). 1976. 2.30. (ISBN 0-85997-190-2) (ISBN 0-85997-191-0). Chivers.

Danger Calling. Patricia Wentworth. LC 31-280443. 1931. J. B. Lippincott Company.

Danger, Dame at Work. Paul Muller. LC 68-26890. 1968. 3.95. Roy Publishers.

Danger: Dinosaurs! Richard Marsten. LC 53-10556. (Science fiction novel). 1953. Winston.

Danger: Explosive True Adventures of the Great Outdoors. Ben East. (Outdoor Life Bks). (Illus.). 1970. 6.50 o.p. (ISBN 0-87468-065-4, Dist. by Dutton). Popular Sci.

Danger Feeds My Fear. Michael Strong. LC 80-7565. 9.95 (ISBN 0-8027-5419-8). Walker.

Danger for Dr. Kerr. Annie L Gelsthorpe. 1975. 4.95. Avalon Books.

Danger for Nurse Vivian. Adelaide Humphries. (YA) 1979. 6.95 (Avalon). Bouregy.

Danger for the Baron. John Creasey. LC 73-93927. 1974. 5.95 (ISBN 0-8027-5297-7). Walker.

Danger for the Baron. Anthony Morris, pseud. LC 73-93927. 192p. 1974. 5.95 o.p. (ISBN 0-8027-5297-7). Walker & Co.

Danger from Deer, a Novel. 1st Ed. Vicki Baum. LC 51-9418. 1951. Doubleday.

Danger; Great Stories of Mystery and Suspense from the Saturday Evening Post. LC 67-10398. 1967. Curtis Books; Distributed by Doubleday, Garden City, N.Y.

Danger: Hospital Zone. (S340). 1968. Avon.

Danger: Hospital Zone. By Ursula Curtiss. Ursula Reilly Curtiss. LC 66-20513. (Red badge mystery). 1966. bds., 3.50. Dodd.

Danger-Human. Gordon R Dickson. LC 77-89082. 1970. 4.95. Doubleday.

Danger in Centerfield. Willie Mays & Jeff Harris. pap. 0.50 o.p. (F116). J L Pratt.

Danger in Eden: By Jennifer Ames Pseud. Maysie Greig. LC 50-8307. 1950. Bouregy & Curl.

Danger in Paradise. Octavus Roy Cohen. LC 46-4405. 1945. The Macmillan Company.

Danger in the Dark. Arthur Minturn Chase. LC 33-16361. 1933. Dodd, Mead & Company.

Danger in the Dark. Mignon Good Eberhart. LC 36-29839. 1936. Doubleday, Doran & Company, Inc.

Danger in the Dark. Mignon Good Eberhart. LC 38-6353. 1937. Doubleday, Doran & Company, Inc.

Danger in the Dark. Mignon Good Eberhart. 1973. (pbk.) 0.95. Popular Lib.

Danger in the Dark. J. E. Wood. 1966. 3.00 o.p. (ISBN 0-682-43128-1). Exposition.

Danger in the Dark: A Tale of Intrigue and Priestcraft. 10th ed. Isaac Kelso. LC 42-26495. 1855. H. M. Rulison, Queen City Publishing House.

Danger in the Deep. Pat Balmes & Julie Balmes. (Perspectives II Ser.). (Illus.). 48p. (gr. 7-12). 1982. pap. 2.50 (ISBN 0-87879-320-8). Acad Therapy.

Danger in the Wind. Margaret Eastvale. 1974. (pbk.) 0.95 (ISBN 0-671-77786-6). Pocket Books.

Danger! Keep Out. Edward Jay Nichols. LC 43-1143. 1943. Houghton Mifflin Company.

Danger Key. Nick Carter. (Nick Carter Ser). (O.s.i.). 192p. 1966. pap. 0.95 o.s.i. (AN1177, Award). Univ Pub & Dist.

Danger Light & Other Stories. Brian Harrison. (Readers Ser.: Stage 4). 1978. pap. text ed. 6.95 (ISBN 0-88377-090-3). Newbury Hse.

Danger Mark. Robert William Chambers. LC 9-24255. 1909. D. Appleton and Company.

Danger Mark. Robert William Chambers. LC 20-18812. 1919. D. Appleton and Company.

Danger Money. Mignon Good Eberhart. LC 74-9091. 1975. 5.95 (ISBN 0-394-49171-8). Random House.

Danger Money. Mignon Good Eberhart. 1976. (pbk.) 1.25. Popular Library.

Danger on the Moon. Michael X. 1970. pap. 3.00 o.p. Saucerian.

Danger Ou Cue. Rebecca Holland. (Raven House Mysteries Ser.). 224p. 1981. pap. 2.25 (ISBN 0-373-63002-6, Pub. by Worldwide). Harlequin Bks.

Danger Patrol. Wayne D. Overholser. LC 81-22837. 1982. 1.95 (ISBN 0-345-30388-1). Ballantine.

Danger Range. Westmoreland Gray. LC 33-14028. The Bobbs-Merrill Company.

Danger Road. Mark Saxton. LC 39-209539. Farrar & Rinehart, Inc.

Danger Signal. Phyllis Bottome. LC 39-174819. 1939. Little, Brown and Company.

Danger Song. Bryant Rollins. LC 67-10370. 1967. Doubleday.

Danger Trail. Johanas L. Bouma. (Orig.). 1981. pap. 1.95 (ISBN 0-505-51725-6). Tower Bks.

Danger Trail. Johanas L. Bouma. (O.s.i.). 1975. pap. 0.95 o.s.i. Tower.

Danger Trail. Max Brand. LC 40-10764. 1940. Dodd, Mead & Company.

Danger Trail. Forrest Raymond Brown. LC 34-36560. Loring & Mussey.

Danger Trail. James Oliver Curwood. LC 10-7478. The Bobbs-Merill Company.

Danger Trail. James Oliver Curwood. LC 30-12327. 1910. Grosset & Dunlap.

Danger Trail. James Oliver Curwood. LC 44-7716. 1944. Triangle Books.

Danger Trail. Frederick Faust. LC 76-40439. 1976. 6.95 (ISBN 0-88411-517-8). Aeonian Press.

Danger Trail. Robert J McCaig. LC 74-33742. (Double D western). 1975. 5.95 (ISBN 0-385-08878-7). Doubleday.

Danger Trail: A Western Novel. Johanas L Bouma. LC 55-17932. (Popular Library eagle books, EB29). 1954. Popular Library.

Danger Tree. Olivia Manning. LC 77-2435. 1977. 8.95 (ISBN 0-689-10802-8). Atheneum.

Danger Under the Moon. 1st Ed. Maurice Walsh. LC 56-11690. 1957. Lippincott.

Danger UXB. Michael Booker. LC 80-24788. 1980. 2.95 (ISBN 0-14-005852-4). Penguin Books.

Danger Valley. Richard Poole. 1969. pap. 0.60 o.p. (0502-06001-060). Curtis.

Danger Valley. Lee E Wells. LC 68-10590. (A Double D western). 1968. Doubleday.

Danger West! Robert J McCaig. LC 54-112435. (Silver star westerns). 1954. Dodd, Mead.

Danger Within. Michael Francis Gilbert. LC 52-7283. 1952. Harper.

Danger Within. Michael Francis Gilbert. (Perennial Library). 1978. (ISBN 0-06-080448-3). Harper & Row.

Danger Within. Ida Geneva Gibson McPherren. LC 42-6834.

Danger Zone. J. M. Flynn. (Inflation Fighters Ser.). 192p. 1982. pap. cancelled o.s.i. (ISBN 0-8439-1139-5, Leisure Bks). Nordon Pubns.

Danger Zone. J. M. Flynn. 1977. pap. 1.50 o.s.i. (ISBN 0-505-51171-1). Tower Bks.

Danger Zone. Pomroy Lee. LC 33-334543. Sears Publishing Company, Inc.

Danger Zone. Maurice Shadbolt. 206p. 1975. 11.45x (ISBN 0-340-20240-8). Intl Pubns Serv.

Dangerfield Talisman. Alfred Walter Stewart. LC 27-405439. 1927. Little, Brown, and Company.

Dangerford. Deirdre Stiles. (Belmont Tower Book). 1977. 1.75 (ISBN 0-505-51212-2). Tower Pubns.

Dangerous. Charlotte Lamb, pseud. (Harlequin Presents Ser.). 192p. 1981. pap. 1.75 (ISBN 0-373-10466-9). Harlequin Bks.

Dangerous Acquaintances. Choderlos De Laclos. Tr. by Richard Aldington from Fr. (Open University Set Text Ser.). (Orig.). 1979. pap. 9.00 (ISBN 0-7100-8858-2). Routledge & Kegan.

Dangerous Acquaintances. Translated by Richard Aldington. Pierre Ambroise Francois Choderlos De Laclos. LC 52-121385. (New Directions book). 1952. J. Laughlin.

Dangerous Age. Ann Rovick Larson. LC 60-510799. (Milestone book). Carlton Press.

Dangerous Age: Letters and Fragments from a Woman's Diary; Translated from the Danish of Karin Michaelis. Karin Michaelis. LC 11-22760. 1911. John Lane Company.

Dangerous Ages. Rose Macaulay. LC 21-15188. Boni and Liveright.

Dangerous American. A. E. Hotchner. LC 58-8762. 1958. Random House.

Dangerous Angel. 1st Ed. Clarence Budington Kelland. LC 54-6017. Harper.

Dangerous Assignment. Jennifer Blair. (Nora Kane Series). (candlelight romance#182)). (Illus.). 1975. (pbk.) 0.75. Dell.

Dangerous Business. Edwin Balmer. LC 27-21348. 1927. Dodd, Mead & Company.

Dangerous by Nature. 1st Ed. Manning Coles, pseud. LC 50-9688. 1950. Publishedfor the Crime Club by Doubleday.

Dangerous Cargo. Hulbert Footner. LC 34-23271. 1934. Harper & Brothers.

Dangerous Cat's-Paw. A Novel. David Christie Murray & Murray, Henry. (On cover: Seaside library. Pocket ed., no. 1177). 1889. G. Munro.

Dangerous Catspaw. David Christie Murray & Murray, Henry. LC 41-33246. 1889. Longmans, Green, and Co.

Dangerous Catspaw: A Novel. David Christie Murray & Murray, Henry. (On cover: Harper's Franklin square library, no. 641). 1889. Harper & Brothers.

Dangerous Corner, a Novel. Edith Holland & Priestley, John Boynton, 1894- Dangerous Corner. LC 33-2864. 1933. Doubleday, Doran & Company, Inc.

Dangerous Cruise. Maysie Greig. 1940. Doubleday, Doran & Company, Inc.

Dangerous Dandy. Barbara Cartland. LC 74-7438. 1974. (pbk.) 0.95. Bantam Books.

Dangerous Davies. Leslie Thomas. (Murder Ink Ser.: No. 39). 1982. pap. 2.25 (ISBN 0-440-12078-0). Dell.

Dangerous Days. Mary Roberts Rinehart. LC 19-10833. George H. Doran Company.

Dangerous Days. Mary Roberts Rinehart. 1921. Grosset & Dunlap.

Dangerous Days of Kiowa Jones. Clifton Adams. LC 63-12966. (Double D western). 1963. Doubleday.

Dangerous Dead. William Brandon. LC 43-2711. 1943. Dodd, Mead & Company.

Dangerous Deceits. Barbara Hazard. (Coventry Romance Ser.: No. 184). 224p. 1982. pap. 1.50 (ISBN 0-449-50286-4, Coventry). Fawcett.

Dangerous Deception. Lilian Peake. (Harlequin Romances Ser.). (Orig.). 1980. pap. 1.50 (ISBN 0-373-10353-0, Pub. by Harlequin). PB.

Dangerous Delight. Christine H. Cott. (Superromances Ser.). 384p. 1983. pap. 2.50 (ISBN 0-373-70050-4). Harlequin Bks.

Dangerous Delights. Andre Theurie & Robins, E. P., Tr. (On cover: Optimus series, no. 4). 1891. Donohue, Henneberry & Co.

Dangerous Design. Lawrence L. Goldman. LC 52-12725. 1952. Arcadia House.

Dangerous Designs. Laura C. Raef. 1981. pap. 6.95 (Avalon). Bouregy.

Dangerous Desire. Aaron Fletcher. 1978. pap. 2.25 (ISBN 0-532-22135-4). Woodhill.

Dangerous Dust. Kim Knight. LC 41-5438. Dodge Publishing Company.

Dangerous Embrace. Donna Vitek. (Candlelight Ecstasy Ser.: No. 136). (Orig.). 1983. pap. 1.95 (ISBN 0-440-12162-0). Dell.

Dangerous Enchantment. Marie Garratt. (ace gothic). 1974. (pbk.) 0.95. Ace Books.

Dangerous Encounter. Darwin Le Ora Teilhet. Orig. Title: Big Runaround. pap. 0.60 o.p. (53-450). Paperback Lib.

Dangerous Engagement. Caroline Courtney. LC 80-21816. 1980. 12.95 (ISBN 0-8161-3094-9). G. K. Hall.

Dangerous Flame. Joye Hockzema. LC 48-28214. 1948. Van Kampen Press.

Dangerous Funeral. Mary McMullen. LC 76-23777. 1977. 5.95 (ISBN 0-385-12344-2). Published for the Crime Club by Doubleday.

Dangerous Funeral. Mary McMullen. LC 81-271. 1981. 9.95 (ISBN 0-89621-269-6). Thorndike Press.

Dangerous Game. William Le Queux. LC 26-7767. The Macaulay Company.

Dangerous Game. Edmund Hodgson Yates. (On cover: Gill's select novels). 1875. W. F. Gill & Company.

Dangerous Games. Warren Murphy. (Destroyer Ser.: No. 40). 192p. (Orig.). 1980. pap. 1.95 (ISBN 0-523-41255-X). Pinnacle Bks.

Dangerous Games. Marta Randall. (Orig.). 1980. pap. 2.95 (ISBN 0-671-82417-1, Timescape). PB.

Dangerous Glamour. Marc Olden. 400p. (Orig.). 1982. pap. 2.95 (ISBN 0-449-14496-8, GM). Fawcett.

Dangerous Gold. Thomas Ernest Mount. LC 34-40671. 1934. W. Morrow & Co.

Dangerous Ground: Or, The Rival Detectives. (On cover: The detective and adventure library, no. 7). 1889. A. T. Loyd & Co.

Dangerous Ground: Or, The Rival Detectives. Emma Murdoch Van Deventer. LC 75-32764. (Literature of Mystery and Detection). (Series: The Great detective series.). (Illus.). 1976. 26.00 (ISBN 0-405-07885-4). Arno Press.

Dangerous Ground: Or, The Rival Detectives. Emma Murdoch Van Deventer. (Great detective series). 1885. A. T. Loyd & Co.

Dangerous Ground: Or, The Rival Detectives. Emma Murdoch Van Deventer. (library of choice fiction, no. 54). 1892. Laird & Lee.

Dangerous Ground: The Rival Detectives. Lawrence L. Lynch. LC 75-32764. (Literature of Mystery & Detection). (Illus.). 1976. Repr. of 1885 ed. 26.00 (ISBN 0-405-07885-4). Ayer Co.

Dangerous Harem. Thompson, John Burton. LC 52-14393. 1952. Arco Pub. Co.

Dangerous Haven. Shirley Hart. (Candlelight Ecstasy Ser.: No. 161). (Orig.). 1983. pap. 1.95 (ISBN 0-440-12032-2). Dell.

Dangerous Honeymoon: Translated from the Swedish Text and the Original Norwegian Manuscript. Axel Kielland & Hannay, Carolyn, Tr. LC 46-3945. 1946. Little, Brown and Company.

Dangerous Hour. Richard Blum & Eva Blum. 1970. 12.50 o.p. (ISBN 0-684-10027-4). Scribner.

Dangerous House. Jan Herbrand. 1975. (pbk.) 0.95 (ISBN 0-446-75719-5). Warner Paperback Library.

Dangerous Inheritance. Veronica Black. 1970. pap. 0.60 o.p. (ISBN 0-446-63457-3, 63-457). Paperback Lib.

Dangerous Inheritance. Georgina Ferrand. (Beagle great gothic). 1974. (pbk.) 0.95. Beagle Books.

Dangerous Inheritance: Or, The Mystery of the Titani Rubies. Izola Louise Forrester. LC 20-18931. 1920. Houghton Mifflin Company.

Dangerous Innocence. Victoria Lincoln. LC 58-6259. 1958. Rinehart.

Dangerous Islands. Mary Dolling Sanders O'Malley. LC 63-20997. 1963. McGraw-Hill.

Dangerous Isles, a Romance of Pearl-Hunger. Basil Carey. LC 28-28029. 1927. L. MacVeagh, The Dial Press.

Dangerous Journey. John Creasey. LC 73-81177. (MW suspense). 1974. 5.95 (ISBN 0-679-50485-0). D. McKay Co.

Dangerous Journeys, 1757. Parrish Wells. LC 41-6373. Free Press Printing Company.

Dangerous Lady. Barbara Hazard. 224p. (Orig.). 1980. pap. 1.75 (ISBN 0-449-50120-5, Coventry). Fawcett.

Dangerous Landing. Patricia McGerr. 1975. (pbk.) 0.95. Dell.

Dangerous Legacy. George Harmon Coxe. 1946. A. A. Knopf.

Dangerous Legacy. Willo Davis Roberts. (Orig.). 1972. pap. 0.95 o.s.i. (75-379). Lancer.

Dangerous Love. Jane Blackmore. 208p. (O.S.I.). 1973. lib. bdg. 4.95 o.s.i. (ISBN 0-7075-0102-4). White Lion Pubs.

Dangerous Magic. Frances Lynch. LC 77-17766. 8.95 (ISBN 0-312-18218-X). St. Martin's Press.

Dangerous Magic. Frances Lynch. 1979. 1.75 (ISBN 0-449-24157-2). Fawcett Crest Books.

Dangerous Marriage. Caroline Fothergill. J. S. Ogilvie and Company.

Dangerous Masquerade. Hermina Black. (Signet book). 1974. (pbk.) 0.95. New American Library.

Dangerous Memory. Lorena Ann Olmsted. 192p. (YA) 1974. 6.95 (Avalon). Bouregy.

Dangerous Memory. Lorena Ann Olmsted. (Avalon nurse romances). 1974. 4.50. Avalon Books.

Dangerous Mission. Bernard Alvin Palmer. LC 45-11434. 1945. Zondervan Publishing House.

Dangerous Mr. Dell. John Victor Turner. LC 35-9321. 1935. D. Appleton-Century Company, Incorporated.

Dangerous Month of May. Edward Henry Russell. LC 76-24130. 1970. 0.95. Pyramid Books.

Dangerous Music. Jessica T. Hagedorn. LC 75-32698. 1975. 10.00x o.p. (ISBN 0-917672-04-6); pap. 4.95x (ISBN 0-917672-03-8). Momos.

Dangerous Obsession. Natasha Peters. 634p. 1981. pap. 3.50 (ISBN 0-441-13705-9). Ace Bks.

Dangerous One: By Robert Ames Pseud. Cover Painting by James Meese. Charles Clifford. LC 55-15740. (Gold medal books, 435). 1954. Fawcett Publications.

Dangerous Paradise. Louise Bergstrom. 192p. (YA) 1975. 6.95 (Avalon). Bouregy.

Dangerous Paradise. Louise Bergstrom. 1975. 4.95. Avalon Books.

Dangerous Paradise. Carl Lyndon Bixby. LC 34-246341. The Macaulay Company.

Dangerous Passenger. Thomas Walsh. LC 58-7864. 1959. Little, Brown.

Dangerous Place to Die. David Wilson. (McCloud,#5). 1975. (pbk.) 0.95. Award Books.

Dangerous Quest. rev. ed. John Creasey. LC 73-83308. (His A Doctor Palfrey thriller). 1974. 5.95 (ISBN 0-8027-5282-9). Walker.

Dangerous Rapture. Sue Peters. (Harlequin Romances Ser.). 192p. 1982. pap. 1.50 (ISBN 0-373-02471-1). Harlequin Bks.

Dangerous Situation. Louis Tracy. LC 32-2876. E. J. Clode, Inc.

Dangerous Splendor. Lucy Fuchs. (YA) 1978. 6.95 (Avalon). Bouregy.

Dangerous Stranger. Marian Martin. 1981. pap. 1.75 (ISBN 0-8439-8024-9, Tiara Bks). Nordon Pubns.

Dangerous Summer. J. H. Rhodes. (YA) 1980. 6.95 (Avalon). Bouregy.

Dangerous to Know. Marian Babson. LC 80-54820. 1981. 9.95 (ISBN 0-8027-5442-2). Walker.

Dangerous to Me. Rae Foley. 1974. (pbk.) 0.95. Dell.

Dangerous Visions. Ed. by Harlan Ellison. (Signet Book). (Illus.). 1975. (pbk.) 1.95. New American Library.

Dangerous Visions; 33 Original Stories. Harlan Ellison. LC 67-19078. (Doubleday science fiction). (Illus.). 1967. Doubleday.

Dangerous Water. Elwyn Whitman Chambers. LC 41-3114. 1941. Doubleday, Doran & Co., Inc.

Dangerous Waters. Berta LaVan Barker. (YA) 1978. 6.95 (Avalon). Bouregy.

Dangerous Woman. Sharon Steele. 384p. (Orig.). 1981. pap. 2.95 (ISBN 0-446-93470-4). Warner Bks.

Dangerous Woman & Other Stories. James Thomas Farrell. 8.95 (ISBN 0-8149-0094-1). Vanguard.

Dangerous Worlds. facs. ed. Joan O'Donovan. LC 72-75783. (Short Story Index Reprint Ser). 1958. 12.00 (ISBN 0-8369-3008-8). Ayer Co.

Dangerous Worlds, Stories and Tales. Joan O'Donovan. LC 58-2442. 1958. W. Morrow.

Dangerous Worlds: Stories and Tales. Joan O'Donovan. LC 72-75783. (Short story index reprint series). 1969. Books for Libraries Press.

Dangerous Years. John Harris. LC 78-72964. 1979. 8.95 (ISBN 0-689-10945-8). Atheneum.

Dangerous Years. Max Hennessy, pseud. 1979. 8.95 (ISBN 0-689-10945-8). Atheneum.

Dangerous Years: A Trilogy. Gilbert Frankau. LC 38-27041. 1938. E. P. Dutton & Co., Inc.

Dangerous Years. 1st American Ed. Richard Church. LC 58-5240. 1958. Dutton.

Dangerous Young Man. George Frank Worts. LC 40-87493. 1940. H. C. Kinsey & Company, Inc.

Dangers of Dining Out: Or, Hints to Those Who Would Make Home Happy. Sarah Stickney Ellis. LC 42-28862. 1873. D. Appleton and Company.

Dangerville Inheritance. Arthur Charles Fox-Davies. LC 6-40211. 1907. J. Lane.

Dangler. Charles Gaines. LC 79-29744. (Illus.). 11.95 (ISBN 0-671-25281-X). Simon and Schuster.

Dangling Man. Saul Bellow. LC 44-3681. 1944. The Vanguard Press.

Daniel Airlie: A Novel. Robert Smythe Hichens. LC 37-25345. 1937. Doubleday, Doran & Company, Inc.

Daniel Boone, Backwoodsman. Charles Harcourt Ainslie Forbes-Lindsay. LC 8-24465. 1908. J. B. Lippincott Company.

Daniel Boone: Westward Trail. Neal Barrett, Jr. (American Explorer Ser.: No. 4). (Orig.). 1982. pap. 2.75 (ISBN 0-440-01654-1, Standish). Dell.

Daniel Defoe, 1660-1731: Commemoration in Stoke Newington of the Tercentenary of His Birth: an Exhibition of Books, Pamphlets, Views, and Portraits and Other Items Presented by the Public Libraries Committee, 7th to 28th May, 1960. Stoke Newington, Eng. Public Libraries. LC 78-21253. 1978. 8.50 (ISBN 0-8414-9710-9). Folcroft Library Editions.

Daniel Deronda. George Eliot. LC 61-1546. (Harper torchbooks. The Academy library, TB1039). (Illus.). 1961. Harper.

Daniel Deronda. George Eliot. LC 42-1413. (Companion books). Hurst & Company.

Daniel Deronda. George Eliot. LC 6-40739. (Added t.-p.,: Novels of George Eliot, v. 8-9). 1876. Harper & Brothers.

Daniel Deronda. George Eliot. (On cover:Seaside library. Pocket ed., no. 34). 1883. G. Munro.

Daniel Deronda. George Eliot. LC 18-434901. (On cover: The Astar prose series). 1917. Thomas Y. Crowell Company.

Daniel Deronda. George Eliot. LC 1-29907. (Half-title: The works of George Eliot. Foleshill edition). 1900. Little, Brown and Company.

Daniel Deronda. George Eliot & Barbara Nathan Hardy. LC 75-308776. (Penguin English library). 1974-1975. 3.95 (ISBN 0-14-043020-2). Penguin Books.

Daniel Deronda. George Eliot & Barbara Nathan Hardy. LC 75-308776. (Penguin English library). 1967. (0.95, 3.95 u.s.) (ISBN 0-14-043020-2). Penguin Books.

Daniel Deronda... Biographical Introduction. George Eliot. LC 1-31173. (Personal edition of George Eliot's works). 1901. Doubleday, Page & Co.

Daniel Deronda. Ed., Introd. by Barbara Hardy. George Eliot. Ed. by Barbara Hardy. (EL20). 1967. pap., 1.95. Penguin.

Daniel Du Luth: Or, Adventuring on the Great Lakes; Bieng the Tale Told by Young Paul Douay of the Long Journey He Made in Indian Canoes in the Company of Daniel Greysolon Du Luth, from Montreal Throught the Great Lakes to Lake Superior, in Quest of His Sister Stolen by the Indians When a Babe...As Set Down in English by Everett McNeil. Everett McNeil. LC 26-15269. E. P. Dutton & Company.

Daniel Everton, Volunteer-Regular: A Romance of the Philippines. Israel Putnam. LC 2-12950. 1902. Funk & Wagnalls Company.

Daniel Hovey: Supposed to Be a Posthumous Romance, of Unknown Authorship, the Manuscript of Which Was Discovered in a Very Peculiar Manner. Ed. by Thomas Bottomley Morton. LC 1-30793. 1901. F. W. Allsopp.

Daniel Martin. John Fowles. LC 77-23343. 12.00 (ISBN 0-316-28959-0). Little, Brown.

Daniel Martin. John Fowles. 1978. 1.95 (ISBN 0-451-08249-4). New American Library.

Daniel North of Wyoming Valley. Samuel Robert Smith. LC 26-22327. 1897. R. Baur & Son.

Daniel Poldertot. A Story, Wherein Is Carefully Recorded the Interesting Adventures of Uncled Dan and His Faithful Friends, Mr. Robert Sturdy, Mr. Harry Cribbler, and Mr. Richard Doolittel. I. E Diekenga. LC 6-36830. 1882. J. H. Earle.

Daniel Quayne, a Morality. Joseph Smith Fletcher. LC 26-20139. 1926. George H. Doran Company.

Daniel Quorm: And His Religious Notions. Mark Guy Pearse. LC 7-33500. 1876. Nelson & Phillips.

Daniel Sweetland. Eden Phillpotts. LC 6-17873. 1906. The Authors and Newspapers Association.

Daniel Trentworthy. A Tale of the Great Fire of Chicago. John McGovern... John McGovern. 1889. Rand, McNally & Company.

Daniel Webster's Horses. Elizabeth Jane Coatsworth. LC 78-130966. (American folk tales). (A Reading shelf book). (Illus.). 1971. 2.39 (ISBN 0-8116-4025-6). Garrard Pub. Co.

Daniele Cortis: A Novel. Antonio Fogazzaro & Tilton, Caroline, "Mrs. J. R. Tilton," Tr. LC 6-41426. (Leisure hour series, no. 202). 1887. H. Holt and Company.

Danira: Ein Gottesurtheil . Elisabeth Burstenbinder. Tr. by Safford, Mary Joanna. LC 7-362302. (On cover: Globe library, no. 75). 1888. Rand, McNally & Company.

Danites in the Sierras. Joaquin Miller. LC 7-25984. 1881. Jansen, McClurg & Company.

Danites in the Sierras. Joaquin Miller. LC 7-25985. (On cover: The household library, v. 6, no 2). 1889. Belford-Clarke Co.

Danju Gig. Carolyn Weston. LC 77-85635. 1969. 4.95. Random House.

Dan'l Boone Kissed Me. Felix Holt. LC 54-5830. 1954. Dutton.

Dannus 1. Mike Sirota. (Prisoner of Reglathium Ser.). 1978. pap. 2.25. Woodhill.

Dannus 2: The Conquerors of Reglathium. Mike Sirota. pap. 2.25 (ISBN 0-532-22125-7). Woodhill.

Dannus 5: The Slaves of Reglathium, 5 pts. Mike Sirota. 1978. pap. 2.25 (ISBN 0-532-22134-6). Woodhill.

Danny. Sara Brown Cunningham. LC 53-9966. 1953. Crown.

Danny. Alfred Ollivant. LC 2-25926. 1902. Doubleday, Page & Company.

Danny and the Boys: Being Some Legends of Hungry Hollow. John Donaldson Voelker. LC 51-2133. 1951. World Pub. Co.

Danny, Delinquent. Rhoda Helen Jefferson. LC 57-42857. 1957. Leecraft Print Co.

Danny's Own Story. Don Marquis. LC 12-352382. 1912. 1.20. Doubleday, Page & Company.

Dans Le Murmure Des Vagues. Flora Kidd. (Collection Harlequin). 192p. 1983. pap. 1.95 (ISBN 0-373-49334-7). Harlequin Bks.

Dan's Ministry. Lewis Erwin Finney. LC 11-519006. Broadway Publishing Co.

Danse de Gengis Cohn see Frere Ocean.

Danse Macabre. Stephen King. 1982. pap. 6.95 (ISBN 0-425-05345-8). Berkley Pub.

Dante & Gentucca: A Love Story. Clayton C Barbeau. LC 75-318418. (Yes! Capra chapbook series; 19). (Illus.). 1974. 1.95 (ISBN 0-912264-95-0) (ISBN 0-912264-94-2). Capra Press.

Danube Runs Red. Ben Haas. LC 68-28576. 1968. 4.95. Random House.

Danube Runs Red. Richard Meade, pseud. LC 68-28576. 1968. 4.95 o.p. Random.

Danvers Jewels and Sir Charles Danvers. Mary Cholmondeley. LC 26-23570. (Harper's Franklin square library. no. 669). 1890. Harper & Brothers.

Danvers Jewels and Sir Charles Danvers. Mary Cholmondeley. LC 6-209719. 1900. Harper & Brothers.

Danvis Folks. Rowland Evans Robinson. 1894. Houghton, Mifflin and Company.

Danvis Folks. Rowland Evans Robinson. LC 4-19008. Houghton, Mifflin and Company.

Danvis Folks, and A Hero of Ticonderoga. Rowland Evans Robinson & Perkins, Liewellyn Rood, Ed. LC 35-67680. The Tuttle Company.

Danvis Pioneer: A Story of One of Ethan Allen's Green Mountain Boys. Rowland Evans Robinson. LC 1564. 1900. Houghton, Mifflin and Company.

Dany & Pleasure. Tr. by L. E. LaBan. (Orig.). pap. 1.75 o.p. (3018). Brandon.

Danza Mitica. John Benteen. Tr. by E. Caballero. (Compadre Collection, Sundnace Ser: No. 6). 1976. pap. 0.95 (ISBN 0-88473-536-2). Fiesta Pub.

Danziger Transcript. Carl Fick. (YA) 1971. 6.95 o.p. (ISBN 0-399-10192-6). Putnam.

Danziger Transcript. Carl Fick. 1974. (pbk.) 1.50. Dell.

Danziger Transcript: A Novel. Carl Fick. LC 75-174634. 1971. 6.95. Putnam.

Daphne. Sarah Carlisle. (Coventry Romance Ser.: No. 67). 224p. 1980. pap. 1.75 (ISBN 0-449-50098-5, Coventry). Fawcett.

Daphne. A Novel. Eliza M. J. Humphreys. (Seaside library, v. 36, no. 749). 1880. G. Munro.

Daphne Adeane. Maurice Baring. LC 27-5841. 1927. Harper & Brothers.

Daphne Adzane. Maurice Baring. 1926. 25.00 (ISBN 0-8274-2142-7). R West.

Daphne, an Autumn Pastoral. Margaret Pollock Sherwood. LC 3-28588. 1903. Houghton, Mifflin & Company.

Daphne and Her Lad. Mary Julia Lagen & Ryland, Cally Thomas. LC 4-15366. 1904. H. Holt and Company.

Daphne Bruno. Ernest Raymond. LC 25-257607. 1925. Cassell and Company, Ltd.

Daphne Bruno. Ernest Raymond. LC 26-6908. George H. Doran Company.

Daphne Deane. Grace Livingston Hill. 1937. 2.95 o.p. (ISBN 0-448-05219-9). G&D.

Daphne Deane, No. 19. Grace L. Hiel. 192p. 1982. pap. 2.25 (ISBN 0-553-22533-2). Bantam.

Daphne Deane: A Novel. Grace Livingston Hill. LC 37-27431. J. B. Lippincott Company.

Daphne in Fitzroy Street. Edith Nesbit Bland. LC 9-4957. 1909. Doubleday, Page & Company.

Daphne Winslow. Elisabeth Finley Thomas. LC 33-170053. Farrar & Rinehart, Incorporated.

Daphne's in Love. Negley Farson. LC 27-17808. 2.00. The Century Co.

Daphnis & Chloe. Tr. by Thornley, George, B. Tr. by Gaselee, Stephen. LC 17-14. (Loeb Classical Library). (Half-title: The Loeb classical library). 1916. W. Heinemann.

Daphnis and Chloe ... LC 4-16441. 1587. Printed by Robert Waldegraue ..

Daphnis and Chloe. Longus. Tr. by Christopher Collins. LC 71-185233. (Illus.). 1972. 40.00 (ISBN 0-87636-028-2). Imprint Society.

Daphnis & Chloe. Longus. LC 68-2113. (Penguin classics). 1968. Penguin Books.

Daphnis & Chloe. Longus. Tr. by Paul Turner. LC 68-118815. (Penguin classics, L59). 1968. Penguin.

Daphnis & Chloe see Three Greek Romances.

Dappled Stallion. Jennie U. Grimstad. 1970. 3.50 o.p. Carlton.

Dar. Vladimir Vladimirovich Nabokov. (Rus.). 1979. pap. 9.00 (ISBN 0-88233-195-7). Ardis Pubs.

Dar. Vladimir Vladimirovich Nabokov. 1975. 12.00 o.p. (ISBN 0-88233-194-9). Ardis Pubs.

Dara, the Cypriot. Louis Paul. LC 58-13174. 1959. Simon and Schuster.

D'Arblay Mystery. Richard Austin Freeman. LC 26-16198. 1926. Dodd, Mead and Company.

Darby and Joan. Maurice Baring. LC 36-27073. 1936. A. A. Knopf.

Darby O'Gill and the Good People. Herminie Templeton Kavanagh. LC 3-10795. 1903. McClure, Phillips & Co.

Darby O'Gill and the Good People. Herminie Templeton Kavanagh. LC 33-2868. 1932. G. P. Putnam's Sons.

Darby Trial. Dick Pearce, pseud. LC 54-10697. 1954. Lippincott.

Darconville's Cat. Alexander Theroux. LC 80-629. 1981. 15.95 (ISBN 0-385-15951-X). Doubleday.

Darcourt: A Novel. Isabelle Holland. LC 76-4830. 8.95 (ISBN 0-679-40133-4). Weybright and Talley.

Darcourt: A Novel. Isabelle Holland. (Fawcett Crest Book). 1977. 1.75 (ISBN 0-449-23224-7). Fawcett Publications.

Darcourt: A Novel of Suspense. Isabelle Holland. 304p. 1976. 8.95 o.p. (ISBN 0-679-40133-4, Weybright). McKay.

D'Arcy of the Guards: Or, The Fortunes of War. Louis Evan Shipman. LC 99-1901. 1899. H. S. Stone and Company.

Darcy Pinckney. Susanna Shulrick Hayne Pinckney. LC 6-38356. 1906. The Neale Publishing Company.

Dardanelles Derelict: A Major North Story. Francis Van Wyck Mason. LC 49-116795. 1949. Doubleday.

Dare. Philip Jose Farmer. (Berkley book). 1979. 1.95 (ISBN 0-425-03953-6). Berkley Pub. Corp.

Dare. Philip Jose Farmer. LC 80-19672. (Series: Gregg Press Science Fiction Series.). 1980. 11.95 (ISBN 0-8398-2621-4). Gregg Press.

Dare. Mary W Glascock. LC 6-43967. 1882. The California Publishing Company.

Dare Devil Pat: Or, The Dashing Rider of the Plains. Harlan Page Halsey. 1872. Independent News Company.

Dare Fairfax. Ada Augusta Gott. LC 6-27638. 1872. E. J. Hale & Son.

Dare to Be Happy. Helen Lowrie Marshall. 1962. 3.50 o.p. (ISBN 0-385-08272-X). Doubleday.

Dare to Dream. Alice M Dodge. 1975. 4.95. Avalon Books.

Dare to Dream. Alice Marie Dodge. LC 37-16931. Arcadia House.

Dare to Love. Glenna Finley, pseud. (Signet Book). 1977. 1.50 (ISBN 0-451-07491-2). New American Library.

Dare to Love. Jennifer Wilde. 560p. (Orig.). 1983. pap. 3.95 (ISBN 0-446-30590-1). Warner Bks.

Daredevil. Rosemary Carter. (Harlequin Presents Ser.). 192p. 1983. pap. 1.75 (ISBN 0-373-10560-6). Harlequin Bks.

Daredevil. Leslie Charteris. LC 29-19786. 1929. Pub. for The Crime Club, Inc., by Doubleday, Doran & Company, Inc.

Daredevil. Maria Thompson Daviess. LC 16-6436. 1.35. The Reilly & Britton Co.

Daredevil Douglass. Amos Moore. LC 35-261227. The Macaulay Company.

Daredevil Heart. Rob Eden. LC 44-5020. 1944. Gramercy Publishing Co.

Dareford. Herbert Edward Bogue. LC 7-15597. 1907. The C. M. Clark Publishing Co.

Darff and His New England Neighbors. Daniel W Howell. LC 35-15317. R. G. Lord.

Dariel: A Romance of Surrey. Richard Doddridge Blackmore. LC 6-13861. (On cover: Seaside library. Pocket ed., no. 625). 1897. Dodd, Mead and Company.

Darien: Or, The Merchant Prince. A Historical Romance. Eliot Warburton. LC 19-2908. 1852. Harper & Brothers.

Darien Venture. Frank Gill Slaughter. 1976. Repr. of 1955 ed. lib. bdg. 15.45x (ISBN 0-89190-532-4). Am Repr-Rivercity Pr.

Darien Venture: By C. V. Terry Pseud. 1st Ed. Frank Gill Slaughter. LC 55-7664. 1955. Hanover House.

Daring Abduction: Or, Nat Ridley's Biggest Fight. Nat Jr Ridley. LC 26-130471. (His Nat Ridley series--5). 1926. Garden City Publishing Co., Inc.

Daring Deeds of Daring Men. A Collection of Graphic Accounts of Deeds of Individual Heroism, Hair-Breadth Escapes, Acts of Bravery, Strategic Movements, and Other Exciting Adventures of the Great Wars of Modern Times. George L Kilmer. (On cover: Leisure-time series. no. 2). W. D. Rowland.

Daring Donald McKay: Or, The Last War Trail of the Modocs. Thomas Augustus Edwards. Ed. by Roland Keith Clark & Donna Clark. LC 74-184573. (Oregon Historical Society Reprint Series). (Illus.). 1971. (ISBN 0-87595-032-9). Oregon Historical Society.

Daring Experiment, and Other Stories. Lillie Devereux Blake. Lovell, Coryell & Company.

Daring Heart. Caroline Courtney. 224p. (Orig.). 1982. pap. 1.95 (ISBN 0-446-90963-7). Warner Bks.

Daring Young Man on the Flying Trapeze and Other Stories. William Saroyan. 1934. Random House.

Daring Young Man on the Flying Trapeze and Other Stories. William Saroyan. LC 41-515363. (Half-title: The modern library of the world's best books). 1941. The Modern Library.

Dario, 1925-1945: A Fictitious Reminiscence. Percy Winner. LC 47-3538. Harcourt.

Dark. Max Franklin, pseud. (Signet Book). (Illus.). 1.75 (ISBN 0-451-08242-7). New American Library.

Dark. James Herbert. 1980. pap. 2.95 (ISBN 0-451-09403-4, E9403, Sig). NAL.

Dark. John McGahern. LC 82-18602. 1983. 4.95 (ISBN 0-14-006237-8). Penguin Books.

Dark. John McGahern. 1966. 3.95 o.p. Knopf.

Dark Abyss. Clifford Knight. LC 49-7019. (Guilt edged mystery)). 1949. E. P. Dutton.

Dark Adventure. Augustus Muir. LC 33-5776. 1933. G. P. Putnam's Sons.

Dark Adventure. Howard Pease. LC 50-10044. 1950. Doubleday.

Dark and Bloody Ground. Betsey Beeler Creekmore. LC 67-12664. (Illus.). 1967. Fell.

Dark & Brilliant Places. Sondra Till Robinson. 1977. pap. 1.75 o.p. (ISBN 0-515-04107-6). BJ Pub Group.

Dark & Deadly Love. Elaine Evans. 1972. Repr. text ed. 0.95 o.s.i. Lancer.

Dark and Lonely Hiding Place. Edith P Begner. 1977. 1.95 (ISBN 0-380-01742-3). Avon Books.

Dark and Lonely Hiding Place. Edith P Begner. LC 68-14044. 1968. Bobbs-Merrill.

Dark and Secret Place. Margaret Summerton. LC 76-42404. 1977. 6.95 (ISBN 0-385-12476-7). Published for the Crime Club by Doubleday.

Dark and Secret Place. Margaret Summerton. 1978. 1.75 (ISBN 0-380-41301-9). Avon Books.

Dark & the Light: Erica & la Garibaldina, Two Short Novels. Elio Vittorini. Tr. by Frances Keene. LC 77-23993. 1977. Repr. of 1961 ed. lib. bdg. 17.25x (ISBN 0-8371-9780-5, VIDL). Greenwood.

Dark Angel. Sean Forestal. (Orig.). 1982. pap. 3.25 (ISBN 0-440-12033-0). Dell.

Dark Angel. Ruby Jean Jensen. 1978. pap. 1.95 (ISBN 0-532-19205-2). Woodhill.

Dark Angel. Gina Kaus. Tr. by Paul, Eden. LC 34-5293. 1934. The Macmillan Company.

Dark Angel Riding. Warren T. Longtree. (Ruff Justice Ser.: No. 7). 1982. pap. 2.50 (ISBN 0-451-11882-0, AE1882, Sig). NAL.

Dark Angel: Translated by Naomi Walford. Mika Toimi Waltari. LC 52-13647. 1953. Putnam.

Dark Arbor. Ione Sandberg Shriber. LC 40-31345. Farrar and Rinehart, Inc.

Dark Are the Shadows. Bernard Alvin Palmer. LC 46-746939. 1945. Zondervan Publishing House.

Dark Arena. Mario Puzo. LC 55-5798. Random House.

Dark Arena: A Novel. Mario Puzo. (Fawcett Crest Book). 1977. 1.95 (ISBN 0-449-23295-6). Fawcett Pubns.

Dark As the Grave Wherein My Friend Is Laid. Malcolm Lowry. Ed. by Douglas Day & Margerie Bonner Lowry. LC 68-26029. 1968. New American Library.

Dark at Noon. Jill Tattersall. LC 80-14123. 1980. 10.95 (ISBN 0-89340-271-0). J. Curley.
Dark Avenues, and Other Stories. Ivan Alekseevich Bunin. LC 76-23875. (Classics Russian literature). (Hyperion library of world literature). 1977. 10.50. (ISBN 0-88355-479-8) (ISBN 0-88355-480-1). Hyperion Press.
Dark Backward. Marie Buchanan. LC 74-30601. 1975. 7.95 (ISBN 0-698-10654-7). Coward, McCann & Geoghegan.
Dark Bahama. Peter Cheyney. LC 51-9129. (Red badge detective). 1951. Dodd, Mead.
Dark Bayou. Juanita Tyree Osborne. (YA) 1980. 6.95 (Avalon). Bouregy.
Dark Before the Rising Sun. Laurie McBain. 528p. 1982. pap. 3.95 (ISBN 0-380-79848-4, 79848). Avon.
Dark Beginnings: The Education of a Lady Doctor, 1875-1918. Katrinka Blickle. LC 77-80877. 1978. 8.95 (ISBN 0-385-12750-2). Doubleday.
Dark Below. Michael T Hinkemeyer. (Fawcett gold medal book). 1975. (pbk.) 0.95. Fawcett.
Dark Beneath the Pines. Lois Dwight Cole. LC 73-7181. 1974. 6.95. Hawthorn Books.
Dark Between the Stairs. Jane Blackmore. (Jane Blackmore Ser.: No. 5). 288p. 1981. pap. 2.25 (ISBN 0-441-13762-8). Ace Bks.
Dark Between the Stars. Poul Anderson. 224p. 1981. pap. 2.25 (ISBN 0-425-04291-X). Berkley Pub.
Dark Birds. Bert Meyers. 1968. 3.95 o.p. Doubleday.
Dark Blood, Dark Terror. Brian Talbot Cleeve. LC 65-21260. 1966. bds., 3.95. Random.
Dark Blue and Dangerous. Jonathan Ross. LC 81-4791. 1981. 9.95 (ISBN 0-684-17021-3). Scribner.
Dark Border: The Lost Prince, Vol. I. Paul E. Zimmer. LC 82-80426. 352p. (Orig.). 1982. pap. 2.95 (ISBN 0-86721-147-4). Playboy Pbks.
Dark Boundary. Anne Purdy. LC 54-9137. 1954. Vantage Press.
Dark Bridwell. Vardis Fisher. 1979. write for info. (ISBN 0-918522-58-7); pap. 5.95. O L Holmes.
Dark Bridwell: By Vardis Fisher... Vardis Fisher. LC 31-14419. 1931. Houghton Mifflin Company.
Dark Bright Water. Patricia Wrightson. 192p. 1981. pap. 2.25 (ISBN 0-345-29486-6, Del Rey). Ballantine.
Dark Brotherhood & Others. Howard Phillips Lovecraft. 5.00 o.p. Arkham.
Dark Brown Is the River. John Maxtone-Graham. LC 75-42365. (O.s.i.). 375p. 1976. 9.95 o.s.i. (ISBN 0-02-582360-4, 58236). Macmillan.
Dark Canyon. Tex Holt, pseud. 1948. Phoenix Press.
Dark Canyon. Louis L'Amour. LC 63-19055. 1963. Bantam Books.
Dark Canyon: A Novel. Walter Leslie River & Wead, Frank Wilber. LC 35-342685. 1935. Frederick A. Stokes Company.
Dark Carnival. Ray Bradbury. LC 47-24598. 1947. Arkham House.
Dark Carnival. Maysie Greig. LC 50-12635. 1950. Random House.
Dark Castle-Silver Strand. Jean English. (Orig.). 1973. pap. 0.75 o.p. (ISBN 0-345-20735-1). Beagle Bks.
Dark Cavalier. Virginia Rath. LC 38-13401. 1938. Pub. for the Crime Club, Inc., by Doubleday, Doran & Co., Inc.
Dark Cedars. Ann Fenton. 1970. pap. 0.75 o.p. (ISBN 0-447-74680-4). Lancer.
Dark Chamber. Leonard Cline. LC 27-18256. 1927. The Viking Press.
Dark Chapter: A Comedy of Class Distinctions. E. J. Rath. LC 24-20556. 1924. G. H. Watt.
Dark Cloud. Thomas Alexander Boyd. LC 24-20723. 1924. C. Scribner's Sons.
Dark Colleen. Harriett Jay. LC 7-10173. (Lovell's library, v. 1, no. 17). J. W. Lovell Company.
Dark Colleen. Harriett Jay. LC 21-13970. (Seaside library, v. 68, no. 1374). 1882. G. Munro.
Dark Comes Early, an American Novel. Pendleton Hogan. LC 34-34745. 1934. I. Washburn.
Dark Comet. Elaine Kimmelman. 1983. pap. 4.95 (ISBN 0-380-81828-0, 81828-0). Avon.
Dark Command: A Kansas Iliad. William Riley Burnett. LC 38-9507. 1938. A. A. Knopf.
Dark Companions. Ramsey Campbell. LC 81-19294. 12.95 (ISBN 0-02-521090-4). Macmillan Pub. Co.
Dark Conquest. William Heyliger. LC 36-9858. 1936. D. Appleton-Century Century Company, Incorporated.
Dark Continent. Richard Sullivan. LC 43-17657. 1943. Doubleday, Doran and Co., Inc.
Dark Corner. Celia Dale. LC 73-161100. 1972. 4.95 (ISBN 0-8027-0351-8). Walker.
Dark Corner. Zach McGhee. LC 8-34812. The Grafton Press.
Dark Corner. Vaclav Rezac. Tr. by Iris Urwin. (Orig.). 1963. pap. 2.50 o.p. (C192). Vanous.
Dark Corner: A Mystery Story. Marie Blizard. LC 50-5306. 1950. Mill.
Dark Crusade. Karl Edward Wagner. 224p. (Orig.). 1983. pap. 2.95 (ISBN 0-446-30679-7). Warner Bks.
Dark Crusade. Karl Edward Wagner (ISBN 0-446-88154-6). Warner Books.
Dark Crusade: A Novel by James M. Fox Pseud. 1st Ed. James M. W. Knipscheer. LC 54-5105. 1953. Brown.
Dark Crystal: A Novel. A. C. H Smith. LC 82-3101. (Illus.). 3.95 (ISBN 0-03-062436-3). Henson Organization Pub.: Holt, Rinehart and Winston.
Dark Cypress. Edwina Noone. 1975. (pbk.) 0.95. Ace Books.
Dark Dame. Wilson Collison. LC 35-4330. C. Kendall & W. Sharp, Inc.
Dark Dancer. Frederic Prokosch. LC 64-11268. 1964. Farrar, Straus.
Dark Dancer. Balachandra Rajan. LC 58-9044. 1958. Simon and Schuster.
Dark Dancer: A Novel. Balachandra Rajan. LC 74-90915. 1970. Greenwood Press.
Dark Dancer, a Novel. Balachandra Rajan. Repr. of 1958 ed. lib. bdg. 15.75x (ISBN 0-8371-3139-1, RADD). Greenwood.
Dark Danger. Sydney Horler. 1945. Mystery House.
Dark Darragh. Edith Rubel Mapother. LC 43-5033. 1943. D. Appleton-Century Company, Incorporated.
Dark Daughters. Rhys Davies. LC 48-5144. 1948. Doubleday.
Dark Dawn. James Gibson Taylor. LC 32-14334. 1932. The Mohawk Press.
Dark Days. Frederick John Fargus. LC 6-38672. (On cover: Lovell's library. v. 9. no. 462). 1884. J. W. Lovell Company.
Dark Days. Frederick John Fargus. (On cover: The seaside library. Pocket ed. no. 301). 1884. G. Munro.
Dark Days and Black Knights. Octavus Roy Cohen. LC 23-12787. 1923. Dodd, Mead and Company.
Dark Days and Black Knights. Octavus Roy Cohen. 1926. Dodd, Mead and Company.
Dark Debts & Other Stories. Ella W. Ramirez. 1968. 2.95 o.p. Vantage.
Dark December. Alfred Coppel. 1970. pap. 0.75 o.p. (T2315, GM). Fawcett World.
Dark Deception. Jane McCarthy. 1974. 4.95. Lenox Hill Press.
Dark Descends. Diana Ramsay. LC 75-4296. 1975. 6.95 (ISBN 0-06-013516-6). Harper & Row.
Dark Descends. Diana Ramsay. 1976. 1.75 (ISBN 0-671-80696-3). Pocket Books.
Dark Design. Philip Jose Farmer. LC 77-5138. (Riverworld series; 3). 9.95 (ISBN 0-399-12031-9). Berkeley Pub. Corp.; Distributed by Putnam.
Dark Design. Philip Jose Farmer. (Berkley Book). (Riverworld series; 3). 1978. 2.25 (ISBN 0-425-03831-9). Berkley Pub. Corp.
Dark Design see Philip Jose Farmer: The Complete Riverworld Novels.
Dark Desires. Parley J Cooper. 1976. (pbk.) 1.95 (ISBN 0-671-80484-7). Pocket Books.
Dark Desires: A Novel. Wilma M Prezzi. 1953. Padell Book Co.
Dark Destiny. Edward Sidney Aarons. pap. 0.95 (ISBN 0-532-95239-1). Woodhill.
Dark Destiny. Edgar E Daniels. LC 54-8335. 1954. Vantage Press.
Dark Destiny. Frank Owen. LC 41-1588. Robert Speller Publishing Corporation.
Dark Destroyers. Manly Wade Wellman. Avalon Books.
Dark Device. Elizabeth Head Fetter. 1947. Harper.
Dark Diamond. Diana Tower. (Birthstone Gothic). (Beagle book: Vol.). 1975. (pbk.) 0.95 (ISBN 0-345-26700-1). Ballantine Books.
Dark Diamonds. Mor Jokai. Tr. by Frances Gerard. 5.00x o.p. (ISBN 0-89918-332-8, H-332). Vanous.
Dark Disciple. 1st Ed. Russell B Shaw. LC 61-8904. 1961. Doubleday.
Dark Dominion. David Duncan. LC 53-130382. 1954. Ballantine Books.
Dark Dominion: A Novel. Marianne Hauser. LC 47-623670. 1947. Random House.
Dark Dominion: Eight Terrifying Tales of Vampires & Werewolves. (Orig.). 1970. pap. 0.60 o.p. (63-438). Paperback Lib.
Dark Don't Catch Me. Vin Packer. 1968. pap. 0.75 o.p. (64-015). Paperback Lib.
Dark Dowry. Willo Davis Roberts. (Black Pearl series; 1). 1978. 1.75 (ISBN 0-445-04224-9). Popular Library.
Dark Dream. Dorothy Phoebe Ansle. LC 77-356489. 1976. 6.95 (ISBN 0-525-08873-3). Dutton.
Dark Dream. Laura Conway. 1977. 6.95 o.p. (ISBN 0-525-08873-3). Dutton.
Dark Dream. Robert Lee Martin. LC 51-11614. (Red badge detective). 1951. Dodd, Mead.
Dark Dreaming. Gene Snyder. LC 81-80778. 304p. (Orig.). 1981. pap. 2.95 (ISBN 0-87216-918-9). Playboy Pbks.
Dark Drums. Wenzell Brown. LC 50-10323. 1950. Appleton-Century-Crofts.
Dark Drums. Wenzell Brown. 1977. 1.95 (ISBN 0-446-89292-0). Warner.
Dark Duel: A Novel. Marguerite Steen. LC 29-19883. 1929. Frederick A. Stokes Company.
Dark Duet. Peter Cheyney. 1971. pap. 0.75 o.p. (B75-2154). Belmont-Tower.
Dark Duet. Peter Cheyney. 1971. pap. 0.95 o.p. (95053). Beagle Bks.
Dark Duet. Barbara Michaels. LC 83-1839. 1983. 14.95 (ISBN 0-86553-083-1). Congdon & Weed.
Dark Duet. Barbara Michaels. 496p. 1983. 14.95 (ISBN 0-312-92119-5). Congdon & Weed.
Dark Echo. Hugh Lawrence Nelson. LC 49-755931. (Murray Hill mystery). 1949. Rinehart.
Dark Ecstasy. Leah Crane. (Superromances Ser.). 384p. 1983. pap. 2.95 (ISBN 0-373-70066-0, Pub. by Worldwide). Harlequin Bks.
Dark Enchantment. 1st Ed. Dorothy Macardle. LC 53-10650. 1953. Doubleday.
Dark Enchantress. Sylvia Thorpe. 224p. 1980. pap. 1.75 (ISBN 0-449-50052-7, Coventry). Fawcett.
Dark Encounter. Suzanna Firth. (Harlequin Romances Ser.). (Orig.). 1980. pap. 1.25 (ISBN 0-373-02307-3). Harlequin Bks.
Dark Encounter. Cathleen Schurr. LC 55-9767. 1955. Rinehart.
Dark Encounter. Florence Stevenson. (Signet Book). 1977. 1.50 (ISBN 0-451-07504-8). New American Library.
Dark Enemy. 1st Ed. Edward J Edwards. LC 54-10862. 1954. Longmans, Green.
Dark Enigma. Rebecca Stratton. (Harlequin Romances Ser.). 192p. 1982. pap. 1.50 (ISBN 0-373-02466-5). Harlequin Bks.
Dark Entry. Eleanor Elliott Carroll. LC 40-35536. The Penn Publishing Company.
Dark-Eyed Queen. Lozania Prole. 1976. (pbk.) 1.50 (ISBN 0-671-80314-X). Pocket Books.
Dark Eyes of London. Edgar Wallace. LC 29-23137. 1929. Pub. for The Crime Club, Inc., by Doubleday, Doran & Company, Inc.
Dark Fantastic. Margaret Echard. LC 47-30292. 1947. Doubleday.
Dark Fantastic. Stanley Ellin. LC 82-60902. 300p. 1983. 13.95 (ISBN 0-89296-059-0); write for info. limited ed. (ISBN 0-89296-060-4). Mysterious Pr.
Dark Fantastic. Whit Masterson, pseud. LC 59-8293. (Red badge detective). 1959. Dodd, Mead.
Dark Fields of Venus. Basile S. Yanovsky. LC 72-88801. (Helen & Kurt Wolff Bk.). 1973. 7.95 o.p. (ISBN 0-15-123880-4). HarBraceJ.
Dark Fire. Elinor Mordaunt, pseud. LC 27-3514. 2.00. The Century Co.
Dark Fire. Linda Murray. LC 76-58848. 1977. 11.95 o.p. (ISBN 0-688-03198-6). Morrow.
Dark Fire: A Novel. Linda Murray. LC 76-58848. 1977. 11.95 (ISBN 0-688-03198-6). Morrow.
Dark Fires. Rosemary Rogers. 1975. pap. 3.50 (ISBN 0-380-00425-9, 80911). Avon.
Dark Flame. Sonia M. Shearer. LC 30-25740. 1930. G. P. Putnam's Sons.
Dark Flames. Arlene Hale. LC 81-5369. 1981. 10.95 (ISBN 0-89340-342-3). J. Curley.
Dark Fleece. Joseph Hergesheimer. LC 22-158531. 1922. A. A. Knopf.
Dark Flight. John Rossiter. LC 80-69390. 1981. 9.95 (ISBN 0-689-11139-8). Atheneum.
Dark Flower. manaton ed. new york, scribner, 1923. ed. John Galsworthy. LC 75-145027. (works of John Galsworthy, v. 10). (Illus.). 1971. (ISBN 0-403-00974-X). Scholarly Press.
Dark Flower. John Galsworthy. LC 13-21704. 1913. C. Scribner's Sons.
Dark Forces. Ed. by Kirby McCauley. 544p. 1981. pap. 3.50 (ISBN 0-553-14801-X). Bantam.
Dark Forces. Ed. by Kirby McCauley. (Illus.). 576p. 1980. 16.95 (ISBN 0-670-25653-6). Viking Pr.
Dark Forces: New Stories of Suspense and Supernatural Horror. Kirby McCauley. LC 79-56287. 1980. 16.95 (ISBN 0-670-25653-6). Viking Press.
Dark Forest. Raymond Foxall. LC 73-87402. 1974. 6.95. St. Martin's Press.
Dark Forest. Raymond Foxall. 1976. 1.75 (ISBN 0-671-80576-2). Pocket Books.
Dark Forest. Hugh Walpole. 1965. 3.50. Hart-Davis.
Dark Forest. Hugh Walpole. LC 16-6603. George H. Doran Company.
Dark Fountain: A Novel of Horror. Jay Robert Nash. LC 81-70464. 13.95 (ISBN 0-89479-102-8). A & W Publishers.
Dark Fountain: A Novel of Horror. Jay Robert Nash. 384p. 1982. 13.95 (ISBN 0-89479-102-8). A & W Pubs.
Dark Frenzy. Buford Guffen. pap. 0.95 o.p. Lancer.
Dark Frigate: Wherein Is Told the Story of Philip Marsham Who Lived in the Time of King Charles and Was Bred a Sailor but Came Home to England After Many Hazards by Sea and Land and Fought for the King at Newbury and Lost a Great Inheritance and Departed for Barbados in the Same Ship, by Curious Chance, in Which He Had Long Before Adventured with the Pirates. Charles Boardman Hawes. LC 23-269282. The Atlantic Monthly Press.
Dark Fury. Helga Moray. LC 57-110759. 1958. D. McKay Co.
Dark Garden. Mignon Good Eberhart. LC 43-15327. 1943. Triangle Books.
Dark Garden... Mignon Good Eberhart. LC 33-28401. 1933. Pub. for the Crime Club, Inc., by Doubleday, Doran & Co., Inc.
Dark Garden. Mignon Good Eberhart. 1973. (pbk.) 0.95. Popular Lib.
Dark Gate. Douglas M. Knight. LC 72-635314. (Quarterly Ser). 1971. 5.95 (ISBN 0-87959-073-4). U of Tex Hum Res.
Dark Gentleman. Gladys Bronwyn Stern. LC 27-5136. 1927. A. A. Knopf.
Dark Geraldine. John Alexander Ferguson. LC 21-120861. 1921. John Lane Company.
Dark Glass. Peggy Morrison. LC 35-904827. 1935. A. A. Knopf.
Dark Glass: A Novel. Charlotte Underwood. LC 44-5031. 1944. Harper & Brothers.
Dark Glasses. Hugh Hood. LC 76-380948. (ISBN 0-88750-208-3) (ISBN 0-88750-209-1). Oberon Press.
Dark Glasses. Francis Henry King. LC 54-34875. 1954. Longmans, Green.
Dark God. Charles De Balzac Rideaux. LC 28-10871. The Century Co.
Dark Goddess. Marvin H Albert. LC 77-76219. 1978. 10.00 (ISBN 0-385-12182-2). Doubleday.
Dark Goddess. Marvin H Albert. (Dell book). 1979. 2.25 (ISBN 0-440-11635-X). Dell Pub. Co.
Dark Gods. Sarah Gertrude Liebson Millin. LC 41-51609. Harper & Brothers.
Dark Gondola. Virginia Coffman. (Ace gothic). 1973. (pbk.) 0.95. Ace.
Dark Green, Bright Red. Gore Vidal. LC 50-9879. 1950. Dutton.
Dark Green Circle. Edward Shanks. LC 36-10525. The Bobbs-Merrill Company.
Dark Guardian. Vanessa Blake. 1974. (pbk.) 0.95 (ISBN 0-671-77709-2). Pocket Books.
Dark Harbor Haunting. Clarissa Ross. (Avon gothic original). 1975. (pbk.) 0.95 (ISBN 0-380-00418-6). Avon.
Dark Harvest. rev. ed. John Creasey. LC 76-53070. 1977. 6.95 (ISBN 0-8027-5362-0). Walker.
Dark Hazard. William Riley Burnett. LC 33-22936. 1933. Harper & Brothers.
Dark Heritage. Dorothy Daniels. (Signet Book). 1976. (pbk.) 1.25. New American Library.
Dark Heritage. Marjorie McEvoy. Ed. by Alice Sachs. 1970. 3.95 o.p. Lenox Hill.
Dark Heritage. Shirland Quin. LC 31-368919. 1931. Little, Brown, and Company.
Dark Heritage - Heritage Hill. Dorothy Daniels. 1983. pap. 2.95 (ISBN 0-451-12075-2, Sig). NAL.
Dark Heritage. Cover Painting by James Meese. John Foster. LC 55-38187. (Gold medal books, 486). 1955. Fawcett Publications.
Dark Hero... Peter Cheyney. LC 46-7097. 1946. Dodd, Mead & Company.
Dark Hester. Anne Douglas Sedgwick. LC 29-7504. 1929. Houghton Mifflin Company.
Dark Hill. Elinore Denniston. LC 74-34117. (Red badge novel of suspense). 1975. 5.95 (ISBN 0-396-07081-7). Dodd, Mead.
Dark Hill. Rae Foley, pseud. 224p. 1975. 5.95 o.p. (ISBN 0-396-07081-7). Dodd.
Dark Hills Rising. Anne Hampson. (Presents Ser.). 1975. pap. 1.25 (ISBN 0-373-70595-6, 70595, Pub by Harlequin). PB.
Dark Hills to Westward: The Saga of Jennie Wiley. Harry M. Caudill. LC 70-79358. (Illus.). 1969. 5.95. Little, Brown.
Dark Hollow. Anna Katharine Green Rohlfs. LC 14-230106. 1914. Dodd, Mead & Company.
Dark Hollow. Anna Katharine Green Rohlfs. LC 19-18169. 1919. A. L. Burt Company.
Dark Homecoming. E. E Somerville. (Empress Gothic). 1973. (pbk) 0.95. Curtis Books.
Dark Homecoming. E. E. Somerville & Martin Ross. 1973. pap. 0.95 o.p. (09183). Curtis.
Dark Horn Blowing. Dahlov Zorach Ipcar. LC 77-16018. 1978. 8.95 (ISBN 0-670-25659-5). Viking Press.
Dark Horn Blowing. Dahlov Zorach Ipcar. LC 79-22649. 1980. 2.95 (ISBN 0-14-005156-2). Penguin Books.
Dark Horse. Rumer Godden. LC 81-10352. 1982. 11.95 (ISBN 0-670-25664-1). Viking Press.
Dark Horse. Rumer Godden. LC 82-7294. 1982. 11.95 (ISBN 0-89340-518-3). J. Curley.
Dark Horse. Fletcher Knebel. 1973. 1.75 (ISBN 0-671-78598-2). Pocket Books.

Dark Horse. Fletcher Knebel. LC 72-75427. 1972. 7.95. Doubleday.
Dark Horse: A Story of the Flying U. Bertha Muzzy Sinclair. LC 43-3846. 1943. Triangle Books.
Dark Horse: A Story of the Younger Chippendales. Robert Grant. LC 31-29821. 1931. Houghton Mifflin Company.
Dark Host. Archie Roy. 1976. 7.95 (ISBN 0-09-126350-6, Pub. by Hutchinson). Merrimack Pub Cir.
Dark House. Warwick Deeping. LC 41-81088. 1941. A. A. Knopf.
Dark House. Ida Alexa Ross Wylie. LC 22-16473. 1922. Cassell and Company, Limited.
Dark House. Ida Alexa Ross Wylie. LC 22-9051. E. P. Dutton & Company.
Dark House: A Knot Unraveled. George Manville Fenn. LC 6-39264. 1885. A. N. Marquis & Company.
Dark House. A Knot Unraveled. George Manville Fenn. LC 6-39265. (On cover: The seaside library. Pocket ed. no. 609). 1885. G. Munro.
Dark House: A Knot Unravelled. George Manville Fenn. LC 6-39266. (Harper's handy series, no. 29). 1885. Harper & Brothers.
Dark House: A Story of the Flying U. Bertha Muzzy Sinclair. LC 31-272202. 1931. Little, Brown, and Company.
Dark House, Dark Road. Carter Wick. (Raven House Mysteries Ser.). 224p. 1982. pap. 2.25 (ISBN 0-373-63035-2, Pub. by Worldwide). Harlequin Bks.
Dark House in Florissant. Reginald Wright Kauffman. LC 27-12824. H. Altemus Company.
Dark Houses. Peter Davison. LC 77-177946. 1971. pap. 4.00 (ISBN 0-912604-07-7). Halty Ferguson.
Dark Hunger. Don James. 1969. pap. 0.75 o.p. (75-261). Manor Bks.
Dark Hunger: Space Probe 6. Charles Huntington, III. 160p. (Orig.). 1972. pap. 0.75 o.p. (A964S, Award). Univ Pub & Dis.
Dark Inheritance. Mary Cecil Hay. LC 7-3760. (On cover: Harper's half-hour series no. 84). 1878. Harper & Brothers.
Dark Inheritance. Mary Cecil Hay. (On cover: Seaside library. Pocket ed., no. 1026). 1887. G. Munro.
Dark Inheritance. Carola Salisbury. LC 75-7256. 1975. 6.95 (ISBN 0-385-11004-9). Doubleday.
Dark Inheritance. Carola Salisbury. 1976. 1.50 (ISBN 0-449-23064-3). Fawcett Crest.
Dark Intent: By Rae Foley Pseud. Elinore Denniston. LC 54-8497. (Red badge detective). 1954. Dodd, Mead.
Dark Interlude. Peter Cheyney. LC 47-31037. 1947. Dodd, Mead.
Dark Interval. Joan Aiken. 1974. (pbk.) 0.95 (ISBN 0-671-77730-0). Pocket Books.
Dark Interval. Joan Aiken. LC 67-14713. 1967. Doubleday.
Dark Is My Destiny. Heather Smith Hurst. (Candlelight gothic). 1974. (pbk.) 0.75. Dell.
Dark Is My Shadow. Dan Ross, pseud. 1970. Repr. pap. 0.60 o.p. (60-450). Manor Bks.
Dark Is My Shadow. William Edward Daniel Ross. 192p. 1976. pap. 1.25 (ISBN 0-532-12369-7). Woodhill.
Dark Is the Mirror: Being an Episode in the Life of John Poorjohn, Sc. D. William Pseud Kinsey. LC 48-6237. 1948. Houghton Mifflin Co.
Dark Is the Sun. Philip Jose Farmer. LC 79-2279. 9.95 (ISBN 0-345-27684-1). Ballantine Books.
Dark Is the Tunnel... Miles Burton. LC 36-15263. 1936. Pub. for the Crime Club, Inc., by Doubleday, Doran and Co., Inc.
Dark Island. Robert Barr. LC 72-9877. (Black Bat mystery). 1973. 6.95. Bobbs-Merrill.
Dark Island. Robert Barr. LC 72-195674. 1972. 1.95 (ISBN 0-491-00632-2). W. E. Allen.
Dark Island. Charles William Collins & Markey, Gene. LC 28-23459. 1928. Doubleday, Doran & Company, Inc.
Dark Island. Grace Corren. 1976. (pbk.) 1.25. Belmont Tower Books.
Dark Island. Victoria Mary Sackville-West. LC 34-41053. 1934. Doubleday, Doran & Company, Inc.
Dark Island: A Novel. Henry Treece. LC 53-6911. 1953. Random House.
Dark Journey. Freeman Wills Crofts. LC 51-13035. (Red badge detective). 1951. Dodd, Mead.
Dark Journey. Julien Green. LC 76-152597. 1972. (ISBN 0-8371-6031-6). Greenwood Press.
Dark Journey. Julien Green. Tr. by Holland, Vyvyan Beresford. LC 29-18002. 1929. Harper & Brothers.
Dark Journey: A Novel. Diana Raymond. LC 79-4404. 1979. 7.95 (ISBN 0-684-16154-0). Scribner.
Dark Journey Home. Patricia Hagan Howell. 1974. (pbk.) 0.95. Avon.
Dark Knight. Margaret Shauers. 1976. 4.95. Avalon Books.
Dark Labyrinth. Lois Barth. Ed. by Alice Sachs. 1971. 3.95 o.p. Lenox Hill.
Dark Labyrinth. Lawrence Durrell. LC 78-15621. 1978. 2.50 (ISBN 0-14-005025-6). Penguin Books.
Dark Labyrinth. Susannah Leigh. (Fawcett gold medal book). 1975. (pbk.) 1.25. Fawcett.
Dark Ladies. Ivor John Carnegie Brown. 1973. Repr. of 1957 ed. 15.00 o.p. R West.
Dark Lady. Louis Auchincloss. LC 77-3666. 1977. 8.95 (ISBN 0-395-25402-7). Houghton Mifflin.
Dark Lady. Doris Miles Disney. LC 60-8862. 1960. Published for the Crime Club by Doubleday.
Dark Lady. Robert Kerr. LC 75-37904. 1976. 7.95 (ISBN 0-8128-1894-6). Stein and Day.
Dark Lady. Gerda Robison. LC 51-3966. 1951. Harper.
Dark Lady: A Novel. Cothburn O'Neal. LC 54-111713. 1954. Crown Publishers.
Dark Lane. William Edward Daniel Ross. (YA) 1979. 6.95 (Avalon). Bouregy.
Dark Lantern. Short, Christopher. LC 61-10777. 1961. Scribner.
Dark Lantern: A Story with a Prologue. Elizabeth Robins. LC 5-14447. 1905. The Macmillan Company.
Dark Laughter. Sherwood Anderson. LC 25-206591. 1925. Boni & Liveright.
Dark Laughter. With an Introd. by Howard Mumford Jones. Sherwood Anderson. LC 60-53556. 1960. Liveright Pub. Corp.
Dark Legacy. Candice Connell. (Orig.). 1980. pap. 1.25 (ISBN 0-440-11771-2). Dell.
Dark Light. Bart Spicer. LC 49-10610. (Red badge mystery). 1949. Dodd, Mead.
Dark Light Years. Brian Wilson Aldiss. 1981. 18.95x (Pub. by Remploy England). State Mutual Bk.
Dark Lightning. Helen Topping Miller. LC 40-31039. 1940. D. Appleton-Century Company, Incorporated.
Dark Love, Dark Magic. O. T. Jackson. 1971. pap. 0.75 o.p. (ISBN 0-447-74739-8). Lancer.
Dark Love, Dark Magic. O. T. Jackson. 1969. pap. 0.75 o.p. (74-577). Lancer.
Dark Lustre. James Whittaker & Ehrich, Edward Price, Joint Author. LC 32-30523. 1932. A. H. King, Inc.
Dark Madonna. Richard Summers. LC 37-7996. 1937. The Caxton Printers, Ltd.
Dark Magic. Michael Norday. LC 54-1455. 1954. Vixen Press.
Dark Man. Robert E. Howard. 5.00 o.p. Arkham.
Dark Man. Robert E. Howard. (Orig.). 1972. pap. 0.95 o.p. Lancer.
Dark Mansion. Caroline Farr. 1974. (pbk.) 0.95. New American Library.
Dark Mansion. H. R. Kaye, pseud. 1968. pap. 1.75 o.p. (3034). Brandon.
Dark Mansion. W. E. Ross. (YA) 1973. 4.50 o.p. (Avalon). Bouregy.
Dark Mansion. William Edward Daniel Ross. (Avalon romances). 1973. 4.50. Avalon Books.
Dark Mare. Damsey Wilson. LC 52-5225. 1952. Doubleday.
Dark Marriage Morn. Charlotte Mary Brame. LC 11-10520. J. S. Ogilvie & Company.
Dark Marriage Morn. Charlotte Mary Brame. LC 44-39940. (On cover: Seaside library. Pocket ed. No. 975). G. Munro.
Dark Marriage Morn. Charlotte Mary Brame. LC 3808. (Bertha M. Clay library, no. 7). 1900. Street & Smith.
Dark Masquerade. LC 39-15716. Green Circle Books.
Dark Masquerade. Patricia Maxwell. (Fawcett Gold Medal). 1974. (pbk.) 0.95. Fawcett.
Dark Masquerade. Elna Stone. (Orig.). 1973. pap. 0.95 o.s.i. (75-426). Lancer.
Dark Master. Raymond Giles, pseud. 224p. 1978. pap. 2.50 (ISBN 0-449-13622-1, GM). Fawcett.
Dark Medallion. Dorothy Langley. LC 45-4370. 1945. Simon and Schuster.
Dark Medallion: A Novel by Dorothy Langley Pseud. Dorothy Langley. 1945. Simon and Schuster.
Dark Memories. Jane Morella. 1971. pap. 0.75 o.p. (ISBN 0-447-74727-4). Lancer.
Dark Memory. Jonathan Latimer. LC 40-6912. 1940. Doubleday, Doran & Company, Inc.
Dark Memory: By Edward Ronns Pseud. Edward Sidney Aarons. LC 51-17396. (Handi-book mystery). 1950. Quinn Pub. Co.
Dark Metropolis. Arthur Joseph. LC 73-18589. 1975. 11.00 (ISBN 0-404-11400-8). AMS Press.
Dark Metropolis. Arthur Joseph. LC 36-33405. 1936. Meador Publishing Company.
Dark Mile: A Sequel to The Flight of the Heron and The Gleam in the North. Dorothy Kathleen Broster. LC 34-28410. 1934. Coward-McCann, Inc.
Dark Mill. Claudette Nicole. (Orig.). 1971. pap. 0.75 o.p. (T2514, GM). Fawcett World.
Dark Millennium. A. J. Merak. LC 66-471. 1966. Arcadia House.
Dark Mind, Dark Heart. Ed. by August William Derleth. 1962. 4.00 o.p. Arkham.
Dark Mirror. Louis Joseph Vance. LC 20-577811. 1920. Doubleday, Page & Company.
Dark Moment. Mary Dolling Sanders O'Malley. LC 51-14992. 1952. Macmillan.
Dark Moon. J. H Brennan. LC 80-20034. 13.95 (ISBN 0-03-058013-7). Holt, Rinehart & Winston.
Dark Moon. Helen Heney. LC 54-8717. 1954. Crowell.
Dark Moon, Lost Lady. Elsie Lee. 1.25. Dell.
Dark Moon of March. Emmett Gowen. LC 33-24534. The Bobbs-Merrill Company.
Dark Moonless Night. Anne Mather. (Presents Ser.). 1975. pap. 1.25 (ISBN 0-373-70600-6, 70600, Pub by Harlequin). PB.
Dark Mosaic. Claire Brooker. LC 58-9282. Arcadia House.
Dark Mother. Waldo David Frank. LC 78-63986. (Gay Experience). Repr. of 1920 ed. 29.50 (ISBN 0-404-61505-8). AMS Pr.
Dark Mother: A Novel. Waldo David Frank. LC 20-19046. Boni and Liveright.
Dark Mountain. Ann Boyle. 1975. 4.95. Avalon Books.
Dark Mountains. Dorothy Richards Bryant. LC 40-3845. Zondervan Publishing House.
Dark Mountains. William Hoffman. LC 63-11386. 1963. Doubleday.
Dark Music. Charlotte Russell. 1972. pap. 0.95 o.s.i. (75-364). Lancer.
Dark Music: And Other Spectral Tales. Jack Snow. LC 47-278517. 1947. Herald Publishing Co.
Dark Nantucket Noon. Jane Langton. LC 74-5799. (Illus.). 1975. 6.95 (ISBN 0-06-012502-0). Harper & Row.
Dark Nantucket Noon. Jane Langton. LC 80-29128. (Illus.). 1981. 2.95 (ISBN 0-14-005836-2). Penguin Books.
Dark Night's Passing. Naoya Shiga. Tr. by Edwin McClellan from Japanese. LC 76-9351. 1976. 15.00 o.p. (ISBN 0-87011-279-1). Kodansha.
Dark Night's Passing. Naoya Shiga. Tr. by Edwin McClellan from Japanese. LC 76-9351. 1980. pap. 6.95 (ISBN 0-87011-362-3). Kodansha.
Dark Night's Work. J. B. Drake. (On cover: Melbourne ser. no. 3). E. A. Weeks & Company.
Dark Number. Edward Boyd & Roger Parkes. LC 73-93933. 1974. 5.95 (ISBN 0-8027-5298-5). Walker.
Dark O' the Moon: A Novel. Samuel Rutherford Crockett. 1902. Harper & Bros.
Dark Oasis. Margaret Pargeter. (Harlequin Presents Ser.). 192p. 1981. pap. 1.50 (ISBN 0-373-10431-6, Pub. by Harlequin). PB.
Dark Odyssey. Florence Stevenson. (Signet book). 1974. (pbk.) 0.95. New American Library.
Dark of Summer. Deanna Dwyer. 1972. pap. 0.95 o.s.i. (75-393). Lancer.
Dark of Summer. 1st American Ed. Eric Robert Russell Linklater. 1957. Harcourt, Brace.
Dark of the Day. Maxine Darity. 1978. pap. 1.75 (ISBN 0-532-17188-8). Woodhill.
Dark of the Moon. John Dickson Carr. LC 67-28824. 1967. Harper & Row.
Dark of the Moon. Margaret Bell Houston & Adams, Gerald Drayson, Joint Author. LC 43-167699. 1943. Arcadia House, Inc.
Dark of the Moon. Dan Ross, pseud. 1969. Repr. pap. 0.60 o.p. (60-421). Manor Bks.
Dark of the Moon: A Peter Clancy Detective Mystery. Lee Thayer. LC 36-182074. 1936. Dodd, Mead and Company.
Dark of the Soul. Ed. by Don Ward. 1970. pap. 0.75 o.p. (T075-3). Tower.
Dark of the Sun. Wilbur A Smith. (Dell Book). 1977. 1.95 (ISBN 0-440-11667-8). Dell Pub. Co.
Dark Omnibus. Peter Cheyney. LC 52-11866. (Red badge detective). 1952. Dodd, Mead.
Dark on the Other Side. Barbara Mertz. LC 78-127169. 1970. 5.95. Dodd, Mead.
Dark on the Other Side. large print ed. Barbara Michaels. LC 82-21364. 1983. 14.95 (ISBN 0-8161-3414-6). G.K. Hall.
Dark on the Other Side. Barbara Michaels. 1977. pap. 1.75 (ISBN 0-449-23239-5, Crest). Fawcett.
Dark on the Other Side. Barbara Michaels. (General Ser.). 1983. lib. bdg. 14.95 (ISBN 0-8161-3414-6, Large Print Bks). G K Hall.
Dark on the Other Side. Barbara Michaels. 1970. 5.95 o.p. (ISBN 0-396-06245-8). Dodd.
Dark Other. Stanley Grauman Weinbaum. LC 50-12836. 1950. Fantasy Pub. Co.
Dark Other Adam Dreaming. Len Fulton. LC 75-28296. (American dust series; no. 4). 8.95. (ISBN 0-913218-48-0) (ISBN 0-913218-49-9). Dustbooks.
Dark Page. Samuel Michael Fuller. LC 44-9240. 1944. Duell, Sloan and Pearce.
Dark Palazzo. Virginia Coffman. LC 72-94015. 1973. 6.95 (ISBN 0-87795-051-2). Arbor House.
Dark Paradise. Berrie Davis. (Orig.). 1980. pap. 1.25 (ISBN 0-440-11354-7). Dell.
Dark Paradise. May Mackintosh. 1978. 1.50 (ISBN 0-440-17583-6). Dell Pub. Co.
Dark Passage. Alice Lent Covert. LC 51-3771. 1951. Bouregy & Curi.
Dark Passage... David Goodis. LC 46-719219. 1946. J. Messner, Inc.
Dark Passage. Andrew York. LC 75-14848. (Crime Club Ser.). 192p. 1975. 5.95 o.p. (ISBN 0-385-11240-8). Doubleday.
Dark Passion: By Gail Jordan Pseud. Peggy Gaddis, pseud. LC 50-7359. 1950. Phoenix Press.
Dark Passions. Holland E Nickerson. LC 51-3123. 1951. Woodford Press.
Dark Passions Subdue. Douglas Sanderson. LC 52-10914. 1952. Dodd, Mead.
Dark Pasture. Jessica Stirling. LC 77-15325. 8.95 (ISBN 0-312-18257-0). St. Martin's Press.
Dark Pasture. Jessica Stirling. 1979. 2.50 (ISBN 0-345-28033-4). Ballantine Books.
Dark Path. Marguerite Neilson, pseud. pap. 1.50 (ISBN 0-532-15260-3). Woodhill.
Dark Patrick. Seumas MacManus. LC 70-178447. (Short story index reprint series). 1971. (ISBN 0-8369-4048-2). Books for Libraries Press.
Dark Patrick. Seumas MacManus. LC 39-299610. 1939. The Macmillan Company.
Dark Philosophers. Gwyn Thomas. LC 47-2976. 1947. Little, Brown and Company.
Dark Pilgrim: Translated by Gerald and Walter Gordon. Francois Alwyn Venter. LC 60-209418. Muhlenberg Press.
Dark Pilgrimage. Jakob Wassermann & Brooks, Cyrus Harry, 1890- Tr. LC 33-33949. 1933. Liveright Publishing Corporation.
Dark Piper. Alice Mary Norton. LC 68-25193. 1968. Harcourt, Brace & World.
Dark Place. Mildred B Davis. LC 55-14828. (Inner sanctum mystery). 1955. Simon and Schuster.
Dark Place. Mildred B. Davis. (Kangaroo Book). (Illus.). 1977. 1.50 (ISBN 0-671-81148-7). Pocket Books.
Dark Places, Deep Regions, and Other Stories. Margaret Sutherland. LC 80-17008. 1980. 9.95 (ISBN 0-916144-53-4). Stemmer House Publishers.
Dark Places of the Heart. Christina Stead. LC 66-21616. 6.95. Holt.
Dark Planet. J. Hunter Holly. 1971. pap. 0.75 o.p. (75-426). Manor Bks.
Dark Plot. Sylvanus Cobb. (On cover: Sunnyside series, no. 14). 1890. J. S. Ogilvie.
Dark Possession. Alice Alison Lide & Margaret Alison Johansen. LC 34-671319. 1934. D. Appleton-Century Company Incorporated.
Dark Power. William Arden, pseud. LC 68-218992. (Red badge mystery). 1968. 3.95. Dodd.
Dark Power. Elisabeth Sanxay Holding. LC 30-3230. The Vanguard Press.
Dark Power. Elisabeth Sanxay Holding. LC 45-4771. (Black cat detective series. No. 14). 1945. Crestwood Publishing Co., Inc.
Dark Power. Dennis Lynds. LC 68-21899. (Red badge mystery). 1968. Dodd, Mead.
Dark Priestess. Juanita Coulson. LC 77-6215. 1977. 1.95 (ISBN 0-345-24958-5). Ballantine Books.
Dark Princess. William Edward Burghardt Du Bois. Repr. of 1928 ed. cancelled o.s.i. (ISBN 0-404-00150-5). AMS Pr.
Dark Princess: A Romance. William Edward Burghardt Du Bois. LC 74-7248. 1974. 12.50 (ISBN 0-527-25295-6). Kraus-Thomson Organization.
Dark Princess: A Romance. William Edward Burghardt Du Bois. LC 28-113190. Harcourt, Brace and Company.
Dark Prism. David Lippincott. (Orig.). 1981. pap. 2.95 (ISBN 0-440-11893-X). Dell.
Dark Promise of Delight. Jessica Logan. (Superromances Ser.). 384p. 1982. pap. 2.50 (ISBN 0-373-70041-5, Pub. by Worldwide). Harlequin Bks.
Dark Prophecy. Marjorie Alan. LC 45-8334. 1945. M. S. Mill Co.
Dark Prophet: A Novel. 1st Ed. Robert Pease. LC 54-11689. 1955. Exposition Press.
Dark Quartet: The Story of the Brontes. Lynne Reid Banks. LC 76-29727. 10.00 (ISBN 0-440-01657-6). Delacorte Press.
Dark Quartet: The Story of the Brontes. Lynne Reid Banks. LC 76-381550. 4.95 (ISBN 0-297-77153-1). Weidenfeld & Nicolson.
Dark Rainbow. Gerald Alfred Butler. LC 45-9502. 1945. Farrar & Rinehart, Inc.
Dark Refuge. Nelle McFather. (Cameo Ser.). 192p. (Orig.). 1976. pap. 1.95 (ISBN 0-441-13808-X). Ace Bks.
Dark Remembrance. Daphne Clair. (Harlequin Presents Ser.). 192p. 1981. pap. 1.75 (ISBN 0-373-10458-8). Harlequin Bks.
Dark Rider. Geraldine Thayer. (Candelight Mystery). 1973. (pbk.) 0.75. Dell.

Dark Rider: A Novel Based on the Life of Stephen Crane. Louis Zara. LC 61-11099. 1961. World Pub. Co.
Dark River. Philip Clark. LC 49-9150. (Inner sanctum mystery). 1949. Simon and Schuster.
Dark River. Philip Clark. LC 81-47335. (Fifty Classics of Crime Fiction, 1950-1975). 1982. 14.95 (ISBN 0-8240-4978-0). Garland.
Dark River. Sarah Gertrude Liebson Millin. LC 21-758. 1920. T. Seltzer.
Dark River. Charles Bernard Nordhoff & Hall, James Norman. LC 38-27506. 1938. Little, Brown and Company.
Dark River. Norman Springer. LC 28-24473. 1928. G. H. Watt.
Dark Road. Harold Bindloss. LC 27-187151. 1927. Frederick A. Stokes Company.
Dark Road. Doris Miles Disney. LC 46-811. 1946. Pub. for the Crime Club by Doubleday & Company, Inc.
Dark Road: By James Cross Pseud. Hugh Jones Parry. (Crest bk. 366). 1960. Fawcett Publications.
Dark Road: By James Cross Pseud. Hugh Jones Parry. LC 59-7015. 1959. Messner.
Dark Road: Further Adventures of Cheri-Bibi. Gaston Leroux. LC 24-18097. The Macaulay Company.
Dark Road. 1st Ed. Clifford Knight. LC 51-12231. (Guilt edged mystery). 1951. Dutton.
Dark Roads. 1st. ed. Leah Ross, pseud. LC 75-1213. 1975. 7.95 (ISBN 0-15-123890-1). Harcourt Brace Jovanovich.
Dark Room. R. K. Narayan. LC 80-39930. 1981. 15.00 (ISBN 0-226-56836-9) (ISBN 0-226-56837-7). University of Chicago Press.
Dark Room. Junnosuke Yoshiyuki. Tr. by John Bester. LC 75-11390. 200p. 1976. 8.95 o.p. (ISBN 0-87011-255-4). Kodansha.
Dark Room. Junnosuke Yoshiyuki. Tr. by John Bester from Japanese. LC 75-11390. 170p. 1980. pap. 3.95 (ISBN 0-87011-361-5). Kodansha.
Dark Rosaleen. Marjorie Bowen. LC 33-316648. 1933. Houghton Mifflin Company.
Dark Rose. Cynthia Harrod-Eagles. (Morland Dynasty Ser.: No. 2). (Orig.). 1982. pap. 3.50 (ISBN 0-440-12105-1). Dell.
Dark Rose: Being the Chronicle of the Wars of Montrose As Seen by Martin Somers, Adjutant of Women in O'Cahan's Regiment. Maurice Walsh. LC 38-6010. 1938. Frederick A. Stokes Company.
Dark Rose: Being the Chronicle of the Wars of Montrose As Seen by Martin Somers, Adjutant of Women in O'Cahan's Regiment. Maurice Walsh. LC 39-32126. 1939. Triangle Books.
Dark Rose the Phoenix. 1st Amer. Ed. William Hutchinson Murray. LC 65-25636. bds., 3.50. McKay.
Dark Sails: A Tale of Old St. Simons. Helen Topping Miller. LC 45-9402. 1945. The Bobbs Merrill Company.
Dark Salvation. Harry V. Richardson. 10.00 o.p. (ISBN 0-385-00245-9). Doubleday.
Dark Saviour; a Novel. Robert Harling. LC 53-5371. 1953. Harper.
Dark Sea Running. George P. Morrill. LC 59-114460. 1959. McGraw-Hill.
Dark Seas of Maltern Manor. Kay Vernon. (Orig.). 1981. pap. 2.50 (ISBN 0-89083-832-1). Zebra.
Dark Season at Aerie. Juanita Tyree Osborne. (Avalon Books). 4.95. Thomas Bouregy.
Dark Seduction. Flora Kidd. (Harlequin Presents Ser.). 192p. 1983. pap. 1.95. Harlequin Bks.
Dark Seed, Dark Flower. Veronica Leigh. 192p. 1974. pap. 0.95 o.p. (ISBN 0-532-95357-6). Woodhill.
Dark Seed, Dark Flower. Veronica Leigh. 192p. 1974. pap. 0.95 o.p. (ISBN 0-532-95357-6). Manor Bks.
Dark Shadow. Ronald Scott Thorn. Orig. Title: Second Opinion. 1970. pap. 0.75 o.p. (75-321). Manor Bks.
Dark Shadow at Bitterhill. Paulette Warren. (Orig.). 1970. pap. 0.75 o.p. (ISBN 0-447-74630-8). Lancer.
Dark Shadows, 8 Vols. pap. 4.80, boxed set o.p. (DS-D). Paperback Lib.
Dark Shadows. Larry McHale. LC 62-11056. 1962. Dorrance.
Dark Shadows. Marilyn Ross. (Orig.). pap. 0.60 o.p. (-63-367). Paperback Lib.
Dark Shadows at Bitterhill. Paulette Warren. 1976. pap. 1.25. Woodhill.
Dark Shadows Book of Vampires & Werewolves. Ed. by Barnabas Collins & Quentin Collins. (Dark Shadows Ser). (Orig.). 1970. pap. 0.60 o.p. (ISBN 0-446-63419-0, 63-419). Paperback Lib.
Dark Ships. Hulbert Footner. LC 37-1710. 1937. Harper & Brothers.
Dark Shore. Susan Howatch. LC 70-185884. 1972. 6.95 (ISBN 0-8128-1457-6). Stein and Day.
Dark Shore. Susan Howatch. (Fawcett crest book). 1975. (pbk.) 1.25. Fawcett.
Dark Shore: A Novel. Philip Freund. LC 41-19189. Ives Washburn, Inc.
Dark Side. Kenn Davis & John Stanley. LC 76-48379 (ISBN 0-380-00829-7). Avon.
Dark Side. Ed. by Damon Francis Knight. LC 65-10606. 4.50. N.Y.
Dark Side of Destiny. Stanley Morgan. 448p. 1982. pap. 3.50 (ISBN 0-449-14456-9, GM). Fawcett.
Dark Side of Glory: By Berta W. Swan. Berta W Swan. LC 79-89518. 1969. 2.95. Zondervan Pub. House.
Dark Side of Love. Peggy Bechko, pseud. (Superromances Ser.). 384p. 1983. pap. 2.50 (ISBN 0-373-70047-4, Pub. by Worldwide). Harlequin Bks.
Dark Side of Love. Oscar Saul, pseud. LC 73-4156. 1974. 6.95 (ISBN 0-06-013771-1). Harper & Row.
Dark Side of Love: Tales of Love and Death. Cornell George Hopley-Woolrich. LC 65-15551. bds., 3.50. Walker.
Dark Side of Nowhere. Dorotha Strayer Kauffman. LC 64-11952. 1965. Zondervan Pub. House.
Dark Side of the Dream. John Starr, pseud. 624p. 1983. pap. 3.95 (ISBN 0-446-30808-0). Warner Bks.
Dark Side of the Dream: A Novel. John Starr, pseud. LC 81-21832. 15.95 (ISBN 0-446-51239-7). Warner Books.
Dark Side of the Island. John Harris. LC 73-7533. 1973. 6.95 (ISBN 0-15-123900-2). Harcourt Brace Jovanovich.
Dark Side of the Island. Jack Higgins, pseud. (Fawcett Gold Medal Book). 1977. 1.75 (ISBN 0-449-13826-7). Fawcett Pubns.
Dark Side of the Moon. William Corlett. LC 77-375462. 1976. 2.90 (ISBN 0-241-89507-3). Hamilton.
Dark Side of the Moon. Don Gray. 1970. pap. 2.50 (Pub. by Twowindows Pr); pap. 10.00x ea. signed ed. SBD.
Dark Side of the Moon: Stories. Phyllis Reynolds Naylor. LC 69-14617. (Illus.). 1969. 1.50. Fortress Press.
Dark Side of the Street. Jack Higgins. (Fawcett gold medal book). 1974. (pbk.) 0.95. Fawcett.
Dark Side of the Sun. Terry Pratchett. LC 75-29644. 1976. 7.95. St. Martin's Press.
Dark Sins, Dark Dreams. Ed. by Barry N. Malzberg & Bill Pronzini. LC 77-76247. 1978. 7.95 o.p. (ISBN 0-385-12832-0). Doubleday.
Dark Sins, Dark Dreams: Crime in Science Fiction. Barry N Malzberg & Bill Pronzini. LC 77-76247. 1978. 7.95 (ISBN 0-385-12832-0). Doubleday.
Dark Soldier. Katherine Myers. (Avon Romance Ser.). 304p. 1983. pap. 2.95 (ISBN 0-380-82214-8, 82214-8). Avon.
Dark Sonata. Evelyn Bond. 1972. pap. 0.75 o.p. (94273). Beagle Bks.
Dark Sonata. Beatrice Murray. 1972. 0.75. Dell.
Dark Splendour. Martha Edith Almedingen, pseud. 1981. 18.95x (Pub. by Remploy England). State Mutual Bk.
Dark Stage. Dorothy Daniels. (Orig.). 1970. pap. 0.60 o.p. (63-376). Paperback Lib.
Dark Stain. Benjamin Appel. LC 43-18559. 1943. The Dial Press.
Dark Star. Robert William Chambers. LC 17-13501. 1917. D. Appleton and Company.
Dark Star. Robert William Chambers. LC 24-28536. 1919. A. L. Burt Company.
Dark Star. Alan Dean Foster. (Illus.). 1974. (pbk.) 1.25 (ISBN 0-345-24267-X). Ballantine Books.
Dark Star. Anne Maybury. LC 76-49495. 8.95 (ISBN 0-394-41114-5). Random House.
Dark Star. Lorna Moon. LC 29-7075. The Bobbs-Merrill Company.
Dark Star: By March Cost Pseud. Peggy Morrison. LC 39-30326. 1939. A. A. Knopf.
Dark Stars & Dragons. Isaac Asimov. LC 78-59069. 1978. pap. 1.75 o.s.i. (ISBN 0-89559-066-2). Dale Books Inc.
Dark Stars and Other Illuminations. Thomas F Monteleone. LC 79-6872. (Doubleday science fiction). 1981. 9.95 (ISBN 0-385-15769-X). Doubleday.
Dark Stars Over Seacrest. William Edward Daniel Ross. LC 74-183375. 1972. 0.95 (ISBN 0-446-65788-3). Paperback Library.
Dark Stone. Mildred Nelson. (Orig.). 1972. pap. 0.75 o.p. (T2652). Pyramid Pubns.
Dark Straits of Reglathium, No. 4. Mike Sirota. 1978. pap. 2.25 (ISBN 0-532-22131-1). Woodhill.
Dark Stranger. Constance Woodbury Dodge. LC 40-27568. The Penn Publishing Company.
Dark Stranger. Julien Gracq. New Directions.
Dark Stranger. John Iggulden. LC 65-238209. bds., 5.50. McGraw.
Dark Stranger. Louis Poirier. LC 50-9035. New Directions.
Dark Stranger. 1st American Ed. Dorothy Charques. LC 56-116651. 1957. Coward-McCann.
Dark Street. Peter Cheyney. LC 44-880211. 1944. Dodd, Mead Company.
Dark Summer. Mark Upton. LC 78-10443. 9.95 (ISBN 0-698-10957-0). Coward, McCann & Geoghegan.
Dark Summer Dawn. Sara Craven. (Harlequin Presents Ser.). 192p. 1982. pap. 1.75 (ISBN 0-373-10487-1). Harlequin Bks.
Dark Summer: Mark Upton. Mark Upton. 1980. 2.25 (ISBN 0-671-82803-7). Pocket Books.
Dark Sun: A Study of D. H. Lawrence. Graham Goulden Hough. LC 57-726263. 1957. Macmillan.
Dark Sun at Midnight. Sharon Wagner. Ace.
Dark Sun, Pale Shadows. Naidra Grey. LC 72-97294. 1973. 6.95 (ISBN 0-399-11143-3). Putnam.
Dark Sun, Pale Shadows. Naidra Grey. (Berkley medallion book). 1974. (pbk.) 0.95 (ISBN 0-425-02560-8). Berkley Pub. Co.
Dark Sunlight. G. A. Broadd. 4.00 o.p. Carlton.
Dark Sunset. John Bodrero. LC 56-6187. 1956. Abelard-Schuman.
Dark Sunshine. Dorothy Lyons. LC 51-11741. 1965. pap. 1.95 (ISBN 0-15-623936-1, VoyB). HarBraceJ.
Dark Surrender. Ronald De Levington Kirkbride. LC 33-855. Sears Publishing Company, Inc.
Dark Surrender. Margaret Pargeter. (Harlequin Romances Ser.). 192p. 1981. pap. 1.25 (ISBN 0-373-02409-6, Pub. by Harlequin). PB.
Dark Swallows. Helen Griffiths. LC 67-11144. 1967. Knopf.
Dark Swan. Ernest Pascal. Brentano's.
Dark Symmetry. Dorothy Phoebe Ansle. LC 73-78647. 1973. 5.95 (ISBN 0-8415-0270-6). Saturday Review Press.
Dark Symmetry. Laura Conway. 1973. 5.95 o.p. (ISBN 0-8415-0270-6). Dutton.
Dark Symphony. Dean R. Koontz. (Orig.). 1970. pap. 0.75 o.p. (ISBN 0-447-74621-9). Lancer.
Dark Talisman. Anne-Marie Brentonne. (queen-size gothic). 1975. (pbk.) 1.25. Popular Library.
Dark Terror. Diane Yale. 1981. pap. 6.95 (Avalon). Bouregy.
Dark Things. Ed. by August William Derleth. LC 71-158720. 1971. 6.50. Arkham House.
Dark Tide. Vera Mary Brittain. LC 36-28916. 1936. The Macmillan Company.
Dark Torrent of Glencoe. Edward Grierson. LC 60-9479. 1960. Doubleday.
Dark Tower. Phyllis Bottome. LC 16-18907. 1916. The Century Co.
Dark Tower. Phyllis Bottome. LC 32-33588. 1917. The Century Co.
Dark Tower, and Other Stories. Clive Staples Lewis. LC 76-52387. (Harvest book; HB354). 1977. 6.95 (ISBN 0-15-123902-9) (ISBN 0-15-623930-2). Harcourt Brace Jovanovich.
Dark Tower: By Francis Brett Young. Francis Brett Young. LC 26-426975. 1926. A. A. Knopf.
Dark Tower: The Gunslinger. Stephen King & Michael Whelan. LC 83-121078. (Illus.). 1982. 20.00 (ISBN 0-937986-50-X) (ISBN 0-937986-51-8). D.M. Grant.
Dark Trade see Death of a Pornographer.
Dark Trade. 1st Ed. in the U. S. A. Anthony Lejeune. LC 66-18614. 1966. 3.50. Pub. for the Crime Club by Doubleday.
Dark Traveler. Josephine Winslow Johnson. LC 63-9269. 1963. Simon and Schuster.
Dark Tunnel. Ross Macdonald & Kenneth Millar. LC 80-36843. (Gregg Press Mystery Fiction Series). 1980. 12.95 (ISBN 0-8398-2657-5). Gregg Press.
Dark Tunnel. Kenneth Millar. LC 44-8261. 1944. Dodd, Mead & Company.
Dark Twin. Marion Campbell. LC 74-7682. 1974. 7.95 (ISBN 0-8415-0345-1). Saturday Review Press.
Dark Universe. Daniel F Galouye. LC 76-10435. (Gregg Press science fiction series). 1976. 8.50 (ISBN 0-8398-2333-9). Gregg Press.
Dark Valley. Jackson Gregory. LC 37-19748. 1937. Dodd, Mead & Company.
Dark Valley. Jackson Gregory. LC 42-10805. 1941. Triangle Books.
Dark Valley Romance. Fannie Janeschek Pike. LC 56-863558. Dorrance.
Dark Victory. Charles E. Israel. 1976. (pbk.) 1.50. Dell.
Dark Villa. Dorothy Daniels. 1967. pap. 0.60 o.p. (73-682). Lancer.
Dark Villa of Capri. William Edward Daniel Ross. LC 68-1545. 1968. Arcadia House.
Dark Voyage. Hugh Addis. LC 44-637566. 1944. Dodd, Mead & Company.
Dark Wanton. Peter Cheyney. LC 49-7656. (Red badge detective). 1949. Dodd, Mead.
Dark Was the Wilderness. P. W O'Grady & Dunn, Dorothy, Joint Author. LC 45-10689. 1945. The Bruce Publishing Company.
Dark Watch. Genevieve St John. 1970. pap. 0.75 o.p. (B75-2007). Belmont-Tower.
Dark Water. Ralph Hayes. (Belmont Tower Book.). 1978. 1.95 (ISBN 0-505-51320-X). Tower Pubns.
Dark Waters. William Corcoran. LC 36-17937. 1936. D. Appleton-Century Company, Incorporated.
Dark Waters. Ardath Wise. 1974. 4.95 (ISBN 0-517-51568-7). Lenox Hill Press.
Dark Waters: A Mystery Novel. Francis Marion Cockrell & Cockrell, Marian, 1909- Joint Author. LC 44-471962. 1944. The World Publishing Company.
Dark Waters of Death. Sharon Wagner. (Beagle books). 1975. (pbk.) 0.95 (ISBN 0-345-26666-8). Ballantine Books.
Dark Way to the Plaza. Hope Hale Davis. LC 68-11774. 1968. Doubleday.
Dark Weather. Marguerite R Baldwin. LC 29-19784. E. P. Dutton & Co., Inc.
Dark Wedding: Eitalamio Del Prieto Trinidad. Ramon Jose Sender & Clark, Eleamor, 1913- Tr. LC 43-6640. 1943. Doubleday, Doran & Company, Inc.
Dark Wheel. C., S M & S. M. C. LC 40-2688. 1939. P. J. Kenedy & Sons.
Dark Wheel. Mary Catherine. LC 40-2688. 1939. P. J. Kenedy & Sons.
Dark Whispers. Claudette Nicole. 1975. pap. 1.25 o.p. (ISBN 0-515-03821-0). BJ Pub Group.
Dark Wind. Tony Hillerman. LC 81-47793. 8.95 (ISBN 0-06-066029-5). Harper & Row.
Dark Window. Robin Skelton. 1962. 3.25 o.p. (ISBN 0-19-211234-1). Oxford U Pr.
Dark Window. 1st Ed. Thomas Walsh. LC 56-5922. 1956. Little, Brown.
Dark Windows. Velia Ercole. LC 34-28963. 1934. D. Appleton-Century Company, Incorporated.
Dark Wing. Arthur John Arbuthnott Stringer. LC 39-13613. The Bobbs-Merrill Company.
Dark Woman. Percival Christopher Wren. LC 43-604. 1943. Macrae-Smith-Company.
Dark Wood. Mona Farnsworth. (O.s.i.). (Orig.). 1976. pap. 1.25 o.s.i. (AQ1610, Award). Univ Pub & Dist.
Dark Wood. Christine Goutiere Weston. LC 46-25254. 1946. C. Scribner's Sons.
Dark World. Hayden Carruth. 1974. pap. 2.00 (ISBN 0-87711-052-2). Kayak.
Dark World. Robert E. Mills. (Star Quest Ser.: No. 4). 224p. pap. cancelled (ISBN 0-505-51810-4). Tower Bks.
Dark World. Robert E. Mills. (Star Quest: No. 4). 224p. (Orig.). 1982. pap. 2.25 o.s.i. (ISBN 0-8439-1178-6, Leisure Bks). Nordon Pubns.
Dark World and Wide. Charles Lee Wilson. LC 37-8758. 1937. The Caxton Printers, Ltd.
Dark. 1st Amer. Ed. John McGahern. LC 66-10527. 1966. bds., 3.95. Knopf.
Darkchild. Sydney J. Van Scyoc. 1982. pap. 4.95 (ISBN 0-425-05644-9). Berkley Pub.
Darke Darrell: The Boy Detective. Francis Henry Stauffer. (secret service series, no. 13). 1888. Street & Smith.
Darkened Rooms. Philip Hamilton Gibbs. LC 29-6174. 1929. Doubleday, Doran & Company, Inc.
Darkened Windows. Cornelia Kane Rathbone. LC 24-8041. 1924. D. Appleton and Company.
Darkening Door. 1st Ed. William Sanborn Ballinger. LC 52-5418. 1952. Harper.
Darkening Green. Compton Mackenzie. LC 34-353162. 1934. Doubleday, Doran & Company, Inc.
Darkening Green. Ruth F. Mintz. 3.75 o.p. (ISBN 0-8040-0062-X). Swallow.
Darkening Green: Notes from the Silent Generation. Peter S. Prescott. LC 72-87591. 288p. (YA) 1974. 6.95 o.p. (ISBN 0-698-10491-9). Coward.
Darkening Island. Christopher Preist. 192p. 1974. pap. 1.25 (ISBN 0-532-12230-5). Woodhill.
Darkening Island. Christopher Priest. 1974. (pbk.) 1.25. Manor Books.
Darkening Island. Christopher Priest. LC 71-181660. 1972. 4.95 (ISBN 0-06-013407-0). Harper & Row.
Darkening Night. Jane Elliott. (queen-size gothic). 1975. (pbk.) 1.25. Popular Library.
Darker Brother. Bucklin Moon. LC 43-512751. 1943. Doubleday, Doran & Company, Inc.
Darker Grows the Valley. Harry Harrison Kroll. LC 47-31027. 1947. Bobbs-Merrill Co.
Darker Heritage. Gerda Cerra. pap. 0.95 o.s.i. (75-294). Lancer.
Darker Places. Parke Godwin. LC 80-82213. 356p. 1980. pap. 2.50 (ISBN 0-87216-757-7). Playboy Pbks.
Darker Places. Parke Godwin. (Orig.). 1973. pap. 0.95 o.p. (09218). Curtis.
Darker Star. Mary Frances Doner. 192p. (YA) 1974. 4.95 o.p. (Avalon). Bouregy.
Darker Star. Mary Frances Doner. (Avalon romances). 1974. 4.50. Avalon Books.
Darker Than Amber. John Dann MacDonald. (Travis McGee Ser.). 1979. pap. 2.50 (ISBN 0-449-14162-4, GM). Fawcett.
Darker Than Amber: A Travis McGee Story. John Dann MacDonald. LC 70-11013. 1970. 4.95. Lippincott.
Darker Than You Think. Jack Williamson. LC 75-440. (Garland Library of Science Fiction). 1975. 11.00 (ISBN 0-8240-1442-1). Garland Pub.
Darker Than You Think. Jack Williamson. LC 49-7348. 1948. Fantasy Press.

Darker the Night. Herbert Brean. LC 49-8286. 1949. W. Morrow.
Darker the Night. Marti Sinclair et al. 1982. pap. 4.95cancelled (ISBN 0-89191-110-3). Cook.
Darker Traffic. Martin Brett. LC 54-10575. (Red badge detective). 1954. Dodd, Mead.
Darker Triumph. Bertram H Appleby. LC 61-9715. 1961. G.J. Rickard.
Darkest Bough. 1st Ed. Anne Chamberlain. LC 58-12905. 1958. Bobbs-Merrill.
Darkest Hour. Hazel Iris Addis. LC 43-6641. 1943. Arcadia House, Inc.
Darkest Hour. William P McGivern. LC 55-523054. (Red badge detective). 1955. Dodd, Mead.
Darkest Hour. Helen Nielsen. LC 69-16636. 1969. 5.95. Morrow.
Darkest Night. Peter Saxon. 1967. pap. 0.50 o.p. (52-562). Paperback Lib.
Darkest Room. Grace Corren, pseud. LC 73-862. (Orig.). 1969. pap. 0.60 o.p. Lancer.
Darkest Room. Grace Corren, pseud. 1973. pap. 0.95 o.s.i. (75-457). Lancer.
Darkest Room. Grace Corren, pseud. (O.s.i.). 1976. pap. 1.25 o.s.i. (BT50901). Belmont-Tower.
Darkest Room. Grace Corren. 1976. (pbk.) 1.25. Belmont Towers.
Darkest Russia: A Novel. Henry Grattan Donnelly. (On cover: Drama series, no. 26). Street & Smith.
Darkest Spot. Lee Thayer. LC 28-5983. 1928. J. H. Sears & Company, Inc.
Darkhaven. Dorothy Daniels. 1969. pap. 0.75 o.p. (ISBN 0-446-64675-X, 64-675). Paperback Lib.
Darkling. Elaine Gottlieb. LC 47-1229. 1947. Reynal & Hitchcock.
Darkling. David Kesterton. LC 82-6671. 12.95 (ISBN 0-87054-093-9). Arkham House.
Darkling Death. Francis Vivian, pseud. LC 57-7189. 1956. Roy Publishers.
Darklings. Julie Cameron. (Berkeley Medallion Book). 1975. (pbk.) 1.25 (ISBN 0-425-02895-X). Berkeley Pub Co.
Darkly the River Flows. John Arthur Macdonald. LC 45-5354. 1945. Coward-McCann, Inc.
Darkness and Dawn. George Allan England. LC 73-13253. (Classics of science fiction). (Illus.). 1974. 13.95 (ISBN 0-88355-108-X) (ISBN 0-88355-108-X). Hyperion Press.
Darkness and Dawn. George Allan England. LC 14-3972. Small, Maynard and Company.
Darkness and Dawn. A Stephens Hurlock. LC 19-278. 1918. Dukes.
Darkness and Dawn. Aleksei Nikolaevich Tolstoi. LC 75-36515. 1977. 28.50 (ISBN 0-8371-8639-0). Greenwood Press.
Darkness and Dawn. Aleksiel Nikolaevich Tolstoi & Bone, Edith, Tr. LC 36-8453. 1936. Longmans, Green and Co.
Darkness and Dawn: Or, Scenes in the Days of Nero. Frederic William Farrar. 1891. Longmans, Green, and Co.
Darkness & Day. Ivy Compton-Burnett. 254p. 1974. 10.00x o.p. (ISBN 0-575-01795-3). Intl Pubns Serv.
Darkness and Day. 1st American Ed. Compton-Burnett, Ivy. LC 51-1832. 1951. Knopf.
Darkness and Daylight. Mary Jane Hawes Holmes. LC 8-11831. G. W. Dillingham Company.
Darkness and Daylight. A Novel. Mary Jane Hawes Holmes. LC 3475. (On cover: Madison square library, no. 26). 1897. G. W. Dillingham Co.
Darkness and the Dawn. Thomas Bertram Costain. 1974. (pbk.) 1.50 (ISBN 0-380-00127-6). Avon.
Darkness and the Dawn: A Novel. Thomas Bertram Costain. LC 59-11583. 1959. Doubleday.
Darkness and the Deep. Vardis Fisher. LC 43-3878. 1943. The Vanguard Press.
Darkness and the Light. William Olaf Stapledon. LC 73-13267. (Classics of science fiction). 1974. (ISBN 0-88355-121-7) (ISBN 0-88355-150-0). Hyperion Press.
Darkness at Dawn. Rebecca Drury. (Women at War Ser.: No. 11). (Orig.). 1983. pap. 3.25 (ISBN 0-440-01663-0, Emerald). Dell.
Darkness at Indian Key. Kamelle Hess. 1978. pap. 1.50 (ISBN 0-532-15338-3). Woodhill.
Darkness at Ingraham's Crest. Frank Yerby. 1980. pap. 2.95 (ISBN 0-440-11640-6). Dell.
Darkness at Ingraham's Crest: A Tale of the Slaveholding South. Frank Yerby. LC 79-4646. 12.95 (ISBN 0-8037-1640-0). Dial Press.
Darkness at Mantia. Iris Barry. (Berkley medallion book). 1974. (pbk.) 0.95 (ISBN 0-425-02542-X). Berkley Pub. Co.
Darkness at Noon. Harry Carlisle. LC 31-7411. 1931. H. Liveright.
Darkness at Noon. unabridged school ed. Arthur Koestler. (Literary heritage; a Macmillan paperback series). 1963. Macmillan.
Darkness at Noon. Arthur Koestler. Tr. by Hardy, Daphne. LC 41-51809. The Macmillan Company.
Darkness at Pemberley. Terence Hanbury White. LC 33-2628. The Century Co.
Darkness at Pemberley. Terence Hanbury White. LC 77-20549. (Illus.). 1978. 3.50 (ISBN 0-486-23613-7). Dover Publications.
Darkness at Sunrise. Rae Brown. 1973. 4.95 (ISBN 0-517-51449-4). Lenox Hill Press.
Darkness Below. Frederic Morton. LC 49-110838. 1949. Crown Publishers.
Darkness: By Evan John Pseud. Evan John Simpson. LC 54-5483. 1954. Putnam.
Darkness Casts No Shadow. Arnost Lustig. LC 76-41232. (His Children of the Holocaust; v. 2). 1976. 8.95 (ISBN 0-87953-406-0). Inscape.
Darkness Casts No Shadow. Arnost Lustig. 1978. 1.75 (ISBN 0-380-01952-3). Avon.
Darkness End. Richard L. Spohn. 5.95 o.p. Vantage.
Darkness Falling. Barbara Kevern. 1974. (pbk.) 0.95 (ISBN 0-523-00325-0). Pinnacle Books.
Darkness in My Soul. Dean R. Koontz. 128p. (Orig.). 1972. pap. 0.95 o.p. (UQ1012). Daw Bks.
Darkness in My Soul. Dean R. Koontz. 1976. pap. 1.25 o.p. (UY1274). DAW Bks.
Darkness in Saint Louis Bearheart. Gerald Robert Vizenor. LC 79-109630. 5.95 (ISBN 0-916562-19-0). Truck Press.
Darkness in St. Louis Bearheart. Gerald Robert Vizenor. 1978. pap. 5.95 (ISBN 0-916562-19-0). Bookslinger.
Darkness in Summer. Takeshi Kaiko. LC 73-7299. 1973. 6.95 (ISBN 0-394-48441-X). Knopf; Distributed by Random House.
Darkness of Slumber. Rosemary Kutak. LC 44-840901. 1944. J. B. Lippincott Company.
Darkness on Diamondia. Alfred Elton Van Vogt. 1982. pap. 2.25 (ISBN 0-87997-724-8, UE1724). DAW Bks.
Darkness on the Stairs. Florence Stevenson. (Signet Book). 1976. (pbk.) 1.25. New American Library.
Darkness Over the Valley. Wendelgard Von Staden. 1982. pap. 4.95 (ISBN 0-14-006316-1). Penguin.
Darkness Visible. William Gerald Golding. LC 79-19206. 1979. (ISBN 0-374-13502-9). Farrar Straus Giroux.
Darkness Visible. Norman Lewis. LC 60-13198. 1960. Pantheon Books.
Darkness Weaves. Karl Edward Wagner. 1978. 1.95 (ISBN 0-446-89598-9). Warner Books.
Darkover Concordance. Walter Breen. LC 79-84472. 1979. 17.95 (ISBN 0-930800-10-9); pap. 8.95 (ISBN 0-930800-07-9). Pennyfarthing.
Darkover Landfall. Marion Zimmer Bradley. LC 78-6874. (Gregg Press science fiction series). (Illus.). 1978. 9.50 (ISBN 0-8398-2404-1). Gregg Press.
Darkroom. Carolyn Banks. LC 79-23240. 1980. 10.95 (ISBN 0-670-25680-3). Viking Press.
Darkwater. Jan Alexander, pseud. 1975. (pbk.) 0.95 (ISBN 0-671-77945-1). Pocket Books.
Darkwater. Dorothy Eden. LC 64-10429. 1964. Coward-McCann.
Darkwater: Voices from Within the Veil. William Edward Burghardt Du Bois. LC 75-1429. 1975. Repr. of 1920 ed. 14.00 (ISBN 0-527-25300-6). Kraus Intl.
Darla and Ken - Infinite Lovers. first ed. Gladys Payne. 1972. 3.95 (ISBN 0-533-00290-7). Vantage.
Darlin' Bill. Jerome Charyn. LC 80-66763. 1980. 11.95 (ISBN 0-87795-283-3). Arbor Hse.
Darling. Harriet Daimler. 176p. (Orig.). 1983. pap. 3.50 (ISBN 0-394-62458-0, B489, BC). Grove.
Darling. rev. ed. Harriet Daimler. pap. 1.25 o.p. (2037). Brandon.
Darling: And Other Stories. Anton Pavlovich Chekhov. Tr. by Garnett, Constance (Black) LC 16-21395. (On cover: The tales of Chekhov. vol. 1). 1916. The Macmillan Company.
Darling Buds of May. 1st Ed. Herbert Ernest Bates. LC 58-78689. 1958. Little, Brown.
Darling Daughter. A Satire. 1st Ed. Helen Tufts Bailie. LC 56-8592. 1956. Greenwich Book Publishers.
Darling Daughters. Elizabeth Troop. LC 80-52354. 1981. 9.95 (ISBN 0-312-18281-3). St. Martin's Press.
Darling Driver. Marieli Benziger. (Illus.). 1978. pap. 9.00x. Benziger Sis.
Darling Fool. Mabel McElliott. LC 33-21389. Grosset & Dunlap.
Darling, I Am Growing Old. Gene Stone. LC 74-5017. 1974. (lib. bdg.) 8.95 (ISBN 0-8161-6205-0). G. K. Hall.
Darling, I Am Growing Old: A Novel. Gene Stone. LC 73-21873. 1974. 5.95 (ISBN 0-395-18489-4). Houghton Mifflin.
Darling, No Regrets. Davidyne S. Mayleas. 544p. (Orig.). 1981. pap. 3.50 (ISBN 0-446-90558-5). Warner Bks.
Darling Pericles. Madelon Dimont. LC 75-190397. 1972. 5.95. Atheneum.
Darling Rebel. Florence Stonebraker. 1949. Arcadia House.
Darling, This Is Death. Albert Leffingwell. LC 45-453320. 1945. Dial Press.
Darling Twins. Robert L. Merriam. (Illus.). 25p. (Orig.). 1976. pap. 2.00. R L Merriam.
Darlingtons. Sylvia Leonora Brett Brooke. LC 50-9330. 1950. Farrar, Straus.
Darlingtons. Elmore Elliott Peake. 1900. McClure, Philips & Co.
Darrel of the Blessed Isles. Irving Bacheller. LC 3-9625. 1903. Lothrop Publishing Company.
Darrell, a Novel. Marion Montgomery. LC 64-13822. 1964. Doubleday.
Darryll Gap: Or, Whether It Paid. Virginia Frances Townsend. LC 3-24515. Lee and Shepard.
Darsham's Tower; a Novel. Harriet Esmond. LC 73-4725. 1973. 6.95. Delacorte Press.
Darshan. Lynn Weinberger & Jon Weinberger. 160p. 1972. pap. 3.95 o.s.i. (0*P*B001). Olympia.
D'artagnan Romances, 5 Vols. Alexandre Dumas. Set. 1ea. 25.00 o.p. (ISBN 0-00-423007-8). Collins-World.
D'Artagnan Signature. Robert S Hopkins. LC 75-30959. 7.95 (ISBN 0-399-11681-8). Putnam.
D'Artagnan Signature. Robert Rostand. LC 75-30959. 1976. 7.95 o.p. (ISBN 0-399-11681-8). Putnam.
D'Artagnan, the King Maker: An Historical Novel. Henry Llewellyn Williams & Dumas, Alexandre, 1802-1870. L'envers D'une Conspiration. LC 1-27101. 1901. Street & Smith.
D'Artagnan: The Sequel to The Three Musketeers. Henry Bedford-Jones. LC 28-22458. 1928. Covici, Friede.
D'Artagnan's Exploit ("Louis Treize") Henry Llewellyn Williams & Dumas, Alexandre, 1802-1870. LC 4-9270. 1904. Street & Smith.
D'Arthez Case. Hans Erich Nossack. LC 76-148711. 1971. 7.95 (ISBN 0-374-13504-5). Farrar, Straus & Giroux.
Darting Rays: And Other Stories. Joseph Loeser. LC 24-28888. 1924. The Author.
Dartmoor a Novel. Maurice H Hervey. LC 7-4659. F. A. Stokes Company.
Dartmoor Enigma. Basil Home Thomson. LC 36-6668. 1936. Pub. for the Crime Club, Inc., by Doubleday, Doran & Co., Inc.
Dartmoor Enigma. Basil Home Thomson. LC 36-32339. 1936. The Sun Dial Press.
Dartmoor Galahad. Olive Katharine Parr. LC 23-17189. 1923. 2.00. Longmans, Green and Co.
Dartmouth Murders. Clifford Orr. LC 29-22681. Farrar & Rinehart Incorporated.
Darwich Castle. Bettina Kingsley. (Dell book). 1974. (pbk.) 0.95. Dell.
Darya of the Bronze Age. Lin Carter. (Science Fiction Ser.). 1981. pap. 1.95 o.p. (ISBN 0-87997-655-1, UJ1655). DAW Bks.
Darzee, Girl of India. Edison Marshall. LC 37-238826. 1937. H. C. Kinsey & Company, Inc.
D.A.'s Daughter. Herman Petersen. LC 43-51063. 1943. Duell, Sloan and Pearce.
Das Edle Blut. Ernst Von Wildenbruch & Schmidt, Friedrich Georg Gottlob, 1868- Ed. LC 12-40235. (Heath's modern language series). 1898. D. C. Heath & Co.
Das Edle Blut: Von Ernst Von Wildenbruch. Ernst Von Wildenbruch & Weigel, John Conrad, 1886- LC 17-21860. (Half-title: Macmillan German series). 1917. The Macmillan Company.
Das Fahnlein der Sieben Aufrechten: Novelle. Gottfried Keller. Ed. by Howard, William Guild & Sturtevant, Albert Morey. LC 7-31169. (Heath's modern language series). 1907. D. C. Heath & Co.
Das Fliegende Klassenzimmer, ein Eoman Von Erich Kastner. Erich Kastner. Ed. by Zeydel, Edwin Hermann. LC 35-24753. 1933. F. S. Crofts & Co.
Das Jahr Des Herrn: Von Karl Heinrich Waggerl. Karl Heinrich Waggerl & Goodloe, Jane Faulkner, 1895- Ed. 1941. F. S. Crofts & Co.
Dash at the Pole. William Lyon Phelps. 1909. The Ball Publishing Company.
Dash for a Throne. Arthur Williams Marchmont. LC 99-2565. 1899. New Amsterdam Book Company; Etc., Etc.
Dash for Freedom: A Novel. Thomas G Jones. LC 51-12916. 1951. Exposition Press.
Dash of Red Paint. Nellie Lowe Willmott. LC 8-36894. 1894. The E. B. Sheldon Co.
Dasha. Martha Edith Almedingen. LC 45-35056. 1945. Harcourt, Brace and Company.
Dashed Against the Rock: A Romance of the Coming Age. William J Colville. LC 6-30670. 1894. Colby & Rich.
Dashes at Life with a Free Pencil. Nathaniel Parker Willis. LC 68-55690. (American short story series, v. 30). 1969. Garrett Press.
Dashes at Life with a Free Pencil. Nathaniel Parker Willis. LC 72-8234. (American short story series, v. 30). 1972. (ISBN 0-8422-8126-6). MSS Information Corp.
Dashes at Life with a Free Pencil. Nathaniel Parker Willis. LC 20-23143. 1845. Burgess, Stringer & Co.
Dashiell Hammett, a Casebook. Nolan. pap. 6.95 o.p. Borden.
Dashiell Hammett: Five Complete Novels. avenel 1980 ed. Dashiell Hammett. LC 80-39931. 1980. 6.98 (ISBN 0-517-33841-6). Avenel Books: Distributed by Crown Publishers.
Dashiell Hammett Omnibus: Red Harvest, The Dain Curse, The Maltese Falcon. Dashiell Hammett. 1935. A. A. Knopf.
Dashiell Hammett's Secret Agent X-9. Dashiell Hammett & Alex Raymond. Ed. by Tony Sparafucile. LC 83-80126. (Illus.). 225p. (Orig.). 1983. pap. 9.95 (ISBN 0-930330-05-6). Intl Polygonics.
Dashing Fugitive: Or, True to His Purpose... Harlan Page Halsey. LC 12-345776. (Old Sleuth's own. no. 100). 1897. The Parlor Car Publishing Co.
Dashing Guardian. Lucia Curzon, pseud. (Second Chance at Love Ser.: No. 123). 1983. pap. 1.75 (ISBN 0-515-07211-7). Jove Pubns.
Dashwoods. Steele Rudd. (O.s.i.). (Illus.). 1970. pap. 2.25x o.s.i. (ISBN 0-7022-0694-6). U of Queensland Pr.
Dashwoods & Grandpa's Selection. Steele Rudd. (Illus.). 1970. 7.25x (ISBN 0-7022-0696-2). U of Queensland Pr.
Datchley Inheritance. Stephen McKenna. LC 29-114428. 1929. Dodd, Mead & Company.
Date for Murder. Louis Trimble. LC 43-203314. 1942. Phoenix Press.
Date with a Dead Man. Brett Halliday. (Mike Shayne mystery). 1974. (pbk.) 0.95. Dell.
Date with Danger. Maysie Greig. LC 52-5153. 1952. Random House.
Date with Danger. Roy Vickers. LC 44-772559. 1944. The Vanguard Press.
Date with Darkness. Donald Hamilton. LC 47-3664. 1947. Rinehart & Company, Inc.
Date with Death. Zenith Jones Brown. LC 48-7682. 1949. C. Scribner's Sons.
Date with Death. Elizabeth Linington. LC 66-10648. bds., 3.95. Harper.
Date with Death. Bradford Scott. pap. 0.50 o.p. (R1978). Pyramid Pubns.
Date with the Dead. Dorothea E. Hammond. 250p. 1983. pap. 6.95 (ISBN 0-942874-00-5). Hammond Records.
Dateless Bargain. Catharine Louisa Pirkis. LC 7-39631. (Lovell's library, no. 1223). J. W. Lovell Company.
Dateline: Europe: By Leonard Ross, Pseud. Leo Calvin Rosten. LC 39-27407. Harcourt, Brace and Company.
Daugher of the Revolution. Esther Singleton. LC 15-26979. 1915. 1.25. Moffat, Yard & Company.
Daughter. Charity Blackstock, pseud. 1970. 5.95 o.p. (ISBN 0-698-10090-5). Coward.
Daughter. Ursula Torday. 1974. (pbk.) 1.25 (ISBN 0-380-00128-4). Avon.
Daughter. Ursula Torday. LC 71-104690. 1970. 5.95. Coward-McCann.
Daughter: A Love Story. Anne Constance Smedley Maxwell Armfield Armfield. LC 8-10433. 1908. Moffat, Yard and Company.
Daughter: A Novel. Bessie Breuer. Simon and Schuster.
Daughter: A Novel Based on the Life of Eleanor Marx. Judith Chernaik. LC 78-69618. 9.95 (ISBN 0-06-010757-X). Harper & Row.
Daughter: A Novel of South Africa. Arthur Markowitz. LC 61-5106. 1951. Farrar, Straus, and Young.
Daughter & Shadow. James B. Johnson. (Science Fiction Ser.). 1981. pap. 1.95 o.p. (ISBN 0-87997-605-5, UJ1605). DAW Bks.
Daughter Buffalo: A Novel. Janet Frame, pseud. LC 72-80014. 1972. 5.95 (ISBN 0-8076-0657-X). G. Braziller.
Daughter in Bondage. Phyllis Kinley. 1974. (pbk.) 1.50 (ISBN 0-87162-171-1). Warner Press.
Daughter-in-Law. Nellie Mabel Fries. LC 35-565871. The Christopher Publishing House.
Daughter of a Hundred Millions. Virginia Niles Leeds. LC 7-12599. 1897. F. T. Neely.
Daughter of a Magnate. Frank Hamilton Spearman. LC 3-25212. 1903. C. Scribner's Sons.
Daughter of a Rebel: A Novel. Georgie Vere Tyler. LC 13-3756. 1913. Duffield & Company.
Daughter of a Republican. Bernie Smade Babcock. LC 6155. 1900. The New Voice Press.
Daughter of a Soldier: A Colleen of South Ireland. Elizabeth Thomasina Meade Smith. LC 16-15131. Hurst & Company.
Daughter of a Star. Frances Christine Tiernan. LC 13-25373. The Devin-Adair Company.
Daughter of a Stoic. Cornelia Atwood Pratt Comer. LC 7-30291. 1896. Macmillan and Co.
Daughter of Adam. Corra May White Harris. LC 23-7005. 1.75. George H. Doran Company.
Daughter of an Egyptian King. Georg Moritz Ebers & Reed, Henry, 1846-1896, Tr. LC 41-38120. 1880. J. B. Lippincott & Co.

TITLE INDEX DAUGHTER OF THE SUN

Daughter of an Egyptian King. Georg Moritz Ebers & Reed, Henry, 1846-1896, Tr. LC 6-36807. 1871. J. B. Lippincott & Co.
Daughter of an Empress. Klara Muller Mundt. (On cover: Lovell's library, no. 1014). 1887. J. W. Lovell Company.
Daughter of an Empress. Klara Muller Mundt. Tr. by Greene, Nathaniel. LC 16-1230. (historical romances of Louisa Muhlbach pseud.). D. Appleton and Company.
Daughter of an Empress: An Historical Novel. Klara Muller Mundt. Tr. by Greene, Nathaniel. LC 7-17268. 1893. D. Appleton and Company.
Daughter of an Outlaw. Agnes Galleberg. 3.75 o.p. Vantage.
Daughter of Anderson Crow. George Barr McCutcheon. LC 7-25508. 1907. Dodd, Mead and Company.
Daughter of Angy. Dora Miranda Merrill Goodwin. LC 11-26948. 1.25. R. G. Badger.
Daughter of Astrea. Edward Phillips Oppenheim. LC 16-22265. D. W. Newton.
Daughter of Brahma. Ida Alexa Ross Wylie. LC 12-18062. The Bobbs-Merrill Company.
Daughter of Brahma: A Tale of the Brahmaputra Country. Ellen Elizabeth Vickland. LC 35-6196. Fleming H. Revell Company.
Daughter of Bugle Ann. MacKinlay Kantor. LC 52-7139. 1953. Random House.
Daughter of Conquest. Robert E Mills. (Leisure books). 1979. 2.25 (ISBN 0-8439-0646-4). Nordon Pubns.
Daughter of Cuba. Helen M Bowen. LC 6-14910. (On cover: The Waldorf series, no. 28). The Merriam Company.
Daughter of Cuba. Helen M Bowen. Rand, McNally & Company.
Daughter of Dale. Emerson Gifford Taylor. LC 4-129751. 1904. The Century Co.
Daughter of Darkness. H. P. Dunne. (Orig.). pap. 2.75 (ISBN 0-451-11265-2, AE1265, Sig). NAL.
Daughter of Darkness. J. R Lowell. LC 72-13803. 1973. 8.95. G. K. Hall.
Daughter of Darkness. Patricia McGerr. 1974. (pbk.) 0.95. Popular Library.
Daughter of Darkness: Novel. J. R Lowell. LC 72-4858. 1972. Delacorte Press.
Daughter of David Kerr. Harry King Tootle. LC 12-20792. 1912. A. C. McClurg & Co.
Daughter of Deep Silence. Catherine Major. 1980. write for info. (ISBN 0-89554-022-3). Brasch & Brasch.
Daughter of Delilah. John Taintor Foote. LC 36-647667. 1936. D. Appleton-Century Co., Incorporated.
Daughter of Delilah. Robert Lee Tyler. (On cover: Criterion series, no. 12). 1895. Street & Smith.
Daughter of Destiny. Stephanie Blake. LC 77-79951. 1977. 1.95. Playboy Press.
Daughter of Divorce. Katharine Haviland Taylor. LC 39-5593. J. B. Lippincott Company.
Daughter of Earth. Agnes Smedley. LC 72-14442. (Feminist Press reprint series). 1973. 8.00. Feminist Press.
Daughter of Earth. Agnes Smedley. LC 29-6445. 1929. Coward-McCann, Inc.
Daughter of Earth. Agnes Smedley. LC 35-271518. 1935. Coward-McCann, Inc.
Daughter of Earth: A Novel. Agnes Smedley. 420p. 1973. 10.00 (ISBN 0-912670-87-8); pap. 5.50. Feminist Pr.
Daughter of Eve. Honore De Balzac. LC 3-23175. (Half-title: The comedy of human life... Scnes from private life). 1895. Roberts Brothers.
Daughter of Eve. Noel Bertram Gerson. LC 58-8091. 1958. Doubleday.
Daughter of Eve. Ellen Warner Olney Kirk. LC 7-12354. 1889. Ticknor and Company.
Daughter of Fanny Hill, Vol. 1. (Orig.). pap. 0.95 o.p. (1024). Brandon.
Daughter of Fanny Hill, Vol. 2. pap. 1.25 o.p. (2054). Brandon.
Daughter of Fanny Hill, Vol. 3. (Illus., Orig.). 1969. pap. 1.95 o.p. (6069). Brandon.
Daughter of Fife. Amelia Edith Huddleston Barr. LC 6-7995. 1886. Dodd, Mead & Company.
Daughter of Fu Manchu. Sax Rohmer, pseud. 1970. pap. 0.60 o.p. (X2149). Pyramid Pubns.
Daughter of Fu Manchu. Sax Rohmer, pseud. 1975. pap. 1.25 o.p. (ISBN 0-515-04024-X). BJ Pub Group.
Daughter of Fu Manchu. Arthur Sarsfield Ward. LC 49-1762. (New Avon library 189). 1949. Avon Pub. Co.
Daughter of Fu Manchu. Arthur Sarsfield Ward. LC 31-6074. 1931. Doubleday, Doran & Company, Inc.
Daughter of Gascony. Noel Bertram Gerson. LC 63-20494. 1963. Macrae Smith.
Daughter of Hassan. Penny Jordan. (Harlequin Ser.). 192p. 1982. pap. 1.75 (ISBN 0-373-10537-1). Harlequin Bks.
Daughter of Helen Kent. Sarah Comstock. LC 21-17911. 1921. Doubleday, Page & Company.
Daughter of Heth. William Black. LC 6-129382. (Lovell's library, v. 2, no. 82). John W. Lovell Company.
Daughter of Heth: A Novel. library ed. William Black. 1903. Harper & Brothers.
Daughter of Humanity: A Novel. Edgar Maurice Smith. LC 8-8633. 1895. Arena Publishing Company.
Daughter of Indra... Reginald Warde. LC 26-2448. The Essene Publishing Co.
Daughter of Israel. Rose Porter. 1899. E. P. Dutton & Company.
Daughter of Jairus. Paul Hervey Fox. LC 51-9205. 1951. Little, Brown.
Daughter of Jehu. Laura Elizabeth Howe Richards. LC 18-18836. 1918. D. Appleton and Company.
Daughter of Jerusalem. Robert G. Pitzer. 1956. 5.95 o.p. (ISBN 0-87140-859-7). Liveright.
Daughter of Jerusalem: A Biblical Novel of the Days of Jeremiah. Robert Claiborne Pitzer. LC 56-755290. 1956. Liveright Pub. Corp.
Daughter of Judas: A Fin-De-Siecle Tale of New York City Life. Richard Henry Savage. LC 8-1996. 1894. F. T. Neely.
Daughter of Mars. Bettina Kingsley. (Berkley Medallion Book.). (Illus.). 1977. 1.50 (ISBN 0-425-03343-0). Berkley Pub.Corp.
Daughter of Maryland. A Narrative of Pickett's Last Charge at Gettysburg. A Novel. George Waldo Browne. LC 6-17381. (On cover: The war series, v. 1, no. 2). Novelist Publishing Co.
Daughter of Maryland. A Narrative of Pickett's Last Charge at Gettysburg. A Novel. George Waldo Browne. LC 6-17231. (On cover: Clover series, no. 68). Street & Smith.
Daughter of Mexico: A Historical Romance Founded on Documentary Evidence. Andrew Edward Breen. LC 16-217136. 1916. 1.50. John P. Smith Printing Company.
Daughter of Music. Gertrude Weaver. (On cover: Appletons' town and country library, no. 145). 1894. D. Appleton and Company.
Daughter of My House. Mair Unsworth. 1973. (pbk) 0.75. Ace Books.
Daughter of Nazareth. Florence Anne Marvyne Bauer. LC 55-136481. 1955. Broadman Press.
Daughter of Neptune: And Other Stories. William Winslow. 1899. Continental Publishing Co.
Daughter of New France: With Some Account of the Gallant Sieur Cadillac and His Colony on the Detroit. Mary Catherine Crowley. LC 1-31715. 1901. Little, Brown, and Company.
Daughter of Night: A Tale of Three Worlds. Lydia Obukhova. Tr. by Mirra Ginsburg. 176p. 1982. pap. 2.95 (ISBN 0-380-61192-9, 61192-9, Bard). Avon.
Daughter of Pan. Cornelia Stratton Parker. LC 26-16354. 1926. Doubleday, Page & Company.
Daughter of Pharaoh. A Tale of the Exodus. Frederick Myron Colby. LC 6-26931. 1886. Phillips & Hunt.
Daughter of Raasay: A Tale of the '45. William MacLeod Raine. LC 2-25518. 1902. F. A. Stokes Company.
Daughter of Ramona: A Heart Appealing Story of Romance, Ambition and Adventure in the West. Robert E Callahan. LC 34-15490. Gaines Publishing Co.
Daughter of Russia. Ivan Sergieevich Turgenev & Scott, George W., Tr. (Seaside library, v. 60, no. 1216). 1882. G. Munro.
Daughter of St. Peter's. A Novel. Janet C Conger. LC 6-30388. J. W. Lovell Company.
Daughter of Satan. Eleanor Hibbert. LC 72-87624. 1973. 6.95 (ISBN 0-399-11077-1). Putnam.
Daughter of Satan. Eleanor Hibbert. LC 73-3149. 1973. 11.95 (ISBN 0-8161-6094-5). G. K. Hall.
Daughter of Satan. Jean Plaidy. (Berkley medallion book). 1974. (pbk.) 1.25 (ISBN 0-425-02561-6). Putnam.
Daughter of Satan. A Sensational Story of the Crescent City. Harry Mills. LC 7-31116. (On cover: New York 10 cent library, no. 12). Katahdin Publishing Company.
Daughter of Shadows. Miranda Seymour, pseud. LC 77-22844. 1977. 8.95 (ISBN 0-698-10784-5). Coward, McCann & Geoghegan.
Daughter of Silence. Morris L West. LC 61-13554. 1961. Morrow.
Daughter of Silence: A Novel. Edgar Fawcett. LC 6-38954. (On cover: The Belford American novel series. no. 25)). 1880. Belford Comapny.
Daughter of Strangers. Elizabeth Boatwright Coker. LC 50-13844. 1950. Dutton.
Daughter of Tehuan: Or, Texas of the Past Century. Alto Sebastian Hoermann & Braun, Alois, Tr. LC 32-258288. 1932. Standard Printing Company.
Daughter of the Badlands. Kate Boyles Bingham & Boyles, Virgil Dillin. LC 22-11851. 1922. The Stratford Company.
Daughter of the Blood. Herbert Bouldin Hawes. LC 30-19832. The Four Seas Company.
Daughter of the Bright Moon. Lynn Abbey. 1979. pap. 6.95 (ISBN 0-441-13877-2). Ace Bks.
Daughter of the Bright Moon. Lynn Abbey. Ed. by Jim Baen. 1980. pap. 2.95 (ISBN 0-441-13875-6). Ace Bks.
Daughter of the Confederacy: A Story of the Old South and the New. Phoebe Hamilton Seabrook. LC 6-43778. 1906. The Neale Publishing Company.
Daughter of the Covenant: A Tale of Louisiana. Littleton Purnell Bowen. LC 1-27716. 1901. The Presbyterian Committee of Publication.
Daughter of the Dawn. William Reginald Hodder. LC 77-84238. (Lost Race and Adult Fantasy Fiction). (Illus.). 1978. 22.00 (ISBN 0-405-10986-5). Arno Press.
Daughter of the Dawn. Marion Randall Parsons. LC 23-8082. 1923. 2.00. Little, Brown, and Company.
Daughter of the Dawn: A Realistic Story of Maori Magic. William Reginald Hodder. Ed. by R. Reginald & Douglas Melville. LC 77-84239. (Lost Race & Adult Fantasy Ser.). (Illus.). 1978. Repr. of 1903 ed. lib. bdg. 22.00x (ISBN 0-405-10986-5). Ayer Co.
Daughter of the Delta. Pearl Elder. LC 52-14829. 1952. Comet Press Books.
Daughter of the Desert. Chloe Gartner. 1978. pap. 2.25 (ISBN 0-89083-375-3). Zebra.
Daughter of the Devil. Lozania Prole. 1974. (pbk.) 0.95 (ISBN 0-671-77748-3). Pocket Books.
Daughter of the Druids. Alice Kimball Hopkins. LC 4-33147. 1892. Printed by A. Mudge & Son.
Daughter of the Elm: A Tale of Western Virginia Before the War. Granville Davisson Hall. LC 50-33208. Arcuri Book Shop.
Daughter of the Elm: A Tale of Western Virginia Before the War. 4th ed. Granville Davisson Hall. LC 46-22355. Arcuri Book Shop.
Daughter of the Gods. Jane Stanley. LC 8-13880. (Harper's handy series. no. 84). 1886. Harper & Brothers.
Daughter of the Gods: Or, How She Came into Her Kingdom; a Romance. Charlotte Clark. LC 37-327803. 1884. White, Stokes, & Allen.
Daughter of the Gods: Or, How She Came into Her Kingdom; a Romance. Charlotte Clark. 1885. Dodd, Mead & Company.
Daughter of the Hawk. Cecil Scott Forester. LC 28-20923. The Bobbs-Merrill Company.
Daughter of the Highlanders. Frances Jones Melton. LC 10-14367. 1.50. The Roxburgh Publishing Company (Incorporated.
Daughter of the Hills. Willie Fain Marmon. LC 9-2039. 1909. The Neale Publishing Company.
Daughter of the Hills: A Woman's Story of Coalmining Life. Myra Page. LC 77-79619. 1977. pap. 4.95 o.p. (ISBN 0-89255-026-0). Persea Bks.
Daughter of the House: A Fleming Stone Story. Carolyn Wells. LC 25-21210. 1925. J. B. Lippincott Company.
Daughter of the House. 1st American Ed. Catherine Gaskin. LC 53-5368. 1953. Harper.
Daughter of the Huguenots. Elizabeth Williams Champney. LC 1-25676. (Her Dames and daughters of colonial days, v. 3). 1901. Dodd, Mead and Co.
Daughter of the King. Louie Alien Baker. LC 6-6887. (On cover: Neely's international library). 1894. F. T. Neely.
Daughter of the Land. Gene Stratton Porter. LC 18-16489. Doubleday, Page & Company.
Daughter of the Land. Gene Stratton Porter. LC 21-13700. 1920. Grosset & Dunlap.
Daughter of the Land. Gene Stratton-Porter. 1974. Repr. of 1918 ed. lib. bdg. 25.00 (ISBN 0-8414-7975-5). Folcroft.
Daughter of the Legend. Jesse Stuart. LC 65-25553. 1965. bds., 4.95. McGraw.
Daughter of the Manse: A Novel. Sophie C. Taylor. LC 10-9701. 1909. 1.50. The John C. Winston Company.
Daughter of the Marionis. new ed.... ed. Edward Phillips Oppenheim. LC 21-146282. 1920. Little, Brown, and Company.
Daughter of the Medici: And Other Stories. Donn Byrne. LC 73-125207. (Short story index reprint series). 1970. Books for Libraries Press.
Daughter of the Medici, and Other Stories. Donn Byrne. LC 35-28927. 1935. D. Appleton-Century Company, Incorporated.
Daughter of the Middle Border see Collected Works.
Daughter of the Misty Gorges. Essie Summers. (Harlequin Romances Ser.). 192p. 1983. pap. 1.50 (ISBN 0-373-02525-4). Harlequin Bks.
Daughter of the Morning. Zona Gale. LC 17-288482. 1.40. The Bobbs-Merrill Company.
Daughter of the Narikin. Etsu Inagaki Sugimoto. LC 32-30025. 1932. Doubleday, Doran and Company, Incorporated.
Daughter of the Navy. Florence Stonebreaker. LC 42-23639. 1942. Gramercy Publishing Co.
Daughter of the Nez Perces. Arthur Henry Paterson. 1894. G. G. Peck.
Daughter of the Nohfu. Etsu Inagaki Sugimoto. LC 35-34911. 1935. Doubleday, Doran & Company, Inc.
Daughter of the North. Nephi Anderson. LC 15-13841. 0.75. Printed by De Utah-Nederlander Pub. Co.
Daughter of the Northwest. Irene Welch Grissom. LC 19-4691. The Cornhill Company.
Daughter of the Ozarks. Alanson Mason Haswell. LC 22-2314. The Cornhill Company.
Daughter of the Pangaran. Arthur Durham Divine. LC 63-18065. 1963. Little, Brown.
Daughter of the People. A Novel. Georgiana Marion Craik May. (Harper's Franklin square library, no. 555). 1886. Harper & Brothers.
Daughter of the People: A Novel. Georgiana Marion Craik May. (On cover: Lovell's library, no. 1006). 1887. J. W. Lovell Company.
Daughter of the Philistines. Hjalmar Hjorth Boyesen. LC 6-15224. (No name series. 3d series, v. 16). 1883. Roberts Brothers.
Daughter of the Philistines. Leonard Merrick. LC 7-25379. R. F. Fenno & Company; Etc., Etc.
Daughter of the Pit. Margaret Doyle Jackson. LC 3-4199. 1903. Houghton, Mifflin and Company.
Daughter of the Plain Folk. S. Earl Dubbel. LC 72-95023. 1973. 3.95 (ISBN 0-8024-1761-2). Moody Press.
Daughter of the Prophets: A Novel. Curtis Van Dyke. The Abbey Press.
Daughter of the Regiment. A Novel. Mary Andrews Denison. (On cover: Manhattan series. no. 3). A. L. Burt.
Daughter of the Regiment. A Novel. Mary Andrews Denison. (select ser. no. 56). 1890. Street & Smith.
Daughter of the Revolution, and Other Stories. John Reed. LC 75-134975. (Short story index reprint series). 1970. Books for Libraries Press.
Daughter of the Revolution: And Other Stories. John Reed & Dell, Floyd, 1887- Ed. LC 27-20761. Vanguard Press.
Daughter of the Riccarees: A Picture of Life in Louisiana. Friedrich Wilhelm Christian Gerstacker. Tr. by Baker, F. M. LC 15-23120. 1851. Z. Baker.
Daughter of the Rich. Mary Ella Waller. LC 3-25720. 1903. Little, Brown, and Company.
Daughter of the Rich. Mary Ella Waller. LC 9-8348. 1908. Little, Brown, and Company.
Daughter of the Rich. Mary Ella Waller. LC 24-19021. (Beacon Hill book shelf). 1924. Little, Brown, and Company.
Daughter of the Rich and Her Friends the Blossoms of Mount Hunger. new ed. illustrated by ellen bernard thompson. ed. Mary Ella Waller. 1905. Little, Brown, and Company.
Daughter of the Sacred Mountain. Mozelle Richardson. LC 76-46415. 1977. 7.95 (ISBN 0-688-03145-5). Morrow.
Daughter of the Sea. Amy Le Feuvre. LC 2-24325. 1902. T. Y. Crowell & Co.
Daughter of the Sierra. Frances Christine Tiernan. LC 3-16062. 1903. B. Herder.
Daughter of the Sioux: A Tale of the Indian Frontier. Charles King. LC 3-7159. 1903. The Hobart Company.
Daughter of the Snows. Jack London. LC 63-14433. (Fitzroy edition of the works of Jack London). 1963. Archer House.
Daughter of the Snows. Jack London. LC 2-242488. 1902. J. B. Lippincott Company.
Daughter of the Soil: A Novel. Mary E. Sweetman Blundell. LC 6-14204. 1895. Harper & Brothers.
Daughter of the South. A Romantic Story Founded Upon Earl Burgess' Successful Play of the Same Name. Helen Burrell D'Apery & Adams, Justin. LC 33-28368. (On cover: Play book series. no. 86). J. S. Ogilvie Publishing Company.
Daughter of the South: A War's End Romance. George Cary Eggleston. LC 5-24192. 1905. Lothrop Publishing Company.
Daughter of the South: And Shorter Stories. Constance Cary Harrison. LC 75-90583. (Short story index reprint series). 1969. Books for Libraries Press.
Daughter of the South: And Shorter Stories. Constance Cary Harrison. LC 7-2882. Cassell Publishing Company.
Daughter of the Stars. Marshall Moore Brice. LC 72-97538. 1973. 8.95. McClure Press.
Daughter of the States. Max Pemberton. 1904. Dodd, Mead & Company.
Daughter of the Storage. William Dean Howells. LC 42-256913. Harper & Brothers.
Daughter of the Sun. Jackson Gregory. LC 77-84233. (Lost Race and Adult Fantasy Fiction). 1978. 18.00 (ISBN 0-405-10981-4). Arno Press.
Daughter of the Sun. Elizabeth D Kennedy. LC 40-2385. Printed by S. B. Newman & Company.
Daughter of the Sun: A Tale of Adventure. LC 21-16183. 1921. C. Scribner's Sons.

Daughter of the Sun: A Tale of Adventure. Jackson Gregory. Ed. by R. Reginald & Douglas Melville. LC 77-842333. (Lost Race & Adult Fantasy Ser.). 1978. Repr. of 1921 ed. lib. bdg. 18.00x (ISBN 0-405-10981-4). Ayer Co.
Daughter of the Sword. Jeanne Williams. 1979. 2.25 (ISBN 0-671-82204-7). Pocket Books.
Daughter of the Tenements. Edward Waterman Townsend. LC 78-104586. (Illus.). 1970. Literature House.
Daughter of the Tenements. Edward Waterman Townsend. LC 8-30423. 1895. Lovell, Coryell & Company.
Daughter of the Union. Lucy Foster Madison. 1903. The Penn Publishing Company.
Daughter of the Vine. Gertrude Franklin Horn Atherton. LC 99-2379. 1899. J. Lane.
Daughter of the Vine. Gertrude Franklin Horn Atherton. LC 24-14936. 1923. Dodd, Mead and Company.
Daughter of This World. Fletcher Williams Battershall. 1893. Dodd. Mead & Company.
Daughter of Time. Elizabeth Mackintosh. LC 52-7599. 1952. Macmillan.
Daughter of Time. Elizabeth MacKintosh. 1.75 (ISBN 0-671-80837-0). Pocket Books.
Daughter of Time. Josephine Tey. 1975. pap. 1.50 (ISBN 0-425-03223-X, Medallion). Berkley Pub.
Daughter of Time. Josephine Tey. 220p. 1976. lib. bdg. 14.95x (ISBN 0-89966-184-X). Buccaneer Bks.
Daughter of Time. Josephine Tey. 1980. pap. 2.95 (ISBN 0-671-41326-0). PB.
Daughter of Time. Nelia Gardner White. LC 42-912614. 1942. The Macmillan Company.
Daughter of to-Day. Mildred Corning Crean. LC 10-23200. 1.00. The C. M. Clark Publishing Company.
Daughter of to-Day. A Novel. Sara Jeannette Duncan Cotes. LC 6-29021. 1894. D. Appleton and Company.
Daughter of Two Nations. Ella Gale McClelland. LC 7-20108. 1897. A. C. McClurg and Company.
Daughter of Two Worlds: A Novel of New York Life. Leroy Scott. LC 19-52741. 1919. 1.60. Houghton Mifflin Company.
Daughter of Tyrconnell. A Tale of the Reign of James the First. Mary Anne Madden Sadlier. LC 8-1649. 1863. D. & J. Sadlier & Co.
Daughter of Valdoro. Evelyn Stewart Armstrong. (Kangaroo Book). 1977. 1.75 (ISBN 0-671-80966-0). Pocket Books.
Daughter of Venice. Ysabel De Witte. LC 28-6768. 1928. R. D. Henkle Co. Inc.
Daughter of Virginia Dare. Mary Virginia Wall. LC 8-16952. 1908. The Neale Publishing Company.
Daughter of Witches. Patricia C. Wrede. 2.50 (Pub. by Ace Science Fiction). Ace Bks.
Daughter Ofis: A Science Fiction Epic. Michael Davidson. (Illus.). 1978. 1.75 (ISBN 0-445-04285-0). Popular Library.
Daughter: Oh, My Daughter! A Novel. Mildred Mesurac Jeffrey. LC 64-15076. 1964. L. Stuart.
Daughter Pays. Gertrude M. Robins Reynolds. LC 17-101220. 1916. George H. Doran Company.
Daughter to Diana. Allene Soule Corliss. LC 35-78075. Farrar & Rinehart, Inc.
Daughter to Philip. Beatrice Kean Stapleton Seymour. LC 33-20519. 1933. A. A. Knopf.
Daughters. Anne Lambton. (Berkley Book). 1.95 (ISBN 0-425-03804-1). Berkley Publishing Corp.
Daughter's a Daughter. Mary Westmacott, pseud. LC 70-184884. 192p. 1972. 5.95 (ISBN 0-87795-030-X). Arbor Hse.
Daughter's a Daughter. Mary Westmacott, pseud. 1982. pap. 2.95 (ISBN 0-440-11674-0). Dell.
Daughter's a Daughter: A Novel of Romance and Suspense. Agatha Miller Christie. LC 70-184884. 1972. 5.95 (ISBN 0-87795-030-X). Arbor House.
Daughters & Fathers. Evan Burke. pap. 1.95 o.p. (ISBN 0-87682-229-4, 7229). Barclay Hse.
Daughters & Sons. Ivy Compton-Burnett. LC 37-7810. 288p. 1974. 9.00x (ISBN 0-575-01796-1). Intl Pubns Serv.
Daughters of Aesculapius. Woman's Medical College of Pennsylvania, Philadelphia. LC 6-32174. 1897. G. W. Jacobs & Co.
Daughters of Albion: A Novel. Alec Brown. LC 36-49880. 1936. Doubleday, Doran and Company, Inc.
Daughters of an Ancient Race. Jack Reynolds. (Writing in Asia Ser.). 1974. pap. text ed. 3.50x (00202). Heinemann Ed.
Daughters of Astaroth. Sandra Shulman. (Orig.). 1968. pap. 0.60 o.p. (53-689). Paperback Lib.
Daughters of Babylon: A Novel. Wilson Barrett & Hichens, Robert Smythe. LC 99-877. 1899. J. B. Lippincott Company.
Daughters of Cain. Miriam Lynch. 1976. pap. 1.25 (ISBN 0-532-12451-0). Woodhill.
Daughters of Cain. Miriam Lynch. (Orig.). 1970. pap. 0.75 o.p. (ISBN 0-447-74661-8). Lancer.
Daughters of Darkness in Sunny India: A Story. Beatrice M Harband. 1903. E. H. Revell Company.
Daughters of Destiny. Schuyler Staunton. LC 6-35621. The Reilly & Britton Co.
Daughters of Earth: Three Novels. Judith Merril. LC 69-20062. (Doubleday science fiction). 1969. 4.95. Doubleday.
Daughters of Erin. Elizabeth Coxhead. (Orig.). pap. text ed. 7.25x (ISBN 0-901072-60-5). Humanities.
Daughters of Eve. Ellery Harding Clark. LC 24-22122. Dorrance & Company.
Daughters of Fire: Sylvie--Emilie--Octavie. Gerard De Nerval. Tr. by Whitall, James. LC 22-115923. (On verso of half-title: The sea gull librart, ed. by O. F. Thesis, vol. iv). 1922. N. L. Brown.
Daughters of Folly. Cosmo Hamilton. LC 28-8409. 1928. G. P. Putnam's Sons.
Daughters of Heaven. Vivian Cory. Brentano's.
Daughters of Heaven. Vivian Cory. LC 21-4092. The Macaulay Company.
Daughters of Incest. Diane Golden. pap. 1.95 o.p. (ISBN 0-87056-185-5). Brandon.
Daughters of India: A Novel. Margaret Wilson. LC 28-10867. 1928. Harper & Brothers.
Daughters of Jasper Clay. Lucille Fletcher, pseud. LC 58-5662. 1958. Holt.
Daughters of Longing: A Novel. Froma Sand. LC 68-13287. 1968. Sherbourne Press.
Daughters of Luxury. Howard Rockey. LC 25-7670. The Macaulay Company.
Daughters of Men. Hannah Lynch. J. W. Lovell Company.
Daughters of Music. large easy-to-read type. ed. Susannah Lawrence. (Queen-size gothic). 1973. 0.95. Popular Library.
Daughters of Nijo: A Romance of Japan. Winnifred Eaton Babcock. LC 4-9961. The Macmillan Company.
Daughters of Old Kentucky. Edna M Black. LC 41-36831. Fortuny's.
Daughters of Richard Heron. Romilly Cavan. LC 35-4721. E. P. Dutton & Co., Inc.
Daughters of Suffolk. William Jasper Nicolls. LC 10-11147. 1910. J. B. Lippincott Company.
Daughters of the Far Islands. Aola Vandergriff. 528p. (Orig.). 1982. pap. 3.50 (ISBN 0-446-30563-4). Warner Bks.
Daughters of the Flame. Julie Grice. 1979. 2.50 (ISBN 0-671-82320-5). Pocket Books.
Daughters of the House. Sarah McGuire. LC 80-21464. 1980. 9.95 (ISBN 0-312-18344-5). St. Martin's Press.
Daughters of the Misty Isles. Aola Vandergriff. 448p. (Orig.). 1981. pap. 2.95 (ISBN 0-446-93929-3). Warner Bks.
Daughters of the Moon. Joan Haggerty. LC 79-161245. 1971. 7.95. Bobbs-Merrill.
Daughters of the Opal Skies. Aola Vandergriff. 496p. (Orig.). 1982. pap. 3.50 (ISBN 0-446-30564-2). Warner Bks.
Daughters of the Revolution and Their Times, 1769-1776: A Historical Romance. Charles Carleton Coffin. LC 4-21707. Houghton, Mifflin and Company.
Daughters of the Rich. Edgar Evertson Saltus. LC 75-116004. 1970. (ISBN 0-404-05540-0). AMS Press.
Daughters of the Rich. Edgar Evertson Saltus. LC 9-13920. M. Kennerley.
Daughters of the Shining City. Aola Vandergriff. 448p. (Orig.). 1982. pap. 3.50 (ISBN 0-446-30180-9). Warner Bks.
Daughters of the South Wind. Aola Vandergriff. 1.95 (ISBN 0-446-89230-0). Warner Books.
Daughters of the Southwind. Aola Vandergriff. 544p. (Orig.). 1982. pap. 3.50 (ISBN 0-446-30561-8). Warner Bks.
Daughters of the Summer Storm. Frances P. Statham. 1979. pap. 2.75 (ISBN 0-449-14201-9, GM). Fawcett.
Daughters of the Sun: And Other Stories. Obi B Egbuna. LC 78-19363. (Three crowns book). 1970. Oxford U.P.
Daughters of the Vicar see Seven Short Novel Masterpieces.
Daughters of the Wild Country. Ada Vandergriff. 1978. 2.25 (ISBN 0-446-82583-2). Warner Books.
Daughter's Portion. Henry Watson Clapp. LC 24-21152. Phelps Publishing Co.
Daughter's Sacrifice: A Novel. Francis Charles Philips & Fendall, Percy. LC 7-36073. (On cover: Lovell's international series, no. 72). F. F. Lovell & Company.
Daughters: The Story of Two Generations. Gabriele Reuter & Tapley, Roberts, 1896- Tr. 1930. The Macmillan Company.
Daughters Who Dare. Rob Eden. LC 43-2346. 1943. Gramercy Publishing Co.
Daunay's Tower: A Novel. Adeline Sergeant. 1901. F. M. Buckles & Company; Etc., Etc.
Dauntless and the Dreamers: A Historical Novel. Frederick Goshe & Goshe, Frank, 1909- LC 63-18242. 1963. T. Yoseloff.
Davault's Mills. A Novel. Charles Henry Jones. LC 7-12132. 1876. J. B. Lippincott & Co.
Dave Sulkin Cares! Fletcher Knebel. LC 77-25600. 1978. 8.95 (ISBN 0-385-13693-5). Doubleday.
Davenant. Albert Kinross. LC 7-13436. 1907. Dodd, Mead and Company.
Davenport. Charles Marriott. LC 16-14843. 1916. John Lane Company.
Davenport Dunn: A Man of Our Day. Charles James Lever. LC 41-42430. G. Routledge and Sons.
Davenport Dunn: A Man of Our Day. Charles James Lever. LC 16-7572. 1904. Little, Brown, and Company.
Davenport Dunn: Or, A Man of Our Day. Charles James Lever. (Seaside library, v. 16, no. 319). 1878. G. Munro.
Dave's Daughter: A Novel. Patience Bevier Cole. LC 13-19333. 4.00. Frederick A. Stokes Company.
Dave's New Girl. Norman Rowcliff. LC 76-2299. 1977. 7.95 (ISBN 0-87949-059-4). Ashley Bks.
David. Carroll Trowbridge Cooney. LC 43-5035. 1943. Howell, Soskin.
David. Aldoph Philip Gouthey. LC 34-1047. Dorrance & Company, Inc.
David: A Tale in Three Parts. Naomi Gwladys Royde-Smith. LC 34-340. 1934. The Viking Press.
David Alden's Daughter: And Other Stories of Colonial Times. Jane Goodwin Austin. LC 71-98556. (Short story index reprint series). 1969. (ISBN 0-8369-3130-0). Books for Libraries Press.
David Aldens' Daughter: And Other Stories of Colonial Times. Jane Goodwin Austin. 1892. Houghton, Mifflin and Company.
David Alden's Daughter: And Other Stories of Colonial Times. Jane Goodwin Austin. LC 4-19036. Houghton, Mifflin and Company.
David Alden's Daughter, & Other Stories of Colonial Times. facsimile ed. Jane Goodwin Austin. LC 71-98556. (Short Story Index Reprint Ser.). 1892. 17.00 (ISBN 0-8369-3130-0). Ayer Co.
David and Anna. Pierre Stephen Robert Payne. LC 47-1793. 1947. Dodd, Mead and Company.
David and Bathsheba: A Novel. Translated by I. M. Lask. Ibn-Sahav, Ari. LC 51-12012. 1951. Crown Publishers.
David and Destiny. John Hay Beith. LC 34-11040. 1934. Houghton Mifflin Company.
David and Diane. Margaretta Brucker. LC 50-7414. 1950. Gramercy Pub. Co.
David and Joanna. George Blake. LC 36-22619. H. Holt and Company.
David and Jonathan. Ernest Temple Thurston. LC 19-216484. 1919. G. P. Putnam's Sons.
David and Max: Based on a Bizarre and Tragic Incident of the Second World War. Peter Simonds. LC 74-75393. (Illus.). 8.95 (ISBN 0-87695-203-1). Aurora Publishers.
David & Susan at the Little Green House. Mary M. Landis. 1975. 6.00. Rod & Staff.
David at Olivet. Wallace Hamilton. LC 78-19437. 10.00. (ISBN 0-312-18366-6) (ISBN 0-312-18367-4). St. Martin's Press.
David Balfour: A Sequel to Kidnapped... Robert Louis Stevenson. LC 5-13038. (Half-title: The biographical edition of the works of Robert Louis Stevenson). 1905. C. Scribner's Sons.
David Balfour: A Sequel to "Kidnapped.". Robert Louis Stevenson. LC 15-23123. (novels and tales of Robert Louis Stevenson. vol. vi). 1895. C. Scribner's Sons.
David Balfour: A Sequel to Kidnapped; Being Memoirs of His Adventures at Home and Abroad... Robert Louis Stevenson. LC 17-220480. (Half-title: Biographical edition of the works of Robert Louis Stevenson). 1915. C. Scribner's Sons.
David Balfour: Being Memoirs of His Adventures at Home and Abroad; the Second Part... Robert Louis Stevenson. 1893. C. Scribner's Sons.
David Balfour: Being Memoirs of His Adventures at Home and Abroad; the Second Part... Robert Louis Stevenson. LC 9-3859. 1895. C. Scribner's Sons.
David Balfour: Being Memoirs of His Adventures at Home and Abroad. The Second Part... Robert Louis Stevenson. LC 4-16579. 1902. C. Scribner's Sons.
David Balfour: Being Memoirs of the Further Adventures of David Balfour at Home and Abroad... Robert Louis Stevenson. LC 24-23373. 1924. C. Scribner's Sons.
David Blaize. Edward Frederic Benson. LC 16-9960. 1916. Hodder and Stoughton.
David Blaize. Edward Frederic Benson. LC 16-11581. George H. Doran Company.
David Blaize of Kings. Edward Frederic Benson. LC 24-22680. 2.00. George H. Doran Company.
David Bran. Morley Roberts. LC 9-32033. 1909. 1.50. L. C. Page & Company.
David Copperfield. a limited ed. Charles Dickens. LC 77-367312. (Illus.). 1976. Franklin Library.
David Copperfield. Charles Dickens. LC 20-23172. (Nelson classics, no. 82, 83). 1912. T. Nelson and Sons.
David Copperfield... Charles Dickens. LC 17-17435. (Harvard classics shelf of fiction, selected by C. W. Eliot. 7-8). P. F. Collier & Son.
David Copperfield. Charles Dickens. (Rittenhouse classics). 1919. G. W. Jacobs & Co.
David Copperfield. Charles Dickens. Ed. by Nevins, Allan. LC 28-27803. (modern readers' series). 1928. The Macmillan Company.
David Copperfield. Charles Dickens. LC 24-27178. (Half-title: The modern library of the world's best books). 1934. The Modern Library.
David Copperfield. Charles Dickens & Becker, May (Lamberton) 1873- LC 43-188390. (On cover: Great illustrated classics). 1943. Dodd, Mead & Company.
David Copperfield. Charles Dickens & Nina Burgis. LC 79-40156. (Clarendon Dickens). (Illus.). 1980. 98.00 (ISBN 0-19-812492-9). Clarendon Press.
David Copperfield. Charles Dickens & Graves, Robert. Ed. by Paine, Merrill, P. LC 34-4066. 1934. Harcourt, Bruce and Company.
David Copperfield. Charles Dickens & Maugham, William Somerset, 1874- Ed. LC 48-4967. (Ten Greatest Novels of the World). 1948. J. C. Winston Co.
David Copperfield. Charles Dickens & Scott, Walter. (Press and poetry individualised program. The novel). 1942. The L. W. Singer Company.
David Copperfield. Adapted by Robert J. Purdy; Edited by Ann Price. Charles Dickens & Robert J Purdy. LC 52-1662. (Classics for enjoyment). Laidlaw Bros.
David Copperfield. Ed. by M. W. & C. Thomas. Orig. Illus. by 'Phiz. Charles Dickens. Ed. by Maurice Walton Thomas & Gladys Thomas. Hablot Knight Browne. LC 66-6336. (Shorter classics). 1966. bds., 2.50. Ginn.
David Copperfield: The Early Years (Chapters 1-14 Complete. Charles Dickens. (Riverside lit ser. R32). 1.80. Houghton.
David Dunne: A Romance of the Middle West. Belle Kanaris Maniates. LC 12-15144. Rand, McNally & Company.
David Elginbrod. George Macdonald. LC 75-1502. (Victorian Fiction: Novels of Faith and Doubt; No. 53). 1975. 35.00 (ISBN 0-8240-1577-0). Garland Pub.
David Elginbrod. George Macdonald. LC 7-15853. 1872. Loring.
David Elginbrod. George Macdonald. (Seaside library. v. 32, no. 668). 1879. G. Munro.
David Elginbrod. George Macdonald. LC 4-16556. G. Routledge & Sons, Limited.
David Elginbrod. George Macdonald. LC 12-18276. 1911. D. McKay.
David Erenberg, Healer. Sarah A Jenison. LC 12-23514. 1912. 1.00. The Shakespeare Press.
David, from Where He Was Lying. Barrington Kaye. LC 61-15319. 1961. Abelard-Schuman.
David, from Where He Was Lying; a Novel. Tom Kaye. Abelard-Schuman.
David Goes to War. William Adair Weldon. LC 43-17619. 1943. Herald Press.
David Golder. Irene Nemirovsky. Tr. by Stuart, Sylvia. LC 30-24849. 1930. H. Liveright, Inc.
David Harum: a Story of American. Edward Noyes Westcott. LC 98-676. 1898. D. Appleton and Company.
David Harum: a Story of American. Edward Noyes Westcott. LC 7-7416. 1899. D. Appleton and Company.
David Harum: a Story of American Life. Edward Noyes Westcott. LC 6731. 1900. D. Appleton & Company.
David Harum: a Story of American Life. Edward Noyes Westcott. Heermans, Forbes, 1856- LC 23-2802. 1923. D. Appleton & Company.
David Harum: a Story of American Life. Edward Noyes Westcott. Ed. by Carrie Belle Parks. LC 31-3837. (Half-title: Appleton modern literature series). D. Appleton and Company.
David Harum: A Story of American Life. Edward Noyes Westcott. pap. 2.00 o.p. (ISBN 0-486-20580-0). Dover.
David Hunt. A Novel. Ann Sophia Winterbotham Stephens. (On cover: The idle hour series, no. 19). 1892. The F. M. Lupton Publishing Company.
David Johnson Passed Through Here: A Novel. John Fairfield. LC 77-170168. (Illus.). 1971. 6.95. Little, Brown.
David Lannarck, Midget: An Adventure Story. George S Harney. LC 51-4042. 1951. Exposition Press.
David Lindsay: A Sequel to "Gloria.". Emma Dorothy Eliza Nevitte Southworth. LC 8-14241. (On cover: Ledger library, no. 49). 1891. R. Bonner's Sons.
David Lindsay: A Sequel to "Gloria.". Emma Dorothy Eliza Nevitte Southworth. LC 20-23139. 1905. A. L. Burt Company.
David Malcolm. Nelson McAllister Lloyd. LC 13-18074. 1913. 1.35. C. Scribner's Sons.

David Meyer Is a Mother. Gail Parent. LC 74-15885. 7.95 (ISBN 0-06-013274-4). Harper & Row.

David of Jerusalem. Louis De Wohl. LC 63-17674. 1963. Lippincott.

David of Sassoun: The Armenian Folk Epic in Four Cycles. Tr. by Artin K. Shalian. LC 64-19874. 1964. 12.00 o.s.i. (ISBN 0-8214-0004-5). Ohio U Pr.

David Penstephen. Richard Pryce. LC 15-248840. 1915. Houghton Mifflin Company.

David Poindexter's Disappearance. Julian Hawthorne. LC 75-32748. (Literature of Mystery and Detection). 1976. 12.00 (ISBN 0-405-07877-3). Arno Press.

David Poindexter's Disappearance: And Other Tales. Julian Hawthorne. LC 9-30157. 1888. D. Appleton and Company.

David Rees, Among Others. Anthony P. West. LC 71-117662. 1970. Random House.

David Rudd. Ralph E Mooney. LC 27-11619. Henry Waterson Company.

David Sherwood. James Hunter Williamson. LC 34-14762. Press of J. H. Williamson.

David Smith by David Smith. Ed. by C. Gray. 1968. pap. text ed. 9.95 (ISBN 0-03-091563-5). HR&W.

David Starr, Space Ranger. 1st. ed. Isaac Asimov. LC 52-5220. 1952. Doubleday.

David Starr, Space Ranger. Isaac Asimov. (Signet science fiction). 1974. (pbk.) 0.75. New American Library.

David Starr, Space Ranger. Isaac Asimov. LC 78-14573. (Lucky Starr Series). ((His). 1978. 7.95 (ISBN 0-8398-2486-6). Gregg Press.

David Strange. Nelia Gardner White. LC 28-8707. 1928. The Penn Publishing Company.

David Strong's Errand. Jennie Maria Drinkwater Conklin. LC 6-30393. Presbyterian Board of Publication.

David, the Boy Harper: A Story of David's Boyhood and Youth. Annie E Smiley. Jennings & Pye.

David the Hero. Sarah Dickson Lowrie. LC 3-10192. 1903. The Westminster Press.

David, the King. Gladys Schmitt. LC 73-164507. (Illus.). 1973. 8.95. Dial Press.

David, the King. Gladys Schmitt. LC 46-25053. 1946. Dial Press.

David, the Son of Jesse. Marjorie Strachey. LC 22-4827. 1922. The Century Co.

David Todd: The Romance of His Life, and Loving. David Maclure. LC 21-8617. Cassell Publishing Company.

David Vallory. Francis Lynde. LC 19-13537. 1919. C. Scribner's Sons.

Davidee Birot. Rene Bazin. LC 12-15740. 1912. C. Scribner's Sons.

Davidian Report. Dorothy Belle Flanagan Hughes. LC 80-12654. 1980. 9.95 (ISBN 0-89340-268-0). J. Curley.

Davidian Report: A Novel of Suspense. Dorothy Belle Flanagan Hughes. LC 52-6789. 1952. Duell, Sloan and Pearce.

David's Day. Denis George Mackail. LC 32-5027. 1932. Houghton Mifflin Company.

David's Heritage: A Novel. Osmond Young Owings. LC 14-16949. 1914. 1.25. The Cosmopolitan Press.

David's Little Lad. Elizabeth Thomasina Meade Smith. LC 8-9015. (Added t.-p.: Harper's half-hour series, no. 54). 1878. Harper & Brothers.

David's Loom: A Story of Rochdale Life in the Early Years of the Nineteenth Century. new ed. John Trafford Clegg. LC 6-21359. 1895. Longmans, Green and Co.

David's Stranger. Tr. by Margaret Benaya. Moshe Shamir. LC 65-101832. 1965. bds., 4.50. Abelard.

Davidson Affair. Stuart Brooke Jackman. LC 67-6100. W. B. Eerdmans Pub. Co.

Davidson File: Compiled from the Personal Papers of His Grace the Lord Caiaphas, High Priest of Jewry. Stuart Brooke Jackman. LC 82-13443. 7.95 (ISBN 0-664-24459-9). Westminster Press.

Davie. Donald McDougall. LC 77-76644. 1977. 7.95 (ISBN 0-312-18385-2). St. Martin's Press.

Davie and Elisabeth: Wonderful Adventures. Muriel Campbell Dyar. LC 8-29338. 1908. Harper & Brothers.

Davina: Or The Romance of Mesmerism. LC 82-84057. (Grove Press Victorian Library). 224p. (Orig.). 1982. pap. 3.95 (BC). Grove.

Davis: A Novel. John Scanlan. LC 69-15166. 1969. 6.95. Doubleday.

Davis Doesn't Live Here Any More. Jack Ripley. LC 76-186041. 192p. 1972. 4.95 o.p. (ISBN 0-385-03324-9). Doubleday.

Davis Doesn't Live Here Any More. John William Wainwright. LC 76-186041. 1972. 4.95. Published for the Crime Club by Doubleday.

Davis Triplets and the Film Action. Bernard Alvin Palmer. LC 75-23332. 1975. 0.75 (ISBN 0-8024-7252-4). Moody Press.

Davor: Ein Stuck in Thirteen Szenen. Gunter Grass. Ed. by Victor Lange & Frances Lange. 182p. (Ger.). 1975. pap. text ed. 4.95 o.p. HarBraceJ.

Davor: Ein Stuck in 13 Szener. Gunter Grass. pap. text ed. 4.50 o.p. (ISBN 0-15-516963-7, HC). HarBraceJ.

Davosers. D Brandon. LC 13-239373. 1912. G. H. Doran Company.

Davy. Edgar Pangborn. LC 75-420. (Garland Library of Science Fiction). 1975. 11.00 (ISBN 0-8240-1425-1). Garland Pub.

Davy. Edgar Pangborn. LC 64-10349. 1964. St. Martin's Press.

Davy and the Goblin: Or, What Followed Reading " Alice's Adventures in Wonderland". 14th impression ed. Charles Edward Carryl. LC 4-18451. Houghton, Mifflin and Company.

Davy and the Goblin: Or, What Followed Reading "Alice's Adventures in Wonderland". Charles Edward Carryl. LC 28-22808. (Riverside bookshelf). 1928. Houghton Mifflin Company.

Davy Jones, I Love You. Frederic Robert Buckley. LC 44-4101. 1944. J. B. Lippincott Company.

Davy Project. Merrill R. Bailey. 1980. 4.95 (ISBN 0-533-04652-1). Vantage.

Daw Science Fiction Reader. Ed. by Donald A. Wollheim. 1976. pap. 1.50 o.p. (UW1242). DAW Bks.

Dawn. Katharine Holland Brown. LC 7-21225. T.Y. Crowell & Co.

Dawn. Henry Rider Haggard. LC 6-45977. (On cover: Lovell'l library. v. 19, no. 941). 1887. J. W. Lovell Company.

Dawn. Tania Langley. 224p. 1980. pap. 1.75 (ISBN 0-449-50049-7, Coventry). Fawcett.

Dawn. Eleanor Hodgman Porter. LC 19-6141. 1919. 1.50. Houghton Mifflin Company.

Dawn. Elie Wiesel. 112p. 1982. pap. 2.95 (ISBN 0-553-22536-7). Bantam.

Dawn. Elie Wiesel. 1961. 3.50 o.p. (ISBN 0-8090-3773-4). Hill & Wang.

Dawn. Sydney Fowler Wright. LC 29-22423. 1929. Cosmopolitan Book Corporation.

Dawn: A Biographical Novel of Edith Cavell. Reginald Cheyne Berkeley. LC 28-15629. J. H. Sears Company, Inc.

Dawn: A Lost Romance of the Time of Christ. Irving Bacheller. LC 27-3174. 1927. The Macmillan Company.

Dawn: A Novel. Mrs. H. A. Adams. LC 5-42957. 1868. Adams & Company.

Dawn, a Novel of Hope. Newman Watts. 1944. Moody Press.

Dawn: A Story of Youth in Quest of the Messiah. Omen Bishop. LC 53-12068. 1954. Exposition Press.

Dawn After Danger. Anne West Strawbridge. LC 34-24352. Coward-McCann.

Dawn Appears. Annie Greene Nelson. LC 76-18799. 135p. 1976. Repr. of 1944 ed. 15.00 (ISBN 0-87152-244-6). Reprint.

Dawn Appears: A Novel. Annie Greene Nelson. LC 44-4354. 1944. Hampton Publishing Company.

Dawn at Noon. 1st Ed. Mark Andrin. LC 59-12364. 1960. Greenwich Book Publishers.

Dawn at Shanty Bay. Robert Edward Knowles. F. H. Revell Company.

Dawn at Twilight: A Novel. Bauerfeind, George L. LC 45-6218. 1945. Dorrance & Company.

Dawn Attack. Brian Callison. LC 72-94260. (Illus.). 1973. 6.95 (ISBN 0-399-11099-2). Putnam.

Dawn Beloved. Jean Crooks Devanny. LC 28-25461. The Macaulay Company.

Dawn Breaks: A Novel from the V-Front. Franz Carl Weiskopf & Norden, Heinz, 1905- Tr. LC 42-10944. 1942. Duell, Sloan and Pearce.

Dawn Breaks the Heart. William Davey. 1941. Howell, Soskin.

Dawn-Builder. John Gneisenau Neihardt. LC 11-946849. 1911. 1.50. M. Kennerley.

Dawn Chorus. Tim Reynolds. LC 80-24377. 1981. 4.00 (ISBN 0-87886-111-4). Ithaca House.

Dawn Comes Soon. Ursula Nightingale. (Orig.). 1973. pap. 0.95 o.p. (09169). Curtis.

Dawn Command. Roland K. Jordon. 1978. pap. 1.75 o.s.i. (ISBN 0-8439-0600-6, Leisure Bks). Nordon Pubns.

Dawn Falcon. Ann Moray. 1976. 1.75 (ISBN 0-449-23004-X). Fawcett Crest.

Dawn Falcon: A Novel of Ancient Egypt. Ann Moray. LC 73-12019. (Illus.). 1974. 7.95 (ISBN 0-688-00217-X). Morrow.

Dawn in Lyonesse. Mary Ellen Chase. LC 38-27053. 1938. The Macmillan Company.

Dawn Is at Hand. Kath Walker. 1966. 3.00 o.s.i. Tri-Ocean.

Dawn Is Silver. Mabel Cleland Widdemer. LC 39-74383. 1939. Arcadia House.

Dawn Meadow. Grace Atherton Dennen. LC 11-10053. 1911. 1.25. R. G. Badger.

Dawn O'Day: By Warren Howard Pseud. James Noble Gifford. 1956. Arcadia House.

Dawn of a New Day. Lee Marlino. LC 41-2814. Savoy Book Publishers, Inc.

Dawn of a New Era. Patrick J Flatley. LC 20-4012. R. G. Badger.

Dawn of a Tomorrow. Frances Hodgson Burnett. LC 6-674431. 1906. C. Scribner's Sons.

Dawn of African Women. John E. Eberegbulam Njoku. LC 77-154067. 5.00 (ISBN 0-682-48862-3). Exposition Press.

Dawn of All. Robert Hugh Benson. LC 11-205458. 1911. B. Herder.

Dawn of Desire. Iris Bancroft. 384p. (Orig.). 1981. pap. 2.75 (ISBN 0-523-41138-3). Pinnacle Bks.

Dawn of Desire. Joyce Verrette. 1976. pap. 1.95 (ISBN 0-380-00562-X, 27375). Avon.

Dawn of Desire. Joyce Verrette. Avon.

Dawn of Flame and Other Stories. Stanley Grauman Weinbaum. LC 37-7081. Ruppert Printing Service.

Dawn of Love. Barbara Cartland. LC 79-14992. 9.95 (ISBN 0-525-08890-3). Dutton.

Dawn of Love. Teri Lester. Bd. with Tania. 1977. pap. 1.75 (ISBN 0-451-07804-7, E7804, Sig). NAL.

Dawn of Passion. Catherine Kay. (Super Romances Ser.). 384p. 1982. pap. 2.50 (ISBN 0-373-70045-8, Pub. by Worldwide). Harlequin Bks.

Dawn of Peace. Geraldine Tolman Wyatt & Book of Mormon. LC 41-13510. Herald Publishing House.

Dawn of Remembered Spring. Jesse Stuart. LC 75-37150. 1972. (ISBN 0-07-062240-X). McGraw-Hill.

Dawn of Romance. Ethel E Bangert. LC 50-12831. 1950. Arcadia House.

Dawn of the Dead. George A. Romero & Susan Sparrow. LC 77-18383. 7.95 (ISBN 0-312-18393-3). St. Martin's Press.

Dawn of the Eighth Day. 1st Ed. Olga Ilyin. LC 51-10776. 1951. Holt.

Dawn of the Morning. Grace Livingston Hill. LC 11-11742. 1911. J. B. Lippincott Company.

Dawn of the Morning. Grace Livingston Hill. 1975. (pbk.) 1.25. Bantam Books.

Dawn of Time: Prehistory Through Science Fiction. Martin Harry Greenberg & Joseph D Olander. LC 79-1254. 7.95 (ISBN 0-525-66624-9). Elsevier/Nelson Books.

Dawn O'Hara: The Girl Who Laughed. 8th ed. Edna Ferber. LC 28-17902. 1911. Grosset & Dunlap.

Dawn O'Hara, the Girl Who Laughed. Edna Ferber. LC 11-112861. 1911. Frederick A. Stokes Company.

Dawn O'Hara: The Girl Who Laughed. 7th ed. Edna Ferber. LC 20-16473. 1911. Frederick A. Stokes Company.

Dawn on Our Darkness: A Novel; Cela S'appelle L'aurore, Translatedfrom the French by Therese Pol. Emmanuel Robles. LC 54-6774. 1954. J. Messner.

Dawn on the Mountains. Charles Ewing Brown. LC 31-14547. The Warner Press.

Dawn Over India. Bankim Chandra Chatterji. Tr. by Roy, Basanta Koomar. LC 41-207220. 1941. The Devin-Adair Company.

Dawn Over the Amazon. Carleton Beals. LC 43-512091. 1943. Duell, Sloan and Pearce.

Dawn Patrol: Novelized. Guy Fowler & Saunders, John Monk. LC 30-16618. Grosset & Dunlap.

Dawn Riders. Frank Gruber. LC 77-2375. 1977. 7.95 (ISBN 0-89340-076-9). J. Curley.

Dawn Riders. William Edward Daniel Ross. LC 68-3976. 1968. Arcadia House.

Dawn Sails North. Robert Dean Frisbie. LC 49-72506. 1949. Doubleday.

Dawn Steals Softly. Anne Hampson. 192p. (Orig.). 1980. pap. 1.50 (ISBN 0-671-57027-7, Pub. by Silhouette Bks). S&S.

Dawn. Translated from the French by Frances Frenaye. 1st American Ed. Eliezer Wiesel. LC 61-8461. 1961. Hill and Wang.

Dawn Wind. David Pickard. 1980. pap. 2.50 (ISBN 0-85363-133-6). OMF Bks.

Dawning; a Novel. John Martin Luther Babcock. LC 6-33404. 1886. Lee and Shepard.

Dawning Light. Robert Randall, pseud. LC 81-4905. 4.95 (ISBN 0-89865-033-X). Donning.

Dawning Light. Robert Silverberg & Randall Garrett. LC 81-4905. (Illus., Orig.). 1981. pap. 5.95 (ISBN 0-89865-034-8, Starblaze). Donning Co.

Dawning Light. 1st Ed. Robert Randall, pseud. LC 59-9316. 1959. Gnome Press.

Dawning of the Day. Elisabeth Ogilvie. LC 53-120551. 1954. McGraw-Hill.

Dawning of the Day. Elisabeth Ogilvie. LC 75-34414. 1975. 6.95 (ISBN 0-88411-186-5). Aeonian Press.

Dawns Are Quiet Here. B. Vassilyev. 287p. 1975. 5.45 (ISBN 0-8285-1950-1, Pub. by Progress Pubs USSR). Imported Pubns.

Dawns Delayed... Joseph McCord. LC 35-1050. 1935. Macrae Smith Company.

Dawn's Early Light. Elswyth Thane. LC 43-51181. 1943. Duell, Sloan and Pearce.

Dawn's Early Light. Elswyth Thane. LC 80-25619. 1981. 16.95 (ISBN 0-8161-3167-8). G. K. Hall.

Dawn's Free Spirit. Dawn Constantine. LC 72-96462. 1973. 2.95 o.p. (ISBN 0-8059-1818-3). Dorrance.

Dawn's Promise. Jo Calloway. (Candlelight Ecstasy Ser.: No. 121). (Orig.). 1983. pap. 1.95 (ISBN 0-440-11619-8). Dell.

Dawson Black: Retail Merchant. Harold Whitehead. LC 18-13453. 1918. The Page Company.

Dawson Pedigree. Dorothy Leigh Sayers. LC 28-2671. 1928. L. MacVeagh, The Dial Press.

Dawson Pedigree and Lord Peter Views the Body. Dorothy Leigh Sayers. LC 38-27668. 1938. Harcourt, Brace and Company.

Dawson '11, Fortune Hunter. John Tinney McCutcheon. LC 12-24462. 1912. Dodd, Mead and Company.

Day After Dark. Emerson Gifford Taylor. LC 22-182352. Small, Maynard & Company.

Day After Doomsday. Rena Marie Vale. (Orig.). pap. 0.60 o.p. (63-479). Paperback Lib.

Day After Judgement. James Blish. 1982. pap. 2.50 (ISBN 0-380-59527-3, 59527). Avon.

Day After Judgment: A Novel. James Blish. LC 74-116190. 1971. 4.95. Doubleday.

Day After Sunday: A Novel. Hollis Spurgeon Summers. LC 68-15979. 1968. Harper & Row.

Day After the Fourth. Turnley Walker. LC 58-9651. 1958. Appleton-Century-Crofts.

Day After Tomorrow. George Franklin Allee. LC 50-4471. 1950. Zondervan.

Day After Tomorrow. Mack Reynolds. 1976. (pbk.) 1.25. Ace Books.

Day and a Night at the Baths. Michael Rumaker. LC 79-15113. 10.00. (ISBN 0-912516-43-7) (ISBN 0-912516-44-5). Grey Fox Press.

Day and a Night in a Forest: By Mary Adrian. Illus. by Genevieve Vaughan-Jackson. Mary Eleanor Venn & Vaughan-Jackson, Genevieve, Illus. LC 67-153418. (Balance of nature ser.). 1967. 3.50. Hastings.

Day & Night. Pierre Berg. pap. 0.95 o.p. (ISBN 0-87067-182-0, 88-182). Holloway.

Day and Night Stories. Algernon Blackwood. LC 17-217934. E. P. Dutton & Co.

Day and Night Stories. Guy De Maupassant. Ed. by Ernest Augustus Boyd. LC 70-157787. (Short story index reprint series). 1971. (ISBN 0-8369-3899-2). Books for Libraries Press.

Day and Night Stories. Thomas Russell Sullivan. LC 8-176642. 1890. C. Scribner's Sons.

Day & Night Stories: Collected Novels & Stories, Vol. 9. facsimile ed. Guy De Maupassant. Ed. by Ernest Boyd. Tr. by Storm Jameson from Fr. LC 70-157787. (Short Story Index Reprint Ser.). Repr. of 1924 ed. 16.00 (ISBN 0-8369-3899-2). Ayer Co.

Day and Night Stories: 2d Series. Thomas Russell Sullivan. LC 8-17663. 1893. C. Scribner's Sons.

Day at Laguerre's and Other Days: Being Nine Sketches. Francis Hopkinson Smith. LC 8-8161. 1892. Houghton, Mifflin and Company.

Day at Laguerre's and Other Days: Nine Sketches by F. Hopkinson Smith. Francis Hopkinson Smith. LC 8-11271. 1892. Houghton, Mifflin and Company.

Day Before; a Romantic Chronicle. Henry Major Tomlinson. G. P. Putnam's Sons.

Day Before Forever: And Thunderhead. Keith Laumer. LC 68-10578. (Doubleday science fiction). 1968. Doubleday.

Day Before Forever: Science Fiction. Kieth Laumer. Bd. with Thunderhead. LC 68-10578. 1968. 3.95 o.p. Doubleday.

Day Before Sunrise: A Novel. Thomas Wiseman. LC 75-21482. (Illus.). 8.95 (ISBN 0-03-015206-2). Holt, Rinehart and Winston.

Day Before Sunrise: A Novel /by Thomas Wiseman. Thomas Wiseman. (Illus.). 1977. 1.95 (ISBN 0-446-89213-0). Warner Books.

Day Before Thunder. Bart Spicer. LC 60-15008. 1960. Dodd, Mead.

Day Before Tomorrow. Gerard Klein. 1982. pap. 1.95 (ISBN 0-87997-767-1, UJ1767). DAW Bks.

Day Before Tomorrow. Gerard Klein. Tr. by P. J. Sokolowski. (Science Fiction Ser.). Orig. Title: Temps n'a pas d'Odeur. 160p. (Orig.). 1972. pap. 0.95 o.p. (UQ1011). DAW Bks.

Day-Books. Mabel E Wotton. LC 8-37219. (On cover: Keynotes series, 26). 1896. Roberts Bros.; Etc., Etc.

Day Breaketh. Fanny Alricks Shugert. LC 8-7320. 1898. H. Altemus.

Day by Night. Tanith Lee. 1980. 2.25 (ISBN 0-87997-576-8). DAW Books.

Day Christ Died. James Alonzo Bishop. (Perennial lib., P67D). 1965. Harper.

Day Christ Died. James Alonzo Bishop. LC 57-6125. 1957. Harper.

Day Claude Buried Mom: And Other Stories. Jessie Bradley Pearson. LC 67-29660. 1968. Dorrance.

Day Comes Round. Ruby Mildred Ayres. LC 51-9290. 1950. Arcadia House.

Day Daddy Died. Alan Burns. (Illus.). 138p. 1982. 13.95 (ISBN 0-8052-8086-3, Pub. by Allison & Busby England); pap. 5.95 (ISBN 0-8052-8085-5). Schocken.

Day-Dreamer: Being the Full Narrative of "The Stolen Story,". Jesse Lynch Williams. LC 6-83102. 1906. C. Scribner's Sons.

Day-Dreams and Nightmares. Fred Grant Young. LC 9-1201. 1894. The Hermitage Publishing Co.

Day for Murder. Katherine McComb. LC 63-6875. 1963. Avalon Books.

Day Fort Larking Fell. Henry Wilson Allen. LC 68-57511. 1968. Chilton Book Co.

Day God Cursed America. Thomas J Tucker. 3.75 o.p. Carlton.

Day He Died. Henry Kuttner. LC 47-30413. 1947. Duell, Sloan and Pearce.

Day I Died. Lawrence Lariar. LC 52-2936. 1952. Appleton-Century-Crofts.

Day I Shot the Mule. Bobby Anderson. 1976. 5.95 o.p. (ISBN 0-8059-2241-5). Dorrance.

Day in a Colonial Home. Della R Prescott. Ed. by Dana, John Cotton. LC 21-15103. 1921. Marshall Jones Company.

Day in Late September. Merle Miller. LC 63-17697. 1963. W. Sloane Associates.

Day in Monte Carlo. Martha Albrand. LC 59-5701. 1959. Random House.

Day in Monte Carlo: By Martha Albrand Pseud. Heidi Huberta Freybe Leewengard. LC 59-5701. 1959. Random House.

Day in Regensburg: Short Stories. Joseph Opatoshu. LC 68-15788. 1968. Jewish Publication Society of America.

Day in San Francisco. Dorothy Bryant. LC 82-73209. 144p. 1983. 12.00 (ISBN 0-931688-09-4); pap. 6.00 (ISBN 0-931688-10-8). Ata Bks.

Day in Shadow: A Novel. Nayantara Pandit Sahgal. LC 72-1432. 1972. (ISBN 0-393-08433-7). Norton.

Day in the Death of Joe Egg. Peter Nichols. 1967. pap. 3.95 o.p. (ISBN 0-571-08369-2). Faber & Faber.

Day in the Life. Ed. by Gardner Dozois. LC 78-160655. 1971. 6.95 (ISBN 0-06-011076-7). Harper & Row.

Day in the Life of Roger Angell. Roger Angell. 1978. pap. 2.95 o.p. (ISBN 0-14-004983-5). Penguin.

Day Is Coming. William Cameron. LC 44-4962. (Full name: William Frederick John Cameron). 1944. The Macmillan Company.

Day Is Dark & Three Travelers. Marie Claire Blais. Tr. by D. Coltman. 1967. 4.95 o.p. FS&G.

Day Is Dark, and Three Travelers: Two Novellas. Marie Claire Blais. LC 67-18971. 1967. Farrar, Straus and Giroux.

Day Israel Died...and Lived. Michael J. Damas. LC 73-89016. 1974. 6.95 (ISBN 0-8059-1949-X). Dorrance.

Day It Rained Diamonds. M. E. Chaber, pseud. LC 66-21636. (Milo March Mystery Ser). 1970. pap. 0.60 o.p. (ISBN 0-446-63231-7, 63-231). Paperback Lib.

Day It Rained Diamonds: A New Milo March Adventure, by M. E. Chaber. 1st Ed. Kendell Foster Crossen. LC 66-21636. (Rinehart suspense novel). 1966. bds., 3.95. Holt.

Day Late. Carolyn Doty. LC 79-23581. 1980. 9.95 (ISBN 0-670-25923-3). Viking Press.

Day Late and a Dollar Short. Gerald A Squibb. LC 57-8719. 1958. Bruce Humphries.

Day Million. Frederik Pohl. LC 70-14827. (Ballantine Books science fiction). 1970. 0.95. Ballantine Books.

Day Miss Bessie Lewis Disappeared. Doris Miles Disney. 1976. (pbk.) 1.50. Ace Books.

Day Miss Bessie Lewis Disappeared. Doris Miles Disney. LC 72-186016. 1972. 4.95. Published for the Crime Club by Doubleday.

Day Must Dawn. Agnes Sligh Turnbull. LC 42-227231. 1942. The Macmillan Company.

Day No Pigs Would Die. Robert Newton Peck. LC 72-259. 1972. 4.95 (ISBN 0-394-48235-2). Knopf.

Day No Pigs Would Die. Robert Newton Peck. LC 73-3147. 1973. 6.95. G. K. Hall.

Day No Pigs Would Die. Robert Newton Peck. 1974. (pbk.) 1.25. Dell Pub. Co.

Day Number One Forty Two. Edgar A. Anderson et al. 132p. 1974. 5.95 o.p. Dorrance.

Day Number 142. Edgar A Anderson. LC 74-80395. 1974. 4.95 (ISBN 0-8059-2035-8). Dorrance.

Day of Atonement. Louis Golding. LC 25-101488. 1925. A. A. Knopf.

Day of Battle. Frederic Franklyn Van De Water. LC 58-6774. 1958. I. Washburn.

Day of Battle: A Novel. Vincent Sheean. LC 38-27602. 1938. Doubleday, Doran & Co., Inc.

Day of Benediction. Ellen G. White. (Newsprint Ser.). 172p. 1982. pap. 0.25 (ISBN 0-8163-0493-9). Pacific Pr Pub Assn.

Day of Chaminuka. William Rayner. LC 76-41329. 1977. 7.95 (ISBN 0-689-10778-1). Atheneum.

Day of Dark Memory. Jean Phillips. (Orig.). 1970. pap. 0.75 o.p. (ISBN 0-447-74647-2). Lancer.

Day of Days: An Extravaganza. Louis Joseph Vance. LC 13-2840. 1913. Little, Brown, and Company.

Day of Escape. Louise Braden. LC 37-1896. Farrar & Rinehart, Inc.

Day of Faith. Arthur Somers Roche. LC 21-19928. 1921. Little, Brown, and Company.

Day of Fate. Theodore A. Cheney. 288p. (Orig.). 1981. pap. 2.50 (ISBN 0-441-13908-6, Pub. by Charter Bks). Ace Bks.

Day of Fate. Edward Payson Roe. LC 7-40222. Dodd, Mead & Company.

Day of Fate. Edward Payson Roe. LC 8-27361. Dodd, Mead and Company.

Day of Fear. John Creasey. LC 77-73867. (Rinehart suspense novel). 1978. 6.95 (ISBN 0-03-022396-2). Holt, Rinehart and Winston.

Day of Fortune. Norman Haghejm Matson. LC 28-9466. 2.50. The Century Co.

Day of His Youth. Alice Brown. LC 6-19371. 1897. Houghton, Mifflin and Company.

Day of Immense Sun. Blair Niles. LC 36-12703. The Bobbs-Merrill Company.

Day of Judgement. Jack Higgins, pseud. 304p. 1980. pap. 2.75 (ISBN 0-553-13202-4). Bantam.

Day of Judgement. Henry Patterson. LC 78-15043. 8.95 (ISBN 0-03-046171-5). Holt, Rinehart, and Winston.

Day of Judgement. Henry Patterson. LC 79-17590. 1979. 13.95 (ISBN 0-8161-6756-7). G. K. Hall.

Day of Judgment. Wayne D. Overholser. LC 65-106659. 3.95. Macmillan.

Day of Miracles. Duane Pederson & Helen Kooiman. 1974. pap. 2.95 o.p. (ISBN 0-8015-1958-6). Hawthorn.

Day of Pleasant Bread. Ray Stannard Baker. LC 42-50213. 1942. Doubleday, Doran and Company, Inc.

Day of Possession. Lilian Peake. (Harlequin Presents Ser.). 192p. 1982. pap. 1.75 (ISBN 0-373-10496-0). Harlequin Bks.

Day of Prosperity. Paul Devinne. LC 73-154439. (Utopian Literature). 1971. (ISBN 0-405-03522-5). Arno Press.

Day of Prosperity: A Vision of the Century to Come. Paul Devinne. LC 73-154439. (Utopian Literature Ser). 1971. Repr. of 1902 ed. 16.00 (ISBN 0-405-03522-5). Ayer Co.

Day of Reckoning. Robert Angel. 1974. 7.50 (ISBN 0-87881-010-2). Mojave Books.

Day of Reckoning. Ray Hogan. Bd. with Dead Man on a Black Horse. 1982. pap. 2.50 (ISBN 0-451-11523-6, AE1523, Sig). NAL.

Day of Reckoning, a Novel. 1st Ed. Ralph De Toledano. LC 54-105318. 1955. Holt.

Day of Reckoning: By John Garden Pseud. 1st Ed. Harry Lutf Verne Fletcher. LC 51-11200. 1951. Lippincott.

Day of Reckoning: Or, She Rode a Bicycle. Ernest Hope. LC 1-30092. 1900. Scroll Publishing Company.

Day of Resis. Lillian Frances Mentor. LC 7-25880. 1897. G. W. Dillingham Co.

Day of Sacrifice. Fereidoun M Esfandiary. LC 59-12434. 1959. McDowell, Obolensky.

Day of St. Anthony's Fire: By John G. Fuller. John Grant Fuller. LC 68-23632. 1968. 5.95. Macmillan.

Day of Small Things... Anna Buchan. 1930. Doubleday, Doran and Company, Incorporated.

Day of Souls: A Novel. Charles Tenney Jackson. LC 10-7175. The Bobbs-Merrill Company.

Day of Temptation. William Le Queux. 1899. G. W. Dillingham Co.

Day of the Ambushers. Stephen E. Fugate. (Orig.). 1979. pap. 1.95 (ISBN 0-532-23158-9). Woodhill.

Day of the Arrow. Philip Loraine. LC 64-12046. 1964. M. S. Mill Co.; Distributed by Morrow.

Day of the Beast. Zane Grey. LC 22-15849. Harper & Brothers.

Day of the Beasts. John E. Muller. (O.s.i.). 1971. pap. 0.75 o.s.i. (532-75407-075). Manor Bks.

Day of the Brown Horde. Richard Tooker. LC 29-24587. 1929. Payson & Clarke, Ltd.

Day of the Bugles. David Bean. LC 64-18484. 1964. Viking Press.

Day of the Burning. Barry N Malzberg. 1974. (pbk.) 0.95. Ace Books.

Day of the Butterfly. Norah Robinson Lofts. LC 79-7566. 1980. 10.00 (ISBN 0-385-15285-X). Doubleday.

Day of the Butterfly. Norah Robinson Lofts. LC 80-12315. 1980. 16.95 (ISBN 0-8186-3097-3). G. K. Hall.

Day of the Comancheros. Steven C. Lawrence, pseud. 176p. 1981. pap. 1.75 (ISBN 0-8439-0999-4, Leisure Bks). Nordon Pubns.

Day of the Conquerors: A Novel. Niven Busch. LC 46-4660. 1946. Harper & Brothers.

Day of the Dead... Murray C. Morgan. LC 46-22833. 1946. David McKay Company.

Day of the Dead. Bart Spicer. LC 55-67144. (Red badge detective). 1955. Dodd, Mead.

Day of the Dog. George Barr McCutcheon. LC 4-7534. 1904. Dodd, Mead & Company.

Day of the Dog. George Barr McCutcheon & Fisher, Harrison, 1875- Illus. LC 16-7544. 1905. Dodd, Mead & Company.

Day of the Dolphin. Robert Merle. LC 73-75865. 1969. 5.95. Simon and Schuster.

Day of the Dragonstar. David F. Bischoff & Thomas F. Monteleone. 352p. (Orig.). 1983. pap. 2.75 (ISBN 0-425-05932-4). Berkley Pub.

Day of the False Dragon. Alice Margaret Huggins. LC 53-6202. 1953. Westminster Press.

Day of the Feast. Margaret Lane. LC 68-12674. 1968. 5.95. Knopf.

Day of the Fox. Norman Lewis. LC 55-946219. 1955. Rinehart.

Day of the Grunion & Other Stories. H. L. Prosser. 16p. 1977. pap. 1.00x o.p. (ISBN 0-918534-01-1). Mafdet.

Day of the Gun. Clifton Adams. 1973. pap. 0.75 o.p. (BT50620). Belmont-Tower.

Day of the Guns. Mickey Spillane, pseud. pap. 1.95 (ISBN 0-451-09653-3, J9653, Sig). NAL.

Day of the Guns. Mickey Spillane, pseud. Bd. with Death Dealers. 1981. pap. 2.95 (ISBN 0-451-09733-5, E9733, Sig). NAL.

Day of the Guns. Mickey Spillane, pseud. 1964. 3.50 o.p. Dutton.

Day of the Halfbreeds. Peter McCurtin. (Sundance Ser.: No. 29). 1979. pap. 1.75 (ISBN 0-8439-0693-6, Leisure Bks). Nordon Pubns.

Day of the Hangman. Ray Hogan. (Shawn Starbuck Western). (Signet Book: Vol. 20). 1975. (pbk.) 0.95. New American Library.

Day of the Harvest. Helen Upshaw. LC 52-14027. 1953. Bobbs-Merrill.

Day of the Jackal. Frederick Forsyth. LC 74-158414. 1971. 7.95 (ISBN 0-670-25936-5). Viking Press.

Day of the Jackal. Frederick Forsyth. LC 72-1453. 1972. 16.95 (ISBN 0-8161-6032-5). G. K. Hall.

Day of the Klesh. M. A. Foster. (Daw Science Fiction Ser.). 1979. pap. 2.25 o.p. (ISBN 0-87997-492-3, UE1492). Daw Bks.

Day of the Lion: A Novel. Translated from the Italian by Ben Johnson. Giose Rimanelli. LC 54-7819. 1954. Random House.

Day of the Locust. Nathanael West. LC 39-125781. Random House.

Day of the Locust: With an Introd. by Richard B. Gehman. Nathanael West. LC 50-9066. (New classics). 1950. New Directions.

Day of the Monkey. David Karp. LC 55-7887. 1955. Vanguard Press.

Day of the Outlaw. Lee E Wells. LC 55-77324. 1955. Rinehart.

Day of the Peacock. 1st Ed. Elizabeth Boatwright Coker. LC 52-5302. 1952. Dutton.

Day of the Peppercorn Kill. John William Wainwright. LC 81-8722. 1981. 9.95 (ISBN 0-312-18420-4). St. Martin's Press.

Day of the Pigeons. Roy Brown. LC 72-78079. 1968. Macmillan.

Day of the Ram. William Campbell Gault. LC 56-8793. 1956. Random House.

Day of the Scorpion. Gene Shelton. 208p. (Orig.). 1982. pap. 2.25 (ISBN 0-505-51787-6). Tower Bks.

Day of the Scorpion: A Novel. Paul Scott. LC 68-58131. 1968. 6.95. Morrow.

Day of the Scorpion: A Novel. Paul Scott. 1979. 2.25 (ISBN 0-380-40923-2). Avon Books.

Day of the Storm. Rosamunde Pilcher. LC 75-26190. 7.95. St. Martin's Press.

Day of the Triffids. John Wyndham, pseud. 192p. 1981. pap. 2.50 (ISBN 0-449-23721-4, Crest). Fawcett.

Day of the Triffids: By John Wyndham Pseud. 1st Ed. John Beynon Harris. LC 51-10046. 1951. Doubleday.

Day of the Trumpet. Miriam Colwell. LC 47-1207. 1947. Random House.

Day of the Trumpet. David Cornel De Jong. LC 41-51891. Harper & Brothers.

Day of the Waxing Moon. Marian Skedgell. LC 65-123691. 3.95. Doubleday.

Day of Their Return. Poul Anderson. (Signet book). 1975. (pbk.) 1.25. New American Library.

Day of Their Wedding: A Novel. William Dean Howells. LC 7-5780. 1896. Harper & Brothers.

Day of Timestop. Philip Jose Farmer. Orig. Title: Woman Day. (Orig.). 1968. pap. 0.60 o.p. (73-715). Lancer.

Day of Trouble. Gerhard Lewis Wind. LC 31-32634. 1931. Concordia Publishing House.

Day of Uniting. Edgar Wallace. LC 30-83335. 1930. The Mystery League, Inc.

Day of Victory. Mary Barrow Linfield. LC 36-7480. 1936. Doubleday, Doran and Company, Inc.

Day of Wrath. William Jeremiah Coughlin. LC 80-11328. 8.95 (ISBN 0-440-02152-9). Delacorte Press.

Day of Wrath. Mor Jokai. LC 6922. 1900. McClure, Phillips & Co.

Day of Wrath. Jonathan Valin. LC 82-1432. 12.95 (ISBN 0-312-92122-5). Congdon & Lattes: Distributed by St. Martin's Press.

Day of Wrath: A Story of 1914. Louis Tracy. LC 16-108392. E. J. Clode.

Day Off. Margaret Storm Jameson. 1981. 18.95x (Pub. by Remploy England). State Mutual Bk.

Day on Campus. Carl Sawyer Downes. LC 50-3301. 1950. Liveright.

Day on Fire: A Novel Suggested by the Life of Arthur Rimbaud. James Ramsey Ullman. LC 58-10060. 1958. World Pub. Co.

Day on Fire: A Novel Suggested by the Life of Arthur Rimbaud. James Ramsey Ullman. LC 70-139068. 1971. 7.95. Doubleday.

Day One. John Maccabee. 1978. (ISBN 0-553-11760-2). Bantam Books.

Day She Died. Helen Kieran Reilly. LC 62-17167. (Random House mystery). 1962. Random House.

Day Star. Mark S. Geston. (Science Fiction Ser.). 128p. (Orig.). 1972. pap. 0.95 o.p. (UQ1006). DAW Bks.

Day Television Died. Don McGuire. 4.50. Doubleday.

Day That Changed the World. Harold Begbie. 1914. Hodder & Stoughton, George H. Doran Company.

Day That I Die: A Novel of Suspense. Paul Frederick Kluge. LC 75-30871. 7.95 (ISBN 0-672-52190-3). Bobbs-Merrill.

Day the Bookies Took a Bath. Arthur P. Hagan. 288p. 1971. 5.95 o.p. (ISBN 0-8202-0017-4). Sherbourne.

Day the Call Came. Thomas Willes Chitty. LC 65-17369. 1965. Vanguard Press.

Day the Cat Jumped. George E. Vandeman. LC 77-91116. (Stories That Win Ser.). 1978. pap. 0.95 (ISBN 0-8163-0009-7, 04135-0). Pacific Pr Pub Assn.

Day the Century Ended. Francis Irby Gwaltney. LC 55-6428. 1955. Rinehart.

Day the Clowns Cried. Richard Goldhurst. 1970. 5.95 o.p. R W Baron.

Day the Cowboys Quit. Elmer Kelton. LC 70-144278. 1971. 5.95. Doubleday.

Day the Cowboys Quit. Elmer Kelton. 1974. (pbk.) 1.25. Ace Books.

Day the Market Crashed. Donald I Rogers. LC 71-154409. (Illus.). 1971. 8.95 (ISBN 0-87000-124-8). Arlington House.

Day the Money Stopped. Brendan Gill. LC 57-5530. 1957. Doubleday.

Day the Music Died: A Novel. Joseph C Smith. LC 80-8914. 1981. 12.95 (ISBN 0-394-51951-5). Grove Press: Distributed by Random House.

Day the Queen Flew to Scotland for the Grouse Shooting: A Document. Arthur Wise. LC 68-6201. 1968. Cavalier Pub.

Day the Sea Rolled by. Mickey Spillane, pseud. 128p. 1981. pap. 1.75 (ISBN 0-553-14597-5). Bantam.

Day the Sparrow Died. William K. Esler. (Orig.). 1980. pap. 2.25 (ISBN 0-532-23313-1). Woodhill.

Day the Sun Died: A Novel. Dale Van Every. LC 73-135437. 1971. 6.95. Little, Brown.

Day the Sun Fell. Robert Lipscomb Duncan. LC 77-107096. 1970. 6.95. Morrow.

Day the Sun Split. Cynthia Cahn. pap. 3.00. Anhinga Pr.

Day the Sun Stood Still - Three Original Novellas of Science Fiction. Poul Anderson et al. LC 77-38748. 1972. 7.95 o.p. (ISBN 0-525-66206-5). Elsevier-Nelson.

Day the Sun Stood Still: Three Original Novellas of Science Fiction. Poul Anderson & Robert Silverberg. LC 77-38748. 1972. 5.95 (ISBN 0-8407-6206-2). T. Nelson.

Day the World Ended. Sax Rohmer, pseud. 1976. Repr. of 1930 ed. lib. bdg. 16.30x (ISBN 0-89190-804-8). Am Repr-Rivercity Pr.

Day the World Ended... Arthur Sarsfield Ward. LC 30-20636. 1930. Pub. for The Crime Club, Inc., by Doubleday, Doran & Company, Inc.

Day the World Ended... Arthur Sarsfield Ward. LC 33-28333. 1931. A. L. Burt Company.

Day the World Went Sane. Harry Barba. LC 78-70762. 1979. 3.95 (ISBN 0-911906-14-2) (ISBN 0-911906-13-4). Harian Creative Press.

Day They Kidnapped Queen Victoria. Horace Kingston Fleming. LC 77-15340. 1978. 7.95 (ISBN 0-312-18457-3). St. Martin's Press.

Day They Stole the Queen Mary. Terence Hughes. 348p. 1983. 13.95 (ISBN 0-688-01935-8). Morrow.

Day They Stole the Queen Mary. Terry Hughes. LC 82-22939. 1983. 13.95 (ISBN 0-688-01935-8). Morrow.

Day to Come. Cateau De Leeuw. LC 44-5304. 1944. Arcadia House, Inc.

Day to Remember to Forget. Rosalind Brackenbury. LC 78-132794. 1971. 4.95 (ISBN 0-395-12092-6). Houghton Mifflin.

Day We Got Drunk on Cake. William Trevor. 1968. 4.50 o.p. (ISBN 0-670-25958-6). Viking Pr.

Day We Got Drunk on Cake: And Other Stories. William Trevor. LC 68-11414. 1968. Viking Press.

Day We Got Drunk on Cake, and Other Stories. William Trevor. LC 73-875622. 1969 (ISBN 0-14-003012-3). Penguin.

Day We Were Mostly Butterflies. Louise W King. 1973. 0.75. Curtis Books.

Day Will Come. Vida Hurst. LC 48-32882. 1948. Gramercy Pub. Co.

Day Will Come. Elizabeth Marion. LC 39-7442. 1939. Thomas Y. Crowell Company.

Day Will Come. Mary Elizabeth Braddon Maxwell. (On cover: Seaside library. Pocket ed., no. 1211). 1889. G. Munro.

Day Will Come: A Novel. Mary Elizabeth Braddon Maxwell. (On cover: Harper's Franklin square library, no. 650). 1889. Harper & Brothers.

Day with a Demon. Julia MacNair Wright. LC 9-9162. 1880. The National Temperance Society and Publication House.

Day with Father. Francis Ellington Leupp. 1914. C. Scribner's Sons.

Day with Nathaniel Hawthorne. May Clarissa Gillington Byron. LC 78-4080. (Illus.). 1978. 8.50 (ISBN 0-8414-0159-4). Folcroft Library Editions.

Day with the Haymakers. Written for the Board of Publication. LC 28-4856. 1856. Presbyterian Board of Publication.

Day with the Risen Lord. Frederick William Eberhardt. LC 13-11561. 1913. 0.35. F. W. Eberhardt.

Day Without End. Van Van Prang. LC 49-9636. 1949. W. Sloane Associates.

Daybreak. LC 13-17334. 1913. 1.25. The Macaulay Company.

Daybreak. Arthur Schnitzler. LC 73-175443. 1972. 9.00 (ISBN 0-404-05615-6). AMS Press.

Daybreak. Arthur Schnitzler & Drake, William A., 1899- Tr. LC 27-24273. 1927. Simon and Schuster.

Daybreak. Frank Gill Slaughter. LC 58-7368. 1958. Doubleday.

Daybreak: A Novel of Adventure in New Guinea. 1st Ed. Winfred B Senior. LC 53-5637. 1953. Exposition Press.

Daybreak: A Romance of an Old World. James Cowan. LC 72-154436. (Utopian Literature). (Illus.). 1971. 15.00 (ISBN 0-405-03519-5). Arno Press.

Daybreak: A Romance of an Old World. James Cowan. LC 6-28867. 1896. G. H. Richmond & Co.

Daybreak: A Story of the Age of Discovery. Elizabeth Jane Miller. LC 15-773490. 1915. C. Scribner's Sons.

Daybreak Man. Jennifer Schneider. LC 74-20386. 1975. 5.95. (ISBN 0-06-025254-5) (ISBN 0-06-025255-3). Harper & Row.

Daybreak, 2250 A. D. By Andre Norton Pseud. Original Title: Star Man's Son. Alice Mary Norton. LC 54-4375. (Ace double novel books, D-69). 1954. Ace Books.

Daybreakers. Louis L'Amour. LC 75-30999. 1975. 10.95 (ISBN 0-8161-6327-8). G. K. Hall.

Daylight and Dark. Agnes Adams Fisher. LC 55-11092. 1955. Funk & Wagnalls.

Daylight Land: The Experiences, Incidents, and Adventures, Humorous and Otherwise, Which Befel Judge John Doe, Tourist, of San Francisco; Mr. Cephas Pepperell, Capitalist of Boston; Colonel Goffe, the Man from New Hampshire, and Divers Others, in Their Parlor-Car Excursion Over Prairie and Mountain. William Henry Harrison Murray. LC 7-32310. 1888. Cupples and Hurd.

Daylight Moon. Thomas Carney. (Signet book). 1979. 1.95 (ISBN 0-451-08755-0). New American Library.

Daylight Moon. Elizabeth C. Forrest. 1937. Repr. 15.00 o.s.i. Finch Pr.

Daylight on Saturday. John Boynton Priestley. LC 43-13164. 1943. Harper & Brothers.

Daymares. Fredric Brown. (Orig.). (YA) (gr. 7-12). 1968. pap. 0.60 o.p. (73-727). Lancer.

Days. Mary Robison. LC 78-20607. 1979. 8.95 (ISBN 0-394-50444-5). Knopf: Distributed by Random House.

Days After Tomorrow: Science Fiction Stories. Ed. by Hans Stefan Santesson. LC 77-129913. 1971. 5.95. Little, Brown.

Days and Moments Quickly Flying. Perry Madoc. LC 59-8352. 1959. Viking Press.

Days and Nights. Konstantin Mikhailovich Simonov. LC 45-35215. 1945. Simon and Schuster.

Days and Nights of a French Horn Player. Murray Schisgal. LC 79-28727. 10.95 (ISBN 0-316-77338-7). Little, Brown.

Days and Nights of Shikar. W. W Baillie. LC 22-16788. 1921. John Lane.

Days and Ways of the Cocked Hats: Or, The Dawn of the Revolution. Mary Andrews Denison. LC 6-33997. 1860. S. A. Rollo.

Days Are As Grass. Wallace McElroy Kelly. LC 41-191911. 1941. A. A. Knopf.

Days Are Fled: A Novel. Percy Marks. LC 39-21784. 1939. Frederick A. Stokes Company.

Days Are Spent: A Novel. George Phillip Griggs. LC 46-3947. 1945. Coward-McCann, Inc.

Days at Cabin John: A Story of Maryland Neighbors Alongthe Chesapeake and Ohio Canal. Illustrated by Florence Martin. 1st Ed. Edith Martin Armstrong. LC 58-4537. 1958. Vantage Press.

Days Before Lent. Hamilton Basso. LC 39-27772. 1939. C. Scribner's Sons.

Days Between: A Novel. Elizabeth Foster. LC 42-12029. 1942. Harper & Brothers.

Days Beyond Recall. Mary Elizabeth Osborn. LC 42-24439. 1942. Coward-McCann, Inc.

Days Beyond Recall: A Novel. Roger Burke Dooley. LC 49-10675. 1949. Bruce Pub. Co.

Days Beyond Recall: A Novel. Roger Burke Dooley. LC 49-10675. 1949. Bruce Pub. Co.

Days Dividing. John Selby. LC 58-9713. 1958. Putnam.

Days Dividing. Stephen Southwold. LC 35-17770. 1935. Little, Brown, and Company.

Day's End & Other Stories. Herbert Ernest Bates. 1971. Repr. of 1928 ed. 24.00 (ISBN 0-403-00504-3). Scholarly.

Day's End for Gunmen. Marion Chrisomalis. 1979. pap. 1.50 o.s.i. (ISBN 0-505-51450-8). Tower Bks.

Day's End for Gunmen. Marion Chrisomalis. (O.s.i.). (Orig.). 1972. pap. 0.75 o.s.i. (BT50215). Belmont-Tower.

Days in the Yellow Leaf. 1st Ed. William Hoffman. LC 58-557538. 1958. Doubleday.

Day's Journey. William Babington Maxwell. LC 23-264376. 1923. Doubleday, Page & Company.

Day's Journey. Netta Syrett. LC 6-33579. 1906. A. C. McClurg & Co.

Days Like These. Edward Waterman Townsend. LC 1-7329. 1901. Harper & Brothers.

Days Long Ago: A Novelette. Sarah A Elliott. LC 6-37577. 1881. Uzzell & Wiley.

Days of a Hireling. 1st Ed. John Gilland Brunini. LC 51-11187. 1951. Lippincott.

Days of Abd-el-Kader: A Tale of Algeria. N. Gerber. Tr. by Ireland, Mary Eliza (Haines) 1900. D. C. Cook Publishing Company.

Days of Auld Lang Syne. John Watson. LC 72-113690. (Short story index reprint series). 1970. Books for Libraries Press.

Days of Auld Lang Syne. John Watson. LC 4-15343. 1895. Dodd, Mead & Company.

Days of Auld Lang Syne. John Watson. LC 8-34347. 1896. Dodd, Mead and Company.

Days of Blood. Charles R. Pike, pseud. LC 80-69749. (Jubal Cade Westerns Ser.). 125p. 1981. pap. 2.95 (ISBN 0-87754-238-4). Chelsea Hse.

Days of Bruce: A Story from Scottish History. Grace Aguilar. LC 7-1626. 1887. D. Appleton and Company.

Days of Bruce: A Story from Scottish History. Grace Aguilar. 1893. D. Appleton and Company.

Days of Bruce: A Story from Scottish History. new ed. Grace Aguilar. LC 4-164876. 1903. D. Appleton and Company.

Days of Bruce: A Story from Scottish History. new ed. Grace Aguilar. 1904. D. Appleton and Company.

Days of Bruce: A Story from Scottish History. Grace Aguilar. 1879. D. Appleton and Company.

Days of Daniel Boone. A Romance of "the Dark and Bloody Ground". Frank Henry Norton. LC 7-33279. The American News Company.

Days of Dust. Halim Isber Barakat. LC 74-77250. 1974. 7.00. (ISBN 0-914456-08-3) (ISBN 0-914456-09-1). Medina University Press International.

Days of Eighty-Nine. Albert Fernandex. LC 33-18479. 1933. Meador Publishing Company.

Days of Gold: A Novel of the Yukon Country. 1st Ed. Irwin R Blacker. LC 61-5804. 1961. World Pub. Co.

Days of Grass: Stories from the Christian Herald. Christian Herald (New York, 1878-) Ed. by Rachel Hartman. LC 65-24853. 1965. Channel Press.

Days of Greatness. Walter Kempowski. LC 80-27695. 1981. 15.00 (ISBN 0-394-50956-0). Knopf: Distributed by Random House.

Days of Her Life: A Novel. Wallace Irwin. LC 30-10088. 1930. Houghton Mifflin Company.

Days of His Grace: A Novel. Eyvind Johnson. LC 77-134666. 1971. 6.95. Vanguard Press.

Days of Jeanne D'Arc. Mary Hartwell Catherwood. LC 4-22071. 1897. The Century Co.

Days of Judgment: A Novel. Harvey Falk. LC 72-189314. 1972. 5.95. Shengold.

Days of Lamb and Coleridge: A Historical Romance. Alice E Lord. LC 7-14797. 1893. H. Holt and Company.

Days of Life and Death and Escape to the Moon. William Saroyan. LC 78-103432. 1970. 5.95. Dial Press.

Days of Madame Pompadour. A Thrilling and Historical Romance of the Reign of Louis Xv. Gabrielle De St. Andre. LC 6-39352. T. B. Peterson & Brothers.

Days of Misfortune. Aaron Marc Stein. LC 49-102507. 1949. Pub. for the Crime Club by Doubleday.

Days of Mohammed. Anna May Wilson. LC 8-37781. D. C. Cook Publishing Company.

Days of My Life. Margaret Oliphant Wilson Oliphant. (On cover: Seaside library. Pocket ed., no. 527). 1885. G. Munro.

Days of My Life. An Autobiography. Margaret Oliphant Wilson Oliphant. LC 7-32618. 1857. Harper & Brothers.

Days of My Love: A Novel. Leonard Bishop. LC 53-5127. 1953. Dial Press.

Days of My Youth. From the French of Francois Coppee. Francois Coppee. Tr. by Kearney, -- LC 6-30881. (On cover: The Belford American novel ser. vol. ii. no. 3). Belford and Company.

Days of Plenty. 1st Ed. Elizabeth Fenwick. LC 56-7918. 1956. Harcourt, Brace.

Days of Power, Nights of Fear: A Novel of Washington. Bynum Shaw. LC 80-14146. 10.95 (ISBN 0-312-18483-2). St. Martin's Press.

Days of Sadness, Years of Triumph. Geoffrey Perrett. (YA) 1973. 10.00 o.p. (ISBN 0-698-10488-9). Coward.

Days of Shoddy: A Novel of the Great Rebellion in 1861. Henry Morford. LC 73-164571. (American fiction reprint series). (Illus.). 1971. (ISBN 0-8369-7048-9). Books for Libraries Press.

Days of Shoddy. A Novel of the Great Rebellion in 1861. Henry Morford. LC 7-18751. T. B. Peterson & Brothers.

Days of Terror. Barbara Claassen Smucker. LC 79-17789. 1979. 7.95 (ISBN 0-8361-1910-X). Herald Press.

Days of the Colonist. Louise Lamprey. LC 22-20540. (Great days in American history series). Frederick A. Stokes Company.

Days of the Commanders. Louise Lamprey. LC 23-13124. (Great days in American history series). 1923. Frederick A. Stokes Company.

Days of the King. Bruno Frank. Tr. by Helen Tracy Porter Lowe. LC 75-121550. (Short story index reprint series). (Illus.). 1970. Books for Libraries Press.

Days of the King. Bruno Frank & Lowe-Porter, H. T., Tr. LC 27-242659. 1927. A. A. Knopf.

Days of the King: A Novel. Bruno Frank. Tr. by Lowe, Helen Tracy (Porter) LC 42-10424. 1942. The Press of the Readers Club.

Days of the Son of Man: A Tale of Syria. Rosamond Dodson Rhone. LC 2-14427. 1902. G. P. Putnam's Sons.

Days of the Swamp Angel. Mary Hall Leonard. LC 14-16945. 1914. The Neale Publishing Company.

Days of Their Youth. Alan Sullivan. LC 26-163521. The Century Co.

Days of Thunder. Michael Hartman. 224p. 1980. 9.95 o.p. (ISBN 0-312-18485-9). St Martin.

Days of Thunder. Michael Hartmann. LC 80-51384. 9.95 (ISBN 0-312-18485-9). St. Martin's Press.

Days of Valor. Willo Davis Roberts. (Orig.). 1983. pap. 3.50 (ISBN 0-445-04752-6). Popular Lib.

Days of Vengeance. C. H. Guenter. (Orig.). 1979. pap. 1.75 (ISBN 0-532-17218-3). Woodhill.

Days of Vengeance. Harry Mark Petrakis. LC 82-45364. 288p. 1983. 14.95 (ISBN 0-385-04921-8). Doubleday.

Days of Winter. Cynthia Freeman. LC 77-79533. 1978. 9.95 (ISBN 0-87795-171-3). Arbor Hse.

Days of Winter. Cynthia Freeman. 1979. pap. 3.50 (ISBN 0-553-20071-2). Bantam.

Days of Wrath. Andre Malraux & Chevalier, Haakon M., Tr. LC 36-11052. 1936. Random House.

Days of '49. Gordon Ray Young. LC 26-26141. George H. Doran Company.

Day's Pleasure, and Other Sketches. William Dean Howells. LC 7-5779. (Modern classics). 1881. Houghton, Mifflin and Company.

Day's Ride. A Life Romance. Charles James Lever. (Seaside library, vo. 27, no. 566). 1879. G. Munro.

Days That Are No More. Elizabeth Bryant Johnston. LC 75-38655. (Black Heritage Library Collection). (Illus.). 1972. 12.75 (ISBN 0-8369-9013-7). Books for Libraries Press.

Days That Are No More. Elizabeth Bryant Johnston. LC 1-19484. The Abbey Press.

Day's Time-Table: Or, Lois Emerson's "Gospel of Guidance,". Emily Steele Elliott. LC 15-21838. (On cover: The renaissance booklets). 1895. F.H. Revell Company.

Days When the House Was Too Small. Dyckman Andrus. LC 74-8079. 1974. 6.95 (ISBN 0-684-13898-0). Scribner.

Days with Ulanova. Albert Eugene Kahn. 1978. pap. 6.95 (ISBN 0-671-24294-6, Fireside). S&S.

Day's Work. Rudyard Kipling. LC 76-37275. (Short story index reprint series). (Illus.). 1971. (ISBN 0-8369-4086-5). Books for Libraries Press.

Day's Work. Rudyard Kipling. LC 98-764. 1898. Doubleday & McClure Co.

Day's Work. Rudyard Kipling. LC 16-6725. 1915. Doubleday, Page & Company.

Day's Work. Rudyard Kipling. LC 46-221218. 1946. Doubleday & Company, Inc.

Daysman. LC 10-2661. 1909. 1.50. Cochrane Publishing Company.

Dayspring. William Francis Barry. LC 3-18312. 1903. Dodd, Mead and Company.

Dayspring. Harry Sylvester. LC 45-2938. 1945. D. Appleton-Century Company Incorporated.

Daystar & Shadow. James B. Johnson. (Science Fiction Ser.). 1981. pap. 2.25 o.p. (ISBN 0-87997-605-5, UE1605, Daw Bks). DAW Bks.

Daytime Affair. Joshua Lorne. 1974. (pbk.) 1.75. Avon.

Daze of Fears. Jan Roffman. (Ace gothic read easy large type). 1973. (pbk.) 0.95. Ace.

Daze of Fears. Margaret Summerton. LC 68-31492. 1968. 3.95. Published for the Crime Club by Doubleday.

Daze to Remember. Georgia H. Ethridge. 4.50 o.p. Vantage.

Dazzle. Dora Landey & Elinor Klein. 416p. 1981. pap. 2.95 (ISBN 0-446-93476-3). Warner Bks.

Dazzling Crystal. Janet Schane. LC 46-6672. 1946. Reynal & Hitchcock.

D.C. Man: Top Secret Kill. James P Cody. (Berkley medallion book). 1974. (pbk.) 0.95 (ISBN 0-425-02639-6). Berkley Pub. Co.

De Abajo: Novela de la Revolucion Mexicana. rev. ed. Mariano Azuela et al. Ed. by J. Englekirk & L. Kiddle. 1971. pap. 8.95 (ISBN 0-13-540690-0). P-H.

De Bercy Affair. Louis Tracy. LC 10-8161. E. J. Clode.

De Clifford: or, The Constant Man. Robert Plummer Ward. LC 8-34857. 1841. Lea and Blanchard.

De Haine et de Passion. Carole Mortimer. (Collection Harlequin). 192p. 1983. pap. 1.95 (ISBN 0-373-49325-8). Harlequin Bks.

De Irlanda a Argentina Con Amor. Oscar Mingorance. 128p. 1981. pap. 4.50 (ISBN 0-311-37025-X). Casa Bautista.

De la Terre a la Lune. Jules Verne. pap. 3.95. French & Eur.

De L'Autre Cote Des Recifs. Marjorie Lewty. (Collection Harlequin Ser.). 192p. 1983. pap. 1.95 (ISBN 0-373-49335-5). Harlequin Bks.

De Lisle: Or, The Sensitive Man. LC 6-34177. 1828. Printed by J. & J. Harper.

De Maisse Journal. Monsieur De Maisse. 1931. 20.00 (ISBN 0-8482-3663-7). Norwood Edns.

De Molai: the Last of the Military Grand Masters of the Order of Templar Knights. A Romance of History. Edmund Flagg. LC 6-41126. T. B. Peterson & Brothers.

De Montfort Legacy. Pamela Bennetts. LC 72-96031. 1973. 5.95. St. Martin's Press.

De Profundis. unexpurgated ed. Oscar Wilde. pap. 1.85 o.p. (ISBN 0-394-70256-5, V256, Vin). Random.

De Profundis: A Tale of the Social Deposits. 2d ed. William Gilbert. 1866. A. Strahan.

De Raptu Proserpinae. Claudius Claudianus & J. B. Hall. LC 69-14395. (Cambridge classical texts and commentaries, no. 11). 1969 (ISBN 0-521-07442-8). Cambridge U.P.

De Rerum Natura. Lucretius Carus, Titus & William Henry Denham Rouse. (Loeb Classical Library: Latin Authors; 181). 1975. 45.00 (ISBN 0-19-814405-9). Harvard University Press.

De Rohan: Or, The Court Conspirator. An Historical Romance. Eugene Sue. (Seaside library, v. 39, no. 800). 1880. G. Munro.

De Time to Live. George Ellington Jorgenson & Nora Jorgenson. LC 54-112279. 1954. Pageant Press.

De Vane: a Story of Plebeians and Patricians. Henry Washington Hilliard. LC 7-1679. 1865. Blelock & Company.

De Vriendt Goes Home. Arnold Zweig & Sutton, Eric, Tr. LC 33-35699. 1933. The Viking Press.

De Witt's War. Hans Koning. LC 82-18826. 1983. 13.95 (ISBN 0-394-52442-X). Pantheon Books.

Deacon Bradbury: A Novel. Edwin Asa Dix. 1900. The Century Co.

Deacon Cranky, the Old Sinner. George Guirey. LC 7-138. The Author's Publishing Company.

Deacon Hackmetack. M. A. MacDonald. 1888. Treager & Lamb.

Deacon Herbert's Bible-Class. James Freeman Clarke. 1890. G. H. Ellis.

Deacon Lysander. Sarah Pratt McLean Green. LC 4-24511. 1904. The Baker & Taylor Co.

Deacon of Dobbinsville. John A. Morrison. 64p. pap. 0.60. Faith Pub Hse.

Deacon Sims' Prayers. Written for the Massachusetts Sabbath School Society. Mary Dwinell Chellis & Massachusetts Sabbath School Society. Committee of Publication. Massachusetts Sabbath School Society.

Deacon White's Ideas. S. W Brown. 1905. Mayhew Publishing Company.

Deaconess Stories. Lucy Jane Rider Meyer. Hope Publishing Co.

Deacons. William Henry Harrison Murray. LC 13-33876. 1875. H. L. Shepard and Company.

Deacons. William Henry Harrison Murray. LC 7-17252. Cupples and Hurd.

Deacon's Daughter. Franz Marshall McConnell. LC 18-17354. 1918. Stealey Book and Publishing Company.

Deacon's Road. Margaret Flint. LC 38-25692. 1938. Dodd, Mead & Company.

Dead. James Augustine Aloysius Joyce. Ed. by William T. Moynihan. LC 65-18896. (Allyn and Bacon casebook series). 1965. Allyn and Bacon.

Dead see Six Great Modern Short Novels.

Dead Against the Lawyers. Roderic Jeffries. LC 65-27970. (Red badge mystery). 1966. bds., 3.50. Dodd.

Dead Aim. Collin Wilcox. LC 72-159388. 1971. 4.95 (ISBN 0-394-46854-6). Random House.

Dead & Buried. Chelsea Quinn Yarbo. (Orig.). 1980. pap. 2.75 (ISBN 0-446-95886-7). Warner Bks.

Dead and Done for. Robert Reeves. LC 39-235262. 1939. A. A. Knopf.

Dead and Dumb: A Detective Story. Robert Bruce Montgomery. LC 47-4897. 1947. J. B. Lippincott Co.

Dead and Not Buried. Hilda Frances Margaret Prescott. LC 54-227895. (Murder revisited mystery novel, no. 5). 1954. Macmillan.

Dead and Not Buried. Hilda Frances Margaret Prescott. LC 38-5596. 1938. Dodd, Mead & Company.

Dead and Trail... Norman A Fox. LC 46-7570. 1946. Dodd, Mead & Company.

Dead Angel. 1st Ed. Jack Dolph. LC 53-934824. 1953. Published for the Crime Club by Doubleday.

Dead Are Discreet. Arthur Lyons. LC 83-103. (Jacob Asch Mystery). ((Series: Lyons, Arthur.). (Jacob Asch mystery.). 1983. 3.95 (ISBN 0-03-060393-5). Holt, Rinehart, and Winston.

Dead Are Mine. James E Ross. LC 63-20064. 1963. D. McKay Co.

Dead As a Dinosaur. Frances Louise Davis Lockridge & Richard Lockridge. LC 75-46601. 1976. 6.95 (ISBN 0-89190-903-6). Rivercity Press.

Dead As a Dinosaur: A Mr. and Mrs. North Mystery. Frances Louise Davis Lockridge & Richard Lockridge. LC 52-5631. (Main line mysteries). 1952. Lippincott.

Dead As They Come. Kin Platt. LC 73-159364. 1972. 4.95 (ISBN 0-394-47154-7). Random House.

Dead at Sunset. Bradford Scott. 1973. pap. 0.75 o.p. (ISBN 0-515-03065-1, T3065). Pyramid Pubns.

Dead at the Take-off. Lester Dent. LC 46-3139. 1946. Pub. for the Crime Club by Doubleday & Company, Inc.

Dead Babies. Martin Amis. LC 75-8216. 1976. 6.95 (ISBN 0-394-49825-9). Knopf.

Dead Beat. Robert Bloch. LC 60-6100. (Inner sanctum mystery). 1960. Simon and Schuster.

Dead Before Docking. Scott Corbett. (Illus.). 147p. (YA) 1973. lib. bdg. 5.95 o.p. (ISBN 0-8161-6066-X, Large Print Bks). G K Hall.

Dead Body in Burtonville: A Story. James Drought. LC 62-20931. 1962.

Dead Bolt. Raymond Obstfeld. (Illus.). 224p. 1982. pap. 2.50 (ISBN 0-441-14102-1, Pub. by Charter Bks). Ace Bks.

Dead Boy and the Comets: Translated by Marianne Ceconi. Goffredo Parise. LC 53-11931. 1953. Farrar, Straus and Young.

Dead Broke: A Western Tale. Dillon O'Brien. LC 7-33166. 1873. Pioneer Company Print.

Dead Butler Caper. Frank Norman. LC 78-21199. 1979. 7.95 (ISBN 0-312-18487-5). St. Martin's Press.

Dead by Now. Margaret Erskine, pseud. 1974. (pbk.) 0.95. Ace Books.

Dead by Now: By Margaret Erskine Pseud. 1st Ed. Wetherby Williams. LC 54-5358. 1954. N. Y., Published for the Crime Club by Doubleday.

Dead by the Light of the Moon. Stanton Forbes, pseud. LC 67-22449. (Illus.). 1967. Published for the Crime Club by Doubleday.

Dead by the Light of the Moon. Tobias Wells. (60-2339). 1968. Popular Lib.

Dead by the Light of the Moon. Tobias Wells. LC 67-22449. 1967. Published for the Crime Club by Doubleday.

Dead Calm. Charles Williams. LC 82-48820. 192p. 1983. pap. 2.84i (ISBN 0-06-080655-9, P 655, PL). Har-Row.

Dead Can Tell. Helen Kieran Reilly. LC 40-33593. Random House.

Dead Canary. James F. Fox. 1979. pap. 1.75 (ISBN 0-89041-265-0, 3265). Major Bks.

Dead Can't Love. Judson Pentecost Philips. LC 63-16247. (Red badge detective). 1963. Dodd, Mead.

Dead Center. Mary Garden Collins. LC 42-4712. 1942. C. Scribner's Sons.

Dead Center. Sarah Langley. LC 68-22512. 1968. 3.95. Published for the Crime Club by Doubleday.

Dead Center. June Pat Wetherell. LC 46-1872. 1946. E. P. Dutton Company, Inc.

Dead Cert. Dick Francis. 1975. (pbk.) 1.50 (ISBN 0-671-78945-7). Pocket Books.

Dead Cert. Dick Francis. LC 81-47383. (Fifty Classics of Crime Fiction, 1950-1975). 1982. 14.95 (ISBN 0-8240-4991-8). Garland.

Dead Circuit see Rook's Gambit.

Dead City. Shane Stevens. LC 73-1567. 1973. 6.95 (ISBN 0-03-010336-3). Holt, Rinehart and Winston.

Dead Command. Vicente Blasco Ibanez & Douglas, Frances, 1870- Tr. LC 19-3786. 1919. Duffield & Company.

Dead Commando. Gordon Landsborough. 1977. pap. 1.50 (ISBN 0-532-15279-4). Woodhill.

Dead Corse. Mary Kelley. LC 67-12582. (Rinehart suspense novel). 1967. Holt, Rinehart and Winston.

Dead Corse. Mary Kelly. LC 67-12582. (Rinehart suspense novel). 1967. Holt, Rinehart and Winston.

Dead Dogs Bite. Elizabeth Curtiss. LC 39-10127. 1939. Simon and Schuster.

Dead Dolls Don't Talk. Day Keene. 1968. pap. 0.60 o.p. (60-329). Manor Bks.

Dead Don't Care. Jonathan Latimer. LC 38-747249. 1938. Pub. for the Crime Club, Inc., by Doubleday Doran & Company, Inc.

Dead Drunk. Aaron Marc Stein. 1973. (pbk) 0.95. Warner.

Dead Drunk: By George Bagby Pseud. 1st Ed. Aaron Marc Stein. LC 53-9981. 1953. Published for the Crime Club by Doubleday.

Dead Easy for Dover: A Novel. Joyce Porter. LC 78-3970. 1979. 7.95 (ISBN 0-312-18492-1). St. Martin's Press.

Dead End. Mark Cruz. (Kill Squad: No. 4). 192p. (Orig.). 1975. pap. 1.25 o.p. (ISBN 0-532-12354-9). Woodhill.

Dead End. Mark Cruz. (Kill Squad: No. 4). 192p. (Orig.). 1975. pap. 1.25 o.p. (ISBN 0-532-12354-9). Manor Bks.

Dead End Killers. Leonard Gribble. 1979. 8.95 (ISBN 0-09-133400-4, Pub. by Hutchinson). Merrimack Pub Cir.

Dead End Option. Raymond Obstfeld. 288p. (Orig.). 1980. pap. 2.25 (ISBN 0-441-14125-0, Pub. by Charter Bks). Ace Bks.

Dead End Street see Callejon Sin Salida.

Dead End Street, No Outlet. Lee Thayer. LC 36-5936. 1936. Dodd, Mead & Company.

Dead Ending. Judson Pentecost Philips. LC 62-17015. (Red badge detective). 1962. Dodd, Mead.

Dead Ernest: A Leonidas Witherall Mystery Reissue by Phoebe Atwood Taylor Writing As Alice Tilton. Phoebe Atwood Taylor. 1966. bds., 3.95. Norton.

Dead Ernest: A Leonidas Witherall Mystery. Phoebe Atwood Taylor. LC 44-4329. 1944. W. W. Norton & Company, Inc.

Dead Eye. John Henry Reese. LC 77-78514. 1978. 6.95 (ISBN 0-385-13396-0). Doubleday.

Dead Fall. Philip Kirk. (Butler Ser.: No. 8). 240p. (Orig.). 1983. pap. 2.50 o.s.i. (ISBN 0-8439-1103-4, Leisure Bks). Dorchester Pub Co.

Dead Fall. Dale Wilmer, pseud. LC 54-71926. 1954-1953. Bouregy & Curl.

Dead Father. Donald Barthelme. LC 75-25566. 1975. 6.95 (ISBN 0-374-13535-5). Farrar, Straus and Giroux.

Dead Father. Donald Barthelme. 1976. 1.95 (ISBN 0-671-80766-8). Pocket Books.

Dead for a Ducat. Helen Kieran Reilly. LC 39-27462. 1939. Pub. for the Crime Club, Inc., by Doubleday, Doran & Co., Inc.

Dead for a Ducat. Helen Kieran Reilly. LC 40-11448. 1940. The Sun Dial Press.

Dead Freight for Piute. Luke Short. LC 40-36104. 1940. Doubleday, Doran and Co., Inc.

Dead Game: A Novel of Suspense. 1st Ed. Michael Avallone. LC 54-5891. 1954. Holt.

Dead Girls. Jorge Ibarguengoitia. Tr. by Asa Zatz. 160p. (Span.). 1983. pap. 2.95 (ISBN 0-380-81612-1, 81612-1, Bard). Avon.

Dead Giveaway. Stella Allan. LC 81-5732. 1981. 10.95 (ISBN 0-312-18497-2). St Martin's Press.

Dead Giveaway. Hugh Lawrence Nelson. LC 50-5425. (Murray Hill mystery). 1950. Rinehart.

Dead Giveaway. Dorothy Wheelock. LC 42-14125. 1942. Phoenix Press.

Dead Giveaway. Dorothy Wheelock. LC 44-28605. 1944. Bard Publishing Corp.

Dead Go Overside. Arthur Douglas Howden Smith. LC 38-31050. The Greystone Press.

Dead God Dancing. Ann Maxwell. 1979. pap. 2.25 (ISBN 0-380-44644-8, 44644). Avon.

Dead Ground. Howard Clewes. LC 46-6548. 1946. E. P. Dutton & Company, Incorporated.

Dead Heart: And, Lady Gwendoline's Dream. Charlotte Mary Brame. (On cover: Seaside library. Pocket ed. no. 305). G. Munro.

Dead Heart; and Lady Gwendoline's Dream. Bertha M. Clay & Brame, Charlotte Mary, 1836-1884. Lady Gwendoline's Dream. LC 44-11666. (On cover: Seaside library. Pocket ed. No. 305). G. Munro.

Dead Heat. Raymond Obstfeld. 224p. (Orig.). 1981. pap. 2.50 (ISBN 0-441-14110-2, Pub. by Charter Bks). Ace Bks.

Dead Heat, a Crime Photographer Mystery: By Paul Ayres Pseud. Edward Sidney Aarons. LC 50-3844. 1950. Bell Pub. Co.

Dead Heat: Love and Money: A Fable of New York. Paul Sann. LC 74-9988. 1974. 6.95 (ISBN 0-8037-1800-4). Dial Press.

Dead Hero. William Campbell Gault. LC 63-13881. 1963. Dutton.

Dead in Aqaba. C. H. Guenter. (Mr. Dynamite Ser.). 1978. pap. 1.50 (ISBN 0-532-15319-7). Woodhill.

Dead in Bed. 3rd ed. Henry Kane. (Orig.). 1969. pap. 0.60 o.p. (73-817). Lancer.

Dead in Guanajuato. Phillip Rock. 1969. 4.95 o.p. (57606). Meredith.

Dead in Guanajuato: A Novel. Phillip Rock. LC 68-9524. 1968. 4.95. Meredith Press.

Dead in the Eye of the Law. (On cover: American author's series. no. 3). 1892. Melbourne Publishing Co.

Dead in the Saddle. Trev Roberts, pseud. LC 59-654784. 1959. Arcadia House.

Dead in the Water. Brock W Yates. LC 75-11657. 1975. (ISBN 0-374-13544-4). Farrar, Straus and Giroux.

Dead Indeed. Marion Rous Hodgkin. LC 56-114487. (Cock Robin mystery). 1956. Macmillan.

Dead Is the Door-Nail: A Mike Warlock Mystery Novel. Henri Weiner, pseud. LC 37-5830. J. B. Lippincott Company.

Dead Knock. Peter Turnbull. LC 82-10700. 1983. 10.95 (ISBN 0-312-18499-9). St. Martin's Press.

Dead Knock. Peter Turnbull. 208p. 1983. 10.95 (ISBN 0-312-18499-9). St Martin.

Dead Letter. Jonathan Valin. LC 82-17964. 1983. 12.95 (ISBN 0-89340-545-0). J. Curley.

Dead Letter. Jonathan Valin. 224p. 1982. pap. 2.50 (ISBN 0-380-61366-2, 61366-2). Avon.

Dead Letter. Metta Victoria Fuller Victor. LC 79-1246. (Gregg Press Mystery Fiction Series). 1979. 9.95. Gregg Press.

Dead Letter: An American Romance. Metta Victoria Victor. 1867. Beadle and Company.

Dead Letters. Maurice Baring. LC 26-11095. 1925. Doubleday, Page & Company.

Dead Level. Russell Gordon. LC 48-5363. 1948. W. Morrow.

Dead Lie Still... William L Stuart. LC 45-9222. 1945. Farrar & Rinehart, Inc.

Dead Lion. John Bonett & Emery Bonett. LC 81-47807. 240p. 1982. pap. 2.40i (ISBN 0-06-080563-3, P 563, PL). Har-Row.

Dead Lion. John Coulson & Carter, Felicity Winifred. LC 49-9323. 1949. Pub. for the Crime Club by Doubleday.

Dead Live. Clark Darlton. (Perry Rhodan,#48). 1974. (pbk.) 0.95. Ace Books.

Dead Look on: A Novel. Gerald Kersh. LC 43-629075. 1943. Reynal & Hitchcock.

Dead Lovers Are Faithful Lovers. Frances Newman. LC 76-51673. (Recovered Fiction by American Women). 1977. 22.00 (ISBN 0-405-10051-5). Arno Press.

Dead Lovers Are Faithful Lovers. Frances Newman. LC 28-12304. 1928. Boni & Liveright.

Dead Lovers Are Faithful Lovers. Frances Newmann. LC 76-51673. (Rediscovered Fiction by American Women Ser). 1977. lib. bdg. 22.00x (ISBN 0-405-10051-5). Ayer Co.

Dead Low Tide. John Dann MacDonald. LC 53-29432. (Gold medal books, 298). 1953. Fawcett Publications.

Dead Low Tide. John Dann MacDonald. LC 81-47338. (Fifty Classics of Crime Fiction, 1950-1975). 1982. 14.95 (ISBN 0-8240-4986-1). Garland Pub.

Dead Man at the Window. Jean Toussaint Samat & Abbott, Elisabeth, Tr. LC 34-19025. J. B. Lippincott Company.

Dead Man Blues. Cornell George Hopley-Woolrich. LC 48-5760. (Main line mysteries). 1948. J. B. Lippincott Co.

Dead Man Calling. Oswald Wynd. LC 62-10333. (Random House mystery). 1962. Random House.

Dead Man Control. Helen Kieran Reilly. LC 36-36432. 1936. Pub. for the Crime Club, Inc., by Doubleday, Doran & Company, Inc.

Dead Man Control. Helen Kieran Reilly. LC 38-3736. 1937. The Sun Dial Press, Inc.

Dead, Man, Dead. 1st Ed. David Alexander. LC 59-7781. (His A Bart Hardin murder mystery). 1959. Lippincott.

Dead Man Dies. Percy Marks. LC 29-4534. The Century Co.

Dead Man in the Silver Market. Aubrey Menen. LC 73-136075. 1971. (ISBN 0-8371-5225-9). Greenwood Press.

Dead Man Inside... Vincent Starrett. LC 31-31230. Pub. for the Crime Club, Inc., by Doubleday, Doran & Company, Inc.

Dead Man Leading. Victor Sawdon Pritchett. LC 37-19450. 1937. The Macmillan Company.

Dead Man Manor. Valentine Williams. LC 36-598. 1936. Houghton Mifflin Company.

Dead Man on a Black Horse see Day of Reckoning.

Dead Man Pass. Peter Dawson. 160p. 1980. pap. 1.75 (ISBN 0-553-14175-9). Bantam.

Dead Man Range. Ernest Haycox. LC 74-22420. 1974. (ISBN 0-8161-6259-X). G. K. Hall.

Dead Man Range. Ernest Haycox. (Signet brand western). 1975. (pbk.) 0.95. New American Library.

Dead Man Running. John Blackburn. pap. 0.60 o.p. (73-446). Lancer.

Dead Man Running. Sam Picard. (Notebooks Ser.). (O.s.i.). 192p. 1971. pap. 1.25 o.s.i. (AQ1515, Award). Univ Pub & Dist.

Dead Man Talks Too Much. Weed Dickinson. LC 37-24274. J. B. Lippincott Company.

Dead Man Twice... Christopher Bush. LC 30-32908. 1930. Pub. for the Crime Club, Inc., by Doubleday, Doran & Company, Inc.

Dead Man's Bay. Catherine Arley. 160p. 1980. pap. 1.95 (ISBN 0-441-14149-8, Pub. by Charter Bks). Ace Bks.

Dead Man's Canyon. John Benteen. (Sundance: No. 2). 1979. pap. 1.75 o.s.i. (ISBN 0-8439-0709-6, Leisure Bks). Nordon Pubns.

Dead Man's Cocktail. Bruce Crowther. LC 77-99216. 1978. 7.95 (ISBN 0-8027-5385-X). Walker.

Dead Man's Court. Maurice H Hervey. LC 11-16145. F. A. Stokes Company.

Dead Man's Diary: Written After His Decease. Coulson Kernahan. LC 32-335985. 1890. Ward, Lock and Co.

Dead Man's Diary. Written After His Decease. Coulson Kernahan. LC 6-1903. J. S. Ogilvie Publishing Company.

Dead Man's Draw. Thomas Charles Buxton. LC 41-8854. House of Field, Inc.

Dead Man's Feud. P. A Bechko. 1976. (pbk.) 0.95 (ISBN 0-523-00790-6). Pinnacle Books.

Dead Man's Float. Amber Dean. LC 44-6665. 1944. Pub. for the Crime Club by Doubleday, Doran and Co., Inc.

Dead Man's Folly. Agatha Miller Christie. LC 56-10056. (Red badge detective). 1956. Dodd, Mead.

Dead Man's Gift. Zelda Popkin. LC 41-23269. 1941. J. B. Lippincott Company.

Dead Man's Gold. Al Cody, pseud. 1980. pap. 1.75 (ISBN 0-8439-0821-1). Nordon Pubns.

Dead Man's Gold. Joseph Allan Elphinstone Dunn. LC 20-13705. 1920. Doubleday, Page & Company.

Dead Man's Gold. William Colt MacDonald. LC 48-8941. (Double D western). 1948. Doubleday.

Dead Man's Hand. Jake Logan. LC 79-88834. (Jake Logan Western Ser.). (Orig.). 1979. pap. 1.95 (ISBN 0-86721-022-2). Playboy Pbks.

Dead Man's Hat. Hulbert Footner. LC 32-31299. 1932. Harper & Brothers.

Dead Man's Knock. 1st Ed. John Dickson Carr. LC 58-8884. 1958. Harper.

Dead Man's Message: An Occult Romance. Florence Marryat Church Lean. LC 75-46290. (Supernatural and Occult Fiction). 1976. 10.00 (ISBN 0-405-08150-2). Arno Press.

Dead Man's Message: An Occult Romance. Florence Marryat Church Lean. LC 7-13589. 1894. C. B. Reed.

Dead Man's Mirror. Agatha Miller Christie. LC 37-27402. 1937. Dodd, Mead & Company.

Dead Man's Mirror. Dame Agatha Miller Christie. 1975. (pbk.) 0.95. Dell.

Dead Man's Music... Christopher Bush. LC 32-761032. Pub. for the Crime Club, Inc., by Doubleday, Doran & Company, Inc.

Dead Man's Noose. Morgan Hill. (Orig.). 1980. pap. 1.95 (ISBN 0-440-12073-X). Dell.

Dead Man's Plack and An Old Thorn. William Henry Hudson. LC 20-23046. E. P. Dutton & Company.

Dead Man's Plans. Mignon Good Eberhart. 1982. 15.00x (ISBN 0-86025-176-4, Pub. by Ian Henry Pubns England). State Mutual Bk.

Dead Man's Range. Allan K. Echols. 1979. pap. 1.25 o.s.i. (ISBN 0-8439-0636-7, Leisure Bks). Nordon Pubns.

Dead Man's Range. Archie Joscelyn. LC 41-258236. Phoenix Press.

Dead Man's Riddle. Mary Kelly. LC 67-23650. 1967. Walker.

Dead Man's Rock, a Romance. Arthur Thomas Quiller-Couch. LC 9-2779. 1906. C. Scribner's Sons.

Dead Man's Rock: A Romance. Arthur Thomas Quiller-Couch. (On cover: Cassell's "rainbow" sereis. v. 1, no. 6). 1887. Cassell & Company, Limited.

Dead Man's Saddle. Llewellyn Perry Holmes. LC 51-1100. (Double D western). 1951. Doubleday.

Dead Man's Saddle. Jon Sharpe. (Trailsman Ser.: No. 9). (Orig.). 1982. pap. 2.25 (ISBN 0-451-11280-6, AE1280, Sig). NAL.

Dead Man's Secret. Mary Plum. LC 31-984. 1931. Harper & Brothers.

Dead Man's Secret: Or, The Adventures of a Medical Student. Jupiter Paeon. (On cover: Seaside library. Pocket ed., no 374). 1855. G. Munro.

Dead Man's Shoes. Evelyn Cameron. LC 39-30546. 1939. Pub. for the Crime Club, Inc., by Doubleday, Doran & Co., Inc.

Dead Man's Shoes: By Michael Innes Pseud. John Innes Mackintosh Stewart. LC 54-10576. (Red badge detective). 1954. Dodd, Mead.

Dead Man's Step. Emma Murdoch Van Deventer. (On cover: Rialto series, no. 6). 1893. Rand, McNally & Company.

Dead Man's Tears. Joel Uman. LC 80-27171. 9.95 (ISBN 0-8253-0035-5). Beaufort Books.

Dead Man's Trail. Hoffman Birney. LC 37-22890. The Penn Publishing Company.

Dead Man's Trail. James Wesley. (YA) 1979. 6.95 (Avalon). Bouregy.

Dead Man's Treasure. Max Brand. LC 73-15034. 1974. 4.95 o.p. (ISBN 0-396-06879-0). Dodd.

Dead Man's Treasure: A Novel of Adventure. Frederick Faust. LC 73-15034. 1974. 4.95 (ISBN 0-396-06879-0). Dodd, Mead.

Dead Man's Walk. Richard S Prather. LC 66-6218. 1965. Pocket Books.

Dead Man's Watch... George Douglas Howard Cole & Margaret Isabel Postgate Cole. LC 32-14331. Pub. for the Crime Club, Inc., by Doubleday. Doran & Comapny, Inc.

Dead March for Penelope Blow. George Bellairs. LC 51-8140. 1951. Macmillan.

Dead Marquise: A Romance. Leonard Kip. LC 7-12538. 1873. G. P. Putnam's Sons.

Dead Matter. Steven Frimmer. LC 81-6535. (Rinehart suspense novel). 12.95. Holt, Rinehart, and Winston.

Dead Men Alive. Desmond Cory, pseud. (Johnny Fedora Ser., No. 6). 1969. pap. 0.60 o.p. (A447X, Award). Univ Pub & Dist.

Dead Men Are Dangerous. Garnett Weston. LC 37-2685. 1937. Frederick A. Stokes Company.

Dead Men at the Folly. Cecil John Charles Street. LC 32-224693. 1932. Dodd, Mead & Company.

Dead Men Do Tell. Keith Trask. LC 31-30256. Farrar & Rinehart, Incorporated.

Dead Men Don't Cry. Yvonne Lehman. 256p. 1972. 4.95 o.p. (10008). Zondervan.

Dead Men Grin... Bruno Fischer. LC 45-9510. 1945. David McKay Company.

Dead Men Leave No Fingerprints. Elwyn Whitman Chambers. LC 35-7313. 1935. Pub. for the Crime Club, Inc., by Doubleday, Doran & Company, Inc.

Dead Men Leave No Fingerprints. Elwyn Whitman Chambers. LC 37-110122. 1937. The Sun Dial Press, Inc.

Dead Men of Sestos. Philip Loraine. LC 68-14502. 1968. Random House.

Dead Men Rise up Never. Christopher Landon. LC 73-153558. 1971. 5.95 (ISBN 0-85617-640-0). White Lion.

Dead Men Rise up Never. Christopher London. LC 62-9865. 1963. W. Sloane Associates.

Dead Men Rising. Kenneth Mackenzie. LC 51-12524. 1951. Harper.

Dead Men Running. D'Arcy Niland. 1978. pap. 2.50 o.p. (ISBN 0-14-004432-9). Penguin.

Dead Men Tell No Tales. W. Hornung. 321p. 1980. lib. bdg. 14.75x (ISBN 0-89968-185-9). Lightyear.

Dead Men Tell No Tales: A Story. Ernest William Hornung. LC 98-1851. 1899. C. Scribner's Sons.

Dead Men's Money. Joseph Smith Fletcher. LC 20-19048. 1920. A. A. Knopf.

Dead Men's Plans. Mignon Good Eberhart. LC 52-5161. 1952. Random House.

Dead Men's Shoes. Mary Elizabeth Braddon Maxwell. (On cover: Lovell's library. no. 890). 1887. J. W. Lovell Company.

Dead Men's Shoes. Lee Thayer. LC 29-4416. J. H. Sears & Company, Inc.

Dead Men's Shoes. A Novel. Mary Elizabeth Braddon Maxwell. (Seaside library. v. 5, no. 95). 1877. G. Munro.

Dead Men's Shoes. A Novel. Mary Elizabeth Braddon Maxwell. (On cover: Seaside library. Pocket ed. no. 567). 1885. G. Munro.

Dead Men's Shoes. A Romance. Jeannette Ritchie Hadermann Walworth. LC 12-10054. 1872. J. B. Lippincott & Co.

Dead Moon. Leo P Kelley. LC 78-68228. (Pacemaker book). (Galaxy 5 series). (Illus.). 3.32 (ISBN 0-8224-3204-8). Fearon Pitman Publishers.

Dead Mrs. Stratton: An Exploit of Mr. Roger Sheringham... Anthony Berkeley Cox. LC 33-27254. 1933. Pub. for the Crime Club, Inc., by Doubleday, Doran & Company, Inc.

Dead Ned and Live and Kicking Ned. John Masefield. LC 41-51978. 1941. The Macmillan Company.

Dead Ned: The Autobiography of a Corpse Who Recovered Life Within the Coast of Dead Ned and Came to What Fortune You Shall Hear. John Masefield. LC 38-27944. 1938. The Macmillan Company.

Dead-Nettle. John Buxton Hilton. LC 77-160. 1977. 7.95. St. Martin's Press.

Dead of Jericho. Colin Dexter. LC 81-5736. 1981. 9.95 (ISBN 0-312-18511-1). St Martin's Press.

Dead of Night. Rudolf Kagey. LC 40-11531. 1940. Little, Brown and Company.

Dead of Night: Horror Stories from Radio, Television, and Films. Peter Haining. LC 81-48444. 1982. 12.95 (ISBN 0-8128-2848-8). Stein & Day.

Dead of Night: The Affair of the Kentucky Casanova. pseud. 1st ed. Prentice Winchell. LC 50-10493. 1950. Dutton.

Dead of Summer. Mary Kelly. LC 63-13222. 1963. M. S. Mill Co.

Dead of Summer: A Mystery. Dana Moseley. LC 53-8364. 1953. Abelard Press.

Dead of the House. Hannah Green. LC 70-172557. 1972. 5.95 o.p. (ISBN 0-385-02557-2). Doubleday.

Dead of the House. Hannah Green. 264p. 1972. Repr. 7.95 o.p. (ISBN 0-8161-6047-3, Large Print Bks). G K Hall.

Dead of the House: A Novel. Hannah Green. LC 72-6489. 1972. 7.95 (ISBN 0-8161-6047-3). G. K. Hall.

Dead of the House: A Novel. Hannah Green. LC 70-172557. 1972. 5.95. Doubleday.

Dead of the Night. Cecil John Charles Street. LC 42-21089. 1942. Dodd, Mead & Company.

Dead of Winter. Dominic Cooper. LC 75-24611. 1976. 7.95. St. Martin's Press.

Dead of Winter. William H Hallahan. 1977. 1.75 (ISBN 0-380-01692-3). Avon Books.

Dead of Winter: A Mystery Story. Frances Moyer Ross Stevens. LC 41-13945. 1941. Pub. for the Crime Club by Doubleday, Doran & Company, Inc.

Dead on Arrival. Aaron Marc Stein. LC 46-1248. 1946. Pub. for the Crime Club by Doubleday & Company, Inc.

Dead on Arrival. Emma Redington Lee Thayer. LC 60-12377. (Red badge detective). 1960. Dodd, Mead.

Dead on the Track. Cecil John Charles Street. LC 43-64521. 1943. Dodd, Mead & Company.

Dead on Time. Owen John. 1969. pap. 0.60 o.p. (63-198). Paperback Lib.

Dead One in Berlin. Ulf Miehe. 1976. (pbk.) 1.50. Bantam Books.

Dead or Alive. Max Brand. LC 38-334022. 1938. Dodd, Mead & Company.

Dead or Alive. Max Brand. 1979. 1.50 (ISBN 0-671-81754-X). Pocket Books.

Dead or Alive. John Creasey. 1974. (pbk.) 0.95. Popular Library.

Dead or Alive. Frederick Faust. LC 76-47537. 1977. 6.95 (ISBN 0-88411-518-6). Aeonian Press.

Dead or Alive. Patricia Wentworth. LC 36-59521. J. B. Lippincott Company.

Dead Parrot... Michael Keyes. LC 33-25366. 1933. Pub. for the Crime Club, Inc., by Doubleday, Doran & Company, Inc.

Dead Past. Jean Scholey. LC 81-47397. (Ifty Classics of Crime Fiction, 1950-1975). 1982. 14.95 (ISBN 0-8240-4964-0). Garland Pub.

Dead Piano. Henry Van Dyke. LC 75-161366. 1971. 5.95 (ISBN 0-374-13550-9). Farrar, Straus & Giroux.

Dead Pigeon: A Mystery. Robert P Hansen. LC 51-12175. 1951. M. S. Mill Co., and W. Morrow.

Dead Pigeon on Beethoven Street. Samuel Fuller. LC 74-19985. 1974. (pbk.) 1.25 (ISBN 0-515-03736-2). Pyramid Books.

Dead Pigeon on Beethoven Street. Samuel Michael Fuller. (Orig.). 1974. pap. 1.25 o.p. (ISBN 0-515-03736-2). Pyramid Pubns.

Dead Reckoning. Bruce Hamilton. LC 37-12768. 1937. Simon and Schuster.

Dead Reckoning. Cyril Northcote Parkinson. LC 78-12050. 1978. 10.95 (ISBN 0-395-27115-0). Houghton Mifflin.

Dead Reckoning. Lee Thayer. LC 54-11239. (Red badge detective). 1954. Dodd, Mead.

Dead Reckoning. Audrey Walz. LC 43-12353. 1943. Duell, Sloan and Pearce.

Dead Ride Hard. Louis Joseph Vance. LC 26-204171. 1926. J. B. Lippincott Company.

Dead Riders. Elliot O'Donnell. 1967. pap. 0.60 o.p. (53-567). Paperback Lib.

Dead Right. Jennette Barbour Perry Lee. LC 25-7073. 1925. C. Scribner's Sons.

Dead Right: A Gil Vine Investigation, by Stewart Sterling Pseud. 1st Ed. Prentice Winchell. LC 56-6414. (Main Line mysteries). 1956. Lippincott.

Dead Ringer. Fredric Brown. LC 48-1133. (A Dutton guilt edged mystery). 1948. E. P. Dutton.

Dead Ringer. Brian Fox. (Alias Smith & Jones Ser). (Orig.). 1971. pap. 0.75 o.p. (A896S, Award). Univ Pub & Dist.

Dead Ringer. Brian Fox. (O.s.i.). (Orig.). pap. 0.75 o.s.i. (A896S, Award). Univ Pub & Dist.

Dead Ringer. Arthur Lyons. LC 83-104. (Jacob Asch mystery). ((Series: Lyons, Arthur.). (Jacob Asch mystery.). 1983. 3.95 (ISBN 0-03-060396-X). Holt, Rinehart, and Winston.

Dead Ringer: A Mystery. Arthur Lyons. LC 77-11684. 1977. 7.95 (ISBN 0-88405-581-7). Mason/Charter.

Dead Ringer: By James Hadley Chase Pseud. Rene Raymond. LC 56-21103. (Ace double novel books, D-135). Ace Books.

Dead Run, a Miss Tessie Mystery. Helen Holley. LC 47-31460. 1947. Pub. for Mystery House by S. Curl.

Dead Run: A Novel of Suspense. Jack Foxx, pseud. LC 73-22661. 6.95 (ISBN 0-672-51939-9). Bobbs-Merrill.

Dead Run: An Inspector Heimrich Mystery. Richard Lockridge. LC 75-37527. 7.95 (ISBN 0-397-01132-6). Lippincott.

Dead Runner. Frank Ross. LC 76-44499. 1977. 8.95 (ISBN 0-689-10774-9). Atheneum.

Dead Runner. Frank Ross. (Fawcett Crest Book). 1978. 1.75. Fawcett Books.

Dead Sea Cipher. Elizabeth Peters, pseud. LC 74-111912. 1970. 4.95. Dodd, Mead.

Dead-Sea Fruit. Mary Elizabeth Braddon Maxwell. (Seaside library. v. 17, no. 322). 1878. G. Munro.

Dead-Sea Fruit. Mary Elizabeth Braddon Maxwell. (On cover: Lovell's library, no. 396). 1885. J. W. Lovell Company.

Dead Seagull. George Barker. LC 51-11466. 1951. Farrar, Straus and Young.

Dead Secret. Wilkie Collins. LC 6-26953. (On cover: Lovell's library. v. 20, no. 957). 1887. J. W. Lovell Company.

Dead Secret. Wilkie Collins. LC 8-31167. 1908. C. Scribner's Sons.

Dead Secret. Wilkie Collins. LC 78-74113. (Illus.). 1979. 4.50 (ISBN 0-486-23775-3). Dover Publications.

Dead Secret. A Novel. Wilkie Collins. LC 3-27268. Harper & Brothers.

Dead Secret. A Novel. Wilkie Collins. LC 6-26954. 1874. Harper & Brothers.

Dead: Senate Office Building. 1st Ed. Margaret Scherf. LC 53-6934. 1953. Published for the Crime Club by Doubleday.

Dead Shot. James M. Fox. 1979. pap. 1.75 (ISBN 0-89041-257-X, 3257). Major Bks.

Dead Side of the Mike. Simon Brett. LC 80-18269. 1980. 8.95 (ISBN 0-684-16729-8). Scribner.

Dead Side of the Mike. 208p. 1981. pap. 2.25 (ISBN 0-425-05049-1). Berkley Pub.

Dead Skip. Joseph N Gores. LC 72-5403. (DKA file novel). 1972. 4.95 (ISBN 0-394-48157-7). Random House.

Dead Solid Perfect. Dan Jenkins. LC 74-81235. 1974. 7.95 (ISBN 0-689-10620-3). Atheneum.

Dead Solid Perfect. Dan Jenkins. LC 74-81235. 1975. (pbk.) 1.95. Warner Paperback Library.

Dead Souls. Nikolai Vasilevich Gogol. Tr. by Bernard Guilbert Guerney. LC 65-15433. (Modern library of the world's best books ML40). 1965. Modern Library.

Dead Souls. Nikolai Vasilevich Gogol. LC 72-30178. (Norton library, N600). 1971. 1.95 (ISBN 0-393-00600-X). W. W. Norton.

Dead Souls. Nikolai Vasilevich Gogol. LC 49-9448. (Novel library). 1948. Pantheon Books.

Dead Souls. Nikolai Vasilevich Gogol. Tr. by Guerney, Bernard Guilbert. LC 48-456949. (Rinehart editions, 5). 1948. Rinehart.

Dead Souls. Nikolai Vasilevich Gogol. Tr. by Hogarth, D. J. Ed. by Cournos, John. (Half-title: Everyman's library, ed. by Ernest Rhys. Fiction). 1916. J. M. Dent & Sons, Ltd.

Dead Souls. Nikolai Vasilevich Gogol. Tr. by Graham, Stephen. LC 16-10452. Frederick A. Stokes Company.

Dead Souls. Nikolai Vasilevich Gogol. Tr. by Garnett, Constance (Black) Odets, Clifford. LC 36-7620. (Half-title: The modern library of the world's best books). The Modern Library.

Dead Souls. Nikolai Vasilevich Gogol. 1915. Frederick A. Stokes Company.

Dead Souls. Translated with an Introd. by Helen Michailoff. Nikolai Vasilevich Gogol. LC 64-4819. 1964. Washington Square Press.

Dead Souls. With an Introd. by Clifford Odets. Nikolai Vasilevich Gogol. LC 36-7620. (Modern library of the world's best books). 1936. Modern Library.

Dead Speak. Robert Sedgwick Minot. LC 7-19689. 1881. A. Mudge & Son, Printers.

Dead Stay Dumb. Rene Raymond. 1973. (pbk) 0.75 (ISBN 0-671-75740-7). Pocket Books.

Dead Stop. Miles Burton. LC 44-524323. 1943. Pub. for the Crime Club by Collins.

Dead Storage. Lee Thayer. LC 35-444. 1935. Dodd, Mead & Company.

Dead Storage: By George Bagby Pseud. 1st Ed. Aaron Marc Stein. LC 56-5596. 1956. Published for the Crime Club by Doubleday.

Dead Straight. Donald MacKenzie. LC 69-11051. 1969. 4.95. Houghton Mifflin.

Dead Straight: Or, Harlow Jack's Life Mystery. Harlan Page Halsey. (Old Sleuth's own, no. 94). 1897. Parlor Car Publishing Co.

Dead Sure: The Affair of the California Cutie. A New Gil Vine Investigation. Prentice Winchell. LC 49-6270. (Dutton guilt edged mystery). 1949. E. P. Dutton.

Dead Survivor. Neal Pizinger. (Orig.). 1979. pap. 2.50 (ISBN 0-89083-470-9). Zebra.

Dead Take No Bows. Richard Burke. LC 41-3532. 1941. Houghton Mifflin Company.

Dead Thing in the Pool. Aaron Marc Stein. 1971. pap. 0.60 o.p. (06135). Curtis.

Dead Thing in the Pool. 1st Ed. Aaron Marc Stein. LC 52-12387. 1952. Published for the Crime Club by Doubleday.

Dead to Rights. Kenn Davis. 224p. 1981. pap. 2.25 (ISBN 0-380-78295-2, 78295). Avon.

Dead to Rights. Elinore Denniston. LC 46-21054. 1946. M. S. Mill Co., Inc.

Dead to Rites. Sylvia Angus. LC 79-17552. 1980. 1.95 (ISBN 0-14-005329-8). Penguin Books.

Dead to Rites. Sylvia Angus. LC 79-17560. 1979. 11.95 (ISBN 0-8161-6759-1). G. K. Hall.

Dead to the World. North Baker & Bolton, William, Novelist, Joint Author. LC 44-2892. 1944. Pub. for the Crime Club by Doubleday, Doran & Co., Inc.

Dead to the World. Francis Durbridge. LC 73-154734. 1972. 5.95 (ISBN 0-85617-962-0). White Lion Publishers Ltd.

Dead to the World. David X Manners. LC 47-30796. 1947. D. McKay Co.

Dead to the World: A Gil Vine Investigation, by Stewart Sterling Pseud. 1st Ed. Prentice Winchell. LC 58-6903. (Main line mysteries). 1958. Lippincott.

Dead Towns of Alabama. W. Stuart Harris. LC 76-29655. (Illus.). 176p. 1977. 9.95 (ISBN 0-8173-5232-5). U of Ala Pr.

Dead Towns of Sunbury & Dorchester. 3rd ed. Paul McIlvaine. LC 75-26008. 1976. 5.95 (ISBN 0-9600410-3-6). P McIlvaine.

Dead Tree Gives No Shelter; a Novel. Virgil Joseph Scott. LC 47-30710. 1947. Swallow Press.

Dead Trouble. Dominic Devine. LC 72-166419. 1971. 4.95. Published for the Crime Club by Doubleday.

Dead Tryst: And A Haunted Life. James Grant. LC 43-26604. G. Routledge and Sons.

Dead Warrior. John Myers Myers. LC 56-5925. 1956. Little, Brown.

Dead Water. Ngaio Marsh. LC 79-28149. 1980. 12.45 (ISBN 0-88411-475-9). Aeonian Press.

Dead Weight. Frank Kane. LC 51-9553. 1951. Washburn.

Dead Weight. Brian Lecomber. LC 76-48310. (Illus.). 1977. 8.95 (ISBN 0-440-01756-4). Delacorte/E. Friede.

Dead Weight. Brian Lecomber. 1979. 2.25 (ISBN 0-440-11861-1). Dell Pub. Co.

Dead Weight. Addison Simmons. LC 47-358. 1946. Phoenix Press.

Dead Woman, and Other Haunting Experiences. Elizabeth Walter. LC 77-76660. 1977. 7.95 (ISBN 0-312-18508-1). St. Martin's Press.

Dead Woman of the Year: A John Jericho Mystery Novel. Judson Pentecost Philips. LC 67-20899. (Red Badge mystery). 1967. Dodd, Mead.

Dead Woman's Ditch: By Simon Nash. Pseud. Raymond Chapman. LC 65-23813. 1966. bds., 2.95. Roy.

Dead Woman's Shoes. Mildred Burcham Hart. LC 32-3293. Thomas Y. Crowell Company.

Dead Wrong. Mark Cruz. (Kill Squad Ser: No. 3). 192p. (Orig.). 1975. pap. 1.25 o.p. (ISBN 0-532-12302-6). Woodhill.

Dead Wrong. Mark Cruz. (Kill Squad Ser: No. 3). 192p. (Orig.). 1975. pap. 1.25 o.p. (ISBN 0-532-12302-6). Manor Bks.

Dead Wrong. William S. Doxey. 1980. pap. 1.75 o.s.i. (ISBN 0-505-51455-9). Tower Bks.

Dead Wrong: By George Bagby Pseud. 1st Ed. Aaron Marc Stein. LC 57-8799. 1957. Published for the Crime Club by Doubleday.

Dead Wrong: The Affair of the Virginia Widow. Prentice Winchell. LC 47-221733. 1947. J. B. Lippincott Company.

Dead Yellow Women. Dashiell Hammett. LC 47-28535. (Jonathan press mystery, no. J29). 1947. L. E. Spivak.

Dead Yesterday. Mary Agnes Hamilton. LC 16-145999. 1.50. George H. Doran Company.

Dead Yesterday. 1st Ed. Ruth Fenisong. LC 51-14368. 1951. Published for the Crime Club by Doubleday.

Dead Zone. Stephen King. LC 79-12785. 1979. 11.95 (ISBN 0-670-26077-0). Viking Press.

Deadest Thing You Ever Saw. Jonathan Ross. 1970. 4.50 o.p. (ISBN 0-8415-0070-3). Sat Rev Pr.

Deadest Thing You Ever Saw. John Rossiter. LC 77-122151. (McCall suspense novel). 1970. 4.50 (ISBN 0-8415-0070-3). McCall Pub. Co.

Deadeye Dick. Kurt Vonnegut. LC 82-13024. 14.95 (ISBN 0-440-01780-7). Delacorte Press/Seymour Lawrence.

Deadfall. Desmond Cory, pseud. LC 65-22137. 4.95. Walker.
Deadfall. Keith Laumer. LC 73-165386. 1971. 4.95. Published for the Crime Club by Doubleday.
Deadfall. Edison Marshall. LC 27-7088. 1927. Cosmopolitan Book Corporation.
Deadfall: A Novel. Jane MacLean. LC 78-13770. 9.95. Dutton.
Deadham Hard: A Romance. Mary St. Leger Kingsley Harrison. LC 19-14230. 1919. Dodd, Mead and Company.
Deadhead. Charles Marquis Warren. LC 49-10478. (Gargoyle mystery). 1949. Coward-McCann.
Deadhorse Express. Walker A Tompkins. Phoenix Press.
Deadlier Sex. Randy Striker. (MacMorgan Ser: No. 4). (Orig.). 1981. pap. 1.95 (ISBN 0-451-09971-0, J9971, Sig). NAL.
Deadlier Than the Male. Jim Conaway. (Belmont Tower Book). 1.50 (ISBN 0-505-51160-6). Tower Pubns.
Deadlier Than the Male. James Edward Gunn. LC 42-14627. 1942. Duell, Sloan and Pearce.
Deadlier Than the Male: By Genevieve Holdenpseud. 1st Ed. Genevieve Long Pou. LC 61-9200. 1961. Published for the Crime Club by Doubleday.
Deadliest Colonel. Thomas N. Moon & Carl F. Eifler. 7.50 o.p. Vantage.
Deadliest Game. Peter McCurtin. (Soldier of Fortune Ser.: No. 2). 192p. 1982. pap. 2.25 (ISBN 0-505-51767-1). Tower Bks.
Deadliest Game. Peter McCurtin. (O.s.i.). 1976. pap. text ed. 1.25 o.s.i. (BT50936). Belmont-Tower.
Deadliest Weapon. Ben Masselink. LC 65-13716. 1965. Little, Brown.
Deadline. Paul Darcy Boles. LC 57-9020. 1957. Macmillan.
Deadline. Thomas Blanchard Dewey. (55002). 1968. Pocket Bks.
Deadline. Thomas Blanchard Dewey. LC 66-24028. (Inner sanctum mystery). 1966. Simon and Schuster.
Deadline. John Dunning. 2.50 (ISBN 0-449-14398-8). Fawcett Books.
Deadline. Tim Heald. LC 74-26955. 1975. 6.95 (ISBN 0-8128-1757-5). Stein and Day.
Deadline. Alexander Irving. LC 47-19085. 1947. Dodd, Mead & Company.
Deadline at Dawn... Cornell George Hopley-Woolrich. LC 44-1706. 1944. J. B. Lippincott Company.
Deadline at Dawn. Cornell Woolrich, pseud. 224p. 1983. pap. 2.25 (ISBN 0-345-30653-8). Ballantine.
Deadline at Durango. 1st Ed. Allan Vaughan Elston. LC 50-6563. 1950. Lippincott.
Deadline for a Dream: A Thane and Moss Case. Bill Knox. LC 76-384020. 1976. 3.25 (ISBN 0-09-123590-1). Long.
Deadline for Destruction. Mary Violet Heberden. LC 42-13998. 1942. Published for the Crime Club by Doubleday, Doran & Company, Inc.
Deadline for Love. Georgia Craig. LC 44-40367. 1944. Arcadia House, Inc.
Deadline for Love. Peggy Gaddis, pseud. LC 44-40367. 1944. Arcadia House.
Deadline for Lovers. Frances Nichols Hanna. LC 38-6964. 1938. Godwin.
Deadline for Macall. Gerard Fairlie. LC 57-515222. 1956. M. S. Mill Co., and W. Morrow.
Deadline for Sheriffs. Leslie Scott. 2.95. Arcadia House.
Deadline in Rome. Max Call. LC 80-66693. 8.95 (ISBN 0-912376-54-6). Chosen Books.
Deadline 2 A.M. Robert L. Pike, pseud. LC 75-17073. (Illus.). 192p. 1976. 6.95 o.p. (ISBN 0-385-03563-2). Doubleday.
Deadline, 2 A.M. A Lieutenant Reardon Novel. Robert L Fish. LC 75-17073. 1976. 6.95 (ISBN 0-385-03563-2). Doubleday.
Deadlock. Ruth Fenisong. pap. 0.95 o.p. (01979, Collier). Macmillan.
Deadlock. Dorothy Miller Richardson. LC 21-20190. 1921. A. A. Knopf.
Deadlock. Vikentii Vikentevich Smidovich. LC 72-90318. 1973. 15.75 (ISBN 0-88355-027-X). Hyperion Press.
Deadlock. 1st Ed. Ruth Fenisong. LC 52-10051. 1952. Published for the Crime Club by Doubleday.
Deadlocked. Leo P. Kelley. (Orig.). 1973. pap. 0.75 o.p. (T2742, GM). Fawcett World.
Deadlocked! Leo P Kelley. 1973. (pbk) 0.75. Fawcett.
Deadly Affair. Ed Lacy. LC 60-349101. (Hillman books, HB146). 1960. Hillman Books.
Deadly Amigos: Two Graves for a Gunman. Barry Cord. 1979. pap. 2.25 o.s.i. (ISBN 0-505-51419-2). Tower Bks.
Deadly Angel. Sarah Holland. (Harlequin Presents Ser.). 192p. 1983. pap. 1.95. Harlequin Bks.
Deadly Beloved. Tillett, Dorothy (Stockbridge) LC 52-511. 1952. Published for the Crime Club by Doubleday.
Deadly Birdmen. (Marc Dean, Mercenary Ser.: No. 3). (Orig.). 1981. pap. 2.25 (ISBN 0-451-11074-9, AE1074, Sig). NAL.
Deadly Chase. Carter Cullen. 1975. (pbk.) 1.25. Belmont Tower Books.
Deadly Climate. Ursula Reilly Curtiss. LC 54-9231. (Red badge detective). 1954. Dodd, Mead.
Deadly Companions. Bob Sang & Dusty Sang. 1978. pap. 1.50 o.s.i. (ISBN 0-505-51243-2). Tower Bks.
Deadly Contact. Amber Dean. LC 63-7846. 1963. Published for the Crime Club by Doubleday.
Deadly Crescent. Marcia Miller. (YA) 1973. 4.95 o.p. (Avalon). Bouregy.
Deadly Deep. Jon Messmann. (Signet Book). 1976. (pbk.) 1.50. New American Library.
Deadly Delight. Aaron Marc Stein. LC 67-12537. 1967. Published for the Crime Club by Doubleday.
Deadly Delusion. Kelly L Segraves. LC 78-1901. 1978. 2.95 (ISBN 0-89293-021-7). Beta Books.
Deadly Ditto. Frances Moyer Ross Stevens. LC 48-5861. 1948. Pub. for the Crime Club by Doubleday.
Deadly Doctor. Stuart Jason. (Butcher series,#10). 1974. (pbk.) 0.95 (ISBN 0-523-00291-2). Pinnacle Books.
Deadly Document. Michael Bar-Zohar. LC 79-19615. 8.95 (ISBN 0-440-00750-X). Delacorte Press.
Deadly Document. Michael Bar-Zohar. 1981. pap. 2.50 (ISBN 0-440-12165-5). Dell.
Deadly Doll. Jay Barbette, pseud. LC 58-5987. (Red badge detective). 1958. Dodd, Mead.
Deadly Doubles. Nick Carter. (Nick Carter Ser.). 192p. (Orig.). 1978. pap. 1.75 o.p. (ISBN 0-441-14163-3). Charter Bks.
Deadly Dove. Rufus King. LC 45-3929. 1945. Pub. for the Crime Club by Doubleday, Doran and Company, Inc.
Deadly Dowager. Edwin Greenwood. LC 35-76733. 1935. Doubleday, Doran & Company, Inc.
Deadly Dream. Theodore S Drachman. LC 82-13824. 9.95 (ISBN 0-8397-1900-0). P.S. Eriksson.
Deadly Duo. Margery Allingham. LC 76-2488. 1976. 6.95 (ISBN 0-89190-193-0). American Reprint Co.
Deadly Duo. Margery Allingham. 1973. (pbk.) 0.95. Manor Books.
Deadly Duo: Wanted, Someone Innocent and Last Act. Margery Allingham. LC 49-8851. 1949. Pub. for the Crime Club by Doubleday.
Deadly Dutchman. John Blaine, pseud. LC 67-20842. (His A Rick Brant science-adventure story, 22). (Illus.). 1967. Grosset & Dunlap.
Deadly Edge. Richard Stark. 1971. 4.95 o.p. (ISBN 0-394-46292-0, 46292). Random.
Deadly Edge. Richard Stark. (Parker). (Berkley medallion book: Vol. 7). 1974. (pbk.) 0.75 (ISBN 0-425-02502-0). Berkley Pub. Co.
Deadly Edge. Donald E Westlake. LC 71-140728. 1971. 4.95 (ISBN 0-394-46292-0). Random House.
Deadly Election. Mort Castle. (Orig.). 1976. pap. 1.50 (ISBN 0-89041-107-7, 3107). Major Bks.
Deadly Eurasian. Alexander Cordell, pseud. LC 68-28271. 1968. 5.50. Weybright and Talley.
Deadly Fog at Dead Man's Landing: Novel. Albert Wass. LC 79-51574. 1979. 5.00 (ISBN 0-87934-020-7). Danubian Press.
Deadly Friend: By Hugh Pentecost Pseud. Judson Pentecost Philips. LC 61-566361. (Red badge detective). 1961. Dodd, Mead.
Deadly Frost. Terrence Moan. LC 78-64797. 9.95 (ISBN 0-89256-089-4). Rawson, Wade Publishers.
Deadly Frost. Terrence Moon. 1980. pap. 2.75 (ISBN 0-394-28947-1). Ballantine.
Deadly Gift. Norah Robinson Lofts. Orig. Title: Afternoon of an Autocrat. 1967. pap. 0.75 o.p. (T1709). Pyramid Pubns.
Deadly Gift. Norah Robinson Lofts. 1976. pap. 1.75 o.p. (ISBN 0-515-04040-1). BJ Pub Group.
Deadly Gold. John Rossiter. LC 75-9134. 1975. 5.95 (ISBN 0-8027-5321-3). Walker.
Deadly Green. Evelyn Harris. LC 81-5766. 1981. 9.95 (ISBN 0-312-18529-4). St Martin's Press.
Deadly Green. John Rossiter. LC 70-142841. 1971. 4.95 (ISBN 0-8027-5221-7). Walker.
Deadly Group Down Under. Patrick Morgan. (Operation Hang Ten Ser). (O.s.i.). (Orig.). 1970. pap. 0.75 o.s.i. (532-75291-075). Manor Bks.
Deadly Hall. John Dickson Carr. LC 72-144194. (Novel of Suspense Ser). 1971. 6.95 o.p. (ISBN 0-06-010607-7, HarpT). Har-Row.
Deadly Hall: A Detective Novel. John Dickson Carr. LC 72-144194. 1971. 6.95. Harper & Row.
Deadly Homecoming. Theodore George. LC 72-3918. (red badge novel of suspense). 1972. 4.95 (ISBN 0-396-06656-9). Dodd, Mead.
Deadly Honeymoon. Lawrence Block. LC 67-19672. (Cock Robin mystery). 1967. Macmillan.
Deadly in the Evil Tongue. Mona Naomi Anne Hocking Messer. LC 40-6341. 1940. Pub. for the Crime Club by Doubleday, Doran & Co. Inc.
Deadly Intent. Anne Von Melborn Rowe. LC 46-19529. 1946. M. S. Mill Company, Inc.
Deadly is the Diamond. Mignon Good Eberhart. 1982. 15.00x (ISBN 0-86025-188-8, Pub. by Ian Henry Pubns England). State Mutual Bk.
Deadly Is the Diamond. Mignon Good Eberhart. 1974. (pbk.) 0.95. Popular Library.
Deadly Is the Diamond: And Three Other Novelettes of Murder: Bermuda Grapevine, The Crimson Paw, Murder in Waltz Time. Mignon Good Eberhart. LC 58-7666. (Random House mystery). 1958. Random House.
Deadly Isles. John Holbrook Vance. LC 69-13101. 1969. 4.95. Bobbs-Merrill.
Deadly Joke. Hugh Pentecost. (Red Badge Mystery Ser.). 1971. 4.95 o.p. (ISBN 0-396-06331-4). Dodd.
Deadly Joke. Hugh Pentecost. 1972. pap. 0.75 o.p. (T2685). Pyramid Pubns.
Deadly Joke. Judson Pentecost Philips. LC 72-147137. (Red badge novel of suspense). 1971. 4.95 (ISBN 0-396-06331-4). Dodd, Mead.
Deadly Joke. Judson Pentecost Philips. LC 74-38829. (Red badge novel of suspense). 1972. 6.95 (ISBN 0-8161-6013-9). G. K. Hall.
Deadly Kind of Lonely. Stanton Forbes, pseud. LC 78-164717. 1971. 4.95. Published for the Crime Club by Doubleday.
Deadly Lady of Madagascar. Frank Gill Slaughter. LC 59-6274. 1959. Doubleday.
Deadly Legacy. William Arden, pseud. LC 72-7920. (Kane Jackson Mystery Novel Ser.). 192p. 1973. 4.95 o.p. (ISBN 0-396-06746-8). Dodd.
Deadly Legacy. Christina Blake. (Raven House Mysteries Ser.). 224p. 1982. pap. cancelled (ISBN 0-373-63045-X, Pub. by Worldwide). Harlequin Bks.
Deadly Legacy. Dennis Lynds. LC 72-7920. (Red badge novel of suspense). 1973. 4.95 (ISBN 0-396-06746-8). Dodd, Mead.
Deadly Litter. James White. 1981. pap. 2.25 (ISBN 0-345-29640-0, Del Rey). Ballantine.
Deadly Meeting. Robert Bernard, pseud. 1971. pap. 0.75 o.p. (07149). Curtis.
Deadly Meeting. Robert Bernard, pseud. LC 77-113477. 1970. 5.95 o.p. (ISBN 0-393-08609-7). Norton.
Deadly Meeting. Robert Bernard Martin. LC 77-113477. 1970. 5.95. Norton.
Deadly Mermaid. James Atlee Phillips. LC 54-7511. (Dell first edition, 26). 1954. Dell Pub. Co.
Deadly Messiah. David Campbell Hill & Albert Fay Hill. LC 76-15036. 1976. 8.95 (ISBN 0-689-10746-3). Atheneum.
Deadly Messiah. David Campbell Hill & Albert Fay Hill. 1977 (ISBN 0-380-00969-2). Avon Books.
Deadly Miss Ashley. 1st Ed. Frederick Clyde Davis. LC 50-6082. 1950. Published for the Crime Club by Doubleday.
Deadly Nightshade. Kate Cameron, pseud. (Holderly Hall Ser). (O.s.i.: No. 4). (Orig.). 1975. pap. 0.95 o.s.i. (LB236NK, Leisure Bks). Nordon Pubns.
Deadly Nightshade. Elizabeth Daly. LC 40-305273. Farrar & Rinehart, Inc.
Deadly Nightshade. James Fraser, pseud. 1970. 4.95 o.p. (ISBN 0-15-124065-5). HarBraceJ.
Deadly Nightshade. Lyda B. Long. 1972. pap. 0.75 o.p. (94223). Beagle Bks.
Deadly Nightshade. Alan White. LC 71-124823. 1970. Harcourt, Brace & World.
Deadly Nightshade: 17 Strange Tales of the Dark. Peter Haining. LC 77-92767. 1978. 8.50 (ISBN 0-8008-2123-8). Taplinger Pub. Co.
Deadly Oasis. Karen Liberatore. (Perspective I Novel Ser.). 48p. 1982. 2.50 (ISBN 0-87879-295-3). Acad Therapy.
Deadly Orbit Mission. Francis Van Wyck Mason. LC 68-10588. 1968. Doubleday.
Deadly Party. Linda DuBreuil. 1979. pap. 1.50 o.s.i. (ISBN 0-505-51374-9). Tower Bks.
Deadly Passion. Gail MacMillan. 192p. (YA) 1975. 4.95 o.p. (Avalon). Bouregy.
Deadly Passion. Gail MacMillan. 1975. 4.95. Avalon Books.
Deadly Patrol. Laurie W Andrews. LC 57-13793. 1957. D. McKay Co.
Deadly Pattern. Douglas Clark. LC 77-122423. 1970. 4.95 (ISBN 0-8128-1327-8). Stein and Day.
Deadly Pearl. Marc Olden. (Black Samurai). (Signet book: Vol. 4). 1974. (pbk.) 0.95. New American Library.
Deadly Percheron. John Franklin Bardin. LC 46-4511. 1946. Dodd, Mead & Company.
Deadly Picnic. John Bingham. 1982. 15.00x (ISBN 0-333-28487-9, Pub. by Macmillan England). State Mutual Bk.
Deadly Place to Stay. Josephine Bell. 224p. 1983. 12.95 (ISBN 0-8027-5496-1). Walker & Co.
Deadly Prey. Ralph Hayes. (Hunter). 1975. (pbk.) 1.25. Leisue Books.
Deadly Professionals. Leonard Gribble. 1976. 7.95 (ISBN 0-09-126650-5, Pub. by Hutchinson). Merrimack Pub Cir.
Deadly Purpose. Robert P Hansen. LC 58-103089. 1958. M. S. Mill Co. and W. Morrow.
Deadly Pursuit. Marcia Miller. 1976. 4.95. Avalon Books.
Deadly Putter. Ted Dexter & Clifford Makins. LC 79-40466. 1979. 12.50 (ISBN 0-04-823167-3). Allen & Unwin.
Deadly Relations. Rosemary Gatenby. LC 71-107972. 1970. 5.95. Morrow.
Deadly Reunion. Jan Ekstrom. LC 82-10455. 1983. 11.95 (ISBN 0-684-17765-X). Scribner.
Deadly Rose. Kathlen Rich. Orig. Title: Jacqueminot. 1972. pap. 0.75 o.p. (BT40120). Belmont-Tower.
Deadly Rose: And Amber Twilight. Miriam Lynch. 1976. (pbk.) 1.25. Ace Books.
Deadly Sea, Deadly Sand. Iris Foster, pseud. (Orig.). 1972. pap. 0.95 o.s.i. (75-394). Lancer.
Deadly Seeds. Warren Murphy. (Destroyer Ser.: No. 21). 192p. (Orig.). 1975. pap. 1.95 (ISBN 0-523-41236-3). Pinnacle Bks.
Deadly Seeds. Richard Sapir & Warren Murphy. (Destroyer#21). 1975. (pbk.) 1.25 (ISBN 0-523-00760-4). Pinnacle Books.
Deadly Sex. Jack Webb. LC 59-10195. (A Father Shanley -- Sammy Golden mystery). 1959. Rinehart.
Deadly Shade of Gold. John Dann MacDonald. LC 73-20286. (Travis McGee series). 1974. 7.50 (ISBN 0-397-01032-X). Lippincott.
Deadly Silents. Lee Killough. LC 80-68218. 2.25 (ISBN 0-345-28780-0). Ballantine Books, C.
Deadly Sky. Doris Piserchia. 176p. 1983. pap. 2.25 (ISBN 0-87997-792-2). NAL.
Deadly Spring. J. C Conaway. Leisure Books.
Deadly Spring. Jim Conaway. 1976. pap. 1.50 o.p. (LB395). Nordon Pubns.
Deadly Streets. Harlan Ellison. 1975. pap. 1.25 o.p. (ISBN 0-515-03931-4). BJ Pub Group.
Deadly Summer. 1st Ed. Glenn M Barns. LC 57-10871. (Main Line Mysteries). 1957. Lippincott.
Deadly the Daring: By William Randall Pseud. William R Gwinn. 1958. Mystery House.
Deadly Trap. Hugh Pentecost. (Julian Quist Mystery Novel & Red Badge Novel of Suspense Ser.). (O.s.i.). 1978. 6.95 o.s.i. (ISBN 0-396-07606-8). Dodd.
Deadly Trap. Judson Pentecost Philips. LC 78-14530. (Red badge novel of suspense). 6.95 (ISBN 0-396-07606-8). Dodd, Mead.
Deadly Truth. Helen McCloy. LC 41-8172. 1941. W. Morrow and Company.
Deadly Weapon. Wade Miller, pseud. LC 46-8396. 1946. Farrar, Straus and Company.
Deadly Welcome. John Dann MacDonald. 1977. pap. 2.25 (ISBN 0-449-13682-5, GM). Fawcett.
Deadly Welcome. Ken Rothrock. 176p. (Orig.). 1976. pap. 1.50 (ISBN 0-89041-083-6, 3083). Major Bks.
Deadly Welcome: An Original Novel. John Dann MacDonald. LC 59-3181. (Dell first edition, B127). 1959. Dell Pub. Co.
Deadman's Gold. Lee Hoffman. 1974. (pbk.) 0.75. Ace Books.
Deadman's Rest. Francis Dorer & Nancy Dorer. 1978. pap. 1.50 (ISBN 0-532-15354-5). Woodhill.
Deadpan. T. A. Schock. (Daniel Keel Ser.: No. 2). 240p. (Orig.). 1982. pap. 2.25 (ISBN 0-8439-0948-X). Leisure Bks CT.
Deadwalk. Ron Goulart. (Vampirella#3). 1976. (pbk.) 1.25. Warner Books.
Deadweight. Hilton-Young, Wayland. LC 52-11326. 1952. Scribner.
Deadweight. Wayland Hilton Young. LC 52-11326. 1952. Scribner.
Deadwood, No. 6. Matthew Braun. (Orig.). 1981. pap. 2.25 (ISBN 0-671-41993-5). PB.
Deadwood Dick, the Prince of the Road. Edward Lytton Wheeler. LC 75-7117. (Garland Library of Narratives of North American Indian Captivities; V. 90). (Illus.). 1979. 29.50 (ISBN 0-8240-1714-5). Garland Pub.
Deadwood Dick's Leadville Lay. facsimile ed. Edward Lytton Wheeler. (Wild & Woolly West Ser., No. 20). (Illus.). 16p. 1971. pap. 1.00 o.p. Filter.
Deaf Spy. A Tale Founded Upon Incidents in the History of Texas. James Wilmer Dallam. LC 6-33184. 1848. W. Taylor.
Deal: A Novel. G. William Marshall. LC 67-30079. 1968. Bartholomew House.
Deal in Violence. William Arden, pseud. LC 71-91275. (Red badge mystery). 1969. 3.95. Dodd, Mead.
Deal in Wheat: And Other Stories of the New and Old West. Frank Norris. LC 74-131788. (Illus.). 1970. Scholarly Press.
Deal in Wheat, and Other Stories of the New and Old West. Frank Norris. LC 77-173797. (Illus.). 1971. (ISBN 0-404-04788-2). AMS Press.

Deal in Wheat: And Other Stories of the New and Old West. Frank Norris. LC 79-113681. (Short story index reprint series). (Illus.). 1970. Books for Libraries Press.
Deal in Wheat: And Other Stories of the New and Old West. Frank Norris. LC 3-21724. 1903. Doubleday, Page & Company.
Deal Me Out. Sam Averbook. 2.75 o.p. Vantage.
Deal Me Out. J S Blazer. LC 73-1733. 1973. 5.95 (ISBN 0-672-51796-5). Bobbs-Merrill.
Deal of the Century. Ian Kennedy Martin. LC 76-43497. 1977. 6.95 (ISBN 0-03-089936-2). Holt, Rinehart and Winston.
Deal Souls. Tr. from Russian, Foreword, by Bernard Guilbert Guerney. Thoroughly. Rev., with Additional New Material, Constituting the Present Tr. the Nearest Approach to a Comprehensive Version in Any Language. Nikolai Vasilevich Gogol. Tr. by Bernard Guilbert Guerney. LC 65-15433. (Mod. lib. of the world's best bks. ML40). 2.45. Random.
Deal with the Devil. Eden Phillpotts. LC 75-46300. (Supernatural and Occult Fiction). 1976. 11.00 (ISBN 0-405-08160-X). Arno Press.
Dealer. Max Collins. (Berkley Medallion) (ISBN 0-425-03259-0). Berkley.
Dealer. (Quarry Ser.). pap. 1.50 (ISBN 0-425-03259-0). Berkley Pub.
Dealer. Malcolm Spade. 160p. pap. 1.95 o.p. (6123). Brandon.
Dealer in Empire: A Romance. Amelia Josephine Burr. LC 15-5596. 1915. Harper & Brothers.
Dealer's Choice. Adrienne Palmer. (Belmont Tower Book). (Illus.). (ISBN 0-505-51323-4). Tower Pubns.
Dealer's Wheels. Steve Wilson. LC 82-5547. 1982. 10.95 (ISBN 0-312-18533-2). St. Martin's Press.
Dealing: Or, The Berkeley-to-Boston Forty-Brick Lost-Bag Blues; a Novel. Michael Douglas. LC 70-127093. 1971. 5.95 (ISBN 0-394-42168-X). Knopf.
Dealing Out Death. Willis Todhunter Ballard. LC 48-602. (Armchair mystery). 1948. D. McKay Co.
Dealings of Captain Sharkey: And Other Tales of Pirates. Arthur Conan Doyle. LC 26-8497. 1925. George H. Doran Company.
Dealings with the Firm of Dombey and Son: Wholesale, Retail, and for Exportation. With Illus. by Henry C. Pitz. Introd. by John T. Winterich. Charles Dickens. LC 57-2348. 1957. Printed for the Members of the Limited Editions Club.
Dealings with the Firm of the Dombey and Son, Wholesale, Retail and for Exportation. Charles Dickens. (Half-title: The centenary edition of the works of Charles Dickens in 36 volumes). 1911. Chapman & Hall, Ltd.
Dean and Jecinora. Victor Lorenzo Whitechurch. LC 26-744258. 1926. Duffield and Company.
Dean Dunham; or, the Waterford Mystery. Horatio Alger. 275p. 1974. Repr. of 1891 ed. lib. bdg. 15.15x (ISBN 0-88411-801-0). Amereon Ltd.
Deanna's Desire. Sylvie F. Sommerfield. (Orig.). 1982. pap. 3.50 (ISBN 0-89083-906-9). Zebra.
Dean's Daughter: Or, The Days We Live in. reprinted entire from the london edition. ed. Catherine Grace Frances Moody Gore. LC 6-27491. (On cover: Lovell's library, v. 2 no. 89). J. W. Lovell Company.
Dean's Death. Alfred Lawrence. (Columbo,#2). 1975. (pbk.) 1.25. Popular Library.
Dean's December. Saul Bellow. LC 80-8705. 12.95 (ISBN 0-06-014849-7). Harper & Row.
Dean's December: A Novel. Saul Bellow. LC 82-9202. 1982. 16.95 (ISBN 0-8161-3404-9). G.K. Hall.
Dean's Elbow. Alfred Edward Woodley Mason. LC 31-12253. 1931. Doubleday, Doran & Company, Inc.
Dean's Watch. Elizabeth Goudge. (YA) 1960. 6.95 o.p. (ISBN 0-698-10091-3). Coward.
Dean's Watch. Elizabeth Goudge. 1973. pap. 1.25 o.p. (ISBN 0-515-03045-7, V3045). Pyramid Pubns.
Dean's Watch. Elizabeth Goudge. 1976. pap. 1.75 o.p. (ISBN 0-515-04142-4). BJ Pub Group.
Dean's Wife. A Novel. Elizabeth C. J. Eiloart Eiloart. (Franklin square library, no. 15). 1881. Harper & Brothers.
Dean's Wife: A Novel. Elizabeth C. J. Eiloart Eiloart. (Seaside library, v. 45, no. 923). 1881. G. Munro.
Dear Abby. A. Van Buren. 1958. price not set o.p. (ISBN 0-13-197004-6). P-H.
Dear and Glorious Physician. Taylor Caldwell. LC 58-12032. 1959. Doubleday.
Dear Angeline: A Novel. Nina Wilkins McCornack. LC 51-12920. 1951. Exposition Press.
Dear Anne, with Love. Norva T. Cummings. 1967. 2.75 o.p. (ISBN 0-8059-0075-6). Dorrance.
Dear Antoine. Jean Anouilh. Tr. by Lucienne Hill. (Pap. ed. 1.95 o.p.). 96p. 1971. 4.95 (ISBN 0-8090-3784-X, New Mermaid). Hill & Wang.
Dear Atoms. Rita Agnes. 1962. 3.75 o.p. (ISBN 0-8283-1150-1). Branden.
Dear Atoms: Story-Essays. Agnes Rita. LC 62-51417. 1962. Bruce Humphries.
Dear Baby. William Saroyan. LC 44-946722. 1944. Harcourt, Brace and Company.
Dear Beast. 1st Ed. Nancy Hale. LC 59-11880. 1959. Little, Brown.
Dear Bill, Remember Me? & Other Stories. Norma F. Mazer. 1978. pap. 1.95 (ISBN 0-440-91749-2, LFL). Dell.
Dear Cathy. William Arthur Neubauer. LC 49-8688. 1949. Arcadia House.
Dear Colleague. Frances Murray. LC 72-90757. 1974. (pbk.) 0.95 (ISBN 0-671-77744-0). Pocket Books.
Dear Daughter Dead. Stanley Bennett Hough. LC 66-16923. 1966. bds., 3.50. Walker.
Dear Dead Days. Jay Barbette, pseud. LC 53-8401. (Red badge detective). 1953. Dodd, Mead.
Dear Dead Days: The 1972 Mystery Writers of America Anthology. Ed. by Edward D. Hoch. Mystery Writers of America. LC 72-80535. 1972. 5.95 (ISBN 0-8027-5267-5). Walker.
Dear, Dead Girls. Nigel Morland. 1977. 5.60 o.p. State Mutual Bk.
Dear, Dead Harry. Milton Scott. LC 49-11936. 1949. Phoenix Press.
Dear Dead Mother-in-Law. Katharine Hill. LC 44-1709. 1944. Books, Inc., Distributed by E. P. Dutton & Co., Inc.
Dear Dead Professor. K. Alison La Roche. LC 45-262. 1944. Phoenix Press.
Dear Dead Woman. Anthony Gilbert, pseud. 256p. 1973. Repr. of 1942 ed. lib. bdg. 5.95 o.s.i. (ISBN 0-85617-261-8). White Lion Pubs.
Dear, Deadly Beloved: By John Flagg Pseud. Cover Painting by Barye Phillips. John Gearon. LC 54-26998. (Gold medal books, 391). 1954. Fawcett Publications.
Dear Deadly Cara. Grace Zaring Stone. LC 68-14537. 1968. Random House.
Dear Deborah. Louise Platt Hauck. LC 39-23639. The Penn Publishing Company.
Dear Deceit: A Novel. 1st American Ed. Christine Brooke-Rose. LC 61-9485. 1961. Doubleday.
Dear Departed. Anne Burton. (Raven House Mysteries Ser.). 224p. 1981. pap. 2.25 (ISBN 0-373-63013-1, Pub. by Worldwide). Harlequin Bks.
Dear Doctor Dick: The Story of a Small-Town Physician. 1st Ed. Joshua Allen Hunter. LC 55-11121. 1955. Exposition Press.
Dear Editor. Watkins Eppes Wright. LC 44-4513. 1944. Arcadia House, Inc.
Dear Ellie. Mac Kay Summers. 64p. 1975. 4.00 o.p. (ISBN 0-682-48208-0). Exposition.
Dear Elsie: A Novel. August Kuhme. Tr. by Safford, Mary Joanna. LC 7-14170. (choice series, no. 65). 1892. R. Bonner's Sons.
Dear Emily: A Novel. Fitz Gibbon, Constantine. LC 52-12424. 1952. Simon and Schuster.
Dear Enemy. Jean Webster. LC 68-28717. (Illus.). 1968. 3.95. Meredith Press.
Dear Enemy. Jean Webster. LC 15-26656. 1915. The Century Co.
Dear Enemy. Jean Webster. LC 33-28339. 1917. Grosset & Dunlap.
Dear Experience. A Tale. Giovanni Domenico Ruffini. LC 1-24865. 1858. Rudd & Carleton.
Dear Family. George Amos Miller. LC 25-15943. The Abingdon Press.
Dear Fatherland. Johannes Mario Simmel. LC 69-16428. 1969. 6.95. Random House.
Dear Faustina. Rhoda Broughton. LC 18-7777. (Macmillan's two shilling library). 1900. Macmillan and Co., Limited.
Dear Faustina. A Novel. Rhoda Broughton. (Half-title: Appleton's town and country library, no. 219). 1897. D. Appleton and Company.
Dear Friend. Peggy Gaddis, pseud. LC 48-440116. 1948. Arcadia House.
Dear Friends. Tom McHale. LC 79-8566. 1982. 16.95 (ISBN 0-385-03503-9). Doubleday.
Dear Guest and Ghost. Josephine Moore Proffitt. LC 50-6705. 1950. Macmillan.
Dear "Herm"-with a Cast of Dozens. Leo Calvin Rosten. LC 73-16226. 1974. 8.95 (ISBN 0-07-053981-2). McGraw-Hill.
Dear Intruder. Ilka Chase. LC 76-3925. 1976. 7.95 (ISBN 0-385-11195-9). Doubleday.
Dear Intruder. Ilka Chase. (Kangaroo Book). 1977. 1.95 (ISBN 0-671-81353-6). Pocket Books.
Dear John. Olle Lansberg. LC 67-22667. 1969. 4.95. Random House.
Dear John. Susan Lee & Sondra Till Robinson. LC 80-15417. 11.95 (ISBN 0-399-90091-8). R. Marek.
Dear John, Dear Coltrane. Michael S. Harper. LC 72-101194. (Pitt Poetry Ser.). 1970. pap. 3.95 o.p. (ISBN 0-8229-5213-0). U of Pittsburgh Pr.
Dear Judgement. John Crosby. LC 77-15971. 1978. 9.95 (ISBN 0-8128-2456-3). Stein and Day.
Dear Judgment. John Crosby. 1978. Pocket Books.
Dear Kate. Suzanne Ebel. (Cameo romance). 1974. (pbk.) 0.75. Fawcett.
Dear Kate. Marcia Miller. 3.25. Avalon Dist. Bouregy.
Dear Laura. Jean Stubbs. LC 72-95551. 1973. 6.95 (ISBN 0-8128-1565-3). Stein and Day.
Dear Life. Herbert Ernest Bates. 1949. Little, Brown.
Dear Lorna. Mike Paul. (O.s.i.). (Orig.). pap. 0.60 o.s.i. (A356X, Award). Univ Pub & Dist.
Dear Love. Amalia Moor. 3.50 o.p. Vantage.
Dear Mad'm. Stella W. Patterson. (Illus.). 264p. 1982. lib. bdg. 11.95 (ISBN 0-87961-130-8); pap. 6.95 (ISBN 0-87961-131-6). Naturegraph.
Dear Me. Edita Morris. LC 67-27522. (O.s.i.). 1967. 5.00 o.s.i. (ISBN 0-8076-0425-9). Braziller.
Dear Me: And Other Tales from My Native Sweden. 1st Ed. Edita Morris. LC 67-27522. 1967. 5.00. G. Braziller.
Dear Miranda. Guthrie Wilson. 1960. 3.50 o.p. (ISBN 0-671-19305-8). S&S.
Dear Mr. Capote: A Novel. Gordon Lish. LC 82-15543. 15.95 (ISBN 0-03-061477-5). Holt, Rinehart, and Winston.
Dear Momma, Please Don't Die. Marilee Horton. 1982. pap. 1.95 (ISBN 0-451-11462-0, AJ1462, Sig). NAL.
Dear Mrs. Boswell. Marie Muir. LC 53-12537. 1953. St. Martin's Press.
Dear Nurse. William Arthur Neubauer. LC 45-4662. 1945. Grammercy Publishing Co.
Dear Old Gentleman. George Goodchild & Roberts, Carl Eric Bechhofer. LC 37-16078. 1936. Harper & Brothers.
Dear Old Gentleman: By George Goodchild and Bechhofer Roberts. George Goodchild & Carl Eric Bechhofer Roberts. LC 54-136895. (Murder revisited mystery novel, no. 9). 1954. Macmillan.
Dear Old Templeton. Alice Brown. LC 27-9310. 1927. The Macmillan Company.
Dear Old Wales: A Patriotic Love Story. Thomas Owen Charles. LC 12-17664. Press of American Printing Co.
Dear Once" A Novel. Zelda Popkin. LC 75-11870. 1975. 9.95 (ISBN 0-397-01053-2). Lippincott.
Dear Papa. Thyra Ferre Bjorn. LC 63-7267. 1963. Holt, Rinehart and Winston.
Dear Plutocrat. Anne Hampson. (Presents Ser.). 1976. pap. 1.25 (ISBN 0-373-70625-1, 70625). Harlequin Bks.
Dear Pretender. Alice Mary Ross Colver. LC 24-510019. 1924. The Penn Publishing Company.
Dear Ruin. Toni Howard. LC 72-75073. 1972. 5.95 (ISBN 0-87645-057-5). Gambit.
Dear Senator. McCready Huston. LC 28-21820. The Bobbs-Merrill Company.
Dear Sooky. Percy Leo Crosby. LC 29-212119. 1929. G. P. Putnam's Sons.
Dear Stranger. Nina Bowyer. LC 47-184270. 1947. Arcadia House, Inc.
Dear Stranger. Nina Conarain. LC 47-18427. 1947. Arcadia House, Inc.
Dear Stranger. Catherine Kidwell. 416p. 1983. pap. 15.50 (ISBN 0-446-51247-8). Warner Bks.
Dear Strangers. Renee Shann. LC 51-13772. 1951. Arcadia House.
Dear Susan Brown. Bennie Caroline Hall. LC 47-185941. 1947. Gramercy Publishing Co.
Dear Teacher: The Hilarious Story of an Old Maid. Louise Rosalie Preysz. LC 42-18152. 1942. Meador Publishing Company.
Dear to This Heart. Doris Kent LeBlanc. LC 42-19937. 1942. G. P. Putnam's Son.
Dear Uncle Bramwell. Thomas Bledsoe. (Orig.). 1963. pap. 1.65 o.p. (ISBN 0-8040-0064-6, 51). Swallow.
Dear Yesterday. Ethel M Sears. LC 40-7597. Suttonhouse.
Dearer Than Life: A Tale of the Times of Wiclif. Emma Leslie. LC 11-16142. 1885. Phillips & Hunt.
Dearest. Mrs. Bridges. LC 6-18270. Tait, Sons & Company.
Dearest Enemy. Sara Woods, pseud. LC 81-8721. 1981. 9.95 (ISBN 0-312-18546-4). St. Martin's Press.
Dearest Father: Stories and Other Writings. Translated by Ernst Kaiser and Eithne Wilkins. Franz Kafka. 1954. Schocken Books.
Dearest Idol. Walter Beckett. LC 29-6452. The Bobbs-Merrill Company.
Dearly Beloved. Alice Lent Covert. LC 52-14350. 1952. Bouregy & Curl.
Dearly Beloved. Margaret Thurston. LC 36-7593. Phoenix Press.
Dearly Beloved: A Novel. Milton George Nicola. LC 51-4592. 1951. Exposition Press.
Dearly Beloved: A Novel. Harry Sylvester. LC 42-4617. 1942. Duell, Sloan and Pearce.
Dearly Beloved: A Theme and Variations. Anne Morrow Lindbergh. LC 60-2225. (60-2225). 1967. Popular Lib.
Dearly Beloved: A Theme and Variations. 1st Ed. Anne Morrow Lindbergh. LC 62-13520. (Helen and Kurt Wolff book). 1962. Harcourt, Brace & World.
Dearly Bought. A Novel. Clara Louise Root Burnham. (On cover: Hammock series. no. 7). 1884. H. A. Sumner & Company.
Death. Ed. by Stuart D. Schiff. LC 81-86260. 240p. (Orig.). 1982. pap. 2.50 (ISBN 0-86721-107-5). Playboy Pbks.
Death a la King. Isabel Woodman Waitt. LC 43-13674. 1943. Phoenix Press.
Death After Breakfast. Hugh Pentecost. 1980. pap. 2.25 (ISBN 0-440-11687-2). Dell.
Death After Breakfast. Hugh Pentecost. (Pierre Chambrun Mystery Novel & Red Badge Novel of Suspense Ser.). 1978. 6.95 o.p. (ISBN 0-396-07554-1). Dodd.
Death After Breakfast. Judson Pentecost Philips. LC 78-5574. (Red badge novel of suspense). 6.95. Dodd, Mead.
Death After Evensong. Douglas Clark. LC 77-104646. (A Stein and Day mystery). 1970. 4.95. Stein and Day.
Death After Lunch. Robert David Abrahams. LC 41-1231. Phoenix Press.
Death Against the Clock. Anthony Gilbert, pseud. 192p. 1973. Repr. of 1958 ed. 5.95 o.s.i. (ISBN 0-85617-580-3). White Lion Pubs.
Death Against the Clock. Lucy Beatrice Malleson. LC 73-153689. 1971. 5.95 (ISBN 0-85617-580-3). White Lion Distributed by White Lion, New York.
Death Against the Clock: By Anthony Gilbert Pseud. Lucy Beatrice Malleson. LC 58-527594. 1958. Random House.
Death Against Venus. abridged ed. by dana chambers pseud.... ed. Albert Leffingwell. LC 47-21044. (Handi-book mysteries 57). 1946.
Death Against Venus. Albert Leffingwell. LC 46-2408. 1946. Dial Press.
Death Ain't Commercial: By George Bagby Pseud. Aaron Marc Stein. LC 51-10815. 1951. Published for the Crime Club by Doubleday.
Death Among Doctors. James William Macqueen. LC 42-150419. 1942. Published for the Crime Club by Doubleday, Doran & Company, Inc.
Death Among the Sands: By Evalina Mack Pseud. Lena Brooke McNamara. LC 57-7714. 1957. Arcadia House.
Death Among the Stars. Kenneth Giles. LC 70-81069. 1968. 4.50. Walker.
Death and Birth of David Markand: An American Story. Waldo David Frank. LC 71-145590. (Series in American studies). 1971. Johnson Reprint Corp.
Death and Birth of David Markand: An American Story. Waldo David Frank. LC 34-33666. 1934. C. Scribner's Sons.
Death and Bitters. Kit Christian. LC 43-13713. 1943. E. P. Dutton & Co., Inc.
Death and Bright Water. James Mitchell. LC 74-16915. 1974. 6.95 (ISBN 0-688-02876-4). W. Morrow.
Death and Bright Water. James Mitchell. LC 75-9840. 1975. 12.95 (ISBN 0-8161-6295-6). G. K. Hall.
Death and Chicanery: A Collection of Tales. 1st Ed. Philip MacDonald. LC 62-16787. 1962. Published for the Crime Club by Doubleday.
Death and Diplomacy in Persia. IUrii Nikolaevich Tynianov. LC 74-10092. (Illus.). 1975. (ISBN 0-88355-178-0). Hyperion Press.
Death and Four Lovers. 1st Ed. Joseph Carter. LC 61-91878. 1961. Doubleday.
Death & I Ching: A Mystery Novel. Lulla Rosenfeld. Ed. by Carol Southern. 192p. 1981. 9.95 (ISBN 0-517-54029-0, C N Potter Bks). Crown.
Death and Letters. Elizabeth Daly. LC 50-7474. (Murray Hill mystery). 1950. Rinehart.
Death and Letters. Elizabeth Daly. LC 81-47376. (Fifty Classics of Crime Fiction, 1950-1975). 1982. 14.95 (ISBN 0-8240-4979-9). Garland.
Death and Life of Harry Goth. D. Keith Mano. LC 75-136326. 1971. 6.95 (ISBN 0-394-46833-3). Knopf.
Death & Lila Fell. Michael J. Johnson. (Orig.). 1981. pap. text ed. 1.95 o.s.i. (ISBN 0-505-51639-X). Tower Bks.
Death and Lilacs. Joanna Jansen. LC 48-110848. 1948. Phoenix Press.
Death and Little Brother. 1st Ed. Clifford Knight. LC 52-6643. (Guilt edged mystery). 1952. Dutton.
Death and Mr. Potter: By Rae Foley Pseud. Elinore Denniston. LC 55-646755. (Red badge detective). 1955. Dodd, Mead.
Death and Mr. Prettyman. Kenneth Giles. LC 69-11441. 1969. 4.50. Walker.
Death and Taxes. Thomas Blanchard Dewey. (Medallion bk., X1527). 1968. Berkley.
Death and Taxes. Thomas Blanchard Dewey. (Red mask mystery). 1967. Putnam.
Death and Taxes. David Dodge. LC 41-106793. 1941. The Macmillan Company.
Death and the Dancing Footman. Ngaio Marsh. LC 41-16489. 1941. Little, Brown and Company.
Death and the Devil. Paul Whelton. LC 44-707246. 1944. J. B. Lippincott Company.

Death & the Dowager. Bertrand Huber. LC 34-213045. (Tired business man's library of adventure, detective, and mystery novels). 1934. D. Appleton-Century Company, Incorporated.

Death and the Dutch Uncle. Patricia Moyes. LC 68-24750. (Rinehart suspense novel). 1968. Holt, Rinehart and Winston.

Death and the Dutch Uncle. Patricia Moyes. LC 82-23259. (Inspector Henry Tibbett mystery). ((Series: Moyes, Patricia.). (Inspector Henry Tibbett mystery.). 1983. 3.95 (ISBN 0-03-063543-8). Holt, Rinehart, and Winston.

Death and the Dutiful Daughter. Anne Morice. LC 73-84678. 1974. 6.95. St. Martin's.

Death and the Gentle Bull, a Captain Heimrich Mystery: By Richard and Frances Lockridge. 1st Ed. Richard Lockridge & Frances Louise Davis Lockridge. (Main line mysteries). 1954. Lippincott.

Death and the Good Life. Richard F Hugo. LC 80-21622. 10.95 (ISBN 0-312-18588-X). St. Martin's Press.

Death and the I Ching. Lulla Rosenfeld. LC 79-27518. 9.95 (ISBN 0-517-54029-0). C. N. Potter: Distributed by Crown Publishers.

Death and the I Ching. Lulla Rosenfeld. LC 82-5185. 1982. 12.95 (ISBN 0-89340-511-6). J. Curley.

Death and the Joyful Woman. Edith Pargeter. LC 61-12569. 1961-1962. Published for Crime Club by Doubleday.

Death and the Leaping Ladies. Kenneth Giles. LC 69-13204. 1969. 4.50. Walker.

Death and the Lover. Hermann Hesse. Tr. by Dunlop, Geoffrey. LC 32-329112. Dodd, Mead & Company.

Death & the Maiden. John Gardner. 1979. 9.80 (ISBN 0-89683-016-0); signed ltd. ed. 50.00 (ISBN 0-89683-017-9). New London Pr.

Death & the Maiden. James K. MacDougall. 240p. 1980. pap. 1.95 (ISBN 0-441-14178-1, Pub. by Charter Bks). Ace Bks.

Death and the Maiden. Q. Patrick, pseud. LC 39-12580. 1939. Simon and Schuster.

Death and the Maiden: A Novel of Suspense. James K MacDougall. LC 78-51084. 1978. 8.95 (ISBN 0-672-52512-7). Bobbs-Merrill.

Death and the Naked Lady: By John Flagg Pseud. John Gearon. LC 51-30212. (Gold medal books, 151). 1951. Fawcett Publications.

Death and the Pleasant Voices. Mary Fitt. LC 47-2349. 1946. G. P. Putnam's Sons.

Death and the Pleasant Voices. Kathleen Freeman. LC 47-2349. 1946. Putnam.

Death and the Pregnant Virgin. S. T Haymon. LC 80-51821. 9.95 (ISBN 0-312-18592-8). St. Martin's Press.

Death and the Princess. Robert Barnard. LC 82-6022. 1982. 10.95 (ISBN 0-684-17759-5). Scribner.

Death and the Princess. large print ed. Robert Barnard. LC 83-115. (Nightingale series). 1983. 9.95 (ISBN 0-8161-3520-7). G.K. Hall.

Death & the Princess. Robert Bernard, pseud. (Nightingale Ser.). 1983. pap. 9.95 (ISBN 0-8161-3520-7, Large Print Bks). G K Hall.

Death and the Professors. Kathleen Sproul. LC 33-6255. E. P. Dutton & Co., Inc.C.

Death and the Spider. Grant Stockbridge. (Spider#4). 1975. (pbk.) 0.95 (ISBN 0-671-77953-2). Pocket Books.

Death & the Visiting Firemen. Henry Reymond Fitzwalter Keating. LC 73-83596. 1973. 4.95 (ISBN 0-385-05876-4). Published for the Crime Club by Doubleday.

Death and Variations. Ivon Baker. LC 77-157. 1977. 7.95 (ISBN 0-312-18880-3). St. Martin's Press.

Death Angel. Clyde B Clason. LC 36-15260. 1936. Pub. for the Crime Club, Inc., by Doubleday, Doran & Co., Inc.

Death Angel. Clyde B Clason. LC 37-17804. 1937. The Sun Dial Press, Inc.

Death-Angel. J. N. Williamson. (Orig.). 1982. pap. 2.95 (ISBN 0-89083-909-3). Zebra.

Death Angel see TaleSpinners I.

Death Angel's Shadow. Karl Edward Wagner. 1983. pap. 2.95 (ISBN 0-446-30749-1). Warner Bks.

Death Angel's Shadow. Karl Edward Wagner. 1973. (pbk.) 0.95. Warner Paperback Lib.

Death Answers the Bell. Valentine Williams. LC 32-2236. 1932. Houghton Mifflin Company.

Death As a Way of Life. Francisco Ayala. LC 64-12270. 1964. Macmillan.

Death-As in Matador. L. V Roper. 1975. (pbk.) 0.95. Popular Library.

Death at a Masquerade. Molly E Corne. LC 36-35021. M. S. Mill Co., Inc.

Death at Ash House. Miles Burton. LC 42-253625. 1942. Published for the Crime Club by Doubleday, Doran & Company, Inc.

Death at Breakfast: A Dr. Priestley Mystery. Cecil John Charles Street. LC 36-15688. 1936. Dodd, Mead & Company.

Death at Crane's Court. Eilis Dillon. LC 63-11468. (Walker mystery). 1963. Walker.

Death at Dakar. Kerry O'Neil. 1942. Pub. for the Crime Club by Doubleday, Doran & Co., Incl.

Death at Dayton's Folly. Virginia Rath. LC 35-18570. 1935. Pub. for the Crime Club, Inc., by Doubleday, Doran & Company, Inc.

Death at Deep End. Patricia Wentworth. pap. 0.95 o.p. (N2894). Pyramid Pubns.

Death at Dusk. Philip Ketchum. LC 38-22136. Phoenix Press.

Death at Eight Bells: A Novel by Frederic Arnold Kummer. Frederic Arnold Kummer. LC 37-344401. 1937. Lothrop, Lee & Shepard Company.

Death at Four Corners. Lucy Beatrice Malleson. LC 29-3135. L. MacVeagh, The Dial Press.

Death at French Creek. Raymond C Borel. LC 75-8954. (Illus.). 1975. 10.95 (ISBN 0-07-006513-6). McGraw-Hill.

Death at Heel. Fred Andreas. LC 33-32186. H. Holt and Company.

Death at Her Elbow. Donald Clough Cameron. LC 40-130894. H. Holt and Company.

Death at Sea (Destination Unknown) a Mystery Novel. Richard Sale. LC 49-525. (Popular library, 163). 1948. Popular Library.

Death at Sea. 1st Ed. LC 61-8467. 1961. Dutton.

Death at Swaythling Court. Alfred Walter Stewart. LC 26-14351. 1926. Little, Brown, and Company.

Death at the Bar. Charles Drummond. LC 72-80527. 1973. 5.95 (ISBN 0-8027-5259-4). Walker.

Death at the Bar. Ngaio Marsh. LC 40-2011. 1940. Little, Brown and Company.

Death at the Bar. Ngaio Marsh. LC 80-25311. 1981. 17.15 (ISBN 0-88411-476-7). Aeonian Press.

Death at "The Bottoms,". Albert Benjamin Cunningham. LC 42-10035. 1942. E. P. Dutton and Company, Incorporated.

Death at the Chase. Michael Innes, pseud. 1970. 4.50 o.p. (ISBN 0-396-06045-5). Dodd.

Death at the Chase. John Innes Mackintosh Stewart. LC 78-99177. (Red badge novel of suspense). 1970. 4.50. Dodd, Mead.

Death at the Dance: By John Rhode Pseud. Cecil John Charles Street. LC 52-12955. (Red badge detective). 1952. Dodd, Mead.

Death at the Depot. Dorothy Grace Hastings. LC 44-9097. 1944. Harper & Brothers.

Death at "The Dog". Joanna Cannan, pseud. LC 41-2804. 1941. Reynal & Hitchcock.

Death at the Door. Lucy Beatrice Malleson. LC 45-2694. 1945. Smith and Durrell.

Death at the Easel: By Marc Miller Pseud. Marceil Genee Kolstad Baker. LC 56-134448. 1956. Arcadia House.

Death at the Furlong Post. Charles Drummond. 1968. Walker.

Death at the Furlong Post. Kenneth Giles. LC 68-13983. 1968. Walker.

Death at the Helm: A Dr. Priestley Mystery. Cecil John Charles Street. LC 41-194688. 1941. Dodd, Mead & Company.

Death at the Inn: A Dr. Thorndyke Detective Story. Richard Austin Freeman. LC 37-21965. 1937. Dodd, Mead & Company.

Death at the Isthmus. George Harmon Coxe. LC 54-8760. 1954. Knopf.

Death at the Manor. Molly E Corne. LC 38-5281. M. S. Mill Co., Inc.

Death at the Mike. Alfred Eichler. LC 46-2152. 1946. Lantern Press, Inc.

Death at War Dance: By Jim O'Mara Pseud. 1st Ed. Vernon L Fluharty. LC 52-6644. (Dutton Diamond D western). 1952. Dutton.

Death at Windward Hill. Helen Joan Hultman. LC 31-11199. 1931. The Fiction League.

Death at Yew Corner. Richard Forrest. LC 80-13285. (Rinehart suspense novel). 1981. 10.95 (ISBN 0-03-053386-4). Holt, Rinehart, and Winston.

Death at 7: 10. Harry F. S Moore. LC 43-142882. 1943. Pub. for the Crime Club by Doubleday, Doran & Co., Inc.

Death Audit. James A. Howard. (Raven House Mysteries Ser.). 224p. 1982. pap. 2.25 (ISBN 0-373-63038-7, Pub. by Worldwide). Harlequin Bks.

Death Be Not Proud and Other Stories. John B. Keane. LC 77-358411. 1976. (ISBN 0-85342-470-5). Mercier Press.

Death Beads. Bette Hagman. 1974. (pbk.) 1.25. Dell.

Death Beam. Robert Moss. 416p. 1982. pap. 3.50 (ISBN 0-425-05655-4). Berkley Pub.

Death Beats the Band. Ida Shurman. LC 43-3884. 1943. Phoenix Press.

Death Bed: A Detective Story. Stephen Greenleaf. LC 80-15437. 9.95 (ISBN 0-8037-1701-6). Dial Press.

Death Bed: A Detective Story. Stephen Greenleaf. 2.50 (ISBN 0-345-30189-7). Ballantine Books,, C.

Death-Bed Marriage. Charlotte M. Stanley McKenna. LC 8-28187. (On cover: Munro's library, v. 1, no. 118). 1884. N. L. Munro.

Death Before Bedtime. Edgar Box, pseud. LC 79-10248. 1979. pap. 1.95 (ISBN 0-394-74053-X, V-53, Vin). Random.

Death Before Bedtime. Gore Vidal. LC 79-10248. 1979. 1.95 (ISBN 0-394-74053-X). Vintage Books.

Death Before Bedtime: By Edgar Box Pseud. 1st Ed. Gore Vidal. LC 52-129675. (Dutton guilt edged mystery). 1953. Dutton.

Death Begs the Question: By Lois Eby and John C. Fleming. 1st Ed. Lois Christine Eby. LC 52-10723. 1952. Abelard Press.

Death Behind the Door. Victor MacClure. LC 33-27438. 1933. Houghton Mifflin Company.

Death Bell. Edison Marshall. LC 24-7116. (Famous authors series. no. 39). 1924. Garden City Publishing Co., Inc.

Death Bell. Guy Smith. 1981. pap. 2.50 (ISBN 0-671-42497-1). PB.

Death Below the Dam. Esther Haven Fonseca. LC 36-12949. 1936. Pub. for the Crime Club, Inc., by Doubleday, Doran & Company, Inc.

Death Below Zero. Helen Smith Head. LC 53-944132. Comet Press Books.

Death Below Zero. Thomas Muir. LC 50-14438. 1950. Published for the Crime Book Society by Hutchinson.

Death Beneath Jerusalem. Paul Winterton. LC 38-199272. 1938. T. Nelson and Sons, Ltd.

Death Benefit. Paul Petersen. (Smuggler,#6). 1975. (pbk.) 0.95 (ISBN 0-671-77987-7). Pocket Books.

Death Beside the Sea. Marian Babson. LC 82-51309. 1983. 12.95 (ISBN 0-8027-5490-2). Walker.

Death Beyond the Go-Thru. Baynard Hardwick Kendrick. LC 38-36505. 1938. Pub. for the Crime Club, Inc., by Doubleday, Doran & Co., Inc.

Death Bids for Corners. Arthur Parkinson Dickson. LC 42-13419. B. Humphries, Inc.

Death Bird Contract. Philip Atlee. (Joe Gall Contract Ser). 1971. pap. 0.75 o.p. (T2289, GM). Fawcett World.

Death Blew Out the Match. Kathleen Moore Knight. LC 35-2489. 1935. Pub. for the Crime Club, Inc., by Doubleday, Doran & Company, Inc.

Death Boards the "Lazy Lady". Ruth Darby. LC 39-4496. 1939. Pub. for the Crime Club, Inc., by Doubleday, Doran & Company, Inc.

Death Box. Basil Godfrey Quin. Greenberg.

Death Breaks the Ring. Virginia Rath. LC 41-118018. 1941. Pub. for the Crime Club by Doubleday, Doran & Co., Inc.

Death-Bringers. Dell Shannon. 1970. pap. 0.75 o.p. (T2262). Pyramid Pubns.

Death-Bringers: By Dell Shannon Pseud. Elizabeth Linington. LC 64-23584. 1965. 3.95. Morrow.

Death Brings a Storke. Anita Boutell. LC 38-5605. 1938. G. P. Putnam's Sons.

Death Brings in the New Year. George Bellairs. LC 51-11315. 1951. Macmillan.

Death Brokers. P. D Ballard. (Fawcett Gold Medal Book). 1973. (pbk) 0.95. Fawcett.

Death by Appointment... Francis Bonnamy. LC 31-22401. Pub. for the Crime Club, Inc., by Doubleday, Doran & Company, Inc.

Death by Appointment ... LC 31-22401. Pub for the Crime Club, Inc., by Doubleday, Doran & Company, Inc.

Death by Arrangement. Laurence Walter Meynell. LC 72-87232. 1972. 4.95. McKay.

Death by Association: A Captain Heimrich Mystery. Richard Lockridge. LC 52-10933. (Main line mysteries). 1952. Lippincott.

Death by Bequest. Mary McMullen. LC 76-50780. 1977. 6.95 (ISBN 0-385-12739-1). Published for the Crime Club by Doubleday.

Death by Bequest. Mary McMullen. LC 78-17285. 1978. 1.95 (ISBN 0-14-004991-6). Penguin Books.

Death by Clue: A Mystery Novel. Henry Charlton Beck. LC 34-2278. E. P. Dutton & Co., Inc.

Death by Design. August William Derleth. LC 53-8569. 1953. Arcadia House.

Death by Design. Anne Nash. LC 44-5689. 1944. Pub. for the Crime Club by Doubleday, Doran and Co., Inc.

Death by Dreaming. Jon Manchip White. 140p. 1981. 10.95 (ISBN 0-918222-27-3). Apple Wood.

Death by Dynamite: A Simon Rolfe Mystery. Joseph L Bonney. LC 40-32552. Carrick & Evans, Inc.

Death by Gaslight. Michael Kurland. 1982. pap. 3.50 (ISBN 0-451-11915-0, AE1915, Sig). NAL.

Death by Hoax. Lionel Black. LC 78-60672. 1978. 1.75 (ISBN 0-380-41376-0). Avon.

Death by Inches. Dell Shannon. 1970. pap. 0.75 o.p. (T2283). Pyramid Pubns.

Death by Inches: By Dell Shannon. Elizabeth. Linington. LC 65-212064. (Luis Mendoza Mystery). bds., 3.95. Morrow.

Death by Invitation. Gail Stockwell. LC 37-15598. 1937. The Macmillan Company.

Death by Night. rev. ed. John Creasey. 1972. Popular Lib.

Death by Sheer Torture. Robert Barnard. LC 81-14569. 1982. 10.95 (ISBN 0-684-17437-5). Scribner.

Death by Sheer Torture. Robert Barnard. LC 82-15638. 1982. 8.05 (ISBN 0-8161-3456-1). G.K. Hall.

Death by Water. Michael Innes, pseud. LC 81-47810. 192p. 1982. pap. 2.40 (ISBN 0-06-080574-9, P574, PL). Har-Row.

Death by Water. Michael Innes, pseud. (Red Badge Mystery Ser). 1968. 3.95 o.p. (ISBN 0-396-05692-X). Dodd.

Death by Water. John Innes Mackintosh Stewart. LC 68-21896. (Red badge mystery). 1968. Dodd, Mead.

Death Calling Collect. Don Tracy. 1976. 1.50 (ISBN 0-671-80704-8). Pocket Books.

Death Came Dancing. Kathleen Moore Knight. LC 40-6299. 1940. Pub. for the Crime Club by Doubleday, Doran & Co., Inc.

Death Came Dancing... Kathleen Moore Knight. LC 41-154449. (Sun dial mysteries). 1941. The Sun Dial Press.

Death Came Softly. Edith Caroline Rivett. LC 44-2700. 1943. Mystery House.

Death Can Be Beautiful. Alfred Hitchcock. 1982. pap. 2.25 (ISBN 0-440-11755-0). Dell.

Death Cancels the Evidence. Robert H Leitfred. LC 38-157281. Green Circle Books.

Death Cap. June Thompson. 1980. pap. 1.95 (ISBN 0-553-13314-4). Bantam.

Death Cap. June Thomson. LC 76-42405. 1977. 6.95 (ISBN 0-385-12473-2). Published for the Crime Club by Doubleday.

Death-Cap Dancers. Gladys Mitchell. LC 81-14519. 1981. 9.95 (ISBN 0-312-18608-8). St. Martin's Press.

Death Car Surfside. Patrick Morgan. (Operation Hang Ten Ser). (Orig.). 1972. pap. 0.75 o.p. (75-460). Manor Bks.

Death Casts a Long Shadow: By Anthony Gilbert Pseud. Lucy Beatrice Malleson. LC 59-10830. (Random House mystery). 1959. Random House.

Death Casts a Lure. Madeleine Johnston. LC 39-23. 1938. Pub. for the Crime Club, Inc., by Doubleday, Doran and Co., Inc.

Death Casts a Vote. Margaret Polk Yates & Bramlette, Paula. LC 47-12526. 1948. E. P. Dutton.

Death Catches up with Mr. Kluck. Xantippe. LC 35-15165. Pub. for the Crime Club, Inc., by Doubleday, Doran & Co., Inc.

Death Cell. Ron Goulart. (Orig.). 1971. pap. 0.95 o.p. (95111). Beagle Bks.

Death Charter. Eustace Lane Adams. LC 43-7236. 1943. Coward-McCann, Inc.

Death Check. Warren Murphy. (Destroyer Ser.: No. 2). 192p. 1980. pap. 2.25 (ISBN 0-523-41757-8). Pinnacle Bks.

Death Checks in. Frederick Clyde Davis. LC 39-8475. 1939. Published for the Crime Club, Inc., by Doubleday, Doran & Co., Inc.

Death Checks in. Stephen Ransome. LC 39-8475. 1939. Pub. for the Crime Club, Inc., by Doubleday, Doran & Co., Inc.

Death Claims. Joseph Hansen. LC 72-80374. 1973. 5.95 (ISBN 0-06-011751-6). Harper & Row.

Death Claims. Joseph Hansen. LC 80-15548. 1980. 2.95 (ISBN 0-03-057484-6). Holt, Rinehart, and Winston.

Death Cloud. Michael Mannion. (O.s.i.). (Orig.). 1976. pap. 1.50 o.s.i. (Leisure Bks). Nordon Pubns.

Death-Coach. J. N. Williamson. (Orig.). 1981. pap. 2.95 (ISBN 0-89083-805-4). Zebra.

Death Collection. Mel Arrighi. 1973. pap. 0.95 o.p. (09227). Curtis.

Death Collection. Mel Arrighi. 1975. (pbk.) 0.95. Popular Library.

Death College. Tom Veitch, pseud. 1970. pap. 1.00 o.s.i. Siamese Banana.

Death Comes As the End:... Agatha Miller Christie. LC 44-8803. 1944. Dodd, Mead & Company.

Death Comes As the End. Agatha Miller Christie. 1973. (pbk.) 0.95 (ISBN 0-671-77445-X). Pocket Books.

Death Comes Easy, a Mystery. Bert Feltner. LC 64-4341. 1964. Carlton Press.

Death Comes for the Archbishop... Willa Sibert Cather. LC 27-18771. 1927. A. A. Knopf.

Death Comes for the Archbishop. Willa Sibert Cather. LC 31-28243. (Half-title: The modern library of the world's best books). 1931. The Modern Library.

Death Comes for the Archbishop... Willa Sibert Cather. LC 45-4223. 1945. A. A. Knopf.

Death Comes for the Archbishop: With Drawings and Designs. Willa Sibert Cather. LC 30-15621. 1929. A. A. Knopf.

Death Comes Grinning. Will Creed. LC 47-17300. (On cover: Five star mystery 47). 1946. Five Star Mysteries, Inc.

Death Comes Grinning. William Long. LC 47-17300. (Five star mystery 47). 1946. Five Star Mysteries.

Death Comes Like a Thief. Virginia Ellis. LC 52-3415. 1952. Arcadia House.

Death Comes on Friday. Lillian Day. LC 37-2175. 1937. E. P. Dutton & Co., Inc.

Death Comes to Casanova. H G Coulter. LC 45-5088. 1945. Manthorne & Burack, Inc.

Death Comes to Perigord. John Alexander Ferguson. LC 31-31744. 1931. Dodd, Mead and Company.

Death Comes to Tea. Theodora McCormick Du Bois. LC 40-14187. 1940. Houghton Mifflin Company.

Death Comes to the Party. first ed. Amanda McAllister. LC 76-51627. 1.50. Playboy Press.

Death Commits Bigamy. James M. W. Knipscheer. LC 48-603. 1947. Coward-McCann.

Death Committee. Noah Gordon. LC 69-18727. 1969. McGraw-Hill.

Death Conducts a Tour. Ruth Darby. LC 40-30177. 1940. Pub. for the Crime Club by Doubleday, Doran and Company, Inc.

Death Connection. Roger Brandt, pseud. LC 76-9596. 1976. pap. 1.50 o.p. (ISBN 0-87216-323-7, C16323). Playboy Pr Pbks.

Death Convention. Diana Winsor. LC 77-21171. 1977. 7.95 (ISBN 0-8128-2425-3). Stein and Day.

Death Counts Five. Henry Leyford Gates. LC 35-304532. 1934. G. H. Watt.

Death Cracks a Bottle. Kenneth Giles. LC 70-97466. 1970. 4.50. Walker.

Death Cries in the Street. Samuel A Krasney. LC 55-58688. 1955. Rinehart.

Death Croons the Blues. James Ronald. LC 40-4094. Phoenix Press.

Death Cruises South. Roger Denbie, pseud. LC 34-5600. 1934. W. Morrow & Company.

Death Cry. Darby Hauck. LC 17-27750. R. J. Shores.

Death Cues the Pageant. Edward Maddin Ainsworth. LC 54-107152. 1954. Arcadia House.

Death Cuts a Caper. David Magarshack. LC 35-11494. H. Holt and Company.

Death Cuts a Silhouette. Dolores Birk Hitchens. LC 39-27930. 1939. Pub. for the Crime Club, Inc., by Doubleday, Doran & Company Inc.

Death Cuts a Silhouette. Dolores Birk Olsen. LC 39-27930. 1939. Pub. for the Crime Club, Inc., by Doubleday, Doran & Company Inc.

Death Cuts the Film. Charles Saxby. LC 39-209544. 1939. E. P. Dutton & Company, Inc.

Death Dance. Peter McCurtin. (Sundance Ser.: No. 27). 1979. pap. 1.75 (ISBN 0-8439-0669-3, Leisure Bks). Nordon Pubns.

Death Dance: Twenty-Five Stories. Angus Wilson. LC 69-15654. 1969. 6.95. Viking Press.

Death Dances: Two Novellas on North American Indians. John Marvin & Raymond Abbott. 1979. 8.95 (ISBN 0-918222-07-9); pap. 3.95 (ISBN 0-918222-08-7). Apple Wood.

Death Deal. George G. Gilman, pseud. (Edge Ser.: No. 35). 160p. 1980. pap. 1.95 (ISBN 0-523-41776-4). Pinnacle Bks.

Death Dealer. Victor James. 1973. pap. 0.95 o.s.i. (75-475). Lancer.

Death Dealers. Mickey Spillane, pseud. 1971. pap. 1.95 (ISBN 0-451-09650-9, J9650, Sig). NAL.

Death Dealers. Ed. by Robert Weinberg. LC 80-8667. 80p. 1980. lib. bdg. 14.95x (ISBN 0-89370-099-1); pap. 5.95x (ISBN 0-89370-097-5). Borgo Pr.

Death Dealers see Day of the Guns.

Death Dealers: By Mickey Spillane. Mickey Spillane, pseud. LC 65-19961. 3.50. Dutton.

Death Dealers: Fantastic Sleuths Battling Diabolical Villains. LC 80-8667. (Pulp classics ; no. 21). 1980. 11.95 (ISBN 0-89370-099-1) (ISBN 0-89370-097-5). Borgo Press.

Death-Dealing Gold: Or, The Miser's Fate. Timothy Shay Arthur. LC 6-2466. (On cover: Columbian library, no. 4). 1890. Columbian Publishing Company.

Death Deals in Diamond: By Bradshaw Jones. Malcolm Henry Bradshaw-Jones. LC 66-12661. 1966. bds., 3.50. Walker.

Death Defies the Doctor. Denis Muir. LC 44-9900. 1944. Phoenix Press.

Death Delivers a Postcard. Judson Pentecost Philips. LC 39-23869. I. Washburn.

Death Delivers a Postcard. Judson Pentecost Philips. LC 42-930843. 1941. Triangle Books.

Death Demands an Audience. Helen Kieran Reilly. 224p. 1974. pap. 1.50 (ISBN 0-532-95365-7). Woodhill.

Death Demands an Audience. Helen Kieran Reilly. 1971. pap. 0.95 o.p. (95-170). Manor Bks.

Death Demands an Audience: An Inspector McKee Story. Helen Kieran Reilly. LC 40-11020. 1940. Pub. for the Crime Club, by Doubleday, Doran & Co., Inc.

Death Department: A Thane and Moss Case. Bill Knox. LC 77-356108. 1976. 3.25 (ISBN 0-09-123580-4). Long.

Death Descending. Karen Campbell, pseud. LC 76-380120. 1976. 3.50 (ISBN 0-00-222444-5). Collins.

Death Descending. Karen Campbell, pseud. LC 77-15550. 1978. 7.95 (ISBN 0-8128-2410-5). Stein and Day.

Death Dines Out. Theodora McCormick Du Bois. LC 39-19157. 1939. Houghton Mifflin Company.

Death Disciple. Robin Moore & Gerald G. Griffin. LC 77-91897. 1978. pap. 2.25 o.s.i. (ISBN 0-89516-024-2). Condor Pub Co.

Death Doctor. J. N. Williamson. (Death Ser.). 1982. pap. 2.95 (ISBN 0-8217-1108-3). Zebra.

Death Dolls of Lyra. Joan H. Holly, pseud. 1977. pap. 1.50 (ISBN 0-532-15290-5). Woodhill.

Death Down East. Hayden Norwood. LC 41-22776. Phoenix Press.

Death Down East. Hayden Norwood. LC 41-227761. Phoenix Press.

Death Down East. Eleanor Blake Atkinson Pratt. LC 40-595301. G. P. Putnam's Sons.

Death Down East. Eleanor Blake Atkinson Pratt. LC 42-17390. 1942. Triangle Books.

Death Draws the Line. Jack Iams. LC 49-7209. 1949. W. Morrow.

Death Drop. B. M Gill. LC 80-11537. 1980. 8.95 (ISBN 0-684-16464-7). Scribner.

Death Drop. B. M Gill. LC 82-7248. 1982. 12.95 (ISBN 0-89340-527-2). J. Curley.

Death Drops Delilah. Queena Mario. LC 44-5666. 1944. E. P. Dutton & Co., Inc.

Death Dupes a Lady... Royce Howes. LC 37-18659. Pub. for the Crime Club, Inc., by Doubleday, Doran & Company, Inc.

Death Elects a Mayor. James William Macqueen. LC 39-9398. 1939. Pub. for the Crime Club, Inc., by Doubleday, Doran & Co., Inc.

Death Enters the Lists. Vivian Collin Brooks. LC 67-24975. 1967. Roy Publishers.

Death Enters the Lists. Osmington Mills. 1967. 3.50 o.p. Roy.

Death Fear. Wyndham Martyn. LC 29-20438. 1929. R. M. McBride & Company.

Death Files for Congress: A Novel of Suspense and Politics. Theda O Henle. LC 72-134670. 1971. 5.95 (ISBN 0-8149-0687-7). Vanguard Press.

Death Finds A Foothold. Glynn Carr, pseud. Ed. by J. Barzun & W. H. Taylor. LC 81-47395. (Crime Fiction 1950-1975 Ser.). 224p. 1982. lib. bdg. 14.95 (ISBN 0-8240-4961-6). Garland Pub.

Death Finds a Target. Mary Fitt. LC 41-10302. 1942. Published for the Crime Club by Doubleday, Doran & Co., Inc.

Death Finds a Target. Kathleen Freeman. LC 42-10302. 1942. Published for the Crime Club by Doubleday, Doran.

Death Finds the Day: 1st Amer. Ed. Alan White. LC 65-21040. 3.95. Harcourt.

Death Fires. Ron Faust. 1980. pap. 1.95 (ISBN 0-449-14376-7, GM). Fawcett.

Death Flies High. Darwin Le Ora Teilhet. LC 31-33683. W. Morrow & Company.

Death Flies West. James Francis Bonnell. LC 41-3323. 1941. C. Scribner's Sons.

Death Flight. Charles Miron. (No. 3). 192p. (Orig.). 1975. pap. 1.25 o.p. (ISBN 0-532-12293-3). Woodhill.

Death Flight. Charles Miron. (No. 3). 192p. (Orig.). 1975. pap. 1.25 o.p. (ISBN 0-532-12293-3). Manor Bks.

Death Flight. rev. and expanded. ed. Domini Wiles. LC 76-57735. 8.95 (ISBN 0-698-10802-7). Coward, McCann & Geoghegan.

Death Flotilla. J. D. Hardin. LC 81-85173. 224p. (Orig.). 1982. pap. 1.95 (ISBN 0-86721-101-6). Playboy Pbks.

Death Follows a Formula. Newton Gayle. LC 35-4298. 1935. C. Scribner's Sons.

Death for Auld Lang Syne. 1st Ed. Jack Sharkey, pseud. LC 62-8016. 1962. Holt, Rinehart and Winston.

Death for Dear Clara. Q. Patrick, pseud. LC 37-23786. 1937. Simon and Schuster.

Death for Hire. Joseph Nazel. (Orig.). 1975. pap. 1.50 (ISBN 0-87067-483-8, BH483). Holloway.

Death for My Neighbor. 1st Ed. Muriel Bradley. LC 51-11421. 1951. Published for the Crime Club by Doubleday.

Death for Sale: An Original Novel. Henry Kane. LC 57-9782. (Dell first edition, A144). 1957. Dell Pub. Co.

Death for the Lady. Stewart Vanderveer. LC 39-8018. Phoenix Press.

Death for the Surgeon. Gilbert Eldredge. LC 39-25707. Phoenix Press.

Death Freak. Clifford Irving & Herbert Burkholz. LC 78-8271. 1978. 8.95 o.p. (ISBN 0-671-40036-3). Summit Bks.

Death Freak. John Luckless, pseud. LC 78-8271. 8.95 (ISBN 0-671-40036-3). Summit Books.

Death from a Top Hat. Clayton Rawson. LC 79-10656. (Gregg Press Mystery Fiction Series). 1979. 9.95 (ISBN 0-8398-2542-0). Gregg Press.

Death from a Top Hat: A Merlini Mystery... Clayton Rawson. LC 38-175634. 1938. G. P. Putnam's Sons.

Death from Below. John Creasey. LC 68-12198. (Rinehart suspense novel). 1968. Holt, Rinehart and Winston.

Death Fuse. Martin James Russell. LC 80-27562. 9.95 (ISBN 0-312-18698-3). St. Martin's Press.

Death Games. Dinah Brooke. LC 75-37524. 6.95 (ISBN 0-15-124093-0). Harcourt Brace Jovanovich.

Death Gets a Head. Adelbert Roland McKenzie. LC 42-21902. 1942. Phoenix Press.

Death Giver: From the Shadow's Private Annals. Walter Brown Gibson. LC 77-93710. (Shadow; 23). 1978. 1.25 (ISBN 0-515-04282-X). Jove Publications.

Death God's Citadel. Juanita Coulson. 400p. (Orig.). 1980. pap. 2.25 (ISBN 0-345-28089-X, Del Rey Bks.). Ballantine.

Death Goes Native. Max Long. LC 41-13233. J. B. Lippincott Company.

Death Goes Native... Max Long. 1944.

Death Goes to a Reunion. 1st Ed. Kathleen Moore Knight. LC 52-5961. 1952. Published for the Crime Club by Doubleday.

Death Goes to School. Q. Patrick, pseud. LC 36-5104. 1936. H. Smith and R. Hass.

Death Gong. Selwyn Jepson. LC 27-22048. 1927. G. H. Watt.

Death Grip: Soldato No. 2. Al Conroy. 1972. pap. 0.95 o.s.i. (75-382). Lancer.

Death Had Two Sons. Yael Dayan. 1967. 4.95 o.p. (ISBN 0-07-016173-9). McGraw.

Death Had Two Sons: A Novel. Yael Dayan. (1823). 1968. Dell.

Death Had Two Sons: A Novel. Yael Dayan. LC 67-27278. 1967. McGraw-Hill.

Death Hall. Mary Reisner. 1971. pap. 0.75 o.p. (B75-2089). Belmont-Tower.

Death Hall. Mary Reisner. (Orig.). pap. 0.75 o.p. (B75-2089). Belmont-Tower.

Death Has a Past. Anita Boutell. LC 39-20730. 1939. G. P. Putnam's Sons.

Death Has a Small Voice. Frances Louise Davis Lockridge & Richard Lockridge. 186p. 1975. Repr. of 1953 ed. lib. bdg. 12.05 sold only to libs & schools (ISBN 0-89190-905-2). Am Repr-Rivercity Pr.

Death Has a Small Voice: A Mr. and Mrs. North Mystery. Frances Louise Davis Lockridge & Richard Lockridge. LC 76-216. 1976. 11.00 (ISBN 0-89190-905-2). Rivercity Press.

Death Has a Small Voice: A Mr. and Mrs. North Mystery, by Frances and Richard Lockridge. 1st Ed. Frances Louise Davis Lockridge & Richard Lockridge. LC 52-137396. (Main line mysteries). 1953. Lippincott.

Death Has a Thousand Doors. Melba Marlett. LC 41-13940. 1941. Pub. for the Crime Club by Doubleday, Doran and Company, Inc.

Death Has a Thousand Doors: A Novel of Suspense. Will Cooper. LC 75-30778. 7.95 (ISBN 0-672-52196-2). Bobbs-Merrill.

Death Has a Will. Amelia Reynolds Long. LC 44-378. 1944. Phoenix Press.

Death Has Deep Roots. Michael Francis Gilbert. LC 51-11916. 1952. Harper.

Death Has Deep Roots. Michael Francis Gilbert. (Perennial Library). 1978. 1.95 (ISBN 0-06-080447-5). Harper & Row.

Death Has Green Fingers. Dudley Barker. LC 74-142842. 1971. 4.95 (ISBN 0-8027-5222-5). Walker.

Death Has Green Fingers. Dudley Barker. LC 82-7537. 1982. 3.50 (ISBN 0-14-006282-3). Penguin Books.

Death Has Green Fingers. Anthony Matthews, pseud. 1971. 4.95 o.p. Walker & Co.

Death Has Many Doors. Susan MacKenzie. (Orig.). 1968. pap. 0.60 o.p. (73-743). Lancer.

Death Has Many Doors. Susan McKenzie. 1973. pap. 0.95 o.s.i. (75-432). Lancer.

Death Has Many Doors. 1st Ed. Fredric Brown. LC 51-2676. (Guilt edged mystery). 1951. Dutton.

Death Has Seven Faces. Hugh Austin Evans. LC 49-5187. 1949. C. Scribner's Sons.

Death Has Three Lives: By Brett Halliday Pseud. Davis Dresser. LC 55-1247. (Torquil book). 1955. Distributed by Dodd, Mead.

Death Haunts the Dark Lane. Albert Benjamin Cunningham. LC 48-10423. (Dutton guilt edged mystery). 1948. E. P. Dutton.

Death Hits the Jackpot: By John Tiger Pseud. Walter H. Wager. LC 54-40765. (Avon, 605). 1954. Avon Publications.

Death Hunt. James Holding. (Orig.). 1979. pap. 1.50 (ISBN 0-532-15399-5). Woodhill.

Death in a Bowl. Raoul Whitfield. LC 31-6790. 1931. A. A. Knopf.

Death in a Cold Climate. Robert Barnard. LC 80-20979. 1981. 8.95 (ISBN 0-684-16795-6). Scribner.

Death in a Cold Climate. Robert Barnard. LC 81-13302. 1981. 12.95 (ISBN 0-8161-3309-3). G.K. Hall.

Death in a Desk Chair... Milward Rodon Burge. LC 31-6071. Pub. for the Crime Club, Inc., by Doubleday, Doran & Company, Inc.

Death in a Domino. Roland Pertwee. LC 32-28019. 1932. Houghton Mifflin Company.

Death in a Downpour. Katherine McComb. 2.95. Arcadia House.

Death in a Lighthouse. Edward Ronns, pseud. LC 38-148909. Phoenix Press.

Death in a Little Town. Ralph Carter Woodthorpe. LC 35-8484. 1935. Pub. for the Crime Club, Inc., by Doubleday, Doran & Company, Inc.

Death in a Little Town. Ralph Carter Woodthorpe. LC 37-19762. 1937. The Sun Dial Press, Inc.

Death in a Million Living Rooms. Patricia McGerr. LC 51-14398. 1951. Published for the Crime Club by Doubleday.

Death in a Pheasant's Eye. James Fraser, pseud. LC 73-188474. 190p. 1972. 4.95 o.p. (ISBN 0-8027-5254-3). Walker & Co.

Death in a Salubrious Place. William John Burley. LC 72-95765. 1973. 5.95 (ISBN 0-8027-5272-1). Walker.

Death in a Small World. Laura Colburn. (Mystery Puzzlers: No. 23). (Illus., Orig.). 1979. pap. 1.95 (ISBN 0-89083-477-6). Zebra.

Death in a Sunny Place. Richard Lockridge. LC 75-159729. 1971-1972. 5.50. Lippincott.

Death in a Tenured Position. Amanda Cross, pseud. LC 80-20565. 10.19. Dutton.

Death in a Tenured Position. Amanda Cross, pseud. LC 81-14504. 10.95 (ISBN 0-89621-321-8). Thorndike Press.

Death in a White Tie. Ngaio Marsh. LC 38-36506. L. Furman, Inc.

Death in a White Tie. Ngaio Marsh. LC 80-25745. 1981. 16.60 (ISBN 0-88411-479-1). Aeonian Press.

Death in Albert Park. Leo Bruce, pseud. 1979. 8.95 o.p. (ISBN 0-684-16267-9, ScribT). Scribner.

Death in Albert Park. Croft-Cooke, Rupert. LC 79-12006. 1979. 8.95 (ISBN 0-684-16267-9). Scribner.

Death in Ancient Egypt. A. J. Spencer. 1983. pap. 5.95 (ISBN 0-14-022294-4, Pelican). Penguin.

Death in Ankara: A Story of Modern Espionage. Clement Wood. LC 44-1212. 1944. Mystery House.

Death in April. Andrew M. Greeley. LC 80-10090. 9.95 (ISBN 0-07-024258-5). McGraw-Hill.

Death in B-Minor... Jean Lilly. LC 34-39741. E. P. Dutton & Co., Inc.

Death in Beirut. Tawfiq Yusuf Awwad. Tr. by Leslie McLoughlin from Arabic. 1978. 10.00 (ISBN 0-914478-86-9); pap. 5.00 (ISBN 0-914478-87-7). Three Continents.

Death in Beirut: A Novel. Tawfiq Yusuf Awwad. LC 77-358078. (Arab authors; 5). (Illus.). 1976. 1.95 (ISBN 0-435-99405-0). Heinemann Educational.

Death in Canaan. Joan Barthel. 1976. 9.95 o.p. (ISBN 0-525-08940-3). Dutton.

Death in Captivity. easy eye ed. Michael Francis Gilbert. 1968. pap. 0.75 o.p. (74-921). Lancer.

Death in Clairvoyance. Josephine Bell. 256p. 1973. 5.95 o.s.i. (ISBN 0-85617-885-3). White Lion Pubs.

Death in Cold Print. John Creasey. 1971. pap. 0.75 o.p. (ISBN 0-447-74738-X). Lancer.

Death in Connecticut. David Linzee. LC 77-467. 7.95 (ISBN 0-679-50742-6). McKay.

Death in Connecticut. David Linzee. (Dell Book). 1978. 2.25 (ISBN 0-440-12298-8). Dell Pub. Co.

Death in Costume. Allan McRoyd. LC 40-35165. The Greystone Press.

Death in Covert. Colin D. Willock. pap. 0.65 o.p. (ISBN 0-14-001934-0, 1934). Penguin.

Death in Dark Glasses. George Bellairs. LC 52-3449. 1952. Macmillan.

Death in Darkness. Charles Bryson. LC 33-36946. E. P. Dutton & Co., Inc.

Death in Darkness. Alan White. LC 76-50801. 1977. 6.95 (ISBN 0-385-12679-4). Published for the Crime Club by Doubleday.

Death in Darkness. Alec Whitney, pseud. LC 76-50801. (Crime Club Ser.). 1977. 6.95 o.p. (ISBN 0-385-12679-4). Doubleday.

Death in Deakins Wood. Rhona Petrie, pseud. LC 63-22480. (Red badge detective). 1964. Dodd, Mead.

Death in Delhi: Modern Hindi Short Stories. Ed. by Gordon C. Roadarmel. LC 74-187871. (UNESCO Collection of Representative Works: Indian Series). 1972. 6.95 (ISBN 0-520-02220-3). University of California Press.

Death in Diamonds. Kenneth Giles. LC 68-25746. (Inner Sanctum Mystery Ser). (O.S.I.). 1968. 4.50 o.s.i. (ISBN 0-671-20105-0). S&S.

Death in Don Mills: A Murder Mystery. Hugh Garner. LC 75-317912. 1975. 7.95 (ISBN 0-07-082178-X). McGraw-Hill Ryerson.

Death in Dwelly Lane. Frank Vigor Morley. LC 52-7293. 1952. Harper.

Death in Ecstasy. Ngaio March. 1977. pap. 1.50 (ISBN 0-425-03644-8, Medallion). Berkley Pub.

Death in Ecstasy. Ngaio Marsh. 1941. Sheridan House.

Death in Egypt. Gerald T. DeFelice. 400p. (Orig.). 1981. pap. 29.95 (ISBN 0-940318-12-1). Une Pub.

Death in Fancy Dress. Joseph Jefferson Farjeon. LC 39-24580. 1939. The Bobbs-Merrill Company.

Death in Five Boxes. Carr, John Dickson. (Belmont Tower Book). 1977. 1.50 (ISBN 0-505-51203-3). Tower Pubns.

Death in Five Boxes. John Dickson. Carr. LC 38-29786. 1938. W. Morrow & Company.

Death in Five Boxes. Carter Dickson, pseud. 1977. pap. 1.50 o.s.i. (ISBN 0-505-51203-3). Tower Bks.

Death in Florence. George Alec Effinger. LC 77-80883. 1978. 6.95 (ISBN 0-385-11190-8). Doubleday.

Death in Four Colors. Brandon Bird. LC 50-5151. (Red badge mystery). 1950. Dodd, Mead.

Death in Four Letters. Francis Beeding. 1935. Harper & Brothers.

Death in Gentle Grove. Francis K Allan. LC 76-5507. 1976. 7.95 (ISBN 0-88405-142-0). Mason/Charter.

Death in Harley Street. Cecil John Charles Street. LC 46-7802. 1946. Dodd, Mead & Company.

Death in High Heels. Christianna Brand, pseud. 1979. 15.00x (Pub. by Ian Henry Pubns England). State Mutual Bk.

Death in High Heels: By Christianna Brand Pseud. Mary Christianna Milne Lewis. LC 54-315. 1954. Scribner.

Death in High Provence. George Bellairs. pap. 0.65 o.p. (1771). Penguin.

Death in Indian Wells. Lewis B Patten. LC 75-123705. (DD western). 1970. 4.50. Doubleday.

Death in Ireland: A Novel. Peter Everett. LC 80-23034. 11.95 (ISBN 0-316-25837-7). Little, Brown.

Death in Lilac Time. Frances Kirkwood Crane. LC 55-581254. 1955. Random House.

Death in Lord Byron's Room. Sally Calkins Wood. LC 48-6730. 1948. W. Morrow.

Death in Midsummer, and Other Stories. Yukio Mishima, pseud. LC 66-17819. 1966. New Directions.

Death in Midwinter. John Buxton Hilton. LC 76-83094. 1969. 4.50. Walker.

Death in Pieces. Judith Milliman. 4.95 o.p. Vantage.

Death in Retirement: By Josephine Bell Pseud. Doris Bell Collier Ball. LC 56-9616. (Cock Robin mystery). 1956. Macmillan.

Death in Rome. Robert Katz. 1973. pap. 1.25 o.p. (ISBN 0-515-03033-3, V3033). Pyramid Pubns.

Death in Rome: A Novel. Translated by Mervyn Savill. Wolfgang Koeppen. LC 61-9013. 1961. Vanguard Press.

Death in Sheep's Clothing. Stella Phillips. 192p. 1983. 12.95 (ISBN 0-8027-5489-9). Walker & Co.

Death in Silver. A Superhero Adventure. Kenneth Robeson. (His the fantastic adventures of Doc Savage, 2). (Illus.). 1975. 1.75. (ISBN 0-307-02376-1). Western Publishing Company.

Death in Slow Motion. Kenneth Robeson. (Avenger #18). 1973. (pbk.) 0.75. Warner Paperback Library.

Death in Stanley Street. William John Burley. LC 74-82397. 1974. 5.95 o.p. (ISBN 0-8027-5309-4). Walker & Co.

Death in That Garden. La Mort En Ce Jardin. Translated by Humphrey Hare. Jose Andre Lacour. LC 59-6566. 1959. Rinehart.

Death in the Air. Agatha Miller Christie. LC 35-4453. 1935. Dodd, Mead & Company.

Death in the Air. Agatha Miller Christie. LC 40-3777. 1939. Triangle Books.

Death in the Air... Agatha Miller Christie. LC 47-423. (New Avon library, 89). 1946.

Death in the Back Seat. Dorothy Cameron Disney. LC 36-22615. Random House.

Death in the Blackout. Lucy Beatrice Malleson. LC 43-4187. 1943. Smith & Durrell.

Death in the Box. Brian Hill. LC 30-9315. 1930. J. B. Lippincott Company.

Death in the Cards. Ann T Smith. LC 45-9506. 1945. Phoenix Press.

Death in the Cards... Ann T Smith. LC 47-79295. (On cover: A Bart house book. 34). 1946.

Death in the Caribbean. John Richard Lane Anderson. LC 77-8748. 1977. 7.95 (ISBN 0-8128-2353-2). Stein and Day.

Death in the Castle. Pearl Sydenstricker Buck. (Cardinal ed., 50288). 1967. Pocket Bks.

Death in the Castle: A Novel. Pearl Sydenstricker Buck. LC 65-13748. 1965. John Day Co.

Death in the Channel. John Richard Lane Anderson. LC 76-13197. 6.95. Stein and Day.

Death in the City. J. R. L Anderson. LC 82-5649. 1982. 10.95 (ISBN 0-684-17758-7). Scribner.

Death in the City: A Colonel Peter Blair Mystery. John Richard Lane Anderson. 192p. 1982. 10.95 (ISBN 0-684-17758-7, ScribT). Scribner.

Death in the Claimshack. John L Sinclair. LC 47-119826. 1947. Sage Books.

Death in the Clouds. Agatha Miller Christie. Incl. N or M; Hercule Poirot's Christmas; Towards Zero. (Greenway Editions). 1974. 8.95 (ISBN 0-396-06961-4). Dodd.

Death in the Crease. Richard Curtis. (Pro/2). 1975. (pbk.) 1.25. Bantam.

Death in the Deep South. Ward Greene. LC 38-34142. (A Mercury book, no. 14). The American Mercury, Inc.

Death in the Deep South: A Novel About Murder. Ward Greene. LC 36-23907. Harisburg, Pa., Stackpole Sons.

Death in the Desert. John Richard Lane Anderson. LC 76-41672. 1977. 7.95 (ISBN 0-8128-2152-1). Stein and Day.

Death in the Desert. Lee E Wells. LC 54-5651. 1954. Rinehart.

Death in the Doll's House. Elizabeth Fetter & Bachmann, Lawrence, Joint Author. LC 43-51069. 1943. Random House.

Death in the Dormitory. Margaretta Brucker. LC 38-942836. Phoenix Press.

Death in the Drawing Room. Richard Adams Rathbone. LC 55-674. Comet Press Books.

Death in the Dunes. Paul H Dobbins. LC 50-8883. 1950. Phoenix Press.

Death in the Dusk. Virgil Markham. LC 28-18571. 1928. A. A. Knopf.

Death in the Family. James Agee. LC 57-121141. 1957. McDowell, Obolensky.

Death in the Family. James Agee. LC 67-6299. 1967. 4.95. Grosset.

Death in the Family. James Agee. LC 67-6299. 1967. Grosset & Dunlap.

Death in the Family see Willis & His Friends Series.

Death in the Fifth Position. Edgar Box, pseud. LC 79-11294. 1979. pap. 1.95 (ISBN 0-394-74054-8, Vin). Random.

Death in the Fifth Position. Gore Vidal. LC 52-7788. (Dutton guilt edged mystery). 1952. Dutton.

Death in the Fifth Position. Gore Vidal. LC 79-11294. 1979. 1.95 (ISBN 0-394-74054-8). Vintage Books.

Death in the Forest. Charles Neville Brand. LC 34-8355. C. Kendall.

Death in the Forest. James Hardy. LC 81-9652. 7.95 (ISBN 0-939834-00-6). Northland Publishers.

Death in the Glass. Newton Gayle. LC 37-34177. 1937. C. Scribner's Sons.

Death in the Greenhouse: A Colonel Peter Blair Mystery. John L. Anderson. 192p. 1983. 11.95 (ISBN 0-684-17872-9, ScribT). Scribner.

Death in the Hands of Talent. William Long. LC 46-6179. (Five star mystery. No. 37). 1946. Green Pub. Co.

Death in the Hands of Talent. Peter Yates. LC 46-6179. (On cover: Five star mystery. No. 37). 1946. Green Publishing Co.

Death in the House. Anthony Berkeley Cox. LC 39-27680. 1939. Pub. for the Crime Club, Inc., by Doubleday, Doran & Company, Inc.

Death in the House. Asnthony Berkeley Cox. LC 42-10298. (Sun dial mysteries). 1940. The Sun Dial Press.

Death in the Inkwell. Joseph Jefferson Farjeon. LC 42-4606. 1942. The Bobbs-Merrill Company.

Death in the Inner Office. Natalie Wight. LC 38-222753. Phoenix Press.

Death in the Lava. John Benteen. (Sundance: No. 4). 1979. pap. 1.75 o.s.i. (ISBN 0-8439-0707-X, Leisure Bks). Nordon Pubns.

Death in the Library. Philip Ketchum. LC 37-549. Thomas Y. Crowell Company.

Death in the Life. Dorothy Salisbury Davis. LC 76-14796. 6.95 (ISBN 0-684-14660-6). Scribner.

Death in the Life. Dorothy Salisbury Davis. 1977. 1.75 (ISBN 0-380-01747-4). Avon Books.

Death in the Limelight. A. E Martin. LC 46-1348. 1946. Simon and Schuster.

Death in the Mind. Richard Lockridge & Estabrooks, George Hoben, 1895- Joint Author. LC 45-6321. 1945. E. P. Dutton & Company, Inc.

Death in the Morning. Sheila Radley. (General Ser.). 1981. lib. bdg. 13.95 (ISBN 0-8161-3199-6, Large Print Bks). G K Hall.

Death in the Morning. Sheila Radley. 1979. 8.95 (ISBN 0-684-16175-3, ScribT). Scribner.

Death in the Morning. Hester Rowan. LC 80-27489. 1981. 13.95 (ISBN 0-8161-3199-6). G. K. Hall.

Death in the Night Watches. George Bellairs. LC 46-805740. 1946. The Macmillan Company.

Death in the North Sea. John Richard Lane Anderson. LC 75-34487. 1976. 6.95 (ISBN 0-8128-1895-4). Stein and Day.

Death in the Past. Richard A. Moore. (Raven House Mysteries). 224p. 1981. pap. 2.25 (ISBN 0-373-63004-2, Pub. by Worldwide). Harlequin Bks.

Death in the Picture: A Cyrus Finnegan Mystery. Moncrieff Williamson. LC 82-4318. 224p. 1982. 12.95 (ISBN 0-8253-0104-1). Beaufort Bks NY.

Death in the Picture: A Superintendent Graham Mystery. Moncrieff Williamson. LC 82-4318. 12.95 (ISBN 0-8253-0104-1). Beaufort Books.

Death in the Quadrangle. Eilis Dillon. 1968. 3.95. Walker.

Death in the Quarry. George Douglas Howard Cole & Margaret Isabel Postgate Cole. LC 34-238523. 1934. Pub. for the Crime Club, Inc. by Doubleday, Doran & Company, Inc.

Death in the Rising Sun. rev. ed. John Creasey. LC 75-34828. (Doctor Palfrey thriller). 1976. 6.95 (ISBN 0-8027-5338-8). Walker.

Death in the Round. Anne Morice. LC 80-13979. 1980. 8.95 (ISBN 0-312-18616-9). St. Martin's Press.

Death in the Round. Anne Morice. LC 81-10678. 1981. 2.95 (ISBN 0-14-005997-0). Penguin Books.

Death in the Saddle. Archie Joscelyn. LC 46-4800. 1946. Arcadia House, Inc.

Death in the Senate. John Franklin Carter. LC 33-8301. 1933. Covici-Friede.

Death in the Snow. Richard Martin Stern. LC 72-7731. 1973. 5.95 (ISBN 0-684-13207-9). Scribner.

Death in the State House. Timothy Knox. LC 34-13991. 1934. Houghton Mifflin Company.

Death in the Stocks. Georgette Heyer. LC 76-108894. 1970. 4.95. Dutton.

Death in the Stocks. Georgette Heyer. LC 35-78111. 1935. Longmans, Green and Co.

Death in the Sun. Charles Saxby. LC 40-855139. 1940. E. P. Dutton & Co., Inc.

Death in the Sunday Supplement. Sam Merwin. LC 42-20332. 1942. Gateway Books.

Death in the Thames. John Richard Lane Anderson. LC 75-9614. 1975. 6.95 (ISBN 0-8128-1824-5). Stein and Day.

Death in the Theatre. James Reginald Wilmot. LC 34-30870. C. Kendall.

Death in the Virgins. Ralph Henry Barbour. LC 40-8355. 1940. D. Appleton-Century Company, Incorporated.

Death in the Wet. Gladys Mitchell. LC 34-516992. 1934. Macrae Smith Company.

Death in the Willows. Richard Forrest. LC 79-4116. (Rinehart suspense novel). 7.95 (ISBN 0-03-049296-3). Holt, Rinehart, and Winston.

Death in the Wind. 1st Ed. Edwin Moultrie Lanham. LC 56-5335. Harcourt, Brace.

Death in the Woods: And Other Stories. Sherwood Anderson. LC 33-23673. Liveright, Inc.

Death in the Wrong Bed. Stewart Farrar. LC 64-23990. 1964. Walker.

Death in the Wrong Room. Lucy Beatrice Malleson. LC 47-122293. 1947. A. S. Barnes.

Death in the Yew Alley. Mari Ervin. LC 38-478. 1937. Phoenix Press.

Death in Time. Mignon Warner. LC 81-43766. 1982. 10.95 (ISBN 0-385-18094-2). Published for the Crime Club by Doubleday.

Death in Venice. Thomas Mann. Tr. by Kenneth Burke. LC 65-12070. (Illus.). 1965. Knopf.

Death in Venice. Thomas Mann. Tr. by Kenneth Burke. Limited Editions Club, Inc., New York. LC 72-172258. (Illus.). 1972. Printed for the Members of the Limited Editions Club, New York by Stinehour Press.

Death in Venice, and Seven Other Stories: Translated from the German by H. T. Lowe-Porter. Thomas Mann. LC 54-12055. (Vintage book, K-3). 1954. Vintage Books.

Death in Venice: Translated from the German. Thomas Mann. Tr. by Helen Tracy Lowe. Lewisohn, Ludwig, 1882- LC 80-305653. 1930. A. A. Knopf.

Death in Venice: Translated from the German of Thomas Mann. Thomas Mann & Burke, Kenneth, 1897- Tr. LC 25-4777. 1925. A. A. Knopf.

Death in View. 1st Ed. Travis Macrae, pseud. LC 60-142516. 1960. Holt, Rinehart and Winston.

Death in Waiting. Jennifer Bland. LC 74-21801. 1975. 7.95. St. Martin's Press.

Death in Wellington Road. Cecil John Charles Street. LC 52-8986. (Red badge detective). 1952. Dodd, Mead.

Death in Willow Pattern. William John Burley. LC 73-98011. 1970. 4.50. Walker.

Death in Zanzibar. M. M. Kaye. 240p. 1983. 12.95 (ISBN 0-312-18623-1). St Martin.

Death in 1-2-3. Robert David Abrahams. LC 42-5119. 1942. Phoenix Press.

Death Inheritance. Phyllis Swan. (Anna J. Ser.: No. 3). (Orig.). 1980. pap. 1.75 o.s.i. (ISBN 0-8439-0731-2, Leisure Bks). Nordon Pubns.

Death Invades the Meeting. Cecil John Charles Street. LC 44-2359. 1944. Dodd, Mead and Company.

Death Is a Cold Keen Edge. Earle Basinsky. LC 56-12515. (Signet book, 1351). 1956. New American Library.

Death Is a Dark Man. Dora Highland. 1974. (pbk.) 0.95. Popular Library.

Death Is a Dirty Trick. Judson Pentecost Philips. LC 79-27738. (Peter Styles mysteries). (Red badge novel of suspense). 7.95 (ISBN 0-396-07820-6). Dodd, Mead.

Death Is a Drum... Beating Forever. John Wyllie. LC 76-50872. 1977. 6.95 (ISBN 0-385-12783-9). Published for the Crime Club by Doubleday.

Death Is a Friend. Donald MacKenzie. LC 67-15528. 1967. 4.50. Houghton.

Death Is a Little Man. Minnie Hite Moody. LC 36-10901. J. Messner, Inc.

Death Is a Lovely Dame: By Matthew Blood Pseud. Cover Painting by Barye Phillips. Davis Dresser. LC 54-38661. (Gold medal books, 423). 1954. Fawcett Publications.

Death Is a Pulpit. Peter Levi. 1971. 3.50 (Pub. by Anvil Pr); signed ltd. ed. 15.00. SBD.

Death Is a Red Rose. Dorothy Enid Eden. 1976. 1.75. Ace Books.

Death Is a Round Black Ball. Mike Pseud Roscoe. LC 52-5673. 1952. Crown Publishers.

Death Is a Ruby Light. Paul Kenyon. (Baroness series,#3). 1974. (pbk.) 0.95. Pocket Books.

Death Is a Silent Room. Jay Bennett. LC 65-11855. (Raven bk.). 3.50. Abelard.

Death Is a Stowaway. Wesley Price. LC 33-47251. 1933. W. Godwin, Inc.

Death Is a Swinger. Jason Morgan. (Orig.). 1968. pap. 0.75 o.p. (74-967). Lancer.

Death Is a Tory. Keats Patrick. LC 35-7381. The Bobbs-Merrill Company.

Death Is Academic. Amanda Mackay. LC 76-40501. 1976. 7.95 (ISBN 0-679-50638-1). D. McKay.

Death Is an Early Riser. John Mason Bigelow. LC 40-6439. 1940. C. Scribner's Sons.

Death Is for Losers. William F. Nolan. LC 68-13285. (His The Bart Challis series). 1968. Sherbourne Press.

Death is Forever. Maxine O'Callaghan. (Raven House Mysteries Ser.). 224p. 1981. pap. 2.25 (ISBN 0-373-63014-X, Pub. by Worldwide). Harlequin Bks.

Death Is in the Garden. Melba Balmat Grimes Marlett. LC 51-10651. 1951. Published for the Crime Club by Doubleday.

Death Is Late to Lunch. Theodora McCormick Du Bois. LC 41-9498. 1941. Houghton Mifflin Company.

Death Is Like That. Cleve Franklin Adams. LC 43-14975. 1943. E. P. Dutton & Co., Inc.

Death Is My Bridegroom. Dominic Devine. LC 69-17395. 1969. 4.50. Walker.

Death Is My Lover. Louis Trimble. LC 48-9070. 1948. M. S. Mill Co.

Death Is My Name. Doris Siegel. LC 42-4719. 1942. C. Scribner's Sons.

Death Is My Name. Susan Wells. LC 42-471912. 1942. C. Scribner's Sons.

Death Is My Shadow. Edward Sidney Aarons. LC 57-12671. 1957. Mystery House.

Death Is My Shadow. Edward Sidney Aarons. 1975. (pbk.) 0.95. Manor Books.

Death Is No Sportsman. Cyril Hare. LC 81-47097. 224p. 1981. pap. 2.40i (ISBN 0-06-080555-2, P555, PL). Har-Row.

Death Is Not a Passing Grade. Victor B Miller. (Kojak series,#5). 1975. (pbk.) 1.25. Pocket Books.

Death Is Not the Final Word. Gerhard Lohfink. Tr. by Robert Cunningham from Ger. LC 77-7299. (Synthesis Ser.). 1977. pap. 0.75. Franciscan Herald.

Death Is Only the Beginning. Robert Curry Ford. LC 79-92145. (ISBN 0-87216-651-1). Playboy Books.

Death Is Skin Deep. Catherine Percy. LC 53-681120. 1953. Abelard Press.

Death Is So Fair. Louis Lynch D'Alton. LC 38-14451. 1938. Doubleday, Doran & Company, Inc.

Death Is So Kind. Liam Redmond. 1959. 4.95 (ISBN 0-8159-5301-1). Devin.

Death Is So Kind: A Novel of Suspense. Liam Redmond. LC 59-12311. 1959. Devin-Adair.

Death Is the Host. Lawrence Lariar. LC 44-3942. Red Circle Magazines, Inc.

Death Is Thy Neighbor. Laurence Dwight Smith. LC 38-3733. J. B. Lippincott Company.

Death Jag. Albert C. Ellis & Jeff Slaten. (Orig.). 1980. pap. 1.95 (ISBN 0-532-23312-3). Woodhill.

Death Joins the Woman's Club. Charles Saxby. LC 40-145009. 1940. E. P. Dutton & Company, Inc.

Death Keeps a Secret. 1st Ed. Clarence Budington Kelland. LC 55-12118. 1956. Harper.

Death Kiss. St. Dennis, Madelon. LC 32-6314. The Fiction League.

Death Kit. Susan Sontag. (Signet bk., Q3597). 1968. New Amer. Lib.

Death Kit. Susan Sontag. LC 67-22434. 1967. Farrar, Straus and Giroux.

Death Kit. Susan Sontag. (Dell Book). 1978. 4.95 (ISBN 0-440-52171-8). Dell Pub. Co.
Death Knell. C. Terry Cline. LC 77-6935. 8.95 (ISBN 0-399-12010-6). Putnam.
Death Knell. C. Terry Cline. 1978. 2.25 (ISBN 0-449-23639-0). Fawcett Books.
Death Knell. Baynard Hardwick Kendrick. LC 48-827. (Duncan Maclain mystery). Triangle Books.
Death Knell. Baynard Hardwick Kendrick. LC 45-35023. 1945. W. Morrow & Company.
Death Knocks Three Times. Lucy Beatrice Malleson. LC 50-5006. 1950. Random House.
Death Lies Deep. Cover Painting by Lu Kimmel. William Guinn. LC 55-42195. (Gold medal books, 503). 1955. Fawcett Publications.
Death Lifts the Latch. Lucy Beatrice Malleson. LC 46-1796. 1946. Smith and Durrell.
Death Lights a Candle. Phoebe Atwood Taylor. LC 32-14531. The Bobbs-Merrill Company.
Death Lights a Candle. Phoebe Atwood Taylor. LC 80-10757. 1980. 9.95 (ISBN 0-89340-260-5). J. Curley & Associates.
Death Like Thunder. Hugh Holman. LC 42-156941. 1942. Phoenix Press.
Death Likes It Hot. Edgar Box, pseud. LC 79-10159. 1979. pap. 1.95 (ISBN 0-394-74055-6, Vin). Random.
Death Likes It Hot. Gore Vidal. LC 79-10159. 1979. 1.95 (ISBN 0-394-74055-6). Vintage Books.
Death Likes It Hot: By Edgar Box Pseud. 1st Ed. Gore Vidal. LC 54-6825. (Guilt edged mystery). 1954. Dutton.
Death List. Ronald Casler. 1975. (pbk.) 1.25 (ISBN 0-523-00683-7). Pinnacle Books.
Death List. Al C Clark. 1974. (pbk.) 1.50 (ISBN 0-87067-443-9). Holloway House.
Death List. Donald Goines. (Orig.). 1974. pap. 1.95 (ISBN 0-87067-626-1, BH626). Holloway.
Death List. Robert Hawkes. (Narc). (Signet Book: Vol. 3). 1974. (pbk.) 0.95. New American Library.
Death List. Robert McKew & DeRouen, Reed. 2.25 (ISBN 0-440-11841-7). Dell Publishing Co.
Death Listened in. Kathleen Sproul. LC 46-42729. 1946. Phoenix Press.
Death Lives in the Mansion. easy eye ed. Douglas Locke. Orig. Title: House of Two Wives. 1969. pap. 0.75 o.p. (74-516). Lancer.
Death Lode. J. D. Hardin. LC 81-47256. (J. D. Hardin Westerns Ser.). 224p. (Orig.). 1981. pap. 1.95 (ISBN 0-87216-911-1). Playboy Pbks.
Death Looks Down. Amelia Reynolds Long. LC 45-3235. 1945. Ziff-Davis Publishing Company.
Death Loves a Shining Mark. Mona Naomi Anne Hocking Messer. LC 43-68272. ("First edition."). 1943. Pub. for the Crime Club by Doubleday, Doran & Co., Inc.
Death Machine. Kenneth Robeson. (Avenger, 32). 1975. 0.95. Warner Paperback Library.
Death Maker. Austin J Small. LC 28-283088. 1926. George H. Doran Company.
Death Makers. Joseph Milton. pap. 0.60 o.p. Lancer.
Death Mask. Hugh Pentecost. LC 83-129. 1982. 9.95 (ISBN 0-8161-3500-2). G.K. Hall.
Death Mask. Hugh Pentecost. LC 80-15717. (Julian Quist Mystery Novel Ser.). 224p. 1980. 8.95 o.p. (ISBN 0-396-07883-4). Dodd.
Death Mask. Hugh Pentecost. (Nightingale Ser.). 1983. pap. 9.95 (ISBN 0-8161-3500-2, Large Print Bks). G K Hall.
Death Mask: A Julian Quist Mystery Novel. Judson Pentecost Philips. LC 80-15717. (Red badge novel of suspense). 8.95 (ISBN 0-396-07883-4). Dodd, Mead.
Death Master. Benjamin Appel. 1974. (pbk.) 1.25. Popular Library.
Death Meets Four Hundred Rabbits. Aaron Marc Stein. 1969. pap. 0.60 o.p. (0502-06023-060). Curtis.
Death Meets the Deadline. David Robinson George. LC 44-9239. 1944. Vulcan Publications.
Death Meets the King's Messenger. Gilbert Collins. LC 34-16900. 1934. Pub. for the Crime Club, Inc., by Doubleday, Doran & Company, Inc.
Death Meets 400 Rabbits. 1st Ed. Aaron Marc Stein. LC 53-6102. 1953. Published for the Crime Club by Doubleday.
Death Merchant, No. 44. Joseph Rosenberger. 192p. (Orig.). 1981. pap. 1.95 (ISBN 0-523-41325-4). Pinnacle Bks.
Death Merchant Billionaire Mission. Joseph Rosenberger. (Death Merchant series). 1974. (pbk.) 0.95. Pinnacle Books.
Death Merchant: Chinese Conspiracy. Joseph Rosenberger. (Death Merchant Ser., No. 4). 192p. (Orig.). 1973. pap. 1.95 (ISBN 0-523-41348-3). Pinnacle Bks.
Death Merchant: No. 1. Joseph N. Rosenberger. 1972. pap. 1.95 (ISBN 0-523-41345-9). Pinnacle Bks.
Death Merchant, No. 10: Mainline Plot. Joseph Rosenberger. (Orig.). 1974. pap. 1.95 (ISBN 0-523-41354-8). Pinnacle Bks.
Death Merchant, No. 2: Operation Overkill. Joseph N. Rosenberger. (Orig.). 1972. pap. 1.95 (ISBN 0-523-41346-7). Pinnacle Bks.
Death Merchant No. 22: The Kondrashev Chase. Joseph Rosenberger. (The Death Merchant Series). 192p. 1977. pap. 1.75 (ISBN 0-523-40827-7). Pinnacle Bks.
Death Merchant, No. 3: The Psychotron Plot. Joseph Rosenberger. 192p. (Orig.). 1972. pap. 1.95 (ISBN 0-523-41347-5). Pinnacle Bks.
Death Merchant No. 34: Operation Mind-Murder. Joseph Rosenberger. 1979. pap. 1.95 (ISBN 0-523-41378-5). Pinnacle Bks.
Death Merchant, No. 5: Satan Strike. Joseph Rosenberger. 1972. pap. 1.95 (ISBN 0-523-41349-1). Pinnacle Bks.
Death Merchant: No. 50-The Hellbomb Theft. Joseph Rosenberger. 208p. (Orig.). 1982. pap. 2.25 (ISBN 0-523-41657-1). Pinnacle Bks.
Death Merchant: No. 51-The Inca File. Joseph Rosenberger. 208p. (Orig.). 1982. pap. 2.25 (ISBN 0-523-41658-X). Pinnacle Bks.
Death Merchant, No. 52: Flight of the Phoenix. Joseph Rosenberger. 208p. (Orig.). 1982. pap. 2.25 (ISBN 0-523-41659-8). Pinnacle Bks.
Death Merchant, No. 6: The Albanian Connection. Joseph Rosenberger. 192p. (Orig.). 1973. pap. 1.95 (ISBN 0-523-41350-5). Pinnacle Bks.
Death Merchant, No. 7: The Castro File. Joseph Rosenberger. 192p. (Orig.). 1974. pap. 1.95 (ISBN 0-523-41351-3). Pinnacle Bks.
Death Merchant, No. 8: Billionaire Mission. Joseph Rosenberger. (Orig.). 1974. pap. 1.95 (ISBN 0-523-41352-1). Pinnacle Bks.
Death Merchant, No. 9: The Laser War. Joseph Rosenberger. 192p. (Orig.). 1974. pap. 1.95 (ISBN 0-523-41353-X). Pinnacle Bks.
Death Merchant: Rim of Fire Conspiracy, No. 45. Joseph Rosenberger. 192p. (Orig.). 1981. pap. 1.95 (ISBN 0-523-41326-2). Pinnacle Bks.
Death Merchants. James H. Readus. (Orig.). 1974. pap. 1.50 (ISBN 0-87067-450-1, BH016). Holloway.
Death Merchants. James Howard Readus. 1974. (pbk.) 1.50 (ISBN 0-87067-450-1). Holloway House.
Death Message: Oil 74-2. Nick Carter. (Nick Carter Ser). (O.s.i.). 176p. 1976. pap. 1.25 o.s.i. (AQ1559, Award). Univ Pub & Dist.
Death Message: Oil 74-2. Nick Carter. (Nick Carter Killmaster AQ 1559). 1976. (pbk.) 1.25. Award Books.
Death, My Darling Daughters. Jonathan Stagge, pseud. LC 46-809. 1945. Pub. for the Crime Club, by Doubleday, Doran & Co., Inc.
Death-Mystery: A Crimson Tale of Life in New York. Edward Zane Carroll Judson. LC 7-11444. F. A. Brady.
Death Near the River. Monte Cooper. LC 28-22144. H. Holt and Company.
Death Never Forgets. Robin Moore, pseud. 1978. pap. 1.95 (ISBN 0-532-19178-1). Woodhill.
Death Never Weeps. Stella Ryan. LC 46-7724. 1946. Coward-McCann, Inc.
Death Notes. Ruth Rendell. LC 81-47211. 9.95 (ISBN 0-394-52078-5). Pantheon Books.
Death Notes. Ruth Rendell. LC 81-20056. 1982. 13.95 (ISBN 0-8161-3335-2). G.K. Hall.
Death of a Banker. Robert McNair Wilson. LC 34-205703. J. B. Lippincott.
Death of a Beekeeper. Lars Gustafsson. LC 81-11182. 12.95 (ISBN 0-8112-0809-5) (ISBN 0-8112-0810-9). New Directions.
Death of a Big Man. John William Wainwright. LC 74-33230. 1975. 6.95. St. Martin's Press.
Death of a Big Man. John William Wainwright. (Berkley book). 1979. 1.75 (ISBN 0-425-04131-X). Berkley Pub. Corp.
Death of a Big Shot. 1st Ed. Clifford Knight. LC 51-9034. (Guilt edged mystery). 1951. Dutton.
Death of a Blue-Eyed Soul Brother. B. B. Johnson. (Orig.). 1970. pap. 0.75 o.p. (64-267). Paperback Lib.
Death of a Bridegroom: By John Rhode. Cecil John Charles Street. LC 58-5980. (Red badge detective). 1958. Dodd, Mead.
Death of a Bridge Expert. Charles Cathcart Nicolet. LC 32-20613. 1932. Simon and Schuster.
Death of a Bullionaire. Albert Benjamin Cunningham. LC 47-5730. 1947. E. P. Dutton.
Death of a Busybody. George Bellairs. LC 43-6818. 1943. The Macmillan Company.
Death of a Busybody. Dell Shannon. 1970. pap. 0.75 o.p. (T2313). Pyramid Pubns.
Death of a Busybody: By Dell Shannon Pseud. Elizabeth Linington. LC 62-15764. 1963. Morrow.
Death of a Call Girl. Leslie Trevor. (Police Woman Ser.). (O.s.i.). 176p. (Orig.). 1975. pap. 1.25 o.s.i. (AQ1487, Award). Univ Pub & Dist.
Death of a Celebrity. Hulbert Footner. LC 38-10327. 1938. Harper & Brothers.
Death of a Chieftain: And Other Stories. John Montague. LC 66-19956. 4.50. Dufor.
Death of a Citizen. Donald Hamilton. (Matt Helm Ser.). 1978. pap. 1.95 (ISBN 0-449-14087-3, GM). Fawcett.
Death of a City. Pritam Amrita. LC 76-903763. 1976. 6.00. Arnold-Heinemann Publishers (India)
Death of a City. Lionel White. LC 77-108164. 1970. 5.95. Bobbs-Merrill Co.
Death of a Con Man. Josephine Bell. 1968. 3.95 o.p. Lippincott.
Death of a Cop. Robert Daley. LC 75-30361. 10.00 (ISBN 0-06-121876-6). Harper's Magazine Press.
Death of a Corinthian. 1st Ed. Edwin Moultrie Lanham. LC 53-7845. 1953. Harcourt, Brace.
Death of a Courier. Robert Hawkes. (Narc#2). 1974. (pbk.) 0.95. New American Library.
Death of a Crow. Ursula Reilly Curtiss. LC 82-19951. 1983. 10.95 (ISBN 0-396-08130-4). Dodd.
Death of a Delegate. George P. Cronin. LC 78-53466. 1978. pap. 1.95 o.s.i. (ISBN 0-89516-032-3). Condor Pub Co.
Death of a Delft Blue. Gladys Mitchell. LC 65-17413. 1965. London House & Maxwell.
Death of a Diplomat. Peter Oldfeld, pseud. LC 28-8130. 1928. I. Washburn.
Death of a Dissident. Stuart M. Kaminsky. 448p. (Orig.). 1981. pap. 2.95 (ISBN 0-441-14204-4). Ace Bks.
Death of a Doll. Hilda Lawrence. 1947. Simon and Schuster.
Death of a Doll. Hilda Lawrence. LC 82-5200. 1982. 3.95 (ISBN 0-14-006307-2). Penguin Books.
Death of a Don. Howard Shaw. LC 81-14408. 1981. 11.95 (ISBN 0-684-17275-5). Scribner.
Death of a Doxy: A Nero Wolfe Novel. Rex Stout. LC 66-22544. bds., 3.75. Viking.
Death of a Dreamer. Douglas Warner. LC 65-15425. 1965. bds., 3.50. Walker.
Death of a Dude. Rex Stout. 160p. 1981. pap. 2.25 (ISBN 0-553-14809-5). Bantam.
Death of a Dude. Rex Stout. (O.s.i.). 1969. 4.50 o.s.i. (ISBN 0-670-26140-8). Viking Pr.
Death of a Dude: A Nero Wolfe Novel. Rex Stout. LC 74-83230. 1969. 4.50. Viking Press.
Death of a Dutchman. Magdalen Nabb. LC 82-16762. 1983. 11.95 (ISBN 0-684-17847-8). Scribner.
Death of a Fat God: By H. R. F. Keating. 1st Ed. Henry Reymond Fitzwalter Keating. LC 66-12257. 1966. 3.95. Dutton.
Death of a Fellow Traveller. Delano L Ames. LC 50-8907. (Murray Hill mystery). 1950. Rinehart.
Death of a First Mate. Charles Bryson. LC 35-21565. E. P. Dutton & Co., Inc.
Death of a Fool. Ngaio Marsh. 1976. Repr. of 1956 ed. lib. bdg. 15.45x (ISBN 0-88411-480-5). Amereon Ltd.
Death of a Fool. Ngaio Marsh. (Ngaio Marsh Mystery Ser.). 288p. 1981. pap. 2.50 (ISBN 0-515-06177-8). Jove Pubns.
Death of a Fool. Ngaio Marsh. 1973. pap. 1.25 o.p. (ISBN 0-515-03184-4, N3184). BJ Pub Group.
Death of a Fool. 1st Ed. Ngaio Marsh. LC 56-10642. 1956. Little, Brown.
Death of a Fox. Jan Roffman. LC 64-18497. 1964. Published for the Crime Club by Doubleday.
Death of a Ghost. Margery Allingham. 1973. 0.95. Manor Books.
Death of a Ghost. Margery Allingham. LC 75-40218. 1975. 9.95 (ISBN 0-89190-195-7). American Reprint Co.
Death of a Ghost. Margery Allingham. LC 34-11032. 1934. Pub. for the Crime Club, Inc., by Doubleday, Doran & Co., Inc.
Death of a God & Other Stories. Osbert Sitwell. 247p. 1981. Repr. of 1949 ed. lib. bdg. 20.00 (ISBN 0-8495-4951-5). Arden Lib.
Death of a Golfer. Robert McNair Wilson. LC 37-142818. J. B. Lippincott Company.
Death of a Gunfighter. Lewis B Patten. LC 68-11775. (Double D western). 1968. Doubleday.
Death of a Hawker. Janwillem Van De Wetering. 1977. 6.95 (ISBN 0-395-25171-0). HM.
Death of a Hawker. Janwillem Van De Wetering. (gr. 12). 1978. pap. 2.25 (ISBN 0-671-81341-2). PB.
Death of a Hawker. Wetering, Janwillem Van De. LC 76-50141. 1977. 6.95 (ISBN 0-395-25171-0). Houghton Mifflin.
Death of a Hawker. Janwillem Van De Wetering. LC 77-15559. 1978. 11.95 (ISBN 0-8161-6527-0). G. K. Hall.
Death of a Hawker. Janwillen Van De Wetering. (Kangaroo Book). 1978. 1.95 (ISBN 0-671-81341-2). Pocket Books.
Death of a Heavenly Twin. Anne Morice. LC 73-93170. 1974. 6.95. St. Martin's Press.
Death of a Hero: A Novel. Richard Aldington. LC 73-144860. 1972. 19.50 (ISBN 0-403-00828-X). Scholarly Press.
Death of a Hero: A Novel. Richard Aldington. LC 34-706236. Garden City Publishing Company, Inc.
Death of a Hero: A Novel. Richard Aldington. LC 29-17387. 1929. Covici, Friede, Inc.
Death of a Hero: Epitaph for Maqbool Sherwani. Mulk Raj Anand. 94p. 1974. pap. 1.50 o.p. (ISBN 0-88253-005-4). InterCulture.
Death of a Highbrow. Frank Arthur Swinnerton. LC 62-9458. 1962. Doubleday.
Death of a Hit Man. Frederick Davies. LC 82-16920. 1982. 10.95 (ISBN 0-312-18640-1). St. Martin's Press.
Death of a Hittite. Sylvia Angus. LC 69-18244. (Cock Robin mystery). 1969. Macmillan.
Death of a Hooker. Henry Kane. 1969. pap. 0.60 o.p. (73-835). Lancer.
Death of a King: Or, The Vigilant Eye. Ottilie Gertrude Boetzkes. LC 57-12164. 1957. Pan Press.
Death of a Lady's Man. Leonard Cohen. LC 79-14435. 1979. 10.00 (ISBN 0-670-26147-5). Viking Press.
Death of a Lady's Man. Leonard Cohen. LC 79-13256. 2.95 (ISBN 0-14-042275-7). Penguin Books.
Death of a Lake. Arthur William Upfield. LC 54-5711. 1954. Published for the Crime Club by Doubleday.
Death of a Legend. Robert Adams. (Horseclans Ser.: No. 8). 1981. pap. 2.75 (ISBN 0-451-12324-7, AE2324, Sig). NAL.
Death of a Legend. Will Henry, pseud. LC 54-7590. 1954. Random House.
Death of a Literary Widow. Robert Barnard. LC 80-13128. 1980. 8.95 (ISBN 0-684-16648-8). Scribner.
Death of a Literary Widow. Robert. Barnard. LC 81-4778. 1981. 11.95 (ISBN 0-8161-3249-6). G.K. Hall.
Death of a Low Handicap Man. Brian N Ball. LC 78-60749. 1978. 8.95 (ISBN 0-8027-5403-1). Walker.
Death of a Lucky Lady. Virginia Rath. LC 40-304061. 1940. Pub. for the Crime Club by Doubleday, Doran & Co., Inc.
Death of a Man. Kay Boyle. LC 36-22179. Harcourt, Brace and Company.
Death of a Man. Lael Tucker Wertenbaker. LC 57-537361. 1957. Random House.
Death of a Man. Lael Tucker Wertenbaker. LC 73-16889. 1974. 7.50. Beacon Press.
Death of a Merchant of Death: A Professor Wells Mystery. Norman Stanley Bortner. LC 37-147353. 1937. Macrae-Smith Company.
Death of a Millionaire. George Douglas Howard Cole & Margaret Isabel Postgate Cole. LC 25-12984. 1925. The Macmillan Company.
Death of a Minor Character. E. X Ferrars, pseud. LC 82-23479. 1983. 11.95 (ISBN 0-385-18839-0). Doubleday.
Death of a Moral Person. Alexandra Roudybush. LC 67-22450. 1967. Published for the Crime Club by Doubleday.
Death of a Mystery Writer. Robert Barnard. LC 79-12090. 1979. 7.95 (ISBN 0-684-16280-6). Scribner.
Death of a Mystery Writer. Robert Barnard. LC 80-11217. 1980. 11.95 (ISBN 0-8161-3081-7). G. K. Hall.
Death of a Nobody. Jules Romains. LC 74-23525. 1975. 10.00. H. Fertig.
Death of a Nobody. Jules Romains & MacCarthy, Desmond, 1878- Tr. 1914. B. W. Huebsch.
Death of a Nobody. Jules Romains & MacCarthy, Desmond, 1878- Tr. LC 44-9587. 1944. A. A. Knopf.
Death of a Nobody. Translated by Desmond MacCarthy and Sidney Waterlow. With a New Introd. by the Author, Translated by Haakon Chevalier. Afterword by Maurice Natanson. Jules Romains. LC 61-4314. (Signet classic, CD54). 1961. New American Library.
Death of a Patriot: A Novel. R. E Harrington. LC 78-27809. 8.95 (ISBN 0-399-12187-0). Putnam.
Death of a Peer. Ngaio Marsh. LC 40-32621. 1940. Little, Brown and Company.
Death of a Perfect Mother. Robert Barnard. LC 81-2815. 9.95 (ISBN 0-684-17019-1). Scribner.
Death of a Perfect Mother. Robert Barnard. LC 82-2840. (Nightingale Series). 1982. 8.95 (ISBN 0-8161-3356-5). G.K. Hall.
Death of a Philanderer. Laurence Walter Meynell. LC 73-78674. 1969. 4.50. Published for the Crime Club by Doubleday.
Death of a Pig. Doyle Bairrington. 6.75 o.p. (ISBN 0-8062-1144-X). Carlton.
Death of a Player. Lillian O'Donnell. LC 64-20873. (Raven bk.). 1965. 3.50. Abelard.
Death of a Poet: A Novel of the Last Years of Alexander Pushkin. Leonid Petrovich Grossman. LC 52-314403. Hutchinson International Authors.
Death of a Poison-Tongue. Josephine Bell. LC 77-21252. 1977. 7.95 (ISBN 0-8128-2409-1). Stein and Day.
Death of a Politican: A Novel. Richard Condon. LC 78-16015. 10.95 (ISBN 0-399-90018-7). R. Marek Publishers.
Death of a Pornographer. Anthony Lejeune. Orig. Title: Dark Trade. pap. 0.60 o.p. (73-627). Lancer.

Death of a Portrait: By Evalina Mack Pseud. Lena Brooke McNamara. LC 52-14404. 1952. Arcadia House.

Death of a Postman. John Creasey. LC 57-11144. Harper.

Death of a Punk. John P Browner. 2.25 (ISBN 0-671-82779-0). Pocket Books.

Death of a Puppeteer. William Gray Beyer. LC 47-17775. 1946. Mystery House.

Death of a Queen: Charles Venables' Fourth Case. Christopher St. John Sprigg. LC 35-26906. 1935. T. Nelson and Sons, Ltd.

Death of a Racehorse. John Creasey. 1971. pap. 0.75 o.p. (ISBN 0-447-74767-3). Lancer.

Death of a Revolutionary. Richard Harris. 1971. pap. 1.95 (ISBN 0-02-073520-0, Collier). Macmillan.

Death of a Revolutionist. Jack Dall. LC 40-33288. 1940. Gateway Books.

Death of a Riverkeeper: And Other Stories. Ernest Schwiebert. (Illus.). 288p. 1981. 14.95 (ISBN 0-525-08947-0). Dutton.

Death of a Saboteur. Hulbert Footner. LC 43-3202. 1943. Harper & Brothers.

Death of a Scavenger. Keith Spore. (Belmont Tower Book). 2.25 (ISBN 0-505-51465-6). Tower Publications.

Death of a Schoolboy. Hans Koning. LC 73-15430. (Helen & Kurt Wolff Bk). 1974. 6.95 (ISBN 0-15-124155-4). HarBraceJ.

Death of a Schoolboy. Hans Koningsberger. LC 73-18324. 1974. 6.95 (ISBN 0-15-124155-4). Harcourt Brace Jovanovich.

Death of a Shipowner. Thomas Henege. LC 80-26917. 8.95 (ISBN 0-396-07952-0). Dodd, Mead.

Death of a Simple Giant & Other Modern Yugoslav Stories. Ed. by Branko Lenski. LC 64-23319. 1964. 10.00 (ISBN 0-8149-0143-3). Vanguard.

Death of a Skin Diver. Simon Jay. LC 64-20984. 1964. Published for the Crime Club by Doubleday.

Death of a Snout. Douglas Warner. LC 62-18736. 1962. Walker.

Death of a Song & Other Stories. Kartar S. Duggal. (Indian Short Stories Ser.). 186p. 1974. 4.95 (ISBN 0-88253-458-0). Ind-US Inc.

Death of A Source. Richard A. Moore. (Raven House Mysteries Ser.). 224p. 1982. pap. 2.25 (ISBN 0-373-63027-1, Pub. by Worldwide). Harlequin Bks.

Death of a Spinster. Frances Riker Duncombe. LC 58-6221. 1958. Scribner.

Death of a Spinster. Dorothy Johnson. LC 31-9714. 1931. Longmans, Green and Co.

Death of a Star... George Douglas Howard Cole & Margaret Isabel Postgate Cole. 1933. Pub. for the Crime Club, Inc., by Doubleday, Doran & Company, Inc.

Death of a Stranger. John Creasey. Orig. Title: Come Here & Die. 192p. (O.S.I.). 1973. Repr. of 1959 ed. lib. bdg. 5.95 o.s.i. White Lion Pubs.

Death of a Stray Cat. Jean Potts. LC 55-9685. 1955. Scribner.

Death of a Supertanker. Antony Trew. LC 77-91887. 1978. 8.95 (ISBN 0-312-18738-6). St. Martin's Press.

Death of a Swagman. Arthur William Upfield. LC 45-9776. 1945. Pub. for the Crime Club by Doubleday, Doran & Co., Inc.

Death of a Tall Man. Frances Louise Davis Lockridge & Richard Lockridge. LC 46-7663. 1946. J. B. Lippincott Company.

Death of a Thin-Skinned Animal. Patrick Alexander. LC 77-372305. 1976. 3.95 (ISBN 0-333-21249-5). Macmillan.

Death of a Thin-Skinned Animal. Patrick Alexander. LC 76-52317. 1977. 7.95 (ISBN 0-525-08949-7). Dutton.

Death of a Train. Freeman Wills Crofts. LC 47-12106. 1947. Dodd, Mead & Company.

Death of a Transplant. S. C. Lee. LC 71-128376. 1971. 4.95 o.p. (ISBN 0-87397-005-5). Strode.

Death of a Voodoo Doll. Margot Arnold, pseud. 224p. (Orig.). 1982. pap. 2.50 (ISBN 0-86721-114-8). Playboy Pbks.

Death of a Wedding Guest. Anne Morice. LC 75-26187. 1976. 7.95. St. Martin's Press.

Death of a White Witch. Inez Hildagard Oellrichs. LC 49-50119. 1949. Published for the Crime Club by Doubleday.

Death of a Wicked Servant. Brian Talbot Cleeve. LC 64-20017. (Random House mystery). 1964. Random House.

Death of a World... Romain Rolland & De Alberti, Amalia, Tr. LC 33-30444. (His The soul enchanted. IV). H. Holt and Company.

Death of a Worldly Woman. Albert Benjamin Cunningham. LC 48-2089. 1945. E. P. Dutton.

Death of a Young Man. Walter Leslie River. LC 27-18267. 1927. Simon and Schuster.

Death of Abbe Didier. Richard Grayson. 180p. 1981. 9.95 o.p. (ISBN 0-312-18648-7). St Martin.

Death of Abbe Didier. Richard Grindal. LC 80-29317. 9.95 (ISBN 0-312-18648-7). St. Martin's Press.

Death of Achilles. Victor Price. LC 63-11895. 1963. Doubleday.

Death of Ahasuerus. Par Fabian Lagerkvist. LC 61-12177. 1962. Random House.

Death of Ahasuerus. Par Fabian Lagerkvist. LC 81-15937. (Illus.). 1982. 2.95 (ISBN 0-394-70820-2). Vintage Books.

Death of Al-Hallaj: A Dramatic Narrative. Herbert Mason. LC 79-4403. 8.95 (ISBN 0-268-00842-6) (ISBN 0-268-00843-4). University of Notre Dame Press.

Death of an Ad Man. Alfred Eichler. LC 54-5235. 1954. Abelard-Schuman.

Death of an Airman... Christopher St. John Sprigg. LC 35-4594. 1935. Pub. for the Crime Club, Inc., by Doubleday, Doran & Company, Inc.

Death of an Airman... Christopher St. John Sprigg. LC 37-17805. 1937. The Sun Dial Press, Inc.

Death of an Angel. Frances Louise Davis Lockridge & Richard Lockridge. LC 55-6720. (Their A Mr. and Mrs. North mystery). 1955. Lippincott.

Death of an Angel. Margaret Lucile Paine Rea. LC 43-58961. 1943. Pub. for the Crime Club by Doubleday, Doran and Company.

Death of an Angel. Pauline Glen Winslow. LC 75-7656. 1975. 7.95. St. Martin's.

Death of an Angel: A Mr. and Mrs. North Mystery. Frances Louise Davis Lockridge & Richard Lockridge. LC 76-217. 1976. (ISBN 0-89190-907-9). Rivercity Press.

Death of an Angel: A New Grant Kirby Adventure. Kendell Foster Crossen. LC 62-19317. 1963. Bobbs-Merrill.

Death of an Artist. Alfred Eichler. LC 55-10199. 1955. Arcadia House.

Death of an Artist: By John Rhode Pseud. Cecil John Charles Street. LC 56-975655. (Red badge detective). 1956. Dodd, Mead.

Death of an Assassin. John Creasey. 1972. pap. 0.95 o.p. (75-288). Lancer.

Death of an Assassin. John Creasey. 1972. pap. 0.95 o.s.i. (75-288). Lancer.

Death of an Author. Edith Caroline Rivett. LC 37-484376. 1937. The Macaulay Company.

Death of an Author. Cecil John Charles Street. LC 48-1230. (Red badge mystery). 1948. Dodd, Mead.

Death of an Editor. John George Haslette Vahey. LC 31-22797. 1931. W. Morrow & Company.

Death of an Eloquent Man: A Jane Amanda Edwards Story. Charlotte Murray Russell, pseud. LC 36-1116. 1936. Pub. by the Crime Club, Inc., by Doubleday, Doran & Company, Inc.

Death of an Englishman. Magdalen Nabb. LC 82-5576. 1982. 10.95 (ISBN 0-684-17757-9). C. Scribner's Sons.

Death of an Expert Witness. P. D James. LC 77-21530. 7.95 (ISBN 0-684-15267-3). Scribner.

Death of an Expert Witness. P. D James. LC 78-308098. 1977. 8.95 (ISBN 0-571-11107-6). Faber.

Death of an Expert Witness. P. D James. LC 78-15952. 1978. 13.95 (ISBN 0-8161-6600-5). G. K. Hall.

Death of an Informer. Will Perry. LC 73-78094. 1973. (pbk.) 1.25 (ISBN 0-515-03133-X). Pyramid Books.

Death of an Intruder: A Tale of Horror in Three Parts. 1st Ed. Nedra Tyre. LC 52-11756. 1953. Knopf.

Death of an Island. Larry Shealy. (Orig.). 1980. pap. text ed. 1.95 o.s.i. (ISBN 0-505-51557-1). Tower Bks.

Death of an Old Girl. Elizabeth Learchand. 224p. 1980. pap. 1.95 o.p. (ISBN 0-441-14179-X). Charter Bks.

Death of an Old Girl. Elizabeth Learchand. 224p. 1980. pap. 1.95 o.p. (ISBN 0-441-14179-X). Charter Bks.

Death of an Old Girl. Elizabeth Lemarchand. (O.s.i.). 1970. pap. 0.75 o.s.i. (A704S, Award). Univ Pub & Dist.

Death of an Old Goat. Robert Barnard. LC 76-57871. 6.95 (ISBN 0-8027-5365-5). Walker.

Death of an Old Goat. Robert Barnard. LC 82-13269. 1983. 2.95 (ISBN 0-14-006537-7). Penguin Books.

Death of an Old Sinner. Dorothy Salisbury Davis. LC 57-6064. Scribner.

Death of Anger. Allan Seager. LC 60-13088. 1960. McDowell, Obolensky.

Death of Artemio Cruz. Carlos Fuentes. LC 64-14685. 1964. Farrar, Straus.

Death of Attila. Cecelia Holland. LC 72-8386. 1973. 6.95 (ISBN 0-394-47309-4). Knopf.

Death of Attila. Cecelia Holland. 1974. (pbk.) 1.50. Ballantine Books.

Death of Christopher. John Sommerfield. LC 30-276843. J. Cape & H. Smith.

Death of Colonel Johns. Kevin Urick. LC 80-51139. (Illus.). 8.95 (ISBN 0-917976-08-8). White Ewe Press.

Death of Cosmo Revere. Christopher Bush. LC 30-177119. 1930. Pub. for the Crime Club, Inc., by Doubleday, Doran & Company, Inc.

Death of Daddy-O: A Marty Land Mystery. 1st Ed. David Alexander. LC 60-5342. (Main line mysteries). 1960. Lippincott.

Death of Descartes. David Bosworth. LC 81-50637. 1981. 9.95 (ISBN 0-8229-3448-5). University of Pittsburgh.

Death of Dickie Draper, and Nine Other Stories. LC 65-11294. 1965. Random House.

Death of Dickie Draper, and Nine Other Stories. Jerome Weidman. LC 65-11294. 5.95. Random.

Death of Dr. Whitelaw. Alexander Wilson. LC 30-28397. 1930. Longmans, Green and Co.

Death of Doxy. Rex Stout. Incl. The Blood Knot; Hello & Good-Bye; Boesman & Lena. 1966. 3.75 o.p. (ISBN 0-670-26126-2). Viking Pr.

Death of Dreams. William Hoffman. LC 72-92222. 1973. 6.95 (ISBN 0-385-07436-0). Doubleday.

Death of Galahad. Rik Davis. 224p. pap. 1.95 o.p. (6125). Brandon.

Death of Grass. John Christopher. (Alpha Books). (Orig.). 1979. pap. text ed. 2.95x (ISBN 0-19-424232-3). Oxford U Pr.

Death of Hewfik Pasha; a Confession. LC 6-32899. 1886. Funk & Wagnalls.

Death of Horn & Hardart: Special Issue 15. Edward Zuckrow. pap. 1.00 o.p. The Smith.

Death of Humpty Dumpty. David Alexander. LC 57-10051. (His A Bart Hardin mystery novel). 1957. Random House.

Death of Innocence. Zelda Popkin. LC 74-146691. 1971. 6.95. Lippincott.

Death of Ivan Iliitch. Lev Nikolaevich Tolstoi. (On cover: Seaside library. Pocket ed. no. 1071). 1888. G. Munro.

Death of Ivan Illyich. Lev Nikolaevich Tolstoi. Bd. with The Power of Darkness; The Fruits of Enlightenment. 1965. pap. text ed. 1.25 o.s.i. (ISBN 0-03-053555-7, HoltC). HR&W.

Death of Ivan Ilych & Other Stories. Lev Nikolaevich Tolstoi. Tr. by Aylmer Maude. 1960. pap. 1.95 (ISBN 0-451-51676-1, CJ1676, Sig Classics). NAL.

Death of Ivan Ilych & Other Stories. Lev Nikolaevich Tolstoi. Tr. by Louise Maude & Aylmer Maude. (World's Classics Ser). 6.50 o.p. (ISBN 0-19-250432-0, 432). Oxford U Pr.

Death of Ivan Ilyich. Lev Nikolaevich Tolstoi. Tr. by Lynn Solotaroff. (Bantam Classics Ser.). 134p. (gr. 9-12). 1981. pap. 1.95 (ISBN 0-553-21035-1). Bantam.

Death of Ivan Ilyitch, and Other Stories. Lev Nikolaevich Tolstoi & Garnett, Mrs. Constance (Black) 1862- Tr. LC 15-18288. 1915. John Lane Company.

Death of Ivan Ilyitch, and Other Stories. Lev Nikolaevich Tolstoi & Garnett, Mrs. Constance (Black) 1862- Tr. LC 27-27795. 1927. Dodd, Mead and Company.

Death of Jason Darby. Georgia Elizabeth Taylor. LC 70-124279. 1970. 6.95. World Pub. Co.

Death of Jezebel. Christianna Brand, pseud. 1979. 15.00x (ISBN 0-86025-072-5, Pub. by Ian Henry Pubns England). State Mutual Bk.

Death of Jezebel. Mary Christianna Milne Lewis. LC 48-8221. (Red badge detective). 1948. Dodd, Mead.

Death of Jim Lonely: By James Welch. James Welch. 1981. Harper & Row.

Death of Jim Loney. James Welch. LC 79-1713. 10.00 (ISBN 0-06-014588-9). Harper & Row.

Death of John Tait. Archibald E. Fielding. LC 32-157575. 1932. H. C. Kinsey & Company, Inc;

Death of King Pellinore. A. Kooyman. 1981. 4.95 (ISBN 0-533-04154-6). Vantage.

Death of Kings. James Leonard Johnson. LC 72-96244. 1974. 6.95 (ISBN 0-385-02884-9). Doubleday.

Death of Kings. Charles Wertenbaker. Random House.

Death of Kyralessa. Constantin Virgil Gheorghiu. LC 75-3992. 1976. 17.00 (ISBN 0-8371-7991-2). Greenwood Press.

Death of Kyralessa. Constantin Virgil Gheorghiu. LC 68-18270. 1968. H. Regnery Co.

Death of Laurence Vining. Alan Ernest Wentworth Thomas. LC 29-138921. 1929. J. B. Lippincott Company.

Death of Lord Haw Haw: No. 1 Personality of World War No. 2; Being an Account of the Last Days of the Foremost Nazi Spy and News Commentator, the Mysterious English Traitor. Elliot Harold Paul. LC 40-13269. Random House.

Death of Lysanda. Yitzhak Orpaz. Tr. by Richard Flint from Heb. LC 73-109282. (Cape Editions Ser). 1970. 3.50 o.p. (ISBN 0-670-26224-2, Grossman). Viking Pr.

Death of Lysanda. Yitzhak Orpaz. Tr. by Richard Flint from Heb. LC 73-109282. (Cape Editions Ser). 1970. pap. 1.50 o.p. (ISBN 0-670-26225-0, Grossman). Penguin.

Death of Mark. Robin Edgerton Spencer. LC 38-6240. The Bobbs-Merrill Company.

Death of Me Yet. Whit Masterson, pseud. 1975. (pbk.) 1.25. Pinnacle Books.

Death of Me Yet. Whit Masterson, pseud. LC 78-124420. (Red badge novel of suspense). 1970. 4.50. Dodd, Mead.

Death of Men. Allan Massie. LC 81-19197. 1982. 10.95 (ISBN 0-395-31854-8). Houghton Mifflin.

Death of Mr. Baltisberger. Bohumil Hrabal. LC 74-4737. 1975. (ISBN 0-385-00692-6). Doubleday.

Death of Monsieur Gallet. Georges Simenon. LC 32-35926. Covici, Fiede.

Death of My Aunt. Clifford Henry Benn Kitchin. LC 30-4655. Harcourt, Brace and Company.

Death of No Lady. Seldon Truss, pseud. LC 52-8055. 1952. Published for the Crime Club by Doubleday.

Death of Nora Ryan. James Thomas Farrell. LC 77-83935. 1978. 10.00 (ISBN 0-385-13450-9). Doubleday.

Death of of an Ambassador: A Tommy Hambledon Story. 1st Ed. Manning Coles, pseud. LC 57-10009. 1957. Published for the Crime Club by Doubleday.

Death of Our Dear One. Margaret Erskine, pseud. Orig. Title: Look Behind You, Lady. 256p. 1973. Repr. of 1956 ed. lib. bdg. 5.95 o.s.i. (ISBN 0-85617-815-2). White Lion Pubs.

Death of Peterson's Wharf. Charles Brooks. LC 63-14194. 1963. Macmillan.

Death of Ruth. Elizabeth Kata. LC 81-21552. 9.95 (ISBN 0-312-18751-3). St. Martin's Press.

Death of Satan. Antonin Artaud. Tr. by Alastair Hamilton. 1980. pap. 3.95 (ISBN 0-7145-1085-8). Riverrun NY.

Death of Society: A Novel of Tomorrow. Florence Roma Muir Wilson O'Brien. LC 21-10336. 2.00. George H. Doran Company.

Death of Society: A Novel of Tomorrow. Florence Roma Muir Wilson O'Brien. LC 21-10336. 2.00. George H. Doran Company.

Death of Society: A Novel of Tomorrow. Florence Roma Muir Wilson O'Brien. LC 28-16622. 1928. A. A. Knopf.

Death of the Adversary. Hans Keilson. Tr. by Ivo Jarosy. 1962. 3.95 o.p. (ISBN 0-670-26119-X, Orion Pr). Grossman.

Death of the Artist. Rudolf Radama Von Abele. 111p. 1980. Repr. of 1955 ed. lib. bdg. 20.00 (ISBN 0-8492-2831-X). R West.

Death of the Claimant. A Richard Martin. LC 29-7497. 1929. R. M. McBride & Company.

Death of the Deputy. Roger Francis Didelot. Tr. by Abbott, Elizabeth. LC 35-105865. J. B. Lippincott Company.

Death of the Detective. Mark Smith. LC 73-20769. 1974. 8.95 (ISBN 0-394-48766-4). Knopf; Distributed by Random House.

Death of the Falcon. Nick Carter. (Nick Carter Ser). (O.s.i.). 192p. (Orig.). 1974. pap. 1.25 o.s.i. (AQ1354, Award). Univ Pub & Dist.

Death of the Fox. George Palmer Garrett. LC 79-139022. 1971. 10.00. Doubleday.

Death of the Fuehrer. Ronald Puccetti. 160p. (Orig.). 1973. pap. 0.75 o.p. (T2897, GM). Fawcett World.

Death of the Fuhrer. Roland Puccetti. (Gold Medal Book, T2897). 1973. (pbk.) 0.75. Fawcett Pubns.

Death of the Fuhrer. Ronald Puccetti. LC 72-90572. 1973. 5.95. St. Martin's Press.

Death of the Gods. Dmitrii Sergeevich Merezhkovskii. Tr. & intro. by Herbert Treuch. LC 82-82473. (Spiritual Fiction Publications: Vol. 8). 464p. 1982. Repr. of 1904 ed. 15.00 (ISBN 0-89345-407-9, Spiritual Fiction). Garber Comm.

Death of the Gods. Dmitrii Sergeevich Merezhkovskil. Tr. by Trench, Herbert. (His Christ and Antichrist. 1st division). 1901. G. P. Putnam's Sons; Etc., Etc.

Death of the Good Samaritan. Owen D. Johnston. 216p. 1979. 6.95 o.p. (ISBN 0-8059-2477-9). Dorrance.

Death of the Heart. Elizabeth Bowen. LC 55-3817. (Vintage book, K-21). 1955. Vintage Books.

Death of the Heart. Elizabeth Bowen. LC 38-32634. 1938. V. Gollancz, Ltd.

Death of the Heart. Elizabeth Bowen. LC 38-29084. 1939. A. A. Knopf.

Death of the Hind Legs: And Other Stories. John Barrington Wain. LC 66-22545. 1966. bds., 4.50. Viking.

Death of the King's Canary. Dylan Thomas & John Davenport. LC 77-352534. 1976. 3.25 (ISBN 0-09-127510-5). Hutchinson.

Death of the King's Canary. Dylan Thomas & John Davenport. LC 78-314472. 1978. 2.50 (ISBN 0-14-004577-5). Penguin Books.

Death of the Lion see Lesson of the Master.

Death of the Novel and Other Stories. Ronald Sukenick. LC 75-76963. 1969. 4.95. Dial Press.

Death of the Orange Trees. Claire Nicolas. LC 62-20124. 1963. Harper & Row.

Death of the Poet King. James H Comey. LC 75-10410. 4.95 (ISBN 0-8283-1614-7). Branden Press.

Death of the Red King. Pamela Bennetts. LC 76-10543. 1976. 7.95 (ISBN 0-7091-5123-3). St. Martin's Press.

Death of Virgil. Hermann Broch & Untermeyer, Jean (Starr) 1886- Tr. LC 45-8650. 1945. Pantheon Books Inc.

Death of Virgil. Tr. from German by Jean Starr Untermeyer. Herman Broch. LC 65-23529. (Universal lib., UI-184). pap., 2.95. Grosses.

Death of Virgil. Tr. from German by Jean Starr Untermeyer. Hermann Broch. (Universal lib. bk. UL184 rebound). 1966. 5.00. P. Smith.

Death of William Posters: 1st Amer. Ed. Alan Sillitoe. LC 65-187516. bds., 4.95. Knopf.

Death on a Back Bench. 1st Ed. Francis Hobson. LC 60-75540. Harper.

Death on a Dude Ranch. Bonnamy. LC 37-3367. 1937. Pub. for the Crime Club, Inc., by Doubleday, Doran & Co., Inc.

Death on a Dude Ranch. Francis Bonnamy. LC 37-336718. 1937. Pub. for the Crime Club, Inc., by Doubleday, Doran & Co., Inc.

Death on a Ferris Wheel. Aylwin Lee Martin. LC 51-32206. (Gold medal books, 170). 1951. Fawcett Publications.

Death on a Quiet Day: By Michael Innes Pseud. John Innes Mackintosh Stewart. LC 57-58676. (Red badge detective). 1957. Dodd, Mead.

Death on a Warm Wind. Douglas Warner. LC 70-82954. 1969. 4.50. Published for the Crime Club by Doubleday.

Death on All Hallows. Alian Campbell McLean. LC 58-12248. 1958. Washburn.

Death on an Island. Gayle Roper. (Chime Suspense Ser.: No. 301). 1980. pap. 2.50 o.p. (ISBN 0-89191-294-0). Cook.

Death on Capitol Hill. Ben Whitehurst & Faith Wiley. 1970. 4.50 o.p. Vantage.

Death on Display. Roger Simons. LC 69-13184. 1969. 3.95 o.p. Roy.

Death on Doomsday. Elizabeth Lemarchand. LC 74-82172. 1975. 5.95 (ISBN 0-8027-5310-8). Walker.

Death on My Left: A Colonel Gethryn Mystery... Philip MacDonald. LC 33-70923. 1933. Pub. for the Crime Club, Inc., by Doubleday, Doran & Company, Inc.

Death on Scurvy Street. Ben Ames Williams. LC 29-10484. E. P. Dutton & Company, Inc.

Death on the Agenda. Patricia Moyes. LC 62-123289. (Rinehart suspense novel). 1962. Holt, Rinehart and Winston.

Death on the Air. Agatha Miller Christie. 1973. 0.95. Popular Library.

Death on the Air. Herman Landon. LC 29-8317. 1929. H. Liveright.

Death on the Aisle: A Mr. and Mrs. North Mystery. Frances Louise Davis Lockridge & Lockridge, Richard. LC 42-10938. 1942. J. B. Lippincott Company.

Death on the Boat Train. Cecil John Charles Street. LC 40-2891. 1940. Dodd, Mead & Company.

Death on the Border. Raymond Peckham Holden. H. Holt and Company.

Death on the Bridge. Royce Howes. LC 35-20678. 1935. Pub. for the Crime Club, Inc., by Doubleday, Doran & Company, Inc.

Death on the Campus. Addison Simmons. LC 35-11493. Thomas Y. Crowell Company.

Death on the Center Court: A McLean of Scotland Yard Mystery. George Goodchild. LC 36-8772. Green Circle Books.

Death on the Clock. Gertrude Knevels. 1940. Pub. for the Crime Club by Doubleday, Doran and Co., Inc.

Death on the Cuff. M G McKnutt. LC 51-12922. 1951. Phoenix Press.

Death on the Deep... Humphrey Meigh Stephenson. LC 30-32386. 1931. Pub. for the Crime Club, Inc., by Doubleday, Doran & Company, Inc.

Death on the Diamond: A Baseball Mystery Story. Cortland Fitzsimmons. LC 34-13763. 1934. Frederick A. Stokes Company.

Death on the Door Mat. Mary Violet Heberden. LC 39-25147. 1939. Pub. for the Crime Club, Inc., by Doubleday, Doran & Co.

Death on the Dragon's Tongue. Margot Arnold, pseud. LC 82-80216. 224p. (Orig.). 1982. pap. 2.50 (ISBN 0-86721-150-4). Playboy Pbks.

Death on the Eno. Amanda Mackay. LC 81-8310. 12.95 (ISBN 0-316-55993-8). Little, Brown.

Death on the Heath. Alan Hunter. LC 81-71199. 1982. 10.95 (ISBN 0-8027-5468-6). Walker.

Death on the High C's. Robert Barnard. LC 78-62353. 1978. 7.95 (ISBN 0-8027-5398-1). Walker.

Death on the Hour. Richard Lockridge. LC 74-2173. 1974. 6.95 (ISBN 0-397-00989-5). Lippincott.

Death on the Installment Plan. Louis-Ferdinand Celine, pseud. Tr. by Ralph Manheim. LC 48-6410. 1971. pap. 8.95 (ISBN 0-8112-0017-5, NDP330). New Directions.

Death on the Installment Plan. Louis Ferdinand Destouches. LC 67-1949. (Signet book). 1966. New American Library.

Death on the Installment Plan. Louis Ferdinand Destouches. LC 66-18692. (New Directions book). 1966. New Directions Pub. Corp.

Death on the Installment Plan. Louis Ferdinand Destouches. Tr. by Marks, John H. P. LC 38-20120. 1938. Little, Brown and Company.

Death on the Last Train. George Bellairs. LC 49-650479. 1949. Macmillan Co.

Death on the Late Show. Jan Michaels. (Mystery Puzzler Ser.: No. 14). (Illus., Orig.). 1979. pap. 1.95 (ISBN 0-89083-434-2). Zebra.

Death on the Lawn: By John Rhode Pseud. Cecil John Charles Street. LC 55-613356. (Red badge detective). Dodd, Mead,

Death on the Limited. Roger Denbie, pseud. LC 33-13643. 1933. W. Morrow & Company.

Death on the Mountain. Dorothy Ogburn. LC 31-961. 1931. Little, Brown, and Company.

Death on the Nile. Agatha Miller Christie. LC 38-27086. 1938. Dodd, Mead & Company.

Death on the Nose. H. Donald Spatz. LC 42-25354. 1942. Phoenix Press.

Death on the Outer Shoal. Anne Fuller & Allen, Marcus. LC 34-145381. E. P. Dutton & Co., Inc.

Death on the Pampas: A Story of Modern Espionage. Clement Wood. LC 44-9754. 1944. Mystery House.

Death on the Reserve. Josephine Bell. 1967. 3.95 o.p. Macmillan.

Death on the Reserve: By Josephine Bell. Doris Bell Collier Ball. LC 67-10303. (Cock Robin mystery). 1966. Macmillan.

Death on the River Kwai. Gerard De Villiers. (Malko,#8). 1975. (pbk.) 1.25 (ISBN 0-523-00541-5). Pinnacle Books.

Death on the Rocks. John Richard Lane Anderson. LC 74-26614. 1975. 6.95 (ISBN 0-8128-1765-6). Stein and Day.

Death on the Set. Victor MacClure. LC 35-7532. J. B. Lippincott Company.

Death on the Slopes. Norma Schier. (Mystery Puzzler Ser.: No. 11). (Illus., Orig.). 1978. pap. 1.95 (ISBN 0-89083-423-7). Zebra.

Death on the Waterfront. Robert Archer. LC 41-22606. 1941. Pub. for the Crime Club by Doubleday, Doran and Co., Inc.

Death on Treasure Trail. Davis Dresser. LC 49-10732. (Triple-A western classic.). 1949. Jefferson House.

Death Out of Darkness. John Creasey. LC 78-148410. (Falcon's head mystery). 1971. 5.95. World Pub. Co.

Death Out of Focus. William Campbell Gault. LC 59-5713. (Random House mystery). 1959. Random House.

Death Out of Season. Emanuel Litvinoff. LC 73-19260. 1974. 6.95 (ISBN 0-684-13755-0). Scribner.

Death Out of the Night. Robert McNair Wilson. LC 33-170009. J. B. Lippincott Company.

Death Out of Thin Air. Clayton Rawson. LC 41-3687. Coward-McCann.

Death Over Deep Water: By Simon Nash Pseud. Raymond Chapman. LC 65-238141. 1965. bds., 2.95. Roy.

Death Over Her Shoulder. Dorothy Cole Meade. LC 39-30685. 1939. C. Scribner's Sons.

Death Over Hollywood. Charles Saxby & Molnar, Louis, Joint Author. LC 37-39103. 1937. E. P. Dutton & Co., Inc.

Death Over London. Malcolm Wheeler-Nicholson. LC 40-89389. 1940. Gateway Books.

Death Over Newark. Alexander Hazard Williams. W. F. Payson.

Death Over San Silvestro. Mike Teagle. LC 37-15597. 1936. Hillman-Curl, Inc.

Death Paints a Picture. Miles Burton. 1978. 11.00x o.p. (ISBN 0-86025-069-5, Pub. by Ian Henry Pubns England). State Mutual Bk.

Death Paints a Picture. Miles Burton. 1977. 6.50 o.p. State Mutual Bk.

Death Paints a Portrait. 1st Ed. William Herber. LC 58-6906. (Main line mysteries). 1958. Lippincott.

Death Paints the Picture. Lawrence Lariar. LC 43-2347. 1943. Phoenix Press.

Death Pays a Dividend. Cecil John Charles Street. LC 39-17422. 1939. Dodd, Mead & Company.

Death Pays the Piper: A Case for Superintendent Slade. Leonard Reginald Gribble. LC 58-77864. Roy Publishers.

Death Plays Solitaire. Raymond Leslie Goldman. LC 39-2157. Coward-McCann, Inc.

Death Plays the Gramophone: A Mystery Novel. Marjorie Stafford. LC 53-5928. 1953. Macmillan.

Death Points a Finger. William Levine. LC 33-8141. 1933. The Mystery League.

Death Pool. John George Haslette Vahey. LC 31-8641. 1931. W. Morrow & Company.

Death Raid. Jon Hart. LC 81-65241. (Mercenaries Ser.). 128p. 1981. pap. 2.95 (ISBN 0-87754-244-9). Chelsea Hse.

Death Range. Eugene A. Clancy. (Orig.). 1971. pap. 0.60 o.p. (06140). Curtis.

Death Rattle. Alfred Betts Caldwell. LC 40-9441. 1940. Pub for the Crime Club by Doubleday, Doran and Company, Inc.

Death Rattle: Translated from the German. Hanns Gobsch. Tr. by Morrow, Ian Fitzherbert Despard. LC 32-12196. 1932. Little, Brown, and Company.

Death Ray Terror, No. 34. Lionel Derrick, pseud. (Penetrator Ser.). (Orig.). 1979. pap. 1.50 (ISBN 0-523-40631-2). Pinnacle Bks.

Death Reign of the Vampire King. Grant Stockbridge. (Spider#1). 1975. (pbk.) 0.95 (ISBN 0-671-77952-4). Pocket Books.

Death Ride. William M. James. (Apache Ser.: No. 24). 208p. (Orig.). 1983. pap. 1.95 (ISBN 0-523-41675-X). Pinnacle Bks.

Death Rider. John H. Hamlin. LC 39-204421. Dodge Publishing Company.

Death Rider. Nina Toye. LC 16-442985. 1916. Cassell and Company, Ltd.

Death Rider: By J. O. Barnwell Pseud. Joseph Caruso. LC 55-135076. 1955. Macmillan.

Death Rider: By J. O. Barnwell Pseud. Joseph Caruso. LC 57-214. (Signet book, 1366). 1957. New American Library.

Death-Riders. Cornelius Cofyn. LC 36-783348. 1935. A. A. Knopf.

Death Rides a Black Horse. Lewis B Patten. LC 77-16851. 1978. 7.95 (ISBN 0-385-14008-8). Doubleday.

Death Rides a Black Horse. Lewis B Patten. LC 79-22192. 1979. 1.50. G. K. Hall.

Death Rides a Black Horse. Lewis B Patten. (Signet Book). 1979. 1.50 (ISBN 0-451-08708-9). New American Library.

Death Rides a Black Steed. Luanna Churchill. LC 75-2138. 1975. 4.95 (ISBN 0-517-52167-9). Lenox Hill Press.

Death Rides a Hobby. Royce Howes. LC 39-22926. 1939. Pub. for the Crime Club, Inc., by Doubleday, Doran and Company, Inc.

Death Rides a Painted Horse. 1st Ed. Robert Patrick Wilmot, pseud. LC 53-102226. (Main line mysteries). 1954. Lippincott.

Death Rides a Sorrel Horse. Albert Benjamin Cunningham. LC 46-17859. 1946. E. P. Dutton & Company, Inc.

Death Rides Tandem. Walbridge McCully. LC 42-24968. 1942. Published for the Crime Club by Doubleday, Doran & Company, Inc.

Death Rides the Air Line. John Murray Cooper. LC 34-38183. C. Kendall.

Death Rides the Desert. Amos Moore. LC 39-30327. I. Washburn, Inc.

Death Rides the Dondrino. 1st Ed. Roe Richmond. LC 54-11118. 1954. Little, Brown.

Death Rides the Dragon. Eugene Thomas. LC 32-313026. Sears Publishing Company, Inc.

Death Rides the Forest: A Gunston Cotton Secret Service Story. Rupert Grayson. LC 38-19639. 1938. E. P. Dutton & Co., Inc.

Death Rides the Mess. Tom Gill. Farrar & Rinehart, Incorporated.

Death Rides the Night: "a Powder Valley Western,". Peter Field. LC 44-8478. 1944. Jefferson House.

Death Rides the Pecos. Davis Dresser. LC 49-799720. (Triple-A western classic). 1949. Jefferson House.

Death Rides the Pecos. Davis Dresser. LC 40-11749. 1941. W. Morrow & Company.

Death Rides the Rails. Jim Hopwood. (Orig.). 1980. pap. 1.95 (ISBN 0-532-23126-0). Woodhill.

Death Rides the Range. Robert Ames Bennet. LC 35-2614. 1935. I. Washburn.

Death Rides the Star Route. Jackson Cole. 1974. (pbk.) 0.95. Popular Library.

Death Rings a Bell. Cortland Fitzsimmons. LC 42-160571. 1942. J. B. Lippincott Company.

Death Rocks the Cradle. Neil Bell. 1978. 9.95 (ISBN 0-86025-050-4). State Mutual Bk.

Death Sails in a High Wind. Theodora McCormick Du Bois. 1945. Pub. for the Crime Club by Doubleday, Doran & Company, Inc.

Death Sails the Bay. John R Feegel. LC 78-55630. 1978. 1.95 (ISBN 0-380-01972-8). Avon.

Death Sails the Nile. Frances Burks McKinley. LC 33-38004. The Stratford Company.

Death Sails with Magellan. Charles Ford. LC 37-356543. Random House.

Death Scene. Betty Suyker. LC 80-29306. 1981. 10.95 (ISBN 0-312-18872-2). St. Martin's Press.

Death-School. J. N. Williamson. 1982. pap. 2.95 (ISBN 0-89083-981-6). Zebra.

Death Schuss. Lillian O'Donnell. LC 63-12466. (Raven book). 1963. Abelard-Schuman.

Death Scouts. Richard Woodley. (Man from Atlantis). (Dell Book: No. 2). 1977. 1.50 (ISBN 0-440-15369-7). Dell Pub. Co.

Death Sends a Cable. Margaret Tayler Yates. LC 38-33209. 1938. The Macmillan Company.

Death Sentence. Maurice Blanchot. Tr. by Lydia Davis from French. LC 78-59907. Orig. Title: L'Arret De Mort. 88p. 1978. 10.00 (ISBN 0-930794-05-2); pap. 4.95 (ISBN 0-930794-04-4). Station Hill Pr.

Death Sentence. Brian Wynne Garfield. 1976. 1.75 (ISBN 0-449-23001-5). Fawcett Crest.

Death Sentence. Leo P. Kelley. LC 79-51081. (Space Police Bks.). 1979. pap. 4.24 (ISBN 0-8224-6382-2). Pitman Learning.

Death Sentence. Alice Duer Miller. LC 35-2810. 1935. Dodd, Mead & Company.

Death Serves an Ace. Helen Wills & Murphy, Robert W., Joint Author. LC 39-27748. 1939. C. Scribner's Sons.

Death Set to Music. John Harris. LC 82-73568. 1983. 12.95 (ISBN 0-8027-5487-2). Walker.

Death Set to Music. Mark Hebden, pseud. 1979. 16.95 (ISBN 0-241-10085-2, Pub. by Hamish Hamilton England). David & Charles.

Death Set to Music. Mark Hebden, pseud. 192p. 1983. 12.95 (ISBN 0-8027-5487-2). Walker & Co.

Death Shall Overcome. Emma Lathen, pseud. LC 66-21159. (Cock robin mystery). 1966. 3.95. Macmillan.

Death Shall Overcome. Emma Lathen, pseud. 1974. (pbk.) 0.95. Pocket Books.

Death Ship. B. Traven. LC 72-96593. 384p. 1973. Repr. of 1934 ed. 12.00 o.s.i. (ISBN 0-88208-034-2). Lawrence Hill.

Death Ship. B. Traven. 1962. pap. 2.25 o.s.i. (ISBN 0-02-025750-3, Collier). Macmillan.

Death Ship: A Strange Story. William Clark Russell. LC 75-46306. (Supernatural and Occult Fiction). 1976. (3 vols. in one) 48.00 (ISBN 0-405-08166-9). Arno Press.

Death Ship. A Strange Story. An Account of a Cruise in the "Flying Dutchman," Collected from the Papers of the Late Mr. Geoffrey Fenton, of Poplar, Master Mariner. William Clark Russell. (On cover: Seaside library. Pocket ed., no. 1129). 1888. G. Munro.

Death Ship: Or The Pirate's Bride, and the Maniac of the Deep. A Nautical Romance. LC 6-32898. 1847. G. H. Williams.

Death Ship: The Story of an American Sailor. B Traven. LC 72-96593. 1973. 8.50 (ISBN 0-88208-034-2). L. Hill.

Death Ship: The Story of an American Sailor. B Traven. LC 34-9916. 1934. A. A. Knopf.

Death Sits in. Harry A Keller. LC 32-24135. 1932. Brentano's.

Death Sits on the Board. Cecil John Charles Street. LC 37-132747. 1937. Dodd, Mead & Company.

Death Slams the Door. Paul Cade. LC 38-2815. (Modern age books. Blue seal books. 23). Modern Age Books, Inc.

Death, Sleep & the Traveler. John Hawkes. LC 73-89481. 1974. 6.95 (ISBN 0-8112-0522-3). New Directions Pub. Corp.

Death Smiles. Russell R Phillips. The Macaulay Company.

Death Solves Nothing. Margaret Sothern & Carter, Barbara Barclay, Tr. LC 38-147031. 1938. Sheed & Ward.

Death Specialists. Gary Paulsen. 1976. pap. 1.50 (ISBN 0-89041-114-X, 3114). Major Bks.

Death Squad. Don Pendleton. (Executioner Ser.: No. 2). 192p. (Orig.). 1982. pap. 2.25 (ISBN 0-523-41714-4). Pinnacle Bks.

Death Squad. Nelson H. Smith. 1976. 5.95 o.p. (ISBN 0-8059-2288-1). Dorrance.

Death Stalk. Thomas Chastain. (O.s.i.). (Orig.). 1971. pap. 0.95 o.s.i. (AN1428, Award). Univ Pub & Dist.

Death Stalk. Richard Grayson. LC 82-16925. 1983. 10.95 (ISBN 0-312-18805-6). St. Martin's Press.

Death Stalk. Richard Grindal. 192p. 1983. 10.95 (ISBN 0-312-18805-6). St Martin.

Death Stalk. Bob Langley. LC 79-22672. (Penguin crime). 1980. 2.50 (ISBN 0-14-005328-X). Penguin Books.

Death Stalk. Robert Langley. LC 77-27710. 1978. 7.95 (ISBN 0-385-14173-4). Published for the Crime Club by Doubleday.

Death Stalk in Spain. Don Smith. (Secret Mission Ser). (O.s.i.). 192p. 1972. pap. 0.95 o.s.i. (AN1040, Award). Univ Pub & Dist.

Death Stalks a Marriage. Russell W Larson. LC 56-8639. 1956. Bellevue Books.

Death Stalks the Cheyenne Trail. William E. Vance. LC 80-926. (Double D Western Ser.). 192p. 1980. 10.95 o.p. (ISBN 0-385-15518-2). Doubleday.

Death Stalks the Cobbled Square. John Newton Chance. LC 46-4291. 1946. R. M. McBride & Company.

Death Stalks the Fleet. Harley Cope. LC 40-3251. Lymanhouse.

Death Stalks the Punjab. Melvin A. Casberg. LC 80-23558. 6.95 (ISBN 0-89407-045-2). Strawberry Hill Press.

Death Stalks the Range: A Western Novel. Brett Rider. LC 45-2149. 1945. Macrae-Smith-Company.

Death Star: A Novel. Robert Moss. LC 81-7772. 13.95 (ISBN 0-517-54487-3). Crown.

Death Stops the Bells: Franklin Russell's Third Case. Richard Merriam Baker. LC 38-7062. 1938. C. Scribner's Sons.

Death Stops the Frolic. George Bellairs. LC 44-374415. 1944. The Macmillan Company.

Death Stops the Manuscript: Franklin Russell's First Case. Richard Merriam Baker. LC 36-171234. 1936. C. Scribner's Sons.
Death Stops the Rehearsal: Franklin Russell's Second Case. Richard Merriam Baker. LC 37-3928. 1937. C. Scribner's Sons.
Death Stops the Show. Lloyd S Thompson. LC 46-19198. 1948. Crown Publishers.
Death Strain. Nick Carter. (Nick Carter Ser.). (O.s.i.). (Orig.). 1970. pap. 0.95 o.s.i. (AN1307, Award). Univ Pub & Dist.
Death Strain. Nick Carter. (Nick Carter Ser.). (O.s.i.). 1976. pap. 1.25 o.s.i. (AQ1615, Award). Univ Pub & Dist.
Death Strikes at Heron House: A Jerry Mooney Story. Kerry O'Neil. LC 44-297818. 1944. Farrar & Rinehart.
Death Strikes Home. Minna Wesselhoft Glidden. LC 37-22494. Phoenix Press.
Death Sty: A Novel. Raymond Cousse. LC 79-2349. 1979. 9.50 (ISBN 0-394-50867-X). Grove Press: Distributed by Random House.
Death Sty: A Pig's Tale. Raymond Cousse. LC 79-2349. Orig. Title: Strategie Pour Deux Jambons. 1980. 5.95 (ISBN 0-394-17573-5, E747, Ever). Grove.
Death Style. J. C. Conaway. 1977. pap. 1.50 o.s.i. (ISBN 0-505-51160-6). Tower Bks.
Death Switch. Henry Henn. (Orig.). 1980. pap. 2.25 (ISBN 0-532-23221-6). Woodhill.
Death Syndicate. Judson Pentecost Philips. LC 39-32629. I. Washburn, Inc.
Death Takes a Bow. Frances Louise Davis Lockridge & Richard Lockridge. LC 48-20688. 1948. Avon Book Co.
Death Takes a Bow. Frances Louise Davis Lockridge & Richard Lockridge. LC 43-4641. 1943. J. B. Lippincott Company.
Death Takes a Dive. Eric Heath. LC 38-13189. 1938. Hillman Curl, Inc.
Death Takes a Dive. Alfred Tack. LC 57-9670. 1957. Roy Publishers.
Death Takes a Gamble: By Richard H. R. Smithies. Richard H. R Smithies. (Signet T3591). 1968. New Amer. Lib.
Death Takes a Partner: By John Rhode. Cecil John Charles Street. LC 56-5738. (Red badge detective). 1959. Dodd, Mead.
Death Takes a Paying Guest. Aaron Marc Stein. LC 47-30472. 1947. Pub. for the Crime Club by Doubleday.
Death Takes a Sabbatical. Robert Bernard Martin. LC 67-11088. 1967. Norton.
Death Takes Small Bites. George Henry Johnston. LC 51-517. (Red badge detective). 1948. Dodd, Mead.
Death Takes the Stage. Charles Rodda. LC 34-22371. 1934. Little, Brown, and Company.
Death Talks Shop. Stephen Longstreet. LC 38-5864. 1938. Hillman-Curl, Inc.
Death Talks Shop. Henri Weiner, pseud. LC 38-5864. 1938. Hillman-Curl, Inc.
Death Tears a Comic Strip. Theodora McCormick Du Bois. LC 39-44951. 1939. Houghton Mifflin Company.
Death, the Knight, and the Lady: A Ghost Story. Henry De Vere Stacpoole. LC 34-3896. 1897. John Lane.
Death, the Red Flower. Oswald Wynd. (P 3460). 1968. New Amer. Lib.
Death, the Red Flower: 1st Amer. Ed. Oswald Wynd. LC 65-21042. 3.95. Harcourt.
Death, the Sure Physician. John Wakefield. LC 66-11459. (Red badge detective). 1966. Dodd, Mead.
Death Therapy see Terapia De Muerte.
Death Through the Looking Glass. Richard Forrest. 1979. 1.75 (ISBN 0-671-82157-1). Pocket Books.
Death Through the Looking Glass: A Novel of Suspense. Richard Forrest. LC 77-15438. 7.95 (ISBN 0-672-52379-5). Bobbs-Merrill.
Death Thumbs a Ride. Jean Lilly. LC 44-167. (Black cat detective series). 1943. Crestwood Publishing Co., Inc.
Death Thumbs a Ride. Jean Lilly. LC 40-2005. 1940. E. P. Dutton & Co., Inc.
Death to a Downbeat. Carter Brown, pseud. (Orig.). 1980. pap. 1.75 (ISBN 0-505-51572-5). Tower Bks.
Death to Drumbeat. Jeremy Lane. LC 44-69402. 1944. Phoenix Press.
Death to My Enemy. Brian Mooney. LC 78-61261. 1978. 2.98 (ISBN 0-913306-02-9). Partridge Publications.
Death to My Killer: By Jeremy York. John Creasey. LC 66-28634. (Cock Robin mystery). 1966. bds., 3.95. Macmillan.
Death to Slow Music. 1st American Ed. Beverley Nichols. LC 56-8297. (Dutton guilt edged mystery). 1956. Dutton.
Death to the Inquisitive! A Story of Sinful Love. Lurana W Sheldon. 1892. W. D. Rowland.
Death to the Landlords! Edith Pargeter. LC 76-170244. 1972. 5.95. W. Morrow.
Death to the Landlords! Ellis Peters. 224p. (YA) 1972. 5.95 o.p. (ISBN 0-688-00093-2). Morrow.
Death to the Ranger. Bradford Scott. (Orig.). 1970. pap. 0.60 o.p. (X2151). Pyramid Pubns.
Death Tolls the Bell. Paul McGuire. LC 34-465. 1938. Coward-McCann, Inc.
Death Took a Greek God. Norman Forrest, pseud. LC 40-23795. 1938. Hillman-Curl, Inc.
Death Took a Publisher. Norman Forrest, pseud. LC 38-24393. 1938. Hillman-Curl, Inc.
Death Tour. David J. Michael. (Signet Book.). 1979. 2.25 (ISBN 0-451-08842-5). New American Library.
Death Tour: A Novel. David J. Michael. LC 78-55652. 1978. 8.95 (ISBN 0-672-52513-5). Bobbs-Merrill.
Death Trail. George G. Gilman, pseud. (Steele: No. 12). 1978. pap. 1.50 (ISBN 0-523-40378-X). Pinnacle Bks.
Death Train. Gordon Davis, pseud. (Sgt. Ser.: No. 1). 256p. (Orig.). 1980. pap. 2.25 (ISBN 0-89083-600-0). Zebra.
Death Train. William M James. (Apache Series, 4). 1975. (pbk.) 1.25 (ISBN 0-523-00692-6). Pinnacle Books.
Death Trap. Harry Carmichael. 1971. 4.95 o.p. (ISBN 0-8415-0137-8). Sat Rev Pr.
Death Trap. Paul H Dobbins. LC 51-4813. 1951. Phoenix Press.
Death Trap. Edith Pinero Green. 1975. (pbk.) 0.95. Dell.
Death Trap. John Dann MacDonald. 256p. 1982. pap. 2.50 (ISBN 0-449-14323-6, GM). Fawcett.
Death Trap. Leopold Horace Ognall. LC 70-160058. (McCall suspense novel). 1971. 4.95 (ISBN 0-8415-0137-8). McCall Pub. Co.
Death Trap. Joseph Rosenberger. (Murder Master Ser.: No. 1). 192p. (Orig.). 1973. pap. 1.25 o.p. (ISBN 0-532-12186-4). Woodhill.
Death Trap. Joseph Rosenberger. (Murder master, #1). 1973. (pbk.) 1.25. Manor Books.
Death Trap: An Original Novel. John Dann MacDonald. LC 57-699643. (Dell first edition, A130). 1957. Dell Pub. Co.
Death Trap on the Platte. Cliff Farrell. LC 68-16887. 1968. Doubleday.
Death Traps. Kay Cleaver Strahan. LC 30-15340. 1930. Pub. for the Crime Club, Inc., by Doubleday, Doran & Company, Inc.
Death Trick. J. F. Burke. LC 74-21813. 1975. 6.95 (ISBN 0-06-010577-1). Harper & Row.
Death Trick. Richard Stevenson. LC 80-29318. 9.95 (ISBN 0-312-18876-5). St. Martin's Press.
Death Turns a Trick. Julie Smith. LC 82-60308. 1982. 11.95 (ISBN 0-8027-5482-1). Walker.
Death Turns Right. Joseph Mathewson. 176p. (Orig.). 1982. pap. 2.25 (ISBN 0-380-79210-9, 79210). Avon.
Death Turns the Tables. John Dickson Carr. LC 42-996. Harper & Brothers.
Death Turns Traitor. Walter S Masterman. LC 36-3539. E. P. Dutton & Co., Inc.
Death Under Par. Janice Law, pseud. LC 80-20307. 1981. 9.95 (ISBN 0-395-30227-7). Houghton Mifflin.
Death Under Sail. Charles Percy Snow. LC 75-46000. (Fifty Classics of Crime Fiction, 1900-1950; 44). 1976. 12.00 (ISBN 0-8240-2393-5). Garland Pub.
Death Under Sail... Charles Percy Snow. LC 32-240618. Pub. for the Crime Club, Inc., by Doubleday, Doran & Company, Inc.
Death Under Sail. Charles Percy Snow. LC 81-50155. 1981. 10.95 (ISBN 0-684-16735-2). Scribners.
Death Under the Moonflower. Todd Downing. LC 39-721150. 1938. Pub. for the Crime Club, Inc., by Doubleday, Doran & Company, Inc.
Death Valley. William M. James, pseud. (Apache Ser.: No. 23). 208p. (Orig.). 1983. pap. 1.95 (ISBN 0-523-41025-5). Pinnacle Bks.
Death Valley Gold. John Benteen. (Fargo series). 1976. (pbk.) 1.25. Belmont Tower Books.
Death Valley Scotty. Henry Johnson. LC 73-87363. 15.00 (ISBN 0-87046-019-6, Pub. by Trans-Anglo). Interurban.
Death Valley Slim. Nelson Nye. 144p. 1976. pap. 1.95 (ISBN 0-441-14196-X). Ace Bks.
Death Visits Downspring. Miles Burton. LC 41-18050. 1941. Pub. for the Crime Club by Doubleday, Doran & Company, Inc.
Death Visits the Apple Hole. Albert Benjamin Cunningham. LC 45-2939. 1945. E. P. Dutton & Company, Inc.
Death Waited at Rialto Creek. Lewis B Patten. LC 66-24312. (A Double D western). 1966. Doubleday.
Death Waits in Sensispace. Kurt Mahr. (Perry Rhodan, 61). (Illus.). 1975. (pbk.) 0.95. Ace Books.
Death Walked in Berlin. Mary Margaret Kay. LC 55-30081. 1955. Staples Press.
Death Walks in Eastrepps. Francis Beeding. LC 66-3628. (Seagull library of mystery and suspense). 1966. Norton.
Death Walks in Eastrepps. Francis Beeding. LC 31-8218. 1931. The Mystery League, Inc.
Death Walks in Eastrepps. Francis Beeding. LC 80-65688. 1980. 4.00 (ISBN 0-486-24014-2). Dover Publications.
Death Walks in Eastrepps. Introd. by Vincent Starrett. Francis Beeding. LC 66-3628. (Seagull lib. of mystery & suspense). 3.95. Norton.
Death Walks on Cat Feet. Henri Weiner, pseud. LC 38-190732. 1938. Hillman-Curl, Inc.
Death Walks on Cat Feet: By D. B. Olsen. 1st Ed. Dolores Birk Hitchens. LC 56-753999. 1956. Published for the Crime Club by Doubleday.
Death Walks Softly. Hazel Christie MacDonald. LC 51-9012. 1950. Phoenix Press.
Death Walks the Dry Tortugas. Margaret Lucile Paine Rea. LC 42-186669. 1942. Published for the Crime Club, by Doubleday, Doran & Company, Inc.
Death Walks the Post. Virginia Hanson. LC 38-14265. 1938. Pub. for the Crime Club, Inc., by Doubleday, Doran & Co., Inc.
Death Walks the Woods. Alfred Alexander Gordon Clark. LC 54-5137. 1954. Little, Brown.
Death Walks the Woods. Cyril Hare. LC 81-47098. 224p. 1981. pap. 2.40i (ISBN 0-06-080556-0, P556, PL). Har-Row.
Death Warmed Over. Mary Garden Collins. 1947. C. Scribner's Sons.
Death Warmed up. Marian Babson. LC 82-60141. 11.95 (ISBN 0-8027-5479-1). Walker.
Death-Watch. John Dickson Carr. LC 35-5657. 1935. Harper & Brothers.
Death Watch. Daoma Winston. (Illus.). 1975. (pbk.) 1.50. Ace Books.
Death Watch: By Ruth and Alexander Wilson. Ruth Wilson & Alexander Wilson. LC 55-225421. (Ace double novel books, D-89). 1955. Ace Books.
Death Watch on the Gazette. Guy Woodward Finney. LC 33-380062. The Press Publishing Co.
Death Wears a Green Hat. Will Creed. LC 46-22511. (Five star mystery 42). 1946. Five-Star Mysteries.
Death Wears a Mask. Therese Benson. LC 35-13544. 1935. Harper & Brothers.
Death Wears a Mask. Douglas Gordon Browne. LC 54-13397. (Murder revisited mystery novel, no. 10). 1954. Macmillan.
Death Wears a Purple Shirt. Ralph Carter Woodthorpe. LC 34-353178. 1934. Pub. for the Crime Club, Inc., by Doubleday, Doran & Co., Inc.
Death Wears a Red Hat. William X Kienzle. LC 79-28353. 9.95 (ISBN 0-8362-6111-9). Andrews and McMeel.
Death Wears a Scarab. Amelia Reynolds Long. LC 43-8701. 1943. Phoenix Press.
Death Wears a White Coat. Theodora McCormick Du Bois. LC 38-6966. 1938. Houghton Mifflin Company.
Death Wears a White Gardenia. Zelda Popkin. LC 38-409823. J. B. Lippincott Company.
Death Wears Cat's Eyes: By D. B. Olsen. 1st Ed. Dolores Birk Hitchens. LC 50-9527. 1950. Published for the Crime Club by Doubleday.
Death Wears Grey. Charles R. Pike, pseud. LC 80-69221. (Jubal Cade Westerns Ser.). 144p. 1981. pap. 2.95 (ISBN 0-87754-237-6). Chelsea Hse.
Death Wears Pink Shoes: By Robert James (Pseud. 1st Ed. Iris Heitner. LC 52-8046. 1952. Published for the Crime Club by Doubleday.
Death Whispers. Joseph Baker Carr. LC 33-17689. 1933. The Viking Press.
Death Will Find Me. Helen Steers Burgess. LC 47-11252. (red badge mystery). 1947. Dodd, Mead.
Death Wind. William C. Heine. 1976. pap. 1.50 o.p. (ISBN 0-515-03961-6). BJ Pub Group.
Death Wind. William C Heine. 1.50 (ISBN 0-515-03961-6). Pyramid Books.
Death Wish. Robert Beck. (Orig.). 1976. pap. 2.25 (ISBN 0-87067-075-1, BH075). Holloway.
Death Wish. Brian Wynne Garfield. (Fawcett crest book). 1974. (pbk.) 1.25. Fawcett.
Death Wish. Brian Wynne Garfield. LC 72-75459. 1972. 4.95. McKay Co.
Death Wish. Elisabeth Sanxay Holding. LC 34-688. 1934. Dodd, Mead & Company.
Death Wish: A Major New Novel. Robert Beck. 1.95. (ISBN 0-87067-609-1). Holloway House Pub. Co.
Death with Blue Ribbon. Leo Bruce, pseud. 1970. 4.50 o.s.i. (ISBN 0-8277-0138-1). British Bk Ctr.
Death Without Battle. Arnold Vieth Von Golssenau. LC 37-6122. 1937. Dodd, Mead & Company.
Death Won the Prize. Ione Montgomery. LC 41-20729. 1941. Pub. for the Crime Club by Doubleday, Doran & Co., Inc.
Death Won't Come: Three Short Stories. Jerry Herman. 1976. pap. 1.50 (ISBN 0-916692-07-8). Black River.
Death Won't Wait: By Anthony Gilbert Pseud. Lucy Beatrice Malleson. LC 54-5969. 1954. Random House.
Death Wore Roses. Charles Saxby. LC 41-26009. 1942. E. P. Dutton & Co., Inc.
Deathbeast. David Gerrold. 1978. 1.75 (ISBN 0-445-04245-1). PopularLibrary.
Deathbed of Roses. Deborah Scott. (Ace Gothic). 1976. (pbk.) 1.25. Ace Books.
Deathbird Stories. Harlan Ellison. 1.75. Dell.
Deathbird Stories: A Pantheon of Modern Gods. Harlan Ellison. LC 73-18663. 1975. 8.95 (ISBN 0-06-011176-3). Harper & Row.
Deathbite. Michael Maryk & Brent Monahan. LC 79-17569. 8.95 (ISBN 0-8362-6104-6). Andrews and McMeel.
Deathblow Hill: An Asey Mayo Mystery of Cape Cod by Phoebe Atwood Taylor. Phoebe Atwood Taylor. LC 35-126787. 1967. bds., 3.95. Norton.
Deathgame. Ron Goulart. (Vampirella #5). 1976. (pbk.) 1.25 (ISBN 0-446-86089-1). Warner Books.
Deathless and the Dead. Anna Clarke. LC 77-360975. 1976. 2.95 (ISBN 0-00-231640-4). Collins for The Crime Club.
Deathless Trumpeter & Other Stories About Young Heroes. A. Gaidar. 165p. 1975. 3.95 (ISBN 0-8285-1130-6, Pub. by Progress Pubs. USSR). Imported Pubns.
Deathlight. Nick Carter. (Nick Carter Ser.). (Illus.). 224p. 1982. pap. 2.50 (ISBN 0-441-14169-2, Pub. by Charter Bks). Ace Bks.
Deathlove. William M. Coffland. 4.75 o.p. Carlton.
Deathmakers. Glen Sire. LC 60-6728. 1960. Simon and Schuster.
Deathman, Do Not Follow Me: A Novel. Jay Bennett. LC 68-22066. 1968. Meredith Press.
Deathmate. Martin Caidin. 240p. 1982. pap. 2.95 (ISBN 0-553-20355-X). Bantam.
Death's Angel. Kathleen Sky. (Star Trek Ser.). 192p. (Orig.). 1981. pap. 2.25 (ISBN 0-553-14703-X). Bantam.
Death's Bounty. George G. Gilman, pseud. (Edge Ser.: No. 12). 1974. pap. 1.75 (ISBN 0-523-41290-8). Pinnacle Bks.
Death's Bright Dart. Clinton-Baddeley, Victor Clinton. LC 69-15874. (Illus.). 1970. 4.95. Morrow.
Death's Clenched Fist: A Paddy Moretti Mystery. James Sherburne. LC 81-7205. 1982. 10.95 (ISBN 0-395-31835-1). Houghton Mifflin.
Death's Deputy. La Fayette Ronald Hubbard. LC 48-10605. 1948. Fantasy Pub. Co.
Death's Echo. Robert B. Hershey. LC 76-127250. 1970. 6.95. Cottonwood Press.
Death's Gray Angel. James Sherburne. LC 82-16202. 1983. 12.95. J. Curley.
Death's Gray Angel. James Sherburne. 216p. 1981. 10.95 (ISBN 0-395-31265-5). HM.
Death's Gray Angel: A Paddy Moretti Mystery. James Sherburne. LC 81-4468. 1981. 10.95 (ISBN 0-395-31265-5). Houghton Mifflin.
Death's Harvest. Bradford Scott. 1973. pap. 0.75 o.p. (ISBN 0-515-03062-7, T3062). Pyramid Pubns.
Death's Head: A Novel. Campbell Black. LC 79-38297. 1972. (ISBN 0-397-00752-3). Lippincott.
Death's Head Conspiracy. Nick Carter. (Nick Carter Ser.). (O.s.i.). (Orig.). 1977. pap. 1.50 o.s.i. (AD 1655, Award). Univ Pub & Dist.
Death's Long Shadow. Katherine Wolffe. LC 46-227243. 1946. Five-Star Mysteries.
Death's Mannikins. Max Afford. LC 37-12726. 1937. D. Appleton-Century Company, Incorporated.
Death's Master. Tanith Lee. 1979. 1.95 (ISBN 0-87997-441-9). DAW Books.
Deaths of Lora Karen. Roman McDougald. LC 44-829. 1944. Simon and Schuster.
Deaths of Lora Karen... Roman McDougald. LC 46-7092. (On cover: Bart house mystery. 17).
Death's Old Sweet Song. Jonathan Stagge, pseud. LC 46-48075. 1946. Pub. for the Crime Club by Doubleday & Company, Inc.
Death's Pale Flag. Edward Wiley. 1981. pap. 1.95 (ISBN 0-8439-0859-9, Leisure Bks). Nordon Pubns.
Death's Pale Horse. large print ed. James Sherburne. LC 82-13971. 1983. 11.95 (ISBN 0-89340-533-7). J. Curley.
Death's Pale Horse: A Novel of Murder in Saratoga in the 1880s. James Sherburne. LC 79-26061. 1980. 8.95 (ISBN 0-395-29087-2). Houghton Mifflin.
Death's Sweet Song. Cover Painting by Barye Phillips. Clifton Adams. LC 55-35940. (Gold medal books, 483). 1955. Fawcett Publications.
Deathstalk. Bruce Clark. 1981. pap. 1.75 (ISBN 0-8439-0897-1). Nordon Pubns.
Deathstar Voyage: A Downtime Mystery Cruise. Ian Wallace. LC 69-18198. 1969. 4.95. Putnam.
Deathstone. Ken Eulo. (Orig.). 1982. pap. 3.95. PB.
Deathtrek. Jeffrey Wallman. (Orig.). 1980. pap. 1.75 o.s.i. (ISBN 0-505-51528-8). Tower Bks.
Deathwalker, No. 2. Roman Castevano. 160p. (Orig.). 1975. pap. 1.25 o.p. (ISBN 0-448-12113-1, Tempo). G&D.

Deathwatch. Robb White. 1973. pap. 2.25 (ISBN 0-440-91740-9, LFL). Dell.

Deathwind. James Powell. LC 78-14654. 1979. 7.95 (ISBN 0-385-14740-6). Doubleday.

Deathwork: A Novel. James McLendon. LC 77-4774. 8.95 (ISBN 0-397-01193-8). Lippincott.

Deathworld. Harry Harrison. LC 60-12456. (Bantam book, A2160). 1960. Bantam Books.

Deathworld Trilogy. Harry Harrison. pap. 2.50 (ISBN 0-425-04859-4). Berkley Pub.

Deathworms of Kratos. Richard Avery. (Expendables). (Fawcett gold medal book: Vol. 1). 1975. (pbk.) 1.25. Fawcett.

Deaves Affair. Hulbert Footner. LC 22-77593. George H. Doran Company.

Deb. Claude H Wiser. LC 52-11900. 1953. Vantage Press.

Debacle. Emile Zola. LC 73-156279. (Penguin classics). 1972. (u.s.) 3.85 (ISBN 0-14-044280-4). Penguin Books.

Debacle. Emile Zola. LC 69-14377. 1969. 8.95. Dufour.

Debatable Ground. Gladys Bronwyn Stern. LC 21-5713. 1921. A. A. Knopf.

Debate. Michael De Forrest. 304p. (Orig.). 1973. pap. 1.25 o.p. (ISBN 0-532-12173-2). Woodhill.

Debate. Michael De Forrest. 304p. (Orig.). 1973. pap. 1.25 o.p. (ISBN 0-532-12173-2). Manor Bks.

Debauched Hospodar. Guillaume Apollinaire. pap. 1.25 o.p. (BH145). Holloway.

Debbie Preston, Teenage Reporter, in The Case of the Superstar Mystery Cruise. Doug Stapleton. 1973. (pbk.) 0.95. New American Lib.

Debbie Preston, Teenage Reporter in the Donny Osmond Mystery. Sylvia Resnick. (official tiger beat publication). 1973. (pbk) 0.95. New American Library.

Debby. 1st Ed. Max Steele. LC 50-6122. 1950. Harper.

Debenham's Vow. Amelia Ann Blandford Edwards. (Seaside library. v. 24, no. 472). 1879. G. Munro.

Debit Account. Oliver Onions. LC 13-4993. 1.25. George H. Doran Company, Publishers in America for Hodder & Stoughton.

Debit and Credit. Gustav Freytâg. Tr. by Cummings, L. C. Bunsen, Christian Karl Josias, Freiherr Von. 1909. W. Abbatt.

Debits and Credits. Rudyard Kipling. LC 26-16150. 1926. Doubleday, Page & Company.

Debonair; the Story of Persephone. Gladys Bronwyn Stern. LC 28-12384. 1928. A. A. Knopf.

Deborah. Marian Castle. LC 46-3685. 1946. W. Morrow and Company.

Deborah. Colette Davenat. LC 73-1673. 6.95. Morrow.

Deborah. Colette Davenat. 1974. (pbk.) 1.25. Bantam Books.

Deborah. Margit Strom Heppenstall. LC 67-19497. 1967. Southern Pub. Association.

Deborah. Elsie Frances Wilson Mack. LC 51-9364. (Avalon books). 1951. Bouregy & Curl.

Deborah. Martin Sampierre. LC 78-69707. 9.95 (ISBN 0-498-02280-3). A. S. Barnes.

Deborah: A Story of the Most Remarkable Woman in History. Effie Lawrence Marshall. LC 58-25378. 1958. L. Tebbetts.

Deborah: A Tale of the Times of Judas Maccabaeus. James Meeker Ludlow. LC 1-23048. F. H. Revell Company.

Deborah and the Many Faces of Love. Colette Davenat. LC 74-11773. 1974. 7.95 (ISBN 0-688-00307-9). William Morrow.

Deborah & the Siege of Paris. Colette Davenat. Tr. by Anne Carter from French. 416p. 1976. 8.95 o.p. (ISBN 0-688-03074-2). Morrow.

Deborah and the Siege of Paris. LC 76-12967. 1976. 8.95 (ISBN 0-688-03074-2). William Morrow.

Deborah Death: A Novel. LC 6-32895. 1889. G. W. Dillingham.

Deborah Leigh. Jeanne Foster. (Frontier Women Saga: No. 2). 352p. 1981. pap. 2.95 (ISBN 0-449-14437-2, GM). Fawcett.

Deborah Moses: Or, Pen Pictures of Colonial Life in New England. Truman Andrew Wellington Weed. LC 15-5561. The Good Will Publishing Co.

Deborah of Tods. 2d impression. ed. Elizabeth Bonham De La Pasture. LC 8-23924. 1908. E. P. Dutton & Company.

Deborah, the Advanced Woman. Mary Ives Todd. 1896. Arena Publishing Company.

Deborah: The Advanced Woman. Mary Van Lennup Ives Todd. LC 8-26756. 1896. Arena Publishing Company.

Deborah's Dreams. 1976. pap. 2.75 o.p. (V00037). Playboy Pr Pbks.

Deborah's Legacy. Stephen Marlowe. 1983. pap. 3.75 (ISBN 0-8217-1153-9). Zebra.

Debriefing. Robert Littell. 1981. pap. 2.75 (ISBN 0-440-11873-5). Dell.

Debriefing: A Novel. Robert Littell. LC 78-22442. 8.95 (ISBN 0-06-012656-6). Harper & Row.

Debris. Brock Brower. LC 67-14327. 1967. Atheneum.

Debs, Dolls & Dope. John Benton. LC 68-28434. 1968. 3.95 o.p. (ISBN 0-8007-0066-X). Revell.

Debt. Olle E. Hogstrand. LC 74-7774. 1975. 5.95 (ISBN 0-394-49191-2). Pantheon Books.

Debt. William Westrup. LC 13-35660. T. Y. Crowell Company.

Debt and Credit: Translated from the German of Gustav Freytag by L. C. C. Gustav Freytag et al. Tr. by C., L. C. LC 6-44729. (Harper's Franklin Square Library). (On cover: Harper's Franklin square library. no. 735: No. 735). 1893. Harper & Brothers.

Debt of Dishonour. Mary Wibberley. (Harlequin Presents Ser.). 192p. 1980. pap. 1.50 (ISBN 0-373-10390-5, Pub. by Harlequin). PB.

Debt of Hatred. Georges Ohnet. Tr. by Robins, E. P. LC 7-32509. Cassell Publishing Company.

Debt of Honor. Diana Brown. 1982. pap. 2.25 (ISBN 0-451-11417-5, AE1417, Sig). NAL.

Debt of Honor No. 16. Barbara Cartland. 1970. pap. 1.25 o.p. (ISBN 0-515-02921-1, V2921). BJ Pub Group.

Debt of Honour. Elizabeth Carey. 192p. (Orig.). 1982. pap. 1.50 (ISBN 0-449-50308-9, Coventry). Fawcett.

Debt of Honour. Mabel Collins Cook. LC 6-28083. J. W. Lovell Company.

Debt of Honour. Adam Kennedy. LC 80-20980. (Illus.). 1981. 12.95 (ISBN 0-440-00012-2). Delacorte Press.

Debt of Vengeance. Emma Augusta Sharkey. (select series, no. 42). 1890. Street & Smith.

Debtor: A Novel. Mary Eleanor Wilkins Freeman. LC 5-34177. 1905. Harper & Brothers.

Debtors' Holiday. Harry A Keller. LC 33-184752. The Macaulay Company.

Debts of Honor. Mor Jokai & Yolland, Arthur Battishill, 1874- Tr. LC 2101. 1900. Doubleday & McClure Co.

Debut. Livingston Biddle. LC 52-13615. 1952. Messner.

Debut. Anita Brookner. LC 80-39772. 1981. 11.95 (ISBN 0-671-42626-5). Linden Press.

Debutante. Edna Walker Malcoskey. LC 23-9167. E. P. Dutton & Company.

Debutante Hill. Lois Duncan. (Willow Bks). 1971. pap. 0.75 o.p. (JT49). Pyramid Pubns.

Debutante in New York Society: Her Illusions and What Became of Them. Abby Buchanan Longstreet. LC 6-19886. 1888. D. Appleton and Company.

Debutante in Uniform. Maysie Greig. LC 38-339432. 1938. Doubleday, Doran & Company, Inc.

Debutante Nurse see Elaine Forrest: Visiting Nurse.

Debutante Nurse: By Margaret Howe Pseud. Margaretta Brucker. 1958. Avalon Books.

Debutante Stand-in. Lois Bull. LC 37-10104. 1937. Hillman Curl, Inc.

Debutantes: A Novel. June Flaum Singer. LC 81-17458. 13.95 (ISBN 0-87131-358-8). M. Evans.

Decade: A Story of Political and Municipal Corruption. Horace Thomas Barnaby. 1908. Wolverine Book Publishing Company.

Decade in Blue. Sid Fuller. LC 32-943120. The Stratford Company.

Decade of Hispanic Literature: An Anniversary Anthology. Ed. by Nicolas Kanellos. LC 82-71653. 320p. (Orig.). 1982. pap. 10.00 (ISBN 0-934770-18-2). Arte Publico.

Decade, the 1940s. Brian Wilson Aldiss & Harry Harrison. LC 77-15865. 1978. 8.95 (ISBN 0-312-18984-2). St. Martin's Press.

Decade, the 1950s. Brian Wilson Aldiss & Harry Harrison. LC 76-376544. 1976. (ISBN 0-333-19001-7). Macmillan.

Decade, the 1950s. Brian Wilson Aldiss & Harry Harrison. LC 77-15866. 1978. 8.95 (ISBN 0-312-18985-0). St. Martin's Press.

Decade the 1950's. Brian Wilson Aldiss & Harry Harrison. LC 79-22925. 1980. 3.95 (ISBN 0-312-18987-7). St. Martin's Press.

Decade, 1929-1939. Stephen Longstreet. LC 38-19073. 1938. Hillman-Curl, Inc.

Decade: 1929-1939. Stephen Longstreet. LC 40-27162. 1940. Random House.

Decade, 1929-1939. Philip Wiener. LC 40-27162. Random House.

Decadence. Maksim Gorkii & Dewey, Veronica, Tr. LC 27-8778. 1927. R. M. McBride & Company.

Decades. Ruth Harris. LC 74-4127. 1974. 7.95 (ISBN 0-671-21799-2). Simon and Schuster.

Decameron. Giovanni Boccaccio. Tr. by George Henry McWilliam. LC 73-150738. (Penguin classics). 1972. (ISBN 0-14-044269-3). Penguin.

Decameron. Giovanni Boccaccio. LC 55-5731. (Modern library of the world's best books 71). 1955. Modern Library.

Decameron. Giovanni Boccaccio. Tr. by George Henry McWilliam. LC 73-150738. (Penguin classics). 1972. 0.90 (ISBN 0-14-044269-3). Penguin.

Decameron. Giovanni Boccaccio. LC 49-11622. 1949. Garden City Pub. Co.

Decameron. Giovanni Boccaccio. LC 50-2051. 1949. Garden City Pub Co.

Decameron. Giovanni Boccaccio & Payne, John, 1842-1916, Tr. LC 31-23429. (Half-title: The modern library of the world's best books). 1931. The Modern Library.

Decameron. new ed. Giovanni Boccaccio & Payne, John, 1842-1916, Tr. LC 47-685442. 1947. Stravon Publishers.

Decameron: A New Translation: 21 Novelle, Contemporary Reactions, Modern Criticism. Giovanni Boccaccio & Mark Musa. LC 77-5664. (Norton critical edition). 10.95 (ISBN 0-393-04458-0) (ISBN 0-393-09132-5). Norton.

Decameron of Boccaccio. Giovanni Boccaccio. Tr. by John Payne. (Black & Gold Lib). 6.95 o.p. Liveright.

Decameron of Giovanni Boccaccio. Giovanni Boccaccio. Tr. by James Macmullen Rigg. Symonds, John Addington, 1840-1893. LC 24-12315. (Half-title: Library of early novelists). G. Routledge & Sons, Limited.

Decameron of Giovanni Boccaccio. Giovanni Boccaccio. Tr. by James Macmullen Rigg. Symonds, John Addington, 1840-1893. LC 30-311757. G. Routledge & Sons, Limited.

Decameron of Giovanni Boccaccio. Giovanni Boccaccio. Tr. by Richard Aldington. Bosschere, Jean De, 1878- LC 30-15310. 1930. Covici, Friede.

Decameron of Giovanni Boccaccio... Giovanni Boccaccio. Tr. by James Macmullen Rigg. LC 37-5676. (Half-title: Everyman's library. ed. by Ernest Rhys. Romance. no. 845-846). 1935. J. M. Dent & Sons, Ltd.

Decameron of Giovanni Boccaccio. Giovanni Boccaccio. Tr. by Richard Aldington. Bosschere, Jean De, 1878- Illus. LC 38-16651. Garden City Publishing Company, Inc.

Decameron of Giovanni Boccaccio. Giovanni Boccaccio & Payne, John, 1842-1916, Tr. LC 31-33518. Blue Ribbon Books.

Decameron of Giovanni Boccaccio. Giovanni Boccaccio & Payne, John, 1842-1916, Tr. LC 46-847922. 1946. Stravon Publishers.

Decameron of Giovanni Boccaccio. Giovanni Boccaccio & Winwar, Frances, Tr. LC 30-14226. 1930. The Limited Editions Club.

Decameron of Giovanni Boccaccio: Faithfully Tr. by J. M. Rigg; with an Essay on Boccaccio As Man and Author, by John Addington Symonds. Giovanni Boccaccio. Tr. by James Macmullen Rigg. Symonds, John Addington, 1840-1893. LC 24-11850. 1905. G. Routledge & Sons, Limited.

Decameron of Giovanni Boccaccio: Including Forty of Its Hundred Novels with an Introduction by Henry Morley... Giovanni Boccaccio. (Half-title: Morley's universal library. 15). 1885. G. Routledge and Sons.

Decameron of Giovanni Boccaccio Including Forty of Its Hundred Novels: With an Introduction by Henry Morley... Giovanni Boccaccio. LC 33-15077. (Half-title: Morley's universal library. 15). 1886. G. Routledge and Sons.

Decameron: Or, Ten Days' Entertainment. Giovanni Boccaccio & Payne, John, 1842-1916, Tr. LC 47-225432. (living library). 1947. World Pub. Co.

Decameron: OrTen Days Entertainment of Boccaccio. india paper ed. Giovanni Boccaccio. LC 20-11592. 1920. Stewart & Kidd Company.

Decameron, Preserved to Posterity. Giovanni Boccaccio & Edward Hutton. LC 73-153500. (Series: The Tudor Translations, 1st Ser., V. 41-44.). 1967. AMS Press.

Decameron Tales. Giovanni Boccaccio & Sears, Joseph Hamblen, 1865- LC 25-24884. (Lettered on cover: The royal collection). J. H. Sears & Company, Inc.

Decameron: The Modell of Wit, Mirth, Eloquence and Conversation, Framed in Ten Dayes, of an Hundred Curious Pieces, by Seven Honourable Ladies, and Three Noble Gentlemen; Preserved to Posterity by the Renowned John Boccaccio, the First Refiner of Italian Prose; Translated into English Anno 1620, with an Introduction by Edward Hutton and Wood-Cuts in the Renaissance Manner by Fritz Kredel. Giovanni Boccaccio. LC 40-6877. The Heritage Club.

Decameron: The Modell of Wit, Mirth, Eloquence and Conversation, Framed in Ten Dayes, of an Hundred Curious Pieces. Giovanni Boccaccio. The Limited Editions Club.

Decameron: Translated by John Payne; Illustrated by Clara Rice... Giovanni Boccaccio & Payne, John, 1842-1916, Tr. LC 26-26987. 1925. Pub. for Subscribers Only by Boni & Liveright.

Decameron: V.2. Introd. by Edward Hutton. Giovanni Boccaccio. (Everyman's lib., 846; Everyman paperback, 1846). 1961. pap., 1.55. Dutton.

Decameron, 1965. Joe Rosenfield. LC 63-24695. 1963. Citadel Press.

Decapitated Chicken, and Other Stories. Horacio Quiroga. LC 75-40167. (Texas Pan American series). (Illus.). 8.95 (ISBN 0-292-77514-8). University of Texas Press.

Decatur and Somers. Molly Elliot Seawell. (On cover: Young heroes of our navy). 1894. D. Appleton and Company.

Decay of the Angel. Yukio Mishima, pseud. LC 73-21525. (His The sea of fertility 4). 1974. 6.95 (ISBN 0-394-46613-6). Knopf; Distributed by Random House.

Decayed Gentlewoman: By E. X. Ferrars Pseud. Morna Doris MacTaggart Brown. LC 63-18213. 1963. Published for the Crime Club by Doubleday.

Deceit: A Novel. Barklie McKee Henry. LC 24-147113. Small, Maynard & Company.

Deceit and Deadly Lies. Franklin Bandy. 1978. 2.25 (ISBN 0-441-06517-1). Charter Books.

Deceit of a Pagan. Carole Mortimer. (Harlequin Presents Ser.). (Orig.). 1980. pap. text ed. 1.50 (ISBN 0-373-10365-4). Harlequin Bks.

Deceitful Marriage, and Other Exemplary Novels. Miguel de Cervantes de Saavedra. LC 63-4443. (Signet classic, CT157). 1963. New American Library.

Deceivers. Joanna Barnes. LC 74-122642. 1970. 6.95 (ISBN 0-87795-007-5). Arbor Hse.

Deceivers. Alfred Bester. LC 82-107886. (Illus.). 6.95 (ISBN 0-671-43432-2). Wallaby Books: Distributed by Pocket Books.

Deceivers. John Dann MacDonald. 208p. 1981. pap. 1.95 (ISBN 0-449-14016-4, GM). Fawcett.

Deceivers: A Novel. Joanna Barnes. LC 72-122642. 1974. (pbk.) 1.25. Pocket Books.

Deceivers: A Novel. Joanna Barnes. LC 74-122642. 1970. 6.95. Arbor House.

Deceivers: A Novel. John Masters. LC 52-1198. 1952. Viking Press.

December Bride. Sam Hanna Bell. LC 51-11686. 1951. Dutton.

December Love. Robert Smythe Hichens. LC 23-472. 1922. George H. Doran Company.

December Nineteen Seventy-Five. Rod Tulloss. (Xtras Ser.: No. 7). 20p. (Orig.). 1978. pap. 1.50 (ISBN 0-89120-037-1). From Here.

December Roses" A Novel. Rosa Caroline Murray-Prior Praed. LC 7-30302. (On cover: Appletons' town and country library, no. 96). 1892. D. Appleton and Company.

December Syndrome. Robert Carson. LC 73-79375. 1969. 7.95. Little, Brown.

Decent Fellows. John Heygate. LC 31-11380. J. Cape & H. Smith.

Deception. Nicolas Born. LC 82-14049. 15.50 (ISBN 0-316-10273-3). Little, Brown.

Deception. Celia Dale. LC 79-2646. 1980. 9.95 (ISBN 0-06-010964-5). Harper & Row.

Deception. Cynthia Kavanaugh. 1972. pap. 0.75 o.p. (ISBN 0-515-02752-9, T2752). Pyramid Pubns.

Deception Area. Sonia Deane. LC 43-1373. 1942. Hutchinson & Co. Ltd.

Deception on Peregrine Island. Lois A. Sunagel. (Orig.). 1979. pap. 1.95 (ISBN 0-532-23331-X). Woodhill.

Deceptions. Judith Michael. LC 81-17787. 1982. 15.95 (ISBN 0-671-42491-2). Poseidon Press.

Deceptive American. William J. Lederer & Eugene Burdick. LC 77-10793. 1977. 9.95 (ISBN 0-393-08802-2). Norton.

Deceptive Cadence. Eugenia Zuckerman. LC 80-15021. 1980. 11.95 (ISBN 0-670-26236-6). Viking Press.

Deceptive Love. Anne N. Reisser. 192p. (Orig.). 1981. pap. 1.75 (ISBN 0-440-11776-3). Dell.

Decimal File. Nina Kahn. (Orig.). 1979. pap. 1.95 (ISBN 0-532-23321-2). Woodhill.

Decision. Allen Drury. LC 82-22231. 1983. 17.95 (ISBN 0-385-18832-3). Doubleday.

Decision. Henry Kane. LC 73-6762. 1973. 6.95. Dial Press.

Decision. Henry Kane. 1974. (pbk.) 1.50. Warner Paperback Library.

Decision. A Tale. 1819. A. T. Goodrich & Co. Etc.

Decision; a Tale. Barbara Wreaks Hoole Hofland. 1867. T. Nelson and Sons.

Decision & Other Stories. Hasel V. Stutsman. 6.95 o.p. Carlton.

Decision at Broken Butte. Harry Sinclair Drago. LC 57-5853. (Permabooks, Western, M-3068 8). 1957. Permabooks.

Decision at Dawn. easy eye ed. Ann Calin. pap. 0.75 o.p. Lancer.

Decision at Delphi. large type ed. complete and unabridged. ed. Helen MacInnes. LC 76-9111. (Illus.). 1969. 9.95. F. Watts.

Decision at Delphi. 1st Ed. Helen MacInnes. LC 60-15705. 1960. Harcourt, Brace.

Decision at Doona. Anne McCaffrey. 256p. 1975. pap. 2.25 (ISBN 0-345-28506-9). Ballantine.

Decision at Doubtful Canyon. Ray Hogan. 1981. pap. 1.95 (ISBN 0-451-11119-2, AJ1119, Sig). NAL.

Decision at Easter. G. P. Gallivan. (Orig.). 1960. pap. 1.00 o.p. (ISBN 0-8283-1139-0). Branden.

Decision at Sea. Ruby C Tolliver. LC 80-65972. 4.95 (ISBN 0-8054-7314-9). Broadman Press.

Decision at Sundown: By Michael Carder Pseud. Vernon L Fluharty. LC 55-6445. (Bull's-eye western). 1955. Macrae Smith.

Decision, from the French of Leon De Tinseau, Tr. by Frank Alvah Dearborn. Leon De Tinseau & Dearborn, Frank Alvah, Tr. G. W. Dillingham Company.

Decision: Historical Novel of the American Revolution. Barbara Bramwell. LC 75-39859. (Illus.). 1976. 7.50 (ISBN 0-916510-01-8). Survey Publications.

Decision in Paris. Jack Welch. 1973. 3.00 (ISBN 0-88027-006-3). Firm Foun Pub.

Decision in Paris. Jack Welch. 1973. Firm Foundation Publishing House.

Decisions and The Furies: Two Narratives of Napoleonic Times. Maurits Ignatius Boas. LC 74-28456. 1975. 6.95 (ISBN 0-8119-0248-X). F. Fell.

Deck Morgan's Winter Carnival. Deck Morgan. LC 35-165863. 1935. J. Messner, Inc.

Deck with Flowers. Elizabeth Cadell. LC 73-9356. 1974. 5.95 (ISBN 0-688-00212-9). Morrow.

Deck with Flowers. Elizabeth Cadell. LC 74-3169. 1974. 9.95 (ISBN 0-8161-6198-4). G. K. Hall.

Decker's Campaign. Jack M Bickham. LC 70-89083. (Double D western). 1970. 4.50. Doubleday.

Declaration of Love: Undiplomatic Correspondence Between Paris and Berlin. Geoffery Pomeroy Dennis. LC 27-20086. 1927. A. A. Knopf.

Declension of Henry D'Albiac. Valentine Francis Taubman-Goldie. LC 13-1309. 1913. Frederick A. Stokes Company.

Decline & Destruction of the Orion Empire, Vol. 1. Ruth E. Norman. (Illus.). 373p. (Orig.). 1979. pap. 7.95 (ISBN 0-932642-50-0). Unarius.

Decline and Fall. Evelyn Waugh. LC 77-88222. (Illus.). 1977. 8.95 (ISBN 0-316-92619-1). Little, Brown.

Decline and Fall: An Illustrated Novelette. Evelyn Waugh. 1929. Doubleday, Doran & Company, Inc.

Decline and Fall of America. Robert De Maria. LC 72-88657. 1973. 8.95 (ISBN 0-8415-0238-2). Saturday Review Press.

Decline and Fall of Samuel Sawbones, M.D., on the Klondike. J. J. Leisher. The Neely Company.

Decline of the Wasp. Peter Schrag. (O.S.I.). 1971. 6.95 o.s.i. (ISBN 0-671-21059-9). S&S.

Decline of the West. David Caute. LC 66-24430. Macmillan.

Declining Gracefully. John Sandman. LC 77-355980. 1976. Coach House Press.

Decorated Corpse. Roy Olin Stratton. LC 62-21340. 1962. M. S. Mill Co. and Morrow.

Decoy. Edward Sidney Aarons. 176p. 1972. pap. 0.75 o.p. (T2588, GM). Fawcett World.

Decoy. Cleve Franklin Adams. LC 41-353120. 1941. E. P. Dutton & Co., Inc.

Decoy. Arthur Maling. LC 72-81876. 1969. 4.95. Harper & Row.

Decoy: A Novel. Francis Dana. LC 2-628318. 1902. J. Lane.

Decoy in Diamonds. Natalie Gates. LC 78-151205. (Red mask mystery). 1971. 4.95. Putnam.

Decoys: A John Denson Mystery. Richard Hoyt. LC 80-17248. 8.95 (ISBN 0-87131-330-8). M. Evans.

Decree. Gertrude Crownfield. LC 37-18660. J. B. Lippincott Company.

Dedicated Man. Joseph Gallina. 5.95 o.p. Vantage.

Dedicated Man. And Other Stories. Elizabeth Taylor. LC 65-21151. bds., 4.95. Viking.

Dedo De Plata. new ed. Glen Chase, pseud. Tr. by Miguel Sarria from Eng. (Pimienta Collection: Cereza Delicias Ser., No. 2). Orig. Title: Silverfinger. 160p. (Span.). 1974. pap. 1.00 o.p. (ISBN 0-88473-212-6). Fiesta Pub.

Deductions of Colonel Gore. Alister McAllister. LC 25-975126. Harper & Brothers.

Dee Dee". Eliot Harlow Robinson. LC 25-20830. Small, Maynard & Company.

Dee Goong an: Three Murder Cases Solved by Judge Dee. Robert Hans Van Gulik, pseud. LC 75-32788. (Literature of Mystery and Detection). (Illus.). 1976. 13.00 (ISBN 0-405-07875-7). Arno Press.

Dee Goong An: Three Murder Cases Solved by Judge Dee. Robert Van Gulik. LC 75-32788. (Literature of Mystery & Detection). (Illus.). 1976. Repr. 13.00x (ISBN 0-405-07875-7). Ayer Co.

Deed Is Drawn: A Christopher Storm Mystery. Willetta Ann Barber & Schabelitz, Rudolph Frederick. LC 49-8800. 1949. C. Scribner's Sons.

Deed of Life: The Novels and Tales of D. H. Lawrence. Julian Moynahan. LC 63-9986. 1963. Princeton University Press.

Deed Without a Name... Dorothy Bowers. LC 40-34000. 1940. Pub. for the Crime Club by Doubleday, Doran and Company, Inc.

Deed Without a Name. Eden Phillpotts. LC 42-18847. 1942. The Macmillan Company.

Deedee. Alison Lord. (Orig.). 1969. pap. 0.75 o.p. (T2016). Pyramid Pubns.

Deeds of Darkness. Blair Ashton. LC 57-11153. 1957. Little, Brown.

Deeds of Denry: The Audacious. Enoch Arnold Bennett. LC 10-3635. 1910. E. P. Dutton & Company.

Deeds of Dr. Deadcert. Joan Margaret Fleming. LC 56-12827. 1957. I. Washburn.

Deeds of Doctor Deadcert. Joan Flernig. pap. 0.50 o.p. Lancer.

Deemster. Hall Caine. (On cover: Lovell's library, no. 1143). 1888. J. W. Lovell Company.

Deemster. Hall Caine. LC 4-15288. 1895. R. F. Fenno and Company.

Deemster. Hall Caine. LC 4-22820. 1897. D. Appleton and Company.

Deemster: A Romance, Upon Which Is Founded the Play, "Ben-My-Chree"... Hall Caine. (On cover: Seaside library, Pocket ed., no. 1284). 1889. G. Munro.

Deenie. Judy Blume. (Laurel Leaf library). 1974. (pbk.) 0.95. Dell.

Deep. Peter Benchley. LC 75-44521. 1976. 7.95 (ISBN 0-385-04742-8). Doubleday.

Deep. Peter Benchley. LC 76-29710. 1976. 10.95 (ISBN 0-8161-6408-8). G. K. Hall.

Deep. Peter Benchley. 1977. 2.25 (ISBN 0-553-10422-5). Bantam Books.

Deep. John Crowley. LC 74-24485. 1975. 5.95 (ISBN 0-385-09098-6). Doubleday.

Deep. John Crowley. 1976. 1.50 (ISBN 0-425-03163-2). Berkley Publishing Corp.

Deep. Kaj Klitgaard. LC 41-5694. 1941. Doubleday, Doran & Co., Inc.

Deep. Mickey Spillane, pseud. pap. 1.95 (ISBN 0-451-11402-7, AJ1402, Sig). NAL.

Deep and Crisp and Even. Peter Turnbull. LC 81-21459. 10.95 (ISBN 0-312-19092-1). St. Martin's Press.

Deep Are the Valleys. Hannah Priebsch Closs. LC 61-901196. 1960. Vanguard Press.

Deep As a Grave. James H Mantinband. LC 50-9962. 1950. Phoenix Press.

Deep Blue Good-by. John Dann MacDonald. LC 75-1092. (His The Travis McGee series). 1975. 6.95 (ISBN 0-397-01090-7). Lippincott.

Deep Blue. Orig.: How the Fishes Live. Joel Lieber. (1891). 1968. Dell.

Deep Channel. Margaret Prescott Montague. LC 23-12709. The Atlantic Monthly Press.

Deep Country. Amory Hare. LC 33-23509. 1933. C. Scribner's Sons.

Deep Cover. Brian Wynne Garfield. (Dell bk., 1865). 1972. 1.25. Dell.

Deep Cover. Brian Wynne Garfield. LC 70-152050. 1971. 7.95. Delacorte Press.

Deep Cover Blast-off. Lionel Derrick, pseud. (Penetrator Ser.: No. 44). 208p. (Orig.). 1981. pap. 1.95 (ISBN 0-523-41407-2). Pinnacle Bks.

Deep Currents. 1st Ed. William Ornstein. LC 54-74957. 1953. Story Book Press.

Deep Dark River. Robert Rylee. LC 35-27234. Farrar & Rinehart, Incorporated.

Deep Deep Freeze. William Garner. LC 68-12098. 1968. Putnam.

Deep End. Fredric Brown. LC 81-47340. (Fifty Classics of Crime Fiction, 1950-1975). 1982. 14.95 (ISBN 0-8240-4990-X). Garland.

Deep End: A Novel. Joseph Arnold Hayes. LC 66-23824. 1967. Viking Press.

Deep End: A Novel, by Joseph Hayes. Joseph Arnold Hayes. (N3713). 1968. Bantam.

Deep End. 1st Ed. Fredric Brown. LC 52-12155. (Guilt edged mystery). 1952. Dutton.

Deep Enough. Malcolm Harrison Ross. LC 27-5838. Harcourt, Brace and Company.

Deep Evening. Eugene William Lohrke. LC 31-113812. J. Cape & H. Smith.

Deep Foot. Richard M. Vixen. LC 77-79739. (Illus.). 1978. pap. 3.00 (ISBN 0-930182-02-2). Avant-Garde CR.

Deep Forest. Norman Eugene Nygaard. LC 47-146100. 1947. Reynal & Hitchcock.

Deep Freeze. H. Walter Whyte. 1977. pap. 1.25 (ISBN 0-532-12527-4). Woodhill.

Deep Freeze & Other Stories. Marcello Maestro. 1977. 5.50 o.p. (ISBN 0-682-48866-6). Exposition.

Deep-Freeze Girls: A Novel. Eva Defago. LC 64-17973. 1964. Coward-McCann.

Deep Furrows. Robert Welles Ritchie. LC 27-3017. Thomas Y. Crowell Company.

Deep Gods. David Mason. 1973. pap. 1.25 o.s.i. (78-762). Lancer.

Deep Grow the Roots. Mari Tomasi. LC 40-30893. J. B. Lippincott Company.

Deep Heart: By Isabel C. Clarke. Isabel Constance Clarke. LC 19-14343. 1919. Benziger Brothers.

Deep Hills: By Matt Stuart Pseud. 1st Ed. Llewellyn Perry Holmes. LC 54-8748. 1954. Lippincott.

Deep Hurt: A Novel. Arthur Mabb Plyer. LC 39-1105. The Welrad Corporation.

Deep in a Dark Country. easy eye ed. Patricia Drew. (Orig.). 1968. pap. 0.60 o.p. (73-756). Lancer.

Deep in a Dark Country. Patricia Drew. 1973. pap. 0.95 o.s.i. (75-444). Lancer.

Deep in Her Heart. Nell Marr Dean. LC 50-11184. 1950. Arcadia House.

Deep in Piney Woods. J. W Church. LC 70-39080. (Black Heritage Library Collection). (Illus.). 1972. (ISBN 0-8369-9018-8). Books for Libraries Press.

Deep in Piney Woods. J. W Church. LC 10-19390. 1910. T. Y. Crowell & Co.

Deep in the Heart. Wyatt Wyatt. LC 80-65986. 1980. 12.95 (ISBN 0-689-11084-7). Atheneum.

Deep in the Hearts of Men. Mary Ella Waller. LC 24-9785. 1924. Little, Brown, and Company.

Deep in the Sky: A Science Fiction Novel. 1st Ed. Helga Nielsen. LC 55-121323. 1955. Exposition Press.

Deep Is the Blue. Max Simon Ehrlich. LC 64-16555. 1964. Doubleday.

Deep Is the Furrow. Kenneth Anderson. 1946. Zondervan Publishing House.

Deep Is the Night. James Howard Wellard. LC 53-9682. 1953. Farrar, Straus & Young.

Deep Is the Shadow: A Novel. 1st Ed. G Arnold Haygood. LC 59-13042. 1959. Doubleday.

Deep Kill. Daniel Da Cruz. (Jock Sargent series,#2). 1974. (pbk.) 0.95. Fawcett.

Deep-Lake Mystery. Carolyn Wells. LC 28-17100. 1928. Pub. for The Crime Club, Inc., by Doubleday, Doran & Company, Inc.

Deep Lay the Dead. Frederick Clyde Davis. LC 42-22575. 1942. Published for the Crime Club by Doubleday, Doran & Company, Inc.

Deep Like the Rivers: Stories of My Negro Friends, Vol. 4. (Texas Folklore Society Paisano Bks.). 1969. 5.00 (ISBN 0-88426-023-2). Encino Pr.

Deep Meadows. Margaret Rivers Larminie Tragett. LC 24-13353. 1924. G. P. Putnam's Sons.

Deep Moat Grange. Samuel Rutherford Crockett. LC 8-91751. 1908. D. Appleton and Company.

Deep Range. Arthur Charles Clarke. LC 57-6214. 1974. (pbk.) 1.25. New American Library.

Deep Range. 1st Ed. Arthur Charles Clarke. LC 57-6214. 1957. Harcourt, Brace.

Deep River. Alton Dowd, Sr. LC 76-56711. 1977. 7.95 o.p. (ISBN 0-87716-047-3). Moore Pub Co.

Deep River. Clement Wood. LC 72-4616. (Black Heritage Library Collection). 1972. 12.25 (ISBN 0-8369-9132-X). Books for Libraries Press.

Deep River. Clement Wood. LC 34-2590. W. Godwin, Inc.

Deep Rivers. Jose Maria Arguedas. LC 77-26243. (Texas Pan American series). 10.00 (ISBN 0-292-71516-1). University of Texas Press.

Deep Run. Ralph Hayes. 288p. (Orig.). 1981. pap. 2.50 (ISBN 0-505-51735-3). Tower Bks.

Deep-Sea Plunderings. Frank Thomas Bullen. LC 75-106251. (Short story index reprint series). (Illus.). 1970. Books for Libraries Press.

Deep Sea Vagabonds. Albert Sonnichsen. LC 3-10934. 1903. McClure, Phillips & Co.

Deep Sea Warriors. Alfred Basil Lubbock. LC 10-2504. 1910. 1.50. Dodd, Mead and Company.

Deep Seam. Jack Bethea. LC 26-6638. 1926. Houghton Mifflin Company.

Deep Sea's Toll. James Brendan Connolly. LC 78-37262. (Short story index reprint series). 1971. (ISBN 0-8369-4073-3). Books for Libraries Press.

Deep Sea's Toll. James Brendan Connolly. LC 5-326962. 1905. C. Scribner's Sons.

Deep Silence. Douglas Reeman. LC 68-12108. 1968. Putnam.

Deep Six. Robert Carse. LC 46-251930. 1946. W. Morrow & Company.

Deep Six. Martin Dibner. LC 53-6942. 1953. Doubleday.

Deep Six. Randy Striker. (Dusky MacMorgan Ser.: No. 2). (Orig.). 1981. pap. 1.95 (ISBN 0-451-09568-5, J9568, Sig). NAL.

Deep Sleep. Wright Morris. LC 75-5746. 1975. 3.95 (ISBN 0-8032-5823-2). University of Nebraska Press.

Deep Sleep. Wright Morris. LC 53-11783. 1953. Scribner.

Deep Snow: An Adventure Story. 1st Ed. Stanley Borucki. LC 53-9784. Exposition Press.

Deep Soundings. Alan Corby. LC 38-1825. 1937. The Caxton Printers, Ltd.

Deep Space; Eight Stories of Science Fiction. Ed. by Robert Silverberg. LC 72-14315. 1973. 5.95 (ISBN 0-8407-6264-X). T. Nelson.

Deep Space: Eight Stories of Science Fiction. Ed. by Robert Silverberg. 1974. (pbk.) 0.95. Dell.

Deep Space. 1st Ed. Eric Frank Russell. LC 54-56903. (Science fiction). 1954. Fantasy Press.

Deep Streets. Benedict Thielen. LC 32-8072. The Bobbs-Merrill Company.

Deep Summer. Gwen Bristow. 1961. Grosset & Dunlap.

Deep Summer. Gwen Bristow. LC 37-1118. Thomas T. Crowell Company C.

Deep Summer. Gwen Bristow. LC 39-4592. 1938. Thomas Y. Crowell Company.

Deep Throat Papers. 1973. pap. 2.95 o.p. (532-29100-295). Manor Bks.

Deep Thunder. Henry W. Coray. (Campus Bks). (YA) (gr. 9-12). 1970. pap. 0.95 o.p. (35-5210). Moody.

Deep Tracks in Africa. Sigurd F. Westberg. 1976. 6.95 o.p. (ISBN 0-910452-28-8); pap. 5.45 o.p. (ISBN 0-910452-41-5). Covenant.

Deep Treasure: Tales of the Oil Fields. J. C Williamson. LC 60-15382. 1960. Crown Publishers.

Deep Valley. Wilder Anthony. LC 40-8381. Dorrance and Company.

Deep Valley. Dan Totheroh. LC 42-36266. 1942. L. B. Fischer.

Deep Valley: The Pomo Indians of California. Burt W. Aginsky & Ethel G. Aginsky. LC 67-15756. 1971. pap. 2.45 o.p. (ISBN 0-8128-1392-8). Stein & Day.

Deep, Very Deep Space. Joseph Nathenson. 1979. pap. 1.75 (ISBN 0-532-17203-5). Woodhill.

Deep Water. Patricia Highsmith. LC 57-8209. (A Harper novel of suspense). 1957. Harper.

Deep Water, Dakota. Mark Vinz. (Juniper Bks: No. 32). pap. 3.00. Juniper Pr WI.

Deep Water, Deep Love. Lynna Cooper, pseud. (Adventures in Love Ser.: No. 29). 1982. pap. 1.75 (ISBN 0-451-11746-8, AE1746, Sig). NAL.

Deep Water Island. Alan Le May. LC 36-7831. Farrar & Rinehart, Incorporated.

Deep Waters. William Hope Hodgson. LC 67-3482. 1967. Arkham House.

Deep Waters. Christine Hunter, pseud. LC 68-27473. 1969. 2.95. Zondervan Pub. House.

Deep Waters. William Wymark Jacobs. LC 19-140017. 1919. C. Scribner's Sons.

Deep Waters. R. Schneider. pap. 1.50 o.p. Adler.

Deep Waters. R. Schneider. pap. 1.50 o.p. Adler.

Deep Waters. Rolf Schneider. pap. 1.25 o.p. Adler.

Deep Waters: An Anthology of Stories of the Sea. Ed. by Charles Wright Gray. LC 28-10300. H. Holt and Company.

Deep Waters: Or A Strange Story. Robert Haskins Crozier. LC 6-31946. 1887. Farris, Smith & Co.

Deep Well. Emil Paul John. LC 67-11853. (Illus.). 1967. Friendship Press.

Deep Well at Noon. Jessica Stirling. 1980. 12.95 o.p. (ISBN 0-312-19090-5). St Martin.

Deep West. Ernest Haycox. LC 37-20891. 1937. Little, Brown and Company.

Deep West. Ernest Haycox. LC 39-32055. 1939. Triangle Books.

Deep West. Ernest Haycox. (Signet Brand Western). 1973. (pbk) 0.75. New American Lib.

Deepdown River. Neill Compton Wilson. LC 64-20297. 1964. Morrow.

Deepening Blue. Sturges Mason Schley. LC 35-17769. 1935. Doubleday, Doran & Company, Inc.

Deepening Purple: A Novel. Louis Isaacson. LC 28-18236. 1928. H. Vinal, Ltd.

Deepening Stream. Francena Harriet Arnold. LC 63-15745. 1963. Zondervan Pub. House.

Deepening Stream. Dorothea Frances Canfield Fisher. LC 30-281756. Harcourt, Brace and Company.

Deepening Stream. Dorothea Frances Canfield Fisher. LC 38-27951. (Half-title: The modern library of the world's best books). 1938. The Modern Library.

Deepening Year. Mabel Louise Robinson. LC 50-9535. 1950. Westminster Press.

Deeper Foot. Richard M. Vixen. LC 77-79740. (Illus.). 1978. pap. 3.00 (ISBN 0-930182-03-0). Avant-Garde CR.

Deeper Foot: Sequel to Deep Foot. Richard M Vixen & Richard M Vixen. LC 77-79740. 1977. 3.95 (ISBN 0-930182-01-4). Avant-Garde Creations.

Deeper Scar. Sinclair Gluck. LC 27-2320. 1927. Dodd, Mead & Company.

Deeper Stain. Frank Hird. LC 9-26958. 1909. D. Appleton and Company.

Deeper the Heritage. Muriel Elwood. LC 47-1203. 1946. C. Scribner's Sons.

Deeper Throat. Warren Bisig. 192p. (Orig.). 1973. pap. 1.95 o.p. (ISBN 0-87682-320-7, 7320). Barclay Hse.

Deeper Yet. Anne Elizabeth Corner. LC 29-93010. 1929. 2.50. Longmans, Green and Co.

Deephaven. Sarah Orne Jewett. LC 72-84601. 1976. Scholarly Press.

Deephaven. Sarah Orne Jewett. LC 34-25494. 1877. J. R. Osgood and Company.

Deephaven. Sarah Orne Jewett. LC 7-9934. 1894. Houghton, Mifflin and Company.

Deephaven. Sarah Orne Jewett. LC 7-9933. 1894. Printed at the Riverside Press.

Deephaven. Sarah Orne Jewett. 1905. Houghton, Mifflin and Company.

Deephaven. 14th ed. Sarah Orne Jewett. LC 44-107103. 1885. Houghton, Mifflin Company.

Deephaven. Sarah Orne Jewett. 1978. Repr. of 1877 ed. lib. bdg. 25.00 (ISBN 0-8495-2729-5). Arden Lib.

Deephaven see Collected Works.

Deephaven & Other Stories. Sarah Orne Jewett. Ed. by Richard Cary. (Masterworks of Literature Ser). 1966. 6.50x (ISBN 0-8084-0099-1); pap. 3.95x (ISBN 0-8084-0100-9, M18). Coll & U Pr.

Deeps of Deliverance. Frederik Willem Van Eeden. LC 74-8923. (Library of Netherlandic literature, v. 5). 1975. (ISBN 0-8057-3419-8). Twayne Publishers.

Deeps of Deliverance. Frederik Willem Van Eeden & Robinson, Margaret, Tr. LC 2-28284. 1902. G. P. Putnam's Sons.

Deeps of Deliverance. Frederik Van Eeden. Tr. by Margaret Robinson. LC 74-8923. (International Studies & Translations Ser.). 1974. lib. bdg. 10.95 o.p. (ISBN 0-8057-3419-8, Twayne). G K Hall.

Deepshaven. 27th impression ed. Sarah Orne Jewett. LC 4-15464. 1900. Houghton, Mifflin and Company.

Deepwater Showdown. Halsey Clark. (Submarine Ser.: No. 2). 320p. (Orig.). 1983. pap. 3.25 (ISBN 0-440-01840-4, Emerald). Dell.

Deepwater Showdown. J. Farragut Jones. (Silent Service Ser.: No. 7). (Orig.). 1982. pap. 2.95 (ISBN 0-440-11971-5, Bryans). Dell.

Deepwood. Blanche Chenery Perrin. LC 50-8167. 1950. Macmillan.

Deepwood. Walter S. J. Swanson. 1981. 12.95 (ISBN 0-316-82476-3). Little.

Deepwood: A Novel. Walter S. J Swanson. LC 80-22361. 10.95 (ISBN 0-316-82476-3). Little, Brown.

Deer Cry: A Novel of Patrick of Eirinn. William Greenough Schofield. LC 48-8715. 1948. Longmans Green.

Deer Hunt. Peter Lefcourt. (Orig.). 1976. pap. 1.50 o.p. (ISBN 0-515-03778-8). Pyramid Pubns.

Deer Hunter. E. M. Corder. 1979. pap. 1.95 (ISBN 0-515-05321-X). Jove Pubns.

Deer Jane,". Isabel Cecilia Williams. LC 11-16888. P. J. Kenedy & Sons.

Deer on the Stairs. Louise Field Cooper. LC 43-18113. 1943. Duell, Sloan and Pearce.

Deer Park. Norman Mailer. LC 55-10093. 1955. Putnam.

Deer Park. Norman Mailer. LC 79-20163. 1980. 16.95 (ISBN 0-86527-235-2). H. Fertig.

Deer Park. Norman Mailer. LC 80-27172. 1981. 4.95 (ISBN 0-399-50531-8). Perigee Books.

Deer Run. Edward Connolly. LC 77-158881. 1971. (ISBN 0-684-12481-5). Scribner.

Deer Stalker. Zane Grey. LC 49-9547. 1949. Harper.

Deerbrook: A Novel, 3 vols. in 2. Harriet Martineau. LC 79-8170. Repr. of 1839 ed. Set. 84.50 (ISBN 0-404-62034-5). AMS Pr.

Deerslayer. James Fenimore Cooper. LC 20-19310. T. Y. Crowell and Company.

Deerslayer. James Fenimore Cooper. LC 7-7573. (Standard literature ser. no. 8). 1896. University Publishing Company.

Deerslayer. James Fenimore Cooper. Ed. by Cooper, Susan Fenimore. LC 6-30179. (Half-title: The Leather stocking sales. Riverside ed.). 1898. Houghton, Mifflin and Company.

Deerslayer. James Fenimore Cooper. LC 1-20324. (Half-title: Macmillan's pocket American and English classics). 1901. The Macmillan Company.

Deerslayer. James Fenimore Cooper. Ed. by Langsin, M. F. LC 11-551. Ginn and Company.

Deerslayer. James Fenimore Cooper. (Fairmount classics). 1924. George W. Jacobe & Company.

Deerslayer. James Fenimore Cooper. Ed. by Paine, Gregory Lansing. LC 27-7932. (Half-title: American authors series, general editor, Stanley T. Williams). Harcourt, Brace and Company.

Deerslayer. James Fenimore Cooper. LC 36-37087. (Half-title: Everyman's library, ed. by Ernest Rhys. Fiction. no. 77). 1934. J. M. Dent & Sons, Ltd.

Deerslayer: A Tale. James Fenimore Cooper. LC 4-15429. (Leather-stocking tales). 1900. Macmillan and Co., Limited.

Deerslayer: A Tale by J. Fenimore Cooper. James Fenimore Cooper. (Half-title: Everyman's library, ed. by Ernest Rhys. Fiction. no. 77). 1906. J. M. Dent & Co.

Deerslayer: Or, The First War-Path. James Fenimore Cooper. (Seaside library. v. 12, no. 224). 1878. G. Munro.

Deerslayer: Or, The First War-Path. James Fenimore Cooper. (On cover: Lovell's library, no. 463). 1884. J. W. Lovell Company.

Deerslayer: Or, The First War-Path. by j. fenimore cooper... ed. James Fenimore Cooper. (On cover: Seaside library. Pocket ed. no. 10.?2). 1888. G. Munro.

Deerslayer: Or, The First War-Path. James Fenimore Cooper. Ed. by Matthews, Brander. LC 6-45531. T. Y. Crowell & Company.

Deerslayer: Or The First War-Path. James Fenimore Cooper. LC 25-21264. 1925. C. Scribner's Sons.

Deerslayer: Or, The First War-Path. a Tale. James Fenimore Cooper. LC 6-30180. 1841. Lea & Blanchard.

Deerslayer: Or, The First War-Path. A Tale. James Fenimore Cooper. LC 26-24696. (Half-title: The choice works of Cooper. Revised and corrected series v. 2). 1856. Stringer & Townsend.

Deerslayer: Or, The First War-Path. A Tale. James Fenimore Cooper. LC 4-13397. 1901. D. Appleton and Company.

Deerslayer: Or, The First War-Path. With a New Introd. James Fenimore Cooper. LC 62-297. (Collier books, AS304). 1962. Collier Books.

Deerslayer: Or, The First Warpath. James Fenimore Cooper. LC 26-274336. Harper & Brothers.

Deerslayer: With a Teacher's Manual and a Reader's Supplement. James Fenimore Cooper. (Reader's enrichment ser. RE 702). Washington Sq.

Deerslayer. With Illus. Reproducing Drawings for Early Editions and Photos. of Historical Scenes, Together with an Introductory Biographical Sketch of the Author and Anecdotal Captions by Basil Davenport. James Fenimore Cooper. LC 52-8076. (Great illustrated classics). 1952. Dodd, Mead.

Deerwander Farm: The Story of Nancy Hartwell. Agnes Barden Dustin. LC 44-21225. 1944. L. G. Page & Company.

Defeat. Geoffrey McNeill-Moss. LC 24-8165. Boni and Liveright.

Defeat Is My Victory. Gregory Aleksis Ptitsin. LC 41-21545. 1941. Murray & Gee.

Defeat of the Bird God. C. Peter Wagner. LC 67-11615. (Illus.). 256p. 1975. Repr. of 1967 ed. 5.95 o.p. (ISBN 0-87808-721-4). William Carey Lib.

Defeat of Youth: And Other Poems. Aldous Leonard Huxley. LC 19-6173. (Colophon: The third of the Iniotiates series of poetry by proved hands). 1918. B. H. Blackwell.

Defeated but Victor Still: Or, Heirs of the Fonca Estate. A Story of the Mysteries of New Orleans, Following the Civil War and Reconstruction. William Vicars Lawrence. F. T. Neely.

Defeated but Victor Still: Or, Heirs of the Fonca Estate, a Story of the Mysteries of New Orleans, Following the Civil War and Reconstruction. 2d ed. William Vicars Lawrence. LC 1-31458. The Abbey Press.

Defection of A. J. Lewinter. Robert Littell. LC 72-5220. 1973. 5.95 (ISBN 0-395-15481-2). Houghton Mifflin.

Defection of A. J. Lewinter. Robert Littell. LC 73-10255. 1973. 9.95 (ISBN 0-8161-6140-2). G. K. Hall.

Defector. Evelyn Anthony. LC 80-25732. 1981. 12.95 (ISBN 0-698-11064-1). Coward, McCann & Geoghegan.

Defector. Evelyn Anthony. (A Signet Book)). 1982. 3.50 (ISBN 0-451-11765-4). New American Library.

Defector. Nick Carter. (Nick Carter Ser.). (O.s.i.). 160p. 1972. pap. 0.95 o.s.i. (AN1264, Award). Univ Pub & Dist.

Defector. Charles Collingwood. LC 77-103133. (Illus.). 1969. 6.95. Harper & Row.

Defector. Rick Raphael. LC 79-6887. 1980. 10.95 (ISBN 0-385-15916-1). Doubleday.

Defend the Rock.". Arthur John Pelham Groom. LC 46-2020. 1945. Jarrolds Limited.

Defender of the Angels; a Black Policeman in Old Los Angeles. Jess Kimbrough. LC 69-14818. 1969. Macmillan.

Defender of the Faith: A Romance. Frank James Mathew. LC 99-3601. 1899. J. Lane.

Defenders. Foy Gillespie. LC 12-6224. 1912. 1.50. The Cosmopolitan Press.

Defenders. Franz Hoellering & Lewisohn, Ludwig, 1882- Tr. LC 40-11889. 1940. Little, Brown, and Company.

Defenders. Edwin P. Hoyt. 3.98 o.p. (ISBN 0-498-06856-0, Encore). A S Barnes.

Defenders: A Novel Stella George Stern Perry. LC 27-19219. 1927. Frederick A. Stokes Company.

Defenders of the Law: Based on the Motion Picture Story. Hampton Del Ruth. LC 31-16445. Jacobsen Publishing Company, Inc.

Defenders of Windhaven. Marie De Jourlet. 448p. (Orig.). 1980. pap. 2.75 (ISBN 0-523-40723-8). Pinnacle Bks.

Defending a Home. A Novel. Ernest A Young. (peerless series, no. 31). 1891. J. S. Ogilvie.

Defense: A Novel by Vladimir Nabokov. Vladimir Vladimirovich Nabokov. LC 64-13017. 1964.

Defense Does Not Rest. Sherry, Edna. LC 59-6192. (Red badge detective). 1959. Dodd, Meade.

Defense of Fort Henry. A Story of Wheeling Creek in 1777, James Otis Kaler. LC 3894. (Illus.). 1900. A. L. Burt.

Defense Rests. Petre Bellu. LC 43-115526. 1943. Jovo Ltd.

Defense Rests. Eleanor Pierson. LC 42-126007. 1942. Howell, Soskin.

Defenseless Daughter. Sterling Harkins. pap. 1.95 o.p. (ISBN 0-87977-134-8, DBB134). Dansk Blue Bk.

Defiance. Oliver Payne. (Northwest Territory Ser.: Bk. 3). 448p. (Orig.). 1983. pap. 3.50 (ISBN 0-425-05846-8). Berkley Pub.

Defiance. D. M Perkins. 1976. (pbk.) 1.75. Warner Books.

Defiance: A Narrative. Myron Lawrence Fagin. LC 8-18408. Imperial Press.

Defiance in the Night: A Novel. 1st Ed. Jean Lacell. LC 54-7042. 1954. Exposition Press.

Defiance Mountain. rev. ed. Frank Bonham. 1981. pap. 1.95 (ISBN 0-425-04932-9). Berkley Pub.

Defiant. Mary Canon. (O'Hara Dynasty Ser.). 1982. pap. 2.95 (ISBN 0-373-89001-X). Harlequin Bks.

Defiant Agents. Andre Norton, pseud. 1979. lib. bdg. 9.95 (ISBN 0-8398-2423-8, Gregg). G K Hall.

Defiant Desire. Anne Carsley. (Orig.). 1982. pap. 3.50 (ISBN 0-440-12019-5). Dell.

Defiant Desire. Kaye Wilson Klem. (Fawcett Gold Medal Book). 1977. 1.75 (ISBN 0-449-13741-4). Fawcett Publications.

Defiant Destiny. Nancy Moulton. 368p. 1982. pap. 2.95 (ISBN 0-380-81430-7, 81430-7). Avon.

Defiant Ecstasy. Janelle Taylor. (Orig.). 1982. pap. 3.50 (ISBN 0-89083-931-X). Zebra.

Defiant Hearts. Bertha Behrens. Tr. by Annie W. Ayer. Slate, Helen T., Joint Tr. LC 6-9753. R. F. Fenno & Company.

Defiant Love. Maura Seger. (Orig.). 1982. pap. 2.50 (ISBN 0-671-45963-5). PB.

Defiant Mistress. Anne Devon. (Second Chance at Love Ser.: No. 105). Date not set. pap. 1.75 (ISBN 0-515-06869-1). Jove Pubns.

Deficient Saints: A Tale of Maine. Marshall Saunders. LC 99-3667. 1899. L. C. Page and Company.

Defiled Daughter. Rodd. pap. 1.95 o.p. (ISBN 0-87977-118-6). Dansk Blue Bk.

Defilement. C. L. Morrison. LC 78-64744. (Illus.). 1979. 12.50 (ISBN 0-932508-02-2). Seven Oaks.

Defilement: A Story of the Art World. C. L Morrison. LC 78-64744. (Illus.). 1978. 9.50 (ISBN 0-932508-02-2). Seven Oaks Press.

Defilers. Intro. by S. George. pap. 1.95 o.p. (6018). Brandon.

Definite Object. Jeffrey Farnol. 1975. lib. bdg. 16.70x (ISBN 0-89966-087-8). Buccaneer Bks.

Definite Object: A Romance of New York. Jeffery Farnol. LC 17-15972. 1917. Little, Brown, and Company.

Definitely Maybe. Arkadii Natanovich Strugatskii & Boris Natanovich Strugatskii. LC 77-16550. (Best of Soviet Science Fiction). 1978. 10.95 o.s.i. (ISBN 0-02-615180-4); pap. 1.95 o.s.i. (ISBN 0-02-025590-X). Macmillan.

Definitely Maybe: A Manuscript Discovered Under Unusual Circumstances. Arkadii Natanovich Strugatskii & Boris Natanovich Strugatskii. LC 77-16550. (Macmillan's Best of Soviet Science Fiction). 7.95. Macmillan.

Definition of Love: A Novel. Catherine Ridgway McCarthy. LC 49-10938. 1949. Houghton Mifflin.

Defoe's Robinson Crusoe. Daniel Defoe. Ed. by Cross, Wilbur Lucius. LC 11-6956. (Half-title: English readings for schools. General editor: W. L. Cross). 1911. 0.50. H. Holt and Company.

DeFord. David Shetzline. LC 67-22650. 1968. bds., 4.95. Random.

DeFord. David Shetzline. LC 67-22650. 1968. Random House.

Defrauded Yeggman... Harry Stephen Keeler. LC 37-4837. E. P. Dutton & Company, Inc.

Defy the Foul Fiend: Or, The Misadventures of a Heart. John Collier. LC 34-24353. 1934. A. A. Knopf.

Defy the Savage Winds. June L. Shiplett. (Orig.). 1980. pap. 2.50 (ISBN 0-451-09337-2, E9337, Sig). NAL.

Defy the Storm. Diana Haviland. 1981. 2.75 (ISBN 0-449-14379-1). Fawcett Gold Medal.

Defy the Tempest. Sylvia G. L. Dannett & Bennett, Edwin, Joint Author. LC 44-49884. 1944. J. Messner, Inc.

Degarmo's Wife & Other Stories. David G. Philips. Ed. by Abe C. Ravitz. (American Authors Ser). 1913. 18.50 o.s.i. (ISBN 0-512-00564-8). Garrett Pr.

Degarmo's Wife, and Other Stories. David Graham Phillips. LC 13-16791. 1913. 1.30. D. Appleton and Company.

Degenerates. Sandra Shulman. (Orig.). 1970. pap. price not set o.p. (64-395). Paperback Lib.

Degradation of Geoffrey Alwith. Morley Roberts. (On cover: Sergel's international library. New series. v. 1, no. 10). 1895. C. H. Sergel Company.

Degree of Difference. J. R. Adams. 1979. cancelled o.s.i.; pap. cancelled o.s.i. Writers West.

Degrees of Love. Rosemary Silverman. (O.s.i.). (Orig.). 1971. pap. 1.25 o.s.i. (B95-2169). Belmont-Tower.

Degrees of Pleasure. David Mason. (Orig.). 1969. pap. 1.95 o.s.i. (OPH165, Ophelia). Olympia.

Deidre of the Sorrows: And the Tinker's Wedding & the Shadow of the Glen. John M. Synge. (Unwin Book). 1967. pap. 3.95 (ISBN 0-04-822033-7). Allen Unwin.

Deirdre. James Stephens. LC 73-10660. (Illus.). 1970. Macmillan.

Deirdre. James Stephens & Longes Mac N Usnig. LC 62-5011. (Signet classic. CP116). 1962. New American Library.

Deirdre. James Stephens & Longes Mac N Usnig. LC 23-12751. 1923. The Macmillan Company.

Deirdre: A Celtic Legend. David Guard & Gretchen Guard. LC 77-23492. (Illus.). 4.95 (ISBN 0-89087-201-5). Celestial Arts.

Deja Vu: A Novel. Saint-Alban, Dominique. LC 77-15341. 7.95 (ISBN 0-312-19183-9). St. Martin's Press.

Dekker. Lou Cameron. (Berkley Medallion Book). 1976. (pbk.) 1.50 (ISBN 0-425-03079-2). Berkley Publishing Corp.

Del Palma, a Novel. Pamela Kellino. LC 48-5173. 1948. E. P. Dutton.

Delafield Affair. Florence Finch Kelly. LC 9-7041. 1909. A. C. McClurg & Co.

Delamer Curse: A Novel. Anne Green. LC 40-14188. Harper & Brothers.

Delaney Rides Out. Charles Stanley Strong. LC 46-19192. 1946. Phoenix Press.

Delano. rev. ed. John Gregory Dunne. 1971. 7.95 o.p. (ISBN 0-374-13697-1). FS&G.

Delaplaine: Or, The Sacrifice of Irene. A Novel. Mansfield Tracy Walworth. LC 12-13319. 1871. G. W. Carleton & Co.

Delaplaine: Or, The Sacrifice of Irene. A Novel. Mansfield Tracy Walworth. LC 42-436091. 1871. G. W. Carleton & Co.

Delay at Parson's Flat. Bob Barrett. LC 76-20835. 1976. 5.95 (ISBN 0-385-12544-5). Doubleday.

Delay En Route. Jerry Weil. LC 56-112525. (Signet books, 1824). 1965. New American Library.

Delay in the Sun. Anthony Thorne. LC 35-441. Doubleday, Doran & Company, Inc.

Delayed Action. Richard Warren Hatch. LC 52-1976. 1951. Rich and Cowan.

Delayed Payment: By John Rhode Pseud. Cecil John Charles Street. LC 56-5738. (Red Badge detective). 1956. Dodd, Mead.

Delayed Steal. Frank Waldman. LC 52-7201. (Illus.). 1952. Houghton Mifflin.

Deldee: Or, The Iron Hand. Florence Alice Price James. (On cover: Lovell's library, v. 20, no. 982). 1887. J. W. Lovell Company.

Delectable Country. Leland Dewitt Baldwin. LC 39-24453. L. Furman, Inc.

Delectable Duchy: Stories, Studies, and Sketches. Quiller-Couch, Arthur Thomas. LC 78-125235. (Short story index reprint series). 1970. Books for Libraries Press.

Delectable Duchy: Stories, Studies and Sketches. Arthur Thomas Quiller-Couch. LC 6-29009. 1893. Macmillan and Co.

Delectable Duchy: Stories, Studies and Sketches. Arthur Thomas Quiller-Couch. LC 4-152922. 1898. C. Scribner's Sons.

Delectable Mountains. Maxwell Struthers Burt. LC 70-144922. 1971. (ISBN 0-403-00885-9). Scholarly Press.

Delectable Mountains. Maxwell Struthers Burt. LC 27-26247. 1927. C. Scribner's Sons.

Delectable Mountains. Arthur Willis Colton. LC 71-86139. (Short story index reprint series). 1969. Books for Libraries Press.

Delectable Mountains. Arthur Willis Colton. LC 1-31605. 1901. C. Scribner's Sons.

Delectable Mountains. Michael Malone. 1977. 8.95 o.p. (ISBN 0-394-49729-5). Random.

Delectable Mountains: A Novel. Michael Malone. LC 76-14189. (Illus.). 8.95 (ISBN 0-394-49729-5). Random House.

Delectable Mountains: And Other Narratives. Berton Roueche. LC 59-763350. 1959. Little, Brown.

Delectable Mountains & Other Narratives. Berton Roueche. 9.95 (ISBN 0-911660-10-0). Yankee Peddler.

Deleplaine: Or, The Sacrifice of Irene; a Novel. Mansfield Tracy Walworth. 1899. G. W. Dillingham Co.

Delfia cada tarde. Edgardo Sanabria. 100p. 1978. pap. 3.00 (ISBN 0-940238-13-6). Ediciones Huracan.

Delft Cat: And Other Stories. Robert Howard Russell. LC 8-1798. 1896. R. H. Russell & Son.

Delgado Killings. Robert Hawkes. (Narc). (Signet book: Vol. 4). 1974. (pbk.) 0.95. New American Library.

Delia. Paul Schneider. 192p. 1971. 4.95 o.p. (ISBN 0-8202-0021-2). Sherbourne.

Delia Blanchflower. Mary Augusta Arnold Humphry Ward Ward. LC 14-13258. Hearst's International Library Co.

Delia Demonstrates. Berton Braley. LC 27-178090. 2.00. The Century Co.
Delia of Valla. Dray Prescot. 192p. 1982. pap. 2.35 (ISBN 0-87997-784-1, UE1784). DAW Bks.
Delia's Doctors: Or, A Glance Behind the Scenes. Hannah Gardner Creamer. LC 6-31613. 1852. Fowler and Wells.
Delicate Ape. Dorothy Belle Flanagan Hughes. LC 44-40089. 1944. Duell, Sloan and Pearce.
Delicate Case of Murder. Sinclair Gluck. LC 27-23783. 1937. The Macmillan Company.
Delicate Darling. Jack Webb. LC 59-5331. (A Father Shanely-Sammy Golden mystery). 1959. Rinehart.
Delicate Deception. Kelly L Segraves. LC 78-1847. 1978. 2.95 (ISBN 0-89293-022-5). Beta Books.
Delicate Dependency: A Novel of Vampire Life. Michael Talbot. 368p. 1982. pap. 2.95 (ISBN 0-380-77982-X, 77982). Avon.
Delicate Fire. Naomi Haldane Mitchison. LC 79-145403. (Short story index reprint series). 1971. (ISBN 0-8369-3778-3). Books for Libraries Press.
Delicate Fire: Short Stories and Poems. Naomi Haldane Mitchison. LC 33-31774. 1933. Harcourt, Brace and Company, Inc.
Delicate Fuss. Flora Klickmann. LC 33-23681. 1932. G. P. Putnam's Sons.
Delicate Geometry. Ken Chowder. LC 81-48052. 12.95 (ISBN 0-06-014973-6). Harper & Row.
Delicate Ground. A Novel. Annie Edwards. LC 6-36597. 1883. G. W. Carleton & Co.
Delicate Prey. Paul Frederic Bowles. LC 72-80780. (Neglected Bks of the 20th Century). 307p. 1981. pap. 7.95 (ISBN 0-912946-01-6). Ecco Pr.
Delicate Prey: And Other Stories. Paul Frederic Bowles. LC 50-10899. 1950. Random House.
Delicate Situation. Elizabeth Chater. (Coventry Romance Ser.: No. 191). 192p. Date not set. pap. 1.50 (ISBN 0-449-50294-5, Coventry). Fawcett.
Delicate Situation. Naomi Gwladys Royde-Smith. LC 31-272272. 1931. Harper & Brothers.
Delicious Life-Saving Kiss, the Quasi-Miraculous Kiss: Or, See What a Seasonable Well-Applied Kiss May Do; a Story of the Spanish-American War and of All Time. C.
Delight. Mazo De La Roche. LC 26-9567. 1926. The Macmillan Company.
Delight. Winifred Mary Scott. LC 33-32598. 1933. Doubleday, Doran & Company, Inc.
Delight Makers. Adolph Francis Alphonse Bandelier. LC 70-28000. (Harvest book). (Illus.). 1971. (ISBN 0-15-625264-3). Harcourt Brace Jovanovich.
Delight Makers. Adolph Francis Alphonse Bandelier. Dodd, Mead and Company.
Delight Makers. With an Introd. by Charles F. Lummis. Adolph Francis Alphonse Bandelier. LC 58-5983. 1960. Dodd, Mead.
Delightful Discipline: Humorous Stories of Woodshed Wisdom & Biblical Principles. Louis R. Goodgame. LC 77-22560. 1977. pap. 3.00 (ISBN 0-915134-43-8). Mott Media.
Delightful Dodd. Elliott Flower. 1904. L.C. Page & Company.
Delightful Road: A Brave Man's Story. Gerhard Lewis Wind. LC 31-32635. 1930. Concordia Publishing House.
Delights of Anna. John Colleton. (Orig.). 1980. pap. 3.50 (ISBN 0-451-12188-0, AE2188, Sig). NAL.
Delights of Detection: Edited with an Introd. Ed. by Jacques Barzun. LC 61-7193. 1961. Criterion Books.
Delights of Turkey: Twenty Tales. Edouard Roditi. LC 77-9588. 1977. 10.95 (ISBN 0-8112-0669-6). New Directions Pub. Corp.
Delilah. Marcus Goodrich. LC 40-35320. Farrar & Rinehart, Incorporated.
Delilah. Marcus Goodrich. LC 41-4441. Farrar & Rinehart Incorporated.
Delilah. Marcus Goodrich. 1979. 2.50 (ISBN 0-445-04433-0). Popular Library.
Delilah. Marcus Goodrich. LC 81-9426. (Time Reading Program Special Edition). 1981. (set) 12.95 (ISBN 0-8094-3646-9) (ISBN 0-8094-3647-7). Time-Life Books.
Delilah: A Novel. Marcus Goodrich. LC 77-26042. (Lost American Fiction Ser.). 520p. 1978. Repr. of 1941 ed. 11.85 (ISBN 0-8093-0739-1). S Ill U Pr.
Delilah of Harlem: A Story of the New York City of to-Day. Richard Henry Savage. LC 12-38250. 1893. The American News Company.
Delilah of the Snows. Harold Bindloss. LC 7-25049. F. A. Stokes Company.
Delilah of the Snows. Harold Bindloss. LC 8-15298. 1908. F. A. Stokes Company.
Delilah's Mountain. Gloria Jahoda. LC 63-13683. 1963. Houghton Mifflin.
Delinquent. Josiah Pitts Woolfolk. LC 34-120821. 1934. W. Godwin, Inc.
Delinquent Chacha. Ved Parkash Mehta. LC 67-15971. Harper & Row.
Delinquent Ghost. Eric Hatch. LC 44-4738. 1944. Bartholomew House, Inc.
Delirium. Barbara Alberti. LC 80-16951. 9.95 (ISBN 0-374-13744-7). Farrar, Straus, Giroux.
Deliver Us from Evil. Achmed Abdullah. LC 39-6260. 1939. G.P. Putnam's Sons.
Deliver Us from Evil. J. F. Sawyer. 1973. 5.95 o.p. Phillips Pub Co.
Deliver Us from Wolves. Leonard Patrick O'Connor Wibberley. LC 62-17926. (Red badge detective). 1963. Dodd, Mead.
Deliver Us to Evil. Joe L. Hensley. LC 79-139030. 1971. 4.50. Published for the Crime Club by Doubleday.
Deliverance. James Dickey. LC 71-100100. 1970. 5.95. Houghton Mifflin.
Deliverance. Ellen Anderson Gholson Glasgow. LC 4-1646. 1904. Doubleday, Page & Co.
Deliverance. Elliot Lovegood Grant Watson. LC 20-3264. 1920. A. A. Knopf.
Deliverance: A Novel. Helen Reimensnyder Martin. LC 25-1087. 1935. Dodd, Mead & Company.
Deliverance: A Romance of the Virginia Tobacco Fields. Ellen Anderson Gholson Glasgow. LC 73-2717. 1973. (ISBN 0-8369-7161-2). Books for Libraries Press.
Delivered from Afar: Or, Hopes Realized in Dakota. Ralph Roberts. LC 7-41202. 1885. Phillips & Hunt.
Delivery. Carolyn Bell. (Outlaws Ser.: Vol. 3). 1980. pap. 4.50x (ISBN 0-917624-19-X). Lame Johnny.
Delivery. Georges Simenon. LC 80-8759. 1981. 10.95 (ISBN 0-15-124655-6). Harcourt Brace Jovanovich.
Delivery of Furies. Victor Canning. LC 61-7803. 1961. W. Sloane Associates.
Della Dare: And Other Stories. Eva Louise Dunning. 0.25. E. L. Dunning.
Della Trewin: A Novel. Florence E Bennett. LC 76-150779. 7.95 (ISBN 0-8059-2330-6). Dorrance.
Della-Wu, Chinese Courtezan: And Other Oriental Love Tales. Frank Owen. LC 32-24980. 1931. The Lantern Press.
Deloraine. William Godwin. LC 1-787. 1833. Carey, Lea & Blanchard.
Delores Divine, Guilty or Innocent? Kenneth M Ellis. LC 31-16337. Grossett & Dunlap.
Delpha: Or, Marriage As a Failure and a Success. A Dramatic Love Story Founded on Life. Isabel Clifton Nye. (Dillingham's globe library, no. 13). 1896. G. W. Dillingham.
Delpha or, Marriage As a Failure and a Success: A Dramatic Love Story Founded on Life. Isabel Clifton Nye. (Dillingham's globe library, no. 13). 1896. G. W. Dillingham.
Delphi Betrayal. Lewis Perdue. 352p. (Orig.). 1983. pap. 2.95 (ISBN 0-523-41728-4). Pinnacle Bks.
Delphine. Mel Arrighi. LC 77-15828. 1978. 10.95 (ISBN 0-689-10862-1). Atheneum.
Delphine. Mel Arrighi. ("A Signet Book".). 1980. 2.50 (ISBN 0-451-09066-7). New American Library.
Delphine. Anne Louise Germaine Necker Stael-Holstein. LC 8-13887. 1836. E. L. Cary & A. Hart.
Delphinium Girl. Mark Smith. LC 79-2660. 9.95 (ISBN 0-06-014018-6). Harper & Row.
Delta Blood. Barbara Ferry Johnson. LC 77-24822. 1.95 (ISBN 0-380-00989-7).
Delta Decision. Wilbur A Smith. LC 79-6660. 1981. 11.95 (ISBN 0-385-13604-8). Doubleday.
Delta Deputies: Adventure Stories of the Bayou Country. 1st Ed. Carl L Martin. LC 59-7892. 1959. Greenwich Book Publishers.
Delta Deputy. Llewellyn Perry Holmes. LC 53-7981. (Double D western). 1953. Doubleday.
Delta Desire: New Orleans II. Miriam Pace. (New Orleans Ser.). 1982. pap. 3.50 (ISBN 0-8217-1021-4). Zebra.
Delta Factor. Mickey Spillane, pseud. 1968. pap. 2.50 (ISBN 0-451-12208-9, AE2208, Sig). NAL.
Delta Factor. Mickey Spillane, pseud. 1967. 3.95 o.p. Dutton.
Delta Factor: By Mickey Spillane. 1st Ed. Frank Morrison Spillane. LC 67-20533. 1967. 3.95. Dutton.
Delta Flame. Marilyn Ross. 1978. 1.95 (ISBN 0-445-04157-9). Popular Library.
Delta Girl. Ethel E Bangert. LC 49-4081. 1949. Arcadia House.
Delta Ladies. Fern Michaels. 1980. pap. 2.75 (ISBN 0-671-83337-5). PB.
Delta of Venus. Anais Nin. 1978. pap. 2.95 (ISBN 0-553-13430-2). Bantam.
Delta of Venus: Erotica. Anais Nin. LC 76-54856. 1977. 10.00 (ISBN 0-15-124656-4). Harcourt Brace Jovanovich.
Delta Q: Stories. Alvin Greenberg. LC 82-20075. (AWP; 5). 1983. 8.95 (ISBN 0-8262-0397-3). University of Missouri Press.
Delta Queen. 1977. pap. 1.95 (ISBN 0-89041-177-8, 3177). Major Bks.
Delta Star. Joseph Wambaugh. 288p. 1983. 15.95 (ISBN 0-688-01912-9). Morrow.
Delta Stud. Stuart Jason. 224p. 1976. pap. 1.50 (ISBN 0-532-15187-9). Woodhill.
Delta Two. James Frew. LC 79-50903. pap. 2.25 o.s.i. (ISBN 0-89516-083-8). Condor Pub Co.
Delta Wedding. Eudora Welty. LC 46-3217. 1946. Harcourt, Brace and Company.
Delta Wedding: A Novel. Eudora Welty. LC 78-23584. (Harvest/HBJ book). 1979. 3.95 (ISBN 0-15-625280-5). Harcourt Brace Jovanovich.
Deltoid Pumpkin Seed. John Angus McPhee. LC 72-84783. 1973. 6.95 (ISBN 0-374-13781-1). Farrar, Straus and Giroux.
Deluge. David Graham Phillips. LC 70-104541. (Illus.). 1970. Literature House.
Deluge. David Graham Phillips. LC 73-79663. (Series in American Studies). (Illus.). 1969. Johnson Reprint Corp.
Deluge. David Graham Phillips. LC 5-34515. 1905. The Bobbs-Merrill Company.
Deluge. Mykolas Vaitkus. 1965. 3.95 o.p. (ISBN 0-87141-011-7). Manyland.
Deluge: A Love Story of Ancient Times. Authorized Tr. from Lithuanian by Abinas Baranauskas, Introd. by Charles Angoff. Mykolas Vaitkus. LC 65-27473. 1966. 3.95. Manyland.
Deluge: A Novel by Ian Niall Pseud. John McNeillie. LC 51-9269. 1951. Duell, Sloan and Pearce.
Deluge: A Novel by Leonardo Da Vinci; Edited by Robert Payne. Pierre Stephen Robert Payne. LC 54-855752. 1954. Twayne Publishers.
Deluge: A Romance. Sydney Fowler Wright. LC 28-676424. 1928. Cosmopolitan Book Corporation.
Deluge; a Romance, and Dawn. Sydney Fowler Wright. LC 74-16527. (Science Fiction). 1975. 42.00 (ISBN 0-405-06335-0). Arno Press.
Deluge: An Historical Novel, 2 Vols. Henryk Sienkiewicz. 1971. Repr. of 1891 ed. Set. 49.00 (ISBN 0-403-00248-6). Scholarly.
Deluge, an Historical Novel of Poland, Sweden, & Russia, 2 vols. Henryk Sienkiewicz. Tr. by Jeremiah Curtin. LC 76-126698. Repr. of 1898 ed. Set. 24.50 (ISBN 0-404-05995-3). AMS Pr.
Deluge: an Historical Novel of Poland, Sweden and Russia: A Sequel to With Fire and Sword. Henryk Sienkiewicz. Tr. by Jeremiah Curtin. LC 76-108539. (Illus.). 1970. Scholarly Press.
Deluge: An Historical Novel of Poland, Sweden, and Russia. A Sequel to "With Fire and Sword". Henryk Sienkiewicz. LC 76-126698. (Illus.). 1971. (ISBN 0-404-05996-1) (ISBN 0-404-05997-X). AMS Press.
Deluge. An Historical Novel of Poland, Sweden, and Russia. A Sequel to "With Fire and Sword.". Henryk Sienkiewicz. Tr. by Jeremiah Curtin. LC 13-33867. 1891. Little, Brown, and Comapny.
Deluge. An Historical Novel of Poland, Sweden, and Russia. A Sequel to "With Fire and Sword.". popular ed. Henryk Sienkiewicz. Tr. by Jeremiah Curtin. LC 98-794. 1898. Little, Brown and Company.
Delusion: Or, The Witch of New England ... LC 6-34170. 1840. Hilliard Gray and Company.
Delusions. John Berryman. 1973. pap. 6.95 o.p. (ISBN 0-374-13798-6, N451, Noonday). FS&G.
Delusion's Master. Tanith Lee. (Science Fiction Ser.). 208p. 1981. pap. 2.25 (ISBN 0-87997-652-7, UE1652). DAW Bks.
Deluxe Tour. Frederic Wakeman. LC 56-9942. 1956. Rinehart.
Deluxe Tour. Frederic Wakeman. LC 57-4265. 1957. Pocket Books.
Dem. William Melvin Kelley. LC 67-19079. 1967. Doubleday.
Dem Good Ole Times. Sallie May Dooley. LC 72-6486. (Black Heritage Library Collection). (Illus.). 1972. (ISBN 0-8369-9166-4). Books for Libraries Press.
Dem Good Ole Times. Sallie May Dooley. LC 6-41718. 1906. Doubleday, Page & Company.
Demagog. William Richard Hereford. 1909. 1.50. H. Holt and Company.
Demagogue. David Ross Locke. LC 73-104515. 1970. (ISBN 0-8398-1163-2). Literature House.
Demagogue: A Political Novel. David Ross Locke. 1891. Lee and Shepard.
Demagogue and Lady Phayre. William John Locke. LC 7-15166. (On cover: The Pioneer series). E. Arnold.
Demanding Land. Giles A Lutz. 1975. (pbk.) 0.95. Ace Books.
Demands of Society. Myra Malinda Johonnot Smith. LC 99-4466. A. I. Bradley & Company.
Demarest Inheritance. Marjorie Chalmers Carleton. Orig. Title: Cry Wolf. 1973. pap. 0.95 o.p. (ISBN 0-515-02970-X, N2970). BJ Pub Group.
Demasque: By Otto M. De Bunnelle-Steiger. Bunnelle-Steiger, Otto M De. LC 29-3968. P.W. Holte.
DeMaury Papers. Isabelle Holland. LC 76-50512. 8.95 (ISBN 0-89256-010-X). Rawson Associates.
DeMaury Papers. large print ed. Isabelle Holland. LC 81-8924. 1981. 12.95. Thorndike.
Demelza: A Novel of Cornwall, 1788-1790. Winston Graham. LC 53-5043. 1953. Doubleday.
Demelza: A Novel of Cornwall, 1788-1790. Winston Graham. LC 78-26791. 1979. 17.95 (ISBN 0-8161-6677-3). G. K. Hall.
Demesne of the Swans: Lebedinyi Stan. Marina Ivanovna Efron TSvetaeva & Robin Kemball. LC 80-12957. (Illus.). 15.00 (ISBN 0-88233-493-X). Ardis.
Demeter Flower. Rochelle Singer. LC 80-14015. 9.95 (ISBN 0-312-19194-4). St. Martin's Press.
Demeter Flower. Rochelle Singer. LC 81-21448. 1982. 6.95 (ISBN 0-312-19195-2). St. Martin's Press.
Demeter's Daughter. Eden Phillpotts. LC 11-644119. 1911. 1.35. John Lane Company.
Demetrain. Ellison Harding. LC 7-15113. 1907. Brentano's.
Demetrio Aguilera-Malta and Social Justice: The Tertiary Phase of Epic Tradition in Latin American Literature. Clementine Christos Rabassa. LC 78-75193. 18.50 (ISBN 0-8386-2079-5). Fairleigh Dickinson University Press.
Demi-Gods. James Stephens. LC 14-188071. 1914. The Macmillan Company.
Demi-Virgins. Marcel Prevost. Tr. by Hornblow, Arthur. LC 7-30110. (On cover: Holland library, no. 2). Holland Publishing Company.
Demi-Widow. Mary Pickford. LC 35-131743. The Bobbs-Merrill Company.
Demian. Hermann Hesse. LC 23-6945. Boni and Liveright.
Demian Notes. Bruce L Marcoon. 1974. (pbk.) 1.25 (ISBN 0-8220-0385-6). Cliffs Notes.
Demian: The Story of a Youth. Hermann Hesse. 1948. H. Holt.
Demian: The Story of Emil Sinclair's Youth. Introd. by Thomas Mann. Tr. from German by Michael Roloff, Michael Lebeck. Hermann Hesse. (Modern classic, NY4054). 1968. Bantam.
Demian: The Story of Emil Sinclair's Youth. Hermann Hesse. LC 64-18078. 1965. Harper & Row.
Demigod: A Novel... Edward Payson Jackson. 1887. Harper & Brothers.
Demigods. John Biggs. LC 26-9110. 1926. C. Scribner's Sons.
Democracy. Henry Adams. Repr. of 1879 ed. lib. bdg. 12.50x o.p. (ISBN 0-89244-021-X). Queens Hse.
Democracy. Shaw Desmond. LC 19-10685. 1919. C. Scribner's Sons.
Democracy: An American Novel. Henry Adams. (CL 164). 1968. Airmont.
Democracy: An American Novel. Henry Adams. LC 82-3147. 1982. 4.95 (ISBN 0-517-54728-7). Harmony Books.
Democracy: An American Novel. Henry Adams & John Hay. LC 7-12165. (Leisure hour series, no. 112). 1880. H. Holt and Company.
Democracy: An American Novel. 16th impression. ed. Henry Adams & John Hay. LC 8-10432. H. Holt and Company.
Democracy: An American Novel. With a Foreword by Henry D. Aiken. Henry Adams. LC 61-3193. (Signet classic, CD48). 1961. New American Library.
Democracy & Esther: Two Novels. Henry Adams. 8.75 (ISBN 0-8446-1008-9). Peter Smith.
Democracy: And, Esther, Two Novels. Introd. by Ernest Samuels. Henry Adams. LC 65-4177. 1965. 4.00. P. Smith.
Democracy & Political Change in Village India. A. H. Somjee. 1972. 7.50x o.p. South Asia Bks.
Democracy at Bay. Alan R Steuer. LC 75-19754. 5.95 (ISBN 0-8283-1630-9). Branden Press.
Democracy Reborn. John Paul Blair. LC 47-17188. 1947. Printed by F. Hubner & Co., Inc.
Democrat. Sam Toperoff. LC 75-12503. 1975. 8.95 (ISBN 0-8415-0386-9). Saturday Review Press.
Democrat: Or, Intrigues and Adventures of Jean le Noir... Henry James Pye. LC 7-42404. 1795. Printed for James Rivington, No. Pearl-Street.
Democratic Rhine-Maid: A Novel. Franklin Kent Gifford. LC 14-11093. 1914. 1.25. The Devin-Adair Company.
Democrats of Yesterday. Josephine Rademaker. LC 35-596263. The John C. Winston Company.
Demolished Man. Alfred Bester. LC 75-396. (Garland Library of Science Fiction). 1975. 11.00 (ISBN 0-8240-1402-2). Garland Pub.
Demolished Man. Alfred Bester. LC 53-7290. 1953. Shasta Publishers.
Demolished Man. Alfred Bester. (Kangaroo Book). 1978. 1.95 (ISBN 0-671-82046-X). Pocket Books.
Demon. Eve Bunting. LC 76-18125. (No Such Things Ser.). (Illus.). 1976. 6.95 (ISBN 0-88436-273-6); pap. 3.95 (ISBN 0-88436-274-4). EMC.
Demon. Hubert Selby. LC 76-41918. 8.95 (ISBN 0-87223-465-7). Playboy Press.

Demon. Hubert Selby. (Signet Book). 1977. 1.95 (ISBN 0-451-07611-7). New American Library.
Demon Caravan. Georges Surdez. LC 27-24671. 1927. L. Macveagh, The Dial Press.
Demon Cosmos. Alan Glasser. 1979. pap. 1.75 (ISBN 0-89041-240-5, 3240). Major Bks.
Demon Device. Robert Saffron. 288p. 1981. pap. 2.50 (ISBN 0-441-14255-9, Pub. by Charter Bks). Ace Bks.
Demon Device. Robert Saffron. As told to Arthur C. Doyle. LC 78-9836. 1979. 10.95 (ISBN 0-399-12285-0). Putnam Pub Group.
Demon Device: A Novel. Robert Saffron & Arthur Conan Doyle. LC 78-9836. (Illus.). 9.95 (ISBN 0-399-12285-0). Putnam.
Demon Fire. Marsha Alexander. 224p. (Orig.). 1982. pap. 2.50 (ISBN 0-523-41636-9). Pinnacle Bks.
Demon Flower. Jo Imog. LC 73-190769. 1973. 6.95 (ISBN 0-8184-0225-3). M. Girodias Associates; Distributed by L. Stuart, Secaucus, N.J.
Demon in My View. Ruth Rendell. LC 76-9486. 1976. 5.95 (ISBN 0-385-12110-5). Doubleday.
Demon in My View. Ruth Rendell. LC 76-381000. 1976. 3.50 (ISBN 0-09-126100-7). Hutchinson.
Demon in My View. Ruth Rendell. LC 78-3824. 1978. 9.95 (ISBN 0-89340-142-0). J. Curley.
Demon in the House. Angela Mackail Thirkell. LC 35-3243. 1935. H. Smith & R. Haas.
Demon in the Sun Parlor. Lester Goran. LC 68-20112. 1968. New American Library.
Demon Island. Kenneth Robeson. (Avenger#36). 1975. (pbk.) 0.95 (ISBN 0-446-75858-2). Warner Paperback Library.
Demon Lover. Victoria Holt, pseud. LC 82-45073. 384p. 1982. 14.95 (ISBN 0-385-18222-8). Doubleday.
Demon of Barnabas Collins. Marilyn Ross. (Orig.). 1969. pap. 0.60 o.p. (ISBN 0-446-63414-X, 63-414). Paperback Lib.
Demon of Cawnpore. Jules Verne. 1959. 3.95 o.p. Assoc Bk.
Demon of Gold. Hendrik Conscience. LC 6-28066. 1857. Murphy & Co.
Demon of Noon. Gordon Merrick. LC 54-6771. 1954. J. Messner.
Demon of Raven's Cliff. Patience Zawadsky. (Orig.). 1971. pap. 0.75 o.p. (B75-2106). Belmont-Tower.
Demon of Scattery. Poul Anderson & Mildred Downey Broxon. LC 80-100034. (Illus.). 4.95 (ISBN 0-441-14252-4). Ace Books.
Demon of the Dark Ones. Robert E. Vardeman & Victor Milan. LC 81-83263. (War of Powers Ser.: Bk. 6). 224p. (Orig.). 1982. pap. 2.50 (ISBN 0-86721-012-5). Playboy Pbks.
Demon of the Darkness. Dana Fuller Ross. 1975. (pbk.) 0.95 (ISBN 0-671-77956-7). Pocket Books.
Demon of the Night. Rita Lakin. (Orig.). 1976. pap. 1.50 o.p. (ISBN 0-515-03939-X). BJ Pub Group.
Demon Prince: The Dissonant Worlds of Jack Vance. Jack Rawlins. LC 81-21600. (Milford Series: Popular Writers of Today; V. 40). 1982. 8.95 (ISBN 0-89370-163-7) (ISBN 0-89370-263-3). Borgo Press.
Demon Samurai. Clay Grant. (Belmont Tower Book). 1.50 (ISBN 0-505-51244-0). Tower Pubns.
Demon Seed. Dean Koontz. LC 73-4817. 1973. 0.95. Bantam Books.
Demon Stalking. Debra Thrall. (Orig.). 1979. pap. 1.95 (ISBN 0-532-23116-3). Woodhill.
Demon Summer. Elaine Booth Selig. 1979. 1.95 (ISBN 0-671-81948-8). Pocket Books.
Demon Trapper of Umbagog. A Thrilling Tale of the Maine Forests. Daniel Pierce Thompson. (On cover: Columbian library, no. 10). 1890. Columbian Publishing Company.
Demon Within. 1st Ed. Brook Hastings. LC 53-9347. 1953. Published for the Crime Club by Doubleday.
Demoniac. authorized ed. Walter Besant. LC 6-12893. (On cover: Lovell's international series, no. 134). United States Book Company.
Demoniacs. 1st Ed. John Dickson Carr. LC 62-15728. 1962. Harper & Row.
Demonic Possession. Hans Holzer. (Orig.). 1980. pap. 2.25 (ISBN 0-532-23128-7). Woodhill.
Demonists. rev. ed. Davis Gurney. 1977. pap. 1.95 (ISBN 0-532-19146-3). Woodhill.
Demons by Daylight. J. Ramsey Campbell. LC 77-169745. 1973. 5.00. Arkham House.
Demon's Feast. Louise Walbrook. (Orlando Ser). 160p. 1972. pap. 1.95 o.s.i. (0*R*L002). Olympia.
Demon's Feast. Illus. by Louise Walbrook. Orig. Title: Gordon. 1968. pap. 1.25 o.s.i. (2221, Travellers Comp). Olympia.
Demon's Mirror. James S Wallerstein. LC 51-20331. 1951. Harbinger House.
Demon's Mirror. 2d ed. James S Wallerstein. LC 52-855. Bellamy Press.
Demons of Highpoint House. Cathy Cunningham. 1973. 0.95. Popular Library.
Demons of Sandorra. Paul Tabori. (O.s.i.). (Orig.). 1970. pap. 0.75 o.s.i. (A716S, Award). Univ Pub & Dist.
Demons of Zammar. Mike Sirota. (Ro-Lan Ser.: No. 4). (Orig.). 1981. pap. 2.50 (ISBN 0-89083-855-0). Zebra.
Demons Within: And Other Disturbing Tales. Ed. by Helen Hoke. LC 77-76473. 1977. 8.95 (ISBN 0-8008-2156-4). Taplinger.
Demophon: A Traveller's Tale. Forrest Reid, pseud. Repr. of 1927 ed. cancelled o.s.i. (ISBN 0-403-01168-X). Scholarly.
Demoralizing Marriage. Edgar Fawcett. LC 6-38953. (On cover: American novels). 1889. J. B. Lippincott Company.
Demos: A Story of English Socialism. a new ed. london, smith, elder, & co., 1892. ed. George Robert Gissing. LC 75-148786. 1971. (ISBN 0-404-02778-4). AMS Press.
Demos: A Story of English Socialism... George Robert Gissing. (Harper's Franklin square library, no. 522). 1886. Harper & Brothers.
Dempsey Diamonds. Allen Arnot. LC 11-269567. 1912. John Lane.
Demu Trilogy. F. M. Busby. (gr. 10-12). 1980. pap. 3.50 (ISBN 0-671-43288-5, Timescape). PB.
Den of the Sixteenth Section. M. E Clements. LC 11-29658. 1.50. Broadway Publishing Co.
Den of Thieves: Or, The Lay-Reader of St. Mark's. Mary Cruger. 1886. Funk & Wagnalies.
Dene Hollow. A Novel. Ellen Price Henry Wood Wood. LC 9-504. T. B. Peterson & Brothers.
Dene Hollow. A Novel. Ellen Price Henry Wood Wood. (Seaside library, v. 4, no. 65). 1877. G. Munro.
Denham Proper. Alfred Slote. LC 52-136449. 1953. Putnam.
Denied a Country. Herman Joachim Bang. Tr. by Marie Busch. Chater, A. G., Joint Tr. LC 27-11720. 1927. A. A. Knopf.
Denis Bracknel. Forrest Reid, pseud. 1947. Faber and Faber.
Denis Dent: A Novel. Ernest William Hornung. LC 4-37333. 1904. F. A. Stokes Company.
Denis Duval. William Makepeace Thackeray. LC 8-28245. (On cover: Lovell's library, v. 4, no. 143). 1883. J. W. Lovell Company.
Denis Duval: The Wolves and the Lamb; Lovel the Widower; and Roundabout Papers. William Makepeace Thackeray & Keene, Charles Samuel, 1823-1891, Illus. LC 12-31113. (Half-title: The biographical edition. The works of... Thackeray... vol. XII). 1899. Harper & Brothers.
Denise. Edward Hunt. (Orig.). 1977. pap. 1.50 (ISBN 0-532-15247-6). Woodhill.
Denise. Arthur Melville. pap. 2.25 o.s.i. (Venus). Grove.
Denise of the Three Pines. Edith Augusta Sawyer. LC 22-13123. 1922. The Page Company.
Denison's Ice Road. Edith Iglaver. LC 74-8810. 1975. 8.95 o.p. (ISBN 0-525-09006-1). Dutton.
Denmam Thompson's Old Homestead. Written from the Celebrated Play of "The Old Homestead.". John Russell Coryell & Thompson, Denman. 1889. Street & Smith.
Denmark Bus. Slater McGurk, pseud. LC 66-224996. 1966. bds., 3.50. Walker.
Denmark's Best Stories: An Introduction to Danish Fiction. Ed. by Hanna Astrup Larsen. LC 28-26939. (Half-title: Scandinavian classics, vol. xxi). The American-Scandinavian Foundation; W. W. Norton & Company, Inc.
Dennecker Code. J. C. Pollock. 224p. 1982. pap. 2.50 (ISBN 0-449-14454-2, GM). Fawcett.
Dennings and Their Beaux: And, Alina Derlay, Etc. Etc. Eliza Leslie. LC 7-14484. 1851. A. Hart.
Dennis Comes Home. Quintin S Scott. LC 42-931093. Harbinger House.
Dennis Horgan: Gentleman, and Other Sketches. P. J McCormack. LC 11-16256. 1911. De Wolfe and Fiske Comapny.
Dennis McGrath--Autocrat: And Other Horseless Tales Hanging Thereby. Edward Porter. LC 4-19642. 1904. H. B. Turner & Co.
Dennis the Menace & His Girls. Hank Ketcham. (Dennis the Menace Ser.). (Illus.). 1978. pap. 1.95 (ISBN 0-449-13795-3, GM). Fawcett.
Dennis the Menace Camps Out. Fred Toole. LC 58-6559. (Tip-top elf book, 1002). Rand McNally.
Dennis the Menace: One More Time! Hank Ketchum. 128p. 1981. pap. 1.50 (ISBN 0-449-14423-2, GM). Fawcett.
Dennis the Menace-Play It Again, Dennis. Hank Ketcham. (Fawcett Gold Medal). 1975. (pbk.) 0.75. Fawcett Pub.
Dennison Hill. Daoma Winston. (Orig.). 1970. pap. 0.60 o.p. (63-349). Paperback Lib.
Denny and the Dumb Cluck. J. P McEvoy. LC 30-200803. 1930. Simon and Schuster.
Denounced. John Banim. LC 79-13089. (Ireland, from the Act of Union, 1800, to the Death of Parnell, 1891). 1979. 96.00 (ISBN 0-8240-3470-8). Garland Pub.
Denounced. John Banim & Michael Banim. LC 6-6110. 1830. Printed by J. & J. Harper.
Denounced: A Romance. John Edward Bloundelle-Burton. LC 6-16697. 1896. D. Appleton and Company.
Denounced: Or, The Last Baron of Crana. a new ed., with introduction and notes, by michael banim, esq.... ed. John Banim. Ed. by Michael Banim. LC 42-531. 1865. D. & J. Sadlier & Co.
Denry the Audacious. Arnold Bennett. LC 74-6208. (collected works of Arnold Bennett). 1974. (ISBN 0-518-19095-1). Books for Libraries Press.
Denry the Audacious. Arnold Bennett. LC 11-2076. E. P. Dutton & Company.
Denton's Army. Ralph Cross. 1979. pap. 1.75 o.s.i. (ISBN 0-505-51388-9). Tower Bks.
Denver. John Dunning. LC 79-19306. 11.95 (ISBN 0-8129-0870-8). Times Books.
Denver in Slices. Louisa W. Arps. LC 59-8214. (Illus.). 268p. 1983. 15.95 (82-76123); pap. 9.95 (82-76131). Ohio U Pr.
Denver Is Missing. Dennis Feltham Jones. (Berkley medallion book). 1974. (pbk.) 1.25 (ISBN 0-425-02509-8). Berkley Pub. Co.
Denver Is Missing. Dennis Feltham Jones. LC 70-161102. 1971. 5.95 (ISBN 0-8027-0355-0). Walker.
Denys the Dreamer: A Novel. Katharine Tynan Hinkson, pseud. LC 21-11101. 1921. Benzinger Brothers.
Denzil Quarrier. George Robert Gissing. LC 6-43982. 1892. Macmillan and Co.
Denzil Quarrier: A Novel. George Robert Gissing. LC 79-80634. 1969. AMS Press.
Deo Gratias. Translated from French. Michel Servin. LC 64-19795. 1965. bds., 3.95. St. Martin's.
Depart This Life: By E. X. Ferrars Pseud. 1st Ed. Morna Doris MacTaggart Brown. LC 58-10047. 1958. Published for the Crime Club by Doubleday.
Departing Friends. Bernard Glemser. LC 78-14703. 1979. 8.95 (ISBN 0-385-14758-9). Doubleday.
Departing Wings. Faith Baldwin Cuthrell. LC 27-23608. 1927. Dodd, Mead & Company.
Department. Gerald Warner Brace. 289p. 1976. Repr. of 1968 ed. lib. bdg. 9.95x o.p. Queens Hse.
Department. Gerald Warner Brace. (Phoenix Fiction Ser.). 290p. 1968. pap. 6.95 (ISBN 0-226-06968-0). U of Chicago Pr.
Department. Gerald Warner Brace. LC 68-15752. 1968. 4.95 o.p. (ISBN 0-393-08442-6). Norton.
Department of Dead Ends: 14 Detective Stories. Roy Vickers & Everett Franklin Bleiler. LC 78-52587. 3.50. Dover Publications.
Department of Death. John Creasey. 1979. 1.75 (ISBN 0-445-04371-7). Popular Library.
Department of Queer Complaints. John Dickson Carr. LC 40-36102. 1940. W. Morrow and Company.
Department of Queer Complaints. John Dickson Carr. LC 81-4839. (Gregg Press Mystery Fiction Series). 1981. 13.95 (ISBN 0-8398-2739-3). Gregg Press.
Department of Queer Complaints. Carter Dickson, pseud. 1981. 13.95 (ISBN 0-8398-2739-3, Gregg). G K Hall.
Department Store. Margarete Bohme & Mayne, Ethel Colburn, Tr. LC 12-6599. 1912. 1.30. D. Appleton and Company.
Department Store Nurse. Rose Dana, pseud. Ed. by Alice Sachs. 1970. 3.95 o.p. Lenox Hill.
Department Store of Global Confinement & Other Entireties. Marvin Cohen. 1978. write for info. o.p. Seagull Pubns.
Departure. Daniel F. Gerber. 1973. p. 7.50_o. (ISBN 0-912090-31-6); pap. 2.45 (ISBN 0-912090-30-8). Sumac Mich.
Departure. Kathryn Martin. LC 62-18755. 1962. Holt, Rinehart and Winston.
Departure: A Novel. Roland Dorgeles & Rush, Pauline E., Tr. LC 28-25462. 1928. Simon and Schuster.
Departure: A Novel. 1st Ed. John Olden Sherry. LC 53-9865. 1953. Bobbs-Merrill.
Departure: And Other Stories. Howard Melvin Fast. LC 49-10734. 1949. Little, Brown.
Departure and Other Stories. Howard Melvin Fast. LC 80-23584. 1980. 7.95 (ISBN 0-915238-37-3) (ISBN 0-915238-40-3). Peace Press.
Departure Deferred. W. Howard Baker. 1966. pap. 0.50 o.p. (50-275). Manor Bks.
Departure Delayed. William Charles Oursler. LC 47-5298. 1947. Simon and Schuster.
Departure from the Rules: A Novel. Anthony Robinson. LC 60-8480. 1960. Putnam.
Departure of Mr. Gaudette. Doris Miles Disney. LC 64-20985. 1964. Published for the Crime Club by Doubleday.
Departures. Jane Bernstein. 304p. 1981. pap. 2.50 (ISBN 0-380-53736-2, 53736). Avon.
Departures: A Novel. Jane Bernstein. LC 79-4060. 9.95 (ISBN 0-03-048216-X). Holt, Rinehart and Winston.
Depends What You Mean by Love. Nicholas Monsarrat. LC 48-5149. 1948-1947. A. A. Knopf.
Deportment & Discipline of a Young Man. Kidrodstock. 1972. pap. 2.25 o.s.i. (V1064R, Venus). Grove.
Deposit Vault Puzzle: Or, The Contents of Box A, No. 39. John Russell Coryell. (On cover: Shield series, no. 36). 1896. Street & Smith.
Depot Master. Joseph Crosby Lincoln. LC 10-14251. 1910. 1.50. D. Appleton and Company.
Depot Master. Joseph Crosby Lincoln. LC 21-13935. 1912. A. L. Burt Company.
Depraved Sleepers and Golden Ophelia. Reimond Karel Maria De Belser. LC 77-1493. (Library of Netherlandic literature; v. 10). 9.95 (ISBN 0-8057-8158-7). Twayne Publishers.
Depression or Bust. Mack Reynolds. (Ace Science fiction). 1974. (pbk.) 0.95. Ace Books.
Depth of Love: Or, A Mother's Sacrifice. Dora Delmar. (On cover: Library of American authors. no. 52). 1893. G. Munro's Sons.
Depths. John Creasey. LC 67-132451. 1967. bds., 3.95. Walker.
Depths of Danger. Halsey Clark. (Periscope Ser.: No. 3). (Orig.). 1983. pap. 3.25 (ISBN 0-440-01888-9). Dell.
Depths of Danger. J. Farragut Jones. (Silent Service Ser.: No. 8). (Orig.). 1981. pap. 2.95 (ISBN 0-440-11972-3). Dell.
Depths of Love. Norma Seely. LC 82-45124. 1982. 10.95 (ISBN 0-385-18208-2). Doubleday.
Depths of Prosperity. Phyllis Bottome & Thompson, Dorothy, Joint Author. LC 25-12734. George H. Doran Company.
Depths of Yesterday. Delphine C. Lyons. 1972. pap. 0.95 o.s.i. (75-355). Lancer.
Depuis Toujours. Daphne Clair. (Harlequin Romantique Ser.). 192p. 1983. pap. 1.95 (ISBN 0-373-41192-8). Harlequin Bks.
Deputies from Hell. Charles Morris Martin. (O.s.i.). 1976. pap. 0.95 o.s.i. Belmont-Tower.
Deputy at Snow Mountain. Edison Marshall. LC 32-5863. 1932. H. C. Kinsey & Company, Inc.
Deputy at Wild Card. Margaret Scaraino. (Perspectives II Ser.). (Illus.). 48p. (gr. 7-12). 1982. pap. 2.50 (ISBN 0-87879-315-1). Acad Therapy.
Deputy from Montana: By Chuck Stanley Pseud. Charles Stanley Strong. LC 55-7153. 1955. Arcadia House.
Deputy of Arcis. Honore De Balzac. Tr. by Katharine Prescott Wormeley. LC 3-23191. (Half-title: The comedy of human life... Scenes from political life). 1896. Roberts Brothers.
Deputy of San Riano. Lawrence A Keating. LC 33-19398. E. J. Clode, Inc.
Deputy Sheriff. Clarence Edward Mulford. LC 73-89652. 1973. 6.95. Aeonian Press.
Deputy Sheriff. Clarence Edward Mulford. LC 30-6807. 1930. Doubleday, Doran & Company, Inc.
Deputy Sheriff. Clarence Edward Mulford. LC 42-508542. 1942. The Sun Dial Press.
Deputy Sheriff. George Washington Ogden. LC 35-1978. 1935. Dodd, Mead & Company.
Deputy Sheriff of Comanche County. Edgar Rice Burroughs. LC 79-16674. (Series: Gregg Press Western Fiction Series.). 1979. 8.95 (ISBN 0-8398-2578-1). Gregg Press.
Deputy Sheriff of Comanche County. Edgar Rice Burroughs. 1975. (pbk.) 1.50. Ace Books.
Deputy Sheriff of Comanche County: By Edgar Rice Burroughs Illustrated by John Coleman Burroughs. Edgar Rice Burroughs. LC 41-5978. E. R. Burroughs, Inc.
Deputy Sheriff of Commanche County. Edgar Rice Burroughs. 320p. 1979. pap. 1.95 (ISBN 0-441-14248-6, Pub. by Charter Bks). Charter Bks.
Deputy Was King. Gladys Bronwyn Stern. LC 26-20059. 1926. A. A. Knopf.
Dequesa By Default. Maura McGiveny. (Harlequin Romances Ser.). 192p. 1982. pap. 1.50 (ISBN 0-373-02511-4). Harlequin Bks.
Der Ketzen Von Soana. Gerhart Johann Robert Hauptmann. Ed. by Lothar Kahn. LC 72-840882. (Holt series in German literature). 1973. (pbk.) 4.25. Holt.
Der Kleine Prinz. Saint Exupery, Antoine De. Tr. by Grete Leitgeb & Josef Leitgeb. LC 73-4886. (Harbrace paperbound library, HPL 60). 1973. (ISBN 0-15-625285-6). Harcourt Brace Jovanovich.
Der Letzte. Ernst Von Wildenbruch & Schmidt, Friedrich Georg Gottlob, 1868- Ed. LC 99-670. (Heath's modern language series). 1899. D. C. Heath & Co.
Der Prozess Um Des Esels Schatten: Die Geschichte der Abderitenm Iv Buch. Ed. by W. E. Yuill. Christoph Martin Wieland. Ed. by William Edward Yuill. LC 65-2140. (Clarendon German ser.) Bibl.). 1965. 1.80. Oxford.
Der Schimmelreiter. Ed. by Willy Schumann. Theodor Storm. Ed. by Willy Schumann. LC 67-11760. 1967. pap., 2.50. Oxford Univ. Pr.

Der Streit Um Den Sergeanten Grischa. (abridged ed.) ed. Arnold Zweig & Peebles, Waldo Cutler, 1895- Ed. LC 39-11449. (Harper's German series). Harper & Brothers.

Derai. E. C. Tubb. (Dumerest of Terra Ser.). 176p. 1982. pap. 2.25 (ISBN 0-441-14261-3). Ace Bks.

Derby Man. Gary McCarthy. LC 76-10519. 1976. 5.95 (ISBN 0-385-12408-2). Doubleday.

Derby Man. Gary McCarthy. 1979. 1.50 (ISBN 0-440-13297-5). Dell Pub. Co.

Derelict. Joseph Thompson Shaw. LC 30-20815. 1930. A. A. Knopf.

Derelict Alley: By M. Coates Webster... Marriott Coates Webster. LC 33-18223. The Macaulay Company.

Derelict: And Also The Liqueur Glass, Mademoiselle L'Anglaise, The Awkward Turn, The Syren's Isle, Iron Stone, The Pace, Brother Leo. Phyllis Bottome. LC 17-141806. 1917. The Century Co.

Derelict: Further Adventures of Charles Selden and His Native Friends Inthe South Seas. Charles Bernard Nordhoff. LC 28-21223. 1928. Little, Brown, and Company.

Derelicts. William John Locke. LC 7-15172. 1897. J. Lane.

Derelicts. Dean T Wilton. LC 28-24703. 1928. Dorrance and Company.

Derelicts: A Novel. William McFee. LC 38-28903. 1839. Doubleday, Doran & Company, Inc.

Derfflinger. Robert Garland. 1978. pap. 1.75 (ISBN 0-532-17181-0). Woodhill.

Dermotts Rampant. Stephen McKenna. LC 31-19570. 1931. Dodd, Mead & Company.

Derrick Tall. Virginia Wilson Lee. LC 72-78399. 1972. 7.50. Sun Mountain Books.

Derrick Vaughan: Novelist. Ada Ellen Bayly. (On cover: Lovell's international series, no. 24.). F.F. Lovell & Company.

Derricks. James Barr. LC 51-13177. 1951. Greenberg.

Derringforth: A Novel. Frank Andrew Munsey. 1894. F. A. Munsey & Company.

Derrumbe. Cesar A. Iglesias. LC 81-68087. 1981. pap. 7.95 (ISBN 0-940238-51-9). Ediciones Huracan.

Deruga Trial. Ricarda Octavia Huch. LC 29-15482. The Macaulay Company.

Derval Hampton: A Story of the Sea. James Grant. LC 44-43129. 1887. G. Routledge and Sons.

Dervorgilla: Or The Downfall of Ireland. Anna C. Scanlan. LC 8-202259. 1895. J. H. Yewdale & Sons Co., Printers.

Deryni Checkmate. Katherine Kurtz. 1976. pap. 2.25 (ISBN 0-345-29224-3). Ballantine.

Deryni Rising. Katherine Kurtz. 1976. pap. 2.25 (ISBN 0-345-29105-0). Ballantine.

Des Bleus a L'ame. Francoise Sagan, pseud. 18.95. French & Eur.

Desalmados. John Benteen. Tr. by Juan A. Rios from Eng. (Compadre Collection: Sundance Ser., No. 2). 160p. (Span.). 1974. pap. 0.75 (ISBN 0-88473-532-X). Fiesta Pub.

Descant for Gossips. Thea Astley. LC 73-482165. 1968. 3.50. Jacaranda.

Descendant. Ellen Anderson Gholson Glasgow. LC 76-51667. (Recovered Fiction by American Women). 1977. 21.00 (ISBN 0-405-10046-9). Arno Press.

Descendant: A Novel... Ellen Anderson Gholson Glasgow. LC 6-43963. 1897. Harper & Brothers.

Descendants of Cyrus Perkins. Charles Bloomer. LC 32-2872. The Christopher Publishing House.

Descendants of Star. Thomas C. Bailey. 96p. 1980. 5.50 (ISBN 0-682-49601-4). Exposition.

Descent. James Whitfield Ellison. LC 78-96309. 1970. 5.95. McCall Pub. Co.

Descent. Arthur Anderson Peters. LC 52-13856. 1952. Farrar, Straus and Young.

Descent into Hell. Charles Williams. LC 75-306793. 1973. 2.45 (ISBN 0-8028-1220-1). Eerdmans.

Descent into Hell. Charles Williams. LC 49-7643. 1949. Pellegrini & Cudahy.

Descent into Hell see Novels.

Descent of Anansi. Larry Niven & Steven Barnes. 288p. (Orig.). 1982. pap. 2.95 (ISBN 0-523-48542-5). Pinnacle Bks.

Descent of Euphues: Three Elizabethan Romance Stories: Euphues, Pandosto and Piers Plainness. Ed. by James Winny. Robert Greene. LC 58-2619. 1957. Eng. University Press.

Descent of Man: And Other Stories. Edith Newbold Jones Wharton. LC 73-110222. (Short story index reprint series). 1970. Books for Libraries Press.

Descent of Man: And Other Stories. Edith Newbold Jones Wharton. 1904. C. Scribner's Sons.

Descent of Man: Stories. T. Coraghessan Boyle. LC 78-23812. 9.95 (ISBN 0-316-10469-8). Little, Brown.

Descent of Man: Stories. T. Coraghessan Boyle. LC 79-26999. 1980. 3.95 (ISBN 0-07-006956-5). McGraw-Hill Book Co.

Descent of the Doves: Camus's Journey to the Spirit. Alfred Cordes. LC 79-3811. 17.50 (ISBN 0-8191-0931-2) (ISBN 0-8191-0932-0). University Press of America.

Descent of the Idol. Jaroslav Durych. Tr. by Hudson, Lynton A. LC 36-24399. E. P. Dutton & Co., Inc.

Descent of Woman. Elaine Morgan. 288p. 1973. pap. 2.50 (ISBN 0-553-12848-5). Bantam.

Descent. 1st Ed. Gina Berriault. LC 60-11944. 1960. Atheneum.

Deschanos. A Thrilling Romance. Junius Lackland Hempstead. LC 5-26125. Ben-Franklin Publishing Co.

Deschooling Kevin Carew. Desmond O'Grady. LC 75-509335. 1974. 4.95 (ISBN 0-85885-108-3). Wren.

Describe a Circle. Zoe Girling. LC 33-253722. 1933. Harper & Brothers.

Description of Millenium Hall. Sarah Robinson Scott & Barbara Montagu. LC 74-16207. (Flowering of the Novel). (Illus.). 1974. (ISBN 0-8240-1161-9). Garland Pub.

Description of Millenium Hall. An 18th Century Novel, Edited by Walter M. Crittenden. Sarah Robinson Scott. LC 55-14664. 1955. Bookman Associates.

Desecration of Susan Browning. Russell W. Martin. LC 80-83567. 1981. 2.50 (ISBN 0-87216-802-6). Playboy Paperbacks.

Desert. Allen Wheelis. LC 72-110778. 1970. 5.95. Basic Books.

Desert: A Legend, by Martin Armstrong... Martin Donisthorpe Armstrong. LC 26-16087. 1926. Harper & Brothers.

Desert Ambush. Jefferson Fraser. LC 55-7931. 1955. Arcadia House.

Desert and Mrs. Ajax. Edward Stewart Moffat. LC 14-9447. 1914. Moffat, Yard and Company.

Desert and the Meadow. Anastasios Aslanis. LC 77-71715. 8.95 (ISBN 0-87949-074-8). Ashley Books.

Desert and the Sown. Mary Hallock Foote. LC 2-14137. 1902. Houghton, Mifflin and Company.

Desert Battle. Rebecca Drury. (Women at War Ser.: No. 15). (Orig.). 1983. pap. 3.25 (ISBN 0-440-02065-4). Dell.

Desert Brew. Bertha Muzzy Sinclair. LC 25-757220. 1925. Little, Brown, and Company.

Desert Campfire: By John Sims Pseud. William L Hopson. LC 51-4814. 1951. Phoenix Press.

Desert Captive. Elliot Tokson. (Fawcett Gold Medal Book). 1.75 (ISBN 0-449-13722-8). Fawcett Publications.

Desert Column. Ion L. Idriess. 1967. Repr. pap. 1.50 o.s.i. Tri-Ocean.

Desert Dan. Elizabeth Jane Coatsworth. (Illus.). 1960. PLB 2.57 o.p. (ISBN 0-670-26720-1). Viking Pr.

Desert Dancer. John Hamlin. LC 31-12373. 1931. L. MacVeagh, The Dial Press.

Desert Democracy. Roy Lemon Smith. LC 40-1920. The Abingdon Press.

Desert Desire. June Jennifer. LC 34-299022. W. Godwin, Inc.

Desert Desperadoes. Nelson Coral Nye. LC 42-25440. 1942. Phoenix Press.

Desert Doctor. H. G. Gunther. (H. G. Gunther Ser.). pap. 1.95 (ISBN 0-515-05675-8). Jove Pubns.

Desert Drama: Being the Tragedy of the Korosko. Arthur Conan Doyle. LC 6-34243. 1898. J. B. Lippincott Company.

Desert Dream. Rosemary Carter. (Harlequin Presents Ser.). 192p. 1980. pap. 1.50 (ISBN 0-373-10397-2). Harlequin Bks.

Desert Dust. Edwin Legrand Sabin. LC 22-89427. G. W. Jacobs & Company.

Desert Episode. George Charles Greenfield. LC 45-8183. 1945. The Macmillan Company.

Desert Fiddler. William Henry Hamby. LC 21-8616. 1921. Doubleday, Page & Company.

Desert Fire. Brooke Hastings. 192p. (Orig.). 1980. pap. 1.50 (ISBN 0-671-57044-7). S&S.

Desert Fires. Lucien Waldo Emerson. LC 54-5841. Arcadia House.

Desert Fires. Joyce Verrette. 1978. 1.95 (ISBN 0-380-01776-8). Avon Books.

Desert Flower. Alice Mary Dicken. LC 28-27812. 1928. G. H. Watt.

Desert Ghost. Thomas Monroe Helm. LC 76-47819. (Double D western). 1977. 5.95 (ISBN 0-385-12889-4). Doubleday.

Desert Gold. Zane Grey. 2.95 o.p. (ISBN 0-448-05108-7). G&D.

Desert Gold. Bradford Scott. LC 46-8176. 1946. Arcadia House, Inc.

Desert Gold: A Romance of the Border. Zane Grey. LC 13-807811. 1913. 1.30. Harper & Brothers.

Desert Gold: A Romance of the Border. Zane Grey. LC 21-13690. 1915. Grosset & Dunlap.

Desert Gold: A Romance of the Border. Zane Grey. LC 40-13044. 1939. T. Nelson and Sons Ltd.

Desert Guns. Steve Frazee. LC 57-775098. (Dell first edition, A135). 1957. Dell Pub. Co.

Desert Haven. Roumelia Lane. (Harlequin Romance Ser.). 192p. 1982. pap. 1.50 (ISBN 0-373-02485-1). Harlequin Bks.

Desert Hawk. Harry Sinclair Drago. LC 27-19628. The Macaulay Company.

Desert Healer. Edith Maude Hull. LC 23-112679. Small, Maynard and Company.

Desert Heritage. Percival Christopher Wren. LC 35-14886. 1935. Houghton Mifflin Company.

Desert Horizon. Grant Watson, Elliot Lovegood. LC 23-8360. 1923. A. A. Knopf.

Desert Hostage. Diane Dunaway. (Orig.). 1982. pap. 3.95 (ISBN 0-440-11963-4). Dell.

Desert in the Heart. Peter Gladwin. LC 54-564874. 1954. Rinehart.

Desert is Fertile. Dom H. Camara. Tr. by McDonagh from Fr. LC 73-89315. (Illus.). 86p. 1981. pap. 4.95 (ISBN 0-88344-093-8). Orbis Bks.

Desert Jungle. Hugh Donnelly. Ed. by Sylvia Ashton. LC 77-80279. 1977. 10.95 o.p. (ISBN 0-87949-091-8). Ashley Bks.

Desert Lake Mystery. Kay Cleaver Strahan. LC 36-934315. The Bobbs-Merrill Company.

Desert Love. Joan Conquest. LC 20-5776. The Macaulay Company.

Desert Love. Translated from the French by Alec Brown. Henry De Montherlant. LC 58-13191. 1957. Noonday Press.

Desert Lure. Jean D'Vicomte Esmenard & Terry, Jane, Tr. LC 32-4112. Sears Publishing Company, Inc.

Desert Madness. Harrison Conrard. LC 28-869931. The Macaulay Company.

Desert Marauders. Gordon Landsborough. pap. 1.50 (ISBN 0-532-15261-1). Woodhill.

Desert Maverick. William L. Hopson. Orig. Title: Border Raider. 1969. pap. 0.50 o.p. (B50-858). Belmont-Tower.

Desert Moon Mystery. Kay Cleaver Strahan. 1928. Pub. for the Crime Club, Inc., by Doubleday, Doran & Company, Inc.

Desert Night: A Novel. Kathryn Cavarly Hulme. LC 32-18954. The Macaulay Company.

Desert of Darkness. Ruth H Wissmann. (Paperback Library gothic). 1973. 0.75. Warner Paperback Lib.

Desert of Darkness. Ruth H Wissmann. LC 77-183018. (Coronet book). 1972. 5.95 (ISBN 0-448-02056-4). Grosset & Dunlap.

Desert of Doom. Donald B. Hobart. 1971. pap. 0.60 o.p. (06127). Curtis.

Desert of Ice. Jules Verne. (Illus.). 1976. Repr. of 1875 ed. lib. bdg. 16.60x (ISBN 0-88411-903-3). Amereon Ltd.

Desert of Love. Francois Mauriac. LC 51-120601. 1951. Pellegrini & Cudahy.

Desert of Love. Francois Mauriac. Tr. by Samuel Putnam. LC 29-22131. 1929. Covici, Friede.

Desert of Salt: By K. R. Butler. K R Butler. LC 64-21157. 1964. M. S. Mill Co. Distributed by Morrow.

Desert of Stolen Dreams. Robert Silverberg. (Illus.). 104p. 1981. 12.50 o.p. (ISBN 0-934438-45-5). Underwood-Miller.

Desert of the Damned. Nelson Coral Nye. LC 52-7208. (Silver star westerns). 1952. Dodd, Mead.

Desert of the Heart. Jane Rule. LC 65-18293. 1965. 4.95. World.

Desert of the Heart. Jane Rule. LC 75-12344. (Homosexuality). 1975. 10.00 (ISBN 0-405-07386-0). Arno Press.

Desert of Wheat. Zane Grey. 2.95 o.p. (ISBN 0-448-05109-5). G&D.

Desert of Wheat: A Novel. Zane Grey. LC 51-18359. Grosset & Dunlap.

Desert of Wheat: A Novel. Zane Grey. LC 21-13687. 1918. Grosset & Dunlap.

Desert of Wheat: A Novel. Zane Grey. LC 19-918. 1919. Harper & Brothers.

Desert of Wheat: A Novel. Zane Grey. LC 22-24780. 1921. Grosset & Dunlap.

Desert Passage: By Richard Poole Pseud. Lee E Wells. LC 53-10478. (Ballantine books, 24). 1953. Ballantine Books.

Desert Places. Kathryn Marshall. LC 77-3796. 8.95 (ISBN 0-06-012849-6). Harper & Row.

Desert Rails. Llewellyn Perry Holmes. LC 49-7776. (Essandess western). 1949. Simon and Schuster.

Desert Rampage. William L. Hopson. (O.s.i.). 1977. pap. 1.25 o.s.i. (BT51134). Belmont-Tower.

Desert Ranger. Jay Lucas. LC 39-12582. L. Furman, Inc.

Desert Rapture. Denise Robins. 1979. 1.75 (ISBN 0-380-42416-9). Avon.

Desert Rider. Leslie Scott. LC 55-7154. 1955. Arcadia House.

Desert Road to Shani Lun: A Romance of Mongolia. Rita Mohler Hanson. LC 39-31196. Binfords & Mont.

Desert Rose... English Moon. Claudette Williams. 256p. (Orig.). 1981. pap. 2.50 (ISBN 0-449-24388-5, Crest). Fawcett.

Desert Sand. Margaret Bass Pedler. LC 32-24284. 1932. Doubleday, Doran and Company, Inc.

Desert Sands. Helen Mary Elizabeth Clamp. LC 32-11119. The Fiction League.

Desert Sentinels. Kenneth Bjorgum. LC 79-6640. 1980. 8.95 (ISBN 0-385-14752-X). Doubleday.

Desert Silver. Thomas Ernest Mount. LC 35-970367. 1935. W. Morrow and Company.

Desert Solitaire. Edward Abbey. 1970. pap. 5.95 (ISBN 0-671-20716-4, Touchstone Bks). S&S.

Desert Stalker. Mike Barry. (Berkley medallion book) (Lone Wolf,#4). 1974. (pbk.) 0.95 (ISBN 0-425-02504-7). Berkley Pub. Co.

Desert Thoroughbred: A Romance of the California Desert Country. Jackson Gregory. LC 26-142202. 1926. C. Scribner's Sons.

Desert Town. Ramona Stewart. LC 46-125279. 1946. W. Morrow and Company.

Desert Trail. Dane Coolidge. LC 15-11003. W. J. Watt & Company.

Desert Valley. Jackson Gregory. LC 21-781042. 1921. C. Scribner's Sons.

Desert Valley Country Club. O. B. Rominger. 255p. 1975. 7.50 o.p. (ISBN 0-682-48294-3). Exposition.

Desert War. Harold Calin. (Orig.). 1967. pap. 0.60 o.p. (73-676). Lancer.

Desert War see Six Days to Suez.

Desert Water. Harry Sinclair Drago. LC 33-285984. The Macaulay Company.

Desert Water, Seven Stories. Victoria Lincoln. LC 63-8958. 1963. Little, Brown.

Desert Wife. Hilda Faunce. LC 80-22163. (Illus.). xiv, 305p. 1981. 19.95x (ISBN 0-8032-1957-1); pap. 5.95 (ISBN 0-8032-6853-X, BB 761, Bison). U of Nebr Pr.

Deserted House. Lidiia Korneevna Chukovskaia. LC 67-26599. 1967. Dutton.

Deserted House. Lidiia Koveneevna Chukovskaia. LC 75-27490. 1977. pap. 7.50 (ISBN 0-913124-16-8). Nordland Pub.

Deserted House. Lidiia Koveneevna Chukovskaia. Tr. by Aline B. Werth. 1967. 4.95 o.p. (ISBN 0-525-09013-4). Dutton.

Deserted Ship: A Story of the Atlantic. Being Adventures in the Early Life of Cupples Howe, Mariner. George Cupples. LC 11-10568. 1873. Shepard and Gill.

Deserted Village. Henry Sherman Boutell. (On cover: Chicago literary club. Club papers)). 1894. Chicago Literary Club.

Deserter. Giuseppe Dessi. LC 62-16735. (Helen and Kurt Wolff book). 1962. Harcourt, Brace & World.

Deserter. Charles King. LC 1-24583. 1902. J. B. Lippincott Company.

Deserter. Gene Thompson. 176p. 1974. pap. 0.95 o.p. (ISBN 0-532-95360-6). Woodhill.

Deserter. Gene Thompson. 176p. 1974. pap. 0.95 o.p. (ISBN 0-532-95360-6). Manor Bks.

Deserter. Lajon Zilahy. LC 32-26389. 1932. Doubleday, Doran and Company, Inc.

Deserter: A Novel. Lowell Barrington. LC 54-10659. 1954. Macmillan.

Deserter, and From the Ranks. Two Novels. Charles King. LC 3-27796. 1893. J. B. Lippincott Company.

Deserter & Other Stories. Harold Frederic. Ed. by Thomas F. O'Donnell. LC 70-96548. (American Authors Ser). 1970. Repr. of 1896 ed. lib. bdg. 21.95 o.s.i. (ISBN 0-512-00199-5). Garrett Pr.

Deserter & Other Stories see Collected Works.

Deserter, and Other Stories: A Book of Two Wars. Harold Frederic. LC 77-99245. (Illus.). 1969. AMS Press.

Deserter, and Other Stories: A Book of Two Wars. Harold Frederic. LC 79-110190. (Short story index reprint series). (Illus.). 1970. Books for Libraries Press.

Deserter, and Other Stories. A Book of Two Wars. Harold Frederic. LC 6-43136. Lothrop Publishing Company.

Deserter & Other Stories, a Book of Two Wars. Harold Frederic. LC 77-99245. (BCL Ser.: I). Repr. of 1898 ed. 15.00 (ISBN 0-404-02572-2). AMS Pr.

Deserter & the Bust. John Bauernfeind. 1979. pap. 3.95 (ISBN 0-89185-204-2). Anthelion Pr.

Deserters. George C Jenks & Chapin, Anna Alice. LC 12-275983. 1.25. The H. K. Fly Company.

Deserters. Luke Short. LC 76-48308. 1977. 7.95 (ISBN 0-89340-041-6). J. Curley.

Deserter's Daughter. W. D. Herrington. LC 77-162220. (Confederate Imprints Collection Ser.). 27p. 1973. Repr. of 1865 ed. 6.00 o.p. (ISBN 0-405-04326-0). Arno.

Desert's Price. William MacLeod Raine. LC 24-7108. 1924. Doubleday, Page & Company.

Desert's Secret. Joan Conquest. LC 33-8304. The Macaulay Company.

Desiderata. Max Ehrmann. (Illus.). 1972. 4.95 (ISBN 0-517-53422-3). Crown.

Desiderata of Happiness. Max Ehrmann. Ed. by Susan P. Schutz. LC 74-27701. (Illus.). 80p. (Orig.). 1975. pap. 3.95 (ISBN 0-88396-009-5). Blue Mtn Pr CO.

Design for a Staircase: A Novel. Guy Noel Pocock. LC 34-381883. 1934. E. P. Dutton & Co., Inc.

Design for Dying... Louise Trimble. LC 46-22423. (On cover: A Bart house mystery. 27). 1946.

Design for Dying. Louise Trimble. LC 45-843933. 1945. Phoenix Press.

Design for Enchantment. Rachel Murray. LC 83-130. (Circle of Love Romance). 1983. 8.95 (ISBN 0-8161-3501-0). G.K. Hall.

Design for Love. Kristin Michaels, pseud. (Orig.). 1981. pap. 1.95 (ISBN 0-451-09821-8, J9821, Sig). NAL.

Design for Love. Nora Powers. 192p. (Orig.). 1980. pap. 1.50 (ISBN 0-671-57042-0, Pub. by Silhouette Bks). S&S.

Design for Murder. Erica Quest. LC 80-43004. 1981. 10.95 (ISBN 0-385-17671-6). Doubleday.

Design for Murder: A Novel. Frederic Arnold Kummer. LC 38-19831. 1936. Lothrop, Lee & Shepard Company.

Design for Murder: A Novel. Percival Wilde. LC 41-13509. Random House.

Design for November. Ronald Elwy Mitchell. LC 47-3619. 1947. Harper & Brothers.

Design for Treachery. Clare Castler Saunders. 1947. C. Scribner's Sons.

Design in Diamonds: A Margot Blair Mystery. Kathleen Moore Knight. LC 44-668. 1944. Pub. for the Crime Club by Doubleday, Doran & Co., Inc.

Design in Evil. Rufus King. LC 42-14998. 1942. Published for the Crime Club by Doubleday, Doran and Company, Inc.

Design of Fiction. Mark Harris & Hester Harris. LC 75-26521. 5.25 (ISBN 0-690-00851-1). Crowell.

Designated Heir. Maxine W Kumin. LC 73-18915. 1974. 6.95 (ISBN 0-670-26896-8). Viking Press.

Designated Hitter. Walter H. Wager. LC 81-71678. 1982. 13.95 (ISBN 0-87795-385-6). Arbor Hse.

Designed for Love. Wright William. Phoenix Press.

Designer of Dawns; and Other Tales: Little Stories of the Here and Thereafter. Gertrude Russell Lewis. LC 17-30267. The Pilgrim Press.

Designing Woman. Elaine R. Chase. (Candlelight Ecstasy Ser.: No. 72). (Orig.). 1982. pap. 1.95 (ISBN 0-440-12091-8). Dell.

Designs: A Novel. Richard Horn. LC 80-26055. 11.95 (ISBN 0-87131-329-4). M. Evans.

Designs in Fiction. Rev. Ed. Ed. by Elizabeth Scheld. LC 68-26861. (Macmillan lit. heritage). 1968. pap., 1.36. Macmillan.

Designs on Life. E. X Ferrars, pseud. LC 79-8283. 1980. 8.95 (ISBN 0-385-15770-3). Published for the Crime Club by Doubleday.

Designs on Love. Gail Everett. (Candlelight romance). 1974. (pbk.) 0.75. Dell.

Desino Me: And Other Stories. Leonhard Frank & Brooks, Cyrus Harry. LC 48-5901. 1948. Penguin Books.

Desirable Aliens: Stories. John Bovey. LC 80-18596. (Illinois short fiction). 10.00 (ISBN 0-252-00837-5) (ISBN 0-252-00838-3). University of Illinois Press.

Desirable Young Men. Patrick Carleton. LC 33-173119. E. P. Dutton & Co., Inc.

Desire. translated from the french by warre b. wells. ed. Jean Fayard & Wells, Warre Bradley, 1892- Tr. LC 32-229791. 2.00. The Century Co.

Desire. Gladys Etta Johnson. LC 29-10430. 1929. Macrae Smith Company.

Desire. Charlotte Lamb, pseud. (Harlequin Presents Ser.). 192p. 1981. pap. 1.75 (ISBN 0-373-10472-3). Harlequin Bks.

Desire & Conquer. Diane Dunaway. (Candlelight Ecstasy Ser.: No. 158). (Orig.). 1983. pap. 1.95 (ISBN 0-440-11779-8). Dell.

Desire & Dawn. Natalie King. (YA) 1974. 4.95 o.p. (Avalon). Bouregy.

Desire, and Other Stories. Clement Wood. LC 50-2902. 1950. Woodford Press.

Desire & Pursuit of the Whole: A Romance of Modern Venice. Frederick C. Rolfe. 1977. Repr. of 1953 ed. lib. bdg. 20.75x (ISBN 0-8371-9808-9, RODP). Greenwood.

Desire & Pursuit of the Whole: A Romance of Modern Venice. Frederick William Rolfe. LC 78-21374. (Gay Experience). Repr. of 1934 ed. 25.50 (ISBN 0-404-61536-8). AMS Pr.

Desire and Pursuit of the Whole: A Romance of Modern Venice, by Frederick Rolfe, Baron Corvo Pseud. With an Introd. by A. J. A. Symons and Foreword by W. H. Auden. Frederick William Rolfe. LC 53-10680. 1953.

Desire for Gold and Conquest: The Story of the Empire of the Incas and the Life of Francisco Pizarro, Compiled, Translated, Edited, and Written by Jose A. Caparo. Jose Angel Caparo. LC 53-231. 1953. Christopher Pub. House.

Desire in New Orleans. Josiah Pitts Woolfolk. LC 52-40857. 1952. Signature Press.

Desire in the Dust. Cover Painting by Barye Phillips. Harry Whittington. LC 57-23231. (Gold medal books, 611). Fawcett Publications.

Desire in the Ozarks. Shelby Steger. pap. 0.95 o.p. (532-95229-095). Manor Bks.

Desire in the Ozarks. Shelby Steger. 1973. (pbk) 0.95. Manor Books.

Desire in the Ozarks see Thorn in His Side.

Desire in the Shadows. Joe L. Houston. pap. 0.75 o.p. (54-942). Paperback Lib.

Desire Is Blind see Bride of Revenge.

Desire Island. Paul Tabori. 1974. (pbk.) 1.50. Warner Paperback Library.

Desire of the Heart. Barbara Cartland. (Historical Romance Ser: No. 1). 1974. pap. 1.25 o.p. (ISBN 0-515-03473-8, V3473). BJ Pub Group.

Desire of the Moth. Eugene Manlove Rhodes. LC 16-9066. 1916. H. Holt and Company.

Desire of the Moth. Mary Gleed Tuttiett. LC 13-20826. 1913. D. Appleton and Company.

Desire of the Moth. Capel Vane. LC 8-30222. (Half-title: Appletons' town and country library, no. 182). 1895. D. Appleton and Company.

Desire to Kill. Alice Ormond Campbell. LC 34-186931. Farrar & Rinehart, Incorporated.

Desire to Kill. Anna Clarke. LC 81-43423. 1982. 10.95 (ISBN 0-385-17992-8). Published for the Crime Club by Doubleday.

Desire Under the Rose. Peggy Gaddis, pseud. LC 48-1830. 1948. Phoenix Press.

Desire Under the Rose. Perry Lindsay. (Signet Book). (Rainbow Romance). 1973. (pbk) 0.60. New American Lib.

Desired. Carter Brown, pseud. 1974. (pbk.) 0.95. New American Library.

Desired Damnations. Peggy Gaddis, pseud. (Alouette Romance Ser.). 128p. (Orig.). 1981. pap. 2.25 (ISBN 0-89531-132-1, 0198-96). Sharon Pubns.

Desired Haven. Evelyn May Fox Richardson. LC 54-6681. 1954. Macrae Smith Co.

Desired Haven. Gladys Henrietta Raphael Schutze. LC 32-225367. 1932. Houghton Mifflin Company.

Desired Haven. Catherine Stadtler. LC 45-4559. 1945. Zondervan Publishing House.

Desired Woman: A Novel. William Nathaniel Harben. LC 13-18722. 1913. Harper & Brothers.

Desiree. Annemarie Selinko. LC 52-9706. 1953. Morrow.

Desires. John L'Heureux. LC 80-20228. 11.95 (ISBN 0-03-058902-9). Holt, Rinehart and Winston.

Desires & Devices. Helen De Guerry Simpson. LC 30-878361. 1930. Doubleday, Doran & Company, Inc.

Desires of the Heart. Le Roy Allen. LC 52-7989. 1952. Zondervan Pub. House.

Desires of the Heart: For Young People. Joan Geisel Gardner. LC 36-4840. Zondervan Publishing House.

Desires of Thy Heart. Joan Carroll Cruz. LC 76-39600. 8.95 (ISBN 0-913024-10-4). Tandem Press Publishers.

Desmond: A Novel. Charlotte Turner Smith. LC 73-22133. (Feminist Controversy in England, 1788-1810). 1974. (ISBN 0-8240-0879-0). Garland Pub.

Desmond Dare: Or, Taking Desperate Chances. The Story of a Great Race. Harlan Page Halsey. (Old Sleuth's own, no. 90). 1897. Parlor Car Publishing Co.

Desmond Hundred... Jane Goodwin Austin. (Round-robin series v. 11). 1882. J. R. Osgood and Company.

Desmond Rourke, Irishman. John George Haslette Vahey. LC 11-23708. 1911. D. Appleton and Company.

Desmonde. Archibald Joseph Cronin. LC 75-8649. 1975. 7.95 (ISBN 0-316-16163-2). Little, Brown.

Desmonde, M.D. Hugh Wakefield. LC 8-32821. (Dillingham's American authors library, no. 30). 1897. G. W. Dillingham Co.

Desmond's Daughter. Katherine Helen Maud Marshall Diver. LC 16-139732. 1916. 1.50. G. P. Putnam's Sons.

Desoeuvre ou l'espion du Boulevard du Temple: Chronique Scandaleuse des Petits Theatres. Francois M. Mayeur de St. Paul. 155p. (Fr.). 1982. Repr. of 1907 ed. lib. bdg. 70.00 (ISBN 0-8287-1790-7). Clearwater Pub.

Desolate Sands. Michael Norday. LC 55-3908. 1955. Vixen Press.

Desolate Splendour. Michael Sadleir. LC 23-7991. 1923. G. P. Putnam's Sons.

Desolation Angels. John Kerouac. LC 77-17879. 1978. (ISBN 0-399-50385-4). Capricorn Books.

Desolation Angels: A Novel. Introd. by Seymour Krim. John Kerouac. LC 65-17524. 5.95. Coward.

Desolation Island. Patrick O'Brian. LC 78-66244. 1979. 9.95 (ISBN 0-8128-2590-X). Stein and Day.

Desolation Pass. Jack Manly. LC 38-387144. Burney Brothers Publishing Co.

Desolation Range. Donald B. Hobart. (Orig.). 1971. pap. 0.60 o.p. (06134). Curtis.

Despair. Vladimir Vladimirovich Nabokov. LC 65-20683. 5.00. Putnam.

Despair. Vladimir Vladimirovich Nabokov. (75258). 1968. Pocket Bks.

Desparados on the Loose see Adios, Bandido!.

Desparate Defiance. Barbara Cartland. (Orig.). 1975. pap. 1.25 o.p. (ISBN 0-515-03996-9). Pyramid Pubns.

Desperado. Clifton Adams. LC 50-12087. (Gold medal book, 121). 1950. Fawcett Publications.

Desperado. Charles Turlock. LC 41-1986. Phoenix Press.

Desperadoes. Ron Hansen. 288p. 1980. pap. 2.50 (ISBN 0-345-28675-8). Ballantine.

Desperadoes: A Novel. Ron Hansen. LC 78-15273. 1979. 8.95 (ISBN 0-394-50350-3). Knopf.

Desperados. Ben Thompson. (Leisure Books). 1977. 1.25 (ISBN 0-8439-0514-X). Nordon Pubns.

Desperado's Gold. Leonard London Foreman. 1979. pap. 1.50 o.s.i. (ISBN 0-505-51431-1). Tower Bks.

Desperado's Gold. Leonard London Foreman. 1970. pap. 0.75 o.p. (B75-2059). Belmont-Tower.

Desperate Adversaries. Jack Hoffenberg. LC 75-16133. 1975. 7.95 (ISBN 0-517-52032-X). Crown Publishers.

Desperate Adversaries. jack hoffenberg. ed. Jack Hoffenberg. 1.95 (ISBN 0-380-00702-9). Avon Books.

Desperate Angel. Helen Topping Miller. LC 42-155431. 1942. D. Appleton-Century Company, Incorporated.

Desperate Asylum. Fletcher Flora. LC 56-26801. (Lion library edition, 44). 1955. Lion Library Editions.

Desperate Chance. James Douglas Jerrold Kelley. LC 7-109719. 1886. C. Scribner's Sons.

Desperate Chance: Or, The Wizard Tramp's Revelation. A Thrilling Narrative. Harlan Page Halsey. 1897. The Parlor Car Publishing Co.

Desperate Character: And Other Stories. Ivan Sergeevich Turgenev. LC 78-10270. (His Novels, v. 14). 1970. AMS Press.

Desperate Character, Etc. Ivan Sergeevich Turgenev. LC 74-132131. (Short story index reprint series). 1970. Books for Libraries Press.

Desperate Characters. Paula Fox. LC 70-95874. 1970. Harcourt, Brace & World.

Desperate Characters: A Novel. Paula Fox. LC 79-90373. 1980. 6.95 (ISBN 0-87923-309-5). Nonpareil Books.

Desperate Children. David Cornel De Jong. LC 49-10219. 1949. Doubleday.

Desperate Cure. Ruth Fenisong. LC 46-59069. 1946. Pub. for the Crime Club by Doubleday & Company, Inc.

Desperate Deed. E. O. Tilburn. (On cover: Pinkerton detective series. Quarterly, no. 43). 1900. Laird & Lee.

Desperate Defiance. Barbara Cartland. 1977. pap. 1.50 o.p. (ISBN 0-515-04382-6). BJ Pub Group.

Desperate Dude. Edwin Booth. 160p. 1980. pap. 1.50 (ISBN 0-448-17140-6, Pub. by Tempo). Ace Bks.

Desperate Games. Pierre Boulle. LC 73-83035. 1973. 6.95 (ISBN 0-8149-0731-8). Vanguard Press.

Desperate Heiress. Marilyn Ross. 1970. pap. 0.60 o.p. (63-294). Paperback Lib.

Desperate Hours. Joseph A. Hayes. 389p. 1981. Repr. lib. bdg. 14.95 (ISBN 0-89968-230-8). Lightyear.

Desperate Hours. Joseph A. Hayes. 1968. pap. 0.60 o.p. (X1904). Pyramid Pubns.

Desperate Hours: A Novel. Joseph A. Hayes. (Signet Book). 1977. 1.95 (ISBN 0-451-07689-3). New American Library.

Desperate Hours: A Novel. Joseph Arnold Hayes. LC 54-5645. 1954. Random House.

Desperate Longings. Frances Flores. (Candlelight Romance Ser.). (Orig.). 1981. pap. 1.75 (ISBN 0-440-12015-2). Dell.

Desperate Love. John E. Cummins. 184p. 1974. 6.95 o.p. (ISBN 0-8059-1933-3). Dorrance.

Desperate Man. Wayne D Overholser. LC 57-7502. 1957. Macmillan.

Desperate Moment. Heidi Huberta Freybe Loewengard. LC 51-1857. 1951. Random House.

Desperate People. Francis Durbridge. LC 73-152732. 1972. 5.95 (ISBN 0-85617-952-3). White Lion.

Desperate Remedies. Thomas Hardy. 1871. 10.95 o.p. (ISBN 0-312-19495-1). St Martin.

Desperate Remedies: A Novel. author's ed. Thomas Hardy. LC 7-1984. (Leisure hour series. no. 32). 1874. H. Holt and Company.

Desperate Remedies: A Novel. Thomas Hardy. (Seaside library, v. 60, no. 1224). 1882. G. Munro.

Desperate Remedies: A Novel. Thomas Hardy. LC 16-7549. 1896. Harper & Brothers.

Desperate Remedies: A Novel. Thomas Hardy. LC 80-24427. (His The new Wessex edition). 1981. 2.95 (ISBN 0-312-19496-X). St. Martin's Press.

Desperate Search. Arthur Mayse. LC 52-5060. 1952. Morrow.

Desperate Season. Diana Davenport. (Illus.). 1978. 1.95 (ISBN 0-449-13981-6). Fawcett Gold Medal Books.

Desperate Voyagers. Marvin Tokayer & Mary Swartz. 1980. pap. 2.75 (ISBN 0-440-12223-6). Dell.

Desperate Wall. Roberta Hill. LC 49-2625. 1949. G. P. Putnam's Sons.

Desperation Valley. Ford Bowne, pseud. 1970. 3.95 o.p. Lenox Hill.

Desperation Valley see Gun-Hawk Valley.

Desperation Valley: A Novel of the Cherokee Strip. Willis Todhunter Ballard. LC 64-17599. 1964. Macmillan.

Desperation Valley, a Western Novel. Philip Ketchum. LC 55-1597. (Popular library, 645). Popular Library.

Despised & Rejected. R Allatini, pseud. LC 75-12314. (Homosexuality). 1975. 12.00 (ISBN 0-405-07389-5). Arno Press.

Despite the Evidence. Peter Alding. LC 70-182472. 1972. 5.95 (ISBN 0-8415-0149-1). Saturday Review Press.

Despot of Broomsedge Cove. Mary Noailles Murfree. LC 7-31841. 1889. Houghton, Mifflin and Company.

Despotic Lady. William Edward Norris. LC 7-33295. 1895. J. B. Lippincott Company.

Despotism and Democracy: A Study in Washington Society and Politics. Molly Elliot Seawell. LC 3-13824. 1903. McClure, Phillips and Company.

Despotism: Or. The Last Days of the American Republic. Reuben Vose. LC 8-32686. 1856. Hall & Wilson.

Desra of the Egyptians: A Romance of the Earlier Century. Ethel Black Kealing. LC 11-2979. 1.50. Printed by Wheeler & Kalb.

Dessert Moon. Jean Helms. LC 43-2264. 1943. Gramercy Publishing Co.

Destination. Peter Caruso. LC 72-118307. 1970. 10.00. Philosophical Library.

Destination Biafra. Buchi Emecheta. 272p. 1982. 14.95 (ISBN 0-8052-8119-3, Pub. by Allison & Busby England). Schocken.

Destination, Danger: A Gregory Quist Story. William Colt MacDonald. LC 55-630920.

Destination Freedom. 1st Ed. John J Lozinak. LC 57-11256. 1958. Vantage Press.

Destination Hell--Standing Room Only! A Christian Allegory of Our Time. 1st Ed. Millard F Day. LC 57-96912. 1957. Greenwich Book Publishers.

Destination Infinity. Henry Kuttner. LC 75-414. (Garland Library of Science Fiction). 1975. 11.00 (ISBN 0-8240-1419-7). Garland Pub.

Destination Moon. Robert Anson Heinlein. LC 79-16538. (Series: Gregg Press Science Fiction Series.). (Illus.). 1979. 15.00 (ISBN 0-8398-2475-0). Gregg Press.

Destination Revenge: By Jim Conroy Pseud. 1st Ed. Joseph Chadwick. LC 53-6944. (Double D western). 1953. Doubleday.

Destination Singapore: From Shanghai to Singapore. Thean Soo Lim. LC 76-941229. 1976. Pan Pacific Book Distributors.

Destination: Terror. Jessyca Paull. (Passport to Danger Ser.). (O.s.i.). 160p. (Orig.). 1968. pap. 0.95 o.s.i. (AN1282, Award). Univ Pub & Dist.

Destination Tokyo. Stephen Gould Fisher. LC 43-16717. 1943. D. Appleton-Century Company, Incorporated.

Destination: Universe? Alfred Elton Van Vogt. LC 52-5053. 1952. Pellegrini & Cudahy.

Destination: Universe! Alfred Elton Van Vogt. 1977. pap. 1.50 o.p. (ISBN 0-515-04412-1). BJ Pub Group.

Destination Unknown. Agatha Miller Christie. (Greenway Edition). 1978. 8.95 (ISBN 0-396-07514-2). Dodd.

Destination: Void. Frank Herbert. 1978. pap. 2.25 (ISBN 0-425-04366-5, Dist. by Putnam). Berkley Pub.

Destination: Void. Frank Herbert. (Orig.). 1973. pap. 1.95 (ISBN 0-425-03922-6, Medallion). Berkley Pub.

Destination: Void. Frank Herbert. (Science Fiction Ser.). 1981. lib. bdg. cancelled o.s.i. (ISBN 0-8398-2550-1, Gregg). G K Hall.

Destination: Void see Worlds Beyond Dune: The Best of Frank Herbert.

Destinations: Two Novels: The Hitchhiker (Feux Rouges) Translated from the French by Norman Denny. The Burial of Monsieur Bouvet (L'enterrement De Monsieur Bouvet) Translated from the French by Eugene MacCown. 1st Ed. Georges Simenon. LC 55-812930. 1955. Doubleday.

Destined. Donald S Stevens. LC 37-808. The Christopher Publishing House.

Destined. Joanna Warren. (Belle Meade Ser.: No. 3). 432p. (Orig.). 1980. pap. 2.50 (ISBN 0-89083-693-0). Zebra.

Destined, Just That. Daisy Lee McDaniel. LC 46-314368. 1946. Dorrance & Company.

Destinies. Charlotte Vale Allen. 1982. pap. 3.25 (ISBN 0-425-05325-3). Berkley Pub.

Destinies. Ed. by James Baen. (Illus.). 1978. 1.95 (ISBN 0-441-14281-8). Ace Books.

Destinies. Peter Bart & Denne Bart Petitclerc. LC 79-11701. 13.95 (ISBN 0-671-24677-1). Simon and Schuster.

Destinies. Francois Mauriac. Tr. by Eric Sutton. LC 29-8315. 1929. Covici, Friede.

Destinies of Darcy Dancer, Gentleman. James Patrick Donleavy. LC 77-22780. 1978. 9.95 (ISBN 0-440-01903-6). Delacorte Press.

Destiny. Charles Neville Buck. LC 16-4582. 1.35. W. J. Watt & Company.

Destiny... Susan Edmonstone Ferrier. LC 6-39366. 1893. Roberts Brothers.

Destiny. Rupert Hughes. LC 25-9752. Harper & Brothers.

Destiny: A New-Thought Novel. Julia Seton. LC 17-22566. E. J. Clode.

Destiny and Desire. Lorinda Hagen. (Leisure book). 1979. 1.95 (ISBN 0-8439-0639-1). Nordon Pubns.

Destiny & the Hero. 2nd ed. Marseille Spetz. 1967. pap. 3.50 (ISBN 0-9600200-0-4). Deuce.

Destiny Bay. Donn Bryne. LC 28-22581. 1928. Little, Brown, and Company.

Destiny Doll. Clifford D. Simak. 1975. pap. 1.25 (ISBN 0-425-02996-4, Medallion). Berkley Pub.

Destiny Doll. Clifford D. Simak. 1982. pap. 2.50 (ISBN 0-87997-772-8, UE1772). DAW Bks.

Destiny Doll: A Science Fiction Novel. Clifford D. Simak. LC 78-136805. 1971. 4.95. Putnam.

Destiny Has Eight Eyes. Willard A Hanna. Harper & Brothers.

Destiny in Dallas. Shirley Seifert. 1976. Repr. of 1958 ed. lib. bdg. 6.95 (ISBN 0-89190-132-9). Am Repr-Rivercity Pr.

Destiny in Dallas. 1st Ed. Shirley Seifert. LC 58-9531. 1958. Lippincott.

Destiny in Rome. Frances Carfi Matranga. 1979. 1.25 (ISBN 0-440-11996-0). Dell Publshing Co.

Destiny News. Robert Fox. LC 76-44192. (Illus.). 4.00 (ISBN 0-913204-07-2). December Press.

Destiny of Fire. Zoe Oldenbourg. 1976. (pbk.) 1.95 (ISBN 0-380-00405-4). Avon.

Destiny of Isabelle Eberhardt. Cecily Mackworth (ISBN 0-380-00886-6). Avon.

Destiny of the Nations. Alice A. Bailey. 1968. 11.00 (ISBN 0-85330-002-X); pap. 5.00 (ISBN 0-85330-102-6). Lucis.

Destiny: Or, Life As It Is. Rosalie Miller Murphy. LC 7-25484. 1867. M. Doolady.

Destiny: Or, The Chief's Daughter. Susan Edmonstone Ferrier. (Seaside library. v. 63, no. 1290). 1882. G. Munro.

Destiny Range. Llewellyn Perry Holmes. LC 36-21195. Greenberg.

Destiny Stone. Robert Vardeman & Victor Milan. LC 80-82223. 224p. (Orig.). 1980. pap. 2.50 (ISBN 0-86721-085-0). Playboy Pbks.

Destiny Waltz. Gerda Charles. LC 72-505. 1972. 7.95 (ISBN 0-684-12936-1). Scribner.

Destiny's Bride. Lucy P. Stewart. 1979. pap. 2.25 (ISBN 0-440-12557-X). Dell.

Destiny's Bride. Diana Stuart. (Berkley Medallion Book). 1978. 1.95. Berkley Pub. Corp.

Destiny's Chickens. Francis Irby Gwaltney. LC 72-89694. 1973. 7.95 (ISBN 0-672-51764-7). Bobbs-Merrill.

Destiny's Chickens. Francis Irby Gwaltney. 1974. (pbk.) 1.50. Bantam Books.

Destiny's Child. Laura M. Brogan. 6.95 o.p. Vantage.

Destiny's Child. Patricia Morton, pseud. 1970. pap. 0.75 o.p. (B75-2071). Belmont-Tower.

Destiny's Children. G. M Warren. 1979. 2.50 (ISBN 0-671-81665-9). Pocket Books.

Destiny's Darling. pap. 2.00 (ISBN 0-89023-013-7). Forrest Printing.

Destiny's Darling. Lita Grabeklis. LC 78-105907. (Illus.). (ISBN 0-89023-013-7). Raven Print.

Destiny's Daughter. Alice Birkhead. LC 15-3872. 1915. 1.25. John Lane.

Destiny's Daughter. Frances Noble. 1980. pap. 2.25 o.s.i. (ISBN 0-505-51462-1). Tower Bks.

Destiny's Duchess. Caroline Courtney. 224p. 1981. pap. 1.95 (ISBN 0-446-30280-5). Warner Bks.

Destiny's Man. Thomas Frederic Tweed. LC 35-749. Farrar & Rinehart, Incorporated.

Destiny's Passion. Lucy Cores. 1982. pap. 3.50 (ISBN 0-8217-1061-3). Zebra.

Destiny's Spell. Susanna Collins. (Second Chance at Love Ser.: No. 19). 192p. (Orig.). (YA) 1981. pap. 1.75 (ISBN 0-515-05705-3). Jove Pubns.

Destiny's Star. Lee Wells. 1982. pap. 2.50 (ISBN 0-451-11414-0, AE1414, Sig). NAL.

Destiny's Women. Willo Davis Roberts. 576p. (Orig.). 1982. pap. 3.50 (ISBN 0-445-04531-0). Popular Lib.

Destroy, She Said. Marguerite Duras. LC 79-18888. 1979. 11.50 (ISBN 0-8357-0448-3). University Microfilms International.

Destroy, She Said. Marguerite Duras & Jean Narboni. LC 70-116170. 1970. 4.95. Grove Press.

Destroyer. Stephen Gould Fisher. LC 41-15439. 1941. D. Appleton Century Company, Incorporated.

Destroyer. William Romaine Paterson. LC 7-34078. F. A. Stokes Company.

Destroyer. Ernest Poole. 1931. The Macmillan Company.

Destroyer: A Tale of International Intrigue. Burton Egbert Stevenson. LC 13-20821. 1913. 1.30. Dodd, Mead and Company.

Destroyer: A Tale of International Intrigue. Burton Egbert Stevenson. LC 21-6905. 1921. Dodd, Mead and Company.

Destroyer at War. 2d impression. ed. George Phillip Griggs. LC 44-2603. 1943. Hutchinson & Co., Ltd.

Destroyer from America. John Fernald. 1942. The Macmillan Company.

Destroyer: Man to Demon, the Devastation of a Life by Strong Drink. Henry Knott. LC 8-35964. W. R. Vansant & Co.

Destroyer, No. 10: Terror Squad. Warren Murphy. (Orig.). 1974. pap. 1.95 (ISBN 0-523-41225-8). Pinnacle Bks.

Destroyer, No. 11: Kill or Cure. Richard Sapir & Warren Murphy. (Orig.). 1974. pap. 2.25 (ISBN 0-523-41856-6). Pinnacle Bks.

Destroyer, No. 12: Slave Safari. Warren Murphy. 1974. pap. 1.95 (ISBN 0-523-41227-4). Pinnacle Bks.

Destroyer, No. 13: Acid Rock. Warren Murphy. (Orig.). 1973. pap. 1.95 (ISBN 0-523-41228-2). Pinnacle Bks.

Destroyer, No. 14: Judgement Day. Warren Murphy. 192p. (Orig.). 1974. pap. 1.95 (ISBN 0-523-41229-0). Pinnacle Bks.

Destroyer, No. 16: Oil Slick. Warren Murphy. 192p. (Orig.). 1974. pap. 1.95 (ISBN 0-523-41231-2). Pinnacle Bks.

Destroyer, No. 17: Last War Dance. Warren Murphy. 192p. (Orig.). 1974. pap. 1.95 (ISBN 0-523-41232-0). Pinnacle Bks.

Destroyer, No. 18: Funny Money. Warren Murphy. 192p. (Orig.). 1975. pap. 1.75 (ISBN 0-523-40894-3). Pinnacle Bks.

Destroyer, No. 19: Holy Terror. Warren Murphy. 192p. (Orig.). 1975. pap. 1.75 (ISBN 0-523-40895-1). Pinnacle Bks.

Destroyer, No. 27: The Last Temple. Warren Murphy. (Orig.). 1977. pap. 1.95 (ISBN 0-523-41242-8). Pinnacle Bks.

Destroyer, No. 28: Ship of Death. Warren Murphy. 192p. 1977. pap. 1.95 (ISBN 0-523-41243-6). Pinnacle Bks.

Destroyer: No. 37, Bottom Line. Warren Murphy. 1979. pap. 1.95 (ISBN 0-523-41252-5). Pinnacle Bks.

Destroyer, No. 43: Midnight Man. Warren Murphy. 192p. (Orig.). 1981. pap. 2.25 (ISBN 0-523-41909-0). Pinnacle Bks.

Destroyer, No. 44: Balance of Power. Warren Murphy. 192p. (Orig.). 1981. pap. 1.95 (ISBN 0-523-40718-1). Pinnacle Bks.

Destroyer, No. 49: Skin Deep. Warren Murphy. (Destroyer Ser.). 208p. (Orig.). 1982. pap. 2.25 (ISBN 0-523-41559-1). Pinnacle Bks.

Destroyer, No. 5: Dr. Quake. Warren Murphy. (Orig.). 1974. pap. 1.95 (ISBN 0-523-41220-7). Pinnacle Bks.

Destroyer, No. 50: Killing Time. Warren Murphy. 208p. (Orig.). 1982. pap. 2.25 (ISBN 0-523-41560-5). Pinnacle Bks.

Destroyer, No. 6: Death Therapy. Warren Murphy. (Orig.). 1974. pap. 1.95 (ISBN 0-523-41221-5). Pinnacle Bks.

Destroyer, No. 7: Union Bust. Warren Murphy. (Orig.). 1974. pap. 1.95 (ISBN 0-523-41222-3). Pinnacle Bks.

Destroyer No. 8: Summit Chase. Warren Murphy. (Orig.). 1974. pap. 2.25 (ISBN 0-523-41814-0). Pinnacle Bks.

Destroyer, No. 9: Murder's Shield. Warren Murphy. (Orig.). 1974. pap. 1.95 (ISBN 0-523-41224-X). Pinnacle Bks.

Destroyers. John F. Carter. LC 8-1780. 1907. The Neale Publishing Company.

Destroyers. A. W. Miller. (Orig.). 1980. pap. 1.75 o.s.i. (ISBN 0-8439-0738-X, Leisure Bks). Nordon Pubns.

Destroyers. Thomas Raste. 4.50 o.p. Vantage.

Destroyers. Douglas Reeman. LC 74-79663. 1974. 7.95 (ISBN 0-399-11399-1). Putnam.

Destroyers. Douglas Reeman. LC 74-79663. (Berkley Medallion Book). 1975. (pbk.) 1.25. Berkley.

Destroyers: A Historical Novel. Edward Roe Eastman. LC 47-19786. 1946. American Agriculturist, Inc.

Destroying Angel. Norman Klein. LC 83-30000. Farrar & Rinehart, Incorporated.

Destroying Angel. Louis Joseph Vance. LC 12-228633. 1912. Little, Brown, and Company.

Destroying Angel. Louis Joseph Vance & Keller, Arthur Ignatius, 1866- Illus. LC 22-4736. 1912. A. L. Burt Company.

Destroying Victor. Carleton Beals. LC 29-201066. 1929. The Macaulay Company.

Destruction of a Nation: A Fascinating and Authentic Account, in Novel Form, of the Great Russian Debacle. Jacob H Rubin & Rubin, Victor. LC 21-17550. Telegraph Printing Co.

Destruction of Crown City. David G McConnell. (Illus.). 1974. 7.50 (ISBN 0-533-00754-2). Vantage Press.

Destruction of Eva. Kathryn Hurst. 1978. pap. 1.50 (ISBN 0-532-15353-7). Woodhill.

Destruction of Gotham. Joaquin Miller. LC 8-31909. 1886. Funk & Wagnalls.

Destruction of the Temple. Barry N Malzberg. 1974. (pbk.) 0.95 (ISBN 0-671-77696-7). Pocket Books.

Destry Rides Again. Max Brand. LC 30-24855. 1930. Dodd, Mead & Company.

Destry Rides Again. Frederick Faust. LC 76-41318. 1976. 6.95 (ISBN 0-88411-515-1). Aeonian Press.

Destry Rides Again. Frederick Faust. LC 79-16675. (Series: Gregg Press Western Fiction Series.). (Illus.). 1979. 9.95 (ISBN 0-8398-2583-8). Gregg Press.

Desultoria: The Recovered Mss. of an Eccentric. LC 6-33403. 1850. Baker and Scribner.

Det Forsoemte Foraar see Stolen Spring.

Details of a Sunset and Other Stories. Vladimir Vladimirovich Nabokov. LC 75-34086. 8.95 (ISBN 0-07-045709-3). McGraw-Hill.

Detainee. Legson Kayira. (African Writers Ser.). 1974. pap. text ed. 4.00x (ISBN 0-435-90162-1). Heinemann Ed.

Detainee. Legson Kayira. (African Writers Ser.: No. 162). 172p. 1974. pap. text ed. 2.50x o.p. (ISBN 0-435-90162-1). Humanities.

Detection Unlimited. Georgette Heyer. LC 77-81983. 1969. 4.95. Dutton.

Detective. Roderick Thorp. LC 66-11630. 1966. Dial Press.

Detective. Louis Joseph Vance. LC 32-11120. 1932. J. B. Lippincott Company.

Detective: A Novel. Paul Ferris. LC 77-358991. 1976. 3.65 (ISBN 0-297-77166-3). Weidenfeld and Nicolson.

Detective and the Poisoner. St. George Rathborne. (On cover: The Pinkerton detective series, no. 5). 1892. Laird & Lee.

Detective and the Somnambulist. The Murderer and the Fortune Teller. Allan Pinkerton. LC 12-37640. (Half-title: Allan Pinkerton's detective stories). 1875. W. B. Keen, Cooke & Co.

Detective Bob Bridger: Or, The Man from Scotland Yard. R. M Taylor. (Secret service series, no. 34). 1890. Street & Smith.

Detective Duff Unravels It. Harvey Jerrold O'Higgins. 1929. H. Liveright.

Detective Fiction: Crime and Compromise. Ed. by Richard Stanley Allen. LC 73-17632. 1974. (pbk.) 4.95 (ISBN 0-15-517408-8). Harcourt Brace Jovanovich.

Detective Johnson of New Orleans. A Tale of Love and Crime. Harrie Irving Hancock. (peerless series, no. 37). 1891. J. S. Ogilvie.

Detective Story Annual. LC 44-34784. Street & Smith Publications, Inc.

Detective Tales of Edgar Allan Poe. Edgar Allan Poe. Ed. by Seaman, George A. LC 950. (On cover: Magnet detective library, no. 115). Street & Smith.

Detective Wore Silk Drawers. Peter Lovesey. LC 75-160858. (Red badge novel of suspense). 1971. 4.95 (ISBN 0-396-06377-2). Dodd, Mead.

Detective's Clew: Or, The Tragedy of Elm Grove. O. S. Adams. LC 6-2526. (secret service series. no. 14). Street & Smith.

Detective's Crime: Or, The Van Peltz Diamonds. Charles Morris. (Globe detective series, no. 2). 1887. Rand, McNally & Company.

Detective's Dilemma. Emile Gaboriau. LC 6-44557. (secret service series. no. 45). 1891. Street & Smith.

Detective's Due: By Lesley Egan Pseud. Elizabeth Linington. LC 65-20990. bds., 3.95. Harper.

Detective's Eye. Fortune Du Boisgobey. LC 6-34425. (On cover: Lovell's library. no. 1146). J. W. Lovell Company.

Detective's Holiday. Charles Bryson. LC 26-15431. 1926. E. P. Dutton & Company.

Detective's Triumph. Emile Gaboriau. LC 6-44556. (secret service series. no. 46). 1891. Street & Smith.

Detective's Wife. Maud Russell. 3.50 o.p. (ISBN 0-8315-0001-8). Speller.

Detective's Wife: 1st Ed. Maud Russell. LC 61-13955. 1961. R. Speller.

Determined Bachelor. Judith Harkness. (Orig.). 1981. pap. 1.95 (ISBN 0-451-09609-6, J9609, Sig). NAL.

Dethroned Heiress. Eliza Ann Dupuy. LC 76-76923. (American fiction reprint series). 1969. Books for Libraries Press.

Dethroned Heiress. Eliza Ann Dupuy. LC 11-10525. T. B. Peterson & Brothers.

Detling Secret. Julian Symons. LC 81-23267. 1982. 11.95 (ISBN 0-89919-096-0). Ticknor & Fields.

Detling Secret. Julian Symons. LC 82-8591. 1983. 14.75 (ISBN 0-670-27063-6). Viking Press.

Detmold: A Romance. William Henry Bishop. LC 6-12715. 1879. Houghton, Osgood and Company.

Detonator. Walter Garys. (Orig.). 1981. pap. 2.50 (ISBN 0-505-51663-2). Tower Bks.

Detour. Michael Brodsky. 1977. 8.95 (ISBN 0-916354-82-2). Urizen Bks.

Detour. Norma Ciraci. LC 47-1456. 1947. Doubleday & Company, Inc.

Detour. Norrell Gregory. LC 27-22955. Greenburg.

Detour. Helen Nielsen. LC 53-7555. 1953. I. Washburn.

Detour. William Wilson. LC 73-87214. 1974. 5.95 (ISBN 0-399-11287-1). Berkley Pub. Corp.: Distributed by Putnam.

Detour: An Extraordinary Tale. Martin M Goldsmith. LC 39-2158. The Macaulay Company.

Detour at Night: An Inner Sanctum Mystery. Guy Endore. (O.S.I.). 1959. 2.95 o.s.i. (19580). S&S.

Detour to a Funeral. V. J Santiago. (Vigilante Series#2). 1975. (pbk.) 1.25 (ISBN 0-523-00766-3). Pinnacle Books.

Detour to Destiny. Renee Shann. 1972. pap. 0.75 o.p. (94260). Beagle Bks.

Detour to Oblivion. Frederick Clyde Davis. LC 47-30698. 1947. Pub. for the Crime Club by Doubleday.

Detour to Romance. Katherine McComb. LC 73-861. (Valentine Ser). (Orig.). 1969. pap. 0.60 o.p. Lancer.

Detours. Octavus Roy Cohen. LC 27-151995. 1927. Little, Brown, and Company.

Detroit at the Century's Turn. George W. Stark. 1951. pap. 0.15 o.p. (ISBN 0-8143-1019-2). Wayne St U Pr.

Detroit Deathwatch. Don Pendleton. (Executioner,#19). 1974. (pbk.) 1.25 (ISBN 0-523-00419-2). Pinnacle Books.

Detroit Massacre. Mike Barry. (Lone Wolf). (Berkley medallion book: Vol. 11). 1975. (pbk.) 0.95 (ISBN 0-425-02793-7). Berkley Pub. Co.

Detroit Unveiled. A Graphic and Startling Revelation of the Mysteries of Michigan's Metropolis. Frederic S Crofoot. LC 6-32167. 1887. Sunday World Print.

Detroiters: A Novel. Harold Livingston. LC 57-107898. 1958. Houghton Mifflin.

Deuce of Diamonds. Charles Morris Martin. LC 37-23529. 1937. Greenberg.

Deuce of Hearts. William Tucker Washburn. LC 1-31079. R. F. Fenno & Company.

Deuces to Open. Zeke Masters, pseud. (Faro Blake Ser.: No. 21). (Orig.). 1982. pap. 2.25 (ISBN 0-671-45180-4). PB.

Deuces Wild. Elizabeth Linington. LC 74-20509. 1975. 5.95 (ISBN 0-688-00335-4). Morrow.

Deuces Wild. Harold MacGrath. LC 13-24979. 1.00. The Bobbs-Merrill Company.

Deuces Wild. Dell Shannon. 1975. 5.95 o.p. (ISBN 0-688-00335-4). Morrow.

Deuces Wild. Dell Shannon. 1976. (pbk.) 1.25 (ISBN 0-671-80308-5). Pocket Books.

Deuda De Sangre. new ed. Don Pendleton. Tr. by O. Blanco from Eng. (Compadre Collection Ser., el Verdugo: No. 13). Orig. Title: Washington: I.O.U. (Illus.). 160p. (Span.). 1975. pap. 0.95 (ISBN 0-88473-313-0). Fiesta Pub.

Deus Irae. Philip K Dick & Roger Zelazny. LC 74-27580. (Doubleday science fiction). 1976. 5.95 (ISBN 0-385-04527-1). Doubleday.

Deutsche Meisternovellen. rev. ed. Ed. by John Theodore Geissendoerfer. Kurtz, John William, 1906- Joint Ed. LC 45-43413. 1945. Prentice-Hall, Inc.

Deutsche Novelle, 2 Vols. Benno Wiese. 7.50 ea. o.p. Adler.

Deutsche Novelle, 1880-1950. expanded ed. Ed. by Harry Steinhauer. 1958. 7.50x o.p. (ISBN 0-393-09515-0, NortonC). Norton.

Deutsche Novellen. Ed. by Albert Van Eerden & B. Ulmer. 1942. 4.80 o.p. (ISBN 0-03-016500-8). HR&W.

Deutsche Novellen Des 19 Jahrhunderts. Robert O. Roseler. 1941. 4.95 o.p. (ISBN 0-03-016210-6). HR&W.

Deutsche Novelletten-Bibliothek: Zur Benutzung in Schulen, Hoheren Lehranstalten, Sowie Fur das Privatstudium Ausgewahlt und Mit Etymologischen, Grammatischen und Erklarenden Noten Versehen. Ed. by Wilhelm Bernhardt. (Added t.-p.: Students' series. German novelettes for school and home...). 1887-88. Heath & Comp.

Deux Cavaliers de l'Orage. Jean Giono. (Coll. Soleil). 13.50. French & Eur.

Deux Testaments. Anna Duval-Thibault. (Novels by Franco-Americans in New England 1850-1940 Ser.). 204p. (Fr.). (gr. 10 up). pap. 4.50x (ISBN 0-911409-15-7). Natl Mat Dev.

Deva. Michael Tobias. 196p. (Orig.). 1982. pap. text ed. 8.95 (ISBN 0-932238-10-6). Avant Bks.

Deva Dasi. Ataullah Mardaan. 176p. 1972. pap. 1.95 o.p. (ISBN 0-87056-266-5, 6266). Brandon.
Devalino Caper. Andrew Joseph Russell. LC 74-26506. 1975. (ISBN 0-394-48999-3). Random House.
Devastating Boys and Other Stories. Elizabeth Taylor. LC 79-181977. 1972. 5.95 (ISBN 0-670-27067-9). Viking Press.
Devastator: A Novel. Arthur John Arbuthnott Stringer. LC 44-733357. 1944. The Bobbs-Merrill Company.
Devastators. Donald Hamilton. (Matt Helm Ser.). 1978. pap. 1.95 (ISBN 0-449-14084-9, GM). Fawcett.
Development: A Novel. Winifred Bryher. LC 21-4134. 1920. The Macmillan Company.
Development of Dan. Andrew Francis Kelley. LC 15-15098. Printed by the J. B. Savage Co.
Developments. Kathleen Conlon. LC 81-14524. 1982. 9.95 (ISBN 0-312-19752-7). St. Martin's Press.
Devereux. Edward George Earle Lytton Bulwer-Lytton Lytton. LC 8-11036. G. Routledge and Sons.
Devereux. Edward George Earle Lytton Bulwer-Lytton Lytton. LC 7-835628. 1883. J. W. Lovell Company.
Devereux. Edward George Earle Lytton Bulwer-Lytton Lytton. LC 7-8354. (Half-title: Novels of Sir Edward Bulwer Lytton. Library ed. Historical romances, vol. I-II). 1893. Little, Brown, and Company.
Devereux: A Tale. Edward George Earle Lytton Bulwer-Lytton Lytton. LC 49-320950. 1878. J.B. Lippincott.
Devereux Lucretia. Edward George Earle Lytton Bulwer-Lytton Lytton. LC 31-32282. (The novels and romances of Edward Bulwer Lytton. v. 2). Aldine Book Publishing Co.
Deveron Hall. Velda Johnston. (Spring Adult Ser.). 1977. lib. bdg. 9.95 o.p. (ISBN 0-8161-6444-4, Large Print Bks). G K Hall.
Deveron Hall. Velda Johnston. LC 76-55334. 1977. 9.95 (ISBN 0-8161-6444-4). G. K. Hall.
Deveron Hall: A Novel of Suspense. Velda Johnston. LC 76-15671. 1976. 7.95. Dodd, Mead.
Deveron Hall: A Novel of Suspense. Velda Johnston. (Signet Book). 1978. 1.75 (ISBN 0-451-08018-1). New American Library.
Deversville. A. W. Hollworth. 3.75 o.p. Carlton.
Deviator. Christopher Nicole. LC 70-82666. 1969. 4.95. Lippincott.
Deviator. Andrew York. LC 70-82666. 1969. 4.95 o.p. (ISBN 0-397-00578-4). Lippincott.
Device and Desire: A Novel of Bad Manners. Mary Fanning Wickham, pseud. LC 49-5950. 1949. J. B. Lippincott Co.
Devices and Desires. Vera Wheatley. LC 26-154301. 1926. E. P. Dutton & Company.
Devices and Desires: By E. Arnot Robertson. Eileen Arbuthnot Robertson. LC 54-11838. 1954. Macmillan.
Devices of Darkness. Jean M English. LC 76-9512. 1976. 5.95. Doubleday.
Devil. Alfred Neumann. Tr. by Paterson, Huntley. LC 28-19006. 1928. A. A. Knopf.
Devil. Lev Nikolaevich Tolstoi & Maude, Aylmer, 1858- Tr. LC 26-7898. 1926. Harper & Brothers.
Devil a Gentleman. Ralston Follett. LC 6-414210. (On Cover: The Waldorf Series. No. 6). 1893. Saalfield & Fitch.
Devil: A Tragedy of the Heart and Conscience. Ferenc Molnar & O'Brien, Joseph. LC 8-28991. (On cover: Play book series, no. 136). J. S. Ogilvie Publishing Company.
Devil & All. Francis Nielson. 2.00 o.s.i. Roseman.
Devil and Aunt Serena. Esther Kellner. LC 68-15811. 1968. 5.00. Bobbs.
Devil & Ben Camden. Heinrich Graat. (Orig.). 1970. pap. 0.75 o.p. (B75-2053). Belmont-Tower.
Devil and Ben Franklin. Theodore Mathieson. LC 61-5842. (Inner sanctum mystery). 1961. Simon and Schuster.
Devil and Danial Webster. Stephen Vincent Benet. LC 38-5407. Farrar & Rinehart.
Devil and Daniel Webster. Stephen Vincent Benet. The Countryman Press.
Devil and Destiny. Theodora McCormick Du Bois. LC 48-6591. 1948. Pub. for the Crime Club by Doubleday.
Devil and Henry Raftin. Howard Singer. LC 67-25409. 1967. Funk & Wagnalls.
Devil and King John. 10th thousand... ed. Philip Lindsay. LC 44-369. 1943. Hutchinson & Co., Ltd.
Devil and Lisa Black. Russell W. Martin. LC 81-83494. 2.95 (ISBN 0-86721-032-X). Playboy Paperbacks.
Devil & Lisa Black. Russell W. Martin. LC 81-83494. 256p. (Orig.). 1982. pap. 2.95 (ISBN 0-86721-032-X). Playboy Pbks.
Devil and Mary Ann. Catherine Cookson. LC 75-24717. 1976. 5.95 (ISBN 0-688-02988-4). W. Morrow.
Devil and Mrs. Devine. Josephine Leslie. 1974. (pbk.) 1.25 (ISBN 0-671-78382-3). Pocket Books.
Devil and the Deep. Sacha Carnegie, pseud. Appleton-Century-Crofts.
Devil and the Deep. Clarice Madeleine Dixon. LC 44-40076. 1944. C. Scribner's Sons.
Devil and the Deep Sea. Elizabeth Garver Jordan. LC 29-6348. 2.00. The Century Co.
Devil and the Doctor. David Henry Keller. LC 75-46284. (Supernatural and Occult Fiction). 1976. 17.00 (ISBN 0-405-08145-6). Arno Press.
Devil and the Doctor. David Henry Keller. LC 40-32082. 1940. Simon and Schuster.
Devil and Webster Daniels. Terrence Lore Smith. LC 74-25125. 1975. 5.95 (ISBN 0-385-00321-8). Published for the Crime Club by Doubleday.
Devil and X.Y.Z... Barum Browne. LC 32-7614. Pub. for the Crime Club, Inc., by Doubleday, Doran & Company, Inc.
Devil at Four O'clock. Max Catto. LC 59-6595. 1959. Morrow.
Devil at the Long Bridge: A Historical Novel ("Il Diavolo Al Pontelungo". Riccardo Bacchelli. Tr. by Williams, Orlo. LC 29-6798. 1929. 2.50. Longmans, Green and Co.
Devil at the Reins. Henry Sharp. 1980. pap. 1.95 (ISBN 0-440-11789-5). Dell.
Devil at Westease: The Story. Victoria Mary Sackville-West. LC 47-303036. 1947. Doubleday & Company, Inc.
Devil at Your Elbow. Dominic Devine. 1967. large type ed. 7.50 o.p. (ISBN 0-8027-5071-0). Walker & Co.
Devil at Your Elbow: By D. M. Devine. Dominic Devine. LC 67-13222. (Walker mystery). 1967. 3.95. Walker.
Devil Beats His Wife. Ben Wasson. LC 29-7083. Harcourt, Brace and Company.
Devil Builds a Chapel. Melba Balmat Grimes Marlett. LC 42-7341. 1942. Pub. for the Crime Club by Doubleday, Doran & Company, Inc.
Devil by the Sea. Nina Bawden. 1973. 0.95. Lancer.
Devil by the Sea. Nina Bawden. LC 59-6432. 1959. Lippincott.
Devil by the Tail. Rocco Fumento. LC 53-12879. 1954. McGraw-Hill.
Devil by the Tail. Langston Moffett. LC 47-175. 1947-1946. J. B. Lippincott Company.
Devil Came on Sunday: A Novel. Oswald Wynd. LC 61-9572. 1961. Doubleday.
Devil Child. Jo Germany. LC 77-23673. 1978. 7.95 (ISBN 0-312-19764-0). St. Martin's Press.
Devil Dances for Gold. May Mackintosh. LC 76-26520. 1.95 (ISBN 0-345-25256-X). Ballantine Books.
Devil, Devil. Michael Avallone. (Satan sleuth no. 3). 1975. (pbk.) 0.95. Bantam.
Devil Dreams, Demon Lovers. Marsha Alexander. 1973. (pbk.) 1.95 (ISBN 0-87056-329-7). Brandon Books.
Devil Drives. Jane Arbor. (Romances Ser.). 192p. (Orig.). 1980. pap. text ed. 1.25 (ISBN 0-373-02342-1, Pub. by Harlequin). PB.
Devil Drives. Virgil Markham. LC 32-6318. 1932. A. A. Knopf.
Devil Drives. Virgil Markham. LC 45-1659. (Bart house books). 1944. Bartholomew House, Inc.
Devil Drives. Ethel Winifred Savi. LC 22-23175. 1922. G. P. Putnam's Sons.
Devil Drums. Clements Ripley. LC 30-10077. 1930. Brewer & Warren Inc. Payson & Clarke Ltd.
Devil Dunes. Mary Sheppard. Ed. by Alice Sachs. 1969. lib. bdg. 3.50 o.p. Arcadia.
Devil Finds Work. Michael Delving, pseud. LC 68-57080. 1969. 4.50. Scribner.
Devil Flotilla. Edwyn Gray. 192p. 1981. pap. 2.25 (ISBN 0-523-41405-6). Pinnacle Bks.
Devil Flower. Alvarez Enriquez, Emigdio. LC 59-8153. 1959. Hill and Wang.
Devil: Founded on Ferenc Molnar's Play. Schade Van Westrum, Adriaan. LC 8-27363. G. W. Dillingham Company.
Devil from Blazing Hill. Bradford Scott. (Orig.). 1969. pap. 0.60 o.p. (X2127). Pyramid Pubns.
Devil Gun. William Edward Syers. LC 75-34380. 8.95. Putnam.
Devil Has Four Faces. John W Jakes. LC 58-7596. 1958. Mystery House.
Devil Herself. Lois Seyster Montross. LC 31-329521. H. Liveright, Inc.
Devil His Due. 1st Ed. William O'Farrell. LC 55-5249. 1955. Published for the Crime Club by Doubleday.
Devil Horse. Max Brand. 202p. Repr. of 1922 ed. lib. bdg. 12.70x (ISBN 0-88411-522-4). Amereon Ltd.
Devil Horse. Max Brand. 1974. (pbk.) 0.95. Warner Paperback Library.
Devil in a Forest. Gene Wolfe. LC 76-5318. 5.95. (ISBN 0-695-40667-1). Follett Pub. Co.
Devil in a Forest. Gene Wolfe. 1977. 1.50 (ISBN 0-441-14288-5). Ace Books.
Devil in Bucks County: A Novel. Edmund Schiddel. LC 59-5491. 1959. Simon and Schuster.
Devil in Command. Helen Bianchin. (Harlequin Presents Ser.). 192p. (Orig.). 1981. pap. 1.50 (ISBN 0-373-10409-X, Pub. by Harlequin). PB.
Devil in Crystal. Erica Lindley. (Signet Book). 1977. 1.75 (ISBN 0-451-07643-5). New American Library.
Devil in Disguise. Jessica Steele. (Harlequin Romances Ser.). 192p. 1981. pap. 1.25 (ISBN 0-373-02424-X). Harlequin Bks.
Devil in Harbour. Catherine Irvine Gavin. LC 68-25963. 1968. 5.95. Morrow.
Devil in Iron. Robert E. Howard. LC 77-87805. (Illus.). 1976. 6.95 (ISBN 0-448-14580-4). Grosset & Dunlap.
Devil in Kansas. Simon Quinn. (Inquisitor, # 1). 1974. (pbk.) 0.95. Dell.
Devil in London. George Robert Sims. LC 9-6850. Dodge Publishing Company.
Devil in Love. Barbara Cartland. 1975. (pbk.) 1.25. Bantam Books.
Devil in Love: From the French of Jacques Cazotte. Jacques Cazotte. LC 26-4213. 1925. Houghton Mifflin Company.
Devil in Miss Jones. David Danziger. (Illus.). 1975. pap. 1.95 o.p. (ISBN 0-8021-0116-X, GP0116, Dist. by Whirlwind). Grove.
Devil in Miss Jones: Special Ser. David Danziger. 160p. (Orig.). 1973. pap. 1.50 o.p. (ERS-2). Grove.
Devil in My Heart: A Romance. Mary Howard, pseud. LC 41-130599. 1941. Doubleday, Doran and Company, Inc.
Devil in Satin... Cecil William Mercer. LC 38-12953. 1938. Doubleday, Doran & Company, Inc.
Devil in Satin. Cecil William Mercer. LC 40-4221. (A Mercury book. no. 23). The American Mercury, Inc.
Devil in Tartan. Elisabeth Ogilvie. LC 79-24296. 10.95 (ISBN 0-07-047678-0). McGraw-Hill.
Devil in Texas & Other Cowboy Tales. John R. Erickson. LC 82-90172. (Illus.). 96p. 1982. pap. 5.95 (ISBN 0-9608612-0-3). Maverick Bks.
Devil in the Belfry. Arthur Russell Thorndike. LC 32-13198. 1932. L. MacVeagh, Dial Press, Inc.
Devil in the Bush. John Edwin Canaday. LC 72-8886. 1973. (ISBN 0-393-08586-4). W. W. Norton.
Devil in the Bush. John Edwin Canaday. LC 45-9497. 1945. Simon and Schuster.
Devil in the Bush: A Mystery. Matthew Head. 184p. 1973. 5.95 o.p. (ISBN 0-393-08586-4). Norton.
Devil in the Desert. 1st Ed. Paul Horgan. LC 52-5918. 1952. Longmans, Green.
Devil in the Flesh. Raymond Radiguet. Tr. by Boyle, Kay. LC 32-5865. 1932. H. Smith.
Devil in the Hills. Cesare Pavese. LC 75-26217. 1975. 12.00 (ISBN 0-8371-8409-6). Greenwood Press.
Devil in the Hills. Translated from the Italian by D. D. Paige. Cesare Pavese. LC 59-151329. (Noonday paperbacks, N152). Noonday Press.
Devil in the Pines. Julie Cameron. (Berkley medallion book). 1975. (pbk.) 0.95 (ISBN 0-425-02777-5). Berkley Pub. Co.
Devil in the Sky. Muriel Bradley. LC 48-5324. 1948. Pub. for the Crime Club by Doubleday.
Devil in the Wind. Charles McLeod. 208p. 1981. 25.00x (ISBN 0-903065-28-2, Pub. by Wright Pub Scotland). State Mutual Bk.
Devil in Velvet. 1st Ed. John Dickson Carr. LC 51-10388. 1951. Harper.
Devil Is a Lonely Man. Morrison Wood. LC 46-602873. 1946. Thomas Y. Crowell Company.
Devil Is an English Gentleman. John Cournos. LC 32-491013. Farrar & Rinehart, Incorporated.
Devil Is Dead. R. A Lafferty. LC 77-5038. (Gregg Press science fiction series). 1977. 11.00 (ISBN 0-8398-2364-9). Gregg Press.
Devil Is Loneliness. Elma K Lobaugh. LC 46-4928. 1946. Current Books, Inc., A. A. Wyn.
Devil Is Loose: A Novel. Graham Shelby. LC 73-10818. (Illus.). 1974. 6.95 (ISBN 0-385-09459-0). Doubleday.
Devil Lord's Daughter. Frederick Ehrenfried Baume. LC 48-6382. 1948. Dodd, Mead.
Devil Lover. Carole Mortimer. (Harlequin Presents Ser.). 192p. 1981. pap. 1.50 (ISBN 0-373-10430-8, Pub. by Harlequin). PB.
Devil Loves Me. Margaret Millar. LC 42-18956. 1942. Published for the Crime Club by Doubleday, Doran and Company, Inc.
Devil Make a Third. William Fields Bailey. LC 48-8168. 1948. E. P. Dutton.
Devil Man... Edgar Wallace. LC 31-312295. Pub. for the Crime Club, Inc., by Doubleday, Doran & Company, Inc.
Devil Mask Mystery. Josephine Kains, pseud. (Mystery Puzzlers Ser.: No. 3). (Illus., Orig.). 1978. pap. 1.95 (ISBN 0-89083-397-4). Zebra.
Devil May Care. Wade Miller, pseud. LC 50-4718. (Gold medal book, 108). 1950. Fawcett Publications.
Devil-May-Care. Elizabeth Peters, pseud. LC 77-378. 7.95 (ISBN 0-396-07413-8). Dodd, Mead.
Devil-May-Care. Elizabeth Peters, pseud. (Fawcet Crest Book). 1978. 1.75 (ISBN 0-396-07413-8). Fawcett Pubns.
Devil-May-Care. Arthur Somers Roche. LC 26-15715. The Century Co.
Devil Must. 1st Ed. Tom Wicker. LC 56-8789. Harper.
Devil of a State. Anthony Burgess. 288p. 1975. pap. 3.95 (ISBN 0-393-00778-2, Norton Lib). Norton.
Devil of a State: A Novel. John Anthony Burgess Wilson. LC 75-20158. (Norton library; N778). 1975. 2.95 (ISBN 0-393-00778-2). Norton.
Devil of a State: A Novel by Anthony Burgess. John Anthony Burgess Wilson. LC 62-7968. 1962. W. W. Norton.
Devil of a State: A Novel. 1st American Ed. Anthony Burgess. LC 62-7968. 1962. Norton.
Devil of a Trip: Or, The Log of the Yacht Champlain. John Armoy Knox. (On cover: The unique series, no. 1). National Literary Bureau.
Devil of Aske. Pamela Hill. (Adult Ser.). 532p. 1973. Repr. lib. bdg. 11.95 o.p. (ISBN 0-8161-6143-7, Large Print Bks). G K Hall.
Devil of Aske: A Novel. Pamela Hill. LC 72-88431. 1973. 6.95. St. Martin's Press.
Devil of Aske: A Novel. Pamela Hill. LC 73-11413. 1973. 11.95 (ISBN 0-8161-6143-7). G. K. Hall.
Devil of Doubt. Daniel Pierce Thompson. 11.95 o.p. (ISBN 0-8062-0790-6). Carlton.
Devil of Pei-Ling. Herbert Asbury. LC 27-20258. 1927. Macy-Masius.
Devil of the Stairs. Pat Root. LC 56-135970. (Inner Sanctum Mystery). 1956. Simon and Schuster.
Devil of the Woods. facs. ed. Paul Annixter, pseud. LC 70-81259. (Short Story Index Reprint Ser., Vol. 1). 1958. 15.00 (ISBN 0-8369-3011-8). Ayer Co.
Devil on Her Tail. Peggy Swenson, pseud. (Orig.). 1969. pap. 1.75 o.p. (3055). Brandon.
Devil on His Trail. John Hawkins & Hawkins, Ward, 1912- Joint Author. LC 44-6706. 1944. E. P. Dutton & Company, Inc.
Devil on Horseback. Eleanor Hibbert. LC 77-72414. 1977. 8.95 (ISBN 0-385-13209-3). Doubleday.
Devil on Horseback. Eleanor Hibbert. LC 77-19153. 1978. 9.95 (ISBN 0-8161-6542-4). G. K. Hall.
Devil on Horseback. Victoria Holt, pseud. LC 77-72414. 1977. 13.95 (ISBN 0-385-13209-3). Doubleday.
Devil on Horseback. Victoria Holt, pseud. 1978. pap. 2.95 (ISBN 0-449-23687-0, Crest). Fawcett.
Devil on Lammas Night. Susan Howatch. LC 72-94532. 1973. 6.95 (ISBN 0-8128-1534-3). Stein and Day.
Devil on Lammas Night. Susan Howatch. (Fawcett crest book). 1974. (pbk.) 1.25. Fawcett.
Devil on Lammas Night. Susan Howatch. (Ace star, 14287). 1973. (pbk.) 0.95. Ace.
Devil on Two Sticks. Wade Miller, pseud. LC 49-11457. 1949. Farrar, Straus.
Devil on Two Sticks: A Translation of Le Diable Boiteux. Alain Rene Le Sage. LC 75-46287. (Supernatural & Occult Fiction). (Illus.). 1976. 17.00 (ISBN 0-405-08148-0). Arno Press.
Devil, Poor Devil: A Novel. Murray Constantine. Ed. by R. Reginald & Douglas Melville. LC 77-84214. (Lost Race & Adult Fantasy Ser.). 1978. Repr. of 1934 ed. lib. bdg. 16.00x (ISBN 0-405-10969-5). Ayer Co.
Devil Rides Out. Dennis Yates Wheatley. 8.95 (ISBN 0-09-025542-9, Pub. by Hutchinson). Merrimack Pub Cir.
Devil Rides Out. Dennis Yates Wheatley. (Black magic ser.). 1972. 1.50. Ballantine.
Devil Rides Outside. 1st Ed. John Howard Griffin. LC 52-9277. 1952. Smiths, Inc.
Devil Soul. Victor Jay. 1972. pap. 0.75 o.p. (BT40127). Belmont-Tower.
Devil Stories: An Anthology. Ed. by Maximilian Josef Rudwin. LC 21-9055. (Half-title: Devil lore; anthologies of diabolical literature, ed. by M. J. Rudwin, i). 1921. A. A. Knopf.
Devil Stories: Modern Man in Search of a Resort. Alan Rosenus. LC 78-64543. (Illus.). 1979. 9.95. (ISBN 0-913522-07-4) (ISBN 0-913522-08-2). Urion Press.
Devil Syndrome. George S. Shortess. 1979. 5.95 o.p. (ISBN 0-533-04018-3). Vantage.
Devil Take All. Alice Brennan. (queen size novel). 1974. (pbk.) 0.95. Popular Library.
Devil Take All. Martin Caidin. (1916). 1967. Dell.
Devil Take All: A Novel. 1st Ed. Martin Caidin. LC 66-13658. 1966. 5.95. Dutton.
Devil Take Her. Fay Nichols. pap. 0.60 o.p. (60-341). Manor Bks.

Devil Take Her, a Realistic Novel: By Fan Nichols. Frances Nichols Hanna. LC 54-318632. (Popular library, 586). 1954. Popular Library.

Devil Take Him. Ralph De Toledano. LC 79-14755. 11.95 (ISBN 0-399-12113-7). Putnam.

Devil Take the Bluetail Fly. John Franklin Bardin. 1967. pap. 0.60 o.p. (60-290). Manor Bks.

Devil Take the Foremost. Curtis Thomas. LC 47-31146. 1947. Pub. for the Crime Club by Doubleday.

Devil Take the Hindmost: A Novel of Suspense. 1st Ed. Harry F Shefter. LC 54-13426. 1955. Exposition Press.

Devil Takes a Hill Town. Charles G Givens. LC 39-31054. The Bobbs-Merrill Company.

Devil Tales. Virginia Frazer Boyle. LC 70-38643. (Black Heritage Library Collection). (Illus.). 1972. (ISBN 0-8369-9001-3). Books for Libraries Press.

Devil Tales by Virginia Frazer Boyle. Virginia Frazer Boyle. LC 6360. 1900. Harper & Brothers.

Devil That Failed. Maurice Samuel. LC 52-8514. 1952. Knopf.

Devil Threw Dice. 1st Ed. Amber Dean. LC 54-934538. 1954. Publishedfor the Crime Club by Doubleday.

Devil Thumbs a Ride. Robert C Du Soe. LC 38-34552. R. M. McBride and Company.

Devil to Pay. Glen Chase, pseud. (Cherry Delight Ser.). 1977. pap. 1.50 o.s.i. (ISBN 0-8439-0473-9, Leisure Bks). Nordon Pubns.

Devil to Pay. Frances Nimmo Greene. LC 18-8988. 1918. C. Scribner's Sons.

Devil to Pay. Cyril Northcote Parkinson. LC 72-6731. (Illus.). 1973. 5.95 (ISBN 0-395-15483-9). Houghton Mifflin Co.

Devil to Pay. Cyril Northcote Parkinson. 1980 (ISBN 0-87216-636-8). Playboy Press.

Devil to Pay. Ellery Queen, pseud. LC 38-5598. 1938. Frederick A. Stokes Company.

Devil to Pay... Ellery Queen, pseud. LC 45-15791. 1944.

Devil to Pay. Earl Thompson. 1981. 14.95 (ISBN 0-453-00404-0, H404). NAL.

Devil to Pay. Earl Thompson. 1982. pap. 3.95 (ISBN 0-451-11909-6, AE1909, Sig). NAL.

Devil to Pay see Door Between.

Devil to Pay: A Novel. Earl Thompson. LC 81-38418. 14.95 (ISBN 0-453-00404-0). New American Library.

Devil to Pay in the Backlands. Joao Guimaraes Rosa. (O.S.I.). 1963. 6.95 o.s.i. (ISBN 0-394-42203-1). Knopf.

Devil to Play. Leonard Holton, pseud. LC 73-11552. (Father Bredder Mystery Novel Ser.). 184p. 1973. 4.95 o.p. (ISBN 0-396-06866-9). Dodd.

Devil to Play. Leonard Patrick O'Connor Wibberley. LC 73-11552. (Red badge novel of suspense). 1974. 4.95 (ISBN 0-396-06866-9). Dodd, Mead.

Devil Tree. Jerzy N. Kosinski. LC 72-88804. 1973. 6.95 (ISBN 0-15-125328-5). Harcourt Brace Jovanovich.

Devil Tree. rev. and expanded ed. Jerzy N. Kosinski. LC 81-5236. 11.95 (ISBN 0-312-19794-2). St. Martin's Press.

Devil-Tree of El Dorado. Frank Aubrey. LC 77-84196. (Lost Race and Adult Fantasy Fiction). (Illus.). 1978. 25.00 (ISBN 0-405-10955-5). Arno Press.

Devil-Tree of el Dorado: A Novel. Frank Atkins. Ed. by R. Reginald & Douglas Melville. LC 77-84196. (Lost Race & Adult Fantasy Ser.). (Illus.). 1978. Repr. of 1897 ed. lib. bdg. 25.00x (ISBN 0-405-10955-5). Ayer Co.

Devil-Tree of El Dorado. A Novel. Frank Aubrey. LC 6-3844. New Amsterdam Book Company.

Devil Walks on Water: A Novel. John F. Murray. LC 69-15072. 1969. 5.95. Little, Brown.

Devil Was Handsome. 1st Ed. Maurice Procter. LC 61-6471. 1961. Harper.

Devil Was Kind. Donald Ross. LC 39-8616. (Half-title: Twentieth century thrillers. 790). Whitman Publishing Company.

Devil Water. Anya Seton. LC 62-7256. 1962. Houghton Mifflin.

Devil Water. Anya Seton. 1976. 1.95 (ISBN 0-449-22888-6). Fawcett Crest.

Devil We Know. May Dikeman. LC 72-13739. 1973. 8.95 (ISBN 0-316-18556-6). Little, Brown.

Devil Wire. Cameron Judd. 1981. pap. 2.25 (ISBN 0-89083-835-6). Zebra.

Devil with Love. Robert Nathan. LC 63-11048. 1963. Knopf.

Devil Within. Fannie Heaslip Lea. LC 48-5577. 1948. Dodd, Mead.

Devil Within Us. Donald Basinger. LC 64-14582. (A London House mystery). 1964. London House & Maxwell.

Devil Wolf. Norma S Schinke. LC 24-3400. Small, Maynard & Company.

Devil Wore Scarlet. Dulcie Gray. 1982. 18.00x (ISBN 0-86025-100-4, Pub. by Ian Henry Pubns England). State Mutual Bk.

Devil Wore Scarlet. Dulcie Gray. 1977. 6.90 o.p. State Mutual Bk.

Devil Worshipper. Frederick Augustus Ray. LC 8-21925. 1908. The C. M. Clark Publishing Company.

Devil You Don't. James Maurice Scott. LC 69-14829. 1968. Chilton Book Co.

Deviled Eggbert. Laf. Date not set. pap. price not set (ISBN 0-671-82191-1, Wallaby). PB.

Devils. Fedor Mikhailovich Dostoevskii. Tr. by David Magarshack. (Classics Ser.). (Orig.). 1954. pap. 5.95 (ISBN 0-14-044035-6). Penguin.

Devil's Admiral. Frederick Ferdinand Moore. LC 13-306982. 1913. 1.25. Doubleday, Page & Co.

Devil's Advocate. Taylor Caldwell. LC 52-5681. 1952. Crown Publishers.

Devil's Advocate. Morris L. West. LC 59-10549. 1959. Morrow.

Devil's Agent: A Novel by Hans Habe Pseud. Translated from the German by Ewald Osers. Jean Bekessy, pseud. LC 58-8741. 1958. F. Fell.

Devil's Alternative. Frederick Forsyth. LC 79-25929. 1980. 12.95 (ISBN 0-670-27081-4). Viking Press.

Devil's Apple Corps. Raymond Barrio. (Illus.). 50p. 1976. pap. 1.50 (ISBN 0-917438-06-X). Ventura Pr.

Devil's Arms. Charlotte Lamb, pseud. (Harlequin Presents Ser.). 1979. pap. 1.25 (ISBN 0-373-70786-X, Pub. by Harlequin). PB.

Devil's Band. Robert McCaig. (Orig.). 1981. pap. 1.95 (ISBN 0-89083-728-7). Zebra.

Devil's Bed. Willi Heinrich. LC 65-15330. 1965. Dial Press.

Devil's Behind You. Henry Edward Helseth. LC 42-14745. 1942. Harper & Brothers.

Devil's Bell. Elsie Mills McMillan. 1974. (pbk.) 1.50 (ISBN 0-89014-114-2). Canyon Books.

Devil's Bondman. Sylvia Thorpe. 1980. pap. 1.75 (ISBN 0-449-50034-9, Coventry). Fawcett.

Devil's Booth: A Novel. Percival Wilde. LC 30-6155. Harcourt, Brace and Company.

Devil's Bowman. Patrick Lee. (Six-Gun Samurai Ser.: No. 5). 192p. (Orig.). 1981. pap. 1.95 (ISBN 0-523-41417-X). Pinnacle Bks.

Devil's Box. Walt Sheldon. (Orig.). 1968. pap. 0.60 o.p. (73-736). Lancer.

Devil's Brand. (Orig.). 1969. pap. 1.75 (ISBN 0-87067-170-7, BH170). Holloway.

Devil's Brand. Ed. by Paul J. Gillette. pap. 1.50 o.p. (ISBN 0-87067-170-7, 88-162). Holloway.

Devil's Breath. Robert Irvine. 288p. 1982. pap. 2.75 (ISBN 0-523-41640-7). Pinnacle Bks.

Devil's Breed. George Smith. LC 79-88835. (American Freedom Ser.). 432p. (Orig.). 1980. pap. 2.50 (ISBN 0-87216-602-3). Playboy Pbks.

Devil's Bride. Noel Bertram Gerson. LC 58-11329. 1958. Doubleday.

Devil's Bride: A Present Day Arraignment of Formalism and Doubt in the Church and in Society, in the Light of the Holy Scriptures. Given in the Form of a Pleasing Story. Milton Henry Stine. LC 10-23319. The Minter Company.

Devil's Bridge. Mary Deasy. LC 52-9780. 1952. Little, Brown.

Devil's Bridge. Mark Aleksandrovich Landau. Tr. by Chamot, Alfred Edward. LC 28-25959. 1928. A. A. Knopf.

Devil's Brigade: The Story of the Hatfield-McCoy Feud. John L. Spivak. LC 30-30242. Brewer and Warren, Inc.

Devil's Brigadier. Don Ryan. LC 54-5799. 1954. Coward-McCann.

Devil's Cameo: A Novel of Suspense and Detection. 1st Ed. William H Dye. LC 56-9558. 1956. Exposition Press.

Devil's Canyon. Eugene E Halleran. LC 56-9289. 1956. Ballantine Books.

Devil's Causeway. Mary Wibberley. (Harlequin Presents Ser.). 192p. 1982. pap. 1.75 (ISBN 0-373-10486-3). Harlequin Bks.

Devil's Cavern. Clarenda Morgan. pap. 0.60 o.p. Lancer.

Devil's Channel. Jeremiah McMahon. (Orig.). 1972. pap. 0.95 o.p. (ISBN 0-515-02793-6, N2793). Pyramid Pubns.

Devil's Chapel: A Novel. Laurence Davis Lafore. LC 64-11292. 1964. Doubleday.

Devil's Chaplain. George Fitzalan Bronson Howard. LC 23-7013. W. J. Watt & Company.

Devil's Children. Michel Parry. (Berkley medallion book). 1976. 1.50 (ISBN 0-425-03202-7). Berkley.

Devil's Children: Tales of Demons and Exorcists. Michel Parry. LC 74-21721. 1975. 7.95 (ISBN 0-8008-5670-8). Taplinger Pub. Co.

Devil's Church. F. Draco, pseud. LC 51-10854. (Murray Hill mystery). 1951. Rinehart.

Devil's Church and Other Stories. Machado De Assis, Joaquim Maria. LC 76-53828. (Texas Pan American series). (Illus.). 10.00 (ISBN 0-292-77535-0). University of Texas Press.

Devil's Churchyard. Godfrey Edmund Turton. LC 79-103782. 1970. 5.95. Doubleday.

Devil's Circus. Louis Berg. LC 34-461931. 1934. W. Godwin, Inc.

Devil's Cockpit. Nick Carter. (O.s.i.). (Orig.). pap. 0.60 o.s.i. (A238X, Award). Univ Pub & Dist.

Devil's Cocktail. Alexander Wilson. LC 28-24154. 1928. Longmans, Green and Co.

Devil's Compact. A Vivid Translation from the French of Emile Zola... Emile Zola. LC 8-37878. (On cover: Fox's sensational series, no. 4). R. K. Fox.

Devil's Cook. Ellery Queen, pseud. (Signet book). 1975. (pbk.) 0.95. New American Library.

Devil's Cook. Ellery Queen. LC 74-4798. 1968. 0.50. Pocket Books.

Devil's Court. Rachel Cosgrove Payes. (Berkley medallion book). 1974. (pbk.) 0.95 (ISBN 0-425-02585-3). Berkley Pub. Co.

Devil's Cradle. Cecily Ullmann Sidgwick. LC 18-13452. W. J. Watt & Company.

Devil's Cross. 1st Ed. Walter O'Meara. LC 57-10309. 1957. Knopf.

Devil's Cub. Georgette Heyer. LC 66-25123. 1966. 4.95. Dutton.

Devil's Cub. Georgette Heyer. (SB4004). 1967. Bantam.

Devil's Cuspidor. Beatrice LaForce. 1981. pap. 1.50. Eldridge Pub.

Devil's Dancing Hour. Sally Purcell. 1968. pap. 0.80 o.p.; pap. 3.50 ea. signed ed. 50 copied o.p. Anvil Pr.

Devil's Dancing Hour. Sally Purcell. 1.00 o.p. Unicorn Pr.

Devil's Daughter. Eleazar Lipsky. LC 73-80279. 1969. 8.95. Meredith Press.

Devil's Daughter. Peter Marsh. LC 42-9306. 1942. J. Swift, Inc.

Devil's Daughter. Marilyn Ross. 1973. 0.95. Warner Paperback Library.

Devil's Daughter. Oscar Schisgall. LC 32-31611. The Fiction League.

Devil's Daughter. Daoma Winston. (Kangaroo Book). 1977. 1.75 (ISBN 0-671-80978-4). Pocket Books.

Devil's Daughter. Frank Yerby. (Dell Book). 1977. 1.95 (ISBN 0-440-11917-0). Dell Pub. Co.

Devil's Defeat. Edwin Stanton De Poncet. LC 38-21706. 1938. Meador Publishing Company.

Devil's Den. Lawrence Saunders. LC 33-32229. Covici, Friede.

Devil's Desire. Laurie McBain. 1975. pap. 3.50 (ISBN 0-380-00295-7, 81802-7). Avon.

Devil's Desire. Laurie McBain. 1975. (pbk.) 1.75 (ISBN 0-380-00295-7). Avon.

Devils' Dice. William Le Queux. LC 7-12855. 1897. Rand, McNally & Ocmpany.

Devil's Dictionary. Ambrose Gwinnett Bierce. LC 62-8606. lib. bdg. 9.50x (ISBN 0-88307-017-0). Gannon.

Devil's Dictionary. Ambrose Gwinnett Bierce. LC 78-13294. (Illus.). 1978. 14.95 (ISBN 0-916144-34-8); pap. 7.95 (ISBN 0-916144-35-6). Stemmer Hse.

Devil's Discharge. Henry Willard French. LC 14-397040. 1914. 1.00. The Neale Publishing Company.

Devil's Ditties. Jeannette Bell Thomas. 1931. Repr. 12.00 o.s.i. Finch Pr.

Devil's Dollar Sign. Joe Millard, pseud. (Dollar Western Ser.). (O.s.i.). 160p. 1973. pap. 0.95 o.s.i. (AN1254, Award). Univ Pub & Dist.

Devil's Door. Robert Neill. LC 79-21302. 8.95 (ISBN 0-312-19807-8). St. Martin's Press.

Devil's Doorstep. Dorinda Kamm. 1972. 4.95. Lenox Hill Pr.

Devil's Doorstep. Paul Evan Lehman. LC 49-6560. (Dutton Diamond D western). 1949. E. P. Dutton.

Devil's Double. Valency Hunter. 1973. (pbk.) 0.95. Dell.

Devil's Dozen. Nick Carter. 1982. pap. 2.50 (ISBN 0-441-14399-7). Ace Bks.

Devil's Dozen. Nick Carter. (Nick Carter Ser.). (O.s.i.). 192p. (Orig.). 1973. pap. 0.95 o.s.i. (AN1133, Award). Univ Pub & Dist.

Devil's Dream. A Termperance Story, Founded on Facts. Evangeline B Blanchard. LC 6-13843. 1889. Funk & Wagnalls.

Devil's Dreamer. Alice Brennan. 1971. pap. 0.75 o.p. (ISBN 0-447-74752-5). Lancer.

Devil's Dress. Mary M. Fletcher. pap. 0.95 o.s.i. (75-282). Lancer.

Devil's Drum see Hellgate.

Devil's Drum: A Gregory Quist Story. 1st Ed. William Colt MacDonald. LC 56-10808. 1956. Lippincott.

Devil's Drummer. Tex Harding & Murphy, James, Tr. LC 34-8351. Reynal & Hitchcock.

Devil's Due. Phyllis Bottome. LC 31-20651. 1931. Houghton Mifflin Company.

Devil's Due. Lanora Miller. (Ace Gothic#). 1975. (pbk.) 0.95. Ace Books.

Devil's Due. 1st Ed. Maurice Procter. LC 60-10450. 1960. Harper.

Devil's Elbow. Brainard Cheney. 1969. 5.95 o.p. Crown.

Devil's Elbow: A Novel. Brainard Cheney. LC 77-75089. 1969. 5.95. Crown Publishers.

Devil's Embrace. Catherine Coulter. 1982. pap. 3.50 (ISBN 0-451-11853-7, AE1853, Sig). NAL.

Devil's Fire, Love's Revenge. Barbara Paul. LC 76-13048. 1976. 7.95 o.p. St Martin.

Devil's Fire, Love's Revenge. Barbara Vstedal. LC 76-13048. 7.95. St. Martin's Press.

Devil's Fire, Love's Revenge. Barbara Vstedal. LC 77-9471. 1977. 12.95 (ISBN 0-8161-6492-4). G. K. Hall.

Devil's Food, a Novel. Dorothy Fremont Grant. LC 49-921956. 1949. Longmans, Green.

Devil's Foot. Christine Goutiere Weston. LC 42-10023. 1942. C. Scribner's Sons.

Devil's Footprints. Evelyn Bond. 1972. pap. 0.75 o.p. (94243). Beagle Bks.

Devil's Footsteps. John Frederick Burke. LC 76-14902. 1976. 7.95 (ISBN 0-698-10765-9). Coward, McCann & Geoghegan.

Devil's Footsteps. John Frederick Burke. 1978. 1.75 (ISBN 0-445-04204-4). Popular Library.

Devil's Gamble: A Novel of Demonology. Frank Gill Slaughter. LC 76-56337. 1977. 8.95 (ISBN 0-385-12851-7). Doubleday.

Devil's Game. Poul Anderson. 1980. pap. 2.50 (ISBN 0-671-83689-7, Timescape). PB.

Devil's Garden. Louise Harvey Gilman. LC 53-101954. 1954. Dorrance.

Devil's Garden. William Babington Maxwell. LC 13-24321. 1913. The Bobbs-Merrill Company.

Devil's Garden. William Babington Maxwell. LC 24-2079. 1924. Dodd, Mead & Company.

Devil's Garden. Bob Reynolds. 1978. pap. 1.25 (ISBN 0-532-12564-9). Woodhill.

Devil's Generation. Ed. by Vic Ghidalia. 1973. pap. 0.95 o.s.i. (75-465). Lancer.

Devil's Gold. Chet Cunningham. (Orig.). 1980. pap. 1.95 o.s.i. (ISBN 0-505-51510-5). Tower Bks.

Devil's Gold. Nicola West. (Harlequin Romances Ser.). 192p. 1983. pap. 1.50 (ISBN 0-373-02526-2). Harlequin Bks.

Devil's Gold: The Story of a Forgotten Race. Oscar F G Day. (On cover: Idylwild series, v. 1, no. 21). 1892. Morrill, Higgins & Co.

Devil's Guard. George R. Elford. 1971. 7.95 o.p. (1867-6). Delacorte.

Devil's Guard. Talbot Mundy. LC 26-15063. The Bobbs-Merrill Company.

Devil's Gunhand. Ray Hogan. Bd. with Guns of Stingaree. 272p. 1980. pap. 1.95 (ISBN 0-451-09355-0, J9355, Sig). NAL.

Devil's Gunhand. Dale London. LC 60-2426. 1960. Arcadia House.

Devil's Half. Ovid Williams Pierce. LC 68-11777. 1968. Doubleday.

Devil's Hand: A Novel. Edith Summers Kelley. LC 74-10552. (Lost American fiction). 1974. 8.95 (ISBN 0-8093-0675-1). Southern Illinois University Press.

Devil's Handmaidens. Mildred I Reid. LC 51-3596. 1951. Humphries.

Devil's Harvest: A Novel. Frank Gill Slaughter. LC 63-8743. 1963. Doubleday.

Devil's Heart. William W. Johnstone. 1983. pap. 2.95 (ISBN 0-8217-1156-3). Zebra.

Devil's Heirloom. Anthony M Rud. LC 24-7117. (Famous authors series. no. 38). 1924. Garden City Publishing Co., Inc.

Devil's Highway. Harold Bell Wright & Gilbert Munger Wright. LC 32-108367. 1932. D. Appleton and Company.

Devil's Holiday. Holland E Nickerson. LC 52-4487. 1952. Woodford Press.

Devil's Horseman. Jean Davison. LC 75-36584. 1976. 5.95 (ISBN 0-385-11587-3). Doubleday.

Devil's House. Julia Tremonte. 1974. (pbk.) 0.95 (ISBN 0-523-00317-X). Pinnacle Books.

Devil's Hunting-Grounds: A Fantasy. Harry Blamires. LC 54-12658. 1954. Longmans, Green.

Devil's Instrument. easy eye ed. Mary M. Fletcher. (Orig.). 1969. pap. 0.75 o.p. (74-987). Lancer.

Devil's Instrument: And Other Danish Stories. Ed. by Sven Holm. LC 72-141038. (Unesco Collection of Contemporary Works). 1971. (ISBN 0-8023-1251-9). Dufour Editions.

Devil's Island: A Novel. Arthur D Hall. LC 99-4073. (On cover: Eagle library, no. 126). Street & Smith.

Devil's Jackpot. Zeke Masters, pseud. (Orig.). 1982. pap. 1.95 (ISBN 0-671-43811-5). PB.

Devil's Jest. Elizabeth Carfrae, pseud. LC 29-6677. 1928. Harper & Brothers.

Devils-Jewish Style. Louis Stricker. 1975. 7.00 o.p. (ISBN 0-682-48222-6). Exposition.

Devils-Jewish Style. Louis Stricker. 1975. 7.00 o.p. (ISBN 0-682-48222-6). Exposition.

Devil's Kiss. William W. Johnstone. (Orig.). 1981. pap. 2.75 (ISBN 0-89083-717-1). Zebra.

Devil's Knee. Irving Shulman. LC 72-76773. 1973. 8.95 (ISBN 0-671-27092-3). Trident Press.

Devil's Knee. Irving Shulman. 1974. (pbk.) 1.50 (ISBN 0-671-78608-3). Pocket Books.

Devil's Lady. Henry Leyford Gates. LC 33-211301. 1933. The Macaulay Company.

Devil's Lady. Linden Howard. LC 79-25391. 10.00 (ISBN 0-312-19823-X). St. Martin's Press.
Devil's Laughter. Frank Yerby. LC 53-9319. 1953. Dial Press.
Devil's Legion. Oscar Schisgall. LC 46-183508. 1946. Arcadia House, Inc.
Devil's Lieutenant. Maria Fagyas. LC 77-105600. 1970. 6.95. Putnam.
Devil's Lottery. Nalbro Isadorah Bartley. LC 31-20805. Farrar & Rinehart, Incorporated.
Devil's Love. Lane Harris. (Orig.). 1981. pap. 3.95 (ISBN 0-440-11915-4). Dell.
Devil's Mansion. Rex Jardin. LC 31-9000. 1931. The Fiction League.
Devil's Mantle. Frank Lucius Packard. LC 28-12554. 1927. George H. Doran Company.
Devil's Marchioness. William Fifield. LC 57-9600. 1957. Dial Press.
Devil's Mess. Clem Edmunds. LC 46-19190. 1946. Phoenix Press.
Devil's Mirror. Miriam Lynch. (ravenswood gothic). 1973. (pbk.) 0.75 (ISBN 0-671-77529-4). Pocket Books.
Devil's Mixture. Milton J. Hinlein. 1975. 5.95 o.p. (ISBN 0-8059-2226-1). Dorrance.
Devil's Necklace. Juliette Benzoni. LC 80-21997. 1980. 11.95 (ISBN 0-399-12515-9). Putnam.
Devils of D-Day. Graham Masterton. 1978. pap. 2.95 (ISBN 0-523-48069-5). Pinnacle Bks.
Devils of Loudun. Aldous Leonard Huxley. 1979. pap. 5.95i o.p. (ISBN 0-06-090210-8, CN-210, CN). Har-Row.
Devil's Own. Peter Curtis, pseud. 1970. pap. 0.95 o.p. (N2371). Pyramid Pubns.
Devil's Own. Christopher Nicole. LC 74-32503. 1975. 10.00. St. Martin's Press.
Devil's Own. Peter Robson. 1975. (pbk.) 0.95. Ace Books.
Devil's Own. Ellsworth Wilson. LC 48-5677. 1947. Christopher Pub. House.
Devil's Own: A Romance of the Black Hawk War. Randall Parrish. LC 17-28849. 1917. A. C. McClurg & Co.
Devil's Own: By Peter Curtis Pseud. 1st Ed. Noran Roninson Lofts. LC 60-7876. 1960. Published for the Crime Club by Doubleday.
Devil's Own Dear Son. James B. Cabell. 238p. Repr. of 1949 ed. lib. bdg. 13.85x (ISBN 0-88411-570-4). Amereon Ltd.
Devil's Owndear Son: A Comedy of the Fatted Calf. James Branch Cabell. LC 49-8665. 1949. Farrar, Straus.
Devil's Paintbrush. Martin Dibner. LC 82-45460. 360p. 1983. 16.95 (ISBN 0-385-15666-9). Doubleday.
Devil's Passkey: A Ruff Morgan Thriller. Jimmy Shannon. LC 52-12546. 1952. Appleton-Century-Crofts.
Devil's Passport. Gordon Ray Young. LC 33-518226. The Century Co.
Devil's Passport. Gordon Ray Young. LC 42-206521. 1942. Triangle Books.
Devil's Paw: A Novel. Edward Phillips Oppenheim. LC 20-168585. 1920. Little, Brown, and Company.
Devil's Paw: A Novel. Edward Phillips Oppenheim. LC 24-204605. 1922. A. L. Burt Company.
Devil's Pit, and Other Stories. Translated by Esther S. Dillon and Angel Flores. Baldomero Lillo. LC 59-65394. (UNESCO Collection of Representative Works: Latin American Series). 1959. Pan American Union, General Secretariat, Organization of American States.
Devil's Pitchfork: By Ruth Artist and Leora Peters. Ruth Hesse Artist & Leora Peters. LC 51-10644. 1951. Dorrance.
Devil's Playground. JoAnna Brandon. (Candlelight Ecstasy Ser.: No. 66). (Orig.). 1982. pap. 1.95 (ISBN 0-440-11985-5). Dell.
Devil's Playground. Cliff Farrell. LC 75-41674. 1976. 5.95 (ISBN 0-385-12079-6). Doubleday.
Devil's Playground: A Story of the Wild Northwest. John Mackie. LC 7-19982. (On cover: Twentieth century series). F. A. Stokes Company.
Devil's Plough: The Romantic History of a Soul Conflict. Anna Farquhar Bergengren. LC 1-30886. 1901. L. C. Page & Company.
Devil's Pool. George Sand & Sedgwick, Jane Minot, Tr. LC 4-23581. 1894. G. H. Richmond & Co.
Devil's Pool. George Sand & Sedgwick, Jane Minot, Tr. LC 4-17503. 1901. Little, Brown & Co.
Devil's Pool and Francois the Waif. George Sand. LC 36-37341. (Half-title: Everyman's library, ed. by Ernest Rhys. Fiction. no. 534). 1939. J. M. Dent & Sons, Ltd.
Devil's Pool. Fourteen Etchings. Tr. by George Burnham Iver. Ives, George Burnham, 1856-1930, Tr. LC 1-12865. (Roman contemporais. Romancists, vol. IX). 1901. G. Barrie & Son.
Devil's Portage. Charles Stoddard. LC 42-20319. 1942. Gateway Books.
Devil's Power: By Charles Rushton Pseud. Charles Rushton Shortt. LC 56-8204. Roy Publishers.
Devil's Princess. Daoma Winston. 1979. 1.75 (ISBN 0-671-80970-9). Pocket Books.
Devil's Pulpit. Henry Brereton Marriott Watson. LC 8-29000. 1908. Dodd, Mead and Company.
Devil's Race-Track: Mark Twain's Great Dark Writings: the Best from Which Was the Dream? and Fables of Man. Samuel Langhorne Clemens & John Sutton Tuckey. LC 78-62865. (Illus.). 15.95 (ISBN 0-520-03780-4). University of California Press.
Devil's Race-Track: Mark Twain's Great Dark Writings: The Best from Which Was the Dream? & Fables of Man. Mark Twain. Ed. by John S. Tuckey. (Illus.). 1980. 15.95 (ISBN 0-520-03780-4); pap. 6.95 (ISBN 0-520-03893-2). U of Cal Pr.
Devil's Rain. Maud Willis. 1975. (pbk.) 1.25. Dell.
Devil's Reception Room. Con De Vlieger. LC 6-33399. C. De Vlieger, Jr.
Devil's Saddle. Norman A. Fox. LC 48-1414. (Silver star westerns). 1948. Dodd, Mead.
Devil's Scrapbook see Call for an Exorcist.
Devil's Shadow. Frank Thiess & Lowe-Porter, H. T., Tr. LC 28-22354. 1928. A. A. Knopf.
Devil's Spawn. Robert Carse. LC 56-8041. (Dell first edition, 95). 1956. Dell Pub. Co.
Devil's Spoon. Theodora McCormick Du Bois. LC 30-5177. 1930. Frederick A. Stokes Company.
Devil's Steps. Arthur William Upfield. LC 46-3409. 1946. Pub. for the Crime Club by Doubleday & Company, Inc.
Devil's Steps: An Inspector Napoleon Bonaparte Mystery. Arthur William Upfield. 1982. pap. 2.95 (ISBN 0-684-17668-8, ScribT). Scribner.
Devil's Stronghold. Zenith Jones Brown. 1948. C. Scribner's Sons.
Devils (The Possessed) Fedor Mikhailovich Dostoevskii. LC 55-3267. (Penguin classics, L35). Penguin Books.
Devil's Tor. David Lindsay. LC 77-84249. (Lost Race and Adult Fantasy Fiction). 1978. 30.00 (ISBN 0-405-10995-4). Arno Press.
Devil's Toy. Anita Stewart. 1935. E. P. Dutton & Co., Inc.
Devil's Vineyard. Barbara Kevern. 1975. (pbk.) 1.25 (ISBN 0-523-00536-9). Pinnacle Books.
Devil's Virtuosos. David Downing. LC 79-89963. (World War II Ser.). 272p. 1980. pap. 2.25 (ISBN 0-87216-609-0). Playboy Pbks.
Devil's Virtuosos. David Downing. (War Bks.). 280p. 1983. pap. 2.25 (ISBN 0-87216-609-0). Jove Pubns.
Devil's Voyage. Jack L Chalker. LC 79-7841. 1981. 11.95 (ISBN 0-385-15284-1). Doubleday.
Devil's Walk. Dimone Hall. (Orig.). 1971. pap. 0.75 o.p. (75-450). Manor Bks.
Devil's Web. Scott Stone. LC 55-208670. 1955. Vixen Press.
Devil's Wind. Patricia Wentworth. 1912. G. P. Putnam's Sons.
Devil's Wind, Nana Saheb's Story: A Novel. Manohar Malgonkar. LC 76-181719. 1972. 7.95 (ISBN 0-670-27102-0). Viking Press.
Devil's Work. John Brunner. LC 70-77400. 1970. 5.95. Norton.
Devil's Work. Carolyn Wells. LC 40-34004. 1940. J. B. Lippincott Company.
Devil's Work. Margaret Yorke. LC 82-5614. 10.95 (ISBN 0-312-19867-1). St. Martin's Press.
Devil's Yard. Ivo Andric. LC 75-15692. 1975. 9.75 (ISBN 0-8371-8218-2). Greenwood Press.
Devil's Yard. Translated by Kenneth Johnstone. Ivo Andric. LC 62-16340. 1962. Grove Press.
Devilweed: 1st Ed. in the U.S.A. Bill Knox. LC 66-11760. 3.50. Pub. for the Crime Club by Doubleday.
Devious Design. Dolores Birk Hitchens. 1948. Pub. for the Crime Club by Doubleday.
Devious Murder. George Bellairs. LC 80-51995. 1980. 9.95 (ISBN 0-8027-5427-9). Walker.
Devious Ones: By Frances and Richard Lockridge. 1st Ed. Frances Louise Davis Lockridge & Lockridge, Richard. LC 64-19015. 1964. Lippincott.
Devious Ways. Gilbert Cannan. LC 10-10778. 1910. 1.50. Duffield and Company.
Devious Ways. Philip Freund. 1963. Repr. 4.50x o.s.i. (ISBN 0-8277-0370-8). British Bk Ctr.
Devlin. Jack Younger. (Orig.). 1976. pap. 1.50 (ISBN 0-532-17140-3). Woodhill.
Devlin the Barber. Benjamin Leopold Farjeon. LC 75-32743. (Literature of Mystery and Detection). 1976. 11.00 (ISBN 0-405-07869-2). Arno Press.
Devlin's Day off. Double D. Western. Amos Moore. LC 42-159777. 1942. Doubleday, Doran & Company, Inc.
Devlin's Triangle. Basil Heatter. 1976. (pbk.) 1.50 (ISBN 0-523-00806-6). Pinnacle Books.
Devlyn. Melissa Clark. (Orig.). 1977. pap. 1.50 o.p. (ISBN 0-515-04330-3). BJ Pub Group.
Devolutioary Notes. Michael Zwerin. (Illus.). 63p. (Orig.). 1980. pap. 2.95 (ISBN 0-937102-01-6). Planet Drum.
Devon Boys: A Tale of the North Shore. George Manville Fenn. LC 6-39268. (Harper's Franklin square library, no. 562). 1887. Harper & Brothers.
Devon Maze. Jean DeWitt Fitz. LC 70-93120. 1969. 4.95. Geron-X.
Devonshers. Honore McCue Willsie Morrow. LC 24-21812. 1924. Frederick A. Stokes Company.
Devonshire Hollow: A Story of Pioneer Life in Wisconsin, 1850-1900. Leora Buckingham Jackson. LC 60-6382. 1960. Pan Press.
Devota... Augusta Jane Evans Wilson. LC 7-21224. 1907. G. W. Dillingham Co.
Devota "J'y Suis, J'y Reste,". Augusta Jane Evans Wilson & De Leon, Thomas Cooper, 1839- G. W. Dillingham Co.
Devoted Bride: Or, Faith and Fidelity. A Love Story. St. George Tucker. LC 8-28275. (On cover: Petersons' dollar series). T. B. Peterson & Brothers.
Devoted Couple: A Novel. J Masterman. LC 7-17807. (On cover: Harper's Franklin square library, no. 745). 1894. Harper & Brothers.
Devoted Friends. Joe Poyer, pseud. LC 81-69139. (Illus.). 1982. 13.95 (ISBN 0-689-11251-3). Atheneum.
Devoted Ladies. Mary Nesta Keane. LC 34-15311. 1934. Little, Brown, and Company.
Devotee and a Darling: Or, The Difference Between Them Also, Something Mother Found on Her Travels. Becca Middleton Samson. LC 8-3751. 1898. D.C.Cook Publishing Company.
Devotion. Botho Strauss. LC 79-9887. 8.95 (ISBN 0-374-13852-4). Farrar, Straus and Giroux.
Devourers. Annie Vivanti Chartres. LC 10-12099. 1910. 1.35. G. P. Putnam's Sons.
Devout Bluebeard. Marie Graham. LC 1-29493. The Abbey Press.
Devs Irae. Philip K Dick. (Dell Book). 1977. 1.75 (ISBN 0-440-11838-7). Dell Pub. Co.
Dew and Mildew: A Loose-Knit Tale of Hindustan. Percival Christopher Wren. LC 27-15394. 1927. Frederick A. Stokes Company.
Dew in April. Henry Bertram Law Webb. LC 35-6718. C. Kendall & W. Sharp, Inc.
Dew of Slumber: A Short Novel. William Dunbar Browne. LC 55-37192. 1955. Christopher Pub. House.
Dew of the Sea: And Other Stories. Horace Annesley Vachell. LC 27-23636. G. P. Putnam's Sons.
Dew of Youth. Carl L L'Amoureux. LC 52-8874. 1952. Vantage Press.
Dew on the Grass. Eiluned Lewis. LC 34-302512. 1934. The Macmillan Company.
Dewer Rides. Leonard Alfred George Strong. LC 30-4842. 1929. C. Boni.
Dewey Decimated. Charles A Goodrum. LC 76-56949. 7.95 (ISBN 0-517-52866-5). Crown Publishers.
Dewey Decimated. Charles A Goodrum. LC 77-13659. 1978. 9.95 (ISBN 0-89340-124-2). J. Curley.
Dewitt Manor. Elizabeth St. Clair. (Signet Book). 1977. 1.50 (ISBN 0-451-07690-7). New American Library.
Dewpond. Charles Marriott. LC 12-14113. 1912. 1.30. John Lane Company.
Dewpond. Theodore Francis Powys. LC 77-12009. (Series: The Woburn Books; No. 2.). 1977. 9.95 (ISBN 0-8383-2187-9). Haskell House Publishers.
Dewy, Dewy Eyes. Babette Rosmond. LC 46-49293. 1946. E. P. Dutton & Company, Inc.
Deynard's Divorce. Edna Goodrich. LC 12-225213. 1.25. R. G. Badger.
Steel Crocodile /D.G. Compton. David Guy Compton. 1980. 2.25 (ISBN 0-671-83078-3). Pocket Books.
Dhalgren. Samuel R Delany. LC 77-13712. (Gregg Press science fiction series). 1977. 35.00 (ISBN 0-8398-2396-7). Gregg Press.
Dhalgren. Samuel R Delany. 1975. (pbk.) 1.95. Bantam Books.
Dhammapada. Tr. by Juan Mascaro. (Classics Ser.). 1973. pap. 2.95 (ISBN 0-14-044284-7). Penguin.
Dhampire. Scott Baker. 1982. pap. 2.95 (ISBN 0-671-44666-5, Timescape). PB.
Dharma Bums. John Kerouac. 192p. 1976. lib. bdg. 14.95x (ISBN 0-89966-135-1). Buccaneer Bks.
Dharma Bums. John Kerouac. pap. 2.50 (ISBN 0-451-12313-1, AE2313, Sig). NAL.
Dharma Bums. John Kerouac. 1971. pap. 4.95 (ISBN 0-14-004252-0). Penguin.
Di Cary. A Novel. M. Jacqueline Thornton. LC 8-19951. (On cover: Appleton's library of American fiction, no. 21). 1879. D. Appleton and Company.
Diable au Corps. Raymond Radiguet. (Coll. Diamant). 11.50. French & Eur.
Diablo Ghost. Wayne D. Overholser. LC 77-94493. 1978. pap. text ed. 1.75 o.s.i. (ISBN 0-89559-017-4). Dale Books Inc.
Diaboliad & Other Stories. Mikhail Bulgakov. Ed. by Ellendea Proffer & Carl R. Proffer. Tr. by Carl R. Proffer. LC 76-172127. (Midland Bks.). (Cloth ed. 10.00x o.p.: No. 153). 256p. 1972. pap. 2.95x (ISBN 0-253-20153-5). Ind U Pr.
Diabolist. Paul Fairman. 1972. pap. 0.95 o.s.i. (75-411). Lancer.
Diabols. R. W. Mackelworth. Orig. Title: Firemantle. 1969. pap. 0.60 o.p. (63-110). Paperback Lib.
Diabolus. Howard Hunt. LC 72-155799. 1971. 4.95. Weybright and Talley.
Diabolus. David St. John, pseud. LC 72-155799. 1971. 4.95 o.p. Weybright.
Diabolus. David St. John, pseud. 160p. 1972. pap. 0.75 o.p. (T1725, Crest). Fawcett World.
Diadem from the Stars. Jo Clayton. 1977. 1.50 (ISBN 0-87997-293-9). DAW Books.
Diagnosis. A Story for Amateur Physicians, As Well As for Regular Practitioners. Duff Child. LC 6-20983. 1872. A. A. Gosnell.
Diagnosis: Homicide: The Casebook of Dr. Coffee. 1st Ed. Lawrence Goldtree Blochman. LC 50-5456. 1950. Lippincott.
Diagnosis Murder. Rufus King. LC 41-726. 1941. Pub. for the Crime Club by Doubleday, Doran and Co.
Diagnosis Positive. Jean Todd Freeman. LC 78-110356. 1970. 6.95. P. H. Wyden.
Dial M for Money. Donald Taggart. 256p. (Orig.). 1972. pap. 0.75 o.p. (T2544, GM). Fawcett World.
Dial "O" for O.R.G.Y. Ted Mark. (man from O.R.G.Y.). 1973. (pbk.) 1.25. Dell.
Dial of Destiny. Frederick Luther Koontz. LC 11-10954. 1.50. The Roxburgh Publishing Company, Incorporated.
Dial 577 R-A-P-E. Lillian O'Donnell. LC 73-93739. (Red mask mystery). 1974. 5.95 (ISBN 0-399-11317-7). Putnam.
Dial 577 R-A-P-E. Lillian O'Donnell. 1976. (pbk.) 1.25. Bantam Books.
Dialect Tales. Katherine Sherwood Bonner McDowell. LC 70-38640. (Black Heritage Library Collection). (Illus.). 1972. (ISBN 0-8369-8998-8). Books for Libraries Press.
Dialect Tales. Katherine Sherwood Bonner McDowell. LC 7-20102. 1883. Harper & Brothers.
Diall of Princes (with the Famous Booke of Marcus Aurelius) Antonio de Guevara. Tr. by T. North. LC 68-54646. (English Experience Ser.: No. 50). 536p. 1968. Repr. of 1557 ed. 69.00 (ISBN 90-221-0050-2). Walter J Johnson.
Dialogue of the Dogs. Miguel de Cervantes de Saavedra & Lewis M Allen. Tr. by Walter Keating Kelly. LC 79-229982. 1969. Deisgned, Printed, and Bound by Lewis & Dorothy Allen at the Allen Press.
Dialogue with Death. Arthur Koestler. 1960. pap. 1.25 o.p. (00435, Collier). Macmillan.
Dialogues. George Barker. 1976. pap. 4.95 o.p. (ISBN 0-571-10834-2). Faber & Faber.
Dialogues. Drawings by Matta. Stanley Berne. LC 62-7479. (Archives of modern literature series). 1962. G. Wittenborn.
Dialogues in a Cave. Charlotte Markman Stein. 1976. 3.49. Double M Press.
Dialogues with the Devil: Novel Dealing with the Conflict Between Good & Evil. Taylor Caldwell. LC 67-11736. (O.s.i.). 4.95 o.s.i. (ISBN 0-385-04573-5). Doubleday.
Dialstone Lane. William Wymark Jacobs. LC 4-321486. 1904. C. Scribner's Sons.
Diamond Beach. Larry Forrester. LC 73-84061. (Illus.). 1974. 7.95 (ISBN 0-679-50413-3). D. McKay Co.
Diamond Bess. Winnie Mims Dean. LC 49-53578. 1949. Mathis, Van Nort.
Diamond Bikini. Charles Williams. LC 57-16784. (Gold medal giant a607). 1956. Fawcett Publications.
Diamond Bogo: An African Idyll. Robert F Jones. LC 76-48901. 8.95 (ISBN 0-13-208579-8). Prentice-Hall.
Diamond Bubble. Robert L Fish. LC 65-15020. (Inner sanctum mystery). 1965. Simon and Schuster.
Diamond Button: Whose Was It? A Tale from the Diary of a Lawyer and the Note-Book of a Reporter. William Cadwalader Hudson. LC 7-5648. Cassell & Company, Limited.
Diamond Button: Whose Was It? A Tale from the Diary of a Lawyer and the Note-Book of a Reporter. William Cadwalader Hudson. LC 99-4657. (On cover: Magnet detective library, no. 100). 1899. Street & Smith.
Diamond Cage. Dwyer-Joyce, Alice. LC 75-9478. 1976. 7.95. St. Martin's Press.
Diamond Coterie. Emma Murdoch Van Deventer. (On cover: The detective and adventure library, no. 10). A. T. Loyd & Co.
Diamond Coterie. Emma Murdoch Van Deventer. (library of choice fiction no. 49). 1892. Laird & Lee.
Diamond Cross: A Tale of American Society. William Barnet Phillips. LC 7-36055. 1866. Hilton & Company.

Diamond Cross Mystery: Being a Somewhat Different Detective Story. Chester K Steele. LC 18-76012. G. Sully & Company.

Diamond Cut Diamond. Jane Bunker. LC 13-19934. 1.25. The Bobbs-Merrill Company.

Diamond Cut Diamond. Jane Donnelly. (Harlequin Romances Ser.). 192p. 1982. pap. 1.50 (ISBN 0-373-02510-6). Harlequin Bks.

Diamond Cut Diamond: A Story of Tuscan Life. Thomas Adolphus Trollope. LC 8-28496. (Harper's Franklin square library. Duodecimo ed.). 1883. Harper & Brothers.

Diamond Exchange. Thomas Chastain. LC 80-1118. 1981. 10.95 (ISBN 0-385-14438-5). Doubleday.

Diamond Feather... Helen Kieran Reilly. LC 30-31187. 1930. Pub. for the Crime Club, Inc., by Doubleday, Doran & Company, Inc.

Diamond Fever. Walter Grunewald. W. P. Grunewald.

Diamond Flush. Zeke Masters, pseud. 1981. pap. 1.95 (ISBN 0-671-43997-9). PB.

Diamond for Christina. Blakely St. James. 240p. (Orig.). 1983. pap. 2.95 (ISBN 0-425-06069-1). Berkley Pub.

Diamond from the Sky: A Romantic Novel. Roy Larcom McCardell. LC 16-8229. 1916. G. W. Dillingham Co.

Diamond Hitch. Frank O'Rourke. LC 56-11040. 1956. Morrow.

Diamond Hook. James Quartermain, pseud. LC 76-111181. 1970. 5.95. Doubleday.

Diamond Hunters. Wilbur A Smith. LC 70-180112. 1974. (pbk.) 1.25. New American Library.

Diamond in the Coalpit. Clement A Taylor. LC 53-12160. 1954. Vantage Press.

Diamond in the Sky. Mary Orr, pseud. LC 56-113694. 1956. Crown Publishers.

Diamond Jo. Daphne Rooke. LC 65-27769. bds., 4.50. Reynal Dist. Morrow.

Diamond Key and How the Railway Heroes Won It. Alvah Milton Kerr. 1907. Lothrop, Lee & Shepard Co.

Diamond Kill. Michael Brett, pseud. LC 76-53026. 7.95 (ISBN 0-399-11869-1) (ISBN 0-399-11869-1). Berkeley Pub. Corp.: Distributed by Putnam.

Diamond Leaves from the Lives of the Dimond Family. Nathan Stone Reed Beal. LC 6-10282. 1872. Pub. by the Author.

Diamond Lens and Other Stories. Fitz James O'Brien. LC 70-109502. (Illus.). 1969. AMS Press.

Diamond Lens and Other Stories. Fitz James O'Brien. LC 76-131791. (Illus.). 1970. Scholarly Press.

Diamond Lens: And Other Stories. Fitz James O'Brien & Seldes, Gilbert Vivian. LC 32-15001. 1932. W. E. Rudge.

Diamond Lens: With Other Stories. new ed. Fitz James O'Brien. Ed. by Winter, William. 1885. C. Scribner's Sons.

Diamond Lil. Mae West. LC 32-32764. The Macaulay Company.

Diamond Master. Jacques Futrelle. LC 9-27746. The Bobbs-Merrill Company.

Diamond Murders. Joseph Smith Fletcher. LC 29-12064. 1929. Dodd, Mead & Company.

Diamond Necklace. Fred Jackson. LC 30-74301. Whitman Publishing Co.

Diamond Necklace: And Four Other Stories. Guy De Maupassant. LC 67-17658. (Illus.). 1967. F. Watts.

Diamond of Desire. Candice Adams. (Orig.). 1983. pap. 2.95 (ISBN 0-440-01990-7). Dell.

Diamond of Years; the Best of the Woman's Home Companion. Edited by Helen Otis Lamont. Woman's Home Companion. Ed. by Helen Otis Lamont. LC 61-9574. 1961. Doubleday.

Diamond Pendant. Ernest Temple Thurston. LC 32-9553. 1932. Doubleday, Doran & Company, Inc.

Diamond Pin. Carolyn Wells. LC 19-5279. 1919. J. B. Lippincott Company.

Diamond Range. James Wesley. 192p. (YA) 1975. 6.95 (Avalon). Bouregy.

Diamond Range. James Wesley. 1975. 4.95. Avalon Books.

Diamond Ransom Murders. Nellise Child. LC 35-4307. 1935. A. A. Knopf.

Diamond River Man. Eugene Cunningham. LC 34-4198. 1934. Houghton Mifflin Company.

Diamond Rock: A Tale of the Paoli Massacre. Clifton Lisle. LC 20-16154. 1920. Harcourt, Brace and Howe.

Diamond Rose Mystery. Gertrude Knevels. LC 28-19240. 1928. D. Appleton and Company.

Diamond Seeker of Brazil: A Novel. Leon Lewis. (On cover: The popular series, no. 10). 1891. R. Bonner's Sons.

Diamond Ship. Max Pemberton. LC 6-28763. D. Appleton and Company,

Diamond Six. Edited by Garland Roark. William Fielding Smith. LC 58-8109. 1958. Doubleday.

Diamond Sky: A Novel. Charles Le Baron. LC 75-20124. 1975. 7.95 (ISBN 0-8037-5397-7). Dial Press.

Diamond Smugglers. Ian Fleming. 1964. pap. 0.95 o.p. (02009, Collier). Macmillan.

Diamond Spider: And Other Stories. Elinor Brotherton Butler. LC 11-473. 1910. 1.00. The Alice Harriman Company.

Diamond Spitfire. James Frew & Robin Moore. LC 78-78063. 1978. pap. 2.25 o.s.i. (ISBN 0-89516-077-3). Condor Pub Co.

Diamond Spitfire. Robin Moore & James Frew. 288p. 1981. pap. 2.75 (ISBN 0-441-14715-1). Ace Bks.

Diamond Stud. Norman Singer. (Shakedown Kid: No. 2). 192p. (Orig.). 1976. pap. 1.25 o.p. (ISBN 0-532-12362-X). Woodhill.

Diamond Stud. Norman Singer. (Shakedown Kid: No. 2). 192p. (Orig.). 1976. pap. 1.25 o.p. (ISBN 0-532-12362-X). Manor Bks.

Diamond-Studded Typewriter: ByCarlton Keith Pseud. Keith Robertson. LC 58-11086. (Cock robin mystery). 1958. Macmillan.

Diamond Thieves. Arthur John Arbuthnott Stringer. LC 23-17185. The Bobbs-Merrill Company.

Diamond Tolls. Raymond Smiley Spears. LC 20-5122. 1920. Doubleday, Page & Company.

Diamond Wedding. Wilbur Daniel Steele. 1973. 0.95. Curtis Books.

Diamond Wedding. 1st Ed. Wilbur Daniel Steele. LC 50-8496. 1950. Doubleday.

Diamonds. Dale Herd. (Orig.). 1975. pap. 2.50 (ISBN 0-914726-14-5). Mudra.

Diamonds. Alan Michaels. LC 79-25275. 10.95 (ISBN 0-312-19923-6). St. Martin's Press.

Diamonds & the Arrogant Rake. Anne Hilary. (Candlelight Regency Ser.: No. 701). (Orig.). 1982. pap. 1.75 (ISBN 0-440-12094-2). Dell.

Diamonds Are Deadly. James Eastwood. LC 70-94499. (MW suspense). 1969. 4.95. McKay.

Diamonds Are for Dying. Paul Kenyon. 1974. (pbk.) 0.95. Pocket Books.

Diamonds Are Forever. Ian Fleming. 1980. 1.95 (ISBN 0-515-05516-6). Jove Publications.

Diamonds Are Forever: Reissue. Ian Fleming. LC 56-11446. 1966. bds., 3.95. Macmillan.

Diamonds Are Trouble. 1st Ed. Scott Corbett. LC 67-17998. 1967. 2.95. Holt.

Diamonds at the Bottom of the Sea and Other Stories. Desmond Hogan. LC 79-13854. 1979. 8.95 (ISBN 0-8076-0934-X). G. Braziller.

Diamonds Bid. Julian Rathbone. LC 67-23107. 1967. Walker.

Diamonds Cut Paste. Agnes Sweetman Castle & Castle, Egerton. LC 9-24954. 1909. 1.50. Dodd, Mead & Company.

Diamonds for Danger. David Esdaile Walker. LC 53-11863. 1954. Harper.

Diamonds Going and Coming. Harrison Gray Dyar. LC 26-957. 1926. The Stratford Company.

Diamonds Grow on Fig Leaves: A Novel of Love and Adventure in the Slums of New York in the '80's. Illustrated by the Author. 1st Ed. Joseph Hallworth. LC 54-13413. 1955. Exposition Press.

Diamonds in the Dumplings. Harriette Ashbrook. LC 46-7634.

Diamonds of Alcazar. Mary Kay Simmons. 1979. 1.95. Pocket Books.

Diamonds of Death. Hilda Willett. LC 30-18662. 1930. Longmans, Green and Co.

Diamonds of Loreta. Ivor Drummond. LC 79-25390. 8.95 (ISBN 0-312-19926-0). St. Martin's Press.

Diamonds of the Night. Arnost Lustig. LC 77-10807. (Lustig, Arnost. Children of the Holocaust). ((His). (Children of the Holocaust; v.). 9.95 (ISBN 0-87953-407-9). INSCAPE.

Diamonds of the Sea. Margarett McKean. (Second Chance at Love Ser.: No. 32). 192p. (Orig.). 1982. pap. 1.75 (ISBN 0-515-06305-3). Jove Pubns.

Diamonds to Amsterdam. Manning Coles, pseud. LC 49-49308. 1949. Published for the Crime Club by Doubleday.

Diamonds to Sit on: A Russian Comedy of Errors. Ilia Arnoldovich Ilf & Evgenii Petrovich Petrov. Tr. by Hill, Elizabeth. LC 31-5073. 1930. Harper & Brothers.

Diamonite Conspiracy. Joseph L. Howard. LC 79-93238. 316p. (Orig.). 1980. pap. 5.95 (ISBN 0-936150-07-6). State St Pubns.

Dian of the Lost Land. Edison Marshall. LC 66-14787. 1966. Chilton Books.

Dian of the Lost Land. Edison Marshall. LC 35-433332. 1935. H. C. Kinsey & Company, Inc.

Dian of the Lost Land see Lost Land.

Diana. Ronald Frederick Delderfield. LC 72-176600. 1972. 1.50 (ISBN 0-671-78532-X). Pocket Books.

Diana. Vida Hurst. LC 28-13446. Grosset & Dunlap.

Diana. Heinrich Mann & Posselt, Erich, Tr. LC 29-104281. 1929. Coward-McCann, Inc.

Diana. Montanye Perry. LC 35-16208. The Abingdon Press.

Diana. Susan Warner. 1877. G. P. Putnam's Sons.

Diana: A Novel by Emil Ludwig, Translated by Eden & Cedar Paul. Emil Ludwig & Paul, Eden, 1865- LC 29-294237. 1929. The Viking Press.

Diana and Persis. Louisa May Alcott. LC 77-11663. 1978. 10.00 (ISBN 0-405-10521-5). Arno Press.

Diana Ardway. Van Zo Post. LC 13-210187. 1913. 1.25. J. B. Lippincott Company.

Diana at the Bath. Elizabeth Hall Yates. LC 28-870923. The Penn Publishing Company.

Diana Carew. Mrs. Bridges. LC 9-814. (On cover: Lovell's library, v. 18, no. 861). 1887. J. W. Lovell Company.

Diana Carew: Or, For a Woman's Sake. Mrs. Bridges. (On cover: Seaside library. Pocket ed., no. 744). 1886. G. Munro.

Diana Dethroned. W. M Letts. LC 9-35848. 1909. J. Lane Company.

Diana Drew: A Romance of India. Isabel Brown Rose. LC 28-19393. Fleming H. Revell Company.

Diana Enamorada: 1564) Together with the English Translation (1598 by Bartholomew Young.,Edited with Notes and Glossary by Raymond L. Grismer and Mildred B. Grismer. Gaspar Gil Polo. Tr. by Bartholomew D Young. LC 59-10565. 1959. pap., 4.50. Dist. by R.,L Grismer, East River Rd.

Diana Fontaine. A Novel. Anna Cogswell Wood. 1891. J. B. Lippincott Company.

Diana Laughs. Florence Ryerson & Clements, Colin Campbell, 1894- Joint Author. LC 32-9428. 1932. R. Long & R. R. Smith, Inc.

Diana of Dobson's. Cicily Mary Hamilton. LC 8-19716. 1908. The Century Co.

Diana of Kara-Kara. Edgar Wallace. LC 24-29076. Small, Maynard and Company.

Diana of Meridor: Or, The Lady of Monsoreau. Alexandre Dumas & Maquet, Auguste. LC 6-43613. 1860. T. B. Peterson and Brothers.

Diana of the Crossways. George Meredith. LC 70-145177. 1971. (ISBN 0-403-01105-1). Scholarly Press.

Diana of the Crossways. George Meredith. LC 1-9339. (On cover: The seaside library. Pocket ed. no. 350). 1885. G. Munro.

Diana of the Crossways. George Meredith. LC 32-3462. (Half-title: The modern library of the world's best books). The Modern Library.

Diana of the Crossways. George Meredith. LC 34-37789. (Half-title: The modern library of the world's best books). 1931. The Modern Library.

Diana of the Crossways: A Novel. rev. ed. George Meredith. LC 73-12362. (Norton library, N700). 1973. 2.95 (ISBN 0-393-00700-6). Norton.

Diana of the Crossways: A Novel. rev. ed. George Meredith. LC 1-19343. 1897. C. Scribner's Sons.

Diana of the Ephesians: A Novel. Eliza M. J. Humphreys. LC 20-2263. Frederick A. Stokes Company.

Diana of the Moorland. Louis Tracy. LC 18-21085. E. J. Clode.

Diana of the North Country. Miriam Monger. LC 28-18287. 1928. Frederick A. Stokes Company.

Diana Stair. Floyd Dell. LC 32-32265. Farrar & Rinehart, Incorporated.

Diana Tempest: A Novel. new ed., with portrait and biographical sketch. ed. Mary Cholmondeley. LC 3322. 1900. D. Appleton and Company.

Diana; the History of a Great Mistake. Margaret Oliphant Wilson Oliphant. United States Book Company.

Diana Victrix: A Novel. Florence Converse. LC 6-27201. 1897. Houghton, Mifflin and Company.

Diana Wakefield. Michael W Figgis. LC 52-11203. 1952. Macmillian.

Diana Wentworth: A Novel. Caroline Fothergill. LC 6-40010. (On cover: Harper's Franklin square library. 658). 1889. Harper & Brothers.

Diana's Daughter. Betty Evelyn Davies. LC 31-12371. 1931. L. Mac Veagh, The Dial Press.

Diana's Debut. Lytton Sinclair. 256p. (Orig.). 1983. pap. 2.75 (ISBN 0-446-30321-6). Warner Bks.

Diana's Discipline. Charlotte Mary Brame. LC 44-11252. (On cover: Lovell's library, no. 1331). John W. Lovell Company.

Diana's Discipline; or, Sunshine and Roses. Charlotte Mary Brame. LC 3809. (Bertha M. Clay library, no. 6). 1900. Street & Smith.

Diana's Hunting. Robert Williams Buchanan. LC 6-19882. (Twentieth century series). F. A. Stokes Company.

Diana's Livery. Eva Wilder McGlasson Brodhead. LC 6-17964. 1891. Harper & Brothers.

Diane. Angela Taylor Ames. 1981. pap. 2.95 (ISBN 0-671-82720-0). PB.

Diane. Herbert Best. LC 54-7101. 1954. Morrow.

Diane: A Romance of the Icarian Settlement on the Mississippi River. Katharine Holland Brown. LC 4-30145. 1904. Doubleday, Page & Company.

Diane and Her Friends. Arthur Sherburne Hardy. LC 14-18303. 1914. Houghton Mifflin Company.

Diane Coryval. Kathleen O'Meara. (Half-title: No name series 3d series, no. 18). 1884. Roberts Brothers.

Diane De Turgis: A Chronicle of the Reign of Charles Ix. Prosper Merimee. Tr. by Bolton, Theodore. LC 25-22283. 1925. The Arnold Company.

Diane Game. Stanley Cohen. LC 73-79417. 1973. 6.95 (ISBN 0-8128-1637-4). Stein and Day.

Diane Looks at Life. Eleanor Browne. LC 35-35684. Arcadia House.

Diane of the Green Van. Leona Dalrymple. LC 14-504178. 1.35. The Reilly & Britton Co.

Diane's Adventure. Ann Sumner. LC 29-5953. A. L. Burt Company.

Diane's Lessons in Bondage. Warren Bisig. 192p. 1972. pap. 1.95 o.p. (ISBN 0-87977-152-6, DBB152). Dansk Blue Bk.

Diantha. Juliet Wilbor Tompkins. LC 15-11872. 1915. The Century Co.

Diapason. Thomas Sullivan. LC 78-53525. 1978. pap. 1.95 o.s.i. (ISBN 0-89516-033-1). Condor Pub Co.

Diaries of Adam and Eve. Samuel Langhorne Clemens. LC 76-168457. (Illus.). 1971. (ISBN 0-07-065610-X). American Heritage Press.

Diaries of Adam & Eve. Mark Twain. 91p. 1971. 6.50x (ISBN 0-87291-012-1). Coronado Pr.

Diary. William Ard. LC 52-6985. (Murray Hill mystery). 1952. Rinehart.

Diary. Judi Lynn. (New Stewardesses Ser.). (O.s.i.). 176p. (Orig.). 1975. pap. 1.25 o.s.i. (AQ1478, Award). Univ Pub & Dist.

Diary. Alice McKay. 222p. (Orig.). 1982. pap. 5.75 (ISBN 0-941474-05-4). A McKay.

Diary of a Bastard. Kriss Lherr. Tr. by L. E. LaBan. 1968. pap. 1.95 o.p. (6011). Brandon.

Diary of a Beauty: A Story. Molly Elliot Seawell. LC 15-773880. 1915. 1.25. J. B. Lippincott Company.

Diary of a Blase. Frederick Marryat. LC 33-24946. 1836. E. L. Carey & A. Hart.

Diary of a Book-Agent. Elizabeth Lindley. LC 12-455985. 1.00. Broadway Publishing Co.

Diary of a Bride. Charlotte S. Martindell. LC 5-26127. T. Y. Crowell & Co.

Diary of a Catholic Bishop. Edward Carben. LC 73-91155. 1974. 6.95 (ISBN 0-517-51444-3). Crown.

Diary of a Chambermaid. Octave Mirbeau. LC 46-5943. 1946. Didier.

Diary of a Communist Schoolboy. Mikhail Gregor'Evich Rozanov. LC 72-90303. 1973. 13.00 (ISBN 0-88355-014-8). Hyperion Press.

Diary of a Communist Schoolboy: Translated from the Russian. Mikhall Grigor'Evich Ro Xanov. Tr. by Werth, Alexander. LC 28-18744. Payson & Clarke Limited.

Diary of a Communist Undergraduate. Mikhail Grigor 'Evich Rozanov. LC 72-90304. 1973. 13.00 (ISBN 0-88355-015-6). Hyperion Press.

Diary of a Communist Undergraduate: Translated from the Russian with an Introduction. Mikhail Grigor 'Evich Rozanov. Tr. by Werth, Alexander. LC 29-26786. Payson and Clarke, Ltd.

Diary of a Country Priest. Georges Bernanos. (Image books). 1974. (pbk.) 1.75 (ISBN 0-385-09600-3). Doubleday.

Diary of a Country Priest: Tr. from French by Pamela Morris. Georges Bernanos. Tr. by Pamela Morris. (126). 1962. pap., 1.95. Macmillan.

Diary of a Country Priest: Translated from the French. Georges Bernanos. Tr. by Morris, Pamela. LC 37-24111. 1937. The Macmillan Company.

Diary of a Country Priest. Translated from the French by Pamela Morris. Georges Bernanos. LC 54-12996. (Doubleday image book, D6). 1954. Image Books.

Diary of a Deaf Mute. David Chagall. LC 76-21092. 1971. 2.00. Millenium House.

Diary of a Drug Fiend. Aleister Crowley, pseud. LC 73-21398. 1974. 29.95 (ISBN 0-87968-110-1). Gordon Press.

Diary of a Drug Fiend. Aleister Crowley, pseud. LC 75-130401. (Illus.). 1970. 7.95. University Books.

Diary of a Drug Fiend. Aleister Crowley, pseud. LC 23-11088. 1923. E. P. Dutton & Company.

Diary of a Dryad. Alice Brown. LC 32-350266. 1932. Press of T. Todd Company.

Diary of a Frantic Kid Sister. Hila Colman. LC 72-92388. 1973. 4.95 (ISBN 0-517-50262-3). Crown.

Diary of a Freshman. Charles Macomb Flandrau. 1901. Doubleday, Page and Company.

Diary of a Freshman. Charles Macomb Flandrau. LC 31-28440. 1931. D. Appleton and Company.

Diary of a Geisha Girl. Kimiko Omura & William Vaneer. 1969. pap. 0.60 o.p. (60-418). Manor Bks.

Diary of a Goose Girl. Kate Douglas Smith Wiggin. LC 2-12956. 1902. Houghton, Mifflin and Company.

Diary of a Line Smasher: Adventures of a College Football Player. Richard Frank Hyland. 1932. A. C. McClurg & Co.

Diary of a Lost One. Margarete Bohme. LC 8-21923. The Hudson Press.
Diary of a Mad Housewife. Sue Kaufman. LC 67-12721. 1967. Random House.
Diary of a Mad Old Man. Tanizaki, Jun'ichiro. LC 65-11115. (UNESCO Collection of Representative Works. Japanese Series). 1965. Knopf.
Diary of a Madman. Nikolai Vasilevich Gogol. Tr. by R. Wilks from Rus. (Classics Ser). 1973. pap. 2.95 (ISBN 0-14-044273-1). Penguin.
Diary of a Madman, and Other Stories. Nikolai Vasilevich Gogol. LC 73-156285. (Penguin classics). 1972. (0.35, 1.75 u.s.) (ISBN 0-14-044273-1). Penguin.
Diary of a Madman, and Other Tales of Horror. Guy De Maupassant. LC 77-374367. 1976. 0.60 (ISBN 0-330-24849-9). Pan Books.
Diary of a Man of Fifty: And A Bundle of Letters. Henry James. LC 7-7556. (On cover: Harper's half-hour sereis. no. 135). 1880. Harper & Brothers.
Diary of a Milliner. Caroline H. Woods. 1867.
Diary of a Minister's Wife. Almedia Morton Brown. 1882. J. S. Ogilvie & Sompany.
Diary of a Minister's Wife. Anna Elizabeth Scott Droke. LC 14-6564. Eaton & Mains.
Diary of a Musician, Ed. Mary Schell Hoke Bacon. LC 4-16166. 1904. H. Holt and Company.
Diary of A. N. The Story of the House on West 104th Street. Julius Horwitz. LC 70-96776. 1970. 5.95. Coward-McCann.
Diary of a Nazi Lady. Gillian Freeman. 1979. 2.50 (ISBN 0-441-14740-2). Ace Books.
Diary of a Nobody. George Grossmith & Weedon Grossmith. LC 75-332640. (Penguin modern classics). (Illus.). 1965. 2.50 (ISBN 0-14-000510-2). Penguin Books.
Diary of a Nobody. George Grossmith & Grossmith, Weedon. LC 7-159. Tait, Sons & Company.
Diary of a Nobody. George Grossmith & Grossmith, Weedon. LC 21-690614. 1921. A. A. Knopf.
Diary of a Papist. Evan S. Connell. (1920). 1967. Dell.
Diary of a Parish Clerk. Steen Steensen Blicher & Sigrid Undset. LC 77-359521. (Illus.). 1976. 85.00 (ISBN 8-7746-8052-8). Poul Kristensen.
Diary of a Pawnbroker: Or, The Tree Golden Balls. LC 6-34205. H. Long & Brothers.
Diary of a "Peculiar" Girl. George Austin Woodward. LC 8-37240. 1896. The P. Paul Book Company.
Diary of a Pensionnaire. Zoe Girling. LC 35-6884. 1935. Harper & Brothers.
Diary of a Physician. Albert Abrams. LC 23-43964. Modern Press Corporation.
Diary of a Pilgrimage. Jerome Klapka Jerome. (Illus.). 160p. 1982. pap. text ed. 4.25x (ISBN 0-86299-010-6, Pub. by Sutton England). Humanities.
Diary of a Pilgrimage: And Six Essays. author's ed. Jerome Klapka Jerome. LC 3-223760. 1891. H. Holt and Company.
Diary of a Provincial Lady. Edmee Elizabeth Monica De La Pasture. LC 31-16917. 1931. Harper & Brothers.
Diary of a Rapist. Evan S. Connell, Jr. 1966. 4.95 o.p. S&S.
Diary of a Rapist: A Novel. Evan S Connell. LC 66-16147. 4.95. S. & S.
Diary of a Seducer. Soren Kierkegaard. Tr. by Gerd Gillhoff. LC 66-17540. 1966. pap. text ed. 4.95 (ISBN 0-8044-6357-3). Ungar.
Diary of a Shirtwaist Striker: A Story of the Shirtwaist Makers' Strike in New York. Theresa Serber Malkiel. LC 10-21020. The Co-Operative Press.
Diary of a Show-Girl. Grace Luce Irwin. LC 9-11150. 1909. Moffat, Yard and Company.
Diary of a Somebody. Christopher Matthew. LC 79-317555. (Illus.). 1978. 8.50 (ISBN 0-09-134360-7). Hutchinson.
Diary of a Soviet Marriage. Panteleimon Sergeevich Romanov. LC 74-10090. 1974. 11.00 (ISBN 0-88355-176-4). Hyperion Press.
Diary of a Superfluous Man: And Other Stories. Ivan Sergeevich Turgenev. LC 70-10268. (His Novels, v. 13). 1970. AMS Press.
Diary of a Superfluous Man, & Other Stories. facsimile ed. Ivan Sergeevich Turgenev. Tr. by I. F. Hapgood from Rus. LC 72-150488. (Short Story Index Reprint Ser). Repr. of 1904 ed. 17.00 (ISBN 0-8369-3829-1). Ayer Co.
Diary of a Superfluous Man: And Other Stories. Ivan Sergeevich Turgenev & Isabel Florence Hapgood. LC 72-150488. (Short story index reprint series). 1971. (ISBN 0-8369-3829-1). Books for Libraries Press.
Diary of a Utah Girl. W. J. McLaughlin. LC 11-29657. Broadway Publishing Co.
Diary of a Virgin. Cindy Peach. LC 78-1325. 1978. 7.95 (ISBN 0-698-10900-7). Coward, McCann & Geoghegan.
Diary of a Warrior King: Adventures from the Odyssey. Frederick James Moffitt & Homerus. LC 67-18717. (Folk literature around the world). (Illus.). 1967. Silver Burdett Co.
Diary of a Woman. Octave Feuillet. LC 6-39524. (Half-title: Collection of foreign authors, no. 16). 1879. D. Appleton and Company.
Diary of a Woman Doctor. Marilyn Gilman. 1981. pap. 2.75 (ISBN 0-89083-718-X). Zebra.
Diary of a Year: Passages in the Life of a Woman of the World. Frances Mary Grogan Brookfield. LC 3-18657. 1903. L. C. Page & Company.
Diary of a Young Lady of Fashion in the Year 1764-1765. King-Hall, Magdalen. LC 67-23850. 1967. Meredith Press.
Diary of a Young Lady of Fashion in the Year 1764-1765. Magdalen King-Hall. LC 26-3115. 1926. D. Appleton and Company.
Diary of Adam and Eve. Samuel Langhorne Clemens. LC 73-82175. (Hallmark crown editions). (Illus.). 5.00 (ISBN 0-87529-360-3). Hallmark Cards.
Diary of an Enlisted Man. Harold Montfort Bush. LC 9-15206. 1908. E. T. Miller.
Diary of an Old Man. Chaim I Bermant. LC 67-11608. 1967. Holt, Rinehart and Winston.
Diary of an Old Man. Jun'Ichiro Tanizaki. LC 80-39940. 1981. 4.95 (ISBN 0-399-50524-5). Perigee Books.
Diary of Death. Wilson Collison. LC 30-292460. 1930. R. M. McBride & Company.
Diary of Delia: Being a Veracious Chronicle of the Kitchen, with Some Side-Lights on the Parlour. Winnifred Eaton Babcock. LC 7-18102. 1907. Doubleday, Page & Company.
Diary of Evil. Violet Hawthorne. 1976. pap. 1.25 o.p. (LB352ZK, Leisure Bks). Nordon Pubns.
Diary of Evil. Violet Hawthorne. 1973. pap. 0.95 o.s.i. (75-483). Lancer.
Diary of Kitty Trevylyan. A Story of the Times of Whitefield and the Wesleys. Elizabeth Rundle Charles. 1868. M. W. Dodd.
Diary of Love. Maude Phelps McVeigh Hutchins. LC 50-10753. 1950. New Directions.
Diary of Love. Maude Phelps McVeigh Hutchins. LC 72-139137. 1971. (ISBN 0-8371-5753-6). Greenwood Press.
Diary of Mad Old Man. Tr. from Japanese by Howard Hibbet. Jun'Ichiro Tanizaki. LC 65-11115. (UNESCO collection of representative works. Japanese ser.). bds., 3.95. Knopf.
Diary of Mrs. Kitty Trevylvan: A Story of the Times of Whitefield and the Wesleys. Elizabeth Rundle Charles. LC 6-24203. 1864. M. W. Dodd.
Diary of Mrs. Kitty Trevylyan. A Story of the Times of Whitefield and the Wesleys. Elizabeth Rundle Charles. LC 42-29933. (On cover: Schonberg-Cotta series). 1886. Etc. T. Nelson and Sons.
Diary of My Honeymoon: Anonymous. LC 10-23771. 1910. 1.20. The Macaulay Company.
Diary of Russell Beresford. Cecil Roberts. LC 27-22944. 1927. George H. Doran Company.
Diary of the War of the Pig. Adolfo Bioy-Casares. 216p. 1972. 5.95 o.p. (ISBN 0-07-073742-8). McGraw.
Diary of the War of the Pig: A Novel. Adolfo Bioy-Casares. LC 72-4217. 1972. 5.95 (ISBN 0-07-073742-8). McGraw-Hill.
Diary of Trilby Frost. Diane Glaser. (YA) 1978. pap. 1.75 (ISBN 0-440-91893-6, LFL). Dell.
Diary of Women. James Mechem. LC 71-124405. 1970. 5.95. Winter House.
Diary Without Dates: A Story. 1st Ed. Dorothy Young. LC 53-11263. 1953. Exposition Press.
Dias Acratas: Sin Ley ni Dios. Alberto Guigou. LC 80-53561. (Senda Narrativa). 276p. (Orig., Span.). 1981. pap. 8.95 (ISBN 0-918454-24-7). Senda Nueva.
Diaspora. Werner Keller. 1969. 10.00 o.p. (ISBN 0-15-125595-4). HarBraceJ.
Diavola: Or, Nobody's Daughter. Mary Elizabeth Braddon Maxwell. (Seaside library. v. 36, no. 734). 1880. G. Munro.
Diavola: Or, Nobody's Daughter. Mary Elizabeth Braddon Maxwell. (On cover: Seaside library. Pocket ed. no. 478). 1885. G. Munro.
D'iavoliada Rasskazy. Mikhail Bulgakov. LC 79-92495. 160p. 1979. pap. 5.95 o.p. (ISBN 0-89830-013-4). Russica Pubs.
Dibble & the Great Blob: A Parable for Children Over & Under 21. Jim Ballard. LC 75-25393. (Mandala Ser. in Education). 1975. pap. 2.50 (ISBN 0-916250-06-7). Irvington.
(Diblos) Notebook. James Ingram Merrill. LC 65-124016. 4.50. Atheneum.
(Diblos) Notebook: By James Merrill. James Ingram Merrill. LC 65-12401. (60-2155). 1966. PopularLib.
Dice Man. Luke Rhinehart. LC 74-151902. 1971. 6.95. W. Morrow.
Dice of God. Joachim G. Joachim. LC 74-78523. 1975. pap. 1.95 (ISBN 0-8128-7003-4). Stein & Day.
Dice of God: A Novel. Joachim G Joachim. LC 74-78523. 1975. 7.95 (ISBN 0-8128-1721-4). Stein and Day.
Dice of God: A Story of South Africa. Cynthia Stockley. LC 26-10312. 1926. G. P. Putnam's Sons.
Dice of God. 1st Ed. Hoffman Birney. LC 56-6191. 1956. Holt.
Dice of War. Andrea Giovene. LC 74-5060. (Series: L'autobiografia Di Giuliano Sansevero. English. 3). 1974. 6.95 (ISBN 0-395-19432-6). Houghton Mifflin.
Dichter see Augustus.
Dick. Bruce Jay Friedman. LC 71-118706. 1970. 6.95. Knopf.
Dick. Wille Drennen Russell. LC 5-42426. 1905. The Neale Publishing Company.
Dick Among the Miners. Anthony Weston Dimock. LC 13-18072. 1913. 1.25. Frederick A. Stokes Company.
Dick Devereux: A Story of the Civil War. David Tod Gilliam. LC 15-22068. 1915. 1.35. Stewart & Kidd Company.
Dick-Dock's Adventures. 1st Ed. Arthur Tane. LC 55-14600. 1955. Pageant Press.
Dick Gibson Show. Stanley Elkin. LC 74-117660. 1971. 6.95 (ISBN 0-394-46215-7). Random House.
Dick Gregory's Bible Tales. Ed. by James R. McGraw. LC 73-91859. 1978. pap. 2.95 o.p. (ISBN 0-8128-2430-X). Stein & Day.
Dick Haley: A Thrilling Story of Poverty, Heroism and Suffering, Dealing with Real Life and a Vital Problem of Our Public Schools. Olivar Barr Whitaker. 1910. Christian Publishing Association.
Dick Heriot's Wife. Doris Mackie. LC 47-20337. 1947. Hurst & Blackett, Ltd.
Dick Netherby. Lucy Bethia Colquhoun Walford. LC 8-328135. (Leisure hour series.--no. 132). 1882. H. Holt and Company.
Dick Rodney: Or, The Adventures of an Eton Boy. James Grant. LC 41-33236. 1875. G. Routledge and Sons.
Dick Rodney: Or, The Adventures of an Eton Boy. James Grant. LC 6-27671. (Seaside library, v. 15, no. 290). G. Munro.
Dick Tracy. William Johnston. LC 67-23813. (Tempo books, 5334). 1970. 0.75. Grosset & Dunlap.
Dick Wick Hall: Stories from "the Salome Sun" by Arizona's Most Famous Humorist. Dick Wick Hall. LC 68-56220. (Illus.). 1968. 6.00 o.p. (ISBN 0-87358-024-9). Northland.
Dicken's A Tale of Two Cities. Charles Dickens. Ed. by Pearce, John William. LC 11-12826. (Eclectic English classics). 0.40. American Book Company.
Dickens: A Tale of Two Cities. Ed. by Ralph W. Elliott. (Macmillan Critical Commentaries). 1966. pap. 1.00 o.p. Fernhill.
Dickens' Christmas Stories for Children. Charles Dickens. Ed. by Bellew, Molly K. Jamieson-Higgins Co.
Dickens-Collins. Christmas Stories, Comprising. No Thoroughfare and the Two Idle Apprentices. Charles Dickens & Collins, Wilkie. LC 42-35082. Belford, Clarke & Company.
Dickens' Cricket on the Hearth, Trial of Pickwick: The Haunted Man, and Dr. Marigold. Charles Dickens. LC 1-438. (Franklin library, no. 7). 1887. Franklin News Co.
Dickens Digest: Four Great Dickens Masterpieces Condensed for the Modern Reader. David Copperfield, Pickwick Papers, Oliver Twist, Martin Chuzzlewit. Charles Dickens. Ed. by Aswell, Mary Louise. LC 43-1780. 1943. Whittlesey House, McGraw-Hill Book Company, Inc.
Dickens Dramatic Reader: Scenes from Pickwick, Scenes from Nicholas Nickleby, The Cricket on the Hearth, A Christmas Carol. Charles Dickens & Comstock, Fanny Amanda. LC 13-11631. 0.60. Etc. Ginn and Company.
Dickens: Hard Times, Great Expectations & Our Mutual Friend. Ed. by Norman Page. 1981. pap. 20.00 (ISBN 0-333-24037-5, Pub. by Macmillan England). State Mutual Bk.
Dickens' Mystery of Edwin Drood. Charles Dickens & A Loyal Dickensian. LC 75-42303. 1975. (ISBN 0-8383-1962-9). Haskell House Publishers.
Dickens' New Stories. Containing The Seven Poor Travellers. Nine New Stories by the Christmas Fire. Hard Times. Lizzie Leigh. The Miner's Daughters. Fortune Wildred, Etc. Charles Dickens. LC 6-26432. T. B. Peterson.
Dickens Reader. Charles Dickens. Ed. by Powers, Ella Marie. LC 11-24099. (Riverside literature series). Houghton Mifflin Company.
Dickens' Stories About Children. Charles Dickens. Ed. by Merchant, Elizabeth Lodor. LC 30-5241. The John C. Winston Company.
Dickens' Stories About Children Every Child Can Read. Charles Dickens. Ed. by Hurlbut, Jesse Lyman. LC 10-9853. (Every child's library). The John C. Winston Co.
Dickens's Doctors. Charles Dickens & David Waldron Smithers. LC 78-40672. 15.00 (ISBN 0-08-023386-4). Pergamon Press.
Dickie's List: A Novel. Ann Birstein. LC 73-78739. 1973. 6.95 (ISBN 0-698-10544-3). Coward, McCann & Geoghegan.
Dickon. Marjorie Bowen. 1971. pap. 1.25 o.p. (96165). Beagle Bks.
Dick's Darling: A Novel. Clarice Lee Izbelle. (On cover: Lenox library, no. 9). Springfield Publishing Company.
Dick's Sweetheart. Margaret Wolfe Hungerford. LC 7-8493. (On cover: Lovell's library. v. 12, no. 618). 1885. J. W. Lovell Company.
Dick's Wandering. Julian Sturgis. (Seaside library, v. 65, no. 1324). 1882. G. Munro.
Dick's Wandering: A Novel. Julian Sturgis. LC 42-33516. 1887. D. Appleton and Company.
Dicky. D. D. Bell. 1970. price not set o.p. (B247, EverBC); pap. 1.45 o.p. (B244). Grove.
Dicky Bird Was Singing: Men, Women, and Black Gold. Robert Lipscomb Duncan. LC 52-8740. (Illus.). 1952. Rinehart.
Dictator: A Novel of Politics and Society. Justin McCarthy. LC 7-15279. 1893. Harper & Brothers.
Did Christ Make Love? A Novel. Chandler Brossard. LC 72-89690. 1973. 6.95 (ISBN 0-672-51730-2). Bobbs-Merrill.
Did Genesis Man Conquer Space? Emil Gaverluk. LC 74-1262. (Illus.). 192p. 1974. pap. 2.95 o.p. (ISBN 0-8407-5553-8). Nelson.
Did She Fail? Anna Fielding. LC 1-31862. The Abbey Press.
Did She Fall? Thorne Smith. LC 30-21179. 1930. Cosmopolitan Book Corporation.
Did She Fall? Thorne Smith. LC 38-3246. 1935. Doubleday, Doran & Company, Inc.
Did You Know They're Beheading Bill Johnson Today? Dave Kelly. 1974. pap. 1.00. Stone Pr Calif.
Did You Love Daddy When I Was Born? Shelley Steinmann List. 1973. (pbk.) 1.25. Popular Library.
Did You Love Daddy When I Was Born? Shelley Steinmann List. LC 77-182471. 1972. 5.95 (ISBN 0-8415-0150-5). Saturday Review Press.
Diddakoi. Rumer Godden. LC 72-11928. 1973. 5.95 (ISBN 0-8161-6067-8). G. K. Hall.
Diddakoi. Rumer Godden. LC 76-184788. 1972. 5.95 (ISBN 0-670-27220-5). Viking Press.
Didman. John Speicher. LC 77-123987. 1971. 12.50 (ISBN 0-89366-108-2). Ultramarine Pub.
Didman: A Novel. John Speicher. LC 77-123987. 1971. 6.95. Harper & Row.
Didn't Anybody Know My Wife? Willo Davis Roberts. LC 74-79664. (Red mask mystery). 1974. 5.95 (ISBN 0-399-11376-2). Putnam.
Dido, Queen of Hearts. Gertrude Franklin Horn Atherton. LC 29-22919. 1929. H. Liveright.
Die a Little Every Day. Lawrence V Fisher. LC 63-7647. (Random House mystery). 1963. Random House.
Die After Dark. Hugh Pentecost. (Red Badge Novel of Suspense). 1976. 6.95 o.p. (ISBN 0-396-07345-X). Dodd.
Die After Dark. Judson Pentecost Philips. LC 76-25558. (Red badge novel of suspense). 1976. 6.95 (ISBN 0-396-07345-X). Dodd, Mead.
Die by Night... Margaret Sharp Marble. LC 47-17696. 1947. Rinehart & Company, Inc.
Die Deutsche Novelle: 1880-1933. Ed. by Harry Steinhauer. LC 36-32603. (Half-title: Gateway books; general editors: Ernst Felse... and R. O. Roseler). W. W. Norton & Company, Inc.
Die Fast, Die Happy. Mark Denning. LC 76-13323. 1976. 1.25. Pyramid Publications.
Die Fast, Die Happy. 1976. pap. 1.25 o.p. (ISBN 0-515-03892-X). BJ Pub Group.
Die Goldeme Truhe see Golden Caskets: Chinese Novellas of Two Millennia.
Die-Hard. Wayne C Lee. 1975. (pbk.) 0.95. Ace Books.
Die in the Country. Stanton Forbes, pseud. LC 72-79429. 1972. 4.95 (ISBN 0-385-01669-7). Published for the Crime Club by Doubleday.
Die in the Country. Tobias Wells. LC 72-79427. 192p. 1972. 4.95 o.p. (ISBN 0-385-01669-7). Doubleday.
Die in the Dark. Anthony Gilbert, pseud. Orig. Title: Missing Widow. 256p. 1973. Repr. of 1948 ed. price not set o.s.i. (ISBN 0-85617-731-8). White Lion Pubs.
Die in the Saddle. Lincoln Drew. LC 56-10593. (Permabooks, 3063. Western, 3). 1956. Permabooks.
Die Jungfrau Von Orleans. Johann Christoph Friedrich Von Schiller. 1927. pap. 2.95 o.p. (ISBN 0-03-016290-4). HR&W.
Die Karawane. Billingual Edition. Wilhelm Hauff & Eaborn, Charles Linus Eugene, 1862- Ed. LC 36-21340. (Harper's German series, under the general editorship of Frederick W. C. Lider). 1936. Harper & Brothers.
Die Laughing. Richard Lockridge. LC 69-11672. 1969. 4.50. Lippincott.
Die Like a Dog. Gwen Moffat. (Illus.). 165p. 1982. 14.95 (ISBN 0-575-03118-2, Pub. by Gollancz England). David & Charles.

Die Like a Dog see Royal Flush: A Nero Wolfe Omnibus.

Die Like a Man. Michael Delving, pseud. LC 72-106541. 1970. 4.95 o.p. (ISBN 0-684-10110-6). Scribner.

Die Like a Man. Michael Delving, pseud. 1971. pap. 0.95 o.p. (B95-2142). Belmont-Tower.

Die Like a Man. Jay Williams. LC 72-106541. 1970. 4.95. Scribner.

Die, Little Goose. David Alexander. LC 56-6349. (His A Bart Hardin murder mystery). 1956. Random House.

Die of a Rose. William Maner. LC 74-89084. 1970. 4.50. Published for the Crime Club by Doubleday.

Die of Gold. Chet Cunningham. 1980. pap. 1.50 o.s.i. (ISBN 0-505-51471-0). Tower Bks.

Die Quickly, Dear Mother. Stanton Forbes, pseud. LC 69-12195. 1969. 3.95. Published for the Crime Club by Doubleday.

Die Quickly, Dear Mother. Tobias Wells. 1970. pap. 0.60 o.p. (0502-06115). Curtis.

Die Quickly, Dear Mother. Tobias Wells. LC 69-12195. 1969. 3.95 o.p. Doubleday.

Die Rich, Die Happy. James Mitchell. 1974. (pbk.) 0.95. Bantam Books.

Die Rich, Die Happy: By James Munro. 1st Amer. Ed. James Mitchell. LC 66-10753. 1966. 4.95. Knopf.

Die She Must. Betsey Riddle Hutton Zum Stolzenberg. LC 36-935681. E. P. Dutton & Co., Inc.

Die Song. Donald T. Lunde & Jefferson Morgan. LC 80-83566. 288p. (Orig.). 1981. pap. 2.95 (ISBN 0-87216-803-4). Playboy Pbks.

Die Stadt see City.

Die the Long Day. Horace Orlando Patterson. LC 79-183360. 1972. 6.95. Morrow.

Die to a Distant Drum. William Arden, pseud. LC 78-180926. (Red Badge Novel of Suspense Ser). 192p. 1972. 4.95 o.p. (ISBN 0-396-06491-4). Dodd.

Die to a Distant Drum. Dennis Lynds. LC 78-180926. (Red badge novel of suspense). 1972. 4.95 (ISBN 0-396-06491-4). Dodd, Mead.

Dieci Novelle Contemporae: Con Esercizi Di Grammatica, Conversazione E Composizione, a Cura Di Michele Cantarella E Di Paul L. Richards. Ed. by Michele Cantarella & Paul Lambert Richarcs. LC 56-3514. Holt.

Died in the Wool. Ngaio Marsh. LC 45-236021. 1945. Little, Brown and Company.

Died O' Wednesday. Paul Townend. LC 61-6953. 1962. Walker.

Died on a Rainy Sunday. Joan Aiken. 192p. (YA) 1973. lib. bdg. 6.50 o.p. (ISBN 0-8161-6073-2, Large Print Bks). G K Hall.

Died on a Rainy Sunday. Joan Aiken. 1973. (pbk) 0.95. Dell.

Diehard. Jon A Jackson. LC 76-44404. 6.96 (ISBN 0-394-41030-0). Random House.

Diehard. Jon A Jackson. 1980. 1.95 (ISBN 0-425-04548-X). Berkley Publishing Corporation.

Diehard. Jean Potts. LC 56-10200. 1956. Scribner.

Diet of Augsburg: A Historical Life Picture. Carl August Wildenhahn & Morris, John Gottlieb, 1803-1895. LC 8-37845. (Half-title: Pictures from the life, v. 5). 1880. J. F. Smith.

Dietegen: Novelle Von. Gottfried Keller. Ed. by Gruener, Gustav. (On cover: International modern language series). 1892. Ginn and Company.

Dieter Bauer. Harold J. Moffie. LC 80-126050. 10.00. Five Seas Press.

Dieux Ont Soif. Anatole France. 1960. 8.50 o.p.; pap. 1.25 pocket ed. o.p. French & Eur.

Dieux Ont Soif see Romans et Contes.

Diez Cuentos Hispanoamericanos. Alejandro Arratia & Carlos D. Hamilton. (Span). 1958. pap. 6.95x (ISBN 0-19-500818-9). Oxford U Pr.

Difference of Design. William Mode Spackman. LC 82-48873. 1983. 10.95 (ISBN 0-394-53130-2). Knopf.

Differences. Hervey White. LC 99-4710. 1899. Small, Maynard & Company.

Different. Alexander Stuart Hunter. LC 18-1722. 1.25. The Gorham Press; Etc., Etc.

Different: An Anthology of Homosexual Short Stories. Ed. by Stephen Wright. LC 74-194372. 1974. 1.95. Bantam Books.

Different Darkness. Gene DeWeese. LC 82-81381. 304p. 1982. pap. 2.95 (ISBN 0-86721-201-2). Playboy Pbks.

Different Dream. Donna K. Vitek. 192p. (Orig.). 1980. pap. 1.50 (ISBN 0-671-57033-1). S&S.

Different Drummer. Donald H Crick. LC 73-162467. 1972. 1.65 (ISBN 0-7260-0006-X). Gold Star Publications.

Different Drummer. William Melvin Kelley. LC 62-11453. 1969. pap. 2.50 (ISBN 0-385-01079-6, Anch). Doubleday.

Different Drummer: Notes, Including Life and Background, Racism: Definition and History, List of Characters, Critical Commentaries, Kelley's Style, Character Analyses, Review Questions. Nathan Garner. 1973. (pbk) 1.25 (ISBN 0-8220-0389-9). Cliff's Notes.

Different Drummers: Readings for Composition. Elizabeth Canar & Cecile R. Vye. 1973. pap. text ed. 7.95 o.p. (ISBN 0-394-31304-6). Random.

Different Face. Olivia Manning. LC 57-114921. 1957. Abelard-Schuman.

Different Face. Joan Mellows. (Regency Romance). 1.75 (ISBN 0-449-24046-0). Fawcett Crest Books.

Different Families. Allison Scott Skelton. LC 79-4890. 11.95 (ISBN 0-87223-610-2). Seaview Books.

Different Fleshes: A Novel-Poem. Albert Goldbarth. 1979. text ed. 7.95 (ISBN 0-934888-00-0); pap. 4.95 (ISBN 0-934888-01-9). Hobart & Wm Smith.

Different Girls... Ed. by William Dean Howells. Alden, Henry Mills, 1836-1919, Joint Ed. LC 6-28758. (Harper's novelettes). 1906. Harper & Brothers.

Different Gods. Violet Quirk. LC 23-11705. 1923. H. Holt and Company.

Different Kind of Rain. DeWitt S Copp. LC 78-3748. 8.95 (ISBN 0-393-08818-9). Norton.

Different Light. Elizabeth A Lynn. (Berkley Book). 1978. 1.75 (ISBN 0-425-03890-4). Berkley Pub. Corp.

Different Music. Mary Milo. LC 78-70868. 1979. 2.25 (ISBN 0-380-43596-9). Avon.

Different Night. Olga Hesky. LC 74-143831. 1971. 5.95 (ISBN 0-394-46883-X). Random House.

Different Seasons. Stephen King. LC 82-70145. 1982. 16.95 (ISBN 0-670-27266-3). Viking Press.

Different Time, Different Place. Lee Damon. (Orig.). 1982. pap. cancelled (Gallen). PB.

Different Woman. Muriel Hine Coxon. LC 36-10529. 1936. D. Appleton-Century Company, Incorporated.

Different World & Other Stories. Carrie W. Foster. 1979. 4.95 o.p. (ISBN 0-533-04084-1). Vantage.

Difficult Act to Follow. Henry J. Korn. LC 79-57461. 80p. 1981. 15.00; pap. 5.95. Assembling Pr.

Difficult Decision. Janet Dailey. (Harlequin Presents Ser.). 192p. 1980. pap. 1.50 (ISBN 0-373-10386-7, Pub. by Harlequin). PB.

Difficult Matter: A Novel. Emily Sharp H. Carmeron. Street & Smith.

Difficult Miss Livingston. Donna Creekmore. (Candlelight Regency Ser.: No. 706). (Orig.). 1982. pap. 1.95 (ISBN 0-440-12164-7). Dell.

Difficult Problem, The Staircase at Heart's Delight, and Other Stories. Anna Katharine Green Rohlfs. LC 72-8087. (American short story series, v. 16). 1972. (ISBN 0-8422-8061-8). MSS Information Corp.

Difficult Problem: The Staircase at the Heart's Delight, and Other Stories. Anna Katharine Green Rohlfs. LC 68-55686. (American short story series, v. 16). 1969. Garrett Press.

Difficult Problem: The Staircase at Heart's Delight, and Other Stories. Anna Katharine Green Rohlfs. LC 2043. 1900. The F. M. Lupton Publishing Company.

Difficult Problems: The Staircase at the Heart's Delight & Other Stories. Anna Katherine Green. Ed. by Clarence Gohdes. (American Short Story Ser., Vol. 16). 1968. Repr. of 1900 ed. lib. bdg. 16.95 o.s.i. (ISBN 0-512-00277-0). Garrett Pr.

Difficult Quest. Harry S Wright. LC 53-12013. 1955. Chapman & Grimes.

Difficult Truce. Joan Wolf. (Orig.). 1981. pap. 1.95 (ISBN 0-451-09973-7, J9973, Sig). NAL.

Difficult Young Man. Martin Boyd. LC 56-7600. 1956. Reynal.

Dig. Frank Clune, pseud. 1967. Repr. pap. 1.20 o.s.i. Tri-Ocean.

Dig a Little Deeper. Ursula Reilly Curtiss. 1982. 15.00 (ISBN 0-333-19761-5, Pub. by Macmillan England). State Mutual Bk.

Dig a Narrow Grave see This Land Turns Evil Slowly.

Dig Another Grave. Donald Clough Cameron. LC 46-3766. 1946. Mystery House.

Dig for Gold. Mildred R. Kodama. 1966. pap. text ed. 4.95x (ISBN 0-8134-0866-0, 866). Interstate.

Dig in Your Own Backyard. Kaye Holden. LC 60-16242. (Carlton milestone book). 1960. Comet Press Books.

Dig Me a Grave. Cleve Franklin Adams. LC 42-50219. 1942. E. P. Dutton & Co., Inc.

Dig Me a Grave. Cleve Franklin Adams. (Black cat detective series. No. 3). 1943. Crestwood Publishing Co., Inc.

Dig Me Later. Miriam Ann Hagan. LC 49-4828. 1949. Pub. for the Crime Club by Doubleday.

Dig the Spurs Deep: A Powder Valley Western. Peter Field. LC 53-100038. 1958. Jefferson House.

Dig: Two Heads Wanted. A Novel. H. Horatio Woodbridge. LC 8-37541. 1876. T. D. Price & Co.

Digby. David Harry Walker. LC 53-5111. 1953. Houghton Mifflin.

Digby: Chess Professor. Charles Edward Barns. LC 6-7221. 1889. Fracker & Company.

Digger: Dead Letter, No. 3. Warren Murphy. (Orig.). 1982. pap. 2.25 (ISBN 0-671-45094-8). PB.

Digger's Game. George V. Higgins. LC 72-10417. 1973. 5.95 (ISBN 0-394-48316-2). Knopf.

Digging for Gold: A Story of California. Horatio Alger. (O.s.i.). 1968. pap. 1.95 o.s.i. (ISBN 0-02-030230-4, Collier). Macmillan.

Digging Out. Anne Richardson. LC 67-10627. 1967. McGraw-Hill.

Digging Out. Anne Richardson Roiphe. LC 67-10627. 1967. McGraw-Hill.

Diggstown Ringers. Leonard Wise. LC 77-27722. 1978. 10.00 (ISBN 0-385-13126-7). Doubleday.

Digit of the Moon & a Draught of blue. Francis William Bain. 1956. pap. 1.00 o.p. (ISBN 0-88253-125-5). InterCulture.

Digit of the Moon and Other Love Stories from the Hindoo: Tr. from the Original Manuscripts. Francis William Bain. LC 5-35303. 1905. G. P. Putnam's Sons.

Dignified Requiem for a Necrophiliac: Greek-Nekros, a Corpse, Jerry Mumford. 1973. 3.50 (ISBN 0-682-47721-4). Exposition Pr.

Dignity: A Springer Spaniel. Sterner St. Paul Meek. LC 37-34171. The Penn Publishing Company.

Dignity of the Despised on Earth. Ed. by Jacques Pohier & Dietmar Mieth. (Concilium Ser.: Vol. 130). 120p. (Orig.). 1980. pap. 4.95 (ISBN 0-8245-0291-4). Crossroad NY.

Dil Dies Hard. Kelly P Gast. LC 74-18799. 1975. 5.95 (ISBN 0-385-01513-5). Doubleday.

Dildo Cay. Nelson Hayes. LC 40-27082. 1940. Houghton Mifflin Company.

Dilemma: A Story of Mental Perplexity. Leonid Nikolaevich Andreev & Cournos, John, Tr. LC 10-7956. 1910. Brown Brothers.

Dilemma. A Tale of the Indian Rebellion. George Tomkyns Chesney. LC 27-13684. (Seaside library, v. 55, no. 1118). G. Munro.

Dilemma for Dax. Marten Cumberland. LC 46-6298. 1946. Pub. for the Crime Club by Doubleday & Company, Inc.

Dilemma in Duet. Margaret Sebastian, pseud. LC 82-7432. 1982. 11.95 (ISBN 0-89340-520-5). J. Curley.

Dilemma of a College Girl. Theodosia B Skinner. LC 70-190181. 1972. 3.95 (ISBN 0-8059-1689-X). Dorrance.

Dilemma of a Ghost. Ama A. Aidoo. (African-American Lib). (O.s.i.). 1971. pap. 1.25 o.s.i. (ISBN 0-02-012020-6, Collier). Macmillan.

Dilemma of Engeltie: The Romance of a Dutch Colonial Maid. Emma Rayner. LC 11-194123. 1911. 1.50. L. C. Page & Company.

Dilemma of Love. Andrea Giovene. LC 72-9019. (His The book of Sansevero, v. 2). 1973. 6.95 (ISBN 0-395-15463-4). Houghton Mifflin.

Dilemmas. Alfred Edward Woodley Mason. LC 35-16058. 1935. Doubleday, Doran & Company, Inc.

Dilemmas; Stories and Studies in Sentiment. Ernest Christopher Dowson. LC 71-157774. (Short story index reprint series). 1971. (ISBN 0-8369-3886-0). Books for Libraries Press.

Dilemmas: Stories and Studies in Sentiment... Ernest Christopher Dowson. LC 12-10683. 1895. E. Mathews.

Diligence. Rene de Goscinny. (Lucky Luke Series). (French.). 1976. 5.95x (ISBN 2-205-00304-6). Intl Learn Syst.

Diligence in Love. Daisy Newman. LC 51-9696. 1951. Doubleday.

Dillinger. Henry Clement. 1973. (pbk.) 0.75. Curtis Books.

Dilson's Key. Charles Lock Davidson. LC 17-2200. 1916. 1.25. The Goldsmith-Woolard Publishing Co.

Dilvish, the Damned. Roger Zelazny. (Orig.). 1982. pap. 2.50 (ISBN 0-345-30625-2, Del Rey). Ballantine.

Dilys! A Novel. Ellie Grossman. LC 82-4598. 13.50 (ISBN 0-02-545840-X). Macmillan.

Dim Lantern. Temple Bailey. LC 23-144463. 1922. The Penn Publishing Company.

Dim Lantern. Temple Bailey. LC 33-17483. 1924. Grosset & Dunlap.

Dim Star. Hannah Yates. LC 30-332651. 1930. W. Morrow & Company.

Dim the Flaring Lamps: A Novel of the Life of John Wilkes Booth. Jan Jordan. LC 72-167625. 1972. 6.95 (ISBN 0-13-214411-5). Prentice-Hall.

Dim View. Basil Heatter. LC 46-11812. 1946. Farrar, Straus and Company.

Dimanche. LC 45-4096. 1945. Brentano's.

Dimbie and I--and Amelia. Mabel Sarah Barnes Grundy. 1907. The Baker & Taylor Company.

Dime. Richard Deutch. 1970. 4.50 (ISBN 0-912284-09-9, Pub. by New Rivers Pr); signed ltd ed 10.00; pap. 2.50. SBD.

Dime to Dance by. Walter Walker. LC 82-48688. 14.95 (ISBN 0-06-015145-5). Harper & Row.

Dimension A. Leslie Purnell Davies. LC 69-10996. 1968. 3.95. Doubleday.

Dimension Demons. 1980. pap. write for info. (ISBN 0-88074-017-5). Metagam.

Dimension of Horror. Jeffrey Lord. (Blade Ser.: No. 30). 1979. pap. 1.50 (ISBN 0-523-40208-2). Pinnacle Bks.

Dimension Search. Kurt Mahr. (Perry Rhodan 60). 1974. (pbk.) 0.95. Ace Books.

Dimension Two. Laurence B. Barrett. 1971. pap. 7.50 o.p. (ISBN 0-02-306120-0, 30612). Macmillan.

Dimension X: Five Science Fiction Novellas. Ed. by Damon Francis Knight. LC 71-122940. 1970. 5.95. Simon and Schuster.

Dimensioneers. Doris Piserchia. 175p. 1982. pap. 2.25 (ISBN 0-87997-738-8). DAW Bks.

Dimensions. Nancy Andrews. LC 76-11400. 96p. 1976. 7.95 (ISBN 0-914628-30-5); pap. 4.95 (ISBN 0-914628-31-3). Graphic Impress.

Dimensions of the Short Story: A Critical Anthology. Ed. by James Edwin Miller. Slote, Bernice, Joint Ed. LC 64-17046. 1964. Dodd, Mead.

Diminishing Circles. Barbara Rees. LC 71-134572. 1971. 4.95. Harcourt, Brace, Jovanovich.

Diminishing Return. A Novel. 1st Ed. Lenard Kaufman. LC 52-5109. 1951. Doubleday.

Diminishing Returns. George William Potter. LC 60-5327. 1960. Rinehart.

Dimitri Donskoi: A Novel Translated from the Russian. Sergei Bordin & Paul, Eden, 1865- LC 45-1213. 1944. Hutchinson's International Authors Ltd.

Dimitri Roudine: A Novel. Ivan Sergeevich Turgenev. LC 8-32678. (On cover: Leisure hour series. no.21). 1873. Holt & Williams.

Dimitrios and Irene: Or, The Conquest of Constantinople, a Historical Romance. Charles Warren Currier. LC 6-31719.

Dimmest Dream. Alice Mary Ross Colver. LC 29-26094. The Penn Publishing Company.

Dimond of Alaska, Adventurer in the Far North. Edward Albert Herron. LC 57-11501. 1957. J. Messner.

Dimpled Racketeer: Published Serially Under the Title "Cotton Stockings". Alma Sioux Scarberry. LC 31-3101. Grosset & Dunlap.

Dina: A Novel. Richard Calhoun. (Berkley Book). 1.95 (ISBN 0-425-03805-X). Berkley Publishing Corp.

Dina Cashman. Kathleen Thompson Norris. LC 42-10312. 1942. Doubleday, Doran and Company, Inc.

Dinah. H. Orlando Patterson. Orig. Title: Children of Sisyphus. 1968. pap. 0.75 o.p. (T1839). Pyramid Pubns.

Dinah, Blow Your Horn. Jack M Bickham. LC 78-14651. 1979. 8.95. Doubleday.

Dinah Faire: A Novel. Coffman, Virginia. LC 78-73863. 9.95 (ISBN 0-87795-218-3). Arbor House.

Dinah Faire: A Novel. Virginia Coffman. LC 80-36759. 1980. 15.95 (ISBN 0-8161-3046-9). G. K. Hall.

Dinan Dauntless: A Romance of the Eighteenth Century. Paul Kester. LC 29-201032. 1929. J. B. Lippincott Company.

Dinarbas: a Tale... Cornelia Knight. LC 4-31643. 1803. Printed for and Sold by Oliver D. Cooke.

Dine and Be Dead. Gwendoline Butler. LC 60-13225. (Cock Robin mystery). 1960. Macmillan.

Dine with the Devil. Janet Gregory Vermandel. LC 77-128861. (Red badge novel of suspense). 1970. 4.50. Dodd, Mead.

Diner on the Other Track. Walter I Frank. LC 55-116481. Vantage Press.

Ding Dong Bell. Helen Kieran Reilly. 160p. 1974. pap. 0.95 (ISBN 0-532-95333-9). Woodhill.

Ding Dong Bell. Helen Kieran Reilly. 1971. pap. 0.95 o.p. (95-160). Manor Bks.

Ding, Dong, Bell: An Inspector McKee Mystery. Helen Kieran Reilly. LC 58-5283. 1958. Random House.

Dingbat of Arcady. Marguerite Ogden Bigelow Wilkinson. LC 22-5815. 1922. The Macmillan Company.

Dingdong. Arthur Maling. LC 73-14316. 1974. 5.95. Harper & Row.

Dingle War. Robert P Davis. LC 68-16320. 1968. Prentice-Hall.

Dingley Falls. Michael Malone. LC 79-3529. (Illus.). 12.95 (ISBN 0-15-125673-X). Harcounrt Brace Jovanovich.

Dingo. James Maurice Scott. LC 67-22759. 1967. Chilton Book Co.

Dingo Boys. George Manville Fenn. LC 6-39267. United States Book Company.

Dingy House at Kensington. Lucy Lane Clifford. (Seaside library, v. 60, no. 1213). 1882. G. Munro.

Dinka Folktales: African Stories from the Sudan. Francis M. Deng. LC 73-82901. (Illus.). 200p. 1974. text ed. 32.50x (ISBN 0-8419-0138-4, Africana). Holmes & Meier.

Dinkelspiel's Letters to Looey. George Vere Hobart. LC 8-12807. G. W. Dillingham Co.

Dink's Blues. Marilyn Hoff. 1966. 4.95 o.p. HarBraceJ.

Dinky Died. Stanton Forbes, pseud. LC 71-97697. (Crime Club). 1970. 4.50. Published for the Crime Club by Doubleday.

Dinky Hocker Shoots Smack. M. E. Kerr. 1973. pap. 1.95 (ISBN 0-440-92030-2, LFL). Dell.

Dinner at Antoine's. Frances Parkinson Wheeler Keyes. (O.s.i.). 1948. 5.95 o.s.i. (ISBN 0-671-19657-X). S&S.

Dinner at Antoine's. Keyes, Frances Parkinson (Wheeler) 1974. (pbk.) 1.50 (ISBN 0-671-78651-2). Pocket Books.

Dinner at Antonine's. Frances Parkinson Wheeler Keyes. LC 48-109975. 1948. J. Messner.

Dinner at Belmont: A Novel of Captured Nashville. Alfred Leland Crabb. LC 42-7627. 1942. The Bobbs-Merrill Company.

Dinner at the Homesick Restaurant. Anne Tyler. LC 81-13694. 1982. 13.50 (ISBN 0-394-52381-4). Knopf: Distributed by Random House.

Dinner at Wyatt's. Victoria Gordon. (Harlequin Romances Ser.). 192p. 1983. pap. 1.50 (ISBN 0-373-02531-9). Harlequin Bks.

Dinner Club. Herman Cyril McNeile. LC 23-12786. George H. Doran Company.

Dinner Club, Stories. Herman Cyril McNeile. LC 23-969532. 1923.

Dinner in Town. Claude Mauriac. Tr. by Richard Howard. 1980. pap. 4.95 (ISBN 0-7145-0199-9). Riverrun NY.

Dinner of Herbs. Marjorie Bartholomew Paradis. LC 28-10868. The Century Co.

Dinner Party (from the Journal of a Lady of Today) Gretchen Damrosch Finletter. LC 81-3517. (Illus.). 1981. 6.95 (ISBN 0-689-70611-1). Atheneum.

Dinner Party: From the Journal of a Lady of Today) 1st Ed. Gretchen Damrosch Finletter. 1955. Harper.

Dinner Party. Translated by Merloyd Lawrence. Claude Mauriac. LC 60-6951. 1960. G. Braziller.

Dinner with James. Heaton Rose Henniker. LC 33-1356. E. P. Dutton & Co., Inc.

Dinner with the Commendatore: Translated from the Itlian by Gwyn Morris and Henry Furst. 1st American Ed. Mario Soldati. LC 52-12179. 1953. Knopf.

Dinosaur. Lawrence Kamarck. LC 68-14533. 1968. Random House.

Dinosaur Beach. Keith Laumer. LC 73-143942. 1971. 4.95 (ISBN 0-684-12374-6). Scribner.

Dinosaur Bite. Ruth Moore. LC 75-37831. 288p. 1976. 7.95 o.p. (ISBN 0-688-03021-1). Morrow.

Dinosaur Bite. Ruth Moore. LC 75-37831. 288p. 1976. 7.95 o.p. (ISBN 0-688-03021-1). Morrow.

Dinosaur Bite: A Novel. Ruth Moore. LC 75-37831. 1976. 7.95 (ISBN 0-688-03021-1). Morrow.

Dinosaur Dilemma. Kelly L Segraves. LC 77-1186. 2.95 (ISBN 0-89293-020-9). Beta Books.

Dinosaur Fund. Vartanig G. Vartan. 480p. 1972. 7.95 o.p. (ISBN 0-07-067206-7). McGraw.

Dinosaur Fund. Vartanig G. Vartan. (O.S.I.). 384p. 1973. pap. 1.50 o.s.i. (0-446-78-063-4). Paperback Lib.

Dinosaur Fund. Vartanig G Vartan. LC 70-178936. 1973. 1.50 (ISBN 0-446-78063-4). Warner Paperback Library.

Dinosaur Planet. Anne McCaffrey. (Del Rey Bks). 1978. 2.25 (ISBN 0-345-29593-5); pap. 1.95 (ISBN 0-345-28509-3). Ballantine.

Dinosaurian Beastiary. Robert Huntoon. (Illus., Orig.). 1978. pap. 7.50 (ISBN 0-913718-10-6). St Heironymous.

Dinosaur's Egg. Edmund Candler. LC 2-12532. 1926. E. P. Dutton & Company.

Dio, the Athenian: Or, From Olympus to Calvary. Enoch Fitch Burr. LC 6-19659. 1880. Phillips & Hunt.

Diomed: The Life, Travels, and Observations of a Dog. John Sergeant Wise. 1897. Lamson, Wolffe and Company.

Diomed: The Life, Travels, and Observations of a Dog. John Sergeant Wise. LC 99-46155. 1899. The Macmillan Company.

Diomede the Centurion: Or, Sowing Scarlet Seed. author's ed. Howard Andrew Millet Henderson. LC 1-12824. 1901. Western Methodist Book Concern.

Dion and the Sibyls. A Classic Christian Novel. Miles Gerald Keon. LC 7-10967. 1875. The Catholic Publication Society.

Dion and the Sibyls. A Classic Novel. Miles Gerald Keon. LC 98-1571. Benziger Bros.

Dionis of the White Veil. Caroline Virginia Krout. LC 11-180661. 1911. 1.50. L. C. Page & Company.

Dionysius "Home Sweet Home". Mariano Leung. 1983. 10.95 (ISBN 0-533-05318-8). Vantage.

Dionysius the Weaver's Heart's Dearest. Blace Willis Howard Von Teuffel. LC 99-5009. 1899. C. Scribner's Sons.

Dionysus. Roderick Thorp. LC 69-14386. 1969. 6.95. Coward-McCann.

Dionysus in Sixty-Nine. Ed. by Richard Schechner. (Illus.). 1970. pap. 4.95 o.p. (ISBN 0-374-50828-3, N382, Noonda). FS&G.

Dionysus: The Ultimate Experience. William S Ruben. 1977. 1.50. Manor Books.

Diosa. Charles Rigdon. (Kangaroo Book). 1.95 (ISBN 0-671-81871-6). Pocket Books.

Diosdado de lo Alto. Odon Betanzos-Palacios. (Illus., Sp.). 1980. pap. 8.80 (ISBN 0-86515-000-1). Edit Mensaje.

Diothas: Or, A Far Look Ahead. John Macnie. LC 70-154449. (Utopian Literature). 1971. (ISBN 0-405-03531-4). Arno Press.

Diothas, Or, a Far Look Ahead. Ismar Thiusen. LC 70-154449. (Utopian Literature Ser). 1971. Repr. of 1883 ed. 20.00 (ISBN 0-405-03531-4). Ayer Co.

Diploids. Katherine MacLean. pap. 0.95 o.p. (ISBN 0-532-95228-6). Woodhill.

Diploids. Katherine MacLean. pap. 0.95 o.p. (ISBN 0-532-95228-6). Manor Bks.

Diploma Was Death. Stephen Jonathan. Ed. by Sylvia Ashton. LC 74-77472. 1975. 7.95 o.p. (ISBN 0-87949-032-2). Ashley Bks.

Diplomat. James Aldridge. 728p. (O.S.I). 1973. Repr. of 1950 ed. lib. bdg. 7.95 o.s.i. (ISBN 0-85617-721-0). White Lion Pubs.

Diplomat and the Gold Piano. Margaret Scherf. LC 63-7847. 1963. Published for the Crime Club by Doubleday.

Diplomat. 1st American Ed. James Aldridge. LC 50-5256. 1950. Little, Brown.

Diplomatic Adventure. Silas Weir Mitchell. 1906. The Century Co.

Diplomatic Bags: An Ambassador's Memoirs. Pietro Quaroni. 1966. 5.95 o.p. (ISBN 0-87250-010-1). D White.

Diplomatic Conclusions. a Novel. Translated by Edward Hyams. Roger Peyrefitte. LC 54-32742. 1954. Thames and Hudson.

Diplomatic Corpse. Taylor, Phoebe Atwood. LC 51-9878. 1951. Little, Brown.

Diplomatic Corpse. Phoebe Atwood Taylor. LC 70-25107. 1971. 5.95 (ISBN 0-393-08634-8). Norton.

Diplomatic Cover. John Branfroot Simpson Pedler. LC 66-19488. 1966. Harcourt, Brace & World.

Diplomatic Disenchantments: A Novel. Edith Evelyn Jaffray Bigelow. 1895. Harper & Brothers.

Diplomatic Diversions: A Novel. Translated by James FitzMaurice. Roger Peyrefitte. LC 53-352467. 1953. Thames and Hudson.

Diplomatic Honeymoon. Maysie Greig. 1942. Doubleday, Doran & Company, Inc.

Diplomatic Immunity: A Novel. Tad Szulc. LC 81-5811. 14.95 (ISBN 0-671-25095-7). Simon and Schuster.

Diplomatic Incident. Judith Kelly. LC 49-9143. 1949. Houghton Mifflin Co.

Diplomat's Folly: A Police Novel by Henry Wade Pseud. Aubrey-Fletcher, Henry Lancelot. LC 52-6595. 1952. Macmillan.

Dippers. Ben Travers. LC 20-19239. 1920. John Lane Company.

Dirdir: Tschai, Planet of Adventure: 3. Jack Vance, pseud. (Science Fiction Ser.). 1979. pap. 1.75 (ISBN 0-87997-478-8, UE1478). DAW Bks.

Direct Descent. Frank Herbert. 192p. 1981. pap. 1.95 (ISBN 0-441-14903-0). Ace Bks.

Directed Study Guides for Stevenson's Treasure Island. Alma Leonhardy & Hogoboom, Grace W., Joint Author. LC 30-24071. 1930. The Macmillan Company.

Director. Henry Denker. LC 77-108976. 1970. 6.95. R. W. Baron.

Director. Henry Denker. (Illus.). 1979. 2.50 (ISBN 0-671-81359-5). Pocket Books.

Director. Oscar Fraley. (O.s.i.). (Orig.). 1976. pap. 1.75 o.s.i. (AR1607, Award). Univ Pub & Dist.

Dirge for a Dog. Jennifer Jones. LC 39-147977. 1939. Pub. for the Crime Club, Inc., by Doubleday, Doran & Co., Inc.

Dirge for a Lady. easy eye ed. Alice N. White. pap. 0.60 o.p. Lancer.

Dirge for Her. Virginia Rath. LC 47-115645. (fingerprint mystery). 1947. Ziff-Davis Pub. Co.

Dirigible. Frank A Andrews & Wead, Frank Wilber. LC 31-1723. A. L. Burt Company.

Dirigo Point. Elizabeth Foster. LC 44-40089. 1944. Houghton Mifflin Company.

Dirks Escape. Charles Brandon Rummer. (Illus.). 191p. 1979. pap. 2.25 o.p. Jeremy Bks.

Dirt. Carolyn Downs. (Illus.). 1980. pap. 9.95 o.p. (ISBN 0-930490-31-2). Future Shop.

Dirt Bike Adventure. W. Wesley Miller. (Perspectives I Novel Ser.). 48p. 1982. 2.50 (ISBN 0-87879-293-7). Acad Therapy.

Dirt Roads. Howard Snyder. LC 27-21021. 2.00. The Century Co.

Dirt Sandwich. Simon Cooper. LC 79-20154. 9.95 (ISBN 0-8037-2185-4). Dial Press.

Dirtiest Book in Town. T. McKerrs & F. Dehn. pap. 1.95 o.s.i. (OPS-43). Olympia.

Dirty Alice. Merril Harris. pap. 1.95 o.s.i. (OPS-14). Olympia.

Dirty Business. Leslie Edgley. LC 68-54852. (Red mask mystery). 1969. 4.50. Putnam.

Dirty Dozen. E. M Nathanson. LC 65-11291. 5.95. Random.

Dirty Dozen. E. M. Nathanson. (1945). 1966. Dell.

Dirty Eddie. Ludwig Bemelmans. LC 47-305709. 1947. Viking Press.

Dirty Friends: Stories. Morris Lurie. 194p. (Orig.). 1983. pap. 4.95 (ISBN 0-14-005825-7). Penguin.

Dirty Game. W. Howard Baker. 1967. pap. 0.60 o.p. (73-659). Lancer.

Dirty Hands. Richard Neely. (Signet book). (Illus.). 1.75 (ISBN 0-451-07381-9). New American Library.

Dirty Harry, No. 1: Duel for Cannons. Dane Hartman. (Men of Action Ser.). 176p. (Orig.). 1981. pap. 1.95 (ISBN 0-446-90793-6). Warner Bks.

Dirty Harry, No. 10: Blood of the Strangers. Dane Hartman. (Men of Action Ser.). 208p. 1982. pap. 1.95 (ISBN 0-446-30053-5). Warner Bks.

Dirty Harry, No. 11: Death in the Air. Dane Hartman. (Men of Action Ser.). 192p. (Orig.). 1983. pap. 1.95 (ISBN 0-446-90853-3). Warner Bks.

Dirty Harry, No. 12: Dealer of Death. Dane Hartman. (Men of Action Ser.). 224p. 1983. pap. 1.95 (ISBN 0-446-30054-3). Warner Bks.

Dirty Harry, No. 2: Death on the Docks. Dane Hartman. (Men of Action Ser.). 192p. (Orig.). 1981. pap. 1.95 (ISBN 0-446-90792-8). Warner Bks.

Dirty Harry, No. 3: Long Death. Dane Hartman. (Men of Action Ser.). 192p. (Orig.). 1981. pap. 1.95 (ISBN 0-446-90848-7). Warner Bks.

Dirty Harry, No. 4: Mexico Kill. Dane Hartman. (Men of Action Ser.). 192p. (Orig.). 1982. pap. 1.95 (ISBN 0-446-90863-0). Warner Bks.

Dirty Harry, No. 5: Family Skeletons. Dane Hartman. (Men of Action Ser.). (Orig.). 1982. pap. 1.95 (ISBN 0-446-90857-6). Warner Bks.

Dirty Harry, No. 6: City of Blood. Dane Hartman. (Men of Action Ser.). 176p. (Orig.). 1982. pap. 1.95 (ISBN 0-446-30051-9). Warner Bks.

Dirty Harry, No. 7: Massacre at Russian River. Dane Hartman. (Men of Action Ser.). 224p. (Orig.). 1982. pap. 1.95 (ISBN 0-446-30052-7). Warner Bks.

Dirty Harry, No. 8: Hatchet Men. Dane Hartman. (Men of Action Ser.). 176p. 1982. pap. 1.95 (ISBN 0-446-30049-7). Warner Bks.

Dirty Harry, No. 9: The Killing Connection. Dane Hartman. (Men of Action Ser.). 192p. (Orig.). 1983. pap. 1.95 (ISBN 0-446-30050-0). Warner Bks.

Dirty Jack. C. J. Floyd. (O.s.i.). 1977. pap. 1.50 o.s.i. (AD1652, Award). Univ Pub & Dist.

Dirty Kids, Dirty Movies. William Horton. pap. 1.95 o.p. (8081). Cameo.

Dirty Me. J. J Savage. LC 76-7578. 1969. 1.95. Ophelia Press.

Dirty Mind Never Sleeps. Max Wilk. LC 68-54970. 1969. Norton.

Dirty Money. Clarke & Tigue. LC 74-30485. (O.s.i.). 1975. 8.95 o.s.i. (ISBN 0-671-21965-0). S&S.

Dirty Money: Or, The Great American Pornographic Money Crisis. Norm Rudman & Ernie Sheldon. LC 76-187692. 1972. 0.95. Paperback Library.

Dirty Old Man. Henry Dupree. 1974. 7.50 o.p. (ISBN 0-682-47990-X). Exposition.

Dirty Old Man: A Novel. Henry Dupree. 1974. 7.50 (ISBN 0-682-47990-X). Exposition Press.

Dirty Pictures from the Prom. Earl Mac Rauch. LC 69-15157. (Doubleday projections books). 1969. 5.95. Doubleday.

Dirty Politics Is Fun. H. B Fox. LC 82-30. 1982. 7.95 (ISBN 0-914842-83-8). Madrona Publishers.

Dirty Pool. George Bagby, pseud. 1969. pap. 0.60 o.p. (0502-06018-060). Curtis.

Dirty Pool. Aaron Marc Stein. LC 66-23772. 1966. Published for the Crime Club by Doubleday.

Dirty Rotten Depriving Ray. Mallory T. Knight. (Man from T.O.M.C.A.T. Ser.). 166p. pap. 0.60 o.p. (A278X, Award). Univ Pub & Dist.

Dirty Rotten Truth. Roy Bernard Sparkia. 1973. 0.75. New American Library.

Dirty Son of a Witch. Sid Jacobson. (Orig.). 1969. pap. 0.75 o.p. (74-523). Lancer.

Dirty Story: A Further Account of the Life and Adventures of Arthur Abdel Simpson. Eric Ambler. LC 67-25468. (Illus.). 1967. Atheneum.

Dirty Street. Henry F. Boucher. 3.95 o.p. Vantage.

Dirty Tricks. George Alec Effinger. LC 76-50306. 1978. 7.95 (ISBN 0-385-12722-7). Doubleday.

Dirty Tricks: A Novel. Chapman Pincher. LC 80-5407. 1980. 10.95 (ISBN 0-8128-2723-6). Stein and Day.

Dirty Tricks: A Novel. Peter Way. LC 76-62798. 8.95 (ISBN 0-312-75127-3). St. Martin's Press.

Dirty Tricks: Or, Nick Noxin's Natural Nobility. John D Seelye. LC 73-89296. 1974. 5.95 (ISBN 0-87140-094-4). Liveright.

Dirty Way to Die. Gene Curry. (Belmont Tower Book). 1979. 1.75 (ISBN 0-505-51398-6). Tower Publications.

Dirty Way to Die. Bruno Rossi, pseud. (Sharpshooter Ser). (Orig.). 1975. pap. 1.25 o.p. (LB276ZK, Leisure Bks). Nordon Pubns.

Dirty Way to Die: By George Bagby Pseud. Aaron Marc Stein. LC 55-840012. 1955. Published for the Crime Club by Doubleday.

Dis-Honourable. facsimile ed.. ed. John David Hennessey. LC 75-330643. (Illus.). 1975. 16.25 (ISBN 0-7022-0898-1). University of Queensland Press.

Disagreeable Man. A Novel. Nevada McNeill. LC 7-20299. 1895. G. W. Dillingham.

Disagreeable Woman: A Social Mystery. Horatio Alger, Jr. 190p. 1978. Repr. of 1895 ed. 24.00. G K Westgard.

Disagreeable Woman. A Social Mystery. Julian Starr. LC 8-13445. 1895. G. W. Dillingham.

Disappearance of Mary Amber. Beulah Poynter. LC 35-4331. Greenberg.

Disappearance. Hollis Alpert. LC 75-1271. 1975. 7.95 (ISBN 0-8037-4834-5). Dial Press.

Disappearance. Robert Carroll, pseud. 1975. 7.95 o.p. (ISBN 0-8037-4834-5). Dial.

Disappearance. Collin Wilcox. pap. 0.95 o.p. (Z1103N, Zebra). Grove.

Disappearance. Philip Wylie. LC 50-11198. 1951. Rinehart.

Disappearance of Flight Nineteen. Larry Kusche. (Illus.). 224p. 1981. 4.95 (ISBN 0-06-464044-2, BN 4044, BN). B&N NY.

Disappearance of Flight Nineteen. Larry Kusche, pseud. LC 79-1669. (Illus.). 1980. 12.95i (ISBN 0-06-012477-6, HarpT). Har-Row.

Disappearance of General Jason. Percival Christopher Wren. 1976. lib. bdg. 18.50x (ISBN 0-89968-139-5). Lightyear.

Disappearance of General Jason. Percival Christopher Wren. 438p. 1973. Repr. of 1940 ed. 15.00. Ultramarine Pub.

Disappearance of John Longworthy. Maurice Francis Egan. LC 77-11281. (American Catholic Tradition). 1978. 18.00 (ISBN 0-405-10818-4). Arno Press.

Disappearance of Kimball Webb. Carolyn Wells. LC 20-819. 1920. Dodd, Mead and Company.

Disappearance of Kit Shane. Leda A Wadsworth. LC 42-184652. 1942. Farrar & Rinehart, Incorporated.

Disappearance of Mr. Derwent: A Mystery. Thomas Cobb. LC 1-259. (On cover: Neely's popular library, no. 78). 1896. F. T. Neely.

Disappearance of Mr. Derwent: A Mystery. Thomas Cobb. LC 6188. (On cover: Magnet detective library, no. 151). Street & Smith.

Disappearance of Odile. Georges Simenon. LC 72-75422. 1972. 5.95 (ISBN 0-15-125720-5). Harcourt Brace Jovanovich.

Disappearance of Penny. Robert Randisi. 256p. (Orig.). 1980. pap. 2.25 (ISBN 0-441-14896-4, Pub. by Charter Bks). Ace Bks.

Disappearance Syndicate and Senator Stanley's Story. Also, Napoleon Wolff and His Newspaper of the Future. Theron Clark Crawford. LC 6-31611. 1894. C. B. Read.

Disappearances. Mary A. Coleman. pap. 3.00. Anhinga Pr.

Disappearances. Howard Frank Mosher. LC 77-22083. 1977. 8.95 (ISBN 0-670-27358-9). Viking Press.

Disappearances. William Wiser. LC 79-55616. 1980. 11.95 (ISBN 0-689-11062-6). Atheneum.

Disappearing Corpse. James Warren. LC 58-12245. (Chantecler mystery novel). 1958. I. Washburn.

Disappearing Dwarf. James P. Blaylock. 288p. (Orig.). 1983. pap. 2.75 (ISBN 0-345-30376-8, Del Rey). Ballantine.

Disappearing Eye. Fergus Hume. LC 9-18023. G. W. Dillingham Company.

Disappearing Parson. 1 st american ed. Miles Burton. LC 49-104838. 1949. Pub. for the Crime Club by Doubleday.

Disarm! Disarm! Adapted from the German Romance "Die Waffen Nieder,". Bertha Felicie Sophie Kinsky Suttner & Proudfoot, Mrs. Andrea (Hofer) LC 14-2356. 1913. Hodder and Stoughton.

Disarmed!" A Novel. Matilda Barbara Bertram Edwards. (On cover: Lovell's library no. 203). 1883. J. W. Lovell Company.

Disaster! Troy Allen. (Illus.). 192p. (Orig.). 1974. pap. 1.95 o.p. (ISBN 0-87682-389-4, 7389). Barclay Hse.

Disaster. Paul Margueritte & Margueritte, Victor. LC 4-16885. 1898. D. Appleton and Company.

Disaster Area Nurse. Arlene Hale. 1976. (pbk.) 0.95. Ace Books.

Disaster Creek. Dwight Bennett. LC 80-1061. 1981. 9.95 (ISBN 0-385-15629-4). Doubleday.

Disaster Nurse. Peggy O'More, pseud. LC 65-7983. 1965. Arcadia House.

Disaster to the Mining Camp at Taboo Valley. Jack H Bont. LC 78-13788. (Illus.). Independant Sic Pub. Co.
Disaster Trail. Archie Joscelyn. LC 48-79974. (Silver star westerns). 1948. Dodd, Mead.
Disaster Valley. Frank Chester Robertson. LC 57-13097. (Ballantine books, 232). 1957. Ballantine Books.
Disastrous Love. Peggy O'More, pseud. (Alouette Romance Ser.). 128p. (Orig.). 1981. pap. 2.25 (ISBN 0-89531-133-X, 0198-96). Sharon Pubns.
Disc of Clear Water. Charlotte Mandel. LC 80-25317. 64p. (Orig.). 1981. pap. 4.00 (ISBN 0-938158-00-7). Saturday Pr.
Discarded Confidante, and Other Stories. Frank Tweedy. LC 18-101731. 1918. The Neale Publishing Company.
Discarded Daughter: Or, The Children of the Isle. Emma Dorothy Eliza Nevitte Southworth. LC 12-38909. 1875. T. B. Peterson & Brothers.
Discarded: Or, Thrown on the World. Mary Grace Halpine. LC 7-1211. (On cover: Munro's library. v. 1 no. 403). N. L. Munro.
Discarded: Or, Thrown on the World. Mary Grace Halpine. LC 7-1210. (On cover: American novelist's series. no. 51). J. W. Lovell Company.
Discarded: Or, Thrown on the World. Mary Grace Halpine. LC 7-120964. (On cover: Clover series, no. 126). Street & Smith.
Disciple. Paul Charles Joseph Bourget. LC 75-28199. 1975. 14.00. H. Fertig.
Disciple. Paul Charles Joseph Bourget. LC 99-4627. (Neely's continental library, no. 13). F. T. Neely.
Disciple. Paul Charles Joseph Bourget. LC 1-30955. 1901. C. Scribner's Sons.
Disciple. Clark Brown. LC 68-11415. 1968. Viking Press.
Disciple of Chance: An Eighteenth-Century Love Story. Sara Dean. LC 10-778420. 1910. 1.50. Frederick A. Stokes Company.
Disciple of Ralph Waldo Emerson. Robert M Grellmann. LC 34-73864. The Christopher Publishing House.
Disciples of Cthulhu. Ed. by Edward P. Berglund. (Science Fiction Ser.). 1976. pap. 1.50 o.p. (ISBN 0-87997-258-0, UW1258). DAW Bks.
Disciples of Cthulhu. Ed. by Edward P. Berglund. Daw Books.
Disciplina Clericalis of Petrus Alfonsi. Petrus Alfonsi & Eberhard Hermes. LC 73-94434. (Islamic World Series). 12.50. University of California Press.
Discipline: A Novel, 3 vols. in 1. Mary Balfour Bruinton. LC 79-8241. Repr. of 1814 ed. 44.50 (ISBN 0-404-61797-2). AMS Pr.
Discipline of Odette. Jean Martinet. pap. 1.95 o.s.i. (Venus). Grove.
Disciplined & the Dead. E. F. Miller, pseud. 1978. pap. 1.50 (ISBN 0-532-15357-X). Woodhill.
Disciplined Daughter. Kip Carmeron. 192p. (Orig.). 1973. pap. 1.95 o.p. (ISBN 0-87977-179-8, DBB179). Dansk Blue Bk.
Discipling of Timothy. William J. Peterson. 144p. 1980. pap. 4.50 (ISBN 0-88207-217-X). Victor Bks.
Disclosures in Scarlet. Carl Jacobi. LC 72-88124. 1972. 5.00. Arkham House.
Disco. Chelsea Farraday. (Leisure Book). 1978. 1.95 (ISBN 0-8439-0599-9). Nordon Pub. Inc.
Disco Candy and Other Stories. L. C Phillips. LC 78-72027. 7.95 (ISBN 0-912282-07-X). Pulse-Finger Press.
Disco Death Beat. Michael Geller. (Bud Dugan Ser.: No. 3). (Orig.). 1981. pap. 1.95 (ISBN 0-505-51596-2). Tower Bks.
Disco Hustle. John M. Faucette. (Orig.). 1978. pap. 1.75 (ISBN 0-87067-537-0, BH537). Holloway.
Disco Inferno: An Illustrated Novel. original ed. Porter Bibb, pseud. LC 79-7486. (Illus.). 1979. 7.95 (ISBN 0-385-15516-6). Dolphin Books.
Discontented. Martin Boris. 288p. 1981. pap. 3.25 (ISBN 0-441-14923-5). Ace Bks.
Discord in Harmony. Paul K McAfee. 1973. 4.95. Lenox Hill Pr.
Discords. Mary Chavelita Bright. LC 6-26735. (On cover: Keynotes series, no. 6). 1894. Roberts Bros.; Etc., Etc.
Discords. Donald Evans. LC 12-251. 1912. 1.00. Brown Brothers.
Discourse Concerning the Mechanical Operation of the Spirit see Tale of a Tub.
Discourse with Shadows. Jean Eileen Malcolm. LC 58-10030. 1958. Doubleday.
Discovered Country. Mary Hall Leonard. 1900. The Editor Publishing Co.
Discovered Country. Carlyle Petersilea. LC 7-36168.
Discovered Country. Carlyle Petersilea. LC 7-36167. Colby & Rich.
Discoveries: 50 Stories of the Quest. Harold Schechter & Jonna Gormely Semeiks. LC 82-22774. 1983. 10.95 (ISBN 0-672-61563-0) (ISBN 0-672-61564-9). Bobbs-Merrill Educational Pub.
Discovering "Evelina" An Old-Fashioned Romance, a Companion Book to "The Jessamy Bride,". Frank Frankfort Moore. LC 13-20581. George H. Doran Company.
Discovering Marin: An Historical Tour by Cities & Towns. Louise Teather. LC 74-77090. (Illus.). 125p. 1976. pap. 3.95 (ISBN 0-912908-02-5). Tamal Land.
Discovery. Willard B. Arnold. 5.95 o.p. Vantage.
Discovery. James Parry. LC 77-1904. 1978. 10.95 o.p. (ISBN 0-690-01166-0, TYC-T). T Y Crowell.
Discovery. Virginia Chase Perkins. 1948. Macmillan Co.
Discovery. James Perry. LC 77-1904. 1977. 8.95 (ISBN 0-690-01166-0). Crowell.
Discovery and Response: The Strategies of Fiction. Ed. by James Hart. LC 75-163998. 1972. (ISBN 0-87626-184-5). Winthrop Publishers.
Discovery of America & Other Tales of Terror & Self-Exploration. Alvin Greenberg. LC 79-13068. 160p. 1980. text ed. 12.95x (ISBN 0-8071-0591-0). La State U Pr.
Discovery of Fiction. Thomas E. Sanders. 1967. pap. 6.95x o.p. (ISBN 0-673-05661-9). Scott F.
Discretion: A Novel. David Linzee. LC 77-25341. 8.95 (ISBN 0-87223-496-7). Seaview Books: Trade Distribution by Simon and Schuster.
Discretion of Dominick Ayres. Matthew Vaughan. LC 77-354254. 1976. 4.50 (ISBN 0-436-55261-2). Secker and Warburg.
Discretion of Dominick Ayres: A Novel. Matthew Vaughan. LC 75-43630. 7.95 (ISBN 0-316-89811-2). Little, Brown.
Discretion of Dominick Ayres: A Novel. Matthew Vaughan. (Kangaroo Book). 1977. 1.75 (ISBN 0-671-81098-7). Pocket Books.
Disenchanted. Pierre Loti. 1906. Repr. lib. bdg. 20.00 (ISBN 0-8414-5886-3). Folcroft.
Disenchanted. Budd Schulberg. LC 50-10247. 1950. Random House.
Disenchanted. Budd Schulberg. LC 74-31325. 1975. 3.95 (ISBN 0-670-00584-3). Viking Press.
Disenchanted: A Love Story. Zahir M Farooqi. LC 76-4210. (Exposition-banner book). 1969. 5.00. Exposition Press.
Disenchanted: Desenchantees. Julien Viaud. Tr. by Bell, Clara Courtenay (Poynter) LC 15-6333. 1912. The Macmillan Company.
Disenchanted: Desenchantees. Julien Viaud. Tr. by Bell, Clara Courtenay (Poynter) 1918. The Macmillan Company.
Disenchanted. (Desenchantees) Julien Viaud & Bell, Mrs. Clara Courtenay (Poynter) 1834-1927, Tr. LC 6-32677. 1906. The Macmillan Company.
Disenchanted Lawyer. Jesse Marcus. 326p. 1971. 6.00 o.p. (ISBN 0-682-47361-8). Exposition.
Disenchanted Lawyer: A Novel. Jesse Marcus. LC 74-191345. 1971. 6.00 (ISBN 0-682-47361-8). Exposition Press.
Disentanglers. Andrew Lang. LC 71-112938. (Illus.). 1970. AMS Press.
Disentanglers. Andrew Lang. LC 2-25928. 1902. Longmans, Green, and Co.
Disenthralled: A Story of My Life. George M Dutcher. LC 6-36409. 1872. Columbian Book Company.
Disguises of Love. Robie Macauley. LC 52-10602. 1952. Random House.
Dish for the Gods. Cyril Hume. LC 29-9373. 1929. Doubleday, Doran and Company, Inc.
Dishonest Murderer. Frances Louise Davis Lockridge & Richard Lockridge. LC 75-46600. 1976. 6.95 (ISBN 0-89190-901-X). Rivercity Press.
Dishonest Murderer. Frances Louise Davis Lockridge & Richard Lockridge. LC 49-481501. (Main line mysteries). 1949. Lippincott Co.
Dishonest Woman. Jessica Steele. (Harlequin Romances Ser.). 192p. 1982. pap. 1.50 (ISBN 0-373-02502-5). Harlequin Bks.
Dishonor Among Thieves: By Spencer Dean Pseud. 1st Ed. Prentice Winchell. LC 58-8115. (Crime Club selection). 1958. Doubleday.
Dishonored. Theodora Havers Boulger. LC 6-15014. (On cover: Lovell's international series, no. 95)). 1890. J. W. Lovell Company.
Dishonored. Frank Vreeland. LC 31-9388. Grosset & Dunlap.
Dishonoured Bones. John Trench. LC 55-1724. (Cock Robin mystery). 1955. Macmillan.
Disillusion, a Story of the Labor Struggle in the Western Woodworking Mills. Ben H Cochrane & Coldiron, William Dean, Joint Author. LC 39-19354. Binfords & Mort.
Disillusion: Or, The Story of Amedee's Youth. translated by e. p. robins and illustrated by emile bayard. ed. Francois Coppee. Tr. by Robins, E. P. LC 6-30863. G. Routledge and Sons.
Disillusioned. Peter Thomas Rohrbach. LC 68-10574. 1968. 5.95. Doubleday.
Disillusioned Occultist. A Drama-Novel. Charles Edward Barns. LC 6-7220. 1889. W. Fracker & Company.
Disinformer. Owen John. 1968. pap. 0.60 o.p. (53-773). Paperback Lib.
Disinherited. Jack Conroy. LC 63-8193. (American century series). 1963. Hill and Wang.
Disinherited. Jack Conroy. LC 34-868. Covici, Friede.
Disinherited. Jack Conroy. LC 78-26296. 1979. 10.00 (ISBN 0-8376-0426-5). R. Bentley.
Disinherited. Jack Conroy. LC 82-15561. 1982. 5.95 (ISBN 0-88208-150-0). L. Hill.
Disinherited. Stella M During. LC 7-20512. 1907. J. B. Lippincott Company.
Disinherited. Clayton Matthews. 1983. pap. 3.50 (ISBN 0-553-22846-3). Bantam.
Disinherited. Milton Waldman. LC 29-6855. 1929. Longmans, Green and Co.
Disinherited: A Novel. Margaret Gorman Nichols. LC 47-11455. 1947. Marcrae-Smith Co.
Disinherited Lady. Benito Perez Galdos. Ed. by Guy E. Smith. 1957. 6.00 o.p. (ISBN 0-682-40117-X). Exposition.
Disinherited Lady: A Novel. A Translation of La Desheredada, with an Introd., by Guy E. Smith. 1st Ed. Benito Perez Galdos. LC 58-53. 1957. Exposition Press.
Disinherited. Translated from the French by Humphrey Hare. Michel Del Castillo. LC 59-15322. 1960. half-cloth, 3.95. Knopf.
Disk: A Tale of Two Passions. Edward A Robinson & Wall, George A., Joint Author. LC 7-41976. 1884. Cupples, Upham and Company.
Dismas, the Good Thief: An Original Novel. Herbert R Clark. LC 72-147914. 1971. (ISBN 0-8407-5030-7). T. Nelson.
Disobedient Daughter. Barbara Hazard. 1982. pap. 2.25 (ISBN 0-451-11557-0, AE1557, Sig). NAL.
Disobedient Nurse. Arlene Hale. (Arlene Hale nurse romance). 1975. (pbk.) 0.75. Ace Books.
Disobedient Son. Translated from the French by Christopher Velel. 1st Ed. Francois Clement. LC 56-10649. 1956. Little, Brown.
Disorder. Simone Benda Porche. Tr. by Marks, Henry Kingdon. LC 31-24137. E. P. Dutton & Co., Inc.
Disorderly Conduct. Charles Stanley Strong. Phoenix Press.
Disorderly Girl. Bruce Stewart. LC 80-52912. 1981. 11.95 (ISBN 0-312-21265-8). St. Martin's Press.
Disorderly Knights. Dorothy Dunnett. LC 66-25075. 6.95. Putnam.
Disoriented Man see Scream & Scream Again.
Disowned. Edward George Earle Lytton Bulwer-Lytton Lytton. LC 8-11037. G. Routledge and Sons.
Disowned. Edward George Earle Lytton Bulwer-Lytton Lytton. LC 7-8353. (Lovell's library, v. 5, no. 222). 1883. J. W. Lovell Company.
Disowned. Edward George Earle Lytton Bulwer-Lytton Lytton. LC 7-8352. (Half-title: Novels of Sir Edward Bulwer Lytton. Library ed. Novels of life and manners, vol. III-IV.). 1893. Little, Brown, and Company.
Disowned, a Novel. John Madison. LC 51-14885. 1951. Exposition Press.
Dispatch from Cadiz. Bruce Weiser. (Chenevix Ser.: No. 2). 1981. pap. 2.25 (ISBN 0-8439-0826-2, Leisure Bks). Nordon Pubns.
Dispensable Man. Wolf Peter Rilla. LC 73-17456. 1974. 6.95 (ISBN 0-200-04019-7). John Day Co.
Dispensable Man. Wolf Peter Rilla. LC 74-166380. 1973. 2.50 (ISBN 0-491-00984-4). W. H. Allen.
Disposable People. Marshall Goldberg & Kenneth Kay. (Orig.). 1980. pap. text ed. 2.25 o.s.i. (ISBN 0-505-51574-1). Tower Bks.
Disposable Woman. Alan C. Miller et al. Ed. by Sylvia Ashton. LC 77-77865. 1977. 12.95 (ISBN 0-87949-077-2). Ashley Bks.
Disposal Unit. John Boland. 1981. 18.95x (Pub. by Remploy England). State Mutual Bk.
Disposing Mind. Richard H. R. Smithies. LC 66-16304. 1966. Horizon Press.
Disposing of Henry. Paul Winterton. LC 47-200031. 1947. Hutchinson & Co., Ltd.
Disposing of Henry. Paul Winterton. LC 47-18230. 1947. Harper & Brothers.
Dispossessed. Ursula K. Le Guin. 1975. pap. 2.95 (ISBN 0-380-00382-1, 62091). Avon.
Dispossessed. Ursula K. Le Guin. LC 73-18667. 352p. (YA) 1974. 11.49i (ISBN 0-06-012563-2, HarpT). Har-Row.
Dispossessed. Geoffrey Atheling Wagner. LC 56-8126. 1956. Devin-Adair Co.
Dispossessed: An Ambiguous Utopia. Ursula K. Le Guin. LC 73-18667. 1974. 7.95 (ISBN 0-06-012563-2). Harper & Row.
Disputed Barier. Elsie Frances Wilson Mack. LC 47-12124. 1947. Arcadia House.
Disputed Barricade. James Hulbert. LC 65-22466. 1966. Holt, Rinehart and Winston.
Disputed Crown. Valerie Anand. LC 82-10279. 14.95 (ISBN 0-684-17629-7). Scribner.
Disputed Inheritance. A Thrilling Story of Love, Mystery, and Intrigue. Telemachus Thomas Timayenis. LC 8-26779. (On cover: American series, no. 2). M. J. Ivers & Co.
Disputed Passage. Lloyd Cassel Douglas. LC 38-29098. 1939. Houghton Mifflin Company.
Disputed Title. Marietta Douglas. LC 28-11531. R. G. Badger.
Disquiet and Peace: A Novel by William Cooper Pseud. Harry Summerfield Hoff. LC 56-4239. Macmillan.
Disquiet and Peace: A Novel by William Cooper Pseud. Harry Summerfield Hoff. LC 57-6238. 1957. Lippincott.
Disraeli in Love. Maurice Edelman. 1973. (pbk.) 1.50. Dell.
Disraeli in Love. Maurice Edelman. LC 70-187303. 1972. 7.95 (ISBN 0-8128-1484-3). Stein and Day.
Disraeli Rising. Maurice Edelman. 1978. 2.25 (ISBN 0-8128-7007-7). Stein & Day.
Disraeli the Novelist. Thom Braun. LC 81-190227. 1981. 19.50 (ISBN 0-04-809017-4). Allen & Unwin.
Disrobing: Sex & Satire. Royal Murdoch. 112p. (Orig.). 1982. limited lettered 30.00 (ISBN 0-917342-95-X); pap. 5.95 (ISBN 0-917342-96-8). Gay Sunshine.
Dissatisfied Soul: And A Prophetic Romancer. Annie Trumbull Slosson. LC 8-19156. 1908. Bonnell, Silver & Co.
Dissector. Hugh Miller. LC 76-5377. 8.95. St. Martin's Press.
Dissemblers. John Creasey. (Medallion bk., X1606). 1968. Berkley.
Dissemblers. John Creasey. LC 67-23684. 1967. Scribner.
Dissent of Dominick Shapiro. Bernard Kops. LC 67-10566. 1967. Coward-McCann.
Dissenter. limited ed. Charles Francis Huston Miller. LC 73-84547. Priv. Print. by Walker, Evans & Cogswell.
Dissenters. Sigurd Jay Simonsen. LC 41-15201. Fortuny's Publishers, Inc.
Dissertation. R. M. Koster. LC 80-20066. 438p. 1981. pap. 7.95 (ISBN 0-688-00043-6). Quill NY.
Dissertation: A Novel. R. M. Koster. LC 74-3899. 1975. 10.95 (ISBN 0-06-125050-3). Harper's Magazine Press.
Dissertation and The Partnership: Short Fiction. Norval Rindfleisch. LC 80-129132. 1980. 3.95. Northern New England Review Press.
Dissolute Years: A Pageant of Stuart England. Eduard Stucken & Harrison, Mrs. Marguerite Elton (Baker) Tr. LC 35-335791. Farrar & Rhinehart, Incorporated C.
Dissolution. A Projected Drama. S. A. Brown. LC 6-18688. 1894. G.W. Dillingham.
Dissolving Circle. William Otis Lillibridge. LC 8-11084. 1908. Dodd, Mead & Company.
Dissolving Views. Leonora Blanche Lang. (On cover: The seaside library. Pocket ed. no. 536). 1885. G. Munro.
Distance and the Dark. Terence De Vere White. LC 72-92630. 1973. 6.95 (ISBN 0-87645-070-2). Gambit.
Distance Man. Samantha Harvey. (Harlequin Romances Ser.). 192p. 1983. pap. 1.50 (ISBN 0-373-02522-X). Harlequin Bks.
Distancing. Nathan Whiting. (New Rivers Chapbook). (Illus.). 1974. wrappers 1.25 (Pub. by New Rivers Pr). SBD.
Distant Clue: A Captain Heimrich Mystery. Richard Lockridge & Frances Louise Davis Lockridge. LC 63-14631. (Main line mysteries). 1963. Lippincott.
Distant Dawn. Margaret Bass Pedler. LC 34-379803. 1934. Doubleday, Doran & Co., Inc.
Distant Drum. Alice Lent Covert. 1974. 4.50. Avalon Books.
Distant Drum. Alice Lent Covert. LC 52-9993. 1952. Bouregy & Curl.
Distant Drum. Charles Bracelen Flood. LC 57-5113. 1957. Houghton Mifflin.
Distant Drum. Dudley Sturrock. LC 13-122828. 1913. John Lane Company.
Distant Eden. Donna Grulndman. (Orig.). 1982. pap. 3.50 (ISBN 0-440-12136-1). Dell.
Distant Laughter. Bryan Forbes. LC 72-79708. (Cass Canfield book). 1972. 6.95 (ISBN 0-06-011308-1). Harper & Row.
Distant Love, Lasting Love. C. O. Lamp. 368p. (Orig.). 1982. pap. 3.50 (ISBN 0-8439-1099-2, Leisure Bks). Nordon Pubns.
Distant Music. Harold Lenoir Davis. LC 57-5424. 1957. Morrow.
Distant Music of Summer. James T. Maher. LC 79-14605. 1979. 9.95 (ISBN 0-316-54384-5). Little.
Distant Princess. Elizabeth Frances Corbett. 1973. pap. 0.95 o.p. (95326). Beagle Bks.
Distant Princess. A T'Serstevens & Riesner, Lawrence, Tr. LC 31-24900. Farrar & Rinehart, Incorporated.
Distant Rainbow. Ed. by M. Ginsburg. 1970. 5.95 o.p. (ISBN 0-03-081847-8). HR&W.
Distant Relations. Carlos. Fuentes. LC 81-9904. 11.95 (ISBN 0-374-14082-0). Farrar Straus Giroux.

TITLE INDEX

DIX CONTES.

Distant Relations. Denice Greenlea. (Coventry Romance Ser.: No. 197). 192p. 1982. pap. 1.50 (ISBN 0-449-50300-3, Coventry). Fawcett.
Distant Shore. Susannah James. 1982. pap. 2.95 (ISBN 0-451-11264-4, AE1264, Sig). NAL.
Distant Shore: A Story of the Sea. Jan De Hartog. LC 52-5443. 1952. Harper.
Distant Song. Iris Bromige. Ed. by Gene DeRoin. (Aston Hall Presents Ser.). (Orig.). pap. 1.50 (ISBN 0-89936-009-2). Aston Hall.
Distant Stars. Elizabeth Carfrae, pseud. LC 29-4641. 1929. Harper & Brothers.
Distant Stations. Jonathan Schwartz. LC 79-116. 1979. 10.00. Doubleday.
Distant Stations. Jonathan Schwartz. LC 77-25607. 1979. 10.00. Doubleday.
Distant Summer. Sarah Patterson. LC 75-45013. 6.95 (ISBN 0-671-22257-0). Simon and Schuster.
Distant Summer. Sarah Patterson. (Kangaroo Book). 1977. 1.50 (ISBN 0-671-81218-1). Pocket Books.
Distant Thunder. Karen A. Bale. (Women at War Ser.: No. 14). 320p. (Orig.). 1983. pap. 3.25 (ISBN 0-440-01899-4, Emerald). Dell.
Distant Trojans. Virginia Hathaway Chapman. LC 48-7830. 1948. Random House.
Distant Trumpet. Paul Horgan. LC 60-7628. 1960. Farrar, Straus and Cudahy.
Distant Wood. Cynthia Harrod-Eagles. (Morland Dynasty Ser.: Bk. III). (Orig.). 1982. pap. 3.50 (ISBN 0-440-11703-8). Dell.
Distant Worlds: The Story of a Voyage to the Planets. Friedrich Wilhelm Mader. LC 75-28859. (Classics of science fiction). (Illus.). 1976. 12.95. (ISBN 0-88355-374-0) (ISBN 0-88355-458-5). Hyperion Press.
Distortions. Ann Beattie. LC 75-46443. 1976. 7.95 (ISBN 0-385-11659-4). Doubleday.
Distortions. Ann Beattie. 1979. 2.50 (ISBN 0-445-04504-3). Popular Library.
Distracted Preacher & Other Tales. Thomas Hardy. Intro. by Susan Hill. (English Library). 1980. pap. 4.95 (ISBN 0-14-043124-1). Penguin.
Distractions. Stanley Middleton. 1975. 8.95 (ISBN 0-09-124840-X, Pub. by Hutchinson). Merrimack Pub Cir.
Distractions of Martha. Mary Virginia Terhune. LC 6-34642. 1906. C. Scribner's Sons.
Distributors. Edward Phillips Oppenheim. LC 8-28064. 1908. The McClure Company.
District Attorney: By William Sage... William Sage. LC 6-17877. 1906. Little, Brown, and Company.
District Bungalow. Cecil Champain Lowis. LC 28-253593. 1928. Doubleday, Doran & Company, Inc.
District Doctor & Other Stories. Ivan Sergeevich Turgenev. pap. 3.95 o.p. (ISBN 0-498-04013-5, Prpta). A S Barnes.
District Nurse. Faith Baldwin Cuthrell. LC 32-13348. Farrar & Rinehart, Incorporated.
District of Columbia. John Dos Passos. LC 52-7617. 1952. Houghton Mifflin.
Distrust Her Shadow. Jessica Steele. (Harlequin Romances Ser.). 192p. 1983. pap. 1.75 (ISBN 0-373-02555-6). Harlequin Bks.
Disturb Not Our Dreams. Hobert Douglas Skidmore. LC 47-4554. 1947. Houghton Mifflin Co.
Disturb Not the Dream. Paula Trachtman. 1982. pap. 3.50 (ISBN 0-345-30170-6). Ballantine.
Disturb Not the Dream: A Novel. Paula Trachtman. LC 80-24463. 11.95 (ISBN 0-517-54322-2). Crown Publishers.
Disturbance in Paris. Carl Fick. LC 82-24. 13.95 (ISBN 0-316-28140-9). Little, Brown.
Disturbance on Berry Hill. Elizabeth Fenwick. LC 68-12538. (Illus.). 1968. Atheneum.
Disturber. L S Davidson. LC 64-14972. 1964. Macmillan.
Disturbers of the Peace: A Novel. Leon Pritcher & Harger, Catharine, Joint Author. LC 45-7215. 1945. B. Humphries, Inc.
Disturbing Affair of Noel Blake. Stephen Southwold. LC 32-266977. 1932. G. P. Putnam's Sons.
Disturbing Charm. Berta Ruck. LC 19-12253. 1919. Dodd, Mead and Company.
Disturbing Death of Jenkin Delaney. Michael Bonner. LC 66-18615. (Double D western). 3.50. Doubleday.
Disturbing Elements. Mabel Charlotte Bradley Birchenough. LC 6-12728. 1896. Macmillian.
Disturbing the Peace. Richard Yates. 1976. 1.95. Dell.
Disturbing the Peace: A Novel. Richard Yates. LC 75-11628. 1975. 7.95 (ISBN 0-440-03390-X). Delacorte Press/S. Lawrence.
Dita. Margaret Elizabeth Lindsay Majendie. (On cover: The seaside library. Pocket ed. no. 185). 1884. G. Munro.
Dita Saxova. Arnost Lustig. LC 78-69505. 10.00 (ISBN 0-06-012712-0). Harper & Row.
Ditch Valley. Daryl Henderson. LC 72-1192. 1972. 5.95 (ISBN 0-684-12995-7). Scribner.
Dithreabhach. Eoghan O'hAnluain. 1977. pap. 3.75 (ISBN 0-85342-476-4). Irish Bk Ctr.
Ditte... Martin Andersen Nexo. LC 31-28473. 1931. P. Smith.
Ditte, Daughter of Man. Martin Andersen Nexo & Chater, Arthur G., Tr. LC 21-18807. 1921. H. Holt and Company.
Ditte: Girl Alive! Martin Andersen Nexo. LC 20-26759. 1920. H. Holt and Company.
Ditte: Towards the Stars. Martin Andersen Nexo & Kenney, Asta., Tr. LC 22-20733. 1922. H. Holt and Company.
Diva. Delacorta. Tr. by Lowell Bair from Fr. 1983. 9.95 (ISBN 0-671-47056-6). Summit Bks.
Diva. Robert F Joseph. (Berkley Medallion Book). 1975. (pbk.) 1.75. Berkley Pub. Co.
Divas. Robert Merrill & Fred G. Jarvis. 1979. 2.50 (ISBN 0-425-04432-7). Berkley Publishing Corp.
Divas: A Novel. Robert Merrill & Fred G. Jarvis. LC 78-19043. 9.95 (ISBN 0-671-24239-3). Simon and Schuster.
Diva's Ruby: A Sequel to "Primadonna" and "Fair Margaret.". Francis Marion Crawford. LC 7-42462. 1908. The Macmillan Company.
Dive Deep for Danger: By H. T. Rothwell. H. T Rothwell. LC 66-242359. 1966. 3.25. Roy.
Dive from the Sky! By Dan Halacy. Daniel Stephen Halacy. LC 67-24952. 1967. 3.95, 3.31 lib. ed.,. McGraw.
Dive in the Sun. Douglas Reeman. (Berkley book). 1979. 1.95 (ISBN 0-425-04020-8). Distributed by Berkley Pub. Corp.
Dive in the Sun, a Novel. 1st American Ed. Douglas Reeman. LC 61-147808. 1961. Putnam.
Dive into Darkness. Lillian O'Donnell. LC 73-141432. (Raven books). 1971. u.s. 5.95 (ISBN 0-200-71801-0). Abelard-Schuman.
Dive into Death. Clayton Matthews. LC 69-20136. 1969. 4.50. Sherbourne Press.
Dive to Danger. Yvind Holmvik & Faye-Lund, Hans. LC 64-17859. 1964. Harcourt, Brace.
Diver Girl. Marilyn Horn. pap. 1.95 o.p. (8027). Cameo.
Diverging Paths: A Story of the Pioneer Days of Missouri, by L. L. Chappelle. L. L. Chappelle. LC 11-78720. 1.50. Broadway Publishing Co.
Diverging Roads. Rose Wilder Lane. LC 19-4791. 1919. The Century Co.
Divers of Arakam. Bert Fisher. LC 77-368397. 1976. B. Fisher.
Divers Women. Isabella Alden & C. M. Livingston. LC 8-22548. Lothrop, Lee & Shepard Co.
Diverse Gathering. Earl P. Nurmi. 1978. pap. 1.50 (ISBN 0-931122-12-0). West End.
Diversey. MacKinlay Kantor. LC 28-18754. 1928. Coward-McCann, Inc.
Diversion of Dawson. Frederick Harcourt Kitchin. LC 24-1640. E. P. Dutton & Company.
Dives & Pauper (1493) LC 73-17391. 1973. Repr. of 1493 ed. lib. bdg. 65.00x (ISBN 0-8201-1111-2). Schol Facsimiles.
Divide and Rule. Lyon Sprague De Camp. LC 48-9738. 1948. Fantasy Press.
Divide by Seven. Robert Chambers. LC 76-81282. 1969. 5.00. Bobbs-Merrill.
Divide by Two. Mildred Evans Gilman. LC 38-196346. Harcourt, Brace and Company.
Divide by Two. Mildred Evans Gilman. LC 40-422263. (A Mercury book. no. 24). The American Mercury, Inc.
Divide the Desolation: A Novel Based on the Life of Emily Bronte. Kathryn J. MacFarlane. 1937. 25.00 (ISBN 0-8274-2192-3). R West.
Divide the Desolation: A Novel Based on the Life of Emily Jane Bronte. Kathryn Jean MacFarlane. LC 36-19832. 1936. Simon and Schuster.
Divide the Heart. R. E Dane. LC 47-1729. 1947. Reynal & Hitchcock.
Divide the Night. Wessel Ebersohn. LC 81-47194. 10.95 (ISBN 0-394-52076-9). Pantheon Books.
Divide the Night. Wessel Ebersohn. LC 82-4756. 1982. 2.95 (ISBN 0-394-70810-5). Vintage Press.
Divide the Night. Donald Honig. 1970. pap. 0.75 o.p. (B75-2055). Belmont-Tower.
Divided: A Novel. Ralph Freedman. LC 48-7529. 1948. E. P. Dutton.
Divided: A Story of the Veldt. Francis Bancroft. LC 13-25051. Small, Maynard & Company.
Divided Allegiance. Stephen McKenna. 1928. Dodd, Mead & Company.
Divided Heart. Angelica Aimes. 352p. (Orig.). 1981. pap. 2.95 (ISBN 0-523-41264-9). Pinnacle Bks.
Divided Heart, and Other Stories. Paul Johann Ludwig Von Heyse. Tr. by Copeland, Constance Stewart. LC 7-6611. Brentano's.
Divided Heaven. Christa Wolf. Tr. by Joan Becker from Ger. 1976. pap. 4.50 (ISBN 0-8417-0002-8). Adler.
Divided Lady. Bruce Marshall. LC 60-7188. 1960. Houghton Mifflin.
Divided Lives: A Novel. Edgar Fawcett. LC 6-38952. (On cover: The household library. no. 1, v. 4). 1888. Belford, Clarke & Co.
Divided Medal. David Skaats Foster. LC 14-22139. 1.25. The Franklin Book Company.
Divided Path: A Novel. William Leroy Thomas. LC 49-11078. 1949. Greenberg.
Divided: The Story of a Poem. Clara Elizabeth Laughlin. LC 4-228358. (Art gift-book series). 1904. F. H. Revell Company.
Dividend. Joseph Knox Stone. LC 27-21342. Dorrance and Company.
Dividend on Death. Davis Dresser. LC 39-23863. H. Holt and Company.
Dividend on Death. Brett Halliday, pseud. (Raven House Mysteries Ser.). 224p. 1982. pap. 2.25 (ISBN 0-373-63033-6, Pub. by Worldwide). Harlequin Bks.
Dividends for Louise. Norman Wright Welsh. LC 42-21647. 1942. House of Field, Inc.
Dividends from Defeat: A Novel. 1st Ed. Dorothy Jane Stone. LC 54-131782. 1955. Exposition Press.
Dividing Line. Kay Thorpe. (Harlequin Presents Ser.). (Orig.). 1980. pap. 1.50 (ISBN 0-373-10360-3, Pub. by Harlequin). PB.
Dividing Lines: A Novel of Love. Joseph S Salzburg. LC 64-25421. 1964. William-Frederick Press.
Dividing Lines: A War Novel. Joseph S. Salzburg. 1975. 6.00 (ISBN 0-87164-084-8). William-F.
Dividing of Time. Elizabeth Missing Sewell. LC 51-9566. 1951. Doubleday.
Dividing Stream. Francis Henry King. LC 51-10967. 1951. Morrow.
Dividing Waters. Ida Alexa Ross Wylie. LC 11-24359. The Bobbs-Merrill Company.
Divine Adventure: A Novel. Theodore Maynard. LC 21-5172. Frederick A. Stokes Company.
Divine Adventure: A Novel. Karl August Meissinger. Tr. by Paul, Eden. LC 36-24397. 1936. The Viking Press.
Divine & the Damned. Robert Vaughan. 1983. pap. 3.50 (Emerald). Dell.
Divine Average: A Historical Novel on That Period of Texas History When "Cow Boy" Was a Phrase with a Controversial Meaning and "Texians" a Nationality. 1st Ed. Elithe Hamilton Kirkland. LC 52-6787. 1952. Little, Brown.
Divine Comedy. Edward G. Davis. 1970. 2.75 o.p. Carlton.
Divine Egotist. Vingie Eve Roe. LC 16-19455. 1916. Dodd, Mead and Company.
Divine Event. William Nathaniel Harben. LC 20-167960. Harper & Brothes.
Divine Fire. May Sinclair. LC 4-25675. 1904. H. Holt and Company.
Divine Fire. May Sinclair. LC 16-70019. 1906. H. Holt and Company.
Divine Gift. Christabel McLaren. LC 29-987314. 1929. Longmans, Green and Co.
Divine Horsemen: The Living Gods of Haiti. Maya Deren. (Illus.). 7.50 o.p. (ISBN 0-8149-0491-2). Vanguard.
Divine Invasion. Philip K. Dick. (Orig.). 1982. pap. 2.95 (ISBN 0-671-44343-7, Timescape). PB.
Divine Lady: A Romance of Nelson and Emma Hamilton. Lily Moresby Adams Beck. LC 24-14710. 1924. Dodd, Mead and Company.
Divine Lady: A Romance of Nelson and Emma Hamilton. Lily Moresby Adams Beck. LC 25-17664. 1925. Dodd, Mead and Company.
Divine Mistress. Frank Gill Slaughter. LC 49-11286. 1949. Doubleday.
Divine Nectar. 2nd ed. Swami Sivananda. 1976. pap. text ed. 16.00x (ISBN 0-8426-0856-7). Verry.
Divine Passion. Vardis Fisher. LC 48-8542. 1948. Vanguard Press.
Divine Queen: Canto Two of the Doom-Quest of Ara Karn, a Dark Romance. Adam Corby. 240p. (Orig.). 1982. pap. 2.95 (ISBN 0-671-41771-1, Timescape). PB.
Divine Right's Trip: A Folk-Tale. Gurney Norman. LC 78-37455. 1972. 7.95. Dial Press.
Divine Seal. Emma Louise Orcutt. LC 9-28695. 1909. 1.50. The C. M. Clark Publishing Company.
Divine Tenement. Robert McDonald. LC 47-4402. 1947. Reynal & Hitchcock.
Divine Wind. Robert Vaughan. (Wartorn Ser.: No. 3). (Orig.). 1983. pap. 3.50 (ISBN 0-440-01992-3). Dell.
Diviner. Marilyn Harris. LC 82-13216. 9.95 (ISBN 0-399-12739-9). Putnam.
Diviners. Margaret Laurence. LC 73-20740. (Illus.). 1974. 7.95 (ISBN 0-394-49156-4). Knopf; Distributed by Random House.
Diviner's Handbook. Tom Graves. (Warner Destiny Book.). (Illus.). 1977. 1.95. Warner Books.
Diving for Roses. Patricia Windsor. LC 75-25402. 5.95. (ISBN 0-06-026519-1). Harper & Row.
Divining Rod. Arthur J. Ellis. LC 77-25879. 1977. lib. bdg. 10.00 (ISBN 0-8414-4103-0). Folcroft.
Divining Rod: A Story of the Oil Regions. Francis Newton Thorpe. LC 5-327363. 1905. Little Brown, and Company.
Divining Rod for Murder. Margot Neville. LC 52-5230. 1952. Published for the Crime Club by Doubleday.
Division Bell Mystery. Ellen Cicely Wilkinson. LC 75-46006. (Fifty Classics of Crime Fiction, 1900-1950; 49). 1976. 12.00 (ISBN 0-8240-2398-6). Garland Pub.
Division of the Spoils: A Novel. Paul Scott. LC 75-879. 1975. 12.50 (ISBN 0-688-02926-4). Morrow.
Division of the Spoils: A Novel. Paul Scott. LC 79-52459. 1979. 3.50 (ISBN 0-380-45054-2). Avon Books.
Divorce. Paul Charles Joseph Bourget. LC 4-357272. 1904. C. Scribner's Sons.
Divorce. Robert P Davis. LC 80-17833. 1980. 10.95 (ISBN 0-688-03725-9). Morrow.
Divorce. Margaret Lee. (On cover: Lovell's library. no. 25). J. W. Lovell Company.
Divorce. Mary Colliver Taylor. LC 8-25667. 1895.
Divorce Contract. Robert J Smith. LC 8-9626. 1898. C. W. Brown.
Divorce Court Murder. Milton Morris Propper. LC 34-11658. 1934. Harper & Brothers.
Divorce Decisions. Constance Cappel, pseud. (Orig.). 1980. pap. 6.95 (ISBN 0-915248-33-6). Vermont Crossroads.
Divorce Las Vegas Style. Linda Dubreuil. 1976. pap. 1.50 o.p. (Leisure Books). Nordon Pubns.
Divorce Las Vegas Style. Linda Dubreuil. Leisure Books.
Divorce Lawyer. Griffith James. LC 39-17418. Phoenix Press.
Divorce of Marcia Moore. Edith Kneipple Roberts. LC 48-658932. 1948. Doubleday.
Divorce Pending, a Novel. William Lindley Grubbs. LC 33-30724. Alamo Printing Company.
Divorce: Tr. and Adapted from the Pekinese of Venerable Lodge, (Pseud. Ch'ing Ch'un Shu. Tr. by Ward, Robert Spencer. LC 48-18747. 1948. King Publications.
Divorce Trap. Harry Sinclair Drago. LC 31-320668. The Macaulay Company.
Divorce Your Wife. Fordin Athearn. 1977. pap. 1.95 o.s.i. (ISBN 0-8439-0503-4, LB503, Leisure Bks). Nordon Pubns.
Divorced. Charlotte Campbell Bury. LC 6-16688. 1837. E. L. Carey & A. Hart.
Divorced. A Novel. Madeleine Vinton Dahlgren. 1887. Belford, Clarke & Co.
Divorced in America: An Anatomy of Loneliness. Joseph Epstein. LC 73-20270. 1974. 10.00 o.p. (ISBN 0-525-09375-3). Dutton.
Divorced Male: The Target for Women. Stephen A. Jones. 192p. 1974. pap. 1.95 o.p. (ISBN 0-87056-389-0, 6389). Brandon.
Divorced Wife: Or, Righted at Last. Mary Grace Halpine. LC 7-120810. (On cover: Munro's library. v. 1. no. 410). N. L. Munro.
Divorcees. O. R Bassett. (Original Brandon Book). 1973. (pbk.) 1.95. Brandon Books.
Divorcees Confess in Celese Jewell's Confession Room. V.1- Ed. by Celese Jewell. LC 53-8095. Pageant Press.
Divorcing. Susan Taubes, pseud. 1969. 5.95 o.p. (ISBN 0-394-42210-4). Random.
Divorcing: A Novel. Susan Feldmann. LC 69-16454. 1972. Popular Lib.
Divots. Pelham Grenville Wodehouse. LC 27-4641. George H. Doran Company.
Divots. Pelham Grenville Wodehouse. LC 35-28582. 1929. A. L. Burt Company.
Diwan 'Abdallah ibn al Mu'tazz. Tr. by Arthur Wormhoudt from Arabic. (Arab Translation Ser.: No. 38). 1978. pap. 6.50x (ISBN 0-916358-88-7). Wormhoudt.
Diwan al Mutanabbi, Farsiyyat. Tr. by Arthur Wormhoudt from Arabic. (Arab Translation Ser.: No. 37). 1978. pap. 6.50 o.p. (ISBN 0-916358-87-9). Wormhoudt.
Diwan al Mutanabbi, Misriyyat. Tr. by Arthur Wormhoudt from Arabic. (Arab Translation Ser.: No. 36). 1978. pap. 6.50 o.p. (ISBN 0-916358-86-0). Wormhoudt.
Diwan al Mutanabbi: Selections. Tr. by Arthur Wormhoudt from Arabic. (Arab Translation Ser.: No. 1). 1968. pap. 2.50 (ISBN 0-916358-51-8). Wormhoudt.
Diwan al Mutanabbi, Shawmiyyat, 3 pts. Tr. by Arthur Wormhoudt from Arabic. (Arab Translation Ser.: No. 31-33). 1978. pap. 6.50 ea. o.p. Pt. 1 (ISBN 0-916358-81-X). Pt. 2 (ISBN 0-916358-82-8). Pt. 3 (ISBN 0-916358-83-6). Wormhoudt.
Diwan al Mutanabbi, Shawmiyyat, 2 pts. Tr. by Arthur Wormhoudt from Arabic. (Arab Translation Ser.: No. 34-35). 1978. pap. 6.50 ea. o.p. Pt. 1 (ISBN 0-916358-84-4). Pt. 2 (ISBN 0-916358-85-2). Wormhoudt.
Diwan Labid. Tr. by Arthur Wormhoudt. (Arab Translation Ser.: No. 25). 1976. pap. 6.50x (ISBN 0-916358-75-5). Wormhoudt.
Dix Contes. John T. Fotos & Edward P. Shaw. (Orig., Fr.). 1961. pap. text ed. 3.25x o.p. Macmillan.

Dix Contes: Selected and Ed. by John T. Fotos, Edward P. Shaw. Ed. by Theodore John & Edward Pease Shaw. LC 61-6862. pap. 2.75, +011. Macmillan.
Dixiana. Winnie Brandon. LC 30-18552. A. L. Burt Company.
Dixiana Moon. William Price Fox. LC 80-51770. 1981. 10.95 (ISBN 0-670-27453-4). Viking Press.
Dixie Convoy. Don Pendleton. (Executioner Ser: No. 27). 1976. pap. 1.95 (ISBN 0-523-41091-3). Pinnacle Bks.
Dixie Death Squad. Lionel Derrick. (Penetrator Series#13). 1976. (pbk.) 1.25 (ISBN 0-523-00825-2). Pinnacle Books.
Dixie Doctor. Ruby Lorraine Radford. LC 55-14333. 1955. Avalon Books.
Dixie Gentleman. A Novel. Frank I. E. William Frank Harrington. LC 7-2844. 1895. The Syndicate Press.
Dixie Gentleman. A Novel. 2d ed. Frank I. E. William Frank Harrington. LC 7-2845. 1895. The Syndicate Press.
Dixie Hart. William Nathaniel Harben. LC 10-22414. 1910. Harper & Brothers.
Dixons: A Story of American Life Through Three Generations. Florence Finch Kelly. LC 21-5655. E. P. Dutton & Company.
DJ. Allan Jefferys & William Hugh Owen. LC 73-167723. 1971. 7.95. Ashley Books.
Djambek the Georgian: A Tale of Modern Turkey. A. Gundaccar Suttner & Jewett, H. M., Tr. LC 8-256509. (On cover: Appleton's town and country library, no. 49). 1890. D. Appleton and Company.
Djinn. Graham Masterton. 192p. 1977. pap. 2.75 (ISBN 0-523-48068-7, 40-523-0). Pinnacle Bks.
Djinn. Robbe-Grillet, Alain. LC 81-86393. 1982. 10.95 (ISBN 0-394-52569-8) (ISBN 0-394-17983-8). Grove Press.
Dmitri. Jamey Cohen. LC 79-67610. 9.95 (ISBN 0-87223-583-1). Seaview Books.
Dmitri Donskoi: A Novel. Sergel Petrovich Borodin. Tr. by Paul, Eden. LC 45-1213. 1944. Hutchinson's International Authors Ltd.
Do a Man Pleasure. Spencer Moore. 160p. 1972. pap. 1.95 o.s.i. (OPH 4156). Olympia.
Do Androids Dream of Electric Sheep? Philip K Dick. LC 68-11779. 1968. Doubleday.
Do Black Patent Leather Shoes Really Reflect up? John R. Powers. LC 75-13247. 240p. 1975. 7.95 o.p. (ISBN 0-8092-8177-5). Contemp Bks.
Do Butlers Burgle Banks? Pelham Grenville Wodehouse. LC 68-22974. 1968. Simon and Schuster.
Do Evil in Return. Margaret Millar. 1974. (pbk.) 0.95 (ISBN 0-380-00033-4). Avon.
Do Evil in Return. Margaret Millar. LC 50-9717. 1950. Random House.
Do Good. William Sayres. LC 66-13096. 1966. Holt, Rinehart and Winston.
Do-Gooders. Alfred Grossman. LC 68-17790. 1968. Doubleday.
Do I Love Her? A Novel... Frank Lee Benedict. LC 7-34454. 1882. G. W. Carleton & Co.; Etc., Etc.
Do I Wake or Sleep. Isabel Bolton. LC 47-1265. 1946. C. Scribner's Sons.
Do, Lord, Remember Me. George Palmer Garrett. LC 65-17253. 1965. Doubleday.
Do Not Defuse. Valery Oistenau. 1980. pap. 2.50 (ISBN 0-9601870-2-2). Pass.
Do Not Disturb. Helen McCloy. LC 43-5525. 1943. W. Morrow & Co.
Do Not Disturb. Lee Thayer. LC 51-10439. (Red badge detective). 1951. Dodd, Mead.
Do Not Do to Others!". Herbert A. Spears. LC 36-8619. The Christopher Publishing House.
Do Not Fold, Spindle, or Mutilate. Doris Miles Disney. LC 72-123687. 1970. 4.50. Published for the Crime Club by Doubleday.
Do Not Go Gentle. 1st Ed. David MacCuish. LC 60-15187. 1960. Doubleday.
Do Not Go, My Love. Denise Robins. (Beagle book). 1974. (pbk.) 0.95 (ISBN 0-345-26602-1). Ballantine Books.
Do Not Murder Before Christmas. Jack Iams. LC 49-11102. (A Morrow mysery). 1949. W. Morrow.
Do Not Worry About the Bear: Stories. Michael Rogers. LC 78-15428. 1979. 8.95 (ISBN 0-394-50191-8). Knopf: Distributed by Random House.
Do Nothin' till You Hear from Me. John William Wainwright. LC 77-284. 1978. 7.95 (ISBN 0-312-21473-1). St Martin's.
Do Unto Others. Doris Miles Disney. LC 52-13560. 1953. Published for the Crime Club by Doubleday.
Do We Agree? Gilbert Keith Chesterton. 1928. lib. bdg. 10.00 (ISBN 0-8414-3021-7). Folcroft.
Do We Need the Church. Richard P. McBrien. LC 69-10476. 1969. 6.50 o.p. (ISBN 0-06-065326-4, HarpR). Har-Row.
Do What You Will: Essays. Aldous Leonard Huxley. LC 75-14273. (Essay index reprint series). 1975. 19.50 (ISBN 0-518-10202-5). Books for Libraries Press.
Do with Me What You Will. Joyce Carol Oates. (Fawcett Crest book). 1974. (pbk.) 1.95. Fawcett.
Do with Me What You Will. Joyce Carol Oates. LC 73-83039. 1973. 7.95 (ISBN 0-8149-0750-4). Vanguard Press.
Do You Hear Them? Nathalie Sarraute. Tr. by Maria Jolas from Fr. LC 72-86680. 178p. 1973. 5.95o.p. (ISBN 0-8076-0663-4); pap. 2.95 (ISBN 0-8076-0739-8). Braziller.
Do You Know This Voice? Evelyn Berckman. LC 60-11930. 1960. Dodd, Mead.
Do You Remember England? Derek Marlowe. 1973. (pbk.) 1.25. Dell.
Do You Remember England? Derek Marlowe. LC 71-181975. 1972. 6.95 (ISBN 0-670-28059-3). Viking Press.
Do You See My Love for You Growing? Ed. by Orde Coombs. LC 72-1538. 750p. 1972. 6.95 o.p. (ISBN 0-396-06518-X). Dodd.
Do Yourself a Favor, Kid. James Stevenson. LC 62-8152. 1962. Macmillan.
Dobachi. Francis Browning Drew Bickerstaffe-Drew. LC 23-7284. 1923. The Macmillan Company.
Dobe Walls: A Story of Kit Carson's Southwest. Stanley Vestal. LC 29-19021. 1929. Houghton Mifflin Company.
Doberman Wore Black. Barbara Moore. 240p. 1983. 13.95 (ISBN 0-312-21474-X). St Martin.
Doble Para Amar. new ed. Jairo Ibero. (Pimienta Collection Ser). 160p. (Span.). 1974. pap. 1.00 (ISBN 0-88473-199-5). Fiesta Pub.
Doc. Pete Hamill. (Illus.). 1971. pap. 0.95 o.p. (ISBN 0-446-65640-2, 65-640). Paperback Lib.
Doc Blakesley: Angler. Arthur Raymond Macdougall. LC 50-102. 1949. Falmouth Pub. House.
Doc Colts' Rebellion. T. W. Ford. LC 47-12085. 1947. Arcadia House.
Doc Dillahay. Paul S Powers. LC 49-7689. 1949. Macmillan Co.
Doc." Gordon. Mary Eleanor Wilkins Freeman. LC 6-256697. McLeod & Allen.
Doc' Horne: A Story of the Streets, and Town. George Ade. 1899. H.S. Stone and Company.
Doc Phoenix. Ted White & Martin Wolfman. Ed. by Byron Preiss. (Weird Heroes Ser.). 1977. pap. 1.50 o.p. (ISBN 0-515-04036-3). BJ Pub Group.
Doc Savage. Philip Jose Farmer. LC 81-80083. 288p. (Orig.). 1981. pap. 2.50 (ISBN 0-87216-854-9). Playboy Pbks.
Doc Savage: His Apocalyptic Life. Philip J. Farmer. LC 72-96236. 240p. 1973. 6.95 o.p. (ISBN 0-385-08488-9). Doubleday.
Doc Savage, Supreme Adventurer. John L. Nauovic. (Illus.). pap. 2.00x (ISBN 0-933752-22-9). Odyssey MA.
Doc Travis. Lou Cameron. 1975. (pbk.) 0.95. Dell.
Doc Williams: A Tale of the Middle West. Charles Henry Lerrigo. LC 13-15520. Fleming H. Revell Company.
Docken Dead. John Trench. (Cock Robin mystery). 1954. Macmillan.
Doctor. Michael Artzibashev. Ed. by Isaac Goldberg. Tr. by Percy Pinkerton. (International Pocket Library). pap. 3.00. Branden.
Doctor. Mary Roberts Rinehart. LC 36-10760. Farrar & Rinehart, Inc.
Doctor. Mary Roberts Rinehart. (Dell Book). 1977. 1.75 (ISBN 0-440-11961-8). Dell Pub. Co.
Doctor. Philip H. Smith. (Orig.). 1979. pap. 1.75 (ISBN 0-532-17210-8). Woodhill.
Doctor: A Tale of the Rockies. Charles William Gordon. LC 6-41274. F. H. Revell Company.
Doctor Addams... Irving Fineman. LC 39-5852. Random House.
Dr. Adriaan. Louis Marie Anne Couperus. Tr. by Teixeira De Mattos, Alexander Louis. LC 18-211635. 1918. 1.50. Dodd, Mead and Company.
Doctor Alice's Daughter: By Kay Hamilton Pseud. Cateau De Leeuw. LC 50-8403. 1950. Macrae Smith.
Doctor and Son: By Richard Gordon Pseud. 1st Ed. Gordon Ostlere. LC 59-6999. 1959. Doubleday.
Doctor and the Corpse. Max Murray. LC 52-13947. 1952. Farrar, Straus and Young.
Doctor & the Dancer. Maysie Greig. 1973. pap. 0.75 o.p. (94345). Beagle Bks.
Doctor & the Devils & Other Scripts. Dylan Thomas. LC 65-15668. 1970. pap. 6.25 (ISBN 0-8112-0206-2, NDP297). New Directions.
Doctor and the Dragon: A Tragi-Comedy of British India. Dennis Gray Stoll. LC 47-304744. 1947. Doubleday.
Doctor and the Lady. Jerome Darwin Engel. LC 40-67366. Gramercy Publishing Co.
Doctor Angel. Peggy O'More, pseud. LC 52-10207. 1952. Arcadia House.
Doctor Antonio. Giovanni Domenico Ruffini. (Seaside library, v. 47, no. 960). 1881. G. Munro.
Doctor Antonio: A Tale. John Ruffini. LC 79-8193. Repr. of 1855 ed. 44.50 (ISBN 0-404-62109-0). AMS Pr.
Doctor Antonio. A Tale of Italy. Giovanni Domenico Ruffini. LC 42-28895. 1859. Rudd & Carleton.
Doctor Antonio: A Tale of Italy. Giovanni Domenico Ruffini. LC 4-16576. G. W. Dillingham Co.
Doctor Arnoldi. Tiffany Thayer. LC 34-7420. 1934. J. Messner, Inc.
Dr. Artz. Robert Smythe Hichens. LC 29-9992. 1929. Cosmopolitan Book Corporation.
Doctor at Coffin Gap. Les Savage. LC 49-11795. (Double D western). 1949. Doubleday.
Doctor at Large: By Richard Gordon Pseud. 1st American Ed. Gordon Ostlere. LC 55-938030. 1956. Harcourt, Brace.
Doctor at Sea. Patrick R. Allanson. 1980. 8.50 (ISBN 0-682-49510-7). Exposition.
Doctor at Sea: By Richard Gordon Pseud. 1st American Ed. Gordon Ostlere. LC 54-524955. Harcourt, Brace.
Doctor at the Crossroads. Elizabeth Seifert. LC 54-576355. 1954. Dodd, Mead.
Doctor at the Crossroads. Elizabeth Seifert. LC 73-791646. 1974. 6.95. Aeonian Press.
Doctor Barbara: By Elizabeth Wesley Pseud. Adeline McElfresh. LC 58-9117. 1958. Avalon Books.
Dr. Barry's Nurse. Arlene Hale. (Arlene Hale Nurse Romance). 1976. (pbk.) 0.95. Ace Books.
Doctor Ben. Douglas Marshall, pseud. LC 41-25825. 1941. Gramercy Publishing Co.
Doctor Ben: An Episode in the Life of a Fortunate Unfortunate... Orlando Witherspoon. LC 8-37126. (Round-robin series. v. 13). 1882. J. R. Osgood and Company.
Doctor Bill. Lucy Agnes Hancock. LC 48-10596. 1948. Macrae-Wmith Co.
Dr. Block and the Human Condition: A Novel. Marjorie Lee. LC 73-181406. 1972. 6.95. Putnam.
Dr. Block and the Human Conditions: A Novel. Marjorie Lee. 1975. (pbk.) 1.25. Dell.
Dr. Bloodmoney. Philip K. Dick. (Orig.). 1980. pap. 2.25 (ISBN 0-440-11489-6). Dell.
Dr. Bloodmoney: Or, How We Got Along After the Bomb. Philip K Dick. LC 77-4508. (Gregg Press science fiction series). 1977. 11.00 (ISBN 0-8398-2365-7). Gregg Press.
Dr. Bloodmoney, or How We Got Along After the Bomb. Philip K. Dick. 1977. Repr. of 1965 ed. lib. bdg. 11.00 o.p. (ISBN 0-8398-2365-7, Gregg). G K Hall.
Doctor Blues. Mark Smith. LC 82-24895. 1983. 15.95 (ISBN 0-688-01553-0). Morrow.
Doctor Blues. Mark Smith. 484p. 1983. 15.95 (ISBN 0-688-01553-0). Morrow.
Doctor Bob. Robert Ravel. LC 34-19651. The Macaulay Company.
Doctor Bradley Remembers. Francis Brett Young. LC 38-27979. 1938. Reynal & Hitchcock.
Dr. Bradley's Nurse. Jerome Darwin Engel. LC 41-7858. Gramercy Publishing Co.
Doctor Brad's Nurse. Jennifer Ames, pseud. (Easy Eye Editions). 1968. pap. 0.60 o.p. (73-776). Lancer.
Doctor Breen's Practice. William Dean Howells. LC 70-131752. 1970. Repr. of 1881 ed. 10.00 (ISBN 0-403-00639-2). Scholarly.
Doctor Breen's Practice: A Novel. William Dean Howells. LC 75-98766. 1969. Greenwood Press.
Doctor Breen's Practice: A Novel. William Dean Howells. LC 7-5778. 1881. J. R. Osgood and Company.
Doctor Breen's Practice: A Novel. William Dean Howells. LC 42-296351. Ticknor and Company.
Dr. Breen's Practice: A Novel. William Dean Howells. LC 16-7564. 1881. Houghton Mifflin Company.
Doctor Breen's Practice: a Novel. William Dean Howells. Repr. of 1881 ed. lib. bdg. 15.00x (ISBN 0-8371-2834-X, HODB). Greenwood.
Doctor Brodie's Report. Jorge Luis Borges. LC 72-158581. 1972. 5.95 (ISBN 0-525-09382-6). E. P. Dutton.
Doctor Brodie's Report. Jorge Luis Borges. LC 79-103906. 1978. 2.50 (ISBN 0-525-47541-9). Dutton.
Dr. Brodie's Report. Jorge Luis Borges. 1979. pap. 2.50 (ISBN 0-525-47541-9). Dutton.
Dr. Bruderstein Vanishes. John Sherwood. LC 49-97334. 1949. Pub. for the Crime Club by Doubleday.
Doctor Bryson: A Novel. Frank Hamilton Spearman. LC 2-23847. 1902. C. Scribner's Sons.
Dr. Caldwell: Or, The Trail of the Serpent. Edward Reynolds Roe. (pastime series, no. 33). 1889. Laird & Lee.
Doctor Carrington. Isabella Cornelia De Vane. LC 1-18537. The Abbey Press.
Doctor Cavallo. Eugene F Baldwin & Eisenberg, Maurice. 1895. Press of J. W. Franks & Sons.
Doctor Charlton: By Norma Newcomb Pseud. William Arthur Neubauer. 1955. Arcadia House.
Dr. Christian's Office. Ruth Adams Yingling Knight & Hersholt, Jean, 1886- Joint Author. LC 44-7186. 1944. Random House.
Doctor Christopher. Peggy Gaddis, pseud. LC 49-119499. 1949. Arcadia House.
Doctor Claudius: A True Story. Francis Marion Crawford. LC 11-10575. 1883. Macmillan and Co.
Doctor Claudius: A True Story. Francis Marion Crawford. LC 33-17495. 1893. Macmillan and Co.
Doctor Claudius: A True Story. Francis Marion Crawford. LC 4-154420. 1901. The Macmillan Company.
Doctor Claudius: A True Story. Francis Marion Crawford. LC 16-19153. (Lettered on cover: Works of F. Marion Crawford). 1912. The Macmillan Company.
Doctor Cobb's Game. Robert Verlin Cassill. LC 72-122880. 1970. 7.95. B. Geis Associates, Distributed by World Pub. Co.
Doctor Comes to Bayard. Elizabeth Seifert. LC 64-21050. 1964. Dodd, Mead.
Doctor Congalton's Legacy: A Chronicle of North Country by-Ways. Henry Johnston. LC 7-10799. 1896. C. Scribner's Sons.
Doctor Copernicus: A Novel. John Banville. LC 76-45754. (Illus.). (ISBN 0-393-08757-3). Norton.
Doctor Copernicus: A Novel. John Banville. LC 77-355057. (Illus.). 1976. 3.90 (ISBN 0-436-03263-5). Secker and Warburg.
Doctor Cox's Couch. Herbert Leon Newbold. LC 79-17738. 10.00 (ISBN 0-8184-0282-2). L. Stuart.
Doctor Cupid. Rhoda Broughton. (On cover: Lovell's Library, v. 17, no. 841). 1887. J. W. Lovell Company.
Doctor Cupid. A Novel. Rhoda Broughton. (On cover: Seaside library. Pocket ed., no. 304). 1886. G. Munro.
Doctor Cupid: A Novel. Rhoda Broughton. LC 18-7779. (Macmillan's two shilling library. no. 14). 1899. Macmillan and Co., Limited.
Dr. Cyclops. Will Garth, pseud. Phoenix Press.
Dr. Dale: A Story Without a Moral. Mary Virginia Terhune & Terhune, Albert Payson, 1872- Joint Author. LC 6477. 1900. Dodd, Mead and Company.
Doctor Danny. Ruth Sawyer. LC 18-22165. 1918. Harper & Brothers.
Dr. Darch's Wife: A Study. Florence Alice Price James. (On cover: The fortnightly library, v. 15, no. 17). P. F. Collier.
Dr. Darwood. John Davidson Frame. LC 51-13427. 1951. Moody Press.
Doctor Darwood. John Davidson Frame. (Orig.). 1964. pap. 1.35 o.p. (38-11). Moody.
Dr. David. Marjorie Benton Cooke. LC 11-235021. 1911. A. C. McClurg & Co.
Doctor De Luxe. Charles Stanley Strong. Phoenix Press.
Dr. Death. Nick Carter. (Espionage Ser). (O.s.i.). (Orig.). 1975. pap. 1.95 o.s.i. (AY1424, Award). Univ Pub & Dist.
Doctor Death. Jerome Hartenfels. LC 70-86818. 232p. 1970. 5.95 (ISBN 0-8090-3919-2). Hill & Wang.
Doctor Death: A Novel. Jerome Hartenfels. 1973. (pbk) 0.95. Popular Library.
Doctor Death: Twelve Must Die. Zorro. LC 80-8666. 80p. 1980. lib. bdg. 14.95x (ISBN 0-89370-083-5); pap. 5.95x (ISBN 0-89370-082-7). Borgo Pr.
Doctor Destiny. Edward Rupen Janjigian. LC 46-19795. 1946. Printed by the Telegraph Press.
Doctor Died at Dusk. Daniel Mainwaring. LC 36-211892. 1936. W. Morrow & Co.
Doctor Disagrees. Elizabeth Seifert. LC 52-141597. 1953. Dodd, Mead.
Doctor Disagrees. Elizabeth Seifert. LC 78-791626. 1974. 6.95. Aeonian Press.
Doctor Dispachemquic: A Story of the Great Southern Plague of 1878. James Dugan. LC 6-346329. 1879. Clark & Hofeline.
Doctor Dna. Nick Carter. 224p. 1982. pap. 2.50 (ISBN 0-441-15676-2, Pub. by Charter Bks). Ace Bks.
Dr. Dodd's School. James Lauren Ford. 1901. International Association of Newspapers and Authors.
Doctor Dogbody's Leg. James Norman Hall. LC 40-9696. 1940. Little, Brown and Company.
Dr. Dumany's Wife: Or, "There Is No Devil," a Romance. Mor Jokai. Tr. by Steinitz, Mme, F. LC 7-12144. (On cover: Cassell's sunshine series. no. 111). 1892. Cassell Publishing Company.
Dr. Dumont. Florence Gilmore. LC 11-12266. 1911. 0.50. B. Herder.
Dr. Ebenezer's Book & Liquor Store. Gerald Rosen. 1980. 8.95 o.p. (ISBN 0-312-21479-0). St Martin.

Dr. Ebenzer's Book and Liquor Store. Gerald Rosen. LC 79-26747. 8.95 (ISBN 0-312-21479-0). St. Martin's Press.

Dr. Ellen. Juliet Wilbor Tompkins. LC 8-2613. 1908. The Baker & Taylor Company.

Doctor Ellison's Decision. Elizabeth Seifert. LC 73-79144. 1973. 5.95. Aeonian Press.

Doctor Ellison's Decision. Elizabeth Seifert. LC 44-826210. 1944. Dodd, Mead & Comapny.

Dr. Endicott's Experiment. Adeline Sergeant. (On cover: The "unknown" library no. 38). The Cassell Publishing Co.

Dr. Erica Werner. H. G. Gunther. (H. G. Gunther Ser.: No. 4). 224p. 1981. pap. 1.95 (ISBN 0-515-05673-1). Jove Pubns.

Dr. Falke of Harley Street. Sidney Herbert Daukes. LC 33-6480. 1933. H. C. Kinsey & Company, Inc.

Dr. Faustus. Christopher Marlowe. Ed. by Rossell H. Robbins. 1948. pap. text ed. 2.25 (ISBN 0-8120-0055-2). Barron.

Doctor Faustus: The Life of the German Composer, Adrian Leverkuhn, As Told by a Friend. Thomas Mann. Tr. by Helen Tracy Lowe. LC 48-8940. 1948. A. A. Knopf.

Dr. Feel Good. Joseph Nazel. 1978. 1.75 (ISBN 0-87067-533-8). Holloway House Pub. Co.

Dr. Fell, Detective: And Other Stories. John Dickson Carr & Queen, Ellery, Pseud., Ed. LC 47-4656. (Mercury mystery). 1947. The American Mercury.

Dr. Finlay Sees It Through. Alan Hart. LC 42-15038. 1942. Harper & Brothers.

Doctor Fischer of Geneva: Or, The Bomb Party. Graham Greene. LC 80-10314. 11.95 (ISBN 0-671-25467-7) (ISBN 0-671-25547-9). Simon and Schuster.

Doctor Flame. Frank R. Wallace. 1971. 6.95 o.p. (ISBN 0-911752-12-9). I & O Pub.

Doctor Fogg. Norman Haghejm Matson. LC 29-16770. 1929. The Macmillan Company.

Doctor for Barbara: By Margaret Howe Pseud. Margaretta Brucker. LC 56-137858. 1956. Avalon Books.

Doctor for Blue Jay Cove. Elizabeth Seifert. LC 56-8361. 1956. Dodd, Mead.

Doctor for Blue Jay Cove. Elizabeth Seifert. LC 73-79149. 1973. 5.95. Aeonian Press.

Doctor for the Dead. Margaret Higgins. 1976. (pbk.) 1.25. Ace Books.

Doctor for the Nurse. Jeanne Judson. LC 54-12600. 1954. Avalon Books.

Doctor Fram. Scobie Mackenzie. 1933. E. P. Dutton & Co., Inc.

Doctor Frigo. Eric Ambler. LC 74-77836. 1974. 8.95 (ISBN 0-689-10609-2). Atheneum.

Doctor Frigo. Eric Ambler. 1976. (pbk.) 1.75. Bantam Books.

Doctor from Cordova: A Biographical Novel About the Great Philosopher Maimonides. Herbert Le Porrier. LC 77-16930. 8.95 (ISBN 0-385-11472-9). Doubleday.

Doctor from Iowa. A Novel. George John Zaffiras. LC 49-9737. 1949. Beechhurst Press.

Doctor from Lhasa. Rampa T. Lobsang. LC 60-8079. Saucerian Books.

Doctor from Lhasa. T. Rampa. pap. 2.95. Weiser.

Dr. Galen's Dilemma. Ruth Burnett. 1976. 4.95. Avalon Books.

Doctor Game: A Novel. Howard A. Olgin. LC 77-20032. 8.95 (ISBN 0-397-01246-2). Lippincott.

Doctor Game: A Novel. Howard A. Olgin. (Dell Book). 1979. 2.50 (ISBN 0-440-12006-3). Dell Publishing Co.

Dr. Gatskill's Blue Shoes. Paul Conant. LC 52-6925. 1952. A. A. Wyn.

Doctor Gion: A Novel. Hans Carossa. Tr. by Scott, Agnes Neill. LC 38-30997. 1933. R. O. Ballou.

Doctor Giovanni: A Novel. Arturo Vivante. LC 69-16966. 1969. 5.95. Little, Brown.

Doctor Glas. Hjalmar Soderberg. (O.s.i.). 1969. pap. 0.60 o.s.i. (A508X, Award). Univ Pub & Dist.

Dr. Glazebrook's Revenge. Andrew Cassels Brown. LC 28-13909. 1928. Dodd, Mead & Company.

Doctor Goodcome. Rosemary Santini. 1971. pap. 1.75 o.p. (ISBN 0-447-79306-3). Lancer.

Dr. Gould: Er, Souls in Despair and The Story of a Criminal. Peter L Bordonaro. LC 26-10317. The Christopher Publishing House.

Dr. Graesler. Arthur Schnitzler. LC 70-175575. 1971. (ISBN 0-404-05618-0). AMS Press.

Dr. Graesler. Arthur Schnitzler. Tr. by Slade, E. C. LC 23-17113. 1923. T. Seltzer.

Dr. Graesler. Arthur Schnitzler. Tr. by Slade, E. C. LC 31-6381. 1930. Simon and Schuster.

Dr. Grass. Grania Davis. LC 77-95097. 1978. 1.75 (ISBN 0-380-01872-1). Avon.

Doctor Grattan. A Novel. William Alexander Hammond. LC 7-561. 1885. D. Appleton and Company.

Doctor Gray's Quest. Francis Henry Underwood. LC 8-32286. 1895. Lee and Shepard.

Doctor Grimshawe's Secret. Nathaniel Hawthorne. LC 52-5392. (Illus.). 1954. Harvard University Press.

Doctor Grimshawe's Secret: A Romance. Nathaniel Hawthorne & Hawthorne, Julian, 1846-1934, Ed. LC 4-18326. 1883. J. R. Osgood and Company.

Doctor Grimshawe's Secret: A Romance. Nathaniel Hawthorne & Hawthorne, Julian, 1846-1934, Ed. LC 9-829. 1884. J. R. Osgood and Company.

Dr. Gulley's Story. Elizabeth Jenkins. (Dell, 2022). 1973. 1.50. Dell.

Dr. Gully's Story. Elizabeth Jenkins. LC 76-179030. 1971. 7.95. Coward, McCann & Geoghegan.

Doctor Happy. Bertha B. Moore McCurry. LC 38-16867. 1938. Wm. B. Eerdmans Publishing Company.

Doctor Hathern's Daughters. A Story of Virginia, in Four Parts. Mary Jane Hawes Holmes. (On cover: Mary J. Holmes' novels). 1895. G. W. Dillingham, Successor to G. W. Carleton & Co.

Dr. Heart: A Novella and Other Stories. Eleanor Clark. LC 74-4754. 1974. 7.95 (ISBN 0-394-49411-3). Pantheon Books.

Dr. Heidegger's Experiment: The Birthmark, Ethan Brand, Wakefield, Drowne's Wooden Image, The Ambitious Guest, The Great Stone Face, The Gray Champion. Nathaniel Hawthorne. LC 7-3877. (Half-title: Little masterpieces). 1897. Doubleday, McClure & Co.

Doctor Heidenhoff's Process. Edward Ballamy. LC 72-84878. (Illus.). 1969. AMS Press.

Dr. Heidenhoff's Process. Edward Bellamy. LC 6-11697. (On cover: Appletons' new handy-volume series v. 54). 1880. D. Appleton and Company.

Doctor Heidenhoff's Process. Edward Bellamy. LC 72-84878. (BCL Ser. I). 1969. Repr. of 1880 ed. 15.00 (ISBN 0-404-00734-1). AMS Pr.

Doctor Helen Rand. Lucy Waite. LC 8-32823. 1891. The Physicians' Publishing Company.

Doctor Hildreth. A Romance. Alfred Ludlow White. 1880. J. B. Lippincott & Co.

Doctor, His Wife and the Clock. Anna Katharine Green Rohlfs. (Half-title: The autonym library, no. 3). 1895. G. P. Putnam's Sons.

Doctor Hudson's Secret Journal. Lloyd Cassel Douglas. LC 39-279756. 1939. Houghton Mifflin Company.

Dr. Hudson's Secret Journey. Lloyd C. Douglas. 2.95 o.p. (ISBN 0-448-01201-4). G&D.

Doctor Huguet. Ignatius Donnelly. LC 75-92230. (American Negro, His History and Literature). 1969. Arno Press.

Doctor Huguet: A Novel. Ignatius Donnelly. LC 6-33726. F. J. Schulte & Company.

Dr. I. R. T. Louise Stickney Tanner. LC 75-46634. 8.95 (ISBN 0-698-10730-6). Coward, McCann & Geoghegan.

Doctor in a Dark Land: A Story of Missions in Africa. Alan Livingstone Wilson. LC 64-22838. bds., 2.50. Zondervan.

Doctor in Buckskin. T. D. Allen, pseud. 1951. Harper.

Doctor in Clover: By Richard Gordon Pseud. 1st Ed. Gordon Ostlere. LC 60-5941. 1960. Doubleday.

Doctor in Court. Abram Stilman. 1968. 5.95 o.s.i. Fountainhead.

Doctor in Court: A Novel. Abram Stilman. LC 66-30455. 1967. 5.95. Fountainhead Pubs.

Doctor in Judgement. Elizabeth Seifert. 1972. pap. 0.95 o.p. (95238). Beagle Bks.

Doctor in Judgment. Elizabeth Seifert. LC 70-143286. 1971. 5.95 (ISBN 0-396-06307-1). Dodd, Mead.

Doctor in Love. Elizabeth Seifert. LC 75-30979. 1975. 11.95 (ISBN 0-8161-6335-9). G. K. Hall.

Doctor in Love. Elizabeth Seifert. LC 74-7770. 1974. 5.95 (ISBN 0-396-06995-9). Dodd, Mead.

Doctor in Love: By Richard Gordon Pseud. 1st Ed. Gordon Ostlere. LC 57-950955. 1958. Doubleday.

Doctor in the Dark. easy eye ed. Carol Gaye, pseud. 1969. pap. 0.60 o.p. (73-821). Lancer.

Doctor in the Family. Elizabeth Seifert. LC 55-646835. 1955. Dodd, Mead.

Doctor in the Family. Elizabeth Seifert. LC 73-791678. 1974. 6.95. Aeonian Press.

Doctor in the Jungle. Alan Livingstone Wilson. LC 60-36410. 1960. Zondervan Pub. House.

Doctor in Ward B. Jean Francis. 1978. pap. 1.50 (ISBN 0-532-15320-0). Woodhill.

Doctor in Ward B. Jean Francis. (Orig.). 1972. pap. 0.95 o.s.i. (75-276). Lancer.

Dr. Inrahim: A Biographical Novel. John Knittel. LC 35-23923. 1935. Frederick. A. Stokes Company.

Doctor Is a Lady. Mary M. Fletcher. pap. 0.75 o.s.i. (01-401). Lancer.

Doctor Is Born. Wallace Dalton Chesney. 1958.

Doctor Is Sick. Anthony Burgess. LC 79-21327. 1979. 3.95 (ISBN 0-393-00959-9). Norton.

Doctor Is Sick. John Anthony Burgess Wilson. LC 65-25931. 1966. Norton.

Doctor Izard. Anna Katharine Green Rohlfs. LC 7-407402. 1895. G. P. Putnam's Sons.

Doctor Jack. A Novel. St. George Rathborne. LC 8-579. (Primrose edition, no. 3). 1890. Street & Smith.

Doctor Jack's Wife. A Novel. St. George Rathborne. LC 8-581. (On cover: Primrose series, no. 33). 1893. Street & Smith.

Doctor Jacob. Matilda Barbara Bertram Edwards. (Half-title: Handy volume ser. no. 2). 1869. Roberts Brothers.

Doctor Jacob. Matilda Barbara Bertram Edwards. (On cover: Seaside library. Pocket ed. no. 594). 1885. G. Munro.

Doctor Jane. Adeline McElfresh. LC 55-14015. 1954. Avalon Books.

Dr. Jane Come Home. Adeline McElfresh. (O.s.i.). 1976. pap. 0.95 o.s.i. (BT50952). Belmont-Tower.

Dr. Jekyl & Mr. Hyde. Robert L. Stevenson. Incl. Merrymen & Other Tales. 1954. 10.50x o.p. (ISBN 0-460-00767-X, Evman); pap. 4.50 o.p. (ISBN 0-460-01767-5). Biblio Dist.

Dr. Jekyll and Mr. Holmes. Loren D Estleman. LC 78-22811. 1979. 8.95 (ISBN 0-385-15257-4). Doubleday.

Dr. Jekyll and Mr. Holmes. Loren D Estleman. LC 80-11325. 1980. 2.95 (ISBN 0-14-005665-3). Penguin Books.

Dr. Jekyll & Mr. Hyde. Robert Louis Stevenson. (Illus.). 1976. lib. bdg. 11.50x (ISBN 0-88411-994-7). Amereon Ltd.

Dr. Jekyll & Mr. Hyde. Robert Louis Stevenson. (Bantam Classics Ser.). 128p. (Orig.). (gr. 7-12). 1981. pap. text ed. 1.95 (ISBN 0-553-21045-9). Bantam.

Dr. Jekyll & Mr. Hyde. Robert Louis Stevenson. (Incl. biography). (gr. 7-12,RL 8). pap. 2.95 (ISBN 0-553-14614-9). Bantam.

Doctor Jekyll & Mr. Hyde. Robert Louis Stevenson. Ed. by Harry Shefter. (Enriched Classics Edition Ser.). 176p. pap. 2.25 (ISBN 0-671-48957-7). WSP.

Doctor Jekyll & Mister Hyde see Stories of the Double.

Dr. Jekyll & Mr. Hyde & Other Tales. new ed. Robert Louis Stevenson. 1976. pap. 0.95 o.p. (ISBN 0-89319-011-X). Andor Pub.

Dr. Jekyll & Mr. Hyde & Other Stories. Robert Louis Stevenson. Ed. by Jenni Calder. (English Library). 1981. pap. 2.95 (ISBN 0-14-005776-5). Penguin.

Dr. Jekyll and Mr. Hyde: & The Merry Men. Robert Louis Stevenson. (Half-title: Everyman's library, ed. by Ernest Rhys. Fiction. no. 767). 1925. J. M. Dent & Sons, Ltd.

Dr. Jekyll and Mr. Hyde & The Suicide Club. Robert Louis Stevenson. LC 64-14043. (Arco juvenile library). (Illus.). 1964. Arco Pub. Co.

Dr. Jekyll and Mr. Hyde: The Merry Men & Other Tales. Robert Louis Stevenson. LC 36-37485. (Half-title: Everyman's library, ed. by Ernest Rhys. Fiction. no. 767). 1932. J. M. Dent & Sons, Ltd.

Doctor Jeremiah. Morris Markey. LC 50-9217. 1950. Dial Press.

Dr. Jeremy's Wife. Elizabeth Seifert. LC 61-15977. 1961. Dodd, Mead.

Dr. Jeremy's Wife. Elizabeth Seifert. LC 73-79181. 1974. 5.95. Aeonian Press.

Dr. Jerry. Peggy Gaddis, pseud. LC 51-5443. 1951. Arcadia House.

Doctor Jim. Margaretta Brucker. LC 49-8613. 1949. Gramercy Pub. Co.

Doctor Joanna. Robert N Webb. LC 36-10118. Arcadia House.

Doctor Joel. Watkins Eppes Wright. LC 45-4051. 1945. Arcadia House, Inc.

Doctor Johns: Being a Narrative of Certain Events in the Life of an Orthodox Minister of Connecticut. Donald Grant Mitchell. 1866. C. Scribner and Company.

Doctor Johns: Being a Narrative of Certain Events in the Life of an Orthodox Minister of Connecticut. new and rev. ed. Donald Grant Mitchell. 1884. C. Scribner's Sons.

Dr. John's Decision. Dorothy Worley. LC 58-7586. 1958. Avalon Books.

Dr. Johnson's "Dear Mistress.". Winifred Carter. LC 50-269472. 1949. Selwyn and Blount.

Doctor Jones' Picnic. Samuel E Chapman. LC 6-23120. The Whitaker & Ray Co.

Doctor Judas. William Rosser Cobbe. LC 80-1218. (Addiction in America). 1981. 29.00 (ISBN 0-405-13574-2). Arno Press.

Doctor Judas. A Portrayal of the Opium Habit. William Rosser Cobbe. 1895. S. C. Griggs and Company.

Dr. Katherine Bell. Evelyn Harter. LC 50-8001. 1950. Doubleday.

Doctor Kerkhoven. Jakob Wassermann. 5.95 o.p. Tudor.

Doctor Kerkhoven. Jakob Wassermann & Brooks, Cyrus Harry, 1890- Tr. LC 32-3192. H. Liveright, Inc.

Dr. Kilbourne Comes Home. Dorothy Worley. LC 54-13266. 1954. Avalon Books.

Dr. Kildare Crisis. Max Brand. 1972. pap. 0.95 o.p. (95276). Beagle Bks.

Dr. Kildare Takes Charge. Max Brand. LC 41-16056. 1941. Dodd, Mead & Company.

Dr. Kildare's Crisis. Frederick Faust. LC 42-2418. 1942. Dodd, Mead & Company.

Dr. Kildare's Search. Max Brand. 1972. pap. 0.95 o.p. (95277). Beagle Bks.

Dr. Kildare's Search and Dr. Kildare's Hardest Case. Frederick Faust. LC 43-985. 1943. Dodd, Mead & Company.

Dr. Kildare's Trial. Max Brand. 174p. Repr. of 1941 ed. lib. bdg. 11.50x (ISBN 0-88411-532-1). Amereon Ltd.

Dr. Kildare's Trial. Max Brand. 1981. 18.95x (Pub. by Remploy England). State Mutual Bk.

Dr. Kildare's Trial. Max Brand. 1972. pap. 0.95 o.p. (95255). Beagle Bks.

Dr. Kildare's Trial. Frederick Faust. LC 42-19430. 1942. Dodd, Mead & Company.

Doctor Kim. Lucy Agnes Hancock. LC 47-31344. 1947. Macrae-Smtih Co.

Dr. Krasinski's Secret. Matthew Phipps Shiel. LC 29-208899. The Vanguard Press.

Doctor Lamar... Elizabeth Phipps Train. T. Y. Crowell & Co.

Dr. Latimer: A Story of Casco Bay. Clara Louise Root Burnham. LC 4-15075. 1893. Houghton, Mifflin and Company.

Doctor Laughs the Doctor Cries. Eric James. (Orig.). 1979. pap. text ed. 3.95 (ISBN 0-912522-69-0). Aero-Medical.

Dr. Laurie's Conquest. Berta LaVan Barker. (YA) 1980. 6.95 (Avalon). Bouregy.

Dr. Lavendar's People. Margaret Wade Campbell Deland. LC 70-90102. (Illus.). 1969. AMS Press.

Dr. Lavendar's People. Margaret Wade Campbell Deland. LC 75-113656. (Short story index reprint series). (Illus.). 1970. Books for Libraries Press.

Dr. Lavendar's People. Margaret Wade Campbell Deland. LC 77-129345. (Illus.). 1970. Scholarly Press.

Dr. Lavendar's People. Margaret Wade Campbell Deland. LC 3-25718. 1903. Harper & Brothers.

Doctor Lavendar's People. Margaret Wade Campbell Deland. Ed. by Clarence Gohdes. LC 69-11888. (American Short Story Ser. Vol. 46). (Illus.). 1969. Repr. of 1903 ed. lib. bdg. 18.25 o.s.i. (ISBN 0-512-00144-8). Garrett Pr.

Doctor, Lawyer... Collin Wilcox. LC 76-47844. 1977. 6.95 (ISBN 0-394-40061-5). Random House.

Dr. Le Baron and His Daughter. A Story of the Old Colony. Jane Goodwin Austin. LC 6-5043. 1890. Houghton, Mifflin and Company.

Dr. Le Baron and His Daughters: A Story of the Old Colony. Jane Goodwin Austin. LC 4-16450. 1901. Houghton, Mifflin and Company.

Dr. Livingstone, I Presume' Henry M. Stanley's Search for David Livingstone in the Jungles of Africa. Harry James Albus. LC 57-13034. 1957. W. B. Eerdmans Pub. Co.

Dr. Llewellyn and His Friends. Caroline Abbot Stanley. LC 14-15790. Fleming H. Revell Company.

Doctor Lochinvar. Jean Carew. pap. 0.75 o.s.i. (01-333). Lancer.

Dr. Logan's Wife. Diana Gaines. LC 51-13243. 1951. Random House.

Doctor Love. Gael Greene. LC 81-21553. 1982. 13.95 (ISBN 0-312-21486-3). St. Martin's Press.

Doctor Luke of the Labrador. Norman Duncan. LC 4-31009. 1904. F. H. Revell Company.

Doctor Luke of the Labrador. Norman Duncan. LC 34-110413. Fleming H. Revell Company.

Doctor Luttrell's First Patient. Rosa Nouchette Carey. 1897. J. B. Lippincott Company.

Doctor Make Love. Danny Land. (Orig.). pap. 0.95 o.p. (1145). Brandon.

Doctor Makes a Choice. Elizabeth Seifert. LC 61-716861. 1961. Dodd, Mead.

Doctor Makes a Choice. Elizabeth Seifert. LC 73-79180. 1974. 6.95. Aeonian Press.

Doctor Mallory. Alan Hart. LC 35-4041. W. W. Norton & Company, Inc.

Doctor Marigold. Two Ghost Stories. The Boy at Mugby. The Seven Poor Travellers. Charles Dickens. LC 6-35894. (On cover: Lovell's library, v. 5, no. 237). 1883. J. W. Lovell Company.

Dr. Marks, Socialist. Marion Couthouy Smith. LC 8-9617. 1897. The Editor Publishing Co.

Doctor Martino and Other Stories. William Faulkner. LC 34-9404. 1934. H. Smith and R. Haas.

Dr. Mary. Jeanne Judson. (Avalon nurse stories). 1964. Avalon Books.

Dr. Meeksneeker & the Bareground Jumper. William Morris. 3.95 o.p. Vantage.

Dr. Merry's Husband. Peggy Gaddis, pseud. LC 47-11776. 1947. Arcadia House.

Doctor Merry's Husband. Peggy Gaddis, pseud. 1970. pap. 0.50 o.p. (50-497). Manor Bks.

Dr. Mirabel's Theory. A Psychological Study. Frederic Henry Balfour. LC 6-6325. (On cover: Harper's Franklin square library, no. 739). 1893. Harper & Brothers.

Dr. Mirabilis. James Blish. 272p. 1982. pap. 2.95 (ISBN 0-380-60335-7, 60335-7). Avon.

Doctor Mirabilis: A Novel. James Blish. LC 79-147136. 1971. 6.95 (ISBN 0-396-06325-X). Dodd, Mead.

Dr. Monte Cristo. Irwin Philip Sobel. LC 77-82773. 1978. 8.95 (ISBN 0-385-12085-0). Doubleday.

Doctor Moon. Catherine Meadows. LC 35-2732. G. P. Putnam's Sons.

Dr. Moore's Legacy. Agnes Brooks Young. LC 73-2316. 1973. 7.95 (ISBN 0-671-21510-8). Simon and Schuster.

Doctor Morath. Max Rene Hesse. Tr. by Crankshaw, Edward. LC 36-40290. 1936. Houghton Mifflin Company.

Dr. Morel. Karen Adler Bramson. LC 27-27963. 1927. Greenberg.

Dr. Morgan. Paul Renard. LC 10-20603. The C. M. Clark Publishing Company.

Dr. Mortimer's Patient. A Novel. Fannie Bean. LC 6-10271. 1878. G.W. Carleton & Co.

Dr. Myra Comes Home. Arlene Hale. (Candlelight Romance, 200). 0.95. Dell.

Dr. Nicholas Stone. Edward Spence De Puy. LC 5-5927. 1905. G. W. Dillingham Company.

Dr. Nick. L M Steele. LC 16-26998. 1.40. Small, Maynard & Company.

Dr. Nikola. Guy Newell Boothby. LC 6-15033. (Half-title: Appletons' town and country library, no. 197). 1896. D. Appleton and Company.

Dr. Nikola Returns. Guy Newell Boothby. LC 80-22358. (Dr. Nikola, master of occult mystery; 2). 1980. 9.95 (ISBN 0-89370-634-5). Borgo Press.

Dr. Nikola Returns: Former Title, Dr. Nikola. Guy Newell Boothby. LC 76-5826. (His Dr. Nikola, master of occult mystery; 2). (Illus.). 1976. 2.95 (ISBN 0-87877-034-8). Newcastle Pub. Co.

Dr. Nikola's Experiment. Guy Newell Boothby. LC 99-2203. 1899. D. Appleton and Company.

Doctor No. Ian Fleming. pap. 3.95 fr. ed; pap. 2.95 span. ed. French & Eur.

Doctor No. Ian Fleming. 240p. 1982. pap. 2.75 (ISBN 0-425-05365-2). Berkley Pub.

Doctor No. Ian Fleming. 1966. 3.95 o.p. (53888). Macmillan.

Doctor No: Reissue. Ian Fleming. LC 66-51. 1966. bds., 3.95. Macmillan.

Dr. North and His Friends. Silas Weir Mitchell. 1900. The Century Co.

Dr. Norton's Wife. Mildred Walker, pseud. LC 38-290391. Harcourt, Brace and Company.

Dr. Norton's Wife. Mildred Walker, pseud. LC 40-11819. 1940. The Sun Dial Press.

Doctor Nye of North Ostable: A Novel. Joseph Crosby Lincoln. LC 23-12002. 1923. D. Appleton and Company.

Doctor Nyet. 2nd ed. Ted Mark, pseud. 1968. pap. 0.75 o.p. (73-477). Lancer.

Dr. Nyet. Ted Mark. (Man from O.R.G.Y.). 1973. (pbk.) 1.25. Dell.

Doctor of Deane. Mary Towle Palmer. LC 7-35773. D. Lothrop Company.

Doctor of Lonesome River. Edison Marshall. LC 31-678539. 1931. Cosmopolitan Book Corporation.

Doctor of Mercy. Elizabeth Seifert. LC 51-13050. 1951. Dodd, Mead.

Doctor of Mercy. Elizabeth Seifert. LC 73-79159. 1973. 6.95. Aeonian Press.

Doctor of Philosophy: A Novel. Cyrus Townsend Brady. LC 3-21723. 1903. C. Scribner's Sons.

Doctor of Pimlico: Being the Disclosure of a Great Crime. William Le Queux. LC 20-270. 1919. Cassell and Company, Ltd.

Doctor of Pimlico: Being the Disclosure of a Great Crime. William Le Queux. LC 20-1211. The Macaulay Company.

Doctor of the Hills. Mary Sydney Burk. (Avalon Books). 4.95. Thomas Bouregyc.

Doctor of the Isles. Helen Murray. (Orig.). 1981. pap. 1.75 (ISBN 0-8439-8026-5, Tiara Bks). Nordon Pubns.

Doctor of the Old School. John Watson. LC 8-36759. 1895. Dodd, Mead & Company.

Doctor on Bean Street: By Simon Kent Pseud. Max Catto. LC 52-10376. 1952. Crowell.

Doctor on Elm Street. Cateau De Leeuw. LC 48-106026. 1948. Triangle Books.

Doctor on Elm Street. Cateau De Leeuw. LC 46-4288. 1946. Macrae-Smith-Company.

Doctor on Toast: By Richard Gordon Pseud. 1st Ed. Gordon Ostlere. 1961. Doubleday.

Doctor on Trial. Elizabeth Seifert. LC 59-13633. 1959. Dodd, Mead.

Doctor on Trial. Elizabeth Seifert. LC 73-79177. 1974. 5.95. Aeonian Press.

Doctor on Trial. Hillary Waugh. (Dell Book). 1977. 1.95. Dell Pub. Co.

Doctor on Wings. Maysie Greig. 1973. pap. 0.75 o.p. (94344). Beagle Bks.

Doctor Onan. Jon Horn. pap. 1.95 o.s.i. (OPS-7). Olympia.

Dr. Orpheus; a Downtime Myth. Ian Wallace. LC 68-25464. 1968. 4.95. Putnam.

Doctor Ox, and Other Stories. authorized ed. Jules Verne & Towle, George Makepeace, 1841-1893, Tr. LC 2-8389. 1874. J. R. Osgood and Company.

Dr. Ox's Experiment. Jules Verne. LC 63-8179. 1963. Macmillan.

Dr. Ox's Experiment: Drama in the Air. Jules Verne. Repr. lib. bdg. 10.60x (ISBN 0-88411-915-7). Amereon Ltd.

Dr. Parrish, Resident. Sydney Thompson. LC 44-5218. 1944. Macrae-Smith-Company.

Doctor Pascal. Emile Zola & Serrano, Mrs. Mary Jane (Christie) D. 1923, Tr. LC 9-1332. (On cover: Cassell's sunshine series. no. 145). 1893. Cassell Publishing Company.

Doctor Pascal. Emile Zola & Serrano, Mrs. Mary Jane (Christie) Tr. LC 98-205. 1898. The Macmillan Company.

Doctor Pascal. Emile Zola & Serrano, Mrs. Mary Jane (Christie) D. 1923, Tr. LC 22-5143. 1901. International Association of Newspapers and Authors.

Doctor Pascal. Tr. from French by Vladimir Kean. Introd. by Hugh Shelley. Emile Zola. 1963. 3.95. Elek Bks. Dist. Chester Springs, Pa., Dufour.

Dr. Paul McKim. Thomas Sawyer Spivey. LC 8-4911. 1908. The Neale Publishing Company.

Dr. Paul's Theory: A Romance. Alice Mangold Diehl. LC 6-36832. (On cover: Appleton's town and country library, no. 112). 1893. D. Appleton and Company.

Dr. Perdue. Stinson Jarvis. LC 7-10346. (On cover: Laird & Lee's prive novels, no. 2). 1892. Laird & Lee.

Dr. Phibes. William Goldstein. (Orig.). 1971. pap. 0.75 o.p. (A869S, Award). Univ Pub & Dist.

Dr. Phibes Rises Again. 160p. (Orig.). 1973. pap. 0.95 o.p. (AN1069, Award). Univ Pub & Dist.

Dr. Phibes Rises Again. William Goldstein. (O.s.i.). (Orig.). 1972. pap. 0.95 o.s.i. (AN1069, Award). Univ Pub & Dist.

Doctor Phoenix Skelton: Or, The Man with a Mystery. Seth S. Wood. LC 8-37545. S. S. Wood.

Dr. Priestley Investigates: A Detective Story. Cecil John Charles Street. LC 30-27756. 1930. Dodd, Mead & Co.

Dr. Priestley Lays a Trap. Cecil John Charles Street. LC 33-1633. 1933. Dodd, Mead & Company.

Dr. Rameau. Georges Ohnet. Tr. by Curtin, J. C. LC 7-32510. 1889. Rand, McNally & Company.

Doctor Rameau. (Le Docteur Rameau) A Novel, by Georges Ohnet. Georges Ohnet. Tr. by Bramwell, Remington. (On cover: The world library, no. 1). 1889. The Waverly Company.

Doctor Rast. James Oppenheim. LC 9-24254. 1909. 1.50. Sturgis & Walton Company.

Doctor Rat. William Kotzwinkle. LC 75-36803. 1976. 7.95 (ISBN 0-394-40080-1). Knopf: Distributed by Random House.

Dr. Ray. Barry Hannah. LC 80-11195. 1980. 7.95 (ISBN 0-394-50972-2). Knopf: Distributed by Random House.

Doctor Red. Thelma Thompson. LC 41-15457. 1941. Arcadia House, Inc.

Doctor Regina: A Novel. Ann Christine Schaefer. LC 78-56581. 6.98. P & A Quill Press.

Doctor Ricardo. William A Garrett. LC 25-118221. 1925. D. Appleton and Company.

Dr. Rocksinger and the Age of Longing: A Novel. Jill Robinson. LC 81-47522. 1981. 12.95 (ISBN 0-394-50951-X). Knopf.

Dr. Rocksinger & the Age of Longing. Jill Robinson. LC 81-47522. 384p. 1982. 13.95 (ISBN 0-394-50951-X). Knopf.

Dr. Roger's Ordeal. Homer Avera. J. H. Hopkins, Inc.

Dr. Rumsey's Patient: A Very Strange Story. Elizabeth Thomasina Meade Smith & Halifax, Clifford, Joint Author. LC 8-8646. The International News Company.

Doctor S. O. S. Lee Thayer. LC 25-919319. 1925. Doubleday, Page & Company.

Dr. Salaam & Other Stories of India. Perera, Padma, Hejmadi. LC 78-23231. 1978. 3.95 (ISBN 0-88496-089-7). Capra Press.

Doctor Sally. Pelham Grenville Wodehouse. 1952. 2.75 o.p. Verry.

Dr. Sam; Johnson, Detector: Being a Light-Hearted Collection of Recently Reveal'd Episodes in the Career of the Great Lexicographer Narrated As from the Pen of James Boswell... Lillian De La Torre, pseud. LC 46-654742. 1946. A. A. Knopf.

Doctor Samaritan. Elizabeth Seifert. LC 65-13918. 1965. Dodd, Mead.

Dr. Samaritan. Elizabeth Seifert. 1974. Repr. of 1965 ed. lib. bdg. 15.45x (ISBN 0-88411-052-4). Amereon Ltd.

Dr. Sara's Vigil. Ruth McCarthy Sears. (Avalon Books). 4.95. Thomas Bouregy.

Doctor Sax. John Kerouac. 245p. 1976. lib. bdg. 14.95x (ISBN 0-89966-133-5). Buccaneer Bks.

Dr. Sax. John Kerouac. 1959. pap. 3.95 (ISBN 0-394-17278-7, B394, BC). Grove.

Doctor Sax; Faust Part Three. John Kerouac. LC 59-9806. 1959. Grove Press.

Dr. Scarlett: A Narrative of His Mysterious Behavior in the East. Alexander Kinnan Laing. LC 36-17947. Farrar & Rinehart, Incorporated.

Dr. Scott: Surgeon on Call. Elizabeth Seifert. 1974. Repr. of 1963 ed. lib. bdg. 14.10x (ISBN 0-88411-049-4). Amereon Ltd.

Doctor Serocold: A Page from His Day-Book. Helen Ashton. LC 30-18555. 1930. Doubleday, Doran and Company, Inc.

Dr. Serocold: A Page from His Day-Book. Helen Ashton. LC 34-37777. 1932. Grosset & Dunlap.

Doctor Sevier. George W. Cable. Ed. by Donald Pizer. LC 74-96489. (American Authors Ser. - Collected Works of George Washington Cable). 1970. Repr. of 1884 ed. lib. bdg. 23.75 o.s.i. (ISBN 0-512-00069-7). Garrett Pr.

Dr. Sevier. George Washington Cable. LC 72-84527. 1974. (lib. ed.) 18.50 (ISBN 0-403-02954-6). Scholarly Press.

Dr. Sevier. George Washington Cable. LC 74-96489. (Works of George W. Cable). 1970. Garrett Press.

Dr. Sevier. George Washington Cable. LC 6-22246. 1885. J. R. Osgood and Company.

Dr. Sevier. George Washington Cable. LC 4-15423. 1902. C. Scribner's Sons.

Dr. Sevier. George Washington Cable. LC 16-6393. 1913. C. Scribner's Sons.

Doctor Sevier see Collected Works.

Dr. Sexy: Or Professor Theobald's Search for the Spark of Electric Ecstasy. Max DeGrundy. 1974. (pbk.) 1.25. Warner Paperback Library.

Doctor Sphinx: A Novel. Caroline C Walch. LC 8-32819. F. T. Neely.

Dr. Strangelove. Peter Bryan George. LC 79-12237. (Gregg Press science fiction series). (Illus.). 1979. 11.00 (ISBN 0-8398-2475-0). Gregg Press.

Dr. Strangelove: Or How I Learned to Stop Worrying and Love the Bomb. Peter Bryan George & Stanley. Dr. Strangelove Kubrick. LC 63-15229. 1964. Bantam Books.

Dr. Suess' Lost World Revisited. Dr. Suess. (O.s.i.). (Orig.). pap. 0.75 o.s.i. (A253, Award). Univ Pub & Dist.

Doctor Syn: A Smuggler Tale of the Romney Marsh. Arthur Russell Thorndike. LC 15-4857. 1915. Doubleday, Page & Company.

Dr. Syn on the High Seas. Arthur Russell Thorndike. (His. the Dr. Syn saga). 1973. (pbk.) 0.95. Ballantine.

Dr. Syn Returns. Russell Thorndyke. 1974. (pbk.) 0.95. Ballantine.

Doctor Takes a Wife. Rona Randall. LC 47-31072. 1947. Arcadia House.

Doctor Takes a Wife. Elizabeth Seifert. LC 52-10269. 1952. Dodd, Mead.

Doctor Takes a Wife. Elizabeth Seifert. LC 73-791614. 1974. 6.95. Aeonian Press.

Doctor Tam and Nurse Morton. Louise Logan. LC 42-2571. 1941. Arcadia House, Inc.

Dr. Tancred Begins: Or, The Pendexter Saga, First Canto Being an Early Episode in the Career of Dr. Benjamin Tancred, Detective, Related by His Friend Paul Graham. George Douglas Howard Cole & Margaret Isabel Postgate Cole. LC 35-14575. 1935. Pub. for the Crime Club, Inc., by Doubleday, Doran & Company, Inc.

Doctor Ted's Clinic. Jennifer Ames, pseud. 1971. pap. 0.75 o.p. (94134). Beagle Bks.

Dr. Temblor. new ed. Richard Sapir & Warren Murphy. Tr. by Margarita O. Castro from Eng. (Compadre Collection, el Destructor: No. 5). 160p. (Span.). 1974. pap. 0.85 (ISBN 0-88473-405-6). Fiesta Pub.

Doctor Therne. Henry Rider Haggard. LC 98-181823. 1898. Longmans, Green and Co.

Doctor Thinkright. Clarence Hawkes. LC 34-33873. Thomas Y. Crowell Company.

Dr. Thorndyke Intervenes. Richard Austin Freeman. LC 33-32224. 1933. Dodd, Mead & Company.

Dr. Thorndyke Omnibus: 38 of His Criminal Investigations. Richard Austin Freeman. LC 32-3421. 1932. Dodd, Mead & Company.

Dr. Thorndyke's Cases. Richard Austin Freeman. LC 31-26721. 1931. Dodd, Mead & Company.

Dr. Thorndyke's Crime File: A Selection of His Most Celebrated Cases, Containing, Also, Hitherto Unpublished Material About the Famous Detective and His Methods. Richard Austin Freeman. Ed. by Stone, Percival Mason. LC 41-1474. 1941. Dodd, Mead & Company.

Dr. Thorndyke's Dilemma. John H. Dirck & Richard Austin Freeman. LC 75-314343. (Illus.). 1974. 5.00. Aspen Press.

Dr. Thorndyke's Discovery. Richard Austin Freeman. LC 32-29497. 1932. Dodd, Mead & Company.

Doctor Thorne. Anthony Trollope. LC 59-3590. (Riverside editions, B43). 1959. Houghton Mifflin.

Doctor Thorne. Anthony Trollope. 1962. Harcourt, Brace & World.

Doctor Thorne. Anthony Trollope. LC 4-24964. (On cover: The chronicles of Barsetshire. iv). 1903. Dodd, Mead & Company.

Doctor Thorne. Anthony Trollope. LC 36-37171. (Half-title: Everyman's library, ed. by Ernest Rhys. Fiction. no. 360). 1930. J. M. Dent & Sons, Ltd.

Doctor Thorne. Anthony Trollope. LC 33-36727. (Half-title: The world's classics. 296). 1931. H. Milford, Oxford University Press.

Dr. Thorne. Anthony Trollope. 1978. Repr. of 1908 ed. 10.95x (ISBN 0-460-00360-7, Evman). Biblio Dist.

Dr. Thorne. Anthony Trollope. (Zodiac Press Ser.). 520p. 1978. 9.95 (ISBN 0-7011-1251-4, Pub. by Chatto Bodley Jonathan). Merrimack Pub Cir.

Doctor Thorne. Anthony Trollope & Thorold, Algar Labouchere, Ed. LC 12-394459. (The new pocket library, vol. III). 1902. John Lane.

Doctor Thorne. A Novel. Anthony Trollope. LC 8-28899. 1858. Harper & Brothers.

Doctor Thorne. A Novel. Anthony Trollope. LC 27-136902. (Seaside library. v. 59, no. 1206). 1882. G. Munro.

Dr. Thorne's Idea. Originally Published As "Gloria Victis". John Ames Mitchell. LC 10-13478. 1910. Life Publishing Company.

Dr. Thorne's Idea: Originally Published As "Gloria Victis,". John Ames Mitchell. LC 41-40516. (pocket books.). George H. Doran Company.

Dr. Time. Kenneth Robeson. (Avenger,#28). 1974. 0.95. Warner Paperback Library.

Doctor to the Stars. Murray Leinster. 1971. pap. 0.75 o.p. (T2367). Pyramid Pubns.

Dr. Toby Finds Murder. Sturges Mason Schley. LC 41-196143. Random House.

Doctor Tom. Peter Wingate. LC 58-5254. 1958. Morrow.

Dr. Tom Gardner: A Story from Life. Virginia Lynch. LC 1-29937. F. Tennyson Neely Co.

Doctor Tom: The Coroner of Brett. John Williams Streeter. 1904. The Macmillan Company.

Dr. Toni's Miracle. Ruth McCarthy Sears. (YA) 1972. 4.50 o.p. (Avalon). Bouregy.

Doctor Tony. Florence Stonebraker. LC 44-3450. 1944. Phoenix Press.

Doctor Transit. Isidor Schneider. LC 25-21767. 1925. Boni & Liveright.

Doctor Trouble. Florence Stonebraker. LC 40-32298. 1940. Phoenix Press.

Dr. Tuck. Elizabeth Seifert. LC 77-14328. 7.95 (ISBN 0-396-07498-7). Dodd, Mead.

Dr. Tuck. Elizabeth Seifert. LC 78-3821. 1978. 8.95 (ISBN 0-89340-147-1). J. Curley.

Dr. Tuppy. Stephen Townesend. LC 12-246861. 1912. Hodder and Stoughton.

Dr. Tuppy. Stephen Townesend. LC 31-35214. 1912.

Doctor Two-Guns. Peter Field. LC 50-8973. (Triple-A western classic). 1950. Jefferson House.

Doctor Two-Guns. Peter Field. LC 39-9036. W. Morrow & Co.

Doctor Upstairs. T. R. Torkelson. LC 70-103126. (Stories That Win Ser.). 64p. 1960. pap. 0.95 o.p. (ISBN 0-8163-0052-6, 04423-0). Pacific Pr Pub Assn.

Doctor Vago. Jordan Brotman. (O.s.i.). (Orig.). 1969. pap. 0.60 o.s.i. (A451X, Award). Univ Pub & Dist.

Doctor Vandyke. A Novel. John Esten Cooke. LC 6-28715. 1872. D. Appleton and Company.

Doctor Villagos: Or, The Nihilist Chief. Fortune Du Boisgobey & Lee, S., Tr. (On cover: Echo series, no. 89). 1889. Pollard & Moss.

Dr. Wallsten's Way. Thomas L Baily. LC 6-5006. 1889. The National Temperance Society and Publication House.

Doctor Warrick's Daughters: A Novel. Rebecca Harding Davis. LC 6-32468. 1896. Harper & Brothers.

Doctor Was a Dame. 1st Ed. Seldon Truss, pseud. 1953. Published for the Crime Club by Doubleday.

Dr. Whitney's Secretary. Dorothy Carle Pierce Walker. LC 44-4516. 1944. Macrae-Smith-Company.

Dr. Who & the Android Invasion. Terrence Dicks. (Dr. Who Ser.: No. 9). (Orig.). 1980. pap. 1.95 (ISBN 0-523-41619-9). Pinnacle Bks.

Dr. Who & the Day of the Daleks. Terrance Dicks. (Dr. Who Ser.: No. 1). 1979. pap. 1.95 (ISBN 0-523-41986-4). Pinnacle Bks.

Dr. Who & the Dinosaur Invasion. Malcolm Hulke. (Dr. Who Ser.: No. 3). 1979. pap. 1.95 (ISBN 0-523-41613-X). Pinnacle Bks.

Dr. Who & the Doomsday Weapon. Malcolm Hulke. (Dr. Who Ser: No. 2). 1979. pap. 1.95 (ISBN 0-523-42005-6). Pinnacle Bks.

Dr. Who & the Genesis of the Daleks. Terrance Dicks. (Dr. Who Ser.: No. 4). 1979. pap. 1.95 (ISBN 0-523-41973-2). Pinnacle Bks.

Dr. Who & the Loch Ness Monster. Terrance Dicks. (Dr. Who Ser.: No. 6). 1979. pap. 1.95 (ISBN 0-523-41791-8). Pinnacle Bks.

Doctor Who & the Masque of Mandragora. Philip Hinchcliffe. (Doctor Who Ser.: No. 8). 1979. pap. 1.95 (ISBN 0-523-41975-9). Pinnacle Bks.

Dr. Who & the Revenge of the Cybermen. Terrance Dicks. (Dr. Who Ser.: No. 5). 1979. pap. 1.95 (ISBN 0-523-41620-2). Pinnacle Bks.

Dr. Who & the Seeds of Doom. Philip Hinchcliffe. (Dr. Who Ser.: No. 10). 1980. pap. 1.95 (ISBN 0-523-41974-0). Pinnacle Bks.

Doctor Who & the Talons of Weng-Chang. Terrance Dicks. (Doctor Who Ser.: No. 7). 1979. pap. 1.75 (ISBN 0-523-40638-X). Pinnacle Bks.

Doctor Who Held Hands: A Madame Storey Novel. Hulbert Footner. LC 29-14380. 1929. Pub. for The Crime Club, Inc., by Doubleday, Doran & Company, Inc.

Doctor Who Made House Calls. Milton R Bass. LC 72-87602. 1972. 6.95 (ISBN 0-399-11063-1). Putnam.

Doctor Who Made House Calls. Milton R Bass. 1974. (pbk.) 1.50. Dell.

Dr. Wilbur's Note Book: The Story of Two Wills. E. O Tilburn. (On cover: Globe library, no. 108). 1889. Rand, McNally & Company.

Doctor Will. Pauline Stiles. LC 49-112761. 1949. Bobbs-Merrill Co.

Dr. Wilmer's Love; or, A Question of Conscience. A Novel. Margaret Lee. LC 7-12625. 1868. D. Appleton and Company.

Dr. Wilmer's Love; or, A Question of Conscience. A Novel. Margaret Lee. (On cover: Lovell's library. no. 7725). 1886. J. W. Lovell Company.

Doctor with a Mission. Elizabeth Seifert. LC 67-26147. 1967. Dodd, Mead.

Doctor with a Mission. Elizabeth Seifert. LC 76-6512. 1976. (ISBN 0-88411-034-6). Aeonian Press.

Doctor Woodward's Ambition. Elizabeth Seifert. LC 73-79145. 1973. 5.95. Aeonian Press.

Doctor Woodward's Ambition. Elizabeth Seifert. LC 45-31320. 1945. Dodd, Mead & Company.

Dr. Woodward's Ambition. Elizabeth Seifert. 1973. Repr. of 1945 ed. lib. bdg. 13.55 (ISBN 0-88411-012-5). Amereon Ltd.

Dr. Wortle's School. Anthony Trollope. LC 29-15487. (Half-title: The World's classics. cccxvii). 1928. Oxford University Press, H. Milford.

Doctor Wortle's School. Anthony Trollope. 6.95 o.p. (ISBN 0-19-250317-0). Oxford U Pr.

Doctor Xavier. Max Pemberton. LC 3-25873. 1903. D. Appleton and Company.

Doctor Zay. Elizabeth Stuart Phelps H. D. Ward Ward. LC 4-15170. 1882. Houghton, Mifflin and Company.

Dr. Zell and the Princess Charlotte. An Autobiographical Relation of Adventures in the Life of a Distinguished Modern Necromancer, Seer and Theosophist. 3d ed. Warren Richardson. LC 7-41226. 1892. L. Kabis and Company.

Dr. Zhivago. Boris Leonidovich Pasternak. 576p. 1981. pap. 3.50 (ISBN 0-345-29310-X). Ballantine.

Doctor Zhivago. Boris Leonidovich Pasternak. LC 60-11762. 1958. 15.95 (ISBN 0-394-42223-6). Pantheon.

Doctor Zhivago. Boris Leonidovich Pasternak. (Modern Library Giants). 4.95 o.p. (G86). Modern Lib.

Doctor Zhivago. Translated from the Russian by Max Hayward and Manya Harari. Boris Leonidovich Pasternak. LC 58-8005. 1958. Pantheon.

Doctora En Lujuria. new ed. Juan Castellanos. (Pimienta Collection Ser). (Illus.). 160p. (Span.). 1976. pap. 1.25 (ISBN 0-88473-247-9). Fiesta Pub.

Doctor's Affair. Elizabeth Seifert. LC 75-29218. 1975. 6.95 (ISBN 0-396-07202-X). Dodd, Mead.

Doctor's Affair. Elizabeth Seifert. (Signet Book). 1977. 1.25 (ISBN 0-451-07281-2). New American Library.

Doctor's Affair. Elizabeth Seifert. LC 80-24470. 1981. 1.50 (ISBN 0-89340-295-8). J. Curley & Associates.

Doctors & Doctors of English. Lyn Lifshin. LC 80-83209. 56p. (Orig.). Date not set. pap. 7.00 (ISBN 0-930012-28-3). Mudborn.

Doctors & Lovers. Garth Brandtson. 192p. (Orig.). 1974. pap. 1.95 o.p. (ISBN 0-87682-390-8, 7390). Barclay Hse.

Doctors & Lovers. Roy Bernard Sparkia. 1968. pap. 0.60 o.p. (60-348). Manor Bks.

Doctors & Sinners. Roy Bernard Sparkia. 1969. pap. 0.60 o.p. (60-378). Manor Bks.

Doctors & Wives. Val Munroe. (O.s.i.). 160p. 1974. pap. 0.95 o.s.i. (AN1252, Award). Univ Pub & Dist.

Doctors & Wives. Ann Pinchot. LC 79-87839. 1980. 10.95 (ISBN 0-87795-236-1). Arbor Hse.

Doctors & Wives. Ann Pinchot. 352p. 1981. pap. 2.75 (ISBN 0-553-14804-4). Bantam.

Doctors and Wives. Benjamin Siegel. LC 76-106605. 1970. 5.95. McKay.

Doctors Are Different. Dorothy Carle Pierce Walker. LC 51-11826. 1951. Macrae Smith.

Doctor's Assistant. William Arthur Neubauer. LC 48-353377. 1948. Arcadia House.

Doctors at Risk. 1st. ed. Frank Gill Slaughter. LC 81-43921. 1983. 15.95 (ISBN 0-385-17876-X). Doubleday.

Doctor's Bed. Jerome Darwin Engel. LC 42-17835. 1942. Phoenix Press.

Doctors, Beware! Walbridge McCully. LC 43-114608. 1943. Printed for the Crime Club by Doubleday, Doran and Company, Inc.

Doctor's Blunder & Other Stories. Flora Dalany. 3.00 o.p. Carlton.

Doctor's Bride. Elizabeth Seifert. 1960. Dodd, Mead.

Doctor's Bride. Elizabeth Seifert. LC 73-79179. 1974. 6.95. Aeonian Press.

Doctors Carry the Keys. Rhoda Truax. LC 33-3745. 1933. E. P. Dutton & Co., Inc.

Doctor's Castle, by Jane England Pseud. Murdock Stuart Jervis. LC 57-771940. 1957. Arcadia House.

Doctor's Choice. Susan Lennox. 1960. Avalon Books.

Doctors' Choice: Sixteen Stories About Doctors and Medicine Selected by Famous Physicians. Edited by Phyllis and Albert Blaustein. With an Introd. by Walter C. Alvarez. Ed. by Phyllis Blaustein & Albert J. Blaustein. LC 57-6513. 1957. W. Funk.

Doctor's Christmas Eve. James Lane Allen. 1977. Repr. of 1910 ed. lib. bdg. 15.00 (ISBN 0-8495-0001-X). Arden Lib.

Doctor's Christmas Eve. James Lane Allen. Repr. of 1910 ed. lib. bdg. 20.00 (ISBN 0-8414-3061-6). Folcroft.

Doctor's Christmas Eve... By James Lane Allen. James Lane Allen. LC 10-2. 1910. The Macmillan Company.

Doctor's Confession. Elizabeth Seifert. LC 68-31334. 1968. 4.95. Dodd, Mead.

Doctor's Daughter. Arlene Hale. (Ace Nurse Romance Series). 1973. (pbk.) 0.75. Ace Books.

Doctor's Daughter. Dorothy Quentin. LC 43-114795. 1942. Arcadia House, Inc.

Doctor's Daughter. Elizabeth Seifert. LC 73-15376. 1974. 5.95 (ISBN 0-396-06890-1). Dodd, Mead.

Doctor's Daughter. Elizabeth Seifert. LC 76-17330. 1976. 8.95 (ISBN 0-89340-042-4). J. Curley & Associates.

Doctor's Daughter: Revised; Sequel to The Pastor's Son. William Wilfred Walter. LC 9-8422. W. W. Walter.

Doctor's Daughter: Sequel to The Pastor's Son. William Wilfred Walter. W. W. Walter.

Doctor's Daughters. Nell Sutton Jordan. LC 72-5841. (Illus.). 1972. 4.95 (ISBN 0-8111-0455-9). Naylor Co.

Doctors Daughters. Frank Gill Slaughter. LC 80-2994. 312p. 1981. 14.95 (ISBN 0-385-17023-8). Doubleday.

Doctor's Daughters. large type ed. Frank Gill Slaughter. LC 82-3362. 446p. 1982. Repr. of 1981 ed. 13.95 (ISBN 0-89621-355-2). Thorndike Pr.

Doctor's Decision. Herbert Nicolo Gerardell. LC 49-11842. 1949. Sheridan House.

Doctor's Defense: The Story of a Lost Reputation. Sidney Herbert Daukes. LC 32-11372. 1932. H. C. Kinsey & Company, Inc.

Doctors' Desires. Adrian Gray. (Signet Book). 1973. (pbk) 0.95. New American Library.

Doctor's Desperate Hour. Elizabeth Seifert. LC 76-8887. (ISBN 0-396-07296-8). Dodd, Mead.

Doctor's Desperate Hour. Elizabeth Seifert. LC 76-48160. 1976. 6.95 (ISBN 0-8161-6438-X). G.K. Hall.

Doctor's Desperate Hour. Elizabeth Seifert. (Signet Book). 1977. 1.50 (ISBN 0-451-07787-3). New American Library.

Doctor's Destiny. Elizabeth Seifert. LC 78-183002. 1972. 5.95 (ISBN 0-396-06493-0). Dodd, Mead.

Doctor's Destiny. Elizabeth Seifert. LC 79-1227. 1979. 10.95 (ISBN 0-89340-204-4). J. Curley.

Doctor's Dilemma. Ethel Matson. LC 60-52133. 1960. Zondervan Pub. House.

Doctor's Double: An Anglo-Australian Sensation. Nathaniel Gould. LC 26-22288. 1919. G. Routledge and Sons, Limited.

Doctor's Family: Or, The Story of the Erlaus. Agnes Breitzmann & Ireland, Mrs. Mary Eliza (Haines) 1834- Tr. LC 7-3042. American Tract Society.

Doctor's First Murder. Robert Hare Hutchinson. LC 33-287292. 1933. Longmans, Green and Co.

Doctor's Hospital. Marilyn Gilman. (Orig.). 1983. pap. 2.95 (ISBN 0-8217-1206-3). Zebra.

Doctor's Husband. Elizabeth Seifert. LC 57-113857. 1957. Dodd, Mead.

Doctor's Husband. Elizabeth Seifert. LC 73-791726. 1974. 6.95. Aeonian Press.

Doctors in Love. Sonia Deane. Ed. by Gene DeRoin. (Aston Hall Presents Ser.). (Orig.). 1979. pap. 1.50 (ISBN 0-89936-005-X). Aston Hall.

Doctor's Kingdom. Elizabeth Seifert. (Signet book). 1974. (pbk.) 1.25. New American Library.

Doctor's Kingdom. Elizabeth Seifert. LC 70-127167. 1970. 4.95. Dodd, Mead.

Doctor's Kingdom. Elizabeth Siefert. LC 76-20814. 1976. 8.95 (ISBN 0-89340-044-0). J. Curley.

Doctor's Lass. Edward Charles Booth. LC 10-359864. 1910. The Century Co.

Doctor's Last Message: A Novel. 1st Ed. Julius Buscher. LC 52-11663. 1953. Exposition Press.

Doctor's Mistake: Or, What Myrta Saw. An Experiment with Life, a Novel. Charles Howard Montague & Hammond, Clement Milton. LC 7-31814. 1888. T. Downey, Jr. & Co.

Doctor's Murder Case. Robert Portner Koehler. LC 39-17107. Phoenix Press.

Doctor's Name Was Mary. Kathleen Harris, pseud. LC 47-31461. 1947. Arcadia House.

Doctor's Office. Elsie Lee. (Orig.). 1968. pap. 0.75 o.p. (74-928). Lancer.

Doctor's Office. Charles Stanley Strong. LC 37-20433. Phoenix Press.

Doctors on Eden Place. Elizabeth Seifert. LC 77-4397. 7.95 (ISBN 0-396-07438-3). Dodd, Mead.

Doctors on Eden Place. Elizabeth Seifert. LC 78-7558. 1978. 10.95 (ISBN 0-8161-6581-5). G. K. Hall.

Doctors on Parade: Including, The Doctor Takes a Wife, The Doctor Disagrees and Lucinda Marries the Doctor. Elizabeth Seifert. LC 60-12975. 1960. Dodd, Mead.

Doctor's Oral. George Rippey Stewart. LC 39-220331. Random House.

Doctor's Orders. Hamilton Johnston. LC 58-9680. 1958. Sloane.

Doctor's Orders. Albert Kovetz. (Orig.). 1981. pap. 2.95 (ISBN 0-89083-877-1). Zebra.

Doctor's Party. Mary Frances Doner. LC 40-34595. The Penn Publishing Company.

Doctors' Passions. Adrian Gray. (Signet Book). 1975. (pbk.) 1.25. New American Library.

Doctor's Pills Are Stardust. Charles G Givens. LC 38-27538. The Bobbs-Merrill Company.

Doctor's Private Life. Elizabeth Seifert. LC 73-6037. 1973. 5.95 (ISBN 0-396-06829-4). Dodd, Mead.

Doctor's Private Life. Elizabeth Seifert. LC 74-3056. 1974. 9.95 (ISBN 0-8161-6196-8). G. K. Hall.

Doctor's Promise. Elizabeth Seifert. LC 79-17675. 7.95 (ISBN 0-396-07726-9). Dodd, Mead.

Doctor's Promise. Elizabeth Seifert. LC 81-5362. 1981. 11.95 (ISBN 0-89340-294-X). J. Curley.

Doctor's Reputation. Elizabeth Seifert. LC 72-3147. 1972. 5.95 (ISBN 0-396-06628-3). Dodd, Mead.

Doctor's Reputation. Elizabeth Seifert. (Signet book). 1974. (pbk.) 0.95. New American Library.

Doctor's Reputation. Elizabeth Seifert. LC 76-20641. 1976. 9.95 (ISBN 0-89340-046-7). J. Curley.

Doctor's Return. Kenneth Anderson. (Orig.). (YA) 1968. pap. 1.75 o.p. (ISBN 0-310-20112-8). Zondervan.

Doctor's Return: A Novel. Kenneth Anderson. LC 43-207. 1942. Zondervan Publishing House.

Doctor's Second Love. Elizabeth Seifert. LC 72-163074. 1971. 5.95 (ISBN 0-396-06388-8). Dodd, Mead.

Doctor's Secret. Dorothy Louise Dern. LC 54-123409. 1954. Pageant Press.

Doctor's Secret. Eliza M. J. Humphreys. (On cover: Lovell's Westminster series, no. 5). 1890. J. W. Lovell Company.

Doctor's Secret. Vera Minshall. LC 65-25958. 1966. Zondervan Pub. House.

Doctor's Secret: Or, The Shadow on the Wall. Frederick William Davis. LC 1-30722. (Magnet detective library, no. 170). 1901. Street & Smith.

Doctor's Secretary. Charles Stanley Strong. LC 43-598. 1943. Phoenix Press.

Doctor's Son: And Other Stories. John O'Hara. LC 35-3041. Harcourt, Brace and Company.

Doctor's Son: And Other Stories. John O'Hara. LC 44-8360. New Avon Library.

Doctor's Strange Legacy. Mary Weller Robbins. (On cover: The pastime series, no. 38). 1896. Laird & Lee.

Doctor's Strange Secret. Elizabeth Seifert. LC 62-16330. 1962. Dodd, Mead.

Doctor's Strange Secret. Elizabeth Seifert. LC 73-79184. 1974. 6.95. Aeonian Press.

Doctor's Sweetheart and Other Stories. Lucy Maud Montgomery & Catherine M McLay. LC 79-317665. 7.95 (ISBN 0-07-082790-7). McGraw-Hill Ryerson.

Doctors: Translated by Oliver Coburn. Andre Soubiran. LC 53-8153. 1953. Putnam.

Doctors: Translated from the French by Oliver Coburn. Andre Soubiran. (Popular Special SP66). 1960. Popular Library.

Doctor's Two Lives. Elizabeth Seifert. LC 76-20802. 1976. 9.95 (ISBN 0-89340-047-5). J. Curley.

Doctor's Two Lives. Elizabeth Seifert. LC 78-108045. 1970. 4.95. Dodd, Mead.

Doctors Wear Scarlet. Simon Raven. 1961. 3.95 o.p. (ISBN 0-671-19825-4). S&S.

Doctors Were Brothers. Elizabeth Seifert. LC 78-12846. 1978. 7.95 (ISBN 0-396-07625-4). Dodd, Mead.

Doctors Were Brothers. Elizabeth Seifert. LC 79-10647. 1979. 7.95 (ISBN 0-8161-6705-2). Dodd, Mead.

Doctor's Wife. Sawako Ariyoshi. LC 79-301318. 1978. 8.95 (ISBN 0-87011-337-2). Kodansha International.

Doctor's Wife. Maysie Greig. LC 37-16382. 1937. Doubleday, Doran and Co., Inc.

Doctor's Wife. Maysie Greig. LC 38-32639. 1938. The Sun Dial Press. Inc.

Doctor's Wife. Millicent Kent. LC 34-34432. W. Godwin, Inc.

Doctor's Wife. Rachel Swete Macnamara. LC 44-3271. 1944. Arcadia House, Inc.

Doctor's Wife. Mary Elizabeth Braddon Maxwell. (On cover: Lovell's library. no. 877). 1887. J. W. Lovell Company.

Doctor's Wife. Brian Moore. ("A Dell Book."). 1977. 2.25 (ISBN 0-440-11931-6). Dell Pub. Co.

Doctor's Wife. A Novel. Mary Elizabeth Braddon Maxwell. (Seaside library. v. 28, no. 459). 1879. G. Munro.

Doctor's Wife. A Novel. Mary Elizabeth Braddon Maxwell. (On cover: Seaside library. Pocket ed. no. 529). 1885. G. Munro.

Doctor's Wife Comes to Stay. Frank Arthur Swinnerton. LC 50-8316. 1950. Doubleday.

Doctor's Wife Comes to Stay. Frank Arthur Swinnerton. 1973. 1.25. Lancer Books.

Doctor's Wife Comes to Stay. Frank Arthur Swinnerton. LC 50-3234. 1949. Hutchinson.

Doctors' Wives. Henry Lieferant & Sylvia Saltzberg Lieferant. LC 30-12741. 1930. Little, Brown, and Company.

Doctors' Wives. Frank Gill Slaughter. LC 67-19080. 1967. Doubleday.

Doctors' Women. Adrian Gray. 1974. (pbk.) 0.95. New American Library.

Doctor's Wooing. Charles Joseph MacConaghy Phillips. LC 26-13989. The Devin-Adair Company.

Doctrine of Selective Depravity. Bruce Cutler. (Inland Seas Ser.: No. 1). 1981. pap. 5.00. Juniper Pr WI.

Documents in the Case. Dorothy Leigh Sayers & Eustace, Robert, Joint Author. LC 30-29256. Brewer & Warren, Inc.

Documents of Murder. T. C. H Jacobs, pseud. LC 33-12428. 1933. The Macaulay Company.

Dodd Cases... Kenneth Livingston. LC 34-36039. 1934. Pub. for the Crime Club, Inc., by Doubleday, Doran & Company, Inc.

Dodd, Mead Gallery of Horror. Charles L. Grant. 1983. 15.95 (ISBN 0-396-08160-6). Dodd.

Dodd the Potter. Cedric Beardmore, pseud. LC 31-23201. 1931. Doubleday, Doran & Company, Inc.

Dodecahedron. Tom Mallin. LC 72-83888. 1972. 4.95 (ISBN 0-87690-085-6). Outerbridge & Lazard; Distributed by Dutton.

Dodeka. John Taggart. LC 79-114049. 1979. 3.00 (ISBN 0-87924-028-8). Membrane Press.

Dodge City Bombers. Lionel Derrick. (Penetrator#9). 1975. (pbk.) 1.25 (ISBN 0-523-00627-6). Pinnacle Books.

Dodge City Darling. Lee D. Willoughby. (Women Who Won the West Ser.: No. 2). (Orig.). 1982. pap. 2.95 (ISBN 0-440-01965-6, Bryans). Dell.

Dodge Club: Or, Italy in Mdccclix. James De Mille. LC 16-938041. Harper & Brothers.

Dodge Club: Or, Italy in 1859. James De Mille. LC 9-812. 1869. Harper & Brothers.

Dodge Club: Or, Italy in 1859. James De Mille. LC 9-813. Harper & Brothers.

Dodo. Edward Frederic Benson. LC 6-11340. (On cover: Seaside library. Pocket ed. no. 2105). G. Munro's Sons.

Dodo. Edward Frederic Benson. LC 78-19214. 14.95 (ISBN 0-690-01782-0). Crowell.

Dodo: A Detail of the Day. 2d ed. Edward Frederic Benson. LC 6-11342. (On Cover: Appletons' town and country library, no. 126). 1893. D. Appleton and Company.

Dodo: A Detail of the Day. 2d ed. Edward Frederic Benson. LC 6-11341. 1894. D. Appleton and Company.

Dodo Wonders-- Edward Frederic Benson. LC 22-119. George H. Doran Company.

Dodo's Daughter: A Sequel to Dodo. Edward Frederic Benson. LC 13-17336. 1913. 1.25. The Century Co.

Dodo's Daughter: A Sequel to Dodo. Edward Frederic Benson. 1914. The Century Co.

Dodsworth. Sinclair Lewis. 1971. pap. 3.50 (ISBN 0-451-51704-0, CE1704, Sig Classics). NAL.

Dodsworth: A Novel. Sinclair Lewis. LC 29-26270. Harcourt, Brace and Company.

Dodu and Other Stories. R. K. Narayan. LC 51-367821. Indian Thought Publications.

Does Anyone Else Have Something Further to Add? Stories About Secret Places and Mean Men. R. A Lafferty. LC 74-4201. 1974. 5.95 (ISBN 0-684-13827-1). Scribner.

Does Crime Pay? Vincent Samuel Stevens. LC 56-7044. 1956. Dorrance & Co.

Does It Always Rain Here, Mr. Hoyt? Murray Hoyt. LC 50-7961. (Illus.). 1950. Rinehart.

Doesn't Everyone. Irving A. Greenfield. 1977. pap. 1.95 (ISBN 0-532-19147-1). Woodhill.

Doesn't Everyone...? Suzanne Topper. (Orig.). 1976. pap. 1.50 o.p. (ISBN 0-8439-0338-4, LB338DK, Leisure Bks). Nordon Pubns.

Doesn't Everyone...? Suzanne Topper. 1976. (pbk.) 1.50. Leisure Books.

Doesticks: What He Says. Mortimer Thomson. LC 8-19955. 1855. E. Livermore.

Doffed Coronet: A True Story. Marguerite De Godart Cunliffe-Owen. LC 2-285141. 1902. Harper & Brothers.

Dog. Roy McKie. (Illus.). 1978. pap. 2.95 (ISBN 0-671-24002-1, Fireside). S&S.

Dog and the Child and the Ancient Sailor Man. Robert Alexander Wason. LC 14-152. Small, Maynard and Company.

Dog & the Fever: A Perambulatory Novella, by Francisco De Quevedo Who Published Under the Name of Pedro Espinosa. Translated by William Carlos Williams and Raquel Helene Williams. Francisco Gomez De Quevedo Y Villegas & Empinosa, Pedro. LC 54-12823. 1954. Shoe String Press.

Dog at Clambercrown. Jocelyn Brooke. 1955. 4.50 o.p. (ISBN 0-8149-0458-0). Vanguard.

Dog Day Afternoon. Leslie Waller. LC 74-13386. 1975. Delacorte Press.

Dog Days of Lank Hank, by T. P. Leaman, Jr. Thomas P. Jr Leaman. LC 37-324172. B. Humphries, Inc.

Dog Eat Dog. Elwyn Whitman Chambers. LC 38-6015. 1938. Pub. for the Crime Club, Inc., by Doubleday, Doran & Co., Inc.

Dog Eat Dog. Mary Garden Collins. LC 49-956948. 1949. C. Scribner's Sons.

Dog in the Manger: A Novel of Suspense. Ursula Reilly Curtiss. LC 82-1501. 8.95 (ISBN 0-396-08057-X). Dodd, Mead.

Dog It Was That Died. Henry Reymond Fitzwalter Keating. 1968. pap. 0.95 o.p. (ISBN 0-14-002443-3, 2443). Penguin.

Dog It Was That Died: By E. C. R. Lorac Pseud. 1st American Ed. Edith Caroline Rivett. LC 52-10405. 1952. Published for the Crime Club by Doubleday.

Dog Kill. Al Dempsey. LC 75-46552. 7.95 (ISBN 0-13-647750-X). Prentice-Hall.

Dog Lane. Lev Ivanovich Gumilevskii. Tr. by Wreden, N. R. LC 30-231850. The Vanguard Press.

Dog Named Wolf. Erik Munsterhjelm. (Laurel-leaf library). 1973. (pbk.) 0.75. Dell Pub. Co.

Dog of Constantinople. Izora Cecilia Chandler. LC 6-28128. 1896. Dodd, Mead and Company.

Dog of Flanders. Louise De La Ramee. LC 14-22442. (Maynard's English classic series. no. 200). Maynard, Merrill & Co.

Dog of Flanders: A Story of Noel. Louise De La Ramee. Ed. by Swart, Rose C. (Half-title: The Canterbury classics...). 0.25. Rand McNally & Company.

Dog of the Desert. Ion Llewellyn Idriess & Moody, J. B. LC 45-9771. 1945. The Bobbs-Merrill Company.

Dog of the High Sierras. Albert Payson Terhune. (Illus.). 1961. Grosset & Dunlap.

Dog of the South. Charles Portis. LC 78-65780. 1979. 8.95 (ISBN 0-394-50614-6). Knopf: Distributed by Random House.

Dog on the Sun: A Volume of Stories. Paul Green. LC 49-11774. 1949. University of North Carolina Press.

Dog Soldiers. Robert Stone. 1975. (pbk.) 1.95. Ballantine.

Dog Soldiers: A Novel. Robert Stone. LC 74-11441. 1974. 8.95 (ISBN 0-395-18481-9). Houghton Mifflin.

Dog Star. Donald Windham. LC 50-7200. 1950. Doubleday.

Dog Tags. Stephen D. Becker. LC 73-3456. 1973. 6.95 (ISBN 0-394-46439-7). Random House.

Dog Tags. Stephen D. Becker. (Berkley Medallion Book). 1978. 1.95 (ISBN 0-425-03664-2). Berkley Pub. Corp.

Dog That Was and Was Not, The Double Guarantee: Two Surrealistic Tales. Maurits Ignatius Boas. LC 74-91100. 1970. 5.95. F. Fell.

Dog Years. Gunter Grass. LC 65-14715. 1965. Harcourt, Brace & World.

Dogfighter. Jonathan Betuel. (Fawcett Gold Medal Book). 1976. (pbk.) 1.25. Fawcett.

Dogo-Graphy. The Life and Adventures of the Celebrated Dog Tiger, Comprising a Variety of Amusing and Instructive Examples, Illustrative of the Happy Effects of the Appropriate Training and Education of Dogs. stereotype ed. Francis Butler. LC 6-16677. 1856. F. Butler.

Dogs. Robert Calder. 1977. 1.95. Dell.

Dogs: A Novel. Robert Calder. LC 75-37568. 7.95 (ISBN 0-440-02050-6). Delacorte Press/Quicksilver Books.

Dogs Bodies. Ralph Steadman. LC 76-62523. (Illus.). 1977. pap. 1.25 o.s.i. (ISBN 0-448-22975-7). Paddington.

Dogs, Cats and People. Harold Charles Le Baron Jackson. 1949. Conjure House.

Dogs Do Bark: A Mystery Novel. Jonathan Stagge, pseud. LC 37-1377. 1937. Pub. for the Crime Club, Inc., by Doubleday, Doran & Company, Inc.

Dog's Head: Translated from the French by Robin Chancellor. Jean Dutourd. LC 53-58673. 1953-1952. Simon and Schuster.

Dogs: Heroes, Adventurers, Friends: A Collection of 30 Outstanding Stories, Selected, Ed. by Florence Peterson. Foreword by Farley Mowat. Illus. by Hamilton Greene. Ed. by Florence K. Peterson. LC 64-14546. 1964. 3.95. Platt & Munk.

Dogs in an Omnibus. Gladys Bronwyn Stern. LC 79-125238. (Short Story Index Reprint Ser). (Illus.). 1942. 15.00 (ISBN 0-8369-3605-1). Ayer Co.

Dog's Life: A Novel. Michael Holroyd. LC 69-10368. 1969. 4.50. Holt, Rinehart and Winston.

Dogs of Fear. Musa Nagenda. (Secondary Readers Ser.). 1971. pap. text ed. 3.00x (ISBN 0-435-92500-8). Heinemann Ed.

Dogs of March. Ernest Hebert. LC 78-26869. 1979. 9.95 (ISBN 0-670-27746-0). Viking Press.

Dogs of March. Ernest Hebert. LC 79-24131. 1980. 2.95 (ISBN 0-14-005560-6). Penguin Books.

Dogs of Want. Mary St. Leger Kingsley Harrison. LC 25-694547. 1925. 2.00. Dodd, Mead and Company.

Dogs of War. Frederick Forsyth. LC 73-19103. 1974. 7.95 (ISBN 0-670-27753-3). Viking Press.

Dogs of War. Frederick Forsyth. LC 74-19206. 1974. (ISBN 0-8161-6245-X). G. K. Hall.

Dogs of War: Wherein the Hero-Worshipper Portrays the Hero and Incidentally Gives and Account of the Greatest Dogs' Club in the World. Walter Lewis Emanuel. LC 7-15118. 1906. C. Scribner's Sons.

Dog's Ransom. Patricia Highsmith. LC 72-2225. 1972. 5.95 (ISBN 0-394-48069-4). Knopf.

Dogwatch: A Mystery. Carlyn Coffin. LC 44-5199. 1944. Farrar & Rinehart, Inc.

Doing His Best. John Townsend Trowbridge. LC 3-11142. (On cover: Jack Hazard series). H. T. Coates & Co.

Doing Time. Amos Brooke. 1.75 (ISBN 0-87067-526-5). Holloway House.

Doing What We Do Best. Jan Kendrick. 1976. (pbk.) 1.50. Warner Books.

Doings in Derryville. Lewis V Price. United Society of Christian Endeavor.

Doings in Maryland: Or Matilda Douglas... Emily Eliza Jours McAlpine. LC 7-15272. 1871. J. B. Lippincott & Co.

Doings of Raffles Haw. Arthur Conan Doyle. LC 72-103507. (Short story index reprint series). 1969. Books for Libraries Press.

Doings of Raffles Haw. Arthur Conan Doyle. J. W. Lovell Company.

Doings of Raffles Haw. Arthur Conan Doyle. LC 16-191663. 1912. Cassell and Company, Limited.

Doings of Raffles Haw. Arthur Conan Doyle. LC 80-67702. (Doyle, Arthur Conan, Sir, 1859-1930. Conan Doyle Centennial Ser.). (Illus.). 1981. 11.95. Gaslight Publications.

Doings of Raffles Haw, & Other Stories. facsimile ed. Arthur Conan Doyle. LC 72-103507. (Short Story Index Reprint Ser.). 1891. 12.50 (ISBN 0-8369-3249-8). Ayer Co.

Doings of the Bodley Family in Town and Country. Horace Elisha Scudder. LC 3-14867. 1903. Houghton, Mifflin and Company.

Doiphan's Ride. 1st Ed. Les Savage. LC 59-6370. 1959. Doubleday.

Dolan Debt. E. R. Slade. (Orig.). 1979. pap. 1.50 (ISBN 0-532-23109-0). Woodhill.

Dolf. Francis Evans Baily. LC 21-21945. Boni and Liveright.

Dolicin. Beatrice May Butt. (Seaside library, v. 28 no. 574). G. Munro.

Dolinda and the Twins: With "Duggie" in the Rear); Being the Memoir of a Naughty Girl. Dora Harvey Munyon. LC 1-30138. The Abbey Press.

Doll. Aleksander Gowacki. LC 75-125261. 1972. Twayne Publishers.

Doll. Ed McBain. 3.50 o.p. Delacorte.

Doll: An 87th Precinct Mystery. by Ed McBain Pseud. Evan Hunter. (2086). 1966. Dell.

Doll: An 87th Precinct Novel, by Ed McBain Pseud. Evan Hunter. LC 65-18625. bds., 3.50. Delacorte, Dist. Dial.

Doll, and One Other. Algernon Blackwood. LC 46-17840. 1946. Arkham House.

Doll Baby. Hugh Barron. (Orig.). pap. 0.75 o.p. (T1920). Pyramid Pubns.

Doll Castle. Martha Monigle. 1975. (pbk.) 0.95 (ISBN 0-345-26702-8). Ballantine Books.

Doll for the Toff. John Creasey. LC 65-186313. (Walker mystery). 1965. bds. 3.50. Walker.

Doll Maker. Marcia Marcoux. (Orig.). 1968. pap. 1.75 o.p. (3048). Brandon.

Doll Who Ate His Mother: A Novel of Modern Terror. J. Ramsey Campbell. LC 76-2363. 8.95 (ISBN 0-672-52236-5). Bobbs-Merrill.

Doll with Opal Eyes. Thomas Eugene DeWeese, pseud. LC 75-21222. 1976. 5.95 (ISBN 0-385-11304-8). Doubleday.

Dollar Covenant. Michael Sinclair. LC 73-8926. 1973. 5.95 (ISBN 0-393-08369-1). Norton.

Dollar Duchess. Rebecca Baldwin, pseud. 192p. (Orig.). 1982. pap. 1.50 (ISBN 0-449-50305-4, Coventry). Fawcett.

Dollar Gold Piece. Virginia Swain. LC 41-256661. Toronto, Farrar & Rinehart, Inc.

Dollar Hunt. From the French. Tr. by Martin, E. G. LC 6-1379. 1905. Benziger Brothers.

Dollar to Die for. Brian Fox. 160p. (Orig.). 1980. pap. 1.95 o.p. (ISBN 0-441-15775-0). Charter Bks.

Dollar to Die For. Brian Fox. (Dollar Western Ser.). (O.s.i.). (Orig.). 1971. pap. 0.95 o.s.i. (AN1464, Award). Univ Pub & Dist.

Dollarocracy: an American Novel. Illustrated by Frank Ver Beck. Oliver Herband Gordon Leigh. (On cover: Broadway series, no. 7). 1891. J. A. Taylor & Co.

Dollars and Cents. Albert Payson Terhune. LC 17-13188. 1917. R. J. Shores.

Dollars and Cents. Anna Bartlett Warner. LC 8-33721. 1852. G. P. Putnam.

Dollars and Cents a Novel. Anna Bartlett Warner. LC 8-337191. 1860. J. B. Lippincott & Co.

Dollars for the Duke. Barbara Cartland. 160p. (Orig.). 1981. pap. 1.95 (ISBN 0-553-14650-5). Bantam.

Dollars or Sense?" A Tale of Every-Day Life in England and America. Arthur Louis Keyser. LC 7-10825. 1886. Brentano Bros.

Dolliver Romance. Nathaniel Hawthorne. Bd. with Fanshawe; Septimius Felton. LC 75-125216. (Short Story Index Reprint Ser.). (With an appendix containing "The Ancestral Footstep"). Repr. of 1883 ed. 18.25 (ISBN 0-8369-3583-7). Ayer Co.

Dolliver Romance: And Other Pieces. Nathaniel Hawthorne. LC 4-16227. (On cover: Hawthorne's works. Little classic edition, vol. xxiii). 1904. Houghton, Mifflin and Company.

Dolliver Romance, Fanshawe, and Septimius Felton: With an Appendix Containing The Ancestral Footstep. Nathaniel Hawthorne. LC 77-125216. (Short story index reprint series). 1970. Books for Libraries Press.

Dolliver Romance, Fanshawe, Septimus Felton: With an Appendix Containing The Ancestral Footstep. Nathaniel Hawthorne. LC 4-16288. (Riverside edition. The complete works of Nathaniel Hawthorne...vol. 11). 1884. Houghton, Mifflin and Company.

Dollmaker. Harriette Louisa Simpson Arnow. LC 54-9223. 1954. Macmillan.

Dollmaker. Maureen E Wakefield. 1974. 4.95. Lenox Hill Press.

Dollmaker: By Harriette Arnow. Harriette Louisa Simpson Arnow. LC 67-6859. 1967. 8.95. Macmillan.

Dollmaster. Rosamond Van Der Zee Marshall. LC 54-5678. 1954. Prentice-Hall.

Dolls. Jessica Free. 408p. (Orig.). 1982. pap. 3.50 (ISBN 0-441-15217-1). Ace Bks.

Dolls. Edwina Lindsay Travers. 1977. 5.50 o.p. (ISBN 0-682-48976-X). Exposition.

Dolls Are Deadly. Davis Dresser. (Mike Shayne Mystery.). 1973. (pbk.) 0.75. Dell.

Doll's House. Henrik Ibsen. LC 24-27959. (Little leather library. no. 20). Little Leather Library Corporation.

Doll's Trunk Murder. Helen Kieran Reilly. LC 32-32264. Farrar & Rinehart, Incorporated.

Dolls with Sad Faces. Conrad Phillips. LC 57-7186. Roy Publishers.

Dolly. Justin Huntly McCarthy. (On cover: Lovell's library, no. 1360). 1889. J. W. Lovell Company.

Dolly: A Love Stroy. Frances Hodgson Burnett. LC 6-19897. (International series of new approved novels). Porter & Coates.

Dolly and the Cooky Bird. Dorothy Dunnett. LC 82-40043. 1982. 2.95 (ISBN 0-394-71174-2). Vintage Books.

Dolly and the Doctor Bird. Dorothy Dunnett. LC 82-40016. 1982. 2.95 (ISBN 0-394-71163-7). Vintage Books.

Dolly and the Nanny Bird. Dorothy Dunnett. LC 82-47814. 1982. 12.95 (ISBN 0-394-52376-8). Knopf.

Dolly and the Singing Bird. Dorothy Dunnett. LC 82-40044. 1982. 2.95 (ISBN 0-394-71162-9). Vintage Books.

Dolly and the Starry Bird. Dorothy Dunnett. LC 82-40045. 1982. 2.95 (ISBN 0-394-71163-7). Vintage Books.

Dolly Diaglogues. Anthony Hope Hawkins. LC 4714. W. B. Conkey Company.

Dolly Dialogues. Anthony Hope Hawkins. LC 72-106288. (Short story index reprint series). (Illus.). 1970. Books for Libraries Press.

Dolly Dialogues. Anthony Hope Hawkins. (On cover: Seaside library. Pocket ed., no. 2098). 1895. G. Munro's Sons.

Dolly Dialogues. Anthony Hope Hawkins. 1901. R. H. Russell.

Dolly Dialogues. Anthony Hope Hawkins. LC 4-16531. 1903. H. Holt and Company.

Dolly Dialogues. Anthony Hope Hawkins. LC 43-212988. E. A. Weeks & Company.

Dolly Dialogues. Anthony Hope Hawkins. LC 42-48598. 1894. H. Holt and Company.

Dolly Dialogues and Comedies of Courtship. Anthony Hope Hawkins. LC 3-24939. (Half-title: Author's edition. Works of Anthony Hope...). D. Appleton and Company.

Dolly Dillenbeck: A Portrayal of Certain Phases of Metropolitan Life and Character. James Lauren Ford. LC 6-41401. 1895. G. H. Richmond & Co.

Dolly, Dolly Spy. Adam Diment. (S3888). 1968. Bantam.

Dolly, Dolly Spy. Adam Diment. LC 67-26600. 1967. Dutton.

Dolly Madison: A Story of the War of 1812. Mary Elizabeth Springer. LC 6-46775. 1906. Bonnell, Silver & Co.

Dolly Purdo. M. M. B Walsh. LC 74-30588. 1975. 7.95 (ISBN 0-399-11524-2). Putnam.

Dolly Purdo. M. M. B Walsh. (berkley Medallion Book). 1977. 1.50 (ISBN 0-425-03299-X). Berkley Pub. Corp: Distributed by Putnam.

Dolores. Mrs. Bridges. (Seaside library, v. 29, no. 600). 1879. G. Munro.

Dolores. Ivy Compton-Burnett. 330p. 1981. 15.00x (ISBN 0-85158-104-8, Pub. by Blackwood & Sons England). State Mutual Bk.

Dolores. Jacqueline Susann. 1977. pap. 2.25 (B13161-3). Bantam.

Dolores. Jacqueline Susann. LC 76-3584. 1976. 6.95 o.p. (ISBN 0-688-03057-2). Morrow.

Dolores: A Tale of Disappointment and Distress. Compiled, Arranged and Edited from the Journal, Letters, and Other Mss. of Roland Vernon, Esq.; and from Contributions by and Conversations with the Vernon Family, of Rushbrook, in Carolina. Benjamin Robinson. 1868. E. J. Hale & Sons.

Dolores: a Tale of Maine and Italy. Rudolph Leonhart. LC 7-13165. 1870. E. Luft, Job Printer.

Dolores! a Tale of Maine and Italy. rev. ed. Rudolph Leonhart. LC 7-13166. 1887. Cassidy., Book and Job Printer.

Dolores. By Mrs. Forrester Pseud. (On cover: Seaside library. Pocket ed., no 721). 1886. G. Munro.

Dolorosa Deal. Blaine Littell. LC 73-76489. 1973. 5.95 (ISBN 0-8415-0261-7). Saturday Review Press.

Dolorosa Deal. Blaine Littell. 1974. (pbk.) 1.25. Ballantine Books.

Dolphin Cottage. Gladys Bronwyn Stern. 1981. 18.95x (Pub. by Remploy England). State Mutual Bk.

Dolphin Crossing: By Jill Paton Walsh. Gillian Paton Walsh. LC 67-17767. 1967. bds., 3.75. Melbourne, Macmillan.

Dolphin in the Wood. Ralph Bates. LC 49-50423. 1950. Random House.

Dolphin Island. Arthur C. Clarke. 192p. 1981. pap. 2.25 (ISBN 0-425-05144-7). Berkley Pub.

Dolphin Island. Arthur C. Clarke. 192p. 1981. pap. 2.25 (ISBN 0-425-04302-9, Medallion). Berkley Pub.

Dolphin Sailed North. Roger Simons. LC 66-9780. (Illus.). 1966. McGraw-Hill.

Dolphin Summer. Michael Butterworth. LC 76-9481. 1976. 7.95 (ISBN 0-385-11679-9). Doubleday.

Dolphin Summer. Carola Salisbury. LC 76-9481. 1977. 7.95 o.p. (ISBN 0-385-11679-9). Doubleday.

Dolphin Summer. Carola Salisbury. LC 76-9481. 1977. 7.95 o.p. (ISBN 0-385-11679-9). Doubleday.

Dolphin Summer: Carola Salisbury. Carola Salisbury. (Fawcett Crest Book). 1.75 (ISBN 0-449-23415-0). Fawcett Books.

Dom Casmurro. Machado De Assis. 1980. pap. 2.95 (ISBN 0-380-49668-2, 49668, Bard). Avon.

Dom Casmurro: A Novel; Tr. from Portuguese by Helen Caldwell. Joaquim Maria Machado De Assis. 1966. 5.50, 1.50 pap.,. Univ. of Calif. Pr.

Dombey and Son. Charles Dickens. Ed. by Peter Fairclough. LC 76-519213. (Penguin English library). (Illus.). 1970. Penguin.

Dombey and Son. diamond ed. Charles Dickens. LC 6-35893. 1867. Ticknor and Fields.

Dombey and Son... Charles Dickens. LC 6-37033. 1867. Hurd and Houghton.

Dombey and Son... Charles Dickens. LC 9-3829. 1867. Hurd and Houghton.

Dombey and Son. illustrated household ed. Charles Dickens. LC 6-35892. 1870. Fields, Osgood & Co.

Dombey and Son... Charles Dickens. LC 15-20303. (Works of Charles Dickens. Globe ed.). 1870. Hurd and Houghton.

Dombey and Son. household ed. Charles Dickens. LC 6-35891. 1873. Harper & Brothers.

Dombey and Son. Charles Dickens. LC 9-3008. (Half-title: Works of Charles Dickens. "Carleton's new illustrated ed." v). 1877. G. W. Carleton & Co.; Etc., Etc.

Dombey and Son. Charles Dickens. LC 6-35890. (On cover: Lovell's library, v. 5, no. 319). 1883. J. W. Lovell Company.

Dombey and Son. Charles Dickens. Ed. by Whipple, Edwin Percy. LC 15-231356. (Half-title: Works of Charles Dickens. New illustrated library ed. vol. xii-xiii). Houghton Mifflin Company.

Dombey and Son. Charles Dickens. LC 36-37125. (Half-title: Everyman's library, ed. by Ernest Rhys. Fiction. no. 240). 1930. J. M. Dent & Sons. Ltd.

Dombey and Son. Charles Dickens. LC 43-434018. 1884. Hurst & Co.

Dombey and Son. Charles Dickens. LC 43-37798. (On cover: The Home library). A. L. Burt Company.

Dombey and Son. Charles Dickens & E. A Horsman. LC 81-16959. (World's classics). 1982. 5.95 (ISBN 0-19-281565-2). Oxford University Press.

Dombey and Son: Illustrated by Henry C. Pitz. Charles Dickens. LC 57-2189. 1957. Heritage Press.

Dome. Lawrence Huff. 1979. pap. 2.50 (ISBN 0-671-83182-8). PB.

Dome in the Forest. Paul Williams. 224p. (Orig.). 1981. pap. 2.25 (ISBN 0-345-30087-4, Del Rey). Ballantine.

Dome of the Rock. Peter Morgan. LC 77-129073. 1970. 3.95. Key Publishers.

Dome World. Dean McLaughlin. 1971. pap. 0.75 o.p. (T2492). Pyramid Pubns.

Domestic Adventurers. Josephine Dodge Daskam Bacon. LC 7-29425. 1907. C. Scribner's Sons.

Domestic Affairs. Miriam Finkelstein. LC 81-6887. 1982. 9.95 (ISBN 0-395-31822-X). Houghton Mifflin.

Domestic Animal. Eric Hatch. LC 20-189429. J. H. Sears & Company, Inc.

Domestic Arrangements: A Novel. Norma Klein. LC 80-28476. 11.95 (ISBN 0-87131-343-X). M. Evans.

Domestic Dramas: Drames De Famille). Paul Charles Joseph Bourget. LC 76-37259. (Short story index reprint series). 1971. (ISBN 0-8369-4070-9). Books for Libraries Press.

Domestic Dramas: Drames En Famille. Paul Charles Joseph Bourget. Tr. by William Marchant. LC 1-30002. 1900. C. Scribner's Sons.

Domestic Particulars: A Family Chronicle. Frederick Busch. LC 76-8904. (New Directions book). 1976. 11.95 (ISBN 0-8112-0605-X) (ISBN 0-8112-0611-4). New Directions Pub. Corp.

Domestic Relations: Stories by Frank O'Connor Pseud. 1st Ed. Michael O'Donovan. LC 57-10558. 1957. Knopf.

Domestic Tranquility. Richard Cohen. LC 80-52675. 12.95 (ISBN 0-87223-670-6). Seaview Books.

Domesticus: A Tale of the Imperial City. William Allen Butler. LC 6-16675. 1886. C. Scribner's Sons.

Domina. Barbara Wood. LC 82-45279. 1983. 15.95 (ISBN 0-385-17653-8). Doubleday.

Dominance. Madge Jenison. LC 28-8514. 1928. Doubleday, Doran & Company, Inc.

Dominance Signals: A Novel. Gerald Kaminski. LC 80-12997. 5.00 (ISBN 0-914974-25-4). Holmgangers Press.

Dominant Blood. Robert E McClure. LC 24-29829. 1924. Doubleday, Page & Company.

Dominant Chord. Edward Kimball. LC 12-5150. 1912. 1.25. L. C. Page & Company.

Dominant Dollar. William Otis Lillibridge. LC 9-24327. 1909. 1.50. A. C. McClurg & Co.

Dominant Fifth. Audrey Louise Laski. LC 72-77394. 1969. 4.95. W. W. Norton.

Dominant Note, and Other Stories. Lucy Lane Clifford. LC 6-20745. 1897. Dodd, Mead and Company.

Dominant Note. 1st Ed. Victor Francis White. LC 56-6782. Bobbs-Merrill.

Dominant Passion: A Novel. Marguerite Bryant. LC 13-24320. 1913. 1.35. Duffield & Company.

Dominant Power. Walter Scott Hill. LC 19-10459. Burton Publishing Company.

Dominant Power. Walter Scott Hill. LC 21-17275. Franklin Book Company.

Dominant Power: A Character Study of the Late 'nineties in Which Cupid and Bacchus Are at Variance. Anna E Satterlee. LC 30-2690. 1930. H. Vinal, Ltd.

Dominant Seventh: A Musical Story. Kate Elizabeth Clark. LC 6-24237. 1890. D. Appelton & Company.

Dominant Seventh. Front. Drypoint by Gene Kloss. Phillips Wray Kloss. LC 51-586. 1950. Caxton Printers.

Dominant Species. George Warren. Ed. by Polly Freas & Kelly Freas. LC 78-15343. (Illus.). 1979. pap. 4.95 o.p. (ISBN 0-915442-63-9, Starblaze). Donning Co.

Dominant Strain. Anna Chapin Ray. 1903. Little, Brown, and Company.

Domination. Ed. by Alkis Kontos. LC 75-37172. 1975. 20.00x o.p. (ISBN 0-8020-2219-7); pap. 7.50 (ISBN 0-8020-6254-7). U of Toronto Pr.

Domination. Jason F. Storm. pap. 2.25 o.s.i. (OPH-211, Ophelia). Olympia.

Dominic Flandry of Terra Series. Poul Anderson. (Science Fiction Ser.). 1979. 72.50 (Gregg). G K Hall.

Dominican Affair. Nick Carter. (Nick Carter Ser.). (Illus.). 224p. 1982. pap. 2.50 (ISBN 0-441-15244-9, Pub. by Charter Bks). Ace Bks.

Dominick Dragon: Or, The Happy Fellow. Charles Norman. LC 51-10005. 1951. Bell Pub. Co.

Dominie Dean: A Novel. Ellis Parker Butler. LC 17-181642. Fleming H. Revell Company.

Dominie of Harlem. Arnold Mulder. LC 13-18720. 1913. 1.25. A. C. McClurg & Co.

Dominie: Or, Reminiscences of a Girl's Life. Sarah Elizabeth Hopkins Bradford. 1890. Hunt & Eaton.

Dominie's Daughter. Joseph McCord. LC 43-4380. 1943. Macrae-Smith-Company.

Dominie's Hope. Amy McLaren. LC 25-3947. 1925. G. P. Putnam's Sons.

Dominie's Legacy: Consisting of a Series of Tales Illustrative of the Scenery and Manners of Scotland... Andrew Picken. LC 7-35919. 1833. Carey, Lea & Blanchard.

Dominie's Son. A Novel. J Hilton Jones. LC 7-11913. 1874. G. P. Putnam's Sons.

Dominion. Pamela Ferguson. LC 77-15829. 1978. 10.95 (ISBN 0-689-10870-2). Atheneum.

Dominion. Fred Saberhagen. 320p. (Orig.). 1982. pap. 2.95 (ISBN 0-523-48536-0). Pinnacle Bks.

Dominion: A Novel of Cecil Rhodes and South Africa. Gladys Skelton. LC 25-6315. 1925. Frederick A. Stokes Company.

Dominion: A Novel of the Early Southwest. Pearl B Mueller. LC 48-946721. 1948. William-Frederick Press.

Dominion of Dreams. Under the Dark Star. William Sharp. LC 72-10968. (Short story index reprint series). 1973. (ISBN 0-8369-4227-2). Books for Libraries Press.

Dominique. Chetwynd-Hayes, R. (Belmont Tower book). 1979. 1.50 (ISBN 0-505-51345-5). Tower Pubns.

Dominique. Eugene Fromentin. Ed. by Stewart, Caroline Taylor. LC 30-31814. (Oxford French series, by American scholars, general editor: R. Weeks). 1930. Oxford University Press.

Dominique: Edited with Introduction, Notes, and Vocabulary. Eugene Fromentin. Ed. by Rhodes, Solomon Alhadef. LC 30-11757. 1930. Prentice-Hall, Inc.

Domino. Phyllis A. Whitney. LC 79-7331. 1979. 10.00 (ISBN 0-385-15419-4). Doubleday.

Domino. Phyllis A. Whitney. LC 79-26483. 1979. 14.95 (ISBN 0-8161-3016-7). G. K. Hall.

Domino. Phyllis A Whitney. 1980. 2.75 (ISBN 0-449-24350-8). Fawcett Crest.

Domino Principle. Adam Kennedy. LC 75-15783. 1975. 5.95 (ISBN 0-670-27812-2). Viking Press.

Domino Principle. Adam Kennedy. (Signet Book)). 1976. 1.95. New American Library.

Domino Spill. William Story. 1981. pap. 2.25 (ISBN 0-8439-0918-8, Leisure Bks). Nordon Pubns.

Dominoes. John William Wainwright. LC 80-14014. 1980. 8.95 (ISBN 0-312-21668-8). St. Martin's Press.

Dominoes: Five-up & Other Games. Dominic C. Armanino. LC 59-12264. 194p. 1972. pap. 4.95 (ISBN 0-679-14009-3). McKay.

Domitia. Sabine Baring-Gould. LC 98-875. Frederick A. Stokes Company.

Domitila: The Romance of an Emperor's Mistress. Paulo Setubal & Richardson, Margaret, Tr. LC 30-21870. 1930. Coward-McCann, Inc.

Domnei. facs. ed. James B. Cabell. LC 75-133517. (Select Bibliographies Reprint Ser). 1920. 16.00 (ISBN 0-8369-5549-8). Ayer Co.

Domnei: A Comedy of Woman-Worship. James Branch Cabell. LC 76-131653. 1970. Scholarly Press.

Domnei: A Comedy of Woman-Worship. James Branch Cabell. LC 75-133517. 1970. (ISBN 0-8369-5549-8). Books for Libraries Press.

Domnei: A Comedy of Woman-Worship. James Branch Cabell. LC 20-201925. 1920. R. M. McBride & Co.

Domnei: A Comedy of Woman-Worship. James Branch Cabell. 1930. R. M. McBride & Company.

Don. Forrest V. Perrin. (O.s.i.). 176p. 1973. pap. 0.95 o.s.i. (AN1083, Award). Univ Pub & Dist.

Don. Goland Ziren. (Orig.). 1972. pap. 0.95 o.p. (T2616). Pyramid Pubns.

Don-a-Dreams: A Story of Love and Youth. Harvey Jerrold O'Higgins. LC 6-29530. 1906. The Century Co.

Don Balasco of Key West: A Novel. Archibald Clavering Gunter. LC 6-46697. The Home Publishing Co.

Don Bartolomeo: A Novel. Jaime De Angulo. LC 73-78140. (Jaime de Angulo library; v. 3). (Illus.). 1974. Turtle Island Foundation.

Don Braulio. Valera y Alcala Galiano, Juan & Bell, Clara, Tr. (On cover: Appletons' town and country library, no. 92). 1892. D. Appleton and Company.

Don Camillo Meets Hell's Angels. Giovanni Guareschi. 1970. 14.95 (ISBN 0-575-00407-X, Pub. by Gollancz England). David & Charles.

Don Camillo Meets the Flower Children. Giovanni Guareschi. LC 70-96146. (Illus.). 1969. 5.95. Farrar, Straus & Giroux.

Don Camillo Takes the Devil by the Tail. Translated by Frances Frenaye. Giovanni Guareschi. LC 57-8937. 1957. Farrar, Straus & Cudahy.

Don Camillo's Dilemma. Translated from the Italian by Frances Frenaye. Giovanni Guareschi. LC 54-9353. 1954. Farrar, Straus and Young.

Don Careless, and Birds of Prey. Rex Ellingwood Beach. LC 28-10876. 1928. Harper & Brothers.

Don Carlos & Other Stories. James A. FitzGerald. LC 81-65342. 168p. 1981. 9.95 (ISBN 0-939296-00-4). Bond Pub Co.

Don Chato. 1st Ed. Anne Sinclair Mehdevi. LC 59-11235. 1959. Knopf.

Don Coronado Through Kansas, 1541, Then Known As Quivira: A Story of the Kansas, Osage, and Pawnee Indians. John Stowell. LC 8-23923. The Don Coronado Co.

Don Coyote: A Novel. Elwyn Whitman Chambers. LC 27-21470. 1927. Rae D. Henkle Co., Inc.

Don Cristobal: By Ernest Goodwin. Ernest Goodwin. LC 29-17047. 1929. Dodd, Mead & Company.

Don Desperado. Leonard London Foreman. LC 41-6793. 1941. E. P. Dutton & Co., Inc.

Don Diego: Or, The Pueblo Indian Uprising of 1680. Albert B Reagan. LC 15-4665. 1914. The Alice Harriman Company.

Don Edwing's Almost Super Heroes. Don Edwing. (Illus.). 192p. 1982. pap. 1.95 (ISBN 0-446-90819-3). Warner Bks.

Don Felipe's Secret. Irene Blight Sands. LC 40-211618. Fortuny's.

Don Finimondone: Calabrian Sketchs. Elizabeth Jones Pullen. LC 3-6819. (Fiction, fact, and fancy series). 1892. C. L. Webster & Co.

Don Flows Home to the Sea. Mikhail Aleksandrovich Sholokhov & Garry, Stephen, Tr. LC 41-5117. 1941. A. A. Knopf.

Don Flows Home to the Sea. Tr. from Russian by Stephen Garry. Mikhail Aleksandrovich Sholokhov. Tr. by Stephen Garry. (Vintage giant. V331). 1966. pap., 2.45. Random.

Don Gastone and the Ladies. Translated from the Italian by Stuart Hood. 1st American Ed. Goffredo Parise. LC 55-9265. 1955. Knopf.

Don Gaucho. Alyce Pollock & Ruth Goode. LC 50-6682. 1950. Whittlesey House.

Don Gesualdo. Louise De La Ramee. (On cover: The seaside library. Pocket ed. no. 671). 1886. G. Munro.

Don Goyo. Aguilera Malta, Demetrio. LC 80-81656. (Contemporary Literature). (Illus.). 12.50 (ISBN 0-89603-019-9). Humana Press.

Don Jim. Charles Horace Snow. LC 32-11202. 1932. Macrae Smith Company.

Don John. Jean Ingelow. (seaside library, v. 48, no. 982). 1881. G. Munro.

Don Juan. George G. Byron. Ed. by L. Marchand. LC 58-14387. (YA) (gr. 9 up). 1958. pap. 5.50 (ISBN 0-395-05138-X, 3-47674, RivEd, B40). HM.

Don Juan. Joseph Delteil. Tr. by Boyle, Kay. LC 31-103823. 1931. J. Cape & H. Smith.

Don Juan. Ludwig Lewisohn. LC 23-14409. Boni and Liveright.

Don Juan and the Wheelbarrow: And Other Stories. Leonard Alfred George Strong. LC 33-14504. 1933. A. A. Knopf.

Don Juan De Marana. Arnold Bennett. (Collected Works of Arnold Bennett: Vol. 15). 1976. Repr. of 1923 ed. 17.25 (ISBN 0-518-19096-X). Ayer Co.

Don Juan in Lourdes. Robert De Maria. LC 66-15327. 1966. bds., 6.50. St. Martin's.

Don Juan in Melanesia. Peter Lawrence. (Illus.). 1967. pap. 4.95x (ISBN 0-7022-0059-X). U of Queensland Pr.

Don Juan in Tulsa. Richard Power. 1982. 12.50 (ISBN 0-916620-54-9). Portals Pr.

Don Juan McQueen. Eugenia Price. LC 74-8941. (Illus.). 1974. 8.95 (ISBN 0-397-01057-5). Lippincott.

Don Juan McQueen. Eugenia Price. 1975. (pbk.) 1.75. Bantam Books.

Don Juan of China: An Amour from the Chin Ping Mei. Kwan Shan-Mei. Tr. by Samuel Buck. LC 60-11511. (Illus.). 1960. 4.15 o.p. (ISBN 0-8048-0142-8). C E Tuttle.

Don Juan: Or, The Continuum of the Libido. Paul Goodman & Taylor Stoehr. LC 79-13657. 1979. 14.00. (ISBN 0-87685-422-6) (ISBN 0-87685-421-8) (ISBN 0-87685-423-4). Black Sparrow Press.

Don Juan: Or, The Elixir of Long Life, and Other Stories. Honore De Balzac. LC 43-43111. The F. M. Lupton Publishing Company.

Don Juan: The Life and Death of Don Miguel De Manars. Toman, Josef. LC 58-10969. 1958. Knopf.

Don Juaneen. John Broderick. 1965. 7.95 (ISBN 0-8392-1156-2). Astor-Honor.

Don Juaneen: A Novel. John Broderick. LC 65-25349. 1965. 3.95. Obolensky.

Don Juan's Bar. Antonio Callado. 1972. 7.95 o.p. (ISBN 0-394-47212-8). Knopf.

Don Juan's Bar: A Novel. Antonio Callado. LC 70-171120. 1972. 7.95 (ISBN 0-394-47212-8). Knopf.

Don Juan's Daughters: Together with Dream Children and The Burden. Irene Flemming Forbes-Mosse & Williams, Oakley, Tr. LC 31-2180. 1930. Dodd, Mead & Co.

Don Lopez De Vere: A Romance. Judith Elizabeth Farley. A. & W. P. Ball Publishing Co.

Don Lorenzo's Bride. Juanita Savage. LC 30-30240. 1930. L. MacVeagh, The Dial Press.

Don Luis' Wife: A Romance of the West Indies, from Her Letters and the Manuscripts of the Padre, the Doctor Caccavelli, Marc Aurele, Curate of Samana. Lillian Hinman Shuey. LC 8-7322. 1897. Lamson, Wolffe and Company.

Don MacGrath: A Tale of the River. Randall Parrish. LC 10-21753. 1910. 1.50. A. C. McClurg & Co.

Don Martin Forges Ahead. Don Martin. (Illus., Orig.). 1977. pap. 1.95 (ISBN 0-446-30447-6). Warner Bks.

Don Miguel, and Other Stories. Edward Sims Van Zile. LC 8-30216. Cassell Publishing Company.

Don Not Inhale It. Emery Balint. LC 49-49189. 1949. Gaer Associates.

Don Orsino. Francis Marion Crawford. LC 4-15089. 1892. Macmillan and Co.

Don Orsino. Francis Marion Crawford. LC 41-42501. 1899. The Macmillan Company.

Don Orsino. Francis Marion Crawford. LC 26-22311. 1912. The Regent Press.

Don Orsino. Francis Marion Crawford. LC 20-18834. 1919. The Macmillan Company.

Don Pedro and the Devil: A Novel of Chivalry Declining. Edgar Maass. LC 42-67601. 1942. The Bobbs-Merrill Company.

Don Pedro's Captain. Pamela Bennetts. LC 77-11740. 1978. 7.95 (ISBN 0-312-21677-7). St. Martin's Press.

Don Q. Jose Lopez-Portillo Y Pacheco. Tr. by Eliot Weinberger & Wilfrido Corral. LC 76-22613. 1976. 8.95 (ISBN 0-8264-0094-9). Continuum.

Don Q: By Jose Lopez-Portillo; Translated from the Spanish by Eliot Weinberger & Wilfrido Corral. Lopez-Portillo y Pacheco, Jose. LC 76-22613. (Continuum book). 8.95 (ISBN 0-8164-9304-9). Seabury Press.

Don Q. in the Sierra. Kate O'Brien Hesketh Prichard & Prichard, Hesketh Vernon Hesketh. 1906. J. B. Lippincott Company.

Don Q's Love Story. Kate O'Brien Hesketh Prichard & Prichard, Hesketh Vernon Hesketh. LC 25-16488. Grosset & Dunlap.

Don Quickshot Looking for Trouble. Stephen Chambers. LC 26-22319. 1926. Garden City Publishing Co., Inc.

Don Quijote. Miguel de Cervantes de Saavedra. (Span). 7.50x. Colton Bk.

Don Quijote De la Mancha. Miguel de Cervantes de Saavedra. Ed. by J. Cano. (Span). 1961. pap. 2.50x o.p. (32052). Macmillan.

Don Quixote. Miguel de Cervantes de Saavedra. Tr. by Jarvis, Charles. Fitzmaurice-Kelly, James. (Half-title: The world's classics, cxxx). 1907. H. Frowde.

Don Quixote. Miguel de Cervantes de Saavedra. Ed. by Howells, William Dean. Tr. by Jarvis, Charles. LC 29-129603. 1923. Harper & Brothers.

Don Quixote... Miguel de Cervantes de Saavedra. Tr. by Motteux, Peter Anthony. Ed. by Lockhart, John Gibson. LC 36-37618. (Half-title: Everyman's library, ed. by Ernest Rhys. Romance. no. 385-386). 1930-32. J. M. Dent & Sons, Ltd.

Don Quixote. Miguel de Cervantes de Saavedra. Ed. by Sheridan, Susan Smith. LC 26-10321. (modern readers' series). 1926. The Macmillan Company.

Don Quixote. unabr. ed. Miguel de Cervantes de Saavedra. Tr. by Walter Starkie. (Orig.). 1957. pap. 4.50 (ISBN 0-451-51682-6, CE1682, Sig Classics). NAL.

Don Quixote. Miguel de Cervantes de Saavedra. (Oxford Progressive English Readers Ser.). (Illus.). 1973. pap. text ed. 3.50x (ISBN 0-19-638224-6). Oxford U Pr.

Don Quixote. Miguel de Cervantes de Saavedra. Tr. by John M. Cohen. (Classics Ser.). (Orig.). (YA) (gr. 9 up). 1951. pap. 5.95 (ISBN 0-14-044010-0). Penguin.

Don Quixote. Miguel de Cervantes de Saavedra. 1981. Repr. lib. bdg. 18.95x (ISBN 0-89966-383-4). Buccaneer Bks.

Don Quixote. Miguel de Cervantes de Saavedra. Tr. & intro. by Samuel Putnam. 10.95 (ISBN 0-394-60438-5). Modern Lib.

Don Quixote. Miguel de Cervantes de Saavedra. Ed. by Crocker. pap. 0.75 o.p. (46901). WSP.

Don Quixote. Miguel de Cervantes de Saavedra. Tr. by Peter A. Motteux. 2.95 o.p. (174). Modern Lib.

Don Quixote. Miguel de Cervantes de Saavedra. Tr. by Peter A. Motteux. pap. 1.60x o.p. (ISBN 0-394-30909-X, T6, Mod LibC). Modern Lib.

Don Quixote. Miguel de Cervantes de Saavedra. (Modern Library Giants). 4.95 o.p. (ISBN 0-394-60715-5, G15). Modern Lib.

Don Quixote. Miquel De Cervantes. LC 76-6691. (Illustrated Classics Ser.). 1976. 10.00 o.p. (ISBN 0-8055-1196-2); pap. 4.95 o.p. (ISBN 0-8055-0282-3). Hart.

Don Quixote De la Mancha. a rev. translation based on those of motteux, jarvis, and smollett... ed. Miguel de Cervantes de Saavedra. LC 16-7014. 1853. D. Appleton and Company.

Don Quixote De la Mancha... Miguel de Cervantes de Saavedra. (Seaside library, v. 34, no. 691). 1880. G. Munro.

Don Quixote De la Mancha. Miguel de Cervantes de Saavedra. LC 6-23331. (On cover: Lovell's library,v. 8, no. 417). 1884. J. W. Lovell Company.

Don Quixote De la Mancha. aldine ed. Miguel de Cervantes de Saavedra. Tr. by Watts, Henry Edward. O'Connor, Joseph. LC 99-247. (Half-title: The world's great books--Aldine ed.). 1898. D. Appleton and Company.

Don Quixote De La Mancha. Miguel de Cervantes de Saavedra. Ed. by Burt, Mary Elizabeth & Bikle, Mrs. Lucy Leffingwell (Cable) LC 2-14857. (Scribner's series of school reading). 1902. C. Scribner's Sons.

Don Quixote De la Mancha. Miguel de Cervantes de Saavedra. Tr. by Motteux, Peter Anthony. Barret, Leighton. LC 39-21689. 1939. Little, Brown & Company.

Don Quixote De la Mancha, Vol. 1. Miguel de Cervantes de Saavedra. 1975. Repr. of 1906 ed. 9.95x (ISBN 0-460-00385-2, Evman). Biblio Dist.

Don Quixote: Designed to Be Read As a Modern Novel. Miguel de Cervantes de Saavedra. Tr. by Peter Anthony Motteux & Charles Jarvis. Ed. by Richard Emery Robert. Book League of America, Inc. LC 46-3828. 1946. The Book League of America.

Don Quixote of America. Charles Hemstreet. LC 21-2386. 1921. Dodd, Mead and Company.

Don Quixote of La Mancha. Miguel de Cervantes de Saavedra. Ed. by Paul Thomas Manchester. LC 72-97515. (Fawcett premier book, P583). 1973. 1.25. Fawcett Publications.

Don Quixote of La Mancha: An Abridged Version Designed to Relate Without Digressions the Principal Adventures of the Knight and His Squire. Translated and Edited with a Biographical Prelude by Walter Starkie. With Decorations from the Drawings by Gustave Dore. Miguel de Cervantes de Saavedra. Ed. by Walter Fitzwilliam Starkie. LC 54-3433. 1954. Macmillan.

Don Quixote of La Mancha. An Abridged Version Designed to Relate Without Digressions the Principal Adventures of the Knight and His Squire. Translated and Edited with an Introd. by Walter Starkie. Miguel de Cervantes de Saavedra. Ed. by Walter Fitzwilliam Starkie. LC 57-3941. (Mentor book, MD207). 1957. New American Library.

Don Quixote of la Mancha: Reissue Tr., Ed., Introd. by Walter Starkie. Miguel de Cervantes de Saavedra. (Mentor bk., MP407). 1964. New Amer. Lib.

Don Quixote of the Mancha. Miguel de Cervantes de Saavedra & Parry, Edward Abbott. 1909. John Lane Company.

Don Quixote of the Mancha. Miguel de Cervantes de Saavedra & Parry, Edward Abbott. LC 11-4938. 1911. John Lane Company.

Don Quixote of the Mancha. Miguel de Cervantes de Saavedra & Sir Edward Abbott Perry. 1960. Dodd, Mead.

Don Quixote. Ozell's Revision of the Tr. of Peter Motteuz. Introd. by Raymond R. Canon. Miguel de Cervantes de Saavedra. (Classics ser., CL153). 1967. pap., 1.25. Airmont.

Don Quixote, U. S. A. By Richard Powell. Richard Pitts Powell. (S3531). 1967. Bantam.

Don Quixote: U.S.A. Richard Pitts Powell. LC 66-20542. 4.95. Scribners.

Don Ricardo. Francis Vere. LC 52-28539. 1952. Staples Press.

Don Rodriguez: Chronicles of Shadow Valley. Edward John Moreton Drax Plunkett Dunsany. LC 70-24745. (Adult fantasy). 1971. 0.95. Ballantine Books.

Don Rogerio: A Grand Romance of Elizabethan Days. Somers Gill. LC 43-185603. 1943. Rich & Cowan.

Don Sagasto's Daughter: A Romance of Southern California. Paul Harcourt Blades. LC 11-16263. R. G. Badger.

Don Sebastian: Or, The House of Braganza. An Historical Romance... Anna Maria Porter. 1835. J. and B. Williams.

Don Segundo Sombra: Shadows on the Pampas. Ricardo Guiraldes. Tr. by Onis, Harriet De. Frank, Waldo David. LC 35-27024. Farrar & Rinehart, Incorporated.

Don Segundo Sombra. Ricardo Guiraldes & Plimpton, Ethel Williams, Ed. LC 45-11164. 1945. H. Holt and Company.

Don Segundo Sombra: Shadows on the Pampas. Translated and with an Afterword by Harriet De Onis. Illustrated by Alberto Guiraldes. Ricardo Guiraldes. Tr. by De Onis, Harriet. LC 66-3412. (Signet classic, CT317). 1966. New American Library.

Don Swashbuckler. Eugene Percy Lyle. LC 98-1585. (Neely's universal library, no. 34). 1898. F. T. Neely.

Don Tarquinio: A Kataleptic Phantasmatic Romance. Frederick William Rolfe. LC 70-480537. 270p. 1969. 8.00x (ISBN 0-7011-1384-7). Intl Pubns Serv.

Don the Burp & Other Stories. Ray Dobbins. (Illus.). 50p. (Orig.). 1982. pap. 5.00 (ISBN 0-930762-06-1). Calamus Bks.

Dona Barbara. Romulo Gallegos. Tr. by Malloy, Robert. LC 31-20843. 1931. J. Cape and H. Smith.

Dona Barbara. Romulo Gallegos & Dunham, Lowell, Ed. LC 42-21906. 1942. F. S. Crofts & Co.

Dona Celestis. Ethel May Dell. LC 33-24663. 1933. G. P. Putnam's Sons.

Dona Eleanora and Lord Edward. Barbara McGraw. LC 81-21241. (Adult Readers Library). (Illus.). 1.98 (ISBN 0-673-24129-7). Scott, Foresman.

Dona Flor and Her Two Husbands. Jorge Amado. (Bard Book). 1977. 2.75 (ISBN 0-380-01796-2). Avon.

Dona Flor and Her Two Husbands: A Moral and Amorous Tale. Jorge Amado. LC 69-10710. 1969. 6.95. Knopf.

Dona Lona: A Story of Old Taos and Santa Fe. Blanche Chloe Grant. LC 41-21541. W. Funk, Inc.

Dona Luz. Valera y Alcala Galiano, Juan. LC 75-1185. 1975. 12.50. H. Fertig.

Dona Luz. Valera y Alcala Galiano, Juan. Tr. by Mary Jane Serrano. LC 43-26796. 1891. D. Appleton and Company.

Dona Perfecta. Galdos Benito Perez. Tr. by Mary Jane Christie D. Serrano. LC 4-16891. 1896. Harper and Brothers.

Dona Perfecta. Galdos Benito Perez. Tr. by Mary Hane Christie D. Serrano. LC 24-11876. (Students' literal translations). The Translation Publishing Company, Inc.

Dona Perfecta. Benito Perez Galdos. Tr. by Mary J. Serrano. 1979. Repr. of 1895 ed. lib. bdg. 30.00 (ISBN 0-8495-2005-3). Arden Lib.

Dona Perfecta: Novela Espanola Contemporance. Benito Perez Galdos. Ed. by Marsh, Arthur Richmond. LC 35-24050. (On cover: International modern language series). 1900. Ginn & Company.

Dona Perfecta. Translation and Introd. by Harriet De Onis. Galdos Benito Perez. LC 60-224216. 1960. Barron's Educational Series, Inc.

Donal Grant. George Macdonald. LC 4-23577. 1883. D. Lothrop and Company.

Donal Grant. George Macdonald. LC 4-17543. (On cover: The home library). A. L. Burt.

Donal Grant. A Novel. George Macdonald. (Harper's Franklin square library, no. 335). 1883. Harper & Brothers.

Donald Campbell's Loyalty. Sara Currie Palmer. LC 22-192. The Bible Institute Colportage Ass'n.

Donald Dyke: The Yankee Detective. Ernest A. Young. LC 3780. (On cover: Magnet detective library. no. 137). 1900. Street & Smith.

Donald Has a Difficulty. Edward Gorey & Peter F. Neumeyer. LC 82-12839. 1982. 4.95 (ISBN 0-88496-175-3). Capra Press.

Donald MacDonald. Josephine Holt Throckmorton. LC 7-20710. 1907. The Neale Publishing Company.

Donald McElroy: Scotch Irishman. Willie Walker Caldwell. LC 18-199842. G. W. Jacobs & Company.

Donald McLane, a Religious Novel. Charles Foster Cole. LC 7-18094. 1907. Republican Printing Company.

Donald McRea. Hanford Montrose Burr. LC 11-215814. 1911. The Seminar Publishing Co.

Donald Marcy. Elizabeth Stuart Phelps H. D. Ward Ward. LC 8-33115. 1893. Houghton, Mifflin and Company.

Donald Moncrieff. Jeanie Oliver Davidson Smith. LC 8-8168. 1893. C. W. Moulton.

Donald Patterson's Daughter. S. K Reeves. LC 7-30661. 1893. The American Sunday-School Union.

Donald Ross of Heimra: A Novel. William Black. LC 6-12966. (On cover: Harper's Franklin square library, no. 703). 1891. Harper & Brothers.

Donald Stephenson's Reminiscences. A True Story. Donald S Mulhern. LC 7-33322. 1891. W. G. Johncton & Co., Printers.

Donald Writes No More. Eddie Stone. (Orig.). 1977. pap. 1.75 (ISBN 0-87067-511-7, BH017). Holloway.

Donavan. Carter Brown, pseud. (Signet book). 1974. (pbk.) 0.95. New American Library.

Donavan's Day. Carter Brown, pseud. (Signet Book). 1975. (pbk.) 1.25. New American Library.

Donavan's Delight. Carter Brown, pseud. 1979. pap. 1.50 (ISBN 0-505-51382-X). Tower Bks.

Donde Termina la Noche. Olga Rosado. LC 78-74598. (Coleccion Caniqui). (Illus.). 1979. pap. 5.95 (ISBN 0-89729-217-0). Ediciones.

Done. Lawrence Huff. 1979. 2.50 (ISBN 0-671-83182-8). Pocket Books.

Done to Death. Sara Woods, pseud. LC 74-15487. (Rinehart suspense novel). 1975. 5.95 (ISBN 0-03-013871-X). Holt, Rinehart and Winston.

Donkey, Daniel: A Christmas Story. Florence Reinhard. 3.95 o.p. Vantage.

Donkey, Daniel: A Christmas Story. Florence Reinhard. (Illus.). 1974. 3.95 (ISBN 0-533-01356-9). Vantage Press.

Donkey of God. Louis Untermeyer. LC 32-270044. Harcourt, Brace and Company.

Donkey Shoe. Gladys Bronwyn Stern. LC 52-10001. 1952. Macmillan.

Donkey Who Always Complained: A Parable for Moderns. Illus. by Johannes Troyer. Francis Beauchesne Thornton. LC 56-10502. 1956. P. J. Kenedy.

Donna Diana. Richard Bagot. LC 2-22730. 1902. Longmans, Green, and Co.

Donna Lisa: An Italian Idyll. Wilfranc Hubbard. LC 24-316825. 1924. The Macmillan Company.

Donna Quixote. Justin McCarthy. (Seaside library. v. 32, no. 663). 1879. G. Munro.

Donna Quixote. A Novel. Justin McCarthy. (Franklin square library, no.95). 1879. Harper & Brothers.

Donnegan: A Western Story. George Owen Baxter. LC 23-1647. 1923. Chelsea House.

Donner People. Lee D. Willoughby. (Making of America Ser.: No. 24). (Orig.). 1982. pap. 2.95 (ISBN 0-440-02084-0, Bryans). Dell.

Donnington Legend. David Beaty. LC 49-10717. 1949. W. Morrow.

Donors. Leslie A. Horvitz & H. Harris Gerhard. 1982. pap. 2.95 (ISBN 0-451-11338-1, AE1338, Sig). NAL.

Donovan. Ada Ellen Bayly. LC 75-1529. (Victorian Fiction: Novels of Faith and Doubt). 1976. 35.00 (ISBN 0-8240-1601-7). Garland Pub.

Donovan: A Modern Englishman. A Novel. Ada Ellen Bayly. LC 4-16491. 1902. D. Appleton and Company.

Donovan, a Novel, 1882. Ada Ellen Bayly. Ed. by Robert L. Wolff. LC 75-1529. (Victorian Fiction Series). 1975. lib. bdg. 66.00 (ISBN 0-8240-1601-7). Garland Pub.

Donovan Pasha: And Some People of Egypt. Gilbert Parker. LC 2-23090. 1902. D. Appleton & Company.

Donovan Rides. Arthur Henry Gooden. LC 37-366543. The Macaulay Company.

Donovan's Brain. Curt Siodmak. LC 43-1291. 1943. A. A. Knopf.

Dons of the Old Pueblo. Percival John Cooney. LC 14-15173. Rand, McNally & Company.

Don't Argue with Death. Leonard Reginald Gribble. LC 59-8450. 1959. Roy Publishers.

Don't Ask Me If I Love: A Novel. Amos Kollek. LC 74-150798. 1971. 5.95. M. Evans; Distributed in Association with Lippincott, Philadelphia.

Don't Be No Hero. Leonard Harris. LC 78-2894. 8.95 (ISBN 0-517-53250-6). Crown Publishers.

Don't Bet on Living, Alice. Kirby Carr. LC 75-14501. 192p. (Orig.). 1975. pap. 1.25 (ISBN 0-89041-017-8, 3017). Major Bks.

Don't Bite off More Than You Can Chew. Troy Conway, pseud. (Coxeman Ser., No. 1). Orig. Title: Berlin Wall Affair. 1971. pap. 0.95 o.p. (ISBN 0-446-65759-X, 65-759-X). Paperback Lib.

Don't Bite the Sun. Tanith Lee. (Science Fiction Ser.). 1976. pap. 1.75 (ISBN 0-87997-486-9, UE1486). DAW Bks.

Don't Blow Your Cool. Marshall Terry, Jr. Orig. Title: Old Liberty. 1967. pap. 0.50 o.p. (52-575). Paperback Lib.

Don't Call Back. Russell O'Neil. (Dell Book). 1.75 (ISBN 0-440-12124-8). Dell Pub. Co., Inc.

Don't Call It Love. Inez Sabastian. LC 30-16613. The Macaulay Company.

Don't Call Me by My Right Name: And Other Stories. With Illus. by the Author. James Purdy. LC 56-686694. 1956. William-Frederick Press.

Don't Call Me Clever: A Novel. Lawrence Drake. LC 29-19777. 1929. Simon and Schuster.

Don't Call Me Madame. Henry Kane. (Peter Chambers Mystery Ser). (Orig.). 1969. pap. 0.60 o.p. (73-858). Lancer.

Don't Catch Me. Richard Pitts Powell. LC 43-51007. 1942. Simon and Schuster.

Don't Come Crying to Me. William Ard. LC 54-5649. (Murray Hill mystery). 1954. Rinehart.

Don't Count Your Chicks. Ingri D' Aulaire & Edgar Parin D' Aulaire. (Zephyr Book). (Illus.). 1973. 0.95. Doubleday.

Don't Crowd. Charles Dickens. 59.95 (ISBN 0-8490-0058-0). Gordon Pr.

Don't Cry for Long. Thomas Blanchard Dewey. LC 64-22417. (Inner sanctum mystery). 1964. Simon and Schuster.

Don't Cry for Me. William Campbell Gault. LC 51-14972. (Guilt edged mystery). 1952. Dutton.

Don't Cry for the Sick. Sketches by W. E. Terry. Frank W Milhening. LC 54-24976. 1952.

Don't Cry, Little Girl. Norman Parker. LC 77-106632. 1970. 4.95. Whitmore Pub. Co.

Don't Cry Little Sister. Jennette Dowling Letton. LC 77-166317. 1971. 4.95 (ISBN 0-8255-5291-5). M. Smith Co.

Don't Drive up a Dirt Road: A Novel. Dorothy Whitney Ball. LC 73-112653. 1970. (ISBN 0-87460-076-6) (ISBN 0-87460-144-4). Lion Press.

Don't Drop Dead Tomorrow. Hugh Pentecost. 1971. 4.95 o.p. (ISBN 0-396-06389-6). Dodd.

Don't Drop Dead Tomorrow. Judson Pentecost Philips. LC 79-163073. (Red badge novel of suspense). 1971. 4.95 (ISBN 0-396-06389-6). Dodd, Mead.

Don't Embarrass the Bureau. Bernard F Conners. LC 74-179638. 1972. 6.95. Bobbs-Merrill.

Don't Ever Forget. Brigid Brophy. 1967. 5.95 o.p. (ISBN 0-03-064145-4). HR&W.

Don't Ever Leave Me. Katharine Brush. LC 35-5828. Farrar & Rinehart, Incorporated.

Don't Feed the Animals: By John Farr Pseud. Jack Webb. LC 55-5042. 1955. Abelard-Schuman.

Don't Fence Me in: A Wilderness Campfire Anthology. Ed. by Dave Foreman & Bart Koehler. Jackson Spurs. (Ned Ludd Book). (Illus.). 400p. (Orig.). 1983. pap. price not set (ISBN 0-942688-03-1). Dream Garden.

Don't Forget the Linens. Sanders et al. 100p. (Orig.). 1981. pap. 4.95. Crossroads Prods.

Don't Get Mad, Get Even. Elvin C. Bell. LC 80-84227. 9.95 (ISBN 0-934086-13-3). JSB Enterprises.

Don't Get Stuck in Our Chimney. Jerry Rosman. 1965. 3.00 o.p. (ISBN 0-682-43127-3); pap. 1.95 o.p. (ISBN 0-682-40121-8). Exposition.

Don't Get Taken Every Time: The Insider's Guide to Buying Your Next Car. Remar Sutton. 382p. 1983. pap. 5.95 (ISBN 0-14-046597-9). Penguin.

Don't Give Up. Dixie Anderson. 1980. 4.95 o.p. (ISBN 0-8062-1446-5). Carlton.

Dont' Give up the Ship!". Charles Seely Wood. LC 12-214011. 1912. The Macmillan Company.

Don't Give up the Ship: A Novel of the Hawaiian Islands. James T Hamada. LC 33-14137. 1933. Meador Publishing Company.

Don't Go Away Dead. Henry Kane. (Peter Chambers Ser). (Orig.). 1970. pap. 0.75 o.p. (ISBN 0-447-74595-6). Lancer.

Don't Go Away Mad. Joseph Arnold Hayes. LC 62-9079. 1962. Random House.

Don't Go Dancing Mother. 2nd, enl. ed. Rose Safran. (Illus.). Date not set. pap. 5.95 (ISBN 0-9602786-3-X). Tide Bk Pub Co.

Don't Go Dancing Mother. Rose Safran. LC 79-64288. (Illus.). 1979. pap. 5.50 (ISBN 0-9602786-1-3). Tide Bk Pub Co.

Don't Go in Alone: By Genevieve Holden Pseud. Genevieve Long Pou. LC 65-13705. 3.50. Pub. for the Crime Club by Doubleday.

Don't Go into the Woods Today. Doris Miles Disney. LC 73-15334. 1974. 7.95 (ISBN 0-385-00471-0). Published for the Crime Club by Doubleday.

Don't Go Near the Water. William Brinkley. LC 56-521977. 1956. Random House.

Don't Go to Sleep in the Dark: A Collection of Short Stories of Suspense. Celia Fremlin, pseud. 1970. 4.95 o.p. (ISBN 0-397-00643-8). Lippincott.

Don't Go to Sleep in the Dark: Short Stories. Celia Fremlin, pseud. LC 71-135360. 1970. 4.95. Lippincott.

Don't Hang Me Too High. James Brendan O'Sullivan. LC 54-10206. 1954. M. S. Mill Co.

Don't Just Die There. 2nd ed. Henry Kane. Orig. Title: Never Give a Millionaire an Even Break. 1969. pap. 0.60 o.p. (73-823). Lancer.

Don't Lie to Me. Tucker Coe. 1972. 4.95 o.p. (ISBN 0-394-47165-2). Random.

Don't Lie to Me. Donald E Westlake. LC 72-3111. 1972. 4.95 (ISBN 0-394-47165-2). Random House.

Don't Look a Gift Shark in the Mouth. Ed. by Alfred Hitchcock. 1976. pap. 1.95 (ISBN 0-440-13620-2). Dell.

Don't Look at Me Like That. Diana Athill. LC 67-26083. 1967. Viking Press.

Don't Look Back. 1st Ed. Miriam Borgenicht. LC 56-5958. 1956. Published for the Crime Club by Doubleday.

Don't Look Behind You. Margaret Erkskine. (Ace gothic). 1974. (pbk.) 0.95. Ace Books.

Don't Look Behind You! Samuel Rogers. LC 44-7923. 1944. Harper & Brothers.

Don't Look Behind You. Marilyn Ross. (Warner Paperback Library Gothic)). 1973. (pbk.) 0.95. Warner Paperback Lib.

Don't Look Now. Daphne Du Maurier. LC 70-163092. 1971. 6.95. Doubleday.

Don't Look Now. Daphne Du Maurier. LC 72-38929. 1972. 9.95 (ISBN 0-8161-6019-8). G. K. Hall.

Don't Look Now. Daphne Du Maurier. 1977. pap. 2.50 (ISBN 0-380-01144-1, 45252). Avon.

Don't Make Waves: Formerly: Muscle Beach. Ira Jan Wallach. (2130). 1967. Dell.

Don't Marry the Man. Peggy O'More, pseud. LC 38-14888. 1938. Hillman-Curl, Inc.

Don't Mention My Name. Eaton K Goldthwaite. LC 42-19129. 1942. Duell, Sloan and Pearce.

Don't Mention the Moon. Richard Cohen. LC 82-19248. 15.95 (ISBN 0-399-31009-6). Seaview/Putnam.

Don't Mind Dying: A Novel of Country Lust and Urban Decay. Steve Chapple. LC 78-22309. 1980. 10.00 (ISBN 0-385-14934-4). Doubleday.

Don't Mr. Disraeli!". Doris Caroline Abrahams & Simon Jasha Skidelsky. LC 41-5366. G.P. Putnam's Sons.

Don't Open the Door. Ursula Reilly Curtiss. LC 68-29806. (Red badge mystery). 1968. 3.95. Dodd, Mead.

Don't Panic. Ruth Winter. 1975. 4.95 o.p. (ISBN 0-307-48720-2, Golden Pr). Western Pub.

Don't Play Us Cheap: A Harlem Party. Melvin Van Peebles. LC 73-4816. (Illus.). 1973. 1.25. Bantam Books.

Don't Push Me Around: A Novel of Suspense. Elliott Gilbert. LC 55-42185. (Popular library, 681). 1955. Popular Library.

Don't Push My Trees Around. Marion Sherrard Oneal. LC 64-19191. 1964. Greenwich Book Publishers.

Don't Put My Name on This Book. Henny Youngman. 192p. 1976. pap. 1.25 o.p. Manor Bks.

Don't Raise the Bridge -- Lower the River: A Novel. Max Wilk. LC 60-5405. 1960. Macmillan.

Don't Rely on Gemini. Marijane Meaker. LC 73-77886. 1969. 4.95. Delacorte Press.

Don't Rely on Gemini. Vin Packer. 1969. 4.95 o.p. (6). Delacorte.

Dont Say Yes When You Want to Say No. Herbert Fensterheim & Jean Baer. 1975. pap. 3.50 (ISBN 0-440-15413-8). Dell.

Don't Shoot Darling. Henry Holt. 2.95 o.p. Roy.

Don't Shut Me Out. Dorothy Phoebe Ansle. LC 77-77925. 1977. 6.95 (ISBN 0-525-09460-1). Dutton.

Don't Shut Me Out. Laura Conway. 1977. 6.95 o.p. (ISBN 0-525-09460-1). Dutton.

Don't Sit Under the Apple Tree. Robin F. Brancato. 128p. 1980. pap. 1.75 (ISBN 0-553-12966-X). Bantam.

Don't Step on It: It Might Be a Writer. Donald MacCampbell. 190p. 1972. 5.95 o.p. (ISBN 0-8202-0093-X). Sherbourne.

Don't Step on My Shadow. Walt Hoster. 1970. 2.95 o.p. Vantage.

Don't Stop for Hooky Hefferman. Laurence Walter Meynell. LC 77-15068. (Jubilee Mystery Ser.). 224p. 7.95 o.s.i. (ISBN 0-8128-2422-9). Stein & Day.

Don't Stop the Carnival. Herman Wouk. LC 64-22324. (Illus.). 1973. 7.95. Doubleday.

Don't Stop the Carnival. Wouk, Herman. 1973. (pbk.) 1.50. Pocket Books.

Don't Talk to Strangers. Beverly Hastings. 224p. 1981. pap. 2.75 (ISBN 0-515-06437-8). Jove Pubns.

Don't Tell Daddy. Barbara Petty. (Orig.). 1982. pap. 2.95 (ISBN 0-440-12096-9). Dell.

Don't Tell Me Your Name: A Novel. Hollis Hodges. LC 78-17235. 7.95 (ISBN 0-517-53472-X). Crown, Publishers.

Don't Tell Me Your Name: A Novel. hollis hodges. ed. Hollis Hodges. 1981. 2.25 (ISBN 0-380-53751-6). Avon Books.

Don't the Moon Look Lonesome. Don Asher. LC 67-18375. 1967. Atheneum.

Don't Touch Me. MacKinlay Kantor. LC 51-12521. 1951. Random House.

Don't Tread on Me: A Novel of the Historic Exploits, Military and Gallant, of Commodore John Paul Jones. Walter Karig. LC 54-7074. (Illus.). 1954. Rinehart.

Don't Wager on Love. Monette Cummings. (Orig.). 1981. pap. 1.95 (ISBN 0-8439-8041-9, Tiara Bks). Nordon Pubns.

Don't Wait for Love. Maysie Greig. LC 37-208. 1936. Doubleday, Doran and Co., Inc.

Don't Wait for Love. Maysie Greig. LC 42-9791. 1941. Traingle Books.

Don't Wait for Me, I'm Already Gone: A Novel. Wal Watkins. LC 73-158950. 1972. 1.65 (ISBN 0-7260-0041-8). Gold Star Publications.

Don't Wait up for Spring. Charles Henry Mergendahl. LC 44-9098. 1944. Little, Brown and Company.

Don't Wake Me up While I'm Driving. Margaret Scherf. LC 76-19622. 1977. 5.95 (ISBN 0-385-12253-5). Published for the Crime Club by Doubleday.

Don't Walk on My Dreams: A Novel. Annie Greene Nelson. LC 76-18308. (Illus.). 1976. 12.00 (ISBN 0-87152-245-4). Reprint Co.

Don't Wear Your Wedding Ring. Lillian O'Donnell. LC 73-76132. (Red mask mystery). 1973. 4.95. Putnam.

Don't Whistle 'Macbeth' David Fletcher, pseud. LC 76-378939. 1976. 2.95 (ISBN 0-333-18780-6). Macmillan.

Don't You Cry for Me: A Novel. John Weld. LC 40-7428. 1940. C. Scribner's Sons.

Don't You Ever Be Afeared. Wilda L Summers. LC 77-104985. 1970. 4.00. Dorrance.

Don't You Weep, Don't You Moan. Richard Coleman. LC 35-3244. 1935. The Macmillan Company.

Dont't Stop for Hooky Hefferman. Laurence Walter Meynell. LC 77-15068. 1977. 7.95 (ISBN 0-8128-2422-9). Stein and Day.

Doobie Doo. Ivan C. Karp. 1968. pap. 0.60 o.p. (73-588). Lancer.

Doobie Doo: A Novel. Ivan C Karp. LC 66-11740. 1966. Doubleday.

Doodab. Harold A Loeb. LC 26-139. 1925. Boni & Liveright.

Dooley's Delusion. Tom McHale. LC 74-161091. 1971. 4.95 (ISBN 0-87667-070-2). Droke House/Hallux.

Doolie's Private Goddess see Up-Tight.

Doom. rev. definitive ed. William Alexander Gerhardie. LC 73-93995. 1975. 7.95. St. Martin's Press.

Doom! an Atlantic Episode. Justin Huntly McCarthy. LC 7-152884. (Harper's handy series, no. 68). 1886. Harper & Brothers.

Doom! An Atlantic Episode. Justin Huntly McCarthy. (On cover: Seaside library. Pocket ed., no. 779). 1886. G. Munro.

Doom Campaign. Mary McMullen. LC 73-20521. 1974. 8.95 (ISBN 0-385-09989-4). Published for the Crime Club by Doubleday.

Doom Castle: A Romance. Neil Munro. LC 1-10020. 1901. Doubleday, Page & Co.

Doom Dealer: An Exploit of The Shadowers, Inc. Isabel Egenton Ostrander. LC 23-9852. 1923. R. M. McBride & Company.

Doom in the Midnight Sun. Eunice Mays Boyd. LC 44-3388. 1944. Farrar & Rinehart, Inc.

Doom-Maker: By B. X. Sanborn Pseud. 1st Ed. William Sanborn Ballinger. LC 59-5823. 1959. Dutton.

Doom of Conaire Mor (Conary the Great) William Emmet Walsh. LC 31-20152. 1931. L. Carrier & Co.

Doom of Glendour. Kate Ostrander. LC 75-12509. 1975. 8.95 (ISBN 0-8415-0390-7). Saturday Review Press.

Doom of the Holy City. Christ and Caesar. Lydia Hoyt Farmer. LC 6-38670. A. D. F. Randolph and Company.

Doom of the Tory's Guard. A Tale. Newton Mallory Curtis. 1843. L Willard.

Doom of Three Planets. Robert Pohle. 1978. pap. 1.50 (ISBN 0-532-15337-5). Woodhill.

Doom of Washakim: A Chapter in King Philip's War. Thomas Cary Rice. 1899. J. S. Wesby and Sons.

Doom Platoon. Nick Brady. 1978. pap. 1.75 o.s.i. (ISBN 0-505-51302-1). Tower Bks.

Doom Star. Edmond Hamilton. (Belmont Tower books). 1979. 1.25 (ISBN 0-505-51336-6). Tower Pubns.

Doom That Came to Sarnath. Howard Phillips Lovecraft. 224p. 1982. pap. 2.50 (ISBN 0-345-30231-1, Del Rey). Ballantine.

Doom Trail. Arthur Douglas Howden Smith. LC 22-5457. Brentano's.

Doom Window: A Novel. Maurice Drake. LC 25-7677. 1925. E.P. Dutton & Company.

Doomed: A Startling Message to the People of Our Day, Interwoven in an Antediluvian Romance of Two Old Worlds and Two Young Lovers. Frank Rosewater. LC 20-20948. 1920. F. Rosewater.

Doomed Chief: Or, Two Hundred Years Ago. Daniel Pierce Thompson. LC 8-28265. 1860. J. W. Bradley.

Doomed City. John R Carling. LC 10-16149. 1.50. E. J. Clode.

Doomed Five. Carolyn Wells. LC 30-93149. 1930. J. B. Lippincott Company.

Doomed in Russia. 1st Ed. Walter Cikalo. LC 60-162743. 1960. Pageant Press.

Doomed Oasis. Hammond Innes. 1978. pap. 2.25 (ISBN 0-345-27418-0). Ballantine.

Doomed Oasis: A Novel of Arabia. 1st American Ed. Hammond Innes. LC 60-14766. 1960. Knopf.

Doomfarers of Coramonde. Brian Daley. LC 76-30343. 1977. 1.95 (ISBN 0-345-25708-1). Ballantine Books.

Dooming Eye: A Novel. Peter Edler. LC 77-92991. 1978. 4.00 (ISBN 0-912292-48-2). The Smith: Distributed by Horizon Press.

Doomrock. Archie Joscelyn. LC 50-7967. 1950. Avalon Books.

Doom's Caravan. Geoffrey Household. LC 79-143705. 1971. 5.95. Little, Brown.

Doomsday. Warwick Deeping. LC 27-2843. 1927. A. R. Knopf.

Doomsday. Myles Hemenway. LC 99-3939. 1898. Copeland and Day.

Doomsday. Marv Wolfman. (Marvel Novel series; #5). 1979. 1.95 (ISBN 0-671-82087-7). Pocket Books.

Doomsday Bells. Miriam Lynch. 256p. 1976. pap. 1.25 (ISBN 0-532-12403-0). Woodhill.

Doomsday Bells. Miriam Lynch. (Orig.). 1968. pap. 0.60 o.p. (73-725). Lancer.

Doomsday Bells. Miriam Lynch. Bd. with Brides of Lucifer; Journey into Twilight. (Orig.). 1972. pap. 1.65 o.s.i. (70-408). Lancer.

Doomsday Book. Julian Maclaren-Ross. LC 61-131761. 1961. I. Obolensky.

Doomsday Bullet. Ray Hogan. LC 80-2839. (Double D Western). 192p. 1981. 10.95 (ISBN 0-385-17554-X). Doubleday.

Doomsday Bullet. Ray Hogan. 1982. pap. 1.95 (ISBN 0-451-11630-5, AJ1630, Sig). NAL.

Doomsday Bullet. Ray Hogan. (General Ser.). 1983. lib. bdg. 11.95 (ISBN 0-8161-3432-4, Large Print Bks). G K Hall.

Doomsday Carrier. Victor Canning. LC 76-47662. 1977. 7.95 (ISBN 0-688-03162-5). Morrow.

Doomsday Clock. Elizabeth S Benoist. LC 75-12703. 1975. 7.95 (ISBN 0-8111-0569-5). Naylor Co.

Doomsday Committee. Richard Gallagher. (O.s.i.). (Orig.). 1970. pap. 0.75 o.s.i. (A670S, Award). Univ Pub & Dist.

Doomsday Conspiracy. Ralph Hayes. (Agent for Cominsec#2). 1974. (pbk.) 0.95. Belmont Tower Books.

Doomsday Contract. Tony Williamson. LC 77-14336. 8.95 (ISBN 0-671-22889-7). Simon and Schuster.

Doomsday Creek. Clifton Adams. LC 64-11379. (double D western). Doubleday,

Doomsday Deposit. Stanley Johnson. LC 79-10509. (Illus.). 9.95 (ISBN 0-525-09468-7). Dutton.

Doomsday Disciples. (Executioner Ser.). 192p. 1983. pap. 1.95 (ISBN 0-373-61049-1, Pub. by Worldwide). Harlequin Bks.

Doomsday England. Michael Cooney. LC 68-13252. 1968. Walker.

Doomsday Formula. Nick Carter. (Nick Carter Ser.). (O.s.i.). (Orig.). 1976. pap. 1.50 o.s.i. (AD 1637, Award). Univ Pub & Dist.

Doomsday Gene. John Boyd. LC 72-95166. 230p. 1973. 5.95 o.p. (ISBN 0-679-40026-5, Weybright). McKay.

Doomsday Gene. John Boyd. LC 72-95166. 1973. (pbk.) 5.95. Weybright and Talley.

Doomsday Marshal. Ray Hogan. LC 74-25106. 1975. 5.95 (ISBN 0-385-08446-3). Doubleday.

Doomsday Marshal. Ray Hogan. (Signet Book). 1976. (pbk.) 1.25. New American Library.

Doomsday Marshal. Ray Hogan. LC 79-16663. 1979. 10.95 (ISBN 0-8161-6754-0). G. K. Hall.

Doomsday Men. Kenneth Bulmer. LC 68-11780. (Doubleday science fiction). 1968. Doubleday.

Doomsday Men, an Adventure. John Boynton Priestley. LC 38-17818. 1938. Harper & Brothers.

Doomsday Morning. Wynwode Reid. LC 66-18114. 1966. bds., 3.95. Rigby.

Doomsday Morning. 1st Ed. Catherine L Moore. LC 57-12471. 1957. Doubleday.

Doomsday Nineteen Ninety-Nine A.D. Charles Berlitz. 1983. pap. 2.95 (ISBN 0-671-44163-9). PB.

Doomsday Posse. Ray Hogan. LC 76-48605. 1977. 5.95 (ISBN 0-385-12925-4). Doubleday.

Doomsday Posse. Ray Hogan. (Signet Book). wps3558. 1.50 (ISBN 0-451-08026-2). New American Library.

Doomsday Posse. Ray Hogan. LC 82-15817. 1982. 10.95 (ISBN 0-8161-3364-6). G.K. Hall.

Doomsday Scroll. Barbara Rogers. LC 79-7101. 8.95 (ISBN 0-396-07655-6). Dodd, Mead.

Doomsday Ship. John-Allen Price. 1982. pap. 3.25 (ISBN 0-8217-1107-5). Zebra.

Doomsday Spiral. Jon Land. 1983. pap. 2.95 (ISBN 0-8217-1175-X). Zebra.

Doomsday Squad. Dom Gober. (Black Cop Ser.: No. 2). 224p. (Orig.). 1975. pap. 1.50 (ISBN 0-87067-465-X, BH465). Holloway.

Doomsday Squad. Clark Howard. LC 74-106031. 1970. 6.95. Weybright and Talley.

Doomsday Square. Ray Ward Taylor. LC 66-13654. 1968. pap. 0.60 o.p. (53-640). Paperback Lib.

Doomsday Square: A Novel. Ray Ward Taylor. LC 66-13654. 1966. Dutton.

Doomsday Trail. Ray Hogan. LC 79-15835. 1979. 7.95 (ISBN 0-385-14841-0). Doubleday.

Doomsday Vendetta. Peter Winston. (Adjusters Ser. No. 3). 160p. pap. 0.60 o.p. (A296X, Award). Univ Pub & Dist.

Doomsman. Harlan Ellison. Bd. with Thief of Thoth. Lin Carter. 1972. pap. 0.75 o.p. (BT 50244). Belmont-Tower.

Doomsman. William Gilbert Van Tassel Sutphen. LC 75-5803. (Gregg Press science fiction series). 1975. 13.50 (ISBN 0-8398-2313-4). Gregg Press.

Doomsman. William Gilbert Van Tassel Sutphen. LC 6-197753. 1906. Harper & Brothers.

Doomsters. Kenneth Millar. LC 58-5829. 1958. Knopf.

Doomswoman. Gertrude Franklin Horn Atherton. LC 71-104406. 1970. Literature House.

Doomswoman. Gertrude Franklin Horn Atherton. LC 6-4514. 1892.

Doomswoman: An Historical Romance of Old California. Gertrude Franklin Horn Atherton. LC 1-29886. 1901. Continental Publishing Company.

Doomtime. Doris Pirserchia. (Science Fiction Ser.). 1981. pap. 2.25 o.p. (ISBN 0-87997-619-5, UE1619). DAW Bks.

Doomway. Evelyn Bond. (Orig.). 1971. pap. 0.75 o.p. (94122). Beagle Bks.

Doonesbury Special. John Hubley & Faith Hubley. 1978. 12.95 o.p. (ISBN 0-8362-1104-9); pap. 5.95 o.p. (ISBN 0-8362-1103-0). Andrews & McMeel.

Door. Mary Roberts Rinehart. LC 30-106131. 1930. Farrar & Rinehart Incorporated.

Door. John F Rossmann. (Mind Masters). (Signet Book: Vol. 3). 1975. (pbk.) 1.25. New American Library.

Door: A Story of the Truth About Mental Hospitals. 1st Ed. Dorothy Michaud. LC 62-14426. 1962. Greenwich Book Publishers.

Door Between. Melanie Harrison. LC 37-1269. Burney Brothers Publishing Co.

Door Between. Geraldine Kitay. LC 59-618759. 1959. Dodd, Mead.

Door Between. Ellery Queen. Bd. with Devil to Pay. 1980. pap. 2.50 (ISBN 0-451-11309-8, AE1309, Sig). NAL.

Door Between: A Problem in Deduction. Ellery Queen, pseud. LC 37-270849. 1937. Frederick A. Stokes Company.

Door Fell Shut. Martha Albrand. LC 66-18812. bds., 4.95. New Amer. Lib.

Door Fell Shut. Martha Albrand. (Signet bk., T3331). 1967. New Amer. Lib.

Door in the Grimming, Paula Grogger & Cunningham, Ccaroline, Tr. LC 37-113. 1936. G. P. Putnam's Sons.

Door in the Hedge. Robin McKinley. 224p. 1982. pap. 2.25 (ISBN 0-441-15313-5). Ace Bks.

Door in the Wall: A Novel of Adventure. Laurence Walter Meynell. LC 37-18255. 1937. Harper & Brothers.

Door in the Wall: And Other Stories. Herbert George Wells. LC 12-2683. 1911. M. Kennerley.

Door in the Wall & Other Stories. Herbert George Wells. LC 79-92211. (Illus.). 1980. 12.95 (ISBN 0-87923-326-5); pap. 6.95 (ISBN 0-87923-327-3). Godine.

Door in the Wall: Stories. Foreword by William Maxwell. Oliver La Farge. LC 64-24641. 1965. 4.95. Houghton.

Door into Fire. Diane Duane. (Dell book). 1979. 1.95 (ISBN 0-440-11874-3). Dell Pub. Co.

Door into Summer. Robert Anson Heinlein. LC 57-5529. (Doubleday science fiction). 1957. Doubleday.

Door into Summer. Robert Anson Heinlein. LC 79-14757. (Gregg Press science fiction series). 1979. 12.50 (ISBN 0-8398-2506-4). Gregg Press.

Door Nails Never Die. Robert McNair Wilson. LC 39-2601. J. B. Lippincott Company.

Door of Death, a Mystery Story. Samuel Shellbarger. LC 28-22871. The Century Co.

Door of Dread: A Secret Service Romance. Arthur John Arbuthnott Stringer. LC 16-12750. The Bobbs-Merrill Company.

Door of Everything. Ruby Nelson. pap. 3.95 (ISBN 0-87516-069-7). De Vorss.

Door of Hope. Joseph S Diamond. LC 51-10646. 1951. Greenberg.

Door of Life. Enid Bagnold. LC 33-29634. 1938. W. Morrow and Co.

Door of the Double Dragon: A Romance of the China of Yesterday and to-Day. Hector Blanding. LC 21-666. W. J. Watt & Company.

Door of the Unreal. Gerald Biss. LC 20-19179. 1920. 1.90. G.P. Putnam's Sons.

Door on Waverly Place. Fannie Harper Rogers. LC 37-23919. Dorrance and Company.

Door Opens. Muriel Hine Coxon. 1935. D. Appleton-Century Company, Incorporated.

Door That Has No Key. Cosmo Hamilton. LC 13-24976. 1.25. George H. Doran Company.

Door Through Space. Marion Zimmer Bradley. Ed. by James P. Baen. 1979. pap. 1.95 (ISBN 0-441-15935-4). Ace Bks.

Door to Anywhere. Ed. by Frederik Pohl. 1970. pap. 0.75 o.p. (0502-07070). Curtis.

Door to Doom. John Dickson Carr. Ed. by Douglas G. Greene. LC 79-1700. 256p. 1980. 12.95i (ISBN 0-06-010628-X, HarpT). Har-Row.

Door to Doom, and Other Detections. John Dickson Carr & Douglas G Greene. LC 79-1700. 9.95 (ISBN 0-06-010628-X). Harper & Row.

Door to Door Nurse. Peggy O'More, pseud. LC 67-5327. 1967. Arcadia House.

Door to the Moor. Millie Bird Vandeburg. LC 25-133002. 1925. Dorrance and Company.

Door to the Tower. Sylvia G. L. Dannett. pap. 0.60 o.p. Lancer.

Door Unlatched. LC 28-108779. 1928. Minton, Balch & Company.

Door Where the Wrong Lay. Mary Ellen Brown Greene. LC 9-12081. 1909. The C. M. Clark Publishing Company.

Door with Seven Locks. Edgar Wallace. LC 26-16197. 1926. Doubleday, Page & Company.

Door with Seven Locks: By Edgar Wallace... Edgar Wallace. LC 29-258971. 1928. A. L. Burt Company.

Door Without a Key. Audrie Manley-Tucker. 1973. (pbk.) 0.75. Pocket Books.

Doorbell Rang: A Nero Wolfe Novel. Rex Stout. LC 65-20319. bds., 3.50. Viking.

Doorbells. Barbara Black. LC 40-9463. 1940. Coward-McCann, Inc.

Doors. Ezra Hannon. LC 75-11833. 1975. 7.95 (ISBN 0-8128-1838-5). Stein and Day.

Doors. Ezra Hannon. 1976. 1.95. Warner Books.

Doors of His Face, the Lamps of His Mouth, and Other Stories. Roger Zelazny. 1974. (pbk.) 1.25. Avon.

Doors of His Face, the Lamps of His Mouth: And Other Stories. Roger Zelazny. LC 70-148921. 1971. 4.95. Doubleday.

Doors of Perception. Aldous Leonard Huxley. 1970. pap. 2.95i (ISBN 0-06-080171-9, P171, PL). Har-Row.

Doors of the Night. Frank Lucius Packard. LC 22-7927. George H. Doran Company.

Doors Open. Michael Francis Gilbert. LC 62-11736. 1962. Walker.

Doorstep Acquaintance, and Other Sketches. William Dean Howells. LC 1546. (Riverside literature series. no. 139). 1900. Houghton, Mifflin & Co.

Doorstep Acquaintance, and Other Sketches. With a Biographical Introd. and Notes. William Dean Howells. LC 72-194930. 1970. Folcroft Library Editions.

Doorstep Acquaintance and Other Sketches: With a Biographical Introduction and Notes. William Dean Howells. LC 75-31982. 1975. 10.00 (ISBN 0-88305-293-8). Norwood Editions.

Doorstep Murders: A Kenneth Carlisle Detective Story. Carolyn Wells. 1930. Pub. for The Crime Club, Inc., by Doubleday, Doran & Company, Inc.

Doorstep to Heaven. Alice Prendergast. LC 58-59855. 1958. T. S. Denison.

Doorway into Time. 2nd ed. Ed. by Samuel Moskowitz. (O.s.i.). pap. 0.95 o.s.i. (532-50311-050). Manor Bks.

Doorway into Time: And Other Stories from Modern Masterpieces of Science Fiction. Ed. by Samuel Moskowitz. (50-311). 1966. Macfadden.

Doorway to Dawn. Roscoe Gilmore Stott. LC 40-34076. 1940. Wm. B. Eerdmans Publishing Company.

Doorway to Death. Helen Arvonen. (Ace gothic read easy large type). 1973. (pbk.) 0.95. Ace.

Doorway to Death. John Creasey. 1972. pap. 0.95 o.s.i. (75-344). Lancer.

Doorway to Dreams. William Arthur Neubauer. LC 56-89793. 1956. Arcadia House.

Doorways in Drumorty. Lorna Moon. LC 25-24062. The Bobbs-Merrill Company.

Doorways in the Sand. Roger Zelazny. 1977. 1.50 (ISBN 0-380-00949-8). Avon.

Doorways to Danger. John Laffin. LC 66-15596. 1966. Abelard-Schuman.

Doorways to Danger. Mark Napier, pseud. 1966. 3.75 o.p. (B20160). Abelard.

Doorways to Space. Wells. 1972. 4.50 o.p. Fantasy Pub Co.

Doowinkle, D. A. Harry M Klingsberg. LC 40-32619. The Dial Press.

Dope. Arthur Sarsfield Ward. LC 19-15081. 1919. R. M. McBride & Co.

Dope. Arthur Sarsfield Ward. LC 21-3916. (Stories of Chinatown). 1920. R. M. McBride & Co.

Dopefiend. Donald Goines. (Orig.). 1971. pap. 1.95 (ISBN 0-87067-659-8, BH044). Holloway.

Dopey Dan. Jack M Bickham. LC 72-76123. (Double D western). 1972. 4.95. Doubleday.

Doppelgangers: An Episode of the Fourth, the Psychological, Revolution, 1997. Gerald Heard. LC 47-1725. 1947. The Vanguard Press, Inc.

Dora. Eleanor Green. LC 48-5765. 1948. Doubleday.

Dora. Julia Kavanagh. LC 34-37778. 1868. D. Appleton and Company.

Dora Bell's Village Cats. Nina Consuelo Epton. LC 77-378252. (Istributed by Michael Joseph, 22 S. Broadway, Salem, NH 03074). 1977-1978. 9.95 (ISBN 0-7181-1584-8). Joseph.

Dora Darling: The Daughter of the Regiment. Jane Goodwin Austin. LC 6-5044. 1865. J. E. Tilton and Company.

Dora Deane; or, The East India Uncle; and Maggie Miller; or, Old Hagar's Secret. Mary Jane Hawes Holmes. LC 5430. (On cover: Madison square library. no. 117). 1897. G. W. Dillingham Co.

Dora Miller: Or, A Young Girl's Love and Pride. Laura Jean Libbey. LC 11-150951. 1892. N. L. Munro.

Dora Thorne. Charlotte Mary Brame. LC 44-16855. (On cover: Seaside library. Pocket ed. No. 51). 1883. G. Munro.

Dora Thorne. Charlotte Mary Brame. LC 12-19581. J. S. Ogilvie & Company.

Dora Thorne. Charlotte Mary Brame. LC 3625. (Bertha M. Clay library, no. 2). 1900. Street & Smith.

Dorance. R E Nelson. LC 7-25784. 1889. J. B. Alden.

Dorando. James Boswell. Ed. by Robert Hunting. LC 73-78276. 1974. 3.50. Puckerbrush Press.

Dorando: A Spanish Tale. James Boswell. LC 72-189745. 1972. Folcroft Library Editions.

Dorando, a Spanish Tale. James Boswell. LC 78-18885. 1978. 10.00 (ISBN 0-8495-0415-5). Arden Library.

Dora's Device. George R Cather. LC 6-22286. T. B. Peterson & Brothers.

Dorcas. A Novel. Georgiana Marion Craik May. (Franklin square library, no. 69). 1879. Harper & Brothers.

Dorcas, the Daughter of Faustina. Nathan Chapman Kouns. LC 13-383. 1911. The Alice Harriman Company.

Dorchester Boy. David S. Viscott. LC 73-82182. 1973. 7.95 (ISBN 0-87795-070-9). Arbor Hse.

Doree. Fannie Heaslip Lea. LC 34-38717. 1934. Dodd, Mead & Company.

Doreen. Barbara Noble. LC 46-7659. 1946. Doubleday & Company, Inc.

Doreen: The Story of a Singer. Ada Ellen Bayly. LC 6-10296. 1894. Longmans, Green and Co.

Dorette: A Post-War Romance of the Land of the Troubadours. Andre Lamande. Tr. by Danforth, A. A. LC 31-25766. H. Vinal, Ltd.

Doria Rafe Case. Hillary Waugh. (Raven House Mysteries Ser.). 224p. 1982. pap. cancelled (ISBN 0-373-63043-3, Pub. by Worldwide). Harlequin Bks.

Dorian. Nephi Anderson. LC 21-21946. 1921. Printed by the Bikuben Publishing Company.

Doris: A Novel. Margaret Wolfe Hungerford. LC 7-9365. (On cover: Lovell's library. v. 9, no. 451). 1884. J. W. Lovell Company.

Doris Drake: A Novel. 1st Ed. Vaughn Albert Fiscus. LC 56-12369. 1956. Exposition Press.

Doris Fein: Murder is No Joke. T. Ernesto Bethancourt, pseud. LC 82-80817. 160p. (YA) 1982. 10.95 (ISBN 0-8234-0468-4). Holiday.

Doris' Fortune. Florence Alice Price James. (On cover: Lovell's library, v. 15, no. 757). 1886. J. W. Lovell Company.

Doris Kingsley, Child and Colonist. Emma Rayner. LC 1-25766. 1901. G. W. Dillingham Co.

Doris's Fortune. Florence Alice Price James. (On cover: Seaside library. Pocket ed., no. 820). 1886. G. Munro.

Dormie One: And Other Golf Stories. Harold Everett Porter. LC 17-24401. 1917. The Century Co.

Dormitory Women. Robert Verlin Cassill. LC 55-16487. (Lion book, 216). 1954. Lion Books.

Dornstein Icon. Janet Louise Roberts. 1978. 1.75 (ISBN 0-671-81380-3). Pocket Books.

Dorothea... Louise Stockton. LC 12-14355. (On cover: Round-robin series). 1882. J. R. Osgood and Company.

Dorothea: A Story of the Pure in Heart. Jozua Marius Willen Van Der Poorten Schwartz. LC 4-11534. 1904. D. Appleton and Company.

Dorothea and Travels in Europe. Katharine Treat Blackledge. LC 24-304530. Cornhill Publishing Company.

Dorothea Kirke: Or, Free to Serve. american ed. Annie S Swan Smith. LC 8-8195. 1890. Cranston and Stowe.

Dorothea's Revenge. Ann Olmstead. 1972. pap. 0.75 o.s.i. (01-354). Lancer.

Dorothy: A Novel. Henriette Hume. (On cover: Dearborn series, no. 37). 1890. Donohue, Henneberry & Co.

Dorothy: A Tale of Two Lands. Elizabeth Sisson. LC 6-42430. Jennings and Graham.

Dorothy, and Other Italian Stories. Constance Fenimore Woolson. LC 8-37231. 1896. Harper & Brothers.

Dorothy Angsleigh: A Story of War Times. Agnes Potter McGee. 1907. W. B. Conkey Company.

Dorothy Delafield. Mary Harriott Norris. LC 44-29288. 1886. Phillips & Hunt.

Dorothy Forster. Walter Besant. LC 11-105373. (On cover: Seaside library. Pocket ed. no. 230). G. Munro.

Dorothy Forster. A Novel. Walter Besant. (Harper's Franklin square library, no. 561). 1887. Harper & Brothers.

Dorothy Fox. Louisa Taylor Parr. LC 7-34718. 1871. J. B. Lippincott & Co.

Dorothy Fox. Louisa Taylor Parr. LC 1-25431. 1901. J. B. Lippincott Company.

Dorothy Quincy. A Story of the American Revolution. Mary Elizabeth Springer. LC 99-2606. (On cover: Neely's imperial library, no. 34). 1899. F. T. Neely.

Dorothy South: A Love Story of Virginia Just Before the War. George Cary Eggleston. LC 2-9792. 1902. Lothrop Pub. Co.

Dorothy the Puritan: The Story of a Strange Delusion. Augusta Campbell Watson. LC 8-34344. 1893. E. P. Dutton and Company.

Dorothy, the Terrified. Katheryn Kimbrough, pseud. (The Saga of the Phenwick Women Ser.: No.19). 1977. pap. 1.50 (ISBN 0-445-04133-1). Popular Lib.

Dorothy Thorn of Thornton. Julia Warth Parsons. LC 7-34093. (On cover: The round World series). D. Lothrop & Company.

Dorothy Vernon of Haddon Hall. Charles Major. LC 2-2762. 1902. The Macmillan Co.

Dorothy Vernon of Haddon Hall. Charles Major. LC 2-11739. 1902. The Macmillan Company.

Dorothy Vernon of Haddon Hall. Charles Major. LC 14-10509. (Half title: Macmillan's standard library). 1913. Grosset & Dunlap.

Dorothy Vernon: Or, The Beauty of Haddon Hall. Henry Hastings. LC 2-19579. 1902. M. A. Donohue & Company.

Dorothy Webb: A Story of Innocence, Credulity, Friendship, Parental Grief, and Paternal Love. Charles Hutchinson Gabriel. LC 24-11235. 1924. McQuiddy Printing Company.

Dorothy's Experience. Adeline Trafton Knox. LC 7-14191. Lee and Shepard.

Dorothy's Islands. Jennie Maria Drinkwater Conklin. Bradley & Woodruff.

Dorothy's Tour. Evelyn Hunt Raymond. LC 12-21316. 0.60. A. L. Chatterton Co.

Dorothy's Venture. A Novel. Mary Cecil Hay. (Harper's Franklin square library, no. 242). 1882. Harper & Brothers.

Dorothy's Vocation. Evelyn Everett Green. LC 6-45545. Bradley & Woodruff.

Dorp. Frieda Arkin. LC 76-80494. 1969. 6.95. Dial Press.

Dorr War. Arthur Mowry. pap. 2.45 o.p. (Chelsea Hse). Random.

Dorrien Carfax: A Game of Hide and Seek. Nowell Griffith. 1909. 1.50. The J. McBride Company.

Dorsai! Gordon R. Dickson. 1982. pap. 2.50 (ISBN 0-441-16016-6). Ace Bks.

Dorsai. Gordon R. Dickson. (Science Fiction Ser). pap. 1.75 o.p. (ISBN 0-87997-342-0, UE1342). DAW Bks.

Dorsai! Gordon R Dickson. (Daw Science Fiction no. 181). 1976. (pbk.) 1.50. Daw Books.

Dorset Dear: Idylls of Country Life. 2d impression.... ed. Mary E. Sweetman Blundell. LC 6-32367. 1905. Longmans, Green, and Co.

Dorset Disaster. Alexander Sidar. LC 79-92637. (Illus.). 10.95 (ISBN 0-448-15713-6). Stonesong Press.

Dorset: Or The Ulterior Marriage. Sarah B. Fitch. LC 6-41106. 1883. Thorp, West & Co., Printers.

Dos Comedias De Azorin. A. Azorin, pseud. Ed. by Francisco Ugarte. LC 52-27526. (Span). 1952. text ed. 4.50 o.p. (ISBN 0-395-05479-6, 3-56985). HM.

Dos Compadres. Deane E. Bostick. LC 75-39876. 1.50 (ISBN 0-914042-11-4). Neptune Books.

Dosadi Experiment see Worlds Beyond Dune: The Best of Frank Herbert.

Dosia. A Russian Story. Alice Marie Celeste Durand. Tr. by Sherwood, Mary (Neal) LC 6-35696. T. B. Peterson & Brothers.

Dosia's Daughter. Alice Marie Celeste Durand. Tr. by Waters, Clara (Erskine) Clement. LC 11-715614. 1886. Ticknor and Company.

Dossie Bell Is Dead: A Novel. Jack Happel Boone. LC 39-5855. 1939. Frederick A. Stokes Company.

Dossier IX. Barry Weil. LC 69-17401. 1969. 5.00. Bobbs-Merrill Co.

Dossier Nine. Barry Weil. 1970. pap. 0.95 o.p. (N2243). Pyramid Pubns.

Dossier 51. Gilles Perrault. LC 73-135149. 1971. 6.95. Morrow.

Dostoevsky Dictionary. Richard L. Chapple. LC 82-18514. 25.00 (ISBN 0-88233-616-9). Ardis Publishers.

Dosvidaniya: A Story of Love in Revolution. Valentina Mueller. LC 73-92808. 192p. 1974. 6.95 o.p. (ISBN 0-8059-1982-1). Dorrance.

Dosvidaniya: A Story of Love in Revolution. Valentina Mueller. LC 73-92808. 192p. 1974. 6.95 o.p. (ISBN 0-8059-1982-1). Dorrance.

Dosvidaniya: A Story of Love in Revolution. Valentina Ratschenko. LC 73-92808. 1974. 6.95 (ISBN 0-8059-1982-1). Dorrance.

Dot & the Line: A Romance in Lower Mathematics. Norton Juster. 1977. pap. 3.95 (ISBN 0-394-73352-5). Random.

Dot & Will. Fannie Kilbourne. LC 29-8647. 1929. Dodd, Mead & Company.

Dot It Down: A Story of Life in the North-West. Alexander Begg. (Toronto Reprint Library of Canadian Prose & Poetry). 1973. Repr. of 1871 ed. 25.00x (ISBN 0-8020-7502-9). U of Toronto Pr.

Dot Sawyers of Arkansaw. Lulu Emma Evarts Keesee Gilbert. LC 39-16742. The Messenger Press.

Doting. Henry Green. LC 52-9321. 1952. Viking Press.

Doting. Henry Green. LC 70-122054. (Viking reprint editions). 1970. A. M. Kelley.

Dotted Line Honeymoon. Joseph McCord. LC 36-10493. 1936. Macrae Smith Company.

Dottie Rambo Cookbook. Dottie Rambo. LC 78-58197. 1978. pap. 4.95 o.p. (ISBN 0-914850-19-9). Impact Tenn.

Doty Dontcare. facsimile ed. Mary Farrington Foster. LC 78-39082. (Black Heritage Library Collection). Repr. of 1895 ed. 13.50 (ISBN 0-8369-9020-X). Ayer Co.

Doty Dontcare; a Story of the Garden of the Antilles. Mary Farrington Foster. LC 78-39082. (Black Heritage Library Collection). 1972. (ISBN 0-8369-9020-X). Books for Libraries Press.

Doty Dontcare. A Story of the Garden of the Antilles. Mary Farrington Foster. LC 6-40008. 1895. Estes & Lauriat.

Double. F. M. Dostoevsky. Tr. by Evelyn Harden from Rus. 1983. 15.00 (ISBN 0-88233-756-4); pap. 6.50 (ISBN 0-88233-757-2). Ardis Pubs.

Double. Edgar Wallace. LC 28-30338. 1928. Pub. for The Crime Club, Inc., by Doubleday, Doran & Company, Inc.

Double see Stories of the Double.

Double see Three Short Novels of Dostoyevsky.

Double Affair. Angela Mackail Thirkell. LC 57-12071. 1957. Knopf.

Double Agent. John Bingham. 1967. 3.95 o.p. Dutton.

Double Agent. John Michael Ward Bingham Clanmorris. LC 67-20535. 1967. Dutton.

Double Agent. Hildegarde Tolman Teilhet. LC 45-6687. 1945. Doubleday, Doran and Company, Inc.

Double Agent-Triple Cross. Johannes Mario Simmel. 1977. 1.95 (ISBN 0-445-04051-3). Popular Library.

Double Axe. Lauren R Stevens. LC 61-7210. 1961. Scribner.

Double Barrel. Nicolas Freeling. (U2133). 1966. Ballantine.

Double-Barrel. Nicolas Freeling. 1975. (pbk.) 1.25 (ISBN 0-14-002585-5). Penguin.

Double Barrel. Nicolas Freeling. LC 65-22161. 1965. Harper & Row.

Double Barrel. Nicolas Freeling. LC 80-6128. 1981. 2.50 (ISBN 0-394-74693-7). Vintage Books.

Double Barrelled Detective Story. Samuel Langhorne Clemens. LC 2-111462. 1902. Harper & Brothers.

Double-Bellied Companion. Akbar Del Piombo. Orig. Title: Traveler's Companion, Orig. pap. 1.25 o.s.i. (OPS44, Travellers Comp). Olympia.

Double Bellied Companion. Akbar Del Piombo pap. 1.95 o.s.i. (OPS-44). Olympia.

Double Bill. Alec McCowen. LC 80-66018. 1980. 10.95 (ISBN 0-689-11070-7). Atheneum.

Double Blackmail. George Douglas Howard Cole & Margaret Isabel Postgate Cole. LC 39-23867. 1939. The Macmillan Company.

Double Blind. 1st American Ed. John Rowan Wilson. LC 60-10266. 1960. Doubleday.

Double Bluff. Elizabeth Linington. LC 63-17683. 1963. Morrow.

Double Bluff. Dell Shannon. 1969. pap. 0.75 o.p. (T2110). Pyramid Pubns.

Double Chance. Joseph Smith Fletcher. LC 28-13910. Dodd, Mead & Company.

Double Circle People. John Terry Robinson. LC 77-124401. 1970. 4.95. Suzanna.

Double Crime. Harlan Page Halsey. LC 12-34573. (On cover: The Calumet series. 34). G. Munro's Sons.

Double Cross. Michael Barak. 1981. 12.95 (ISBN 0-453-00408-3, H408). NAL.

Double Cross. Michael Barak. 1982. pap. 2.95 (ISBN 0-451-11547-3, AE1547, Sig). NAL.

Double Cross. Charles R. Pike, pseud. LC 80-68160. (Jubal Cade Westerns Ser.). 128p. 1980. pap. 2.95 (ISBN 0-87754-231-7). Chelsea Hse.

Double Cross. Albert Ellsworth Thomas. LC 24-206105. 1924. Dodd, Mead and Company.

Double Cross: A Novel. Michael Bar-Zohar. LC 81-9559. 1981. 12.95 (ISBN 0-453-00408-3). New American Library.

Double Cross: A Romance of Mystery and Adventure in Mexico of to-Day. Gilson Willets. LC 10-22802. G. W. Dillingham Company.

Double-Cross Canyon: A Powder Valley Western. Peter Field. 1974. (pbk.) 0.75. Pocket Books.

Double-Cross Circuit: A Novel. Michael Dorland. LC 78-54630. 10.00 (ISBN 0-448-15162-6). Grosset & Dunlap.

Double-Cross Ranch. Stuart Brock, pseud. 256p. (YA) 1974. 6.95 (Avalon). Bouregy.

Double-Cross Ranch. Stuart Brock, pseud. (Avalon westerns). 1974. 4.50. Avalon Books.

Double Cross Ranch. Lee Floren. (Orig.). 1981. pap. 1.95 (ISBN 0-8439-0922-6, Leisure Bks). Nordon Pubns.

Double Cross Ranch. Charles Alden Seltzer. LC 32-2234. 1932. Doubleday, Doran & Company, Inc.

Double-Cross Ranch. Louis Trimble. LC 54-13264. 1954. Avalon Books.

Double Cross Ranch: By Will Watson Pseud. Lee Floren. LC 51-9004. 1950. Phoenix Press.

Double-Cross System. John Cecil Masterman. 1982. pap. 2.50 (ISBN 0-345-29743-1). Ballantine.

Double Cross Trail. Eugene E. Halleran. LC 44-21400. 1946. Macrae-Smith-Company.

Double Crossfire. Don Pendleton. (Executioner Ser.). 192p. 1982. pap. 1.95 (ISBN 0-373-61040-8, Pub. by Worldwide). Harlequin Bks.

Double-Crostics, No. 70. Ed. by Thomas H. Middleton. 1973. 2.95 (ISBN 0-671-21634-1, Fireside). S&S.

Double-Crostics, No. 71. Ed. by Thomas H. Middleton. (O.s.i.). 1974. 2.95 o.s.i. (ISBN 0-671-21749-6). S&S.

Double Dagger: Or, Nat Ridley's Mexican Trail. Nat Jr Ridley. LC 27-17586. (His Nat Ridley series--no.13). 1926. Garden City Publishing Co., Inc.

Double Dare. Edward Keyes. LC 80-28183. 10.95 (ISBN 0-07-034450-7). McGraw-Hill.

Double Darkness. Edward Fenton. LC 47-4220. 1947. Doubleday.

Double Dealers. Helen Tucker. (Coventry Romance Ser.: No. 168). 224p. 1982. pap. 1.50 (ISBN 0-449-50269-4, Coventry). Fawcett.

Double Dealing. M. Arthur Bogen. 160p. 1983. pap. 2.25 (ISBN 0-380-83394-8, Flare). Avon.

Double Death. Freeman Wills Crofts. LC 32-24981. 1932. Harper & Brothers.

Double Death of Frederic Belot. Claude Aveline. LC 73-22631. 1974. 4.95 (ISBN 0-385-05195-6). Doubleday.

Double Death of Frederick Belot. Claude Aveline. Tr. by Shields, Archibald Kenneth. LC 40-82609. H. Holt and Company.

Double Deception. Louise Landis. (Griffon Ser). (Orig.). 1969. pap. 0.50 o.p. (Golden Pr). Western Pub.

Double Deception. Amanda Troy. 192p. 1982. pap. 1.75. Jove Pubns.

Double Decker. Richard Edward Wormser. 1974. (pbk.) 0.95. Manor Books.

Double Defector. Patrick Wayland. LC 64-23220. 1964. Published for the Crime Club by Doubleday.

Double Delight. Aston Cantwell. (Erotica Ser.). 256p. (Orig.). 1983. pap. 2.75 (ISBN 0-446-30298-8). Warner Bks.

Double Diamond Brand. Archie Joscelyn. LC 40-8385. Phoenix Press.

Double Doom: By Josephine Bell Pseud. Doris Bell Collier Ball. LC 58-5740. (Cock Robin mystery). 1958. Macmillan.

Double Door. Theodora Keogh. LC 51-387. Creative Age Press.

Double, Double. Ellery Queen, pseud. LC 77-14541. 1977. 9.95 (ISBN 0-89340-106-4). J. Curley.

Double Double. Jose Yglesias. LC 73-15473. 1974. 6.95 (ISBN 0-670-28051-8). Viking Press.

Double, Double: A New Novel of Wrightsville. Ellery Queen, pseud. LC 50-8227. 1950. Little, Brown.

Double, Double: A New Novel of Wrightsville. Ellery Queen, pseud. 1975. (pbk.) 1.25 (ISBN 0-345-24431-1). Ballantine Books.

Double, Double, Oil and Trouble. Emma Lathen, pseud. LC 78-5151. 7.95 (ISBN 0-671-24215-6). Simon and Schuster.

Double, Double, Toil and Trouble. Lion Feuchtwanger & Oram, Caroline, Tr. LC 43-59432. 1943. The Viking Press.

Double Dunk. Beckham. 224p. (Orig.). 1980. pap. 1.95 (ISBN 0-87067-678-4). Holloway.

Double-E Document. first ed. Carlos B Valrand. 1973. 6.00 (ISBN 0-682-47664-1). Exposition Press.

Double-E Document. Carlos B. Varland. 192p. 1973. 6.00 o.p. (ISBN 0-682-47664-1). Exposition.

Double Eagle. Mr. X. (Espionage-Intelligence Library). 288p. 1983. pap. 2.95 (ISBN 0-345-30192-7). Ballantine.

Double-Eagles. Mark Stanislaus Gross. LC 19-26. 1919. The Stratford Company.

Double Entry: A Spirited Tale. Bert Kopperl. 1980. 6.00 (ISBN 0-682-49537-9). Exposition.

Double Event: A Tale of the Melbourne Cup. Nathaniel Gould. LC 24-11839. 1920. G. Routledge and Sons, Limited.

Double Exposure. Theodore Fleischman. 1956. 3.50 o.p. (ISBN 0-8149-0525-0). Vantage.

Double Exposure. Donald MacKenzie. 1963. 3.75 o.p. (ISBN 0-395-07941-1). HM.

Double Exposure. Hugh McLeave. LC 79-67331. 8.95 (ISBN 0-684-16310-1). Scribner.

Double Exposure: A Novel. Translated from the French by Elisabeth Abbott. Theodore Fleischman. LC 56-7887. 1956. Vanguard Press.

Double Fault. Dan Brennan. 1979. pap. 2.25 o.s.i. (ISBN 0-8439-0654-5, Leisure Bks). Nordon Pubns.

Double Fault. Judith Chernaik. LC 75-2122. 1975. 9.95. Putnam.

Double Feature. Anthony Fowles. LC 72-88052. (Simon and Schuster novel of suspense). 1973. 6.95 (ISBN 0-671-21461-6). Simon and Schuster.

Double for Death. G. Ashe. (Rinehart Suspense Novels). 1968. 3.95 o.p. (ISBN 0-03-081837-0). HR&W.

Double for Death. John Creasey. LC 73-80331. (Rinehart suspense novel). 1969. Holt, Rinehart and Winston.

Double for Death: A Tecumseh Fox Mystery. Rex Stout. LC 39-30067. Farrar and Rinehart, Inc.

Double for the Toff. John Creasey. LC 65-18632. 1965. bds., 3.50. Walker.

Double Fortune. Bertha Ladd Hoskins. LC 10-3290. 1909. The Neale Publishing Company.

Double Garden. Maurice Maeterlinck & Teixeira De Mattos, Alexander Louis, 1865-1921, Tr. LC 4-13663. 1904. Dodd, Mead and Company.

Double Griffin. Patricia Blake. 288p. (Orig.). 1981. pap. 2.75 (ISBN 0-515-06005-4). Jove Pubns.

Double Harness. Anthony Hope Hawkins. LC 3-32406. 1904. McClure, Phillips & Co.

Double Harness. Gussie D Ogden. LC 31-134842. H. Harrison.

Double Honeymoon. Evan S Connell. LC 75-34386. 7.95 (ISBN 0-399-11663-X). Putnam.

Double Honeymoon. Evan S. Connell. 1977. 1.75 (ISBN 0-380-01743-1). Avon Books.

Double House. Elizabeth Dejeans. LC 24-8652. 1924. Doubleday, Page & Company.

Double Identities. LC 50-6987. 1950. Dodd, Mead.

Double Identity. Nick Carter. (Nick Carter Ser.). (O.s.i.). (Orig.). 1972. pap. 0.75 o.s.i. (A923S, Award). Univ Pub & Dist.

Double Identity. George Harmon Coxe. 1974. (pbk.) 1.25. Manor Books.

Double Identity. George Harmon Coxe. LC 76-98655. 1970. 4.95. Knopf.

Double Identity--Strike of the Hawk. (Nick Carter Ser.). 320p. (Orig.). 1980. pap. 2.25 (ISBN 0-441-79072-0, Pub. by Charter Bks). Ace Bks.

Double Image. Arthur Herbert Bryant. LC 47-1333. 1947. Farrar, Straus and Company.

Double Image. Helen MacInnes. (Crest bk., t1013). 1967. Fawcett.

Double Image. Helen MacInnes. LC 66-12370. (Illus.). 1966. Harcourt, Brace & World.

Double in Space. Fletcher Pratt. 1969. pap. 0.75 o.p. (0502-07043-075). Curtis.

Double in Space: Two Novels. Fletcher Pratt. LC 51-14187. 1951. Doubleday.

Double in Trouble. Richard Prather & Stephen Marlowe. 1970. pap. 0.95 o.p. (M2364, GM). Fawcett World.

Double Indemnity. James Mallahan Cain. LC 48-1239. (New Avon library, 137). 1947. Avon Book Co.

Double Indemnity. James Mallahan Cain. LC 77-92631. 1978. 1.65 (ISBN 0-394-72581-6). Vintage Books.

Double Jeopardy. Martin L. Friedland. 470p. 1969. 21.00x o.p. (ISBN 0-19-825187-4). Oxford U Pr.

Double Jeopardy. Martin M Goldsmith. LC 38-58721. The Macaulay Company.

Double Jeopardy. Fletcher Pratt. LC 52-8057. (Doubleday science fiction). 1952. Doubleday.

Double Jeopardy. Michael Underwood. LC 81-8821. 1981. 9.95 (ISBN 0-312-21814-1). St Martin's Press.

Double Jeopardy! A Novel. William Curtis Stiles. The Home Publishing Company.

Double Jeopardy: A Skeleton Keyne Mystery. Clement Wood. LC 47-203724. 1947. Arcadia House.

Double Jeopardy. 1st Ed. Edwin Moultrie Lanham. LC 59-6421. 1959. Harcourt, Brace.

Double Knot, and Other Stories. Mary Teresa Waggaman. LC 5-37584. 1905. Benziger Brothers.

Double Know. A Novel. George Manville Fenn. LC 6-39269. (Lovell's international series, no. 141). United States Book Company.

Double Life. Gaston Leroux. LC 9-32370. J. E. Kearney.

Double Life. Karolina Karlovna IAnish Pavlova. LC 78-104806. (Illus.). 10.00. (ISBN 0-88233-223-6) (ISBN 0-88233-224-4) (ISBN 0-88233-224-4). Ardis.

Double Life. Ella Wheeler Wilcox. (sunnyside series, no. 25). 1891. J. S. Ogilvie.

Double Life, a Novel. Grant Richards. LC 20-18767. 1920. Dodd, Mead and Company.

Double Life of Mr. Alfred Burton. Edward Phillips Oppenheim. 1913. 1.25. Little, Brown, and Company.

Double Life: Or, Starr Cross; an Hypnotic Romance. Herbert E Chase. LC 6-23441. 1884. S. W. Green's Son.

Double Lives. Jane Barnes. LC 79-7795. 1981. 11.95 (ISBN 0-385-15647-2). Doubleday.

Double Love: Or, The Romance of a Beauty. Laura A. E. White. (On cover: The red cover series, no. 21). J. S. Ogilvie.

Double M Factor. Peggye Swenson. LC 76-53254. 2.25 (ISBN 0-915392-04-6). Domina Books.

Double Man. Eando Binder, pseud. 1971. pap. 0.75 o.p. (07167). Curtis.

Double Man. Helen Kieran Reilly. LC 52-5170. 1952. Random House.

Double Man: A Novel. Elinor Pryor. LC 57-5501. 1957. Norton.

Double Masquerade. Karen Lynn. LC 80-2944. 1981. 9.95 (ISBN 0-385-17467-5). Doubleday.

Double Mobius Sphere. P. S Nim. 1978. 1.75 (ISBN 0-671-81131-2). Pocket Books.

Double Mort De Frederic Belot. Claude Aveline. Ed. by R. W. Torrens & J. B. Sanders. 1958. 3.50x o.p. (ISBN 0-679-30126-7). McKay.

Double Muscadine. Frances Ormond Jones Gaither. LC 49-1163. 1949. Macmillan Co.

Double Negative. David Carkeet. LC 81-17934. (Penguin crime fiction). 1982. 2.95 (ISBN 0-14-006070-7). Penguin Books.

Double Negative: A Novel. David Carkeet. LC 80-16383. 9.95 (ISBN 0-8037-6578-9). Dial Press.

Double Occupancy. Elaine Chase. (Candlelight Ecstasy Ser.: No. 56). (Orig.). 1982. pap. 1.95 (ISBN 0-440-11732-1). Dell.

Double or Nothing: A Novel. Raymond Federman. LC 82-72983. 203p. 1971. 8.95x (ISBN 0-8040-0543-5); pap. 4.95x (ISBN 0-8040-0544-3). Swallow.

Double or Nothing: A Real Fictitious Discourse. Raymond Federman. LC 71-171875. 1971. 6.00 (ISBN 0-8040-0543-5). Swallow Press.

Double or Quits. Erle Stanley Gardner. LC 41-25663. 1941. W. Morrow.

Double or Quits. Erle Stanley Gardner. LC 47-19982. 1946. Blakiston Co.

Double Overture. Edward Frederic Benson. LC 6-11339. (On cover: Sergel's international library. New series. v. l, no. 2). 1894. C. H. Sergel Company.

Double Ring: The Proud Generation. Ava Ruth Hochstatter. LC 76-370229. 10.00 (ISBN 0-8059-2267-9). Dorrance.

Double Road. Michael Wood. LC 16-17424. 1915. Longmans, Green and Co.

Double Room. James Noble Gifford. LC 44-9902. 1944. Phoenix Press.

Double Run. Roderic Jeffries. LC 73-83193. 1973. 4.95 (ISBN 0-8027-5288-8). Walker.

Double Secret. Shoshone Beauxdette. 1979. 5.95 (ISBN 0-533-02020-4). Vantage.

Double Seven. Maxwell Grant, pseud. (Shadow Ser.: No. 5). 1975. pap. 0.95 o.p. (ISBN 0-515-03700-1, N3700). BJ Pub Group.

Double Shadow. Frances Adrian. (Fawcett Gold Medal Book). 1977. 1.75 (ISBN 0-449-13867-4). Fawcett Pubns.

Double Shadow. Frederick Turner. (Berkley book). 1979. 1.75 (ISBN 0-425-03951-X). Berkley Pub. Corp.

Double Shadow: Fiction. Frederick Turner. LC 77-17938. 7.95. Berkley Pub. Corp.: Distributed by Putnam.

Double Shadow Murders. Allan McRoyd. LC 40-3853. Greystone Press.

Double Shuffle. Donald Bayne Hobart. LC 28-29081. E. J. Clode, Inc.

Double Shuffle: By James Hadley Chase Pseud. 1st Ed. Rene Raymond. LC 52-121565. (Guilt edged mystery). 1953. Dutton.

Double Sin, and Other Stories. Agatha Miller Christie. LC 61-11721. (Red badge detective). 1961. Dodd, Mead.

Double Sin and Other Stories. Dame Agatha Miller Christie. 1974. (pbk.) 0.95. Dell.

Double Snare. Rosemary Harris. LC 75-6568. (Simon and Schuster novel of suspense). 1975. 7.95 (ISBN 0-671-22036-5). Simon and Schuster.

Double Solution: A Tale of Inspector Higgins. Cecil Freeman Gregg. LC 32-3494. 1932. L. MacVeagh, Dial Press, Inc.

Double Squeeze. Henry Beach Needham. LC 75-150557. (Short story index reprint series). (Illus.). 1971. (ISBN 0-8369-3854-2). Books for Libraries Press.

Double Squeeze. Henry Beach Needham. LC 15-8001. 1915. 1.25. Doubleday, Page & Company.

Double Standard. Linda Dubreuil. 1980. pap. 2.25 (ISBN 0-8439-0801-7). Nordon Pubns.

Double Standard. Alan Williams. LC 38-307949. 1938. Godwin.

Double Standards. Aviva Hellman. LC 80-1861. 1981. 14.95 (ISBN 0-385-17358-X). Doubleday.

Double Star. Robert Anson Heinlein. LC 78-5569. (Gregg Press science fiction series). (Illus.). 1978. 10.00 (ISBN 0-8398-2446-7). Gregg Press.

Double Star. 1st Ed. Robert Anson Heinlein. LC 56-596117. (Doubleday science fiction). 1956. Doubleday.

Double Suicide. The True History of the Lives of the Twin Sisters, Sarah and Maria Williams. Containing an Account of Maria's Love, Mock Marriage, Suffering and Degradation, Together with Sarah's Love and Suffering ... 1855. G. C. Holbrook.

Double Take. David Craig. LC 72-186217. 1972. 5.95 o.p. (ISBN 0-8128-1462-2). Stein & Day.

Double Take. Roy Huggins. LC 45-111495. 1946. W. Morrow & Company.

Double Take. Vardis Margener. LC 82-80210. 288p. (Orig.). 1982. pap. 2.95 (ISBN 0-86721-078-8). Playboy Pbks.

Double Take. Allan James Tucker. LC 72-186217. 1972. 5.95 (ISBN 0-8128-1462-2). Stein and Day.

Double Take. Ellen Violett. LC 73-83679. 1977. 7.95 (ISBN 0-385-07440-9). Doubleday.

Double Thirteen. Robert McNair Wilson. LC 26-7015. 1926. J. B. Lippincott Company.

Double Thread. Ellen Thorneycroft Fowler. LC 99-2095. 1899. D. Appleton and Company.

Double Tragedy. Odessa Bond. 1970. 3.00 o.p. Vantage.

Double Tragedy: An Inspector French Story. Freeman Wills Crofts. LC 43-11955. 1943. Dodd, Mead & Company.

Double Traitor. Edward Phillips Oppenheim. LC 15-11000. 1915. 1.35. Little, Brown, and Company.

Double Traitor. Edward Phillips Oppenheim. LC 19-6146. Hodder and Stoughton.

Double Traitor. Edward Phillips Oppenheim. LC 21-137173. 1920. A. L. Burt Company.

Double Trap. Elliot West. 1974. (pbk.) 1.25. Bantam Books.

Double Treasure. Clarence Budington Kelland. LC 47-30246. 1946. Harper.

Double Trouble. Elliott Lewis. (Bennett Ser.: No. 4). 192p. (Orig.). 1981. pap. 1.95 (ISBN 0-523-41438-2). Pinnacle Bks.

Double Trouble. Roosevelt Mallory. (Radcliff#3). 1975. (pbk.) 1.50 (ISBN 0-87067-455-2). Holloway House.

Double Trouble. Doreen Tovey. (Illus.). 144p. 1972. 5.95 (ISBN 0-393-08547-3). Norton.

Double Trouble: Or, Every Hero His Own Villain. Herbert Quick. LC 6-31241. 1906. The Bobbs-Merrill Company.

Double Turn. Audrey Lucas. E. P. Dutton & Co., Inc.

Double View. Chandler Brossard. (O.s.i.). pap. 0.50 o.s.i. (A150F, Award). Univ Pub & Dist.

Double View: A Novel. Chandler Brossard. LC 60-12544. 1960. Dial Press.

Double Vision. Noel Bertram Gerson. LC 74-180077. 1972. 5.95. Doubleday.

Double Vision: An Anthology of Twentieth-Century Stories in English. Rudy Henry Wiebe. LC 77-358008. (ISBN 0-7705-1344-1). Macmillan of Canada.

Double Wedding. Adelaide Humphries. 1946. Arcadia House, Inc.

Double Wedding. Alix Melbourne. (Coventry Romance Ser.: No. 180). 224p. 1982. pap. 1.50 (ISBN 0-449-50281-3, Coventry). Fawcett.
Double Wedding: Or, How She Was Won. Catherine Ann Ware Warfield. LC 8-34838. T. B. Peterson & Brothers.
Double Wedding Ring. Josephine Lawrence. LC 46-6102. 1946. D. Appleton-Century Company, Inc.
Double Wrong: Or, A Broken Life. Georges Ohnet. Tr. by Curtin, J. C. (On cover: Echo series, no. 90). 1889. Pollard & Moss.
Double Z. Maxwell Grant. (Shadow,#5). 1975. (pbk.) 0.95 (ISBN 0-515-03700-1). Pyramid Books.
Doublecross. Armstrong Livingston. LC 29-10176. R. D. Henkle Co., Inc.
Doublecross Gun. Jim Kane. Ed. by Alice Sachs. 1970. 3.95 o.p. Lenox Hill.
Doubled in Diamonds. Victor Canning. LC 67-15152. 1967. W. Morrow.
Doubleday's Children. Dutton Cook. LC 6-28072. 1877. G.P. Putnam's Sons.
Doublefields. Elizabeth Enright. LC 66-23806. 1966. 4.75 o.p. (ISBN 0-15-126408-2). HarBraceJ.
Doubles. V. Mikhanovsky. 512p. 1981. 5.50 (ISBN 0-8285-2039-9, Pub. by Progress Pubs USSR). Imported Pubns.
Doubles. Tom Seligson. 1982. 3.50 (ISBN 0-440-11819-0). Dell Publishiing Co.
Doubles in Death: By William Grew Pseud. 1st Ed. William O'Farrell. LC 53-6630. 1953. Published for the Crime Club by Doubleday.
Doubloons. Eden Phillpotts & Bennett, Enoch Arnold. 1906. McClure, Phillips & Co.
Doubloons--and the Girl. John Maxwell Forbes. LC 17-10668. Sully & Kleinteich.
Doubly Damned. O. C. Lott. (Orig.). 1981. pap. 2.75 (ISBN 0-505-51720-5). Tower Bks.
Doubly Dead. John M Patterson. LC 69-10959. (Crime Club selection). 1969. 3.95. Published for the Crime Club by Doubleday.
Doubly Dead: By E. X. Ferrars Pseud. Morna Doris MacTaggart Brown. LC 63-11896. 1963. Published for the Crime Club by Doubleday.
Doubly Wronged. Also, Ruth's Holiday. Adah M Howard. (On cover: Munro's library, v. 1, no. 107). N. L. Munro.
Doubtfire. Robert Nye. 1968. 4.95 o.p. (ISBN 0-8090-3960-5). Hill & Wang.
Doubtful Character. Gertrude M. Robins Reynolds. LC 13-24449. Hodder and Stoughton.
Doubtful Character. Gertrude M. Robins Reynolds. LC 13-25055. Hodder & Stoughton, Geroge H. Doran Company.
Doubtful Guest. Edward Gorey. LC 57-10200. (Illus.). 1978. 5.95 o.p. (ISBN 0-396-07628-9). Dodd.
Doubtful Guest. Edward Gorey. (Illus.). 64p. 1982. pap. 5.95 (ISBN 0-312-92145-4). Congdon & Weed.
Doubtful Joy. Elizabeth Jenkins. LC 35-12776. 1935. Doubleday, Doran & Co., Inc.
Doubtful Valley: A Novel of Traitor Whites and Apaches in 1880. Garland Roark. LC 51-2265. 1951. Houghton Mifflin.
Doubtful Year. Gilbert Munger Wright. LC 28-18235. 1928. D. Appleton & Company.
Doubting Castle. Elinor Chipp. LC 22-18398. Boni and Liveright.
Doubting Castle: A Religious Novelette. Roswell Alphonzo Benedict. LC 7-34447. 1891. J. B. Alden.
Doubting Heart. Annie Keary & Macquoid, Katherine Sarah (Gadsden) LC 9-3339. 1895. Macmillan and Co.
Doubting Heart. A Novel. Annie Keary & Macquoid, Katherine Sarah (Gadsden) (Franklin square library. no. 93). Harper & Brothers.
Doubting Heart. A Novel. Katherine Sarah Macquoid & Macquoid, Katharine Sarah (Gadsden) (Seaside library, v. 33, no. 681). G. Munro.
Doubting Thomas. Winston Brebner. LC 56-10183. 1956. Rinehart.
Dough Boys. Patrick MacGill. LC 18-23223. George H. Doran Company.
Douglas. Hiram Wallace Hayes. LC 12-24631. 1.25. The Howerton Press.
Douglas Convolution. Edward Llewellyn. (Daw Science Fiction Ser.). 1979. pap. 1.75 o.p. (ISBN 0-87997-495-8, UE1495). Daw Bks.
Douglas; Tender and True. Susanna Shulrick Hayne Pinckney. LC 7-35889. 1892. Nixon-Jones Printing Co.
Douglass Farm. Mary Emily Neely Bradley. LC 74-37584. (Black heritage library collection). (Illus.). 1972. (ISBN 0-8369-8960-0). Books for Libraries Press.
Doulbe Agent. John Michael Ward Bingham. LC 67-10535. 1967. Dutton.
Dournof. A Russian Story. Alice Marie Celeste Durand. Tr. by Stewart, Marie. T. B. Peterson & Brothers.
Dove: A Novel. Barbara Hanrahan. LC 81-10952. 203p. 1982. 14.95 (ISBN 0-7022-1880-4); pap. 7.95 (ISBN 0-7022-1890-1). U of Queensland Pr.
Dove Against Death. Christopher Wood. LC 82-19991. 1983. 15.75 (ISBN 0-670-28066-6). Viking Press.
Dove and Roebuck. Ena Limebeer. LC 33-15941. E. P. Dutton & Co., Inc.
Dove and the Dart. 1st Ed. Patricia Campbell. LC 50-11403. 1950. Superior Pub. Co.
Dove Brings Peace. Richard Hagopian. LC 44-3159. 1944. Farrar & Rinehart Inc.
Dove Creek Rodeo. Alden Stevens. LC 36-6958. 1936. W. Morrow & Company.
Dove Flies South. James Aloysius Hyland. LC 57-413327. 1957. Bruce Pub. Co.
Dove Flies South. James Aloysius Hyland. LC 43-172354. 1943. The Bruce Publishing Company.
Dove Found No Rest. Dennis Gray Stoll. LC 47-1636. 1947. Doubleday & Company, Inc.
Dove in the Eagle's Nest. Charlotte Mary Yonge. LC 4-22085. 1866. D. Appleton and Company.
Dove in the Eagle's Nest. Charlotte Mary Yonge. (On cover: Seaside library. Pocket ed. no. 665). 1886. G. Munro.
Dove in the Eagle's Nest. Charlotte Mary Yonge. (On cover: Lovell's library, no. 1355). 1889. J. W. Lovell Company.
Dove in the Eagle's Nest. Charlotte Mary Yonge. LC 41-42517. (The home library). A. L. Burt.
Dove in the Eagle's Nest. Charlotte Mary Yonge. LC 4-16596. 1901. Macmillan and Co., Limited.
Dove in the Eagle's Nest. Charlotte Mary Yonge. LC 24-21072. 1924. Duffield and Company.
Dove in the Eagle's Nest. Charlotte Mary Yonge. LC 26-17974. (The Macmillan children's classics). 1926. The Macmillan Company.
Dove in the Eagle's Nest. Charlotte Mary Yonge. LC 36-37158. (Half-title: Everyman's library, ed. by Ernest Rhys. Fiction. no. 329). 1929. J. M. Dent & Sons, Ltd.
Dove of the East. Mark Helprin. 1981. pap. 5.95 (ISBN 0-440-52151-3, Delta). Dell.
Dove of the East, and Other Stories. Mark Helprin. LC 75-8215. 1975. 6.95 (ISBN 0-394-49659-0). Knopf: Distributed by Random House.
Dove Persists. Kathryn Zinn. 3.75 o.p. Vantage.
Dove Tree. 1st Ed. L. D. Clark. LC 61-7640. 1961. Doubleday.
Dove with the Bough of Olive. Dunstan Thompson. LC 54-5817. 1954. Simon and Schuster.
Dovebury Murders: By John Rhode Pseud. Cecil John Charles Street. LC 54-8495. (Red badge detective). 1954. Dodd, Mead.
Dovecote: Or, The Heart of the Homestead. George Canning Hill. LC 7-4692. 1854. J. P. Jewett and Company.
Dover and the Unkindest Cut of All. Joyce Porter. LC 67-13309. 1967. Scribner.
Dover Goes to Pott. Joyce Porter. LC 68-19306. 1968. Scribner.
Dover One. Joyce Porter. LC 64-21296. 1964. Scribner.
Dover Strikes Again. Joyce Porter. LC 73-77297. 1973. 4.95. D. McKay Co.
Dover the Unkindest Cut. Joyce Porter. 1981. 15.00x (ISBN 0-86025-144-6, Pub. by Ian Henry Pubns England). State Mutual Bk.
Dover Three. Joyce Porter. LC 66-13088. 1966. 3.50. Scribners.
Dover Train Mystery. Lucy Beatrice Malleson. LC 36-19977. The Dial Press.
Dover Two. Joyce Porter. LC 65-155405. bds., 3.50. Scribners.
Doves' Nest: And Other Stories. Katherine Mansfield. LC 23-11811. 1923. A. A. Knopf.
Doves of Venus, a Novel. Olivia Manning. LC 56-11324. 1956. Abelard-Schuman.
Doves of War. Paul Evan Lehman. LC 52-5312. (Dutton Diamond D western). 1952. Dutton.
Dovisch in the Wilderness, and Other Stories. Herbert Wilner. LC 68-11142. 1968. 5.50. Bobbs-Merrill.
Dowager. Elise Ayers Sanguinetti. LC 68-25420. 1968. 5.95. Scribner.
Dowager Countess and the American Girl. Lilian Lida Bell. 1903. Harper & Brothers.
Dowager: Or, The New School for Scandal. Catherine Grace Frances Moody Gore. LC 6-27493. 1841. Lea and Blanchard.
Dower Chest. Amber Dean. LC 77-124172. (Red mask mystery). 1970. 4.95. G. P. Putnams's Sons.
Dower House Mystery. Patricia Wentworth. LC 25-191705. Small, Maynard & Company.
Dowie Elder. Mortimer A Dittenhoefer. LC 1-29292. 1900. The News Printery.
Down. Walt Grove. LC 53-10778. (Dell first edition, 1E). 1953. Dell Pub. Co.
Down a Dark Alley. Genevieve Holden. LC 75-20748. (Crimeclub Ser.). 192p. 1976. 5.95 o.p. (ISBN 0-385-11188-6). Doubleday.
Down a Dark Alley. Genevieve Long Pou. LC 75-20748. 1976. 5.95 (ISBN 0-385-11188-6). Published for the Crime Club by Doubleday.
Down a Dark Road. Sallie Lee Bell. LC 68-55323. 1968. 2.95. Zondervan.
Down All the Days. Christy Brown. LC 70-104644. 1970. 6.95. Stein and Day.
Down All Your Streets: A Novel. Leonard Bishop. LC 52-5945. 1952. Dial Press.
Down Among Men. Will Levington Comfort. LC 13-23881. 1.25. George H. Doran Company.
Down Among the Crackers. Rosa Pendleton Chiles. LC 8-7682. 1900. The Editor Publishing Co.
Down Among the Dead Men. Michael Hartland. LC 82-22875. 13.95 (ISBN 0-02-548520-2). Macmillan.
Down Among the Dead Men. Michael Hartland. (Illus.). 320p. 1983. 13.95 (ISBN 0-02-548520-2). Macmillan.
Down Among the Dead Men. Patricia Moyes. LC 61-5296. 1961. Holt, Rinehart and Winston.
Down Among the Dead Men. Prentice Winchell. LC 43-1550. 1943. G. P. Putnam's Sons.
Down among the Donkey. Elizabeth Svendsen. (Illus.). 1982. pap. 10.00x (ISBN 0-330-26316-1, Pub. by Pan Bks). State Mutual Bk.
Down Among the Jocks. Ralph Dennis. (Hardman, No. 5.). 1974. (pbk.) 0.95. Popular Library.
Down Among the Women. Fay Weldon. 1974. (pbk.) 1.50. Warner Paperback Library.
Down and Dirty. W. B Murphy. (Razoni & Jackson detective series,#4). 1974. (pbk.) 0.95 (ISBN 0-523-00346-3). Pinnacle Books.
Down and Dirty: A Novel. Frank King. (signet book). 1979. 1.95 (ISBN 0-451-08699-6). New American Library.
Down and Down and Down. LC 52-67083. 1952. Signature Press.
Down and Out in Cambridge. Douglas Fairbairn. LC 81-7782. 13.95 (ISBN 0-698-11089-7). Coward, McCann & Geoghegan.
Down & Out in Paris & London. George Orwell. LC 65-67354. 1972. pap. 3.95 (ISBN 0-15-626224-X, Harv). HarBraceJ.
Down at Cross Timbers. Patrick Sylvester McGeeney. LC 10-1780. 1909. Angel Guardian Press.
Down at Stein's Pass: A Romance of New Mexico. Patrick Sylvester McGeeney. LC 10-178136. 1909. Angel Guardian Press.
Down Bound Train. Bill Garnett, pseud. LC 72-92402. 1973. 4.95 (ISBN 0-385-01820-7). Doubleday.
Down by the Old Blood Stream. Alfred Hitchcock. 1981. pap. 2.25 (ISBN 0-440-12127-2). Dell.
Down by the Rio Grande. Henry Spofford Canfield. 1901. Hurst & Company.
Down Come the Trees. Anthony Thorne. LC 36-15259. 1936. Doubleday, Doran & Company, Inc.
Down-East Duchess. Ruth Blodgett. LC 39-273553. Harcourt, Brace and Company.
Down East Master's First School. Edward Augustus Rand. LC 8-219. D. Lothrop Company.
Down East Nurse. William Edward Daniel Ross. LC 67-6866. 1967. Arcadia House.
Down-Easters, 2 vols. John Neal. LC 78-64083. Repr. of 1833 ed. 75.00 (ISBN 0-404-17310-1). AMS Pr.
Down-Easters, &C., &C., &C. John Neal. 1833. Harper & Brothers.
Down from the Mountain. Louis H Charbonneau. LC 69-20063. 1969. 5.95. Doubleday.
Down Here in the Dream Quarter. Barry N Malzberg. LC 76-14706. 1976. 5.95 (ISBN 0-385-12268-3). Doubleday.
Down Home. George Mettler. 2.95 (ISBN 0-449-14403-8). Fawcett Gold Medal Books.
Down Home. Laurie Lee Simmons. (O.s.i.). 1976. pap. 1.50 o.s.i. (BT50991). Belmont-Tower.
Down Home with Jennie Allen. Grace Donworth. LC 10-19623. 1.50. Small, Maynard and Company.
Down I Go: A Novel of Suspense by Ben Kerr Pseud. William Ard. LC 55-328299. (Popular library, 653). 1955. Popular Library.
Down in Arkansas a Story. Charles Henry Rand Hibler. LC 2-20643. 1902. The Abbey Press.
Down in Flames. Ben Ray Redman. LC 30-2761. 1930. Payson & Clarke Ltd.
Down in Maryland. Gus Ward. LC 30-3871. J. W. Stowell Printing Company.
Down in the Black Gang: And Others; a Story Collection. Philip Jose Farmer. LC 79-26326. 1971. Nelson Doubleday.
Down in the Canyon. Walter Samuel Cramp. LC 13-256122. 1.25. R. G. Badger.
Down in the Valley. Harold Webber Freeman. LC 30-262693. H. Holt and Company.
Down in the World. Florence Alice Price James. (sunnyside series, no. 59). 1892. J. S. Ogilvie.
Down on the Farm. Jack Richards. Whitman Publishing Company.
Down on the Old Plantation: Original Sketches of Everyday Life on a Mississippi Cotton Plantation. Samuel Martha Caldwell Scogin & Howe, John Dicks. LC 9-2766. 1908.
Down Our Way. Lilla Mar Hall Smith. LC 11-23503. 1911. Dodd, Mead and Company.
Down Our Way: Stories of Southern and Western Character. Mary Jameson Judah. LC 7-11896. Way & Williams.
Down River. Richard Anderson. 1950. 6.50 (ISBN 0-8323-0107-8). Binford.
Down River. Richard Church. LC 57-7892. 1957. J. Day Co.
Down River. Ambrose Elwell. LC 26-151351. Small, Maynard & Company.
Down River. Lona Rae. 1981. 2.25 (ISBN 0-505-51607-1). Tower Books.
Down River: A Novel. Richard Anderson. LC 50-7849. 1950. Binfords & Mort.
Down Second Avenue. Ezekiel Mphahlele. LC 75-139080. (Orig.). 1971. pap. 1.95 o.p. (ISBN 0-385-03111-4, Anch). Doubleday.
Down Stream (A Vau-L'eau) and Other Works, Including Marthe, A Dish of Spices (Le Drageoir Aux Epices), Critical Papers (from Certains and L'art Moderne), and a Twenty-Year-After Preface (to A Rebours) Joris Karl Huysmans. LC 75-1383. 1975. 14.00. H. Fertig.
Down Stream (A Vau-L'eau) And Other Works, Including Marthe, A Dish of Spices (Le Drageoir Aux Epices) Critical Papers (from Certains and L'art Moderne), and a Twenty-Year-After Preface (to A Rebours). Joris Karl Huysmans. Tr. by Putnam, Samuel. LC 28-67538. 1927. P. Covici.
Down the American River & Other Stories. Rose G. Ignatow. (Illus., Orig.). 1979. pap. 5.50 (ISBN 0-914278-27-4). Copper Beech.
Down the Bath Rocks: A Boy's Own Penny Wonder. Patrick O'Connor. LC 73-170260. 1971. 1.95 (ISBN 0-7171-0530-X). Gill and Macmillan.
Down the Dark Alley. Bertrand William Sinclair. LC 36-1532. 1936. Little, Brown, and Company.
Down the Dark Street. Jessie M. Chase Fenton. LC 37-38113. 1937. Houghton Mifflin Company.
Down the Line with John Henry. George Vere Hobart. LC 1-24857. 1901. G. W. Dillingham Co.
Down the Long Hills. Louis L'Amour. (Louis L'amour Westerns Ser). 1978. pap. 1.95 (ISBN 0-553-13722-0, Y13722-0). Bantam.
Down the Long Slide. Henry Thomas Hopkinson. LC 50-7622. 1950. Morrow.
Down the Mother Lode. Vivia Hemphill. LC 22-12086. 1922. Purnell's.
Down the O-Hi-O,". Charles Humphrey Roberts. LC 7-41029. 1891. A. C. McClurg and Company.
Down the Proud Stream. Carl Fallas. LC 37-23082. 1937. Longmans, Green and Co.
Down the Rabbit Hole. Winifred Lear. LC 74-18734. 1975. 7.95 o.p. (ISBN 0-312-21875-3). St Martin.
Down the Ravine: A Story. Mary Noailles Murfree. 1885. Houghton, Mifflin and Company.
Down the Road a Piece. Margaret Flint. LC 41-5297. 1941. Dodd, Mead & Company.
Down the Sky: An Entertainment. Edward Verrall Lucas. LC 30-31185. 1930. J. B. Lippincott Company.
Down the Styx. Lawrence Durrell. (Illus.). 1971. pap. 2.50 o.p. (ISBN 0-912264-20-9). Capra Pr.
Down There. Cover Painting by Mitchell Hooks. David Goodis. LC 57-20928. (Gold medal book 623). 1956. Fawcett Publications.
Down There: La Bas. Joris Karl Huysmans. Tr. by Wallis, Keene. LC 24-7729. 1924. A. & C. Boni.
Down There (La Bas) A Study in Satanism. Joris Karl Huysmans. LC 56-13015. 1958. University Books.
Down There on a Visit. Christopher Isherwood. 1978. 2.50 (ISBN 0-380-01883-7). Avon Books.
Down to a Sunless Sea. David Graham. LC 80-25603. 13.95 (ISBN 0-671-41217-5). Simon and Schuster.
Down to Seven. 1st Ed. Walter P Henderson. LC 56-127693. 1957. Vantage Press.
Down to the Bone. Alan Sillitoe. LC 76-373358. (Literature for life series). (Illus.). 1976. 0.80 (ISBN 0-08-019799-X). Wheaton.
Down to the Sea. Morgan Robertson. LC 71-101289. (Short story index reprint series). 1969. Books for Libraries Press.
Down to the Sea. Morgan Robertson. LC 5-7380. 1905. Harper & Brothers.
Down to the Sea. autograph ed. Morgan Robertson. LC 16-11585. 1914. McClure's Magazine and Metropolitan Magazine.
Down-Trodden: Or, Black Blood and White. Walter Sketch. LC 22-4769. 1853. J. Miller, Jr.

Down Under. Patricia Wentworth. LC 37-17231. J. B. Lippincott Company.
Down Under & Dirty. Dan Streib. (Hawk Ser.: No. 9). (Orig.). 1981. pap. 1.95 (ISBN 0-515-05874-2). Jove Pubns.
Down Where the Moon Is Small. LC 66-12205. 1966. Doubleday.
Down Wild Goose Canyon. Charles Elmer Upton. LC 10-27742. 1910. C. E. Upton.
Down Yonder with Judge Priest and Irvin S. Cobb. Irvin Shrewsbury Cobb. LC 32-8074. 1932. R. Long & R. R. Smith, Inc.
Downbeat for a Dirge. Brandon Bird. LC 52-10161. (Red badge detective). 1952. Dodd, Mead.
Downbelow Station. C. J Cherryh. 1981. 2.75 (ISBN 0-87997-594-6). DAW Books.
Downey of the Mounted. James Beardsley Hendryx. LC 26-9578. 1926. G. P. Putnam's Sons.
Downfall. Zalman Shneur. LC 44-5462. 1944. Roy Publishers.
Downfall: By Harold W. Brecht. Harold W Brecht. LC 29-8540. 1929. Harper & Brothers.
Downfall (La Debacle) A Story of the Horrors of War. Emile Zola & Vizetelly, Ernest Alfred, 1853-1922, Tr. LC 26-26871. 1925. A. & C. Boni.
Downfall (La Debacle) The Smash-up. Emile Zola. LC 9-3426. (On cover: Cassell's sunshine series. no. 117, extra). 1892. Cassell Publishing Company.
Downfall (La Debacle) The Smash-up. Emile Zola & Robins, E. P., Tr. LC 9-3426. 1898. The Macmillan Company.
Downfall of a Politician; or, Death or Destiny. A Story of Politics, Religion, and Society. H. H. Smith. LC 8-8164. 1891. J. P. Morton and Company.
Downfall of the Gods. Hugh Charles Clifford. LC 12-14119. 1911. E.P. Dutton and Company.
Downfall: Tr. from the French of Emile Zola. Emile Zola. LC 3-8443. (Half-title: A century of French romance. Puritan ed. Edited by E. Goma. Vol. XVII). D. Appleton & Co.
Downhill Racers. Oakley M Hall. LC 63-7563. 1963. Viking Press.
Downing Legends. John William De Forest. Ed. by Donald Pizer. LC 77-96523. (American Authors Ser). 1970. Repr. of 1901 ed. lib. bdg. 14.25 o.s.i. (ISBN 0-512-00141-3). Garrett Pr.
Downland Corner. Victor L Whitechurch. LC 13-352746. 1913. H. Holt and Company.
Downrenter's Son. Ruth Hall. 1902. Houghton, Mifflin and Company.
Downright Dencey. Caroline Dale Parke Snedeker. LC 27-15114. 1927. Doubleday, Page & Co.
Downriver: A Novel. Peter Collier. LC 78-2423. 8.95 (ISBN 0-03-043826-8). Holt, Rinehart and Winston.
Downstairs at Ramsey's: A Novel. James Leigh. LC 67-28819. 1968. Harper & Row.
Downstairs Room: And Other Speculative Fiction. Kate Wilhelm. LC 68-22513. 1968. 4.95. Doubleday.
Downstream. Paul Brodeur. LC 70-175292. 1972. 6.95. Atheneum.
Downstream. Sigfrid Siwertz. LC 23-8080. 1923. A. A. Knopf.
Downstream: A Modern Story of Men and a River. Paul William Burres. LC 61-182265. 1961. Concordia Pub. House.
Downstream (A vau-l'Eau) & Other Works, Including Marthe. Joris Karl Huysmans. Tr. by S. Putnam. LC 75-1383. 343p. 1975. Repr. of 1927 ed. 21.50 (ISBN 0-86527-240-9). Fertig.
Downtown Lady. Cissy Lacks, pseud. LC 76-41077. 1976. pap. 2.95 (ISBN 0-933530-00-5). Beanie Bks.
Downward: A "Slice of Life,". Maud Churton Braby. LC 12-10816. 1912. 1.25. W. Rickey & Company.
Downward Path. Cliff Towner. LC 54-118974. Vantage Press.
Downward Path. From the French of Emile Gaboriau... Emile Gaboriau. LC 6-44555. Estes and Lauriat.
Downward to the Earth. Robert Silverberg. LC 76-16689. 1970. Doubleday.
Dowry. Maggy Gould. 1975. pap. 1.25 o.p. (ISBN 0-515-03624-2, V3624). Pyramid Pubns.
Dowry: A Novel. Maggy Gould. LC 49-10310. 1949. W. Morrow.
Dowry. 1st Ed. Margaret Culkin Banning. LC 54-11999. 1955. Harper.
Dozen Deadly Dragons of Joy. Mallory T. Knight. (Man from T.O.M.C.A.T. Ser.). 176p. pap. 0.60 o.p. (A212X, Award). Univ Pub & Dist.
Dracula. Ed. by Tom Barling. pap. 1.99 o.p. (ISBN 0-448-12637-0, G&D). Putnam Pub Group.
Dracula. Russ Jones Production. (Illus.). 160p. (Orig.). 1975. pap. 1.25 o.p. (ISBN 0-532-12356-5). Woodhill.
Dracula. Russ Jones Production. (Illus.). 160p. (Orig.). 1975. pap. 1.25 o.p. (ISBN 0-532-12356-5). Manor Bks.
Dracula. Bram Stoker. LC 59-1336. Garden City Books.
Dracula. Bram Stoker. LC 73-11899. 1973. 6.95 (ISBN 0-385-09580-5). Doubleday.
Dracula. Bram Stoker. LC 75-99187. (Great illustrated classics). (Illus.). 1970. Dodd, Mead.
Dracula. Bram Stoker. LC 1-24939. 1899. Doubleday & McClure Co.
Dracula. Bram Stoker. LC 15-6319. 1913. Doubleday, Page & Company.
Dracula. Bram Stoker. LC 18-174. 1917. Doubleday, Page & Company.
Dracula. Bram Stoker. LC 20-14560. 1919. Doubleday, Page & Company.
Dracula. Bram Stoker. LC 21-153375. 1920. Doubleday, Page & Company.
Dracula. Bram Stoker. LC 29-252831. 1927. Doubleday, Page & Company.
Dracula. Bram Stoker. LC 27-22762. (The Lambskin library, no. 6). 1927. Doubleday, Page & Company.
Dracula. Bram Stoker. LC 28-24705. (Sundial library). 1928. Garden City Publishing Company, Inc.
Dracula. Bram Stoker. LC 30-2772. 1928. Grosset & Dunlap.
Dracula. Bram Stoker. LC 31-51308. Grosset & Dunlap.
Dracula. Bram Stoker. LC 32-26376. (Half-title: The modern library of the world's best books). 1932. The Modern Library.
Dracula. Bram Stoker. (Jove Book). 1979. 2.50 (ISBN 0-515-05347-3). Jove Publications.
Dracula: A Mystery Story. Bram Stoker. LC 25-23778. (international adventure library). W. R. Caldwell.
Dracula Archives. Raymond Rudorff. LC 73-183380. 1973. (pbk) 0.95 (ISBN 0-671-77678-9). Pocket Books.
Dracula Began. Gail Kimberly. (Orig.). 1976. pap. 1.25 o.p. (ISBN 0-515-03741-9). BJ Pub Group.
Dracula Book of Great Horror Stories. Leslie Shepard. LC 80-29656. 12.00 (ISBN 0-8065-0765-9). Citadel Press.
Dracula Book of Great Vampire Stories. Leslie Shepard. LC 76-51732. 10.00 (ISBN 0-8065-0565-6). Citadel Press.
Dracula in Love. John Shirley. (Orig.). 1979. pap. 1.95 (ISBN 0-89083-443-1). Zebra.
Dracula. Introd. by Anthony Boucher. Illus. with Wood Engravings by Felix Hoffmann. Bram Stoker & Felix Illus Hoffman. LC 66-3512. 1966. 6.95. Heritage Dist. Dial.
Dracula Made Easy. J. Youngson. 4.00 o.p. (ISBN 0-8062-0945-3). Carlton.
Dracula Spectacula. John Gardiner & Andrew Parr. 1981. script 15.00x (ISBN 0-237-75012-0, Pub. by Evans Bros); score 15.00x. State Mutual Bk.
Dracula Tape. Fred Saberhagen. Ed. by Jim Baen. 1980. pap. 2.25 (ISBN 0-441-16599-0). Ace Bks.
Dracula Was a Woman: In Search of the Blood Countess of Transylvania. Raymond T. McNally. LC 82-17264. (Illus.). 288p. 1983. 14.95 (ISBN 0-07-045671-2). Galley OR.
Dracula's Children. Richard Lortz. LC 80-85346. 1981. 12.95 (ISBN 0-932966-15-2). Permanent Press.
Dracula's Daughter. Carl Dreadstone & Stoker, Bram. (Berkley Medallion Book). (Illus.). 1977. 1.25 (ISBN 0-425-03463-1). Berkley Pub. Corp.
Dracula's Guest. Bram Stoker. LC 88-10621. 1937. Hillman-Curl, Inc.
Dracutwig. Bernhardt J. Hurwood. (O.s.i.). (Orig.). 1969. pap. 0.95 o.s.i. (AN1325, Award). Univ Pub & Dist.
Draft Bride. Adelaide Humphries. LC 42-290604. 1941. Arcadia House, Inc.
Draft Dodger. Louis Caron. Tr. by David T. Homel from Fr. (Fiction Ser: No. 42). 150p. (Orig.). 1980. pap. 8.95 (ISBN 0-88784-085-X, Pub. by Anansi Pr Canada). U of Toronto Pr.
Drag: A Comedy. William Dudley Pelley. LC 25-4857. 1925. 2.00. Little, Brown, and Company.
Drag" Harlan. Charles Alden Seltzer. LC 21-9056. 1921. A. C. McClurg & Co.
Drag" Harlan. Charles Alden Seltzer. 1922. Grosset & Dunlap.
Drag Me Down: A Realistic, Modern Novel by E. B. Stuart Pseud. Eugene Stuart Brown. LC 55-39732. (Popular library, 671). 1955. Popular Library.
Drag-Net: A Prison Story of the Present Day. Elizabeth Baker Bohan. LC 9-29504. 1909. The C. M. Clark Publishing Company.
Drag the Dark. Frederick Clyde Davis. LC 54-356844. (Ace double novel books, D-63). 1954. Ace Books.
Drag the Dark. 1st Ed. Frederick Clyde Davis. LC 53-6100. 1953. Published for the Crime Club by Doubleday.
Dragnet. Evelyn Snead Barnett. 1909. 1.50. B. W. Huebsch.
Dragnet, Case No. 561. David Knight. LC 56-9703. (Pocket book 1120. Mystery O). 1956. Pocket Books.
Dragoman: A Novel. George Kean Stiles. LC 13-2575. 1913. Harper & Brothers.
Dragoman Pass: An Adventure in the Balkans. 1st American Ed. Eric Ernest Williams. LC 59-8740. 1959. Coward-McCann.
Dragon. Alfred Coppel. LC 76-54584. 10.00 (ISBN 0-15-126500-3). Harcourt Brace Jovanovich.
Dragon. Jane Gaskell. LC 76-62772. (Gaskell, Jane, 1941-. The Atlan Ser.: No. 2). 1977. 7.95 (ISBN 0-312-21892-3). St. Martin's Press.
Dragon. Jane Gaskell. (Her the Atlan Series;). 1979. 1.75 (ISBN 0-671-82545-3). Pocket Books.
Dragon. Evgenii Ivanovich Zamiatin. Ed. & tr. by Mirra Ginsburg. LC 75-27415. 312p. 1976. 20.00x (ISBN 0-226-97867-2). U of Chicago Pr.
Dragon, and Other Stories. Evgeny Ivanovich Zamyatin & Mirra Ginsburg. LC 75-325706. (Penguin modern classics). 1975. 0.45 (ISBN 0-14-003785-3). Penguin.
Dragon & the George. Gordon R. Dickson. 1978. pap. 2.25 (ISBN 0-345-29514-5). Ballantine.
Dragon and the Pearl. Barbara Cartland. LC 77-670160. 1977. 6.95 (ISBN 0-87272-074-8). Duron Books.
Dragon & the Phoenix. E. Chou. (O.s.i.). 1971. 8.95 o.s.i. (ISBN 0-87795-016-4). Arbor Hse.
Dragon and the Rose. Roberta Gellis. LC 76-43400. (Illus.). 1.95. Playboy Press.
Dragon and the Tea-Kettle: An Experience; and The Doppleganger! Julia MacNair Wright. LC 9-915. 1885. National Temperance Society and Publication House.
Dragon Boat Mystery. John Bechtel. LC 43-15177. 1943. Wm. B. Eerdmans Publishing Company.
Dragon Breath Papers. Richard M Gardner. LC 75-40135. 1976. 8.95 (ISBN 0-670-63000-4). Viking Press.
Dragon Cove. Noel Bertram Gerson. LC 64-13825. 1964. Doubleday.
Dragon Feast. John Elliott. (O.s.i.). 1970. pap. 0.95 o.s.i. (B95-2009). Belmont-Tower.
Dragon: Fifteen Stories. Evgeny Ivanovich Zamyatin. LC 75-27415. 1976. 3.95 (ISBN 0-226-97868-0). University of Chicago Press.
Dragon; Fifteen Stories. Evgeny Ivanovich Zamyatin. Tr. by Mirra Ginsburg. LC 66-12281. 1967. Random House.
Dragon Flame. Nick Carter. (Nick Carter Espionage Ser.). (O.s.i.). (Orig.). pap. 0.60 o.s.i. (A311, Award). Univ Pub & Dist.
Dragon for Christmas. Gavin Black. LC 63-10614. 1979. pap. 1.95i (ISBN 0-06-080473-4, P 473, PL). Har-Row.
Dragon for Christmas. Oswald Wynd. (Perennial library). 1979. 1.95 (ISBN 0-06-080473-4). Harper & Row.
Dragon for Edward. Pamela Bennetts. LC 74-33915. 1975. 6.95 (ISBN 0-7091-4588-8). St. Martin's Press.
Dragon Harvest. Upton Beall Sinclair. (His Lanny Budd series, 6). 1973. 1.50. Curtis Books.
Dragon Harvest. Upton Beall Sinclair. LC 45-35107. 1945. The Viking Press.
Dragon in Paradise. John Vincent McNally. LC 63-20502. 1963. Doubleday.
Dragon in Shallow Waters. Victoria Mary Sackville-West. LC 22-2219. 1922. G. P. Putnam's Sons.
Dragon in Spring. Albert Barker. (Hawk Macrae Ser, No. 3). 1973. pap. 0.95 o.p. (09241). Curtis.
Dragon in the Sea. Frank Herbert. LC 56-5586. 1956. Doubleday.
Dragon in the Sea. Frank Herbert. LC 80-19867. (Gregg Press Science Fiction Series). 1980. 13.95 (ISBN 0-8398-2646-X). Gregg Press.
Dragon Keepers. Rodney Hughes. 1974. (pbk.) 0.95. Popular Library.
Dragon Lady: A Novel. Donald Cameron. LC 80-486996. 1980. 13.95 (ISBN 0-7710-1833-9). McClelland and Stewart.
Dragon Lensman. David A. Kyle. 192p. (Orig.). 1980. pap. 2.25 (ISBN 0-553-20461-0). Bantam.
Dragon Lord. David Drake. LC 79-10298. 8.95 (ISBN 0-399-12381-4). Berkley Pub. Corp.: Distributed by Putnam.
Dragon Lord of the Savage Empire. Jean Lorrah. LC 82-82000. 224p. 1982. pap. 2.75 (ISBN 0-86721-221-7). Playboy Pbks.
Dragon Magic. Andre Norton, pseud. 192p. 1982. pap. 1.95 (ISBN 0-441-16644-X). Ace Bks.
Dragon Masters. John Holbrook Vance. LC 76-9747. (Gregg Press science fiction series). 1976. 7.50 (ISBN 0-8398-2323-1). Gregg Press.
Dragon Murder Case: A Philo Vance Story. Willard Huntington Wright. LC 33-29645. 1933. C. Scribner's Sons.
Dragon of Destiny. Emma Drummond. (Orig.). 1982. pap. 2.95 (ISBN 0-440-11975-8). Dell.
Dragon of Ishtar Gate. Lyon Sprague De Camp. LC 82-5024. 5.95 (ISBN 0-89865-196-4). Donning Co.
Dragon of Lung Wang. Marion Harvey. LC 23-7953. E. J. Clode, Inc.
Dragon Painter. Mary McNeil Fenollosa. 1906. Little, Brown, and Company.
Dragon Rises. Adrienne Martine-Barnes. 2.75 (ISBN 0-441-16655-5, Pub. by Ace Science Fiction). Ace Bks.
Dragon Road. Henry Gibbs. LC 69-11440. 1969. 4.50. Walker.
Dragon Road. Simon Harvester. 1971. pap. 0.75 o.p. (75-402). Manor Bks.
Dragon Road. Simon Harvester. LC 69-11440. 1969. 4.50 o.p. Walker & Co.
Dragon Seed. Pearl Sydenstricker Buck. The John Day Company.
Dragon Seed. Pearl Sydenstricker Buck. 1943. The Sun Dial Press.
Dragon Shadows. James W Bennett. LC 28-11971. 1928. Duffield & Company.
Dragon Slayers. Andrew DeQuasie. 3.50 o.p. Carlton.
Dragon Star. Olivia O'Neill. 336p. 1983. pap. 2.95 (ISBN 0-441-16663-6, Pub. by Charter Bks). Ace Bks.
Dragon Strikes Back. Tom Roan. LC 36-6813. J. Messner, Inc.
Dragon Tales. Isaac Asimov & Martin Harry Greenberg. 320p. 1982. pap. 2.95 (Crest). Fawcett.
Dragon Thread. Laura Beheler. LC 80-84202. 9.95 (ISBN 0-937884-00-6). Hystry Mystry House.
Dragon Treasure. Adolph Paschang. LC 32-23566. 1932. Longmans, Green and Co.
Dragon Tree. Victor Canning. LC 58-6663. 1958. W. Sloane Associates.
Dragon Under the Hill. Gordon Honeycombe. (Fawcett crest book). 1974. (pbk.) 1.50. Fawcett.
Dragon Variation. Anthony Geoffrey Leo Simon Glyn. 1973. (pbk) 0.95. Popular Library.
Dragon Watch. 1st Ed. William Harrison Hays. LC 54-5719. 1954. Doubleday.
Dragon Winter. Niel Hancock. 1978. pap. 2.50 (ISBN 0-445-04191-9). Popular Lib.
Dragon Winter: Niel Hancock. Niel Hancock. 1.95 (ISBN 0-445-04191-9). Popular Library.
Dragon World. Ed. by Byron Preiss & Alfredo Alcala. (Fiction Illustrated Ser.: No. 5). 1977. pap. write for info o.p. BJ Pub Group.
Dragonard Blood. Rupert Gilchrist. LC 78-316393. (Illus.). 1977. 11.95 (ISBN 0-285-62283-8). Souvenir Press.
Dragondrums. Anne McCaffrey. (gr. 9 up). 1980. pap. 2.25 (ISBN 0-553-13189-3). Bantam.
Dragonfire. Peter G. Scott. 288p. 1982. pap. 2.95 (ISBN 0-523-41697-0). Pinnacle Bks.
Dragonfire: A "Nameless Detective" Mystery. Bill Pronzini. 208p. 1982. 10.95 (ISBN 0-312-21893-1). St Martin.
Dragonflame & Other Bedtime Nightmares. Don McGregor & David Anthony Kraft. LC 80-19775. 1980. 10.95. Borgo Press.
Dragonflight. Anne McCaffrey. LC 69-14239. 1969. 4.95. Walker.
Dragonflight. Anne McCaffrey. LC 78-16707. (McCaffrey, Anne. The Dragonriders of Pern). 8.95 (ISBN 0-345-27749-X). Ballantine Books.
Dragonfly. K. R. Dwyer. 256p. 1975. 7.95 o.p. (ISBN 0-394-49214-5). Random.
Dragonfly. Dean Koontz. LC 75-9877. 1975. 7.95 (ISBN 0-394-49214-5). Random House.
Dragonhead Deal: A Novel. Richard J Harper. 1975. (pbk.) 1.50. Warner Paperback Library.
Dragonmede. Rona Randall. LC 73-17619. 1974. 7.95 (ISBN 0-671-21712-7). Simon and Schuster.
Dragonquest. Anne McCaffrey. LC 78-19721. (McCaffrey, Anne. The Dragonriders of Pern). 1979. 8.95 (ISBN 0-345-28030-X). Ballantine Books.
Dragonriders of Pern, 3 vols. Anne McCaffrey. Date not set. pap. 6.75 (ISBN 0-345-28416-X, Del Rey). Ballantine.
Dragons & Nightmares. Robert Bloch. LC 75-1060. 1969. pap. 0.75 o.p. (B75-1060). Belmont-Tower.
Dragons & Nightmares. Robert Bloch. (O.s.i.). 1972. pap. 0.75 o.s.i. (BT40119). Belmont-Tower.
Dragons and Nightmares: Four Short Novels. Robert Bloch. LC 78-14533. (Voyager series). (Illus.). 1968. 4.00. Mirage Press.
Dragons at the Gate. Robert Lipscomb Duncan. (Signet Book). 1976. (pbk.) 1.95. New American Library.
Dragons at the Gate: A Novel. Robert Lipscomb Duncan. LC 75-11572. 1975. (ISBN 0-688-02937-X). Morrow.
Dragon's Blood. Henry Milner Rideout. LC 9-9507. 1909. Houghton Mifflin Company.
Dragon's Blood: Conte De Fee ! Deuxieme. Florence Roma Muir Wilson O'Brien. LC 26-20057. 1926. A. A. Knopf.
Dragon's Breath. Frank Smith. LC 80-21818. 12.95 (ISBN 0-8253-0007-X). Beaufort Books.
Dragon's Brood. William Henry Warner. LC 34-2647. 1934. H. C. Kinsey & Company, Inc.

Dragon's Cave: A Theocritus Lucius Westborough Story. Clyde B Clason. LC 40-4190. 1939. Pub. for the Crime Club by Doubleday, Doran & Co., Inc.

Dragon's Claw. Peter O'Donnell. 1979. 10.50 (ISBN 0-285-62381-8, Pub. by Souvenir Pr). Intl Schol Bk Serv.

Dragon's Daughter. Clyde C Westover. LC 12-27200. 1912. The Neale Publishing Company.

Dragons Drive You. Edwin Balmer. LC 34-1362. 1934. Dodd, Mead & Company.

Dragon's Egg. Robert L Forward. LC 79-21269. (Illus.). 1980. 9.95 (ISBN 0-345-28646-4). Ballantine Books.

Dragon's Egg. Robert L Forward. 1981. 2.25 (ISBN 0-345-28349-X). Ballantine Books.

Dragon's End. Josephine Hope Westervelt. LC 24-352. The Sunday School Times Company.

Dragon's Eye. Jennie Melville, pseud. LC 76-15616. 7.95 (ISBN 0-671-22309-7). Simon and Schuster.

Dragon's Eye. Jennie Melville, pseud. LC 77-9449. 1977. 10.95 (ISBN 0-8161-6491-6). G. K. Hall.

Dragon's Eye. Scott C. S. Stone. (Orig.). 1969. pap. 0.60 o.p. (R2554, GM). Fawcett World.

Dragon's Fire. Ralph Hayes. (Leisure Book). 1.95 (ISBN 0-8439-0630-8). Nordon Publications.

Dragon's Fists. Jim Dennis. (Kung Fu Master Ser). (O.s.i.). 192p. (Orig.). 1974. pap. 1.25 o.s.i. (AQ1358, Award). Univ Pub & Dist.

Dragon's Island. Jack Williamson. LC 51-10321. (A Science fiction adventure). 1951. Simon and Schuster.

Dragon's Jaws: A Million-Dollar Ransom in Diamonds. Frank Lucius Packard. LC 37-5993. 1937. Pub. for the Crime Club, Inc. by Doubleday Doran & Company, Inc.

Dragon's Lair. easy eye ed. Isabel D. Wenzell. pap. 0.60 o.p. Lancer.

Dragon's Mount. Deirdre Rowan. (Fawcett Gold Medal Book). 1973. (pbk) 0.75. Fawcett.

Dragon's Mouth. La Selle Gilman. LC 54-7085. 1954. W. Sloane Associates.

Dragons of Darkness. Orson Scott Card. LC 81-215874. (Ace science fiction). (Illus.). 6.95 (ISBN 0-441-16662-8). Ace Books.

Dragons of Eden. Carl Sagan. 1978. pap. 2.50 (ISBN 0-345-28153-5). Ballantine.

Dragons of Eden. Carl Sagan. 1977. 10.95 (ISBN 0-394-41045-9). Random.

Dragons of Light. Orson Scott Card. LC 81-129331. (Ace science fiction). (Illus.). 7.95 (ISBN 0-441-16660-1). Ace Books.

Dragons of Mist & Torrent. Teo Savory. LC 74-76907. 1974. 6.00 (ISBN 0-87775-042-4). Unicorn Pr.

Dragon's Smile: Novel. Michael P Knopl. LC 26-22409. 1926. Eastern Printing Company.

Dragon's Teeth. Keith Miles. (Frankenstein Horror Series). 1973. (pbk.) 0.95. Popular Lib.

Dragon's Teeth. Ellery Queens. Bd. with Calamity Town. 1980. pap. 2.50 (ISBN 0-451-11310-1, AE1310, Sig). NAL.

Dragon's Teeth. Upton Beall Sinclair. LC 42-106. 1942. The Viking Press.

Dragon's Teeth: A Novel. Jose Maria de. Eca de Queiros. Tr. by Mary J. Serrano from Port. LC 70-98833. 516p. Repr. of 1889 ed. lib. bdg. 20.75x (ISBN 0-8371-3089-1, ECDT). Greenwood.

Dragon's Teeth: A Novel. Jose Maria de. Eca de Queiros & Serrano, Mrs. Mary Jane (Christie) Tr. LC 8-15523. 1889. Ticknor and Company.

Dragons Teeth: A Novel from the Portuguese. Jose Maria de. Eca de Queiros. Tr. by Mary Jane Christie Serrano. LC 70-98833. 1972. (ISBN 0-8371-3089-1). Greenwood Press.

Dragon's Teeth: A Problem in Deduction. Ellery Queen, pseud. 1939. Frederick A. Stokes Company.

Dragon's Teeth: The Record of a Nobleman of France During the French Revolution. Arthur Hood. LC 25-10220. 1925. Cassel and Company, Ltd.

Dragon's Village: An Autobiographical Novel of Revolutionary China. Yuan-Tsung Chen. 1980. 10.00 (ISBN 0-394-50791-6). Pantheon.

Dragonseeds. Barbara Banks. LC 76-29854. 1977. 8.95 (ISBN 0-312-21927-X). St. Martin's Press.

Dragonship. Michael Kirk, pseud. LC 76-18355. (Crime Club Ser.). 1977. 5.95 o.p. (ISBN 0-385-12152-0). Doubleday.

Dragonship. Bill Knox. LC 76-18355. 1977. 5.95 (ISBN 0-385-12152-0). Published for the Crime Club by Doubleday.

Dragonship. Bill Knox. LC 77-358191. 1976. 3.25 (ISBN 0-09-126630-0). Long.

Dragonsinger. Anne McCaffrey. 1978. Repr. pap. 2.50 (ISBN 0-553-14127-9). Bantam.

Dragonslayer. Wayland Drew. (Orig.). 1981. pap. 2.75 (ISBN 0-345-29694-X, Del Rey). Ballantine.

Dragonsong. Anne McCaffrey. (gr. 6 up). 1977. pap. 2.50 (ISBN 0-553-14204-6). Bantam.

Dragonworld. Byron Preiss & J. Michael Reaves. 1979. pap. 7.95 (ISBN 0-553-01077-8). Bantam.

Dragonwyck. Anya Seton. LC 44-40044. 1944. Houghton Mifflin Company.

Dragoons of La Guerche. Louis Amedee Eugene Archard & Duffy, Richard, Tr.

Drake, by George! Ernest George Henham. LC 16-23091. 1916. A. A. Knopf.

Drakestail. Jan Wahl & Byron Barton. (Greenwillow read-alone). (Illus.). Greenwillow Books.

Drakor Memoranda. Jon Winters. LC 79-52461. 2.25 (ISBN 0-380-47563-4). Avon Books.

Dram of Poison. Charlotte Armstrong. (Berkley medallion book). 1975. (pbk.) 0.95 (ISBN 0-425-02152-1). Berkley Pub. Co.

Dram of Poison. Charlotte Armstrong. LC 56-5986. 1956. Coward-McCann.

Dram Tree. Hamilton Cochran. LC 61-15136. 1961. Bobbs-Merrill.

Drama in Dutch. Louis Zangwill. LC 8-83408. 1894. Macmillan and Co.

Drama in Pokerville. Joseph M. Field. LC 76-91078. (American humorists series). (Illus.). 1969. Literature House.

Drama in Pokerville: The Bench and Bar of Jurytown, and Other Stories. Joseph M. Field. 1847. Carey and Hart.

Drama in Pokerville: The Bench and Bar of Jurytown, and Other Stories. Joseph M. Field. LC 6-41199. (With Thompson, W. T. Chronicles of Pineville...Philadelphia, 1852). 1850. A. Hart.

Drama of the Hills. Alanson Mason Haswell. LC 24-3458. The Cornhill Publishing Company.

Dramas of Life. authorized ed. George Robert Sims. LC 8-9003. (On cover: Lovell's international series, no. 127). 1890. United States Book Company.

Dramatic Scenes from Real Life. Sydney Owenson Morgan. LC 78-31713. (Ireland, from the Act of Union, 1800, to the Death of Parnell, 1891). 1979. 64.00 (ISBN 0-8240-3459-7). Garland Pub.

Dramatist. Anthony Gibbs. LC 35-25389. 1935. Doubleday, Doran & Company, Inc.

Dramaturges of Yan. John Brunner. 208p. 1982. pap. 2.50 (ISBN 0-345-30677-5, Del Rey). Ballantine.

Dramocles. Robert Sheckley. LC 82-15864. 14.45 (ISBN 0-03-059037-X). Holt, Rinehart and Winston.

Draudziba Uz Sparna. Janina Babris. (Illus.). 80p. 1975. 4.75 (ISBN 0-89023-006-4). Res Publs.

Draught of the Blue, Together with An Essence of the Dusk: Tr from the Original Manuscripts. Francis William Bain. LC 7-6406. 1907. G. P. Putnam's Sons.

Draw Batons! Bill Knox. LC 73-79685. 1973. 4.95 (ISBN 0-385-03600-0). Published for the Crime Club by Doubleday.

Draw Near to Battle. Jere Hungerford Wheelwright. LC 53-6184. 1953. Scribner.

Draw or Drag. Wayne D Overholser. LC 50-5515. 1950. Macmillan.

Draw the Curtain Close. Thomas Blanchard Dewey. LC 47-11466. 1947. Jefferson House.

Drawback to Murder: A Christopher Storm Mystery. Willetta Ann Barber & Schabelitz, Rudolph Frederick, 1884- Joint Author. LC 47-3786. 1947. G. Scribner's Sons.

Drawbridge. Donald F. Drummond. 2.50 o.p. (ISBN 0-8040-0070-0). Swallow.

Drawn Blanc. Reg Gadney. LC 79-146076. 1971. 4.95. Coward-McCann.

Drawn Conclusion: A Christopher Storm Mystery. Willetta Ann Barber & Schabelitz, Rudolph Frederick, 1884- Joint Author. LC 42-203. 1942. Pub. for the Crime Club by Doubleday, Doran & Company, Inc.

Drawn Game. Richard Ashe King. (On cover: Seaside library. Pocket ed., no. 585). 1885. G. Munro.

Draycott Murder Mystery. Molly Thynne. LC 28-7869. 1928. Frederick A. Stokes Company.

Drayton. A Story of American Life. Thomas H. Shreve. LC 8-7327. 1851. Harper & Brothers.

Draytons and the Davenants: A Story of the Civil Wars. Elizabeth Charles. LC 42-48589. 1867. T. Nelson and Sons.

Draytons and the Davenants: A Story of the Civil Wars. Elizabeth Rundle Charles. LC 41-29681. Dodd & Mead.

Draytons and the Davenants: A Story of the Civil Wars. author's ed. Elizabeth Rundle Charles. LC 6-24202. 1867. M. W. Dodd.

Dread and Fear of Kings. John Breckenridge Ellis. LC 2609. 1900. A. C. McClurg & Co.

Dread Dwelling. Richmal Crompton Lamburn. LC 26-15272. 1926. Boni & Liveright.

Dread Journey. Dorothy Belle Flanagan Hughes. LC 45-880944. 1945. Duell, Sloan and Pearce.

Dread the Sunset. Marjorie Chalmers Carleton. LC 62-9863. 1962. Morrow.

Dreadful Hollow. Nicholas Blake. LC 53-7730. 1979. pap. 1.95i (ISBN 0-06-080493-9, P 493, PL). Har-Row.

Dreadful Hollow. Day-Lewis, Cecil. LC 74-192878. 1973. 1.80 (ISBN 0-85617-284-7). White Lion Publishers.

Dreadful Hollow. Irina Karlova. LC 42-209892. 1942. The Vanguard Press.

Dreadful Hollow (a Spine-Chiller) Irina Karlova. LC 45-302354. 1942. Hurst & Blackett.

Dreadful Hollow: By Nicholas Blake Pseud. Cecil Day-Lewis. LC 53-7730. 1953. Harper.

Dreadful Lemon Sky. John D Macdonald. 1975. (pbk.) 1.50. Fawcett.

Dreadful Lemon Sky. John Dann MacDonald. LC 74-23085. (His The Travis McGee series). 1975. 6.95 (ISBN 0-397-01074-5). Lippincott.

Dreadful Lemon Sky. John Dann MacDonald. LC 75-19112. 1975. 11.95 (ISBN 0-8161-6308-1). G. K. Hall.

Dreadful Night. Ben Ames Williams. LC 28-5864. 1928. Dutton.

Dreadful Reckoning. Charlotte Murray Russell, pseud. LC 41-3914. 1941. Pub. for the Crime Club by Doubleday, Doran & Company, Inc.

Dreadful Sanctuary. Eric Frank Russell. LC 51-10363. (Fp science fiction). 1951. Fantasy Press.

Dreadful Summit. Stanley Ellin. (Foul Play Press Ser.). 192p. pap. 4.95 (ISBN 0-914378-66-X). Countryman.

Dreadful Summit: A Novel of Suspense. Stanley Ellin. LC 48-5820. (Inner sanctum suspense special). 1948. Simon and Schuster.

Dreadful Temptation, and Countess Vera. Alexander McVeigh Miller. (On cover: Clover series, no. 117). 1896. Street & Smith.

Dreadful Temptation: Or, A Young Wife's Ambition. Alexander McVeigh Miller. (On cover: Munro's library, v. 1, no. 1). N. L. Munro.

Dreads and Drolls. Arthur Machen. LC 67-28757. (Essay index reprint series). 1967. Books for Libraries Press.

Dream. Lucy Freeman. LC 79-167746. 1971. 6.50 (ISBN 0-87795-020-2). Arbor House.

Dream. Lucy Freeman. 1974. (pbk.) 1.25. Dell.

Dream: A Novel. Herbert George Wells. LC 24-7679. 1924. The Macmillan Company.

Dream Adventure. Ed. by Roger Caillois. LC 63-9524. 1963. Onion Press.

Dream and a Forgetting. Julian Hawthorne. LC 7-3898. Belford, Clarke & Co.

Dream & a Promise. Doraine Moore. 1964. 2.95 o.p. Concordia.

Dream and the Business. Pearl Mary Teresa Richards Craigie. LC 6-36053. 1906. D. Appleton and Company.

Dream and the Desert. Uys Krige. LC 54-3650. 1954. Houghton Mifflin.

Dream and the Destiny: A Novel. Alexander Cordell, pseud. LC 73-11629. (Illus.). 1975. 8.95 (ISBN 0-385-00128-2). Doubleday.

Dream Apart. large print ed. Lesley Egan, pseud. LC 81-9002. 1981. 10.95 (ISBN 0-89621-302-1). Thorndike Press.

Dream Apart. Elizabeth Linington. LC 77-82756. 1978. 6.95 (ISBN 0-385-13412-6). Published for the Crime Club by Doubleday.

Dream Boat. Norval Richardson. LC 29-922. 1929. Little, Brown, and Company.

Dream-Boaters: A Story of Young Dope Addicts. 1st Ed. Larry Frisch. LC 53-11262. 1953. Exposition Press.

Dream Buyers. Myrick Land. LC 80-13967. 9.95 (ISBN 0-393-01393-6). Norton.

Dream Chariots. Manning Norvil. 1977. 1.50 (ISBN 0-87997-328-5). DAW Books.

Dream-Charlotte: A Story of Echoes. Matilda Barbara Bertram Edwards. LC 6-36583. 1896. Macmillan and Co.

Dream Chasers. David Rogers. (Dell Book). 1978. 1.95 (ISBN 0-440-18302-2). Dell Publishing Co., Inc.

Dream Children. Ed. by Elizabeth B Brownell. LC 1-26596. 1901. The Bowen-Merrill Co.

Dream Children. Gail Godwin. 256p. 1983. pap. 3.50 (ISBN 0-380-62406-0, Bard). Avon.

Dream Children: Stories. Gail Godwin. LC 75-26722. 1976. 7.95 (ISBN 0-394-47894-0). Knopf.

Dream Chintz. By the Author of "A Trap to Catch a Sunbeam," "Only"... Matilda Anne Planche Mackerness. LC 7-16441. 1851. J. Munroe and Company.

Dream Come True. Elaine R. Chase. (Candlelight Ecstasy Ser.: No. 43). (Orig.). 1982. pap. 1.75 (ISBN 0-440-11697-X). Dell.

Dream Come True. Winifred Mary Scott. LC 35-7670. 1935. Doubleday, Doran & Company, Inc.

Dream Come True. Betty Weels. (Harlequin Romance Ser.). 192p. 1983. pap. 1.75 (ISBN 0-373-02550-5). Harlequin Bks.

Dream Come True: The Life of Winifred La Prise. Winnie Allred Goad. LC 54-38445. 1954. New Voices Pub. Co.

Dream Comes True. Bethea Creese. Orig. Title: My Heart Is Fast. pap. 0.50 o.p. (52-928). Paperback Lib.

Dream Dancer. Janet Morris. LC 80-22584. 12.95 (ISBN 0-399-12591-4). Berkeley Pub. Corp.: Distributed by Putnam.

Dream Days. Kenneth Grahame. LC 4-16306. 1899. J. Lane.

Dream Days. Kenneth Grahame. 1902. John Lane.

Dream Days. Kenneth Grahame. 1931. Dodd, Mead & Co.

Dream Days. Kenneth Grahame. (Equinox edition). (Illus.). 1975. (pbk.) 4.95 (ISBN 0-380-00288-4). Avon.

Dream Days. Kenneth Grahame & Maxfield Parrish. LC 75-32201. (Classics of Children's Literature, 1621-1932). 1976. 27.00 (ISBN 0-8240-2311-0). Garland Publishing.

Dream-Detective. Sax Rohmer, pseud. LC 77-77454. 1977. pap. 3.50 (ISBN 0-486-23504-1). Dover.

Dream-Detective. Arthur Sarsfield Ward. LC 77-77454. 1977. 3.00 (ISBN 0-486-23504-1). Dover Publications.

Dream Detective: Being Some Account of the Methods of Moris Klaw. Arthur Sarsfield Ward. LC 25-9821. 1925. Doubleday, Page & Company.

Dream Doctor: The New Adventure of Craig Kennedy, Scientific Detective. Arthur Benjamin Reeve. LC 17-22302. Harper & Brothers.

Dream Doctor: The New Adventures of Craig Kennedy, Scientific Detective. Arthur Benjamin Reeve. LC 14-769130. 1914. Hearst's International Library Co.

Dream Ends in Fury: A Novel Based on the Life of Joaquin Murrieta. Samuel Anthony Peeples. 1949. Harper.

Dream for Tomorrow. Marilyn Austin. (YA) 1980. 6.95 (Avalon). Bouregy.

Dream from the Night. Barbara Cartland (ISBN 0-553-02972-X). Bantam.

Dream Gate. Marcus Bach. LC 49-10583. 1949. Bobbs-Merrill Co.

Dream Girl. Ethel Gertrude Hart. LC 12-25201. 1912. Doubleday, Page & Company.

Dream Girls. William Murray. LC 71-158597. 1972. 5.95 (ISBN 0-525-09570-5). Dutton.

Dream Hero. Elizabeth Oldfield. (Harlequin Presents Ser.). 192p. 1983. pap. 1.95 (ISBN 0-373-10604-1). Harlequin Bks.

Dream House. Victoria Gordon. (Harlequin Romances Ser.). 192p. 1982. pap. 1.50 (ISBN 0-373-02458-4). Harlequin Bks.

Dream House: By Warren Howard Pseud. James Noble Gifford. LC 53-702846. 1953. Arcadia House.

Dream House for Nurse Rhonda. Berta LaVan Barker. (YA) 1979. 6.95 (Avalon). Bouregy.

Dream in the Flesh. Dan Levin. LC 52-9842. 1953. Putnam.

Dream in the Stone. Dana Faralla. LC 48-10237. 1948. J. Messner.

Dream Is Deadly. Carter Brown, pseud. Bd. with Savage Salome. 1981. pap. 2.50 (ISBN 0-451-09776-9, E9776, Sig). NAL.

Dream Island. Roumelia Lane. (Harlequin Romances Ser.). 192p. 1982. pap. 1.50 (ISBN 0-373-02460-6). Harlequin Bks.

Dream Island. Florence Riddell. LC 33-18225. J. B. Lippincott Company.

Dream Journal. Howard Schwartz. pap. 3.00 o.p. Tree Bks.

Dream Journey. James Hanley. LC 76-17428. 1976. 8.95 (ISBN 0-8180-0623-4). Horizon Press.

Dream Journey. James Hanley. LC 77-351680. 1976. 3.95 (ISBN 0-233-96708-7). Deutsch.

Dream Killers. Donna Winston. 1976. 1.95. Ace Books.

Dream Kiss. Ann Sumner. LC 29-22203. A. L. Burt Company.

Dream-Land by Daylight: A Panorama of Romance. 2d ed. Caroline Chesebro' LC 6-24217. 1852. Redfield.

Dream. (Le Reve.) authorized ed. Emile Zola. LC 8-37877. (On cover: The illustrated series. no. 4). 1888. Rand, McNally & Company.

Dream Life. Donald Grant Mitchell. LC 43-445423. Donohue, Henneberry & Co.

Dream Life. Donald Grant Mitchell. LC 4601. W. B. Conkey Company.

Dream Life: A Fable of the Season. Donald Grant Mitchell. LC 13-180753. The Bobbs-Merrill Company.

Dream Life: A Fable of the Seasons. Donald Grant Mitchell. LC 9-3854. 1857. C. Scribner.

Dream Life: A Fable of the Seasons. Donald Grant Mitchell. LC 20-23141. 1869. C. Scribner and Company.

Dream Life: A Fable of the Seasons. new ed. Donald Grant Mitchell. LC 3-17121. 1874. Scribner, Armstrong & Co.

Dream Life: A Fable of the Seasons. a new ed. Donald Grant Mitchell. LC 8-21281. 1876. Scribner, Armstrong & Co.

Dream Life: A Fable of the Seasons. Donald Grant Mitchell. LC 42-273701. (On cover: The Home library). A. L. Burt Company.

Dream Life. A Fable of the Seasons. Donald Grant Mitchell. LC 3-17123. (On cover: Seaside library. Pocket ed. no. 2141). 1895. G. Munro's Sons.

Dream Life: A Fable of the Seasons. Donald Grant Mitchell. LC 4341. T. Y. Crowell & Co.

Dream Life and Real Life: A Little African Story. Olive Schreiner. LC 12-10051. 1893. Roberts Brothers.

Dream Life and Real Life: A Little African Story. Olive Schreiner. LC 77-21347. 1977. 5.50 (ISBN 0-915864-32-0) (ISBN 0-915864-31-2). Cassandra Editions.
Dream Life of Balso Snell. Nathanael West. LC 31-19679. Contact Editions.
Dream Life of Balso Snell & A Cool Million. Nathanael West. Bd. with Cool Million. 179p. 1963. pap. 5.95 (ISBN 0-374-50292-7, N244). FS&G.
Dream Lover. Mark Upton. LC 77-10107. 8.95 (ISBN 0-698-10855-8). Coward, McCann & Geoghegan.
Dream Machines. Compiled by Peter Haining. 1973. 7.50 o.p. (ISBN 0-690-00341-2). T Y Crowell.
Dream Maker. Helen Fitzgerald Sanders. LC 18-21377. The Cornhill Company.
Dream-Maker Man. Fannie Heaslip Lea. LC 25-19728. 1925. Dodd, Mead and Company.
Dream Man. Winifred Mary Scott. LC 29-13898. 1929. The Macaulay Company.
Dream Master. Roger Zelazny. LC 76-10718. (Gregg Press science fiction series). 1976. 8.50 (ISBN 0-8398-2345-2). Gregg Press.
Dream Merchant. Carter Brown, pseud. (Signet Book). 1976. 1.25. New American Library.
Dream Merchants. Harold Robbins. 1980. pap. 3.95 (ISBN 0-671-41710-X). PB.
Dream Merchants. Harold Rubins. LC 49-657736. 1949. A. A. Knopf.
Dream Millennium. James White. LC 74-6206. 1974. 1.25 (ISBN 0-345-24012-X). Ballantine Books.
Dream Museum. Seymour Epstein. LC 77-157588. 1971. 6.95. Doubleday.
Dream No More. Joseph Calvitt Clarke. LC 38-6344. Gramercy Pub. Co.
Dream No More. Joseph Calvitt Clarke. LC 33-6344. 1937. Gramercy Publishing Co.
Dream No More. Mamie A. Sutherland. 1967. 2.50 o.p. (ISBN 0-8059-0280-5). Dorrance.
Dream of a Throne: The Story of a Mexican Revolt. Charles Fleming Embree. LC 2972. 1900. Little, Brown, and Company.
Dream of a Woman: Translated from the French. Remy De Gourmont. Tr. by Galantiere, Lewis. LC 27-205861. 1927. Boni and Liveright.
Dream of Africa. Camara Laye. LC 70-156991. (American Library). 1971. 1.50. Collier Books.
Dream of Blue Roses. Edith Noel Daniell Barclay. LC 12-24923. (Illus.). 1912. Hodder and Stoughton.
Dream of Blue Roses. Edith Noel Daniell Barclay. LC 12-27195. 1.25. Hodder & Stoughton, George H. Doran Company.
Dream of Danger. Ann Nolder. (Orig.). 1981. pap. 1.75 (ISBN 0-8439-8030-3, Tiara Bks). Nordon Pubns.
Dream of Destiny. J. H Brennan. LC 79-8555. 1980. 10.00 (ISBN 0-385-14983-2). Doubleday.
Dream of Dragonflies. Noel Langley. LC 70-134510. 1971. Macmillan.
Dream of Empire: Or, The House of Blennerhassett. William Henry Venable. LC 1-31933. 1901. Dodd, Mead and Company.
Dream of Fair Serpents. Catherine Darby, pseud. 1979. 1.95 (ISBN 0-445-04436-5). Popular Library.
Dream of Fair Woman. Armstrong, Charlotte. LC 66-10427. Coward-McCann.
Dream of Fair Women. Henry Williamson. LC 24-23493. E. P. Dutton & Company.
Dream of Fair Women. Henry Williamson. LC 31-209196. E. P. Dutton & Co., Inc.
Dream of Falling. Mary O. Rank. pap. 0.60 o.p. (60-363). Manor Bks.
Dream of Freedom. Ellen Catt Philtine. LC 38-21326. 1938. D. Appleton-Century Company, Incorporated.
Dream of Innocence. Turnley Walker. LC 52-8415. 1952. McKay.
Dream of Kings. Davis Grubb. LC 55-9671. 1955. Scribner.
Dream of Kings. Harry Mark Petrakis. LC 66-23600. 1966. D. McKay Co.
Dream of Kinship. Richard Cowper, pseud. (Orig.). 1981. pap. 2.50 (ISBN 0-671-43304-0, Timescape). PB.
Dream of Love: A Realistic Novel. authorized ed. Emile Zola & Valcourt-Vermont, Edgar De, Tr. LC 9-1329. (On cover: The pastime series v. 39). 1890. Laird & Lee.
Dream of Mansions. Norris Lloyd. LC 61-12143. 1962. Random House.
Dream of Silence: A Novel. Bruce Jewell & Wanda Jewell. LC 72-108057. 1970. 4.95. Crown Publishers.
Dream of the Red Chamber. Tsao Hsueh-Chin. LC 58-13296. pap. 5.50 (ISBN 0-385-09379-9, Anch). Doubleday.
Dream of the Red Chamber. abridged ed. Chan Tsao. LC 58-13296. (Doubleday anchor books, A159). 1958. Doubleday.
Dream of the Red Chamber. Chan Ts'Ao & E. Fi Kao. LC 58-1761. 1958. Twayne Publishers.
Dream of the Red Chamber: Hung Lou Meng: a Chinese Novel of the Early Ching Period. Chan Tsao & Florence McHugh. LC 75-8833. (Illus.). 1975. 26.00 (ISBN 0-8371-8113-5). Greenwood Press.
Dream of the Red Chamber. Hung Lou Meng. Chan Tsao. Tr. by Florence McHugh. LC 58-6097. 1958. Pantheon Books.
Dream of the Traveler. Richard McCann. 1976. pap. 3.50 (ISBN 0-87886-070-3, Pub. by Ithaca Hse). SBD.
Dream of Thee. Mary Wibberley. (Harlequin Presents Ser.). 192p. 1981. pap. 1.50 (ISBN 0-373-10419-7, Pub. by Harlequin). PB.
Dream of Things That Were. Katherine A. Taras. (Orig.). 1979. pap. 1.95 (ISBN 0-532-19235-4). Woodhill.
Dream of Treason. Maurice Edelman. LC 55-6292. 1955. Lippincott.
Dream of Treason. Marshall Pugh. LC 73-78751. 1974. 6.95. Coward, McCann & Geoghegan.
Dream of Treason. Marshall Pugh. 1975. (pbk.) 1.25 (ISBN 0-523-00557-1). Pinnacle Books.
Dream of Unicorns. Marion Naismith. LC 72-387233. 1975. (pbk.) 0.95. Pocket Books.
Dream Palaces: Malcolm the Nephew & 63: Dream Palace. James Purdy. 1980. 19.95 (ISBN 0-670-28463-7). Viking Pr.
Dream Palaces: Three Novels. James Purdy. LC 79-23025. 14.95 (ISBN 0-670-28463-7). Viking Press.
Dream Park. Larry Niven & Steven Barnes. LC 81-157646. 1981. 35.00 (ISBN 0-932096-09-3). Phantasia Press.
Dream Peddlers. Norman Phillips. 1970. pap. 0.95 o.p. (B95-1092). Belmont-Tower.
Dream Peddlers. Norman Phillips. (O.s.i.). 1975. pap. 1.25 o.s.i. Tower.
Dream Pirate see TaleSpinners I.
Dream Prevails: A Story of India... Katherine Helen Maud Marshall Diver. LC 38-9976. 1938. Houghton Mifflin Company.
Dream Quest of Unknown Kadath. Introd. by George T. Wetzel. 1st Ed. Howard Phillips Lovecraft. LC 56-276114. 1955. Shroud.
Dream Seeker. William Arthur Neubauer. LC 63-22948. Arcadia House.
Dream Seeker. Joseph S. Salzburg. 162p. 1972. 5.00 o.p. (ISBN 0-682-47559-9). Exposition.
Dream Seekers. Stephen Longstreet. 448p. 1981. pap. 2.50 (ISBN 0-523-40501-4). Pinnacle Bks.
Dream Sleepers & Other Stories. Patricia Grace. (Pacific Paperperbacks Ser.). 106p. (Orig.). (gr. 10-12). 1980. pap. 6.00x (ISBN 0-582-70620-3). Three Continents.
Dream Song of Olaf Asteson: An Ancient Norwegian Folk-Song of the 13 Holy Nights. Eleanor C. Merry. 1977. pap. 1.95 (ISBN 0-916786-22-6). St George Bk Serv.
Dream Squad. Kenneth W. Hassler. Ed. by Alice Sachs. 1970. 3.95 o.p. Lenox Hill.
Dream Street. Robert Sylvester. LC 46-7784. 1946. The Dial Press.
Dream Tales and Prose Poems. Ivan Sergeevich Turgenev. LC 76-10267. (His Novels, v. 10). 1970. AMS Press.
Dream Tales, and Prose Poems. illustrated ed. translated from the russian by constance garnett. ed. Ivan Sergeevich Turgenev. LC 79-103530. (Short story index reprint series). (Illus.). 1969. Books for Libraries Press.
Dream Team. Joe McGinniss. 1973. (pbk.) 1.25. Dell.
Dream Team. Joe McGinniss. LC 73-38589. 1972. 5.95 (ISBN 0-394-47992-0). Random House.
Dream to the Moon: A Metaphysical Fantasy in Two Parts. Harry Perlowitz. LC 79-66165. 92p. 1980. 5.95 (ISBN 0-533-04365-4). Vantage.
Dream Walker. Charlotte Armstrong. LC 54-10138. Coward-McCann.
Dream Walker. Charlotte Armstrong. LC 63-50136. (Ace giant double novel book, G-526). 1963. Ace Books.
Dream Walker. Charlotte Armstrong. LC 74-166712. 1973. 1.80 (ISBN 0-85617-262-6). White Lion Publishers.
Dream Weaver. Martin Brooks. LC 77-94413. 1978. 10.95 (ISBN 0-89662-001-8). Summers Books.
Dream Weaver. Millie J Ragosta. LC 82-45266. 1983. 11.95 (ISBN 0-385-18077-2). Doubleday.
Dream Weaver. Millie J. Ragosta. LC 82-45266. (Starlight Romance Ser.). 192p. 1983. 11.95 (ISBN 0-385-18077-2). Doubleday.
Dream Weavers: Short Stories by the Pre-Raphaelite Poet-Painters. Ed. by John Weeks. LC 79-26749. (Orig.). 1980. pap. 4.95 (ISBN 0-912800-73-9, Banquo Bks). Woodbridge Pr.
Dream with No Stump Roots in It: Stories. David Huddle. LC 74-22229. (Breakthrough book). 1975. 6.00 (ISBN 0-8262-0174-1). University of Missouri Press.
Dream Within. Barbara Cartland. 1974. pap. 1.25 o.p. (ISBN 0-515-03271-9, V3271). Pyramid Pubns.
Dream Within. Barbara Cartland. 1976. pap. 1.25 o.p. (ISBN 0-515-04118-1). BJ Pub Group.
Dream Without End. Grace Jamison Breckling. LC 50-6820. 1950. Westminster Press.
Dream Without Ending. Katherine Ursula Parrott. LC 35-16312. 1935. Longmans, Green and Co.
Dream Years. Virginia Akin. LC 64-14289. 1964. Chilton Books.
Dreamboat. Arthur Watterson Hoppe. LC 64-19232. 1964. Doubleday.
Dreamboat. Rick Lucas. LC 55-258563. 1955. Vixen Press.
Dreambook for Our Time: Translated by David Welsh; Introd. by Leszek Kolakowski. Tadeusz Konwicki. (Writers from the other europe). 1976. 2.95 (ISBN 0-14-004115-X). Penguin Books.
Dreamer. Emma Downing Coolidge. LC 15-18912. 0.50. The Pilgrim Press.
Dreamer. Julien Green. Tr. by Holland, Vyvyan Beresfrod. LC 34-10333. 1934. Harper & Brothers.
Dreamer: A Tale of the Sioux. Bill Martino. LC 74-84199. 1975. 4.95 (ISBN 0-8283-1593-0). Branden Press.
Dreamer & Other Stories. Krishan Chander. Tr. by Jai Ratan. 160p. 1970. pap. 2.50 (ISBN 0-88253-025-9, 4027). Ind-US Inc.
Dreamer and the Worker. Douglas William Jerrold. LC 7-9926. 1847. Burgess, Stringer and Company.
Dreamer Beware. Ruth Wissmann. 1978. 1.50 (ISBN 0-445-04167-6). Popular Library.
Dreamer Beware. Ruth H Wissmann. LC 76-18375. 1977. 5.95 (ISBN 0-385-12345-0). Doubleday.
Dreamer of Dreams. Queen Consort Of Charles I King Of Rumania Elisabeth & Dulac, Edmund, Illus. LC 16-8076. 1915. Hodder & Stoughton.
Dreamer of Dreams. Holbrook Jackson. 283p. 1980. Repr. of 1948 ed. lib. bdg. 30.00 (ISBN 0-8482-1397-1). Norwood Edns.
Dreamer of Dreams: A Modern Romance. Joseph Shield Nicholson. LC 41-313335. (On cover: Appletons' town and country library). 1889. D. Appleton and Company.
Dreamer of the Vine: A Novel About Nostradamus. Liz Greene. 1981. 12.95 (ISBN 0-393-01434-7). Norton.
Dreamer Under Arms. Francis Gordon Hurrell. LC 18-185262. E. P. Dutton and Company.
Dreamers. Vera Caspary. 1975. (pbk.) 1.50 (ISBN 0-671-78867-1). Pocket Books.
Dreamers. John Bigelow Clark. LC 45-8185. 1945. Doubleday, Doran & Co., Inc.
Dreamers. Dorothy Fletcher. 1973. (pbk.) 1.25. Lancer Books.
Dreamers. Ellen Bromfield Geld. LC 73-79669. 1973. 6.95 (ISBN 0-385-06473-X). Doubleday.
Dreamers. James E. Gunn. LC 80-19146. 10.95 (ISBN 0-671-25280-1). Simon and Schuster.
Dreamers. Knut Hamsun & Worster, William W., Tr. LC 21-201893. 1921. A. A. Knopf.
Dreamers, a Club. facsimile ed. John Kendrick Bangs. LC 72-98559. (Short Story Index Reprint Ser.). 1899. 16.00 (ISBN 0-8369-3133-5). Ayer Co.
Dreamers; a Club: Being a More or Less Faithful Account of the Literary Exercises of the First Regular Meeting of That Organization. John Kendrick Bangs. LC 72-98559. (Short story index reprint series). (Illus.). 1969. Books for Libraries Press.
Dreamers: a Club: Being a More or Less Faithful Account of the Literary Exercises of the First Regular Meeting of That Orginization, Reported. John Kendrick Bangs. LC 90-249250. 1899. Harper & Brothers.
Dreamers, a Novel. Roger Manvell. 1958. Simon and Schuster.
Dreamer's Clay. George Abbe. LC 40-800951. H. Holt and Company.
Dreamers in a Haunted House. Marc Lovell, pseud. LC 75-14990. 1975. 5.95 (ISBN 0-385-11100-2). Published for the Crime Club by Doubleday.
Dreamers of Dreams: An Anthology of Fantasy. Douglas Alver Menville & R Reginald. LC 77-84280. (Lost Race and Adult Fantasy Fiction). (Illus.). 1978. 35.00 (ISBN 0-405-11017-0). Arno Press.
Dreamers of the Ghetto. Israel Zangwill. LC 77-125240. (Short story index reprint series). 1970. (ISBN 0-8369-3607-8). Books for Libraries Press.
Dreamers of the Ghetto: By I. Zangwill... Israel Zangwill. LC 4-15346. 1898. Harper & Brothers.
Dreamer's Tales. Edward John Moreton Drax Plunkett Dunsany. LC 70-101803. (Short story index reprint series). (Illus.). 1969. (ISBN 0-8369-3191-2). Books for Libraries Press.
Dreamer's Tales. Edward John Moreton Drax Plunkett Dunsany. LC 17-4466. J. W. Luce & Company.
Dreamer's Tales. Edward John Moreton Drax Plunkett Dunsany. LC 79-84655. (Illus.). 1979. 12.75 (ISBN 0-913896-13-6). Owlswick Press.
Dreamer's Tales: And Other Stories. Edward John Moreton Drax Plunkett Dunsany. LC 21-2379. (Half-title: The modern library of the world's best books). Boni and Liveright, Inc.
Dreamer's Tales & Other Stories. Lord Dunsany. 1978. Repr. lib. bdg. 25.00 (ISBN 0-8482-0621-5). Norwood Edns.
Dreaming Dragons. Damien Broderick. 1980. 2.25 (ISBN 0-671-83150-X). Pocket Books.
Dreaming Earth. John Brunner. 1970. pap. 0.75 o.p. (T2325). Pyramid Pubns.
Dreaming Earth. John Brunner. 1974. pap. 0.95 o.p. (ISBN 0-515-03457-6, N3457). Pyramid Pubns.
Dreaming in the Dawn. Ed. by Ruth W. Schuler. 50p. (Orig.). 1980. pap. 3.00 (ISBN 0-910083-07-X). Heritage Trails.
Dreaming Jewels. Theodore Sturgeon. LC 78-10733. (Gregg Press Science Fiction Series). 1978. 11.00 (ISBN 0-8398-2467-X). Gregg Press.
Dreaming Jewels. Edward Hamilton Waldo, pseud. LC 50-9541. (Corwin book). 1950. Greenberg.
Dreaming Jewels. Edward Hamilton Waldo, pseud. (Dell book). 1978. 1.75 (ISBN 0-440-11803-4). Dell Pub. Co.
Dreaming of Babylon. Richard Brautigan. 1978. pap. 6.95 (ISBN 0-440-52059-2, Delta). Dell.
Dreaming of Babylon: A Private Eye Novel, 1942. Richard Brautigan. LC 77-7476. 7.95 (ISBN 0-440-02146-4). Delacorte Press/S. Lawrence.
Dreaming of Babylon: A Private Eye Novel, 1942. Richard Brautigan. (Delta book). 1978. 3.95 (ISBN 0-440-52059-2). Dell Pub. Co.
Dreaming River. Barr Moses. LC 9-3051. 1909. F. A. Stokes Company.
Dreaming Spires: A Novel. by diana patrick pseud.... ed. Desemea Wilson. LC 25-6198. E. P. Dutton & Company.
Dreaming Suburb. Ronald Frederick Delderfield. LC 69-14281. 1976. (pbk.) 1.95 (ISBN 0-671-80278-X). Pocket Books.
Dreaming Swimmer. Elisabeth Ogilvie. LC 76-5511. 8.95 (ISBN 0-07-047598-9). McGraw-Hill.
Dreaming Tree: A Novel. Allan W Eckert. LC 68-24242. 1968. Little, Brown.
Dreaming True. Cecily Bowman. 1945. Arcadia House.
Dreaming True. Alma Newton. LC 21-15334. 1921. John Lane Company.
Dreamland. George V. Higgins. LC 77-4499. 8.95 (ISBN 0-316-88745-5). Little, Brown.
Dreamland. Clarence Budington Kelland. LC 35-105903. 1935. Harper & Brothers.
Dreamland. Newton Thornburg. 1983. 14.95 (ISBN 0-87795-444-5). Arbor Hse.
Dreamlovers. Pete Fisher. LC 81-97. 224p. (Orig.). 1982. pap. 8.95x (ISBN 0-933322-07-0). Sea Horse.
Dreamrider. Sandra Miesel. 304p. (Orig.). 1982. pap. 2.75 (ISBN 0-441-15679-7). Ace Bks.
Dreamrise. 2nd ed. Ondra The Sixth. 1977. pap. 2.95 (ISBN 0-930472-00-4). G Stempien.
Dreams. author's ed. Olive Schreiner. LC 46-40166. 1915. Little, Brown, and Company.
Dreams and Delights. Lily Moresby Adams Beck. LC 26-17630. 1926. Dodd, Mead and Company.
Dreams and Dream Stories. Anna Bonus Kingsford. (On cover: Lovell's occult series. no. 2). F. F. Lovell & Company.
Dreams and Memories. George McLean Harper. LC 22-12041. 1922. Princeton University Press; Etc., Etc.
Dreams and Realities in the Life of a Pastor and Teacher. Samuel Hayes Elliot. LC 6-37260. 1856. J.C. Derby.
Dreams and Scars. Neene Mills. LC 51-14178. 1951. Exposition Press.
Dreams and Tales. 1st Ed. Brigitta Valentine. LC 58-12660. Greenwich Book Publishers.
Dreams Are for Tomorrow. Agnes Mary White Sandford. 1963. 3.95 o.p. (ISBN 0-397-00278-5). Lippincott.
Dreams Come True. Solomon Philip Elias. 1923. L. M. Morris Company.
Dreams Come True. Gerhard Lewis Wind. LC 38-19599. Zondervan Publishing House.
Dreams Die First. Harold Robbins. 1981. pap. 3.95. PB.
Dreams Die First: A Novel. Harold Robbins. LC 77-23846. 9.95 (ISBN 0-671-22590-1). Simon and Schuster.
Dreams Do Come True, No. 141. Barbara Cartland. (Orig.). 1981. pap. 1.95 (ISBN 0-553-14750-1). Bantam.
Dream's Edge: Science Fiction Stories About the Future of Planet Earth. Ed. by Terry Carr. LC 80-13389. 12.95 (ISBN 0-87156-232-4) (ISBN 0-87156-238-3). Sierra Club Books.
Dream's End. Joseph McCord. LC 34-32211. The Penn Publishing Company.
Dream's End. Thorne Smith. LC 27-8781. 1927. R. M. McBride & Company.

Dreams from Bunker Hill. John Fante. LC 81-15533. 1981. 14.00 (ISBN 0-87685-529-X) (ISBN 0-87685-528-1) (ISBN 0-87685-530-3). Black Sparrow Press.

Dreams from R'lyeh. Lin Carter. LC 74-78131. 1975. 5.00 (ISBN 0-87054-067-X). Arkham.

Dreams: Gateway to the Unconscious. Hans Holzer. (Orig.). 1979. pap. 2.25 (ISBN 0-532-23219-4). Woodhill.

Dreams Get You Nowhere. Maysie Greig. LC 37-3290. 1937. Doubleday, Doran and Co., Inc.

Dreams Get You Nowhere. Maysie Greig. LC 38-7214. The Sun Dial Press, Inc.

Dreams of a Young Girl. David Hamilton & Alain Robbe-Grillet. 1971. 22.50 (ISBN 0-688-01482-8). Morrow.

Dreams of Billy Joe. John E. Sutphin, Sr. 3.50 o.p. Carlton.

Dreams of Chang: And Other Stories. Ivan Alekseevich Bunin & Guerney, Bernard Guilbert, Tr. LC 23-13889. 1923. A.A. Knopf.

Dreams of Day. James Noble Gifford. LC 47-115316. 1947. Gramercy Pub. Co.

Dreams of Glory. Thomas J. Fleming. 496p. 1983. pap. 3.95 (ISBN 0-446-80655-2). Warner Bks.

Dreams of Life. Timothy T. Fortune. LC 72-168125. Repr. of 1905 ed. 9.00 (ISBN 0-404-00051-7). AMS Pr.

Dreams of Norn: Four Fiction Stories. Illus. by the Author. Paul Anton Broste. LC 58-225901. 1958.

Dreams of Reason. Xavier Domingo. Tr. by L. Kemp. LC 65-10198. (O.s.i.). 1966. 5.00 o.s.i. (ISBN 0-8076-0344-9). Braziller.

Dreams of Reason: A Novel. Tr. from Spanish by Lysander Kemp. Xavier Domingo. LC 65-101986. bds., 5.00. Braziller.

Dreams of the Dead. Edward Stanton Huntington. LC 7-9378. (On cover: Good company series, no. 15). 1892. Lee and Shepard.

Dreams of Yesterday. Henry Elliot Harman. LC 12-9929. 1.00. The State Company.

Dreams of Youth. Philip Freund. 1938. Pilgrim House.

Dream's on Me: A Love Story. Dotson Rader. (Signet Book). 1977. 1.75 (ISBN 0-451-07536-6). New American Library.

Dreams That Burn in the Night. Craig Strete. LC 81-43660. 192p. 1982. 10.95 (ISBN 0-385-17188-9). Doubleday.

Dreams to Come. Melanie Ward. LC 77-91253. (Jove/HBJ Book). 1978. 2.25 (ISBN 0-515-04474-1). Jove Publications.

Dreams to Give. Therese Martini, pseud. 2.25 (ISBN 0-445-04347-4). Popular Library.

Dreams to Mend. Joseph McCord. LC 40-85502. 1940. Macrae, Smith Company.

Dreams Within Dreams: A Plagiarism of the Seventeenth Century; Being Like Most Visions of the Night, a Medley of Old Things and New. Edmund D Griffin. LC 6-45420. 1864. P. O'Shea.

Dreamsnake. Vonda N McIntyre. LC 77-18891. 1978. 8.95 (ISBN 0-395-26470-7). Houghton Mifflin.

Dreamstone. C. J. Cherryh. 1983. pap. 2.75 (ISBN 0-87997-808-2). DAW Bks.

Dreamthorp, a Book of Essays Written in the Country. Alexander Smith. LC 45-25822. 1913. T. B. Mosher.

Dreamtigers. Jorge Luis Borges. 1970. pap. 2.45 o.p. (ISBN 0-525-47269-X). Dutton.

Dreamtime. Robert Louis Nathan. LC 74-21584. 1975. 8.95 (ISBN 0-87951-028-5). Overlook Press.

Dreamwalker. Janine Fitzpatrick. 1975. (pbk.) 0.95 (ISBN 0-671-77991-5). Pocket Books.

Dreamy Hollow. Sumner Charles Britton. LC 21-15335. World Syndicate Company, Inc.

Dreamy Rivers. Henry Philip Bernard Baerlein. LC 31-26524. 1930. Simon and Schuster.

Drearloch. Dorinda Kamm. (Orig.). 1978. pap. 1.95 (ISBN 0-89083-379-6). Zebra.

Dred: A Tale of the Great Dismal Swamp. Harriet Elizabeth Beecher Stowe. LC 72-127450. 1970. (ISBN 0-404-06290-3). AMS Press.

Dred, a Tale of the Great Dismal Swamp, 2 Vols. Harriet Elizabeth Beecher Stowe. LC 72-127450. Repr. of 1856 ed. 27.50 (ISBN 0-404-06290-3). AMS Pr.

Dred, a Tale of the Great Dismal Swamp, 2 Vols. Harriet Elizabeth Beecher Stowe. LC 8-16126. 1969. Repr. of 1856 ed. Set. 35.00 (ISBN 0-403-00052-1). Scholarly.

Dred: Tale of the Great Dismal Swamp. Harriet Elizabeth Beecher Stowe. LC 70-5460. 1968. 24.00. Scholarly Press.

Drei Erzahlungen: Edited by Waldo C. Peebles. Hermann Hesse. LC 51-37. 1950. American Book Co.

Drei Manner Im Schnee. Erich Kastner. Ed. by Bell, Clair Hayden. 1937. F. S. Crofts & Co.

Drei Manner Im Schnee: Ed. by Clair Hayden Bell. Erich Kastner. Ed. by Clair Hayden Bell. 1961. pap., 1.95. Appleton-Century-Crofts.

Drei Marchenspiele. Emma Meyer Rendtorff. LC 18-105. (Heath's modern language series). D. C. Heath & Co.

Dremer's Search for Happiness. Leon R Searles. LC 56-25011. 1956. Meador Pub. Co.

Drender's Daughter. Netta Syrett. LC 11-17101. 1911. 1.25. John Lane Company.

Dresden Finch: A Novel. Jessica Stirling. LC 75-35805. 6.95. Delacorte Press.

Dresden Green. Nicolas Freeling. (71107). 1968. Ballantine.

Dresden Green. Nicolas Freeling. LC 67-22518. 1967. Harper & Row.

Dress Gray. Lucian K. Truscott. LC 78-1250. 1979. 10.95 (ISBN 0-385-13475-4). Doubleday.

Dress Her in Indigo. John Dann MacDonald. LC 75-20451. (Travis McGee series). 1971. 5.50. Lippincott.

Dress Her in Indigo. John Dann MacDonald. LC 79-6840. (Fawcett gold medal book). 1969. 0.75. Fawcett Publications.

Dress Rehearsal: A Novel. Monica Stirling. LC 52-10116. 1952. Simon and Schuster.

Dress to Die in. Marion Cooper. LC 79-66264. 142p. 1980. 7.95 (ISBN 0-533-04368-9). Vantage.

Dressed All in Pink. Dudley Randall. (Broadside Ser., No. 2). broadsheet. 0.50 o.p. Broadside.

Dressed in Black. Victor Hull. LC 73-90095. 1974. 6.95 (ISBN 0-8059-1963-5). Dorrance.

Dressed to Kill. Brian DePalma & Campbell Black. 192p. 1980. pap. 2.25 (ISBN 0-553-12977-5). Bantam.

Dressed to Kill. Emma Lou Fetta. LC 41-77982. 1941. Pub. for the Crime Club by Doubleday, Doran and Company, Inc.

Dresser. Ronald Harwood. LC 81-47637. 128p. (Orig.). 1982. pap. 5.95 (ISBN 0-394-17936-6, E769, Ever). Grove.

Dressing of Diamond. Nicolas Freeling. LC 73-18710. 1974. 5.95 (ISBN 0-06-011352-9). Harper & Row.

Dressing of Diamond. Nicolas Freeling. (Penguin crime fiction)). 1976. 1.95 (ISBN 0-14-004131-1). Penguin.

Dressing Room Murder. Joseph Smith Fletcher. LC 31-1717. 1931. A. A. Knopf.

Drewitt's Dream: A Story. William Livingston Alden. LC 2-100175. (Half-title: Appleton's town and country library, no. 310). 1902. D. Appleton and Company.

D'ri and I: A Tale of Daring Deeds in the Second War with the British. Being the Memoirs of Colonel Ramon Bell, U. S. A. Irving Bacheller. LC 1-17686. Lothrop Publishing Company.

D'ri and I: A Tale of Daring Deeds in the Second War with the British. Being the Memoirs of Colonel Ramon Bell, U. S. A. Irving Bacheller. Grosset & Dunlap.

Drieu la Rochelle: Decadence in Love. Robert B. Leal. 208p. 1973. 20.00x (ISBN 0-7022-0800-0). U of Queensland Pr.

Drift. Mary Reynolds Aldis. LC 18-8490. 1918. Duffield & Company.

Drift. Lloyd Kropp. LC 68-17792. 1969. 4.95. Doubleday.

Drift. Marguerite Mooers Marshall. LC 11-23060. 1911. 1.10. D. Appleton and Company.

Drift: A Story of Old Ukraine. Gustav Gotlieb Wenzlaff. LC 34-33125. The Grindal Publishers.

Drift Fence. Walt Coburn. Orig. Title: Rope Law. 1978. pap. 1.25 o.s.i. (ISBN 0-505-51236-X). Tower Bks.

Drift Fence. Walt Coburn. 1970. pap. 0.60 o.p. (60-458). Manor Bks.

Drift Fence. Zane Grey. LC 33-973. 1932. Harper & Brothers.

Drift from Two Shores. Bret Harte. LC 73-113669. (Short story index reprint series). 1970. Books for Libraries Press.

Drift from Two Shores. Bret Harte. LC 7-3641. 1878. Houghton, Osgood and Company.

Drift from Two Shores. Bret Harte. LC 6-18351. Houghton, Mifflin and Company.

Drift of Pinions. Robert Keable. LC 20-15963. 1919. E. P. Dutton & Co.

Drift Wood; The Bull. N. P. Muhammad. LC 76-902191. 1976. 6.50. Orient Longman.

Drift. 1st Ed. Rose Sutton. LC 55-7184. 1955. Vantage Press.

Drifted Ashore: Or, A Child Without a Name. Evelyn Everett Green. LC 6-45546. Bradley & Woodruff.

Drifted Asunder: Or, The Tide of Fate. Amanda Minnie Douglas. LC 6-33489. 1876. W. F. Gill & Co.

Drifted Together: A Novel... Maria Elizabeth Jourdan Westmoreland. 1880. G. W. Carleton & Co.; Etc., Etc.

Drifter. Burt Arthur, pseud. (Illus.). 192p. 1975. pap. 1.25 (ISBN 0-532-12359-X). Woodhill.

Drifter. Thomas Albert Curry. (YA) 1973. 4.95 o.p. (Avalon). Bouregy.

Drifter. Daniel Pratt Mannix. LC 74-1172. 1974. 6.95. Readers Digest Press; Distributed by Dutton.

Drifter. Daniel Pratt Mannix. (Fawcett crest book). 1975. (pbk.) 1.25. Fawcett.

Drifter: By Burt Arthur. Herbert Arthur, pseud. LC 55-270820. (Ace double novel books, D-92). 1955. Ace Books.

Drifters. James A. Michener. 1978. pap. 3.50 (ISBN 0-449-23862-8, Crest). Fawcett.

Drifters. James A. Michener. (Ltd. ed. 20.00 o.p.). 1971. 16.95 (ISBN 0-394-46200-9). Random.

Drifters. B. Miller. (O.s.i.). 1972. pap. 1.95 o.s.i. (ISBN 0-02-061320-2, Collier). Macmillan.

Drifters: A Novel. James Albert Michener. LC 75-117655. (Illus.). 1971. 10.00 (ISBN 0-394-46200-9). Random House.

Drifter's Gold. William E Vance. LC 78-3260. 1979. 7.95 (ISBN 0-385-14240-4). Doubleday.

Drifter's Luck. Alex Hawk, pseud. 1970. pap. 0.60 o.p. (63-291). Paperback Lib.

Drifter's Vengeance. Max Brand. LC 72-1540. 190p. 1972. 4.95 o.p. (ISBN 0-396-06626-7). Dodd.

Drifter's Vengeance. Max Brand. 1973. lib. bdg. 9.95 o.p. (ISBN 0-8161-6068-6, Large Print Bks). G K Hall.

Drifter's Vengeance. Frederick Faust. LC 72-12513. 1973. 9.95 (ISBN 0-8161-6068-6). G. K. Hall.

Drifter's Vengeance. Frederick Faust. LC 72-1540. 1975. (pbk.) 0.95 (ISBN 0-446-75363-7). Warner Paperback Library.

Driftglass. Samuel R Delany. LC 71-27226. 1971. N. Doubleday.

Driftglass. Samuel R Delany. LC 77-13809. (Gregg Press science fiction series). 1977. 13.00 (ISBN 0-8398-2395-9). Gregg Press.

Drifthaven. Clarissa Ross. (Avon gothic). 1974. (pbk.) 0.95 (ISBN 0-380-00016-4). Avon.

Drifting: A Story. Thomas Hayden Hawkins. LC 7-2188. 1892. Printed by the Chain & Hardy Co.

Drifting: A Tale True to Life. W W Breese. 1879. South Western Publishing House.

Drifting Along: With Tales of Past and Present Happenings. Benjamin Nason Hamlin. LC 39-23560. 1939. Priv. Print. at the Plimpton Press.

Drifting and Resisting. Atwood Bond Meservey. 1897. R. A. Carver.

Drifting Cities. Strates Tsirkas. LC 73-19937. 1974. 10.00 (ISBN 0-394-46971-2). Knopf; Distributed by Random House.

Drifting Diamond. Lincoln Colcord. LC 12-23931. 1912. The Macmillan Company.

Drifting Kid. Harry Sinclair Drago. LC 47-4640. 1947. Doubleday.

Drifting Man. Giles A. Lutz. 1976. pap. 1.25 (ISBN 0-532-12416-2). Woodhill.

Drifting of the Cavashaws. Robert Norman Griswood. LC 13-247922. 1.25. R. F. Fenno & Company.

Drifting on Sunny Seas. Detached Fragments Selected at Random from an Old Sailor's Journal... Thomas Robinson Warren. LC 8-33482. 1893. G. W. Dillingham.

Drifting Waters. Rachel Swete Macnamara. LC 15-27926. 1915. G. P. Putnam's Sons.

Drifting Where the Dark Begins. Toivo Puustinen. 5.00 o.p. Carlton.

Drifting (with Browne) Albert Byers Fletcher. LC 18-26325. 1918. Dodd, Mead and Company.

Driftings from Mid-Ocean. Character Studies. A Sequel to Summer Drift-Wood and The Winter Fire. Rose Porter. LC 15-62961. A. D. F. Randolph & Company.

Driftwood. Ida Adaline Powell. LC 13-13961. Printed by R. R. Donnelley and Sons Company.

Driftwood. Wilson Rockwell. LC 40-35998. 1940. The World Press, Inc.

Driftwood. Dudley Hilton Taylor. LC 40-11756. 1940. Pegasus Publishing Company.

Driftwood and Other Stories. J. H. Sutherland. LC 77-362154. (Illus.). 1976. Sutherland.

Driftwood Beach. Samantha Harvey. (Harlequin Romances Ser.). 192p. 1982. pap. 1.50 (ISBN 0-373-02481-9). Harlequin Bks.

Driftwood Spars: The Stories of a Man, a Boy, a Woman, and Certain Other People Who Strangely Met Upon the Sea of Life. Percival Christopher Wren. LC 17-54047. 1916. Longmans, Green and Co.

Driftwood Spars: The Stories of a Man, a Boy, a Woman, and Certain Other People Who Strangely Met Upon the Sea of Life. Percival Christopher Wren. LC 28-3981. 1927. Frederick A. Stokes Company.

Drill a Crooked Hole. Garland Roark. LC 68-14181. 1968. 5.95. Doubleday.

Drill Is Death: By Frances and Richard Lockridge. 1st Ed. Frances Louise Davis Lockridge & Richard Lockridge. LC 61-122423. (Main line mysteries). 1961. Lippincott.

Drilling for Death. John Wolfe. (Raven House Mysteries Ser.). 224p. 1981. pap. 2.25 (ISBN 0-373-63007-7, Pub. by Worldwide). Harlequin Bks.

Drink: A Love Story on a Great Question. Hall Caine. LC 7-13438. 1907. D. Appleton and Company.

Drink for Mr. Cherry. Dorothy Gardiner. LC 34-8979. 1934. Pub. for the Crime Club, Inc., by Doubleday, Doran & Company, Inc.

Drink for the Bridge: A Novel of the Tay Bridge Disaster. Alanna Knight. LC 76-363642. 1976. 3.95 (ISBN 0-333-18515-3). Macmillan.

Drink: Or, Unto the Third and Fourth Generation; a Narrative Ed. from the Papers of the Late Mr. Justice Harcourt. Hall Caine. LC 6-199013. 1895. D. Appleton and Company.

Drink the Green Water; or Young Caldwell's Toe. Hugh Austin Evans. LC 48-5175. (His A Sultan's harem mystery). 1948. C. Scribner's Sons.

Drink This. Eileen Dewhurst. LC 80-2320. 1981. 9.95 (ISBN 0-385-17457-8). Published for the Crime Club by Doubleday.

Drink to Me Only... Ethel Powelson Hueston. LC 43-18238. 1943. The Bobbs-Merrill Company.

Drink to the Hunted. Ellen Marsh. LC 45-3505. 1945. E. P. Dutton & Company, Inc.

Drink to Yesterday. Manning Coles, pseud. LC 67-18686. (Seagull library of mystery and suspense). 1967. Norton.

Drink to Yesterday. Manning Coles, pseud. LC 48-15979. (Bantam books, 76). 1947. Bantam Books.

Drink to Yesterday. Manning Coles, pseud. LC 41-2202. 1941. A. A. Knopf.

Drinkers of Darkness. Gerald Hanley. LC 55-3470. 1955. Macmillan.

Drinking Sapphire Water. Tanith Lee. (Science Fiction Ser.). 1977. pap. 1.75 o.p. (ISBN 0-87997-565-2, VE1565). DAW Bks.

Drinking Sapphire Water. Tanith Lee (ISBN 0-87997-277-7). Daw.

Drinking Well. Neil Miller Gunn. LC 47-30332. 1947. G. W. Stewart.

Drinks on the Victim. Mary Violet Heberden. LC 47-125104. 1948. Pub. for the Crime Club by Doubleday.

Drip-Dried Tourist. Willard Temple. LC 69-18197. 1969. 5.95. Putnam.

Driscoll's Diamonds. Ian MacAlister. (Fawcett Gold Medal Book). 1973. (pbk) 0.95. Fawcett.

Drive-a-Way Man. Tom Huth. LC 81-166106. 6.95 (ISBN 0-440-52149-1). Dell Pub. Co.

Drive for the Green. Anthony Tuttle. LC 77-79412. 1969. 5.95. Doubleday.

Drive, He Said. Jeremy Larner. LC 64-25945. 1964. Distributed by the Dial Press.

Drive Slowly-Six Dogs. Ilse Bischoff. LC 53-8819. (Illus.). 1953. Viking Press.

Driven. Donald Stuart. LC 62-14159. 1962. St Martin's Press.

Driven: A Novel. Richard Gehman. LC 54-1011. 1954. D. McKay Co.

Driven Afar. Betty Swinford. (Diamond Ser). Orig. Title: Driven Afar & Shadow Across the Sun. (YA) 1969. pap. 1.35 o.p. (38-23). Moody.

Driven Afar & Shadow Across the Sun see Driven Afar.

Driven Flesh. Lawrence Easton. LC 55-44659. (Ace books, S-119). 1955. Ace Books.

Driven from Sea to Sea: Or, Just a Campin.' Charles Cyrel Post. LC 7-30320. 1884. J. E. Downey & Co.

Driven from the Path. A Novel. Charles Smart. LC 8-90079. 1873. D. Appleton and Company.

Driven Out by Flame. Eldora Rodenbeek Hallett. LC 22-21571. 1922. Dorrance.

Driven to Bay. A Novel. Florence Marryat Church Lean. (On cover: Seaside library. Pocket ed. no. 1022). 1887. G. Munro.

Driven to the Wall: Or, A Forced Confession. Frederick William Davis. LC 6520. (On cover: Magnet detective library, no. 154). 1900. Street & Smith.

Driver. Garet Garrett. LC 22-20878. E. P. Dutton & Company.

Driver. Pat Winter. 320p. (Orig.). 1982. pap. 2.95 (ISBN 0-523-41278-9). Pinnacle Bks.

Driver Dallas. Henrietta Eliza Vaughan Stannard. (On cover: Seaside library. Pocket ed. no. 1039). 1887. G. Munro.

Driver Dallas: A Novel. Henrietta Eliza Vaughan Stannard. LC 8-13866. (Harper's handy series, no. 157). 1887. Harper & Brothers.

Driver, Give a Soldier a Lift. Susan Berman. LC 76-7597. 7.95. Putnam.

Driver Give a Soldier a Lift. Susan Berman. (Berkley Medallion Book). 1977. 1.50 (ISBN 0-425-03500-X). Berkley Pub. Corp.

Driver's Seat. Muriel Spark. 1975. (pbk.) 1.25. Bantam Books.

Driver's Seat. Muriel Spark. LC 79-111242. 1970. 4.95. Knopf.

Drives and Puts: A Book of Golf Stories. Walter Chauncey Camp & Brooks, Lilian, Joint Author. LC 99-4048. 1899. L. C. Page.

Drives My Green Age. 1st Ed. Josephine Carson. LC 57-820019. 1957. Harper.

Drivin' Woman. Elizabeth Pickett Chevalier. LC 42-16185. 1942. The Macmillan Company.

Driving at Night. Samuel Kashner. 1976. pap. 3.50 (ISBN 0-914610-07-4). Hanging Loose.

Driving Axle: A Novel of Socialist Construction. Casilil Pavlovich Il'Enkov. LC 35-6726. 1933. International Publishers.
Driving Through the Clouds & Other Stories. Jo Stanchfield. LC 72-92846. (Highway Holidays Ser). 1973. pap. text ed. 3.54 o.p. (ISBN 0-8372-0798-3). Bowmar-Noble.
Driving Wheel & My House Is Dark. Tony Hozeny. LC 74-82345. 1974. pap. 5.95 (ISBN 0-88361-033-7). Stanton & Lee.
Driving Wheel and My House Is Dark: Two Novels. Tony Hozeny. LC 74-82345. 4.95 (ISBN 0-88361-033-7). Wisconsin House.
Drogas, Lujuria y Muerte. new ed. Rod Gray. Tr. by Juan Castellanos from Eng. (Pimienta Collection Ser). (Illus.). 160p. (Span.). 1975. pap. 1.25 (ISBN 0-88473-240-1). Fiesta Pub.
Droles De Journal. Carl Rakosi. LC 80-28307. 25.00 (ISBN 0-915124-43-2) (ISBN 0-915124-44-0). Toothpaste Press.
Droll Peter: A Novel. Felix Timmermans & Darnton, Mrs. Maida (Castelhun) Tr. LC 30-8176. 1930. Coward-McCann, Inc.
Droll Stories. Honore De Balzac. LC 31-28422. (Half-title: The modern library of the world's best books). 1931. The Modern Library.
Droll Stories. Honore De Balzac. Ed. by Ernest Augustus Boyd. Barton, Ralph, 1891- Illus. LC 47-7153. 1946. Garden City Pub. Co.
Droll Stories. Honore De Balzac. Tr. by Alec Brown. 1958. 5.95 o.p. Dufour.
Droll Stories. Honore De Balzac. 2.95 o.p. (193); PLB 2.69 o.p. Modern Lib.
Droll Stories: Collected in the Monasteries of Touraine and Given to the Light by Honore De Balzac. Tr. by Alec Brown. Engravings by Gustave Dore. Honore De Balzac. Tr. by Alec Brown. Gustave Dore. LC 65-7365. (Masterpieces of World Lit., 2). 1965. 5.00. Elek Bks.
Droll Stories: Ed by Ernest Boyd; Illus. by Ralph Barton. Honore De Balzac. Ed. by Ernest Augustus Boyd. Ralph Barton. (Black cat bk., BD-20). 1962. Grove.
Droll Stories of Honore De Balzac. Honore De Balzac. LC 47-2345. 1946. Blue Ribbon Books.
Droll Stories: Thirty Tales. Honore De Balzac. Tr. by Jacques Georges Clemenceau Le Clerq. Limited Editions Club, Inc., New York. LC 32-16326. 1932. The Limited Editions Clubs.
Droll Stories: Thirty Tales. Honore De Balzac & Le Clercq, Jacques Georges Clemenceau, 1898- Tr. LC 39-25741. 1939.
Droll Stories: Thirty Tales Tr. from French by Jacques Le Clercq Reissue Illus. by Boris Artzybasheff. Honore De Balzac. LC 65-7377. 1965. 6.00. Heritage Dist. Dial.
Droll Tales of Reno. Bessemer Slingsbee. LC 45-1551. 1944. Wetzel Publishing Co., Inc.
Drolls from Shadowland. Joseph Henry Pearce. LC 1-21244. 1893. Macmillan and Co.
Drome: Illustrated by John Martin Leahy. John Martin Leahy. LC 53-39520. 1952. Fantasy Pub. Co.
Dromina. Francis Browning Drew Bickerstaffe-Drew. LC 9-8577. 1909. 1.50. G. P. Putnam's Sons.
Drone and a Dreamer. Nelson McAllister Lloyd. LC 1-18531. 1901. J. F. Taylor & Company.
Drones Must Die. Max Simon Nordau. LC 7-33472. 1897. G. W. Dillingham Co.
Drop City. Peter Rabbit. (Orig.). 1972. pap. 1.50 o.s.i. (OPS6131). Olympia.
Drop Dead. June Drummond. LC 75-40759. 1976. 6.95 (ISBN 0-8027-5344-2). Walker.
Drop Dead in Havana. C. H. Guenter. (Mr. Dynamite Ser.). 1978. pap. 1.25 (ISBN 0-532-12529-0). Woodhill.
Drop in Infinity. Gerald Grogan. LC 15-486496. 1915. 1.25. John Lane.
Drop-Ins. Warren Mild. LC 68-13602. 1968. Judson Press.
Drop into Hell. Lou Cameron. (Gold Medal Book) (ISBN 0-449-13611-6). Fawcett.
Drop of a Hat. Ruth Fenisong. LC 74-123690. 1970. 4.50. Published for the Crime Club by Doubleday.
Drop of Patience. William Melvin Kelley. LC 65-106095. 4.50. Doubleday.
Drop of Patience. William Melvin Kelley. LC 72-95319. 1973. 7.50. Chatham Bookseller.
Drop One, Carry Four. Fredric Sinclair. LC 47-4266. 1947. Pub. for the Crime Club by Doubleday.
Drop Out Drops Back. R. P. Turner. 5.95 o.p. (ISBN 0-8062-0792-2). Carlton.
Drop the Hook: A Novel About the Wartime Navy. Taylor, Jim. LC 51-11871. 1952. Exposition Press.
Dropout. Martin Yoseloff. Orig. Title: Girl in the Spike-Heeled Shoes. 1968. pap. 0.60 o.p. (73-770). Lancer.
Dropped from the Clouds. Jules Verne & Kingston, William Henry Giles, 1814-1880, Tr. LC 41-351472. (Half-title: Everyman's library, ed. by Ernest Rhys. For young people. no. 367). 1914. J. M. Dent & Sons, Ltd.
Dropped from the Clouds. Jules Verne & Kingston, William Henry Giles, 1814-1880, Tr. LC 36-37177. (Half-title: Everyman's library, ed. by Ernest Rhys. For young people no. 367). 1930. J. M. Dent & Sons, Ltd.
Dropped from the Fast Express: Or, A Daughter's Sacrifice. Fred Merrick White. LC 11-1521. Laird & Lee.
Dropped Living Room. Frances Y. McHugh. 192p. 1972. 3.95 o.p. Lenox Hill.
Drops of Blood. Lily Curry. (Fireside Ser. No. 22). 1877. J. S. Ogilvie & Company.
Dross. Hugh Stowell Scott. LC 8-20114. 1896. H. S. Stone & Co.
Drought. J. G. Ballard. LC 76-10445. (Gregg Press science fiction series). 1976. (ISBN 0-8398-2341-X). Gregg Press.
Drought! Ralph Hayes. 1981. pap. 2.95 (ISBN 0-89083-774-0). Zebra.
Drought. Iwan Simatupang. Tr. by Harry Aveling. (Writing in Asia Ser.). 1978. pap. text ed. 4.50x (00210). Heinemann Ed.
Drought: A New Dr. Palfrey Story. John Creasey. LC 67-23103. 1967. Walker.
Drought and Other North Carolina Yarns. Edith Hutchins Smith. LC 55-9091. 1955. J. F. Blair.
Drove Rider. Orlando Rigoni. Ed. by Alice Sachs. 1971. 3.95 o.p. Lenox Hill.
Drover's Daughter. Ruth Windsheimer. LC 53-6485. 1953. Vantage Press.
Drown the Wind. Margaret Page Hood. LC 61-156634. 1961. Coward-McCann.
Drowned Gold: Being the Story of a Sailor's Life. Roy Norton. LC 19-15315. 1919. 1.65. Houghton Miffin Company.
Drowned Man's Lode: A Novel of the Old West. Robert J McCaig. LC 60-8574. 1960. Macmillan.
Drowned Rat. E. X Ferrars, pseud. LC 74-33640. 1975. 5.95 (ISBN 0-385-07292-9). Published for the Crime Club by Doubleday.
Drowned World. J. G. Ballard. 1976. pap. 1.95 o.p. (ISBN 0-14-002229-5). Penguin.
Drowned World, and The Wind from Nowhere. J. G. Ballard. LC 65-12820. 1965. 4.50. Doubleday.
Drowner. John Dann MacDonald. 160p. 1982. pap. 2.25 (ISBN 0-449-13582-9, GM). Fawcett.
Drowning Day. Alan Dipper. LC 76-381832. (Illus.). 1976. 3.95 (ISBN 0-7181-1496-5). Joseph.
Drowning of an Old Cat, and Other Stories. Chun-Ming Huang. LC 80-7494. (Chinese Literature in Translation). 27.50 (ISBN 0-253-32452-1). Indiana University Press.
Drowning of an Old Cat & Other Stories. Chun-ming Hwang. Tr. by Howard Goldblatt. LC 80-7494. (Chinese Literature in Translation Ser.-Midland Bks: No. 253). 288p. 1980. 27.50x (ISBN 0-253-32452-1); pap. 9.95x (ISBN 0-253-20253-1). Ind U Pr.
Drowning Pool. Ross MacDonald. LC 75-44990. (Crime Fiction Ser). (O.s.i.). 1976. Repr. of 1950 ed. lib. bdg. 17.50 o.s.i. (ISBN 0-8240-2382-X). Garland Pub.
Drowning Pool. Kenneth Millar. LC 50-13124. 1950. Knopf.
Drowning Pool. Kenneth Millar. LC 75-44990. (Fifty Classics of Crime Fiction, 1900-1950; 33). 1976. 12.00 (ISBN 0-8240-2382-X). Garland Pub.
Drowning Season. Alice Hoffman. LC 78-21252. 8.95 (ISBN 0-525-09577-2). Dutton.
Drowning Season. Alice Hoffman. 1980. 2.50 (ISBN 0-449-24352-4). Fawcett Crest Books.
Drowning, the Dancing. Jerome Nilssen. LC 68-23990. 1968. 3.50. Fortress Press.
Drowsy. John Ames Mitchell. LC 74-16512. (Science Fiction). 1974-1975. 17.00 (ISBN 0-405-06306-7). Arno Press.
Drowsy. John Ames Mitchell. LC 17-25378. Frederick A. Stokes Company.
Druce. Mark Dunster. (Rin: Part 2). 1976. pap. 4.00 (ISBN 0-89642-015-9). Linden Pubs.
Drug of Choice. John Lange. 1974. (pbk.) 1.25. Bantam Books.
Drug on the Market. Henry Brinton. LC 57-671445. 1957. Macmillan.
Drug on the Market. Nigel G. Tranter. 1981. 18.95x (Pub. by Remploy England). State Mutual Bk.
Drug Slave. Mary Lake. LC 13-7803. 1913. Cassell and Company, Ltd.
Drug Store: A Novel. Morris Perman. LC 54-7844. 1954. Citadel Press.
Drug Tales. Duncan Fallowell. LC 79-22918. 1980. 8.95 (ISBN 0-312-21977-6). St. Martin's Press.
Drugged Cornet and Other Mystery Stories. Ed. by Susan Dickinson. LC 73-77452. (Illus.). 1973. 5.95 (ISBN 0-525-28928-3). Dutton.
Drugie Beraga. Vladimir Vladimirovich Nabokov. (Rus.). 1978. 15.00 o.p. (ISBN 0-88233-325-9); pap. 8.00 (ISBN 0-88233-326-7). Ardis Pubs.
Drugoth: The Biography of a Private Person. James Drought. LC 65-252909. 1965. 5.00, 2.50pap.,. Skylight Pr.
Drugstore Bandit of Horseshoe Bend. Linda Boorman. 120p. 1982. pap. 2.50 (ISBN 0-88207-492-X). Victor Bks.
Drugstore: The Saga of an American Institution. Abraham L. Furman & Hadley, Harold. LC 35-91190. The Macaulay Company.
Druid. Leonard Mosley. 256p. 1982. pap. 2.95 (ISBN 0-425-05663-5). Berkley Pub.
Druid Path. Marah Ellis Martin Ryan. LC 73-130071. (Short story index reprint series). (Illus.). 1970. Books for Libraries Press.
Druid Path. Marah Ellis Martin Ryan. LC 17-4311. 1917. A. C. McClurg & Co.
Druid Stone. Simon Majors. 1970. pap. 0.60 o.p. (63-359). Paperback Lib.
Druida. John Towner Frederick. LC 23-14431. 1923. A. A. Knopf.
Drum. with an introduction by henry seidel canby... ed. James Boyd. LC 36-7118. (Modern standard authors). C. Scribner's Sons.
Drum. Kyle Onstott. LC 62-176889. 1962. Dial Press.
Drum and Monkey. George Manning-Sanders. LC 30-3869. 1930. H. Liveright.
Drum Beat. Ed. by Leonard Okola. 1967. pap. 2.00 o.p. (Pub. by East African Publ Hse). Northwestern U Pr.
Drum Beat: Marianne. Stephen Marlowe. (Chester Brem Series). (Orig.). 1968. pap. 0.50 o.p. (D1909, GM). Fawcett World.
Drum Calls West. Grover C Gulick. LC 52-6919. 1952. Houghton Mifflin.
Drum Concerto: Stories. Emily Katharine Harris. LC 78-31137. 7.95 (ISBN 0-916078-05-1). Iris Press.
Drum Goes Dead. Bess Streeter Aldrich. LC 75-29112. 1975. 6.95. Aeonian Press.
Drum Goes Dead. Bess Streeter Aldrich. LC 41-22352. 1911. D. Appleton-Century Company, Incorporated.
Drum-Runnin' Fool. Donna Alverson. LC 76-21838. 1976. 8.95 (ISBN 0-88349-095-1). Reader's Digest Press: Distributed by Crowell.
Drum Say Be: An Anthology of African Literature. Ed. by Joseph A. Walker. pap. price not set o.p. (Prem). Fawcett World.
Drum Singers, by Lau Shaw (S. Y. Shu) Ch'ing Ch'un Shu. LC 52-6438. 1952. Harcourt, Brace.
Drum Taps. Leaves from the Diary of a Commercial Traveler... William H Maher. 1890. The Toledo Book Company.
Drum up the Dawn. Arthur Hawthorne Carhart. LC 37-17513. 1937. Dodd, Mead & Company.
Drumbeat of Desire. Diana Summers. LC 82-82115. 368p. 1982. pap. 2.95 (ISBN 0-86721-208-X). Playboy Pbks.
Drumbeat. 1st Ed. Dudley Pope. LC 67-22467. 1968. 4.95. Doubleday.
Drumbeater & Other Stories. Esther V. Daroy. 144p. (Orig.). 1982. pap. 5.75 (Pub. by New Day Philippines). Cellar.
Drumbuie House. Marianne D. Scott. 1972. pap. 0.95 o.s.i. (75-381). Lancer.
Drumfire. Peter McCurtin. (Sundance Ser.: No. 38). 192p. 1982. pap. 1.95 o.s.i. (ISBN 0-8439-0976-5, Leisure Bks). Nordon Pubns.
Drumfire. 1st Ed. Tom J Hopkins. LC 51-10648. (Double D western). 1951. Doubleday.
Drummer Boy. Cyprian Ekwensi. 1960. text ed. 3.50x (ISBN 0-521-04882-6). Cambridge U Pr.
Drummer in the Dark. Francis Clifford. LC 75-34223. 7.95 (ISBN 0-15-126580-1). Harcourt Brace Jovanovich.
Drummond Tradition. Charles E Mercer. LC 57-11714. 1957. Putnam.
Drums. James Boyd. LC 68-7241. (Scribner school paperbacks, SSP1). (Illus.). 1968. Scribner.
Drums. James Boyd. LC 25-8792. 1925. C. Scribner's Sons.
Drums. James Boyd. LC 26-63385. 1926. C. Scribner's Sons.
Drums. James Boyd. LC 28-21487. C. Scribner's Sons.
Drums Afar: An International Romance. John Murray Gibbon. LC 18-16375. 1918. John Lane Company.
Drums Against Frontenac. Harvey Chalmers. LC 64-8326. 1965. 6.00. Twayne.
Drums Against Frontenac. Harvey Chalmers. LC 65-9056. 1949. Twayne Publishers.
Drums Against Frontenac. Harvey Chalmers. LC 49-50078. 1949. R. R. Smith.
Drums Along the Khyber. Duncan MacNeil. LC 72-96135. 1973. 6.95. St. Martin's Press.
Drums Along the Mohawk. Walter Dumaux Edmonds. LC 36-16924. 1936. Little, Brown, and Company.
Drums Along the Mohawk. Walter Dumaux Edmonds. LC 37-926240. 1937. Little, Brown, and Company.
Drums Along the Mohawk. An Educational Ed., by Hope Brewer. Walter Dumaux Edmonds. LC 54-2641. 1954. Globe Book Co.
Drums at Dusk: A Novel by Arna Bontemps. Arna Wendell Bontemps. LC 39-10640. 1939. The Macmillan Company.
Drums for Rancas. Manuel Scorza. LC 72-9177. 8.95 (ISBN 0-06-013814-9). Harper & Row.
Drums in the Dawn. John Thomas McIntyre. LC 32-3608. 1932. Doubleday, Doran & Company, Inc.
Drums in the Dawn. John Thomas McIntyre. LC 38-12699. 1938. The Sun Dial Press, Inc.
Drums in the Forest. Allan Dwight, pseud. LC 36-21649. 1936. The Macmillan Compaby.
Drums of April: A Novel. Charles Henry Mergendahl. LC 63-9666. 1963. Putnam.
Drums of Aulone. Robert William Chambers. LC 27-5940. 1927. D. Appleton and Company.
Drums of Dambala. Henry Bedford-Jones. LC 32-58082. Covici-Friede.
Drums of Darkness. Elizabeth Lane. 304p. (Orig.). 1981. pap. 2.75 (ISBN 0-515-05664-2). Jove Pubns.
Drums of Darkness: An Astrological Gothic Novel, Leo. Marion Zimmer Bradley. LC 76-7974. 1976. 1.25 (ISBN 0-345-25108-3). Ballantine Books.
Drums of December. Sharon Anne Salvato. 1983. pap. 5.95 (ISBN 0-440-52534-9, Dell Trade Pbks). Dell.
Drums of Destiny. Graham Montague Jeffries. LC 47-30855. 1947. G. P. Putnam's Sons.
Drums of Doom. Robert Welles Ritchie. LC 23-6378. 1923. 1.75. Dodd, Mead and Company.
Drums of Doomsday. Thornwell Jacobs. LC 42-2421. 1942. E. P. Dutton & Co., Inc.
Drums of Dracula. Robert Lory. (Dracula horror series,#5). 1974. (pbk.) 0.95 (ISBN 0-523-00322-6). Pinnacle Books.
Drums of Fu Manchu. Sax Rohmer, pseud. (Adventure Ser). 1971. pap. 0.60 o.p. (X2531). Pyramid Pubns.
Drums of Fu Manchu. Sax Rohmer, pseud. 1976. pap. 1.25 o.p. (ISBN 0-515-04030-4). BJ Pub Group.
Drums of Fu Manchu. Arthur Sarsfield Ward. LC 39-21858. 1939. Pub. for the Crime Club, Inc., by Doubleday, Doran & Co., Inc.
Drums of Fun Manchu. Arthur Sarsfield Ward. LC 40-14088. 1940. The Sun Dial Press.
Drums of Jeopardy. Harold MacGrath. LC 20-179602. 1920. Doubleday, Page & Company.
Drums of Khartoum. Chole Gartner. LC 67-16373. 1967. bds., 4.95. Morrow.
Drums of Kufu. Japhet Delft. LC 76-377385. 1976. 3.95 (ISBN 0-7043-2082-7). Quartet Books.
Drums of Love. Barbara Cartland. LC 78-31719. 1979. 6.95 (ISBN 0-87272-049-7). Duron Books.
Drums of Mer. Ion L. Idriess. pap. 2.00 o.s.i. Tri-Ocean.
Drums of Morning. Philip Van Doren Stern. LC 42-18496. 1942. Doubleday, Doran and Company, Inc.
Drums of Panic. Martin Feinstein. LC 27-19782. 1927. Macy-Masius.
Drums of Paradise Woods. 1st Ed. George G Price. LC 56-12785. 1957. Vantage Press.
Drums of Tapajos. Sterner St. Paul Meek. LC 61-65993. 1961. Avalon Books.
Drums of the Dark Gods. W. A. Ballinger, pseud. 1967. pap. 0.50 o.p. (52-584). Paperback Lib.
Drums of the Fore and Aft. Rudyard Kipling. LC 18-11994. 1898. Brentanos.
Drums of the Fore and Aft. Rudyard Kipling. LC 99-424715. 1899. Doubleday and McClure Company.
Drums of the Night. Norma Patterson. LC 35-30054. Farrar & Rinehart, Incorporated.
Drums of the North. A De Herries Smith. LC 28-13913. The Macaulay Company.
Drums of Ungara: 1st Ed. Bill Knox. LC 63-12967. 1963. Published for the Crime Club by Doubleday.
Drums of War. Roy Clews. LC 79-2130. 8.95 (ISBN 0-312-22022-7). St. Martin's Press.
Drums of War. Henry De Vere Stacpoole. LC 10-27674. 1910. 1.20. Duffield & Company.
Drums of Winter. Sandra Paretti. LC 73-80176. 1974. 7.95 (ISBN 0-87131-129-1). M. Evans.
Drums. Pen Drawings by N. C. Wyeth. Introd., Study Guide by John C. Adler. James Boyd. LC 65-17548. 1968. pap., 2.84. Scribners.
Drum's Story, and Other Tales. Delavan S Miller. LC 9-28272. Hungerford-Holbrook Company.
Drums Without Warriors. Fred Grove. LC 76-5337. 1976. 5.95 (ISBN 0-385-09689-5). Doubleday.
Drumsticks: A Little Story of a Sinner and a Child. Katharine Mary Cheever Meredith. LC 7-26232. The Transatlantic Publishing Company.
Drumsticks: A Little Story of a Sinner and a Child. Katharine Mary Cheever Meredith. 1897. Continental Publishing Company.
Drunk Before Dawn. Shirley Lees. 1979. pap. 3.50 (ISBN 0-85363-128-X). OMF Bks.
Drunk in Madrid. Joyce Elbert. LC 72-80329. 1972. 6.95 (ISBN 0-87795-037-7). Arbor House.
Drunk in Madrid. Joyce Elbert. (Signet Book, W5657). 1973. (pbk.) 1.50. New American Library.

Drunkard. Cyril Arthur Edward Ranger Gull. LC 12-1161. 1.35. Sturgis & Walton Company.
Drunkard. Emile Zola. 200p. 1980. 17.95x (ISBN 0-8464-1237-3). Beekman Pubs.
Drunkard. Emile Zola. 1958. 9.95 o.p. (ISBN 0-236-31008-9, Pub. by Paul Elek). Merrimack Pub Cir.
Drunkards Dream. Mary A. Baker. 3.50 o.p. Carlton.
Drunkard's End. Thurman Warriner. LC 61-6958. 1961. Walker.
Drunks. Donald Newlove. LC 74-4027. 1974. 8.95. Saturday Review Press.
Drury Affair. Ivy Valdes. (Orig.). 1975. pap. 1.25 o.p. (ISBN 0-515-03850-4). Pyramid Pubns.
Drury Club Case. Sidney Clark Williams. 1927. The Penn Publishing Company.
Drury Lane Boy's Club. Frances Hodgson Burnett. LC 6-16421. 1892. Press of "The Moon,
Drury Lane's Last Case, the Tragedy of 1599: A Drury Lane Mystery. Ellery Queen, pseud. LC 33-25371. 1933. The Viking Press.
Drury Randall. Mary Johnston. 1934. Little, Brown, and Company.
Drusilla with a Million. Elizabeth Cooper. LC 16-3306. 1916. Frederick A. Stokes Company.
Druskin. Grace Livingston Hill. LC 29-9031. 1929. J. B. Lippincott Company.
Drustan the Wanderer: A Novel Based on the Legend of Tristan and Isolde. Anna Taylor. LC 70-186428. 1972. 5.95 (ISBN 0-8415-0165-3). Saturday Review Press.
Dry Bones in the Valley. William MacLeod Raine. LC 53-5064. 1953. Houghton Mifflin.
Dry Bread: Or, The Reign of Selfishness. A Novel for Men. 2d ed. Samuel Walker. LC 99-2858. (Dillingham's metropolitan library. no. 49). 1899. G. W. Dillingham Co.
Dry County, a Novel. Earl Lueallen Young. LC 50-33207. 1950. Enterprise Press.
Dry Gulch. Galen C. Colin. LC 42-21230. 1942. Phoenix Press.
Dry-Gulch Adams. Peter Field. LC 34-38182. 1934. W. Morrow & Company.
Dry Gulcher 1. Wayne D. Overholser. 1977. 0.95 (ISBN 0-440-12169-8). Dell Pub. Co.
Dry Hustle. Sarah Kernochan. LC 76-50918. 1977. 8.95 (ISBN 0-688-03149-8). Morrow.
Dry Hustle. Sarah Kernochan. (Berkley Medallion Book). 1978. 1.95 (ISBN 0-425-03661-8). Berkley Pub. Corp.
Dry Lake Ranch. Francis Mitchell. LC 57-979655. 1957. Arcadia House.
Dry Martini: A Gentleman Turns to Love. John Thomas. LC 73-14675. (Lost American fiction). 1974. 7.95 (ISBN 0-8093-0661-1). Southern Illinois University Press.
Dry Martini: A Gentleman Turns to Love. John Thomas. LC 26-218943. George H. Doran Company.
Dry Points: Studies in Black and White. Henry Martyn Hoyt & Benet, William Rose, 1886-LC 22-22287. 1921. F. Shay.
Dry Ridge Gang. Bertha Muzzy Sinclair. LC 35-2491. 1935. Little, Brown, and Company.
Dry Ridge Gang. Bertha Muzzy Sinclair. LC 44-783049. 1944. Triangle Books.
Dry Season. Dan Wickenden. LC 50-13667. 1950. Morrow.
Dry Tortugas. Elwyn Whitman Chambers. LC 40-30394. 1940. Doubleday, Doran & Company, Inc.
Dry White Season. Andre Philippus Brink. LC 79-91518. 1980. 9.95 (ISBN 0-688-03568-X). Morrow.
Dry Wood. Frances Caryll Houselander. LC 47-11634. 1947. Sheed & Ward.
Dryad: A Novel. Justin Huntly McCarthy. 1905. Harper & Brothers.
Drygulchers. Ford Bowne, pseud. 1977. pap. 1.25 (ISBN 0-532-12504-5). Woodhill.
Drygulchers! Ford Bowne, pseud. 1973. 4.95. Lenox Hill Pr.
Drylake Desperadoes. Ernest Finlay. LC 44-6123. 1944. Phoenix Press.
Du Mauriers. Daphne Du Maurier. 1974. (pbk.) 1.50 (ISBN 0-380-00125-X). Avon.
Dual Alliance. Marjorie Benton Cooke. LC 15-21421. 1915. 1.00. Doubleday, Page & Company.
Dual Destiny. Karen Lynn. LC 82-45204. 1983. 11.95 (ISBN 0-385-18219-8). Doubleday.
Dual Role: A Romance of the Civil War. William Issac Yopp. J. F. Worley.
Dual Role: And Other Stories. Anthony Joseph Drexel Biddle. LC 6-131063. 1894. The Warwick Book Publishing Company.
Duane of the F. B. I. John Benton. LC 37-34923. Dodge Publishing Company.
Dubai. Robin Moore, pseud. LC 74-33654. 1976. 10.00 (ISBN 0-385-04927-7). Doubleday.
Dubin's Lives. Bernard Malamud. LC 78-23897. 10.00 (ISBN 0-374-14414-1). Farrar Straus Giroux.
Dubin's Lives. Bernard Malamud. 1980. 2.50 (ISBN 0-380-48413-7). Avon Books.
Dubious Persuasions: Short Stories by Jack Matthews. Jack Matthews. LC 81-47591. (Poetry & Fiction Ser.). 168p. 1981. 10.95 (ISBN 0-8018-2692-6). Johns Hopkins.
Dublin Letters. Lee Harriman. LC 31-9377. 1931. I. Washburn.
Dublin Pawn. John Keckhut. LC 77-1173. 8.95 (ISBN 0-393-08761-1). Norton.
Dubliners. James Augustine Aloysius Joyce. LC 68-3294. (Viking compass book, C41). 1967. Viking Press.
Dubliners. James Augustine Aloysius Joyce. Ed. by Robert E. Scholes & A. Walton Litz. LC 69-15934. (Viking critical library, 5). (Illus.). 1969. 1.95. Viking Press.
Dubliners. James Augustine Aloysius Joyce. LC 17-24698. 1916. B. W. Huebsch.
Dubliners. James Augustine Aloysius Joyce. LC 25-23228. 1925. B. W. Huebsch, Inc.
Dubliners. James Augustine Aloysius Joyce. LC 27-3416. (Half-title: The Modern library of the world's best books). The Modern Library.
Dubliners. Corrected Text, Ed. by Robert Scholes with Richard Ellmann. James Augustine Aloysius Joyce. (C41). 1967. pap., 1.45. Viking.
Dubrovnik Massacre. Nick Carter. (Nick Carter Ser.). 224p. (Orig.). 1981. pap. 2.25 (ISBN 0-441-17014-5, Pub. by Charter Bks). Ace Bks.
Dubu: A Novel of New Guinea Conquest. Maslyn Williams. 1971. 6.95 o.p. (ISBN 0-688-01489-5). Morrow.
Dubu; a Novel of New Guinean Conquest. Maslyn Williams. 1973. (pbk) 0.95 (ISBN 0-671-77439-5) (ISBN 0-671-77439-5). Pocket Books,
Dubu: A Novel of New Guinean Conquest. Maslyn Williams. LC 71-132874. 1971. 6.95. Morrow.
Duca and the Milan Murders. Giorgio Scerbanenco. LC 74-120404. 1970. 4.95. Walker.
Ducal Skeleton: A Story. Heloise Durant Rose. F. T. Neely.
Duchess. Josephine Edgar, pseud. LC 76-10551. 1977. 8.95 o.p. (ISBN 0-312-22085-5). St Martin.
Duchess. Mary Howard, pseud. 1978. 2.25 (ISBN 0-446-82423-2). Warner Books.
Duchess. Margaret Wolfe Hungerford. LC 7-83283. (On cover: Lovell's library. no. 1072). 1887. J. W. Lovell Company.
Duchess and Her Daughter. Alfred Bishop Mason. 1929. A. & C. Boni.
Duchess by Appointment. Mary Lady Cameron. LC 34-19484. A. H. King.
Duchess De Langeais: With An Episode Under the Terror, The Illustrious Gaudissart, A Passion in the Desert, and The Hidden Masterpiece. Honore De Balzac. Tr. by Katharine Prescott Wormeley. LC 3-23183. (Half-title: The comedy of human life... Scenes from Parisan life). 1889. Roberts Brothers.
Duchess Disappeared. Barbara Cartland. LC 79-21293. 1979. 6.95 (ISBN 0-87272-084-5, Duron Bks). Brodart.
Duchess Emilia: A Romance. Barrett Wendell. 1885. J. R. Osgood and Company.
Duchess Emilia: A Romance. Barrett Wendell. LC 8-36241. 1896. C. Scribner's Sons.
Duchess Hotspur. Rosamond Van Der Zee Marshall. LC 46-266878. 1946. Prentice-Hall, Inc.
Duchess in Disguise. Caroline Courtney. LC 79-22200. 1979. 12.50 (ISBN 0-8161-3002-7). G. K. Hall.
Duchess Intervenes. Marie Adelaide Belloc Lowndes. LC 33-970. 1933. G. P. Putnam's Sons.
Duchess Laura: Further Days of Her Life. Marie Adelaide Belloc Lowndes. LC 33-32012. 1933. Longmans, Green and Co.
Duchess of Baden: A Tale of the French Revolution. With a History of the Fall of the Marquis Louis De Beauharnais, and the Flight and Perils of His Family in France, Spain, Saint Domingo, and Philadelphia. Edward Ford. LC 6-414031. 1849. Carey & Hart.
Duchess of Bloomsbury Street. Helene Hanff. LC 73-1801. 144p. 1973. 6.95i (ISBN 0-397-00976-3). Har-Row.
Duchess of Denver. Lee D. Willoughby. (Women Who Won the West Ser.: No. 3). (Orig.). 1982. pap. 2.95 (ISBN 0-440-02172-3). Dell.
Duchess of Dreams. Edith Macvane. 1908. J. B. Lippincott Company.
Duchess of Duke Street: A Novel. Mollie Hardwick. LC 76-29903. 1977. 8.95 (ISBN 0-03-018291-3). Holt, Rinehart and Winston.
Duchess of Few Clothes: A Comedy. Philip Payne. LC 4-10477. Rand, McNally & Company.
Duchess of Glover. Herbert Kubly. LC 74-3552. 1975. 8.95 (ISBN 0-385-04822-X). Doubleday.
Duchess of Siona. Ernest Goodwin. LC 19-46927. 1919. 1.60. Hougton Mifflin Company.
Duchess of Vidal. Dawn Lindsey. LC 77-11777. 1978. 7.95 (ISBN 0-385-12939-4). Doubleday.
Duchess of Wrexe; Her Decline and Death: A Romantic Commentary. Hugh Walpole. LC 14-5432. (His The rising city: I). George H. Doran Company.
Duchess Says No. Frank O'Rourke. LC 65-9108. 1965. W. Morrow.
Duchesse De Langeais: With An Episode Under the Terror, The Illustrious Gaudissart, A Passion in the Desert, and The Hidden Masterpiece. Honore De Balzac. Tr. by Katharine Prescott Wormeley. LC 6-6306. (Half-title: The comedy of human life... Scenes from Parisian life). 1885. Roberts Brothers.
Duchesse Undine: Or, Slain by a Woman's Lie. Hanson Penn Diltz. LC 6-36824. T. B. Peterson & Brothers.
Ducie Diamonds. C Blatherwick. LC 6-13837. (On cover: The seaside library. Pocket ed., no. 151). 1883. G. Munro.
Duck Hunt. Translated from the French by George Libaire. Hugo Claus. LC 55-5794. Random House.
Duck Hunting. Aleksandr Valentinovich Vampilov & Alma H Law. LC 80-121665. (Illus.). 2.25. Dramatists Play Service.
Duck May Be Somebody's Mother. George Moorse. LC 67-3206. 1967. Delacorte Press.
Duck to Water. Gladys Bronwyn Stern. LC 50-6888. 1950. Macmillan.
Duck You Sucker. James Lewis. (Orig.). 1971. pap. 0.75 o.p. (A831S, Award). Univ Pub & Dist.
Duckfoot. William Scoales. LC 76-142470. 1971. 5.95 (ISBN 0-672-51264-5). Bobbs.
Duckfoot: A Novel. William Scoales. LC 76-142470. 1971. 5.95. Bobbs-Merrill.
Duck's Back. Kate Mary Maugham Bruce. LC 34-7610. The John Day Company.
Ducks in Thunder. Jay Dratler. LC 40-90306. Reynal & Hitchcock.
Ducky, Ucky, and Mucky. Robert Oechsle. (Illus.). 1975. (pbk.) 2.50. Flourtown Pub. Co.
Dud Dean and His Country. Arthur Raymond Macdougall. LC 46-5161. 1946. Coward-McCann, Inc.
Dud Dean and the Enchanted. Arthur Raymond Macdougall. LC 54-7447. 1954. Falmouth Pub. House.
Dud Dean Yarns. Arthur Raymond Macdougall. LC 35-184. 1934. The Bingham Press.
Dude. Max Brand. 1940. Dodd, Mead & Company.
Dude. Frederick Faust. LC 76-40440. 1976. 6.95 (ISBN 0-88411-519-4). Aeonian Press.
Dude: Or, The Adventures of Verdant Green... Edward Bradley. LC 6-16075. 1883. G. W. Carleton & Co.; Etc., Etc.
Dude Ranch. Milton Krims. LC 31-11287. The Macaulay Company.
Dude Ranch Nurse. Diana Douglas. (Signet Nurse Books). 1973. (pbk) 0.60. New American Lib.
Dude Ranch Nurse. Arlene Hale. 1975. (pbk.) 0.75. Ace Books.
Dude Rancher: A Story of Modern Ranching. Stephen B Strang. LC 41-200522. (Career books). 1941. Dodd, Mead & Company.
Dude Ranger. Grey, Zane. (Great western edition 11). 1962. Grosset & Dunlap.
Dude Ranger. Zane Grey. 1981. 1.95 (ISBN 0-671-83591-2). Pocket Books.
Dude Ranger. Zane Grey. LC 81-20090. 1982. 13.95 (ISBN 0-8161-3220-8). G.K. Hall.
Dude Woman. Peter Bernard Kyne. LC 40-4887. 1940. H. C. Kinsey & Company, Inc.
Dude Wrangler. Caroline Lockhart. LC 21-8308. 1921. Doubleday, Page & Company.
Dude Wrangler: Hunter: Line Rider. Floyd C. Bard & Agnes W. Spring. pap. 1.35 o.p. (ISBN 0-8040-0071-9, 19, SB). Swallow.
Dudley & Gilderoy: N Nonsense. Algernon Blackwood. LC 29-25037. 1929. E. P. Dutton & Co., Inc.
Dudley Carleon; or, The Brother's Secret. And George Caulfield's Journey. Mary Elizabeth Braddon Maxwell. (On cover: Seaside library. Pocket ed. no. 549). 1885. G. Munro.
Dudley Smithwright & the Phantom Voice. Marcus Steinour. 96p. 12.95x (ISBN 0-943864-09-7); pap. 3.95x (ISBN 0-943864-04-6). MD Bks.
Duds. Henry Cottrell Rowland. LC 20-1699. Harper & Brothers.
Dud's House: A Success Story. Jack Keary. LC 67-24543. 1967. Dorrance.
Due for a Hangin' Caddo Cameron. LC 39-15603. 1939. Doubleday, Doran & Company, Inc.
Due Mondi. Nat Scammacca. (Orig.). 1979. 15.00x (ISBN 0-89304-562-4, CCC123); pap. 8.00 (ISBN 0-89304-561-6). Cross Cult.
Due Preparations for the Plague, As Well for Soul As Body. Daniel Defoe. LC 74-13434. (Illus.). 1974. (ISBN 0-404-07925-3). AMS Press.
Due Reckoning: Being the Third and Last Part of 'The Realists' Stephen McKenna. LC 28-329. 1928. Little, Brown, and Company.
Duedame. John Cowper Powys. LC 25-619991. 1925. Doubleday, Page & Company.
Duel. Aleksandr Ivanovich Kuprin. LC 76-23881. (Classics of Russian literature.). (Hyperion library of world literature). 1977. 4.95 (ISBN 0-88355-492-5). Hyperion Press.
Duel. Donald Seaman. LC 78-22819. 1979. 10.95 (ISBN 0-385-15221-3). Doubleday.
Duel. Donald Seaman. 220p. 1981. pap. 2.50 (ISBN 0-445-04601-5). Popular Lib.
Duel: And Other Stories. Anton Pavlovich Chekhov. Tr. by Garnett, Constance (Black) LC 16-23209. (Half-title: The tales of Chekhov, vol. ii). 1916. 1.50. The Macmillan Company.
Duel, and Selected Stories. Newly Translated, and with an Afterword, by Andrew R. MacAndrew. Aleksandr Ivanovich Kuprin. LC 61-1898. (Signet classic, CD45). 1961. New American Library.
Duel at Dodge City. Jackson Flynn, pseud. (Gunsmoke Ser.). (O.s.i.: No. 3). (Orig.). 1974. pap. 0.95 o.s.i. (AN1328, Award). Univ Pub & Dist.
Duel at Freemark. Spencer Knight. (Orig.). 1979. pap. 1.50 (ISBN 0-532-15404-5). Woodhill.
Duel at Gold Buttes. William Jeffrey. 1981. 1.75 (ISBN 0-505-51674-8). Tower Publications Inc.
Duel in Herne Wood. Wilkie Collins. (standard short story series...). F. Harrison & Co.
Duel in the Snow. Hans Otto Meissner. LC 70-142392. 1972. 5.95. Morrow.
Duel in the Sun. Niven Busch. LC 44-40001. 1944. The Hampton Publishing Co., Distributed by W. Morrow and Company.
Duel in the Sun. forum books ed. Niven Busch. LC 47-46434. 1947. World Pub. Co.
Duel of Hearts. Barbara Cartland. 1974. pap. 1.25 o.p. (ISBN 0-515-03537-8, V3537). BJ Pub Group.
Duel of Hearts. Elizabeth Mansfield, pseud. (Orig.). 1980. pap. 2.25 (ISBN 0-425-04677-X). Berkley Pub.
Duel of the Queens: A Romance of Mary, Queen of Scotland. Lily Moresby Adams Beck. LC 30-24775. 1930. Doubleday, Doran & Company, Inc.
Duel on the Wind: A Novel of the America's Cup Challenge. Richard A Duprey. LC 76-5370. 10.00. St. Martin's Press.
Duel: Translated from the Norwegian. Ronald Fangen. Tr. by Wiking, Paula. LC 34-27188. 1934. The Viking Press.
Duel with Destiny. Hattie Semones. LC 75-37226. 6.95 (ISBN 0-89227-001-2). Commonwealth Press.
Duelling Fire. Anne Mather. (Harlequin Presents Ser.). 192p. 1982. pap. 1.75 (ISBN 0-373-10490-1). Harlequin Bks.
Duellist. Gordon Williams. (Kangaroo Book). 1.75 (ISBN 0-671-81930-5). Pocket Books.
Duelo En el Paraiso. Juan Goytisolo. Ed. by D. W. Bleznick. 1967. 5.95x o.p. (ISBN 0-536-00201-0). Xerox College.
Duelo En el Paraiso. Ed. by Donald W. Bleznick. Juan Goytisolo. Ed. by Donald William Bleznick. LC 67-19535. (Blaisdell bk. in the modern languages). 1967. 5.25. Blaisdell.
Duenna of a Genius. Mary E. Sweetman Blundell. LC 6-142034. 1898. Litton, Brown, and Company.
Duet. Wendy Susans. 1981. pap. 2.75 o.s.i. (ISBN 0-8439-0914-5, Leisure Bks). Nordon Pubns.
Duet, 3 bks, No. 2. Benjamin Benedict. (Eggs Benedict Ser.). (Illus., Orig.). 1982. pap. 2.95 (ISBN 0-942764-02-1). Falcon Pub Venice.
Duet for Three Spies. H. T Rothwell. LC 67-20233. 1967. Roy Publishers.
Duet in Discord. Elma Napier. LC 37-13273. 1937. A. A. Knopf!
Duet: The Flight of the Falcon and The Scapegoat. Daphne Du Maurier. LC 68-2890. 1968. Nelson Doubleday.
Duet: With an Occasional Chorus. Arthur Conan Doyle. 1899. D. Appleton and Company.
Duffels. Edward Eggleston. LC 72-5868. (Short story index reprint series). 1972. (ISBN 0-8369-4216-7). Books for Libraries Press.
Duffels. Edward Eggleston. LC 75-38708. 1976. (ISBN 0-403-03158-3). Scholarly Press.
Duffels. Edward Eggleston. LC 6-37565. 1893. D. Appleton and Company.
Dugmar the Egyptian. M C Colson. LC 27-18299. The Christopher Publishing House.
Dugout. Zoe A Tilghman. LC 25-22284. 1925. Harlow Publishing Company.
Dugout Brother. J. Jason Grant. 1978. 1.75 (ISBN 0-87067-534-6). Holloway House.
Duino Elegies. Rainer Maria Rilke & Gary Miranda. LC 81-67299. 8.95 (ISBN 0-932576-08-7). Breitenbush Books.
Duke. Joseph Storer Clouston. LC 6762. 1900. Longmans, Green and Co.
Duke. Hal Ellson. LC 49-8025. 1949. C. Scribner's Sons.
Duke. John Hunter. 1970. pap. 0.60 o.p. (ISBN 0-446-63317-8, 63-317). Paperback Lib.
Duke and His Double. with frontispiece by florence scovel shinn. ed. Edward Sims Van Zile. 1903. H. Holt and Company.

Duke and the Preacher's Daughter. Barbara Cartland. LC 78-27088. 1979. 6.95 (ISBN 0-87272-048-9). Duron Books.

Duke Comes Back. Lucian Cary. LC 33-173883. 1933. Doubleday, Doran & Co., Inc.

Duke Decides. Francis Edward Grainger. LC 3-28590. 1903. A. Wessels Company.

Duke Herring. Maxwell Bodenheim. LC 31-185903. H. Liveright, Inc.

Duke Jones. Ethel Sidgwick. LC 15-26657. 1915. Small, Maynard & Company.

Duke of Albany's Own Highlanders: A Novel. James Grant. LC 44-43267. 1881. G. Routledge and Sons.

Duke of Arcanum: A Novel. Frank Carleton Long. LC 7-15147. (On cover: Library of choice fiction. no. 74). 1894. Laird & Lee.

Duke of Chaos. Ellery Queen, pseud. LC 64-4079. 1964. Pocket Books.

Duke of Chatham Square. John Hubert Larkin. LC 39-181589. Author & Publisher.

Duke of Chimney Butte. George Washington Ogden. LC 20-64279. 1920. A. C. McClurg & Co.

Duke of Deception. Geoffrey Wolff. 1980. pap. 2.75 (ISBN 0-425-04660-5). Berkley Pub.

Duke of Gaalodoro: A Novel. Aubrey Menen. LC 52-7055. 1952. Scribner.

Duke of Kandos: From the French of A. Mathey Pseud. Arthur Arnould & Clark, Frank Pinckney, Tr. LC 6-2073. John W. Lovell Company.

Duke of Oblivion. John Reed Scott. LC 14-164733. 1914. 1.25. J. B. Lippincott Company.

Duke of Sin. Charles M. Wayne. LC 54-9131. Vantage Press.

Duke of Stockbridge. Edward Bellamy. Repr. of 1901 ed. lib. bdg. 35.00 (ISBN 0-8414-1636-2). Folcroft.

Duke of Stockbridge: A Romance of Shay's Rebellion. Ed. by Joseph Schiffman. Edward Bellamy. LC 62-172155. (John Harvard lib., JHL9). 1966. pap., 1.95. Belknap Pr. of Harvard.

Duke of Stockbridge: A Romance of Shay's Rebellion. Edward Bellamy. LC 6504. 1900. Silver, Burdett and Company.

Duke of War. Walter O'Meara. LC 66-12374. 4.50. Harcourt.

Duke of York's Steps. Henry Wade. LC 81-48023. 350p. 1982. pap. cancelled o.p. (ISBN 0-06-080588-9, P-588, PL). Har-Row.

Duke Steps Out. Lucian Cary. LC 29-499425. 1929. Doubleday, Doran & Company, Inc.

Dukes. Malcolm Ross. 1981. 14.95 o.p. (ISBN 0-671-25111-2). S&S.

Dukes: A Novel. Ross-Macdonald, Malcolm. LC 80-27950. (Illus.). 14.95 (ISBN 0-671-25111-2). Simon and Schuster.

Duke's Chase: Or, The Diamond Ring Vs. the Gold Ring. M. E. McCormick. LC 7-15298. 1871. R. Clarke & Co., Printers.

Duke's Children. Anthony Trollope. LC 74-188259. (His Palliser novels). (Illus.). 1973. 12.50 (ISBN 0-19-254616-3) (ISBN 0-19-281148-7). Oxford University Press.

Duke's Children. Anthony Trollope. LC 4-16849. (On cover: The parliamentary novels. v). 1893. Dodd, Mead & Company.

Duke's Children. Anthony Trollope. LC 4-16586. (On cover: The parliamentary novels). 1903. Dodd, Mead & Company.

Duke's Children. Anthony Trollope. LC 38-27978. (Half-title: The world's classics. 462-468). 1938. Oxford University Press, H. Milford.

Duke's Children. With a Pref. by Chauncey B. Tinker; Illus. by Charles Mozley. Anthony Trollope. LC 56-2169. (Oxford Trollope. Crown ed.). 1954. Oxford University Press.

Duke's Daughter. Angela Mackail Thirkell. LC 51-11080. 1951. Knopf.

Duke's Daughter. Angela Mackail Thirkell. 1973. 1.25. Pyramid.

Duke's Daughter. 1st Ed. Elizabeth Frances Corbett. LC 50-6296. 1950. Doubleday.

Duke's Day. Alec Tavis. LC 76-108693. 1970. 4.95. Houghton Mifflin.

Duke's Diamonds. Marion Chesney. 160p. (Orig.). 1983. pap. 2.25 (ISBN 0-449-20085-X, Crest). Fawcett.

Duke's Messenger. Vanessa Gray, pseud. 1982. pap. 2.25 (ISBN 0-451-11868-5, AE1868, Sig). NAL.

Duke's Mistress. Frank Wilson Kenyon. 1978. pap. 1.95 o.s.i. (ISBN 0-505-51299-8). Tower Bks.

Duke's Mistress. Frank Wilson Kenyon. Orig. Title: No Lady, This. 1969. 5.95 o.p. (ISBN 0-396-05974-0). Dodd.

Duke's Mistress. Frank Wilson Kenyon. 272p. (YA) 1972. pap. 0.95 o.p. (T-095-145). Tower.

Duke's Mistress: The Story of Mary Ann Clarke. Frank Wilson Kenyon. LC 72-469069. 1969. 4.00. Hutchinson of Australia.

Duke's Mistress: The Story of Mary Ann Clarke. Frank Wilson Kenyon. LC 78-80824. 1969. 5.95. Dodd, Mead.

Duke's Motto: A Melodrama. Justin Huntly McCarthy. 1908. Harper & Brothers.

Dukes of Hazzard: Gone Racin' Eric Alter. 224p. Date not set. pap. 2.50 (ISBN 0-446-30324-0). Warner Bks.

Duke's Price. Demetra Vaka Brown & Brown, Kenneth, 1868- Joint Author. LC 10-7932. 1910. Houghton, Mifflin Company.

Duke's Secret. Charlotte Mary Brame. (On cover: Lovell's library. no. 1064). J. W. Lovell Company.

Duke's Secret. Charlotte Mary Brame. (On cover: Seaside library. Pocket ed. no. 982). G. Munro.

Duke's Secret. Charlotte Mary Brame. LC 1-3006. (Bertha Clay library, no. 47). 1900. Street & Smith.

Duke's Wager. Edith Layton. 224p. 1983. pap. 2.25 (ISBN 0-451-12067-1, Sig). NAL.

Dukesborough Tales. Richard Malcolm Johnston. LC 3-21968. 1871. Turnbull Brothers.

Dukesborough Tales. Richard Malcolm Johnston. LC 7-10532. (Harper's Franklin square library, no. 290). 1883. Harper & Brothers.

Dukesborough Tales: The Chronicles of Mr. Bill Williams. Richard Malcolm Johnston. LC 68-20015. (Americans in Fic.). 1968. 10.00. Gregg Pr.

Dukesborough Tales: The Chronicles of Mr. Bill Williams. Richard Malcolm Johnston. LC 3-21967. 1892. D. Appleton and Company.

Dulany-Furlong & Kindred Families. R. Furlong. 1975. 25.00 (ISBN 0-87012-209-6). McClain.

Dulcarnon. Henry Milner Rideout. LC 25-171539. 1925. Duffield and Company.

Dulce Pecadora. new ed. Franklin D. Reeve. (Pimienta Collection Ser). (Illus.). 160p. 1975. pap. 1.25 (ISBN 0-88473-235-5). Fiesta Pub.

Dulcibel: A Tale of Old Salem. Henry Peterson. LC 7-12980. 1907. The J. C. Winston Co.

Dulcie Bligh. Gail Clark. 1979. 1.95 (ISBN 0-671-82251-9). Pocket Books.

Dulcie Carlyon: A Novel. James Grant. LC 42-27124. 1886. G. Routledge and Sons.

Dulcimer Boy. Tor Seidler & David Hockney. LC 78-31351. 1979. 7.95 (ISBN 0-670-28609-5). Viking Press.

Dulcimer Street. Norman Collins. LC 47-30035. 1947. Duell, Sloan and Pearce.

Dull Miss Archinard. Anne Douglas Sedgwick. LC 8-6434. 1898. C. Scribner's Sons.

Dull Miss Archinard. Anne Douglas Sedgwick. 1902. The Century Co.

Dull the Sharp Edge: By Ellen Marsh. Ellen Marsh. LC 47-4136. 1947. E. P. Dutton & Company, Inc.

Dull Thud. Manning Long. LC 47-305641. 1947. Duell, Sloan and Pearce.

Dull Tree. Harry Canelstein. 1970. 3.95 o.p. Vantage.

Duluth. Gore Vidal. LC 82-40126. 13.95 (ISBN 0-394-52738-0). Random House.

Dumachas and Sheba: The Greatest Love Story Ever Told. Leonard Wise. LC 77-82975. 1979. 8.95 (ISBN 0-385-13127-5). Doubleday.

Dumaresq's Daughter. Grant Allen. LC 6-72. (On cover: Harper's Franklin square library, no. 910)). 1891. Harper & Brothers.

Dumaresq's Temptation. Charlotte Mary Brame. LC 44-38281. (On cover: Seaside library. Pocket ed. No. 1195). G. Munro.

Dumb-Animal and Other Stories. Osbert Sitwell. LC 31-930320. 1931. J. B. Lippincott Company.

Dumb-Bell and Others: The Great Dog Stories of John Taintor Foote. John Taintor Foote. 1946. D. Appleton-Century Co., Inc.

Dumb-Bell of Brookfield. John Taintor Foote. 1917. D. Appleton and Company.

Dumb-Bell of Brookfield. John Taintor Foote. LC 22-18649. 1922. D. Appleton and Company.

Dumb Dutch, by One of Them. Illus. by Frederic De Peyster Rothermel, Jacket Designed by Dorothy Rothermel. Special Bicentennial Ed. Abraham Heckman Rothermel. LC 48-18943. 1948. Church Center Press.

Dumb Foxglove: And Other Stories. Annie Trumbull Slosson. LC 79-142278. (Short story index reprint series). (Illus.). 1970. (ISBN 0-8369-3762-7). Books for Libraries Press.

Dumb Gods Speak. Edward Phillips Oppenheim. LC 37-854. 1937. Little, Brown, and Company.

Dumb Man. Isabel Adams. LC 33-21522. D. Appleton Century Company, Incorporated.

Dumb Witness. T. Arthur Plummer. LC 36-151606. The Macaulay Company.

Dumdum Murder. Carter Brown, pseud. LC 62-529441. (Carter Brown Mystery Series). New American Library of World Literature.

Dummy Murder Case. Milton K Ozaki. LC 51-25334. (Graphic mystery, 33). 1951. Graphic Pub. Co.

Dumpling: A Detective Love Story of a Great Labour Rising. Coulson Kernahan. LC 8-8306. 1907. B. W. Dodge and Company.

Dumps. authorized ed. Louisa Taylor Parr. LC 7-34717. (Lovell's international series, no. 122). J. W. Lovell Company.

Dunallan; or, Know What You Judge. Grace Kennedy. LC 7-11109. (On cover: Lovell's library, v. 3. no. 106). J. W. Lovell Company.

Dunbar's Cove. Borden Deal. LC 57-116634. 1957. Scribner.

Duncan Adair: Or, Captured in Escaping. A Story of One of Morgan's Men. Jane T. H Cross. LC 16-3404. 1864. Burke, Boykin & Company.

Duncan & Clotilda. Giovanni Guareschi. Tr. by L. K. Conrad. LC 68-14598. 1968. 4.95 o.p. (ISBN 0-374-14481-8). FS&G.

Duncan & Clotilda: An Extravaganza with a Long Digression. Giovanni Guareschi. LC 68-24598. 1968. 4.95. Farrar, Straus & Giroux.

Duncan Davidson. W. A. King. LC 28-113133. Dorance and Company.

Duncan Polite: The Watchman of Glenoro. Mary Esther MacGregor. LC 5-16118. F. L. Revell Company.

Duncan's Colony: A Novel. Natalie L. M. Petesch. LC 82-75463. 220p. 1982. 21.95 (ISBN 0-8040-0401-3); pap. 9.95 (ISBN 0-8040-0402-1). Swallow.

Duncraig. Monica Heath. 1974. (pbk.) 0.95. New American Library.

Duncton Wood. playboy books, ed. William Horwood. 2.75 (ISBN 0-87216-769-0).

Dune. Frank Herbert. LC 65-22547. 5.95. Chilton.

Dune Girl. Paul Largo. pap. 2.25 o.s.i. (Venus). Grove.

Dune House: A Story of Summer People in the Long Island Hamptons. Geraldine Trotta. LC 60-5168. (Red badge detective). 1960. Farrar, Straus and Cudahy.

Dune Messiah. Frank Herbert. (Berkley medallion book). 1975. (pbk.) 1.50 (ISBN 0-425-02952-2). Berkley Pub. Co.

Dune Witch. Evelyn Minshull. (Illus.). 218p. (YA) 1973. lib. bdg. 8.95 o.p. (ISBN 0-8161-6075-9, Large Print Bks). G K Hall.

Dunes: A Novel. Walter J Sheldon. LC 74-82010. 1974. 7.95 (ISBN 0-679-50477-X). McKay.

Dunes of Pradai. Tony R. Wayman. 1971. pap. 0.75 o.p. (07178). Curtis.

Dunfords Travels Everywheres. William Melvin Kelley. LC 70-118849. 1970. 5.95. Doubleday.

Dungeon Rock: Or, The Pirate's Cave, at Lynn. Nannette Snow Emerson. LC 6-37833. 1885. C. M. A. Twitchell, Printer.

Dunkerley's. Howard Spring. LC 47-30053. 1947. Harper & Brothers.

Dunkirk Directive. Donald Richmond. LC 79-65119. 1980. 10.95 (ISBN 0-8128-2687-6). Stein and Day.

Dunkirk Vikingess, and Other Stories. Lillian Mathilda Svenson. LC 52-25165. 1956. Story Book Press.

Dunleath Abbey: Or, The Fatal Inheritance. Hanson Penn Diltz. 1889. G. W. Dillingham.

Dunne Family. James Thomas Farrell. LC 75-36621. 1976. 8.95 (ISBN 0-385-11263-7). Doubleday.

Dunninger's Secrets. Walter Gibson. (O.s.i.). 8.95 o.s.i. Wehman.

Dunny, a Mountain Romance. Philip Verrill Mighels. 1906. Harper & Brothers.

Dunnybrook. Gladys Hasty Carroll. LC 43-16037. 1943. The Macmillan Company.

Dunnybrook. Gladys Hasty Carroll. LC 78-18801. (Illus.). 11.95 (ISBN 0-393-08822-7). Norton.

Dunnybrook. Rev. Ed. Gladys Hasty Carroll. LC 52-10381. 1952. Macmillan.

Dunwich Horror... Howard Phillips Lovecraft. LC 45-4136. (Bart house books. 12). 1945.

Dunwich Horror: And Others. Howard Phillips Lovecraft. LC 63-4565. 1963. Arkham House.

Dunwich Horror & Others. Howard Phillips Lovecraft. 1963. 12.95 (ISBN 0-87054-026-2). Arkham.

Duo. Sidonie Gabrielle Colette. Tr. by Blossom, Frederick Augustus. LC 36-17720. Farrar & Rinehart, Incorporated.

Duo and Le Toutounier: Two Novels. Sidonie Gabrielle Colette. LC 76-376518. 1976. 3.75 (ISBN 0-7206-0273-4). Owen.

Duo: The Girl with a Secret. Incident at a Corner. Charlotte Armstrong. LC 59-7121. 1959. Coward-McCann.

Dupe. Liza Cody. LC 81-9238. 9.95 (ISBN 0-684-17153-8). Scribner.

Dupe: A Story of the Sea. Robert S. Close. LC 47-11613. 1947. Vanguard Press.

Dupe Negative. Anthony Fowles. LC 73-150293. 1970 (ISBN 0-491-00225-4). W. H. Allen.

Dupe Negative. Anthony Fowles. LC 76-185340. (Inner sanctum mystery). 1972. 5.95 (ISBN 0-671-21164-1). Simon and Schuster.

Duplicate. H. Baldwin Taylor. LC 64-21726. 1964. Published for the Crime Club by Doubleday.

Duplicate Death. Arthur Charles FoxDavis. LC 10-9074. 1910. 1.50. The Macaulay Company.

Duplicate Death. Georgette Heyer. LC 69-13351. 1969. 4.95. Dutton.

Duplicate Keys. Jon Bracker. LC 77-3451. (Orig.). 1977. pap. 3.00x (ISBN 0-914476-61-0). Thorp Springs.

Duplicate Stiff. Archie O'Neill. (Jeff Pride series,#2). 1974. (pbk.) 0.95. Bantam Books.

Duplications. Kenneth Koch. 1977. 6.95 o.p. (ISBN 0-394-40614-1); pap. 3.95 (ISBN 0-394-73368-1). Random.

Dupree Blues. Dale Curran. LC 48-5943. 1948. A. A. Knopf.

Durable Fire. Dorothy James Roberts. LC 45-5349. 1945. The Macmillan Company.

Durable Fire. Howard Swiggett. LC 56-11576. 1957. Houghton Mifflin.

Durable Fire: A Novel of Elizabethan England 1577-1584. Sheila Bishop. 1976. 1.75. Ace.

Durango Street. Frank Bonham. 192p. 1972. pap. 2.25 (ISBN 0-440-92183-X, LFL). Dell.

Duration. George Palmer Putnam. LC 43-15968. 1943. Doubleday, Doran & Company, Inc.

Durawald. Theodore E Shea. LC 30-3952. The Stratford Company.

Durer's Angel: A Novel. Marie Claire Blais. LC 77-357898. 1976. 4.95 (ISBN 0-88922-111-1). Talonbooks.

Durez City Bonanza. Dan Roberts. LC 65-29982. 1965. Arcadia House.

Durian Tree. Michael Keon. LC 60-6093. 1960. Simon and Schuster.

During the Reign of the Queen of Persia: A Novel. Joan Chase. LC 82-48680. 14.95 (ISBN 0-06-015136-6). Harper & Row.

Durkett Sperret: A Novel. Sarah Barnwell Elliott. 1898. H. Holt and Company.

Durner's Spring. James J Rush. LC 79-26732. 9.95 (ISBN 0-8065-0732-2). Citadel Press.

Durrell Towers. Clarissa Ross, pseud. 1971. pap. 0.75 o.p. (T2505). Pyramid Pubns.

Durrell Towers. Clarissa Ross, pseud. 1976. pap. 1.25 o.p. (ISBN 0-515-04092-4). BJ Pub Group.

Dusantes: A Sequel to "The Casting Away of Mrs. Lecks and Mrs. Aleshine". Frank Richard Stockton. LC 8-15665. The Century Co.

Duse of the Beautiful Hands: An Imaginative Life. Sofia McQuaide De Bonis. LC 32-18952. Farrar & Rinehart, Incorporated.

Dusha. Jean L Backus. LC 71-142836. 1971. 5.95 (ISBN 0-8027-0345-3). Walker.

Dusk at the Grove. Samuel Rogers. LC 34-27218. 1934. Little, Brown, and Company.

Dusk of Day. Catherine Clark. LC 26-9670. 1926. T. Seltzer.

Dusk of Moonrise: A Novel. Desemea Wilson. LC 23-2882. E. P. Dutton & Company.

Duskin. Grace Livingston Hill. Repr. lib. bdg. 15.95x (ISBN 0-89190-038-1). Am Repr-Rivercity Pr.

Dusky Flesh see Sweet Humiliation.

Dusky Rose. Joanna Scott. 192p. (Orig.). 1980. pap. 1.50 (ISBN 0-671-57050-1). S&S.

Dust. Yael Dayan. LC 63-8773. 1963. World Pub. Co.

Dust. Emanuel Haldeman-Julius & Haldeman-Julius, Mrs. Anna Marcet (Haldeman) 1888- Joint Author. LC 21-4909. Brentano's.

Dust: A Novel. Julian Hawthorne. LC 7-3897. (On cover: Our continent library. v. 3). 1883. Fords, Howard & Hulbert.

Dust: A Novel of Hawaii. Armine Von Tempski. LC 28-608124. 1928. Frederick A. Stokes Company.

Dust Above the Sage. Vingie Eve Roe. LC 42-89092. 1942. M. S. Mill Co., Inc.

Dust and Laurels: A Study in Nineteenth Century Womanhood. Mary Lucy Pendered. LC 7-36374. 1894. D. Appleton and Company.

Dust and Sun. Clements Ripley. LC 29-16080. 1929. Payson & Clarke Ltd.

Dust Bowl Sailor. Gordon Wenczel Schindler. LC 44-4708. 1944. Arnold Press.

Dust Devil. Parris Afton Bonds. 320p. 1981. pap. 2.95 (ISBN 0-445-04667-8). Popular Lib.

Dust Devil. Walter S James, pseud. LC 57-12163. 1957. Abelard-Schuman.

Dust Flower. Basil King. LC 22-20345. 1922. Harper & Brothers.

Dust in the Afternoon. Holmes Moss Alexander. LC 40-30571. Harper & Brothers.

Dust in the Balance. George Knight. LC 7-14179. B. F. Fenno & Company.

Dust in the Wind. Richard O'Brien. (Jazz Age Ser.: No. 5). (Orig.). 1983. pap. 3.25 (ISBN 0-440-02158-8). Dell.

Dust in the Wind: Translated from the French by Mary Glasgow. Emile Danoen. LC 52-30191. 1952. Staples Press.

Dust Is My Pillow. Phyllis Hastings. LC 55-5639. 1955. Dutton.

Dust of Conflict. Harold Bindloss. LC 7-7189. 1907. F. A. Stokes Company.

Dust of Desire. Margaret Peterson. LC 23-6843. 1922. R. M. McBride & Company.

Dust of Dreams. Denise Robins. 1976. (pbk.) 1.25 (ISBN 0-380-00623-5). Avon.

Dust of Far Suns. Jack Vance, pseud. (Science Fiction Ser.). 1981. pap. 1.75 o.p. (ISBN 0-87997-588-1, UE1588). Daw Bks.

Dust of Mexico. Ruth Comfort Mitchell. LC 41-3909. 1941. D. Appleton-Century Company, Incorporated.

Dust of New York. Konrad Bercovici. LC 19-18642. 1919. Boni and Liveright.

Dust of Our Brothers' Blood," A Tale of Poland. Jona Konopko. Ed. by Calhoun, Earle C. The White Eagle Press.

Dust of the Desert. Robert Welles Ritchie. LC 22-17775. 1922. 1.75. Dodd, Mead and Company.
Dust of the Desert: Plain Tales of the Desert and the Border. Jack Weadock. LC 36-19561. 1936. D. Appleton-Century Company, Incorporated.
Dust of the Earth: A Historical Novel of Texas. 1st Ed. Londa Pickett Ogletree. LC 53-11267. 1953. Exposition Press.
Dust of the Road. Marjorie Patterson. LC 13-18222. 1913. 1.30. H. Holt and Company.
Dust of the Trail. Bennett Foster. LC 41-3118. 1941. Doubleday, Doran and Company, Inc.
Dust of the Trial. Bennett Foster. LC 42-17385. 1942. The Sun Dial Press.
Dust of the Yellow Sea. E. Beach. 6.95 o.p. (ISBN 0-03-076390-8). HR&W.
Dust on the King's Highway. Helen Constance White. 1947. The Macmillan Company.
Dust on the Sea. Edward Latimer Beach. LC 79-155503. 1972. 7.95 (ISBN 0-03-076390-8). Holt, Rinehart, and Winston.
Dust on the Sea. Edward Latimer Beach. 1973. (pbk) 1.75. Dell.
Dust Out Your Attic. Dusty Miller. 2.50 o.p. Carlton.
Dust Over the City. Translated by John Latrobe and Robert Gottlieb. Andre Langevin. LC 54-10484. 1955. Putnam.
Dust Over the Ruins. Helen Ashton. LC 36-785. 1936. The Macmillan Company.
Dust to Diamonds. Mary S. Craig. (Chicagoans Ser.: Bk. 1). 304p. (Orig.). 1981. pap. 2.95 (ISBN 0-515-05486-0). Jove Pubns.
Dust to Dust. Isabel Egenton Ostrander. LC 24-15680. 1924. R. M. McBride & Company.
Dust to Dust. Maris Randel. 1975. pap. 1.25 o.p. (ISBN 0-515-03664-1). Pyramid Pubns.
Dust Tracks on a Road. Zora Neale Hurston. LC 70-94133. (American Negro, His History and Literature). 1969. Arno Press.
Dust Under the Rug: Six Stories. 1st Ed. Joyce Gourfain. LC 53-208756. 1952. Pageant Press.
Dust Within the Rock. Frank Waters. LC 40-3857. Liveright Publishing Corporation.
Dusty. Frank Dalby Davison. LC 74-30243. 224p. 1975. 7.95 o.p. (ISBN 0-8092-8286-0). Contemp Bks.
Dusty: A Novel. Frank Dalby Davison. LC 74-30243. 1975. 7.95. Regnery.
Dusty: A Novel. Frank Dalby Davison. LC 46-630097. 1946. Coward-McCann, Inc.
Dusty Answer. Rosamond Lehmann. LC 74-17031. (Harvest book HB 307). 1975. (pbk.) 3.95 (ISBN 0-15-626290-8). Harcourt Brace Jovanovich.
Dusty Answer. Rosamond Lehmann. LC 27-20342. 1927. H. Holt and Company.
Dusty Answer. Rosamond Lehmann. LC 47-23771. 1947. Reynal & Hitchcock.
Dusty Boots: By Lee Thomas Pseud. Lee Floren. LC 50-12638. 1950. Phoenix Press.
Dusty Dan Delaney. Clement Yore. LC 30-5068. The Macaulay Company.
Dusty Dawn. Anne Duffield. 1953. Arcadia House.
Dusty Dawn. Anne Duffield. 1975. (pbk.) 1.25 (ISBN 0-425-02714-7). Berkley Pub. Co.
Dusty Death. Clifton Robbins. LC 32-7345. 1932. D. Appleton and Company.
Dusty Death: By Osmington Mills. Vivian Collin Brooks. LC 66-22227. 1966. bds., 3.25. Roy.
Dusty Death: Peter Clancy and Wiggar Solve a Unique Case. Lee Thayer. LC 66-11701. (Red badge detective). 1966. Dodd, Mead.
Dusty Godmother: A Novel. Michael Foster. LC 49-10595. 1949. Rinehart.
Dusty Highway. Christine Whiting Parmenter. LC 29-25608. Hale, Cushman & Flint.
Dusty Rivers. Raymond A Berry. LC 34-35321. 1934. Macrae-Smith Company.
Dusty Road. McDonald Feader. LC 34-30250. 1934. The Reilly & Lee Co.
Dusty Road. Therese Pauline Coles Tyler. LC 15-458920. 1915. J. B. Lippincott Company.
Dusty Spring. Elizabeth Seifert. LC 73-79148. 1973. 5.95. Aeonian Press.
Dusty Spring. Elizabeth Seifert. LC 46-76583. 1946. Dodd, Mead & Company.
Dusty Spurs. William Dudley Cotton. LC 57-771662. 1957. Arcadia House.
Dusty Wagons. Llewellyn Perry Holmes. LC 49-11610. 1949. Lippincott Co.
Dusty Wheels: By Lew Smith Pseud. Lee Floren. LC 55-793653. 1955. Arcadia House.
Dutch Courage. Ritchie Perry. 192p. 1982. pap. 2.25 (ISBN 0-345-29213-8). Ballantine.
Dutch Dominie of the Catskills: Or, The Times of the "Bloody Brandt.". David Murdoch. LC 7-25485. 1861. Derby & Jackson.
Dutch Interior. Frank O'Connor, pseud. LC 40-82087. 1940. A. A. Knopf.
Dutch Interior. Michael O'Donovan. LC 40-32087. 1940. A. A. Knopf.
Dutch Shea, Jr. A Novel. John Gregory Dunne. LC 81-19355. 1982. 16.50 (ISBN 0-671-41292-2). Linden Press/Simon & Schuster.
Dutch Shoe Mystery. Ellery Queen. 305p. 1976. lib. bdg. 15.75x (ISBN 0-89966-149-1). Buccaneer Bks.
Dutch Shoe Mystery. Ellery Queen, pseud. LC 79-19761. (Ellery Queen mystery). 1980. 10.95 (ISBN 0-89340-233-8). J. Curley.
Dutch Shoe Mystery: A Problem in Deduction. Ellery Queen, pseud. LC 31-25232. 1931. Frederick A. Stokes Company.
Dutch Treat: A Novel of World War II. Tristan Jones. LC 79-18856. 9.95 (ISBN 0-8362-6107-0). Andrews and McMeel.
Dutch Uncle. Marilyn Durham. LC 73-6601. 1973. 7.50 (ISBN 0-15-126930-0). Harcourt Brace Jovanovich.
Dutch Uncle. Marilyn Durham. LC 73-23115. 1974. (ISBN 0-8161-6189-5). G. K. Hall.
Dutch Vet: A Novel, Translated from the Dutch. A Roothaert & Renier, Fernand G., Tr. LC 40-30888. 1940. The Macmillan Company.
Dutch. 1st Ed. Theodore Bonnet. 1955. Doubleday.
Dutchess Hotspur. Rosamond Van Der Zee Marshall. 1971. pap. 0.75 o.p. (T2431). Pyramid Pubns.
Dutchess of Glover. Herbert Kubly. (Illus.). 1976. 1.95 (ISBN 0-380-00595-6). Avon Books.
Dutchman's Fireside. James Kirke Paulding. LC 5518. (Standard literature series. no. 44). University Publishing Company.
Dutchman's Fireside. A Tale. James Kirke Paulding. LC 7-34069. (Harper's stereotype ed.). 1831. J. & J. Harper.
Dutchman's Fireside. A Tale. 5th ed.... ed. James Kirke Paulding. 1837. Harper & Brothers.
Dutchman's Fireside. A Tale. James Kirke Paulding. Ed. by Paulding, William Irving. 1868. C. Scribner and Company.
Dutchman's Fireside. Ed. for the Modern Reader by Thomas F. O'Donnell. James Kirke Paulding. Ed. by Thomas Francis O'Donnell. LC 66-24151. (Masterworks of lit. ser.). 5.00, 2.25 pap.. College & Univ. Pr.
Dutiful Daughter. Vanessa Gray, pseud. LC 81-4815. 1981. 11.95 (ISBN 0-89340-327-X). J. Curley.
Dutiful Daughter. Thomas Keneally. LC 78-138491. 1971. 5.95 (ISBN 0-670-28661-3). Viking Press.
Duty Elsewhere. John William Wainwright. LC 78-21200. 7.95 (ISBN 0-312-22280-7). St. Martin's Press.
Duty First. Enzena Smith Williams. LC 50-3846. 1949. Humphries.
Duty Target. Barrie Anderson. 1977. 6.95 o.p. (ISBN 0-533-02895-7). Vantage.
Duty to Live. Emmett Dedmon. LC 46-1514. 1946. Houghton Mifflin Company.
Duty. With Illustrations of Courage, Patience and Endurance. Samuel Smiles. LC 21-15370. (Seaside library, v. 44, no. 891). 1880. G. Munro.
Duveen Letter. Edwin Leather. LC 80-624. 1980. 8.95 (ISBN 0-385-17038-6). Published for the Crime Club by Doubleday.
Duxberry Doings. Caroline Bigelow Le Row. LC 7-12829. Congregational Sunday School and Publishing Society.
Dva svetova see Two Worlds.
Dwarf. Par Fabian Lagerkvist. Tr. by Sibyl Alexandra Erikson. LC 45-10478. 1945. L. B. Fischer.
Dwarf Pine. 1st Ed. A Reiser. LC 55-10623. 1955. C. E. Tuttle Co.
Dwarf's Blood. Edith Olivier. LC 31-16668. 1931. The Viking Press.
Dwarf's Legacy. Tolly Kizilos. LC 76-2302. 8.95 (ISBN 0-87949-065-9). Ashley Books.
Dwasuparna: A Novel in Two Parts, 2 vols. Nishi Khanolkar. (Greenbird Bk.). 1976. Set. text ed. 20.00 (ISBN 0-89253-120-7); flexible bdg. 12.00 (ISBN 0-89253-136-3). Ind-US Inc.
Dwell Deep: Or, Hilda Thorn's Life Story. Amy Le Feuvre. LC 7-12603. F. H. Revell Company.
Dwell in the Wilderness. Alvah Cecil Bessie. LC 35-142414. Covici, Friede.
Dweller in the Hills. Sidney J. Taylor. 4.95 o.p. Vantage.
Dweller on the Borderland. Clara Hammond Lanza. LC 9-31674. 1909. 1.50. J. J. McVey.
Dweller on the Threshold. Robert Smythe Hichens. LC 11-4602. 1911. The Century Co.
Dweller on Two Planets: Or, The Dividing of the Way. Frederick Spencer Oliver. 1905. Baumgardt Publishing Company.
Dweller on Two Planets: Or, The Dividing of the Way. Frederick Spencer Oliver. LC 20-5581. 1920. Poseid Publishing Company.
Dweller on Two Planets: Or, The Dividing of the Way. 4th ed. Frederick Spencer Oliver. LC 24-28667. 1924. Poseid Publishing Company.
Dweller on Two Planets or the Dividing of the Way. Frederick Spencer Oliver. LC 73-94420. (Spiritual Fiction Publications: Vol. 2). 432p. 1982. Repr. of 1974 ed. 15.00 (ISBN 0-89345-402-8, Spiritual Fiction). Garber Comm.
Dwellers Beyond the Styx: Or, Tragedies of Love. Lincoln Hulley. LC 25-382. E. O. Painter Printing Co.
Dwellers in Arcady: The Story of an Abandoned Farm. Albert Bigelow Paine. LC 19-6662. 1919. Harper & Brothers.
Dwellers in Darkness. August William Derleth. LC 75-44848. 1976. 6.50 (ISBN 0-87054-074-2). Arkham House.
Dwellers in Five-Sisters Court. Horace Elisha Scudder. LC 8-3393. 1876. Hurd and Houghton.
Dwellers in Gotham: A Romance of New York. James Wesley Johnston. LC 98-2159. 1898. Eaton & Mains.
Dwellers in the Hills: A Novel. Melville Davisson Post. LC 1-31357. 1901. G. P. Putnam's Sons.
Dwellers in the Mirage. Abraham Merritt. LC 32-17144. Liveright, Inc.
Dwellers in the Mirage. Abraham Merritt. LC 44-47305. (Murder mystery monthly. No. 24). 1944. Avon Book Company.
Dwellers in the Mirage. Abraham Merritt. Bd. with Face in the Abyss. 1953. 5.95 o.s.i. (ISBN 0-87140-875-9). Liveright.
Dwellers of Riven Oak. Juanita Tyree Osborne. (YA) 1978. 6.95 (Avalon). Bouregy.
Dwelling of Playful Goddesses. Chang Wen-Ch'eng. Tr. by Howard S. Levy. 18.00. Oriental Bk Store.
Dwelling of Playful Goddesses. Tr. by Howard S. Levy. (Illus.). 1965. 4.50x o.p.; with Chinese text. 6.50x o.p. Paragon.
Dwelling of Playful Goddesses: China's First Love Novelette. Tsu Chang. 1965. 5.00 o.p. Levy.
Dwelling Place. Catherine Cookson. LC 78-142476. 1971. 6.95. Bobbs-Merrill.
Dwelling-Place of Light. Winston Churchill. LC 17-25746. 1917. The Macmillan Company.
Dwelling Places. Burke Davis. LC 80-11283. 10.95 (ISBN 0-684-16598-8). Scribner.
Dwight Craig. Donald MacRae. LC 47-3828. 1947. Houghton Mifflin Company.
Dybbuk. S. Ansky. Tr. by S. Morris Engel from Yiddish. LC 79-63047. (Illus.). 1979. Repr. of 1974 ed. pap. 5.95 (ISBN 0-89526-904-X). Regnery-Gateway.
Dyed for Death. Warrick W. Rider. (Orig.). 1980. pap. 1.95 o.s.i. (ISBN 0-505-51497-4). Tower Bks.
Dying Alderman. Aubrey-Fletcher, Henry Lancelot. LC 75-46004. (Fifty Classics of Crime Fiction, 1900-1950; 47). 1976. 12.00 (ISBN 0-8240-2396-X). Garland Pub.
Dying Alderman. Henry Lancelot Aubrey-Fletcher. LC 30-32332. Brewer & Warren, Inc.
Dying Alderman. Henry Wade. LC 75-46004. (Crime Fiction Ser). 1976. Repr. of 1930 ed. lib. bdg. 17.50 (ISBN 0-8240-2396-X). Garland Pub.
Dying Day. Wiodzimierz Odojewski. LC 64-15775. 1964. Harcourt, Brace & World.
Dying Earth. Jack Vance, pseud. (Kangaroo Book)). 1977. 1.25 (ISBN 0-671-81092-8). Pocket Books.
Dying Earth: By Jack Vance Pseud. Henry Kuttner. LC 50-58129. 1950. Hillman Periodicals.
Dying Echo: Adventure and Death in the Ancient Maya Cities of Yucatan. Kathleen Moore Knight. LC 49-8387. 1949. Pub. for the Crime Club by Doubleday.
Dying Fall. Hildegarde Dolson. LC 78-11282. 1981. 7.95 (ISBN 0-89340-181-1). J. Curley & Associates.
Dying Fall. Henry Wade. LC 80-8719. 256p. 1981. pap. 2.84i (ISBN 0-06-080543-9, P543, PL). Har-Row.
Dying Fall. Henry Wade. pap. 0.95 o.p. (02631, Collier). Macmillan.
Dying Fall: A Mystery Novel. Hildegarde Dolson. LC 72-14240. 1973. 5.95 (ISBN 0-397-00955-0). Lippincott.
Dying Fall: By Henry Wade Pseud. Harry Lancelot Aubrey-Fletcher. LC 55-3966. (Cock Robin mystery). 1955. MacMillan.
Dying for Tomorrow. Michael Moorcock. (Science Fiction Ser). 1978. pap. 1.50 o.p. (ISBN 0-87997-366-8, UW1366). DAW Bks.
Dying in the Night. Jan Roffman. LC 73-83665. (Crime Club Ser.). 192p. 1974. 4.95 o.p. (ISBN 0-385-07197-3). Doubleday.
Dying in the Night. Margaret Summerton. (Ace gothic). 1975. (pbk.) 0.95. Ace Books.
Dying in the Sun. P. Palangyo. (African Writers Ser.). 1968. pap. text ed. 4.00x (ISBN 0-435-90053-6). Heinemann Ed.
Dying Inside. Robert Silverberg. LC 72-1231. 1972. 6.95 (ISBN 0-684-13083-1). Scribner.
Dying Inside. Robert Silverberg. 1973. (pbk.) 1.25 (ISBN 0-345-23563-0). Ballantine Books.
Dying Light. Evan Chandler. (Signet Book). 1979. 1.95 (ISBN 0-451-08465-9). New American Library.
Dying of Fright. Les Daniels. (Encore Edition). 1976. 5.95 o.p. (ISBN 0-684-15399-8). Scribner.
Dying of Fright: Masterpieces of the Macabre. Les Daniels. LC 75-43969. (Illus.). 12.95 (ISBN 0-684-14624-X). Scribner.
Dying of the Light. Brian Glanville. LC 76-379373. 1976. 3.50 (ISBN 0-436-18111-8). Secker and Warburg.
Dying of the Light. George R. R Martin. LC 77-22833. 9.95 (ISBN 0-671-22861-7). Simon & Schuster.
Dying of the Light. George R. R Martin. (Pocket Book). 1978. 1.95 (ISBN 0-671-81130-4). Pocket Books.
Dying Room. Manning Lee Stokes. LC 47-11532. Phoenix Press.
Dying Space. Warren Murphy. (Destroyer Ser.: No. 47). 208p. (Orig.). 1982. pap. 2.25 (ISBN 0-523-41557-5). Pinnacle Bks.
Dyke Controversy: "a Story of Politics and the Dykelands". Alfred Scott Burns. LC 35-1812. 1934. Meador Publishing Company.
Dyke Darrel, the Railroad Detective: Or The Crime of the Midnight Express. A. Frank Pinkerton. LC 7-39638. (On cover: The Pinkerton detective series). F. C. Laird.
Dyke's Corners. E Clarence Oakley. LC 9-14215. 1909. R. G. Badger.
Dynamite. Louis Adamic. (Cherry Pie Ser.). (O.s.i.). pap. 2.45 o.s.i. (ISBN 0-394-70602-1). Chelsea Hse.
Dynamite. Thomas F Sullivan. LC 72-86215. 1973. 4.00 (ISBN 0-8059-1741-1). Dorrance.
Dynamite Cartridge. By Mrs. Frances Grant Teetzel... Frances Grant Teetzel. 1885. Cleaves, Macdonald & Co.
Dynamite Freaks. Donald Ryan. 160p. 1972. pap. 0.95 o.p. (532-95187-095). Woodhill.
Dynamite Freaks. Donald Ryan. 160p. 1972. pap. 0.95 o.p. (532-95187-095). Manor Bks.
Dynamite Monster Boogie Concert. Paul Ross. 1975. (pbk.) 0.95. Popular Library.
Dynamite Ship. Donald Mackay. LC 7-199873. 1888. Manhattan Publishing House.
Dynamiter. Robert Louis Stevenson & Fanny Van De Grift Osbourne Stevenson. LC 77-152959. (Short story index reprint series). 1971. (ISBN 0-8369-3874-7). Books for Libraries Press.
Dynamiter. authors' ed. Robert Louis Stevenson & Fanny Van De Grift Osbourne Stevenson. LC 8-160895. (Leisure hour series, no. 162). 1885. H. Holt and Company.
Dynamiter. Robert Louis Stevenson & Fanny Van De Grift Osbourne Stevenson. (On cover: Lovell's library, no. 770). 1886. J. W. Lovell Company.
Dynamiter. Robert Louis Stevenson & Fanny Van De Grift Osbourne Stevenson. (On cover: Seaside library. Pocket ed. bo. 855). 1886. G. Munro.
Dynamiter: More New Arabian Nights. Robert Louis Stevenson & Stevenson, Fanny (Van De Grift) LC 6-18296. (biographical edition of the works of Robert Louis Stevenson). 1905. Scribner.
Dynast. Paul Erikson. 1982. pap. 2.95 (ISBN 0-425-05304-0). Berkley Pub.
Dynasty. Jack Ansell. 1976. 1.75 (ISBN 0-515-03827-X). Pyramid Publications.
Dynasty. Robert S. Elegant. 864p. 1982. pap. 3.50 (ISBN 0-449-23655-2, Crest). Fawcett.
Dynasty. Robert S. Elegant. 672p. 1977. 10.95 (ISBN 0-07-019172-7, GB). McGraw.
Dynasty. Clarence Budington Kelland. LC 29-59578. 1929. Harper & Brothers.
Dynasty. Tony Morphett. LC 68-24167. 1968. 6.50. D. McKay Co.
Dynasty: A Medical Novel. 1st Ed. Charles H Knickerbocker. LC 62-7654. N. Y.
Dynasty of Air. Jack Ansell. LC 74-187807. 1974. 7.95 (ISBN 0-87795-094-6). Arbor House.
Dynasty of Death. Taylor Caldwell. LC 79-111147. 1970. 7.95. Doubleday.
Dynasty of Death. Taylor Caldwell. LC 38-27629. 1938. C. Scribner's Sons.
Dynasty of Death. Taylor Caldwell. LC 47-20000. 1946. The Sun Dial Press.
Dynasty of Death. An Abridged Ed. Taylor Caldwell. LC 57-379227. (Cardinal edition, C-252. Fiction, 2). 1957. Pocket Books.
Dynasty of Death: Novel About a Great Munitions Empire. Taylor Caldwell. (O.s.i.). 7.95 o.s.i. (ISBN 0-385-01066-4). Doubleday.
Dynasty of Decadence. Nick Allan. (Orig.). pap. 0.95 o.p. (999). Brandon.
Dynasty of Desire. Elizabeth Zachary. 1978. pap. 2.50 (ISBN 0-440-02024-7). Dell.
Dynasty of Doom. P. A Foxall. LC 72-3667. 1972. 3.95 (ISBN 0-87749-315-4). Drake Publishers.
Dynasty of Fear. Joyce Claypool Sprague. 1973. 4.95 (ISBN 0-517-51506-7). Lenox Hill Press.
Dynasty of Power. David Thoreau. LC 81-71677. 1982. 14.50 (ISBN 0-87795-383-X). Arbor Hse.
Dynasty of Spies. Dan Sherman. LC 79-54012. 11.95 (ISBN 0-87795-255-8). Arbor House.
Dynevor Terrace: Or, The Clue of Life. Charlotte Mary Yonge. LC 41-42362. 1857. D. Appleton and Company.
Dynostar Menace. Kit Pedler & Gerry Davis. LC 75-40937. 7.95 (ISBN 0-684-14604-5). Scribner.

Dyskolos. Menander. Tr. by Carroll Moulton. (Orig.). 1977. pap. 1.50 (ISBN 0-451-61540-9, MW1540, Ment). NAL.
Dystopian Visions. Roger Elwood. LC 75-25544. 1975. 7.95 (ISBN 0-13-222216-7). Prentice-Hall.
Dzintara Gredzens. Ed. by Apgads. (Latvian). 6.80 o.p. (ISBN 0-87908-301-8). Rota Pr.

E

E" Company. Frank O'Rourke. LC 45-6826. 1945. Simon and Schuster.
E. K. Means. Eldred Kurtz Means. LC 72-8554. (Black Heritage Library Collection). 1972. (ISBN 0-8369-9190-7). Books for Libraries Press.
E. K. Means. Is This a Title? It Is Not. It Is the Name of a Writer of Negro Stories, Who Has Made Himself So Completely the Writer of Negro Stories That His Book Needs No Title. Illustrated by Kemble. Eldred Kurtz Means. LC 18-15875. 1918. G. P. Putnma's Sons.
E Pluribus Bang! David Lippincott. LC 70-123027. 1970. 5.95. Viking Press.
E Pluribus Unicorn. Theodore Sturgeon. 1979. pap. 1.95 (ISBN 0-671-83149-6, Timescape). PB.
E Pluribus Unicorn: A Collection of Short Stories. Edward Hamilton Waldo, pseud. (Kangaroo Book). 1977. 1.50 (ISBN 0-671-81355-2). Pocket Books.
E Pluribus Unum: A Story of Today and of Today's Tomorrow. Quain. LC 37-104928. Patriot Publishing Company.
E. Q's Big Book. Containing the Two Complete Mystery Stories: The Siamese Twin Mystery; The Greek Coffin Mystery. Ellery Queen, pseud. Grosset & Dunlap.
E S P Coed. Rudell R. Grissett. 2.95 o.p. Carlton.
E. S. P. Worm. Robert Margroff & Piers Anthony. (Orig.). 1970. pap. 0.60 o.p. (ISBN 0-446-63357-7, 63-357). Paperback Lib.
E. S. Pionage. William S Doxey. (Belmont Tower Book). 1.95 (ISBN 0-505-51363-3). Tower Publications.
E. T. The Extra-Terrestrial. William Kotzwinkle. 1982. 12.95 (ISBN 0-399-12730-5). Putnam Pub Group.
E. T. The Extra Terrestrial. William Kotzwinkle. 256p. 1982. pap. 2.95 (ISBN 0-425-05453-5). Berkley Pub.
E: The Complete and Somewhat Mad History of the Family of Montague Vincent, Esq., Gent. Julian Hinckley. LC 14-78730. 1914. 1.35. Duffield & Company.
Each Alone. Harriet Ball. LC 42-12026. 1942. Harper & Brothers.
Each and All: The Seven Little Sisters Prove Their Sisterhood; a Companion to "The Seven Little Sisters Who Live on the Round Ball That Floats in the Air", "Ten Boys Who Lived on the Road from Long Ago to Now"... Etc. Jane Andrews. LC 5-37587. Ginn & Company.
Each Bright River: A Novel of the Oregon Country. Mildred Masterson McNeilly. LC 50-6117. 1950. Morrow.
Each Dawn I Die. Jerome Odlum. LC 38-103372. The Bobbs-Merrill Company.
Each Day Is New. Orville Steggerde. LC 57-23338. Zondervan Pub. House.
Each Day's Proud Battle. Josephine Hornik Winn. LC 61-5825. New York.
Each for All. Iuri Nagibin. LC 45-10365. 1945. Hutchinson & Co., Ltd.
Each in His Darkness. Julien Green. LC 61-14977. 1961. Pantheon Books.
Each Life to Live. Richard Gehman. LC 54-24192. (Gold medal books. Red seal books, 8). 1952. Fawcett Publications.
Each Life Unfulfilled: A Novel of to-Day Dealing with American Life. Anna Chapin Ray. LC 99-1351. 1899. Little, Brown, and Company.
Each Man's Son. Hugh MacLennan. LC 51-10097. 1951. Little, Brown.
Each Moment Is Measured. Mozelle Ferguson. LC 66-24870. 1966. Dorrance.
Each One Was Alone. Donald Barr Chidsey. LC 38-27267. 1938. A. A. Knopf.
Each Purple Curtain. Wallace Perry. LC 54-10176. 1954. Naylor Co.
Each Shadow Moving: A Novel. Howard Jones. LC 52-17544. 1951. T. V. Boardman.
Each Shining Hour. Lida Larrimore Turner Thomas. LC 48-5317. 1948. Macrae-Smith Co.
Each Thief Passing by. E. M Swift. LC 81-5997. 11.95 (ISBN 0-316-82540-9). Little, Brown.
Each to His Own Ground. John S. Wade. 1979. signed ed. 20.00; 10.00; pap. 4.50. Juniper Pr WI.
Eager Love. May Christie. LC 29-18415. Grosset & Dunlap.
Eager Vines. Bonnie Melbourne Busch. LC 26-12836. W. J. Watt & Co.
Eagle. Dorothy Hamilton. LC 74-13069. 1974. 4.95 (ISBN 0-8361-1748-4). Herald Press.
Eagle and His Egg. Mark Rascovich. 1966. bds., 4.95. Atheneum.
Eagle and the Cross. Hubertus Prince Loewenstein. LC 47-2842. 1947. The Macmillan Company.
Eagle and the Dove. Douglas Kent Hall. LC 76-5831. 1976. (ISBN 0-690-01171-7). Crowell.
Eagle and the Dove. Ruth Freeman Solomon. LC 73-97081. 1971. 7.95. Putnam.
Eagle and the Iron Cross. Glendon Fred Swarthout. LC 66-26042. 1966. New American Library.
Eagle & the Raven. Pauline Gedge. 480p. 1978. 10.95 (ISBN 0-8037-2328-8). Dial.
Eagle & the Raven. Pauline Gedge. 1980. pap. 2.95 (ISBN 0-445-04511-6). Popular Lib.
Eagle and the Rock. 1st Ed. Frances Winwar. LC 52-11699. 1953. Harper.
Eagle & the Serpent. Lee Jackson. 304p. (Orig.). 1982. pap. 2.95 (ISBN 0-515-05733-9). Jove Pubns.
Eagle and the Sword. Harvey K Schreiber. 1979. 1.75 (ISBN 0-445-04346-6). Popular Library.
Eagle and the Wind. Herbert E Stover. LC 53-8404. 1953. Dodd, Mead.
Eagle and the Wren. Roland Pertwee. LC 24-10850. 1923. Cassell and Company, Ltd.
Eagle at My Eyes. Norman Katkov. LC 48-4453. 1948. Doubleday.
Eagle at the Gate. Rona Randall. LC 77-10062. 1978. 8.95 (ISBN 0-698-10863-9). Coward, McCann & Geoghegan.
Eagle at the Gate. Rona Randall. LC 78-16485. 1978. 13.95 (ISBN 0-8161-6601-3). G. K. Hall.
Eagle at the Gate. Rona Randall. 1979. 2.25 (ISBN 0-380-42846-6). Avon Books.
Eagle Badge: Or. The Skokums of the Allagash. Holman Francis Day. LC 8-29336. 1908. Harper & Brothers.
Eagle Blood. James Creelman. LC 2-23845. 1902. Lothrop Publishing Company.
Eagle Eye. Hortense Calisher. LC 73-82181. 1973. 7.50 (ISBN 0-87795-062-8). Arbor House.
Eagle-Feather. Catherine Isabel Dodd. LC 33-33463. 1933. D. Appleton and Company.
Eagle Flight: A Filipino Novel. Jose Rizal Y Alonso. LC 6301. 1900. McClure, Phillips & Co.
Eagle Fur. Robert Newton Peck. LC 77-13103. 1978. 7.95 (ISBN 0-394-42785-8). Knopf.
Eagle Has Landed. Jack Higgins, pseud. 368p. 1976. pap. 2.75 (ISBN 0-553-13848-0, A13848-0). Bantam.
Eagle Has Landed. Jack Higgins, pseud. (Adult Series). 1975. Repr. lib. bdg. 14.95 o.p. (ISBN 0-8161-6330-8, Large Print Bks). G K Hall.
Eagle Has Landed. Henry Patterson. LC 74-15475. 1975. 8.95 (ISBN 0-03-013746-2). Holt, Rinehart and Winston.
Eagle Has Landed. Henry Patterson. LC 75-30977. 1975. 14.95 (ISBN 0-8161-6330-8). G. K. Hall.
Eagle in a Butterfly Net. Charles N. Aronson. LC 74-22641. (Illus.). 1975. 12.50. C. N. Aronson Book Publisher.
Eagle in the Air: A Novel. Rose Robinson. LC 73-76235. 1969. 4.95. Crown Publishers.
Eagle in the Sky. Francis Van Wyck Mason. (Berkley medallion book). 1975. (pbk.) 1.95 (ISBN 0-425-02993-X). Berkley.
Eagle in the Sky. Francis Van Wyck Mason. LC 48-5212. 1948. J. B. Lippincott Co.
Eagle in the Sky. Wilbur A Smith. LC 73-22792. 1974. 7.95 (ISBN 0-385-06648-1). Doubleday.
Eagle in the Sky. Wilbur A. Smith. 1975. (pbk.) 1.95. Dell.
Eagle in the Sky. F. Van Wyck Mason. 1975. pap. 1.95 (ISBN 0-425-02993-X, Medallion). Berkley Pub.
Eagle in the Snow: A Novel. Wallace Breem. LC 76-124275. (Illus.). 1970. 5.95. Putnam.
Eagle in the Sun. Hoffman Birney. LC 35-19676. 1935. G. P. Putnam's Sons.
Eagle King. Henry Treece. LC 65-10178. 1965. Random House.
Eagle Man. H. V. Elkin. (Cutler Ser.: No. 1). 1978. pap. 1.50 o.s.i. (ISBN 0-505-51295-5). Tower Bks.
Eagle of the Empire: A Story of Waterloo. Cyrus Townsend Brady. LC 15-800435. George H. Doran Company.
Eagle of the Gredos. Claude Jack Osgood. LC 42-21437. 1942. Reynal & Hitchcock.
Eagle on the Coin. Robert Verlin Cassill. LC 50-9546. 1950. Random House.
Eagle on the Plain: A Novel. Victor Wolfson. LC 47-470046. 1947. Simon and Schuster.
Eagle on the Sun. Julia Davis. LC 56-72533. 1956. Rinehart.
Eagle Pass. Lauran Paine. LC 68-550. 1967. Arcadia House.
Eagle Song: A Novel, Based on True Events. James A. Houston. LC 82-15759. 14.95 (ISBN 0-15-127117-8). Harcourt Brace Jovanovich.
Eagle Wing. J. A. McLeod. 3.50 o.p. Carlton.
Eagles. Maggie Hill Davis. LC 80-14471. 1980. 13.95 (ISBN 0-688-03727-5). W. Morrow.
Eagles Depart. John Gloag. LC 72-96494. (Illus.). 1973. 7.25. St. Martin's Press.
Eagle's Eye: A True Story of the Imperial German Government's Spies and Intrigues in America from Facts Furnished by William J. Flynn, Recently Retired Chief of the U. S. Secret Service. Courtney Ryley Cooper & Flynn, William James. LC 19-1338. 1.50. Prospect Press, Inc.
Eagle's Feather. Emily Price Post. LC 10-271913. 1910. 1.25. Dodd, Mead and Company.
Eagle's Feather: A Novel. William Campbell Douglass. LC 66-23934. 1966. Free Men Speak.
Eagles Fly. Sean Flannery, pseud. 320p. 1982. pap. 3.25 (ISBN 0-441-18018-3, Pub. by Charter Bks). Ace Bks.
Eagles Fly High: A Novel. Elizabeth Bartol Dewing Kaup. LC 29-14906. 1929. Frederick A. Stokes Company.
Eagles Fly West. Edward Maddin Ainsworth. 1946. The Macmillan Company.
Eagles Gather. Taylor Caldwell. LC 40-2382. 1940. C. Scribner's Sons.
Eagle's Gift. Carlos Castaneda. 1981. 14.95 o.s.i. (ISBN 0-671-23087-5). S&S.
Eagle's Gift. Carlos Castenada. 1982. pap. 3.95 (ISBN 0-671-44226-0). PB.
Eagle's Gift. Carlos Castenada. 1983. pap. text ed. write for info. (ISBN 0-671-47070-1, Touchstone Bks). S&S.
Eagle's Heart. sunset edition. new york, harper. ed. Hamlin Garland. LC 72-84702. (Illus.). 1974. (lib. ed.) 14.95 (ISBN 0-403-02987-2). Scholarly Press.
Eagle's Heart. Hamlin Garland. 1900. D. Appleton and Company.
Eagle's Mate. Anna Alice Chapin. LC 14-1106. 1.25. W. J. Watt & Company.
Eagle's Mile. James Dickey. 1981. 6.00 (ISBN 0-89723-028-0); ltd. ed. 20.00 (ISBN 0-89723-029-9). Bruccoli.
Eagle's Nest. easy eye ed. Dorothy Daniels. (Orig.). 1968. pap. 0.75 o.p. (74-970). Lancer.
Eagle's Nest. Dorothy Daniels. 1973. pap. 0.95 o.s.i. (75-453). Lancer.
Eagle's Nest. Anna Kavan. 180p. 1982. 12.95 (ISBN 0-7206-2835-0, Pub. by Peter Owen). Merrimack Pub Cir.
Eagles of Malice. Alan Scholefield. LC 68-25486. (Illus.). 1968. 5.50. W. Morrow.
Eagles of the East: Short Stories. Mary R. Cline. 96p. 1975. 4.50 o.p. (ISBN 0-682-48215-3). Exposition.
Eagles of Two Continents: A Civil War Story. Leslie Konnyu. 1963. pap. 1.25 o.p. (ISBN 0-911862-05-6). Hungarian Rev.
Eagles Over Big Sur. Jack Curtis. 144p. (Orig.). 1981. pap. 7.95 (ISBN 0-88496-160-5). Capra Pr.
Eagles Pawn. Clare F. Holmes. 216p. 1981. pap. 1.95 (ISBN 0-441-18021-3). Ace Bks.
Eagle's Quest; a Prince's Fight for Freedom. Charlotte Bacskay Lederer. LC 39-27919. 1939. Doubleday, Doran & Company, Inc.
Eagle's Shadow. James Branch Cabell. 69.95 (ISBN 0-87968-088-1). Gordon Pr.
Eagle's Shadow. Arthur Douglas Howden Smith. LC 31-30502. 1931. J. B. Lippincott Company.
Eagle's Shadow: A Comedy of Purse-Strings. rev. ed. James Branch Cabell. LC 24-127. 1923. R. M. McBride & Company.
Eagle's Song. Anne Miller Downes. LC 49-8193. 1949. J. B. Lippincott Co.
Eagle's Talon. Georges Ohnet. Tr. by Meyer, Helen. LC 13-22214. 1913. 1.25. G. P. Putnam's Sons.
Eagles: the Hill of the Dead see Hill of the Dead.
Eagles Where I Walk. 1st Ed. Stephen Longstreet. LC 61-12549. 1961. Doubleday.
Eagle's Wing: A Story of the Colorado. Bertha Muzzy Sinclair. LC 24-345621. 1924. Little, Brown, and Company.
Eagle's Wings. William Hardwick Ruth. LC 45-100844. (Contemporary poets of Dorrance (292).
Eagle's Wings to Higher Places. Hannah Hurnard. LC 82-48406. 160p. 1983. pap. 4.76i (HarpR). Har-Row.
Eagle's Wings to the Higher Places. Hannah Hurnard. 160p. 1983. pap. 4.95 (HarpJ). Har-Row.
Eagles' Wings to the Higher Places. Hannah Hurnard. LC 82-48406. 4.76 (ISBN 0-06-064084-7). Harper & Row.
Eagles' Wings to the Higher Places. Hannah Hurnard. (Orig.). 1983. pap. 4.95 (ISBN 0-06-064084-7). Har-Row.
Eaglescliffe. Marjorie McEvoy. Ed. by Alice Sachs. 1971. 3.95 o.p. Lenox Hill.
Eaglesmere Trio. Edwin MacMinn. LC 7-20115. 1883. American Baptist Publication Society.
Ealdwood. C. J Cherryh. LC 81-185895. (Illus.). 1981. 25.00. D.M. Grant.
Eames-Erskine Case: A Detective Novel. Archibald E. Fielding. LC 25-9299. 1925. A. A. Knopf.
Ear: By Stewart Sterling Pseud. 1st Ed. Prentice Winchell. LC 52-10420. 1953. Dutton.
Ear in the Wall. Arthur Benjamin Reeve. LC 16-23090. 1916. Hearst's International Library Co.
Ear Witness: Fifty Characters. Elias Canetti. LC 78-31192. (Continuum book). 1979. 8.95 (ISBN 0-8164-9357-X). Seabury Press.
Earhart Betrayal. James Stewart Thayer. LC 79-25888. 10.95 (ISBN 0-399-12485-3). Putnam.
Earhart Legacy. Peter Tanous. (O.s.i.). 1979. 8.95 o.s.i. (ISBN 0-671-24265-2). S&S.
Earhart Mission. Peter Tanous. LC 78-15793. 8.95 (ISBN 0-671-24265-2). Simon and Schuster.
Earl. Cecelia Holland. LC 78-154913. 1971. 6.95 (ISBN 0-394-46189-4). Knopf.
Earl Derr Biggers Tells Ten Stories. Earl Derr Biggers. LC 33-24658. The Bobbs-Merrill Company.
Earl Derr Biggers' The House Without a Key; a Charlie Chan Mystery Play in Three Acts, Dramatized from the Novel. Jean Lee Latham. LC 42-51153. 1942. The Dramatic Publishing Company.
Earl of Chicago. Brock Williams. LC 37-3288. The Bobbs-Merrill Company.
Earl of Hell. Joseph Gray Kitchell. LC 24-887839. The Century Co.
Earl of Mayfield. A Novel. Thomas P. May. T. B. Peterson & Brothers.
Earl of Mayfield. An Historical Novel. 8th ed. rev. by the author... ed. Thomas P May. LC 7-26238. T. B. Peterson & Brothers.
Earl of Rossville Hall. Lady Lois Pinkston. LC 6-25176. 1906. The Neale Publishing Company.
Earl Stimson. Phebe Consalus Bullard. LC 6-19662. The American News Company.
Earl T. Jackson. T. O McLendon. LC 30-12691. The Christopher Publishing House.
Earle Wayne's Nobility. A Novel. Sarah Elizabeth Forbush Downs. LC 6-45945. 1882. G. W. Carleton & Co. Etc.
Earlier Stories. 1st- 2d series... ed. Frances Hodgson Burnett. LC 6-16429. 1891. C. Scribner's Sons.
Earlier Stories. 1st-2d series... ed. Frances Hodgson Burnett. LC 6-27354. 1906. C. Scribner's Sons.
Earlier Stories. 1st-series... ed. Frances Hodgson Burnett. LC 7-5684. C. Scribner's Sons.
Earliest Dreams. Nancy Hale. LC 36-8548. 1936. C. Scribner's Sons.
Earl's Atonement. Bertha M. Clay. LC 44-39235. (On cover: Lovell's library, v. 9, no. 465). J. W. Lovell Company.
Earl's Atonement. Bertha M. Clay. LC 44-39238. (On cover: The Primrose series. No. 28). Street & Smith.
Earl's Atonement. A Novel. G. Munro.
Earl's Daughter. Elizabeth Missing Sewell & Sewell, William, 1804-1874, Ed. LC 31-19519. 1850. D. Appleton & Company.
Earl's Error. Charlotte Mary Brame. LC 44-112531. (On cover: Lovell's library, no. 1042). John W. Lovell Company.
Earl's Error; and, Arnold's Promise. Charlotte Mary Brame. LC 44-38089. (On cover: Seaside library. Pocket ed. No. 990). G. Munro.
Earl's Fancy. Charlotte Hines. (Second Chance at Love Ser.: No. 93). 1982. pap. 1.74 (ISBN 0-515-06855-1). Jove Pubns.
Earl's Heirs. A Tale of Domestic Life. Ellen Wood. T. B. Peterson & Brothers.
Early Americana and Other Stories. Conrad Richter. LC 36-21011. 1836. A. A. Knopf.
Early Americana and Other Stories. Conrad Richter. LC 78-14505. (Gregg Press Western Fiction Series). 1978. 10.95 (ISBN 0-8398-2468-8). Gregg Press.
Early Asimov. Isaac Asimov. LC 72-76116. 528p. 1972. 10.00 (ISBN 0-385-03979-4). Doubleday.
Early Asimov, Bk. 1. Isaac Asimov. 1978. pap. 2.25 (ISBN 0-449-23873-3, Crest). Fawcett.
Early Asimov, Bk. 2. Isaac Asimov. 304p. 1978. pap. 2.25 (ISBN 0-449-23700-1, Crest). Fawcett.
Early Asimov: Book One. Isaac Asimov. LC 72-76116. (Fawcett crest book). 1974. (pbk.) 1.25. Fawcett.
Early Autumn. Louis Bromfield. 264p. Repr. of 1926 ed. lib. bdg. 14.65x (ISBN 0-88411-508-9). Amereon Ltd.
Early Autumn. Robert B. Parker. (O.s.i.). 1981. 10.95 o.s.i. (ISBN 0-440-02248-7, Sey Lawr). Delacorte.
Early Autumn. Robert B. Parker. 1981. pap. 2.50 (ISBN 0-440-12214-7). Dell.
Early Autumn: A Spenser Novel. Robert B. Parker. LC 80-17736. 9.95 (ISBN 0-440-02248-7). Delacorte Press/S. Lawrence.
Early Autumn: A Story of a Lady. Louis Bromfield. LC 26-17996. 1926. Frederick A. Stokes Company.
Early Bird: A Business Man's Love Story. George Randolph Chester. LC 10-11878. 1.50. The Bobbs-Merrill Company.

Early Boyd. Carter Brown, pseud. (Signet book). 1975. (pbk.) 0.95. New American Library.
Early Candlelight, a Novel. minnesota territorial centennial ed. Maud Hart Lovelace. LC 49-8656. 1949. University of Minnesota Press.
Early Candlelight: A Novel. Maud Hart Lovelace. LC 29-17999. The John Day Company.
Early Closing. D. Wynne Willson. LC 32-6664. 1932. Doubleday, Doran & Company, Inc.
Early Dawn: Or, Sketches of Christian Life in England in the Olden Time. Elizabeth Rundle Charles & Smith, Henry Boynton. LC 6-20157. 1864. Dodd, Mead & Co.
Early Dawn: Or, Sketches of Christian Life in England in the Olden Time. Elizabeth Rundle Charles & Smith, Henry Boynton. LC 6-20156. 1864. M. W. Dodd.
Early Del Rey. Lester Del Rey. LC 74-9484. 1975. 7.95 (ISBN 0-385-02740-0). Doubleday.
Early Engagements: And Florence. (a Sequel. Sarah Marshall Hayden. LC 7-3752. 1854. Moore, Anderson, Wilstach & Keys.
Early English Prose Romances. new ed., rev. and enl. ed. Ed. by William John Thoms. Morley, Henry, 1822-1894, Ed. LC 24-11848. (Library of early novelists, ed. by E. A. Baker. v.11). 1906. G. Routledge and Sons, Limited.
Early English Versions of the Tales of Guiscardo and Ghismonda and Titus and Gisippus from the Decameron. Giovanni Boccaccio et al. LC 38-13659. (Early English Text Soceity Original Ser.). (Half-title: Early English text society. Original series, no. 205. 1935 (for 1936: No. 205). 1937. Pub. for the Early English Text Society by H. Milford, Oxford University Press.
Early Essays. George Eliot. LC 77-6728. 1977. 10.00 (ISBN 0-8414-3965-6). Folcroft Library Editions.
Early Frost. Clare Jaynes, pseud. LC 52-5150. 1952. Random House.
Early History of a Sewing-Machine Operator. Nathan Reznikoff & Reznikoff, Charles, 1894- Joint Author. LC 36-15978. C. Reznikoff.
Early History of Jacob Stahl. John Davys Beresford. LC 11-9900. 1.35. Little, Brown, and Company.
Early in the Morning. Introd. by John Mason Brown. 1st Ed. Marion Edey. LC 54-6703. 1954. Harper.
Early in the Summer of 1970. Abraham B Yehoshua. LC 76-16262. 1977. 5.95 (ISBN 0-385-02590-4). Doubleday.
Early Italian Love Stories. Una Taylor. Repr. of 1899 ed. 17.50 (ISBN 0-8414-8030-3). Folcroft.
Early Italina Love Stories Taken from the Originals. Una Taylor. 144p. 1980. Repr. of 1899 ed. lib. bdg. 50.00 (ISBN 0-89760-882-8). Telegraph Bks.
Early Joys. K. Fedin. 398p. 1973. 5.95 (ISBN 0-8285-0963-8, Pub. by Progress Pubs USSR). Imported Pubns.
Early Joys. Konstantin Aleksandrovich Fedin. (Vintage Russian Library Ser). (Orig.). pap. 1.65 o.p. (ISBN 0-394-70709-5, V709, Vin, V709). Random.
Early Life and Adventures of Sylvia Scarlett. Compton Mackenzie. LC 18-16486. 1918. Harper & Brothers.
Early Life of Stephen Hind. Margaret Storm Jameson. LC 66-20750. 1966. Harper & Row.
Early Long. Frank Belknap Long. LC 75-11075. 1975. 7.95 (ISBN 0-385-05563-3). Doubleday.
Early Losses. Pat Burch. LC 73-86274. 1973. 3.00 (ISBN 0-913780-03-0). Daughters, Inc.
Early Modern Town. Ed. by Peter Clark. LC 76-7041. (Open University set book). 1976. text ed. 18.95x (ISBN 0-582-48404-9); pap. text ed. 8.95x (ISBN 0-582-48405-7). Longman.
Early Morning Wind, and Other Stories. Dale Herd. LC 74-166134. (Writing, 29). 1972. 2.50 (ISBN 0-87704-019-2). Four Seasons Foundation Distributed by Book People. Berkeley, Calif.
Early One Morning. Walter De La Mare. 1977. Repr. of 1935 ed. lib. bdg. 42.50x (ISBN 0-374-92098-2). Octagon.
Early Pohl. Frederik Pohl. LC 75-14837. 1976. 5.95 (ISBN 0-385-11014-6). Doubleday.
Early Rain. Campbell Long. LC 61-1397. 1961. Brethren Press.
Early Reaping. Cale Young Rice. LC 29-19523. The Century Co.
Early Reminiscences. A Poem, Recounting Incidents Occurring in the Youth of the Author. And Describing Country Life in the Province of New Brunswick, Forty Years Ago. Leonard Scott. LC 30-10788. 1864. Printed by the Author for Private Distribution.
Early Routines. William S. Burroughs. LC 79-54919. 1981. 10.00 (ISBN 0-932274-02-1) (ISBN 0-932274-03-X). Cadmus Editions.
Early Science Fiction Stories of Thomas M. Disch. Thomas M Disch. LC 77-4934. (Gregg Press science fiction series). 1977. 13.00 (ISBN 0-8398-2370-3). Gregg Press.
Early Sorrow: Translated from the German. Thomas Mann & Scheffauer, Herman George, 1878-1927, Tr. LC 30-15223. 1930. A. A. Knopf.
Early Spring. Robert Hazel. LC 70-139380. 1971. 5.95 (ISBN 0-393-08643-7). Norton.
Early Stories of the Coyote State. Chloe Garber. 3.75 o.p. Vantage.
Early Stories of the Great Lakes. W. S. Harwood et al. LC 75-39086. Orig. Title: Stories of the Great Lakes. (Illus.). 186p. 1981. pap. 7.75 (ISBN 0-912382-18-X). Black Letter.
Early Stories of Willa Cather. Willa Sibert Cather. Ed. by Mildred R. Bennett. pap. 1.95 o.p. (ISBN 0-8152-0130-3, A130). Apollo Eds.
Early Stories. Selected and with Commentary by Mildred R. Bennett. Willa Sibert Cather. Ed. by Mildred R. Bennett. LC 57-6787. 1957. Dodd, Mead.
Early Stories... 1st Ed. Elizabeth Bowen. LC 50-58028. 1951. Knopf.
Early Summer. Elizabeth Frances Corbett. LC 42-21238. 1942. D. Appleton-Century Company, Incorporated.
Early Summer. Jan MacLean. (Harlequin Romance). 1979. pap. 1.25 (ISBN 0-373-02295-6, Pub. by Harlequin). PB.
Early Tales & Sketches. Samuel Langhorne Clemens et al. LC 75-46045. (Works of Mark Twain). (works of Mark Twain; v. 15: Vol. 15). (Illus.). 37.50 (ISBN 0-520-03186-5). Published for the Iowa Center for Textual Studies by the University of California Press.
Early Tales & Sketches, Vol. 1. Mark Twain. Ed. by Edgar M. Branch & Robert H. Hirst. (Iowa-California Works of Mark Twain). 1980. 42.50 (ISBN 0-520-03186-5). U of Cal Pr.
Early Tales & Sketches, Vol. 2: Eighteen Sixty-Four to Eighteen Sixty-Five. Mark Twain. Ed. by Edgar M. Branch & Robert H. Hirst. 1981. 37.50 (ISBN 0-520-04382-0). U of Cal Pr.
Early Times in Texas. John Crittenden Duval. LC 68-5771. 1967. Steck-Vaughn Co.
Early Times in Texas. John Crittenden Duval. LC 6-34600. H. P. N. Gammel & Co.
Early Times in Texas. John Crittenden Duval. (Original narratives of Texas history and adventure). 1935. The Steck Company.
Early to Bed. Geoffrey Harwood. LC 32-18242. 1932. I. Washburn.
Early to Bed... Wood Kahler. LC 28-17095. 1928. A. A. Knopf.
Early to Rise. Arnold Ellis Grisman. LC 57-11797. 1958. Harper.
Early Warning. Christopher Fitzsimmons. 1981. 2.25 (ISBN 0-380-50179-1). Avon Books.
Early Warning. Christopher Fitzsimons. LC 78-24151. 1979. 8.95 (ISBN 0-670-28717-2). Viking Press.
Early Williamson. Jack Williamson. LC 74-25130. 1975. 5.95 (ISBN 0-385-02722-2). Doubleday.
Earlyriders. Ed. by Lou Kimzey. (Paisano Bks.). 1982. pap. 7.95 (ISBN 0-440-02117-0, Dell Trade Pbks). Dell.
Earnest Leighton. A F Smith. LC 8-81873. 1881. Christian Publishing Company.
Earnest Trifler. Mary Alpin Sprague. LC 8-14048. 1880. Houghton, Osgood and Company.
Earnestness: The Sequel to "Thankfulness.". Charles Benjamin Tayler & Protestant Episcopal Book Society. LC 42-27068. Protestant Episcopal Book Society.
Earnshaw Neighborhood. Erskine Caldwell. LC 70-151724. 1971. 6.95. World Pub. Co.
Ear's Chamber. Ed. by Stacy Tuthill. (SCOP Ser.: No. V). 1981. pap. 5.00 (ISBN 0-930526-04-X). SCOP Pubns.
Ears from Harvested Sheaves. J. C. Philpot. 3.50 o.p. Reiner.
Ears of the Jungle. Pierre Boulle. LC 72-83350. 1972. 6.95 (ISBN 0-8149-0720-2). Vanguard Press.
Earth. 4th ed. Muriel Hine Coxon. LC 12-31384. 1912. 1.25. John Lane.
Earth. Marie C Farca. LC 74-175604. 1972. 4.95. Doubleday.
Earth. Emile Zola. LC 55-17018. 1954. Elek.
Earth. Emile Zola. LC 81-467802. (Penguin classics). 1980. 4.95 (ISBN 0-14-044387-8). Penguin.
Earth Abides. George Rippey Stewart. LC 49-11267. 1949. Random House.
Earth Again Redeemed: May 26 to July 1, 1984, on This Earth of Ours and Its Alter Ego: a Science Fiction Novel. Martin Burgess Green. LC 76-54834. (Illus.). 9.95 (ISBN 0-465-01762-2). Basic Books.
Earth and All It Holds. Victor J Banis. LC 79-22789. 12.95 (ISBN 0-312-22467-2). St. Martin's Press.
Earth and High Heaven. Gwethalyn Graham Erichsen Brown. LC 44-7997. 1944. J. B. Lippincott Company.
Earth & High Heaven. Gwethalyn Graham. pap. 1.25 o.s.i. (78-677). Lancer.
Earth and the Fullness Thereof: A Romance of Modern Styria. Peter Rosegger. Tr. by Skinner, Frances E. LC 2-24241. 1902. G. P. Putnam's Sons.
Earth Angels. Susan Cahill. 1978. 1.95 (ISBN 0-445-04205-2). Popular Library.
Earth Angels: Portraits from Childhood and Youth. Susan Cahill. LC 75-23875. 8.95 (ISBN 0-06-010621-2). Harper & Row.
Earth Beneath. Harold Heslop. LC 47-24202. 1946. T. V. Boardman.
Earth Beneath. Harold Heslop. LC 47-113814. 1947. J. Day Co.
Earth Book of Stormgate. Poul Anderson. LC 77-28774. 8.95 (ISBN 0-399-12144-7). Berkley Pub. Corp.: Distributed by Putnam.
Earth Book of Stormgate. Poul Anderson. 1979. 2.25 (ISBN 0-425-04090-9). Berkley Pub. Corp.
Earth-Born! earthborn ed. George W. Hanna. (On cover: Psycho series, no. 1). 1889. The Press Bureau.
Earth-Born: A Novel of the Plantation. Howard Snyder. LC 29-635036. 2.00. The Century Co.
Earth-Bound: Nine Stories of Ireland. Dorothy Macardle. LC 25-4209. 1924. The Harrigan Press.
Earth Descended. Fred Saberhagen. 288p. (Orig.). 1981. pap. 2.95 (ISBN 0-523-48564-6). Pinnacle Bks.
Earth Dies. Clark Darlton. (Perry Rhodan,#41). 1974. (pbk.) 0.75. Ace Books.
Earth Dreams. Janet Morris. LC 81-15818. 14.95 (ISBN 0-399-12686-4). Putnam.
Earth Eagles. Marguerite Farlee Bayliss. LC 47-22233. 1947. H. Holt and Company.
Earth Enslaved. Gregory Kern. (Cap Kennedy#9). 1974. (pbk.) 0.95. DAW Books.
Earth Factor X. (Science Fiction Ser.). pap. 1.25 o.p. (UY1250). DAW Bks.
Earth Factor X. Alfred Elton Van Vogt. (Science Fiction Ser.). 1978. pap. 1.50 o.p. (ISBN 0-87997-412-5, UW1412). DAW Bks.
Earth Factor X. Alfred Elton Van Vogt. 1.25. Daw Books.
Earth Giant. 1st Ed. Edison Marshall. LC 60-11387. 1960. Doubleday.
Earth Gone Mad: By Roger Dee Pseud. Roger D Aycock. LC 55-18984. (Ace double novel books, D-84). 1954. Ace Books.
Earth Has Been Found: A Novel /by D.F. Jones. D. F Jones. (Dell book). 1979. 2.25. Dell Pub. Co.
Earth: His Mistress. Peggy Gaddis, pseud. LC 35-11486. Godwin.
Earth Horizon. Mary Austin. 1932. lib. bdg. 15.00 (ISBN 0-8414-1681-8). Folcroft.
Earth Invader. Randall Garrett. 192p. 1982. pap. 2.25 (ISBN 0-8439-1059-3, Leisure Bks). Nordon Pubns.
Earth Is Heaven. E. C. Tubb. (Dumarest of Terra Ser.: No. 27). 160p. 1982. pap. 2.25 (ISBN 0-87997-786-8, UE1786). DAW Bks.
Earth Is Laughing: A Novel. 1st Ed. John Fell Scott. LC 56-9567. 1956. Exposition Press.
Earth Is Mine. Luther Cox. 1968. 6.00 o.p. (ISBN 0-682-46778-2). Exposition.
Earth Is Our Heritage: Translated by Robert Maxwell. Ernst Emil Wiechert. LC 51-21601. 1950. Nevill.
Earth Is Ours: A Novel. Vilhelm Moberg & Bjorkman, Edwin August, 1866- LC 41-8612. 1940. Simon and Schuster.
Earth Is Room Enough. Isaac Asimov. 1979. pap. 2.50 (ISBN 0-449-24125-4, Crest). Fawcett.
Earth Is Room Enough: Science Fiction Tales of Our Own Planet. Isaac Asimov. LC 57-11410. 1957. Doubleday.
Earth Is the Alien Planet: J. G. Ballard's Four-Dimensional Nightmare. David Pringle. LC 79-13065. (Popular writers of today; v. 26). (Milford series). 1979. 8.95. (ISBN 0-89370-138-6) (ISBN 0-89370-238-2). Borgo Press.
Earth Is the Lord's. Taylor Caldwell. 1979. pap. 2.75 (ISBN 0-515-05094-6). Jove Pubns.
Earth Is the Lords. Taylor Caldwell. 1973. pap. 1.50 o.p. (ISBN 0-515-03159-3, A3159). Pyramid Pubns.
Earth Is the Lord's. Taylor Caldwell. 1976. pap. 1.95 o.p. (ISBN 0-515-04062-2). BJ Pub Group.
Earth Is the Lord's. Carobeth Laird. pap. 2.00 o.p. (ISBN 0-87516-035-2). De Vorss.
Earth Is the Lord's. Mary J. McFadyen. (Illus., Orig.). 1967. pap. 3.95 o.p. (ISBN 0-8042-9864-5). John Knox.
Earth Is the Lord's: A Tale of the Rise of Genghis Khan. Taylor Caldwell. LC 75-700. 1975. 9.95 (ISBN 0-88411-154-7). Aeonian Press.
Earth Is the Lord's: A Tale of the Rise of Genghis Khan. Taylor Caldwell. LC 41-1125. 1941. C. Scribner's Sons.
Earth Is the Lord's: A Tale of the Rise of Genghis Kahn. Taylor Caldwell. 1974. Repr. of 1941 ed. lib. bdg. 24.90x (ISBN 0-88411-154-7). Amereon Ltd.
Earth Is the Strangest Planet: Ten Stories of Science Fiction. Robert Silverberg. LC 76-55728. 6.95 (ISBN 0-8407-6528-2). T. Nelson.
Earth Is Your Spaceship. Nat Dring, pseud. LC 67-17565. 1967. 2.95 o.p. (ISBN 0-911412-00-X). Space Age.
Earth Is Your Spaceship: The Story of Man. 1st Ed. Nat Dring, pseud. LC 67-17565. 1967. 2.95. Space Age Pr.
Earth Movers: A Novel. David Grinstead. LC 79-20270. 10.95 (ISBN 0-316-26001-0). Little, Brown.
Earth Music. Lyman V. Rutledge. 5.95 o.p. (ISBN 0-8283-1280-X). Branden.
Earth Never Tires. Darragh Aldrich. LC 56-19440. 1936. H. C. Kinsey & Company, Inc.
Earth Never Tires. Darragh Aldrich. LC 36-19440. 1936. H. C. Kinsey & Company, Inc.
Earth: Our Crowded Spaceship. Isaac Asimov. 1978. pap. 1.95 (ISBN 0-449-23172-0, Crest). Fawcett.
Earth. Pref. by Angus Wilson. Translated from the French by Ann Lindsay. Emile Zola. LC 55-6275. Grove Press.
Earth Revisited. Byron Alden Brooks. LC 44-27437. 1893. Arena Publishing Company.
Earth-Shaker. Lin Carter. LC 76-42320. (Science Fiction Ser.). 192p. 1982. 10.95 (ISBN 0-385-12477-5). Doubleday.
Earth Shaker. Nick Carter. (Nick Carter Ser.). (Illus.). 224p. 1982. pap. 2.50 (ISBN 0-441-18124-4, Pub. by Charter Bks). Ace Bks.
Earth Ship & Star Song. Ethan I. Shedley. 224p. 1981. pap. 1.95 (ISBN 0-445-04639-2). Popular Lib.
Earth Ship and Star Song: A Novel. Ethan I Shedley. LC 78-26861. 1979. 8.95 (ISBN 0-670-28720-2). Viking Press.
Earth Song. Sharon Webb. LC 82-16298. 1983. 12.95 (ISBN 0-689-30964-3). Atheneum.
Earth to Earth. Clotilde Inez Mary Graves. LC 16-22629. 1916. Frederick A. Stokes Company.
Earth Told Me. Thames Ross Williamson. LC 30-20159.
Earth: Tr. by Ann Lindsay Pref. by Angus Wilson. Emile Zola. LC 55-17018. 1965. bds., 4.50. Elek Bks.
Earth Trembled. Edward Payson Roe. (On cover: Dodd, Mead & company's library of fiction, no. 5). Dodd, Mead, and Company.
Earth Trembled. Edward Payson Roe. LC 7-402253. Dodd, Mead and Company.
Earth Tripper. Leo P. Kelley. 1973. pap. 0.75 o.p. (T2719, GM). Fawcett World.
Earth-Tube. George Edward Pendray. LC 74-15967. (Science Fiction). 1975. 17.00 (ISBN 0-405-06287-7). Arno Press.
Earth-Tube. George Edward Pendray. LC 29-19452. 1929. D. Appleton & Company.
Earth Two. Leo P. Kelley. LC 79-51077. (Space Police Bks.). 1979. pap. 4.24 (ISBN 0-8224-6379-2). Pitman Learning.
Earth Unaware. Mack Reynolds. (Leisure book). 1979. 1.50 (ISBN 0-8439-0628-6). Nordon Pubns.
Earth Waits for Dawn. 1st Ed. Larry Clinton O'Brien. LC 56-10544. 1956. Vantage. Press.
Earth Will Shake: A Novel. lst ed. Robert Anton Wilson. LC 82-10490. 14.95 (ISBN 0-87477-211-7). J.P. Tarcher.
Earthblood. Keith Laumer & Rosel George Brown. LC 66-24313. (Doubleday science fiction). 1966. Doubleday.
Earthbound. Richard Matheson. LC 82-80213. 224p. (Orig.). 1982. pap. 2.50 (ISBN 0-86721-144-X). Playboy Pbks.
Earthbound. Dalton S Reymond. LC 48-613536. 1948. Ziff-Davis Pub. Co.
Earthbound: A Novel. 1st Ed. John W Combs. LC 55-12329. Pageant Press.
Earthbound. Jacket Illus. by Peter Poulton; Endpaper Design by Alex Schomburg. 1st Ed. Milton Lesser. LC 52-5493. (Science fiction novel).
Earthbreakers. Ernest Haycox. LC 52-6067. 1972. 1.25. New Amer. Lib.
Earthbreakers. Ernest Haycox. LC 76-6520. 1976. 9.95 (ISBN 0-89190-977-X). Rivercity Press.
Earthbreakers. Ernest Haycox. LC 79-14924. (Gregg Press Western Fiction Series). 1979. 9.95 (ISBN 0-8398-2576-5). Gregg Press.
Earthbreakers. 1st Ed. Ernest Haycox. LC 52-6067. 1952. Little, Brown.
Earthchild. Doris Piserchia. (Science Fiction Ser.). 1977. pap. 1.50 (ISBN 0-87997-308-0, UW1308). DAW Bks.
Earthchild. Sharon Webb. LC 82-1791. 1982. 11.95 (ISBN 0-689-30945-7). Atheneum.
Earthdivers: Tribal Narratives on Mixed Descent. Gerald Robert Vizenor. LC 81-150279. (Illus.). 14.95 (ISBN 0-8166-1048-7). University of Minnesota Press.
Earthen Lot. Bradda Field. LC 28-5639. Harcourt, Brace and Company.
Earthen Mold: The Evolution of a Girl. Edward Powhatan Buford. LC 14-9276. 1.25. The Gorham Press; Etc., Etc.
Earthenware: A Group of Stories. Murrell Edmunds. LC 30-7671. The Little Bookshop.
Earthjacket. Jon Hartridge. LC 71-130810. 1970. 4.95 (ISBN 0-8027-5532-1). Walker.
Earthlight. Arthur Charles Clarke. LC 55-69371. 1955. Ballantine Books.

Earthlight. Arthur Charles Clarke. LC 72-188459. 1972. 5.95 (ISBN 0-15-127225-5). Harcourt Brace Jovanovich.

Earthlove. Neil McAleer. (Orig.). 1979. pap. 7.95 o.p. (ISBN 0-89407-027-4). Strawberry Hill.

Earthlove. Neil McAleer. (Orig.). 1979. pap. 7.95 o.p. (ISBN 0-89407-027-4). Strawberry Hill.

Earthlove: A Novel. Neil McAleer. LC 78-18906. 11.95. (ISBN 0-89407-031-2) (ISBN 0-89407-027-4). Strawberry Hill Press.

Earthly Bread. Michael Mewshaw. LC 76-7991. 7.95 (ISBN 0-394-49925-5). Random House.

Earthly Creatures, Ten Stories. Charles Reginald Jackson. LC 53-9678. 1953. Farrar, Straus and Young.

Earthly Creatures: Ten Stories. facsimile ed. Charles Reginald Jackson. LC 76-157778. (Short Story Index Reprint Ser.). Repr. of 1953 ed. 15.00 (ISBN 0-8369-3890-9). Ayer Co.

Earthly Creatures: Ten Stories by Charles Jackson. Charles Reginald Jackson. LC 76-157778. (Short story index reprint series). 1971. (ISBN 0-8369-3890-9). Books for Libraries Press.

Earthly Paragon: A Novel. Eva Wilder McGlasson Brodhead. 1892. Harper & Brothers.

Earthly Possessions. Anne Tyler. LC 76-41222. 1977. 8.95 (ISBN 0-394-41147-1). Knopf: Distributed by Random House.

Earthly Possessions. Anne Tyler. LC 77-20916. 1978. 10.95 (ISBN 0-8161-6532-7). G. K. Hall.

Earthly Possessions. Anne Tyler. LC 76-41222. 1978. 1.95 (ISBN 0-445-04214-1). Popular Library.

Earthly Powers. Anthony Burgess. LC 80-20978. 15.95 (ISBN 0-671-41490-9). Simon and Schuster.

Earthly Powers. Anthony Burgess. 3.95. (ISBN 0-380-56903-5). Avon Books,, C.

Earthly Watchers at the Heavenly Gates. The False and the True Spiritualism. John Chester. LC 6-24210. Presbyterian Board of Publications.

Earthman, Come Home. James Blish. LC 55-5662. Putnam.

Earthman's Burden: By Poul Anderson and Gordon R. Dickson. Poul Anderson & Gordon R. Dickson. LC 57-7111. 1957. Gnome Press.

Earthmen and Strangers: Nine Stories of Science Fiction. Ed. by Robert Silverberg. (2206). 1968. Dell.

Earthmen and Strangers: Nine Stories of Science Fiction. 1st Ed. Ed. by Robert Silverberg. LC 66-813595. 1966. 3.95. Duell.

Earthmother Drinks Blood: A Novel About Chief Joseph and the Nez Perce Tribe. Richard Gibson Hubler. LC 75-16025. 7.95. Creek House.

Earthquake. Milton Berle & John Roeburt. (O.s.i.). 192p. 1972. pap. 0.95 o.s.i. (532-95188-095). Manor Bks.

Earthquake: A Novel by Milton Berle and John Roeburt. Milton Berle & John Roeburt. LC 59-9482. 1959. Random House.

Earthquake in the Triangle. Joseph Walter Cove. LC 35-6158. H. Holt and Company.

Earthquake Machine. Mitchelson & Utechin. (O.s.i.). 1976. pap. 1.50 o.s.i. (BT50939). Belmont-Tower.

Earthquake. The Story of a Movie. George Fox. (Signet Film Ser.). (Signet book). 1974. (pbk.) 1.50. New American Library.

Earthquake: Translated by Rita Eldon. Heinz Risse. LC 53-121745. 1953. Farrar, Straus & Young.

Earth's Enigmas. Charles George Douglas Roberts. LC 72-94742. (Short story index reprint series). (Illus.). 1969. Books for Libraries Press.

Earth's Enigmas. Charles George Douglas Roberts. LC 3-13615. 1903. L. C. Page & Company.

Earth's Enigmas: A Volume of Stories. Charles George Douglas Roberts. 1896. Lamson, Wolffe and Company.

Earth's Last Citadel. C. L. Moore & Henry Kuttner. pap. 2.25 (ISBN 0-441-18112-0, Pub. by Ace Science Fiction). Ace Bks.

Earth's Other Shadow: Nine Science Fiction Stories. Robert Silverberg. (Signet, Q5538). 1973. (pbk.) 0.95. New American Lib.

Earth's Quality. Winifred G Birkett. LC 36-16196. 1936. Dodd, Mead & Company.

Earth's Works. Brian Wilson Aldiss. 1980. pap. 1.95 (ISBN 0-380-52159-8, 52159). Avon.

Earthshaker. Robert W Krepps. 1958. Macmillan.

Earthshapers. Karen Speerstra & George Douglas Armstrong. LC 80-16237. (Illus.). 7.95 (ISBN 0-87961-108-1) (ISBN 0-87961-109-X). Naturegraph Publishers.

Earthsound. Arthur Herzog. LC 75-6702. 1975. 7.95 (ISBN 0-671-21993-6). Simon and Schuster.

Earthwind. Robert Holdstock. 1978. 1.95 (ISBN 0-671-82265-9). Pocket Books.

Earthworks. Brian Wilson Aldiss. LC 66-12206. (Doubleday science fiction). 1966. Doubleday.

Earthworms in Europe: Alexander Botts Makes the Old World Tractor-Conscious. William Hazlett Upson. LC 31-607519. 1931. Farrar & Rinehart, Incorporated.

Earthworms Through the Ages: The Wisdon of Alexander Botts. William Hazlett Upson. LC 47-6043. 1947. Rinehart.

Earthwreck! Thomas N. Scortia. 224p. 1981. pap. 2.50 (ISBN 0-449-14435-6). Fawcett.

Earthwreck! Thomas N. Scortia. 224p. (Orig.). 1974. pap. 0.95 o.p. (M2963, GM). Fawcett World.

Earthwreck! Thomas N Scortia. (Fawcett gold medal book). 1974. (pbk.) 0.95. Fawcett.

Earwax. Carolyn Balducci. 197p. (YA) 1973. lib. bdg. 5.95 o.p. (ISBN 0-8161-6077-5, Large Print Bks). G K Hall.

Easiest Way: A Story of Metropolitan Life. Eugene Walter & Hornblow, Arthur, 1865- Joint Author. LC 11-4600. G. W. Dillingham Company.

Easily Persuaded. Elizabeth Deane. LC 29-6450. 1929. H. Liveright.

East All the Way. John Gilbert Lockhart. LC 28-21968. 1928. D. Appleton & Company.

East and West. Pearl Sydenstricker Buck. LC 75-26840. 9.95 (ISBN 0-8161-6303-0). G. K. Hall.

East and West. Daphne Smith Giles Jenkins. LC 41-20688. 1857. Printed by Davis & Cole.

East and West. Talbot Mundy. LC 37-23784. 1937. D. Appleton-Century Company, Incorporated.

East and West. Aleksandr Isaevich Solzhenitsyn. LC 79-5222. (Perennial library). 1.95 (ISBN 0-06-080508-0). Harper & Row.

East and West. A Novel. Frederick William Thomas. LC 8-27049. 1836. Carey, Lea & Blanchard.

East and West: A Story of New-Born Ohio. Edward Everett Hale. LC 6-46171. Cassell Publishing Company.

East and West: A Temperace Story. by daphne s. giles... ed. Daphne Smith Giles Jenkins. LC 6-44053. 1853. Printed by R. Craighead.

East and West: Stories. Pearl Sydenstricker Buck. LC 75-11609. 1975. 7.95 (ISBN 0-381-90015-0). John Day Co.

East and West: The Collected Short Stories of W. Somerset Maugham. William Somerset Maugham. LC 34-272284. 1934. Doubleday, Doran & Company, Inc.

East and West: The Collected Short Stories of W. Somerset Maugham. de luxe ed. William Somerset Maugham. LC 37-48454. 1937. Garden City Publishing Company, Inc.

East Angels, a Novel. Constance Fenimore Woolson. LC 9-5211. Harper & Brothers.

East by Day. Blair Niles. LC 40-29653. Farrar & Rinehart Incorporated.

East by Southwest. Neil Claremon. 1970. pap. 1.95 o.p. (ISBN 0-671-20602-8, Touchstone Bks). S&S.

East by Southwest. Christopher La Farge. LC 44-6865. 1944. Coward-McCann, Inc.

East Came West. Peter J. Huxley-Blythe. LC 64-15391. (Illus.). 1964. pap. 2.50 (ISBN 0-87004-072-3). Caxton.

East End Power and Light: A Novel. Russ Wellen. LC 82-90160. (Illus.). 1982. 4.95 (ISBN 0-9608364-0-3). Littoral Pub.

East Florida Romance. Caroline Washburn Rockwood. LC 7-39800. New Amsterdam Book Company.

East German Short Stories: An Introductory Anthology. Tr. by Peter E. Firchow & Evelyn S. Firchow. (International Studies & Translations Program). 1979. lib. bdg. 15.00 (ISBN 0-8057-8159-5, Twayne). G K Hall.

East India and Company. Paul Morand. LC 27-98640. 1927. A. & C. Boni.

East India Sketch-Book: Comprising an Account of the Present State of Society in Calcutta, Bombay, &C. ... LC 6-36386. 1836. T. Foster.

East Indiaman. Ellis K Meacham. LC 68-25906. (Illus.). 1968. 6.95. Little, Brown.

East Indiaman. Frank Pollard. LC 36-754. 1936. Little, Brown, and Company.

East Is Always East. Winifred Mary Scott. LC 31-4510. Doubleday, Doran & Company, Inc.

East Is East. Elaine Read Henry. LC 60-14384. 1969. Dorrance.

East Lies the Sun. Alla Crone. (Orig.). 1982. pap. 3.50 (ISBN 0-440-12229-5). Dell.

East Lynne. Arline De Haas & Wood, Ellen (Price) "Mrs. Henry Wood,". LC 31-6858. Grosset & Dunlap.

East Lynne. Ellen Price Henry Wood Wood. LC 24-24995. T. Nelson & Sons.

East Lynne. Ellen Price Henry Wood Wood. LC 17-13024. (Half-title: The new universal library. The works of Mrs Henry Wood, II). 1913. G. Routledge & Sons, Limited.

East Lynne: Or, The Earl's Daughter. Ellen Price Henry Wood Wood. (Seaside library, v. 20, no. 381). 1878. G. Munro.

East Lynne: Or, The Earl's Daughter. Ellen Price Henry Wood Wood. Rand, McNally & Company.

East of Broadway. Octavus Roy Cohen. LC 38-72052. 1938. D. Appleton Century Company, Incorporation.

East of Desolation. Jack Higgins, pseud. LC 69-10945. 1969. 3.95. Published for the Crime Club by Doubleday.

East of Desolation. Jack Higgins. (Fawcett gold medal book). 1975. (pbk.) 1.25. Fawcett.

East of Eden. Isa Glenn. LC 32-258423. 1932. Doubleday, Doran and Company, Inc.

East of Eden. Lynn Montross. LC 25-18057. 1925. Harper & Brothers.

East of Eden. Israel Joshua Singer & Samuel, Maurice, 1895- LC 39-271562. 1939. A. A. Knopf.

East of Eden. John Steinbeck. LC 52-12297. 1952. Viking Press.

East of Eden. autographed 1st ed. John Steinbeck. LC 52-4118. 1952. Viking Press.

East of Eden. John Steinbeck. LC 79-14915. 1979. 1.95 (ISBN 0-14-004997-5). Penguin Books.

East of Farewell. Howard Hunt. LC 42-19935. 1942. A. A. Knopf.

East of Jamaica. Kaye Wilson Klem. 1980. 2.50. Fawcett Gold Medal Books.

East of Katahdin. John Franklin Day. LC 50-624. 1949. Dirigo Edition.

East of Mansion House. Thomas Burke. LC 26-123200. George H. Doran Company.

East of Midnight. Forrest Rosaire. LC 45-1696. 1945. A. A. Knopf.

East of Singapore: A Novel of Adventure. Sydney Muller Parkman. LC 32-10942. 1932. Macrae Smith Company.

East of the Giants: A Novel. George Rippey Stewart. LC 38-278881. H. Holt and Company.

East of the Setting Sun: A Story of Graustark. George Barr McCutcheon. LC 24-19665. 1924. Dodd, Mead and Company.

East of the Shadows. Edith Noel Daniell Barclay. 1.25. Hodder & Stoughton, George H. Doran Company.

East of the Shadows. Paul Hutchens. LC 79-175490. 1972. 3.95 (ISBN 0-8024-2300-0). Moody Press.

East River. Borden Chase. LC 35-1202. Thomas Y. Crowell Company.

East River: A Novel. Shalom Asch. Tr. by Gross, A. H. LC 46-736533. 1946. G. P. Putnam's Sons.

East Side General. Frank Gill Slaughter. LC 52-5549. 1952. Doubleday.

East Side General. Frank Gill Slaughter. LC 75-33039. 1975. 9.95 (ISBN 0-89190-282-1). American Reprint Co.

East Side, West Side. Marcia Gluck Davenport. LC 78-74647. 1979. 12.50 (ISBN 0-8376-0428-1). R. Bentley.

East Side, West Side. Marcia Gluck Davenport. 1.75 (ISBN 0-445-04323-7). Popular Library.

East Side, West Side. Margaret Maitland, pseud. (Belmont Tower Book). 1.75 (ISBN 0-505-51210-6). Tower Pubns.

East Side, West Side. Felix Riesenberg. LC 27-2317. 1927. Harcourt, Brace and Company.

East South East. Frank Vigor Morley. LC 29-13476. 1929. Longmans, Green and Co.

East South East. Frank Vigor Morley. LC 29-18168. Harcourt, Brace and Company.

East to Montana. Al Cody. 1974. 4.95 (ISBN 0-517-51566-0). Lenox Hill Press.

East-West. Karen Swenson. 1980. pap. 3.25 o.p. (ISBN 0-917652-23-1). Confluence Pr.

East Wind. Julie Ellis. 1983. 15.95 (ISBN 0-87795-498-4). Arbor Hse.

East Wind. Compton Mackenzie. LC 37-2385. 1937. Dodd, Mead & Company.

East Wind: And Other Stories. Hugh MacNair Kahler. LC 78-167455. (Short story index reprint series). 1971. (ISBN 0-8369-3981-6). Books for Libraries Press.

East Wind, and Other Stories. Hugh MacNair Kahler. LC 23-280569. 1923. 2.00. G. P. Putnam's Sons.

East Wind Coming. Arthur B. Cover. 1979. pap. 2.25 (ISBN 0-425-04439-4). Berkley Pub.

East Wind Coming. 2.25 (ISBN 0-425-04439-4). Berkley Pub. Corp.

East Wind on Friday. Elizabeth Margaret Scott Smith. LC 39-153876. 1938. Longmans, Green and Co.

East Wind, Rain. N. Richard Nash. LC 76-40433. 1977. 9.95 (ISBN 0-689-10773-0). Atheneum.

East Wind: West Wind. Pearl Sydenstricker Buck. LC 30-109865. The John Day Company.

East Wind: West Wind. Pearl Sydenstricker Buck. LC 39-20731. (A Mercury book, no. 19). The American Mercury, Inc.

East Wind: West Wind. Pearl Sydenstricker Buck. (John Day Bk.). 1973. 14.37i (ISBN 0-381-98026-X, A21660). T Y Crowell.

East 57th Street. 1870-1970. Alan R Jackson. LC 61-583622. 1961. Simon and Schuster.

Easter Egg Hunt. Gillian Freeman. LC 81-3092. 1981. 9.95 (ISBN 0-86553-022-X) (ISBN 0-312-92169-1). Congdon & Lattes: Distributed by St. Martin's Press.

Easter Egg Hunt: A Novel. Speed Lamkin. LC 53-7078. 1954. Houghton Mifflin.

Easter Fleet: Translated from the French by Katharine Woods. Roger Vercel. LC 50-6024. 1950. Random House.

Easter Holiday. Ruth Blodgett. LC 35-354092. Harcourt, Brace and Company.

Easter House. David Rhodes. LC 73-14322. 1974. 7.95 (ISBN 0-06-013544-1). Harper & Row.

Easter in Modern Story. Ed. by Maud Van Buren. Bemis, Katharine Isabel, Joint Ed. LC 29-6673. The Century Co.

Easter Island: A Novel. Philip Freund. LC 47-3708. 1947. The Beechhurst Press.

Easter-Lilies. Alfred Almond McKay. 1896. The Peter Paul Book Company.

Easter of Darkness. With an Introd. Written Specially for This Ed. Robert Myron Coates. LC 59-15150. (Putnam Capricorn book, CAP18). 1959. Capricorn Books.

Easter Parade. Richard Yates. (Dell Book). 1977. 1.95 (ISBN 0-440-12274-0). Dell Pub. Co.

Easter Parade: A Novel. Richard Yates. LC 76-16198. 1976. 7.95 (ISBN 0-440-02197-9). Delacorte Press.

Easter Party. Sackville-West, Victoria Mary. LC 70-139147. 1972. (ISBN 0-8371-5763-3). Greenwood Press.

Easter Party. 1st Ed. LC 52-13374. 1953. Doubleday.

Easter Sun. Peter Neagoe. LC 34-6042. Coward-McCann, Inc.

Easter Vigil and Other Poems. John Paul II. LC 79-73. 5.00 (ISBN 0-394-50628-6) (ISBN 0-394-50650-2). Random House.

Easterly Inheritance. Robin Anne Selby. (Regency Romance). 1975. (pbk.) 1.25. Belmont Tower Books.

Eastern Lion in the West: Or, Marvelous Find of an Ideal. Ludwig Nicolovius. LC 9-18721. Broadway Publishing Company.

Eastern Red. Helen Manchester Gates Granville-Barker. LC 18-5212. 1918. 1.50. G. P. Putnam's Sons.

Eastern Shame Girl, and Other Stories: Classic Tales of Oriental Love. LC 48-1235. (New Avon library, 127). 1947. Avon Book Co.

Eastern Shore. James Noble Gifford. LC 35-23328. 1935. Arcadia House.

Eastern Shore by Coach-and-Four & Other Stories. Dorothy N. Harr. LC 76-6025. (Illus.). 1976. pap. 5.00 (ISBN 0-87033-217-1, Pub. by Tidewater). Cornell Maritime.

Eastern Tradition. Phyllis Birnbaum. LC 79-3783. 10.95 (ISBN 0-87223-605-6). Seaview Books.

Eastern Window. Sidney Williams. LC 18-16558. 1918. Marshall Jones Company.

Eastford: Or, Household Sketches. George Lunt. LC 7-14512. 1855. Crocker & Brewster.

Easthampton. Richard Hubbard. (Orig.). 1973. pap. 1.25 o.p. (01045). Curtis.

Eastover Court House: A Novel. Henry Burnham Boone & Brown, Kenneth, 1868- Joint Author. LC 1-30456. 1901. Harper & Brothers.

Eastover Parish: A Tale of Yesterday. Margaret Elizabeth Munson Sangster. LC 12-25992. Fleming H. Revell Company.

Eastward Drift: A Novel. Edward Percy Smith. LC 32-11461. 1932. H. C. Kinsey & Company, Inc.

Eastward Ha! Sidney J. Perelman. 1978. pap. 3.95 (ISBN 0-671-24410-8, Touchstone Bks). S&S.

Eastward in Eden. David Garth. LC 39-940040. 1939. H. C. Kinsey & Company, Inc.

Eastward in Eden. Philomene De Laforest-Divonne. Tr. by Evelyn Maud Hatch. LC 45-11151. 1945. Creative Age Press.

Eastward: Or, A Buddhist Lover; a Novel. Lucy Klinck Rice Hosea. LC 7-715723. J. G. Cupples Co.

Eastward Sweeps the Current: A Saga of the Polynesian Seafarers. Alida Sims Malkus. LC 38-1502. The John C. Winston Company.

Eastward the Sea. Charles Fry Haywood. LC 59-28755. 1959. Jackson & Phillips.

Easy. James Noble Gifford. LC 36-8454. Phoenix Press.

Easy. Beatrice Burton Morgan. LC 30-8778. Grosset & Dunlap.

Easy. Nina Wilcox Putnam. LC 24-48680. Harper & Brothers.

Easy & Hard Ways Out. Robert Grossbach. LC 74-4863. 258p. 1974. 6.95 o.p. (ISBN 0-06-122608-4). Harper Mag Pr.

Easy and Hard Ways Out: A Novel. Robert Grossbach. 1976. (pbk.) 1.75. Warner Books.

Easy and Hard Ways Out: A Novel. Robert Grossbach. LC 74-4863. 1974. 6.95 (ISBN 0-06-122608-4). Harper's Magazine Press.

Easy Answers. Judith Greber. LC 81-43371. 1982. 14.95 (ISBN 0-385-17857-3). Doubleday.

Easy Come. Andrew Miller. pap. 1.95 o.s.i. (Venus). Grove.

Easy Come. Gordon Wheeler. LC 74-9094. 1974. 5.95 (ISBN 0-394-49324-9). Random House.

Easy Come, Easy Love. Philip Tremont. 1969. pap. 0.60 o.p. (60-403). Manor Bks.

Easy Company & the Bible Salesman, No. 25. John W. Howard. 192p. 1983. pap. 2.25 (ISBN 0-515-06357-6). Jove Pubns.
Easy Company & the Big Blizzard, No. 15. John W. Howard. (Orig.). 1982. pap. 1.95 (ISBN 0-515-06032-1). Jove Pubns.
Easy Company & the Big Game Hunter, No. 28. John W. Howard. 192p. 1983. pap. 2.25 (ISBN 0-515-06360-6). Jove Pubns.
Easy Company & the Blood Feud, No. 26. John W. Howard. 192p. pap. 2.25 (ISBN 0-515-06358-4). Jove Pubns.
Easy Company & the Bloody Flag. John W. Howard. (Easy Company Ser.: No. 12). 192p. (Orig.). 1982. pap. 1.95 (ISBN 0-515-05953-6). Jove Pubns.
Easy Company & the Bootleggers. John W. Howard. (Easy Company Ser.: No. 9). (Orig.). 1981. pap. 1.95 (ISBN 0-515-05951-X). Jove Pubns.
Easy Company & the Bootleggers, No. 17. John W. Howard. (Orig.). 1982. pap. 1.95 (ISBN 0-515-05949-8). Jove Pubns.
Easy Company & the Cardsharps, No. 18. John W. Howard. 192p. 1982. pap. 1.95 (ISBN 0-515-06350-9). Jove Pubns.
Easy Company & the Cherokee Beauty. John W Howard. (Easy Company Ser.: No. 14). 192p. (Orig.). 1982. pap. 1.95 (ISBN 0-515-06031-3). Jove Pubns.
Easy Company & the Cow Country, No. 24. John W. Howard. 192p. 1983. pap. 2.25 (ISBN 0-515-06356-8). Jove Pubns.
Easy Company & the Dog Soldiers. John W. Howard. 192p. 1983. pap. 2.25 (ISBN 0-515-06359-2). Jove Pubns.
Easy Company & the Engineers. John W. Howard. (Easy Company Ser.: No. 11). (Orig.). 1981. pap. 1.95 (ISBN 0-515-05952-8). Jove Pubns.
Easy Company & the Green Arrows. John W. Howard. (Easy Company Ser.: No. 3). 192p. (Orig.). 1981. pap. 1.95 (ISBN 0-515-05887-4). Jove Pubns.
Easy Company & the Headline Hunter. John W. Howard. (Easy Company Ser.: No. 10). 192p. (Orig.). 1981. pap. 1.95 (ISBN 0-515-06030-5). Jove Pubns.
Easy Company & the Long Marchers, No. 16. John W. Howard. (Orig.). 1982. pap. 1.95 (ISBN 0-515-06033-X). Jove Pubns.
Easy Company at the Longhorns. John W. Howard. (Easy Company Ser.: No. 5). 192p. (Orig.). 1981. pap. 1.95 (ISBN 0-515-05946-3). Jove Pubns.
Easy Company & the Medicine Gun. John W. Howard. (Easy Company Ser.: No. 2). 240p. (Orig.). 1981. pap. 1.95 (ISBN 0-515-05804-1). Jove Pubns.
Easy Company & the Mystery Trooper, No. 23. John W. Howard. 192p. 1982. pap. 2.25 (ISBN 0-515-06355-X). Jove Pubns.
Easy Company & the Sheep Ranchers, No. 21. John W. Howard. 192p. (Orig.). 1982. pap. 2.25 (ISBN 0-515-06353-3). Jove Pubns.
Easy Company & the Suicide Boys. John W. Howard. (Easy Company Ser.: No. 1). 224p. (Orig.). 1981. pap. 1.95 (ISBN 0-515-05761-4). Jove Pubns.
Easy Company & the Twilight Sniper. John W. Howard. 192p. 1982. pap. 2.25 (ISBN 0-515-06352-5). Jove Pubns.
Easy Company & the White Man's Path. John W. Howard. (Easy Company Ser.: No. 4). 192p. (Orig.). 1981. pap. 1.95 (ISBN 0-515-05945-5). Jove Pubns.
Easy Company at Hat Creek Station, No. 22. John W. Howard. 208p. 1982. pap. 2.25 (ISBN 0-515-06354-1). Jove Pubns.
Easy Company in the Back Hills, No. 7. John W. Howard. 1981. pap. 1.95 (ISBN 0-515-05948-X). Jove Pubns.
Easy Company on the Bitter Trail. John W. Howard. (Easy Company Ser.: No. 8). (Orig.). 1981. pap. 1.95 (ISBN 0-515-05952-8). Jove Pubns.
Easy Company on the Oklahoma Trail. John W. Howard. (Easy Company Ser.: No. 13). 192p. (Orig.). 1982. pap. 1.95 (ISBN 0-515-06215-4). Jove Pubns.
Easy Dream Book. Toby Mussman. (Illus.). 12p. 1972. 15.00 o.p. (ISBN 0-911156-28-3). Porter.
Easy Favors. Neil Claremon. LC 79-26161. 1980. 9.95 (ISBN 0-07-011121-9). McGraw-Hill.
Easy Gun. E. M. Parsons. 128p. 1977. pap. 1.50 (ISBN 0-449-14293-0, GM). Fawcett.
Easy Gun. E. M. Parsons. (Orig.). 1970. pap. 0.50 o.p. (D2195, GM). Fawcett World.
Easy Lady. Henry Leyford Gates. LC 32-330521. 1932. The Macaulay Company.
Easy Life. Charlotte Mayerson. LC 80-18189. 1980. 9.95 (ISBN 0-531-09561-4). D. Elliott: Distributed by Watts.
Easy Money. Sam Koperwas. LC 82-14399. 1983. 13.95 (ISBN 0-688-01550-6). Morrow.
Easy Money. Arthur R. Mather. 1982. pap. 3.50 (ISBN 0-440-12211-2). Dell.
Easy Money. Frank Roderus. LC 78-52121. 1978. 7.95 o.p. (ISBN 0-385-14423-7). Doubleday.
Easy Money. Jane Snodgrass. LC 59-14788. 1959. Meador Pub. Co.
Easy Money: A Novel in Three Parts; Sequel to the Tangled Lives. Anna M Lucas. LC 45-858950. 1945. Buechler Publishing Company.
Easy Money: By Frank Peace Pseud. Will Cook. LC 56-5320. (Perma books, M-3026. Western, 6). 1956. Permabooks.
Easy Money. 1st Ed. William McKendrick Douglas. LC 54-12702. 1954. Pageant Press.
Easy Payments. Novel. Raymond Doyle. LC 54-10971. 1954. Hermitage House.
Easy Pickings. Alexander Hill. LC 31-24263. 1931. Brentano's.
Easy Prey, by Josephine Bell: Pseud. Doris Bell Collier Ball. LC 59-12474. (Cook Robin mystery). 1959. Macmillan.
Easy Ride. Rod Gray. (Lady from L. U. S. T. Ser). (Orig.). 1970. pap. 0.95 o.p. (B95-2076). Belmont-Tower.
Easy Ride. Rod Gray. (The Lady from L.U.S.T. Ser.). (O.si.). 1974. pap. 0.95 o.s.i. (BT50727). Belmont-Tower.
Easy Score. Joan Sherman. Orig. Title: Strangers in the Dark. 1970. pap. 0.75 o.p. (75-352). Manor Bks.
Easy Street. Susan Berman. 1983. pap. 2.95 (ISBN 0-553-22935-4). Bantam.
Easy Street. Elisabeth Stancy Payne. LC 30-28172. The Penn Publishing Company.
Easy Terms. 1st Ed. Bernard Phillips. LC 66-20964. 1966. 4.95. Doubleday.
Easy to Kill. Agatha Miller Christie. LC 39-227398. 1939. Dodd, Mead & Company.
Easy to Kill. Hulbert Footner. LC 31-23967. 1931. Harper & Brothers.
Easy to Know. Florence Stonebreaker. LC 45-3095. 1945. Phoenix Press.
Easy to Murder. Nancy Rutledge. LC 51-10862. 1951. Published for the Crime Club by Doubleday.
Easy Travel to Other Planets. Ted Mooney. LC 81-5571. 11.95 (ISBN 0-374-12631-3). Farrar, Straus, Giroux.
Easy Victories. James Trowbridge. LC 72-9018. 1973. 5.95 (ISBN 0-395-15569-X). Houghton Mifflin.
Easy Warren and His Cotemporaries: Sketched for Home Circles. William Turner Coggeshall. LC 6-26741. 1854. Redfield.
Easy Way. Kay Cicellis. LC 50-14688. 1950. Scribner.
Easy Way Out. Martin Meyers. (Orig.). 1973. pap. 1.25 o.p. (01045). Curtis.
Easy Way to Go. George Harmon Coxe. LC 69-10801. 1969. 4.50. Knopf.
Easy Way to Sexual Success. Adrian Y. Meadows. 192p. (Orig.). 1973. pap. 1.95 o.p. (ISBN 0-87682-331-2, 7331). Barclay Hse.
Eat a Bowl of Tea. Louis Chu. LC 60-6351. 1961. L. Stuart.
Eat a Bowl of Tea. Louis Chu. LC 78-21209. 1979. 6.95 (ISBN 0-295-95607-0). University of Washington Press.
Eat, Drink, and Be Buried. Edited, and with an Introd., by Rex Stout. Mystery Writers of America. LC 56-10479. 1956. Viking Press.
Eat, Drink and Be Merry. David Esdaile Walker. LC 34-1166. 1933. Longmans, Green and Co.
Eat, Drink & Make Mary. William F. Brett. (O.s.i.). 80p. 1974. pap. 1.50 o.s.i. (ISBN 0-912852-08-9). Echo Pubs.
Eat Not Thy Heart. Julie Grinnell Cruger. LC 6-31587. 1897. H. S. Stone & Co.
Eat of Me, I Am the Savior. Arnold Kemp. LC 73-182454. 1972. 6.95. Morrow.
Eat Them Alive. Pierce Nace. 1977. pap. 1.75 (ISBN 0-532-17157-8). Woodhill.
Eater of Darkness. Robert Myron Coates. LC 29-15568. 1929. The Macaulay Company.
Eater of Worlds. Gregory Kern. (Cap Kennedy#8). 1974. (pbk.) 0.95. DAW Books.
Eaters of the Dead. Michael Crichton. (YA) 1976. 8.95 o.s.i. (ISBN 0-394-49400-8). Knopf.
Eating Cake. Meredith Marsh. LC 78-20955. 10.95 (ISBN 0-698-10985-6). Coward, McCann & Geoghegan.
Eating Valley: A Novel. Augusta Walker. LC 56-12129. 1956. Dial Press.
Eavesdropper. Peter Boynton. LC 79-78871. 1969. Harcourt, Brace & World.
Eavesdropper: An Unparalleled Experience. James Payn. LC 7-33776. (On cover: Harper's Franklin square library, no. 626). 1888. Harper & Brothers.
Eavesdropper: An Unparalleled Experience. James Payn. (On cover: Lovell's library, no. 1227). 1888. J. W. L. Lovell Company.
Eavesdropper: By Lin Tai-Yi. 1st Ed. Wu-Shuang Lin. LC 59-5922. 1959. World Pub. Co.
Eavesdropping on Death. Carroll Cox Estes. LC 52-2441. 1952. Arcadia House.
Eb Peechcrap and Wife at the Fair: Being the Experience of Residents of 'Possum Ridge, Arkansaw, in St. Louis... Herbert Pierce Lewis. LC 6-9621. 1906. The Neale Publishing Company.
Ebb and Flo: And Other Short Stories. Amelia Willard Hillier. LC 8-29736. 1908. J. M. Williams & Son, Printers.
Ebb and Flow. Lydia L Rouse. 1892. Hunt & Eaton.
Ebb of the River. Richard C. Mears. LC 80-10658. (Illus.). 10.95 (ISBN 0-671-61032-5). Wyndham Books.
Ebb Tide: A Trio & Quartette. Robert Louis Stevenson. LC 8-16088. 1894. Stone & Kimball.
Ebb-Tide: A Trio and Quartette... Robert Louis Stevenson & Osbourne, Lloyd. LC 5-27091. (Half-title: The biographical edition of the works of Robert Louis Stevenson). 1905. C. Scribner's Sons.
Ebb-Tide, and Other Stories. Frances Christine Tiernan. 1872. D. Appleton and Company.
Ebb-Tide, and Other Stories. Frances Christine Tiernan. LC 2901. 1899. D. Appleton & Co.
Ebbing of the Tide: South Sea Stories. Louis Becke. LC 5-41006. 1900. J. B. Lippincott Company.
Ebbing Tide. Elisabeth Ogilvie. LC 75-34424. 1975. 6.95 (ISBN 0-88411-185-7). Aeonian Press.
Ebbing Tide. Elisabeth Ogilvie. 1976. (pbk.) 1.75 (ISBN 0-380-00577-8). Avon.
Ebbing Tide. Elisabeth Ogilvie. LC 47-4042. 1947. Thomas Y. Crowell Company.
Eben Erskine: Or, The Traveller. John Galt. LC 6-44475. 1833. Carey, Lea & Blanchard.
Eben Holden: A Tale of the North Country. Irving Bacheller. LC 70-5183. 1968. Scholarly Press.
Eben Holden: A Tale of the North Country. Irving Bacheller. LC 74-128934. 1970. (ISBN 0-404-00439-3). AMS Press.
Eben Holden: A Tale of the North Country. Irving Bacheller. LC 4258. Lothrop Publishing Company.
Eben Holden: A Tale of the North Country. special limited ed. Irving Bacheller. LC 9-32309. Grosset & Dunlap.
Eben Holden: A Tale of the North Country. Irving Bacheller. LC 41-26676. 1901. Lothrop Publishing Company.
Eben Holden: A Tale of the North Country. Irving Bacheller. LC 3-32793. 1903. Lothrop Publishing Company.
Eben Holden's Last Day a-Fishing. Irving Bacheller. LC 7-29429. 1907. Harper and Brothers.
Ebenezer Walks with God. George Baker. LC 31-252267. 1931. The Macmillan Company.
Ebon and Gold. A Novel. McIlvain, Charlotte L. 1874. G. W. Carleton & Co.
Ebon and Gold: A Novel. Charlotte L McIlvain & C. L. M. LC 79-38648. (Black Heritage Library Collection). 1972. (ISBN 0-8369-9006-4). Books for Libraries Press.
Ebon & Gold: Novel by C.L.M. facsimile ed. Charlotte L. McAlvain. LC 79-38648. (Black Heritage Library Collection). Repr. of 1874 ed. 18.25 (ISBN 0-8369-9006-4). Ayer Co.
Ebony and Ivory. Llewelyn Powys. LC 75-144168. (Short story index reprint series). 1971. (ISBN 0-8369-3783-X). Books for Libraries Press.
Ebony and Ivory. Llewelyn Powys. LC 23-994569. 1923. American Library Service.
Ebony Bed Murder. Rufus Hamilton Gillmore. LC 32-20151. 1932. The Mystery League, Inc.
Ebony Classics, 4 Vols. 1970. Set. 25.00 (ISBN 0-87485-080-0). Johnson Chi.
Ebony Idol. G. M. Flanders. LC 75-83915. (Illus.). 1969. Mnemosyne Pub. Co.
Ebony Idol... G. M. Flanders. LC 6-41131. 1860. D. Appleton & Company.
Ebony Image. Earl J Zentmyer. LC 80-10666. 1980. 9.95 (ISBN 0-87949-133-7). Ashley Books.
Ebony Madonna. Martha B. Bowman. 240p. 1962. 3.00 o.p. (ISBN 0-87178-207-3). Brethren.
Ebony Tower. John Fowles. LC 74-10952. 1974. 7.95 (ISBN 0-316-29093-9). Little, Brown.
Ecce Femina: Or, The Woman Zoe. Ellen Peck. LC 7-364833. 1875. G. W. Carleton & Co.; Etc., Etc.
Eccentricity Factor: A Novel. Dolly Thakore. LC 80-903747. (Vikas Library of Modern Indian Writing; 4). 10.00. Vikas.
Echo. Sybil Irene Eleanor Taylor Cookson. LC 20-7528. 1919. J. Lane.
Echo. Kenneth Jupp. LC 80-20289. 1981. 10.95 (ISBN 0-316-47703-6). Little, Brown.
Echo. Giles A Lutz. LC 79-7120. 1979. 7.95 (ISBN 0-385-15403-8). Doubleday.
Echo. Lilla Van Saher. LC 47-2027. 1947. E. P. Dutton & Company Inc.
Echo. Margaret Rivers Larminie Tragett. LC 23-7994. 1923. G. P. Putnam's Sons.
Echo. Sydney Tremayne. LC 20-75283. 1919. John Lane.
Echo Answers. Margaret Culkin Banning. 1973. (pbk.) 1.25. Manor Books.
Echo Answers. Elswyth Thane. LC 27-26567. 1927. Frederick A. Stokes Company.
Echo Answers Murder. Nigel FitzGerald. LC 65-12486. (Cock Robin mystery). 1965. Macmillan.
Echo Answers. 1st Ed. Margaret Culkin Banning. LC 59-13302. 1960. Harper.
Echo My Tears. Jan Foster. LC 48-7949. 1948. Dial Press.
Echo of a Bomb. Mark Derby. LC 57-5130. 1957. Viking Press.
Echo of a Bomb. Hilda Van Siller. LC 43-4270. 1943. Pub. for the Crime Club by Doubleday, Doran and Company, Inc.
Echo of a Dream. Juanita Franks. LC 76-99940. 1970. 3.00. Dorrance.
Echo of Evil. Manuel Komroff. 1948. Farrar, Straus.
Echo of Love. Vida Hurst. LC 50-2506. 1950. Gramercy Pub. Co.
Echo of Passion. George Parsons Lathrop. LC 41-31113. 1882. Houghton, Mifflin and Company.
Echo of Sin. Gin Le Conte Menssen. LC 51-5906. 1951. Vantage Press.
Echo of the Flute. 1st Ed. Mildred A Jordan. LC 58-100270. 1958. Doubleday.
Echo of Their Cries. Pierre V. Daigle. 1978. 9.95 (ISBN 0-914216-04-X); pap. 7.95 (ISBN 0-914216-06-6). Acadian Pub.
Echo of Treason. Jonathan Burke. LC 66-137014. (Red badge mystery). 1966. bds., 3.50. Dodd.
Echo of Union Chapel: A Tale of the Ozark Low Hill Country. Clarence E Hatfield. LC 13-32520. 1.50. Broadway Publishing Co.
Echo of Voices... Richard Curle. LC 17-13448. 1917. 1.50. A. A. Knopf.
Echo the Halls. Robert R. Edgington. 1970. 4.50 o.p. Vantage.
Echo Without Sound. Larry Smith & Stephen Smigocki. LC 80-81747. (Illus.). 1980. 13.50 (ISBN 0-89002-162-7); pap. 3.50 (ISBN 0-89002-161-9). Northwoods Pr.
Echo X. Ben Barzman. Orig. Title: Twinkle Twinkle Little Star. 1968. pap. 0.75 o.p. (ISBN 0-446-54684-4, 54-684). Paperback Lib.
Echoes. Bettie Wysor. 288p. 1983. pap. 2.95 (ISBN 0-515-06122-0). Jove Pubns.
Echoes & Embers. Patricia Gallagher. 1983. pap. 3.50 (ISBN 0-380-80929-X, 80929-7). Avon.
Echoes from Heaven. Flora B Foster. LC 13-19030. 0.60. Pentecostal Publishing Company.
Echoes From the Hills. Barbara Ferry Johnson. 464p. 1983. pap. 3.50 (ISBN 0-446-90834-7). Warner Bks.
Echoes from the Hills: A Novel. Alma Elder. LC 51-386. 1950. Exposition Press.
Echoes from the Macabre: Selected Stories. Daphne Du Maurier. LC 76-42325. 1977. 8.95 (ISBN 0-385-12655-7). Doubleday.
Echoes from the Macabre: Selected Stories. Daphne Du Maurier. LC 77-352855. 1976. 4.50 (ISBN 0-575-02181-0). Gollancz.
Echoes from the Macabre: Selected Stories. Daphne Du Maurier. (Kangaroo Book). 1978. 1.95 (ISBN 0-380-01953-1). Pocket Books.
Echoes from the Past. Marjorie McEvoy. LC 78-18141. 1979. 7.95 (ISBN 0-385-13410-X). Doubleday.
Echoes in the Wind. Dona Le'Man. LC 75-14903. 96p. 1975. 5.00 o.p. (ISBN 0-912760-12-5). Valkyrie Pr.
Echoes of a Belle: Or, A Voice from the Past. Ben Shadow. LC 8-4789. 1853. G. P. Putnam & Co.
Echoes of a Summer. William Johnston. 1975. (pbk.) 1.25 (ISBN 0-345-24713-2). Ballantine Books.
Echoes of an Ancient Love. Sharon Wagner. 1976. (pbk.) 1.25. Ballantine.
Echoes of Celandine. Derek Marlowe. LC 70-104139. 1970. 5.95. Viking Press.
Echoes of Evil. Kate Cameron, pseud. (Whispering Hills gothic,#6). 1974. (pbk.) 0.95. Leisure Books.
Echoes of Evil. Iris Tracy Comfort. LC 76-23754. 1977. 5.95 (ISBN 0-385-12599-2). Doubleday.
Echoes of Evil. Iris Tracy Comfort. 1978. 1.50 (ISBN 0-523-40323-2). Pinnacle Books.
Echoes of Love. Elisabeth Beresford. 1979. 1.25 (ISBN 0-440-17757-X). Dell Pub. Co.
Echoes of Myself: Romantic Studies of the Human Soul. studio ed. Ivan Narodny. LC 9-28955. 1909. 3.00. The Liberty Publishing Company.
Echoes of the Heart. Ann Bernadette. (Orig.). 1981. pap. 2.50 (ISBN 0-8439-8042-7, Tiara Bks). Nordon Pubns.
Echoes of the Past: New Mexico's Ghost Towns. Patricia F. Meleski. LC 72-80753. (Illus.). 288p. 1972. 15.00 o.p. (ISBN 0-8263-0219-X). U of NM Pr.
Echoes of the Tide. Sara Ware Bassett. LC 51-11273. 1951. Doubleday.
Echoes of the Unlocked Odyssey. Ed. by Salvatore St. John Buttaci & Susan L. Gerstle. 1974. pap. 7.95 (ISBN 0-917398-01-7). New Worlds.
Echoes of Yesterday. Nomi Berger. LC 80-82848. 384p. (Orig.). 1981. pap. 2.95o.p. (ISBN 0-87216-777-1). Playboy Pbks.
Echoes of Zero. Ross H Spencer. LC 80-29354. 1981. 9.95 (ISBN 0-312-22552-0). St. Martin's Press.
Echoes on the Wind. Dallas W. Green. 1973. 5.00 o.p. (ISBN 0-914330-03-9). Pioneer Pub Co.

TITLE INDEX

EDGE OF THE ALPHABET.

Echoing Cliffs. Hjalmar Thesen. (Illus.). 1964. 3.50 o.p. McKay.
Echoing Green: A Novel. Eleanor Estes. LC 47-11773. 1947. Macmillan Co.
Echoing Grove. Rosamond Lehmann. LC 79-24170. (Harvest/HBJ book). 1980. 5.95 (ISBN 0-15-627487-6). Harcourt Brace Jovanovich.
Echoing Grove. 1st American Ed. Rosamond Lehmann. LC 53-5646. 1953. Harcourt, Brace.
Echoing Shore. Robert Lee Martin. LC 55-6715. (Red badge detective). 1955. Dodd, Mead.
Echoing Silence. Audrey Curling. (Interlude Romance Ser.). 192p. 1981. pap. 1.95 (ISBN 0-441-20403-1). Ace Bks.
Echoing the Father's Love. Sadhu Ittyavirah. LC 68-1557. (Illus.). 1968. Franciscan Publishers.
Eclectic Musings of a Brooklyn Bum, Robert A. Frauenglas. LC 79-93225. 72p. (Orig.). 1980. pap. 4.00 o.p. (ISBN 0-9603950-0-8). Somrie Pr.
Eclipse. Alexander H Carasso. LC 33-29648. 1933. The Dial Press, Inc.
Eclipse. Paul Hutchens. LC 42-191633. 1942. Wm. B. Eerdmans Publishing Company.
Eclipse. Stuart Pretre Brodie Mais. LC 25-18696. Brentano's.
Eclipse. Dirk Wittenborn. LC 77-24285. 1977. 7.95 (ISBN 0-396-07383-2). Dodd, Mead.
Eclipse. Nicholas Wollaston. LC 73-93926. 1974. 6.95 (ISBN 0-8027-0458-1). Walker.
Eclipsing Binaries. E. E. Smith & Stephen Goldin. (Family d'Alembert Ser.: No. 8). 192p. (Orig.). 1983. pap. 2.50 (ISBN 0-425-05848-4). Berkley Pub.
Eclogues & Georgics of Virgil. Publius Vergilius Maro & Royds, Thomas Fletcher, 1880- Tr. LC 36-37264. (Half-title: Everyman's library, ed by E. Rhys. Classical 222). 1924. J. M. Dent & Sons; Ltd.
Eclogues: Eight Stories. Guy Davenport. LC 80-29027. (Illus.). 1981. 15.00 (ISBN 0-86547-029-4) (ISBN 0-86547-030-8). North Point Press.
Eclogues: Eight Stories by Guy Davenport. Guy Davenport. LC 80-29027. (Illus.). 256p. 1981. 20.00 (ISBN 0-86547-029-4); pap. 11.00 (ISBN 0-86547-030-8). N Point Pr.
Eclogues, Georgics, and Moretum of Virgil. With Explanatory Notes and a Lexicon. rev. ed. Publius Vergilius Maro & Stuart, George, 1831-1897, Ed. LC 30-17138. (Chase and Stuart's classical series). 1885. Eldredge & Brother.
Eclogues of Vergil. Herbert Jennings Rose. LC 42-37410. (Half-title: Sather classical lectures, v. 16). 1942. University of California Press.
Eco-Fiction. Ed. by John Stadler. LC 78-23628. 1971. 0.95 (ISBN 0-671-47845-1). Washington Square Press.
Eco-Spasm Report. Alvin Toffler. 128p. (Orig.). 1980. pap. 2.50 (ISBN 0-553-14474-X). Bantam.
Ecodeath. William Jon Watkins & Eugene V. Snyder. LC 71-171327. (Doubleday science fiction). 1972. 5.95. Doubleday.
Ecola! Jacland Marmur. LC 28-9739. 1928. Doubleday, Doran & Company, Inc.
Ecole Des Femmes: Nouvelles. Andre Paul Guillaume Gide. 1961. pap. 4.95. French & Eur.
Ecological Fantasies: Death from Falling Watermelons. Cy A. Adler. LC 73-80695. (Illus., Orig.). 1978. 11.95 (ISBN 0-914018-02-7). Green Eagle Pr.
Ecological Sanity. George Claus & Karen Bolander. LC 73-94190. 624p. 1977. 16.95 o.p. (ISBN 0-679-50388-9). McKay.
Ecological Sanity. George Claus & Karen Bolander. LC 73-94190. 624p. 1977. 16.95 o.p. (ISBN 0-679-50388-9). McKay.
Economic Feminism in American Literature Prior to 1848. Augusta V. Violette. LC 79-165410. (Research & Source Works Ser.). (O.s.i.: No. 339). 1971. Repr. of 1925 ed. 11.50 o.s.i. (ISBN 0-8337-4714-2). B Franklin.
Economy Must Be Our Watchword. Joyce Dennys. LC 32-292088. 1932. Putnam.
Economy Spinning Faster and Faster: Poems. Goran Sonnevi. LC 82-16719. 1982. 6.00 (ISBN 0-915342-39-1) (ISBN 0-915342-40-5). SUN.
Ecotopia. Ernest Callenbach. (gr. 10 up). 1977. pap. 2.95 (ISBN 0-553-14691-2). Bantam.
Ecotopia Emerging. Ernest Callenbach. LC 81-10821. 1981. 7.95 (ISBN 0-9604320-3-5) (ISBN 0-9604320-4-3). Banyan Tree Books.
Ecotopia: The Notebooks and Reports of William Weston. Ernest Callenbach. LC 74-84366. 1975. 7.95. Banyan Tree Books: Distributed by Bookpeople.
Ecotopian Sketchbook. Judith Clancy. 48p. 1981. pap. 4.25 (ISBN 0-9604320-2-7). Banyan Tree.
Ecrits Louisianais Du Dix-Neuvieme Siecle: Nouvelles, Contes, et Fables. Ed. by Gerard L. St. Martin & Jacqueline K. Voorhies. LC 78-24295. 1979. 20.00x (ISBN 0-8071-0353-5). La State U Pr.
Ecstasia. Richard Roe. LC 79-87688. (Orig.). Date not set. pap. 3.95 (ISBN 0-9602100-1-6). R Hart.
Ecstasy: A Study of Happiness. Louis Marie Anne Couperus. Tr. by Teixeira De Mattos, Alexander Louis. LC 19-15679. 1919. 1.50. Dodd, Mead and Company.
Ecstasy Business. Richard Condon. (Signet bk. T3615). 1968. New Amer. Lib.
Ecstasy Business. 1st Amer. Ed. Richard Condon. LC 67-14467. 1967. 5.95. Dial.
Ecstasy Connection. Paul Kenyon. (Baroness,#1). 1974. (pbk.) 0.95. Pocket Books.
Ecstasy Girl. Josiah Pitts Woolfolk. LC 48-10599. (Novel library, 2). 1948. Novel Publications.
Ecstasy Girl. Josiah Pitts Woolfolk. LC 37-206412. 1937. Godwin.
Ecstasy Reclaimed. Brandy Larue. (Second Chance at Love Ser.: No. 97). 192p. 1983. pap. 1.75 (ISBN 0-515-06861-6). Jove Pubns.
Ecstasy's Captive. Nelle McFather. 416p. 1982. pap. 3.50 o.p. (ISBN 0-505-51861-9). Tower Bks.
Ecstasy's Captive. Nelle McFather. 416p. 1983. pap. 3.50 (ISBN 0-8439-2006-8, Leisure Bks). Dorchester Pub Co.
Ecstasy's Dawn. Rochelle Wayne. (Orig.). 1983. pap. 3.75 (ISBN 0-8217-1192-X). Zebra.
Ecstasy's Empire. Gimone Hall. (Orig.). 1980. pap. 2.75 (ISBN 0-451-09292-9, E9292, Sig). NAL.
Ecstasy's Fury. Linda Benjamin. 1983. pap. 3.50 (ISBN 0-8217-1126-1). Zebra.
Ecstasy's Promise. Constance O'Banyon. 1982. pap. 3.50 (ISBN 0-89083-978-6). Zebra.
Ecstasy's Torment. Olivia Sinclair. 1982. pap. 3.50 (ISBN 0-8217-1089-3). Zebra.
Ecstasy's Treasure. Jean Haught. (Orig.). 1982. pap. 3.50 (ISBN 0-7217-1053-0). Zebra.
Ecstatic Thief. Gilbert Keith Chesterton. LC 80-2760. 1930. Dodd, Mead & Company.
Ecumenism & the Evangelical. J. Marcellus Kik. 2.50 o.p. Presby & Reformed.
Ed Dean Is Queer. N. A. Diaman. LC 78-57153. (1978 pap. ed. 5.00 o.p.). (Illus.). 224p. (Orig.). 1978. pap. 5.95 o.p. (ISBN 0-931906-00-8). Persona Pr.
Ed Dean Is Queer. 2nd ed. N. A. Diaman. LC 78-57153. (Illus.). 175p. 1981. pap. 7.95 (ISBN 0-931906-02-4). Persona Pr.
Ed Dean Is Queer: A Novel. N. A Diaman. LC 78-57153. 5.00 (ISBN 0-931906-00-8). Persona Press.
Ed. Somers, the Pinkerton Detective: Or, The Murdered Miser. Ernest Stark. (On cover: The eureka detective series). J. S. Ogilvie and Company.
Edarstone, a Kentucky Manor. Pearl Smith Truman. LC 37-158897. Burney Brothers Publishing Co.
Edda's Birthright: A Novel. Harriet Lewis. (choice series, no. 24). 1890. R. Bonner's Sons.
Eddie and the Archangel Mike. Barry Benefield. LC 43-166. 1943. Reynal & Hitchcock.
Eddie and the Cruisers. Paul Frederick Kluge. LC 80-14786. 1980. 10.95 (ISBN 0-670-28850-0). Viking Press.
Eddie Macon's Run. James McLendon. LC 79-22865. (Illus.). 1980. 9.95 (ISBN 0-670-28855-1). Viking Press.
Eddie Macon's Run. McLendon, James. 1980. 2.95 (ISBN 0-451-09518-9). New American Library.
Eddie of Jackson's Gang. Ernest. LC 43-1556. 1941. St. Anthony Guild Press.
Eddy: A Novel of to-Day. Clarence Louis Cullen. LC 10-841973. 1.50. G. W. Dillingham Company.
Eddy and Edouard. Betsey Riddle Hutten Zum Stolzenberg. LC 29-10007. 1929. Doubleday, Doran & Company, Incl.
Eddyite: A Christian Science Tale. George William Louttit. LC 8-30705. 1908. The Colonial Press.
Edelsteine: Six Select Stories by Baumbach, Seidel and Volkmann-Leander. Ed. by Richard Alexander Von Minckwitz & Frida Von Unwerth. Baumbach, Rudolf, 1840-1906 & Seidel, Heinrich, 1842-1906. LC 1-31644. (International Modern Language Ser.). (On cover: International modern language series). 1901. Ginn & Company.
Edelweiss. A Story. Berthold Auerbach. Tr. by Frothingham, Ellen. LC 6-4503. (Half-title: Handy-volume series, no 4). 1869. Roberts Brothers.
Edelweiss of the Sierras, Golden-Rod: And Other Tales. Constance Cary Harrison. LC 78-94730. (Short story index reprint series). 1969. Books for Libraries Press.
Edelweiss of the Sierras: Golden-Rod, and Other Tales. Constance Cary Harrison. LC 7-2883. 1892. Harper & Brothers.
Eden. Julie Ellis. LC 75-4835. 1975. 8.95 (ISBN 0-671-22028-4). Simon and Schuster.
Eden. Julie Ellis. (Fawcett Crest Book). 1976. (pbk.) 1.75. Fawcett.
Eden. Murray Sheehan. LC 28-971. E. P. Dutton & Company.
Eden: An Episode. Edgar Evertson Saltus. LC 72-116006. 1970. AMS Press.
Eden: An Episode. Edgar Evertson Saltus. LC 8-3741. Belford, Clarke & Company.
Eden Burning. Belva Plain. LC 82-1452. 15.95 (ISBN 0-440-02412-9). Delacorte Press.
Eden Burning. Belva Plain. LC 82-15802. 1982. 16.95 (ISBN 0-8161-3424-3). G.K. Hall.
Eden for One: An Amusement. John Gunther. LC 27-20253. 1927. Harper & Brothers.
Eden II. Edd Doerr. LC 74-25179. 1974. Aquarius Press.
Eden Motel; and To Love Flaminio. Nina Galen. LC 82-71905. 4.95 (ISBN 0-943628-00-8). East Palace Pub. Co.
Eden of Labor, or, the Christian Utopia. T. Wharton Collens. LC 79-154435. (Utopian Literature Ser). (Illus.). 1971. Repr. of 1876 ed. 15.00 (ISBN 0-405-03518-7). Ayer Co.
Eden Passion. Marilyn Harris. LC 78-21602. 11.95 (ISBN 0-399-12269-9). Putnam.
Eden Prairie. Frederick Feikema Manfred. LC 68-26708. 1968. 6.95. Trident Press.
Eden Rising. Marilyn Harris. LC 81-19893. 14.95 (ISBN 0-399-12687-2). Putnam.
Eden Seekers. Rose Breitfeld. LC 48-5986. 1948. Meador Pub. Co.
Eden Tree. Clyde Ware. LC 76-172510. 1971. 7.95. Touchstone Pub. Co.
Eden Two. Richard G. Eli. 3.95 o.p. Vantage.
Edens Lost. Sumner Locke Elliott. LC 78-81872. 1969. 5.95. Harper & Row.
Edgar Allan. John Neufeld. LC 68-3117. 1968. 3.95. S. G. Phillips.
Edgar Allan Poe and Ambrose Bierce. Anthony Adams. LC 77-373639. (Pegasus library). (Illus.). 1976. 1.60 (ISBN 0-245-52813-X). Harrap.
Edgar Allan Poe and Others: Representative Short Stories of the Nineteenth Century. Ed. by Maurice Baudin, Jr. LC 53-927. (American heritage series, no. 4). 1953. Liberal Arts Press.
Edgar Allan Poe: Centenary. D. M. Barnes. 1977. 16.50. Porter.
Edgar Allan Poe: Tales of the Folio Club & Three Other Stories. Ed. by Sybille Haage. (Studien und Texte zur Amerikanistik: Vol. 3). xii, 127p. 1978. pap. write for info. (ISBN 3-261-02679-0). P Lang Pubs.
Edgar Allan Poe's Tales of Mystery and Imagination. Edgar Allan Poe. (Half-title: Everyman's library, ed. by Ernest Rhys. Fiction). 1908. J. M. Dent & Co.
Edgar Allan Who--? Peter Van Greenaway. 176p. 1981. 14.95 (ISBN 0-575-02998-6, Pub. by Gollancz England). David & Charles.
Edgar Allen. John Neufeld. LC 68-31175. (novel for young readers.). 1968. 3.95. S. G. Phillips.
Edgar Chirrup. Peggy Webling. LC 15-154293. 1915. G. P. Putnam's Sons.
Edgar Fairfax. A Story of West Point. Florence Nightingale Craddock. LC 6-31146. (Dillingham's metropolitan library, no. 17). 1896. G. W. Dilligham Co.
Edgar Henry: Novel. Paul Snider. LC 66-23602. 1967. Beis Associates; Distributed by Random House.
Edgar Huntly. Charles Brockden Brown. Ed. by David Stineback. (Masterworks of Literature Ser). 1973. 7.50x (ISBN 0-8084-0359-1); pap. 4.95x (ISBN 0-8084-0360-5, M42). Coll & U Pr.
Edgar Huntly: Or, Memoirs of a Sleep-Walker. Brown, Charles Brockden. LC 63-24274. (His Novels, v. 4). 1963. Kennikat Press.
Edgar Huntly: Or Memoirs of a Sleep-Walker. Charles Brockden Brown. LC 5-41074. 1799. Printed by H. Maxwell, No. Letitia Court, and Sold by Thomas Dobson, Asbury Dickins, and the Principal Booksellers.
Edgar Huntly: Or, Memoirs of a Sleep-Walker. Charles Brockden Brown. LC 6-19638. 1857. M. Polock.
Edgar Huntly: Or, Memoirs of a Sleep-Walker. Charles Brockden Brown. LC 17-130411. (Half-title: Charles Brockden Brown's novels, vol. iv). 1887. D. McKay.
Edgar Huntly: Or, Memoirs of a Sleep Walker. Charles Brockden Brown. LC 43-399537. 1827. S. G. Goodrich.
Edgar Huntly: Or, Memoirs of a Sleep-Walker. Charles Brockden Brown & Arthur Mervyn, Wieland,-Ormond, &C., Author of. LC 79-144587. 37.50 (ISBN 0-404-01130-6). AMS Press.
Edgar Huntly: Or, Memoirs of a Sleep-Walker. Charles Brockden Brown & Clark, David Lee, 1887- Ed. LC 28-13915. (modern readers' series). 1928. The Macmillan Company.
Edgar Livingston: A Story of New York. Edmond Gastineau. LC 6-444678. (national series, no. 1). National Publishing Company.
Edgar Wallace Reader: Of Mystery and Adventure. Edgar Wallace. LC 43-9094. 1943. The World Publishing Company.
Edgar Winners: 33rd Annual Anthology of the Mystery Writers of America. Bill Pronzini & Mystery Writers of America. LC 79-5546. 11.95 (ISBN 0-394-50830-0). Random House.
Edge. George G. Gilman, pseud. (Edge Ser., No. 5). 160p. 1973. pap. 1.95 (ISBN 0-523-41836-1). Pinnacle Bks.
Edge. John Vliet Lindsay. LC 75-35670. 7.95 (ISBN 0-393-08732-8). Norton.
Edge. John Vliet Lindsay. (Berkley Medallion). 1.75 (ISBN 0-425-03240-X). Berkley.
Edge. Shirley Mezvinsky. LC 65-13096. 1965. Doubleday.
Edge: A Novel. John Corbin. LC 15-4585. 1915. 1.35. Duffield & Company.
Edge: A Novel. Page Stegner. LC 67-25307. 1967-1968. Dial Press.
Edge-Hill: Or, The Family of the Fitzroyals. A Novel. LC 7-8475. 1828. T. W. White.
Edge Meets Steele: Matching Pair. George G. Gilman, pseud. 208p. (Orig.). 1982. pap. 2.25 (ISBN 0-523-41894-9). Pinnacle Bks.
Edge, Number Thirty-Six: Town on Trial. George G. Gilman, pseud. 160p. 1981. pap. 1.95 (ISBN 0-523-41799-3). Pinnacle Bks.
Edge of Beauty. Betty Ferm. 1974. (pbk.) 1.25. Dell.
Edge of Belonging. Dorothy McKay Martin. 1963. pap. 2.95 (ISBN 0-8024-0114-7). Moody.
Edge of Beyond. James Beardsley Hendryx. LC 39-324898. 1939. Doubleday, Doran & Company, Inc.
Edge of Beyond. James Beardsley Hendryx. LC 40-33291. 1940. The Sun Dial Press.
Edge of Circumstance: A Story of the Sea. Edward Noble. LC 5-28011. 1905. Dodd, Mead & Company.
Edge of Danger. Michael Storm. LC 57-8739. 1957. Mystery House.
Edge of Darkness. Mary Ellen Chase. LC 57-10637. 1957. Norton.
Edge of Darkness. William Howard Woods. LC 42-361674. 1942. J. B. Lippincott Company.
Edge of Decision. T. Poole-Tombs. 3.00 o.p. Carlton.
Edge of Despair. M. L. Heinkel. 1978. pap. 1.50 (ISBN 0-532-15340-5). Woodhill.
Edge of Doom. Henry Francis Prevost Battersby. LC 20-7652. 1919. John Lane.
Edge of Doom. Leo Brady. LC 49-4829. 1949. E. P. Dutton.
Edge of Eden. 1st Ed. Dick Pearce, pseud. LC 62-10540. 1962. Lippincott.
Edge of Eternity. Aida Rodman De Milt. LC 26-11206. 1926. The Reader Publications.
Edge of Fear. Joyce Morton. (Avalon Books). 4.95. Thomas Bouregy.
Edge of Fear. Jack Pearl, pseud. price not set o.p. Norton.
Edge of Forever. Chad Oliver. 1978. pap. 4.95 o.s.i. (ISBN 0-8202-5030-9). Sherbourne.
Edge of Forever. Chad Oliver. 312p. 1971. 7.50 o.p. (ISBN 0-8202-0051-4). Sherbourne.
Edge of Glass. Catherine Gaskin. 240p. 1981. pap. 2.50 (ISBN 0-553-14362-X). Bantam.
Edge of Glass. Catherine Gaskin. 1979. pap. 1.95 (ISBN 0-449-23846-6, Crest). Fawcett.
Edge of Glass. 1st Ed. Catherine Gaskin. LC 67-13784. 1967. 4.95. Doubleday.
Edge of Grass. James B Kelly. 1973. 4.95 (ISBN 0-517-51391-9). Lenox Hill Press.
Edge of Greatness. Winthrop Neilson & Neilson, Frances Fullerton. LC 51-9837. 1951. Putnam.
Edge of Gunsmoke. Matt Harding, pseud. 1978. pap. 1.25 (ISBN 0-532-12576-2). Woodhill.
Edge of Hazard. George Horton. LC 6-6488. 1906. The Bobbs-Merrill Company.
Edge of Never: Classic and Contemporary Tales of the Supernatural. Ed. by Robert Hoskins. LC 73-76986. (Fawcett premier book). 1973. 0.95. Fawcett Publications.
Edge of Night. August William Derleth. 1945. 2.00 o.p. Arkham.
Edge of Panic. Henry Kane. LC 50-7747. (Inner sanctum mystery). 1950. Simon and Schuster.
Edge of Piracy: A Novel. Donald Barr Chidsey. LC 64-23816. 1964. Crown Publishers.
Edge of Running Water. William Milligan Sloane. LC 55-7243. 1955. Dodd, Mead.
Edge of Running Water. William Milligan Sloane. LC 39-13357. 1939. Farrar & Rinehart, Incorporated.
Edge of Sadness. Edwin O'Connor. LC 61-5738. 1961. Little, Brown.
Edge of Space: Three Original Novellas of Science Fiction. Phyllis Bloom Gotlieb et al. Ed. by Robert Silverberg. LC 79-4406. (Science Fiction Ser.). 1979. 8.95 o.p. (ISBN 0-525-66625-7). Lodestar Bks.
Edge of Space: Three Original Novellas of Science Fiction. Robert Silverberg. LC 79-4406. 7.95 (ISBN 0-525-66625-7). Elsevier/Nelson Books.
Edge of Spring. Helen Bianchin. (Harlequin Presents Ser.). 192p. 1981. pap. 1.50 (ISBN 0-373-10415-4, Pub. by Harlequin). PB.
Edge of Temptation. Anne Mather. (Harlequin Presents Ser.). 192p. (Orig.). 1981. pap. 1.50 (ISBN 0-373-10405-7, Pub. by Harlequin). PB.
Edge of the Alphabet. Janet Frame, pseud. LC 62-16268. 1962. 4.95 o.p. (ISBN 0-8076-0194-2). Braziller.

Edge of the Chair: Anthology. Joan Kahn. LC 67-22500. 1967. Harper & Row.
Edge of the City: Novelization by Ffrederik Pohl, Based Upon the Screenplay by Robert Allan Aurthur. Frederik Pohl. LC 57-8246. (Ballantine books, 199). 1957. Ballantine Books.
Edge of the Desert. Gifford Paul Cheshire. LC 58-7353. (Double D western). 1958. Doubleday.
Edge of the Desert. easy eye ed. Matt Stuart. pap. 0.60 o.p. Lancer.
Edge of the Forest. Decorations by Roberta Moynihan. Agnes Smith. LC 59-2113. 1959. Viking Press.
Edge of the Land. Steven C Lawrence. 1974. (pbk.) 0.75. Ace Books.
Edge of the Nest. Philip Stevenson. LC 29-9287. 1929. Coward-McCann, Inc.
Edge of the Pond. Robin Moore & Ronald Van Duren. 1978. pap. 1.95 (ISBN 0-532-19140-4). Woodhill.
Edge of the Pond. Robin Moore & Ronald Van Duren. 1977. pap. 1.95 o.p. (ISBN 0-532-19140-4). Manor Bks.
Edge of the Storm. Augustin Yanez. Tr. by Ethel Brinton from Sp. LC 63-7434. (Texas Pan American Ser.). Orig. Title: Al filo del agua. (Illus.). 342p. 1963. 14.95x (ISBN 0-292-73221-X); pap. 7.95x (ISBN 0-292-70131-4). U of Tex Pr.
Edge of the Storm (Al Filo Del Agua) A Novel. Agustin Yanez. LC 63-7434. (Texas Pan-American series). 1963. University of Texas Press.
Edge of the Sword. Vladimir Pozner. Tr. by Chevalier, Haakon Maurice. LC 42-154250. 1942. Modern Age Books.
Edge of the Tightrope. John H. Drew. LC 79-13285. 7.95 (ISBN 0-918880-04-1). Communication Creativity.
Edge of the Woods. Heather Ross Miller. LC 64-21528. 1964. Atheneum.
Edge of the World. Edith Blinn. LC 19-2847. 1.50. Britton Publishing Company.
Edge of the World. George Brydges Rodney. LC 31-252144. Duffield and Green.
Edge of the World: A Novel. David Malouf. LC 77-27506. 1978. 11.95 (ISBN 0-8076-0884-X). G. Braziller.
Edge of Things. William Edmund Barrett. 1974. (pbk.) 1.50. Avon.
Edge of Things. Elia Wilkinson Peattie. LC 3-20060. 1903. F. H. Revell Company.
Edge of Things. 1st Ed. William Edmund Barrett. 1960. Doubleday.
Edge of Time. Loula Grace Erdman. LC 50-14306. 1950. Dodd, Mead.
Edge of Time. Loula Grace Erdman. LC 81-597. (Gregg Press Western Fiction Series). 1981. 13.95 (ISBN 0-8398-2675-3). Gregg Press.
Edge of Time. David Grinnell, pseud. LC 58-12513. 1958. Avalon Books.
Edge of Time: Historical Novel of the Texas Panhandle. Loula Grace Erdman. 1950. 4.95 o.p. (ISBN 0-396-03186-2). Dodd.
Edge of Tomorrow. Reinhold Schmidt. 1975. pap. 3.00 o.p. Saucerian.
Edge of Twilight. Paula Christian. LC 78-103689. 1978. 4.50 (ISBN 0-931328-00-4). Timely Books.
Edge of Violence. Dorris Riter. LC 64-19402. (Illus.). 1964. D. McKay Co.
Edgell's Island: A Novel. Robert Pressnell. LC 51-9914. 1951. Dial Press.
Edges. Alice Woods. LC 2-23993. 1902. The Bowen-Merrill Company.
Edges: Thirteen New Tales from the Borderlands of the Imagination. Ursula K Le Guin & Kidd, Virginia. 1980. 2.50 (ISBN 0-671-83532-7). Pocket Books.
Edgewater People. Mary Eleanor Wilkins Freeman. LC 13-215281. Harper & Brothers.
Edging Through. James Bertolino. 1972. pap. 1.50 o.p. Stone-Marrow Pr.
Edible Woman. Margaret Eleanor Atwood. 1976. (pbk.) 1.50. Popular Library.
Edict. Max Simon Ehrlich. LC 71-31653. 1971. Doubleday.
Edie Tells. John Wheatcroft. 8.95 (ISBN 0-8453-1605-2). Cornwall Bks.
Edie Tells: A Portrait of the Artist As a Middle-Aged Cleaning Woman. John Wheatcroft. LC 74-9304. 1975. 8.95 (ISBN 0-498-01605-6). A. S. Barnes.
Edificare My Iglesia. Melvin Hodges. (Spanish Bks.). 1979. 1.75 (ISBN 0-8297-0544-9); wkbk. 01.00 (ISBN 0-8297-0545-7). Life Pubs Intl.
Edifice. Kole Omotoso. (African Writers Ser.). 1971. pap. text ed. 4.00x (ISBN 0-435-90102-8). Heinemann Ed.
Edina: Or, Missing Since Midnight. Ellen Price Henry Wood Wood. (Seaside library, v. 34, no. 467). 1879. G. Munro.
Edinburgh Caper: A One-Man International Plot. 1st Ed. St. Clair McKelway. LC 62-18756. 1962. Holt, Rinehart and Winston.
Edinburgh Stories. Arthur Conan Doyle. Compiled by Owen D. Edwards. 96p. 1981. 30.00x (ISBN 0-904919-49-8, Pub. by Polygon Bks Scotland). State Mutual Bk.
Edison's Conquest of Mars: With an Introd. by A. Langley Searles. Garrett Putnam Serviss. 1947. Carcosa House.
Edit with Lead. George Madison Grooms. LC 57-13076. 1958. Macmillan.
Edith: A Story of Chinatown. Harry M Johnson. LC 7-105423. (On cover: Beacon series). 1895. Arena Publishing Co.
Edith: A Tale of the Present Time. Mary Elizabeth A'Court Herbert Herbert. LC 7-4299. (On cover: Premium library). H. L. Kilner & Co.
Edith and John: A Story of Pittsburgh. Franklin Smith Farquhar. LC 12-13464. 1912. 1.00. Printed by Commercial Bindery and Printing Co.
Edith Bonham. Mary Hallock Foote. LC 17-858239. 1917. Houghton Miffling Company.
Edith Lyle. A Novel. Mary Jane Hawes Holmes. LC 1-1176. 1876. G. W. Carleton.
Edith Lyle. A Novel. Mary Jane Hawes Holmes. LC 1-1177. 1888. G. W. Dillingham, Successor to G. W. Carleton & Co.
Edith Lyle. A Novel. Mary Jane Hawes Holmes. (On cover: Madison square library. no. 72). 1897. G. W. Dillingham Co.
Edith Murray. A Story. Joanna Hooe Mathews. LC 44-34782. 1878. G. W. Carleton & Co.
Edith: Or, A Time to Weep. A Sketch of Real Life... Abby Bent. 1842. Massachusetts Sabbath School Society.
Edith: Or, The Light of Home. Eliza B Davis. LC 6-32494. 1856. Crosby, Nichols and Company.
Edith Percival. A Novel. May Agnes Early Fleming. LC 6-39993. 1893. G. W. Dillingham.
Edith Travor's Secret. A Novel. Harriet Lewis. (On cover: The choice series, no. 59). 1892. R. Bonner's Sons.
Edith Vernon: Or, Crime and Retribution. A Tragic Story of New England, Founded Upon Fact. Francis Alexander Durivage. LC 6-36560. 1845. F. Gleason.
Edith Wharton Omnibus. Edith Newbold Jones Wharton. LC 78-12686. 12.50 (ISBN 0-684-15973-2). Scribner.
Edith Wharton Reader. Ed. by Louis Auchincloss. Edith Newbold Jones Wharton. LC 65-14613. bds., 7.50. Scribners.
Edith Wharton Treasury: Edited and with an Introd. by Arthur Hobson Quinn. Edith Newbold Jones Wharton. LC 50-2775. 1950. Appleton-Century-Crofts.
Editha's Burglar. A Story for Children. Frances Hodgson Burnett. LC 6-16417. 1888. Jordan, Marsh & Company.
Edith's Diary. Patricia Highsmith. LC 76-58867. 8.95 (ISBN 0-671-22686-X). Simon and Schuster.
Edith's Diary. Patricia Highsmith. 1978. 1.95. Pocket Books.
Edith's Ministry. Harriet Burn McKeever. LC 7-16316. 1864. Lindsay & Blakiston.
Edith's Mistake; or, Left to Herself. By Jennie Woodville Pseud. Jennie Latham Stabler. LC 9-935. J. B. Lippincott & Co.
Edith's Strange Desire. pap. 1.95 o.p. (V1012T, Venus). Grove.
Editor. Sam Post. (Belmont Tower books). 1979. 1.95 (ISBN 0-505-51375-7). Tower Pubns.
Editor. Don Tracy. 1973. Pocket Books.
Editorial Wild Oats. Samuel Langhorne Clemens. LC 77-125685. (American journalists). (Illus.). 1970. (ISBN 0-405-01662-X). Arno.
Editors & Writers. Ed. by Betty J. Breyer. LC 79-19986. (Anthony Trollope; The Complete Short Stories Ser.: Vol. II). 1979. 17.50 (ISBN 0-912646-57-8). Tex Christian.
Editors and Writers. Anthony Trollope & Betty Jane Breyer. LC 79-19986. (Anthony Trollope, the complete short stories; v. 2). 12.50 (ISBN 0-912646-57-8). Texas Christian University Press.
Editor's Choice. Ed. by Alfred Dashiell. LC 34-35693. G. P. Putnam's Sons.
Editor's Choice in Science Fiction. Ed. by Samuel Moskowitz. LC 54-7374. 1954. McBride.
Editor's Choice: 26 Modern Short Stories from Good Housekeeping, Edited by Herbert R. Mayes. Good Housekeeping. Ed. by Herbert Raymond Mayes. LC 56-7076. 1956. Random House.
Editor's Tales. Anthony Trollope. Ed. by N. John Hall. LC 80-1888. (Selected Works of Anthony Trollope Ser.). 1981. Repr. of 1870 ed. lib. bdg. 45.00 (ISBN 0-405-14155-6). Ayer Co.
Edleen Vaughan: Or, Paths of Peril. Elisabeth. Cassell Publishing Company.
Edmond Dante, the Count of Monte Cristo. Alexandre Dumas & Maquet, Auguste. Tr. by Williams, Henry Llewellyn, Jr. LC 11-16151. The F. M. Lupton Publishing Company.
Edmond Dantes... A Sequel to The Count of Monte-Cristo. Edmund Flagg. LC 6-41127. T. B. Peterson & Brothers.
Edmond Dantes: The Count of Monte Cristo. Alexandre Dumas & Maquet, Auguste. Tr. by Williams, Henry Llewellyn. LC 6-42820. (On cover: The eureka series. no. 41). 1892. W. H. Davis.
Edmond Dantes: The Count of Monte Cristo. Alexandre Dumas & Maquet, Auguste. Tr. by Thiese, William. LC 6-42819. (American series. no. 288). M. J. Ivers & Co.
Edmond Dantes: The Count of Monte Cristo. a new translation from the latest french edition by henry l. williams. ed. Alexandre Dumas & Auguste Maquet. LC 11-16151. The F. M. Lupton Publishing Company.
Edmond Dantes. The Sequel to Alexandre Dumas' Celebrated Novel of The Count of Monte-Cristo. an entire new and enl. ed... ed. Edmund Flagg. LC 6-41144. T. B. Peterson & Brothers.
Edmond Peyre. Charles Blanton Roberts. LC 36-4308. Fleming H. Revell Company.
Edmund Daw: Or, Ever Forgive. Charles Washington Beebe. LC 6-9764. 1873. G.W. Carleton & Co.; Etc., Etc.
Edna Carlisle: Or, Flossie's Violet. C. W. Doyle. LC 5-34234. 1887. C. W. Doyle.
Edna, His Wife: An American Idyll. Margaret Ayer Barnes. LC 35-23926. 1935. Houghton Mifflin Company.
Edna Lee. A Novel. Hattie Weller Worden. LC 1-29614. 1900. Scroll Publishing Company.
Edna the Inebriate Woman. Jeremy Sandford. (Illus.). 128p. 1978. 9.95 (ISBN 0-7145-2548-0, Pub. by M Boyars); pap. 5.95 (ISBN 0-7145-2549-9, Pub. by M Boyars). Merrimack Pub Cir.
Edna, the Pretty Typewriter. A Thrilling Story Founded Upon a Play of the Same Name. Grace Miller White & Woods, Albert Herman. LC 33-28360. (On cover: Play book series, no. 113). 1907. J. S. Ogilvie Publishing Company.
Edna's Fruit Hat: And Other Stories. John Pudney. LC 47-30476. 1947. Harper.
Edrie's Legacy. Sarah Elizabeth Forbush G. S. Downs Downs. LC 6-45946. (On cover: The select series. no. 98). 1892. Street & Smith.
Edsel. Karl Jay Shapiro. LC 72-153743. 1971. 6.95. B. Geis Associates.
Eduardo Mallea. Astur Morsella. LC 57-40113. 1957. Editorial MAC--CO.
Education Before Verdun. Arnold Zweig & Sutton, Eric, Tr. LC 36-10347. 1936. Viking Press.
Education Before Verdun. Arnold Zweig & Sutton, Eric, Tr. Title. LC 38-31837. 1938. The Sun Dial Press, Inc.
Education in Blood: A Novel. Richard M Elman. LC 72-140771. 1971. 7.95 (ISBN 0-684-10139-4). Scribner.
Education of Anthony Dare. Archibald Marshall. LC 24-9129. 1924. Mead and Company.
Education of Don Juan. Robin Hardy. 1980. 12.95 (ISBN 0-671-25335-2, Wyndham Bks). S&S.
Education of Eric Lane. Stephen McKenna. LC 21-10607. (His The sensationalists, II). 1.90. George H. Doran Company.
Education of Ernest Wilmerding: a Story of Opening Flowers. Edward Chichester Wentworth. LC 24-2626. 1924. Covici--McGee Co,
Education of Hyman Kaplan Leo Calvin Rosten. LC 37-27486. Harcourt, Brace and Company.
Education of Hyman Kaplan . Leo Calvin Rosten. LC 65-2725. (Harvest book, HB87).
Education of Jacqueline. Claire De Pratz. LC 10-11874. 1910. 1.50. Duffield and Company.
Education of Jonatgan Beam: A Novel. Russell Brantley. LC 62-927561. 1962. Macmillan.
Education of Lydia. Charles Wolffe. (O.s.i.). 1974. pap. 0.95 o.s.i. (AN1355, Award). Univ Pub & Dist.
Education of Oversoul No. 7. Jane Roberts. 1976. pap. 2.75 (ISBN 0-671-80794-3). PB.
Education of Oversoul Seven. Jane Roberts. LC 73-446. (Illus.). 1973. 6.95 (ISBN 0-13-240440-0). Prentice-Hall.
Education of Patrick Silver. Jerome Charyn. LC 76-8633. 8.95 (ISBN 0-87795-142-X). Arbor House.
Education of Patrick Silver. Jerome Charyn. 1977. 1.75 (ISBN 0-380-01698-2). Avon Books.
Education of Peter: A Novel of the Younger Generation. John Wiley. LC 24-470420. 1924. Frederick A. Stokes Company.
Education of Pretty Boy. Drawings by Arthur D. Fuller. 1st Ed. Havilah Babcock. LC 60-7334. 1960. Holt.
Education of Sallie May. Fannie Kilbourne. LC 25-194279. 1925. G. P. Putnam's Sons.
Education of Winnie D. Wendy Owen. LC 78-27167. 1979. 8.95 (ISBN 0-8008-2365-6). Taplinger.
Education of Winnie D. A Novel. Wendy Owen. LC 78-27171. 1979. 7.95 (ISBN 0-8008-2365-6). Taplinger Pub. Co.
Education Sentimentale. Gustave Flaubert. Ed. by Maynial. (Coll. Prestige). 27.95. French & Eur.
Edward Austin: Or, The Hunting Flask. A Tale of the Forest and Town... Joseph Holt Higraham. LC 7-10357. 1842. F. Gleason.
Edward Barry, South Sea Pearler. Louis Becke. LC 3315. 1900. L. C. Page & Co. (Incorporated.
Edward Berner Is Alive Again! Herbert D Kastle. LC 75-15556. 1975. 8.95 (ISBN 0-13-240770-1). Prentice-Hall.
Edward Burton: A Novel. Henry Wood. LC 8-37556. 1890. Lee and Shepard.
Edward De Bono Science Fiction Collection. George Hay. LC 77-365382. 1976. 4.95 (ISBN 0-7057-0068-2). Elmfield Press.
Edward, Edward. Lolah Burford. LC 73-182446. (O.s.i.). 576p. 1973. 8.95 o.s.i. (ISBN 0-02-518200-5). Macmillan.
Edward, Edward: A Part of His Story and of History, 1795-1816, Set Out in Three Parts in This Form of a New-Old Picaresque Romance That Is Also a Study in Grace. Lolah Burford. LC 73-182446. 1973. 8.95. Macmillan.
Edward, Edward: A Part of His Story and of History, 1795-1816, Set Out in Three Parts in This Form of a New-Old Picaresque Romance That Is Also a Study in Grace. Lolah Burford. 1974. (pbk.) 1.75. Bantam Books.
Edward: Edward the Seventh, King and Emperor; a Novel. Tyler-Whittle, Michael Sidney. LC 75-10001. (Illus.). 8.95. St. Martin's Press.
Edward King & Emperor. Tyler Whittle, pseud. LC 75-10001. 320p. 1975. 8.95 o.p. (ISBN 0-312-23835-5). St Martin.
Edward Manning: Or, The Bride and the Maiden. Joseph Holt Ingraham. 1847. Williams Brothers; Etc., Etc.
Edward. Various Views of Human Nature, Taken from Life and Manners, Chiefly in England... John Moore. LC 25-2815. 1798. Printed by W. Durell, for J. Harrisson, C. Davis, E. Duyckinck & Co., W. Milns, A. Somerville, R. Macgill, Gaine & Teneyck, Spencer & Webb, Thomas, Andrews, & Penniman, and Carter, & Wilkinson.
Edward Vernon: My Cousin's Story. Edward Vernon Childe. LC 6-20978. 1848. Harper & Brothers.
Edward Wortley Montagu. An Autobiography Fictitious... Edward Vaughan Hyde Kenealy. LC 7-10985. 1870. Turner & Co.
Edward Zoltan. Philip Freund. LC 48-8829. 1948. Beechhurst Press.
Edward Zoltan: A Novel. Philip Freund. LC 46-20798. 1946. The Beechhurst Press.
Edwardians. Sackville-West, Hon. Victoria Mary. (Compass bk. C87). 1961. pap., 1.45. Viking.
Edwardians. Victoria Mary Sackville-West. (Compass bk. C87). 1961. 1.45pap. Viking.
Edwardians. Victoria Mary Sackville-West. LC 30-26888. 1930. Doubleday, Doran & Company, Inc.
Edwardians. Victoria Mary Sackville-West. 1975. (pbk.) 1.50 (ISBN 0-380-00326-0). Avon.
Edward's Fancy. Monica Dickens. LC 44-1896. 1944. Harper & Brothers.
Edwin Brothertoft. 3d ed. Theodore Winthrop. LC 9-947. 1862. Ticknor and Fields.
Edwin Brothertoft. Theodore Winthrop. LC 4-35645. (Leisure hour series). 1876. H. Holt and Company.
Edwin Drood: & Master Humphrey's Clock. Charles Dickens. LC 37-30958. (Half-title: Everyman's library, ed. by Ernest Rhys. Fiction. no. 725). 1916. J. M. Dent. & Sons, Ltd.
Edwin Drood & Master Humphrey's Clock. Charles Dickens. 1970. Repr. of 1915 ed. 9.95x (ISBN 0-460-00725-4, Evman). Biblio Dist.
Edwin Drood: And Master Humphrey's Clock. Charles Dickens & Chesterton, Gilbert Keith. (Half-title: Everyman's library, ed. by Ernest Rhys. Fiction. no. 723). 1909. J. M. Dent & Co.
Edwin Mullhouse. Steven Millhauser. 1978. pap. 2.50 (ISBN 0-380-01946-9, 37952, Bard). Avon.
Edwin Mullhouse: The Life and Death of an American Writer 1943-1954. Steven Millhauser. LC 72-2230. 1973. (pbk) 1.25. Popular Lib.
Edwin of the Iron Shoes. Marcia Muller. (McKay-Washburn Mystery Ser.). 1977. 7.95 o.p. (ISBN 0-679-50782-5). McKay.
Edwin of the Iron Shoes. Marcia Muller. (Crime Ser). 1978. pap. 1.95 o.p. (ISBN 0-14-004915-0). Penguin.
Edwin of the Iron Shoes: A Novel of Suspence. Marcia Muller. LC 77-8564. (MW suspence). 7.95 (ISBN 0-679-50782-5). McKay.

TITLE INDEX EIGHTH DAY.

Edwin of the Iron Shoes: A Novel of Suspense. Marcia Muller. LC 78-1967. 1978. 1.95 (ISBN 0-14-004915-0). Penguin Books.
Ee-Dah-How. Tracy Coker. LC 33-30723. 1933. The Caxton Printers, ltd.
Eel Pie Murders. Zenith Jones Brown. LC 33-4549. Farrar & Rinehart, Incorporated.
Eelgrass. Joe Ashby Porter. LC 77-4996. 1977. 4.95 (ISBN 0-8112-0655-6). New Directions Pub.
Eenie, Meenie, Minie--Murder! William Gray Beyer. LC 45-9671. 1945. Mystery House.
Eerie He and She. Alfred J. Cohen. LC 6-267391. 1889. G. W. Dillingham.
Eferding Diaries: A Novel. Gordon Shepherd. LC 66-23286. 1967. Lippincott.
Effendi: A Romance of the Soudan. Florence Brooks Whitehouse. LC 4-212. 1904. Little, Brown, and Company.
Effervescence, Excerpts from Mark Twain. Mark Twain. (Illus.). 32p. 1978. pap. write for info o.p. Turtles Quill.
Effi Briest. Theodor Fontane. Tr. by Douglas Parmee. (Penguin classics.). 1976. 1.95 (ISBN 0-14-044190-5). Penguin Books.
Effi Briest. Theodor Fontane. LC 66-25107. 1966. F. Ungar Pub. Co.
Effi Briest. Tr., with an Introd., by Douglas Parmee. Theodor Fontane. LC 67-7236. (Penguin classics, L190). 1967. pap., 1.45. Penguin.
Efficiency Edgar. Clarence Budington Kelland. LC 20-7299. Harper & Brothers.
Efficiency Expert. authorized 1st ed. Edgar Rice Burroughs. LC 68-555. (Illus.). 1966. House of Greystoke.
Efficiency in Hades: The Romantic Adventures of an Enterprising Expert in the Lower World. Robert B Vale. LC 23-12224. 1923. Frederick A. Stokes Company.
Effie Hetherington. Robert Williams Buchanan. LC 6-19880. 1896. Roberts Brothers.
Effie Ogilvie. The Story of a Young Life. Margaret Oliphant Wilson Oliphant. (On cover: Seaside library. Pocket ed., no. 827). 1886. G. Munro.
Effie Ogilvie: The Story of a Young Life. Margaret Oliphant Wilson Oliphant. (Harper's handy series, no. 82). 1886. Harper & Brothers.
Effie Wingate's Work. Mary Dwinell Chellis. LC 6-23416. H. A. Young & Co.
Effigies. William K. Wells. (Orig.). 1980. pap. 2.95 (ISBN 0-440-12245-7). Dell.
Effinghams: Or Home As I Found It... Frederick Jackson. LC 11-354. 1841. S. Colman.
Efraim's Book. Alfred Andersch. LC 72-121946. 1970. 6.95. Doubleday.
Efuru. Flora Nwapa. (African Writers Ser.). 1966. pap. text ed. 3.00x (ISBN 0-435-90026-9). Heinemann Ed.
Egan. Harold Everett Porter. LC 20-15701. 1920. 1.90. Dodd, Mead and Company.
Egan Rendy. John Cromwell. LC 43-57. 1942. The Non-Pragmatic Press.
Egbert. William Aubrey Darlington. LC 25-6194. 1925. The Penn Publishing Company.
Egg of the Glak: And Other Stories. Harvey Jacobs. LC 75-81874. 1969. 5.95. Harper & Row.
Egg: Or, The Memoirs of Gregory Giddy, Esq. LC 74-20515. (Flowering of the Novel). (Illus.). 1974. (ISBN 0-8240-1198-8). Garland Pub.
Egg-Shaped Thing. Hodder-Williams, Christopher. LC 67-15110. 1967. Putnam.
Egghead Republic. Arno Schmidt. Ed. by Ernst Krawehl & Marion Boyars. Tr. by Michael Horovitz from Ger. 160p. 1982. pap. 7.95 (ISBN 0-7145-2592-8, Pub. by M Boyars). Merrimack Pub Cir.
Egghead Republic: A Short Novel from the Horse Latitudes. Arno Schmidt. LC 80-670270. 1979. 12.00 (ISBN 0-7145-2591-X). M. Boyars.
Eggheads in the End Zone: A Novel. 1st Ed. Robert L Scribner. LC 57-139560. 1957. Exposition Press.
Eggheads in the End Zone, a Novel. 1st Ed. Robert L Scribner. LC 57-13956. 1957. Exposition Press.
Eggnog Riot: The Christmas Mutiny at West Point. James B Agnew. LC 78-21641. (Illus.). 12.95 (ISBN 0-89141-036-8). Presidio Press.
Eggs and Baker: Or, The Days of Trial. John Masefield. LC 36-24952. 1936. The Macmillan Company.
Eggs, Beans and Crumpets. Pelham Grenville Wodehouse. LC 40-79247. 1940. Doubleday, Doran & Company, Inc.
Eglee, a Girl of the People. William Rutherford Hayes Trowbridge. LC 2-29266. 1902. A. Wessels Company.
Ego: A Novel. Henry Willard French. LC 11-16161. 1880. Lee and Shepard.
Egoist. George Meredith. LC 79-52414. 1979. 14.95 (ISBN 0-915864-98-3) (ISBN 0-915864-97-5). Academy Chicago Ltd.
Egoist: A Comedy in Narrative. George Meredith. LC 1-19344. (Franklin square library. no. 90). 1879. Harper & Brothers.
Egoist: A Comedy in Narrative. rev. ed. George Meredith. LC 1-193460. 1897. C. Scribner's Sons.
Egoist: A Comedy in Narrative. rev. ed. George Meredith. LC 17-503. 1913. C. Scribner's Sons.
Egoist: A Comedy in Narrative. Edited with an Introd. and Notes by Lionel Stevenson. George Meredith. LC 58-1477. (Riverside editions B27). 1958. Houghton Mifflin.
Egoist: An Authoritative Text, Background, Criticism. George Meredith. Ed. by Robert Martin Adams. LC 77-25313. (Norton critical edition). 14.95 (ISBN 0-393-04431-9). Norton.
Egoists: A Novel. Bonaventura Tecchi. LC 64-12435. 1964. Appleton-Century.
Egomaniac. Christian Iber & Jane Iber. 1970. 7.00 o.p. (ISBN 0-682-47130-5). Exposition.
Egrin and the Painted Wizard. Amanda Walsh. (Picture Puffin original.). (Illus.). 1973. (pbk.) 1.00 (ISBN 0-14-050081-2). Penguin Books.
Egypt Ennis; or, Prisons Without Walls. A Novel. William B Smith. LC 8-963564. (On cover: Satchel series, no. 2). 1876. The Authors' Publishing Company.
Egyptian. Mika Toimi Waltari. 1978. Repr. 2.50 (ISBN 0-425-03721-5, Medallion). Berkley Pub.
Egyptian: A Novel. Mika Toimi Waltari. LC 49-9830. 1949. G. P. Putnam's Sons.
Egyptian Bondage, and Other Stories. Jascha Frederick Kessler. LC 67-22133. 1967. Harper & Row.
Egyptian Childhood. Taha Hussein. (Arab Writers Series). 200p. (Orig.). 1980. 12.00x (ISBN 0-89410-210-9); pap. 6.00x (ISBN 0-89410-211-7). Three Continents.
Egyptian Cross Mystery. Ellery Queen. 334p. 1976. lib. bdg. 15.95x (ISBN 0-89966-150-5). Buccaneer Bks.
Egyptian Cross Mystery. Ellery Queen, pseud. LC 40-32564. 1940. Triangle Books.
Egyptian Cross Mystery: A Problem in Deduction. Ellery Queen, pseud. LC 32-28037. 1932. Frederick A. Stokes Company.
Egyptian Dove. Konstantin Leontiev. Ed. by George Ivask. Tr. by George Reavey. LC 68-31244. 1969. 7.50 o.p. Weybright.
Egyptian Interlude. Jolan Foldes. Tr. by Alexander G. Kenedi. LC 39-29835. Farrar & Rinehart, Inc.
Egyptian Love. Stephen Haweis. LC 24-24691. 1924. Doubleday, Page & Company.
Egyptian Love Spell. Edith S. Billings. LC 14-14257. 1914. 0.50. The Central Publishing Co.
Egyptian Portrait. C. W Grudy. LC 31-29783. 1930. J. M. Dent & Sons, Ltd.
Egyptian Princess. Georg Moritz Ebers. (On cover: Seaside library. Pocket ed., no. 1101). 1888. G. Munro.
Egyptian Princess... Georg Moritz Ebers. Tr. by Grove, Eleanor. LC 16-15706. (historical romance by Georg Ebers. vol. ii). 1915. D. Appleton and Company.
Egyptian Princess. Georg Moritz Ebers & Grove, Eleanor, Tr. LC 4-16859. 1901. D. Appleton and Company.
Egyptian Princess. Georg Moritz Ebers & Grove, Eleanor, Tr. LC 4-23583. 1880. W. S. Gottsberger.
Egyptian Short Stories. Tr. by Denys Johnson-Davies from Arabic. 1978. 10.00 (ISBN 0-89410-038-6); pap. 5.00 (ISBN 0-89410-039-4). Three Continents.
Egyptologists. Kingsley Amis & Robert Conquest. LC 66-10310. 1966. Random House.
Ehrengard. Karen Blixen. LC 74-17033. 1975. (pbk.). 1.95 (ISBN 0-394-71431-8). Vintage Books.
Ehrengard. Karen Blixen. LC 77-355892. 1976. 3.60 (ISBN 0-226-15293-6). University of Chicago Press.
Ehrengard. Isak Dinesen, pseud. LC 74-17033. (O.s.i.). 1975. pap. 1.95 o.s.i. (ISBN 0-394-71431-8, Vin). Random.
Eichhofs: A Romance. Valeska Bethusy-Huc. Tr. by Wister, Annie Lee (Furness) LC 8-155291. 1881. J. B. Lippincott & Co.
Eichmann Syndrome. Uri Dan & Edward Radley. 1977. pap. 1.75 o.p. (ISBN 0-8439-0466-6, Leisure Bks). Nordon Pubns.
Eiger Sanction. Trevanian. LC 72-84293. 1972. 6.95 (ISBN 0-517-50034-5). Crown Publishers.
Eight Against Utopia. Douglas R. Mason. 1970. pap. 0.60 o.p. (ISBN 0-446-63496-4, 63-496). Paperback Lib.
Eight & One Half. Nobella Arthur. 192p. pap. 1.95 o.p. (6122). Brandon.
Eight April Days. Scott Hart. LC 49-10343. 1949. Coward-McCann.
Eight Candles Glowing. Patricia Muse. LC 76-7542. 1.25 (ISBN 0-345-25092-3). Ballantine Books.
Eight Cents: 1st. Ed. Richard Pike Bissell. LC 52-12642. 1953. Little, Brown.
Eight Crooked Trenches. Francis Beeding. LC 36-6804. 1936. Harper & Brothers.
Eight Days. authorized ed. Robert Edward Forrest & Robert Edward Forrest. LC 6-40378. (Lovell's international series, no. 154). 1891. United States Book Company.
Eight Days: By Gabriel Fielding Pseud. Alan Gabriel Barnsley. LC 59-5134. 1959. Morrow.
Eight Faces at Three. Craig Rice. LC 30-32376. 1939. Simon and Schuster.
Eight Fantasms & Magics. Jack Vance, pseud. (Science Fiction Adventure Ser). (O.s.i.). 1969. 5.95 o.s.i. (ISBN 0-02-621510-1). Macmillan.
Eight Fantasms and Magics: A Science Fiction Adventure. John Holbrook Vance. LC 75-80798. 1969. Macmillan.
Eight for Eternity. Cecil Roberts. LC 48-6725. 1948. Doubleday.
Eight Great American Short Novels: Ed., Introd. by Philip Rahv. Ed. by Philip Rahv. (Medallion DQ1553). 1968. pap., 1.25. Berkley.
Eight Great Hebrew Short Stories. Ed. by Alan Lelchuk & Gerson Shaked. 1983. pap. 7.95 (ISBN 0-452-00605-8, Mer). NAL.
Eight Hours from England. Anthony Quayle. LC 46-4005. 1946. Doubleday & Company, Inc.
Eight Hundred Thirteen. Maurice Leblanc. Tr. by Teixeira De Mattos, Alexander Louis. 1910. 1.20. Doubleday, Page & Company.
Eight Hundred Thirteen. Maurice Leblanc. Tr. by Teixeira De Mattos, Alexander Louis. LC 14-10513. Hurst & Company.
Eight Hundred Thirteen. Maurice Leblanc. Tr. by Teixeira De Mattos, Alexander Louis. LC 22-5163. 1911. Doubleday, Page & Company.
Eight Is Enough. Tom Braden. 1977. pap. 2.25 (ISBN 0-449-23002-3, Crest). Fawcett.
Eight Keys to Eden. Mark Clifton. LC 60-9470. 1960. Doubleday.
Eight Keys to Eden. Mark Clifton. LC 82-12871. 5.95 (ISBN 0-89865-258-8). Donning Co.
Eight Men. Richard Wright. LC 61-5636. 1961. World Pub. Co.
Eight Million Ways to Die. Lawrence Block. LC 81-71698. 13.50 (ISBN 0-87795-405-4). Arbor House.
Eight Mortal Ladies Possessed: A Book of Stories. Tennessee Williams. LC 73-89484. (New Directions book). 1974. 6.00 (ISBN 0-8112-0530-4) (ISBN 0-8112-0531-2). New Directions Pub. Corp.
Eight-Oared Victors: A Story of College Water Sports. Lester Chadwick. LC 13-752122. (His The college sports series). 1.00. Cupples & Leon Company.
Eight O'clock Alibi. Christopher Bush. LC 37-1603. H. Holt and Company.
Eight of Swords. John Dickson Carr. LC 63-288. (Collier mystery). 1962. Collier Books.
Eight of Swords. John Dickson Carr. LC 34-3536. 1934. Harper & Brothers.
Eight Panes of Glass: A Novel of the Scottish Highlands. Robert Simpson. LC 24-4871. 1924. Frederick A. Stokes Company.
Eight Plus One. Robert Cormier. 192p. 1982. pap. 2.25 (ISBN 0-553-22690-8). Bantam.
Eight Rainbows of 'Umi, Ku'ulei Ihara & 'Iliahi Johnson. Illus. by Marcia Morse. (Illus.). 1976. pap. 4.95 (ISBN 0-914916-14-9). Topgallant.
Eight Short Novels. Ed. by Dean S. Flower. 1979. pap. 2.50 (ISBN 0-449-30842-1, Prem). Fawcett.
Eight Short, Short Stories & Sketches. James Thomas Farrell. LC 81-10855. (Nostoc Magazine; No. 10). 10.00 (ISBN 0-933292-08-2) (ISBN 0-933292-07-4). Arts End Books.
Eight Short Stories. Jerry Bumpus et al. (Illus., Orig.). 1975. pap. 2.50 (ISBN 0-930866-02-9). Helix Hse.
Eight Short Stories. Anne Paolucci. LC 76-53274. 6.95 (ISBN 0-918680-04-2). H. Prim Co.
Eight Short Stories, Edited, with Introduction, Notes, Exercises, and Vocabulary. Guy De Maupassant. Ed. by Blondheim, David Simon. LC 33-25351. 1933. The Macmillan Company.
Eight Stories by Chinese Women. Nieh Hau-Ling. 148p. 1980. 7.50 (ISBN 0-89955-172-6, Pub. by Mei Ya China). Intl Schol Bk Serv.
Eight Stories from the Rest of the Robots. Isaac Asimov. 1971. pap. 0.75 o.p. (T2565). Pyramid Pubns.
Eight Strange Tales. Ed. by Vic Ghidalia. 192p. (Orig.). 1972. pap. 0.75 o.p. (T2624, GM). Fawcett World.
Eight Strokes of the Clock. Maurice Leblanc. LC 74-10487. (Illus.). 1975. 10.50 (ISBN 0-88355-202-7). Hyperion Press.
Eight Strokes of the Clock. Maurice Leblanc. Tr. by Teixeira De Mattos, Alexander Louis. LC 22-9053. The Macaulay Company.
Eight Swinging Cats. Robert Chambers. 5.95 o.p. Bobbs.
Eight Tales. Walter John De La Mare. LC 73-25846. 1971. 4.00. Arkham House.
Eight Tales from the Major Phase. Henry James. 1969. pap. 7.95 (ISBN 0-393-00286-1, Norton Lib). Norton.
Eight Times Ten: Or, Much Ado About Nothing by Penfield Williams Pseud. 1st Ed. Joseph C Wilson. LC 54-12358. 1954. Pageant Press.
Eight Uncollected Tales. facsimile ed. Henry James. Ed. by Edna Kenton. LC 71-160936. (Short Story Index Reprint Ser.). Repr. of 1950 ed. 18.00 (ISBN 0-8369-3915-8). Ayer Co.
Eight Uncollected Tales: Edited with an Introd. by Edna Kenton. Henry James. Ed. by Edna Kenton. LC 50-9190. 1950. Rutgers University Press.
Eight Uncollected Tales of Henry James. Henry James. LC 71-160936. (Short story index reprint series). 1971. (ISBN 0-8369-3915-8). Books for Libraries Press.
Eight Wells of Elim. Esther Loewen Vogt. LC 73-12396. 1974. 3.95 (ISBN 0-8361-1721-2). Herald Press.
Eight Years of His Life a Blank: A Story of the Pioneer Days of South Dakota; a Novel. Levi Judson Ross. LC 16-375. 1.00. W. R. Lambert.
Eighteen Best Stories of Edgar Allan Poe. Edgar Allan Poe. Ed. by Richard Wilbur. (Orig.). pap. 2.95 (ISBN 0-440-32227-8, LE). Dell.
Eighteen-Carat Kid, and Other Stories. Pelham Grenville Wodehouse & David A Jasen. LC 80-14012. 1980. 10.95 (ISBN 0-8264-0012-4). Continuum.
Eighteen Fifty-One: Or, The Adventures of Mr. and Mrs. Sandboys, Their Son and Daughter, Who Came up to London to Enjoy Themselves and to See the Great Exhibition. Henry Mayhew & Cruikshank, George, 1792-1878, Joint Author. LC 49-41822. Stringer and Townsend.
Eighteen Forty-Four; or, the Power of the "S.F." A Tale; Developing the Secret Action of Parties During the Presidential Campaign of 1844. Thomas Dunn English. LC 6-38407. (Mirror library--new ser.). 1847. Burgess, Stringer & Co. Etc.
Eighteen Fourty-Four. Etienne Leroux. LC 71-80423. 1972. 4.95 (ISBN 0-395-13647-4). Houghton Mifflin.
Eighteen Great Stories of Today. Ed. by Whit Burnett. LC 44-8265. (Avon annual. Special anniversary number). 1944. Avon Book Company.
Eighteen Hole Course. Harry Paul. pap. 1.95 o.p. (8009). Cameo.
Eighteen Miles from Home. William Thomas Hodge. 1904. Small, Maynard & Company.
Eighteen Seventy-Six. Gore Vidal. 448p. 1982. pap. 3.95 (ISBN 0-345-30674-0). Ballantine.
Eighteen Seventy-Six: A Novel. Gore Vidal. 1976. 14.95 (ISBN 0-394-49750-3). Random.
Eighteen Sixty to Eighteen Sixty-Five. Emma Lyon Bryan. LC 6-19895. J. Taliaffero.
Eighteen Stories: By Heinrich Boll. Tr. from German by Leila Vennewitz. 1st Ed. Heinrich Boll. LC 66-23273. 1966. 5.50. McGraw.
Eighteen Twelve: A Tale of Cape Cod. Michael Fitzgerald. LC 12-23707. 1912. 1.25. C. W. Swift.
Eighteen Visits to Mars. 1st Ed. Winthrop Allen Rember. LC 56-121889. 1956. Vantage Press.
Eighteen Wheeler Hijack. Avin Harry Johnston. (Orig.). 1979. pap. 1.95 (ISBN 0-532-23139-2). Woodhill.
Eighteenth Century English Novel in French Translation. Harold W. Streeter. LC 69-13251. 1969. Repr. of 1936 ed. 15.00 (ISBN 0-405-09011-0, Pub. by Blom). Ayer Co.
Eighteenth Century Russian Reader. Ed. by C. L. Drage & W. N. Vickery. (Oxford Readings in Philosophy Ser). (Pap. ed. 7.25x o.p.). 1969. 9.00x o.p. (ISBN 0-19-872011-4). Oxford U Pr.
Eighteenth-Century Shorter Novels. Ed. by Philip Henderson. 3.25x o.p. (ISBN 0-460-00856-0, Evman). Dutton.
Eighteenth Commandment: An Epic of the Prohibition Era. Clifton Carlisle Osborne. LC 28-9734. City Publishing Company.
Eighteenth Summer. Lillie Holland. (Orig.). 1973. pap. 0.95 o.s.i. (75-437). Lancer.
Eighth A-J Assembling. Ed. by Richard Kostelanetz & Henry J. Korn. (Illus.). 1978. pap. 4.95. Assembling Pr.
Eighth-Best-Dressed Man in the World. 1st Ed. Keith Botsford. LC 57-100702. 1957. Harcourt, Brace.
Eighth Circle. Stanley Ellin. 1975. (pbk.) 1.50 (ISBN 0-345-24462-1). Ballantine Books.
Eighth Circle. Stanley Ellin. LC 79-11705. (Gregg Press Mystery Series). 1979. 9.95 (ISBN 0-8398-2532-3). Gregg Press.
Eighth Day. Robert C Goldston. LC 56-9501. 1956. Rinehart.
Eighth Day. Thornton Niven Wilder. (95-180). 1968. Popular Lib.
Eighth Day. Thornton Niven Wilder. 1973. 1.25. Popular Lib.
Eighth Day. Thornton Niven Wilder. 1976. (pbk.) 2.25 (ISBN 0-380-00639-1). Avon.
Eighth Day. large type ed. Thornton Niven Wilder. LC 77-3835. 1969. 9.95. Harper & Row.

Eighth Day: By Thornton Wilder. 1st Ed. Thornton Niven Wilder. LC 67-15972. 1967. 6.95. Harper.
Eighth Day of Genesis. Al Jessep. LC 78-54133. 1979. 8.95 (ISBN 0-87949-128-0). Ashley Books.
Eighth Day of the Week. Marek Hasko. LC 74-27462. 1975. (ISBN 0-8371-7896-7). Greenwood Press.
Eighth Day of the Week. Marek Hlasko. LC 58-958594. 1958. Dutton.
Eighth Dwarf. Ross Thomas. LC 78-24578. 9.95 (ISBN 0-671-24653-4). Simon and Schuster.
Eighth Husband. May Howell Beecher. LC 13-20749. 1913. Sherman, French & Company.
Eighth K-Z Assembling. Ed. by Richard Kostelanetz & Henry J. Korn. (Illus.). 1978. pap. 4.95 (ISBN 0-915066-31-9). Assembling Pr.
Eighth Mrs. Bluebeard. Hillary Waugh. LC 58-7372. 1958. Published for the Crime Club by Doubleday.
Eighth Pan Book of Horror Stories. Ed. by H. Van Thal. 1982. pap. 10.00x (ISBN 0-330-10699-6, Pub. by Pan Bks). State Mutual Bk.
Eighth Plague. Denys Rhodes. LC 57-63. 1956. Longmans, Green.
Eighth Sacrament. Thomas Cullinan. LC 77-4189. 1977. 7.95 o.p. (ISBN 0-399-12011-4). Putnam.
Eighth Sin. Stefan Kanfer. LC 77-90254. 8.95 (ISBN 0-394-41476-4). Random House.
Eighth Sin. Stefan Kanfer. 1979. 2.50 (ISBN 0-425-04263-4). Berkley Publishing Corp.
Eighth Square. Herbert H. Lieberman. LC 72-95160. 1973. 6.95. McKay.
Eighth Square. Herbert H. Lieberman. (Kangaroo Book). 1978. 1.95 (ISBN 0-671-81425-7). Pocket Books.
Eighth Veil. Ellis Kadison. 384p. (Orig.). 1981. pap. 2.75 (ISBN 0-553-14893-1). Bantam.
Eighth Wonder: And Other Stories. Arthur Stuart-Menteth Hutchinson. LC 23-13375. 1923. Little, Brown, and Company.
Eighth Year: A Vital Problem of Married Life. Philip Hamilton Gibbs. LC 13-19940. 1.25. The Devin-Adair Company.
Eighty Dollars to Stamford. Lucille Fletcher, pseud. LC 75-8536. 1975. 6.95 (ISBN 0-394-47544-5). Random House.
Eighty Dollars to Stamford. Lucille Fletcher, pseud. LC 77-17907. 1978. 1.95 (ISBN 0-14-004788-3). Penguin Books.
Eighty-Eight More Stories. Guy de Maupassant. 1964. 3.50 o.p. Dufour.
Eighty Million Eyes: An 87th Precinct Mystery Novel, by Ed McBain Pseud. Evan Hunter. LC 65-18628. 3.50. Delacorte Dist. Dial.
Eighty Minute Hour. Brian Wilson Aldiss. (O.s.i.). 1975. pap. 1.25 o.s.i. (LB237ZK, Leisure Bks). Nordon Pubns.
Eighty-Minute Hour: A Space Opera. Brian Wilson Aldiss. LC 73-82241. (Doubleday science fiction). 1974. 5.95 (ISBN 0-385-08430-7). Doubleday.
Eighty-Nne. Edgar Henry. LC 7-41299. 1891. Cassell & Company.
Eighty-Seven Days. Andrew Angarsky. 1963. 6.50 o.p. Knopf.
Eighty-Six Proof Pro. Philip Chabody & Florence Chabody. 160p. 1974. 5.50 o.p. (ISBN 0-682-47753-2). Exposition.
Eilean More. Arthur Aitken Davidson. LC 28-16855. 1928. Longmans, Green and Co.
Eileen Alanna. Dennis O'Sullivan. (On cover: Munro's library, popular novels, v. 1, no. 502). N. L. Munro.
Eileen Duggan. Peggy Gaddis, pseud. LC 52-14852. 1952. Arcadia House.
Eileen McCullough. Alice Boissonneau. LC 77-359943. 9.95 (ISBN 0-88924-052-3). Simon & Pierre Pub. Co.
Eileen of the Trees. Henry De Vere Stacpoole. LC 29-16787. 1929. Doubleday, Doran & Company, Inc.
Eileen's Love Letters. Thomas Ignatius Reilly. LC 42-17636. 1942. Meador Publishing Company.
Eilene: Or, The Invisible Side of a Visible Character. Bessie Lee Blease. 1901. F.T. Neely.
Ein Abend in Den Munchner Kammerspielen: Das Haus Erinnering: By Frank Wedekin. edited by conrad p. homberger. ed. Ed. by Conrad P Homberger. Kastner, Erich & Wedekind, Frank. LC 65-268667. 1966. Scribner.
Ein Marsch in der Sonne. Harry Peter M'Nab Brown. LC 47-544997. (Overseas editions. German translations 18). 1945.
Ein Vierteljahrhundert. Frau Betty Young. 1882. G. Munro.
Einstein Intersection. Samuel R Delany. LC 75-402. (Garland Library of Science Fiction). 1975. 11.00 (ISBN 0-8240-1407-3). Garland Pub.
Einstein Intersection. Samuel R. Delany. Ed. by Lester Del Rey. LC 75-402. (O.s.i.). (Library of Science Fiction). 1975. lib. bdg. 17.50 o.s.i. (ISBN 0-8240-1407-3). Garland Pub.
Einstein Plot. Basil Heatter. (Orig.). 1982. pap. 3.50 (ISBN 0-440-12385-2). Dell.
Einstein's Brain. Mark Olshaker. 1982. pap. 3.50 (ISBN 0-671-43210-9). PB.
Einstein's Brain: A Novel. Mark Olshaker. LC 80-28662. 10.95 (ISBN 0-87131-342-1). M. Evans.
Eirene: Or, A Woman's Right. Mary Clemmer Ames. LC 6-263936. 1871. G. P. Putnam & Sons.
Eisenhower Deception. Clive Egleton. LC 80-69397. 1981. 10.95 (ISBN 0-689-11127-4). Atheneum.
Eisenhower, My Eisenhower. Jerome Charyn. LC 79-117289. 1973. 2.45 (ISBN 0-03-085055-X). Holt.
Either, or. Rudolph Leonhart. LC 7-13205. 1893. Roller Printing Co.
Ekkehard: A Novel. Joseph Viktor Von Scheffel. Ed. by Rudolf Tombo. LC 64-20049. 1965. F. Ungar Pub. Co.
Ekkehard: A Tale of the Tenth Century. Joseph Victor Von Scheffel & Dole, Nathan Haskell, 1852- 1895. T. Y. Crowell & Company.
Ekkehard: A Tale of the Tenth Century. Joseph Viktor Von Scheffel. LC 8-2028. 1890. W. S. Gottsberger & Co.
Ekkehard, a Tale of the Tenth Century. Joseph Viktor Von Scheffel & Dale, Nathan Haskell, 1852-1935. LC 4-16865. 1895. T. Y. Crowell & Company.
Ekkehard: A Tale of the 10th Century. Joseph Viktor Von Scheffel & Easson, Helena, Tr. (Half-title: Everyman's library, ed. by Ernest Rhys. Fiction. no. 529). 1911. J. M. Dent & Sons, Ltd.
Ekkehard: A Tale of the 10th Century. Joseph Viktor Von Scheffel & Easson, Helena, Tr. LC 36-37336. (Half-title: Everyman's library, ed. by Ernest Rhys. Fiction. no. 529). 1927. J. M. Dent & Sons, Ltd.
Ekkehard. Eine Geschichte Aus Dem Zehnten Jahrhundert, Von Joseph Victor Van Scheffel... Joseph Viktor Von Scheffel. LC 17-8823. (Die deutsche library, bd. 2, no. 100). 1882. G. Munro.
El Alferez Real. Eustaquio Palacios & Martin, John Lewis, 1911- Ed. LC 41-16924. (Half-title: Oxford library of Spanish texts). 1941. Oxford University Press.
El bordo see Precipice.
El Bronx Remembered: A Novella and Stories. Nicholasa Mohr. LC 75-6306. 5.95 (ISBN 0-06-024313-9) (ISBN 0-06-024314-7). Harper & Row.
El Cristo De Espaldas: Ed. by Roberto Esquenazi-Mayo, Carmen Esquenazi-Mayo. Eduardo Caballero Calderon. LC 66-25503. (Macmillan modern Spanish Amer. lit. ser.). 1967. 2.25. Macmillan.
El Diablo. Brayton Norton. LC 21-18885. The Bobbs-Merrill Company.
El Diablo Blanco. Luis De Oteyza. Ed. by Jones, Willis Knapp. LC 32-242610. (On cover: The Macmillan Hispanic series). 1932. The Macmillan Company.
El Diablo Cojo: The Limping Devil. texas centennial ed., 1836-1936. ed. Patrick Sylvester McGeeney. LC 36-12119. Standard Printing Company.
El Doncel De Don Enrique el Doliente: Por Mariano Jose De Larra. Mariano Jose De Larra. Ed. by Nunemaker, John Horace. LC 42-160844. (Half-title: The Dryden press. Modern language publications; general editor, Frederic Ernst). 1942. The Dryden Press.
El Dorado. Maggie Mackeever. 288p. 1981. pap. 2.95 (ISBN 0-449-24449-0). Fawcett.
El Estranjero (The Stranger) A Story of Southern California. Russell Judson Waters. LC 10-23665. 1910. Rand, McNally & Company.
El Fureidis. Maria Susanna Cummins. LC 6-31940. 1860. Ticknor and Fields.
El Fureidis. Maria Susanna Cummins. LC 6-31939. 1888. Houghton, Mifflin and Company.
El Goes South. MacKinlay Kantor. LC 30-218678. 1930. Coward-McCann, Inc.
El Gran Galeoto. Echegaray y Eizaguirre, Jose & Beardsley, Wilfred Attwood, 1889- Ed. LC 30-28704. (Heath's modern language series). D. C. Heath and Company.
El Greco Puzzle. John Murphy. LC 73-16821. 1974. 6.95 (ISBN 0-684-13712-7). Scribner.
El Hidalgo De la Mancha: Aventuras De Don Quijote. Miguel de Cervantes de Saavedra. Ed. by Daniel Quilter. LC 72-11249. (Illus.). 1973. (pbk.) 2.88 (ISBN 0-395-13390-4). Houghton.
El Humo Dormido. Introd., Notes by Edmund L. King. Gabriel Miro Ferrer. (Laurel lang. lib., Spanish ser., 5663). 1967. Dell.
El Indio. Translated by Anita Brenner. Illus. by Diego Rivera. Lopez y Fuentes, Gregorio. LC 61-17563. 1961. F. Ungar Pub. Co.
El Ingenioso Hidalgo Don Quijote De la Mancha. Miguel de Cervantes de Saavedra. Ed. by Cano, Juan. LC 32-345192. (On cover: The Macmillan Hispanic series). 1932. The Macmillan Company.
El Matadero (The Slaughter House) Echeverria, Esteban Jose Esteban Antonio Echeverria. (Cypress book). 1959. 1.00pap. Las American Pub. Co.
El Mesquite; a Story of the Early Spanish Settlements Between the Nueces and the Rio Grande: As Told by "La Posta Del Palo Alto". Elena Zamora O'Shea. LC 35-9851. Mathis Publishing Co.
El Miedo. 1st Ed. Earl Cloud. LC 55-11780. 1955. Comet Press Books.
El norte see Norther.
El Ombu: Together with the Story of a Piebald Horse, Pelino Viera's Confession, Nino Diablo, Marta Riquelme, and Ralph Herne. William Henry Hudson. LC 72-181621. (collected works of W. H. Hudson). 1968. AMS Press.
El Paso. Matthew Braun. 1978. 1.75 (ISBN 0-671-82029-X). Pocket Books.
El Paso. Matthew Braun. (Fawcett Gold Medal Book). 1973. (pbk) 0.95. Fawcett.
El Penon De las Animas. Orlando R. Lopez. (Romance Real Ser.). 192p. (Orig.). pap. 1.50 (ISBN 0-88025-007-0). Roca Pub.
El Periquillo Sarniento: Edited by Erwin K. Mapes and Frances M. Lopez-Morillas. Jose Joaquin Fernandez de Lizardi. LC 52-13688. 1952. Appleton-Century-Crofts.
El Rancho Rio. Mignon Good Eberhart. LC 70-117659. 1970. 4.95. Random House.
El Reshid: A Novel. LC 6255. Rand, McNally & Company.
El Reshid: A Novel, Anonymous. David Patterson Hatch. LC 99-2835. 1899. B. R. Baumgardt & Co.
El Sargento Felipe: Edited with Introduction, Cuestionario, Notes, and Vocabulary by Guillermo Rivera... Drawings by Rafael D. Palacios. Gonzalo Picon-Febres & Rivera, Guillermo, 1885- Ed. LC 42-14353. (Spanish American series). 1942. D. C. Heath and Company.
El Segundo. Thomas Wakefield Blackburn. 1974. (pbk.) 0.95. Dell.
El Sistema Expresivo De Ricardo Guiraldes. 1. ed. Curet De De Anda, Miriam. LC 76-8166. (Coleccion Mente y palabra). 1976. 5.00. (ISBN 0-8477-0532-3) (ISBN 0-8477-0533-1). Editorial Universitaria, Universidad De Puerto Rico.
El Sombra. Edward Beverly Mann. LC 36-16930. 1936. W. Morrow & Company.
El Sombrero De Tres Picos. 2d ed. Pedro Antonio De Alarcon. Ed. by Edmund De Chasca. LC 65-14558. (Blaisdell bk. in the humanities) Bibl.). pap., 2.75. Blaisdell.
El Sombrero De Tres Picos. Pedro Antonio De Alarcon. LC 53-801. (Illus.). 1952. Ginn.
El Supremo: A Romance of the Great Dictator of Paraguay. Edward Lucas White. LC 16-21974. E. P. Dutton & Company.
El Supremo: A Romance of the Great Dictator of Paraguay. Introd. by Wayne G. Broehl, Jr. Edward Lucas White. LC 67-14714. 10.00. Dutton.
El Tigre! Mexican Short Stories. Illustrated by Elizabeth Toth Spencer. Edith Hutchins Smith. LC 56-9352. 1956. J. F. Blair.
El Vago. Laurence Gonzales. LC 82-71057. 320p. 1983. 14.95 (ISBN 0-689-11330-7). Atheneum.
El Zarco, Episodios De la Vida Mexicana En 1861-1863, Por Ignacio Manuel Altamirano: Edited with Notes and Vocabulary by Raymond L. Grismer... and Miguel Ruelas... Ignacio Manuel Altamirano & Grismer, Raymond Leonard, Ed. LC 33-28392. (Norton Spanish series. vol. ii). W. W. Norton and Company, Inc.
Elaghin Affair and Other Stories. Ivan Alekseevich Bunin. LC 68-55946. (Illus.). 1969. 5.95. Funk & Wagnalls.
Elaghin Affair and Other Stories. Ivan Alekseevich Bunin. LC 35-1982. 1935. A. A. Knopf.
Elaine at the Gates. William Babington Maxwell. LC 24-29530. 1924. Doubleday, Page & Company.
Elaine Forrest, Visiting Nurse. Lois Hobart. LC 59-7134. (Romance for young moderns). 1959. Messner.
Elaine Forrest: Visiting Nurse. Lois Hobart. Orig. Title: Debutante Nurse. pap. 0.50 o.p. (52-465). Paperback Lib.
Elbow Lane. Altogether Jane, Author of. LC 15-6453. 1915. M. Kennerley.
Elbow of the Snake. 1st Ed. Sarah McNeil Lockwood. LC 58-8100. 1959. Doubleday.
Elbow-Room: A Novel Without a Plot. LC 6-25362. (On cover: Lovell's library. v. 6, no. 325). 1883. John W. Lovell Company.
Elbow Room: Stories. James Alan McPherson. LC 77-7268. 8.95 (ISBN 0-316-56328-5). Little, Brown.
Elder Boise; a Novel. Everett Titsworth Tomlinson. LC 1-12873. 1901. Doubleday, Page & Co.
Elder Boise; a Novel. Everett Titsworth Tomlinson. 1907. American Baptist Publication Society.
Elder Brother. Anthony Gibbs. LC 26-16147. 1926. L. MacVeagh, The Dial Press.
Elder Brother: A Dawn Thought Sketch. Charles Louis Brewer. LC 8-7670. 1907. To-Morrow Publishing Co.
Elder Brother: A Novel in Which Are Presented the Vital Questions Now Confronting the South Growing Out of Reconstruction, and in Which the Author Defines the True Relations Between the Races Now Existing in the South. Theodore Dehon Jervey. LC 5-15688. 1905. The Neale Publishing Company.
Elder Conklin. Frank Harris. LC 79-104475. 1970. Literature House.
Elder Conklin: And Other Stories. Frank Harris. LC 7-2624. 1894. Macmillan and Co.
Elder Conklin & Other Stories. Frank Harris. 1978. Repr. of 1895 ed. lib. bdg. 25.00 (ISBN 0-8492-5259-8). R West.
Elder MacGregor. Charles Hannan. R. F. Fenno & Company.
Elder Miss Ainsborough. Marion Ames Taggart. LC 15-3645. 1915. Benziger Brothers.
Elder Northfield's Home: Or, Sacrificed on the Mormon Altar. Jennie Bartlett Surtzer. LC 12-11054. The J. H. Brown Company.
Elder Northfield's Home: Or, Sacrificed on the Mormon Altar; the Story of the Blighting Curse of Polygamy. Jennie Bartlett Switzer. LC 71-164576. (American fiction reprint series). 1971. (ISBN 0-8369-7053-5). Books for Libraries Press.
Elder Northfield's Home: Or, Sacrificed on the Mormon Altar; a Story of the Blighting Curse of Polygamy. Jennie Bartlett Switzer. LC 15-12465. 1891. The J. Howard Brown Company.
Elder Northfield's Home: Or, Sacrificed on the Mormon Altar. A Story of Utah. Jennie Bartlett Switzer. LC 8-25590. B. B. Russell & Co.
Elder Northfield's Home; or, Sacrificed on the Mormon Altar. facsimile ed. Jennie Bartlett Switzer. LC 71-164576. (American Fiction Reprint Ser). Repr. of 1882 ed. 23.00 (ISBN 0-8369-7053-5). Ayer Co.
Elder or Poetic Edda: Commonly Known As Saemund's Edda. LC 76-43949. 1982. 49.00 (ISBN 0-404-60012-3). AMS Press.
Elder Sister. Maysie Greig. LC 39-217873. 1939. Doubleday, Doran & Company, Inc.
Elder Sister. Maysie Greig. LC 45-40834. 1941. The Sun Dial Press.
Elder Sister. Frank Arthur Swinnerton. LC 25-21415. George H. Doran Company.
Elderberry Flute Song: Contemporary Coyote Tales. Peter B. Cloud. LC 82-4965. (Illus.). 1982. 14.95 (ISBN 0-89594-070-1); pap. 6.95 (ISBN 0-89594-069-8). Crossing Pr.
Elderberry Tree. Irving Petite. (Illus.). 160p. 1976. pap. 3.95 o.p. Seattle Bk.
Elders & Betters. Ivy Compton-Burnett. 1944. 14.95 (ISBN 0-575-02371-6, Pub. by Gollancz England). David & Charles.
Elders & Betters. Ivy Compton-Burnett. 1981. 20.00x (ISBN 0-575-02371-6, Pub. by Gollancz England). State Mutual Bk.
Elder's People. Harriet Elizabeth Prescott Spofford. LC 70-130073. (Short story index reprint series). (Illus.). 1970. (ISBN 0-8369-3654-X). Books for Libraries Press.
Elder's People. Harriet Elizabeth Prescott Spofford. LC 20-54053. 1920. Houghton Mifflin Company.
Eldest Son. Archibald Marshall. LC 11-117412. 1911. Dodd, Mead and Company.
Eldorado. Emmuska Orczy. 435p. 1980. Repr. of 1913 ed. lib. bdg. 15.95x (ISBN 0-89968-195-6). Lightyear.
Eldorado: An Adventure of the Scarlet Pimpernel. Emmuska Orczy. LC 13-6257. 1.35. Hodder & Stoughton, George H. Doran Company.
Eldorado Network. Derek Robinson. LC 79-23640. 1980. 10.95 (ISBN 0-393-01322-7). Norton.
Eldorado of Socialism, Communism and Anarchism: Or, A Trip to the Planet Jupiter. John Hugh Reynaert. LC 17-13360. Reporter-Star Pub. Co.
Eldorado Red. Donald Goines. (Orig.). pap. 1.95 (ISBN 0-87067-647-4, BH067). Holloway.
Eldorado Red. Donald Goines. 1974. (pbk.) 1.50 (ISBN 0-87067-447-1). Holloway House.
Eleanor: A Novel. Rhoda Lerman. LC 78-15140. 10.00. Holt, Rinehart, and Winston.
Eleanor: A Novel. Mary Augusta Arnold Humphry Ward Ward. LC 697720. 1900. Harper & Brothers.
Eleanor and I. A Tale of the Days of King Richard II. Mary Ellen Bamford. LC 6-6298. Congregational Sunday-School and Publishing Society.
Eleanor: By Colin Ross Pseud. Harry Roskolenko. LC 53-1634. 1953. Woodford Press.
Eleanor Dayton. Nathaniel Wright Stephenson. LC 3-20902. 1903. John Lane.

TITLE INDEX ELISE: OR, THE REAL

Eleanor Gwynn. Mary Greenway McClelland. LC 44-24015. (On cover: American novelists' series. No. 56). 1890. United States Book Company.
Eleanor Lee; a Novel: By Margaret E. Sangster. Margaret Elizabeth Munson Sangster. LC 3-22512. 1903. F. H. Revell Company.
Eleanor Maitland: A Novel. Clara Erskine Clement Waters. LC 8-36764. 1881. J. R. Osgood and Company.
Eleanor: Or Life Without Love. Hannah Gardner Creamer. LC 6-31614. 1850. J. French.
Eleanor Roosevelt's Niggers. David J. Williams. LC 76-22608. 1976. pap. 1.75 (ISBN 0-914042-15-7, Neptune Bks). Coral Reef.
Eleanor the Queen. Norah Robinson Lofts. 1977. pap. 2.50 (ISBN 0-449-22848-7, Q2848, Crest). Fawcett.
Eleanora Duse. Jean Stubbs. LC 79-104641. 1970. 6.95. Stein and Day.
Eleanore. Alex Austin. LC 75-3253. 1969. 3.95. Olympia Press.
Eleanor's Victory. A Novel. Mary Elizabeth Braddon Maxwell. 1877. G. Munro.
Elect. Gerald Suster. LC 82-82003. 256p. 1982. pap. 2.95 (ISBN 0-86721-224-1). Playboy Pbks.
Elect Lady. George Macdonald. LC 7-17780. (On cover: Appletons' town and country library, no. 11). 1888. D. Appleton and Company.
Elect Lady. George Macdonald. (On cover: Lovell's library, no. 1221). 1888. J. W. Lovell Company.
Elect Lady. George Macdonald. (On cover: Seaside library. Pocket ed., no. 1118). 1888. G. Munro.
Electa. Jennie Maria Drinkwater Conklin. LC 6-30398. 1881. R. Carter & Brothers.
Election. Sherwin Markman. LC 79-117672. 1970. 6.95. Random House.
Election Booth Murder. Milton Morris Propper. LC 35-19673. 1935. Harper & Brothers.
Election by Murder. Alfred Eichler. LC 47-247724. 1947. Lantern Press.
Election on Academy Hill: A Story Drawn from the Novel, Seasoned Timber. Dorothea Frances Canfield Fisher. LC 40-88175. Harcourt, Brace and Company.
Elective Affinities. Johann Wolfgang Von Goethe. LC 75-40993. 1976. 16.50 (ISBN 0-8371-8709-5). Greenwood Press.
Elective Eclat. John V. Willis. Ed. by M. Rabatine. LC 76-58124. (Illus., Orig.). (gr. k-12). 1978. pap. text ed. 9.95x washable cover (ISBN 0-913732-08-7). J V Willis.
Electra. Elisabeth Schmidt-Wolf. (60-2129). 1966. Popular Lib.
Electra. Gladys Schmitt. LC 65-19068. 1965. Harcourt, Brace & World.
Electra. A Story of Love and Malice. Laura C Ford. LC 6-41398. (On cover: Munro's library. v. 1, no. 211). 1884. N. L. Munro.
Electric Banana. LC 75-33678. 1976. pap. 1.50x o.p. (ISBN 0-916156-07-9). Cherry Valley.
Electric Book. Malcolm Hall. LC 75-10454. (Illus.). 1975. 5.95. (ISBN 0-698-20339-9). Coward, McCann & Geoghegan.
Electric Cotillion. Don Asher. LC 79-105614. 1970. 5.95. Doubleday.
Electric Delights. William Plomer. LC 78-57682. 1978. 10.00 (ISBN 0-87923-248-X). Godine.
Electric Forest. Tanith Lee. (Daw Science Fiction Ser.). (Orig.). 1979. pap. 1.75 (ISBN 0-87997-482-6, UE1482). Daw Bks.
Electric Horseman. H. B Gilmour. 2.25 (ISBN 0-671-83409-6). Pocket Books.
Electric Kool-Aid Acid Test. Tom Wolfe, pseud. 1969. pap. 2.95 (ISBN 0-553-14094-9). Bantam.
Electric Love. Vivian Cory. LC 29-28507. The Macaulay Company.
Electric Sensation. Leslie Adirondack. (Orig.). 1969. pap. 1.95 o.s.i. (TC459, Travellers Comp). Olympia.
Electric Theft. Neil Wynn Williams. LC 7-37715. 1906. Small, Maynard & Company.
Electric Torch. Ethel May Dell. LC 34-25923. 1934. G. P. Putnam's Sons.
Electronic Revolution & the Book of Breathing. William Burroughs. 180p. 1982. pap. 8.95 o.p. (ISBN 0-7145-3683-0). Riverrun NY.
Electronic Teabowl. Dale Carlson. (Griffon Ser). (Orig.). 1969. pap. 0.50 o.p. (Golden Pr). Western Pub.
Elegant Infidelities of Madame Li Pei Fou. Charles Pettit. H. Liveright.
Elegant Journey. John Selby. LC 44-8724. 1944. Farrar & Rinehart, Inc.
Elegant Peccadillo. George Rheims & Putnam, Samuel, Tr. LC 31-244458. H. Holt and Company.
Elegant Witch. Robert Neill. LC 52-5227. 1952. Doubleday.
Elegy for a Revolutionary. C. J Driver. LC 77-97216. 1970. 5.95. Morrow.
Elegy of Innocence. Richard Shaw. LC 78-71419. 11.95 (ISBN 0-87973-643-7). Our Sunday Visitor.
Element of Risk. Mark Derby. 1977. 15.00. State Mutual Bk.
Element of Risk: By Mark Derby Pseud. Harry Wilcox. LC 52-12085. 1952. Viking Press.
Element 79. Fred Hoyle. LC 67-14726. (Signet bk., P 3463). 1968. New Amer. Liib.
Elementals. Michael McDowell. 1981. pap. 2.95 (ISBN 0-380-78360-6, 78360). Avon.
Elementary Jane. Richard Pryce. LC 7-30085. 1897. G. P. Putnam's Sons.
Elementary Latin. Minnie Louise Smith. LC 20-10388. Allyn and Bacon.
Elements of a Coffee Service: A Book of Stories. Robert Gluck. LC 81-20143. 5.95 (ISBN 0-912516-67-4). Grey Fox Press.
Elements of Fiction: Introduction to the Short Story. Ed. by Jack Carpenter. LC 73-93149. 1974. (pbk.) 4.95 (ISBN 0-697-03713-4). W. C. Brown Co.
Elena. Emily Francis. (Leisure Books). 1977. 1.50 (ISBN 0-8439-0502-6). Nordon Pubns.
Elena: A Love Story of the Russian Revolution. Judith Egan. LC 80-39613. 1981. 11.95 (ISBN 0-89919-028-6). Ticknor & Fields.
Elena. The Story of a Russian Woman. Roman Ivanovitch Zubof. LC 8-37861. 1894. G. W. Dillingham.
Eleonore. After the German of E. Von Rothenfels Pseud. Emilie Von Loga Von Ingersleben. Tr. by Bennett, Frances Elizabeth. LC 7-8848. 1872. J. B. Lippincott & Co.
Elephant. Sawomir Mrozek. LC 75-11428. (Illus.). 1975. 10.75 (ISBN 0-8371-8182-8). Greenwood Press.
Elephant; a Novel of the Civil War. Robert Gray. LC 78-1711. 1968. Madison House.
Elephant Across Border. Colin Burke. LC 68-22965. (O.S.I.). 1968. 4.95 o.s.i. (ISBN 0-671-20011-9). S&S.
Elephant Across Border: A Novel. Colin Burke. LC 68-22965. (Illus.). 1968. Simon and Schuster.
Elephant and Castle: A Reconstruction. Ray Coryton Hutchinson. LC 71-106695. 1970. Greenwood Press.
Elephant and Castle: A Reconstruction. Ray Coryton Hutchinson. LC 49-7231. 1949. Rinehart.
Elephant and the Kangaroo. Terence Hanbury White. LC 47-2147. 1947. G. P. Putnam's Sons.
Elephant Bangs Train. William Kotzwinkle. LC 71-132779. 1971. 5.95 (ISBN 0-394-46047-2). Pantheon Books.
Elephant for Aristotle. Lyon Sprague De Camp. 1971. pap. 0.95 o.p. (09059). Curtis.
Elephant God. Gordon Casserly. LC 21-18317. 1921. 1.90. G. P. Putnam's Sons.
Elephant Grass. Jack Denton Scott. LC 69-12046. 1969. Harcourt, Brace & World.
Elephant in Eden. Kelly L. Segraves. 1974. pap. 3.49 with cassette o.s.i. Creation Sci.
Elephant Is White. Doris Caroline Abrahams & Simon Jasha Skidelsky. LC 40-408736. Farrar & Rinehart, Inc.
Elephant Murders. 1st Ed. Elwood S Brown. LC 55-10860. Vantage Press.
Elephant Never Forgets. Ethel Lina White. LC 38-2268. 1938. Harper & Brothers.
Elephant School. John Stewart. LC 81-20796. (Illus.). 56p. (gr. 8-12). 1982. 10.95 (ISBN 0-394-85085-8); PLB 10.99 (ISBN 0-394-95085-2). Pantheon.
Elephant Song. Barry B. Longyear. (Orig.). 1982. pap. 2.50 (ISBN 0-425-05167-6). Berkley Pub.
Elephant Valley. Finis Farr. LC 66-25068. 1967. Arlington House.
Elephant Walk. Digby George Gerahty. LC 49-9454. 1949. Macmillan Co.
Elephant Walk. Robert Standish. Repr. lib. bdg. 15.45x (ISBN 0-88411-827-4). Amereon Ltd.
Elephants Can Remember. Agatha Miller Christie. LC 73-1180. 1973. 9.95 (ISBN 0-8161-6086-4). G. K. Hall.
Elephants Can Remember. Agatha Miller Christie. 1976. 1.75. Dell.
Elephants Can Remember. Agatha Miller Christie. LC 72-7788. 1972. 6.95 (ISBN 0-396-06742-5). Dodd, Mead.
Elephants Can Remember. Dame Agatha Miller Christie. 1973. (pbk) 1.25. Dell.
Elephants Have the Right of Way. J. H. McCown. LC 74-15319. 1974. pap. 1.95 o.p. Liguori Pubns.
Elephant's Track: And Other Stories. Mary Evelyn Moore Davis. LC 78-94714. (Short story index reprint series). (Illus.). 1969. Books for Libraries Press.
Elephant's Track, and Other Stories. Mary Evelyn Moore Davis. LC 6-32472. 1897. Harper & Brothers.
Elephant's Work: An Enigma. 1st American Ed. Edmund Clerihew Bentley. LC 50-8751. 1950. Knopf.
Elevated Railroad Mystery, The Sleeping-Car Puzzle. A Fortune in a Photograph; Three Complete Stories of the Exploits of Nicholas Carter, America's Greatest Detective. John Russell Coryell. LC 2004. (On cover: Magnet detective library. no. 123). 1900. Street & Smith.
Elevator Man. Leslie Adirondack. 176p. (Orig.). 1972. pap. 1.95 o.s.i. (OPH 4496). Olympia.
Eleven. Roger Lovin. 192p. pap. 1.95 o.p. (6116). Brandon.
Eleven Bullets for Mohammed. Harry Arvay. 1975. (pbk.) 1.25. Bantam Books.
Eleven Came Back. Mabel Seeley. LC 43-4864. 1943. Pub. for the Crime Club by Doubleday, Doran & Co., Inc.
Eleven Declarations of War. Len Deighton. LC 74-13068. 1975. 6.95. Harcourt Brace Jovanovich.
Eleven Declarations of War. Len Deighton. 1976. 1.50 (ISBN 0-446-88125-2). Warner.
Eleven Harrowhouse. Gerald A. Browne. LC 70-183382. 1972. 6.95 (ISBN 0-87795-024-5). Arbor Hse.
Eleven Harrowhouse: A Novel. Gerald A Browne. (Dell book). 1979. 2.25. Dell Pub. Co.
Eleven Kinds of Loneliness. Richard Yates. 208p. 1982. pap. 6.95 (ISBN 0-440-52366-4, Delta). Dell.
Eleven Kinds of Loneliness: Short Stories. 1st Ed. Richard Yates. LC 69-9538. 1962. Little, Brown.
Eleven Kinds of Loneliness: Short Stories. Richard Yates. LC 72-603. 1972. 10.25 (ISBN 0-8371-5727-7). Greenwood Press.
Eleven Modern Short Novels. Ed. by Leo Hamalian & Edmond L. Volpe. 1971. pap. 7.95 (ISBN 0-399-30004-X). Putnam Pub Group.
Eleven of Diamonds. Baynard Hardwick Kendrick. LC 36-22618. 1936. Greenberg.
Eleven of the World's Great War & Spy Stories. Ed. by Marjorie Barrows. LC 45-5362. Consolidated Book Publishers.
Eleven Stories. Anton Pavlovich Chekhov. LC 76-377657. (Oxford paperbacks; 356). 1975. 5.95 (ISBN 0-19-281184-3). Oxford University Press.
Eleven Were Brave. Francis Beeding. LC 41-34178. 1941. Harper & Brothers.
Eleventh Commandment. Lester Del Rey. 192p. 1981. pap. 2.50 (ISBN 0-345-29641-9, Del Rey). Ballantine.
Eleventh Commandment. Melville Shavelson. LC 77-23071. 1977. 7.95. Reader's Digest Press: Distributed by Crowell.
Eleventh Commandment: A Romance. Antonio Giulio Barrili. Tr. by Bell, Clara Courtney (Poynton) LC 6-411. 1882. W. S. Gottsberger.
Eleventh Commandment & Other Short Stories. Mary Silberman. 1978. pap. 4.00 o.p. (ISBN 0-682-49163-2). Exposition.
Eleventh Galaxy Reader. Frederik Pohl. 1969. 4.95 o.p. Doubleday.
Eleventh Hour. Robert Clive. LC 38-38718. 1937. W. W. Norton & Company, Inc.
Eleventh Hour. Ethel May Dell. LC 15-12873. 1915. 1.00. G. P. Putnam's Sons.
Eleventh Hour. David Potter. LC 10-7303. 1910. 1.50. Dodd, Mead and Company.
Eleventh Hour. Robert B Sinclair. LC 51-432. 1951. M. S. Mill Co. and W. Morrow.
Eleventh Hour: A Novel. Donald Forbes. LC 55-9302. 1955. Roy Publishers.
Eleventh Hour: Being the Second of the Further Adventures of Ronald Camberwell. Joseph Smith Fletcher. LC 35-3365. 1935. A. A. Knopf.
Eleventh Little Indian. Yves Jacquemard. LC 79-28634. 1980. 12.50 (ISBN 0-8161-3058-2). G. K. Hall.
Eleventh Little Indian. Yves Jacquemard & Jean Michael Senecal. (General Ser.). 1980. pap. 8.95 (ISBN 0-8161-3058-2, Large Print Bks). G K Hall.
Eleventh Little Indian. Yves Jacquemard & Jean Michel Senecal. LC 79-15093. 1979. 8.95 (ISBN 0-396-07717-X). Dodd, Mead.
Eleventh Pan Book of Horror Stories. Ed. by H. Van Thal. 1982. pap. 10.00x (ISBN 0-330-02562-7, Pub. by Pan Bks). State Mutual Bk.
Eleventh Plague. L. T Peters. LC 73-11540. 1973. 6.95 (ISBN 0-671-21613-9). Simon and Schuster.
Eleventh Virgin. Dorothy Day. LC 24-8256. 1924. A. and C. Boni.
Elfa: A Romance. Arthur Williams Marchmont. LC 11-12128. Hodder and Stoughton.
Elfin Ship. James P. Blaylock. 352p. 1982. pap. 2.75 (ISBN 0-345-29491-2, Del Rey). Ballantine.
Elfquest: The Novel. Wendy Pini & Richard Pini. LC 82-81384. 320p. 1982. pap. 5.95 (ISBN 0-86721-172-5). Playboy Pbks.
Elfquest, The Novel: Raid at Sorrow's End. Richard Pini & Wendy Pini. (Elfquest Ser.). (Illus.). 320p. 1982. 4.95 o.p. (ISBN 0-934438-63-3). Underwood-Miller.
Elfreda. A Sequel to Leofwine. Emma Leslie. LC 7-14498. (Church history stories, v. 6). Nelson & Phillips.
Elfrida: The Red Rover's Daughter. A New Mystery of New York. Edward Zane Carroll Judson. LC 7-11445. F. A. Brady.
Elfstones of Shannara. Terry Brooks. LC 81-69187. (Illus.). 1982. 15.95 (ISBN 0-345-30253-2) (ISBN 0-345-28555-7). Ballantine Books.
Elfwin: A Romance of History. Sydney Fowler Wright. LC 30-24851. 1930. Longmans, Green and Co.
Elgar on the Journey to Hanley. Keith Alldritt. LC 78-19445. 1979. 8.95 o.p. (ISBN 0-312-24214-X). St Martin.
Elgar on the Journey to Hanley: A Novel. Keith Alldritt & Edward William Elgar. LC 78-19445. 8.95 (ISBN 0-312-24214-X). St. Martin's Press.
Elgar Variation. Michael Kenyon. LC 80-19037. 11.95 (ISBN 0-698-11057-9). Coward, McCann & Geoghegan.
Eli & the Tiger. Bruce Van Blair. 4.95 o.p. Vantage.
Eli of the Downs. C. M. A Peake. LC 20-187680. 2.00. George H. Doran Company.
Elia: Or, Spain Fifty Years Ago. Fernan Caballero. LC 6-2430. 1868. D. Appleton and Company.
Eliane. from the french by lady georgiana fullerton. ed. Pauline Marie Armande Aglae Ferron De La Ferronnays Craven. Tr. by Fullerton, Georgiana Charlotte (Leveson-Gower) LC 1-2419. 1882. W. S. Gottsberger.
Eliane: A Novel. Pauline Marie Armande Aglae Ferron De La Ferronnays Craven. Tr. by Fullerton, Georgiana Charlotte. (Seaside library, v. 64, no. 1304). G. Munro.
Elidor. Alan Garner. 160p. 1981. pap. 1.95 (ISBN 0-345-29042-9, Del Rey). Ballantine.
Eligible Bachelor. Humphrey Pakington. LC 35-5928. W. W. Norton & Company, Inc.
Eligible Connection. Elsie Lee. 1980. pap. 1.95 (ISBN 0-440-12821-8). Dell.
Eligible Connection. Elsie Lee. 1975. (pbk.) 0.95. Dell.
Eligible Connection. Maggie MacKeever. 1980. pap. 1.75 (ISBN 0-449-50029-2, Coventry). Fawcett.
Elijah. Jerry McGuire. LC 73-75202. (Illus.). 112p. 1973. 7.95 (ISBN 0-87358-104-0). Northland.
Elijah: A Novel. Jerry McGuire. LC 73-75202. (Illus.). 1973. 7.95 (ISBN 0-87358-104-0). Northland Press.
Elijah Conspiracy. Charles Robertson. 320p. (Orig.). 1980. pap. 2.95 (ISBN 0-553-20414-9). Bantam.
Elijah Jeremiah Phillips' Great Journey. Paul Ricchiuti. (Hello World Ser.). 1975. pap. 1.65 o.p. (ISBN 0-8163-0185-9, 05303-3). Pacific Pr Pub Assn.
Elijah the Prophet: A Dream of the Christ. Joel Bunyan Lemon. LC 99-4420. F.H. Revell Company.
Eliminate the Middle Man. Max Wilk. LC 73-14810. 1974. 6.95 (ISBN 0-393-08684-4). Norton.
Eliminator. Christopher Nicole. LC 66-23250. 1967. Lippincott.
Eliminator. Andrew York. 1968 (74-931, 6-74-931). pap. 0.75 o.p. (74-931). Lancer.
Eline Vere. Louis Marie Anne Couperus & Grein, James Thomas, 1862-1935, Tr. LC 45-22316. (Holland fiction series). 1892. D. Appleton and Co.
Elinor Belden: Or, The Step Brothers. Lucy Cecil White Lillie. LC 7-19386. 1896. H. T. Coates & Co.
Elinor Colhouse. Stephen Hudson. LC 22-6311. 1922. A. A. Knopf.
Elinor Dryden. A Novel. Katharine Sarah Gadsden Macquoid. (Franklin square library, no. 31). Harper & Brothers.
Elinor Fenton: An Adirondack Story. David Skaats Foster. LC 6-40006. 1893. J. B. Lippincott Company.
Elinor Fulton. 9th ed. Farnham Hannah. LC 7-12621. (On cover: Stories from real life. no. 2). 1837. Whipple & Damrell.
Elinor Fulton. 11th ed. Farnham Hannah. LC 7-12620. (On cover: Stories from real life. no. 2). 1837. Whipple & Damrell.
Eli's Children: The Chronicles of an Unhappy Family. George Manville Fenn. (On cover: Lovell's international series, no. 88). J. W. Lovell Company.
Eli's Road: A Novel. Lucas Webb. LC 71-151762. 1971. 6.95. Doubleday.
Elisa. Edmond De Goncourt. Tr. by M. Crosland from Fr. 190p. 1975. Repr. of 1959 ed. 19.75 o.p. (ISBN 0-86527-242-5). Fertig.
Elisa. Edmond Louis Antoine Huot De Goncourt. LC 74-5136. 1975. H. Fertig.
Elisabeth: His Dream Child. A. Elisabeth Upton Kirk. LC 28-11923. Simpson Printing Company.
Elisabeth Koett. Rudolf Hans Bartsch. Tr. by Lewisohn, Ludwig. LC 10-300342. 1.20. D. FitzGerald, Inc.
Elise. Ken Grimwood. LC 79-7072. 1979. 8.95 (ISBN 0-385-13631-5). Doubleday.
Elise: Or, The Real Life. Claire Etcherelli. LC 69-17629. 1969. 5.95. Morrow.

Elise or the Real Life. Claire Etcherelli. Tr. by June P. Wilson & Walter B. Michaels. (Orig., Title Elise ou la Vraie Vie). 1969. 5.95 o.p. Morrow.
Elissa: The Doom of Zimbabwe. Black Heart and White Heart; a Zulu Idyll. Henry Rider Haggard. LC 3198. 1900. Longmans, Green, and Co.
Elixir. Robert Nathan. LC 76-38098. 1971. 6.95 (ISBN 0-8161-6007-4). G. K. Hall.
Elixir: A Novel. Robert Nathan. LC 73-154936. 1971. 5.95 (ISBN 0-394-47175-X). Knopf.
Elixir: And Other Tales. authorized ed. Georg Moritz Ebers. Tr. by Clara Courtenay Bell. LC 6-36806. 1890. W. S. Gottsberger & Co.
Elixir of Hate. George A. England. 1976. lib. bdg. 12.95x (ISBN 0-89968-176-X). Lightyear.
Elixir of Life: An Historical Novel of New Orleans. Albert E Cowdrey. LC 65-17254. 4.95. Doubleday.
Elixir of Life: Or, Robert's Pilgrimage. An Allegory. H. M. Stowe. LC 8-16283.
Eliza. Paula Allardyce, pseud. 1975. (pbk.) 0.95. Dell.
Eliza. Jean Anne Bartlett. (torment of Aaron Burr; 3). 1977. 1.75 (ISBN 0-445-04012-2). Popular Library.
Eliza. Barry Eric Odell Pain. D. Estes & Company.
Eliza Callaghan. Robert S Close. LC 57-11413. 1958. Doubleday.
Eliza for Common. Anna Buchan. LC 28-143176. 1928. Doubleday, Doran & Company, Inc.
Eliza of Wappoo; a Tale of Indigo,by Nell S. Graydon, Illustrated with Photos. by Eugene B. Sloan. Nell S Graydon. LC 67-31726. R. L. Bryan Co.,
Eliza: Or, The Pattern of Women. A Moral Romance. Roche, Mrs. Regina Maria (Dalton) 1764?-1845, Supposed Author. LC 6-39361. 1802. Printed by Henry Grimler, for Chr. Jac. Hutter.
Eliza Stanhope. Joanna Trollope. LC 78-74023. 1979. 8.95 (ISBN 0-525-09750-3). E. P. Dutton.
Eliza Woodson: Or, The Early Days of One of the World's Workers. A Story of American Life... Eliza Woodson Burhans Faraham. 1864. A. J. Davis & Co.
Elizabeth. Jessica Hamilton. 1977. 1.75 (ISBN 0-445-04013-0). Popular Library.
Elizabeth. Brian Swann. Ed. by Michael McCurdy. (Fiction Ser.: No. 3). (Illus.). 1981. 12.00x o.p. (ISBN 0-915778-35-1); ltd. signed ed. 40.00x (ISBN 0-915778-34-3). Penmaen Pr.
Elizabeth: A Novel of the Unnatural. Jessica Hamilton. LC 75-33018. 6.95 (ISBN 0-394-49875-5). Random House.
Elizabeth: A Story in Six Parts. Frank Arthur Swinnerton. LC 34-360457. 1934. Doubleday, Doran & Company, Inc.
Elizabeth Abbott: A Novel of Southern Illinois. Mae Connie Trovillion Smith. LC 56-12286. Exposition Press.
Elizabeth Alone. William Trevor. LC 73-16937. 1974. 7.95 (ISBN 0-670-29189-7). Viking Press.
Elizabeth & Her German Garden. Elizabeth. 1973. pap. 0.95 o.p. (09185). Curtis.
Elizabeth and Her German Garden. Mary Annette Russel. LC 43-39949. J. S. Ogilvie Publishing Company.
Elizabeth and Her German Garden. Mary Annette Beauchamp Russell Russell. LC 1-305618. Laird & Lee.
Elizabeth and Her German Garden. Mary Annette Beauchamp Russell Russell. LC 7-3075. 1900. The Macmillan Company.
Elizabeth and Her German Garden. Mary Annette Beauchamp Russell Russell. LC 32-19527. 1900. Macmillan and Co., Limited.
Elizabeth and Her German Garden. Mary Annette Beauchamp Russell Russell. LC 1-31587. 1901. The Mershon Company.
Elizabeth and Her German Garden. New Ed., with Additions. Mary Annette Beauchamp Russell Russell. LC 4185. 1900. The Macmillan Company.
Elizabeth and Her German Garden: With Twelve Photogravure Illustrations from Photographs. Mary Annette Beauchamp Russell Russell. LC 6572. 1900. The Macmillan Company.
Elizabeth and Son. Gladys M Schuldt. LC 40-13630. Dorrance and Company.
Elizabeth and the Archdeacon. James Owen Hannay. LC 33-2851. The Bobbs-Merrill Company.
Elizabeth and the Prince of Spain. Margaret Emma Faith Irwin. LC 66-2776. 1966. bds., 3.95. Chatto & Windus.
Elizabeth and the Prince of Spain. Margaret Emma Faith Irwin. LC 53-10633. 1953. Harcourt, Brace.
Elizabeth Ann and Uncle Doctor. Josephine Lawrence. LC 28-14005. Barse & Co.
Elizabeth Appleton. John O'Hara. 1974. (pbk.) 1.50. Popular Library.
Elizabeth Appleton: A Novel. John O'Hara. LC 63-14140. 1963. Random House.
Elizabeth Bennet; or, Pride and Prejudice: A Novel... Jane Austen. LC 36-21377. 1832. Carey & Lea.
Elizabeth, by Name. Will C. Cook. (Illus.). 320p. 1982. pap. 1.95 (ISBN 0-441-20391-4, Pub. by Charter Bks). Ace Bks.
Elizabeth: Captive Princess. Margaret Emma Faith Irwin. LC 48-9521. 1948. Harcourt, Brace.
Elizabeth, Christian Scientist. Matt Crim. LC 6-316087. 1893. C. L. Webster & Co.
Elizabeth Crane: A Novel. Henry Ellsworth Curtis. LC 10-30579. 1.50. Broadway Publishing Co.
Elizabeth Gail & the Handsome Stranger. Hilda Stahl. 128p. 1983. pap. 2.95 (75-0707-9). Tyndale.
Elizabeth Gaskell: The Artist in Conflict. Margaret Ganz. LC 68-24279. 1969. 6.00. Twayne Publishers.
Elizabeth Gaskell's Cranford: Ed. with Notes and an Introduction. Elizabeth Cleghorn Stevenson Gaskell. Ed. by Franklin Thomas Baker. (Half-title: Longmans' English classics...). 1905. Longmans, Green, and Co.
Elizabeth Goudge Reader, Compiled and Arranged, with an Introduction. Elizabeth Goudge & Dobbs, Rose, Comp. LC 46-827829. 1946. Doward-McCann, Inc.
Elizabeth in Retreat. Margaret Westrup. LC 12-15818. 1912. John Lane.
Elizabeth Morley: A Novel. Katharine Sarah Gadsden Macquoid. LC 7-20288. F. F. Lovell & Company.
Elizabeth, My Daughter. Ann Katherine Gilliland Ritner. LC 40-35463. M. S. Mill Co., Inc.
Elizabeth Newt. Harold Fleming. LC 67-17786. 1967. 4.95. Red Dust.
Elizabeth: Or, The Exiles of Siberia. Marie Risteau Cottin. LC 6-29012. (On cover: Fitch's popular library, no. 12). 1879. G. W. Fitch.
Elizabeth: Or, The Exiles of Siberia: a Tale, Founded Upon Facts. From the French of Madame Cottin. Marie Risteau Cottin. LC 9-32312. Printed by Ann Cochran, For Mathew Carey.
Elizabeth, Queen and Woman. Helen Thorpe. LC 72-176405. 1972. 5.95. Roy Publishers.
Elizabeth Rip. Dan Lees. LC 75-16212. 1975. 7.95. St. Martin's Press.
Elizabeth: The Polish Exile, a Story Founded on Fact; Tr. from the French of Madame Sophia Ristand Cottin. Marie Risteau Cottin. LC 22-24759. 1916. W. B. Conkey Company.
Elizabeth, the Woman: A Novel. Amanda Mae Ellis. LC 51-12226. 1951. Dutton.
Elizabeth Visits America. Elinor Sutherland Glyn. LC 9-13919. 1909. Duffield & Company.
Elizabethan Fiction. Ed. by Robert Paul Ashley & Edwin M. Moseley. LC 52-13061. (Rinehard editions, 64). 1953. Rinehart.
Elizabethan Garden. Pamela Sykes. LC 72-10808. 224p. 1973. 6.95 o.p. (ISBN 0-381-98233-5, A23330). John Day.
Elizabethan Garden: A Novel. Pamela Sykes. LC 72-10808. 1973. 6.95 (ISBN 0-381-98233-5). John Day Co.
Elizabethan Love Stories. Terence John Bew Spencer. LC 68-3908. (Penguin Shakespeare library, SL3). 1968. Penguin Books.
Elizabethan Lover. Barbara Cartland. 1975. pap. 1.25311 o.p. Pyramid Pubns.
Elizabethan Lover, No. 28. Barbara Cartland. 1975. pap. 1.25 o.p. (ISBN 0-515-03907-1, V3907). BJ Pub Group.
Elizabethan Shorter Novels. Ed. by Philip Henderson. 3.25x o.p. (ISBN 0-460-00824-2, Evman). Dutton.
Elizabethan Tales. Ed. by Edward Joseph Harrington O'Brien. LC 70-178452. (Short story index reprint series). 1971. (ISBN 0-8369-4053-9). Books for Libraries Press.
Elizabeth's Campaign. Mary Augusta Arnold Humphry Ward Ward. LC 18-19923. 1918. Dodd, Mead and Company.
Elizabeth's Fortune. Bertha Thomas. (On cover: Seaside library. Pocket ed. no. 960). 1887. G. Munro.
Elizabeth's Fortune. A Novel. Bertha Thomas. (Harper's Franklin square library, no. 564). 1887. Harper & Brothers.
Elizabeth's Greeting. Rosemary Haughton. LC 68-26675. (Illus.). 1968. 5.95. Lippincott.
Elizabeth's Story. Grace Howard Peirce. LC 10-236726. 0.50. Printed by Beber Printing Co.
Elizabeth's Tower. Margaret Weymouth Jackson. LC 26-10072. The Bobbs-Merrill Company.
Eliza's Galiardo. James Gollin. LC 82-17057. 1983. 10.95 (ISBN 0-312-24244-1). St. Martin's Press.
Elk and the Evidence. Margaret Scherf. LC 52-6365. 1952. Published for the Crime Club by Doubleday.
Elk-Dog Heritage. Don Coldsmith. LC 80-2849. 1982. 10.95 (ISBN 0-385-17501-9). Doubleday.
Elkan Lubliner, American. Montague Marsden Glass. LC 12-24207. 1912. 1.20. Doubleday, Page & Company.
Elkhorn Tavern. Douglas C Jones. LC 81-270. 1981. 12.95 (ISBN 0-89621-273-4). Thorndike Press.
Ella. Hubert Nicholson. 1974. (pbk.) 0.95. Popular Library.
Ella. Elisabeth Wilkins Thomas. LC 30-26379. 1930. The Viking Press.
Ella: A Narrative. William H Graham. 1931. Printed by W. H. Graham.
Ella: A Story of the White Slave Traffic. John Couchois Wright. LC 11-26644. Pub. Priv. by J. C. Wright.
Ella Barnwell: A Historical Romance of Border Life. Emerson Bennett. LC 27-13672. W. P. James.
Ella Barnwell: A Historical Romance of Border Life. Emerson Bennett. LC 7-36495. 1854. J. A. & U. P. James.
Ella; Book of Magic Love. Miguel Serrano. LC 70-184377. 1972. 5.00 (ISBN 0-06-013829-7). Harper & Row.
Ella Cinders in Hollywood: A Novel. Bill Conselman. LC 30-15704. The Stratford Company.
Ella Keeps House. Jessie Champion. LC 21-20541. 1921. John Lane.
Ella Lincoln: Or, Western Prairie Life, an Autobiography. H., Mrs. E.A.W. LC 6-46688. 1857. J. French & Company.
Ella Price's Journal. Dorothy Bryant. LC 75-39758. (Signet Book). 1973. (pbk) 1.25. New American Lib.
Ella Stratford: Or, The Orphan Child. A Thrilling Novel, Founded on Facts. Marguerite Power Farmer Gardiner Blessington. T.B. Peterson.
Ella V-- Or, The July Tour. F. Taylor. LC 8-256623. 1841. D. Appleton & Co.
Elle et Lui. George Sand. LC 75-41240. 1977. 14.00 (ISBN 0-404-14796-8). AMS Press.
Ellen: A Short Life Long Remembered. Rose Levit. 1974. (pbk.) 1.25. Bantam Books.
Ellen Adair. Frederick John Niven. LC 25-170623. 1925. Boni & Liveright.
Ellen and Mr. Man. Gouverneur Morris. LC 4-29783. 1904. The Century Co.
Ellen De Vere: Or, The Way of the Will. John Frederick Smith. LC 27-13686. (Seaside library. v. 59, no. 1202). 1882. G. Munro.
Ellen Durand. Euphemia Barnes. LC 6-7205. 1855. Moore, Wilstach, Keys & Co.
Ellen Grafton: The Lily of Lexington; or, The Bride of Liberty. Benjamin Barker. LC 6-3857. 1846. Gleason's Publishing Hall.
Ellen Levis: A Novel. Elsie Singmaster. LC 21-2816. 1921. Houghton Mifflin Company.
Ellen Middleton. A Tale. from the last london ed. Georgiana Charlotte Leveson-Gower Fullerton. LC 7-3512. 1854. D. Appleton & Company.
Ellen Middleton, a Tale, 1844. Georgiana Charlotte Leveson-Gower Fullerton. Ed. by Robert L. Wolff. LC 75-471. (Victorian Fiction Ser). 1975. lib. bdg. 66.00 (ISBN 0-8240-1549-5). Garland Pub.
Ellen Monroe. A Sequel to "Life in London." Illustrated with Twenty-Two Engravings. George William McArthur Reynolds. LC 42-26424. Dick & Fitzgerald.
Ellen Norbury: Or, The Adventures of an Orphan. Emerson Bennett. LC 7-34431. T. B. Peterson.
Ellen of the Plains Country: A Novel of Catholic Life in the Great Southwest. Sue Mildred Lee Johnston. LC 32-23275. 1932. Benziger Brothers.
Ellen: Or, The Chained Mother; and Pictures of Kentucky Slavery. Drawn from Real Life. Mary B Harlan. 1853. For the Author, by Applegate & Co.
Ellen: Or, The Fanatic's Daughter. V. G. Cowdin. LC 21-8688. 1860. S. H. Goetzel & Compny.
Ellen Parry: Or, Trials of the Heart. Emily Edson Briggs. LC 7-24103. 1850. D. Appleton & Co.
Ellen Rogers. James Thomas Farrell. LC 41-176126. The Vanguard Press.
Ellen Seymour: Or, The Bud and the Flower. Anne Houlditch Shepherd. LC 49-57556. 1850. J. W. Moore.
Ellen Spring. Elizabeth Marion. LC 41-51947. Thomas Y. Crowell Company.
Ellen Story: A Novel. Edgar Fawcett. LC 6-38050. 1876. E. J. Hale & Son.
Ellen Wareham; or, Love and Duty. A Thrilling Novel of Real Life. Ellen Pickering. LC 6-35104. T. B. Peterson.
Ellerby Case. Cecil John Charles Street. LC 27-13598. 1927. Dodd, Mead and Company.
Ellery Queen, Master Detective. Ellery Queen, pseud. LC 41-333695. Grosset & Dunlap.
Ellery Queen, Master Detective see Vanishing Corpse.
Ellery Queen Omnibus: The Roman Hat Mystery; The French Powder Mystery; The Egyptian Cross Mystery. Ellery Queen, pseud. 1936. Grosset & Dunlap.
Ellery Queen Presents Erle Stanley Gardner: The Amazing Advetures of Lester Leith. 1981. 9.95 (ISBN 0-8037-1653-2). Dial.
Ellery Queen Presents Erle Stanley Gardner's The Amazing Adventures of Lester Leith. Erle Stanley Gardner. LC 81-107616. 1981. (pbk.) 1.75. Davis Publications.
Ellery Queen Presents Julian Symons' How to Trap a Crook, and 12 Other Mysteries. Julian Symons. LC 77-357566. (First book publication; no. 7). 1977. 1.35. Davis Publications.
Ellery Queen Selects: The Riddles of Hildegarde Withers. Stuart Palmer & Queen, Ellery, Pseud., Ed. LC 47-20363. (On cover: A Jonathan press mystery, no. J26). 1947.
Ellery Queen's A Multitude of Sins: 21 Stories from Ellery Queen's Mystery Magazine. Ellery Queen, pseud. LC 78-54103. (EQMM Annual: 32). 8.95 (ISBN 0-8037-2256-7). Dial Press.
Ellery Queen's Aces of Mystery. Ed. by Ellery Queen, pseud. 320p. 1975. 8.95 o.p. (ISBN 0-8037-4515-X). Dial.
Ellery Queen's All-Star Lineup. 1st- 1946- ed. LC 67-21802.
Ellery Queen's All-Star Lineup: 22 Stories from Ellery Queen's Mystery Magazine. Ed. by Ellery Queen, pseud. LC 67-21802. (EQMM Annual: 22). 1967. New American Library.
Ellery Queen's Awards, 11th & 12th Series. Ed. by Ellery Queen, pseud. 3.50 ea. o.p. S&S.
Ellery Queen's Book of First Appearances. Ellery Queen & Eleanor Sullivan. LC 82-221616. (Illus.). 12.95 (ISBN 0-385-27774-1). Dial Press: Davis Publications.
Ellery Queen's Challenge to the Reader: An Anthology. Ed. by Ellery Queen, pseud. LC 38-34127. 1938. Frederick A. Stokes Company.
Ellery Queen's Challenge to the Reader: An Anthology. Ed. by Ellery Queen, pseud. 1940. Blue Ribbon Books.
Ellery Queen's Circumstantial Evidence. 288p. 1980. 9.95 (ISBN 0-8037-2213-3). Dial.
Ellery Queen's Cops & Capers. Ed. by Ellery Queen, pseud. LC 77-81935. 1977. pap. 1.50 o.s.i. (ISBN 0-89559-001-8). Davis Pubns.
Ellery Queen's Crime Carousel. 1st- 1946- ed. LC 66-24426. New American Library Etc.
Ellery Queen's Crime Carousel: 21 Stories from Ellery Queen's Mystery Magazine. Ed. by Ellery Queen, pseud. LC 66-24426. 1966. New American Library.
Ellery Queen's Crime Cruise Round the World. Ed. by Ellery Queen, pseud. 288p. 1981. 9.95 (ISBN 0-385-27191-3). Davis Pubns.
Ellery Queen's Crime Cruise Round the World. Ed. by Ellery Queen, pseud. 1981. 9.95 (Dist. by Doubleday). Dial.
Ellery Queen's Crime Wave: 24 Stories from Ellery Queen's Mystery Magazine. Ellery Queen, pseud. LC 75-43963. (EQMM Annual: 30). 8.95 (ISBN 0-399-11737-7). Putnam.
Ellery Queen's Crime Wave: 30th Mystery Annual. Ed. & intro. by Ellery Queen. LC 75-43963. 1976. 8.95 o.p. (ISBN 0-399-11737-7). Putnam Pub Group.
Ellery Queen's Crime Wave: 30th Mystery Annual. Ed. & intro. by Ellery Queen. LC 75-43963. 1976. 8.95 o.p. (ISBN 0-399-11737-7). Putnam.
Ellery Queen's Crimes & Consequences. Ed. by Ellery Queen, pseud. LC 77-82626. 1977. pap. 1.50 o.s.i. (ISBN 0-89559-002-6). Davis Pubns.
Ellery Queen's Crookbook: 25 Stories from Ellery Queen's Mystery Magazine. Ed. by Ellery Queen, pseud. LC 73-5418. (EQMM Annual: 28). 1974. 7.95 (ISBN 0-394-48850-4). Random House.
Ellery Queen's Doors to Mystery. Ellery Queen, pseud. LC 81-156655. 9.95 (ISBN 0-8037-2194-3). Dial Press: Davis Publications.
Ellery Queen's Eyes of Mystery. 1981. 9.95 (ISBN 0-385-27199-9, Dist. by Doubleday). Dial.
Ellery Queen's Eyes of Mystery. Ellery Queen, pseud. LC 82-109214. 9.95. Dial Press: Davis Publications.
Ellery Queen's Eyewitnesses. Ellery Queen, pseud. LC 83-126200. 12.95 (ISBN 0-385-27911-6). Dial Press.
Ellery Queen's Giants of Mystery. 1976. 8.95 o.s.i. (ISBN 0-8037-4362-9). Davis Pubns.
Ellery Queen's Giants of Mystery. Ellery Queen, pseud. LC 76-374243. (Ellery Queen's Anthology; V. 31). 8.95. Dial Press.
Ellery Queen's Grand Slam. Ed. by Ellery Queen, pseud. 1970. 6.95 o.p. (ISBN 0-529-00604-9, A3263). World Pub.
Ellery Queen's Grand Slam: 25 Stories from Ellery Queen's Mystery Magazine. Ed. by Ellery Queen, pseud. LC 75-115800. 1970. 6.95. World Pub. Co.
Ellery Queen's Headliners: 20 Stories from Ellery Queen's Mystery Magazine. Ed. by Ellery Queen, pseud. LC 75-149582. (EQMM Annual: 26). 1971. 6.95. World Pub. Co.

TITLE INDEX EMBEZZLED HEAVEN.

Ellery Queen's Japanese Golden Dozen: The Detective Story World in Japan. Ellery Queen, pseud. LC 77-83615. (Illus.). 8.50 (ISBN 0-8048-1254-3). C. E. Tuttle Co.
Ellery Queen's Magicians of Mystery. 1976. 8.95 o.s.i. (ISBN 0-8037-4362-9). Davis Pubns.
Ellery Queen's Masks of Mystery. Ellery Queen, pseud. LC 78-105494. (Illus.). 8.95. Davis Publications.
Ellery Queen's Masters of Mystery. Ellery Queen, pseud. LC 76-357060. (Ellery Queen's Anthology; V. 30). 8.95 (ISBN 0-8037-5398-5). Dial Press.
Ellery Queen's Maze of Mysteries. Ellery Queen, pseud. LC 82-147654. 12.95 (ISBN 0-385-27619-2). Dial Press.
Ellery Queen's Minimysteries. Ed. by Ellery Queen, pseud. 1969. 6.95 o.p. (A3262). World Pub.
Ellery Queen's Minimysteries: 70 Short-Short Stories of Crime, Mystery, and Detection. Ed. by Ellery Queen, pseud. LC 69-18523. 1969. 6.95. World Pub. Co.
Ellery Queen's Murder-in Spades! Ed. by Ellery Queen, pseud. LC 71-16677. 1969. 0.75. Pyramid Books.
Ellery Queen's Murder Menu. Ed. by Ellery Queen, pseud. LC 70-75367. 1969. 6.95 o.p. (A3262). World Pub.
Ellery Queen's Murder Menu: 22 Stories from Ellery Queen's Mystery Magazine. Ed. by Ellery Queen, pseud. LC 70-75367. (EQMM Annual, 24). 1969. World Pub. Co.
Ellery Queen's Murdercade: 23 Stories from Ellery Queen's Mystery Magazine. Ed. by Ellery Queen, pseud. LC 74-30352. (EQMM Annual: 29). 1975. 7.95 (ISBN 0-394-49674-4). Random House.
Ellery Queen's Mystery Bag. Ellery Queen, pseud. 256p. 1972. 6.95 o.p. (ISBN 0-529-04562-1, A4190). World Pub.
Ellery Queen's Mystery Bag: 25 Stories from Ellery Queen's Mystery Magazine. Ed. by Ellery Queen, pseud. LC 75-183098. (EQMM Annual: 27). 1972. 6.95 (ISBN 0-529-04562-1). World.
Ellery Queen's Mystery Bag: 27th Mystery Annual 1972. Ed. by Ellery Queen, pseud. 368p. 1973. pap. 1.25 o.p. (ISBN 0-532-12153-8). Woodhill.
Ellery Queen's Mystery Bag: 27th Mystery Annual 1972. Ed. by Ellery Queen, pseud. 368p. 1973. pap. 1.25 o.p. (ISBN 0-532-12153-8). Manor Bks.
Ellery Queen's Mystery Jackpot. Ed. by Ellery Queen, pseud. (Orig.). 1970. pap. 0.75 o.p. (T2207). Pyramid Pubns.
Ellery Queen's Mystery Mix:...; 20 Stories from Ellery Queen's Mystery Magazine. Ed. by Ellery Queen, pseud. LC 70-7406. 1963. Random House.
Ellery Queen's Mystery Parade: 19 Stories from Ellery Queen's Mystery Magazine. Ed. by Ellery Queen, pseud. LC 68-21367. (EQMM Annual, 23). 1968. New American Library.
Ellery Queen's Poetic Justice: 23 Stories of Crime, Mystery, and Detection by World-Famous Poets from Geoffrey Chaucer to Dylan Thomas. Ed. by Ellery Queen, pseud. LC 67-26239. 1967. New American Library.
Ellery Queen's Searches & Seizures. 1977. 8.95 o.s.i. (ISBN 0-8037-2224-9). Davis Pubns.
Ellery Queen's Searches and Seizures: 27 Stories from Ellery Queen's Mystery Magazine. Ellery Queen, pseud. LC 76-57910. (EQMM Annual: 31). 1977. 8.95. Dial Press.
Ellery Queen's Secrets of Mystery. Ellery Queen, pseud. LC 79-119688. 9.95 (ISBN 0-8037-3070-5). Dial Press.
Ellery Queen's Shoot the Works. Ed. by Ellery Queen, pseud. (Orig.). 1969. pap. 0.75 o.p. (T2129). Pyramid Pubns.
Ellery Queen's the Golden 13: 13 First Prize Winners from Ellery Queen's Mystery Magazine. Ed. by Ellery Queen, pseud. LC 73-129841. 1970. World Pub. Co.
Ellery Queen's The Tragedy of X: Reintroducing Mr. Drury Lane, Originally Published As by Barnaby Ross. Ellery Queen, pseud. LC 40-35542. 1940. Frederick A. Stokes Company.
Ellery Queen's The Tragedy of Y: A Drury Lane Mystery. Ellery Queen, pseud. LC 41-4818. 1941. Frederick A. Stokes Company.
Ellery Queen's Veils of Mystery. 288p. 1980. 9.95 o.p. (ISBN 0-8037-2224-9). Dial.
Ellery Queen's Veils of Mystery. Ellery Queen, pseud. LC 80-123828. 9.95 (ISBN 0-8037-2201-X). Dial Press.
Ellery Queen's Windows of Mystery. Ellery Queen, pseud. LC 80-140100. 9.95 (ISBN 0-8037-2368-7). Dial Press.
Ellery Queen's Wings of Mystery. Ellery Queen, pseud. LC 79-106979. (Illus.). 8.95 (ISBN 0-8037-2300-8). Dial Press.
Ellery Queen's X Marks the Plot. Ed. by Ellery Queen, pseud. LC 77-81937. pap. 1.95 o.s.i. (ISBN 0-89559-004-2). Davis Pubns.
Ellery Queen's 15th Mystery Annual: The Year's Best from Ellery Queen's Mystery Magazine. Edited by Ellery Queen Psued. of Frederic Dannay and Manfred Bennington Lee. Ed. by Ellery Queen, pseud. LC 46-8129. half cloth, 3.95. Random House.
Ellery Queen's 20th Anniversary Annual: 20 Stories from Ellery Queen's Mystery Magazine. Ed. by Ellery Queen, pseud. LC 73-222741. 1965. Random House.
Ellice Larrabee: A Tale of the Olden Time. Mary E A Brown. LC 6-18689. 1889. Elm Street Printing Co.
Ellie. Herbert Kastle. 1974. (pbk.) 1.50. Dell.
Ellie: A Novel. Herbert D Kastle. LC 72-10573. 1973. 7.95. Delacorte Press.
Ellie: Or, The Human Comedy. John Esten Cooke. 1855. A. Morris.
Ellington Brat. Berthe Knatvold Mellett. LC 28-12797. 1928. Dodd, Mead & Company.
Ellinor: Or, The World As It Is. Mary Anne Hanway. LC 73-22145. (Feminist Controversy in England, 1788-1810). 1974. (4 vols.) 88.00 (ISBN 0-8240-0867-7). Garland Pub.
Ellis Island: A Novel. Fred Mustard Stewart. LC 82-14301. 1983. 15.95 (ISBN 0-688-01622-7). Morrow.
Ellis Island & Other Stories. Mark Helprin. 1981. 10.95 (ISBN 0-440-02204-5, Sey Lawr). Delacorte.
Ellis Island & Other Stories. Mark Helprin. 1982. pap. 5.95 (ISBN 0-440-52204-8, Delta). Dell.
Ellison Wonderland. Harlan Ellison. (Signet book). 1974. (pbk.) 1.25. New American Library.
Ellison Wonderland. Ed. by Harlan Ellison. (RL 7). 1974. pap. 1.50 (ISBN 0-451-07717-2, W7717, Sig). NAL.
Elltradonnic City. Ondra The Sixth. 1979. pap. 3.95 (ISBN 0-930472-02-0). G Stempien.
Elltradonnic Sun. Omdra the Sixth. (Orig.). 1979. pap. cancelled (ISBN 0-930472-03-9). G Stempien.
Elltradonnic Sun. Omdra the Sixth. (Orig.). 1979. pap. 3.95 o.p. (ISBN 0-930472-03-9). G Stempien.
Ellwoods. Charles Stuart Welles. LC 4-18173. Simpkins Marshall, Hamilton, Kent & Co., Ltd.
Elm Is Green. Charles B McLaughlin. (Illus.). 1974. 4.50 o.p. Dnomro Pubns.
Elm Manor Mystery. Louise Barry. 9.75 o.p. (ISBN 0-8062-1164-4). Carlton.
Elm Tree Murder. Cecil John Charles Street. LC 39-303211. 1939. Dodd, Mead & Company.
Elmer Gantry. Sinclair Lewis. LC 27-476127. Harcourt, Brace and Company.
Elmer Gantry. Sinclair Lewis. LC 79-15937. 1979. 12.50 (ISBN 0-8376-0441-9). R. Bentley.
Elmira College Stories. Sylvia Chatfield Bates. LC 11-318942. 1.50. Broadway Publishing Co.
Elmwood: Or, Helen and Emma. Cora Mayfield. LC 7-19154. 1856. J. Munroe and Company.
Eloisa, or, A Series of Original Letters Collected and Published: Translated from the French Together with the Sequel of Julia; or, The New Eloisa (Found Amongst the Author's Papers After His Decease. Jean Jacques Rousseau. LC 51-49319. 1796. Printed for S. Longcope.
Eloise. E. C. Tubb. (Science Fiction Ser). 1975. pap. 1.25 o.p. (UY1162). DAW Bks.
Eloise. E. C Tubb. (Dumarest of Terra:#12). 1975. (pbk.) 1.25. DAW Books.
Elope If You Must. E. J Rath. LC 26-16326. 1926. G. H. Watt.
Elope to Death. John Creasey. LC 76-43493. (Rinehart suspense novel). 1977. 6.95 (ISBN 0-03-020621-9). Holt, Rinehart and Winston.
Elopement. Phyllis Ann Karr. (Coventry Romance Ser.: No. 190). 192p. 1982. pap. 1.50 (ISBN 0-449-50293-7, Coventry). Fawcett.
Elopement. Elsie Frances Wilson Mack. LC 52-13528. 1952. Bouregy & Curl.
Elopement into Exile. Victor Sawdon Pritchett. LC 32-12197. 1932. Little, Brown, and Company.
Eloquent Silence. Rachel Ryan. (Candlelight Ecstasy Ser.: No. 49). (Orig.). 1982. pap. 1.75 (ISBN 0-440-12106-X). Dell.
Elric of Melnibone. Michael Moorcock. 1976. 1.25. Daw Books.
Elroy Bode's Sketchbook II: Portraits in Nostalgia. Elroy Bode. LC 70-170986. (Illus.). 1972. 5.00 (ISBN 0-87404-032-9). Texas Western Press.
Elsa: A Novel. Edward McQueen Gray. (Half-title: Harper's Franklin square library, no. 711). 1891. Harper & Brothers.
Elsa. A Romance. Alfred C Hogbin. LC 7-6596. 1879. J. B. Lippincott & Co.
Elsa, the Mark Woman. C. F. Herm. 3.00 o.p. Carlton.
Else Von der Tanne. With Translation and Commentary and an Introd. to Raabe's Life and Work. Wilhelm Karl Raabe. Ed. by James C. O'Flaherty & Janet K. King. LC 78-181895. 1972. (ISBN 0-8173-8554-1). University of Alabama Press.
Elsewhere, Vol. II. Terri Windling & Mark A. Arnold. 384p. 1982. pap. 2.95 (ISBN 0-441-20404-X, Pub. by Ace Science Fiction). Ace Bks.
Elsewhere, Vol. I. Ed. by Terry Windling & Mark Arnold. 384p. (Orig.). 1982. pap. 2.75 (Pub. by Ace Science Fiction). Ace Bks.
Elsewhere, Elsewhen, Elsehow: Collected Stories. Miriam Allen De Ford. LC 77-147792. 1971. 5.95 (ISBN 0-8027-5540-2). Walker.
Elsewhere Land. Gertrude Ethel Mallette. LC 10-5689. 1909. Press of the Department of Journalism, University of Washington.
Elsewhere, Perhaps. Amos Oz. LC 73-8628. 1973. 7.95 (ISBN 0-15-183746-5). Harcourt Brace Jovanovich.
Elsewhere, Perhaps. Translated from the Hebrew by Nicholas De Lange in Collaboration with the Author. Amos Oz. 1974. (pbk.) 1.50. Bantam Books.
Elsie. Bertha Behrens. Tr. by Hettie E. Miller. LC 6-9752. (On cover: Globe library, v. 1, no. 161). 1891. Rand, McNally & Company.
Elsie: a Christmas Story. From the Norwegian of Alexander L. Kjelland. Alexander Lange Kielland & Dawson, Miles Meanander, 1863- Tr. LC 7-10947. 1894. C. H. Kerr & Company.
Elsie: A Story for the Home. Annie E Thompson. LC 8-19974. 1892. J. H. Earle.
Elsie and Her Loved Ones. Martha Finley. LC 3-29273. Dodd, Mead & Company.
Elsie and the Child: And Other Stories. Arnold Bennett. LC 24-269383. 2.50. George H. Doran Company.
Elsie Venner.--A Romance of Destiny. Oliver Wendell Holmes. LC 5-2441. 1883. Houghton, Mifflin and Company.
Elsie Venner.--A Romance of Destiny. 35th ed. Oliver Wendell Holmes. 1889. Houghton, Mifflin and Company.
Elsie Venner, a Romance of Desitny. Oliver Wendell Holmes. LC 37-328110. 1883. New York Publishing Company.
Elsie Venner: A Romance of Destiny. Oliver Wendell Holmes. LC 75-46279. (Supernatural and Occult Fiction). 1976. 29.00 (ISBN 0-405-08137-5). Arno Press.
Elsie Venner; a Romance of Destiny. Oliver Wendell Holmes. LC 16-9382. (Half-title: The writings of Oliver Wendell Holmes. Reiverside edition. vol. v). Houghton Mifflin Company.
Elsie Venner: A Romance of Destiny. With an Afterword by Miriam R R Small. Oliver Wendell Holmes. LC 61-667461. (Signet classic, CT78). 1961. New American Library.
Elsieville, a Tale of Yesterday. Charles Bassett Holmes. 1903. C. B. Holmes.
Elsingham Portrait. Elizabeth Chater. (Orig.). 1980. pap. 1.75 (ISBN 0-449-50018-7, Coventry). Fawcett.
Elsinor: A Novel. Charles Richard Webb. LC 76-20804. 7.95. McGraw-Hill.
Elsket, and Other Stories. Thomas Nelson Page. LC 73-85693. (Short story index reprint series). 1969. Books for Libraries Press.
Elsket and Other Stories. Thomas Nelson Page. 1891. C. Scribner's Sons.
Elster's Folly. Ellen Price Henry Wood Wood. (Seaside library, v. 18, no. 340). 1878. G. Munro.
Elstones: A Novel. Isabel Constance Clarke. LC 19-4694. 1919. Benziger Brothers.
Eltham House. Mary Augusta Arnold Humphry Ward Ward. LC 15-19970. 1915. Hearst's International Library Company.
Elusive Clue. Jacquelyn Aeby. (Candlelight mystery). 1974. (pbk.) 0.75. Dell.
Elusive Desire. Anne Mather. (Harlequin Presents Ser.). 192p. 1983. pap. 1.95 (ISBN 0-373-10586-X). Harlequin Bks.
Elusive Earl. Barbara Cartland. (Bantam Barbara Cartland Library#36). 1976. (pbk.) 1.25. Bantam Books.
Elusive Harmony. Mary Burchell. (Alpha Books). (Orig.). 1978. pap. text ed. 2.95x (ISBN 0-19-424163-7). Oxford U Pr.
Elusive Heart. Eva Zumwalt. LC 82-45373. (Starlight Romance Ser.). 192p. 1983. 11.95 (ISBN 0-385-18273-2). Doubleday.
Elusive Hildegarde: A Novel. Helen Reimensnyder Martin. LC 3514. 1900. R. F. Fenno & Company.
Elusive Isabel. Jacques Futrelle. LC 9-13428. 1909. 1.18. The Bobbs-Merrill Company.
Elusive Lover. Virna Woods. LC 8-37244. 1898. Houghton, Mifflin and Company.
Elusive Mrs. Pollifax. Dorothy Gilman Butters. LC 76-144266. 1971. 5.95. Doubleday.
Elusive Mrs. Pollifax. Dorothy Gilman. 1974. (pbk.) 0.95. Fawcett Publications.
Elusive Mrs. Pollifax. Dorothy Gilman. LC 82-23339. 1983. 8.95 (ISBN 0-8161-3370-0). G.K. Hall.
Elusive Pimpernel. Emmuska Orczy. LC 8-33437. 1908. Dodd, Mead & Company.
Elva. Durward Grinstead. LC 29-21209. 1929. Covic, Friede.
Elverno. Joseph Maiolo. LC 72-77868. 1972. Blairwood Publishers.
Elves & the Otterskin. Elizabeth Boyer. 1981. pap. 2.50 (ISBN 0-345-29212-X, Del Rey). Ballantine.
Elvira Hopkins of Tompkin's Corner. Izora Cecilia Chandler. LC 99-4792. W. B. Ketcham.
Elvis & Gladys. Elaine Dundy. 320p. 1983. 15.95 (ISBN 0-02-553910-8). Macmillan.
Elvis, Why Don't They Leave You Alone? Mary Mann. 1982. pap. 2.95 (ISBN 0-451-11877-4, AE1877, Sig). NAL.
Elya. Edmond Jabes. Tr. by Rosmarie Waldrop. pap. 3.00. Tree Bks.
Elyria. Elsie Leigh Whittlesey. LC 8-36534. 1877. Claxton, Remsen & Haffelfinger.
Elysian. Michael H Kennedy. LC 80-16570. 1982. 11.95 (ISBN 0-87949-186-8). Ashley Books.
Elysium. William K. Carlson. LC 81-43542. (Science Fiction Ser.). 192p. 1982. 10.95 (ISBN 0-385-17273-7). Doubleday.
Elyza. Clare Darcy. LC 75-36245. 1976. 8.95 (ISBN 0-8027-0516-2). Walker.
Elyza. Clare Darcy. LC 76-45452. 1976. 10.95 (ISBN 0-8161-6414-2). G. K. Hall.
Elyza. Clare Darcy. (Signet Book). 1977. 1.75 (ISBN 0-451-07540-4). New American Library.
Em." A Novel. Emma Dorothy Eliza Nevitte Southworth. (On cover: Ledger library, no. 74). 1892. R. Bonner's Sons.
Emancipated. George Robert Gissing. LC 77-80328. 1977-1978. 14.50 (ISBN 0-8386-2171-6). Fairleigh Dickinson University Press.
Emancipated: A Novel. George Robert Gissing. LC 79-75983. 1969. AMS Press.
Emancipation of Miss Susana. Margaret Hannis. LC 7-24766. 1907. Funk & Wagnalls Company.
Emancipation: The Key... Gertrude Elizabeth Miles. LC 22-19909. The University Press.
Emanicipated: A Novel, 3 Vols. in 1. George Robert Gissing. LC 74-75983. Repr. of 1890 ed. 30.00 (ISBN 0-404-02785-7). AMS Pr.
Embarkation. Murray Gitlin. LC 50-5772. 1950. Crown Publishers.
Embarkation. J. R Salamanca. LC 73-7292. 1973. 6.95 (ISBN 0-394-46028-6). Knopf; Distributed by Random House.
Embarkation. J. R Salamanca. 1975. (pbk.) 1.75. Bantam Books.
Embarrassed Murderer. Gail Stockwell. LC 38-1967. 1938. The Macmillan Company.
Embarrassing Death. Roderic Jeffries. LC 65-12847. (Red badge detective). 1965. bds., 3.50. Dodd.
Embarrassing Orphan. William Edward Norris. (The Griffin series of new fiction). The J. C. Winston Co.
Embarrassment of Riches. Marjorie Fischer. LC 44-338933. 1944. Random House.
Embarrassments. Henry James. LC 79-110202. (Short story index reprint series). 1970. Books for Libraries Press.
Embassy. Stephen Coulter. LC 69-18914. 1969. 5.95. Coward-McCann.
Embassy Ball. Charles Stanley Strong. LC 38-15715. 1935. Gramercy Publishing Co.
Embassy Madonna. Lydia Kirk. LC 74-144279. 1971. 4.95. Doubleday.
Embattled: A Novel of the Spanish Civil War. Translated from the Spanish by Daniel Crabb. With Illus. by Antonio Cobos. Javier Martin-Artajo. LC 56-11417. 1956. Newman Press.
Embedding. Ian Watson. LC 75-947. 1975. 6.95 (ISBN 0-684-13896-4). Scribner.
Ember Days. Margaret Wander Bonanno. LC 79-3629. 10.95 (ISBN 0-87223-590-4). Seaview Books.
Ember in the Ashes. Jane Lane. 1971. pap. 1.25 o.p. (96025-125). Beagle Bks.
Ember Lane: A Winter's Tale. Sheila Kaye-Smith. LC 40-10190. Harper Brothers.
Ember Light: A Novel. Roy Rolfe Gilson. LC 11-26601. 1911. 1.30. The Baker & Taylor Company.
Embers: A Novel. Jeffrey Deprend. LC 19-367. 1919. J. W. Wallace and Company.
Embers: A Winter Tale. Frank Baker. LC 46-2684. 1946. Coward-McCann, Inc.
Embers of Dawn. Patricia Matthews. LC 81-17549. 1982. 6.95 (ISBN 0-553-01368-8). Bantam Books.
Embers of Love: Anonymous. Herman Alfred Kasen. LC 33-3296. 1932. G. H. Watt.
Embers of Old Russia. Otto Peter Peterson. LC 36-1716. City College Co-Operative Store.
Embers on the Hearth: A Story of William's Family. 1st Ed. Charles Rudolph Tobie. LC 53-7373. 1953. Exposition Press.
Embezzled Heaven. Franz V. Werfel. Tr. by William Rose. LC 40-11821. 1940. The Viking Press.

Embezzled Heaven. Franz V. Werfel. Tr. by William Rose. LC 42-256788. 1942. The Sun Dial Press.

Embezzled Heaven: A Play in a Prologue and Three Acts. Laszlo Bus Fekete & Fay, Mary Helen, Joint Author. LC 45-1620. 1945. The Viking Press.

Embezzler. Louis Auchincloss. (2275). 1967. Dell.

Embezzler. Louis Auchincloss. 1974. (pbk.) 1.50. Avon.

Embezzler. Louis Auchincloss. LC 66-11231. 1966. Houghton Mifflin Co.

Embezzler... James Mallahan Cain. LC 47-20918. (On cover: New Avon library. 99). 1946.

Embezzler. James Mallahan Cain. LC 44-8266. (Murder mystery monthly. No. 20). 1944. Avon Book Company.

Embezzler and Double Indemnity: Two Novels. James Mallahan Cain. LC 48-10851. 1948. Triangle Books.

Embezzlers. Valentin Petrovich Kataev. LC 72-90295. 1973. (ISBN 0-88355-005-9). Hyperion Press.

Embezzlers. Valentin Petrovich Kataev. LC 75-309700. 1975. 13.95. Ardis.

Embezzlers. Valentin Petrovich Kataev. Tr. by Zarin, Leonid Sergreevich. LC 29-21421. 1929. L. MacVeagh, The Dial Press.

Embezzlers & Envy. Valentin Petrovich Kataev & Yury Olesha. (Cloth ed. 13.95 o.p.). 300p. 1975. 13.95 o.p. (ISBN 0-88233-090-X). Ardis Pubs.

Embezzlers & Envy. Valentin Petrovich Kataev & Yury Olesha. Tr. by C. Rougle & T. Berczynski. 300p. 1974. 13.95 o.p. (ISBN 0-88233-090-X); pap. 3.25 o.p. (ISBN 0-88233-091-8). Ardis Pubs.

Emblems of Fidelity. James Lane Allen. Repr. of 1919 ed. lib. bdg. 20.00 (ISBN 0-8414-3062-4). Folcroft.

Emblems of Fidelity: A Comedy in Letters. James Lane Allen. LC 19-4848. 1919. Doubleday, Page & Company.

Embrace and Stories. Eleanor Glaze. LC 72-98279. 1970. 5.95. Bobbs-Merrill.

Embrace of the Butcher. Anthony Burton. LC 82-5068. 10.95 (ISBN 0-396-08059-6). Dodd, Mead.

Embrace the Fury. Jessica March. 1.95 (ISBN 0-449-13973-5). Fawcett Gold Medal Books.

Embrace the Wind. Melinda Harris. (Second Chance at Love Ser.: No. 98). 192p. 1983. pap. 1.75 (ISBN 0-515-06862-4). Jove Pubns.

Embrace the Wind. Blaine Stevens, pseud. 352p. (Orig.). 1982. pap. 2.95 (ISBN 0-515-05621-9). Jove Pubns.

Embrace Tomorrow. T. J. Feely. 352p. Date not set. pap. 2.95. PB.

Embraceable. Florence Stonebraker. LC 49-119570. 1949. Phoenix Press.

Embraced by Destiny. Simone Hadary. 192p. 1982. pap. 1.75 (ISBN 0-515-06596-X). Jove Pubns.

Embraces. Sharon Wagner. (Orig.). 1980. pap. 2.50 (ISBN 0-89083-666-3). Zebra.

Embroidered City. Lewis David Gelfan. LC 50-6378. 1950. Little, Brown.

Embroidered Sunset. Joan Aiken. LC 77-116180. 1970. 5.95. Doubleday.

Embryo. Louis Charbonneau. 1976. (pbk.) 1.25. Warner Books.

Embryo. Daniel M. Klein. LC 80-709. 284p. 1981. 11.95 (ISBN 0-385-15797-5). Doubleday.

Embryo. Daniel M. Klein. 288p. 1981. pap. 2.95 (ISBN 0-445-04688-0). Popular Lib.

Emelie. Melissa Mather. (Orig.). 1982. pap. 3.50 (ISBN 0-345-28540-9). Ballantine.

Emerald. Helen Ashfield. 192p. 1983. 10.95 (ISBN 0-312-24386-3). St Martin.

Emerald. Suzan Jarvis. (Orig.). 1980. pap. 1.95 (ISBN 0-532-23120-1). Woodhill.

Emerald. Mario Soldati. Tr. by William Weaver. LC 76-54764. (Helen & Kurt Wolff Bk). 1977. 8.95 o.p. (ISBN 0-15-128530-6). HarBraceJ.

Emerald. Phyllis A. Whitney. LC 82-45369. 1982. 14.95 (ISBN 0-385-18285-6). Doubleday.

Emerald. Phyllis A. Whitney. LC 83-235. 1983. 17.95 (ISBN 0-8161-3512-6). G.K. Hall.

Emerald: A Novel. Mario Soldati. LC 76-54764. 8.95 (ISBN 0-15-128530-6). Harcourt Brace Jovanovich.

Emerald and Ermine: A Tale of the Argoat. Marquerite De Godart Cunliffe-Owen. LC 7-33591. 1907. Harper & Brothers.

Emerald Bay. Winter Ames. (Second Chance at Love, Contemporary Ser.: No. 7). 192p. (Orig.). 1981. pap. 1.75 (ISBN 0-515-05694-4). Jove Pubns.

Emerald Buddha. Elizabeth Morse. LC 35-4722. 1935. E. P. Dutton & Co., Inc.

Emerald Canyon. Jack M Bickham. LC 73-19313. 1974. 4.95 (ISBN 0-385-03977-8). Doubleday.

Emerald Canyon. Jeff Clinton, pseud. LC 73-19313. (Double D Western Ser.). 192p. 1974. 4.95 o.p. (ISBN 0-385-03977-8). Doubleday.

Emerald Canyon. Jeff Clinton, pseud. (O.s.i.). 1975. pap. 0.95 o.s.i. (BT50809). Belmont-Tower.

Emerald Canyon. Jeff Clinton. 1975. (pbk.) 0.95. Belmont Tower Books.

Emerald Cave. Gloria Bevan. 192p. 1982. pap. write for info. (ISBN 0-373-02455-X). Harlequin Bks.

Emerald Clasp. Francis Beeding. LC 33-15248. 1938. Little, Brown, and Company.

Emerald Crown. Theodora McCormick Du Bois. LC 55-7587. 1955. Funk &Wagnalls.

Emerald Decision. David Grant, pseud. 352p. 1982. pap. 2.75 (ISBN 0-345-29645-1). Ballantine.

Emerald Decision. David Grant, pseud. LC 80-13759. 396p. 1980. 11.95 (ISBN 0-03-056909-5). HR&W.

Emerald Decision. Craig Thomas. LC 80-13759. 11.95 (ISBN 0-03-056909-5). Holt, Rinehart and Winston.

Emerald Embrance. Diane Du Pont. 1980. pap. 2.50 (ISBN 0-449-14316-3, GM). Fawcett.

Emerald Enchantment. Nomi Berger. (Interlude Romance Ser.). 208p. (Orig.). 1982. pap. 1.95 (ISBN 0-441-20479-1). Ace Bks.

Emerald Fire. Julia Grice. LC 78-57624. 1978. 2.25 (ISBN 0-380-38596-1). Avon Books.

Emerald. From the German of William Redenbacher. Wilhelm Redenbacher. Tr. by Lochman, Augustus Hoffman. Lutheran Board of Publication. LC 41-267036. (Half-title: The fatherland series). 1872. Lutheran Board of Publication.

Emerald Kiss. Christopher Reeve. LC 31-30598. 1931. W. Morrow & Co.

Emerald Land. Livia James. 368p. (Orig.). 1983. pap. 2.95 (ISBN 0-449-12410-X, GM). Fawcett.

Emerald Lizard: Tales and Legends of Guatemala. Samayoa Chinchilla, Carlos. LC 56-12348. (Illus.). 1957. Falcon's Wing Press.

Emerald Mountain. Frances Y. McHugh. 1970. 3.95 o.p. Lenox Hill.

Emerald Murder Case. Dennis Dean. LC 40-89339. Phoenix Press.

Emerald Murder Trap: The Third Case of Mr. Paul Savoy. Jackson Gregory. 1934. C. Scribner's Sons.

Emerald Necklace. Diana Brown. LC 79-23126. 1980. 10.95 (ISBN 0-312-24385-5). St. Martin's Press.

Emerald Necklace. Agnes Russell Weekes & Weekes, Rose Kirkpatrick, 1874- Joint Author. LC 31-24899. 1931. Dodd, Mead & Company.

Emerald Necklace: A Novel. Elise Fraser. LC 50-11056. 1950. Van Kampen Press.

Emerald of Catherine the Great. Hilaire Belloc. LC 26-20761. 1926. Harper & Brothers.

Emerald of Henry. Ann Carry Taylor. bds. 3.00. Pageant.

Emerald Oil Caper. James D. Lawrence. (Dark Angel Ser: No. 2). (Orig.). 1975. pap. 1.25 o.p. (ISBN 0-515-03629-3, V3629). BJ Pub Group.

Emerald Peacock. Katharine Gordon. LC 78-27489. 9.95 (ISBN 0-688-03394-6). Morrow.

Emerald Route. R. K. Narayan. 115p. 1980. pap. 4.95 (ISBN 0-86578-075-7). Ind-US Inc.

Emerald Station. Daoma Winston. 1983. pap. 3.50 (ISBN 0-380-00738-X, 63933-5). Avon.

Emerald Station. Daoma Winston. 1974. (pbk.) 1.50. Avon.

Emerald Tiger. Edgar Jepson. LC 28-12996. 1928. Macy-Masius.

Emerald Trails. Jackson Gregory. LC 28-812555. 1928. C. Scribner's Sons.

Emerald Trap. Leonard St. Clair. LC 73-87206. 1973. 6.95 (ISBN 0-399-11269-3). Putnam.

Emergence. Robert D. San Souci. 288p. 1981. pap. 2.95 (ISBN 0-380-77792-4, 77792). Avon.

Emergence: Tales. Anthony J Summers. LC 77-362600. (Illus.). 1977. 3.00 (ISBN 0-917146-06-9). The Cauldron Press.

Emergency. Wilfred Charles Heinz. LC 72-89315. 1974. 6.95 (ISBN 0-385-06245-1). Doubleday.

Emergency. Wilfred Charles Heinz. (Fawcett crest book). 1975. (pbk.) 1.50. Fawcett.

Emergency: A Novel. Richard Rive. LC 65-66476. 1964. Faber and Faber.

Emergency: A Novel. Richard Rive. LC 70-102973. (American Library). 1970. 1.50. Collier Books.

Emergency Call. Elizabeth Harrison. 1974. (pbk.) 0.95 (ISBN 0-671-77735-1). Pocket Books.

Emergency Calling Nurse Mallon. Peggy O'More, pseud. LC 64-25955. 1964. Arcadia House.

Emergency Exit. Alfred Edgar Coppard. LC 34-34946. Random House.

Emergency Exit. Clarence Major. LC 79-52031. (Illus.). 9.95 (ISBN 0-914590-58-8) (ISBN 0-914590-59-6). Fiction Collective: Distributed by G. Braziller.

Emergency Exit: A Dr. Hailey Story. Robert McNair Wilson. LC 44-3475. 1944. J. Messner, Inc.

Emergency in the Pyrenees. Ann Bridge, pseud. 1965. 5.50 o.p. (ISBN 0-07-007743-6). McGraw.

Emergency in the Pyrenees: By) Ann Bridge Pseud. Mary Dolling Sanders O'Malley. LC 64-66286. bds., 5.50. McGraw.

Emergency Nurse. Peggy Gaddis, pseud. pap. 0.50 o.p. (50-412). Manor Bks.

Emergency Nurse. Rosamund Hunt. LC 64-7420. 1964. Avalon Books.

Emergency Nurse. Patricia Rae. 1981. pap. 2.75 (ISBN 0-89083-761-9). Zebra.

Emergency Nurse. Patricia Rae. (Orig.). 1982. pap. 2.95 (ISBN 0-8217-1045-1). Zebra.

Emergency Nurse. Carlton Williams. LC 40-4893. The Penn Publishing Company.

Emergency Nurse: By Georgia Craig Pseud. Peggy Gaddis, pseud. LC 63-6704. 1963. Arcadia House.

Emergency Procedure. Macdowell Fredericks. LC 70-96784. 1970. 5.95. Coward-McCann.

Emergency Room. James Kerr. LC 74-19360. 1975. 7.95 (ISBN 0-440-03384-5). Delacorte Press.

Emergency Room. James Kerr. 1976. (pbk.) 1.50. Dell.

Emergency Ten Thirty-Three on Channel Eleven. Hilary H. Milton. 1978. pap. 1.50 (ISBN 0-440-92325-5, LFL). Dell.

Emergency Wife. Helen Marion Edginton. LC 37-36090. Green Circle Books.

Emerson Hough. Delbert E Wylder. LC 80-25897. (Twayne's United States authors series; TUSAS 397). (Illus.). 1981. 13.95 (ISBN 0-8057-7328-2). Twayne Publishers.

Emes Morris. Milt Weiner. LC 62-22277. 1963. Rocket Book Press.

Emigrant. Lubov' Fedorovna Dostoevskaia & Margolies, Vera, Tr. LC 17-22563. 1916. Brentano's.

Emigrant. Frederick James Howard. LC 28-11711. 1928. Longmans, Green and Co. Ltd.

Emigrant Ship: A Novel. William Clark Russell. LC 8-1801. The Cassell Publishing Co.

Emigrant Squire. Peter Hamilton Myers. LC 7-23123. T. B. Peterson.

Emigrant Trail. Geraldine Bonner. LC 10-9922. 1910. Duffield & Company.

Emigrants. Johan Bojer. LC 73-21338. 1974. 15.00 (ISBN 0-8371-6194-0). Greenwood Press.

Emigrants. Johan Bojer. LC 78-9813. 1978. 4.95 (ISBN 0-8032-6051-2). University of Nebraska Press.

Emigrants. Johan Bojer & Jayne, Arthur Garland, 1882- Tr. LC 25-269963. The Century Co.

Emigrants. George Lamming. 1955. McGraw-Hill.

Emigrants. Vilhelm Moberg. (Emigrants Saga: No. 1). 1971. pap. 2.75 (ISBN 0-445-08561-4). Popular Lib.

Emigrants: A Novel; Translated from the Swedish by Gustaf Lannestock. Vilhelm Moberg. LC 51-11040. 1951. Simon and Schuster.

Emigrant's Daughter: A Tale of the West. LC 34-36440. (Half-title: Youth's western library no. 2). 1849. C. Cropper & Son.

Emigrant's Mother: A True Story of the Last Fifty Years, for the Old and the Young... With a Prefatory Authentication. Rufus Babcock. LC 42-48291. (On cover: Good girl's library). 1871. Sheldon & Company.

Emigrants of Ahadarra: A Tale of Irish Life. William Carleton. Ed. by Robert L. Wolff. (Ireland Nineteenth Century Fiction Ser. Two: Vol. 42). 320p. 1979. lib. bdg. 32.00 (ISBN 0-8240-3491-0). Garland Pub.

Emigrants (1793) Traditionally Ascribed to Gilbert Imlay, but, More Probably by Mary Wollstonecraft. A Fasimile Reproduction of the Dublin Ed. (1794. Gilbert Imlay & Wollstonecraft, Mary. LC 64-10668. 1964. Scholars'Facsimiles & Reprints.

Emigration of Sergey Ivanovich. Richard Freeborn. LC 65-11042. 1965. 4.00. Morrow.

Emil und Die Detektive. Erich Kastner & Stroebe, Lilian Luise, 1875- Ed. LC 44-45292. 1936. H. Holt and Company.

Emil und Die Detektive, Von Erich Kastner. Erich Kastner. Ed. by Stroebe, Lilian Luise & Hofrichter, Ruth J. LC 33-15674. H. Holt and Company.

Emil und Die Drei Zwillinge; Edited with Notes, Exercises and Vocabulary by Lilian L. Stroebe and Gabriele Humbert Parker... Erich Kastner. Ed. by Stroebe, Lilian Luise & Humbert, Gabriele. LC 38-16426. H. Holt and Company.

Emile et les Detectives. Erich Kastner. Tr. by Faisans-Maury, Louise. Ed. by Bovee, Arthur Gibbon. LC 36-7431. (Heath's modern language series). D. C. Heath and Company.

Emile Zola: An Introductory Study of His Novels. Angus Wilson. (A-28). 1961. pap., 1.50. Apollo Eds.

Emile Zola's First Love Story and Others. (On cover: Famous stories, v. 1, no. 2). 1895. Jewett & Buchanan.

Emilia Galotti. Gotthold E. Lessing. Tr. by Anna G. Von Aesch. (YA) 1959. pap. text ed. 1.95 (ISBN 0-8120-0063-3). Barron.

Emily. Paula Allardyce, pseud. 1976. (pbk.) 1.25. Dell Books.

Emily. Sally Benson. LC 38-18018. Covici Friede.

Emily. Jilly Cooper. 192p. 1981. pap. 1.95 (ISBN 0-449-24410-5, Crest). Fawcett.

Emily. MacGregor Jenkins. LC 30-242404. The Bobbs-Merrill Co.

Emily. A Tale of the Empire State. Clara Loring. Bogart. LC 6-14190. 1894. Printed by Andrus & Church.

Emily Bellefontaine. Christopher Yerf. LC 8-179991. 1908. W. B. Conkey Company.

Emily Chester. A Novel... Anne Moncure Crane Seemuller. LC 8-6444. 1864. Ticknor and Fields.

Emily Chester. A Novel... Anne Moncure Crane Seemuller. LC 43-427061. 1871. J. R. Osgood and Company.

Emily Davis. Miss Read, pseud. 1972. 4.95 o.p. (ISBN 0-395-13524-9). HM.

Emily Davis. Dora Jessie Saint. LC 73-177543. (Illus.). 1972. 4.95 (ISBN 0-395-13524-9). Houghton Mifflin.

Emily Does Her Best. Horace Tremlett. LC 17-30043. 1917. John Lane.

Emily Hamilton, a Novel. Founded on Incidents in Real Life. Eliza Vicery. LC 8-32804. 1803. I. Thomas, Jun.

Emily Mayland: Or, The Faithful Governess. M H Cox. LC 6-28858. 1864. Printed by J. B. Rodgers.

Emily of New Moon. Lucy Maud Montgomery. LC 23-12112. 1923. Frederick A. Stokes Company.

Emily, Part 1: Charles. Mark Dunster. 46p. (Orig.). 1975. pap. 4.00 (ISBN 0-89642-017-5). Linden Pubs.

Emily Roe of Baltimore. 2d ed.... ed. Julia Frances Graham. LC 11-147219. 1911. 1.35. F. T. Borden.

Emily Stone. Anne Redmon, pseud. LC 74-17726. 1975. 7.95 (ISBN 0-275-05150-1). Praeger.

Emily Will Know. Nancy Rutledge. LC 49-822094. 1949. Pub. for the Crime Club by Doubleday.

Emily's Destiny. Whitney Faulkner. (American Dream: Bk. 1). (Orig.). 1983. pap. 3.50 (ISBN 0-8217-1203-9). Zebra.

Emily's Quest. Lucy Maud Montgomery. LC 27-18262. 1927. Frederick A. Stokes Company.

Eminent Yachtsman and the Whorehouse Piano Player. Don Asher. LC 73-75241. 1973. 6.95. Coward, McCann & Geoghegan.

Emir's Education in the Proper Use of Magical Powers. Jane Roberts & Lynne Cherry. LC 79-15444. (Illus.). 7.95. Delacorte Press/E. Friede.

Emma. Jane Austen. (Harcourt library of English and American classics). 1962. Harcourt, Brace & World.

Emma. Jane Austen. LC 62-21620. 1965. Collier Books.

Emma. Jane Austen. LC 66-768062. (Penguin English Library, ELIO) 6/-). 1966. Penguin.

Emma. Jane Austen. LC 78-870114. (Oxford English novels). 1971. 2.25 (ISBN 0-19-255344-5). Oxford University Press.

Emma. Jane Austen. LC 6-3864. 1892. Roberts Brothers.

Emma. Jane Austen. LC 4-15273. 1896. Macmillan and Co., Ltd.

Emma. Jane Austen. Ed. by Dobson, Austin. LC 16-25062. 1897. Macmillan and Co., Limited.

Emma. Jane Austen. LC 25-27470. (Rittenhouse classics). 1925. Macrae, Smith Company.

Emma. Jane Austen. LC 36-37050. (Half-title: everyman's library, ed. by Ernest Rhys. Fiction. no. 24). 1934. J. M. Dent & Sons, Ltd.

Emma. Jane Austen & John Cann Bailey. LC 29-243875. 1928. Dodd, Mead & Company.

Emma. Jane Austen & James Kinsley. LC 79-17305. (World's classics). 1980. 2.95 (ISBN 0-19-281504-0). Oxford University Press.

Emma. Jane Austen & Fritz Kredel. LC 65-2032. 1964. Printed for the Members of the Limited Editions Club at the Thistle Press.

Emma. Jane Austen & Van Doren, Carl Clinton. LC 38-24568. (modern readers' series). 1928. The Macmillan Company.

Emma. Charlotte Bronte. 224p. 1981. 11.95 (ISBN 0-89696-114-1, An Everest House Book). Dodd.

Emma... Louis Paul. LC 37-17353. 1937. Doubleday, Doran & Company, Inc.

Emma see Oxford Illustrated Jane Austen.

Emma Blue. Beverly Lowry. LC 77-17003. 1978. 7.95 (ISBN 0-385-13135-6). Doubleday.

Emma Blue. Beverly Lowry. 1979. 1.95 (ISBN 0-445-04467-5). Popular Library.

Emma Conquest. Rene Ray. LC 51-13046. 1951. Putnam.

Emma Corbett: Exhibiting Henry and Emma, the Faithful Modern Lovers; As Delineated by Themselves, in Their Original Letters. Samuel Jackson Pratt. LC 9-32311. 1782. Printed and Sold by R. Bell.

Emma: Ed., Introd. by Ronald Blythe. Jane Austen. LC 66-33624. (Penguin Eng lib., EL 10). 1966. pap., 1.25. Penguin.

Emma Hamilton. Betty Alice Martin King. LC 77-369985. 1976. 3.25 (ISBN 0-7091-5612-X). Hale.

Emma. Illus. by Philip Gough. Jane Austen. LC 66-5540. (Macdonald illus. classics, 4). 1966. 3.50. Macdonald.

Emma: Introd. by Alexander Welsh. Jane Austen. (Collateral classic, CC505). Washington Sq., C.

Emma Lou--Her Book. Mary Martha Mears. LC 7-258649. 1896. H. Holt and Company.

Emma McChesney & Co. Edna Ferber. LC 71-169548. (Short story index reprint series). (Illus.). 1971. (ISBN 0-8369-4010-5). Books for Libraries Press.

Emma McChesney & Co. Edna Ferber. LC 15-26558. 1915. Frederick A. Stokes Company.

Emma: My Lord Admiral's Mistress. Frank Wilson Kenyon. LC 56-3607. (Avon, T-128). Avon Publications.

Emma: New Introd. by John Dennis Duffy. Jane Austen. (Classics ser., CL102). 1966. Airmont.

Emma: Notes, Including Life and Background, Introduction to Emma, Feneral Plot Summary, List of Characters, Chapter Summaries and Commentaries, Critical Analysis... Consulting Ed.: James L. Roberts. Thomas J Rountree. 1967. pap., 1.00. Cliff S.

Emma. Pref. by Stella Gibbons, Illus. by Fritz Kredel. Jane Austen & Fritz Kredel. 1968. 7.50. Heritage.

Emma Smith, the Elect Lady: A Novel Based on Her Life. Margaret Wilson Gibson. LC 54-791023. 1954. Herald House.

Emma Walton: Or, Trials and Triumph. Eliza Ann Dupuy. LC 5-35860. 1854. J. A. & U. P. James.

Emma. With an Introd. by Lionel Trilling. Jane Austen. LC 57-13918. (Riverside editions, B17). 1957. Houghton Mifflin.

Emma. With Illus. of the Author and Her Environment and Pictures from Early Editions of the Book, Together with an Introd. by Frederic E. Faverty. Jane Austen. LC 61-117153. (Great illustrated classics). 1961. Dodd, Mead.

Emmanuel: A Novel. Tr. from French by Eric Earnshaw Smith. Nicole Vidal. LC 65-169029. bds., 4.95. Viking.

Emmanuel Burden: Merchant, of Thames St., in the City of London, Exporter of Hardware; a Record of His Lineage, Speculations, Last Days and Death. Hilaire Belloc. LC 4-34562. 1904. C. Scribner's Sons.

Emmanuel Burden, Merchant of Thames St. in the City of London, Exporter of Hardware: A Record of His Lineage, Speculations, Last Days, and Death. Hilaire Belloc. LC 75-41024. (Illus.). 1979. 15.00 (ISBN 0-404-14642-2). AMS Press.

Emmanuel-Philibert: Or, The European Wars of the Xvith Century. Alexandre Dumas. LC 6-43609. 1854. D. Appleton and Company.

Emmanuel: The Story of the Messiah. William Forbes Cooley. LC 6-301973. 1889. Dodd, Mead and Company.

Emmanuelle. Emmanuelle Arsan. LC 78-139255. (v. 1) 6.95. Grove Press.

Emmanuelle II. Emmanuelle Arsan. LC 73-21049. 1974. (ISBN 0-394-49271-4) (ISBN 0-8021-0053-8). Grove.

Emmanuelle Two. Emmanuelle Arsan. Tr. by Anselm Hollo from Fr. LC 74-24995. 1974. 3.95 (ISBN 0-394-17891-2, B453, BC). Grove.

Emmeline. Judith Rossner. LC 80-15553. 11.95 (ISBN 0-671-22938-9). Simon and Schuster.

Emmeline. Elsie Singmaster. LC 16-5189. 1916. Houghton Mifflin Company.

Emmeline: the Orphan of the Castle. Charlotte Turner Smith. LC 77-591127. (Oxford English novels). (Illus.). 1971. 4.00 (ISBN 0-19-255322-4). Oxford University Press.

Emmeline: The Orphan of the Castle. Charlotte Turner Smith. LC 8-8629.

Emmerton Mills. E S Goff. LC 16-23089. 1.00. The Roxburgh Publishing Company, Inc.

Emmet Twelve. Pamela L. Clark. 1970. 4.50 o.p. Vantage.

Emmett Bonlore. Opie Percival Read. F. J. Schulte & Company.

Emmett Lawler. Jim Tully. LC 22-4922. 1922. Harcourt, Brace and Company.

Emmie's Love. Janette Seymour. 1981. 2.75 (ISBN 0-671-83129-1). Pocket Books.

Emmy Untamed: A Novel of the Pennsylvania Dutch. Helen Reimensnyder Martin. LC 37-3023. 1937. D. Appleton-Century Company, Incorporated.

Emotion Denied. Lawrence Nelson. LC 37-39536. 1937. Hillman-Curl, Inc.

Emotion Mixed with Love. Erma Kriedeman. 1976. 2.95 o.p. (ISBN 0-8059-2382-9). Dorrance.

Emotional Journey. William Babington Maxwell. LC 37-1709. 1937. D. Appleton-Century Company, Incorporated.

Emotionalist: The Romance of an Awakening to Temperament. Stanley Olmsted. LC 8-30250. 1908. D. Appleton & Company.

Emotions in Abstract: A Collections of Short Stories. Jimmy Orr. LC 81-90671. 83p. 1983. 7.95 (ISBN 0-533-05297-1). Vantage.

Emotions of a Black Sheep. Richard E. Nowack. 3.50 o.s.i. (ISBN 0-8181-0116-4). Pageant-Poseidon.

Emotions of Suzette. Victor Cravat. 1972. pap. 1.75 o.s.i. (V1083K, Venus). Grove.

Emperor... Georg Moritz Ebers. Tr. by Bell, Clara Courtenay (Poynter) LC 16-157075. (historical romances of Georg Ebers. vol. v). 1915. D. Appleton and Company.

Emperor. Ryszard. Kapuscinski. LC 82-47670. 10.95. Harcourt Brace Jovanovich.

Emperor: A Romance. Georg Moritz Ebers. Tr. by Clara Courtenay Bell. LC 6-43720. 1881. W. S. Gottsberger.

Emperor. A Romance. Georg Moritz Ebers. Tr. by Storrs, Catharine H. (Seaside library. v. 55. no. 1120). 1881. G. Munro.

Emperor. A Romance. Georg Moritz Ebers & Storrs, Mrs. Catharine H., Tr. (On cover: Seaside library. Pocket ed., no. 1106). 1888. G. Munro.

Emperor; a Romance of the Camp and Court of Alexander the Great. The Love of Statira, the Persian Queen. Marshall Monroe Kirkman. LC 13-222123. Cropley Phillips Company.

Emperor & the Actress. Joan Haslip. 352p. 1982. 18.95 (ISBN 0-385-27457-2). Dial.

Emperor and the Monster. William Voltz. (Perry Rhodan, 107). (Illus.). Ace.

Emperor Arthur. Godfrey Edmund Turton. LC 67-23825. 1967. Doubleday.

Emperor Brims. Herbert Ravenel Sass. LC 41-982. 1941. Doubleday, Doran and Company, Inc.

Emperor Falls in Love: The Romance of Josephine and Napoleon. Octave Aubry. Tr. by Stuart, Henry Longan. LC 28-5536. 1928. Harper & Brothers.

Emperor Fu Manchu. Sax Rohmer, pseud. 1976. pap. 1.25 o.p. (ISBN 0-515-03946-2). BJ Pub Group.

Emperor Fu Manchu: An Original Gold Medal Novel. Arthur Sarsfield Ward. LC 59-1894. (Gold medal books, a929). 1959. Fawcett Publications.

Emperor in the Dock. Willem De Veer. LC 15-4214. 1915. John Lane.

Emperor of America. Sax Rohmer, pseud. 1976. Repr. of 1929 ed. lib. bdg. 16.30x (ISBN 0-89190-805-6). Am Repr-Rivercity Pr.

Emperor of America. Arthur Sarsfield Ward. LC 29-28788. 1929. Pub. for the Crime Club, Inc., by Doubleday, Doran & Company, Inc.

Emperor of Death. G. Wayman Jones & Robert Weinberg. LC 80-8668. (Pulp classic; no. 20). 1980. 11.95 (ISBN 0-89370-085-1) (ISBN 0-89370-084-3). Borgo Press.

Emperor of Elam: And Other Stories. Harrison Griswold Dwight. LC 20-19763. 1920. Doubleday, Page & Company.

Emperor of Evil. Carroll John Daly. LC 37-1873. 1937. Frederick A. Stokes Company.

Emperor of Ice-Cream. Brian Moore. LC 77-23322. 1977. 1.95 (ISBN 0-14-004449-3). Penguin Books.

Emperor of Ice-Cream: A Novel. Brian Moore. LC 65-20780. 1965. Viking Press.

Emperor of Kings. Mary L. Burkhalter. 1980. pap. 2.50 (ISBN 0-934284-01-6). Jolean Pub Co.

Emperor of Portugallia: From the Swedish of Selma Lagerlof. Selma Ottiliana Lovisa Lagerlof. Tr. by Howard, Velma (Swanston) LC 16-21127. 1916. Doubleday, Page & Company.

Emperor of the Amazon. Marcio Souza. 192p. 1980. pap. 2.75 (ISBN 0-380-76240-4, 76240, Bard). Avon.

Emperor of the Sea. Obi B. Egbuna. 1974. pap. 1.25 o.p. (ISBN 0-531-06054-3, Fontana Pap). Watts.

Emperor Shaka the Great: A Zulu Epic. Mazisi Kunene & United Nations Educational, Scientific and Cultural Organization. LC 80-479284. (UNESCO collection of representative works: African author series). (Illus.). 1979. 25.00 (ISBN 0-435-90648-8) (ISBN 0-435-90211-3). Heinemann.

Emperor, Swords, Pentacles. Phyllis Bloom Gotlieb. 304p. 1982. pap. 2.75 (ISBN 0-441-18067-1, Pub. by Ace Science Fiction). Ace Bks.

Emperor: The Sages and Death. Translated from the German by William Wolf. Introd. by Theodor Reik. Rachel Berdach. LC 62-131533. 1962. T. Yoseloff.

Emperor's Candlesticks. Emmuska Orczy. 1976. lib. bdg. 13.75x (ISBN 0-89968-075-5). Lightyear.

Emperor's Candlesticks. Emmuska Orezy. 1908. Repr. lib. bdg. 20.00 (ISBN 0-8414-9226-3). Folcroft.

Emperor's Candlesticks: A Romance. Emmuska Orczy. LC 8-18369. C. H. Doscher & Co.

Emperor's Charioteer: A Tale of the Great Days of Constantinople. W. H Spears. LC 65-16279. 3.95. Adams Pr., W. Washintoning St.

Emperor's Duchess. Rosie Goldschmidt Waldeck. LC 48-9163. 1948. Doubleday.

Emperor's Ladies. Noel Bertram Gerson. LC 59-10667. 1959. Doubleday.

Emperor's Lady: A Novel Based on the Life of the Empress Josephine. Frank Wilson Kenyon. LC 53-5082. 1953. Crowell.

Emperor's Old Clothes. Frank Heller. 388p. 1981. pap. text ed. write for info. (ISBN 0-86649-062-0). Twentieth Century.

Emperor's Old Clothes. Gunnar Serner & Lee, Robert Emmons, Tr. LC 23-8078. Thomas Y. Crowell Company.

Emperor's Pearl. Robert Van Gulik. 1982. 3.50 (ISBN 0-434-82559-X, Pub. by Heinemann). David & Charles.

Emperor's Pearl, a Chinese Detective Story: By Robert Van Gulik. With Eight Illus. Drawn by the Author in Chinese Style. Robert Hans Van Gulik, pseud. LC 64-20052. 1964. Scribner.

Emperor's Pearl: A Chinese Detective Story. Robert Van Gulik. LC 64-20052. 1974. (pbk.) 0.95. Warner Paperback Library.

Emperor's Pearl: A Judge Dee Mystery. Robert Van Gulik. 160p. 1981. pap. 2.50 (ISBN 0-684-17318-2, ScribT). Scribner.

Emperor's Physician. Jacob Randolph Perkins. LC 44-5266. 1944. The Bobbs-Merrill Company.

Emperor's Shadow. J. C. Brown. 4.75 o.p. Carlton.

Emperor's Snuff Box. John Dickson Carr. LC 68-113837. (B67-24872). 1967. Penguin in Association with H. Hamilton.

Emperor's Snuff-Box. John Dickson Carr. LC 42-24671. 1942. Harper & Brothers.

Emperor's Snuff-Box. John Dickson Carr. LC 47-27904. (Pocket Book 372). 1946. Pocket Books.

Emperor's Tea. Edwin P. Geauque. (Illus.). 1978. 2.95 (ISBN 0-87482-095-2); pap. 1.25 o.p. (ISBN 0-87482-096-0). Wake-Brook.

Emperor's Virgin: A Novel. Sylvia Fraser. LC 80-486998. 14.95 (ISBN 0-7710-3175-0). McClelland and Stewart.

Emphyrio. Jack Vance, pseud. (Science Fiction Ser.). (Orig.). 1979. pap. 2.25 (ISBN 0-87997-504-0, UE1504). Daw Bks.

Empire. George De Mare. LC 56-6488. 1956. Putnam.

Empire. Patricia Matthews & Clayton Matthews. 368p. 1982. pap. 3.50 (ISBN 0-553-22577-4). Bantam.

Empire. H. Beam Piper. 320p. (Orig.). 1981. pap. 2.50 (ISBN 0-441-20557-7). Ace Bks.

Empire. Etta Revesz. (Orig.). 1981. pap. 2.95 (ISBN 0-451-09564-2, E9564, Sig). NAL.

Empire: A Visual Novel. Samuel R Delany & Howard V Chaykin. LC 78-19575. (Berkley/Windhover books). (Illus.). 1978. 19.95. (ISBN 0-399-12245-1) (ISBN 0-425-03900-5). Berkley Pub. Corp.: Distributed by Putnam.

Empire Blues: A Novel. Taylor Branch. LC 80-27295. 12.95 (ISBN 0-671-23096-4). Simon and Schuster.

Empire Builder. Paul R. Rothweiler. (Westward Rails Ser.: No. 3). (Orig.). 1982. pap. 2.75 (ISBN 0-440-02089-1, Banbury). Dell.

Empire Builders. Francis Lynde. LC 7-260192. 1907. The Bobbs-Merrill Company.

Empire Celeste. Francoise Mallet-Joris. 1968. pap. 1.10 o.s.i. Paris Pubns.

Empire City. Paul Goodman. LC 76-41277. 1977. 4.95 (ISBN 0-394-72277-9). Vintage Books.

Empire City. George Lippard. LC 70-76927. (American fiction reprint series). 1969. Books for Libraries Press.

Empire for a Lady. Alan Le May. LC 37-20206. Farrar & Rinehart, Inc.

Empire of Crime! Nick Carter. LC 45-667423. 1945. Vital Publications, Inc.

Empire of the Ants: Novelization. Lindsay West. (Illus.). 1977. 1.95 (ISBN 0-441-20560-7). Ace Books.

Empire of the Atom. Alfred Elton Van Vogt. LC 56-12564. 1957. Shasta Publishers.

Empire of the East. Fred Saberhagen. LC 80-116503. (Illus.). 1980. 2.95. Ace Books.

Empire of the Invisibles. Harriet E Orcutt. LC 33-28357. 1899. The Metaphysical Publishing Co.

Empire of the Nairs (1811) James Henry Lawrence. LC 76-21346. 1976. 63.00 (ISBN 0-8201-1270-4). Scholars' Facsimiles & Reprints.

Empire of the World. Charles John Cutcliffe Wright Hyne. LC 74-16385. (Science Fiction). (Illus.). 1975. 18.00 (ISBN 0-405-06298-2). Arno Press.

Empire of Things: And Other Stories. H. L Mountzoures. LC 68-17335. 1968. Scribner.

Empire of Things & Other Stories. H. L. Mountzoures. LC 68-17335. 1968. 4.50 o.p. Scribner.

Empire of Time. Crawford Kilian. LC 78-60701. (Dell Rey Book). 1978. 1.75 (ISBN 0-345-27938-7). Ballantine Books.

Empire of Two Worlds. Barrington J. Bayley. 160p. 1980. 11.95 (ISBN 0-8052-8016-2, Pub. by Allison & Busby England); pap. 4.95 (ISBN 0-8052-8015-4, Pub. by Allison & Busby England). Schocken.

Empire Star. Samuel R Delany. LC 77-13735. (Gregg Press science fiction series). 1977. 8.00 (ISBN 0-8398-2394-0). Gregg Press.

Empire Strikes Back. illustrated ed., 1st ed. Donald F Glut & George Lucas. LC 80-81062. (Illus.). 4.95 (ISBN 0-345-28831-9). Ballantine Books.

Empire West. Leonard Lupton. 192p. 1972. 4.95 o.p. Lenox Hill.

Empire West. Leonard Lupton. 1972. 4.95. Lenox Hill Pr.

Empress. Carola Mary Anima Oman Lenanton, pseud. LC 32-32125. H. Holt and Company.

Empress. Sylvia Wallace. LC 80-11197. 1980. 12.95 (ISBN 0-688-03655-4). Morrow.

Empress Josephine. Klara Muller Mundt. Tr. by Binet, W. LC 16-1244. (historical romances of Louisa Muhlbach pseud.). D. Appleton and Company.

Empress Josephine. An Historical Sketch of the Days of Napoleon. Klara Muller Mundt. Tr. by Binet, W. LC 7-25466. 1867. D. Appleton and Company.

Empress Josephine. An Historical Sketch of the Days of Napoleon. Klara Muller Mundt. Tr. by Binet, W. LC 15-174021. 1911. D. Appleton and Company.

Empress Might-Have-Been: The Love Story of Marie Valevska and Napoleon. Octave Aubry. Tr. by Dwight, Harry Griswold. LC 27-4651. 1927. Harper & Brothers.

Empress Octavia: A Romance of the Reign of Nero; Translated from the German of Wilhelm Walloth... Wilhelm Walloth & Safford, Mary Joanna, D. 1916, Tr. LC 2661. 1900. Little, Brown, and Company.

Empress of Byzantium. Helen A Mahler. LC 52-8027. 1952. Coward-McCann.

Empress of Desire. Jack Mertes. (Orig.). 1982. pap. 2.95 (ISBN 0-671-82915-7). PB.

Empress of Hearts. Lily Moresby Adams Beck. LC 28-23920. 1928. Dodd, Mead & Company.

Empress of the Earth. Matthew Phipps Shiel. Bd. with Purple Cloud. LC 79-88149. 1979. Repr. of 1901 ed. 35.00x (ISBN 0-934236-00-3). Reynolds Morse.

Empress of the Isles: Or, The Lake Bravo. A. Romance of the Canadian Struggle in 1837. Charley Clewline. LC 6-20751. 1853. Stringer & Townsend.

Empress of the Isles: Or, The Lake Bravo. A Romance of the Canadian Struggle in 1837. George S Raymond. LC 48-32637. U. P. James.

Empress's Ring: Stories. Nancy Hale. LC 55-9672. 1955. Scribner.

Emprey: A Story of Love and Battle in Rupert's Land. Samuel Alexander White. LC 13-4987. 1913. Outing Publishing Company.

Empty Bed. Herbert Adams. LC 26-16886. 1928. J. B. Lippincott Company.

Empty Canvas. Alberto Moravia. LC 81-83495. 288p. 1982. pap. 2.95 (ISBN 0-86721-038-9). Playboy Pbks.

Empty Canvas. Alberto Morravia. Tr. by Angus Davidson. LC 61-17265. 320p. 1973. pap. 1.50 (ISBN 0-532-15112-7). Woodhill.

Empty Canvas. Alberto Pincherle. 1973. (pbk.) 1.50. Manor Books.

Empty Canvas: By Alberto Moravia Pseud. Translated by Angus Davidson. Alberto Pincherle. LC 61-172658. 1961. Farrar, Straus and Cudahy.

Empty Copper Sea. John Dann MacDonald. LC 78-17868. 8.95 (ISBN 0-397-01220-9). Lippincott.

Empty Copper Sea. John Dann MacDonald. LC 79-10651. 1979. 13.50 (ISBN 0-8161-6702-8). G. K. Hall.

Empty Cottage at Silver Falls: And Another Story. Paul Rader. LC 17-167270. The Book Stall.

Empty Cradles. Marque Trayde. LC 36-84523. Covent Garden Press.

Empty Day. Richard Lockridge. 1965. bds., 5.95. Lippincott.

Empty Face. Katharina Havekamp. LC 78-12154. 9.95 (ISBN 0-399-90031-4). R. Marek.

Empty Hands. Saverio Strati. LC 64-10129. 1964. Abelard-Schuman.

Empty Hands. Arthur John Arbuthnott Stringer. LC 24-7319. The Bobbs-Merrill Company.

Empty Heart: Or, Husks. "For Better, for Worse.". Mary Virginia Terhune. LC 11-8214. 1871. Carleton; Etc. Etc.

Empty Holsters. Archie Joscelyn. 1974. 4.50. Avalon Books.

Empty Holsters. Edward Earl Repp. LC 37-425. 1936. Godwin.

Empty Hours. Ed McBain. 1982. pap. 2.25 (ISBN 0-451-11835-9, AE1835, Sig). NAL.

Empty Hours. Maureen Oswin. 7.50 o.p. (ISBN 0-7139-0231-0, AL231). Allen Lane.

Empty Hours: An 87th Precinct Mystery. Evan Hunter. (Signet Book). 1977. 1.25 (ISBN 0-451-07287-1). New American Library.
Empty House. Algernon Blackwood. LC 65-8408. 1965. 4.00. J. Baker for the Richards Pr.
Empty House. LC 17-17515. 1917. 1.40. The Macmillan Company.
Empty House. Michael Francis Gilbert. LC 78-69501. 1979. 10.00 (ISBN 0-06-011502-5). Harper & Row.
Empty House. Francis Durham Grierson. LC 34-7410. 1934. D. Appleton-Century Company, Incorporated.
Empty House. Rosamunde Pilcher. LC 74-81470. 1975. 6.95. St. Martin's Press.
Empty House: A Spine-Chiller. Irina Karlova. LC 44-45327. 1944. Hurst & Blackett Ltd.
Empty House & Nine Other Stories. Algernon Blackwood. 1964. Repr. of 1906 ed. 4.00 o.p. Verry.
Empty House, and Other Stories. Elizabeth Stuart Phelps Ward. LC 10-250653. 1910. Houghton Mifflin Company.
Empty House: By Jeanne Bowman Pseud. Peggy O'More, pseud. LC 56-12455. 1956. Arcadia House.
Empty Land. Louis L'Amour. (Orig.). 1969. pap. 2.25 (ISBN 0-553-14589-4). Bantam.
Empty Man. Melvin Leighton Heimer. LC 70-139533. 1971. 6.50 (ISBN 0-8415-0098-3). McCall Pub. Co.
Empty Meadow. Ben Logan. LC 82-17060. 14.95 (ISBN 0-88361-087-6). Stanton & Lee.
Empty Nest. 1st Ed. Josephine Lawrence. LC 56-8527. 1956. Harcourt, Brace.
Empty People. K. M. O'Donnell, pseud. pap. 0.75 o.p. Lancer.
Empty Pews: A Novel of the World War II Based on the Life of Immigrants Who Found Hope, Love, and Happiness in America. Herman Taube. LC 62-1060. 1958. N. A. Gossmann Pub. Co.
Empty Pews: The Story of a Weak Unthinking People, by Harley Rosso Pseud.... Harvey Ross McClure. LC 25-15264. 1925. Hollywood, Calif., McClure Publishing Co.
Empty Pews: The Story of a Week Unthinking People. Harley Rosso. LC 25-15264. Hollywood, Calif., McClure Publishing Co.
Empty Pockets. Rupert Hughes & Flagg, James Montgomery, 1877- Illus. LC 19-113443. 1915. A. L. Burt Company.
Empty Pockets: A Novel. Rupert Hughes. LC 15-11449. 1915. Harper & Brothers.
Empty Pockets, Empty Hands. Marvin E. Purser. 3.50 o.p. Vantage.
Empty Room. Charles Morgan. LC 41-21283. 1941. The Macmillan Company.
Empty Sack. Basil King. LC 21-15434. Harper & Brothers.
Empty Saddles. Burt Arthur, pseud. 1976. pap. 1.25 (ISBN 0-532-12383-2). Woodhill.
Empty Saddles. Archie Joscelyn. LC 47-2346. 1946. Dodd, Mead & Company.
Empty Saddles. Donald S. Rowland. 1972. 3.95 o.s.i. Lenox Hill.
Empty Saddles: By Chuck Stanley. Charles Stanley Strong. LC 56-12458. 1956. Arcadia House.
Empty Shrine. 1st Ed. William Edmund Barrett. LC 58-132706. 1958. Doubleday.
Empty Shrines. Elisabeth Finley Thomas. LC 27-19194. The Bobbs-Merrill Company.
Empty Street: Stories Sydney Angus and Robertson. Peter Cowan. LC 65-9055. bds., 3.15. Tri-Ocean.
Empty Throne. Lori Kamae. 1980. 18.95 (ISBN 0-914916-44-0). Topgallant.
Empty Tiger. Max Catto. LC 77-291. 1977. 7.95 (ISBN 0-312-24490-8). St. Martin's Press.
Empty Trap. John Dann MacDonald. 144p. 1982. pap. 2.25 (ISBN 0-449-14185-3, GM). Fawcett.
Empty Trap. John Dann MacDonald. (Orig.). 1969. pap. 0.75 o.p. (T2497, GM). Fawcett World.
Empty Villa. Jessie Louisa Rickard. LC 30-19717. 1930. H. Liveright.
Empty Villa. Jessie Louisa Moore Rickard. LC 30-19717. 1929. H. Liveright.
Em's Husband. A Novel. Emma Dorothy Eliza Nevitte Southworth. LC 8-14243. (Ledger library, no. 75). 1892. R. Bonner's Sons.
Emu in the Fowl Pen. Ruth Hawker. LC 67-21782. (Illus.). 1967. 6.50 o.s.i. Tri-Ocean.
En Attendant Godot. Samuel Beckett. LC 68-1645. 1967. French and European Publications.
En Garde! Samuel Morse. LC 28-113189. Payson & Clarke Ltd.
En la Ardiente Obscuridad. A. Buero Vallejo. Bd. with Madrugada; Hoy Es Fiesta; Cartas Boca Abajo. (Span.). pap. 2.25 o.s.i. French & Eur.
En la Senda De los Renegados. new ed. John Benteen. Tr. by E. Caballero from Eng. (Compadre Collection: Sundance Ser., No. 1). Orig. Title: Bronco Trail. 160p. (Span.). 1974. pap. 0.75 o.p. (ISBN 0-88473-531-1). Fiesta Pub.
En marge des vieux livres: Contes, 2 vols. Jules Lemaitre & Godegroy Cavaignac. LC 75-41173. (French.). Repr. of 1924 ed. 35.00 set (ISBN 0-404-15020-9). AMS Pr.
En Nueva York y Otras Desfracias. Jose L. Gonzalez. LC 81-65310. 172p. 1981. pap. 4.25 (ISBN 0-940238-14-4). Ediciones Huracan.
En Posicion Horizontal. Rogelio Rios. (Pimienta Collection Ser). (Illus.). 160p. 1975. pap. 1.25 (ISBN 0-88473-234-7). Fiesta Pub.
En Route. Joris Karl Huysmans. LC 76-15215. 1976. 14.00. H. Fertig.
En Route. 4th ed. Joris Karl Huysmans. Tr. by Paul, Charles Kegan. LC 19-11343. 1918. K. Paul, Trench, Trubner & Co., Ltd.
En Route. Joris Karl Huysmans. Tr. by Paul, Charles Kegan. LC 20-28488. 1920. E. P. Dutton & Company.
En Sus Pasos. Charles Monroe Sheldon. Tr. by Ruth Reuben from Eng. Orig. Title: In His Steps. 92p. (Span.). 1981. pap. 1.75 (ISBN 0-311-37011-X). Casa Bautista.
Enameled Wishbone, and Other Touchstones. Robert Henderson. LC 63-15683. 1963. Macmillan.
Enardo and Rosael, an Allegorical Novella. Tapia y Rivera, Alejandro. LC 52-14466. 1952. Philosophical Library.
Enbury Heath. Stella Gibbons. LC 35-14388. Longmans, Green and Co.
Enchanted. Elizabeth Jane Coatsworth. LC 68-12652. 1975. (pbk.) 0.95 (ISBN 0-380-00329-5). Avon.
Enchanted. Vina Delmar. LC 65-14717. 4.95. Harcourt.
Enchanted. Martin Flavin. LC 47-30295. 1947. Harper & Brothers.
Enchanted Acres. Ella Booker Cook. LC 41-225171. 1940. Pegasus Publishing Company.
Enchanted: An Authenic Account of the Strange Origin of the New Physical Club. John Bell Bouton. LC 11-10517. 1891. Cassell Publishing Company.
Enchanted: An Incredible Tale. Elizabeth Jane Coatsworth. LC 51-10514. 1951. Pantheon.
Enchanted: An Incredible Tale. Elizabeth Jane Coatsworth. LC 68-12649. (Illus.). 1968. Pantheon Books.
Enchanted April. Elizabeth. 1973. pap. 0.95 o.p. (09198). Curtis.
Enchanted April. Mary Annette Beauchamp Russell Russell. LC 23-2809. 1923. Doubleday, Page & Company.
Enchanted Avenue. Constance Noyes Robertson. LC 31-25218. 1931. Longmans, Green and Co.
Enchanted Barn. Grace Livingston Hill. LC 18-10533. 1918. J. B. Lippincott Company.
Enchanted Beggar. Norman Haghejm Matson. 1959. Lippincott.
Enchanted Boathouse. Rosalind Bowen. LC 48-3721. 1948. Meador Pub. Co.
Enchanted Burro: And Other Stories As I Have Known Them from Maine to Chile and California. new ed., with many new stories and illustrations. ed. Charles Fletcher Lummis. 1912. A. C. McClurg & Co.
Enchanted Burro: Stories of New Mexico and South America. Charles Fletcher Lumis. LC 7-14505. 1897. Way and Williams.
Enchanted Burro: Stories of New Mexico and South America. Charles Fletcher Lummis. LC 72-3373. (Short story index reprint series). (Illus.). 1972. 14.50 (ISBN 0-8369-4154-3). Books for Libraries Press.
Enchanted Canyon: A Novel of the Grand Canyon and the Arizona Desert. Honore McCue Willsie Morrow. LC 21-602978. Frederick A. Stokes Company.
Enchanted Castle: A Novel. Harvey Q Brown. LC 51-6200. 1951. Humphries.
Enchanted Circle. Alicia Grace. 192p. 1976. pap. 1.25 (ISBN 0-532-12398-0). Woodhill.
Enchanted Circle. Alicia Gray. Bd. with Enchanted Circle; Wharf Sinister; Mass for a Dead Witch. 1972. pap. 1.65 o.s.i. (70-405). Lancer.
Enchanted Cottage. Dean F. Du Vall. LC 80-65176. (Derek Dax Adventure Ser.: No. 1). 228p. 1981. pap. 6.95 (ISBN 0-931232-21-X). Du Vall Financial.
Enchanted Country. Joan Sutherland. LC 23-9489. 1923. George H. Doran Company.
Enchanted Cup. Dorothy James Roberts. LC 53-5608. 1953. Appleton-Century-Crofts.
Enchanted Dawn. Anne Dee. LC 53-9106. 1953. Meador Pub. Co.
Enchanted Dust. Frances Mocatta. LC 29-17789. 1929. G. H. Watt.
Enchanted Garden. Beatrice C. Baskerville. LC 21-15821. W. J. Watt & Company.
Enchanted Garden. Iris Bromige. 1972. pap. 0.75 o.p. (94262). Beagle Bks.
Enchanted Garden. John Erskine. LC 25-27966. 1925. The Bookfellows.
Enchanted Garden. Henry James Forman. LC 23-11804. 1923. Little, Brown, and Company.
Enchanted Golf Clubs. Robert Marshall. LC 20-3577. Frederick A. Stokes Company.
Enchanted Ground. Temple Bailey. LC 33-22829. The Penn Publishing Company.
Enchanted Ground: An Episode in the Life of a Young Man. Harry James Smith. LC 10-18381. 1910. Houghton Mifflin Company.
Enchanted Harbor. Dorothy Worley. LC 56-58194. 1956. Avalon Books.
Enchanted Hat. Harold MacGrath. LC 5-33005. 1908. The Bobbs-Merrill Company.
Enchanted Heart. Marjorie Muir Worthington. LC 49-7936. 1949. Doubleday.
Enchanted Hearts. Darragh Aldrich. LC 17-25127. 1917. Doubleday, Page & Company.
Enchanted Highway. Elsie Frances Wilson Mack. LC 51-14013. 1951. Bouregy & Curl.
Enchanted Hill. Peter Bernard Kyne. LC 24-251791. 1924. Cosmopolitan Book Corporation.
Enchanted Hours. Louise Hathaway. LC 41-2382. J. J. Newbegin.
Enchanted Interlude. Kathleen Rollins. LC 35-35374. Arcadia House.
Enchanted Island. Anne Mather. pap. 0.75 o.p. Lancer.
Enchanted Island. Denise Robins. 1974. (pbk.) 0.95 (ISBN 0-380-00129-2). Avon.
Enchanted Isle. James Mallahan Cain. LC 77-81174. 1977. cancelled o.s.i. (ISBN 0-88373-073-1). Stonehill Pub Co.
Enchanted Isle. Marjorie McEvoy. Ed. by Alice Sachs. (OSI). 1971. 3.95 o.s.i. Lenox Hill.
Enchanted Journey. Kristin Michaels. (Signet Book). 1977. 1.25 (ISBN 0-451-07628-1). New American Library.
Enchanted Journey see Special Kind of Love.
Enchanted Land. Jude Deveraux, pseud. 1978. 2.25 (ISBN 0-380-40063-4). Avon Books.
Enchanted Land. Beth McHenry Myers. LC 53-11886. 1953. Avalon Books.
Enchanted Life: A Novel. Mary Foster Main. LC 48-8514. 1948. Harcourt, Brace.
Enchanted Moment. Barbara Cartland. 1976. pap. 1.25 o.p. (ISBN 0-515-04145-9). BJ Pub Group.
Enchanted Moment, No. 40. Barbara Cartland. 1972. pap. 1.25 o.p. (ISBN 0-515-02795-2, V2795). Pyramid Pubns.
Enchanted Oasis. Faith Baldwin Cuthrell. LC 38-51383. Farrar & Rinehart, Incorporated.
Enchanted Park. Archie Joscelyn. LC 37-25341. Gramercy Publishing Co.
Enchanted Pilgrim, and Other Stories. Nikolai Semenovich Leskov. LC 76-23886. (Classics of Russian literature). (Hyperion library of world literature). 1977. 11.50. (ISBN 0-88355-497-6) (ISBN 0-88355-498-4). Hyperion Press.
Enchanted Pilgrimage. Clifford D. Simak. LC 74-16617. 1975. 6.95 (ISBN 0-399-11477-7). Berkley Pub. Corp.: Distributed by Putnam.
Enchanted Pilgrimage: Science Fiction. Clifford D. Simak. LC 76-383419. 1976. 3.50 (ISBN 0-283-98230-6). Sidgwick and Jackson.
Enchanted Pillowcase, and Other Stories. Josephine Cunnington Edwards. LC 53-39526. Review and Herald Pub. Association.
Enchanted Planet. Pierre Barbet, pseud. (Science Fiction Ser). 1975. pap. 1.25 o.p. (UY1181). DAW Bks.
Enchanted Quill. Autumn Stanley. 1978. pap. 1.00 o.p. (ISBN 0-931832-10-1). No Dead Lines.
Enchanted Sea-Gull. Harriet Bartnett & Keene, Roxroy. The Roxburgh Publishing Company Incorporated.
Enchanted Spring. Lily Clive Nutt. LC 35-9074. The Bobbs-Merrill Company.
Enchanted Spring. Lily Clive Nutt. LC 35-907480. The Bobbs-Merrill Company.
Enchanted Stone. Charles Lewis Hind. LC 98-1547. 1899. Dodd, Mead and Company.
Enchanted Summer. Gabrielle Carbotte Roy. LC 76-380621. 7.95 (ISBN 0-7710-7831-5). McClelland and Stewart.
Enchanted Things. Kathie. 1975. 3.95. Libra.
Enchanted Twilight. Kristin Michaels. (Signet Book). 1976. (pbk.) 0.95. New American Library.
Enchanted Type-Writer. John Kendrick Bangs. LC 73-94702. (Short story index reprint series). (Illus.). 1969. Books for Libraries Press.
Enchanted Typewriter. John Kendrick Bangs. 1899. Harper & Brothers.
Enchanted Villa. Marjorie Vernon. 1966. pap. 0.60 o.p. (60-263). Manor Bks.
Enchanted Village. Edward Shanks. LC 33-32917. The Bobbs-Merrill Company.
Enchanted Voyage. William P. McKenzie. 4.50 o.p. Vantage.
Enchanted Voyage. Robert Nathan. LC 36-18874. 1936. A. A. Knopf.
Enchanted Waltz, No. 26. Barbara Cartland. (Barbara Cartland Romance Ser., No. 26). (O.S.I). 1971. pap. 0.95 o.s.i. (N3048). Pyramid Pubns.
Enchanted Wanderer & Other Stories. Nikolai Semenovich Leskov. 352p. 1974. 5.45 (ISBN 0-8285-1007-5, 180641, Pub. by Progress Pubs USSR). Imported Pubns.
Enchanted Wanderer: Translated from the Russian. Nikolai Semenovich Lieskoy. Tr. by Pashkov, A. G. LC 25-9750. 1924. Robert M. McBride & Company.
Enchanted Winter. Zoe Girling. LC 33-270562. 1933. Harper & Brothers.
Enchanted Year. Anne Tedlock Brooks. LC 49-2534. 1949. Arcadia House.
Enchanter. Robert Newman. LC 62-11485. 1962. Houghton Mifflin.
Enchanters. Romain Gary, pseud. LC 74-30552. 1975. 8.95 (ISBN 0-399-11488-2). Putnam.
Enchanters. Katherine Yorke. 2.50 (ISBN 0-671-83165-8).
Enchanter's Nightshade. Mary Dolling Sanders O'Malley. LC 37-28683. 1937. Brown and Company.
Enchanting Clementina. Sophia Cleugh. LC 31-3501. 1931. Houghton Mifflin Company.
Enchanting Courtesan. Lozania Prole. 1975. (pbk.) 0.95 (ISBN 0-671-77957-5). Pocket Books.
Enchanting Danger. Vera Wheatley. LC 28-25354. E. P. Dutton & Co., Inc.
Enchanting Evil. Barbara Cartland. LC 79-388560. 1968. 2.90. Hutchinson of Australia.
Enchanting Witch: By M. J. Farrell Pseud. Mary Nesta Skrine Keane. LC 51-13062. 1951. Crowell.
Enchantment. Anne Duffield. LC 38-12850. 1937. Hillman-Curl, Inc.
Enchantment. Harold MacGrath. LC 5-11603. (On cover: The pocket books). 1905. The Bobbs-Merrill Company.
Enchantment. Grace Therese Mitchell. LC 27-27455. Kohnke Printing Co.
Enchantment. Ernest Temple Thurston. LC 17-13720. 1917. D. Appleton and Company.
Enchantment, No. 143. Barbara Cartland. 160p. (Orig.). 1981. pap. 1.95 (ISBN 0-553-20301-0). Bantam.
Enchantment: A Novel. Ruth Cross. LC 30-6543. 1930. Longmans, Green and Co.
Enchantment: A Novel. Linda Grace Hoyer. LC 77-132791. 1971. 5.95 (ISBN 0-395-12044-6). Houghton Mifflin.
Enchantress. Guy Reginald Bolton. LC 63-20512. 1964. Doubleday.
Enchantress: And Other Stories. Herbert Ernest Bates. LC 61-13897. 1961. Little, Brown.
Enchantress of World's End. Lin Carter. 1975. (pbk.) 1.25. DAW Books.
Enclaves: A Novel. Felix Bastian. LC 65-13997. 4.50. Doubleday.
Enclosure. 1st Ed. Ethan Ayer. LC 51-10509. 1951. Little, Brown.
Encore. Margaret Wade Campbell Deland. LC 7-325623. 1907. Harper & Brothers.
Encore. Monique Raphel High. LC 80-26120. 13.95 (ISBN 0-440-02351-3). Delacorte Press.
Encore for Love: A Novel. Katharine Dunlap. LC 37-1871. 1937. W. Morrow & Co.
Encore the Lone Wolf. Louis Joseph Vance. LC 33-10153. J. B. Lippincott Company.
Encores for a Dilettante. Ursule Molinaro. LC 77-81003. 8.95. (ISBN 0-914590-44-8) (ISBN 0-914590-45-6). Fiction Collective: Distributed by G. Braziller.
Encounter, 31 Vols. 1953-68. Set. 557.00 o.p.; 27.50 ea. o.p.; pap. 25.00 ea. o.p.; Set. pap. 775.00 o.p. AMS Pr.
Encounter. Anne Douglas Sedgwick. LC 14-181133. 1914. The Century Co.
Encounter. Anne Douglas Sedgwick. LC 30-264052. Houghton Mifflin Company.
Encounter. Ursula Torday. LC 72-146085. 1971. 6.95. Coward, McCann & Geoghegan.
Encounter at Alpenrose. Iris Bromige. 1973. pap. 0.75 o.p. (ISBN 0-345-20742-4). Beagle Bks.
Encounter at Kharmel. Robert Dentry, pseud. 228p. 1973. 3.50 o.p. (ISBN 0-85885-004-4). David & Charles.
Encounter Darkness. Stanton Forbes, pseud. 1969. pap. 0.60 o.p. (0502-06003-060). Curtis.
Encounter Darkness. 1st Ed. Stanton Forbes, pseud. LC 67-167967. 1967. 3.95. Pub. for the Crime Club by Doubleday.
Encounter in Key West. Richard Lockridge. LC 66-12339. 1966. Lippincott.
Encounter Program. Robert Enstrom. LC 77-74300. 1977. 7.95 (ISBN 0-385-13068-6). Doubleday.
Encounter: Reissue. Crawford Francis Power. LC 50-811665. 1965. 5.00. Sloane Dist. Morrow.
Encounters. Stephen Spender et al. (O.s.i.). 1965. pap. 2.45 o.s.i. (ISBN 0-671-22551-0, Fireside). S&S.
Encounters with the Archdruid. John Angus McPhee. (Walden Editions). 1972. 1.25 (ISBN 0-345-02934-8). Ballantine.
Encumbrances. Aylwin Lee Martin. LC 32-6323. 1931. A. H. King.
Encyclopedia. Richard Horn. LC 76-84887. 1969. 4.95. Grove Press.
Encyclopedia of Modern American Humor. Drawings by Doug Anderson. 1st Modern Library Giant Ed. Ed. by Bennett Alfred Cerf. LC 58-6366. (Modern library of the world's best books. A reader-check). 1958. Modern Library.

Encyclopedia of Science Fiction & Fantasy, Vol. 1. Donald H. Tuck. LC 73-91828. 1974. 30.00 (ISBN 0-911682-20-1). Advent.

End". Carol Sturm Smith. LC 78-53128. 1978. 1.75 (ISBN 0-380-01978-7). Avon Books.

End and a Beginning. James Hanley. LC 58-135521. 1958. Horizon Press.

End and Beginning. Kenneth Edgar. LC 72-2898. 1972. 6.95 (ISBN 0-13-277145-4). Prentice-Hall.

End As a Man. Calder Willingham. LC 47-1581. 1947. The Vanguard Press, Inc.

End Bringers. Douglas R Mason. 1973. (pbk.) 1.25. Ballantine.

End-Game. Michael Francis Gilbert. LC 81-48053. 5.95 (ISBN 0-06-014976-0). Harper & Row.

End Game in Paris: A Novel. Ian Adams. LC 78-22767. 1979. 8.95 (ISBN 0-385-14935-2). Doubleday.

End: How the Great War Was Stopped. Louis Pope Gratacap. LC 17-10858. 1917. T. Benton.

End Is Known. Geoffrey Holiday Hall. LC 49-17234. 1949. Simon and Schuster.

End Is Not Yet. L. Ron Hubbard. Ed. by Virgil Wilhite. (Illus.). 1979. write for info. Theta Bks.

End Is Not Yet: A Novel of Hatred and Love; of Darkness and Light; of Despair and Hope; of Death and Life; of War and a New Courage. Fritz Von Unruh. LC 47-3352. 1947. Storm Publishers.

End of a Childhood. Henry Handel Richardson. LC 34-35880. 1934. W. W. Norton.

End of a Coil. Susan Warner. LC 8-33707. 1880. R. Carter and Brothers.

End of a Day. Translated from the Spanish by A. D. Towers. Beatriz Guido. LC 66-16689. 1966. Schribner.

End of a Dream. A M N Jenkin. LC 20-74294. 1919. John Lane.

End of a Mission. Heinrich Boll. (McGraw-Hill paperbacks). 1974. (pbk.) 2.95 (ISBN 0-07-006410-5). McGraw-Hill.

End of a Mission. Heinrich Boll. LC 68-11926. 1967. McGraw-Hill.

End of a Party. Hillary Waugh. LC 65-12821. 1965. Published for the Crime Club by Doubleday.

End of a Skein: A Novel. N. Cleona Flowers. LC 6-41666. 1896. Hartman & Cadick.

End of a Song. Jeannette Augustus Marks. LC 11-4935. 1911. 1.15. Houghton Mifflin Company.

End of a War. Edward Loomis. LC 57-14682. 1958. Ballantine Books.

End of a World. Jean Schopfer. Tr. by Marsion, Jeffery Eardley. LC 27-17657. 1927. A. A. Knopf.

End of All Men. Charles Ferdinand Ramuz & Macdougall, Allan Ross, Tr. LC 44-51046. 1944. Pantheon Books Inc.

End of All Songs. Michael Moorcock. LC 75-25092. (His The dancers at the end of time; v. 3). 8.95 (ISBN 0-06-012999-9). Harper & Row.

End of an Ancient Mariner. George Douglas Howard Cole & Margaret Isabel Postgate Cole. LC 34-2349. 1934. Pub. for the Crime Club, Inc., by Doubleday, Doran & Company, Inc.

End of an Old Song: A Romance. John Dick Scott. LC 53-9482. 1954. Knopf.

End of Chapter. Nicholas Blake. 1977. pap. 1.95i (ISBN 0-06-080397-5, P397, PL). Har-Row.

End of Chapter. Cecil Day-Lewis. (Perennial Library). (Illus.). 1977. 1.75 (ISBN 0-06-080397-5). Harper & Row.

End of Chapter: By Nicholas Blake Pseud. 1st Ed. Cecil Day-Lewis. LC 57-958921. 1957. Harper.

End of Cornwall. Richard Preston, pseud. LC 40-8315. 1938. The Vanguard Press.

End of Days: A Novel of the Jewish War Against Rome 66-73 C.E. Daniel Gavron. LC 77-105067. (Illus.). 1970. 5.50. Jewish Publication Society of America.

End of Desire. Robert Herrick. LC 72-85668. 1976. (ISBN 0-403-03195-8). Scholarly Press.

End of Desire. Robert Herrick. LC 32-767. Farrar & Rinehart, Incorporated.

End of Desire see Collected Works.

End of Dreams. Orrie Lashin. LC 47-21944. 1947. Gramercy Publishing Co.

End of Dreams. Wood Levette Wilson. LC 9-31675. M. Kennerley.

End of Dreams: A Novel of New England. Philip Jerome Cleveland. LC 43-5356. 1943. The Ingland Co.

End of Eternity. Isaac Asimov. LC 55-9227. 1966. 3.95. Doubleday.

End of Eternity. Isaac Asimov. LC 81-4758. 1981. 10.95 (ISBN 0-89340-338-5). J. Curley.

End of Her Honeymoon. Marie Adelaide Belloc Lowndes. LC 75-32763. (Literature of Mystery and Detection). 1976. 13.00 (ISBN 0-405-07884-6). Arno Press.

End of Honeymoon. Marie Adelaide Belloc Lowndes. LC 13-19506. 1913. 1.25. C. Scribner's Sons.

End of Illusion. Homer William Smith. LC 35-4103. 1935. Harper & Brothers.

End of Innocence. Jacqueline Cummins. 1961. 8.95 (ISBN 0-8392-1028-0). Astor-Honor.

End of Innocence. Christopher Shaft. pap. 1.95 o.s.i. (Venus). Grove.

End of Innocence. Abra Taylor. (Superromances Ser.). 384p. 1980. pap. 2.50 (ISBN 0-373-70001-6, Pub. by Worldwide). Harlequin Bks.

End of It. Mitchell Goodman. LC 79-66117. 286p. 1980. 16.95 (ISBN 0-933256-10-8); pap. 8.95 (ISBN 0-933256-11-6). Second Chance.

End of Loving. Beatrice Joy Chute. LC 53-8247. 1953. Dutton.

End of Man? Olof Johannesson. LC 68-11869. (O.s.i.). Orig. Title: Tale of the Big Computer. 1969. pap. 0.60 o.s.i. (A448X, Award). Univ Pub & Dist.

End of Me. Alfred Hayes. LC 68-12539. 1968. Atheneum.

End of Mr. Garment... Vincent Starrett. LC 32-30019. Pub for the Crime Club, Inc., by Doubleday, Doran & Company, Inc.

End of My Career. Miles Franklin. LC 81-8772. 1981. 10.95 (ISBN 0-312-25075-4). St. Martin's.

End of Pity: And Other Stories. Robie Macauley. LC 57-105174. 1957. McDowell, Obolensky.

End of Reckoning. Alice Lent Covert. LC 42-19158. 1942. H. C. Kinsey & Company, Inc.

End of Reckoning. Clayton Moore. (River Falls Series). (Berkley medallion book): Vol. 3). 1974. (pbk.) 1.25 (ISBN 0-425-02619-1). Berkley Pub. Co.

End of Roaming. Alexander Kinnan Laing. LC 30-23891. Farrar & Rinehart Incorporated.

End of Solomon Grundy. Julian Symons. 1971. pap. 0.95 o.p. (95065). Beagle Bks.

End of Someone Else's Rainbow. Robert Rossner. LC 73-16399. 1974. 5.95. Saturday Review Press.

End of Someone Else's Rainbow. Robert Rossner. LC 72-16399. 1975. (pbk.) 1.25 (ISBN 0-446-76750-6). Warner Paperback Library.

End of Something Nice: A Novel. Angus Wolfe Murray. LC 67-21891. 1967. Viking Press.

End of Steel. Courtney Ryley Cooper. LC 31-6382. 1931. Farrar & Rinehart, Incorporated.

End of Summer. Nancy Lamb. (Orig.). 1981. pap. 3.25 (ISBN 0-440-12372-0). Dell.

End of the Affair. Graham Greene. LC 51-13559. 1951. Viking Press.

End of the Affair. Graham Greene. LC 51-13559. 1975. (pbk.) 1.95 (ISBN 0-671-80039-6). Pocket Books.

End of the Affair. Graham Greene. LC 77-10024. 1977. 1.95 (ISBN 0-14-004696-8). Penguin Books.

End of the Avenue. Winifred Mary Scott. LC 30-3536. 1930. Doubleday, Doran & Company, Inc.

End of the Battle. Evelyn Waugh. 1979. 9.95 (ISBN 0-316-92621-3); pap. 5.95 (ISBN 0-316-92620-5). Little.

End of the Battle. Evelyn Waugh. (A novel). 1962. 6.95 o.p. (ISBN 0-316-92586-1). Little.

End of the Beginning. Jeanette Martin Bass. LC 56-8624. Dorrance.

End of the Beginning. Clara Jones. (O.s.i.). 1968. pap. 0.60 o.s.i. (A355X, Award). Univ Pub & Dist.

End of the Beginning. Charles Francis Richardson. LC 7-41216. 1896. Little, Brown, and Company.

End of the Cattle Trail. J. L. Hill. LC 73-94430. (Illus.). 1969. 8.95 (ISBN 0-8363-0030-0). Jenkins.

End of the Chapter. John Galsworthy. LC 72-112973. (His The Forsyte chronicles, v. 7-9). 12.50. Scribner.

End of the Chapter. John Galsworthy. LC 34-284145. 1934. C. Scribner's Sons.

End of the Corduroy. Ellen Lenore Minahan. LC 47-26192. 1947. Christopher Pub. House.

End of the Dream. Philip Wylie. (Daw sf books, UQ1079). 1973. (pbk.) 0.95. Daw Books.

End of the Dream. Philip Wylie. LC 73-186051. 1972. 5.95. Doubleday.

End of the Dreams: Three Short Novels. James E. Gunn. 220p. 1975. 6.95 o.p. (ISBN 0-684-14352-6). Scribner.

End of the Dreams: Three Short Novels About Space, Happiness, and Immortality. James E. Gunn. LC 75-12887. 1975. 6.95 (ISBN 0-684-14352-6). Scribner.

End of the Feud, and Other Kentucky Legends. 1st Ed. James William Jewell. LC 52-9239. 1952. Exposition Press.

End of the Flight. Burton Kline. LC 17-11708. 1917. 1.50. John Lane Company.

End of the Game. Friedrich Durrenmatt, pseud. (pbk.) 1.25. Warner Books.

End of the Game: A Novel. Arthur Hornblow. LC 7-14587. 1907. G. W. Dillingham Company.

End of the Game, and Other Stories. Julio Cortazar. LC 66-10413. 1967. Pantheon Books.

End of the Game: And Other Stories. Julio Cortazar. 1978. pap. 6.25i (ISBN 0-06-090637-5, CN 637, CN). Har-Row.

End of the Gun. Henry A De Rosso. LC 55-8715. (Permabooks, M-30144). 1955. Permabooks.

End of the House of Alard. Sheila Kaye-Smith. LC 23-12671. E. P. Dutton & Company.

End of the Journey. Marie Florence Giles. (Dillingham's metropolitan library, no. 23). 1897. G. W. Dillingham Co.

End of the Journey. Jules Verne. 3.95. Assoc Bk.

End of the Lane. James Noble Gifford. LC 39-2152. 1939. Arcadia House.

End of the Lane. Warren Howard. 1939. Arcadia House.

End of the Line. Stanley Wade Baron. LC 51-11058. 1951. Knopf.

End of the Line. Monica Dickens. LC 70-116201. 1970. 5.95. Doubleday.

End of the Line. Shannon O'Cork. LC 81-8755. 1981. 10.95 (ISBN 0-312-25102-5). St. Martin's.

End of the Line: By Bert and Dolores Hitchens. 1st Ed. Hubert Hitchens & Dolores Birk Hitchens. LC 57-11088. 1957. Published for the Crime Club by Doubleday.

End of the Matter. Alan Dean Foster. LC 77-6128. 1977. 1.95 (ISBN 0-345-25861-4). Ballantine Books.

End of the Night. John Dann MacDonald. LC 60-109947. 1960. Simon and Schuster.

End of the Old Times. Tr. from Czech by Edith Pargeter. Vladislav Vancura. LC 65-29737. (Artia pocket bks.). pap., 1.80. Artia.

End of the Party. Marvin Barrett. LC 75-44089. 7.95 (ISBN 0-399-11745-8). Putnam.

End of the Rainbow. Stella M During. LC 10-9700. 1910. 1.50. J. B. Lippincott Company.

End of the Rainbow. Diane E. Finley. 192p. (YA) 1975. 6.95 (Avalon). Bouregy.

End of the Rainbow. Francis D. Gray. 1970. 2.50 o.p. (ISBN 0-8059-1462-5). Dorrance.

End of the Rainbow. Mary Esther MacGregor. LC 14-119. 1.25. Hodder & Stoughton, George H. Doran Company.

End of the Rainbow. George G. Rutherford. (O.s.i.). 3.50 o.s.i. (ISBN 0-8181-0283-7). Pageant-Poseidon.

End of the Rawhide: A Fictional Biography of Uriah Philip Sic Levy. Sol Blumrosen. LC 51-7930. 1951. Seaboard Books.

End of the River. Desmond Holdridge. LC 40-68049. Harcourt, Brace and Company.

End of the Road. rev. ed. John Barth. LC 67-19082. 1967. Doubleday.

End of the Road. Helen A Carey. LC 40-633814. House of Field, Inc.

End of the Road. John Margolies. Ed. by C. Ray Smith. (Illus.). 96p. 1981. 22.95 (ISBN 0-670-29482-9, Studio). Viking Pr.

End of the Road. Holland E Nickerson. LC 52-25503. 1952. Woodford Press.

End of the Road: A Novel. Stanley Portal Hyatt. LC 9-218673. 1909. 1.50. D. Appleton and Company.

End of the Road. 1st Ed. John Barth. LC 58-9381. 1958. Doubleday.

End of the Rug. Richard Llewellyn. LC 67-12863. 1968. 5.95 o.p. Doubleday.

End of the Rug. 1st Ed. Richard Llewellyn. LC 67-12863. 1968. 5.95. Doubleday.

End of the Summer. Rosamunde Pilcher. LC 74-12637. 1975. 6.95. St. Martin's Press.

End of the Tiger & Other Stories. John Dann MacDonald. 192p. 1982. pap. 2.25 (ISBN 0-449-14241-8, GM). Fawcett.

End of the Track: By Andrew Garve Pseud. 1st American Ed. Paul Winterton. LC 56-6046. 1956. Harper.

End of the Tracks. Stack Sutton. LC 80-2463. 1981. 9.95 (ISBN 0-385-17470-5). Doubleday.

End of the Trail: "a Powder Valley Western,". Peter Field. LC 45-81808. 1945. Jefferson House.

End of the Trail. Illus. by George Phippen. Gene Hoopes. LC 59-8850. 1959. Naylor Co.

End of the Web. George Sims. LC 75-32833. 1976. 6.95 (ISBN 0-8027-5345-0). Walker.

End of the Web. George Sims. LC 76-376599. (Illus.). 1976. 2.90 (ISBN 0-575-02049-0). Gollancz.

End of the Week: A Novel. Virginia Chase Perkins. LC 53-12773. 1953. Macmillan.

End of the World. Vina Delmar. LC 35-32771. 1934. International Magazine Co., Inc.

End of the World. Edward Eggleston. 1872. lib. bdg. 30.00 (ISBN 0-8414-3888-9). Folcroft.

End of the World. Edward Eggleston. Ed. by Donald Pizer. LC 75-96528. (American Authors Ser). 1970. lib. bdg. 16.95 o.s.i. (ISBN 0-512-00159-6). Garrett Pr.

End of the World. A Love Story. Edward Eggleston. LC 75-94925. (Illus.). 1969. AMS Press.

End of the World: A Love Story. Edward Eggleston. LC 75-144996. (Illus.). 1970. (ISBN 0-403-00923-5). Scholarly Press.

End of the World. A Love Story. Edward Eggleston. LC 24-25486. 1872. O. Judd and Company.

End of the World. A Love Story. Edward Eggleston. 1908. Orange Judd Company.

End of the World and Other Stories. Bryan MacMahon. LC 77-357517. 1976. 1.32 (ISBN 0-905169-03-4). Poolbeg Press.

End of the World: California Stories. Frederick Waage. 56p. 1977. pap. text ed. 3.00 (ISBN 0-916300-08-0). Gallimaufry.

End of the World Is Los Angeles: Stories. Francois Andre Camoin & Associated Writing Programs. LC 81-16166. 1982. 6.95 (ISBN 0-8262-0365-5). University of Missouri Press.

End of the World News. Anthony Burgess. LC 82-17159. 15.95 (ISBN 0-07-008965-5). McGraw-Hill.

End of the World: Stories. Ed. by Donald A. Wollheim. LC 56-10384. (Ace books, S-183). 1956. Ace Books.

End of Track. Francis Van Wyck Mason. LC 43-114623. 1943. Reynal & Hitchcock.

End of Violence: A Ralph Lindsey Mystery. Ben Benson. LC 59-5532. 1959. M. S. Mill Co. and W. Morrow.

End Over End. Nelson Gidding. LC 46-6985. 1946. The Viking Press.

End to Chivalry: A Short Novel and Five Stories. Tom Cole. LC 65-20744. 1965. Little, Brown.

End to Comedy: A Novel. Robert Carson. LC 63-18985. 1963. Bobbs-Merrill.

End to Dying, a Novel. Samuel Astrachan. LC 56-616113. 1956. Farrar, Straus, and Cudahy.

End to Fury: A Novel. Edward Mannix. LC 58-12774. 1959. Dial Press.

End to Glory. Pierre Henri Simon. LC 61-12234. 1961. Harper.

End to Innocence. Leslie A. Fiedler. LC 72-82145. 1972. pap. 4.95 (ISBN 0-8128-1478-9). Stein & Day.

End to Mirth. Ben Ames Williams. LC 31-11731. E. P. Dutton & Co., Inc.

End to Ordinary History: A Novel. Michael Murphy. LC 81-51040. 11.95 (ISBN 0-87477-204-4). J.P. Tarcher.

End to Patience. Mary B Durant. LC 65-14711. 1965. Harcourt, Brace & World.

End to Summer. Roe Richmond. 1980. pap. 2.25 (ISBN 0-8439-0825-4). Nordon Pubns.

End Zone. Don Delillo. 1973. (pbk) 1.25. Pocket Books.

End Zone. Don DeLillo. LC 77-177544. 1972. 5.95 (ISBN 0-395-13645-8). Houghton Mifflin.

Endangered. Barnaby Conrad & Mortensen, Niels. 1980. 2.25 (ISBN 0-425-04298-7). Berkkley Publishing Co.

Endangered Species. Sandra Hochman. 8.95. Putnam.

Endangered Species. Sandra Hochman. 1979. 2.25 (ISBN 0-380-42366-9). Avon Books.

Endangered Species & Other Fables with a Twist. Fritz Eichenberg. LC 79-15247. (Illus.). 1979. 27.50 (ISBN 0-916144-42-9); pap. 14.95 (ISBN 0-916144-43-7). Stemmer Hse.

Endeavor Doin's Down to the Corners. John Franklin Cowan. LC 6-28866. 1893. D. Lothrop Company.

Enderby. Anthony Burgess. LC 68-13483. 1968. 5.95 (ISBN 0-393-08444-2). Norton.

Enderby. John Anthony Burgess Wilson. LC 68-13483. 1968. W. W. Norton.

Endgame. Harvey Ardman. 1975. (pbk.) 1.75 (ISBN 0-380-00352-X). Avon.

Ending. Hilma Wolitzer. LC 74-3473. 1974. 6.95 (ISBN 0-688-00304-4). Morrow.

Ending. Hilma Wolitzer. 1975. (pbk.) 1.75. Bantam Books.

Ending up. Kingsley Amis. LC 74-10678. 1974. 6.50 (ISBN 0-15-128796-1). Harcourt Brace Jovanovich.

Ending up. Kingsley Amis. 1976. 1.95 (ISBN 0-14-004151-6). Penguin.

Endings and Beginnings. John Michael Drinkrow Hardwick. LC 79-23371. 1979. 10.95 (ISBN 0-8161-6799-0). G. K. Hall.

Endless Adventure. Coman. 1978. pap. 3.95 (ISBN 0-89272-041-7). Down East.

Endless Colonnade: A Novel. 1st American Ed. Robert Harling. LC 59-12003. 1959. Putnam.

Endless Frontier, Vol. II. Jerry Pournelle. 432p. (Orig.). 1982. pap. 2.95 (ISBN 0-441-20666-2). Ace Bks.

Endless Frontier, Vol. 1. Jerry Pournelle. 384p. 1982. pap. 2.75 (ISBN 0-441-20667-0). Ace Bks.

Endless Furrow. Arthur George Street. LC 35-33168. 1935. E. P. Dutton & Co., Inc.

Endless Love. Scott Spencer. LC 79-2089. 10.95 (ISBN 0-394-50605-7). Knopf.

Endless Night. Agatha Miller Christie. LC 68-13598. 1968. Dodd, Mead.

Endless Orgy. Richard E. Geis. (Orig.). pap. 1.25 o.p. (2061). Brandon.

Endless Passion. Carol Finch. 1983. pap. 3.50 (ISBN 0-8217-1155-5). Zebra.

Endless River. Felix Riesenberg. LC 31-24495. Harcourt, Brace and Company.

Endless Road. Roger L Treat. LC 60-6840. 1960. Barnes.

Endless Summer: An Adventure Story of Time. Marsha D. Wellein. 4.50 o.p. Vantage.

Endless Tunnel. Howard H. Hilton. (Orig.). 1980. pap. text ed. 2.25 o.s.i. (ISBN 0-505-51591-1). Tower Bks.

Endplay. Ray Grant Toepfer. (Fawcett gold medal). 1975. (pbk.) 0.95. Fawcett.

Ends. James Hughes. LC 72-123427. 1971. 5.95. Knopf.

Ends and Means. Stanley Middleton. LC 78-309690. 1977-1978. 8.95 (ISBN 0-09-131110-1). Hutchinson.

Ends of the Circle. Paul O. Williams. 208p. (Orig.). 1981. pap. 2.25 (ISBN 0-345-29551-X, Del Rey). Ballantine.

Ends of Things. Mary Dixon Thayer. LC 27-23508. 1928. E. P. Dutton & Company.

Ends of Time: Eight Stories of Science Fiction. Ed. by Robert Silverberg. LC 74-121775. 1970. 5.95. Hawthorne Books.

Endurance. Henry Gibson. LC 46-6606. 1946. The Hobson Book Press.

Endure My Heart. Joan Smith. 224p. (Orig.). 1980. pap. 1.75 (ISBN 0-449-50051-9, Coventry). Fawcett.

Endure No Longer. Martha Albrand. LC 44-3607. 1944. Little, Brown.

Endure No Longer. Heidi Huberta Loewengard. LC 44-3607. 1944. Little, Brown and Company.

Enduring As the Camphor Tree. R. J. Oakes. 1967. pap. 6.50x o.p. (ISBN 0-522-83806-5, Pub by Melbourne U Pr). Intl Schol Bk Serv.

Enduring Flame. Denise Robins. (Beagle romance#39). 1975. (pbk.) 0.95. Ballantine Books.

Enduring Flame. Nigel G. Tranter. 1981. 18.95x (Pub. by Remploy England). State Mutual Bk.

Enduring Hills. 2d ed., with a new foreword by the author. ed. Janice Holt Giles. LC 74-132793. 1971. 6.95. Houghton Mifflin.

Enduring Hills. Janice Holt Giles. LC 50-6822. 1950. Westminster Press.

Enduring Love: A Romantic Novel. Ida Schaaf Regelman. LC 49-48765. 1949. Exposition Press.

Enduring Old Charms. Doris Miles Disney. LC 47-113998. 1947. Pub. for the Crime Club by Doubleday.

Enduring Riches. Margaret Flint. LC 42-22578. 1942. Dodd, Mead & Company.

Enduring Years: A Novel. Claire Rayner. LC 82-10045. (Illus.). 15.95 (ISBN 0-440-02460-9). Delacorte Press.

Endymion. Benjamin Disraeli Beaconsfield. LC 76-12442. (Works of Benjamin Disraeli, Earl of Beaconsfield; v. 19-20). 1976. (ISBN 0-404-08800-7). AMS Press.

Endymion... Benjamin Disraeli Beaconsfield. LC 4-23567. 1882. G. Routledge & Sons.

Endymion. Benjamin Disraeli Beaconsfield. LC 4-21547. 1900. Longmans, Green, and Co.

Endymion. Benjamin Disraeli Beaconsfield. Ed. by Edmund William Gosse. LC 5-7378. 1905. The Cambridge Society.

Endymion: A Novel. Benjamin Disraeli Beaconsfield. (Franklin square library, no. 150). 1880. Harper & Brothers.

Endymion and Falconet. Benjamin Disraeli Beaconsfield. (In his The Bradenham edition of the novels and tales. New York, 1934? vol. XII). Alfred A. Knopf.

Endymion... By the Right Honorable the Earl of Beaconsfield... Benjamin Disraeli Beaconsfield. LC 4-15281. 1880. D. Appleton and Company.

Endymion: The Man in the Moon. John Lyly. Ed. by George P. Baker. 1977. Repr. lib. bdg. 20.00 (ISBN 0-8414-2292-3). Folcroft.

Enema. Ed. by Medical Academic Press. LC 79-91913. (Illus.). 1980. lib. bdg. 14.95 o.s.i. (ISBN 0-918944-01-5); pap. 9.95 o.s.i. (ISBN 0-918944-02-3). Wildwood.

Enemies. Richard Harris. 320p. 1980. pap. 2.75 (ISBN 0-345-28435-6). Ballantine.

Enemies. George W Proctor. LC 82-45334. 1983. 11.95 (ISBN 0-385-17654-6). Doubleday.

Enemies. Brian James Royal. (Leisure book). 1.75 (ISBN 0-8439-0644-8). Nordon Pubns.

Enemies, a Love Story. Isaac Bashevis Singer. (Crest Book, P1877). 1973. (pbk.) 1.25. Fawcett.

Enemies: A Love Story. Isaac Bashevis Singer. LC 78-189337. 1972. 6.95 (ISBN 0-374-14830-9). Farrar, Straus and Giroux.

Enemies: A Novel. Richard Harris. LC 78-27831. 9.95 (ISBN 0-399-90040-3). R. Marek.

Enemies and Friends. 1st Ed. William Harrison Prosser. LC 58-106844. 1958. Little, Brown.

Enemies Born: Or, A Heritage of Hate. Laura C Ford. LC 6-41397. (On cover: Munro's library. v. 1, no. 164). 1884. N. L. Munro.

Enemies from Beyond. Keith Laumer. (Orig.). 1967. pap. 0.60 o.p. (X1689). Pyramid Pubns.

Enemies in the Rear: Or, A Golden Circle Squared. A Story of Southeastern Pennsylvania in the Time of the Civil War. Francis Trout Hoover. LC 7-5260. 1895. Arena Publishing Company.

Enemies of the Bride: By Osmington Mills. Vivian Collins Brokks. LC 67-17180. 1967. bds., 3.50. Roy.

Enemies of the System. Brian Wilson Aldiss. 112p. 1981. pap. 1.95 (ISBN 0-380-53793-1, 53793). Avon.

Enemies of the System: A Tale of Homo Uniformis. Brian Wilson Aldiss. LC 77-11541. 7.95 (ISBN 0-06-010054-0). Harper & Row.

Enemies of the System: A Tale of Homo Uniformis. Brian Wilson Aldiss. 1981. 1.95 (ISBN 0-380-53793-1). Avon Books.

Enemies of Women: Los Enemigos De la Mujer. Vicente Blasco Ibanez & Brown, Irving Henry, 1888- Tr. LC 20-19241. E. P. Dutton & Company.

Enemies Within. Michael Z Lewin. LC 74-7277. 1974. 5.95 (ISBN 0-394-49031-2). Knopf; Distributed by Random House.

Enemies Within. Michael Z Lewin. 1979. 1.75 (ISBN 0-425-04029-1). Berkley Pub. Corp.

Enemy. Desmond Bagley. LC 76-42058. 1978. 7.95 (ISBN 0-385-04873-4). Doubleday.

Enemy. George Randolph Chester & Chester, Lillian, Joint Author. LC 15-9201. 1.25. Hearst's International Library Co.

Enemy. James Drought. LC 64-8056. 5.00, 2.50 pap.,. Skylight.

Enemy. Felix Greene. 1972. 8.95 o.p. (ISBN 0-394-46279-3). Random.

Enemy. Wirt Williams. LC 51-6511. 1951. Houghton Mifflin.

Enemy: A Novel. Desmond Bagley. 1978. 1.95 (ISBN 0-449-23906-3). Fawcett Crest Books.

Enemy and Brother. Dorothy Salisbury Davis. LC 67-11439. 1967. Scribner.

Enemy at Home. Meriol Trevor. 1974. (pbk.). 0.95 (ISBN 0-671-77778-5). Pocket Books.

Enemy Below. Denys Arthur Rayner. LC 56-11164. 1957. Holt.

Enemy Blood. Luis Spota. LC 61-5984. 1961. Doubleday.

Enemy Camp: A Novel. Weidman, Jerome. LC 58-5258. 1958. Random House.

Enemy from the Past. Lilian Peake. (Harlequin Presents Ser.). (Orig.). 1979. pap. 1.50 (ISBN 0-373-70830-0, Pub. by Harlequin). PB.

Enemy Gods. Oliver La Farge. LC 75-17377. (Zia book). 1975. 3.45 (ISBN 0-8263-0395-1). University of New Mexico Press.

Enemy Gods. Oliver La Farge. LC 37-25757. 1937. Houghton Mifflin Company.

Enemy Guest. Vivian D. Gunderson. 1964. pap. 1.25 (11-0). Rapids Christian.

Enemy: In an English Version by Edward Hyams. Tibor Meray. LC 58-8784. 1959. Criterion Books.

Enemy in Camp. Janet Dailey. (Harlequin Presents Ser.). 192p. 1980. pap. 1.50 (ISBN 0-373-10373-5, Pub. by Harlequin). PB.

Enemy in Sight. Bill Bragg. (Orig.). 1980. pap. 1.75 o.s.i. (ISBN 0-505-51530-X). Tower Bks.

Enemy in Sight! Alexander Kent. (Berkley medallion book). (Richard Bolitho adventure). 1975. (pbk.) 1.25 (ISBN 0-425-02748-1). Putnam.

Enemy in Sight! Alexander Kent. LC 71-105584. 1970. 5.95. Putnam.

Enemy in the Dark. Kurt Mahr. (Perry Rhodan#85). 1975. (pbk.) 1.25. Ace Books.

Enemy in the House. Mignon Good Eberhart. 1973. (pbk) 0.75. Popular Library.

Enemy in the Mirror. Eli Cantor. LC 77-7897. 8.95 (ISBN 0-517-53112-7). Crown Publishers.

Enemy Joy. Ben Belitt. (O.s.i.). 1964. 4.50x o.s.i. (ISBN 0-226-04191-3). U of Chicago Pr.

Enemy: Novelized from the Play. Channing Pollock. LC 26-11040. Brentanos.

Enemy of the State. Francis Paul Wilson. LC 79-7883. (Doubleday science fiction.). 1980. 10.00 (ISBN 0-385-15422-4). Doubleday.

Enemy Outpost. James Saxon Childers. LC 42-19138. 1942. D. Appleton-Century Company, Incorporated.

Enemy Sea. Abraham Polonsky. LC 43-8212. 1943. Little, Brown and Company.

Enemy Sighted. Wilfred Jay Holmes. LC 41-51572. 1941. The Macmillan Company.

Enemy Sky. Peter Saxon. 1971. pap. 0.75 o.p. (94035-075). Beagle Bks.

Enemy Stars. Poul Anderson. 160p. pap. 1.95 (ISBN 0-425-04339-8). Berkley Pub.

Enemy Stars. 1st Ed. Poul Anderson. LC 59-7102. 1959. Lippincott.

Enemy to Society: A Romance of New York of Yesterday and Today. George Fitzalan Bronson Howard. LC 11-26639. 1911. Doubleday, Page & Company.

Enemy to the King: From the Recently Discovered Memoirs of the Sieur De la Tournoire. Robert Neilson Stephens. LC 4-31653. (Fleur de lis library, no. 1). 1900. L. C. Page & Company.

Enemy Unseen... Freeman Wills Crofts. LC 45-3502. 1945. Dodd, Mead & Company.

Enemy Within. Guy Eugene Morton. LC 19-1030. Saulsbury Publishing Company.

Enemy Within the Skull. A "Cap Kennedy" Novel. Gregory Kern. 1974. (pbk.) 0.75. Daw Books.

Enemy's Country. Robert Gamble. 1972. 12.95 o.p. (ISBN 0-8059-1576-1). Dorrance.

Enemy's Country: A Novel of the American Revolution. Robert H Gamble. LC 72-159684. (Illus.). 1972. 12.95 (ISBN 0-8059-1576-1). Dorrance.

Enemy's Gates. Richmond Brooks Barrett. LC 26-4779. 1926. Boni & Liveright.

Enfants du Capitaine Grant, 2 vols. Jules Verne. Set. pap. 7.90. French & Eur.

Enfants et Petites Gens: Stories and Selections from the Works of Charles-Louis Philippe. Charles Louis Philippe. Ed. by Harvitt, Helene Josephine & Doub-Kerr, William Clarke. LC 25-24030. (Oxford French series, by American scholars; general editor: R. Weeks). 1925. Oxford University Press.

Enfermia. 2nd ed. Lwerne W. Lewis. 608p. 1982. pap. text ed. write for info. (ISBN 0-06-315016-6, Pub. by HarLA Mexico). Har-Row.

Enforcer. Benjamin Appel. (O.s.i.). 1972. pap. 0.95 o.s.i. (BT50283). Belmont-Tower.

Enforcer. Wesley Morgan (ISBN 0-446-88366-2). Warner Books.

Enforcer. Andrew Sugar. 1973. pap. 0.95 o.s.i. (75-443). Lancer.

Enforcer: Calling Doctor Kill. Andrew Sugar. 1976. pap. 1.25 o.p. (ISBN 0-532-12363-8). Woodhill.

Enforcer: Calling Doctor Kill. Andrew Sugar. 1976. pap. 1.25 o.p. (ISBN 0-532-12363-8). Manor Bks.

Enforcer: Caribbean Kill. Andrew Sugar. (Action Novel Ser: No.3). 224p. (Orig.). 1975. pap. 1.25 o.p. (ISBN 0-532-12336-0). Woodhill.

Enforcer: Caribbean Kill. Andrew Sugar. (Action Novel Ser: No.3). 224p. (Orig.). 1975. pap. 1.25 o.p. (ISBN 0-532-12336-0). Manor Bks.

Enforcer, No. 5: Kill City. Andrew Sugar. (Orig.). 1976. pap. 1.25 o.p. (ISBN 0-532-12373-5). Woodhill.

Enforcer, No. 5: Kill City. Andrew Sugar. (Orig.). 1976. pap. 1.25 o.p. (ISBN 0-532-12373-5). Manor Bks.

Enforcer No. 6 (Kill Deadline) Andrew Sugar. 1979. pap. 1.50 (ISBN 0-532-15385-5). Woodhill.

Engaged Girl Sketches. Emily Calvin Blake. LC 10-15195. 1910. Forbes & Company.

Engaged in Writing, and, The Fool and the Princess. Stephen Spender. LC 58-10544. 1958. Farrar, Straus and Cudahy.

Engaged in Writing: Two Novels. Stephen Spender. 10.00x (ISBN 0-87556-519-0). Saifer.

Engaged to Jarrod Stone. Carole Mortimer. (Harlequin Presents Ser.). 192p. pap. 1.50 (ISBN 0-373-10388-3, Pub. by Harlequin). PB.

Engaged to Murder. Mary Violet Heberden. LC 49-105642. 1949. Pub. for the Crime Club by Doubleday.

Engaged to Murder. Mary Violet Heberden. LC 81-47341. (Fifty Classics of Crime Fiction, 1950-1975). 1982. 14.95 (ISBN 0-8240-4992-6). Garland Pub.

Engagement. Bryan Walter Guinness Moyne. LC 70-856725. (Illus.). 1970 (ISBN 0-902591-00-2). Rampant Lions Press.

Engagement. Robert Peel. F. A. Stokes Company.

Engagement. Eloise R Weld. LC 74-28107. 1975. 8.95 (ISBN 0-394-49679-5). Random House.

Engangement. Eloise R Weld. (Signet Book). 1976. 1.75. New American Library.

Engine Summer. John Crowley. LC 78-62601. 1979. 7.95 (ISBN 0-385-12831-2). Doubleday.

Engineer Writes: About People & Places & Projects. Eldred Harrington. 1967. 6.50 o.p. (ISBN 0-910750-13-0). C Horn.

Engineer's Vision of the Promised Land. Wilner Ensign Butler. LC 40-10516. 1939. Fortuny's.

England and Always: Tolkien's World of the Rings. Jared Lobdell. LC 81-12651. (Illus.). 4.95 (ISBN 0-8028-1898-6). W.B. Eerdmans Pub. Co.

England Invaded: A Collection of Fantasy Fiction. Ed. by Michael Moorcock. 245p. 1977. 10.00 o.p. (ISBN 0-491-02191-7). Ultramarine Pub.

England Is My Village. John Llewelyn Rees. LC 72-152955. (Short story index reprint series). 1971. (ISBN 0-8369-3870-4). Books for Libraries Press.

England Is My Village. John Llewelyn Rees. LC 41-51904. Reynal & Hitchcock.

England Is My Village. facsimile ed. John Llewelyn Rhys. LC 72-152955. (Short Story Index Reprint Ser.). Repr. of 1941 ed. 13.00 (ISBN 0-8369-3870-4). Ayer Co.

England Made Me. Graham Greene. 1974. (pbk.) 1.25 (ISBN 0-671-78378-5). Pocket Books.

England Made Me see Ship Wrecked.

England Made Me: A Novel. Graham Greene. LC 35-15620. 1935. Doubleday, Doran & Company, Inc.

England, My England. David Herbert Lawrence. LC 72-3279. (Short story index reprint series). 1972. 10.50 (ISBN 0-8369-4153-5). Books for Libraries Press.

England, My England: And Other Stories. David Herbert Lawrence. LC 22-21569. 1922. T. Seltzer.

England Swings SF: Stories of Speculative Fiction. Ed. by Judith Merril. LC 68-17793. 1968. 5.95. Doubleday.

England, Their England. Archibald Gordon Macdonnell. LC 57-13998. (St. Martin's library). 1957. Macmillan.

England, Their England. Archibald Gordon Macdonnell. LC 33-18663. 1933. The Macmillan Company.

England to America. Margaret Prescott Montague. LC 20-8625. 1920. Doubleday, Page & Company.

English Air. 2d ed. Dorothy Emily Stevenson. LC 75-29720. 1976. 7.95 (ISBN 0-03-016841-4). Holt, Rinehart and Winston.

English Air. Dorothy Emily Stevenson. LC 40-10777. Farrar and Rinehart Inc.

English-American. Emma Homan Thayer. 1890. Donohue, Henneberry & Co.

English Assassin: A Romance of Entropy. Michael Moorcock. LC 73-19949. (Illus.). 1972. 6.95 (ISBN 0-06-013003-2). Harper & Row.

English Captain. Simon White. LC 77-3191. 1977. 7.95 (ISBN 0-312-25357-5). St. Martin's Press.

English Captain and Other Stories. Leonard Alfred George Strong. LC 31-280642. 1931. A. A. Knopf.

English Country Short Stories. Ronald Lewin. Repr. of 1949 ed. 15.00 (ISBN 0-89987-146-1). Darby Bks.

English "Daisy Miller". Virginia Wales Johnson. 1882. Estes and Lauriat.

English Gentleman's Wife. Douglas Sutherland. 96p. 1981. pap. 3.50 (ISBN 0-14-005734-X). Penguin.

English Girl in Paris. A Story. J. Lane.

English Heiress. Roberta Gellis. (Orig.). 1980. pap. 2.50 (ISBN 0-440-12141-8). Dell.

English in England: Short Stores. Rudyard Kipling. LC 63-13086. (Doubleday Anchor original). 1963. Anchor Books.

English in England: Short Stories. Rudyard Kipling. 5.00. Doubleday.

English in England: Short Stories by Rudyard Kipling. Rudyard Kipling. 8.50 (ISBN 0-8446-4000-X). Peter Smith.

English Lady. William Harrington. LC 81-52071. 13.95 (ISBN 0-87223-750-8). Seaview Books.

English Lover. Marguerite Duras. Tr. by Barbara Bray. LC 68-31618. Orig. Title: Amante Anglaise. 1968. 3.95 o.p. (GP517). Grove.

English Maiden, Parable of a Happy Life. Frank Arthur Swinnerton. LC 46-23134. Hutchinson & Co. Ltd.

English Medieval Town. Colin Platt. (Illus.). 1976. 17.95 o.p. (ISBN 0-679-50584-9). McKay.

English Miss. Ralph Hale Mottram. LC 28-21225. 1928. L. MacVeagh, The Dial Press.

English Murder. Alfred Alexander Gordon Clark. LC 51-11286. 1951. Little, Brown.

English Murder. Cyril Hare. (Perennial library). 1978. 1.95 (ISBN 0-06-080455-6). Harper & Row.

English Nun: Or, The Sorrows of Edward and Louisa. A Novel. Catharine Selden. LC 8-11249. 1806. Printed by J. Swaine.

English Orphans; or, A Home in the New World. Mary Jane Hawes Holmes. LC 11-16153. Carleton.

English Review Book of Short Stories. Intro. by Horace Shipp & Ford M. Ford. 1978. Repr. lib. bdg. 20.00 (ISBN 0-8495-4835-7). Arden Lib.

English Rue. Zoe Girling. LC 38-25846. 1938. The Macmillan Company.

English Serfdom and American Slavery: Or, Ourselves--As Others See Us. Lucien Bonaparte Chase. LC 15-21834. H. Long & Brother.

English Serfdom and American Slavery: Or, Ourselves, As Others See Us. Lucien Bonaparte Chase. LC 68-58052. 1968. Negro Universities Press.

English Serfdom and American Slavery: Or, Ourselves-As Others See Us. Lucien Bonaparte Chase. LC 77-83929. 1969. Mnemosyne Pub. Co.

English Short Stories. pap. 3.95 o.p. (ISBN 0-460-01743-8, Evman). Biblio Dist.

English Short Stories. Ernest Rhys. Repr. 8.50 (ISBN 0-8414-7425-7). Folcroft.

English Short Stories: Fifteenth to Twentieth Centuries. Ed. by Richard Wilson. 1957. 5.00x o.p. (ISBN 0-460-00743-2, Evman); pap. 2.25 o.p. (ISBN 0-460-01743-8). Biblio Dist.

English Short Stories: Fifteenth to Twentieth Centuries. Ed. by Richard Wilson. 1957. 5.00x o.p. (ISBN 0-460-00743-2, Evman); pap. 2.25 o.p. (ISBN 0-460-01743-8). Dutton.

English Short Stories of My Time. David Cecil. LC 73-566240. (Oxford paperbacks). 1970 (ISBN 0-19-281095-2). Oxford U.P.

English Short Stories of the Nineteenth Century. Ed. by Heinz Bergner. LC 75-549474. (Olms Studien, Bd. 16). 1969. 39.80. G. Olms.

English Short Stories, 1888-1937. Ed. by Phyllis Maud Jones. LC 73-180459. (Oxford paperbacks). 1973. 0.95 (ISBN 0-19-281135-5). Oxford University Press.
English Short Story, Pts. 1-2. Thomas Owen Beachcroft. 1964. 3.95x ea. o.s.i.; Pt. 1. (ISBN 0-8277-6168-6, WTW168 & 169); Pt. 2. (ISBN 0-8277-6169-4, W*T*W168 & 169); pap. 1.95 ea. o.s.i. British Bk Ctr.
English Short Story in Transition: 1880-1920. Ed. by Helmut E. Gerber. Ed. by Helmut E. Gerber. LC 67-25503. 1967. pap., 3.95. Pegasus.
English Silver. Jessie M. Dennis. 4.50 o.p. (ISBN 0-8027-2211-3). Walker & Co.
English Squire. A Novel. Christabel Rose Coleridge. (On cover: Seaside library. Pocket ed., no. 403). 1885. G. Munro.
English Stories. Ed. by Edward Everett Hale. LC 78-98571. (Hawthorne Classics.). (Short story index reprint series). 1969. (ISBN 0-8369-3145-9). Books for Libraries Press.
English Stories. Ed. by Edward Everett Hale. (Hawthorne classics). 1903. Globe School Book Company.
English Stories. Arturo Vivante. LC 75-19938. 2.45 (ISBN 0-914908-27-8). Street Fiction Press.
English Summer. Cornelia S. Parker. 1934. 3.50 o.p. (ISBN 0-87140-800-7). Liveright.
English Tales and Sketches. Camilla Dufour Toulmin Crosland. LC 6-31963. 1853. Ticknor, Reed, and Fields.
English Tradition: Fiction. Ed. by Kubat et al. (Macmillan Lit. Heritage Ser. Gr. 12: English Tradition). pap. text ed. 2.08, s.p. 1.56 o.p. Macmillan.
English Tradition: (The). Fiction Ed. by Marjorie Wescott Barrows, Others. Ed. by Marjorie Wescott Barrows. LC 68-268938. (Macmillan lit. heritage). 1968. pap., 2.40. Macmillan.
English Wife. Ursula Torday. LC 64-13063. 1964. Coward-McCann.
English Wife: By Charity Blackstock Pseud. Ursula Torday. 1965. Macfadden.
English Yankee. Donna L. Schenk. LC 77-13573. 3.95 (ISBN 0-89293-046-2). Beta Books.
Englishman of the Rue Cain. H. Freeman Wood. LC 16-1251. 1889. Rand, McNally & Company.
Englishman's Breakfast. Derek Barton. LC 77-353621. 1976. 4.25 (ISBN 0-304-29636-8). Cassell.
Englishman's Haven. William John Gordon. LC 6-27488. 1892. D. Appleton and Company.
Englishman's Mistress. Jean Bartholomew. 1974. (pbk.) 0.75. Dell.
Englishwoman's Love-Letters. Laurence Housman. LC 1-2481. 1900. Doubleday, Page and Co.
Englishwoman's Love-Letters. Laurence Housman. LC 1-31614. The Mershon Company.
Engrafted Rose: A Novel. Emma Frances Brooke. 1900. H. S. Stone and Company.
Enigma. Michael Barak. LC 78-6599. 1978. 8.95 o.p. (ISBN 0-688-03358-X). Morrow.
Enigma Sacrifice. Michael Bar-Zohar. LC 78-6599. 1978. 8.95 (ISBN 0-688-03358-X). Morrow.
Enigma Variations. Brian Murphy. LC 81-9344. 1981. 11.95 (ISBN 0-684-17291-7). Scribner.
Enigmas of Euphoria. Elizabeth W. Johnson. 3.95 o.p. Vantage.
Enit for a Dame. Richard Ellington. LC 51-2020. 1951. Morrow.
Enjoying Life: And Other Literary Remains of W. N. P. Barbellion Pseud.... Bruce Frederick Cummings. LC 20-16882. George H. Doran Company.
Enjoying What Comes Naturally. Gustave Telschow. LC 75-35298. 6.85. Telschow.
Enjoyment of Amy. John Colleton. 1980. pap. 2.50 (ISBN 0-671-83659-5). PB.
Enjoyment of Murder. William Roughead. LC 38-22020. Sheridan House.
Enlightenment of Olivia. Lucy Bethia Colquhoun Walford. LC 7-312305. 1907. Longmans, Green, and Co.
Enlightenment of Paulina; a Novel. Ellen Wilkins Tompkins. LC 17-28187. E. P. Dutton & Co.
Ennemonde. Jean Giono. 14.95 (ISBN 0-7206-2801-6). Dufour.
Ennemonde et Autres Caracteres: Roman. Jean Giono. (Coll. Soleil). 13.50. French & Eur.
Ennui. Maria Edgeworth. LC 25-23771. (Half-title: The novels of Maria Edgeworth, vol. iv). 1893. J. M. Dent & Co.
Enoch Crane. Francis Hopkinson Smith & Smith, Frank Berkeley, 1869- LC 16-182907. 1916. C. Scribner's Sons.
Enoch Storne: A Master of Men. Edward Phillips Oppenheim. LC 16-25043. 1907. Little, Brown, and Company.
Enoch Strone: A Novel. Edward Phillips Oppenheim. LC 2-94512. 1902. G. W. Dillingham Co.
Enoch, the Philistine: A Traditional Romance of Philistia, Egypt, and the Great Pyramid. Le Roy Hooker. LC 98-8831. Rand, McNally & Company.
Enoch Willoughby: A Novel. James Alexander Wickersham. LC 2365. 1900. C. Scribner's Sons.
Enola: Or, Her Fatal Mistake. Mary Young Ridenbaugh. LC 7-41439. 1886. For the Author.
Enone: A Tale of Slave Life in Rome. Leonard Kip. LC 7-12539. 1866. J. Bradburn.
Enormous Bed. Henry Jones. pap. 1.25 o.p. (2027). Brandon.
Enormous Changes at the Last Minute: Stories. Grace Paley. LC 73-87691. 1974. 6.95 (ISBN 0-374-14851-1). Farrar, Straus, Giroux.
Enormous Changes at the Last Minute: Stories. Grace Paley. 1975. (pbk.) 1.25. Dell.
Enormous Hour Glass. Ron Goulart. (O.s.i.). 160p. (Orig.). 1975. pap. 1.25 o.s.i. (AQ1510, Award). Univ Pub & Dist.
Enormous Hourglass. Ron Goolart. 1976. (pbk.) 1.25. Award Books.
Enormous Radio: And Other Stories. John Cheever. (Colophon bks., CN48). 1965. pap., 1.60. Harper.
Enormous Radio, and Other Stories. John Cheever. LC 53-6976. 1953. Funk & Wagnalls.
Enormous Room. new ed. E. E. Cummings. LC 77-114387. 1950. 5.95 o.s.i. (ISBN 0-87140-956-9); pap. 3.25 o.s.i. (L-001). Liveright.
Enormous Shadow. Robert Harling. LC 80-8714. 224p. 1981. pap. 2.50i (ISBN 0-06-080545-5, P545, PL). Har-Row.
Enormous Shadow. 1st American Ed. Robert Harling. LC 56-8782. 1959. Putnam.
Enormous Shadow. 1st American Ed. Robert Harling. 1956. Harper.
Enormous Turtle. Kenneth Neill Cameron. LC 54-9490. (Illus.). 1954. Bobbs-Merrill Co.
Enough! Donald E Westlake. LC 76-48712. 8.95 (ISBN 0-87131-226-3). M. Evans.
Enough. Donald E Westlake. 1978. 1.75 (ISBN 0-449-23768-0). Fawcett Crest Books.
Enough Good Men. Charles E Mercer. LC 59-11443. 1960. Putnam.
Enough Good Men. Charles E. Mercer. (Berkley Medallion Book)). 1976. 1.95 (ISBN 0-425-03157-8). Berkley Publishing Corp.
Enough of Dreams. Francesco Perri. Tr. by Tutt, Charles H. LC 29-20888. 1929. Brentano's.
Enough of This Lovemaking: Two Short Novels. David George Rubin. LC 75-101882. 1970. 5.95. Simon and Schuster.
Enough to Kill a Horse: By E. X. Ferrars Pseud. 1st Ed. Morna Doris MacTaggart Brown. LC 55-11627. 1955. Published for the Crime Club by Doubleday.
Enough to Live on. Margaret Culkin Banning. LC 40-18548. Harper & Brothers.
Enquiries of Doctor Eszterhazy. Avram Davidson. (Illus.). 1975. (pbk.) 1.25. Warner Books.
Enquiry. Dick Francis. LC 76-96007. 1969. 4.95. Harper & Row.
Enquiry see Across the Board: Three Harper Novels of Suspense.
Enquiry into the Existence of Vampires. Marc Lovell, pseud. LC 73-15354. 1974. (ISBN 0-385-04655-3). Doubleday.
Enrique Amorim, the Passion of a Uruguayan. K. E. A Mose. LC 73-163400. (Coleccion Scholar, 17). (Illus.). 1972. Plaza Mayor.
Enriquillo: Leyenda Historica Dominicana. Cata Prologo De Jose Marti. Manuel De Jesus Galvan. LC 64-4128. 1964. pap., 3.50. Las Americas.
Enrollment Cancelled: By D. B. Olsen. 1st Ed. Dolores Birk Hitchens. LC 52-11624. 1952. Published for the Crime Club by Doubleday.
Ensign Flandry. Poul Anderson. LC 77-363095. 1976. 0.65 (ISBN 0-340-19864-8). Coronet.
Ensign Flandry. Poul Anderson. LC 79-12735. (Gregg Press science fiction series). (Illus.). 1979. 10.00 (ISBN 0-8398-2526-9). Gregg Press.
Ensign Flandry. 1st Ed. Poul Anderson. LC 66-27598. 1966. 4.50. Chilton.
Ensign Knightley: And Other Stories. Alfred Edward Woodley Mason. LC 70-103525. (Short story index reprint series). 1969. Books for Libraries Press.
Ensign Knightley: And Other Stories. Alfred Edward Woodley Mason. F. A. Stokes Company.
Ensign Knightley & Other Stories. Alfred Edward Woodley Mason. LC 70-103525. (Short Story Index Reprint Ser.). 1901. 17.00 (ISBN 0-8369-3267-6). Ayer Co.
Ensign Merrill. Lionel Lounsberry. LC 99-3974. (On cover: Medal library, no. 17). Street & Smith.
Ensign O'toole & Me. William J. Lederer. pap. 0.50 o.p. (52-630). Paperback Lib.
Ensign Russell. David Gray. LC 74-130058. (Short story index reprint series). (Illus.). 1970. Books for Libraries Press.
Ensign Russell. David Gray. LC 12-139001. 1912. 1.00. The Century Co.
Entail of the Lairds of Grippy. John Galt. Ed. by Ian A. Gordon. (Oxford English Novels Ser). 1970. 8.00x o.p. (ISBN 0-19-255334-8). Oxford U Pr.
Entail: Or, The Lairds of Grippy. John Galt. LC 72-172251. (His Works, v. 5-6). (Illus.). 1968. AMS Press.
Entail: Or, The Lairds of Grippy. John Galt. Ed. by Meldrum, David Storrar. LC 17-488. (Works of John Galt. Ed. by D. Storrar Meldrum). 1896. Roberts Brothers.
Entail: Or, The Lairds of Grippy. John Galt & Ian Alistair Gordon. LC 70-480151. (Oxford English novels). 1970. Oxford U.P.
Entailed Hat: Or, Patty Cannon's Times. George Alfred Townsend. LC 6-36634. 1884. Harper & Brothers.
Entailed Hat: Or Patty Cannon's Times; a Romance. George Alfred Townsend. (On cover: Harper's Franklin square library. New series, no. 679). 1890. Harper & Brothers.
Entailed Hat: Or, Patty Cannon's Times, a Romance, by George Alfred Townsend, 'Gath.' George Alfred Townsend. LC 55-14663. 1955. Tidewater Publishers.
Entangled. Paul Jason & Jeffrey Sager. LC 81-22420. 12.95 (ISBN 0-453-00414-8). New American Library.
Entangled. A Novel. E. Fairfax Byrrne. (Harper's Franklin square library, no. 481). 1885. Harper & Brothers.
Entangled. A Novel. E. Fairfax Byrrne. (On cover: Seaside library. Pocket ed., no. 521). 1885. G. Munro.
Entangled Web. John V. Ritchie. 1979. pap. 2.95 (ISBN 0-89185-179-8). Anthelion Pr.
Entanglement. George Buchanan. LC 39-10128. 1939. D. Appleton-Century Company, Incorporated.
Enter a Gentlewoman. Sara Woods, pseud. LC 81-14518. 9.95 (ISBN 0-312-25691-4). St. Martin's Press.
Enter a Goldfish: Memoirs of an Irish Actor, Young and Old. Micheal Mac Liammoir. LC 77-367032. 8.95 (ISBN 0-500-01181-8). Thames & Hudson.
Enter: A Messenger. Richard Blaker. LC 27-7178. George H. Doran Company.
Enter a Murder see Ngaio Marsh.
Enter a Murderer. Ngaio Marsh. 1942. Sheridan House.
Enter a Murderer. Ngaio Marsh. LC 80-14424. 1980. 11.60 (ISBN 0-88411-483-X). Aeonian Press.
Enter a Strange Country. F. McKeldon Smith. 80p. 1974. 4.00 o.p. (ISBN 0-682-47935-7). Exposition.
Enter a Strange Country:: a Novella. 1st. ed. F. McKelden Smith. 1974. 4.00 (ISBN 0-682-47935-7). Exposition Press.
Enter Certain Murderers. Sara Woods, pseud. LC 66-20756. 1966. Harper & Row.
Enter Craig Kennedy. Arthur Benjamin Reeve. LC 35-18841. The Macaulay Company.
Enter David Garrick. Anna Bird Stewart. LC 51-11179. 1951. Lippincott.
Enter Dr. Nikola! Guy Newell Boothby. LC 80-22357. (Dr. Nikola, master of occult mystery; 1). 1980. 9.95 (ISBN 0-89370-632-9). Borgo Press.
Enter Dr. Nikola! Former Title, A Bid for a Fortune. Guy Newell Boothby. LC 75-23091. (Dr. Nikola, master of occult mystery; 1). 1975. (ISBN 0-87877-032-1). Newcastle Pub. Co.
Enter Jerry. Edwin Meade Robinson. LC 21-19200. 1921. The Macmillan Company.
Enter Laughing. Carl Reiner. 1958. Simon and Schuster.
Enter Mrs. Belchamber. Elizabeth Cadell. LC 51-12171. 1951. Morrow.
Enter Murderers. Henry Slesar. LC 60-12122. (Random House mystery). 1960. Random House.
Enter Nurse Marian. Emily Thorne. LC 56-1105. Avalon Books.
Enter Psmith. Pelham Grenville Wodehouse. LC 35-33170. 1935. The Macmillan Company.
Enter Sir John. Winifred Ashton & Simpson, Helen, 1897-1940, Joint Author. LC 28-29961. 1928. Cosmopolitan Book Corporation.
Enter Sir Robert. 1st American Ed. Angela Mackail Thirkell. 1955. Knopf.
Enter Sir Robert (18) Angela Mackail Thirkell. 1973. pap. 1.25 o.p. (ISBN 0-515-03117-8, V3117). Pyramid Pubns.
Enter, Sleeping. 1st Ed. David Karp. LC 60-7431. 1960. Harcourt, Brace.
Enter the Corpse. Sara Woods, pseud. LC 74-54. (Rinehart suspense novel). 1974. 5.95 (ISBN 0-03-012266-X). Holt, Rinehart and Winston.
Enter the Dragon. Mike Roote. (O.s.i.). 160p. (Orig.). 1973. pap. 0.95 o.s.i. (AN1210, Award). Univ Pub & Dist.
Enter the Dragon Lady. Milton Caniff. Ed. by Bill Chadbourne. LC 77-75670. (Milton Coniff's Terry & the Pirates Ser.: Vol. 4). (Illus.). 1977. pap. 6.95 (ISBN 0-87897-016-9). Nostalgia Pr.
Enter the G-Men: Johnny Barton Pitted Against "Monk the Fiend". William Engle. LC 40-32556. (On cover: Bantam books, 9). Bantam Publications.
Enter the Lion. Michael P Hodel & Wright, Sean M. (Playboy paperback). 1980. 2.50 (ISBN 0-8015-5286-9). Playboy Press.
Enter the Lion: A Posthumous Memoir of Mycroft Holmes. Michael P Hodel & Sean M. Wright. LC 78-65407. 9.95 (ISBN 0-8015-5286-9). Hawthorn Books.
Enter the Saint... Leslie Charteris. LC 31-11279. Pub. for the Crime Club, Inc., by Doubleday, Doran & Company, Inc.
Enter Three Witches. Paul McGuire. LC 40-27252. 1940. W. Morrow & Co.
Enter: Toni's Father. Clarke Hammond. pap. 1.95 o.p. (ISBN 0-87056-187-1, 6187). Brandon.
Entering Ephesus. Daphne Athas. LC 75-150120. 1971. 7.95 (ISBN 0-670-29716-X). Viking Press.
Entering Wedge: a Romance of the Heroic Days of Kansas. William Kennedy Marshall. 1904. Jennings & Graham.
Enterprising Burglar. Hearnden Balfour. LC 28-20730. 1928. Houghton Miffin Company.
Entertainer. John Jay Osborn. LC 58-6810. 1958. 8.95 (ISBN 0-87599-082-7). S G Phillips.
Entertainer. John Jay Osborn. 1983. pap. 4.95 (ISBN 0-14-048178-8). Penguin.
Entertaining Angel. Samuel Merwin. LC 26-14676. J. H. Sears & Company, Inc.
Entertaining Mr. Sloane. Joe Orton. 1965. pap. 2.95 o.p. (ISBN 0-394-17416-X, E393, Ever). Grove.
Entertaining Strangers. Albert Ramsdell Gurney. LC 76-19752. 1977. 7.95 (ISBN 0-385-12551-8). Doubleday.
Entertaining Strangers. Albert Ramsdell Gurney. 1979. 1.95 (ISBN 0-380-44313-9). Avon.
Entertaining the Islanders. Maxwell Struthers Burt. LC 33-235147. 1933. C. Scribner's Sons.
Entertainment: And Other Stories. Edmee Elizabeth Monica De La Pasture. LC 27-14704. Harper & Brothers.
Entertainments of Gallantry or Remedies of Love see Court & City Vagaries, or Intrigues, of Both Sexes.
Enthisiastic Spring. Hamlin Etheredge. Pegasus Publishing Company.
Enthralled. Ann Cristy. (Second Chance at Love Ser.: No. 103). Date not set. pap. 1.75 (ISBN 0-515-06867-5). Jove Pubns.
Enthralled: A Story of International Life Setting Forth the Curious Circumstances Concerning Lord Cloden and Oswald Quain. Edgar Evertson Saltus. LC 75-93534. 1969. AMS Press.
Enthralled and Released. Elisabeth Burstenbinder. Tr. by Raphael, Henry. LC 6-19399. 1885. T. R. Knox & Co.
Enthusiast. Peter Hill. LC 78-12039. 1979. 7.95 (ISBN 0-395-27543-1). Houghton Mifflin.
Enthusiast. Edith Anna CEnone Somerville & Violet Florence Martin. LC 21-11496. 1921. Longmans, Green, and Co.
Enthusiasts. Robert Musil. Tr. by Andrea Simon from Ger. LC 82-62098. 1983. 15.95 (ISBN 0-933826-46-X); pap. 5.95 (ISBN 0-933826-47-8). Performing Arts.
Enthusiasts in Love. Audrey Curling. 1978. 1.75 (ISBN 0-445-04260-5). Popular Library.
Entibiame la Cama. Luisa Estrella. (Pimienta Collection Ser). (Sp.). 1977. pap. 1.00 (ISBN 0-88473-255-X). Fiesta Pub.
Enticement. Lily Clive Nutt. LC 24-23481. The Bobbs-Merrill Company.
Enticement of Cindy. John Colleton. 1981. pap. 2.95 (ISBN 0-451-11019-6, AE1019, Sig). NAL.
Entire Stranger. Thomas L Baily. LC 6-5007. T Y. Crowell & Co.
Entirely Different Woman. Georg Froschel. Tr. by Darnton, Maida Castelhun. 1931. Brentano's.
Entirely New Feature of a Thrilling Novel! Entitled, The Social War of the Year 1900; or The Conspirators and Lovers! Simon Mohler Landis. LC 41-41840. 1872. Landis Publishing Society.
Entirely Surrounded. Charles Brackett. LC 34-255290. 1934. A. A. Knopf.
Entity: A Novel. Frank De Felitta. LC 78-9811. (Illus.). 10.95. Putnam.
Entombed Man of Thule: Stories. Gordon Weaver. LC 70-185952. 1972. 6.95 (ISBN 0-8071-0245-8). Louisiana State University Press.
Entrance to Porlock. Frederick Buechner. LC 79-97132. 1970. 5.95. Atheneum.
Entranced. Grace C. Hodgson Flandrau. LC 24-25526. Harcourt, Brace and Company.
Entrapment Memo. David Allen. write for info. (ISBN 0-937884-04-9); pap. write for info. (ISBN 0-937884-05-7). Hyst'ry Myst'ry.
Entrapped. A Love Story. John Russell Coryell. LC 6-39929. (On cover: Munro's library, v. 1, no. 592). 1886. N. L. Munro.

Entreat Me Not: A Novel Showing the Young How to Prolong Youth and the Aged How to Regain Youth. Floyd T Dodd. LC 56-56375. 1956. Lone Star Print. Co.

Entremeses. Miguel de Cervantes de Saavedra. (O.s.i.). (Span). 4.50x o.s.i. Colton Bk.

Entretiens avec Georges Charbonnier. Michel Butor. pap. 8.95. French & Eur.

Entropy Effect. Vonda N. McIntyre. 224p. (Orig.). 1981. pap. 2.50 (ISBN 0-671-83692-7, Timescape). PB.

Entry. Hans Holzer. 1981. pap. 2.50 (ISBN 0-505-51661-6, T51661). Tower Bks.

Entry E. Richard Frede. LC 57-10034. 1958. Random House.

Entry of Death. Kenneth Giles. LC 79-81071. 1969. 4.50. Walker.

Entry of Death. Edmund McGirr. LC 79-81071. (Mystery Ser). 1969. 4.50 o.p. (ISBN 0-8027-5085-0, 21054). Walker & Co.

Entry to Elsewhen. John Brunner. 1972. pap. 0.95 o.p. (UQ1026). DAW Bks.

Entry to Elsewhen. John Brunner. (Science Fiction Ser). 1975. pap. 1.25 o.p. (ISBN 0-87997-154-1, UY1154). DAW Bks.

Entwined Lives of Miss Gabrielle Austin, Daughter of the Late Rev. Ellis C. Austin: And of Redmond, the Outlaw, Leader of the North Carolina "Moonshiners.". Edward B Crittenden. Barclay & Co.

Entwining. Richard Condon. LC 80-14981. 12.50 (ISBN 0-399-90089-6). R. Marek.

Envious Casca. Georgette Heyer. LC 41-252571. 1941. Pub. for the Crime Club by Doubleday, Doran & Company, Inc.

Envious Time. Dale Van Dalsem. (Illus.). 16p. 1970. pap. 1.00 o.p. Christopher Bks.

Environment. Phyllis Eleanor Bentley. LC 36-7190. 1935. Hillman-Curl, Inc.

Environment. A Story of Modern Society. Florine Thayer McCray. LC 7-15415. 1887. Funk & Wagnalls.

Envolee. college ed. R. Cadoux. 1973. 13.95 (ISBN 0-02-318020-X). Macmillan.

Envoy Extraordinary. Edward Phillips Oppenheim. LC 37-12722. 1937. Little, Brown and Company.

Envoy from Elizabeth. Pamela Bennetts. LC 73-76757. 1973. 5.95. St. Martin's Press.

Envoy from Elizabeth. Pamela Bennetts. LC 77-3681. 1977. 9.95 (ISBN 0-89340-071-8). John Curley.

Envoy from Heaven: A Novel. Obolensky. Joseph Tusiani. LC 65-17403. bds., 4.95. World.

Envoys. Hoffman Reynolds Hays. LC 53-9967. 1953. Crown Publishers.

Envy. Iurii Olesha. Tr. by Thomas Berczynski from Rus. (Orig.). 1979. pap. 4.50 (ISBN 0-88233-091-8). Ardis Pubs.

Envy: A Tale. Ernst Wildenbruch & Traut, Elise, Tr. LC 22-2865. 1921. The Four Seas Company.

Envy, and Other Works. IUrii Karlovich Olesha. LC 81-2583. 1981. 5.95 (ISBN 0-393-00042-7). Norton.

Eoline: Or, Magnolia Vale, a Novel. Caroline Lee Whiting Hentz. LC 77-164564. (American fiction reprint series). (Illus.). 1971. (ISBN 0-8369-7041-1). Books for Libraries Press.

Eoline; or, Magnolia Vale: A Novel. facsimile ed. Caroline Lee Whiting Hentz. LC 77-164564. (American Fiction Reprint Ser.). 1825. 20.00 (ISBN 0-8369-7041-1). Ayer Co.

Eoneguski: Or, The Cherokee Chief (1839); Two-Volume Historical Novel. Foreword by Richard Walser. Facsimile Ed. Robert Strange. LC 61-112. 1960. MaNally.

Ephesian Matron (1668) Walter Charleton. LC 75-622975. (Augustan Reprint Society. Publication: No. 172-173). (Illus.). 1975. William Andrews Clark Memorial Library, University of California.

Ephesian Tale see Three Greek Romances.

Ephod & Ark. William R. Arnold. LC 17-18713. 1917. pap. 7.00 (ISBN 0-527-01003-0). Kraus Repr.

Ephraim of Israel, the Unknown Apostle. Paul Constant. LC 57-198. 1956. Philosophical Library.

Ephraim the Jew. A. Norton Raybould. LC 39-317866. B. Humphries, Inc.

Epic Joy: A Novel Based on the Life of Rubens. Donald Braider. LC 75-135258. 1971. 7.95. Putnam.

Epic of Ebenezer: A Christmas Story. Florence Tinsley Cox. LC 12-21598. 1912. 1.00. Dodd, Mead and Company.

Epic of Gilgamesh. revised ed., incorporating new material. ed. Nancy K Sandars. LC 78-318052. (Penguin classics). (Illus.). 1978. 1.95 (ISBN 0-14-044100-X). Penguin.

Epic of Gilgamish. R. Campbell Thompson. LC 78-72736. 1981. 45.00 (ISBN 0-404-18175-9). AMS Press.

Epic of Life: Poems of a Lifetime. Albert Fletcher Bridges. LC 30-14115. Printed for the Author by the Caxton Press.

Epic Peters, Pullman Porter. Octavus Roy Cohen. 1930. D. Appleton & Company.

Epic Stories of Adventure. Patrick Pringle. LC 66-70567. (B 66-2976). 1965. Evans Bros.

Epicenter. Basil Jackson. LC 78-125862. 1971. 6.95. Norton.

Epickall Quest of the Brothers Dichtung and Other Outrages. Richard Carter Higgins. LC 78-9344. (Illus.). 1978. 19.95. (ISBN 0-914162-26-8) (ISBN 0-914162-27-6). Printed Editions.

Epicurean, a Tale. Thomas Moore. LC 48-34214. 1827. Olive-Branch Book Store.

Epicurean, a Tale. a new ed., rev. and cor. by the author, with notes. ed. Thomas Moore. 1841. C. S. Francis; Boston, J. H. Francis.

Epicurean: A Tale. a new edition, revised and corrected by the author, with notes. ed. Thomas Moore. LC 31-352181. 1862. J. Miller.

Epicurean: A Tale. new american ed. Thomas Moore. (Half-title: Laurel crowned tales). 1890. A. C. McClurg and C Omapny.

Epicurus My Master. Max Radin. LC 49-8114. 1949. Univ. of North Carolina Press.

Epidemic. Jean Todd Freeman. 1970. 7.95 o.p. Wyden.

Epidemic! Larry R. Leichter. (Orig.). 1981. pap. 2.50 (ISBN 0-89083-860-7). Zebra.

Epidemic! Larry R. Leichter. 368p. (Orig.). 1980. pap. 2.50 (ISBN 0-89083-644-2). Zebra.

Epidemic! Frank Gill Slaughter. LC 61-5982. 1961. Doubleday.

Epidemic! Frank Gill Slaughter. (Permabk., M5044). 1962. Pocket Bks.

Epidemic Center: Aralon. Clark Darlton. (Perry Rhodan#37). 1974. (pbk.) 0.75. Ace Books.

Epidemic 9. Richard A Lerner & Max Gunther. LC 79-21759. 1980. 10.95 (ISBN 0-688-03585-X). Morrow.

Epiphanies. James Augustine Aloysius Joyce. LC 76-43258. 1976. 10.00 (ISBN 0-8414-7740-X). Folcroft Library Editions.

Epiphany. Nicholas Yermakov. 1982. pap. 2.50 (ISBN 0-451-11884-7, AE1884, Sig). NAL.

Epiplectic Bicycle. Edward Gorey. LC 75-93550. 1968. 4.95 o.p. (ISBN 0-396-06012-9). Dodd.

Epiplectic Bicycle. Edward Gorey. (Illus.). 64p. 1983. pap. 6.95 (ISBN 0-312-92185-3). Congdon & Weed.

Episode. Eric Hodgins. (Fireside Paperback Ser.). 1971. pap. 2.95 (ISBN 0-671-21043-2, Fireside). S&S.

Episode: A Record of Five Hundred Lost Days. 1st Ed. Peter W Denzer. LC 53-10848. Dutton.

Episode at Toledo. Ann Bridge, pseud. 1966. 5.95 o.p. McGraw.

Episode at Toledo: By Ann Bridge. Mary Dolling Sanders O'Malley. (S1477). 1967. Berkley.

Episode at Toledo: By Ann Bridge. 1st Ed. Mary Dolling Sanders O'Malley. LC 66-24578. 1966. bds., 5.95. McGraw.

Episode in Luxor and Other Stories. John Kent. LC 29-256061. 1929. Brentano's.

Episode in Palmetto. Erskine Caldwell. 1965. pap. 0.50 o.p. (50-232). Manor Bks.

Episode in Palmetto. 1st Ed. Erskine Caldwell. LC 50-9621. 1950. Duell, Sloan and Pearce.

Episode in the Doings of the Dualized... Eveleen Laura Mason. 1898. Press of Fish & Libby.

Episode in the Transvaal: A Novel. Harry Bloom. LC 55-9499. 1955. Doubleday.

Episode of Sparrows. Rumer Godden. LC 81-47095. 246p. 1981. pap. 2.95i (ISBN 0-06-080562-5, P 562, PL). Har-Row.

Episode of Sparrows: A Novel. Rumer Godden. LC 56-5069. 1955. Viking Press.

Episode of the Wandering Knife. Mary Roberts Rinehart. 1975. (pbk.) 1.25. Dell.

Episode of the Wandering Knife. Mary Roberts Rinehart. LC 81-726. 1981. 15.95 (ISBN 0-8161-3234-8). G.K. Hall.

Episode of the Wandering Knife: Three Mystery Tales. Mary Roberts Rinehart. LC 59-4139. 1950. Rinehart.

Episode on Beacon Hill. Louis Joseph Gallagher. LC 50-2689. 1950. Benziger.

Episode on West 8th Street. Jule Brousseau. LC 41-7325. 1941. Smith & Durrell.

Episodes. George Slythe Street. LC 8-16886. The Merriam Company.

Episodes from Sans Famille. Hector Henri Malot & Spiers, Isidore Henry Bowles, Ed. LC 8-12546. (Heath's modern language series). 1899. D. C. Heath & Co.

Episodes in a Widow's Life and Two Monkey Stories. Sarah Godwin. LC 39-4493. The Christopher Publishing House.

Episodes in an Obscure Life. Richard Rowe. LC 9-3856. 1871. G. Routledge & Sons.

Episodes in Van Bibber's Life. Richard Harding Davis. LC 75-101795. (Short story index reprint series). (Illus.). 1969. Books for Libraries Press.

Episodes in Van Bibber's Life. Richard Harding Davis. LC 99-5620. (Little books by famous writers). 1899. Harper & Brothers.

Episodes of Fiction: Or, Choice Stories from the Great Novelists, with Biographical Introductions; Numerous Original Illustrations. LC 6-38405. 1869. Virtue & Yorston.

Episodes of Life. MacDonald Givin. 1972. pap. 1.95 o.s.i. (V1078T, Venus). Grove.

Episodes of Vathek. William Beckford. LC 74-4883. 1975. 12.50 (ISBN 0-8386-1128-1). Fairleigh Dickinson University Press.

Epitaph for a Lobbyist. R. B Dominic. LC 73-9021. 1974. 4.95 (ISBN 0-385-08556-7). Published for the Crime Club by Doubleday.

Epitaph for a Nurse. Anne Hocking. Orig. Title: Victim Must Be Found. 224p. 1973. Repr. of 1959 ed. lib. bdg. 5.95 o.s.i. (ISBN 0-85617-583-8). White Lion Pubs.

Epitaph for a Spy. Eric Ambler. 201p. Repr. of 1952 ed. lib. bdg. 12.70x (ISBN 0-89190-462-X). Am Repr-Rivercity Pr.

Epitaph for a Spy: With a Footnote by the Author. Eric Ambler. LC 51-13217. 1952. Knopf.

Epitaph for a Tramp see Fannin.

Epitaph for an Enemy. George Barr. LC 58-11389. (Illus.). 1959. Harper.

Epitaph for Emily. D. W. Christner. (Mystery Puzzler Ser.: No. 13). (Illus., Orig.). 1979. pap. 1.95 (ISBN 0-89083-433-4). Zebra.

Epitaph for Lemmings. Henry Gibbs. LC 44-75252. 1943. Rich & Cowan.

Epitaph for Lemmings. Henry Gibbs. LC 44-47042. 1944. The Macmillan Company.

Epitaph for Love: A Novel. Howard Clewes. LC 53-7973. 1953. Doubleday.

Epitaph for Lydia. Virginia Rath. LC 42-361014. 1942. Published for the Crime Club by Doubleday, Doran & Co., Inc.

Epitaph for Mister Wynn. Keith Wheeler. LC 78-139606. 1971. 6.95. Putnam Sons.

Epitaph for the Giants (the Story of the Tillamook Burn) J. Larry Kemp. LC 67-29848. (Illus.). 128p. 1967. 4.95 (ISBN 0-911518-08-8). Touchstone Pr Ore.

Epitaph for Three Women. Jean Plaidy. (The Plantagenet Saga Ser.: Vol. 12). 336p. 1983. 12.95 (ISBN 0-399-12782-8, Putnam). Putnam Pub Group.

Epitaph of a Small Winner. Machado De Assis, Joaquim Maria. LC 52-36198. (Illus.). 1952. Noonday Press.

Epitaph of a Small Winner. Joaquim Maria Machado De Assis. (Bard Book). 1978. 2.25 (ISBN 0-380-01712-1). Avon.

Epitaph to a Bad Cop. John Fredman. LC 73-76560. (MW suspense). 1973. 4.95. D. McKay.

Epitaph Universal: And Other Verses. Robert E Farley. LC 22-7118. Brieger Press, Inc.

Eplow in Wallenstein. Richard George Sturgeon. LC 66-789179. (B 66-13257). 1966. Semaphore Publications.

Epoch. Robert Silverberg & Roger Elwood. LC 75-20343. 1975. 9.95 (ISBN 0-399-11460-2). Berkley Pub. Corp.: Distributed by Putnam.

Epoch. Ed. by Robert Silverberg & Roger Elwood. (Berkley medallion Book). 1977. 1.95. Berkley Pub. Corp.

Eppie: The Story of Ann Landers. Margo Howard. (Illus.). 1983. pap. 3.50 (ISBN 0-523-42016-1). Pinnacle Bks.

Eppworth Case. Innis Patterson. LC 30-27759. Farrar & Rinehart, Incorporated.

Epsilon: A Journey Along the Epsilon River from the Eastern Mountains to the Sea. Vern Swansen. LC 74-79852. (Illus.). 1974. (pbk.) 4.50 (ISBN 0-914598-00-7). Padre Productions.

Equal Danger. Leonardo Sciascia. LC 72-9176. 1973. 5.95 (ISBN 0-06-013809-2). Harper & Row.

Equal Partners. Charles Witherle Hooke. LC 1-23035. G. W. Dillingham Company.

Equalities of Para-Para. Written from the Dictations of George Rambler, M.D.; F.R.G.S. Paul Haedicke. LC 6-45971. (On cover: Progressive series. v. 1, no. 1). 1895. The Schuldt-Gathmann Co.

Equality. Edward Bellamy. (BCL Ser. II). (Illus.). 1970. Repr. of 1897 ed. 10.00 (ISBN 0-404-00735-X). AMS Pr.

Equality. William Ryan. LC 81-52258. 256p. 1982. pap. 6.95 (ISBN 0-394-71185-8). Random.

Equilibrium. Tonino Guerra. LC 69-16515. 1970. 4.95. Walker.

Equinox: A Novel. Lorna Pegram. LC 76-376905. 1976. 4.25 (ISBN 0-575-02127-6). Gollanoz.

Equinox: A Novel. Allan Seager. LC 43-10497. 1943. Simon and Schuster.

Equinox: A Novel of Rome in the Time of Commodus. Carol Saylor. LC 66-111624. 1966. 4.95. Lippincott.

Equisite Thing. Joyce MacIver. 1977. 1.75 (ISBN 0-380-00923-4). Avon Books.

Equitania, or the Land of Equity. W. O. Henry. LC 76-154445. (Utopian Literature Ser). 1971. Repr. of 1914 ed. 13.00 (ISBN 0-405-03528-4). Ayer Co.

Equivocal Men: Tales of the Establishment. Holmes Moss Alexander. LC 65-28197. 1964. Western Islands.

ER: Or, The Brassbound Beauty, the Bearded Bicyclist, and the Gold-Colored Teen-Age Grandfather; a Novel. Shepherd Mead. LC 72-79636. 1969. 5.95. Simon and Schuster.

Er: Or the Monumental Mistress. Shepherd Mead. LC 72-79636. (O.S.I.). 1969. 5.95 o.s.i. (ISBN 0-671-20329-0). S&S.

Erase My Name. Jackson Donahue. LC 64-12056. 1964. World Pub. Co.

Erasers. Alain Robbe-Grillet. LC 61-11766. 1964. Grove Press.

Erasmus -- with Freckles. Haase, John. LC 63-12571. 1963. Simon and Schuster.

Erasmus Magister. Charles Sheffield. 224p. (Orig.). 1982. pap. 2.25 (ISBN 0-441-21526-2). Ace Bks.

Erb" A Story. William Pett Ridge. LC 2-25929. (Half-title: Appletons' town and country library, no. 317). 1902. D. Appleton and Company.

Erckmann-Chatrian's Le Tresor Du Vieux Seigneur. Emile Erckmann & Chatrian, Alexandre, 1826-1890, Joint Author. LC 28-28597. H. Holt and Company.

Ere the Rosebuds Withered. James A. Wyld. 1969. 3.95 o.p. (ISBN 0-8059-1390-4). Dorrance.

Erebus. Robert Hunter. LC 75-78444. 1969. 5.95. Grove Press.

Erec. Von Aue Hartman. Tr. by J. W. Thomas from Ger. LC 81-7471. viii, 146p. 1982. 11.95x (ISBN 0-8032-4408-8). U of Nebr Pr.

Erection Set. Frank Morrison Spillane. LC 79-158600. 1972. (ISBN 0-525-09945-X). Dutton.

Erections, Ejaculations, Exhibitions, and General Tales of Ordinary Madness. Charles Bukowski. LC 75-164498. 1972. 3.95. City Lights Books.

Erema: Or, My Father's Sin. Richard Doddridge Blackmore. (On cover:Lovell's library, no. 1040). J. W. Lovell Company.

Erema: Or, My Father's Sin. A Novel. Richard Doddridge Blackmore. LC 6-13861. (On cover: Seaside library. Pocket ed., no. 625). G. Munro.

Erev: By Elya Schechtman. Tr. from Yiddish by Joseph Singer. Elye Shekhtman. LC 67-17706. 1967. 4.50. Crown.

Erewhon. Samuel Butler. Ed. by Peter Mudford. (Penguin English library). (Illus.). 1976. 1.95 (ISBN 0-14-043057-1). Penguin Books.

Erewhon. Introd. by Mary M. Threapleton. Samuel Butler. (Classics ser., CL130). 1967. Airmont.

Erewhon; Or, Over the Range, by Samuel Butler. 2nd ed. Ed. by Hans-Peter Breuer & Daniel F. Howard. LC 77-92568. 280p. 1981. Repr. of 1872 ed. 29.50 (ISBN 0-87413-142-1). U Delaware Pr.

Ergo. Jakov Lind. LC 67-22649. 1967. Random House.

Ergo. Tr. from German by Ralph Manheim. 1st Amer. Ed. Jakov Lind. LC 67-22649. 1967. bds., 3.95. Random.

Eric Braddon's Love. Alexander McVeigh Miller. (On cover: The library of American authors, no. 46). 1892. G. Munro.

Eric Brighteyes. with numerous illustrations by lancelot speed, and an introduction especially prepared for this authorized ed. Henry Rider Haggard. (Lovell's international series, no. 163). 1891. United States Book Company.

Eric Brighteyes. Henry Rider Haggard. LC 80-24107. 1980. 10.95. Borgo Press.

Eric Brighteyes, a Novel. Henry Rider Haggard. LC 6-46135. (On cover: Harper's Franklin square library. no. 698). 1891. Harper & Brothers.

Eric Brighteyes: Full Page Illus. from Originals by Lancelot Speed. Henry Rider Haggard. LC 66-5444. 1966. bds., 2.95. Macdonald.

Eric Brighteyes Two: A Witch's Welcome. Sigfriour Skaldaspillir. (Orig.). 1979. pap. 2.25 (ISBN 0-89083-557-8). Zebra.

Eric Flame. Frank R Wallace. LC 76-139225. 1970. 6.95. I & O Pub. Co.

Eric John Stark: Outlaw of Mars. Leigh Brackett. 208p. 1982. pap. 2.25 (ISBN 0-345-30515-9, Del Rey). Ballantine.

Eric Mattson. Norman Katkov. LC 64-16220. 1964. Doubleday.

Eric: Or, The Black Finger. Mary Teresa Waggaman. LC 10-26229. H. L. Kilner & Co.

Erica's Return. Louise De Vilmorin & Scott, Sarah (Fisher) 1909- LC 48-496689. 1948. Random House.

Eric's Image. Owen S. Rachleff. 304p. 1982. pap. 2.95 (ISBN 0-505-51794-9). Tower Bks.

Eridahn. Robert F. Young. (Orig.). 1983. pap. 1.95 (Del Rey). Ballantine.

Erie Kerrelly: A Novel. Ann Payne Savage. 1944. Dorrance & Company.

Erie Train Boy. Horatio Alger. 249p. 1974. Repr. of 1890 ed. lib. bdg. 15.15x (ISBN 0-88411-802-9). Amereon Ltd.

Erie Water. Walter Dumaux Edmonds. LC 33-3217. 1933. Little, Brown, and Company.

Erik Dorn. Ben Hecht. LC 21-1858. 1921. G.P. Putnam's Sons.

Erik Dorn: A Novel. Ben Hecht. LC 63-22588. (Chicago in fiction). 1963. University of Chicago Press.

Erik Dorn: By Ben Hecht. Introduction by Burton Rascoe. Ben Hecht. (Half-title: The modern library of the world's best books)). The Modern Library.

Erin. Jerry B Jenkins. LC 81-22368. (Jenkins, Jerry B. A Margo Mystery: 6). 2.95 (ISBN 0-8024-4316-8). Moody Press.

Erin Go Bragh!... Mary Andrews Denison. LC 11-10511. 1879. Globe Printing and Publishing House.

Erin Mor: The Story of Irish Republicanism. John Brennan. LC 6-17394. 1892. P. M. Diers & Company.

Erin's Ecstasy. Sylvie F. Sommerfield. (Orig.). 1981. pap. 2.50 (ISBN 0-89083-861-5). Zebra.

Erin's Ecstasy. Sylvie F. Sommerfield. 320p. (Orig.). 1980. pap. 2.50 (ISBN 0-89083-656-6). Zebra.

Eris. Robert William Chambers. LC 23-131253. 2.00. George H. Doran Company.

Erl King. Edwin Granberry. LC 30-23442. 1930. The Macaulay Company.

Erl Queen. Nataly Von Eschstruth & Howard, Emily S., Tr. LC 6-38157. (On cover: Worthington's international library. no. 27). 1892. Worthington Company.

Erlach Court. Lula Kirschner. Tr. by Wister, Annie Lee (Furness) LC 7-12819. 1889. J. B. Lippincott Company.

Erle Stanley Gardner, Seven Complete Novels. Erle Stanley Gardner. LC 79-16338. 1979. 5.98 (ISBN 0-517-29363-3). Avenel Books.

Erma at Perkins. Ruth Rodman Hayden. LC 44-4112. 1944. Chapman & Grimes.

Ermyntrude and Esmeralda. Giles Lytton Strachey. LC 76-84828. (Illus.). 1969. 5.95. Stein and Day.

Erna Stark; a Story of Conscience. Tr. from the German of Elise Von Fernhain. Elise Von Fernhain & Ireland, Mrs. Mary Ellza (Haines) 1834-1927, Tr. LC 6-38986. American Baptist Publication Society.

Erna Vitek. Alfred Kreymborg. LC 14-13578. 1914. 1.00. A. and C. Boni.

Ernest Carroll: Or Artist-Life in Italy. A Novel... Henry Greenough. LC 7-3515. 1858. Ticknor and Fields.

Ernest Carroll: Or, Artist-Life in Italy. A Novel... 2d ed. Henry Greenough. LC 6-44858. 1859. Ticknor and Fields.

Ernest Grey; or, The Sins of Society. A Story of New York Life. Maria Maxwell. LC 7-17920. 1855. T. W. Strong.

Ernest Hemingway, Cub Reporter: Kansas City Star Stories. Ed. by Matthew J. Bruccoli. (Illus.). 1969. 4.95 o.p. (ISBN 0-8229-3193-1). U of Pittsburgh Pr.

Ernest Hemingway, Knut Hamsun and Hermann Hesse. Ernest Hemingway & Knut Hamsun. LC 73-27607. (Nobel Prize Library). (Illus.). 1971. A. Gregory.

Ernest Hemingway: the Man and His Work. Ed. by John K. M. McCaffery. LC 69-17516. 1969. 7.50. Cooper Square Publishers.

Ernest Linwood: A Novel. Caroline Lee Whiting Hentz. LC 7-4132. 1856. J. P. Jewett and Company.

Ernest Linwood: Or, The Inner Life of the Author. Caroline Lee Whiting Hentz. T. B. Peterson.

Ernest Maltravers. a new edition. ed. Edward George Earle Lytton Bulwer-Lytton Lytton. LC 7-8351. 1877. G. Routledge and Sons.

Ernest Maltravers. Edward George Earle Lytton Bulwer-Lytton Lytton. G. Routledge and Sons.

Ernest Maltravers. Edward George Earle Lytton Bulwer-Lytton Lytton. (Lovell's library, v. 1, no. 31). 1882. J. W. Lovell Company.

Ernest Maltravers, Alice: Or, The Mysteries. Edward George Earle Lytton Bulwer-Lytton Lytton. LC 31-32283. (The novels and romances of Edward Bulwer Lytton. v. 3). Aldine Book Publishing Co.

Ernest Maltravers: Or, The Eleusinia. Edward George Earle Lytton Bulwer-Lytton Lytton. LC 7-8349. (Half-title: Novels of Sir Edward Bulwer Lytton. Library ed. Novels of life and manners, vol. VIII). 1893. Little, Brown, and Company.

Ernest Marble: The Labor Agitator. Milton Robinson Scott. LC 8-2905. 1895. Tribune Book Print.

Ernest Pontifex: Or, The Way of All Flesh. Samuel Butler & Howard, Daniel Francis, Ed. LC 64-5779. 1964. Houghton Mifflin.

Ernest Quest: Or, The Search for Truth. Sallie Rochester Ford. LC 6-41390. 1878. Sheldon & Company.

Ernestine: A Novel. Wilhelmine Birch Von Hillern & Gould, Sabine Barine-, 1834- Tr. LC 7-4744. 1881. W.S. Gottsberger.

Ernestine Sophie. Sophia Cleugh. LC 25-21211. 1925. The Macmillan Company.

Ernestine Takes Over. Walter Rollin Brooks. LC 35-30403. 1935. W. Morrow and Company.

Ernie's Group. E. B. Grafling. pap. 1.95 o.p. (8090). Cameo.

Ernie's Group. John O'Donnel. pap. 1.95 o.p. (8091). Cameo.

Ernst Ellert Returns. Clark Darlton. (Perry Rhodan 83). 1975. (pbk.) 1.25. Ace Books.

Ernst in Civilian Clothes. Mavis Gallant. LC 72-12585. 1973. Random House.

Eroica. Mara Rostov. LC 76-30824. 1977. 8.95 (ISBN 0-399-11926-4). Putnam Pub Group.

Eroica: A Novel. Mara Rostov. LC 76-30824. 7.95 (ISBN 0-399-11926-4). Putnam.

Eroica: A Novel. Mara Rostov. (Jove / HBJ Book). 1978. 1.95 (ISBN 0-515-04469-5). Jove Pubns.

Eroica: A Novel Based on the Life of Ludwig Van Beethoven. Samuel Chotzinoff. LC 72-1021. 1975. 12.50 (ISBN 0-404-01529-8). AMS Press.

Eroica: A Novel Based on the Life of Ludwig Van Beethoven. Samuel Chotzinoff. LC 30-6433. 1930. Simon and Schuster.

Eros. Laura Deintery. Belford, Clarke & Co.

Eros and Anteros: Or, The Bachelor's Ward. Juliet H. Lewis Campbell. LC 6-21479. 1857. Rudd & Carleton.

Eros in Orbit. Ed. by Joseph Elder. 1973. 6.95 o.p. (27102). S&S.

Eros in Orbit: A Collection of All New Science Fiction Stories About Sex. Joseph Elder. LC 72-96813. 1973. 6.95 (ISBN 0-671-27102-4). Trident Press.

Eros in Order. new ed. Ed. by Joseph Elder. 1973. 6.95 o.s.i. (ISBN 0-671-27102-4). Trident.

Eros Invincible. Ricarda Octavia Huch. LC 76-50128. 1976. 14.00. H. Fertig.

Eros' Revenge: The Brave New World of American Sex. Boye De Mente. LC 78-78307. (Phoenix Books original). 6.95 (ISBN 0-914778-21-8). Phoenix Books/Publishers.

Eros, Two Thousand A. D. H. R. Kaye, pseud. 176p. pap. 1.95 o.p. (6099). Brandon.

Erotic Anthology. Ed. by P. H. Porosky. LC 72-170336. (Signet book). 1972. 1.25. New American Library.

Erotic Comedies. Vassi. 1982. 16.95; pap. 8.98 (ISBN 0-531-07433-1). Watts.

Erotic Faculty. Odette Newman. LC 71-9891. (Traveller's companion series, TC-438). 1.75. Traveller's Companion, Inc.

Erotic Indian Tales from the Sanskrit Classic Suksaptati. Tr. by G. L. Mathur. 202p. 1971. pap. 2.00 o.p. (ISBN 0-88253-059-3). InterCulture.

Erotic Killer. Jack Matcha. (Orig.). pap. 0.95 o.p. (1138). Brandon.

Erotic Massage Parlor. Ted Hudson. 192p. (Orig.). 1973. pap. 1.95 o.p. (ISBN 0-87056-306-8, 6306). Brandon.

Erotic Spectacles. Genghis Cohen. 160p. (Orig.). 1971. pap. 1.95 o.s.i. (O*P*H265, Ophelia). Olympia.

Erotic Tool. Akbar Del Piombo. pap. 1.95 o.s.i. (OPS-25). Olympia.

Erotic Variations. John Barry. (Orig.). pap. 0.95 o.p. (1109). Brandon.

Erotica. Donna Ippolito & Adele Aldridge. LC 75-10058. (Illus.). 1975. pap. 5.95 (ISBN 0-8040-0752-7). Swallow.

Erotica Caper. Jay Martin. (Orig.). 1968. pap. 0.60 o.p. (73-753). Lancer.

Errand Girl: A Romance of New York Life. Evelyn Kimball Johnson. LC 7-10540. 1889. G. W. Dillingham.

Errant Heart: A Novel. Henriette Pascar. LC 50-14612. 1950. Island Press.

Errant Knight. Monica Mugan. (Signet book). 1.25. New American Library.

Errant Knights. John Harris. LC 68-24391. 1968. Harcourt, Brace & World.

Errant Wooing. Constance Cary Harrison. LC 7-2884. 1895. The Century Co.

Errata: Or, The Works of Will, Adams. A Tale. John Neal. LC 7-23109. 1823. For the Proprietors.

Erratic Flame. Ysabel De Teresa. LC 26-15190. The Macaulay Company.

Erring, Yet Noble. A Tale of and for Women... Isaac George Reed. LC 7-309503. 1865. J. Bradburn.

Erring Yet Noble. The Story of a Woman's Life... Isaac George Reed. LC 7-30949. T. B. Peterson & Brothers.

Error of Judgement. Henry Denker. (O.s.i.). 1979. 10.95 o.s.i. (ISBN 0-671-24130-3). S&S.

Error of Judgement. 1st American Ed. Pamela Hansford Johnson. LC 62-14469. 1962. Harcourt, Brace & World.

Error of Judgement. 1st Ed. Pamela Hansford Johnson. LC 62-51478. 1962. Macmillan.

Error of Judgment. Henry Denker. LC 78-21220. 9.95 (ISBN 0-671-24130-3). Simon and Schuster.

Error of Judgment. Stanley A. Wolpert. LC 70-99901. (Illus.). 1970. 6.95. Little, Brown.

Error of Sexton Jones. Robert Edward Gard. LC 64-24486. 1964. Duell, Sloan and Pearce.

Errors; or, The Rightful Master. A Novel. Sarah Franklin Davis Robertson. 1879. G. W. Carleton & Co.; Etc., Etc.

Erskine Dale: Pioneer. John Fox. LC 20-16857. 1920. C. Scribner's Sons.

Erudia, the Foreign Missionary to Our World: Or, The Dream of Orphanos. William Allen. LC 6-52. 1890. Publishing House of the M.E. Church, South.

Eruption. Paul Patchick. 480p. (Orig.). 1980. pap. 2.75 (ISBN 0-89083-614-0). Zebra.

Esarhaddon: And Other Tales. Lev Nikolaevich Tolstoi. LC 74-113688. (Short story index reprint series). 1970. Books for Libraries Press.

Esarhaddon & Other Tales. Lev Nikolaevich Tolstoi. (Short Story Index Reprint Ser.). 1903. 11.00 (ISBN 0-8369-3417-2). Ayer Co.

Esau & Jacob. Joaquim Maria Machado de Assis. Tr. by Helen Caldwell. 1965. 14.95 (ISBN 0-520-00788-3). U of Cal Pr.

Esau and Jacob. Tr. Introd. by Helen Caldwell. Joaquim Maria Machado De Assis. LC 65-19249. 5.00. Univ. of Calif. Pr.

Esau Hardery: A Novel of American Life. William Osborn Stoddard. LC 8-16303. 1881. White & Stokes.

Esau: Or, The Banker's Victim. Thomas Augustus Bland. LC 6-13840. 1892. Pub. by the Author.

ESBAE: A Winter's Tale. Linda Haldeman. 224p. (Orig.). 1981. pap. 2.50 (ISBN 0-380-78758-X, 78758). Avon.

Escalante: Wilderness Path. (American Explorers Ser.: No. 10). 336p. (Orig.). 1983. pap. 2.95 (ISBN 0-440-02402-1, Banbury). Dell.

Escapade. Regis Rivald. Tr. by Lowell Blair. 1971. pap. 0.95 o.p. (N2485). Pyramid Pubns.

Escapade. Evelyn Scott. LC 78-145285. 1971. (ISBN 0-403-01199-X). Scholarly Press.

Escapade. Evelyn Scott. LC 23-11263. 1923. T. Seltzer.

Escapade. Evelyn Scott. LC 29-30200. 1929. J. Cape and H. Smith.

Escapade: A Novel. Joan Smith. (Fawcett Crest Book). 1977. 1.50 (ISBN 0-449-23232-8). Fawcett Pubns.

Escapade of Roger Drew. Frank Dilnot. 1923. The Stratford Company.

Escapades of Condy Corrigan: An Amusing Series of Irish Fireside Stories by Cahir Healy. Cahir Healy. LC 10-2602. Society of the Divine Word.

Escape! Benjamin Bova. LC 70-98920. 1970. 3.50. Holt, Rinehart and Winston.

Escape. Alden Brooks. LC 24-10844. 1924. C. Scribner's Sons.

Escape. Royla Brown. LC 38-8833. 1938. E.P. Dutton & Co. Inc.

Escape! Gladys Moon Cook. LC 74-143472. 1971. 3.95. Moody Press.

Escape. Fritz Jordan. 1971. pap. 0.75 o.p. (07152). Curtis.

Escape... Philip MacDonald. LC 32-13054. Pub. for the Crime Club, Inc., by Doubleday, Doran & Company, Inc.

Escape. Jeffery Eardley Marston. LC 22-21567. 1922. T. Seltzer.

Escape. James Purvis & Bernard Lipman. 1979. pap. 1.95 (ISBN 0-532-19155-2). Woodhill.

Escape. James Purvis & Bernard Lipman. 1977. pap. 1.95 o.p. Woodhill.

Escape. James Purvis & Bernard Lipman. 1977. pap. 1.95 o.p. Manor Bks.

Escape. Grace Zaring Stone. LC 39-27762. 1939. Little, Brown, and Company.

Escape a Killer. Judson Pentecost Philips. LC 70-156861. (Red badge novel of suspense). 1971. 4.95 (ISBN 0-396-06313-6). Dodd, Mead.

Escape Artist. David Wagoner. 1982. pap. 2.50 (ISBN 0-345-29738-5, Ballantine Books). Ballantine.

Escape Artist: A Novel. David Wagoner. LC 65-13728. bds., 4.95. Farrar.

Escape Attempt. Arkadii Natanovich Strugatskii & Boris Natanovich Strugatskii. LC 82-29. (MacMillan's Best of Soviet Science Fiction). 14.95 (ISBN 0-02-615250-9). Macmillan.

Escape Attempt. Arkadii Natanovich Strugatskii & Boris Natanovich Strugatskii. Tr. by Roger DeGaris. 360p. 1982. 14.95 (ISBN 0-02-615250-9). Macmillan.

Escape from Anatolia. Panos N Panais. LC 40-9908. Fortuny's.

Escape from Death Row. Omar Fletcher. 1979. 1.95 (ISBN 0-87067-635-0). Holloway House.

Escape from Desire. Penny Jordan. (Harlequin Presents Ser.). 192p. 1983. pap. 1.75 (ISBN 0-373-10569-X). Harlequin Bks.

Escape from Devil's Island. Peter McCurtin. (Orig., Osi). 1971. pap. 0.75 o.s.i. (B75-2168). Belmont-Tower.

Escape from Eden. Catherine Lee Clay. LC 77-77112. 9.95 (ISBN 0-86533-005-0). Amber Crest Books.

Escape from Evil. Ernest Becker. LC 75-12059. 1975. 11.95 (ISBN 0-02-902300-9). Free Pr.

Escape from Five Shadows. Elmore Leonard. LC 55-119880. 1956. Houghton Mifflin.

Escape from Flint Corners. Ford Bowne, pseud. Ed. by Alice Sachs. 1970. 3.95 o.p. Lenox Hill.

Escape from Hell. Abas Korchari. 4.95 o.p. Vantage.

Escape from Hell. V. A Stuart. (Hazard series, 8) (ISBN 0-523-00895-3). Pinnacle Books.

Escape from Java. 1st Ed. Harvey Haislip. LC 62-7641. 1962. Doubleday.

Escape from Konigstein. LC 44-693519. 1944. C. Scribner's Sons.

Escape from Loneliness. Paul Tournier. LC 61-14599. 1976. pap. 6.95 (ISBN 0-664-24592-7). Westminster.

Escape from Love. Rosemary Frances Rees. LC 38-15217. 1937. Hillman-Curl, Inc.

Escape from Macho. John Cleve, pseud. LC 81-86031. (Spaceways Ser.: No. 3). 224p. (Orig.). 1982. pap. 2.50 (ISBN 0-86721-066-4). Playboy Pbks.

Escape from Mindanao. Lawrence Cortesi, pseud. 1978. pap. 1.75 o.s.i. (ISBN 0-8439-0584-0, Leisure Bks). Nordon Pubns.

Escape from New York. Mike McQuay. 192p. (Orig.). 1981. pap. 2.50 (ISBN 0-553-14914-8). Bantam.

Escape from Nowhere. Jeannette Eyerly. LC 69-11995. 1969. 3.95. Lippincott.

Escape from Paradise. Katharine Newlin Burt. LC 52-10736. 1952. Scribner.

Escape from Passion. Barbara Cartland. 1977. pap. 1.50 o.p. (ISBN 0-515-03995-0). BJ Pub Group.

Escape from Philistia. A Novel. Russell P Jacobus. LC 7-7424. J. G. Cupples Company.

Escape from Pimlico: A Novel, by Robert Standish Pseud. Digby George Gerahty. LC 55-976. 1955. Macmillan.

Escape from Rage. Marie Chapian. 1982. pap. 4.95 (Pub. by Logos). Bridge Pub.

Escape from Sonora. Will Bryant. LC 76-37031. 1973. 5.95 (ISBN 0-394-46995-X). Random House.

Escape from Sonora. Will Bryant. LC 76-37031. (Fawcett world library). 1974. (pbk.) 1.25. Fawcett.

Escape from the Icecap: A Tale of Huskie and Spareribs. Bertrand Leslie Shurtleff. LC 52-5819. (Illus.). 1952. Bobbs-Merril.

Escape from the Planet Karaxe. William B. Dunn. 1970. 3.75 o.p. Vantage.

Escape from the Planet of the Apes. Jerry Pournelle. (O.s.i.). 160p. (Orig.). 1974. pap. 0.95 o.s.i. (AN1240, Award). Univ Pub & Dist.

Escape from Vermont. James Melvin Stewart Gordon. LC 48-10683. 1948. H. Holt.

Escape from Youth. Edith Mendel Stern. LC 35-13560. Coward-McCann.

Escape in Vain. Georges Simenon & Gilbert, Stuart, Tr. LC 44-40031. 1944. Harcourt, Brace and Company.

Escape into Danger. Marguerite S Gaffney. LC 77-80973. 6.95 (ISBN 0-89343-019-6). Ermine Publishers.

Escape Machine. James McQueen. LC 81-4786. 1981. 16.95 (ISBN 0-7022-1591-0) (ISBN 0-7022-1592-9). University of Queensland Press.

Escape Me--Never. Gladys Skelton. LC 28-18291. 1928. D. Appleton & Company.

Escape of Mr. Trimm: His Plight and Other Plights. Irvin Shrewsbury Cobb. LC 13-22283. George H. Doran Company.

Escape of Socrates. Robert Pick. LC 53-9480. 1954. Knopf.

Escape of the Leopard. John Moffit. LC 73-11415. 1974. 5.95 (ISBN 0-15-129050-4). HarBraceJ.

Escape on Venus. Edgar Rice Burroughs. LC 63-21730. 1963. Canaveral Press.

Escape on Venus. Edgar Rice Burroughs. LC 46-8465. 1946. E. R. Burroughs, Inc.

Escape Orbit. James White. pap. 2.50 (ISBN 0-441-21590-4, Pub. by Ace Science Fiction). Ace Bks.

Escape Room. Airey Neave. 1982. pap. 2.50 (ISBN 0-89083-922-0). Zebra.

Escape the Night. Mignon Good Eberhart. LC 44-4878. 1944. Random House.

Escape the Night. Mignon Good Eberhart. LC 47-28536. (Bantam book, 46). 1946. Bantam Books.

Escape the Night. Mignon Good Eberhart. 1974. (pbk.) 0.95. Popular Library.

Escape the Thunder. William Laurence Coleman. 1944. E. P. Dutton & Co., Inc.

Escape to Adventure. Fran Priddy. (Orig.). 1979. pap. 1.95 (ISBN 0-532-23194-5). Woodhill.

Escape to Cairo. James Rives Childs. LC 38-5600. 1938. The Bobbs-Merrill Company.

Escape to China. Anna Lincoln. (Illus.). 271p. 1983. 10.95 (ISBN 0-87141-076-1). Manyland.

Escape to Ecstasy. Yvonne Gordon. Ed. by Gene DeRoin. (Aston Hall Presents Ser.). (Orig.). 1979. pap. 1.50 (ISBN 0-89936-001-7). Aston Hall.

Escape to Fort Bridger. John Earl Lewis. (YA) 1980. 6.95 (Avalon). Bouregy.

Escape to Happiness. Elisabeth Beresford. (Orig.). 1980. pap. 1.75 (ISBN 0-8439-8007-9, Tiara Bks). Nordon Pubns.
Escape to Life. Ferenc Kormendi. Tr. by Holt, Eugene I. LC 33-304434. 1933. W. Morrow & Company.
Escape to Love. Edward Sidney Aarons. 1970. pap. 0.75 o.p. (T2223, GM). Fawcett World.
Escape to Love. Anne Benson. LC 81-47251. (Anne Benson Ser.). 192p. (Orig.). 1981. pap. 1.95 (ISBN 0-87216-896-4). Playboy Pbks.
Escape to Love. Denise Robins. 1.50 (ISBN 0-380-00657-X). Avon.
Escape to Nowhere: By Ralph A. Jason Pseud. Maurits Ignatius Boas. LC 54-8366. 1954. Vantage Press.
Escape to Romance. Pamela Nichols & Teri Lester. Bd. with Everything But Love. 1982. pap. 2.50 (ISBN 0-451-11879-0, AE1879, Sig). NAL.
Escape to the Andes: A Novel. Rupert Croft-Cooke. LC 38-134003. J. Messner, Inc.
Escape to the Gunflint. James R Sherman, pseud. LC 82-82206. (Illus.). 3.95 (ISBN 0-935538-04-6). Pathway Books.
Escape to the Gunflint. James R. Sherman, pseud. (Illus.). 175p. (Orig.). 1982. pap. 3.95 (ISBN 0-935538-03-8). Pathway Bks.
Escape to the Hills. James Wittenmeyer Chapman & Chapman, Ethel R., Joint Author. LC 47-11603. 1947. J. Cattell Press.
Escape to the Inner Earth. Raymond Bernard. 1974. pap. 4.95. G Barker Bks.
Escape to the Land. 1st Ed. Melvin Ned Holland. LC 56-12314. 1957. Vantage Press.
Escape to Tomorrow. George Alec Effinger. (Planet of the Apes#2). 1975. (pbk.) 0.95. Award Books.
Escape to Victory. Yabo Yablonsky. 224p. (Orig.). 1981. pap. 2.25 (ISBN 0-553-20124-7). Bantam.
Escape While I Can. Melba Balmat Grimes Marlett. LC 44-513263. 1944. Pub. for the Crime Club by Doubleday, Doran and Company, Inc.
Escaped Cock. David Herbert Lawrence. Ed. by Gerald M. Lacy. LC 73-12739. 1973. 10.00 (ISBN 0-87685-171-5) (ISBN 0-87685-171-5). Black Sparrow Press.
Escaped Cock. David Herbert Lawrence. LC 30-14395. Black Sun Press.
Escaped from Sing Sing. John A Fraser. LC 6-43149. (Globe detective series. no. 7). 1888. The Eagle Publishing Co.
Eschatus: Nostradamus' Prophecies of Our Future. Bruce Pennington. (O.s.i.). (Illus.). 1978. 19.95 o.s.i. (ISBN 0-671-22911-7); pap. 8.95 o.s.i. (ISBN 0-671-22933-8). S&S.
Esclava de Su Sexo. Jacinto Lopez. (Pimienta Collection Ser). (Span.). 1977. pap. 1.00 (ISBN 0-88473-262-2). Fiesta Pub.
Escritoire of Yolande. Intro. by S. George. pap. 1.95 o.p. (6027). Brandon.
Eshek the Oppressor. Gertrude Potter Daniels. LC 2-27734. 1902. Rand, McNally & Company.
Eskimo. Peter Freuchen & Branden, Albrecht Paul Maerker. 1931. H. Liveright.
Esme. Dirk Wittenborn. 1983. 15.95 (ISBN 0-440-02138-3, Sey Lawr). Delacorte.
Esmeralda: Or, Every Little Bit Helps. Nina Wilcox Putnam & Jacobsen, Norman. LC 18-21825. 1918. J. B. Lippincott Company.
Esme's Sons. Agnes Russell Weeks. LC 30-29826. Dodd, Mead & Co.
Esmond. Una Troy. LC 62-7820. 1962. Dutton.
Esmond in India: A Novel. 1st Ed. Ruth Prawer Jhabvala. LC 58-10476. 1958. W. W. Norton.
Especially at Christmas. Celestine Sibley. LC 76-78672. (Illus.). 1969. 2.95. Doubleday.
Especially for You. Walter J. Sepaniac. 1974. 3.50 o.s.i. (ISBN 0-8181-0337-X). Pageant-Poseidon.
Especially When They Drink. 1st Ed. William J Harl. LC 56-12779. 1957. Vantage Press.
Espejo - the Mirror: Selected Chicano Literature. Ed. by Octavio I. Romano-V & Herminio Rios. 284p. 1972. 6.75 o.p. (ISBN 0-88412-055-4); pap. 3.75 o.p. (ISBN 0-88412-054-6). Tonatiuh-Quinto Sol Intl.
Esper Transfer. George W. Proctor. 1978. pap. 1.50 (ISBN 0-89041-204-9, 3204). Major Bks.
Esperance. Margaret Oliver Woods Lawrence. LC 7-13230. 1865. Sheldon and Company.
Esperanza. Susan L Valerga. LC 11-31636. Press of Brown & Power Stationery Co.
Esperie. Frederic Bradlee. LC 67-11449. 1967. Houghton Mifflin.
Espers. Steven M. Souza. Ed. by Alice Sachs. 192p. (OSI). 1972. 3.95 o.s.i. Lenox Hill.
Espeshilly Lem: A Tale of a Lonesome Heart. Harrie Victor Schieren. LC 25-25122. McDevitt-Wilson's.
Espesor Del Pellejo De un Gato Ya Cadaver. Celedonio Gonzalez. LC 77-88536. 1978. pap. 5.00 (ISBN 0-89729-170-0). Ediciones.
Espionage & Sex. Ted Hudson. 192p. (Orig.). 1973. pap. 1.95 o.p. (ISBN 0-87682-339-8, 7339). Barclay Hse.
Espionage Double Book. Paul Richards. (Hot Line Ser.). (O.s.i.). 320p. 1975. pap. 1.50 o.s.i. (AD1491, Award). Univ Pub & Dist.
Espiritista. H. Wendey Joy. 192p. 1982. pap. 10.00 (Pub. by New Day Philippines). Cellar.
Espiritu Santo: A Novel. Henrietta Channing Dana Skinner. LC 99-848. 1899. Harper & Brothers.
Esprit De Corps. Lawrence Durrell. Bd. with Stiff Upper Lip. pap. 1.95 o.p. (ISBN 0-525-47078-6). Dutton.
Essays & Fiction. George Robert Gissing. Ed. by Pierre Coustillas. LC 78-100702. (Illus.). 1970. 8.50. Johns Hopkins Press.
Essays and Soliloquies: Translated from the Spanish with an Introductory Essay. Unamuno y Jugo, Miguel De & Flitch, John Ernest Crawford, Tr. LC 25-9001. 1925. A. A. Knopf.
Essays, Lovecraftian. Darrell Schweitzer. LC 80-19213. 1980. 9.95 (ISBN 0-89370-096-7). Borgo Press.
Essence of Honeymoon. Harry Perry Robinson. LC 11-10952. 1911. Harper & Brothers.
Essence of Life. Minnie Merochnik. LC 56-42788. (Arrowhead Press book). 1956. Storm Publishers.
Essential Dracula. Bram Stoker & Raymond T. McNally. LC 79-2413. 1979. 9.98 (ISBN 0-8317-2993-7). Mayflower Books.
Essential Dreams. Charley Langfur. LC 81-82776. 52p. 1981. 8.50 (ISBN 0-941566-01-3); pap. text ed. 5.00 (ISBN 0-941566-00-5). Sky Pubns NJ.
Essential Fly Tier. J. Edson Leonard. 262p. 1982. pap. 11.95 (ISBN 0-13-286112-7). P-H.
Essential Man. Al Morgan. 1977. 8.95 o.p. (ISBN 0-671-16973-4, Dist. by S&S). Playboy.
Essential Man: A Novel. Albert Morgan. LC 77-14925. 8.95 (ISBN 0-671-16973-4). Playboy Press.
Essential Thing. Arthur Hodges. LC 12-4136. 1912. 1.60. Dodd, Mead and Company.
Establishment. Howard Melvin Fast. LC 79-1186. (Illus.). 1979. 10.95 (ISBN 0-395-28160-1). Houghton Mifflin.
Establishment. Howard Melvin Fast. LC 79-21328. (Illus.). 1979. 16.95 (ISBN 0-8161-3003-5). G. K. Hall.
Establishment. Robin Moore, pseud. 1977. pap. 1.95 (ISBN 0-532-19139-0). Woodhill.
Establishment of Innocence. Harvey Aronson & Mike McGrady. LC 75-21938. 8.95 (ISBN 0-399-11540-4). Putnam.
Establishment of Innocence. Harvey Aronson & Mike McGrady. (Berkely Medallion Book). 1977. 1.95 (ISBN 0-425-03288-4). Berkley Pub. Corp.: Distributed by Putnam.
Establishment of Madame Antonia. Edith Gyorgy. LC 32-666133. Liveright, Inc.
Estadistica Para Ciencias e Incenieria. 2nd ed. John B. Kennedy. Ed. by Adam M. Neville. 560p. (Span.). 1982. pap. text ed. write for info. (ISBN 0-06-314490-5, Pub. by HarLA Mexico). Har-Row.
Estampas Puertorriquenas; un Libro Bilinqe, Cuentos En Espanol y En Ingles: Stories in Spanish and English for All Ages. Jose Padin. LC 67-26941. 1967.
Estate. Isaac Bashevis Singer. LC 73-88782. 1969. 6.95. Farrar, Straus and Giroux.
Estate of Grace. James Powers. LC 78-22445. 8.95 (ISBN 0-06-013452-6). Harper & Row.
Estate of Memory. Ilona Karmel. LC 69-12503. 1969. 6.95 o.p. (ISBN 0-395-07840-7). HM.
Estate of Memory: A Novel. Ilona Karmel. LC 69-12503. 1969. 6.95. Houghton Mifflin.
Estate of the Beckoning Lady. Margery Allingham. 1975. (pbk.) 0.95. Manor Books.
Estate of the Beckoning Lady. Margery Allingham. LC 55-5587. 1955. Doubleday.
Estella's Husband: Or, Thrice Lost, Thrice Won. May Agnes Early Fleming. LC 6-41675. (On cover: The library of American authors. no. 34). 1891. G. Munro.
Estelle. A Novel. Annie Edwards. 1874. Sheldon and Company.
Estelle Grant: Or, The Lost Wife... LC 6-38144. 1855. Garrett & Co.
Ester: The Story of a Small Ghost. Ruth Lynn. LC 81-69693. (Illus.). 12.95 (ISBN 0-941674-00-2). Woodcock Press.
Estevan: A Story of the Spanish Conquests. John Roy Musick. LC 7-33330. (On cover: Columbian historicals novels v. 2). 1892. Funk & Wagnalls Company.
Esther. Agnes Eliza Jacomb. LC 12-24204. 1911. H. Ober.
Esther. Norah Robinson Lofts. LC 50-10143. 1950. Macmillan.
Esther. M. A. MacDonald. 1887. Reformed Episcopal Publication Society (Limited.
Esther. Nathaniel Norsen Weinreb. LC 55-9996. 1955. Doubleday.
Esther: A Book for Girls. Rosa Nouchette Carey. 1887. J. B. Lippincott Company.
Esther: A Novel. Henry Adams & Spiller, Robert Ernest, 1896- LC 38-18393. (Scholars facsimiles & reprints). 1938. Scholars' Facsimiles & Reprints.
Esther: A Sequel to Ben-Hur; or, The Lost Epistles of the First and Second Centuries, and the Lost Records of the Great International Camp Meeting, Held at Alexandrea Troas, in Asia Minor, A.D. 80, in the Reign of the Emperor Titus. J. O. A Clark. 1892. Publishing House of the M.E. Church, South.
Esther Damon. Cora Miranda Baggerly Older. LC 11-14712. 1911. 1.25. C. Scribner's Sons.
Esther De Warren: The Story of a Mid-Victorian Maiden. Marshall Saunders. LC 27-18961. George H. Doran Company.
Esther Pennefather. A Novel. Alice Perry. (On cover: Library of American fiction. no. 1). 1878. Harper & Brothers.
Esther the Gentile. Mary Worrell Smith Hudson. LC 7-116827. 1888. G. W. Crane & Co., Printers.
Esther Vanhomrigh. Margaret Louisa Bradley Woods. LC 8-37530. J. W. Lovell Company.
Esther-Vashti. Laurel Boardman. 1944. The Harvard Press.
Esther Waters. rev. and enl. ed. George Moore. LC 45-32981. 1899. H. S. Stone and Company.
Esther Waters: A Novel. George Moore. LC 64-9787. (Riverside editions, B80). Houghton Mifflin.
Esther Waters: A Novel. rev. and enl. ed. George Moore. LC 4-30951. 1901. H. S. Stone and Company.
Esther Waters. A Novel. George Moore. LC 26-223045. 1917. Brentano's.
Esther Waters: An English Story. George Moore. LC 32-17147. (The black and gold library). Liveright, Inc.
Esther Waters: Novel Introd. by Malcolm Brown. George Moore. LC 59-24417. (Norton library, N6). 1958. Norton.
Esther's Altar: A Novel. Paul Smith. LC 59-11838. 1960. Abelard-Schuman.
Esty Family. Sara E Hervey. 1889. Published by the Author.
Et Al: A Collection of Short Stories. Gary Peterson. 64p. 1982. 5.00 (ISBN 0-682-49833-5). Exposition.
Etched in Moonlight. James Stephens. 1928. The Macmillan Company.
Etchingham Letters. Frederick Pollock & Maitland, Ella Fuller. LC 99-5722. 1899. Dodd, Mead & Company.
Etelka's Vow: A Novel. Dorothea Gerard Longard De Longgarde. (On cover: Appletons' town and country library. no. 98). 1892. D. Appleton and Company.
Eteocles: a Tale of Antioch. Jessie Agnes Andrews. LC 6-2458. 1889. A. D. F. Randolph and Co.
Eternal Boy: Being the Story of the Prodigious Hickey. Owen McMahon Johnson. LC 9-2772. 1909. Dodd, Mead & Company.
Eternal Call. A. Ivanov. 770p. 1978. 9.95 (ISBN 0-8285-1568-9, Pub. by Progress Pubns USSR). Imported Pubns.
Eternal Champion: A Fantastic Romance. Michael Moorcock. LC 77-3797. 8.95 (ISBN 0-06-013014-8). Harper & Row.
Eternal Circle. Jay William Hudson. LC 25-212601. 1925. D. Appleton and Company.
Eternal City. Hall Caine. LC 1-20945. 1901. D. Appleton and Company.
Eternal City. theatre ed. Hall Caine. LC 2-249303. 1902. D. Appleton and Company.
Eternal City. Hall Caine. LC 16-6830. 1916. D. Appleton and Company.
Eternal Compromise. Mona Naomi Anne Hocking Messer. LC 32-5867. 1932. G. P. Putnam's Sons.
Eternal Conflict. David Henry Keller. LC 50-7068. 1949. Prime Press.
Eternal Covenant. Aletha Burgess. LC 42-17630. 1942. Wm. B. Eermans Publishing Co.
Eternal Curse on the Reader of These Pages. Manuel Puig. LC 81-51034. 13.50 (ISBN 0-394-52151-X). Random House.
Eternal Curse on the Reader of These Pages. Manuel Puig. LC 82-40431. 240p. 1983. pap. 3.95 (ISBN 0-394-71384-2, Vin). Random.
Eternal Deeps. Sara Ware Bassett. LC 36-15267. 1936. Doubleday, Doran & Company, Inc.
Eternal Deeps. Sara Ware Bassett. LC 37-38314. 1937. The Sun Dial Press, Inc.
Eternal Destinies. Charles Harold Rogers. LC 37-39121.
Eternal Dream. Leonardas Andriekus. 1980. 6.00 (ISBN 0-87141-061-3). Manyland.
Eternal Dream: Selected Poems. Leonardas Andriekus & Jonas Zdanys. LC 77-72585. 6.00 (ISBN 0-87141-061-3). Manyland Books.
Eternal Feminine: And Other Stories. Mary Raymond Shipman Andrews. LC 16-22256. 1916. C. Scribner's Sons.
Eternal Fire. Poul Hoffmann. LC 62-8204. 1962. Muhlenberg Press.
Eternal Fire. Calder Willingham. LC 63-7498. 1963. Vanguard Press.
Eternal Fire. Calder Willingham. 1974. (pbk.) 1.75. Dell.
Eternal Fires. Nancy Musselman Schoonmaker. LC 10-10576. 1.50. Broadway Publishing Company.
Eternal Fires: A Novel. Vivian Cory. LC 10-79503. M. Kennerley.
Eternal Flame: A Novelette. Edwin Carlile Litsey. LC 38-8334. 1937. The Standard Printing Company, Incorporated.
Eternal Flight. Lotte Lehmann & Krauch, Elsa, Tr. LC 37-35649. G. P. Putnam's Sons.
Eternal Forest Under Western Skies. George Stanley Godwin. LC 29-117496. 1929. D. Appleton & Company.
Eternal Frontiers. James H. Schmitz. LC 72-87627. 1973. 5.95 (ISBN 0-399-11073-9). Putnam.
Eternal Heritage. Margaret Jessup Van Briggle. LC 55-14598. 1955. Beacon Hill Press.
Eternal Huntress. Rayner Seelig. LC 24-32087. 1924. A. A. Knopf.
Eternal Husband see Three Short Novels of Dostoyevsky.
Eternal Husband: And Other Stories. Fedor Mikhailovich Dostoevskii & Garnett, Mrs. Constance (Black) 1862- Tr. LC 17-170806. (Half-title: The novels of Fyodor Dostoevsky. vol. VIII). 1917. The Macmillan Company.
Eternal Husband and Other Stories. Fedor Mikhailovich Dostoevskii & Garnett, Mrs. Constance (Black) 1862- Tr. LC 32-31875. (Half-title: The novels of Fyodor Dostoevsky. vol. VIII). 1932. The Macmillan Company.
Eternal Life: A Novel. Donald Newlove. LC 79-51730. (Illus.). 4.95 (ISBN 0-380-46458-6). Avon Books.
Eternal Lover. Edgar Rice Burroughs. LC 25-194371. 1925. A. C. McClurg & Co.
Eternal Magdalene. Robert H McLaughlin. LC 16-377. George H. Doran Company.
Eternal Masculine: Stories of Men and Boys. Andrews, Mary Raymond Shipman. LC 13-22209. 1913. C. Scribner's Sons.
Eternal Moment, and Other Stories. Edward Morgan Forster. LC 64-25972. (Universal library, UL 172). 1964. Grosset & Dunlap.
Eternal Moment: And Other Stories. Edward Morgan Forster. LC 76-19262. (Harvest book, HB 180). 1970. 1.85. Harcourt Brace Jovanovich.
Eternal Moment, and Other Stories. Edward Morgan Forster. LC 28-11816. Harcourt, Brace & Company.
Eternal Mountain. Alice Lent Covert. LC 44-5269. 1944. Doubleday, Doran & Co., Inc.
Eternal Priestess: A Novel of China Manners. Bertram Lenox Simpson. LC 14-17922. 1914. Dodd, Mead and Company.
Eternal Quest. Telesphore Boucher De Montville. LC 17-4197. The Roxburgh Publishing Company, Inc.
Eternal Quest. David Ferdinand Nygren. LC 38-442655. Zondervan Publishing House.
Eternal Quest. John Alexander Steuart. LC 1-5445. 1901. Dodd, Mead & Company.
Eternal Rectangle of Race. E. W. Leatherman.. 4.50 o.p. Vantage.
Eternal Reich. Jerome M. Knopp. (Orig.). 1981. pap. 1.95 (ISBN 0-505-51684-5). Tower Bks.
Eternal Rose: A Story Without a Beginning or an End. Melville Chater. LC 10-209022. 1.00. Etc. Fleming H. Revell Company.
Eternal Savage. Edgar Rice Burroughs. 1982. pap. 2.25 (ISBN 0-441-21806-7). Ace Bks.
Eternal Smile. Par Lagerkvist. Tr. by Erik Mesterton & David O'Gorman. LC 78-145810. (Cloth ed. 5.95 o.p.). 206p. 1971. pap. 5.95 o.p. (ISBN 0-8090-1358-4). Hill & Wang.
Eternal Smile, and Other Stories: Translated by Alan Blair and Others. Par Fabian Lagerkvist. LC 53-5017. 1954. Random House.
Eternal Smile, Three Stories. Par Fabian Lagerkvist. LC 78-145810. 1971. 5.95 (ISBN 0-8090-4309-2). Hill and Wang.
Eternal Spring: A Novel. Neith Boyce. LC 6-3511. 1906. Fox, Duffield & Company.
Eternal Time. Nevzat Karsak. 3.75 o.p. Vantage.
Eternal Tomorrow. Ursula Bloom. LC 29-16917. 1929. G. H. Watt.
Eternal Trio. Stephen Cupchalk. 3.50 o.p. Carlton.
Eternal Voyagers. Robert F Mirvish. LC 53-7673. 1953. Sloane.
Eternity. Harry Jasper Harris. LC 15-1888. 1914. 0.25. Royce-Clark Printing Co.
Eternity Brigade. Stephen Goldin. 256p. (Orig.). 1982. pap. 2.50 (ISBN 0-449-14336-8, GM). Fawcett.
Eternity in Their Heart. Lon Riley Woodrum. LC 55-135298. 1955. Zondervan Pub. House.
Eternity Ring. Patricia Wentworth. LC 48-6429. (Main line mysteries). 1948. J. B. Lippincott Co.
Eternity Stone. Aden F. Romine & Mary C. Romine. 336p. (Orig.). 1981. pap. 2.50 (ISBN 0-505-51742-6). Tower Bks.
Ethan Bowles, Dirty Old Man. Michael Jerome. 160p. (Orig.). 1972. pap. 1.95 o.s.i. (OPS6160). Olympia.

Ethan Brand: A Chapter from an Abortive Romance. Nathaniel Hawthorne & Holmes, Oliver Wendell, 1809-1894. Houghton, Mifflin & Co.

Ethan Brand: Or, The Unpardonable Sin. Nathaniel Hawthorne. LC 9-2682. (On cover: Arundel series). The Arundel Print.

Ethan Frome. Edith Newbold Jones Wharton. LC 63-6738. Scribner.

Ethan Frome. Edith Newbold Jones Wharton. LC 11-25015. 1911. C. Scribner's Sons.

Ethan Frome. Edith Newbold Jones Wharton. LC 21-4132. 1919. C. Scribner's Sons.

Ethan Frome. Edith Newbold Jones Wharton. (modern student's library). C. Scribner's Sons.

Ethan Frome. Edith Newbold Jones Wharton. LC 34-1838. 1931. C. Scribner's Sons.

Ethan Frome. Edith Newbold Jones Wharton. LC 36-36227. 1936. C. Scribner's Sons.

Ethan Frome. Edith Newbold Jones Wharton & De Voto, Bernard Augustine, 1897- LC 38-9978. 1938. C. Scribner's Sons.

Ethan Frome. Edith Newbold Jones Wharton & Poor, Henry Varnum, 1888- Illus. LC 39-4553. 1939. Printed for Members of the Limited Editions Club.

Ethan Frome see Three Great American Novels.

Ethan Frome. Foreword and Study Guide by Helen T. Munn. Edith Newbold Jones Wharton. (Scribner sch. paperbacks, SSP10). 1968. pap., 1.44. Scribners.

Ethan Frome. Introd. by Mrs. Wharton. Edith Newbold Jones Wharton. (Keith Jennison bk., large type ed.). 1965. 6.95, 4.95 lib. ed.,. Watts.

Ethan Frome. The Story, with Sources and Commentary. Edith Newbold Jones Wharton. Ed. by Blake Nevius. LC 68-13290. (Scribner research anthologies). 1968. Scribner.

Ethan Frome. With a Foreword and a Study Guide by Helen T. Munn. Edith Newbold Jones Wharton. LC 60-209555. 1960. Scribner.

Ethan Quest: His Saga. Harry Hervey. LC 25-9753. 1925. Cosmopolitan Book Corporation.

Ethe Innocents: A Novel, by Henry Kitchell Webster. Henry Kitchell Webster. LC 24-22461. The Bobbs-Merrill Company.

Ethel Ernestine. Hattie Bassett. LC 24-22124. 1924. H. Bassett.

Ethel Hamilton: Or, Lights and Shadows of the War of Independence Also Life Pictures. Anna Theresa Sadlier. LC 8-1369. 1877. D. & J. Sadlier & Co.

Ethel Holbrook: Or, The Mysterious Clue. Charles Manoah Delling. LC 99-2712.

Ethel Mildmay's Follies. A Story. Katharine King. (On cover: Seaside library. Pocket ed. no. 786). 1886. G. Munro.

Ethel Opens the Door: An Exploit of the Shadowers, Inc. Isabel Egenton Ostrander. LC 22-1719. 1922. R. M. McBride & Company.

Ethel Somers: Or The Fate of the Union. James M Smythe. LC 8-10192. 1857. H. D. Norrell.

Ethel Vale, the White Slave. Guy Fitch Phelps. LC 10-20181. The Christian Witness Co.

Ethel Wright: Or, Only a Music Teacher. Minnie Lahr Corwin. LC 9-27258. 1909. 1.00. Cochrane Publishing Co.

Ethelind. Clara E. Ballou. LC 6-6000. J. S. Ogilvie & Company.

Ethelind. Clara E. Ballou. LC 99-464. (Criterion library, no. 37). Dike Book Company.

Ethel's Perplexity. F. W Leggett. LC 7-12592. (On cover: Satchel series. no. 31). W. B. Smith & Co.

Ethel's Triumph: From Fifteen to Twenty-Five. Mary Andrews Denison. LC 6-33996. Bradley & Woodruff.

Ethelyn's Mistake; or, The Home in the West: A Novel. Mary Jane Hawes Holmes. LC 5431. (On cover:Madison square library. No. 62). 1897. G. W. Dillingham Co.

Ether and Me: Or "Just Relax.". Will Rogers. LC 73-79456. (Writings of Will Rogers, I, 1). (Illus.). 1973. 6.50. Oklahoma State University Press.

Ethiopia, the Land of Promise: A Book with a Purpose. Charles Henry Holmes. LC 75-158224. 1973. 5.50 (ISBN 0-404-00133-5). AMS Press.

Ethiopia, the Land of Promise: A Book with a Purpose. Charles Henry Holmes. LC 17-242834. 1917. The Cosmopolitan Press.

Ethiopian... Clarence L Blakely. LC 32-2464. 1931. Independence Pub. Co.

Ethiopian Romance. Heliodorus of Emesa. Tr. by Moses Hadas. LC 76-28171. 1976. Repr. of 1957 ed. lib. bdg. 20.50x (ISBN 0-8371-9085-1, HEER). Greenwood.

Ethiopian Story. Heliodorus of Emesa. Tr. by Walter Lamb. 1961. 3.95x o.p. (ISBN 0-460-00276-7, Evman). Dutton.

Ethne: Being a Truthful Historie of the Great and Final Settlement of Ireland by Oliver Cromwell, and Certain Other Noteworthy Events, from the Records of Ethne O'Conner and of Roger Standfast, Captain in the Army of the Commons of England. Louise Frances Field. LC 6-41200. W. Gardner, Darton & Co.

Etidorhpa; or, The End of Earth. The Strange History of a Mysterious Being and the Account of a Remarkable Journey As Communicated in Manuscript to Llewellyn Drury Who Promised to Print the Same, but Finally Evaded the Responsibility, Which Was Assumed. author's ed., limited. ed. John Uri Lloyd. LC 9-2488. J. U. Lloyd.

Etidorhpa; or, The End of Earth. The Strange History of a Mysterious Being and the Account of a Remarkable Journey As Communicated in Manuscript to Llewellyn Drury Who Promised to Print the Same, but Finally Evaded the Responsibility Which Was Assumed. 2d ed. John Uri Lloyd. LC 7-19398. The Robert Clarke Company.

Etidorhpa; or, The End of Earth: The Strange History of a Mysterious Being and the Account of a Remarkable Journey. 11th ed., rev. and enl. ed. John Uri Lloyd. LC 1-31751. 1901. Dodd, Mead & Company.

Etienne Mayran. Hippolyte Adolphe Taine & Henry, Blossom Lids, Ed. LC 31-7167. 1931. Prentice-Hall, Inc.

Etna Vandemir: A Romance of Kentucky and "the Great Uprising". Sallie J Hancock. 1863. Cutter, Tower & Co.

Eto- Ya- Edichka. Edward Limonov. 280p. (Orig., Rus.). pap. 6.95 o.p. (ISBN 0-934692-00-9). Index Pubs.

Etowah. A Romance of the Confederacy. Francis Fontaine. LC 37-21876. 1887. F. Fontaine.

Etranger. A. Camus. 1955. pap. 6.95 o.p. (ISBN 0-13-530790-2). P-H.

Etranger. A. Camus. 1955. pap. 6.95 o.p. (ISBN 0-13-530790-2). P-H.

Etranger. Albert Camus. (Coll. Blanche). 1942. 7.50; pap. 3.95. French & Eur.

Etruscan. Mika Toimi Waltari. LC 56-13140. 1956. Putnam.

Etruscan Bull. Frank Gruber. LC 69-13345. 1969. 4.50. Dutton.

Etruscan Smile: A Novel of Suspense. Velda Johnston. LC 77-3727. 7.95 (ISBN 0-396-07421-9). Dodd, Mead.

Etta at Night. LC 78-161896. 1971. 0.95. Playboy Press.

Ettore Fieramosca: Or The Challenge of Barletta, an Historical Romance of the Times of the Medici. Massimo Tapparelli Azeglio. Tr. by Lester, Charles Edwards. LC 6-3853. (On cover: The Medici series of Italian prose. no. 1). 1845. Paine & Burgess.

Etudes. Maurits Ignatius Boas. LC 80-70949. 1981. 9.95 (ISBN 0-8119-0344-3). F. Fell.

Etwas Neues. Ed. by Ernest Raymond Dodge & Viereck, Margaret H. LC 36-3835. American Book Company.

Eudocia (a Comedy Royal) Eden Phillpotts. LC 21-180942. 1921. The Macmillan Company.

Eudora's Men. Mabel Osgood Wright. LC 31-257679. 1931. The Macmillan Company.

Eugen Aram. A Tale. Edward George Earle Lytton Bulwer-Lytton Lytton. LC 4-15321. (Half-title: Novels of Sir Edward Bulwer Lytton. Library ed. Romances, vol. I). 1893. Little, Brown, and Company.

Eugen Daubigny. G. P Hardin. LC 77-9019. 1969. 6.95. Pageant Press International Corp.

Eugene Aram. A Novel. Edward George Earle Lytton Bulwer-Lytton Lytton. LC 41-35142. J. B. Smith & Co.

Eugene Aram. A Tale. Edward George Earle Lytton Bulwer-Lytton Lytton & Aram, Eugene, 1704-1759--Fiction. LC 42-26815. (On cover: Library of select novels. No. XIX-XX). 1832. J. & J. Harper.

Eugene Aram: A Tale. Edward George Earle Lytton Bulwer-Lytton Lytton. LC 9-15661. 1851. G. Routledge and Sons.

Eugene Aram: A Tale. library ed. Edward George Earle Lytton Bulwer-Lytton Lytton. LC 7-8346. (Half-title: Novels of Sir Edward Bulwer Lytton. Library ed. Romances. Vol. XXII-XXIII). 1862. J. B. Lippincott & Co.

Eugene Aram: A Tale. Edward George Earle Lytton Bulwer-Lytton Lytton. LC 7-83452. (On cover: Lovell's library, v. 5, no. 204). J. W. Lovell Company.

Eugene Aram... And Zanoni. caxton ed. Edward George Earle Lytton Bulwer-Lytton Lytton. LC 8-7703. G. Routledge and Sons.

Eugene Norton: A Tale of the Sagebrush Land. Anne Shannon Monroe. Rand, McNally & Company.

Eugene Onegin. Aleksandr Sergeevich Pushkin. Tr. by Charles Hepburn Johnston. LC 80-511119. (Penguin classics). 1979. 3.95 (ISBN 0-14-044394-0). Penguin.

Eugene Onegin: A Novel in Verse. Aleksandr Sergeevich Pushkin. Tr. by Vladimir Nabokov from Russ. LC 80-8730. (Bollingen Ser.: Vol. LXXII). 1460p. 1981. Set Of 4 Vols. 100.00x (ISBN 0-691-09744-5); Set Of 2 Vols. pap. 19.50 (ISBN 0-691-01837-5). Princeton U Pr.

Eugene Onegin: A Novel in Verse: the Bollingen Prize Translation in the Onegin Stanza, Extensively Revised. 2nd ed., rev. ed. Aleksandr Sergeevich Pushkin. Tr. by Walter W. Arndt. LC 79-50763. 6.25 (ISBN 0-525-47591-5). E.P. Dutton.

Eugenia. Clare Darcy. LC 76-39591. 8.95 (ISBN 0-8027-0556-1). Walker.

Eugenia. Clare Darcy. LC 77-29205. 1978. 10.95 (ISBN 0-8161-6576-9). G. K. Hall.

Eugenia, a Friend's Victim: A Tale of Italy. Walter Palmer Hoxie. LC 7-5668. (elite library. no. 2). The Welles Publishing Company.

Eugenia's Embrace. Cassie Edwards. (Orig.). 1982. pap. 3.25 (ISBN 0-89083-952-2). Zebra.

Eugenie. Beatrice May Butt. LC 41-27424. (Leisure hour series). 1877. H. Holt and Company.

Eugenie: A Novel. 1st Ed. Hester W Chapman. LC 61-12815. 1961. Little, Brown.

Eugenie Grandet. Honore De Balzac. Tr. by Katharine Prescott Wormeley. LC 3-23176. (Half-title: The comedy of human life... Scenes from provincial life). 1889. Roberts Brothers.

Eugenie Grandet. Honore De Balzac. Tr. by Ellen Marriage. LC 4-18467. (Half-title:... Comedie humaine...). 1901. J. M. Dent and Co.

Eugenie Grandet. Honore De Balzac. Tr. by Ellen Marriage. Saintsbury, George Edward Bateman, 1845-1933. (Half-title: Everyman's library, ed. by Ernest Rhys. Fiction. no. 169). 1907. J. M. Dent & Co.

Eugenie Grandet. Honore De Balzac. Tr. by Ellen Marriage. LC 36-37081. (Half-title: Everyman's library, ed. by Ernest Rhys. Fiction. no. 169). 1930. J. M. Dent & Sons, Ltd.

Eugenie Grandet. Honore De Balzac & Wormeley, Katharine Prescott, 1830-1908, Tr. 1932. The Book League of America.

Eugenie Grandet. rev. ed. H. De Balzac. (Fr). 1925. 4.55 o.p. (ISBN 0-03-014925-8). HR&W.

Eugenie Grandet. Honore De Balzac. Ed. by Castex. (Coll. Prestige). 27.95. French & Eur.

Eugenie Grandet. Honore De Balzac. Ed. by Gilbert Quenelle. (Illus., Fr.). 1967. 3.25x o.p. St Martin.

Eugenie Grandet. Honore De Balzac. Ed. by H. J. Hunt. 1967. 3.50x o.p. Oxford U Pr.

Eugenie Grandet. A Novel. from the french of honore de balzac. ed. Honore De Balzac. LC 6-6304. (Choice series, no. 37). 1891. R. Bonner's Sons.

Eugenie Grandet and The Cure of Tours. Honore De Balzac. LC 64-1446. (Riverside editions) "c72."). 1964. Houghton Mifflin.

Eugenie Grandet. Ed. by Gilbert Quenelle. Honore De Balzac. Ed. by Gilbert Quenelle. LC 67-152898. (Macmillan's modern lang. texts). 1967. bds., 2.50. Macmillan.

Eugenie Grandet: Or, The Miser's Daughter. From the French of. Honore De Balzac. Tr. by Orlando Williams Wight. Goodrich, Frank Boott, 1826-1894, Tr. LC 6-6300. (Half-title: Novels of M. Honore de Balzac. Library ed., v. 4). 1861. Rudd & Carleton.

Eugenie Grandet. Pierrette... Honore De Balzac. Tr. by Katharine Prescott Wormeley. LC 26-269813. (Half-title: The works of Balzac. Centenary ed. vol. vii). Little, Brown, and Company.

Eugenie Grandet, The Country Parson, and Other Stories. Honore De Balzac. Tr. by Ellen Marriage. 1899. The Gebbie Publishing Co., Ltd.

Eugenie Grandet. Translated by Lowell Bair. Honore De Balzac. LC 59-5173. (Bantam classic). 1959. Bantam Books.

Eugenie Grandet. Translated by Marion Ayton Crawford. Honore De Balzac. LC 57-16791. (Penguin classics, L50). 1955. Penguin Books.

Eulalie. Julie Ellis. 1978. pap. 1.95 (ISBN 0-449-23550-5, Crest). Fawcett.

Euloowirree Walkabout. John Kiddell. LC 68-15860. 1968. Chilton Book Co.

Eumeemie: A Legend of Cannon Falls. Silas S Lewis. LC 12-250. 1911. The Red Wing Printing Company.

Eunice: A Novel. Isabel Constance Clarke. LC 19-161523. 1919. Benziger Brothers.

Eunice Hussey: A Nantucket Story. Louise Southard Baker. LC 38-465174. The Inquirer and Missor Press.

Eunice Lathrop, Spinster. Annette Lucile Noble. LC 7-334819. (On cover: Knickerbocker novels). 1882. G. P. Putnam's Sons.

Eunice Loyd: Or, The Struggle and Triumph of an Honest Heart... Robert Neill Moody. LC 10-1692. 1909. F. L. Rowe.

Eunice; or, As Ye Would. Clara Elizabeth Ward. LC 8-33119. (On cover: Crown series). 1894. American Baptist Publication Society.

Eunice Quince: A New England Romance. L. P. M Curran. LC 6-31723. Lovell, Coryell & Company.

Eunuch of Stamboul. Dennis Yates Wheatley. LC 35-23313. 1935. Little, Brown, and Company.

Eunuch of Time & Other Stories. Sunita Jain. (Vikas Library of Modern Indian Writing: No. 24). 100p. 1982. text ed. 15.00x (ISBN 0-7069-1881-9, Pub. by Vikas India). Advent NY.

Euphrates: And Other Poems. Edward Clarence Farnsworth. LC 16-6803. 1916. Smith & Sale, Printers.

Euphues: The Anatomy of Wit; Euphues & His England. Ed. by Morris William Croll, Harry Clemons. John Lyly. Ed. by Morris William Croll & Harry Clemons. LC 64-150408. 1964. 10.00. Russell & Russell.

Eurasian Girl. Joseph Calvitt Clarke. LC 35-18233. 1935. Godwin.

Eurasian Girl. Joseph Calvitt Clarke. LC 35-162339. 1935. Godwin.

Eureka,". Eva Jane Washburn. LC 10-99166. 1910. Sun Publishing Co.

Euro-Killers. Julian Rathbone. LC 79-3007. 7.95 (ISBN 0-394-50902-1). Pantheon Books.

Europa. Robert Briffault. 1967. pap. 0.95 o.p. (95-113). Manor Bks.

Europa. Romain Gary, pseud. LC 77-90812. 1978. 8.95 (ISBN 0-385-01986-6). Doubleday.

Europa in Limbo. Robert Briffault. 1937. C. Scribner's Sons.

Europa: The Days of Ignorance. Robert Briffault. LC 35-15469. 1935. C. Scribner's Sons.

Europe see Author of Beltraffio.

Europe After the Rain. Alan Burns. 1980. pap. cancelled (ISBN 0-7145-0222-7). Riverrun NY.

Europe After the Rain. Alan Burns. 1965. 4.00 o.p. Fernhill.

Europe After the Rain. Alan Burns. 1965. 4.00 o.p. Hillary.

Europe After the Rain: A Novel. Alan Burns. LC 70-120864. 1970. 4.95. John Day.

Europe at Love. Paul Morand. LC 27-25542. 1927. Boni and Liveright.

Europe on a Saturday Night. John Gould. 308p. 1979. pap. 3.95 (ISBN 0-89272-056-5, 430). Down East.

Europe: Or, Up and Down with Schreiber and Baggish. Richard G Stern. LC 61-12037. 1961. McGraw-Hill.

Europe That Was. Geoffrey Household. LC 78-20671. 1979. 8.95 (ISBN 0-312-27058-5). St. Martin's Press.

Europe to Let: The Memoris of an Obscure Man. Margaret Storm Jameson. LC 40-4885. 1940. The Macmillan Company.

Europe Was in Flames. Conan Spaderna. 2.50 o.p. Vantage.

European see Four Selected Novels of Henry James.

European Relations: A Tirolese Sketch. Talmage Dalin. LC 6-33186. ("Unknown" library. v. 9). Cassell Publishing Company.

European War Fiction & Personal Narratives. Loleta I. Dawson & Marion D. Huntting. 1921. 1.75 o.p. (ISBN 0-87305-025-8). Faxon.

Europeans. Henry James. (Penguin Modern classics). (Pelican book). 1975. (pbk.) 1.95 (ISBN 0-14-002070-5). Penguin Books.

Europeans. Henry James. LC 77-16343. 1978. 7.50. Queens House.

Europeans. A Sketch. Henry James. LC 7-7445. 1879. Houghton, Osgood and Company.

Europeans. A Sketch. Henry James. Houghton, Mifflin and Company.

Europeans, Washington Square see Bodley Head Henry James.

Euskal Jai: Or, In Guest of Health and Happiness, by the Euskal Jai Company. Joseph Marion Hans. 1904.

Eustace & Hilda: A Trilogy. Leslie Poles Hartley. 1961. 6.95 o.p. Dufour.

Eustace Chisholm and the Works. James Purdy. (N3797). 1968. Bantam.

Eustace Chisholm and the Works. James Purdy. LC 67-15008. 1967. Farrar, Straus & Giroux.

Eustace Conyers: A Novel, 3 vols. in 2. James Hannay. LC 79-8128. Repr. of 1855 ed. Set. 84.50 (ISBN 0-404-61895-2). Vol. 1 (ISBN 0-404-61896-0). Vol. 2 (ISBN 0-404-61897-9). AMS Pr.

Eustace Diamonds. Anthony Trollope. LC 75-318783. (Penguin English library). (Illus.). 1973. 3.50 (ISBN 0-14-043041-5). Penguin Books.

Eustace Diamonds. Anthony Trollope. LC 51-5023. (Illus.). 1951. Doubleday.

Eustace Diamonds. Anthony Trollope. LC 4-24965. (On cover: The parliamentary novels). 1903. Dodd, Mead & Company.

Eustace Diamonds. A Novel. Anthony Trollope. LC 8-28898. 1872. Harper & Brothers.

Eustace Diamonds. A Novel. Anthony Trollope. LC 42-27379. 1873. Harper & Brothers.

Eustis: A Novel. Robert Apthorp Boit. LC 6-14182. 1884. J. R. Osgood and Company.

Eutaw. William Gilmore Simms. 1974. Repr. of 1888 ed. lib. bdg. 30.00 (ISBN 0-8414-8060-5). Folcroft.

Eutaw: A Sequel to The Forayers, or, The Raid of the Dog-Days: a Tale of the Revolution. William Gilmore Simms. LC 76-9055. (Simms, William Gilmore, 1806-1870. Simms Revolutionary War Novels: Vol. 7). 1976. 22.50 (ISBN 0-87152-241-1). Reprint Co.

Eutaw: a Sequel to The Forayers: Or, The Raid of the Dog-Days. A Tale of the Revolution. new and rev. ed. William Gilmore Simms. LC 73-116009. (Illus.). 1970. (ISBN 0-404-06018-8). AMS Press.

Eutaw, a Sequel to The Forayers; or, The Raid of the Dogdays, a Tale of the Revolution. William Gilmore Simms. LC 3-11020. 1882. A. C. Armstrong.

Eutaw: a Sequel to The Forayers; or, The Raid of the Dogdays. A Tale of the Revolution. new and rev. ed. William Gilmore Simms. (On cover: Lovell's library. v. 14, no. 703). 1886. J. W. Lovell Company.

Eva. Meyer Levin. LC 59-11198. 1959. Simon and Schuster.

Eva. A Novel. Hattie Weller Worden. LC 6-25691. 1906. Sunflower Publishing Co.

Eva: A Novel of the Holocaust. Meyer Levin. LC 79-14440. (Jewish legacy book). 1979. 5.95. Behrman House.

Eva and The Derelict Boat. Ferenc Molnar. Tr. by Lengyel, Emil. LC 26-833419. The Bobbs-Merrill Company.

Eva Gay: A Romantic Novel. Evelyn Scott. LC 33-271028. H. Smith & R. Haas.

Eva May: The Foundling; or, The Secret Dungeon. A Romance of New York. M. M. Huet. LC 7-5641. 1853. Garrett & Co.

Eva: Or, The Interrupted Diary. Jacques Chardonne. Tr. by Garvin, Viola Gerard. LC 31-659441. 1931. Simon and Schuster.

Eva Trout. Elizabeth Bowen. 1968. 6.95 o.p. (ISBN 0-394-42384-4). Knopf.

Eva Trout: Or, Changing Scenes. Elizabeth Bowen. LC 68-12685. 1968. 5.95. Knopf.

Eva Trout; or Changing Scenes. Elizabeth Bowen. 1978. 1.95 (ISBN 0-380-39016-7). Avon Books.

Evacuation of England: The Twist in the Gulf Stream. Louis Pope Gratacap. LC 8-18410. 1908. Brentano's.

Evaders. Betty McKim. 4.50 o.p. Carlton.

Evalore. Eva Jones. LC 77-26788. 1978. 7.95 (ISBN 0-397-01259-4). Lippincott.

Evalore. Eva Jones. 1978. 1.95 (ISBN 0-449-23912-8). Fawcett Crest Books.

Evan Dale... F. Keyes. LC 7-10824. 1864. A. Williams & Co.

Evan Harrington: A Novel. rev. ed. George Meredith. LC 1-19349. 1896. C. Scribner's Sons.

Evan Harrington: A Novel. George Meredith. LC 22-10238. (modern student's library). C. Scribner's Sons.

Evan Harrington: Or, He Would Be a Gentleman. George Meredith. LC 16-7000. 1860. Harper & Brothers.

Evander. Eden Phillpotts. 1919. The Macmillan Company.

Evangel Ahvallah: Or, The White Spectrum. A Novel Whose Incidents Are Linked Together by a Chain of Metaphysical Deductions. C Josephine Barton. LC 6-9102. 1895. The Author.

Evangelical Cockroach. Josiah Pitts Woolfolk. LC 30-24044. 1929. L. Carrier & Co.

Evangelical Cockroach. Josiah Pitts Woolfolk. LC 30-33617. W. B. Simon.

Evangeline. Henry Wadsworth Longfellow. (Pocket Classics). 2.25 o.p. (ISBN 0-679-50022-7). McKay.

Evangeline of Ole Virginia. Margaret Roberts Ely. LC 23-10587. 1923. J. P. Morton & Company (Incorporated.

Evangelist, Manning Lee Stokes. Lyle Engle. 1974. pap. 1.25 o.p. (V3446). Pyramid Pubns.

Evangelist. 1st Ed. Howard Otway. LC 54-8980. 1954. Harper.

Evans and Sontag, the Famous Bandits of California. Hu Maxwell. (On cover: The California library, no. 1). 1893. San Francisco Printing Company.

Evans of Suffolk. Anna Farquhar Bergengren. LC 4-3950. 1904. L. C. Page & Company.

Eva's Apples: A Story of Jazz and Jasper. William Alexander Gerhardie. LC 28-14828. 1928. Duffield and Company.

Eva's Man. Gayl Jones. LC 75-40565. 6.95. Random House.

Evasion. Eugenia Brooks Frothingham. LC 6-10023. 1906. Houghton, Mifflin and Company.

Evasion Line: A Novel. Alfred W Satterthwaite. LC 78-185476. 1972. 9.75 (ISBN 0-912838-01-9). Toll & Armstrong.

Eve. Angela Taylor Ames. 1979. 2.25 (ISBN 0-671-81839-2). Pocket Books.

Eve. Katharine Howard. LC 13-24133. 1913. Sherman, French & Company.

Eve. Rene Raymond. LC 45-10699. 1945. Jarrolds Limited.

Eve. A Novel. Sabine Baring-Gould. (On cover: Seaside library. Pocket ed., no. 1122). 1888. G. Munro.

Eve and Christopher. Elizabeth Frances Corbett. LC 49-7588. 1949. Doubleday.

Eve and the Evangelist: A Romance of A.D. 2108. Harry E Rice. LC 8-31692. The Roxburgh Publishing Company, Incorporated.

Eve and the Others. Edith Thomas. LC 75-36694. 3.50 (ISBN 0-916868-01-X). Continental Editions.

Eve Cameron: M. D. Ann Rush. LC 57-12667. 1957. Avalon Books.

Eve Cameron, M. D. Ann Rush. LC 57-12667. 1957. Avalon Books.

Eve De Paris. Hugh King. (A Berkley Medallion Book). 1977. 1.95 (ISBN 0-425-03541-7). Berkley Pub. Co.

Eve Dorre: The Story of Her Precarious Youth. Emily Viele Strother. LC 15-19072. E. P. Dutton & Company.

Eve in the Garden. Peggy Gaddis, pseud. LC 35-8483. Godwin.

Eve, Junior. Reginald Heber Patterson. 1917. 1.25. The Macaulay Company.

Eve of Evil. George G. Gilman, pseud. (Edge Ser.: No. 28). 1978. pap. 1.50 (ISBN 0-523-40204-X, Dist. by Independent News Co.). Pinnacle Bks.

Eve of Pascua: And Other Stories. Clotilde Inez Mary Graves. LC 20-124509. 1.90. George H. Doran Company.

Eve of St. Venus. Anthony Burgess. (Illus.). 1970. 4.95 o.p. (ISBN 0-393-08602-X). Norton.

Eve of Saint Venus. John Anthony Burgess Wilson. LC 79-108328. (Illus.). 1970. 4.95. Norton.

Eve of the Wedding. Lionel Black. 160p. 1981. pap. 2.25 (ISBN 0-380-55996-X, 55996). Avon.

Eve: The Factory Girl; or, An Undisciplined Heart. Lucy Randall Comfort. (On cover: The library of American authors. no. 28). 1891. G. Munro.

Eve to the Rescue. Ethel Powelson Hueston. LC 20-19182. The Bobbs-Merrill Company.

Eve Today. Playboy Editors. LC 74-81186. 1974. pap. 2.50 o.p. (Z00029). Playboy Pr Pbks.

Eveleen Wilson: Or, The Trials of an Orphan Girl. 1853. H. Long & Brother.

Eveless Eden. Allen Eppes. LC 40-31179. 1940. Gateway Books.

Evelina. Fanny Burney. 1958. 5.00x o.p. (ISBN 0-460-00352-6, Evman). Biblio Dist.

Evelina. Fanny Burney. 1965. pap. 6.95 (ISBN 0-393-00294-2, Norton Lib). Norton.

Evelina. Fanny Burney. Ed. & intro. by Edward A. Bloom. (World's Classics Ser.). 480p. 1982. pap. 6.95 (ISBN 0-19-281596-2). Oxford U Pr.

Evelina. Frances Burney D'Arblay. (Half-title: Everyman's library, ed. by Ernest Rhys. Fiction. no. 352). 1909. J. M. Dent & Co.

Evelina. Frances Burney D'Arblay. LC 36-37164. (Half-title: Everyman's library, ed. by Ernest Rhys. Fiction. no. 352). 1929. J. M. Dent & Sons, Ltd.

Evelina; or, The History of a Young Lady's Entrance into the World. Fanny Burney & Edward Alan Bloom. LC 81-18758. (World's classics). 1982. 6.95 (ISBN 0-19-281596-2). Oxford University Press.

Evelina: Or, A Young Lady's Entrance into the World... Frances Burney D'Arblay. LC 43-34718. 1812. Published by William Fessenden.

Evelina: Or, A Young Lady's Entrance into the World... Printed at Worcester, Massachusetts. Frances D'Arblay, pseud. LC 6-2059.

Evelina: Or, A Young Lady's Entrance into the World. In Two Volumes... Frances D'Arblay, pseud. 1797. Printed by Jacob S. Mott, No. Vesey-Street.

Evelina: Or, The History of a Young Lady's Entrance into the World. Frances Burney D' Arblay & Bjorkman, Edwin August, 1866- Ed. LC 21-1281. (Living literature series, R. Burton, PH.D., editor-in-chief). The Gregg Publishing Company.

Evelina: Or, the History of a Young Lady's Entrance into the World. Frances Burney. Ed. by Edward A. Bloom. (Oxford English Novels Ser & Oxford Paperbacks Ser). 1968. pap. 4.95x o.p. (ISBN 0-19-281075-8). Oxford U Pr.

Evelina: Or the History of a Young Lady's Entrance into the World by Fanny Burney. Frances Burney D'Arblay. LC 65-188791. (Norton lib., N249. Classics in Eng. lit.). 1965. pap., 1.65. Norton.

Evelina: Or, The History of a Young Lady's Entrance into the World. Frances Burney D'Arblay. Ed. by Edward Alan Bloom. LC 78-575765. (Oxford paperbacks, 208). (Illus.). 1970 (ISBN 0-19-281075-8). Oxford U.P.

Evelina: Or, The History of a Young Lady's Entrance into the World. Frances Burney D'Arblay. LC 6-115433. (Half-title: The English Comedie humaine. 2d series). 1906. The Century Co.

Evelina: Or, The History of a Young Lady's Entrance into the World. Frances Burney D'Arblay. LC 26-269776. (The Cranford series). 1925. Macmillan & Co., Limited.

Evelina: Or, The History of a Young Lady's Introduction to the World. Frances Burney D' Arblay & Macaulay, Thomas Babington, 1st Baron, 1800-1859. LC 6-2062. 1858. Derby & Jackson.

Evelina: Or, The History of a Young Lady's Introduction to the World. Frances D'Arblay, pseud. 1852. Harper & Brothers.

Evelina: Or, The History of a Young Lady's Introduction to the World. Frances Burney D'Arblay. LC 25-15498. 1857. Derby & Jackson.

Evelina: Or, The History of a Young Lady's Introduction to the World. Frances Burney D'Arblay. (Franklin square library, no. 22). 1910. Little, Brown and Company.

Evelina: Or, The History of Ayoung Lady's Entrance into the World by Frances Burney; Ed., Introd. by Edward A. Bloom. Frances Burney D'Arblay. Ed. by Edward Alan Bloom. LC 68-73843. (Oxford English novels). 1968. 4.80. Oxford Univ. Pr.

Evelina's Garden. Mary Eleanor Wilkins Freeman. LC 99-5777. (Little books by famous writers). 1899. Harper & Brothers.

Eveline, 2 Vols. Intro. by G. Lowndes. pap. 1.75 ea. o.p. (3027, 3030). Brandon.

Eveline II. Intro. by Patrick Henden. LC 81-48545. 208p. (Orig.). 1982. pap. 2.95 (ISBN 0-394-17972-2, B-473, BC). Grove.

Eveline Neville: Or, "A Spirit, Yet a Woman Too.". 1845. Burgess, Stringer & Co.

Eveline: The Amorous Adventures of a Victorian Lady. LC 80-8915. 352p. 1981. pap. 3.25 (ISBN 0-394-17892-0, B45, BC). Grove.

Evelyn Byrd. George Cary Eggleston. LC 4-115369. 1904. Lothrop Publishing Company.

Evelyn Grainger. George Frederick Hummel. LC 27-6811. 1927. Boni & Liveright.

Evelyn Innes. George Moore. LC 7-25299. 1898. D. Appleton and Company.

Evelyn Innes. George Moore. LC 34-38287. (Half-title: Appleton dollar library). 1927. D. Appleton and Company.

Evelyn Innes. George Moore. LC 42-47278. 1920. D. Appleton and Company.

Evelyn Innes, and Sister Teresa. George Moore. LC 75-464. (Victorian Fiction: Novels of Faith and Doubt; V. 8). 1975. 35.00 (ISBN 0-8240-1542-8). Garland Pub.

Evelyn Prentice. William E. Woodward. LC 33-15495. 1933. A. A. Knopf.

Evelyn: Something More Than a Story. James Francis Dwyer. LC 29-27799. The Vanguard Press.

Evelyn, the Ambitious. Katheryn Kimbrough, pseud. (saga of the Phenwick Women;). 1978. 1.75 (ISBN 0-445-04265-6). Popular Library.

Evelyn, the Child of the Revolution. A Romance of Real Life. John Hovey Robinson. LC 7-41991. 1850. Hotchkiss & Company.

Evelyn Van Courtland. William Henry Carson. LC 7-29570. R. F. Fenno & Company.

Evelyn's Career: A Novel by the Author of "My Wife's Niece," "Dr. Edith Romney," "An Old Man's Favor" Etc. (On cover: Harper's Franklin square library. no. 712). 1891. Harper & Brothers.

Evelyn's Folly. Charlotte Mary Brame. LC 4364. (Bertha M. Clay library, no. 18). 1900. Street & Smith.

Evelyn's Folly. A Novel. Charlotte Mary Brame. LC 12-19580. 1881. G. W. Carleton & Co.

Evelyn's Folly. A Novel. Charlotte Mary Brame. (On cover: Lovell's library. v. 14. no. 744). 1886. J. W. Lovell Co.

Evelyn's Folly. A Novel. Charlotte Mary Brame. LC 44-12290. (On cover: Seaside library. Pocket ed. No. 470). G. Munro.

Even As You Love. Elizabeth Borton Trevino. LC 57-11093. 1957. Crowell.

Even Bishops Die. Charles Saxby. LC 42-17638. 1942. E. P. Dutton and Company, Inc.

Even Cowgirls Get the Blues. Tom Robbins. LC 75-46633. 1976. 10.00 (ISBN 0-395-24305-X) (ISBN 0-395-24510-9). Houghton Mifflin.

Even Doctors Die. Lindsay Anson. LC 39-4288. 1939. Pub. for the Crime Club, Inc., by Doubleday, Doran and Company, Inc.

Even Hand. Caroline Wright. LC 12-22251. The Pilgrim Press.

Even If You Run. Desmond Cory, pseud. LC 77-180067. (Crime Club Ser). 192p. 1972. 4.95 o.p. (ISBN 0-385-02371-5). Doubleday.

Even If You Run. Shaun McCarthy. LC 77-180067. 1972. 4.95. Published for the Crime Club by Doubleday.

Even in a Hundred Years. Katherine Ursula Parrott. LC 44-2188. 1944. Dodd, Mead & Company.

Even in Death. 1st Ed. Stewart Devine. LC 50-6840. 1950. Published for the Crime Club by Doubleday.

Even in Laughter. Constance Cassady & Cardwell, Ruth. LC 35-6100. The Bobbs-Merrill Company.

Even in the Depths: A Novel. Amy Winifred Cramp Wilkinson. LC 65-14950. 1965. Reynal.

Even Jericho, a Novel. Warner Hall. LC 44-46610. 1944. Macrae-Smith-Company.

Even Keel. Rayne Kruger. LC 55-35184. 1955. Longmans, Green.

Even My Own Brother. John Burgan. LC 42-21684. 1942. The Bobbs-Merrill Company.

Even So to Them" "the Law and the Prophets")... James G. Ellis. LC 43-13642. 1943. Wetzel Publishing Co., Inc.

Even Steven. 1st Ed. Patric Knowles. LC 60-50304. 1960. Vantage Press.

Even Such Is Time. Doreen Eileen Agnew Wallace, pseud. LC 34-31983. 1934. The Macmillan Company.

Even Temperature in the Cave: And Other Stories. Mary Nash. LC 63-8952. 1963. Little, Brown.

Even the Rich Girl. Henry Leyford Gates. LC 34-5280. 1934. The Macaulay Company.

Even the Wicked. Ed McBain. 1982. pap. 2.25 (ISBN 0-451-11872-3, AE1872, Sig). NAL.

Even the Wicked. Ed McBain. (Signet Book)). 1977. 1.25 (ISBN 0-451-07402-5). New American Library.

Even Tide. Larry Woiwode. 1977. pap. 3.95 o.p. (ISBN 0-374-51475-5). FS&G.

Even to the End: A Prophecy. Ray Maier. 52p. 1975. 4.00 o.p. (ISBN 0-682-48304-4). Exposition.

Evening and the Morning. Virginia Eggertsen Sorensen. LC 49-85150.

Evening Edged in Gold. Arno Schmidt. LC 79-3373. (Illus.). 75.00 (ISBN 0-15-129376-7). Harcourt Brace Jovanovich.

Evening Faces: A Novel. Diana Cobbold. LC 81-71688. 13.95 (ISBN 0-87795-404-6). Arbor House.

Evening Heron. Philip Freund. LC 37-157839. 1937. Pilgrim House.

Evening in Byzantium. Irwin Shaw. LC 72-12856. 1973. 7.95. Delacorte Press.

Evening in Byzantium. Irwin Shaw. 1974. (pbk.) 1.50. Dell.

Evening in Pisa. Pierre Rossi. LC 72-14043. 1973. 4.95 (ISBN 0-87955-902-0). J. P. O'Hara.

Evening in Spring. August William Derleth. LC 41-15438. 1941. C. Scribner's Sons.

Evening in Spring. August William Derleth. LC 46-781. 1945. Stanton and Lee.

Evening Land: Aftonland. Par Lagerkvist. Tr. by W. H. Auden & Leif Sjoberg. LC 75-16172. 192p. (Eng. & Swedish.). 1975. 12.95x (ISBN 0-8143-1542-9). Wayne St U Pr.

Evening of a Martinet: A Novel. Jane Oliver, pseud. LC 35-528. 1935. Doubleday, Doran & Company, Inc.

Evening of the Holiday. Shirley Hazzard. LC 66-10073. 1966. bds., 3.95. Knopf.

Evening of the Holiday. Shirley Hazzard. LC 67-92530. 1966. Macmillan; New York, St. Martin's P.

Evening of the Holiday. Shirley Hazzard. LC 81-80087. 1981. 2.25 (ISBN 0-87216-874-3). Playboy Paperbacks.

Evening Out. David Walton. 180p. 1982. cancelled (ISBN 0-88233-670-3); pap. cancelled (ISBN 0-88233-671-1). Ardis Pubs.

Evening Star. Nellie Graf. LC 39-15273. Gramercy Publishing Co.

Evening Street. Katrina Johnson. LC 47-120073. 1947. G. P. Putnam's Sons.

Evening Tales. authorized ed. Jean Baptiste Frederic Ortoli. Tr. by Harris, Joel Chandler. 1893. C. Scribner's Sons.

Evening Tales. Mihail Sadoveanu. Tr. by E. Farca et al from Rumanian. LC 62-9873. 1962. lib. bdg. 24.00x (ISBN 0-8057-5172-6). Irvington.

Evening Tales. Mihail Sadoveanu. (International Studies & Translations Ser.). lib. bdg. 5.95 o.p. (ISBN 0-8057-5172-6). Twayne.

Evening Tales for the Winter: Being a Selection of Wonderful & Supernatural Stories. Ed. by St. Clair, Henry. LC 14-5703. 1856. R. Marsh.

Evening Tales. Translated from the Rumanian by E Farca and Others. Mihail Sadoveanu. LC 62-9873. 1962. Twayne Publishers.

Evening with Scott... Walter Scott & Cody, Sherwin. LC 28-17090. (nutshell library, ed. by S. Cody). Sherwin Cody School of English.

Evening Wolves: A Novel. Marie McCall. LC 49-9284. 1949. J. Day Co.

Evenings at Donaldson Manor: Or, The Christmas Guest. Maria Jane McIntosh. LC 7-16452. 1851. D. Appleton & Company.

Evenings at Haddon Hall: A Series of Romantic Tales of the Olden Time. Ed. by E C De Calabrella. LC 16-1246. (Half-title: Bohn's illustrated library). 1893. G. Bell & Sons.

Evenings at Home: Or, The Juvenile Budget Opened. John Aikin & Barbauld, Mrs. Anna Letitia (Aikin) 1743-1825, Joint Author. LC 26-750816. 1879. G. Routledge and Sons.

Evenings at Woodlawn. Elizabeth Fries Lummis Ellet. LC 6-37263. 1849. Baker and Scribner.

Evenings on a Farm Near Dikanka. Nikolai Vasilevich Gogol. LC 26-14495. (Added t.-p.: The collected works on Nikolay Gogol, tr. by Constance Garnett). 1926. A. A. Knopf.

Evensong: A Novel. Beverley Nichols. LC 32-26069. 1932. Doubleday, Doran & Company, Inc.

Event One Thousand. David Lavallee. 1971. 5.95 o.p. (ISBN 0-03-085969-7). HR&W.
Event 1000: A Novel. David Lavallee. LC 73-138881. (Illus.). 1971. 5.95 (ISBN 0-03-085969-7). Holt, Rinehart and Winston.
Event 1000: A Novel. David Lavallee. LC 70-38809. 1972. (ISBN 0-8161-6017-1). G. K. Hall.
Eventful Night: A Comedy of a Western Mining Town. Clara Parker. 1900. Doubleday & McClure Co.
Eventide. Betty Ferm. 1974. (pbk.) 0.75. Dell.
Events Echo. Norma Hamilton. 7.00 o.p. Vantage.
Events of That Week. Nicolas Bentley. LC 72-78184. 1972. 5.95. St. Martin's Press.
Eventually Yours. Watkins Eppes Wright. LC 42-29192. 1941. Arcadia House, Inc.
Ever After. Janet McNeill, pseud. LC 75-17793. 1975. 5.95 (ISBN 0-316-56302-1). Little, Brown.
Ever After. Elswyth Thane. LC 45-9327. 1945. Duell, Sloan and Pearce.
Ever After. Elswyth Thane. LC 80-25631. 1981. 17.95 (ISBN 0-8161-3165-1). G. K. Hall.
Ever After. Juliet Wilbor Tompkins. LC 13-10540. 1913. Doubleday, Page & Company.
Ever After. Phyllis A. Whitney. 1979. pap. 1.95 (ISBN 0-449-24128-9, Crest). Fawcett.
Ever After. Phyllis A. Whitney. (Orig.). pap. 0.60 o.p. (73-686). Lancer.
Ever Faithful: Jessica Versus Literality. Ann Dee. LC 49-507649. 1948. Exposition Press.
Ever-Loving Blues. Carter Brown, pseud. LC 61-1928. (Signet books, S1919). 1961. New American Library of World Literature.
Ever-Loving Blues. Alan Geoffrey Yates. LC 61-1928. (Signet books, S1919). 1961. New American Library of World Literature.
Ever-Loving Blues see Sad-Eyed Seductress.
Ever One God: A Novel. Robert W Lutnes. LC 55-9789. 1955. Augsburg Pub. House.
Ever-Present Past. Edith Hamilton. 1964. 5.00 (ISBN 0-393-04264-2, Norton Lib); pap. 2.95x (ISBN 0-393-00425-2). Norton.
Ever the Winds Blow. Elliott Merrick. LC 36-138805. 1936. C. Scribner's Sons.
Ever to Love. William Arthur Neubauer. LC 50-519435. 1949. Arcadia House.
Ever Tomorrow. Eleanor Saltzman. LC 36-8546. Coward, McCann.
Everafter. Phyllis A. Whitney. (Fawcett crest book). 1974. (pbk.) 1.25. Fawcett.
Everbreeze. Sarah Pratt McLean Greene. LC 13-1900. 1913. 1.30. D. Appleton and Company.
Evered. Ben Ames Williams. LC 21-14135. E. P. Dutton & Company.
Everglades Assault. Randy Striker. (Macmorgan Ser.: No. 6). (Orig.). 1982. pap. 1.95 (AJ1344, Sig). NAL.
Everglades: River of Grass. Marjory Stoneman Douglas. 1981. pap. 2.75 (ISBN 0-89176-029-6, 6029). Mockingbird Bks.
Evergreeen: A Novel. Belva Plain. LC 80-16734. 1980. 23.95 (ISBN 0-8161-3114-7). G. K. Hall.
Evergreen. Belva Plain. 1979. pap. 3.95 (ISBN 0-440-13278-9). Dell.
Evergreen, a Novel. Edward Nils Holstius. LC 48-9522. 1949. Doubleday.
Evergreen: A Novel. Belva Plain. LC 77-20778. 9.95 (ISBN 0-440-02661-X). Delacorte Press.
Evergreen Castles. Laurie B. Clifford. 1983. pap. 2.95 (ISBN 0-8423-0779-6). Tyndale.
Evergreen Cottage. Louis Arthur Cunningham. LC 49-41288. 1949. Arcadia House.
Evergreen Death. James Fraser, pseud. LC 69-14833. 1969. 4.50 o.p. (ISBN 0-15-129385-6). HarBraceJ.
Evergreen Death. Alan White. LC 69-14833. 1969. Harcourt, Brace & World.
Evergreen Gallant. Eleanor Hibbert. LC 73-86857. 1973. 6.95 (ISBN 0-399-11285-5). Putnam.
Evergreen Gallant. Jean Plaidy. 384p. (YA) 1973. 6.95 o.p. (ISBN 0-399-11285-5). Putnam.
Evergreen Girl. Anne T. Broods. (Alouette Romance Ser.). 224p. (Orig.). 1981. pap. 2.25 (ISBN 0-89531-125-9, 0198-96). Sharon Pubns.
Evergreen House. Louise Platt Hauck. LC 43-3658. 1943. Dodd, Mead & Company.
Evergreen Tree. Gladys Bagg Taber. LC 37-6301. 1937. Macrae-Smith Company.
Evergreens & Other Short Stories. Jerome Klapka Jerome. 128p. 1982. pap. text ed. 3.25x (ISBN 0-86299-011-4, Pub. by Sutton England). Humanities.
Everlasting. Leonard Bishop. LC 81-17808. 14.95 (ISBN 0-671-44154-X). Poseidon Press.
Everlasting Arms. Albert Benjamin Cunningham. LC 52-12945. 1953. Dutton.
Everlasting Fire. 1st Ed. Jonreed Lauritzen. LC 62-11366. 1962. Doubleday.
Everlasting Harpers. Mildred Wasson. LC 29-172635. 1929. Coward-McCann, Inc.
Everlasting Man. Gilbert Keith Chesterton. pap. 2.25 o.p. (ISBN 0-396-06561-9). Dodd.
Everlasting Struggle: A Novel by Johan Bojer. Johan Bojer & Heni, Arna. Tr. LC 31-26710. The Century Co.
Everlasting Whisper. Jackson Gregory. 1976. Repr. of 1922 ed. lib. bdg. 18.55x (ISBN 0-88411-282-9). Amereon Ltd.
Everlasting Whisper: A Tale of the California Wilderness. Jackson Gregory. LC 22-2312. 1922. C. Scribner's Sons.
Evermore. Barbara Steward & Dwight Steward. LC 77-13768. 1978. 7.95. Morrow.
Every Bet's a Sure Thing. Thomas Blanchard Dewey. LC 52-4980. (Inner sanctum mystery). Simon and Schuster.
Every Body's Ready to Die. Macdowell Frederics. LC 66-21633. (Rinehart suspense novel). 1966. Holt, Rinehart and Winston.
Every Cloud. Margaret Peterson. LC 32-843280. 1932. Sears Publishing Company, Inc.
Every Crazy Wind. John Wallace Pritchard. LC 52-7346. 1952. Dodd, Mead.
Every Crime in the Book. Ed. by Robert L. Fish & Mystery Writers of America. LC 75-10502. 1975. 7.95 o.p. (ISBN 0-399-11536-6). Putnam.
Every Crime in the Book: An Anthology of Mystery Stories. Mystery Writers of America & Robert L Fish. LC 75-10502. 1975. 7.95 (ISBN 0-399-11536-6). Putnam.
Every Day by Storm. Michael O'Malley. LC 66-20288. 1967. Putnam.
Every-Day Heroine: A Story for Girls. Mary Andrews Denison. LC 6-33995. 1896. The Penn Publishing Company.
Every Day Is Sunday. Willard Temple. LC 59-9168. 1959. Crown Publishers.
Every Day's News... C. E. Francis. LC 8-4787. (On cover: Incognito library v. 7). 1895. G. P. Putnam's Sons.
Every Ecstasy. June Pat Wetherell. LC 41-5580. Phoenix Press.
Every Inch a King. A Story Illustrating the Reigns of David and Solomon, Kings of Israel. Celia Emmeline Gardner. LC 7-15172. 1876. Nelson & Phillips.
Every Inch a King: The Romance of Henry of Monmouth, Sometime Prince of Wales. Josephine Caroline Sawyer. LC 1-31782. 1901. Dodd, Mead & Company.
Every Inch a Lady. Joan Margaret Fleming. LC 78-12825. 1979. 10.95 (ISBN 0-89340-166-8). J. Curley.
Every Inch a Lady: A Murder of the Fifties. Joan Margaret Fleming. LC 77-10423. 7.95 (ISBN 0-399-12087-4). Putnam.
Every Inch a Man. Joseph Turner Wilson. LC 37-142766. The Warner Press.
Every Inch a Soldier. Henrietta Eliza Vaughan Stannard. LC 8-13865. (On cover: Lippincott's series of select novels). 1894. J. B. Lippincott Company.
Every Island Fled Away. John B Sanford. LC 64-11149. 1964. Norton.
Every Little Crook & Nanny. Evan Hunter. LC 71-164718. 1972. 5.95 o.p. (ISBN 0-385-08574-5). Doubleday.
Every Little Crook and Nanny: A Novel. Evan Hunter. LC 71-164718. (Signet book). 1974. (pbk.) 1.25. New American Library.
Every Little Sin. James Noble Gifford. LC 50-563052. 1949. Phoenix Press.
Every Man a King: A Novel of Suspense. Anne Worboys. LC 76-26742. 1976. 7.95 (ISBN 0-684-14702-5). Charles Scribner's Sons.
Every Man a Murderer. Heimito Von Doderer. 1964. 6.95 o.p. Knopf.
Every Man a Phoenix. Margaret Bottrall. (gr. 9 up). 5.00 o.p. Transatlantic.
Every Man an Eagle. Richard H. Curtis. (Skymasters Ser.: No. 8). (Orig.). 1983. pap. 3.25 (ISBN 0-440-02276-2, Emerald). Dell.
Every Man an Enemy. W. Howard Baker. 1967. pap. 0.50 o.p. (50-354). Manor Bks.
Every Man for Himself. Norman Duncan. LC 8-26677. 1908. Harper & Brothers.
Every Man His Chance: A Novel. Matilda Woods Stone. LC 8-37195. C.
Every Man His Price. Max Rittenberg. LC 14-15564. 1.25. G. W. Dillingham Company.
Every Man His Sword. Irving Schwartz. LC 51-10227. 1951. Doubleday.
Every Man Is God. Raymond William Postgate. LC 60-6095. 1960. Simon and Schuster.
Every Man Is My Father. William Edward Wilson. LC 72-94799. 1973. 8.95 (ISBN 0-8415-0239-0). Saturday Review Press.
Every Man's Brother. John Elwood Cutler. LC 6-32238.
Every Man's Brother. Norman Lewis. LC 68-18585. 1968. W. Morrow.
Every Man's Desire. Geoffrey Uther Ellis. LC 25-18582. 1925. Dodd, Mead and Company.
Every Mother's Son. Norman Lindsay. LC 30-23199. 1930. Cosmopolitan Book Corporation.
Every Night's a Festival. John E Gardner. LC 79-170226. 1972. (ISBN 0-688-00050-9). Morrow.
Every One His Own Way. Edith Franklin Wyatt. LC 70-37572. (Short story index reprint series). 1972. (ISBN 0-8369-4131-4). Books for Libraries Press.
Every One His Own Way. Edith Franklin Wyatt. LC 1-6334. 1901. McClure, Phillips and Company.
Every Politician and His Wife. Adele Steiner Burleson. LC 21-5710. Dorrance and Company, Inc.
Every Second Thursday. Emma Page. LC 81-51978. 9.95 (ISBN 0-8027-5451-1). Walker.
Every Secret Thing: A Novel. John Rowan Wilson. LC 55-9997. 1955. Morrow.
Every Soul Hath Its Song. Fannie Hurst. LC 16-20440. 1916. 1.30. Harper & Brothers.
Every Wall a Door. Anne Dooley. 1974. pap. 2.95 o.p. (ISBN 0-525-47380-7). Dutton.
Every Wall Shall Fall. Helen Battle. 1972. pap. 0.95 o.p. (N2692). Pyramid Pubns.
Every Whit Whole: The Adventure of Spiritual Healing. Michael Drury. LC 78-18389. 1978. 5.95 o.p. (ISBN 0-396-07578-9). Dodd.
Every Wife: An Amusement. Grant Richards. LC 25-224538. E. J. Clode, Inc.
Every Wise Woman. William Mestrezat John. LC 31-24071. Sears Publishing Company, Inc.
Every Woman's Man. Maysie Greig. pap. 0.50 o.p. (50-276). Manor Bks.
Every Woman's Right: A Novel. Nina Miller Elliott. LC 19-18225. Thos. W. Jackson Publishing Co.
Everybody Adored Cara. Ann Head, pseud. LC 63-9180. (Signet book). 1975. (pbk.) 1.25. New American Library.
Everybody Adored Cara. Ann Head, pseud. LC 63-9180. 1963. Published for the Crime Club by Doubleday.
Everybody Had a Gun. Richard S. Prather. 1970. pap. 0.60 o.p. (R2201, GM). Fawcett World.
Everybody Knows and Nobody Cares: A Novel. Mason Smith. LC 70-136330. 1971. 5.95 (ISBN 0-394-42382-8). Knopf.
Everybody Makes Mistakes... Margaret Sharp Marble. LC 46-3128. 1946. Rinehart & Company, Inc.
Everybody's All-American. Frank Deford. LC 81-65287. 1981. 13.95 (ISBN 0-670-30035-7). Viking Press.
Everybody's Birthright: A Vision of Jeanne D'Arc. Clara Elizabeth Laughlin. LC 14-162115. 0.75. Fleming H. Revell Company.
Everybody's Husband. Gilbert Cannan. LC 19-14221. 1919. B. W. Huebech.
Everybody's Husband. Gilbert Cannan. LC 20-10540. B. W. Huebsch.
Everybody's Secret. Dion Clayton Calthrop. LC 9-20662. G. W. Dillingham Company.
Everybody's Studying Us: The Irony of Aging in the Pepsi Generation. Irene Paull. LC 76-15149. (Orig.). 1976. pap. 3.95x (ISBN 0-917154-01-0). CA Assn Older.
Everyday. Philip Whalen. pap. 1.75 o.p. Coyote.
Everyday Animals. Gertrude E Allen. (Sandpiper book). (Illus.). 1974. (pbk.) 0.95 (ISBN 0-395-18563-7). Houghton, Mifflin.
Everyday Aphasia. Ric Barthelme. (Illus.). 1970. pap. 2.95 o.p. (Anch). Doubleday.
Everyday Cameos. Ralph Leslie Finn. LC 46-23201. 1946. Rich & Cowan.
Everyday Heroes. Frank Hughes. 1981. pap. 2.50 o.s.i. (ISBN 0-8439-0885-8, Leisure Bks). Nordon Pubns.
Everyday People. Harriet Winton Davis. LC 31-12759. University Press.
Everyman Book of Classic Horror Stories. Ed. by Peter Haining. 1976. pap. 2.50x (ISBN 0-460-01158-8, Evman). Biblio Dist.
Everyman's Land. Charles Norris Williamson & Alice Muriel Livingston Williamson. LC 18-203242. 1918. Doubleday, Page & Company.
Everyman's Land. Charles Norris Williamson & Alice Muriel Livingston Williamson. LC 22-516032. 1919. Doubleday, Page & Company.
Everyone Is a King. Ermando J. Bruno. 1968. 3.95 o.p. Vantage.
Everyone Suspect. Nedra Tyre. LC 64-12176. (Cock Robin mystery). 1964. Macmillan.
Everything but a Husband. Jeanette Kamins. LC 62-17421. 1962. St Martin's Press.
Everything But Love see Escape to Romance.
Everything Else, 3 pts. Daniel L. Klauck. Incl. Pt. 1. But the Wolves'll Get You Here Too; Pt. 2. In the Sun's Angry Clutch; Pt. 3. Poetry in Painless Birth. LC 76-22907. 1976. pap. 3.00 perfect bdg. (ISBN 0-917676-01-7). King Pubns.
Everything Goes. Charles Grayson. LC 32-9432. The Macaulay Company.
Everything Happened to Susan. Barry N. Malzberg. 1978. pap. 1.50 o.s.i. (ISBN 0-505-51221-1). Tower Bks.
Everything Happens for the Best. Sarah Winston. LC 68-27212. 1969. 4.95. T. Yoseloff.
Everything Has Its Price. Hans Hellmut Kirst. LC 75-37124. 1976. 8.95 (ISBN 0-698-10719-5). Coward, McCann & Geoghegan.
Everything in Its Path. Kai T. Erikson. 1978. pap. 6.75 (ISBN 0-671-24067-6, Touchstone Bks). S&S.
Everything in Rhyme. Robert W. Deneke. 3.95 o.p. Vantage.
Everything in the Window: A Novel. Shirley Faessler. LC 80-300. 10.95 (ISBN 0-316-25986-1). Little, Brown.
Everything Is Quite All Right. Wendell Wilcox. LC 45-9220. 1945. B. Ackerman, Incorporated.
Everything Is Thunder. Jocelyn Lee Hardy. LC 35-135510. Doubleday, Doran & Company, Inc.
Everything Must Go. Keith Waterhouse. LC 68-25466. 1969. 4.95. Putnam.
Everything Rustles. Mannix Walker. LC 45-6728. 1945. Dodd, Mead & Company.
Everything That Has Been Shall Be Again: The Reincarnation Fables of John Gilgun. John Gilgun & Michael McCurdy. LC 81-10194. (Illus.). 1981. (pbk.) 7.95 (ISBN 0-931460-13-1) (ISBN 0-931460-11-5). Bieler Press.
Everything That Moves. Budd Schulberg. LC 79-7809. 1980. 10.00 (ISBN 0-385-00521-0). Doubleday.
Everything That Rises Must Converge. Flannery O'Connor. LC 65-137262. bds., 4.95. Farrar.
Everything That Rises Must Converge. Flannery O'Connor. (Signet bk., T3177). 1967. New Amer. Lib.
Everything to Live for. Paul Horgan. LC 68-23740. 1968. Farrar, Straus and Giroux.
Everything's the Same. Suzanne Klotz & Jeffrey Powers. LC 79-12485. 1979. 5.95. (ISBN 0-89807-001-5) (ISBN 0-89807-000-7). Illuminati.
Everywhere I Roam. Ben Lucien Burman. LC 49-11670. 1949. Doubleday.
Everywhere Man. Victoria Gordon. (Harlequin Romances Ser.). 192p. 1981. pap. 1.50 (ISBN 0-373-02438-X). Harlequin Bks.
Everywhere the Light. Neal Biship. Ed. by Billie Young. LC 78-14861. 1979. 12.95 (ISBN 0-87949-137-X). Ashley Bks.
Everywoman: A Novel. Gilbert Frankau. LC 34-6585. E. P. Dutton & Co., Inc.
Everywoman's Road: A Morality of Woman, Creator, Worker, Waster, Joy-Giver and Keeper of the Flame. Josephine Hammond. LC 14-2505. M. Kennerley.
Eve's Daughter. June Jennifer. LC 36-10117. Godwin.
Eve's Delight. Cindy Nemser. 320p. (Orig.). 1982. pap. 3.75 (ISBN 0-523-41755-1). Pinnacle Bks.
Eve's Diary. Mark Twain. 109p. 1981. Repr. of 1906 ed. lib. bdg. 15.00 (ISBN 0-8495-5207-9). Arden Lib.
Eve's Diary: Tr, from the Original Ms. Samuel Langhorne Clemens. 1906. Harper & Brothers.
Eve's Doctor. Signe Toksvig. LC 37-331182. 1937. Harcourt, Brace and Company.
Eve's Hollywood. Eve Babitz. LC 73-17458. (Illus.). 1974. 7.95 (ISBN 0-440-02339-4). Delacorte Press/S. Lawrence.
Eve's Hollywood. Eve Babitz. 1975. (pbk.) 1.50. Dell.
Eve's Hour. Norma Newcomb, pseud. (Alouette Romance Ser.). 224p. (Orig.). 1981. pap. 2.25 (ISBN 0-89531-127-5, 0198-96). Sharon Pubns.
Eve's Lover, and Other Stories. Lucy Lane Clifford. LC 70-128724. (Short story index reprint series). 1970. Books for Libraries Press.
Eve's Lover, and Other Stories. Lucy Lane Clifford. LC 24-7681. 1924. C. Scribner's Sons.
Eve's Orchard. Margaret Widdemer. LC 35-20667. Farrar & Rinehart, Incorporated.
Eve's Ransom. George Robert Gissing. LC 80-67317. 1981. 3.00 (ISBN 0-486-24016-9). Dover Publications.
Eve's Ransom: A Novel. George Robert Gissing. LC 74-87055. 1969. AMS Press.
Eve's Ransom: A Novel. George Robert Gissing. LC 6-43981. 1895. D. Appleton and Company.
Eve's Second Apple. Herbert Silvette. LC 46-5410. 1946. E. P. Dutton and Company, Inc.
Eve's Second Husband. Corra May White Harris. LC 11-2078. Henry Altemus Company.
Eve's Temptation. Lucy Walling. LC 34-20348. A. L. Burt Company.
Eve's Tower. May Martin Van Wye. LC 61-14519. Dorrance.
Evidence: A Novel. John Weisman. LC 79-20562. 1980. 10.95 (ISBN 0-670-30041-1). Viking Press.
Evidence: A Novel. John Weisman. ("A Signet Book)). 1981. 2.95 (ISBN 0-451-09892-7). New American Library.
Evidence Circumstantial. Alfred Sohland. LC 55-11656. 1956. Vantage Press.
Evidence Code of California. Ed. by Parker & Son Staff. 1975. pap. 5.00x o.p. Parker & Son.
Evidence of Love. Shirley Ann Grau. LC 76-47920. 1977. 7.95 (ISBN 0-394-41115-3). Knopf: Distributed by Random House.
Evidence of Love. ltd. 1st ed. Shirley Ann Grau. LC 77-367158. (Illus.). 1977. 1.95 (ISBN 0-449-23766-4). Franklin Library.
Evidence of Love. Shirley Ann Grau. 1978. 1.95 (ISBN 0-449-23766-4). Fawcett Crest Books.

Evidence of Love: A Novel. 1st Ed. Dan Jacobson. LC 60-587356. 1960. Little, Brown.

Evidence of Things Seen. Elizabeth Daly. LC 43-9416. 1943. Farrar & Rinehart, Inc.

Evidence Unseen. Lavinia Riker Davis. LC 45-3921. 1945. Pub. for the Crime Club, by Doubleday, Doran & Co., Inc.

Evidence You Will Hear. Hamilton Jobson. LC 75-15334. 6.95 (ISBN 0-684-14424-7). Scribner.

Evidently Murdered. Jay Hall. LC 43-8272. 1943. Dorrance and Company.

Evie's Fortune in Paris. (Signet Book). 1.50 (ISBN 0-451-08267-2). New American Library.

Evil. Hugh Barnett Cave. 320p. (Orig.). 1981. pap. 3.25 (ISBN 0-441-21850-4). Ace Bks.

Evil Among Us. Jeanne Crecy. (Signet Book). 1975. (pbk.) 1.25. New American Library.

Evil at Queen's Priory. Virginia Coffman. 1973. pap. 0.95 o.s.i. (75-424). Lancer.

Evil at Roger's Cross. Catherine Marchant, pseud. 1970. pap. 0.75 o.p. (ISBN 0-447-74716-9). Lancer.

Evil Became Them. Pat Root. LC 52-7943. (Inner sanctum mystery). 1952. Simon and Schuster.

Evil Cargo. Ken Stanton. (Aquanaut Ser.). (Orig.). 1973. pap. 0.95 o.p. (ISBN 0-532-95248-0). Woodhill.

Evil Cargo. Ken Stanton. (Aquanauts #9). 1973. (pbk) 0.95. Manor Books.

Evil Chateau. Sydney Horler. LC 31-21543. 1931. A. A. Knopf.

Evil Children. Willo Davis Roberts. 1973. pap. 0.95 o.s.i. (75-449). Lancer.

Evil Come(Evil Go. Whit Masterson, pseud. LC 61-83113. (Red badge detective). 1961. Dodd, Mead.

Evil Companions. Michael Perkins. pap. 1.95 o.p. (0109). Essex Hse.

Evil Cousin. Martin Neil. 192p. (Orig.). 1973. pap. 1.95 o.p. (ISBN 0-87682-312-6, 7312). Barclay Hse.

Evil Day. Errol Brathwaite. LC 67-97426. (B 67-14348). 1967. Collins.

Evil Days. Bruno Fischer. LC 73-5055. 1974. 5.95 (ISBN 0-394-48409-6). Random House.

Evil Earths: An Anthology of Way-Back-When Futures. Brian Wilson Aldiss. LC 79-52182. 1979. 2.50 (ISBN 0-380-44636-7). Avon Books.

Evil Empress: A Romance of the Court of Catherine the Great. Aleksandr Mikhailovich. LC 34-4569. 1934. J. B. Lippincott Company.

Evil Eye. Theophile Gautier. Tr. by Alexina Loranger Donovan. Maupassant, Guy De, 1850-1893. (On cover: Idylwild series, v. 1, no. 18). 1892. Morrill, Higgins & Co.

Evil Eye and Other Stories. Natacha Stewart. LC 70-186341. 1972. 5.95 (ISBN 0-395-13693-8). Houghton Mifflin.

Evil Friendship. Vin Packer. 1970. pap. 0.75 o.p. (75-299). Manor Bks.

Evil Genius. George Bagby, pseud. 1969. pap. 0.60 o.p. (0502-06027-060). Curtis.

Evil Genius. Wilkie Collins. LC 6-26950. (On cover: Lovell's library. v. 14, no. 722). 1886. John W. Lovell Company.

Evil Genius. Aaron Marc Stein. LC 61-9558. 1961. Published for the Crime Club by Doubleday.

Evil Genius: A Domestic Story. Wilkie Collins. (On cover: The seaside library. Pocket ed., no. 764). 1886. G. Munro.

Evil Genius: A Domestic Story. Wilkie Collins. LC 6-26951. (Harper's handy series, no. 72). 1886. Harper & Brothers.

Evil Gnome. Kenneth Robeson. (Doc Savage Adventure#82). 1976. (pbk.) 1.25. Bantam Books.

Evil Guest. Joseph Sheridan Le Fanu. LC 76-4605. (collected works of Joseph Sheridan Le Fanu). ((Series: Le Fanu, Joseph Sheridan, 1814-1873.). (Works. 1976.). 1976. 17.00 (ISBN 0-405-09206-7). Arno Press.

Evil Heart: Or, The Flirt. Bertha M. Clay. LC 48-40649. (Bertha Clay library, no. 162). 1902. Street & Smith.

Evil in the Family. Grace Corren, pseud. (Orig.). 1972. pap. 0.95 o.s.i. (75-402). Lancer.

Evil in the Family. Grace Corren, pseud. (O.s.i.). 1975. pap. 1.25 o.s.i. Tower.

Evil in the House. easy eye ed. Evelyn Bond. (Orig.). 1969. pap. 0.75 o.p. (74-515). Lancer.

Evil in the House: By Elbur Ford Pseud. Eleanor Hibbert. LC 54-509752. 1954. Morrow.

Evil in Waiting: By Renate Chapman. Renate Chapman. 1974. 4.50. Avalon Books.

Evil Is a Quiet Word. Theodus Carroll. 1975. (pbk.) 1.50. Warner Books.

Evil Is As Evil Does. Rosemary Gatenby. LC 67-12987. 1967. M. S. Mill Co.; Distributed by Morrow.

Evil Is the Night. Jocelyn Chadwick. (Avon gothic). 1974. (pbk.) 0.95. Avon.

Evil Island. Jennifer Blair. (candlelight mystery). 1974. (pbk.) 0.75. Dell.

Evil Lives Here. Helen Nuelle. 192p. 1974. pap. 0.95 o.p. (ISBN 0-532-12464-2). Woodhill.

Evil Lives Here. Helen Nuelle. 192p. 1974. pap. 0.95 o.s.i. (ISBN 0-532-12464-2). Manor Bks.

Evil Lives Here. Helen Nuelle. (Avalon romances). 1973. 4.50. Avalon Books.

Evil Lives Here. Helen Nuelle. 1974. (pbk.) 0.95. Manor Books.

Evil Men Do. Cortland Fitzsimmons. LC 41-610. 1941. Frederick A. Stokes Company.

Evil Mistress. Weldon Matthews. LC 34-223683. 1934. W. Godwin, Inc.

Evil of Dark Harbor. Clarissa Ross. 1975. (pbk.) 1.25 (ISBN 0-380-00478-X). Avon.

Evil of the Day. Thomas L. Sterling. LC 55-14404. (Inner sanctum mystery). 1955. Simon and Schuster.

Evil of Time. Evelyn Berckman. LC 54-605119. (Red badge detective). 1954. Dodd, Mead.

Evil of Time. Evelyn Berckman. LC 54-6051. (Signet book). 1975. (pbk.) 0.95. New American Library.

Evil One. C. Scott Mackie. LC 73-77535. 1973. 4.95 (ISBN 0-8059-1855-8). Dorrance.

Evil One. J. N. Williamson. (Orig.). 1982. pap. 2.95 (ISBN 0-89083-966-2). Zebra.

Evil Ones. James Mitchell. 224p. 1983. 14.95 (ISBN 0-241-10837-3, Pub. by Hamish Hamilton England). David & Charles.

Evil Place. Wayne Welty. (Orig.). 1979. pap. 1.95 (ISBN 0-532-23153-8). Woodhill.

Evil Root. Lee Thayer. LC 49-7843. (Red badge mystery). 1949. Dodd, Mead.

Evil Saint. Karl May. 1979. 12.95 (ISBN 0-8264-0101-5). Continuum.

Evil Saint: A Novel. Karl Friedrich May. LC 79-14965. (collected works of Karl May; ser. 3, v. 4). (Continuum book). 12.95 (ISBN 0-8164-9362-6). Seabury Press.

Evil Shepherd. Edward Phillips Oppenheim. LC 22-18397. 1922. Little, Brown, and Company.

Evil Side of Eden. Sara North, pseud. LC 77-15849. (Orig.). 1978. pap. 1.50 o.p. (ISBN 0-87216-451-9, C16451). Playboy Pr Pbks.

Evil Star. Cleve Franklin Adams. LC 44-410021. 1944. E. P. Dutton & Company, Inc.

Evil Streak. Andrea Newman. LC 76-40636. 1977. 7.95 (ISBN 0-385-12641-7). Doubleday.

Evil Streak. Andrea Newman. 1979. 1.95 (ISBN 0-671-82193-8). Pocket Books.

Evil That Men Do. Edgar Fawcett. (On cover: Belford American novel series, no. 7). 1889. Belford Company.

Evil That Men Do. R. Lance Hill. LC 78-53302. 1978. 9.95 (ISBN 0-8129-0769-8). Times Books.

Evil That Men Do. Eric Cyril Egerton Leadbitter. LC 23-11975. New York Etc.

Evil That Men Do. Hugh Pentecost. 1973. pap. 0.75 o.p. (ISBN 0-515-02892-4, T2892). Pyramid Pubns.

Evil That Men Do: By Hugh Penntcost Pseud. Judson Pentecost Philips. LC 66-18347. (Red badge mystery). bds., 3.50. Dodd.

Evil Tongue. Preston Harriman. 192p. (Orig.). 1973. pap. 1.95 o.p. (ISBN 0-87056-283-5, 6283). Brandon.

Evil Under the Sun. Agatha Miller Christie. LC 41-197163. 1941. Dodd, Mead & Company.

Evil Under the Sun. Agatha Miller Christie. LC 45-5365. (On cover: Pocket book. 285). 1945. Pocket Books, Inc.

Evil Under the Sun. the greenway ed. Agatha Miller Christie. LC 81-67343. 1981. 8.95 (ISBN 0-396-08017-0). Dodd, Mead.

Evil Under the Sun. Agatha Miller Christie. 1973. (pbk.) 0.95. Pocket Books.

Evil Under the Sun. Anton Myer. LC 51-13135. 1951. Random House.

Evil Vineyard. Marie Hay. LC 24-4865. 1923. G. P. Putnam's Sons.

Evil Wish. Jean Potts. LC 62-14035. 1962. Scribner.

Evolution of a Trade Unionist. Frank Keyes Foster. LC 2-1090. 1901. Allied Printing Trades Council.

Evolution of "Dodd" A Pedagogical Story Giving His Struggle for the Survival of the Fittest: Tracing His Chances, His Changes, and How He Came Out. William Hawley Smith. LC 34-38295. 1890. Rand, McNally & Company.

Evolution of "Dodd" A Pedagogical Story. William Hawley Smith. Rand, McNally & Company.

Evolution of "Dodd," In His Struggle for the Survival of the Fittest in Himself: Tracing His Chances, His Changes, and How He Came Out. William Hawley Smith. LC 8-9636. 1884. Henderson & Smith.

Evolution of Dodd's Sister: A Tragedy of Everyday Life. Charlotte Whitney Eastman. LC 6-36813. 1897. Rand, McNally & Company.

Evolution of Fredda. Edward Harold Crosby. LC 11-1853. 1.50. The C. M. Clark Publishing Co.

Evolution of Helen Bright. George H Eisenhart. LC 27-14608. Durrance and Company.

Evolution of Peter Moore. Dale Drummond. LC 19-2846. 1.50. Britton Publishing Company.

Evolution of Rose. Ellen Snow. LC 8-276. 1907. R. G. Badger.

Evvie. Vera Caspary. LC 73-175670. 1973. 1.80 (ISBN 0-85617-734-2). White Lion Publishers.

Evvie. 1st Ed. Vera Caspary. LC 60-10440. 1960. Harper.

Ewa, a Tale of Korea. William Arthur Noble. LC 6-36433. Eaton & Mains.

Ewe Lamb. Margaret Erskine. (Ace gothic). 1974. (pbk.) 0.95. Ace Books.

Ewe Lamb. Wetherby Williams. LC 68-18078. 1968. Published for the Crime Club by Doubleday.

Ewings. John O'Hara. LC 78-31494. 1972. 6.95 (ISBN 0-394-47404-X). Random House.

Ewing's Lady. Harry Leon Wilson. LC 7-38598. 1907. D. Appleton and Company.

Ewings of Dallas. 384p. (Orig.). 1980. pap. 2.75 (ISBN 0-553-14439-1). Bantam.

Ex-Detective. Edward Phillips Oppenheim. LC 77-150481. (Short story index reprint series). 1971. (ISBN 0-8369-3822-4). Books for Libraries Press.

Ex-Detective. Edward Phillips Oppenheim. LC 33-30451. 1933. Little, Brown, and Company.

Ex-"It" Anonymous. LC 30-21182. The Vanguard Press.

Ex-Judge. LC 30-27925. Brentano's.

Ex-Love. Mateel Howe Farnham. LC 37-17365. 1937. Dodd, Mead & Company.

Ex-Magician and Other Stories. Murilo Rubiao. LC 78-2064. 10.00 (ISBN 0-06-013708-8). Harper & Row.

Ex-Mistress. Grace Perkins Oursler. LC 30-3867. 1930. Brentano's.

Ex-Nun. William Wilfrid Whalen. LC 27-2303. 1927. B. Herder Book Co.

Ex Officio. Timothy J Culver. LC 75-106590. 1970. 6.95. M. Evans.

Ex-Wife. Katherine Ursula Parrott. LC 29-17090. 1929. J. Cape & H. Smith.

Ex-Wife. Katherine Ursula Parrott. LC 30-21164. 1930. Grosset & Dunlap.

Exact and Very Strange Truth. Ben Daniel Piazza. LC 64-18968. 1964. Farrar, Straus.

Exaggerations of Peter Prince. Steve Katz. LC 68-11389. 281p. 1968. 6.95 o.p. HR&W.

Exagggerations Sic of Peter Prince: The Novel. Steve Katz. LC 68-11389. (Illus.). 1968. Holt, Rinehart and Winston.

Exaltation of Stars: Transcendental Adventures in Science Fiction. Ed. by Terry Carr. Robert Silverberg et al. LC 72-89253. 191p. 1973. 12.50 (ISBN 0-671-21469-1). Ultramarine Pub.

Exaltation of Stars: Transcendental Adventures in Science Fiction. Ed. by Terry Carr. LC 72-89253. (O.s.i.). 1973. 6.95 o.s.i. (ISBN 0-671-21469-1). S&S.

Exaltation of Stars: Transcendental Adventures in Science Fiction. Robert Silverberg & Roger Zelazny. Ed. by Terry Carr. LC 72-89253. 1973. 6.95 (ISBN 0-671-21469-1). Simon and Schuster.

Exalted Valley. Marjorie Babbage. 1979. 7.95 (ISBN 0-533-03983-5). Vantage.

Example of Richard Wright. Dan McCall. LC 69-14837. 1969. Harcourt, Brace & World.

Excalibur! Kane & Jakes. 1980. pap. 3.50 (ISBN 0-440-12213-9). Dell.

Excalibur. Sanders Anne Laubenthal. (Original adult fantasy). 1973. (pbk.) 1.25. Ballantine Books.

Excalibur Disaster. Jack M Bickham. LC 77-25577. 1978. 10.00 (ISBN 0-385-14169-6). Doubleday.

Excalibur Disaster. Jack M Bickham. 1980. 2.75 (ISBN 0-87216-756-9). Playboy Paperbacks.

Excavating a Husband. Ella Bell Wallis. LC 17-172861. The McLean Company.

Excellency. David Beaty. LC 77-14130. 1978. 8.95 (ISBN 0-688-03269-9). Morrow.

Excellent Knave. Joseph Fitzgerald Molloy. LC 7-25314. Lovell, Coryell & Company.

Excellent Night for Murder... Virginia Rath. LC 37-257594. 1937. Pub. for the Crime Club, Inc., by Doubleday, Doran & Co., Inc.

Excellent Women. Barbara Pym. LC 78-19877. 1978. 7.95 (ISBN 0-525-10116-0). Dutton.

Excelsior! Paul Hyde Bonner. LC 55-7191. 1955. Scribner.

Excelsior. Alberto Ongaro. LC 68-18272. 1968. H. Regnery Co.

Except for Me & Thee. Jessamyn West. LC 69-17171. 1969. 8.50 (ISBN 0-15-129454-2). HarBraceJ.

Except the Lord: A Novel. 1st Ed. Joyce Cary. LC 53-7728. 1953. Harper.

Exception. Oliver Onions. LC 11-14104. 1911. 1.50. John Lane Company.

Exceptional Case. Itti Kinney Reno. LC 7-39783. (On cover: American novels). 1891. J. B. Lippincott Company.

Exceptional Child Through Literature. Elliott D Landau & Sherrie Landau Epstein. LC 77-16317. 7.95. Prentice-Hall.

Exceptional Man. Michael Blankfort. LC 80-66008. 1980. 10.95 (ISBN 0-689-11072-3). Atheneum.

Excerpts from L-Seven: A New World Mythos. new ed. Michael Gosney. (Illus., Orig.). 1979. pap. 8.00 o.p. (ISBN 0-932238-02-5). Avant Bks.

Excerpts from Visions of Cody. John Kerouac. LC 60-4490. 1959. New Directions.

Excess Baggage. Hilary Mason Raleigh. LC 32-202325. E. P. Dutton & Co., Inc.

Excess of Love. Jac Lenders. LC 68-22008. 1968. 5.95. Grove Press.

Exchange. R. L. Brent. (Liquidator Ser.). (O.s.i.). (Orig.). 1977. pap. 1.50 o.s.i. (AD1661, Award). Univ Pub & Dist.

Exchange of Clowns. Theodore Wilden. LC 81-82072. 12.95 (ISBN 0-316-94051-8). Little, Brown.

Exchange of Eagles. Owen Sela. LC 76-62711. 8.95 (ISBN 0-394-41132-3). Pantheon Books.

Exchange of Joy: 1st American Ed. Isabel Quigly. LC 55-10152. 1955. Harcourt, Brace.

Exciting Short Stories. Ed. by Greta A Clark. LC 60-8084. Hart Pub. Co.

Exciting Western Stories. Illustrated by Frank Kramer. Ed. by Chet Beatty. LC 60-6581. (World-famous book, 206). 1960. Hart Pub. Co.

Excitment Circle R. B. Palmer. (Danny Orlis Ser.). pap. 0.95 o.p. Believers Bkshelf.

Excluded from the Cemetery. Peter Marshall. LC 67-20296. 1967. Bobbs-Merrill.

Exclusively Yours. Peggy O'More, pseud. LC 52-13533. 1952. Arcadia House.

Excursion. Francis Pollini. (Signet bk., T3498). 1968. New Amer. Lib.

Excursion to Lilliput: A Novel by Lewis Gibbs Pseud. Joseph Walter Cove. LC 34-1945. 1934. D. Appleton-Century Company, Incorporated.

Excursion to the Sky. Translated from the Serbo-Crostian by Kenneth Johnstone. 1st Ed. Grozdana Olujie. LC 61-503716. 1961. Dutton.

Excursion to Tilsit. Hermann Sudermann & Galantiere, Lewis, 1893- Tr. LC 30-8170. 1930. H. Liveright.

Excursion: 1st Amer. Ed. Francis Pollini. LC 66-202916. 1966. bds., 4.95. Putnam.

Excuse Book. Marcia Jacobs. 1978. pap. 2.50 (ISBN 0-8431-0432-5). Price Stern.

Excuse It, Please. Oliver Herford. LC 30-5089. J. B. Lippincott Company.

Excuse Me! Rupert Hughes. LC 11-23409. The H. K. Fly Company.

Excuse Me, Mrs. Meigs. Elizabeth Frances Corbett. LC 43-1683. 1943. D. Appleton-Century Company, Incorporated.

Excuse My Feet! Being the Full Adventures of Herbert Simkins of the 2nd N. Z. E. F. by the Sarge. The Sarge. LC 52-32081. Printed by the Otago Daily Times and Witness Newspapers Co.

Execution. Marie Claire Blais. LC 77-361738. (Talonplays). 1976. (ISBN 0-88922-103-0). Talonbooks.

Execution. Miranda Cambanis. LC 75-2079. (Orig.). 1975. pap. 2.00x (ISBN 0-914476-35-1). Thorp Springs.

Execution. Oliver Crawford. LC 77-9225. 1978. 8.95 (ISBN 0-312-27422-X). St. Martin's Press.

Execution. Colin McDougall. LC 58-130510. 1958. St. Martin's Press.

Execution. Robert Mayer. LC 78-13652. 1979. 8.95 (ISBN 0-670-30050-0). Viking Press.

Execution: A Novel. Oliver Crawford. 1979. 2.25 (ISBN 0-445-04409-8). Popular Library.

Execution of Adolf Hitler and Other Stories. R. W. Robinson. 2.75 o.p. Vantage.

Execution of Mayor Yin, and Other Stories from the Great Proletarian Cultural Revolution. Jo-Hsi Ch'En. LC 78-1956. (Chinese Literature in Translation). 8.95 (ISBN 0-253-12475-1). Indiana University Press.

Execution of Mayor Yin & Other Stories from the Great Proletarian Cultural Revolution. Jo-hsi Chen. Tr. by Nancy Ing & Howard Goldblatt. LC 78-1956. (Midland Bks: Chinese Literature in Translation Ser: No. 231). 248p. 1978. 10.95x (ISBN 0-253-12475-1); pap. 5.95x (ISBN 0-253-20231-0). Ind U Pr.

Executioner. Jay Bennett. 176p. 1982. pap. 2.25 (ISBN 0-380-79160-9, 79160, Flare). Avon.

Executioner. Pierre Boulle. LC 61-15474. 1961. Vanguard Press.

Executioner: A Parable of Man in Our Century. Richard B Webb. LC 67-19157. 1967. Naylor Co.

Executioner: Assault on Soho. Don Pendleton. (Executioner Ser, No. 6). (Orig.). 1971. pap. 2.25 (ISBN 0-523-41831-0). Pinnacle Bks.

Executioner: Boston Blitz. Don Pendleton. (Executioner Ser., No. 12). 192p. (Orig.). 1972. pap. 2.25 (ISBN 0-523-41833-7). Pinnacle Bks.

Executioner: California Hit. Don Pendleton. (Executioner Ser.: No. 11). 192p. (Orig.). 1972. pap. 2.25 (ISBN 0-523-41832-9). Pinnacle Bks.

Executioner: Caribbean Kill. Don Pendleton. (The Executioner Ser. No. 10). 1972. pap. 1.95 (ISBN 0-523-41074-3). Pinnacle Bks.

Executioner: Chicago Wipeout. Don Pendleton. (Executioner Ser., No. 8). (Orig.). 1971. pap. 2.25 (ISBN 0-523-41763-2). Pinnacle Bks.

TITLE INDEX

EXPEDITION: A NOVEL.

Executioner: Continental Contract. Don Pendleton. (Executioner Ser.: No. 5). (Orig.). 1971. pap. 2.25 (ISBN 0-523-41918-X). Pinnacle Bks.
Executioner: Detroit Deathwatch. Don Pendleton. (Executioner der.: No. 19). (Orig.). 1974. pap. 2.25 (ISBN 0-523-41830-2). Pinnacle Bks.
Executioner: Firebase Seattle. Don Pendleton. (Executioner Ser.: No. 21). 192p. 1975. pap. 1.75 (ISBN 0-523-40757-2). Pinnacle Bks.
Executioner: Jersey Guns. Don Pendleton. (Executioner Ser., No. 17). 1974. pap. 2.25 (ISBN 0-523-41882-5). Pinnacle Bks.
Executioner: Miami Massacre. Don Pendleton. (Executioner Ser.: No. 4). 1970. pap. 2.25 (ISBN 0-523-41823-X). Pinnacle Bks.
Executioner: New Orleans Knockout. Don Pendleton. (Executioner Ser.: No. 20). (Orig.). 1974. pap. 2.25 (ISBN 0-523-41853-1). Pinnacle Bks.
Executioner: Nightmare in New York. Don Pendleton. (Executioner Ser, No. 7). (Orig.). 1971. pap. 2.25 (ISBN 0-523-42014-5). Pinnacle Bks.
Executioner of Venice: A Novel. William Henry Peck. LC 7-36479. (popular series. no. 24). 1892. R. Bonner's Sons.
Executioner: Panic in Philly. Don Pendleton. (Executioner Ser., No. 15). 192p. (Orig.). 1973. pap. 1.95 (ISBN 0-523-41079-4). Pinnacle Bks.
Executioner: San Diego Siege. Don Pendleton. (The Executioner Ser. No. 14). 192p. (Orig.). 1972. pap. 1.95 (ISBN 0-523-41078-6). Pinnacle Bks.
Executioner: Savage Fire. Don Pendleton. (Executioneer Ser: No. 28). 1977. pap. 1.95 (ISBN 0-523-41092-1). Pinnacle Bks.
Executioner: Texas Storm. Don Pendleton. (Executioner Ser.: No. 18). 192p. (Orig.). 1974. pap. 2.25 (ISBN 0-523-41764-0). Pinnacle Bks.
Executioner: Vegas Vendetta. Don Pendleton. (Executioner Ser. No. 9). (Orig.). 1971. pap. 2.25 (ISBN 0-523-42015-3). Pinnacle Bks.
Executioner Waits. Josephine Herbst. LC 74-26115. (Labor Movement in Fiction and Non-Fiction). 1977. 27.50 (ISBN 0-404-58440-3). AMS Press.
Executioner Waits. Josephine Herbst. LC 34-354682. Harcourt, Brace and Company.
Executioner: Washington I.O.U. Don Pendleton. (Executioner Ser., No. 13). 194p. (Orig.). 1972. pap. 2.25 (ISBN 0-523-41855-8). Pinnacle Bks.
Executioners. Nick Carter. (Nick Carter Ser). (O.s.i.). 160p. 1975. pap. 1.25 o.s.i. (AQ1493, Award). Univ Pub & Dist.
Executioners. John Creasey. LC 67-136531. 1967. 3.95. Scribners.
Executioners. John Dann MacDonald. LC 58-9046. 1958. Simon and Schuster.
Executioner's Knife: Or, Joan of Arc; a Tale of the Inquisition. Eugene Sue & De Leon, Daniel, 1852-1914, Tr. LC 10-9819. 1910. New York Labor News Company.
Executioner's Revenge. Leonoe Ferret. LC 6-39234. 1883. Rand, McNally & Co.
Executioner's Song. Norman Mailer. LC 79-17193. 16.95 (ISBN 0-316-54417-5). Little, Brown.
Executioners: The Story of Smersh. Ronald Seth. 1970. pap. 0.75 o.p. (5333, Tempo). G&D.
Executive Bed. George T Dickens. 1973. (pbk.) 1.95 (ISBN 0-87056-355-6). Brandon Books.
Executive Lesbian. Stanley Curson. (Orig.). pap. 0.95 o.p. (1151). Brandon.
Executive Privilege. Geoffrey Perrett. LC 73-88541. 1974. 6.95 (ISBN 0-698-10579-6). Coward, McCann & Geoghegan.
Executive Privilege: A Washington Novel. Lynne Cheney. LC 78-27325. 8.95 (ISBN 0-671-24060-9). Simon and Schuster.
Executive Reader. Playboy Press Editors. pap. 1.25 o.p. (BB127). Playboy.
Executive Suite. Cameron Hawley. LC 52-9588. 1952. Houghton Mifflin.
Executive Wife. Robert Colby. 1970. pap. 0.75 o.p. (75-311). Manor Bks.
Executives. Alexander Fullerton. LC 78-118074. 1970. Putnam.
Executor. A Novel. Annie French Hector. (On cover: Lovell's library, v. 5, no. 209). 1883. J. W. Lovell Company.
Exemplary Life. Siegfried Lenz. LC 76-23113. 1976. 12.50 (ISBN 0-8090-4322-X). Hill and Wang.
Exemplary Life. Siegfried Lenz. LC 77-354923. 1976. 4.90 (ISBN 0-436-24423-3). Secker and Warburg.
Exemplary Novels by Cervantes. 1640. ed. Miguel de Cervantes de Saavedra. Tr. by Mabbe, James. Ed. by Orson, S. W. LC 3-1775. 1900. Gibbings & Company.
Exemplary Novels. Illustrated by Kenneth Hassrick. Translation by Walter K. Kelly. Selected by J. I. Rodale and David M. Glixon. Miguel de Cervantes de Saavedra. LC 53-511. 1952. Story Classics.
Exemplary Novels of Cervantes. Miguel de Cervantes de Saavedra. pap. 3.95 o.p. (ISBN 0-498-04014-3, Prpta). A S Barnes.
Exemplary Novels of Miguel De Cervantes Saavedra; to Which Are Added "The Serpent" & "The Pretended Aunt". Miguel De Cervantes Saavedra. Tr. by Walter K. Kelly. LC 77-91713. (Short Story Index in Reprint Ser.). 1978. Repr. of 1882 ed. 26.75x (ISBN 0-8486-5001-8). Core Collection.
Exemplary Novels of Miguel De Cervantes Saavedra. Miguel de Cervantes de Saavedra. Tr. by Kelly, Walter Keating. LC 16-21304. (Half-title: Bonn's standard library). 1894. G. Bell & Sons.
Exemplary Stories. Miguel de Cervantes de Saavedra. Ed. by Cyril A. Jones. LC 72-171239. (Penguin classics). 1972. 0.40 (ISBN 0-14-044248-0). Penguin.
Exemplary Stories. Miguel de Cervantes Saavedra. Tr. by C. A. Jones. (Classics Ser.). pap. 2.15 o.p. (ISBN 0-14-044248-0, L248). Penguin.
Exercise for Madmen. Barbara Paul. (Berkley Medallion book). 1.50 (ISBN 0-425-03809-2). Berkley Pub. Corp.
Exercise Hoodwink. Maurice Procter. LC 67-28826. 1967. Harper & Row.
Exerciser. Sol Weinstein & Howard Albrect. 1974. (pbk.) 1.95. Ballantine Books.
Exeter Hall. A Theological Romance. William McDonnell. LC 7-16588. 1869. The American News Company.
Exeter Hall. A Theological Romance. 10th ed. William McDonnell. LC 37-18309. 1885. Colby and Rich.
Exhaustive Parallel Intervals. Richard Kostelanetz. LC 79-51581. 1980. 15.00; signed & lettered, A-Z 50.00; pap. 6.00 (ISBN 0-918406-09-9). Future Pr.
Exhibit. Leslie Hollander. 384p. (Orig.). 1981. pap. 2.75 (ISBN 0-523-48000-8). Pinnacle Bks.
Exhibitionist. David R. Slavitt. LC 67-13097. 1967. B. Geis Associates; Distributed by Crown Publishers.
Exhibitionist: A Novel. Henry Sutton, pseud. LC 67-13097. 1967. B. Geis Associates; Distributed by Crown Publishers.
Exil et le Royaume: Nouvelles. Albert Camus. (Coll. Soleil). 1957. 13.25; pap. 3.95. French & Eur.
Exile. Warwick Deeping. 1930. A. A. Knopf.
Exile. Mary Johnston. LC 27-191983. 1927. Little, Brown, and Company.
Exile. Madison Jones. LC 67-20292. 1967. Viking Press.
Exile. Robert Nichols. LC 79-15330. (His Daily lives in Nghsi-Altai; book 4). 3.95 (ISBN 0-8112-0732-3). New Directions Pub. Corp.
Exile: A Novel. Peter Weiss. LC 68-11669. (Seymour Lawrence book.). 1968. Delacorte Press.
Exile, an Out Post of Empire. Dolf Wyllarde. LC 16-6610. 1916. John Lane Company.
Exile and the Kingdom. Albert Camus. LC 58-6531. 1958. Knopf.
Exile from London: A Novel. Richard Henry Savage. LC 8-1997. 1896. The Home Publishing Co.
Exile in Deep Space. Cahill Black. 1979. pap. 1.75 (ISBN 0-89041-239-1, 3239). Major Bks.
Exile of Capri. Foreword by Jean Cocteau. Tr. from French by Edward Hyams. Roger Peyrefitte. LC 65-237794. 1965. 4.95. Fleet.
Exile of Ellendon. William Marden. LC 73-19023. (Doubleday science fiction). 1974. 4.95 (ISBN 0-385-01526-7). Doubleday.
Exile of Erin: A Novel... Elizabeth Gunning Plunkett. LC 2-2048. 1809. Printed by Cotton and Stewart and Sold at Her Book-Stores in Alexandria, and Fredericksburg.
Exile of Tadmor, and Other Tales. Ed. by Mary Anne Madden Sadlier. LC 12-38413. (On cover: Catholic youth's library). D. & J. Sadlier & Co.
Exile of the Lariat. Honore McCue Willsie Morrow. LC 23-11708. 1923. Frederick A. Stokes Company.
Exile to the Stars. Ed Mack Miller. LC 63-12968. 1963. Doubleday.
Exile to the Stars see Handful of Lightning.
Exile Waiting. Vonda N McIntyre. LC 75-328415. N. Doubleday.
Exiled! Steven Greene. 224p. 1982. pap. 2.50 (ISBN 0-445-04700-3). Popular Lib.
Exiled: A Story of an English Parsonage. Charles Hartley. LC 748. Printed for Author by M. W. Knapp.
Exiled, a True Story. Joseph Spillmann. 1963. St. Paul Publications.
Exiled for Lese Majeste. James Thomas Whittaker. LC 8-36536. 1898. Press of Curts & Jennings.
Exiled from Earth. Benjamin Bova. (Dutton anytime books, AB08). 1973. (pbk.) 0.95 (ISBN 0-525-45016-5). Dutton.
Exiled from Earth. Benjamin Bova. LC 74-133120. 1971. 4.95 (ISBN 0-525-29425-2). Dutton.
Exiled from Two Lands a Story. Everett Titsworth Tomlinson. (The hearthstone series). 1898. Lee and Shepard.
Exiled to Heaven. Eugene Thomas. LC 38-7057. R. Speller.
Exiles. Michael J Arlen. LC 70-109553. 1970. 6.95. Farrar, Straus & Giroux.
Exiles. Ed. by Ben Bova & Benjamin Bova. LC 78-3974. 1978. 7.95 o.p. (ISBN 0-312-27493-9). St Martin.
Exiles. James M. Fox. LC 70-90406. 1970. 6.95 o.p. Weybright.
Exiles. James M. W. Knipscheer. LC 70-90406. (Illus.). 1970. 6.95. Weybright and Talley.
Exiles. William Stuart Long. LC 80-111047. (Long, William Stuart, The Australians). 1980. 2.75 (ISBN 0-440-12369-0). Dell Pub. Co.
Exiles. A Russian. Victor Tissot & Amero, Constant, Joint Author. T. B. Peterson & Brothers.
Exiles: And Other Stories. Richard Harding Davis. LC 68-55671. (American short story series, v. 11). (Illus.). 1968. Garrett Press.
Exiles, and Other Stories. Richard Harding Davis. LC 72-8179. (American short story series, v. 11). 1972. (ISBN 0-8422-8034-0). MSS Information Corp.
Exiles, and Other Stories. Richard Harding Davis. LC 6-32462. 1894. Harper & Brothers.
Exiles at the Well of Souls. Jack L Chalker. LC 78-14847. 1978. 1.95 (ISBN 0-345-27701-5). Ballantine Books.
Exiles from Paradise. Sara Mayfield. (O.s.i.). 1971. 8.95 o.s.i. (ISBN 0-440-02379-3, 2379-6). Delacorte.
Exiles of Time. Nelson Slade Bond. LC 50-104. 1949. Prime Press.
Exile's Romance: Or Realities of Australian Life. Arthur Louis Keyser. LC 7-108276. 1887. G. W. Dillingham; Etc., Etc.
Exiles to Glory. Jerry Pournelle. 1.75 (ISBN 0-441-22215-3). Ace Books.
Exiles Trilogy. Benjamin Bova. 1980. pap. 2.50 (ISBN 0-425-04525-0). Berkley Pub.
Exiles: 3 Novellas. Benjamin Bova. LC 78-3974. 1978. 7.95 (ISBN 0-312-27493-9). St. Martin's Press.
Exilius; or The Banish'd Roman. Jane Barker. LC 70-170536. (Foundations of the Novel Ser.: Vol. 25). lib. bdg. 50.00 (ISBN 0-8240-0537-6). Garland Pub.
Existential Errands. Norman Mailer. (Signet, E5422). 1973. 1.75. New American Lib.
Existential Errands. Norman Mailer. LC 76-175476. 1972. 7.95. Little, Brown.
Existential Imagination. Ed. by Frederick Robert Karl & Leo Hamalian. LC 63-3184. (premier book, t188). 1963. Fawcett Publications.
Exit. George Deaux. LC 66-161566. 4.95. S. & S.
Exit. Harold Bell Wright. LC 30-19835. 1930. D. Appleton and Company.
Exit a Dictator. Edward Phillips Oppenheim. LC 39-20163. 1939. Little, Brown and Company.
Exit a Star: A Margot Blair Mystery. Kathleen Moore Knight. LC 41-25824. 1941. Pub. for the Crime Club by Doubleday, Doran & Company, Inc.
Exit, Actors Dying. Margot Arnold, pseud. LC 79-65196. 176p. 1982. pap. 2.50 (ISBN 0-86721-181-4). Playboy Pbks.
Exit and Curtain: A Chico Brett Thriller, by Kevin O'Hara Pseud. Marten Cumberland. LC 52-64153. 1952. Hurst & Blackett.
Exit Betty. Grace Livingston Hill. LC 75-38997. 1975. 9.95 (ISBN 0-89190-007-1). American Reprint Co.
Exit Betty. Grace Livingston Hill. LC 20-13974. 1920. J. B. Lippincott Company.
Exit Charlie. Alex Atkinson. LC 56-5717. 1956. Knopf.
Exit Charlie. Alex Atkinson. LC 81-47402. (Fifty Classics of Crime Fiction, 1950-1975). 1982. 14.95 (ISBN 0-8240-4970-5). Garland Pub.
Exit Dying. Harry Olesker. LC 59-10814. (Random House mystery). 1959. Random House.
Exit Harlequin. Jessica Ryan. LC 47-627. 1947. Pub. for the Crime Club by Doubleday & Company, Inc.
Exit Humanity. Leo Brett, pseud. LC 65-7360. 1965. Arcadia House.
Exit in Green. Martin Brett. (Red badge detective). 1953. Dodd, Mead.
Exit Murderer. Sara Woods, pseud. LC 77-17767. 1978. 7.95 (ISBN 0-312-27587-0). St. Martin's Press.
Exit of Caliban and Shylock: A Ta le of Captive Lady, Knight, Tourney and Crusade ... 1868. A. Winch.
Exit, Running. Bart Spicer. LC 59-13635. (Red Badge Detective). 1959. Dodd, Mead.
Exit Screaming. Herbert Dalmas. LC 66-17230. bds., 3.50. Walker.
Exit Screaming. Frances Moyer Ross Stevens. LC 42-15003. 1942. Published for the Crime Club by Doubleday, Doran & Company, Inc.
Exit Sherlock Holmes. Robert Lee Hall. 288p. 1979. pap. 2.95 (ISBN 0-86721-162-8). Playboy Pbks.
Exit Sherlock Holmes: The Great Detective's Final Days. Robert Lee Hall. LC 76-56152. 1977. 7.95 (ISBN 0-684-14849-8). Scribner.
Exit Sherlock Holmes: The Great Detective's Final Days. Robert Lee Hall. 1979. 1.95 (ISBN 0-87216-511-6). Playboy Press.
Exit Simeon Hex. J. M. Walsh. LC 32-154401. 1931. Brewer, Warren & Putnam, Inc.
Exit the Prince. Lucy Poate Stebbins. LC 35-170973. 1935. The Penn Publishing Company.
Exit Thirty Six: A Fictional Chronicle. Robert Farrar Capon. 250p. 1975. 7.95 o.p. (ISBN 0-8164-0262-0). Seabury.
Exit This Way. 1st Ed. Mary Violet Heberden. LC 50-14985. 1950. Published for the Crime Club by Doubleday.
Exit with Drums. Joseph A Daley. LC 79-125593. (Illus.). 1970. 6.95. St. Martin's Press.
Exit 36: A Fictional Chronicle. Robert Farrar Capon. LC 74-32129. 1975. 7.95 (ISBN 0-8164-0262-0). Seabury Press.
Exodus. Konrad Bercovici. LC 47-3983. 1947. Beechhurst Press.
Exodus. P J Clyde Randall. LC 19-17074. 1919. Peoples Printing Company.
Exodus. Leon M Uris. LC 62-16691. 1962. Doubleday.
Exodus. Leon M. Uris. LC 58-11328. (Illus.). 1958. Doubleday.
Exodus to a Hidden Valley. Eugene Morse. 1974. 8.95 o.p. (ISBN 0-88349-021-8). Readers Digest Pr.
Exodus '43. John Goldsmith. LC 81-19468. (Illus.). 1982. 17.95 (ISBN 0-698-11129-X). Coward, McCann & Geoghegan.
Exorcism. Eth Natas. 192p. 1974. pap. 1.25 o.p. (ISBN 0-532-12206-2). Woodhill.
Exorcism. Eth Natas. 192p. 1974. pap. 1.25 o.p. (ISBN 0-532-12206-2). Manor Bks.
Exorcism of Jenny Slade. Dorothy Daniels. 1974. (pbk.) 1.50 (ISBN 0-671-78747-0). Pocket Books.
Exorcismo de Angela Gray. new ed. Norman T. Vane. Tr. by Javier Lopez from Eng. (Compadre Collection Ser). (Illus.). 160p. (Span.). 1975. pap. 0.95 (ISBN 0-88473-615-6). Fiesta Pub.
Exorcist. William Peter Blatty. LC 73-144189. 1971. 6.95 (ISBN 0-06-010365-5). Harper & Row.
Exotic. Albert Haley. LC 81-9786. 1982. 14.50. Dutton.
Exotic: A Novel. Albert Haley. 352p. 1982. 13.95 (ISBN 0-525-03053-0, 01355-400). Dutton.
Exotic Japanese Stories. Ryunosuke Akutagawa. LC 71-92702. (Illus.). 1972. 3.95 (ISBN 0-87140-069-3). Liveright.
Exotic Japanese Stories, the Beautiful and the Grotesque: 16 Unusual Tales and Unforgettable Images. Ryunosuke Akutagawa. LC 64-14894. 1964. Liveright Pub. Corp.
Exotic Japanese Stories: The Grotesque & the Beautiful. Ryunosuke Akutagawa. (Illus.). 6.95 o.p. (ISBN 0-8148-0099-8). Tudor.
Exotic Nudes. Andre De Dienes. (Illus.). 4.95 (ISBN 0-910550-04-2). Elysium.
Exotic Tea. Yvonne L. Rusiniak. 1970. 2.95 o.p. Vantage.
Exotica in the Desert. Nat Freedland. pap. 0.95 o.p. (1162). Brandon.
Expanded Moment, a Short Story Anthology. Ed. by Robert Coningsby Gordon. LC 63-5055. 1963. Heath.
Expanded Universe. Robert Anson Heinlein. 544p. 1981. pap. 8.95 (ISBN 0-441-21883-0). Ace Bks.
Expanded Universe. Robert Anson Heinlein. 592p. 1982. pap. 3.50 (ISBN 0-441-21888-1). Ace Bks.
Expanded Universe: The New Worlds of Robert A. Heinlein. Robert Anson Heinlein. LC 80-67367. (Illus.). 12.95 (ISBN 0-448-11916-1). Grosset & Dunlap.
Expatriate. Bjrn Robinson Rye. LC 74-17681. 1975. 7.95 (ISBN 0-672-52006-0). Bobbs-Merrill.
Expatriates. Marian Edna Sharrock. LC 32-5037. 1932. D. Appleton and Company.
Expatriates: A Novel. Lilian Lida Bell. LC 5905. 1900. Harper & Brothers.
Expatriates at Large. Charles Beadle. LC 31-4336. 1930. The Macaulay Company.
Expatriation: A Novel. LC 6-38131. (On cover: Appleton's town and country library. no. 56). 1890. D. Appleton and Company.
Expectancy: A Novel. John Seymour Eyton. LC 24-20376. The Century Co.
Expectant Mother. Redbook Editors. pap. 2.75 (ISBN 0-671-42413-0). PB.
Expecting. Christine Lehner. LC 82-8120. 192p. 1982. 12.95 (ISBN 0-8112-0848-6). New Directions.
Expecting Miracles. Linda Howard. LC 79-28571. 10.95 (ISBN 0-399-12496-9). G. P. Putnam.
Expedition. Stanley Wolpert. 1971. pap. 1.25 o.p. (B12-2187). Belmont-Tower.
Expedition: A Novel. Stanley A. Wolpert. LC 68-11520. 1968. Little, Brown.

Expedition of Humphrey Clinker. Ed. Introd., by Angus Ross. Tobias George Smollett. Ed. by Angus Ross. LC 67-981782. (Penguin English lib., EL21). 1967. pap., 1.25. Penguin.

Expedition of Humphry Clinker. Tobias George Smollett. (Dolphin bk., C120). 1961. Doubleday.

Expedition of Humphry Clinker. Tobias George Smollett. Ed. by Lewis Mansfield Knapp. LC 66-66694. (Oxford English novels). 1966. 7.00. Oxford Univ. Pr.

Expedition of Humphry Clinker. Tobias George Smollett. Ed. by Lewis Mansfield Knapp. LC 73-174665. (Oxford English novels). (Oxford paperbacks, no. 287). 1972. 6.95 (ISBN 0-19-281132-0). Oxford University Press.

Expedition of Humphry Clinker. Tobias George Smollett. Ed. by Andre Parreaux. LC 68-5601. (Riverside editions, B67). (Illus.). 1968. 1.75. Houghton Mifflin.

Expedition of Humphry Clinker. Tobias George Smollett. Ed. by Angus Ross. LC 67-9817. (Penguin English library, EL21). (Illus.). 1967. Penguin Books.

Expedition of Humphry Clinker. Tobias George Smollett. LC 2-29255. (English Comedie humaine. 1st ser., v. 4). 1902. The Century Co.

Expedition of Humphry Clinker. Tobias George Smollett. LC 43-17350. (Half-title: Everyman's library, ed. by Ernest Rhys. Fiction. No. 975). 1943. J. M. Dent & Sons Ltd.

Expedition of Humphry Clinker. Tobias George Smollett & Machen, Arthur. LC 29-26915. (Half-title: The modern library of the world's best books). 1929. The Modern Library.

Expedition of Humphry Clinker. Tobias George Smollett & Thomas R Preston. LC 76-20336. (works of Tobias Smollett; v. 6). 15.00 (ISBN 0-87413-121-9). University of Delaware Press.

Expedition of Humphry Clinker. Tobias George Smollett & Roscoe, Thomas. 1836. Harper & Brothers.

Expeditions of Humphry Clinker. Tobias George Smollett. 1972. pap. 2.95 o.p. (ISBN 0-460-01975-9, EP1975, Evman). Biblio Dist.

Expeditions of Humphry Clinker. Tobias George Smollett. 1972. pap. 2.95 o.p. (ISBN 0-460-01975-9, EP1975, Evman). Dutton.

Expeditions of Humphry Clinker. Tobias George Smollett. 3.95x o.p. (ISBN 0-460-00975-3, Evman). Dutton.

Expedition of Humphry Clinker. Ed., Introd., Notes by Andre Parreaux. Tobias George Smollett. Ed. by Andre Parreaux. (Riverside eds., B67). 1968. pap., 1.75. Houghton.

Expedition of Humphry Clinker. Edited with an Introd. by Robert Gorham Davis. Tobias George Smollett. LC 50-12247. (Rinehart editions, 48). 1950. Rinehart.

Expedition to Earth. Arthur Charles Clarke. LC 78-95868. 1970. Harcourt, Brace & World.

Expedition to Earth: Eleven Science-Fiction Stories. Arthur Charles Clarke. LC 53-12766. 1953. Ballantine Books.

Expendable. Willo Davis Roberts. LC 75-21497. 1976. 5.95 (ISBN 0-385-11386-2). Published for the Crime Club by Doubleday.

Expendable Man. Dorothy Belle Flanagan Hughes. LC 63-7639. (Random House mystery). 1963. Random House.

Expendable Spy. Jack D Hunter. LC 65-19968. 1965. Dutton.

Expense Account. Joe Morgan. LC 58-527148. 1958. Random House.

Expensive Habits. Robin Vigfusson. LC 81-50322. 13.50 (ISBN 0-87223-708-7). Seaview Books.

Expensive Halo. Elizabeth Mackintosh. LC 31-24141. 1931. D. Appleton and Company.

Expensive Lady. Helen Marion Edginton. LC 34-8988. The Macaulay Company.

Expensive Miss Du Cane. Sarah Broom Macnaughton. LC 7-66541. 1906. P. R. Reynolds.

Expensive Miss Du Cane: An Episode in Her Life. Sarah Broom Macnaughton. LC 9-35331. 1908. E. P. Dutton and Company.

Expensive People. Joyce Carol Oates. LC 68-8084. 1968. 5.95. Vanguard Press.

Expensive Place to Die. Len Deighton. 1980. 2.25 (ISBN 0-425-04470-X). Berkley Publishing Corp.

Expensive Place to Die: A Novel. Len Deighton. LC 67-12334. (Illus.). 1967. Putnam.

Expensive Pleasures. Stephen Lewis. 1981. pap. 2.95 (ISBN 0-8439-0929-3, LB929). Leisure Bks CT.

Expensive Women. Wilson Collison. LC 31-21904. 1931. R. M. McBride & Company.

Experience. Cecil Henley. LC 60-8162. 1960. Horizon Press.

Experience and Expression: Reading and Responding to Short Fiction. John Lansing Kimmey. LC 75-37901. 5.95 (ISBN 0-673-15016-X). Scott, Foresman.

Experience of Fiction. Marvin Klotz & Richard Abcarian. LC 74-23048. (Illus.). 1975. 4.95. St. Martin's Press.

Experience of India. Ruth Prawer Jhabvala. LC 70-163372. 1972. 6.95 (ISBN 0-393-08659-3). Norton.

Experience of Life; or, Aunt Sarah, 1852 see Margaret Percival, 1847.

Experiences of a Barrister. Samuel Warren. LC 8-33684. 1852. Cornish, Lamport & Co.

Experiences of a Barrister, and Commissions of an Attorney. Samuel Warren. LC 8-33484. 1880. Estes and Lauriat.

Experiences of a Barrister and Confessions of an Attorney. Samuel Warren. LC 75-32790. (Literature of Mystery and Detection). 1976. 21.00 (ISBN 0-405-07906-0). Arno Press.

Experiences of a Country Girl. 1971. pap. 1.75 o.p. (V1017K, Venus). Grove.

Experiences of a Lady Help. Henrietta Eliza Vaughan Stannard. LC 8-13864. Lovell, Coryell & Company.

Experiences of an Irish R.M. Edith Anna Œnone Somerville & Violet Florence Martin. LC 44-53470. (Half-title: Everyman's library, ed. by Ernest Rhys Fiction. No. 978). 1944. J. M. Dent & Sons Ltd.

Experiment. Patrick Skene Catling. LC 67-25380. 1968. Trident Press.

Experiment. Henry Denker. 1977. 1.95 (ISBN 0-671-80848-6). Pocket Books.

Experiment. W. D. Musser. 3.50 o.p. Carlton.

Experiment. Richard Setlowe. 1983. pap. 2.75 (ISBN 0-445-04753-4). Popular Lib.

Experiment. Dolf Wyllarde. LC 33-20826. The Macaulay Company.

Experiment: A Novel. Henry Denker. LC 75-45437. 7.95 (ISBN 0-671-22268-6). Simon and Schuster.

Experiment: A Novel. Richard Setlowe. LC 79-19905. 10.95 (ISBN 0-03-041745-7). Holt, Rinehart, and Winston.

Experiment at Proto. Philip Oakes. LC 72-94114. 1973. 6.95 (ISBN 0-698-10528-1). Coward, McCann & Geoghegan.

Experiment: Four Short Novels. Helen Rose Hull. LC 40-27085. Coward-McCann, Inc.

Experiment in Altruism. Margaret Pollock Sherwood. LC 8-8159. 1895. Macmillan and Co.

Experiment in Crime. Cecil John Charles Street. LC 47-1969. 1947. Dodd, Mead & Company.

Experiment in Crime. easy eye ed. Philip Wylie. 1967. pap. 0.60 o.p. (73-675). Lancer.

Experiment in Marriage. a facsim. reproduction / with an introd. by joel nydahl. ed. Charles Joseph Bellamy. LC 77-16040. 1977. 25.00 (ISBN 0-8201-1304-2). Scholars' Facsimiles & Reprints.

Experiment in Marriage. A Romance. Charles Joseph Bellamy. 1889. Albany Book Company.

Experiment in Perfection. Marion T Davis Barton. LC 7-11589. 1907. Doubleday, Page & Company.

Experiment in Springtime. Margaret Millar. LC 47-1632. 1947. Random House.

Experiment Perilous. Margaret Carpenter. LC 43-4264. 1943. Little, Brown and Company.

Experiment Perilous... Margaret Carpenter. LC 45-422064. 1945.

Experiment with Death. E. X Ferrars, pseud. LC 80-2739. 1981. 9.95 (ISBN 0-385-17523-X). Published for the Crime Club by Doubleday.

Experimental Wooing. Thomas Winthrop Hall. LC 99-45. E. B. Herrick & Company.

Experiments in Crime and Other Stories. Gilbert Frankau. LC 37-2682. 1937. E. P. Dutton & Co., Inc.

Expert Dreamers. 1st Ed. Ed. by Frederik Pohl. LC 62-11295. 1962. Doubleday.

Expert in Murder. Mary Violet Heberden. LC 45-7085. 1945. Pub. for the Crime Club by Doubleday, Doran and Co., Inc.

Experts. 1st American Ed. Martin Mayer. LC 54-12192. Harper.

Expiation. Alice French. LC 6-40030. 1890. C. Scribner's Sons.

Expiation. Mary Annette Beauchamp Russell Russell. LC 29-3495. 1929. Doubleday, Doran & Company, Inc.

Expiation and Naboth's Vineyard. Edward Frederic Benson. LC 24-6740. George H. Doran Company.

Exploding Cow & Other Combustibles: Collected Writings of Sam P. Davis. Samuel P. Davis. Compiled by Daniel E. Small. pap. write for info. (ISBN 0-930830-08-3). Great Basin.

Exploit of Death. Dell Shannon. LC 82-21649. 1983. 11.95 (ISBN 0-688-02018-6). Morrow.

Exploiters. Samuel Edwards, pseud. LC 73-19435. 378p. 1974. 8.95 o.p. (ISBN 0-275-05140-4). Praeger.

Exploiters. Noel Bertram Gerson. LC 73-19435. 1974. 8.95 (ISBN 0-275-05140-4). Praeger.

Exploiters. Noel Bertram Gerson. (Fawcett crest book). 1975. (pbk.) 1.50. Fawcett.

Exploits of a Physician Detective. George Frank Butler. LC 8-30249. 1908. Clinic Publishing Co.

Exploits of Arsene Lupin. Maurice Leblanc. LC 75-32758. (Literature of Mystery and Detection). 1976. 18.00 (ISBN 0-405-07881-1). Arno Press.

Exploits of Arsene Lupin. Maurice Leblanc. Tr. by Teixeira De Mattos, Alexander Louis. LC 7-31976. 1907. Harper & Brothers.

Exploits of Bilge and Ma. Peter Clark Macfarlane. LC 19-14798. 1919. Little, Brown, and Company.

Exploits of Brigadier Gerard. Arthur Conan Doyle. LC 76-376872. 1976. 3.25 (ISBN 0-7195-3227-2). J. Murray: Cape.

Exploits of Brigadier Gerard. Arthur Conan Doyle. LC 21-4129. (Longmans' colonial library). 1896. Longmans, Green and Co.

Exploits of Brigadier Gerard. Arthur Conan Doyle. LC 6-34242. 1896. D. Appleton and Company.

Exploits of Brigadier Gerard. Arthur Conan Doyle. 15.95 (ISBN 0-7195-3227-2). Transatlantic.

Exploits of Captain O'Hagan. Sax Rohmer, pseud. 1968. 6.00. Bookfinger.

Exploits of Elaine: A Detective Novel. Arthur Benjamin Reeve. LC 15-12253. Hearst's International Library Co.

Exploits of Hans Solo, 3 vols. Brian Daley. 1982. pap. 6.75 (ISBN 0-345-29699-0, Del Rey). Ballantine.

Exploits of Juve: Being the Second of the Series of the "Fantomas" Detective Tales. Pierre Souvestre & Allain, Marcel, Joint Author. LC 17-24693. 1917. Brentano's.

Exploits of King Whossis. Edmund G Creeth. LC 43-157557. 1943. The Christopher Publishing House.

Exploits of Sherlock Holmes. John Dickson Carr & Adrian C. Doyle. 1954. 7.95 o.p. (ISBN 0-394-41210-9). Random.

Exploits of Sherlock Holmes. facsimile ed. Arthur Conan Doyle & John D. Carr. LC 75-157775. (Short Story Index Reprint Ser.). Repr. of 1954 ed. 21.00 (ISBN 0-8369-3887-9). Ayer Co.

Exploits of Sherlock Holmes. Arthur Conan Doyle & John Dickson Carr. 1976. 1.95 (ISBN 0-671-80604-1). Pocket Books.

Exploits of Sherlock Holmes. Arthur Conan Doyle & John Dickson Carr. LC 75-157775. (Short story index reprint series). (Illus.). 1971. (ISBN 0-8369-3887-9). Books for Libraries Press.

Exploits of Sherlock Holmes. Arthur Conan Doyle & John Dickson Carr. LC 54-5387. (Illus.). 1954. Random House.

Exploits of the Chevalier Dupin. Michael Harrison. LC 68-7907. (Illus.). 1968. 3.50. Mycroft & Moran.

Exploration of Space. rev. ed. Arthur C. Clarke. (gr. 10-12). 1979. pap. 2.50 (ISBN 0-671-82140-7). PB.

Explorations. Poul Anderson. 320p. 1980. pap. 2.50 (ISBN 0-523-48517-4). Pinnacle Bks.

Explorations. William Butler Yeats. LC 63-9338. (Illus.). 1973. (pbk.) 2.95. Collier Books.

Explorer. Frances Parkinson Wheeler Keyes. 1977. pap. 1.95 (ISBN 0-449-22791-X, C2791, Crest). Fawcett.

Explorer. William Somerset Maugham. LC 75-25353. (Maugham, William Somerset, 1874-1965. Works. 1976). 1976. 15.00 (ISBN 0-405-07810-2). Arno Press.

Explorer. William Somerset Maugham. LC 78-432446. 1969. Penguin.

Explorer. William Somerset Maugham. LC 9-3205. 1909. The Baker & Taylor Co.

Explorer. William Somerset Maugham. LC 20-7650. 1920. George H. Doran Company.

Explorer. Philip Temple. LC 76-365359. 19.70 (ISBN 0-340-20623-3). Hodder & Stoughton.

Explorers. William Stuart Long. (Australians Ser.: Vol. IV). 512p. (Orig.). 1982. pap. 3.50 (ISBN 0-440-12391-7). Dell.

Explorers of Gor. John Norman. 1979. 2.25 (ISBN 0-87997-449-4). DAW Books.

Explorers of the Dawn. Mazo De La Roche. LC 22-4825. 1922. A. A. Knopf.

Explorers of the Infinite. Ed. by Samuel Moskowitz. LC 73-15068. (Classics of Science Fiction Ser.). 353p. 1974. 14.50 (ISBN 0-88355-130-6); pap. 4.95 (ISBN 0-88355-159-4). Hyperion Conn.

Explorers, Short Stories. Cyril M Kornbluth. LC 54-9671. (Ballantine books, 86). 1954. Ballantine Books.

Exploring Other Worlds. Ed. by Samuel Moskowitz. LC 63-10800. 1963. Collier Books.

Explosion. Dorothy Cameron Disney. LC 48-55651. 1948. Random House.

Explosion. Francis Wallace. LC 43-450. 1943. W. Morrow and Co.

Explosion. Eva-Lis Wuorio. Orig. Title: Midsummer Lokki. 1968. pap. 0.75 o.p. (74-945). Lancer.

Explosion at Donner Pass. Gary McCarthy. (Orig.). 1981. pap. 1.95 (ISBN 0-553-14745-5). Bantam.

Explosion in a Cathedral. Alejo Carpentier. Tr. by John Sturrock from Span. 1979. pap. 4.95i o.p. (ISBN 0-06-090651-0, CN 651, CN). Harper & Row.

Explosion in a Cathedral: A Novel. Alejo Carpenter. (Harper Colophon books). 1979. 4.95 (ISBN 0-06-090651-0). Harper & Row.

Explosion in a Cathedral: A Novel. Alejo Carpentier. LC 63-14955. 1963. Little, Brown.

Explosive Assembly. William D Waddell & Hamilton Beazley. LC 67-19126. 1967. Doubleday.

Explosive Assembly: By William D. Waddell, Hamilton Beazley, Jr. William D Waddell & Hamilton Beazley. (75-213). 1968. Macfadden.

Expo Summer. Eileen Fitzgerald. 3.95 o.p. Doubleday.

Expositio in Cantica Canticorum of Williram, Abbot of Ebersberg, 1048-1085. Erminnie H. Bartelmez. (Memoirs Ser.: Vol. 69). (Illus.). 1967. 13.00 o.p. (ISBN 0-87169-069-1). Am Philos.

Express Messenger, and Other Tales of the Rail. Cy Warman. LC 4-15173. 1897. C. Scribner's Sons.

Express of '76: A Chronicle of the Town of York in the War for Independence. Lindley Murray Hubbard. LC 6-38054. 1906. Little, Brown, and Company.

Express Riders. Lee D. Willoughby. (Making of America Ser.: No. 28). 368p. 1982. pap. 3.25 (ISBN 0-440-02249-5, Bryans). Dell.

Express to the East. C. Spoelstra & De Jong, David Cornel, Tr. LC 36-1045. 1935. H. Smith and R. Haas.

Expressions from Inner Space. Ronald B. Avington. 3.50 o.p. Vantage.

Expressway. Howard North. LC 72-90398. 1973. 7.95 (ISBN 0-671-21473-X). Simon and Schuster.

Expurgator. Christopher Nicole. LC 72-84955. 1973. 4.95 (ISBN 0-385-02241-7). Published for the Crime Club by Doubleday.

Expurgator. Andrew York. LC 72-84955. (Crime Club Ser). 192p. 1973. 4.95 o.p. (ISBN 0-385-02241-7). Doubleday.

Exquisite Corpse: A Novel. Alfred Chester. LC 67-10897. 1967. Simon & Schuster.

Exquisite Fool: A Novel. Eleanor Frances Poynter. LC 7-30306. (On cover: Harper's Franklin square library, no. 727). 1892. Harper & Brothers.

Exquisite Perdita. Lily Moresby Adams Beck. LC 26-13798. 1926. Dodd, Mead and Company.

Exquisite Siren: The Romance of Peggy Shippen and Major John Andre. Edwin Ervin Haines. LC 38-281824. J. B. Lippincott Company.

Exquisite Thing. Joyce MacIver. LC 68-19933. 1968. Putnam.

Extenuating Circumstances. Eda Lord. LC 75-154915. 1971. 5.95 (ISBN 0-394-46621-7). Knopf.

Exterior to the Evidence. Joseph Smith Fletcher. LC 23-8756. 1923. A. A. Knopf.

Exterminating Angel. Luis Bunuel. 3.95 o.p. (21276). S&S.

Exterminator. W. A. Ballinger, pseud. 1967. pap. 0.50 o.p. (50-342). Manor Bks.

Exterminator! William S. Burroughs. 1979. pap. 4.95 (ISBN 0-14-005003-5). Penguin.

Exterminator. Patrick Skene Catling. LC 71-79676. 1969. 5.95. Trident Press.

Exterminator! A Novel. William S. Burroughs. LC 72-9736. 1973. 6.95 (ISBN 0-670-30281-3). Viking Press.

Exterminator! A Novel. William S. Burroughs. LC 78-25920. 1979. 2.95 (ISBN 0-14-005003-5). Penguin Books.

External Evidence for Interpolation in Homer. George Melville Bolling. LC 26-14651. 1925. The Clarendon Press.

Exton Manor: By Archibald Marshall... Archibald Marshall. 1908. Dodd, Mead and Company.

Extortioners. John Creasey. LC 74-14013. 1974. 5.95 (ISBN 0-684-13927-8). Scribner.

Extra Body, No. 3. Richard Reinsmith. (Bodyguard Ser.). (Orig.). 1980. pap. text ed. 1.95 o.s.i. (ISBN 0-505-51597-0). Tower Bks.

Extra Day. Algernon Blackwood. LC 15-19806. 1915. The Macmillan Company.

Extra-Girl: A Novel. Stella George Stern Perry. LC 29-17394. 1929. Frederick A. Stokes Company.

Extra Girl: Published Serially Under the Title The Hollywood Story. Ernest Lynn. LC 31-19271. Grosset & Dunlap.

Extra Kill. Dell Shannon. (Lt. Luis Mendoza Mystery Ser). 1971. pap. 0.75 o.p. (T2503). Pyramid Pubns.

Extra Kill: By Dell Shannon Pseud. Elizabeth Linington. LC 62-7927. 1962. W. Morrow.

Extra: L3. Gary Gabriel. Ed. by Jean McConochie. (Regents Readers Ser.). (Illus.). 68p. (gr. 7-12). 1982. pap. text ed. 1.95 (ISBN 0-88345-458-0, 20898). Regents Pub.

Extract from Captain Stormfield's Visit to Heaven. Samuel Langhorne Clemens. LC 9-27263. 1909. Harper & Brothers.

Extracts from the Diary of a Country Pastor. H. C. Gardner. LC 7-3077. 1864. Poe & Hitchcock.

Extracts from the Diary of Moritz Svengali. Alfred Welch. LC 8-36735. 1897. H. Holt and Company.

Extraordinary Adventures of Arsene Lupin, Gentleman-Burglar. Maurice Leblanc. Tr. by George Morehead. LC 76-163040. (Short story index reprint series). 1971. (ISBN 0-8369-3954-9). Books for Libraries Press.

Extraordinary Adventures of Arsene Lupin: Gentleman-Burglar. Maurice Leblanc. Tr. by Morehead, George. LC 10-266019. 0.25. M. A. Donohue & Co.

Extraordinary Adventures of Arsene Lupin: Gentlemen Burglar. Maurice Leblanc. Tr. by D'Apery, Helen (Burrell) LC 10-11876. 0.75. J. S. Ogilvie Publishing Company.

Extraordinary Adventures of Arsene Lupin, Gentleman-Burgler. facsimile ed. Maurice Leblanc. Tr. by George Morehead from Fr. LC 76-163040. (Short Story Index Reprint Ser.). Repr. of 1910 ed. 17.00 (ISBN 0-8369-3954-9). Ayer Co.

Extraordinary Adventures of Julio Jurenito and His Disciples, Translated. Ilya Grigorevich Ehrenburg & Vanzler, Usick, Tr. LC 30-19512. 1930. Covici-Friede.

Extraordinary and All-Absorbing Journal of Wm. N. Seldon: One of a Party of Three Men Who Belonged to the Exploring Expedition of Sir John Franklin, and Who Left the Ship Terror, Frozen up in Ice, in the Arctic Ocean, on the 10th Day of June, 1850...Together with an Account of the Discovery of a New and Beautiful Country, Inhabited by a Strange Race of People... William N. Seldon. LC 10-22482. 1851. E. E. Barclay, A. R. Orton & Co.

Extraordinary Case of Mr. Bell. William John Budd. LC 36-23272. 1936. J. H. Hopkins & Son, Inc.

Extraordinary Experience: Or, The Romance of an Alter Ego. a new ed. Lloyd Stephens Bryce. LC 6-19893. 1891. Brentano's.

Extraordinary House. Rosita Torr Forbes. LC 35-2971. 1935. Frederick A. Stokes Company.

Extraordinary Mary. Evelyn Whitell. LC 20-11896. Master Mind Publishing Company.

Extraordinary Professor. W Kreupp. LC 45-368. 1944. The Colt Press.

Extraordinary Seaman. Phillip Rock. LC 67-21289. 1967. Meredith Press.

Extraordinary Tales. Ed. by Jorge Luis Borges. Adolfo Bioy-Casares. LC 70-150301. 1971. 5.50. Herder and Herder.

Extraordinary Women: Theme and Variations. Compton Mackenzie. LC 28-22880. 1928. Macy-Masius.

Extrapolasis. Alexander Malec. 1969. pap. 0.75 o.p. (0502-07007-075). Curtis.

Extrapolasis: Stories. Alexander Malec. LC 67-11166. 1967. Doubleday.

Extraterrestrial. Julian Shock. (Orig.). 1982. pap. 2.95. Zebra.

Extraterrestrial Report. John H. Butterfield & Robert Siegel. (Illus.). 160p. 1978. 15.00 o.s.i. (ISBN 0-89104-107-9, A & W Visual Library); pap. 7.95 o.s.i. (ISBN 0-89104-093-5). A & W Pubs.

Extraterrestrials. Ed. by Roger Elwood. LC 74-7667. 160p. Date not set. 5.95 (ISBN 0-8255-3054-7). Macrae.

Extreme Friendship. Henri Troyat. LC 66-28104. 1968. Phaedra Publishers.

Extreme License. 1st Ed. Jerome Barry. LC 58-132712. 1958. Published for the Crime Club by Doubleday.

Extreme Magic: A Novella and Other Stories. Hortense Calisher. LC 64-15045. 1964. Little, Brown.

Extreme Occasion. Alec Dixon. LC 27-15117. 1927. Dodd, Mead and Company.

Extreme Occident. Petru Dumitriu. 1966. 6.95 o.p. (ISBN 0-03-054620-6). HR&W.

Extreme Remedies. Miriam Borgenicht. LC 67-12538. 1967. Published for the Crime Club by Doubleday.

Extreme Remedies. John Hejinian. 1975. (pbk.) 1.75. Bantam Books.

Extreme Remedies. Ellen H. Meyer. (Orig.). 1982. pap. 3.50 (ISBN 0-440-12428-X). Dell.

Extreme Remedies: A Novel. John Hejinian. LC 73-87406. 1974. 7.95. St. Martin's Press.

Extreme Unctions and Other Last Rites. Ed. by Robert Bonazzi. LC 74-77663. (New departures in fiction). (Illus.). (pbk.) 3.00. Latitudes Press; Distributed by Serendipity Books, Berkeley, Calif.

Extremes Meet. Compton Mackenzie. LC 28-21579. 1928. Doubleday, Doran & Company, Inc.

Extricating Obadiah. Joseph Crosby Lincoln. LC 21-139369. 1919. A. L. Burt Company.

Extricating Obadiah. Joseph Crosby Lincoln. LC 17-258183. 1917. D. Appleton and Company.

Eye. Vladimir Vladimirovich Nabokov. LC 65-25317. 1965. Phaedra.

Eye Among the Blind. Robert Holdstock. LC 76-381821. 1976. 3.95 (ISBN 0-571-10883-0). Faber.

Eye Among the Blind. Robert Holdstock. LC 76-26350. 1977. 6.95 (ISBN 0-385-12681-6). Doubleday.

Eye Among the Blind. Robert Holdstock. (Signet book). 1979. 1.75 (ISBN 0-451-08480-2). New American Library.

Eye at the Window. Richard E. Geis. (Orig.). pap. 0.95 o.p. (1119). Brandon.

Eye for a Tooth. Cecil William Mercer. LC 44-2599. 1944. G. P. Putnam's Sons.

Eye for a Tooth. Lorne Schemmer. LC 68-56171. 1969. 4.95. Dorrance.

Eye for an Eye. Oliver Weld Bayer, pseud. LC 45-59863. 1945. Pub. for the Crime Club by Doubleday, Doran and Co., Inc.

Eye for an Eye. Clarence Seward Darrow. LC 76-79093. 1969. 5.95. Moore Pub. Co.

Eye for an Eye. Clarence Seward Darrow. LC 5-32855. 1905. Fox, Duffield & Company.

Eye for an Eye. Frances Hickok. LC 29-9991. Hale, Cushman & Flint.

Eye for an Eye. Graham Seton Hutchison. LC 33-293775. Farrar & Rinehart, Incorporated.

Eye for an Eye. V. J Santiago. (Vigilante Series,#1). 1975. (pbk.) 1.25 (ISBN 0-523-00714-0). Pinnacle Books.

Eye for an Eye. Anthony Trollope. LC 66-24802. (Doughty library, no. 1). 1967. Stein and Day.

Eye for an Eye. Anthony Trollope. LC 78-12534. (Ireland, from the Act of Union, 1800, to the Death of Parnell, 1891). 1980. 32.00 (ISBN 0-8240-3505-4). Garland Pub.

Eye for an Eye. reprint ed. / introduction by james r. kincaid. ed. Anthony Trollope. LC 80-1897. 1981. 45.00 (ISBN 0-405-14169-6). Arno Press.

Eye for an Eye. 1st Ed. Leigh Brackett. LC 57-13015. 1957. Published for the Crime Club by Doubleday.

Eye in Attendance. Valentine Williams. LC 27-137956. 1927. Houghton Mifflin Company.

Eye in the Museum. Alfred Walter Stewart. LC 30-125914. 1930. Little, Brown, and Company.

Eye in the Pyramid. Robert Shea & Robert Anton Wilson. (Illuminatus, Part 1). 1975. (pbk.) 1.50. Dell.

Eye in the Ring. Robert J. Randisi. 256p. 1982. pap. 2.75 (ISBN 0-380-81455-2, 81455-2). Avon.

Eye in the Sky. Philip K Dick. LC 79-18395. (Gregg Press science fiction series). (Illus.). 1979. 14.95 (ISBN 0-8398-2481-5). Gregg Press.

Eye la View. Willam Benton. (Capra Chapbook Ser.). (Cloth ed. 10.00 o.p.: No. 33). 1975. pap. 2.50 o.p. (ISBN 0-88496-023-4). Capra Pr.

Eye of a God: And Other Tales of East and West. William Alexander Fraser. LC 79-121551. (Short story index reprint series). 1970. Books for Libraries Press.

Eye of a God and Other Tales of East and West. William Alexander Fraser. LC 99-1964. 1899. Doubleday & McClure Co.

Eye of Cat. Roger Zelazny. LC 82-10433. 13.95 (ISBN 0-671-25519-3). Timescape Books: Distributed by Simon and Schuster.

Eye of Cat. Roger Zelazny. 1982. 13.95 (ISBN 0-671-25519-3, Timescapape). PB.

Eye of Dread. Payne Erskine. LC 13-22282. 1913. Little, Brown, and Company.

Eye of God: A Novel. Ludwig Bemelmans. LC 49-112874. 1949. Viking Press.

Eye of Istar. William Le Queux. LC 77-84247. (Lost Race and Adult Fantasy Fiction). 1978. 25.00 (ISBN 0-405-10993-8). Arno Press.

Eye of Istar: A Romance of the Land of No Return. William Le Queux. LC 7-12854. F. A. Stokes Ocmpany.

Eye of Love. 1st American Ed. Margery Sharp. LC 57-5516. 1957. Little, Brown.

Eye of Lucifer. Frederic Franklyn Van De Water. LC 27-2307. 1927. D. Appleton and Company.

Eye of Night. John L. Brom. 1970. pap. 0.95 o.p. (M1480, Crest). Fawcett World.

Eye of Night. John L. Brom. 6.95 o.p. Delacorte.

Eye of Night: A Novel. John L Brom. LC 72-79435. 1969. 6.95. Bartholomew House.

Eye of Osiris. Richard Austin Freeman. LC 28-244831. (S. S. Van Dine detective library). 1928. C. Scribner's Sons.

Eye of Osiris: A Detective Romance. Richard Austin Freeman. LC 11-31136. Hodder and Stoughton.

Eye of Reason. Paul L. Bennett. 1976. pap. 3.00. Orchard.

Eye of Shiva. Lee Grimes. 1974. (pbk.) 1.25. Warner Paperback Library.

Eye of Summer. Marjorie Lee. LC 61-15126. 1961. Simon and Schuster.

Eye of the Beholder. Marc Behm. LC 79-17064. 8.95 (ISBN 0-8037-2377-6). Dial Press.

Eye of the Beholder. Marc Behm. 1981. 2.95 (ISBN 0-345-29260-X). Ballantine Books.

Eye of the Beholder. Philip Glazebrook. LC 76-11586. 1976. 7.95. Atheneum.

Eye of the Beholder. John William Wainwright. LC 79-27317. 8.95 (ISBN 0-312-27920-5). St. Martin's Press.

Eye of the Beholder, and Other Stories. Elizabeth Baynes De Vegh. LC 57-6461. 1957. Random House.

Eye of the Cat. Dorothy Gladys Spicer. pap. 0.75 o.s.i. (01-340). Lancer.

Eye of the Devil. easy eye ed. Philip Loraine. pap. 0.60 o.p. Lancer.

Eye of the Gods. Richard Owen. LC 77-24399. 7.95 (ISBN 0-525-10196-9). Dutton.

Eye of the Heart. Ed. by Barbara Howes. 1974. pap. 3.95 (ISBN 0-380-00163-2, 54346, Bard). Avon.

Eye of the Heart: Short Stories from Latin America. Ed. by Barbara Howes. LC 72-9879. 1973. 10.95 (ISBN 0-672-51637-3) (ISBN 0-672-51637-3). Bobbs-Merrill.

Eye of the Heron. Ursula K. Le Guin. LC 82-48146. 12.95 (ISBN 0-06-015086-6). Harper & Row.

Eye of the Hurricane. Fergus Reid Buckley. LC 67-10373. 1967. Doubleday.

Eye of the Kite. Archibald Fleming MacLiesh. LC 52-5151. 1952. Random House.

Eye of the Lens. Langdon Jones. LC 76-177438. 1972. 5.95. Macmillan.

Eye of the Lion: A Novel Based on the Life of Mata Hari. Lael Tucker Wertenbaker. LC 64-10956. 1964. Little, Brown.

Eye of the Mind. Lynn Biederstadt. LC 80-28717. 12.95 (ISBN 0-399-90108-6). R. Marek Publishers.

Eye of the Monster. Andre Norton, pseud. 1980. pap. 1.95 (ISBN 0-441-22376-1). Ace Bks.

Eye of the Monster. Andre Norton. 1975. (pbk.) 1.25. Ace Books.

Eye of the Needle. Ken Follett. (Signet Book). 1979. 2.95 (ISBN 0-451-08746-1). New American Library.

Eye of the Needle. Ken Follett. LC 78-21575. 1979. 16.50 (ISBN 0-8161-6655-2). G. K. Hall.

Eye of the Needle. Garland Roark. LC 72-103452. (DD western). 1970. 4.50. Doubleday.

Eye of the Needle. Neilma Sidney, pseud. LC 72-175071. 1970. 3.75 (ISBN 0-85550-021-2). Lloyd O'Neil.

Eye of the Needle. Thomas Walsh. LC 61-15121. 1961. Simon and Schuster.

Eye of the Needle: A Novel. Ken Follett. LC 77-90670. 8.95 (ISBN 0-87795-186-1). Arbor House.

Eye of the Needle: By Ben Stoltzfus. Ben Frank Stoltzfus. LC 67-11265. bds., 4.50. Viking.

Eye of the Scarecrow. Wilson Harris. 108p. (Orig.). 1974. pap. 3.95 (ISBN 0-571-10557-2). Faber & Faber.

Eye of the Storm. Patrick White. LC 73-3501. 1974. 8.95 (ISBN 0-670-30374-7). Viking Press.

Eye of the Storm. 1st American Ed. John Hearne. LC 58-7858. 1958. Little, Brown.

Eye of the Tiger. Wilbur A Smith. LC 75-14841. 1976. 7.95 (ISBN 0-385-11264-5). Doubleday.

Eye of the Tornado. Chapman Pincher. cancelled o.s.i. (ISBN 0-7181-1494-9, Pub. by Michael Joseph). Merrimack Pub Cir.

Eye of the Wolf. Theodore V Olsen. LC 75-161315. 1971. 4.95. Doubleday.

Eye of the Zodiac. E. C. Tubb. (Science Fiction Ser). 1975. pap. 1.25 o.p. (UY1194). DAW Bks.

Eye of the Zodiac. E. C Tubb. (Dumarest of terra#13). 1975. (pbk.) 1.25. Daw Books.

Eye of Zeitoon. Talbot Mundy. LC 20-495907. The Bobbs-Merrill Company.

Eye Opener. Geoffrey Dutton. LC 81-14633. 1982. 14.95 (ISBN 0-7022-1622-4) (ISBN 0-7022-1623-2). University of Queensland Press.

Eye Stones. Harriet Esmond. LC 75-6770. 1975. 6.95 (ISBN 0-440-02425-0). Delacorte Press.

Eye to Eye. Diana C Chang. LC 74-4857. 1974. 6.95 (ISBN 0-06-010704-9). Harper & Row.

Eye Witness. Eric Levison. The Bobbs-Merrill Company.

Eye Witness. John S. Strange. 1970. pap. 0.60 o.p. (0502-06080). Curtis.

Eye-Witness! Tiffany Thayer. LC 31-5218. The John Day Company.

Eye Witness. Tillett, Dorothy (Stockbridge) LC 61-956128. 1961. Published for the Crime Club by Doubleday.

Eye-Witness: Or, Life Scenes in the Old North State... eyewitness ed. A. O Wheeler & A. O. W. LC 72-1510. (Black Heritage Library Collection). (Illus.). 1972. 12.50 (ISBN 0-8369-8994-5). Books for Libraries Press.

Eye-Witness: Or, Life Scenes in the Old North State, Depicting the Trials and Sufferings of the Unionists During the Rebellion. A. O. Wheeler. LC 8-34339. 1865. B. B. Russell and Company.

Eyeless in Gaza. Aldous Leonard Huxley. LC 36-14923. 1936. Harper & Brothers.

Eyeless in Gaza. Aldous Leonard Huxley. (Perennial library). 1974. (pbk.) 1.25 (ISBN 0-06-080317-7). Harper & Row.

Eyelids of the Morn. Wijnant Johnston. LC 29-1809. 1929. D. Appleton and Company.

Eyes. Felice Picano. LC 75-13409. 1976. 8.95 (ISBN 0-87795-123-3). Arbor House.

Eyes. Felice Picano. (Dell Book). 1977. 1.95 (ISBN 0-440-12427-1). Dell Pub. Co.

Eyes: A Novel. Janet Burroway. LC 66-16687. 1966. Little, Brown.

Eyes & Objects. Ronald Johnson. LC 75-37296. pap. 4.00 (ISBN 0-912330-34-1, Dist. by Inland Bk). Jargon Soc.

Eyes Around Me. Gavin Black. LC 64-18085. 1980. pap. 1.95i o.p. (ISBN 0-06-080485-8, P 485, PL). Har-Row.

Eyes Around Me. Gavin Black. 1981. 18.95x (Pub. by Remploy England). State Mutual Bk.

Eyes Around Me. Oswald Wynd. LC 64-18085. 1964. Harper & Row.

Eyes at the Window. Olivia Smith Cornelius. 1.50. Broadway Publishing Co.

Eyes at the Window. George Selmark, pseud. LC 66-20965. 1966. Published for the Crime Club by Doubleday.

Eyes in the Dark. Zenobia Bird. LC 30-30578. 1930. Fleming H. Revell Company.

Eyes in the Night. Caroline M Howarth. LC 53-11182. 1953. Pageant Press.

Eyes in the Wall. Carolyn Wells. LC 34-116559. J. B. Lippincott Company.

Eyes Like the Sea: A Novel. Mor Jokai. Tr. by Bain, Robert Nisbet. LC 9-3336. (The Hudson library. 19). 1901. G. P. Putnam's Sons.

Eyes of Amber & Other Stories. Joan D. Vinge. (Orig.). 1979. pap. 1.95 (J8863, Sig). NAL.

Eyes of Amber & Other Stories. Joan D. Vinge. 1983. pap. 2.75 (ISBN 0-451-12083-3, Sig). NAL.

Eyes of Boyhood. Clyde Brion Davis. 1953. 3.95 o.p. Lippincott.

Eyes of Buddha. John Dudley Ball. LC 76-205. 7.95 (ISBN 0-316-07952-9). Little, Brown.

Eyes of Darkness. Leigh Nichols. (Orig.). 1980. pap. 2.75 (ISBN 0-671-82784-7). PB.

Eyes of Death. John Bentley. LC 34-41049. 1934. Pub. for the Crime Club, Inc., by Doubleday, Doran & Company, Inc.

Eyes of Green. Nina Bawden. LC 53-10168. 1953. Morrow.

Eyes of Heisenberg. Frank Herbert. (Orig.). 1973. pap. 1.95 (ISBN 0-425-04338-X, Medallion). Berkley Pub.

Eyes of Horus. Joan Marshall Grant. LC 78-20220. (Grant, Joan Marshall, 1907-. Works). (Illus.). 1980. 26.00 (ISBN 0-405-11782-5). Arno Press.

Eyes of Innocence. Maurice Leblanc. Tr. by Teixeira De Mattos, Alexander Louis. LC 20-19765. 1920. The Macaulay Company.

Eyes of Love. Charles Beardsley. 2.50 (ISBN 0-445-04482-9). Popular Library.

Eyes of Love. Corra May White Harris. LC 22-145775. 1.75. George H. Doran Company.

Eyes of Love. Jean Woodward. 1982. pap. 6.95 (Avalon). Bouregy.

Eyes of Love: A Novel. Warwick Deeping. LC 33-8993. R. M. McBride & Company.

Eyes of Max Carrados. Ernest Bramah Smith. LC 24-5830. George H. Doran Company.

Eyes of Reason: A Novel. 1st Ed. Stefan Heym. LC 51-122. 1951. Little, Brown.

Eyes of Sarsis. Andrew J. Offut & Richard K. Lyon. (Orig.). 1980. pap. 2.25 (ISBN 0-671-82679-4, Timescspe). PB.

Eyes of the Blind. Arthur Somers Roche. LC 19-5200. George H. Doran Company.

Eyes of the Blind. Arthur Somers Roche. 1922. A. L. Burt Company.

Eyes of the Gull. Margaret Duley. LC 77-353619. 1976. 4.95 (ISBN 0-88760-083-2). Griffin House.

Eyes of the Hawk. large print ed. Elmer Kelton. LC 82-10542. 1982. 9.95 (ISBN 0-89621-384-6). Thorndike Press.

Eyes of the Hawk. Lee McElroy. LC 80-2945. 1981. 10.95 (ISBN 0-385-17611-2). Doubleday.

Eyes of the Interred. Miguel Angel Asturias. LC 72-10815. 1973. 10.00. Delacorte Press.

Eyes of the Overworld. Jack Vance. (Kangaroo Book). 1977. 1.50 (ISBN 0-671-80904-0). Pocket Books.

Eyes of the Overworld. John Holbrook Vance. LC 77-4492. (Gregg Press science fiction series; 3). 1977. 11.00 (ISBN 0-8398-2366-5). Gregg Press.

Eyes of the Panther: Tales of Soldiers and Civilians. Ambrose Gwinnett Bierce. LC 76-169541. (Short story index reprint series). 1971. (ISBN 0-8369-4002-4). Books for Libraries Press.

Eyes of the Proud. Translated by Delano Ames. 1st American Ed. Mercedes Salisachs. LC 60-10931. 1960. Harcourt, Brace.

Eyes of the Tiger. Nick Carter. (Nick Carter Ser.). (O.s.i.). 1973. pap. 0.95 o.s.i. (AN1132, Award). Univ Pub & Dist.

Eyes of the Tiger. Virginia Evans. 1970. 4.00 (ISBN 0-8233-0139-7). Golden Quill.

Eyes of the Village. Anice Morris Stockton Terhune. LC 22-5072. The Macaulay Company.

Eyes of the Wilderness. Charles George Douglas Roberts. LC 33-25975. 1933. The Macmillan Company.

Eyes of the Woods. Joseph Alexander Altsheler. 1976. lib. bdg. 12.95x (ISBN 0-89968-145-X). Lightyear.
Eyes of the World. Harold Bell Wright. LC 17-389038. 1914. A. L. Burt Company.
Eyes of the World: A Novel. Harold Bell Wright. LC 14-13881. 1914. The Book Supply Company.
Eyes of the World: A Novel. Harold Bell Wright. LC 21-139438. 1916. A. L. Burt Co.
Eyes on Utopia Murders. Barbara D'Amato. (Orig.). 1981. pap. 2.50 (ISBN 0-441-22416-4). Ace Bks.
Eyes That Do Not See. Hilton Hill. LC 7-4695. R. F. Fenno and Company.
Eyes That See Not. Emma Lewis Thomson Southwick. LC 25-24579. 1925. Siebel Publishing Corporation.
Eyes That Watch You: By William Irish Pseud. Hopley-Woolrich, Cornell George. LC 52-8732. (Murray Hill mystery). 1952. Rinehart.
Eyes Through the Tree. Maude C Keator. LC 30-4726. 1930. D. Appleton and Company.
Eyes Unto the Hills. Bertha B. Moore McCurry. LC 51-8589. 1951. W. B. Eerdmans Pub. Co.
Eyes,Etc. A Memoir. Eleanor Clark. 1979. 1.95 (ISBN 0-671-82516-X). Pocket Books.
Eyewitness. John Harris. LC 67-10763. 1967. Harcourt, Brace & World.
Eyewitness. John Minahan. 176p. (Orig.). 1981. pap. 2.25 (ISBN 0-380-77388-0, 77388). Avon.
Eyewitness: The Testimony of John. Mary Ronalds. LC 67-17380. 1967. 4.50. Abingdon.
Eyewitness to Disaster. Dan Perkes. (Illus.). 256p. 1976. 12.95 o.p. (ISBN 0-8437-3000-5). Hammond Inc.
Eyrbyggja Saga. Tr. by Hermann Palsson & Paul Edwards. LC 72-97525. 1973. 15.00 o.p. (ISBN 0-8020-1942-0). U of Toronto Pr.
Eyre's Acquittal. Helen Buckingham Mathers Reeves. (On cover: Lovell's library, v. 4, no. 165). 1883. J. W. Lovell Company.
Eyrie. Also, The Mystery of a Young Girl. Court Howard. LC 7-7127. (On cover: Munro's library. v. 1. no. 108). N. L. Munro.
Eyrie of an Eagle. Andrea Delmonico. (Ace gothic). 1974. (pbk.) 0.95. Ace Books.
Ezekiel. Lucy Pratt. LC 9-148259. 1909. 1.00. Doubleday, Page & Company.
Ezekiel Expands. Lucy Pratt. LC 14-32499. 1914. 1.25. Houghton Mifflin Company.
Ezekiel of Bethlehem: Or, From Bethlehem to Calvary. Fanny Alricks Shugert. LC 8-7319. 1896. Presbyterian Committee of Publication.
Ezekiel's Sin: A Cornish Romance. Joseph Henry Pearce. LC 98-1256. 1898. G. H. Richmond & Son.
Ezekiel's Sin: A Cornish Romance. Joseph Henry Pearce. LC 99-4763. 1899. J. F. Taylor & Company.
Ezra. Perlita Wolff. LC 11-30045. 1911. Reid Publishing Company.
Ezra Hardman, M. A. of Wayback College. facsimile ed. Sarah Bulkley Rogers. LC 78-163046. (Short Story Index Reprint Ser.). Repr. of 1900 ed. 15.00 (ISBN 0-8369-3960-3). Ayer Co.
Ezra Hardman, M.A., of Wayback College: And Other Stories. Sarah Bulkley Rogers. LC 78-163046. (Short story index reprint series). (Illus.). 1971. (ISBN 0-8369-3960-3). Books for Libraries Press.
Ezra Hardman, M.A. Of Wayback College, and Other Stories. Sarah Bulkley Rogers. LC 2137. Dodge Publishing Company.

F

F As in Flight. Lawrence Treat. LC 48-58798. 1948. W. Morrow.
"F" Certificate. Patrick Bair. LC 69-12361. 1969. 5.95. B. Geis Associates.
F Certificate. David Gurney. LC 69-12361. 1969. 5.95 o.p. Geis.
F Corridor. James William MacQueen. LC 36-10494. 1936. Pub. for the Crime Club, Inc., by Doubleday, Doran & Company, Inc.
F. O. B. Detroit. Wessel Smitter. LC 38-334057. 1938. Harper & Brothers.
F. O. B. Murder: By Bert and Dolores Hitchens. 1st Ed. Hubert Hitchens & Dolores Birk Hitchens. LC 55-8403. 1955. Published for the Crime Club by Doubleday.
F. Quantmeyer Hose No. 7. William G. Herron. 80p. 1972. 3.50 o.p. (ISBN 0-682-47412-6). Exposition.
F. Scott Fitzgerald's Screenplay for Three Comrades by Erich Maria Remarque. Francis Scott Key Fitzgerald & Matthew Joseph Bruccoli. LC 77-28077. (Screenplay Library). (Illus.). 1978. 10.00. (ISBN 0-8093-0854-1) (ISBN 0-8093-0853-3). Southern Illinois University Press.
F. Scott Fitzgerald's Tender Is the Night: And This Side of Paradise a Critical Commentary. Stanley Cooperman. LC 66-1862. (Monarch notes and study guides, 668-4). 1966. 2.50. Monarch Pr.
F 1,000,000 Bank-Note. Samuel Langhorne Clemens. LC 17-13620. 1917. 0.50. Harper & Brothers.
Faber; or, The Lost Years. Jakob Wassermann & Hansen, Harry, 1884- Tr. LC 25-20408. Harcourt, Brace and Company.
Fabia. Olive Higgins Prouty. LC 51-4590. 1951. Houghton Mifflin.
Fabian Dimitry: A Novel. Edgar Fawcett. LC 6-38798. (On cover: The Rialto series. v. 1, no. 25)). 1890. Rand, McNally & Company.
Fabian: The Story of a Moralist. Erich Kastner. Tr. by Brooks, Cyrus Harry. LC 32-32912. 1932. Dodd Mead & Company.
Fabians. Norman MacKenzie & Jeanne MacKenzie. (Illus.). 1978. pap. 6.95 o.p. (ISBN 0-671-24072-2, Touchstone Bks). S&S.
Fabiola. Wiseman, Nicholas Patrick Stephen, Cardinal & Edward Joseph Doherty. LC 51-4712. 1951. Kenedy.
Fabiola: Or, The Church of the Catacombs. Nicholas Patrick Stephen Cardinal - Wiseman. LC 62-53254. 1962. Newman Press.
Fabiola: Or, The Church of the Catacombs. Nicholas Patrick Stephen Wiseman. LC 75-454. (Victorian Fiction: Novels of Faith and Doubt). 1976. 40.00 (ISBN 0-8240-1533-9). Garland Pub.
Fabiola: Or, The Church of the Catacombs. Nicholas Patrick Stephen Wiseman. 1855. D. & J. Sadlier & Co.
Fabiola: Or, The Church of the Catacombs. Nicholas Patrick Stephen Wiseman. LC 3-19541. 1874. D. & J. Sadlier & Co.
Fabiola: Or, The Church of the Catacombs. Nicholas Patrick Stephen Wiseman. LC 7-742. 1896. Benziger Brothers.
Fabiola: Or, The Church of the Catacombs. Nicholas Patrick Stephen Wiseman & Brennan, Richard. LC 24-21030. 1886. Benziger Brothers.
Fabiola: Or, The Church of the Catacombs. Nicholas Patrick Stephen Wiseman & Hagan, John Raphael, Ed. LC 32-29093. 1932. Longmans, Green and Co.
Fabiola; or, the Church of the Catacombs, 1854. Nicholas P. Wiseman. Ed. by Robert L. Wolff. LC 75-454. (Victorian Fiction Ser). 1975. lib. bdg. 66.00 (ISBN 0-8240-1533-9). Garland Pub.
Fabiola's Sisters: A Tale of the Christian Heroines Martyred at Carthage in the Commencement of the Third Century. A. C Clarke. LC 6-21380. 1898. Benziger Bros.
Fabius, the Roman: Or, How the Church Became Militant. Enoch Fitch Burr. LC 6-161149. The Baker & Taylor Company,C.
Fable. William Faulkner. LC 77-356141. (Illus.). 1976. Franklin Library.
Fable. William Faulkner. LC 54-6651. 1954. Random House.
Fable. William Faulkner. LC 77-3039. 1978. 2.95 (ISBN 0-394-72413-5). Vintage Books.
Fable. James J Kavanaugh. LC 80-66799. (Illus.). 8.95 (ISBN 0-525-93154-6). Dutton.
Fable and Fiction: Frank Stockton. Frank Richard Stockton. LC 49-9768. 1949. Story Classics.
Fable: By William Faulkner. Introd. by Michael Novak. William Faulkner. (Signet modern classic, CY412). 1968. pap., 1.25. New Amer. Lib.
Fable for Wives. Robert E McClure. LC 32-14332. 1932. Doubleday, Doran and Company, Incorporated.
Fable in Gothic. Lois Foster Winter. LC 40-5948. 1940. The Caxton Printers, Ltd.
Fable of Cupid and Psyche. Apuleius Madaurensis & Thomas Taylor. LC 77-114. 12.50 (ISBN 0-89314-411-8). Philosophical Research Society.
Fable of the Bees. Bernard Mandeville. 5.25 o.p. (ISBN 0-8446-0193-4). Peter Smith.
Fables. Jean Anouilh. 1966. 20.95. French & Eur.
Fables, 2 tomes. Jean de La Fontaine. Incl. Tome I, Livre I-VI; Tome II, Livres VII-XII. (Fr.). 1962. Set. pap. 9.90. French & Eur.
Fables. Jean De La Fontaine. Tr. by Edward Marsh. 1966. 3.95x o.p. (ISBN 0-460-00991-5, Evman). Dutton.
Fables. Theodore Francis Powys. LC 79-145245. 1972. (ISBN 0-403-01160-4). Scholarly Press.
Fables. Theodore Francis Powys. LC 29-24039. The Viking Press.
Fables. Mikhail Evgrafovich Saltykov. LC 76-23898. (Series: Phoenix Library.). (Classics of Russian literature). (Hyperion library of world literature). 1977. 10.95. (ISBN 0-88355-516-6) (ISBN 0-88355-517-4). Hyperion Press.
Fables, & Fables Volume Two. John Gay. 1975. Repr. of 1727 ed. text ed. 35.00x o.s.i. (ISBN 0-8277-3837-4). British Bk Ctr.
Fables & Fairy Tales. Lev Nikolaevich Tolstoi. 1972. pap. 3.95 (ISBN 0-452-25302-0, Z5302, Plume). NAL.
Fables at Life's Expense. Marvin Cohen. 1975. 5.00 (Pub. by Latitudes Pr). SBD.
Fables for Parents. Dorothea Frances Canfield Fisher. LC 37-28503. Harcourt, Brace and Company.
Fables for the Fair. Josephine Dodge Daskam Bacon. 1901. C. Scribner's Sons.
Fables for the Fair: Cautionary Tales for Damsels Not Yet in Distress. One Of Them. (Illus.). 1967. 2.95 o.p. (ISBN 0-03-061560-7). HR&W.
Fables in Slang. George Ade. LC 20-23148. 1901. H.S. Stone and Company.
Fables in Slang. George Ade. LC 45-26353. 1900. H. S. Stone and Company.
Fables in Slang. George Ade. LC 99-5367. 1900. H.S. Stone & Co.
Fables in Slang: And More Fables in Slang. Illus. by Clyde J. Newman. With an Introd. by E. F. Bleiler. George Ade. 1960. Dover Publications.
Fables of Aesop. Aesop. Tr. by S. A. Handford. (Classics Ser.). (Orig.). 1964. pap. 3.95 (ISBN 0-14-044043-7). Penguin.
Fables of Avianus. Avianus. Ed. by Robinson Ellis. 1966. Repr. of 1887 ed. 8.70 o.p. Adler.
Fables of Field and Staff. James Albert Frye. LC 6-44719. 1894. The Colonial Company.
Fables of Jean De La Fontaine. Frances J. Brewer. (Illus.). 13p. (With a leaf from the Fables Choises & three original leaves of the 1755-59 printing). 1964. bds. 24.00 o.p. Dawsons.
Fables of la Fontaine. Jean D. La Fontaina. Tr. by Marianne Moore. 1964. pap. 1.65 o.p. (ISBN 0-670-00146-5, Comp). Viking Pr.
Fables of La Fontaine. rev. ed. Jean de La Fontaine. Tr. by Marianne Moore. 1964. pap. 1.65 o.p. (ISBN 0-670-00146-5, Comp). Viking Pr.
Fables of Phonecius. Yvonne Grozny & Phonecius. LC 78-68416. 1978. 10.00 (ISBN 0-932364-00-4). Ann Arbor Book Co.
Fables of Wit and Elegance. Ed. by Louis Auchincloss. LC 73-37198. 1972. 7.95 (ISBN 0-684-12745-8). Scribner.
Fables on Four Modern and Four Ancient Sciences. George G Haydu. LC 75-101263. 1970. 3.00 (ISBN 0-8283-1270-2). Branden Press.
Fables, Tales, Stories. Lev Nikolaevich Tolstoi. 122p. 1973. pap. text ed. 1.95 (ISBN 0-8285-0616-7, Pub. by Progress Pubs USSR). Imported Pubns.
Fabliaux: Ribald Tales from the Old French. Illus. by Ashley Bryan et al. Robert Hellman & Richard O'Gorman. (YA) (gr. 9-12). pap. 2.25 o.p. (ISBN 0-8152-0134-6, A134). Apollo Eds.
Fabliaux: Ribald Tales from the Old French. Tr. by Robert Hellman. LC 65-12509. 1965. Crowell.
Fabliaux: Ribald Tales from the Old French. Tr. by Robert Hellman. Richard F. O'Gorman. LC 75-3993. (Illus.). 1976. 13.50 (ISBN 0-8371-7414-7). Greenwood Press.
Fabliaux: Ribald Tales from the Old French. Tr., Notes, Afterword by Robert Hellman, Richard O'Gorman. Illus. by Ashley Bryan. Tr. by Robert Hellman. 1966. pap., 1.95. Apollo Eds.
Fablus Train. Frederic Wakeman. LC 55-8990. 1955. Rinehart.
Fabric of the Loom. Mary Stanbery Watts. LC 24-243451. 1924. The Macmillan Company.
Fabrications. Michael Ayrton. 224p. 1973. 6.95 o.p. (ISBN 0-03-001001-2). HR&W.
Fabrications. Mars-Jones, Adam. LC 81-47514. 1981. 10.95 (ISBN 0-394-51998-1). A.A. Knopf: Distributed by Random House.
Fabricator. Hollis Hodges. LC 75-40314. 7.95 (ISBN 0-517-52511-9). Crown Publishers.
Fabricator. Hollis Hodges. 1978. 1.75 (ISBN 0-380-01918-3). Avon Books.
Fabrizio's Book. Carlo Coccioli. LC 66-17254. 1966. Shorecrest.
Fabula De Jemima Anate Aquatica: Liber Omnibus Notus Beatricis Potter. In Latinum Conversus Est Aucture Jonathan Musgrave. Beatrix Potter. LC 65-157252. bds., 1.25. Warne.
Fabulae Aesopi. C. P. Watson. text ed. 1.75 o.p. Transatlantic.
Fabularum Liber: Basel, 1535. Hyginus & C. Julius Hyginus. LC 75-27848. (Renaissance and the Gods; No. 6). 1976. 40.00 (ISBN 0-8240-2055-3). Garland Pub.
Fabulous Ancestor. Donald Demarest. LC 53-12290. 1954. Lippincott.
Fabulous Buccaneer. Robert Carse. LC 57-73533. (Dell first edition, B109). 1957. Dell Pub.
Fabulous Clipjoint. Fredric Brown. LC 47-17762. 1947. E. P. Dutton & Company, Inc.
Fabulous Clipjoint. Fredric Brown. LC 79-10908. (Gregg Press Mystery Series). 1979. 9.95 (ISBN 0-8398-2619-2). Gregg Press.
Fabulous Concubine: A Novel. Hsin-Hai Chang. LC 56-9930. 1956. Simon and Schuster.
Fabulous Fallacies. Thaddeus Tuleja. 240p. 1982. 15.95 (ISBN 0-517-54348-6, Harmony); pap. 6.95 (ISBN 0-517-54700-7). Crown.
Fabulous Finn. Cover Painting by Lu Kimmel. Dan Cushman. LC 54-27000. (Gold medal books, 392). 1954. Fawcett Publications.
Fabulous Gunman. Wayne D Overholser. LC 52-7344. 1952. Macmillan.
Fabulous Gunman. Wayne D. Overholser. 1974. (pbk.) 0.95. Dell.
Fabulous John Gray: A Novel. Russ Marker. LC 68-901. (Illus.). 1968. Book Craft.
Fabulous Journey of Hieronymus Meeker. Willy Johns. LC 54-6889. 1954. Little, Brown.
Fabulous Mrs. V. H. E. Bates. 1981. 18.95x (Pub. by Remploy England). State Mutual Bk.
Fabulous People: By Robert Norman Hubner. Robert Norman Hubner. LC 42-140843. 1942. A. A. Knopf.
Fabulous Riverboat. Philip Jose Farmer. LC 80-13013. 1980. 13.50 (ISBN 0-8398-2619-2). Gregg Press.
Fabulous Riverboat see Philip Jose Farmer: The Complete Riverworld Novels.
Fabulous Riverboat: A Science Fiction Novel. Philip Jose Farmer. LC 79-174635. (Riverworld series). 1971. Putnam.
Fabulous Showman. Irving Wallace. pap. 2.95 (ISBN 0-451-11385-3, AE1385, Sig). NAL.
Fabulous Valley: A Novel. Cornelia Stratton Parker. LC 56-649425. 1956. Putnam.
Fabulous Wink. Kem Bennett. LC 51-12417. 1951. Pellegrini & Cudahy.
Fabulous Year. Elisabeth Ogilvie. Repr. lib. bdg. 13.25x (ISBN 0-88411-330-2). Amereon Ltd.
Facade. Theodora Benson. LC 33-27190. 1933. W. Morrow & Company.
Facade. Douglas Goldring. LC 28-597926. 1928. R. M. McBride & Company.
Facades. Bill Cunningham. (Large Format Ser.). (Illus.). 1978. pap. 8.95 o.p. (ISBN 0-14-004948-7). Penguin.
Facades. Bill Cunningham. (Large Format Ser.). (Illus.). 1978. pap. 8.95 o.p. (ISBN 0-14-004948-7). Penguin.
Facades. Stanley Levine & Bud Knight. (Orig.). 1979. pap. 2.50 (ISBN 0-89083-500-4). Zebra.
Face. John Petty. 192p. 1972. 10.50x o.p. (ISBN 0-85614-018-X). Intl Pubns Serv.
Face. Jack Vance, pseud. (Science Fiction Ser.). (Orig.). 1979. pap. 1.95 o.p. (ISBN 0-87997-498-2, UJ1498). Daw Bks.
Face. Jack Vance, pseud. (Demon Prince Ser.: Bk. 4). (Illus.). 224p. 1980. 15.00 (ISBN 0-934438-23-4). Underwood-Miller.
Face and the Mask. Robert Barr. LC 6-9071. (Twentieth century series). 1895. F. A. Stokes Company.
Face at the Window. Willo Davis Roberts. (Raven House Mysteries Ser.). 224p. 1983. pap. cancelled (ISBN 0-373-63054-9, Pub. by Worldwide). Harlequin Bks.
Face Behind the Face: Poems. Evgenii Aleksandrovich Evtushenko. LC 78-17749. 10.00. (ISBN 0-399-90027-6) (ISBN 0-399-90028-4). R. Marek Publishers.
Face Behind the Image. Richard S. Usem. 1968. 6.00 o.p. (ISBN 0-682-46836-3). Exposition.
Face Behind the Image: Politics Hollywood Style, a Novel. Richard S Usem. LC 72-576. 1968. 6.00. Exposition Press.
Face Beside the Fire: A Novel. Laurens Van Der Post. LC 52-9707. 1953. Morrow.
Face Cards. Carolyn Wells. LC 25-902331. 1925. G. P. Putnam's Sons.
Face Divine; the Book of the Centuries: A Septilogy. Illustrated by the Author. Cover and Special Illus. by Venetia Epler. Paul Caesar Rinaudo De Ville & Rt Work by Florence Daphne Huntington. Limited Ed. LC 57-39904.
Face Down in a Coffin. J. D. Hardin. LC 79-89964. (J. D. Hardin Ser.). 208p. (Orig.). 1980. pap. 1.95 (ISBN 0-87216-843-3). Playboy Pbks.
Face Illumined. Edward Payson Roe. LC 7-40226. (On cover: Dodd, Mead & company's library of fiction, no. 13). Dodd, Mead & Company.
Face Illumined. Edward Payson Roe. LC 7-40227. (On cover: Roe's works). Dodd, Mead and Company.
Face in the Abyss. Abraham Merritt. LC 31-15685. H. Liveright, Inc.
Face in the Abyss see Dwellers in the Mirage.
Face in the Clouds: By John Gilbert Pseud. John Gilbert Harrison. LC 59-510832. 1959. Morrow.
Face in the Fog. Marilyn Ross. (empress gothic.). 1973. (pbk.) 0.95. Curtis Books.
Face in the Frost. John Bellairs. (Illus.). 1978. 1.75 (ISBN 0-441-22528-4). Ace Books.
Face in the Girandole: A Romance of Old Furniture. William Frederick Dix. LC 6-39023. 1906. Moffat, Yard & Company.
Face in the Mirror. Denys Val Batter. LC 78-140124. 1971. 3.75. Arkham House.
Face in the Night. Edgar Wallace. LC 29-26572. 1929. Pub. for The Crime Club, Inc., by Doubleday, Doran & Company, Inc.

TITLE INDEX FAIR COUNTRY MAID.

Face in the Portrait. Rosemary Carter. (Harlequin Presents Ser.). 192p. (Orig.). 1981. pap. 1.50 (ISBN 0-373-10410-3, Pub. by Harlequin). PB.
Face in the Shadows. Velda Johnston. LC 78-156863. (Red badge novel of suspense). 1971. 4.95 (ISBN 0-396-06303-9). Dodd, Mead.
Face in the Shadows. Peter Ordway. LC 51-11700. 1952. A. A. Wyn.
Face in the Shadows. Marilyn Ross. 1973. (pbk) 0.95. Warner.
Face Me When You Walk Away. Brian Freemantle. LC 74-83096. 1975. 6.95 (ISBN 0-399-11410-6). Putnam.
Face of a Hero. unabridged school ed. Pierre Boulle. LC 63-6628. (Literary heritage; a Macmillan paperback series). 1963. Macmillan.
Face of a Hero: Translated from the French by Xan Fielding. Pierre Boulle. LC 56-12030. 1956. Vanguard Press.
Face of a Hero. 1st Ed. Louis Falstein. LC 50-8821. 1950. Harcourt, Brace.
Face of a Nation: Poetical Passages from the Writings of Thomas Wolfe. Thomas Wolfe. 1939. C. Scribner's Sons.
Face of Air. George Leonard Knapp. LC 12-22590. 1912. 1.00. John Lane Company.
Face of an Angel. Dorothy Eden. 192p. 1976. pap. 1.95 (ISBN 0-441-22545-4). Ace Bks.
Face of Another. Kobo Abe. LC 80-15074. 1980. 4.95 (ISBN 0-399-50482-6). Perigee Books.
Face of Another. Tr. from Japanese by E. Dale Saunders. 1st Amer. Ed. Kobo Abe. LC 66-17968. 1966. bds., 4.95. Knopf.
Face of Clay: An Interpretation. Horace Annesley Vachell. 1906. Dodd, Mead & Company.
Face of Danger. Regina Ross. 288p. 1982. pap. 2.95 (ISBN 0-380-80135-3, 80135, Flare). Avon.
Face of Evil. John McPartland. 192p. 1973. pap. 0.95 o.p. (ISBN 0-532-95236-7). Woodhill.
Face of Evil. John McPartland. 192p. 1973. pap. 0.95 o.p. (ISBN 0-532-95236-7). Manor Bks.
Face of Evil. Cover Painting by Ray Johnson. John McPartland. LC 54-270034. (Gold medal books, 396). 1954. Fawcett Publications.
Face of Fear. Brian Coffey. LC 76-46164. 1977. 8.95 o.p. Bobbs.
Face of Fear. Brian Coffey. LC 76-46164. 1977. 8.95 o.p. Bobbs.
Face of Fear: A Novel. Dean Koontz. LC 76-46164. 1977. 8.95 (ISBN 0-672-52312-4). Bobbs-Merrill.
Face of Fear. 1st Ed. Louise Eskrigge Crump. LC 54-7474. 1954. Longmans, Green.
Face of Guilt. Kathryn K Ecenbarger. LC 68-27467. 1968. 2.95. Zondervan Pub. House.
Face of Hate. Theodora McCormick Du Bois. 1948. Pub. for the Crime Club by Doubleday.
Face of Him. Irving A. Greenfield. 1976. pap. 1.50 (ISBN 0-532-15202-6). Woodhill.
Face of Innocence. Elisabeth Ogilvie. LC 74-106232. 1970. McGraw-Hill.
Face of Jalanath. Ronald Hardy. LC 72-92305. 1973. 6.95 (ISBN 0-399-10980-3). Putnam.
Face of Love. Lenore Coffee. LC 59-9166. 1959. Crown Publishers.
Face of Love. Marianne Steiff Finton Meisel. LC 49-10108. 1949. C. Scribner's Sons.
Face of Love. Anne N. Reisser. (Candlelight Ecstacy Ser.: No. 20). (Orig.). 1981. pap. 1.50 (ISBN 0-440-12496-4). Dell.
Face of My Assassin: A Novel, by Jan Huckins and Carolyn Weston. Jan Huckins & Carolyn Weston. LC 59-10801. 1959. Random House.
Face of Night. Bernard Brunner. LC 67-20434. 1967. F. Fell.
Face of Rosenfel. A Novel. Charles Howard Montague. LC 7-31813. (On cover: Manhattan series, v. 1, no. 6). A. L. Burt.
Face of Rosenfel: A Novel. Charles Howard Montague. LC 7-31812. (Street & Smith's select series. no. 54). 1890. Street & Smith.
Face of Terror. Emanuel Litvinoff. LC 78-5732. 1978. (ISBN 0-688-03334-2). Morrow.
Face of the Clam. Luther Whiteman. LC 47-664. 1947. Random House.
Face of the Crime. Lillian O'Donnell. LC 68-15222. (Raven Book Mystery Ser). 1969. 4.25 o.p. (24150). Abelard.
Face of the Deep. Jacob Twersky. LC 52-13246. 1953. World Pub. Co.
Face of the Enemy. Thomas Walsh. (Inner sanctum mystery). 1967. bds., 3.95. S.&S.
Face of the Foe. Patricia Power. LC 72-94758. 1973. 4.95 (ISBN 0-385-03669-8). Published for the Crime Club by Doubleday.
Face of the King. Robert James Shores. LC 18-13114. R. J. Shores.
Face of the Lion. John Blackburn. LC 76-379548. 1976. 2.60 (ISBN 0-224-01184-7). Cape.
Face of the Man from Saturn. Harry Stephen Keeler. LC 33-31657. E. P. Dutton & Co., Inc.
Face of the Tiger. Ursula Reilly Curtiss. 1975. (pbk.) 0.95. Dell.
Face of the World. Johan Bojer & Muir, Jessie, Tr. LC 19-15684. 1919. Moffat, Yard and Company.
Face of Things. Ann Katherine Gilliland Ritner. LC 44-3320. 1944. Dodd, Mead & Company.
Face of Time. James Thomas Farrell. LC 53-10805. 1953. Vanguard Press.
Face of Trespass. Ruth Rendell. LC 73-10817. 1974. 4.95. Published for the Crime Club by Doubleday.
Face of Trespass. Ruth Rendell. LC 78-3816. 1978. 9.95 (ISBN 0-89340-144-7). J. Curley.
Face of Trespass. Ruth Rendell. 1975. (pbk.) 0.95. Bantam Books.
Face on the Cutting-Room Floor. Ernest Borneman. LC 81-2759. (Gregg Press Mystery Fiction Series). 1981. 19.95 (ISBN 0-8398-2738-5). Gregg Press.
Face on the Cutting Room Floor. Cameron McCabe. 1981. 14.95 (ISBN 0-8398-2738-5, Gregg). G K Hall.
Face to Face. Ingmar Bergman. Tr. by Alan Blair. (Illus.). 1976. 7.95 o.p. (ISBN 0-394-40452-1); pap. 1.95 (ISBN 0-394-73206-5). Pantheon.
Face to Face. Ellery Queen. Bd. with House of Brass. 1982. pap. 2.75 (ISBN 0-451-11464-7, AE1464, Sig). NAL.
Face to Face. Robert Grant. LC 74-22786. (Labor Movement in Fiction and Non-Fiction). 1976. 23.50 (ISBN 0-404-58433-0). AMS Press.
Face to Face... Robert Grant. LC 31-32276. 1886. C. Scribner's Sons.
Face to Face. Ellery Queen, pseud. LC 67-14727. 1967. New American Library.
Face to Face. Edward A. Rogers. (O.s.i.). 1968. pap. 0.95 o.s.i. (532-95116-095). Manor Bks.
Face to Face. Fons Van Woerkom. (O.s.i.). 1973. pap. 4.95 o.s.i. (ISBN 0-394-70628-5). Knopf.
Face to Face. Jeanne E Wylie. LC 52-5787. 1952. W. Morrow.
Face to Face: A Fact in Seven Fables. Robert Edward Francillon. LC 6-43268. (On cover: Seaside library. Pocket ed. no. 319). G. Munro.
Face to Face. Novel. Edward A Rogers. LC 62-11895. 1962. Morrow.
Face to the Sun. Arthur R McGratty & Husslein, Joseph Casper, 1873- Ed. LC 42-21899. 1942. The Bruce Publishing Company.
Face Towards the Spring. Faith Baldwin. 219p. Repr. of 1956 ed. lib. bdg. 13.25x (ISBN 0-88411-628-X). Amereon Ltd.
Face Value. J. L Campbell. LC 27-16579. E. P. Dutton & Company.
Face Value. Ron Powers. LC 79-773. 9.95 (ISBN 0-440-01649-5). Delacorte Press.
Face Value: By Robert Standish Pseud. 1st Ed. Digby George Gerahty. LC 55-5260. 1955. Doubleday.
Face Your Lover. Hubert Nicholson. LC 35-21562. H. Holt and Company.
Faced with Love. Adrianne Marcus. (Illus., Orig.). 1978. pap. 4.50 (ISBN 0-914278-13-4). Copper Beech.
Faceless Adversary: By Frances and Richard Lockridge. 1st Ed. Frances Louise Davis Lockridge & Richard Lockridge. LC 56-8194. (Main line mysteries). 1956. Lippincott.
Faceless Enemy. Frances Shelley Wees. LC 66-14111. 1966. Published for the Crime Club by Doubleday.
Faceless Man. Carter Wick. LC 74-28110. 1975. 7.95. Saturday Review Press.
Facemaker. Gordon Ostlere. LC 69-12264. 1968. 6.95. McGraw-Hill.
Faces in a Dusty Picture... Gerald Kersh. LC 45-2061. 1945. Whittlesey House, McGraw-Hill Book Company, Inc.
Faces in the Dawn. Hermann Hagedorn. LC 14-15363. 1914. 1.35. The Macmillan Company.
Faces in the Flames. Peter Tate. LC 75-21246. 207p. 1976. 10.00 o.p. (ISBN 0-385-01860-6). Ultramarine Pub.
Faces in the Flames. Peter Tate. LC 75-21246. (Science Fiction Ser.). 216p. 1976. 5.95 o.p. (ISBN 0-385-01860-6). Doubleday.
Faces in the Flames: Fourth in a Series of Small Wars. Peter Tate. LC 75-21246. 1976. 5.95 (ISBN 0-385-01860-6). Doubleday.
Faces in the Water. paperback reprint ed. Janet Frame, pseud. LC 79-25441. 1982. 5.95 (ISBN 0-8076-0957-9). G. Braziller.
Faces of Blood Kindred: A Novella and Ten Stories. William Goyen. LC 60-12124. 1960. Random House.
Faces of Destiny. Precioso M Nicanor. LC 76-52059. 7.95 (ISBN 0-918458-00-5). Pre-Mer Pub. Co.
Faces of Fear. Hugh L. Cayce. 1982. pap. 2.50 (ISBN 0-425-05204-4). Berkley Pub.
Facial Justice. Leslie Poles Hartley. 1969. pap. 0.75 o.p. (0502-07028-075). Curtis.
Facial Justice. Leslie Poles Hartley. 7.95 o.p. (ISBN 0-241-90168-5). Dufour.
Facing the Dawn. P. Spillman. 3.00 o.p. Carlton.
Facing the Flag. Jules Verne. LC 1-981430. (On cover: Neely's library of choice literature. no. 61). F. T. Neely.
Facing the Footlights. Florence Marryat Church Lean. LC 7-13590. (On cover: Lovell's library. v. 19. no. 942). 1887. J. W. Lovell Company.
Facing the Lions. Tom Wicker. LC 72-11065. 1973. 7.95 (ISBN 0-670-30448-4). Viking Press.
Facing the Lions. Tom Wicker. 1974. (pbk.) 1.75 (ISBN 0-380-00045-8). Avon.
Facing the Tree. David Ignatow. 1975. pap. 3.95 (ISBN 0-316-41491-3, Pub. by Atlantic Monthly Pr). Little.
Fact & Fiction. Bertrand Russell. (O.S.I.). 1962. 4.95 o.s.i. (ISBN 0-671-23975-9). S&S.
Fact and Fiction: A Collection of Stories. Lydia Maria Francis Child. LC 6-20981. 1847. C. S. Francis & Co.
Fact of Fiction: Social Relevance in the Short Story. Ed. by Cyril M. Gulassa. LC 75-184742. 1972. 3.95. Canfield Press.
Factory. Vera Fedorovna Panova. LC 75-39006. (Early Soviet literature). 1977. 18.00 (ISBN 0-88355-409-7). Hyperion Press.
Factory Ship" and "The Absentee Landlord.". Takiji Kobayashi. LC 73-6947. (UNESCO Collection of Representative Works: Japanese Series). 1973. 6.95 (ISBN 0-295-95285-7). University of Washington Press.
Factotum. Charles Bukowski. LC 75-34231. 1975. 10.00. (ISBN 0-87685-264-9) (ISBN 0-87685-263-0) (ISBN 0-87685-265-7). Black Sparrow Press.
Facts in a Clergyman's Life. Charles Benjamin Tayler. LC 8-20128. (On cover: C. B. Tayler's works). 1849. Stanford and Swords.
Facts in the Curious Case of H. Hyrtl, Esq. Edgar Evertson Saltus. LC 70-137311. 1972. 10.00 (ISBN 0-404-05519-2). AMS Press.
Facts of Life. Paul Goodman. LC 45-6866. 1945. The Vanguard Press.
Facts of Life. Richard Gordon. 1971. pap. 0.95 o.p. (N2459). Pyramid Pubns.
Facts of Life. Richard Gordon. 1970. 5.95 o.p. (ISBN 0-07-023797-2). McGraw.
Facts of Life. Maureen Howard. LC 79-27356. 1980. 2.95 (ISBN 0-14-005500-2). Penguin Books.
Facts of Life. Gordon Ostlere. LC 71-91965. 1970. McGraw-Hill.
Facts of Life: Stories, 1940-1949. Paul Goodman & Taylor Stroehe. LC 79-9289. (His The collected stories; v. 3). (Illus.). 1979. 7.50 (ISBN 0-87685-357-2) (ISBN 0-87685-356-4) (ISBN 0-87685-358-0). Black Sparrow Press.
Facts of Life Stories 1940-1949: The Collected Stories of Paul Goodman, Vol. 3. Paul Goodman. Ed. by Taylor Stoehr. 329p. 1979. 14.00 (ISBN 0-87685-357-2); deluxe ed. 25.00 (ISBN 0-87685-358-0); pap. 7.50 (ISBN 0-87685-356-4). Black Sparrow.
Facts of Love. 1st American Ed. Stanley Wade Baron. LC 56-85264. 1956. Harcourt, Brace.
Facts of Wife (for Teenage Girls from 13 to 53) Robert Warren. (Illus.). (YA) 1968. 3.95 (ISBN 0-913830-01-1). Rodney.
Faculty Swap Circle. Michael Word. pap. 1.95 o.p. (8071). Cameo.
Fade Out. Naomi Ellington Jacob. LC 37-16538. 1937. The Macmillan Company.
Fade-Out. Patrick Tilley. LC 74-34400. (Illus.). 1975. 8.95 (ISBN 0-688-02905-1). Morrow.
Fade Out. Douglas Woolf. LC 59-5415. 1959. Grove Press.
Fade Out the Stars. 1st Ed. Marten Cumberland. LC 52-10050. 1952. Published for the Crime Club by Doubleday.
Faded Banners: A Treasury of Nineteenth-Century Civil War Fiction. Ed. by Eric Solomon. LC 60-6839. 1960. T. Yoseloff.
Faded Elegance. Paul Hackett. LC 76-123227. 1970. 6.50 o.p. Bobbs.
Faded Mezzuzoth. Gershon Kranzler, pseud. saddle-stitched 3.00 (ISBN 0-87559-134-5). Shalom.
Faded Portraits. Robert Nieuwenhuys. LC 81-19653. (Library of the Indies). 1982. 15.00 (ISBN 0-87023-363-7). University of Massachusetts Press.
Faded Sun: Kesrith. C. J. Cherryh. (Science Fiction Ser). (Orig.). 1978. pap. 2.95 (ISBN 0-87997-813-9, UE1813). DAW Bks.
Faded Sun: Kutath. C. J. Cherryh. (Science Fiction Ser.). (Orig.). 1980. pap. 2.50 (ISBN 0-87997-743-4, UE1743). DAW Bks.
Faded Sun: Shon'jir. C. J Cherryh. 1.95 (ISBN 0-87997-453-2). DAW Books Inc.,, C.
Faded Sun: Shon'jir. C. J. Cherryh. (Science Fiction Ser.). 1979. pap. 2.50 (ISBN 0-87997-753-1, UE1753). DAW Bks.
Fadeless Stars. Edwin Arnold. LC 42-50080. 1942. Alpha Law Brief Company.
Fadeout. Joseph Hansen. LC 75-122889. 1970. 4.95. Harper & Row.
Fadeout. Joseph Hansen. LC 80-15549. 1980. 2.95 (ISBN 0-03-057486-2). Holt, Rinehart, and Winston.
Fadette. George Sand & Lancaster, Mrs. James M., Tr. LC 6-34612. T. Y. Crowell & Company.
Fadette (La Petite Fadette) George Sand & Sedgwick, Jane Minot, Tr. LC 4-17504. 1899. Little, Brown, & Co.
Fadette (La Petite Fadette) Tr. by Jane Minot Sedgwick. Sedgwock, Jane Minot, Tr. LC 4-23582. 1893. G. H. Richmond & Co.
Faeries. Ed. by David Larkin. (Illus.). 1979. pap. 9.95 (ISBN 0-553-01159-6, M01159-6). Bantam.
Fafhrd & the Gray Mouser Saga. Fritz Leiber. (Science Fiction Ser.). 1977. 50.00 o.p. (ISBN 4-4444-7010-0, Gregg). G K Hall.
Faggots. Larry Kramer. 1979. pap. 2.75 (ISBN 0-446-95153-6). Warner Bks.
Faggots: A Novel. Larry Kramer. LC 77-5998. 10.95 (ISBN 0-394-41095-5). Random House.
Faggots & Their Friends Between Revolutions. Larry Mitchell. LC 77-88125. (Illus.). 1978. pap. 5.00 (ISBN 0-930762-00-2). Calamus Bks.
Fagin: A Novel. Pat Graversen. 300p. 1982. 11.95 (ISBN 0-89479-087-0, A & W Visual Library). A & W Pubs.
Fago. Berton Roueche. LC 77-3804. 8.95 (ISBN 0-06-013689-8). Harper & Row.
Fagots on the Fire, a Novel. Ethel Symonds Low. LC 50-4469. 1950. Zondervan.
Faguhar: The Beaux Stratagem & the Recruiting Office. Ed. by Raymond A. Anselment. 1981. pap. 15.00x (ISBN 0-333-21146-4, Pub. by Macmillan England). State Mutual Bk.
Fahnsworth Manor. Elisabeth Welles. 1976. (pbk.) 1.50 (ISBN 0-671-80257-7). Pocket Books.
Fahrenheit Four Fifty-One. Ray Bradbury. (Orig.). 1979. pap. 2.25 (ISBN 0-345-29234-0). Ballantine.
Fahrenheit Four Fifty One. Ray Bradbury. 176p. 1981. pap. 5.95 (ISBN 0-345-29466-1, Del Rey). Ballantine.
Fahrenheit 451. Ray Bradbury. LC 67-14240. 1967. Simon and Schuster.
Fahrenheit 451. Ray Bradbury. LC 53-11280. (Illus.). 1953. Ballantine Books.
Faience Violin. Jules Fleury & Bishop, William Henry, 1847- Tr. LC 6-41672. 1893. D. Appleton and Company.
Fail-Safe. Eugene Bordick & Wheeler, Harvey. (Dell book). 1978. 1.95 (ISBN 0-440-12459-X). Dell Pub. Co.
Fail-Safe. Eugene Burdick & John Harvey Wheeler. LC 62-19642. 1962. McGraw-Hill.
Failure of Elisabeth. Eleanor Frances Poynter. LC 7-30305. (On cover: Lovell's international series, no. 87). J. W. Lovell Company.
Failure of Sibyl Fletcher: A Novel. Adeline Sergeant. LC 8-6849. (On cover: Lippincott's select novels, no. 179). 1896. J. B. Lippincott Company.
Failure to Rescue. Herbert Druks. 1977. 7.95 (ISBN 0-8315-0175-8); pap. 3.50. Speller.
Failure (Un Uomo Finito) Giovanni Papini. LC 76-137070. (Series: The European Library (New York). 1972. 13.25 (ISBN 0-8371-5533-9). Greenwood Press.
Fainalls of Tipton. Virginia Wales Johnson. 1884. C. Scribner's Sons.
Faint Echo. Natalie King. pap. 0.75 o.s.i. (01-344). Lancer.
Faint Harmony. Vivian Ellis. LC 34-16905. 1934. Frederick A. Stokes Company.
Faint Perfume. Zona Gale. LC 23-6139. 1923. D. Appleton and Company.
Fair. Juan Jose Arreola. LC 76-48981. (Texas Pan American series). (Illus.). 10.00 (ISBN 0-292-72417-9). University of Texas Press.
Fair. Robert Nathan. LC 64-12322. 1964. A A. Knopf.
Fair American. Pierre Sales & Kendall, Laura E., Tr. LC 8-3736. (On cover: Rialto series, no. 35). 1891. Rand, McNally & Company.
Fair Are the Meadows, a Novel: By J. Wesley Ingles. James Wesley Ingles. LC 41-193109. Augsburg Publishing House.
Fair As the Moon. Temple Bailey. LC 35-15158. The Penn Publishing Company.
Fair Barbarian. Frances Hodgson Burnett. LC 6-16428. 1881. J. R. Osgood and Company.
Fair Barbarian. Frances Hodgson Burnett. LC 16-6321. 1915. C. Scribner's Sons.
Fair Blows the Wind. Louis L'Amour. LC 77-25189. 7.95. Dutton.
Fair Blows the Wind. Louis L'Amour. LC 79-11598. 1979. 14.95 (ISBN 0-8161-6719-2). G. K. Hall.
Fair Blows the Wind. William H. Mulcahy. 6.95 o.p. (ISBN 0-8283-1306-7). Branden.
Fair Bride: A Novel. Bruce Marshall. LC 52-11826. 1953. Houghton Mifflin.
Fair Brigand. George Horton. 1899. H. S. Stone and Company.
Fair, but Faithless. Bertha M. Clay. LC 44-39236. (On cover: Street & Smith's select series, no. 96). Street & Smith.
Fair but False. Charlotte Mary Braeme. (On cover: Lovell's library, v. 11. no. 558). J. W. Lovell Company.
Fair Company. Doris Oppenheim Leslie, pseud. LC 36-192263. 1936. The Macmillan Company.
Fair Country Maid. A Novel. E. Fairfax Byrrne. LC 6-16398. (Harper's Franklin square library, no. 381). 1884. Harper & Brothers.

Fair Country Maid: A Novel. E. Fairfax Byrrne. (On cover: Seaside library, Pocket ed., no. 538). 1885. G. Munro.

Fair Day & Another Step Begun. Katie L. Lyle. 144p. 1975. pap. 1.50 (ISBN 0-440-95968-3, LFL). Dell.

Fair Days Along the Talbert. Dennis T. Patrick Sears. LC 77-354864. 1976. 11.95. (ISBN 0-7737-0031-5) (ISBN 0-7737-1010-8). Musson Book Co.

Fair Day's Work. Nicholas Monsarrat. LC 64-15478. 1964. W. Sloane Associates.

Fair Device. Wolcott Balestier. LC 6-632729. (On cover: Lovell's library, v. 7, no. 38). J. W. Lovell Company.

Fair Devil. Edwin Greenwood. LC 35-18420. 1935. Doubleday, Doran & Company, Inc.

Fair Dinkum. Douglas Lockwood. pap. 1.75 o.s.i. Tri-Ocean.

Fair Exchange. by harry p. bailey. ed. Harry P Bailey. LC 64-10910. (Tempo books, T47). 1964. Grossett & Dunlap.

Fair Exchange. Palma Harcourt. LC 75-34974. 1976. 7.95 (ISBN 0-679-50591-1). McKay.

Fair Exchange: A Novel in the First Person. Grant Richards. LC 27-18959. George H. Doran Company.

Fair Exchange: A Novel of International Intrigue. Palma Harcourt. 224p. 1976. 7.95 o.p. (ISBN 0-679-50591-1). McKay.

Fair, Fair Ladies of Chantres Street. Christopher Stanislas Blake. 1965. pap. 3.95 (ISBN 0-87651-203-1). Southern U Pr.

Fair Fair Ladies of Chartres Street. Christopher Stanislas Blake. LC 65-29793. 4.95. Beale Pr.

Fair Flowering. Erika Zastrow. LC 38-22279. Gramercy Publishing Co.

Fair Game. George Bartram. LC 73-7354. 1973. 6.95. Macmillan.

Fair Game. Paula Gosling. LC 78-5819. 1978. 8.95 (ISBN 0-698-10921-X). Coward, McCann & Geoghegan.

Fair Game. Paula Gosling. 1979. 1.95 (ISBN 0-445-04470-5). Popular Library.

Fair Game. Gerald Hammond. LC 81-21505. 9.95 (ISBN 0-312-27961-2). St. Martin's Press.

Fair Game. Marjorie Erskine Smith. LC 43-5929. 1943. Smith & Durrell.

Fair Game. Olive Wadsley. LC 27-240071. 1927. Dodd, Mead & Company.

Fair Game: A Novel. Diane Johnson. LC 65-19061. 1965. Harcourt, Brace & World.

Fair God: A Tale of the Conquest of Mexico. Lewis Wallace & Pape, Eric, 1870-1938, Illus. LC 93-1698. 1899. Houghton, Mifflin and Company.

Fair God: Or, The Last of the Tzins. A Tale of the Conquest of Mexico. Lewis Wallace. LC 8-34322. 1873. J. R. Osgood and Company.

Fair God: Or, The Last of the 'Tzins, a Tale of the Conquest of Mexico. 31st ed. Lewis Wallace. LC 37-32812. 1887. Houghton, Mifflin and Company.

Fair God: Or, The Last of the 'Tzins; a Tale of the Conquest of Mexico. Lewis Wallace. (Warne's "Crown" library. 16). 1887. F. Warne and Co.

Fair God: Or, The Last of the 'Tzins, a Tale of the Conquest of Mexico. 38th ed. Lewis Wallace. LC 32-33603. 1888. Houghton, Mifflin and Company.

Fair God: Or, The Last of the 'Tzins; a Tale of the Conquest of Mexico. Lewis Wallace. LC 8-34323. 1892. Houghton, Mifflin and Company.

Fair God: Or, The Last of the 'Tzins; a Tale of the Conquest of Mexico. Lewis Wallace. LC 1-20209. Houghton, Mifflin and Company.

Fair God: Or, The Last of the 'Tzins; a Tale of the Conquest of Mexico. Lewis Wallace. LC 21-168554. Grosset & Dunlap.

Fair-Haired Alda, Florence Marryat Church Lean. (On cover: Lovell's library. v.19. no. 948). J. W. Lovell Company.

Fair-Haired Alda. A Novel. Florence Marryat Church Lean. (Seaside library. v. 40 no. 820). 1880. G. Munro.

Fair Harbor: A Novel. Joseph Crosby Lincoln. LC 22-19481. 1922. D. Appleton and Company.

Fair Harvard: a Story of American College Life... William Tucker Washburn. LC 8-33475. 1869. G. P. Putnam & Son; Etc., Etc.

Fair Haven and Foul Strand. August Strindberg. LC 70-39048. 1972. (ISBN 0-8383-1396-5). Haskell House Publishers.

Fair Havens. Bradley Carter Jefferson. LC 48-8706. 1948. Macmillan Co.

Fair House. Hugh De Selincourt. LC 11-5481. 1911. 1.50. John Lane.

Fair Imposter: One Hundred Fifty Dollars. Miriam Lynch. 224p. 1981. pap. 1.50 (ISBN 0-449-50223-6, GM). Fawcett.

Fair Irish Maid. Justin Huntly McCarthy. LC 11-25435. 1911. Harper & Brothers.

Fair Is My Love. Elsie Frances Wilson Mack. LC 50-6728. 1950. Avalon Books.

Fair Jewess. Benjamin Leopold Farjeon. LC 6-38640. The Cassell Publishing Company.

Fair Lady. Helen Marion Edginton. LC 32-222133. 1932. Amour Press, Inc.

Fair Lady of Halifax: Or, Colmey's Six Hundred. John Alfred Pollock. LC 20-51915. 1920. Edwards & Broughton Printing Co.

Fair Land, Fair Land. large print ed. A. B Guthrie. LC 82-19484. 14.95 (ISBN 0-89621-417-6). Thorndike Press.

Fair Land, Fair Land. Alfred Bertram Guthrie. LC 82-3055. 1982. 14.95 (ISBN 0-395-32511-0). Houghton Mifflin.

Fair Laurel. Peggy O'More, pseud. LC 43-10330. 1943. Grammercy Publishing Co.

Fair Lavinia: And Others. Mary Eleanor Wilkins Freeman. LC 7-34778. 1907. Harper & Brothers.

Fair Lilias. A Novel. Pierce Egan. (Seaside library, v. 79, no. 1600). 1883. G. Munro.

Fair Maid. A Novel. Frederick William Robinson. LC 7-41962. (Harper's Franklin square library, no. 389). 1884. Harper & Brothers.

Fair Maid. A Novel. Frederick William Robinson. (On cover: The seaside library. Pocket ed. no. 261). 1884. G. Munro.

Fair Maid of Florida. Mary Moncure Parker. LC 7-34982. 1898.

Fair Maid of Graystones. Beulah Marie Dix. LC 5-30571. 1905. The Macmillan Company.

Fair Maid of Marblehead. By Mrs. Kate Tannatt Woods... Kate Tannatt Woods. LC 8-37533. (On cover: American authors' series, no. 1). 1889. F. F. Lovell & Company.

Fair Maid of Perth. A Romance. Walter Scott. (On cover: Seaside library. Pocket ed. no. 417). 1885. G. Munro.

Fair Maid of Perth: Or, St. Valentine's Day; Chronicles of the Canongate--2d Ser. Walter Scott. (On cover: Lovell's library, no. 638). 1885. J. W. Lovell Company.

Fair Maids Missing. Pierre Audemars. LC 65-110551. 1965. 3.50. Pub. for Crime Club by Doubleday.

Fair Margaret: A Portrait. Francis Marion Crawford. LC 5-35302. 1905. The Macmillan Company.

Fair Margaret: A Portrait. Francis Marion Crawford. LC 16-191491. (Lettered on cover: Works of F. Marion Crawford). 1910. The Macmillan Company.

Fair Mississippian: A Novel. Mary Noailles Murfree. 1908. Houghton Mifflin Company.

Fair Moon of Bath". Elizabeth Ellis. LC 8-8093. 1908. Dodd, Mead and Company.

Fair Moralist. Charlotte McCarthy & John Nelson. LC 74-23586. (Flowering of the Novel). 1974. (ISBN 0-8240-1115-5). Garland Pub.

Fair Mystery. G. Munro.

Fair Mystery. The Story of a Coquette. Charlotte Mary Braeme. (On cover: Lovell's library. v. 15 no. 764). J. W. Lovell Company.

Fair of St. James. Eleanor Farjeon. LC 32-216678. 1932. Frederick A. Stokes Company.

Fair Philosopher. Henrietta Hardy Hammond. LC 7-5679. (Kasterskill series). 1882. G. W. Harlan & Co.

Fair Pioneer: Or, Fighting for Love's Sake. A Novel. James Milford Merrill. (On cover: Flag series, no. 3). 1896. Street & Smith.

Fair Plebeian. Mary E. Stone Bassett. LC 6-9097. (On cover: "The hammock series." no. 5). 1883. H. A. Summer and Company.

Fair Prisoner. Iris Bromige. 1974. pap. 0.75 o.p. (26555-6-075). Beagle Bks.

Fair Puritan. A New England Tale. Mary Johnson Holmes. LC 7-12589. 1891. Hurst and Company.

Fair Rebel: A Tale of Colonial Times. Emerson Bennett. LC 7-36494. 1853. H. M. Rulison.

Fair Revolutionist: A Romance of the Central American Republics. St. George Rathborne. LC 8-582. (On cover: Criterion series, no. 22). Street & Smith.

Fair Rewards. Thomas Beer. LC 22-4213. 1922. A. A. Knopf.

Fair Sailing. Anne Tedlock Brooks. LC 48-3514. 1948. Arcadia House.

Fair Shine the Day. Sylvia Thorpe. (Fawcett Crest Book). 1977. 1.75 (ISBN 0-449-23229-8). Fawcett Pubns.

Fair Shine the Day. Sylvia Thorpe. LC 78-3751. 1978. 8.95. J. Curley.

Fair Shines the Day. Margaret Kathleen Avern Maddocks. LC 52-36193. 1952. Hurst & Blackett.

Fair Sister: A Novel. William Goyen. LC 63-17274. 1963. Doubleday.

Fair Slaughter. Howard Barker. 1980. pap. 3.95 (ISBN 0-7145-3654-7). Riverrun NY.

Fair Stood the Wind for France... Herbert Ernest Bates. LC 44-401197. 1944. Little, Brown and Company.

Fair Stranger. Cecile Gilmore. LC 47-4068. 1947. S. Curl, Inc.

Fair Syrian. Robert Bage. LC 78-60845. (Novel, 1720-1805). 56.00 (ISBN 0-8240-3659-X). Garland Pub.

Fair to Look Upon. Mary Belle Freeley. LC 6-42851. Morrill, Higgins & Co.

Fair to Middling. Nalbro Isadorah Bartley. LC 21-15950. 1921. Doubleday, Page & Company.

Fair to See. A Novel. Laurence William Maxwell Lockhart. (seaside library. v. 60, no. 1211). 1882. G. Munro.

Fair Tomorrow. Emilie Baker Loring. LC 31-27237. The Penn Publishing Company.

Fair Trial. Translated from the French by David Hughes. 1st Ed. Jean Laborde. LC 62-7655. 1962. Doubleday.

Fair Violet. Florence Stonebraker. LC 49-953732. 1949. Arcadia House.

Fair Warning. Mignon Good Eberhart. LC 36-27265. 1936. Doubleday, Doran & Co., Inc.

Fair Warning. Mignon Good Eberhart. LC 42-763053. 1942. Triangle Books.

Fair Warning. Mignon Good Eberhart. 1975. (pbk.) 0.95. Popular Library.

Fair Warning. George E. Simpson & Neal R. Burger. (O.s.i.). 1980. 10.95 o.s.i. (ISBN 0-440-02474-9). Delacorte.

Fair Warning. George P. Simpson & Neal R. Burger. 1981. pap. 3.50 (ISBN 0-440-12478-6). Dell.

Fair Warning: A Novel. George E Simpson & Neal R. Burger. LC 79-26627. 9.95 (ISBN 0-440-02474-9). Delacorte Press.

Fair Weather North: A Novel. Osborn, Mary Elizabeth. LC 52-18686. 1950-1951. Sage Books.

Fair Were the Days. Christine Whiting Parmenter. LC 47-5858. 1947. T. Y. Crowell Co.

Fair Wind Home. Ruth Moore. LC 53-7781. 1953. Morrow.

Fair Wind of Love. Barbara Douglas. LC 76-18356. (Romantic Suspense Ser.). 1980. 8.95 o.p. (ISBN 0-385-08998-8). Doubleday.

Fair Wind of Love. Barbara Vstedal. LC 76-18356. 1980. 8.95 (ISBN 0-385-08998-8). Doubleday.

Fair Wind to Java. Garland Roark. LC 48-8114. 1948. Doubleday.

Fair Wind to Malabar. Stanley White. LC 78-314462. 1978. 9.75 (ISBN 0-09-132050-X). Hutchinson.

Fair Winds & Far Places. Zane Mann. LC 78-543. (Illus.). 1978. 12.95 (ISBN 0-87518-159-7). Dillon.

Fair with Rain: A Novel. Ann Head, pseud. (Signet, Q5526). 1973. (pbk.) 0.95. New American Lib.

Fair with Rain: A Novel. Ann Head, pseud. LC 56-10315. 1957. McGraw-Hill.

Fair Woman. Hilda Vaughan. LC 42-5690. 1942. Duell, Sloan and Pearce.

Fair Women. Mrs. Bridges. (Seaside library, v. 20, no. 395). 1879. G. Munro.

Fair Women. Mrs. Bridges. (On cover: Seaside library. Pocket ed. no. 727). 1886. G. Munro.

Fair Women. Mrs. Bridges. (On cover: Lovell's library, v. 13, no. 760). 1886. J. W. Lovell Company.

Fairacre Festival. Dora Jessie Saint. LC 69-15027. (Illus.). 1969. 4.00. Houghton Mifflin.

Fairacres: A Novel of the Shephard Family and the Founding of Independence, Missouri. Gladys Poe Waters. LC 52-7756. 1952. University of Denver Press.

Fairbrothers: A Novel. Clark McMeekin. LC 61-103309. 1961. Putnam.

Faire Damzell. A Novel. Amelie Claire Leroy. (Harper's Franklin square library, no. 533).

Fairest of All. Peggy Gaddis, pseud. LC 47-185931. 1947. Gramercy Publishing Co.

Fairfax and His Pride: A Novel. Marie Van Vorst. LC 20-40108. Small, Maynard & Company.

Fairfax: Or, The Master of Greenway Court. A Chronicle of the Valley of the Shenandoah. John Esten Cooke. LC 6-28758. 1868. Carleton & Co.

Fairfax: Or, The Master of Greenway Court. A Chronicle of the Valley of the Shenandoah. John Esten Cooke. LC 44-25789. 1871. Carleton.

Fairly Good Time. Mavis Gallant. 1973. (pbk) 0.95. Popular Library.

Fairly Good Time. Mavis Gallant. LC 73-102352. 1970. 5.95. Random House.

Fairly Honourable Defeat. Iris Murdoch. LC 75-89509. (Fawcett crest book, P1779). 1973. (449-01779-125) 1.25. Fawcett Publications.

Fairly Honourable Defeat. Iris Murdoch. LC 75-89509. 1970. 6.95. Viking Press.

Fairly Innocent Little Man. Laurence Walter Meynell. LC 77-15005. 1977. 7.95 (ISBN 0-8128-2421-0). Stein and Day.

Fairoaks. Frank Yerby. (Dell Book). 1977. 1.95. (ISBN 0-440-12455-7). Dell Pub. Co.

Fairoaks: A Novel. Frank Yerby. LC 57-11707. 1957. Dial Press.

Fairoaks, a Novel. Frank Yerby. LC 57-11707. 1957. Dial Press.

Fairview Idea: A Story of the New Rural Life. Herbert Quick. LC 19-300515. The Bobbs-Merrill Company.

Fairview's Mystery. George Hersey Marquis. LC 2-1091. 1901. The Abbey Press.

Fairway and Folly. James J Reno. 1881. Ramsey, Millett & Hudson.

Fairy & Folk Tales of the Irish Peasantry. Ed. by William Butler Yeats. 416p. 1973. 13.95 (ISBN 0-02-632640-X). Macmillan.

Fairy Bells Tinkle Afar. Violet Windell. 3.95 o.p. Vantage.

Fairy Fingers. A Novel. Anna Cora Ogden Mowatt Ritchie. LC 7-41655. 1865. Carleton.

Fairy Godmother. Charles Baxter Clement. LC 80-29340. 8.95 (ISBN 0-89803-035-8). Caroline House Publishers.

Fairy Gold. Compton Mackenzie. LC 26-14515. George H. Doran Company.

Fairy Gold. Frances Christine Tiernan. LC 8-19815. 1897. The Ave Maria.

Fairy Gold. A Novel. Ellen Warner Olney Kirk. 1883. J. B. Lippincott & Co.

Fairy Goose: And Two Other Stories. Liam O'Flaherty. LC 27-25830. 1927. C. Gaige.

Fairy Leapt Upon My Knee. Bea Howe. LC 28-1741. 1928. The Viking Press.

Fairy Legends & Traditions of the South of Ireland, 3 Vols. in 1. Thomas C. Croker. LC 75-110295. 1971. Repr. lib. bdg. 27.50 o.s.i. (ISBN 0-87696-012-3). Lemma.

Fairy Man. Leslie Cope Cornford. LC 20-7531. 1919. J. M. Dent & Sons, Ltd.

Fairy of the Alps: A Novel. Elisabeth Burstenbinder. Tr. by Wister, Anuls Lee (Furness) LC 3-6867. (Seaside library. Pocket ed., no. 1181). 1889. G. Munro.

Fairy of the Snows. Francis James Finn. LC 13-23729. 1913. Benziger Brothers.

Fairy Prince: And Other Stroies. Eleanor Hallowell Abbott. LC 22-21208. E.P. Dutton & Company.

Fairy Princess. Joe E. Pierce. LC 82-83473. 125p. (Orig.). 1982. pap. 5.95 (ISBN 0-913244-58-9). Hapi Pr.

Fairy Stories That Did Not Come True: Containing Also Miss Loomis' Legacy and The Symphony in G Minor. Annie Pupin. LC 13-19421. 0.60. Madame A. Pupin.

Fairy Story That Came True: Showing That All Modern Inventions Were Foreshadowed in Fairy Stories; Containing Also "The Three Famous F's"; a Story of the Time of Chopin, Mendelssohn and Liszt. Annie Pupin. LC 13-19420. 0.60. Madame A. Pupin.

Fairy Tale. Erich W Segal. LC 72-9101. (Illus.). 1973. 4.95 (ISBN 0-06-013828-9). Harper & Row.

Fairy Tale. S. Steinberg. 1981. pap. 2.50 (ISBN 0-440-10181-6). Dell.

Fairy Tale: A Novel. S Steinberg. LC 79-24823. 8.95 (ISBN 0-440-00011-4). Delacorte Press.

Fairy Tale of New York. James Patrick Donleavy. (Laurel edition). 1974. (pbk.) 1.75. Dell.

Fairy Tales for Computers. Edward Morgan Forster. LC 77-93091. 1969. 2.95. Eakins Press.

Fairy Tales for Computers. Intro. by Leslie G. Katz. LC 78-58450. 1978. pap. 8.95 (ISBN 0-87923-245-5, Nonpareil Bk). Godine.

Fairy Tales from Grandfather's Big Book: Jewish Legends of Old Retold for Young People. Edith Lindeman Calisch. LC 30-22. 1938. Behrman's Jewish Book House.

Fairy Tales, Legends, Etc., Illustrative of Shakespeare. Joseph Ritson. 1879. Repr. 13.00 o.s.i. Finch Pr.

Fairy Tales of My Mind: Or, The Love Story of Tom and John and Annette and Nanette. REbecca Rass. LC 78-53828. (Illus.). 8.00. (ISBN 0-931642-03-5). Lintel.

Fairy Tales of Oscar Wilde. Oscar Wilde. (Illus.). 192p. (Orig.). 1978. pap. 4.95 o.s.i. (ISBN 0-89104-231-8). A & W Pubs.

Fairy Tales of Oscar Wilde. Oscar Wilde. (Hart Illustrated Classics). (Illus.). 156p. 1976. 4.95 o.p. (ISBN 0-8055-1186-5); pap. 2.95 o.p. (ISBN 0-8055-0228-9). Hart.

Fairytales: A Novel. Cynthia Freeman. LC 76-50340. 8.95 (ISBN 0-87795-163-2). Arbor House.

Fais et Concquestes Du Noble Roy Alexandre: Edition Du Manuscrit 836 De la Bibliotheque Municipale De Besancon. Renee N. Liscinsky. LC 80-12745. 592p. (Orig.). 1980. pap. 24.75 (ISBN 0-8357-0512-9, SS-00133). Univ Microfilms.

Faith. Martha Cabanne Kayser. LC 31-33891. 1931. Meador Publishing Company.

Faith. Palacio Valdes, Armando & Hapgood, Isabel Florence, 1850- Tr. (On cover: Cassell's sunshine series, no. 119). 1892. Cassell Publishing Company.

Faith & Doubt in Victorian England see Gains & Losses.

Faith and Fiction: The Modern Short Story. Robert Detweiler & Glenn Meeter. LC 78-32082. 6.95 (ISBN 0-8028-1737-8). W. B. Eerdmans.

Faith & Fried Potatoes. Grayce Confer. 184p. 1982. pap. 4.95 (ISBN 0-8341-0732-5). Beacon Hill.

Faith and Inquisitions: A Novel by Susanne Carwin Pseud. Herta Schubart-Karpeles. LC 50-1980. 1950. Hutchinson International Authors.
Faith and the Flame. June Dimmitt Houston. LC 58-11091. 1958. W. Sloane Associates.
Faith and the Good Thing. Charles Johnson. LC 74-11. 1974. 6.95 (ISBN 0-670-30569-3). Viking Press.
Faith and Unfaith: A Novel. Margaret Wolfe Hungerford. LC 7-8494. (On cover: Lovell's library. v. 4, no. 162). 1883. J. W. Lovell Company.
Faith and Unfaith. A Novel. Margaret Wolfe Hungerford. LC 14-5757. 1906. J. B. Lippincott Company.
Faith Brandon: A Novel. Henrietta Channing Dana Skinner. LC 12-9510. 1912. D. Appleton and Company.
Faith Creek. 1st Ed. Sherman A Noyes. LC 56-684495. 1956. Vantage Press.
Faith Desmond's Last Stand: A Story of Love, Courage, and a Miracle. Elizabeth Garver Jordan. LC 24-28118. 1924. Extension Press.
Faith Doctor. Edward Eggleston. LC 68-20011. (Americans in Fiction Ser). 1968. Repr. of 1891 ed. lib. bdg. 10.50x o.p. (ISBN 0-8398-0453-9). Gregg.
Faith Doctor: A Story of New York. Edward Eggleston. LC 68-20011. (Americans in fic.). 1968. 10.00. Gregg Pr.
Faith Doctor: A Story of New York. Edward Eggleston. LC 73-144997. 1973. Scholarly Press.
Faith Doctor: A Story of New York. Edward Eggleston. LC 6-37564. 1891. D. Appleton and Company.
Faith, Hope and a Horse. John Benton. LC 40-4881. 1940. D. Appleton-Century Company, Incorporated.
Faith, Hope and Charity. Irvin Shrewsbury Cobb. LC 34-23853. The Bobbs-Merrill Company.
Faith, Hope and Death. Allan James Tucker. LC 77-357889. 1976. 2.95 (ISBN 0-333-19437-3). Macmillan.
Faith, Hope, No Charity. Margaret Lane. LC 36-6805. 1936. Harper & Brothers.
Faith of His Fathers: A Story of Some Idealists. Agnes Eliza Jacomb. LC 9-35907. 1909. Dodd, Mead & Company.
Faith of Men: And Other Stories. Jack London. LC 73-122729. (Short story index reprint series). 1970. Books for Libraries Press.
Faith of Men: And Other Stories. Jack London. 1904. The Macmillan Company.
Faith of Men, & Other Stories. Jack London. LC 73-122729. (Short Story Index Reprint Ser). 1904. 16.00 (ISBN 0-8369-3562-4). Ayer Co.
Faith of Mrs. Kelleen. Drawings by Daniel Rasmusson. Katherine Mary O'Fallon Flannigan. LC 51-9159. 1951. Coward-McCann.
Faith of Our Fathers. Merlin L Neff. LC 30-32903. Review and Herald Publishing Association.
Faith of Our Fathers. Dorothy Walworth. LC 25-5771. 1925. Harper & Brothers.
Faith of Our Fathers. Spiro Bernard Zavos. LC 82-2060. (Paperback prose,). 1982. 14.50 (ISBN 0-7022-1751-4) (ISBN 0-7022-1761-1). University of Queensland Press.
Faith of Tarot. Anthony Piers. 256p. (Orig.). 1982. pap. 2.50 (ISBN 0-425-05720-8). Berkley Pub.
Faith on the Frontier. Edmund March Vittum. LC 8-32697. Congregational Sunday School and Publishing Society.
Faith the Root. Barbara Frances Fleury. LC 42-10423. 1942. E. P. Dutton & Co., Inc.
Faith Tresilion. Eden Phillpotts. LC 14-11355. 1914. 1.35. The Macmillan Company.
Faith White's Letter Book. 1620-1623. Plymouth, New England... M. H. Whiting. LC 8-343171. H. Hoyt.
Faithful. Nancy E Kline. LC 68-22430. 1968. W. Morrow.
Faithful Achates. Anthony Gould. LC 6-27639. (On cover: Judge's novels, no. 3). 1889. The Judge Publishing Company.
Faithful Are the Wounds. May Sarton. LC 55-5304. 1955. Rinehart.
Faithful Are the Wounds. May Sarton. LC 72-1812. 1972. (ISBN 0-393-08439-6). Norton.
Faithful Company: A Winter's Tale. Frank Arthur Swinnerton. LC 48-7140. 1948. Doubleday.
Faithful Dog. Miguel de Cervantes de Saavedra. 3.00 o.p. Branden.
Faithful for Eight Hours. Alfred Blake. (O.s.i.). (Orig.). pap. 0.60 o.s.i. (A227X, Award). Univ Pub & Dist.
Faithful Forever. Ethel Symonds Low. LC 47-25851. 1947. Zondervan Pub. House.
Faithful in My Fashion: A Novel. John Coates. LC 53-7815. 1953. Macmillan.
Faithful Jenny Dove, & Other Stories. Eleanor Farjeon. LC 78-128734. (Short Story Index Reprint Ser.). 1925. 15.00 (ISBN 0-8369-3625-6). Ayer Co.
Faithful Jenny Dove: And Other Tales. Eleanor Farjeon. LC 78-128734. (Short story index reprint series). 1970. Books for Libraries Press.
Faithful Lover. A Novel... Alfred W. Arrington. LC 6-2427. 1884. G. W. Carleton & Co.; Etc., Etc.
Faithful Lovers. John Davys Beresford. LC 36-37300. L. Furman, Inc.
Faithful Margaret. A Novel. Jim Simpson. ("New York weekly" series no. 3). 1877. G. W. Carleton & Co.
Faithful Ruslan: The Story of a Guard Dog. Georgii Nikolaevich Vladimov. LC 78-11087. (Illus.). 9.95 (ISBN 0-671-24633-X). Simon and Schuster.
Faithful Servants. Margery Sharp. LC 74-26370. 1975. 6.95. Little, Brown.
Faithful Shepherd. Lucette Finas. LC 63-7503. 1963. Pantheon Books.
Faithful Slave. Robert Morris. LC 72-1562. (Black Heritage Library Collection). (Illus.). 1972. 9.75 (ISBN 0-8369-9039-0). Books for Libraries Press.
Faithful Stranger, and Other Stories. Sheila Kaye-Smith. LC 38-13103. 1938. Harper & Brothers.
Faithful Wife. Sigrid Undset & Chater, Arthur G., Tr. LC 37-23347. 1937. A. A. Knopf.
Faithless. Clayton Matthews. 1970. pap. 0.75 o.p. (75-293). Manor Bks.
Faithless Guardian: Or, Out of the Darkness into the Light. A Story of Struggles, Trials, Doubts, and Triumphs. J. William Van Namee. LC 37-327914. 1870. W. White and Company.
Fak, Tavak, Tengerek. Tibor Denes. LC 66-29554. (Hungarian). 1967. 5.00 (ISBN 0-911050-29-9). Occidental.
Faked Passports. Dennis Yates Wheatley. (His Gregory Sallust series, 2). 1973. (pbk.) 1.50 (ISBN 0-345-03352-3). Ballantine.
Faked Passports: A Novel. Dennis Yates Wheatley. LC 43-11140. The Macmillan Company.
Fakers. Samuel George Blythe. LC 14-184593. 1.35. George H. Doran Company.
Faking It, Making It. Jake Danjo. pap. 1.95 o.p. (8078). Cameo.
Faking It: Or, The Wrong Hungarian. Gerald Green. LC 70-138430. 1971. 7.95 (ISBN 0-671-27073-7). Trident Press.
Falaise of the Blessed Voice: A Tale of the Youth of St. Louis, King of France. William Stearns Davis. LC 4-256838. 1904. London, Macmillan & Co., Ltd.
Falcon. Nigel Slater. LC 78-73106. 1979. 9.95 (ISBN 0-689-10968-7). Atheneum.
Falcon. Nigel Slater. 1982. 2.95 (ISBN 0-425-05197-8). Berkley Books.
Falcon & the Snowman: A True Story of Friendship & Espionage. Robert Lindsey. 1980. pap. 3.50 (ISBN 0-671-41160-8). PB.
Falcon: Black Pope, No. 2. Mark Ramsey. 1982. pap. 2.50 (ISBN 0-451-11771-9, AE1771, Sig). NAL.
Falcon Cuts in. Drexel Drake. LC 37-5410. J. B. Lippincott Company.
Falcon for a Queen. Catherine Gaskin. LC 77-175373. 1972. 6.95. Doubleday.
Falcon Fury. Katherine Yorke. 384p. (Orig.). 1982. pap. 3.25 (ISBN 0-523-41746-2). Pinnacle Bks.
Falcon Gold. Katherine Yorke. 352p. 1981. pap. 2.95 (ISBN 0-523-41341-6). Pinnacle Bks.
Falcon Meets a Lady: By Drexel Drake. Drexel Drake. LC 38-67552. J. B. Lippincott Company.
Falcon, No. 1: The Falcon Strikes. Mark Ramsey. 1982. pap. 2.50 (ISBN 0-451-11770-0, AE1770, Sig). NAL.
Falcon, No. 3: The Bloody Cross. Mark Ramsay. 1982. pap. 2.50 (ISBN 0-451-11917-7, AE1917, Sig). NAL.
Falcon of Eden. Graham Diamond. LC 80-80985. 288p. (Orig.). 1980. pap. 2.25 (ISBN 0-87216-717-8). Playboy Pbks.
Falcon of Langeac. Isabel Nixon Whiteley. LC 99-274655. 1897. Copeland and Day.
Falcon of Sqnawtooth: A Western Story. Arthur Preston Hankins. LC 23-13732. Chelsea House.
Falcon Road. Chris Massie. LC 36-30703. 1936. Longmans, Green and Co.
Falcon Royal. Catherine Darby, pseud. (Falcon Ser.: No. 5). 256p. 1976. pap. 1.25 (ISBN 0-445-00357-X). Popular Lib.
Falcon Sunset. Catherine Darby, pseud. (Falcon Ser.: No. 9). 256p. 1976. pap. 1.25 (ISBN 0-445-00421-5). Popular Lib.
Falcon; the Autobiography of His Grace James the 4, King of Scots. A. J. Stewart. LC 77-127359. (Illus.). 1970. 5.95. Delacorte Press.
Falcon to the Lure. Catherine Darby, pseud. 1978. 1.75 (ISBN 0-445-04322-9). Popular Library.
Falconberg. Hjalmar Hjorth Boyesen. 1879. C. Scribner's Sons.
Falconberg. Hjalmar Hjorth Boyesen. LC 22-5155. 1899. C. Scribner's Sons.
Falconer. John Cheever. LC 77-22619. 1977. 10.95 (ISBN 0-8161-6506-8). G. K. Hall.
Falconer. John Cheever. LC 76-19382. 1977. 7.95 (ISBN 0-394-48347-2). Knopf.
Falconer. John Cheever. 1977. 2.25 (ISBN 0-345-27300-1). Ballantine Books.
Falconer's Voyage. Hugh Hickling. LC 56-7010. 1956. Houghton Mifflin.
Falconhurst Fancy. Kyle Onstott. 1978. lib. bdg. 14.30x (ISBN 0-89966-248-X). Buccaneer Bks.
Falconhurst Fancy. Kyle Onstott & Lance Horner. (Falconhurst Plantation Ser.). 448p. 1978. pap. 2.25 (ISBN 0-449-13685-X, GM). Fawcett.
Falconlough. Monica Heath. pap. 1.50 (ISBN 0-451-07627-3, W7627, Sig). NAL.
Falcon's Flight. Donald Douglas. LC 29-13946. 1929. Doubleday, Doran & Company, Inc.
Falcon's Island. Antonia Scott. 1973. (pbk.) 1.25 (ISBN 0-671-78285-1). Pocket Books.
Falcons of France. Charles Bernard Nordhoff & James Norman Hall. LC 79-7290. (Flight, Its First Seventy-Five Years). (Illus.). 1980. 26.00 (ISBN 0-405-12198-9). Arno Press.
Falcons of France: A Tale of Youth and the Air. Charles Bernard Nordhoff & Hall, James Norman. LC 29-185539. 1929. Little, Brown, and Company.
Falcons of Narobedla: The Dark Intruder and Other Stories. Marion Zimmer Bradley. (Ace Double, 22576). 1972. 0.95. Ace Books.
Falcon's Prey. Drexel Drake. LC 36-18974. J. B. Lippincott Company.
Falcon's Prey. Penny Jordan. (Harlequin Presents Ser.). 192p. 1981. pap. 1.75 (ISBN 0-373-10471-5). Harlequin Bks.
Falcon's Shadow. Anne Maybury. 256p. 1981. pap. 2.25 (ISBN 0-441-22583-7). Ace Bks.
Falk; Amy Foster; To-Morrow. Joseph Conrad. LC 3-11676. 1903. McClure, Phillips and Company.
Falk; Amy Foster; To-Morrow. Joseph Conrad. LC 25-7165. 1921. Doubleday, Page & Company.
Falkenhorst. Mark Rascovich. LC 72-78143. 1974. 8.95 (ISBN 0-03-001431-X). Holt, Rinehart and Winston.
Falkland. A Novel. only cheap edition ever printed. ed. Edward George Earle Lytton Bulwer-Lytton Lytton. LC 9-1824. (With Beasley, S. The roue. Philadelphia, 185-?). 1852. T. B. Peterson.
Falkner: A Novel. Mary Wollstonecraft Godwin Shelley. LC 75-11752. 1975. 75.00 (ISBN 0-8414-7840-6). Folcroft Library Editions.
Falkner: A Novel. Mary Wollstonecraft Godwin Shelley. LC 31-17951. 1837. Harper & Brothers.
Falkner of the Inland Seas. James Oliver Curwood. Ed. by Bryant, Dorothea A. LC 31-68693. The Bobbs-Merill Company.
Fall Among Thieves. L. H. Evers. 1968. 8.45 o.s.i. Tri-Ocean.
Fall, & Exile and the Kingdom. Albert Camus. LC 64-55583. (Modern library of the world's best books 352). 1964. Modern Library.
Fall, and Other Stories. Grigori Gerenstain. LC 75-25083. 7.95 (ISBN 0-06-011492-4). Harper & Row.
Fall & Rise of Jimmy Hoffa. Walter Sheridan. 1973. 10.95 o.p. (ISBN 0-8415-0202-1). Dutton.
Fall: Being a True Account of What Happened in Paradise, for the Benefit of All Scandal-Mongers, with a New Interpretation of Sacred History, Vindicating Snakes and Apples. George Seibel. LC 18-23507. 1918. The Lessing Company.
Fall Collection. Antoine-Dariaux, Genevieve. LC 71-157581. 1973. 6.95 (ISBN 0-385-05934-5). Doubleday.
Fall Collection. Genevieve A. Dariaux, pseud. Tr. by Helen Eustis from Fr. LC 71-157581. 288p. 1973. 6.95 o.p. (ISBN 0-385-05934-5). Doubleday.
Fall Darkness, Fall! Laura Brighton. (large print gothic). 1975. (pbk.) 0.95. Leisure Books.
Fall Flight. Eleanor M. Patterson Gizycka. LC 28-23918. 1928. Minton, Balch & Company.
Fall Forward, My Son. Don Ingle. 4.95 o.p. Carlton.
Fall from Aloft. Brian Burland. LC 75-85577. 1969. 4.95. Random House.
Fall from Grace. Victor Canning. LC 80-83325. 1981. 9.95 (ISBN 0-688-00195-5). Morrow.
Fall Girl. Watkins Eppes Wright. LC 49-8628. 1949. Phoenix Press.
Fall Guy. Jerome Barry. LC 60-15167. 1960. Published for the Crime Club by Doubleday.
Fall Guy. Jay Cronley. LC 77-89880. 1978. 6.95 (ISBN 0-385-13316-2). Doubleday.
Fall Guy. Joe Barry Lake. LC 45-4535. 1945. Mystery House.
Fall Guy. Ritchie Perry. LC 72-574. (Midnight novel of suspense). 1972. 5.95 (ISBN 0-395-13941-4). Houghton Mifflin Co.
Fall Guy. Timothy Trent, pseud. LC 36-1013. Godwin.
Fall Guy. Brand Whitlock. LC 12-11709. The Bobbs-Merrill Company.
Fall Guy for Murder. Lawrence L. Goldman. LC 43-17042. (On cover: Prize mystery novels). 1943. Crestwood Publishing Co., Inc.
Fall Guy for Murder. Lawrence L. Goldman. LC 42-50771. 1943. E. P. Dutton & Company, Inc.
Fall of a Nation: A Sequel to The Birth of a Nation. Thomas Dixon. LC 74-15965. (Science Fiction). (Illus.). 1975. 20.00 (ISBN 0-405-06286-9). Arno Press.
Fall of a Nation: A Sequel to The Birth of a Nation, by Thomas Dixon... Illustated by Charles Wrenn. Thomas Dixon. 1916. 1.35. D. Appleton and Company.
Fall of a Sparrow. Nigel Balchin. LC 56-5720. 1956. Rinehart.
Fall of a Titan. Igor Gouzenko. LC 54-10351. 1954. Norton.
Fall of an Eagle. Jon Cleary. LC 64-22510. 1964. Morrow.
Fall of Angels. Elizabeth Savage. LC 74-154955. 1971. 5.95. Little, Brown.
Fall of Asgard: A Novel. Julian Stafford Corbett. (Harper's handy ser. no. 86). 1886. Harper & Brothers.
Fall of Bethar: A Historical Romance, Adopted from the Hebrew. Samuel Maier & Schulman, Kalman, 1819-1899. LC 8-28092. Press of M. Stern, Goldsmith & Co.
Fall of Casa Malvado. Sarah Chisom. (Orig.). 1969. pap. 1.95 o.p. (6033). Brandon.
Fall of Chronopolis. Barrington J Bayley. 1974. (pbk.) 0.95. DAW Books.
Fall of Colossus. Dennis Feltham Jones. LC 73-87195. 1974. 5.95 (ISBN 0-399-11282-0). Putnam's.
Fall of Constantinople. John Mason Neale. (Half-title: Everyman's library, ed. by Ernest Rhys. Fiction. no. 655). 1913. J. M. Dent & Sons, Ltd.
Fall of Damascus. An Historical Novel. Charles Wells Russell. LC 8-1332. 1878. Lee and Shepard.
Fall of El Dorado, a Novel. 1st ed. William Rittenour. LC 54-13427. 1955. Exposition Press.
Fall of Fort Sumter: Or, Love and War in 1860-61. Newbrough, J. B. LC 9-3444. F. A. Brady.
Fall of Heaven. William Leftschatz. LC 82-83494. 384p. (Orig.). 1983. pap. 6.95 (ISBN 0-86666-122-0). GWP.
Fall of Kilman Kon. Arthur Cummings. 1889. G. W. Dillingham.
Fall of Man. Croft-Cooke, Rupert. LC 76-383282. 1976. 3.25 (ISBN 0-7274-0056-8). White Lion Publishers.
Fall of Midas. Juliet Astley, pseud. 256p. 1975. 7.95 o.p. (ISBN 0-698-10680-6, Coward). Putnam Pub Group.
Fall of Midas. Juliet Astley, pseud. (General Ser.). 1979. 14.50 (ISBN 0-8161-6727-3, Large Print Bks). G K Hall.
Fall of Midas. Norah Robinson Lofts. LC 75-10462. 1975. 7.95 (ISBN 0-698-10680-6). Coward, McCann & Geoghegan.
Fall of Midas. Norah Robinson Lofts. 1976. 1.95 (ISBN 0-671-80698-X). Pocket Books.
Fall of Midas. Norah Robinson Lofts. LC 79-10646. 1979. 14.50 (ISBN 0-8161-6727-3). G. K. Hall.
Fall of Moondust. Arthur Charles Clarke. LC 61-12345. 1974. (pbk.) 1.25. New American Library.
Fall of Moondust. 1st Ed. Arthur Charles Clarke. LC 61-123452. 1961. Harcourt, Brace & World.
Fall of New York. Miles Donis. LC 78-149091. 1971. 5.95. D. McKay Co.
Fall of Paris. Ilia Grigorevich Ehrenburg & Shelley, Gerard, Tr. LC 43-69024. 1943. A. A Knopf.
Fall of Paris. Ilya Grigorevich Ehrenburg & Shelley, Gerard, Tr. LC 43-3874. 1942. Hutchinson & Co. Ltd.
Fall of the Crimea. Edmund Spencer. LC 41-405214. 1854. G. Routledge & Co.
Fall of the Curtain. Harold Begbie. LC 1-9999. The Bowen-Merrill Company.
Fall of the Great Republic. Henry Standish Coverdale. LC 15-12481. 1885. Roberts Brothers.
Fall of the House of Usher. Edgar Allan Poe. Ed. by Eric W. Carlson. LC 73-166123. (Merrill literary casebook series). 1971. (ISBN 0-675-09641-3). Merrill.
Fall of the House of Usher: And Four Other Tales: The Black Cat, Ms. Found in a Bottle, Three Sundays in a Week, The Oval Portrait. Illus. by Rick Schreiter. Edgar Allan Poe. LC 67-14248. 1967. 2.95, 2.21 lib. ed.,. Watts.
Fall of the House of Usher, and Other Tales. Edgar Allan Poe. LC 60-50786. (Signet classic, CD29). (Illus.). 1960. New American Library.
Fall of the House of Usher & Other Tales of Horror. new ed. Edgar Allan Poe. Ed. by Joseph W. Nash. 1976. pap. 0.95 o.p. (ISBN 0-89319-001-2). Andor Pub.

Fall of the House of Usher: Ligeia; The Cask of Amontillado; The Assignation; Ms. Found in the Bottle; The Black Cat; The Gold Bug. Edgar Allan Poe. Ed. by Perry, Bliss. LC 7-38187. (Little masterplaces; ed. by Bliss Perry). 1897. Doubleday & McClure Co.
Fall of the King. Johannes Vilhelm Jensen. Tr. by Federspiel, P. T. LC 33-29194. H. Holt and Company.
Fall of the Nibelungs. Margaret Armour. 1897. Repr. 10.00 (ISBN 0-8274-2329-2). R West.
Fall of the Russian Empire. Donald James. LC 81-21175. (Illus.). 14.95 (ISBN 0-399-12689-9). Putnam.
Fall of the Shell. Paul O. Williams. LC 82-6670. 1982. 2.50 (ISBN 0-345-30595-7). Ballantine Books.
Fall of the Sparrow. Marie Clothilde Balfour. LC 6-6324. (On cover: The Hudson library, no. 25). 1897. G. P. Putnam's Sons.
Fall of the Staincliffes. Alfred Colbeck. LC 6-25422. F. H. Revell Company.
Fall of the Towers. Samuel R. Delancy. 224p. 1982. pap. 2.50 (ISBN 0-553-20309-6). Bantam.
Fall of the Towers. Samuel R Delany. LC 77-5842. (Gregg Press science fiction series). 1977. 16.00 (ISBN 0-8398-2372-X). Gregg Press.
Fall of the Towers: A Classic Science Fiction Trilogy. Samuel R Delany. 1976. (pbk.) 1.95. Ace Books.
Fall of Ulysses: An Elephant Story. Charles Dwight Willard. LC 12-16894. 1912. George H. Doran Company.
Fall of Utopia. Charles Joseph Bayne. Eastern Publishing Company.
Fall of Valor. Charles Reginald Jackson. 320p. 1974. pap. 1.50 (ISBN 0-532-15133-X). Woodhill.
Fall of Valor: A Novel. Charles Reginald Jackson. LC 46-6208. 1946. Rinehart & Co., Inc.
Fall of Worlds. Francine Mezo. 320p. 1980. pap. 2.50 (ISBN 0-380-75564-5, 75564). Avon.
Fall Over Cliff: By Josephine Bell Pseud. Doris Bell Collier Ball. LC 56-8582. (Murder revisited mystery novel, no. 15). 1956. Macmillan.
Fall Roundup: By Members of the Western Writers of America. Edited, with an Introd., by Harry E. Maule; Jacket Painting and Line-Drawing Illus. by Charles M. Russell. Western Writers of America. Ed. by Harry Edward Maule. LC 55-10638. 1955. Random House.
Fall. Translated from the French by Justin O'Brien. 1st American Ed. Albert Camus. LC 57-565263. 1957. Knopf.
Fallback. Peter Niesewand. LC 81-11252. 1982. 14.50 (ISBN 0-688-00819-4). Morrow.
Fallen. Juan Marse. LC 79-13856. 9.95 (ISBN 0-316-54676-3). Little, Brown.
Fallen Among Thieves. A Summer Tour. Martha Louise Rayne. LC 7-36628. 1879. G. W. Carleton & Co.; Etc., Etc.
Fallen Angel. Michael Avallone. (Satan sleuth#1). 1974. (pbk.) 0.95. Warner Paperback Library.
Fallen Angel. Marty Holland. LC 45-3537. 1945. E. P. Dutton & Company, Inc.
Fallen Angel. Anne Mather. (Harlequin Presents Ser.). 1979. pap. 1.25 (ISBN 0-373-70787-8). Harlequin Bks.
Fallen Angel. Sally Mitchell. LC 79-92711. 1981. 15.95 (ISBN 0-87972-155-3); pap. 8.95 (ISBN 0-87972-156-1). Bowling Green Univ.
Fallen Angel. Diana Summers. LC 81-81984. 368p. (Orig.). 1981. pap. 2.95 (ISBN 0-87216-950-2). Playboy Pbks.
Fallen Angel, and Other Stories. William Tannahill Polk. LC 56-13842. 1956. University of North Carolina Press.
Fallen Angel: By Walter Ericson Pseud. 1st Ed. Howard Melvin Fast. LC 52-5001. 1952. Little, Brown.
Fallen Angels. Ursula Holden. LC 79-15597. 12.95 (ISBN 0-416-00021-5). Methuen.
Fallen Angels: Turnstiles. Ursula Holden. 192p. 1982. pap. 2.25 (ISBN 0-523-41275-4). Pinnacle Bks.
Fallen Away. 1st Ed. Margaret Culkin Banning. LC 51-12203. 1951. Harper.
Fallen Badge. John Earl Lewis. 1982. pap. 6.95 (Avalon). Bouregy.
Fallen Curtain. Ruth Rendell. 192p. 1981. pap. 2.25 (ISBN 0-553-20039-9). Bantam.
Fallen Curtain, and Other Stories. Ruth Rendell. LC 77-357664. 1976. 3.75 (ISBN 0-09-127270-X). Hutchinson.
Fallen Curtain: Eleven Mystery Stories by an Edgar-Award Winning Writer. Ruth Rendell. LC 75-40739. 1976. 5.95 (ISBN 0-385-11605-5). Published for the Crime Club by Doubleday.
Fallen Fortunes. A Novel. James Payn. (Seaside library. v. 33, no. 687). 1880. G. Munro.
Fallen Gods: An Italian Tragedy. Lillian Michalczewska Bond. LC 65-2094. Exposition Press.
Fallen Idol. Thomas Anstey Guthrie. (On cover: Lovell's library. v. 15, no. 755). 1866. J. W. Lovell Company.
Fallen Idol. Thomas Anstey Guthrie. (On cover: Seaside library. Pocket ed. no. 819). 1886. G. Munro.
Fallen Man. Mark Sadler, pseud. pap. 0.95 o.p. (Z1098N, Zebra). Grove.
Fallen Ones. Robert E. Vardeman & Victor Milan. LC 81-82361. (War of Powers Ser.). 224p. (Orig.). 1982. pap. 2.50 (ISBN 0-87216-986-3). Playboy Pbks.
Fallen Priest. Story Founded on Fact. Key and Sequel to "Boston Inside Out"... Book I.--The Story... Book II.--Catholic Church in Politics: for Sale or to Let. Book III.--Key and Appendix. 3d ed. 11 extra chapters. ed. Henry Morgan, pseud. LC 7-25996. Shawmut Pbulishing Company.
Fallen Race: A Story. Austyn Granville. (On cover: Neely's library of choice literature v. l. no. 15). 1892. F. T. Neely.
Fallen Sparrow. Dorothy Belle Flanagan Hughes. LC 42-21967. 1942. Duell, Sloan and Pearce.
Fallen Staircase. Kamelle Hess. 1978. pap. 1.25 (ISBN 0-532-12579-7). Woodhill.
Fallen Star. James Blish. 192p. 1983. pap. 2.50 (ISBN 0-380-62463-X, 62463-X). Avon.
Fallen Star Mystery. Bob Wright. (Tom & Ricky Mystery Ser.: No. 2). (Illus.). 48p. 1983. pap. 2.00 (ISBN 0-87879-341-0). Acad Therapy.
Fallen Woman. Albert Quandt. LC 36-19259. 1936. Godwin.
Fallen Woman. Leona Slottman. 1947. Phoenix Press.
Fallible Fiend. Lyon Sprague De Camp. (Del Rey Book). 1981. 1.95 (ISBN 0-345-29367-3). Ballantine Books.
Fallible Fiend. Lyon Sprague DeCamp. 1973. pap. 0.95. New American Library.
Fallible Plot. Mary F. Halbash. LC 81-85572. 144p. 1983. pap. 5.95. GWP.
Fallina: A Tale of Modern American Social Life. Rosa Meyers Mumma. LC 6-36879. 1906. The Roxburgh Publishing Company.
Falling. Harris Dulany. LC 75-139529. 1971. 4.95 (ISBN 0-8415-0087-8). McCall Pub. Co.
Falling. Susan Fromberg Schaeffer. LC 72-87159. 1973. 6.95. Macmillan.
Falling Angel. William Hjortsberg. LC 78-53866. 8.95 (ISBN 0-15-130118-2). Harcourt Brace Jovanovich.
Falling Bodies. Sue Kaufman. LC 73-83644. 1974. 7.95 (ISBN 0-385-05132-8). Doubleday.
Falling Hills. Perry Lentz. LC 67-154912. 1967. 6.95. Scribners.
Falling in Love Again. Pamela Wallace. 288p. (Orig.). 1981. pap. 2.75 (ISBN 0-523-41055-7). Pinnacle Bks.
Falling in Place. Ann Beattie. 2.95 (ISBN 0-445-04650-3). Fawcett Popular Library,, C.
Falling in Place: A Novel. Ann Beattie. LC 79-3880. 10.95 (ISBN 0-394-50323-6). Random House.
Falling Man. Warren Forma. LC 73-8990. 1973. 4.95 (ISBN 0-690-00089-8). Crowell.
Falling Man. Mark Sadler, pseud. 1974. (pbk.) 1.25. Manor Books.
Falling Man. Mark Sadler, pseud. LC 78-102348. 1970. 4.95. Random House.
Falling off. Kathleen Thompson Norris. 1971. 4.95 o.p. (ISBN 0-695-80257-7); pap. 2.95 o.p. (ISBN 0-695-80256-9). Follett.
Falling Out. Charles Cohen. LC 80-54527. 10.95 (ISBN 0-87223-675-7). Seaview Books.
Falling Place. Elizabeth Bailey. (Orig.). 1981. pap. 1.95 (ISBN 0-8439-8040-0, Tiara Bks). Nordon Pubns.
Falling Seeds. Elisabeth Cobb Chapman. LC 27-7730. 1927. Doubleday. Page & Company.
Falling Star. Vicki Baum. Tr. by Zeltlin, Ida. LC 34-5588. 1934. Doubleday, Doran & Comapny, Inc.
Falling Star. Patricia Moyes. LC 64-14364. (Rinehart suspense novel). 1964. Holt, Rinehart and Winston.
Falling Star. Patricia Moyes. LC 81-7030. 1982. 3.50 (ISBN 0-03-059784-6). Holt, Rinehart, and Winston.
Falling Star. Lillian O'Donnell. LC 79-11060. 8.95 (ISBN 0-399-12407-1). Putnam.
Falling Star see Ceasar Dies.
Falling Through the Night. Alexander Federoff. 1964. 8.95 (ISBN 0-8392-1030-2). Astor-Honor.
Falling Torch. Algis Budrys, pseud. 1974. pap. 0.95 o.p. (ISBN 0-515-03430-4, N3430). BJ Pub Group.
Falling up. Miles Donis. LC 72-130750. 1970. 5.95. D. McKay Co.
Falling Uphill. Nan F. Salerno. LC 81-5839. 12.95 (ISBN 0-13-301804-0). Prentice-Hall.
Falling World of Tristram Pocket. David F Kellum. LC 77-352510. 1976. 7.95. (ISBN 0-88967-014-5) (ISBN 0-88967-015-3). Tree Frog Press.
Fallon. Louis L'Amour. LC 63-8934. (Bantam western). 1963. Bantam Books.
Fallon. Louis L'Amour. LC 81-24437. 1982. 11.95 (ISBN 0-8161-3359-X). G.K. Hall.
Fallon Legacy. Reagan O'Neal. 480p. (Orig.). 1982. pap. 3.50 (ISBN 0-523-48029-6). Pinnacle Bks.
Fallon Pride. Reagan O'Neal. (Fallon Chronicles Ser.: Vol. 2). 1981. pap. 2.95 (ISBN 0-523-48002-4). Pinnacle Bks.
Fallow Ground. Meredith Reed. LC 36-19443. The Penn Publishing Company.
Fallow Land. Herbert Ernest Bates. LC 79-144867. 1971. (ISBN 0-403-00854-9). Scholarly Press.
Fallow Land. Herbert Ernest Bates. LC 33-27019. 1933. R. O. Ballou.
Falls of Rabbor. Jess Carr. LC 73-75340. 1973. 10.95 (ISBN 0-87716-042-2, Pub. by Moore Pub Co). F Apple.
Falls the Shadow. Regina Ross. LC 73-13966. 1974. 6.95. Delacorte Press.
Falmont Claimants. Alfred Bercovici. (Orig.). 1973. pap. 0.95 o.p. (09225). Curtis.
Falmouth Massacre in 1676. Charles Pomeroy Sherman. LC 43-7362. 1942. Country Life Press Corporation.
Falsche Agentin: Reader 4. Rita M. Walbruck. LC 80-22162. (Auf Heisser Spur Ser.). (gr. 9-12). 1981. pap. 1.95 (ISBN 0-88436-853-X). EMC.
False. John Russell Coryell. LC 6-39928. (On cover: Lovell's library, no. 1257). 1888. John W. Lovell Company.
False. Geraldine Fleming. LC 6-39928. (On cover: Lovell's library, no. 1257). 1888. J. W. Lovell Company.
False Alarm. Manning Long. LC 43-7896. 1943. Duell, Sloan and Pearce.
False Beards. Alan Williams. LC 65-14665. 1965. 4.95. Harper.
False Bounty. Frederick Clyde Davis. LC 48-6123. 1948. Pub. for the Crime Club by Doubleday.
False Coin, a Novel. Harvey Swados. LC 59-11099. 1960. Little, Brown.
False Coin or True! Frances Frederica Montresor. LC 7-31804. 1896. D. Appleton and Company.
False Colors. Richard Pitts Powell. LC 55-14250. (Inner sanctum mystery). 1955. Simon and Schuster.
False Colours. Georgette Heyer. 1964. 4.95 o.p. (ISBN 0-525-10271-X). Dutton.
False Colours. Georgette Heyer. (A Fawcett Crest Book). 1977. 1.50 (ISBN 0-449-23169-0). Fawcett Publications.
False Couple. A Novelization of the Drama. "A False Couple"... Eugene Sheridan. LC 8-5123. Exchange Publishing Company.
False Dawn. Arden Coombs. LC 29-22918. J. Lamothe.
False Dawn. Chelsea Quinn Yarbro. LC 77-82777. 1978. 6.95 (ISBN 0-385-13144-5). Doubleday.
False Dawn. Chelsea Quinn Yarbro. 1979. 1.95 (ISBN 0-446-90077-X). Warner Books.
False Dawn see Old New York.
False Dawn: The 'forties. Edith Newbold Jones Wharton. LC 24-11471. (Her Old New York. v. 1). 1924. D. Appleton and Company.
False Entry: A Novel. Hortense Calisher. LC 58-7861. 1961. Little, Brown.
False Entry: And Other Stories About Schools. Charles William Bardeen. LC 6-139. (School bulletin publication). 1905. C. W. Bardeen.
False Evidence. Leopold Horace Ognall. LC 77-77951. 1977. 6.95 (ISBN 0-525-10275-2). Dutton.
False Face. Leslie Edgley. LC 47-1649. 1947. Simon and Schuster.
False-Face. Sydney Horler. LC 26-18316. George H. Doran Company.
False Face. Jean Lilly. LC 29-27527. E. P. Dutton & Co., Inc.
False Face. Seldon Truss, pseud. LC 55-9994. 1955. Published for the Crime Club by Doubleday.
False Face of Death. Anita Allen, pseud. LC 78-55844. 1979. 7.95 (ISBN 0-385-12721-9). Doubleday.
False Faces. Theodore S Drachman. LC 31-9824. Newland Press.
False Faces. Anita Blackmon Smith. LC 34-33132. W. Goodwin, Inc.
False Faces: Further Adventures from the History of the Lone Wolf. Louis Joseph Vance. LC 18-2606. 1918. Doubleday, Page & Company.
False Flags: A Novel. Noel Hynd. LC 78-23872. 1979. 8.95 (ISBN 0-8037-2591-4). Dial Press.
False Front. Clark Darlton. (Perry Rhodan, 103). (Illus.). Ace.
False Front. Lawrence Meyer. LC 78-26873. 1979. 9.95 (ISBN 0-670-30607-X). Viking Press.
False Front. Lawrence Meyer. 1980. 1.95 (ISBN 0-445-04522-1). Fawcett Popular Library.
False Gods. George Horace Lorimer. LC 6-12858. 1906. D. Appleton and Company.
False Gods: A Novel. Will Scarlet. LC 24-10215. 1924. Benziger Brothers.
False Idols. Betty Ferm. LC 74-81702. 1974. 6.95 (ISBN 0-399-11405-X). Putnam.
False Idols. Betty Ferm. LC 74-81702. (Fawcett crest book). 1975. (pbk.) 1.25. Fawcett.
False Inspector Dew. Peter Lovesey. LC 81-18706. 12.50 (ISBN 0-394-52304-0). Pantheon Books.
False Joanna. John Fredman. LC 71-142477. 1971. 4.95. Bobbs-Merrill.
False Love. Marcia Miller. 1973. pap. 0.75 o.s.i. (01-397). Lancer.
False Match. Henry Bean. LC 81-21096. 13.95 (ISBN 0-671-44251-1). Poseidon Press.
False Measure: A Satirical Novel of the Lives and Objectives of Upper Middle- Class Negroes. Charles A Smythwick. LC 53-10280. 1954. William-Frederick Press.
False Night. Algis Budrys, pseud. LC 55-21031. (Lion book, 230). 1954. Lion Books.
False Prophets. Sean Flannery, pseud. Date not set. pap. price not set (Pub. by Charter Bks). Ace Bks.
False Purple. Sydney Horler. LC 32-2662. 1932. The Mystery League, Inc.
False Scent. Joseph Smith Fletcher. LC 25-18352. 1925. A. A. Knopf.
False Scent. Annie French Hector. (On cover: Lovell's library, no. 1361). 1889. J. W. Lovell Company.
False Scent. Annie French Hector. (On cover: Seaside library. Pocket ed. no. 1199). 1889. G. Munro.
False Scent. Ngaio Marsh. 1976. Repr. of 1959 ed. lib. bdg. 15.45x (ISBN 0-88411-484-8). Amereon Ltd.
False Scent. Ngaio Marsh. (Ngaio Marsh Mystery Ser.). 214p. 1981. pap. 2.50 (ISBN 0-515-06007-0). Jove Pubns.
False Spring. Beatrice Kean Stapleton Seymour. LC 30-850. 1930. A. A. Knopf.
False Star. Anne Duffield. LC 40-9007. 1939. Arcadia House.
False Star: A Tale of the Occident. Abram Dale Gash. 1899. W. B. Conkey Company.
False Summer. 1st Ed. Amanda Brooks. LC 61-176615. 1961. T. Gaus' Sons.
False to Any Man. Zenith Jones Brown. LC 39-27679. 1939. C. Scribner's Sons.
False Trees. Rochelle Ratner. 1973. 5.00 (Pub. by New Rivers Pr); signed ltd. ed. 10.00; pap. 2.50. SBD.
False Witness. Helen Nielsen. LC 59-10383. (Ballantine suspense novel, 310K). 1959. Ballantine Books.
False Witness. Dorothy Uhnak. 288p. 1982. pap. 3.50 (ISBN 0-449-24512-8). Fawcett.
False Witness, a Novel. Irving Stone. LC 40-6545. 1940. Doubleday, Doran and Company, Inc.
False Witness: A Novel. Dorothy Uhnak. LC 81-1591. 12.95 (ISBN 0-671-23076-X). Simon & Schuster.
False Youth. Lawrence Rising. LC 29-29432. 1929. H. Liveright.
Falsehood and Truth; Conformity. Charlotte Elizabeth Browne Tonna. LC 75-488. 1975-1976. 35.00 (ISBN 0-8240-1564-9). Garland Pub.
Falsely Accused: A Story of Russian Intrigue. William Frank Roll. LC 20-2649. Citizen Print Shop.
Falstaff. Robert Nye. 1976. 8.95 o.p. (ISBN 0-316-61738-5). Little.
Falstaff: Being the Acta Domini Johannis Fastolfe, or Life and Valiant Deeds of Sir John Faustoff, or The Hundred Days War, As Told by Sir John Fastolf, K. G., to His Secretaries, William Worcester, Stephen Scrope, Fr Brackley, Christopher Hanson, Luke Nanton, John Bussard, and Peter Basset. Robert Nye. LC 76-27765. 8.95. Little, Brown.
Falstaff: Being the Acta Domini Johannis Fastolfe, or Life and Valiant Deeds of Sir John Faustoff, or The Hundred Days War, As Told by Sir John Fastolf, K.G., to His Secretaries William Worcester, Stephen Scrope, Fr. Brackley, Christopher Hanson, Luke Nanton, John Bussard, and Peter Basset. Robert Nye. LC 77-352232. 1976. 3.95 (ISBN 0-241-89429-8). Hamilton.
Fame. Leonore Fleischer. 1980. pap. 2.25 (ISBN 0-449-14359-7, GM). Fawcett.
Fame. Micheline Keating. LC 25-10060. 1925. G. P. Putnam's Sons.
Fame and Fancy, or, Voltaire Improved. Containing the Story of Candid--Revised... Francois Marie Arouet De Voltaire & Thorel De Campigneulles, Charles Claude Florent De, 1737-1809. LC 8-32691. 1826.
Fame & Fortune. Joanne Kaye. LC 81-81146. (Garment Center Ser.). 224p. (Orig.). 1981. pap. 2.25 (ISBN 0-87216-921-9). Playboy Pbks.
Fame & Obscurity. Gay Talese. 1981. pap. 3.25 (ISBN 0-440-12620-7). Dell.

Fame and Sorrow. With Colonel Chabert. The Atheist's Mass. La Grande Breteche. The Purse. La Grenadiere. Honore De Balzac. Tr. by Katharine Prescott Wormeley. LC 12-135163. (HalfTitle: The comedy of human life... Scenes from private life). 1890. Roberts Brothers.
Fame for a Woman: Or, Splendid Mourning. Cranstoun Metcalfe. LC 2-18737. 1902. G. P. Putnam's Sons.
Fame Game. Rona Jaffe. LC 76-85553. 1969. 6.95. Random House.
Fame Is the Spur. Howard Spring. LC 40-33709. 1940. The Viking Press.
Fame-Seekers: By Alice Woods... with Illustrations by May Wilson Preston. Alice Woods. LC 12-8667. George H. Doran Company.
Famed Fontenoy: Or, The Brothers of the Bivouac. Dennis O'Sullivan. (On cover: Munro's library, popular novels, v. 1, no. 415). N. L. Munro.
Fame's Pathway: A Romance of a Genius. Hobart Chatfield Chatfield-Taylor. LC 9-8576. 1909. Duffield & Company.
Familiar Faces: Best Contemporary American Short Stories. Ed. by Pat McNees. 1979. pap. 2.25 (ISBN 0-449-24078-9, Crest). Fawcett.
Familiar Faces: Stories of People You Know. Mary Roberts Rinehart. LC 41-10775. Farrar & Rinehart, Inc.
Familiar Letters Betwixt a Gentleman & a Lady see Reform'd Coquet.
Familiar Letters of Peppermint Perkins... Reprinted from the Boston "Saturday Evening Gazette.". Peppermint Perkins. LC 11-7176. 1886. Ticknor and Company.
Familiar Spirits. Lisa Tuttle. 208p. (Orig.). 1983. pap. 2.95 (ISBN 0-425-05854-9). Berkley Pub.
Familiar Strangers. Bettina Montgomery. 384p. (Orig.). 1981. pap. 3.25 (ISBN 0-441-22696-5). Ace Bks.
Familiar Touch, No. 85. Lynn Lawrence. 1982. pap. 1.75. Jove Pubns.
Families and Survivors. Alice Boyd Adams. LC 74-7751. 1974-1975. 6.95 (ISBN 0-394-49167-X). Knopf; Distributed by Random House.
Familistere. Marie Howland. LC 74-32134. (American Utopian Adventure Ser). iv, 547p. Repr. of 1918 ed. lib. bdg. 27.50x (ISBN 0-87991-024-0). Porcupine Pr.
Familistere: A Novel. 3d ed.... ed. Marie Howland. LC 18-13454. Christopher Publishing House.
Family. Elinor Sutherland Glyn. LC 19-4969. 1919. D. Appleton and Company.
Family. Herbert Gold. 224p. 1983. pap. 2.75 (ISBN 0-523-41887-6). Pinnacle Bks.
Family. Fannie Hurst. 1975. pap. 1.50 o.p. (ISBN 0-515-03898-9). Pyramid Pubns.
Family. Caroline Ivey. LC 52-9735. 1952. Sloane.
Family. Fei-Kan Li. LC 72-79433. 1972. 2.50 (ISBN 0-385-05787-3). Anchor Books.
Family. Elinor Mordaunt, pseud. LC 15-7737. 1915. 1.35. John Lane Company.
Family. David Plante. LC 78-4189. 1978. 8.95 (ISBN 0-374-15218-7). Farrar, Straus, Giroux.
Family. Antonina Riasnowsky. LC 40-27600. 1940. Little, Brown and Company.
Family. Toson Shimazaki. LC 76-380063. 16.00 (ISBN 0-86008-165-6). University of Tokyo Press.
Family: A Novel. Leslie Waller. LC 68-25465. 1968. 6.95. Putnam.
Family: A Novel. Wayland Wells Williams. LC 23-68388. 1923. Frederick A. Stokes Company.
Family: A Novel in the Form of a Memoir. Herbert Gold. LC 81-66964. 11.95 (ISBN 0-87795-332-5). Arbor House.
Family! A Novel. 1st Ed. Fannie Hurst. LC 60-6882. 1960. Doubleday.
Family: A Story. Gregory Morton. LC 79-25723. (Illus.). 8.95 (ISBN 0-8065-0691-1). Citadel Press.
Family: A Story of Forgiveness, from the Play of Robert Hobart Davis. Edward Marshall & Davis, Robert Hobart. LC 11-27298. 1.25. G. W. Dillingham Company.
Family Affair. Mignon Good Eberhart. LC 80-6029. 9.95 (ISBN 0-394-51899-3). Random House.
Family Affair. Mignon Good Eberhart. LC 81-13160. 1981. 13.95 (ISBN 0-8161-3297-6). G.K. Hall.
Family Affair. Frederick John Fargus. LC 6-38439. (On cover: Lovell's library. v. 12. no. 631). 1885. J. W. Lovell Company.
Family Affair. Lilian Gill. LC 32-255972. The Macaulay Company.
Family Affair. Melvin Leighton Heimer. LC 65-23378. 1965. Trident Press.
Family Affair. Joan Mellows (ISBN 0-449-22967-X). Fawcett Crest.
Family Affair. Rex Stout. LC 77-28760. 1978. 9.95 (ISBN 0-8161-6561-0). G. K. Hall.
Family Affair. Nelia Gardner White. LC 34-27070. 1934. Frederick A. Stokes Company.
Family Affair: A Mystery. Ione Sandberg Shriber. LC 41-19315. Farrar & Rinehart, Incorporated.
Family Affair: A Nero Wolfe Novel. Rex Stout. LC 75-15526. 1975. 5.95 (ISBN 0-670-30611-8). Viking Press.
Family Affair: A Nero Wolfe Novel. Rex Stout. 1976. 1.50 (ISBN 0-553-02614-3). Bantam Books.
Family Affair: A Novel. Mary Fassett Hunt. LC 48-7707. 1948. Harper.
Family Affairs. Edward Cartwright. 1972. pap. 1.95 o.s.i. (V10557, Venus). Grove.
Family Affairs. Catherine Gaskin. LC 79-8832. 1980. 12.95 (ISBN 0-385-13468-1). Doubleday.
Family Affairs. John L'Heureux. LC 73-18777. 1974. 6.95 (ISBN 0-385-03671-X). Doubleday.
Family Affairs. Jane Watkins. LC 77-3807. 8.95 (ISBN 0-06-014574-9). Harper & Row.
Family Affairs. Jane Watkins. 1979. 2.25 (ISBN 0-06-014574-9). Pocket Books.
Family Album. David D. Galloway. 1980. pap. 6.95 (ISBN 0-7145-3785-3). Riverrun NY.
Family Album. Antonia Ridge. LC 52-11695. Harper.
Family Album: A Novel. David D Galloway. LC 77-84387. 8.95 (ISBN 0-15-130153-0). Harcourt Brace Jovanovich.
Family & a Fortune. Ivy Compton-Burnett. 1939. 11.95 (ISBN 0-575-02579-4, Pub. by Gollancz England). David & Charles.
Family & a Fortune. Ivy Compton-Burnett. 304p. 1983. pap. 4.95 (ISBN 0-14-001713-5). Penguin.
Family and a Fortune, and More Women Than Men: Two Novels 1st Amer. Ed. Ivy Compton-Burnett. LC 65-10942. (Essandess paperback). 1965. pap., 2.45. S. & S.
Family & Sexual Deviation. Edward Small, Jr. 192p. (Orig.). 1973. pap. 1.95 o.p. (ISBN 0-87682-301-0, 7301). Barclay Hse.
Family Arsenal. Paul Theroux. LC 76-10212. 1976. 8.95 (ISBN 0-395-24400-5). Houghton Mifflin.
Family Arsenal: A Novel. Paul Theroux. LC 76-376475. 1976. 3.75 (ISBN 0-241-89380-1). Hamilton.
Family at Gilje: A Domestic Story of the Forties. Jonas Lauritz Idemil Lie. LC 21-26552. (Half-title: Scandinavian classics, vol. xiv). The American-Scandinavian Foundation.
Family at Tammerton. Margaret Erskine. (Ace gothic). 1974. (pbk.) 0.95. Ace Books.
Family at Tammerton: By Margaret Erskine Pseud. 1st Ed. in U.S.A. Wetherby Williams. LC 66-12189. 1966. 3.95. Pub. for the Crime Club by Doubleday.
Family at War. Kathleen Baker. (Signet book). (Family at war,#1). 1975. (pbk.) 1.50. New American Library.
Family Bed. Lester Heath. pap. 1.95 o.p. (ISBN 0-87682-258-8, 7258). Barclay Hse.
Family Book of Best Loved Short Stories: Edited by Leland W. Lawrence Pseud. Ed. by Lawrence Lamb. LC 54-5421. 1954. Hanover House.
Family Burial Murders. Milton Morris Propper. LC 34-37831. 1934. Harper & Brothers.
Family Business. Anthony Blond. LC 77-3784. 12.95 (ISBN 0-06-010364-7). Harper & Row.
Family Business: A Novel by Anthony Blond. Anthony Blond. 1979. Popular Library.
Family Carnovsky. Israel Joshua Singer. (Harrow books, HW7053). 1973. (pbk.) 1.50 (ISBN 0-06-087053-2). Harper & Row.
Family Carnovsky. Israel Joshua Singer. LC 68-8089. 1969. 6.95. Vanguard Press.
Family Circle. Muriel Hine Coxon. LC 39-861385. 1939. D. Appleton-Century Company, Incorporated.
Family Circle. Inez Haynes Irwin. LC 31-63761. The Bobbs-Merrill Company.
Family Circle. Andre Maurois. Tr. by Miles Hamish. LC 32-20046. 1932. D. Appleton and Company.
Family Cruise: A Marine Comedy. Helen Ashton. LC 34-8137. 1934. Doubleday, Doran and Company, Inc.
Family Cupboard: A Novel from the Play. Owen Davis. 1914. 1.25. The Macaulay Company.
Family Curse. Simpson John Frederick Norman Hampson. LC 36-18257. 1936. Dodd, Mead & Company.
Family Difficulty. Sarah Doudney. (On cover: Seaside library. Pocket ed., no. 338). 1885. G. Munro.
Family Doom: Or, The Sin of a Countess. Emma Dorothy Eliza Nevitte Southworth. LC 8-10817. 1888. T. B. Peterson & Brothers.
Family Doom: Or, The Sin of a Countess. Emma Dorothy Eliza Nevitte Southworth. LC 99-1613. (Southworth series. No. 31). The F. M. Lupton Publishing Company.
Family Failing. Oliver Knox. LC 77-351882. 1976. 3.95 (ISBN 0-00-222243-4). Collins.
Family Failing. Bertha Muzzy Sinclair. LC 40-358880. 1941. Little, Brown and Company.
Family Failing. authorized ed. Hawley Smart. (On cover: Lovell's Westminster series, no. 33). 1891. United States Book Company.
Family Failure. Renate Rasp. Tr. by Eva Figes from Ger. LC 74-10631. 1970. 5.95 o.p. (ISBN 0-670-30618-5, Orion Pr). Grossman.
Family Failure: A Novel. Renate Rasp. LC 74-106303. 1970. 5.95 (ISBN 0-670-30618-5). Orion Press.
Family Favorites. Alfred Leo Duggan. LC 60-11764. 1961. Pantheon Books.
Family Feeling. Suzanne Ebel. 1975. (pbk.) 0.95. Fawcett.
Family Feeling. Helen Yglesias. LC 75-33831. 1976. 8.95 (ISBN 0-8037-5365-9). Dial Press.
Family Feud: After the German of Ludwig Harder. Ludwig Harder & Wister, Mrs. Annis Lee (Furness) 1830-1908, Tr. 1905. J. B. Lippincott Company.
Family Fortune. Mignon Good Eberhart. LC 76-12436. 8.95 (ISBN 0-394-40723-7). Random House.
Family Fortune. Mignon Good Eberhart. 1978. 1.75 (ISBN 0-445-04203-6). Popular Library.
Family Fortune. Mignon Good Eberhart. LC 79-13138. 10.95 (ISBN 0-89340-215-X). J. Curley.
Family Fortune. Jerome Weidman. LC 77-26922. 10.95 (ISBN 0-671-24106-0). Simon and Schuster.
Family Fortune. Jerome Weidman. 1979. 2.50 (ISBN 0-671-82384-1). Pocket Books.
Family Fortunes. A Domestic Story. Isabella Fyvie Mayo. LC 7-18483. 1881. T. Nelson and Sons.
Family Fortunes: A Novel. Gwen Davenport. LC 49-10485. 1949. Doubleday.
Family, Friends & Other Funny People: Memories of Growing up Southern. William H. Willimon & Harriet W. Cabell. LC 80-80511. (Illus.). 94p. (Orig.). 1980. pap. 5.95 (ISBN 0-87716-115-1). R L Bryan.
Family from Vietnam. Tana Reiff. LC 78-75218. (Lifetimes Ser.). 1979. pap. 3.32 (ISBN 0-8224-4320-1). Pitman Learning.
Family Goldschmitt: Poems. Henri Coulette. LC 70-158882. 1971. 4.95 (ISBN 0-684-12482-3). Scribner.
Family Group. Iris Bromige. (Beagle Book). 1975. (pbk.) 0.95. Ballantine Books.
Family Group. Desemea Wilson. LC 29-16555. E. P. Dutton & Co., Inc.
Family Happiness: A Novel. Laurie Colwin. LC 82-23. 1982. 12.95 (ISBN 0-394-52511-6). Knopf.
Family Happiness: A Romance, from the Russian of Count Lyof N. Tolstoi. Lev Nikolaevich Tolstoi & Dole, Nathan Haskell, 1852- Tr. LC 8-26747. T. Y. Crowell & Co.
Family History. Victoria Mary Sackville-West. LC 32-305103. 1932. Doubleday, Doran & Company, Inc.
Family Holiday. Patricia Burstein. LC 81-16865. 1982. 13.50 (ISBN 0-688-03023-8). Morrow.
Family Honeymoon. Homer Croy. LC 42-15423. 1942. Harper & Brothers.
Family Hour. Joseph Corrado. 1975. 1.25 (ISBN 0-936426-05-5). Play Schs.
Family Installments: Memories of Growing up Hispanic. Edward Rivera. LC 82-2236. 1982. 14.50 (ISBN 0-688-01231-0). Morrow.
Family Jewels. Franz T Hansell. LC 75-7611. 1969. 1.95. Ophelia Press.
Family Jewels. Tr. by L. E. LaBan. pap. 1.95 o.p. (6039). Brandon.
Family Jewels. Joanne Stonebridge. (Orig.). 1969. pap. 1.75 o.s.i. (OPH153, Ophelia). Olympia.
Family Kingdom. Samuel W. Taylor. 350p. 1974. 9.95 (ISBN 0-914740-14-8). Western Epics.
Family (Les Peloueyres) Francois Mauriac. Tr. by Lewis Galantiere. LC 30-197249. 1930. Covici, Friede.
Family Lie. Georges Simenon. LC 78-53898. 1978. 7.95 (ISBN 0-15-156247-4). Harcourt Brace Jovanovich.
Family Likeness. Anna Gilbert, pseud. LC 77-22725. 8.95 (ISBN 0-312-28144-7). St. Martin's Press.
Family Likeness: A Novel. Janis P Stout. LC 82-4888. 11.95 (ISBN 0-932012-26-4). Texas Monthly Press.
Family Likeness: A Sketch in the Himalayas. Beatrice M. Sheppard Croker. LC 6-32164. (On cover: Lippincott's series of select novels. no. 140). 1893. J. B. Lippincott Company.
Family Man. John M. Gale. LC 69-11063. 1969. 4.95. Coward-McCann.
Family Man. Joseph Monninger. LC 81-12870. 1982. 11.95 (ISBN 0-689-11235-1). Atheneum.
Family Man. large print ed. Joseph Monninger. LC 83-1953. 1983. 11.95 (ISBN 0-89340-601-5). J. Curley.
Family Man. Robin Moore & Milt Machlin. LC 74-1575. 1974. (ISBN 0-515-03443-6). Pyramid Books.
Family Man, a Novel. Sidney Sulkin. LC 62-13704. 1962. R. B. Luce.
Family Man: A Victorian Novel. Lucy Beatrice Malleson. LC 42-22717. 1942. Howell, Soskin.
Family Mark Twain. Samuel Langhorne Clemens. LC 76-156502. 1972. 12.50 (ISBN 0-06-010121-0). Harper & Row.
Family Matter. Janet Macfarlane. LC 49-10578. 1949. S. Scribner's Sons.
Family Matter. James Roosevelt & Sam Toperoff. LC 80-11759. 10.95 (ISBN 0-671-24621-6). Simon and Schuster.
Family Matters. Kitty Burns Florey. LC 79-66076. 9.95 (ISBN 0-87223-558-0). Seaview Books.
Family Matters. Louise Platt Hauck. LC 34-31077. The Penn Publishing Company.
Family Members. Martin Yoseloff. LC 48-100653. 1948. E. P. Dutton.
Family Moskat. Isaac Bashevis Singer. LC 50-14988. (Fawcett crest book). 1975. (pbk.) 1.95. Fawcett.
Family Moskat. Tr. from Yiddish by A. H. Gross. Isaac Bashevis Singer. (Q3464). 1967. pap., 1.25. Bantam.
Family Moskat. Tr. from Yiddish by A. H. Gross Reissue. Isaac Bashevis Singer. 1965. 5.95, 2.25 pap.,. Farrar.
Family Moskat. Translated from the Yiddish by A. H. Gross. Isaac Bashevis Singer. LC 50-14988. 1950. Knopf.
Family Name. Arnold Henry Moore Lunn. LC 32-9439. 1932. L. MacVeagh, The Dial Press, Inc.
Family Number Three. Leila Andrews & Jay Presson Allen. LC 76-56770. 1977. 1.50 (ISBN 0-345-25706-5). Ballantine Books.
Family Occasions. George R Clay. LC 78-27161. 1979. 13.50 (ISBN 0-8161-6684-6). G. K. Hall.
Family Occasions: A Novel. George R Clay. LC 78-57137. 8.95 (ISBN 0-394-50188-8). D. Obst Books.
Family of Chung Song. Ruth Kim. 4.95 o.p. Vantage.
Family of Destiny. 1st Ed. Charles L Tarter. LC 54-123447. 1954. Pageant Press.
Family of Jaspard. Doris Almon Ponsonby. LC 51-3179. 1951. Hutchinson.
Family of Jaspard. Doris Almon Ponsonby. LC 51-13095. 1951. Crowell.
Family of Noblemen. Mikhail Evgrafovich Saltykov & Yarmolinsky, Avrahm, 1890- Tr. LC 18-549718. 1917. Boni & Liveright, Inc.
Family of Pascual Duarte. Camilo Jose Cela. LC 64-17474. 1964. Little, Brown.
Family of Strangers. Marian M. Poe. (Orig.). 1981. pap. 2.50 o.s.i. (ISBN 0-505-51648-9). Tower Bks.
Family of the Black Forest: A Tale of the Peasants' War. Maria Frances Hill Anderson. LC 7-25802. 1883. American Baptists Publ. Society.
Family on Maple Street. Gladys Bagg Taber. LC 46-816. 1946. Macrae-Smith-Company.
Family on the Hill: A Novel. Ambrose Flack. LC 45-1422. 1945. Thomas Y. Crowell Company.
Family on Vendetta Street. Lucas Longo. LC 68-14196. 1968. Doubleday.
Family Orchestra. Mary Howard, pseud. LC 45-5014. 1945. Arcadia House, Inc.
Family Orgy. Myrle Kaye. pap. 1.95 o.p. (ISBN 0-87682-214-6, 7214). Barclay Hse.
Family O'Rourke. Helene Thornton. (Orig.). 1980. pap. 2.50 (ISBN 0-449-14353-8, GM). Fawcett.
Family Party. John O'Hara. LC 56-10932. 1956. Random House.
Family Physician. Oliver Herbrand Gordon Leigh. LC 7-14298. (On cover: Leisure-time series. no. 13). 1892. W. D. Rowland.
Family Portrait. 1st Ed. Elizabeth Frances Corbett. LC 54-6114. 1955. Lippincott.
Family Reunion. Joyce Harrington. LC 81-14562. 13.95 (ISBN 0-312-28146-3). St. Martin's Press.
Family Reunion. Rose Moss. LC 73-19556. 1974. 5.95 (ISBN 0-684-13734-8). Scribner.
Family Reunion. Janet Curren Owen. LC 33-9095. 1933. Harper & Brothers.
Family Romance. Richard Wollheim. LC 77-82625. 1969. 5.95. Farrar, Straus & Giroux.
Family Secret. Janet Agle. LC 57-10872. 1957. Lippincott.
Family Secret. A Novel. Eliza Frances Andrews. LC 6-51314. 1876. J. B. Lippincott & Co.
Family Secrets. Henri Docimo. 160p. pap. 1.95 o.p. (MP-114). Montmartre.
Family Secrets. Rona Jaffe. 1975. (pbk.) 1.95. Bantam Books.
Family Secrets: A Novel. Rona Jaffe. LC 74-9893. 1974. 9.95 (ISBN 0-671-21842-5). Simon and Schuster.
Family Skeleton. Doris Miles Disney. 1949. Pub. for the Crime Club by Doubleday.
Family Skeletons. Patrick Quentin. LC 65-11292. bds., 3.95. Random.
Family Style. Karle Wilson Baker. LC 37-28658. Coward McCann, Inc.
Family Style. David Eames. LC 74-20349. 1975. 8.95 (ISBN 0-689-10647-5). Atheneum.
Family Swap Games. McCambridge. pap. 1.95 o.p. (ISBN 0-87682-158-1). Barclay Hse.

Family Swap Games. Kyle McCambridge. 192p. pap. 1.95 o.p. (7158). Barclay Hse.
Family Symphony. Isabel Constance Clarke. LC 37-144916. 1936. Longmans, Green & Co.
Family Takes a Wife. 1st Ed. Ethel Powelson Hueston. LC 50-9301. 1950. Bobbs-Merrill.
Family That Overtook Christ. Raymond. LC 42-25364. (His The sage of Citeauz. 2d epoch). 1942. P. J. Kenedy & Sons.
Family That Was. Ernest Raymond. LC 30-141933. 1930. D. Appleton and Company.
Family Ties. Syrell Rogovin Leahy. LC 82-9835. 14.95 (ISBN 0-399-12741-0). Putnam.
Family Ties. Clarice Lispector. LC 72-412. (Texas pan-American series). (Illus.). 1972. 5.75 (ISBN 0-292-72404-7). University of Texas Press.
Family Ties. Marguerite Steen. LC 39-23857. 1971. 7.50x (ISBN 0-7182-0873-0). Intl Pubns Serv.
Family Tomb. Michael Francis Gilbert. LC 79-83636. (Novel of Suspense Ser). 1970. 5.95 o.p. (ISBN 0-06-011524-6, HarpT). Har-Row.
Family Trade. James Carroll. LC 82-21361. 1983. 18.95 (ISBN 0-8161-3483-9). G.K. Hall.
Family Tree. Albany De Grenier Fonblanque. LC 6-41416. Estes & Lauriat.
Family Tree: A Novel. Florence Maple. LC 45-3926. 1945. A. A. Knopf.
Family Tree: A Novel. Dorothy Yates. LC 67-15009. 1967. Farrar, Straus and Giroux.
Family Tree: And Other Stories. Brander Matthews. LC 7-25563. 1889. Longmans, Green & Co.
Family Trouble. William McFee. LC 49-7302. 1949. Random House.
Family Trouble. Joseph Masiello. (Kangaroo Book). 1.95 (ISBN 0-671-81764-7). Pocket Books.
Family Trust: A Novel. Ward S Just. LC 77-25160. 8.95 (ISBN 0-316-47723-0). Little, Brown.
Family Vault. Charlotte MacLeod. LC 78-14687. 1979. 7.95 (ISBN 0-385-14871-2). Published for the Crime Club by Doubleday.
Family Vault. Charlotte MacLeod. 1980. 2.25 (ISBN 0-380-49080-3). Avon Books.
Family Vault. Charlotte MacLeod. LC 80-24581. 1981. 12.95 (ISBN 0-89340-299-0). J. Curley & Associates.
Family Way. Myron Brinig. LC 42-9118. 1942. Farrar and Rinehart, Inc.
Family Web. Iris Bromige. 1972. pap. 0.75 o.p. (94280). Beagle Bks.
Family Web: A Story of India. Sarah Hobson. (Illus.). 284p. 1981. 14.95 (ISBN 0-89733-049-8); pap. 6.95 (ISBN 0-89733-050-1). Academy Chi LTD.
Famine. John Creasey. 1970. pap. 0.75 o.p. (ISBN 0-447-74652-9). Lancer.
Famine. John Creasey. 1968. 3.95 o.p. Walker & Co.
Famine. Graham Masterton. 384p. (Orig.). 1981. pap. 3.25 (ISBN 0-441-22744-9). Ace Bks.
Famine. Liam O'Flaherty. LC 37-14924. Random House.
Famine: A New Story of Dr. Palfrey. John Creasey. LC 68-13253. 1968. Walker.
Famine: A Novel. Liam O'Flaherty. LC 81-7161. (Nonpareil Book; No. 25). 1982. 18.95 (ISBN 0-87923-412-1). D.R. Godine.
Famine of Hearts" And Other Selections ... LC 99-4261. (Tales from Town topics, no. 33). 1899. Town Topics Publishing Company.
Famine Plot. John Freivalds. LC 77-20488. 1978. 8.95 (ISBN 0-8128-2436-9). Stein and Day.
Famished Land. Elizabeth Byrd. LC 72-3878. 1972. 6.95 (ISBN 0-397-00949-6). Lippincott.
Famished Land. Elizabeth Byrd. 1978. 1.95 (ISBN 0-380-39313-1). Avon Books.
Famous" A Novel. Steve Zousmer & Liebmann-Smith, Richard. LC 79-16216. 4.95 (ISBN 0-02-633600-6). Macmillan.
Famous" A Novel. Steve Zousmer & Liebmann-Smith, Richard. LC 79-16217. 9.95 (ISBN 0-02-026900-5). Collier Books.
Famous All Over Town. Danny Santiago. LC 82-19468. 14.95 (ISBN 0-671-43249-4). Simon and Schuster.
Famous American Stories. Ed. by John A. Burrell & Bennett Cerf. 1953. 5.95 o.p. (60777). Modern Lib.
Famous Blue Stockings. Ethel R. Wheeler. Repr. of 1910 ed. 18.00 o.s.i. Finch Pr.
Famous Boy: Or, Tom and the Missing Beauty. The Story of a Homeless Hero. Harlan Page Halsey. (Old Sleuth's own, no. 88). 1897. Parlor Car Publishing Co.
Famous Chinese Short Stories. Lin Yutang. LC 78-10746. 1979. 21.00 (ISBN 0-8371-9062-2). Greenwood Press.
Famous Chinese Short Stories. Lin Yutang. LC 78-10746. 1979. Repr. of 1952 ed. lib. bdg. 21.00x (ISBN 0-8371-9062-2, YUFC). Greenwood.
Famous Chinese Short Stories. Lin Yutang. pap. 0.60 o.p. (W532). WSP.
Famous Chinese Short Stories: Retold by Lin Yutang. Hutang Lin. LC 52-6175. 1952. J. Day Co.
Famous Detective Stories. Ed. by Joseph Walker McSpadden. LC 20-15065. Thomas Y. Crowell Company.
Famous Dog Stories. Ed. by Page Cooper. LC 48-9168. 1948. Doubleday.
Famous Fantastic Classics, No. 2. LC 74-20652. 1975. 14.95x (ISBN 0-913960-20-9); pap. 5.00x (ISBN 0-913960-11-X). Fax Collect.
Famous Fantastic Classics No. 1. LC 74-20652. 1974. 5.00 o.p. (ISBN 0-913960-10-1). Fax Collect.
Famous Fantastic Classics No. 2. LC 74-20652. 1975. 5.00 o.p. (ISBN 0-913960-11-X). Fax Collect.
Famous Flyers and Their Famous Flights. Elsie N. Wright. LC 32-25311. 1932. The World Syndicate Publishing Company.
Famous Ghost Stories. Bennett Alfred Cerf. Repr. lib. bdg. 18.55x (ISBN 0-88411-146-6). Amereon Ltd.
Famous Ghost Stories. Bennett Alfred Cerf. 1944. 3.95 (ISBN 0-394-60073-8, 73). Modern Lib.
Famous Ghost Stories. Bennett Alfred Cerf. 1956. pap. 2.95 (ISBN 0-394-70140-2, Vin, V140). Random.
Famous Ghost Stories. Ed. by Joseph Walker McSpadden. LC 70-152949. (Short story index reprint series). (Illus.). 1971. (ISBN 0-8369-3808-9). Books for Libraries Press.
Famous Ghost Stories. Ed. by Joseph Walker McSpadden. LC 18-180982. Thomas Y. Crowell Company.
Famous Ghost Stories: Compiled and with an Introductory Note. Bennett Alfred Cerf. LC 44-5432. (Half-title: The Modern library of the world's best books). 1944. The Modern Library.
Famous Ghost Stories: Compiled, and with an Introductory Note. Ed. by Bennett Alfred Cerf. LC 46-11858. (Illustrated modern library). 1946. Random House.
Famous Historical Mysteries. Leonard Gribble. 1971. 5.95 o.p. (ISBN 0-584-62015-2). Transatlantic.
Famous Last Words: A Novel. Timothy Findley. LC 82-1430. 1982. 13.95 (ISBN 0-440-02477-3). Delacorte Press/Seymour Lawrence.
Famous Modern Ghost Stories: Selected, with an Introduction. Ed. by Dorothy Scarborough. LC 21-8835. 1921. G. P. Putnam's Sons.
Famous Monster Tales. Ed. by Basil Davenport. LC 67-27991. 1967. Van Nostrand.
Famous Mysteries: By Walter Brooks and Others Illustrated by Don Merrick. Ed. by Mary Yost Sandrus. LC 55-1362. 1955. Scott, Foresman.
Famous Mystery and Detective Stories. Ed. by Joseph Walker McSpadden. 1938. Blue Ribbon Books.
Famous Mystery Stories. Ed. by Joseph Walker McSpadden. LC 22-5893. Thomas Y. Crowell Company.
Famous or Infamous: A Novel. authorized ed. Bertha Thomas. LC 8-28191. (Lovell's international series, no. 129). 1890. United States Book Company.
Famous Potatoes. Joe Cottonwood. LC 78-56001. (Illus.). 1978. 4.95. No Dead Lines Press.
Famous Potatoes: A Novel. Joe Cottonwood. LC 78-11145. (Illus.). 1979. 8.95 (ISBN 0-440-03098-6) (ISBN 0-440-52334-6). Delacorte Press.
Famous Psychic and Ghost Stories. Ed. by Joseph Walker McSpadden. LC 73-77. (Short story index reprint series). 1973. 10.50 (ISBN 0-8369-4248-5). Books for Libraries Press.
Famous Psychic and Ghost Stories. Ed. by Joseph Walker McSpadden. 1938. Blue Ribbon Books.
Famous Psychis Stories. Ed. by Joseph Walker McSpadden. LC 20-16801. Thomas Y. Crowell Company.
Famous Pulp Classics, No. 1. LC 74-20653. 1975. 14.95x (ISBN 0-913960-21-7); pap. 5.00x (ISBN 0-913960-12-8). Fax Collect.
Famous Romances of Voltaire... Francois Marie Arouet De Voltaire. LC 8-32689. 1893. Laird & Lee.
Famous Science-Fiction Stories. Ed. by Healy. 1957. 5.95 o.s.i. (ISBN 0-394-60731-7, G31). Modern Lib.
Famous Science-Fiction Stories: Adventures in Time and Space. Ed. by Raymond J Healy & J. Francis McComas. LC 57-11402. (Modern library of the world's best books G31). 1957. Random House.
Famous Short Stories. Ed. by Kurt D. Singer. LC 68-21246. Denison.
Famous Short Stories Analysed: Foreword and Commentaries. Reginald Francis Foster. LC 76-6162. (Series: The Writer's Library.). 1976. (ISBN 0-88305-691-7). Norwood Editions.
Famous Short Stories from Liberty. Liberty (New York) LC 32-5033. 1932. Liberty Pub. Corp.
Famous Short Stories of H. G. Wells. de luxe ed. Herbert George Wells. LC 38-27474. 1938. Garden City Publishing Co., Inc.
Famous Stories by Famous Authors: For Junior High School Reading. Ed. by Norma Helen Deming. LC 22-19683. The Atlantic Monthly Press.
Famous Stories from Foreign Countries: Austrian, Armenian, Bohemian, Czech, Dutch, Finnish, Hungarian, Norwegian. Edna Worthley Underwood. pap. 3.00 (ISBN 0-8283-1433-0, IPL34, IPL). Branden.
Famous Stories from Foreign Countries. Edna Worthley Underwood. LC 64-22333. (IPL, 34). 1965. Intl. Pocket Lib.
Famous Stories of Code and Cipher. Raymond Tostevin Bond. LC 47-383186. 1947. Rinehart and Company, Incorporated.
Famous Stories of Code and Cipher. Ed. by Raymond Tostevin Bond. LC 64-20659. 1966. Collier Books.
Famous Stories of Detective Adventure... Charles J. McKeon. LC 11-15074. (Happy hours library, no. 58). J. F. Hill & Co.
Famous Stories of Five Centuries. Ed. by Hugh Walpole. Partington, Wilfred George, 1888- Joint Ed. LC 34-38912. 1934. Farrar & Rinehart, Incorporated.
Famous Stories of Joseph Conrad. Joseph Conrad. LC 33-11066. 1938. Doubleday, Doran & Company, Inc.
Famous Tales of Barbarians and Savages. Ed. by Frederick Brigham De Berard. LC 72-5688. (Black Heritage Library Collection). 1972. (ISBN 0-8369-9138-9). Books for Libraries Press.
Famous Tales of Sherlock Holmes. Arthur Conan Doyle. (Great Il. Classics). (Illus.). 4.50 o.p. (ISBN 0-396-04160-4). Dodd.
Famous Tales of the Fantastic. Ed. by Herbert Van Thal. Illus. by Edward Pagram. Ed. by Herbert Maurice Van Thal. LC 65-24719. 1965. 3.95. Hill & Wang.
Famous Tragedy of the Queen of Cornwall. Thomas Hardy. 76p. 1980. Repr. of 1923 ed. lib. bdg. 12.50 (ISBN 0-8414-4890-6). Folcroft.
Famous Victory... E. Goodman Holden. LC 7-6122. 1880. Jansen, McClurg & Company.
Fan. Bob Randall. LC 76-53491. 7.95 (ISBN 0-394-41203-6). Random House.
Fan. Bob Randall. 1978. 2.25 (ISBN 0-446-82471-2). Warner Books.
Fan Club. Irving Wallace. 640p. 1975. pap. 3.50 (ISBN 0-553-14699-8). Bantam.
Fan Club: A Novel. Irving Wallace. LC 73-19095. 1974. 9.95 (ISBN 0-671-21717-8). Simon and Schuster.
Fan Dance at Cockcrow: A Novel. Daniel Carson Goodman. LC 41-4550. W. Funk.
Fan Man. William Kotzwinkle. LC 73-89748. (Equinox books). 1974. 2.45. Avon.
Fan Man. William Kotzwinkle. LC 74-17339. 1974. 5.95 (ISBN 0-517-51503-2). Harmony Books.
Fan Man: The Novel. William Kotzwinkle. LC 79-116061. (Illus.). 1979. 4.95 (ISBN 0-380-43125-4). Avon.
Fan: The Story of a Young Girl's Life. William Henry Hudson. LC 72-181622. (collected works of W. H. Hudson). 1968. AMS Press.
Fan: The Story of a Young Girl's Life. William Henry Hudson. LC 23-15894. (Half-title: The collected works of W. H. Hudson). 1923. J. M. Dent & Sons, Ltd.
Fan: The Story of a Young Girl's Life. William Henry Hudson. LC 24-1309. 1923. E. P. Dutton & Co.
Fanatic. Meyer Levin. (Cardinal ed., 75054). 1965. Pocket Bks.
Fanatic of Christian? A Story of the Pennsylvania Dutch. Helen Reimensnyder Martin. LC 18-5504. 1918. Doubleday, Page & Company.
Fanatic of Fez. Mary Violet Heberden. LC 43-9681. 1943. Pub. for the Crime Club by Doubleday, Doran & Company, Inc.
Fanatic: Or The Perils of Peter Pliant, the Poor Pedagogue. LC 9-3814. 1846. Office of the American Citizen.
Fanatics. Paul Laurence Dunbar. LC 70-81110. 1969. Mnemosyne Pub. Inc.
Fanatics. Paul Laurence Dunbar. LC 70-84687. 1969. Negro Universities Press.
Fanatics. Paul Laurence Dunbar. LC 72-104441. 1970. (ISBN 0-8398-0370-2). Literature House.
Fanatics. Paul Laurence Dunbar. LC 1-30976. 1901. Dodd, Mead & Company.
Fanatics. Peter Hill. LC 78-53482. 1978. 7.95 (ISBN 0-684-15821-3). Scribner.
Fanatics of Al Asad. Nick Carter. (Nick Carter Ser). (O.s.i.). 176p. (Orig.). 1976. pap. 1.25 o.s.i. (AQ1575, Award). Univ Pub & Dist.
Fancher Train. Amelia Bean. LC 58-7349. 1958. Doubleday.
Fanchette. John Esten Cooke. LC 6-28719. (Round-robin series. v. 15). 1883. J. R. Osgood and Company.
Fanchon the Cricket. George Sand. LC 6-34611. 1864. J. Bradburn.
Fanchon the Cricket (of Fadette) mary pickford ed. George Sand & Sedgwick, Jane Minot, Tr. LC 15-20592. 1915. Duffield & Company.
Fanchon the Cricket: Or, La Petite Fadette. George Sand. LC 6-34607. T. B. Peterson & Brothers.
Fanchon's Book. Zane Pella. pap. 1.95 o.s.i. (V1072T, Venus). Grove.
Fancies and Goodnights. 1st Ed. John Collier. LC 51-14145. 1951. Doubleday.
Fanciful Tales. Frank Richard Stockton & Langworthy, Julia Elizabeth, Ed. LC 4-18940. (On verso of half-title: Scribner's series of school reading). 1904. C. Scribner's Sons.
Fanciful Tales of Time & Space. Howard Phillips Lovecraft et al. 1977. pap. 4.95. Necronomicon.
Fancy. Genevieve Davis. 320p. (Orig.). 1982. pap. 2.95 (ISBN 0-515-05654-5). Jove Pubns.
Fancy. John London. LC 95-1049. (Orig.). 1969. pap. 0.95 o.p. (B95-1048). Belmont-Tower.
Fancy: A Novel. Robert W. Krepps. LC 69-16970. 1969. 5.95. Little, Brown.
Fancy Dancer. Patricia Nell Warren. LC 75-38996. 1976. 7.95 (ISBN 0-688-03022-X). Morrow.
Fancy Dress Party. Alberto Moravia. Tr. by Angus Davidson from It. 1973. pap. 1.50 (ISBN 0-532-15116-X). Woodhill.
Fancy Dress Party. Alberto Pincherle. 1973. (pbk.) 1.50. Manor Books.
Fancy Dress Party: By Alberto Moravia Pseud. Alberto Pincherle. LC 52-11469. 1952. Farrar, Straus and Young.
Fancy Lady. Homer Croy. LC 27-19215. 1927. Harper & Brothers.
Fancy of Hers; The Disagreeable Woman: Two Lost Novels for Adults by the Man Loved for His Rags-to-Riches Tales for Juveniles. Horatio Alger. LC 80-13018. (Illus.). 14.95 (ISBN 0-442-24716-8). Van Nostrand Reinhold.
Fancy Strut. Lee Smith. LC 73-4158. (Cass Canfield book). 1973. 7.95 (ISBN 0-06-013928-5). Harper & Row.
Fancy's Knell. Babs H Deal. LC 66-209669. 3.95. Doubleday.
Fandango. Robert Briffault. LC 40-711176. 1940. C. Scribner's Sons.
Fandango. John Masters. LC 58-12471. 1959. Harper.
Fandango Involvement. Thomas Mahon. 224p. 1981. pap. 2.25 (ISBN 0-449-14427-5, GM). Fawcett.
Fandora's Story. Betty Hale Hyatt. LC 81-80089. 192p. (Orig.). 1981. pap. 1.95 (ISBN 0-87216-790-9). Playboy Pbks.
Fane. David M. Alexander. 1981. pap. 3.50 (ISBN 0-671-83154-2, Timescape). PB.
Fanfare. Richard Halliday. LC 29-18150. 1929. G. P. Putnam's Sons.
Fanfare for a Witch. William Vaughan Wilkins. LC 54-9389. 1954. Macmillan.
Fanfare for Tin Trumpets. Margery Sharp. LC 33-49934. 1933. G. P. Putnam's Sons.
Fangs of the Sea. Norman Caldwell. 1967. Repr. pap. 1.65 o.s.i. Tri-Ocean.
Fangs of the Serpent. George R Fox. LC 24-11332. 1924. Minton, Balch & Company.
Fangs of the Vampire. Richard LeBlanc. LC 78-65867. 1979. 7.95 o.p. (ISBN 0-533-04117-1). Vantage.
Fanina. Pierre Sabbagh & Antoine Graziani. LC 68-16871. 1968. 0.95. Bantam Books.
Fann Marlow. 1st Ed. Jane Hardy. LC 54-885919. 1954. Dutton.
Fannie Davenport: A Story. Jessie A Schley. LC 8-2033. 1890. The Pioneer Press Company.
Fannie St. John: a Romantic Incident of the American Revolution. Emily Pierpont De Lesdernier. LC 12-12829. 1874. Hurd and Houghton.
Fannin. David Markson. Orig. Title: Epitaph for a Tramp. 1971. pap. 0.75 o.p. (B75-2109). Belmont-Tower.
Fanny. Norma Lee Clark. 1980. pap. 1.75 (ISBN 0-449-50030-6, Coventry). Fawcett.
Fanny. Ernest Aime Feydeau & Janin, Jules Gabriel, 1804-1874. LC 6-39532. E. D. Long & Co.
Fanny. Erica Jong. 1981. pap. 6.95 (ISBN 0-452-25273-3, Z5273, Plume). NAL.
Fanny. Erica Jong. 1981. pap. 3.95 (ISBN 0-451-11200-8, AE 1200, Sig). NAL.
Fanny & Alexander. Ingmar Bergman. 220p. 1983. 13.95; pap. 5.95. Pantheon.
Fanny: Being the True History of the Adventures of Fanny Hackabout-Jones: a Novel. Erica Jong. LC 80-14386. (Mentor book). 1980. 12.95. New American Library.
Fanny by Gaslight. Michael Sadleir. LC 40-340743. D. Appleton-Century Company, Incorporated.
Fanny Campbell: The Female Pirate Captain. A Tale of the Revolution. Maturin Murray Ballou. LC 6-8632. 1845. F. Gleason.
Fanny Comes Across. Norman Jackson. (Orig.). 1969. pap. 0.75 o.p. (74-989). Lancer.
Fanny for Free. Norman Jackson. pap. 0.60 o.p. Lancer.

TITLE INDEX

FAR FROM THE SEA.

Fanny G. Lou Graham. (Orig.). 1980. pap. text ed. 2.25 o.s.i. (ISBN 0-505-51569-5). Tower Bks.
Fanny Hell. Norman Jackson. (Orig.). 1968. pap. 0.60 o.p. (73-749). Lancer.
Fanny Hell Meets Captain Sex. Norman Jackson. LC 75-99. (Fanny Hell Captain Sex Ser). (Orig.). 1969. pap. 0.95 o.p. Lancer.
Fanny Herself. Edna Ferber. LC 74-27979. (Modern Jewish Experience). (Illus.). 1975. 21.00 (ISBN 0-405-06708-9). Arno Press.
Fanny Herself. Edna Ferber. Frederick A. Stokes Company.
Fanny Hill. John Cleland. 256p. 1982. pap. 2.95 (ISBN 0-440-05555-5). Dell.
Fanny Hill: Memoirs of a Woman of Pleasure. John Cleland. 1963. pap. 0.95 o.p. (901). Brandon.
Fanny Lovers. R. T. Powers. 192p. (Orig.). 1973. pap. 1.95 o.p. (ISBN 0-87682-321-5, 7321). Barclay Hse.
Fanny of the Forty Frocks. Frances Aymar Mathews. LC 13-20755. 1.20. The John C. Winston Company.
Fanny's Autobiography: A Story of Home Missionary Life on the Frontier. Mary Evaline McArthur Drake. LC 6-34278. Congregational Sunday-School and Publishing Society.
Fanny's Double Feature. Norman Jackson. (Orig.). 1969. pap. 0.60 o.p. (73-837). Lancer.
Fanny's First Novel. Frank Frankfort Moore. LC 13-8321. 1.25. Hodder & Stoughton, George H. Doran Company.
Fan's Notes. Frederick Exley. 1977. pap. 2.95 (ISBN 0-671-81182-7). PB.
Fan's Notes. Frederick Exley. 1975. 10.00 (ISBN 0-394-49641-8). Random.
Fan's Notes. Frederick Exley. LC 67-22514. 1968. 6.95 o.p. (ISBN 0-06-011203-4, HarpT). Har-Row.
Fan's Notes: A Fictional Memoir. Frederick Exley. LC 74-23352. 1975. 10.00 (ISBN 0-394-49641-8). Random House.
Fan's Notes: A Fictional Memoir. Frederick Exley. LC 67-22514. 1968. 6.95. Harper & Row.
Fanshawe see Dolliver Romance.
Fanshawe: A Tale... Nathaniel Hawthorne. LC 7-3780. 1828. Marsh & Capen.
Fanshawe: And Other Pieces. Nathaniel Hawthorne. LC 4-16228. Houghton, Mifflin and Company.
Fanshawe of the Fifth: Being Memoirs of a Person of Quality. Ashton Hilliers. LC 7-415936. 1907. McClure, Phillips & Co.
Fanshawe, The Dolliver Romance: And Other Pieces. Nathaniel Hawthorne. LC 7-3775. (Hawthorne's Works. Illustrated library edition). 1876. J. R. Osgood and Company.
Fantasia on a Theme of Frank. Graham H Whiting. LC 73-128765. 1970. Pariah Press.
Fantasias. Mary Chavelita Bright. LC 6-25389. 1898. J. Lane.
Fantasies. Mel Spivak. 1975. 5.00. (ISBN 0-87881-025-0). Mojave Books.
Fantasies of Harlan Ellison. Harlan Ellison. LC 79-17453. (Gregg Press science fiction series). (Illus.). 1979. 15.00 (ISBN 0-8398-2411-4). Gregg Press.
Fantasies Two. William Griffith, Jr. LC 79-55742. (Illus.). 160p. (gr. 7 up). 1980. 9.95 (ISBN 0-89742-039-X, Dawne-Leigh). Celestial Arts.
Fantastic Bouquet. Anca Vrbovska. Ed. by Alfred Dorn. (Fiction Ser.). 164p. (Orig.). 1980. 6.50x (ISBN 0-917608-03-8). New Orlando.
Fantastic Dilemma. Fausto Lage. LC 52-367. Dorrance.
Fantastic Fables. Ambrose Gwinnett Bierce. 160p. 1976. Repr. of 1911 ed. lib. bdg. 10.85x (ISBN 0-89190-184-1). Am Repr-Rivercity Pr.
Fantastic Fables. Ambrose Gwinnett Bierce. LC 73-92026. 1970. pap. 2.50 (ISBN 0-486-22225-X). Dover.
Fantastic Folklore & Fact: New England Tales of Land & Sea. Edward R. Snow. (Illus.). 1968. 5.95 o.p. (ISBN 0-396-05844-2). Dodd.
Fantastic Four. (Super Hero Collection). (Illus., Orig.). 1968. pap. 0.50 o.p. (72-111). Lancer.
Fantastic Four Return. (Illus., Orig.). 1968. pap. 0.50 o.p. (72-169). Lancer.
Fantastic Holiday. Berta Ruck. LC 53-9611. 1953. Dodd, Mead.
Fantastic Imagination: An Anthology of High Fantasy. Robert H Boyer & Kenneth J Zahorski. LC 76-55545. 1977. 2.25 (ISBN 0-380-00956-0). Avon.
Fantastic Journey of Walther Von Windsack: A Novel. Hugh W Hosch. (Illus.). 1973. 6.50 (ISBN 0-682-47621-8). Exposition Pr.
Fantastic Journey Through the Cosmos. J. L. Morens. 12.00 o.p. Beacon Hse.
Fantastic Memories. Maurice Yves Sandoz. LC 57-9512. 1957. Doubleday.
Fantastic Memories. Maurice Yves Sandoz. LC 70-85695. (Short story index reprint series). 1969. Books for Libraries Press.
Fantastic Memories. Maurice Yves Sandoz & Dali, Salvador, 1904- Illus. LC 44-41882. 1944. Doubleday, Doran and Co., Inc.
Fantastic Planet. Steven Caldwell. LC 79-52718. 3.98 (ISBN 0-517-29225-4). Crescent Books.
Fantastic Pulps. Peter Haining. LC 75-29638. 1976. 10.00. St. Martin's Press.
Fantastic Pulps. Peter Haining. LC 76-9056. (Illus.). 1976. 2.95 (ISBN 0-394-72109-8). Vintage Books.
Fantastic Saint. Leslie Charteris & Martin Harry Greenberg. LC 81-43614. (Doubleday Science Fiction). 1982. 10.95 (ISBN 0-385-17331-8). Doubleday.
Fantastic Stories. Andrei Donatevich Siniavskii. LC 62-14263. 1963. Pantheon Books.
Fantastic Stories. Abram Tertz, pseud. pap. 2.45 o.p. (ISBN 0-448-00219-1, UL). G&D.
Fantastic Tales of Fitz-James O'Brien. 1980. 9.95 (ISBN 0-7145-3617-2). Riverrun NY.
Fantastic Traveller. Maude Meagher. LC 31-29820. 1931. Houghton Mifflin Company.
Fantastic Voyage. Isaac Asimov & Harry. Fantastic Voyage Kleiner. LC 66-14718. 1966. Bantam.
Fantastic Voyage: A Novel. Isaac Asimov & Harry Kleiner. LC 66-12593. 1966. Houghton Mifflin.
Fantastica: Being The Smile of the Sphinx, and Other Tales of Imagination. Robert Malise Bowyer Nichols. LC 75-128744. (Short story index reprint series). 1970. Books for Libraries Press.
Fantastica: Being The Smile of the Sphinx, and Other Tales of Imagination. Robert Malise Bowyer Nichols. LC 23-13195. 1923. The Macmillan Company.
Fantastics and Other Fancies. Lafcadio Hearn. LC 75-46276. (Supernatural and Occult Fiction). 1976. 14.00 (ISBN 0-405-08134-0). Arno Press.
Fantasy. Poul Anderson. 336p. 1981. pap. 2.50 (ISBN 0-523-48515-8). Pinnacle Bks.
Fantasy: A Cartoon Novella. Joan Altabe. 94p. (Orig.). 1982. pap. 9.95 (ISBN 0-931494-36-2). Brunswick Pub.
Fantasy: A Novel. Matilde Serao & Harland, Henry, 1861-1905, Tr. LC 8-6451. (On cover: Lovell's series of foreign literature, no. 8). 1890. United States Book Company.
Fantasy and Fugue. Roy Fuller. LC 56-8446. (Cock Robin mystery). 1956. Macmillan.
Fantasy & Science Fiction, April Nineteen Sixty-Five. Ed. by Edward L. Ferman. (Alternatives Ser.). (Illus.). 160p. 1981. 16.95 (ISBN 0-8093-1007-4). S Ill U Pr.
Fantasy Annual, No. IV. Ed. by Terry Carr. 1981. pap. 3.50 (ISBN 0-671-41273-6, Timescape). PB.
Fantasy Annual V. Ed. by Terry Carr. 1982. pap. 2.95 (Timescape). PB.
Fantasy Master's Codex. (Fantasy Trip Ser.). 1981. pap. write for info. (ISBN 0-88074-475-8). Metagam.
Fantasy Master's Screen. (Fantasy Trip Ser.). 1981. pap. write for info. (ISBN 0-88074-476-6). Metagam.
Fantasy of Truth. Irene Lincoln. 3.75 o.p. Vantage.
Fantasy Sketches. Maurice Sendak. 24p. 1970. pap. 3.95 (ISBN 0-939084-02-3, Pub. by Rosenbach Mus & Lib). U Pr of Va.
Fantasy Stories of George Macdonald, 4 vols. Ed. by Glenn Sadler. 1980. pap. 12.95 set (ISBN 0-8028-1858-7); pap. 2.95 ea. Eerdmans.
Fantasy Trip: Death Test, No. 2. S. Jackson. (Microquest Ser.: No. 1). 1980. pap. write for info. (ISBN 0-88074-081-7). Metagam.
Fantasy Trip: Master of the Amulets. M. Monastero. (Microquest Ser.: No. 7). 192p. 1982. pap. 4.95 (ISBN 0-88074-087-6). Metagam.
Fantasy Trip: Melee. S. Jackson. (Microgame Ser.: No. 3). 192p. 1982. pap. 4.95 (ISBN 0-88074-003-5). Metagam.
Fantasy Trip: Security Station. J. W. Colbert. (Microquest Ser.: No. 5). 1980. pap. write for info. (ISBN 0-88074-085-X). Metagam.
Fantasy Trip: Wizard. S. Jackson. (Microgame Ser.: No. 6). 192p. 1982. pap. 4.95 (ISBN 0-88074-006-X). Metagam.
Fantasy Voyages--Great Science Fiction from the Saturday Evening Post. Saturday Evening Post Editors. LC 79-55717. 300p. 1979. 7.95 (ISBN 0-89387-036-6, Co-Pub by Sat Eve Post). Curtis Pub Co.
Fantasy Worlds of Peter S. Beagle. Peter S Beagle. LC 78-14545. 1978. 12.95 (ISBN 0-670-30725-4). Viking Press.
Fantasy Worlds of Peter Stone: And Other Fables. Malcolm Boyd. LC 69-17006. 1969. 3.95. Harper & Row.
Fantazius Mallare. Ben Hecht. 12.95 o.p. Wehman.
Fantazius Mallare: A Mysterious Oath. Ben Hecht. LC 78-6637. (Harvest/HBJ book). 1978. 3.95 (ISBN 0-15-630160-1). Harcourt Brace Jovanovich.
Fantazius Mallare, a Mysterious Oath and The Kingdom of Evil, a Continuation of the Journal of Fantazius Mallare. Ben Hecht. LC 75-46277. (Supernatural and Occult Fiction). 1976. 24.00 (ISBN 0-405-08135-9). Arno Press.
Fantazius Mallare: A Mysterious Oath & the Kingdom of Evil, 2 vols. in one. Ben Hecht. Ed. by R. Reginald & Douglas Menville. 1976. Repr. of 1924 ed. 12.00x (ISBN 0-405-08135-9). Ayer Co.
Fantine Avenel. Lucie Lacoste. LC 22-22776. 1922. The Cornhill Publishing Company.
Fantod Press Set Number Three, 3 vols. Edward Gorey. Incl. The Eleventh Episode; The Deranged Cousins; The Untitled Book. Set. pap. 7.50 o.p. Gotham.
Fantomas Captured: By Marcel Allain; Translated and Edited by A. R. Allinson. Marcel Allain. LC 27-1099. 1926. David McKay Company.
Far Above Rubies. Agnes Sligh Turnbull. LC 26-14724. Fleming H.Revell Company.
Far and Away: Eleven Fantasy and Science-Fiction Stories, by Anthony Boucher Pseud. William Anthony Parker White. LC 56-2173. 1955. Ballantine Books.
Far and Near; Stories of Japan, China, and America. Pearl Sydenstricker Buck. LC 47-119189. 1947. J. Day Co.
Far & Wide. Douglas Reed. 398p. pap. 5.00 (ISBN 0-913022-22-5). Angriff Pr.
Far Arena. Richard Sapir. LC 78-8270. 8.95 (ISBN 0-87223-506-8). Seaview Books: Trade Distribution by Simon and Schuster.
Far Away & Long Ago. William Henry Hudson. Repr. of 1923 ed. 21.50 (ISBN 0-404-03408-X). AMS Pr.
Far Away & Long Ago. William Henry Hudson. 1976. 9.95x (ISBN 0-460-00956-7, Evman). Biblio Dist.
Far Away & Long Ago. William Henry Hudson. 1972. pap. 2.95 o.p. (ISBN 0-460-01956-2, Evman). Biblio Dist.
Far Away & Long Ago. William Henry Hudson. 1972. pap. 2.95 o.p. (ISBN 0-460-01956-2, Evman). Dutton.
Far Away and Long Ago. Frances Anne Kemble. LC 7-10983. (Leisure hour series. no. 225). 1889. H. Holt and Company.
Far-Away Bride. Stella Benson. LC 77-138606. 1972. 14.50 (ISBN 0-8371-5714-5). Greenwood Press.
Far-Away Bride. Stella Benson. LC 30-30775. 1930. Harper & Brothers.
Far-Away Bride. Stella Benson. LC 41-8353. The Press of the Readers Club.
Far Away Music. Arthur Meeker. LC 47-20335. Houghton Mifflin Company.
Far-Away Princess. Frances Christine Tiernan. LC 14-21432. The Devin-Adair Company.
Far-Away Stories. William John Locke. LC 19-14480. 1916. John Lane.
Far Bayou. J Max McMurray. LC 51-13112. 1951. Rinehart.
Far Below and Other Horrors. Ed. by Robert Weinberg. LC 74-82615. 1974. 6.95 (ISBN 0-913960-05-5). Fax Collector's Editions.
Far Beyond Desire. Barbara Riefe. LC 77-82173. 464p. 1978. pap. 2.95 (ISBN 0-86721-056-7). Playboy Pbks.
Far Blue Horizons. Mary Howard, pseud. LC 42-734005. 1942. Doubleday, Doran and Company, Inc.
Far Boundaries: 20 Science-Fiction Stories. Ed. by August William Derleth. LC 51-10782. 1951. Pellegrini & Cudahy.
Far Call. Gordon R Dickson. LC 77-94500. (Quantum Science Fiction). 1978. 8.95 (ISBN 0-8037-2501-9). Dial Press.
Far Call. Gordon R Dickson. (Dell boo). 1978. 1.95 (ISBN 0-440-12284-8). Dell Pub. Co.
Far Call. Jackson Gregory. LC 40-325593. 1940. Dodd, Mead & Company.
Far Call. Edison Marshall. LC 28-858916. 1928. Cosmopolitan Book Corporation.
Far Command. Elinor Chamberlain. LC 53-9111. 1953. Ballantine Books.
Far Country. Winston Churchill. LC 15-11876. 1915. The Macmillan Company.
Far Country. Marthedith Furnas. LC 47-31466. 1947. Harper.
Far Country. Nevil Shute Norway. LC 52-9696. 1952. Morrow.
Far Cry. Fredric Brown. LC 51-8424. 1951. Dutton.
Far Cry. Henry Milner Rideout. LC 16-22404. 1916. Duffield and Company.
Far Cry. Earl H Rovit. LC 67-11975. 1967. Harcourt, Brace & World.
Far Cry. Emma Smith. LC 49-50363. 1950. Random House.
Far Down. Elizabeth Frances Corbett. LC 39-611175. 1939. D. Appleton-Century Company, Incorporated.
Far Down the Road, Stranger. Clyde I. Swanson. 4.75 o.p. Carlton.
Far End. May Sinclair. LC 26-149136. 1926. The Macmillan Company.
Far Ends of Time & Earth: The Collected Fiction of Isaac Asimov, Vol. 1. Isaac Asimov. LC 77-25574. 1979. 12.95 (ISBN 0-385-13269-7). Doubleday.
Far Enough: A Story of the Great Trek. Eugenie De Kalb. LC 35-13550. Frederick A. Stokes Company.
Far Face of the Moon. George Henry Johnston. LC 64-13265. 1964. Morrow.
Far Family. Wilma Dykeman. LC 65-10131. 1966. Holt, Rinehart and Winston.
Far, Far the Mountain Peak: A Novel. John Masters. LC 57-6435. 1957. Viking Press.
Far Flies the Eagle. Eve Stephens, pseud. (Signet Book, Y5751). 1974. (pbk.) 1.25. New American Library.
Far Flies the Eagle: By Evelyn Anthony Pseud. Eve Stephens, pseud. LC 55-9191. 1955. Crowell.
Far Flight of Love. 1st Ed. Robert Raynolds. LC 57-11457. 1957. Pageant Press.
Far Forest. Francis Brett Young. LC 36-19171. Reynal & Hitchcock.
Far from Cibola. Paul Hogan. LC 75-37272. (Short story index reprint series). 1971. (ISBN 0-8369-4083-0). Books for Libraries Press.
Far from Cibola. Paul Horgan. LC 74-84235. (Zia book). 1974. 2.45 (ISBN 0-8263-0360-9). University of New Mexico Press.
Far from Cibola. Paul Horgan. LC 38-27181. 1938. Harper & Brothers.
Far from Heaven. Morrie Raymond. LC 62-10302. 1962. Abelard-Schuman.
Far from Home... Robert H Newman. LC 41-3423. J. B. Lippincott Company.
Far from Home. Walter S Tevis. LC 80-1073. 1981. 9.95 (ISBN 0-385-17036-X). Doubleday.
Far from Home: From the German of Johannes Van Derval Pseud. August Kuhne. Tr. by Hamilton, Katharine. LC 8-29983. (On cover: V. I. F. series). D. Lothrop and Company.
Far from Home: From the German of Johannes Van Derval Pseud. August Kuhne. Tr. by Hamilton, Kathrine. LC 8-29982. (On cover: The household library, no. 4). 1886. D. Lothrop and Company.
Far from Porcelain the Human Clay: Episodes. 1st Ed. E. Wahlert McCourt. Pageant Press.
Far from the Blessed Land. Ian Kavanaugh. (O'Donnell's Ser.: No. 3). (Orig.). 1983. pap. 3.50 (ISBN 0-440-02483-8, Emerald). Dell.
Far from the Customary Skies. Warren Eyster. LC 53-5010. 1953. Random House.
Far from the Maddening Girls. Guy Wetmore Carryl. LC 4-34126. 1904. McClure, Phillips & Co.
Far from the Madding Crowd. Thomas Hardy. LC 66-1379. (Premier world classic). 1963. Fawcett Publications.
Far from the Madding Crowd. Thomas Hardy. LC 67-27222. 1967. Bantam Books.
Far from the Madding Crowd. Thomas Hardy. (On cover: Seaside library, Pocket ed., no. 690). 1886. G. Munro.
Far from the Madding Crowd. Thomas Hardy. (On cover: Lovell's library, v. 20, no. 964). 1887. J. W. Lovell Company.
Far from the Madding Crowd. Thomas Hardy. LC 41-32217. (On cover: The home library). 1894. A. L. Burt.
Far from the Madding Crowd. Thomas Hardy. LC 16-7548. 1895. Harper & Brothers.
Far from the Madding Crowd. Thomas Hardy. LC 18-165512. (Added t.-p.: Harper's modern classics, ed. for educational use, by W. T. Brewster). 1918. Harper & Brothers.
Far from the Madding Crowd. Thomas Hardy. Ed. by Weber, Carl Jefferson. LC 37-675. 1937. Oxford University Press.
Far from the Madding Crowd. Thomas Hardy. LC 80-22887. (His The New Wessex edition). 1981. 2.95 (ISBN 0-312-28247-8). St. Martin's.
Far from the Madding Crowd. Thomas Hardy & Ronald Blythe. LC 79-303130. (Penguin English library). (Illus.). 1978. 2.50 (ISBN 0-14-043126-8). Peguin Books.
Far from the Madding Crowd. Edited with an Introd. and Notes by Richard L. Purdy. Thomas Hardy. LC 57-13919. (Riverside editions, B18). 1957. Houghton Mifflin.
Far from the Madding Crowd: Introd. by Francis R. Gemme. Thomas Hardy. (Classics ser., CL136). 1967. Airmont.
Far from the Madding Crowd. New Introd. by Mary Ellen Chase. Thomas Hardy. LC 51-7374. (Everyman's library, 644A. Fiction). 1951. Dutton.
Far from the Madding Crowd. Photos. of the Author, His Environment & the Setting of the Book. Introd. by E. P. Lawrence. Thomas Hardy. LC 68-161814. (Great illustrated classics). 1968. 3.59. Dodd.
Far from the Madding Crowd. With an Introd. by Robert Cantwell and Engravings by Agnes Miller Parker. Thomas Hardy. LC 58-14875. 1958. Heritage Press.
Far from the Sea. Evan Hunter. LC 82-71564. 320p. 1983. 12.95 (ISBN 0-689-11338-2). Atheneum.

Far from to-Day. Gertrude Hall Brownell. LC 7-1489. 1892. Roberts Brothers.

Far Frontier. William Rotsler. LC 79-90926. 240p. (Orig.). 1980. pap. 1.95 (ISBN 0-87216-633-3). Playboy Pbks.

Far High Ridge. C. R. Hanley. 192p. (Orig.). 1982. pap. 1.95 (ISBN 0-8439-0954-4). Leisure Bks Ct.

Far Horizon. Polan Banks. LC 36-130482. Green Circle Books.

Far Horizon. Mary St. Leger Kingsley Harrison. LC 7-983. 1907. Dodd, Mead & Company.

Far Horizon. Mary St. Leger Kingsley Harrison. LC 42-29486. A. L. Burt Company.

Far Horizons. Michael Wagman. LC 80-11790. 11.95 (ISBN 0-440-02815-9). Delacorte Press.

Far in the Forest. A Story. Silas Weir Mitchell. LC 18-20851. 1889. J. B. Lippincott Company.

Far in the Forest: A Story. Silas Weir Mitchell. 1898. The Century Co.

Far into the Sound. Michael Boylan. 1973. 1.50 o.p. (ISBN 0-912852-03-8). Echo Pubs.

Far into the Sound, a Novel. Michael Boylan. 1973. (pap.) 1.00. Echo Publishers.

Far Islanders. Lee D. Willoughby. (Making of America Ser.: No. 18). (Orig.). 1981. pap. 2.75 (ISBN 0-440-02581-8, Bryans). Dell.

Far Journey. Loula Grace Erdman. LC 55-9923. 1955. Dodd, Mead.

Far Lands Other Days. E. Hoffmann Price. (Illus.). 587p. 1975. 15.00 (ISBN 0-913796-01-8). Carcosa.

Far Lands. 1st Ed. James Norman Hall. LC 50-14871. 1950. Little, Brown.

Far Morning. Brenda Clarke. 416p. 1982. pap. 3.50 (ISBN 0-445-04719-4). Popular Lib.

Far Morning. 1st American Ed. Edward Grierson. LC 54-8766. 1955. Knopf.

Far Mountains. Frank O'Rourke. 1959. Morrow.

Far-off Place. Laurens Van Der Post. LC 74-7632. 1974. 7.95 (ISBN 0-688-00286-2). Morrow.

Far-off Place. Laurens Van Der Post. LC 78-5639. (Harvest/HBJ book). 1978. 3.95 (ISBN 0-15-630198-9). Harcourt Brace Jovanovich.

Far-off Rhapsody. Anne Marie Sheridan. (Kangaroo Book). 1978. 1.95 (ISBN 0-671-82014-1). Pocket Books.

Far-off Rhapsody: A Novel. Anne Marie Sheridan. LC 76-54898. 8.95 (ISBN 0-671-22601-0). Simon and Schuster.

Far off Rhapsony. Anne-Marie Sheridan. LC 76-54898. (O.s.i.). 1977. 8.95 o.s.i. (ISBN 0-671-22601-0). S&S.

Far Pavilions. Mary Margaret Kaye. LC 78-3975. 1978. 12.95 (ISBN 0-312-28259-1). St. Martin's Press.

Far Place. 1st Ed. Blair Fuller. LC 56-11102. 1957. Harper.

Far Rainbow - The Second Invasion from Mars. Arkadii Natanovich Strugatskii & Boris Natanovich Strugatskii. (Best of Soviet Science Fiction Ser.). 1979. 9.95 o.s.i. (ISBN 0-02-615200-2). Macmillan.

Far Rainbow-Second War of the Worlds. Arkadii Natanovich Strugatskii & Boris Natanovich Strugatskii. Tr. by Antonina W. Bouis & Gary Kern. (Best of Soviet Science Fiction Ser.). 252p. 1980. pap. 3.95 o.s.i. (ISBN 0-02-025610-8, Collier). Macmillan.

Far Rainbow: The Second Invasion from Mars. Arkadii Natanovich Strugatskii & Boris Natanovich Strugatskii. LC 80-298. (Macmillan's Best of Soviet science fiction series). 1980. 9.95 (ISBN 0-02-615200-2). Collier Books.

Far Rainbow, Translated from the Russian by Antonina W. Bouis; The Second Invasion from Mars, Translated from the Russian by Gary Kern. Arkadii Natanovich Strugatskii & Boris Natanovich Strugatskii. LC 79-13628. (Series: Macmillan's Best of Soviet Science Fiction.). 9.95. Macmillan.

Far Reader-Check: Validity Card Update -Cards Punched Out 53 Out. Damon Francis Knight. LC 61-583833. 1961. Simon and Schuster.

Far Sands. Andrew Garve. 1978. pap. 1.95 o.p. (ISBN 0-06-080442-4, P 442, PL). Har-Row.

Far Sands. Andrew Garve. pap. 0.50 o.p. (72-693). Lancer.

Far Sands. Paul Winterton. (Perennial library). 1978. 1.95 (ISBN 0-06-080442-4). Harper & Row.

Far Sands: By Andrew Garve Pseud. 1st Ed. Paul Winterton. LC 60-15341. 1960. Harper.

Far Side. DeWitt S Copp. LC 75-16219. 1975. 6.95 (ISBN 0-393-08723-9). Norton.

Far Side. Wirt Williams. LC 79-188190. 1972. 6.95 (ISBN 0-8180-0612-9). Horizon Press.

Far Side of Home. Maggie Hill Davis. LC 63-14191. 1963. Macmillan.

Far Side of the Dollar. Ross Macdonald. LC 79-25721. 1980. 11.95 (ISBN 0-89340-248-6). J. Curley & Associates.

Far Side of the Dollar: By Ross MacDonald Pseud. Kenneth Millar. LC 65-10103. 1965. bds., 3.95. Knopf.

Far Side of the Dollar: By Ross MacDonald Pseud. Kenneth Millar. (F3159). 1966. Bantam.

Far Side of the Hill. Belle Turnbull. LC 53-9969. 1953. Crown Publishers.

Far Side of the Sky: A Novel. Maslyn Williams. LC 67-15154. (Illus.). 1967. Morrow.

Far Side of the Storm. Ed. by Gary Elder. 216p. 1975. pap. 5.95 o.p. (ISBN 0-914974-32-7). Holmgangers.

Far Side of the Storm: New Ranges of Western Fiction. Gary Elder. LC 75-330358. 4.00 (ISBN 0-88235-025-0). San Marcos Press.

Far Side of Time. Roger Elwood. LC 73-9272. 192p. 1973. 5.95 o.p. (ISBN 0-396-06857-X). Dodd.

Far Side of Time, Thirteen Original Stories: A Science Fiction Anthology. Ed. by Roger Elwood. LC 73-9272. 1974. 5.95 (ISBN 0-396-06857-X). Dodd, Mead.

Far Sunset. Edmund Cooper. (Medallion bk., X1607). 1968. Berkley.

Far Sunset. Edmund Cooper. LC 67-23100. 1967. Walker.

Far to Go: A Novel of Suspense. Mary Louise White Aswell. LC 57-9094. 1957. Farrar, Straus and Cudahy.

Far to Seek: A Romance of England and India. Katherine Helen Maud Marshall Diver. LC 21-163151. 1921. Houghton Mifflin Company.

Far Tortuga. Peter Matthiessen. 1976. (pbk.) 2.25. Bantam Books.

Far Tortuga. Peter Matthiessen. LC 74-20576. 1975. (ISBN 0-394-49461-X). Random House.

Far Traveler. A. Bertram Chandler. 1979. 1.50 (ISBN 0-87997-444-3). DAW Books.

Far Traveller. 1st Ed. Manning Coles, pseud. LC 56-8494. 1956. Doubleday.

Far Triumph. Elizabeth Dejeans. LC 11-25676. 1911. J. B. Lippincott Company.

Far Trouble. Thomas Bowyer Campbell. LC 32-10937. Macrae Smith Company.

Far Wandering Men. John Russell. LC 29-26571. W. W. Norton & Company, Inc.

Far Whistle: And Other Stories. Warren Beck. LC 51-11342. 1951. Antioch Press.

Faragon Fairingay. Niel Hancock. (Circle of light; 2). 1977. 1.95 (ISBN 0-445-08618-1). Popular Library.

Faragon Faringay. Niel Hancock. (Circle of Light Ser: No. 2). 352p. 1981. pap. 2.95 (ISBN 0-445-08618-1). Popular Lib.

Farang. Dean Boyd & Marjorie Martin. LC 64-18280. 1964. Harcourt, Brace & World.

Faraway. John Boynton Priestley. LC 32-15758. 1932. Harper & Brothers.

Faraway: A Novel. Translated from the French by Stephen Becker. Andre Dhotel. LC 57-109731. 1957. Simon and Schuster.

Faraway Drummer: A Novel. Robert O'Neil Bristow. LC 72-96674. 1973. 6.95 (ISBN 0-517-50407-3). Crown Publishers.

Faraway Drums. Jon Cleary. LC 81-14091. 1982. 13.50 (ISBN 0-688-00790-2). W. Morrow.

Faraway Haven. Lida Larrimore Thomas. LC 50-5065. 1950. Macrae Smith Co.

Faraway Hills Are Green. Charles Dranker. LC 53-11591. 1953. Vantage Press.

Faraway Island. Elizabeth Garver Jordan. LC 41-7653. 1941. D. Appleton-Century Company, Incorporated.

Faraway Love. Virginia Nielsen, pseud. 256p. 1982. pap. 2.75 (ISBN 0-449-14477-1, GM). Fawcett.

Faraway the Spring. Richard Hagopian. LC 52-8355. 1952. Scribner.

Fardel of Facetious Tales. George Brakeley White. LC 28-303391. 1928. Printed by H. S. Jacobs & Company, Inc.

Fardorougha the Miser. William Carleton. LC 78-11950. (Ireland, from the Act of Union, 1800, to the Death of Parnell, 1891). 1979. 32.00 (ISBN 0-8240-3486-4). Garland Pub.

Fardorougha the Miser; or, the Convicts of Lisnamona. William Carleton. LC 79-8245. Repr. of 1839 ed. 44.50 (ISBN 0-404-61805-7). AMS Pr.

Fardorougha, the Miser; or, the Convicts of Lisnamona. William Carleton. Ed. by Robert L. Wolff. (Ireland Nineteenth Century Fiction - Ser. Two: Vol. 37). 481p. 1979. lib. bdg. 32.00 (ISBN 0-8240-3486-4). Garland Pub.

Farewell, Babylon. Naim Kattan. LC 77-463729. 9.95 (ISBN 0-7710-4470-4). McClelland and Stewart.

Farewell, Babylon. Naim Kattan. LC 79-25580. 1980. 9.95 (ISBN 0-8008-2598-5). Taplinger.

Farewell Companions. James Plunkett. LC 77-26829. 1978. 10.95 (ISBN 0-698-10901-5). Coward, McCann & Geoghegan.

Farewell Crown and Goodbye King. Margot Bennett. 1961. Walker.

Farewell, Earth's Bliss. David Guy Compton. LC 79-12824. 1979. 10.95. (ISBN 0-89370-135-1) (ISBN 0-89370-235-8). Borgo Press.

Farewell, Frank Merriwell. George Zuckerman. LC 74-179847. 1973. 6.95 (ISBN 0-525-10345-7). Dutton.

Farewell from Nowhere. Vladimir Emelianovich Maksimov, pseud. LC 76-42374. 1979. 10.00 (ISBN 0-385-09569-4). Doubleday.

Farewell Great King. Paton Walsh, Jill. LC 72-75025. (Illus.). 1972. 6.95. Coward, McCann & Geoghegan.

Farewell, Great King. Jill Paton Walsh. 256p. (YA) 1972. 6.95 o.p. (ISBN 0-698-10445-5). Coward.

Farewell, Little Mother Russia: A Novel. 1st Ed. Brund M Stracke. LC 55-572489. 1955. Exposition Press.

Farewell, Love! A Society Novel; from the 40th Italian Ed. By Matilde Serao. Matilde Serao. (On cover: The Marco-Botzaris series, no. 51). 1892. The Minerva Publishing Co.

Farewell, Miss Julie Logan: A Wintry Tale. James Matthew Barrie. LC 82-28185. 1932. C. Scribner's Sons.

Farewell. Miss Julie Logan: A Wintry Tale. James Matthew Barrie. LC 33-155048. 1933. C. Scribner's Sons.

Farewell, My General. Shirley Seifert. 1976. Repr. of 1954 ed. lib. bdg. 7.95 (ISBN 0-89190-133-7). Am Repr-Rivercity Pr.

Farewell, My General. 1st Ed. Shirley Seifert. LC 54-6109. 1954. Lippincott.

Farewell My Heart. Ferenc Molnar & Rice, Elinor, Tr. LC 45-5598. 1945. Simon and Schuster.

Farewell, My Lovely. Raymond Chandler. LC 76-10606. 1976. 1.95 (ISBN 0-394-72138-1). Vintage Books.

Farewell, My Lovely. Raymond Chandler. LC 40-145357. 1940. A. A. Knopf.

Farewell, My Lovely, & The Lady in the Lake. Raymond Chandler. LC 67-11591. (Modern library of the world's best books 337). 1967. Modern Library.

Farewell, My Slightly Tarnished Hero. Edwin Corley. LC 74-162616. 1971. 6.95 (ISBN 0-396-06364-0). Dodd, Mead.

Farewell, My Son: A Novel. Elmer Grossberg. LC 46-8059. 1946. Julian Messner, Inc.

Farewell Party. Franklin Bandy. 320p. (Orig.). 1980. pap. 2.50 (ISBN 0-441-22832-1, Pub. by Charter Bks). Ace Bks.

Farewell Party. June Drummond. LC 72-7921. (Red badge novel of suspense). 1973. 4.95 (ISBN 0-396-06624-0). Dodd, Mead.

Farewell Party. June Drummond. 1974. (pbk.) 0.95. Dell.

Farewell Party. Milan Kundera. LC 76-13675. 1976. 7.95 (ISBN 0-394-49660-4). Knopf Distributed by Random House.

Farewell Performance. Ernest Lehman. LC 82-7871. 14.95 (ISBN 0-07-037074-5). McGraw-Hill.

Farewell Pretty Ladies. Chris Massie. LC 42-7200. Random House.

Farewell Romance: A Novel. Gilbert Frankau. LC 36-24681. 1936. E. P. Dutton & Co., Inc.

Farewell Supper. Arthur Schnitzler. Ed. by Edmund R. Brown. (International Pocket Library). pap. 3.00. Branden.

Farewell the Stranger. Frankie Lee Griggs Zelley. LC 56-7343. 1956. Morrow.

Farewell the Tranquil Mind by. Ronald Frederick Delderfield. 1973. 1.50 (ISBN 0-671-78590-7). Pocket Books.

Farewell the Tranquil. 1st Ed. Ronald Frederick Delderfield. LC 50-10468. 1950. Dutton.

Farewell the Trumpets: The Decline of an Empire. James Morris. LC 79-24253. (Illus.). 576p. 1980. pap. 8.95 (ISBN 0-15-630286-1, Harv). HarBraceJ.

Farewell to Arms. Ernest Hemingway. LC 53-7687. 1953. Scribner.

Farewell to Arms. Hemingway, Ernest. 1948. C. Scribner's Sons.

Farewell to Arms. Ernest Hemingway. LC 49-41317. (Modern standard authors). 1949. C. Scribner's Sons.

Farewell to Arms. Ernest Hemingway. LC 29-20658. 1929. C. Scribner's Sons.

Farewell to Arms. Ernest Hemingway. LC 32-140239. (Half-title: The modern library of the world's best books). 1932. The Modern Library.

Farewell to Arms see Three Great American Novels.

Farewell to Arms. Introd., Study Guide by John C. Schweitzer. School Ed. Ernest Hemingway. LC 67-13157. 1967. 4.50. Scribners.

Farewell to Dreams. Lee Muiron Rousseau. LC 46-21103. 1946. The Colt Press.

Farewell to Europe: A Novel. Walter Ze'Er Laqueur. LC 81-80377. 12.95. Little, Brown.

Farewell to Freedom. Willis Gale Gray. LC 32-11570. The Macaulay Company.

Farewell to India. Edward John Thompson. LC 31-16667. E. P. Dutton & Co., Inc.

Farewell to Love. Rose Meadows. 1973. (pbk) 0.95 (ISBN 0-671-77690-8). Pocket Books.

Farewell to Matyora: A Novel. Valentin Grigorevich Rasputin. LC 79-19072. 1979. 9.95 (ISBN 0-02-601160-3). Macmillan.

Farewell to Military Profession, 1581. Edited by Thomas Mabry Cranfill. Barnabe Rich. Ed. by Thomas Mabry Cranfill. 1959. University of Texas Press.

Farewell to Nova Scotia. Jeffrey Holmes. LC 75-312296. 1974. Lancelot Press.

Farewell to Otterley. 1st. ed. Humphrey Pakington. LC 51-9699. 1951. Norton.

Farewell to Paradise. Frank Thiess & Lowe, Mrs. Helen Tracy (Porter) Tr. LC 29-16428. 1929. A. A. Knopf.

Farewell to Samaria: A Story of the Last Years of the Kingdom of Israel. Harry H Fein. LC 55-14308. 1955. Verndale Pub. Co.

Farewell to Tharrus. Catherine Macdonald Maclean. LC 44-4609. 1944. The Macmillan Company.

Farewell to the Admiral. Peter Cheyney. LC 43-511419. 1943. Dodd, Mead & Company.

Farewell to the Castle. Jane Corby. 1976. (pbk.) 1.25. Belmont Tower Books.

Farewell to the Castle. Jane Irenita Corby. LC 67-9246. 1967. Arcadia House.

Farewell to the Coast. Alejandro Murguia. LC 79-88207. 1980. 4.00 (ISBN 0-915970-03-1). Heirs Press.

Farewell to the King. Pierre Schoendoerffer. LC 70-122424. 1970. 6.95. Stein and Day.

Farewell to the Westerns. G. M. Kichenside. LC 75-2915. 1975. 6.95 (ISBN 0-7153-7069-3). David & Charles.

Farewell to the White Cockage. Jane Lane. 1971. pap. 1.25 o.p. (96026-125). Beagle Bks.

Farewell to Thee. Marian Forrester. 1978. pap. 2.25 o.s.i. (ISBN 0-505-51309-9). Tower Bks.

Farewell to Valley Forge. David Taylor. LC 55-10454. (Illus.). 1955. Lippincott.

Farewell to Vienna. Dorothy Fletcher. 1973. pap. 0.95 o.s.i. (75-466). Lancer.

Farewell to Women: A Comedy About Sex. Wilson Collison. LC 32-642360. 1932. R. M. McBride & Company.

Farewell to Yesterday's Tomorrow. Alexei Panshin. LC 74-30574. 1975. 6.95 (ISBN 0-399-11505-6). Berkley Pub. Corp.: Distributed by Putnam.

Farewell to Yesterday's Tomorrow. Alexei Panshin. (Berkley medallion book). 1976. 1.25. Berkley.

Farewell to Youth... Margaret Storm Jameson. LC 28-18499. 1928. A. A. Knopf.

Farewell Toinette: A Footnote to History. Bertita Leonarz Harding, pseud. LC 38-272908. The Bobbs-Merrill Company.

Farewell Victoria. Terence Hanbury White. LC 34-2031. 1934. H. Smith & R. Haas.

Farewell Yesterday: A Comedy of Manners Good and Bad Played in Bath. Horace Annesley Vachell. LC 47-87. Hutchinson & Co., Ltd.

Fargo. John Benteen. 1971. pap. 0.75 o.p. (B75-2135). Belmont-Tower.

Fargo. John Benteen. LC 60-1056. (Orig.). 1969. pap. 0.60 o.p. (B60-1056). Belmont-Tower.

Fargo. E. M. Parsons. 144p. 1980. pap. 1.95 (ISBN 0-449-13874-7, GM). Fawcett.

Fargo. E. M. Parsons. 1971. pap. 0.60 o.p. (R2425, GM). Fawcett World.

Fargo, No. 1. John Benteen. 1980. pap. 1.75 o.s.i. (ISBN 0-505-51481-8). Tower Bks.

Fargo & the Texas Rangers. John Benteen. 1977. pap. 1.25 o.s.i. (ISBN 0-505-51126-6, BT51126). Tower Bks.

Fargo and the Texas Rangers. John Benteen. (Belmont Tower Books). 1.25. Tower Publications.

Fargo Bandolero. John Benteen. (Fargo Ser.). 1977. pap. 1.25 o.s.i. (ISBN 0-505-51144-4). Tower Bks.

Fargo Is His Name, Violence Is His Game see Campeon De Violencia.

Fargo Killer's Moon. John Benteen. (O.s.i.). 1976. pap. 1.25 o.s.i. (BT50970). Belmont-Tower.

Fargo, No. 1. John Benteen. (Fargo Ser.). (O.s.i.: No. 1). 144p. 1973. pap. 0.75 o.s.i. (BT50526). Belmont-Tower.

Fargo No. 3: Alaska Steel. John Benteen. (Orig.). 1980. pap. 1.50 o.s.i. (ISBN 0-505-51502-4). Tower Bks.

Fargo No. 4: Massacre River. John Benteen. (Orig.). 1980. pap. 1.50 (ISBN 0-505-51521-0). Tower Bks.

Fargo: Panama Gold, No. 2. John Benteen. 1980. pap. 1.75 o.s.i. (ISBN 0-505-51482-6). Tower Bks.

Fargus Technique. David Mangum. LC 73-1897. 1973. 5.95 (ISBN 0-690-28964-2). Crowell.

Farm. Louis Bromfield. LC 76-6462. 1976. (ISBN 0-88411-501-1). Aeonian Press.

Farm. Louis Bromfield. LC 33-212768. 1933. Harper & Brothers.

Farm. Louis Bromfield. LC 46-22069. 1946. Harper & Brothers.

Farm. Louis Bromfield. 1980. 2.50 (ISBN 0-380-41715-4). Avon Books.

Farm. Louis Bromfield & Rogers, Windfield Heyaev, Ed. LC 35-1175. (Harper's modern classics). Harper & Brothers.

Farm. Clarence I. Cooper, Jr. (O.s.i.). 1970. pap. 0.75 o.s.i. (A659S, Award). Univ Pub & Dist.

Farm: A Novel, by Clarence I. Sic Cooper, Jr. Clarence I. Cooper, Jr. LC 67-17702. 1967. 4.95. Crown.

Farm at Paranao. Eric Andrew Simson. LC 35-11015. 1935. Doubleday, Doran & Company, Inc.

Farm at Paranao. Eric Andrew Simson. LC 36-32343. The Sun Dial Press.
Farm Boy's Adventure in the Mines. Paul Robert Lynch. 88p. 7.95 (ISBN 0-8059-2857-X). Dorrance.
Farm Fresh Eggs & Other Stories. Lester Beberfall. 1970. 3.50 o.p. Carlton.
Farm-House Cobweb: A Novel. Emory James Haynes. LC 7-3750. 1895. Harper & Brothers.
Farm in Provence: Tr. from the French. Henri Bosco. LC 47-5762. 1947. Doubleday.
Farm of Muiceron. Tr. from the French of Marie Rheil. Marie Rheil & Storrs, Mrs. Annie Blount, Tr. LC 6-34214. (With Dubois, C. Madame Agnes. New York, 1874). 1874. The Catholic Publication Society.
Farm of the Dagger. Eden Phillpotts. LC 4-26249. 1904. Dodd, Mead and Company.
Farm Philosopher: A Love Story. Ada Harriet Miser Kepley. LC 12-15630. Worman's Printery.
Farm That Blew Away: A Collection of Bush Ballads and Sundry Humorous Verse. Wilbur Gordon Howcroft. LC 74-182625. 1973. 3.95 (ISBN 0-7256-0092-6). Hawthorn.
Farmer. James Harrison. LC 76-10214. 1976. (ISBN 0-670-30838-2). Viking Press.
Farmer and the Lord. George Hughes Hepworth. LC 7-4279. 1896. E. P. Dutton and Company.
Farmer Bibbins. Hypkin Brown. LC 14-15365. 1.25. R.G. Badger; Etc., Etc.
Farmer Giles of Ham. John Ronald Reuel Tolkien. 1978. pap. 4.95 (ISBN 0-395-26799-4). HM.
Farmer in the Dell. Philip Duffield Stong. LC 35-10317. Harcourt, Brace and Company.
Farmer of New-Jersey: Or, A Picture of Domestic Life. A Tale. John Davis. LC 6-33060. 1800. Furman and London's Type.
Farmer of Roaring Run. Mary C Johnson Dillon. LC 20-1892. 1920. The Century Co.
Farmer Takes a Wife. Sheila Turner. LC 64-14351. (Illus.). 1964. Holt, Rinehart and Winston.
Farmer's Daughter. Herman Milton Appel. LC 36-420264. Godwin.
Farmer's Daughter. James Noble Gifford. LC 40-322947. Phoenix Press.
Farmer's Daughter. Rodney Stanton. 192p. pap. 1.95 o.p. (2013). Intimate Lib.
Farmer's Daughter of Essex. Containing an Account of Her Distress, Wonderful Adventures, Manner of Being Courted and Seduced by a Nobleman in London, Who After Living with Her Some Years, Parted in the Most Dishonorable Manner.--With an Account of Her Meeting Him a Second Time, and Many Particular Occurrences That Happened During the Remainder of Their Lives. James Penn. 1798. Printed by Jacob S. Mott.
Farmers' Daughters: Collected Short Stories. William Carlos Williams. LC 61-12776. (Orig.). 1961. 7.00 o.p. (ISBN 0-8112-0428-6); pap. 7.95 (ISBN 0-8112-0228-3, NDP106). New Directions.
Farmers' Daughters; Collected Stories. Introd. by Van Wyck Brooks. William Carlos Williams. LC 61-127761. 1961. New Directions.
Farmer's Friend: Or The History of Mr. Charles Worthy. Who, from Being a Poor Orphan, Rose, Through Various Scenes of Distress and Misfortune, to Wealth and Eminence, by Industry, Economy and Good Conduct. Interspearsed with Many Useful and Entertaining Narratives... Enos Hitchcock. LC 7-4951. By I. Thomas and E. T. Andrews, Faust's Statue, No., Newbury Street.
Farmer's Hotel. John O'Hara. 1951. 4.00 o.p. (ISBN 0-394-42444-1). Random.
Farmers Hotel: A Novel. John O'Hara. LC 51-14121. 1951. Random House.
Farmhouse. Helen Kieran Reilly. LC 47-4557. 1947. Random House.
Farmhouse Virgins. Robert Earliton. 192p. (Orig.). 1974. pap. 1.95 o.p. (ISBN 0-87056-373-4, 6373). Brandon.
Farming. Richard Kendall Munkittrick. LC 7-32286. 1891. Harper & Brothers.
Farming for Fun: Or, Back-Yard Grangers. George G. Small. 1874. Collin & Small.
Farmington. Clarence Seward Darrow. LC 4-25700. 1904. A. C. McClurg & Co.
Farmington. 3d ed. Clarence Seward Darrow. LC 20-26097. 1919. B. W. Huebsch.
Farmington. Clarence Seward Darrow. LC 25-11587. 1925. Boni and Liveright.
Farmington: By Clarence Darrow. Clarence Seward Darrow. LC 32-27259. 1932. C. Scribner's Sons.
Farnham's Freehold. Robert Anson Heinlein. pap. 2.75 (ISBN 0-425-04856-X, Dist. by Putnam). Berkley Pub.
Farnham's Freehold. Robert Anson Heinlein. 1971. pap. 1.95 (ISBN 0-425-03568-9, Medallion). Berkley Pub.
Farnham's Freehold: A Novel. Robert Anson Heinlein. LC 64-18007. 1964. Putnam.
Farnsbee South. Helen Hudson. LC 77-138866. 1971. 5.95 (ISBN 0-03-085997-2). Holt, Rinehart and Winston.
Farnsworth Score. Rex Burns. (Berkley Book). 1978. 1.75 (ISBN 0-425-03749-5). Berkley Pub. Corp.
Faro Kid. Leslie Charles Ernenwein. LC 44-3533. 1944. Phoenix Press.
Faro Nell and Her Friends: Wolfville Stories. Alfred Henry Lewis. LC 73-163042. (Short story index reprint series). (Illus.). 1971. (ISBN 0-8369-3956-5). Books for Libraries Press.
Faro Nell and Her Friends: Wolfville Stories. Alfred Henry Lewis. LC 13-9238. 1.25. G. W. Dillingham Company.
Faroese Short Stories. Ed. by Hedin Brnner. LC 73-155592. (Library of Scandinavian Literature V. 16). 1972. 7.50. Twayne Publishers.
Faroese Short Stories. Tr. by Hedin Bronner. (Library of Scandinavian Literature). 1972. lib. bdg. 18.50x (ISBN 0-8057-3308-6). Irvington.
Faroese Short Stories. Tr. by Hedin Bronner. (International Studies & Translations Ser.). lib. bdg. 8.50 o.p. (ISBN 0-8057-3308-6). Twayne.
Faro's Daughter. Georgette Heyer. LC 67-20529. 1967. Dutton.
Faro's Daughter. Georgette Heyer. LC 42-13732. 1942. Doubleday, Doran & Company, Inc.
Farquharson's Physique and What It Did to His Mind. David James Knight. LC 73-149824. 1971. 7.95 (ISBN 0-8128-1362-6). Stein and Day.
Farquharson's Physique & What It Did to His Mind: A Novel. David James Knight. (Crest Book, P2016). 1973. (pbk.) 1.25. Fawcett Pubns.
Farragan's Retreat. Tom McHale. LC 73-132861. 1971. 6.95 o.p. (ISBN 0-670-30846-3). Viking Pr.
Farrago. Max Ehrmann. LC 6-37548. 1898. Cooperative Publishing Company.
Farramonde. Anne Maybury. LC 68-18471. 1968. D. McKay Co.
Farramonde. Katherine Troy. 1968. 4.95 o.p. McKay.
Farringdons. Ellen Thorneycroft Fowler. LC 2085. 1900. D. Appleton and Company.
Farther Adventures of Robinson Crusoe, Being the Second and Last Part of His Life. Daniel Defoe. LC 74-13446. (Illus.). 1974. (ISBN 0-404-07912-1). AMS Press.
Farther Afield. LC 74-23173. (Illus.). 1975. 6.95 (ISBN 0-395-20427-5). Houghton Mifflin.
Farther Afield. Read. LC 74-23173. 224p. 1975. 6.95 o.p. (ISBN 0-395-20427-5). HM.
Farther Shore. Robert Myron Coates. LC 55-10148. 1955. Harcourt, Brace.
Farthest Eden. Louise O'Flaherty. 1979. pap. 2.50 (ISBN 0-345-27400-8). Ballantine.
Farthest Reaches. Joseph Elder. LC 68-26712. 1968. 4.95. Trident Press.
Farthest Shore. Ursula K. Le Guin. 1975. (pbk.) 1.50. Bantam Books.
Farthest Shore. Ursula K. Le Guin. LC 72-75273. (Illus.). 1972. 6.25. Atheneum.
Farthest Star: The Saga of Cuckoo. Frederik Pohl & Jack Williamson. LC 75-322351. 1975. 1.50 (ISBN 0-345-24330-7). Ballantine Books.
Farthing Hall. Hugh Walpole & Priestley, John Boynton, 1894- Joint Author. LC 29-6351. 1929. Doubleday, Doran and Company, Inc.
Farthing's Fortunes. Richard Bruce Wright. LC 76-11860. 1976. 9.95 (ISBN 0-689-10756-0). Atheneum.
Fascinating Brute. Baker. pap. 1.95 o.p. (ISBN 0-87977-154-2, DBB154). Dansk Blue Bk.
Fascinating Girl. Helen B. Andelin. 306p. 6.95 o.s.i. (ISBN 0-911094-03-2). Pacific Pr.
Fascinating Mrs. Halton. Edward Frederic Benson. LC 10-7176. 1910. 1.20. Doubleday, Page & Company.
Fascinating Sin. George P Dillenback. LC 14-13020. 1.50. H. N. Halsey.
Fascinating Stranger: And Other Stories. Booth Tarkington. LC 23-8938. 1923. Doubleday, Page & Company.
Fascinating Traitor: An Anglo-Indian Story. Richard Henry Savage. LC 8-1998. (On cover: The welcome series, no. 26). 1897. The Home Publishing Co.
Fascinating Woman. (Laide). Juliette Lamber La Messine Adam & Sherwood, Mary Neal, Tr. LC 5-426153. T.B. Peterson & Brothers.
Fascination. Candice Adams. LC 82-8789. 1982. 1.75 (ISBN 0-345-30524-8). Ballantine Books.
Fascination. Cecil Champain Lowis. LC 13-24451. 1913. 1.25. John Lane.
Fascination. Olive Wadsley. LC 31-11946. 1931. Dodd, Mead & Company.
Fascination: A Novel ... LC 6-38989. 1882. G. W. Carleton & Co.; Etc., Etc.
Fascination... A Novel. Jean Pedrick. LC 47-236333. 1947. Houghton Mifflin Company.
Fascinator. Theodora Keogh. 160p. 1973. pap. 0.75 o.p. (532-00486-075). Manor Bks.
Fascinator. Christopher Nicole. LC 74-25131. 1975. 5.95 (ISBN 0-385-08443-9). Published for the Crime Club by Doubleday.
Fascinator. Andrew York. 1976. (ISBN 0-425-03165-9). Berkley Publishing Corp.
Fascinator. Line Drawings by Tom Keogh. Theodora Keogh. LC 54-5684. 1954. Farrar, Straus & Young.
Fashion and Famine. Ann Sophia Winterbotham Stephens. 1854. Bunce & Brothers.
Fashion and Famine. Ann Sophia Winterbotham Stephens. LC 8-14275. T. B. Peterson & Brothers.
Fashion and Famine. Ann Sophia Winterbotham Stephens. LC 8-12415. T. B. Peterson & Brothers.
Fashion Game. Marcia Miller. pap. 0.75 o.s.i. (01-404). Lancer.
Fashion in Shrouds. Margery Allingham. LC 75-40009. 1975. 9.95 (ISBN 0-89190-194-9). American Reprint Co.
Fashion in Shrouds. Margery Allingham. LC 74-168672. 1973. 0.40 (ISBN 0-14-000771-7). Penguin.
Fashion in Shrouds. Margery Allingham. LC 39-32049. 1939. The Sun Dial Press, Inc.
Fashion in Shrouds. Margery Allingham. LC 38-27954. 1938. Doubleday, Doran & Company, Inc.
Fashion in Shrouds. Margery Allingham. 1973. (pbk.) 0.95. Manor Books.
Fashion of This World. Helen Buckingham Mathers Reeves. (On cover: The seaside library. Pocket ed. no. 798). 1886. G. Munro.
Fashion: Or, Siska Von Roosemael. From the Flemish of Hendrik Conscience. With 30 Illustrations. Hendrik Conscience. (Half-title: Dunigan's home library, no. XI). 1849. E. Dunigan & Brother.
Fashionable Adventures of Joshua Craig. David Graham Phillips. Ed. by Abe C. Ravitz. LC 79-96683. (American Authors Ser). 1970. lib. bdg. 21.50 o.s.i. (ISBN 0-512-00558-3). Garrett Pr.
Fashionable Adventures of Joshua Craig: A Novel. David Graham Phillips. LC 72-84635. 1974. (ISBN 0-403-03157-5). Scholarly Press.
Fashionable Adventures of Joshua Craig: A Novel. David Graham Phillips. LC 9-2260. 1909. D. Appleton and Company.
Fashionable Adventures of Joshua Craig: A Novel. David Graham Phillips. LC 16-936222. 1914. D. Appleton and Company.
Fashionable Life. Mary Henderson Eastman. LC 6-368150. 1856. J. B. Lippincott and Co.
Fashionable Marriage. Alexander Fraser. LC 12-32861. (On cover: Lovell's Westminister series. no. 35). John W. Lovell Company.
Fashionable Sins. A Novel. Stella Chapman. LC 6-23119. (On cover: Minerva series, no. 42). 1891. The Minerva Publishing Company.
Fashionable Sufferer: Or, Chapters from Life's Comedy. Augustus Hoppin. LC 7-52391. 1883. Houghton, Mifflin and Company.
Fashioned Anew. Frank L Gale. LC 31-6990. 1931.
Fashioned for Murder. George Harmon Coxe. LC 47-5388. 1947. A. A. Knopf.
Fashions in Marriage. Claude Farrere. Tr. by Strauss, Harold. LC 30-28402. A. H. King.
Fashion's Lady. Sandra Heath. 1982. pap. 2.25 (ISBN 0-451-11829-4, AE1829, Sig). NAL.
Fashions of the Heart. Yvonne Lehman. (Chime Ser.). (YA) 1981. pap. 2.50 (ISBN 0-89191-372-6, 53728). Cook.
Fashions of the Heart. Yvonne Lehman. (Chime Ser.). 1982. pap. 2.50 o.p. Caroline Hse.
Fast and Loose. Ann Lawrence. LC 35-8038. Godwin.
Fast and Loose. A Novel. Arthur George Frederick Griffiths. (On cover: Seaside library. Pocket ed. no. 680). 1886. G. Munroe.
Fast and Loose: A Novel. new ed. Arthur George Frederick Griffiths. 1886. Rand, McNally & Co.
Fast and Loose: A Novelette. Edith Newbold Jones Wharton. LC 76-58438. (Illus.). 1977. 17.50 (ISBN 0-8139-0599-0). University Press of Virginia.
Fast & Loose: A Novelette by David Olivieri. Edith Newbold Jones Wharton. LC 76-58438. 1977. ltd. boxed 50.00x o.p. (ISBN 0-8139-0599-0). U Pr of Va.
Fast As the Wind: A Novel. Nathaniel Gould. LC 18-18335. Frederick A. Stokes Company.
Fast Company. Harry Kurnitz. LC 38-19401. 1938. Dodd, Mead & Company.
Fast Company. Marco Page. LC 38-19401. 1938. Dodd, Mead & Company.
Fast Curve. Justin Kent. 1953. Vixen Press.
Fast Eddie. Neil Bayne & Wes Sarginson. 320p. (Orig.). 1983. pap. 3.50 (ISBN 0-8439-1070-4, Leisure Bks). Dorchester Pub Co.
Fast Forward. Ann Berk. LC 82-45238. 264p. 1983. 14.95 (ISBN 0-385-17906-5). Doubleday.
Fast Friends. Joy Darlington. LC 78-22732. 1979. 8.95 (ISBN 0-385-15158-6). Doubleday.
Fast Friends. John Townsend Trowbridge. LC 3-11143. (On cover: Jack Hazard series). H. T. Coates & Co.
Fast Friendship. Joy Darlington. (Berkley Books). 1980. 2.50 (ISBN 0-425-04742-3). Berkley Publishing Corp.
Fast Game. Kirk Parson. LC 10-16324. The Roxburgh Publishing Company (Incorporated.
Fast Girl: A Novel, by Token West Pseud. Adelaide Humphries. LC 52-2188. 1952. Woodford Press.
Fast Gun. Walt Coburn. 1978. pap. 1.25 o.s.i. (ISBN 0-505-51227-0). Tower Bks.
Fast Gun Grass. Lee Floren. (Orig.). 1979. pap. 1.75 (ISBN 0-532-23214-3). Woodhill.
Fast Life. Cynthia Wilkerson. (Belmont Tower book). 1.95 (ISBN 0-505-51350-1). Tower Pubns.
Fast Man with a Dollar. Robert Avery. LC 47-24311. 1947. Arcadia House.
Fast One. Paul Cain. LC 49-276993. (New Avon library, 178). 1948. Avon Pub. Co.
Fast One. Paul Cain. LC 33-354813. 1933. Doubleday, Doran & Company, Inc.
Fast One. Paul Cain. 1980. 2.50 (ISBN 0-445-04526-4). Fawcett Popular Library.
Fast One. Robert Daley. LC 77-8570. 8.95 (ISBN 0-517-53140-2). Crown.
Fast One: A Novel. Paul Cain. LC 77-28030. (Lost American fiction). 8.95 (ISBN 0-8093-0872-X). Southern Illinois University Press.
Fast Shuffle, No. 14. Zeke Masters, pseud. (Orig.). 1982. pap. 1.95 (ISBN 0-671-43812-3). PB.
Fast Start, Fast Finish. Stephen Birmingham. LC 66-18836. 5.95. New Amer. Lib.
Fast Track. Charlie Avery Harris. (Orig.). 1978. pap. 1.75 (ISBN 0-87067-529-X, BH050). Holloway.
Faster! Faster!". Edmee Elizabeth Monica De La Pasture. LC 36-3545. 1936. Harper & Brothers.
Faster, Faster. Edward Newman Horn. LC 46-2672. 1946. Coward-McCann, Inc.
Faster! Faster! A Novel. Patrick Bair. LC 50-9238. 1950. Viking Press.
Faster Than Light. Jack Dann & George Zebrowski. 352p. 1982. pap. 2.95 (ISBN 0-441-22825-9, Pub. by Ace Science Fiction). Ace Bks.
Faster Than Light: An Original Anthology About Interstellar Travel. Jack Dann & George Zebrowski. LC 74-15865. (Illus.). 8.95 (ISBN 0-06-010952-1). Harper & Row.
Faster They Go: A Novel of Motor Racing. 1st Ed. John Bentley. LC 57-10870. 1957. Lippincott.
Fastest Boy in New York. Harlan Page Halsey. LC 7-1190. (On cover: The calumet series, no. 14). G. Munro.
Fastest Gun. Dan Cushman. LC 55-114722. (Dell first edition,67). 1955. Dell Pub. Co.
Fastest Gun. Charles Morris Martin. (O.s.i.). 1976. pap. 0.95 o.s.i. Belmont-Tower.
Fat and the Brave. Frank Wright Moxley. LC 32-8805. Liveright, Inc.
Fat and the Thin: Le Ventre De Paris. sole authorized english version... ed. Emile Zola & Vizetelly, Ernest Alfred, 1853-1922, Tr. LC 9-1328. (Neely's library of choice literature, no. 53). 1895. F. T. Neely.
Fat Chance. 1975. (pbk.) 1.25 (ISBN 0-671-78899-X). Pocket Books.
Fat City. Leonard Gardner. LC 70-85234. 1969. 5.50. Farrar, Straus and Giroux.
Fat Death. Michael Avallone. (Orig.). 1972. pap. 0.75 o.p. (07231). Curtis.
Fat Emily. Susan Ries Lukas. LC 73-79416. 1974. 6.95 (ISBN 0-8128-1639-0). Stein and Day.
Fat Lady's Ghost. Charlotte MacLeod. LC 68-12864. 1968. Weybright and Talley.
Fat Like Me: A Satire on Dieting. Bob Tramonte. LC 81-65584. (Illus.). 3.95 (ISBN 0-939602-00-8). Blue Star Press.
Fat Man in History, and Other Stories. Peter Carey. LC 79-5519. 1980. 8.95 (ISBN 0-394-51072-0). Random House.
Fat People: A Novel. Carol Sturm Smith. LC 77-81004. 3.95 (ISBN 0-914590-46-4) (ISBN 0-914590-47-2). Fiction Collective: Distributed by G. Braziller.
Fat Tuesday. R. Wright Campbell. LC 82-19264. 1983. 14.95 (ISBN 0-89919-158-4). Ticknor & Fields.
Fat Woman. Leon Rooke. LC 80-21893. 1981. 9.95 (ISBN 0-394-51642-7). Knopf.
Fata Morgana. William Kotzwinkle. LC 76-43292. 1977. 7.95 (ISBN 0-394-40905-1). Knopf.
Fata Morgana: A Romance of Art Student Life in Paris. Andre Castaigne. LC 4-30589. 1904. The Century Co.
Fata Morgana." A Vision of Empire--the Burr Conspiracy in Mississippi Territory and the Great Southwest--Natchez Love Story of Ex-Vice President Aaron Burr; a Historical Novel. Elizabeth Brandon Stanton. LC 17-30729. Printed by the Signal Publishing Co.
Fatal Amateur. D. L. Mathews. LC 59-7413. 1959. Rinehart.
Fatal Attraction. Shirley Hart. (Candlelight Ecstacy Ser.: No. 78). 224p. 1982. pap. 1.95 (ISBN 0-440-12842-0). Dell.

Fatal Attraction: A Novel. Craig Jones. 1983. 11.95 (ISBN 0-517-54926-3). Crown.
Fatal Bacon. Ferdinande Brackel. LC 4-6877. 1904. Benziger Brothers.
Fatal Boots: And Other Sketches. William Makepeace Thackeray. LC 8-28203. (On cover: Lovell's library, v. 5, no. 262). 1883. J. W. Lovell Company.
Fatal Card. Arthur D Hall & Chambers, Haddon. The Fatal Card. (On cover: Drama series, no. 10). Street & Smith.
Fatal Demonstrations. Elizabeth Moulton. LC 78-20213. 9.95 (ISBN 0-06-013054-7). Harper & Row.
Fatal Descent. Cecil John Charles Street & Carr, John Dickson, Joint Author. LC 39-2161. 1939. Dodd, Mead & Company.
Fatal Diamonds. Eleanor Cecilia Donnelly. LC 6-33729. 1897. Benziger Brothers.
Fatal Dower... Sophy Beckett. LC 6-9772. (On cover: The seaside library. Pocket edition, no. 246). 1884. G. Munro.
Fatal Element. Edward C Clark. LC 34-14906. Empire Publishing Company.
Fatal Fetish. Peter Hochstein. (Berkley Medallion Book). 1977. 1.50 (ISBN 0-425-03449-6). Berkley Pub.
Fatal Feud: Or, Passion and Piety. A Moral Tale. George A Raybold. LC 7-36639. 1850. Lane & Scott.
Fatal Finale. Paul H Dobbins. LC 50-5375. 1949. Phoenix Press.
Fatal Flaw. Laurence Walter Meynell. LC 77-17997. (Jubilee mystery). 1978. 7.95 (ISBN 0-8128-2419-9). Stein and Day.
Fatal Flourishes. S. S Rafferty. LC 78-61899. 1979. 1.95 (ISBN 0-380-41772-3). Avon.
Fatal Footsteps. Wilburn O. Hague. LC 48-4908. 1943. Phoenix Press.
Fatal Friday. Francis Gerard. LC 37-22964. H. Holt and Company.
Fatal Friendship. A Lady. LC 75-5722. (Flowering of the Novel). 1975. (ISBN 0-8240-1194-5). Garland Pub.
Fatal Garden. Cecil John Charles Street. LC 49-11315. (Red badge mystey). 1949. Dodd, Mead.
Fatal Gesture. John Taintor Foote. LC 33-17934. 1933. D. Appleton-Century Company, Incorporated.
Fatal Gift. Katharine Newlin Burt. LC 41-15432. 1941. Macrae-Smith Company.
Fatal Gift. Frank Frankfort Moore. LC 98-2098. 1898. Dodd, Mead and Company.
Fatal Gift. Alec Waugh. 1974. (pbk.) 1.75. Manor Books.
Fatal Gift: A Novel. Alec Waugh. LC 72-97081. 1973. 6.95 (ISBN 0-374-15380-9). Farrar, Straus and Giroux.
Fatal Gift: A Novel. Alec Waugh. LC 73-175344. 1973. 2.50 (ISBN 0-491-01170-9). W. H. Allen.
Fatal Gift of Beauty: And Other Stories. Elizabeth Robins. LC 7-41969. 1896. H. S. Stone & Co.
Fatal Glimpse. Robert K. Wilcox. 1981. pap. 2.25 (ISBN 0-8439-0899-8, Leisure Bks). Nordon Pubns.
Fatal Glove. A Novel. Also Constitutionally Bashful. Clara Augusta Jones. LC 7-12138. (On cover: The idle hour series. no. 12). 1892. The F. M. Lupton Publishing Company.
Fatal Harvest: By Alan Amos Pseud. 1st Ed. Kathleen Moore Knight. LC 57-124687. 1957. Published for the Crime Club by Doubleday.
Fatal in My Fashion. Patricia McGerr. 1969. pap. 0.60 o.p. (60-369). Manor Bks.
Fatal in My Fashion. 1st Ed. Patricia McGerr. LC 54-10772. 1954. Published for the Crime Club by Doubleday.
Fatal Intrigue. Josephine E Barry. LC 6-9407. (On cover: Dearborn series, no. 107). 1895. Donohue, Henneberry & Co.
Fatal Kiss Mystery. Rufus King. LC 28-14551. 1928. Pub. for the Crime Club, Inc., by Doubleday, Doran & Company, Inc.
Fatal Ladder: Or, Harry Linford ... LC 6-38965. American Sunday School Union.
Fatal Lady: A Mr. Potter Mystery. Elinore Denniston. LC 64-10951. 1964. Dodd, Mead.
Fatal Lilies, and, A Bride from the Sea. Charlotte Mary Brame. LC 44-12257. (On cover: Seaside library. Pocket ed. No. 299). G. Munro.
Fatal Lozenge. Edward Gorey. (Illus.). 1960. pap. 4.75 (ISBN 0-8392-1031-0). Astor-Honor.
Fatal Marriage. Emma Dorothy Eliza Nevitte Southworth. LC 8-14244. T. B. Peterson & Brothers.
Fatal Marriage: And The Shadow in the Corner. Mary Elizabeth Braddon Maxwell. (On cover: Seaside library. Pocket ed. no. 548). 1885. G. Munro.
Fatal Misunderstanding: And Other Stories. Bertha Behrens. Tr. by Elise L. Lathrop. (Worthington's international library, no. 33). 1893. Worthington Company.
Fatal Obsession. Stephen Greenleaf. LC 82-22226. 264p. 1983. 14.95 (ISBN 0-385-27886-1). Dial.
Fatal Odds. John Halkin. 1981. pap. 2.25 (ISBN 0-8439-0935-8). Nordon Pubns.
Fatal Past. Dora Russell. LC 8-1335. (On cover: Lovell's international series, no. 170). 1891. J. W. Lovell Company.
Fatal Phryne. Francis Charles Philips & Wills, Charles James. LC 7-36072. (On cover: Lovell's international series, no. 20). F. F. Lovell & Company.
Fatal Picnic. Bernice Carey Martin. LC 55-9976. 1955. Published for the Crime Club by Doubleday.
Fatal Pool: By John Rhode. Cecil John Charles Street. LC 60-15148. (Red badge detective). 1961. Dodd, Mead.
Fatal Purchase. Anne Van Melborn Rowe. LC 45-4222. 1945. M. S. Mill Co., Inc.
Fatal Request. A. L. Harris. LC 7-2623. Cassell Publishing Company.
Fatal Revenge: Or, The Family of Montorio: a Romance. Charles Robert Maturin. LC 73-22767. (Gothic Novels II). 1974. (ISBN 0-405-06018-1). Arno Press.
Fatal Revenge: The Family of Montorio, 3 vols. Charles Robert Maturin. LC 73-22767. (Gothic Novels II Ser.). 1974. Repr. of 1807 ed. Set. 66.00 (ISBN 0-405-06018-1). Ayer Co.
Fatal Ruby. Charles Garvice. LC 9-28211. G. H. Doran Company.
Fatal Secret. Emma Dorothy Eliza Nevitte Southworth & Frances Henshaw Baden. LC 12-38912. T. B. Peterson & Brothers.
Fatal Shadows. Sara George. 1982. 15.00x (ISBN 0-333-19296-6, Pub. by Macmillan England). State Mutual Bk.
Fatal Shadows. Eleanor Stanley Lockwood. LC 49-10541. 1949. Humphries.
Fatal Shadows. Dorothy Cole Meade. LC 33-332683. 1933. R. Long & R. R. Smith.
Fatal Skin. Honore De Balzac. LC 64-96. (Signet classic). 1963. New American Library.
Fatal Skin. Honore De Balzac. LC 49-9449. (Novel Library). 1949. Pantheon Books.
Fatal Step. Clarissa Fairchild Cushman. LC 52-12651. 1953. Little, Brown.
Fatal Step. Wade Miller, pseud. LC 48-5401. 1948. Farrar, Straus.
Fatal Susan: A Tale of Sophistication. Florence Helm. LC 32-1319. The Chelmsford Press.
Fatal Trip. Michael Underwood. LC 77-76655. 1977. 7.95 (ISBN 0-312-28507-8). St. Martin's Press.
Fatal Voyage. Francois Ponthier. LC 67-24978. 1967. D. McKay Co.
Fatal Wooing. Laura Jean Libbey. (On cover: Munro's library, popular novels, v. 1, no. 91). N. L. Munro.
Fatal Wooing. Laura Jean Libbey. (On cover: Lovell's library, no. 1239). 1888. J. W. Lovell Company.
Fatal 5 Minutes. Robert Alfred John Walling. LC 32-656. 1932. W. Morrow & Company.
Fatalist, or, The Fortunes of Godolphin. Nicholas Michell. LC 43-26707. 1840. Lea & Blanchard.
Fatback Odes. J. D. Reed. 1972. 7.50 (ISBN 0-912090-26-X); pap. 2.45 (ISBN 0-912090-25-1). Sumac Mich.
Fate and a Marionette. Hanna Rion Ver Beck. LC 24-22462. E. J. Clode, Inc.
Fate & Dreams. Leslie Arlen. (Borodins Ser.: No. 3). 384p. (Orig.). 1981. pap. 3.50 (ISBN 0-515-06898-5). Jove Pubns.
Fate and the Butterfly. Forrest Halsey. LC 9-9466. 1909. B. W. Dodge & Company.
Fate at the Door. A Novel. Jessie Perry Van Zile Belden. LC 6-9422. 1895. J. B. Lippincott Company.
Fate Cannot Harm Me. John Cecil Masterman. LC 41-10145. (On cover: Penquin books. 252). 1940. Penquin Books Limited.
Fate Cries Out: Nine Tales. Winifred Ashton. LC 35-31971. 1935. Doubleday, Doran & Company, Inc.
Fate Directs. Mark Avery Walser. LC 27-246725. Sentinel Publishing Company.
Fate Is a Fool. Harriet Theresa Smith Comstock. LC 30-32907. 1930. Doubleday, Doran & Company, Inc.
Fate Is a Woman. Clarke Robinson. LC 37-548367. 1937. Godwin.
Fate Knocks at the Door: A Novel. Will Levington Comfort. LC 12-996126. 1912. J. B. Lippincott Company.
Fate Laughs. Herbert Adams. LC 35-12656. J. B. Lippincott Company.
Fate of a Crown. Schuyler Staunton. LC 5-17289. 1905. The Reilly & Britton Co.
Fate of a Fairy. Ellen E Jack. LC 11-469. 1.50. W. B. Conkey Company.
Fate of a Fool. Emma Ghent Curtis. LC 6-317123. 1888. J. A. Berry & Company.
Fate of a Soldier. Henryk Sienkiewicz & Bay, Jens Christian, 1871- Tr. (sunnyside series. no. 103). J. S. Ogilvie Publishing Company.
Fate of Esther Fox. David Emerson. LC 76-376184. 1976. 8.95 (ISBN 0-09-125220-2). Hutchinson.
Fate of Father Sheehy. A Tale of Tipperary Eighty Years Ago. Mary Anne Madden Sadlier. LC 3-165049. D. & J. Sadlier & Co.
Fate of Felix Brand. Florence Finch Kelly. LC 13-20752. The John C. Winston Company.
Fate of Fenella: A Novel. LC 6-38963. Cassell Publishing Company.
Fate of Freeman. Tom Kapanka. 1981. pap. 1.50. Eldridge Pub.
Fate of Innocence. Gerald Jay Goldberg. 1965. pap. text ed. 7.50x o.p. (ISBN 0-13-308189-3). P-H.
Fate of Jane McKenzie... Nancy Barr Mavity. LC 33-5920. 1933. Pub. for the Crime Club, Inc., by Doubleday, Doran & Company, Inc.
Fate of Madame La Tour: A Tale of Great Salt Lake. Cornelia Paddock. 1881. Fords, Howard, & Hulbert.
Fate of Mansfield Humphreys: With the Episode of Mr. Washington Adams in England, and an Apology. Richard Grant White. LC 8-36567. 1884. Houghton, Mifflin and Company.
Fate of Marcel. Caleb Harlan. LC 7-190964. 1883. J. B. Lippincott & Co.
Fate of Mary Rose. Caroline Blackwood. LC 81-1129. 11.95 (ISBN 0-671-42321-5). Summit Books.
Fate of O'Loughlin. Dudley McCarthy. 1980. 12.95 (ISBN 0-07-093549-1). McGraw.
Fate of Sister Jessica. Frederick William Robinson. LC 7-41961. (On cover: Lovell's Westminster series no. 46). 1891. J. W. Lovell Company.
Fate of the Black Eagle: And Other Stories. Russell Duryee Smith. LC 99-2159. (Neely's universal library. no. 60). F. T. Neely.
Fate of the Dane: And Other Stories. Anna Hanson McKenney Dorsey. LC 6-33712. J. Murphy & Co.
Fate of the Dane, and Other Stories. Anna Hanson McKenney Dorsey. LC 43-215450. John Murphy Company.
Fate of the Lovers. Angela Gordon. 1972. pap. 0.75 o.p. (94290). Beagle Bks.
Fate of the Malous. Georges Simenon. LC 67-73519. 1966. Penguin in Association with Hamilton.
Fate of the Phoenix. Sondra Marshak & Myrna Culbreath. 1979. pap. 1.95 (ISBN 0-553-12779-9). Bantam.
Fate or Law? The Story of an Optimist. Warren Anson Rodman. LC 99-1356. 1899. Lee and Shepard.
Fate, the Fiddler. Herbert C MacIlwaine. LC 3053. 1901. J. B. Lippincott Company.
Fated Lovers: And Other Beautiful Stories. George Morley Vickers. LC 8-32803. (current library). 1891. The Current Publishing Co.
Fated Promise. A Novel. O P Caylor. LC 6-222773. 1890. G. W. Dillingham.
Fated to Be Free. A Novel. Jean Ingelow. LC 7-88546. 1875. Roberts Brothers.
Fated to Be Free. A Novel. Jean Ingelow. LC 21-13969. (Seaside library, v. 41, no. 839). 1880. G. Munro.
Fated to Be Free. A Novel. Jean Ingelow. LC 16-131224. 1907. Little, Brown, and Company.
Fated to Win (The Soul of a Serf) Intensely Dramatic and True to Life: A Romance of Love and Valor. John Breckenridge Ellis. LC 11-635917. 1.50. Laird & Lee.
Fated Woman. William La Varre. LC 34-14640. The Macaulay Company.
Fateful Hand: Or, Saved by Lightning a Thrilling Romance of the St. Louis Cyclone. E. O. Tilburn. (On cover: The pastime series, no. 42 184). 1896. Laird & Lee.
Fateful Promise. Lorena Ann Olmsted. (Candlelight romance). 1974. (pbk.) 0.75. Dell.
Fateful Star Murder. Herbert Kerkow. LC 31-21749. 1931. The Mohawk Press.
Fateful Summer. Velda Johnston. LC 81-7771. 8.95 (ISBN 0-396-08015-4). Dodd, Mead.
Fateful Summer. Velda Johnston. LC 81-23526. 1982. 11.95 (ISBN 0-8161-3350-6). Hall.
Fate's a Fiddler. Edwin George Pinkham. LC 8-18409. 1908. Small, Maynard & Company.
Fates Are Laughing. William Percival Crozier. LC 45-6993. 1945. Harcourt, Brace and Company.
Fate's Captive. Ethel Winifred Savi. LC 34-424142. 1933. G. H. Watt.
Fate's Passion. Anne Gaynor. (Orig.). 1982. pap. 3.25 (ISBN 0-8217-1022-2). Zebra.
Father. Katharine Holland Brown. LC 28-294251. 1928. The John Day Company.
Father. Charles J Calitri. LC 61-15799. 1962. Crown Publishers.
Father. Elizabeth. 1973. pap. 0.95 o.p. (09211). Curtis.
Father. Mary Annette Beauchamp Russell Russell. LC 31-268732. 1931. Doubleday, Doran & Company, Inc.
Father Abraham: A Tale of the Last Years of Abraham Lincoln. Irving Bacheller. LC 25-5539. The Bobbs-Merrill Company.
Father Ambrose: The Revelation of May 3d '68. copyright ed.... ed. Steele Mackaye. LC 7-19985. (On cover: Belt line series). 1894. The Deshler Welch Publishing Co.
Father and Daughter: A Portraiture from the Life. Fredrika Bremer. Tr. by Mary Botham Howitt. LC 7-1232. T.B. Peterson and Brothers.
Father and Daughter: A Tale. Amelia Alderson Opie. LC 45-32781. 1812. Published by William Cooper; and By Joseph Milligan, Georgetown.
Father & His Fate. Ivy Compton-Burnett. 1957. 11.95 o.p. (ISBN 0-575-01580-2, Pub. by Gollancz England). David & Charles.
Father & His Fate. Ivy Compton-Burnett. 1981. 20.00x (ISBN 0-575-01580-2, Pub. by Gollancz England). State Mutual Bk.
Father: And Other Stories. Robert Verlin Cassill. LC 65-11980. 1965. Simon and Schuster.
Father, & Others Stories. Robert Verlin Cassill. 1965. 4.95 o.p. S&S.
Father and Son. James Thomas Farrell. LC 76-6340. (Irish-Americans). 1976. 29.00 (ISBN 0-405-09335-7). Arno Press.
Father and Son. James Thomas Farrell. LC 40-32291. The Vanguard Press.
Father and Son: A Novel. William Gundry Broughton. LC 72-79469. 1972.
Father and Son: With a New Introd. James Thomas Farrell. LC 47-5505. 1947. World Pub. Co.
Father and Sons. Tr. by Rosemary Edmonds. Ivan Sergeevich Turgenev. LC 65-2787. (Penguin classics, L147). pap., 1.25. Penguin.
Father Anthony: A Romance of to-Day. Robert Williams Buchanan. LC 3425. 1900. G. W. Dillingham Company.
Father Bernard's Parish. Florence Olmstead. LC 16-117347. 1916. C. Scribner's Sons.
Father Bombo's Pilgrimage to Mecca, 1770. Hugh Henry Brackenridge & Philip Morin Freneau. LC 75-5391. (Illus.). 10.00 (ISBN 0-87811-020-8). Princeton University Library.
Father Bredder Mystery Story see Problem in Angels.
Father Brown Omnibus... Gilbert Keith Chesterton. LC 33-27022. 1933. Dodd, Mead & Company.
Father Brown Omnibus. Gilbert Keith Chesterton. LC 46-38952. Dodd, Mead & Company.
Father Brown Omnibus. Gilbert Keith Chesterton. LC 83-1807. 1983. 13.95 (ISBN 0-396-08159-2). Dodd, Mead.
Father Brown Omnibus... New and Rev. Ed. Gilbert Keith Chesterton. LC 51-11019. 1951. Dodd, Mead.
Father Brown Stories. Gilbert Keith Chesterton. 718p. 1982. Repr. of 1929 ed. lib. bdg. 45.00 (ISBN 0-8495-0867-3). Arden Lib.
Father Butler; The Lough Dearg Pilgrim. William Carleton. LC 78-32163. (Ireland, from the Act of Union, 1800, to the Death of Parnell, 1891; 33). (Illus.). 1980. 32.00 (ISBN 0-8240-3482-1). Garland Pub.
Father by Proxy: A Novel of Reconstruction Days in Florida, Based on Actual Events. 1st Ed. James H Whitney. LC 54-13412. 1955. Exposition Press.
Father Catich's Visit with Bill Dwiggins. Dwight Agner. 16p. 1982. pap. 12.50 (ISBN 0-912960-14-0). Nightowl.
Father Christmas Letters. rev. ed. John Ronald Reuel Tolkien. Ed. by Baille Tolkien. 1979. pap. 4.95 (ISBN 0-395-28262-4). HM.
Father Clement. Grace Kennedy. LC 75-445. (Victorian Fiction: Novels of Faith and Doubt; No. 1). 1976. 35.00 (ISBN 0-8240-1525-8). Garland Pub.
Father Clement, a Roman Catholic Story. from the 6th edinburgh ed. Grace Kennedy. LC 7-3076. 1827. E. Duyckinck.
Father Clement, a Roman Catholic Story. Grace Kennedy. 1848. Stanford and Swords.
Father Clement: A Roman Catholic Story. from the last edinburgh ed. Grace Kennedy. LC 7-11110. 1856. R. Carter & Brothers.
Father Clement. A True and Touching Story. Grace Kennedy. LC 7-111118. 1850. T. B. Peterson.
Father Coldstream. Julian Duguid. 1938. D. Appleton-Century Company, Incorporated.
Father Confessor. Marie Samms. LC 57-70221. (Milestone book). 1957. Comet Press Books.
Father Connell: A Romance of Ireland. John Banim & Michael Banim. LC 1-1526. (Brother Jonathan. Extra. v. 2, no. 3. June 25, 1842). 1842. Wilson and Company.
Father Daughter. Jasper Evian. LC 80-16658. 9.95 (ISBN 0-02-536700-5). Macmillan.
Father Drummond and His Orphans: Or, The Children of Mary. Mary C Edgar. LC 6-26310. 1854. H. & C. McGrath.
Father Eustace: A Tale of the Jesuits. Frances M. Trollope. Ed. by Robert L. Wolff. LC 75-448. (Victorian Fiction Ser.). (O.s.i.). 1975. Repr. of 1847 ed. lib. bdg. 66.00 o.s.i. (ISBN 0-8240-1528-2). Garland Pub.
Father Flynn. George Carter Needham. LC 7-25790. J. A. O'Connor.
Father Gabriel's Daughter. Corinne Johnson Kern. LC 31-33068. 1931. California Graphic Press.

Father Goriot, Ursule Mirouet, and Other Stories: Tr. by Ellen Marriage and Clara Bell; with Prefaces by George Saintsbury. Honore De Balzac. Tr. by Ellen Marriage. Bell, Mrs. Clara Courtenay (Poynter) 1834-1927, Joint Tr & Ursule Mirouet. LC 8-7688. 1899. The Gebbie Publishing Co., Ltd.

Father Gregory: A Tale of Hindostan. Percival Christopher Wren. LC 26-24136. 1926. Frederick A. Stokes Company.

Father Hilary's Holiday. Bruce Marshall. LC 65-19883. 3.95. Doubleday.

Father Hilary's Holiday. Bruce Marshall. (Echo bk., E35). 1966. Doubleday.

Father Hollis of Long Shot, Minnesota. Lillian Kay Anderson. LC 51-21608. 1951. Vantage Press.

Father Hunt. Rex Stout. 160p. 1980. pap. 1.95 (ISBN 0-553-14453-7). Bantam.

Father Hunt. Rex Stout. 1968. 4.50 o.p. (ISBN 0-670-30945-1). Viking Pr.

Father Hunt: A Nero Wolfe Novel. Rex Stout. LC 68-21584. 1968. Viking Press.

Father Hunter. John Gemma. 1968. 3.75 o.p. Vantage.

Father Ildefonso: Or, The Priests of St. Omers. John Hovey Robinson. LC 7-42157. 1847. Williams Brothers; Etc., Etc.

Father in a Fix. Peter De Rosa. LC 80-15258. 1980. 9.95. Morrow.

Father in Modern Story. Ed. by Maud Van Buren. Bemis, Katharine Isabel, Joint Ed. LC 29-183369. Century Co.

Father in the Family. Louis Paul. LC 51-12359. 1951. Crown Publishers.

Father John: Or, Ruth Webster's Quest. Anna Johnson. LC 7-32843. American Tract Society.

Father Jonathan: Or, the Scottish Converts. A Catholic Tale. John McDermott. LC 7-15419. 1853. H. & C. M'Grath.

Father Joseph, and Other Stories. Josephine Byrne Sullivan. LC 20-19313. The Michigan Catholic.

Father Juniper and the General: By James Norman Pseud. James Norman Schmidt. LC 56-106060. 1957. Morrow.

Father Kelly of the Rosary. Edward Everett Rose. LC 10-232069. 1910. 0.50. The Rosary Publishing Co.

Father Lambert's Family. A Story of Old-Time France. Mary Ellen Bamford. LC 6-6297. 1888. Phillips & Hunt.

Father Laval: Or, The Jesuit Missionary. by james mcsherry... ed. James McSherry. LC 7-168142. 1860. J. Murphy & Co.; Etc., Etc.

Father Malachy's Miracle: A Heavenly Story with an Earthly Meaning. Bruce Marshall. 1931. Doubleday, Doran & Company, Inc.

Father Malachy's Miracle: A Heavenly Story with an Earthly Meaning. Bruce Marshall. LC 33-14296. 1933. Garden City Publishing Co., Inc.

Father Malachy's Miracle: A Heavenly Story with an Earthly Meaning. Bruce Marshall. LC 36-331415. The Sun Dial Press.

Father Means Well. Hugh MacNair Kahler. LC 30-217773. 1930. Farrar & Rinehart Incorporated.

Father Merrill... Mary Dwinell Chellis. LC 6-23415. (Added t.-p.: $500 prize series of illustrated books). C.

Father Noodle: A Narrative of the Glory of the Everlasting Gospel. Albert Friedrich Wilhelm Grimm. Tr. by Musller, John Theodore. LC 19-1337. 1.00. Antigo Publishing Company.

Father O'Brien and His Girls. David Chandler. LC 63-16823. 1963. Appleton-Century.

Father of Fires. Kenneth M Cameron. 2.95 (ISBN 0-445-04640-6). Fawcett Popular Library.

Father of Six: And An Occasional Holiday; from the Original of N. E. Potapeeko; Tr. Ignatii Nikolaevich Potapenko. Tr. by Gaussen, William Frederick Armytage. LC 7-30051. ("unknown" library no. 26). Cassell Publishing Company.

Father of the Bride. Edward Streeter. LC 49-876093. 1949. Simon and Schuster.

Father of Waters. Veronica Murphy Pennington. LC 52-180924. 1953. Dorrance.

Father Oswald: A Genuine Catholic Story ... LC 6-38961. 1843. Casserly & Sons.

Father Owned a Circus. Sherlock Holmes Evans. LC 51-10902. 1951. Dorrance.

Father Paul: And Other Pretty Stories. LC 44-313339. (On cover: Little Catholic children stories). P. J. Kennedy & Sons.

Father Pig.". Burt Hirschfeld. 1973. (pbk) 1.50. Dell Pub. Co.

Father Pig.". Burt Hirschfeld. LC 76-184883. 1972. 6.95 (ISBN 0-87795-028-8). Arbor House.

Father Pink. Alfred Wilson Barrett. LC 6-41278. 1906. Small, Maynard & Company.

Father Rowland: A North American Tale... 2d ed., enl. ed. Charles Constantine Pise. LC 7-38202. F. Lucas, Jr.

Father Rowland: A North American Tale. Charles Constantine Pise. LC 77-11305. (American Catholic Tradition). 1978. 11.00 (ISBN 0-405-10847-8). Arno Press.

Father Sergius: And Other Stories and Plays. Lev Nikolaevich Tolstoi. LC 76-132129. (Short story index reprint series). (Illus.). 1970. Books for Libraries Press.

Father Sergius, & Other Stories & Plays. facs. ed. Lev Nikolaevich Tolstoi. (Short Story Index Reprint Ser). 1911. 18.00 (ISBN 0-8369-3686-8). Ayer Co.

Father Sky: A Novel. Devery Freeman. LC 79-18562. 1979. 8.95 (ISBN 0-688-03557-4). Morrow.

Father Spike. Kim P. Yu. 3.50 o.p. Vantage.

Father Stafford. Anthony Hope Hawkins. LC 7-2180. Cassell Publishing Company.

Father Stafford. Anthony Hope Hawkins. LC 7-21816. (On cover: Neely's prismatic library). 1895. F. T. Neely.

Father Time's Children, a Novel. Foreword by Harry J. Beardsley. Muriel Hallett Gallant. LC 51-12335. 1951. Exposition Press.

Father to the Stars. Philip Jose Farmer. 320p. (Orig.). 1981. pap. 2.75 (ISBN 0-523-48504-2). Pinnacle Bks.

Father Tom and the Pope: Or, A Night at the Vaticon... Samuel Ferguson & William Maginn. LC 6-38983. T. B. Peterson & Brothers.

Father Tom and the Pope: Or A Night in the Vatican. Samuel Ferguson & William Maginn. LC 15-23124. 1868. Moorhead, Simpson & Bond.

Father Tom of Connemara. Elizabeth O'Reilly Neville. 1902. Rand, McNally & Company.

Father Under Fire. Neil Boyd. LC 81-2458. 1981. 9.95 (ISBN 0-688-03643-0). Morrow.

Father Vikenty: A Novel About a Russian Priest and His New York Parish. Paul Chavchavadze. LC 55-6554. 1955. Houghton Mifflin.

Father William: A Comedy of Father and Son. Donald Ogden Stewart. LC 29-9487. 1929. Harper & Brothers.

Father William, a Comedy of Father & Son. Donald Ogden Stewart. 202p. 1981. Repr. of 1929 ed. lib. bdg. 15.00 (ISBN 0-89987-784-2). Darby Bks.

Fathering. Nicholas Delbanco. LC 73-10105. 1973. 7.95 (ISBN 0-688-00213-7). Morrow.

Fatherland, Farewell! Gosta Larsson. LC 38-27132. Harcourt, Brace and Company.

Fathers. Herbert Gold. LC 66-12012. 1980. pap. 6.95 (ISBN 0-916870-26-X). Creative Arts Bk.

Fathers. Herbert Gold. 1971. pap. 0.95 o.p. (M1597, Crest). Fawcett World.

Fathers. Allen Tate. LC 60-3394. 1960. A. Swallow.

Fathers. Allen Tate. LC 38-277561. 1938. G. P. Putnam's Sons.

Fathers: A Novel in the Form of a Memoir. Herbert Gold. LC 66-12012. 1967. Random House.

Fathers and Children. Ivan Segeevich Turgenev & Hare Richard, Tr. LC 49-307449. (Rinehart editions, 17). 1948. Rinehart.

Fathers and Children: A Novel. Ivan Sergeevich Turgenev. LC 70-10320. (His Novels, v. 4). 1970. AMS Press.

Fathers and Children, and Rudin: Tr. from the Russian. Ivan Sergeevich Turgenev & Hare, Richard, Tr. LC 47-28682. 1947. Hutchinson International Authors.

Fathers and Dreamers. Harry Dallas Miller. LC 66-18616. 1966. Doubleday.

Fathers, and Other Fiction. Allen Tate. LC 77-22617. (Library of Southern civilization). 17.50. (ISBN 0-8071-0381-0). Louisiana State University Press.

Fathers and Sons. new ed. Theodore Edward Hook. LC 41-31107. G. Routledge and Sons.

Fathers and Sons. Ivan Sergeevich Turgenev. LC 58-13194.

Fathers and Sons. Ivan Sergeevich Turgenev. LC 50-12193. (Modern Library college editions, T38). 1950. Modern Library.

Fathers and Sons. Ivan Sergeevich Turgenev. LC 51-6234. (Harper's modern classics). 1951. Harper.

Fathers and Sons. Ivan Sergeevich Turgenev. Tr. by Rosemary Edmonds. LC 65-2787. (Penguin classics, L147). 1965. Penguin Books.

Fathers and Sons. Ivan Sergeevich Turgenev. 1975. (pbk.) 1.95 (ISBN 0-14-044147-6). Penguin Books.

Fathers and Sons. Ivan Sergeevich Turgenev. LC 60-12161. (Modern library of the world's best books 21). 1961. Modern Library.

Fathers and Sons. Ivan Sergeevich Turgenev. Tr. by Constance Garnett. Eichenberg, Fritz, 1901- Illus. LC 41-19317. 1941. The Heritage Press.

Fathers and Sons. Ivan Sergeevich Turgenev & Cores, Lucy Michaella, 1914- Ed. LC 42-7971. (On cover: Classics club library). 1942. Published for the Classics Club by W. J. Black.

Fathers and Sons. Ivan Sevgeevich Turgenev & Rosemary Edmonds. LC 76-375072. (Penguin classics; L147). 1975. 2.50 (ISBN 0-14-044147-6). Penguin.

Fathers and Sons. Ivan Sergieevich Turgenev. Tr. by Constance Garnett. LC 20-5235. (Half-title: The modern library of the world's best books). 1917. Boni and Liveright, Inc.

Fathers and Sons. Ivan Sergieevich Turgenev & Hogarth, C.J., Tr. (Half-title: Everyman's library, ed. by Ernest Rhys. Fiction. no. 742). 1921. J. M. Dent & Sons, Ltd.

Fathers and Sons. Ivan Sergieevich Turgenev & Hogarth, C. J., Tr. LC 36-58258. (Half-title: Everyman's library, ed. by Ernest Rhys.). 1934. J. M. Dent & Sons, Ltd.

Fathers & Sons-a Nest of the Gentry. Ivan Sergeevich Turgenev. 388p. 1974. 5.45 (ISBN 0-8285-1063-6, Pub. by Progress Pubs USSR). Imported Pubns.

Fathers & Sons: A Novel, 3 vols. in 2. Theodore Edward Hook. LC 79-8131. Repr. of 1842 ed. Set. 84.50 (ISBN 0-404-61904-5). AMS Pr.

Fathers and Sons: A Novel. Ivan Sergieevich Turgenev & Schuyler, Eugene, 1840-1890, Tr. LC 20-123516. 1867. Leypoldt & Holt.

Fathers and Sons: A Novel. Ivan Sergieevich Turgenev & Schuyler, Eugene, 1840-1890, Tr. LC 22-108363. (On cover: Leisure hour series). 1872. H. Holt and Company.

Fathers and Sons. The Author on the Novel, Contemporary Reactions, Essays in Criticism. Ivan Sergeevich Turgenev. Ed. by Ralph E. Matlaw. LC 66-11789. (Norton critical edition). 1966. Norton.

Fathers & Sons, Translated from the Russian. Ivan Sergeevich Turgenev. Tr. by Constance Garnett. Eichenberg, Fritz, 1901- Illus. LC 43-14367. (Heritage reprints). 1943. The Press of the Readers Club.

Fathers and Sons. With a New Foreword by Avrahm Yarmolinsky. Ivan Sergeevich Turgenev. LC 62-11021. (Classic Collier books, AS198V). 1962. Collier Books.

Father's Curse: A Historical Romance of the Time of Sir Walter Raleigh. Alphonse Maria Grussi. LC 31-11243. The Christopher Publishing House.

Father's Curse: And Other Stories. Honore De Balzac. Tr. by James Waring. 1898. J. M. Dent and Company.

Father's Day. William Goldman. LC 76-134568. 1970. Harcourt Brace Jovanovich.

Father's Day. Eugene C. Kennedy. 1982. pap. 3.75 (ISBN 0-671-43242-7). PB.

Father's Day: A Novel. Eugene C Kennedy. LC 80-2560. 1981. 13.95 (ISBN 0-385-15415-1). Doubleday.

Father's Day: A Novel of Power, Passion & Conscience. Eugene C. Kennedy. LC 80-2560. 504p. 1981. 14.95 o.p. (ISBN 0-385-15415-1). Doubleday.

Father's Days. Katherine Brady. 1981. pap. 3.25 (ISBN 0-440-12475-1). Dell.

Father's Generation Gap. Junius Willis Rogers. LC 70-163726. 1971. 4.00 (ISBN 0-8059-1591-5). Dorrance.

Father's Love. Jacques Chessex. LC 74-17654. 6.96 (ISBN 0-672-52068-0). Bobbs-Merrill.

Father's Love. Jacques Chessex. (Leisure Book). 1977. 1.25. Nordon Publications.

Father's Love. Joseph Francis Perez. LC 81-17522. 14.95 (ISBN 0-385-27200-6). Dial Press.

Fathers of Men. Ernest William Hornung. LC 12-5153. 1912. C. Scribner's Sons.

Fathers of Their People. Harold Webber Freeman. LC 32-26241. H. Holt and Company.

Fathomless. Aylward Edward Dingle. LC 27-11211. 1927. Henry Waterson Company.

Fathoms Deep. Elisabeth Stancy Payne. LC 23-9850. 1923. The Penn Publishing Company.

Fathoms Deep: By Michael Dawson. Michael Dawson. LC 43-16217. 1943. Sheridan House.

Fatima: A Dream of Passion. Abi S Jackman. LC 7-9477.

Fatima & the Seven Sorrows. 80p. 1.25 (ISBN 0-911988-08-4). AMI Pr.

Fatima: Or, Always Pick a Fool for Your Husband; Being the Strange Adventures of a Woman Who Was the Most Beautiful Creature, and Quite, Quite the Cleverest Creature Ever Was, and Knew It. Rowland Thomas. LC 13-20207. 1913. Little, Brown, and Company.

Fatkat. Jerry Marcus. 128p. 1981. pap. 1.75 (ISBN 0-523-49021-6). Pinnacle Bks.

Faucit of Balliol. Herman Charles Merivale. LC 30-12346. (Seaside library. v. 67. no. 1355). 1882. G. Munro.

Faulkner Reader. William Faulkner. (Modern Library Giants). 1959. 5.95 o.p. (ISBN 0-394-60782-1, G82). Modern Lib.

Faulkner Reader: Selections from the Works of William Faulkner. William Faulkner. LC 54-5959. 1954. Random House.

Faulkner Reader: Selections from the Works of William Faulkner. William Faulkner. LC 59-5911. (Modern library of the world's best books. A Modern library giant, G82). 1959. Modern Library.

Faulkner's As I Lay Dying. rev. and enl. ed. Andre Bleikasten. LC 72-79904. (Midland book, MB-159). 1973. 2.95 (ISBN 0-253-32150-6) (ISBN 0-253-32150-6). Indiana University Press.

Faulkner's Folly. Carolyn Wells. LC 17-285993. George H. Doran Company.

Faulkner's Folly. Carolyn Wells. LC 20-115035. 1919. Grosset & Dunlap.

Faulkner's Light in August. rev. and enl. ed. translated by gillian e. cook with the collaboration of the author. ed. Francois Pitavy. LC 72-79909. (Midland book, MB-166). 1973. (pbk) 2.25 (ISBN 0-253-32153-0) (ISBN 0-253-32153-0). Indiana University Press.

Fault Lines. James Carrol. 1982. pap. 3.50 (ISBN 0-440-12436-0). Dell.

Fault Lines. James Carroll. LC 80-36756. 11.95 (ISBN 0-316-13012-5). Little, Brown.

Fault Lines. Alvah Reida. LC 76-183090. 1972. 7.95 (ISBN 0-529-04557-5). World Pub.

Fault Lines. Kate Wilhelm. LC 76-26282. 1977. 8.95i o.p. (ISBN 0-06-014656-7, HarpT). Har-Row.

Fault Lines. Kate Wilhelm. 176p. (Orig.). 1981. pap. 2.25 (ISBN 0-671-42425-4, Timescape). PB.

Fault Lines: a Novel: Kate Wilhelm. Kate Wilhelm. (Kangaroo Book). 1978. 1.95. Pocket Books.

Fault Lines: A Novel. Kate Wilhelm. LC 76-26282. 9.95 (ISBN 0-06-014656-7). Harper & Row.

Fault of Angels. Paul Horgan. LC 33-22307. 1933. Harper & Brothers.

Fault of One. Effie Adelaide Maria Albanesi. LC 7-12330. (On cover: Lippincott's select novels, no 189). 1897. J. B. Lippincott Company.

Fault of the Apple. Frederic Wakeman. 1961. 4.95 o.p. (ISBN 0-671-24750-6). S&S.

Faultline: A Novel. Sheila Ortiz Taylor. LC 81-16922. 1982. 6.95 (ISBN 0-930044-24-X). Naiad Press.

Faun: And Other Poems. Genevieve Browne Farnell-Bond. LC 13-24132. 1913. 1.00. Sherman, French & Company.

Faun & the Naughtiest Pig. Anne Townsend. 1974. pap. 1.15 (ISBN 0-85363-093-3). OMF Bks.

Fauna. Denise Robins. 1978. pap. 2.25 (ISBN 0-380-37580-X, 37580). Avon.

Faust. Robert Nye. LC 80-39696. 1981. 12.95 (ISBN 0-399-12606-6). Putnam.

Faust: A Tragedy. Johann Wolfgang Von Goethe. Tr. by Taylor, Bayard. LC 6-39766. 1906. Houghton, Mifflin and Company.

Faustin. Edmond De Goncourt. Tr. by G. Monkshood from Fr. 1976. Repr. of 1906 ed. 19.50x (ISBN 0-86527-267-0). Fertig.

Faustina. A Novel. Translated from the German of Ida, Countess Hahn-Hahn. Ida Marie Louise Sophie Friedrika Gustava Hahn-Hahn. LC 2-8393. 1872. G. W. Carleton & Co.

Faustine: A Novel. Eliza M. J. Humphreys. (On cover: Lovell's library, no. 1158). 1888. J. W. Lovell Company.

Fausto and Anna. Carlo Cassola. LC 75-3795. 1975. 15.25 (ISBN 0-8371-8074-0). Greenwood Press.

Fausto and Anna. Translated by Isabel Quigly. Carlo Cassola. LC 60-6793. 1960. Pantheon Books.

Fausto's Keyhole. 1st Ed. Jean Arnaldi. LC 62-9407. 1962. Atheneum.

Faustrecht. Hans Hellmut Kirst. 1971. Repr. 6.95 o.p. Coward.

Faustula N. A. D. 340. Francis Browning Drew Bickerstaffe-Drew. LC 12-25462. 1912. Benziger Brothers.

Favor. Nicholas Guild. LC 80-21817. 12.95 (ISBN 0-312-28512-4). St. Martin's Press.

Favor of Kings. Mary Hastings Bradley. 1912. 1.30. D. Appleton and Company.

Favor the Runner. Jay Richard Kennedy. LC 63-8975. bds., 5.95. World.

Favor the Runner. Jay Richard Kennedy. (Signet bk., W5315). 1973. 1.50. New Amer. Lib.

Favorite Doctor Stories: Fact and Fiction. Ed. by A. K. Adams. LC 63-8496. 1963. Dodd, Mead.

Favorite Dog Stories: Illustrated by Robert Doremus. Ed. by Marguerite Bloch. LC 50-6624. 1950. World Pub. Co.

Favorite Game. Leonard Cohen. 1963. 4.50 o.p. (ISBN 0-670-31085-9). Viking Pr.

Favorite Game: A Novel. Leonard Cohen. LC 63-17072. 1963. Viking Press.

Favorite Huey Long Stories. Hugh M. Blain. 1972. 3.00; pap. 1.00. Claitors.

Favorite Novels of H. Rider Haggard. One Volume Edition. Henry Rider Haggard. LC 33-33954. 1933. Blue Ribbon Books, Inc.

Favorite Short Stories. Ed. by Henry Gilfond. LC 67-26131. 1967. Walker.

Favorite Short Stories. Ed. by Lewis George Sterner. LC 58-929. 1958. Globe Book Co.

Favorite Short Stories in Large Print. large print ed. Virginia S Reiser. LC 82-18520. 1982. 17.95 (ISBN 0-8161-3434-0). G.K. Hall.

Favorite Short Stories of H. G. Wells. Herbert George Wells. LC 75-33090. 1975. 9.95 (ISBN 0-89190-443-3). American Reprint Co.

Favorite Short Stories of H. G. Wells. Herbert George Wells. 1937. Doubleday, Doran & Company, Inc.

Favorite Short Stories of W. Somerset Maugham. William Somerset Maugham. LC 37-11011. 1937. Doubleday, Doran & Company, Inc.

Favorite Short Stories of W. Somerset Maugham. William Somerset Maugham. LC 40-9077. The Book League of America, Inc.

Favorite Sister. Sheila Bishop. 192p. 1981. pap. 1.95 (ISBN 0-441-22861-5). Ace Bks.

Favorite Sleuths: Ellery Queen, Doctor Alcazar, Lord Peter Wimsey, Nero Wolfe, Miss Marple, The Saint, Mr. Campion, Tommy Hambledon, Perry Mason, Mr. Fortune. Illus. by Harvey Kidder. Ed. by John Ernst. LC 65-17268. 1965. 3.95. Doubleday.

Favorite Son. Bethany Strong. Date not set. price not set. Parable Pr.

Favorite Stories by Famous Writers. Burton, Harry Payne, 1886 & Cosmopolitan. LC 32-20304. 1832.

Favorite Stories of Hypnotism. Commentaries by Milton V. Kline. Ed. by Don Ward. Milton V Kline. LC 65-156364. 4.50. Dodd.

Favorite Tales from Shakespeare: By Charles and Mary Lamb. Edited for Modern Readers by Morris Schreiber. Illustrated by Donald Lynch. Charles Lamb & Shakespeare. William. Paraphrases, Tales, Etc. LC 56-14294. Grosset & Dunlap.

Favorite Trial Stories: Fact and Fiction, Compiled by A. K. Adams. A K Adams. LC 66-12968. 1966. Dodd, Mead.

Favorite Wife. Helen Marion Edginton. LC 36-15377. The Macaulay Company.

Favorites of Fate: A Novel. Malcolm MacDonald. LC 54-12474. 1954. Exposition Press.

Favourite Short Stories. Herbert George Wells. 1976. Repr. of 1937 ed. lib. bdg. 20.80x (ISBN 0-89190-443-3). Am Repr-Rivercity Pr.

Favourite Sories from Persia. Cynthia Helms. (Favourite Stories Ser.). (Illus.). ix, 61p. (Orig.). 1982. pap. text ed. 2.00x (ISBN 9971-64-041-4). Heinemann Ed.

Favourite Stories. Henry Archibald Hertzberg Lawson & Walter W Stone. LC 77-352435. (Illus.). (ISBN 0-17-005036-X). Nelson.

Favourite Stories From Taiwan. Leon Comber & Charles Shuttleworth. (Orig.). 1975. pap. text ed. 2.00x (00317). Heinemann Ed.

Favourite. Translated from the French by Herma Briffault. Francoise Mallet-Joris. 1962. Farrar, Straus and Cudahy.

Favours: A Novel by Bernice Rubens. Bernice Rubens. LC 78-32086. 8.95 (ISBN 0-671-40080-0). Summit Books.

Fawn: A Novel. Robert Newton Peck. LC 74-19078. 1975. 6.95 (ISBN 0-316-69652-8). Little, Brown.

Fawn of Spring-Vale, the Clarionet, & Other Tales, 3 vols. William Carleton. Ed. by Robert L. Wolff. (Ireland Nineteenth Century Fiction - Ser. Two: Vol. 38). 1068p. 1979. Set. lib. bdg. 96.00 (ISBN 0-8240-3487-2). Garland Pub.

Fawn of the Pale Faces: Or, Two Centuries Ago. John Pierce Brace. LC 6-15214. 1853. D. Appleton & Company.

Fax. Middleton Kiefer. LC 58-9872. 1958. Random House.

Fay. Edwin Baird. LC 23-14563. E. J. Clode.

Fay Banning: By Will J. Bloomfield. A Novel. Will J Bloomfield. LC 6-14210. 1893. Dibble Publishing Company.

Faye's Folly. Elizabeth Frances Corbett. LC 41-159155. 1941. D. Appleton-Century Company, Incorporated.

Fay's Circus. Katharine Susannah Prichard. LC 31-26739. W. W. Norton & Company, Inc.

FBI Story. Mildred Gordon & Gordon Gordon. LC 50-9519. 1950. Published for the Crime Club by Doubleday.

Fear. Thomas Keneally. 12.50x o.p. (LTB). Soccer.

Fear Among the Shadows. Louise Hoffman. (Ace Gothic). 1974. (pbk.) 0.95. Ace Books.

Fear & Loathing in Las Vegas. Hunter S. Thompson. 1975. pap. 2.95 (ISBN 0-445-08431-6). Popular Lib.

Fear & Loathing in las Vegas. Hunter S. Thompson. 1972. 5.95 o.p. (ISBN 0-394-46435-4). Random.

Fear and Loathing in Las Vegas: A Savage Journey to the Heart of the American Dream. Hunter S Thompson. 1973. (pbk) 1.50. Popular Library.

Fear & Mrs. Crusoe. Martha Groves McKelvie. (Illus.). 1962. 3.00 o.p. (ISBN 0-8059-0187-6). Dorrance.

Fear and Tenderness. Eleanor Glaze. LC 72-89693. 1973. 8.95 (ISBN 0-672-51777-9). Bobbs-Merrill.

Fear and Tenderness. Eleanor Glaze. (Fawcett crest book). 1974. (pbk.) 1.50. Fawcett.

Fear and the Guilt: By Wilene Shaw Pseud. Virginia M Harrison. LC 55-189923. (Ace books, S-80). 1954. Ace Books.

Fear and Trembling; Shivery Stories. Ed. by Alfred Hitchcock. LC 49-5664. (Dell book, 264). 1948. Dell Pub. Co.

Fear at My Heart. Mary Kathleen Harris. LC 51-3419. 1951. Sheed and Ward.

Fear at My Heart. Mary Kathleen Harris. LC 51-6942. 1951. Sheed and Ward.

Fear by Night. Patricia Wentworth. LC 34-2145. J. B. Lippincott Company.

Fear Came First. Vera Kelsey. LC 45-2948. 1945. Pub. for the Crime Club by Doubleday, Doran and Company, Inc.

Fear Comes to Chalfont. Freeman Wills Crofts. LC 42-194287. 1942. Dodd, Mead & Company.

Fear Dealers. Robin Cade. (O.s.i.). 1974. 6.95 o.s.i. (ISBN 0-671-21710-0). S&S.

Fear Dealers. Christopher Nicole. LC 73-14092. (Simon and Schuster novel of suspense). 1974. 6.95 (ISBN 0-671-21710-0). Simon and Schuster.

Fear Haunts the Summer. Gayle G Roper. LC 77-163445. 1971. 2.95. Moody Press.

Fear in a Handful of Dust. John Ives. LC 77-24296. 8.95 (ISBN 0-525-10420-8). Dutton.

Fear in a Handful of Dust. John Ives. (Jove Book). 1979. 1.95 (ISBN 0-515-04845-3). Jove Publications.

Fear in Borzano. Willa Jay. (Orig.). pap. 0.60 o.p. (73-613). Lancer.

Fear Is the Hunter: The Terrified Society. Hildegarde Tolman Teilhet. LC 51-33992. (Permabooks, P 116). 1951. Permabooks.

Fear Is the Key. Alistair MacLean. LC 75-31573. 1975. 9.95 (ISBN 0-89190-171-X). American Reprint Co.

Fear Is the Key. 1st Ed. Alistair MacLean. LC 61-125533. 1961. Doubleday.

Fear Is the Parent: A Novel. Mathilde Ferro. LC 48-517835. 1948. Doubleday.

Fear Is the Same: By Carter Dickson Pseud. John Dickson Carr. LC 56-5393. 1956. Morrow.

Fear Island. J. H. Rhodes. 1981. pap. 6.95 (Avalon). Bouregy.

Fear Itself: A Novel. Stefan Kanfer. LC 81-5872. 12.95 (ISBN 0-399-12607-4). Putnam.

Fear Makers. Wilfrid Schilling. LC 60-947451. 1960. Doubleday.

Fear Makers. Darwin Le Ora Teilhet. LC 45-6549. 1945. D. Appleton-Century Company Incorporated.

Fear No Evil. Alice Brennan. 256p. 1973. pap. 0.95 o.s.i. (75-467). Lancer.

Fear No Evil. John Gordon Davis. LC 81-20874. (Illus.). 12.95 (ISBN 0-02-529920-4). Macmillan.

Fear No Evil. John Leach. 3.75 o.p. Vantage.

Fear No Evil. Hugh Massingham. LC 49-10602. 1949. Random House.

Fear No More. Hester W. Chapman. LC 68-57445. 1968. 6.95. Reynal.

Fear No More. Leslie Edgley. LC 46-6855. 1946. Simon and Schuster.

Fear Not, My Son: A Novel. 1st Ed. Jack Piner. LC 55-12031. 1955. Pageant Press.

Fear of a Stranger. Elinore Denniston. (Ace gothic). 1973. (pbk.) 0.95. Ace.

Fear of a Stranger. Elinore Denniston. LC 67-12289. (Red badge mystery). 1967. Dodd, Mead.

Fear of a Stranger. Rae Foley. (Red Badge Mystery Ser). 1967. 3.95 o.p. Dodd.

Fear of Fear. Florence Ryerson & Clements, Colin Campbell, 1894- Joint Author. LC 31-21757. 1931. D. Appleton and Company.

Fear of Flying. Erica Jong. 1975. pap. 4.95 (ISBN 0-452-25106-0, Z5106, Plume). NAL.

Fear of Flying. Erica Jong. 1974. pap. 3.50 (AE1329, Sig). NAL.

Fear of Flying: A Novel. Erica Jong. LC 73-3697. 1973. 6.95 (ISBN 0-03-010731-8). Holt, Rinehart and Winston.

Fear of God. Derry Quinn. LC 78-19388. 1979. 7.95 (ISBN 0-312-28517-5). St. Martin's Press.

Fear of Heights. Virginia Coffman. (Orig.). 1973. pap. 0.95 o.s.i. (75-438). Lancer.

Fear of Love. Carole Mortimer. (Harlequin Presents Ser.). 192p. 1980. pap. 1.50 (ISBN 0-373-10377-8). Harlequin Bks.

Fear of the World: Or, Living for Appearances. Henry Mayhew & Mayhew, Augustus Septimus, 1826-1875, Joint Author. LC 43-45738. 1850. Harper & Brothers.

Fear Rides the Fog. Elinore Cowan Stone. LC 37-1371. 1937. D. Appleton-Century Company, Incorporated.

Fear Round About. George Bellairs. LC 80-54821. 1981. 9.95 (ISBN 0-8027-5441-4). Walker.

Fear Sign. Margery Allingham. 192p. Repr. of 1933 ed. lib. bdg. 12.05x (ISBN 0-89190-190-6). Am Repr-Rivercity Pr.

Fear Sign. Margery Allingham. 1976. pap. 1.50 (ISBN 0-532-12419-7). Woodhill.

Fear Sign. Margery Allingham. 1971. pap. 0.75 o.p. (75-422). Manor Bks.

Fear Sign. 2nd ed. Margery Allingham. 192p. 1974. pap. 0.95 o.p. (532-95308-095). Manor Bks.

Fear Stalks the Bayou. large print ed. Juanita Coulson. LC 76-20657. (Zodiac gothic: Aries). 1976. 8.95 (ISBN 0-89340-009-2). J. Curley.

Fear Stalks the Bayou: An Astrological Gothic Novel, Aries. Juanita Coulson. LC 75-44258. 1976. 1.25 (ISBN 0-345-24909-7). Ballantine Books.

Fear Stalks the Village. Ethel Lina White. LC 42-36220. 1942. Harper & Brothers.

Fear the Light. Morna Doris MacTaggart Brown. 1974. (pbk.) 0.75. Dell.

Fear the Light: By E. X. Ferrars Pseud. 1st Ed. Morna Doris MacTaggart Brown. LC 60-949400. 1960. Published for the Crime Club by Doubleday.

Fear to Tread. Michael Francis Gilbert. LC 53-8749. 1953. Harper.

Fear to Tread. Michael Francis Gilbert. LC 80-20661. 1981. 12.95 (ISBN 0-89340-290-7). J. Curley.

Fear Today-Gone Tomorrow. Robert Bloch. (O.s.i.). 160p. 1975. pap. 1.25 o.s.i. (AQ1469, Award). Univ Pub & Dist.

Fear Waits on Cypress Road. Ruth H Wissmann. LC 75-14850. 1975. 5.95 (ISBN 0-385-11278-5). Doubleday.

Fear Was the Pursuer: An Engrossing Account of a Flight to Freedom Across the Deadly Gobic Desert. Goldie M Down. LC 80-21915. (Illus.). 4.95. Review and Herald Pub. Association.

Fear Without Childbirth. Irene Kampen. LC 77-19272. 8.95 (ISBN 0-397-01277-2). Lippincott.

Feared and the Fearless. Guthrie Wilson. LC 53-9046. 1953. Putnam.

Fearful Joy: A Novel. Joyce Cary. LC 50-14742. Harper.

Fearful Joy, a Novel. Joyce Cary. LC 73-428. 343p. 1973. Repr. of 1949 ed. lib. bdg. 17.50x (ISBN 0-8371-6777-9, CAFJ). Greenwood.

Fearful Passage. Henry C Branson. LC 45-103634. 1945. Simon and Schuster.

Fearful Pleasures. Alfred Edgar Coppard. LC 52-32076. 1951. P. Nevill.

Fearful Pleasures. Alfred Edgar Coppard. LC 46-227781. 1946. Arkham House.

Fearful Responsibility. William Dean Howells. LC 72-104492. 1970. (ISBN 0-8398-0797-X). Literature House.

Fearful Responsibility: And Other Stories. William Dean Howells. LC 73-131750. 1970. (ISBN 0-403-00637-6). Scholarly Press.

Fearful Responsibility: And Other Stories. William Dean Howells. LC 79-98767. 1970. (ISBN 0-8371-2820-X). Greenwood Press.

Fearful Responsibility, and Other Stories. William Dean Howells. LC 7-5777. 1881. J. R. Osgood and Company.

Fearful Responsibility, and Other Stories. William Dean Howells. LC 42-26171. Ticknor and Company.

Fearful Responsibility, and Other Stories. William Dean Howells. LC 16-756371. Houghton, Mifflin and Company.

Fearful Symmetry. David E. Fisher. LC 73-9025. 1974. 6.95 (ISBN 0-385-08459-5). Doubleday.

Fearful Void. Geoffrey Moorhouse. LC 73-19977. (Illus.). 1974. 10.00 o.p. (ISBN 0-397-01019-2). Lippincott.

Fearful Way to Die. Jeannette Covert Nolan. LC 56-13789. (Her A Lace White mystery). 1956. Washburn.

Fearless Investigator: A Novel. Frances U. Eaton. LC 6-368118. 1896. A. C. McClurg and Company.

Fearless Spectator. Charles McCabe. LC 78-133452. 1970. 6.95 o.p. (ISBN 0-87701-006-4). Chronicle Bks.

Fearns of Audley Street. Audrey Blanshard. 224p. 1980. pap. 1.75 (ISBN 0-449-50035-7, Coventry). Fawcett.

Fears. Charles L. Grant. 288p. (Orig.). 1983. pap. 2.95 (ISBN 0-425-06066-7). Berkley Pub.

Fearsome Island: Being a Modern Rendering of the Narrative of One Silas Fordred, Master Mariner of Hythe... Albert Kinross. 1896. H. S. Stone & Company.

Fearsome Riddle. Max Ehrmann. LC 1-23018. The Bowen-Merrill Company.

Feast. Margaret Kennedy. LC 50-5698. 1950. Rinehart.

Feast for Spiders. Kenneth L Evans. LC 78-22458. 9.95 (ISBN 0-690-01805-3). Crowell.

Feast for the Forgiven. Vurrell Yentzen. LC 54-7694. 1954. Appleton-Century-Crofts.

Feast in the Morning. Hugh Preston. LC 76-28053. 1977. 8.95 (ISBN 0-312-28525-6). St. Martin's Press.

Feast of All Saints. Anne Rice. LC 79-16680. 13.95 (ISBN 0-671-24755-7). Simon and Schuster.

Feast of Ashes. Sally Rosenbluth. LC 80-13195. 1980. 12.95 (ISBN 0-689-11071-5). Atheneum.

Feast of Fat Things. Hugh Zachary. LC 67-31272. 1968. 5.95 (ISBN 0-911676-01-5). Harris-Wolfe.

Feast of Fear. Ed. by Vic Ghidalia. 1977. pap. 1.50 (ISBN 0-532-15245-X). Woodhill.

Feast of Freedom. Leonard Patrick O'Connor Wibberley. LC 64-17615. 1964. Morrow.

Feast of Jackals. Robert Charles Sherman. 1.95 (ISBN 0-8439-0534-4). Leisure Books.

Feast of July. Herbert Ernest Bates. LC 54-8288. 1954. Little, Brown.

Feast of Leviathan: Tales of Adventure, Faith, and Love from Jewish Literature. Ed. by Leo Walder Schwarz. LC 56-7480. 1956. Rinehart.

Feast of Lupercal. Brian Moore. LC 57-7837. (Illus.). 1957. Little, Brown.

Feast of Passions. Carol Norris. 1980. 2.50 (ISBN 0-671-83332-4). Pocket Books.

Feast of Pikes. Bjrn Robinson Rye. LC 75-29963. 7.95 (ISBN 0-672-52142-3). Bobbs-Merrill.

Feast of Pikes: A Novel. Robinson Rye. LC 75-29963. 224p. 1976. 7.95 o.p. (ISBN 0-672-52142-3). Bobbs.

Feast of Reason. Dorothy Walworth. LC 41-312557. Farrar & Rinehart, Inc.

Feast of Saint Barnabas. Jesse Hill Ford. LC 69-12630. 1969. 6.95. Little, Brown.

Feast of St. Dionysus: Five Science Fiction Stories. Robert Silverberg. LC 74-11078. 1975. (ISBN 0-684-13998-7). Scribner.

Feast of St. Dionysus: Five Science Fiction Stories, with a New Introduction by the Author. Robert Silverberg. 1979. 1.95 (ISBN 0-425-04174-3). Berkley Pub. Co.

Feast of Snakes. Harry Crews. LC 76-8206. 1976. 7.95 (ISBN 0-689-10729-3). Atheneum.

Feast of the Jesters. Manuel Komroff. LC 47-11414. 1947. Farrar, Straus.

Feast of the Midnight Sun: A Story of the Canadian Arctic. Jack David Ford. LC 58-12097. 1958. Greenwich Book Publishers.

Feast of Vultures. Peter G. Scott. (Orig.). 1983. pap. 2.95. Pinnacle Bks.

Feast of Vultures. Charles Weissner. (Orig.). 1981. pap. 2.50 (ISBN 0-505-51719-1). Tower Bks.

Feast Unknown. Philip Jose Farmer. LC 79-88843. 288p. 1980. pap. 2.50d (ISBN 0-87216-951-0). Playboy Pbks.

Feast Unknown. Philip Jose Farmer. pap. 1.95 o.p. (0121). Essex Hse.

Feasting Dead. John Metcalfe. LC 54-9265. 1954. Arkham House.

Feather. Ruby Mildred Ayres. LC 37-16232. 1937. The Sun Dial Press.

Feather Bed Jane. Helen Mary Elizabeth Clamp. LC 32-4634. 1932. L. MacVeagh, Dial Press, Inc.

Feather Castles. Patricia Veryan. LC 81-21542. 13.95 (ISBN 0-312-28532-9). St. Martin's Press.

Feather Cloak Murders: The Second Adventure of the Baron Von Kaz. Darwin L. Teilhet & Teilhet, Mrs. Hildegarde (Tolman) Joint Author. LC 36-10526. 1936. Pub. for the Crime Club, Inc., by Doubleday, Doran & Co., Inc.

Feather Cloak Murders: The Second Adventure of the Baron Von Kaz. Darwin L. Teilhet & Teilhet, Mrs. Hildegarde (Tolman) LC 36-362269. 1936. The Sun Dial Press.

Feather in Her Cap. Barbara Worsley-Gough. LC 36-339832. G. P. Putnam's Sons.

Feather in Her Hat. Ida Alexa Ross Wylie. LC 34-8135. 1934. Doubleday, Doran & Company, Inc.

Feather in the Wind. Robert MacLeod. 1976. 1.50 (ISBN 0-671-80553-3). Pocket Books.

Feather in the Wind: A Novel. Madelyn Galbraith. 1952. Herald House.

Feather Merchants. Max Shulman. LC 44-396562. 1944. Doubleday, Doran and Co., Inc.

Feather of Doubt. Cecile Gilmore. LC 45-2493. 1945. S. Curl, Inc.

Feather of the Dawn. Sarojini Naidu. 3.00x o.p. (ISBN 0-210-33855-5). Asia.

Feather Your Nest. Gladys Greenaway. 1973. (pbk.) 0.75. Ace.

Feathered Nest. Margaret Leech. LC 28-242671. 1928. H. Liveright.

Feathered Serpent. Edgar Wallace. LC 29-172009. 1928. Pub. for The Crime Club, Inc., by Doubleday, Doran & Company, Inc.

Feathered Shaft, Wildfire Quest: The Flower on the Rock. Jane Arbor. (Harlequin Romances Ser.). 576p. 1982. pap. 3.50 (ISBN 0-373-20056-0). Harlequin Bks.

Feathered Sombrero. Norman A. Fox. LC 48-7430. (Silver star westerns). 1948. Dodd, Mead.

Feathered Water. Edith Austin Holton. LC 37-15782. The Penn Publishing Company.

Featherlys: A Virginia Tapestry. Virginia Cruse Watson. LC 36-14623. 1936. E. P. Dutton & Co., Inc.

Feathers for the Toff. John Creasey. LC 77-103385. 1970. 4.50. Walker.
Feathers in the Fire. Catherine Cookson. 288p. 1981. pap. 2.25 (ISBN 0-553-13936-3). Bantam.
Feathers in the Fire. Catherine Cookson. LC 72-173202. 6.95 o.p. (ISBN 0-672-51591-1). Bobbs.
Feathers in the Wind, Bk. 1. Wilma Ross Westphal. (Orion Ser.). 160p. 1981. pap. write for info. (ISBN 0-8127-0309-X). Review & Herald.
Feathers in the Wind, Bk. 2. Wilma Westphal & Chester Westphal. (Orion Ser.). 160p. 1981. pap. write for info. (ISBN 0-8127-0322-7). Review & Herald.
Feathers Left Around. Carolyn Wells. LC 23-5365. 1923. J. B. Lippincott Company.
Feathers of Death. Simon Raven. 1960. 3.75 o.p. (ISBN 0-671-24950-9). S&S.
Feather's Weight: A Story of Mystery. Amarala Arter Martin. LC 99-3812. F. T. Neely.
Feather's Weight: A Story of Mystery. Amarala Arter Martin. LC 1-30343. The Abbey Press.
Feats on the Fiord. new ed. Harriet Martineau. LC 7-17935. 1865. Routledge, Warne, and Routledge.
Feats on the Fiord. Harriet Martineau. (Half-title: Tales for children from many lands, ed. by F. C. Tilney). 1916. J. M. Dent & Sons, Limited.
Feats on the Fiord. Harriet Martineau. LC 24-28115. (The Macmillan children's classics). 1924. The Macmillan Company.
Feats on the Fjord. Harriet Martineau. LC 7-25841. 1894. J. Knight Company.
Feats on the Fjord: And Merdhin. Harriet Martineau. (Half-title: Everyman's library, ed. by Ernest Rhys. For young people no. 429). 1910. J. M. Dent & Sons, Ltd.
Featured on Broadway. Ann Knox. LC 30-24841. 2.50. The Century Co.
Featuring the Saint. Leslie Charteris. 1980. pap. 1.95 (ISBN 0-441-23155-1, Pub. by Charter Bks). Ace Bks.
Featuring the Saint. Leslie Charteris. 192p. 1973. Repr. of 1931 ed. 5.95 o.s.i. (ISBN 0-85617-993-0). White Lion Pubs.
Febechi & Group in Cave Adventure. Anezi N. Okoro. 82p. 1971. pap. 1.00 o.p. (ISBN 0-911860-20-7). Chatham Bkseller.
February Hill. Victoria Lincoln. LC 34-34751. Farrar & Rinehart, Incorporated.
February Hill. Victoria Lincoln. LC 39-7932. 1938. Modern Age Books, Inc.
February Plan. James Hall Roberts. 1971. pap. 0.95 o.p. (M1590, Crest). Fawcett World.
February Plan: A Novel. James Hall Roberts. LC 67-11634. 1967. Morrow.
Fecondite see Quatre Evangiles.
Fed up. James Owen Hannay. LC 31-27223. The Bobs-Merrill Company.
Feder; or the Moneyed Husband. Marie Henri Beyle. Tr. by H. R. Edwards. 7.95 (ISBN 0-85036-091-9). Dufour.
Federal Bullets: A Mystery Story. George Fielding Eliot. LC 37-2460. The William Caslon Company, Inc.
Federal Judge: A Novel. Charles Keeler Lush. 1897. Houghton, Mifflin and Company.
Federal Triangle. Hardee Mumms. LC 77-22831. 8.95 (ISBN 0-525-10425-9). Dutton.
Federati of Italy: A Romance of Caucasian Captivity. George Leighton Ditson. LC 6-33873. 1871. W. White and Company.
Federation. H. Beam Piper. LC 81-147315. 5.95 (ISBN 0-441-23188-8). Ace Books.
Federigo: Or, The Power of Love. 1st Ed. Howard Nemerov. LC 54-11120. 1954. Little, Brown.
Fedor. Laura Daintrey. 1889. The Empire City Publishing Co.; Etc., Etc.
Fedora. Founded on the Famous Play of the Same Name. John Russell Coryell & Sardou, Victorien. (On cover: Sea and shore series, no. 17). Street & Smith.
Fedora: Or, The Tragedy in the Rue De la Paix. Adolphe Belot. Tr. by H., A. D. LC 6-11686. 1883. Rand, McNally & Co.
Feed My Sheep. Mildred Mansfield. LC 35-19276. Armenia Press, Inc.
Feed Them Thrice. Lorol E. Toy. 106p. 1956. 3.00 o.s.i. (ISBN 0-910348-02-2). Channel Pub.
Feel Free. David R. Slavitt. LC 68-10040. 1968. Delacorte Press.
Feel-It Book. Charles Hurch. pap. 1.95 o.s.i. (OPS-26). Olympia.
Feelers. Mitchell Sisskind. 192p. (Orig.). 1981. pap. 2.25 (ISBN 0-523-41527-3). Pinnacle Bks.
Feelgood; a Trip in Time and Out. Peter De Lissovoy. LC 69-15020. 1970. 6.95. Houghton Mifflin.
Feeling It. L. H Whittemore. LC 72-129656. 1971. 5.95. Morrow.
Feet in Chains. Kate Roberts. Tr. by Idwal Walters & John I. Jones. 1977. 3.50 (ISBN 0-89733-005-6). Academy Chi Ltd.
Feet of Clay. with illustrations by h. r. ballinger. ed. Margaretta Muhlenberg Perkins Tuttle. LC 23-126705. 1923. Little, Brown, and Company.
Feet of Clay: A Novel. Ellen Martin. LC 7-24376. 1882. Brown & Derby.
Feet of Love. Anne Reeve Aldrich. LC 6-497. 1890. Worthington Co.
Feet of the Years. John Dallison Hyde. LC 10-28798. 1910. 1.25. The Metropolitan Press.
Feet Upon the Mountains and Uncertain Star. 8th Thousand. Isabel Constance Clarke. LC 35-4457. 1934. Longmans, Green & Co.
Felding Castle. 1st American Ed. Edith De Born. LC 59-5428. 1959. Knopf.
Feleen Brand. Henry Allen. LC 62-20936. (Bantam books). 1962. Bantam Books.
Felembe: A Novel. 1st Ed. Jens Peter Mouritz Larsen. LC 57-95927. 1957. Muhlenberg Press.
Felembe, a Novel. 1st Ed. Jens Peter Mouritz Larsen. LC 57-9592. 1957. Muhlenberg Press.
Felice. Davis-Gardner, Angela. LC 81-40234. 13.00 (ISBN 0-394-52009-2). Random House.
Felice. John Luther Long. LC 8-28990. 1908. Moffat, Yard & Company.
Felice Constant: Or, The Master Passion, a Romance. William Cyrus Sprague. LC 4-10849. 1904. F. A. Stokes Company.
Felicia. Leonora Blythe. 1.75 (ISBN 0-449-23754-0). Fawcett Crest.
Felicia. George Alec Effinger. LC 76-14933. 8.95 (ISBN 0-399-11792-X). Berkley Pub. Corp.: Distributed by Putnam.
Felicia. George Alec Effinger. (Berkley Medallion Book). 1978. 1.75 (ISBN 0-425-03654-5). Berkley Pub. Corp.
Felicia. Elizabeth Mayhew. 1974. (pbk.) 0.95 (ISBN 0-671-77770-X). Pocket Books.
Felicia: A Novel. Fanny Noailles Dickinson Murfee. LC 7-31842. 1891. Houghton, Mifflin and Company.
Felicia to Charlotte. Mary Mitchell Collyer. LC 74-16308. (Flowering of the Novel). 1974. (ISBN 0-8240-1112-0). Garland Pub.
Feliciana. Stark Young. LC 35-12198. 1935. C. Scribner's Sons.
Felicidad: The Romantic Adventures of an Enthusiastic Young Pessimist. Rowland Thomas. LC 14-6192. 1914. Little, Brown, and Company.
Felicita. Robin Edgerton Spencer. LC 37-22975. The Bobbs-Merrill Company.
Felicitas: A Romance. Felix Ludwig Sophus Dahn. Tr. by Safford, Mary Joanna. LC 3-8557. 1903. A. C. McClurg & Co.
Felicitas: From the German of Felix Dahn. Felix Ludwig Sophus Dahn. Tr. by Lansdale, Mary Gowen. 1903. The Neale Publishing Company.
Felicity Crofton. Marguerite Bryant. LC 16-1395. 1916. Duffield & Company.
Felicity: The Making of a Comedienne. Clara Elizabeth Laughlin. 1907. C. Scribner's Sons.
Felix: A Novel. Robert Smythe Hichens. LC 3-13017. 1903. F. A. Stokes Company.
Felix and Anne: A Novel. Raymond William Postgate. LC 33-2936. 1933. The Vanguard Press.
Felix Factor: A Novel. Richard Stiller. LC 68-9085. 1968. 5.95. Crown Publishers.
Felix Holt... George Eliot. LC 26-26894. (Half-title: The writings of George Eliot. Riverside ed. vol. x-xi) $2.00). Houghton Mifflin Company.
Felix Holt, the Radical. George Eliot. LC 70-24248. (Norton library, N517). 1970. 1.85 (ISBN 0-393-00517-8). Norton.
Felix Holt, the Radical. George Eliot. LC 73-159199. (Penguin English library). (Illus.). 1972. 0.50 (ISBN 0-14-043084-9). Penguin.
Felix Holt, the Radical. George Eliot. LC 6-41700. 1866. Harper & Brothers.
Felix Holt, the Radical. George Eliot. (On cover: Seaside library. Pocket ed., no. 603). 1886. G. Munro.
Felix Holt, the Radical. new ed.... ed. George Eliot. New York Etc.
Felix Holt, the Radical. George Eliot. (Half-title: Everyman's library, ed. by Ernest Rhys. Fiction no. 353). 1909. J. M.Dent & Co.
Felix Holt, the Radical. George Eliot. LC 31-35234. (On cover: The home library). A. L. Burt.
Felix Holt, the Radical. George Eliot. LC 36-37165. (Half-title: Everyman's library, ed. by Ernest Rhys. Fiction. no. 353)). 1923. J. M. Dent & Sons, Ltd.
Felix Holt, the Radical. George Eliot & Fred C Thomson. LC 79-42922. (Series: Clarendon Edition of the Novels of George Eliot.). (Illus.). 1980. 79.00 (ISBN 0-19-812561-5). Clarendon Press.
Felix Holt, the Radical: Biographical Introduction. George Eliot. LC 14-193443. (personal edition of George Eliot's works). 1901. Doubleday, Page & Co.
Felix Holt, the Radical: Biographical Introduction. George Eliot. LC 1-31174. (Personal edition of George Eliot's works. v. 5)). 1901. Doubleday, Page & Co.
Felix Lanzberg's Expiation. Lula Kirschner. Tr. by Lathrop, Elise L. LC 7-12820. (On cover: The rose library, no. 13). 1892. Worthington Company.
Felix O'Day. Francis Hopkinson Smith. LC 15-18694. 1915. C. Scribner's Sons.
Felix Tells It. Lucy Pratt. LC 15-4805. 1915. D. Appleton and Company.
Felix Walking. Hilary Ford, pseud. (O.S.I.). 1958. 3.50 o.s.i. (25040). S&S.
Fell of Dark. Judson Jerome. LC 66-105612. 4.95. Houghton.
Fell of Dark: By James Norman Pseud. 1st Ed. James Norman Schmidt. LC 60-7649. 1960. Lippincott.
Fell Purpose. August William Derleth. (His The Judge Peck mysteries). 1953. Arcadia House.
Fellow Mortals. Marion Strobel. LC 35-2815. Farrar & Rinehart, Incorporated.
Fellow of Infinite Jest. Thomas Yoseloff. LC 77-106703. 1970. Greenwood Press.
Fellow of Trinity. Frances Bridges Marshall & Wheeler, Walt. 1890. Rand, McNally & Co.
Fellow-Townsmen. Thomas Hardy. LC 3-22852. (On cover: Harper's half-hour series, no. 136). 1880. Harper & Brothers.
Fellow-Traveler. David Montross, pseud. LC 65-11804. 3.95. Pub. for the Crime Club by Doubleday.
Fellow Travellers. Margaret Georgiana Todd. (Half-title: Appletons' town and country library, no. 206). 1896. D. Appleton and Company.
Fellow Travellers: A Story. Edward Fuller. LC 6-44585. 1886. Cupples, Upham and Company.
Fellowe and His Wife. Blanche Willis Howard Von Teuffel & Sharp, William, 1855-1905, Joint Author. LC 8-26067. 1892. Houghton, Mifflin and Company.
Fellowship of Fear. Aaron J Elkins. LC 82-60145. 1982. 11.95 (ISBN 0-8027-5478-3). Walker.
Fellowship of Hearts. Mary Fenton Bigelow. 1892. Hunt & Eaton.
Fellowship of the Craft: Conrad on Ships and Seamen and the Sea. Chester Francis Burgess. LC 75-31644. (National University Publications). (Literary criticism series). (National university publications). 1976. 9.95 (ISBN 0-8046-9116-9). Kennikat Press.
Fellowship of the Hand. Edward D. Hoch. LC 72-83115. 1973. 5.95 (ISBN 0-8027-5553-4). Walker.
Fellowship of the Mystery. John N. Figgis. 1914. 15.00 o.p. (ISBN 0-8337-1125-3). B Franklin.
Fellowship of the Ring. John Ronald Reuel Tolkien. 1967. 11.95 (ISBN 0-395-08254-4). HM.
Fellowship of the Ring: Being the First Part of The Lord of the Rings. silver anniversary ed. John Ronald Reuel Tolkien. LC 81-166135. (Tolkien, John Ronald Reuel, 1892-1973. Lord of the Rings: Pt. 1). (Illus.). 1981. 11.95 (ISBN 0-395-31267-1). Houghton Mifflin.
Fellowship of the Stars: Nine Science Fiction Stories. Ed. by Terry Carr. Alan Dean Foster. LC 74-12154. 1974. 6.95 (ISBN 0-671-21881-6). Simon and Schuster.
Fellowship of the Talisman. Clifford D. Simak. LC 78-16657. 1978. 8.95 (ISBN 0-345-27751-1). Ballantine Books.
Felmeres. A Novel. Sarah Barnwell Elliott. LC 6-375769. 1879. D. Appleton and Company.
Felony at Random. Elizabeth Linington. LC 78-27317. 1979. 8.95 (ISBN 0-688-03474-8). W. Morrow.
Felony at Random. Dell Shannon. 224p. 1980. pap. 1.95 (ISBN 0-553-13954-1). Bantam.
Felony at Random. Dell Shannon. LC 78-27317. 1979. 8.95 o.p. (ISBN 0-688-03474-8). Morrow.
Felony File. Elizabeth Linington. LC 79-22033. 1980. 9.95 (ISBN 0-688-03593-0). Morrow.
Felony File. Elizabeth Linington. LC 81-5635. 1981. 10.95 (ISBN 0-89621-281-5). Thorndike Press.
Felony File. Dell Shannon. 1980. 9.95 (ISBN 0-688-03593-0). Morrow.
Felony File. large print ed. Dell Shannon. LC 81-5635. 374p. 1981. Repr. of 1980 ed. 10.95x (ISBN 0-89621-281-5). Thorndike Pr.
Felony Tank. Malcolm Braly. 1.75 (ISBN 0-671-80619-X). Pocket Books.
Female. Donald Henderson Clarke. LC 32-5475. The Vanguard Press.
Female: A Novel of Another Time. Paul Iselin Wellman. 3.95 o.p. Doubleday.
Female: A Novel of Another Time. 1st Ed. Paul Iselin Wellman. 1953. Doubleday.
Female American. Unca Eliza Winkfield. LC 72-104598. 1970. (ISBN 0-8398-2171-9). Literature House.
Female American. Unca Eliza Winkfield. LC 74-17288. (Flowering of the Novel). 1974. (ISBN 0-8240-1178-3). Garland Pub.
Female Bluebeard: Or, Le Morne-Au-Diable. Eugene Sue. LC 8-17680. J. Winchester.
Female Complaints. Leslie Tonner. LC 81-52069. 12.95 (ISBN 0-87223-741-9). Seaview Books.
Female Critick: Letters in Drollery from Ladies to Their Humble Servants. Bd. with Iter-Lunare: A Voyage to the Moon. Davis Russen. LC 71-17054. (Foundations of the Novel Ser.: Vol. 4). lib. bdg. 50.00 o.s.i. (ISBN 0-8240-0516-3). Garland Pub.
Female Deserters see Love's Intrigues.
Female Friends: A Novel. Fay Weldon. LC 74-80844. 1974. 7.95. St. Martin's Press.
Female Jesuit: Or, The Spy in the Family. Jemima Thompson Luke. LC 1-6274. 1851. M. W. Dodd.
Female Man. Joanna Russ. LC 77-23498. (Gregg Press science fiction series III). 1977. 11.00 (ISBN 0-8398-2351-7). Gregg Press.
Female Man. Joanna Russ. 1975. (pbk.) 1.25. Bantam Books.
Female Menagerie. Jay G. Brenter. pap. 0.95 o.p. (1161). Brandon.
Female Minister: Or, A Son's Revenge. Lies, Eugene, Tr & Plunkett, Eugene, Tr. LC 6-38969. 1846. Harper & Brothers.
Female of the Species. Alexandra Roudybush. LC 77-12872. 1978. 6.95 (ISBN 0-385-13652-8). Published for the Crime Club by Doubleday.
Female of the Species: By H. C. McNeile. Herman Cyril McNeile. LC 28-29069. 1928. Pub. for the Crime Club, Inc., by Doubleday, Doran & Company, Inc.
Female of the Species: The Great Women Detectives and Criminals. Ed. by Ellery Queen, pseud. LC 43-104244. 1943. Little, Brown and Company.
Female Quixote. Charlotte Ramsay Lennox. LC 79-104511. 1970. (ISBN 0-8398-1155-1). Literature House.
Female Quixote. Charlotte Ramsay Lennox. LC 74-16200. (Flowering of the Novel). 1974. (ISBN 0-8240-1135-X). Garland Pub.
Female Quixote: Or, The Adventures of Arabella. Charlotte Ramsay Lennox. LC 73-526120. (Oxford English novels). (Oxford pbks., 305). 1973. (pbk) 4.50. Oxford Univ. Pr.
Female Quixote: or the Adventures of Arabella, 1752, 2 vols. in 1. Charlotte Ramsay Lennox. Ed. by Michael F. Shugrue. (Flowering of the Novel, 1740-1775 Ser.: Vol. 36). 1974. lib. bdg. 50.00 (ISBN 0-8240-1135-X). Garland Pub.
Female Quixote; or, the Adventures of Arabella, 2 Vols. in 1. Charlotte Ramsay Lennox. LC 79-104511. 1971. Repr. of 1752 ed. lib. bdg. 15.50x o.p. (ISBN 0-8398-1155-1). Gregg.
Female Quixote; or, the Adventures of Arabella. Charlotte Ramsay Lennox. Ed. & intro. by Margaret Dalziel. (Oxford Paperbacks Ser). (Illus.). 452p. 1973. pap. 4.50x o.p. (ISBN 0-19-281140-1, OPB305). Oxford U Pr.
Female Quixotism: Exhibited in the Romantic Opinions and Extravagant Adventures of Dorcasina Sheldon... Tabitha Tenney. LC 5-401882. 1829. J. P. Peaslee.
Female Robinson Crusoe: A Tale of the American Wilderness ... LC 8-30426. 1837. Printed by J. W. Bell.
Female Spy: Or, Treason in the Camp. by emerson bennett... ed. Emerson Bennett. LC 7-36493. L. Stratton.
Female Volunteer. Eliza Allen Billings. 1851.
Feminine Finance. Frances Crouch. 1907. B. W. Dodge & Company.
Feminine Plural. Benoite Groult & Flora Groult. LC 68-12701. 1968. Prentice-Hall.
Feminine Plural: Stories by Women About Growing up. Ed. by Stephanie Spinner. LC 76-187798. 1972. Macmillan.
Feministas. new ed. Parley J. Cooper. Tr. by Javier Lopez from Eng. (Compadre Collection Ser.). Orig. Title: Feminists. 160p. (Span.). 1974. pap. 0.75 (ISBN 0-88473-607-5). Fiesta Pub.
Feminists see Feministas.
Femme Fatale: Erotic & Fatal Muse. Virginia M. Allen. 300p. 1983. 25.00X (ISBN 0-87875-267-6). Whitston Pub.
Femmes Fatales. Claude Mauriac. Tr. by Henry Wolff. 1980. pap. 4.95 (ISBN 0-7145-0232-4). Riverrun NY.
Fen Country. Edmund Crispin, pseud. 176p. 1980. 9.95 (ISBN 0-8027-5424-4). Walker & Co.
Fen Country: Twenty-Six Stories. Edmund Crispin, pseud. LC 81-10545. 1981. 3.95 (ISBN 0-14-005946-6). Penguin.
Fen Country: Twenty-Six Stories. Robert Bruce Montgomery. LC 80-51723. 1980. 9.95 (ISBN 0-8027-5424-4). Walker.
Fen Tiger. Catherine Cookson. LC 79-84694. 1979. 8.95. Morrow.
Fen Tiger. Catherine Marchant, pseud. LC 79-84694. 1979. 8.95 o.p. (ISBN 0-688-03448-9). Morrow.
Fen Tiger see House on the Fens.
Fence. Bruce McGinnis. LC 80-105133. 10.00 (ISBN 0-8149-0821-7). Vanguard Press.
Fence. Hugh Lawrence Nelson. LC 53-5356. (Murray Hill mystery). 1953. Rinehart.
Fence & Other Stories. Elena Calderon. 1970. 3.50 o.p. Vantage.
Fenced Off. Harry Sinclair Drago. 1969. pap. 0.60 o.p. (0502-06031-060). Curtis.
Fenced Water. George Washington Ogden. LC 31-21890. 1931. Dodd, Mead & Company.
Fenceless Meadows: Tales of the Sea. Bertram Martin Adams. LC 23-141121. 1923. Frederick A. Stokes Company.

Fenceless Range. Illus. by John W. Hampton. Martha Groves McKelvie. LC 60-10542. 1960. Dorrence.

Fencing Master: And Other Stories. Gilbert Rogin. LC 65-11288. 4.95. Random.

Fencing with Shadows. Hattie Tyng Griswold. LC 7-165. (On cover: Idylwild series. v. 1, no. 24). Morrill, Higgins & Co.

Fenella: A Novel. Henry Longan Stuart. LC 11-9898. 1911. Doubleday, Page & Company.

Fenella in the South of France. David Gentleman. 1.50 o.p. (ISBN 0-87556-099-7). Saifer.

Fenella Phizackerley. Margaret Forster. LC 76-130471. 1971. 6.50. Simon and Schuster.

Fengriffen: A Chilling Tale. David Case. LC 73-106962. 1970. 5.00 o.p. (ISBN 0-8090-4442-0). Hill & Wang.

Fengriffin. David Case. 1971. pap. 0.95 o.p. (75-312). Lancer.

Fenist the Falcon. Illus. by I. Bilibin. 16p. 1979. pap. 2.45 (ISBN 0-8285-1135-7, Pub. by Goznak Pubs USSR). Imported Pubns.

Fennel and Rue: A Novel. William Dean Howells. LC 8-9174. 1908. Harper & Brothers.

Fenner. George Harmon Coxe. LC 75-136334. 1971. 4.95 (ISBN 0-394-42462-X). Knopf.

Fenner. George Harmon Coxe. LC 77-38102. 1971. 7.95 (ISBN 0-8161-6003-1). G. K. Hall.

Fennister Affair. Josephine Bell. LC 77-21305. 1977. 7.95 (ISBN 0-8128-2408-3). Stein and Day.

Fenris Device. Brian M Stableford. 1974. (pbk.) 0.95. DAW Books.

Fenris Option. R. D. Jones. (Orig.). 1981. pap. 2.50 (ISBN 0-505-51640-3). Tower Bks.

Fenton's Quest. Mary Elizabeth Braddon Maxwell. (On cover: Seaside library. Pocket ed. no. 542). 1885. G. Munro.

Fenton's Quest. Mary Elizabeth Braddon Maxwell. (On cover: Lovell's library. no. 893). 1887. J. W. Lovell Company.

Fenwick's Career. Mary Augusta Arnold Humphry Ward Ward. 1906. Harper & Brothers.

Fenwick's Trail. Harold Bindloss. LC 33-787419. 1938. Frederick A. Stokes Company.

Feo: A Romance. Max Pemberton. LC 2301. 1900. Dodd, Mead & Company.

Fer-De-Lance. Rex Stout & Nero Wolfe, Fer-De-Lance. LC 80-29560. 1981. 13.50 (ISBN 0-8161-3222-4). G.K. Hall.

Fer-De-Lance see Royal Flush: A Nero Wolfe Omnibus.

Fer-De-Lance: A Nero Wolfe Mystery. Rex Stout. LC 34-34975. Farrar & Rinehart, Inc.

Fer-De-Lance: A Nero Wolfe Mystery. Rex Stout. LC 47-278994. (Pocket books, 112). 1946.

Fer Shur! How to be a Valley Girl-Totally! Mary Corey & Victoria Westermark. 64p. 1982. pap. 2.50 (ISBN 0-553-23237-1). Bantam.

Feral. Berton Roueche. LC 74-1894. 1974. 5.95 (ISBN 0-06-013688-X). Harper & Row.

Feral. Berton Roueche. LC 74-1894. 1975. (pbk.) 1.50 (ISBN 0-671-80152-X). Pocket Books.

Feral Child. Eric Sundell. (Illus.). 1971. 4.95 o.p. (ISBN 0-200-71834-7, B25230). Abelard.

Feramontov. Desmond Cory, pseud. (O.s.i.). 1968. pap. 0.75 o.s.i. (A322S, Award). Univ Pub & Dist.

Feramontov: By Desmond Cory. Shaun McCarthy. (Award Bks. A322S). 1968. Universal Pub. & Dist.

Feramontoy: By Desmond Cory Pseud. Shaun McCarthy. LC 66-16920. bds., 3.95. Walker.

Ferdinand. Louis Zukofsky. Bd. with It Was. LC 72-385527. (Cape Edition). 1968. pap. 1.95 o.p. (ISBN 0-670-31166-9, Grossman). Penguin.

Ferdinand and Isabella: A Novel. Hermann Kesten. LC 46-11819. 1946. A. A. Wyn, Inc.

Ferdydurke. 2d ed. Witold Gombrowicz. LC 67-3519. 1967. Grove Press.

Ferdydurke: By Witold Gombrowicz. Tr. by Eric Mosbacher. Witold Gombrowicz. LC 66-29765. (Evergreen, E464). 1968. pap., 2.45. Grove.

Fergus. Brian Moore. 1977. pap. 1.95 o.p. (ISBN 0-14-004270-9). Penguin.

Fergus, a Novel. Brian Moore. LC 77-121635. 1970. 5.95. Holt, Rinehart and Winston.

Fergus Lamont. Robin Jenkins. LC 79-63120. 1979. 12.95 (ISBN 0-8008-2622-1). Taplinger Pub. Co.

Fergus Lamont. Robin Jenkins. LC 79-63120. 1979. 3.95 (ISBN 0-8008-2623-X). Taplinger Pub. Co.

Ferguson. Rayne Kruger. LC 57-779431. 1957. Appleton-Century-Crofts.

Ferguson. Rayne Kruger. 1956. Longmans, Green.

Ferguson Affair. Ross Macdonald. 1960. 4.95 o.p. Knopf.

Ferguson Affair: By Ross Macdonald Pseud. 1st Ed. Kenneth Millar. LC 60-9990. 1960. Knopf.

Ferguson Rifle. Louis L'Amour. LC 72-13698. 1973. 0.95. Bantam Books.

Ferguson's Trail. Charles Alden Seltzer. (Belmont Tower book). 1979. 1.25 (ISBN 0-505-51357-9). Tower Pubns.

Fergy the Guide, and His Moral and Instructive Lies About Beasts, Birds and Fishes. Henry Spofford Canfield. LC 4-19060. 1904. H. Holt and Company.

Feria de Amantes. new ed. Juan Castellanos. (Pimienta Collection Ser.). 160p. (Span.). 1974. pap. 1.00 (ISBN 0-88473-207-X). Fiesta Pub.

Ferment. John Thomas McIntyre. LC 74-26117. (Labor Movement in Fiction and Non-Fiction). 1977. 25.00 (ISBN 0-404-58448-9). AMS Press.

Ferment. John Thomas McIntyre. LC 37-14928. Farrar & Rinehart, Inc.

Fern Gatherer. Belva Clayton. (Geneva Books). 1968. 2.50 o.p. Carlton.

Fern Leaves from Fanny's Port-Folio: Second Series. Sara Payson Willis Parton. LC 77-164572. (American fiction reprint series). (Illus.). 1971. (ISBN 0-8369-7049-7). Books for Libraries Press.

Fern Leaves from Fanny's Portfolio. With Original Designs by Fred M. Coffin. Sara Payson Willis Parton. LC 32-6622. 1854. Miller, Orton & Mulligan.

Fern Seed. Henry Milner Rideout. LC 21-104014. 1921. Duffield and Company.

Fernanda. Victor B Miller. 1976. 1.50 (ISBN 0-671-80774-9). Pocket Books.

Fernande. William Babington Maxwell. LC 25-17539. 1925. Dodd, Mead and Company.

Fernando. Francis Browning Drew Bickerstaffe-Drew. LC 19-13964. 1919. P. J. Kenedy & Sons.

Fernando De Lemos. Truth and Fiction. A Novel. Charles Etienne Arthur Gayarre. LC 6-44263. 1872. G. W. Carleton & Co.; Etc., Etc.

Fernando: Or, The Moor of Castile. A Romance of Old Spain. Sylvanus Cobb. LC 7-11438. (With Judson, Edward Z. C. The black avenger of the Spanish Main. New York, c1847). 1853. F. Gleason's Publishing Hall.

Ferne Fleming. A Novel. Catherine Ann Ware Warfield. LC 3-34837. T. B. Peterson & Brothers.

Fernhurst, Q.E.D., and Other Early Writings. Gertrude Stein. LC 71-148663. 1973. 3.45, (ISBN 0-87140-082-0). Liveright.

Fernley Manor: Or, Edith the Inconstant. Robert Mackenzie Daniel. LC 6-33163. H. Long and Brother.

Fernwood. Marcella Thum. LC 73-81416. 1973. 4.95 (ISBN 0-385-05310-X). Published for the Crime Club by Doubleday.

Ferragus, Chief of the Devorants. The Last Incarnation of Vautrin. Honore De Balzac. Tr. by Katharine Prescott Wormeley. LC 11-7158. (Half-title: The comedy of human life... Scenes from Parisian life). 1895. Roberts Brothers.

Ferret Fancier. Anthony C West. LC 65-11982. 1965. Simon and Schuster.

Ferrol Bond. John Easton. LC 33-137613. 1933. G. P. Putnam's Sons.

Ferry of Fate: A Tale of Russian Jewry. Samuel Gordon. 1907. Duffield & Company.

Ferryboat Across the Kirenga: Stories. IU. A Lopusov. LC 81-112063. 8.95. Progress Publishers.

Ferrybridge Mystery. Derek Vane. LC 20-17412. 1920. Moffat, Yard and Company.

Ferryman, Take Him Across! Virginia Rath. LC 36-23266. 1936. Pub. for the Crime Club, Incorporated, by Doubleday, Doran & Company, Inc.

Fertig. Sol Yurick. LC 66-16178. 1966. Trident Press.

Fertile Four-Poster: A Novel. Kimball McIlroy. LC 72-75085. 1969. 4.95. Crown.

Fertile Plain. Esther Polianowsky Salaman. LC 57-9061. 1957. Abelard-Schuman.

Festin De Sexo. new ed. Rogelio Rios. (Pimienta Collection Ser.). 160p. (Span.). 1975. pap. 1.00 o.p. (ISBN 0-88473-226-6). Fiesta Pub.

Festival. John Richard Lane Anderson. LC 79-5336. 1979. 8.95 (ISBN 0-312-28759-3). St. Martin's Press.

Festival. Maxwell Struthers Burt. LC 31-26357. 1931. C. Scribner's Sons.

Festival. Brian Hay. 1973. (pbk.) 0.95 (ISBN 0-671-77536-7). Pocket Books.

Festival. John Boynton Priestley. LC 51-2104. 1951. Harper.

Festival. Bart Spicer. LC 71-124961. 1970. 7.95. Atheneum.

Festival. Lael Tucker, pseud. LC 54-7811. 1954. Random House.

Festival at Meron. Harry Sackler. LC 35-18078. Covici, Friede.

Festival for Christina. Blakely St. James. LC 82-60694. 1983. pap. 2.95 (ISBN 0-86721-240-3). Playboy Pbks.

Festival of Darkness. Marie Garratt. 1975. (pbk.) 0.95. Ace Books.

Festival of Flora. Godfrey Turton. LC 74-171325. 1972. 6.95 o.p. (ISBN 0-385-09462-0). Doubleday.

Festival of Flora: A Story of Ancient and Modern Times. Godfrey Edmund Turton. LC 74-171325. 1972. 6.95. Doubleday.

Fetch. Peter Everett. LC 67-10523. 1967. Simon and Schuster.

Fetch Over the Canoe: A Story of a Song. William Lightfoot Visscher. 1908. Atwell Printing and Binding Co.

Fete. Translated from the French by Peter Wiles. Roger Vailland. LC 60-530124. 1961. half cloth, 3.95. Knopf.

Fetish. Christine Garnier. LC 52-9832. 1952. Putnam.

Fetish. Alberto Morravia. 1973. pap. 1.25 (ISBN 0-532-12157-0). Woodhill.

Fetish, & Other Stories. Alberto Moravia. LC 75-28668. 1976. 15.00 (ISBN 0-8371-8487-8). Greenwood Press.

Fetish: And Other Stories by Alberto Moravia Pseud. Tr. from Italian by Angus Davidson. Alberto Pincherle. LC 65-142686. 1965. 4.95. Farrar.

Fetish Girl. Sylvia Bayer. pap. 1.95 o.s.i. (Venus). Grove.

Fetish Murders. Avon Curry. 1973. (pbk) 0.95. Ace Books.

Fettered. A Novel. Frances Campbell Sparhawk. 1899. F. T. Neely.

Fettered for Life. Frank Barrett. LC 6-9065. (On cover: Seaside library. Pocket ed. no. 1245). G. Munro.

Fettered for Life; or, Lord and Master. A Story of Today. By Lillie Devereux Blake... Lillie Devereux Blake. LC 6-138493. 1874. Sheldon & Company.

Fettered for Life: Or, Lord and Master. A Story of Today. Lillie Devereux Blake. LC 6-13848. (On cover: Lovell's library, v. 11, no. 597). 1885. J. W. Lovell Company.

Fettered Past. Netta Muskett. 1974. pap. 0.75 o.p. (26559-9-075). Beagle Bks.

Fettered Yet Free. A Novel... Burleigh Kimball. 1884. G. W. Carleton & Co.

Fetters Fall. John Bechtel. 1945. W. H. Dietz, Inc.

Fetters of Eve. Lily Clive Nutt. LC 31-23466. The Bobbs-Merrill Company.

Fetters of Freedom. Cyrus Townsend Brady. LC 13-788018. 1913. Dodd, Mead and Company.

Feud. Amelia Bean. LC 60-8853. 1960. Doubleday.

Feud. Giles A Lutz. LC 81-43293. 1982. 10.95 (ISBN 0-385-17685-6). Doubleday.

Feud: A Novel. Thomas Berger. LC 82-22139. 1983. 14.95 (ISBN 0-440-02833-7). Delacorte Press.

Feud at Five Rivers. Frederick Schlick. LC 55-9919. (Silver star westerns). 1955. Dodd, Mead.

Feud at Mendoza. Grover Marshall. LC 60-1070. 1969. Repr. pap. 0.60 o.p. (B60-1070). Belmont-Tower.

Feud at Mendoza: Marshall Grover. Marshall Grover. (Belmont Tower Book). 1977. 1.25 (ISBN 0-505-51187-8). Tower Pubns.

Feud at Silver Bend. Jesse Edward Grinstead. LC 39-11267. Dodge Publishing Company.

Feud at Silvermine. Peter Field. LC 66-11239. (His A Powder Valley western). 1965. Jefferson House; Distributed by W. Morrow.

Feud at Single Shot. Luke Short. LC 36-400436. Farrar & Rinehart, Incorporated.

Feud at Sleepy Cat. Drake C. Denver, pseud. LC 40-10293. 1940. Phoenix Press.

Feud at Sleepy Cat. Nelson Coral Nye. (Leisure book). 1979. 1.50 (ISBN 0-8439-0611-1). Nordon Pubns.

Feud at Spanish Ford. Frank Bonham. LC 54-9670. (Ballantine books, 85). Ballantine Books.

Feud at Sundown. Robert J. Hogan. 1976. pap. 1.25 (ISBN 0-532-12447-2). Woodhill.

Feud at Sundown. easy eye ed. Robert J. Hogan. 1968. pap. 0.60 o.p. (73-796). Lancer.

Feud at Sundown: By Bob Jasper Pseud. Robert J Hogan. LC 51-12148. 1951. Houghton Mifflin.

Feud at Twin Mountain. Jesse Edward Grinstead. LC 42-158221. 1942. Dodge Publishing Company.

Feud of Cattle Kings. Robert Ames Bennet. LC 33-239313. 1933. I. Washburn.

Feud of Oakfield Creek. Josiah Royce. LC 71-104560. 1970. (ISBN 0-8398-1770-3). Literature House.

Feud of Oakfield Creek: A Novel of California Life. Josiah Royce. LC 77-111996. (Series in American Studies). 1970. Johnson Reprint Corp.

Feud of Oakfield Creek: A Novel of California Life. Josiah Royce. LC 8-95620. 1887. Houghton, Mifflin and Company.

Feud on the Range. Clay Bridger. LC 40-33060. Dodge Publishing Company.

Feuders' Gold. Kim Knight. LC 40-344268. Dodge Publishing Company.

Feuding Postmasters. Neill Compton Wilson. LC 69-16316. 1969. 4.95. Morrow.

Feudists. Ernest Haycox. LC 78-23988. 1978. 10.50 (ISBN 0-8161-6636-6). G. K. Hall.

Fever. Robin Cook. LC 82-12147. 1982. 15.95 (ISBN 0-8161-3420-0). G.K. Hall.

Fever. Charlotte Lamb, pseud. (Presents Ser.). (Orig.). 1980. pap. 1.50 (ISBN 0-373-10350-6). Harlequin Bks.

Fever: A Novel. 1st Ed. John Hazard Wildman. LC 52-11678. 1953. Exposition Press.

Fever Called Living. Barbara Moore. LC 76-2807. 1976. 8.95 (ISBN 0-385-12081-8). Doubleday.

Fever for Living. Robert A Roripaugh. LC 61-5788. 1961. Morrow.

Fever Grass. John Morris. LC 70-85285. 1969. 5.95. Putnam.

Fever Heat. Henry Gregor Felsen. 1972. pap. 0.75 o.p. (07215). Curtis.

Fever House. Walther Georg Heinrich Von Hollander & Jenkins, Susan, Tr. LC 29-21213. 1929. The Macauley Company.

Fever in the Blood. William Pearson. LC 59-14675. 1959. St. Martin's Press.

Fever of Life. Fergus Hume. LC 7-5796. J. W. Lovell Company.

Fever of Life. Fergus Hume. LC 2-12483. (Lettered on cover: Sea shore & mountain series). Street & Smith.

Fever of Love. Harcourt-Smith, Rosamond. LC 52-12695. 1952. Longmans, Green.

Fever of Love. 1st American Ed. Rosamund Harcourt-Smith. LC 53-6523. 1953. Longmans, Green.

Fever on the Wind. Adrien Lloyd. (Orig.). 1980. pap. 2.50 (ISBN 0-440-12613-4). Dell.

Fever Pitch. Betty Fern. 2.75 (ISBN 0-671-82155-5). Pocket Books.

Fever Pitch. Sarah Holland. (Harlequin Presents Ser.). 192p. 1983. pap. 1.95 (ISBN 0-373-10601-7). Harlequin Bks.

Fever Pitch. Frank Waters. LC 30-10704. H. Liveright.

Fever. Tr. from French by Daphne Woodward. 1st Amer. Ed. Jean Marie Gustave Le Clezio. LC 66-16359. 1966. bds., 4.95. Atheneum.

Fever Tree. 1st ed. Richard Lakin Mason. LC 62-10621. 1962. World Pub. Co.

Fever Tree and Other Stories. Ruth Rendell. LC 82-19014. 1983. 11.95 (ISBN 0-394-52916-2). Pantheon Books.

Fever Tree & Other Stories. Ruth Rendell. 191p. 1983. 11.95. Pantheon.

Feversham. Diane Davidson. 1971. pap. 0.95 o.p. (N2441). Pyramid Pubns.

Feversham. Diane Davidson. 1977. pap. 1.75 o.p. (ISBN 0-515-04298-6). BJ Pub Group.

Feversham: A Novel. Diane Davidson. LC 75-93392. 1969. 6.50. Crown Publishers.

Fevre Dream. George R. R Martin. LC 82-7711. 15.95 (ISBN 0-671-45577-X). Poseidon Press.

Few and the Many. Hans Sahl. LC 62-9444. 1962. Harcourt, Brace & World.

Few Days in Athens: Being the Translation of a Greek Manuscript Discovered in Herculaneum. Frances Wright D'Arusmont. LC 72-4984. (Romantic Tradition in American Literature). 1972. 10.00 (ISBN 0-405-04653-7). Arno Press.

Few Days in Athens: Being the Translation of a Greek Manuscript Discovered in Herculaneum. Frances Wright D'Arusmont. LC 6-33063. 1825. E. Blise & E. White.

Few Days in Athens: Being the Translation of a Greek Manuscript Discovered in Herculaneum. Part 1. Frances Wright D'Arusmont. 1835. G. W. & A. J. Matsell.

Few Days in Athens: Being the Translation of a Greek Manuscript Discovered in Herculaneum. Part I. ... republished from the original london ed. Frances Wright D'Arusmont. LC 44-10703. 1831. Wright & Owen.

Few Days in Endel. Diana Gordon. (Ace Gothic). 1973. (pbk.) 0.95. Ace Books.

Few Days in Madrid: By Audrey and William Roos. Audrey Kelley Roos & William Roos. LC 65-19751. 4.50. Scribners.

Few Days in Weasel Creek. Joanna Brent. LC 79-66082. 8.95 (ISBN 0-87223-566-1). Seaview Books.

Few Days to See the World. Edward S. Hanlon. 1965. 5.00 o.p. (ISBN 0-525-10458-5). Dutton.

Few Days to See the World: A Novel. Edward S Hanlon. LC 64-19530. 1965. Dutton.

Few Die Well. Sterling Noel. LC 53-7080. 1953. Farrar, Straus and Young.

Few Drops of Murder. Isabel Capeto. LC 55-11880. 1955. Arcadia House.

Few Fiends to Tea. Virginia Coffman. 1969. pap. 0.75 o.p. (1031). Belmont-Tower.

Few Flowers for Shiner. Richard Llewellyn. LC 50-5029. 1950. Macmillan.

Few Foolish Ones. Gladys Hasty Carroll. LC 35-27137. 1935. The Macmillan Company.

Few Good Men. Tom Suddick. LC 77-18336. 1978. 1.95 (ISBN 0-380-01866-7). Avon Books.

Few Green Leaves. Barbara Pym. LC 80-18905. 1980. 10.95 (ISBN 0-525-10450-X). Dutton.

Few Hours of Sunlight. Francoise Quiorez. LC 70-138796. 1971. 5.95 (ISBN 0-06-013747-9). Harper & Row.

Few Hours of Sunlight. Francoise Sagan, pseud. LC 70-138796. 1971. 5.95 o.p. (ISBN 0-06-013747-9, HarpT). Har-Row.

Few Hours of Sunlight. Francoise Sagan, pseud. pap. 1.25 o.p. (ISBN 0-06-087020-6, HW). Har-Row.

Few Kind Words. Donald Spatz. LC 77-1109. (Illus.). 1978. pap. text ed. 4.95 (ISBN 0-910254-19-2). Bodine.

Few Last Words. James Sallis. LC 71-122293. 1970. 4.95. Macmillan.

Few Little Lives. Clara Thropp. LC 8-19946. 1896.

Few Neighbors. Henry Augustus Shute. LC 6-15430. 1906. Doubleday, Page & Company.

Few Nights & Days. Mbella S. Dipoko. (African Writers Ser.). 1970. pap. text ed. 4.00x (ISBN 0-435-90082-X). Heinemann Ed.

Few Painted Feathers. 1st ed. Stephen Longstreet. LC 63-20503. 1963. Doubleday.

Few Pianos. Robert Collen. LC 77-83731. 1978. pap. 2.00 (ISBN 0-89924-016-X). Lynx Hse.

Few Quick Ones. Pelham Grenville Wodehouse. LC 59-9497. 1959. Simon and Schuster.

Few Short Blocks Between. John Selby. LC 59-12496. 1959. Crowell.

Few Virtuous Men (Li Cornuti) A Novel of Sicily. Ben Morreale. LC 73-76300. 1973. 7.50 (ISBN 0-912766-07-7). Tundra Books.

Few Were Left. Harold Rein. (O.s.i.). 219p. 1976. Repr. of 1955 ed. lib. bdg. 8.50 o.s.i. Queens Hse.

Few Were Left: A Novel. Harold Rein. J. Day Co.

Ffollots of Redmarley. Lizzie Allen Harker. LC 13-12596. 1913. C. Scribner's Sons.

Fia Fia: A Novel of the South Pacific. James Ramsey Ullman. LC 62-9045. 1962. World Pub. Co.

Fiametta. Anne Duffield. (Berkley medallion book). 1974. (pbk.) 1.25 (ISBN 0-425-02702-3). Berkley Pub. Co.

Fiammetta: A Summer Idyl. William Wetmore Story. LC 8-16287. 1886. Houghton, Mifflin and Company.

Fiance on Trail. Francis Tillou Buck. LC 6-19655. The Merriam Company.

Fiancees Are Relatives. Berta Ruck. LC 41-10776. 1941. Dodd, Mead & Company.

Fiander's Widow: A Novel. Mary E. Sweetman Blundell. LC 1-7285. Longmans, Green, and Co.,

Fibble,D. D. Irvin Shrewsbury Cobb. LC 16-22854. George H. Doran Company.

Ficciones. Jorge Luis Borges. Ed. & intro. by Anthony Kerrigan. 1962. pap. 4.95 (ISBN 0-394-17244-2, E368, Ever). Grove.

Ficciones. Edited and with an Introd. by Anthony Kerrigan. Jorge Luis Borges. LC 62-13054. 1962. Grove Press.

Fickle. Rob Eden. LC 33-293476. Grosset & Dunlap.

Fickle Fate. K. Alice Rowland. 1892. Roberts & Son, Printers.

Fickle Fortune: A Romance of Life Among the Ozarks. Rose L Hamilton. LC 29-7496. The Grafton Press.

Fickle Fortune: A Story of Place La Greve. Christine Faber. LC 6-37857. 1878. D. & J. Sadlier & Co.

Fickle Moment. Peter Blackmore. LC 47-7279. 1948. G. P. Putnam's Sons.

Fickle Smile of Destiny. Michael Bertone. LC 72-96807. 1973. 6.95 (ISBN 0-8059-1827-2). Dorrance.

Fiction. Ed. by Jerome Beaty. LC 73-260. (Norton Introduction to Literature). 1973. (pbk.) 3.45 (ISBN 0-393-09359-X). W. W. Norton.

Fiction & Poetry by Texas Women. LC 75-31388. (Illus.). 1975. 9.95 o.s.i. (ISBN 0-916092-03-8). Tex Ctr Writers.

Fiction and Process: Comp. by Carl Hartman, Hazard Adams. Ed. by Carl Hartman. LC 68-16187. 1968. pap., 4.95. Dodd.

Fiction As Experience: An Anthology. Irving Howe. LC 77-85190. 5.95 (ISBN 0-15-527281-0). Harcourt Brace Jovanovich.

Fiction As Process. Ed. by Carl Hartman. LC 68-16187. 1968. Dodd, Mead.

Fiction Fields of Australia. Frederick Sinnett. Ed. by Cecil Hadgraft. (Illus.). 1966. pap. 4.75x o.p. (ISBN 0-7022-0046-8). U of Queensland Pr.

Fiction Fights the Civil War. Robert A. Lively. LC 73-11751. 230p. 1973. Repr. of 1957 ed. lib. bdg. 15.00x (ISBN 0-8371-7084-2, LIFF). Greenwood.

Fiction Fights the Civil War. Robert A. Lively. 1957. 6.00 o.p. (ISBN 0-8078-0708-7). U of NC Pr.

Fiction Goes to Court: Favorite Stories of Lawyers and the Law Selected by Famous Lawyers. Ed. by Albert P. Blaustein. LC 77-2827. 1977. 19.00 (ISBN 0-8371-9522-5). Greenwood Press.

Fiction Goes to Court: Favorite Stories of Lawyers & the Law. Ed. by Albert P. Blaustein. pap. 0.95 o.p. (04864, Collier). Macmillan.

Fiction Illustrated. Byron Preiss. (Star Fawn Ser.: Vol. 2). 1976. pap. 1.00 o.p. (ISBN 0-515-04077-0). BJ Pub Group.

Fiction Illustrated. Byron Preiss. (Chandler Ser: No. 3). 1976. pap. 1.00 o.p. (ISBN 0-515-04078-9). BJ Pub Group.

Fiction Illustrated, Vol. 3. Byron Preiss. (Orig.). 1976. pap. 4.95 o.p. BJ Pub Group.

Fiction of James Tiptree, Jr. Gardner Dozois. 1977. pap. 2.50 (ISBN 0-916186-04-0). Algol Pr.

Fiction of the Absurd: Pratfalls in the Void: a Critical Anthology. Dick Penner. LC 80-82620. (Mentor book). 3.50 (ISBN 0-451-61904-8). New American Library.

Fiction of the Fifties: A Decade of American Writing; Stories. Ed. by Herbert Gold. LC 59-13967. 1959. Doubleday.

Fiction One Hundred: An Anthology of Short Stories. 2nd ed. Ed. by James H. Pickering. 1978. pap. 7.50x o.p. (ISBN 0-02-395330-6, 39533). Macmillan.

Fiction: The Narrative Art. James W. Kirkland & Paul W. Dowell. LC 76-50081. 7.95 (ISBN 0-13-314310-4). Prentice-Hall.

Fiction, the Universal Elements. Ed. by Pearl Gasarch. LC 75-183938. (Illus.). 1972. Van Nostrand Reinhold.

Fiction 100: an Anthology of Short Stories. Ed. by James H. Pickering. LC 72-12748. 1974. 4.95 (ISBN 0-02-395290-3). Macmillan.

Fiction 100: An Anthology of Short Stories. 2d ed. Ed. by James H. Pickering. LC 76-50594. 5.95 (ISBN 0-02-395330-6). Macmillan.

Fictional Children of Henry James. Muriel G. Shine. 1969. 9.25 o.p. (ISBN 0-8078-1118-1). U of NC Pr.

Fictional Lives. Hugh Fleetwood. 166p. 1981. 15.95 (ISBN 0-241-10434-3, Pub. by Hamish Hamilton England). David & Charles.

Fiction's Journey: 50 Stories. Barbara McKenzie. LC 77-83621. 6.95 (ISBN 0-15-527320-5). Harcourt Brace Jovanovich.

Fidalgos of Casa Mourisca. Coelho Joaquim Guilherme Gomes. Tr. by Dabney, Roxana L. LC 7-2177. D. Lothrop Company.

Fiddle-Back Ranch. Nelson Coral Nye. LC 45-263. 1944. Phoenix Press.

Fiddle for Eighteen Pence. Sybil Bolitho. LC 27-18435. George H. Doran Company.

Fiddle Hill. James P. McCague. LC 60-153841. 1960. Crown Publishers.

Fiddle Longspay. Warren Bledsoe. LC 42-14047. 1942. Little, Brown and Company.

Fiddle-Maker. Carl F. Meyer. 1970. 3.50 o.p. Vantage.

Fiddlefoot. Frederick Dilley Glidden. LC 49-8810. 1949. Houghton Mifflin Co.

Fiddlefoot Fugitive. James R. Dowler. Ed. by Alice Sachs. 1970. 3.95 o.p. Crown.

Fiddleheads & Mustard Blossoms. Derevitzky. (Illus.). 1979. pap. 4.50 (ISBN 0-89272-074-3). Down East.

Fiddler. David King. LC 77-12861. 1978. 7.95 (ISBN 0-385-13438-X). Doubleday.

Fiddler. Sarah Gertrude Liebson Millin. LC 29-16597. 1929. H. Liveright.

Fiddler in Barly. Robert Nathan. LC 26-19675. 1926. R. M. McBride & Company.

Fiddler of the Ritz. Armand Vecsey. LC 31-250433. W. F. Payson.

Fiddler's Coin. Jane Ludlow Drake Abbott. LC 34-179738. J. B. Lippincott Company.

Fiddler's Fee. Josiah Pitts Woolfolk. LC 34-20020. W. Godwin, Inc.

Fiddler's Folly and Encores. Robert Haven Schauffler. LC 43-115. 1942. H. Holt & Co.

Fiddler's Green. Ernest Kellogg Gann. LC 50-8111. 1950. Sloane.

Fiddlers' Green: Or, The Strange Adventures of Tommy Lawn; a Tale of the Great Divide of the Sailormen. Albert Richard Wetjen. LC 31-12456. 1931. Little, Brown, and Company.

Fiddler's Luck: The Gay Adventures of a Musical Amateur. Robert Haven Schauffler. LC 20-94752. 1920. Houghton Mifflin Company.

Fiddlers 'n Fishermen. Benjamin Frederick Clark. LC 46-7638. 1946. Crown Publications.

Fiddling Cowboy. Adolph Casper Regli. LC 49-11372. 1949. McKay Co.

Fiddling Girl: The Story of Virginia Hammond. Daisy Rhodes Campbell. LC 14-6193. 1914. 1.25. The Page Company.

Fidelia. Edwin Balmer. LC 24-6459. 1924. Dodd, Mead and Company.

Fidelio Score. Gerald Sinstadt. pap. 0.60 o.p. Lancer.

Fidelis: A Novel. Ada Cambridge Cross. LC 6-39308. 1895. D. Appleton and Company.

Fidelite. Edna Verne. LC 14-224343. 1877. A. L. Bancroft and Company.

Fidelity: A Novel. Susan Glaspell. LC 15-10490. 1.35. Small, Maynard and Company.

Fidelity's Flight. Sandra DuBay. 448p. (Orig.). 1982. pap. cancelled o.p. (ISBN 0-505-51825-2). Tower Bks.

Fiedler Reader. Leslie A Fiedler. LC 76-54437. 15.00 (ISBN 0-8128-2190-4) (ISBN 0-8128-2192-0). Stein and Day.

Field. Dola De Jong. LC 79-84437. 1979. 12.50 (ISBN 0-933256-02-7) (ISBN 0-933256-05-1). Second Chance Press.

Field. Dola De Jong. Ed. by Maxwell Perkins. Tr. by A. V. Van Duyn from Dutch. LC 79-84437. 1979. 16.95 (ISBN 0-933256-02-7); pap. 8.95 (ISBN 0-933256-05-1). Second Chance.

Field. Dola De Jong. 1979. 15.95 (ISBN 0-531-07309-2); pap. 7.95 (ISBN 0-531-07327-0). Watts.

Field. Dola De Jong. Tr. by A. V. Van Duym. LC 79-84437. 215p. 1983. pap. 4.95 (ISBN 0-933256-39-6). Second Chance.

Field Clover and Beach Grass. Susan Hartley Swett. LC 28-1649. 1896. Estes and Lauriat.

Field Full of People. Robert Hazel. LC 54-8176. 1954. World Pub. Co.

Field Marshal's Memoirs: A Novel. John Masters. LC 74-33685. 1975. 8.95 (ISBN 0-385-00160-6). Doubleday.

Field of Death. Stephen Overholser. LC 77-75875. 1977. 6.95 (ISBN 0-385-13204-2). Doubleday.

Field of Forty Footsteps. Phyllis Hastings. LC 78-19446. 1978. 7.95 (ISBN 0-312-28825-5). St. Martin's Press.

Field of Glory. An Historical Novel. Henryk Sienkiewicz & Britoff, Henry, Tr. LC 6-10652. J. S. Ogilvie Publishing Company.

Field of Honor. Donn Byrne. LC 29-185498. The Century Co.

Field of Honor. St. John, Adela Rogers. LC 38-21551. 1938. E. P. Dutton and Co., Inc.

Field of Honor: A Novel. Timeri Murari. LC 81-928. 13.95 (ISBN 0-671-42375-4). Simon and Schuster.

Field of Honour. Harold Fielding-Hall. LC 16-16157. 1915. Houghton Mifflin Company.

Field of Life and Death and Tales of Hulan River: Two Novels. Nai-Ying Chang. LC 78-19549. (Chinese Literature in Translation). 14.95 (ISBN 0-253-15821-4). Indiana University Press.

Field of Mustard. Alfred Edgar Coppard. LC 27-2562. 1927. A. A. Knopf.

Field of Night. Robert W Krepps. LC 48-242. Rinehart.

Field of Tares: A Novel. Clotilde Inez Mary Graves. LC 6-45445. (On cover: Harper's Franklin square library, no. 696). 1891. Harper & Brothers.

Field of Thistle. Thomas G. Jones. 5.95 o.p. Vantage.

Field of Vision. Wright Morris. (Bison book, BB577). 1974. (pbk.) 2.95 (ISBN 0-8032-5789-9). University of Nebraska Press.

Field of Vision. Wright Morris. LC 56-8525. 1956. Harcourt, Brace.

Field of Women: By Alan Caillou Pseud. 1st Ed. Alan Lyle-Smythe. LC 62-15453. 1962. Appleton- Century-Crofts.

Fielder's Choice. Jerome Holtzman. LC 79-24261. (Harvest/HBJ book). 1980. 12.95 (ISBN 0-15-130681-8). Harcourt Brace Jovanovich.

Fielder's Choice: An Anthology of Baseball Fiction. Jerome Holtzman. LC 79-24261. 408p. 1980. pap. 4.95 (ISBN 0-15-630652-2, Harv). HarBraceJ.

Fielding. Hamilton Macallister. LC 70-123551. (Arco literary critiques). (Illus.). 1971. 1.95. Arco.

Fielding Gray. Simon Raven. (Alms for Oblivion Ser.: No. 4). 1967. 12.50x (ISBN 0-85634-995-X). Intl Pubns Serv.

Fielding Sargent: A Novel. Elsa Barker. LC 22-20879. E. P. Dutton & Company.

Fielding Selections: With Essays by Hazlitt, Scott, Thackeray. Henry Fielding. LC 79-21044. 1979. 17.50 (ISBN 0-8414-7404-4). Folcroft Library Editions.

Fielding's Folly. Frances Parkinson Wheeler Keyes. 1975. (pbk.) 1.95 (ISBN 0-671-80137-6). Pocket Books.

Fielding's Folly. Frances Parkinson Wheeler Keyes. LC 40-326184. J. Messner, Inc.

Fielding's Folly. Frances Parkinson Wheeler Keyes. LC 42-254391. 1942. The Sun Dial Press.

Fields. Conrad Richter. LC 46-2155. 1946. A. A. Knopf.

Fields. Conrad Richter. 1975. (pbk.) 1.25. Bantam.

Fields Above the Sea. William Lavendar. (Orig.). pap. 2.75 (ISBN 0-515-05390-2). Jove Pubns.

Fields Are White. Beatrice Joy Chute. LC 50-5075. 1950. Dutton.

Fields at Evening. Ethel Edith Mannin. LC 52-3376. 1952. Jarrolds.

Fields of Battle. Kate Alexander. LC 80-29348. 1981. 13.95 (ISBN 0-312-28842-5). St. Martin's Press.

Fields of Dulditch. Mary E. Rackham Mann. LC 77-368789. (Norfolk library). 1976. 7.50 (ISBN 0-85115-056-X). Boydell Press.

Fields of Eden. Michael T Hinkemeyer. LC 77-23754. 7.95. Putnam.

Fields of Fate. Fernando Namora. 1970. 5.95 o.p. Crown.

Fields of Fate: A Novel. Fernando Namora. LC 79-101299. 1970. 5.95. Crown.

Fields of Fire. James H. Webb, Jr. 1979. pap. 2.95 (ISBN 0-553-14927-X). Bantam.

Fields of Fire: A Novel. James H Webb, Jr. LC 78-4046. (Illus.). 9.95 (ISBN 0-13-314286-8). Prentice-Hall.

Fields of Gomorrah: A Novel. Nelia Gardner White. LC 35-15746. 1935. Frederick A. Stokes Company.

Fields of Paradise. Ralph Bates. LC 40-31175. E. P. Dutton & Co., Inc.

Fields on the Hoof: Nexus of Tibetan Nomadic Pastoralism. R. B. Ekvall. LC 68-8603. (Case Studies in Cultural Anthropology). 1968. pap. text ed. 4.95 o.s.i. (ISBN 0-03-072910-6, HoltC). HR&W.

Fieldwork. Maria Danielle. 224p. 1981. pap. 2.25 (ISBN 0-380-78162-X, 78162). Avon.

Fiend. LC 70-147940. (Playboy science fiction). 1971. 0.75. Playboy Press.

Fiend. Margaret Millar. LC 64-14835. 1964. Random House.

Fiend. Margaret Millar. 1974. (pbk.) 1.25. Avon.

Fiend in Need. Milton K Ozaki. LC 47-3523. 1947. Ziff-Davis Publishing Company.

Fiend Incarnate. David Malcolm. (On cover: The Zenda series). J. S. Tait & Sons.

Fiend's Delight. Ambrose Gwinnett Bierce. 1873. Repr. of 1873 ed. lib. bdg. 18.50 (ISBN 0-8398-0165-3). Irvington.

Fierce and Beautiful World. Andrei Platonovich Platonov. LC 71-87195. 1970. 6.95. E. P. Dutton.

Fierce and Gentle Warriors: Three Stories. Mikhail Aleksandrovich Sholokhov. (Illus.). 1967. Doubleday.

Fierce Dispute. Helen Hooven Santmyer. LC 29-8837. 1929. Houghton Mifflin Company.

Fierce Meadows. Tony Quagliano. 24p. 1981. pap. 2.50 (ISBN 0-932136-04-4). Petronium Pr.

Fierce Metronome: The One-Page Novels & Other Short Fiction. Carol Berge. 44p. (Orig.). 1981. signed ed. 25.00 (ISBN 0-939290-05-7); pap. 6.00 (ISBN 0-939290-04-9). Window Edns.

Fierceheart the Soldier: A Romance of 1745. John Collis Snaith. (Half-title: Appleton's town and county librartym no. 217). 1897. D. Appleton and Company.

Fiercest Heart. Stuart Cloete. LC 60-8762. 1960. Houghton Mifflin.

Fierry Flower. Paul Iselin Wellman. 1971. pap. 0.95 o.p. (09093). Curtis.

Fiery Angel, a Sixteenth Century Romance. Valery I. Briusov. Tr. by Ivor Montagu & Sergei Nalbandov. LC 70-114475. 392p. Repr. of 1930 ed. 15.00 o.p. (ISBN 0-8371-4815-4). Greenwood.

Fiery Dawn. Coleridge, Mary Elizabeth. LC 1-25419. 1901. Longmans, Green, and Co.

Fiery Dive and Other Stories. Martin Donisthorpe Armstrong. LC 30-6150. Harcourt, Brace and Company.

Fiery Flower, a Novel. Paul Iselin Wellman. LC 59-12660. 1959. Doubleday.

Fiery Furnace. Lawrence Williams. LC 60-6731. 1960. Simon and Schuster.

Fiery Ordeal. Charlotte Mary Braeme. (On cover: Seaside library. Pocket ed. no. 1185). G. Munroe.

Fiery Ordeal. Charlotte Mary Brame. LC 44-12245. (On cover: Seaside library. Pocket ed. No. 1185). G. Munro.

Fiery Ordeal. Mary Craig. LC 6-28871. (Half-title: Appletons' town and country library, no. 233). 1898. D. Appleton and Company.

Fiery Ordeal. By Tasma Pseud.... Jessie Catherine Huybers Covreur. LC 6-28872. 1898. D. Appleton and Company.

Fiery Particles. Charles Edward Montague. LC 79-131781. 1970. Scholarly Press.

Fiery Particles. Charles Edward Montague. LC 26-16262. 1926. Doubleday, Page & Company.

Fiery Trials. Or A Story of an Infidel's Family. Robert Haskins Crozier. LC 6-31944. 1882. Rogers & Co., Printers.

Fiesta. Georgie Brassell. LC 41-14430. 1941. The Naylor Company.

Fiesta: A Captivating Novel of Adventure, Mystery and Romance in the Colorful Days of Eary Santa Barbara. Ruth Parsons & Verne, Valcour. LC 40-13266. The Odyssey Book House, Pacific Coast Division.

Fiesta: A Novel. Robert Waddy Ramsey. LC 55-11197. 1955. J. Day Co.

Fiesta: A Novel of Modern Spain. Prudencio De Pereda. LC 53-9428. 1953. A. A. Wyn.

Fiesta at Anderson's House. Scott Graham Williamson. LC 47-177823. 1947. H. Holt and Company.

Fiesta De Abril. Berta Savariego. LC 81-67772. (Coleccion Caniqui Ser.). 117p. (Orig.). 1981. pap. 9.95 (ISBN 0-89729-297-9). Ediciones.

Fiesta in Manhattan: A Novel. Charles Kaufman. LC 39-27138. 1939. W. Morrow & Company.

Fiestas. Introd., Notes by Kessel Schwartz. Juan Goytisolo. LC 64-56131. (Alurel lang. lib.: Spanish ser.; 2945). Dell.

Fiestas. Translated from the Spanish by Herbert Weinstock. Juan Goytisolo. LC 60-9321. half cl., 3.95. Knopf.

Fievre A Malte. Valerie Lafargue. (Collection Colombine Ser.). 192p. 1983. pap. 1.95 (ISBN 0-373-48065-2). Harlequin Bks.

Fife and Drum. Mary Dwinell Chellis. LC 6-23414. (On cover: Fife and drum series, no. 1). 1881. National Temperance Society and Publication House.

Fifteen and Five. Abraham Bernstein. LC 32-12598. Liveright, Inc.

Fifteen by Maupassant. Guy De Maupassant. LC 73-169929. 1972. 3.95. Doubleday.

Fifteen by Three: R. V. Cassill, Herbert Gold and James B. Hall. Short Stories. Robert Verlin Cassill. LC 57-13082. (New Directions paperbook 68). 1957. New Directions.

Fifteen Days. An Extract from Edward Colvil's Journal... Mary Lowell Putnam. LC 7-42401. 1866. Ticknor and Fields.

Fifteen Detective Stories. LC 1-651. (The Champion detective, series, no. 24). J. S. Ogilvie & Company.

Fifteen Detective Stories. LC 6527. (On cover: Magnet detective library, no. 152). 1900. Street & Smith.

Fifteen Finest Short Stories. Ed. by John Cournos. LC 28-206103. 1928. Dodd, Mead & Company.

Fifteen Flags. Richards L Hardman. LC 68-17269. (Illus.). 1968. Little, Brown and Co.

Fifteen Great Russian Short Stories. Ed. by John W. Strahan. LC 73-7387. (Washington Square Press classics W925). 0.75. Washington Square Press; Distributed in the U.S. by Affiliated Publishers.

Fifteen Great Russian Short Stories. Tr. by John W. Strahan. (Orig.). pap. 0.75 o.p. (W0925). WSP.

Fifteen Modern Polish Short Stories: An Annotated Reader & a Glossary. Alexander M. Schenker. LC 74-123394. (Linguistic Ser). 1970. text ed. 14.95x o.p. (ISBN 0-300-01325-6); pap. text ed. 8.95x (ISBN 0-300-01326-4). Yale U Pr.

Fifteen Rabbits. Felix Salten & Chambers, Whittaker, Tr. LC 30-31598. 1930. Simon and Schuster.

Fifteen Rabbits: A Celebration of Life. Felix Salten & John Freas. LC 75-35808. (Illus.). 1976. 7.95 (ISBN 0-440-02563-X). Delacorte Press/Eleanor Friede.

Fifteen Selected Stories. James Thomas Farrell. LC 44-7520. 1943. Avon Book Company.

Fifteen Seventy-Two, a Chronicle of the Times of Charles the Ninth. Prosper Merimee. 1830. G. & C. & H. Carvill.

Fifteen Short Stories. Edited and with an Introd. by Morton Dauwen Zabel. Henry James. LC 61-197296. (Bantam classic, SC84). 1961. Bantam Books.

Fifteen Stories. Ed. by Herbert Barrows. LC 50-9405. 1950. Heath.

Fifteen Strings of Cash. Ed. by Kuang Rong. (Illus., Orig.). 1982. pap. 4.95 (ISBN 0-8351-1103-2). China Bks.

Fifteen Tales. Ivan Alekseevich Bunin & Bernard Guilbert Guerney. LC 77-91708. (Short Story Index in Reprint). 1978. 21.50 (ISBN 0-8486-5000-X). Core Collection Books.

Fifteen Tales: Fifteen Tales. Stacy Aumonier. LC 25-4778. 1924. Doubleday, Page & Company.

Fifteen Terse Stories. Roger E. Hyde. (Illus.). 1976. signed & numbered 5.00 (ISBN 0-89376-001-3); pap. 3.00 (ISBN 0-89376-000-5). Washoe.

Fifteenth Pan Book of Horror Stories. Ed. by H. Van Thal. 1982. pap. 10.00x (ISBN 0-330-24149-4, Pub. by Pan Bks). State Mutual Bk.

Fifteenth Pelican. Teresa Rios, pseud. LC 65-19885. (Illus.). 1965. Doubleday.

Fifteenth Pelican see Flying Nun.

Fifth Ace. Isabel Egenton Ostrander. LC 18-12303. W. J. Watt & Company.

Fifth Assembling. new ed. Ed. by Richard Kostelanetz & Henry J. Korn. (Illus.). 300p. (Orig.). 1974. pap. 4.95. Assembling Pr.

Fifth Avenue. facs. ed. Fred Rothermell. LC 76-134978. (Short Story Index Reprint Ser.). 1930. 16.00 (ISBN 0-8369-3708-2). Ayer Co.

Fifth Avenue Store Only. Isabel Glass. LC 73-93181. 1974. 6.95 (ISBN 0-399-11330-4). Putnam.

Fifth Avenue: Twenty-Eight X-Rays of a Street. Fred Rothermell. LC 76-134978. (Short story index reprint series). (Illus.). 1970. Books for Libraries Press.

Fifth Avenue, Twenty-Eight X-Rays of a Street. Fred Rothermell. LC 30-6537. Harcourt, Brace and Company.

Fifth Business. William Robertson Davies. LC 76-48960. 1977. 1.95 (ISBN 0-14-004387-X). Penguin Books.

Fifth Caller. Helen Nielsen. LC 59-5529. 1959. Morrow.

Fifth Column: A Play in Three Acts. Ernest Hemingway. 1940. C. Scribner's Sons.

Fifth Column, and Four Stories of the Spanish Civil War. Ernest Hemingway. LC 70-182369. (Scribner library. Contemporary classics). 1972. 2.45 (ISBN 0-684-10238-2) (ISBN 0-684-12723-7). Scribner.

Fifth Column, and the First Forty-Nine Stories. Ernest Hemingway. LC 38-27930. 1938. C. Scribner's Sons.

Fifth Cord. Dominic Devine. LC 67-23101. 1967. Walker.

Fifth Cord. Dominic Devine. 1967. Walker.

Fifth Criterion. Bruce Zortman. LC 78-71802. (Orig.). 1979. pap. 6.95x (ISBN 0-9602498-0-X). Firestein Bks.

Fifth Dagger. Dorothy Quick. LC 47-1624. 1947. C. Scribner's Sons.

Fifth Daughter. 1st Ed. Hal C Gurney. LC 57-630312. 1957. Doubleday.

Fifth Estate. Robert Lowell Moore. LC 72-92231. 1973. 7.95 (ISBN 0-385-04920-X). Doubleday.

Fifth Estate. Robert Lowell Moore. 1974. (pbk.) 1.75. Bantam Books.

Fifth Fontana Book of Great Horror Stories. Ed. by Mary Danby. 1972. pap. 0.95 o.p. (95199). Beagle Bks.

Fifth Generation: Translated from the Italian by Adrienne Foulke. Dante Arfelli. LC 53-6155. 1953. Scribner.

Fifth Head of Cerberus: Three Novellas. Gene Wolfe. LC 77-38283. 1972. 5.95 (ISBN 0-684-12830-6). Scribner.

Fifth Head of Cerberus: Three Novellas. Wolfe, Gene. 1976. 1.75. Ace Books.

Fifth Horseman. Nathan M Adams. LC 67-12728. 1967. Random House.

Fifth Horseman. Robert William Chambers. LC 37-147373. 1937. D. Appleton-Century Company, Incorporated.

Fifth Horseman. Larry Collins & Dominique Lapierre. 496p. 1981. pap. 3.50 (ISBN 0-380-54734-1, 60889-8). Avon.

Fifth Horseman. Lauran Paine. LC 59-3954. (Foulsham western story). 1959. W. Foulsham.

Fifth Horseman. Jose Antonio Villarreal. LC 73-81452. 1974. 7.95 (ISBN 0-385-07883-8). Doubleday.

Fifth Horseman: A Novel. Larry Collins & Dominique Lapierre. LC 80-14643. 13.95 (ISBN 0-671-24316-0). Simon and Schuster.

Fifth Horseman: By Nathan M. Adams. Nathan M Adams. (72005). 1968. Ballantine.

Fifth Jade of Heaven. Marilyn Granbeck. 352p. 1982. pap. 2.95 (ISBN 0-515-04628-0). Jove Pubns.

Fifth Key. George Harmon Coxe. LC 47-803. 1947. A. A. Knopf.

Fifth Latchkey. Natalie Sumner Lincoln. LC 29-143001. 1929. D. Appleton and Company.

Fifth Man. Manning Coles, pseud. LC 46-805561. 1946. Pub. for the Crime Club by Doubleday & Company, Inc.

Fifth Man. Manning Coles, pseud. LC 47-19985. 1947. The Sun Dial Press.

Fifth Miracle: A Novel. William Joyce Cowen. LC 54-10861. 1954. Longmans, Green.

Fifth Mystery Book: Four Short Mysteries. LC 44-920. 1944. Farrar & Rinehart, Inc.

Fifth of a Century. Arthur Bernard Winter & Hill, Harry Emerson, 1898- Joint Author. The Falcon Press.

Fifth of November; a Romance of the Stuarts. Charles S Bentley & Scribner, Frank Kimball. LC 96-1108. Rand, McNally & Company.

Fifth of the Medlocks. David P Allison. 1940. Wm. B. Eerdmans Publishing Company.

Fifth Pan Book of Horror Stories. Ed. by H. Van Thal. 1982. pap. 10.00x (ISBN 0-330-02079-X, Pub. by Pan Bks). State Mutual Bk.

Fifth Passenger. Edward Preston Young. LC 63-10618. 218p. 1981. pap. 2.25i (ISBN 0-06-080544-7, P 544, PL). Har-Row.

Fifth Passenger. 1st Ed. Edward Preston Young. LC 63-10618. 1963. Harper & Row.

Fifth Pestilence, Together with The History of the Tinkling Cymbal and Sounding Brass, Ivan Semyonovitch Stratilatov. Aleksei Mikhailovich Remizov. LC 76-23895. (Classics of Russian literature). (Hyperion library of world literature). 1977. 11.50. (ISBN 0-88355-511-5) (ISBN 0-88355-512-3). Hyperion Press.

Fifth Planet. Fred Hoyle & Hoyle, Geoffrey. LC 63-20284. 1963. Harper & Row.

Fifth Planet. Fred Hoyle & Geoffrey Hoyle. (Perennial library). 1979. 1.95 (ISBN 0-06-080487-4). Harper & Row.

Fifth Queen: The Fifth Queen, Privy Seal, The Fifth Queen Crowned. Ford Madox Ford. LC 63-13786. 1963. Vanguard Press.

Fifth Sally. Daniel Keyes. LC 80-12026. 1980. 10.95. Houghton Mifflin Co.

Fifth Seal. Mark Aleksandrovich Aldanov. Tr. by Wreden, Nicholas R. LC 43-6454. 1943. C. Scribner's Sons.

Fifth Season. Joseph Tusiani. 1964. 8.95 (ISBN 0-8392-1032-9). Astor-Honor.

Fifth Simenon Omnibus. Georges Simenon. LC 73-155173. 1972. 0.50 (ISBN 0-14-003432-3). Penguin.

Fifth Son of the Shoemaker. Donald Corley. LC 30-293437. 1930. R. M. McBride & Company.

Fifth String. John Philip Sousa. LC 2-4951. 1902. The Bowen-Merrill Co.

Fifth String. John Philip Sousa. LC 7-29567. The Bobbs-Merrill Company.

Fifth Tumbler: Introducing Professor Theocritus Lucius Westborough... Clyde B Clason. LC 36-749. 1936. Pub. for the Crime Club, Inc., by Doubleday, Doran & Company, Inc.

Fifth Week. John O'Malley. LC 75-43583. 1976. 2.95 (ISBN 0-8294-0248-9). Loyola.

Fifth Wheel: A Novel. Olive Higgins Prouty. LC 16-6605. 1.35. Frederick A. Stokes Company.

Fifth Woman. Maria Fagyas. LC 63-20515. 1963. Published for the Crime Club by Doubleday.

Fifth World of Forster Bennett: Portrait of a Navaho. Vincent Crapanzano. LC 77-184547. 256p. 1973. pap. 2.25 o.p. (ISBN 0-670-00378-6). Penguin.

Fifties. Isaac Asimov et al. Afterword by Barry Malzburg & Bill Pronzini. (Analog Science Fiction Ser.). 1979. pap. 5.95 (ISBN 0-89437-073-1). Baronet.

Fifty & His Friends. W. W. Williams. 3.50 o.p. Carlton.

Fifty Best Amercan Short Stories: 1915-1965. Ed. by Martha Foley. Best American Short Stories (The) Ed. by Martha Foley. LC 65-11538. 6.95. Houghton.

Fifty Best American Short Stories: 1915-1965. Ed. by Martha Foley. LC 65-11538. 1965. Houghton Mifflin.

Fifty Best American Short Stories: 1915-1939. Ed. by Edward Joseph Harrington O'Brien. Schramm, Wilbur Lang. LC 39-232903. Houghton Mifflin Company.

Fifty Candles. Earl Derr Biggers. LC 26-4065. The Bobbs-Merrill Company.

Fifty Dollars a Night. Don James. pap. 0.60 o.p. (60-400). Manor Bks.

Fifty-Eight Short Stories. O. Henry. 3.00 o.p. (ISBN 0-00-422549-X). Collins-World.

Fifty Famous Stories Retold. James B. Baldwin. 1970. pap. 1.25 o.p. (ISBN 0-486-22421-X). Dover.

Fifty Fathom Klondike. Prentice Winchell. LC 59-940567. (Illus.). 1959. Funk & Wagnalls.

Fifty Feelings. Franz H. Denghausen. 4.75 o.p. (ISBN 0-8283-1285-0). Branden.

Fifty-Fifty: A Blend of Old and New. Albert Michael Neil Lyons. LC 73-178445. (Short story index reprint series). 1971. (ISBN 0-8369-4046-6). Books for Libraries Press.

Fifty-Five Days at Peking: A Novel. Noel Bertram Gerson & Philip. Days At Peking Yordan. LC 63-8932. (Bantam fifty, F2561). 1963. Bantam Books.

Fifty-Five Short Stories from the New Yorker, 1940-1949. The, New Yorker Magazine. 1965. pap. 2.50 o.p. (68928). S&S.

Fifty-Four Forty or Fight. Emerson Hough. LC 9-2775. 1909. The Bobbs-Merrill Company.

Fifty Golden Years. Albert Aloysius Maas & Maas, Rose Anne (Smith) 1889- Joint Author. LC 45-6642. 1945. Printed by the Consolidated Publishing Company.

Fifty Great American Short Stories. Ed. by Milton Crane. LC 65-13863. (Bantam classic, WC265) Bibl.). Bantam.

Fifty Great American Short Stories. Ed. by Milton Crane. (Orig.). (gr. 9 up). pap. 2.95 (ISBN 0-553-14528-2). Bantam.

Fifty Great Ghost Stories. Ed. by John Canning. LC 67-17807. (Illus.). 1967. Taplinger Pub. Co.

Fifty Great Ghost Stories. Ed. by John Canning. 560p. (gr. 9 up). 1973. pap. 2.50 (ISBN 0-553-13499-X, 13499-X). Bantam.

Fifty Great Horror Stories. Ed. by John Canning. LC 69-18368. (Illus.). 1969. 5.95. Taplinger Pub. Co.

Fifty Great Horror Stories. Ed. by John Canning. 512p. (gr. 9 up). 1973. pap. 2.50 (ISBN 0-553-13762-X, C 13762-X). Bantam.

Fifty Great Oriental Stories. Ed. by Gene Z Hanrahan. LC 65-13862. (A Bantam classic, NC266). 1965. Bantam Books.

Fifty Great Sea Stories. Joseph Conrad et al. 768p. 1980. Repr. lib. bdg. 35.00 (ISBN 0-8495-1712-5). Arden Lib.

Fifty Great Short Stories. Ed. by Milton Crane. LC 52-43293. (Bantam giant, A950). 1952. Bantam Books.

Fifty Great Short Stories. Ed. by Milton Crane. (gr. 9 up). pap. 2.75 (ISBN 0-553-20142-5); tchr's guide avail. Bantam.

Fifty Missionary Stories. Ed. by Belle Marvel Brain. LC 3-29836. 1903. F. H. Revell Company.

Fifty Modern Stories: By Warren Beck and Others. Ed. by Thomas Marshall Howe Blair. LC 60-1534. 1960. Row, Peterson.

Fifty-One Tales. Lord Dunsany. 1978. Repr. of 1919 ed. lib. bdg. 20.00 (ISBN 0-8482-0619-3). Norwood Edns.

Fifty-One Tales see Food of Death: Fifty-One Tales.

Fifty Pounds for a Wife. Anna L Glyn. LC 11-16156. 1892. H. Holt and Company.

Fifty Roads to Town. Earl Hamner, Jr. LC 53-6912. 1969. pap. 0.95 o.p. (65-042). Paperback Lib.

Fifty Roads to Town. Frederick Nebel. LC 36-154023. 1936. Little, Brown, and Company.

Fifty Roads to Town: A Novel. Earl Hamner. LC 53-6912. 1953. Random House.

Fifty-Seventh Franz Kafka. Rudy Rucker. 1983. pap. 2.50 (ISBN 0-441-23516-6, Pub. by Ace Science Fiction). Ace Bks.

Fifty-Seventh Street. George Selcamm. LC 76-77395. 1971. 6.95 (ISBN 0-393-08633-X). Norton.

Fifty Short Science Fiction Tales. Ed. by Isaac Asimov. Conklin, Groff, 1904- Joint Ed. LC 62-21646. 1963. Collier Books.

Fifty Short Shorts, an Omnibus of Short Stories. Ed. by Mary Anne Howard. LC 45-9731. 1945. The World Publishing Company.

Fifty Stories. Kay Boyle. LC 78-22151. 1980. 15.95 (ISBN 0-385-14996-4). Doubleday.

Fifty Stories. Kay Boyle. LC 81-7361. 1981. 7.95 (ISBN 0-14-005922-9). Penguin Books.

Fifty Thousand Dollars Ransom: A Novel. David Malcolm. (On cover: The Zenda series). 1896. J. S. Tait & Sons.

Fifty-Two Pickup. Elmore Leonard. LC 73-20098. 1974. 6.95 (ISBN 0-440-03153-2). Delacorte Press.

Fifty-Two Pickup. Elmore Leonard. 1975. (pbk.) 1.50. Dell.

Fifty-Two West: A Novel of Success in Our Time. Ann Pinchot. LC 62-16282. 1962. Farrar, Straus and Cudahy.

Fifty Wall Street. Vartanig G Vartan. LC 68-12269. 1967. McGraw-Hill.

Fifty Years a Woman. Ishbel Ross. LC 38-255074. 1938. Harper & Brothers.

Fifty Years Ago. A Story of New England Life. Clara A. Willard. LC 8-37012. 1871. A. D. F. Randolph & Company.

Fifty Years & the Stars. Lola I. Bryan. 3.50 o.p. Carlton.

Fifty Years in Medicine: The Story of New England Doctor. 1st Ed. Mary Styrska Carlton. LC 56-549161. Vantage Press.

Fifty Years in the Wilderness: A Pioneer Tale of Eastern New York; from the German; with an Appendix--An Appreciation of the German Character. Frederick Mayer & Reinhard, August William, 1856- Tr. LC 33-33686. 1931. Wetzel Publishing Company, Inc.

Fifty Years of the American Short Story: From the O. Henry Awards, 1919-1970. Ed. by William Miller Abrahams. LC 71-111137. 1970. Doubleday.

Fifty Years, Three Months, Two Days. A Tale of the Neckar Valley. Julius Wolff & Winslow, W. Henry, Tr. LC 9-2515. T. Y. Crowell & Co.

Fifty Years to Erase. Joseph DeMario. 3.00 o.p. Carlton.

Fig in Winter: A Novel. Willa Gibbs. LC 63-13709. 1963. Morrow.

Fig Leaves. Mildred Evans Gilman. LC 25-21363. 1925. Siebel Publishing Corporation.

Fig Leaves. 3d ed. Mildred Evans Gilman. LC 29-146. The Avondale Press.

Fig Tale. Tony Johnston. (Illus.). 1974. 4.97 (ISBN 0-399-60908-3). Putnam.

Fig Tree. Aubrey Menen. LC 59-7197. 1959. Scribner.

Fig Tree. Francoise Xenakis. 1971. 4.50 o.p. (ISBN 0-8027-0358-5). Walker & Co.

Fig Tree John. Edwin Corle. LC 79-148665. 1971. 6.95 (ISBN 0-87140-518-0). Liveright.

Fig Tree John. Edwin Corle. LC 35-9122. Liveright Publishing Corporation.

Fig Tree John. Foreword by Lawrence Clark Powell. Illus. by Don Perceval. Edwin Corle. LC 55-33526. 1955. W. Ritchie Press.

Fig Tree. Obolensky. Nancy Bruff Gardner. LC 64-23766. 3.95. World.

Figaro Fiction: A Collection Short Stories. LC 7-1231. 1892. W. J. F, Dailey.

Fight at Sun Mountain. Kenneth Fowler. LC 57-8245. 1957. Ballantine Books.

Fight for a Throne. Josiah Turner Newcomb. LC 98-2194. F. T. Neely.

Fight for Arkenvald. Thomas Johnston. (Illus.). 1973. 4.50. Doubleday.

Fight for Powder Valley! Peter Field. LC 42-11449. 1942. W. Morrow & Company.

Fight for the Crown: A Novel. William Edward Norris. LC 7-33294. 1897. Harper & Brothers.

Fight for the Sweetwater: By Bliss Lomax Pseud. Harry Sinclair Drago. LC 50-6527. (Silver star westerns). 1950. Dodd, Mead.

Fight for the Valley. Lee Deighton. 160p. 1981. pap. 1.75 (ISBN 0-345-29076-3). Ballantine.

Fight Night on a Sweet Saturday: A Novel. Mary Lee Settle. LC 64-12226. 1964. Viking Press.

Fight of the Few. Richard Alexander Hough. LC 79-3728. 1980. 9.95 (ISBN 0-688-03606-6). Morrow.

Fight on the Standing Stone. Francis Lynde. LC 25-7669. 1925. C. Scribner's Sons.

Fight or Die. Willis Todhunter Ballard. (Belmont Tower Books). 1977. 1.50 (ISBN 0-505-51184-3). Tower Pubns.

Fight the Wild River. William Edmunds Claussen. LC 54-9230. (Silver star westerns). 1954. Dodd, Mead.

Fight with Fate. Annie French Hector. 1896. J. B. Lippincott Company.

Fighter. Len Deighton. 1982. pap. 9.95 (ISBN 0-345-29821-7). Ballantine.

Fighter. Albert Payson Terhune. LC 9-32367. F. F. Lovell Company.

Fighter Pilots: A Novel. Kelly Rollins. LC 81-5978. 12.95 (ISBN 0-316-75453-6). Little, Brown.

Fighters: A Panoramic Novel About the Fighter War in the West-1939-1945. Colin D Willock. LC 73-77055. 1973. 7.95. St. Martin's Press.

Fighters and Lovers: Theme in the Novels of John Updike. Joyce B Markle. LC 72-96469. 1973. 8.95 (ISBN 0-8147-5361-2). New York University Press.

Fighters for Freedom. Clara K Curtis. LC 33-7197. 1938.

Fighters in the Sky: Adventure Tales of Fighter Pilots in Three Wars, by Arch Whitehouse. 1st Ed. Arthur George Joseph Whitehouse. LC 59-5555. Duell, Sloan, and Pearce.

Fightin' Fool. Max Brand. LC 39-15604. 1939. Dodd, Mead & Company.

Fightin' Sons of Texas. 1st Ed. Paul Evan Lehman. LC 52-10421. (Dutton Diamond D western). 1953. Dutton.

Fighting Against Millions: Or, The Detective in the Jewel Caves of Kurm. A Detective Story. John Russell Coryell. (On cover: Secret service series, no. 57). 1892. Street & Smith.

Fighting American: A War-Chest of Stories of American Soldiers, from the French and Indian Wars Through the First World War. Francis Van Wyck Mason. LC 43-9679. 1943. Reynal & Hitchcock.

Fighting American: A War-Chest of Stories of American Soldiers, from the French and Indian Wars Through the First World War. Francis Van Wyck Mason. 1945. Garden City Publishing Co., Inc.

Fighting Araucanians. Maria P Dillon. LC 64-16508. 1964. Dorrance.

Fighting Back. Charles Alverson. LC 73-1732. (Black Bat Mysteries Ser). 192p. 1974. 5.95 o.p. (ISBN 0-672-51759-0). Bobbs.

Fighting Back. Meyer Barkai. 279p. (Orig.). 1981. pap. 8.95 (ISBN 0-86649-050-7). Twentieth Century.

Fighting Back. Ronni Sandroff. LC 77-20372. 1978. 8.95 (ISBN 0-394-41310-5). Knopf: Distributed by Random House.

Fighting Back. Ronni Sandroff. 1979. 1.95 (ISBN 0-515-05120-9). Jove Publications.

Fighting Back: A Sequel to "The Leather Pusher". Harry Charles Witwer. LC 24-24343. Grosset & Dunlap.

Fighting Bishop. Herbert Muller Hopkins. LC 2-75629. 1902. The Bowen-Merrill Co.

Fighting Blade. Beulah Marie Dix. LC 12-7964. 1912. 1.30. H. Holt and Company.

Fighting Blood. Harry Charles Witwer. LC 23-6557. 1923. G. P. Putnam's Sons.

Fighting Blood. Gordon Ray Young. LC 32-266797. 1932. Doubleday, Doran & Company, Inc.

Fighting Breed. Lawrence P Cain. LC 60-2721. 1960. Avalon Books.

Fighting Breed. David Case. (Orig.). 1979. pap. 1.95 (ISBN 0-89083-541-1). Zebra.

Fighting Byng: A Novel of Mystery, Intrigue and Adventure. A Stone. LC 19-2848. 1919. Britton Publishing Co.

Fighting Caravans. Zane Grey. LC 29-20110. 1929. Harper & Brothers.

Fighting Chance. Robert William Chambers. 1906. D. Appleton and Company.

Fighting Chance: The Romance of an Ingenue. Gertrude Lynch. LC 3-12968. 1903. The Smart Set Publishing Co.

Fighting Danites. Dane Coolidge. 1934. E. P. Dutton & Co., Inc.

Fighting Doctor. Helen Reimensnyder Martin. LC 12-4354. 1912. The Century Co.

Fighting Dr. Diana. Isabel S. Way. 1973. 4.50 o.p. (Avalon). Bouregy.

Fighting Edge. William MacLeod Raine. LC 22-17939. 1922. Houghton Mifflin Company.

Fighting Edge. William MacLeod Raine. 1973. 0.75. Popular Lib.

Fighting Fantastic. Yvonne Marie Aimee Moyse. LC 29-3270. 1929. Longmans, Green and Co.

Fighting Fool: A Tale of the Western Frontier. Dane Coolidge. LC 18-9490. E. P. Dutton & Company.

Fighting for Favour: A Romance. W. G Tarbet. LC 8-25562. 1898. H. Holt and Company.

Fighting Four. Max Brand. 1981. 15.00x (ISBN 0-86025-157-8, Pub. by Ian Henry Pubns England). State Mutual Bk.

Fighting Four: A Silvertip Story. Frederick Faust. LC 44-719598. 1944. Dodd, Mead & Company.

Fighting from Baltimore: A Bloody Picaresque Through the Bowels of America. Howard Gould. 6.95 o.p. Vantage.

Fighting Hearts. James French Dorrance. LC 32-659737. The Macaulay Company.

Fighting Horse Valley. William Fitzgerald Jenkins. LC 34-31988. A. H. King.

Fighting Jack Warbonnet. Frank Chester Robertson. LC 39-4057. 1939. E. P. Dutton & Company, Inc.

Fighting Littles. Booth Tarkington. LC 41-21285. 1941. Doubleday, Doran and Company, Inc.

Fighting Livingstons. Leonard Hastings Nason. LC 31-481130. 1931. Doubleday, Doran & Company, Inc.

Fighting Man. Frank Gruber. LC 48-7555. 1948. Rinehart.

Fighting Man. Frank Gruber. 1974. (pbk.) 0.75. New American Library.

Fighting Man of Mars. Edgar Rice Burroughs. LC 31-12974. Metropolitan Books, Inc.

Fighting Man of Mars. Illustrated by Mahlon Blaine. Edgar Rice Burroughs. 1962. Canaveral Press.

Fighting Men. Alden Brooks. LC 17-21873. 1917. C. Scribner's Sons.

Fighting Men. Willard Manus. 200p. 1982. 12.95 (ISBN 0-915572-55-9); pap. 6.95 (ISBN 0-915572-54-0). Panjandrum.

Fighting Men: A Novel. Willard Manus. LC 81-14092. 12.95 (ISBN 0-915572-55-9) (ISBN 0-915572-54-0). Panjandrum Books.

Fighting Men, U.S.A. James Warner Bellah. LC 63-6019. 1963. Regency Books.

Fighting Parson: A Novel. Alice Lent Covert. LC 41-22773. 1941. H. C. Kinsey & Company, Inc.

Fighting Parson of Barbary Coast. Franklin Rhinaldo Wedge. 1912. Tribune Printing Company.

Fighting Ramrod. Lee Floren. (Leisure book). 1978. 1.25 (ISBN 0-8439-0547-6). Nordon Pubns.

Fighting Ramrod. Charles N Heckelmann. LC 51-10819. (Double D western). 1951. Doubleday.

Fighting Rawhider. W J Reynolds. LC 57-7722. 1957. Arcadia House.

Fighting Sheepman. Ray Palmer Tracy. LC 51-9551. 1951. Little, Brown.

Fighting Shepherdess. Caroline Lockhart. LC 19-5695. 1.50. Small, Maynard & Company.

Fighting Sheriff. James Lyon Rubel. LC 39-12001. 1939. Phoenix Press.

Fighting Ships. Arch Whitehouse. 1972. pap. 0.95 o.p. (09115). Curtis.

Fighting Slave of Gor. John Norman. (Gor Ser.: No. 14). 1980. pap. 2.95 (ISBN 0-87997-681-0, UE1681). Daw Bks.

Fighting Sons of Texas. Paul Evan Lehman. 1968. Repr. pap. 0.50 o.p. (50-417). Manor Bks.

Fighting Sons of Texas. Paul Evan Lehman & Chuck Martin. (Manor Books double Western). 1973. (pbk.) 0.95. Manor Books.

Fighting Sons of Texas: Box Star Buckaroo. Paul E. Lehman & Chuck Martin. 256p. 1973. pap. 0.95 o.p. (532-95274-095). Manor Bks.

Fighting Starrs of Oregon. Sabra Conner. LC 32-232869. The Reilly & Lee Co.

Fighting Stars. Hiram Alfred Cody. LC 28-15624. George H. Doran Company.

Fighting Submarine. Edwyn Gray. 192p. 1981. pap. 2.25 (ISBN 0-523-41399-8). Pinnacle Bks.

Fighting Temeraire. John Winton. LC 70-154769. 1971. 6.95. Coward, McCann & Geoghegan.

Fighting Tenderfoot. William MacLeod Raine. LC 29-18935. Doubleday, Doran & Company, Inc.

Fighting Tenderfoot. William MacLeod Raine. LC 44-21956. 1944. Triangle Books.

Fighting Terhunes. Peggy Gaddis, pseud. LC 42-224493. 1942. Arcadia House, Inc.

Fighting Terms. Thom Gunn. 39p. 1970. pap. 1.95 o.p. (ISBN 0-571-09390-6). Faber & Faber.

Fighting Texan: A Western Novel. Will Cook. LC 56-26714. (Popular library, 722). 1956. Popular Library.

Fighting the Air. Florence Marryat Church Lean. LC 7-135948. (On cover: Lovell's library. v. 20, no. 999). 1887. J. W. Lovell Company.

Fighting the Sea: Or, Winter at the Life-Saving Station. Edward Augustus Rand. LC 8-2205. (Fighting the sea series, no. 1). 1887. T. Whittaker.

Fighting Troubadour: A Novel. Archibald Clavering Gunter. LC 99-4649. (On cover: The welcome series, no. 50). The Home Publishing Company.

Fighting Under the Southern Cross: A Story of the Chile-Peruvian War. Claude Hazeltine Wetmore. LC 1-23102. W. A. Wilde Company.

Fighting Vengeance. Jake Logan. LC 80-80995. (Jake Logan Ser.). 192p. (Orig.). 1980. pap. 1.95 (ISBN 0-86721-006-0). Playboy Pbks.

Fighting Wagons to Santa Fe! A Tale of Adventure and Romance on the Old Trail to the Southwest. John W Tait. LC 54-7408. 1954. Vantage Press.

Fighting with Fremont: A Tale of the Conquest of California. Everett McNeil. LC 10-19382. E. P. Dutton & Company.

Fighting Words: Stories and Cartoons by Members of the Armed Forces of America, Published Under the Auspices of the Armed Forces Service League. Ed. by Warfield Lewis. Armed Forces Service League. LC 44-8479. 1944. J. B. Lippincott Company.

Figs and Thistles. Albion Winegar Tourgee. LC 73-104582. 1970. (ISBN 0-8398-1964-1). Literature House.

Figs and Thistles: A Western Story. Albion Winegar Tourgee. LC 8-298474. Fords, Howard & Hulbert.

Figs in Frost. Denise Robins. 1975. (pbk.) 1.25. Bantam Books.

Figure Away. Phoebe Atwood Taylor. (Foul Play Press Bks.). 1979. pap. 4.50 (ISBN 0-914378-48-1). Countryman.

Figure Away. Phoebe Atwood Taylor. 1970. pap. 0.60 o.p. (X2175). Pyramid Pubns.

Figure Away: An Asey Mayo Mystery. Phoebe Atwood Taylor. LC 37-10143. W. W. Norton & Company, Inc.

Figure Away: The Story of the Yale Puppeteers and the Turnabout Theatre. Phoebe Atwood Taylor. LC 80-10663. 1980. 9.95 (ISBN 0-89340-259-1). J. Curley.

Figure Eight: Or, The Mystery of Meredith Place. Metta Victoria Victor. Beadle & Company.

Figure in the Carpet see Lesson of the Master.

Figure in the Door. Arthur Gregor. 1968. 1.49 o.p. Doubleday.

Figure in the Dusk. John Creasey. LC 53-7729. 1953. Harper.

Figure in the Sand. Jacquelin Ambler Caskie. LC 24-155503. American Library Service.

Figure It Out for Yourself: By James Hadley Chase. Rene Raymond. LC 51-10418. (A Bloodhound mystery). 1951. Duell, Sloan and Pearce.

Figure 8: A Novel. Mark Dintenfass. LC 74-4131. 1974. 6.95 (ISBN 0-671-21795-X). Simon and Schuster.

Figured Flame. Jane Darrow Tallman. LC 28-20924. 1928. Century Co.

Figurehead. Owen Burke. LC 78-11784. 1979. 10.95 (ISBN 0-698-10958-9). Coward, McCann & Geoghegan.

Figurehead. Owen Burke. 1980. 2.50 (ISBN 0-449-24218-8). Fawcett Crest Books.

Figurehead. Bill Knox. LC 68-27812. 1968. 3.95. Published for the Crime Club by Doubleday.

Figures in a Landscape. Barry England. LC 68-14500. 1968. 4.95. Random House.

Figures in a Landscape. Paul Horgan. LC 40-7419. Harper & Brothers.

Figures in the Straw: An Allegorical Novel. 1st Ed. Count Dillon Gibson. LC 57-921955. 1957. Exposition Press.

Figures of Earth. James B. Cabell. 1927. 8.00 o.p. (ISBN 0-404-01351-1). AMS Pr.

Figures of Earth: A Comedy of Appearance. James Branch Cabell. LC 21-3415. 1921. R. M. McBride & Co.

Filament Winding. D. Rosato & S. Grove. (O.s.i.). 1964. 23.00 o.s.i. (ISBN 0-87245-282-4). Textile Bk.

Filaree. Marguerite Noble. 272p. 1980. pap. 2.50 (ISBN 0-345-28709-6). Ballantine.

Filaree: A Novel of an American. Marguerite Noble. LC 78-57099. 9.95 (ISBN 0-394-50228-0). Random House.

File for Record: A Leonidas Witherall Mystery by Alice Tilton Pseud. Phoebe Atwood Taylor. LC 43-51060. 1967. bds., 3.95. Norton.

File No. 113. Emile Gaboriau. LC 75-32793. (Literature of Mystery and Detection). (Illus.). 1976. 30.00 (ISBN 0-405-07871-4). Arno Press.

File No. 113. Emile Gaboriau. Tr. by Ives, George Burnham. LC 99-5072. 1899. Little, Brown and Company.

File No. 113. From the French of Emile Gaboriav. Emile Gaboriau. LC 6-44553. (On cover: Lovell's library. v. 5, no. 258). 1883. J. W. Lovell Company.

File No. 113: Tr. from the French of Emile Gaboriau. Emile Gaboriau. LC 16-250299. 1916. C. Scribner's Sons.

File No. 113: Tr. from the French of Emile Gaboriau. Emile Gaboriau. LC 2819. 1900. C. Scribner's Sons.

File No. 113: Translated from the French of Emile Gaboriau. Emile Gaboriau. LC 26-222942. 1923. C. Scribner's Sons.

File No. 114. A Sequel to File 113. Ernest A. Young. G. W. Ogilvie.

File No. 115: Or, A Man of Steel. Harry Harper. LC 7-2857. J. S. Ogilvie and Company.

File on Charlie. Bill Copeland, pseud. (Orig.). 1968. pap. 0.60 o.p. (X1870). Pyramid Pubns.

File on Death: A Novel. Kenneth Giles. LC 72-95799. 1973. 5.95 (ISBN 0-8027-5278-0). Walker.

File on Devlin. Catherine Gaskin. LC 65-18391. 4.50. Doubleday.

File on Devlin. Catherine Gaskin. (Crest bk., R960). 1966. Fawcett.

File on Stanley Patton Buchta. Irvin Faust. LC 74-102312. 1970. 5.95. Random House.

Files on Parade. John O'Hara. LC 39-23749. Harcourt, Brace and Company.

Filibuster: A Novel of Adventure. Baldwyn Dyke Acland. LC 30-75682. R.M. McBride & Company.

Filigree Ball. Anna Katharine Green Rohlfs. LC 75-32778. (Literature of Mystery and Detection). 1976. 24.00 (ISBN 0-405-07873-0). Arno Press.

Filigree Ball: Account of the Solution of the Mystery Concerning the Jeffrey-Moore Affair. Anna Katherine Green. LC 75-32778. (Literature of Mystery & Detection). (Illus.). 1976. Repr. of 1903 ed. 24.00x (ISBN 0-405-07873-0). Ayer Co.

Filigree Ball: Being a Full and True Account of the Solution of the Mystery Concerning the Jeffrey-Moore Affair. Anna Katharine Green Rohlfs. LC 3-8441. 1903. The Bobbs-Merrill Company.

Fill the World with Phantoms. Earle W. Emerson. (Orig.). 1979. pap. 1.75 (ISBN 0-532-17215-9). Woodhill.

Fillets of Plaice. Gerald Durrell. 1977. pap. 1.95 o.p. (ISBN 0-14-004338-1). Penguin.

Fillies Don't Win. Herman Milton Appel. Godwin.

Filling His Own Shoes. Henry Cottrell Rowland. LC 16-20499. 1916. 1.35. Houghton Mifflin Company.

Filling Your Love Cup. Kay Kuzma. 90p. (Orig.). 1982. 9.95x (ISBN 0-910529-01-9); pap. 5.95 (ISBN 0-910529-00-0). Parent Scene.

Fillliou Sampler. Robert Filliou. (Orig.). 1967. pap. 2.50 o.p. (ISBN 0-89366-078-7). Ultramarine Pub.

Film Mystery. Arthur Benjamin Reeve. LC 21-2589. Harper & Brothers.

Film of Fear. Frederic Arnold Kummer. LC 17-14950. 1.35. W. J. Watt & Company.

Film of Memory: A Novel. Translated from the French by Moura Budberg. Maurice Druon. LC 55-12046. 1955. Scribner.

Filmi, Filmi, Inspector Ghote. 1st. ed. in the u.s.a. ed. Henry Reymond Fitzwalter Keating. LC 76-23770. 1977. 5.95 (ISBN 0-385-12521-6). Published for the Crime Club by Doubleday.

Filo Del Agua. Agustin Yanez. (Span). pap. 2.25 o.p. U of Tex Pr.

Filostrato of Giovanni Boccaccio: A Translation with Parallel Text by Nathaniel Edward Griffin and Arthur Beckwith Myrick; with an Introduction by Nathaniel Edward Griffin. Giovanni Boccaccio & Griffin, Nathaniel Edward, 1873- Tr. LC 29-22938. 1929. University of Pennsylvania Press.

Fils De Personne. Henri De Montherlant. Ed. by France Anders. (Fr). 1964. pap. text ed. 2.25x o.p. (38240). Macmillan.

Filthy Liars. L. S. Baier. 1968. 4.00 o.p. (ISBN 0-682-46786-3). Exposition.

Final Act. Christopher Hudson. LC 80-13822. 1981. 10.95 (ISBN 0-03-057476-5). Holt, Rinehart, and Winston.

Final Adventures of Sherlock Holmes. A Definitive Text. Arthur Conan Doyle. Ed. by Edgar Wadsworth Smith. Limited Editions Club, Inc., New York. LC 71-21892. (Illus.). 1952. For the Members of the Limited Editions Club.

Final Amendment. Ted Perry. LC 79-79363. 1969. 5.95. Little, Brown.

Final Analysis. Lois Gould. LC 73-18304. 1974. 5.95 (ISBN 0-394-48240-9). Random House.

Final Appearance. Jeannette Covert Nolan. LC 43-431685. 1943. Duell, Sloan and Pearce.

Final Appearances... Jeanette Covert Nolan. LC 45-276. 1944.

Final Appointment. Marcia Blair. (Mystery Puzzlers Ser.: No. 17). (Illus., Orig.). 1979. pap. 1.95 (ISBN 0-89083-452-0). Zebra.

Final Approach. Peter Griffiths. LC 78-459. 1978. 7.95 (ISBN 0-312-28938-3). St. Martin's Press.

Final Approach. First Ed. in U. S. A. Christopher Hodder-Williams. LC 60-50768. 1960. Doubleday.

Final Assembly. Edmund Harry Leftwich. LC 44-233851. 1944. The Dispatch Press.

Final Awakening. Egbert Brown. LC 23-946154. Overstreet & Co.

Final Beast. Frederick Buechner. LC 65-13812. 4.50. Atheneum.

Final Beast. Frederick Buechner. (SP35). 1967. pap., 2.45. Seabury.

Final Beast. Frederick Buechner. LC 81-47438. 1982. 10.95 (ISBN 0-06-061159-6). Harper & Row.

Final Blackout. La Fayette Ronald Hubbard. LC 75-411. (Garland Library of Science Fiction). 1975. 11.00 (ISBN 0-8240-1416-2). Garland Pub.

Final Blackout. La Fayette Ronald Hubbard. LC 48-17797. 1948. Hadley Pub. Co.

Final Circle of Paradise. Arkadi Strugatski & Boris Strugatski (ISBN 0-87997-264-5). Daw Books.

Final Circle of Paradise. Arkadii Natanovich Strugatskii & Boris Natanovich Strugatskii. (Science Fiction Ser.). 1976. pap. 1.25 o.p. (ISBN 0-87997-264-5, UY1264). DAW Bks.

Final Conflict: Omen III. Gordon McGill. (Orig.). 1980. pap. 2.95 (ISBN 0-451-12258-5, AE2258, Sig). NAL.

Final Copy. Jay Barbette, pseud. LC 50-10152. (Red badge detective). 1950. Dodd, Mead.

Final Count. Herman Cyril McNeile. LC 26-357102. George H. Doran Company.

Final Countdown. Martin Caidin. 240p. (Orig.). 1980. pap. 2.50 (ISBN 0-553-20441-6). Bantam.

Final Curtain. J. Eddie Infante. LC 74-151482. 1972. 0.75. Facilities Pub.

Final Curtain. Ngaio Marsh. LC 47-17766. 1947. Little, Brown and Company.

Final Cut: A Novel. Pamela Herbert Chais. LC 81-2455. 12.95 (ISBN 0-671-25196-1). Simon and Schuster.

Final Cut: A Novel. Daniel Stern. LC 74-4799. 1975. 8.95 (ISBN 0-670-31333-5). Viking Press.

Final Death, No. 29. Warren Murphy. (Destroyer Ser.). 1977. pap. 1.75 (ISBN 0-523-40905-2). Pinnacle Bks.

Final Deduction. Rex Stout. 144p. 1981. pap. 1.95 (ISBN 0-553-12205-3). Bantam.

Final Deduction: A Nero Wolfe Novel. Rex Stout. LC 61-16847. 1961. Viking Press.

Final Diagnosis. Arthur Hailey. LC 78-1510. 1969. 5.95. Doubleday.

Final Diagnosis: Pseud. Arthur Hailey. LC 59-128215. 1959. A Novel. St Ed.

Final Doors. Joe L. Hensley. LC 81-43254. (Crime Club Ser.). 192p. 1981. 10.95 (ISBN 0-385-17800-X). Doubleday.

Final Echo: Selected Short Stories. James Melvin Reinhardt. LC 73-165012. 1971. (ISBN 0-910814-35-X). Johnsen Pub. Co.

Final Edition. Arthur Miller. 384p. (Orig.). 1981. pap. 2.75 (ISBN 0-523-41170-7). Pinnacle Bks.

Final Encounter. Ed. by Frederik Pohl. 1970. pap. 0.75 o.p. (0502-07071). Curtis.

Final Exposure. Paul H Mansfield. LC 58-7139. (Cock Robin mystery). 1958. Macmillan.

Final Fair. Marcia Blair. (Mystery Puzzler Ser.: No. 21). (Illus., Orig.). 1979. pap. 1.95 (ISBN 0-89083-476-8). Zebra.

Final Fire. Dennis Smith. LC 75-6811. 1975. 7.95 (ISBN 0-8415-0385-0). Saturday Review Press.

Final Fire. Dennis Smith. (Signet book). 1976. 1.95. New American Library.

Final Guest. Marcia Blair. (Mystery Puzzler Ser.: No. 16). (Illus., Orig.). 1979. pap. 1.95 (ISBN 0-89083-436-9). Zebra.

Final Harbor. Harry Homewood. LC 79-24174. 10.95 (ISBN 0-07-029694-4). McGraw-Hill.

Final Hosting: A Novel. Patrick Welch, pseud. LC 40-5228. 1940. Frederick A. Stokes Company.

Final Hour. Taylor Caldwell. LC 75-564. 1975. 11.95 (ISBN 0-88411-152-0). Aeonian Press.

Final Hour. Taylor Caldwell. LC 44-3238. 1944. C. Scribner's Sons.

Final Hour. Taylor Caldwell. (Fawcett crest book). 1974. (pbk.) 1.75. Fawcett.

Final Hours. Suarez Carreno, Jose. LC 52-12195. 1954. Knopf.

Final Initiation. David A. Wilson. 44p. 1973. pap. 1.50 (ISBN 0-934852-11-1). Lorien Hse.

Final Island: The Fiction of Julio Cortazar. Jaime Alazraki & Ivar Ivask. LC 77-21912. (Illus.). 12.95 (ISBN 0-8061-1436-3). University of Oklahoma Press.

Final Judgment. Mitchell Benjoya. LC 77-23689. 8.95 (ISBN 0-8092-7834-0). Contemporary Books.

Final Landscapes. Kirk Keller. 1981. pap. 2.25 (ISBN 0-8439-0931-5). Nordon Pubns.

Final Lie. Marcia Blair. (Mystery Puzzler Ser.: No. 6). (Illus., Orig.). 1978. pap. 1.95 (ISBN 0-89083-409-1). Zebra.

Final Mission. Mark Druck. (Orig.). 1978. pap. 2.25 (ISBN 0-89083-386-9). Zebra.

Final Night. 1st Ed. Robert Gaines. LC 50-6149. 1950. Doubleday.

Final Notice. Joseph N Gores. LC 73-4291. (DKA file novel). 1973. 4.95 (ISBN 0-394-48706-0). Random House.

Final Notice. Jonathan Valin. LC 80-16654. 8.95 (ISBN 0-396-07898-2). Dodd, Mead.

Final Notice. Jonathan Valin. LC 81-5496. 1981. 11.95 (ISBN 0-89340-354-7). J. Curley & Associates.

Final Payment. Valery Shore. 1979. pap. 1.75 (ISBN 0-89041-236-7, 3236). Major Bks.

Final Payment: A Novel. Searn Leonard Rodgers. LC 33-15943. 1933. Hicks Publishing Company Priv. Print. by the Author.

Final Payments. Mary Gordon. LC 77-90259. 8.95 (ISBN 0-394-42793-9). Random House.

Final Phase. William Meyerowitz. 159p. 1972. 5.50 o.p. (ISBN 0-682-47634-X). Exposition.

Final Phase. first ed. William Meyerowitz. 1973. 5.50 (ISBN 0-682-47634-X). Exposition Press.

Final Pose. Marcia Blair. (Mystery Puzzler Ser.: No. 10). (Illus.). 1978. pap. 1.95 (ISBN 0-89083-422-9). Zebra.

Final Programme. Michael Moorcock. LC 76-9846. (Gregg Press science fiction series). 1976. 9.50 (ISBN 0-8398-2335-5). Gregg Press.

Final Proof. Marie R Reno. LC 75-30355. 7.95 (ISBN 0-06-013564-6). Harper & Row.

Final Proof. Julia Savarese. LC 76-116110. 1971. 6.95 (ISBN 0-393-08618-6). Norton.

Final Proof: Or, The Value of Evidence. Rodrigues Ottolengui. LC 98-1145. (The Hudson library, no. 33). 1898. G. P. Putnam's Sons.

Final Quest. Richard Monaco. LC 80-12685. 12.95 (ISBN 0-399-12501-9). Putnam.

Final Reckoning. Barry Nazarian. LC 82-19234. 15.95 (ISBN 0-399-31011-8). Seaview/Putnam.

Final Ring. Marcia Blair. (Mystery Puzzler Ser.: No. 2). (Illus.). 1978. pap. 1.95 (ISBN 0-89083-396-6). Zebra.

Final Score. Martha Albrand. LC 78-3962. 8.95 (ISBN 0-312-28941-3). St. Martin's Press.

Final Score. Warren Beck. LC 44-692205. 1944. A. A. Knopf.

Final Score. Emmett Grogan. LC 76-3979. 8.95 (ISBN 0-03-014041-2). Holt, Rinehart and Winston.

Final Season. Edna M. Manley. 192p. (Orig.). 1982. pap. 1.50 (ISBN 0-449-50306-2, Coventry). Fawcett.

Final Shot. George G. Gilman, pseud. (Edge Ser.: No. 16). 160p. (Orig.). 1975. pap. 1.75 (ISBN 0-523-41294-0). Pinnacle Bks.

Final Solution. Richard E Peck. LC 72-89340. (Doubleday science fiction). 1973. 4.95 (ISBN 0-385-08744-6). Doubleday.

Final Stage; the Ultimate Science Fiction Anthology. Ed. by Edward L. Ferman. LC 73-91122. 1974. 7.95 (ISBN 0-88327-035-8). Charterhouse.

Final Stage: The Ultimate Science Fiction Anthology. Ed. by Edward L. Ferman & Barry N. Malzberg. 1975. pap. 2.50 o.p. (ISBN 0-14-004039-0). Penguin.

Final Stage: The Ultimate Science Fiction Anthology. Ed. by Edward L. Ferman & Barry N. Malzberg. 1975. pap. 2.50 o.p. (ISBN 0-14-004039-0). Penguin.

Final Things. Richard Bruce Wright. LC 80-11492. 8.95 (ISBN 0-525-10495-X). Dutton.

Final Verdict: Six Stories of Men and Women. Sidney Lauer Nyburg. LC 15-4795. 1915. 1.00. J. B. Lippincott Company.

Final War. Louis Tracy. 1896. G. P. Putnam's Sons.

Final Witness. Roger E. Swaybill. 256p. 1983. pap. 2.75 (ISBN 0-380-81422-6). Avon.

Finale. Calvin Miller. LC 78-70810. (Illus.). 4.25 (ISBN 0-87784-627-8). InterVarsity Press.

Finalists. Russell Braddon. LC 77-3869. 1977. 7.95 (ISBN 0-689-10801-X). Atheneum.

Finalities: A Novelette & 5 Short Stories. Edilberto K. Tiempo. 132p. (Orig.). 1982. pap. 6.00x (Pub. by New Day Philippines). Cellar.

Finally... I'm a Doctor. Neil Shulman. LC 76-14605. 7.95 (ISBN 0-684-14601-0). Scribner.

Financial Expert. R. K. Narayan. LC 59-9457. (Noonday paperbacks, N142). 1959. Noonday Press.

Financial Expert. R. K. Narayan. LC 81-3020. 1981. 4.50 (ISBN 0-226-56841-5). University of Chicago in Association with W. Heinemann.

Financial Expert: A Novel. R. K. Narayan. LC 53-1131. 1953. Michigan State College Press.

Financier. Theodore Dreiser. LC 67-29733. (Signet classic CY376). 1967. New American Library.

Financier. John Burland Harris-Burland. LC 6-6268. 1906. G. W. Dillingham Company.

Financier: A Noval. Theodore Dreiser. LC 19-944374. 1919. Harper & Brothers.

Financier: A Novel. completely rev. ed. Theodore Dreiser. LC 27-151167. 1927. Boni & Liveright.

Finch's Fortune. Mazo De La Roche. LC 31-24146. 1931. Little, Brown, and Company.

Finch's Fortune. Mazo De La Roche. 1976. pap. 1.50 (ISBN 0-449-23053-8, Crest). Fawcett.

Find a Crooked Sixpence. Estelle Thompson. LC 76-57853. 1977. 6.95 (ISBN 0-8027-5366-3). Walker.

Find a New Heaven. first american ed. Josephine Delves-Broughton. LC 54-8302. 1954. Little, Brown.

Find a Victim: By John Ross Macdonald Pseud. 1st Ed. Kenneth Millar. LC 53-9478. 1954. Knopf.

Find Him! Elaine Kraf. LC 77-70899. (Illus.). 9.95. (ISBN 0-914590-38-3) (ISBN 0-914590-39-1). Fiction Collective: Distributed by G. Braziller.

Find Me in Fire. Robert James Collas Lowry. LC 48-7932. 1948. Doubleday.

Find My Killer. Manly Wade Wellman. LC 47-1837. 1947. Farrar, Straus and Company.

Find Sherri ! Phyllis Pettit. (Leisure book). 1.75 (ISBN 0-8439-0641-3). Nordon Pubns.

Find Sherri! Phyllis Swan. 1979. pap. 1.75 o.s.i. (ISBN 0-8439-0641-3, Leisure Bks). Nordon Pubns.

Find the Body. John Creasey. LC 67-24786. (Cock Robin mystery). 1967. Macmillan.

Find the Body. Jeremy York. (O.s.i). 1967. 4.50 o.s.i. (63324). Macmillan.

Find the Boy: A Novel. W. H Canaway. LC 61-9863. 1961. Viking Press.

Find the Changeling. Gregory Benford & Gordon Eklund. 1980. pap. 2.50 (ISBN 0-440-12604-5). Dell.

Find the Clock: A Detective Mystery of Newspaper Life. Harry Stephen Keeler. LC 28-5531. E. P. Dutton & Company.

Find the Don's Daughter. Jeff Jacks. 224p. (Orig.). 1974. pap. 0.95 o.p. (449-02912-95, GM). Fawcett World.

Find the Don's Daughter. Jeff Jacks. (Gold medal book. M2912). 1973. (pbk.) 0.95. Fawcett Books.

Find the Dreamers, 1954. Peter W Denzer. LC 55-564008.

Find the Feathered Serpent. Evan Hunter. 1979. lib. bdg. 9.50 (ISBN 0-8398-2519-6, Gregg). G K Hall.

Find the Feathered Serpent. Jacket Design by Henry Enoch Sharp; Endpaper Design by Alex Schomburg. 1st Ed. Evan Hunter. LC 52-5495. (Science fiction novel). 1952. Winston.

Find the Motive. Josiah Pitts Woolfolk. LC 32-23724. 1932. R. Long & R. R. Smith, Inc.

Find the Woman. Gelett Burgess. LC 11-28812. The Bobbs-Merrill Company.

Find the Woman. Helen Joan Hultman. LC 29-11676. 1929. Pub. for The Crime Club, Inc., by Doubleday, Doran & Company, Inc.

Find the Woman. Arthur Somers Roche. LC 21-4551. 1921. Cosmopolitan Book Corporation.

Find This Woman. Richard S. Prather. (Orig.). 1969. pap. 0.75 o.p. (T2683, GM). Fawcett World.

Finders Keepers. Lucienne S Bloch. LC 81-23518. 1982. 11.95 (ISBN 0-395-32040-2). Houghton Mifflin.

Finders Keepers. Gloria Gibbs & Nicolette Clark. 1978. pap. 1.95 (ISBN 0-532-19169-2). Woodhill.

Finders Keepers. Daniel Mainwaring. LC 40-9812. 1940. W. Morrow & Company.

Finding a Girl in America. Andre Dubus. LC 79-90371. 1981. 12.95 (ISBN 0-87923-311-7); pap. 6.95 (ISBN 0-87923-393-1). Godine.

Finding a Girl in America: Ten Stories & a Novella. Andre Dubus. LC 79-90371. 1980. 10.95 (ISBN 0-87923-311-7). D. R. Godine.

Finding a Home. Kate Douglas Smith Wiggin. LC 7-34181. (Riverside literature series no. 174). Houghton, Mifflin and Company.

Finding His Stride. John Harbottle. LC 15-4797. 1915. D. Appleton and Company.

Finding Home. Frances Duncan. 192p. 1982. pap. 2.75 (ISBN 0-380-80143-4, 80143, Flare). Avon.

Finding Maubee. Albert H. Z Carr. LC 74-136804. (Red mask mystery). 1971. 4.95. Putnam.

Finding Maubee. Albert H. Z Carr. LC 81-47334. (Fifty Classics of Crime Fiction, 1950-1975). 1982. 14.95 (ISBN 0-8240-4977-2). Garland.

Finding of Jasper Holt. Grace Livingston Hill. LC 61-4967. 1961. Grosset & Dunlap.

Finding of Jasper Holt. Grace Livingston Hill. LC 75-33131. 1975. 9.95 (ISBN 0-89190-008-X). American Reprint Co.

Finding of Jasper Holt. Grace Livingston Hill. LC 16-12235. 1916. J. B. Lippincott Company.

Finding of Lot's Wife. Alfred Clark. LC 6-25364. F. A. Stokes Company.

Finding of Norah. Eugenia Brooks Frothingham. LC 18-41543. 1918. 0.75. Houghton Mifflin Company.

Finding of the Gentian. Alice Marland Wellington Rollins. LC 7-40754. 1895. Press of J. J. Little & Co.

Finding Out. Thomas P. Baird. LC 67-16089. 1967. Harcourt, Brace & World.

Finding the Groove. Hal Higdon. (YA) 1973. 7.95 o.p. (ISBN 0-399-11144-1). Putnam.

Finding the Lamb. Rebecca Newth. 1982. pap. 4.95 (ISBN 0-940170-05-1). Open Bk Pubns.

Finding True North. W. M. Ransom. LC 73-92744. 51p. 1973. pap. 3.50 (ISBN 0-914742-02-7). Copper Canyon.

Finding Words in Winter. John Judson. 1973. pap. 6.00 o.p. (Pub. by Elizabeth Pr). SBD.

Findings Is Keepings. John Boyd Clarke. LC 27-9365. 1927. E. J. Clode, Inc.

Findlay's Landing. Margaret Chittenden. (Ace Gothic#17). 1975. (pbk.) 0.95. Ace Books.

Fine. Ann Hebson. LC 58-6961.

Fine and Handsome Captain. Frances Lynch. (Fawcett Crest Book). 1977. 1.50 (ISBN 0-449-23269-7). Fawcett Pubns.

Fine & Private Place. Peter S. Beagle. 256p. 1976. pap. 2.25 (ISBN 0-345-29001-1). Ballantine.

Fine & Private Place. Peter S. Beagle. 1960. 3.95 o.p. (ISBN 0-670-31424-2). Viking Pr.

Fine and Private Place. Morley Callaghan. 1977. 1.95 (ISBN 0-445-08553-3). Popular Library.

Fine and Private Place. Kathleen Freeman. LC 47-4733. 1947. Putnam.

Fine and Private Place. Ellery Queen, pseud. LC 74-136603. 1971. 5.95. World Pub. Co.

Fine and Private Place. Ellery Queen, pseud. LC 75-314628. (Penguin crime fiction). 1974. 0.35 (ISBN 0-14-003881-7). Penguin.

Fine & Private Place: A Madman Theory. Ellery Queen, pseud. 1982. pap. 2.25 (ISBN 0-451-11855-3, AE1855, Sig). NAL.

Fine and Private Place: A Novel. Morley Callaghan. LC 75-4545. 1975. 7.95 (ISBN 0-88405-110-2). Mason/Charter.

Fine Clay: A Novel. Isabel Constance Clarke. LC 14-16758. 1914. Benziger Brothers.

Fine Day for Dying. J. T. MacCargo. (Mannix Ser). (O.s.i.: No. 2). (Orig.). 1975. pap. 1.25 o.s.i. (BT50823). Belmont-Tower.

Fine Feathers. Webster Denison & Walter, Eugene. LC 14-3977. 1914. 1.25. A. C. McClurg & Co.

Fine Feathers. Margery H Lawrence. LC 28-12997. The Curtiss Press.

Fine Fellows. Laurie York Erskine. LC 29-112557. 1929. D. Appleton and Company.

Fine Figure of a Girl: Fifteen Tales of War, Postwar, Peace, and Adventure (Former Title: A Role in Manila. Eugene Burdick. (Signet bk., T3255). 1967. New Amer. Lib.

Fine Flowers in the Valley. Donald Wayne. LC 37-291663. 1937. C. Scribner's Sons.

Fine Frenzy. Noel Woodin. LC 59-15320. 1960. Knopf.

Fine Furniture. Theodore Dreiser. LC 75-22164. 1976-1975. 7.95 (ISBN 0-8383-2107-0). Haskell House Publishers.

Fine Furniture. Theodore Dreiser. LC 76-28778. 1976. 7.50 (ISBN 0-8414-3708-4). Folcroft Library Editions.

Fine Furniture. Theodore Dreiser. LC 31-8183. 1930. Random House.

Fine Gossoon: Saga of a Proud Irishman. Ellen Hayes. 160p. 1981. 8.00 (ISBN 0-682-49782-7). Exposition.

Fine in the Blood. Mary Kay Simmons. (Kangaroo Book). 1977. 1.95. Pocket Books.

Fine Madness. Elliott Baker. LC 63-17548. 1964. Putnam.

Fine Me Love! Jane Roth. LC 34-110362. J. Messner, Inc.

Fine of 200 Francs. Elsa Triolet. LC 47-30883. 1947. Reynal & Hitchcock.

Fine Romance... Herman Irving Bloom. LC 38-13184. 1938. Hillman-Curl, Inc.

Fine Romance. Cynthia Propper Seton. LC 79-19617. 1980. 9.95 (ISBN 0-89340-229-X). J. Curley.

Fine Romance: A Novel. Cynthia Propper Seton. LC 75-40497. 7.95 (ISBN 0-393-08742-5). Norton.

Fine Romance: A Novel. Cynthia Propper Seton. (Signet Book). 1977. 1.50 (ISBN 0-451-07455-6). New American Library.

Fine to Look at. Sophie Kerr. LC 37-229600. Farrar & Rinehart, Incorporated.

Fine Tooth Comb. Paul M. Hollister. LC 47-4404. 1947. Doubleday.

Fine White Linen: A Novel of the First Christians in Jerusalem. Polly Hulsey. LC 63-6090. 1963. Exposition Press.

Fineman: A Novel. William Link & Richard Levinson. LC 72-76809. 1972. 6.95. Laddin Press.

Finer Grain. Henry James. LC 10-22859. 1910. C. Scribner's Sons.

Finer Things of Life. Frances Gray Patton. LC 51-13488. 1951. Dodd, Mead.

Finest Baby in the World: Being Letters from a Man to Himself About His Child. Theadorer. LC 4-23722. 1904. F. H. Revell Company.

Finest Stories of Sean O'Faolain. Sean O'Faolain. 1957. 5.95 o.p. (ISBN 0-316-63286-4). Little.

Finest Stories. 1st Ed. Sean O'Faolain. LC 57-5828. 1957. Little, Brown.

Finest Story in the World" and Other Stories. Rudyard Kipling. LC 22-24786. (On cover: Little leather library. no. 55). Little Leather Library Corporation.

Finger. Aaron Marc Stein. LC 72-84946. 1973. 4.95 (ISBN 0-385-08518-4). Published for the Crime Club by Doubleday.

Finger and the Moon. Geoffrey Ashe. LC 73-19068. 1974. 6.95 (ISBN 0-381-98269-6). John Day Co.

Finger! Finger! A Mystery Novel. Harry Stephen Keeler. LC 38-5755. 1938. E. P. Dutton & Co., Inc.

Finger in the Candle Flame. Giorgio Saviane. Tr. by L. Edwards. 1964. 5.50x o.p. Verry.

Finger Man, and Other Stories. Raymond Chandler. LC 47-4654. (Murder mystery monthly. No. 43). 1947. Avon Book Co.

Finger of Fate. Thomas Mayne Reid. (On cover: Seaside library. Pocket ed. no. 575). G. Munro.

Finger of Fate: Fourteen Thrilling Short Stories... Herman Cyril McNeile. LC 31-2156. Pub. for the Crime Club, Inc., by Doubleday, Doran & Company, Inc.
Finger of Providence. Ed. by Robert M. Myers. (The Children of Pride Ser: Vol. 2). 1977. pap. 1.95 (ISBN 0-445-08614-9). Popular Lib.
Finger of Saturn. Victor Canning. LC 73-16586. 1974. 6.95 (ISBN 0-688-00233-1). Morrow.
Finger of Saturn. Victor Canning. LC 74-9898. 1974. (lib. bdg.) 11.95 (ISBN 0-8161-6225-5). G. K. Hall.
Finger of Unreason. Willa Benton. LC 53-10284. Vantage Press.
Finger Points. Guy Fowler & Saunders, John Monk. LC 31-10980. Grosset & Dunlap.
Finger-Post. Alice Dudeney. LC 24-31100. 1924. Minton, Balch & Company.
Finger to Her Lips. Evelyn Berckman. LC 72-116187. 1971. 5.95. Doubleday.
Fingered City. Denison Hatch. LC 73-83179. 1973. 7.95 (ISBN 0-8397-2240-0). P. S. Eriksson.
Fingerprint. Patricia Wentworth. 240p. 1980. pap. 1.95 (ISBN 0-553-13948-7). Bantam.
Fingerprint: A Miss Silver Mystery. 1st Ed. Patricia Wentworth. LC 56-10813. (Main line mysteries). 1956. Lippincott.
Fingerprints. Hunter Stinson. LC 25-8415. 1925. H. Holt and Company.
Fingerprints & Other Stories. Seth Gilkerson. 1979. 8.00 (ISBN 0-682-49430-5). Exposition.
Fingers in the Door: And Other Stories. Frank Tuohy. LC 77-123822. 1970. 5.95. Scribner.
Fingers of Death. Maxwell Grant, pseud. (Shadow Ser.: No. 17). 1977. pap. 1.25 o.p. (ISBN 0-515-04279-X). BJ Pub Group.
Fingers of Fear. John Urban Nicolson. LC 37-14279. Covici. Friede.
Fingers of Night. Hubert Creekmore. LC 46-376725. 1946. D. Appleton-Century Company, Inc.
Fingers That See. Nancy Buskett & Grey, Cynthia, Ed. LC 14-7076. 1914. 1.00. The Stuff Printing Concern.
Finish Line. R. E Sebenthall. LC 68-22970. (Inner sanctum mystery). 1968. 4.50. Simon and Schuster.
Finish Me off. Hillary Waugh. LC 75-109438. 1970. 5.95. Doubleday.
Finish Me Off. Hillary Waugh. (Belmont Tower Book). 1978. 1.75 (ISBN 0-505-51324-2). Tower Pubns.
Finish'd Rake: Or, Gallantry in Perfection (Anonymous) The Secret History of Mama Oello, Princess Royal of Peru (Anonymous) The Masterpiece of Imposture. LC 70-170584. (Foundations of the Novel). 1973. 22.00 (ISBN 0-8240-0569-4). Garland Pub.
Finished. Henry Rider Haggard. LC 16-23622. 1916. 0.50. Paget Literary Agency.
Finished. Henry Rider Haggard. LC 17-24205. 1917. 1.40. Longmans, Green and Co.
Finished. Illus. by Hookway Cowles. Henry Rider Haggard. LC 66-5445. 1966. bds., 2.95. Macdonald.
Finished Man. George Palmer Garrett. 1971. pap. 0.95 o.p. (09076). Curtis.
Finished Product: And Other Selections. Elza Ivan Edwards. LC 18-12038. 1918. Edwards and Shurtleft.
Finished Rake: or Gallantry in Perfection. Bd. with Secret History of Mama Oella, Princess Royal of Peru; Masterpiece of Imposture. Elizabeth Harding; Temple Rakes: or Innocence Preserved. LC 73-170585. (Foundations of the Novel Ser.: Vol. 57). lib. bdg. 50.00 (ISBN 0-8240-0569-4). Garland Pub.
Finisher. Richard Nesbitt. (Orig.). 1979. pap. 1.95 (ISBN 0-532-23142-2). Woodhill.
Finishing Stroke. Ellery Queen, pseud. LC 58-6271. (Inner sanctum mystery). 1958. Simon and Schuster.
Finishing Touch. Mona Naomi Anne Hocking Messer. LC 48-6481. 1948. Pub. for the Crime Club by Doubleday.
Finishing Touch: And Other Stories. Ora Mae Campbell Willing. LC 57-447421. 1957. White Wing Pub. House.
Finishing Touches. Jean Kerr. LC 74-3474. 192p. 1974. 6.95 o.p. (ISBN 0-385-02713-3). Doubleday.
Finistere. 3rd ed. Fritz Peters, pseud. 1968. pap. 0.75 o.p. (74-947). Lancer.
Finistere: A Novel. Arthur Anderson Peters. LC 51-9378. 1951. Farrar, Straus.
Finland Family: Or, Francis Taken for Facts. A Tale of the Past for the Present. Susan Peyton Cornwall. LC 6-28731. 1853. M. W. Dodd.
Finnegan's Dilemma. Charles Belmar. LC 51-897. 1950. Vantage Press.
Finnegan's Wake. James Augustine Aloysius Joyce. LC 59-354. 1957. Viking Press.
Finnegans Wake. James Augustine Aloysius Joyce. LC 39-11411. 1939. The Viking Press.
Finnegans Wake: A Facsimile of Buffalo Notebooks VI.B.33-36. James Augustine Aloysius Joyce. LC 78-1112. (Joyce, James, 1882-1941. The James Joyce Archive). (Illus.). 1978. 85.00 (ISBN 0-8240-2836-8). Garland Pub.
Finnegans Wake, Book I, Chapter 1: A Facsimile of Drafts, Typescripts & Proofs. James Augustine Aloysius Joyce. LC 78-896. (Joyce, James, 1882-1914. The James Joyce Archive). (Illus.). 1978. 85.00 (ISBN 0-8240-2843-0). Garland Pub.
Finnegans Wake, Book I, Chapter 8: A Facsimile of Drafts, Typescripts & Proofs. James Joyce & Danis Rose. LC 78-4039. (Joyce, James, 1882-1914. The James Joyce Archive). 1978. 85.00 (ISBN 0-8240-2862-7). Garland Pub.
Finnegans Wake, Book I, Chapters 2 and 3: A Facsimile of Drafts, Typescripts & Proofs. James Augustine Aloysius Joyce. LC 78-4140. (Joyce, James, 1882-1941. The James Joyce Archive). 1978. 85.00 (ISBN 0-8240-2844-9). Garland.
Finnegans Wake, Book I, Chapters 4 and 5: A Facsimile of Drafts, Typescripts & Proofs. James Augustine Aloysius Joyce. LC 78-4138. (Joyce, James, 1882-1941. The James Joyce Archive). 1978. 85.00 (ISBN 0-8240-2860-0). Garland.
Finnegans Wake, Book I, Chapters 6 and 7: A Facsimile of Drafts, Typescripts & Proofs. James Augustine Aloysius Joyce. LC 78-8958. (Joyce, James, 1882-1914. The James Joyce Archive). 1978. 85.00 (ISBN 0-8240-2861-9). Garland Pub.
Finnegans Wake, Book II, Chapter 1: A Facsimile of Drafts, Typescripts, & Proofs. James Augustine Aloysius Joyce. LC 77-11681. (Joyce, James, 1882-1914. The James Joyce Archive). (Illus.). 1977. 85.00 (ISBN 0-8240-2849-X). Garland Pub.
Finnegans Wake, Book II, Chapter 2: A Facsimile of Drafts, Typescripts, & Proofs. James Augustine Aloysius Joyce. LC 78-721. (Joyce, James, 1882-1914. The James Joyce Archive). 1978. 85.00 (ISBN 0-8240-2853-8) (ISBN 0-8240-2854-6). Garland Pub.
Finnegans Wake, Book II, Chapter 3: A Facsimile of Drafts, Typescripts, & Proofs. James Augustine Aloysius Joyce. LC 77-10573. (Joyce, James, 1882-1914. The James Joyce Archive). (Illus.). 1978. 85.00 (ISBN 0-8240-2850-3). Garland Pub.
Finnegans Wake, Book II, Chapter 4: A Facsimile of Drafts, Typescripts, & Proofs. James Augustine Aloysius Joyce. LC 77-84971. (Joyce, James, 1882-1914. The James Joyce Archive). (Illus.). 1978. 85.00 (ISBN 0-8240-2852-X). Garland Pub.
Finnegans Wake Book III: A Facsimile of the Galley Proofs. James Augustine Aloysius Joyce. LC 77-22951. (Joyce, James, 1882-1914. The James Joyce Archive). (Illus.). 1978. 85.00 (ISBN 0-8240-2847-3). Garland Pub.
Finnegans Wake, Book III, Chapter 3: A Facsimile of Drafts, Typescripts, & Proofs. James Augustine Aloysius Joyce. LC 78-899. (Joyce, James, 1882-1914. The James Joyce Archive). 1978. per vol. 85.00 (ISBN 0-8240-2856-2) (ISBN 0-8240-2857-0). Garland Pub.
Finnegans Wake, Book III, Chapter 4: A Facsimile of Drafts, Typescripts & Proofs. James Augustine Aloysius Joyce. LC 78-4465. (Joyce, James, 1882-1914. The James Joyce Archive). (Illus.). 1978. 85.00 (ISBN 0-8240-2858-9). Garland Pub.
Finnegans Wake, Book III, Chapters 1 - 2: A Facsimile of Drafts, Typescripts, & Proofs. James Joyce & Danis Rose. LC 78-898. (Joyce, James, 1882-1914. The James Joyce Archive). (Illus.). 1978. 85.00 (ISBN 0-8240-2855-4). Garland Pub.
Finnegans Wake, Book III, Chapters 1-4: A Facsimile of Transition Pages. James Augustine Aloysius Joyce. LC 78-17968. (Joyce, James, 1882-1914. The James Joyce Archive). 1978. 85.00 (ISBN 0-8240-2859-7). Garland Pub.
Finnish Short Stories. Tr. by Inkeri Vaananen-Jensen from Finnish. 238p. (Orig.). 1982. pap. text ed. 11.75 (ISBN 0-938500-00-7). Nordic Trans.
Finnish Short Stories. Vaananen-Jensen, Inkeri & K. Borje Vahamaki. LC 82-131437. 1982. 11.75 (ISBN 0-938500-00-7). Nordic Translators.
Finnley Wren: His Notions and Opinions, Together with a Haphazard History of His Career and Amours in These Moody Years, As Well As Sundry Rhymes, Fables, Diatribes and Literary Misdemeanors; a Novel in a New Manner. Philip Wylie. LC 34-8134. 1934. Farrar & Rinehart.
Finns and Finnicans. Walter Mattila. LC 78-286323. 1970. 5.00.
Fiona. Catherine Gaskin. LC 69-15173. 1970. Doubleday.
Fionn and His Companions. Standish O'Grady. LC 77-287553. (Illus.). 1970. Talbot Press.
Fir and the Palm. Olive Mary Briggs. LC 10-7788. 1910. C. Scribner's Sons.
Fir and the Palm: A Novel. Elizabeth Asquith Bibescu. 1924. 2.00. G. P. Putnam's Sons.
Fire! Anita Deyneka. LC 74-17731. (Illus.). 1.25 (ISBN 0-912692-49-9). D. C. Cook Pub. Co.
Fire. George Rippey Stewart. LC 73-151078. (Illus.). 1971. 7.50 (ISBN 0-395-12548-0). Houghton Mifflin.
Fire. A Novel. George Rippey Stewart. LC 48-624780. 1948. Random House.
Fire: A Novel of Hawaii. Armine Von Tempski. LC 29-67944. 1929. Frederick A. Stokes Company.
Fire & Flesh. Barbara Riefe. LC 78-55738. 464p. (Orig.). 1978. pap. 2.95 (ISBN 0-86721-057-5). Playboy Pbks.
Fire and Frost. Maud Cruttwell. LC 13-8083. 1913. 1.25. John Lae.
Fire & Ice. Barry Devlin. LC 52-43296. 1952. Vixen Press.
Fire and Ice. Johannes Vilhelm Jensen. Tr. by Chater, Arthur G. LC 23-3133. (His The long journey. i-ii). 1923. A. A. Knopf.
Fire and Ice. Ray Kytle. LC 74-21994. 1975. 7.95 (ISBN 0-679-50534-2). D. McKay Co.
Fire and Ice. Wallace Earle Stegner. LC 41-5677. Duell, Sloan and Pearce.
Fire & Iron. Kenneth M. Cameron. (Arms Saga: Book III). 384p. 1982. pap. 3.25 (ISBN 0-445-04708-9). Popular Lib.
Fire and Morning. Francis W Leary. 1957. Putnam.
Fire & Shadow. Penn - Smith. 3.00 o.p. Vantage.
Fire and the Gold. Phyllis A Whitney. LC 56-5324. Crowell.
Fire and the Gold. Phyllis A Whitney. LC 56-5324. 1974. (pbk.) 1.25. New American Library.
Fire and the Hammer: A Tale of Love and Viqlence. Shirley Barker. LC 53-9971. 1953. Crown Publishers.
Fire & the Offering: The English Language Novel of India, Vol. 1. S. C. Harrex. (Writers Workshop Greybird Book). 1977. 16.00 (ISBN 0-86578-049-8); flexible bndg. 12.00 (ISBN 0-86578-048-X). Ind-US Inc.
Fire & the Offering: The English Language Novel of India, Vol. 2. S. C. Harrex. (Writers Workshop Greybird Book). 1978. 16.00 (ISBN 0-86578-051-X); flexible bndg. 12.00 (ISBN 0-86578-050-1). Ind-US Inc.
Fire & the Rope. Alison Yorke. 1979. pap. 2.50 (ISBN 0-425-04045-3). Berkley Pub.
Fire & the Rose. Ursula Bloom. 1977. pap. 1.95 (ISBN 0-89041-169-7, 3169). Major Bks.
Fire and the Wood: A Love Story. Ray Coryton Hutchinson. Farrar & Rinehart, Inc.
Fire & Water: Short Stories. Elisabeth Stevens. LC 82-203. (Illus.). 100p. 1983. pap. 5.25 (ISBN 0-912288-20-5). Perivale Pr.
Fire Ants. Saul Wernick. 320p. (Orig.). 1978. pap. 1.95 o.p. (ISBN 0-441-23833-5). Charter Bks.
Fire Ants. Saul Wernick. (O.s.i.). (Orig.). 1976. pap. 1.50 o.s.i. (AD1644, Award). Univ Pub & Dist.
Fire at Greycombe Farm. Cecil John Charles Street. LC 32-3191. Dodd, Mead & Company.
Fire at the Center. George W. Proctor. 224p. (Orig.). 1981. pap. 2.25 (ISBN 0-449-14417-8, GM). Fawcett.
Fire at Will. Doris Miles Disney. 1976. pap. 1.25 (ISBN 0-532-12377-8). Woodhill.
Fire at Will. Doris Miles Disney. (O.s.i.). 1971. pap. 0.75 o.s.i. (532-75424-075). Manor Bks.
Fire at Will. 1st Ed. Doris Miles Disney. LC 50-7588. 1950. Published for the Crime Club by Doubleday.
Fire Balloon. Ruth Moore. LC 48-9197. 1948. W. Morrow.
Fire Beds to Mecca. Rod Gray. (The Lady from L.U.S.T. Ser.). (O.s.i.). 1973. pap. 0.95 o.s.i. (BT50566). Belmont-Tower.
Fire Bell in the Night. Constance Noyes Robertson. LC 44-304854. 1944. H. Holt and Company.
Fire-Brain. Max Brand. LC 26-734002. 1926. G. P. Putnam's Sons.
Fire Brain. Frederick Faust. 1974. (pbk.) 0.95. Warner Paperback Library.
Fire Bringers. Francis Lynde. 1921. C. Scribner's Sons.
Fire, Burn! John Dickson Carr. 1975. (pbk.) 1.50. Award Books.
Fire, Burn! 1st Ed. John Dickson Carr. LC 57-713523. 1957. Harper.
Fire Child. Salambo Forest. (Orig.). 1968. pap. 1.75 o.s.i. (122, Ophelia). Olympia.
Fire Circle. William Leonard Marshall. LC 77-466943. 1969. 2.95. Macmillan.
Fire Cloud. Kenneth McKenney. LC 79-13104. 10.95 (ISBN 0-671-24628-3). Simon and Schuster.
Fire Dancer. Ann Maxwell. 208p. 1982. pap. 2.50 (ISBN 0-451-11939-8, AE1939, Sig). NAL.
Fire Dawn. Virginia Coffman. LC 80-12198. 1980. 10.95 (ISBN 0-89340-273-7). J. Curley.
Fire Dawn: A Novel. Virginia Coffman. LC 76-39720. 8.95 (ISBN 0-87795-159-4). Arbor House.
Fire: Devoted to Younger Negro Artists, Vol. 1. Repr. of 1926 ed. 25.00 (ISBN 0-8371-3048-4, Pub. by Negro U Pr). Greenwood.
Fire Door and Other Stories. William Lobell. LC 37-1374. 1937. The Reader Press.
Fire Down Below. Margaret Emma Faith Irwin. LC 28-24955. 1928. Harcourt, Brace and Company.
Fire Drills: Stories. Barbara L. Greenberg. LC 81-69837. (Breakthrough Book; No. 38). 1982. 6.95 (ISBN 0-8262-0363-9). University of Missouri Press.
Fire-Dwellers. Margaret Laurence. LC 69-14736. 1969. 5.95. Knopf.
Fire-Dwellers. Margaret Laurence. LC 74-174581. 1973. 0.40 (ISBN 0-586-03618-0). Panther.
Fire Engine That Disappeared. Maj Sjowall & Per Wahloo. LC 76-42997. (Their A Martin Beck police mystery; 5). 1977. 1.65 (ISBN 0-394-72340-6). Vintage Books.
Fire Engine That Disappeared. Maj Sjowall & Per Wahloo. LC 76-128771. 1970. 4.95. Pantheon Books.
Fire Escape. Joyce Reason. 1971. pap. 0.95 o.p. (ISBN 0-87508-669-1). Chr Lit.
Fire Flingers. William Jonathan Neidig. LC 19-4849. 1919. 1.50. Dodd, Mead and Company.
Fire from Heaven. Mary Renault, pseud. 1973. (pbk) 1.25. Popular Library.
Fire from Heaven. Mary Renault, pseud. LC 76-48317. (Illus.). 1977. 2.95 (ISBN 0-394-72291-4). Vintage Books.
Fire from Heaven. Mary Renault, pseud. LC 72-98035. (Illus.). 1969. 7.95. Pantheon Books.
Fire from Heaven: A Novel, Tr. from French by Arthur Train. Jr. Michel Bataille. LC 67-17707. 1967. bds., 5.95. Crown.
Fire from the Fountains. Pauline B Innis. LC 68-20067. 1968. Harcourt, Brace & World.
Fire from the Wine-Dark Sea. Somtow Sucharitkul. LC 82-12827. 5.95 (ISBN 0-89865-252-9). Donning.
Fire Goddess. Ava Maria Molnar & Daniel Whiteside. LC 71-141559. 1971. 6.95 (ISBN 0-200-71776-6). Abelard-Schuman.
Fire Goddess: By Sax Rohmer Pseud. Arthur Sarsfield Ward. LC 53-26224. (Gold medal books, 283). 1953. Fawcett Publications.
Fire in His Bones. Ruthanne Garlock. 1981. pap. 2.95 (ISBN 0-88270-451-6, Pub. by Logos). Bridge Pub.
Fire in His Hand. J. C. Sheers. (Orig.). 1968. pap. 0.60 o.p. (R2015, GM). Fawcett World.
Fire in His Hand. 1st Ed. Michael Grieg. LC 63-8768. 1963. Doubleday.
Fire in My Blood. Deniso. 3.50 o.p. Wehman.
Fire in My Blood. Edward Hunt. 192p. (Orig.). 1974. pap. 1.25 o.p. (ISBN 0-532-12205-4). Woodhill.
Fire in My Blood. Edward Hunt. 1974. (pbk.) 1.25. Manor Books.
Fire in Summer. Robert Ramsey. LC 42-39548. 1942. The Viking Press.
Fire in the Barley. Frank Parrish. LC 78-27819. (Dan Mallet Novel of Suspense Ser.). 1979. 7.95 o.p. (ISBN 0-396-07684-X). Dodd.
Fire in the Barley. Frank Parrish. LC 82-48815. 160p. 1983. pap. 2.84i (ISBN 0-06-080651-6, P651, PL). Har-Row.
Fire in the Barley: A Novel of Suspense. Frank Parrish. LC 78-27819. 1979. 7.95 (ISBN 0-396-07684-X). Dodd, Mead.
Fire in the Bush: A Novel of Africa. Translated from the French by Roch Le Page. Paul Bernier. LC 58-7326. P. J. Kenedy.
Fire in the Canebrake. Reuben Herring. LC 79-56694. (Illus.). 2.95 (ISBN 0-8054-5171-4). Broadman Press.
Fire in the Desert: By Ford Logan Pseud. Dwight Bennett Newton. LC 54-11985. 1954. Ballantine Books.
Fire in the Embers. Burt Hirschfeld. 1972. pap. 2.75 (ISBN 0-380-00312-0, 76885). Avon.
Fire in the Flesh. Garibaldi Marto Lapolla. LC 74-17935. (Italian American Experience). 1975. 20.00 (ISBN 0-405-06407-1). Arno Press.
Fire in the Flesh see My Shame, My Degradation.
Fire in the Flesh: A Novel. Garibaldi Marto Lapolla. LC 31-7636. The Vanguard Press.
Fire in the Flint. Walter Francis White. LC 74-75545. 1969. Negro Universities Press.
Fire in the Flint. Walter Francis White. LC 24-214009. 1924. A. A. Knopf.
Fire in the Forest. John Tedman & Alison Tedman. (New Oxford Supplementary Readers Ser). (Illus.). 96p. 1960. pap. text ed. 0.75x o.p. (ISBN 0-19-422431-7). Oxford U Pr.
Fire in the Heart. 1st. ed. Henrietta Henkle. LC 48-8791. 1948. Harcourt, Brace.
Fire in the Heavens. George Oliver Smith. LC 58-9134. 1958. Avalon Books.
Fire in the Hole. Glen Chase, pseud. (Cherry delight, 12). 1974. (pbk.) 1.25. Leisure Books.
Fire in the Hole. S. W. Karl. 1978. pap. 1.50 (ISBN 0-532-15355-3). Woodhill.
Fire in the Ice. 1st Ed. Dorothy James Roberts. LC 61-12814. 1961. Little, Brown.

Fire in the Morning. Elizabeth Spencer. LC 68-20057. 1968. McGraw-Hill.
Fire in the Morning. Elizabeth Spencer. LC 48-8392. 1948. Dodd, Mead.
Fire in the Night. Raymond Otis. LC 34-186874. Farrar and Rinehart, Incorporated.
Fire in the Rain. William Lodewick Doty. LC 51-5873. 1951. Bruce.
Fire in the Sky. Tarleton Collier. LC 41-15914. 1941. Houghton Mifflin Company.
Fire in the Sky. Chris L. Wolf & Michael F. Maikowski. 1978. pap. 1.75 (ISBN 0-89041-220-0, 3220). Major Bks.
Fire in the Snow. Ralph Hammond-Innes. LC 47-2978. 1947. Harper & Brothers.
Fire in the Snow. Hammond Innes. pap. 0.95 o.p. (02127, Collier). Macmillan.
Fire in the Stone. Colin Thiele. LC 74-2610. 1974. 6.95 (ISBN 0-06-026102-1). Harper & Row.
Fire in the Streets. Jon Messmann. (Revenger,#2). 1974. (pbk.) 0.95. New American Library.
Fire in the Sun: By Kathrine Talbot Pseud. Ilse Eva Louise Gross Barker. LC 52-6150. 1952. Putnam.
Fire in the Thatch: A Chief Inspector Macdonald Mystery. pseud. ed. Edith Caroline Rivett. LC 47-18544. 1946. Mystery House.
Fire in the Water. Peggy Simson Curry. LC 51-10094. 1951. McGraw-Hill.
Fire in the Wind. Anne Tedlock Brooks. LC 50-7413. 1950. Arcadia House.
Fire in the Wind. Alexandra Sellers. (Superromances Ser.). 384p. 1982. pap. 2.50 (ISBN 0-373-70042-3, Pub. by Worldwide). Harlequin Bks.
Fire Kill. Daniel Da Cruz. (Gold Medal) (ISBN 0-449-13676-0). Fawcett.
Fire Mission. William Mulvihill, pseud. LC 57-7298. 1957. Ballantine Books.
Fire Mountain. Janet Cullen-Tanaka. 288p. (Orig.). 1980. pap. 2.50 (ISBN 0-89083-646-9). Zebra.
Fire Mountain: A Thrilling Sea Story. Norman Springer. 1923. G. H. Watt.
Fire Next Time. James B. Baldwin. 1970. pap. 1.75 (ISBN 0-440-32542-0). Dell.
Fire of Life: A Novel. Charles Kennett Burrow. LC 6-19657. 1893. H. Holt and Company.
Fire of Spring. Dorothy Coursen. LC 28-236602. H. Holt and Company.
Fire of Spring. Edward Noble. LC 26-5145. 1926. Houghton Mifflin Company.
Fire of Spring. Margaret Horton Potter. LC 5-6284. 1905. D. Appleton and Company.
Fire of the Lord. Norman Nicholson. LC 46-4957. 1946. E. P. Dutton & Company, Inc.
Fire of the Soul. Ginger Chambers. (Candlelight Ecstasy Ser.: No. 83). (Orig.). 1982. pap. 1.95 (ISBN 0-440-12540-5). Dell.
Fire of Youth. Margaret Bass Pedler. LC 30-17703. 1930. Doubleday, Doran & Company, Inc.
Fire of Youth, a Novel. Henry James Forman. LC 20-3795. 1920. Little, Brown, and Company.
Fire on Fear Street: A Marshal Pedley Mystery. Prentice Winchell. LC 58-13182. 1958. Lippincott.
Fire on the Cliffs. Chris Waynar. (Ace gothic no. 10). 1975. (pbk.) 0.95. Ace Books.
Fire on the Ice. John Burnett. 352p. (Orig.). 1979. pap. 2.25 (ISBN 0-441-23876-9, Pub. by Charter Bks). Ace Bks.
Fire on the Mountain. Edward Abbey. LC 62-18846. 1962. Dial Press.
Fire on the Mountain. Edward Abbey. LC 77-89434. (Zia book). 1978. 3.95 (ISBN 0-8263-0457-5). University of New Mexico Press.
Fire on the Mountain. Anita Desai. LC 77-3788. 8.95 (ISBN 0-06-011066-X). Harper & Row.
Fire on the Rock. Norman Partington. LC 76-378971. 1976. 3.95 (ISBN 0-333-18028-3). Macmillan.
Fire on the Snow. Barbara Cartland. (Bantam Barbara Cartland Library 30). 1976. (pbk.) 1.25. Bantam Books.
Fire on the Wind. David Garth. LC 51-3332. 1951. Putnam.
Fire Opal. Robert Fraser. LC 11-151806. 1.25. E. J. Clode.
Fire Opal. Pamela Hill. LC 79-28424. 10.00 (ISBN 0-312-29111-6). St. Martin's Press.
Fire Opals: By Rebecca Danton. Rebecca Danton. (Fawcett Crest Book). 1977. 1.50 (ISBN 0-449-23112-7). Fawcett Publications.
Fire Over England. Alfred Edward Woodley Mason. LC 36-21642. 1936. Doubleday, Doran & Company, Incorporated.
Fire Pool Seven. Claire Macfarlane. LC 78-70481. 1980. 8.95 (ISBN 0-936632-00-3) (ISBN 0-936632-03-8). Mann Publishers.
Fire-Raisers: A Novel. Marris Murray. 1954. Farrar, Straus & Young.
Fire Rock. Wood, James. LC 66-28727. 1966. Vanguard Press.
Fire Sale. Robert Klane. LC 75-13501. (Illus.). 1975. 6.95 (ISBN 0-689-10675-0). Atheneum.
Fire Sermon. Wright Morris. LC 73-156563. 1971. 5.95 (ISBN 0-06-013066-0). Harper & Row.
Fire Sermon. Wright Morris. LC 79-14763. 1979. 9.75 (ISBN 0-8032-3055-9) (ISBN 0-8032-8104-8). University of Nebraska Press.
Fire Storm. Robert Lipscomb Duncan. LC 78-6747. 1978. 9.95 (ISBN 0-688-03363-6). Morrow.
Fire That Burns. Mark Tryon. LC 54-1242. 1954. Vixen Press.
Fire That Will Not Die. Michele McBride. (Illus.). 250p. 1979. 10.00 (ISBN 0-88280-066-3). Chicago Review.
Fire, the Sword & the Devil. Dennis Adair & Janet Rosenstock. 382p. 1982. 14.95 (ISBN 0-920510-44-2, Pub. by Personal Lib). Dodd.
Fire Throne Mountain. F. Rew Bixby. 208p. (Orig.). 1982. pap. 2.25 (ISBN 0-505-51723-X). Tower Bks.
Fire Time. Poul Anderson. 1975. (pbk.) 1.50. Ballantine Books.
Fire Time. Poul Anderson. LC 74-5928. (Doubleday science fiction). 1974. (ISBN 0-385-05582-X). Doubleday.
Fire-Tongue. Arthur Sarsfield Ward. LC 22-3191. 1922. Doubleday, Page & Company.
Fire Trap. Owen Cameron. LC 57-13640. (Inner sanctum mystery). 1957. Simon and Schuster.
Fire Waits. Michael I. Hecht. 9.95x. Hartmore.
Fire Watch: A Novel. Alan Dennis Burke. LC 79-25666. 12.95 (ISBN 0-316-11683-1). Little, Brown.
Fire Will Freeze. Margaret Millar. LC 44-3680. 1944. Random House.
Fire Within. Ann Coombs. 1978. pap. 2.25 (ISBN 0-532-22137-0). Woodhill.
Fire Within. Joe David. LC 81-65447. 245p. 1981. 10.95x (ISBN 0-939360-00-4); pap. 4.95x (ISBN 0-939360-01-2). Bks for All Times.
Fire Within. Pierre Drieu La Rochelle. 1965. 4.95 o.p. Knopf.
Fire Within. George Fort Gibbs. LC 30-224322. 1930. D. Appleton and Company.
Fire Within. Patricia Wentworth. LC 13-169992. 1913. G. P. Putnam's Sons.
Fire Within. Tr. from French by Richard Howard 1st Amer. Ed. Drieu la Rochelle, Pierre. LC 65-10062. 1965. bds., 3.95. Knopf.
Fire Woman. William Pinkney Lawson. LC 25-11515. 1925. Boni & Liveright.
Fireball. Vic Mayhew & Doug Long. LC 77-376204. 8.95 (ISBN 0-458-92400-8). Methuen.
Fireball. Vic Mayhew & Long, Doug. (Signet Book). 1979. 1.95 (ISBN 0-451-08701-1). New American Library.
Fireball Assignment. Andrew Sugar. (Israeli Commandos Ser: No. 2). 192p. (Orig.). 1974. pap. 1.25 o.p. (ISBN 0-532-12224-0). Woodhill.
Fireball Assignment. Andrew Sugar. (Israeli Commandos Ser: No. 2). 192p. (Orig.). 1974. pap. 1.25 o.p. (ISBN 0-532-12224-0). Manor Bks.
Fireball Assignment. Andrew Sugar. (Israeli commandoes,#2). 1974. (pbk.) 1.25. Manor Books.
Fireball at the Lake. Jay Groves. 1967. 3.00 o.p. (ISBN 0-682-45729-9). Exposition.
Firebase. John Crowther. LC 75-9489. 7.95. St. Martin's Press.
Firebase Seattle. Don Pendleton. (Executioner,#21). 1975. (pbk.) 1.25 (ISBN 0-523-00499-0). Pinnacle Books.
Firebird. Charles L. Harness. (Orig.). 1981. pap. 2.95 (ISBN 0-671-83577-7, Timescape). PB.
Firebird: A Novel. William Marchant. LC 79-28174. 10.00 (ISBN 0-517-53922-5). Crown Publishers.
Firebird of Unlimited Happiness. Dorothea Condry. (Illus.). 116p. 1981. pap. 7.50 (ISBN 0-942316-01-0). Pueblo Pub Pr.
Firebird One. 336p. 1982. 35.00x o.p. (ISBN 0-7139-1492-0, Pub. by Penguin Bks). State Mutual Bk.
Firebolt. Patrick Clay. (Sargeant Hawk Ser.: No. 5). 240p. (Orig.). 1982. pap. 2.25 o.s.i. (ISBN 0-8439-1169-7, Leisure Bks). Nordon Pubns.
Fireborn. Chane Safran. LC 64-2017. 1963. Vantage Press.
Firebrand. George Challis. LC 50-1204. Harper.
Firebrand. Samuel Rutherford Crockett. LC 1-27054. 1901. McClure, Phillips & Co.
Firebrand. Georgia Di Donato. LC 81-47860. 1982. 16.50 (ISBN 0-385-15886-6). Doubleday.
Firebrand. Tom Gill. LC 39-27289. Farrar & Rinehart, Inc.
Firebrand from Burnt Creek. Frank Chester Robertson. LC 40-33107. 1940. E. P. Dutton & Co., Inc.
Firebrand of the Indies: A Romance of Francis Xavier. Elsie K Seth-Smith. LC 23-131112. 1922. Society for Promoting Christian Knowledge.
Firebrand" Trevison. Charles Alden Seltzer. LC 18-188838. 1918. A. C. McClurg & Co.
Firebrand" Trevison. Charles Alden Seltzer. LC 29-307738. 1918. Grosset & Dunlap.
Firebrands. J. T. Richards. 272p. 1982. pap. 2.95 (ISBN 0-515-05633-2). Jove Pubns.
Firebrands. Berhane Marian Sahle Sellassie. LC 79-313767. (Longman Drumbeat). 1980. 2.95 (ISBN 0-582-64243-4). Longman.
Firebrands. George Smith. LC 80-82222. 400p. (Orig.). 1980. pap. 2.95 (ISBN 0-87216-765-8). Playboy Pbks.
Firebrands. A Temperance Tale. Julia MacNair Wright. LC 9-914. 1879. National Temperance Society and Publication House.
Firebrand's Woman. Vanessa Royall. (Orig.). 1980. pap. 2.95 (ISBN 0-440-12597-9). Dell.
Firebug: A Regency Novel of Terror. Robert Bloch. LC 62-5101. 1961. Regency Books.
Firebugs. Tr. from German by Arnold J. Pomerans. 1st Amer. Ed. Peter Faecke. LC 65-11108. 1966. 3.95. Knopf.
Fireclown see Winds of Limbo.
Firecracker Jane: A Novel. Alice Calhoun Haines. LC 18-193013. 1918. 1.50. H. Holt and Company.
Firecrackers: A Realistic Novel. Carl Van Vechten. LC 25-16657. 1925. A. A. Knopf.
Firecrest. Victor Canning. LC 78-170215. 1972. 5.95. Morrow.
Fired! Karl Aloys Schenzinger & Endore, S. Guy, 1901- LC 32-24675. The Century Co.
Firedrake. Cecelia Holland. LC 66-11393. 1966. bds., 5.00. Atheneum.
Firedrake. Cecelia Holland. 1973. (pbk) 1.25. Ballantine.
Firedrake: A Novel. Elgin Earl Groseclose. LC 42-394911. 1942. J. B. Lippincott Company.
Fireflies. Shiva Naipaul. LC 70-874450. 1971. 0.50 (ISBN 0-14-003150-2). Penguin.
Fireflies. Shiva Naipaul. LC 79-136327. 1971. 7.95 (ISBN 0-394-42493-X). Knopf.
Fireflies. Rabindranath Tagore. (Illus.). 1928. 13.95 (ISBN 0-02-615980-5). Macmillan.
Fireflood and Other Stories. Vonda N McIntyre. LC 79-17774. 1979. 10.95 (ISBN 0-395-28422-8). Houghton Mifflin.
Fireflood and Other Stories. vonda n. mcintyre. ed. Vonda N McIntyre. (Timescape Book). 2.25 (ISBN 0-671-83631-5). Pocket Books.
Firefly: A Novel. Desemea Wilson. LC 26-1061. E. P. Dutton & Company.
Firefly of France. Marion Polk Angellotti. LC 18-692335. 1918. The Century Co.
Firefox. Craig Thomas. LC 77-71356. (Illus.). 8.95 (ISBN 0-03-020791-6). Holt, Rinehart and Winston.
Firefox. Craig Thomas. LC 78-7332. (Illus.). 1978. 13.95 (ISBN 0-8161-6560-2). G. K. Hall.
Firegold. Jeffrey R Daniels. LC 75-10476. 1975. 7.95 (ISBN 0-698-10679-2). Coward, McCann & Geoghegan.
Firehall. J. Adin Mann. LC 49-5740. 1949. B. Humphries.
Firelight. Burton L Spiller & Hunt, Lynn Bogue, Illus. LC 37-10975. The Derrydale Press.
Firelord. Parke Godwin. LC 80-497. 1980. 12.95 (ISBN 0-385-17070-X). Doubleday.
Firemakers: A Novel of Environment. Rollo Walter Brown. LC 74-22770. Repr. of 1931 ed. 24.00 (ISBN 0-404-58409-8). AMS Pr.
Fireman Flower: And Other Stories. William Sansom. LC 45-5348. 1945. The Vanguard Press.
Fireman's Heart. Beatrice Marean. LC 7-20444. (On cover: The Marguerite series, no. 38). 1894. E. A. Weeks & Company.
Firemantle see Diabols.
Fireplay. William Wingate. LC 77-4980. 8.95 (ISBN 0-698-10846-9). Coward, McCann & Geoghegan.
Firepower. S. W. Karl. (Orig.). 1979. pap. 2.25 (ISBN 0-532-23182-1). Woodhill.
Fires. Marguerite. Yourcenar & Dori Katz. LC 81-1097. 1981. 10.95 (ISBN 0-374-15765-0). Farrar, Straus, Giroux.
Fires at Fitch's Folly. Kenneth Whipple. LC 35-4006. Thomas Y. Crowell Company.
Fires Burn Blue. Andrew Caldecott. LC 49-804076. 1948. Longmans, Green.
Fires in May. Ruth Feiner & Alexander, Norman, Tr. LC 36-666121. J. B. Lippincott Company.
Fires of Ambition. George Fort Gibbs. LC 23-13126. 1923. D. Appleton and Company.
Fires of Arcadia. George Bagshawe Harrison. LC 65-19057. 1965. Harcourt, Brace & World.
Fires of Autumn. Helen Huntington Howe. LC 59-6335. 1959. Harper.
Fires of Azeroth. C. J Cherryh. 1979. 1.95 (ISBN 0-87997-466-4). DAW Books.
Fires of Ballymorris. Vivian Connolly. 1975. (pbk.) 0.95. Dell.
Fires of Desire: A Tragedy of Modern India. Lawrence Rogers Mansfield. LC 7-16746. 1907. The C. M. Clark Publishing Co.
Fires of Faith: The Romance of a Salvation Army Lassie. Charles Kenmore Ulrich. LC 19-7917. Grosset & Dunlap.
Fires of Fate: A Mystery Novel. Wilbur Finley Fauley. LC 23-6151. Metropolitan Book Service.
Fires of Glenlochy. Constance Heaven. LC 75-44091. 1976. 7.95 (ISBN 0-698-10726-8). Coward, McCann & Geoghegan.
Fires of Heaven: A Novel. Beulah Montgomery Miller. LC 72-87749. 1974. 7.95 (ISBN 0-913264-06-7). Douglas-West.
Fires of Hell. Harvey R Saunders. LC 72-164911. 1972. 7.50 (ISBN 0-8022-2060-6). Philosophical Library.
Fires of July, Bk. 1. Sharon Anne Salvato. (Orig.). 1983. pap. 5.95 (ISBN 0-440-52680-9, Dell Trade Pbks). Dell.
Fires of Lan-Kern. Peter Tremayne, pseud. LC 79-28396. 1980. 10.95 (ISBN 0-312-29209-0). St. Martin's Press.
Fires of Lust. Jean Francis. (Orig.). 1968. pap. 0.60 o.p. (73-771). Lancer.
Fires of Oakheath. Andrea Robbins. (Orig.). 1981. pap. 2.95 (ISBN 0-89083-867-4). Zebra.
Fires of Oakhurst. Walter Reed Johnson. 1980. pap. 2.95 (ISBN 0-451-11100-1, AE1100, Sig). NAL.
Fires of Paratime. L. E. Modessit. 205p. 1982. pap. 2.95 (Timescape). PB.
Fires of Paris. Zachary Hughes. (Hotel Destiny, Paris Ser.: No. 3). 304p. (Orig.). 1982. pap. 2.95 (ISBN 0-515-06049-6). Jove Pubns.
Fires of Passion. Arlene Hale. (Orig.). 1981. pap. 1.95 (ISBN 0-8439-8047-8, Tiara Bks). Nordon Pubns.
Fires of Rapture. Lisa Beaumont. 384p. (Orig.). 1982. pap. 2.95 (ISBN 0-449-24549-7, Crest). Fawcett.
Fires of September. Thomas J. Kearns. 3.75 o.p. Carlton.
Fires of Spring. Hettie Grimstead. (Cameo Romance#30). 1975. (pbk.) 0.95. Fawcett.
Fires of Spring. James Albert Michener. LC 49-7426. 1949. Random House.
Fires of the Heart. Stephanie Blake. LC 81-84140. 368p. (Orig.). 1982. pap. 2.95 (ISBN 0-86721-059-1). Playboy Pbks.
Fires of Tjepo: A Novel. 1st Ed. Allison Ind. LC 55-5706. 1955. Vantage Press.
Fires of Winter. Johanna Lindsey. 368p. 1980. pap. 3.50 (ISBN 0-380-75747-8, 82909-6). Avon.
Fires of Youth. Edward De Roo. LC 55-338243. (Ace books, S-105). 1955. Ace Books.
Fires of Youth. Margaret B McGee. LC 59-10535. 1959. Muhlenberg Press.
Fires on the Plain. Shohei Ooka. LC 78-16916. 1978. 28.00 (ISBN 0-313-20567-1). Greenwood Press.
Fires on the Plain. Translated from the Japanese by Ivan Morris. 1st Ed. Shohei Ooka. LC 57-5651. 1957. A. A. Knopf.
Fires Underground: A Narrative of the Secret Struggle Carried on by the Illepal Organizations in Germany Under Penalty of Death. Heinz Liepmann. Tr. by Clark, Robert Thomson. LC 36-185634. 1936. J. B. Lippincott Company.
Fireship. Adam Hardy. (Fox series no. 11). 1976. (pbk.) 1.25 (ISBN 0-523-00845-7). Pinnacle Books.
Fireship. Cyril Northcote Parkinson. LC 75-11670. (Illus.). 1975. 7.95 (ISBN 0-395-20428-3). Houghton Mifflin.
Fireside Book of Flying Stories: Short Stories, Fragments, Vignettes, Observations, Reports, Essays, a Novelette, and a Science Fiction Story, Selected from the Writings of the Age of Flight. Ed. by Paul Jensen. LC 51-14883. 1951. Simon and Schuster.
Fireside Book of Ghost Stories. Ed. by Edward Charles Wagenknecht. LC 47-23606. 1947. The Bobbs-Merrill Company.
Fireside Book of Romance. Ed. by Edward Charles Wagenknecht. LC 48-5723. 1948. Bobbs-Merrill Co.
Fireside Book of Suspense. Stories. Ed. by Alfred Hitchcock. 1947. Simon and Schuster.
Fireside Dickens. A Cyclopedia of the Best Thoughts of Charles Dickens. Comprising a Careful Selection of His Best Writings. Arranged in Subjects and in Alphabetical Order, with a Complete Index... Charles Dickens. Ed. by De Fontaine, Felix Gregory. LC 24-31720. 1883. G. W. Carleton & Co.
Fireside Ideals. Ed. by James A. Kuse & Ralph D. Luedke. 1977. pap. 2.50 o.p. (ISBN 0-89542-312-X). Ideals.
Fireside Mystery Book, Edited by Frank Owen. Ed. by Frank Owen. LC 47-2028. 1947. Lantern Press, Inc.
Fireside Reader: A Treasury of Outstanding Short Stories. LC 77-76319. (Illus.). 11.98. Reader's Digest Association.
Fireside Stories, Old and New, Collected. Ed. by Henry Troth Coates. LC 7-1234. 1897. H. T. Coates and Co.
Firestar. Robert E. Mills. (Star Quest Ser.: No. 5). 224p. (Orig.). 1982. pap. cancelled (ISBN 0-505-51817-1). Tower Bks.
Firestarter. Stephen King. LC 80-14793. 1980. 13.95 (ISBN 0-670-31541-9). Viking Press.
Firestorm. Peter Rand. LC 76-84371. 1969. 4.95. Doubleday.
Firewall. Alan Clark. LC 40-141847. Random House.
Fireweed. Joslyn Gray. LC 20-5583. 1920. C. Scribner's Sons.

Fireweed. Frances Sarah Moore. LC 45-4920. 1945. Arcadia House, Inc.

Fireweed. Paton Walsh, Jill. LC 73-109554. (Ariel book). 1970. 3.95. Farrar, Straus & Giroux.

Fireweed. Mildred Walker, pseud. LC 34-270261. Harcourt, Brace and Company.

Firewind. Henry Hunt Searls. LC 80-648. (Illus.). 1981. 12.95 (ISBN 0-385-17084-X). Doubleday.

Firework for Oliver. John Edward Sanders. LC 65-23266. 1965. Walker.

Firework Nights & Ice Cream Days. Evelyn Wisner. 3.00 o.p. Carlton.

Fireworks: A Novel. Rosemary Edelman. LC 78-72923. 9.95 (ISBN 0-87795-213-2). Arbor House: Distributed by Dutton.

Fireworks for a Hot Fourth see Football.

Fireworks: Nine Stories in Various Disguises. Angela Carter. LC 80-8706. 144p. 1982. pap. 4.09i (ISBN 0-06-090920-X, CN 920, CN). Har-Row.

Fireworks: Nine Stories in Various Disguises. Angela Carter. LC 80-8706. 144p. 1981. 10.53i (ISBN 0-06-014852-7, HarpT). Har-Row.

Firing Line. Robert William Chambers. LC 8-23561. 1908. D. Appleton and Company.

Firing Line. Robert William Chambers. LC 15-218581. 1909. D. Appleton and Company.

Firing Line. Warren Murphy. (Destroyer Ser.: No. 41). 192p. (Orig.). 1980. pap. 2.25 (ISBN 0-523-41766-7). Pinnacle Bks.

Firing of Rabbi Levi. Hyman Agress & Frances Agress. 1978. pap. 1.75 (ISBN 0-532-17190-X). Woodhill.

Firing Squad. James Barnett. LC 81-11011. 1981. 10.95 (ISBN 0-688-03380-6). Morrow.

Firing Squad. Franz Carl Weiskopf & Galston, James Austin, 1881- Tr. LC 44-5267. 1944. A. A. Knopf.

Firing Squad: A Novel of Revenge. James Barnett. LC 81-11011. 276p. 1981. Repr. 11.95 (ISBN 0-688-00843-7). Morrow.

Firm of Girdlestone. Arthur Conan Doyle. LC 6-34241. (On cover: Fenno's illustrated ser. no. 6). R. F. Fenno and Company.

Firm of Girdlestone. Arthur Conan Doyle. LC 80-65205. (Conan Doyle Centennial Ser.). (Illus.). 364p. 1981. 16.95 (ISBN 0-934468-42-7). Gaslight.

Firm of Girdlestone. A Romance of the Unromantic. Arthur Conan Doyle. 1890. J. W. Lovell Company.

Firm of Girdlestone: A Romance of the Unromantic. Arthur Conan Doyle. LC 80-65205. (Doyle, Arthur Conan, Sir, 1859-1930. Conan Doyle Centennial Ser.). (Illus.). 1980. 16.95 (ISBN 0-934468-42-7). Gaslight Publications.

Firm of Nan & Sue, Stenographers. Harriet Carpenter Cullaton. LC 5-10052. 1904. Broadway Publishing Co.

Firm Word or Two. Nathaniel Benchley. LC 65-22954. bds., 3.95. McGraw.

Firmly by the Tail. P. N. Gwynne. LC 76-21053. (YA) 1976. 8.95 o.p. (ISBN 0-399-11767-9). Putnam.

First a Murder. John Creasey. LC 72-87142. (MW suspense). 1972. 4.95. D. McKay Co.

First Affair: And Other Sketches. 6th ed. John Ames Mitchell. LC 22-16066. 1910. C. Scribner's Sons.

First American King. George Gordon Hastings. LC 4-26241. 1904. The Smart Set Publishing Company.

First American King. George Gordon Hastings. LC 43-427094. 1905. The Smart Set Publishing Company.

First and Last. Victor Lorenzo Whitechurch. LC 30-6540. 1930. Duffield and Company.

First & Last Loves. John Betjeman. pap. 2.50 o.p. Transatlantic.

First and Last Murder. Robert Leigh. LC 82-17068. 1983. 10.95 (ISBN 0-312-29222-8). St. Martin's Press.

First and the Second Marriages: Or, The Courtesies of Wedded Life. 5th thousand. ed. Harriette Newell Woods Baker. LC 6-68831. 1856. Shepard, Clark & Co.

First and Vital Candle. Rudy Henry Wiebe. LC 66-18726. 4.95. Eerdmans.

First Assembling. Ed. by Richard Kostelanetz & Henry J. Korn. (Illus.). 1970. pap. 4.95. Assembling Pr.

First Blood. Lou Cameron. (Orig.). 1972. pap. 0.95 o.p. (75-289). Lancer.

First Blood. Lou Cameron. 1972. pap. 0.95 o.s.i. (75-289). Lancer.

First Blood. Peter McCurtin. (Soldier of Fortune Ser.: No. 5). 160p. 1982. pap. 1.95 (ISBN 0-505-51800-7). Tower Bks.

First Blood. Peter McCurtin. (Soldier of Fortune Ser.). (O.s.i.). 1977. pap. 1.25 o.s.i. (BT511337). Belmont-Tower.

First Blood. David Morrell. 256p. 1981. pap. 2.50 (ISBN 0-449-22976-9, Crest). Fawcett.

First Blood. David Morrell. LC 73-186591. 256p. 1972. 5.95 (ISBN 0-87131-048-1). M Evans.

First Blood. Jack Warner Schaefer. LC 52-10605. 1953. Houghton Mifflin.

First Blood. large type ed., complete and unabridged. ed. Jack Warner Schaefer. LC 68-3610. F. Watts.

First Blood: A Novel. David Morrell. LC 73-186591. 1972. 5.95. M. Evans; Distributed in Association with Lippincott, Philadelphia.

First Book Edition of The Man Without a Country. Edward Everett Hale. LC 60-10807. (Illus.). 1960. F. Watts.

First Book of Eppe. Roderick Macleish. 384p. 1981. pap. 2.95 (ISBN 0-449-24405-9, Crest). Fawcett.

First Book of Eppe: An American Romance. Roderick MacLeish. LC 79-26560. 10.95 (ISBN 0-394-50424-0). Random House.

First Book of Ghost Stories: Widdershins. Oliver Onions. LC 77-20545. 1978. pap. 3.00 (ISBN 0-486-23608-0). Dover.

First Book of Swords. Fred Saberhagen. 309p. 1983. pap. 6.95. Pinnacle Bks.

First Book of Swords. Fred Saberhagen. 320p. (Orig.). 1983. pap. 6.95 (ISBN 0-523-48560-3). Tor Bks.

First Book of the Neo-Narrative: Containing Sections from Three Novels: Bodies Continents by Stanley Berne; Grounds for Possibilities, with a Pref. by Donald Sutherland, and Hemispheres by Arlene Zekowski. Stanley Berne & Zekowaki, Ariene, 1922--Hemispheres. LC 55-19322. 1954. Metier Editions.

First-Born: A Novel. Georges Simenon & Sainsbury, Geoffrey, Tr. LC 47-4014. 1947. Reynal & Hitchcock.

First-Born of Egypt. Alain Demouzon. LC 78-54648. (Midnight library). 1979. 8.95 (ISBN 0-85690-077-X). Peebles Press International: Distributed in the United States by Farrar, Strauss & Giroux.

First Bus Out. Eugene William Lohrke. LC 35-8978. 1935. D. Appleton-Century Company, Incorporated.

First Cap'n General of Liberty Tree. Jane Johnston Mills. LC 79-90388. 324p. 1979. pap. 5.95 (ISBN 0-935344-00-4). Jupiter Bks.

First Cardinal. Edward M Hughes. LC 39-22441. 1939. New System Printing.

First Casualty. William Powell. LC 79-17454. 10.00 (ISBN 0-8184-0291-1). L. Stuart.

First Channel. Jacqueline Lichtenberg & Jean Lorrah. LC 80-82658. 368p. 1981. pap. 2.50 (ISBN 0-87216-772-0). Playboy Pbks.

First Channel. Jean Lorrah & Jacqueline Lichtenberg. LC 79-7200. 1980. 10.00 (ISBN 0-385-14766-X). Doubleday.

First Christmas. Theodore V. Kundrat. 1978. 28.00x (ISBN 0-88020-090-1). Coach Hse.

First Christmas Dinner. Julian Lee Rayford. 1947. Haunted Book Shop.

First Christmas: From "Ben-Hur". Lewis Wallace. LC 99-5769. (Little books by famous writers). 1899. Harper & Brothers.

First Christmas: From "Ben-Hur,". Lewis Wallace & Johnson, William Martin, 1892- Illus. LC 42-1555. 1902. Harper & Brothers.

First Christmas Tree. Henry Van Dyke. LC 6-34077. 1906. C. Scribner's Sons.

First Christmas-Tree. Henry Van Dyke & Pyle, Howard, 1853-1911, Illus. 1897. C. Scribner's Sons.

First Church's Christmas Barrel. Caroline Abbot Stanley. LC 12-21146. Thomas Y. Crowell Company.

First Circle. Aleksandr Isaevich Solzhenitsyn. LC 68-54547. 1968. 10.00. Harper & Row.

First Citizen. Richard Sullivan. LC 48-8550. 1948. H. Holt.

First Claim. M Hamilton. LC 7-5067. 1907. Doubleday, Page & Company.

First Clash. Andre Stil. LC 55-3065. International Publishers.

First-Class Men: A Novel of German Army Life. unabridged american ed. Wolf Ernst Hugo Emil Baudissin. LC 4-14891. 1904. M. Schnitzer Publishing Co.

First Come, First Kill. Francis K Allan. 1945. Reynal & Hitchcock.

First Come, First Kill: A Captain Heimrich Mystery. Richard Lockridge & Frances Louise Davis Lockridge. LC 62-10534. (Main line mysteries). 1962. Lippincott.

First Comes Courage (The Commandos) Elliott Arnold. LC 43-15323. 1943. Triangle Books.

First Cousin to a Dream. Cyril Harcourt. LC 15-702. 1915. John Lane.

First Cycle. Ed. by H. Bedm Pipers & Michael Kurland. 224p. (Orig.). 1982. pap. 2.25 (ISBN 0-441-23919-6). Ace Bks.

First Day of Friday: A Novel. Honor Lilbush Wingfield Tracy. LC 63-11622. 1963. Random House.

First Day of Spring: Stories and Other Prose. Raymond Knister. LC 76-10475. (Literature of Canada, poetry and prose in reprint). (Illus.). 22.50. (ISBN 0-8020-2069-0) (ISBN 0-8020-6198-2). University of Toronto Press.

First Deadly Sin. Lawrence Sanders. LC 73-82018. 1973. 8.95 (ISBN 0-399-11228-6). Putnam.

First Deadly Sin. Lawrence Sanders. (Berkley medallion book). 1974. (pbk.) 1.95 (ISBN 0-425-02506-3). Putnam.

First Death. William M James. (Apache,#1). 1974. (pbk.) 0.95 (ISBN 0-523-00306-4). Pinnacle Books.

First-Draft Version of Finnegans Wake. James Joyce & David Hayman. LC 62-14501. (Illus.). 1963. University of Texas Press.

First Earl of Lothair. Benjamin Disraeli Beaconsfield. 1981. Repr. lib. bdg. 29.00 (ISBN 0-403-00458-6). Scholarly.

First Earl of Tancred, or the New Crusade. Benjamin Disraeli Beaconsfield. 1981. Repr. lib. bdg. 14.00 (ISBN 0-403-00457-8). Scholarly.

First Encounter. Boris Nikolaevich Bugaev & Gerald J Janecek. LC 78-70276. (Illus.). 10.00 (ISBN 0-691-06381-8). Princeton University Press.

First Estate. Charles Alfred Lee Reed. LC 27-8663. 1927. The Stratford Company.

First Falls on Monday. Arthur L. Murphy. LC 72-80709. (Canadian Play Ser.). 100p. 1972. pap. 3.00 o.p. (ISBN 0-8020-6151-6). U of Toronto Pr.

First Families: A Tale of North and South. Richard Mace. LC 7-20099. 1897. F. A. Munsey.

First Families of the Sierras. Joaquin Miller. LC 7-25986. 1876. Jansen, McClurg & Co.

First Family. Patrick Anderson. 1980. pap. 2.50 (ISBN 0-445-04545-0). Popular Lib.

First Family. Patrick Anderson. (O.s.i.). 1979. 9.95 o.s.i. (ISBN 0-671-24037-4). S&S.

First Family. Richard Scowcroft. LC 50-5979. 1950. Houghton Mifflin.

First Family: A Novel. Patrick Anderson. LC 78-14358. 9.95 (ISBN 0-671-24037-4). Simon and Schuster.

First Family of Tasajara. Bret Harte. LC 39-19451. 1891. Macmillan and Co.

First Family of Tasajara. Bret Harte. LC 7-3642. 1892. Houghton, Mifflin and Company.

First Fast Draw. Louis L'Amour. LC 59-516819. (Bantam western, 1905). 1959. Bantam Books.

First Fiddle. Margaret Weymouth Jackson. LC 32-49036. The Bobbs-Merrill Company.

First Fish, and Other Stories. Warren Beck. LC 47-123513. 1947. Anticoch Press.

First Fleet Family. Louis Becke. LC 6-9779. 1896. Macmillan & Co.

First Fleet Family. A Hitherto Unpublished Narrative of Certain Remarkable Adventures Compiled from the Papers of Sergeant William Dew of the Marines. Louis Becke. LC 6-9778. 1896. Macmillan & Co.

First Flight. Jeffery R Daniels. LC 73-86856. 1973. 5.95 (ISBN 0-698-10571-0). Coward, McCann & Geoghegan.

First Flight see Now Begins Tomorrow.

First Flight: Maiden Voyages in Space & Time. Ed. by Damon Francis Knight. (Orig.). pap. 0.50 o.p. (72-145). Lancer.

First Flights to the Moon. Ed. by Harry C. Stubbs. LC 74-103738. (Doubleday science fiction). 1970. 4.95. Doubleday.

First for Freedom. Maxville Burt Williams. LC 76-25333. 1976. 9.95 (ISBN 0-87716-067-8, Pub. by Moore Pub Co). F Apple.

First for Freedom: A Story About the First Official Act for Independence by Any Colonial Government. Maxville Burt Williams. LC 76-25333. (Illus.). 7.95 (ISBN 0-87716-067-8). Moore Pub. Co.

First Four Years. Laura Ingalls Wilder. LC 76-135774. (Illus.). 1971. 4.95 (ISBN 0-06-026426-8). Harper & Row.

First Freedom. Nat Hentoff. 1981. pap. 2.50 (ISBN 0-440-33850-6, LE). Dell.

First Garden. C. Z. Guest. LC 75-34655. (Illus.). 1976. 8.95 o.p. (ISBN 0-399-11712-1). Putnam Pub Group.

First Garden. C. Z. Guest. LC 75-34655. (Illus.). 1976. 8.95 o.p. (ISBN 0-399-11712-1). Putnam.

First Gentleman of America: A Comedy of Conquest. James Branch Cabell. LC 42-16202. (His Heirs and assigns, v. 3). 1942. Farrar & Rinehart, Inc.

First Gentleman of America: A Comedy of Conquest. James Branch Cabell. LC 42-3407. (His Heirs and assigns, v. 3). Farrar & Rinehart, Inc.

First Girl. Jean Carew. LC 45-9832. 1945. Arcadia House, Inc.

First Gravedigger. Barbara Paul. LC 80-1126. 1980. 8.95 (ISBN 0-385-17270-2). Published for the Crime Club by Doubleday.

First Harvest. Vladimir Pozner & Chevalier, Haakon Maurice, 1902- Tr. LC 43-7229. 1943. The Viking Press.

First Hunt. Dennis Crafton. 208p. (Orig.). 1982. pap. 1.95 (ISBN 0-523-41639-3). Pinnacle Bks.

First Hurdle: And Others. John Reed Scott. LC 12-25993. 1912. 1.25. J. B. Lippincott Company.

First I Must Forget. Tempest, Jan. LC 51-10930. 1951. Arcadia House.

First Impressions: Or, Hints to Those Who Would Make Home Happy. Sarah Stickney Ellis. LC 51-52458. (Tales for the people and their children). 1842. Appleton.

First in My Heart. Archie Joscelyn. LC 36-7590. Phoenix Press.

First in the Field: A Story of New South Wales. George Manville Fenn. LC 6-39271. Dodd, Mead & Company.

First Lady. Ron Nessen. LC 79-4876. 1979. 9.95 o.p. (Playboy). Putnam Pub Group.

First Lady: A Novel. Ron Nessen. LC 79-4876. 9.95 (ISBN 0-87223-537-8). Playboy Press.

First Lady Brendon: A Novel in a Prologue and Two Parts. Robert Smythe Hichens. LC 31-33325. 1931. Doubleday, Doran & Company, Inc.

First Lady Chatterley. David Herbert Lawrence. LC 44-3755. 1944. Dial Press.

First Lady Chatterley: The First Version of Lady Chatterley's Lover. David Herbert Lawrence. LC 75-324621. 1973. 0.35 (ISBN 0-14-003731-4). Penguin.

First Lady in the Land: Or, When Dolly Todd Took Boarders. Acton Davies & Nirdlinger, Charles Frederic. LC 12-27597. 1.25. The H. K. Fly Company.

First Lady: My Thirty Days Upstairs in the White House. Edward Everett Tanner. LC 64-5557. 1964. W. Morrow.

First Law: A Romance. Gilson Willets. LC 11-13981. G. W. Dillingham Company.

First Lensman. Edward Elmer Smith. LC 50-5730. 1950. Fantasy Press.

First Lesson. James Aston, pseud. 1973. pap. 0.75 o.p. (07273). Curtis.

First Long Kiss. Denise Robins. 1.25 (ISBN 0-380-00653-7). Avon.

First Love. Dorothy Black. LC 40-4661. The Penn Publishing Company.

First Love. D. J. Cryle. 3.00 o.p. Carlton.

First Love. Edmee Elizabeth Monica De La Pasture. LC 29-1964. 1929. Harper & Brothers.

First Love. Peggy Gaddis, pseud. LC 44-289761. 1944. Arcadia House, Inc.

First Love. Ed. by Joseph Ingham Greene. Abell, Elizabeth. LC 48-4525. (Bantam Books, 503). 1948. Bantam Books.

First Love. Charles Morgan. LC 29-5699. 1929. A. A. Knopf.

First Love. Phyllis Speshock. LC 55-187. 1954. Zondervan Pub. House.

First Love. Bethany Strong. LC 76-17950. 1977. 8.95 (ISBN 0-917250-03-6). Parable Press.

First Love. Ivan Sergeevich Turgenev. LC 78-303371. (Peacock books). 1977. 1.50 (ISBN 0-14-047095-6). Penguin.

First Love. Marie Van Vorst. LC 10-22858. The Bobbs-Merrill Company.

First Love see Seven Short Novel Masterpieces.

First Love and Last: A Novel. Howard Coxe. LC 34-146893. Harcourt, Brace and Company.

First Love and Last Love. A Tale of the Indian Mutiny. James Grant. LC 44-15526. 1868. G. Routledge and Sons.

First Love and Last Love. A Tale of the Indian Mutiny. James Grant. LC 42-47097. (Routledge's railroad library). 1869. G. Routledge and Sons.

First Love & Other Shorts. Samuel Beckett. Tr. by Samuel Beckett from Fr. 180p. 1974. 10.00 (ISBN 0-394-49149-1, GP731). Grove.

First Love and Other Sorrows. Harold Brodkey. LC 57-14668. 1957. Dial Press.

First Love & Other Tales. Ivan Sergeevich Turgenev. Tr. by David Magarshack. Orig. Title: Selected Tales of Ivan Turgenev. 1968. pap. 6.95 (ISBN 0-393-00444-9, Norton Lib). Norton.

First Love, Farewell. Graeme Lorimer & Lorimer, Sarah. LC 40-33066. 1940. Little, Brown and Company.

First Love Is Best. A Sentimental Sketch. Mary Abigail Dodge. LC 6-33860. (Cobweb series of choice fiction). Estes and Lauriat.

First Love, Last Love. Carole Mortimer. (Harlequin Presents Ser.). 192p. 1981. pap. 1.50 (ISBN 0-373-10443-X, Pub. by Harlequin). PB.

First Love, Last Rites. Ian McEwan. LC 74-30218. 1975. 6.95 (ISBN 0-394-49422-9). Random House.

First Love: Three Short Novels. Ivan Sergeevich Turgenev. LC 76-29154. (Classics of Russian literature). (Hyperion library of world literature). 1977. 12.50. Hyperion Press.

First Love: Three Short Novels. Ivan Sergeevich Turgenev. LC 48-75394. 1948. Lear.

First Love: Three Short Novels; First Love; the Diary of a Superfluous Man; Acia. Ivan Sergeevich Turgenev. Tr. by Constance Garnett from Rus. LC 76-29154. (Classics of Russian Literature). 1977. 13.50 (ISBN 0-88355-523-9); pap. 4.95 (ISBN 0-88355-524-7). Hyperion Conn.

First Lover and Other Stories. Kay Boyle. LC 33-27080. 1933. H. Smith & R. Haas.

First Loves of Perilla. John Corbin. 1903. Fox, Duffield and Company.

First Loves: With Sketches of the Poets... Samuel M Kennedy. LC 15-631892. 1867. S. M. Kennedy.
First Man, Last Man. Josephine Carson. 1967. 5.95 o.p. McGraw.
First Man, Last Man. 1st Ed. Josephine Carson. LC 66-17868. 1966. 5.95. McGraw.
First Man on the Sun: A Novel. Richard H. W. Dillard. 304p. 1983. 19.95 (ISBN 0-8071-1090-6); pap. 8.95 (ISBN 0-8071-1098-1). La State U Pr.
First Marian Reader: Folktales, Legends, and Short Stories. The Marian. LC 51-7074. 1951. Lithuanian Catholic Press Society.
First Mate of the Henry Glass. Robert A Hill. LC 59-118738. 1959. Vantage Press.
First Medicine Man: The Tale of Yobaghu-Talyonunh. Arthur R. Wright. LC 77-99137. (World Discovery Books). (Illus.). 1977. 10.00 (ISBN 0-930766-03-2); pap. 4.95 (ISBN 0-930766-04-0). O W Frost.
First Men in the Moon. Herbert George Wells. LC 66-657. (airmont classic, CL78). 1965. Airmont Pub. Co.
First Men in the Moon. Herbert George Wells. LC 1-23101. The Bowen-Merrill Company.
First Mrs. Fraser, a Novel. St. John Greer Ervine. LC 31-32085. 1931. The Macmillan Company.
First Mrs. Winston. Elinore Denniston. LC 72-3925. (Red badge novel of suspense). 1972. 4.95 (ISBN 0-396-06696-8). Dodd, Mead.
First Mrs. Winston. Rae Foley. 224p. 1972. 4.95 o.p. (ISBN 0-396-06696-8). Dodd.
First Mrs. Winston. Rae Foley. 1973. (pbk) 0.95. Dell.
First Night. Emil Michael Rasmussen. LC 50-55519. 1947. W. Malliet.
First Night. Lorna Rea. LC 32-258433. 1932. Harper & Brothers.
First Night Murder. F G Parke. LC 31-22904. 1931. L. MacVeagh, The Dial Press.
First of January. Lee Head. LC 73-87192. 1973. 6.95 (ISBN 0-399-11221-9). Putnam.
First of the English: A Novel. Archibald Clavering Gunter. LC 6-46698. The Home Publishing Co.
First of the Great Detective Stories. LC 70-180258. Repr. 7.95 (ISBN 0-912092-48-3). Educator Bks.
First of the Hoosiers. Edward Eggleston. 1903. lib. bdg. 25.00 (ISBN 0-8414-3889-7). Folcroft.
First of the Knickerbocker: A Tale of 1673. 2d ed. Peter Hamilton Myers. LC 7-24124. (On cover: Putnam's choice library). 1849. G. P. Putnam; Etc., Etc.
First of the Knickerbockers: A Tale of 1673... Peter Hamilton Myers. (On cover: Putnam's choice library). 1848. G. P. Putnam; Etc., Etc.
First of the Knickerbockers: A Tale of 1673. Peter Hamilton Myers. (On cover: The Sunny side series. no. 1). 1866. Chapman & Co.
First Officer Sue. Peggy O'More, pseud. LC 43-5569. 1943. Grammercy Publishing Co.
First Ophelia, and Other Stories. Louis Paul Kirby. LC 71-144159. (Short story index reprint series). 1971. (ISBN 0-8369-3774-0). Books for Libraries Press.
First Ophelia and Other Stories. Louis Paul Kirby. LC 37-388722. 1937. Meador Publishing Company.
First or the Second: Or, A Mistake Marriage. Florence Blackburn White Schoeffel. LC 8-2039. 1888. The American News Co.
First Pan Book of Horror Stories. Ed. by H. Van Thal. 1982. pap. 10.00x (ISBN 0-330-10045-9, Pub. by Pan Bks). State Mutual Bk.
First Papers. Laura Keane Zametkin Hobson. 1964. 8.95 o.p. (ISBN 0-394-42501-4). Random.
First Papers: By Laura Z. Hobson. Laura Keane Zametkin Hobson. LC 64-20029. 1964. Random House.
First Part of the Delightful History of the Most Ingenious Knight Don Quixote of the Mancha. Miguel de Cervantes de Saavedra. Tr. by Shelton, Thomas. LC 10-2921. (Harvard classics, ed. by C. W. Eliot. vol. xiv). P. F. Collier & Son.
First Part of the Life and Achievements of the Renowned Don Quixote De la Mancha. Miguel de Cervantes de Saavedra. Tr. by Motteux, Peter Anthony. LC 41-9355. 1941. Random House.
First Part of the Life & Achievements of the Renowned Don Quixote De la Mancha. Miguel de Cervantes de Saavedra. Tr. by Peter Motteux from Sp. LC 78-27832. (Illus.). 587p. 1979. Repr. 17.95 o.p. (ISBN 0-89659-023-2). Abbeville Pr.
First Part of the Life and Achievements of the Renowned Don Quixote De la Mancha. Miguel de Cervantes de Saavedra & Motteux, Peter Anthony, 1663-1718, Tr. LC 46-118594. (illustrated modern library). 1946. Random House, Inc.
First Part of the Life and Achievements of the Renowned Don Quixote De la Mancha. Miguel de Cervantes de Saavedra & Peter Anthony Motteux. LC 78-27832. (Series: The Illustrated Modern Library.). (Illus.). 1979. 17.95 (ISBN 0-89659-023-2). Abbeville Press.
First Patient: A Story, Written in Aid of the Fair for the "Channing Home"... Caterine Tilden. LC 8-27029. 1859. J. Wilson and Son.
First Person. Richard Mealand. LC 50-5841. 1950. Doubleday.
First Person Rural: Essays of a Sometime Farmer. Noel Perrin. LC 79-14257. (Illus.). 1979. 8.95 (ISBN 0-89340-214-1). J. Curley.
First Person Singular. William Rose Benet. LC 71-144873. 1971. (ISBN 0-403-00860-3). Scholarly Press.
First Person Singular. William Rose Benet. LC 22-8941. George H. Doran Company.
First Person, Singular. Vida Demas. LC 73-85660. 1973. 6.95 (ISBN 0-399-11241-3). Putnam.
First Person Singular. David Christie Murray. (On cover: Seaside library. Pocket ed., no. 674). 1886. G. Munro.
First Person Singular. A Novel. David Christie Murray. (Harper's Franklin square library, no. 503). 1885. Harper & Brothers.
First Persons: A Novel. Austin McGiffert Wright. LC 73-4167. 1973. 7.95 (ISBN 0-06-014759-8). Harper & Row.
First Player. Ivor John Carnegie Brown. 1973. Repr. of 1927 ed. 10.00 o.p. R West.
First Port of Call. Elizabeth Garver Jordan. LC 40-7420. 1940. D. Appleton-Century Company, Incorporated.
First Prize Stories from the O. Henry Memorial Awards, 1919 - 1966. Ed. by Harry Hansen. 5.95 o.p. Doubleday.
First-Prize Stories: 1916-1966. The O. Henry Awards. Introd. by Harry Hansen. Ed. by Blanche Colton Williams & Harry Hansen. Society of Arts and Sciences, New York. LC 21-9372. 1966. 5.95. Doubleday.
First-Prize Stories, 1919-1954: From the O. Henry Memorial Awards. Introd. by Harry Hansen. 1st Ed. Prize Stories. The O. Henry Awards. LC 54-11451. 1954. Hanover House.
First-Prize Stories, 1919-1957: From the O. Henry Memorial Awards. Introd. by Harry Hansen. Prize Stories. The O. Henry Awards. LC 57-8118. Hanover House.
First Quarrels and First Discords in Married Life: To Which Is Added a Matrimonial Peace-Offering. James H Burk. LC 7-1504. 1864. Applegate & Company.
First Quarrels and First Discords in Married Life: To Which Is Added a Matrimonial Peace-Offering. Ed. by James H Burk. 1860. Applegate & Company.
First Reader of Contemporary American Short Fiction. Ed. by Patrick Gleeson. LC 74-158946. 1971. (ISBN 0-675-09826-2). Merrill.
First Republic: Or, The Whites and the Blues... Alexandre Dumas. LC 6-42818. 1894. Estes and Lauriat.
First Rituals. Elinor Klein & Dora Landey. LC 79-13656. 10.95 (ISBN 0-399-12343-1). Putnam.
First Rose of Summer. Josef Ben-Porat. 302p. (Orig.). 1980. pap. cancelled (ISBN 0-9603256-1-1). Brighton House.
First Round Murder. John Victor Turner. LC 32-21435. (London edition (G. P. Putnam's sons) has title: Death must have laughed.). H. Holt and Company.
First Saint Omnibus: An Anthology of Saintly Adventures. Leslie Charteris. LC 30-32999. 1939. Pub. for the Crime Club by Doubleday, Doran & Company, Inc.
First Saint Omnibus: An Anthology of Saintly Adventures by Leslie Charteris. Leslie Charteris. 1941. The Sun Dial Press.
First Season. Timothy Houghton. LC 67-15159. 1967. W. Morrow.
First Secretary: A Novel. Demetra Vaka Brown & Brown, Kenneth, 1868- Joint Author. 1907. B. W. Dodge & Company.
First Sentimental Education. Gustave Flaubert. LC 77-149947. 1972. 8.95 (ISBN 0-520-01967-9). University of California Press.
First Series of Representative Russian Stories. Janko Lavrin. 1946. 15.00. Havertown Bks.
First Series of Representative Russian Stories, Pushkin to Gorky. Ed. by Janko Lavrin. LC 74-114539. (Illus.). 1975. 12.75 (ISBN 0-8371-4740-9). Greenwood Press.
First Series of Representative Russian Stories: Pushkin to Gorky. Ed. by Janko Lavrin. 1978. Repr. of 1946 ed. lib. bdg. 15.00 (ISBN 0-8495-3227-2). Arden Lib.
First Series of Representative Russian Stories: Pushkin to Gorky. Ed. by Janko Lavrin. 1979. Repr. of 1946 ed. lib. bdg. 22.50 (ISBN 0-8495-3308-2). Arden Lib.
First Settlers of Virginia: An Historical Novel. 2nd ed. John Davis. LC 78-64070. Repr. of 1805 ed. 37.50 (ISBN 0-404-17059-5). AMS Pr.
First Sheriff. Gary McCarthy. LC 78-14706. 1979. 7.95 (ISBN 0-385-14781-3). Doubleday.
First Simenon Omnibus. Georges Simenon. LC 76-352249. (Penguin crime books). 1975. 0.90 (ISBN 0-14-003184-7). Penguin.
First Sip of Wine. Jane Gale Pattison. LC 60-11537. 1960. Crowell.
First Sir Percy: An Adventure of the Laughing Cavalier. Emmuska Orczy. LC 21-26083. George H. Doran Company.
First Soprano. Mary Hitchcock. LC 13-10047. 0.50. Gospel Publishing House.
First Star. Mary Howard, pseud. 1949. Arcadia House.
First Step: A Novel. Eliza Orne White. LC 14-5195. 1914. Houghton Mifflin Company.
First Steps to Health. Oliver Erasmus Byrd. LC 64-57357. (New road to health series). Laidlaw Bros.
First Stone: And Other Stories. William Tucker Washburn. LC 4-22985. 1904. R. F. Fenno & Company.
First Story Job: By E. P. Maxwell Pseud. Elva Publicker Mangold. LC 61-10033. 1961. Pilot Industries.
First Strike. D. Terman. LC 79-16759. (Illus.). 9.95 (ISBN 0-684-16383-7). Scribner.
First Team. John Dudley Ball. 1973. 1.50. Bantam.
First Team. John Dudley Ball. LC 79-154959. 1971. 7.95. Little, Brown.
First Temptation of Saint Anthony. Gustave Flaubert. Ed. by Rene Francis. LC 65-59703. 1932. Privately Printed for Rarity Press.
First the Blade. May Merrill Miller. LC 38-320101. 1928. A. A. Knopf.
First the Blade. Katherine Drayton Mayrant Simons. LC 50-10389. 1950. Appleton-Century-Crofts.
First the Blade: A Comedy of Growth. Winifred Ashton. LC 18-9289. 1918. The Macmillan Company.
First, the Field. Charles Barnett Wood. The University of North Carolina Press.
First Thing in the Field: Poems. Chris McCawley. LC 82-12061. (Kestrel; 1). (Illus.). 3.00 (ISBN 0-914974-33-5). Holmgangers Press.
First Thunder. Vian Smith. LC 65-10614. 1965. Doubleday.
First Time I Live: A Romantic Book About the Writing of a Book and the Birth of a Writer. Discursive Introd. by Henry Miller. Will Slotnikoff & Henry - Miller. LC 66-6198. 1966. pap., lim. ed., 2.25,. Manchester Lane Eds.
First Time Incest. Marsha Alexander. pap. 1.95 o.p. (ISBN 0-87682-239-1, 7239). Barclay Hse.
First Time: Initial Sexual Experiences in Fiction. Ed. by Lawrence R. Broer. LC 74-9903. 1974-1975. (pbk.) 5.95 (ISBN 0-672-61355-7). Bobbs-Merrill.
First Time Swappers. Del Val. pap. 1.95 o.p. (ISBN 0-87682-195-6). Barclay Hse.
First to Awaken. Granville Hicks & Richard M. Bennett. LC 70-154446. (Utopian Literature). (Illus.). 1971. (ISBN 0-405-03529-2). Arno Press.
First to Awaken. Granville Hicks & Bennett, Richard M. LC 40-11300. 1940. Modern Age Books.
First to Know. Anne Bernays. 1975. (pbk.) 1.25. Popular Library.
First Train to Babylon. Max Simon Ehrlich. LC 55-9692. 1955. Harper.
First Treasury of Herman. Jim Unger. LC 79-84409. (O.s.i.). 224p. 1979. 10.95 o.s.i. (ISBN 0-8362-1121-9); pap. 6.95 o.s.i. (ISBN 0-8362-1122-7). Andrews & McMeel.
First Trilogy: Herself Surprised. To Be a Pilgrim. The Horse's Mouth. Joyce Cary. LC 57-8201. 1958. Harper.
First Valley, a Novel. Mary Farley Sanborn Sanborn. LC 20-8860. 1920. The Four Seas Company.
First Vice-President: A Novel. Joan Transue, pseud. LC 53-5291. 1953. Doubleday.
First Violin: A Novel. Jessie Fothergill. (Leisure hour series, no. 101). 1878. H. Holt and Company.
First Violin. A Novel. Jessie Fothergill. LC 4-15310. A. L. Burt.
First Violin: A Novel. Jessie Fothergill. LC 11-3198. Grosset & Dunlap.
First Violin: A Novel. Jessie Fothergill. LC 16-340212. (On cover: The home library). 1915. A. L. Burt Company.
First Violin: A Novel. Jessie Fothergill. LC 4-19640. R. F. Fenno & Company.
First Virginians. Allan Dwight, pseud. LC 36-4001. (Our changing world). 1936. T. Nelson & Sons.
First Waltz. Janet Louise Roberts. (candlelight regency). 1974. (pbk.) 0.75. Dell.
First Whisper of "The Wind in the Willows,". Kenneth Grahame & Grahame, Elspeth, Ed. LC 45-2713. 1945. J. B. Lippincott Company.
First Wife and Other Stories. Pearl Sydenstricker Buck. LC 33-174018. The John Day Company.
First Wine. Jack Dunphy. LC 82-7326. 14.95 (ISBN 0-8071-1046-9). Louisiana State University Press.
First Wine: A Novel. Jack Dunphy. 232p. 1982. 14.95 (ISBN 0-8071-1046-9). La State U Pr.
First Woman. Margaret Culkin Banning. LC 35-34328. 1935. Harper & Brothers.
First Women. Adelaide Wilson. LC 33-7198. The Macaulay Company.
First You Have to Find Him. Eaton K Goldthwaite. LC 81-43002. 1981. 9.95 (ISBN 0-385-17697-X). Published for the Crime Club by Doubleday.
First You Steal Two Eggs. Hedda Hendrix. LC 75-6013. 1976. 9.50 (ISBN 0-915494-02-7, Dist. by Media-America); pap. 7.95 (ISBN 0-915494-03-5). Fibonacci Corp.
First Your Penny. Desemea Wilson. LC 32-14328. E. P. Dutton & Co., Inc.
Firstborn. Roland Cutler. 1978. pap. 2.75 (ISBN 0-449-14002-4, GM). Fawcett.
Firstborn: A Novel. Roland Cutler. 1978. 1.75. Fawcett Gold Medal Books.
Firstfruits: A Harvest of 25 Years of Israeli Writing. Ed. by James Albert Michener. LC 72-14199. 1973. 6.95 (ISBN 0-8276-0018-6). Jewish Publication Society of America.
Firsts of the Famous. Ed. by Whit Burnett. LC 62-4224. (Ballantine books, F508). 1962. Ballantine Books.
Fish. Monroe Engel. LC 81-7975. 1981. 12.95 (ISBN 0-689-11219-X). Atheneum.
Fish and Company. Ralph Arnold. LC 51-4265. 1951. Macmillan.
Fish and Tin Fish: Crunch and Des Strike Back. Philip Wylie. LC 44-9586. 1944. Farrar & Rinehart, Inc.
Fish Can Sing. Halldor Kiljan Laxness. LC 67-13745. 1967. Crowell.
Fish Dinner in Memison. Eric Rucker Eddison. LC 41-9033. 1941. E. P. Dutton & Co., Inc.
Fish Flake Hill. Beverly C Carlman. LC 67-29138. (Illus.). 1967. Christopher Pub. House.
Fish Flying Through Air: A Novel. Roswell Gray Ham. LC 57-6727. 1957. Putnam.
Fish for Murder. Edward Lee Fouts. LC 44-200. 1944. Pub. for the Crime Club by Doubleday, Doran and Co., Inc.
Fish Hawk. Edison Marshall. LC 29-7494. 1929. Cosmopolitan Book Corporation.
Fish in a Stream in a Cave: Stories. Ralph Maloney. LC 72-3865. 1972. (ISBN 0-393-08455-8). Norton.
Fish in the Sea. Elizabeth Carfrae, pseud. LC 37-270551. 1937. G. P. Putnam's Sons.
Fish in the Sea. John McGrath. 96p. (Orig.). 1981. pap. 3.95. Pluto Pr.
Fish Lane. Louis Corkill. LC 51-6229. 1951. Bobb-Merrill.
Fish on the Steeple. Ed Bell. LC 35-34919. Farrar & Rinehart, Incorporated.
Fish or Cut Bait. A. A. Fair, pseud. 1963. 3.95 o.p. Morrow.
Fish or Cut Bait. Erle Stanley Gardner. LC 63-9962. (A. Donald Lam-Bertha Cool mystery). 1963. Morrow.
Fish Pond. Peggy O'More, pseud. LC 63-6715.
Fish Preferred. Pelham Grenville Wodehouse. LC 70-4719. (P. G. Wodehouse classic). 1969. 4.95. Simon and Schuster.
Fish Preferred: A Novel. Pelham Grenville Wodehouse. LC 29-14150. 1929. Doubleday, Doran & Company, Inc.
Fish Tales & Ocean Odd Balls. William B. Gray. LC 79-88265. (Illus.). 1970. 6.95 o.p. (ISBN 0-498-07440-4); pap. 2.95 o.p. (ISBN 0-498-07812-4). A S Barnes.
Fish the Strong Waters. With a Foreword by Richard Bissell. N. C. McDonald. 1956. Ballantine Books.
Fisher Boy. Alonzo Tripp. LC 75-164577. (American fiction reprint series). (Illus.). 1971. (ISBN 0-8369-7054-3). Books for Libraries Press.
Fisher Girl of France: From the French of Fernand Calmettes. Fernand Calmettes. Dodd, Mead & Company.
Fisher Maiden. author's ed. Bjornstjerne Bjornson & Anderson, Rasmus Bjorn, 1846- Tr. LC 4-23585. 1882. Houghton, Mifflin and Company.
Fisher of Men: A Novel of Simon Peter. Kurt Frieberger. LC 54-12137. 1954. Appleton-Century-Crofts.
Fisher Village. Anne Beale. LC 6-10281. (On cover: Seaside library. Pocket ed., no. 199). G. Munro.
Fisherman. Tom Okoyo. (Secondary Readers Ser.). 1971. pap. text ed. 3.00x (ISBN 0-435-92506-7). Heinemann Ed.
Fisherman and His Soul. Oscar Wilde & Dean, Mallette, 1907- Illus. LC 44-38516. 1939. The Grabhorn Press.
Fisherman of Auge. A Story. Katharine Sarah Gadsden Macquoid. LC 7-20827. (Appleton's new handy-volume series v. 5). 1878. D. Appleton and Company.
Fisherman's Beach. Vukelich, George. LC 62-16183. 1962. St. Martin's Press.

Fisherman's Daughter. Anne Kendrick Benedict. LC 7-34455. American Baptist Publication Society.

Fisherman's Daughter. Hendrik Conscience. LC 6-28065. 1878. J. Murphy & Co.

Fisherman's Daughter. Valentine Vattier & Monroe, Mrs. Mary C., Tr. LC 8-30120. (Catholic premium-book library, 1st series). 1875. Benziger Brothers.

Fisherman's Dwarf. Raymond Barrio. (Illus.). 1970. pap. text ed. 1.00 o.p. Ventura.

Fisherman's Gat (The Issue) A Story of the River Thames. Edward Noble. LC 7-13441. 1907. Doubleday, Page & Company.

Fisherman's Lady. George Macdonald & Michael Phillips. LC 82-1322. (Illus.). 5.95 (ISBN 0-87123-197-2). Bethany House Publishers.

Fisherman's Luck. Tom Pace. LC 77-156580. 1971. 5.95 (ISBN 0-06-013260-4). Harper & Row.

Fisherman's Luck: And Some Other Uncertain Things. Henry Van Dyke. LC 5-32463. 1905. C. Scribner's Sons.

Fisherman's Pier. James Clifford Safley. LC 48-217117. 1948. Stanford Univ. Press.

Fisherman's Whore. Dave Smith. LC 73-85445. 74p. 1974. 7.50 (ISBN 0-8214-0137-8, 82-81404). Ohio U Pr.

Fishermen. Dmitrii Vasil'Evich Grigorovich. Tr. by Rappoport, Angelo S. LC 26-26502. (The International library, ed. by F. L. L. Johnston). 1926. 1.25. S. Paul & Co., Ltd.

Fishermen. Ella Pieper. 3.95 o.p. Vantage.

Fisher's Hornpipe. Todd McEwen. LC 82-48684. 12.95 (ISBN 0-06-015164-1). Harper & Row.

Fishers of Men. Samuel Rutherford Crockett. LC 6-7395. 1906. D. Appleton and Company.

Fishers of Men. Maxence Van Der Meersch. LC 47-11745. 1947. Sheed & Ward.

Fishery Imbroglio: Treating of a Question in the Domain of Intersexual Politics: a Sketch. Charles William Woolsey. LC 8-372333. Gilliss Brothers & Turnure.

Fishes, Birds, and Sons of Men. Jesse Hill Ford. LC 67-11233. 1967. Little, Brown.

Fishin' Jimmy. Annie Trumbull Slosson. A. D. F. Randolph & Co.

Fishin' Jimmy. Annie Trumbull Slosson. 1903. C. Scribner's Sons.

Fishing Trip. Bruce Dexter. LC 66-13374. 1966. New American Library.

Fishing Widows. Nick Lyons. LC 73-91524. 1974. 5.95 (ISBN 0-517-51480-X). Crown Publishers.

Fishing's Just Luck: And Other Stories. Elmer Inglesby Ransom. 1945. Howell, Soskin.

Fishkill Landing. Roy Russell. 1970. 5.00 o.p. (ISBN 0-682-47100-3). Exposition.

Fishmans. H. W. Katz. Tr. by Samuel, Maurice. LC 38-16755. 1938. The Viking Press.

Fishmonger's Fiddle. Alfred Edgar Coppard. LC 25-26898. 1925. A. A. Knopf.

Fishmonger's Fiddle. Alfred Edgar Coppard. LC 45-6829. (On cover: Penguin books. 336). 1943. Penguin Books.

Fishmonger's Fiddle: Tales. Alfred Edgar Coppard. LC 78-106276. (Short story index reprint series). 1970. Books for Libraries Press.

Fishpingle: A Romance of the Countryside. Horace Annesley Vachell. LC 17-15975. George H. Doran Company.

Fist of Fatima. Paul Edwards. (John Eagle, expeditor, no. 4). 1973. (pbk.) 0.95 (ISBN 0-515-03157-7). Pyramid Books.

Fistful of Fig Newtons. Jean Shepherd. LC 80-2872. 1981. 14.95 (ISBN 0-385-17503-5). Doubleday.

Fistful of Stars. Sarah McNeil Lockwood. LC 47-314134. 1947. D. Appleton-Century Co.

Fit. William Wood. LC 60-13965. 1960. Macmillan.

Fit As a Filly. Jennifer Ramage. LC 54-10306. (Illus.). 1954. W. Morrow.

Fit to Kill. Davis Dresser. 1976. 1.25. Dell.

Fit to Kill. Louis Trimble. LC 41-16495. Phoenix Press.

Fittest: By J. T. McIntosh Pseud. 1st Ed. James Murdoch Macgregor. LC 55-5503. (Doubleday science fiction). 1955. Doubleday.

Fitzboodle Papers: Also The Wolves and the Lamb. William Makepeace Thackeray. LC 8-28202. (Lovell's library, v. 5, no. 280). 1883. J. W. Lovell Company.

Fitzcarraldo: The Original Story. Werner Herzog. Tr. by Martje Herzog & Alan Greenberg. 160p. (Orig.). 1982. pap. 8.00 (ISBN 0-940242-04-4). Fjord Pr.

Fitzempress' Law. Diana Norman. LC 80-52656. 1980. 11.95 (ISBN 0-312-29419-0). St. Martin's Press.

Fitzgerald Reader. Ed. by Arthur Mizener. Francis Scott Key Fitzgerald. LC 62-96323. (SL118). 1965. pap., 2.95. Scribners.

Fitzgerald's The Great Gatsby: A Critical Commentary. Austin Fowler. LC 66-30243. (Bar notes literature study and examination guides). Barrister Pub. Co.

Five. Temple Field. LC 31-14413. Farrar & Rinehart, Incorporated.

Five. C. M Naim. LC 77-902304. 1976. 5.00. Bhasha Prakashan.

Five A. M. Jean Dutourd. (O.S.I.). 1956. 3.00 o.s.i. (26160). S&S.

Five Acres & Dementia. Augusta Mutchler. (Illus.). 96p. 1983. pap. 8.95 (ISBN 0-931722-18-7). Corona Pub.

Five Adventure Novels: Each Complete and Unabridged. Henry Rider Haggard. LC 52-8569. Dover Publications, Inc.

Five Against the House: 1st Ed. Jack Finney. LC 54-5366. 1954. Doubleday.

Five Against the Law. Thomas Ernest Mount. LC 36-169331. 1936. W. Morrow & Co.

Five Against the Law: By Stone Cody Pseud. Thomas Ernest Mount. LC 58-6666. (Triple-A western classic). 1958. Jefferson House.

Five Against Vensus: By Philip Latham Pseud. Jacket. Design by Virgil Finlay; Endpaper Design by Alex Schomburg. 1st Ed. Robert Shirley Richardson. LC 52-5496. (Science fiction novel). 1952. Winston.

Five Against Venus. Philip Latham, pseud. (Winston Science Fiction Ser). 1952. 2.95 o.p. (ISBN 0-03-033935-9). Hr&W.

Five Against Venus. Robert Shirley Robinson. LC 52-5496. (Science fiction novel). 1952. Winston.

Five Alarm Funeral. Stewart Sterling. LC 42-7205. 1942. G. P. Putnam's Sons.

Five Alarm Funeral: A Thrilling New Kind of Detective Mystery. Prentice Winchell. LC 44-3409. (Hand-book mysteries). 1944. Quinn Publishing Company, Inc.

Five & Dime Murders. Richard Reinsmith. (Orig.). 1980. pap. text ed. 2.25 o.s.i. (ISBN 0-505-51604-7). Tower Bks.

Five and Ten. Fannie Hurst. LC 29-18149. 1929. Harper & Brothers.

Five and the Rope. Alison York. (Berkley Medallion Book). 1979. 2.50 (ISBN 0-425-04045-3). Berkley Pub. Corp.

Five Arrows. Allan Chase. LC 44-8152. 1944. Random House.

Five-Barred Gate. Ernest Temple Thurston. LC 16-22598. 1916. Hodder and Stoughton.

Five-Barred Gate. Ernest Temple Thurston. LC 16-221446. 1916. D. Appleton and Company.

Five Beds to Mecca. Rod Gray. (Lady from L.U.S.T. Ser). 1970. pap. 0.95 o.p. (B95-2052). Belmont-Tower.

Five Blind Men. Dan Gerber et al. 1969. 7.50 o.p. (ISBN 0-912090-01-4); pap. 2.45 o.p. (ISBN 0-912090-00-6). Sumac.

Five Brothers in Four Countries. Lila Watson & Robert T. Allan. 3.95 o.p. Vantage.

Five Bullets. Lee Thayer. LC 44-8264. 1944. Dodd, Mead & Company.

Five Children and It. Edith Nesbit Bland. LC 3-36814. 1905. Dodd, Mead & Company.

Five Christmas Novels. Charles Dickens. LC 40-2549. 1939. The Heritage Club.

Five Complete Novels. avenal 1981 ed. Edna Ferber. LC 81-8059. 6.98 (ISBN 0-517-34874-8). Avenel Books: Distributed by Crown.

Five-Day Nightmare. Fredric Brown. LC 62-9705. 1962. Dutton.

Five Day Week. Sylvia Palmer Wynne. LC 53-366843. 1953. Rich and Cowan.

Five Days. Eric Hatch. LC 33-176726. 1933. Little, Brown, and Company.

Five Days at Sea. Anne Weale. (Harlequin Presents Ser.). 192p. 1981. pap. 1.50 (ISBN 0-373-10444-8, Pub. by Harlequin). PB.

Five Days in June: A Novel. Stefan Heym. LC 77-26374. 1978. 14.95 (ISBN 0-87975-107-X). Prometheus Books.

Five Days to Love. Daisy H. Thomson. 1974. pap. 0.95 o.p. (ISBN 0-515-03338-3, N3338). BJ Pub Group.

Five Days to Oblivion. David O. Woodbury. 1963. pap. 2.50 (ISBN 0-8159-5505-7). Devin.

Five Days to Paradise. Orlando R. Petrocelli. 1977. pap. 2.25 (ISBN 0-532-22110-9). Woodhill.

Five Deadly Guns. Ralph Hayes. (Orig.). 1980. pap. write for info. o.s.i. (ISBN 0-505-51522-9). Tower Bks.

Five Deceivers. Flora Armitage. LC 63-19268. 1963. Dodd, Mead.

Five Destinies. Anna Reiner & Owens, Philip, Tr. LC 39-23527. 1939. A. A. Knopf.

Five Devils of Kilmainham. Esther Morgan McCullough. LC 55-6132. 1955. C. Taylor.

Five Diamond Brand. Nelson Coral Nye. LC 41-4548. Phoenix Press.

Five Dollars a Scalp: The Last Mighty War Whoop of the Creek Indians. David P Mason. LC 75-23633. (Illus.). 6.95 (ISBN 0-87397-086-1). Strode Publishers.

Five Down & Glory. Gene Gurney. (War Library). 288p. 1983. pap. 2.95 (ISBN 0-345-30799-2). Ballantine.

Five Eyes: Stories. Abdeslam Boulaich & Paul Frederic Bowles. LC 79-16941. 1979. 14.00 (ISBN 0-87685-409-9) (ISBN 0-87685-408-0) (ISBN 0-87685-410-2). Black Sparrow Press.

Five Faces of Incest. Deena Winters. 192p. pap. 1.95 o.p. (7148). Barclay Hse.

Five Fairies. Parlee Clyde Grose. LC 18-3015. 1.25. Fifth Avenue Publishing Co.

Five Fatal Days. Josiah Pitts Woolfolk. LC 33-32592. 1933. Carlyle House.

Five Fatal Letters. Constance Noyes Robertson. LC 37-17246. Farrar & Rinehart, Inc.

Five Fatal Words. Edwin Balmer & Philip Wylie. LC 32-29208. 1932. R. Long & R. R. Smith, Inc.

Five Fates. Keith Laumer. LC 76-111173. (Doubleday science fiction). 1970. 4.95. Doubleday.

Five Fathers of Pepi. Ira Avery. LC 55-10893. 1955. Bobbs-Merrill.

Five Fingers. Gayle Rivers & James Hudson. LC 77-80910. (Illus.). 1978. 8.95 (ISBN 0-385-12963-7). Doubleday.

Five Flamboys. Francis Beeding. LC 29-13890. 1929. Little, Brown, and Company.

Five Flights of the Starfire. Edwin Mumford. 1974. pap. 3.00 (ISBN 0-682-47882-2). Exposition.

Five Folk Tales, Level 1. Lise Winer. Ed. by Jean McConochie. (Regents Readers Ser.). (gr. 7-12). 1982. pap. text ed. 1.75 (ISBN 0-88345-452-1). Regents Pub.

Five for Bridge. Ernest Ward. LC 40-7254. 1940. Thomas Y. Crowell Company.

Five for Infinity. Thomas W. Barker. LC 75-36892. 176p. (Orig.). 1976. pap. 1.25 (ISBN 0-89041-050-X, 3050). Major Bks.

Five for Sorrow, Ten for Joy. Rumer Godden. LC 79-12822. 9.95 (ISBN 0-670-31701-2). Viking Press.

Five Forts. John Ankenbruck. LC 72-91181. 1976. pap. 1.95. Lions Head.

Five Fragments. George Dyer. LC 32-12520. 1932. Houghton Mifflin Company.

Five Fridays. Frank Ramsay Adams. LC 15-17133. Small, Maynard & Company.

Five from Life: Short Stories. John A Millington. LC 25-353922. Chilusk Publishers.

Five Furies of Leaning Ladder. Bertha Muzzy Sinclair. LC 36-404. 1936. Little, Brown, and Company.

Five Gallons of Gasoline. Morris Benjamin Wells. LC 11-11313. 1911. Dodd, Mead & Company.

Five Gates to Armageddon. John Christian. 1976. 1.75 (ISBN 0-671-80772-2). Pocket Books.

Five Gates to Armageddon: A Novel. John Christian. LC 75-9472. 1975. 7.95. St. Martin's Press.

Five Generations Hence. Lillian B Jones. LC 16-16264. 1916. 0.50. Printed by Dotson-Jones Pt'g Co.

Five Go Down. William C. Spatari. (Illus., Orig.). 1969. pap. 1.75 o.p. (3072). Brandon.

Five Gold Bands. Jack Vance, pseud. (Science Fiction Ser.). 1980. pap. 1.95 o.p. (ISBN 0-87997-518-0, UJ1518). DAW Bks.

Five Good Boys. Leo Rutman. LC 81-52152. 1982. 13.95 (ISBN 0-670-31704-7). Viking Press.

Five Graves for Lassiter. Jack Slade, pseud. 1979. pap. 1.50 o.s.i. (ISBN 0-505-51409-5). Tower Bks.

Five Graves to Boot Hill. Gordon D. Shirreffs. 1977. pap. 1.25 o.s.i. (ISBN 0-505-51157-6). Tower Bks.

Five Great Dog Novels: Jack London: The Call of the Wild John Brown: Rab and His Friends; Alfred Ollivant: Bob, Son of Battle; Marshall Saunders: Beautiful Joe and Ouida (Louise De la Ramee): A Dog of Flanders. Ed. by Blanche Cirker. LC 61-19809. 1961. Dover Publications.

Five Hours from Isfahan. William Copeland. LC 74-16586. 1975. 7.95 (ISBN 0-399-11431-9). Putnam.

Five Hundred Dollars: And Other Stories of New England Life. Heman White Chaplin. LC 6-23126. 1887. Little, Brown, and Company.

Five Hundred Dollars & Other Stories of New England Life. facsimile ed. Heman White Chaplin. LC 79-106260. (Short Story Index Reprint Ser.). 1887. 16.00 (ISBN 0-8369-3297-8). Ayer Co.

Five Hundred Majority: Or, The Days of Tammany. John Ferguson Hume. LC 7-25776. 1872. G. P. Putnam & Sons.

Five in Family. Eileen Harriet Anstruther Wilkinson Squire. LC 25-26163. 1925. Dodd, Mead and Company.

Five Jars. Montague Rhodes James. LC 75-46282. (Supernatural and Occult Fiction). 1976. 10.00 (ISBN 0-405-08141-3). Arno Press.

Five Jars. Montague Rhodes James. LC 23-26134. 1922. Longmans, Green & Co.

Five Jewels. Allan Dowling. LC 49-13599. 1948. Added Enterprises.

Five Knots. Fred Merrick White. LC 8-12766. 1908. Little, Brown, and Company.

Five Legs & Communion. Graeme Gibson. 333p. (Orig.). 1979. pap. 5.95 o.p. (ISBN 0-88784-073-6, Pub. by Hse Anansi Pr Canada). U of Toronto Pr.

Five Little Foxes and Other Folks of Land and Sea. Nellie Lathrop Helm. LC 12-18644. Educational Publishing Company.

Five Little Gifts. Paul Ricchiuti. (Hello World Ser.). 1975. pap. 1.65 o.p. (ISBN 0-8163-0186-7, 06265-3). Pacific Pr Pub Assn.

Five Little Heiresses. Alice Duer Miller. LC 36-59354. 1936. Dodd, Mead and Company.

Five Long Short Stories: From "It Takes All Kinds"... Louis Bromfield. LC 45-206985. (On cover: Avon modern short story monthly. 24). 1945.

Five Man War. Chuck Belanger. LC 76-22271. 1976. pap. 1.50 o.p. (ISBN 0-87216-346-6, C16346). Playboy Pr Pbks.

Five Masks of Incest. Lydia Wilkinson. 192p. 1971. pap. 1.95 o.p. (ISBN 0-87056-215-0, 6215). Brandon.

Five Men. Tiffany Boots. LC 77-7329. (Venus library, V-1003). 1969. 1.50. Grove Press.

Five Million in Cash... O. B King. LC 32-93687. Pub. for the Crime Club, Inc., by Doubleday, Doran & Company, Inc.

Five-Minute Girl and Other Stories. Mary Hastings Bradley. LC 36-12815. 1936. D. Appleton-Century Company, Incorporated.

Five-Minute Marriage. Joan Aiken. LC 77-72443. 1978. 8.95 (ISBN 0-385-12990-4). Doubleday.

Five-Minute Marriage. Joan Aiken. LC 77-72443. 1979. 1.75 (ISBN 0-446-84682-1). Warner Books.

Five-Minute Marriage. Joan Aiken. LC 78-23876. 1978. 14.50 (ISBN 0-8161-6649-8). G. K. Hall.

Five Minutes to Midnight. Sabi Shabtai. 1981. pap. 2.95 (ISBN 0-440-12534-0). Dell.

Five Minutes to Midnight. Sabi H Shabtai. LC 79-21897. 9.95 (ISBN 0-440-02569-9). Delacorte Press.

Five Minutes to Midnight. Sabi H. Shabtai. (O.s.i.). 1980. 9.95 o.s.i. (ISBN 0-440-02569-9). Delacorte.

Five Murderers. Raymond Chandler. (Murder mystery monthly. No. 19). Avon Book Company.

Five Mystery Classics: Tales of Murder & Detection from England's Golden Age of Mystery, 1918-1938, 5 vols. J. S. Fletcher et al. (Illus.). 1369p. 1982. Set. pap. cancelled (ISBN 0-486-24328-1). Dover.

Five Myths of the Passionate Poseidon. Weinstein De Gracia, Alexandra. LC 66-11537. 1966. Dutton.

Five Nights. Vivian Cory. LC 8-2612. M. Kennerley.

Five Nights at the Five Pines. Harriette Lester Avery Gaul. LC 22-17452. 1922. The Century Co.

Five Nights of St. Albans. A Romance of the Sixteenth Century. William Mudford. LC 7-4446. 1833. Baltimore, E. L. Carey & A Hart.

Five Novelettes. Charlotte Bronte. Ed. by Winifred Gerin. (Illus.). 367p. 1971. boxed 18.75x o.p. (ISBN 0-87471-300-5). Rowman.

Five Novellas. Jerome Bahr. LC 76-53357. 8.95. Trempealeau Press.

Five Novels. Arthur Annesley Ronald Firbank. LC 49-48966. New Directions.

Five Novels by Alberto Moravia: Pseud.: Mistaken Ambitions. Agostino. Luca. Conjugal Love. A Ghost at Noon. With an Introd. by Charles J. Rolo. Alberto Pincherle. LC 55-11187. 1955. Farrar, Straus and Cudahy.

Five O'clock Girl. Edna Robb Webster. LC 33-32013. A. L. Burt Company.

Five O'clock Lightning. William L DeAndrea. LC 81-21534. 11.95 (ISBN 0-312-29498-0). St. Martin's Press.

Five O'clock Surgeon. Dorothy Carle Pierce Walker. LC 48-106089. 1948. Macrae-Smith.

Five O'clock Whistle. Ramona Herdman. LC 38-32007. 1938. Harper & Brothers.

Five-Odd. Ed. by Groff Conklin. 1971. pap. 0.75 o.p. (T2450). Pyramid Pubns.

Five of a Kind: The Third Nero Wolfe Omnibus. Rex Stout. LC 61-10444. 1961. Viking Press.

Five of a Kind: The Third Nero Wolfe Omnibus. Rex Stout. LC 74-38723. (Short story index reprint series). 1972. (ISBN 0-8369-4136-5). Books for Libraries Press.

Five on Parade. Doris Peel. LC 30-29244. 1930. Houghton Mifflin Company.

Five Oriental Tales. Joseph Arthur Gobineau. LC 25-17541. 1925. The Viking Press.

Five Passengers from Lisbon. Mignon Good Eberhart. LC 46-25202. 1946. Random House.

Five Passengers from Lisbon. Mignon Good Eberhart & Roden, Henry Wisdon, 1895- Wake for a Lady. LC 46-8604. 1946. Pub. for the Detective Book Club by W. J. Black.

Five Patients. Michael Crichton. 224p. 1981. pap. 2.75 (ISBN 0-380-57364-4, 57364). Avon.

Five Pieces of Jade. John Dudley Ball. LC 70-175477. 1972. 5.95. Little, Brown.

Five Plays. Edmund Wilson. 1969. 7.50 o.p. FS&G.

Five Ports to Danger. Vivian Connolly. (Orig.). 1980. pap. 1.75 o.s.i. (ISBN 0-505-51518-0). Tower Bks.

Five Pounds Satisfying Joy. J. I. Smith. 3.00 o.p. Carlton.

Five Red Fingers. Brian Flynn. LC 38-31623. 1938. M.S. Mill Co., Inc.
Five Red Herrings. Dorothy L. Sayers. (Reader's Request Ser.). 1980. lib. bdg. 15.95 (ISBN 0-8161-3044-2, Large Print Bks). G K Hall.
Five Red Herrings. Dorothy Leigh Sayers. 1968. pap. 2.95 (ISBN 0-380-01187-5, 62109-6). Avon.
Five Red Herrings. Dorothy Leigh Sayers. LC 58-8894. 1958. 14.37i (ISBN 0-06-013775-4, HarpT). Har-Row.
Five Red Herrings see Wimsey Set II.
Five Red Herrings (Suspicious Characters) Dorothy Leigh - Sayers. LC 58-8894. 1958. Harper.
Five Red Herrings: Suspicious Characters. Dorothy Leigh Sayers. LC 80-20861. 1980. 15.95 (ISBN 0-8161-3044-2). Hall.
Five Rivers to Death. Melvin A. Casberg. LC 82-5814. (Illus.). 6.95 (ISBN 0-89407-051-7). Strawberry Hill Press.
Five Roads to Death. Judson Pentecost Philips. LC 77-22467. (Red badge novel of suspense). 7.95 (ISBN 0-396-07472-3). Dodd, Mead.
Five Science Fiction Novels. Ed. by Martin Greenberg. LC 52-9500. 1952. Gnome Press.
Five Seasons. Roger Angell. 1978. pap. 3.50 (ISBN 0-445-04199-4). Popular Lib.
Five Seasons. Roger Angell. (O.s.i.). 1977. 9.95 o.s.i. (ISBN 0-671-22743-2). S&S.
Five Seasons: A Novel. Translated by Robert Kee. Karl Eska. LC 54-95943. 1954. Viking Press.
Five Seasons of a Golden Year: A Chinese Pastoral. Cheng-Ta Fan & Gerald William Bullett. LC 81-670010. (Renditions Book). (Illus.). 12.95. Chinese University Press.
Five Senses for One Death: Special Issue 18. Adi. pap. 1.00 o.p. The Smith.
Five-Seven-Five. James D. Andrews. 1974. 5.00 (ISBN 0-8233-0210-5). Golden Quill.
Five Short Novels. Translated and with an Introd. by Franklin Reeve. Turgenev, Ivan Sergeevich. LC 62-289. (Bantam classic, SC92). 1961. Bantam Books.
Five Signs from Ruby. Hugh C. McDonald. 1976. pap. 1.75 o.p. (ISBN 0-515-03983-7). BJ Pub Group.
Five Silver Buddhas: A Mystery Novel. Harry Stephen Keeler. LC 35-2098. E. P. Dutton & Co., Inc.
Five Silver Daughters. Louis Golding. LC 34-10389. Farrar & Rinehart, Incorporated.
Five Sinister Characters. Raymond Chandler. LC 45-162323. (Murder mystery monthly. No. 28). 1945.
Five Sinister Characters... Raymond Chandler. LC 46-21778. 1946.
Five Sisters: Women Against the Tsar. Ed. by Barbara A. Engel & Clifford N. Rosenthal. 1975. 8.95 o.p. (ISBN 0-394-48553-X). Knopf.
Five Smooth Stones. Ann Fairbairn, pseud. 944p. 1975. pap. 3.50 (ISBN 0-553-14949-0). Bantam.
Five Smooth Stones. Ann Fairbairn, pseud. 1966. 10.95 (ISBN 0-517-50687-4). Crown.
Five Smooth Stones: A Novel. Ann Fairbairn, pseud. LC 66-26196. 1966. Crown Publishers.
Five Spy Novels. Ed. by Howard Haycraft. LC 62-19184. 1962. Doubleday.
Five Star Finish. J. Julius Fanta. LC 70-116627. 1971. 6.95 (ISBN 0-912214-03-1). Sea Lore Pub. Co.
Five Steps to Tomorrow. Eando Binder, pseud. 1970. pap. 0.75 o.p. (0502-07106). Curtis.
Five Stories. Willa Sibert Cather. LC 56-13685. (Vintage books, K28). 1956. Vintage Books.
Five Stories. Catherine McKenna. 1981. 15.00x (ISBN 0-7223-1357-8, Pub. by Stockwell). State Mutual Bk.
Five Stories. Frank Luther Mott. LC 62-15379. 1962. Prairie Press.
Five Stories of Ferrara. Giorgio Bassani. LC 76-153681. 1971. 5.95 (ISBN 0-15-131400-4). Harcourt Brace Jovanovich.
Five Stories of Man. David Gordon. LC 48-10999. 1948. Christopher Pub. House.
Five Tales. John Galsworthy. LC 79-145028. 1971. (ISBN 0-403-00975-8). Scholarly Press.
Five Tales. John Galsworthy. LC 18-7035. 1918. C. Scribner's Sons.
Five Tales. John Galsworthy. LC 31-19500. 1929. C. Scribner's Sons.
Five Tales. Emile Verhaeren. LC 71-132133. (Short story index reprint series). (Illus.). 1970. Books for Libraries Press.
Five Tales. Emile Verhaeren & Wallis, Keene, Tr. LC 25-3196. 1924. A. & C. Boni.
Five Tales from Tuscany. Ouida, pseud. 192p. 1982. 30.00x (ISBN 0-284-98633-X, Pub. by C Skilton Scotland). State Mutual Bk.
Five Tales: Retold by D. Fullerton & J. Oxley. Oscar Wilde. (Oxford Progressive English Readers Ser.). (Illus.). 1975. pap. text ed. 1.95x o.p. (ISBN 0-19-580723-5). Oxford U Pr.
Five Tales. With Illus. of the Author and His Environment, Together with an Introd. by James H. Pickering. Herman Melville. Ed. by James H. Pickering. LC 67-14088. (Great illus. classics). 1967. 3.95. Dodd.
Five Thirty to Midnight: A Novel. Ruth Willock. LC 41-176195. Harper & Brothers.
Five Thousand an Hour: How Johnny Gamble Won the Heiress. George Randolph Chester. LC 12-622320. The Bobbs-Merrill Company.
Five Thousand Dollar Reward: Or, The Missing Bride. Geraldine Fleming. LC 6-39927. (Munro's library. v. 50, no. 802). 1887. N. L. Munro.
Five Thousand Dollar Reward: Or, The Missing Bride. Geraldine Fleming. LC 6-39926. (On cover: American novelists' series, no. 46). 1890. J. W. Lovell Company.
Five to Twelve. Edmund Cooper. LC 71-83504. 1969. 4.50. Putnam.
Five Towns. Leslie Tonner. LC 80-52418. 12.95 (ISBN 0-87223-652-8). Seaview Books.
Five Victorian Ghost Novels. Ed. by Everett Franklin Bleiler. LC 77-102771. (Illus.). 1971. 3.50 (ISBN 0-486-22558-5). Dover Publications.
Five Way Secret Agent and Mercenary from Tomorrow. Mack Reynolds. 1975. (pbk.) 1.25. Ace Books.
Five Weeks in a Balloon. Jules Verne. LC 64-9537. (Fitzroy edition of Jules Verne). 1962. Associated Booksellers.
Five Weeks in a Balloon. Jules Verne. LC 50-130529. Didier.
Five Weeks in a Balloon: An Abridged Translation of Jules Verne's Stirring Romance. Jules Verne & Finger, Charles J., Tr. (Pocket series, no. 482, ed. by E. Haldeman-Julius). Haldeman-Julius Company.
Five Weeks in a Balloon: & Around the World in Eighty Days. Jules Verne & Chambers, Arthur, Tr. (Half-title: Everyman's library, ed. by Ernest Rhys. For young people. no. 779). 1926. J. M. Dent & Sons, Ltd.
Five Weeks in a Balloon: Or, Journeys and Discoveries in Africa by Three Englishmen. Jules Verne. LC 76-2140. 1976. 9.95. Aeonian Press.
Five Weeks in a Balloon: Or, Journeys and Discoveries in Africa, by Three Englishmen. Jules Verne & Lackland, William, Tr. LC 1-9792. 1869. D. Appleton & Co.
Five Were Called. Edward Morrell Massey. LC 41-6657. The Penn Publishing Company.
Five Who Vanished. George Frank Worts. LC 45-2791. 1945. R. M. McBride & Co.
Five Windows. Dorothy Emily Stevenson. LC 53-9237. 1953. Rinehart.
Five Wives of Silverbeard: Adda, Francesca & Nella. 32p. 4.95 (ISBN 0-904613-60-7). Writers & Readers.
Five Women in Three Novels. Faith Baldwin Cuthrell. LC 42-196502. 1942. Farrar & Rinehart, Inc.
Five Women on a Gallery. Suzanne Normand. Tr. by Taylor, G. S. LC 29-5951. 1929. The Vanguard Press.
Five Women. Tr. from German by Eithne Wilkins, Ernst Kaiser. Pref. by Frank Kermode. 1st Amer. Ed. Robert Musil & Robert Musil. LC 66-12663. (Seymour Lawrence bk.). 5.00. Delacorte Dist. Dial.
Five Women. Tr. from German by Eithne Wilkins, Ernst Kaiser. Pref. by Frank Kermode. Robert Musil & Robert Musil. (Delta bk., 2575). 1966. pap., 1.75. Dell.
Five Women Who Loved Love. Ihara Saikaku. Tr. by William T. De Bary. LC 55-10619. (Illus.). 1955. pap. 5.95 (ISBN 0-8048-0184-3). C E Tuttle.
Five Women Who Loved Love. Translated by Wm. Theodore De Bary, with a Background Essay by Richard Lane, and the 17-Century Illus. by Yoshida Hambei. 1st Ed. Saikaku Ibara. LC 55-106198. 1956. C. E. Tuttle Co.
Five Years a Captive. Sylvester Crakes. LC 75-7099. (Garland library of narratives of North American Indian captivities; v. 74). (Illus.). 1976. 21.00 (ISBN 0-8240-1698-X). Garland Pub.
Five Years to Find Out. Ida Alexa Ross Wylie. LC 14-5313. The Bobbs-Merrill Company.
Fives Wild. Walter Winward. LC 75-41850. 1976. 8.95 (ISBN 0-689-10711-0). Atheneum.
Fives Wild. Walter Winward. (Kangaroo Book). 1978. 1.75 (ISBN 0-671-81102-9). Pocket Books.
Fivescourt: A Novel in Reverse. Hilya Harsch, pseud. 1979. 6.50 (ISBN 0-682-49382-1). Exposition.
Fivesquare City. James Dougherty. 178p. 1980. 12.95 (ISBN 0-268-00946-5). U of Notre Dame Pr.
Fix. Leo Clancy. LC 79-63808. 1979. 8.95 (ISBN 0-394-50815-7). Knopf: Distributed by Random House.
Fix. Dorian Fliegel. LC 78-9475. 1978. 8.95 (ISBN 0-395-25700-X). Houghton Mifflin.
Fix. Jack Usher. LC 59-11710. 1959. M. S. Mill Co., and W. Morrow.
Fix Bayonets! And Other Stories. John William Thomason. LC 74-123824. (Illus.). 1970. 8.95. Scribner.
Fix Bayonets & Other Stories. John William Thomason. LC 74-123824. (Illus.). 1970. 8.95 o.p. (ISBN 0-684-10603-5). Scribner.
Fix Like This. K. C Constantine. LC 75-5949. 1975. 6.95 (ISBN 0-8415-0391-5). Saturday Review Press.
Fixation. John London. LC 12-1059. (Orig.). 1969. pap. 1.25 o.p. (B12-1059). Belmont-Tower.
Fixed Stars: Or, The Goddess of Truth and Justice... E. W Deen. LC 6-32891. 1865. J. Miller.
Fixer. Bernard Malamud. (2573). 1967. Dell.
Fixer. Bernard Malamud. 1976. 2.25 (ISBN 0-671-80100-7). Pocket Books.
Fixer. Bernard Malamud. LC 66-20164. 1966. Farrar, Straus and Giroux.
Fixions. Taban Lo Liyong. (African Writers Ser.). 1969. pap. text ed. 4.00x (ISBN 0-435-90069-2). Heinemann Ed.
Fixions & Other Stories by a Ugandan Writer. Taban Lo Liyong. (African Writers Ser: No. 69). (Orig.). 1969. pap. text ed. 1.75x o.p. (ISBN 0-435-90369-1). Humanities.
Fizzles. Samuel Beckett. LC 76-17479. (Evergreen book). 1976. 1.95 (ISBN 0-8021-4029-7). Grove Press: Distributed by Random House.
Flag. Robert Shaw. LC 65-11996. 1965. Harcourt, Brace & World.
Flag. Robert Shaw. LC 77-381521. 1968. Penguin, in Association with Chatto & Windus.
Flag. John Toombs. (Orig.). 1979. pap. 1.95 (ISBN 0-89083-481-4). Zebra.
Flag Captain. Alexander Kent. LC 74-163412. (Illus.). 1971. 6.95. Putnam.
Flag for Sunrise. Robert Stone. 448p. 1982. pap. 3.95 (ISBN 0-345-30650-3). Ballantine.
Flag for Sunrise: A Novel. Robert Stone. LC 81-47507. 1981. 13.95 (ISBN 0-394-40757-1). Knopf: Distributed by Random House.
Flag Full of Stars. Don Robertson. 1969. pap. 0.95 o.p. (M1316, Crest). Fawcett World.
Flag Full of Stars: A Novel. Don Robertson. LC 64-18014. 1964. Putnam.
Flag in the City. Christopher Landon. LC 54-13166. 1954. Macmillan.
Flag in the Wind. Alfred Boller Stanford. LC 30-14005. 1930. W. Morrow & Company.
Flag on the Hilltop. Mary Tracy Earle. LC 49-40497. 1930. Printed by the Herrin News.
Flag on the Hilltop. Mary Tracy Earle. LC 2-221728. 1902. Houghton, Mifflin and Company.
Flag on the Island: By V. S. Naipaul. 1st Amer. Ed. Vidiadhar Surajprasad Naipaul. LC 68-19698. 5.95. Macmillan.
Flag on the Mill. Mary Breck Sleight. LC 8-980125. 1887. Funk & Wagnalls.
Flag-Raising. Kate Douglas Smith Wiggin. LC 7-34312. (Riverside literature series no. 173). Houghton, Mifflin and Company.
Flag the Hawk Flies. Ned O'Gorman, pseud. 1972. 4.95 o.p. (ISBN 0-394-47317-5). Knopf.
Flagellants. Carlene Hatcher Polite. (2580). 1968. Dell.
Flagellants. Carlene Hatcher Polite. LC 67-15013. 1967. Farrar, Straus & Giroux.
Flagellator. Alan Geoffrey Yates. LC 78-11602. (Signet book). 1969. New American Library.
Flagrant Years: A Novel of the Beauty Market. Samuel Hopkins Adams. LC 29-10429. 1929. H. Liveright.
Flags at Doney. Harris Greene. LC 64-19252. 1964. Doubleday.
Flags in the Dust. William Faulkner. LC 73-1781. 1973. 8.95 (ISBN 0-394-46591-1). Random House.
Flags in the Dust. William Faulkner. LC 74-3315. 1974. (pbk.). 1.95 (ISBN 0-394-71239-0). Vintage Books.
Flags Were Three: A Novel of Old New Orleans. Leo Margulies & Merwin, Samuel, 1910- Joint Author. LC 45-1817. 1945. S. Curl, Inc.
Flagstone Walk. Thad Stem. LC 68-27772. 1968. McNally and Loftin.
Flail. Newton A Fuesle. LC 19-5138. 1919. Moffat, Yard & Company.
Flake of Snow: A Novel. Edward Sagarin. LC 74-80308. 1974. 6.95 (ISBN 0-517-51663-2). Crown Publishers.
Flambards. K. M. Peyton, pseud. LC 68-123692. (B 67-19260). 1967. Oxford U. P.
Flambeau Jim. Frank Hamilton Spearman. LC 27-218862. 1927. C. Scribner's Sons.
Flamboyant Tree: A Portrait. Carl Sevening. LC 42-16026. 1942. Margent Press.
Flame. Robert Verlin Cassill. LC 80-66505. 1980. 11.95 (ISBN 0-87795-280-9). Arbor Hse.
Flame. Jim Hunter. LC 66-11712. 1966. Pantheon Books.
Flame. Kenneth Roberts. (Orig.). 1970. pap. 0.95 o.p. (65-303). Paperback Lib.
Flame. Charles Elbert Scoggins. LC 32-15438. 1932. W. Morrow & Co.
Flame. Louise E Taber. LC 11-26416. 1911. 1.35. The Alice Harriman Company.
Flame: A Novel. Robert Verlin Cassill. LC 80-66505. 11.95 (ISBN 0-87795-280-9). Arbor House.
Flame: A Novel. Josiah Pitts Woolfolk. LC 49-11905. 1949. Woodford Press.
Flame & Shadow, Selected Stories. David Campbell. 1977. 14.95x (ISBN 0-7022-1394-2); pap. 7.95x (ISBN 0-7022-1400-0). U of Queensland Pr.
Flame and Shadow: Selected Stories. David Watt Ian Campbell. LC 77-360679. 1977. 7.90 (ISBN 0-7022-1394-2). University of Queensland Press.
Flame & the Dagger. Arthur Moore. (California Saga Ser.: No. 2). 1979. pap. 1.95 (ISBN 0-445-04419-5). Popular Lib.
Flame and the Fire. Elizabeth Hanely. (Belmont Tower Book.). 1978. 1.95 (ISBN 0-505-51251-3). Tower Pubns.
Flame & the Fire. Elizabeth Hanley, pseud. 272p. 1982. pap. write for info o.p. (ISBN 0-505-51858-9). Tower Bks.
Flame & the Flower. Kathleen E. Woodiwiss. 1972. pap. 3.95 (ISBN 0-380-00525-5, 82750-6). Avon.
Flame & the Fury. Lionel Webb, pseud. 1977. pap. 1.50 o.s.i. (ISBN 0-8439-0436-4, Leisure Bks). Nordon Pubns.
Flame and the Fury. Lionel Webb. (Leisure Books). 1977. 1.50. Nordon Publications.
Flame and the Serpent. Hilda Marie Osterhout. LC 48-9204. (Intercollegiate Literary Fellowship prize novel). 1948. Dodd, Mead.
Flame and the Shadow-Eater. Henrietta Weaver. LC 17-141359. 1917. H. Holt and Company.
Flame Burns on. 1972. pap. 1.95 o.p. Peoples Pr.
Flame Dancer. Frances Aymar Mathews. LC 8-244670. G. W. Dillingham Company.
Flame for Doubting Thomas. Richard Llewellyn. LC 53-12957. 1953. Macmillan.
Flame from an Ash. Lydia Rijos. 264p. 1975. 10.00 o.p. (ISBN 0-682-48350-8). Exposition.
Flame from the Rock. Adet Lin. LC 43-17617. 1943. The John Day Company.
Flame-Gatherers. Margaret Horton Potter. LC 4-12095. 1904. The Macmillan Company.
Flame (Il-Fuoco) ed. de luxe ed. Gabriele D' Annunzio & Ranous, Mrs. Dora Knowlton (Thompson) 1859-1916, Tr. LC 7-3182. (Added t.p.: The literature of Italy, 1265-1907. Ed by Rossiter Johnson and Dora Knowlton Ranous). The National Alumni.
Flame in a High Wind. Jacqueline Kidd. (Leisure Books). 1977. 1.50 (ISBN 0-8439-0500-X). Nordon Pubns.
Flame in the Dark. Basil Bonallack. LC 76-367190. (Illus.). 1976. 3.50 (ISBN 0-7011-2166-1). Chatto & Windus.
Flame in the Forest. Al Cody, pseud. 1977. pap. 1.50 (ISBN 0-532-15287-5). Woodhill.
Flame in the Forest. Harold Titus. LC 33-316591. Macrae Smith Company.
Flame in the Icebox. Charles T. Morrison. 1968. 4.00 o.p. (ISBN 0-682-46788-X). Exposition.
Flame in the Mist. Pierre Audemars. 1971. pap. 0.60 o.p. (06125). Curtis.
Flame in the Wind. James Noble Gifford. LC 32-297654. 1932. W. Godwin, Inc.
Flame in the Wind. Janis Harrison. (Orig.). 1981. pap. 2.50 (ISBN 0-8439-8025-7, Tiara Bks). Nordon Pubns.
Flame in the Wind. Margaret Bass Pedler. LC 37-8143. 1937. Doubleday, Doran & Company, Inc.
Flame in the Wind. Margaret Bass Pedler. LC 38-9516. 1938. The Sun Dial Press, Inc.
Flame Is Green. R. A Lafferty. LC 75-142837. 1971. 5.95 (ISBN 0-8027-0346-1). Walker.
Flame of Anger: A Novel of Africa in Ferment. Eric Clark. LC 66-29417. (Illus.). 1966. Zondervan Pub. House.
Flame of Chandrapore. Aaron Fletcher. 1979. pap. 2.25 o.s.i. (ISBN 0-505-51342-0). Tower Bks.
Flame of Courage. George Fort Gibbs. LC 26-157864. 1926. D. Appleton and Company.
Flame of Desire. Carole Mortimer. (Harlequin Presents Ser.). 192p. 1981. pap. 1.50 (ISBN 0-373-10418-9, Pub. by Harlequin). PB.
Flame of Diablo. Sara Craven. (Harlequin Presents Ser.). (Orig.). 1980. pap. 1.50 (ISBN 0-373-70831-9, Pub. by Harlequin). PB.
Flame of Fidelity. Sandra DuBay. 288p. (Orig.). 1981. pap. 2.50 (ISBN 0-505-51741-8). Tower Bks.
Flame of Fire. 1st American Ed. Jane Oliver & Tyndale, William, D. 1536--Fiction. LC 61-127401. 1961. Putnam.
Flame of Forgotten Guns. Ralph Page. LC 33-20520. 1933. Doubleday, Doran and Company, Inc.
Flame of Frost. Alice Jones. LC 14-14914. 1914. 1.30. D. Appleton and Company.
Flame of Happiness. Florence Jeannette Baier Ward. LC 24-30620. G. W. Jacobs & Company.
Flame of Hercules: The Story of a Fugitive Galley Slave. 1st Ed. Richard Llewellyn. LC 55-8408. (Cavalacade books). 1955. Doubleday.

Flame of Life: A Novel. Gabriele D' Annunzio & Sindici, Magda, Tr. LC 4819. (romances of the pomegranate). 1900. L. C. Page & Company.

Flame of Life: A Novel. Gabriele D'Annunzio. LC 73-21841. 1974. H. Fertig.

Flame of Love. Clarissa Ross, pseud. 1978. pap. 1.95 o.s.i. (ISBN 0-8439-0583-2, Leisure Bks). Nordon Pubns.

Flame of New Orleans. Frances Patton Statham. (Fawcett Gold Medal Book). 1.95 (ISBN 0-449-13720-1). Fawcett Publications.

Flame of Sunset. Llewellyn Perry Holmes. LC 47-30661. 1947. S. Curl.

Flame of the Border. Vingie Eve Roe. LC 33-173903. 1933. Doubleday, Doran and Company, Incorporated.

Flame of the Borgias. Jean Briggs. LC 74-15864. 1975. 7.95 (ISBN 0-06-010463-5). Harper & Row.

Flame of the Desert. Joseph Bushnell Ames. LC 28-9840. 1928. Duffield and Company.

Flame of the Forest: A Novel. Constance E Bishop. LC 21-3628. 1920. Benziger Brothers.

Flame of the South. Constance Gluyas. (Orig.). 1979. pap. 2.50 (ISBN 0-451-08648-1, E8648, Sig). NAL.

Flame of Tournay. Lisa Beaumont. 320p. 1981. pap. 2.25 (ISBN 0-449-24397-4, Crest). Fawcett.

Flame on Ethirdova. Hector Bolitho. LC 31-28058. 1931. D. Appleton and Company.

Flame on the Water: By E. M. Almedingen. Martha Edith Almedingen. LC 52-25498. 1952. Hutchinson.

Flame on the Wind. Irving A Greenfield. 1975. (pbk.) 1.50. Dell.

Flame Out of Dorset. Clifford J Stevens. LC 64-19249. 1964. Doubleday.

Flame Tree. Theodore Pratt. LC 50-5175. 1950. Dodd, Mead.

Flame Tree Planet: An Anthology of Religious Science Fantasy. Ed. by Roger Elwood. LC 72-91153. 1973. 1.35 (ISBN 0-570-03144-3). Concordia Pub. House.

Flame Tree Planet & Other Stories. G. Smith et al. Ed. by R. Elwood. LC 72-91153. 176p. 1973. pap. 1.95 o.p. (ISBN 0-570-03144-3, 12-2528). Concordia.

Flame Trees of Thika. Elspeth Joscelin Grant Huxley. 1982. pap. 3.95 (ISBN 0-14-001715-1). Penguin.

Flame Vine. Effie Lawrence Marshall. 1964. 3.95. House of Falmouth, Preble St.

Flame Vine. Helen Topping Miller. LC 48-668049. 1948. Appleton-Century-Crofts.

Flame Winds. Norvell W Page. (Berkley book). 1978. 1.75 (ISBN 0-425-03898-X). Berkley Pub. Corp.

Flamehair the Skald: A Tale of the Days of Hardrede. Henry Bedford-Jones. LC 13-21256. 1913. A. C. McClurg & Co.

Flamenco. Eleanor Furneaux Smith. LC 31-8325. The Bobbs-Merrill Company.

Flamenco Love Song. Ena Young. pap. 0.50 o.p. (52-352). Paperback Lib.

Flamenco Nights. Susanna Collins. (Second Chance at Love, Contemporary Ser.: No. 1). 192p. (Orig.). 1981. pap. 1.75 (ISBN 0-515-05703-7). Jove Pubns.

Flamenco Rose. Janet Louise Roberts. 416p. (Orig.). 1981. pap. 2.75 (ISBN 0-446-95583-3). Warner Bks.

Flameout. Basil Jackson. LC 76-13578. (Illus.). 7.95 (ISBN 0-393-08740-9). Norton.

Flameout. Basil Jackson. (Dell Book). 1977. 1.75 (ISBN 0-440-12529-4). Dell Pub. Co.

Flameout. Colin D Peel. LC 77-15918. 7.95 (ISBN 0-312-29546-4). St. Martin's Press.

Flames. Elisabeth Burstenbinder. (On cover: Dearborn series no. 41). 1891. Donohue, Henneberry & Co.

Flames. Robert Smythe Hichens. LC 13-12019. 1906. Duffield & Company.

Flames. Robert Smythe Hichens. LC 41-28182. 1906. Grosset & Dunlap.

Flames and Ashes. Alice De Carret. LC 98-326. 1898. G. W. Dillingham Co.

Flames Coming Out of the Top. Norman Collins. LC 38-101192. 1938. Harper & Brothers.

Flames of Desire. Leonard Noel Barker. LC 28-4089. The Curtiss Press.

Flames of Desire. Vanessa Royall. (Dell Book). 1978. 2.25 (ISBN 0-440-14637-2). Dell Pub. Co.

Flames of Empire. Graham Montague Jeffries. LC 49-10973. 1949. G. P. Putnam's Sons.

Flames of Faith: A Novel. Samuel Harden Church. LC 24-73131. Boni and Liveright.

Flames of Glory. Hervey Smith McCowan. LC 19-3593. The Character Building Company.

Flames of Glory. Patricia Matthews. 1983. pap. 6.95. Bantam.

Flames of Moscow. Ivan Sozontovich Lukash & Duddington, Mrs. Natalie Alexandrovna (Ertel) Tr. LC 30-29337. 1930. The Macmillan Company.

Flames of Passion. Sheryl Flourney. (Tapestry Romance Ser.). (Orig.). 1982. pap. 2.50. PB.

Flames of Rome. Paul L. Maier. 1982. pap. 3.95 (ISBN 0-451-11737-9, AE1737, Sig). NAL.

Flames of the Blue Ridge. Ethel Arnold Smith Dorrance. LC 19-159769. The Macaulay Company.

Flames of Time. Baynard Hardwick Kendrick. LC 48-7055. 1948. C.Scribner's Sons.

Flames Over the Castle. Diane La Point. (Ace gothic). 1975. (pbk.) 0.95. Ace Books.

Flamethrowers. Gordon Friesen. LC 36-596. 1936. The Caxton Printers, Ltd.

Flaming Arrow. Carl Moon. LC 27-182972. 1927. Frederick A. Stokes Company.

Flaming Canyon: A Westernnovel. Walker A Tompkins. LC 48-8358. 1948. Macrae-Smith-Co.

Flaming Cross: A Novel of the Klan in Alabama in the 1880's. 1st Ed. Katherine Porter Alligood. LC 56-12668. 1956. Exposition Press.

Flaming Desire: A Novel About Our Young People Today. 1st Ed. Charles J Krivachek. LC 59-13685. 1959. Greenwich Book Publishers.

Flaming Feud: By Tom West Pseud. 1st Ed. Fred East. LC 51-11541. (Dutton Diamond D western). 1951. Dutton.

Flaming Forest. James Oliver Curwood. LC 46-4566. 1946. Triangle Books, the Blakiston Company.

Flaming Forest: A Novel of the Canadian Northwest. James Oliver Curwood. LC 21-13417. 1921. Cosmopolitan Book Corporation.

Flaming Gahagans. Helen Topping Miller. LC 33-23508. The Penn Publishing Company.

Flaming Guns. Burt Arthur, pseud. 1978. pap. 1.25 o.s.i. (ISBN 0-505-51278-5). Tower Bks.

Flaming Guns. Jesse Edward Grinstead. LC 38-77993. The Dodge Publishing Company.

Flaming Hand. Hal Corell. LC 30-9468. David C. Cook Publishing Co.

Flaming Heart. Deborah Deutsch. pap. 0.75 o.p. (54-906). Paperback Lib.

Flaming Heart. Deborah Deutsch. 1964. 4.95 o.s.i. Guild Pr Ltd.

Flaming Irons. Max Brand. 256p. 1976. pap. 1.95 (ISBN 0-446-30260-0). Warner Bks.

Flaming Irons. Frederick Faust. 1976. 1.25 (ISBN 0-446-76318-7). Warner Books.

Flaming Irons. Frederick Faust. LC 48-5580. (Silver star westerns). 1948. Dodd, Mead.

Flaming Jewel. Robert William Chambers. LC 22-15214. 1922. George H. Doran Company.

Flaming Jewel. Robert William Chambers. LC 42-258974. 1942. Triangle Books.

Flaming Lance. Clair Huffaker. 1970. pap. 0.60 o.p. (ISBN 0-446-63330-5, 63-330). Paperback Lib.

Flaming Lance: A Novel of the West. Clair Huffaker. LC 58-13754. 1958. Simon and Schuster.

Flaming Lead. William Colt MacDonald. (Pyramid books, 231). 1956. Pyramid Books.

Flaming Man. M. E. Chaber, pseud. (Milo March Mystery Ser). 1970. pap. 0.60 o.p. (ISBN 0-446-63353-4, 63-353). Paperback Lib.

Flaming Man. M. E. Chaber, pseud. LC 69-10228. (Rinehart Suspense Novel Ser). 1969. 3.95 o.p. (ISBN 0-03-072485-6). HR&W.

Flaming Man. Kendell Foster Crossen. LC 69-10228. (Rinehart suspense novel). 1969. 3.95. Holt, Rinehart and Winston.

Flaming Passions. Bjorne Peterson. 1972. pap. 2.25 o.s.i. (V1087R, Venus). Grove.

Flaming River: A Tale of the Great Titusville Oil Fire of 1892. Reuben E Stainbrook. LC 40-29471. The Tribune Publishing Company.

Flaming Sands. Albert M Treynor. LC 30-1938. 1930. Dodd, Mead & Company.

Flaming Stallion. Johnston McCulley. LC 32-3497. 1932. G. H. Watt.

Flaming Sword. Thomas Dixon. LC 39-20781. 1939. Monarch Publishing Company.

Flaming Sword. George Fort Gibbs. LC 14-16477. 1914. 1.30. D. Appleton and Company.

Flaming Torch. John Alvin Blair. LC 55-13508. 1955. Comet Press Books.

Flaming Wilderness. Ridgwell Cullum. LC 34-145421. 1934. J. B. Lippincott Company.

Flaming Youth. Warner Fabian. LC 23-3136. Boni and Liveright.

Flamingo: A Novel. Mary Borden. LC 27-23862. 1927. Doubleday, Page & Company.

Flamingo Feather. Laurens Van Der Post. LC 54-10305. Morrow.

Flamingo Park. Margaret Way. (Harlequin Romances). 192p. 1981. pap. 1.25 (ISBN 0-373-02400-2, Pub. by Harlequin). PB.

Flamingo Road. Robert Wilder. LC 42-11046. 1942. G. P. Putnam's Sons.

Flamingos: A Novel. Robert Somerlott. LC 67-14458. 1967. Little, Brown.

Flamingo's Nest: A Honolulu Story. Roger Sprague. LC 18-266. 1917. Lederer, Street and Zeus.

Flaminia: And Other Stories. LC 7-1230. 1876. The Catholic Publication Society.

Flamsted Quarries. Mary Ella Waller. LC 10-20852. 1910. Little, Brown, and Company.

Flamsteed. Brian K. Avison. 3.50 o.p. Carlton.

Flanagan's Run. Tom McNab. LC 81-22574. (Illus.). 1982. 14.50 (ISBN 0-688-01198-5). Morrow.

Flander Mare see Ann of Cleves.

Flanders' Folly. Sara Christy. LC 37-20618. M. S. Mill Co., Inc.

Flandry of Terra. Poul Anderson. LC 65-20904. 1965. Chilton Books.

Flandry of Terra. Poul Anderson. LC 79-12734. (Gregg Press science fiction series). (Illus.). 1979. 12.50 (ISBN 0-8398-2519-6). Gregg Press.

Flanigan: Anatomy of a Railroad Ghost Town. Eric N. Moody. LC 78-53152. (Illus.). 1978. pap. 4.00 (ISBN 0-930830-03-2). Great Basin.

Flannel Morning. Sonya Jones. 1977. pap. 3.00 o.s.i. Vanity.

Flannery O'Connor: A Critical Essay. Robert Drake. LC 66-22944. (Contemporary writers in Christian perspective). 1966. Eerdmans.

Flannigan's Folly. George Milburn. LC 47-2786. 1947. Whittlesey House, McGraw-Hill Book Company, Inc.

Flap. Clair Huffaker. Orig. Title: Nobody Loves a Drunken Indian. 1970. pap. 0.95 o.p. (ISBN 0-446-65477-9, 65-477). Paperback Lib.

Flapper Anne. Corra May White Harris. LC 26-9754. 1926. Houghton Mifflin Company.

Flapper Wife. Beatrice Burton Morgan. LC 25-20406. Grosset & Dunlap.

Flappers and Philosophers. Francis Scott Key Fitzgerald. LC 59-13358. 1959. Scribner.

Flappers and Philosophers. Francis Scott Key Fitzgerald. LC 20-26757. 1920. C. Scribner's Sons.

Flappers and Philosophers. Francis Scott Key Fitzgerald. LC 22-247496. 1921. C. Scribner's Sons.

Flapper's Daughter. Beatrice Burton Morgan. LC 33-24662. Farrar & Rinehart, Incorporated.

Flapper's Mother. Madge Mears. LC 19-1777. 1918. John Lane.

Flare Path. Tod Claymore. LC 42-21633. 1942. W. Morrow & Company.

Flash. Mel Juffe. LC 73-2336. 1974. 7.95 (ISBN 0-670-31743-8). Viking Press.

Flash. John Henry Van Dyke. LC 28-22869. R. G. Badger.

Flash and Filigree: A Novel. Southern, Terry. LC 58-12116. 1958. Coward-McCann.

Flash Casey... Detective. George Harmon Coxe. LC 48-10748. (New Avon library, 143). 1948. Avon Book Co.

Flash Casey...Dectective. George Harmon Coxe. LC 47-101. (Murder mystery monthly, no. 39). 1946. Avon Book Company.

Flash for Freedom. George MacDonald Fraser. LC 70-11739. 1973. (pbk) 1.25. New American Library.

Flash for Freedom! George MacDonald Fraser. LC 70-171139. 1972. 6.95 (ISBN 0-394-47947-5). Knopf.

Flash Gordon. Arthur B. Cover. (Orig.). pap. 2.50 (ISBN 0-515-05848-3). Jove Pubns.

Flash Gordon Escapes to Arboria, Vol. 3. Alex Raymond. Ed. by David Kaler. 1978. 9.95 (ISBN 0-517-53359-6). Crown.

Flash Gordon in the Ice Kingdom of Mongo. Alex Raymond. Ed. by Leonard Brown. LC 67-28204. (Illus.). 1967. 12.95 (ISBN 0-87897-008-8). Nostalgia Pr.

Flash Gordon in the Planet Mongo. Alex Raymond. (Illus.). 160p. (YA) 1974. 14.95 o.p. (ISBN 0-517-51581-4). Crown.

Flash Gordon Joins the Power Men, Vol. 5. Alex Raymond. Ed. by David Kaler. 1978. pap. 9.95 (ISBN 0-517-53361-8). Crown.

Flash Gordon: Massacre in the 22nd Century. David Hagberg. (Flash Gordon Novel Ser.: No. 1). 208p. 1980. pap. 2.25 (ISBN 0-448-12963-9, Pub. by Tempo). Ace Bks.

Flash Gordon Versus Frozen Horrors, Vol. 4. Alex Raymond. Ed. by David Kaler. 1978. pap. 9.95 o.p. (ISBN 0-517-53360-X). Crown.

Flash Gordon: War of the Citadels. David Hagberg. (Flash Gordon Novel Ser.: No. 2). 208p. 1980. pap. 2.25 (ISBN 0-448-17254-2, Pub. by Tempo). Ace Bks.

Flash of Gold. Francis Rufus Bellamy. LC 22-186513. 1922. Doubleday, Page & Company.

Flash of Green. John Dann MacDonald. LC 62-16387. 1962. Simon and Schuster.

Flash of Scarlet. Sylvia Thorpe. LC 81-22218. 1982. 12.95 (ISBN 0-89340-399-7). J. Curley.

Flash of Summer: A Novel. Lucy Lane Clifford. LC 6-20744. 1894. D. Appleton and Company.

Flash of Summer: The Story of a Simple Woman's Life. Lucy Lane Clifford. LC 6-20743. (Half-title: Appletons' town and country library, no. 189). 1896. D. Appleton and Company.

Flash of Swallows. William C. Stevens. 3.95 o.p. G&D.

Flash of the Firefly. Parris Afton Bonds. (Orig.). 1979. pap. 2.25 (ISBN 0-445-04497-7). Popular Lib.

Flash Point. Jane Donnelly. 192p. 1982. pap. 1.50 (ISBN 0-373-02456-8). Harlequin Bks.

Flash Point. Michael Francis Gilbert. LC 74-5798. 1974. 6.95 (ISBN 0-06-011518-1). Harper & Row.

Flashback. Roger Burke Dooley. LC 69-15169. 1969. 4.50. Published for the Crime Club by Doubleday.

Flashes from the Furnace,". C. H Rutledge. LC 12-16613. Printed by the Keweenaw Printing Compan.

Flashes in the Night: A Collection of Stories from Contemporary Hungary, Edited by William Juhasz and Abraham Rothberg, Under the Auspices of the East Europe Institute. Ed. by William Juhasz & Abraham Rothberg. LC 58-10949. 1958. Random House.

Flashing Spikes. Frank O'Rourke. LC 48-9006. (Barnes sport novel). 1948. A. S. Barnes.

Flashing Swords! Ed. by Lin Carter. LC 73-169817. 1973. (pbk.) 0.95. N. Doubleday.

Flashman. George MacDonald Fraser. 1971. pap. 2.50 (ISBN 0-451-11658-5, AE1658, Sig). NAL.

Flashman. George MacDonald Fraser. 1969. 6.95 o.p. (NAL). Norton.

Flashman. George MacDonald Fraser. 1969. 6.95 o.p. (A3335). World Pub.

Flashman and the Redskins. George MacDonald Fraser. LC 82-47828. 1982. 13.95 (ISBN 0-394-52852-2). Knopf: Distributed by Random House.

Flashman at the Charge. George MacDonald Fraser. LC 73-7260. (Illus.). 1973. 6.95 (ISBN 0-394-48756-7). Knopf; Distributed by Random House.

Flashman at the Charge. George MacDonald Fraser. (Signet Book). (Illus.). 1974. (pbk.) 1.25. New American Library.

Flashman: From the Flashman Papers 1839-1842. George Macdonald Fraser. LC 70-80439. 1969. 5.95. World Pub. Co.

Flashman in the Great Game. George MacDonald Fraser. LC 75-8247. 1975. 8.95 (ISBN 0-394-49893-3). Knopf.

Flashman in the Great Game. George MacDonald Fraser. (Signet Book). 1977. 1.95 (ISBN 0-451-07429-7). New American Library.

Flashman's Lady. George MacDonald Fraser. LC 77-20365. 1978. 8.95 (ISBN 0-394-50135-7). Knopf: Distributed by Random House.

Flashman's Lady. George MacDonald Fraser. (Signet book). 1979. 2.25 (ISBN 0-451-08514-0). New American Library.

Flashpoint. George La Fountaine. LC 76-3622. 6.95 (ISBN 0-698-10742-X). Coward, McCann & Geoghegan.

Flashpoint. Dan J. Marlowe. 1970. pap. 0.75 o.p. (T2446, GM). Fawcett World.

Flashy Fists. Michael Norday. LC 55-351888. 1955. Vixen Press.

Flask for the Journey: A Novel. Frederick Lawrence Green. LC 48-5094. 1948. Reynal & Hitchcock.

Flat Tire. Alma Sioux Scarberry. LC 30-242399. Grosset & Dunlap.

Flat 2. Edgar Wallace. LC 24-71215. (Famous authors series. no. 41). 1924. Garden City Publishing Co., Inc.

Flateyjarbok, 3 vol. set. Ed. by C R Unger & Guthbrandr Vigfusson. LC 80-1973. 215.00 (ISBN 0-404-18638-6). AMS Pr.

Flatland. Edwin A. Abbott. (Illus.). 144p. 1983. pap. 3.80i (ISBN 0-06-463573-2, EH 573). B&N NY.

Flats: A Novel. Rudolph Wurlitzer. LC 70-122787. 1970. 4.95. Dutton.

Flats Fixed-Among Other Things: A Giff Speer Story. Don Tracy. 1974. (pbk.) 0.95 (ISBN 0-671-77920-6). Pocket Books.

Flattery's Foal: Translated from the Russian. Petr Alekseevich Shiriaev & Fremantle, Alfred, Tr. LC 38-11078. 1938. A. A. Knopf.

Flavia: Or, "Loyal Unto the End." A Tale of the Church in the Second Century. Emma Leslie. LC 7-14490. (Church history stories, v. 2). Nelson & Phillips.

Flaw: A Novel. Antones Samarakes. LC 70-85152. 1969. 5.95. Weybright and Talley.

Flaw Dexter. Thomas E Doremus. LC 47-3874. 1947. Little, Brown and Company.

Flaw in the Crystal. May Sinclair. LC 12-15568. E. P. Dutton & Company.

Flaw in the Crystal. Godfrey Smith. LC 54-7866. 1954. Putnam.

Flaw in the Iron: Or, The Weak Place in the Character That Failed in Temptation. John A Davis. LC 6-32481. Presbyterian Board of Publication and Sabbath-School Work.

Flaw in the Marble. (Twentieth century series). F. A. Stokes Company.

Flaw in the Sapphire. Charles McCoy Snyder. LC 9-24257. 1909. 1.00. The Metropolitan Press.

Flawed Blades: Tales from the Foreign Legion. Percival Christopher Wren. LC 33-28669. 1933. Frederick A. Stokes Company.

Flawed Escape. Boris Kidel. LC 73-91841. 1974. 6.95. St. Martin's Press.

Flawed Marriage. Penny Jordan. (Harlequin Presents Ser.). 192p. 1983. pap. 1.95 (ISBN 0-373-10584-3). Harlequin Bks.
Flawless Play Restored. Gilbert Sorrentino. 80p. (Orig.). 1974. pap. 3.00 (ISBN 0-87685-197-9). Black Sparrow.
Flaws". James Paxton Voorhees. LC 25-4610. 1925. The Caverns of Dawn Medium.
Flaws. Henry S. Wilcox. 1885. G. S. Cline.
Flaws in the Glass. Patrick White. 1983. pap. 5.95 (ISBN 0-14-006293-9). Penguin.
Flea Circus. Bettina Linn. LC 36-6667. 1936. H. Smith and R. Hass.
Flea of Sodom. Edward Dahlberg. price not set o.s.i. Croton Pr.
Fleagle: The Son of a Ruddy Duck. Stan Hardison. LC 77-15075. (Illus.). 1977. pap. 2.50 o.p. (ISBN 0-915442-45-0). Donning Co.
Flecker's Magic. Norman Haghejm Matson. LC 26-79063. 1926. Boni & Liveright.
Fledgling. Elizabeth Cadell. LC 74-17473. 1975. 5.95 (ISBN 0-688-02880-2). Morrow.
Fledgling. Elizabeth Cadell. LC 75-8641. 1975. 10.95 (ISBN 0-8161-6292-1). G. K. Hall.
Fledgling Outlaw. Robert Pohle. 1978. pap. 1.25 (ISBN 0-532-12569-X). Woodhill.
Flee from the Past. Carolyn G Hart. 1975. (pbk.) 1.25. Bantam Books.
Flee Seven Ways. James Burke. LC 64-19810. 1964. Pantheon Books.
Flee the Angry Strangers. George Mandel. LC 52-5811. 1952. Bobbs-Merrill.
Flee the Night in Anger: A Tough Suspense Novel by Dan Keller Pseud. Louis Kaufman. LC 55-18986. (Popular library 625). 1954. Popular Library.
Fleeced. Stuart Buchan. LC 74-16578. (Red mask mystery). 1975. 6.95 (ISBN 0-399-11423-8). Putnam.
Fleet Hall Inheritance. Clifford James Wheeler Hosken. LC 31-22243. 1931. Harper & Brothers.
Fleet in the Forest. Lane, Carl Daniel. LC 43-16383. 1943. Coward-McCann, Inc.
Fleet in the Window: A Novel. David Bergamini. LC 60-125816. 1961. Simon and Schuster.
Fleet Rabble: A Novel of the Nez Perce War. Frank Boroen Hanes. LC 61-11316. 1961. L. C. Page.
Fleet Surgeon to Pharaoh. Sheldon A. Jacobson. LC 71-126923. (Illus.). 1971. (ISBN 0-87071-316-7). Oregon State University Press.
Fleet Wedding. Rachelle Edwards. (Coventry Romance Ser.: No. 196). 192p. 1982. pap. 1.50 (ISBN 0-449-50299-6, Coventry). Fawcett.
Fleetfoot: And Other Stories. 1st Ed. William E Davis. LC 56-553429. 1956. Vantage Press.
Fleetfoot,and Other Stories. William E. Davis. LC 56-5534. 1956. Vantage Press.
Fleeting Breath. Ivy Preston. 1971. pap. 0.75 o.p. (94181). Beagle Bks.
Fleeting Thoughts. Caroline Edwards Prentiss. LC 28-22647. 1893. G. P. Putnam's Sons.
Fleet's in! Russell Holman. LC 28-235362. Grosset & Dunlap.
Fleetwood: Or, The New Man of Feeling. rev., corr., and illustrated with a new pref. / by the author. ed. William Godwin. LC 72-162889. 1975. 14.50 (ISBN 0-404-54422-3). AMS Press.
Fleetwood: Or, The New Man of Feeling. William Godwin. LC 78-60852. (Series: Novel, 1720-1805.). 1979. 84.00 (ISBN 0-8240-3663-8). Garland Pub.
Fleming Field: Or, The Young Artisan. A Tale of the Days of the Stamp Act. Joseph Holt Ingraham. LC 46-35748. 1845. Burgess, Stringer and Company.
Fleming, John Chester. Eby, Lois Christine, 1908- Joint Author. LC 44-8151. 1944. Arcadia House, Inc.
Fleming's Folly. Lawrence A Keating. E. J. Clode, Inc.
Flemmings: A True Story. Anna Hanson McKenney Dorsey. LC 77-11280. (American Catholic Tradition). (Series: The Notre Dame series of Catholic novels.). 1978. 26.00 (ISBN 0-405-10817-6). Arno Press.
Flemmings: Or, Truth Triumphant. Anna Hanson McKenney Dorsey. LC 44-14749. (Notre Dame series of Catholic novels). 1870. P. O'Shea.
Flesh. Brigid Brophy. 144p. 1980. 12.95 (ISBN 0-85031-318-X, Pub. by Allison & Busby England); pap. 4.95 (ISBN 0-85031-319-8, Pub. by Allison & Busby England). Schocken.
Flesh. Philip Jose Farmer. LC 68-11784. (Doubleday science fiction). 1968. Doubleday.
Flesh Altar. H. R. Kaye, pseud. (Orig.). 1969. pap. 1.95 o.p. (6-42). Brandon.
Flesh and Blood. Pete Hamill. LC 77-5979. 8.95 (ISBN 0-394-49437-7). Random House.
Flesh and Blood. Bruce Palmer. LC 60-109869. 1960. Simon and Schuster.
Flesh and Blood. Anna Winter. LC 68-59643. 1969. 3.95. Olympia Press.
Flesh and Blood (La Chair et le Sang) Francois Mauriac. LC 55-7211. 1955. Farrar, Straus.
Flesh and Blood Man. Almus Day Jameson. LC 25-25989. Cokesbury Press.
Flesh & Ecstasy. Gisele De Roseaux. 160p. pap. 1.95 o.p. (MP-101). Montmartre.
Flesh & Fantasy. Penny Stallings & Howard Mandelbaum. LC 78-19391. (Illus.). 1978. 19.95 o.p. (ISBN 0-312-29586-3); pap. 9.95 (ISBN 0-312-29587-1). St Martin.
Flesh and Mary Ducan. Monte Sohn. LC 48-8729. 1948. Dodd, Mead.
Flesh and Mr. Rawlie. Cover Painting by Barye Phillips. Morton Cooper. LC 56-230707. (Gold medal books, 538). 1955. Fawcett Publications.
Flesh and Other Stories. Clement Wood. LC 31-305090. 1931. Priv. Print. The Panurge Press.
Flesh and Phantasy. Newton A Fuessle. LC 20-7057. The Cornhill Company.
Flesh and Spirit. Elizabeth Christman. LC 78-26805. 1979. 7.95 (ISBN 0-688-03435-7). Morrow.
Flesh and Spirit. Elizabeth Christman. LC 80-12542. 1981. 11.50 (ISBN 0-89340-274-5). J. Curly.
Flesh & Spirit. A Novel. George James Atkinson Coulson. (The "Odd trump" series of novels). 1876. E. J. Hale & Son.
Flesh and the Devil. Teresa Denys. LC 80-29307. 1981. 12.95 (ISBN 0-312-29583-9). St. Martin's Press.
Flesh Dealers. Hugh Morgan. (Orig.). 1969. pap. 1.75 o.p. (3054). Brandon.
Flesh Eaters. L. A. Morse. 240p. 1979. pap. 2.25 (ISBN 0-446-82633-2). Warner Bks.
Flesh Is Heir: An Historical Reomance. Lincoln Kirstein. LC 32-6899. 1932. Brewer, Warren & Putnam.
Flesh Is Heir: An Historical Romance. Lincoln Kirstein. LC 75-9584. 1975. 7.95 (ISBN 0-8093-0730-8). Southern Illinois University Press.
Flesh Is Not All. Iris Petroff. LC 42-15697. 1942. Phoenix Press.
Flesh Is Not Life... Hilary Leighton Barth. LC 38-35018. The Bruce Publishing Company.
Flesh Is Weak. John Held. LC 31-252695. The Vanguard Press.
Flesh Is Willing. Alvin Winston. LC 35-13817. Phoenix Press.
Flesh Mast. Rod Sawyers. (Illus., Orig.). 1969. pap. 1.75 o.p. (3073). Brandon.
Flesh of the Wild Ox: A Riffian Chronicle of High Valleys and Long Rifles. Carleton Stevens Coon. LC 32-28986. 1932. W. Morrow & Company.
Flesh on Fire. Lloyd Darden. pap. 2.25 o.s.i. (Venus). Grove.
Flesh Peddlers: A Novel. Stephen Longstreet. LC 62-17323. 1962. Simon and Schuster.
Flesh Remembers. Vivien Grey. LC 49-4126. 1949. Phoenix Press.
Flesh Wager. Ann Griffin. pap. 1.95 o.p. (8066). Cameo.
Flesheaters. Frederick Price. LC 67-183792. 1967. 5.00. Dimensions Pr.
Fleshmonger's Woman. Jackson Dunn. pap. 1.95 o.s.i. (Venus). Grove.
Fleshpots. Anna Weber Robeson. LC 37-5366. 1937. Margent Press.
Fleshpots. Florence Stonebraker. LC 44-5955. 1944. Phoenix Press.
Fleshwound. F. W. Belland. 224p. (Orig.). 1981. pap. 2.25 (ISBN 0-515-05652-9). Jove Pubns.
Fletch. Gregory McDonald. LC 74-3884. 6.50 (ISBN 0-672-52020-6). Bobbs-Merrill.
Fletch. Gregory McDonald. LC 75-31502. 1975. 10.95 (ISBN 0-8161-6329-4). G. K. Hall.
Fletch & the Man Who. Gregory Mcdonald. 1983. pap. 2.95. Warner Bks.
Fletch and the Widow Bradley. Gregory McDonald. LC 81-23964. 1982. 11.95 (ISBN 0-8161-3377-8). G.K. Hall.
Fletch and the Widow Bradley. warner books ed. Gregory McDonald. LC 81-215881. 2.95 (ISBN 0-446-90922-X). Warner Books.
Fletcher Omnibus... Joseph Smith Fletcher. LC 33-27086. 1933. A. A. Knopf.
Fletch's Fortune. Gregory McDonald. LC 78-56902. 1.95 (ISBN 0-380-37978-3). Avon.
Fletch's Moxie. Gregory McDonald. 288p. (Orig.). 1982. pap. 3.25 (ISBN 0-446-90923-8). Warner Bks.
Fleur. Rachel Delauney. 1979. 2.25 (ISBN 0-446-82656-1). Warner Books.
Fleur Dans le desert. Margaret Rome. (Harlequin Romantique Ser.). 192p. 1983. pap. 1.95 (ISBN 0-373-41181-2). Harlequin Bks.
Fleur-De-Lis: And Other Stories. by melvin l. severy. ed. Melvin Linwood Severy. LC 8-6875. 1889. The Esoteric Publishing Company.
Fleur de Lys Affair. Hal Ross. LC 75-11076. 250p. 1975. 7.95 o.p. (ISBN 0-385-11194-0). Doubleday.
Fleur De Lys, the Story of a Crime. Geraldine Gordon Salmon. LC 29-20967. 1929. Pub. for The Crime Club, Inc., by Doubleday, Doran & Company, Inc.
Fleurange. A Novel from the French of Mme. Augustus Craven... Pauline Marie Armande Aglae Ferron De La Ferronnays Craven. Tr. by R., M. M. LC 6-31068. (Leisure hour series, v. 10). 1873. Holt & Williams.
Fleurette: The History of a French Flower-Girl. Augustin Eugene Scribe. Tr. by Clark, Frank Pinckney. LC 8-3394. (On cover: Lovell's library). J. W. Lovell Company.
Flex. Marc Rubel. LC 83-2926. 1983. 14.95 (ISBN 0-312-29592-8). St. Martin's Press.
Flexible Ferdinand. Julie Mathilde Lippmann. LC 19-6865. George H. Doran Company.
Flexible Morals. Ruth Louise Sheldon. LC 3-1278. 1898. H. I. Kimball.
Flicker of Doom. Paul Kenyon. 1974. (pbk.) 0.95 (ISBN 0-671-77961-3). Pocket Books.
Flickering Death. Bill Knox. LC 75-150924. 1971. 4.95. Published for the Crime Club by Doubleday.
Flickering Death. Noah Webster, pseud. LC 75-150924. (Crime Club Ser). 1971. 1.95 o.p. (ISBN 0-385-04432-1). Doubleday.
Flickers: A Novel. Phillip Rock. LC 77-22577. 8.95 (ISBN 0-396-07506-1). Dodd, Mead.
Flickers: A Novel. Phillip Rock. (Signet Book). 1979. 2.25 (ISBN 0-451-08839-5). New American Library.
Fliehendes Pferd. Martin Walser. (Suhrkamp Taschenbuecher: St 600). 176p. (Ger.). 1980. pap. text ed. 3.90 (ISBN 3-518-37100-2, Pub. by Suhrkamp Verlag Germany). Suhrkamp.
Fliers of Antares. Alan Burt Akers. (Science Fiction Ser). 1975. pap. 1.25 o.p. (UY1165). DAW Bks.
Fliers of Antares. Dray Prescot. 1982. pap. 2.25 (ISBN 0-87997-733-7, UE1733). DAW Bks.
Flight. Edgar Jean Bracco. (Berkeley medallion bk. G291). Berkley Pub. Corp.
Flight. Muriel Hine Coxon. LC 23-5620. 1923. 2.00. Dodd, Mead and Company.
Flight. Edmund Fuller. LC 76-117658. 1970. 5.95. Random House.
Flight. Norman Mailer. LC 75-15824. 1975. 7.95 (ISBN 0-316-54416-7). Little.
Flight. Richard Olsenius. Ed. by Susan Winter. (Illus.). 1977. pap. 5.95 (ISBN 0-916320-03-0). Red Studio.
Flight. Arthur Omre. Tr. by Bateson, Solvi. LC 40-4666. 1940. D. Appleton-Century Company, Incorporated.
Flight. Walter Francis White. LC 78-75546. 1969. Negro Universities Press.
Flight. Walter Francis White. LC 26-9564. 1926. A. A. Knopf.
Flight, a Novel. 1st Ed. Evelyn Sybil Mary Eaton. LC 54-6054. 1954. Bobbs-Merrill.
Flight: A Romance of Gypsy O'Malley--a Girl Who Lived Down Her Family-- Alma Sioux Scarberry. LC 32-129892. Grosset & Dunlap.
Flight Against the Wind. Karen Millberg. LC 47-5372. 1947. Odyssey Press.
Flight, an Epic of the Air. Irwin R Franklyn. LC 29-22689. Grosset & Dunlap.
Flight Erotica. Joe Crawford. pap. 1.95 o.p. (8011). Cameo.
Flight for Dreamers. Jane Converse. LC 81-5661. 8.95 (ISBN 0-89621-283-1). Thorndike Press.
Flight from a Dark Equator. Norman Lewis. LC 72-83332. 1972. 6.95 (ISBN 0-399-11012-7). Putnam.
Flight from a Firing Wall. Baynard Hardwick Kendrick. LC 66-21824. (Special inner sanctum mystery). 1966. Simon and Schuster.
Flight from Ashiya. Elliott Arnold. 1973. 1.25 (ISBN 0-515-02991-2). Pyramid.
Flight from Ashiya. 1st Ed. Elliott Arnold. LC 59-857710. 1959. Knopf.
Flight from Bucharest. R. T Stevens. LC 77-76266. 1978. 8.95 (ISBN 0-385-12850-9). Doubleday.
Flight from Eden Key. Dorinne Moore. (Berkley medallion book). 1974. (pbk.) 0.75 (ISBN 0-425-02531-4). Berkley Pub. Co.
Flight from Love. Peggy Gaddis, pseud. LC 57-7725. Arcadia House.
Flight from Montego Bay. Alec Haig. LC 72-6880. (Red badge novel of suspense). 1972. 4.95 (ISBN 0-396-06714-X). Dodd, Mead.
Flight from Natchez. 1st Ed. Frank Gill Slaughter. LC 55-550865. 1955. Doubleday.
Flight from the Enchanter. Iris Murdoch. (Compass bk. C182). 1965. pap., 1.65. Viking.
Flight from the Enchanter. Iris Murdoch. LC 56-6280. 1956. Viking Press.
Flight from the Enchanter. Iris Murdoch. 1973. 1.25. Warner Paperback Lib.
Flight from the Hunter: A Novel. Siegfried Stander. LC 77-76653. 8.95 (ISBN 0-312-29598-7). St. Martin's Press.
Flight from Time One. Deane Romano. LC 72-83116. 1972. 5.95 (ISBN 0-8027-5554-2). Walker.
Flight from Woman. Karl Stern. 1965. pap. 2.95 o.p. (ISBN 0-374-50504-7, N298, Noonday). FS&G.
Flight from Yesterday. Peggy Gaddis, pseud. LC 42-171475. 1942. Arcadia House, Inc.
Flight from Yesterday. Barbara Webb. LC 37-202032. 1937. Doubleday, Doran & Company, Inc.
Flight from Youth. William E Barrett. LC 39-28870. J. B. Lippincott Company.
Flight Hostess. Emily Thorne. LC 58-9124. 1958. Avalon Books.
Flight in Darkness. Henry Gibbs. LC 65-154223. 1965. 3.50. Walker.
Flight Instructor Murders. George Redder, pseud. 1977. 8.00 o.p. (ISBN 0-682-48941-7). Exposition.
Flight into Camden. David Storey. LC 61-11950. 1961. Macmillan.
Flight into Darkness. Philip Clark. LC 48-5409. (Inner sanctum mystery). 1948. Simon and Schuster.
Flight into Darkness. Arthur Schnitzler. LC 78-175577. 1971. (ISBN 0-404-05620-2). AMS Press.
Flight into Darkness. Arthur Schnitzler. Tr. by Drake, William A. LC 31-31326. 1931. Simon and Schuster.
Flight into Egypt: A Fantasy. Philippe Jullian. LC 75-83225. 1970. 5.95. Viking Press.
Flight into Egypt. Translated from the French by Frances Frenaye. Jean Bloch-Michel. LC 55-9669. 1955. Scribner.
Flight into Fear. Duncan Kyle. LC 72-183290. 1972. 5.95. St. Martin's Press.
Flight into Fear: By Jennifer Ames Pseud. Maysie Greig. LC 54-14580. 1954. Avalon Books.
Flight into Love. Jane Blackmore. pap. 0.45 o.p. (56-950). Paperback Lib.
Flight into Morning. Amelia Elizabeth Walden. LC 57-12054. 1957. Appleton-Century-Crofts.
Flight into Peril. James Douglas Rutherford McConnell. LC 52-10922. (Red badge detective). 1952. Dodd, Mead.
Flight into Space: Great Science-Fiction Stories of Interplanetary Travel. Ed. by Donald A. Wollheim. LC 50-8318. (Fell's science fiction library). 1950. Fell.
Flight into Terror. Lionel White. LC 57-108315. (Signet book, 1378). 1957. New American Library.
Flight into Terror. 1st Ed. Lionel White. LC 55-832755. (Guilt edged mystery). 1955. Dutton.
Flight into Yesterday. 1st Ed. Charles Leonard Harness. LC 53-118829. 1953. Bouregy & Curl.
Flight Nurse. Peggy Gaddis, pseud. LC 45-3453. 1945. Arcadia House.
Flight Nurse: By Kathleen Harris Pseud. Adelaide Humphries. LC 60-3080. Avalon Books.
Flight of a Dragon. Lee R Bobker. LC 80-22670. 1981. 10.50 (ISBN 0-688-03759-3). Morrow.
Flight of a Moth. Emily Price Post. 1904. Dodd, Mead & Company.
Flight of an Angel. Verne Chute. LC 46-1253. 1946. W. Morrow and Company.
Flight of Birds. 1st Amer. Ed. Cecil Roberts. LC 65-253989. 1966. 4.50. Coward.
Flight of Chariots. Jon Cleary. LC 63-20925. 1963. Morrow.
Flight of Cranes. Christine Bruckner. LC 81-22176. 14.95 (ISBN 0-88064-001-4). Fromm International Pub. Corp.
Flight of Dragons. Peter Dickinson & Wayne Anderson. LC 78-22450. (Illus.). 1979. 17.50i (ISBN 0-06-011074-0, HarpT). Har-Row.
Flight of Exiles. Benjamin Bova. LC 72-78092. 1972. 4.95 (ISBN 0-525-29865-7). Dutton.
Flight of Falcons: Translated from the French by Naomi Walford. Francoise D' Eaubonne. LC 51-13541. 1951. McGraw-Hill.
Flight of Fallen Angel. Daoma Winston. (Kangaroo Book). 1977. 1.50 (ISBN 0-671-80953-9). Pocket Books.
Flight of Fancy. Jacquelyn Aeby. 192p. (YA) 1975. 4.95 o.p. (Avalon). Bouregy.
Flight of Faviel. Robert Ernest Vernede. LC 12-21144. 1912. H. Holt and Company.
Flight of Georgianna: A Story of Love and Peril in England in 1746. Robert Neilson Stephens. LC 5-28005. 1905. L. C. Page & Company.
Flight of Hawks. Matthew Eden. (Raven Book). 1970. 5.95 o.p. (B26150). Abelard.
Flight of Icarus. Raymond Queneau. LC 73-76900. (New Directions book). 1973. 7.50 (ISBN 0-8112-0482-0) (ISBN 0-8112-0482-0). New Directions Pub. Corp.
Flight of Icarus: An Idyl of Printing-House Square. Jay Robin. LC 98-16521. (Neely's universal library. no. 29). 1898. F. T. Neely.
Flight of Jenny Bird. Monica Mugan. (Signet book). 1974. (pbk.) 1.25. New American Library.
Flight of Lies. Gavin Scott. LC 80-52654. 9.95 (ISBN 0-312-29614-2). St. Martin's Press.
Flight of Peter Fromm. Martin Gardner. LC 73-1932. 1973. 8.95 (ISBN 0-913232-04-1). W. Kaufmann.
Flight of Splendor. Joellyn Carroll. (Candlelight Ecstasy Ser.: No. 159). (Orig.). 1983. pap. 1.95 (ISBN 0-440-12858-7). Dell.
Flight of Steps. Robert Nicolson. LC 66-19391. 1967. Knopf.

Flight of the Aerofix. Maurice Renard. LC 32-23573. (Science fiction series, no. 14). Stellar Publishing Corporation.

Flight of the Bamboo Saucer. Fritz Gordon. (O.s.i.). (Orig.). 1967. pap. 0.60 o.s.i. (A244X, Award). Univ Pub & Dist.

Flight of the Bat. Donald Gordon, pseud. 1964. 4.50 o.p. Morrow.

Flight of the Bat. Donald Gordon Payne. LC 64-12526. 1964. Morrow.

Flight of the Cormoran. Herbert T. Ward. 3.95 o.p. Vantage.

Flight of the Dancing Bear. 1st Ed. Mark Rascovich. LC 59-10686. 1959. Doubleday.

Flight of the Eagle. M. M. Rendon. 1970. 3.50 o.p. Vantage.

Flight of the Eagle. Per Olof Sundman. LC 69-20190. (Illus.). 1970. 6.95. Pantheon Books.

Flight of the Eagle. Donald Thomas. LC 75-30655. 1976. 8.95 (ISBN 0-670-31830-2). Viking Press.

Flight of the Endeavor. Robert Petyo. 1979. pap. 1.75 (ISBN 0-532-17204-3). Woodhill.

Flight of the Falcon. Daphne Du Maurier. LC 65-7425. 4.95. Doubleday.

Flight of the Falcon. Wilbur A. Smith. LC 81-43328. 1982. 15.95 (ISBN 0-385-17833-6). Doubleday.

Flight of the Feathered Serpent. Peter Balin. (Illus.). 184p. 1983. pap. 10.95 (ISBN 0-910261-01-6). Arcana Pub.

Flight of the Grey Goose. Victor Canning. LC 73-1448. 1973. 5.95 (ISBN 0-688-00176-9). Morrow.

Flight of the Hawk, No. 4. Leigh F. James. 352p. 1982. pap. 3.50 (ISBN 0-553-22578-2). Bantam.

Flight of the Henny. Jan De Hartog. LC 80-8228. 10.95 (ISBN 0-06-010983-1). Harper & Row.

Flight of the Heron. Dorothy Kathleen Broster. LC 27-1245. 1926. Dodd, Mead and Company.

Flight of the Heron. Dorothy Kathleen Broster. LC 30-7303. 1930. Coward-McCann, Inc.

Flight of the Horse. Larry Niven. 1973. (pbk.) 1.25 (ISBN 0-345-23487-1). Ballantine.

Flight of the Innocents. Lin Yutang. LC 64-211155. 1964. Putnam.

Flight of the Phoenix. Elleston Trevor. LC 64-12689. 1964. Harper & Row.

Flight of the Raven. Robert Charles, pseud. 1975. (pbk.) 1.25 (ISBN 0-523-00659-4). Pinnacle Books.

Flight of the Seabird: A Novel. William Lavender. LC 76-53793. 8.95 (ISBN 0-671-22662-2). Simon and Schuster.

Flight of the Shadow. Laura M Dake. 1899. The Editor Publishing Co.

Flight of the Shadow. George Macdonald. LC 12-182788. (With his Home again, New York 1911). 1911. G. Routledge and Sons, Limited.

Flight of the Shadow. George Macdonald. LC 82-48407. 1983. 6.68 (ISBN 0-06-250563-7). Harper & Row.

Flight of the Shadow a Story. George Macdonald. LC 7-18781. (On cover: Appletons' town and country library, no. 85). 1891. D. Appleton and Company.

Flight of the "Swallow". Emily Malbone Morgan. LC 7-26000. A. D. F. Randolph & Company (Incorporated).

Flight One. Charles Carpentier. LC 72-83896. 1974. (pbk.) 1.50. Warner Paperback Lib.

Flight Plan Aquarius. Joan Cassity. LC 77-86488. 7.95 (ISBN 0-87949-088-8). Ashley Books.

Flight Seaward. Andrew Jones. LC 78-6735. 1978. 8.95 (ISBN 0-688-03359-8). Morrow.

Flight Seven: A Story of the Airlines. Robert Elliott Johnson. LC 40-35815. (Career books). 1940. Dodd, Mead & Company.

Flight South. Charles Grayson. LC 35-201543. The Macaulay Company.

Flight Surgeon. Cameron Rogers & Halland, Herman E., Joint Author. LC 40-14084. Duell, Sloan and Pearce.

Flight Through Hell: A Novel. Michael D'Avranches. LC 51-10017. 1951. Exposition Press.

Flight to Afar. Translated from the German by Michael Bullock. Alfred Andersch. LC 58-9701. 1958. Coward-McCann.

Flight to Africa: Translated from the German by Richard and Clara Winston. 1st Ed. Johanna Moosdorf. LC 54-7900. 1954. Brace.

Flight to Canada. Ishmael Reed. LC 76-15598. 6.95 (ISBN 0-394-48754-0). Random House.

Flight to Canada. Ishmael Reed. (Bard Book). 1977. 2.25. Avon.

Flight to Eden: A Florida Romance. Harrison Rhodes. LC 7-30836. 1907. H. Holt and Company.

Flight to Falconhurst. Kyle Onstott & Lance Horner. (Falconhurst Plantation Ser.). 1978. pap. 2.50 (ISBN 0-449-14257-4, GM). Fawcett.

Flight to France; or, The Memoirs of a Dragoon. A Tale of the Day of Dumouriez. Jules Verne. LC 1-9790. (On cover: Seaside library. Pocket edition. no. 1168). G. Munro.

Flight to Freedom. new ed. Kent Durden. (Adult Ser). 220p. 1974. Repr. lib. bdg. 6.95 o.p. (ISBN 0-8161-6226-3, Large Print Bks). G K Hall.

Flight to Freedom. Hugh Zachary. (Sierra Leone Ser.: No. 1). 320p. (Orig.). 1981. pap. 2.75 (ISBN 0-440-02614-8, Banbury). Dell.

Flight to Glory. Douglas Cecil Percy. LC 67-22684. 1967. Zondervan Pub. House.

Flight to Happiness: By Jennifer Ames Pseud. Maysie Greig. LC 51-520. 1950. Bouregy & Curl.

Flight to Landfall. Gerald M. Glaskin. LC 80-14214. 12.95 (ISBN 0-312-29624-X). St. Martin's Press.

Flight to Lucifer: A Gnostic Fantasy. Harold Bloom. LC 78-31897. 1979. 8.95 (ISBN 0-374-15644-1). Farrar, Straus, Giroux.

Flight to Lucifer: A Gnostic Fantasy. Harold Bloom. LC 79-22095. 1979. 3.95 (ISBN 0-394-74323-7). Vintage Books.

Flight to Opar. Philip Jose Farmer. (Science Fiction Ser.). 1976. pap. 1.50 o.p. (UW1238). DAW Bks.

Flight to Opar. Philip Jose Farmer. (Daw Science Fiction #197). 1976. 1.50. Daw Books.

Flight to Paradise. Sara Orwig. 1979. pap. 1.95 (ISBN 0-89041-237-5, 3237). Major Bks.

Flight to Safety. Richard Rosenfeld. LC 57-5400. 1957. Dorrance.

Flight to the Hills. Charles Neville Buck. LC 26-7846. 1926. Doubleday, Page & Company.

Flight to Utopia. Carleton Matthews. LC 47-23058. 1947. Mount Eyre Publishing Company.

Flight Without End: A Report. Joseph Roth. Tr. by Zeitlin, Ida. LC 30-11277. 1930. Doubleday, Doran and Company, Inc.

Flight. 1st Ed. Ruth Walgreen Stephan. LC 56-891355. 1956. Knopf.

Flight 311. Robert D Neff. (Pyramid fiction, V3155). 1973. (pbk.) 1.25 (ISBN 0-515-03155-0). Pyramid Books.

Flight 902 Is Down. Hal Fishman & Barry J Schiff. LC 82-5795. 1982. 13.95 (ISBN 0-312-29612-6). St. Martin's Press.

Flight's End. Lillian Taft Maize. LC 35-7524. The Penn Publishing Company.

Flights Inside and Outside Paradise. George Cullen Pearson. LC 2-24104. 1886. G. P. Putnam's Sons.

Flights of Icarus. Donald Lehmkuhl et al. (Illus.). 160p. 1978 (A & W Visual Library). pap. 12.50 o.s.i. (ISBN 0-89104-117-6). A & W Pubs.

Flighty Arethusa. David Skaats Foster. LC 10-22412. 1910. 1.50. Press of J. B. Lippincott Company.

Flim-Flam Man and Other Stories. Guy Owen. LC 79-90651. 9.95 (ISBN 0-87716-109-7). Moore Pub. Co.

Flim-Flam Man & the Apprentice Grifter. Guy Owen. LC 72-84305. 1972. 5.95 (ISBN 0-517-50061-2). Crown Publishers.

Fling Out the Banners. Robert H Newman. LC 41-18900. J. B. Lippincott Company.

Flint. Gil Dodge. LC 57-111336. (Signet book, 1414). 1957. New American Library.

Flint. Louis L'Amour. LC 60-12457. (Bantam western, 3). 1960. Bantam Books.

Flint. Charles Gilman Norris. 1944. Doubleday, Doran and Company, Inc.

Flint. M. Herbert Wolf. LC 29-16767. Gage & Moran, Inc.

Flint Anchor: A Novel. Sylvia Townsend Warner. LC 54-8615. 1954. Viking Press.

Flint: His Faults, His Friendships and His Fortunes. Maud Wilder Goodwin. LC 6-27480. 1897. Little, Brown and Company.

Flint Spears: Cowboy Rodeo Contestant. Will James. LC 38-32855. 1938. C. Scribner's Sons.

Flints to Diamonds. Scott Anderson. LC 40-3025. Printed by the Pioneer Press.

Flinx of the Commonwealth, 3 vols. Alan Dean Foster. 1982. pap. 6.25 (ISBN 0-345-26200-X, Del Rey). Ballantine.

Flip, and Other Stories. Bret Harte. LC 78-37270. (Short story index reprint series). 1971. (ISBN 0-8369-4081-4). Books for Libraries Press.

Flip-Flop Spy. Tommy C. Brooks. 1983. 10.95 (ISBN 0-533-05251-3). Vantage.

Flirt. Booth Tarkington. LC 13-4422. 1913. Doubleday, Page & Company.

Flirt. Booth Tarkington. LC 21-13947. 1915. Grosset & Dunlap.

Flirt. Booth Tarkington. LC 22-160143. 1920. Doubleday, Page & Company.

Flirt. Rajendra Yadav. LC 75-903521. 1975. 1.50 (ISBN 0-88253-769-5). Orient Paperback: Distributed by Hindi Pocket Books.

Flirt. A Story of Parisian Life. Paul Ernest Hervieu. Tr. by Craig, Hugh. (On cover: Worthington's international library, no. 12). 1890. Worthington Company.

Flirt: Or, The Life of a Young Lady of Fashion. Elizabeth Caroline Grey. (Seaside library, v. 83, no. 1688). 1884. G. Munro.

Flirt to Death. A Novel. Luke Leary. LC 7-14293. (Sunnyside series. no. 95). 1896. J. S. Ogilvie Publishing Company.

Flirtation Camp: Or, The Rifle, Rod, and Gun in California; a Sporting Romance. Theodore Strong Van Dyke. LC 8-30223. 1881. Fords, Howard, & Hulbert.

Flirtations of a Beauty: Or, A Summer's Romance at Newport... Laura Jean Libbey. LC 11-15067. 1890. N. L. Munro.

Flirting Wives: A Novel. May Christie. LC 31-10979. Grosset & Dunlap.

Flitters, Tatters, & the Counsellor & Other Sketches. May Laffan Hartley. (Nineteenth Century Fiction Ser.: Ireland: Vol. 67). 1979. lib. bdg. 46.00 (ISBN 0-8240-3516-X). Garland Pub.

Flivver King. Upton Beall Sinclair. LC 79-92589. 1969. Phaedra.

Floater. Calvin Trillin. LC 80-17337. 1980. 10.95 (ISBN 0-89919-017-0). Ticknor & Fields.

Floating Admiral. LC 32-26150. 1932. Pub. for the Crime Club, Inc., by Doubleday, Doran & Company, Inc.

Floating Admiral. LC 79-10776. (Series: Gregg Press Mystery Fiction Series.). (Illus.). 1979. 9.95 (ISBN 0-8398-2540-4). Gregg Press.

Floating Admiral. The, Detection Club. 320p. pap. 2.50 (ISBN 0-441-24095-X, Pub. by Charter Bks). Ace Bks.

Floating City. Jules Verne. 1958. 3.95. Assoc Bk.

Floating Dragon. Peter Straub. LC 82-15057. 15.95 (ISBN 0-399-12772-0). Putnam.

Floating Dredges. A. Roorda. 55.00 o.p. Fla St U Pr.

Floating Dutchman. Nicolas Bentley. LC 51-9610. 1951. Duell, Sloan and Pearce.

Floating Fancies Among the Weird and the Occult. Clara H Holmes. LC 33-7784. 1898. F. T. Neely.

Floating Fancies Among the Weird and the Occult. Clara H Holmes. LC 99-278. (Lettered on cover: Neely's universal library. v. 37). 1898. F. T. Neely.

Floating Gods. M. John Harrison. (Orig.). 1983. pap. 2.50 (ISBN 0-671-41513-1, Timescape). PB.

Floating Opera. John Barth. LC 56-10340. 1956. Appleton-Century-Crofts.

Floating Opera. rev. ed. John Barth. LC 67-12864. 1967. Doubleday.

Floating Outfit. John Thomas Edson. 1974. (pbk.) 0.75. Bantam Books.

Floating Peril. Edward Phillips Oppenheim. LC 36-27121. 1936. Little, Brown, and Company.

Floating World in Japanese Fiction. Howard Hibbett. LC 75-28976. (Illus.). 1974. pap. 5.95 (ISBN 0-8048-1154-7). C E Tuttle.

Floating Worlds. Cecelia Holland. LC 75-36781. 1976. 10.95 (ISBN 0-394-49330-3). Knopf: Distributed by Random House.

Floating Worlds. Cecelia Holland. (Kangaroo Book.). 1977. 1.95. (ISBN 0-671-80867-2). Pocket Books.

Floating Worlds. Cecelia Holland. 1980. 2.95 (ISBN 0-671-83147-X). Pocket Books.

Floating Zombie. D. F Jones. 1975. (pbk.) 1.25 (ISBN 0-425-02980-8). Berkley Pub. Co.

Flock of Birds. Kathleen Coyle. LC 30-16617. E. P. Dutton & Co., Inc.

Flock of Ships. Brian Callison. LC 79-105594. 1970. 5.95. Putnam.

Flockmaster of Poison Creek. George Washington Ogden. LC 21-507537. 1921. A. C. McClurg & Co.

Flood. Dudley Barker. LC 74-122425. (A Stein and Day mystery). 1971. 4.95 (ISBN 0-8128-1311-1). Stein and Day.

Flood. Lionel Black. LC 74-122425. 1970. 4.95 o.p. (ISBN 0-8128-1311-1). Stein & Day.

Flood. John Creasey. 1970. pap. 0.75 o.p. (ISBN 0-447-74675-8). Lancer.

Flood. John Creasey. Ed. by Alice Bosk. LC 69-11778. (Doctor Palfrey Ser). 1969. 4.50 o.p. (L/). Walker & Co.

Flood. Jean Marie Gustave Le Clezio. Tr. by Peter Green. LC 67-25471. 1968. 5.95 o.p. (ISBN 0-689-10165-1). Atheneum.

Flood. George Moore. LC 73-18131. 1973. Folcroft Library Editions.

Flood. George Moore. LC 30-333371. 1930. G. C. at the Harbor Press.

Flood. Robert Neumann. Tr. by Drake, William A. LC 30-10605. 1930. Covici, Friede.

Flood. Richard Martin Stern. LC 79-7456. 1979. 10.00. Doubleday.

Flood: A Romance of Our Time. Robert Penn Warren. LC 64-10357. 1964. Random House.

Flood and Field: Or, Tales of Battles on Sea and Land. William Starbuck Mayo. LC 7-18479. 1855. W. P. Hazard.

Flood Crest. Hodding Carter. LC 47-12033. 1947. Rinehart.

Flood of Passion: The Story of a Brother and Sister. Ursula Bloom. LC 33-11098. 1932. E. P. Dutton & Co., Inc.

Flood Tide. Bassett, Sara Ware. LC 21-431729. 1921. Little, Brown, and Company.

Flood Tide. Daniel Chase. LC 18-6518. 1918. The Macmillan Company.

Flood-Tide. Sarah Pratt McLean Greene. LC 1-23672. 1901. Harper & Brothers.

Flood Tide. Frank Yerby. 1976. 1.75. Dell.

Flood Tide, a Novel. Olive Wadsley. LC 34-8153. 1933. Dodd, Mead and Company.

Flood Tide and Stars. Mary Wentworth King. LC 42-500755. 1942. M. S. Mill Co., Inc.

Flood Tides, a Novel. Louis Cochran. LC 33-33959. B. Humphries, Inc.

Floods of Fear: By John and Ward Hawkins. John Hawkins & Ward Hawkins. LC 56-10057. (Red badge detective). 1956. Dodd, Mead.

Floods of Spring. Henry Bellamann. LC 42-132663. 1942. Simon and Schuster.

Floodtide. Kay Thorpe. (Harlequin Presents Ser.). 192p. 1981. pap. 1.50 (ISBN 0-373-10425-1, Pub. by Harlequin). PB.

Floodtide. Frank Yerby. LC 50-9227. 1950. Dial Press.

Floodtide. large print ed. Frank Yerby. LC 81-21354. 1982. 13.95 (ISBN 0-89621-334-X). Thorndike Press.

Floodtide of Fate. Olav Duun. (Orig.). 1970. 7.50x o.p. (ISBN 0-8002-0814-5). Intl Pubns Serv.

Floor of Heaven. Sylvia Chatfield Bates. LC 40-5954. Harcourt, Brace and Company.

Flor de Estrella. span. ed. Jim Kelly. (Small Star Stories). (Illus.). 1975. 5.95 o.p. (ISBN 0-02-645730-X, 64573). Glencoe.

Flora. Arnold Bennett. LC 74-5325. (Collected Works of Arnold Bennett: Vol. 17). 1976. Repr. of 1933 ed. 14.75 (ISBN 0-518-19098-6). Ayer Co.

Flora. Anne Weale. 512p. 1983. pap. 3.95 (ISBN 0-373-97004-8). Harlequin Bks.

Flora Lyndsay: Or, Passages in an Eventful Life. Susannah Strickland Moodie. LC 7-19149. (On cover: Lovell's library. no. 1068). 1887. J. W. Lovell Company.

Flora Mac-Alpin: An Episode of the Court of James VI. of Scotland and Mary Stuart, Queen of Scots. Mary Monica Maxwell-Scott. LC 8-2910. (On cover: Premium library). H. L. Kilner & Co.

Flora Shawn. Samuel Rogers. LC 42-6836. 1942. J. Messner, Inc.

Flora Sweet. Jeannie Sakol. LC 77-6210. 1977. 1.95 (ISBN 0-345-25055-9). Ballantine Books.

Florabel's Lover: Or, Rival Belles. A Novel. Laura Jean Libbey. (On cover: The choice series, no. 57). 1892. R. Bonner's Sons.

Floralie, Where Are You? Roch Carrier. Tr. by Sheila Fischman from Fr. LC 75-152413. (Anansi Fiction Ser.: No. 17). 108p. 1971. pap. 4.95 (ISBN 0-88784-317-4, Pub. by Hse Anansi Pr Canada). U of Toronto Pr.

Flora's Dream. Martin Cruz Smith. LC 75-179858. 1972. 6.95 (ISBN 0-525-10650-2). Dutton.

Flora's Fairy Forget Me Not. Laura Rountree Smith. LC 23-15587. Stanton & Van Vliet Co.

Florence, 2 vols. Grant Allen. Repr. of 1901 ed. lib. bdg. 40.00 (ISBN 0-8414-3054-3). Folcroft.

Florence Betrayed: Or. The Last Days of the Republic. Massimo Tapparelli Azeglio. LC 6-15460. 1856. W. V. Spencer.

Florence Dalbiac: And Other Tales. S. C. H. Tremayne. LC 8-29718. 1840. Printed by S. W. Benedict.

Florence De Lacey: Or, The Coquette. A Novel. LC 7-4202. (With Herbert, H. W. Marmaduke Wyvil. New York c1843). 1845. E. Winchester.

Florence Erwin's Three Homes: A Tale of North and South. LC 77-38650. (Black Heritage Library Collection). 1972. (ISBN 0-8369-9008-0). Books for Libraries Press.

Florence Fables. William Jermyn Florence. LC 6-39998. (On cover: The household library, no. 2. v. 4). 1888. Belford, Clarke & Company.

Florence Falkland: Or, The Shrouded Life. Nathan D. Urner. (On cover: Street & Smith's select series, no. 14). 1888. Street & Smith.

Florence MacCarthy: An Irish Tale. Morgan Sydney Owenson. Ed. by Robert L. Wolff. (Ireland Nineteenth Century Fiction, Ser. Two: Vol. 8). 1979. lib. bdg. 46.00 (ISBN 0-8240-3457-0). Garland Pub.

Florence O'Neil: The Rose of St Germains; or, The Siege of Limerick. Agnes M Stewart. LC 8-15695. 1872. Kelly, Piet and Company.

Florence, the Parish Orphan: And A Sketch of the Village in the Last Century. Eliza Buckminster Lee. LC 7-16032. 1852. Ticknor and Fields.

Florentine. Sandra Shulman. LC 73-8511. 1973. 11.95 (ISBN 0-8161-6116-X). G. K. Hall.

Florentine. Carl J Spinatelli. LC 53-5735. 1953. Prentice-Hall.

Florentine Dagger: A Novel for Amateur Detectives. Ben Hecht. LC 28-267702. Boni and Liveright.

Florentine Finish. Cornelius Hirschberg. LC 63-16533. 1963. Harper & Row.

Florentine Finish. Cornelius Hirschberg. (Jove/HBJ Book). 1978. 1.75 (ISBN 0-515-04652-3). Jove Publications.

Florentine Frame. Elizabeth Robins. LC 9-28705. 1909. 1.50. Moffat, Yard and Company.
Florentine Ring. Stanley Jackson. pap. 0.60 o.p. (53-305). Paperback Lib.
Florentine Ring. Jackson Stanley. LC 62-7684. 1962. Doubleday.
Florentine Table. Paul Durst. LC 80-14779. 8.95 (ISBN 0-684-16526-0). Scribner.
Florentine Woman. Ross Williamson, Hugh. LC 72-93323. (Illus.). 1973. 6.50. St. Martin's Press.
Florian Mayr Der Kraft-Mayr: A Humorous Tale of Musical Life. Ernst Ludwig Wolzogen Und Neuhaus & Genung, Charles Harvey, Joint Tr. LC 14-12286. 1914. B. W. Huebsch.
Florian Signet. Harriet Esmond. (Fawcett Gold Medal Book). 1.75 (ISBN 0-449-13743-0). Fawcett Publications.
Florian Signet. Harriet Esmond. (Fawcett Gold Medal Book). 1.75 (ISBN 0-449-13743-0). Fawcett Publications.
Florian Slappey. Octavus Roy Cohen. LC 38-183870. 1938. D. Appleton Century Company, Incorporated.
Florian Slappey Goes Abroad. Octavus Roy Cohen. LC 70-130054. (Short story index reprint series). 1970. Books for Libraries Press.
Florian Slappey Goes Abroad. Octavus Roy Cohen. LC 28-108630. 1928. Little, Brown and Company.
Florian: The Emperor's Stallion. Felix Salten & Posselt, Erich, Tr. LC 34-28428. The Bobbs-Merrill Company.
Florian: The Lippizaner. Felix Salten. 8.75 (ISBN 0-85131-127-X, Dist. by Sporting Book Center). J A Allen.
Florians. Brian M. Stableford. (Science Fiction Ser.). 1976. pap. 1.25 (ISBN 0-87997-255-6, UY1255). DAW Bks.
Florida Alexander: A Kentucky Girl. Eleanor Talbot Kinkead. 1898. A. C. McClurg and Company.
Florida Enchantment: A Novel. Archibald Clavering Gunter. LC 6-467010. 1892. The Home Publishing Company.
Florida Fishing and Other Stories. Nathan Kushin. LC 52-6771. 1952. Exposition Press.
Florida Frenzy. Harry Crews. LC 82-1997. 6.00 (ISBN 0-8130-0726-7). University Presses of Florida.
Florida Historical Tales... Story of the Huguenots; a Sixteenth Century Narrative Wherein the French, Spaniards and Indians Were the Actors. author's rev. ed. (3d thousand) ed. Florian Alexander Mann. LC 12-3794. 1912. Press of Will A. Kistler Company.
Florida Is Closed Today. Jack D. Hunter. 304p. (Orig.). 1982. pap. 3.50 (ISBN 0-8439-1115-8). Leisure Bks CT.
Florida Nurse. easy eye ed. Peggy Dern, pseud. Orig. Title: Leona Gregory R. (N). 1968. pap. 0.60 o.p. (73-763). Lancer.
Florida Roundabout. 1st Ed. Theodore Pratt. LC 59-5561. 1959. Duell, Sloan and Pearce.
Florida Wilds: Being Tales of Adventure and Romance from a Land of Romance, with Stories of Plantation Life. Albert Edwin Philips. LC 6-38889. 1906. The Neale Publishing Company.
Florilegio De Cuentos Hispanoamericanos. Ed. by Paul Rogers. (Orig., Span). 1968. pap. text ed. 3.95x o.p. (ISBN 0-02-403120-8). Macmillan.
Florine: Or, The Inner Life of One of the "Four Hundred.". Linda Marguerite Allen. LC 6-43. 1891. G. W. Dillingham.
Floris and the Belle of Louisiana. Jacqueline Monsigny. LC 76-40701 (ISBN 0-380-00802-5). Avon.
Floris, My Love. Jacqueline Monsigny. (Illus.). 1976. 1.75 (ISBN 0-380-00586-7). Avon Books.
Florizel. Isabel McReynolds Gray. LC 33-17482. 1910. 1.25.
Flossie, After Dark. Florence H. 1972. pap. 1.95 o.s.i. (V1084T, Venus). Grove.
Flossie the Florist. Katherine Eubanks. pap. 2.95 (ISBN 0-89185-104-6). Anthelion Pr.
Flotilla Attack. Duncan Harding. 192p. (Orig.). 1981. pap. 1.95 (ISBN 0-505-51758-2). Tower Bks.
Flotsam: The Study of a Life. Hugh Stowell Scott. LC 8-2918. 1896. Longmans, Green and Co.
Flotsam: Translated from the German. Erich Maria Remarque. Tr. by Denver Lindley. LC 41-516781. 1941. Little, Brown and Company.
Flounder. Gunter Grass. LC 78-53891. 10.95 (ISBN 0-15-131486-1). Harcourt Brace Jovanovich.
Flour Is Dusty. Curtis Lucas. LC 44-368. 1943. Dorrance & Company.
Flow My Tears, the Policeman Said. Philip K Dick. LC 73-83625. 1974. 6.95. Doubleday.
Flow on Lovely River. Francis MacManus. LC 77-99169. 1978. 1.95 (ISBN 0-87973-202-4). Our Sunday Visitor.
Flow to the Leaf. Elizabeth Abell. LC 47-118343. 1947. Macmillan Co.
Flower and Jewel: Or, Daisy Forrest's Daughter. Alexander McVeigh Miller. (On cover: The library of American authors, no. 50). 1893. G. Munro's Sons.
Flower and Market Girls of Paris. Emile Zola & Sherwood, Mrs. Mary (Neal) Tr. LC 9-1327. T. B. Peterson & Brothers.
Flower and Thorn. Beatrice Whitby. LC 1-24824. 1901. Dodd, Mead & Company.
Flower and Thorn. Beatrice Whitby. LC 2-88624. 1902. Dodd, Mead & Company.
Flower Basket: Or, A Selection of Interesting Stories. Samuel Griswold Goodrich. LC 42-47435. Nafis & Cornish.
Flower Beneath the Foot see Two Novels.
Flower Beneath the Foot: Being a Record of the Early Life of St. Laura De Nazianzi and the Times in Which She Lived. Arthur Annesley Ronald Firbank. LC 24-28341. Brentano's.
Flower-Covered Corpse. Michael Avallone. (Orig.). 1972. pap. 0.75 o.p. (07241). Curtis.
Flower De Hundred: The Story of a Virginia Plantation. Constance Cary Harrison. LC 7-2885. 1890. Cassell Publishing Company.
Flower De Hundred: The Story of a Virginia Plantation. Constance Cary Harrison. LC 99-5414. 1899. The Century Co.
Flower Fables. Louisa May Alcott. LC 31-16496. 1855. G. W. Briggs & Co.
Flower for Catherine. Frank Arthur Swinnerton. LC 51-286. 1950. Hutchinson.
Flower for Catherine. Frank Arthur Swinnerton. LC 51-1621. 1951. Doubleday.
Flower-Garden: A Collection of Short Tales and Historical Sketches, from the French of Emile Souvestre. Emile Souvestre & Donaldson, S. J., Jr., Tr. LC 8-12377. 1864. J. Murphy & Co.
Flower Girl of Paris (Das Kind der Strasse) Hedwig Harnisch Schobert. Tr. by Kendall, Laura E. LC 8-2036. (On cover: Rialto series, no. 51). 1893. Rand, McNally & Company.
Flower Girls. Winifred Ashton. LC 55-14626. 1955. Norton.
Flower Girls of Marseilles. Emile Zola & Cox, George D., Tr. LC 41-41848. 1888. T. B. Peterson & Brothers.
Flower in Her Hair. James Gould Cozzens. LC 76-355211. 1974. Bruccoli Clark.
Flower in the Gutter. 1st Ed. Ion Braby. LC 51-7228. 1951. Dutton.
Flower Mat. Shugoro Yamamoto. LC 76-6031. 8.50 (ISBN 0-8048-1181-4). C. E. Tuttle Co.
Flower-O'-the-Corn. Samuel Rutherford Crockett. LC 3-10623. 1903. McClure, Phillips & Co.
Flower O' the Lily: A Romance of Old Cambray. Emmuska Orczy. LC 19-1032. 1918. Hodder and Stoughton.
Flower O' the Lily: A Romance of Old Cambray. Emmuska Orczy. 1.50. George H. Doran Company.
Flower O' the Orange: And Other Tales of Bygone Days. Agnes Sweetman Castle & Castle, Egerton. LC 8-5883. 1908. The Macmillan Company.
Flower O' the Peach. Perceval Gibbon. LC 11-27455. 1911. 1.30. The Century Co.
Flower of Crime. Adolphe Belot. Tr. by M., J. LC 6-11684. (On cover: Garden City series, no. 1). 1892. Newberry Publishing Co.
Flower of Desire. S. Andrew Wood. LC 27-854585. E. P. Dutton & Company.
Flower of Destiny: An Episode. William Dana Orcutt. LC 5-12394. 1905. A. C. McClurg & Co.
Flower of Destiny: Old Days of the Serail. Margaret Mordecai. LC 10-127848. 1910. 1.50. G. P. Putnam's Sons.
Flower of Doom: And Other Stories. Matilda Barbara Bertram Edwards. (Harper's handy ser. no. 24). 1885. Harper & Brothers.
Flower of Doom and Other Stories. Matilda Barbara Bertram Edwards. (On cover: Lovell's library. no. 663). 1885. J. W. Lovell Company.
Flower of Doom and Other Stories. Matilda Barbara Bertram Edwards. (On cover: Seaside library. Pocket ed. no. 579). 1885. G. Munro.
Flower of Evil. Delphine C. Lyons. pap. 0.75 o.p. (ISBN 0-515-02859-2). Pyramid Pubns.
Flower of Fate. Joseph Allan Elphinstone Dunn. LC 77-84219. (Lost Race and Adult Fantasy Fiction). 1978. 18.00 (ISBN 0-405-10974-1). Arno Press.
Flower of Forgiveness. Flora Annie Webster Steel. LC 8-134390. 1894. Macmillan and Co.
Flower of Fortune. Emilie Benson Knipe & Knipe, Alden Arthur. LC 22-17942. 1922. 1.75. The Century Co.
Flower of France. Justin Huntly McCarthy. LC 6-16303. 1906. Harper & Brothers.
Flower of France. Marah Ellis Martin Ryan. LC 14-14262. Rand, McNally & Company.
Flower of France: A Story of Old Louisana. Marah Ellis Martin Ryan. LC 8-1354. 1894. Rand, McNally & Company.
Flower of France: A Story of Old Louisiana. Marah Ellis Martin Ryan. LC 72-2930. (Black Heritage Library Collection). 1972. 14.50 (ISBN 0-8369-9078-1). Books for Libraries Press.
Flower of Gala Water. A Novel. Amelia Edith Huddleston Barr. (Ledger library, no. 119). R. Bonner's Sons.
Flower of Gold. Kenn Smith. 304p. (Orig.). 1982. pap. 3.25 o.p. (ISBN 0-505-51836-8). Tower Bks.
Flower of Life. Thomas Burke. LC 31-27222. 1931. Little, Brown, and Company.
Flower of Life: A Christmas Fable. Thomas Burke. LC 30-534221. 1930. Doubleday, Doran & Company, Inc.
Flower of Light. Josephine Abbott Peck. LC 52-11798. 1952. R. R. Smith.
Flower of Love. Rachel North. (Orig.). 1980. pap. 2.50 o.s.i. (ISBN 0-505-51525-3). Tower Bks.
Flower of May. 1st Ed. Kate O'Brien. LC 53-7741. 1953. Harper.
Flower of Monterey: A Romance of the California. Katherine Bernie King Mrs. - Hamill. LC 21-12702. 1921. The Page Company.
Flower of Silence. Joanne Marshall. (Avon original gothic). 1975. (pbk.) 0.95 (ISBN 0-380-00304-X). Avon.
Flower of Smoke. Felicia Gizycka. LC 39-8725. 1939. C. Scribner's Sons.
Flower of the Chapdelaines. George Washington Cable. LC 72-84540. (Illus.). 1974. (lib. ed.) 14.50 (ISBN 0-403-02991-0). Scholarly Press.
Flower of the Chapdelaines. George Washington Cable. LC 18-7034. 1918. C. Scribner's Sons.
Flower of the Chapdelaines see Collected Works.
Flower of the Chippewa. Evan Henry Jones. LC 74-78672. 1974. 5.95 (ISBN 0-8059-2021-8). Dorrance.
Flower of the Desert. Roberta Leigh. 1979. pap. 1.75 (ISBN 0-449-14150-0, GM). Fawcett.
Flower of the Dusk. Myrtle Reed. LC 8-24448. 1908. G. P. Putnam's Sons.
Flower of the Dust. John Oxenham, pseud. LC 15-25351. 1915. Hodder and Stoughton.
Flower of the Flame. Louise Gerard. LC 26-143. The Macaulay Company.
Flower of the Gods. Achmed Abdullah & Oursler, Fulton. LC 36-4846. Green Circle Books.
Flower of the Gods. Eden Phillpotts. LC 43-103238. 1943. The Macmillan Company.
Flower of the Gorse. Louis Tracy. LC 15-5150. E. J. Clode.
Flower of the Grass: A Novel. Dee Olsen. LC 77-77640. (Illus.). 5.95. Ketron-Davis Pub. Co.
Flower of the Land: A Tapestry of the Great War. Ellanore J Parker. LC 41-7945. De Vorss & Co.
Flower of the Marshland. Virginia Gregory. LC 35-82206. 1935. The Peter Reilly Company.
Flower of the North: A Modern Romance. James Oliver Curwood. LC 24-27991. 1914. Grosset & Dunlap.
Flower of the North: A Modern Romances. James Oliver Curwood. LC 12-5673. 1912. 1.30. Harper & Brothers.
Flower of the Republic. Raymond A Kennedy. LC 82-47834. 1982. 12.50 (ISBN 0-394-52539-6). Knopf.
Flower of the Season. Nannie Deaderick Betts. LC 12-14399. 1912. 1.50. Broadway Publishing Co.
Flower of the World. Alice Calhoun Haines. E. P. Dutton & Company.
Flower of Thorn. Marie Conway Oemler. LC 31-24060. 2.50. The Century Co.
Flower of Youth: A Romance. Roy Rolfe Gilson. 1904. Harper & Brothers.
Flower-Patch Among the Hills. Flora Klickmann. LC 17-26323. Frederick A. Stokes Company.
Flower Phantoms. Ronald Fraser. LC 26-24556. 1926. Boni and Liveright.
Flower Power. Ernest Tidyman. (Orig.). 1968. pap. 0.50 o.p. (52-643). Paperback Lib.
Flower Shadows Behind the Curtain. Translated by Vladimir Kean from Franz Kuhn's German Version of the Original Chinese. With an Introd. by Franz Kuhn. LC 59-11955. 1959. Pantheon.
Flower Show. Denis George Mackail. LC 27-15203. 1927. Houghton Mifflin Company.
Flower Show; The Toth Family. Istvan Orkeny. LC 81-22373. 1982. 14.95 (ISBN 0-8112-0836-2) (ISBN 0-8112-0837-0). New Directions.
Flower Song, the Romance of Jane Alden. Helen Catheryn Willis. LC 29-9935. The Stratford Company.
Flower That Grew in the Sand, and Other Stories. Ella Rhoads Higginson. LC 72-3276. (Short story index reprint series). 1972. (ISBN 0-8369-4150-0). Books for Libraries Press.
Flower That Grew in the Sand, and Other Stories. Ella Rhoads Higginson. LC 7-4769. 1896. The Calvert Company.
Flower That Grew in the Sand: And Other Stories. Ella Rhoads Higginson. LC 72-3276. (Short Story Index Reprint Ser.). Repr. of 1896 ed. 17.00 (ISBN 0-8369-4150-0). Ayer Co.
Flower Thoughts. 1967. 2.95 o.p. (ISBN 0-442-82220-0). Peter Pauper.
Flower Wagon and Other Stories. Margaret Elizabeth Sangster. LC 37-4268. 1937. Round Table Press, Inc.
Flowerdown. Ann Knox. LC 28-22468. 1928. 2.50. The Century Co.
Flowered Box: A Novel of Suspense. Thomas J. Green. LC 80-22442. 192p. 1980. 9.95 (ISBN 0-8253-0010-X). Beaufort Bks NY.
Flowering. Agnes Sligh Turnbull. LC 72-75613. (Fawcett crest book). 1974. (pbk.) 0.95. Fawcett.
Flowering Aloe. Sylvia Stevenson. LC 37-16073. H. Holt and Company.
Flowering Green. Miriam Lynch. 400p. (Orig.). 1981. pap. 2.95 (ISBN 0-441-24101-8). Ace Bks.
Flowering Harvest. Vera Murdock Stuart Jervis. LC 42-17988. 1941. Arcadia House, Inc.
Flowering Judas. Katherine Anne Porter. LC 30-25819. Harcourt, Brace and Company.
Flowering Judas and Other Stories. Katherine Anne Porter. LC 35-19672. Harcourt, Brace and Company.
Flowering Judas and Other Stories. Katherine Anne Porter. LC 40-27678. (Half-title: The Modern library of the world's best books). 1940. The Modern Library.
Flowering Judas: And Other Stories. With a New Introd. by the Author. Katherine Anne Porter. LC 53-5342. (Modern library of the world's best books). 1953. Modern Library.
Flowering Quince. Dorothy Graffe Van Doren. LC 27-17785. George H. Doran Company.
Flowering Thorn. Margery Sharp. LC 52-10940. 1952. Little, Brown.
Flowering Thorn. Margery Sharp. LC 34-862. 1934. G. P. Putnam's Sons.
Flowering Vine see Three Loves for Cecily.
Flowering Wilderness. John Galsworthy. LC 77-113923. (His The Forsyte chronicles, v. 8). (Scribner library. Contemporary classics.). 1970. 2.45. Scribner.
Flowering Wilderness. John Galsworthy. LC 32-280873. 1932. C. Scribner's Sons.
Flowers & Shadows. Benjamin Okri. (Drum Beat Ser.). 274p. 1980. pap. 6.00 o.s.i. (ISBN 0-582-64301-5). Three Continents.
Flowers at Her Feet. Marie Blizard. 1939. Arcadia House.
Flowers by Request. Leonard Patrick O'Connor Wibberley. LC 63-20004. (Red badge detective). 1964. Dodd, Mead.
Flowers for a Dead Witch. Michael Butterworth. LC 75-144255. 1971. 4.95. Published for the Crime Club by Doubleday.
Flowers for Algernon. Daniel Keyes. LC 66-12366. 1966. Harcourt, Brace & World.
Flowers for Dorothy: By Jeanne Bowman Pseud. Peggy O'More, pseud. Arcadia House.
Flowers for Lilian. Anna Gilbert. LC 80-21358. 1980. 9.95 (ISBN 0-312-29653-3). St. Martin's Press.
Flowers for Lilian. Anna Gilbert. LC 82-9177. 1982. 13.95 (ISBN 0-8161-3399-9). G.K. Hall.
Flowers for My Love. Katrina Britt. (Romances Ser.). 192p. (Orig.). 1980. pap. text ed. 1.25 (ISBN 0-373-02343-X, Pub. by Harlequin). PB.
Flowers for the Executioner. Bernardo Teixeira. 272p. (Orig.). 1982. pap. 2.75 (ISBN 0-380-79376-8, 79376). Avon.
Flowers for the God of Love. Barbara Cartland. 1979. 7.95 o.p. (ISBN 0-525-10720-7). Dutton.
Flowers for the Judge. Margery Allingham. LC 36-10524. 1936. Doubleday, Doran & Company, Inc.
Flowers for the Judge. Margery Allingham. LC 36-33416. 1936. The Sun Dial Press.
Flowers for the Judge. Margery Allingham. 1973. (pbk) 0.95. Manor Books.
Flowers for the Living. Charles Ray. LC 37-708438. 1937. Godwin.
Flowers from the Tree of Night. Maria Gillan. LC 81-18087. 64p. (Orig.). 1981. pap. 5.00 (ISBN 0-941608-00-X). Chantry Pr.
Flowers Gang. Garnett Radcliffe. LC 30-7784. 1930. Houghton Mifflin Company.
Flowers in the Attic. Virginia C. Andrews. 2.50 (ISBN 0-671-82531-3). Pocket Books.
Flowers in the Attic. Virginia C Andrews. LC 80-13307. 12.95 (ISBN 0-671-41124-1). Simon and Schuster.
Flowers in the Attic. large print ed. Virginia C. Andrews. LC 82-23315. 1983. 18.95 (ISBN 0-8161-3428-6). G.K. Hall.
Flowers in the Mirror. Ju-Chen Li. LC 65-28004. 1965. University of California Press.
Flowers in the Mirror. Li, Ju-chen. Ed. & tr. by Tai-yi Lin. 1965. 30.00x (ISBN 0-520-00747-6). U of Cal Pr.
Flowers in the Sky. Kok Liang Lee. (Writing in Asia Ser.). (Orig.). 1982. pap. text ed. 5.50x (00268). Heinemann Ed.
Flowers of Adonis. Rosemary Sutcliff. LC 76-96780. (Illus.). 1970. 6.95. Coward-McCann.
Flowers of Darkness. Elizabeth Barr. (Orig.). 1980. pap. 1.25 (ISBN 0-440-12624-X). Dell.
Flowers of Eden. Joan Smith. 1979. pap. 2.50 (ISBN 0-449-24210-2, Crest). Fawcett.

Flowers of Evil. Charles Pierre Baudelaire. 1.95 o.p. (ISBN 0-442-82222-7). Peter Pauper.

Flowers of Evil. Robert Charles, pseud. 256p. (Orig.). 1981. pap. 2.50 (ISBN 0-553-20297-9). Bantam.

Flowers of Evil: From the French of Charles Baudelaire. Edna St. Vincent Millay. 1936. 6.00 o.p. (ISBN 0-06-012960-3, HarpT). Harper Row.

Flowers of Fire. Stephanie Blake. LC 76-49400. 448p. 1977. pap. 2.95 (ISBN 0-87216-891-3). Playboy Pbks.

Flowers of Fire: Twentieth-Century Korean Stories. Ed. by Peter H. Lee. LC 73-90853. 1974. 12.00 (ISBN 0-8248-0302-7). University Press of Hawaii.

Flowers of Hell. Morgan Drake. pap. 1.95 o.s.i. (OPH-189, Ophelia). Olympia.

Flowers of Hiroshima. Edita Morris. LC 59-134124. 1959. Viking Press.

Flowers of Our Lost Romance. Charles Fletcher Lummis. 1929. Houghton Mifflin Company.

Flowers of the Desert. C. A. Haddad. (Orig.). 1982. pap. 3.50 (ISBN 0-440-12718-1). Dell.

Flowers of the Field. Sarah Harrison. LC 79-25790. 11.95 (ISBN 0-698-11008-0). Coward, McCann & Geoghegan.

Flowers of the Forest. Ruth Doan MacDougall. LC 80-22415. 1981. 11.95 (ISBN 0-689-11124-X). Atheneum.

Flowers on the Grass: A Novel. Monica Dickens. LC 50-9410. 1950. McGraw-Hill.

Flowing Gold. Rex Ellingwood Beach. LC 22-175610. Harper & Brothers.

Flowing Valley: An Historical Novel of California in 1846. Orville J Harrell. LC 53-8721. 1953. BcBride Co.

Floyd Grandon's Honor. Amanda Minnie Douglas. LC 6-33488. 1884. Lee and Shepard.

Floyd Ireson. Henry Colford Gauss. LC 2-1763. 1901. Newcomb & Gauss.

Floyd's Flowers. Silas X. Floyd. LC 78-168050. (Illus.). Repr. of 1905 ed. 23.50 (ISBN 0-404-00048-7). AMS Pr.

Fluger. Doris Perschia. (Science Fiction Ser.). 1980. pap. 1.95 o.p. (ISBN 0-87997-577-6, UJ1577). DAW Bks.

Fluger. Doris Piserchia. 1980. 1.95 (ISBN 0-87997-577-6). DAW Books.

Fluke. James Herbert. (Signet book). 1978. 1.95 (ISBN 0-451-08394-6). New American Library.

Flurry in Diamonds. Thomas E Price. LC 7-30102. (On cover: Globe library, no. 52). 1888. Rand, McNally & Company.

Flush As May. Philip Maitland Hubbard. 1963. 4.50 o.s.i. (ISBN 0-8277-0048-2). British Bk Ctr.

Flush Times. 1st Ed. Warren Miller. LC 62-17943. 1962. Little, Brown.

Flute Across the Pond. Frederic Wakeman. LC 66-14046. 4.95. World.

Flute & Violin. James Lane Allen. Repr. of 1891 ed. lib. bdg. 20.00 (ISBN 0-8414-3063-2). Folcroft.

Flute & Violin & Other Kentucky Tales & Romances. facsimile ed. James L. Allen. LC 78-98555. (Short Story Index Reprint Ser.). 1891. 14.00 (ISBN 0-8369-3129-7). Ayer Co.

Flute and Violin: And Other Kentucky Tales and Romances. James Lane Allen. LC 78-98555. (Short story index reprint series). (Illus.). 1969. Books for Libraries Press.

Flute and Violin: And Other Kentucky Tales and Romances. James Lane Allen. LC 6-42. 1891. Harper & Brothers.

Flute and Violin: And Other Kentucky Tales and Romances. biographical ed. James Lane Allen. LC 99-4617. 1899. Harper & Brothers.

Flute Boy of the Navajos. Florence Romaine. LC 35-14581. (Our changing world). 1935. T. Nelson and Sons.

Flute of Pan. Pearl Mary Teresa Richards Craigie. LC 5-33648. 1905. D. Appleton and Company.

Flute of the Gods. Marah Ellis Martin Ryan. LC 9-25977. 1909. F. A. Stokes Company.

Flute-Player. D. M. Thomas. 224p. 1982. pap. 3.50 (ISBN 0-671-44211-2). WSP.

Flute-Player: A Novel. D. M Thomas. LC 79-2582. 1979. 8.95 (ISBN 0-525-10727-4). Dutton.

Flutes of Shanghai. Louise Jordan Miln. LC 28-20728. 1928. Frederick A. Stokes Company.

Flutter of an Eyelid. Myron Brinig. LC 33-251935. Farrar & Rinehart, Incorporated.

Flux. Ron Goulart. 1974. (pbk.) 0.95. DAW Books.

Fly. Richard Chopping. LC 65-13729. 1965. Farrar, Straus & Giroux.

Fly Away Blackbird. Jerrard Tickell. LC 36-10345. 1936. W. Morrow and Company.

Fly Away Home. Carolyn Doty. LC 81-51882. 1982. 14.95 (ISBN 0-670-64310-6). Viking Press.

Fly Away Home. Mary Hedin. LC 79-28524. (Iowa School of Letters Award for Short Fiction Ser.: 10). 257p. 1980. 9.95 (ISBN 0-87745-099-4); pap. 5.95 (ISBN 0-87745-100-1). U of Iowa Pr.

Fly Away Home. Gillian Tindall. LC 78-161104. 1971. 5.95 (ISBN 0-8027-0357-7). Walker.

Fly Away, Jill. Max Byrd. 224p. (Orig.). 1981. pap. 2.50 (ISBN 0-553-20232-4). Bantam.

Fly Away Paul. Victor Canning. LC 36-19834. 1936. Reynal & Hitchcock.

Fly Away, Paul. Peter Davies. 1974. 5.95. Crown.

Fly Bird, Fly. Jacob Hill. LC 79-182075. 1972. 4.50 (ISBN 0-8059-1652-0). Dorrance.

Fly Boys: Sky-Jacked. Stanley Morgan. LC 76-376883. 1976. 2.95 (ISBN 0-491-01826-6). W. H. Allen.

Fly-by-Night. Eric Hatch. LC 35-8104. 1935. Little, Brown, and Company.

Fly for Your Life. Larry Forrester. 320p. (Orig.). 1981. pap. 2.50 (ISBN 0-553-20391-6). Bantam.

Fly Girl. Matt Harding, pseud. 1970. pap. 0.75 o.p. (75-329). Manor Bks.

Fly in the Martini. Parke Cummings. (Illus.). 1961. 3.95 o.p. (ISBN 0-8090-4580-X). Hill & Wang.

Fly in the Pigment. Sidney Peterson. pap. 1.95 o.p. (ISBN 0-87465-029-1). Pacific Coast.

Fly in the Pigment. 1st Ed. Sidney Peterson. LC 61-11003. (Contact editions, 1). 1961. Contact Editions.

Fly Now, Falcon. Pamela Frankau. LC 35-20904. 1935. Houghton Mifflin Company.

Fly on the Wall. Tony Hillerman. LC 78-156575. 1971. 5.95 (ISBN 0-06-011897-0). Harper & Row.

Fly on the Wall. Tony Hillerman. LC 81-47384. (Fifty Classics of Crime Fiction, 1950-1975). 1982. 14.95 (ISBN 0-8240-4993-4). Garland Pub.

Fly on the Wall. Tony Hillerman. 1974. (pbk.) 1.25. Dell.

Fly on the Wheel. Katherine Cecil Thurston. LC 8-27495. 1908. Dodd, Mead and Company.

Flyaway. Desmond Bagley. LC 78-22226. 1979. 9.95 (ISBN 0-385-14911-5). Doubleday.

Flyaway Ned: Or, The Old Detective's Pupil. Harlan Page Halsey. LC 74-15747. (Popular Culture in America). 1974. 7.00 (ISBN 0-405-06382-2). Arno Press.

Flyer. Gail Kimberly. 1975. (pbk.) 1.25. Popular Library.

Flyers. Robert French. (Orig.). 1979. pap. 1.95 (ISBN 0-532-23157-0). Woodhill.

Flyers. George Barr McCutcheon. LC 7-12643. 1907. Dodd, Mead & Company.

Flyin' M Buckaroo. Galen C Colin. LC 39-330866. Phoenix Press.

Flying Artillerist: Or, The Child of the Battlefield. A Tale of Mexican Treachery. Justin Jones. LC 8-2123. T. B. Peterson & Brothers.

Flying Artillerist: Or, The Child of the Battle-Field. A Tale of Mexican Treachery. Justin Jones. LC 7-11897. 1853. H. Long & Brother.

Flying Beast. Walter S Masterman. LC 32-143264. E. P. Dutton & Co., Inc.

Flying Blood. Thomson Burtis. LC 32-11204. 1932. The Fiction League.

Flying Bo'sun: A Mystery of the Sea. Arthur Mason. LC 20-192368. 1920. H. Holt and Company.

Flying Boys in the Sky. Edward Sylvester Ellis. LC 11-13139. (Half-title: The flying boys series v. 1). 0.60. The John C. Winston Company.

Flying Boys to the Rescue. Edward Sylvester Ellis. LC 11-13140. (Half-title: The flying boys series v. 2). 0.60. The John C. Winston Company.

Flying Buccaneer: A Novel of Adventure in the Skies. Jack Binns. LC 23-169761. 1923. N. L. Brown.

Flying Chinaman. Harry H Fein. LC 38-217023. 1938. A. A. Knopf.

Flying Cloud: A Story of the Sea. Morley Roberts. LC 7-15115. 1907. L. C. Page & Company.

Flying Clues. Charles Judson Dutton. LC 27-123526. 1927. Dodd, Mead & Company.

Flying Colors. Cecil Scott Forester. (Hornblower Saga,#7). 1975. (pbk.) 1.25 (ISBN 0-523-00387-0). Pinnacle Books.

Flying Colours. Cecil Scott Forester. LC 38-29010. 1939. Little, Brown and Company.

Flying Courtship. E. J. Rath. LC 28-24474. 1928. G. H. Watt.

Flying Cromlech. Aodh Sandrach De Blacam. LC 30-13208. The Century Co.

Flying Dagger Murder. Joan A Cowdroy. LC 32-172681. 1932. R. M. McBride & Company.

Flying Death. Samuel Hopkins Adams. LC 8-3520. 1908. The McClure Company.

Flying Death. Edwin Balmer. LC 27-124019. 1927. Dodd, Mead & Company.

Flying Dutchman. Michael Arlen. LC 39-20966. 1939. Doubleday, Doran & Company, Inc.

Flying Dutchman. new ed. William Johnson Neale. LC 7-23102. 1868. G. Routledge & Sons.

Flying Dutchman: Or, The Death Ship. William Clark Russell. (On cover: Lovell's library, no. 1232). 1888. J. W. Lovell Company.

Flying Dutchman: Or, The Wedding Guest of Amsterdam. A Mysterious Tale of the Sea. Captain Merry. H. Long & Brother.

Flying Elbows. Ernest Lockridge. LC 75-8857. 1975. 8.95 (ISBN 0-8128-1812-1). Stein and Day.

Flying Emerald. Ethelreda Lewis. LC 26-6812. George H. Doran Company.

Flying Ferry. John Tedman & Alison Tedman. (New Oxford Supplementary Readers Ser). (Illus.). 78p. 1965. pap. text ed. 0.75x o.p. (ISBN 0-19-422409-0). Oxford U Pr.

Flying Finish. Dick Francis. LC 67-13702. 1967. Harper & Row.

Flying Finish. Dick Francis. LC 67-13702. 1975. (pbk.) 1.50 (ISBN 0-671-80088-4). Pocket Books.

Flying Finish see Across the Board: Three Harper Novels of Suspense.

Flying Footballs. Jacket Drawing and Illus. by William B. Ricketts. 1st Ed. Bertrand Leslie Shurtleff. LC 53-10764. 1953. Bobbs-Merrill.

Flying Fox. William Fisher Alder. LC 21-4511. 1921. Wayside Press.

Flying Fox in a Freedom Tree. 149p. (gr. 10 up). 1979. pap. 6.00x (ISBN 0-582-71734-5, Pub. by Longman Paul New Zealand). Three Continents.

Flying Fox. 1st American Ed. Mary McMinnies. LC 57-5298. Harcourt, Brace.

Flying Game. William Carigan. LC 74-13775. 1974. 7.95. Juniper Publishers.

Flying Girl. Edith Van Dyne, pseud. LC 11-24130. The Reilly & Britton Co.

Flying Halcyon: A Mystery of the Pacific Ocean. new version. ed. Richard Henry Savage. LC 8-2000. 1894. F. T. Neely.

Flying Halcyon: A Mystery of the Pacific Ocean. new version. ed. Richard Henry Savage. LC 8-2001. 1894. G. Routledge and Sons, Limited.

Flying Heels. Hugh Lundsford. LC 30-3229. The Curtise Press.

Flying High. Sally Wentworth. (Harlequin Presents Ser.). 192p. 1983. pap. 1.95 (ISBN 0-373-10581-9). Harlequin Bks.

Flying Horse. Henry Gibbs. LC 64-16804. 1964. Walker.

Flying Horseman. Gustave Aimard & St. John, Percy Bolingbroke, 1821-1889, Ed. LC 5-42195. (On cover: Lovell's library, no. 1079). 1887. J.W. Lovell Company.

Flying Horses: Tales from China. Jo Manton & Robert Gittings. LC 77-6344. 6.95 (ISBN 0-03-022701-1). Holt, Rinehart and Winston.

Flying Inland. Kathleen Spivack. LC 73-79713. 80p. 1973. Softbound 2.50 o.p. (ISBN 0-385-05128-X). Doubleday.

Flying Inn. Gilbert Keith Chesterton. LC 55-7483. (New World Chesterton). 1955. Sheed and Ward.

Flying Inn. Gilbert Keith Chesterton. LC 14-2211. 1914. John Lane Company.

Flying Kestrel. Aylward Edward Dingle. LC 27-131251. 1927. G. H. Watt.

Flying Legion. George Allan England. LC 20-12813. 1920. A. C. McClurg & Co.

Flying Lovers. Charles Stanley Strong. LC 39-8473. Phoenix Press.

Flying Mail. Meir Goldschmidt & Thoresen, Magdalene I. E. Anna Magdalene. Tr. by Larsen, Carl. LC 6-43741. 1870. Sever, Francis, & Co.

Flying Marquis. Richards Jarden. LC 44-9746. 1944. Dorrance & Company.

Flying Mercury. Eleanor Marie Ingram. LC 10-25793. 1.50. The Bobbs-Merrill Company.

Flying Nun. Tererios. Orig. Title: Fifteenth Pelican. 1965. 3.50 o.p. Doubleday.

Flying Osip: Stories of New Russia. Lidia Nikolaevna Seifullina. LC 76-122700. (Short story index reprint series). 1970. Books for Libraries Press.

Flying Osip: Stories of New Russia. Lidia Nikolaevna Seifullina et al. LC 76-122700. (Short Story Index Reprint Ser). 1925. 15.00 (ISBN 0-8369-3533-0). Ayer Co.

Flying Osip: Stories of New Russia. Seifullina, Lidia Nikolaevna, 1889- & Kasatkin, Ivan Mikhailovich. Tr. by Louis S. Friedland & Iosif R. Pirozhnikov. LC 25-4773. 1925. International Publishers.

Flying Poilu: A Story of Aerial Warfare. Marcel Nadaud. Tr. by Huard, Mme, Frances, (Wilson) LC 18-11942. George H. Doran Company.

Flying Porcupine. Richard Haligon. 288p. 1982. pap. 2.95 (ISBN 0-445-04715-1). Popular Lib.

Flying Red Horse. Frances Kirkwood Crane. LC 49-9271. 1949. Random House.

Flying Sand. Peter Norden. (Orig.). 1981. pap. 2.25 (ISBN 0-505-51680-2). Tower Bks.

Flying Saucer. Bernard Newman. LC 49-511107. 1949. Gollancz.

Flying Saucer Revelations. Michael X. 1969. pap. 6.95. G Barker Bks.

Flying Saucers. Isaac Asimov et al. 352p. 1982. pap. 2.95 (ISBN 0-449-24503-9, Crest). Fawcett.

Flying Saucers Are Watching You. John C. Sherwood. pap. 3.95 o.p. Saucerian.

Flying Saucers Closeup. John W. Dean. (Illus., Orig.). 1970. pap. 7.95 o.p. Saucerian.

Flying Saucers in Fact & Ficton. Ed. by Hans S. Santesson. 1968. pap. 0.75 o.p. (74-953). Lancer.

Flying Saucers in the Bible. Virginia Brasington. (Illus.). 1965. pap. 3.95 o.p. Saucerian.

Flying Snowshoes. Drawings by David Hunt. Evelyn Dangberg Teal. LC 57-5246. 1957. Caxton Printers.

Flying Sorcerers. David Gerrold & Larry Niven. 1976. Repr. of 1971 ed. lib. bdg. 16.60x (ISBN 0-88411-194-6). Amereon Ltd.

Flying Sorcerers. David Gerrold & Larry Niven. 1982. pap. 2.75 (ISBN 0-345-30494-2, Del Rey). Ballantine.

Flying South. Nancy Geyer. LC 82-5766. 10.95 (ISBN 0-684-17599-1). Scribner.

Flying Squad. Edgar Wallace. LC 28-299242. 1929. Pub. for The Crime Club, Inc., by Doubleday, Doran & Company, Inc.

Flying Staircase. a dirigo ed. Alice Mariett. LC 50-432017. Falmouth Pub. House, C.

Flying Swans. Padraic Colum. LC 56-11378. 1957. Crown Publishers.

Flying Tavern & Other Tales. Brigitta Valentiner. 180p. 1978. 6.95 o.p. (ISBN 0-8059-2451-5). Dorrance.

Flying Teuton: And Other Stories. Alice Brown. LC 18-7292. 1918. The Macmillan Company.

Flying U Ranch. Bertha Muzzy Sinclair. LC 14-5351. G. W. Dillingham Company.

Flying U Strikes. Bertha Muzzy Sinclair. LC 34-12031. 1934. Little, Brown, and Company.

Flying U Strikes. Bertha Muzzy Sinclair. LC 41-130630. 1941. Triangle Books.

Flying U's Last Stand. B. M. Bower. 1975. lib. bdg. 16.30x (ISBN 0-89966-020-7). Buccaneer Bks.

Flying U's Last Stand. Bertha Muzzy Sinclair. LC 15-5556. 1915. Little, Brown and Company.

Flying Visit. Peter Fleming & Low, David, 1891- Illus. LC 40-303979. 1940. C. Scribner's Sons.

Flying Wildcats. Ed. by Leo Margulies. LC 44-1333. 1943. The Hampton Publishing Company.

Flying Y Brand. Jesse Edward Grinstea. LC 40-312901. Dodge Publishing Company.

Flying Yorkshiremen, Novellas... With a Note. Knight, Eric Mowbray, 1897- et al. LC 38-10450. 1938. Harper & Brothers.

Flynn. Gregory McDonald. LC 77-84403. 1.95 (ISBN 0-380-01764-4). Avon.

Flypaper War. Richard Starnes. LC 69-18268. 1969. 5.95. Trident Press.

Fo' Meals a Day. Hugh Wiley. LC 75-163048. (Short story index reprint series). 1971. (ISBN 0-8369-3962-X). Books for Libraries Press.

Fo' Meals a Day. Hugh Wiley. LC 27-175288. 1927. A. A. Knopf.

Foam. Mary Dixon Thayer. LC 26-176253. Dorrance and Company.

Foam of the Sea: And Other Tales. Gertrude Hall Brownell. LC 7-1490. 1895. Roberts Brothers.

Foaming Fore Shore. Samuel Alexander White. LC 20-163445. 1920. Doubleday, Page & Company.

Foc's'le Boy. Carl Driver. (Orig.). 1969. pap. 1.95 o.p. (7056). Barclay Hse.

Focus. Arthur Miller. LC 45-9586. 1945. Reynal & Hitchcock.

Focus All. Alastair Galt. 192p. (Orig.). 1971. pap. 1.95 o.s.i. (O*P*H258, Ophelia). Olympia.

Focus Changes of August Previco: A Novel. Dale Worsley. LC 80-19515. 10.00 (ISBN 0-8149-0841-1). Vanguard Press.

Focus on Murder. Ronal Kayser. LC 43-2940. 1943. J. B. Lippincott Company.

Focus on Murder. 1st Ed. George Harmon Coxe. LC 54-5262. 1954. Knopf.

Focus: The Cry for Bread. Anna Josephine Lindgren. LC 62-22366. Moody Press.

Foe in the Household. Caroline Chesebro' LC 6-24216. 1871. J. R. Osgood and Company.

Foe of Barnabas Collins. Marilyn Ross. (Dark Shadows No. 7). (Orig.). 1969. pap. 0.50 o.p. (62-135). Paperback Lib.

Foes: A Novel. Mary Johnston. LC 18-19300. 1918. Harper & Brothers.

Foes in Ambush. Charles King. LC 3-22372. 1893. J. B. Lippincott Company.

Foes in Law. Rhoda Broughton. LC 4982. 1900. The Macmillan Company.

Foes of Her Household. Amanda Minnie Douglas. LC 6-33487. 1887. Lee and Shepard.

Fog. Dennis Etchison. 224p. (Orig.). 1980. pap. 2.25 (ISBN 0-553-13825-1). Bantam.

Fog. James Herbert. (Orig.). 1975. pap. 1.95 (ISBN 0-451-09193-0, J9193, Sig). NAL.

Fog. James Herbert. (Signet Book). 1975. (pbk.) 1.50. New American Library.

Fog. Valentine Williams & Sims, Mrs. Dorothy Rice, Joint Author. LC 33-6260. 1933. Houghton Mifflin Company.

Fog: A Novel. William Dudley Pelley. LC 21-163195. 1921. 2.00. Little, Brown, and Company.

Fog Comes. Mary Garden Collins. LC 41-529519. 1941. C. Scribner's Sons.

Fog Island. Dorothy Osborne. (Berkley medallion book). 1975. (pbk.) 1.25 (ISBN 0-425-02801-1). Berkley Pub.
Fog Island Horror. Marilyn Ross. 1978. 1.50 (ISBN 0-445-04239-7). Popular Library.
Fog Island Secret. Marilyn Ross. (Queen-size gothic). 1975. (pbk.) 1.25. Popular Library.
Fog Magic. Julia L Sauer. (Archway Paperback). 1977. 1.25 (ISBN 0-671-29817-8). Pocket Books.
Fog Maiden. Jane Toombs. LC 75-38995. 1.25 (ISBN 0-345-25210-1). Ballantine Books.
Fog of Doubt. Christianna Brand, pseud. 1979. lib. bdg. 9.95 (ISBN 0-8398-2535-8, Gregg). G K Hall.
Fog of Doubt. Mary Christianna Milne Lewis. LC 79-661. (Series: Gregg Press Mystery Fiction Series.). 1979. 9.95 (ISBN 0-8398-2535-8). Gregg Press.
Fog of Doubt: By Christianna Brand Pseud. Mary Christianna Milne Lewis. LC 53-6189. 1953. Scribner.
Fog on the Mountain. Frederica De Laguna. 1938. Pub. for the Crime Club, Inc., by Doubleday, Doran & Co., Inc.
Fog Over Fund. Louis Arthur Cunningham. LC 36-30324. The Penn Publishing Company.
Fog Over Hong Kong. Kenneth Anderson. LC 45-4534. 1945. Zondervan Publishing House.
Fog Princes. Florence Alice Price James. LC 7-7420. (On cover: Lovell's international series, no. 18). 1889. F. F. Lovell & Company.
Fog Princes: A Romance of the Dark Metropolis. Florence Alice Price James. (On cover: Seaside library. Pocket ed., no. 1193). 1889. G. Munro.
Fog Sinister. Marc Lovell, pseud. 1977. pap. 1.50 (ISBN 0-532-15295-6). Woodhill.
Fogarty & Co. Joe Flaherty. LC 70-146095. 1973. 6.95 (ISBN 0-698-10440-4). Coward, McCann & Geoghegan.
Fogarty & Co. Joe Flaherty. 1973. (pbk.) 1.25. Popular Library.
Fogbound. Clarissa Ross, pseud. LC 67-3716. 1967. Arcadia House.
Foggy, Foggy Death: A Captain Heimrich Mystery. Richard Lockridge & Frances Louise Davis Lockridge. LC 50-10759. (Main line mysteries). 1950. Lippincott.
Foggy Foggy Dew. Amber Dean. LC 47-11519. 1947. Pub. for the Crime Club by Doubleday.
Foggy, Foggy Dew and Dewey Death. Ursula Torday. LC 60-113. 1959. London House & Maxwell.
Foghorn. Gertrude Franklin Horn Atherton. LC 34-37996. 1934. Houghton Mifflin Company.
Foghorn: Stories. Gertrude Franklin Horn Atherton. LC 78-116928. (Short story index reprint series). 1970. Books for Libraries Press.
Foiled. Robert H Cowdrey. 1885. Clark & Longley, Printers.
Foiled by Love. Bertha N Clay. LC 6-21370. (On cover: The Melbourne ser., no. 9). 1893. Melbourne Publishing Co.
Folcarinia, a Political Love Story. Adam Dixon Warner & Bell, Theodore A. LC 8-22242. 1908. Smith-Brooks Printing Co.
Folded Hills. Stewart Edward White. LC 34-28323. 1934. Doubleday, Doran & Company, Inc.
Folded Hills. Stewart Edward White. LC 36-364355. Doubleday, Doran & Company, Inc.
Folded Leaf. William Maxwell. LC 46-31472. 1945. Harper & Brothers.
Folded Leaf. William Maxwell. LC 80-67031. (Nonpareil Books; 20). 1980. 7.95 (ISBN 0-87923-351-6). Godine.
Folded Leaf. William Maxwell. LC 78-63992. 1982. 26.50 (ISBN 0-404-61510-4). AMS Press.
Folded Leaf. Slight Revisions Have Been Made by the Author. William Maxwell. LC 59-850. (Vintage book, K78). 1959. Vintage Books.
Folgen der Verfolgung: Das Ueberlebenden-Syndrom. William G. Niederland. (Edition Suhrkamp. Neue Folge: esNF 15). 280p. (Orig., Ger.). 1980. pap. text ed. 7.80 (ISBN 3-518-11015-2, Pub. by Suhrkamp Verlag Germany). Suhrkamp.
Folio Club Presents R. L. S: Three Stories. Robert Louis Stevenson & Folio Club, Philadelphia. LC 37-31444. 1937. Printed by the Eldon Press.
Folio Forty-One. Michael Sinclair. LC 72-175274. 1972. 5.95. Putnam.
Folio on Florence White. William Charles Oursler. LC 42-17637. 1942. Simon and Schuster.
Folk Afield. Eden Phillpotts. LC 76-128747. (Short story index reprint series). 1970. Books for Libraries Press.
Folk Afield. Eden Phillpotts. LC 7-32550. 1907. G. P. Putnam's Sons.
Folk of Furry Farm: The Romance of an Irish Village. Katherine Frances Purdon. LC 14-8474. 1914. 1.35. G. P. Putnam's Sons.
Folk-Story and Verse. William Adams. LC 98-1509. (Lakeside literature series, book II). 1899. Western Publishing House.
Folk Tales from Korea. Ed. & tr. by Zong In-Sob. LC 53-12953. 1979. 6.95 (ISBN 0-394-17096-2, E738, Ever). Grove.
Folk Tales from Portugal. Alan S. Feinstein. LC 74-146754. (Illus.). 160p. 1972. 5.95 o.p. (ISBN 0-498-01031-7). A S Barnes.
Folkhouse: The Autobiography of a Home. Ruth Sawyer. LC 32-3005. 1932. D. Appleton and Company.
Folklore from the Adirondack Foothills: Phases of Life in the Foothills. Howard Thomas. 1958. 4.95 (ISBN 0-913710-02-4). Prospect.
Folklore of Kissing Games. Susan McDonald & David J. Gerrick. 84p. (Orig.). 1981. pap. 3.00 (ISBN 0-916750-77-9). Dayton Labs.
Folklore of Love & Courtship. Duncan Emrich. (New Gift Book Ser). (Illus.). 1969. 1.95 o.p. (ISBN 0-07-019522-6). McGraw.
Folklore of Weddings & Marriage. Duncan Emrich. (New Gift Book Ser). (Illus.). 1970. 1.95 o.p. (ISBN 0-07-019523-4). McGraw.
Folks. Ruth Suckow. LC 34-322147. Farrar & Rinehart, Inc.
Folks Back Home. Eugene Wood. LC 8-8099. 1908. The McClure Company.
Folks from Dixie. Paul Laurence Dunbar. LC 72-101281. (Short story index reprint series). (Illus.). 1969. Books for Libraries Press.
Folks from Dixie. Paul Laurence Dunbar. LC 73-81111. (Illus.). 1969. Mnemosyne Pub. Inc.
Folks from Dixie. Paul Laurence Dunbar. LC 78-78572. (Illus.). 1968. Gregg Press.
Folks from Dixie. Paul Laurence Dunbar. LC 72-75531. (Illus.). 1969. Negro Universities Press.
Folks from Dixie. Paul Laurence Dunbar. LC 6-35871. 1898. Dodd, Mead and Company.
Folktales Told Around the World. Richard M. Dorson. (Illus.). xxvi, 622p. 1978. pap. 9.95 (ISBN 0-226-15874-8, P781, Phoen). U of Chicago Pr.
Folktales Told Around the World. Richard M. Dorson. LC 74-33515. (O.s.i.). xxvi, 622p. 1976. 17.50x o.s.i. (ISBN 0-226-15872-1). U of Chicago Pr.
Follain Initiation. Frank Graziano & Jean Follain. Tr. by Mary Feeney. (O.s.i). 1979. pap. 27.50 o.s.i. (ISBN 0-931460-07-7). Bieler.
Folle-Farine. Louise De La Ramee. LC 42-26417. 1871. J. B. Lippincott & Co.
Folle-Farine. Louise De La Ramee. (Seaside library. v. 4, no. 62). 1877. G. Munro.
Follies of the King. Jean Plaidy. LC 81-23454. (Plaidy, Jean, 1906-. Plantagenet Saga). 1982. 12.95 (ISBN 0-399-12690-2). Putnam.
Follow a Shadow... Ruby Mildred Ayres. LC 37-5992. 1937. Doubleday, Doran and Company, Inc.
Follow a Shadow. Joanne Marshall, pseud. LC 73-87197. 1973. 6.95 (ISBN 0-399-11260-X). Putnam.
Follow, As the Night... Patricia McGerr. LC 50-8209. 1950. Published for the Crime Club by Doubleday.
Follow, Follow. Alice Darling Glenday & Auckland, N.Z. City Council. LC 74-179793. 1973-1974. Collins in Conjunction with the Auckland City Council.
Follow Me. 1976. 5.95 o.p. (ISBN 0-88270-200-9, Pub. by Logos); pap. 3.95 o.p. (ISBN 0-88270-201-7). Bridge Pub.
Follow Me! Charles Hunter. 184p. (Orig.). 1975. pap. 2.95 (ISBN 0-86694-020-0). Omega Pubns OR.
Follow Me. Mabel Dana Lyon. LC 36-4303. Godwin.
Follow Me. Helen Kieran Reilly. LC 60-12117. (Random House mystery). 1960. Random House.
Follow Me Down. Shelby Foote. LC 50-8530. 1950. Dial Press.
Follow Me Down. Shelby Foote. LC 78-57120. 1978. 8.95 (ISBN 0-394-40875-6). Random House.
Follow Me Ever: A Novel. Charles Edward Butler. LC 51-9404. 1951. Pantheon.
Follow Me, Love. Harriette Sheffer Abels. (YA) 1978. 6.95 (Avalon). Bouregy.
Follow the Circus. Raymond Hoy. LC 73-101312. (Illus.). 1969. 4.95. Pacific Pub. Group.
Follow the Drinking Gourd. Frances Gaither. 1972. Curtis Bks.
Follow the Drinking Gourd. Frances Ormond Jones Gaither. LC 40-5534. 1940. The Macmillan Company.
Follow the Drum. James Leasor. 1975. (pbk.) 1.50. Dell.
Follow the Drum. Andre Norton, pseud. 224p. 1981. pap. 2.25 (ISBN 0-449-24434-2, Crest). Fawcett.
Follow the Drum: A Novel. James Leasor. LC 72-7477. 1973. 7.95. Morrow.
Follow the Free Wind. LC 63-12969. (Ballantine western epic). 1974. (pbk.) 1.25 (ISBN 0-345-24013-8). Ballantine.
Follow the Furies. Eleanor Carroll Chilton. LC 85-4605. The Bobbs-Merrill Company.
Follow the Heart. Heather Sinclair. Bd. with For the Love of a Stranger. 1978. pap. 2.50 (ISBN 0-451-11594-5, AE1594, Sig). NAL.
Follow the Heart. Heather Sinclair. (Signet Book). 1976. (pbk.) 0.95. New American Library.
Follow the Leader. Clyde Brion Davis. LC 42-18360. 1942. Farrar & Rinehart, Inc.
Follow the Leader. Linda DuBreuil. 1979. pap. 1.95 o.s.i. (ISBN 0-505-51433-8). Tower Bks.
Follow the Leader. John Logue. LC 78-21028. 8.95 (ISBN 0-517-53645-5). Crown Publishers.
Follow the Little Pictures! Alan Graham. LC 20-13547. 1920. 1.75. Little, Brown, and Company.
Follow the New Grass. Cliff Farrell. LC 54-538219. 1954. Random House.
Follow the North Star. Harriette DeJarnette. 384p. (Orig.). 1982. pap. 3.25 (ISBN 0-8439-1073-9, Leisure Bks). Nordon Pubns.
Follow the River. James Alexander Thom. LC 80-66552. (Illus.). 1981. (6.95, 8.25 can) (ISBN 0-345-28480-1). Ballantine Books.
Follow the River. Frances Wright Turner. LC 57-9841. 1957. Christopher Pub. House.
Follow the Running Grass. Georgia McKinley. LC 76-82945. ("A Houghton Mifflin literary fellowship book."). 1969. 4.95. Houghton Mifflin.
Follow the Saint. Leslie Charteris. LC 75-46605. 1975. 9.95 (ISBN 0-89190-382-8). American Reprint Co.
Follow the Saint. Leslie Charteris. LC 39-113. 1938. Pub. for the Crime Club, Inc., by Doubleday, Doran & Co., Inc.
Follow the Saint. Leslie Charteris. LC 40-2687. 1939. The Sun Dial Press, Inc.
Follow the Setting Sun. Clement Jeanotte. 3.50 o.p. Vantage.
Follow the Seventh Man: By Robert Standish Pseud. Digby George Gerahty. LC 50-9485. 1950. Macmillan.
Follow the Shadows. Jocelyn Carew, pseud. 1979. pap. 2.75 (ISBN 0-380-44776-2, 44776). Avon.
Follow the Toff. John Creasey. LC 67-13218. 1967. 3.95. Walker.
Follow the Wind. Don Coldsmith. LC 82-45391. (DD Western Ser.). 192p. 1983. 11.95 (ISBN 0-385-17502-7). Doubleday.
Follow This Fair Corpse. Laurence Dwight Smith. LC 42-2914. 1941. Mystery House.
Follow Through to Love. Elsie W Strother. (Avalon Books). 1977. 4.95. Thomas Bouregy.
Follow Your Dream: By Jennifer Ames Pseud. Maysie Greig. LC 57-87310. 1957. Avalon Books.
Follow Your Heart. Emilie Baker Loring. LC 82-15398. 1982. 12.95 (ISBN 0-8161-3418-9). G.K. Hall.
Follow Your Heart. Carol Morris. LC 45-9781. 1945. Arcadia House, Inc.
Follow Your Heart. Albert Quandt. LC 38-5365. 1938. Gramercy Pub. Co.
Follow Your Heart. Virginia Randall. pap. 0.75 o.s.i. (01-402). Lancer.
Follow Your Heart. Natalie Shipman. LC 50-10728. 1950. Avalon Books.
Follow Your Star. Lucy Walker, pseud. 1976. pap. 1.75 (ISBN 0-345-29279-0). Ballantine.
Followed Man. Thomas Williams. LC 78-16629. 10.95 (ISBN 0-399-90025-X). R. Marek Publishers.
Follower. Henry Bromell. 1982. cancelled (ISBN 0-671-43271-0). S&S.
Follower. Patrick Quentin. LC 50-10987. (Inner sanctum mystery). 1950. Simon and Schuster.
Followers of the Sun: A Trilogy of the Santa Fe Trail: Wolf Song, In Those Days, The Blood of the Conquerors. Harvey Fergusson. LC 36-15256. 1936. A. A. Knopf.
Following Ann. Kenneth Robert Gordon Browne. LC 25-10303. Cassell and Company, Ltd.
Following Footsteps. Joseph Jefferson Farjeon. LC 30-8261. 1930. L. MacVeagh, The Dial Press.
Following Footsteps. Louise Gerard. LC 36-5927. The Macaulay Company.
Following Mad Anthony: Or, The Drums of Germantown. Thomas Chalmers Harbaugh. LC 12-9564. D. McKay.
Following of the Star: A Romance. Florence Louisa Charlesworth Barclay. LC 11-262575. 1911. G. P. Putnam's Sons.
Following the Grass. Harry Sinclair Drago. LC 24-19214. 1924. The Macaulay Company.
Following the Star: Or, The Story of the Wise Men. Henry Bushnell. LC 6-166802. 1894. The American Sunday School Union.
Folly. Martha Edith Rickert. LC 6-6490. 1906. The Baker & Taylor Co.
Folly. Clement Wood. LC 25-19108. Small, Maynard & Company.
Folly, a Novel. Maureen Brady. LC 82-17235. (Crossing Press Feminist Series). 15.95 (ISBN 0-89594-091-4) (ISBN 0-89594-090-6). Crossing Press.
Folly Corner. Alice Dudeney. LC 851. 1899. Henry Holt and Company.
Folly for the Wise. Carolyn Wells. 1904. Repr. 11.00 o.s.i. Finch Pr.
Folly Island. Warwick Deeping. LC 39-29837. 1939. A. A. Knopf.
Folly of Eustace, and Other Stories. Robert Smythe Hichens. LC 78-37550. (Short story index reprint series). 1972. (ISBN 0-8369-4109-8). Books for Libraries Press.
Folly of Eustace, and Other Stories. Robert Smythe Hichens. LC 7-4759. 1896. D. Appleton and Company.
Folly of Foley in Fort Lauderdale. W. McGill. 3.50 o.p. Carlton.
Folly of Henrietta Dale. Laurence Walter Meynell. LC 76-361582. 1976. 2.90 (ISBN 0-7091-5103-9). Hale.
Folly of Others. Neith Boyce. LC 73-122690. (Short story index reprint series). (Illus.). 1970. Books for Libraries Press.
Folly of Others. Neith Boyce. LC 4-10537. 1904. Fox, Duffield & Company.
Folly of Pen Harrington: A Novel. Julian Sturgis. LC 8-16861. (Half-title: Appletons' town and country library, no. 221). 1897. D. Appleton and Company.
Folly of Pride. Anne Maguire. 192p. (YA) 1974. 4.95 o.p. (Avalon). Bouregy.
Folly's Gold. Leroy Scott. LC 26-18623. 1926. Houghton Mifflin Company.
Folsom Flint: And Other Curious Tales. David Henry Keller. LC 77-9323. 1969. 5.00. Arkham House.
Foma Gordeyev. Maksim Gorkii. LC 74-10361. (Series: Library of Contemporary Soviet Novels.). 1974. (ISBN 0-8371-7670-0). Greenwood Press.
Foma Gordeyev. A Novel. Maksim Gorkii & Bernstein, Herman, 1876-1935, Tr. LC 28-12313. 1928. Bee De Publishing Co., Inc.
Foma Gordyeeff. Maksim Gorkii & Hapgood, Isabel Florence, 1850-1928, Tr. LC 1-19483. 1901. C. Scribner's Sons.
Fombombo. Thomas Sigismund Stribling. LC 23-12967. 1923. The Century Co.
Fond Adventures: Tales of the Youth of the World. Maurice Henry Hewlett. LC 71-152944. (Short story index reprint series). (Illus.). 1971. (ISBN 0-8369-3803-8). Books for Libraries Press.
Fond Adventures: Tales of the Youth of the World. Maurice Henry Hewlett. LC 5-10541. 1905. Harper & Brothers.
Fond Farewell to Dying. Syd Logsdon. (Orig.). 1981. pap. 2.50 (ISBN 0-671-41099-7, Timescape). PB.
Fonder Heart. Watkins Eppes Wright. LC 42-20569. 1942. Arcadia House, Inc.
Fondie. Edward Charles Booth. LC 16-158436. 1916. 1.40. D. Appleton and Company.
Fondle with Care. Jay Martin. (Orig.). 1968. pap. 0.60 o.p. (73-803). Lancer.
Fong and the Indians. Paul Theroux. LC 68-23030. 1968. 4.95. Houghton Mifflin.
Fong and the Indians: A Novel. Paul Theroux. LC 76-377389. 1976. 3.50 (ISBN 0-241-89379-8). Hamilton.
Fontamara. Ignazio Silone. LC 81-81590. 2.95 (ISBN 0-451-51525-0). New American Library.
Fontamara. Ignazio Silone & Wharf, Michael, Tr. LC 34-28402. 1934. H. Smith & R. Haas.
Fontamara. Translated from the Italian by Harvey Fergusson II. Foreword by Malcolm Cowley. Ignazio Silone. LC 60-7773. 1960. 4.00. Athenum Pblishers.
Fontana Book of Great Ghost Stories. Ed. by Robert Aickman. 1971. pap. 0.95 o.p. (95094). Beagle Bks.
Fontana Book of Great Horror Stories. Ed. by Christine Bernard. 1971. pap. 0.95 o.p. (95142). Beagle Bks.
Fontego's Folly. Paul Winterton. LC 50-7724. 1950. Harper.
Fontelroy: Or, The Web of Crime. Francis Alexander Durivage. (On cover: The select series, no. 26). 1889. Street & Smith.
Fontenay, the Swordsman: A Military Novel. Fortune Du Boisgobey & Williams, Henry Llewellyn, Jr., Tr. (On cover: Rialto series. no. 36). 1891. Rand, McNally & Company.
Fonthill: A Comedy. Aubrey Menen. LC 74-79660. 1974. 6.95 (ISBN 0-399-11368-1). Putnam.
Foo Dog. Stanton Forbes, pseud. LC 71-157636. 1971. 4.95. Published for the Crime Club by Doubleday.
Foo Dog. Tobias Wells. LC 71-157636. (Crime Club Ser). 1971. 1.95 o.p. (ISBN 0-385-00181-9). Doubleday.
Food of Death: Fifty-One Tales. Edward John Moreton Drax Plunkett Dunsany. LC 74-6394. (Newcastle Forgotten Fantasy classic F-102). 1974. (pbk.) 2.45 (ISBN 0-87877-102-6). Newcastle Pub. Co.
Food of Death: Fifty-One Tales. Edward John Moreton Drax Plunkett Dunsany. LC 80-19151. 1980. 9.95 (ISBN 0-87877-502-1). Borgo Press.
Food of Death: Fifty-One Tales. new ed. Lord Dunsany. (Forgotten Fantasy Library: Vol. 3). Orig. Title: Fifty-One Tales. 138p. 1974. pap. 3.95 (ISBN 0-87877-102-6, F-102). Newcastle Pub.

Food of Love. Anthony P Cavallo. LC 73-106071. 1970. 5.00. Dorrance.

Food of Love." And Other Selections. LC 1-29844. (Tales from Town topics. no. 38). 1900. Town Topics Publishing Company.

Food of the Gods. Herbert George Wells. LC 65-2726. Airmont Pub. Co.

Food of the Gods and How It Came to Earth. Herbert George Wells. LC 24-27741. 1924. C. Scribner's Sons.

Fool. Henry Christopher Bailey. LC 27-14207. E. P. Dutton & Company.

Fool: A Novel from the Play. Channing Pollock. LC 26-19264. Grosset & Dunlap.

Fool and His Money. George Barr McCutcheon. LC 13-19326. 1913. Dodd, Mead and Company.

Fool, Be Still. Fannie Hurst. LC 64-11609. 1964. Doubleday.

Fool Beloved. Jeffery Farnol. 1981. 18.95x (Pub. by Remploy England). State Mutual Bk.

Fool Divine. Edith J. Lyttleton. LC 17-25376. George H. Doran Company.

Fool Errant. Patricia Wentworth. LC 29-267879. 1929. J. B. Lippincott Company.

Fool Errant: Being the Memoirs of Francis-Antony Strelley, Esq., Citizen of Lucca: Ed. Maurice Henry Hewlett. LC 5-21566. 1905. The Macmillan Company.

Fool for Love. Robert Norcross. LC 39-11568. Phoenix Press.

Fool for Love. Wright Williams. 1971. pap. 0.60 o.p. (60-483). Manor Bks.

Fool in Christ: Emanuel Quint. Gerhart Johann Robert Hauptmann & Seltzer, Thomas, Tr. LC 26-100743. 1926. The Viking Press.

Fool in Christ, Emanuel Quint: A Novel. Gerhart Johann Robert Hauptmann. LC 76-28694. 1976. 18.00. H. Fertig.

Fool in Christ. Emanuel Quint: A Novel. Gerhart Johann Robert Hauptmann & Seltzer, Thomas, Tr. LC 11-35965. 1911. B. W. Huebsch.

Fool in the Forest. Agnes Russell Weekes & Weekes, Rose Kirkpatrick, 1874- Joint Author. LC 28-11394. 1928. Dodd, Mead & Company.

Fool Killer. Edward D. Coxe. 1885. American Publishers' Association.

Fool Killer. Helen Eustis. (Laurel-leaf library). 1974. (pbk.) 0.95. Dell.

Fool Killer. 1st Ed. Helen Eustis. LC 54-5167. 1954. Doubleday.

Fool of April. Justin Huntly McCarthy. LC 13-26564. 1914. John Lane Company.

Fool of God: A Historical Novel. Andrew Francis Klarmann. LC 12-16610. 1912. F. Pustet & Co.

Fool of God: A Novel Based Upon the Life of Alexander Campbell. 1st Ed. Louis Cochran. LC 58-5562. 1958. Duell, Sloan and Pearce.

Fool of Nature: A Novel. Julian Hawthorne. LC 7-3896. 1896. C. Scribner's Sons.

Fool of Quality. Henry Brooke. LC 78-60842. (Novel, 1720-1805: 6). 1979. per vol. 28.00 (ISBN 0-8240-3656-5). Garland Pub.

Fool of Quality. Henry Brooke & Baker, Ernest Albert, 1869- (Library of early novelists; ed. by E. A. Baker. v. 7). 1906. G. Routledge & Sons, Limited.

Fool of Quality: Or, The History of Henry, Earl of Moreland. Henry Brooke & Strickland, William Peter, 1809-1884. LC 6-19387. 1860. Derby & Jackson.

Fool of Quality: Or The History of Henry, Earl of Moreland, by Henry Brooke. Henry Brooke & Coutts, Francis Burdett Thomas Money, 1852- LC 11-5646. (Half-title: The new pocket library). 1909. John Lane.

Fool of the Family. Margaret Kennedy. 1972. pap. 0.95 o.p. (95237). Beagle Bks.

Fool of the Family: Continuing the Story of Sanger's Circus from "The Constant Numph". Margaret Kennedy. LC 30-29828. 1930. Doubleday, Doran & Company, Inc.

Fool of the Nineteenth Century: And Other Tales. Heinrich I. E. Johann Heinrich Daniel Zschokke & Strack, Louis, Tr. LC 8-37803. 1845. D. Appleton & Co.

Fool of Time. Beatrice Kean Stapleton Seymour. LC 41-9968. 1941. The Macmillan Company.

Fool of Venus: The Story of Peire Vidal. George William Cronyn. 1934. Covici-Friede.

Fool Repents. Florig, Beatrix. LC 55-2679. 1955. Comet Press Books.

Fool-Spy. John Richard Kuehl. LC 68-3939. 1967. For Now Press.

Fool the Toff. John Creasey. LC 66-22502. 1966. 3.95. Walker.

Fool There Was. Porter Emerson Browne. LC 9-30113. 1.50. The H. K. Fly Company.

Foolish Fire. Virginia Swain. LC 29-20976. J. H. Sears & Company, Inc.

Foolish Gentlewoman. Margery Sharp. LC 48-246966. 1948. Little, Brown.

Foolish Giant. Robert Westerby. LC 37-16643. Harcourt, Brace and Company.

Foolish Immortals. Paul Gallico. 1973. pap. 1.25 o.s.i. (78-732). Lancer.

Foolish Immortals. 1st Ed. Paul Gallico. LC 53-5963. 1953. Doubleday.

Foolish Lovers. St. John Greer Ervine. 1920. The Macmillan Company.

Foolish Virgin. Kathleen Thompson Norris. LC 28-21582. 1928. Doubleday, Doran and Company, Inc.

Foolish Virgin. Kathleen Thompson Norris. LC 32-33596. A. L. Burt Company.

Foolish Virgin. Margaret Penn. LC 80-41545. 1981. 8.95 (ISBN 0-521-28297-7). Cambridge University Press.

Foolish Virgin: A Romance of Today. Thomas Dixon. LC 15-18728. 1915. 1.35. D. Appleton and Company.

Foolish Wife. Watkins Eppes Wright. LC 45-1138. 1945. Phoenix Press.

Foolish Wind: A Novel. Francis Askham, pseud. LC 47-11464. 1947. Macmillan Co.

Foolishness of Lilian. Jessie Champion. LC 18-8169. 1918. John Lane.

Fools and Their Folly; Originally Titled "Then and Now.". William Somerset Maugham. LC 49-23214. (Avon, 188). 1949. Avon Pub. Co.

Fool's Apple. Sara Cardiff. LC 79-159336. 1971. 5.95 (ISBN 0-394-47267-5). Random House.

Fool's Apple. Sara Cardiff. LC 72-5502. 1972. 8.95 (ISBN 0-8161-6043-0). G. K. Hall.

Fool's Apprentice. Martin Munkacsi. LC 45-9988. 1945. The Readers Press.

Fools Die. Mario Puzo. 1979. pap. 3.50 (ISBN 0-451-08881-6, E8881, Sig). NAL.

Fools Die: A Novel. Mario Puzo. LC 78-9608. 10.95. Putnam.

Fools Die on Friday. Erle Stanley Gardner. LC 47-31433. 1947. W. Morrow.

Fool's Effort: An Echo of Civic Administrations. Charles T. Palmer. 1891. Barnard & Gunthrope.

Fool's Errand. Marc Norman. 1978. 8.95 o.p. (ISBN 0-03-019301-X). HR&W.

Fool's Errand. Jessie Louisa Moore Rickard. LC 22-6517. George H. Doran Company.

Fool's Errand. Albion Winegar Tourgee. LC 8-34328. 1879. Fords, Howard & Hulbert.

Fool's Errand. Albion Winegar Tourgee. LC 4-16473. 1902. Fords, Howard, & Hulbert.

Fool's Errand. Frederic Franklyn Van De Water. LC 45-5347. 1945. Duell, Sloan and Pearce.

Fool's Errand: A Novel. Marc Norman. LC 77-13608. 8.95 (ISBN 0-03-019301-X). Holt, Rinehart and Winston.

Fool's Errand: A Novel of the South During Reconstruction. Albion Winegar Tourgee. Ed. by George M. Fredrickson. pap. 5.95xi (ISBN 0-06-133074-4, TB3074, Torch). Har-Row.

Fool's Errand: A Novel of the South During Reconstruction. Introd. to the Torchbook Ed. by George M. Fredrickson. Albion Winegar Tourgee. LC 66-6634. (Amer. perspectives). 1966. pap., 2.75. Harper.

Fool's Errand: By One of the Fools; the Famous Romance of American History. New, Enl., and Illustrated Ed. To Which Is Added, by the Same Author, Part II. The Invisible Empire: a Concise Review of the Epoch on Which the Tale Is Based. With Many Thrilling Personal Narratives and Startling Facts of Life at the South Never Before Narrated for the General Reader... Albion Winegar Tourgee. LC 13-12927. 1880. Fords, Howard, & Hulbert.

Fool's Errand. Ed. by John Hope Franklin. Albion Winegar Tourgee. LC 61-13744. (John Harvard lib. JHL 5). 1965. pap., 2.25. Belknap Pr. of Harvard.

Fool's Goal. Bertha Muzzy Sinclair. LC 48-2933. 1947. Triangle Books.

Fool's Goal. Bertha Muzzy Sinclair. LC 30-1261. 1930. Little, Brown, and Company.

Fool's Gold. Therese Benson. LC 32-1080. 1932. Dodd, Mead & Company.

Fools' Gold. Margaret Greco. 1973. pap. 0.75 o.s.i. (01-391). Lancer.

Fool's Gold. William M. James, pseud. (Apache Ser.: No. 12). 1978. pap. 1.50 (ISBN 0-523-40355-0, Dist. by Independent News Co.). Pinnacle Bks.

Fool's Gold. Simon Marawille. LC 73-20981. 1974. 6.95 (ISBN 0-684-13776-3). Scribner.

Fool's Gold. Stanley Hart Page. LC 33-10969. 1933. A. A. Knopf.

Fool's Gold: A Study in Values. Annie Raymond Stillman. LC 2-23306. 1902. F. H. Revell Company.

Fool's Haven. Clifford Comer Cawley. LC 53-8713. 1953. House of Edinboro.

Fool's Haven. Mary Howard, pseud. LC 55-7940. Arcadia House.

Fool's Heart. Lise Roche. LC 71-94845. 1970. 4.95. Viking Press.

Fool's Hell. Rosita Torr Forbes. LC 24-10644. 1924. H. Holt and Company.

Fool's Hill. Leona Dalrymple. LC 22-192184. 1922. R. M. McBride & Company.

Fools in Mortar. Doris Oppenheim Leslie. LC 28-17644. The Century Co.

Fools in Town Are on Our Side. Ross Thomas. LC 78-118058. 1971. 6.95. Morrow.

Fool's Mate. Ritchie Perry. LC 81-47210. 10.95 (ISBN 0-394-51916-7). Pantheon Books.

Fool's Melody. Miss Tiverton Goes Out, Author of & Cape-Meadows, Michael, Joint Author. The Bobbs-Merrill Company.

Fool's Mercy. Henry Allen. LC 81-13366. 1982. 12.95 (ISBN 0-395-32039-9). Houghton Mifflin.

Fools of Nature: A Novel. Alice Brown. LC 11-7139. 1887. Ticknor and Company.

Fools of the Trade. Paul Petersen. (Smuggler#2). 1974. (pbk.). 0.95 (ISBN 0-671-77763-7). Pocket Books.

Fools of Time: A Novel. William Edmund Barrett. LC 63-11202. 1963. Doubleday.

Fools' Parade. Davis Grubb. LC 69-18518. 1969. 6.95. World Pub. Co.

Fools' Parade: Stories. John Womack Vandercook. LC 72-142279. (Short story index reprint series). (Illus.). 1970. (ISBN 0-8369-3763-5). Books for Libraries Press.

Fools' Parade: Stories by John W. Vandercook with Drawings by Mahlom Blaine. John Womack Vandercook & Blaine, Mahlon, Illus. LC 30-7098. 1930. Harper & Brothers.

Fool's Paradise. Ann Cooper. (Harlequin Romances Ser.). 192p. (Orig.). 1981. pap. 1.25 (Pub. by Harlequin). PB.

Fools Paradise. Christopher Leopold. LC 79-7605. 1980. 10.95 (ISBN 0-385-14389-3). Doubleday.

Fool's Paradise. Linda Vail. (Candlelight Ecstasy Ser.: No. 160). (Orig.). 1983. pap. 1.95 (ISBN 0-440-12852-8). Dell.

Fool's Paradise. Translation from the French by Cornelia Schaeffer. 1st American Ed. Bertrand Poirot-Delpech. LC 59-10616. 1959. Harper.

Fool's Pilgrimage: A Novel. Herbert J Scheibl. LC 29-28636. 1929. B. Herder Book Co.

Fool's Proof. Alberta Simpson Carter. (Queen-size gothic). 1975. (pbk.) 1.25. Popular Library.

Fools Rush in. Anne Green. LC 34-290418. E. P. Dutton & Co., Incl. C.

Fools Say". Nathalie Sarraute. LC 76-16696. 1977. 7.95 (ISBN 0-8076-0837-8). G. Braziller.

Fool's Year. Edward Herbert Cooper. (Half-title: Appletons' town and country library, no. 308). 1902. D. Appleton and Company.

Foolscap Rose. Joseph Hergesheimer. LC 34-34747. 1934. A. A. Knopf.

Foot in a Field of Men: Short Stories. Pat E. Taylor. 132p. pap. write for info. o.p. (ISBN 0-941720-12-8). Slough Pr TX.

Foot in the Grave. Morna Doris MacTaggart Brown. LC 72-79387. 1972. 4.95 (ISBN 0-385-02556-4). Published for Crime Club by Doubleday.

Foot in the Grave. E. X. Ferrars. 176p. 1981. pap. 1.95 (ISBN 0-553-14794-3). Bantam.

Foot in the Grave. E. X. Ferrars, pseud. LC 72-79387. 192p. 1972. 4.95 o.p. (ISBN 0-385-02556-4). Doubleday.

Foot of Clive. John Berger. 160p. 1981. 9.95 (ISBN 0-906495-09-1); pap. 3.95 (ISBN 0-904613-88-7). Writers & Readers.

Foot-Path Way. Henry Milner Rideout. LC 20-6491. 1920. Duffield and Company.

Football. Jon Swan. Bd. with Fireworks for a Hot Fourth; Short Sacred Right of Search & Destruction. 1969. pap. 1.95 o.p. (E491, Ever). Grove.

Football Dreams. David Guy. LC 80-50551. 10.95 (ISBN 0-87223-624-2). Seaview Books.

Football Fever. Curtis Kent Bishop. LC 52-11191. 1952. Steck Co.

Football Gravy Train. Frank O'Rourke. LC 51-13353. (Barnes sports novel). 1951. A.S. Barnes.

Football Stories. Ed. by Josh Furman. LC 74-21888. (Lantern press book) (ISBN 0-671-80677-7). Pocket Books.

Footbridge to Death. Kathleen Moore Knight. LC 47-630. 1947. Pub. for the Crime Club by Doubleday & Company, Inc.

Footbridges & Abysses. Aloyzas Baronas. 1965. 5.00 o.p. (ISBN 0-87141-014-1). Manyland.

Footbridges and Abysses. Introd. by Charles Angoff. Tr. from Lithuanian by J. Zemkalnis. Aloyzas Baronas. LC 65-28126. 1966. 5.00. Manyland.

Foothold: By Grigory Baklanov. Tr. from Russian by R. Ainsztein. Grigorii IAkovlevich Baklanov. LC 64-254655. 1965. bds., 3.95. Dufour.

Foothold of Earth. Richard Matthews Hallet. LC 44-941238. 1944. Doubleday, Doran and Company, Inc.

Footlight Fever. Berta Ruck. LC 42-23437. 1942. Dodd, Mead & Company.

Footlights. Rita Weiman. LC 23-7015. 1923. Dodd, Mead and Company.

Footlights and Fools: Novelized. Wilton Chalmers. LC 29-30409. Efrus & Bennett, Inc.

Footlights on a Hero. Sydney Thompson. LC 39-23291. 1939. Thomas Y. Crowell Company.

Footloose. Irving Stettner. (Illus.). 160p. (Orig.). 1981. pap. 5.95 (ISBN 0-918154-12-X). Stroker.

Footloose and Free. Stephen Chalmers. LC 12-239193. 1912. 1.25. Outing Publishing Company.

Footloose McGarnigal. Harvey Fergusson. 1930. A. A. Knopf.

Footloose: Sequel to "The Flapper Wife". Beatrice Burton Morgan. LC 26-2811. Grosset & Dunlap.

Footman in Powder. Helen Ashton. LC 54-8498. 1954. Dodd, Mead.

Footnote to Life. Eleanor Arnett Nash. LC 44-7587. 1944. D. Appleton-Century Company, Incorporated.

Footnote to Murder. L. A. Taylor. 192p. 1983. 12.95 (ISBN 0-8027-5486-4). Walker & Co.

Footnote to Youth: Tales of the Philippines and Others. Jose Garcia Villa. LC 33-28937. 1933. C. Scribner's Sons.

Footpath Murder. Mary Bringle. LC 75-6153. 1975. 5.95 (ISBN 0-385-11043-X). Published for the Crime Club by Doubleday.

Footprint, and Other Stories. Gouverneur Morris. LC 70-142270. (Short story index reprint series). 1970. Books for Libraries Press.

Footprint: And Other Stories. Gouverneur Morris. LC 8-6985. 1908. C. Scribner's Sons.

Footprint of Cinderella. Philip Wylie. LC 31-19095. Farrar & Rinehart, Incorporated.

Footprints. Kay Cleaver Strahan. LC 29-261709. 1929. Pub. for the Crime Club, Inc., by Doubleday, Doran & Company, Inc.

Footprints Beneath the Snow: A Novel. Henry Bordeaux & Houghton, Mary Seymour, Tr. LC 13-19945. 1913. Duffield & Company.

Footprints: Chilling Drama of Two Bigfoot. Gordon Jones. 1977. 7.00 o.p. (ISBN 0-682-48829-1). Exposition.

Footprints in a Darkened Forest. Fulton J. Sheen. 1967. 4.95 o.p. Hawthorn.

Footprints in the Sands of Time. Mary Bibb. LC 82-90338. (Illus.). 215p. (Orig.). pap. 8.95 (ISBN 0-9608778-0-0). M Bibb.

Footprints in the Sands of Time. Gladys Z. Petersen. 1968. 3.75 o.p. Vantage.

Footprints of Young Explorers. Ed. by Todd Tarbox. LC 77-92359. (Illus.). 1978. 6.95 (ISBN 0-89297-015-4). Todd Tarbox.

Footprints on the Ceiling. Clayton Rawson. LC 39-13883. 1939. G. P. Putnam's Sons.

Footprints on the Ceiling. Clayton Rawson. LC 79-10655. (Gregg Press Mystery Fiction Series). 1979. 9.95 (ISBN 0-8398-2543-9). Gregg Press.

Footsteps. Theodora DuBois. 1976. (pbk.) 1.25. Leisure Books.

Footsteps. Theodora McCormick Du Bois. LC 47-4218. 1947. Pub. for the Crime Club by Doubleday.

Footsteps. Robert Irvine. 320p. (Orig.). 1982. pap. 2.95 (ISBN 0-523-41609-1). Pinnacle Bks.

Footsteps. Hamilton Maule. LC 61-12138. 1961. Random House.

Footsteps. Hamilton Maule. 1973. Manor Bks.

Footsteps. Dorothy Percival. LC 18-220336. 1918. 1.40. John Lane.

Footsteps Behind Her. Mitchell A Wilson. LC 42-2918. 1941. Simon and Schuster.

Footsteps Behind Her: A Mystery Novel. Mitchell A Wilson. LC 43-13675. (Handi-book mysteries. 17). 1943. Quinn Publishing Company, Inc.

Footsteps in the Air. Doris Siegel. LC 40-4895. 1940. Simon and Schuster.

Footsteps in the Dark. Georgette Heyer. 1976. Repr. of 1932 ed. lib. bdg. 16.95x (ISBN 0-89966-122-X). Buccaneer Bks.

Footsteps in the Dark. Lyon Mearson. LC 27-18258. The Macaulay Company.

Footsteps in the Dark: A Novel of Mystery. Georgette Heyer. LC 32-10448. 1932. Longmans, Green and Co.

Footsteps in the Fog. Pamela Bennetts. LC 79-26748. 8.95 (ISBN 0-312-29782-3). St. Martin's Press.

Footsteps in the Fog. Margaret James. 182p. 1980. 8.95 o.p. (ISBN 0-312-29782-3). St Martin.

Footsteps in the Night. Cicely Fraser-Simson. LC 27-13127. 1927. E. P. Dutton & Company.

Footsteps in the Rain. Frank H Lovegrove. LC 73-82565. 1973. 5.95 (ISBN 0-8059-1888-4). Dorrance.

Footsteps of a Throne: Being the Story of an Idler, and of His Work; and of What He Did in Moscow in the House of Exile. Max Pemberton. LC 1-29956. 1900. D. Appleton and Company.

Footsteps on Old Floors: True Tales of Mystery, by Thomas H. Raddall. 1st Ed. Thomas Head Raddall. LC 68-117855. 1968. 4.95. Doubleday.

Footsteps on the Stair. Myron Brinig. LC 50-8266. 1950. Rinehart.

Footsteps on the Stairs. Jean Potts. LC 66-20541. 1966. Scribner.

Footsteps That Follow. Mona Farnsworth. 1976. pap. 1.25 (ISBN 0-532-12380-8). Woodhill.

Footsteps That Stopped. Archibald E. Fielding. LC 26-18503. 1926. A. A. Knopf.

Footsteps to Freedom. Levi O Keidel. LC 68-59628. 1969. 3.95. Moody Press.

Footsteps to Romance. William Arthur Neubauer. LC 66-4336. 1966. Arcadia House.

Foozles. Pat Fortunato. 1978. pap. 1.25 (ISBN 0-440-92740-4). Dell.

For a Dream Cometh. Lily Barr. LC 77-99161. 1979. 12.95 (ISBN 0-87949-083-7). Ashley Bks.

For a Dream Cometh. Inez Marschal. LC 51-21214. 1951. Vantage Press.

For a Free Conscience. Lydia Cope Wood. LC 5-12704. 1905. F. H. Revell Company.

For a Living. Frances Phillips. 1981. pap. 4.50 (ISBN 0-914610-26-0). Hanging Loose.

For a Maiden Brave. Chauncey Crafts Hotchkiss. LC 2-28811. 1902. D. Appleton & Company.

For a Mess of Pottage. Sidney Lyon. LC 7-19408. 1890. J. B. Lippincott Company.

For a New Era of Hate. James Boyer May. LC 47-5408. 1947. A. Swallow.

For a Rainy Day. J. B. Burns. LC 79-54314. (Illus., Orig.). 1979. pap. 6.00 (ISBN 0-9602998-0-7). J B Burns.

For a Song... Konrad Bercovici. LC 31-5683. Dodd, Mead & Company.

For a Woman: A Novel. Nora Perry. LC 43-34446. 1886. Ticknor.

For All But One. Stella March. 1981. 18.95x (Pub. by Remploy England). State Mutual Bk.

For All Men Born: A Novel. Margaret Mackprang Mackay. LC 43-603. 1943. The John Day Company.

For All of Our Lives. Katherine Ursula Parrott. LC 38-23206. 1938. Dodd, Mead & Company.

For All That I Found There. Caroline Blackwood. LC 73-92762. 144p. 1974. 6.95 (ISBN 0-8076-0742-8). Braziller.

For All the Wrong Reasons. John Neufeld. 1980. 7.95 (ISBN 0-453-00361-3, AE2355, Sig); pap. 2.25 (ISBN 0-451-12355-7). NAL.

For All the Wrong Reasons: A Novel. John Neufeld. LC 73-75999. 1973. 5.95. New American Library.

For All We Know. Gladys Bronwyn Stern. LC 56-7336. 1956. Macmillan.

For All Your Life. Emilie Baker Loring. LC 77-6770. 1977. 9.95 (ISBN 0-89340-084-X). J. Curley.

For All Your Life. Emilie Baker Loring. LC 80-25175. 1981. 14.10 (ISBN 0-88411-355-8). Aeonian Press.

For All Your Life. 1st Ed. Emilie Baker Loring. LC 52-10947. 1952. Little, Brown.

For Always Only. Ellen Prescott Davidson. LC 73-6753. 1973. 5.95 (ISBN 0-393-08374-8). Norton.

For Andromeda. Fred Hoyle & John Elliot. 1975. (pbk.) 1.25 (ISBN 0-380-00299-X). Avon.

For Andromeda; a Novel of Tomorrow by Fred Hoyle and John Elliot. Fred Hoyle & John Elliot. LC 62-13768. 1962. Harper.

For Another's Sin: Or, A Struggle for Love, a Story of Real Life. Charlotte Mary Brame. (On cover: Lovell's library. v. 14 no. 727). J. W. Lovell Company.

For Another's Sin: Or, A Struggle for Love. Charlotte Mary Brame. LC 44-12244. (On cover: Lovell's library, v. 14, no. 727). J. W. Lovell Company.

For Another's Sin: Or, A Struggle for Love. Charlotte Mary Brame. LC 44-378313. (On cover: Seaside library. Pocket ed. No. 745). G. Munro.

For Another's Sin: Or, A Struggle for Love. Charlotte Mary Brame. LC 4365. (Bertha M. Clay library, no. 11). 1900. Street & Smith.

For Anything. Damon Francis Knight. LC 70-141817. 1970. 4.95 (ISBN 0-8027-5533-X). Walker.

For Better and for Worse. Myrna Blyth. LC 78-16874. 8.95 (ISBN 0-399-12166-8). Putnam.

For Better and for Worse. Myrna Blyth. 1980. Fawcett Crest Books.

For Better, for Worse. Wyatt Blassingame. LC 51-2764. 1951. Crowell.

For Better for Worse. Lewis M. Boland. LC 6-14181. 1879. E. E. Rettig.

For Better, for Worse. Ed. by Esther B. Kling. Kling, Samuel G., 1910- Joint Comp. LC 47-353037. 1947. H. Holt and Company.

For Better, for Worse. William Babington Maxwell. LC 20-8240. 1920. Dodd, Mead and Company.

For Better, for Worse: A Novel. Martin Jerome Scott. LC 23-15030. 1923. Benziger Brothers.

For Cash Only. A Novel. James Payne. (Harper's Franklin square library, no. 243). 1882. Harper & Brothers.

For Chloe with Love. Jacket and Decorations by Roger Duvoisin. Harry Harrison Kroll. LC 59-131624. 1959. Lothrop, Lee Shepard Co.

For Christ and the Church. Charles Monroe Sheldon. LC 99-3209. 1899. Fleming H. Revell Company.

For Daily Bread, and Other Stories. Henryk Sienkiewicz & Young, Iza, Tr. LC 98-1668. 1898. H. Altemus.

For Dying You Always Have Time. Sally M Singer. LC 79-135259. (Red mask mystery). 1970. 4.95. Putnam.

For Each a Woman. Duane R. Hopkins. 4.95 o.p. Vantage.

For Each and for All: Or, Letitia and Maria. Harriet Martineau. (On cover: Lovell's library, v. 7, no. 363). 1884. J. W. Lovell Company.

For Each Other. A Novel ... 1878. G. W. Carleton & Co., Etc., Etc.

For Ever Wilt Thou Love. Ludwig Lewisohn. LC 49-54706. (N. A. L. Signet books, 749). 1949. New American Library.

For Ever Wilt Thou Love. Ludwig Lewisohn. LC 39-55902. 1939. The Dial Press.

For Every Favour. 1st American Ed. Ruby Ferguson. 1957. Little, Brown.

For Every Hero: A Novel of the WAVES in World War II. 1st Ed. Sylvia Wilcox. LC 61-174461. 1961. D. McKay Co.

For Every Red Sea. Crawford, Matsu. LC 64-8851. bds., 2.95. Zondervan.

For Fair Virginia. Arthur Hall. LC 7-536. (On cover: Drama series, no. 25). Street & Smith.

For Faith and Freedom. Walter Besant. (On cover: Seaside library. Pocket ed., no. 1151). 1889. G. Munro.

For Faith and Freedom: A Novel. Walter Besant. LC 6-12408. (On cover: Harper's Franklin square library, no. 634). 1888. Harper & Brothers.

For Faith and Freedom: Novel. Walter Besant. LC 4-16296. 1889. Harper & Brothers.

For Frank O'Hara's Birthday. Alice Notley. 1976. pap. 3.00 (Pub. by St Edns). SBD.

For Freedom's Cause: Or, On to Saratoga. Thomas Chalmers Harbaugh. LC 10-8940. (Boys of liberty library). D. McKay.

For Freedom's Sake. Arthur Henry Paterson. LC 7-34083. 1896. J. B. Lippincott Company.

For Friends to Share. Gayle Lawrence. (Illus.). 1978. boxed 4.95 (ISBN 0-8378-1739-0). Gibson.

For Ginger's Sake. Ethel Powelson Hueston. LC 30-231978. The Bobbs-Merrill Company.

For Godmother & Country. R. T. Larkin, pseud. (Orig.). 1972. pap. 1.25 o.s.i. (78-709). Lancer.

For Goodness' Sake. pseud. ed. Elsie Peterson. LC 51-8666. 1951. Vantage Press.

For Goodness' Sake. Carolyn Wells. J. B. Lippincott Company.

For Granted. Cid Corman, pseud. 1967. pap. 4.00 (Pub. by Elizabeth Pr). SBD.

For Her Daily Bread. Lillian E. Sommers. LC 8-10215. (On cover: Globe library, no. 34). 1887. Rand, McNally & Company.

For Her Dear Sake. Mary Cecil Hay. (Seaside library, v. 35, no. 724). 1880. G. Munro.

For Her Dear Sake. A Novel. Mary Cecil Hay. (Franklin square library, no. 116). 1880. Harper & Brothers.

For Her Life: A Story of St. Petersburg. Richard Henry Savage. LC 8-20028. (On cover: Rialto series, no. 79). 1897. Rand, McNally & Company.

For Her No Name. Alice Warfield Hayes Robertson. LC 48-17430. 1947. Lincoln.

For Her to Decide. Richard Posner. (Lucas Tanner Ser.: No. 3). (Orig.). 1976. pap. 1.25 o.p. (ISBN 0-515-04042-8). BJ Pub Group.

For Her to See. Joseph Shearing. LC 47-5198. 1947. Hutchinson.

For Her to See. Joseph Shearing. LC 47-7246. 1947. Harper.

For Here Is My Fortune. Amos R Harlin. LC 46-7191. 1946. Whittlesey House, McGraw-Hill Book Company, Inc.

For Him: Or, A Promise Given and a Promise Kept. Frankie B. Sherman. LC 8-6416. 1887. Brentano Bros.

For Himself Alone. A Tale of Reversed Identities. Thomas Wilkinson Speight. (On cover: The seaside library. Pocket ed. no. 150). 1884. G. Munro.

For Hire. Irwin R Franklyn. LC 32-4109. 1932. W. Godwin, Inc.

For His Brother's Sake. Telemachus Thomas Timayenis. (On cover: Fireside series, no. 42). J. S. Ogilvie.

For His Sake. A Novel. Annie French Hector. (On cover: Lippincott's series of select novels, no. 136). 1892. J. B. Lippincott Company.

For Honor and Life. William MacLeod Raine. LC 33-24191. 1933. Houghton Mifflin Company.

For Honor and Life: A Novel. William Westall. LC 8-36229. 1894. Harper & Brothers.

For Honor's Sake. B. Sim Cunningham. LC 6-31730. 1879. J. B. Lippincott & Co.

For I Am! The Reading. Aroen. (For I Am Ser.). 1980. 8.50 (ISBN 0-682-49512-3). Exposition.

For Immediate Release. Rion Bercovici. LC 37-18436. Sheridan House.

For Infamous Conduct. Derek Lambert. LC 73-104688. 1970. 6.95. Coward-McCann.

For Jacinta. Harold Bindloss. 1908. F. A. Stokes Company.

For Kicks. Dick Francis. LC 65-14668. 1975. (pbk.) 1.50 (ISBN 0-671-80109-0). Pocket Books.

For King and Company. Ellis K Meacham. LC 76-27578. (Illus.). 7.95. Little, Brown.

For Kings Only. Curt Siedmak. LC 61-10313. 1961. Crown Publishers.

For Lack of Gold. by charles gibbon... ed. Charles Gibbon. (Seaside library, v. 38, no. 776). 1880. G. Munro.

For Land's Sake. Georgia L Nichols. LC 54-41714. 1954. New Voices Pub. Co.

For Life: A Novel by Nathalie Colby. Nathalie Sedgwick Colby. LC 35-16786. 1935. W. Morrow & Co.

For Life and Love. Alison. (On cover: Seaside library. Pocket ed., no. 276). G. Munro.

For Life and Love: A Story of the Rio Grande... Richard Henry Savage. LC 12-12212. F. T. Neely.

For Lilias. A Novel. Rosa Nouchette Carey. (On cover: Seaside library. Pocket ed. no. 608). G. Munro.

For Lilias: A Novel. Rosa Nouchette Carey. LC 16-191398. 1915. A. L. Burt Company.

For Lizzie & Harriet. Robert Lowell. 48p. 1973. 6.95 (ISBN 0-374-15729-4); pap. 2.95 (ISBN 0-374-51291-4). FS&G.

For Love Alone. James Harris. 3.50 o.p. Carlton.

For Love Alone. Christina Stead. LC 66-28952. 1966. 5.75. Augus & Robertson.

For Love Alone. Christina Stead. LC 44-8969. 1944. Harcourt, Brace and Company.

For Love Alone. Christina Stead. LC 78-23847. (Harvest/HBJ book). 1979. 5.95 (ISBN 0-15-632535-7). Harcourt Brace Jovanovich.

For Love and Gold. Evan John David. LC 34-368413. The Macaulay Company.

For Love and Honor. Frank Barrett. LC 6-9064. United States Book Company.

For Love and Honor. Antonia Van-Loon. LC 77-18384. 10.00 (ISBN 0-312-29795-5). St. Martin's Press.

For Love and Life. Margaret Oliphant Wilson Oliphant. (Seaside library, v. 25, no. 497). 1879. G. Munro.

For Love & Valcour. Dorothy Daniels. 480p. 1983. pap. 3.50 (ISBN 0-446-30256-2). Warner Bks.

For Love of a Bedouin Maid. Rosa Nouchette Carey. LC 42-210831. Rand, McNally & Company.

For Love of a Doctor. Elizabeth Seifert. LC 76-18866. 1976. 8.95 (ISBN 0-89340-043-2). J. Curley & Associates.

For Love of a Doctor. Elizabeth Seifert. LC 73-88068. 1969. 4.95. Dodd, Mead.

For Love of a Painted Lady. Heller Toren. 1976. (pbk.) 1.75 (ISBN 0-671-80405-7). Pocket Books.

For Love of a Pirate. Anthony Esler. LC 78-17287. 1978. 9.95 (ISBN 0-688-03375-X). Morrow.

For Love of a Sinner: A Tale with Villain for Hero. Robert Gordon Anderson. LC 24-11236. 1924. Minton, Balch & Company.

For Love of a Sinner: Being a Tale of the Loves and Sorrows of Francois Villon. Robert Gordon Anderson. 2.00. The Century Co.

For Love of a Woman. James Francis Dwyer. LC 14-7075. 1914. Minden-Burkert Printing Co.

For Love of Anne. Claude De Leusse. 1976. pap. 1.25 (ISBN 0-532-12332-8). Woodhill.

For Love of Anne. Claude De Leusse. 192p. 1975. pap. 1.25 o.p. (532-12332-125). Manor Bks.

For Love of Audrey Rose. Frank De Felitta. 464p. (Orig.). 1982. pap. 3.95 (ISBN 0-446-30206-6). Warner Bks.

For Love of Country: A Story of Land and Sea in the Days of the Revolution. Cyrus Townsend Brady. LC 48-35769. 1911. C. Scribner's Sons.

For Love of Country. A Story of Land and Sea in the Days of the Revolution. Cyrus Townsend Brady. LC 6-16080. 1898. C. Scribner's Sons.

For Love of Crannagh Castle. Brian Talbot Cleeve. LC 75-13687. 1975. 8.95 (ISBN 0-525-10767-3). Dutton.

For Love of Gold. 5th ed. Marie Walsh. (On cover: Mascot library, no. 2). 1894. The Mascot Publishing Co.

For Love of Imabelle. Chester B. Himes. 192p. 1973. Repr. of 1965 ed. 7.95x (ISBN 0-911860-33-9). Chatham Bkseller.

For Love of Imabelle. Chester B. Himes. 1974. (pbk.) 1.25. New American Library.

For Love of Mother-Not. Alan Dean Foster. 256p. (Orig.). 1983. pap. 2.95 (ISBN 0-345-30511-6, Del Rey). Ballantine.

For Love of Two Men. Maude Johnson. (Dear Miss Lonelyhearts,#3). 1974. (pbk.) 0.95 (ISBN 0-523-00324-2). Pinnacle Books.

For Love or Crown: A Romance. Arthur Williams Marchmont. LC 1-25450. Frederick, A. Stokes Company.

For Love or Money. Harriet Works Corley. LC 32-28826. Grosset & Dunlap.

For Love or Money. Roy Doliner. LC 74-8835. 1974. 6.95 (ISBN 0-671-21818-2). Simon and Schuster.

For Love or Money. Vivian Donald. 1974. (pbk.) 0.75. New American Library.

For Love or Money: The 1957 Anthology of the Mystery Writers of America. 1st Ed. Ed. by Dorothy Gardiner. LC 57-12465. 1957. Published for the Crime Club by Doubleday.

For Love or Money. 1st Ed. Tim Jeal. LC 67-144639. 1967. bds., 4.50. McGraw.

For Love's Sake Only: A Novel. Margaret Gorman Nichols. LC 43-126886. 1943. Macrae-Smith-Company.

For Love's Sake Only: By Elizabeth Hoy Pseud. Nina Conarain. LC 51-1596. 1951. Arcadia House.

For Maimie's Sake. A Tale of Love and Dynamite. Grant Allen. LC 6-73. (On cover: Seaside library. Pocket ed. no. 712)). 1886. G. Munro.

For Maimie's Sake: A Tale of Love and Dynamite. Grant Allen. LC 2589. (On cover: Arrow library, no. 115)). 1900. Street & Smith.

For Maryland's Honor: A Story of the War for Southern Independence. Lloyd Tilghman Everett. LC 22-3016. The Christopher Publishing House.

For Maurice: Five Unlikely Stories. Violet Paget. LC 76-1462. (Supernatural and Occult Fiction). 1976. (ISBN 0-405-08423-4). Arno Press.

For Me Alone (Pour Moi Seule) A Novel by Andre Corthis Pseud.; Tr. from the French by Frederick Taber Cooper. Audree Lecuyer & Cooper, Frederic Taber, 1864- Tr. Frederick A. Stokes Company.

For Me and My Friends. David Rottenberg. LC 73-171034. (Zebra books, Z-1083-Z). 1971. 1.25. Grove Press.

For Me to Live. Alice M Ardagh. LC 96-16006. The Bible Institute Colportage Ass'n.

For Men Only. Beth Brown. LC 30-323368. 1930. C. Kendall.

For Men Only: A Collection of Short Stories. James Mallahan Cain. LC 44-202121. 1944. The World Publishing Company.

For My Country: "Pour la Patrie": an 1895 Religious and Separatist Vision of Quebec in the Mid-Twentieth Century. Jules Paul Tardivel. LC 75-6862. (Social History of Canada: 27). 1975. 15.00. (ISBN 0-8020-2183-2) (ISBN 0-8020-6267-9). University of Toronto Press.

For My Great Folly. Thomas B Costain. 1974. (pbk.) 1.75 (ISBN 0-380-00174-8). Avon.

For My Great Folly: A Novel. Thomas Bertram Costain. LC 42-178017. 1942. G. P. Putnam's Sons.

For My Great Folly: A Novel. Thomas Bertram Costain. LC 47-6111. 1947. Sun Dial Press.

For My Own Sake. (Um Meinetwillen.) A Romance from the German. Marie Bernhard. Tr. by Smith, Mary Stuart (Harrison) LC 1-17909. (On cover: The author's library. no 3). 1893. The International News Company.

For Nights Like This One: Stories of Loving Women. Becky Birtha. 128p. (Orig.). 1983. pap. 4.75 (ISBN 0-9603628-4-3). Frog in Well.

For Old Crime's Sake. Delano L. Ames. LC 82-47790. 256p. 1983. pap. 2.84i (ISBN 0-06-080629-X, P 629, PL). Har-Row.

For Old Crime's Sake. 1st Ed. Delano L Ames. LC 59-6439. (Main line mysteries). 1959. Lippincott.

For Old Times' Sake: A Story. Charles Albert Macfarlane. 1905. The Macfarlane Company.

For Once in My Life. Shebe Stuart & Trish Douglas. 1974. 5.95 (ISBN 0-533-00925-1). Vantage.

For One and the World. Matilda Barbara Bertram Edwards. LC 6-36587. (On cover: Lovell's international ser. no. 115). J. W. Lovell Company.

For One Moment. Christmas Carol Miller Kauffman. 1964. pap. 4.95 (ISBN 0-8024-3808-3). Moody.

For One Moment: A Biographical Story. Christmas Carol Miller Kauffman. LC 60-13935. 1960. Herald Press.

For One Sweet Grape. Kate O'Brien. LC 46-4402. 1946. Doubleday & Company, Inc.

For Our Vines Have Tender Grapes. George Victor Martin. LC 40-315291. W. Funk, Inc.

For Peace Comes Dropping Slow. Donoghue, Gerald T. LC 48-28255. 1948. Naylor Co.

For Pete's Sake. Pete Finley. (Illus.). 114p. (Orig.). 1981. pap. 4.50 (ISBN 0-941718-00-X). Master Writers.

For Pete's Sake. M. Vincent Guarino & James F Collier. LC 72-83341. (Word paperback, 90031). 1972. 1.25. Word Books.

For Pity's Sake: A Story for the Times, Being Reminiscences of a Guest at a Country Inn. Sarah Nelson Carter. LC 6-23111. De Wolfe, Fiske & Company.

For Plain Women Only. Julia Constance Fletcher. (Half-title: The Mayfair set, iv). 1896. The Merriam Co.; Etc., Etc.

For Promised Joy. Trudy Hamilton. LC 47-24597. 1947. Phoenix Press.

For Rent--One Pedestal. Marjorie Shuler. LC 17-781127. 1917. National Woman Suffrage Publishing Co., Inc.

TITLE INDEX FORBIDDEN PATH.

For Richer, for Poorer. Harold Hunter Armstrong. LC 22-17448. 1922. A. A. Knopf.
For Richer, for Poorer. Edward Stewart. LC 81-43112. 1981. 14.95 (ISBN 0-385-11492-3). Doubleday.
For Richer, for Poorer, till Death. Patricia McGerr. LC 78-87998. 1974. (pbk.) 0.95. Manor Books.
For Sale. Compton Mackenzie. LC 31-28031. 1931. Doubleday, Doran & Company, Inc.
For Sale--Murder. William Levine. LC 32-9885. 1932. The Mystery League, Inc.
For Special Services. John E Gardner. LC 82-1485. 9.95 (ISBN 0-698-11163-X). Coward, McCann & Geoghegan.
For Special Services. large print ed. John E Gardner. LC 82-18524. 1982. 13.95 (ISBN 0-8161-3477-4). G.K. Hall.
For Students & Others Fed Up. Alberta Z. Brown. LC 79-105054. 1970. 3.95 o.p. (ISBN 0-8272-1000-0). Bethany Pr.
For Sully's Sake. Harris Jameson. 1970. 3.75 o.p. Carlton.
For the Ahkoond. Ambrose Bierce. 1.00 o.p. Necronomicon.
For the Allinson Honor. Harold Bindloss. LC 13-203403. Frederick A. Stokes Company.
For the Blue and Gold: A Tale of Life at the University of California. Joy Lichtenstein. 1901. A. M. Robertson.
For the Cause. Stanley John Weyman. LC 76-103532. (Short story index reprint series). 1969. Books for Libraries Press.
For the Cause. Stanley John Weyman. LC 8-36220. C. H. Sergel Company.
For the Defence. Benjamin Leopold Farjeon & Gould, Sabine Baring- LC 6-38639. (On cover: Lovell's international series. 16). 1891. J. W. Lovell Company.
For the Defense, Dr. Thorndyke. Richard Austin Freeman. LC 34-37084. 1934. Dodd, Mead & Company.
For the Delight of Antonio. Beatrice Curtis Brown, pseud. LC 32-19272. 1932. Houghton Mifflin Company.
For the Flag. Jules Verne. 3.95. Assoc Bk.
For the Flag. A Tale of Western Adventure. Win C Livingstone. (On cover: New York 10 cent library, no. 11). 1896. Katahdin Publishing Company.
For the Freedom of the Sea: A Romance of the War of 1812. Cyrus Townsend Brady. LC 234. 1899. C. Scribner's Sons.
For the French Lilies: A.D. 1511-1512. Isabel Nixon Whiteley. 1899. B. Herder.
For the Glory of God. Helen Norris. 1958. Macmillan.
For the Glory of God: A Love Story. Josephine Lurie Jessup. LC 58-14976. 1958. Whitland Press.
For the Glory of Venice. Denton Whitson. LC 74-99298. 1970. 6.95 (ISBN 0-87716-027-9). Moore Pub. Co.
For the Going. Joel Bernstein. LC 74-24492. (Illus.). 1974. 3.95 o.s.i. (ISBN 0-915298-00-7). Sagarin Pr.
For the Good of the Party: Or, The Fortunes of "the Blackville Star,". Herman Hine Brinsmade. LC 17-101182. 1916. Sherman, French & Company.
For the Good of the Race: And Other Stories. Bert Levy. LC 21-21949. Ad Press.
For the Grape Season. Harry Barba. LC 60-6843. 1960. Macmillan.
For the Hangman. Dorothy Stockbridge Tillet. LC 35-260. 1934. Pub. for the Crime Club, Inc., by Doubleday, Doran & Company, Inc.
For the Honor of a Child. Beulah Downey Hanks. LC 99-371. 1899. Continental Publishing Co.
For the King. Alan Douglas. LC 26-10561. Macrae Smith Company.
For the Love of a Stranger. Heather Sinclair. (Signet Book). 1976. (pbk.) 1.25. New American Library.
For the Love of a Stranger see Follow the Heart.
For the Love of Dying. George Sidney. LC 70-79097. 1969. 4.95. Morrow.
For the Love of Kate: Further Adventures of Henri Rochard Pseud. Roger Henri Charlier. LC 63-23559. 1963. Exposition Press.
For the Love of Mike. Thomas Connolly, Jr. 4.00 o.p. Carlton.
For the Love of Tonita: & Other Tales of the Mesas. Charles Fleming Embree. LC 35-334084. 1897. H.S. Stone & Co.
For the Major: A Novelette. Constance Fenimore Woolson. LC 70-126703. (Illus.). 1970. AMS Press.
For the Major: A Novelette. Constance Fenimore Woolson. LC 9-5210. Harper & Brothers.
For the Major: A Novelette. Constance Fenimore Woolson. LC 35-28556. 1883. Harper & Brothers.
For the Major: And Selected Short Stories. Ed. for the Modern Reader by Rayburn S. Moore. Constance Fenimore Woolson. Ed. by Rayburn S. Moore. LC 67-17940. (Masterworks of lit. ser.). 1967. 2.75 pap., 6.50. College & Univ. Pr.
For the Major & Selected Short Stories. Constance Fenimore Woolson. Ed. by Rayburn S. Moore. (Masterworks of Literature Ser). 1967. 7.50x (ISBN 0-8084-0131-9); pap. 4.45x (ISBN 0-8084-0132-7, M26). Coll & U Pr.
For the Ohio Country. Jim Baker. (Illus.). 1976. pap. 1.95 (ISBN 0-914482-12-2). Ohio Hist Soc.
For the Old Sake's. Frances Bridges Marshall. LC 7-24663. (On cover: Rialto series, no. 39). 1891. Rand, McNally & Company.
For the Patriarch. Angelo Loukakis. LC 81-1935. (Paperback prose). 13.25 (ISBN 0-7022-1599-6) (ISBN 0-7022-1600-3). University of Queensland Press.
For the Pleasure of His Company: An Affair of the Misty City, Thrice Told. Charles Warren Stoddard. LC 3-13058. 1903. A. M. Robertson.
For the President's Eyes Only: A Novel. Richard Sale. LC 71-139658. 1971. 7.95 (ISBN 0-671-20885-3). Simon and Schuster.
For the Prime Minister: The Paul Zwilling Papers. Josef Gert Vondra. 1975. 4.95 (ISBN 0-85885-082-6). David & Charles.
For the Queen in South Africa. Caryl Davis Haskins. LC 2526. 1900. Little, Brown and Company.
For the Right. Karl Emil Franzos & MacDonald, George. Tr. by Sutter, Julie. LC 3-14808. (Harper's Franklin square library. no. 616). 1888. Harper & Brothers.
For the Right. Karl Emil Franzos & Sutter, Julie, Tr. LC 44-366153. 1888. Harper & Brothers.
For the Sake of a Name. A Story for Our Times. Elizabeth Grinnell. LC 29-8258. 1900. D. C. Cook Publishing Company.
For the Sake of a Name: A Story of Our Times. Elizabeth Grinnell. LC 3680. (New Sabbath library, v. 3, no. 2). D. C. Cook Publishing Co.
For the Sake of Heaven. Martin Buber. LC 77-97311. 1970. (ISBN 0-8371-2592-8). Greenwood Press.
For the Sake of Heaven; a Chronicle. Martin Buber. (temple book). 1969. Atheneum.
For the Sake of Heaven. Tr. from German by Ludwig Lewisohn. Martin Buber. (Torchbk., TB801N. Temple Lib.). 1966. pap., 2.45. Harper.
For the Sake of Heaven. Translated Form the German by Ludwig Lewisohn. Martin Buber. LC 58-8531. 1958. Meridian Books.
For the Sake of Heaven: Translated from the German by Ludwig Lewisohn. 2d Ed. Martin Buber. LC 53-760419. 1953. Jewish Publication Society of America.
For the Sake of the Duchesse: A Page from the Life of the Vicomte De Championnet. Samuel Walkey. F. A. Stokes Company.
For the Sake of the Faith: Four Stories of the Times of the Reformation. Minna Waack Rudiger. LC 5-6940. (Reformation series, vol. i). 1905. The German Literary Board.
For the Sake of the Family. Maria Henrietta De La Cherois Crommelin. LC 6-31978. J. W. Lovell Company.
For the Sins of His Youth. A Novel. Jane Kavanagh. LC 7-111133. 1887. G. W. Dillingham; Etc., Etc.
For the Soul of Rafael. Marah Ellis Martin Ryan. LC 6-17869. 1906. A. C. McClurg & Co.
For the Term of His Natural Life. Marcus Andrew Hislop Clarke. LC 74-580789. (Australian classics). 1970. 2.50. Lloyd O'Neil.
For the Term of His Natural Life see Australian Classics.
For the Term of His Natural Life. With an Introd. by L. H.,Allen. Marcus Andrew Hislop Clarke. LC 52-14675. (World's classics, 527). 1952. Oxford University Press.
For the Time Being. Julia Siebel. LC 61-12344. 1961. Harcourt, Brace & World.
For the Whie Christ: A Story of the Days of Charlemage. Robert Ames Bennet. LC 5-9656. 1905. A. C. McClurg & Co.
For the White Rose. Katharine Tynan Hinkson, pseud. LC 5-35596. 1905. Benzinger Brothers.
For the White Rose of Arno. Owen Vaughan. 1896. Longmans, Green and Co.
For the Witch, a Stone. Salambo Forest. 160p. (Orig.). 1971. pap. 1.95 o.s.i. (O*P*H262, Ophelia). Olympia.
For the Witch of the Mists. David C. Smith & Richard L. Tierney. (Bran Mak Morn Ser.: No. 3). 240p. 1981. pap. 2.25 (ISBN 0-441-24806-3). Ace Bks.
For Thee the Best. Mark Aleksandrovich Aldanov. Tr. by Wreden, Nicholas R. LC 45-9645. 1945. C. Scribner's Sons.
For Them That Trespass. Ernest Raymond. LC 76-12609. 1976. 8.95 (ISBN 0-8415-0442-3). Dutton.
For Thinking Out Loud. Martha M. Hoskins. 1967. 2.50 o.p. (ISBN 0-8059-0137-X). Dorrance.
For This I Went to College? Bil Keane. (Family Circus Ser.). (Illus.). 1978. pap. 1.50 (ISBN 0-449-14069-5, GM). Fawcett.
For This My Glory: A Story of a Mormon Life. Paul Dayton Bailey. LC 40-33286. Lyman House.
For This My Mother Wrapped Me Warm. Eunice Lee Caesar. LC 47-11547. 1947. D. Appleton-Century Co.
For This One Hour: A Historical Novel. E. Lee North. LC 68-25325. 1968. 4.95. William-Frederick Press.
For Time and All Eternity. Paul Dayton Bailey. LC 64-11395. 1964. Doubleday.
For to End Yet Again and Other Fizzles. Samuel Beckett. LC 77-356280. 1976. 3.50. (ISBN 0-7145-3599-0) (ISBN 0-7145-3600-8). Calder.
For to Forget the Pain. Patricia E Jenkins. LC 74-82752. 5.95. Libra Publishers.
For Today Only. Margaret Lee Runbeck. London.
For Tommy, and Other Stories. Laura Elizabeth Howe Richards. LC 79-110210. (Short story index reprint series). 1970. Books for Libraries Press.
For Tommy, and Other Stories. Laura Elizabeth Howe Richards. LC 1-29374. D. Estes & Company.
For Us in the Dark: A Novel. Naomi Gwladys Royde-Smith. LC 37-36386. 1937. The Macmillan Company.
For Us, the Living. Haakon Maurice Chevalier. LC 48-117143. 1949. A. A. Knopf.
For Us the Living. Bruce Lancaster. LC 75-31891. 1975. 9.95 (ISBN 0-89190-882-X). Rivercity Press.
For Us the Living. Bruce Lancaster. LC 40-33786. 1940. Frederick A. Stokes Company.
For Us the Living. Antonia Van-Loon. LC 75-10002. 8.95. St. Martin's Press.
For Us the Living: By Antonia Van-Loon. Antonia Van-Loon. (Dell Book). 1977. 1.95 (ISBN 0-440-12673-8). Dell Pub. Co.
For Want of a Nail: If Burgoyne Had Won at Saratoga. Robert Sobel. (O.s.i.). (Illus.). 384p. 1973. 12.95 o.s.i. (ISBN 0-02-612250-2). Macmillan.
For Want of a Nail. 1st Amer. Ed. Melvyn Bragg. LC 65-187508. bds., 4.95. Knopf.
For Whom the Angels Sing. James R. Randles. 4.50 o.p. Vantage.
For Whom the Bell Tolls. Ernest Hemingway. LC 40-27782. 1940. C. Scribner's Sons.
For Whom the Bell Tolls. Ernest Hemingway. 482p. 1983. 14.95 (ISBN 0-684-10239-0, ScribT). Scribner.
For Whom the Bell Tolls. Ernest Hemingway & Ward, Lynd Kendall, 1905- Illus. LC 42-51223. 1942. Princeton University Press.
For Whom the Cloche Tolls. Angus Wilson. 1973. pap. 0.95 o.p. (09164). Curtis.
For Whom the Cloche Tolls. Angus Wilson. LC 73-555. (O.s.i.). (Illus.). 128p. 1973. 6.95 o.s.i. (ISBN 0-670-32460-4). Viking Pr.
For Woman's Love. A Novel. Emma Dorothy Eliza Nevitte Southworth. LC 8-14245. (Ledger library, no. 18). R. Bonner's Sons.
For Women Only. J J Markey. LC 32-2226. The Macaulay Company.
For You I Commit Murder. Dominick Rocke Sperduti. LC 57-16790. 1956. Christopher Pub. House.
For Your Eyes Only. Ian Fleming. pap. 3.95 fr. ed. French & Eur.
For Your Eyes Only. Ian Fleming. 192p. 1982. pap. 2.75 (ISBN 0-425-05366-0). Berkley Pub.
For Your Eyes Only - Read & Destroy. Louis Honig. Ed. by Walter Schmidt. LC 72-83313. 300p. 1972. 6.95 o.p. (ISBN 0-912880-02-3). Charles Pub.
For Your Eyes Only: Read and Destroy! A Novel of Modern Intrigue. Louis Honig. LC 72-83313. 1972. 6.95 (ISBN 0-912880-02-3). Charles Pub.
For Zion's Sake: A Tale of Real Life. Frank Willoughby. LC 11-28687. Broadway Publishing Co.
Foragers. Ben Haas. LC 62-754838. 1962. Simon and Schuster.
Forayers. William Gilmore Simms. 1974. Repr. of 1890 ed. lib. bdg. 30.00 (ISBN 0-8414-8061-3). Folcroft.
Forayers: Or, The Raid of the Dog-Days. William Gilmore Simms. LC 76-8932. (Simms Revolutionary War novels; v. 6). 1976. 22.50 (ISBN 0-87152-240-3). Reprint Co. Publishers.
Forayers: Or, The Raid of the Dog-Days. new and rev. ed. William Gilmore Simms. LC 76-116015. (Illus.). 1970. (ISBN 0-404-06038-2). AMS Press.
Forayers; or, The Raid of the Dog-Days. William Gilmore Simms. (With his Woodcraft. New York, 1882). 1882. A. C. Armstrong & Son.
Forayers; or, The Raid of the Dog-Days. new and rev. ed. William Gilmore Simms. (On cover: Lovell's library, v. 13, no. 697). 1885. J. W. Lovell Company.
Forbidden. Joan Conquest. LC 27-16672. The Macaulay Company.
Forbidden. Edward S. Hanlon. (Orig.). 1970. pap. 0.75 o.p. (64-220). Paperback Lib.
Forbidden. Arthur Housman & Capra, Frank. LC 32-3412. Grosset & Dunlap.
Forbidden. Judith Cabot Priest. LC 52-25664. 1952. Woodford Press.
Forbidden Area. 1st Ed. Pat Frank. LC 56-6417. Lippincott.
Forbidden Blessing. Lucy Casselman. (Orig.). 1980. pap. 1.50 (ISBN 0-440-12638-X). Dell.
Forbidden Castle. Edward Packard. 128p. 1982. 1.75 (ISBN 0-553-22515-4). Bantam.
Forbidden Castle. William Edward Daniel Ross. 192p. (OSI). 1972. 4.95 o.s.i. Lenox Hill.
Forbidden City. Anthony Esler. LC 77-6743. 1977. 9.95 (ISBN 0-688-03219-2). Morrow.
Forbidden City. Anthony Esler. 1979. 1.95 (ISBN 0-449-23836-9). Fawcett Crest Books.
Forbidden City. Muriel Molland Jernigan. LC 54-12072. 1954. Crown Publishers.
Forbidden City. Idella Purnell. LC 32-10938. 1932. The Macmillan Company.
Forbidden Colors. Yukio Mishima, pseud. LC 80-14679. 1980. 5.95 (ISBN 0-399-50490-7). Perigee Books.
Forbidden Colors. Tr. from the Japanese by Alfred H. Marks. 1st Amer. Ed. Yukio Mishima, pseud. LC 67-18594. 1968. 6.95. Knopf.
Forbidden Desire. Kathie Reed. 1969. pap. 0.60 o.p. (60-420). Manor Bks.
Forbidden Desires. Jan Hammer. pap. 1.95 o.s.i. (Venus). Grove.
Forbidden Destiny. Paula Fairman. 1977. 1.95. Pinnacle Books.
Forbidden Door. Herman Landon. LC 27-2045. 1927. L. MacVeagh, The Dial Press.
Forbidden Ecstasy. Janelle Taylor. (Orig.). 1982. pap. 3.50 (ISBN 0-8217-1014-1). Zebra.
Forbidden Embrace. Cassie Edwards. 1982. pap. 3.50 (ISBN 0-8217-1105-9). Zebra.
Forbidden Family Game. Ward Fulton. 192p. (Orig.). 1973. pap. 1.95 o.p. (ISBN 0-87682-299-5, 7299). Barclay Hse.
Forbidden Flame. Anne Mather. (Harlequin Presents Ser.). 192p. 1981. pap. 1.50 (ISBN 0-373-10436-7, Pub. by Harlequin). PB.
Forbidden Flame. Marilyn Ross. (Orig.). 1982. pap. 2.95 (ISBN 0-445-04738-0). Popular Lib.
Forbidden Flowers. Nancy Friday. 1981. pap. 3.50. PB.
Forbidden Forest. Mircea Eliade. Tr. by Mac L. Ricketts & Mary P. Stevenson. LC 76-51618. 1978. text ed. 25.00x (ISBN 0-268-00943-0, 85-09432). U of Notre Dame Pr.
Forbidden Frontier. Archie Joscelyn. LC 68-2761. 1968. Arcadia House.
Forbidden Fruit. 1971. pap. 1.75 o.p. (Z1059K, Zebra). Grove.
Forbidden Fruit. A Novelization of the Celebrated Play. Arthur D. Hall & Boucicault, Dion, 1822?-1890. Forbidden Fruit. LC 7-535. (On cover: Drama series, no. 16). Street & Smith.
Forbidden Fruit. From the German of F. W. Hacklander... Friedrich Wilhelm Hacklander & Kaufman, Rosalie, Tr. LC 6-45969. (cobweb series of choice fiction). Estes and Lauriat.
Forbidden Fruit. From the German of F. W. Hacklander... Friedrich Wilhelm Hacklander & Kaufman, Rosalie, Tr. LC 6-45970. (On cover: Lovell's library. v. 12, no. 606). 1885. J. W. Lovell Company.
Forbidden Fruit: Luscious and Exciting Story, and More Forbidden Fruit; or, Master Percy's Progress in and Beyond the Domestic Circle. LC 71-139256. (Zebra books). 1971. 1.75. Grove Press.
Forbidden Garden. Eric Temple Bell. LC 47-6283. 1947. Fantasy Press.
Forbidden Ground. Neil Harmon Swanson. LC 38-13187. Farrar & Rinehart, Inc.
Forbidden Ground. Gilbert Watson. LC 10-162362. 1910. John Lane Company.
Forbidden Heart. Vivien Grey. LC 51-1595. 1951. Arcadia House.
Forbidden Land. Bertha Hettleman. LC 47-392057. 1947. Margent Press.
Forbidden Land. Hunter Ingram. 1975. (pbk.) 0.95 (ISBN 0-345-24281-5). Ballantine Books.
Forbidden Lips. Robert Terry Shannon. LC 29-177324. E. J. Clode, Inc.
Forbidden Love. Caroline Courtney. 224p. 1980. pap. 1.75 (ISBN 0-446-94297-9). Warner Bks.
Forbidden Love. Ho-Ching Ling. LC 70-28393. 1971. 6.95. Continental Book Co.
Forbidden Love. Karen Robards. 384p. 1983. pap. 3.50 (ISBN 0-8439-2024-6, Leisure Bks). Dorchester Pub Co.
Forbidden Man. William Wilfrid Whalen. LC 27-20087. 1927. B. Herder Book Co.
Forbidden Man: A Novel. 1st Ed. Gina Allen. LC 61-702214. 1961. Chilton Co., Book Division.
Forbidden Marriage: Or, In Love with a Handsome Spendthrift; a Novel. Laura Jean Libbey. LC 7-14311. 1888. The American News Company.
Forbidden Miracle. Stasius Budavas. 1955. Comet Press Books.
Forbidden Mountain. Hebe Weenolsen. LC 82-14302. 288p. 1983. 13.95 (ISBN 0-688-01630-8). Morrow.
Forbidden Path. William J Walters. LC 38-20486. 1938. Dodd, Mead & Company.

Forbidden Places. Mary Napier. LC 81-3222. 1981. 11.95 (ISBN 0-698-11091-9). Coward, McCann & Geoghegan.
Forbidden Planet. W. J Stuart. LC 56-5755. 1956. Farrar, Staus and Cudahy.
Forbidden Planet. W. J Stuart. LC 77-27544. (Gregg Press science fiction series). (Illus.). 1978. 10.00 (ISBN 0-8398-2409-2). Gregg Press.
Forbidden Ranch. Claude Rister. LC 33-86307. E. J. Clode, Inc.
Forbidden Range. Louis Trimble. LC 56-58406. 1956. Avalon Books.
Forbidden Range: A Romance of the Yellowstone. James French Dorrance. LC 39-17937. The Macaulay Company.
Forbidden Rapture. Kate Nevins. (Second Chance at Love Ser.: No. 90). 1982. pap. 1.75 (ISBN 0-515-06852-7). Jove Pubns.
Forbidden Reunion. Marjorie H. Gardner. (YA) 1980. 6.95 (Avalon). Bouregy.
Forbidden River. Harold Bindloss. LC 36-813513. 1936. Frederick A. Stokes Comapny.
Forbidden River. Al Cody, pseud. (YA) 1973. 6.95 (Avalon). Bouregy.
Forbidden River. Al Cody, pseud. 192p. 1977. pap. 1.25 (ISBN 0-532-12472-3). Woodhill.
Forbidden River. Al Cody. 1974. (pbk.) 0.95. Manor Books.
Forbidden River: By Al Cody Pseud. Archie Joscelyn. LC 52-8061. 1952. Bouregy & Curl.
Forbidden Road. Effie Adelaide Maria Albanesi. LC 7-42010. Empire Book Company.
Forbidden Room. Arthur Russell Thorndike. LC 33-172769. 1933. L. MacVeagh, Dial Press, Inc.
Forbidden Sanctuary. Richard Bowker. 240p. 1982. pap. 2.50 (ISBN 0-345-29871-3, Del Rey). Ballantine.
Forbidden Surrender. Carole Mortimer. (Harlequin Presents Ser.). 192p. 1982. pap. 1.75 (ISBN 0-373-10547-9). Harlequin Bks.
Forbidden Talents. Katia Baden. LC 29-212154. Dorrance and Company.
Forbidden Territory. Dennis Yates Wheatley. LC 33-160621. E. P. Dutton & Co., Inc.
Forbidden Territory. Dennis Yates Wheatley. 1973. (pbk.) 1.50. Ballantine.
Forbidden Tower. Marion Zimmer Bradley. LC 78-21226. (Gregg Press science fiction series). (Illus.). 1979. 14.00 (ISBN 0-8398-2405-X). Gregg Press.
Forbidden Tower. Eugenia Cook. 1973. (pbk.) 0.75. Dell Books.
Forbidden Town. Mary Eliza Bakewell Gaunt. LC 26-18096. 1926. E.J. Clode, Inc.
Forbidden Trail. Honore McCue Willsie Morrow. LC 19-171812. Frederick A. Stokes Company.
Forbidden Trail. Honore McCue Willsie Morrow. LC 22-474518. 1921. A. L. Burt Company.
Forbidden Trails. Frank Chester Robertson. LC 35-2613. 1935. I. Washburn, Inc.
Forbidden Tree. Elizabeth Moorhead Vermorcken. LC 33-670626. The Bobbs-Merrill Company.
Forbidden Valley. William Byron Mowery. LC 33-657686. 1933. R. Long & R. R. Smith, Inc.
Forbidden Valley. 1st Ed. Allan Vaughan Elston. LC 55-6310. 1955. Lippincott.
Forbidden Way. George Fort Gibbs. LC 11-244021. 1911. 1.25. D. Appleton and Company.
Forbidden Wine. Frederic Arnold Kummer. Sears Publishing Company, Inc.
Forbidden Woman. Frances Mocatta. LC 28-13447. 1928. G. H. Watt.
Forbidden World. Ted White & Dave Bischoff. 1978. 1.50 (ISBN 0-445-04328-8). Popular Library.
Forbidden Years. Charles Wadsworth Camp. LC 30-31195. 1930. Doubleday, Doran & Company, Inc.
Forbush and the Penguins. Graham Billing. LC 66-13079. 1966. Holt, Rinehart and Winston.
Force of Circumstances. Elizabeth Caramossi Wright. LC 50-14608. 1950. Exposition Press.
Force Play. Anthony Stuart, pseud. LC 78-73870. 1979. 8.95 (ISBN 0-87795-224-8). Arbor Hse.
Force Play. Anthony Stuart, pseud. 192p. 1981. pap. 1.95 (ISBN 0-445-04658-9). Popular Lib.
Force Play: A Novel. Julian Anthony Stuart Hale. LC 78-73870. 8.95 (ISBN 0-87795-224-8). Arbor House.
Force Red: A Novel. Milton R Bass. LC 70-112932. 1970. 5.95. Putnam.
Force Ten from Navarone. Alistair MacLean. LC 68-18084. 1968. 4.95 (ISBN 0-385-02759-1). Doubleday.
Force Ten from Navarone. Alistair MacLean. 1979. pap. 2.50 (ISBN 0-449-23934-9, Crest). Fawcett.
Forced Down. B. Palmer. (Danny Orlis Ser.). pap. 0.95 o.p. Believers Bkshelf.
Forced Entry. Michael Scott. (O.s.i.). 1976. pap. 1.50 o.s.i. (BT50926). Belmont-Tower.
Forced Feedings. Maxine Herman. 1980. pap. 2.50 (ISBN 0-425-04560-9). Berkley Pub.
Forced Feedings: A Novel. Maxine Herman. LC 78-31140. 8.95 (ISBN 0-87131-283-2). M. Evans.
Forced March: Selected Poems. Miklos Radnoti & Clive Wilmer. LC 79-322107. 1979. 6.95 (ISBN 0-85635-275-6). Carcanet New Press.
Forced Marriage. A Novel. Frederick W Pearson. (sunnyside series, no. 11). 1890. J. S. Ogilvie.
Ford. Mary Hunter Austin. LC 17-11466. 1917. 1.50. Houghton Mifflin Company.
Ford Policy: Or, A True Life Insurance Story. John H Shumard. LC 8-7318. 1890. Standard Publishing Company.
Fordham Castle see Author of Beltraffio.
Fore! Charles Emmett Van Loan. LC 18-11940. George H. Doran Company.
Fore-Hitchin' Thurlow Weed Hoffman. LC 33-16738. The Christopher Publishing House.
Forecast for Love. Kristin Michaels. 1981. pap. 1.95 (ISBN 0-451-11124-9, AJ1124, Sig). NAL.
Forecast for Love. Renee Shann. 1972. pap. 0.75 o.p. (94281). Beagle Bks.
Forecastle Yarns. John W Gould. Ed. by Gould, Edward Sherman. LC 9-3822. 1854. Stringer & Townsend.
Foregone Conclusion. William Dean Howells. LC 77-131751. 1972. 14.50 (ISBN 0-403-00638-4). Scholarly Press.
Foregone Conclusion. William Dean Howells. LC 79-104491. 1970. Literature House.
Foregone Conclusion. William Dean Howells. LC 7-5776. 1875. J. R. Osgood and Company.
Foregone Conclusion. William Dean Howells. LC 7-5775. 1877. J. R. Osgood and Company.
Foregone Conclusion. William Dean Howells. LC 2-274201. 1902. Houghton, Mifflin and Company.
Foreign Affair. Andrew Graham. LC 59-8666. 1959. Doubleday.
Foreign Affair: By John Baxter Pseud. Complete and Unabridged. Howard Hunt. LC 54-26996. (Avon red-and-gold library, T- 78). 1954. Avon Publications.
Foreign Affairs. Hugh Fleetwood. LC 73-91852. 1974. 6.95 (ISBN 0-8128-1676-5). Stein and Day.
Foreign Affairs. Hugh Fleetwood. 1.50 (ISBN 0-671-80829-X). Pocket Books.
Foreign Affairs, and Other Stories. Sean O'Faolain. LC 76-382617. 1976. 2.95 (ISBN 0-09-460760-5). Constable.
Foreign Bodies: A Novel. Jean Cayrol. LC 60-5263. 1960. Putnam.
Foreign Body. Moira Field. LC 51-12303. 1951. Macmillan.
Foreign Body. Roderick Mann. LC 74-18284. 1975. 6.95 (ISBN 0-02-579420-5). Macmillan.
Foreign Constellations. John Brunner. LC 79-92183. 1980. 8.95x (ISBN 0-89696-094-3, An Everest House Book). Dodd.
Foreign Devil. Carter Hixson. LC 41-2809. C.
Foreign Devils: A Novel. Irvin Faust. LC 72-97685. 1973. 7.95 (ISBN 0-87795-056-3). Arbor House.
Foreign Exchange. Jimmy Sangster. LC 68-28250. 1968. 4.95 o.p. (ISBN 0-393-08573-2). Norton.
Foreign Fictions: 25 Contemporary Stories from Canada, Europe, Latin America. John Biguenet. LC 77-25469. 1978. 4.95 (ISBN 0-394-72493-3). Vintage Books.
Foreign Marriage: Or, Buying a Title; a Novel. Virginia Wales Johnson. LC 7-10554. (On cover: Harper's library of American fiction, no. 13). 1880. Harper & Brothers.
Foreign Match. Marie Healy Bigot. LC 6-12736. 1890. A. C. McClurg and Company.
Foreign Matter. Christopher Byron. LC 79-7666. 1980. 10.00 (ISBN 0-385-14284-6). Doubleday.
Foreign Minister: Novel by Leo Lania Pseud. Translated by James Stern. Lazar Herrmann. LC 56-9500. 1956. Houghton Mifflin.
Foreigner. Arun Joshi. 1968. Asia Pub. House.
Foreigner. Nahid Rachlin. LC 78-1603. 8.95 (ISBN 0-393-08819-7). Norton.
Foreigner. Desmond Stewart. (Illus.). 181p. 1982. 24.95 (ISBN 0-241-10686-9, Pub. by Hamish Hamilton England). David & Charles.
Foreigner: A Novel. Arun Joshi. 1969. 6.00x (ISBN 0-210-98113-X). Asia.
Foreigner. A Tale of Saskatchewan. Charles William Gordon. LC 9-28400. Hodder & Stoughton.
Foreigner in the Family. Wilfrid Benson. LC 29-299774. Harcourt, Brace and Company.
Foreigner. 1st Ed. Ralph Blum. LC 61-127914. 1961. Atheneum.
Foreigners. Eleanor C Price. LC 7-30106. (On cover: Seaside library. Pocket ed. no. 173). 1884. G. Munro.
Foreigners. Preston Schoyer. LC 42-86121. 1942. Dodd, Mead & Company.
Forelady. Ann Harbage. LC 41-39042. 1941. Meador Publishing Company.
Forelopers: A Romance of Colonial Days. Isaac Newton Phipps. LC 12-27850. 1912. 1.25. The Neale Publishing Company.
Foreman of Circle B. Stanley Burnett Reynolds. LC 40-1418. House of Field.
Foreman of the Forty-Bar. Frank Chester Robertson. LC 25-17150. Barse & Hopkins.
Foreman of the JA6: A Novel. E. Joy Johnson. LC 11-28685. 1911. 1.50. Wyoming Publishing Co.
Foreordained: With Other Stories. Everhardt Armstrong. LC 13-6892. 1913. The John C. Winston Co.
Forerunner. Neith Boyce. LC 3-25410. 1903. Fox, Duffield & Company.
Forerunner. Andre Norton, pseud. 288p. (Orig.). 1981. pap. 2.75 (ISBN 0-523-48558-1). Pinnacle Bks.
Forerunner Foray. Andre Norton, pseud. 1975. pap. 2.50 (ISBN 0-441-24621-4). Ace Bks.
Forerunner Foray. Andre Norton, pseud. 288p. 1982. pap. 2.50 (ISBN 0-441-24623-0, Pub. by Ace Science Fiction). Ace Bks.
Forerunners. Reed M. Holmes. (Illus.). 1981. pap. 13.00 (ISBN 0-8309-0315-1). Herald Hse.
Foreshadowed. Florence Ethel Mills Young. LC 21-147093. 1921. George H. Doran Company.
Forest and Fairy Fancies. William Harper Huff. LC 27-24865. 1927. The Miles and Dryer Printing Company.
Forest and Prairie: Or, Life on the Frontier. Emerson Bennett. LC 20-23150. 1860. J. E. Potter and Company.
Forest and Shore: Or, Legends of the Pine-Tree State. 4th thousand. ed. Charles Parker Ilsley. LC 7-8842. 1856. J. P. Jewett and Company.
Forest and the Fort. Hervey Allen. LC 43-4731. 1943. Farrar & Rinehart, Inc.
Forest and the Fort. Hervey Allen. 1973. 1.25. Popular Lib.
Forest Cavalier: A Romance of America's First Frontier and of Bacon's Rebellion. Roy Catesby Flannagan. LC 52-5810. 1952. Bobbs-Merrill.
Forest Creek. William Arthur Neubauer. LC 63-6809. 1963. Arcadia House.
Forest Fire. David James. (O.s.i.). 1975. pap. 1.50 o.s.i. (BT50865). Belmont-Tower.
Forest Fire. David James. 1975. (pbk.) 1.50. Belmont Tower Books.
Forest Fire. Rex Stout. LC 33-9099. Farrar & Rinehart, Incorporated.
Forest Fortune and Ted Jones. Alexis Francois Gillet. LC 34-41604. 1934. Meador Publishing Company.
Forest Goddess: A Novel. M. Basu. 5.25x (ISBN 0-210-33862-8). Asia.
Forest Goddess. Translated by Barindra Nath Dass from the Bengali Novel Jalajangal. Manoje Basu. LC 61-182201. 1961. Asia Pub. House.
Forest Hearth: A Romance of Indiana in the Thirties. Charles Major. LC 3-26166. 1903. The Macmillan Company.
Forest Idyl. Jeanie Oliver Davidson Smith. LC 13-265576. 1913. Sherman, French & Company.
Forest King: Or, The Wild Hunter of the Adaca. A Tale of the Seventeenth Century. Hervey Keyes. 1878. Wheat & Cornett.
Forest Life. Caroline Matilda Stansbury Kirkland. LC 72-104504. 1970. Literature House.
Forest Life. Caroline Matilda Stansbury Kirkland. LC 7-13208. 1844. C. S. Francis & Co.
Forest Lily. A Novel. James Donald Dunlop. LC 98-723. F. T. Neely.
Forest Lord: A Romantic Adventure of 18th Century Charleston. Noel Bertram Gerson. LC 54-10766. 1955. Doubleday.
Forest Lovers: A Romance. Maurice Henry Hewlett. LC 75-41136. 1976. 17.50 (ISBN 0-404-14783-6). AMS Press.
Forest Lovers: A Romance. Maurice Henry Hewlett. LC 7-4662. 1898. The Macmillan Company.
Forest Lovers: A Romance. Maurice Henry Hewlett. LC 7-4663. 1899. The Macmillan Company.
Forest Lovers: A Romance. Maurice Henry Hewlett. LC 1-3098. 1899. The Macmillan Company.
Forest Maiden. Lee Robinet. LC 14-13682. 1914. 1.25. Browne & Howell Company.
Forest of Adventure. Raymond Lee Ditmars. LC 33-30729. 1933. The Macmillan Company.
Forest of Eyes. Victor Canning. LC 50-5966. 1950. Mill.
Forest of Fear. Alfred Gordon Bennett. LC 24-256410. The Macaulay Company.
Forest of Fear. Gail MacMillan. 1974. 4.50. Avalon Books.
Forest of Feathers. Margaret Jones Hoffmann. LC 66-12365. 1966. Harcourt, Brace & World.
Forest of the Dead. Ernst Emil Wiechert & Stechow, Ursula, Tr. LC 47-7082. 1947. Greenberg.
Forest of the Hanged. Liviu Rebreanu. Tr. by Wise, A. V. LC 30-24951. 1930. Duffield & Company.
Forest of the Night. 1st Ed. Madison Jones. LC 60-5427. 1960. Harcourt, Brace.
Forest of the South. Caroline Gordon. LC 45-9169. 1945. C. Scribner's Sons.
Forest of Tigers. 1st Ed. Robert Shaplen. LC 55-9269. 1956. Knopf.
Forest on the Hill. Richard Girling. LC 81-69973. 1982. 13.95 (ISBN 0-670-39187-5). Viking Press.
Forest on the Hill. Eden Phillpotts. LC 12-98587. 1912. 1.30. John Lane Company.
Forest Orchid, and Other Stories. Ella Rhoads Higginson. LC 7-4770. 1897. The Macmillan Company.
Forest Playfellow: A Story. Ella Katharine Sanders. LC 8-30020. 1907. E. P. Dutton and Company.
Forest Princess. Harriet Herman. (Illus.). 1974. (pbk.) 2.95. Over the Rainbow Press.
Forest Rose. Frank Edwin Wilson & Bennett, Emerson. LC 48-35062. 1929. Brown Pub. Co.
Forest Rose: A Tale of the Frontier. Emerson Bennett. LC 72-96394. 1973. 7.50 (ISBN 0-8214-0128-9). Ohio University Press.
Forest Rose: A Tale of the Frontier. new ed., rev. by the author. ed. Emerson Bennett. LC 50-495678. City News Agency.
Forest Rose: A Tale of the Frontier. Emerson Bennett. LC 7-34430. 1850. J. A. & U. P. James.
Forest Rose: A Tale of the Frontier. new ed. rev. by the author. ed. Emerson Bennett. 1852. J. A. & U. P. James.
Forest Rose: A Tale of the Ohio Frontier. Emerson Bennett. LC 59-65029. 1959. Business and Professional Women's Club.
Forest Runners. Joseph Alexander Altsheler. 1976. lib. bdg. 16.30x (ISBN 0-89968-002-X). Lightyear.
Forest Schoolmaster: By Peter Rosegger, Authorized Translation by Frances E. Skinner. Peter Rosegger. Tr. by Skinner, Frances E. LC 1-30818. 1901. G. P. Putnam's Sons.
Forest Spy: A Tale of the War of 1812. Edward Sylvester Ellis. LC 10-27857. Hurst & Company.
Forest Things. Gerald DiPego. LC 79-311. 8.95 (ISBN 0-440-02338-6). Delacorte Press.
Forest Things. Gerard Di Pego. 1980. pap. 2.50 (ISBN 0-440-12593-6). Dell.
Forest Tragedy: And Other Tales. Sara Jane Clarke Lippincott. LC 7-16037. 1856. Ticknor and Fields.
Forest Voices. Gustav Heinrich Gans Putlitz. Ed. by Smith, Charles Adam. LC 8-15526. 1866. J. Munsell.
Forest World. Felix Salten & Milton, Paul Robert, 1904- Tr. LC 42-50435. 1942. The Bobbs-Merrill Company.
Forestalled: Or, The Life Quest. authorized ed. Matilda Barbara Bertram Edwards. LC 6-36588. (Lovell's international ser. no. 147). United States Book Company, Successors to J. W. Lovell Company.
Forester: A Novel. Translated from the Polish by H. C. Stevens. Maria Szczepanska Kuncewiczowa. 1954. Roy Publishers.
Foresters. Jeremy Belknap. LC 78-104413. 1970. (ISBN 0-8398-0159-9). Literature House.
Foresters. Alexandre Dumas. LC 6-42337. 1854. D. Appleton & Co.
Foresters. A Novel. Berthold Auerbach. LC 6-4504. (Appleton's new handy-volume series, v. 62). 1880. D. Appleton and Company.
Foresters. A Tale of Domestic Life. John Wilson. LC 10-3732. 1845. Saxton & Kelt.
Foresters, an American Tale, 1792. Jeremy Belknap. LC 71-100127. 1969. Repr. of 1792 ed. 30.00x (ISBN 0-8201-1071-X). Schol Facsimiles.
Forester's Daughter see Collected Works.
Forester's Daughter: A Romance of the Bear-Tooth Range. Hamlin Garland. LC 14-2897. 1914. 1.25. Harper & Brothers.
Forestfield, a Story of the Old South: In Two Periods. Robert Thomson Bentley. LC 3-32591. 1903. The Grafton Press.
Forestman of Vimpek: His Neighbors, His Doings, and His Reflections. Flora Pauline Wilson Kopta. LC 1834. 1900. Lothrop Publishing Company.
Forests of Gleor. Jeffrey Lord. (Blade, 22). 1.25 (ISBN 0-523-00993-3). Pinnacle Books.
Forests of Norbio. Giuseppe Dessi. LC 74-30087. 1975. (ISBN 0-15-132505-7). Harcourt Brace Jovanovich.
Forests of the Night. Elliott Arnold. 1973. 1.50 (ISBN 0-515-02882-7). Pyramid Bks.
Forests of the Night. Elliott Arnold. LC 70-162745. 1971. (ISBN 0-684-12533-1). Scribner.
Forests of the Night. J. P. S Brown. LC 74-7007. 1974. 7.95 (ISBN 0-8037-3212-0). Dial Press.
Forests of the Night. Jon Cleary. LC 63-10893. 1963. Morrow.
Forests of the Night. Cary Morgan. 1982. pap. 3.50 (ISBN 0-451-11733-6, AE1733, Sig). NAL.
Forests of the Night: Translated from the French by Nora Wydenbruck. Jean Louis Curtis. LC 51-140853. 1951. Putnam.
Foretaste of Glory. Jesse Stuart. LC 46-110994. 1946. E. P. Dutton & Company, Inc.
Foretelling. Caroline Crane. LC 82-1409. 8.95 (ISBN 0-396-08056-1). Dodd, Mead.

Forever... Judy Blume. 1976. 1.75 (ISBN 0-671-80588-6). Pocket Books.
Forever. Mildred Cram. LC 35-5819. 1935. A. A. Knopf.
Forever... A Novel. Judy Blume. LC 74-22850. 6.95 (ISBN 0-87888-079-8). Bradbury Press.
Forever After. Florence Jacquelin La Farge. LC 35-6276. The Dial Press, Inc.
Forever After. William Arthur Neubauer. LC 46-21126. 1946. Grammercy Publishing Co.
Forever After: A Novel. Kate Lazlo. LC 80-26881. 10.95 (ISBN 0-8037-2679-1). Dial Press.
Forever Amber. Kathleen Winsor. LC 45-3612. 1945. The Macmillan Company.
Forever Amber: By Kathleen Winsor. Kathleen Winsor. LC 44-848920. 1944. The Macmillan Company.
Forever Amber: Kathleen Winsor. Kathleen Winsor. (Signet Book). 1.95 (ISBN 0-451-07360-6). New American Library.
Forever and a Day. Emilie Baker Loring. LC 65-109058. 1965. 3.95. Little.
Forever and a Day. Emilie Baker Loring. (6342). 1966. 1.95. Grosset.
Forever and a Day. Emilie Baker Loring. LC 79-10512. 1979. 12.50 (ISBN 0-8161-6729-X). G. K. Hall.
Forever and a Day. A Novel. Edward Fuller. LC 6-46669. 1882. J. B. Lippincott & Co.
Forever and Ever: A Novel. William Charles Langel. LC 32-2228. 1932. A.H. King.
Forever & Ever & a Wednesday. Menke Katz. LC 79-90500. 6.50; pap. 5.00 (ISBN 0-912292-58-X). The Smith.
Forever Autumn. Ursula Bloom. 1979. pap. 1.95 (ISBN 0-89041-246-4, 3246). Major Bks.
Forever Damned. Marina Cisternas. LC 54-118839. 1955. Vantage Press.
Forever Dear. Ruth Dewey Groves. LC 38-16694. Phoenix Press.
Forever Ecstasy. Tor Kung. (Orig.). 1968. pap. 1.95 o.s.i. (OPS-30, Ophelia). Olympia.
Forever Eden. Noelle B. McCue. (Candlelight Ecstasy Ser.: No. 88). (Orig.). 1982. pap. 1.95 (ISBN 0-440-12619-3). Dell.
Forever Engaged. Horace Coon. LC 32-8077. 1932. W. Godwin, Inc.
Forever Flowing. Vasilii Semenovich Grossman. LC 72-181655. 1972. 6.95 (ISBN 0-06-011613-7). Harper & Row.
Forever Free: A Novel of Abraham Lincoln. Honore McCue Willsie Morrow. LC 27-3820. 1927. W. Morrow & Company.
Forever Glory: A Novel by Steve Fisher... Stephen Gould Fisher. LC 36-1119. The Macaulay Company.
Forever in My Heart. Vivien Grey. LC 40-29465. 1940. Arcadia House, Inc.
Forever Is So Long. Alice Mary Ross Colver. LC 42-79543. 1912. Macrae-Smith-Company.
Forever Island: A Novel. Patrick D. Smith. (Laurel Leaf Library). 1974. (pbk.) 0.95. Dell.
Forever More: A Love Story. Mary Frances Doner. LC 34-40098. Chelsea House.
Forever My Love. Rebecca Brandewyne. 560p. (Orig.). 1983. pap. 2.95 (ISBN 0-446-90981-5). Warner Bks.
Forever Panting. Peter De Vries. LC 72-10989. 1973. 7.95 (ISBN 0-316-18187-0). Little, Brown.
Forever Panting. Peter De Vries. 1973. (pbk.) 1.25. Popular Library.
Forever Panting. Peter De Vries. LC 81-19916. 1982. 3.95 (ISBN 0-14-006188-6). Penguin Books.
Forever Panting. Peter De Vries. 288p. 1973. 7.95 (ISBN 0-316-18187-0). Little.
Forever Panting. Peter De Vries. 288p. 1982. pap. 3.95 (ISBN 0-14-006188-6). Penguin.
Forever Passion. Karen A. Bale. (Orig.). 1980. pap. 2.50 (ISBN 0-89083-563-2). Zebra.
Forever Possess... Alexandra Phillips. LC 46-1163. 1946. E. P. Dutton & Company, Inc.
Forever Rainbows. Cynthia Blair. 224p. 1982. pap. 2.50 (ISBN 0-449-14468-2, GM). Fawcett.
Forever Sad the Hearts. Patricia L. Walsh. 400p. 1982. pap. 2.95 (ISBN 0-380-78378-9, 78378). Avon.
Forever Spell. Robyn Anzelon. (Superromances Ser.). 384p. 1983. pap. 2.50 (ISBN 0-373-70049-0, Pub. by Worldwide). Harlequin Bks.
Forever Springtime. Kit O'Malley. (Second Chance at Love Ser.: No. 22). 192p. (Orig.). 1982. pap. 1.75 (ISBN 0-515-06279-0). Jove Pubns.
Forever Strangers. 1st Ed. Eleanor R Mayo. LC 57-106398. 1958. W. W. Norton.
Forever the Song. Milford E Anness. LC 67-9227. 1967. Printed by Caxton Printers.
Forever Timeless. Devereaux Rochester. 3.95 o.p. Vantage.
Forever to Remain. E. V. Timms. 1975. pap. 1.25 o.p. (ISBN 0-515-03559-9). BJ Pub Group.
Forever to Remain. E. V. Timms. 1967. Repr. pap. 1.80 o.s.i. Tri-Ocean.
Forever Tomorrow. Anne Duffield. LC 55-185. 1951. Arcadia House.
Forever Tomorrow. Anne Duffield. (Berkley medallion book). 1974. (pbk.) 1.25 (ISBN 0-425-02672-8). Berkley Pub. Co.
Forever Ulysses: A Novel by C. P. Rodocanachi. Konstantinos P Rhodokanakes & Leigh-Fermor, Patric, Tr. LC 38-27031. 1938. The Viking Press.
Forever War. Joe Haldeman. 1976. (pbk.) 1.50 (ISBN 0-345-24767-1). Ballantine Books.
Forever War. Joe W Haldeman. LC 74-81241. 1975. 7.95. St. Martin's Press.
Forever Wilt Thou Die. Barbara Ninde Byfield. LC 75-40715. 1976. 5.95 (ISBN 0-385-11512-1). Published for the Crime Club by Doubleday.
Forever Young: A Novel by Zoe Akins. Zoe Akins. LC 41-7324. 1941. C. Scribner's Sons.
Forever Young, Forever Free. Hettie Jones. (Berkley Medallion) (ISBN 0-425-03203-5). Berkley.
Forever Yours. Cecily Bowman. 1946. Arcadia House.
Forever Yours. Harriett Thurman. LC 38-19635. 1938. Macrae-Smith Company.
Foreward Ho! A Story of the Argonne. Perry Newberry. LC 27-18768. 1927. Frederick A. Stokes Company.
Foreward the Nation. Donald Culross Peattie. LC 42-140542. 1942. G. P. Putnam's Sons.
Forewarners: A Novel. Giovanni Cena. Tr. by Rossetti, Olivia Agresti. LC 9-3334. 1908. Doubleday, Page & Company.
Forfeit. Ridgwell Cullum. LC 17-112141. G. W. Jacobs & Company.
Forfeit. Dick Francis. 1975. (pbk.) 1.50. Pocket Books.
Forfeit. Dick Francis. LC 69-15289. 1969. 4.95. Harper & Row.
Forfeit: A Novel. Clara Lathrop Strong. LC 12-23211. 1912. Houghton Mifflin Company.
Forge. Thomas Sigismund Stribling. LC 70-145319. 1971. (ISBN 0-403-01230-9). Scholarly Press.
Forge. Thomas Sigismund Stribling. LC 31-6082. 1931. Doubleday, Doran & Company, Inc.
Forge. Thomas Sigismund Stribling. LC 34-13712. 1933. Doubleday, Doran & Company, Inc.
Forge and Furnace: A Novel. Florence Alice Price James. LC 7-741932. (On cover: Netherland library, no. 8). 1896. New Amsterdam Book Company.
Forge in the Forest: Being the Narrative of the Acadian Ranger. Jean De Mer, Seigneur De Briart; and How He Crossed the Black Abbe; and of His Adventures in a Strange Fellowship. Charles George Douglas Roberts. LC 7-41026. 1896. Lamson, Wolffe and Company; Etc., Etc.
Forge in the Forest: Being the Narrative of the Acadian Ranger, Jean De Mer, Seigneur De Briart; and How He Crossed the Black Abbe; and of His Adventures in a Strange Fellowship. Charles George Douglas Roberts. LC 4-15469. Silver, Burdett and Company.
Forge of Destiny. George E Crater. LC 14-154049. 1.35. The Dominion Publishing Company, Limited.
Forged Coupon, and Other Stories. Lev Nikolaevich Tolstoi & Bernstein, Herman, 1876- Tr. LC 12-4138. J. S. Ogilvie Publishing Company.
Forged Coupon, and Other Stories and Dramas. Lev Nikolaevich Tolstoi & Wright, Charles Theodore Hagberg, 1862- Ed. LC 12-327. T. Nelson and Sons.
Forged Coupon, and Other Stories and Dramas. Lev Nikolaevich Tolstoi & Wright, Charles Theodore Hagberg, 1862- Ed. 1911. Dodd, Mead and Company.
Forged in Blood. Robert Leckie. (Americans at War Ser.: No. 2). (Orig.). 1982. pap. 2.95 (ISBN 0-451-11337-3, AE1337, Sig). NAL.
Forged in Fury. Evan H. Rhodes. 400p. 1982. pap. 3.25 (ISBN 0-425-05624-4). Berkley Pub.
Forged in Strong Fires. John Ironside. LC 11-599748. 1911. Little, Brown, and Company.
Forged Souls. John Henry Wilson. LC 39-29250. Dorrance and Company.
Forger. Edgar Wallace. LC 75-303147. (Illus.). 1974. 1.80 (ISBN 0-85617-697-4). White Lion Publishers.
Forger. 1st Ed. Williams, Jay. LC 61-6745. 1961. Atheneum.
Forgers and Confidence Men: Or, The Secrets of the Detective Service Divulged. George S McWatters. (On cover: The Pinkerton detective series. no. 3). 1892. Laird & Lee.
Forget Harry. Carrie Smith. LC 80-25858. 11.95 (ISBN 0-671-42590-0). Simon and Schuster.
Forget If You Can, a Novel. John Erskine. LC 35-2492. The Bobbs-Merrill Company.
Forget It,". Ida Von Claussen. LC 11-474. 1.50. Broadway Publishing Co.
Forget-Me-Not. Chester E Dobosz. LC 52-7313. 1952. Meador Pub. Co.
Forget-Me-Nots of Love. Audrey McDaniel. LC 64-22742. (Illus.). 1964. boxed 3.50 o.p. (ISBN 0-8378-1733-1). Gibson.
Forget My Fate. Ruth Otis Sawtell Wallis. LC 50-10158. (Red badge mystery). 1950. Dodd, Mead.
Forget Not Ariadne. LC 67-14281. 1967. 4.95. A.S. Barnes.
Forget That I Remember. Denise Robins. LC 41-7868. 1940. Arcadia House, Inc.
Forget Tomorrow. Desiree Meyler. LC 81-14595. 16.95 (ISBN 0-312-29894-3). St. Martin's Press.
Forget What You Saw by Jeffrey Ashford. Roderic Jeffries. LC 67-14264. 1967. bds., 3.95. Walker.
Forgetmenot: Or, Sunshine in Affliction. A Story from Life. Alice Hallowell. LC 7-1213. 1893. Gibson Bros.
Forgetting Elena. Edmund White. LC 72-10807. 1973. 5.95 (ISBN 0-394-48341-3). Random House.
Forgetting Elena. Edmund White. LC 81-7331. 1981. 5.95 (ISBN 0-14-005983-0). Penguin Books.
Forging of the Pikes: A Romance of the Upper Canadian Rebellionof 1837. Anison North. LC 20-4710. 1.75. George H. Doran Company.
Forging the Fetters. Annie French Hector. (On cover: Lovell's library, no. 1044). 1887. J. W. Lovell Company.
Forging the Fetters, and The Australian Aunt. Annie French Hector. (On cover: Seaside library. Pocket ed., no. 997). 1887. G. Munro.
Forgive Adam. Michael Foster. LC 35-2258. 1935. W. Morrow & Company.
Forgive and Forget. Ernst Lingen. LC 9-5204. 1909. 1.50. Benziger Brothers.
Forgive Me, Dr. Johnson. Irene Patterson. 4.00 o.p. Carlton.
Forgive Us Our Happiness. Walton Hall Smith. LC 29-29527. 1930. H. Liveright.
Forgive Us Our Trepasses. Lloyd Cassel Douglas. LC 62-50. 1961. Grosset & Dunlap.
Forgive Us Our Trespasses. Lloyd Cassel Douglas. LC 32-31306. 1932. Houghton Mifflin Company.
Forgive Us Our Trespasses. Lloyd Cassel Douglas. LC 39-17473. 1932. Grosset & Dunlap.
Forgive Us Our Trespasses. Lloyd Cassel Douglas. 1935. Houghton Mifflin Company.
Forgive Us Our Virtues: A Comedy of Evasion. Vardis Fisher. LC 38-6752. 1938. The Caxton Printers, Ltd.
Forgiven at Last. Jeannette Ritchie Hadermann Walworth. 1870. J. B. Lippincott & Co.
Forgiveness. Jennifer Allyn. (Love & Life Romance Ser.). 176p. (Orig.). 1983. pap. 1.75 (ISBN 0-345-31082-9). Ballantine.
Forgiving. Shelley Steinmann List. LC 82-2495. 12.95. Dutton.
Forgiving Kiss;" Or, Our Destiny. A Novel. Moritz Loth. LC 7-14766. 1874. G. W. Carleton & Co; Etc., Etc.
Forgone Conclusions. William Dean Howells. 1973. lib. bdg. 25.00 (ISBN 0-8414-5140-0). Folcroft.
Forgotten Bride. Lillian Marsh. (Second Chance at Love Ser.: No. 99). 1983. pap. 1.75. Jove Pubns.
Forgotten Canon. Hoffman Birney. LC 34-31807. The Penn Publishing Company.
Forgotten Children. Julia Colliton Flewellyn. LC 29-15126. Gospel Trumpet Company.
Forgotten Debt (Dette Oubliee); Tr. from the French of Leon De Tinseau. authorized ed. Leon De Tinseau & Gilmour, Florence Belknap, Tr. LC 8-26769. 1895. J. B. Lippincott Company.
Forgotten Doors, & Other Stories. Maria P. Dillon. 4.50 o.p. Vantage.
Forgotten Family. Ann Burkhart. LC 40-340017. The Pyramid Press.
Forgotten Family Jewels. 1st. ed. Doris M Burk. 1974. 3.95 (ISBN 0-533-01010-1). Vantage Press.
Forgotten Fleet Mystery. Francis Van Wyck Mason. LC 36-23524. Dodge Publishing Company.
Forgotten Gods. Theodore Acland Harper & Harper, Winifred. LC 29-18948. 1929. Doubleday, Doran & Company, Inc.
Forgotten Image. Eleanor Scott. LC 21-727713. 1930. Doubleday, Doran & Company, Inc.
Forgotten Impulses. Todd Walton. LC 80-10464. 15.00 (ISBN 0-8093-0947-5). Simon and Schuster.
Forgotten Island. Arthur Olney Friel. LC 33-117893. 1931. The Fiction League.
Forgotten Lady. Norval Richardson. LC 37-33904. J. B. Lippincott Company.
Forgotten Legend of Sleepy Hollow. E. R. Welles & J. P. Evans. LC 73-77815. (Key book). (Illus.). 1973. (pbk.) 2.00 (ISBN 0-913692-03-4) (ISBN 0-913692-03-4). Learning Incorporated.
Forgotten Love. Lynna Cooper, pseud. (Signet book). 1979. 1.75 (ISBN 0-451-08569-8). New American Library.
Forgotten Lover. Carole Mortimer. (Harlequin Presents Ser.). 192p. 1982. pap. 1.75 (ISBN 0-373-10539-8). Harlequin Bks.
Forgotten Memories. Floyd E Willison. LC 48-4145. 1948. Craft Press.
Forgotten Mission. Gus Leodas. (Orig.). 1982. pap. 2.95 (ISBN 0-89083-970-0). Zebra.
Forgotten Music. Cecil John Eustace. LC 74-196928. (Illus.). 1974. (ISBN 0-07-082202-6). McGraw-Hill Ryerson.
Forgotten News: The Crime of the Century & Other Lost Stories. Jack Finney. LC 81-43561. (Illus.). 304p. 1983. 14.95 (ISBN 0-385-17721-6). Doubleday.
Forgotten Passion. James Noble Gifford. LC 45-2951. 1945. Phoenix Press.
Forgotten Place. John Fores. LC 56-10501. 1956. Coward-McCann.
Forgotten Planet. William Fitzgerald Jenkins. LC 54-7255. 1954. Gnome Press.
Forgotten Planet: By Murray Leinster Pseud. William Fitzgerald Jenkins. LC 56-26719. (Ace double novel books, D-146). 1956. Ace Books.
Forgotten Prophet. Francis McKenna. 3.95 o.p. Vantage.
Forgotten Prose. Isaak Emmanuilovich Babel & Nicholas Stroud. LC 78-57175. (Illus.). 1978. 10.95 (ISBN 0-88233-307-0). Ardis.
Forgotten Race. Julius P Newton. LC 67-2532. 1967. Arcadia House.
Forgotten Road. Simon Harvester. LC 73-93934. 224p. 1974. 5.95 o.p. (ISBN 0-8027-5299-3). Walker & Co.
Forgotten Season. Kathleen Conlon. LC 80-53088. 1981. 9.95 (ISBN 0-312-29899-4). St. Martin's Press.
Forgotten Shrines. John Chipman Farrar. LC 20-3703. (On cover: The Yale series of younger poets). 1919. Etc., Etc.
Forgotten Sin: A Novel. Dorothea Gerard Longard De Longgarde. (Half-title: Appletons' town and country library, no. 237). 1898. D. Appleton and Company.
Forgotten Story. Winston Graham. LC 82-45109. 1982. 14.95 (ISBN 0-385-18181-7). Doubleday.
Forgotten Sweetheart. Mary Raymond. LC 34-19183. A. L. Burt Company.
Forgotten Yesterday. Adel Pryor, pseud. LC 65-25957. 1966. Zondervan Pub. House.
Forgotten Yesterdays: A Tale of Early Michigan. Merritt Greene. LC 64-17629. 1964. Hillsdale School Supply.
Fork River Space Project. Wright Morris. LC 77-3798. 1977. 8.95 o.p. (ISBN 0-06-013106-3, HarpT). Har-Row.
Fork River Space Project. Wright Morris. LC 81-7540. vi, 185p. 1981. pap. 5.95 (ISBN 0-8032-8112-9, BB 781, Bison). U of Nebr Pr.
Fork River Space Project: A Novel. Wright Morris. LC 77-3798. 8.95 (ISBN 0-06-013014-8). Harper & Row.
Fork River Space Project: A Novel. Wright Morris. LC 81-7540. 1981. 5.95 (ISBN 0-8032-8112-9). University of Nebraska Press.
Forked Lightning: The Green Flag); a Comedy. John Keble Bell. LC 16-8461. 1916. 1.25. John Lane.
Forked Tongue. Giles A. Lutz. 160p. 1981. pap 1.75 (ISBN 0-345-29220-0). Ballantine.
Forlorn Island. Edison Marshall. LC 32-22974. 1932. Kinsey & Company, Inc.
Forlorn River. Zane Grey. LC 58-42040. Grosset & Dunlap.
Forlorn River. Zane Grey. LC 77-20784. 1978. 11.95 (ISBN 0-8161-6526-2). G. K. Hall.
Forlorn River. Zane Grey. 1974. (pbk.) 0.75 (ISBN 0-671-75792-X). Pocket Books.
Forlorn River: A Romance. Zane Grey. LC 27-23151. 1927. Harper & Brothers.
Forlorn Sunset. Michael Sadleir. LC 46-7876. 1946. Farrar, Straus and Company.
Form Divine. Hildegarde Dolson. LC 51-9489. 1951. Random House.
Form Line of Battle! Alexander Kent. LC 69-18182. (Illus.). 1969. 5.95. Putnam.
Form Line of Battle! Alexander Kent. LC 74-446071. (Illus.). 1969. 3.80. Hutchinson of Australia.
Former Countess: A Romance of the French Revolution. Annie Fields Vila. LC 13-625. 1912. Sherman, French & Company.
Former King: Canto One of the Doom-Quest of Ara Karn-A Dark Romance. Adam Corby. (Orig.). 1981. pap. 2.50 (ISBN 0-671-41770-3, Timescape). PB.
Former People: A Novel. 1st American Ed. Boris Watson. LC 54-5883. 1954. J. Day Co.
Forms of Prose Fiction. Ed. by James L. Calderwood. Harold E. Toliver. LC 70-167635. (Prentice-Hall English literature series). 1972. 4.95 (ISBN 0-13-329219-3). Prentice-Hall.
Forms of the Novella: 10 Short Novels. David Richter. 833p. 1981. pap. text ed. 9.95 (ISBN 0-394-32030-1). Knopf.
Formula. Gordon Sager. LC 52-5086. 1952. Lippincott.
Formula. Steve Shagan. 352p. 1982. pap. 2.75 (ISBN 0-553-13801-4). Bantam.
Formula. Steve Shagan. LC 79-14600. 1979. 10.95 (ISBN 0-688-03532-9). Morrow.

Formula. Gordon Soger. pap. 0.60 o.p. Lancer.
Formula for Death. L. E. Bramwell. (Orig.). 1981. pap. 2.25 (ISBN 0-505-51710-8). Tower Bks.
Formula for Murder. Amelia Reynolds Long. LC 47-123068. 1947. Phoenix Press.
Fornaldar Sogur Nordrlanda Eptir Gomlum Handritum Utgefnar, 3 vol. set. Ed. by C C Ratn. LC 80-1971. 195.00 (ISBN 0-404-18643-2). AMS Pr.
Fornicator. Peggy Stewart. pap. 1.95 o.p. (8076). Cameo.
Fornmanna Sogur, 12 vol. set. Ed. by C C Rafn. LC 80-1970. 610.00 (ISBN 0-404-18650-5). AMS Pr.
Fornsogur Suthrlanda, 2 vol. set. Ed. by Gustaf Cederschiold. LC 80-1969. Repr. of 1884 ed. 62.50 (ISBN 0-404-18663-7). AMS Pr.
Vengeance Trial of Josey Wales.. /Forrest Carter. Forrest Carter. 1977. 1.50 (ISBN 0-440-19344-3). Dell.
Forrest House. A Novel. Mary Jane Hawes Holmes. LC 6-228229. 1883. G. W. Carleton & Co.
Forrest House, As Published in the New York Weekly, Vol. 32, No. 12. Mary Jane Hawes Holmes. LC 7-19043. G. W. Dillingham Company.
Forrestal: Or, The Light of the Reef. A Romance of the Blue Waters. Joseph Holt Ingraham. 1850. Morning Star Office.
Forsaken. George Hatfield Dingley Gossip. LC 10-14650. 1910. 1.00. Cochrane Publishing Company.
Forsaken. Terence Kingsley-Smith. 1975. (pbk.) 1.25. Pocket Books.
Forsaken. Cameron Read. 320p. (Orig.). 1982. pap. 2.95 (ISBN 0-523-41595-8). Pinnacle Bks.
Forsaken: A Tale, 2 vols. Richard Penn Smith. LC 78-64097. Repr. of 1831 ed. 75.00 set (ISBN 0-404-17380-2). AMS Pr.
Forsaken Bride. A Novel. Sarah Elizabeth Forbush G. S. Downs Downs. LC 6-45947. 1886. G. W. Dillingham Etc.
Forsaken Inn: A Novel. Anna Katharine Green Rohlfs. LC 78-164575. (American fiction reprint series). (Illus.). 1971. (ISBN 0-8369-7052-7). Books for Libraries Press.
Forsaken Inn. A Novel. Anna Katharine Green Rohlfs. LC 7-40742. (choice series, no. 22). 1890. R. Bonner's Sons.
Forsaken Inn. A Novel. Anna Katharine Green Rohlfs. (ledger library, no. 22). 1890. R. Bonner's Sons.
Forsaking All Others. Jimmy Breslin & New York (N.Y.). Homicide Zone, 8th. Team C. LC 82-3274. 16.50 (ISBN 0-671-25248-8). Simon and Schuster.
Forsaking All Others. Emilie Baker Loring. LC 70-152401. 1971. 5.95. Little, Brown.
Forsaking All Others. Emilie Baker Loring. LC 72-1476. 1972. 9.95 (ISBN 0-8161-6033-3). G. K. Hall.
Forsaking All Others. Frances Best Simpson. LC 49-50142. 1949. Meador Pub. Co.
Forsaking All Others. Pamela Windsor. (Berkley Medallion Book). 1977. 1.50 (ISBN 0-425-03392-9). Berkley Publishing Corp.
Forsaking All Others: A Story of Sherman's March Through Georgia. Sylla Withers Thomas Hamilton & Sherman, William Tecumseh, 1820-1891--Fiction. 1905. The Neale Publishing Company.
Forsyte Saga. John Galsworthy. 1922. C. Scribner's Sons.
Forsyte Saga. John Galsworthy. LC 41-32210. 1926. C. Scribner's Sons.
Forsyte Saga. John Galsworthy. LC 28-17909. 1927. C. Scribner's Sons.
Forsyte Saga. John Galsworthy. LC 30-12324. 1929. C. Scribner's Sons.
Forsyte Saga. John Galsworthy. LC 33-28739. 1933. C. Scribner's Sons.
Forsyte Saga. John Galsworthy. LC 20-5204. 1928. C. Scribner's Sons.
Forsyte Saga... With Introduction. John Galsworthy. LC 34-18689. (Modern standard authors). C. Scribner's Sons.
Forsythia Intrigued by the Stars. Azerlea P. Barton. 208p. 1976. 7.50 o.p. (ISBN 0-682-48577-2). Exposition.
Forsyth's Three. omnibus ed. Frederick Forsyth. LC 80-14790. 1980. 15.95 (ISBN 0-670-52410-7). Viking Press.
Fort. Margaret Storm Jameson. LC 41-19311. 1941. The Macmillan Company.
Fort Apache. Hunter Ingram. 1975. (pbk.) 0.95 (ISBN 0-345-24413-3). Ballantine Books.
Fort Apache, the Bronx. Heywood Gould. 224p. (Orig.). 1981. pap. 2.75 (ISBN 0-446-95618-X). Warner Bks.
Fort at the Dry. Al Cody, pseud. (Avalon Books). 4.95. Thomas Bouregy.
Fort Bliss. Irving A. Greenfield. 1977. pap. 1.95. Woodhill.
Fort Braddock Letters. John Gardiner Calkins Brainard. LC 6-17940. (Fugitive tales, no. 1). 1830. C. Gaplin.
Fort Braddock Letters: A Tale of the Old French War, or, The Adventure of Du Quesne, Dudley, and Van Tromp: with the Capture of Captain Kidd. John Gardiner Calkins Brainard. 1832. Huestis & Brewer, Printers.
Fort Braddock Letters: Or, A Tale of the French and Indian Wars, in America, at the Beginning of the Eighteenth Century. John Gardiner Calkins Brainard. LC 10-14254. 1827. Dorr & Howland.
Fort Despair. George G. Gilman, pseud. (Steele Ser.: No. 23). 192p. 1983. pap. 1.95 (ISBN 0-523-41914-7). Pinnacle Bks.
Fort Everglades. Frank Gill Slaughter. LC 51-1834. 1951. Doubleday.
Fort Fear. Archie Joscelyn. LC 67-9487. 1967. Arcadia House.
Fort Fisher: Or, The Thunder of Siege Guns. by major a. f. grant. ed. A. F Grant. LC 6-27665. (War library Pocket ed. v. 1, no. 10). 1883. Novelist Publishing Co.
Fort Frayne. Charles King. LC 3-129748. The Hobart Company.
Fort Hogan. Frank Bonham. (Orig.). 1982. pap. 1.95 (ISBN 0-425-05619-8). Berkley Pub.
Fort in the Jungle: The Extraordinary Adventures of Sinbad Dysart in Tonkin. Percival Christopher Wren. LC 36-20443. 1936. Houghton Mifflin Company.
Fort in the Wilderness: Or, The Soldier Boys of the Indian Trails. Edward Stratemeyer. LC 5-32728. (On cover: Colonial series). 1905. Lee and Shepard.
Fort Lafayette: Or, Love and Secession. A Novel. Benjamin Wood. 1862. Carleton.
Fort Starke. Wade Everett. 160p. (Orig.). 1980. pap. 1.75 (ISBN 0-345-28851-3). Ballantine.
Fort Starvation. Frank Gruber. LC 52-12102. Rinehart.
Fort Sun Dance. Manly Wade Wellman. LC 54-12492. (Dell first edition 52). 1955. Dell Pub. Co.
Fort Terror Murders... Francis Van Wyck Mason. LC 32-331. Pub. for the Crime Club, Inc., by Doubleday, Doran & Company, Inc.
Fortas Case & the Struggle for the Supreme Court. Barnett & Harvey. (Illus.). 1972. 7.95 o.p. Bobbs.
FORTEC Conspiracy. Richard M. Garvin & Edmond G. Addeo. LC 68-13286. 1968. Sherbourne Press.
Fortenberry Rites. Margaret Ogan. 1976. pap. 1.25 (ISBN 0-89041-118-2, 3118). Major Bks.
Forth into Light. Gordon Merrick. 1974. pap. 2.75 (ISBN 0-380-01195-6, 76869). Avon.
Forthcoming Marriages. Mary Lutyens. LC 33-30446. E. P. Dutton & Co., Inc.
Fortieth Door. Mary Hastings Bradley. LC 20-22641. 1920. D. Appleton and Company.
Fortitude. V. Ketlinskaya. 558p. 1975. 7.95 (ISBN 0-8285-0993-X, Pub. by Progress Pubs USSR). Imported Pubns.
Fortitude. Hugh Walpole. LC 31-261231. (Half-title: The modern library of the world's best books). 1930. The Modern Library.
Fortitude. Hugh Walpole. LC 37-18323. (Half-title: The modern library of the world's best books). 1930. The Modern Library.
Fortitude: Being a True and Faithful Account of the Education of an Adventurer. Hugh Walpole. LC 13-5068. George H. Doran Company.
Fortitude: Being a True and Faithful Account of the Education of an Adventurer. abridged ed. Hugh Walpole. LC 38-4653. Doubleday, Doran & Company, Inc.
Fortnight in Old Vincennes. 1st Ed. Emily Adams Emison. LC 56-129230. 1957. Vantage Press.
Fortnight in September: A Novel. Robert Cedric Sherriff. LC 32-5862. 1932. Frederick A. Stokes Company.
Fortnight of Folly. Maurice Thompson. LC 8-19967. 1888. J. B. Alden.
Fortnight's Anger. R. Scruton. 224p. 1981. text ed. 15.00x (ISBN 0-85635-376-0, Pub. by Carcanet Pr England). Humanities.
Fortress. Catherine Irvine Gavin. LC 64-19254. 1964. Doubleday.
Fortress. Henry Jaeger. LC 65-20985. Harper & Row.
Fortress. Gabrielle Lord. LC 80-29322. 8.95 (ISBN 0-312-29978-8). St. Martin's Press.
Fortress. Siegfried Stander. LC 72-9073. 1973. 5.95 (ISBN 0-395-15464-2). Houghton Mifflin.
Fortress. Hugh Walpole. 1932. 5.50 o.p. St Martin.
Fortress. Hugh Walpole. 1972. pap. 1.25 o.p. (01032). Curtis.
Fortress: A Novel. Hugh Walpole. LC 32-27005. 1932. Doubleday, Doran & Company, Inc.
Fortress Atlantis. K. H Scheer. (Perry Rhoda#52). (Illus.). 1974. (pbk.) 0.95. Ace Books.
Fortress Besieged. Chung-Shu Chien. LC 78-24846. (Chinese Literature in Translation). 17.50 (ISBN 0-253-16518-0). Indiana University Press.
Fortress Fury: By Carter A. Vaughan Pseud. Noel Bertram Gerson. LC 66-17397. 4.50. Doubleday.
Fortress in the Forth. Jane Lane. LC 78-21465. 1967. 5.25x o.p. Intl Pubns Serv.
Fortress in the Forth. Jane Lane. 1971. pap. 0.95 o.p. (95131). Beagle Bks.
Fortress in the Rice. 1st Ed. Benjamin Appel. LC 51-13642. 1951. Bobbs-Merrill.
Fortress in the Skies: A Tale... Peter Mendelssohn. LC 43-14281. 1943. Doubleday, Doran and Company, Inc.
Fortress London. Zachary Hughes. (Hotel Destiny Ser.: No 2). 320p. (Orig.). 1981. pap. 2.95 (ISBN 0-515-06047-X). Jove Pubns.
Fortress Within. Sylvia D Holcomb. LC 46-233. 1945. Dorrance & Company.
Fortuna. Perez Escrich, Enrique. Ed. by Barnes, Gladys Aspasia. (Harlow Spanish series). 1936. Harlow Publishing Corporation.
Fortunata: A Novel. Marjorie Patterson. LC 11-1962. 1911. 1.30. Harper & Brothers.
Fortunata and Jacinta: Two Stories of Married Women. translated by lester clark. ed. Benito Perez Galdos. 1973. (ISBN 0-14-044277-4). Penguin Books.
Fortunate Belle. Maggie Gladstone, pseud. LC 78-58392. 208p. 1978. pap. 1.50 (ISBN 0-87216-483-7). Playboy Pbks.
Fortunate Failure. Caroline Bigelow Le Row. LC 11-16150. D. Lothrop and Company.
Fortunate Failure. Caroline Bigelow Le Row. LC 7-12828. (On cover: The household library. no. 7). 1886. D. Lothrop and Company.
Fortunate Foundlings. Eliza Fowler Haywood. LC 74-17293. (Flowering of the Novel). 1974. (ISBN 0-8240-1109-0). Garland Pub.
Fortunate Island. Enid S Russell. LC 72-96255. 1973. 4.95 (ISBN 0-385-02838-5). Published for the Crime Club by Doubleday.
Fortunate Lady: A Dramatic Chronicle. Frank Arthur Swinnerton. LC 41-181182. 1934. Doubleday, Doran & Co., Inc.
Fortunate Madness. Susan Richards Shreve. LC 74-5213. 1974. 5.95 (ISBN 0-395-18500-9). Houghton Mifflin.
Fortunate Man. Frank Tilsley. LC 53-8491. 1953. J. Messner.
Fortunate Man: The Story of a Country Doctor. John Berger. (Illus.). 176p. (Orig.). 1981. pap. 3.95 (ISBN 0-904613-11-9). Writers & Readers.
Fortunate Marriage. Meriol Trevor. LC 75-32662. 7.95 (ISBN 0-525-10770-3). Dutton.
Fortunate Marriage. Meriol Trevor. (Fawcett Crest Book.). 1976. 1.50 (ISBN 0-449-23137-2). Fawcett Publications.
Fortunate Mary. Eleanor Hodgman Porter. LC 28-21586. 1928. Doubleday, Doran & Company, Inc.
Fortunate Miss East. Laurence Meynell. LC 73-93758. (Signet book). 1975. (pbk.) 1.50. New American Library.
Fortunate Miss East. Laurence Walter Meynell. LC 73-93758. 256p. (YA) 1974. 6.95 o.p. (ISBN 0-698-10604-0). Coward.
Fortunate Mistress: Or, A History of the Life of Mademoiselle De Beleau, Known by the Name of the Lady Roxana. Daniel Defoe. LC 74-13447. (Illus.). 1974. (ISBN 0-404-07922-9). AMS Press.
Fortunate Pilgrim. Mario Puzo. LC 65-10917. 1965. bds., 5.75. Atheneum.
Fortunate Prisoner. Max Pemberton. LC 9-26144. 1.50. G. W. Dillingham Company.
Fortunate Wayfarer. Edward Phillips Oppenheim. LC 28-12654. 1928. Little, Brown, and Company.
Fortunate Youth. William John Locke. LC 14-55126. 1914. John Lane Company.
Fortune. Doug Bailey. 320p. (Orig.). 1981. pap. 3.25 (ISBN 0-441-24871-3). Ace Bks.
Fortune... Robert Raynolds. LC 35-18687. 1935. W. Morrow & Company.
Fortune. John Collis Snaith. LC 10-9820. 1.50.
Fortune. John Collis Snaith. LC 10-105113. 1910. 1.50. Moffat, Yard and Company.
Fortune. Albert Payson Terhune. LC 18-18402. 1918. Doubleday, Page & Company.
Fortune: A Romance of Friendship. Douglas Goldring. LC 20-5. 1919. Scott and Seltzer.
Fortune and Men's Eyes. George William Cronyn. LC 35-8858. Covici, Friede.
Fortune at Bandy's Flat. Camilla Kenyon. LC 21-17268. The Bobbs Merrill Company.
Fortune Finders. Jacquin Sanders. LC 56-6005. 1956. Appleton-Century-Crofts.
Fortune Finders. Jacquin Sanders. LC 81-69102. 9.95 (ISBN 0-8027-4003-0). Walker.
Fortune for Kregan. Dray Prescot. (Science Fiction Ser.). (Illus., Orig.). 1979. pap. 1.95 o.p. (ISBN 0-87997-505-9, UJ1505). Daw Bks.
Fortune Hunter. Ira J Morris. LC 72-79034. (Fawcett crest book). 1974. (pbk.) 1.25. Fawcett.
Fortune Hunter. David Graham Phillips. LC 72-84629. 1976. (ISBN 0-403-03163-X). Scholarly Press.
Fortune Hunter. David Graham Phillips. 1906. The Bobbs-Merrill Company.
Fortune Hunter. Louis Joseph Vance & Smith, Winchell, 1871-1933. LC 10-4592. 1910. Dodd, Mead and Company.
Fortune Hunter: A Novel of New York Society. Anna Cora Ogden Mowatt Ritchie. T. B. Peterson.
Fortune Hunter: Or, The Old Stone Corral. A Tale of the Santa Fe Trail. John Dunloe Carteret. LC 6-20173. 1888. The Author.
Fortune Hunters. Joan Aiken. LC 65-11056. 1965. Published for the Crime Club by Doubleday.
Fortune Hunters. Joan Aiken. 1973. Pocket Bks.
Fortune Hunters. John Thomas Edson. 1983. pap. 2.25 (ISBN 0-425-05753-4). Berkley Pub.
Fortune in Death. Leonard St. Clair. (Orig.). 1972. pap. 0.75 o.p. (T2636, GM). Fawcett World.
Fortune in Dimes: A Novel. Mary Arkley Carter. LC 63-8305. (Atlantic Monthly Press book). 1963. Little, Brown.
Fortune in Romance. Maysie Greig. LC 40-40101. 1940. Doubleday, Doran and Company, Inc.
Fortune in Your Hand. Elizabeth D. Scuire. pap. 1.75 (ISBN 0-451-08061-0, E8061, Sig). NAL.
Fortune Is a Woman. Winston Graham. LC 53-7980. 1953. Doubleday.
Fortune Machine. Sam Ross. LC 71-96996. 1970. 5.95. Delacorte Press.
Fortune Made His Sword: A Novel. Martha Rofheart. 1973. (pbk.) 1.75. Dell.
Fortune Made His Sword: A Novel. Martha Rofheart. LC 78-175254. 1972. 8.95. Putnam.
Fortune My Foe. Audrey Lindop. LC 47-1579. 1947. Harper & Brothers.
Fortune of a Day. Grace Ellery Channing Stetson. LC 5153. 1900. H. S. Stone & Company.
Fortune of Bridget Malone. Marie Adelaide Belloc Lowndes. LC 37-230844. 1937. Longmans, Green and Co.
Fortune of Christina M'Nab. Sarah Broom Macnaughtan. LC 1-27699. (Half-title: Appleton's town and country library. no. 306). 1901. D. Appleton and Company.
Fortune of War: Being Portions of Many Letters and Journals Written to and for Her Cousin Mistress Dorothea Engel... Elizabeth N. Barrow. 1900. H. Holt and Company.
Fortune Road. Edward Hunt. (Orig.). 1971. pap. 0.75 o.p. (75-380). Manor Bks.
Fortune Road. James P. McCague. LC 65-209879. 4.95. Harper.
Fortune Seeker. Denice Greenlea. (Fawcett Crest Book). 1977. 1.50 (ISBN 0-449-23301-4). Fawcett Pubns.
Fortune Seeker. Emma Dorothy Eliza Nevitte Southworth. LC 11-7151. T. B. Peterson & Brothers.
Fortune, Smile Once More! Mary Floyd Williams. LC 46-733256. 1946. The Bobbs-Merrill Company.
Fortune Stick. Bob Stanley. pap. 1.95 o.s.i. (OPH-214, Ophelia). Olympia.
Fortune Teller of Killarney: Or, The Spirit of Revenge, and Ever in Danger. M. J. McGlynn. LC 7-20005. 1876. Ottaway & Colbert, Printers.
Fortune-Teller of New Orleans: Or, The Two Lost Daughters. William Henry Peck. LC 7-36478. (sea and shore series, no. 14). 1889. Street & Smith.
Fortune Tellers. 1st Ed. Berry Fleming. LC 51-11202. 1951. Lippincott.
Fortune Wheel. Valerie Bradstreet. 160p. 1981. pap. 2.25 (ISBN 0-380-78303-7, 78303). Avon.
Fortunes. Mary Bringle. LC 80-397. 11.95 (ISBN 0-399-12458-6). Putnam.
Fortunes. James Ferguson. (Orig.). 1982. pap. 3.95 (ISBN 0-440-12765-3). Dell.
Fortunes & Misfortunes of Moll Flanders. Daniel Defoe. 3.25x o.p. (ISBN 0-460-00837-4, Evman). Dutton.
Fortunes and Misfortunes of the Famous Moll Flanders. Daniel Defoe. LC 74-13449. (Illus.). 1974. 11.00 ea. (ISBN 0-404-07917-2). AMS Press.
Fortunes & Misfortunes of the Famous Moll Flandera. Daniel Defoe. LC 49-507210. (Rinehart editions, 25). 1949. Rinchart.
Fortunes and Misfortunes of the Famous Moll Flanders. Daniel Defoe. LC 23-15254. (Borzoi classics). 1923. A. A. Knopf.
Fortunes and Misfortunes of the Famous Moll Flanders. Daniel Defoe. LC 27-26623. (Half-title: The modern library of the world's best books). 1926. The Modern Library.
Fortunes & Misfortunes of the Famous Moll Flanders. Daniel Defoe. (Half-title: Everyman's library, ed. by Ernest Rhys. Fiction.. no. 837). 1930. J. M. Dent & Sons, Ltd.
Fortunes and Misfortunes of the Famous Moll Flanders... a new ed., with illustrations by alexander king. ed. Daniel Defoe. LC 32-987176. The Hogarth Press, Inc.

Fortunes and Misfortunes of the Famous Moll Flanders. Daniel Defoe & Marsh, Reginald, 1898- Illus. LC 43-5944. 1942. The Heritage Press.

Fortunes and Misfortunes of the Famous Moll Flanders. Daniel Defoe & Juliet Mitchell. LC 78-314286. (Penguin English library). 1978. 1.95 (ISBN 0-14-043107-1). Penguin.

Fortunes and Misfortunes of the Famous Moll Flanders: &C..... Introd. by Edward Wagenknecht. Daniel Defoe. LC 65-664610. (Perennial classic P3034A). 1.50, .50 pap.,. Harper.

Fortunes and Misfortunes of the Famous Moll Flanders, &C... Daniel Defoe. LC 72-181436. (Oxford English novels). 1971. 2.50 (ISBN 0-19-255352-6). Oxford University Press.

Fortunes and Misfortunes of the Famous Moll Flanders &C.... Introd. by Mark Schorer. Daniel Defoe. LC 50-12239. (Modern Library college editions, T8). 1950. Modern Library.

Fortunes and Misfortunes of the Famous Moll Flanders and The Fortunate Mistress: Or, The Lady Roxana. Daniel Defoe. 1906. G. Routledge & Sons, Ltd.

Fortune's Child, No. 149. Rachelle Edwards. 224p. 1981. pap. 1.50 (ISBN 0-449-50222-8, Coventry). Fawcett.

Fortune's Cup. Gordon Malherbe Hillman. LC 41-19309. 1941. Thomas Y. Crowell Company.

Fortune's Fool. Julian Hawthorne. LC 7-38958. 1883. J. R. Osgood and Company.

Fortune's Fool. Rafael Sabatini. LC 23-11978. 1923. Houghton Mifflin Company.

Fortune's Foot-Ball: Or, The Adventures of Mercutio. Founded on Matters of Fact. A Novel... James Butler. LC 6-166763. 1797-98. Printed by J. Wyeth.

Fortune's Footballs. George Brown Burgin. LC 6-186614. (Half-title: Appletons' town and country library, no. 236). 1897. D. Appleton and Company.

Fortune's Gift. Elizabeth Burton. LC 47-3636. 1947. Dodd, Mead & Company.

Fortunes, Good and Bad of a Sewing-Girl: Or, "Out of Darkness into Light.". Charlotte M. Stanley McKenna. (On cover: The seaside library. Pocket ed. no. 468). 1885. G. Munro.

Fortune's Marriage. A Novel. Georgiana Marion Craik May. (Harper's Franklin square library, no. 266). 1882. Harper & Brothers.

Fortune's Mistress. Marilyn Ross. 288p. 1981. pap. 2.75 (ISBN 0-445-04673-2). Popular Lib.

Fortune's My Foe: A Romance. John Edward Bloundelle-Burton. LC 14-22443. 1899. D. Appleton and Company.

Fortunes of a Factory Girl. A Tale of the Manchester Mills. Erwin L Coolidge. LC 31-35337. (Hub ten cent library, v. 1, no. 4). 1894. Atlantic News Company.

Fortunes of a Fool. Translated from the Hebrew by Hebrew Hodes. With a Foreword to the English Ed. by Max Brod. Aharon Megged. LC 62-127265. 1962. Random House.

Fortunes of a Free-Lance: Or, Brakespeare. George Alfred Lawrence. LC 4-30149. 1904. The Saalfield Publishing Company.

Fortunes of a Household. Herman Johan Robbers. Tr. by Chilton, Helen. LC 24-15068. 1924. A. A. Knopf.

Fortunes of Betty. A Sweet and Tender Romance of an Old Soldier's Daughter. Cecil Spooner. LC 10-256793. J. S. Ogilvie Publishing Company.

Fortunes of Captain Blood. Rafael Sabatini. LC 36-30932. 1936. Houghton Mifflin Company.

Fortunes of Colonel Torlogh O'Brien: A Tale of the Wars of King James. Joseph Sheridan Le Fann & Browne, Hablot Knight, 1815-1882, Illus. LC 17-13046. G. Routledge and Sons.

Fortunes of Colonel Torlogh O'Brien: A Tale of the Wars of King James. Joseph Sheridan Le Fanu. LC 76-4603. (Le Fanu, Joseph Sheridan, 1814-1873. Works. 1976). 1976. 26.00 (ISBN 0-405-09207-5). Arno Press.

Fortunes of Conrad: A Novel. Sylvanus Cobb. (On cover: The popular series, no. 9). 1891. R. Bonner's Sons.

Fortunes of Fifi. Molly Elliot Seawell. LC 3-23048. 1903. The Bobbs-Merrill Company.

Fortunes of Fingel. Simon Raven. LC 77-356360. (Illus.). 1976. 3.50 (ISBN 0-85634-055-3). Blond and Briggs.

Fortunes of Garin. Mary Johnston. LC 15-21626. 1915. Houghton Mifflin Company.

Fortunes of Glencore. Charles James Lever. LC 42-29444. G. Routledge and Sons.

Fortunes of Glencore. To Which Is Added A Rent in a Cloud. Charles James Lever. LC 24-118568. (Half-title: The novels of Charles Lever. Library edition. Novels of foreign life). 1901. Little, Brown, and Company.

Fortunes of Hector O'Halloran & His Man, Mark Anthony O'Toole. William Hamilton Maxwell. Ed. by Robert L. Wolff. (Ireland Nineteenth Century Fiction - Ser. Two: Vol. 51). 416p. 1979. lib. bdg. 32.00 (ISBN 0-8240-3500-3). Garland Pub.

Fortunes of Hugo. Denis George Mackail. LC 26-14677. 1926. Houghton Mifflin Company.

Fortunes of Laurie Breaux: A Novel. 1st Ed. Charlotte Painter. LC 61-138995. 1961. Little, Brown.

Fortunes of Lolita: The Dancer. Kate O'Brien Hesketh Prichard & Prichard, Hesketh Vernon Hesketh. LC 10-4640.

Fortunes of Love. Caroline Courtney. LC 80-29449. 1981. 12.95 (ISBN 0-8161-3138-4). G. K. Hall.

Fortunes of Margaret Weld. Sarah M. H Gardner. LC 7-295296. 1894. Arena Publishing Company.

Fortunes of Maurice O'Donnell: An Irish-American Story. James F. Murphy. LC 7-31832. 1887. A. E. & R. E. Ford; Etc., Etc.

Fortunes of Nigel. Walter Scott. (On cover: Lovell's library, no. 504). 1885. J. W. Lovell Company.

Fortunes of Nigel. Walter Scott. (Half-title: Everyman's library, edited by Ernest Rhys 71). 1906. J. M. Dent & Co.

Fortunes of Nigel. Walter Scott. LC 36-37081. (Half-title: Everyman's library, ed. by Ernest Rhys. Fiction. no. 71). 1929. J. M. Dent & Sons, Ltd.

Fortunes of Nigel... Walter Scott. LC 43-37799. (Waverley novels. Illustrated library ed.). 1875. J. R. Osgood and Company.

Fortunes of Nigel. Walter Scott. LC 43-42356. Rand, McNally & Company.

Fortunes of Nigel. Ed., Introd. by Frederick M. Link. Walter Scott. Ed. by Frederick M. Link. LC 65-18715. (Bison bk., BB321). pap., 1.90. Univ. of Neb. Pr.

Fortunes of Oliver Horn. Francis Hopkinson Smith. LC 2-20817. 1902. C. Scribner's Sons.

Fortunes of Perkin Warbeck: A Romance. Mary Wollstonecraft Godwin Shelley & Author Of Frankenstein. LC 75-33814. 1975. 100.00 (ISBN 0-8414-7576-8). Folcroft Library Editions.

Fortunes of Rachel. Edward Everett Hale. LC 6-46172. (On cover: Standard library. no. 115). 1884. Funk & Wagnalls.

Fortunes of Richard Mahoney. Henrietta Richardson. LC 41-92783. The Press of the Readers Club.

Fortunes of Richard Mahony. Henry Handel Richardson. LC 17-23332. 1917. H. Holt.

Fortunes of Richard Mahony. Henry Handel Richardson. LC 31-28159. 1931. W. W. Norton.

Fortunes of Richard Mahony. Henry Handel Richardson. LC 41-9278. 1941. Press of the Readers Club.

Fortunes of Richard Mahony see Australian Classics.

Fortunes of the Colville Family: Or, A Cloud with Its Silver Lining. Francis Edward Smedley. LC 41-27434. G. Routledge and Sons.

Fortunes of the Faradays. Amanda Minnie Douglas. LC 6-33486. 1888. Lee and Shepard.

Fortunes of the Landrays. Vaughan Kester. LC 5-32850. 1905. McClure, Phillips & Co.

Fortunes of the Pasquiers. Georges Duhamel. Tr. by Putnam, Samuel. LC 35-287341. 1935. Harper & Brothers.

Fortune's Tide. Gene Lancour. (Carlisle Saga: No. 2). 336p. 1981. pap. 2.75 (ISBN 0-440-02755-1, Standish). Dell.

Fortune's Wheel. Rhoda Edwards. LC 78-7752. (Illus.). 8.95 (ISBN 0-385-11582-2). Doubleday.

Fortune's Wheel. Agnes Louise Provost. LC 34-35304. 1934. Macrae Smith Company.

Fortune's Wheel: A Novel. Alexander Innes Shand. LC 8-4792. (Harper's handy series, no. 54). 1886. Harper & Brothers.

Fortune's Wheel: And Other Stories. Eliza M. J. Humphreys & Cudlip, Annie Hall (Thomas) "Mrs. P. H. Cudlip," 1838- (On cover: The seaside library, Pocket ed., no. 171). 1884. G. Munro.

Fortune's Yellow. Evelyn Schuyler Schaeffer. LC 25-5848. 1925. C. Scribner's Sons.

Fortunes's Mistress. Paul R. Rothweiler. (Westward Rails Ser.: No. 2). (Orig.). 1982. pap. 2.75 (ISBN 0-440-02761-6, Banbury). Dell.

Fortunoff's Child. Leslie Tonner. LC 79-27138. 9.95 (ISBN 0-8037-5792-1). Dial Press.

Forty Acres & No Mule. 2d ed.,with a new prologue by the author. ed. Janice Holt Giles. LC 66-22126. (Illus.). 1967. Houghton Mifflin.

Forty Acres & No Mule. Janice Holt Giles. LC 52-8129. 1952. Westminster Press.

Forty Brothers. Jean Francis Webb. LC 35-19154. The Collegiate Press.

Forty Centuries Look Down: A Biographical Novel of Napoleon. Frederick Britten Austin. LC 37-2689. 1937. Frederick A. Stokes Company.

Forty Days. first american ed. Oswald Wynd. LC 72-88800. 1973. 6.95 (ISBN 0-15-132680-0). Harcourt.

Forty Days of Muna Dagh. Franz V. Werfel. Tr. by Geoffrey Dunlop. LC 34-28461. 1934. The Viking Press.

Forty Days of Musa Dagh. Franz V. Werfel. Tr. by Geoffrey Dunlop. 1967. pap., 2.25. Viking.

Forty Days of Musa Dagh. Franz V. Werfel. Tr. by Geoffrey Dunlop. LC 37-27273. (Half-title: The modern library of the world's best books). 1937. The Modern Library.

Forty Days till Dawn: Memoirs of the Apostle Paul. Wesley Shrader. LC 78-170913. 1972. 3.95. Word Books.

Forty-Eight Bernard Street. Susanna Rebecca Graham Clark. LC 24-32085. C.

Forty-Eight Guns for the General. Eddie Iroh. LC 77-368288. (African writers series). (H.E.B. paperback). 1976-1977. 2.50 (ISBN 0-435-90189-3). Heinemann.

Forty-Eight Hours to Hammelburg. Charles Whiting. LC 82-81389. 224p. 1982. pap. text ed. 2.95 (ISBN 0-86721-200-4). Playboy Pbks.

Forty-Eight Saroyan Stories. William Saroyan. LC 43-7714. (Avon pocket-size books). 1942. The Avon Book Company.

Forty Fathoms Down. Lawrence Cortesi, pseud. 1979. pap. 1.75 o.s.i. (ISBN 0-505-51445-1). Tower Bks.

Forty Fathoms Down (The Silent Service No. 2) Jones J. Farragut. (Orig.). 1981. pap. 2.75 (ISBN 0-440-12655-X). Dell.

Forty First. hyperion reprint ed. Boris Andreevich Lavrenev. LC 75-39003. (Early Soviet Literature in English Translation). 1978. 16.00 (ISBN 0-88355-406-2). Hyperion Press.

Forty-First Thief. Edward A. Pollitz. 1975. 8.95 o.p. (ISBN 0-440-04837-0). Delacorte.

Forty-First Thief: A Novel. Edward A. Pollitz. LC 74-31106. 1975. 8.95 (ISBN 0-440-04837-0). Delacorte Press.

Forty-Five. Alexandre Dumas. 1893. Little, Brown, & Company.

Forty-Five. Alexandre Dumas & Maquet, Auguste. LC 6-42120. (Half-title: The Valois romances). 1889. Little, Brown and Company.

Forty-Five. Alexandre Dumas & Maquet, Auguste. LC 36-37257. (Half-title: Everyman's library, ed. by Ernest Rhys. Fiction. no. 420). 1932. J. M. Dent & Sons, Ltd.

Forty-Five Guardsmen. Alexandre Dumas & Maquet, Auguste. LC 5699. 1900. T. Y. Crowell & Company.

Forty-Five Guardsmen. Alexandre Dumas & Maquet, Auguste. LC 4564. T. Y. Crowell & Company.

Forty-Five Guardsmen. A Novel. Alexandre Dumas & Maquet, Auguste. LC 6-42119. (Seaside library, v. 14, no. 268). G. Munro.

Forty-Five Guardsmen: A Sequel to "Marguerite De Valois", and "Chicot the Jester". Alexandre Dumas & Maquet, Auguste. LC 3-27811. G. Routledge and Son, Limited.

Forty-Five Guardsmen: A Sequel to "Marguerite De Valois" and "Chicot, the Jester.". Alexandre Dumas & Maquet, Auguste. (American series no. 330). 1894. M. J. Ivers & Co.

Forty-Five Guardsmen. A Sequel to "Marguerite De Valois" and "Chicot, the Jester.". Alexandre Dumas & Maquet, Auguste. (On cover: Seaside library. Pocket ed. no. 2117). G. Munro's Sons.

Forty Footers. Avin Harry Johnston. (Orig.). 1980. pap. 1.95 (ISBN 0-532-23215-1). Woodhill.

Forty-Four Caliber. Jimmy Breslin & Richard Schaap. LC 78-3864. 1978. 9.95 (ISBN 0-670-32432-9). Viking Press.

Forty Four Gravel Street. Ben Maddow. LC 52-5506. 1952. Little, Brown.

Forty-Four Hungarian Short Stories. Intro. by Charles Percy Snow. 733p. 1979. 13.50x (ISBN 963-13-6510-7). Intl Pubns Serv.

Forty-Four Irish Short Stories: An Anthology of Irish Short Fiction from Yeats to Frank O'Connor. Ed. by Devin A. Garrity. 1980. 10.95 (ISBN 0-517-34295-2). Devin.

Forty-Four Irish Short Stories: Anthology of Irish Short Fiction from Yeats to Frank O Connor. Ed. by Devin A. Garrity. LC 54-10817. 1955. Devin-Adair Co.

Forty-Four Vintage. Anthony Price. LC 77-92229. 1978. 7.95 (ISBN 0-385-14028-2). Published for the Crime Club by Doubleday.

Forty-Four Years of the Life of a Hunter," Being Reminiscences of Meshach Browning, a Maryland Hunter. Meshach Browning & Edward Stabler. LC 43-2511. 1942. Winston Printing Company.

Forty-Four Years of the Life of a Hunter: Being Reminiscences of Meshach Browning, a Maryland Hunter. Meshach Browning & Stabler, Edward, 1794-1833, Ed. LC 7297. 1860. J. B. Lippincott & Co.

Forty Is...!? Jim Everhart, pseud. (Orig.). 1969. pap. 2.95 (ISBN 0-8220-1468-8). Cliffs.

Forty Lashes Less One. Elmore Leonard. 176p. (Orig.). 1981. pap. 1.95 (ISBN 0-553-20578-1). Bantam.

Forty Minutes Late: And Other Stories. Francis Hopkinson Smith. LC 9-25819. 1909. C. Scribner's Sons.

Forty Modern Fables. George Ade. LC 1-270464. 1901. R.H. Russell.

Forty Modern Fables. George Ade. LC 21-129703.

Forty-Nine: A Novel of Gold. George William Cronyn. LC 25-4213. Dorrance & Company.

Forty-Nine Cuentos Minimos y una Triste Leyenda. Andres Rivero. LC 79-51379. (Short Stories in Spanish Ser.). 48p. (Orig., Span.). (gr. 11). 1980. pap. 3.00x o.p. (ISBN 0-933648-01-4). Cruzada Span Pubns.

Forty-Nine Days of Death. Bill S. Ballinger. 224p. 1969. 4.95 o.p. (ISBN 0-8202-0055-7). Sherbourne.

Forty-Nine Stories. John O'Hara. (Modern Library Giants). 1963. 4.95 o.p. (G88). Modern Lib.

Forty-Nine: The Gold-Seekers of the Sierras. Joaquin Miller. LC 78-104527. 1970. (ISBN 0-8398-1258-2). Literature House.

Forty-Niner, the Gold-Seeker of the Sierras. Joaquin Miller. LC 7-25987. (On cover: Standard library, no. 123). 1884. Funk & Wagnalls.

Forty-Niners. (Frontier Rakers Ser.: No. 2). (Orig.). 1981. pap. 2.95 (ISBN 0-89083-883-6). Zebra.

Forty-Niners. David Norman. (Frontier Rakers Ser.: No. 2). 384p. (Orig.). 1980. pap. 2.50 (ISBN 0-89083-634-5). Zebra.

Forty-Niners. John Toombs. (Dell / Bryans Book). (Illus.). 1979. 2.50 (ISBN 0-440-02535-4). Dell Pub. Co.

Forty-One Grove Street. Rosemarie Santini. (Orig.). 1973. pap. 0.95 o.p. (09177). Curtis.

Forty-One Thieves: A Tale of California. Angelo Hall. LC 19-14697. The Cornhill Company.

Forty Pounds of Gold. Philip Duffield Stong. LC 51-12485. 1951. Doubleday.

Forty-Second Parallel. John Dos Passos. 3.50 o.p. HM.

Forty-Second Street. Bradford Ropes. LC 32-23426. A. H. King.

Forty-Second Year of Mrs. Charles Prescott. Jain McNab. 1976. pap. 1.50 o.p. (ISBN 0-515-04099-1). BJ Pub Group.

Forty Seven Days & a Night. Virda B. Wilkins. 4.95 o.p. Vantage.

Forty-Seven Ronin Story. John Allyn. LC 70-121274. 1970. 3.95 (ISBN 0-8048-0196-7). C.E. Tuttle Co.

Forty Stay in: A Novel by John W. Vandercook. John Womack Vandercook. LC 31-23968. 1931. Harper & Brothers.

Forty-Two Days for Murder. Roger Torrey. LC 38-4574. 1938. Hillman-Curl, Inc.

Forty Whacks. Fanny Howe. LC 69-15017. 1969. 4.95. Houghton Mifflin.

Forty Whacks. Daniel Mainwaring. LC 41-21404. 1941. W. Morrow and Company.

Forty Years of Psychic Research see Collected Works.

Forty Years of Silence. Clifford A. Brown. 2.00 o.p. (ISBN 0-8338-0017-5). M Jones.

Forum Stories. The Forum. Ed. by Hooley, Arthur. LC 14-14460. 1914. M. Kennerley.

Forward Ever! Maurice Bishop. 280p. 1982. lib. bdg. 23.00 (ISBN 0-909196-16-8); pap. 6.95 (ISBN 0-909196-17-6). Path Pr NY.

Forward from Babylon. Louis Golding. LC 32-229859. Farrar & Rinehart, Incorporated.

Forward, Gunner Asch. Hans Hellmut Kirst. 1968. pap. 0.75 o.p. (T1845). Pyramid Pubns.

Forward, Gunner Asch! Translated from the German by Robert Kee. 1st American Ed. Hans Hellmut Kirst. LC 56-10646. 1956. Little, Brown.

Forward, Gunner Ash. Hans Hellmut Kirst. 1976. pap. 1.50 o.p. (ISBN 0-515-03930-6). BJ Pub Group.

Forward House: A Romance. 'William Scoville Case. LC 6-22798. 1895. C. Scribner's Sons.

Forward in Time. Benjamin Bova. 288p. 1982. pap. 2.75 (ISBN 0-445-08310-7). Popular Lib.

Forward in Time: A Science Fiction Story Collection. Benjamin Bova. LC 73-83312. 1973. 6.95 (ISBN 0-8027-5562-3). Walker.

Foster & Laurie. Al Silverman. 1974. 7.95 (ISBN 0-316-79116-4). Little.

Foster Brothers: A Novel. Edward Percy Frankland. LC 54-10457. (Illus.). 1954. J. Day Co.

Foster Child. Marion Dane Bauer. (Laurel Leaf Library Book). 1978. 1.25 (ISBN 0-440-92861-3). Dell Publishing Co., Inc.

Foster Child - What Then. Barbara H. Smith. 1970. 2.00 o.p. Carlton.

Foster Father. Harry Ellis Madden. LC 75-28567. (Illus.). 1975. Madden.

Foster-Mother. Martin Donisthorpe Armstrong. LC 34-1944. Harcourt, Brace and Company.

Fostina Woodman: The Wonderful Adventurer... Avis A. Burnham Stanwood. LC 8-28091. 1850. Redding and Company.

Fostina Woodman: The Wonderful Adventurer... Avis A. Burnham Stanwood. 1854. Boston Stereotype Foundry.

Fothergill: Or, The Man of Enterprise. J. Austin Sperry. LC 8-14066. 1850. Printed at "the Great West" Office.

Foul Matter. Joan Aiken. LC 82-45536. 264p. 1983. 14.95 (ISBN 0-385-18371-2). Doubleday.
Foul Play. Charles Reade. LC 42-309140. (His Works. Library edition). 1895. Metropolitan Publishing Company.
Foul Play. Charles Reade & Boucicault, Dion. (On cover: Lovell's library, v. 15, no. 759). 1886. J. W. Lovell Company.
Foul Play. Charles Reade & Boucicault, Dion. LC 41-32442. (On cover: The home library). 1903. A. L. Burt Company.
Foul Play. Charles Reade & Boucicault, Dion. LC 18-26178. 1917. G. P. Putnam's Sons.
Foul Play. A Novel. household ed. Charles Reade & Boucicault, Dion. LC 7-39662. 1869. Fields, Osgood, & Co.
Foul Play. A Novel. Charles Reade & Boucicault, Dion. (On cover: Seaside library. Pocket ed., no. 216). 1884. G. Munro.
Foul Play & Other Puzzles of All Kinds. Ivan Morris. 1974. pap. 1.95 o.p. (ISBN 0-394-71050-9, Vin). Random.
Foul Up. Ritchie Perry. LC 82-45547. (Crime Club Ser.). 1982. 11.95 (ISBN 0-385-18358-5). Doubleday.
Foul Weather. George Fort Gibbs. LC 33-1349. 1938. London, D. Appleton and Company.
Found and Lost. Mary Putnam Jacobi. LC 7-9465. (Half-title: Autonym library. no. ii). 1894. G. P. Putnam's Sons.
Found Dead: Or, The Charles River Mystery. Clara Augusta Jones. LC 7-12141. (On cover: The secret service series. no. 53). 1892. Street & Smith.
Found Drowned". Eden Phillpotts. LC 75-44998. (Fifty Classics of Crime Fiction, 1900-1950; 42). 1976. 12.00 (ISBN 0-8240-2391-9). Garland Pub.
Found Drowned". Eden Phillpotts. LC 81-112807. 1931. The Macmillan Company.
Found Floating: An Inspection French Z Detective Story. Freeman Wills Crofts. LC 37-21642. 1937. Dodd, Mead & Company.
Found Guilty. Frank Barrett. LC 6-9063. Lovell, Coryell & Company.
Found Guilty. Frank Barrett. LC 6-9062. United States Book Company.
Found in the Philippines: The Story of a Woman's Letters. Charles King. LC 3-12973. The Hobart Company.
Found, Lost, Found: Or, The English Way of Life. John Boynton Priestley. LC 76-48159. 1976. 7.95 (ISBN 0-8161-6436-3). G. K. Hall.
Found Money. James Owen Hannay. LC 23-12110. The Bobbs-Merrill Company.
Found on the Beach. John Russell Coryell. LC 99-2394. (On cover: Magnet detective library. no. 65). 1898. Street & Smith.
Found Out. A Story. Helen Buckingham Mathers Reeves. (On cover: The seaside library. Pocket ed. no. 438). 1885. G. Munro.
Found Treasure. Grace Livingston Hill. 1976. Repr. of 1928 ed. lib. bdg. 14.40x (ISBN 0-89190-009-8). Am Repr-Rivercity Pr.
Found Treasure. Grace Livingston Hill. 1928. 2.95 o.p. (ISBN 0-448-05223-7). G&D.
Found Wanting. A Novel. Annie French Hector. LC 7-5163. 1893. J. B. Lippincott Company.
Found, Yet Lost. Edward Payson Roe. LC 7-40228. Dodd, Mead & Company.
Foundation. Isaac Asimov. LC 79-10906. 1979. 10.95 (ISBN 0-89340-209-5). J. Curley.
Foundation. Briant Sayre Young. LC 34-30044. The Maribeck Press.
Foundation and Empire. Isaac Asimov. LC 79-10907. 1979. 10.95 (ISBN 0-89340-210-9). J. Curley.
Foundation and Empire. 1st Ed. Isaac Asimov. LC 52-12466. 1952. Gnome Press.
Foundation Pit. Andrei Platonovich Platonov. LC 73-122788. 1975. 7.50 (ISBN 0-525-10775-4). Dutton.
Foundation Pit. Kotlovan (Romanized Form. bi-lingual ed. Andrei Platonovich Platonov. LC 74-166468. 10.00 (ISBN 0-88233-044-6) (ISBN 0-88233-045-4). Ardis.
Foundation Rock: A Story of Facts and Factors. Sarah M De Line. LC 1-31719. 1901. Jennings & Pye.
Foundation Stone. Lella Warren. LC 40-11820. 1940. A. A. Knopf.
Foundation Trilogy. Isaac Asimov. 1974. pap. 7.95 (ISBN 0-380-00101-2, 54403). Avon.
Foundation Trilogy: Three Science Fiction Classics. Isaac Asimov. LC 82-19919. 1982. 17.95 (ISBN 0-385-18830-7). Doubleday.
Foundation. 1st Ed. Isaac Asimov. LC 51-13439. Gnome Press.
Foundation's Edge. Isaac Asimov. LC 82-45450. 1982. 17.95 (ISBN 0-385-17725-9). Doubleday.
Foundations: Or, Castles in the Air. Rose Porter. LC 7-37749. A. D. F. Randolph & Co.
Founded on Paper: Or Uphill and Downhill Between the Two Jubilees. Charlotte Mary Yonge. LC 9-1216. 1897. T. Whittaker.
Founder of the House. Naomi Ellington Jacob. LC 36-27305. 1936. The Macmillan Company.
Founder's Praise. Joanne Greenberg. LC 76-3968. 8.95. Holt, Rinehart and Winston.
Founder's Praise. Joanne Greenberg. 1977. 1.95 (ISBN 0-380-01757-1). Avon Books.
Founding. Cynthia Harrod-Eagles. (Orig.). 1982. pap. 3.50 (ISBN 0-440-12677-0). Dell.
Founding of Belgrade: A Translation from the French. Jennings, W & F., M. De. LC 11-351. Printed & Published by D. Longworth, at the Shakspeare-Glalleryno., Park.
Founding of Fortunes. Jane Barlow. 1902. Dodd, Mead & Company.
Founding of the Mohawk. A Tale of the Revolution. Newton Mallory Curtis. 1848. Williams Brothers.
Foundling. Georgette Heyer. (Berkley Medallion Book). 1977. 1.95 (ISBN 0-425-03325-2). Berkley Pub. Corp.
Foundling. Georgette Heyer. LC 48-586649. 1948. G.P. Putnam's Sons.
Foundling. Francis Joseph Spellman. LC 51-10798. 1951. Scribner.
Foundlings. Lev Hakak. 1982. pap. write for info. (ISBN 0-86628-028-6). Ridgefield Pub.
Foundry. Albert Halper. LC 34-287786. 1934. The Viking Press.
Fountain. Charles Morgan. LC 32-14111. 1932. A. A. Knopf.
Fountain Affair. Andrew L. Lange. 1977. pap. 1.95 (ISBN 0-915602-04-0). Hill Hse Pr.
Fountain at Marlieux. Claude Aveline. LC 75-97647. 1970. 4.95. Doubleday.
Fountain at Marlieux. Translated from the French by Peter Green. Claude Aveline. LC 54-10464. 1954. Roy Publishers.
Fountain Boy. Neil Brant. LC 33-20821. The Vanguard Press.
Fountain of Arethusa. Translated from the French by Anne and Christopher Fremantle. 1st American Ed. Maurice Zermatten. LC 60-13752. 1960. Doubleday.
Fountain of Death. Hugh Lawrence Nelson. LC 48-7721. (Murray Hill mystery). Rinehart.
Fountain of Fire. Joyce Verrette. 448p. 1981. pap. 2.95 (ISBN 0-449-14425-9, GM). Fawcett.
Fountain of Youth. Ellsworth Wilson. LC 32-1938. The Book Krafters.
Fountain of Youth: Stories to Be Told. Padraic Colum. Repr. of 1927 ed. 12.00 o.s.i. Finch Pr.
Fountain Overflows: A Novel. Rebecca West. LC 56-10406. 1956. Viking Press.
Fountain Sealed. Margaret E Epp. LC 65-19505. 1965. Zondervan Pub. House.
Fountain Sealed. Anne Douglas Sedgwick. LC 42-27489. Houghton Mifflin Company.
Fountain Sealed. Anne Douglas Sedgwick. LC 7-30436. 1907. The Century Co.
Fountain Sealed. A Novel. Walter Besant. C.
Fountain Sealed. A Novel. Walter Besant. LC 6-12404. F. A. Stokes Company.
Fountainhead. 25th anniversary ed. Ayn Rand. LC 68-11314. (Illus.). 1968. 8.00. Bobbs-Merrill.
Fountainhead. Ayn Rand. LC 46-427515. The Bobbs-Merrill Company.
Fountainhead. Ayn Rand. LC 46-565652. The Blakiston Company.
Fountains. Sylvia Wallace. LC 76-1007. 1976. 8.95 (ISBN 0-688-03040-8). Morrow.
Fountains of Glory. Fiona Harrowe, pseud. 1979. pap. 2.50 (ISBN 0-449-14244-2, GM). Fawcett.
Fountains of Paradise. Arthur Charles Clarke. LC 78-14072. 10.00 (ISBN 0-15-132773-4). Harcourt Brace Jovanovich.
Fountains of Paradise. large print ed. Arthur Charles Clarke. LC 80-17924. 1980. 2.50 (ISBN 0-8161-3039-6). G. K. Hall.
Four Against the Bank of England. Ann Huxley. LC 80-82216. 240p. 1980. pap. 2.50 incl. insert (ISBN 0-87216-750-X). Playboy Pbks.
Four Against the Mob. Oscar Fraley. (O.s.i.). 1976. pap. 1.50 o.s.i. (AD1638, Award). Univ Pub & Dist.
Four-and-Forty Fairies. Nathaniel Moore Banta & Benson, Alphha Banta, Joint Author. LC 23-5919. 1923. A. Flanagan Company.
Four & Growing. Pearl W. Clark. 3.50 o.p. Carlton.
Four and the Fire: Or, Five Nights in a Yacht Club. Thomas Fleming Day. LC 8-5577. 1907. The Rudder Publishing Company.
Four-and-Twenty Blackbirds. Howard Vincent O'Brien. LC 28-16626. 1928. Pub. for the Crime Club, Inc., by Doubleday, Doran & Company, Inc.
Four-&-Twenty Bloodhounds: Short Stories Plus Biographies of Fictional Detectives, Amateur and Professional, Public and Private, Created by Members of Mystery Writers of America. Mystery Writers of America & William Anthony Parker - Ed White. LC 50-10532. 1950. Simon and Schuster.
Four Armourers. Francis Beeding. LC 30-20814. 1930. Little, Brown, and Company.
Four Before Richardson: Selected English Novels, 1720-1727. Ed. by William H. McBurney. LC 63-9095. (Landmark Edition). xxxvi, 375p. 1963. 24.95x (ISBN 0-8032-0114-1). U of Nebr Pr.
Four Before Richardson: Selected English Novels, 1720-1727. Ed. by William H. McBurney. Incl. Luck at Last, or the Happy Unfortunate. A. Blackamore; Jamaica Lady, or the Life of Baria; Philidore & Placentia, or l'Amour Trop Delicat. Eliza Haywood; Accomplished Rake, or Modern Fine Gentleman. M. Davys. 1963. 6.50 o.p. (ISBN 0-8032-0114-1). U of Nebr Pr.
Four Bells: A Tale of the Caribbean. Ralph Delahaye Paine. LC 24-4862. 1924. Houghton Mifflin Company.
Four Blind Mice. Donald Joseph. LC 32-24136. 1932. Frederick A. Stokes Company.
Four Blind Mice. Cecil Champain Lowis. LC 20-195093. 1920. John Lane.
Four Blocks Apart. Arthur Somers Roche. LC 31-2905. Sears Publishing Company, Inc.
Four Boys and a Gun. Willard Wiener. LC 44-3946. 1944. Dial Press.
Four by Four. Incl. Stairway to the Sea. Thomas F. Jones; This Night in Sodom. Charles J. Reiter; Custom. John Schultz; The Apostate Heriger. Anthony Shafton. (Black Circle Books). 1967. 5.00 o.p. (GP415). Grove.
Four Came Back: A Novel. Martin Caidin. LC 68-29629. 1968. 5.50. D. McKay Co.
Four-Chambered Heart. Anais Nin. LC 66-6825. 3.50, 1.45 pap.,. Swallow.
Four-Chambered Heart. Anais Nin. LC 50-5129. 1950. Duell, Sloan and Pearce.
Four-Chambered Villain. Gary Madderom. LC 79-131477. 1971. Macmillan.
Four-Chimneys: A Novel. Sarah Broom Macnaughton. 1912. T. Nelson and Sons.
Four Classic American Novels. Intro. by Willard Thorp. Incl. Scarlet Letter. Nathaniel Hawthorne; Adventures of Huckleberry Finn. Mark Twain; Red Badge of Courage. Stephan Crane; Billy Budd. Herman Melville. 1969. pap. 3.95 (ISBN 0-451-51765-2, CL1765, Sig Classics). NAL.
Four Color Person. Max Luscher. (gr. 11-12). 1980. pap. 2.95 (ISBN 0-671-83457-6). PB.
Four-Colored Hoop. M. M. B Walsh. LC 75-34381. 7.95. Putnam.
Four Complete Adventure Novels: Ed. by Jessie Alford Nunn. Ed. by Jessie Alford Nunn. with a teacher's guide. 3.96. Globe.
Four Complete Modern Novels. Ed. by Willian M Popp. LC 62-163. Globe Book Co.
Four Complete Novels. James Mallahan Cain. LC 81-19079. 1982. 6.98 (ISBN 0-517-36249-X). Avenel: Distributed by Crown.
Four Complete Novels. avenel 1981 ed. Trevanian. LC 81-3564. 6.98 (ISBN 0-517-34796-2). Avenel: Distributed by Crown.
Four Complete Novels of Character and Courage: Ed. by Lilian M. Popp. Lilian M Popp. 3.96. Globe.
Four Complete Novels of Drama and Suspense. school ed. Ed. by Lawrence H Feigenbaum. LC 64-57265. 1964. Globe Book Co.
Four Complete World Novels: Edited by Richard L. Loughlin and Lilian M. Popp. Ed. by Richard L Loughlin & Lilian M. Popp. LC 61-527. 1961. Globe Book Co.
Four Cornered Story. Frank Albert Chittenden. LC 51-6513. 1951. T. V. Boardman.
Four Corners. Clifford Samuel Raymond. LC 21-10333. 1.90. George H. Doran Company.
Four Corners of the House. Abraham Rothberg. LC 81-10464. (Illinois Short Fiction Ser.). 120p. 1981. 11.95 (ISBN 0-252-00922-3); pap. 4.95 (ISBN 0-252-00926-6). U of Ill Pr.
Four Corners of the House: Stories. Abraham Rothberg. LC 81-10464. (Illinois Short Fiction). 11.95 (ISBN 0-252-00922-3) (ISBN 0-252-00926-6). University of Illinois Press.
Four Corners of the World. Alfred Edward Woodley Mason. LC 17-25588. 1917. C. Scribner's Sons.
Four-Day Planet. H. Beam Piper. LC 61-8242. 1961. Putnam.
Four Day Work Week & Other Stories. Gerald Locklin. 1977. 3.00 (ISBN 0-917554-06-X). Maelstrom.
Four Days. John Buell. LC 62-8933. 1962. Farrar, Straus and Cudahy.
Four Days. William Crook. LC 79-55600. 1980. 8.95 (ISBN 0-689-11033-2). Atheneum.
Four Days. Gloria Goldreich. LC 79-3352. 10.95 (ISBN 0-15-132802-1). Harcourt Brace Jovanovich.
Four Days. Harold King. 1980. pap. 2.95 (ISBN 0-671-81999-2). PB.
Four Days. Harold King. LC 75-30888. 352p. 1976. 8.95 o.p. (ISBN 0-672-52183-0). Bobbs.
Four Days. Paddy Kitchen. LC 79-2739. 160p. 1980. 9.95i (ISBN 0-06-012406-7, HarpT). Har-Row.
Four Days: A Novel of Burma 1945. William Crook. LC 79-55600. 1980. 9.95 o.p. (ISBN 0-689-11033-2). Atheneum.
Four Days; the Story of a War Marriage. Hetty Laurence Hemenway. LC 17-24973. 1917. Little, Brown, and Company.
Four Days to the Fireworks. Philip Purser. LC 65-22131. 1965. bds., 3.50. Walker.
Four Days' Wonder. Alan Alexander Milne. LC 33-284031. E. P. Dutton & Co., Inc.
Four Dead Mice. Thomas B Black. LC 54-7925. (Murray Hill mystery). 1954. Rinehart.
Four Defences. Alfred Walter Stewart. LC 40-13052. 1940. Little, Brown and Company.
Four Devils. Herman Joachim Bang & Fowler, Guy. LC 26-30259. Grosset & Dunlap.
Four Doctors: A Novel. Benjamin Siegel. LC 74-19069. 1975. 7.95 (ISBN 0-440-04563-0). Delacorte Press.
Four Doctors, Four Wives. Elizabeth Seifert. LC 74-34439. 1975. 5.95 (ISBN 0-396-07083-3). Dodd, Mead.
Four Doctors, Four Wives. Elizabeth Seifert. (Signet Book). 1976. (pbk.) 1.25. New American Library.
Four Doctors, Four Wives. Elizabeth Seifert. LC 79-1159. (Seifert, Elizabeth, 1897-. An Elizabeth Seifert Romance). 1979. 10.95 (ISBN 0-89340-203-6). J. Curley.
Four Ducks on a Pond. Alice Brainerd Nelson. LC 51-14507. 1951. Vermont Book Shop.
Four Ducks on a Pond. Ruth Sawyer. LC 28-25817. 1928. Harper & Brothers.
Four Early Stories. limited ed. James Agee. (Illus.). mor. lea. 30.00 o.p. Cummington.
Four Elements: A Creative Approach to the Short Story. Anne Sherrill & Paula Robertson. LC 74-23934. 1975. 4.95 (ISBN 0-03-011311-3). Holt, Rinehart and Winston.
Four English Novels: By J. B. Priestley and O. B. Davis. Ed. by John Boynton Priestley & O. B. Davis. LC 60-16110. 1960. Harcourt, Brace.
Four Faces. Suyin Han. LC 63-16179. 1963. Putnam.
Four Faces, Wobbly Mirror. Chester Eagle. LC 76-374060. 1976. (ISBN 0-85885-206-3). Wren.
Four Fallen Women. Joris Karl Huysmans. LC 53-29499. (Dell book, 667). 1953. Dell Pub.Co.
Four False Weapons. John Dickson Carr. 1962. pap. 1.95 (ISBN 0-02-018710-6, Collier). Macmillan.
Four False Weapons: Being the Return of Bencolin. John Dickson Carr. LC 37-22965. 1937. Harper & Brothers.
Four Famous Adventures. Ed. Frank G. Jennings, Eric W. Johnson. Frank G Jennings. (Adventures in good bks ser.). 1963. 3.48. Harcourt.
Four Fates: A Novel. Margaret Mackprang Mackay. 1955. J. Day Co.
Four Faultless Felons. Gilbert Keith Chesterton. LC 62-17711. (G. K. Chesterton reprint series, v. 4). 1962. Dufour Editions.
Four Faultless Felons. Gilbert Keith Chesterton. LC 30-24048. 1930. Dodd, Mead & Company.
Four Favorite Books. Christopher Darlington Morley. LC 39-276782. 1939. Garden City Publishing Co.
Four Feathers. Alfred Edward Woodley Mason. LC 2-25599. 1902. The Macmillan Company.
Four Feathers. Alfred Edward Woodley Mason. LC 12-31383. 1911. The Macmillan Company.
Four Feathers. Alfred Edward Woodley Mason. (Macmillan's fiction library). 1913. The Macmillan Company.
Four Feathers. Alfred Edward Woodley Mason. LC 24-11858. 1922. Grosset & Dunlap.
Four Feathers. Illustrated by Frank Kramer. abridgement. ed. Alfred Edward Woodley Mason. LC 60-11502. (World-famous book, 209). 1960. Hart Pub. Co.
Four Feet in the Grave. Amelia Reynolds Long. LC 41-119813. Phoenix Press.
Four Feet in the Grave. Amelia Reynolds Long. LC 45-5978. (On cover: Bart house mystery. 13). 1945.
Four-Fifty from Paddington. Agatha Miller Christie. LC 82-73250. (Greenway Edition). 1982. 9.95 (ISBN 0-396-08110-X). Dodd.
Four, Five & Six by Tey. Josephine Tey. (O.s.i.). 1958. 8.95 o.s.i. (ISBN 0-02-617060-4). Macmillan.
Four, Five, and Six: By Tey, by Josephine Tey Pseud. Elizabeth Mackintosh. LC 58-731315. (Cock Robin mystery). 1958. Macmillan.
Four Flirts: Their Cards and How They Played Them. Ernest Warren. (On cover: Round table books). Rhodes & McClure.
Four-Flusher. John Edward Hazzard. G. W. Dillingham Company.
Four-Flusher: The Story of a Woman of Action. by elizabeth jordan. ed. Elizabeth Garver Jordan. LC 31-7376. 2.00. The Century Co.
Four for a Fortune: A Tale. Albert Lee. LC 7-12606. 1898. Harper & Brothers.
Four for Texas: Based on the Screen-Play Written by Teddi. Sherman and Robert Aldrich. Dan Cushman & Teddi. For Texas Sherman. LC 63-21963. (Bantam fifty). 1963. Bantam Books.
Four for Tomorrow. Roger Zelazny. LC 75-442. (Garland Library of Science Fiction). 1975. 11.00 (ISBN 0-8240-1444-8). Garland Pub.

Four-Four-Four: Short Fiction by Laurence Gonzales, Grant Lyons, & Roger Rath. Laurence Gonzales et al. LC 76-56873. (Breakthrough Bks.). 200p. 1977. 12.95 (ISBN 0-8262-0207-1). U of Mo Pr.

Four Friends. Robert Grossbach. 1982. pap. 2.25 (ISBN 0-345-29872-1). Ballantine.

Four Frightened People. Eileen Arbuthnot Robertson. LC 31-28334. 1931. Doubleday, Doran & Company, Inc.

Four Frightened People. Eileen Arbuthnot Robertson. LC 33-16070. 1933. Garden City Publishing Company, Inc.

Four Frightened Women. George Harmon Coxe. LC 38-290674. 1939. A. A. Knopf.

Four from Gila Bend. Merle Constiner. 1974. (pbk.) 0.95. Ace Books.

Four Futures: Four Original Novellas of Science Fiction. Isaac Asimov & R. A Lafferty. LC 79-158024. 1971. 5.95. Hawthorn Books.

Four Futures: Four Original Novellas of Science Fiction. R. A. Lafferty et al. 1971. 5.95 o.p. Hawthorn.

Four Gardens. Margery Sharp. LC 35-15739. 1935. G. P. Putnam's Sons.

Four-Gated City. Doris May Lessing. LC 69-16611. (Her Children of violence). 1969. 7.50. Knopf Distributed by Random House.

Four Generation. Naomi Ellington Jacob. LC 34-20029. 1934. The Macmillan Company.

Four Generations. Naomi Ellington Jacob. (Gollantz Saga). (Signet Book, Y5661: Vol.). 1973. (pbk.) 1.25. New American Library.

Four German Stories. Ed. by Margaret W. Pfaffle. Danton, George Henry, 1860- Joint Ed. LC 47-5084. (Harper's German series). 1947.

Four Gordons. Edna Adelaide Brown. LC 11-12124. 1911. Lothrop, Lee & Shepard Co.

Four Graces. Dorothy Emily Stevenson. LC 46-32167. 1946. Rinehart & Company, Incorporated.

Four Graves to Jericho. Orlando Rigoni. 1974. 4.95. Lenox Hill Press.

Four Great American Novels... Ed. by Raymond Wright Short. Hawthorne, Nathaniel, 1804-1864. The Scarlet Letter et al. LC 46-316291. 1946. H. Holt and Company.

Four Great Oaks. Mildred McNaughton. LC 46-41200. 1946. Creative Age Press, Inc.

Four Handsome Negresses: The Record of a Voyage. by r. hernekin baptist... ed. R. Hernekin Baptist. LC 31-21315. 1931. J. Cape.

Four Handsome Negresses, the Record of a Voyage. R. Hernekin Baptist. LC 31-21494. J. Cape & H. Smith.

Four Hoofs & a Heartbeat. Carl W. Swanson. 4.50 o.s.i. (ISBN 0-8181-0014-1). Pageant-Poseidon.

Four Horse-Players Are Missing. Alexander Rose. LC 60-12495. 1960. Coward-McCann.

Four Horsemen of the Apocalypse. Vicente Blasco Ibanez. 1918. 8.95 o.p. (ISBN 0-525-10798-3). Dutton.

Four Horsemen of the Apocalypse. Vicente Blasco Ibanez. 1982. Repr. lib. bdg. 24.95x (ISBN 0-89966-384-2). Buccaneer Bks.

Four Horsemen of the Apocalypse. Los Cuatro Jinetes Del Apocalipsis. Vicente Blasco Ibanez & Jordan, Mrs. Charlotte Brewster, Tr. LC 18-16490. 1918. E. P. Dutton & Company.

Four Hundred. Stephen Sheppard. 1980. 2.75 (ISBN 0-425-04665-6). Berkley Publishing Corporation.

Four Hundred: A Novel. Stephen Sheppard. LC 79-12362. 10.95 (ISBN 0-671-40071-1). Summit Books.

Four Hundred Brattle Street. George Wolk. LC 78-13423. 1979. 9.95 (ISBN 0-88326-154-5). Wyden Book; Trade Distribution by Simon and Schuster.

Four Hundred Ninety-Nine Scottish Stories: For the Price of Five Hundred. B. C. Forbes. Repr. lib. bdg. 10.00 o.p. Folcroft.

Four Hundred Ninety-One: A Novel. Translated from the Swedish by Anselm Hollo. Lars Gorling, pseud. LC 66-14098. 1966. Grove Press.

Four in Family. Humphrey Pakington. LC 31-27201. W. W. Norton & Company, Inc.

Four in Family: The Story of How We Look from Where the Dog Sits. Florida Pope Sumerwell. LC 11-3946. The Bobbs-Merrill Company.

Four-in-Hand: A Group of Short Stories; Mr. Durbar's Toast; Mrs. Billy's Baby and the Professor; From Dolly to Dick; Poetry and Life. Frank Joseph McCormick. LC 6-42925. 1906. Press of United Brethren Publishing House.

Four in Hand: A Novel by Mrs. A. M. Castello. Almeda Merchant Castello. LC 2-3568. The Pilgrim Press.

Four-in-Hand: A Story of Smart Life in New York and at a Country Club. Geraldine Anthony. LC 3-25207. 1903. D. Appleton and Company.

Four in Love. Albert Quandt. LC 49-49120. 1949. Arcadia House.

Four in Paradise. Peggy Gaddis, pseud. LC 46-782. 1946. Arcadia House.

Four Infantrymen. Ernst Johannssen. Tr. by Wheen, Arthur Wesley. LC 30-9239. 1930. A. H. King.

Four Johns. Ellery Queen, pseud. LC 64-3117. 1964. Pocket Books.

Four Johns. Ellery Queen. 1974. (pbk.) 0.95. New American Library.

Four Just Men. Edgar Wallace. LC 20-159573. Small, Maynard & Company.

Four-Leaved Clover; an Everyday Romance. Mary Gleed Tuttiett. LC 1-20335. (Half-title: Appletons' town and country library, no. 301). 1901. D. Appleton and Company.

Four-Legged Duck. Frederic Clark. LC 67-27230. 1968. 5.95 o.p. Bobbs.

Four-Legged Duck: A Novel. Frederic Clark. LC 67-25175. 1968. 5.95. Bobbs.

Four Lives of Mundy Tolliver. Ben Lucien Burman. LC 53-10498. 1953. J. Messner.

Four Lost Ladies: A Miss Withers Mystery. Stuart Palmer. LC 49-10497. 1949. M. S. Mill Co.

Four Loves. Clive Staples Lewis. LC 60-10920. 1971. pap. 2.95 (ISBN 0-15-632930-1, Harv). HarBraceJ.

Four Macnicols: And Other Tales. William Black. LC 6-129335. (Lovell's library, v. 5, no. 217). J. W. Lovell Company.

Four Mad Monarchs. Rachael E Cooke. LC 54-8379. 1954. Vantage Press.

Four Marys. Fannie Heaslip Lea. LC 37-2389. 1937. Dodd, Mead & Company.

Four Marys. Agnes Sligh Turnbull. LC 33-492724. 1932. Fleming H. Revell Company.

Four-Masted Cat-Boat, and Other Truthful Tales. Charles Battell Loomis. LC 73-110206. (Short story index reprint series). (Illus.). 1970. Books for Libraries Press.

Four-Masted Cat-Boat: And Other Truthful Tales. Charles Battell Loomis. LC 158. 1899. The Century Co.

Four Masterworks of American Indian Literature. John Bierhorst. 1975. 6.95 o.p. (ISBN 0-374-51105-5). FS&G.

Four Meetings see Author of Beltraffio.

Four Men. Paul Hervey Fox. LC 46-3948. 1946. C. Scribner's Sons.

Four Men and a Prayer. David Garth. LC 37-238786. 1937. H. C. Kinsey & Company, Inc.

Four Miles from Tarrytown. Fannie H Gallagher. LC 6-44491. Congregational Sunday-School and Publishing Society.

Four Million. O. Henry. 1908. 3.95 o.p. (ISBN 0-385-04146-2). Doubleday.

Four Million. William Sydney Porter. LC 15-17417. 1914. Doubleday, Page & Company.

Four Million. William Sydney Porter. LC 19-135234. 1918. Doubleday, Page and Company.

Four Million. William Sydney Porter. LC 22-16018. 1919. Doubleday, Page & Company, for Review of Reviews Co.

Four Million. William Sydney Porter. LC 21-13703. 1920. Doubleday, Page & Company.

Four Million. William Sydney Porter. LC 24-149342. 1922. Doubleday, Page & Company.

Four Million. William Sydney Porter. LC 25-219192. 1925. Doubleday, Page & Company.

Four Million, and Other Stories. William Sydney Porter. LC 66-1373. 1964. Airmont Pub. Co.

Four Million Stories. William Sydney Porter. LC 6-12856. 1906. McClure, Phillips & Co.

Four Million Stories. William Sydney Porter. LC 10-6185. 1909. Doubleday, Page & Company.

Four Modes; a Rhetoric of Modern Fiction. Ed. by James M. Mellard. LC 72-75150. (Illus.). 1973. 4.95. Macmillan.

Four Months Among the Gold-Finders of California. Henry Vizetelly. LC 71-104587. (Illus.). 1971. (ISBN 0-8398-2050-X). Literature House.

Four Months at Glencairn. Katharine Theus Obear. LC 14-231. 1.25. Broadway Publishing Co.

Four Musketeers. John Michael Drinkrow Hardwick. 1975. (pbk.) 1.25. Bantam Books.

Four Musketeers. Michael Hardwick. 1978. 9.95 o.p. (ISBN 0-86025-125-X). State Mutual Bk.

Four Musketeers. E. A. Van Dyke, Jr. 4.50 o.p. Vantage.

Four Must Die. Bradford Scott. (Orig.). 1973. pap. 0.75 o.p. (ISBN 0-515-02794-4, T2794). Pyramid Pubns.

Four Novelists of the Old Regime: Crebillon, Laclos, Diderot, Restif de la Bretonne. John Palache. LC 73-132443. (Studies in French Literature, No. 45). 1970. Repr. of 1926 ed. lib. bdg. 53.95x (ISBN 0-8383-1193-8). Haskell.

Four Novels. Marguerite Duras. Tr. by Richard Seaver et al from Fr. Incl. Afternoon of Mr. Andesmas; Ten-Thirty on a Summer Night; Moderato Cantabile; Square. 1965. pap. 9.95 (ISBN 0-394-17987-0, E808, Ever). Grove.

Four Novels of Eliza Haywood: Photoreprints. Eliza Fowler Haywood. LC 81-24000. 1983. 45.00 (ISBN 0-8201-1376-X). Scholar's Facsimiles & Reprints.

Four-Oaks: A Novel. Elizabeth Whitfield Croom Bellamy. 1870. Carleton; Etc., Etc.

Four Oaks Farm: By Phyllis Yahnke. Phyllis Yahnke. LC 46-2499. 1946. Gramercy Publishing Co.

Four O'Clock. Virginia Cantwell. 1970. 2.75 o.p. Vantage.

Four O'clock: And Other Stories. Mary Borden. LC 27-8280. 1927. Doubleday, Page & Company.

Four of a Kind. John Phillips Marquand. LC 23-5823. 1923. C. Scribner's Sons.

Four of a Kind. Zeke Masters, pseud. (Orig.). 1981. pap. 1.95 (ISBN 0-671-42617-6). PB.

Four of Hearts: A Problem in Deduction. Ellery Queen, pseud. LC 38-27879. 1938. Frederick A. Stokes Company.

Four of Them. Layne Shroder. LC 57-5314. 1957. Houghton Mifflin.

Four-Part Setting. Mary Dolling Sanders O'Malley. LC 39-29729. 1939. Little, Brown and Company.

Four Past Four. Roy Vickers. 1945. Jefferson House.

Four People: A Novel of South Africa. Gerald Gordon. LC 66-32834. 1966. 6.95. Macdonald.

Four Philanthropists. Edgar Jepson. LC 7-16752. 1907. The Authors and Newspapers Association.

Four-Pools Mystery. Jean Webster. LC 8-8103. 1908. The Century Co.

Four Portraits. Tabitha Froneberger. LC 72-179398. (Illus.). 1972.

Four Post Bed. Charles Fielding Marsh. LC 27-123643. 1927. D. Appleton and Company.

Four Rivers of Paradise. Helen Constance White. LC 55-14609. 1955. Macmillan.

Four Roads. Sheila Kaye-Smith. LC 19-27518. 1919. George H. Doran Company.

Four Roads. Sheila Kaye-Smith. LC 21-16318. George H. Doran Company.

Four Roads to Death. Benjamin Appel. LC 35-8749. 1935. A.A. Knopf.

Four Roads to Death see Gold & Flesh.

Four Roads to Happiness: A Story of Hoosier Life. Mary Nantz McCrae Culter. LC 3843. The Union Press.

Four Roads to Paradise. Maud Wilder Goodwin. LC 4-10476. 1904. The Century Co.

Four Roger Zelazny Novels. Roger Zelazny. 1979. 48.00 (ISBN 0-444-47120-0, Gregg). G K Hall.

Four Romantic Tales from 19th Century German. Ed. by Helene Scher. LC 75-1428. 1975. 6.50. (ISBN 0-8044-2769-0) (ISBN 0-8044-6804-4). F. Ungar Pub. Co.

Four Seasons. (Haiku Ser.: No. 2). 1958. 3.95 (ISBN 0-88088-174-7). Peter Pauper.

Four Seek Love. with an introd. by jack woodford. ed. Gloria Goddard & Wood, Clement. LC 49-11918. 1949. Woodford Press.

Four Selected Novels of Henry James. Henry James. Incl. American; European; Daisy Miller; International Episode. 1958. pap. 2.45 o.p. (ISBN 0-448-00039-3, UL). G&D.

Four Sensational Adventure Novels. Francis B. Young. 15.00. Havertown Bks.

Four Sergeants. Zeno. LC 76-25232. 1977. 7.95 (ISBN 0-689-10765-X). Atheneum.

Four Sergeants. Zeno. LC 76-383580. (Illus.). 1976. 3.95 (ISBN 0-333-14573-9). Macmillan.

Four Short Mysteries. English Language Services. (Collier-Macmillan English Readers Ser.). pap. 1.40 (ISBN 0-02-971470-2). Macmillan.

Four Short Novels. David Herbert Lawrence. LC 65-2786. (Compass books, C180). 1965. Viking Press.

Four Short Novels. David Herbert Lawrence. 1976. 2.50 (ISBN 0-14-003726-8). Penguin.

Four Short Stories. Charlie Brown. 2.50 o.p. Carlton.

Four Short Stories. William Somerset Maugham. LC 71-27112. (Illus.). 1971. 2.50 (ISBN 0-87529-120-1). Hallmark Editions.

Four Short Stories: Quattro Novelle. Luigi Pirandello. Tr. by V. M. Jeffery from Italian. (Harrap's Bilingual Ser.). 58p. 1955. 5.00 (ISBN 0-911268-44-8). Rogers Bk.

Four-Sided Triangle. Temple, William F. LC 51-10086. (Fell's science-fiction library). 1951. F. Fell.

Four Sisters. Stephen Byko. (Orig.). 1980. pap. 2.95 o.p. (ISBN 0-89260-164-7). Hwong Pub.

Four Sisters. James Fritzhand. LC 81-878. 1981. 14.95 (ISBN 0-688-00457-1). W. Morrow.

Four Sisters. A Tale of Social and Domestic Life in Sweden. authorized american ed. Fredrika Bremer. Tr. by Mary Botham Howitt. LC 6-17404. T.B. Peterson and Brothers.

Four Soviet Masterpieces: Translated and with an Introd. by Andrew R. MacAndrew. Ed. by Andrew Robert MacAndrew. LC 65-11848. 1965. Bantam Books.

Four-Squard. Short Stories. Dorothea Frances Canfield Fisher. LC 49-11288. 1949. Harcourt, Brace.

Four-Square. Dorothea Frances Canfield Fisher. LC 71-167448. (Short story index reprint series). 1971. (ISBN 0-8369-3974-3). Books for Libraries Press.

Four States Corner: Including Dwarf of Four States Corner, and Firebird Without Wings. Leondine Morgan Pelmounter. LC 54-497356. 1954. Naylor Co.

Four Stories. Ingmar Bergman. LC 76-2754. 1976. 7.95 (ISBN 0-385-00778-7). Anchor Press.

Four Stories. Ingmar Bergman. 1977. 3.50 (ISBN 0-385-02747-8). Anchor Press /Doubleday.

Four Stories. Hugo Hofmann Hofmannsthal. Ed. by Margaret Jacobs. LC 77-535547. (Clarendon German series). (Illus.). 1968 (ISBN 0-19-832453-7). Oxford U.P.

Four Stories. Gabriel Josipovici. 1977. pap. 3.00 (Pub. by Menard Pr). SBD.

Four Stories. Sigrid Undset. LC 59-7982. 1959. Knopf.

Four Stories. Sigrid Undset. LC 78-16903. 1978. 18.50 (ISBN 0-313-20566-3). Greenwood Press.

Four Stragglers. Frank Lucius Packard. LC 23-9234. George H. Doran Company.

Four-Stroke. Donald Grant Mitchell. LC 73-19599. 1974. 6.95 o.p. (ISBN 0-316-57505-4). Little.

Four-Stroke: A Novel. Donald Grant Mitchell. LC 73-19599. 1974. 6.95 (ISBN 0-316-57505-4). Little, Brown.

Four Studs for the Bride. Ward Fulton. pap. 1.95 o.p. (ISBN 0-87977-138-0, DBB138). Dansk Blue Bk.

Four Sunday Suits, and Other Stories. Alan Marshall. LC 75-9680. 1975. 5.95 (ISBN 0-8407-6424-3). T. Nelson.

Four Swans: A Novel of Cornwall, 1795-1797. Winston Graham. LC 76-18347. 1977. 8.95 (ISBN 0-385-12338-8). Doubleday.

Four Swans: A Novel of Cornwall, 1795-1797. Winston Graham. LC 79-10636. 1979. 19.95 (ISBN 0-8161-6681-1). G. K. Hall.

Four Swans: A Novel of Cornwall 1795-7. Winston Graham. LC 76-370520. (Illus.). 1976. 3.95 (ISBN 0-00-222246-9). Collins.

Four Tales. Isabella Agneta Van Tuyll Zuylen De Charriere. LC 75-140327. (Short story index reprint series). (Illus.). 1970. Books for Libraries Press.

Four Tales. Isabella Agneta Van Tuyll De Charriere. Tr. by Lubback, Sybil Marjorie (Cuffe) LC 26-264013. 1926. C. Scribner's Sons.

Four Tales by Bergengruen. Werner Bergengruen. Ed. by William Eickhorst. LC 66-22256. (Orig., Ger.). 1966. pap. 1.95x o.p. (ISBN 0-672-63037-0). Odyssey Pr.

Four Tales by Zelide. facs. ed. Isabella A. De Charriere. LC 75-140327. (Short Story Index Reprint Ser.). 1926. 16.00 (ISBN 0-8369-3719-8). Ayer Co.

Four Texans North. Lee Floren. LC 55-33827. (Ace double novel books, D-106). 1955. Ace Books.

Four Times a Widower. Adam Bliss. LC 36-10497. 1936. Macrae Smith Company.

Four Tools of Thales. 30p. 1976. pap. 0.35. Thales Microuniv.

Four Ugly Guns. Ralph Hayes. (Buffalo Hunter Ser.: No. 2). 160p. 1982. pap. 1.75 (ISBN 0-8439-1032-1, Leisure Bks). Nordon Pubns.

Four Ugly Guns. Ralph Hayes. (Orig.). 1970. pap. 0.75 o.p. (B75-2077). Belmont-Tower.

Four Way Payoff. Richard A Henriquez. LC 51-21217. 1951. Phoenix Press.

Four-Way Triangle. Marcia Marcoux. (Orig.). pap. 0.95 o.p. (1169). Brandon.

Four Were Possessed. Helena Frost. LC 34-34022. 1934. R. M. McBride & Company.

Four-Wheeling Bastard. George Anthony. (Orig.). 1969. pap. 1.25 o.p. (2090). Brandon.

Four Window Girl: Cr, How to Make More Money Than Men a Novel. Illustrated by John Huehnergarth. Shepherd Mead. LC 59-8048. 1959. Simon and Schuster.

Four Winds. David Beaty. LC 54-10300. 1955. Morrow.

Four Winds. Sinclair Gluck. LC 26-11488. 1926. Dodd, Mead and Company.

Four Winds. Charles Edward Hayes. LC 42-25513. 1942. The Macmillan Company.

Four Winds: A Novel. Roland Pertwee. LC 35-150405. 1935. Little, Brown, and Company.

Four Winds of Heaven. Monique Raphel High. LC 79-21753. (Illus.). 10.95 (ISBN 0-440-02573-7). Delacorte Press.

Four Wise Men. Michel Tournier. LC 81-43550. 1982. 15.95 (ISBN 0-385-17723-2). Doubleday.

Four Witnesses. Mary Reisner. LC 47-5387. 1947. Dodd, Mead.

Four Wives. Carlos Keith. LC 32-18238. 1932. The Vanguard Press.

Four Women. Marie B. Coffrey. (Orig.). 1980. pap. text ed. 2.25 o.s.i. (ISBN 0-505-51578-4). Tower Bks.

Four Women. Edward Loomis. LC 68-4995. (Work in progress, 2). (Illus.). Printed by N. Young; Distributed by Unicorn Press.

Four Words - Four Lives. new ed. James Serino. LC 75-43432. 96p. 1976. pap. 1.98 o.p. (ISBN 0-89144-015-1). Crescent Pubns.

Four Years As a Nun & Other Stories. R. Worlds. 2.00 o.p. Carlton.

Four Years Voyages of Captain George Roberts. Daniel Defoe & George Roberts. LC 72-170566. (Foundations of the Novel). (Illus.). 1972. 22.00 (ISBN 0-8240-0559-7). Garland Pub.

Fourflush Island. Louis Charles Douthwaite. LC 29-16169. 1929. Brentano's Ltd.

Fourfold. Jennie Maria Drinkwater Conklin. 1889. R. Carter & Brothers.

Fourscore. Sidney Herschel Small. LC 24-225652. The Bobbs-Merrill Company.

Foursquare. Grace Louise Smith Richmond. LC 22-18891. 1922. Doubleday, Page & Company.

Foursquare. Grace Louise Smith Richmond. LC 33-1969. 1924. A. L. Burt Company.

Foursquare Murder. John Victor Turner. LC 33-8986. 1933. R. M. McBride & Company.

Fourteen-Carat Roadster. P. Howard. Tr. by Patricia Bozso. 1.50x o.p. Vanous.

Fourteen-Day Conspiracy: A Novel. Jean Gilliland. LC 80-51212. (Illus.). 6.95 (ISBN 0-934616-09-4). Valkyrie Press.

Fourteen Dilemma. Hugh Pentecost. (Pierre Chambrun Mystery Novel Ser). 1976. 5.95 o.p. (ISBN 0-396-07287-9). Dodd.

Fourteen Dilemma. Judson Pentecost Philips. LC 76-942. (Red badge novel of suspense). 1976. 5.95 (ISBN 0-396-07287-9). Dodd, Mead.

Fourteen for Now: A Collection of Contemporary Stories. Ed. by John Ivan Simon. LC 68-24320. 1969. 4.95. Harper & Row.

Fourteen for Tonight. 1st Ed. Steve Allen. LC 55-9874. 1955. Holt.

Fourteen Great Detective Stories. Howard Haycraft. 2.95 o.p. (144); PLB 2.69 o.p. Modern Lib.

Fourteen Great Detective Stories. rev. ed. Ed. by Howard Haycraft. Starrett, Vincent, 1896- Ed. Fourteen Great Detective Stories. LC 49-6111. (Modern library of the world's best books 144). 1949. Modern Library.

Fourteen Great Detective Stories: Edited, with an Introduction. Ed. by Vincent Starrett. LC 28-10874. (Half-title: The modern library of the world's best books). The Modern Library.

Fourteen Great Short Stories: By Soviet Authors. Ed. by George Reavey. LC 60-2060. (Avon, G1040). Avon Book Division, Hearst Corp.

Fourteen Great Short Stories from The Long Valley. John Steinbeck. LC 49-347978. (New Avon library, 132). 1947. Avon Book Co.

Fourteen Great Tales of ESP. Ed. by Idella P. Stone. 288p. 1973. pap. 0.95 o.p. (M2679, GM). Fawcett World.

Fourteen Ninety-Two. Mary Johnston. LC 22-22437. 1922. Little, Brown, and Company.

Fourteen-O-Seven Broadway. Joel Gross. 1980. pap. 2.50 (ISBN 0-440-12819-6). Dell.

Fourteen of My Favorites in Suspense. Alfred Hitchcock. 1982. pap. 2.25 (ISBN 0-440-13630-X). Dell.

Fourteen Points, Tales of Craig Kennedy: Master of Mystery. Arthur Benjamin Reeve. LC 25-6947. 1925. Harper & Brothers.

Fourteen Seconds to Hell. Nick Carter. (Nick Carter Ser.). (O.s.i.). 192p. 1972. pap. 1.25 o.s.i. (AQ1448, Award). Univ Pub & Dist.

Fourteen-Seven Broadway. Joel Gross. LC 78-18806. 8.95 (ISBN 0-87223-511-4). Seaview Books Trade Distribution by Simon and Schuster.

Fourteen Seven Broadway. Joel Gross. LC 78-18806. 1978. 8.95 o.p. (ISBN 0-87223-511-4, Seaview Bks). Putnam Pub Group.

Fourteen Stories. Stephen Dixon. LC 80-14911. (Johns Hopkins Poetry & Fiction Program). 145p. 1980. 11.50 (ISBN 0-8018-2445-1). Johns Hopkins.

Fourteen Stories see In the Cage & Other Tales.

Fourteen Stories from One Plot. Ed. by John Milton Berdan. Fothergill, John. LC 32-31721. 1932. Oxford University Press.

Fourteen Stories from One Plot, Based on "Mr. Fothergill's Plot.". Ed. by John Milton Berdan. John Forthergill. LC 74-4054. (Short story index reprint series). 1974. 15.25 (ISBN 0-8369-4262-0). Books for Libraries Press.

Fourteen Stories from One Plot: Based on "Mr. Fothergill's Plot.". Ed. by John Milton Berdan. John Fothergill. LC 76-131629. 1971. (ISBN 0-403-00844-1). Scholarly Press.

Fourteen Stories from One Plot, Based on Mr. Fothergill's Plot. Ed. by John Milton Berdan. LC 70-137047. xvi, 287p. Repr. of 1932 ed. 12.25 o.p. (ISBN 0-8371-5508-8). Greenwood.

Fourteen Thumbs of St. Peter. Joice M Nankivell. LC 27-3016. E. P. Dutton & Company.

Fourteen to One. Elizabeth Stuart Phelps H. D. Ward Ward. 1891. Houghton, Mifflin and Company.

Fourteenth Agent. David Coxe Cooke. 1967. 4.95 o.p. (ISBN 0-396-05591-5). Dodd.

Fourteenth Duchess. Mollie Aghadjian. 1978. pap. 2.25 (ISBN 0-532-22138-9). Woodhill.

Fourteenth Key. Carolyn Wells. LC 24-19920. 1924. G. P. Putnam's Sons.

Fourteenth of October. Winifred Bryher. 1951. 5.95 o.p. (ISBN 0-394-42553-7). Pantheon.

Fourteenth of October:, a Novel. Winifred Bryher. LC 52-7393. 1952. Pantheon Books.

Fourteenth Pan Book of Horror Stories. Ed. by H. Van Thal. 1982. pap. 10.00x (ISBN 0-330-23729-2, Pub. by Pan Bks). State Mutual Bk.

Fourteenth Point. John Dudley Ball. LC 73-10460. 1973. 7.95 (ISBN 0-316-07949-9). Little, Brown.

Fourteenth Trump. Judson Pentecost Philips. LC 42-22859. 1942. Dodd, Mead & Company.

Fourteenth Trump. Judson Pentecost Philips. LC 43-13633. (Handi-book mysteries. 16). 1943. Quinn Publishing Company, Inc.

Fourth. Frank Samperi. 1973. pap. 6.00 (Pub. by Elizabeth Pr). SBD.

Fourth Agency. John Fredman. LC 79-123225. 1970. 4.95. Bobbs-Merrill.

Fourth Angel. John Rechy. LC 72-11085. 1973. 5.95 (ISBN 0-670-32630-5). Viking Press.

Fourth Angel. John Rechy. 1975. (pbk.) 1.25 (ISBN 0-523-00533-4). Pinnacle Books.

Fourth Angel. John Rechy. LC 73-169258. 1972. 1.75 (ISBN 0-491-00913-5). W. H. Allen.

Fourth Assembling. Ed. by Richard Kostelanetz et al. (Illus.). 274p. (Orig.). 1973. pap. 4.95 (ISBN 0-915066-04-1). Assembling Pr.

Fourth at Bridge: And Other Stories. Walter Edward Duncan. LC 13-379. 1912. 1.00. The Shakespeare Press.

Fourth at Junction. Joseph Baker. LC 79-28479. 8.95 (ISBN 0-312-30181-2). St. Martin's Press.

Fourth at Junction. Joseph Barker. 1980. 8.95 o.p. (ISBN 0-312-30181-2). St Martin.

Fourth Blow. Charles Beardsley. 1980. pap. 2.50 (ISBN 0-445-04623-6). Popular Lib.

Fourth Bomb. Cecil John Charles Street. LC 42-1116. 1942. Dodd, Mead & Company.

Fourth Book of Jorkens. Edward John Moreton Drax Plunkett Dunsany. 1948. Arkham House.

Fourth Day of Fear. Berrie Davis. LC 73-81027. (Red mask mystery). 1973. 4.95 (ISBN 0-399-11232-4). Putnam.

Fourth Degree: A Mystery Novel. K. S Dalger. LC 31-5704. Macrae Smith Company.

Fourth Dimension. Horace Annesley Vachell. LC 21-264231. George H. Doran Company.

Fourth Down Pass: By Jack Paulson Pseud. Illustrated by Joseph Bolden. 1st Ed. Caary Paul Jackson. LC 50-11538. 1950. Winston.

Fourth Down to Death. Brett Halliday. (Mike Shayne Mystery). 1975. (pbk.) 0.95. Dell.

Fourth Estate. Palacio Valdes, Armando & Challice, Rachel, Tr. LC 1-31388. 1901. Brentano's.

Fourth Estate & the Queen Bees. Henry Burchfiel. 3.75 o.p. Vantage.

Fourth Finger. Robert McNair Wilson. 1929. J. B. Lippincott Company.

Fourth Flight of the Starfire. Edwin Mumford. 1972. 4.00 (ISBN 0-682-47574-2). Exposition.

Fourth Floor. Hal Boswell. 1981. 8.95 (ISBN 0-533-04772-2). Vantage.

Fourth Fontana Book of Great Horror Stories. Ed. by Christine Bernard. 1971. pap. 0.95 o.p. (95185). Beagle Bks.

Fourth Gear City Limits. Renny Pritikin. 1976. pap. 4.25 (Pub. by Twowindows Pr). SBD.

Fourth Generation. Walter Besant. LC 4971. Frederick A. Stokes Company.

Fourth Generation Preacher's Kid. Colleen L. Reese. LC 81-2943. 1982. pap. 7.00 (ISBN 0-8309-0314-3). Herald Hse.

Fourth Ghost Book. Barbara C. Turner. 1965. 5.95 o.p. Dufour.

Fourth Ghost Book. Ed. by James Turner. 1971. pap. 0.95 o.p. (95174). Beagle Bks.

Fourth Gift. Elizabeth B. De Trevino. 1971. pap. 0.75 o.p. (07123). Curtis.

Fourth Gift. Elizabeth Borton Trevino. LC 66-11765. 1966. Doubleday.

Fourth Horseman. Will Henry, pseud. 208p. 1981. pap. 1.95 (ISBN 0-553-14989-X). Bantam.

Fourth Horseman. Alan Edward Nourse. LC 81-48056. 13.95 (ISBN 0-06-038034-9). Harper & Row.

Fourth Horseman: A Novel. Geoffrey Bocca. LC 79-5223. 9.95 (ISBN 0-89256-117-3). Rawson, Wade Publishers.

Fourth Horseman, a Novel of Old Arizona. Will Henry, pseud. LC 54-5386. 1954. Random House.

Fourth Horseman of Miami Beach: A Novel. 1st Ed. Albert Halper. LC 66-18080. 1966. bds., 4.95. Norton.

Fourth King. Harry Stephen Keeler. LC 30-13233. E. P. Dutton & Co., Inc.

Fourth King. Harry Stephen Keeler. LC 44-46606. 1931. A. L. Burt Company.

Fourth Letter. Frank Gruber. LC 47-11648. (Murray Hill mystery). 1947. Rinehart.

Fourth Lovely Lady. Therese Benson. LC 32-288271. The Bobbs-Merrill Company.

Fourth Man. Andrew Boyle. 464p. 1980. pap. 3.50 (ISBN 0-553-14245-3). Bantam.

Fourth Man. Lou Smith. (Signet Book). 1978. 1.75 (ISBN 0-451-07880-2). New American Library.

Fourth Man on the Rope. Evelyn Berckman. 1973. (pbk) 0.95. Dell.

Fourth Man on the Rope. Evelyn Berckman. LC 74-175359. 1972. 5.95. Doubleday.

Fourth Mystery Book: Six Short Mysteries. LC 42-51185. 1942. Farrar & Rinehart, Inc.

Fourth Napoleon: A Romance. Charles Benham. LC 7-34445. 1897. H. S. Stone & Co.

Fourth Night Watch. Johan Falkberget. LC 68-9016. (Nordic translation series). 1968. 6.95. University of Wisconsin Press.

Fourth Norwood. Robert Eugene Pinkerton. LC 25-19111. The Reilly & Lee Co.

Fourth of Forever. William Sanborn Ballinger. LC 62-20127. 1963. Harper & Row.

Fourth-of-July Kid. William Robert Cox. (Orig.). 1981. pap. 2.25 (ISBN 0-505-51621-7). Tower Bks.

Fourth of June. 1st American Ed. David Benedictus. LC 62-20495. 1962. Dutton.

Fourth Physician: A Christmas Story. Montgomery B Pickett. LC 11-24973. 1911. A. C. McClurg & Co.

Fourth Plague... Edgar Wallace. LC 30-27774. 1930. Pub. for the Crime Club, Inc., by Doubleday, Doran & Company, Inc.

Fourth Point of the Star. Hazel Walsh. LC 49-4492. (Publisher's library, v. 2). L. L. Morrison.

Fourth Postman. Craig Rice. LC 48-4687. (Inner sanctum mystery). 1948. Simon and Shuster.

Fourth Queen. Isabel Bowler Paterson. LC 26-106895. 1926. Boni & Liveright.

Fourth "R.". George Oliver Smith. LC 59-11151. (Ballantine books, 316K). 1959. Ballantine Books.

Fourth Reich. Martin Hale. 3.75 o.p. Saifer.

Fourth Reich. Joseph Rosenberger. (Death Merchant Ser.: No. 39). 192p. (Orig.). 1980. pap. 1.95 (ISBN 0-523-41383-1). Pinnacle Bks.

Fourth Reich Death Squad. Axel Kilgore. (They Call Me the Mercenary Ser.: No. 3). 1981. pap. 2.25 (ISBN 0-89083-753-8). Zebra.

Fourth Round: Stories for Men, an Anthology. Ed. by Charles Grayson. LC 53-5265. 1953. Holt.

Fourth Shot. L. Christian Balling. LC 82-12670. 14.50 (ISBN 0-316-07968-5). Little, Brown.

Fourth Side of the Triangle. Ellery Queen. LC 65-18108. (Random House mystery). 1965. Random House.

Fourth Side of the Triangle. Ellery Queen. 1975. (pbk.) 1.50. Ballantine Books.

Fourth Stage of Gainsborough Brown. Clarissa Watson. LC 76-45651. (MW suspense). 6.95 (ISBN 0-679-50667-5). D. McKay Co.

Fourth Stage of Gainsborough Brown. Clarissa Watson. LC 77-28634. 1978. 1.95 (ISBN 0-14-004789-1). Penguin Books.

Fourth Star, a Quinny Hite Mystery. Richard Burke. LC 46-6625. 1946. Mystery House.

Fourth Street East: A Novel of How It Was. Jerome Weidman. LC 75-117698. 1970. 5.95. Random House.

Fourth Wall. N. A Diaman. LC 79-92284. 4.95 (ISBN 0-931906-01-6). Persona Press.

Fourth Wall. Barbara Paul. LC 79-7715. (Crime Club Ser.). 1979. 8.95 o.p. (ISBN 0-385-15638-3). Doubleday.

Fourth Wall. Barbara Paul. 474p. 1980. Repr. of 1979 ed. large print ed. 12.95x (ISBN 0-89621-254-8). Thorndike Pr.

Fourth Wall. Barbara Vstedal. LC 80-22946. 1980. 12.95 (ISBN 0-89621-254-8). Thorndike Press.

Fourth Watch. Hiram Alfred Cody. LC 11-246812. Hodder & Stoughton, George H. Doran Company.

Fourth Wise Man. Illustrated by Charles B. Vukovich. 1st Ed. Wadeeha Atiyeh. LC 59-13904. 1959. R. Speller.

Fourth World: A Novel. Daphne Athas. LC 56-6487. 1956. Putnam.

Fourways. Alice Mary Ross Colver. LC 44-4517. 1944. Macrae-Smith-Company.

Fowl Murder: The Mystery of Between the Lines. Robert Howard Lindsay. 1941. Little, Brown and Company.

Fowl Play. Theodora McCormick Du Bois. LC 51-12100. 1951. Published for the Crime Club by Doubleday.

Fowler... Beatrice Harraden. LC 99-1846. 1899. Dodd, Mead and Company.

Fowler Formula. Herbert Dalmas. LC 67-20917. 1967. Published for the Crime Club by Doubleday.

Fowler Formula. Herbert Damas. 1969. pap. 0.60 o.p. (0502-06034-060). Curtis.

Fowlers End. Gerald Kersh. LC 57-7305. 1957. Simon and Schuster.

Fox. Lee Hoffman. LC 75-21229. 1976. 5.95 (ISBN 0-385-11035-9). Doubleday.

Fox & Hare. Chester Anderson. LC 80-66869. (Illus.). 192p. 1980. 13.95 (ISBN 0-9601428-0-0); pap. 6.95 (ISBN 0-9601428-9-4). Entwhistle Bks.

Fox and His Vixen. Sally M Singer. LC 77-6205. 1.95 (ISBN 0-345-27325-7). Ballantine Books.

Fox and the Camellias. Ignazio Silone. LC 61-6467. 1961. Harper.

Fox Dancer. Robert J. Steelman. LC 74-11818. 1975. 4.95 (ISBN 0-385-00364-1). Doubleday.

Fox Dancer. Robert J Steelman. 1976. 0.95. Leisure Books.

Fox-Fables. Edited and Translated by Bernard M. Knab. Illus. by James Brunsman. Otto Joseph Michael Knab. LC 67-542. 1966. Washington State University Press.

Fox Farm. Warwick Deeping. LC 11-24827. 1911. 2.60. Cassell and Company, Ltd.

Fox Farm. Warwick Deeping. LC 11-278117. 1.20. Cassell and Company, Limited.

Fox Fire. Anya Seton. 1975. (pbk.) 1.50. Fawcett.

Fox Fire: A Novel. Jeanne De Lavigne & Rutherford, Jacques. LC 29-261191. 1929. Duffield and Company.

Fox from His Lair. Elizabeth Cadell. LC 66-10705. 1966. bds., 3.95. Morrow.

Fox Hill Way. Arthur A. Cusano. 5.95 o.p. Vantage.

Fox Hill Way: By Arthur J. Cusano. 1st. ed. Arthur J Cusano. 1974. 5.95 (ISBN 0-533-01210-4). Vantage Press.

Fox in One Bite. Elizabeth Scofield. LC 65-19185. (Illus.). 1966. 3.95 o.p. (ISBN 0-87011-014-4). Kodansha.

Fox in the Attic. Richard Arthur Warren Hughes. LC 61-12232. 1962. Harper.

Fox in the Cloak. Harry Lee. LC 38-357448. 1938. The Macmillan Company.

Fox Prowls. Valentine Williams. LC 39-19152. 1939. Houghton Mifflin Company.

Fox Running: A Novel. H. Rozanne Knudson. (Illus.). 1977. 1.25 (ISBN 0-380-00930-7). Avon.

Fox Trap. Robert Arthur Smith. 1978. 1.75 (ISBN 0-449-14073-3). Fawcett Gold Medal Books.

Fox Valley Murders. John Holbrook Vance. LC 66-18283. 1966. Bobbs-Merrill.

Fox Woman. Nalkbro Isadorah Bartley. LC 28-16625. 1928. Doubleday, Doran & Company, Inc.

Fox-Woman. John Luther Long. LC 99-5099. 1900. J. B. Lippincott Company.

Fox Woman & Other Stories. Abraham Merritt. LC 77-80562. 1977. 1.50 (ISBN 0-380-01744-X). Avon Books.

Fox Woman & Other Stories. Abraham Merritt. LC 77-84256. (Lost Race and Adult Fantasy Fiction). 1978. 12.00 (ISBN 0-405-11000-6). Arno Press.

Fox Woman & the Blue Pagoda & the Black Wheel, 2 vols. in one. LC 75-46293. (Supernatural & Occult Fiction Ser.). 1976. Repr. of 1947 ed. lib. bdg. 15.00x (ISBN 0-405-08153-7). Ayer Co.

Fox Woman and The Blue Pagoda and The Black Wheel. Abraham Merritt. LC 75-46293. (Supernatural and Occult Fiction). 1976. 15.00 (ISBN 0-405-08153-7). Arno Press.

Foxbait. Peter Cave. LC 78-70787. 1979. 1.95 (ISBN 0-515-04878-X). Jove/HBJ.

Foxes. Robert Preston Harriss. LC 36-7116. 1936. Houghton Mifflin Company.

Foxes of Harrow. Frank Yerby. LC 48-3512. 1946. Dial Press.

Foxes of Harrow. Frank Yerby. LC 46-250303. 1946. The Dial Press.

Foxes of Harrow. Frank Yerby. LC 47-561341. 1947. Sun Dial Press.

Foxes of Harrow: Frank Yerby. Frank Yerby. 1976. 1.95. Dell.

Foxes on the Hill. Serena Sue Hilsinger. LC 69-12585. 1969. 5.95. Gambit.

Foxfire. Cecile Gilmore. LC 45-94939. 1945. S. Curl, Inc.

Foxfire. Anya Seton. LC 50-11177. (Illus.). 1951. Houghton Mifflin.

Foxfire Light. large print ed. Janet Dailey. LC 82-23316. (Nightingale Series). 1983. 8.95 (ISBN 0-8161-3494-4). G.K. Hall.

Foxglove Country. Linden Howard. LC 76-5374. 8.95. St. Martin's Press.

Foxglove Hollow. Dennis P. Brown. 192p. (Orig.). 1982. pap. 2.50 (ISBN 0-449-14484-4, GM). Fawcett.

Foxglove Manor. Robert Williams Buchanan. LC 75-483. (Victorian Fiction: Novels of Faith and Doubt; V. 35). 1975. 35.00 (ISBN 0-8240-1560-6). Garland Pub.

Foxglove Manor, Eighteen Eighty-Four. Robert William Buchanan. Ed. by Robert Lee Wolff. LC 75-483. (Victorian Fiction Ser.). 1975. lib. bdg. 66.00 (ISBN 0-8240-1560-6). Garland Pub.

Foxglove Saga. Auberon Waugh. 1961. 3.95 o.p. (ISBN 0-671-27070-2). S&S.

Foxglove Summer. Naidra Grey. LC 76-26086. 1976. 7.95. Putnam.

Fox's Earth. Anne Rivers Siddons. LC 81-1920. 14.95 (ISBN 0-671-24962-2). Simon and Schuster.

TITLE INDEX FRANKENSTEIN: OR, THE MODERN

Fox's Paw La Pata De la Raposa: A Novel of Spanish Life. Ramon Perez De Ayala. Tr. by Walsh, Thomas. LC 24-22265. E. P. Dutton & Co.

Foxway: A Novel. Richard Jessup. LC 71-161854. 1971. 6.95. Little, Brown.

Foxx's Foe. Zack Tyler. (Orig.). 1982. pap. 2.50 (ISBN 0-440-12526-X). Dell.

Foxx's Herd. Zack Tyler. (Orig.). 1981. pap. 2.25 (ISBN 0-440-12730-0). Dell.

Foxx's Vixen. Zack Taylor. (Orig.). 1982. pap. 2.25 (ISBN 0-440-12781-5). Dell.

Foxy's Lion Tales. Arnold C Schueren. LC 43-228573. 1943.

F.P.1 Does Not Reply. Curt Siodmak & Farrell, Henry William, Tr. LC 33-28929. 1933. Little, Brown, and Company.

Fra Angelo Bomberto in the Underworld of Art... John Gilmore Wolcott & Coburn, Frederick William, 1870- LC 46-6887. 1946. N. M. Hill Press.

Fra Lippo Lippi: A Romance. Margaret Vere Farrington Livingston. LC 7-19396. 1890. G. P. Putnam's Sons.

Fracas Factor. Mack Reynolds. (Leisure Book). 1978. 1.50 (ISBN 0-8439-0602-2). Nordon Pub. Inc.

Fracas in the Foothills: A Homer Evans Western Murder Mystery and Open Space Adventure. Elliot Harold Paul. LC 40-34748. Random House.

Fracasso. Voldemar Lestienne. LC 74-81459. 8.95. St. Martin's Press.

Fractionally Awake Monad. Gus Blaisdell. 1974. signed ed. o.p. 7.50; pap. 3.50. Sand Dollar.

Fractions. Andrew Field. LC 73-165542. 1972. 0.30 (ISBN 0-14-003516-8). Penguin.

Fractions: A Novel. Andrew Field. LC 75-75860. 1969. 4.95. Simon and Schuster.

Fracture. Clayton Eshleman. 140p. 1983. 14.00 (ISBN 0-87685-580-X); pap. 7.50 (ISBN 0-87685-579-6); (signed cloth edition) 25.00 (ISBN 0-87685-581-8). Black Sparrow.

Fraeulein Von Scuderi. Ernst Theodor Amadeus Hoffmann. (Insel Taschenbuecher: It 410). (Illus.). 126p. (Ger.). 1980. pap. text ed. 3.25 (ISBN 3-458-32110-1, Pub. by Insel Verlag Germany). Suhrkamp.

Fragile Armour. Desemea Wilson. LC 37-26836. E. P. Dutton & Co., Inc.

Fragile Bark. Joseph P Benante. LC 79-154092. 1971. (ISBN 0-671-20861-6). Simon and Schuster.

Fragile Chain. Annie Morecroft. LC 54-6123. 1954. Dodd, Mead.

Fragile Years. 1st Ed. Rose Franken. LC 52-10410. 1952. Doubleday.

Fragment from a Lost Diary and Other Stories: Women of Asia, Africa, and Latin America. Ed. by Naomi Katz. LC 73-7014. 1974. 10.00 (ISBN 0-394-48475-4). Pantheon Books.

Fragment from a Lost Diary and Other Stories: Women of Asia, Africa, and Latin America. Ed. by Naomi Katz. LC 74-26792. (Beacon paperback 508). 1975. 3.95 (ISBN 0-8070-6385-1). Beacon Press.

Fragment of a Novel. Jane Austen. Repr. of 1925 ed. lib. bdg. 15.00 (ISBN 0-8414-1676-1). Folcroft.

Fragment of a Novel see Castle of Otranto (Three Gothic Novels).

Fragment of a Novel see Three Gothic Novels.

Fragment of Fear. John Michael Ward Bingham Clanmorris. LC 66-21317. 1966. Dutton.

Fragmented Life of Don Jacobo Lerner. Isaac Goldemberg. LC 76-15056. 8.95 (ISBN 0-89255-002-3). Persea Books.

Fragmented, the Empty, the Love. Patti Bard. LC 70-81066. 1969. 3.50. Zondervan Pub. House.

Fragments. Ayi Kwei Armah. LC 77-91062. 1970. 5.95. Houghton Mifflin.

Fragments. Lou Graham. 288p. (Orig.). 1981. pap. 2.50 (ISBN 0-505-51708-6). Tower Bks.

Fragments. C. Jinarajadasa. Ed. by Elithe Nieswanger. LC 79-3663. (Orig.). 1980. pap. 3.50 (ISBN 0-8356-0533-7, Quest). Theos Pub Hse.

Fragments & Splinters. Edgar Fraley. LC 75-11144. 147p. 1975. 5.95 (ISBN 0-89227-007-1). Commonwealth Pr.

Fragments: Essays and Poems. Fannie May Barbee Hughs. LC 20-10534. Christopher Publishing House.

Fragments of Perseus. Michael McClure. 1983. pap. 6.25 (ISBN 0-8112-0867-2, NDP554). New Directions.

Fragments of Stained Glass. Joan C. Westcott. 1965. 3.00 o.p. (ISBN 0-8059-0298-8). Dorrance.

Fragments of the History of Bawlfredonia. Jonas Clopper. LC 79-91076. (American Humorists Ser.). 1979. Repr. of 1819 ed. lib. bdg. 18.75 (ISBN 0-8398-0268-4). Irvington.

Fragoletta: A Novel. Eliza M. J. Humphreys. (On cover: Lovell's library. no. 116). 1888. J. W. Lovell Company.

Fragrance of Geraniums. Louise H. Kohr. LC 78-174490. 1971. 5.95 (ISBN 0-913264-04-0). Douglas-West.

Fragrance of Lilacs. Betty C. Mowery. 1982. pap. 6.95 (Avalon). Bouregy.

Fragrant Death. (Raven House Mysteries Ser.). 224p. 1981. pap. 2.25 (ISBN 0-373-63001-8, Pub. by Worldwide). Harlequin Bks.

Fragrant Flower. Barbara Cartland. (Bantam Cartland Library#35). 1976. (pbk.) 1.25. Bantam Books.

Frail Barrier. Philip Gillon. LC 52-6777. 1952. Vanguard Press.

Frailty: A Novel. Olive Wadsley. LC 17-3857. 1917. Cassell and Company, Ltd.

Frame for Murder: A Detective Novel. Kirke Mechem. LC 36-15381. 1936. Pub. for the Crime Club, Inc., by Doubleday, Doran & Company, Inc.

Frame of Dreams. Barbara Cartland. (Bantam Barbara Cartland Library#34). 1976. (pbk.) 1.25. Bantam Books.

Frame-Up. easy eye ed. Andrew Garve. 1967. pap. 0.75 o.p. (74-900). Lancer.

Frame-up. Paul Winterton. LC 64-12693. 1964. Harper & Row.

Frame-Up: The Incredible Case of Tom Mooney & Warren Billings. Curt Gentry. (Illus.). 1967. 7.50 o.p. (ISBN 0-393-05308-3). Norton.

Framed. Art Powers & Mike Misenheimer. 1974. (pbk.) 1.25 (ISBN 0-523-00359-5). Pinnacle Books.

Framed for Hanging. Constance Lindsay Taylor. LC 56-8195. (Main line mysteries). 1956. Lippincott.

Framed in Blood: By Brett Halliday Pseud. Davis Dresser. LC 51-10018. (Red badge detective). 1951. Dodd, Mead.

Framed in Hardwood. Eric Lowe. LC 40-4192. Reynal & Hitchcock.

Framed in Quilt. Day Keene. LC 49-7010. M.S. Mill Co.

Framework of Fate: Or, The One in Twenty. John Russell Coryell. LC 1-29676. (On cover: Magnet detective library, no. 159). Street & Smith.

Framley Parsonage. Anthony Trollope. (His The chronicles of Barsetshire, 4). 1962. Harcourt, Brace & World.

Framley Parsonage. Anthony Trollope. LC 12-394463. (new pocket library). 1903. John Lane.

Framley Parsonage. Anthony Trollope. LC 4-24966. (On cover: The chronicles of Barsetshire. xxi). 1903. Dodd, Mead & Company.

Framley Parsonage. Anthony Trollope. (Half-title: The world's classics. cccv). 1926. H. Milford, Oxford University Press.

Framley Parsonage. Anthony Trollope. LC 38-168741. (Half-title: Everyman's library, ed. by Ernest Rhys. Fiction. no. 832, 833). 1932. J. M. Dent & Sons, Ltd.

Framley Parsonage. Anthony Trollope. LC 80-40830. (World's classics). 1980. 7.95 (ISBN 0-19-251020-7) (ISBN 0-19-281545-8). Oxford University Press.

Framley Parsonage. A Novel. Anthony Trollope. LC 24-285409. 1873. Harper & Brothers.

Framley Parsonage. With an Introd. by Sir Arthur Quiller-Couch. Anthony Trollope. LC 64-9044. T. Nelson.

Frampton--of "the Yard"! T. Arthur Plummer. LC 35-335886. The Macaulay Company.

Fran. John Breckenridge Ellis. LC 12-7626. 1.25. The Bobbs-Merrill Company.

Franc Elliott, a Story of Society and Bohemia. Clarence Herbert New. (Dillingham's metropolitan library, no. 5). 1895. G. W. Dillingham.

Frances: A Novel. Catherine Hubbell. LC 49-11915. 1950. Norton.

Frances: A Story for Men and Women. by florence finch kelly. ed. Florence Finch Kelly. LC 7-10973. 1889. Sanfred & Company.

Frances Kane's Fortune. Elizabeth Thomasina Meade Smith. (On cover: Lovell's Westminster series, no. 8). J. W. Lovell Company.

Frances Sanders Lesson & Two Related Works. Eli Siegel. LC 74-79604. 1974. pap. 1.50 (ISBN 0-910492-19-0). Definition.

Frances Waldeaux: A Novel. Rebecca Harding Davis. LC 6-32469. 1897. Harper & Brothers.

Frances Woldeaux: A Novel. Rebecca Harding Davis. 1897. Harper & Brothers.

Francesca. Dorothy Phoebe Ansle. LC 72-88648. 1973. 5.95 (ISBN 0-8415-0221-8). Saturday Review Press.

Francesca. Laura Conway. LC 72-88648. 1973. 5.95 o.p. (ISBN 0-8415-0221-8). Dutton.

Francesca. Laura Conway. 1975. (pbk.) 1.25. Bantam Books.

Francesca. Florence Morse Kingsley. LC 11-26609. R. G. Badger.

Francesca and Carlotta Rondoli, and Short Stories: By Guy De Maupassant. Guy De Maupassant. LC 10-7486. 1910. The Pearson Publishing Co.

Francesca Da Rimini. Ernst Wildenbruch & Kannida, Pseud., Tr. (library of choice fiction no. 29). 1891. Laird & Lee.

Franchise Affair. Elizabeth Mackintosh. LC 49-7347. 1949. Macmillan Co.

Franchise Affair. Elizabeth MacKintosh. LC 79-19129. 1981. 10.00 (ISBN 0-8376-0446-X). R. Bentley.

Franchise Affair. Josephine Tey. LC 79-19129. 1981. Repr. of 1948 ed. lib. bdg. 10.00x (ISBN 0-8376-0446-X). Bentley.

Franchise Affair. Josephine Tey. 1971. pap. 1.25 (ISBN 0-425-01962-4, Medallion). Berkley Pub.

Franchise Affair. Josephine Tey. 1977. pap. 2.50 (ISBN 0-671-41527-1). PB.

Franchise Affair. Josephine Tey. (Kangaroo Book). 1977. 1.75 (ISBN 0-671-80906-7). Pocket Books.

Franchiser. Stanley Elkin. LC 76-4867. 8.95 (ISBN 0-374-15833-9). Farrar, Straus, Giroux.

Franchiser. Stanley Elkin. LC 79-92109. 1980. 6.95 (ISBN 0-87923-323-0). Nonpareil Books.

Francie Again. Emily Hahn. LC 53-9927. 1953. F. Watts.

Francie Again. Emily Hahn. 1961. Grosset & Dunlap.

Francis. David Stern. LC 46-11914. 1946. Farrar, Straus and Company.

Francis. A Socialistic Romance. Being for the Most Part an Idyll of England and Summer. M Dal Vero. LC 7-1513. (Harper's handy series, no. 93). 1886. Harper & Brothers.

Francis Abbott: Or, The Hermit of Niagara. A Tale of the Old and New World. LC 6-43164. 1846. Gleason's Publishing Hall.

Francis Abbott; or, The Hermit of Niagara. A Tale of the Old and New World. LC 43-30739. 1846. Gleason's Publishing Hall.

Francis Berrian: Or The Mexican Patriot... 2d ed.... ed. Timothy Flint. LC 1-684. 1834. Key & Biddle.

Francis Berrian, or the Mexican Patriot. Timothy Flint. Ed. by Douglas B. Hill, Jr. LC 72-93615. (American Fiction Ser). 1970. lib. bdg. 26.95 o.s.i. (ISBN 0-512-00178-2). Garrett Pr.

Francis Goes to the Seashore. Barry Gifford. LC 81-14538. 1982. 10.95 (ISBN 0-312-30358-0). St. Martin's Press.

Francis Goes to Washington. David Stern. LC 48-84406. 1948. Farrar, Straus.

Francis Parkman: Dakota Legend. Randall King. (American Explorers Ser.: No. 9). (Orig.). 1982. pap. 2.95 (ISBN 0-440-02752-7, Bryans). Dell.

Francis Stuart. J. H. Natterstad. LC 70-168817. (Irish writers series). 1974. 4.50 (ISBN 0-8387-7895-X) (ISBN 0-8387-7895-X). Bucknell University Press.

Francis the Waif (Francois le Champi. George Sand & Masson, Gustave, 1819-1888, Tr. LC 7-3310. 1889. G. Routledge and Sons.

Francisca, and Other Stories. Translated by Clavia Goodman and Bayard Qunicy Morgan, with an Appreciation by Emil Strauss. Johann Peter Hebel. LC 57-46638. (Anvil Press publication 6). Anvil Press.

Franciscan. Forrester Blake. LC 63-18201. 1963. Doubleday.

Francisco. Alison Mills. LC 73-83190. 1974. 3.95. Reed, Cannon & Johnson Communications Co.

Francois the Waif. George Sand & Sedgwick, Jane Minot, Tr. LC 4-17505. 1894. G. H. Richmond & Co.

Francotirador. Pedro Juan Soto. (Sur Ser.). 298p. 1978. pap. 4.00 (ISBN 0-940238-16-0). Ediciones Huracan.

Frangipani Garden. Barbara Hanrahan. (Illus.). 224p. 1981. text ed. 19.25 (ISBN 0-7022-1562-7); pap. 9.75 (ISBN 0-7022-1563-5). U of Queensland Pr.

Frank & Fearless; or, the Fortunes of Jasper Kent. Horatio Alger. 322p. 1974. Repr. of 1897 ed. lib. bdg. 17.15x (ISBN 0-88411-803-7). Amereon Ltd.

Frank & Hazel. Glen Williamson. 1972. 2.25 o.p. Light & Life.

Frank" and I. Dolly Morton. LC 68-56363. 1968. 7.50. Grove Press.

Frank & I. 1969. pap. 1.50 o.p. (Z1033D, Zebra). Grove.

Frank Bear. Spencer Knight. (Orig.). 1979. pap. 1.95 (ISBN 0-532-23112-0). Woodhill.

Frank Blake. Dillon O'Brien. LC 7-331641. 1876. The Pioneer-Press Company.

Frank Brown, Sea Apprentice. Frank Thomas Bullen. LC 7-25665. 1907. E. P. Dutton and Company.

Frank City (Goodbye) A Novel. Joe Cottonwood. LC 80-25549. 9.95 (ISBN 0-440-02910-4) (ISBN 0-440-52906-9). Delacorte Press /Seymour Lawrence.

Frank Fairlegh: Or, Scences from the Life of a Private Pupil. A Novel. Francis Edward Smedley. (On cover: Seaside library. Pocket ed. no. 333). 1885. G. Munro.

Frank Fairlegh: Or, Scenes from the Life of a Private Pupil. Francis Edward Smedley. G. Routledge and Sons.

Frank Fairlegh: Or, Scenes from the Life of a Private Pupil. A Novel. Francis Edward Smedley. (Harper's Franklin square library, no. 398). 1884. Harper & Brothers.

Frank Forester's Sporting Scenes and Characters. Embracing "The Warwick Woodlands", "My Shooting Box", "The Quondon Hounds", and "The Deerstalkers". with a life of the author by will wildwood, pseud.... and illustrations... by darley and frank forester pseud. ed. Henry William Herbert. LC 7-4287. T. B. Peterson & Brothers.

Frank Freeman's Barber Shop: A Tale. Baynard Rush Hall. LC 7-323. 1852. C. Scribner.

Frank Hall's Hard Hits in His Ragged Edge Rambles. Marcus Lafayette Byrn. (Rattlehead's humorous series, no. 4). The Coast City Publishing Co.

Frank Hilton: Or, "The Queen's Own,". James Grant. LC 41-381239. G. Routledge and Sons.

Frank Merriwell's Schooldays. Burt L. Standish. Ed. by Jack Rudman. (Merriwell Ser.). 3.95 (ISBN 0-8373-9301-9); pap. 1.95 (ISBN 0-8373-9001-X). F Merriwell.

Frank Mildmay: Or, The Naval Officer. Frederick Marryat & Lean, Florence (Marryat) Church. LC 42-15824. G. Routledge & Sons.

Frank Mildmay: Or, The Naval Officer. Frederick Marryat & Millar, H. R, Illus. 1897. Macmillan and Co., Limited.

Frank Norris of "The Wave" Stories & Sketches from the San Francisco Weekly, 1893 to 1897. Frank Norris. LC 78-131789. (Illus.). 1972. 19.50 (ISBN 0-403-00676-7). Scholarly Press.

Frank Norris of "The Wave" Stories & Sketches from the San Francisco Weekly, 1893 to 1897. Frank Norris. LC 74-23591. (Illus.). 1974. 20.00 (ISBN 0-8414-6272-0). Folcroft Library Editions.

Purple Sea /Frank Owen. Frank Owen. LC 77-84262. (Lost Race and Adult Fantasy Fiction). 1978. 12.00 (ISBN 0-405-11003-0). Arno Press.

Frank Reade Jr.'s New Electric Terror "The Thunderer"; or, the Search for the Tartar's Captive. Ed. by Everett Franklin Bleiler. (Frank Reade Library: Vol. 2). 1980. lib. bdg. 44.00 (ISBN 0-8240-3541-0). Garland Pub.

Frank Warrington. Miriam Coles Harris. LC 13-12902. 1871. C. Scribner & Company.

Frank Warrington. Miriam Coles Harris. LC 7-2902. Houghton, Mifflin and Company.

Frank Weston: The Real West of the Past, "Quite a Much" of It Based on Fact. Sullivan Calvin Richardson. LC 39-5763. Zion's Printing & Publishing Co.

Frankenstein. John Gardner. 1979. 9.95 (ISBN 0-89683-010-1); signed ltd. ed. 60.00 (ISBN 0-89683-009-8). New London Pr.

Frankenstein. Ed. by David Rider. pap. 1.99 o.p. (ISBN 0-448-12638-9, G&D). Putnam Pub Group.

Frankenstein. Ed. by David Rider. pap. 1.99 o.p. (ISBN 0-448-12638-9, Crimson Press). G&D.

Frankenstein. Mary Wollstonecraft Godwin Shelley. (Everyman's lib., 1616). 1961. 1.05pap. Dutton.

Frankenstein Diaries. Hubert Venables. LC 80-14806. 1980. 10.00 (ISBN 0-670-32710-7). Viking Press.

Frankenstein Factory: A Novel of the Future. Edward D Hoch. 1975. (pbk.) 1.25. Warner Paperback Library.

Frankenstein Lives Again. Donald F Glut & Hank Stine. LC 80-23272. (His The New adventures of Frankenstein; v. 1). (Starblaze editions). ((Series: Glut, Donald F.). (New Adventures of Frankenstein; v. 1.). 20.00 (ISBN 0-89865-082-8) (ISBN 0-89865-081-X). Donning Co.

Frankenstein Nineteen Sixty-Nine. Ed Martin. (Orig.). 1969. pap. 1.75 o.s.i. (TC440, Travellers Comp). Olympia.

Frankenstein: Or, The Modern Prometheus. Mary Wollstonecraft Godwin Shelley. LC 72-80409. (Library of literature). (Illus.). 1974. 7.50 (ISBN 0-672-51457-5). Bobbs-Merrill.

Frankenstein: Or, The Modern Prometheus. Mary Wollstonecraft Godwin Shelley. LC 70-889893. (Oxford paperbacks 264). 1971. 0.60 (ISBN 0-19-281116-9). Oxford University Press.

Frankenstein: Or The Modern Prometheus. 1831 ed.; edited with an introduction by m. k. joseph. ed. Mary Wollstonecraft Godwin Shelley. Ed. by M. K. Joseph. LC 71-432987. (Oxford English novels). (Illus.). 1969. Oxford U.P.

Frankenstein: Or, The Modern Prometheus. Mary Wollstonecraft Godwin Shelley. LC 50-3334. (Illustrated library). Halcyon House.

Frankenstein: Or, The Modern Prometheus. Mary Wollstonecraft Godwin Shelley. (Half-title: Everyman's library, ed. by Ernest Rhys. Fiction. no. 616). J. M. Dent & Sons, Ltd.

Frankenstein: Or, The Modern Prometheus. Mary Wollstonecraft Godwin Shelley. LC 7-3049. (On cover: New library of standard novels. no. 1). 1845. H. G. Daggers.

Frankenstein: Or, The Modern Prometheus. Mary Wollstonecraft Godwin Shelley. (On cover: Lovell's library, no. 5). J. W. Lovell Company.
Frankenstein: Or, The Modern Prometheus. Mary Wollstonecraft Godwin Shelley. LC 4-17550. G. Routledge & Sons, Limited.
Frankenstein: Or, The Modern Prometheus. Mary Wollstonecraft Godwin Shelley. LC 13-9374. ("gem" classics). 1910. J. Pott & Company.
Frankenstein: Or, The Modern Prometheus. Mary Wollstonecraft Godwin Shelley & Carbe, Nino, Illus. LC 32-18953. Illustrated Editions Company.
Frankenstein: Or, The Modern Prometheus. Mary Wollstonecraft Godwin Shelley. LC 36-37606. (Half-title: Everyman's library, ed. by Ernest Rhys. Fiction. no. 616). 1933. J. M. Dent & Sons, Ltd.
Frankenstein: Or, The Modern Prometheus. Mary Wollstonecraft Godwin Shelley & Pearson, Edmund Lester, 1880- LC 34-10901. 1934. The Limited Editions Club.
Frankenstein, or, The Modern Prometheus. Mary Wollstonecraft Godwin Shelley & Jane Furth. LC 80-54132. (Silver classics). (Illus.) (ISBN 0-382-03440-6). Silver Burdett Co.
Frankenstein: Or, The Modern Prometheus. (The 1818 Text. Mary Wollstonecraft Godwin Shelley. (Illus.). 1976. (pbk.) 1.95 (ISBN 0-671-80413-8). Pocket Books.
Frankenstein or the Modern Prometheus: The 1818 Text with a New Preface. Mary Wollstonecraft Godwin Shelley. Ed. by James Rieger. LC 81-19722. xliv, 288p. 1982. Repr. of 1974 ed. pap. 6.95 (ISBN 0-226-75227-5). U of Chicago Pr.
Frankenstein: the True Story. Christopher Isherwood & Don Bachardy. LC 73-890130. 1973. (pbk.) 1.25. Avon.
Frankenstein Unbound. Brian Wilson Aldiss. LC 73-20581. 1974. 5.95 (ISBN 0-394-49079-7). Random House.
Frankie and Johnnie: A Love Story. Meyer Levin. LC 30-100906. The John Day Company.
Frankie: Or, The Little Conqueror... E. M. Whittemore. LC 8-36535. Door of Hope Repository.
Frankincense. Guy Fletcher. LC 30-17095. E. J. Clode, Inc.
Frankincense and Murder. Baynard Hardwick Kendrick. LC 61-9869. (Red badge detective). 1961. Dodd, Mead.
Frankincense: Or, The Bride of Clairemont. Mel-Inda Jennie Porter. 1887. G. W. Dillingham; Etc., Etc.
Frankley. Alice Marie Celeste Durand. (On cover: Lovell's library, no. 1001). 1887. J. W. Lovell Company.
FRANKLIN Comes Home. A. A. Hoehling. 1974. 6.95 o.p. (ISBN 0-8015-2820-8). Hawthorn.
Franklin Evans. Walter Whitman. Ed. by Jean Downey. (Masterworks of Literature Ser). 1967. 6.00x (ISBN 0-8084-0135-1); pap. 2.45x (ISBN 0-8084-0136-X, M22). Coll & U Pr.
Franklin Evans: Or, The Inebriate; a Tale of the Times. Walt Whitman. Ed. by Jean Downey. LC 66-28900. (Masterworks of literature series). 1967. College & University Press.
Franklin Returns. Robert R. Leichtman. LC 81-69138. (From Heaven to Earth Ser.). 96p. (Orig.). 1982. pap. 3.00 (ISBN 0-89804-069-8). Ariel OH.
Franklin Scare. Jerome Charyn. LC 77-79529. 8.95 (ISBN 0-87795-167-5). Arbor House.
Franklin Winslow Kane. Anne Douglas Sedgwick. LC 10-9696. 1910. The Century Co.
Franklin Winslow Kane. Anne Douglas Sedgwick. LC 25-27476. 1925. Houghton Mifflin Company.
Franklin's Folly. Georgina Grey, pseud. (Orig.). 1980. pap. 1.75 (ISBN 0-449-50026-8, Coventry). Fawcett.
Frankly McCarthy. Carol Eisen Rinzlen. pap. 1.00 o.p. (ISBN 0-8183-0168-6). Pub Aff Pr.
Franny and Zooey. J. D. Salinger. LC 61-14542. 1961. Little, Brown.
Franny & Zooey: Two Novellas. J. D. Salinger. 1961. 10.95 (ISBN 0-316-76954-1). Little.
Franny: The Queen of Provincetown. John Preston. 96p. (Orig.). 1983. pap. 4.95 (ISBN 0-932870-31-7). Alyson Pubns.
Frantic Young Man. Charles Samuels. LC 29-5413. 1929. Coward McCann, Inc.
Fraser Butts in. Clevely, Hugh. LC 32-2873. 1931. E. J. Clode, Inc.
Fraternally Yours. Henry Von Rhau. LC 49-11113. 1949. Houghton Mifflin Co.
Fraternity. John Galsworthy. LC 72-145029. (His The works of John Galsworthy. Manaton ed., v. 7). (Illus.). 1971. (ISBN 0-403-00976-6). Scholarly Press.
Fraternity. John Galsworthy. LC 9-6848. 1909. G. P. Putnam's Sons.
Fraternity: A Romance ... LC 6-43129. (On cover: Harper's Franklin square library, no. 645). 1899. Harper & Brothers.
Fraternity Row. Lynn Montross & Montross, Lois Seyster. LC 26-15179. George H. Doran Company.
Fraternity Village. Ben Ames Williams. LC 49-9914. 1949. Houghton Mifflin Co.
Fraters. John Rogers Stewart. LC 16-14561. 1916. Publishing House of the M.E. Church, South, Smith & Lamar, Agents.
Fratricides. Maurice Edelman. LC 63-13548. 1963. Random House.
Fratricides. Nikos Kazantzakis. LC 64-24331. 1964. Simon and Schuster.
Fratricides. Nikos Kazantzakis. pap. 4.95 (ISBN 0-671-27221-7, Touchstone Bks). S&S.
Frau Jenny Treibel: Ed., by H. B. Garland. Theodor Fontane. Ed. by Henry Burnand Garland. LC 68-153087. (Macmillan's modern lang. texts). 1968. 2.95. Macmillan.
Frau Wilhelmine: The Concluding Part of the Bucholz Family. Julius Ernst Wilhelm Stinde & Powell, Harriet F., Tr. LC 8-15674. 1887. C. Scribner's Sons.
Fraud: A Novel. Paul Rader. LC 61-7274. 1961. Viking Press.
Fraulein. Mario De Andrade & Hollingsworth, Margaret Richardson, Tr. LC 33-14291. The Macaulay Company.
Fraulein. James McGovern. LC 56-7184. Crown Publishers.
Fraulein Else. Arthur Schnitzler. Tr. by Robert A. Simon from Ger. 145p. 1981. Repr. of 1928 ed. lib. bdg. 15.00 (ISBN 0-89987-771-0). Darby Bks.
Fraulein Else: A Novel. Arthur Schmitzler. Tr. by Simon, Robert Alfred. LC 25-21494. 1925. Simon and Schuster.
Fraulein Else: A Novel. Arthur Schnitzler. Tr. by Robert A. Simon from Ger. 1979. Repr. of 1925 ed. lib. bdg. 12.50 (ISBN 0-8495-4918-3). Arden Lib.
Fraulein Lili Marlene: And Other Stories. James Wakefield Burke. LC 53-4305. 1953. World Wide Productions.
Fraulein Schmidt and Mr. Anstruther. Mary Annette Beauchamp Russell Russell. 1907. C. Scribner's Sons.
Fraulein Spy. Nick Carter. (Nick Carter Ser.). (O.s.i.). (Orig.). 1970. pap. 0.95 o.s.i. (AN1101, Award). Univ Pub & Dist.
Fray Mario. Irvine Helen Douglas. LC 39-273789. 1939. Longmans, Green and Co.
Fraycar's Fist. Mary Marvin Heaton Vorse. LC 24-9266. Boni and Liveright.
Frayne of the Lying Y. George Brydges Rodney. LC 42-10314. 1942. Phoenix Press.
Frazer Acquittal: By Stephen Ransome Pseud. 1st Ed. Frederick Clyde Davis. LC 55-549829. 1955. Published for the Crime Club by Doubleday.
Freak. Michael Collins, pseud. 216p. 1983. 10.95 (ISBN 0-396-08104-5). Dodd.
Freak: A Novel of Suspense. William Arden, pseud. LC 82-12869. 9.95 (ISBN 0-396-08104-5). Dodd, Mead.
Freak-Out. Mel Arrighi. LC 68-17475. (Red mask mystery). 1968. Putnam.
Freak Show. Andrei Mikhailovich Sobel. LC 72-90314. (Illus.). 1973. (ISBN 0-88355-024-5). Hyperion Press.
Freak Show: Freaks, Monsters, Ghouls, Etc. Ed. by Peter Haining. LC 72-1436. 1972. (ISBN 0-8407-6244-5). T. Nelson.
Freak Show: Translated from the Russian of Andre Sobol. Andrei Mikhailovich Sobol. Tr. by Covan, Jenny. LC 30-11280. C. Kendall.
Freaked Out Stranger. Patrick Morgan. (Hang Ten Ser.: No. 10). 192p. 1973. pap. 0.95 o.p. (ISBN 0-532-95271-5). Woodhill.
Freaked Out Stranger. Patrick Morgan. (Hang Ten Ser.: No. 10). 192p. 1973. pap. 0.95 o.p. (ISBN 0-532-95271-5). Manor Bks.
Freaks' Amour. Tom De Haven. LC 78-10277. 1979. 9.95 (ISBN 0-688-03408-X) (ISBN 0-688-08408-7). Morrow.
Freaks of Fortune: Or, The History and Adventures of Ned Lorn. John Beauchamp Jones. LC 7-11915. T. B. Peterson.
Freaks of Lady Fortune. authorized ed. Maria Henrietta De La Cherois Crommelin. LC 6-31977. (Lovell's international series. no. 168). 1891. J. W. Lovell Company.
Freaks of Mayfair. Edward Frederic Benson. LC 77-150536. (Short story index reprint series). (Illus.). 1971. (ISBN 0-8369-3833-X). Books for Libraries Press.
Freaks of Mayfair. Edward Frederic Benson. LC 17-316541. 1917. George H. Doran Company.
Freakshow. 1st Ed. Jacquin Sanders. LC 54-686877. 1954. Little, Brown.
Freckle Juice. Judy Blume. 1978. pap. 1.75 (ISBN 0-440-42813-0, YB). Dell.
Freckles. Gene Stratton Porter. LC 74-145241. 1973. 19.50 (ISBN 0-403-01156-6). Scholarly Press.
Freckles. Gene Stratton Porter. LC 77-154033. (Illus.). 1977. Museum Shop, Indiana State Museum.
Freckles. Gene Stratton Porter. LC 4-29191. 1904. Doubleday, Page & Company.
Freckles. Gene Stratton Porter. LC 10-732364. 1909. Doubleday, Page & Company.
Freckles. Gene Stratton Porter. LC 12-22382. 1912. Doubleday, Page & Company.
Freckles. Gene Stratton Porter. LC 16-8696. 1916. 1.28. C. Scribner's Sons.
Freckles. Gene Stratton Porter. LC 21-137023. 1917. Grosset & Dunlap.
Freckles. Gene Stratton Porter. LC 21-8680. 1921. Doubleday, Page & Company.
Freckles.". Rebecca Fergus Redd. LC 7-309548. (On cover: Lovell library). J. W. Lovell Company.
Freckles. Gene Stratton-Porter. 1974. Repr. of 1904 ed. lib. bdg. 25.00 (ISBN 0-8414-7976-3). Folcroft.
Freckles Comes Home. Jeannette Porter Meehan. LC 29-178199. 1929. Doubleday, Doran & Company, Inc.
Freckles. Illus. by Michael Lowenbein. Unabridged. Gene Stratton Porter. LC 65-11920. (Whitman classics lib.). 1965. 1.00. Whitman Pub. Co.
Freckles. Illustrated by Ruth Ives. Gene Stratton Porter. LC 57-1581. 1957. Junior Deluxe Editions.
Fred Winsted, a College Man. Stephen Wood McClave. LC 19-10522. The Roxbury Publishing Company, Incorporated.
Freddy Hill. Patrick Shene Catling. (O.S.I.). 1970. 6.50 o.s.i. (ISBN 0-671-20524-2). S&S.
Freddy's Book. John Champlin Gardner. LC 79-16681. (Illus.). 1980. 10.00 (ISBN 0-394-50920-X). Knopf.
Frederica. Georgette Heyer. LC 65-11392. bds., 4.95. Dutton.
Frederica. Georgette Heyer. (V2157). 1966. Avon.
Frederica. Georgette Heyer. 1973. (pbk.) 1.25. Bantam.
Frederica Dennison, Spinster. Elizabeth Robinson Walker Price. LC 16-22938. 1.25. The Pilgrim Press.
Frederick: A Novel. Lucy Bethia Colquhoun Walford. LC 8-32814. 1895. Macmillan and Co.
Frederick De Algerov. The Hero of Camden Plains. A Revolutionary Tale. Giles Gazer. LC 6-44260. 1825. Collins and Hannay Etc.
Frederick Lonton. Desmond Warrick Croft. LC 26-2817. 1926. 2.25. Longmans, Green and Co.
Frederick Pohl's Favorite Stories: Four Decades As a Science Fiction Editor. Frederik Pohl. 504p. 1981. cancelled (ISBN 0-399-12592-2). Putnam Pub Group.
Frederick the Great and His Court. tr. from the 8th rev. ed. Klara Muller Mundt. (On cover: Lovell's library, no. 1000). 1887. J. W. Lovell Company.
Frederick the Great and His Court. Klara Muller Mundt. (On cover: The gentleman's library). 1887. Mervill and Baker.
Frederick the Great and His Court. Klara Muller Mundt. Tr. by Coleman, Ann Mary Butler (Crittenden) LC 16-1231. (historical romances of Louisa Muhlbach pseud.). D. Appleton and Company.
Frederick the Great and His Court. An Historical Romance. Klara Muller Mundt. Tr. by Coleman, Ann Mary Butler (Crittenden) LC 7-24119. 1866. D. Appleton and Company.
Frederick the Great and His Court. An Historical Romance. Klara Muller Mundt. Tr. by Coleman, Ann Mary Butler (Crittenden) LC 17-230057. 1890. D. Appleton and Company.
Frederick the Great and His Family. Klara Muller Mundt. Tr. by Coleman, Ann Mary Butler (Crittenden) LC 16-1226. (historical romances of Louisa Muhlbach pseud.). D. Appleton and Company.
Frederick the Great and His Family: An Historical Novel. Tr. by Coleman, Ann Mary Butler (Crittenden) Mundt, KlaraMuller. LC 7-172673. 1893. D. Appleton and Company.
Frederick the Great and His Family. An Historical Novel. Klara Muller Mundt. Tr. by Coleman, Ann Mary Butler (Crittenden) 1867. D. Appleton and Company.
Frederick the Great and His Family: An Historical Novel. Klara Muller Mundt. Tr. by Coleman, Ann Mary Butler (Crittenden) 1891. D. Appleton and Company.
Frederick Young: A Novel. Charles Lincoln Phillips. LC 1-31773. H. A. Dickerman & Son.
Fredericksburg: Or, The Great Tunnel at Libby. A Story of Battlefield and Prison Pen. by aleck forbes pseud.... ed. St. George Rathborne. (War library Pocket ed. no. 6). 1883. Novelist Publishing Co.
Frederik Pohl Omnibus. Frederik Pohl. LC 74-157270. (Panther science fiction). 1973. 0.40. Panther.
Frederika and the Convict. Lilliam M Robertson. LC 65-23790. 1965. Published for the Crime Club by Doubleday.
Fredi & Shirl & the Kids: The Autobiography in Fables of Richard M. Elman; a Novel. Richard M Elman. LC 70-37201. 1972. 6.95 (ISBN 0-684-12749-0). Scribner.
Free. Elizabeth Irons Folsom. LC 25-16972. The Macaulay Company.
Free. Blair Niles. LC 30-4237. Harcourt, Brace and Company.
Free Agent. Paul Cooper Murray. LC 51-11942. 1952. Holt.
Free Agent. Frederic Wakeman. 1963. 4.95 o.p. (ISBN 0-671-27240-3). S&S.
Free Air. Sinclair Lewis. LC 72-145140. 1970. Scholarly Press.
Free Air. Sinclair Lewis. LC 28-179418. 1919. Grosset & Dunlap.
Free Air. Sinclair Lewis. 1919. Harcourt, Brace and Howe.
Free and Clear. Marguerite Pearman McIntire. LC 39-33011. Farrar & Rinehart, Inc.
Free and Easy. Ann Lawrence. LC 36-10116. 1936. Godwin.
Free, and Other Stories. Theodore Dreiser. LC 70-144984. 1971. (ISBN 0-403-00949-9). Scholarly Press.
Free: And Other Stories. Theodore Dreiser. LC 18-26757. 1918. Boni and Liveright.
Free: And Other Stories. Theodore Dreiser. (Half-title: The modern library of the world's best books). The Modern Library.
Free & the Brave. John Cornwell. 1978. pap. 2.25 o.s.i. (ISBN 0-8439-0591-3, Leisure Bks). Nordon Pubns.
Free Are the Dead. Stuart Friedman. LC 54-5234. 1954. Abelard-Schuman.
Free As the Wind. Georgia Atwood White. LC 42-8902. 1942. Liveright Publishing Corporation.
Free Association: A Novel. Paul Buttenwieser. LC 80-21751. 11.95 (ISBN 0-316-11899-0). Little, Brown.
Free at Last. Jane S Collins. LC 71-37586. (Black Heritage Library Collection). (Illus.). 1972. (ISBN 0-8369-8962-7). Books for Libraries Press.
Free at Last. Jane S Collins. LC 6-25417. 1896. Press of Murdoch, Kerr & Co.
Free Born: An Unpublishable Novel. Scott Nearing. LC 72-4737. (Black Heritage Library Collection). 1972. 11.25 (ISBN 0-8369-9115-X). Books for Libraries Press.
Free Born: An Unpublishable Novel. Scott Nearing. LC 32-142319. Urquhart Press.
Free Country. Warren Dearden. LC 70-156905. (Evergreen black cat book). 1971. 1.25. Grove Press.
Free Drinks. John Dolben Mackworth. LC 26-201367. 1926. Cassell and Company, Ltd.
Free Fall. Gerald Jay Goldberg. LC 60-5431. (YA) (gr. 9-12). 1962. pap. 2.95 (ISBN 0-15-633468-2, Harv). HarBraceJ.
Free Fall: A Novel. J. D. Reed. LC 79-15776. 8.95 (ISBN 0-440-02724-1). Delacorte Press.
Free Fall in Crimson. John Dann MacDonald. LC 80-7871. 10.95 (ISBN 0-06-014833-0). Harper & Row.
Free Fall in Crimson. John Dann MacDonald. LC 81-6858. 1981. 13.50 (ISBN 0-8161-3272-0). G.K. Hall.
Free Fire Zone: Short Stories by Vietnam Veterans. LC 72-5875. 1973. pap. 4.00 o.p. (ISBN 0-9607554-2-X). Packrat Pr.
Free Fire Zone: Short Stories by Vietnam Veterans. Wayne Karlin & Basil T. Paquet. LC 72-13881. (Illus.). 1973. 2.95 (ISBN 0-07-033326-2) (ISBN 0-07-033326-2). McGraw-Hill.
Free Fishers. John Buchan. LC 34-227592. 1934. Houghton Mifflin Company.
Free Flight. Douglas C. Terman. 1981. pap. 2.95 (ISBN 0-671-42735-0). PB.
Free for All. Evan Shipman. LC 78-140341. (Short story index reprint series). (Illus.). 1970. Books for Libraries Press.
Free for All. Evan Shipman. LC 35-36772. 1935. C. Scribner's Sons.
Free for All. 1st Ed. Viola Rowe. LC 59-8306. 1959. Longmans, Green.
Free for 3 Months Only. Dorothy Dwight Power Hutchison. LC 39-27496. 1939. Stephen Daye Press.
Free Forester: A Novel of Pioneer Kentucky. Horatio Colony. LC 35-19420. 1935. Little, Brown, and Company.
Free Grass. Ernest Haycox. LC 29-4996. 1929. Doubleday, Doran and Company, Inc.
Free Grass: By Jim O'Mara Pseud. 1st Ed. Vernon L Fluharty. LC 51-11778. (Dutton Diamond D western). 1951. Dutton.
Free Joe, and Other Georgian Sketches. Joel Chandler Harris. LC 67-29268. (Americans in fiction). 1967. Gregg Press.
Free Joe: And Other Georgian Sketches, by Joel Chandler Harris... Joel Chandler Harris. LC 7-366342. 1887. C. Scribner's Sons.
Free Joe & Other Sketches. Joel C. Harris. LC 67-29268. (Americans in Fiction Ser: No. 11). 1967. Repr. of 1887 ed. lib. bdg. 8.00x o.p. (ISBN 0-8398-0762-7). Gregg.

Free Lady. Cecil Strange. LC 32-5082. 1932. Covici, Friede.
Free Lance. George Shipway. LC 75-2379. 1975. 7.95 (ISBN 0-15-133476-5). Harcourt Brace Jovanovich.
Free Lance Lover. Ross Sloane. LC 35-100479. Godwin.
Free-Lance Murder. Vic Rodell. LC 57-12677. 1957. Mystery House.
Free-Lance Pallbearers. Ishmael Reed. LC 67-19084. 1967. Doubleday.
Free-Lance Pallbearers. Ishmael Reed. (Bard Book). 1977. 1.75 (ISBN 0-380-00987-0). Avon Books.
Free-Lance Spy. Victor Armstrong. LC 75-36123. 176p. (Orig.). 1976. pap. 1.25 (ISBN 0-89041-051-8, 3051). Major Bks.
Free Land. Rose Wilder Lane. LC 38-8223. 1938. Longmans, Green and Co.
Free Lovers. Josiah Pitts Woolfolk. LC 48-105984. (Novel library, 3). 1948. Diversey Pub. Corp.
Free Lovers: A Novel of to-Day. Reginald Wright Kauffman. LC 25-23589. The Macaulay Company.
Free Man. Conrad Richter. LC 43-11545. 1943. A. A. Knopf.
Free Man's Heritage. Lester L. Roush. 3.50 o.p. Vantage.
Free Not Bound. Kate Nichols Trask. LC 3-26966. 1903. G. P. Putnam's Sons.
Free of a Dream. Adel Pryor, pseud. LC 70-87855. 1969. 2.95. Zondervan Pub. House.
Free Prisoners. A Story of California Life. Jane W Bruner. LC 6-16709. 1877. Claxton, Remsen & Haffelfinger.
Free Range. Francis William Sullivan. LC 13-18003. W. J. Watt & Company.
Free Range Lanning: A Western Story. George Owen Baxter. LC 21-18588. 1921. Chelsea House.
Free Range Lanning: A Western Story. George Owen Baxter. LC 25-15494. 1924. A. L. Burt Company.
Free Range Wife. Michael Kenyon. LC 82-23480. (Crime Club Ser.). (Illus.). 192p. 1983. pap. 11.95 (ISBN 0-385-18838-2). Doubleday.
Free Rangers. Joseph Alexander Altsheler. 350p. 1981. Repr. lib. bdg. 14.95 (ISBN 0-89968-225-1). Lightyear.
Free Soil. Marguerite Allis. LC 57-6719. 1958. Putnam.
Free Soil. Margaret Lynn. LC 20-20945. 1920. The Macmillan Company.
Free Soil Prophet of the Verdigris. R. E Heller. 1894.
Free Soul. St. John, Adela Rogers. LC 27-5836. 1927. Cosmopolitan Book Corporation.
Free Spirit. David Rook. 1978. pap. 1.75 (ISBN 0-425-03728-2, Medallion). Berkley Pub.
Free to Live. Alan Williams. LC 34-168007. 1934. W. Godwin, Inc.
Free to Love: Published Serially Under the Title City Girl. Jane Dixon. LC 32-22973. Grosset & Dunlap.
Free to Serve, a Tale of Colonial New York. Emma Rayner. LC 4-15151. 1897. Copeland and Day.
Free to Serve: A Tale of Colonial New York. new ed., with a frontispiece in full colour by george gibbs. ed. Emma Rayner. LC 11-19411. 1911. 1.50. L. C. Page & Company.
Free Woman. Terry N. Bonner. (Australians Ser.: No. 3). 352p. (Orig.). 1983. pap. 3.50 (ISBN 0-440-01072-1, Emerald). Dell.
Free, Yet Forging Their Own Chains. Mary Abigail Roe. LC 7-40255. Dodd, Mead & Company.
Freebie and the Bean: A Novel. Paul B Ross. 1974. (pbk.) 1.25. Warner Paperback Library.
Freebody Heiress. Ethel Edison Gordon. LC 74-82981. 1975. 6.95 (ISBN 0-679-50515-6). D. McKay Co.
Freebody Heiress. Ethel Edison Gordon. (Dell Book). 1977. 1.50. Dell Pub Corp.
Freebooter of the Baltic. Viktor Rydberg & Broomall, Caroline L., Tr. LC 8-1348. 1891. Cooper & Vernon, Printers.
Freebooters. Elleston Trevor. LC 67-12865. 1967. Doubleday.
Freebooters. A Novel. Robert Wernick. LC 49-7844. 1949. C. Scribner's Sons.
Freebooty. Jack Foxx. LC 76-1987. 1976. 8.95 o.p. (ISBN 0-672-52213-6). Bobbs.
Freebooty: A Novel of Suspense. Jack Foxx. LC 76-1985. 8.95 (ISBN 0-672-52213-6). Bobbs-Merrill.
Freeburgers. A Novel. literary school ed. Denton Jaques Snider. 1889. Press of Nixon-Jones Printing Co.
Freeburgers. A Novel. Denton Jaques Snider. LC 9-2685. 1890. The Sigma Publishing Co.
Freedom at Midnight. Larry Collins & Dominique Lapierre. 608p. 1976. pap. 4.95 (ISBN 0-380-00693-6, 617471). Avon.
Freedom at Midnight. Larry Collins & Dominique Lapierre. LC 75-16123. (O.s.i.). (Illus.). 613p. 1975. 12.50 o.s.i. (ISBN 0-671-22088-8). S&S.
Freedom Dues: Or, A Gentleman's Progress in the New World. Robert H. Abel. LC 79-29755. (Illus.). 9.95 (ISBN 0-8037-2575-2). Dial Press.
Freedom, Farewell. Phyllis Eleanor Bentley. LC 36-27113. 1936. The Macmillan Company.
Freedom Front. Clara Worth Baker. LC 50-8319. 1950. Meador.
Freedom Next Time: A Novel. Florence Chanock Cohen. LC 70-147861. 1971. 3.95 (ISBN 0-671-32413-6). J. Messner.
Freedom Observed. Gwyn Griffin. LC 63-7245. 1963. Holt, Rinehart and Winston.
Freedom of Henry Meredyth. M Hamilton. (Half-title: Appletons' town and country library. no 230). 1897. D. Appleton and Company.
Freedom or Death: A Novel. Translated by Jonathan Griffin. Pref. by A. Den Doolaard. Nikos Kazantzakes. LC 55-880918. 1956. Simon and Schuster.
Freedom Road. Howard Melvin Fast. LC 44-401611. 1944. Duell, Sloan and Pearce.
Freedom Run. Burt Arthur, pseud. 1971. pap. 0.60 o.p. (60-464). Manor Bks.
Freedom Run: By Arthur Herbert Pseud. Herbert Arthur, pseud. LC 51-14306. 1951. Rinehart.
Freedom Song. With Line Drawings by Dexter F. Knox. 1st Ed. Neill Compton Wilson. LC 55-5954. 1955. Holt.
Freedom to Do Right. Nellie Smeenk De Mots. LC 47-219495.
Freedom to Love. Carole Mortimer. (Harlequin Presents Ser.). 192p. 1981. pap. 1.75 (ISBN 0-373-10473-1). Harlequin Bks.
Freedom to Love. Sabrina Myles. (Candlelight Ecstasy Ser.: No. 25). (Orig.). 1981. pap. 1.75 (ISBN 0-440-12530-8). Dell.
Freedom Trail to Greystone. Louisa Bronte. LC 75-41384. 1.50. Ballantine Books.
Freedom Trail to Greystone. large print ed. Louisa Bronte. LC 76-20646. (Greystone Tavern series). 1976. 9.95 (ISBN 0-89340-002-5). J. Curley.
Freedom Trap. Desmond Bagley. LC 72-5799. 1972. 9.95 (ISBN 0-8161-6045-7). G. K. Hall.
Freedom Trap. Desmond Bagley. 1973. 0.95. Fawcett Crest.
Freedom Trap. Desmond Bagley. LC 70-171277. 1972. 5.95. Doubleday.
Freedom's Flag: The Story of Francis Scott Key. Rupert Sargent Holland. LC 43-7869. 1943. Macrae-Smith-Company.
Freedom's Flame. Dee Stuart. (Orig.). 1980. pap. text ed. 2.50 (ISBN 0-440-12532-4). Dell.
Freedom's Gateway. James P Lynyse. LC 57-7963. 1957. Creative Press.
Freedom's Passion. Hugh Zachary. (Sierra Leone Ser.: No. 2). (Orig.). 1981. pap. 2.75 (ISBN 0-440-02769-1, Bryans). Dell.
Freedom's Thunder. Michael Foster. 1976. 1.95 (ISBN 0-380-00660-X). Avon Books.
Freedom's Way. Theodora McCormick Du Bois. LC 53-698275. 1953. Funk &Wagnalls.
Freefall into Hell. Hal Hennesey. (Orig.). pap. 0.50 o.p. (B50-780). Belmont-Tower.
Freeholder. Joe David Brown. 1976. (pbk.) 1.50. New American Library.
Freeholder. Joe David Brown. LC 49-10481. 1949. W. Morrow.
Freehooters of the Wilderness. Agnes Christina Laut. LC 10-25213. 1910. 1.35. Moffat, Yard and Company.
Freelance in Kashmir: A Tale of the Great Anarchy. George Fletcher MacMunn. LC 15-16239. 1914. E. P. Dutton & Company.
Freelance the Buccaneer. Prentiss Ingraham. LC 31-10366. The Arthur Westbrook Company.
Freelands. John Galsworthy. LC 15-16896. 1915. C. Scribner's Sons.
Freeman Cooper. William R. Hopkins. 3.95 o.p. Vantage.
Freeman in Bondage: Or, Twelve Years a Slave. (Companion Story to "Uncle Tom's Cabin.) A True Tale of Slavery Days. Solomon Northup. (On cover: Columbian library, no. 6). 1890. Columbian Publishing Company.
Freemartin. David Keith Cohler. LC 81-8283. 12.95 (ISBN 0-316-15023-1). Little, Brown.
Freer's Cove. Ethel Edison Gordon. LC 79-187142. 1972. 6.95. Coward, McCann & Geoghegan.
Freer's Cove. Ethel Edison Gordon. 1974. (pbk.) 1.25. Dell.
Freewater Range. Frank Chester Robertson. LC 33-6577. 1933. I. Washburn.
Freeway. Deanne Barkley. LC 77-17829. 8.95 (ISBN 0-02-507210-2). Macmillan.
Freeway. Peter Nichols. 88p. 1975. pap. 4.95 (ISBN 0-571-10744-3). Faber & Faber.
Freeways. Vina Delmar. LC 70-153685. 1974. (pbk.) 1.25. Manor Books.
Freezing Down. Anders Bodelsen. LC 77-122892. 1971. 5.95 (ISBN 0-06-010401-5). Harper & Row.
Freezing Point. Ayako Miura. Tr. by H. Shimizu & J. Terry. 250p. 1982. pap. 5.95 (ISBN 0-933704-29-1). Dawn Pr.
Freighter: A Novel. Suzette Telenga. LC 57-5985. 1957. J. Day Co.
Freighter: A Tale of the Pittsburgh Frontier. Andrew Lyle Russell. LC 15-19191. 1.50. The Roxburgh Publishing Company, Inc.
Freighters West. Judy M. Frank. 4.95 o.p. Vantage.
Fremde, Erzaehlung. Sinclair. (Edition Suhrkamp. Neue Folge: es. NF 7). 150p. (Orig., Ger.). 1980. pap. text ed. 4.55 (ISBN 3-518-11007-1, Pub. by Suhrkamp Verlag Germany). Suhrkamp.
French. W. Maureen Miller. 640p. (Orig.). 1983. pap. 3.95 (ISBN 0-440-02737-3, Emerald). Dell.
French Adventurer: The Life and Exploits of La Salle. Maurice Constantin-Weyer. LC 31-22065. The Macaulay Company.
French and Italian Notebooks. Nathaniel Hawthorne & Thomas Woodson. LC 81-122144. (centenary edition of the works of Nathaniel Hawthorne; v. 14). ((Series: Hawthorne, Nathaniel, 1804-1864.). (1962). (Works.). (V. 14.). 36.00 (ISBN 0-8142-0256-X). Ohio State University Press.
French and Oriental Love in a Harem. With Decorations by Paul Avril. Mario Uchard. LC 52-32132. Priv. Issued by Faltstaff Press.
French Atlantic Affair. Ernest Lehman. LC 77-4709. 1977. 9.95 (ISBN 0-689-10803-6). Atheneum.
French Atlantic Affair. Ernest Lehman. 1978. 2.50 (ISBN 0-446-81562-4). Warner Books.
French Bandello: A Selection; the Original Text of Four of Belleforest's Histoires Tragiques. Matteo Bandello. Ed. by Hook, Frank Scott. (University of Missouri Studies, V. 22,No. 1). 1948. Univ. of Missouri.
French Boy. Andrew McCall. LC 69-18188. 1969. 5.95. Putnam.
French Bride. Evelyn Anthony. 1977. pap. 1.95 (ISBN 0-451-07683-4, J7683, Sig). NAL.
French Bride. Eve Stephens, pseud. LC 64-16222. 1964. Doubleday.
French Bride. Eve Stephens, pseud. (Signet Book). 1977. 1.95 (ISBN 0-451-07683-4). New American Library.
French Connection II. Robin Moore & Milt Machlin. 1975. (pbk.) 1.50. Dell.
French Consul. Lucien Bodard. LC 76-41767. (Illus.). 1977. 10.00 (ISBN 0-394-49321-4). Knopf: Distributed by Random House.
French Country Family. Henriette Elizabeth Guizot Witt. LC 30-12312. 1868. Harper & Brothers.
French Decision. David Osborn. LC 79-6873. 1980. 10.95 (ISBN 0-385-15904-8). Doubleday.
French Doll: A Novel of Suspense. Vincent McConnor. LC 65-14529. 3.95. Hill & Wang.
French Dragoon. Translated from the French by Hugo Charteris. Roger Rudigoz. LC 59-11003. 1959. Coward- McCann.
French Farce... Edwin Greenwood. LC 37-4080. Doubleday, Doran & Company, Inc.
French Fiction: Honore De Balzac, George Sand, Alfred De Musset, Alphonse Daudet, Guy De Maupassant.., The/harvard Classics Shelf Of Fiction. Balzac, Honore De et al. LC 17-174303. (Harvard Classics Shelf of Fiction). (Harvard classics shelf of fiction. selected by C. W. Eliot. 13: 13). P. F. Collier & Son.
French Finish. Robert Ross. LC 76-48309. 7.95 (ISBN 0-399-11884-5). Putnam.
French Follies & Other Follies: 20 Stories from 'The New Yorker. Francis Steegmuller. LC 46-6851. 1946. Reynal & Hitchcock.
French Girls Are Vicious & Other Stories. James Thomas Farrell. 1955. 11.95 (ISBN 0-8149-0095-X). Vanguard.
French Girls of Killini: Twenty-One Short Stories 1st Ed. Arturo Vivante. LC 67-144521. 1967. 5.95. Little.
French Husband. Kathleen Coyle. LC 32-26562. E. P. Dutton & Co., Inc.
French Husband. Ethel Edison Gordon. LC 76-27349. 1977. 7.95 (ISBN 0-690-01207-1). Crowell.
French Imposter, No. 1. Bruce Weiser. (Chenevix Ser.). 1980. pap. 2.25 (ISBN 0-8439-0815-7). Nordon Pubns.
French Inheritance. Anne Stevenson, pseud. LC 73-87209. 1974. 6.95 (ISBN 0-399-11271-5). Putnam.
French Jade. Rebecca Danton, pseud. (Coventry Romance Ser.: No. 177). 224p. 1982. pap. 1.50 (ISBN 0-449-50278-3, Coventry). Fawcett.
French Janet: A Novel. Henrietta Keddie. LC 7-11138. (On cover: Harper's Franklin square library, no. 640). 1889. Harper & Brothers.
French Key. Frank Gruber. LC 40-5222. Farrar & Rinehart, Inc.
French Key Mystery. Frank Gruber. LC 43-123137. (Murder of the month. No. 4). 1942. The Avon Book Company.
French Key Mystery... Frank Gruber. LC 46-22078. 1946.
French Killing. James P Cody. (D.C. Man Series). 1975. (pbk.) 0.95 (ISBN 0-425-02921-2). Berkley Publishing Corp.
French Kiss. Mark Logan. (Signet Book). (Illus.). 1978. 1.95 (ISBN 0-451-07876-4). New American Library.
French Kiss. J. J. Montague. (Black Swan Ser). 192p. 1974. pap. 1.50 o.p. (ISBN 0-89014-113-4, CB-113). Canyon Bks.
French Kiss. J. J Montague. (Black swan#3). 1974. (pbk.) 1.50 (ISBN 0-89014-113-4). Canyon Books.
French Kiss: A Novel. Peter Israel. LC 76-6549. 6.95 (ISBN 0-690-01099-0). Crowell.
French Kiss: A Tongue-in-Cheek Political Fantasy. Eric Koch. LC 73-470793. (Illus.). 1969. 5.95. McClelland and Stewart.
French Lady's Lover. Barbara Annandale, pseud. LC 77-10786. 1978. 9.95 o.p. (ISBN 0-698-10880-9, Coward). Putnam Pub Group.
French Lady's Lover. Jean Bowden. LC 77-10786. 9.95 (ISBN 0-698-10880-9). Coward, McCann & Geoghegan.
French Leave. Pelham Grenville Wodehouse. LC 59-13139. 1959. Simon and Schuster.
French Lieutenant's Woman. John Fowles. (Signet novel, W4479). 1973. 1.50. New American Lib.
French Lieutenant's Woman. John Fowles. LC 77-86616. 1969. 7.95. Little, Brown.
French Mademoiselle. Eva McDonald. 1973. pap. 0.75 o.p. (07281). Curtis.
French Passion. Diane Du Pont. (Fawcett Gold Medal Book). 1977. 1.95 (ISBN 0-449-13888-7). Fawcett Pubns.
French Powder Mystery. Ellery Queen. 316p. 1976. lib. bdg. 15.75x (ISBN 0-89966-148-3). Buccaneer Bks.
French Powder Mystery. Ellery Queen, pseud. LC 42-10941. 1941. Triangle Books.
French Powder Mystery. Ellery Queen, pseud. LC 79-19450. (Illus.). 1980. 10.95 (ISBN 0-89340-235-4). J. Curley & Associates.
French Powder Mystery: A Problem in Deduction. Ellery Queen, pseud. LC 30-18208. 1930. Frederick A. Stokes Company.
French Quarter. Herbert Asbury. 1981. pap. 2.50 (ISBN 0-89176-028-8, 6028). Mockingbird Bks.
French Short Stories. Ed. by Lyon. 1966. pap. 3.95 (ISBN 0-14-002385-2). Penguin.
French Short Stories. Ed. by Pamela Lyon. (Orig., Bilingual). (YA) (gr. 9 up). 1966. pap. 1.45 o.p. (ISBN 0-14-002385-2, 2385). Penguin.
French Short Stories. Ed. by Harry Christian Schweikert. LC 18-16983. (Lake English classics). Scott, Foresman and Company.
French Short Stories, Vol. 2. Ed. by Simon Lee. (Orig., Bilingual). 1972. pap. 1.95 o.p. (ISBN 0-14-003414-5, 3414). Penguin.
French Short Stories, Edited with Introductions, Vocabulary and Notes. abridged ed. Ed. by Elijah Clarence Hills. Holbrook, Richard Thayer, 1870-1934, Joint Ed & Humphreys, Harold Llewelyn, 1894- LC 45-6246. 1945. D. C. Heath and Company.
French Short Stories: Nouvelles Francaises. Ed. by Pamela Lyon. LC 66-5018. (Penguin parallel texts, 2385). Penguin.
French Short Stories of the Nineteenth & Twentieth Centuries. Compiled by Frederick Charles Green. 1971. Repr. of 1906 ed. 8.95x (ISBN 0-460-00896-X, Evman); pap. 3.95x (ISBN 0-460-01896-5). Biblio Dist.
French Short Stories of the Nineteenth Century. Ed. by Edwin Bucher Williams. LC 33-299429. 1933. F. S. Crofts & Co.
French Short Stories of the 19th and 20th Centuries. Ed. by Green, Frederick Charles. (Half-title: Everyman's library, ed. by Ernest Rhys. Fiction. no. 896). 1933. J. M. Dent & Sons, Ltd.
French Short Stories of the 19th and 20th Centuries. Selected, with Introd. by F.C. Green. Ed. by Frederick Charles Green. (Everyman's lib., 896). 1962. 1.95. Dent.
French Short Stories of to-Day. Ed. by Margaret W. Watson. LC 22-12849. C. Scribner's Sons.
French Short Story in the Nineteenth Century. Ed. by Murray Sachs. 1969. pap. 4.00x o.p. (ISBN 0-19-501042-6). Oxford U Pr.
French Short Story in the Nineteenth Century. Ed. by Murray Sachs. 1969. pap. 4.00x o.p. (ISBN 0-19-501042-6). Oxford U Pr.
French Short Story in the Nineteenth Century: A Critical Anthology. Ed. by Murray Sachs. LC 69-17773. 1969. Oxford University Press.
French Slippers. Deborah Chester. LC 80-27266. 11.95 (ISBN 0-698-11071-4). Coward, McCann & Geoghegan.
French Stories and Tales. Ed. by Stanley Geist. LC 53-6842. (Borzoi series of stories and tales). 1954. Knopf.
French Stories from New Writing. John Lehmann. 1947. 15.00. Havertown Bks.
French Stories of the Past and Present. Ed. by Clifford Stetson Parker. LC 33-33103. H. Holt and Company.
French Summer. Guy Gilpatric. LC 49-2768. (New Avon library, 180). 1948. Avon Pub. Co.

French Summer. Guy Gilpatric. LC 33-19880. 1933. Dodd, Mead & Company.
French Tales of Love and Passion. Guy De Maupassant. LC 68-19059. 1969. 3.00. Young Publications.
French, They Are a Funny Race. Lyon Mearson. LC 31-21622. The Mohawk Press.
French Touch. Bruce J. Brooks. pap. 1.95 o.p. (ISBN 0-87056-236-3). Brandon.
French Wife. Dorothy Graham. LC 28-2879. 1928. Frederick A. Stokes Company.
French Windows. 4th impression. ed. Francis Browning Drew Bickerstaffe-Drew. LC 17-24699. 1917. Longmans, Green & Co.; Etc., Etc.
French Windows. Geraldine Symons. LC 52-4746. 1952. Longmans, Green.
Frenchman. Velda Johnston. LC 76-17620. 1976. 8.95 (ISBN 0-8161-6389-8). G. K. Hall.
Frenchman. Velda Johnston. (Signet Book). 1977. 1.50 (ISBN 0-451-07519-6). New American Library.
Frenchman: A Novel of Suspense. Velda Johnston. LC 76-3462. 6.95 (ISBN 0-396-07301-8). Dodd, Mead.
Frenchman Must Die. Kay Boyle. LC 46-1435. 1946. Simon and Schuster.
Frenchman's Creek. Daphne Du Maurier. LC 70-184730. 1971. 8.50 (ISBN 0-8376-0412-5). R. Bentley.
Frenchman's Creek. Daphne Du Maurier. LC 42-207. 1942. Doubleday, Doran & Company, Inc.
Frenchman's Creek. Daphne Du Maurier. LC 47-23775. 1946. Triangle Books, the Blakiston Company.
Frenchman's Mistress. Irene Michaels. (Orig.). 1980. pap. 2.75 (ISBN 0-440-12545-6). Dell.
Frenchman's River: By Will Ermine Pseud. Harry Sinclair Drago. LC 55-10040. (Permabooks, M3024. Western, 4). 1955. Permabooks.
Frenchwoman. Barbara Paul. 1977. 8.95 o.p. (ISBN 0-312-30537-0). St Martin.
Frenchwoman. Barbara Vstedal. LC 76-62787. 8.95 (ISBN 0-312-30537-0). St. Martin's Press.
Frenchy & Cuban Pete & Other Stories. Bobbie L. Hawkins. (O.s.i.). 1976. pap. 3.50 o.s.i. (ISBN 0-939180-05-7). Tombouctou.
Frenchy: The Story of a Gentleman. William Sage. LC 4-13658. 1904. Scott-Thaw Company.
Frenesi: A Novel. Harvey Deakin. LC 45-5190. 1945. Centaur Publishing Co.
Frenological Finance: Being a True History of the Life and Adventures of Mortimer Kensington Queen. James Francis Davis. LC 8-22612. 1907. The C. M. Clark Publishing Company.
Frenzied Fiction. Stephen Butler Leacock. LC 78-125227. (Short story index reprint series). 1970. Books for Libraries Press.
Frenzy. Arthur J. La Bern. 1971. pap. 0.95 o.p. (65-713). Paperback Lib.
Frenzy: By Jack Woodford Pseud. & Todd Marshall. Josiah Pitts Woolfolk & Todd Marshall. LC 53-405178. 1953. Signature Press.
Frenzy in the Flesh. Desmond Reid. pap. 0.60 o.p. (60-353). Manor Bks.
Frequent Hearses. Edmund Crispin, pseud. LC 82-9836. 1982. 2.95 (ISBN 0-14-006325-0). Penguin Books.
Frequent Hearses: A Detective Story. Robert Bruce Montgomery. LC 72-146322. (London House & Maxwell mystery). 1971. 4.95 (ISBN 0-8277-0251-5). London House & Maxwell.
Frere Ocean, 3 tomes. Romain Gary, pseud. Incl. Tome I. Pour Sganarelle Recherche d'un Personnage et d'un Roman. 11.25; Tome II. Danse de Gengis Cohn; Tome III. Tete Coupable. (Coll. Soleil). 11.25 ea. French & Eur.
Freres: A Novel. author's ed. Annie French Hector. LC 7-5164. (On cover: Leisure hour series no. 134). 1882. H. Holt and Company.
Frescati: A Page from Virginia History. Nettie Gray Daingerfield. 1909. The Neale Publishing Company.
Frescoe. Louise De La Ramee & Fenn, George Manville. (seaside library. v. 78, no. 1586). G. Munroe.
Fresh Air Child. George Edward Hawes. LC 15-5348. 1914. Fleming H. Revell Company.
Fresh and Open Sky, and Other Stories. Richard Sullivan. LC 50-10694. 1950. Holt.
Fresh and the Salt. Olga Stringfellow. LC 59-10692. 1959. Doubleday.
Fresh Every Hour: Detailing the Adventures, Comic and Pathetic of One Jimmy Martin, Purveyor of Publicity, a Young Gentlemen Possessing Sublime Nerve, Whimsical Imagination, Colossal Impudence, and, Withal, the Heart of a Child. John Peter Toohey. Boni and Liveright.
Fresh Fields. John Burroughs. Repr. of 1885 ed. 15.00 o.s.i. Finch Pr.
Fresh from the Barrens. Blanche Jane Smith. LC 15-6070. 1915. Smith Printing Company.
Fresh from the Country. Read. 221p. 1960. 10.95 o.p. (ISBN 0-7181-0141-3, Pub. by Michael Joseph). Merrimack Pub Cir.
Fresh from the Laundry. pap. 0.75 o.p. (07095). Curtis.
Fresh Furrow. Burris Atkins Jenkins. LC 36-13188. 1936. Willett, Clark & Company.
Fresh Gleanings. Donald Grant Mitchell. 1847. Repr. lib. bdg. 25.00 (ISBN 0-8414-6627-0). Folcroft.
Fresh Leaves from Western Woods. Metta Victoria Fuller Victor. LC 10-3730. 1852. G. H. Derby & Co.
Fresh off the Bus: Teenage Hookers. Stephen Lewis. 1974. (pbk.) 1.50. Ace Books.
Fresh Waters and Other Stories. Richard Washburn Child. LC 24-27994. E. P. Dutton & Company.
Freshman at Large. Alan Bentel. pap. 0.60 o.p. (JX36). Pyramid Pubns.
Freshman at McDonough. William Talbott Childs. LC 47-17769. 1946. The Maurice Leeser Co.
Freshman, Novelized. Russell Holman. LC 25-198316. Grosset & Dunlap.
Freshwater, a Panorama. Richard Warner Borst. LC 54-10235. 1954. Vantage Press.
Frey and His Wife. Maurice Henry Hewlett. LC 16-7919. 1916. 1.00. R. M. McBride & Company.
Freydis and Gudrid. Elizabeth Boyer. LC 76-23353. (Illus.). 9.95. Veritie Press.
Friar of Wittenberg. William Stearns Davis. LC 12-12133. 1912. The Macmillan Company.
Friar Tuck: Being the Chronicles of the Reverend John Carmichael, of Wyoming, U.S.A. Robert Alexander Wason. LC 12-20796. 1912. Small, Maynard and Company.
Friars and Filipinos: An Abridged Translation of Dr. Jose Rizal's Tagalog Novel, "Noli Me Tangere.". Jose Rizal Y Alonso. Tr. by Gannett, Frank Ernest. LC 1-30162. The St. James Press.
Friar's Daughter: A Story of the American Occupation of the Philippines. Charles Lincoln Phifer. LC 17-7991. 1909. The Author.
Friar's Summoner's & Pardoner's Tales. Geoffrey Chaucer. Ed. by N. R. Havely. LC 75-19090. (London Medieval & Renaissance Ser.). 164p. 16.50x (ISBN 0-8419-0220-8); pap. 9.00x (ISBN 0-8419-0224-0). Holmes & Meier.
Friarsyurd. William Neilson Brown. LC 29-17790. 1929. Longman, Green and Co.
Friary's Dor. Betty Hale Hyatt. (Candlelight Regency). 1973. 0.60. Candlelight Regency.
Friday. Robert Anson Heinlein. LC 81-13221. (Illus.). 14.95. Holt, Rinehart and Winston.
Friday. Michel Tournier. LC 69-12202. 1969. 4.95. Doubleday.
Friday & Saturday Nights. Michael De Forrest. (O.s.i.). 160p. 1974. pap. 0.95 o.s.i. (AN1179, Award). Univ Pub & Dist.
Friday at Noon. Benedict Thielen. LC 47-633344. 1947. H. Holt.
Friday Bus. Natalja Wendel. 208p. 1979. 9.95 (ISBN 0-8119-0313-3). Fell.
Friday for Death. Lawrence Lariar. LC 49-10690. 1949. Crown Publishers.
Friday in the Basement, Rosemary, The Fortunes of Little Phil, The Thanksgiving Story. Lilian Walker Hale. LC 17-392. Printed by Cooper Journal Company.
Friday Market. Catherine Meadows. LC 38-7575. 1938. The Macmillan Company.
Friday Run. James Wood. LC 76-141319. 1971. 5.95. Vanguard Press.
Friday, Thank God! Fern Rives. LC 43-3841. 1943. G. P. Putnam's Sons.
Friday the Rabbi Slept Late. Harry Kemelman. LC 64-17836. 1964. Crown.
Friday the Thirteenth, Pt. 3. Michael Avallone. (Illus.). 208p. 1982. pap. 2.25 (ISBN 0-8439-1164-6, Leisure Bks). Nordon Pubns.
Friday, the Thirteenth: A Novel. Thomas William Lawson. 1907. Doubleday, Page & Company.
Friday the 13th. Joseph Jefferson Farjeon. LC 40-70106. The Bobbs-Merrill Company.
Friday to Monday. William A. Garrett. LC 23-133252. 1923. D. Appleton and Company.
Friday to Monday. Nancy Ross. LC 32-636934. Liveright, Inc.
Friday's Business. Maurice Baring. LC 33-10150. 1933. A. A. Knopf.
Friday's Child. Louise Platt Hauck. The Penn Publishing Company.
Friday's Child. Georgette Heyer. (Berkley medallion book). 1975. (pbk.) 1.50 (ISBN 0-425-02840-2). Berkley Pub. Co.
Friday's Child. 2d american ed. Georgette Heyer. LC 79-178232. 1971. 6.95. Putnam.
Friday's Child. Georgette Heyer. LC 46-235. 1946. G. P. Putnam's Sons.
Friday's Child. Isabel Smith Olson. LC 54-9632. 1954. Vantage Press.
Friday's Child. Ruth McCarthy Sears. Ed. by Alice Sachs. (OSI). 1971. 3.95 o.s.i. Lenox Hill.
Friday's Child: A Story. Fannie V. Wright. LC 8-37130. 1890. E. P. Dutton & Company.
Friday's Feast. Don Pendleton. (Executioner Ser.: No. 37). (Orig.). 1979. pap. 2.25 (ISBN 0-523-41883-3). Pinnacle Bks.
Friday's Footprint: Twelve Stories & a Novella. Nadine Gordimer. 1960. 3.95 o.p. (ISBN 0-670-32952-5). Viking Pr.
Fridericus: A Novel. Frederic F Flach. LC 79-24769. 9.95 (ISBN 0-690-01891-6). Lippincott & Crowell.
Fridericus Testament. Frederic F. Flach. 256p. 1980. 9.95 o.p. (ISBN 0-690-01891-6). Harper-Row.
Fridolin's Mystical Marriage: A Study of an Original, Founded on Reminiscences of a Friend. Wilbrandt, Adolf Von. LC 12-40095. 1884. W. S. Gottsberger.
Friedemann Bach. Translated by Emanuel W. Hammer. Albert Emil Brachvogel. LC 60-681. 1960. 3.00. Pageant Press.
Friedrich. Hans Peter Richter. (Laurel leaf library, 2721). 1973. (pbk.) 0.95. Dell.
Friedrich. Hans Peter Richter. LC 78-119098. 1970. 3.97. Holt, Rinehart and Winston.
Friend: A Novel. Perry Sidney Wolff. LC 50-7436. 1950. Crown Publishers.
Friend Alice. Illus. by Amelia Reinmann. 1st Ed. Mary Ellis Lottmann. LC 56-11349. 1956. Pageant Press.
Friend and Lover. A Novel. Iza Duffus Hardy. (Franklin square library, no. 104). 1880. Harper & Brothers.
Friend at Court. Leon Thomas Stern & Stern, Elizabeth Gertrude (Levin) 1890- Joint Author. LC 23-8403. 1923. The Macmillan Company.
Friend Fritz: A Tale of the Banks of the Lauter. Emile Erckmann & Chatrian, Alexandre, 1826-1890, Joint Author. LC 4-46877. 1899. C. Scribner's Sons.
Friend in Deed. Robert Jagoda. LC 77-22445. 7.95 (ISBN 0-393-08789-1). Norton.
Friend in Need. Margaret Morley. LC 77-350212. 1976. 3.25 (ISBN 0-903895-73-0). Robson Books.
Friend in the Police. John Givens. LC 79-1822. 10.95 (ISBN 0-15-133538-9). Harcourt Brace Jovanovich.
Friend Is for Always. Patricia Benton. 1963. pap. 1.00 o.p. (ISBN 0-8119-0064-9). Fell.
Friend ("L'aimce. Alice Marie Celeste Durand. Tr. by Stanley, Helen. LC 6-35694. T. B. Peterson & Brothers.
Friend of Antaeus: A Comedy of Fantastic People. Gerard Hopkins. LC 28-11974. E. P. Dutton & Company.
Friend of Caesar. William Stearns Davis. (Illus.). 1919. 7.95 o.s.i. (ISBN 0-02-529980-8). Macmillan.
Friend of Caesar: A Tale of the Fall of the Roman Republic, Time, 50-47 B. C. William Stearns Davis. LC 2962. The Macmillan Company; London, Macmillan & Co., Ltd.
Friend of Caesar: A Tale of the Fall of the Roman Republic Time, 50-47 B. C. William Stearns Davis. LC 16-6483. The Macmillan Company.
Friend of Death. A Fantastic Tale. Pedro Antonio De Alarcon & Serrano, Mrs. Mary Jane (Christie) Tr. (On half-title: The "unknown" library v. 4). Cassell Publishing Company.
Friend of Kafka & Other Stories. Isaac Bashevis Singer. LC 70-115752. 311p. 1970. 12.95 (ISBN 0-374-15880-0); pap. 5.95 (ISBN 0-374-51538-7). FS&G.
Friend of My Springtime: A Classic Story of Friendship. Willa Sibert Cather. LC 73-76065. (Hallmark crown editions). (Illus.). 1974. 4.00 (ISBN 0-87529-342-5). Hallmark Cards.
Friend of the Bride. Marsha Manning. Ed. by Alice Sachs. 1970. Repr. of 1868 ed. 3.95 o.p. Lenox Hill.
Friend of the Family. Fedor Mikhailovich Dostoevskii. LC 49-8597. 1949. Macmillan Co.
Friend of the Family, No. 154. Denice Greenlea. 224p. 1981. pap. 1.50 (ISBN 0-449-50227-9, Coventry). Fawcett.
Friend of the Family: A Novel. Oswald Wynd. LC 49-10504. 1949. Doubleday.
Friend of the Family: And The Eternal Husband. Fedor Mikhailovich Dostoevskii & Fedor Mikhailovich Dostoevskii. LC 63-10850. 1963. Holt, Rinehart and Winston.
Friend of the Family: Or, Stepantchikovo and Its Inhabitants, and Another Story. Fedor Mikhailovich Dostoevskii & Garnett, Mrs. Constance (Black) 1862- Tr. LC 21-4911. (Half-title: The novels of Fyodor Dostoevsky. vol. XII). 1920. The Macmillan Company.
Friend of the Family: Or, Stepantchikovo and Its Inhabitants, and Another Story. Fedor Mikhailovich Dostoevskii & Garnett, Mrs. Constance (Black) 1862- Tr. LC 33-175004. (Half-title: The novels of Fyodor Dostoevsky. vol. XII). 1923. The Macmillan Company.
Friend of the Friends see Altar of the Dead.
Friend of the People: A Tale of the Reign of Terror. Mary C Rowsell. LC 8-971. F. A. Stokes Company.
Friend of the Seminole. George Ethelbert Walsh. LC 11-303601. The David C. Cook Publishing Co.
Friend Olivia. Amelia Edith Huddleston Barr. 1898. Dodd. Mead and Company.
Friend or Foe: A Tale of Connecticut During the War of 1812. Frank Samuel Child. LC 6185. 1900. Houghton, Mifflin and Company.
Friend or Lover: A Novel... Millicent Fawcett. 1881. G. W. Carleton & Co., Etc., Etc.
Friend to Mankind. William Voltz. (Perry Rhodan Series#91). 1976. (pbk.) 1.25. Ace Books.
Friend to the Widow. William Loring Spencer. LC 8-15503. 1888. Belford, Clarke & Co.
Friend with the Countersign. Blackwood Ketcham Benson. LC 1-22982. 1901. The Macmillan Company.
Friendin Power. Carlos Heard Baker. LC 58-7517. 1958. Scribner.
Friendly Air. Elizabeth Cadell. 1974. (pbk.) 0.95. Bantam Books.
Friendly Air. Elizabeth Cadell. LC 76-130534. 1971. 5.95. Morrow.
Friendly Cove. Irving Brant. LC 63-11633. (Illus.). 1963. Bobbs-Merrill.
Friendly Enemy. Peggy O'More, pseud. LC 49-624435. 1949. Arcadia House.
Friendly Evil. Marceil Genee Kolstad Baker. 1972. pap. 0.75 o.s.i. (01-365). Lancer.
Friendly Four: And Other Stories. Charles William Gordon. LC 27-2043. George H. Doran Company.
Friendly Little House: And Other Stories. Marion Ames Taggart. LC 10-221353. 1910. Benziger Brothers.
Friendly Persuasion. Jessamyn West. LC 45-35221. 1945. Harcourt, Brace and Company.
Friendly Relations. Jane Stern & Michael Stern. LC 79-4798. 8.95 (ISBN 0-394-50358-9). Random House.
Friendly Relations: A Novel. Audrey Lucas. LC 36-15265. 1936. E. P. Dutton & Co., Inc.
Friendly Road: New Adventures in Contentment. Ray Stannard Baker. LC 13-22869. 1913. Doubleday, Page & Company.
Friendly Tree. Cecil Day-Lewis. LC 38-178. 1937. Harper and Brothers.
Friendly U.F.O. Carlo Juzzinno. 1983. 5.95 (ISBN 0-533-05575-X). Vantage.
Friends. Elieba Levine. 288p. (Orig.). 1980. pap. 2.25 (ISBN 0-89083-645-0). Zebra.
Friends. Godfrey Smith. LC 68-31521. 1968. 5.95 o.p. (ISBN 0-8128-1064-3). Stein & Day.
Friends; a Duet. Elizabeth Stuart Phelps Ward. LC 8-33114. 1881. Houghton, Mifflin and Company.
Friends; a Duet. Elizabeth Stuart Phelps H. D. Ward Ward. LC 9-10495. Houghton Mifflin Company.
Friends: A True Story of Male Love. Alexander Douglas. LC 73-78754. 1973. 6.95 (ISBN 0-698-10535-4). Coward, McCann, and Geoghegan.
Friends & Betrayers. Carl Johnes. (Orig.). 1981. pap. 2.50 (ISBN 0-440-12570-7). Dell.
Friends and Enemies. Kate Alexander. LC 83-2890. 1983. 12.95 (ISBN 0-312-30545-1). St. Martin's Press.
Friends and Heroes. 1st Ed. in the U. S. A. Olivia Manning. LC 66-16918. 1966. 4.95. Doubleday.
Friends & Lovers. Jennie Gallant. (Coventry Romance Ser.: No. 179). 224p. 1982. pap. 1.50 (ISBN 0-449-50280-5, Coventry). Fawcett.
Friends and Lovers. Helen MacInnes Highet. LC 47-475686. 1947. Little, Brown.
Friends & Lovers. Helen MacInnes. 320p. 1978. pap. 2.95 (ISBN 0-449-23538-6, Crest). Fawcett.
Friends & Lovers. Helen MacInnes. LC 47-4756. 1971. 6.95 o.p. (ISBN 0-15-133550-8). HarBraceJ.
Friends & Lovers. Liz Marsh. (O.s.i.). Orig. Title: Vixens. 1969. pap. 0.75 o.s.i. (A493S, Award). Univ Pub & Dist.
Friends and Lovers. Oscar Pinkus. LC 63-8777. 1963. World Pub. Co.
Friends & Lovers. Playboy Press Editors. LC 71-174999. (Illus.). 1972. pap. 0.95 o.p. (ISBN 0-87216-153-6, A16153). Playboy Pr Pbks.
Friends & Lovers. Walter Rinder. Ed. by Celestial Arts. LC 78-54474. (Illus.). 1978. pap. 5.95 (ISBN 0-89087-223-6). Celestial Arts.
Friends and Lovers: 10 Sensuous Short Stories. LC 71-174999. 1972. Playboy Press.
Friends & Neighbors. Florence Schulz. 1962. pap. 1.50 o.p. United Church.
Friends: And Other Stories. Stacy Aumonier. LC 17-233345. 1917. The Century Co.
Friends and Relations. Elizabeth Bowen. LC 31-24657. 1931. L. Mac Veagh, The Dial Press.
Friends & Relations. Mira Stables. 1979. pap. 1.75 (ISBN 0-449-50019-5, Coventry). Fawcett.
Friends and Relations: A Collection of Stories. Daniel Menaker. LC 76-12053. 1976. 6.95 (ISBN 0-385-03896-8). Doubleday.

Friends and Romans. Virginia Faulkner. LC 34-19652. 1934. Simon and Schuster.

Friends and Vague Lovers. Jack Dunphy. LC 52-8674. 1952. Farrar, Straus and Young.

Friends Ashore see Mate of the Daylight.

Friends at Court. 1st American Ed. Henry Cecil. LC 57-614712. 1957. Harper.

Friends Come in Boxes. Michael G. Coney. (Science Fiction Ser.). (Orig.). 1973. pap. 0.95 o.p. (UQ1056). DAW Bks.

Friends for Life. Ellen E. White. 176p. 1983. pap. 2.25 (ISBN 0-380-82578-3, Flare). Avon.

Friends for Simon. Jean A. Davis. 1973. pap. 1.50 (ISBN 0-87508-676-4). Chr Lit.

Friends in Exile: A Tale of Diplomacy, Coronets, and Hearts. Lloyd Stephens Bryce. LC 6-19892. Cassell Publishing Company.

Friends in Exile. A Tale of Diplomacy, Coronets, and Hearts. Lloyd Stephens Bryce. LC 99-3471. (On cover: Neely's popular library. no. 143). F. T. Neely.

Friends in Exile: A Tale of Diplomacy, Coronets, and Hearts. 3d ed. Lloyd Stephens Bryce. LC 4868. 1900. Harper & Brothers.

Friends in High Places. John Weitz. LC 82-10072. 15.75 (ISBN 0-02-625920-6). Macmillan.

Friends in High Places: A Novel. Lucianne Goldberg & Sondra Till Robinson. LC 78-26187. 10.95 (ISBN 0-399-90039-X). R. Marek Publishers.

Friends in Low Places. Simon Raven. (Alms for Oblivion Ser.: No. 2). 1972. Repr. of 1965 ed. 12.50x (ISBN 0-85634-993-3). Intl Pubns Serv.

Friends in Low Places: 1st Amer. Ed. Simon Raven. LC 66-155896. 4.95. Putnam.

Friends of Eddie Coyle. George V. Higgins. LC 71-163134. 1972. 5.95 (ISBN 0-394-47327-2). Knopf.

Friends of Eddie Coyle. George V. Higgins. LC 72-6065. 1972. 7.95 (ISBN 0-8161-6044-9). G. K. Hall.

Friends of Mr. Sweeney. Elmer Holmes Davis. LC 25-23368. 1925. R. M. McBride & Company.

Friends of the People. Alfred Neumann & Purtscher, Nora (Grafin Von Wydenbruck) 1894- Tr. 1942. The Macmillan Company.

Friendship. Louise De La Ramee. (On cover: Lovell's library. v. 18. no. 852). 1887. J. W. Lovell Company.

Friendship. Ralph Woods. 1980. pap. 3.95 (ISBN 0-89293-008-X). Beta Bk.

Friendship. A Story of Society. Louise De La Ramee. 1878. J. B. Lippincott & Co.

Friendship and Folly: A Novel. Maria Louise Pool. 1898. L. C. Page and Company (Incorporated.

Friendship on the Wing. Janina Babris. LC 74-25969. (Illus.). 80p. 1975. 5.95 (ISBN 0-89023-005-6). Res Publs.

Friendship Village. Zona Gale. LC 8-305349. 1908. The Macmillan Company.

Friendship Village Love Stories. Zona Gale. LC 9-29428. 1909. The Macmillan Company.

Friendships, Secrets & Lies. Babs Deal. 1979. pap. 2.25 (ISBN 0-449-24253-6, Crest). Fawcett.

Friendship's Test. Zwei Freundinnen. Bertha Behrens & Burdette, Amelia, Tr. LC 6-9430. (On cover: Ogilvie, Fireside series. 84). 1889. J. S. Ogilvie.

Frigate Captain. Showell Styles. LC 56-50330. Vanguard Press.

Frigate's Namesake. Alice Balch Abbot. LC 1-24054. 1901. The Century Co.

Fright: By George Hopley Pseud. Cornell George Hopley-Woolrich. LC 50-5392. 1950. Rinehart.

Fright in the Forest. Benn Sowerby. LC 51-11065. 1951. Knopf.

Frightened Amazon. 1st Ed. George A. Stinson. LC 50-9263. 1950. Published for the Crime Club by Doubleday.

Frightened Angels. Joanna Cannan, pseud. LC 36-7371. 1936. Harper & Brothers.

Frightened Bride. Barbara Cartland. (Barbara Cartland library, 18). 1975. (pbk.) 1.25. Bantam Books.

Frightened Chameleon. Leonard Reginald Gribble. LC 57-6612. Roy Publishers.

Frightened Child. Mabel Dana Lyon. LC 48-6377. 1948. Harper.

Frightened Dove: By Peter Hardin Pseud. Louis Charles Vaczek. LC 51-981. 1951. Scribner.

Frightened Fiancee. George Harmon Coxe. LC 50-9943. 1950. Knopf.

Frightened Fingers: By Spencer Dean Pseud. Prentice Winchell. LC 55-412. 1954. I. Washburn.

Frightened Girl. Michael Crombie. LC 44-847787. (Prize mystery novels. No. 11). 1944. Crestwood Publishing Co., Inc.

Frightened Gun, No. Thirty Two. George G. Gilman, pseud. (Edge Ser.). (Orig.). 1979. pap. 1.75 (ISBN 0-523-41314-9). Pinnacle Bks.

Frightened Hare. F. Russell. 1966. 3.00 o.p. (ISBN 0-03-057445-5). HR&W.

Frightened Man: A Mystery Novel. Albert Leffingwell. LC 44-11967. (Handi-book mysteries). 1944. Quinn Publishing Co., Inc.

Frightened Man: A New Jim Steele Mystery. Albert Leffingwell. LC 42-14045. 1942. The Dial Press.

Frightened Murderer. Nancy Rutledge. LC 57-5385. 1957. Random House.

Frightened Nurse. Arlene Hale. 1976. (pbk.) 0.95. Ace Books.

Frightened Ones; Five Stories. 1st Ed. Melba Balmat Grimes Marlett. LC 56-5442. 1956. Doubleday.

Frightened Ones: Five Stories.1st Ed. Melba Balmat Grimes Marlett. LC 56-5442. 1956. Doubleday.

Frightened Pigeon. Richard Burke. LC 44-41845. 1944. G. P. Putnam's Sons.

Frightened Stiff. Kelley Roos. LC 42-22619. 1942. Dodd, Mead & Company.

Frightened Wife: And Other Murder Stories. Mary Roberts Rinehart. LC 53-5353. 1953. Rinehart.

Frightened Wife & Other Murder Stories. Mary Roberts Rinehart. 1953. 3.00 o.p. (ISBN 0-03-029840-7). HR&W.

Frightening Talent. Louis Golding. LC 73-175317. 1973. 1.75 (ISBN 0-491-01220-9). W. H. Allen.

Frightful Sin of Cisco Newman. Gilbert A. Newhafer & Richard Ralston. LC 72-5359. 1973. 6.95 o.p. (ISBN 0-13-331389-1). P-H.

Frightful Sin of Cisco Newman. Gilbert A. Ralston & Richard L. Newhafer. LC 72-5359. 1972. 6.95 (ISBN 0-13-331389-1). Prentice-Hall.

Frights: New Stories of Suspense and Supernatural Terror. Kirby McCauley. LC 75-40798. 8.95. St. Martin's Press.

Frights: New Stories of Suspense and Supernatural Terror. Kirby McCauley. 1977. 1.95 (ISBN 0-446-79815-0). Warner Books.

Frills and Thrills: The Career of a Young Fashion Designer, by Louise Barnes Gallagher. Louise Barnes Gallagher. LC 40-32614. (Career books). 1940. Dodd, Mead & Company.

Fringe of Heaven. Lee Belvedere, pseud. 1972. 4.50 o.p. (Avalon). Bouregy.

Fringe of Leaves. Patrick White. LC 76-18961. 1977. 10.00 (ISBN 0-670-33073-6). Viking Press.

Fringe of Leaves. Patrick White. LC 76-380628. 1976. 4.50 (ISBN 0-224-01290-8). Cape.

Fringe of Leaves. Patrick White. 1978. 1.95 (ISBN 0-380-01826-8). Avon.

Fringe of the Desert. Rachel Swete Macnamara. LC 13-80586. 1913. G. P. Putnam's Sons.

Fringilla: Or, Tales in Verse. Richard Doddridge Blackmore. LC 18-8461. 1895. The Burrows Brothers Co.

Fringilla: Or, Tales in Verse. Richard Doddridge Blackmore. LC 18-8460. 1895. The Burrows Brothers Company.

Frisco Epic. Gerald Locklin. 1978. 1.50 (ISBN 0-917554-07-8). Maelstrom.

Frisco Kid. Jerry Kamstra. LC 74-1889. 1975. 7.95 (ISBN 0-06-012251-X). Harper and Row.

Frisco Kid: A Novelization. Robert Grossbach. 1979. 1.95 (ISBN 0-446-90205-5). Warner Books.

Frisco Lady. Chet Cunningham. (Pinkerton Agent Brad Spear Ser.: No. 4). 320p. (Orig.). 1981. pap. 2.25 (ISBN 0-440-02583-4, Banbury). Dell.

Frisco Sweetheart. Gerald Foster. LC 42-7959. 1942. J. Swift.

Frisette and Faazil: A Novel. May DeWitt Hopkins. LC 39-5851. Dorrance and Company.

Fritz, the Emigrant. A Story of New York Life. Founded Upon Mr. Gayler's Drama of "Fritz"... Charles Gayler. LC 6-44262. (On cover: Frank Leslie's popular library). 1876. F. Leslie's Publishing House.

Fritz, the German Detective. Judson R Taylor. LC 3773. (On cover: Magnet detective library. no. 139). 1900. Street & Smith.

Frivolous Cupid. Anthony Hope Hawkins. LC 75-94732. (Short story index reprint series). (Illus.). 1969. Books for Libraries Press.

Frivolous Cupid. Anthony Hope Hawkins. 1895. Platt, Bruce & Company.

Frivolous Cupid. Anthony Hope Hawkins. (On cover: Arrow library, no. 64). Street & Smith.

Frog Face. Horace Winston Stokes. LC 46-587161. 1946. G. P. Putnam's Sons.

Frog in the Bottom of the Well. F. X Mathews. LC 71-141358. 1971. 5.95 (ISBN 0-395-12100-0). Houghton Mifflin.

Frog in the Moonflower. Ivor Drummond. LC 72-79065. 1973. 6.50. St Martins.

Frog in the Reeds: A Novel. Kit Marshall. LC 37-2573. 1936. T. Nelson & Sons, Limited.

Frog in the Throat. E. X Ferrars, pseud. LC 80-1033. 1980. 8.95 (ISBN 0-385-17207-9). Published for the Crime Club by Doubleday.

Frog Lamps. Wendell E. Wilson. LC 81-84374. (Illus.). 140p. (Orig.). 1982. pap. 9.75x (ISBN 0-917422-05-8). Rushlight Club.

Frog Murders. Leonard Serrester. LC 55-5906. 1955. Dorrance.

Frog Pond. Joyce MacIver. 1969. pap. 1.50 o.s.i. (71-359). Lancer.

Frog Salad. Sally George. LC 80-24827. 9.95 (ISBN 0-684-16766-2). Scribner.

Frogs at the Bottom of the Well: A Novel. Ken Edgar. LC 75-40705. 1.75. Playboy Press.

Frogs Die in Earnest: A Novel. Douglas Boot. LC 36-4469. 1934. C. Scribner's Sons.

Froler Case. A Novel. From the French of J. L. Jacolliot. Tr. by H. O. Cooke. Louis Jacolliot. Tr. by Cooke, H. O. (On cover: The choice series, no. 89). 1893. R. Bonner's Sons.

Frolic of His Own: A Novel. Clement R Hoopes. LC 70-102875. 1969. 5.95. Devin-Adair Co.

Frolic Wind. Richard Oke. LC 30-21636. 1930. Payson & Clarke Ltd.

Frolics of Cupid; or, Love's Vagaries. Tr. from the French by Henry Llewellyn Williams. Paul Lelen & Williams, Henry Llewellyn, 1842- Tr. (On cover: Pollard's popular publications, no. 7). 1891. The Pollard Publishing Company.

Frolicsome Girl. John Calvin Wallis. (Leisure series. v. 1, no. 6). 1887. G. W. Ogilvie.

Frolik Defection. Josef Frolik. 1979. pap. 3.50 o.p. (ISBN 0-88264-147-6). Diane Bks.

From a Bench in Our Square. Samuel Hopkins Adams. LC 72-103487. (Short story index reprint series). 1969. Books for Libraries Press.

From a Bench in Our Square. Samuel Hopkins Adams. LC 22-23262. 1922. Houghton Mifflin Company.

From a Crooked Rib. Nuruddin Farah. (African Writers Ser.). 1970. pap. text ed. 3.00x (ISBN 0-435-90080-3). Heinemann Ed.

From a Crooked Rib. Nuruddin Farah. (African Writers Ser.: No. 80). (Orig.). 1970. pap. text ed. 1.75x o.p. (ISBN 0-435-90380-2). Humanities.

From a Land Where Other People Live. Audre Lorde. 1973. pap. 1.50 (ISBN 0-910296-94-4). Broadside.

From a Presbytery Window. Maurice Browne. LC 73-170388. (Illus.). 1971. 2.00. Talbot Press.

From a Surgeon's Diary. Clifford Ashdown. LC 77-151744. (Illus.). 1977. 7.00. O. Train.

From a Swedish Homestead. Selma Ottiliana Lovisa Lagerlof. LC 73-116959. (Short story index reprint series). 1970. Books for Libraries Press.

From a Swedish Homestead. Selma Ottiliana Lovisa Lagerlof. Tr. by Brochner, Jessie. LC 1-31331. 1901. McClure, Phillips & Co.

From a Swedish Notebook. Samuel B. Charters. 1973. 5.00 (Pub. by Oyez); pap. 2.50. SBD.

From A to Z. San Antonio. Tr. by Hugh Campbell. (San Antonio Ser). 1970. pap. 0.60 o.p. (ISBN 0-446-63352-6, 63-352). Paperback Lib.

From a Turkish Harim. Tr. by Kraemer, John C. LC 30-9472. 1930. The Lotus Society.

From a View to a Death. Anthony Dymoke Powell. LC 68-11178. 1968. Little, Brown.

From a View to a Death. Anthony Dymoke Powell. 2.25 (ISBN 0-445-04295-8). Popular Library,.

From an Altar Screen: El Retablo: Tales from New Mexico. Angelico Chavez. LC 72-85690. (Short story index reprint series). (Illus.). 1969. Books for Libraries Press.

From an Altar Screen, el Retablo: Tales from New Mexico. facs. ed. Angelico Chavez. LC 72-85690. (Short Story Index Reprint Ser). 1957. 12.00 (ISBN 0-8369-3031-2). Ayer Co.

From an Altar Screen: El Retablo: Tales from New Mexico.Illustrated by Peter Hurd. Angelico Chavez. LC 57-12157. 1957. Farrar, Straus and Cudahy.

From an Oregon Ranch. Louise G. Stephens. LC 16-23143. 1916. 1.00. A. C. McClurg & Co.

From an Ozark Holler: Stories of Ozark Mountain Folk. Vance Randolph. LC 33-28931. The Vanguard Press.

From Baseball to Boches. Harry Charles Witwer. LC 18-26326. 1918. Small, Maynard & Company.

From Bed to Worse. Ed. by Phil Hirsch. (Orig.). 1969. pap. 0.60 o.p. (X2071). Pyramid Pubns.

From Beginning to End. Jozsef Lengyel. LC 68-11913. (Illus.). 1968. Prentice-Hall.

From Beneath the Hill of the Three Crosses: Procesion De Navidad. Pat M Esslinger. LC 77-11520. 2.75. South and West.

From Berlin to Bagdad: An Historical Romance. William Rutledge McGarry. LC 15-23060. 1915. International Publishing Company.

From Bondage They Came. George Peter Crump. LC 54-9633. 1954. Vantage Press.

From Boniface to Bank Burglar: Or, The Price of Persecution; How a Successful Business Man, Through the Miscarriage of Justice, Became a Notorious Bank Looter. George Miles White. LC 7-26958. 1907. The Seaboard Publishing Company.

From Boston, Mass., to Sodom, N.B., on a Bicycle. Mayhew B. Cleveland. LC 6-20753. 1887.

From Carthage Then I Came. Douglas R Mason. LC 66-24315. 1966. Doubleday.

From Claudia No David. 1st Ed. Rose Franken. LC 50-5821. 1950. Harper.

From Clouds to Sunshine: Or, The Evolution of a Soul. E Thomas Kaven. LC 1-29336. 1900. The Abbey Press.

From Darkness to Light. Gertrude McGovern Cummings. LC 34-6718. 1934. Printed by Snow & Farnham Co.

From Dawn to Daylight: Or, The Simple Story of a Western Home. Eunice White Becher. LC 6-9761. 1859. Derby & Jackson.

From Dawn to Noon. Mary Montgomery Lamb Singleton Currie. LC 49-42843. 1886. G. W. Carleton.

From Day to Day. Ferdynand Goetel. Tr. by Cooper, Winifred. LC 31-11282. 1931. The Viking Press.

From Death to Morning. Thomas Wolfe. LC 35-25839. 1935. C. Scribner's Sons.

From Death to Morning. Thomas Clayton Wolfe. 1965. pap., 1.65. Scribners.

From Different Standpoints. Isabella Macdonald Alden. Foster, Mrs. Theodosia Marie (Toll) 1838- Joint Author & Foster, Mrs. Theodosia Marie (Toll) 1835-Joint Author. LC 6-12563. Lothrop, Lee & Shepard Co.

From Director C.I.A-Burn Agent Scorpio. Mike Roote. (O.s.i.). 160p. 1975. pap. 1.25 o.s.i. (AQ1514, Award). Univ Pub & Dist.

From Distant Shores. Bruce Nicolaysen. 480p. 1980. pap. 2.50 (ISBN 0-380-75424-X, 75424). Avon.

From Doon with Death. Ruth Rendell. LC 76-24852. 1976. 7.95 (ISBN 0-89340-022-X). J. Curley.

From Doon with Death: 1st. Ed. in the U.S. Ruth Rendell. LC 65-11057. 1965. 3.50. Pub. for the Crime Club by Doubleday.

From Door to Door: A Book of Romances, Fantasies, Whimsies, and Levities. Bernard Edward Joseph Capes. LC 2792. Frederick A. Stokes Company.

From Dusk till Dawn. William A Garrett. LC 29-104360. 1929. D. Appleton and Company.

From Dusk to Dawn: A Story. Katharine Pearson Woods. LC 8-37246. 1892. D. Appleton and Company.

From Dust to Ashes. A Romance of the Confederacy. George P C Rumbough. LC 8-965. The Brown Printing Company.

From Error's Chains: Or, The Story of the Religious Struggles of an Accomplished Young Lady. Lovelace Savidge Foster. LC 6905. 1899. Baptist Orphanage Press.

From Every Mountain Side. Lillie T. Wallace. 3.50 o.p. Carlton.

From Every Mountainside. Norman Wright Welsh. LC 45-7611. 1945. Harbinger House.

From Evil's Pillow. Basil Copper. LC 73-81266. 1973. 6.00. Arkham House.

From Exile. A Novel. James Payn. (Franklin square library, no. 176). 1881. Harper & Brothers.

From Exile. A Novel. James Payn. (Seaside library. v. 48, no. 981). 1881. G. Munro.

From Far Dakota, and Otherwhere. Hendry Durie Ross. LC 5-38489. The Grafton Press.

From Father to Son. Mary Dwinell Chellis. LC 11-10564. (On cover: The Chellis library). 1879. National Temperance Society and Publication House.

From Father to Son. Mary Stanbery Watts. LC 19-11154. 1919. The Macmillan Company.

From Fjord to Prairie: Or, In the New Kingdom. Simon Johnson. Tr. by Solberg, C. O. LC 17-5817. 1916. 0.75. Augsburg Publishing House.

From Flax to Linen. Jennie Maria Drinkwater Conklin. 1888. R. Carter and Brothers.

From Flushing to Calvary. Edward Dahlberg. LC 32-28968. Harcourt, Brace and Company.

From Four Corners to Washington: A Little Story of Home Love, War, and Politics. Cyrenus Cole. LC 20-17524. 1920. The Torch Press.

From Four Corners to Washington: A Little Story of Home, Love, War, and Politics. Cyrenus Cole. LC 25-23749. 1920. The Torch Press.

From Fourteen to Fourscore. Susan W Jewett. LC 7-9730. 1871. Hurd and Houghton.

From "Gallegher" to "The Deserter" The Best Stories of Richard Harding Davis. Richard Harding Davis. Ed. by Burlingame, Roger. LC 27-228420. 1927. C. Scribner's Sons.

From Generation to Generation. Augusta Keppel Noel. Ed. by Gore, John. LC 30-12152. (Half-title: The rescue series vi). 1929. Frederick A. Stokes Company.

From Gloom to Sunlight. Charlotte Mary Brame. LC 44-12248. (On cover: Seaside library. Pocket ed. No. 288). G. Munro.

From Gloom to Sunlight: Or, From Out the Gloom. Charlotte Mary Brame. LC 44-378303. (On cover: Seaside library. Pocket ed. No. 955). G. Munro.

From Green Hills of Galilee. Cathal O'Byrne. LC 71-167464. (Short story index reprint series). 1971. (ISBN 0-8369-3990-5). Books for Libraries Press.

From Green Hills of Galilee. Cathal O'Byrne. LC 35-6201. P. J. Kenedy & Sons.

From Hand to Hand: A Novel, from the German of Golo Raimund Pseud.... Bertha Heyn Frederich. Tr. by Wister, Annie Lee (Furness) LC 6-42856. 1882. J. B. Lippincott & Co.

From Hand to Mouth. Amanda Minnie Douglas. Lothrop, Lee & Shepard Co.

From Hawthorne Hall: An Historical Story, 1885. William Lyman Johnson. LC 22-22158. The Homewood Press.

From Headquarters: Odd Tales Picked up in the Volunteer Service. James Albert Frye. LC 6-44588. 1893. Estes and Lauriat.

From Heaven to New York. by isaac george reed, jr.... ed. Isaac George Reed. LC 7-30948. (On cover: American authors' series, no. 1).

From Heaven to New York: Or, The Good Hearts and the Brown Stone Fronts. A Fact Founded on a Fancy. Isaac George Reed. (On cover: Paragon library of modern books, no. 7). 1894. Optimus Printing Company.

From Hell to Breakfast. Edward Kimbrough. LC 41-426319. J. B. Lippincott Company.

From Hell to Heaven, No. 133. Barbara Cartland. 160p. (Orig.). 1981. pap. 1.75 (ISBN 0-553-14361-1). Bantam.

From Hell to Texas. Dwight Bruckner. (Belmont Tower Book). 1977. 1.50 (ISBN 0-505-51207-6). Tower Pubns.

From Here to Eternity. James Jones. LC 51-9228. 1951. Scribner.

From Here to Eternity. James Jones. LC 80-12571. 1980. 12.95 (ISBN 0-440-02751-9). Delacorte Press.

From Here to the Bugle. Frank Clay Jennings. LC 49-6832. 1949. Thoroughbred Press.

From Heroin to San Quentin. Clinton T. Duffy & Eva Irene Linkletter. LC 77-151039. 10.00. Java Books.

From Hide & Horn. John Thomas Edson. 192p. 1982. pap. 2.25 (ISBN 0-425-05760-7). Berkley Pub.

From Hollow to Hilltop. Mary Lowe Dickinson. LC 6-370275. 1896. American Baptist Publication Society.

From Honey to Ashes. Claude Levi-Strauss. 1969. price not set o.p. (ISBN 0-06-012593-4, HarpT). Har-Row.

From Inhale & Exhale: Thirty-One Selected Stories. William Saroyan. LC 44-10080. (Avon modern short story monthly, no. 4). 1943. Avon Book Company.

From Jerusalem to Jericho. Edward Gholson. LC 43-150693. 1943. Chapman & Grimes.

From Jest to Earnest. Edward Payson Roe. LC 4-35664. (On cover: Dodd, Mead & company's library of fiction. no. 8). 1890. Dodd, Mead and Company.

From Jest to Earnest. Edward Payson Roe. LC 3-22819. 1903. Dodd, Mead & Company.

From Jordan's Delight. R. P. Blackmur. LC 73-16284. 1937. lib. bdg. 10.00 (ISBN 0-8414-9883-0). Folcroft.

From Jungle Roots. Marcos Spinelli. LC 38-18016. Covici Friede.

From Karamzin to Bunin: An Anthology of Russian Short Stories. Ed. by Carl R. Proffer. LC 79-85097. 1969. 12.50. Indiana University Press.

From Karen with Love. Barbara Thorn, pseud. 1981. 18.95x (Pub. by Remploy England). State Mutual Bk.

From Kingdom to Colony. Mary Devereux. LC 99-5055. 1899. Little, Brown and Company.

From Kingdom to Colony. Mary Devereux. LC 4-15447. 1904. Little, Brown, and Company.

From Lake to Lake; or, A Trip Across Country. A Narrative on the Wilds of Maine. With Thirty Illustrations, Drawn by Reder, Garrett, Reed, and Myrick. Charles Alden John Farrar. LC 6-38663. 1887. Jamaica Publishing Co.

From Lake to Wilderness: Or, The Cruise of the Yolande. William Murray Graydon. LC 99-4800. (Medal library, no. 22). 1899. Street & Smith.

From Lands of Exile. Julien Viaud & Bell, Mrs. Clara Courtenay (Poynter) 1834-1927, Tr. LC 8-29997. 1888. W. S. Gottsberger.

From Lima to Leticia: The Peruvian Novels of Mario Vargas Llosa. Marvin A. Lewis. LC 83-1057. 182p. (Orig.). 1983. lib. bdg. 21.75 (ISBN 0-8191-3049-4); pap. text ed. 10.00 (ISBN 0-8191-3050-8). U Pr of Amer.

From London Far. Michael Innes, pseud. (Crime Ser.). 320p. 1976. pap. 2.95 (ISBN 0-14-001692-9). Penguin.

From London Far. Michael Innes, pseud. (Orig.). 1969. pap. 0.95 o.p. (ISBN 0-14-001692-9, 1692). Penguin.

From Madge to Margaret. Caroline Gardiner Cary Curtis. 1880. Lee and Shepard.

From Malaga to the Mountain: The Story of Matilda. Robert E Jones. LC 72-200881. (Illus.). 1971. Jones & Holt.

From Man to Man. Olive Schreiner. LC 77-21242. 1977. 7.50. (ISBN 0-915864-48-7) (ISBN 0-915864-47-9). Cassandra Editions.

From Man to Man; or, Perhaps Only... Olive Schreiner. LC 71-38697. (Belles lettres in English). 1972. Johnson Reprint Corp.

From Man to Man: Or Perhaps Only... by olive schreiner; with an introduction by s. c. cronwright-schreiner... ed. Olive Schreiner. Ed. by Cronwright-Schreiner, Samuel Cron. LC 27-6809. 1927. Harper & Brothers.

From May to October. Jennifer Lash. LC 82-108878. 1980. 14.95 (ISBN 0-241-10470-X). Hamish Hamilton.

From Midnight to Morning. Maurice Leblanc. LC 33-4544. The Macaulay Company.

From Moment to Moment. Esther Sager. 1983. pap. 3.50 (ISBN 0-515-06221-9). Jove Pubns.

From Monkey to Man: Or, Society in the Tertiary Age. A Story of the Missing Link, Showing the First Steps in Industry, Commerce, Government, Religion and the Arts; with an Account of the Great Expedition from Cocoanut Hill and the Wars in Alligator Swamp. Austin Bierbower. LC 6-12746. 1894. Dibble Publishing Co.

From Monkey to Man: Or, Society in the Tertiary Age. A Story of the Missing Link, Showing the First Steps in Industry, Commerce, Government, Religion and the Arts; with an Account of the Great Expedition from Cocoanut Hill and the Wars in Alligator Swamp. Austin Bierbower. 1906. Ingersoll Beacon Co.

From My Highest Hill: Carolina Mountain Folks. Olive Tilford Dargan. LC 41-17085. J. B. Lippincott Company.

From My Window. William Lindsay Robbins. LC 43-17225. 1943. The Messenger Press.

From My Youth up. Mary Virginia Terhune. LC 8-26049. 1874. G. W. Carleton & Co.; Etc., Etc.

From Night to Light. Emma Elizabeth Brown. LC 7-3313. D. Lothrop & Co.

From Night to Light. Emma Elizabeth Brown. LC 6-16397. (On cover: The young folks' library, no. 22). 1886. D. Lothrop & Co.

From Nine to Five. Mary Badger Wilson. LC 38-7565. The Penn Publishing Company.

From Nine to Nine. Leo Perutz. Tr. by Lore, Lily. LC 26-151810. 1926. The Viking Press.

From Nine O'clock to Jamaica Bay. Daniel Broun. (Rinehart Suspense Novel). 1964. 3.50 o.p. (ISBN 0-03-044610-4). HR&W.

From Noon till Three: The Possibly True and Certainly Tragic Story of an Outlaw and a Lady Whose Love Knew No Bounds. Frank Daniel Gilroy. LC 73-82254. 1973. 4.95 (ISBN 0-385-08295-9). Doubleday.

From Noon till Three: The Possibly True and Certainly Tragic Story of an Outlaw and a Lady Whose Love Knew No Bounds. Frank Daniel Gilroy. 1976. 1.25 (ISBN 0-380-00728-2). Avon.

From Now on. Frank Lucius Packard. LC 20-61937. George H. Doran Company.

From off This World: Gems of Science Fiction... Ed. by Leo Margulies. Friend, Oscar Jerome, 1897- Joint Ed. LC 49-49116. 1949. Merlin Press.

From Olympus to Hades. Mrs. Bridges. (Seaside library, vo. 78, no. 1588). 1883. G. Munro.

From Olympus to Hades. Mrs. Bridges. (On cover: Seaside library. Pocket ed., no. 732). 1886. G. Munro.

From Olympus to Hades. Mrs. Bridges. (On cover: Lovell's library, v. 18, no. 862). 1887. J. W. Lovell Company.

From One Generation to Another. Hugh Stowell Scott. LC 8-2917. 1893. Harper & Brothers.

From Other Days. Walter Allen Harris. LC 75-314364. 1975. Great Outdoors Press.

From Out Magdala. Lucille Papin Borden. LC 27-192175. 1927. The Macmillan Company.

From Out of the Past: The Story of a Meeting in Touraine... Emily Howland Hoppin. LC 7-5237. Dodd, Mead & Company.

From Out of the West. Henrietta R Hinckley. LC 6-4643. 1905. Mayhew Publishing Company.

From Out the Flame: A Story of the Re-Creation. autograph ed. William Richard Burrell. LC 5-16125. 1905. Burr Printing House.

From Out the Gloom. Charlotte Mary Brame. J. S. Ogilvie & Company.

From Out the Gloom. Charlotte Mary Brame. LC 44-37829. J. S. Ogilvie & Company.

From Out the Gloom. Charlotte Mary Brame. LC 44-122438. (On cover: Lovell's library, v. 17, no. 806). J. W. Lovell Company.

From Out the Shadows. Tried by Fire. G. Filer. LC 6-41208.

From Out the Vasty Deep. Marie Adelaide Belloc Lowndes. LC 21-26289. George H. Doran Company.

From Out This House. Alice Wheeler Greve. LC 46-177. 1945. Binfords & Mort.

From Over the Border: Or, Light on the Normal Life of Man. Benjamin George Smith. LC 8-8623. 1890. C. H. Kerr & Company.

From Oxford to Rome, & How It Fared with Some Who Lately Made the Journey, 1847. Elizabeth F. Harris. Ed. by Robert L. Wolff. Bd. with Rest in the Church, 1848. LC 74-449. (Victorian Fiction Ser.). 1975. lib. bdg. 66.00 (ISBN 0-8240-1529-0). Garland Pub.

From Oxford to Rome and Rest in the Church. Elizabeth F. Harris. LC 75-449. (Victorian Fiction: Novels of Faith and Doubt; V. 5). 1975. 35.00 (ISBN 0-8240-1529-0). Garland Pub.

From Palms to Pines. Bertha B. Moore McCurry. LC 47-12096. 1947. W. B. Eerdmans Pub. Co.

From Peace to Chaos: A Forgotten Story. Kaity Argyropoulo. 5.95 o.p. Vantage.

From Pillar to Post. John Kendrick Bangs. Repr. of 1916 ed. lib. bdg. 25.00 (ISBN 0-8414-1666-4). Folcroft.

From Pillar to Post. Helen Reimensnyder Martin. LC 33-22236. 1933. Dodd, Mead & Company.

From Pillar to Post. Martha Wylie. LC 27-24660. The John C. Winston Company.

From Pit to Palace: A Romantic Autobiography. James Joseph Lawler. LC 6-21390. The Palace Publishing Company.

From Place to Place. Irvin Shrewsbury Cobb. LC 20-2846. George H. Doran Company.

From Post to Finish. A Racing Romance. Hawley Smart. (Harper's Franklin square library, no. 436). 1884. Harper & Brothers.

From Post to Finish. A Racing Romance. Hawley Smart. (On cover: Seaside library. Pocket ed. no. 348). 1885. G. Munro.

From Riva Ridge to Riva. Julius Keller. 4.95 o.p. Vantage.

From Russia: With Love. Ian Fleming. LC 57-102928. 1957. Macmillan.

From Russia with Love. Ian Fleming. pap. 3.95 fr. ed.; pap. 2.95 span. ed. French & Eur.

From Russia with Love. Ian Fleming. 256p. 1982. pap. 2.75 (ISBN 0-425-05367-9). Berkley Pub.

From Russia, with Love: Reissue. Ian Fleming. 1966. bds., 3.95. Macmillan.

From Sand Creek. Simon J. Ortiz. 96p. (Orig.). 1981. 10.95 (ISBN 0-938410-03-2); pap. 4.95 (ISBN 0-938410-00-8). Thunder's Mouth.

From Sand Hill to Pine. Bret Harte. LC 78-113670. (Short story index reprint series). (Illus.). 1970. Books for Libraries Press.

From Sand Hill to Pine. Bret Harte. LC 3201. 1900. Houghton, Mifflin and Company.

From Scenes Like These. Gordon M. Williams. LC 69-14303. 1969. 5.95. Morrow.

From School-Room to Bar: A Novel. W. H. W Moran. LC 7-262120. 1892. J. B. Lippincott Company.

From Secret Places. Miriam Lynch. (Ravenswood Gothic). 1973. (pbk) 0.95 (ISBN 0-671-77634-7). Pocket Books.

From Shadow to Sunlight: By the Marquis of Lorne... John George Edward Henry Douglas Sutherland Campbell Argyll. LC 6-23095. 1891. D. Appleton and Company.

From Side Streets and Boulevards: A Collection of Chicago Stories. Ella L. McDougalol. 1893. R. R. Donnelley & Sons Company.

From Six to Six. Walter Bertram Foster. LC 27-71770. E. J. Clode, Inc.

From Sleep Unbound. Andree Chedid. Tr. by Sharon Spencer from Fr. LC 82-75430. 170p. 1983. 18.95 (ISBN 0-8040-0399-8); pap. 8.95 (ISBN 0-8040-0837-X). Swallow.

From Solitude with Love. Daisy H. Thomson. 1976. pap. 1.25 o.p. (ISBN 0-515-04038-X). BJ Pub Group.

From Son-Lit Shores. James Falk. LC 39-260231. 1939. Meador Publishing Company.

From Stewardess to Captain's Wife. Sybil R. Parker. (Orig.). 1980. pap. 3.95 o.p. (ISBN 0-89260-151-5). Hwong Pub.

From Sunlight to Shade. Grenville Atkins. LC 1-30562. The Neely Company.

From Sunup to Sundown. Corra May White Harris & Leech, Faith Harris. LC 19-4851. 1919. Doubleday, Page & Company.

From Surabaya to Armageddon: Indonesian Short Stories. Harry Aveling. LC 76-940752. (Writing in Asia series). 1976. Heinemann Educational Books (Asia)

From the Academy Bridge: A Novel. P. M Pasinetti. LC 77-85572. 1970. 6.95. Random House.

From the Archives of Evil. Ed. by Christopher Lee. 1976. (pbk.) 1.25. Warner Books.

From the Ashes of Hell. Cannon Cole. LC 73-82973. 1973. 4.95 (ISBN 0-88419-062-5). Creation House.

From the Ashes: Voices of Watts. Ed. by Budd Schulberg. 1969. pap. 3.95 o.p. (M272, Mer). World Pub.

From the Backyard of the Diaspora. 2nd ed. Myra Sklarew. 1981. pap. 4.75 (ISBN 0-931848-40-7). Dryad Pr.

From the Berkeley Hills. George P. Elliott. LC 68-28193. 1969. 9.00 (ISBN 0-89366-093-0). Ultramarine Pub.

From the Bitter Land. Maisie Mosco. 1981. pap. 2.95 (ISBN 0-553-13913-4). Bantam.

From the Bottom Up. Leigh A. Wilson. LC 82-15975. (Flannery O'Connor Award for Short Fiction Ser.). 160p. 1983. text ed. 12.95 (ISBN 0-8203-0647-9). U of Ga Pr.

From the Broken Tree. Lee Langley. LC 78-7813. 10.95 (ISBN 0-525-10988-9). E. P. Dutton.

From the Car Behind. Eleanor Marie Ingram. LC 12-5553. 1912. 1.25. J. B. Lippincott Company.

From the City: From the Plough. Alexander Baron. LC 49-7627. 1949. I. Washburn.

From the City, from the Plough. Alexander Baron. 1949. 3.00 o.p. Washburn.

From the Cliffs of Croaghaun. Robert Cromie. LC 4-13659. 1904. The Saalfield Publishing Company.

From the Clouds to the Mountains: Comprising Narratives of Strange Adventures by Air, Land, and Water, by Jules Verne. Jules Verne & Paul Verne. LC 1-9805. 1874. W. F. Gill.

From the Country of Eight Islands. Tr. by Hiroaki Sato & Burton Watson. LC 80-1077. 480p. 1981. pap. 11.95 (ISBN 0-385-14030-4, Anch). Doubleday.

From the Dark Tower. Ernst Pawel. LC 57-8103. 1957. Macmillan.

From the Deep of the Sea. Charles E. Smith. LC 78-51909. 1978. 9.95 (ISBN 0-87021-932-4). Naval Inst Pr.

From the Desert. John W. Holloway. LC 73-18578. Repr. of 1919 ed. 15.00 (ISBN 0-404-11389-3). AMS Pr.

From the Diary of a Snail. Gunter Grass. LC 73-6680. (Illus.). 1973. 7.95 (ISBN 0-15-133800-0). Harcourt Brace Jovanovich.

From the Diary of a Snail. Gunter Grass. LC 75-29309. (Harvest book; HB 330). 1976. 3.95 (ISBN 0-15-633950-1). Harcourt Brace Jovanovich.

From the Earth to the Moon. Jules Verne. LC 67-1095. (Bantam pathfinder editions, FP161). 1967. Bantam Books.

From the Earth to the Moon. Jules Verne. LC 1-9801. (Lovell's library, no. 1294). 1888. J. W. Lovell Company.

From the Earth to the Moon. All Around the Moon. Jules Verne. LC 68-1422. (His Space novels). (Illus.). 1960. Dover Publications.

From the Earth to the Moon and A Tour of the Moon. new rev. ed. Jules Verne. LC 50-582116. Didier.

From the Earth to the Moon: And a Trip Around It. Jules Verne. LC 58-940. Lippincott.

From the Earth to the Moon: And All Around the Moon. Space Novels by Jules Verne; Tr. from the French by Edward Roth. Jules Verne. (T633). 1960. pap., 1.75. Dover Pubns.

From the Earth to the Moon: And Around the Moon. Jules Verne & Limited Editions Club, Inc., New York. LC 72-281686. (Illus.). 1970. Printed for the Members, the Limited Editions Club.

From the Earth to the Moon: And Round the Moon. Jules Verne. LC 63-7412. (Great illustrated classics). 1962. Dodd, Mead.

From the Earth to the Moon and Round the Moon. Jules Verne. (Publisher's lettering: The home library). A. L. Burt Company.

From the Earth to the Moon: Direct in Ninety-Seven Hours and Twenty Minutes; and a Trip Round It. Jules Verne. LC 36-29340. 1908. C. Scribner's Sons.

From the Earth to the Moon in 97 Hours and 20 Minutes. Jules Verne. LC 1-9802. (Seaside library. Pocket ed. no 1152). 1889. G. Munro.

From the Earth to the Moon, Including the Sequel, Round the Moon. Jules Verne & Mercier, Lewis Page, Tr. LC 47-3317. 1947. Didier.

From the East Side to the West Side. Evalyn Knickerbocker. LC 46-224989. 1946. The Hobson Book Press.

From the Ends of the Earth. Lambert Williams. LC 38-20797. 1938. D. Appleton-Century Company, Incorporated.

From the Far Side of Now. Lynne Schilder. LC 72-186722. 64p. 1972. pap. 2.25 o.p. (ISBN 0-911842-07-1). Valley Sun.

From the Fifteenth District: A Novella and Eight Short Stories. Mavis Gallant. LC 79-4774. 10.00 (ISBN 0-394-50719-3). Random House.

From the Five Rivers. Flora Annie Webster Steel. LC 8-13438. (On cover: Appletons' town and country library, no. 121). 1893. D. Appleton and Company.

From the Foothills of Song. Charlotte Mellen Packard. LC 8-17698. 1908. R. G. Badger.

From the Fury of the Northmen: And Other Stories of Events That Shaped Our Destiny in 8th to 19th Century England. Rhoda D Power. LC 56-8269. (Illus.). 1957. Houghton Mifflin.

From the Hand of the Hunter. John Braine. 1960. 3.75 o.p. HM.

From the Heart. Sherman Burns. 64p. (Orig.). 1981. pap. 3.95. Vistula Pr.

From the Heart of England: A Story of the Dawn of Modern Missions. L. M. N & N., L. M. LC 7-25801. American Baptist Publication Society.

From the Heart of Israel: Jewish Tales and Types. Bernard Drachman. LC 72-110183. (Short story index reprint series). (Illus.). 1970. (ISBN 0-8369-3334-6). Books for Libraries Press.

From the Heart of the Country. J. M. Coetzee. LC 76-50168. 7.95 (ISBN 0-06-010841-X). Harper & Row.

From the Heat of the Day. Roy A. Heath. 160p. 1980. 9.95 (ISBN 0-8052-8003-0, Pub. by Allison & Busby England); pap. 5.95 (ISBN 0-8052-8071-5). Schocken.

From the Hills. Martha Bussert Hoyt. LC 14-12790. 1914. J. H. Abbott.

From the House Tops: A Pastor Speaks to Adults. E. Stevens. 1965. 4.95 o.p. (ISBN 0-03-053680-4). HR&W.

From the Housetops. George Barr McCutcheon. LC 16-180263. 1916. Dodd, Mead and Company.

From the Kingdom of Necessity. Isidor Schnelder. LC 35-19990. G. P. Putnam's Sons.

From the Land of the Shamrock. Jane Barlow. LC 5192. 1900. Dodd, Mead and Company.

From the Land of the Snow-Pearls: Tales from Puget Sound. Ella Rhoads Higginson. LC 70-122720. (Short story index reprint series). 1970. Books for Libraries Press.

From the Land of the Snow-Pearls: Tales from Puget Sound. Ella Rhoads Higginson. LC 7-4771. 1897. The Macmillan Company.

From the Legend of Biel. Mary Staton. (Ace science fiction special 1). 1975. (pbk.) 1.25. Ace Books.

From the Life: Imaginary Portraits of Some Distinguished Americans. Harvey Jerrold O'Higgins. LC 75-130069. (Short story index reprint series). 1970. Books for Libraries Press.

From the Life of the Marionettes. Ingmar Bergman. LC 80-7698. (Illus.). 1980. 8.95 (ISBN 0-394-51317-7) (ISBN 0-394-73970-1). Pantheon Books.

From the Marais Des Cygnes. William Oscar Atkeson. LC 20-13066. Burton Publishing Company.

From the Melting Pot into the Mold. David A Driscoll. LC 23-11442. The Christopher Publishing House.

From the Memoirs of a Minister of France. Stanley John Weyman. LC 77-113694. (Short story index reprint series). (Illus.). 1970. Books for Libraries Press.

From the Memoirs of a Minister of France. Stanley John Weyman. 1895. Longmans, Green, and Co.

From the Nets of a Salmon Fisherman. Eric Forrer. LC 72-79436. (Illus.). 168p. 1973. 5.95 o.p. (ISBN 0-385-01761-8); pap. 2.50 o.p. (ISBN 0-385-02179-8). Doubleday.

From the Ocean, from the Stars. Arthur C. Clarke. LC 62-8058. 1962. 8.50 o.p. (ISBN 0-15-133881-7). HarBraceJ.

From the Ocean, from the Stars: An Omnibus Containing the Complete Novels: The Deep Range and The City and the Stars, and Twenty-Four Short Stories. Arthur Charles Clarke. LC 62-8058. 1962. Harcourt, Brace & World.

From the Old Pueblo, and Other Tales. LC 6-24361. 1902.

From the Old World to the New: Or, A Christmas Story of the World's Fair, 1893... Being the Christmas Number of the "Review of Reviews.". William Thomas Stead. LC 7-1644. 1892. Office Review of Reviews.

From the Other Side. Henry Blake Fuller. LC 78-90581. (Short Story Index Reprint Ser.). 1898. 15.00 (ISBN 0-8369-3064-9). Ayer Co.

From the Other Side. Henry Blake Fuller. Ed. by Donald Pizer. LC 70-96556. (American Authors Ser). 1970. lib. bdg. 14.50 o.s.i. (ISBN 0-512-00215-0). Garrett Pr.

From the Other Side. Frances Eliza Millett Notley. (On cover: Lovell's library, no. 1095). 1887. J. W. Lovell Company.

From the Other Side see Collected Works.

From the Other Side: Stories of Transatlantic Travel. Henry Blake Fuller. LC 78-90581. (Short story index reprint series). 1969. Books for Libraries Press.

From the Other Side: Stories of Transatlantic Travel. Henry Blake Fuller. LC 6-44577. 1898. Houghton, Mifflin and Company.

From the Ranks. Paul Alwyn Platz. LC 99-4683. (On cover: Neely's authors' library, no. 6). 1899. F. T. Neely.

From the Ranks. A Novel. Charles King. LC 11-150866. J. B. Lippincott Company.

From the Ranks: A Novel. Charles King. 1902. J. B. Lippincott Co.

From the "S" File. LC 77-136581. (Playboy science fiction). 1971. 0.75. Playboy Press.

From the "S" File. Playboy Editors. LC 77-136581. 1971. pap. 0.75 o.p. (ISBN 0-87216-110-2, D16110). Playboy Pr Pbks.

From the Sea and the Jungle. Robert Carse. LC 51-2441. 1951. Scribner.

From the Shamrock Shore. Ian Kavanaugh. 1982. pap. 3.50 (ISBN 0-440-02798-5, Emerald). Dell.

From the Shores of Ladoga. Tauna Hammar & Ritari, Emilia, 1895- Tr. LC 47-230234. 1947. Meador Publishing Company.

From the Snare of the Hunters. Jane Lane. LC 75-419675. 1968. 6.25x o.p. (ISBN 0-584-31034-X). Intl Pubns Serv.

From the Soil of Two Continents. Roland G. Kaiser. 3.50 o.p. Carlton.

From the South of France: The Roses of Monsieur Alphonse, The Poodle of Monsieur Gaillard, The Recrudescence of Madame Vic, Madame Jolcoeur's Cat. A Consolate Giantess. Thomas Allibone Janvier. LC 12-11160. 1912. Harper & Brothers.

From the Terrace: A Novel. John O'Hara. LC 58-12336. 1958. Random House.

From the Torrid Past. Ann Christy. (Second Chance at Love Ser.: No. 49). (Orig.). 1982. pap. 1.75 (ISBN 0-515-06540-4). Jove Pubns.

From the Unknown. Nancy Dorer & Frances Dorer. (Orig.). 1979. pap. 1.95 (ISBN 0-532-23225-9). Woodhill.

From the Unsounded Sea: A Romance... Nellie K Blissett. LC 1-31827. 1901. D. Appleton and Co.

From the Valley of the Missing. Grace Miller White. LC 11-20313. 1911. W. J. Watt & Company.

From the West to the West: Across the Plains to Oregon. Abigall Scott Duniway. LC 5-13281. 1905. A. C. McClurg & Co.

From the Wings. A Novel. Bertha H Leupold Buxton. LC 26-24710. (Seaside library, v. 43, no. 873). 1880. G. Munrow.

From These Beginnings. Jane Levington Comfort, pseud. LC 37-1000. 1937. E. P. Dutton & Co. Inc.

From These Hills, from These Valleys: Selected Fiction About Western Pennsylvania. David P Demarest. LC 75-15088. (Illus.). (ISBN 0-8229-1123-X). University of Pittsburgh Press.

From These Shores. abr. ed. Helga Skogsbergh. 1975. pap. 1.50 o.p. (ISBN 0-515-03711-7, FA3711). Pyramid Pubns.

From this Beloved Hour. Willa Lambert. (Superromances Ser.). 384p. 1982. pap. 2.50 (ISBN 0-373-70023-7, Pub. by Worldwide). Harlequin Bks.

From This Dark Stairway... Mignon Good Eberhart. LC 31-285804. Pub. for the Crime Club, Inc., by Doubleday, Doran & Company, Inc.

From This Day Forward. Jolene Adams. (Second Chance at Love Ser.: No. 38). 192p. (Orig.). 1982. pap. 1.75 (ISBN 0-515-06408-4). Jove Pubns.

From This Day Forward. Ruby Mildred Ayres. LC 34-28962. 1934. Doubleday, Doran & Company, Inc.

From This Day Forward. John Brunner. LC 76-186009. (Doubleday science fiction). 1972. 5.95. Doubleday.

From This Day Forward. Elswyth Thane. LC 76-18874. 1976. 6.95 (ISBN 0-88411-960-2). Aeonian Press.

From This Day Forward. Elswyth Thane. LC 41-176182. Duell, Sloan and Pearce.

From This Day Forward, a Junior Novel: By Jessica Lyon Pseud. Cateau De Leeuw. LC 51-9829. 1951. Macrae Smith.

From This Day on. Cecily Spaulding. LC 43-172219. 1942. Arcadia House, Inc.

From This Death Forward: By Robert Bloomfield Pseud. 1st Ed. Leslie Edgley. LC 52-5544. 1952. Published for the Crime Club by Doubleday.

From This Hill Look Down. Elliott Merrick. LC 34-30224. 1934. Stephen Daye Press.

From This Valley. Adelmann. 1981. 4.95 (ISBN 0-934860-18-1). Adventure Pubns.

From This White Island. Willis Barnstone. 1959. 2.75 (ISBN 0-8084-0374-5). Coll & U Pr.

From Thunder Bay. Arthur Maling. LC 80-8397. 10.00 (ISBN 0-06-014832-2). Harper & Row.

From Thunder to Breakfast. Hube Yates & Gene K. Garrison. LC 77-80295. (Illus.). 1978. 10.50 o.p. (ISBN 0-87358-175-X); pap. 7.50 o.p. (ISBN 0-87358-178-4). Northland.

From Timber to Town: Down in Egypt. R Perley. LC 7-36189. 1891. A. C. McClurg and Company.

From Van Dweller to Commuter: The Story of a Strenuous Quest for a Home and a Little Hearth and Garden. Albert Bigelow Paine. LC 7-40002. 1907. Harper & Brothers.

From Vaquero to Dominie. Schufle. 1977. pap. 4.95 o.p. Rydal.

From Vilna to Hollywood. Leon Zolotkoff. LC 32-25170. 1932. Block Publishing Co.

From Violent Men: A Novel. Daniel Curzon. (Orig.). 1983. pap. write for info. (ISBN 0-930650-04-2). D Brown Bks.

From Washington to Four Corners: A Second Story of Home, Love, War and Politics. Cyrenus Cole. LC 22-170672. 1922. The Torch Press.

From West to East. Benjamin Subercaseaux & Underhill, John Garrett, 1876- Tr. LC 40-34430. 1940. G.P. Putnam's Sons.

From West to East: Five Stories. Benjamin Subercaseaux & Underhill, John Garrett, 1876- Tr. LC 40-34430. 1940. G. P. Putnam's Sons.

From What Dark Roots... Francine Findley. LC 40-9519. Harper & Brothers.

From Where I Stood. Ora Pate Stewart. 1.25 o.p. (ISBN 0-87747-092-8). Deseret Bk.

From Where the Sun Now Stands. Henry Wilson Allen. LC 78-14512. (Gregg Press Western Fiction Series). 1978. 9.95 (ISBN 0-8398-2461-0). Gregg Press.

From Where the Sun Now Stands. Will Henry, pseud. 256p. 1981. pap. 1.95 (ISBN 0-553-14182-1). Bantam.

From Where the Sun Now Stands. Will Henry, pseud. (Western Fiction Ser.). 1978. lib. bdg. 9.95 (ISBN 0-8398-2461-0, Gregg). G K Hall.

From Where the Sun Now Stands: By Will Henry Pseud. Henry Allen. LC 59-108252. 1960. Random House.

From Whose Bourne. Robert Barr. F. A. Stokes Conmpany.

From Women's Tears: A Novel. Mabel Millen. 1973. 3.00 (ISBN 0-682-47688-9). Exposition Pr.

From 18 to 20. A Novel. LC 8-6450. 1888. J. B. Lippincott Company.

Fromont and Risler: "Fromont Jeune et Risler Aine". Alphonse Daudet. Tr. by Ives, George Burnham. LC 99-69439. 1899. Little, Brown, and Company.

Front. Robert Alley (ISBN 0-671-80739-0). Pocket Books.

Front for Murder. Russell Guy Emery. LC 47-2066. 1947. Macrae-Smith-Company.

Front Man. Francis Wallace. LC 52-8737. 1952. Rinehart.

Front Office Nurse. Ruth Dorset, pseud. 1968. Repr. pap. 0.50 o.p. (50-416). Manor Bks.

Front Page. Ira Wallach. 1975. (pbk.) 1.25. Warner Paperback Library.

Front Page Deadline: The Fictional Story of a Pulitzer Prize-Winning Newspaper Crusade, by Jack Kofoed and Hal Leyshon. John Christian Kofoed & Harold I Leyshon. LC 50-6906. 1950. Merlin Press.

Front Page Girl. Nell Marr Dean. LC 52-6489. 1952. Arcadia House.

Front Porch. Reginald Wright Kauffman. LC 33-176774. The Macaulay Company.

Front Runner. Patricia Nell Warren. LC 73-14774. 1974. 7.95 (ISBN 0-688-00235-8). Morrow.

Front Yard: And Other Italian Stories. Constance Fenimore Woolson. LC 76-101826. (Short story index reprint series). (Illus.). 1969. Books for Libraries Press.

Front Yard, and Other Italian Stories. Constance Fenimore Woolson. LC 4-15058. 1895. Harper & Brothers.

Fronteras. Max Espinoza. 224p. (Orig.). 1980. pap. 2.25 (ISBN 0-87067-007-7, BH007). Holloway.

Frontier. Maurice Leblanc. Tr. by Teixeira De Mattos, Alexander Louis. LC 12-866625. 1.20. Hodder & Stoughton, George H. Doran Company.

Frontier Angel: A Romance of Kentucky Rangers' Life. Edward Sylvester Ellis. Hurst & Company.

Frontier Army Sketches. James William Steele. LC 73-99567. 1969. (ISBN 0-8263-0159-2). University of New Mexico Press.

Frontier Blood. Ernest Haycox. 1974. (pbk.) 0.75. Ace Books.

Frontier Doctor. Bradford Scott. LC 47-1674. 1946. Arcadia House, Inc.

Frontier Dynasty. Elizabeth I. Riseden. (Orig.). 1982. pap. 3.50 (ISBN 0-89083-935-2). Zebra.

Frontier Feud. Max Brand. LC 73-1659. 186p. 1973. 4.95 o.p. (ISBN 0-396-06804-9). Dodd.

Frontier Feud. Max Brand. (Adult Ser.). 384p. 1974. Repr. lib. bdg. 9.95 o.p. (ISBN 0-8161-6180-1, Large Print Bks). G K Hall.

Frontier Feud. Frederick Faust. LC 73-21927. 1974. 4.95 (ISBN 0-8161-6180-1). G. K. Hall.

Frontier Feud. Frederick Faust. LC 73-1659. (Silver star westerns). 1973. 4.95 (ISBN 0-396-06804-9). Dodd, Mead.

Frontier Healers. Lee D. Willoughby. (Making of America Ser.). (Orig.). 1981. pap. 2.75 (ISBN 0-440-02608-3). Dell.

Frontier Incident. Stanley Bennett Hough. LC 52-816. 1952. Crowell.

Frontier Justice. George Brydges Rodney. LC 36-21196. Greenberg.

Frontier Lawman. Lee Floren. LC 81-6852. 1981. 11.50 (ISBN 0-8161-3238-0). G.K. Hall.

Frontier Legion. Jackson Cole, pseud. LC 45-830. 1945. Arcadin House, Inc.

Frontier Life: Or Scenes and Adventures in the South West. Charles Sealsfield. Ed. by Hardman, Frederick. 1856. Miller, Orton & Mulligan.

Frontier Life: Or, Scenes and Adventures in the South West. Charles Sealsfield. Ed. by Hardman, Frederick. LC 17-130688. 1857. Miller, Orton & Co.

Frontier Life: Or, Tales of the South-Western Border. Charles Sealsfield. Ed. by Hardman, Frederick. LC 7-1926. 1859. C. M. Saxton.

Frontier Life: Or, Tales of the South-Western Border. Charles Sealsfield & Hardman, Frederick, 1814-1874, Ed. LC 45-26350. (On cover: Alta edition). 1886. Porter & Coates.

Frontier Life: Or, Tales of the South-Western Border. Charles Sealsfield & Hardman, Frederick, 1814-1874, Ed. LC 45-26349. H. T. Coates & Co.

Frontier Nurse. Watkins Eppes Wright. LC 43-15358. 1943. Arcadia House, Inc.

Frontier of the Deep: A Tale of the Great Northeast. Will Beale. LC 26-12470. Chelsea House.

Frontier: One Hundred & Fifty Years of the West. (Orig.). 1980. pap. cancelled (ISBN 0-553-13748-4). Bantam.

Frontier Passage. Mary Dolling Sanders O'Malley. LC 42-36305. 1942. Little, Brown and Company.

Frontier Rakers. David Norman. (Orig.). 1981. pap. 2.75 (ISBN 0-89083-859-3). Zebra.

Frontier Rakers. David Norman. (Frontier Rakers Ser.: No. 1). 512p. (Orig.). 1980. pap. 2.50 (ISBN 0-89083-633-7). Zebra.

Frontier Rakers, No. 5. David Norman. (Montana Pass Ser.). (Orig.). 1982. pap. 2.95 (ISBN 0-89083-954-9). Zebra.

Frontier Rakers, No. 3: Gold Fever. David Norman. (Montana Pass Ser.). 1981. pap. 2.95 (ISBN 0-89083-903-4). Zebra.

Frontier Renegade: By Chuck Stanley Pseud. Charles Stanley Strong. LC 55-89823. 1955. Arcadia House.

Frontier Scout. Charles Stanley Strong. LC 48-3916. 1948. Phoenix Press.

Frontier Steel. Nevada Carter. 160p. 1982. 10.95 (ISBN 0-8027-4008-1). Walker & Co.

Frontier Steel. Lauran Paine. LC 81-71198. 1982. 10.95 (ISBN 0-8027-4008-1). Walker.

Frontier. Stories. Marvin De Vries. LC 56-11535. 1956. Ballantine Books.

Frontier Stories. Bret Harte. LC 73-3476. (Short story index reprint series). 1973. (ISBN 0-8369-4256-6). Books for Libraries Press.

Frontier Stories. Bret Harte. LC 11-16158. 1887. Houghton, Mifflin and Company.

Frontier Stories. Cy Warman. LC 70-94747. (Short story index reprint series). 1969. Books for Libraries Press.

Frontier Stories. Cy Warman. LC 8-37850. 1898. C. Scribner's Sons.

Frontier Street: By Brad Ward Pseud. Samuel Anthony Peeples. LC 58-5120. 1958. Macmillan.

Frontier: Tales of the American Adventure. MacKinlay Kantor. LC 59-3664. (Signet book, S1703). 1959. New American Library.

Frontier Trader: By Chuck Stanley Pseud. Charles Stanley Strong. LC 53-112938. 1953. Arcadia House.

Frontier War. Jonathan Scofield, pseud. (Freedom Fighters Ser.: No. 8). (Orig.). 1981. pap. 2.95 (ISBN 0-440-02622-9, Bryans). Dell.

Frontiers. John Strachey. LC 52-9579. 1952. Random House.

Frontiers: A Novel. Bernard Ledwidge. LC 79-5037. 1979. 10.00 (ISBN 0-312-30910-4). St. Martin's Press.

Frontiers of Love. Diana C Chang. LC 56-8805. 1956. Random House.

Frontiers of the Heart. Victor Margueritte. Tr. by Lees, Frederic. LC 13-1381. 1913. 1.25. Frederick A. Stokes Company.

Frontiers of the Sea. Peter Ustinov. (A collection of short stories). 1966. 5.95 o.p. (ISBN 0-316-89046-4, Pub. by Atlantic Monthly Pr). Little.

Frontier's Secret. Ian Francis Turek. 1973. (pbk.) 0.95. Popular Library.

Frontiers West. Western Writers of America. Ed. by Squire Omar Barker. LC 76-113691. (Short story index reprint series). 1970. (ISBN 0-8369-3420-2). Books for Libraries Press.

Frontiers West: By Members of the Western Writers of America. Western Writers of America. LC 59-13986. 1959. Doubleday.

Frontiersman. Harold Bindloss. LC 29-5218. 1929. Frederick A. Stokes Company.

Frontiersman. Allan W. Eckert. 768p. 1980. pap. 3.50 (ISBN 0-553-13944-4). Bantam.

Frontiersman, a Tale of the Yukon. Hiram Alfred Cody. LC 10-20606. Hodder & Stoughton, George H. Doran Company.

Frontiersmen. Allan W. Eckert. (Winning of America Ser.). (The epic history of the first American frontier). 1967. 17.50 (ISBN 0-316-20856-6). Little.

Frontiersmen. Mary Noailles Murfree. LC 79-116963. (Short story index reprint series). 1970. Books for Libraries Press.

Frontiersmen. Mary Noailles Murfree. LC 4-85793. 1904. Houghton, Mifflin and Company.
Froomb! John Lymington, pseud. LC 66-11754. 1966. 3.95. Doubleday.
Froomb! John Lymington, pseud. (60-287). 1967. Macfadden.
Frossia. Martha Edith Almedingen. LC 44-40080. 1944. Harcourt, Brace and Company.
Frossia: A Novel of Russia. Martha Edith Almedingen. LC 73-80035. 1969. 4.95. Meredith Press.
Frost. Richard Amory. pap. 1.95 o.s.i. (TC-510, Travellers Comp). Olympia.
Frost. Andrew Hall. LC 67-10955. 1967. Putnam.
Frost and Fire. Elliott Merrick. LC 39-29243. 1939. C. Scribner's Sons.
Frost and the Fire. Ruth Park. LC 58-5795. 1958. Houghton Mifflin.
Frost at Morning. Beatrice Kean Stapleton Seymour. LC 35-150362. 1935. Little, Brown, and Company.
Frost Fair. Elizabeth Mansfield, pseud. (Orig.). 1982. pap. 2.25 (ISBN 0-425-05362-8). Berkley Pub.
Frost Flower. Helen Rose Hull. LC 39-27000. Coward-McCann, Inc.
Frost in April. Peggy Gaddis, pseud. LC 44-699161. 1944. Arcadia House, Inc.
Frost in April. Mary Whitaker. LC 73-140348. (Short story index reprint series). 1970. Books for Libraries Press.
Frost in April. Mary Whitaker. LC 31-8958. 1930. J. Cape & H. Smith.
Frost in May. Antonia White. LC 34-8994. 1934. The Viking Press.
Frost in May. Antonia White. LC 80-20015. 1980. 4.95 (ISBN 0-8037-2697-X). Dial Press.
Frost in the Orchard. Donald R. Marshall. LC 77-22654. (Illus.). 4.95 (ISBN 0-8425-0760-4). Brigham Young University Press.
Frost of Summer. Jess Carr. LC 75-4257. 244p. 1975. 8.95 (Pub. by Moore Pub Co). F Apple.
Frost of Summer: A Novel. Jess Carr. LC 75-4257. 1975. 7.95 (ISBN 0-87716-042-2). Moore Pub. Co.
Frostworld and Dreamfire. John Morressy. LC 76-57515. 1977. 6.95 (ISBN 0-385-12256-X). Doubleday.
Frosty Ferguson: Strategist. Lowell Edwin Hardy. LC 13-23493. 1913. 0.50. John Lane Company.
Frosty Roberts & the Golden Jade Mystery. Bernard Alvin Palmer. pap. 1.95 o.p. (ISBN 0-8024-2883-5). Moody.
Frozen Assets. Pelham Grenville Wodehouse. LC 77-366877. 1976. 3.95 (ISBN 0-257-65835-1). Barrie and Jenkins.
Frozen Deep. Wilkie Collins. LC 6-26949. 1875. W. F. Gill and Company.
Frozen Fire. Charlotte Lamb, pseud. (Harlequin Presents Ser.). 192p. 1980. pap. 1.50 (ISBN 0-373-10380-8, Pub. by Harlequin). PB.
Frozen Fortune. Frank Lillie Pollock. LC 10-23749. 1910. 1.20. The Macaulay Company.
Frozen Frontier. Walter William Liggett. LC 27-4642. The Macaulay Company.
Frozen Humor: or, Trains That Met in the Blizzard. The Adventures of Twelve Men and a Young Widow Two and a Half Days in a Snowstorm. Robert Pitcher Woodward. (Dillingham's metropolitan library, no. 20). 1896. G. W. Dillingham Co.
Frozen Inlet Post. James Beardsley Hendryx. LC 27-175333. 1927. Doubleday, Page & Company.
Frozen Jungle. Lawrence Earl. LC 56-5292. 1956-1955. A.A. Knopf.
Frozen Justice: A Story of Alaska, Tr. from the Danish. Ejnar Mikkelsen & Jayne, Arthur Garland, 1882- Tr. LC 22-19485. 1922. A. A. Knopf.
Frozen Lady. Susan Arnout. LC 81-71662. 581p. 1983. 15.95 (ISBN 0-87795-368-6). Arbor Hse.
Frozen Pirate. William Clark Russell. LC 74-16518. (Science Fiction). 1975. 33.00 (ISBN 0-405-06311-3). Arno Press.
Frozen Pirate. William Clark Russell. (On cover: Lovell's library, no. 1087). 1887. J. W. Lovell Company.
Frozen Pirate. A Novel. William Clark Russell. (Harper's Franklin square library, no. 607). 1887. Harper & Brothers.
Frozen Planet. A. J. Merak. 192p. Date not set. pap. cancelled o.p. (ISBN 0-505-51827-9). Tower Bks.
Frozen Planet. A. J. Merak. LC 60-1071. 1969. pap. 0.60 o.p. (B60-1071). Belmont-Tower.
Frozen Planet. Pel Torro, pseud. LC 67-9819. 1967. Arcadia House.
Frozen Planet, an Anthology from Galaxy Magazine. Galaxy Magazine Editors. (Galaxy Science Fiction Collection Ser., No. 2). 1970. pap. 0.75 o.p. (75-340). Manor Bks.
Frozen Trail. Roy Norton. LC 32-342304. E. J. Clode, Inc.
Frozen Trail. Austin J Small. LC 24-12284. 1924. Houghton Mifflin Company.
Frozen Year. James Blish. LC 57-9039. (Ballantine books, 197). Ballantine Books.
Fruit for Tomorrow. Francena Harriet Arnold. LC 49-49575. 1949. Zondervan.
Fruit in His Season. Helen Corse Barney. LC 51-10823. 1951. Crown Publishers.
Fruit in Season. Anthony Thorne. LC 38-178221. Random House.
Fruit of Eden. Louise Gerard. LC 27-907031. The Macaulay Company.
Fruit of Experiment. Henry Howard Harper. LC 37-807. Priv. Print., The Torch Press.
Fruit of Folly. Violet Craig. LC 13-167859. 1913. 1.25. The Macaulay Company.
Fruit of Folly. Lillian Bennet Thompson & Hubbard, George, 1884- Joint Author. LC 34-186880. The Macaulay Company.
Fruit of the Desert. Richard Hayes Barry. LC 20-7295. 1920. Doubleday, Page & Company.
Fruit of the Desert. Everett Titsworth Tomlinson. 1907. The Griffith & Rowland Press.
Fruit of the Poppy: A Novel. Robert Wilder. LC 65-19737. 1965. Putnam.
Fruit of the Tree. Henry Hamilton Fyfe. 1922. T. Seltzer.
Fruit of the Tree. Edith Newbold Jones Wharton. LC 7-32842. 1907. C. Scribner's Sons.
Fruit of the Tree: A Novel. Helen Marion Edginton. LC 47-1994. 1947. Macrae-Smith-Company.
Fruit of the Tree: A Novel. Mabel Adelaide Farnum. LC 14-21624. 1914. 1.00. B. Herder.
Fruit Out of Rock. Frances Gillmor. LC 40-14496. Duell, Sloan and Pearce.
Fruit Stoners. Algernon Blackwood. LC 77-84200. (Lost Race and Adult Fantasy Fiction). 1978. 18.00. Arno Press.
Fruit Stoners; Being the Adventures of Maria Among the Fruit Stoners. Algernon Blackwood. LC 35-5814. 1935. E. P. Dutton & Co., Inc.
Fruit Stoners: Being the Adventures of Maria Among the Fruit Stoners. Algernon Blackwood. Ed. by R. Reginald & Douglas Melville. LC 77-84200. (Lost Race & Adult Fantasy Ser.). 1978. Repr. of 1935 ed. lib. bdg. 18.00x (ISBN 0-405-10958-X). Ayer Co.
Fruit Tramp. 1st Ed. Vinnie Williams. LC 56-122395. 1957. Harper.
Fruitful Vine. Robert Smythe Hichens. LC 11-24406. 1911. 1.40. Frederick A. Stokes Company.
Fruitfulness: Fecondite. Emile Zola & Vizetelly, Ernest Alfred, 1853-1922, Ed. and Tr. LC 3156. 1900. Doubleday, Page & Co.
Fruitless Repentance: Or, The History of Miss Kitty Le Fever. LC 74-19404. (Flowering of the Novel). 1974. 25.00 (ISBN 0-8240-1185-6). Garland Pub.
Fruits: A Story About Small Town Mill People. Stella Lovisa Olmstead. LC 32-16873. 1932. Meador Publishing Company.
Fruits of Winter. Bernard Clavel. LC 72-81013. 1969. 6.95. Coward-McCann.
Fruits of Yesterday: A Novel Tracing Three Generations of a Southern Family. Clara Cox Roth. LC 78-85390. 1970. 5.00. William-Frederick Press.
Fruits of Yesterday: A Southern Novel. Clara Cox Roth. 1973. 5.00 (ISBN 0-87164-106-2). William-F.
Frustrated Martyr: A Novel Ofa Medical Missionary in West China. 1st Ed. James Lincoln McCartney. LC 53-5141. 1953. Exposition Press.
Fry the Little Fishes. Matt McGinn. 160p. 1982. 10.00 (ISBN 0-7145-0992-2). Riverrun NY.
FSO-1. Harris Greene. LC 76-27040. 1977. 7.95 (ISBN 0-385-12453-8). Doubleday.
Fu Manchu's Bride... Arthur Sarsfield Ward. LC 33-33461. 1933. Pub. for the Crime Club, Inc., by Doubleday, Doran & Company, Inc.
Fuck-a-Doodle-Doo. J. Fabian Daly. 1976. 2.95. Birchfield Press.
Fudge Doings: Being Tony Fudge's Record of the Same... Donald Grant Mitchell. LC 7-25327. 1855. C. Scribner.
Fuego en la Nieve. new ed. Evelio Rios. (Pimienta Collection Ser). 160p. (Span.). 1974. pap. 1.00 o.p. (ISBN 0-88473-195-2). Fiesta Pub.
Fuel of Fire. Ellen Thorneycroft Fowler. LC 2-23304. 1902. Dodd, Mead & Company.
Fuga. Enrique A. Imbert. Ed. by John V. Falconieri. 99p. 1980. pap. text ed. 6.95x (ISBN 0-8290-0223-5). Irvington.
Fugitive. Pierre Gascar, pseud. LC 64-10215. 1964. Little, Brown.
Fugitive. John Grane. Tr. by Blewitt, Trevor Eaton. LC 40-27442. 1940. Harper & Brother.
Fugitive. Richard Warren Hatch. LC 38-32606. 1938. Dodd, Mead & Company.
Fugitive. Marion Montgomery. LC 73-14319. 1974. 8.95 (ISBN 0-06-012998-0). Harper & Row.
Fugitive. Louise Redfield Peattie. LC 35-253940. The Bobbs-Merrill Company.
Fugitive. Pramoedya A. Toer. Tr. by Harry Aveling. (Writing in Asia Ser.). 1975. pap. text ed. 4.50x (00208). Heinemann Ed.
Fugitive: A Tale of Adventure in the Days of Clipper Ships and Slavers. John Randolph Spears. LC 99-4115. 1899. C. Scribner's Sons.
Fugitive Affair: A Novel of Suspense. Rosemary Gatenby. LC 76-2740. (Red badge novel of suspense). 5.95 (ISBN 0-396-07312-3). Dodd, Mead.
Fugitive Anne. Rosa Caroline Murray-Prior Praed. LC 4-1817. 1903. New Amsterdam Book Company.
Fugitive: Being Memoirs of a Wanderer in Search of a Home... Ezra Selig Brudno. LC 4-3583. 1904. Doubleday, Page & Company.
Fugitive Blacksmith. Charles David Stewart. LC 5-5068. 1905. The Century Co.
Fugitive: Crime Impuni) Translated from the French by Louise Varese. 1st Ed. Georges Simenon. LC 55-9992. 1955. Doubleday.
Fugitive Crosses His Tracks. Aksel Sandemose & Gay-Tifft, Eugene, Tr. LC 36-15689. 1936. A. A. Knopf.
Fugitive Eye: By Charlotte Jay Pseud. 1st American Ed. Geraldine Jay. LC 54-6016. Harper.
Fugitive from Love. Barbara Cartland. LC 77-25534. 1978. 6.95 (ISBN 0-87272-033-0). Duron Books.
Fugitive from Murder. Mary Violet Heberden. LC 40-30400. 1940. Pub. for the Crime Club by Doubleday, Doran & Co., Inc.
Fugitive Group. Louise Cowan. LC 59-14394. xxiii, 277p. 1959. pap. 7.95x (ISBN 0-8071-0129-X). La State U Pr.
Fugitive Heart. Janet Doran. LC 41-9276. Gramercy Publishing Co.
Fugitive Heart. Emily Mesta. (Superromances Ser.). 384p. 1982. pap. 2.50 (ISBN 0-373-70034-2, Pub. by Worldwide). Harlequin Bks.
Fugitive Love. Negley Farson. LC 29-75008. 2.00. The Century Co.
Fugitive Love. Negley Farson. LC 47-33617. 1939. D. Appleton-Century Company Incorporated.
Fugitive Millionaire. Gladys Alexandra Milton. LC 22-16744. 1922. Houghton Mifflin Company.
Fugitive Pigeon. Donald E Westlake. (2774). 1968. Dell.
Fugitive Pigeon. Donald E Westlake. LC 65-11295. (Random House mystery). 1965. Random House.
Fugitive Pigeon. Donald E Westlake. 1979. Charter.
Fugitive Romans. William Murray. 1955. Vanguard Press.
Fugitive Trail. Zane Grey. LC 57-9590. 1957. Harper.
Fugitive Trail. Zane Grey. LC 78-2654. 1978. 9.95. J. Curley.
Fugitive Wife. Sara Craven. (Presents Ser.). 192p. (Orig.). 1980. pap. text ed. 1.50 (ISBN 0-373-10368-9, Pub. by Harlequin). PB.
Fugitives. John M. Bradbury. 1958. pap. 3.95 (ISBN 0-8084-0139-4, L15). Coll & U Pr.
Fugitives. John Broderick. 1962. 7.95 (ISBN 0-8392-1036-1). Astor-Honor.
Fugitives. Belle Willey Gue. LC 23-112663. Dorrance.
Fugitives. Meriol Trevor. 1974. (pbk.) 0.95 (ISBN 0-671-77779-3). Pocket Books.
Fugitives: A Novel. John Broderick. LC 62-18200. 1962. I. Obolensky.
Fugitives. A Story. Margaret Oliphant Wilson Oliphant. (Franklin square library, no. 86). 1879. Harper & Brothers.
Fugitives & Their Women. Carl Schubbe. 192p. 1974. pap. 1.95 o.p. (ISBN 0-87056-398-X, 6398). Brandon.
Fugitives and Their Women. Carl Schubbe. 1974. (pbk.) 1.95 (ISBN 0-87056-398-X). Brandon Books.
Fugitive's Canyon. Hal George Evarts. 1973. (pbk.) 0.75. Pocket Books.
Fugitives from Passion. Coningsby William Dawson. LC 30-12986. 1930. Doubleday, Doran and Company, Inc.
Fugitives of the Pearl. John Henry Paynter. LC 72-170846. (Illus.). 1971. (ISBN 0-404-00205-6). AMS Press.
Fugitives of the Pearl. John Henry Paynter. LC 31-1514. The Associated Publishers, Inc.
Fugitive's Return. Susan Glaspell. LC 29-22913. 1929. Frederick A. Stokes Company.
Fugitives. 1st Ed. Robert Gutwillig. 1959. Little, Brown.
Fugue. Theresa De Kerpely. LC 77-24943. 1977. 7.95 (ISBN 0-8128-2356-7). Stein and Day.
Fugue. Olive Moore. LC 32-25854. 1932. L. MacVeagh, Dial Press, Inc.
Fugue for a Darkening Island. Christopher Priest. LC 72-186800. 1972. (ISBN 0-571-09794-4). Faber and Faber Ltd.
Fugue in Time. Rumer Godden. LC 76-380179. 1976. 3.25 (ISBN 0-333-19366-0). Macmillan.
Fugitive Heiress. Besse Sprague. LC 39-9822. M. S. Mill Co., Inc.
Fuhrer Seed: A Novel. Gus Weill. LC 79-385. 1979. 9.95 (ISBN 0-688-03452-7). Morrow.
Fulfilling of the Law. ... 1st ed. Alvan Cavala Halphide. LC 7-31977. M. A. Donohue & Company.
Fulfillment. James McKinley Bryant. 1976. pap. 6.50. J M Bryant.
Fulfillment. James McKinley Bryant. 1975. pap. 5.00. Rocket Pub Co.
Fulfillment. Cosmo Hamilton. LC 35-10042. 1935. Dodd, Mead & Company.
Fulfillment. Elizabeth Newport Hepburn. LC 24-10642. 1924. H. Holt and Company.
Fulfillment. Elsie Lee. (Orig.). 1968. pap. 0.60 o.p. (73-804). Lancer.
Fulfillment. Alice P Raphael. LC 10-9523. 1910. 1.50. Sturgis & Walton Company.
Fulfillment. LaVyrle Spencer. 1979. pap. 2.25 (ISBN 0-380-47084-5, 47084). Avon.
Fulfillment: A California Novel. Emma Wolf. LC 16-90689. 1916. H. Holt and Company.
Fulfillment: Doctor Marston's Secret. by mary elizabeth campbell. ed. Mary Elizabeth Campbell. LC 37-10649. 1936. Renaissance Book Company.
Fulfilment of Daphne Bruno. Ernest Raymond. LC 26-109252. 1926. Cassell and Company, Ltd.
Fulfilment of Daphne Bruno. Ernest Raymond. LC 26-13533. George H. Doran Company.
Full and by. David Stanley Livingstone & McFee, William. Dodge Publishing Company.
Full and Faithful Report of the Memorable Trial of Bardell Against Pickwick: Extracted from The Pickwick Papers. Charles Dickens. LC 75-310035. (Illus.). 1974. S.N.
Full and Particular Account of the Life and Transactions of Roger Johnson. LC 74-31332. (Flowering of the Novel). 1975. 25.00 (ISBN 0-8240-1102-3). Garland Pub.
Full and True Account of the Wonderful Mission of Earl Lavender. John Davidson. LC 76-20049. (Decadent Consciousness). 1977. 26.00 (ISBN 0-8240-2756-6). Garland Pub.
Full Cargo: More Stories. Wilbur Daniel Steele. LC 75-36514. 1976. 19.75 (ISBN 0-8371-8636-6). Greenwood Press.
Full Cargo; More Stories. 1st Ed. Wilbur Daniel Steele. LC 51-14516. 1951. Doubleday.
Full Circle. John Collier. LC 33-109782. 1933. D. Appleton & Company.
Full Circle. Stephen E. Fugate. (Orig.). 1979. pap. 1.50 (ISBN 0-532-15401-0). Woodhill.
Full Circle. Rhoda Hoff. LC 47-2367. 1947. Dodd, Mead & Company.
Full Circle. J. E. Johnson. (War Book Ser.). 288p. 1980. pap. 2.50 (ISBN 0-553-13568-6). Bantam.
Full Circle. Grace Lumpkin. LC 63-212. Western Islands.
Full Circle. Erich Maria Remarque. LC 74-1190. 116p. 1974. pap. 2.95 o.p. (ISBN 0-15-634020-8, HB282, Harv). HarBraceJ.
Full Circle. Mary H Wiseman. 1973. 4.50 (ISBN 0-533-00679-1). Vantage Press.
Full Circle of the Travelling Cuckoo. Renato Amato. 1967. 3.90 o.s.i. Tri-Ocean.
Full Circle Three. Vivian M. Loken et al. (Annual Anthology Ser.). 66p. (Orig.). 1982. pap. 3.50 (ISBN 0-940248-10-7). Guild Pr.
Full Crash Dive. Allan R. Bosworth. LC 42-5131. 1942. Duell, Sloan and Pearce.
Full Day in a Village Postoffice. Ruby McAdam Barnes. LC 40-332872. Printed by Johnston & Bordewyk, Inc.
Full Disclosure: A Novel. William L Safire. LC 76-18365. 1977. 10.95 (ISBN 0-385-12115-6). Doubleday.
Full Fare for a Corpse: Murder on a Transcontinental Train Snowbound on the Great Divide. Tech Davis. LC 37-16372. 1937. Pub. for the Crime Club, Inc., by Doubleday, Doran & Co., Inc.
Full Fathom Five. John Stewart Carter. LC 65-121738. 1965. 4.95. Houghton.
Full Fathom Five. J. E. MacDonnell. 1979. pap. 1.25 o.s.i. (ISBN 0-8439-0663-4, Leisure Bks). Nordon Pubns.
Full Fathom Five. Jonathan Valin. LC 81-3112. 9.95 (ISBN 0-396-07981-4). Dodd, Mead.
Full Flavour. Doris Oppenheim Leslie. LC 34-25164. 1934. The Macmillan Company.
Full Flight. Illus. by Jerry Lazare. Ed. by L. Ruth Godwin. (Passport to reading; a multi-level reading ser.). 1966. 3.80. Macmillan.
Full Flood. Percy Marks. LC 42-19936. 1942. Reynal & Hitchcock.
Full Glory of Diantha. Ella Sterling Clark Mighels. LC 9-15516. 1909. Forbes & Company.
Full Harvest. Dora Aydelotte. LC 39-27174. 1939. D. Appleton-Century Company, Incorporated.
Full House. Mary Nesta Keane. LC 35-19274. 1935. Little, Brown, and Company.
Full House. Zeke Masters, pseud. (Faro Blake Western Ser.: No. 14). pap. 1.95 (ISBN 0-671-43813-1). PB.
Full House. Feenie Ziner, pseud. (O.S.I.). 1967. 4.95 o.s.i. (ISBN 0-671-27434-1). S&S.
Full House: A Nero Wolfe Omnibus. Rex Stout. LC 55-7629. 1955. Viking Press.

Full Measure. Hans Otto Storm. LC 29-164300. 1929. The Macmillan Company.

Full Measure of Devotion. Dana Gatlin. LC 18-3839. 1918. Doubleday, Page & Company.

Full Meridian. Naomi Ellington Jacob. LC 40-724502. 1940. The Macmillan Company.

Full Moon. Talbot Mundy. LC 35-4294. 1935. D. Appleton-Century Company, Incorporated.

Full Moon. Wodehouse. 11.95 o.s.i. (ISBN 0-8277-4258-4). British Bk Ctr.

Full Moon: Illustrated by Paul Galdone. Pelham Grenville Wodehouse. LC 47-30327. 1947. Doubleday and Company, Inc.

Full of Grace. Nancy Henderson. LC 82-45396. 1983. 15.95 (ISBN 0-385-18303-8). Doubleday.

Full of Life. 1st Ed. John Fante. LC 52-5518. 1952. Little, Brown.

Full of Love. Beatrix. 6.95 o.p. Vantage.

Full of the Moon. Caroline Lockhart. 1914. 1.25. J. B. Lippincott Company.

Full Personality. John Taintor Foote. LC 35-511434. 1935. D. Appleton-Century Company, Incorporated.

Full Proof of the Ministry: A Sequel to The Boy Who Was Trained up to Be a Clergyman. John Nicholas Norton. LC 7-33177. 1855. Redfield.

Full Score. Frank Baker. LC 42-13383. 1942. Coward-McCann Inc.

Full Stature of a Man: A Life Story. Julia Warth Parsons. LC 7-34092. (On cover: The round world series). D. Lothrop and Company.

Full Stop. Gilroy Mitcham, pseud. LC 57-11355. (Blue lamp mystery). 1957. Roy Publishers.

Full Swing. Julia Davis Frankau. LC 14-8472. 1914. 1.35. J. B. Lippincott Company.

Full Term: A Novel. John Innes Mackintosh Stewart. LC 79-124284. (His A staircase in Surrey). 1979. 10.95 (ISBN 0-393-01282-4). W. W. Norton.

Full-Time Restless. Dave Goldman. LC 79-20098. 12.50 (ISBN 0-399-90063-2). R. Marek Publishers.

Full up. Molly Parkin. LC 76-28048. 8.95. St. Martin's Press.

Full up. Molly Parkin. LC 77-355889. 1976. 3.95 (ISBN 0-7181-1498-1). Joseph.

Fullback. Lawrence Perry. LC 16-22054. 1916. C. Scribner's Sons.

Fuller's Earth. Carolyn Wells. LC 32-242781. J. B. Lippinocott Company.

Fully Automated Love Life of Henry Keanridge. LC 79-155834. (Playboy science fiction). 1971. 0.75. Playboy Press.

Fully Automated Love Life of Henry Keanridge. Playboy Editors. LC 79-155834. (Orig.). 1971. pap. 0.75 o.p. (D16135). Playboy.

Fully Dressed and in His Right Mind. Michael Fessler. LC 35-7172. 1935. A. A. Knopf.

Fully Processed Cheese. Norman Ward. LC 64-66440. (Illus.). 1965. Crown.

Fumbler. Phillips Russell. LC 28-23669. The Macaulay Company.

Fume. Lajos Ruff. 1965. 3.50 o.p. Regnery.

Fume: A Novel. Lajos Ruff. LC 65-269049. 3.50. Regnery.

Fume of Poppies. Jonathan Kozol. LC 58-11762. 1958. Houghton Mifflin.

Fun and Earnest. Frederic Townsend. 1853. J. S. Taylor.

Fun and Fact. F. H Chambers. LC 6-23340. (On cover: The red cover series no. 33). J. S. Ogilvie.

Fun Begins at Fifty, with Other Stories: By Frances G. Rogers and Johanne K. Sundergaard. Frances G Rogers & Johanne K Sundergaard. LC 55-33528. 1955. Clover House.

Fun City. Hugh Barron. (Orig.). 1968. pap. 0.75 o.p. (T1844). Pyramid Pubns.

Fun Couple. John Haase. LC 61-5834. 1961. Simon and Schuster.

Fun for Doctors and Their Patients: Fifty Authentics Ghost Stories by Fifty Experienced Physicians... Ed. by John L. Short. 1901. J. L. Short.

Fun House. Philip Reid, pseud. LC 73-20329. (Midnight novel of suspense). 1974. 5.95. Houghton Mifflin.

Fun House: A Novel. William Brinkley. LC 61-121754. 1961. Random House.

Fun in a Teacup. new ed. Ian McKinnie. (Your Complete Guide to Tea Leaf Reading). (Illus.). 96p. 1974. pap. 2.95 o.p. (ISBN 0-912310-61-8). Celestial Arts.

Fun-Jottings: Or Laughs I Have Taken a Pen to. Nathaniel Parker Willis. LC 8-36902. 1853. C. Scribner.

Fun-Jottings: Or, Laughs I Have Taken a Pen to. Nathaniel Parker Willis. LC 34-38308. Alden, Beardsley & Co.

Fun of It: A Love Story. John Neufeld. LC 77-18658. 8.95 (ISBN 0-399-11993-0). Putnam.

Fun on the Farm: in Old Kentucky. Ollis Craveison. LC 10-3292. 1.25. The Kuyahora Press.

Fun Was Where You Found It: A Sojourn in Fantasy Down Memory Lane. 1st. ed. Dare Harrington. 1974. 5.00 (ISBN 0-682-47914-4). Exposition Press.

Fun with Your New Head. Thomas M Disch. LC 72-132503. (Doubleday science fiction). 1971. 4.95. Doubleday.

Funcionario Publico. Dolores Medio. LC 63-7868. 1963. Oxford University Press.

Funco File. Burt Cole. LC 69-12203. 1969. 4.95. Doubleday.

Fundamental Disch. Thomas M. Disch. Ed. by Samuel R. Delany. 416p. (Orig.). 1980. pap. 2.50 (ISBN 0-553-13670-4). Bantam.

Funeral. George Abbe. LC 67-30057. 1967. The Smith; by Arrangement with Horizon Press.

Funeral at Egg Hill. Leslie Clare Manchester. LC 11-27917. 1911. Sherman, French & Company.

Funeral Bend. Jack Slade, pseud. (Lassiter, No. 11). (Orig.). 1970. pap. 0.60 o.p. (B60-2050). Belmont-Tower.

Funeral for a Commissar. Ronald Magowan. LC 76-103717. 1970. 3.95. Roy Publishers.

Funeral for Sabella. Robert John Travers. LC 52-9860. 1952. Harcourt, Brace.

Funeral for the Eyes of Fire. Michael Bishop. 1975. (pbk.) 1.50 (ISBN 0-345-24350-1). Ballantine Books.

Funeral Games. Mary Renault, pseud. LC 81-47273. 1981. 12.95 (ISBN 0-394-52068-8). Pantheon Books.

Funeral in Berlin. Len Deighton. 1980. pap. 2.75 (ISBN 0-425-06123-X). Berkley Pub.

Funeral in Berlin. Len Deighton. (YA) 1964. 6.95 o.p. Putnam.

Funeral in Berlin. Len Deighton. (Keith Jennison Book). 7.95 o.p. (ISBN 0-531-00187-3). Watts.

Funeral in Berlin: A Novel. Len Deighton. LC 65-10849. 1965. Putnam.

Funeral in Eden. Paul McGuire. LC 75-44992. (Fifty Classics of Crime Fiction, 1900-1950; 35). 1976. 12.00 (ISBN 0-8240-2357-9). Garland Pub.

Funeral in Eden. Paul McGuire. LC 38-20487. 1938. W. Morrow and Company.

Funeral Is Tomorrow. Peter Dyke. 4.95 o.p. Vantage.

Funeral of Gondolas. Timothy Holme. LC 82-5094. 13.95 (ISBN 0-698-11179-6). Coward, McCann & Geoghegan.

Funeral Rites. Jean Genet. LC 68-58157. 1969. 7.50. Grove Press.

Funeral Rites, Stark No. 1. Joseph Hedges. (Stark Ser.: No. 1). 1974. pap. 0.95 o.p. (ISBN 0-515-03534-3, N3534). Pyramid Pubns.

Funeral Sites. Jessica Mann. LC 81-43616. 1982. 10.95 (ISBN 0-385-18045-4). Published for the Crime Club by Doubleday.

Funeral Urn: A Novel. June Drummond. LC 76-57858. 1977. 6.95 (ISBN 0-8027-5363-9). Walker.

Funerals Are Fatal. Agatha Miller Christie. LC 53-5095. (Red badge detective). (Illus.). 1953. Dodd, Mead.

Fungi from Yuggoth. Howard Phillips Lovecraft. 2.50. Necronomicon.

Fungus the Bogeyman. Raymond Briggs. LC 78-20712. (Illus.). 1979. pap. 4.95 (ISBN 0-394-73820-9, BYR). Random.

Funhouse. Philip Reid, pseud. (Penguin crime fiction). 1976. 1.50 (ISBN 0-14-004103-6). Penguin Books.

Funhouse. Owen West. 288p. 1980. pap. 2.75 (ISBN 0-515-05726-6). Jove Pubns.

Funky. Barbara H. Herrera. LC 77-80685. (Destiny Ser.). 1978. pap. 4.95 o.p. (ISBN 0-8163-0001-1, 06829-6). Pacific Pr Pub Assn.

Funniest Killer in Town. Hampton Stone, pseud. (Hampton Stone Mystery Ser.). 1971. pap. 0.75 o.p. (ISBN 0-446-64503-6, 64-503). Paperback Lib.

Funniest Killer in Town: By Hampton Stone. Aaron Marc Stein. LC 67-253854. (Inner sanctum mystery). 1967. 3.95. S. & S.

Funny Bone: New Humorous Stories. Ed. by Cynthia Mary Evelyn Charteris Asquith. LC 28-27587. 1928. C. Scribner's Sons.

Funny, Jonas, You Don't Look Dead. Mary McMullen. LC 76-2797. 1976. 5.95 (ISBN 0-385-11415-X). Published for the Crime Club by Doubleday.

Funny Lady. Leonore Fleischer. (Illus.). 1975. (pbk.) 1.75. Bantam Books.

Funny Money. Richard Sapir & Warren Murphy. (Destroyer, #18). 1975. (pbk.) 1.25 (ISBN 0-523-00538-5). Pinnacle Books.

Funny Philosophers, or Wags and Sweethearts. A Novel. George Yellott. LC 9-1221. 1872. J. B. Lippincott & Co.

Funny Thing Happened... and a Hunt in the Yukon. 1st. ed. George Witter. 1974. 6.00 (ISBN 0-682-47934-9). Exposition Press.

Funny Thing Happened on the Way to the Moon: By Lois C. Philmus. Illus. by Natalie Bigelow. Lois C Philmus. 1966. 3.95. Books. Inc.

Fur and Feather Tales. Joseph Hamblen Sears. LC 99-1753. 1899. Harper & Brothers.

Fur Brigade: A Story of the Trappers of the Early West. Hal George Evarts. LC 28-19246. 1928. Little, Brown, and Company.

Fur Briugers: A Story of the Canadian Northwest. Hulbert Footner. LC 20-8241. 1920. The James A. McCann Company.

Fur Country: Or, Seventy Degrees North Latitude. Jules Verne. 1874. J. R. Osgood.

Fur Country: Or, Seventy Degrees North Latitude. Jules Verne. LC 76-2507. 1976. Aeonian Press.

Fur, Fin & Feather Fables. Philip White. (Illus.). cancelled o.s.i. (Pub. by Haverford). Rittenhouse.

Fur Magic. Andre Norton, pseud. (Archway paperback). (Illus.). 1978. 1.50 (ISBN 0-671-29902-6). Pocket Books.

Fur Masters. Alan Sullivan. LC 47-8864. 1947. Coward-McCann, Inc.

Fur Person. May Sarton. LC 68-2140. (Illus.). 1968. W. W. Norton.

Fur Person. May Sarton. LC 78-8240. (Illus.). 8.95 (ISBN 0-393-08841-3). Norton.

Fur Person. May Sarton. LC 79-25188. (Illus.). 1980. 8.95 (ISBN 0-8161-3010-8). G. K. Hall.

Fur Person. Illus. by Barbara Knox. May Sarton. LC 57-5055. 1957. Rinehart.

Fur Pie in the Sky. Ray Kainen. LC 77-28550. (Traveller's companion series, TC-482). 1.95. Traveller's Companion, Inc.

Furia: A Novel Based on the Murder of the Poet Garcia Lorca. Jose Luis De Vilallonga. LC 76-382479. 1976. 3.50 (ISBN 0-297-77105-1). Weidenfeld and Nicolson.

Furies. Niven Busch. LC 48-8461. 1948. Dial Press.

Furies. book club ed.. ed. John W. Jakes. LC 78-105290. (Jakes, John W., 1932-. The American Bicentennial Ser.). (His The Kent chronicles; v. 4: Vol. 4). (Illus.). 1977. 3.99. N. Doubleday.

Furiosa. Voldemar Lestienne. 1974. (pbk.) 1.75. Warner Paperback Library.

Furioso. Voldemar Lestienne. LC 73-162315. 1972. 2.50 (ISBN 0-491-00663-2). W. H. Allen.

Furious Old Women. Leo Bruce, pseud. Ed. by J. Barzun & W. H. Taylor. LC 81-47375. (Crime Fiction 1950-1975 Ser.). 191p. 1982. lib. bdg. 14.95 (ISBN 0-8240-4976-4). Garland Pub.

Furious Old Women. Croft-Cooke, Rupert. LC 81-47375. (Fifty Classics of Crime Fiction, 1950-1975). 1982. 14.95 (ISBN 0-8240-4976-4). Garland.

Furious Seasons and Other Stories. Raymond Carver. LC 77-22672. 1977. 10.00. (ISBN 0-88496-116-8) (ISBN 0-88496-115-X). Capra Press.

Furious Winter. Louise Roedocker. LC 50-3233. 1950. Crown Publishers.

Furious Young Man. Ida Alexa Ross Wylie. LC 36-480. 1936. Little, Brown, and Company.

Furlough: A Novel. Franz Hoellering. LC 44-6672. 1944. The Viking Press.

Furlough Bride. Peggy Gaddis, pseud. LC 42-21233. 1942. Gramercy Publishing Co.

Furlough from Heaven: A Novel. Jerome Dreifuss. LC 46-810. 1946. Crown Publishers.

Furnace. Daniel Alfred Poling. LC 25-103065. 2.00. George H. Doran Company.

Furnace for a Foe. Shortt, Charles Rushton. LC 57-6613. Roy Publishers.

Furnace for Gold. Emma Sarah Gage Allen. LC 19-15972. American Tract Society.

Furnace of Earth. Hallie Erminie Rives. LC 5555. 1900. The Camelot Company.

Furnace of Gold. Philip Verrill Mighels. LC 10-1471. Desmond FitzGerald, Inc.

Furnace of Iron. Andrew Firth. LC 17-419816. 1915. Brentano's.

Furono Amati: A Romance. Louise C Ellsworth. United States Books Company.

Furrow's End: An Anthology of Great Farm Stories. Ed. by David Benjamin Greenberg. LC 46-7719. 1946. Greenberg.

Further Adventures of Brunhild. Rebecca Kavaler. LC 78-50811. (Associated Writing Program Award Winner Ser.: No. 1). 172p. 1978. 10.95 (ISBN 0-8262-0249-7). U of Mo Pr.

Further Adventures of Brunhild: Stories. Rebecca Kavaler. LC 78-50811. 1978. 10.00 (ISBN 0-8262-0249-7). University of Missouri Press.

Further Adventures of Captain Gregory Dangerfield. Jeremy Lloyd. LC 73-87413. 1974. 6.50. St. Martin's Press.

Further Adventures of Halley's Comet. John Calvin Batchelor. LC 80-67858. 12.95 (ISBN 0-312-92231-0). Congdon & Lattes: Distributed by St. Martin's Press.

Further Adventures of Jimmie Dale. Frank Lucius Packard. LC 28-179169. 1919. A. L. Burt Company.

Further Adventures of Jimmie Dale. Frank Lucius Packard. LC 19-686620. George H. Doran Company.

Further Adventures of Jungle John. John Austin Budden. LC 29-18951. 1929. 2.50. Longmans, Green and Co.

Further Adventures of Lad. Albert Payson Terhune. 208p. 1983. pap. 2.25 (ISBN 0-451-12086-8, Sig Vista). NAL.

Further Adventures of Oversoul Seven. Jane Roberts. LC 78-26860. 1979. 8.95 o.p. (ISBN 0-13-345306-5). P-H.

Further Adventures of Quincy Adams Sawyer and Mason Corner Folks: A Novel. Charles Felton Pidgin. LC 9-13543. 1909. L. C. Page & Company.

Further Adventures of the One-Eyed Poacher. Edmund Ware Smith. LC 47-7029. 1947. Crown Publishers.

Further Annals of the Girl in the Slumber-Boots. Adah Viola Rohrer Bienz. LC 12-25071. 1.35. Press of Jennings and Graham.

Further Chronicles of Avonlea. Lucy Maud Montgomery. LC 53-3913. (Thrushwood book). 1953. Grosset & Dunlap.

Further Chronicles of Avonlea, Which Have to Do with Many Personalities and Events in and About Avonlea... Lucy Maud Montgomery. LC 54-37. (Illus.). 1953. L. C. Page.

Further Chronicles of Avonlea: Which Have to Do with Many Personalities and Events in and About Avonlea... Lucy Maud Montgomery. LC 20-5578. 1920. The Page Company.

Further Confessions of a Pimp. 1970. pap. 1.25 o.p. (B12-1087). Belmont-Tower.

Further E. K. Means. Eldred Kurtz Means. LC 72-4648. (Black Heritage Library Collection). (Illus.). 1972. 14.00 (ISBN 0-8369-9111-7). Books for Libraries Press.

Further E. K. Means. Is This a Title? It Is Not. It Is the Name of a Writer of Negro Stories, Who Has Make Himself So Completely the Writer of Negro Stories That This Third Book, Like the First and Second, Needs No Title. Illustrated by Kemble. Eldred Kurtz Means. G. P. Putnam's Sons.

Further Education of Oversoul Seven. Jane Roberts. LC 78-26860. 8.95 (ISBN 0-13-345306-5). Prentice-Hall.

Further Experiences of an Irish R. M. Edith Anna CEnone Somerville & Violet Florence Martin. LC 8-23093. 1908. Longmans, Green, and Co.

Further Fables for Our Time. James Thurber. 1956. 9.95 (ISBN 0-671-27880-0, Fireside). S&S.

Further Nonsense Verse and Prose. Charles Lutwidge Dodgson. Ed. by Reed, Langford. LC 26-19905. 1926. D. Appleton and Company.

Further Rivals of Sherlock Holmes. Ed. by Hugh Greene. LC 73-7020. 1973. 6.95 (ISBN 0-394-48827-X). Pantheon Books.

Further Rivals of Sherlock Holmes. Ed. by Hugh Greene. 1974. (pbk.) 1.50 (ISBN 0-14-003891-4). Penguin.

Further Side of Fear. Helen McCloy. LC 67-12712. (Red badge mystery). 1967. Dodd, Mead.

Further Side of Silence. Hugh Charles Clifford. LC 79-110182. (Short story index reprint series). (Illus.). 1970. Books for Libraries Press.

Further Side of Silence. Hugh Charles Clifford. LC 16-21130. 1916. Doubleday, Page & Company.

Further Side of Silence: By Hugh Clifford...Illustrated by Mahlon Blaine. Hugh Charles Clifford. LC 27-24485. 1927. Doubleday, Page & Comapny.

Further Stories of Ireland. Samuel Lover & David James O'Donoghue. LC 79-19247. (Series: Irish Heritage Series (Wilmington, Del.). 1980. 25.00 (ISBN 0-934204-03-9). M. P. Browne.

Further Story of Lieutenant Sandy Ray. Charles King. LC 6-24576. H. F. Fenno & Company.

Further Tales of the City. Armistead Maupin. LC 81-48059. 16.30 (ISBN 0-06-014991-4) (ISBN 0-06-090916-1). Harper & Row.

Further Waters: A Novel, by William J. Arthurs. William J Arthurs. LC 65-24772. Dresser, Chapman & Grimes.

Furthest Fury: A Fleming Stone Story. Carolyn Wells. LC 24-594681. 1924. J. B. Lippincott Company.

Fury. John Farris. LC 76-3628. 8.95 (ISBN 0-87223-456-8). Playboy Press.

Fury. John Farris. 1978. 2.50 (ISBN 0-445-08620-3). Popular Library.

Fury. Edmund Goulding. LC 22-24225. 1922. 1.75. Dodd, Mead and Company.

Fury. Henry Kuttner. 1972. 0.95. Lancer Books.

Fury. Mark Swanson. (Orig.). 1969. pap. 0.95 o.p. (65-221). Paperback Lib.

Fury. Alice Thorne. (YA) (gr. 7 up). 1.00 o.p. G&D.

Fury. E. V. Timms. 1975. pap. 1.25 o.p. (ISBN 0-515-03834-2). BJ Pub Group.

Fury. E. V. Timms. 1967. Repr. pap. 1.80 o.s.i. Tri-Ocean.

Fury: A Novel. John Farris. 1977. 2.25 (ISBN 0-445-08620-3). Popular Library.

Fury & the Passion. Paula Fairman. (Orig.). 1979. pap. 2.95 (ISBN 0-523-41798-5). Pinnacle Bks.

Fury at Painted Rock: A Western Novel. Will Cook. LC 55-32832. (Popular library, 652). 1955. Popular Library.

Fury Bombs. Robert Hoskins. (Phoenix Force Ser.). 192p. 1983. pap. 1.95 (ISBN 0-373-61305-9, Pub. by Worldwide). Harlequin Bks.

Fury from Earth. Dean McLaughlin. 1971. pap. 0.75 o.p. (T2542). Pyramid Pubns.

Fury in the Earth: A Novel of the New Madrid Earthquake. Harry Harrison Kroll. LC 45-2362. 1945. The Bobbs-Merrill Company.

Fury of Rachel Monette. Peter Abrahams. 224p. 1980. 10.95 o.s.i. (ISBN 0-02-500130-2). Macmillan.

Fury of Rachel Monette. 352p. 1982. pap. 3.50 (ISBN 0-671-41906-4). PB.

Fury of the Norsemen. 1980. pap. text ed. write for info. (ISBN 0-88074-163-5). Metagam.

Fury on Sunday. Richard Matheson. LC 54-27798. (Lion book, 180). 1954. Lion Books.

Fury on the Plains: By Chad Merriman Pseud. Cover Painting by Leslie Ross. Gifford Paul Cheshire. LC 54-24970. (Gold medal books, 381). 1954. Fawcett Publications.

Fury Out of Time. Lloyd Biggle, Jr. LC 65-17255. (Doubleday science fiction). 1965. Doubleday.

Fury, Stallion of Broken Wheel Ranch: Illus. by James W. Schucker. Albert G Miller. 1963. bds., 1.25. Grossett.

Furys: A Novel. James Hanley. LC 35-9548. 1935. The Macmillan Company.

Furze the Cruel. Ernest George Henham. LC 13-1156. 1908. Moffat, Yard & Company.

Fuseli: The Nightmare. Nicholas Powell. (Art in Context Ser). (Illus.). 1973. 7.50 o.p. (ISBN 0-670-33285-2). Viking Pr.

Fusing Force: An Idaho Idyl. Katharine Hopkins Chapman. LC 11-25438. 1911. 1.35. A. C. McClurg & Co.

Fusion & Faster Than Light. Ed. by Isaac Asimov. 1979. pap. 1.75 o.s.i. (ISBN 0-89559-160-X). Dale Books Inc.

Futile Alibi. Freeman Wills Crofts. LC 38-204860. 1938. Dodd, Mead and Company.

Futile Life of Pito Perez. Jose Ruben Romero. LC 67-12200. (Illus.). 1967. Prentice-Hall.

Futility. Morgan Robertson. M. F. Mansfield.

Futility: A Novel on Russian Themes. William Alexander Gerhardie. LC 73-92457. (Revised definitive edition of the works of William Gerhardie). 1974. 7.95. St. Martin's Press.

Futility: A Novel on Russian Themes. William Alexander Gerhardie. LC 75-305890. (Penguin modern classics). 1974. 0.40 (ISBN 0-14-000391-6). Penguin.

Futility: A Novel on Russian Themes. William Alexander Gerhardie. LC 28-471. 1922. Duffield and Company.

Future, Vol. I. Ed. by Martin Harry Greenberg et al. 384p. (Orig.). 1981. pap. 2.50 (ISBN 0-449-24366-4, Crest). Fawcett.

Future at War: The Spear of Mars, Vol. II. Ed. by Reginald Bretnor. 1980. pap. 2.25 (ISBN 0-441-25971-5). Ace Bks.

Future City. Ed. by Roger Elwood. LC 72-96814. 1973. 7.95 (ISBN 0-671-27103-2). Trident Press.

Future Corruption. Ed. by Roger Elwood. 1975. (pbk.) 1.25 (ISBN 0-446-76571-6). Warner Paperback Library.

Future Dark Ages. A Story of a Trip Through a Dark Continent. Milton Worth Ramsey. (nation library. v. 7, no. 11). 1900.

Future Glitter. Alfred Elton Van Vogt. 1973. (pbk.) 0.95. Ace Books.

Future Glitter: Science Fiction. Alfred Elton Van Vogt. LC 76-378606. 1976. 3.50. Sidgwick and Jackson.

Future in Question. Isaac Asimov et al. (Orig.). 1980. pap. 2.50 (ISBN 0-449-24266-8, Crest). Fawcett.

Future Is Not What It Used to Be. Patricia Browning Griffith. LC 78-130477. 1970. 5.95. Simon and Schuster.

Future Is Now. William F. Nolan. 1978. pap. 4.95 o.s.i. (ISBN 0-8202-5028-7). Sherbourne.

Future Is Now. William F. Nolan. 288p. 1971. 6.50 o.p. (ISBN 0-8202-0056-5). Sherbourne.

Future Leaders. Mwangi Ruheni. (African Writers Ser.). 1973. pap. text ed. 4.00x (ISBN 0-435-90139-7). Heinemann Ed.

Future Life: Or, Scenes in Another World. George Wood. 1858. Derby & Jackson.

Future Makers. Ed. by Peter Haining. 1971. pap. 0.75 o.p. (B75-2125). Belmont-Tower.

Future Mister Dolan: A Novel. Charles O Gorham. LC 48-7961. 1948. Dial Press.

Future Now: Saving Tomorrow. Ed. by Robert Hoskins. (Fawcett Crest Book). 1.75 (ISBN 0-449-23227-1). Fawcett Pubns.

Future Nurse. Peggy Gaddis, pseud. 128p. 1972. pap. 0.60 o.p. (60-495). Manor Bks.

Future Nurse & Student Nurse. Peggy Gaddis, pseud. Orig. Title: Grass Roots Nurse. 256p. 1972. pap. 0.95 o.p. (532-00209-095). Manor Bks.

Future Nurse, and Student Nurse. Peggy Gaddis & Peggy Gaddis. 0.95. Manor Books.

Future Pastimes. Scott Edelstein. LC 76-54881. 1977. 6.95 (ISBN 0-87695-181-7). Aurora Publishers.

Future Perfect: American Science Fiction of the Nineteenth Century. rev. ed. Howard Bruce Franklin. LC 77-22010. 1978. 15.00. (ISBN 0-19-502322-6) (ISBN 0-19-502323-4). Oxford University Press.

Future Power: A Science Fiction Anthology. Jack Dann & Gardner R Dozois. LC 75-33362. 7.95 (ISBN 0-394-49420-2). Random House.

Future Sex. Saul Kent. 1974. (pbk.) 1.50. Warner Paperback Library.

Future Tense. John Brosnan. 1979. pap. 7.95 o.p. (ISBN 0-312-31489-2). St Martin.

Future Tense: New and Old Tales of Science Fiction. Ed. by Kendell Foster Crossen. LC 52-928234. 1952. Greenberg.

Future to Let, a Novel. Jerzy Pietrkiewicz. LC 59-7107. 1959. Lippincott.

Future Without Future. Jacques Sternberg. LC 73-6427. (Continuum book). 1974. 6.95 (ISBN 0-8164-9170-4). Seabury Press.

Futurelove: A Science Fiction Triad. Gordon R Dickson. LC 78-17896. 8.95 (ISBN 0-672-52032-X). Bobbs-Merrill.

Futurelove: A Science Fiction Triad. Anne McCaffery & Joan C. Holly. LC 76-11625. 1977. 8.95 o.p. (ISBN 0-672-52032-X). Bobbs.

Futurelove: A Science Fiction Triad. Anne McCaffery & Joan C. Holly. LC 76-11625. 1977. 8.95 o.p. (ISBN 0-672-52032-X). Bobbs.

Future's Advocate. Edwin George Carr. LC 74-82187. 1975. 10.00 (ISBN 0-8309-0121-3). Herald Pub. House.

Futures Past. James White. 240p. (Orig.). 1982. pap. 2.50 (ISBN 0-345-30433-0, Del Rey). Ballantine.

Futures to Infinity. Ed. by Samuel Moskowitz. (Orig.). 1970. pap. 0.75 o.p. (T2312). Pyramid Pubns.

Futurological Congress (from the Memoirs of Ijon Tichy). Stanislaw Lem. LC 74-12079. (Continuum book). 1974. 5.95 (ISBN 0-8164-9222-0). Seabury Press.

Futurological Congress (from the Memoirs of Ijon Tichy). Stanislaw Lem. 1976. (pbk.) 1.25 (ISBN 0-380-00584-0). Avon Books.

Fuzz. Ed McBain. LC 68-12156. (Eighty-Seventh Precint Ser). 1968. 4.95 o.p. Doubleday.

Fuzz; an 87th Precinct Mystery. Evan Hunter. LC 68-12156. 1968. 4.95. Doubleday.

Fuzzies: A Folk Fable for All Ages. first ed. Richard Lessor. (Illus.). 1971. 2.50. Argus Communications.

Fuzzy Bones. William Tuning. 320p. (Orig.). 1981. pap. 2.50 (ISBN 0-441-26181-7). Ace Bks.

Fuzzy Papers. H. Beam Piper. 1982. pap. 2.75 (ISBN 0-441-26193-0). Ace Bks.

Fuzzy Pink Nightgown. Sylvia Tate. LC 56-6051. 1956. Harper.

G

G. John Berger. LC 72-77006. 1972. 7.95 (ISBN 0-670-33341-7). Viking Press.

G. A Novel. John Berger. LC 80-8031. (Illus.). 1980. 5.95 (ISBN 0-394-73967-1). Pantheon Books.

G. B." A Story of the Great War. Walter Frederick Morris. LC 29-197753. 1929. Dodd, Mead & Company.

G. E. Falkland. Edward Bulwer-Lytton. Ed. by Herbert V. Thal. (First Novel Library). 1967. 7.95 (ISBN 0-304-92027-4); pap. 4.95 (ISBN 0-8023-9054-4). Dufour.

G for Gunsmoke. K McComb. LC 57-4897. 1957. Arcadia House.

G Man. Charles Francis Coe. LC 35-9551. J. B. Lippincott Company.

G. O. G. 666: By John Taine Pseud. Decorations by John T. Brooks. 1st Ed. Eric Temple Bell. LC 53-12941. 1954. Fantasy Press.

G. P. William A Block. LC 76-127644. 1971. 6.95 (ISBN 0-13-362111-1). Prentice-Hall.

G. P. R. James's Novels. George Payne Rainsford James. LC 45-52365. G. Routledge and Sons.

G Stands for Gun. Nelson Coral Nye. LC 38-5136. Greenberg.

G-String Murders. Gypsy Rose Lee. LC 41-20725. 1941. Simon and Schuster.

G. T. T. Or, The Wonderful Adventures of a Pullman. Edward Everett Hale. LC 6-46173. (Half-title: Town and country series). 1877. Roberts Brothers.

G. T. T. Or, The Wonderful Adventures of a Pullman. Edward Everett Hale. LC 5-31823. 1892. Roberts Brothers.

Gabby. Clella H. Holland. 1970. 2.95 o.p. Vantage.

Gabriel. Justus E Wyman. LC 46-22363. 1946. The Beechhurst Press.

Gabriel: A Novel. Harry J. Pollock. LC 76-353968. 7.95 (ISBN 0-07-082242-5). McGraw-Hill Ryerson.

Gabriel and the Angels. Theresa Townsend. LC 42-114528. 1942. The John C. Winston Company.

Gabriel & the Creatures. Gerald Heard. LC 52-5445. 1952. 4.95 (ISBN 0-87481-697-1). Vedanta Pr.

Gabriel and the Creatures: Illustrated by Susanne Suba. Gerald Heard. LC 52-5445. 1952. Harper.

Gabriel Conroy. Bret Harte. LC 70-104478. (Illus.). 1970. (ISBN 0-8398-0769-4). Literature House.

Gabriel Conroy. Bret Harte. LC 34-30574. 1876. American Publishing Company.

Gabriel Conroy. Bret Harte. LC 3-13616. (Half-title: The works of Bret Harte. Riverside edition). Houghton, Mifflin and Company.

Gabriel Conroy. Bret Harte. LC 12-27752. (Half-title: The works of Bret Harte. Riverside edition... v. 4). 1882. Houghton, Mifflin and Company.

Gabriel Conroy: Bohemian Papers, Stories of and for the Young. Bret Harte. LC 4-22486. (Half-title: Riverside edition. The writings of Bret, vol. xiii). 1902. Houghton, Mifflin and Company.

Gabriel Da Costa. Jacob Samuel Minkin. LC 68-27256. 1969. A. S. Barnes.

Gabriel Denver. Oliver Madox Brown. LC 72-129368. 1972. 11.00 (ISBN 0-404-01137-3). AMS Press.

Gabriel Horn. Felix Holt. LC 51-6671. 1951. Dutton.

Gabriel Hounds. Mary Stewart. LC 67-7309. 1967. M. S. Mill Co.; Distributed by Morrow.

Gabriel Over the White House: A Novel of the Presidency. Thomas Frederic Tweed. LC 33-5769. Farrar & Rinehart, Incorporated.

Gabriel Praed's Castle. Alice Jones. LC 4-22983. 1904. H. B. Turner & Co.

Gabriel Renville, Young Sioux Warrior: The Adventures of an Indian Boy in Early Minnesota. Donald D. Parker. LC 73-86547. 1973. 7.00 o.p. (ISBN 0-682-47719-2, Lochinvar). Exposition.

Gabriel Samara: Peacemaker. Edward Phillips Oppenheim. LC 25-20258. 1925. Little, Brown, and Company.

Gabriel Tolliver. Joel Chandler Harris. LC 67-29269. (Americans in Fiction Ser.). Repr. of 1902 ed. lib. bdg. 14.00 (ISBN 0-8398-0763-5). Irvington.

Gabriel Tolliver: A Story of Reconstruction. Joel Chandler Harris. LC 67-29269. (Americans in fiction). 1967. Gregg Press.

Gabriel Tolliver: A Story of Reconstruction. Joel Chandler Harris. LC 2-18736. 1902. McClure. Phillips & Co.

Gabriel Vane: His Fortune and His Friends. Jeremy Loud. LC 7-14773. 1856. Derby & Jackson.

Gabriela, Clove and Cinnamon. Jorge Amado. (Bard book). 1974. (pbk.) 1.95. Avon.

Gabriela, Clove and Cinnamon. Translated from the Portuguese by James L. Taylor and William L. Grossman. 1st American Ed. Jorge Amado. LC 62-8688. 1962. Knopf.

Gabrielle. Theresa Conway. (Fawcett Gold Medal Book). 1977. 1.95 (ISBN 0-449-13916-6). Fawcett Books.

Gabrielle. Louise McCarty. (On cover: Munro's library, v. 1, no. 109). N. L. Munro.

Gabrielle. William Babington Maxwell. LC 26-77650. 1926. Dodd, Mead and Company.

Gabrielle. Kathleen Thompson Norris. Orig. Title: Black Flemings. 1968. pap. 0.75 o.p. (54-797). Paperback Lib.

Gabrielle De Bergerac. Henry James. LC 19-1493. 1918. Boni and Liveright.

Gabrielle De Bourdaine. A Novel. Lilian Headland Spender. (Harper's Franklin square library. no. 289). 1883. Harper & Brothers.

Gabrielle of the Lagoon: A Romance of the South Seas. Arnold Safroni-Middleton. LC 19-12611. 1919. Lippincott.

Gabrielle: Or, The House of Maureze. Alice Marie Celeste Durand. LC 6-35693. T. B. Peterson & Brothers.

Gabrielle: Transgressor. Harris Dickson. 1906. J. B. Lippincott Company.

Gabrielle's Girls. Peggy Gaddis, pseud. LC 42-457. 1943. Phoenix Press.

Gabriel's Search. Della Thompson Lutes. LC 40-14080. 1940. Little, Brown and Company.

Gabriel's Vocation. Camille Debans. (On cover: Cassell's sunshine series, no. 94). 1892. Cassell Publishing Company.

Gabriel's Wooing. Andrew Jackson Graham. The Young Churchman Co.

Gad. Stephen Geller. LC 78-69620. 1979. 11.49i (ISBN 0-06-011493-2, HarpT). Har-Row.

Gadfly. Ethel Lillian Boole Voynich. LC 61-32650. 1961. Pyramid Books.

Gadget. Nicolas Freeling. LC 77-24130. 1977. 8.95 (ISBN 0-698-10810-8). Coward, McCann & Geoghegan.

Gadget Maker. 1st Ed. Maxwell Griffith. LC 54-94225. 1954. Lippincott.

Gadget Man. Ron Goulart. LC 72-135714. 1971. 4.95. Doubleday.

Gad's Hall. Norah Robinson Lofts. LC 77-92220. 1978. 8.95 (ISBN 0-385-12988-2). Doubleday.

Gad's Hall. Norah Robinson Lofts. (Fawcett Crest book). 1979. 2.25 (ISBN 0-449-24040-1). Fawcett Crest.

Gadsby: A Story of Over 50,000 Words Without Using the Letter "E". Ernest Vincent Wright. LC 40-613172. Wetzel Publishing Co., Inc.

Gael Over Glasgow. Edward Shiels. 1937. Sheed & Ward.

Gaelic Source of the Bronte Genius. Cathal O'Byrne. LC 72-102621. (Kennikat Press scholarly reprints. Series in Irish history and culture). (Illus.). 1970. Kennikat Press.

Gage. David Chacko. LC 73-89569. 1974. 6.95. St. Martin's Press.

Gail Donner: A Novel. victory ed. Frank J McDonald. LC 7-18779.

Gail Weston. Susanna Rebecca Graham Clark. LC 7-31978. 1907. Griffith & Rowland Press.

Gain with God: A Novel. Thomas Savage. LC 53-105335. 1953. Simon and Schuster.

Gaining the Heights. Jessie C Glasier. LC 6-43962. 1890. Standard Publishing Company.

Gains & Losses. Robert L. Wolff. (Victorian Fiction Ser). Orig. Title: Faith & Doubt in Victorian England. 1975. lib. bdg. 66.00 (ISBN 0-8240-1617-3). Garland Pub.

Gainst Wind and Tide. Eleanor Talbot Kinkead. LC 7-12530. (On cover: Rialto series, no. 49). 1892. Rand, McNally & Company.

Gaints' Bread. Agatha Miller Christie. LC 72-97688. 1982. pap. 5.95 (ISBN 0-87795-387-2). Arbor Hse.

Gala: A Fictional Sequel. Paul West. LC 76-9212. 10.00 (ISBN 0-06-014569-2). Harper & Row.

Gala Day. Robert De Vries. LC 54-11509. 1954. Vanguard Press.

Galactic Bodies, Strange Stars: The Fantastic Worlds of John Brunner. John Brunner. LC 79-92183. 8.95 (ISBN 0-89696-094-3). Everest House.

Galactic Derelict. Andre Norton, pseud. 1979. lib. bdg. 9.95 (ISBN 0-8398-2422-X, Gregg). G K Hall.

Galactic Diplomat: Nine Incidents of the Corps Diplomatique Terrestrienne. Keith Laumer. LC 65-115367. (Doubleday sci. fic.). 1965. 3.95. Doubleday.

Galactic Dreamers: Science Fiction As Visionary Literature. Robert Silverberg. LC 77-1597. 8.95 (ISBN 0-394-49479-2). Random House.

Galactic Effectuator. Jack Vance, pseud. 224p. (Orig.). 1981. pap. 2.25 (ISBN 0-441-27232-0). Ace Bks.

Galactic Empire: An Anthology of Way-Back-When Futures. Brian Wilson Aldiss. 1979. 2.25 (ISBN 0-380-42341-3). Avon Books.

Galactic Empires, Vol. 1. Brian Wilson Aldiss. LC 77-76626. 1977. 8.95 o.p. (ISBN 0-312-31527-9). St Martin.

Galactic Empires, Vol. 2. Brian Wilson Aldiss. LC 77-76626. 1977. 8.95 o.p. (ISBN 0-312-31528-7). St Martin.

Galactic Empires: An Anthology of Way-Back-When Futures. Brian Wilson Aldiss. LC 77-76626. 1977. per vol. 8.95 (ISBN 0-312-31527-9). St. Martin's Press.

Galactic Empires: An Anthology of Way-Back-When Futures. Brian Wilson Aldiss. LC 77-355186. 1976. per vol. 4.95 (ISBN 0-297-77108-6). Weidenfeld and Nicolson.

Galactic Empires: An Anthology of Way-Back-When Futures. Brian Wilson Aldiss. LC 77-76626. 1977. per vol. 8.95 (ISBN 0-312-31527-9). St. Martin's Press.

Galactic Gambit. Roy C. Dudley. 192p. (OSI). 1972. 3.95 o.s.i. Lenox Hill.

Galactic Patrol. 1st. ed. Edward Elmer Smith. LC 51-9107. 1950. Fantasy Press.

Galactic Pot-Healer. Philip K Dick. (Berkley medallion book). 1974. (pbk.) 0.95 (ISBN 0-425-02569-1). Berkley Pub. Co.

Galactic Rejects. Andrew J Offutt. (Laurel leaf library). 1974. (pbk.) 0.95. Dell.

Galactic Rift. R. D. Warner & Michael Warner. (Orig.). 1979. pap. 1.75 (ISBN 0-532-17233-7). Woodhill.

Galactic Whirlpool. David Gerrold. (Star Trek Ser.). 240p. (Orig.). 1980. pap. 2.25 (ISBN 0-553-14242-9). Bantam.

Galahad. Edmund Wilson. Bd. with I Thought of Daisy. 316p. 1967. pap. 1.95 o.p. (ISBN 0-374-50588-8). FS&G.

Galahad. Edmund Wilson. Bd. with I Thought of Daisy. 316p. 1967. pap. 1.95 o.p. (ISBN 0-374-50588-8). FS&G.

Galahad. Edmund Wilson. Incl. I Thought of Daisy. 1967. pap. 1.95 o.p. (ISBN 0-374-50588-8, Noonday). FS&G.

Galahad & I Thought of Daisy. Edmund Wilson. 316p. 1967. pap. 1.95 o.p. (ISBN 0-374-50588-8, N319, Noonday). FS&G.

Galahad and I Thought of Daisy: Rev. Edmund Wilson. LC 67-15012. 1967. 5.50. Farrar.

Galahad; Enough of His Life to Explain His Reputation. John Erskine. LC 26-275872. The Bobbs-Merrill Company.

Galahad of the Creeks: The Widow Lamport. Sidney Kilner Levett-Yeats. (Half-title: Appletons' town and country library, no. 214). 1897. D. Appleton and Company.

Galantrys. Margery Allingham. LC 43-150712. 1943. Little, Brown and Company.

Galanty Gold. Victor MacClure. LC 30-317907. 1931. W. Morrow and Company.

Galapagos Kid. Luke Walton, pseud. LC 76-155276. (O.s.i.). 1971. 6.95 o.s.i. (ISBN 0-87874-000-7, Nautilus). Galloway.

Galapagos Kid; or, the Last Great All-American Boy. Luke Walton, pseud. LC 76-155276. 168p. 1973. pap. 1.95 (ISBN 0-916366-00-6). Pushcart Pr.

Galapagos Kid: Or, The Spirit of 1976; a Novel. Luke Walton, pseud. LC 76-155276. 1971. 4.95 (ISBN 0-87874-000-7). Nautilus Books.

Galaski. A Novel. George Middleton Bayne. LC 6-10287. (On cover: Lovell's library, v. 9, no. 460.). J.W. Lovell Company.

Galatea. Margaret Rivers Larminie Tragett. LC 28-196783. 1928. Houghton Mifflin Company.

Galatea: A Novel. Philip Pullman. LC 78-70518. 1979. 8.95 (ISBN 0-525-11125-5). Dutton.

Galatea. A Pastoral Romance. Miguel de Cervantes de Saavedra. Tr. by Gyll, Gordon Willoughby James. LC 16-12454. 1892. G. Bell & Sons.

Galatea. 1st Ed. James Mallahan Cain. LC 53-6839. 1953. Knopf.

Galaxies. Barry N Malzberg. LC 75-16918. 1975. 1.25 (ISBN 0-515-03734-6). Pyramid Books.

Galaxies. Barry N Malzberg. LC 79-13852. (Gregg Press science fiction series). 1979. 9.00 (ISBN 0-8398-2548-X). Gregg Press.

Galaxies Like Grains of Sand. Brian Wilson Aldiss. LC 77-4496. (Gregg Press science fiction series). (Reprint of the ed. published by New American Library, New York, in series: A Signet book.). 1977. 9.00 (ISBN 0-8398-2376-2). Gregg Press.

Galaxy. Susan Ertz. LC 29-16163. 1929. D. Appleton & Company.

Galaxy, Vol. 1. Ed. by Frederik Pohl et al. LC 81-80783. 240p. 1981. pap. 2.50 (ISBN 0-87216-917-0). Playboy Pbks.

Galaxy, Vol. 2. Ed. by Frederik Pohl et al. LC 81-80783. 240p. 1981. pap. 2.50 (ISBN 0-87216-926-X). Playboy Pbks.

Galaxy of Black Writing. Ed. by R. Baird Shuman. LC 70-99294. 1970. 11.95 (ISBN 0-87716-018-X, Pub. by Moore Pub Co); pap. 5.95. F Apple.

Galaxy of Ghouls. Ed. by Judith Merril. LC 55-58950. (Lion Library edition, LL25). 1955. Lion Library Edition, by Arrangement with Non Pareil Pub. Corp.

Galaxy of Strangers. Lloyd Biggle, Jr. LC 76-2992. 1976. 5.95 (ISBN 0-385-12246-2). Doubleday.

Galaxy of the Lost. Gregory Kern. (Cap Kennedy Ser). 1973. pap. 0.75 o.p. (UT1073). DAW Bks.

Galaxy Reader of Science Fiction: Edited and with an Introd. by H. L. Gold. Galaxy Science Fiction. Ed. by H. L Gold. LC 52-5675. 1952. Crown Publishers.

Galaxy: The Best of My Years. Ed. by Jim Baen. 1980. pap. 2.25 (ISBN 0-441-27296-7). Ace Bks.

Galaxy, Thirty Years of Innovative Science Fiction. Frederik Pohl & Martin Harry Greenberg. LC 79-4891. 10.95. Playboy Press.

Galaxy, Thirty Years of Innovative Science Fiction. Frederik Pohl & Martin Harry Greenberg. LC 80-29410. 1981. 2.50 (ISBN 0-87223-647-1). Wideview Books.

Galaxy 666. Pel Torro, pseud. LC 68-3381. 1968. Arcadia House.

Gale Force. Elleston Trevor. LC 57-8106. 1957. Macmillan.

Gale Warning. Ralph Hammond-Innes. LC 48-6095. 1948. Harper.

Gale Warning. Cecil William Mercer. 1940. G. P. Putnam's Sons.

Galeotes see Amores y Amorios.

Galician Girl's Romance... Pardo Bazan, Emilia. (Holly library, no. 179). 1900. The Mershon Co.

Galileans. Frank Gill Slaughter. (Kangaroo Book.). 1977. 1.95. (ISBN 0-671-80987-3). Pocket Books.

Galileans: A Novel of Mary Magdalene. Frank Gill Slaughter. (Waymark bks., W8). 1967. pap., 1.95. Doubleday.

Gallagher Plot. Nick Carter. (Nick Carter Ser). (O.s.i.). 1976. pap. 1.50 o.s.i. (AD1647, Award). Univ Pub & Dist.

Gallant Adventures. Therese Benson. LC 33-22826. 1933. Dodd, Mead and Company.

Gallant and Game. Amory Hare Hutchinson. LC 63-23506. 1964. Dorrance.

Gallant Came Late. Marian Storm. LC 28-21486. 1923. G. P. Putnam's Sons.

Gallant Captain: A Biographical Novel Based on the Life of John Paul Jones. 1st Ed. Pearl Frye. Little, Brown.

Gallant Dust. Ronald Currie Lee. LC 36-192488. The Penn Publishing Company.

Gallant Fight. Mary Virginia Terhune. LC 8-26050. Dodd, Mead & Company.

Gallant Fraud. Edith Austin Holton. LC 40-136289. The Penn Publishing Company.

Gallant Gesture. Adelaide Humphries. LC 37-7126. 1937. Arcadia House.

Gallant Harvest. Peggy Gaddis, pseud. LC 43-1148. 1943. Arcadia House, Inc.

Gallant Heart: The Story of a Race Horse. Susanne McMasters. LC 54-9829. (Illus.). 1954. Doubleday.

Gallant Horses: Great Horse Stories of Our Days. Ed. by Frances Elizabeth Clarke. LC 38-7725. 1938. The Macmillian Company.

Gallant Lady. Percy James Brebner. LC 19-6326. 1919. Duffield & Company.

Gallant Lady. Elizabeth Chater. 288p. 1981. pap. 1.50 (ISBN 0-449-50217-1, GM). Fawcett.

Gallant Lady. Hebe Elsna. 1971. pap. 0.95 o.p. (95176). Beagle Bks.

Gallant Lords of Bois-Dore. George Sand & Clovis, Steven, Tr. LC 6-34610. 1890. Dodd, Mead & Company.

Gallant Mrs. Stonewall: A Novel Based on the Lives of General and Mrs. Stonewall Jackson. 1st Ed. Harnett Thomas Kane. LC 57-11426. 1957. Doubleday.

Gallant Mrs. Stonewall: A Novel Based on the Lives of General and Mrs. Stonewall Jackson. Harnett Thomas Kane. LC 77-16213. (Illus.). 1978. 10.95 (ISBN 0-89244-075-9). Queens House.

Gallant Refuge. James Noble Gifford. LC 40-31527. 1940. Arcadia House.

Gallant Rogue. Burton Kline. LC 21-6907. 1921. Little, Brown, and Company.

Gallant Spirit. Willo Davis Roberts. 512p. 1982. pap. 3.50 (ISBN 0-445-04732-1). Popular Lib.

Gallant Spy. Betty Hale Hyatt. (Candlelight Regency, 210). Dell.

Gallant: The Story of Storm Veblen. Ruth Sawyer. LC 36-9860. 1936. D. Appleton-Century Company, Incorporated.

Gallant Warrior: A Biographical Novel. 1st Ed. Helen R Mann. LC 54-123341. 1954. W. B. Eerdmans Pub. Co.

Gallant Widow. Emma D. Price. 4.50 o.p. Vantage.

Gallant Years. Anne Powers, pseud. 1974. (pbk.) 1.25 (ISBN 0-523-00314-5). Pinnacle Books.

Gallant Years: A Novel. Anne Powers, pseud. LC 46-3410. 1946. The Bobbs-Merrill Company.

Gallantry: Dizain Des Fetes Galantes. James Branch Cabell. LC 22-14571. 1922. R. M. McBride & Company.

Gallants, Following According to Their Wont the Ladies! Lily Moresby Adams Beck. LC 76-128207. (Essay index reprint series). (Illus.). 1970. Books for Libraries Press.

Gallants: Following According to Their Wont the Ladies! Lily Moresby Adams Beck. LC 24-21588. The Atlantic Monthly Press.

Gallegher, and Other Stories. Richard Harding Davis. LC 68-55670. (American short story series, v. 10). (Illus.). 1968. Garrett Press.

Gallegher, and Other Stories. Richard Harding Davis. LC 70-92174. (Illus.). 1969. AMS Press.

Gallegher, and Other Stories. Richard Harding Davis. LC 71-131684. (Illus.). 1970. Scholarly Press.

Gallegher, and Other Stories. Richard Harding Davis. LC 72-8158. (American short story series, v. 10). 1972. (ISBN 0-8422-8035-9). MSS Information Corp.

Gallegher, and Other Stories. Richard Harding Davis. LC 4-15096. 1891. C. Scribner's Sons.

Gallegher, and Other Stories. Richard Harding Davis. LC 99-4896. 1899. C. Scribner's Sons.

Gallegher and Other Stories. Richard Harding Davis. 1910. C. Scribner's Sons.

Gallegher, and Other Stories. Richard Harding Davis. LC 16-6989. 1915. C. Scribner's Sons.

Galleon Bay. Neill Compton Wilson. 1968. 4.95 o.p. Morrow.

Galleon Bay: A Novel. Neill Compton Wilson. LC 68-14808. (Illus.). 1968. Morrow.

Galleon Treasure. Percy Keese Fitzhugh. LC 8-23543. T. Y. Crowell & Co.

Gallery. John Horne Burns. LC 47-4090. 1947. Harper & Brothers.

Gallery of a Random Collector. Clinton Ross. LC 8-670. 1888. G. P. Putnam's Sons.

Gallery of Modern Fiction: Stories from the Kenyon Review, Edited by Robie Macauley. Associate Editors: George Lanning, David Madden. 1st Ed. The Kenyon Review. Ed. by Macauley, Robie. LC 66-19517. 1966. Salem Press.

Gallery of Nudes. J. Hume Parkinson. pap. 1.75 o.p. (3015). Brandon.

Gallery of Women. Theodore Dreiser. LC 29-27599. 1929. H. Liveright.

Gallery of Women. Bernard Glemser. LC 57-5377. 1957. Random House.

Gallery of Women: By Theodore Dreiser. Theodore Dreiser. LC 29-27590. 1962. Premier Books.

Gallery Slave. Translated from the German of Heinrich Zschokke. from the 45th german ed. Heinrich Zschokke & Sullivan, John Turner Sargent, 1813-1838, Tr. LC 8-37802. 1849. H. N. Joy & Co.

Galley Slave: The Story of "Most Excellent Theophilus.". Joseph Stephens. LC 47-29237. 1947. W. B. Eerdmans Pub. Co.

Galley Slave's Ring: Or, The Family of Lebrenn: a Tale of the French Revolution of 1848. Eugene Sue & De Leon, Daniel, 1852-1914, Tr. LC 11-9154. 1911. New York Labor News Company.

Galley to Mytilene, Stories 1949-1960: The Collected Stories of Paul Goodman, Vol. 4. Paul Goodman. Ed. by Taylor Stoehr. 315p. (Orig.). 1980. 14.00 (ISBN 0-87685-360-2); deluxe ed. 25.00 (ISBN 0-87685-361-0); pap. 7.50 (ISBN 0-87685-359-9). Black Sparrow.

Gallia. Menie Muriel Dowie. LC 7-33308. (On cover: Lippincott's select novels, no. 166). 1895. J. B. Lippincott Company.

Galliard's Hay. Clare Rossiter. 256p. (Orig.). 1981. pap. 1.95 (ISBN 0-441-27246-0). Ace Bks.

Gallico Magic: 7 Complete Books. Paul Gallico. LC 67-9350. (Illus.). 1967. Doubleday.

Gallie Girl. (Le Mariage De Chiffon). Sybille Gabrielle Marie Antoinette De Riquetti De Mirabeau Martel De Janville. Tr. by Pene Du Bois, Henri. LC 7-243851. (modern life library v. 1). Brentano's.

Gallions Reach. Henry Major Tomilson. LC 27-19641. 1927. Harper & Brothers.

Gallions Reach. Henry Major Tomlinson. (Mariners Library). 1949. text ed. 4.75x (ISBN 0-246-63589-4). Humanities.

Gallipoli. Jack Bennett & Peter Weir. LC 81-213600. 11.95 (ISBN 0-312-31572-4). St. Martin's Press.

Gallivant: A Novel. Ronald Roose. LC 78-14980. 7.95 (ISBN 0-8037-3182-5). Dial Press.

Galloping Broncos. Max Brand. 1974. (pbk.) 0.95. Warner Paperback Library.

Galloping Danger. Max Brand. LC 82-12150. 1982. 12.95 (ISBN 0-8161-3431-6). G.K. Hall.

Galloping Danger. Frederick Faust. LC 79-9164. (Silver star westerns). 1979. 7.95 (ISBN 0-396-07707-2). Dodd, Mead.

Galloping Dawns. Arthur Tuckerman. LC 24-12762. 1924. Doubleday, Page & Company.

Galloping Dick. Henry Brereton Marriott Watson. 1896. J. Lane.

Galloping Down. Brainerd Beckwith, pseud. LC 31-112811. The Century Co.

Galloping Ghost: A Three Mesquiteers Story. William Colt MacDonald. LC 52-5769. (Double D western). 1952. Doubleday.

Galloping Preacher: Being Some Experiences of a Clergyman. Yandell Smythe Beans. LC 27-137650. Dorrance and Company.

Gallops. David Gray. LC 73-75778. (Short story index reprint series). 1969. Books for Libraries Press.

Gallops. David Gray. LC 98-483. 1898. The Century Co.

Gallops 2. David Gray. 1903. The Century Co.

Galloway. Louis L'Amour. 160p. (Orig.). 1974. pap. 2.25 (ISBN 0-553-20273-1). Bantam.

Galloway Case. Andrew Garve. pap. 0.50 o.p. (72-716). Lancer.

Galloway Case: By Andrew Garve Pseud. 1st Ed. Paul Winterton. LC 58-12477. 1958. Harper.

Galloway Herd. Samuel Rutherford Crockett. R. F. Fenno and Company.

Gallowglass. Howard Breslin. LC 58-12289. 1958. Crowell.

Gallows Are Waiting. John Creasey. LC 73-81180. (McKay-Washburn suspense). 1973. 4.95. D. McKay Co.

Gallows Are Waiting. Jeremy York. LC 73-81180. 1973. 4.95 o.p. (ISBN 0-679-50402-8). McKay.

Gallows at Graheros. Lewis B. Patten. LC 75-7254. 192p. 1975. 5.95 o.p. (ISBN 0-385-11110-X). Doubleday.

Gallows at Graneros. Lewis B Patten. LC 75-7254. 1975. 5.95 (ISBN 0-385-11110-X). Doubleday.

Gallows at Graneros. Lewis B Patten. (Signet Book). 1977. 1.25 (ISBN 0-451-07290-1). New American Library.

Gallows Brand. Weston Clay. LC 47-23205. 1947. Arcadia House.

Gallows Child. Pauline Glen Winslow. LC 77-73018. 1978. 7.95 (ISBN 0-312-31583-X). St. Martin's Press.

Gallows for the Groom. Dolores Birk Hitchens. LC 47-2097. 1947. Pub. for the Crime Club by Doubleday & Company, Inc.

Gallows Garden. M. E. Chaber, pseud. (Milo March Mysteries Ser). 1971. pap. 0.60 o.p. (63-549). Paperback Lib.

Gallows Ghost and the Long Wire. Barry Cord. (Ace double western). 1974. (pbk.) 0.95. Ace Books.

Gallows Gold. Donald B. Hobart. 1970. pap. 0.60 o.p. (0502-06079). Curtis.

Gallows Gold. James Parrette. (Orig.). 1980. pap. 1.95 (ISBN 0-89083-687-6). Zebra.

Gallow's Gulch. Tom West. 288p. 1981. pap. 1.95 (ISBN 0-441-27252-5). Ace Bks.

Gallows Hill. Frances Vinciguerra Grebanier. LC 37-38174. H. Holt and Company.

Gallows Hill. Frances Winwar. LC 44-4851. 1937. H. Holt and Company.

Gallows in My Garden. Richard Deming. LC 52-5570. (Murray Hill mystery). 1952. Rinehart.

Gallows Land. Bill Pronzini. LC 82-51102. 1983. 11.95 (ISBN 0-8027-4016-2). Walker and Co.

Gallows of Chance. Edward Phillips Oppenheim. LC 34-182225. 1934. Little, Brown, and Comany.

Gallows' Orchard. Claire Spencer. LC 30-9491. J. Cape & H. Smith.

Gallows' Seed. Marie Troubetzkoy. LC 35-12682. C. Kendall & W. Sharp, Inc.

Gallows Trail. Garth Davis. LC 57-11462. 1957. Arcadia House.

Gallows Waits. William John Budd. LC 32-21185. 1932. G. P. Putnam's Sons.

Gallows Way. Daoma Winston. LC 76-23114. 8.95 (ISBN 0-671-22345-3). Simon and Schuster.

Gallows Wedding. Rhona Martin. LC 78-14974. 1978. 9.95 (ISBN 0-698-10951-1). Coward, McCann & Geoghegan.

Gallows Wedding, Rhona Martin. 1980. Berkley Books.

Gallybird: A Novel. Sheila Kaye-Smith. LC 34-378281. 1934. Harper & Brothers.

Gals They Left Behind. Margaret Hammel Shea & Files, Rebecca, Illus. LC 44-6987. 1944. I. Washburn.

Galsworthy Reader. John Galsworthy. Ed. by Anthony West. LC 67-24054. 1968. Scribner.

Galton Case. Ross Macdonald. LC 81-1933. 1981. 10.95 (ISBN 0-89340-334-2). J. Curly.

Galton Case: By Ross Macdonald Pseud. 1st Ed. Kenneth Millar. LC 59-622299. 1959. Knopf.

Galusha the Magnificent: A Novel. Joseph Crosby Lincoln. LC 21-11027. 1921. D. Appleton and Company.

Galvanized Reb. Richard J. Steelman. 192p. 1981. pap. 2.25 (ISBN 0-441-27298-3, Pub. by Charter Bks). Ace Bks.

Galvanized Reb. Robert J. Steelman. LC 77-78515. 1977. 6.95 o.p. (ISBN 0-385-13011-2). Doubleday.

Galvanized Reb. Robert Stoelman. LC 77-78515. 1977. 6.95 (ISBN 0-385-13011-2). Doubleday.

Galveston. Suzanne Morris. LC 75-38168. 512p. 1976. 12.95 (ISBN 0-385-11534-2). Doubleday.

Galveston: A Novel. Suzanne Morris. LC 75-38168. 1976. 10.00 (ISBN 0-385-11534-2). Doubleday.

Gam: Being a Group of Whaling Stories. Charles Henry Robbins. LC 99-4302. 1899. H. S. Hutchinson & Company.

Gam: Being a Group of Whaling Stories. rev. ed.... ed. Charles Henry Robbins. LC 42-26744. 1913. Newcomb & Gauss.

Gamailis, and Other Tales from Stalin's Russia. Vladimir Andreyev. LC 75-17671. 1975. 12.75 (ISBN 0-8371-8231-X). Greenwood Press.

Gamailis, and Other Tales from Stalin's Russia. Vladimir Andreyev. LC 63-9949. 1963. Regnery.

Gambier's Advocate. Ronald MacDonald. LC 14-14459. 1914. John Lane Company.

Gambit. Rex Stout. 160p. 1981. pap. 2.25 (ISBN 0-553-14646-7). Bantam.

Gambit: A Nero Wolfe Novel. Rex Stout. LC 62-17936. 1962. Viking Press.

Gambit for Mr. Groode: By George Griswold Pseud. 1st Ed. Robert George Dean. LC 52-7791. (Guilt edged mystery). 1952. Dutton.

Gamble My Last Game. Robert W Krepps. LC 58-10244. 1958. Macmillan.

Gamble with Hearts. Barbara Cartland. (Bantam Barbara Cartland Library#32). 1976. (pbk.) 1.25. Bantam Books.

Gambler. Max Brand. 1976. Repr. of 1954 ed. lib. bdg. 14.40x (ISBN 0-88411-520-8). Amereon Ltd.

Gambler. Fedor Mikhailovich Dostoevskii. Tr. by MacAndrew, Andrew Robert. LC 64-4276. 1964. Bantam Books.

Gambler. Fedor Mikhailovich Dostoevskii. Tr. by Andrew R. MacAndrew. 192p. 1981. pap. 3.95 (ISBN 0-393-00044-3). Norton.

Gambler. Frederick Faust. LC 76-40296. 1976. 6.95 (ISBN 0-88411-520-8). Aeonian Press.

Gambler. Olle E. Hogstrand. LC 73-7028. 1974. 4.95 (ISBN 0-394-48506-8). Pantheon Books.

Gambler. Aylwin Lee Martin. LC 29-5217. 1929. Thomas Y. Crowell Company.

Gambler see Poor Folk & the Gambler.

Gambler, a Novel. Katherine Cecil Thurston. LC 5-29988. 1905. Harper & Brothers.

Gambler: A Story of Chicago Life. Franc Bangs Wilkie. LC 8-37020. T. S. Denison.

Gambler and Notes from Underground. Fedor Mikhailovich Dostoevskii. Tr. by Constance Black Garnett. LC 67-6147. (Illus.). 1967. Printed at the Sign of the Stone Book for the Members of the Limited Editions Club.

Gambler: And Other Stories. Fedor Mikhailovich Dostoevskii & Garnett, Mrs. Constance (Black) 1862- Tr. LC 32-31876. (Half-title: The novels of Fyodor Dostoevsky. vol. IX). 1931. The Macmillan Company.

Gambler-Bobok: A Nasty Story. Fyodor Dostoyevsky. Tr. by Jesse Coulson. Bd. wit. (Classics Ser.). (Orig.). 1966. pap. 3.95 (ISBN 0-14-044179-4). Penguin.

Gambler, Bobok. A Nasty Story. Tr. Introd., by Jessie Coulson. Fedor Mikhailovich Dostoevskii. LC 66-7736. (Penguin classics, L179). pap., 1.25.

Gambler, Bobok and A Nasty Story. Fedor Mikhailovich Dostoevskii. LC 66-77172. (Penguin classics, L179). 1966. Penguin.

Gambler Takes a Wife. Myron Brinig. LC 43-7891. 1943. Farrar & Rinehart, Inc.

Gambler, the Minstrel, and the Dance Hall Queen. Warwick Downing. LC 76-6540. 1976. Saturday Review Press/E. P. Dutton.

Gambler with a Gun. Lee Floren. 1971. pap. 0.60 o.p. (ISBN 0-447-73209-9). Lancer.

Gambler. 1st Ed. William Krasner. LC 50-9650. 1950. Harper.

Gamblers. Lee Hays. 1.75 (ISBN 0-445-04354-7). Popular Library.

Gamblers: A Story of to-Day. Charles Klein & Hornblow, Arthur. LC 11-13138. G. W. Dillingham Company.

Gambler's Chance. Bar-H Books. James Beardsley Hendryx. LC 41-25426. Carlton House.

Gambler's Companion. George G. Blakey. LC 78-27529. (Illus.). 10.00 (ISBN 0-448-22071-7). Paddington Press; Distributed by Grosset & Dunlap.

Gambler's Gadget & Other Stories. Edward White. 2.75 o.p. Vantage.

Gambler's Gold. Peter Field. LC 47-24. 1946. Jefferson House.

Gambler's Guns: By Lee Thomas Pseud. Lee Floren. LC 53-11300. 1953. Arcadia House.

Gambler's Love. Amii Lorin. (Candlelight Ecstasy Ser.: No. 99). (Orig.). 1982. pap. 1.95 (ISBN 0-440-13029-8). Dell.

Gamblers' Syndicate. The Story of a Great Swindle. John Russell Coryell. (On cover: Secret service series, no. 62). 1892. Street & Smith.

Gambler's Throw. Eustace L Adams. LC 30-24348. 1930. L. MacVeagh, The Dial Press.

Gambler's Wax Finger: And Other Startling Detective Experiences. Culled from the Private Records of Government Officers in Europe and America. George S McWatters. (On cover: The Pinkerton detective series. no. 2). Laird & Lee.

Gambler's Wife. Elizabeth Gertrude Levin Stern. LC 31-8327. 1931. The Macmillan Company.

Gambler's Wife. A Novel... Elizabeth Caroline Grey. (On cover: Seaside library. Pocket ed. no. 285). 1884. G. Munro.

Gamble's Hundred. Clifford Dowden. LC 39-27531. 1939. Little, Brown and Company.

Gamblin' Kid. William Fitzgerald Jenkins. LC 33-140278. A. H. King.

Gamblin' Man. Edward Beverly Mann. 1934. W. Morrow & Company.

Gambling Man: A Novel. Catherine Cookson. LC 75-12578. 1975. 7.95 (ISBN 0-688-02937-X). Morrow.

Gambling on Love. Peggy Gaddis. LC 47-250328. 1947. Phoenix Press.

Gambling on Love. Gail Jordan. (Starlight Romance Ser). 1971. pap. 0.60 o.p. (60-477). Manor Bks.

Gambolling with Galatea: A Bucolic Romance. Curtis Dunham. LC 9-13921. 1909. Houghton Mifflin Company.

Gambrinus, and Other Stories. Aleksandr Ivanovich Kuprin. LC 75-128736. (Short story index reprint series). 1970. Books for Libraries Press.

Gambrinus and Other Stories: Translated from the Russian of Alexandre Kuprin. Aleksandr Ivanovich Kuprin. Tr. by Guerney, Bernard Guilbert. LC 25-16719. 1925. Adelphi Company.

Game. Izzy Abrahami. LC 72-1215. 1973. 5.95 (ISBN 0-684-13024-6). Scribner.

Game. Gerald Hammond. LC 82-16800. 1982. 10.95 (ISBN 0-312-31590-2). St. Martin's Press.

Game. Michael Hastings. LC 58-8040. 1958. McGraw-Hill.

Game. Jack London. LC 71-96890. (Illus.). 1969. Literature House.

Game. Jack London. LC 5-17288. 1905. The Macmillan Company.

Game. Lyn Phillips. 256p. (Orig.). 1982. pap. 2.95 (ISBN 0-523-48037-7). Pinnacle Bks.

Game: A Novel. Antonia Susan Drabble Byatt. LC 68-12487. 1968. Scribner.

Game: And The Abysmal Brute. Jack London. LC 69-12447. (Horizon edition of the works of Jack London). 1969. 3.95. Horizon Press.

Game and the Candle. Audrey De Graff. LC 36-296088. 1936. Godwin.

Game and the Candle. Eleanor Marie Ingram. LC 9-28032. 1909. 1.50. The Bobbs-Merrill Company.

Game and the Candle. Eleanor Marie Ingram. LC 14-193525. Grosset & Dunlap.

Game and the Ground: A Novel. Peter Vansittart. LC 57-5568. 1957. Abelard-Schuman.

Game at Platonics, and Other Stories. Francis Charles Philips. LC 7-36071. (On cover: Union square series, no. 2). Cleveland Publishing Company.

Game Bet. Stockton Woods. 256p. 1981. pap. 2.50 (ISBN 0-449-14430-5, GM). Fawcett.

Game Called Love. Angela Gordon. 1971. pap. 0.75 o.p. (94171). Beagle Bks.

Game Cock & Other Stories. Michael McLaverty. (Illus.). 1947. 6.50 (ISBN 0-8159-5600-2). Devin.

Game for Children. William Bloom. LC 72-82733. 1974. (pbk) 1.75. Ballantine Books.

Game for Eagles. Oakley M Hall. LC 73-121693. 1970. 5.95. Morrow.

Game for Empires: A Biographical Novel (1793-1798) 1st Ed. Pearl Frye. LC 50-8817. 1950. Little, Brown.

Game for Heroes. James Graham, pseud. Ed. by Lawrence P. Ashmead. 1970. 5.95 o.p. Doubleday.

Game for Heroes. Henry Patterson. LC 70-116209. (Illus.). 1970. 5.95. Doubleday.

Game for One Player. Vera Benedicta Gage Birch. LC 47-300694. 1947. C. Scribner's Sons.

Game for the Living. 1st Ed. Patricia Highsmith. LC 58-124783. 1958. Harper.

Game for Three Losers. Edgar Marcus Lustgarten. LC 59-11397. 1952. Scribner.

Game for Vultures. Michael Hartmann. 304p. 1976. 7.95 o.p. (ISBN 0-690-01072-9). T Y Crowell.

Game in Diamonds. Elizabeth Cadell. LC 75-34334. 1976. 6.95 (ISBN 0-688-03015-7). Morrow.

Game in Diamonds. Elizabeth Cadell. LC 76-20498. 1976. 10.95 (ISBN 0-8161-6399-5). G. K. Hall.

Game in Heaven with Tussy Marx. 1st Ed. Piers Paul Read. LC 67-26173. bds., 4.95. McGraw.

Game Is Played. Amii Lorin. (Orig.). 1981. pap. 1.75 (ISBN 0-440-12835-8). Dell.

Game Men Play: A Novel. Vance Nye Bourjaily. LC 79-19660. 9.95 (ISBN 0-8037-0092-X). Dial Press.

Game of Chance. Anne Sheldon Coombs. LC 6-30191. 1887. D. Appleton and Company.

Game of Chess. Thomas Middleton. 1980. pap. text ed. 25.00x (ISBN 0-391-02145-1). Humanities.

Game of Consequences. Shelley Smith. 1982. 15.00x (ISBN 0-333-23778-1, Pub. by Macmillan England). State Mutual Bk.

Game of Consequences: A Comedy-Novel. Albert Kinross. LC 7-12535. The Merriam Company.

Game of Doeg: A Story of the Hebrew People. Elanor E Harris. LC 14-12637. 1914. 1.00. The Jewish Publication Society of America.

Game of Dostoevsky. Samuel Astrachan. LC 65-10923. 1965. Farrar, Straus and Giroux.

Game of Flesh. John Trinian. 1970. pap. 0.75 o.p. (75-360). Manor Bks.

Game of Gloris ... LC 4429. (Tales from Town topics. no. 37). 1900. Town Topics Publishing Company.

Game of Hearts. James Noble Gifford. LC 40-10300. 1940. Gramercy Publishing Co.

Game of Hearts. Troy S Green. 1976. 5.95 (ISBN 0-8059-2320-9). Dorrance.

Game of Hearts. Marlaine Kayle. (Candlelight Regency Ser.: No. 705). 1982. pap. 1.95 (ISBN 0-440-12912-5). Dell.

Game of Hearts. Emily Noble. LC 40-10800. Gramercy Publishing Co.

Game of Kings. Dorothy Dunnett. 1970. pap. 2.95 (ISBN 0-445-08571-1). Popular Lib.

Game of Life. Francesca Maria Steele. LC 8-13429. (On cover: Once a week library, v. 12, no. 4, 5). P. F. Collier.

Game of Life & Death. facsimile ed. Lincoln Colcord. LC 76-106270. (Short Story Index Reprint Ser). 1914. 16.00 (ISBN 0-8369-3307-9). Ayer Co.

Game of Life and Death: Stories of the Sea. Lincoln Colcord. LC 14-16217. 1914. The Macmillan Company.

Game of Love. William Romaine Paterson. LC 2-10714. 1902. C. Scribner's Sons.

Game of Patience. Lorna Pegram. 1970. 4.95 (ISBN 0-87645-024-9). Gambit.

Game of Patience. Lorna Pegram. LC 78-118216. 1970. 4.95 o.p. (ISBN 0-87645-024-9). Gambit.

Game of Secrets. Thomas Wiseman. LC 78-26971. 9.95. Delacorte Press.

Game of Shadows. Marianne Ruuth. (Ace gothic). 1974. (pbk.) 0.95. Ace Books.

Game of Soldiers. Stuart Brooke Jackman. LC 81-14950. (Illus.). 1982. 11.95 (ISBN 0-689-11237-8). Atheneum.

Game of Statues. Anne Stevenson, pseud. (Fawcett crest book). 1974. (pbk.) 1.25. Fawcett.

Game of Statues. Anne Stevenson, pseud. LC 71-175255. 1972. 6.95. Putnam.

Game of Survival. Marijane Meaker. LC 68-20118. 1968. New American Library.

Game of the Golden Ball. Elizabeth Johnson & Johnson, Adrian. LC 10-9917. 1910. 1.50. The Macaulay Company.

Game of Titans: A Novel. Gary Alan Ruse. LC 76-27370. 8.95 (ISBN 0-13-346080-0). Prentice-Hall.

Game of Troy. Jon Ewbank Manchip White. LC 70-149003. (MW suspense). 1971. 4.95. McKay.

Game of Wits. J. Healey & B. Cassiday. 1973. 6.95 o.p. (ISBN 0-679-50421-4). McKay.

Game of Wits. John J Healy. LC 75-20275. 1975. 8.95 (ISBN 0-679-50559-8). D. McKay Co.

Game of X. Robert Sheckley. LC 65-219363. 3.95. Delacorte Dist. Dial.

Game Park Holiday. George Orwell. 1967. pap. 0.50 o.p. Northwestern U Pr.

Game Plan. Casey Taylor. LC 75-6830. 1975. 5.95 (ISBN 0-689-30486-2). Atheneum.

Game Plan. Casey Taylor. 1976. 1.50 (ISBN 0-449-22943-2). Fawcett Crest.

Game Player. Rafael Yglesias. LC 77-76270. 1978. 7.95 (ISBN 0-385-12448-1). Doubleday.

Game Players of Titan. Philip K Dick. LC 79-1290. (Gregg Press science fiction series). 1979. 13.95 (ISBN 0-8398-2482-3). Gregg Press.

Game Poachers & Other Stories. Ralph F. Guire & Mavis Guire. 1982. 6.95 (ISBN 0-533-04755-2). Vantage.

Game, Set, and Danger. Anna Clarke. LC 81-43135. 1981. 10.95. Published for the Crime Club by Doubleday.

Game That Must Be Lost. Adrian Stokes. 160p. 1975. 8.95x o.p. (ISBN 0-85635-069-9). Dufour.

Game Without Rules. Michael Francis Gilbert. LC 67-13703. 1967. Harper & Row.

Gamekeeper's Gallows. John Buxton Hilton. LC 77-364239. 1976. 2.95 (ISBN 0-333-19880-8). Macmillan.

Gamemaker. David Keith Cohler. LC 79-6035. 1980. 10.00 (ISBN 0-385-15650-2). Doubleday.

Gameplayers of Zan. M. A Foster. 1977. 1.95 (ISBN 0-87997-287-4). DAW Books.

Games. Hugh Atkinson. LC 68-11009. 1968. Simon and Schuster.

Games. Bill Pronzini. LC 76-25413. 7.95 (ISBN 0-399-11588-9). Putnam.

Games. Bill Pronzini. (Fawcett Crest Book). 1978. 1.75 (ISBN 0-449-23484-3). Fawcett Books.

Games at Twilight. Anita Desai. LC 79-4943. 1980. 9.95i (ISBN 0-06-011079-1, HarpT). Har-Row.

Games at Twilight. Anita Desai. 144p. 1983. pap. 3.95 (ISBN 0-14-005348-4). Penguin.

Games Cats Play & Other Scrivelsby Tales. Marshall E. Dimock. LC 77-14515. 7.95. Countryman Press.

Games in Room 401. Gus Stevens. pap. 1.95 o.s.i. (OPH-248, Ophelia). Olympia.

Games in the Darkening Air. Peter Boynton. LC 66-12356. 1966. Harcourt. Brace & World.

Games Murderers Play. Carleton Carpenter. 1973. 0.75. Curtis Books.

Games of Chance. Peter Delacorte. LC 80-5192. 10.95. Seaview Books.

Games of Chance. Thomas Hinde. LC 66-29207. (Two complete novels). 1966. 8.95 o.s.i. (ISBN 0-8149-0119-0). Vanguard.

Games of Chance: The Interviewer, the Investigator, by Thomas Hinde. Thomas Willes Chitty. LC 66-29207. 1967. 4.95. Vanguard.

Games of Chance with Strangers. Malissa Redfield, pseud. LC 76-144290. 1971. 5.95. Doubleday.

Games of 'Eighty. W. H. Mefford. (Orig.). 1980. pap. 1.95 o.s.i. (ISBN 0-505-51494-X). Tower Bks.

Games of Love and War. Dinah Brooke. LC 77-354271. 1976. 3.50 (ISBN 0-224-01196-0). Cape.

Games Psyborgs Plays. Pierre Barbet, pseud. (Science Fiction Ser.). 1973. pap. 0.95 o.p. (UQ1087). DAW Bks.

Games. Res., Background by Phillip Knightley. Hugh Atkinson. (N3951). 1968. Bantam.

Games Satan Plays. Stan Baldwin. 32p. 1971. pap. 0.59 o.p. (ISBN 0-88207-351-6). Victor Bks.

Games They Paid Michael to Play. Elizabeth Shinn Terrell. LC 79-14344. 1979. 10.95 (ISBN 0-87949-149-3). Ashley Books.

Games Were Coming. Michael Anthony. LC 68-16269. 1968. Houghton Mifflin.

Gamesman. Barry N Malzberg. 1975. (pbk.) 1.25 (ISBN 0-671-80174-0). Pocket Books.

Gamester. Elizabeth Chater. (Orig.). 1980. pap. 1.75 (ISBN 0-449-50047-0, Coventry). Fawcett.

Gamester. Rafael Sabatini. LC 49-10448. 1949. Houghton Mifflin. Co.

Gamesters. Henry Christopher Bailey. LC 19-6414. 1919. 1.75. E. P. Dutton and Company.

Gamesters. Peter De Polnay. LC 62-18734. 1962. Walker.

Gamiani or Two Nights of Excess. Alfred De Musset. (O.s.i.). 1968. pap. 0.95 o.s.i. (A349N, Award). Univ Pub & Dist.

Gamiani, or Two Nights of Excess see Libertine Reader.

Gaming Lady. Alden Hatch. LC 31-17273. Farrar & Rinehart, Incorporated.

Gandle Follows His Nose. Heywood Campbell Broun. LC 26-9261. 1926. Boni & Liveright.

Gang. Joseph Anthony. LC 21-20268. 1921. H. Holt and Company.

Gang. Herbert Kastle. Dell.

Gang: A Story of the Middle West. Fred Brasted. LC 10-9259. 1910. 1.25. The Griffith & Rowland Press.

Gang of Ten. Erika Mann. LC 42-50077. 1942. L. B. Fischer.

Gang-Smasher. Hugh Clevely. LC 30-8174. E. J. Clode, Inc.

Gang That Couldn't Shoot Straight. Jimmy Breslin. LC 71-83232. 1969. 5.95. Viking Press.

Gang War. Frank Colter. (Death squad#1). 1975. (pbk.) 1.25. Belmont Tower Books.

Gang War. Paul Kropp. LC 82-12928. (Encounter Ser.). (Illus.). 96p. 1982. pap. text ed. 3.95 (ISBN 0-88436-963-3); wkbk. 1.20 (ISBN 0-88436-967-6). EMC.

Gang Wars of the Twenties. Allen. (Illus.). pap. 1.95 o.p. (6376). Brandon.

Gang Way. Marcus Van Heller, pseud. (Orig.). 1968. pap. 1.95 o.s.i. (OPH-213, Ophelia). Olympia.

Gangland Killers. George Carpozi, Jr. (Orig.). 1979. pap. 1.95 (ISBN 0-532-19256-7). Woodhill.

Gangrene. Jef Geeraerts. LC 74-4806. 1975. 7.95 (ISBN 0-670-33400-6). Viking Press.

Gang's All Here. Harvey Hassall Smith. LC 41-6550. 1941. Princeton University Press.

Gangster Girl. Jack Lait. LC 31-113. Grosset & Dunlap.

Gangsters. David Chandler. 1976. 1.75. Pyramid Publications.

Gangsters: A Novel. David Chandler. LC 74-8727. 1975. (ISBN 0-688-00314-1). Morrow.

Gangsters' Glory. Edward Phillips Oppenheim. LC 31-28129. 1931. Little, Brown, and Company.

Gangway. Donald E Westlake & Brian Wynne Garfield. LC 72-97504. 1973. 5.95 (ISBN 0-87131-116-X). M. Evans; Distributed in Association with J. B. Lippincott, Philadelphia.

Gangway for Love. Vida Hurst. LC 42-141204. 1942. Gramercy Publishing Co.

Gannon's Line. John Whitlatch (ISBN 0-671-80743-9). Pocket Books.

Gantenbein. Max Frisch. LC 82-48033. (Harvest/HBJ book). 1982. 7.95 (ISBN 0-15-634407-6). Harcourt Brace Jovanovich.

Ganton & Co. A Story of Chicago Commercial and Social Life. Arthur Jerome Eddy. LC 74-22780. (Labor Movement in Fiction and Non-Fiction). (Illus.). 1976. 28.50 (ISBN 0-404-58421-7). AMS Press.

Ganton & Co. A Story of Chicago Commercial and Social Life. Arthur Jerome Eddy. LC 8-28058. 1908. A. C. McClurg & Co.

Ganymede Takeover. Philip K Dick & Ray Nelson. 1977. 1.50. Ace.

Gap in the Curtain. John Buchan. LC 32-20526. 1932. Houghton Mifflin Company.

Gap in the Garden. Vanda Wathen- Bartlett. LC 3-7661. 1903. John Lane.

Gap in the Wall. Gabrielle Estivals. 1963. 4.95 o.p. Knopf.

Gaptown Law. Louis Trimble. LC 52-6275. 1951-1952. Macrae Smith.

Garan the Eternal. Norton. 1972. 6.50. Fantasy Pub Co.

Garan the Eternal. Andre Norton, pseud. Date not set. 6.50 (ISBN 0-87505-274-6). Borden.

Garan the Eternal. Andre Norton, pseud. (Science Fiction Ser.). 1973. pap. 1.50 (ISBN 0-87997-431-1, UW1431). DAW Bks.

Garan the Eternal. Andre Norton. 1973. (pbk.) 0.95. Daw Books.

Garbage & the Goddess. Bubba Free John. LC 74-19796. 1974. pap. 4.95 o.p. (ISBN 0-913922-10-2). Dawn Horse Pr.

Garbage World. Charles Platt. 1977. pap. 1.25 o.s.i. (ISBN 0-505-51164-9). Tower Bks.

Garber of Thunder Gorge. John Mersereau & Chambers, E. Whitman. LC 24-14709. Small, Maynard & Company.

Garbo & the Night Watchman. Alistair Cooke. 1972. 7.95 o.p. (ISBN 0-07-012490-6). McGraw.

Garcilago. John Breckenridge Ellis. LC 1-31433. 1901. A. C. McClurt & Co.

Garda. Rose Cecil O'Neill. LC 29-8724. 1929. Doubleday, Doran & Company, Inc.
Garde a Vous! (On Guard!) A Novel... John Dimmock Newsom. LC 28-10801. 1928. Doubleday, Doran & Company, Inc.
Garde du Coeur. Francoise Sagan, pseud. 13.95. French & Eur.
Garde of Happy Valley: A Mid-West Tale. William Henry Collier Taylor. LC 25-35529. Retail Lumberman Publishing Co.
Garden. Yves Berger. LC 63-19572. 1963. G. Braziller.
Garden. Hollis Spurgeon Summers. LC 72-79713. 1972. 6.95 (ISBN 0-06-014174-3). Harper & Row.
Garden: A Novel. Leonard Alfred George Strong. LC 31-16666. 1931. A. A. Knopf.
Garden, Ashes. Danilo Kis. LC 75-15769. 1975. 7.95 (ISBN 0-15-134287-3). Harcourt Brace Jovanovich.
Garden, Ashes. Danilo Kis. LC 78-7508. (Harvest/HBJ book). 1978. 2.95 (ISBN 0-15-634548-X). Harcourt Brace Jovanovich.
Garden at 19. Edgar Jepson. LC 10-12780. 1910. 1.50. Wessels & Bissell Co.
Garden Club Murders. Delia Van Deusen. LC 41-7871. The Bobbs-Merrill Company.
Garden Game. Jon Manchip White. LC 73-22662. 1973-1974. 6.50 (ISBN 0-672-51960-7). Bobbs-Merrill.
Garden in Iran. Georgia Dunn. LC 41-2313. Fortuny's, Publishers, Inc.
Garden in Pink. Blanche Elizabeth Wade. LC 5-375817. 1905. A. C. McClurg and Company.
Garden in the Sky. Jean Carew. LC 42-3944. 1941. Aroadia House, Inc.
Garden Murder Case: A Philo Vance Story. Willard Huntington Wright. LC 35-27366. 1935. C. Scribner's Sons.
Garden Oats. Faith Baldwin. 1976. Repr. of 1929 ed. lib. bdg. 15.45x (ISBN 0-88411-607-7). Amereon Ltd.
Garden Oats. Faith Baldwin Cuthrell. LC 74-82147. 1974. Aeonian Press.
Garden Oats. Faith Baldwin Cuthrell. LC 29-54113. 1929. Dodd, Mead & Company.
Garden Oats. Alice Herbert. LC 14-2273. 1914. John Lane.
Garden of a Commuter's Wife. Mabel Wright. LC 1-27071. 1901. The Macmillan Company.
Garden of Adonis. Caroline Gordon. LC 70-164530. 1971-1972. 7.00 (ISBN 0-8154-0399-2). Cooper Square Publishers.
Garden of Adonis. Caroline Gordon. LC 37-33903. 1937. C. Scribner's Sons.
Garden of Allah. Robert Smythe Hichens. LC 5-2776. F. A. Stokes Company.
Garden of Allah. Robert Smythe Hichens. LC 7-25672. 1905. F. A. Stokes Company.
Garden of Allah. Robert Smythe Hichens. LC 24-149266. 1907. Grosset & Dunlap.
Garden of Allah. Robert Smythe Hichens. LC 7-80108. 1907. F. A. Stokes Company.
Garden of Allah. Robert Smythe Hichens. LC 41-88242. 1911. Frederick A. Stokes Company.
Garden of Armida. Anne Sheldon Coombs. LC 11-10560. Cassell & Company, Limited.
Garden of Cucumbers. Poyntz Tyler. LC 59-5715. 1960. Random House.
Garden of Delights. Roch Carrier. Tr. by Sheila Fischman from Fr. (Anansi Fiction Ser.: No. 38). 173p. (Orig.). 1978. pap. 7.95 (ISBN 0-88784-066-3, Pub. by Hse Anansi Pr Canada). U of Toronto Pr.
Garden of Desire. rev. ed May Christie. LC 26-7119. Grosset & Dunlap.
Garden of Doctor Persuasion. Francis Neilson. LC 42-23430. 1942. C. C. Nelson Publishing Company.
Garden of Doctor Persuasion: A Novel for the Practical Mystic. Francis Nielson. 6.50 o.s.i. Roseman.
Garden of Dreams. Clarice Vallette McCauley. LC 12-21405. 1912. A. C. McClurg & Co.
Garden of Earthly Delights. Joyce Carol Oates. LC 67-19288. 1967. Vanguard Press.
Garden of Earthly Pleasures. Ary C. Phillips. 1970. pap. 0.95 o.p. (B95-1072). Belmont-Tower.
Garden of Eden. Frederick Faust. LC 63-20473. 1963. Dodd, Mead.
Garden of Eden. Frederick Faust. LC 63-20473. 1976. (pbk.) 1.25. Warner Books.
Garden of Eden. Blanche Willis Howard Von Teuffel. LC 2156. 1900. C. Scribner's Sons.
Garden of Eden, U.S.A. A Very Possible Story. William Henry Bishop. LC 6-12714. 1895. C. H. Kerr & Company.
Garden of Eros. Dorothy Bryant. LC 78-73215. 1979. pap. 6.00 (ISBN 0-931688-03-5). Ata Bks.
Garden of Evil. Ruth Calif. 1977. pap. 1.95 (ISBN 0-89041-164-6, 3164). Major Bks.
Garden of Evil. Bram Stoker. Repr. 12.95x (ISBN 0-88411-133-4). Amereon Ltd.
Garden of Faith. Clifton E Re Vere. LC 17-1013. The McLean Company.
Garden of Fate. Roy Norton. LC 10-16983. 1910. 1.50. W. J. Watt & Company.

Garden of Fear. Robert E. Howard. pap. 4.95x. Wehman.
Garden of Flames. Linda DuBreuil. LC 27-179072. 1927. Frederick A. Stokes Company.
Garden of Ghosts. Marilyn Ross. (queen-size gothic). 1974. (pbk.) 1.25. Popular Library.
Garden of Girls: A Story. Marian A Hilton. LC 9-12623. 1909. The Tandy-Thomas Company.
Garden of God. Henry De Vere Stacpoole. LC 23-14803. 1923. 2.00. Dodd, Mead and Company.
Garden of God's. 4th rev. ed. Paul W. Nesbit. (Illus.). 1982. pap. 4.00x (ISBN 0-911746-07-2). Nesbit.
Garden of Grief. Helen Arvonen. (Ace gothic). 1974. (pbk.) 0.95. Ace Books.
Garden of Hope. Audrey McDaniel. (Illus.). 2.95 o.p (ISBN 0-385-00186-X). Doubleday.
Garden of Indra. Michael Alfred Edwin White. LC 12-147858. 1912. Duffield & Company.
Garden of Lies: A Romance. Justus Miles Forman. LC 2-23839. 1902. F. A. Stokes Company.
Garden of Love. Thompson, John Burton. LC 52-5791. 1952. Arco Pub. Co.
Garden of Luzon. Julian Scott Bryan. LC 12-23754. 1.00. R. G. Radger.
Garden of Mars. John Kolyer. LC 75-36483. 1976. pap. 3.75 o.p. (ISBN 0-8283-1673-2). Branden.
Garden of Memories. Henry St. John Cooper. LC 22-6514. 1.75. George H. Doran Company.
Garden of Paradise. Stella Morton. 1981. 18.95x (Pub. by Remploy England). State Mutual Bk.
Garden of Peril: A Story of the African Veld. Cynthia Stockley. LC 24-1973. 1924. G. P. Putnam's Sons.
Garden of Persephone. Cesar J Rotondi. LC 81-14608. 18.95 (ISBN 0-312-31682-8). St Martin's Press.
Garden of Redemption. William E Royden. LC 27-877970. 1927. R. M. McBride & Company.
Garden of Resurrection: Being the Love Story of an Ugly Man. Ernest Temple Thurston. LC 11-28815. 1911. M. Kennerley.
Garden of Romance: Romantic Tales of All Time. Ed. by Ernest Rhys & Ernest Rhys. LC 7-41410. 1897. New Amsterdam Book Company.
Garden of Sand. Earl Thompson. LC 79-126444. 1971. 7.95. Putnam.
Garden of Satan. Claire Vincent. 1973. pap. 0.95 o.s.i. (75-482). Lancer.
Garden of Shadows. Virginia Coffman. 1973. pap. 0.95 o.s.i. (75-476). Lancer.
Garden of Silvery Delights. Sharon Francis. (Second Chance at Love Ser.: No. 42). (Orig.) 1982. pap. 1.75 (ISBN 0-515-06424-6). Jove Pubns.
Garden of Spices. Aylmer Keith Fraser. 1.25. Hodder & Stoughton, George H. Doran Company.
Garden of Spices. Aylmer Keith Fraser. LC 13-17096. 1913. 0.60. Hodder and Stoughton.
Garden of Stones. M. M. Parker. LC 80-13966. 224p. 1980. 8.95 (ISBN 0-396-07858-3). Dodd.
Garden of Swords. Max Pemberton. 1899. Dodd, Mead and Company.
Garden of the Brave in War. Terence O'Donnell. LC 80-14656. 232p. 1980. 10.95 (ISBN 0-89919-016-2). Ticknor & Fields.
Garden of the Finzi-Continis. Giorgio Bassani. LC 77-77261. (Harvest/HBJ book). 1977. 2.95 (ISBN 0-15-634570-6). Harcourt Brace Jovanovich.
Garden of the Finzi-Continis. Tr. from Italian by Isabel Quigly 1st Amer. Ed. Giorgio Bassani. 1965. 4.95. Atheneum.
Garden of the Gods Romance. William Lee Popham. LC 11-32419. 1.00. The World Supply Company.
Garden of the Incubus. John Tigges. 320p. 1982. pap. 3.25 (ISBN 0-8439-1085-2, Leisure Bks). Nordon Pubns.
Garden of the Okapi. Richard A Johns. LC 68-29095. 1968. 2.95. Zondervan Pub. House.
Garden of the Prophet. Kahlil Gibran. LC 33-32404. 1933. A. A. Knopf.
Garden of the Sun: A Novel. Thomas J Powers. LC 11-18561. 1.25. Small, Maynard & Company.
Garden of Tortures see Chinese Torture Garden.
Garden of Unicorns. J. C Conaway. LC 76-8213. 1976. 1.25 (ISBN 0-345-25303-5). Ballantine Books.
Garden of Vision: A Story of Growth. Lily Moresby Adams Beck. LC 29-22425. 1928. Cosmopolitan Book Corporation.
Garden of Weapons. John E Gardner. LC 80-21573. 1981. 11.95. McGraw-Hill.
Garden of Winter. Gordon Eklund. 1980. pap. 1.95 (ISBN 0-425-04568-4). Berkley Pub.
Garden on the Moon. Pierre Boulle. LC 65-10229. 1965. Vanguard Press.
Garden Party. Katherine Mansfield. LC 31-26991. (Half-title: The modern library of the world's best books). 1931. The Modern Library.

Garden Party: And Other Stories. Katherine Mansfield. LC 22-11444. 1922. A. A. Knopf.
Garden Party: And Other Stories. Katherine Mansfield. LC 28-6757. 1923. A. A. Knopf.
Garden Path. Kitty Burns Florey. LC 82-19267. 1983. 16.95 (ISBN 0-399-31019-3). Seaview/Putnam.
Garden Plot. Henry Goldingham. (Roxburghe Club Publications). 1972. Repr. of 1825 ed. text ed. 12.75x o.p (ISBN 0-8277-0819-X). British Bk Ctr.
Garden Shower. Corinne Running. LC 48-5349. 1948. Swallow Press.
Garden State: A Novel. Julian Moynahan. LC 73-5529. 1973. 6.95 (ISBN 0-316-58697-8). Little, Brown.
Garden Street: A Novel. Eric Felderman. LC 76-907. (Illus.). 2.95 (ISBN 0-914974-09-2). Holmgangers Press.
Garden to the Eastward. Harold Lamb. LC 47-30195. 1947. Doubleday & Company, Inc.
Garden to the Sea. 1st American Ed. Philip Toynbee. LC 54-6249. 1954. Doubleday.
Garden Where the Brass Band Played. Simon Vestdijk. LC 64-22596. (Bibliotheca Neerlandica). 1965. London House & Maxwell.
Garden Where the Brass Band Played: Bibliotheca Neerlandica Ser. Simon Vestdijk. Tr. by A. Brotherton. 1965. 10.00x o.s.i. (ISBN 0-8277-0129-2). British Bk Ctr.
Garden Without Flowers. Willa Thompson. LC 57-6525. 1957. Beacon Press.
Garden Without Walls. Coningsby William Dawson. LC 13-19939. 1913. 1.25. H. Holt and Company.
Garden. 1st Ed. Kathrin Perutz. LC 62-7934. 1962. Atheneum.
Gardener of Evil: A Portrait of Baudelaire & His Times. Pierre Loving. Brewer and Warren Inc.
Gardener Who Saw God. Edward James. LC 37-33907. 1937. C. Scribner's Sons.
Gardenia Angel. Doris Knight. LC 47-167584. 1947. Arcadia House, Inc.
Gardenia: The Curious Cat. Laura Beesley Hudgins. LC 48-17536. 1948. Story Book Press.
Gardenias for Sue. Louise Platt Hauck. LC 42-675907. 1942. Dodd,Mead & Company.
Gardens. John Graham Jackson. LC 76-383484. 1976. 3.95 (ISBN 0-920000-02-9). Catalyst.
Gardens Immortal. Curtis G. Gentry. 192p. 1976. 7.50 o.p (ISBN 0-682-48440-7). Exposition.
Gardens of Delight. Ian Watson. 1982. pap. 2.50 (ISBN 0-671-41604-9, Timescape). PB.
Gardens of Omar: Yamile Sous les Cedres. Henry Bordeaux & Stuart, Henry Longan, D. 1928, Tr. LC 24-8792. E. P. Dutton & Company.
Gardens of Silihdar & Other Writings. Zapel Esayian. LC 81-10920. 7.50 (ISBN 0-935102-07-8). Ashod Press.
Gardens of the Casino. Stuart Evans. LC 76-381335. 1976. 4.25 (ISBN 0-09-124630-X). Hutchinson.
Gardens of the World see Collected Works.
Gardens of This World. Henry Blake Fuller. LC 72-84599. 1974. (lib. ed.) 9.50 (ISBN 0-403-02964-3). Scholarly Press.
Gardens of This World. Henry Blake Fuller. LC 29-19020. 1929. A. A. Knopf.
Gardens One to Five. Peter Tate. LC 76-139067. (Doubleday science fiction). 1971. 4.95. Doubleday.
Gardner Street. Amy Allison. (O.s.i.). pap. 3.00 o.s.i. (ISBN 0-910266-32-8). Bk Page.
Garfield at Large. Jim Davis, pseud. 1981. pap. 4.95 (ISBN 0-345-29796-2). Ballantine.
Garfield Gains Weight. Jim Davis, pseud. 128p. (Orig.) 1981. pap. 4.95 (ISBN 0-345-28844-0). Ballantine.
Garfield Honor. Frank Yerby. LC 61-15505. 1961. Dial Press.
Garfield Honor. Frank Yerby. 1973. (pbk) 1.50. Dell.
Gargantua and Pantagruel. Francois Rabelais. Tr. by Thomas Urquhart & Peter Anthony Motteux. Charles Whibley. LC 73-153564. (Series: The Tudor Translations, 1st Ser., V. 24-26.). 1967. AMS Press.
Gargantua and Pantagruel: Selections. Tr., Ed. by Floyd Gray. Francois Rabelais. Ed. by Floyd Francis Gray. LC 66-12976. (Crofts classics). Appleton.
Gargoyle Conspiracy. Marvin H Albert. LC 74-18777. 1975. 7.95 (ISBN 0-385-08562-1). Doubleday.
Gargoyle Conspiracy. Marvin H Albert. 1976. 1.95. Dell Publishing Co.
Gargoyle Conspiracy. Marvin H Albert. (Dell book). 1979. 1.95 (ISBN 0-440-15239-9). Dell Pub. Co.
Gargoyles. Thomas Bernhard. LC 70-106630. 1970. 5.95. Knopf.
Gargoyles. Ben Hecht. LC 22-18299. Boni and Liveright.
Garh City. Robert Nichols. LC 77-13196. (His Daily lives in Nghsi-Altai; book 2). 1978. 3.95 (ISBN 0-8112-0654-8). New Directions Pub. Corp.

Garibaldi and the New Italy... Ricarda Octavia Huch & Phillips, Mrs. Catherine Alison, 1884- Tr. LC 28-21745. 1928-29. A. A. Knopf.
Garies and Their Friends. Frank J Webb. LC 69-18595. (Afro-American Culture Series). (American Negro, his history and literature.). 1969. Arno Press.
Garies and Their Friends. Frank J Webb. LC 71-144700. 1971. (ISBN 0-404-06884-7). AMS Press.
Garland of Bays. Gwyn Jones. LC 38-33946. 1938. The Macmillan Company.
Garland of Country Song. Sabine Baring-Gould. LC 76-16147. 1976. Repr. of 1895 ed. lib. bdg. 15.00 (ISBN 0-8414-3311-9). Folcroft.
Garland of Defeat. Florence Mary Bennett Anderson. LC 27-17792. 1927. H. Vinal Limited.
Garland of Straw. Sylvia Townsend Warner. LC 43-13072. 1943. The Viking Press.
Garland of Straw: Twenty-Eight Stories. Sylvia Townsend Warner. LC 75-38726. (Short story index reprint series). 1972. (ISBN 0-8369-4139-X). Books for Libraries Press.
Garlic, Grapes, & a Pinch of Heroin. Elaine Turner. 1978. pap. 1.50 (ISBN 0-532-15301-4). Woodhill.
Garlic in My Shoes. Marion Sherrard Oneal. 1969. 4.00 o.p (ISBN 0-8059-1330-0). Dorrance.
Garlic Kid. Thomas Starling, pseud. LC 77-91896. 1.95 (ISBN 0-914864-01-7). Spindrift Press.
Garlic Tree. Ellen Bromfield Geld. LC 78-89093. 1970. 6.95. Doubleday.
Garment. Catherine Cookson. (Signet book.). 1974. (pbk.) 1.25. New American Library.
Garment District Girls. Warren Bisig. 192p. (Orig.). 1973. pap. 1.95 o.p (ISBN 0-87056-288-6, 6288). Brandon.
Garments of Caean. Barrington J Bayley. LC 74-33675. 1976. 5.95 (ISBN 0-385-04397-X). Doubleday.
Garnelle: Or The Rover's Oath of Blood. An Exciting Tale of the Ocean and the Land and Other Stories. Charles Powell Bickley & Roberts, Edwin F. LC 6-129053. 1853. Garrett & Co.
Garnered Sheaves. Elizabeth Holaday Emerson. LC 48-791058. 1948. Longmans, Green.
Garnered Sheaves. An Intensely Interesting Narration of the Good Deeds of a Young Lady of Wealth and Fashion. Sherman N Aspinwall & Parker, Theodore, 1810-1860. LC 6-4531. 1886. W. W. Hart, Printer.
Garnet. Petra Leigh. 1978. 2.25 (ISBN 0-446-82788-6). Warner Books.
Garnet Bracelet. Aleksandr Ivanovich Kuprin. 379p. 1982. pap. 4.00 (ISBN 0-8285-2288-X, Pub. by Progress Pubs USSR). Imported Pubns.
Garonsky Missile. Alan Caillou, pseud. (Tobin's War Series #7). 1976. (pbk.) 1.25 (ISBN 0-523-00798-1). Pinnacle Books.
Garret Van Horn: Or, The Beggar on Horseback. John S. Sauzade. LC 8-1835. 1863. Carleton.
Garretson Chronicle. Gerald Warner Brace. 1964. pap. 1.65x (ISBN 0-393-00272-1, Norton Lib). Norton.
Garretson Chronicle: A Novel. Gerald Warner Brace. LC 47-4753. 1947. W. W. Norton.
Garrick Year. Margaret Drabble. 1977. 1.95 (ISBN 0-445-04018-1). Popular Library.
Garrick Year: A Novel. Margaret Drabble. LC 65-14949. 1965. bds., 3.95. Morrow.
Garrick's Pupil: By Augustin Filon. Pierre Marie Augustin Filon & Prichard, J. V., Tr. LC 6-41206. 1893. A. C. McClurg & Company.
Garrison Gossip: Gathered in Blankhampton. A Novel. Henrietta Eliza Vaughan Stannard. (Harper's Franklin square library, no. 578). 1887. Harper & Brothers.
Garrison Gossip: Gathered in Blankhampton. A Novel. Henrietta Eliza Vaughan Stannard. 1887. G. Munro.
Garrison Hospital, by Alex Stuart Pseud. Violet Vivian Mann. LC 58-1144. 1958. Arcadia House.
Garrison Tales from Tonquin. James O'Neill. LC 7-24097. 1895. Copeland and Day.
Garrison Tangle. Charles King. LC 7-12230. 1896. F. T. Neely.
Garrison's Finish: A Romance of the Race-Course. William Blair Morton Ferguson. Street & Smith.
Garrison's Finish: A Romance of the Race-Course. William Blair Morton Ferguson. 1907. G. W. Dillingham Company.
Garryowen. Henry De Vere Stacpoole. LC 9-32683. 1909. 1.50. Duffield & Company.
Garston Bigamy. Linn Boyd Porter. LC 7-37772. (On cover: The albatross novels). 1892. G. W. Dillingham.
Garston Murder Case... Henry Christopher Bailey. LC 30-25379. 1930. Pub. for the Crime Club, Inc., by Doubleday, Doran & Company, Inc.
Garth, Able Seaman. Edith Ballinger Price. LC 23-12518. 1923. 1.75. The Century Co.

Garthowen: A Story of a Welsh Homestead. Beynon Puddicombe. LC 2309. 1900. D. Appleton and Company.
Gas. Charles Platt. LC 73-27150. 1970. 1.95. Ophelia Press.
Gas--Drive in: A High-Powered Comedy-Romance That Hits on Every Cylinder. E. J. Rath. LC 25-19432. 1925. G. H. Watt.
Gas Buggy. Robert Paterson. LC 33-33458. 1933. Napier & Noyes, Incorporated.
Gas-House McGinty: A Novel. James Thomas Farrell. LC 33-5767. 1933. The Vanguard Press.
Gas Office. Morgan Lewis Davis. LC 6-30470. Broadway Publishing Co.
Gascoyne. Stanley G. Crawford. LC 66-10465. 4.95. Putnam.
Gaseoigne's "Ghost" A Novel. George Brown Burgin. LC 6-18660. 1896. Harper & Brothers.
Gashlycrumb Tinies. Edward Gorey. 1981. 5.95 (ISBN 0-396-08007-3). Dodd.
Gaslight. Patrick Hamilton. pap. 0.60 o.p. (53-333). Paperback Lib.
Gaslight Sonatas. Fannie Hurst. LC 18-7293. 1918. 1.40. Harper & Brothers.
Gasoline: The Automotive Adventures of Charlie Bates. James D Houston. LC 79-28425. (Illus.). 1980. 8.95 (ISBN 0-88496-144-3). Capra Press.
Gasoline Wars. Jean Thompson. LC 79-19579. (Illinois Short Fiction Ser.). 1979. 11.95 (ISBN 0-252-00782-4); pap. 4.95 (ISBN 0-252-00783-2). U of Ill Pr.
Gasp: A Novel. Romain Gary, pseud. LC 72-89771. 1973. 6.95 (ISBN 0-399-11090-9). Putnam.
Gaspar Desmond's Passion: Also, Kreutzer Sonata Bearing Fruit. Pauline Grayson. (peerless series, no. 29). 1891. J. S. Ogilvie.
Gaspards of Pine Croft: A Romance of the Windermere. Charles William Gordon. LC 23-16463. 1923. George H. Doran Company.
Gasparilla Story: A Life of Jose Gaspar, the Pirate of Florida, with Frequent Reference to History. Jack Beater. LC 53-16717.
Gasteropod. Maggie Ross. LC 69-15655. 1969. 5.95. Viking Press.
Gaston De Blondeville: A Romance. St. Alban's Abbey: a Metrical Tale with Some Poetical Pieces. Ann Ward Radcliffe. LC 76-473537. (Anglistica & Americana; 160). 1976. (ISBN 3-487-05904-5). Olms.
Gaston De Blondeville: Or, The Court of Henry III Keeping Festival in Ardenne; a Romance. Ann Ward Radcliffe. LC 71-131337. (Gothic novels). 1972. (ISBN 0-405-00815-5). Arno Press.
Gaston De Blondeville, Or, the Court of Henry 3rd, Keeping Festival in Ardenne, 2 Vols. Ann Ward Radcliffe. LC 71-131337. (Gothic Novels Ser). 1972. Repr. of 1826 ed. Set. 38.00 (ISBN 0-405-00815-5). Ayer Co.
Gaston De Latour: An Unfinished Romance. library ed. reprinted. ed. Walter Horatio Pater. Ed. by Charles Lancelot Shadwell. LC 68-70815. 1967. Blackwell.
Gaston De Latour: An Unfinished Romance. Walter Horatio Pater. Ed. by Shadwell, Charles Lancelot. LC 4-15329. 1896. The Macmillan Company.
Gaston Olaf. Henry Oyen. LC 17-25377. George H. Doran Company.
Gastronomic Murder. Alexandra Roudybush. LC 73-79707. 1973. 4.95 (ISBN 0-385-03926-3). Published for the Crime Club by Doubleday.
Gat Heat. Richard S Prather. (55021). 1968. Pocket Bks.
Gat Heat: By Richard S. Prather. Richard S Prather. LC 67-13573. 1967. 3.95. Trident.
Gate. James Noble Gifford. LC 42-20329. 1942. Arcadia House.
Gate. Warren Howard. LC 42-20329. 1942. Arcadia House, Inc.
Gate: A Novel. Peter Sourian. LC 65-210383. (Helen and Kurt Wolff bk.). 5.75. Harcourt.
Gate Is Down: A Novel of the Alabama Hills. William H Yancey. LC 56-9574. 1956. Exposition Press.
Gate Marked "Private". Ethel May Dell. LC 28-24953. 1928. G. P. Putnam's Sons.
Gate of a Strange Field. Harold Heslop. LC 29-8004. 1929. Brentano's, Ltd.
Gate of a Strange Field. Harold Heslop. LC 29-142988. 1929. D. Appleton and Company.
Gate of Eden. William Corlett. LC 75-16892. 1975. 6.95 (ISBN 0-87888-090-9). Bradbury Press.
Gate of Fulfillment. Knowles Ridsdale. LC 20-6634. 1920. 1.50. G. P. Putnam's Sons.
Gate of Happy Sparrows. Daniele Vare. LC 37-19344. 1937. Doubleday, Doran & Co., Inc.
Gate of Heaven. Ralph M McInerny. LC 74-15877. 1975. 7.95 (ISBN 0-06-012941-7). Harper & Row.
Gate of Heaven. Ralph M. McInerny. 1976. (pbk.) 1.75 (ISBN 0-380-00568-9). Avon.
Gate of Hell. Alfred Coppel. LC 67-20305. 1967. Harcourt, Brace & World.
Gate of Horn. Beulah Marie Dix. LC 12-17665. 1912. 1.25. Duffield & Company.
Gate of Ivory. Sidney Lauer Nyburg. LC 20-19577. 1920. A. A. Knopf.
Gate of Ivory, Gate of Horn. Philip Craig. LC 69-20068. 1969. 4.50. Published for the Crime Club by Doubleday.
Gate of Ivrel. C. J. Cherryh. (Science Fiction Ser.). 1976. pap. 1.75 (ISBN 0-87997-615-2, UE1615). DAW Bks.
Gate of Ivrel. C. J Cherryh. (Daw Science Fiction#188). 1976. (pbk.) 1.25. Daw Books.
Gate of the Kiss: A Romance in the Days of Hezekiah, King of Judah. John William Harding. LC 2-13791. 1902. Lothrop Publishing Company.
Gate of Time. Philip Jose Farmer. (Osi). 1970. pap. 0.75 o.s.i. (B75-2016). Belmont-Tower.
Gate Swings Open. Daisy Fisher. LC 32-16961. 1932. Doubleday, Doran & Company, Inc.
Gate Through the Mountain. Hugh Pendexter. LC 29-707694. The Bobbs-Merrill Company.
Gate to the Sea. Winifred Bryher. LC 58-11776. 1958. Pantheon.
Gatehouse. Richard Dohrman. (Dell 2812). 1973. 1.50. Dell.
Gatehouse. Richard Dohrman. LC 71-164848. 1971. 7.95. Delacorte Press.
Gateless Barrier. Mary St. Leger Kingsley Harrison. LC 4578. 1900. Dodd, Mead & Company.
Gates Ajar. Elizabeth Steward Phelps. Ed. by Helen S. Smith. LC 64-16068. (John Harvard Library). 1964. 10.00x (ISBN 0-674-34150-3). Harvard U Pr.
Gates Ajar. Elizabeth Stuart Phelps Ward. LC 64-16068. (John Harvard Library). 1964. Belknap Press of Harvard University Press.
Gates Ajar. Elizabeth Stuart Phelps Ward. LC 34-255117. 1870. Fields, Osgood, & Co.
Gates Ajar. 80th thousand. ed. Elizabeth Stuart Phelps Ward. LC 4-16477. 1896. Houghton, Mifflin and Company.
Gates Ajar. Elizabeth Stuart Phelps H. D. Ward Ward. LC 8-33113. 1869. Fields, Osgood, & Co.
Gates Between. Elizabeth Stuart Phelps Ward. LC 8-33112. 1887. Houghton, Mifflin and Company.
Gates of Aulis. Gladys Schmitt. LC 42-14052. 1942. The Dial Press.
Gates of Brass. McCready Huston. LC 56-819378. 1956. Lippincott.
Gates of Bronze. Haim Hazaz. LC 74-15463. 1975. 7.95 (ISBN 0-8276-0059-3). Jewish Publication Society of America.
Gates of Chance. William Gilbert Van Tassel Sutphen. LC 4-11530. 1904. Harper & Brothers.
Gates of Creation. Philip Jose Farmer. 224p. 1981. pap. 2.50 (ISBN 0-441-27389-0). Ace Bks.
Gates of Dawn. Fergus Hume. LC 7-5797. (Lettered on cover: Neely's international library). 1894. F. T. Neely.
Gates of Destiny. Edna G Cornell. LC 30-15404. 1930. Meador Publishing Company.
Gates of Disappearance. G. P. Skratz. LC 81-4386. (Illus.). 60p. 1982. 14.00 (ISBN 0-916906-36-1); pap. 7.50 (ISBN 0-916906-37-X). Konglomerati.
Gates of Eden. A Story of Endeavour. Annie S Swan Smith. LC 8-8196. 1890. Cranston and Stowe.
Gates of Eden. 1st American Ed. Allan Campbell McLean. LC 62-8057. 1962. Harcourt, Brace & World.
Gates of Epidorus: Cap Kennedy No. 14. Gregory Kern. (Science Fiction Ser). pap. 0.95 o.p. (UQ1159). DAW Bks.
Gates of Fire. Elwyn M Chamberlain. LC 77-18319. 1978. 12.95 (ISBN 0-394-50162-4). Grove Press: Distributed by Random House.
Gates of Fire. Elwyn M Chamberlain. 1979. 2.75 (ISBN 0-553-12113-8). Bantam Books.
Gates of Flame. Roe Raymond Hobbs. LC 6-37928. 1906. The Neale Publishing Company.
Gates of Heaven. Paul Preuss. 224p. 1980. pap. 2.25 (ISBN 0-553-20063-1). Bantam.
Gates of Hell. Harrison Evans Salisbury. LC 75-10291. 1975. 10.00 (ISBN 0-394-49953-0). Random House.
Gates of Hell. Harrison Evans Salisbury. (Signet book). (Bernard Geis associates book). 1976. 2.25 (ISBN 0-451-07213-8). New American Library.
Gates of Hell. Calder Willingham. LC 51-11152. 1951. Vanguard Press.
Gates of Hell: An Historical Novel of the Present Day. Erik Maria Von Kuhnelt-Leddihn. Tr. by Collins, I. J. LC 34-6716. 1934. Sheed & Ward, Inc.
Gates of Ivory, the Gates of Horn. With a Foreword by Charles Humboldt. Thomas McGrath. LC 58-14524. 1957. Mainstream Publishers.
Gates of Kamt. Emmuska Orczy. 1907. Dodd, Mead & Company.
Gates of Kunarja. Duncan MacNeil. LC 72-96138. 1973. 6.95 o.p. St Martin.
Gates of Kunarja: An Ogilvie Novel. Duncan MacNeil. LC 72-96138. 1974. 6.95. St. Martin's Press.
Gates of Life. Edwin August Bjorkman. LC 75-144882. 1971. (ISBN 0-403-00868-9). Scholarly Press.
Gates of Life. Bram Stoker. LC 8-14957. Cupples & Leon Company.
Gates of Living. 1st Ed. Josephine Lawrence. LC 55-563755. 1955. Harcourt, Brace.
Gates of Living. 1st Ed. Josephine Lawrence. LC 55-563755. 1957. Harcourt, Brace.
Gates of Morning. Henry De Vere Stacpoole. LC 25-29643. 1925. Dodd, Mead and Company.
Gates of Olivet. Lucille Papin Borden. LC 23-121649. 1922. The Macmillan Company.
Gates of Sagittarius. Roland Cutler. LC 80-10631. 9.95 (ISBN 0-8037-3268-6). Dial Press.
Gates of the Forest. Elie Wiesel. LC 81-16547. 1982. 5.95 (ISBN 0-8052-0698-1). Schocken Books.
Gates of the Forest. Tr. from French by Frances Frenaye. Eliezer Wiesel. LC 66-102610. bds., 4.95. Holt.
Gates of the Mountain. Henry Allen. LC 63-16851. 1963. Random House.
Gates of the Mountains. Henry Wilson Allen. LC 80-13082. (Series: Gregg Press Western Fiction Series.). 1980. 13.95 (ISBN 0-8398-2689-3). Gregg Press.
Gates of the Mountains. Will Henry, pseud. 1980. lib. bdg. 13.95 (ISBN 0-8398-2689-3, Gregg). G K Hall.
Gates of Wrath. Arnold Bennett. LC 74-5322. (Collected Works of Arnold Bennett: Vol. 21). 1976. Repr. of 1903 ed. 19.75 (ISBN 0-518-19102-8). Ayer Co.
Gates Shall Not. E. E. Cleveland. (Horizon Ser.). 96p. 1980. pap. write for info. (ISBN 0-8127-0325-1). Review & Herald.
Gates to the New City. Ed. by Howard Schwartz. 800p. 1982. 12.95 (ISBN 0-380-81091-3, 81091-3). Avon.
Gates to the New City: A Treasury of Modern Jewish Tales. Howard Schwartz. LC 82-11532. 12.95 (ISBN 0-380-81091-3). Avon Books.
Gates Wide Open: Or, Scenes in Another World. George Wood. LC 8-37560. 1869. Lee and Shepard.
Gateway. Ned McCune. 1973. (pbk.) 1.25. Dell.
Gateway. Frederik Pohl. LC 76-10561. 8.95 (ISBN 0-312-31780-8). St. Martin's Press.
Gateway to Empire. Allan W. Eckert. 1982. 20.00 (ISBN 0-316-20821-1). Little.
Gateway to Fortune: By Peter Bourne Pseud. Graham Montague Jeffries. LC 52-9829. 1952. Putnam.
Gateway to Heaven. Sheldon Vanauken. 336p. 1981. pap. 2.95 (ISBN 0-553-14648-3). Bantam.
Gateway to Heaven: A Novel. Sheldon Vaunauken. LC 79-3600. (Illus.). 304p. 1980. 9.95i (ISBN 0-06-068822-X). Har-Row.
Gateway to Hell. Dennis Yates Wheatley. 1973. (pbk.) 1.50. Ballantine Books.
Gateway to Life. Frank Thiess & Lowe-Porter, H. T., Tr. LC 27-22157. 1927. A. A. Knopf.
Gateway to Limbo. Chris Lampton. LC 77-12864. 1979. 7.95 (ISBN 0-385-13142-9). Doubleday.
Gateway to Love. Arlene Hale. (Signet Book). 1977. 1.50 (ISBN 0-451-07803-9). New American Library.
Gateway to the Heart. Debbie Camp. (Orig.). 1980. pap. 1.95 (ISBN 0-532-23208-9). Woodhill.
Gather, Darkness! Fritz Leiber. LC 50-6699. 1950. Pellegrini & Cudahy.
Gather, Darkness! Fritz Leiber. 1975. (pbk.) 1.50 (ISBN 0-345-24585-7). Ballantine Books.
Gather, Darkness! Fritz Leiber. LC 80-23604. (Series: Gregg Press Science Fiction Series). 1980. 14.95 (ISBN 0-8398-2639-7). Gregg Press.
Gather No Moss. Sarah Shears. 1972. 7.95 (ISBN 0-236-17694-3, Pub. by Paul Elek). Merrimack Pub Cir.
Gather No Moss: An Apocryphal Autobiography. Sean O'Hanlon. LC 59-9775. 1959. Harper.
Gather the Stars! Desemea Wilson. LC 30-1704. E. P. Dutton & Co., Inc.
Gather Ye Rosebuds. Jeannette Covert Nolan. LC 46-3701. 1946. D. Appleton-Century Company, Incorporated.
Gathered in: A Novel. Catherine Helen Spence. LC 78-300455. (Australian literary reprints). 1977. 12.00 (ISBN 0-424-00041-5). Sydney University Press.
Gathered into One. William Robertson Davies. 1975. pap. 3.50 o.p. (ISBN 0-8192-1191-5). Morehouse.
Gatherer. Owen Brookes. LC 81-23735. 13.95 (ISBN 0-03-059531-2). Holt, Rinehart and Winston.
Gathering. Virginia Hamilton. 160p. 1981. pap. 1.95 (ISBN 0-380-56135-2, 56135, Flare). Avon.
Gathering at Greystone. Louisa Bronte. LC 76-18869. (Greystone Tavern series). 1976. 9.95 (ISBN 0-89340-001-7). J. Curley.
Gathering at Greystone. Louisa Bronte. LC 75-31538. 1976. 1.50 (ISBN 0-345-24766-3). Ballantine Books.
Gathering Clouds: A Tale of the Days of St. Chrysostom. Frederic William Farrar. LC 6-386613. 1895. Longmans, Green and Co.
Gathering Darkness. 1st Ed. Thomas Michael Gallagher. LC 52-10693. 1952. Bobbs-Merrill.
Gathering Fire. Mary Gilliland. LC 82-13022. 65p. 1982. pap. 5.00 (ISBN 0-87886-119-X). Ithaca Hse.
Gathering Force. Leslie Newman. (O.s.i.). 1974. 7.95 o.s.i. (ISBN 0-671-21850-6). S&S.
Gathering Force: A Novel. Leslie Newman. LC 74-10551. 1974. (ISBN 0-671-21850-6). Simon and Schuster.
Gathering of Evil. Marilyn Ross. 1970. pap. 0.60 o.p. (63-314). Paperback Lib.
Gathering of Ghosts. Roy Lewis. LC 83-2958. 1983. 10.95 (ISBN 0-312-31788-3). St. Martin's Press.
Gathering of Ghosts: A Treasury: Field and Others. Ed. by Seon Manley. LC 74-119787. 1970. 5.95. Funk & Wagnalls.
Gathering of Lambs: A Story from World War II. Gertrude F. Johnson. LC 74-31719. (Illus.). 1975. 5.95 (ISBN 0-570-03241-5). Concordia Pub. House.
Gathering of Rosebuds. Kassandra Hansen. 1972. pap. 1.95 o.s.i. (OPH4024, Ophelia). Olympia.
Gathering of Stones. Richard E. Baker. 150p. (Orig.). (YA) 1981. pap. 3.95 (ISBN 0-939066-01-7). Rapier Pr.
Gathering of the West. John Galt. Ed. by Booth, Bradford Allen. LC 39-11751. 1939. The Johns Hopkins Press.
Gathering of the West. John Galt & Bradford Allen Booth. LC 78-19324. (Johns Hopkins University Press reprints). 1979. 12.00 (ISBN 0-405-10585-1). Arno Press.
Gathering of Thoughts. Naomi Freggiaro. LC 78-6908. 1978. 3.95 (ISBN 0-89293-018-7). Beta Book Co.
Gathering of Wolves. Michael Hammonds. LC 74-33741. 1975. 5.95 (ISBN 0-385-09690-9). Doubleday.
Gathering of Wolves. Michael Hammonds. 1976. 1.25 (ISBN 0-8439-0039-3). Leisure Books.
Gathering Passion. Julie Davis. (Leisure Book). 1.95 (ISBN 0-8439-0527-1). Nordon Pubns.
Gathering Storm: A Story of the Black Belt. Dorothy Myra Page. LC 32-339948. 1932. International Publishers.
Gathering Wave. Alvaro Cardona-Hine. pap. 0.75 o.p. (ISBN 0-8040-0132-4). Swallow.
Gaucho". Eustace Hale Ball & Thomas, Elton. LC 28-5530. Grosset & Dunlap.
Gaudeamus Igitur. Alois Jirasek. LC 76-58010. 1977. 11.75 (ISBN 0-8371-9469-5). Greenwood Press.
Gaudentius: A Story of the Colosseu,. Gerald Stanley Davies & Society for Promoting Christian Knowledge London, General Literature Committee. LC 35-35479. Society for Promoting Christian Knowledgez.
Gaudy. John Innes Mackintosh Stewart. LC 74-23150. 1975. 6.95 (ISBN 0-393-08712-3). Norton.
Gaudy Empire: A Novel. Alfred Neumann. Tr. by Paul, Eden. LC 37-6526. 1937. A. A. Knopf.
Gaudy Image. William Talsman. 1968. pap. 1.75 o.s.i. (302, Travellers Comp). Olympia.
Gaudy Night. Dorothy Leigh Sayers. LC 36-27125. Harcourt, Brace and Company.
Gaudy Night. large print ed. Dorothy Leigh Sayers. LC 81-6792. 1981. 18.95 (ISBN 0-8161-3295-X). G.K. Hall.
Gaudy Place. Fred Chappell. LC 72-91834. 1973. 5.95 (ISBN 0-15-134590-2). Harcourt Brace Jovanovich.
Gaudy Shadows. John Brunner. (Orig.). 1971. pap. 0.95 o.p. (95158). Beagle Bks.
Gaudy's Ladies. Clark McMeekin. LC 48-6756. 1948. Appleton-Century-Crofts.
Gauge of Deception. Holly Roth. LC 63-17271. 1963. Published for the Crime Club by Doubleday.
Gaul Is Divided: An Historical Novel of Caesar's Time and of Vercingetorix, Arvernian Chieftain. Esther Fisher Brown. LC 52-9951. 1952. William-Frederick Press.
Gaunt Woman. John Blackburn. LC 62-169627. 1962. M. S. Mill Co.
Gaunt Woman. Edmund Gilligan. LC 42-36433. 1943. C. Scribner's Sons.
Gaunt Women. John Blackburn. pap. 0.60 o.p. Lancer.
Gauntlet. James Howell Street. LC 45-9403. 1945. Doubleday, Doran & Co., Inc.
Gauntlet. James Howell Street. LC 47-24300. 1947. The Sun Dial Press.
Gauntlet: A Novel. Michael Butler & Dennis Shryack. 1.95 (ISBN 0-446-89470-2). Warner Books.
Gauntlet of Alceste. Herbert Joseph Moorhouse. LC 22-95745. The James A McCann Company.
Gauri. Mulk Raj Anand. LC 76-911147. 7.50. Orient Paperbacks.

Gaut Gurley: Or, the Trappers of Umbagog. A Tale of Border Life. Daniel Pierce Thompson. 1857. J. P. Jewett and Company.
Gautran: Or, The House of White Shadows. Benjamin Leopold Farjeon. (Lovell's library. v. 5, no. 243). 1883. J. W. Lovell Company.
Gaverocks. A Tale of the Cornish Coast. Sabine Baring-Gould. LC 3-28162. 1888. J. B. Lippincott Company.
Gavin Douglas. John Sillars. LC 24-17902. Small, Maynard and Company.
Gavroche: the Gamin of Paris. From "Les Miserables". Victor Marie Hugo & Pyle, M. C., Tr. LC 7-5884. Porter & Coates.
Gay. Ruth Pine Furniss. LC 28-207298. Harcourt, Brace and Company.
Gay Agony. Harold Alfred Manhood. LC 31-14059. 1931. The Viking Press.
Gay and Festive Claverhouse: An Extravaganza. Anne Warner French. 1914. 1.00. Little, Brown, and Company.
Gay and Melancholy Sound. Merle Miller. LC 61-7969. 1961. W. Sloane Associates.
Gay Bait. Norma Gilbert. (Orig.). pap. 1.25 o.p. (2043). Brandon.
Gay Bandit of the Border. Tom Gill. LC 31-15551. 1931. Cosmopolitan Book Corporation.
Gay Brotherhood. Brad Tempus. 192p. 1974. pap. 2.25 o.s.i. (ISBN 0-89053-110-2, LB-110). Lambda Pr.
Gay Captain. Metta Victoria Fuller Victor. (select series. no. 79). 1891. Street & Smith.
Gay Cockade. Temple Bailey. LC 21-18891. 1921. The Penn Publishing Company.
Gay Courage. Emilie Baker Loring. LC 28-24954. 1928. The Penn Publishing Company.
Gay Crusader. Charles William Gordon. LC 37-3418. 1936. Dodd, Mead & Company.
Gay Crusader. Magdalen King-Hall. LC 34-31649. 1934. D. Appleton-Century Company, Incorporated.
Gay Deceiver. Peter Leslie. LC 67-15763. 1967. pap., 4.95. Stein & & Day.
Gay Defeat. Denise Robins. 1973. pap. 0.75 o.p. (26548-3-075). Beagle Bks.
Gay Deserters. Ronald Victor Courtenay Bodley. LC 45-10123. 1945. Creative Age Press, Inc.
Gay-Dombeys: A Novel. Harry Hamilton Johnston. LC 19-6771. 1919. The Macmillan Company.
Gay-Dombeys: A Novel. Harry Hamilton Johnston. LC 46-30077. 1920. The Macmillan Company.
Gay Dreamers: An Idyl of Paris. Roger Devigne. Tr. by Cooper, Frederic Taber. LC 27-20260. 1927. Frederick A. Stokes Company.
Gay Family. Ethel Mary Young Boileau. LC 33-22937. 1933. E. P. Dutton & Co., Inc.
Gay Family. Ethel Mary Young Boileau. LC 42-470944. 1936. E. P. Dutton & Co., Inc.
Gay Fiction Anthology. Ed. by Winston Leyland. (Gay Sunshine Journal Ser.: No. 47). (Illus.). 192p. 1982. 20.00x (ISBN 0-917342-00-3); pap. 7.95 (ISBN 0-917342-01-1). Gay Sunshine.
Gay Fiesta. Anne Duffield. LC 39-16971. 1938. Arcadia House.
Gay Galliard: The Love Story of Mary, Queen of Scots. Margaret Emma Faith Irwin. 1942. Harcourt, Brace and Company.
Gay Girl. Robert Emmet MacAlarney. LC 33-6711. 1933. L. MacVeagh, Dial Press, Inc.
Gay Haunt. Victor Jay. LC 76-28566. (Traveller's companion series, TC-484). 1.95. Traveller's Companion.
Gay Head Conspiracy. Carlos Heard Baker. LC 72-11111. 192p. 1973. 5.95 o.p. (ISBN 0-684-13297-4). Scribner.
Gay Head Conspiracy: A Novel of Suspense. Carlos Heard Baker. LC 72-11111. (Illus.). 1973. 5.95 (ISBN 0-684-13297-4). Scribner.
Gay Highway. Mary Chase. LC 33-7380. The Penn Publishing Company.
Gay Insider. John F. Hunter. pap. 2.95 o.s.i. (TC-504, Travellers Comp). Olympia.
Gay Is Life. Mary Howard, pseud. LC 43-14287. 1943. Doubleday, Doran and Company, Inc.
Gay Life. John Keble Bell. LC 17-653625. 1917. 1.30. John Lane Company.
Gay Life. Max Ehrmann. LC 25-18597. (On cover: Scarlet women series). Indiana Publishing Company.
Gay Lord Robert. Eleanor Hibbert. LC 79-161533. 1971. 6.95. Putnam.
Gay Lord Waring. Houghton Townley. LC 10-11366. W. J. Watt & Company.
Gay Love Letters. Jock Stein. pap. 1.95 o.p. (8042). Cameo.
Gay Morning. Annie Edith Foster Jameson. LC 14-5430. 1.25. Hodder & Stoughton, George H. Doran Company.
Gay Mortician. Milton Michael Raison. LC 46-4853. 1946. Murray & Gee, Inc.
Gay Ones. Charles Hanson Towne. The Century Co.
Gay Phoenix. Michael Innes, pseud. LC 81-5147. 1981. 2.95 (ISBN 0-14-004701-8). Penguin Books.
Gay Phoenix. John Innes Mackintosh Stewart. LC 77-74674. (Red badge novel of suspense). 1977. 6.95 (ISBN 0-396-07442-1). Dodd, Mead.
Gay Phoenix: A Sir John Appleby Mystery Novel. Michael Innes, pseud. 1977. 6.95 o.p. (ISBN 0-396-07442-1). Dodd.
Gay Place. William Brammer. 1978. 11.95 (ISBN 0-932012-05-1). Texas Month Pr.
Gay Place: Being Three Related Novel: The Flea Circus. Room Enough to Caper. Country Pleasures. William Brammer. LC 61-524566. 1961. Houghton Mifflin.
Gay Pretending. Lucy Agnes Hancock. LC 36-19258. The Penn Publishing Company.
Gay Procession. Norma Patterson. LC 30-20074. Farrar & Rinehart Incorporated.
Gay Pursuit. Elizabeth Cadell. LC 48-3513. 1948. W. Morrow.
Gay Rebellion. Robert William Chambers. LC 74-15953. (Science Fiction). (Illus.). 1975. 17.00. Arno Press.
Gay Rebellion. Robert William Chambers. LC 13-376424. 1913. 1.30. D. Appleton and Company.
Gay Ritual. Angelo Balthazar. (Orig.). pap. 0.95 o.p. (1147). Brandon.
Gay Rivers. William Gilmore Simms. 1974. Repr. of 1882 ed. lib. bdg. 30.00 (ISBN 0-8414-8062-1). Folcroft.
Gay Saint. Paul Dayton Bailey. LC 44-665. 1944. Murray & Gee, Inc.
Gay Sisters. Stephen Longstreet. LC 42-5834. 1942. Random House.
Gay Sisters. Stephen Longstreet. LC 42-5834. 1942. Random House.
Gay Soldier. Jonathan Martin. 192p. 1974. pap. 2.25 o.s.i. (ISBN 0-89053-107-2, LB-107). Lambda Pr.
Gay Source. Dennis Sanders. 1977. pap. 6.95 (Windhover). Berkley Pub.
Gay Summer: By Warren Howard Pseud. James Noble Gifford. LC 51-12915. 1951. Arcadia House.
Gay Touch: Short Stories. Peter Robins. LC 82-12704. 11.95 (ISBN 0-89594-085-X) (ISBN 0-89594-084-1). Crossing Press.
Gay Tradition. Norman Venner. LC 27-19646. George H. Doran Company.
Gay Voyager. Scot Torey. 192p. (Orig.). 1974. pap. 2.25 o.s.i. (ISBN 0-89053-101-3, LB101). Lambda Pr.
Gay Waters. Oci Kendall Monahan. LC 36-19437. Dorrance and Company.
Gay Way. Amy Irwin. (Orig.). pap. 0.95 o.p. (1164). Brandon.
Gay Year. M. De F. pap. 0.75 o.p. (74-919). Lancer.
Gay Year. Dorothy Speare. LC 23-13319. George H. Doran Company.
Gay Year. Dorothy Speare. LC 31-16245. 1925. A. L. Burt Company.
Gay Year: A Novel. Michael Jean De Forrest. LC 49-4559. 1949. Woodford Press.
Gayle Langford: Being the Romance of a Troy Belle and a Patriot Captain. Harold Morton Kramer. LC 7-25081. 1907. Lothrop, Lee & Shepard Co.
Gaylord's Badge. Ben Haas. LC 75-3643. 1975. 5.95 (ISBN 0-385-09952-5). Doubleday.
Gaylord's Badge. Ben Haas. LC 76-20492. 1976. 8.95 (ISBN 0-8161-6397-9). G. K. Hall.
Gaylord's Badge. Ben Haas. 1976. 1.25. Belmont Tower Books.
Gaylord's Badge. Richard Meade, pseud. 1976. pap. 1.25 o.p. (ISBN 0-505-50974-1, BT50974). Tower Bks.
Gaylord's Badge. Richard Meade, pseud. LC 75-3643. (Double D Western Ser). 192p. 1975. 5.95 o.p. (ISBN 0-385-09952-5). Doubleday.
Gaynor Women. Virginia Coffman. 1979. pap. 1.95 (ISBN 0-449-24075-4, Crest). Fawcett.
Gaynor Women. Virginia Coffman. (Reader's Request Ser.). 1980. lib. bdg. 16.95 (ISBN 0-8161-3047-7, Large Print Bks). G K Hall.
Gaynor Women: A Novel. Coffman, Virginia. LC 77-90664. 8.95 (ISBN 0-87795-180-2). Arbor House.
Gaynor Women: A Novel. Virginia Coffman. LC 80-36758. 1980. 16.95 (ISBN 0-8161-3047-7). G. K. Hall.
Gaynor Women: A Novel. Virginia Coffman. 1.95 (ISBN 0-449-24075-4). Fawcett Crest.
Gayworthys: A Story of Threads and Thrums. 3d ed. Adeline Dutton Train Whitney. 1865. Loring.
Gayworthys: A Story of Threads and Thrums. Adeline Dutton Train Whitney. LC 8-36571. 1893. Houghton, Mifflin and Company.
Gaywyck. Vincent Virga. 384p. 1980. 2.95 (ISBN 0-380-75820-2, 75820). Avon.
Gaza Intercept. E. Howard Hunt. LC 80-6171. 1981. 12.95 (ISBN 0-8128-2804-6). Stein and Day.
Gazapo. Gustavo Sainz. Tr. by Hardie St. Martin. LC 67-15014. 1968. 4.95 o.p. (ISBN 0-374-16076-7). FS&G.
Gazapo. Tr. from Spanish by Hardie St. Martin. Gustavo Sainz. LC 67-15014. 1968. 4.95. Farrar.
Gazebo. Patricia Wentworth. LC 56-5862. (Her A Miss Silver mystery). 1956. Lippincott.
Gazebo: By D. A. Ponsonby. Doris Almon Ponsonby. LC 46-5864. (New York, Liveright publishing corporation) has title: If my arms could hold.). 1945. Hutchinson & Co. Ltd.
Gazella. Stuart Cloete. LC 58-9059. 1958. Houghton Mifflin.
Gazelle on the Lawn. Douglas Fairbairn. LC 64-10534. 1964. Random House.
Geber: A Tale of the Reign of Harun Al Raschid, Khalif of Baghdad. Kate A Benton. LC 1236. 1900. Frederick A. Stokes Company.
Gebo; Successor to Man. Joseph H. Simons. LC 71-170397. (Illus.). 1971. 5.00 (ISBN 0-87141-043-5). Manyland Books.
Gee-Boy. Cyrus Lauron Hooper. 1903. J. Lane.
Gee Raff's Chap Book... George Raffalovich. The Conger Printing Company.
Geek. Craig Nova. LC 74-15884. (Illus.). 1975. 8.95 (ISBN 0-06-013209-4). Harper & Row.
Gees' First Case. Jack Mann. LC 70-39010. 285p. 1972. Repr. 5.00 o.p. ALA.
Gee's Trap: Or, The Lambs and Field Street. Josephine R Baker. Congregational Sunday-School and Publishing Society.
Geese Fly South. Mary Bourn. LC 23-9228. 1923. Doubleday, Page & Company.
Geese in the Forum. Lawrence Edward Watkin. LC 40-11452. 1940. A. A. Knopf.
Gehenna. Conrad Potter Aiken. LC 73-4672. Repr. of 1930 ed. lib. bdg. 8.50 (ISBN 0-8414-1734-2). Folcroft.
Gehlen Portfolio. Thomas Douglas. 2.25 (ISBN 0-505-51654-3). Tower Publications.
Geier-Wally: A Tale of the Tyrol. Wilhelmina Birch Von Hillern. LC 7-4745. 1876. D. Appleton and Company.
Geier-Wally. A Tale of the Tyrol. Wilhelmine Birch Von Hillern. LC 7-47461. (On cover: Library of choice novels. no. 49). 1876. D. Appleton and Company.
Geier-Wally. A Tale of the Tyrol. Wilhelmine Birch Von Hillern. LC 7-4747. (Appletons' new handy-volume series v. 33). 1879. D. Appleton and Company.
Geisha. Stephen Longstreet. (Kangaroo Book). 1977. 1.75 (ISBN 0-671-81168-1). Pocket Books.
Geisha: A Novel, by Stephen and Ethel Longstreet. Stephen Longstreet & Ethel Longstreet. LC 60-6701. 1960. Funk & Wagnalls Co.
Geisha Diary. Ken Noyle. LC 76-5430. (A Berkley Medallion Book.). 1977. 1.75 (ISBN 0-425-03494-1). Berkley Pub. Corp.
Geisha in Rivalry. Kafu Nagai. LC 63-7963. (Library of Japanese literature). 1963. C. F. Tuttle Co.
Gelebt und Gelitten. Roman Von Hans Wachenhusen... Hans Wachenhusen. LC 17-7788. (Die deutsche library, bd. 1, no. 20). 1881. G. Munro.
Gelignite. William Leonard Marshall. LC 77-1402. (Rinehart suspense novel). 1977. 6.95 (ISBN 0-03-016906-2). Holt, Rinehart and Winston.
Gelignite Gang. 1st American Ed. John Creasey. LC 56-110992. Harper.
Gem of Earh. Marjorie Booth. LC 29-173257. Harcourt, Brace and Company.
Gem of the Lake. A Novel. Sarah Ann Wright. LC 9-1477. 1868. American News Company.
Gem of the Mines. A Thrilling Narrative of California Life. Composed of Scenes and Incidents Which Passed Under the Immediate Observation of the Author During Five Years Residence in That State in the Early Days. Jennett Blakeslee Frost. 1866. The Authoress.
Gem of Youth: Or, Fireside Tales. Maggie Roberts. LC 7-410363. 1876. Lange, Little & Co.
Gemas Fatales. Glen Chase, pseud. Tr. by Jairo Ibero from Eng. (Pimienta Collection, Cereza Delicias Ser: No. 8). Orig. Title: Hot Rocks. (Illus., Span.). 1976. pap. 1.25 (ISBN 0-88473-249-5). Fiesta Pub.
Gemini. Margaret Elizabeth Atkins. 178p. 1964. 12.95x (ISBN 0-8464-0445-1). Beekman Pubs.
Gemini. Emily Fox. LC 7-964. (No name series. v. 12). 1878. Roberts Brothers.
Gemini. Emily Fox. LC 17-498. (No name series. v. 12). 1880. Roberts Brothers.
Gemini. Michel Tournier. LC 76-42406. 1981. 14.95 (ISBN 0-385-11449-4). Doubleday.
Gemini: A Novel. Margaret Elizabeth Atkins. LC 66-12086. 1966. Morrow.
Gemini Contenders. Robert Ludlum. LC 75-33821. 1976. 8.95 (ISBN 0-8037-3064-0). Dial Press.
Gemini Contenders. Robert Ludlum. LC 77-361823. 1976. 3.50 (ISBN 0-246-10957-2). Hart-Davis, MacGibbon.
Gemini in Darkness. Clarissa Ross, pseud. (Orig.). 1970. pap. 0.75 o.p. (ISBN 0-447-74598-0). Lancer.
Gemini in Darkness. Clarissa Ross, pseud. (Orig.). 1972. pap. 0.95 o.s.i. (75-351). Lancer.
Gemini Rising. J. S. Filbrun. 192p. (Orig.). 1982. pap. 2.25 (ISBN 0-449-14493-3, GM). Fawcett.
Gemini Smile, Gemini Kill. Robert Lory. (Horrorscope,#4). 1975. (pbk.) 1.25 (ISBN 0-523-00524-5). Pinnacle Books.
Gemini Trip. Janice Law, pseud. LC 77-7614. 1977. 7.95 (ISBN 0-395-25703-4). Houghton Mifflin.
Gemini. 1st Ed. William Kelley. LC 59-12633. 1959. Doubleday.
Gemma. A Novel. Thomas Adolphus Trollope. LC 8-284979. T. B. Peterson & Brothers.
Gemmo: A Novel. Kemal Bilbasar. LC 77-358076. (Unesco Collection of Representative Works: Turkish Ser.). 1976. 4.75 (ISBN 0-7206-0424-9). P. Owen.
Gems of Romance: A Treasury of Tales, Legends, and Traditions ... LC 9-182120. Cassell Publishing Company.
Gems of the Bog: A Tale of the Irish Peasantry. Jane Dunbar Chaplin & American Tract Society. LC 42-290196. 1869. The American Tract Society.
Gems of the Prairies: First Collection. Alfred O Halvorson.
Gems of the Vieux Carre: The Story of Four Historical Romances of the Frence ! Quarter of Old New Orleans, Depicting Living Conditions and Home Life of the Creole and Their Slaves in Pre-Civil War Days. Pierre Paul Ebeyer. LC 46-1111. 1945. Windmill Publishing Company.
Gems Without Polish: A Story of the Country Week. Alice May Douglas. LC 6-35886. 1890. Hunt & Eaton.
Gena of the Appalachians. Clarence Monroe Wallin. LC 11-1519. 1910. Cochrane Publishing Company.
Gender in Satin. Eliza M. J. Humphreys. LC 7-5789. (Half-title: The incognito library no. 6). 1895. G. P. Putnam's Sons.
Gene Autry and the Big Valley Grab: An Original Story Featuring Gene Autry, Famous Motion Picture, Radio, and Television Star, As the Hero. Illustrated by Randy Steffen Authorized Ed. W H Hutchinson. LC 52-43297. 1952. Whitman Pub. Co.
Gene Wolfe's Book of Days. Gene Wolfe. LC 80-1074. 1981. 9.95 (ISBN 0-385-15991-9). Doubleday.
Gen'eman of De South. Anna Walker Robinson. LC 44-2098. 1943. Broadman Press.
General. Cecil Scott Forester. LC 36-5508. 1936. Little, Brown and Company.
General. Cecil Scott Forester. LC 38-17008. (On cover: A Mercury book, no. 10). The American Mercury, Inc.
General. Cecil Scott Forester. 1947. Little, Brown and Company.
General. Cecil Scott Forester. LC 82-80140. 1982. 11.95 (ISBN 0-933852-27-4). Nautical & Aviation Pub. Co.
General. Stephen Longstreet. (Berkley Medallion Book.). 1977. 1.75. (ISBN 0-425-03312-0). Berkley Pub. Corp.
General; a Farcical Novel with an Historical Background Based on Buster Keaton's Comedy Spectacle Film of the Same Name: Inspired by a Glorious Exploit of the American Civil War, Wherein a Lad Chased a Lass and a Locomotive and a Good Time Was Enjoyed by All. Joseph Warren. LC 27-79300. Grosset & Dunlap.
General: A Novel. Stephen Longstreet. LC 74-79656. 1974. 7.95 (ISBN 0-399-11390-8). Putnam.
General and the Co-Ed: A Novel. Robert Lipscomb Duncan. LC 63-11214. 1963. Doubleday.
General Besserley's Puzzle Box. Edward Phillips Oppenheim. LC 35-20903. 1935. Little, Brown, and Company.
General Besserley's Second Puzzle Box. Edward Phillips Oppenheim. LC 40-3663. 1940. Little, Brown and Company.
General Blastem. Bob Robinson. 128p. 1973. 5.00 o.p. (ISBN 0-682-47733-8). Exposition.
General Blastem: A Novel. Bob Robinson. 1973. 5.00 (ISBN 0-682-47733-8). Exposition Pr.
General Bounce: Or, The Lady and the Locusts. new ed. George John Whyte-Melville. LC 41-424396. 1873. Longmans, Green, and Co.
General Bramble. Andre Maurois. Tr. by Jules Castier. Boswell, Ronald, Joint Tr. LC 22-930. 1921. John Lane.
General Bramble. Andre Maurois. Tr. by Jules Castier. Boswell, Ronald, Joint Tr. LC 22-8046. 1922. Dodd, Mead and Company.
General Buntop's Miracle and Other Stories. Martin Donisthorpe Armstrong. LC 34-259281. Harcourt, Brace and Company.
General Claxton: A Novel. Cornelius Holgate Hanford. LC 17-31025. 1917. The Neale Publishing Company.
General Crack. George Preedy, pseud. LC 28-20759. 1928. Dodd, Mead & Company.
General Danced at Dawn, and Other Stories. George MacDonald Fraser. LC 75-154923. 1973. 5.95 (ISBN 0-394-47435-X). Knopf.

General Della Rovere. Translated from the Italian by Adrienne Foulke. 1st Ed. in the U. S. A. Indro Montanelli. LC 61-125594. 1961. Doubleday.
General Duty Nurse. Lucy Agnes Hancock. LC 45-9509. 1945. Macrae-Smith-Company.
General Duty Nurse. Lucy Agnes Hancock. LC 47-3060. 1947. Triangle Books, the Blakiston Company.
General from the Jungle. B Traven. LC 72-81292. 1972. 8.95 (ISBN 0-8090-4904-X). Hill and Wang.
General Goes Too Far. Lewis George Robinson. LC 36-10605. 1936. G. P. Putnam's Sons.
General John Regan. James Owen Hannay. LC 13-238781. Hodder & Stoughton, George H. Doran Company.
General Manpower. John Stuart Martin. LC 39-5400. 1938. Simon and Schuster, Inc.
General of the Dead Army: A Novel. Ismail Kadare. LC 73-157867. 1972. 7.95 (ISBN 0-670-33630-0). Grossman.
General Piesc or, The Case of the Forgotten Mission. Stefan Themerson. LC 76-378976. 1976. (ISBN 0-85247-113-0). Gaberbocchus.
General Sheridan's Squaw Spy and Clara Blynn's Captivity. LC 75-40452. (Garland Library of Narratives of North American Indian Captivities ; V. 81). 1976. 21.00 (ISBN 0-8240-1705-6). Garland Pub.
General. Translated from the German by Constantine Fitzgibbon. 1st American Ed. Karlludwig Opitz. LC 57-5983. 1957. J. Day Co.
General Utility" Or, The Trials of Manon the Actress. Florence Blackburn White Schoeffel. (On cover: Munro's library v. 50: no. 807). 1888. N. L. Munro.
General Zapped an Angel: New Stories of Fantasy and Science Fiction. Howard Melvin Fast. LC 70-94385. 1970. 4.95. Morrow.
Generales y Doctores: By Carlos Loveira. Edited by Shasta M. Bryant and J. Riis Owre. Loveira y Chirino, Carlos. Ed. by Owre, J. Rils. LC 65-11528. 1965. Oxford University Press.
Generales y Doctores: By Carlos Loveira. Edited by Shasta M. Bryant and J. Riis Owre. Loveira y Chirino, Carlos. Ed. by Bryant, Shasta M. & Owre, J. Rils. LC 65-11528. 1965. Oxford University Press.
Generally Speaking. Carl Jackson. 3.00 o.p. Carlton.
Generals. Per Wahloo. LC 73-18730. 1974. 5.95. Pantheon Books.
General's Daughter. Ignatii Nikolaveich Potapenko. Tr. by Gaussen, William Frederick Armytage. LC 7-30050. (On cover: Cassell's sunshine series, no, 126 extra). Cassell Publishing Company.
Generals Die in Bed. Charles Yale Harrison. LC 30-16259. 1930. W. Morrow & Co.
General's Double: A Story of the Army of the Potomac. Charles King. LC 7-13214. 1898. J. B. Lippincott Company.
General's Lady. Esther Forbes. LC 38-27638. Harcourt, Brace and Company.
General's Mess. Tom H. Bates. 1981. 18.00x (ISBN 0-7223-1396-9, Pub. by Stockwell). State Mutual Bk.
General's Ring. Selma Ottiliana Lovisa Lagerlof. Tr. by Martin, Francesca. LC 28-103952. 1928. Doubleday, Doran & Company, Inc.
General's Spy: A Tale of the American Revolution by Ella C. Eckert with Frances E. Whitney. 1st Ed. Ella C Eckert. LC 56-8080. 1956. Vantage Press.
General's Wench. Rosamond Van Der Zee Marshall. Prentice-Hall.
General's Wife. Peter Straub. (Illus.). 128p. 1983. 25.00 (ISBN 0-937986-54-2). D M Grant.
Generalship: Or, How I Managed My Husband; a Tale. George Roy. LC 7-35778. 1875. R. Clarke & Co.
Generation Apart. J. T. Richards. (Whitmarsh Chronicles Ser.: Vol. 1). 416p. (Orig.). 1981. pap. 2.75 (ISBN 0-515-05242-6). Jove Pubns.
Generation-Degeneration-Regeneration. Irwin L. Brown. 5.95 o.p. Vantage.
Generation of Blood. I. A. Grenville. 1978. pap. 1.50 (ISBN 0-532-15318-9). Woodhill.
Generation of Blood. I. A. Grenville. (Orig.). 1969. pap. 0.95 o.p. (B95-1016). Belmont-Tower.
Generation of Blood. I. A. Grenville. 1976. pap. 1.25 o.p. (LB340ZK, Leisure Bks). Nordon Pubns.
Generation of Blood. I. A Grenville. 1976. (pbk.) 1.25. Leisure Books.
Generation of Rust: A Novel. Endre Fejes. LC 70-107287. 1970. McGraw-Hill.
Generation of Victors. Burt Hirschfeld. LC 73-82180. 1973. 7.95 (ISBN 0-87795-061-X). Arbor House.
Generation of Vipers. Philip Wylie. 1979. Repr. of 1942 ed. 18.00 (ISBN 0-89783-013-X). Larlin Corp.
Generation Removed. Gary K Wolf. LC 76-23802. 1977. 6.95 (ISBN 0-385-11549-0). Doubleday.
Generation Untamed. J. T. Richards. (Whitmarsh Chronicles: Vol. 2). (Orig.). 1981. pap. 2.95 (ISBN 0-515-05632-4). Jove Pubns.
Generation Unto Generation. Fayth Sone. LC 41-2816. 1940. The Naylor Company.
Generation Without Farewell. Kay Boyle. 1960. 3.95 o.p. Knopf.
Generations. David Alman. LC 78-143832. 1971. 6.95. H. Regnery Co.
Generations. Neela Padmanabhan. Tr. by Ka N. Subramanyam from Tamil. (Orient Paperback Ser). 192p. 1972. pap. 2.50 (ISBN 0-88253-110-7). Ind-US Inc.
Generations: A Memoir. Lucille Clifton. LC 75-38758. (Illus.). 5.95 (ISBN 0-394-46155-X). Random House.
Generations of Men. John Clinton Hunt. 1973. Curtis Bks.
Generations of Men: A Novel. John Clinton Hunt. LC 56-5928. (Atlantic Monthly Press book). 1956. Little, Brown.
Generations of Noah Edon. David Pinsky. LC 31-200771. 1931. The Macaulay Company.
Generous Cow. Bijou Le Tord. 4.96 (ISBN 0-8193-0853-6). Parents' Magazine Press.
Generous Heart: A Novel. 1st Ed. Kenneth Fearing. LC 54-598127. 1954. Harcourt, Brace.
Generous Man. Reynolds Price. LC 66-16357. 4.95. Atheneum.
Generous Man. Reynolds Price. (Signet bk., T3072). 1967. New Amer. Lib.
Generous Rivals or Love Triumphant. LC 72-170531. (Foundations of the Novel Ser.: Vol. 20). lib. bdg. 50.00 (ISBN 0-8240-0532-5). Garland Pub.
Generous Rivals: Or, Love Triumphant (Anonymous). LC 72-170531. (Foundations of the Novel). 1973. 22.00 (ISBN 0-8240-0532-5). Garland Pub.
Genesee Castle. Paul Bernard. LC 72-94253. 1970. 3.95. Dorrance.
Genesee Fever. Carl Lamson Carmer. LC 72-146479. 1971. 6.95. D. McKay Co.
Genesee Fever. Carl Lamson Carmer. LC 41-25661. Farrar & Rinehart, Inc.
Genesis Five. Henry Wilson Allen. LC 68-54873. 1968. 5.95. Morrow.
Genesis Machine. James P Hogan. LC 77-25166. 1978. 1.75 (ISBN 0-345-27519-5) (ISBN 0-345-27231-5). Ballantine Books.
Genesis of a Revolution: An Anthology of Modern Chinese Short Stories. Stanley R Munro. LC 79-941656. (Writing in Asia series). (Illus.). 1979. 5.95. Heinemann Educational Books (Asia)
Genesis of Nam: A New Earth with Its Own Blue Heaven. Charles Goodrich. LC 56-862942. Dorrance.
Genesis Rock. Edwin Corley. 1981. pap. 2.75 (ISBN 0-440-12877-3). Dell.
Genesis Rock. Edwin Corley. LC 79-7045. 1980. 12.95 o.p. (ISBN 0-385-15018-0). Doubleday.
Genesis Two. Leslie Purnell Davies. LC 72-111156. 1970. 4.95. Doubleday.
Genetha. Roy A. Heath. 176p. 1982. 13.95 (ISBN 0-8052-8100-2, Pub. by Allison & Busby England); pap. 5.95 (ISBN 0-8052-8101-0). Schocken.
Genetic Babies. Valcoulon MeMoyne Ellicott. LC 76-15445. 1.95. Job Productions.
Genetic Bomb. Andrew J Offutt & D. Bruce Berry. 1975. (pbk.) 1.25. Warner Paperback Library.
Genetic Buccaneer. Gregory Kern. (Cap Kennedy,#12). 1974. (pbk) 0.95. DAW Books.
Geneva. Mark Dunster. (Rin: Part 41). 1977. pap. 4.00 (ISBN 0-89642-020-5). Linden Pubs.
Geneva Crisis: A Novel. Matti Golan. LC 80-66677. 11.95 (ISBN 0-89479-073-0). A & W Publishers.
Geneva Mystery. Francis Durbridge. 1982. 18.00x (ISBN 0-86025-211-6, Pub. by Ian Henry Pubns England). State Mutual Bk.
Geneveive: A Story of Southern Life Before the War of the States. Eva Holmes Mrs Hall. LC 14-329096. 1913. The Neale Publishing Company.
Genevieve: A Tale of Oregon. Frederic Homer Balch. LC 32-34227. 1932. Metropolitan Press.
Genevieve and Alexander. Marjorie Franco. LC 81-69147. 1982. 12.95 (ISBN 0-689-11259-9). Atheneum.
Genevieve De Brabant: An Original Novel of Fact and Fiction; a Romance of Love, Travel, Self-Sacrifice, Adventure and War in France, England, Italy, Malta and South Africa... James Qallan Dixon. LC 5-21565.
Genevra. Charles Marriott. 1904. D. Appleton and Company.
Genevra's Money. Edward Verrall Lucas. LC 23-81813. George H. Doran Company.
Genghis Coppersmith. Robert J. Griffin. (Orig.). 1972. pap. 0.95 o.p. (N2703). Pyramid Pubns.
Genial Idiot: His Views and Reviews. John Kendrick Bangs. LC 3-29647. 1908. Harper & Brothers.
Genial Stranger. Donald MacKenzie. LC 62-7388. 1962. Houghton Mifflin.
Genie du Lieu. Michel Butor. pap. 8.95. French & Eur.
Genius. Patrick Dennis, pseud. 1962. 4.50 o.p. (ISBN 0-15-134900-2). HarBraceJ.
"Genius". Theodore Dreiser. 1915. John Lane Company.
"Genius". Theodore Dreiser. LC 26-22295. 1925. Boni and Liveright.
Genius. Margaret Horton Potter. LC 6-69705. 1906. Harper & Brothers.
"Genius." Afterword by Larzer Ziff. Theodore Dreiser. LC 67-29732. (Signet classic, CW375). 1967. pap., 1.50. New Amer. Lib.
Genius & Lust. Henry Miller. 1978. 17.50 o.p. Porter.
Genius and the Goddess: A Novel. Aldous Leonard Huxley. 1973. (pbk.) 0.95 (ISBN 0-06-080310-X). Harper & Row.
Genius and the Goddess: A Novel. 1st Ed. Aldous Leonard Huxley. 1955. Harper.
Genius: By Patrick Dennis Pseud. Edward Everett Tanner. LC 62-19585. 1962. Harcourt, Brace & World.
Genius in Murder. Ernest Robertson Punshon. LC 33-29201. 1933. Houghton Mifflin Company.
Genius of America. Stuart Pratt Sherman. LC 65-27130. Repr. of 1923 ed. 11.00 (ISBN 0-8046-0416-9). Kennikat.
Genius of American Fiction. William Wasserstrom. LC 78-101095. 1970. Allyn and Bacon.
Genius of Elizabeth Anne. Mabel Hotchkiss Robbins. LC 16-22897. 1.25. The Pilgrim Press.
Genius of Galilee: An Historical Novel. Anson Uriel Hancock. LC 7-555901. 1891. C. H. Kerr & Company.
Genius of John Ruskin. Ed. by John D. Rosenberg. 1967. pap. 1.85x o.p. (B87, RivEd, 3-47721). HM.
Genius Unlimited. John T. Phillifuet. (Science Fiction Ser). pap. 0.95 o.p. (UQ1016). Daw Bks.
Genji Monogatari. Murasaki Shikibu. LC 72-77523. (Tut books. L). 1974. (pbk.) 3.75 (ISBN 0-8048-1045-1). C. E. Tuttle.
Genji Monogatari. Murasaki Shikibu. Tr. by Kencho Suematsu. LC 72-77523. 1973. pap. 5.25 (ISBN 0-8048-1045-1). C E Tuttle.
Genki Boys. Terence Kelly. LC 66-73994. 1966. Macmillan; New York, St. Martin's P.
Genoa Ferry. Ronald Harwood. 1977. 7.95 (ISBN 0-442-80591-8). Van Nos Reinhold.
Genoa Ferry: A Novel. Ronald Harwood. LC 77-22455. 1977. 7.95 (ISBN 0-88405-590-6). Mason/Charter.
Genocides. Thomas M Disch. LC 78-106269. (Gregg Press Science Fiction Series). (Illus.). 1978. 10.00 (ISBN 0-8398-2436-X). Gregg Press.
Gente Sencilla. Roberto Hosne. LC 57-43996. 1957. Buenos Aires, Editorial Stilcograf.
Genteel Female: An Anthology. Clifton J. Furness. 1931. Repr. 14.50 o.s.i. Finch Pr.
Genteel Murderer. Charles Norman. pap. 0.95 o.p. (02319, Collier). Macmillan.
Gentian Hill. Elizabeth Goudge. LC 49-503203. 1949. Coward-McCann.
Gentian Violet: A Romance of Political Life. Edward S Hyams. LC 53-427521. 1953. Longmans, Green.
Gentile: By Sylvia and Henry Lieferant. Sylvia Saltzberg Lieferant & Henry Lieferant. LC 58-89473. 1958. Muhlenberg Press.
Gentle Albatross. Elizabeth Foote-Smith. LC 75-44098. (Red mask mystery). 6.95 (ISBN 0-399-11730-X). Putnam.
Gentle Annie. MacKinlay Kantor. LC 79-25149. (Series: Gregg Press Western Fiction Series.). 1980. 11.95 (ISBN 0-8398-2688-5). Gregg Press.
Gentle Annie: A Western Novel. MacKinlay Kantor. LC 42-362633. 1942. Coward-McCann, Inc.
Gentle Art of Cooking Wives. Elizabeth Strong Worthington. LC 2-1781. Dodge Publishing Company.
Gentle Art of Murder: The Detective Fiction of Agatha Christie. Earl F Bargainnier. LC 80-83187. 16.95 (ISBN 0-87972-158-8) (ISBN 0-87972-159-6). Bowling Green University Popular Press.
Gentle Art of Pleasing. Mary E Bennett. LC 98-1524. The Baker and Taylor Company.
Gentle Assassin. Kendell Foster Crossen. LC 64-25305. 1964. Bobbs-Merrill.
Gentle Asylum: Life at a Mental Hospital. Isabelle Andersen. LC 76-23426. (Continuum book). 8.95 (ISBN 0-8164-9292-1). Seabury Press.
Gentle Awakening. Marianne Cole. (Second Chance at Love Ser.: No. 101). Date not set. pap. 1.75 (ISBN 0-515-06865-9). Jove Pubns.
Gentle Belle. A Novel. Frances Christine Tiernan. LC 8-19814. (On cover: Appletons' library of American fiction no. 29). 1879. D. Appleton and Company.
Gentle Benefactress. Hattie E Colter. LC 6-30674. D. Lothrop Company.
Gentle Boy and Other Tales. Nathaniel Hawthorne. LC 6916. (Riverside literature series. no. 145). Houghton, Mifflin and Company.
Gentle Breadwinners: The Story of One of Them. Helen Alice Matthews Nitsch. LC 7-33483. 1888. Houghton, Mifflin and Company.
Gentle Bush. Barbara Giles. LC 47-30271. 1947. Harcourt, Brace and Company.
Gentle Captain. With Drawings by David Cobb. Arthur Kennard Davis. LC 55-5475. 1955. Rinehart.
Gentle Degenerates. Marco Vassi. 1976. pap. 2.25 (ISBN 0-532-22104-4). Woodhill.
Gentle Desperado: With a Complete Max Brand Bibliography. Frederick Faust. LC 80-26072. (Series: Max Brand Popular Classic.). 1981. 7.95 (ISBN 0-88496-157-5). Capra Press.
Gentle Enchanter. Theophile Gautier. Tr. by Brian Hill. (Fr. & Eng.). 1961. 2.95 o.p. Dufour.
Gentle Folk: A Novel. Alexander Baron. LC 76-365329. 1976. 3.95 (ISBN 0-333-18649-4). Macmillan.
Gentle Fury. Noel Bertram Gerson. LC 61-8640. 1961. Holt, Rinehart and Winston.
Gentle Fury. Peter Thomas Rohrbach. (Echo bk., E4). 1956. Doubleday.
Gentle Fury. 1st Ed. Paul Lewis, pseud. LC 61-8640. 1961. Holt, Rinehart and Winston.
Gentle Fury. 1st Ed. Peter Thomas Rohrbach. LC 59-12878. 1959. Hanover House.
Gentle Grafter. O. Henry. (Literature of Mystery & Detection). (Illus.). 1976. Repr. of 1908 ed. 14.00x (ISBN 0-405-07889-7). Ayer Co.
Gentle Grafter. William Sydney Porter. LC 75-32770. (Literature of Mystery and Detection). (Illus.). 1976. 14.00 (ISBN 0-405-07889-7). Arno Press.
Gentle Grafter. William Sydney Porter. LC 8-31472. 1908. 1.00. The McClure Company.
Gentle Grafter. William Sydney Porter. LC 15-17416. 1913. Doubleday, Page & Company.
Gentle Grafter. William Sydney Porter. LC 19-135391. 1918. Doubleday, Page & Company.
Gentle Grafter. William Sydney Porter. LC 22-16017. 1919. Doubleday, Page & Company, for Review of Reviews Co.
Gentle Greaves. Ernest Raymond. LC 72-79035. 1972. 8.95 (ISBN 0-8415-0173-4). Saturday Review Press.
Gentle Greaves. Ernest Raymond. 1973. (pbk) 1.75. Dell.
Gentle Gunman. Max Brand. 1981. 15.00x (ISBN 0-86025-156-X, Pub. by Ian Henry Pubns England). State Mutual Bk.
Gentle Gunman. Max Brand. 1976. pap. 1.75 (ISBN 0-446-94291-X). Warner Bks.
Gentle Gunman. Frederick Faust. 1976. (pbk.) 1.25. Warner Books.
Gentle Hangman: By James M Fox Pseud. 1st Ed. James M. W. Knipscheer. LC 50-8348. 1950. Little, Brown.
Gentle Infidel. Lawrence L Schoonover. LC 50-6237. 1950. Macmillan.
Gentle Insurrection, and Other Stories. Doris Betts. LC 54-8709. 1954. Putnam.
Gentle Intruder. Irene Hunter Steiner. (Red rose romance,#145). 1974. (pbk.) 0.75. Bantam Books.
Gentle Invaders. Ed. by Hans S. Santesson. (Orig.). 1969. pap. 0.60 o.p. (B60-1011). Belmont-Tower.
Gentle Julia. Booth Tarkington. LC 22-9877. 1922. Doubleday, Page & Company.
Gentle Julia. Booth Tarkington. LC 35-33397. Grosset & Dunlap.
Gentle Kingdom of Giscomo. Evelyn Wells. LC 52-13373. 1953. Doubleday.
Gentle Knight of Old Brandenburg. Charles Major. LC 9-26322. 1909. The Macmillan Company.
Gentle Libertine. Sidonie Gabrielle Colette. Tr. by Benet, Rosemary (Carr) LC 31-3864. 1931. Farrar & Rinehart, Inc.
Gentle Libertine. Sidonie Gabrielle Colette. Tr. by Benet, Rosemary (Carr) LC 41-347923. 1931. Grosset & Dunlap.
Gentle Lover. Beth Gorman. Ed. by Gene DeRoin. (Aston Hall Presents Ser.). (Orig.). 1980. pap. 1.50 (ISBN 0-89936-019-X). Aston Hall.
Gentle Lover: A Comedy of Middle Age. Forrest Reid, pseud. 1971. Repr. of 1913 ed. 25.00 o.s.i. (ISBN 0-403-01169-8). Scholarly.
Gentle Murderer. Dorothy Salisbury Davis. LC 50-11035. 1951. Scribner.
Gentle Murderer. Dorothy Salisbury Davis. LC 80-17169. (Gregg Press Mystery Fiction Series). 1980. 11.95 (ISBN 0-8398-2650-8). Gregg Press.
Gentle Neighbor; Poems. Lee Tucker. LC 59-24460. Vantage Press.
Gentle Obsession. Frances Cowen. Ed. by Gene DeRoin. (Aston Hall Presents Ser.). (Orig.). 1980. pap. 1.50 (ISBN 0-89936-020-3). Aston Hall.
Gentle Occupation. Dirk Bogarde. LC 79-3617. 1980. 9.95 (ISBN 0-394-51121-2). Knopf: Distributed by Random House.

Gentle People. Lavinia T. Bentley. 3.50 o.p. Vantage.

Gentle Persuasion. Maude E Butler. LC 68-54479. 1968. 3.00. Dorrance.

Gentle Pioneers. a book for tired hours, either to cause, or to relieve them. ed. Robert Habersham Barnwell. LC 15-7109. R. G. Badger; Etc., Etc.

Gentle Pirate. Jayne Castle. 1980. pap. 1.75 (ISBN 0-440-12981-8). Dell.

Gentle Pirate, an Entertainment. Oswald Wynd. LC 51-10659. 1951. Doubleday.

Gentle Powers. Stella Gibbons. LC 46-7633. 1946. Dodd, Mead & Company.

Gentle Savage. Edward King. LC 11-15087. 1883. J. R. Osgood and Company.

Gentle Stranger. Charlotte Vale Allen. 1977. 1.50 (ISBN 0-446-88264-X). Warner Books.

Gentle Tigress. C. O. Lamp. (Orig.). 1980. pap. 2.25 o.s.i. (ISBN 0-8439-0727-4, Leisure Bks). Nordon Pubns.

Gentle Torment. Johanna Phillips. (Second Chance at Love Ser.: No. 20). 192p. (Orig.). 1981. pap. 1.75 (ISBN 0-515-06106-9). Jove Pubns.

Gentle Tyrant. Berta Ruck. LC 49-8735. 1949. Dodd, Mead.

Gentle Tyrants. Melanie L. Pflaum. 4.50 o.p. Carlton.

Gentle Vengeance. Charles Le Baron. 1982. pap. 4.95 (ISBN 0-14-006106-1). Penguin.

Gentle Whisper. Eleanor Woods. (Candlelight Ecstasy Ser.). (Orig.). 1983. pap. 1.95 (ISBN 0-440-12997-4). Dell.

Gentle Wife. Ann Falwell Ellis. LC 39-32122. 1939. Carlyle House.

Gentlehands. M. E. Kerr. 144p. (gr. 8 up). 1981. pap. 1.95 (ISBN 0-553-12577-X). Bantam.

Gentleman. Edison Marshall. LC 56-5753. 1956. Farrar, Straus and Cudahy.

Gentleman: A Romance of the Sea. Alfred Ollivant. LC 8-28998. 1908. The Macmillan Company.

Gentleman Adventurer: A Story of the Hudson's Bay Company. Mary Esther MacGregor. LC 24-308578. George H. Doran Company.

Gentleman and Courtier. Florence Marryat Church Lean. (On cover: Seaside library. Pocket ed. no. 1126). 1888. G. Munro.

Gentleman and Ladies. uniform ed. Susan Hill. LC 76-382130. 1976. 3.50 (ISBN 0-241-89409-3). Hamilton.

Gentleman and Ladies. Susan Hill. LC 69-14638. 1969. 5.95. Walker.

Gentleman & the Jew. Maurice Samuel. LC 70-163541. 325p. Repr. of 1950 ed. lib. bdg. 17.25x (ISBN 0-8371-6201-7, SAGJ). Greenwood.

Gentleman Born. Edward Charles Kane. 1900. G. W. Dillingham Co.

Gentleman Callers. Nancy Lamb. LC 78-31725. 1979. 9.95 o.p. (ISBN 0-87223-530-0, Seaview Bks). Putnam Pub Group.

Gentleman Comrade: A Novel of Romance and Intrigue in the World of a Generation Ago. 1st Ed. Ferenc Imrey. LC 57-14804. Greenwich Book Publishers.

Gentleman for the Gallows. Sydney Horler. LC 39-7931. 1938. Hillman-Curl, Inc.

Gentleman from America. Polan Banks. LC 30-22761. J. Cape & H. Smith.

Gentleman from America. Paul Benton. LC 57-10472. 1957. Crowell.

Gentleman from Brazil. Silvino Da Silva. 5.95 o.p. Vantage.

Gentleman from California: A Novel. Niven Busch. LC 65-22261. 5.95. S & S.

Gentleman from Chicago: Being an Account of the Doings of Thomas Neill Cream, M.D. (M'Gill), 1850-1892. John Cashman, pseud. LC 73-4145. 1973. 6.95 (ISBN 0-06-010663-8). Harper & Row.

Gentleman from Chicago: Being an Account of the Doings of Thomas Neill Cream, M.D. (M'Gill), 1850-1892. John Cashman, pseud. 1973-1974. (pbk.) 1.50. Popular Library.

Gentleman from England. Lawrence Edward Watkin. LC 41-173274. 1941. A. A. Knopf.

Gentleman from Glascony. A Romance of the Huguenota. Bicknell Dudley. LC 6-35669. (On cover: Criterion series, no. 11). 1895. Street & Smith.

Gentleman from Indiana. Booth Tarkington. LC 73-121843. 1970. AMS Press.

Gentleman from Indiana. Booth Tarkington. LC 75-129453. 1970. Scholarly Press.

Gentleman from Indiana. Booth Tarkington. LC 99-5008. 1899. Doubleday & McClure Co.

Gentleman from Indiana. Booth Tarkington. 1900. Doubleday & McClure Co.

Gentleman from Indiana. Booth Tarkington. LC 22-14538. 1904. McClure, Phillips & Co.

Gentleman from Indiana. Booth Tarkington. LC 35-28562. Grosset & Dunlap.

Gentleman from Indiana. one-by-one ed. Booth Tarkington. LC 35-17775. 1935. Doubleday, Doran & Company, Inc.

Gentleman from Indiana. Booth Tarkington & Full Name: Newton Booth Tarkington. 1920. Doubleday, Page & Company.

Gentleman from Indianapolis: A Treasury of Booth Tarkington. Booth Tarkington. LC 57-12460. 1957. Doubleday.

Gentleman from Maryland. Raymond Pue Day. LC 24-11017. R. G. Badger.

Gentleman from Parnassus. Josiah Pitts Woolfolk. LC 37-22462. Godwin.

Gentleman from San Francisco. Ivan Alekseevich Bunin. LC 80-23694. 1981. 17.50 (ISBN 0-374-91093-6). Octagon Books.

Gentleman from San Francisco. Ivan Alekseevich Bunin & Guerney, Bernard Guilbert, Tr. LC 33-27457. 1934. A.A. Knopf.

Gentleman from San Francisco: And Other Stories. Ivan Alekseevich Bunin & Lawrence, David Herbert, 1885-1930, Tr. 1923. T. Seltzer.

Gentleman from San Francisco, and Other Stories. Ivan Alekseevich Bunin & Lawrence, David Herbert, 1885-1930, Tr. LC 23-3218. 1923. T. Seltzer.

Gentleman from Texas. Hearnden Balfour. LC 27-20428. 1927. Houghton Mifflin Company.

Gentleman from Virginia. Charles Alden Seltzer. LC 76-28476. 1976. 6.95 (ISBN 0-88411-111-3). Aeonian Press.

Gentleman from Virginia. Charles Alden Seltzer. LC 26-14383. 1926. Doubleday, Page & Company.

Gentleman from Virginia. Charles Alden Seltzer. LC 32-335898. 1928. Grosset & Dunlap.

Gentleman Grizzly. Reginald Charles Barker. LC 28-124299. L. C. Page & Company.

Gentleman Hangs: A Detective Novel. John Dollond. LC 41-341965. 1940. Longmans, Green and Co.

Gentleman in Armor: How Rene of Bar, Duke of Lorraine, Pursued My Lady of the Firelight, Found Joan of Arc and Led the Army of the Dead. Robert J Casey. LC 27-23689. J. H. Sears & Company, Inc.

Gentleman in Black. LC 75-46265. (Supernatural and Occult Fiction). 1976. 18.00 (ISBN 0-405-08123-5). Arno Press.

Gentleman in Hades: The Story of a Damned Debutante. Frederic Arnold Kummer. LC 30-21418. Sears Publishing Company, Inc.

Gentleman in Pajamas. Charles Neville Buck. LC 24-4267. 2.00. The Century Co.

Gentleman in Paradise. Harper McBride. (Orig.). 1981. pap. 1.75 (ISBN 0-440-12186-8). Dell.

Gentleman in the Parlour: A Record of a Journey from Rangoon to Haiphong. William Somerset Maugham. LC 48-1424. (New Avon library, 129). 1947. Avon Book Co.

Gentleman in Waiting. Cornelius V. V Sewell. LC 99-4111. F. T. Neely.

Gentleman Jack. A Naval Story. William Johnson Neale. LC 7-23101. 1837. E. L. Carey & A. Hart.

Gentleman Johnny. Showell Styles. LC 63-8510. 1963. Macmillan.

Gentleman Junkie. Harlan Ellison. (Ace Ellison Ser.: No. 6). 256p. 1983. pap. 2.50 (ISBN 0-441-27938-4). Ace Bks.

Gentleman Junkie. Harlan Ellison. 1975. pap. 1.25 o.p. (ISBN 0-515-03933-0). BJ Pub Group.

Gentleman Junkie and Other Stories of the Hung-up Generation. Harlan Ellison. LC 75-324342. 1975. 1.25 (ISBN 0-515-03933-0). Pyramid Books.

Gentleman of China: A Novel by Robert Standish Pseud. Digby George Gerahty. LC 53-6766. 1953. Macmillan.

Gentleman of Courage: A Novel of the Wilderness. James Oliver Curwood. LC 24-16563. 1924. Cosmopolitan Book Corporation.

Gentleman of Fortune. Henry Christopher Bailey. LC 7-33910. 1907. D. Appleton and Company.

Gentleman of France: Being the Memoirs of Gaston De Bonne, Sieur De Marsac. Stanley John Weyman. 1894. Longmans, Green, and Co.

Gentleman of France: Being the Memoirs of Gaston De Bonne, Sieur De Marsac. Stanley John Weyman. LC 3-26180. 1895. Longmans, Green, and Co.

Gentleman of France: Being the Memoirs of Gaston De Bonne, Sieur De Marsac. Stanley John Weyman. LC 20-13347. 1908. A. L. Burt Company.

Gentleman of France: Being the Memoirs of Gaston De Bonne, Sieur De Marsac. Stanley John Weyman. LC 22-16039. 1921. Longmans, Green and Co.

Gentleman of Leisure. P. G. Wodehouse. 1962. 11.95 o.s.i. (ISBN 0-8277-0201-9). British Bk Ctr.

Gentleman of Leisure. P. G. Wodehouse. 1962. 11.95 o.s.i. (ISBN 0-8277-0201-9). British Bk Ctr.

Gentleman of Quality. Frederic Van Rensselaer Dey. LC 9-795020. 1909. 1.50. L. C. Page & Company.

Gentleman of Stratford. John Brophy. LC 40-3844. 1940. Harper & Brothers.

Gentleman of the Jungle. Tom Gill. LC 40-6701. 1940. G. P. Putnam's Sons.

Gentleman of the Party. Arthur George Street. LC 37-163862. 1937. E. P. Dutton & Co.

Gentleman of the Road. Horace William Bleackley. LC 11-5480. 1911. 1.50. John Lane.

Gentleman of the Slums: Being the Autobiography of a Charwoman. Annie Wakeman Lathrop. LC 1-25453. 1901. L. C. Page & Company.

Gentleman of the South: A Memory of the Black Belt, from the Manuscript Memoirs of the Late Colonel Stanton Elmore. William Garrott Brown. LC 3-12961. 1903. The Macmillan Company.

Gentleman on Horseback. Bernard McConville. LC 35-22663. 1935. Trayor Lane.

Gentleman Overboard. Herbert Clyde Lewis. LC 37-9720. 1937. The Viking Press.

Gentleman Pirate. Jawette Radcliffe. (Candlelight Regency Romance#185). 1975. (pbk.) 0.75. Dell.

Gentleman Player: His Adventures on a Secret Mission for Queen Elizabeth. Robert Neilson Stephens. LC 99-2607. 1899. L. C. Page and Company.

Gentleman Ragman: Johnny Thompson's Story of the Emigger. Wilbur Dick Nesbit. LC 6-33585. 1906. Harper & Brothers.

Gentleman Ranker. John Edward Jennings. LC 42-200974. 1942. Reynal & Hitchcock.

Gentleman Riches. Lucille Papin Borden. LC 25-182782. 1925. The Macmillan Company.

Gentleman Rogue. Cover Painting by Walter Baumhofer. Gardner F Fox. LC 54-26999. (Gold medal books, 394). 1954. Fawcett Publications.

Gentleman Traitor. Alan Williams. LC 75-15791. 1975. 8.95 (ISBN 0-15-135015-9). Harcourt Brace Jovanovich.

Gentleman Upcott's Daughter. Walter Raymond. LC 7-36634. (On cover: The "Unknown" library. no. 19,). Cassell Publishing Company.

Gentleman Vagabond: And Some Others. Francis Hopkinson Smith. LC 69-11915. (American short story series, v. 74). 1969. Garrett Press.

Gentleman Vagabond, and Some Others. Francis Hopkinson Smith. LC 72-8152. (American short story series, v. 74). 1972. (ISBN 0-8422-8109-6). MSS Information Corp.

Gentleman Vanishes. William Marchant. LC 78-21404. 1979. 10.00 (ISBN 0-312-32108-2). St. Martin's Press.

Gentleman with the Walrus Mustache. Guy Gilpatric. LC 39-7081. 1839. Dodd, Mead & Company.

Gentleman's Agreement. Laura Keane Zametkin Hobson. LC 47-30138. 1947. Simon and Schuster.

Gentleman's Agreement: A Novel. Laura Keane Zametkin Hobson. LC 79-27243. 1979. 15.00 (ISBN 0-89783-010-5). Larlin Corp.

Gentleman's Agreement: A Novel. Laura Keane Zametkin Hobson. LC 81-21243. 1982. 12.95 (ISBN 0-89621-332-3). Thorndike Press.

Gentleman's Gentleman: Being Certain Pages from the Life and Strange Adventures of Sir Nicolas Steele, Bart. Max Pemberton. LC 7-36381. 1896. Harper & Brothers.

Gentlemen All. William F Fitzgerald. LC 39-270671. 1930. Longmans, Green and Co.

Gentlemen All and Merry Companions. Ralph Wilhelm Bergengren. LC 23-885. 1922. B. J. Brimmer Company.

Gentlemen at Arms, by "Centurion" Pseud. a Captain in the British Army Who Has Served in France... John Hartman Morgan. LC 18-26820. 1918. Doubleday, Page & Company.

Gentlemen at Large. John Boland. (O.s.i.). 1968. pap. 0.60 o.s.i. (A332, Award). Univ Pub & Dist.

Gentlemen Callers. Nancy Lamb. LC 78-31725. 9.95 (ISBN 0-87223-530-0). Seaview Books: Trade Distribution by Simon and Schuster.

Gentlemen from England: A Novel. Maud Hart Lovelace & Lovelace, Delos W. LC 37-4879. 1937. The Macmillan Company.

Gentlemen from Mississippi. Frederick R. Toombs & Wise, Thomas Alfred, 1865-1928. LC 9-31678. J. S. Ogilvie Publishing Company.

Gentlemen Go by: Being an Exciting Interlude in the Life of a Young Man. Laurence Walter Meynell. LC 34-6043. 1934. J. B. Lippincott Company.

Gentlemen, Hush! Henry Herbert Knibbs & Lummis, Turbese. LC 38-285972. 1933. Houghton Mifflin Company.

Gentlemen, Hush! Jere Hungerford Wheelwright. LC 48-9118. 1948. C. Scribner's Sons.

Gentlemen: I Address You Privately. Kay Boyle. LC 33-34143. 1933. H. Smith and R. Haas.

Gentlemen in Black. 2nd ed. Dalton. Ed. by R. Reginald & Douglas Menville. LC 75-46265. (Supernatural & Occult Fiction Ser.). (Illus.). 1976. Repr. of 1831 ed. lib. bdg. 18.00x (ISBN 0-405-08123-5). Ayer Co.

Gentlemen in Their Season: By Gabriel Fielding Pseud. Alan Gabriel Barnsley. LC 66-17183. bds., 5.95. Morrow.

Gentlemen March. Roland Pertwee. LC 27-15525. 1927. Houghton Mifflin Company.

Gentlemen of Adventure. Ernest Kellogg Gann. 312p. 1983. 15.95 (ISBN 0-87795-465-8). Arbor Hse.

Gentlemen of Sixteen July. Rene L. Maurice & Ken Follett. 192p. 1982. pap. 2.75 (ISBN 0-523-41655-5). Pinnacle Bks.

Gentlemen of Sorts. Everett Young, pseud. LC 23-9243. 1923. H. Holt and Company.

Gentlemen of the North. Hugh Pendexter. LC 20-18928. 1920. Doubleday, Page & Company.

Gentlemen of Valor: And Other Stories. Thomas M Evans. LC 51-5876. 1951. Exposition Press.

Gentlemen Prefer Blondes. Anita Loos. (Illus.). 1963. 5.95 (ISBN 0-87140-888-0). Liveright.

Gentlemen Prefer Blondes. Anita Loos. (Illus.). 4.50 o.p. Tudor.

Gentlemen Prefer Blondes. Anita Loos. 1967. pap. 0.60 o.p. (60-299). Manor Bks.

Gentlemen Prefer Blondes. Anita Loos. 1974. pap. 1.25 o.p. (01064). Curtis.

Gentlemen Prefer Blondes," The Illuminating Diary of a Professional Lady. Anita Loos. LC 63-9284. 1963. Liveright Pub. Corp.

Gentlemen Prefer Blondes" The Illuminating Diary of a Professional Lady. Anita Loos. LC 25-23371. 1925. Boni & Liveright.

Gentlemen Prefer Slaves. Lucille Kallan. Orig. Title: Outside There, Somewhere. 1972. pap. 0.95 o.p. (95190). Beagle Bks.

Gentlemen Reform. John Boland. (O.s.i.). 1968. pap. 0.60 o.s.i. (A331, Award). Univ Pub & Dist.

Gentlemen Rogue. Ursula Torday. 1975. (pbk.) 1.25. Dell.

Gentlemen Should Marry. Florence Antoinette Kilpatrick. LC 46-17427. 1946. Arcadia House, Inc.

Gentlemen Traitor. Alan Williams. 1977. pap. 1.95 o.p. (ISBN 0-515-04333-8). BJ Pub Group.

Gentlemen's Agreement. Betsey Riddle Hutton Zum Stolzenberg. LC 36-123129. E. P. Dutton Co., Inc.

Gentlemen's Relish. James Graham, pseud. 1968. pap. 0.95 o.p. (A396N, Award). Univ Pub & Dist.

Gentlewomen of Evil: An Anthology of Rare Supernatural Stories from the Pens of Victorian Ladies. Ed. by Peter Haining. LC 67-19279. (Illus.). 1967. Taplinger Pub. Co.

Gently Between Tides. Alan Hunter. 1982. 11.95 (ISBN 0-8027-5480-5). Walker & Co.

Gently by the Hand. Michael Trauner. 1976. (pbk.) 1.95 (ISBN 0-671-80440-5). Pocket Books.

Gently by the Shore. Alan Hunter. LC 56-7007. 1956. Rinehart.

Gently Does It: A Detective Story. Alan Hunter. LC 55-80077. 1955. Rinehart.

Gently Down the Stream. Alan Hunter. LC 60-110181. 1957. Roy Publishers.

Gently Falls the Rain: A Novel. William Harry Cannon. LC 45-99838. 1945. The Highland Press.

Gently in an Omnibus. A. Hunter. Incl. Gently Does It; Gently Through the Mill; Gently in the Sun. 1972. 6.95 o.p. (G06800). St Martin.

Gently in Another Omnibus: Three Complete Novels. Alan Hunter. LC 73-166525. (His The Gently series). (Crime connoisseur book). 1972. 7.95. St. Martin's Press.

Gently in the Highlands. Alan Hunter. LC 74-18254. 1975. 5.95 (ISBN 0-02-557550-3). Macmillan.

Gently Through the Woods. (Scene of the Crime Ser.: No. 46). 1982. pap. 2.25 (ISBN 0-440-13055-7). Dell.

Gently Through the Woods. Alan Hunter. LC 75-15852. 1975. 6.95. Macmillan.

Gently Where the Birds Are. Alan Hunter. LC 77-368793. 1976. 3.25 (ISBN 0-304-29752-6). Cassell.

Gently with the Innocents. Alan Hunter. (Scene of the Crime Mystery Ser.: No. 28). 1981. pap. 2.25 (ISBN 0-440-12834-X). Dell.

Gently with the Innocents. Alan Hunter. LC 73-16602. 1974. 5.95. Macmillan.

Gently with the Ladies. american ed. Alan Hunter. LC 74-477. 1974. 5.95. Macmillan.

Gently with the Painters. Alan Hunter. LC 75-43639. 1976. 6.95 (ISBN 0-02-557570-8). Macmillan.

Genuine Article: A Novel. Alfred Bertram Guthrie. LC 77-2248. 1977. 7.95 (ISBN 0-395-25361-6). Houghton Mifflin.

Genuine Girl. Jeanie Thomas Gould Lincoln. 1896. Houghton, Mifflin and Company.

Genuine Memoirs of the Celebrated Miss Maria Brown. John Cleland. LC 74-28329. (Flowering of the Novel). 1975. 25.00. Garland Pub.

Genuis Loci: And Other Tales. Clark Ashton Smith. LC 48-11586. 1948. Arkham House.

Geoffery Castleton, Passenger: A Romance of the Little Things. Richard Blaker. LC 24-9358. 1924. George H. Doran Company.

Geoffrey Hampstead: A Novel. Stinson Jarvis. LC 7-10347. (On cover: Appleton's town and country library, no. 57). 1890. D. Appleton and Company.

Geoffrey Moncton: Or, The Faithless Guardian. Susannah Strickland Moodie. LC 7-19148. (On cover: Lovell's library. no. 1067). 1887. J. W. Lovell Company.
Geoffrey Strong. Laura Elizabeth Howe Richards. LC 1-13908. D. Estes & Company.
Geography. Edward Dorn. 1964. 7.50 (ISBN 0-89760-133-5). Telegraph Bks.
Geometries Bright & Dark. Federico L. Espino, Jr. 112p. 1981. pap. 5.00x. New Day NY.
Geordie. David Harry Walker. LC 50-6580. 1950. Houghton Mifflin.
George Allender. James William Chilton. LC 41-5872. Fortuny's.
George and Anna. Barbara Rees. LC 75-25097. 7.95 (ISBN 0-06-013528-X). Harper & Row.
George and Georgina: A Mystery Story. Eden Phillpotts. LC 52-2478. 1952. Hutchison.
George and Other Parables. Patricia Ryan. (Illus.). 1972. 1.95. Argus Communications.
George and the Crown. Sheila Kaye-Smith. LC 25-8269. E. P. Dutton & Company.
George Arbuthnott Jarrett: 1st Amer. Ed. Bernard Toms. LC 65-14707. bds., 4.75. Harcourt.
George Bailey: A Tale of New York Mercantile Life. Oliver Oldboy. LC 7-32515. 1880. Harper & Brothers.
George Balcombe. A Novel ... 1836. Harper & Brothers.
George Beneath a Paper Moon. Nina Bawden. LC 74-1876. 6.95 (ISBN 0-06-010246-2). Harper & Row.
George Blake: Double Agent. E. H. Cookridge, pseud. (Espionage-Intelligence Library). 256p. 1982. pap. 2.75 (ISBN 0-345-30264-8). Ballantine.
George Brandt. James Seguin De Benneville. LC 41-1584. The Christopher Publishing House.
George Brown: A Profile. Cassandra, pseud. price not set o.p. Pergamon.
George Canterbury's Will. Ellen Price Henry Wood Wood. (Seaside library. v. 11, no. 220). 1878. G. Munro.
George Christy: Or, The Fortunes of a Minstrel. Harlan Page Halsey. (On cover: Seaside library. Pocket ed., no. 365). G. Munro.
George Eliot and Her Readers: A Selection of Contemporary Reviews, Eds.: John Holmstrom, Laurence Lerner. With a Linking Commentary by Laurence Lerner. Ed. by John Holmstrom & Laurence Joint Lerner. LC 66-5739. bds., 6.00. Barnes & Noble.
George Eliot Miscellany: A Supplement to Her Novels. George Eliot & F. B Pinion. LC 81-7974. 1982. 28.50 (ISBN 0-389-20225-8). Barnes & Noble.
George Eliot's Mill on the Floss, Edited. George Eliot & Herzberg, Max John. 1886- LC 29-13156. (Golden Key Series). D. C. Heath and Company.
George Eliot's Scenes of Clerical Life. Thomas A Noble. LC 65-19755. (Yale studies in Eng., v.159) Bibl.). 5.00. Yale.
George Eliot's Silas Marner. George Eliot. LC 11-6715. (Eclectic English classics). American Book Company.
George Eliot's Silas Marner, Ed. By Ellen E. Garrigues... George Eliot & Garrigues, Ellen E., Ed. LC 11-17626. (Half-title: English readings for schools. General editor: W.L. Cross). 1911. 0.40. H. Holt and Company.
George Eliot's Silas Marner: Ed. for School Use by Arthur Hobston Quinn... George Eliot & Quinn, Arthur Hobson, 1875- Ed. LC 4184. (English Classics--Star Series). Globe School Book Company.
George Eliot's Silas Marner: Ed. with Introduction and Notes. George Eliot & Witham, Rose Adelaide, 1873- Ed. 1898. Ginn & Company.
George Eliot's Silas Marner: Ed. with Introduction and Notes by Carroll Lewis Maxcy... George Eliot & Maxcy, Carroll Lewis, 1865- Ed. LC 1-23020. (Silver Series of English and American Classics). 1901. Silver, Burdett and Company.
George Eliot's Silas Marner: Ed. with Notes and an Introduction. George Eliot & Herrick, Robert, 1888- Ed. LC 6-40728. (Half-title: Longman's English classics. no.2). 1895. Longmans, Green, and Co.
George Eliot's Silas Marner: Ed., with Notes and an Introduction by M.A. Eaton, B.A. George Eliot & Whiting, Mrs. Margaret Abbott (Eaton) 1876- Ed. Educational Publishing Company.
George Eliot's Silas Marner, the Weaver of Raveloe, Edited. George Eliot & Harrington, Evaline, Ed. LC 30-9739. (Golden Key Series). D.C. Heath and Company.
George Eliot's Silas Marner, the Weaver of Raveloe; with an Introduction by George Armstrong Wauchope... George Eliot. LC 99-3350. (On cover: Heath's English classics). 1899. D.C. Heath & Co.
George Eliot's The Mill on the Floss, Edited: By Myron R. Williams... George Eliot & Williams Myron Richards, Ed. LC 27-13375. (Half-title: English readings). H. Holt and Company.
George Eliot's The Mill on the Floss, Edited. George Eliot & Hayward, Mary Sully, Ed. LC 29-21545. (Eclectic English classics). American Book Company.
George Forest. A Story of the Present Day. Waverly Greene. (Dillingham's metropolitan library, no. 33). 1897. G. W. Dillingham Co.
George Geith of Fen Court. A Novel. Charlotte Eliza Lawson Riddell. 1865. T. O. H. P. Burnham,
George Helm. David Graham Phillips. LC 72-84640. 1974. (lib. ed.) 12.00 (ISBN 0-403-02999-6). Scholarly Press.
George Helm. David Graham Phillips. LC 12-21733. 1912. D. Appleton, and Company.
George: His Place to Be. Evelyn Keane. 1978. pap. 5.00 (ISBN 0-89502-020-3). FEB.
George MacDonald. Richard H. Reis. LC 72-125820. (Twayne's English Authors Series, TEAS119). 1972. 4.95. Twayne.
George Malcolm. Thomas Nicoll Hepburn. LC 7-4144. F. Warne & Co.
George Mandeville's Husband. Elizabeth Robins. LC 7-41970. 1894. D. Appleton and Company.
George Mason. Timothy Flint. LC 76-93616. (American Fiction Ser). 1970. lib. bdg. 10.95 o.s.i. (ISBN 0-512-00179-0). Garrett Pr.
George Mason, the Young Backwoodsman: Or, 'Don't Give up the Ship.' A Story of the Mississippi. Timothy Flint. 1829. Hilliard, Gray, Little and Wilkins.
George Meek: Bath Chair-Man. George Meek & Wells, Herbert George. LC 10-163906. 1910. 1.50. E. P. Dutton & Company.
George Melville. An American Novel... C. Hatch Smith. LC 8-8625. 1858. W. R. C. Clark & Co.
George Mills: A Novel. Stanley Elkin. LC 82-2494. 15.95. Dutton.
George Mueller: Young Rebel in Bristol. Faith Bailey. 1958. pap. 1.95 o.p. (ISBN 0-8024-0031-0). Moody.
George Orwell and the Origins of 1984. William R Steinhoff. LC 74-78989. 1975. 12.50 (ISBN 0-472-87400-4). University of Michigan Press.
George Orwell's Animal Farm: Notes. Ralph A Ranald. LC 66-1780. (Monarch notes and study guides, 718-7). 1966. 2.50. Monarch Pr.
George Thorne. Norval Richardson. LC 11-9940. 1911. 1.25. L. C. Page & Company.
George Washington Jones: A Christmas Gift That Went a-Begging. Ruth McEnery Stuart. LC 72-2068. (Black Heritage Library Collection). (Illus.). 1972. 9.75 (ISBN 0-8369-9068-4). Books for Libraries Press.
George Washington Jones: A Christmas Gift That Went a-Begging. Ruth McEnery Stuart. LC 3-27518. 1903. H. Altemus Company.
George Washington September, Sir! Ronald Harwood. LC 61-150293. 1961. Farrar, Straus and Cudahy.
George Wendern Gave a Party. John Inglis. LC 12-12011. 1912. 1.25. C. Scribner's Sons.
George Westover. Eden Phillpotts. LC 26-4778. 1926. The Macmillan Company.
George Whitefield & the Great Awakening. John Pollock. LC 72-76198. 288p. 1972. 7.95 o.p. (ISBN 0-385-03466-0). Doubleday.
Georges Lewys' The "Charmed American" Francois, L'American) a Story of the Iron Division of France. Georges Lewys. LC 19-641316. 1919. John Lane Company.
Georges Lewys' "The House of Love" "La Maitresse De Son Mari") Drawing by Steindl from Life. Georges Lewys. LC 36-610. 1935. Pub. for the Paris Book Club of New York by Lavater-Dorette, Inc.
George's Mother. Stephen Crane. 1896. E. Arnold.
George's Steam Locomotive. Helena Chambers. 3.75 o.p. Vantage.
George's Women. Catherine MacArthur. LC 79-3991. 1979. 8.95 (ISBN 0-312-32461-8). St. Martin's Press.
Georgette. Marion Hill. LC 12-13193. Small, Maynard and Company.
Georgette. From the French of Th. Bentzon Pseud. Tr. by E. P. Robins. Marie Therese Blanc & Robins, E. P., Tr. LC 6-13845. (On cover: The optimus series, no. 16). 1892. Donohue, Henneberry & Co.
Georgette Heyer Compendium. Harmony Raine. 95p. (Orig.). 1981. pap. 4.95x (ISBN 0-89966-325-7). Buccaneer Bks.
Georgette Heyer Omnibus. Georgette Heyer. LC 77-158585. 1973. 8.95 (ISBN 0-525-11265-0). Dutton.
Georgia Bequest. Manolia: Or, The Vale of Tallulah. W. R. Rembert. LC 7-30964. 1854. McKinne & Hall.
Georgia Boy. autograph ed. Erskine Caldwell. 1961. Grosset & Dunlap.
Georgia Boy. Erskine Caldwell. LC 43-511372. 1943. Duell, Sloan and Pearce.
Georgia Boy: And Other Stories. Erskine Caldwell. LC 48-1427. (New Avon library, 134). 1947. Avon Book Co.
Georgia Boy: And Other Stories. Erskine Caldwell. LC 46-6706. (On cover: Avon modern short story monthly, no. 30). 1946. Avon Book Company.
Georgia Clay. Hazel Higgins Gobay. LC 48-6063. 1948. Beechhurst Press.
Georgia Girl: By Token West Pseud. Adelaide Humphries. LC 53-2257. 1953. Woodford Press.
Georgia Jekyl & Hyde. E. C. Bruffey. Repr. of 1911 ed. 11.00 o.s.i. Finch Pr.
Georgia Nigger. John Louis Spivak. LC 69-14948. (Patterson Smith reprint series in criminology, law enforcement, and social problems. Publication no. 32). (Illus.). 1969. Patterson Smith.
Georgia Nigger. John Louis Spivok. LC 32-30643. 1932. Brewer, Warren and Putnam.
Georgia Scenes. Augustus Baldwin Longstreet. LC 70-91087. (American humorists series). (Illus.). 1969. Literature House.
Georgia Scenes, Characters, Incidents, &C. In the First Half Century of the Republic. Augustus Baldwin Longstreet. LC 17-6124. 1835. Printed at the S. R. Sentinel Office.
Georgia Scenes, Characters, Incidents, &C. In the First Half Century of the Republic. 2d ed. with original illustrations. ed. Augustus Baldwin Longstreet. LC 7-14374. 1840. Harper & Brothers.
Georgia Scenes, Characters, Incidents, &C. In the First Half Century of the Republic. 2d ed.... ed. Augustus Baldwin Longstreet. LC 17-6123. 1842. Harper & Brothers.
Georgia Scenes, Characters, Incidents, &C. In the First Half Century of the Republic. 2d ed.... ed. Augustus Baldwin Longstreet. LC 16-13106. 1846. Harper & Brothers.
Georgia Scenes, Characters, Incidents, &C. In the First Half Century of the Republic. 2d ed. with original illustrations. ed. Augustus Baldwin Longstreet. LC 18-173127. 1850. Harper & Brothers.
Georgia Scenes, Characters, Incidents, &C. In the First Half Century of the Republic. 2d ed.... ed. Augustus Baldwin Longstreet. LC 17-6122. 1854. Harper & Brothers.
Georgia Scenes, Characters, Incidents, &C. In the First Half Century of the Republic. 2d ed. with original illustrations. ed. Augustus Baldwin Longstreet. LC 3-6813. 1857. Harper & Brothers.
Georgia Scenes, Characters, Incidents, &C. In the First Half Century of the Republic. 2d ed. with original illustrations. ed. Augustus Baldwin Longstreet. 1860. Harper & Brothers.
Georgia Scenes: Characters, Incidents, Etc., in the First Half Century of the Republic. Introd. by B. R. McElderry, Jr. Augustus Baldwin Longstreet. LC 57-12444. (American century series, S-24). 1957. Sagamore Press.
Georgia Scenes, Characters, Incidents, Etc. In the First Half Century of the Republic. Augustus Baldwin Longstreet. LC 7-23205. (Harper's Franklin square library. no. 391). 1884. Harper & Brothers.
Georgia Scenes, Characters, Incidents, Etc. In the First Half Century of the Republic. Augustus Baldwin Longstreet. LC 7-14789. 1894.
Georgia Scenes, Characters, Incidents, Etc. In the First Half-Century of the Republic. new ed., from new plates, with the original illustrations. ed. Augustus Baldwin Longstreet. LC 8-26638. 1897. Harper & Brothers.
Georgia Whirlwind. Ray Landrum. LC 79-172874. 1972. 6.95 (ISBN 0-8059-1619-9). Dorrance.
Georgian Actress. Pauline Bradford Mackie Cavendish. LC 4193. 1900. L. C. Page & Company (Incorporated.
Georgian Actress. Pauline Bradford Mackie Hopkins. LC 4193. 1900. L. C. Page & Company (Incorporated.
Georgian House: A Tale in Four Parts. Frank Arthur Swinnerton. LC 32-30788. 1932. Doubleday, Doran & Company, Inc.
Georgian Love Story. Ernest Raymond. LC 78-160060. 1971. 6.95 (ISBN 0-8415-0118-1). McCall Pub. Co.
Georgian Rake. Alice C. Ley. 1974. pap. 0.95 o.p. (26590-4-095). Beagle Bks.
Georgian Stories ... With Portraits of the Authors. LC 23-4899. G. P. Putnam's Sons.
Georgiana. Marian P. Rettke. (Regency Romance Ser.). 224p. (Orig.). 1981. pap. 2.25 (ISBN 0-515-05656-1). Jove Pubns.
Georgiana: A Novel. Maude Phelps McVeigh Hutchins. LC 48-794602. 1948. New Directions.
Georgians. M. W Fuller. LC 71-39083. (Black Heritage Library Collection). 1972. (ISBN 0-8369-9021-8). Books for Libraries Press.
Georgians. Henrietta Hardy Hammond. LC 7-56496. 1881. J. R. Osgood and Company.
Georgians. Cynthia Van Hazinga. (Dell / James A. Bryans Book.). 1978. 2.25 (ISBN 0-440-04271-2). Dell Pub Co.
Georgians: A Novel. William Nathaniel Harben. LC 78-38653. (Black Heritage Library Collection). 1972. (ISBN 0-8369-9011-0). Books for Libraries Press.
Georgics. Maro Publius Vergilius. Tr. by L. P. Wilkinson. 1983. pap. 3.95 (ISBN 0-14-044414-9). Penguin.
Georgie May. Maxwell Bodenheim. LC 28-157901. 1928. Boni & Liveright.
Georgie May. Maxwell Bodenheim. LC 38-127663. 1928. H. Liveright.
Georgie Papers: Giving the Humorous Adventures and Experiences of Georgie, Bill Johnson, Marie and Several Other Persons. George E Booram. LC 6-15038. (sunnyside series, no 96.). 1897. J. S. Ogilvie Publishing Company.
Georgie Winthrop. Sloan Wilson. LC 62-20125. 1963. Harper & Row.
Georgina. Clare Darcy. (Dell Book.). (Illus.). 1977. (ISBN 0-440-12837-4). Dell Pub. Co.
Georgina. Clare Darcy. LC 78-150259. 1971. 5.95 (ISBN 0-8027-0348-8). Walker.
Georgina's Service Stars. Annie Fellows Johnston. LC 18-17914. 1.35. Britton Publishing Company.
Georgina's Service Stars. Annie Fellows Johnston. LC 20-17963. 1920. D. Appleton and Company.
Gerait's Daughter. Millie J Ragosta. LC 80-2759. 1981. 9.95 (ISBN 0-385-17274-5). Doubleday.
Geral-Milco: Or, The Narrative of a Residence in a Brazilian Valley of the Sierra-Paricis. A. R. Middletoun Payn. LC 2-29987. 1852. C. B. Norton.
Gerald. Eleanor C Price. (On cover: Seaside library. Pocket ed., no. 331). 1884. G. Munro.
Gerald. A Novel. Eleanor C Price. (Harper's Franklin square library, no. 458). 1885. Harper & Brothers.
Gerald: A Story of to-Day. Emma Leslie. LC 7-14491. (Church history stories, 2d ser., v. 6). 1881. Phillips & Hunt.
Gerald and Elizabeth. Dorothy Emily Stevenson. LC 78-80335. 1969. 5.95. Holt, Rinehart and Winston.
Gerald and Elizabeth. Dorothy Emily Stevenson. 1978. 1.95 (ISBN 0-441-28075-7). Ace Books.
Gerald Barry: Or The Joint Venture, a Tale in Two Lands. E A Fitzsimon. LC 6-41122. 1881. J. Sheehy.
Gerald Cranston's Lady. Gilbert Frankau. LC 24-4266. 2.00. The Century Co.
Gerald De Lacey's Daughter: An Historical Romance of Colonial Days. Anna Theresa Sadlier. LC 17-5452. 1916. P. J. Kenedy & Sons.
Gerald Ffrench's Friends. George Henry Jessop. LC 7-9928. 1889. Longmans, Green & Co.
Gerald Fitzgeald: "the Chvalier.". Charles James Lever. LC 52-46781. Harper.
Gerald Fitzgerald: "The Chevalier.". Charles James Lever. (Seaside library, v. 24, no. 464). G. Munro.
Gerald Northrop: A Novel. Claude Carlos Washburn. LC 14-17094. 1914. Duffield & Company.
Geraldine Bradshaw. Calder Willingham. LC 50-6253. 1950. Vanguard Press.
Geraldine: Or, The Gipsey of Germantown. A National and Military Romance. Harry Halyard. 1848. F. Gleason.
Geraldine's Saints: And Other Stories About School. Charles William Bardeen. LC 15-16234. 1.00. C. W. Bardee.
Geranium Lady. Sylvia Chatfield Bates. LC 16-2877. 1916. 1.25. Duffield & Company.
Geranium Leaf: An Original Tale. George Flagg Man. LC 44-34786. 1840. Marsh, Capen, Lyon, & Webb.
Gerard De Nevers: Prose Version of the Roman De la Violette, Ed. by L. F. H. Lowe. (Elliott monographs in the Romance langs. & lit., 22). 1966. pap., 8.50. Kraus Reprint.
Gerard, the Call of the Church-Bell. A Story. Lucinda Barbour Helm. LC 7-4116. 1884. Southern Methodist Publishing House, for the Author.
Gerardo the Unfortunate Spaniard: A Pattern for Lascivious Lovers. Gonzalo Cespedes y Meneses. Tr. by Leonard Digges. LC 80-2475. 1981. Repr. of 1622 ed. 142.40 (ISBN 0-404-19107-X). AMS Pr.
Gerard's Marriage: A Novel, from the French of Andre Theuriet. Andre Theuriet. LC 8-27744. (Half-title: Collection of foreign authors, no. II). 1877. D. Appleton and Company.
Gerda: Or, The Children of Work. Marie Sofie Birath Schwartz. Tr. by Borg, Selma & Shipley, Marie Adelaide (Brown) LC 8-2898. 1874. Porter & Coates.
Gerfalcon. Leslie Barringer. LC 76-6464. (His The Neustrian cycle; book 1). (Newcastle Forgotten Fantasy library; v. 7). (Illus.). 1976. 3.45 (ISBN 0-87877-106-9). Newcastle Pub. Co.
Gerfalcon. Leslie Barringer. LC 27-15196. 1927. Doubleday, Page & Company.

TITLE INDEX GETTING OUT.

Gerfalcon. Leslie Barringer. LC 80-19243. (His The Neustrian cycle; book 1). 1980. 10.95. Borgo Press.
Gerfalcon: The Neustrian Cycle, Book One. Leslie Barringer. (Forgotten Fantasy Library: Vol. 7). (Illus.). 310p. 1976. pap. 4.95 (ISBN 0-87877-106-9, F-106). Newcastle Pub.
Gerhard's Gold. Raymond W. Becker. (Orig.). 1979. pap. 1.95 (ISBN 0-532-23317-4). Woodhill.
Gerhardt's Children. Jerrold J Mundis. LC 76-7359. (Illus.). 1976. 9.95 (ISBN 0-689-10732-3). Atheneum.
Gerhart Hauptmann's "Before Daybreak" A Translation & an Introduction. Peter Bauland. (Studies in the Germanic Languages & Literatures: No. 92). xxiv, 87p. 1978. 9.95x (ISBN 0-8078-8092-2). U of NC Pr.
Germaine's Marriage. A Tale of Peasant Life in France. George Sand. 1892. Richmond, Croscup & Co.
German Affair. Theodore Weesner. LC 76-14201. 7.95 (ISBN 0-394-48433-9). Random House.
German Bracelet. J. Farrer Graydon. 1908. The Neale Publishing Company.
German Classics, 20 Vols. Ed. by Kuno Francke. Repr. of 1914 ed. Set. 695.00 (ISBN 0-404-02600-1); 34.75 ea. AMS Pr.
German Family. L. C. N Stone. LC 34-14544. The Bobbs-Merrill Company.
German Fiction: J. W. Von Goethe, Gottfried Keller, Theodor Fontane, Theodor Storm... c1917 ed. Goethe, Johann Wolfgang Von & Keller, Gottfried. LC 17-17428. (Harvard classics shelf of fiction, selected by C. W. Eliot. 15). P. F. Collier & Son.
German Humanism & Reformation: Selected Writings. Erasmus et al. Ed. by Reinhard P. Becker. LC 82-7278. (German Library: Vol. 6). 299p. 1982. 17.50 (ISBN 0-8264-0251-8); pap. 8.95 (ISBN 0-8264-0261-5). Continuum.
German Immigrant. Caroline Langman Converse. LC 53-12283. Bruce Humphries.
German Lesson. Siegfried Lenz. LC 77-163567. 1972. 8.95 (ISBN 0-8090-4907-4). Hill and Wang.
German Lieutenant: And Other Stories. August Strindberg. LC 15-23641. 1915. A. C. McClurg & Co.
German Love Story. Rolf Hochhuth. LC 80-13077. 10.95 (ISBN 0-316-36765-6). Little, Brown.
German Narrative Prose. Ed. by Eva J. Engel & William Edward Yuill. LC 66-13842. Dufour Editions.
German Narrative Prose: Ed. by E. J. Engel. Ed. by Eva J Engel & William Edward Yuill. LC 66-13842. v.3 bds., 6.95. Dufour.
German Narrattive Prose: V.1 Tr. from German by J. F. Hargreaves & J. G. Cumming. Ed. by Eva J. Engel. LC 66-13842. 1966. bds., 6.95. Dufour.
German Officer. Translated by Antonia White. Serge Groussard. LC 55-100911. 1955. Putnam.
German Pioneers: A Tale of the Mohawk. Friedrich Spielhagen & Sternberg, Levi, Tr. LC 8-16311. (On cover: Dearborn series, no. 55). 1891. Donohue, Henneberry & Co.
German Popular Stories Translated from the Kinder und Haus Marchen. Grimm Brothers. Tr. by Edgar Taylor. 1975. Repr. of 1823 ed. 12.95x o.s.i. (ISBN 0-8277-3854-4). British Bk Ctr.
German Requiem. Heike Doutine. LC 75-19335. 1975. 9.95. Scribner.
German Romance: Specimens of Its Chief Authors; with Biographical and Critical Notices. Thomas Carlyle et al. LC 7-3335. 1841. J. Munro and Company.
German Short Stories. Ed. by Harold Herman Bender. Blau, Julia E LC 20-11696. H. Holt and Company.
German Short Stories. Ed. by Hermann Georg Fiedler. Fiedler, Herma Ethelfried. LC 29-24505. 1928. The Clarendon Press.
German Short Stories. Ed. by Richard Newnham. (Orig., Bilingual.). (YA) (gr. 9 up). 1965. pap. 1.95 o.p. (ISBN 0-14-002040-3). Penguin.
German Short Stories, Vol. 2. Ed. by David Constantine. 320p. 1976. pap. 2.95 o.p. (ISBN 0-14-004119-2). Penguin.
German Short Stories, Vol. 1. 1900-1945, Vol. 2. 1945-1955, Vol. 3. 1955-1965. H. M. Waidson. Vol. 1. text ed. 5.50 (ISBN 0-521-06717-0); Vol. 2. text ed. 5.25 o.p. (ISBN 0-521-06718-9); Vol. 3. text ed. 6.50 (ISBN 0-521-07180-1). Cambridge U Pr.
German Short Stories: Contemporary Authors, German & English. bilingual ed. 155p. (Eng. & Ger.). 1975. pap. 5.20 (ISBN 3-4230-9097-9). Adler.
German Short Stories. Deutsche Kurzgeschichten. Ed. by Richard Newnham. LC 65-3835. (Penguin parallel texts, 2040). 1965. Penguin.
German Short Stories of Today. Ed. by E Hildegard Schumann & G. M. Wolff. LC 51-3549. 1951. Heath.
German Short Stries: Selected and Translated. Ed. by Ernest Nathaniel Bennett. LC 34-27180. (Half-title: The world's classics, 415). H. Milford. Oxford Uniersity Press.
German Spy. Bernard Newman. LC 37-20326. 1936. Hillman-Curl, Inc.
German Stories and Tales. Ed. by Robert Pick. LC 53-9481. (Borzoi series of stories and tales). 1954. Knopf.
German Tales. Berthold Auerbach. LC 6-4506. (Half-title: Handy-volume series, no. 7). 1869. Roberts Brothers.
German Women Writers of the Twentieth Century. Elisabeth Rutschi Herrmann & Edna Huttenmaier Spitz. LC 78-7016. (Pergamon international library of science, technology, engineering, and social studies). 1978. 16.00 (ISBN 0-08-021827-X) (ISBN 0-08-021828-8). Pergamon Press.
Germanna: An Historical Novel; Based Upon the "Ghost Stories" and Traditions Which Haunt the One-Time Home of "Parson" John Thompson and His Wife, the Former Lady Spotwood. Jennie Thornley Grayson. LC 31-13712. 1930. Shenadoah Publishing House, Inc.
Germinal. Emile Zola. LC 62-56471. 1924. Boni and Liveright.
Germinal. Emile Zola. LC 64-9652. 1961. Dolphin Books.
Germinal. Emile Zola. LC 68-5566. 1968. P. Smith.
Germinal. Emile Zola. Tr. by Stanley Hochman & Eleanor Hochman. LC 71-115136. (Signet classic). 1970. 1.50. New American Library.
Germinal. Emile Zola & Carlynme, --Tr. LC 22-514400. 1885. Belford, Clarke & Co.
Germinal. Emile Zola & Ellis, Havelock, 1859-Tr. LC 25-3548. (Borzoi classics). 1925. A. A. Knopf.
Germinal. Emile Zola & Ellis, Havelock, 1859-Tr. LC 37-18102. (Alblabooks). 1937. A. A. Knopf.
Germinal: By Emile Zola. Emile Zola & Ellis, Havelock, 1859- Tr. LC 37-31203. (Half-title: Everyman's library, ed. by Ernest Rhys. Fiction. no. 897). 1933. J. M. Dent & Sons, Ltd.
Germinal: Ed. by Elliott M. Grant. Emile Zola. (Modern student's lib.). 1962. 1.50. Scribners.
Germinal. Tr. from French Havelock Ellis. Emile Zola. (Doubleday dolphin bk. rebound). 1962. 3.50. Peter Smith.
Germinal. Translated from the French by Havelock Ellis, with an Introd. by Henri De Montherlant and Illus. by Berthold Mahn. Emile Zola. LC 56-14039. 1956. Heritage Press.
Germinie. Edmond Louis Antoine Huot De Goncourt & Jules Alfred Huot De Goncourt. LC 69-13911. (Illus.). 1969. (ISBN 0-8371-2011-X). Greenwood Press.
Germinie: By Edmond and Jules De Goncourt. With Front. by Anthony Gross. Introd. by Martin Turnell. Edmond Louis Antoine Huot De Goncourt & Jules Alfred Huot De Goncourt. LC 55-9929. 1955. Grove Press.
Germinie Lacerteux. Edmond Louis Antoine Huot De Goncourt & Goncourt, Jules Alfred Huot De. Tr. by M., H. E. (library of choice fiction no. 15). 1891. Laird & Lee.
Germinie Lacerteux. Edmond Louis Antoine Huot De Goncourt & Jules Alfred Huot De Goncourt. LC 5-32474. (Added T.-P.; Comedie D'amour Series). 1905. Societe Des Beaux-Arts.
Ge..inie Lacerteux; Ten Etchings. Edmond Louis Antoine Huot De Goncourt & Goncourt, Jules Alfred Huot De. Tr. by Chestershire, John. LC 6-43728. (Half-title: Chefs d'oeuvre du roman contemporain. Realists. v. 4). 1897. Printed by G. Barrie & Son.
Gernsback Awards, Vol. 1, 1926. Ed. by Forrest J. Ackerman. LC 82-50927. (Gernsback Awards Ser. 1926-1954). (Illus.). 320p. 1982. 14.95 (ISBN 0-943958-01-6). Triton Bks.
Geronimo Rex. Barry Hannah. 1973. 1.25. Avon.
Geronimo Rex. Barry Hannah. LC 70-174665. 1972. 7.95 (ISBN 0-670-33728-5). Viking Press.
Geronimo Rex. Barry Hannah. LC 82-22416. 1983. 5.95 (ISBN 0-14-006472-9). Penguin Books.
Gershon Kranzler's Ten Stories. Gershon Kranzler, pseud. 12.50 (ISBN 0-87559-126-4). Shalom.
Gershwin Song Book. George Gershwin. 1941. 4.95 o.p. S&S.
Gertrude. Hermann Hesse. LC 73-22196. 1974. 9.95 (ISBN 0-8161-6183-6). G. K. Hall.
Gertrude. Hermann Hesse. 1974. (pbk.) 1.50. Bantam Books.
Gertrude. rev. translation ed. Hermann Hesse. LC 69-13738. 1969. 4.95. Farrar, Straus and Giroux.
Gertrude: A Novel. Edward Hungerford. LC 13-8393. 1913. 1.25. McBride, Nast & Company.
Gertrude and I. Hermann Hesse. Tr. by Lewisohn, Adele (Guggenheimer) LC 16-10119. 1.00. The International Monthly, Inc.
Gertrude & the Mermaid. Richard Arthur Hughes. (Illus.). 4.95 (ISBN 0-8252-3115-9). Quist.
Gertrude Dorrance: A Story by Mary Fisher. Mary Fisher. LC 2-122963. 1902. A. C. McClurg & Co.
Gertrude Elliot's Crucible. Sarah Elizabeth Forbush G. S. Downs Downs. LC 8-4910. 1908. G. W. Dillingham Company.
Gertrude Haddon. "Only a Girl's Heart." 3d Series. Emma Dorothy Eliza Nevitte Southworth. LC 8-14246. (Ledger library, no. 101). 1894. R. Bonner's Sons.
Gertrude Haviland's Divorce. Inez Haynes Irwin. LC 25-208271. 1925. Harper & Brothers.
Gertrude Kloppenberg, Private. Ruth Hooker. (gr. 3-5). 1973. pap. 0.60 o.p. (ISBN 0-671-29334-6). Archway.
Gertrude Morgan: Or, Life and Adventures Among the Indians of the Far West. Barclay & Co.
Gertrude Stein. Avis Burnett. LC 72-75264. (Illus.). 1972. 5.95. Atheneum.
Gertrude, the Governess: Or, The Finger of Fate. A Tale of Retribution and Reward. William Mason Turner. (On cover: Munro's library, popular novels, v. l., no. 73). N. L. Munro.
Gertrude Wyoming: Or, The Splendors of a New World... Illustrated... Sidney Howard Vaughan. (Twentieth century series). Authors' Publishing Co.
Gertrude's Marriage. Bertha Behrens. Tr. by Mrs. J. W. Davis. LC 6-9748. 1889. Worthington Co.
Gertrude's Marriage. Bertha Behrens & Ford, Marian, Tr. LC 6-9747. (On cover: Seaside library. Pocket ed. no. 1270). G. Munro.
Gervaise. (L'assommoir). The Natural and Social Life of a Family Under the Second Empire. A Novel. Emile Zola & Binsse, Edward, Tr. LC 9-1326. 1879. G. W. Carleton & Co.; Etc., Etc.
Gervase. Ann Moray. LC 75-126198. (Illus.). 1970. 4.50. Morrow.
Gervase Castonel: Or, The Six Gray Powders. Ellen Price Henry Wood Wood. LC 9-502. Dick & Fitzgerald.
Gesammelte Kleine Schriften, 4 vols. Johann M. Von Loen. Ed. by J. C. Schneider & J. B. Muller. (Illus.). Repr. of 1752 ed. Set. 180.00 (ISBN 0-384-33788-0). Johnson Repr.
Gessar Khan. Ida Zeitlin. LC 77-79162. (Mythology). (Illus.). 1978. 12.00 (ISBN 0-405-10570-3). Arno Press.
Gesta Romanorum: Entertaining Moral Stories. Invented by the Monks As As a Fire-Side Recreation... Gesta Romanorum. Tr. by Swan, Charles. LC 24-11845. (Library of early novelists, ed. by E. A. Baker, v. 6). 1905. G. Routledge & Sons, Limited.
Gesta Romanorum: Or, Entertaining Moral Stories. rev. ed. Charles Swan. Ed. by Wynnard Hooper. (Illus.). 1876. pap. 3.00 o.p. (ISBN 0-486-20535-5). Dover.
Gesta Romanorum or Entertaining Moral Stories Invented by the Monks. Ed. by Wynnard Hooper. Tr. by Charles Swan. LC 75-136377. (Bohn's Antiquarian Lib). Repr. of 1894 ed. 37.50 (ISBN 0-404-50009-9). AMS Pr.
Geste of Duke Jocelyn. Jeffery Farnol. LC 20-1694. 1920. 2.25. Little, Brown, and Company.
Geste of Duke Jocelyn. Jeffery Farnol. LC 20-169308. 1920. 2.50. Little, Brown, and Company.
Gesture. John Cobb Cooper. LC 48-5368. 1948. Harper.
Gestures. Francis Poole. pap. 3.00. Anhinga Pr.
Get a Horse. Bellamy Partridge. LC 37-191530. Arcadia House.
Get a Little Lost, Tia. Phyllis A. Wood. 1979. pap. 1.75 (ISBN 0-451-09872-2, E9872, Sig). NAL.
Get Buchanan! Jonas Ward. 1978. pap. 1.50 (ISBN 0-449-14062-8, GM). Fawcett.
Get Buchanan! Jonas Ward. (Fawcett gold medal book). 1974. (pbk.) 0.95. Fawcett.
Get Home Free. John Clellon Holmes. LC 64-11074. 1964. Dutton.
Get Judge Parker! Albert Butler. 1982. 18.00x (ISBN 0-86025-171-3, Pub. by Ian Henry Pubns England). State Mutual Bk.
Get Judge Parker! Albert Butler. (Orig.). 1980. pap. 1.75 o.s.i. (ISBN 0-505-51500-8). Tower Bks.
Get Me to the Wake on Time. Ed. by Alfred Joseph Hitchcock. 1975. (pbk.) 0.95. Dell.
Get Next! George Vere Hobart. LC 5-26126. 1905. G. W. Dillingham Co.
Get Nookie. Ross Webb. (Nookie: No. 2). 192p. (Orig.). 1975. pap. 1.50 (ISBN 0-532-15168-2). Woodhill.
Get off My World. Eando Binder, pseud. (Orig.). 1970. pap. 0.75 o.p. (07121). Curtis.
Get off the Unicorn. Anne McCaffrey. LC 77-1709. 1977. 1.75 (ISBN 0-345-25666-2). Ballantine Books.
Get Out and Get Under. Max Wilk. LC 80-26051. 12.95 (ISBN 0-393-01425-8). Norton.
Get Out, Dr. Fogg! Thomas Edward Law. LC 50-54782. 1950. Story Book Press.
Get Out of the Draft or You Will Catch Your Death. Douglas B. Miller. 4.95 o.p. Vantage.
Get Ready for Battle. Ruth Prawer Jhabvala. 1963. 3.95 o.p. Norton.
Get-Rich-Quick Wallingford. A Cheerful Account of the Rise and Fall of an American Business Buccaneer. George Randolph Chester. LC 12-203413. 1908. A. L. Burt Company.
Get-Rich-Quick Wallingford: A Cheerful Account of the Rise and Fall of an American Business Buccaneer. George Randolph Chester. LC 8-128043. 1908. H. Altemus Company.
Get Smart! William Johnston. LC 65-24485. (Tempo books). 1965. Grosset & Dunlap.
Get Smart Once Again. William Johnston. LC 66-5286. (Tempo books orginal). 1966. Grosset & Dunlap.
Get the Woman ("M'sieu Sweetheart") Helen Barham Shipman. LC 30-35168. 1930. L. MacVeagh, The Dial Press.
Get These Men Out of the Hot Sun. Herbert Mitgang. LC 71-188941. 1972. 6.00 (ISBN 0-87795-035-0). Arbor House.
Get Wallace! Alexander Wilson. LC 35-8755. 1934. H. Jenkins, Limited.
Get Your Man: A Canadian Mounted Mystery. Ethel Arnold Smith Dorrance & Dorrance, James French, 1879- Joint Author. LC 21-7332. The Macaulay Company.
Getaway. Leslie Charteris. 1975. Repr. of 1933 ed. lib. bdg. 16.30x (ISBN 0-89190-388-7). Am Repr-Rivercity Pr.
Getaway: The New Saint Mystery. Leslie Charteris. LC 33-439155. 1933. Pub. for the Crime Club, Inc., by Doubleday, Doran & Company, Inc.
Getaway World. E. E. Smith & Stephen Goldin. (Family D'alembert Ser.: No. 4). 1977. pap. 1.25 o.p. (ISBN 0-515-04004-5). BJ Pub Group.
Gettin' in Society. George Blake. LC 28-131658. 1928. Harper & Brothers.
Getting Away with It. Leslie Glass. LC 76-2774. 1976. 7.95 (ISBN 0-385-12113-X). Doubleday.
Getting Away with It. Leslie Glass. 1977. 1.75 (ISBN 0-380-01703-2). Avon Books.
Getting Away with Murder. Alan Dennis Burke. LC 81-2345. 12.95 (ISBN 0-316-11688-2). Little, Brown.
Getting Better. Kenneth Klein. 1982. pap. 2.25 (ISBN 0-451-11558-9, AE1558, Sig). NAL.
Getting Down. Gail Anderson. 1973. pap. 1.95 o.s.i. (76-322). Lancer.
Getting Even. Woody Allen, pseud. 128p. Date not set. pap. 2.95 (ISBN 0-394-72640-5, V-640, Vin). Random.
Getting Even. Edward Behr. LC 80-5206. 10.00 (ISBN 0-06-010331-0). Harper & Row.
Getting Even: Gripping Tales of Revenge. LC 77-15441. 1978. 8.95 o.p. (ISBN 0-672-52397-3). Bobbs.
Getting Even: Gripping Tales of Revenge. LC 77-15441. 1978. 8.95 o.p. (ISBN 0-672-52397-3). Bobbs.
Getting Even: Gripping Tales of Revenge. Diana King. LC 77-15441. 1978. 8.95 (ISBN 0-672-52397-3). Bobbs-Merrill.
Getting Free. Lee Wotherspoon. 1976. pap. 3.50 o.p. Dear Kids.
Getting George Married. Florence Antoinette Kilpatrick. LC 33-1957.
Getting High in Government Circles. Art Buchwald. LC 76-158365. 1971. 5.95. Putnam.
Getting into Death. Thomas M. Disch. (Kangaroo Book)). 1977. 1.75 (ISBN 0-671-80926-1). Pocket Books.
Getting into Death and Other Stories. Thomas M Disch. LC 75-30998. 1976. 7.95 (ISBN 0-394-49803-8). Knopf: Distributed by Random House.
Getting It Right. Elizabeth Jane Howard. LC 82-70125. 1982. 13.95 (ISBN 0-670-33759-5). Viking Press.
Getting Married. August Strindberg. LC 72-11063. 1973. 7.95 (ISBN 0-670-33760-9). Viking Press.
Getting Mary Married. Jean Carew. LC 40-29644. 1940. Arcadia House, Inc.
Getting of Wisdom. Henrietta Richardson. LC 10-22804. 1910. Duffield & Company.
Getting of Wisdom. Henry Handel Richardson. LC 10-22804. 1910. Duffield.
Getting of Wisdom. rev. ed. Henry Handel Richardson. LC 32-26075. 1931. W. W. Norton.
Getting of Wisdom. Henry Handel Richardson. LC 81-9701. (Virago Modern Classic). 1981. 5.95 (ISBN 0-385-27189-1). Dial Press.
Getting of Wisdom see Australian Classics.
Getting off. Paul Rosner. 1973. pap. 0.95 o.p. (09249). Curtis.
Getting off: A Novel. Don Carpenter. LC 70-133588. 1971. 5.95 (ISBN 0-525-11330-4). Dutton.
Getting Out. Morton Redner. 1971. 5.95 o.p. (ISBN 0-8027-0350-X). Walker & Co.

Getting Out: A Novel. Morton Redner. LC 74-150258. 1971. 5.95. Walker.
Getting Pretty on the Table. Robert Gover. LC 75-9549. (Capra chapbook series; no. 31). 1975. 10.00. (ISBN 0-88496-032-3) (ISBN 0-88496-031-5). Capra Press.
Getting Rid of Richard. Joyce Elbert. LC 77-183381. 1972. 6.95 o.p. (ISBN 0-87795-026-1, A4314). Arbor Hse.
Getting Rid of Richard: A Novel. Joyce Elbert. (Signet Book, Y5421). 1973. 1.25. New American Lib.
Getting Serious. Gordon Weaver. LC 80-17737. 144p. 1980. 12.95x (ISBN 0-8071-0777-8); pap. 7.95 (ISBN 0-8071-0778-6). La State U Pr.
Getting Shafted. Jackson Short. 1973. (pbk) 1.25. Dell.
Getting Straight. Ken Kolb. LC 67-14173. 1967. Chilton Books.
Getting Straight. 1st Ed. Ken Kolb. (S3684). 1968. Bantam.
Getting There. William Bloom. LC 73-21005. 6.95 (ISBN 0-394-49294-3). Grove Press; Distributed by Random House.
Getting Through. John McGahern. LC 79-3667. 8.95 (ISBN 0-06-013043-1). Harper & Row.
Getting Together. Toby Stein. LC 79-23724. 1980. 9.95 (ISBN 0-689-11027-8). Atheneum.
Getting Together, No. 3. (The Bobby Sherman Show). (Orig.). 1972. pap. 0.75 o.p. (502-07191). Curtis.
Getting up and Going Home. Robert Woodruff Anderson. LC 77-16359. 8.95 (ISBN 0-671-22853-6). Simon and Schuster.
Getting up and Going Home. Robert Woodruff Anderson. (Berkley Book). 1979. 2.25 (ISBN 0-425-04186-7). Berkley Pub. Corp.
Gettysburg: A Novel. Stephen Longstreet. LC 61-6991. 1961. Farrar, Straus and Cudahy.
Gettysburg: Stories of the Red Harvest and the Aftermath. Elsie Singmaster. LC 13-94763. 1913. Houghton Mifflin Company.
Gettysburg: Stories of the Red Harvest and the Aftermath. new and enl. ed. Elsie Singmaster. LC 30-29560. 1930. Houghton Mifflin Company.
Gewehre der Frau Carrar. Bertolt Brecht. (Edition Suhrkamp: Bd. 219). 72p. (Ger.). 1980. pap. text ed. 3.25 (ISBN 3-518-10219-2, Pub. by Suhrkamp Verlag Germany). Suhrkamp.
GG 2 Deception. C. R. Duggan. (Orig.). 1981. pap. 2.50 (ISBN 0-505-51619-5). Tower Bks.
G'hals of New York: A Novel. Edward Zane Carroll Judson. LC 7-11446. R. M. De Witt.
Ghetto Comedies: By Israel Zangwill... Israel Zangwill. LC 7-151208. 1907. The Macmillan Company; Etc., Etc.
Ghetto Fighters. Tr. by Meyer Barkai. 1977. pap. text ed. 1.75 o.s.i. (ISBN 0-505-51159-2). Tower Bks.
Ghetto Fire Fighter. Harry J. Ahearn. 1977. 5.95 o.p. (ISBN 0-533-02447-1). Vantage.
Ghetto Messenger. sixty tales of a unique seventy year old telegraph messenger "boy". ed. Abraham Burstein. LC 29-5968. 1928. Bloch Publishing Company.
Ghetto Messenger: Sixty Tales of a Unique Seventy Year Old Messenger 'Boy' facsimile ed. Abraham Burstein. LC 72-150540. (Short Story Index Reprint Ser). Repr. of 1928 ed. 16.00 (ISBN 0-8369-3837-2). Ayer Co.
Ghetto Nurse. Ruth McCarthy Sears. 192p. (OSI). 1972. 3.95 o.s.i. Lenox Hill.
Ghetto Silhouettes. David Warfield & Hamm, Margherita Arlina, 1871- Joint Author. LC 2-21989. 1902. J. Pott & Company.
Ghetto Sketches. Odie Hawkins. 256p. (Orig.). 1972. pap. 1.50 (ISBN 0-87067-425-0, BH425). Holloway.
Ghetto Tragedies. Israel Zangwill. LC 19-5139. The Jewish Publication Society of America.
Ghitza and Other Romances of Gypsy Blood. Konrad Bercovici. LC 21-16538. Boni and Liveright.
Gholan Gate. Gregory Kern. (Cap Kennedy,#7). 1974. (pbk.) 0.95. DAW Books.
Ghost. Arnold Bennett. LC 7-24288. 1907. H. B. Turner & Co.
Ghost. William Douglas O'Connor. LC 7-44519. 1867. G. P. Putnam & Son; Etc., Etc.
Ghost: A Fantasia on Modern Themes. Arnold Bennett. LC 74-5392. (collected works of Arnold Bennett). 1974. (ISBN 0-518-19103-6). Books for Libraries Press.
Ghost: A Legend. Clara Sicard. LC 76-3975. (Supernatural and Occult Fiction). 1976. 15.00 (ISBN 0-405-09160-5). Arno Press.
Ghost: A Modern Fantasy. Arnold Bennett. LC 11-1448. 1911. 1.20. Small, Maynard & Company.
Ghost and Flesh: Stories and Tales. William Goyen. LC 52-5143. 1952. Random House.
Ghost & Horror Stories of Ambrose Bierce. Ambrose Gwinnett Bierce. Ed. by E. F. Bleiler. (Orig.). 1964. pap. 3.00 (ISBN 0-486-20767-6). Dover.
Ghost and Mrs. Muir. Alice Denham. LC 75-6097. 1968. 0.60. Popular Library.
Ghost & Mrs. Muir. R. A. Dick, pseud. 180p. 1972. Repr. of 1945 ed. 6.95 o.s.i. (ISBN 0-85617-000-3). White Lion Pubs.
Ghost and Mrs. Muir. Josephine Leslie. 1974. (pbk.) 0.95 (ISBN 0-671-77761-0). Pocket Books.
Ghost and Mrs. Muir. Josephine A. Leslie. 1945. Ziff-Davis Publishing Company.
Ghost & Shadow Towns of the Glory Road. Thomas W. Moore. LC 76-92040. (Illus.). 1970. 10.00 o.p. (ISBN 0-498-07427-7). A S Barnes.
Ghost and the Garnet. Marilyn Ross. (Birthstone Gothic). (Beagle book: Vol. 5). 1975. (pbk.) 0.95 (ISBN 0-345-26665-X). Ballantine Books.
Ghost at Lost Lover's Lane. large easy-to-read type. ed. Joy Ann Blackwood. (Queen-Size Gothic). 1973. (pbk) 0.95. Popular Lib.
Ghost at Ravenkill Manor. easy eye ed. Paulette Warren. pap. 0.60 o.p. Lancer.
Ghost at Stagmere. Alice Brennan. 1973. (pbk) 0.95. Warner Paperback Library.
Ghost at the Wedding. Elna Stone. 1977. pap. 1.25 o.s.i. (ISBN 0-505-51145-2). Tower Bks.
Ghost Blonde. Mark Derby. 1960. 3.50 o.p. (ISBN 0-670-33770-6). Viking Pr.
Ghost Blonde: By Mark Derby Pseud. Harry Wilcox. LC 60-140850. 1960. Viking Press.
Ghost Book: Stories. Ed. by Cynthia Mary Evelyn Charteris Asquith. LC 27-5135. 1927. C. Scribner's Sons.
Ghost Books. Cynthia Mary Evelyn Charteris Asquith. (Orig.). 1971. pap. 0.95 o.p. (95155). Beagle Bks.
Ghost Breaker: A Novel Based Upon the Play. Charles W Goddard & Dickey, Paul. LC 15-186213. 1915. 0.50. Hearst's International Library Company.
Ghost Bullet Range. Johnston McCulley. LC 45-1219. 1945. Arcadia House, Inc.
Ghost Car. Bill Knox. LC 66-209688. 3.50. Pub. for the Crime Club by Doubleday.
Ghost Child. Duffy Stein. (Orig.). 1982. pap. 3.50 (ISBN 0-440-12955-9). Dell.
Ghost Dance. John Norman. (Science Fiction Ser.). 1979. pap. 2.75 (ISBN 0-87997-633-0, UE1633). Daw Bks.
Ghost Dance Messiah: The Jack Wilson Story. Paul Bailey. 1971. 6.95 o.p. (ISBN 0-87026-025-1). Westernlore.
Ghost Dancers. John Benteen. (Sundance Ser.: No. 10). 176p. 1982. pap. 2.25 (ISBN 0-8439-1117-4, Leisure Bks). Nordon Pubns.
Ghost Flowers. Margaret Summerton. LC 72-89348. 1973. 4.95 (ISBN 0-385-07736-X). Published for the Crime Club by Doubleday.
Ghost Flowers. Margaret Summerton. 1977. 1.75 (ISBN 0-441-28555-4). Ace Books.
Ghost Fox. James A. Houston. LC 76-24907. 8.95 (ISBN 0-15-135300-X). Harcourt Brace Jovanovich.
Ghost Fox. James A. Houston. 1978. 1.95 (ISBN 0-380-01816-0). Avon.
Ghost, Gales & Gold. Edward R. Snow. LC 72-3936. (Illus.). 288p. 1972. 6.95 (ISBN 0-396-06658-5). Dodd.
Ghost Girl. Edgar Evertson Saltus. LC 79-116005. 1970. (ISBN 0-404-05546-X). AMS Press.
Ghost Girl. Edgar Evertson Saltus. LC 22-15848. Boni and Liveright.
Ghost Girl. Henry De Vere Stacpoole. LC 18-18341. 1918. John Lane Company.
Ghost Girl. Henry Kitchell Webster. LC 13-1901. D. Appleton and Company.
Ghost Gold: By Tom West Pseud. 1st Ed. Fred East. LC 49-50348. (Dutton Diamond D western). 1950. Dutton.
Ghost Gun: By Tom West Pseud. 1st Ed. Fred East. LC 52-8242. (Dutton Diamond D western). 1952. Dutton.
Ghost House. Norman Berrow. LC 79-2533. 1980. 8.95 (ISBN 0-312-32651-3). St. Martin's Press.
Ghost House. Foxhall Daingerfield. LC 26-15136. 1926. D. Appleton and Company.
Ghost House. Claire McNally. (Orig.). 1980. pap. 2.95 (ISBN 0-553-20472-6). Bantam.
Ghost House. Conde Benoist Pallen. LC 28-242751. 1928. Manhattanville Press.
Ghost House. Lois Simmie. LC 77-362602. (Illus.). 3.00 (ISBN 0-919926-03-7). Coteau-Books.
Ghost House Revenge. Claire McNally. 240p. (Orig.). 1981. pap. 2.50 (ISBN 0-553-14624-6). Bantam.
Ghost-Hunter and His Family. John Banim. LC 7-19677. (library of romance, v. 1). 1833. Carey, Lea, & Blanchard.
Ghost-Hunter and His Family. Michael Banim. LC 78-12230. (Ireland, from the Act of Union, 1800, to the Death of Parnell, 1891; 22). 1978. 42.00 (ISBN 0-8240-3471-6). Garland.
Ghost Hunters. Ralph Aiken. LC 34-8577. 1934. R. M. McBride & Company.
Ghost Hunters. Arthur Tofte. 1978. pap. 1.75 (ISBN 0-89041-224-3, 3224). Major Bks.
Ghost Images. Stephen Minot. LC 78-69509. 10.95 (ISBN 0-06-012978-6). Harper & Row.
Ghost in Monte Carlo (Number Forty Eight) Barbara Cartland. 1973. pap. 1.25 o.p. (ISBN 0-515-03019-8, V3019). BJ Pub Group.
Ghost in the Capitol. Idella Bodie. LC 75-32397. 1976. pap. 3.95 (ISBN 0-87844-028-3). Sandlapper Store.
Ghost in the Garret, and Other Stories. Mary Ann Fisher. LC 11-471. Aberdeen Publishing Company.
Ghost in the Music. John Treadwell Nichols. LC 79-657. 8.95 (ISBN 0-03-042576-X). Holt, Rinehart and Winston.
Ghost in the Sloss Furnaces. Kathryn T. Windham. (Illus.). 24p. 1978. pap. 3.00. Birmingham Hist Soc.
Ghost in the Tower: An Episode in Jacobia. Earl H Reed. LC 21-223260. 1921. Priv. Print.
Ghost It Was. Richard Henry Sampson. LC 37-2461. G. P. Putnam's Sons.
Ghost Kings. with eight illustrations by a. c. michael. 4th impression. ed. Henry Rider Haggard. LC 9-16804. 1908. Cassell and Company, Limited.
Ghost Lane. Edwin Palmer Hoyt. LC 73-165071. 1971. 6.95. R. B. Luce.
Ghost Legion. A Superhero Adventure. Kenneth Robeson, pseud. (His The fantastic adventures of Doc Savage, 3). (Illus.). 1975. 1.75. (ISBN 0-307-02377-X). Golden Press.
Ghost Lover. Dennis M. Clausen. 1982. pap. write for info. Bantam.
Ghost Lover. Patricia Theofan. (Orig.). 1979. pap. 1.95. Woodhill.
Ghost Mansion. J. N. Williamson. (Orig.). 1981. pap. 2.95 (ISBN 0-89083-884-4). Zebra.
Ghost Mesa. C. W. Thurlow Craig. LC 44-394319. 1944. Hutchinson & Co., Ltd.
Ghost Mine Gold. Walker A. Tompkins. (Orig.). 1971. pap. 0.60 o.p. (06149). Curtis.
Ghost Mountain Guns. William Frederick Bragg. LC 55-11875. 1955. Arcadia House.
Ghost of a Chance. Kelley Roos. LC 47-3150. 1947. A.A. Wyn, Inc.
Ghost of a Gunfighter. Wayne C. Lee. (Orig.). 1979. pap. 1.95 (ISBN 0-89083-559-4). Zebra.
Ghost of Africa: A Novel. William Stevenson. LC 80-7943. (Illus.). 14.95 (ISBN 0-15-135338-7). Harcourt Brace Jovanovich.
Ghost of an Idea. Mary Challis. (Raven House Mysteries Ser.). 224p. 1983. pap. cancelled (ISBN 0-373-63055-7, Pub. by Worldwide). Harlequin Bks.
Ghost of Bayou Tigre. Mary A. Fontenot. 1965. 2.95. Claitors.
Ghost of Black Hawk Island. August William Derleth. 1961. 3.00 o.p. (ISBN 0-696-61767-6). Hawthorn.
Ghost of Channing House. easy eye ed. Genevieve St. John. pap. 0.60 o.p. Lancer.
Ghost of Charlotte Cray: And Other Stories. Florence Marryat Church Lean. (On cover: The seaside library. Pocket ed. no. 208). 1884. G. Munro.
Ghost of Coquina Key. Jean Bellemy. (Orig.). 1970. pap. 0.75 o.p. (ISBN 0-447-74597-2). Lancer.
Ghost of Dark Harbor. Clarissa Ross. 1974. (pbk.) 0.95. Avon.
Ghost of Gallows Hill. Stanley Hart Cauffman. LC 26-7267. 1926. The Penn Publisheing Company.
Ghost of Guir House. Charles Willing Beale. LC 1-31821. 1897. The Editor Publishing Co.
Ghost of Guy Thyrle. Edgar Fawcett. LC 6-38797. (On cover: Once-a-week semi-monthly library. v. 12. no. 19)). 1895. P.F. Collier.
Ghost of Hamlet. Jennie Dethloffs Klein. LC 42-17634. 1942. Dorrance and Company.
Ghost of Hemlock Canyon. Harold Bindloss. LC 27-337651. 1927. Fredrick A. Stokes Company.
Ghost of Henry James. David Plante. LC 71-118217. 1970. 5.95. Gambit.
Ghost of Megan. Marc Lovell, pseud. LC 68-17796. 1968. Published for the Crime Club by Doubleday.
Ghost of Monsieur Scarron. Janet Lewis, pseud. LC 65-16520. 1965. 4.00, 1.95 pap.,. Swallow.
Ghost of Monsieur Scarron. 1st Ed. Janet Lewis, pseud. LC 59-63653. 1959. Doubleday.
Ghost of My Husband. A Tale of the Crescent City... William Gilmore Simms. LC 8-13062. (On cover: The sunny side series, no. 2). Chapman & Company.
Ghost of Oaklands. William Edward Daniel Ross. LC 67-9489. 1967. Arcadia House.
Ghost of Redbrook: A Novel. George James Atkinson Coulson. LC 6-28998. (The "Odd trump" series of novels). 1879. J. B. Lippincott & Co.
Ghost of Riverdale Hal. May Agnes Early Fleming. LC 15-21859. (arm chair library, no. 74). F. M. Lupton.
Ghost of Sir Francis Whynn Baronet: By L. A. Griffin Brownlee. Louisa Alberta Griffin Brownlee. LC 22-21187. 1922. The Austin Publishing Co.
Ghost of Staghorn. Auriel Douglas. 192p. (Orig.). 1981. pap. 1.95 (ISBN 0-523-41323-8). Pinnacle Bks.
Ghost of the Glen Gorge. Grace Miller White. LC 25-5618. The Macaulay Company.
Ghost of Whitaker Mountain. Emily Cary. (YA) 1979. 6.95 (Avalon). Bouregy.
Ghost Omnibus. Kurt D. Singer. 1974. pap. 0.75 o.p. (LB20S). Leisure Bks.
Ghost on the Balcony. Dwight Marfield. LC 39-11999. 1939. E. P. Dutton & Co., Inc.
Ghost Pirates. William Hope Hodgson. LC 75-28856. (Classics of science fiction). 1976. 12.50. (ISBN 0-88355-370-8) (ISBN 0-88355-455-0). Hyperion Press.
Ghost Plane: A Novel of the North. Arthur John Arbuthnott Stringer. LC 40-138083. The Bobbs-Merrill Company.
Ghost Rider. Max Brand. 212p. Repr. of 1920 ed. lib. bdg. 12.95x (ISBN 0-88411-521-6). Amereon Ltd.
Ghost Rig. Cliff Patton. (Orig.). 1981. pap. 3.50 (ISBN 0-89083-865-8). Zebra.
Ghost River. Frances Moyer Ross Stevens. LC 37-39257. 1937. Pub. for the Crime Club, Inc., Doubleday, Doran & Company, Inc.
Ghost River Inn. Cynthia Van Hazinga. (Queen-size gothic). 1973. (pbk) 0.95. Popular Library.
Ghost Road. George Washington Ogden. LC 36-18970. 1936. Dodd, Mead & Company.
Ghost Ship. R. W. Schooley. 2.75 o.p. Carlton.
Ghost Ships of the Great Lakes. Dwight Boyer. LC 68-23094. (Illus.). 1968. 8.95 (ISBN 0-396-05783-7). Dodd.
Ghost Song. Dorothy Daniels. LC 77-3723. 1977. 9.95 (ISBN 0-89340-083-1). J. Curley.
Ghost Song. Dorothy Daniels. 1974. (pbk.) 0.95 (ISBN 0-671-77777-7). Pocket Books.
Ghost Stories. Michael Arlen. LC 75-46249. (Supernatural and Occult Fiction). 1976. 10.00 (ISBN 0-405-08109-X). Arno Press.
Ghost Stories. Ed. by John Hampden. LC 43-423642. (Half-title: Everyman's library, ed. by Ernest Rhys. Fiction. No. 952). 1939. J. M. Dent & Sons Ltd.
Ghost Stories. Herbert Russell Wakefield. LC 75-46311. (Supernatural & Occult Fiction). 1977. 16.00 (ISBN 0-405-08173-1). Arno Press.
Ghost Stories and Mysteries. Joseph Sheridan Le Fanu. LC 74-75845. 1975. 4.00 (ISBN 0-486-20715-3). Dover Publications.
Ghost Stories and Tales of Mystery. Joseph Sheridan Le Fanu. LC 76-6013. (Le Fanu, Joseph Sheridan, 1814-1873. Works. 1976). 1976. 21.00 (ISBN 0-405-09254-7). Arno Press.
Ghost Stories of an Antiquary. Montague Rhodes James. LC 74-160855. (Illus.). 1971. 1.75 (ISBN 0-486-22758-8). Dover Publications.
Ghost Stories of an Antiquary. Montague Rhodes James. LC 76-358127. 1974-1911. (0.80, 2.95 u.s.) (ISBN 0-14-003892-2). Penguin Books.
Ghost-Stories of an Antiquary. Montague Rhodes James. LC 77-81269. (Short story index reprint series). (Illus.). 1969. (ISBN 0-8369-3021-5). Books for Libraries Press.
Ghost Stories of Edith Wharton. Edith Newbold Jones Wharton. LC 72-12148. (Illus.). 1973. 8.95 (ISBN 0-684-13338-5). Scribner.
Ghost Stories of M. R. James. M. R. James. LC 74-16222. 1975. 15.00 o.p. (ISBN 0-312-32655-6). St Martin.
Ghost Stories of M. R. James. M. R James. 1974. (ISBN 0-7131-5757-7). Edward Arnold.
Ghost Stories of Old New Orleans. Jeanne De Lavigne. LC 46-7188. 1946. Rinehart & Company, Inc.
Ghost Stories of Texas. W. C. Syles. 1981. 10.95. Texian.
Ghost Stories Round the World. Geoffrey Palmer & Noel Lloyd. LC 68-12414. (Illus.). Roy Publishers.
Ghost Story. Richard Hill. LC 79-162427. (Liveright new writer). 1971. 3.95 (ISBN 0-87140-538-5). Liveright.
Ghost Story. Peter Straub. LC 78-27120. 10.95. Coward, McCann & Geoghegan, Inc.
Ghost Sub. Roger E. Herst. 384p. 1980. pap. 2.50 (ISBN 0-89083-655-8). Zebra.
Ghost Sub. Roger E. Herst. 1982. pap. 2.50 (ISBN 0-8217-1060-5). Zebra.
Ghost Tales and Legends. H. Drummond Gauld. 1930. Frederick A. Stokes Company.
Ghost Tales of Cripple Creek. Chas. Clifton. (Illus.). 30p. (Orig.). 1983. pap. write for info. (ISBN 0-936564-24-5). Little London.
Ghost Town. Ursula Torday. LC 76-6906. 1976. 7.95 (ISBN 0-698-10735-7). Coward, McCann & Geoghegan.
Ghost Town Album. Lambert F. Florin. (Illus.). 1962. 12.95 o.p. (ISBN 0-87564-302-7). Superior Pub.
Ghost Town Bonanza: A Gay Novel. Rosemary Drachman Taylor. LC 54-6335. 1954. Crowell.
Ghost-Town Gold. William Colt MacDonald. LC 35-199869. Covici-Friede.
Ghost Town Gold. William Colt MacDonald. 1974. (pbk.) 0.95 (ISBN 0-380-00130-6). Avon.
Ghost Towns & Back Roads. Donald E. Bower. 256p. 1974. pap. 4.95 o.p. Stackpole.

TITLE INDEX GIANTS UNLEASHED.

Ghost Towns & Mining Camps: Selected Papers. B. R. Nelson et al. (Illus.). 1977. 3.50 o.p. (ISBN 0-89133-055-0). Preservation Pr.
Ghost Towns of Australia. George Farwell. (Illus.). 1965. 7.50 o.s.i. Tri-Ocean.
Ghost Towns of British Columbia (1975) Bruce Ramsay. (Illus.). pap. 7.50 o.p. Heinman.
Ghost Towns of New Mexico. Michael Jenkinson & Karl Kernberger. LC 67-29684. (Illus.). 1967. 7.50 o.p. (ISBN 0-8263-0056-1). U of NM Pr.
Ghost Towns of Southern Illinois. Glenn J. Sneed. (Illus.). 1977. 16.95 o.p. G J Sneed.
Ghost Towns of the West. 2nd ed. Sunset Editors. LC 77-72507. (Illus.). 224p. 1978. pap. 9.95 (ISBN 0-376-05314-3, Sunset Bks.). Sunset-Lane.
Ghost Towns of the West. Sunset Editors. Ed. by William Carter. LC 78-157170. (Illus.). 1971. 14.95 o.p. (ISBN 0-376-05311-9, Sunset). Lane.
Ghost Trails. Wilbur C Tuttle. LC 40-4667. 1940. Houghton Mifflin Company.
Ghost Trails to Ghost Towns. rev. ed. Inez Hunt & Wanetta W. Draper. (Orig., Photos). pap. 1.00 o.p. (ISBN 0-8040-0134-0, CB1, SB). Swallow.
Ghost Train. Ruth Rogers. LC 26-21489. Small, Maynard & Company.
Ghost Wanted. Finlay McDermid. LC 43-73814. 1943. Simon and Schuster.
Ghost Who Fell in Love. Barbara Cartland. LC 77-28768. 6.95. Dutton.
Ghost Winds. Muriel O'Brien. 1974. 4.95 o.p. (ISBN 0-89002-024-8); pap. 2.00 o.p. (ISBN 0-89002-025-6). Northwoods Pr.
Ghost Wore Black. Frances Y. McHugh. Ed. by Alice Sachs. 1970. 3.95 o.p. Lenox Hill.
Ghost Wore Black. Frances Y. McHugh. pap. 0.75 o.s.i. (01-348). Lancer.
Ghost Writer. Diana Carter. LC 74-15366. 1975. 6.95. Macmillan Publishing Co. Inc.
Ghost Writer. Philip Roth. LC 79-13146. 8.95 (ISBN 0-374-16189-5). Farrar, Straus and Giroux.
Ghost Writer. Philip Roth. LC 79-28657. 1980. 10.95 (ISBN 0-8161-3069-8). G. K. Hall.
Ghostboat. George Simpson & Neal Burger. 1976. pap. 3.95 (ISBN 0-440-15421-9). Dell.
Ghostboat. George E Simpson & Burger, Neal R. (Illus.). 1976. (pbk.) 1.95. Dell.
Ghosting. Robert Goulart. (Raven House Mysteries Ser.). 224p. 1982. pap. 2.25 (ISBN 0-373-63025-5, Pub. by Worldwide). Harlequin Bks.
Ghostland: A Novel. Fred Rothermell. LC 40-30889. J. B. Lippincott Company.
Ghostlight. Clare McNally. 1982. pap. 2.95 (ISBN 0-553-22520-0). Bantam.
Ghostly Bridegroom. Leona Collier. (Orig.). 1981. pap. 1.75 (ISBN 0-8439-8015-X, Tiara Bks). Nordon Pubns.
Ghostly by Gaslight. Ed. by Samuel Moskowitz & Alden Norton. (Orig.). 1971. pap. 0.75 o.p. (T2416). Pyramid Pubns.
Ghostly Gentlewomen: Two Centuries of Spectral Tales by the Gentle Sex. Seon Manley & Gogo Lewis. 7.95 (ISBN 0-688-41782-5). Lothrop, Lee & Shepard Co.
Ghostly, Grim and Gruesome: An Anthology. Ed. by Helen Hoke. LC 76-54258. 6.95 (ISBN 0-8407-6545-2). T. Nelson.
Ghostly Hoofbeats. Norman A Fox. LC 52-8080. (Silver star westerns). 1952. Dodd, Mead.
Ghostly Lover. Elizabeth Hardwick. LC 45-4283. 1945. Harcourt, Brace and Company.
Ghostly Lover. Elizabeth Hardwick. LC 81-9679. 1982. 12.95 (ISBN 0-912946-95-4). Ecco Press.
Ghostly Tales & Mysterious Happenings of Old Monterey. Randall A. Reinstedt. LC 79-110356. (Illus.). 64p. 1977. pap. 3.95 (ISBN 0-933818-04-1). Ghost Town.
Ghostly Tales of Henry James. Henry James & Edel, Leon Joseph, 1907- Ed. LC 49-7759. 1948-1949. Rutgers Univ. Press.
Ghostly Tales of Washington Irving. Ed. by Michael Hayes. 1980. 9.95 (ISBN 0-7145-3739-X). Riverrun NY.
Ghostly Tales to Be Told: A Collection of Stories from the Great Masters, Arranged for Reading and Telling Aloud. Ed. by Basil Davenport. LC 50-10165. 1950. Dodd, Mead.
Ghosts. Ed McBain. 176p. 1981. pap. 2.25 (ISBN 0-553-14518-5). Bantam.
Ghosts. Ed McBain. 212p. 1980. 9.95 (ISBN 0-670-33806-0). Viking Pr.
Ghosts. Marsha Parker. LC 81-19497. 12.95. E.P. Dutton.
Ghosts. Ursula Perrin. (H3714). 1968. Bantam.
Ghosts. Ursula Perrin. LC 67-11125. 1967. Knopf; Distributed by Random House.
Ghosts. Edith Newbold Jones Wharton. LC 37-24569. 1937. D. Appleton-Century Company, Incorporated.
Ghosts: A Samuel Lyle Mystery Story. Arthur Crabb. LC 21-45505. 1921. 2.00. The Century Co.
Ghosts: A Treasury of Chilling Tales Old and New. Marvin Kaye & Saralee Kaye. LC 81-43065. 2.95 (ISBN 0-385-18506-5). Doubleday.
Ghosts About Us. rev. ed. Clara Burke. (Illus.). 1969. 2.95 o.p. (ISBN 0-8059-1358-0). Dorrance.
Ghosts: An 87 Precinct Novel. Evan Hunter. LC 79-26557. 1980. 9.95 (ISBN 0-670-33806-0). Viking Press.
Ghosts: An 87th Precinct Novel. Evan Hunter. LC 80-23791. 1980. 12.95 (ISBN 0-8161-3128-7). G. K. Hall.
Ghosts & Goosebumps: Supernatural Stories from Alabama. Jack Solomon & Olivia Solomon. (Illus.). 240p. 1981. 17.95 (ISBN 0-8173-0075-9). U of Ala Pr.
Ghosts & Greasepaint. W. MacQueen-Pope. 334p. 1980. Repr. lib. bdg. 30.00 (ISBN 0-8492-6753-6). R West.
Ghosts & Grinning Shadows. Helen Adam. 1979. pap. 4.00 (ISBN 0-914610-10-4). Hanging Loose.
Ghosts & Legends of Fredrick County. Timothy L. Cannon & Nancy F. Whitmore. LC 79-64285. (Illus., Orig.). 1979. pap. 2.95 (ISBN 0-9602816-0-6). T L Cannon & N F Whitmore.
Ghosts and Marvels: A Selection of Uncanny Tales from Daniel Defoe to Algernon Blackwood. Ed. by Vere Henry Collins. LC 72-6075. (Short story index reprint series). 1972. (ISBN 0-8369-4203-5). Books for Libraries Press.
Ghosts, Castles, and Victims: Studies in Gothic Terror. Ed. by Jack Wolf. Barbara H. Wolf. LC 74-76209. (Fawcett Crest book). 1974. (pbk.) 1.50. Fawcett Publications.
Ghost's Companion: A Haunting Anthology. Peter Haining. LC 75-30227. (Illus.). 1976. 7.95 (ISBN 0-8008-3228-0). Taplinger Pub. Co.
Ghosts Go Haunting. Geoffrey Palmer & Noel Lloyd. LC 68-12413. (Illus.). Roy Publishers.
Ghosts, Grim and Gentle: A Collection of Moving Ghost Stories. Ed. by Joseph Lewis French. LC 26-16192. 1926. Dodd, Mead and Company.
Ghosts' High Noon. John Dickson Carr. LC 71-85927. 1969. 5.95 o.p. (ISBN 0-06-010606-9, HarpT). Har-Row.
Ghosts' High Noon. Carolyn Wells. LC 30-277721. 1930. J. B. Lippincott Company.
Ghosts' High Noon: A Detective Novel. John Dickson Carr. LC 71-85927. 1969. 5.95. Harper & Row.
Ghosts I Have Met. John Kendrick Bangs. Repr. of 1899 ed. lib. bdg. 10.00 (ISBN 0-8414-1667-2). Folcroft.
Ghosts I Have Met. John Kendrick Bangs. 1971. pap. 4.95 (ISBN 0-87877-005-4, P-5). Newcastle Pub.
Ghosts I Have Met and Some Others. John Kendrick Bangs. LC 68-55663. (American short story series, v. 3). (Illus.). 1968. Garrett Press.
Ghosts I Have Met and Some Others. John Kendrick Bangs. LC 72-8203. (American short story series, v. 3). 1972. (ISBN 0-8422-8004-9). MSS Information Corp.
Ghosts I Have Met and Some Others. John Kendrick Bangs. LC 80-19172. 1980. 9.95 (ISBN 0-87877-305-3). Borgo Press.
Ghosts I Have Met and Some Others. By By John Kendrick Bangs. With Illustrations by Newell, Frost, & Richards. John Kendrick Bangs. LC 6-6290. 1898. Harper & Brothers.
Ghosts in the Valley. Adi-Kent T. Jeffrey. LC 75-4658. 96p. 1971. pap. 1.50 o.p. (ISBN 0-915460-00-9). New Hope.
Ghosts Incorporated. 1st Ed. Marjorie Hamilton Talbot. LC 57-9949. 1957. Pageant Press.
Ghosts Never Die. Rufus Heed. LC 54-837635. 1954. Vantage Press.
Ghosts of Buttonwillow: & Other Stories. Violet Keller. LC 75-129776. 1971. 3.95. Dorrance.
Ghosts of Buttonwillow & Other Stories. Violet Keller. 1970. 3.95 o.p. (ISBN 0-8059-1482-X). Dorrance.
Ghosts of Devils," I'm Done. Francis Marion Moore. LC 9-15518. Press of O. C. Cole & Son.
Ghosts of Elkhorn. Kerry Newcomb & Frank Schaefer. LC 81-51890. 1982. 12.95 (ISBN 0-670-33819-2). Viking Press.
Ghosts of Epidoris. Gregory Kern. (Science Fiction Ser). 1975. pap. 0.95 o.p. (UQ1159). DAW Bks.
Ghosts of Epidoris. Gregory Kern. (Cap Kennedy,#14). 1975. (pbk.) 0.95. DAW Books.
Ghosts of Fleet Street. John Gore. 1973. 17.50 (ISBN 0-8274-0734-3). R West.
Ghosts of Forever. Ray Bradbury. (Illus.). 130p. 1981. 60.00 o.p. (ISBN 0-8478-0358-9). Rizzoli Intl.
Ghosts of Kings. Ariadne Pritchett. (Orig.). 1972. pap. 0.75 o.p. (T2528, GM). Fawcett World.
Ghosts of My Study: A Book of Short Stories. Lou Hampton. LC 27-28083. Authors & Publishers Corporation.
Ghosts of Old Berkshire. Willard Douglas Coxey. LC 34-35319. 1934-35. The Berkshire Courier.
Ghosts of Palo Duro Canyon: A Historical Novel About the Wild Plains Indians. Robert S. Sprague. LC 73-173380. (Illus.). 1973. 5.95.
Ghosts of Red Hill: The Mystery of the Haunted House. Ira McKoger. 4.95 o.p. Carlton.
Ghosts of Slave Driver's Bend. Harry Harrison Kroll. LC 37-6381. The Bobbs-Merrill Company.
Ghosts of the Adobe Walls. Nell Murbarger. (Illus.). 7.50 o.p. Westernlore.
Ghosts of the Adobe Walls: Human Interest & Historical Highlights from 400 Ghost Haunts of Old Arizona. Nell Murbarger. 1977. pap. Treasure Chest.
Ghosts of the Air-Waves. Antonio Luigi Tauro. LC 49-2292. 1949. Meador Pub. Co.
Ghosts of the Assassins. Ian Todd. LC 76-274. 7.95 (ISBN 0-912458-58-5). E. A. Seeman Pub.
Ghosts of the Gold Rush. George Koenig. (Illus.). 1968. wrappers 1.95 o.p. (ISBN 0-910856-27-3). La Siesta.
Ghosts of the Golden West. Hans Holzer. LC 68-11149. (Illus.). 1968. 5.00 o.p. (ISBN 0-672-50683-1). Bobbs.
Ghosts of the Heart. John Logan. LC 60-7239. (O.s.i.). 1960. 4.50x o.s.i. (ISBN 0-226-49110-2). U. of Chicago Pr.
Ghosts of the Hilo Hills. William D. Westervelt. (Illus.). 1967. pap. 1.25 o.p. (ISBN 0-912180-02-1). Petroglyph.
Ghosts of Their Ancestors. Weymer Jay Mills. LC 6-12130. 1906. Fox, Duffield & Co.
Ghosts of Yesterday. Georgia M. Shewmake. 1983. 6.95 (Avalon). Bouregy.
Ghosts on the Range Tonight. Caddo Cameron. LC 41-679139. Carlton House.
Ghosts, Spooks, and Spectres. Ed. by Charles Molin. (David White collection). 1967. D. White Co.
Ghosts: Stories of the Supernatural. Elliot O'Donnell. LC 69-18113. 1969. 4.95 o.p. (ISBN 0-8008-3225-6). Taplinger.
Ghost's Touch: A New Story. Wilkie Collins. LC 6-26948. (On cover: Lovell's library. v. 13, no. 683). 1885. J. W. Lovell Company.
Ghosts: Washington's Most Famous Ghost Stories. John Alexander. LC 75-27691. (Illus.). 160p. cancelled o.s.i. (ISBN 0-915168-08-1); pap. cancelled o.s.i. (ISBN 0-915168-07-3). Washingtonian.
Ghosts with Southern Accents. Flo H. Scott. 1969. 3.95 o.p. Southern U Pr.
Ghostwater. Eden Phillpotts. LC 41-18114. 1941. The Macmillan Company.
Ghostwood. Ina Fargason. LC 71-134694. 1970. 2.95 o.p. (ISBN 0-8111-0382-X). Naylor.
Ghoul. Frank King. LC 29-7492. 1929. G. H. Watt.
Ghoul see Bird.
Ghouling Around. Ed. by Phil Hirsch & Paul Laikin. (Orig.). 1975. pap. 0.95 o.p. (ISBN 0-515-03871-7). BJ Pub Group.
Ghouls. Ed. by Peter Haining. LC 70-150254. (Illus.). 1971. 7.95. Stein and Day.
G.I. Wives. Alvin Homer Lowe. LC 46-22357. 1946. Meador Publishing Company.
Giafar Al Barmeki, a Tale of the Court of Haroun Al Raschid... Samuel Spring & Spring, Gardiner, Jr., Supposed Author. LC 8-14045. 1836. Harper & Brothers.
Giannella. Mary Crawford Fraser. LC 9-24234. 1909. 1.50. B. Herder.
Giannetto. Margaret Elizabeth Lindsay Majendie. LC 7-16809. (Leisure hour series v. 69). 1876. H. Holt and Company.
Giant. Edna Ferber. LC 52-10412. 1952. Doubleday.
Giant Afraid. George Pattillo. LC 58-163449. 1957. Printed by Naylor Co.
Giant Anthology of Science Fiction: 10 Complete Short Novels, Edited by Leo Margulies and Oscar J. Friend. Ed. by Leo Margulies & Oscar Jerome Friend. LC 54-11439. 1954. Merlin Press.
Giant, Behind the Brick Wall, Love: Three Stories. Tibor Dery. 1964. 4.50 o.p. Fernhill.
Giant: By Feike Feikema. 1st Ed. Frederick Feikema Manfred. LC 51-14783. 1951. Doubleday.
Giant Cat: Or, The Quest of Aoun and Zouhr. J. H. Rosny. Tr. by Whitehead, Lady Marian Cecilia (Brodrick) LC 25-9024. 1924. R. M. McBride & Company.
Giant Detective in France: Or, The Beautiful Mystery of Paris... Harlan Page Halsey. LC 7-11897. (calumet series, no. 15). G. Munro.
Giant Dwarf. Wood Kahler. LC 42-25512. 1942. Liveright Publishing Corporation.
Giant Dwarfs: A Contribution. Tr. from German by Joel Carmichael. Gisela Elsner. LC 65-14206. 5.95. Grove.
Giant in Gray. Manly Wade Wellman. 1980. 15.00 (ISBN 0-89029-054-7). Pr of Mornings.
Giant Joshua. Maurine Whipple. LC 40-355444. 1941. Houghton Mifflin Company.
Giant Kill. Kin Platt. LC 73-16396. 1974. 4.95 (ISBN 0-394-48707-9). Random House.
Giant Killer. Elmer Holmes Davis. LC 28-234645. The John Day Company.
Giant Killer. Vernon T. Hyman. 352p. 1981. 12.95 o.s.i. (ISBN 0-399-90099-3, Marek). Putnam Pub Group.
Giant Killer. Walter D. Mosher. 3.75 o.p. Vantage.
Giant Killer. Richard Vasquez. 1978. pap. 1.75 (ISBN 0-532-17173-X). Woodhill.
Giant Killer: A Novel. Elmer Holmes Davis. LC 43-51182. 1943. The Press of the Readers Club.
Giant of Oldborne. John Owen. LC 27-12827. 1926. Houghton Mifflin Company.
Giant of Red Millrun. (Illus.). 1975. 4.95. Teapot.
Giant of Worlds' End. Lin Carter. (Orig.). 1969. pap. 0.50 o.p. (B50-853). Belmont-Tower.
Giant on Horseback. Lewis B Patten. LC 64-19256. (Double D western). 1964. Doubleday.
Giant on Horseback. Lewis B Patten. 1973. (pbk.) 0.75. Ace.
Giant Raft... Jules Verne. LC 1-98364. (Lovell's library. v. 2, no. 34-35). J. W. Lovell Company.
Giant Rat of Sumatra: /Richard L. Boyer. Richard L Boyer. 1976. 1.50. Warner Books.
Giant Steps. Barry N. Kauffman. 352p. 1980. pap. 2.50 (ISBN 0-449-24290-0, Crest). Fawcett.
Giant Swing. William Riley Burnett. LC 32-22541. 1932. Harper & Brothers.
Giant Wakes: A Novel About Samuel Gompers. 1st Ed. Rupert Hughes. LC 50-8854. 1950. Borden Pub. Co.
Giants. Jean Marie Gustave Le Clezio. LC 75-13628. 1975. 10.00 (ISBN 0-689-10661-0). Atheneum.
Giants: A Novel. Jack Ansell. LC 75-11149. 9.95 (ISBN 0-87795-111-X). Arbor House.
Giants: A Novel. Cora Miranda Baggerly Older. LC 5-32693. 1905. D. Appleton and Company.
Giant's Arrow. Samuel Youd. LC 60-6083. 1960. Simon and Schuster.
Giants' Bread. 1st ed. Agatha Miller Christie. LC 30-20635. 1930. Doubleday, Doran.
Giant's Bread. Dame Agatha Miller Christie. 1975. (pbk.) 1.25. Dell.
Giants Bread. Mary Westmacott, pseud. LC 72-97688. 1973. 6.95 o.p. (ISBN 0-87795-058-X). Arbor Hse.
Giant's Bread. Mary Westmacott. 320p. 1982. pap. 2.50 (ISBN 0-440-12871-4). Dell.
Giants Bread. Mary Westmacott. LC 72-97688. 1973. 6.95 o.p. (ISBN 0-87795-058-X). Arbor Hse.
Giants' Bread: A Novel of Romance and Suspense. Agatha Miller Christie. LC 72-97688. 1973. 6.95 (ISBN 0-87795-058-X). Arbor House.
Giants from Eternity. Manly Wade Wellman. (Avalon books). Thomas Bouregy and Co.
Giant's Gate: A Story of a Great Adventure. Max Pemberton. LC 1-18535. F. A. Stokes Company.
Giant's House. Frederick Laing. LC 55-11201. 1955. Dial Press.
Giants in the Dust. Chad Oliver. (Orig.). 1976. pap. 1.25 o.p. (ISBN 0-515-03670-6). BJ Pub Group.
Giants in the Earth. Ole Edvart Rolvaag. LC 64-6326. (Harper's Modern Classics). 1964. Harper & Row.
Giants in the Earth. Ole Edvart Rolvaag. LC 65-6531. (Perennial classic). 1965. Harper & Row.
Giants in the Earth. Ole Edvart Rolvaag & Parrington, Vernon Louis, 1871-1929, Ed. LC 29-22808. (Harper's modern classics). Harper & Brothers.
Giants in the Earth: A Saga of the Prairie. Ole Edvart Relvaag. LC 64-375. (Harper torchbooks. The University library) "TB3504."). 1964. Harper & Row.
Giants in the Earth: A Saga of the Prairie. Ole Edvart Rolvaag. Tr. by Lincoln Colcord. LC 27-125130. 1927. Harper & Brothers.
Giants in the Earth: A Saga of the Prairie. Ole Edvart Rolvaag. Tr. by Lincoln Colcord. LC 28-179333. 1928. Harper & Brothers.
Giants in the Shadows. Gloria V. Basile. 512p. 1982. pap. 3.50 (ISBN 0-523-41898-1). Pinnacle Bks.
Giants in the Wings. Louise Bergstrom. 192p. (YA) 1974. 4.95 o.p. (Avalon). Bouregy.
Giants in the Wings. Louise Bergstrom. (Avalon romances). 1974. 4.50. Avalon Books.
Giant's Partner. Clark Darlton. (Perry Rhodan, #33). 1973. (pbk.) 0.75. Ace Books.
Giant's Robe. Thomas Anstey Guthrie. LC 3-21965. 1884. D. Appleton and Company.
Giants Should Be Gelded. Bogart Carlaw. LC 32-25724. 1932. G. P. Putnam's Sons.
Giant's Strength. Basil King. LC 7-11209. 1907. Harper & Brothers.
Giants Unleashed. Ed. by Groff Conklin. LC 65-21854. 2.95. Grosset.
Giants Unleashed. pap. 0.50 o.p. (4811, Tempo). G&D.

Gibbeted Gods. Lillian Barrett. LC 21-15823. 1921. 1.90. The Century Co.

Gibby of Clamshell Alley. Jasmine Stone Van Dresser. LC 16-6722. 1916. Dodd, Mead and Company.

Giddy Moment. Ernestine Moller Gilbreth Carey. LC 58-6035. 1958. Little, Brown.

Giddy Mrs. Goodyer. Horace Tremlett. LC 17-117945. 1916. John Lane.

Gideon. Inez Haynes Irwin. LC 27-15517. 1927. Harper & Brothers.

Gideon, a Boy Who Hates Learning in School. Gladys Natchez. LC 74-25909. (Illus.). 1975. 8.95 (ISBN 0-465-02676-1). Basic Books.

Gideon Drevell's Millions: Or, A Puzzling As. John Russell Coryell. LC 99-2535. (On cover: Magnet detective library, no. 99). 1899. Street & Smith.

Gideon Fleyce. A Novel. Henry William Lucy. LC 7-14738. (On cover: Lovell's library. v. 3. no. 96). 1883. J. W. Lovell Company.

Gideon Giles the Roper. Thomas Miller. LC 41-311200. G. Routledge and Sons.

Gideon Planish. Sinclair Lewis. 448p. 1974. pap. 1.95 (ISBN 0-532-19105-6). Woodhill.

Gideon Planish: A Novel. Sinclair Lewis. LC 43-51122. 1943. Random House.

Gideon S Day: By J. J. Marric Pseud. 1st Ed. John Creasey. LC 55-8046. 1955. Harper.

Gideon's Art. John Creasey. 1973. (pbk) 0.75. Popular Library.

Gideon's Art. John Creasey. LC 79-156578. 1971. 5.95 (ISBN 0-06-012781-3). Harper & Row.

Gideon's Art. J. J. Marric, pseud. (Gideon Detective Ser.). 1979. pap. 1.75 (ISBN 0-445-04444-6). Popular Lib.

Gideon's Art. J. J. Marric, pseud. LC 79-156578. (Novel of Suspense). 1971. 5.95 o.p. (ISBN 0-06-012781-3, HarpT). Har-Row.

Gideon's Badge: By J. J. Marric Pseud. John Creasey. LC 65-213821. bds., 3.95. Harper.

Gideon's Band: A Tale of the Mississippi. George Washington Cable. LC 72-84537. (Illus.). 1974. 29.00 (ISBN 0-403-02959-7). Scholarly Press.

Gideon's Band: A Tale of the Mississippi. George Washington Cable. LC 76-83934. (Illus.). 1969. Mnemosyne Pub. Co.

Gideon's Band: A Tale of the Mississippi. George Washington Cable. LC 14-16204. 1914. C. Scribner's Sons.

Gideon's Band: A Tale of the Mississippi see Collected Works.

Gideon's Children. Jane Stuart. LC 75-33628. 7.95 (ISBN 0-07-062211-6). McGraw-Hill.

Gideon's Day. J. J. Marric, pseud. (Gideon Detective Ser.). 1979. pap. 1.75 (ISBN 0-445-04475-6). Popular Lib.

Gideon's Drive. 1st. u.s. ed. John Creasey. LC 76-5544. 7.95 (ISBN 0-06-012821-6). Harper & Row.

Gideon's Drive. J. J. Marric. LC 76-5544. (Harper Novel of Suspense). (YA) 1976. 7.95 o.p. (ISBN 0-06-012821-6, HarpT). Har-Row.

Gideon's Fire: By J. J. Marric Pseud. John Creasey. LC 61-6210. 1972. Popular Lib.

Gideon's Fog. John Creasey. LC 74-5801. 1974. 5.95 (ISBN 0-06-012798-8). Harper & Row.

Gideon's Fog. J. J. Marric, pseud. (Harper Novel of Suspense). 188p. 1974. 7.95 o.p. (ISBN 0-06-012798-8, HarpT). Har-Row.

Gideon's Fog. J. J. Marric, pseud. 1981. pap. 1.95 (ISBN 0-445-08530-4). Popular Lib.

Gideon's Lot. John Creasey. LC 64-25134. 1964. Harper & Row.

Gideon's Lot. J. J. Marric, pseud. (Gideon Detective Ser.). 1979. pap. 1.75 (ISBN 0-445-04462-4). Popular Lib.

Gideon's March. J. J. Marric, pseud. (Gideon Detective Ser.). 1977. pap. 1.25 (ISBN 0-445-02579-4). Popular Lib.

Gideon's Men. John Creasey. LC 72-409. 1972. 5.95 (ISBN 0-06-012786-4). Harper & Row.

Gideon's Men. J. J. Marric, pseud. LC 72-409. (A Harper Novel of Suspense Ser.). 192p. (YA) 1972. 5.95 o.p. (ISBN 0-06-012786-4, HarpT). Har-Row.

Gideon's Power. John Creasey. LC 76-81877. 1969. 4.95. Harper & Row.

Gideon's Power. J. J. Marric, pseud. 160p. 1981. pap. 1.95 (ISBN 0-445-00451-7). Popular Lib.

Gideon's Power. J. J. Marric, pseud. LC 76-81877. (Suspense Ser). 1969. 4.95 o.p. (ISBN 0-06-012789-9, HarpT). Har-Row.

Gideon's Press. John Creasey. LC 73-4154. 1973. 5.95 (ISBN 0-06-012787-2). Harper & Row.

Gideon's Press. J. J. Marric, pseud. LC 73-4154. (Harper Novel of Suspense). (O.s.i.). 192p. (YA) 1973. 7.95i (ISBN 0-06-012787-2, HarpT). Har-Row.

Gideon's Press. J. J. Marric, pseud. (Gideon Detective Ser.). 192p. 1981. pap. 1.95 (ISBN 0-445-00426-6). Popular Lib.

Gideon's Ride. John Creasey. LC 62-20129. Harper & Row.

Gideon's Risk. John Creasey. LC 59-13313. 1972. Popular Lib.

Gideon's Risk. J. J. Marric, pseud. (Gideon Detective Ser.). 1979. pap. 1.75 (ISBN 0-445-04412-8). Popular Lib.

Gideon's River. John Creasey. LC 68-26546. 1968. Harper & Row.

Gideon's River. John Creasey. LC 81-47347. (Fifty Classics of Crime Fiction, 1950-1975). 1982. 14.95 (ISBN 0-8240-4956-X). Garland.

Gideon's River. J. J. Marric, pseud. Ed. by J. Barzun & W. H. Taylor. LC 81-47347. (Crime Fiction 1950-1975 Ser.). 143p. 1982. lib. bdg. 14.95 (ISBN 0-8240-4956-X). Garland Pub.

Gideon's River. J. J. Marric, pseud. LC 68-26546. (Harper Novel of Suspense). 1968. 4.95 o.p. (ISBN 0-06-012796-1, HarpT). Har-Row.

Gideon's Sport. John Creasey. LC 76-123992. 1970. 4.95. Harper & Row.

Gideon's Sport. J. J. Marric, pseud. (Gideon Detective Ser.). 1979. pap. 1.75 (ISBN 0-445-04459-4). Popular Lib.

Gideon's Sport. J. J. Marric, pseud. LC 76-123992. (Novel of Suspense Ser.). 1970. 6.95 o.p. (ISBN 0-06-012797-X, HarpT). Har-Row.

Gideon's Vote. John Creasey. LC 63-20311. Harper & Row.

Gideon's Wrath: By J. J. Marric. 1st U.S. Ed. John Creasey. LC 67-13704. 1967. bds., 4.50. Harper.

Gidget Goes to Rome: A Novel. Frederick Kohner & Flippen, Ruth Brooks. Gidget Goes to Rome. LC 63-17443. 1963. Bantam Books.

Gidget. Illus. by Ronald Wing. Frederick Kohner. LC 57-12212. 1957. Putnam.

Giemonda. Arthur D Hall. LC 7-533. (On cover: Drama series, no. 1). 1895. Street & Smith.

Gift. Hilda Doolittle. LC 82-8027. 160p. 1982. 14.95 o.p. (ISBN 0-8112-0853-2); pap. 5.95 o.p. (ISBN 0-8112-0854-0, NDP546). New Directions.

Gift. Pete Hamill. LC 73-3981. 1973. 4.95 (ISBN 0-394-47338-8). Random House.

Gift. H. D, pseud. LC 82-8027. 1982. 14.95 (ISBN 0-8112-0853-2). New Directions.

Gift. Margaret Prescott Montague. LC 19-8321. E. P. Dutton & Company.

Gift. Madeena S. Nolan. (Orig.). 1981. pap. 2.50 (ISBN 0-440-12875-7). Dell.

Gift. Madeleine Nuttall. LC 51-9698. 1951. A. A. Wyn.

Gift: A Novel. Vladimir Vladimirovich Nabokov. LC 63-9667. 1963. Putnam.

Gift and the Giver: A Novel. Nelia Gardner White. LC 57-11122. 1957. Viking Press.

Gift & the Promise: In the Fourth Dimension. Durbin H. Downey. LC 82-90787. (Illus.). 176p. (Orig.). 1983. pap. 9.95 (ISBN 0-9610006-0-0). Four D Pub Co.

Gift Bearers: A Novel, by Henry Berman... Henry Berman. LC 7-36097. The Grafton Press.

Gift Bearers. 1st Amer. Ed. David Walder. LC 67-152819. 1967. 4.00. Coward.

Gift for Gomala: By John Baxter Pseud. 1st Ed. Howard Hunt. LC 62-9341. 1962. Lippincott.

Gift from a Stranger. Ivy Valdes. Bd. with Over My Shoulder. 1978. pap. 1.75 (ISBN 0-451-08181-1, E8181, Sig). NAL.

Gift from Berlin. Albert Barker. 160p. 1980. pap. 1.95 (ISBN 0-441-28828-6, Pub. by Charter Bks). Ace Bks.

Gift from Berlin. Albert Barker. (Rufus King Ser). (O.s.i.). (Orig.). 1969. pap. 0.60 o.s.i. (A540X, Award). Univ Pub & Dist.

Gift from Earth. Larry Niven. LC 70-103859. 1970. 4.95. Walker.

Gift from God: The Story of a Mongoloid Boy. Maria A. Lum. 3.50 o.p. Vantage.

Gift from the Boys. 1st Ed. Buchwald, Art. LC 58-888318. 1958. Harper.

Gift from the Sea. Anne Morrow Lindbergh. LC 77-14351. (25th Anniversary Ed.). 1978. pap. 1.95 (ISBN 0-394-72455-0, Vin). Random.

Gift Horse: A Johnny Fletcher Mystery. Frank Gruber. LC 42-22696. 1942. Farrar & Rinehart, Inc.

Gift Horse, and Other Stories. Kate Cruise O'Brien. LC 80-14996. 8.95 (ISBN 0-8076-0976-5). G. Braziller.

Gift in the Gauntlet. Gertrude M. Robins Reynolds. LC 27-20430. George H. Doran Company.

Gift of a Cow: A Translation from the Hindi Novel Godaan. rev. ed. Premchand. Tr. by Gordon C. Roadarmel. LC 68-16783. (Midland Bks.: No. 136). 1968. 12.50x o.p. (ISBN 0-253-13000-X); pap. 3.95x o.p. (ISBN 0-253-20136-5). Ind U Pr.

Gift of a Cow: A Translation of the Hindi Novel, Godaan. Dhanpat Rai Srivastava. LC 68-16783. (UNESCO Collection of Representative Works: Indian Series). 1968. 7.95. Indiana University Press.

Gift of a Home. Beverley Nichols. LC 73-7575. (Illus.). 1973. 8.95 (ISBN 0-396-06855-3). Dodd, Mead.

Gift of a Home. Beverley Nichols. LC 73-150216. (Illus.). 1972. 3.50 (ISBN 0-491-00703-5). W. H. Allen.

Gift of Abou Hassan. Francis Perry Elliott. LC 12-20789. 1912. 1.25. Little, Brown, and Company.

Gift of Acabar. Og Mandino & Buddy Kaye. LC 78-9816. 5.95 (ISBN 0-397-01296-9). Lippincott.

Gift of Acabar. Og Mandino & Buddy Kaye. LC 79-11000. 1979. 8.95 (ISBN 0-8161-6697-8). G. K. Hall.

Gift of Autumn. Ed. by James A. Kuse. (Illus.). 1979. pap. 4.95 (ISBN 0-89542-072-4). Ideals.

Gift of Bonaparte: A Novel, by Robert Shortz... Robert Shortz. (On cover: The welcome series, no. 33). 1898. The Home Publishing Company.

Gift of Christmas. Myra Scovel. LC 72-78335. 1972. 4.95 (ISBN 0-06-067171-8). Harper & Row.

Gift of Death. Edward Sidney Aarons. 160p. 1974. pap. 0.95 o.p. Woodhill.

Gift of Death. Edward Sidney Aarons. 1970. Repr. pap. 0.75 o.p. (75-374). Manor Bks.

Gift of Death. Edward Sidney Aarons. 160p. 1974. pap. 0.95 o.p. Manor Bks.

Gift of Death: A Jerry Benedict Novel. Edward Sidney Aarons. LC 48-9915. (Armchair mystery). 1948. D. McKay Co.

Gift of Desire. Ivy St. David. 320p. 1982. pap. 2.95 (ISBN 0-440-02971-6, Emerald). Dell.

Gift of Echoes. Robert Harlow. LC 65-25068. 1966. bds., 4.95. St. Martin's.

Gift of Glory. William Carroll Munro. LC 50-5353. 1950. Scribner.

Gift of Gold. Beverly Butler. 393p. (YA) 1973. lib. bdg. 9.95 o.p. (ISBN 0-8161-6076-7, Large Print Bks). G K Hall.

Gift of Guns. Buck Gilmore. LC 57-873248. 1957. Avalon Books.

Gift of Indifference. Tr. from French by Margaret Crosland. Cecile Arnaud, pseud. LC 65-11276. bds., 3.95. Random.

Gift of Life, a Novel. Charles E Mercer. LC 63-16186. 1963. Putnam.

Gift of Love. Romen Basu. (Greenbird Bk.). 176p. 1975. 12.00 (ISBN 0-88253-823-3); pap. 5.00 (ISBN 0-88253-824-1). Ind-US Inc.

Gift of Love. Gordon E. Hoffman. LC 76-50848. (Illus.). 1977. pap. 3.50 (ISBN 0-9601120-1-4). Aspen Art.

Gift of Love. Portia Maxwell. LC 43-150682. 1943. Gramercy Publishing Company.

Gift of Onyx. Jocelyn Kettle. LC 73-78641. 1974. 6.95 (ISBN 0-399-11189-1). Putnam.

Gift of Orchids. Patti Moore. (Second Chance at Love Ser.: No. 25). 192p. (Orig.). 1982. pap. 1.75 (ISBN 0-515-06160-3). Jove Pubns.

Gift of Paul Clermont. Francis Warrington Dawson. LC 21-17270. 1921. Doubleday, Page & Company.

Gift of Peace. St. Dawn, Grace. LC 74-32435. (Illus.). 1975. 4.95. Naylor Co.

Gift of Rome: A Novel. John Wagner & Wagner, Esther. LC 61-5733. 1961. Little, Brown.

Gift of the Deer. Helen Hoover. 1981. pap. 4.95 (ISBN 0-395-30534-9). HM.

Gift of the Desert. Randall Parrish. LC 22-16873. 1922. A. C. McClurg & Co.

Gift of the Drum. Dorothy J. Goulding. 1955. in collection of 3 christmas plays 3.00x (ISBN 0-88020-097-9). Coach Hse.

Gift of the Gods. Flora Annie Webster Steel. LC 13-2081. 1897. J. Chartres.

Gift of the Gods, No. 147. Barbara Cartland. (Orig.). 1981. pap. 1.95 (ISBN 0-553-20014-3). Bantam.

Gift of the Grass: Being the Autobiography of a Famous Racing Horse. John Trotwood Moore. LC 11-1008. 1911. Little, Brown, and Company.

Gift of the Magi. O. Henry. LC 78-55660. (Illus.). 1978. Repr. 7.95 (ISBN 0-672-52296-9). Bobbs.

Gift of the Magi. William Sydney Porter. LC 74-179130. (Illus.). 1972. 2.95. Hawthorn Books.

Gift of the Magi, and Five Other Stories. William Sydney Porter. LC 67-15764. 1967. F. Watts.

Gift of the Morning Star: A Story of Sherando. Armistead Churchill Gordon. LC 5-12158. 1905. Funk & Wagnalls Company.

Gift of the River. Lou Ricketts Matlock. LC 47-203361. 1947. Mayes Printing Company Incorporated.

Gift of the Sea. Ruth McCarthy Sears. 1973. 4.95. Lenox Hill Pr.

Gift of Time. Phyllis Brett Young. pap. 0.75 o.p. (54-809). Paperback Lib.

Gift of Time: A Novel. Phyllis Brett Young. LC 61-10327. 1961. Putnam.

Gift of Violets. Janette Radcliffe. 1977. 0.95 (ISBN 0-440-12891-9). Dell Pub. Co.

Gift of Wings. Richard Bach. 1979. pap. 2.50 (ISBN 0-440-34571-5). Dell.

Gift Shop. Charlotte Armstrong. LC 67-15272. 1967. 4.95. Coward.

Gift Shop. Charlotte Armstrong. (Berkley medallion book). 1974. (pbk.) 0.95 (ISBN 0-425-02577-2). Berkley Pub. Co.

Gift Supreme. Ramsey Cowley. LC 29-6353. 1929. G. P. Putnam's Sons.

Gift Supreme. George Allan England. LC 17-29331. George H. Doran Company.

Gift-Wife. Rupert Hughes. LC 10-23130. 1910. Moffat, Yard and Company.

Gifted. Roswell Gray Ham. LC 52-5669. 1952. Crown Publishers.

Gifts: A Story of the Boyhood of Jesus. 1st Ed. Dorothy Clarke Wilson. LC 57-11876. 1957. McGraw- Hill.

Gifts Divine. Ethel Tompkins Moose. LC 26-133. The C. A. Brewton Press.

Gifts from Eykis: A Novel of Self-Discovery. Wayne W Dyer. LC 82-17066. 12.95 (ISBN 0-671-46066-8). Simon and Schuster.

Gifts from God, Two Stories. 1st Ed. Easterling, Narena. LC 53-12927. 1953. Pageant Press.

Gifts of Love: A Novel by Andrina Iverson. Andrina Iverson. LC 46-8000. 1946. Farrar, Straus and Company, Inc.

Gifts of Sheba. Walter Lionel George. LC 26-3793. 1926. G. P. Putnam's Sons.

Gifts of the Child Christ: Fairytales and Stories for the Childlike. George Macdonald. LC 72-96406. (Illus.). 1973. per vol. 6.95. W. B. Eerdmans Pub. Co.

Gifts of the Spirit. Robert E. Picirilli. 1980. pap. 1.39 (ISBN 0-89265-065-6). Randall Hse.

Gifts That We Bear. Winston Weathers. (Illus.). 1976. pap. 2.95 (ISBN 0-912484-06-3). Joseph Nichols.

Gig. James D Houston. LC 78-80501. 1969. 4.95. Dial Press.

Gigantic Meddler: A Tale Gathered from the Files of the Court of Uncommon Pleas... Edward Belcher Callender. LC 3636. The Blaxton Press.

Gigantic Shadow. Julian Symons. 1971. pap. 0.95 o.p. (95093). Beagle Bks.

Gigantick History of the Two Famous Giants and Other Curiosities in Guildhall, London. Thomas Boreman. LC 75-32140. (Classics of Children's Literature, 1621-1932). (Illus.). 1979. 27.00 (ISBN 0-8240-2256-4). Garland Pub.

Gigging. Bert Stratton. pap. 4.95 (ISBN 0-9604194-0-3). Acorn OH.

Gigging: A Novel. Bert Stratton. LC 80-129162. 4.00 (ISBN 0-9604194-0-3). Acorn.

Gigi, and Selected Writings. Sidonie Gabrielle Colette. LC 64-2843. (Signet classic, CT196). 1963. New American Library.

Gigi, and The Cat. Sidonie Gabrielle Colette. 1961. Penguin Books.

Gigi, Julie De Carneilhan. Chance Acquaintances. Sidonie Gabrielle Colette. LC 52-138453. 1952. Farrar, Straus and Young.

Gigolo. Edna Ferber. LC 75-169549. (Short story index reprint series). 1971. (ISBN 0-8369-4011-3). Books for Libraries Press.

Gigolo. Edna Ferber. LC 22-26970. 1922. Doubleday, Page & Company.

Gil Blas. Translated by Tobias Smollett. A Modern Abridgment, with an Introd. by Bergen Evans. Alain Rene Le Sage. Tr. by Toblas George Smollett. Ed. by Bergen Evans. LC 62-3517. (Premler world classic, t157). 1962. Fawcett Publications.

Gilbert, a Comedy of Manners. Judith Martin. LC 82-71060. 1982. 12.95 (ISBN 0-689-11327-7). Atheneum.

Gilbert Elgar's Son. Harriet Riddle Davis. LC 6-32485. 1890. G. P. Putnam's Sons.

Gilbert Frankau's Self-Portrait: A Novel of His Own Life. Gilbert Frankau. LC 40-6700. 1940. E. P. Dutton & Co., Inc.

Gilbert Neal: A Novel. William Nathaniel Harben. LC 8-278053. 1908. Harper & Brothers.

Gilbert: Or, Then and Now. J. Cabaniss Underwood. LC 72-3012. (Black Heritage Library Collection). (Illus.). 1972. (ISBN 0-8369-9086-2). Books for Libraries Press.

Gilbert St. Maurice. Lorenzo Dow Whitson. 1875. Bradley & Gilbert, Printers.

Gilbert Thorndyke: Or, A Man of His Word. William G Henry. (On cover: Green paper series. no. 19). De Wolfe, Fiske & Co.

Gilberto Freyre Reader. Gilberto Freyre. 1974. 7.95 o.p. (ISBN 0-394-48325-1). Knopf.

Gilbert's Last Toothache. Margaret Scherf. LC 49-7642. 1949. Pub. for the Crime Club by Doubleday.

Gilded Age. Mark Twain & Charles D. Warner. Ed. by Herbert Van Thal. 1873-1967. 4.95 o.p.; pap. 2.95 o.p. Dufour.

Gilded Age. Mark Twain & Charles D. Warner. LC 64-16578. (O.s.i.). Orig. Title: Gilded Age: A Tale of Today. (Illus.). 1968. pap. 3.95 o.s.i. (ISBN 0-295-78556-X, WP40). U of Wash Pr.

Gilded Age. A Novel. Samuel Langhorne Clemens & Charles Dudley Warner. LC 3-19530. 1883. G. Routledge and Sons.

Gilded Age: A Tale of to-Day. Samuel Langhorne Clemens & Charles Dudley Warner. Ed. by Bryant Morey French. LC 76-183110. (Library of literature, no. 38). (Illus.). 1972. 10.00. Bobbs-Merrill.

Gilded Age: A Tale of to-Day. Samuel Langhorne Clemens & Charles Dudley Warner. LC 17-6111. 1874. American Publishing Company.

Gilded Age: A Tale of to-Day. Samuel Langhorne Clemens & Charles Dudley Warner. LC 31-255. 1887. American Publishing Company.

Gilded Age: A Tale of to-Day. Samuel Langhorne Clemens & Charles Dudley Warner. LC 1-31842. 1901. The American Publishing Company.

Gilded Age: A Tale of to-Day. Mark Twain. Ed. by Bryant M. French. LC 76-183110. 1972. 8.95 o.p. (ISBN 0-672-61028-0). Bobbs.

Gilded Age, a Tale of to-Day. By Mark Twain Pseud....and Charles Dudley Warner...Fully Illustrated from New Designs by Hoppin, Stephens, Williams, White, Etc., Etc.... Samuel Langhorne Clemens & Charles Dudley Warner. 1888. American Publishing Company.

Gilded Age: A Tale of Today. Samuel Langhorne Clemens & Charles Dudley Warner. LC 64-16578. (Illus.). 1964. Trident Press.

Gilded Age: a Tale of Today. Samuel Langhorne Clemens & Charles Dudley Warner. LC 70-80901. (Signet classic). (Illus.). 1969. 1.50. New American Library.

Gilded Age: A Tale of Today. Samuel Langhorne Clemens & Charles Dudley Warner. LC 24-222064. 1902. The American Publishing Company.

Gilded Age: A Tale of Today. Samuel Langhorne Clemens & Charles Dudley Warner. LC 28-1683. 1915. Harper & Brothers.

Gilded Age: A Tale of Today see Gilded Age.

Gilded Bat. Edward St. John Gorey. LC 80-114600. (Illus.). 1979. 4.95 (ISBN 0-396-07688-2). Dodd, Mead.

Gilded Cage. Rob Eden. LC 40-4089. Gramercy Publishing Col.

Gilded Caravan. Alice Woods. LC 27-21141. 1927. Balch & Company.

Gilded Chair: A Novel. Melville Davisson Post. LC 10-11875. 1910. 1.50. D. Appleton and Company.

Gilded Challenge. Elsie Frances Wilson Mack. LC 50-11224. 1950. Avalon Books.

Gilded Chyrsalis: A Novel. Gertrude Pahlow. LC 14-14801. 1914. 1.25. Duffield & Company.

Gilded Clique. Emile Gaboriau. (On cover: Lovell's library. v. 4. no. 138. July 16, 1883). 1884. J. W. Lovell Company.

Gilded Dust. Blanche Smith Ferguson. LC 88-83392. The Penn Publishing Company.

Gilded Fly, a Political Satire. George C. Kelly. (On cover: Idle moment series. no. 18). 1892. The Price-McGill Company.

Gilded Fool. A Novelization of the Popular Comedy. Henry Guy Carleton. LC 6-16685. (On cover: Drama series, no. 19). Street & Smith.

Gilded God: A Novel. Emma Augusta Sharkey. (On cover: The advance library, no. 46). Springfield Publishing Co.

Gilded Halo. Cosmo Hamilton. LC 32-22558. 1932. R. Long & R. R. Smith, Inc.

Gilded Hearse. Charles O Gorham. LC 48-5213. 1948. Creative Age Press.

Gilded Hideaway: By Peter Twist Pseud. Chester P Hewitt. LC 55-37188. (Ace books, S-107). 1955. Ace Books.

Gilded Lily. Janet Doran. LC 38-307933. 1938. Hillman-Curl, Inc.

Gilded Man. John Dickson Carr. LC 42-14099. 1942. W. Morrow and Company.

Gilded Man: A Romance of the Andes. Clifford Smyth. LC 18-188939. 1918. Boni and Liveright.

Gilded Needles. Michael McDowell. 352p. 1980. pap. 2.50 (ISBN 0-380-76398-2, 76398). Avon.

Gilded Nightmare. Hugh Pentecost. LC 68-21901. (Red Badge Mystery Ser). 1968. 3.95 o.p. Dodd.

Gilded Nightmare. Hugh Pentecost. 1972. pap. 0.75 o.p. (ISBN 0-515-02757-X, T2757). Pyramid Pubns.

Gilded Nightmare: A Pierre Chambrun Mystery Novel. Judson Pentecost Philips. LC 68-21901. (Red badge mystery). 1968. Dodd, Mead.

Gilded Rooster. Richard Emery Roberts. LC 47-3529. 1947. G. P. Putnam's Sons.

Gilded Rose: A Novel. May Christie. LC 25-166569. 1925. G.P. Putnam's Sons.

Gilded Sin. Charlotte Mary Brame. LC 44-38091. (On cover: Lovell's library, v. 14, no. 718). J. W. Lovell Company.

Gilded Sin, and, A Bridge of Love. Charlotte Mary Brame. LC 44-12242. (On cover: Seaside library. Pocket ed. No. 300). G. Munro.

Gilded Splendour. LC 81-43457. 1982. 16.95 (ISBN 0-385-17540-X). Doubleday.

Gilded Splendour. Rosalind Laker. LC 82-18680. 1982. 17.95 (ISBN 0-8161-3476-6). G.K. Hall.

Gilded Splendour. Rosalind Laker. LC 81-43457. 384p. 1982. 16.95 (ISBN 0-385-17540-X). Doubleday.

Gilded Splendour. Rosalind Laker. (General Ser.). 1982. lib. bdg. 17.95 (ISBN 0-8161-3476-6, Large Print Bks). G K Hall.

Gilded Spurs. Grace Ingram. LC 77-17104. 1978. 8.95 (ISBN 0-8128-2335-4). Stein and Day.

Gilded Spurs: A Novel. Grace Ingram. 1.95 (ISBN 0-449-23910-1). Fawcett Crest Books.

Gilded Torch. Iola Fuller, pseud. LC 57-6731. 1957. Putnam.

Gilded Vanity. Clotilde Inez Mary Graves. LC 16-177276. 1.40. George H. Doran Company.

Gilded Way: A Novel. Victor Mapes. LC 10-30033. 1910. 1.50. The Neale Publishing Company.

Gilden-Fire. Stephen R. Donaldson. (Illearth War ("Thomas Covenant the Unbeliever") Ser.). (Illus.). 70p. 1982. lib. bdg. 11.95 o.p. (ISBN 0-934438-54-4). Underwood-Miller.

Gildenford. Valerie Anand. LC 76-30661. 9.95 (ISBN 0-684-14896-X). Scribner.

Gildenford. Valerie Anand. 1979. 2.50 (ISBN 0-445-04336-9). Popular Library.

Gilderoy, the Freebooter. A Tale of Daring Adventure. Dewitt & Davenport.

Gilead: Or, The Vision of All Souls' Hospital. An Allegory. John Hyatt Smith. LC 8-8171. 1863. C. Scribner.

Giles Goat-Boy. John Barth. (Windstone Ser.). 768p. 1981. pap. text ed. 4.95 (ISBN 0-553-14705-6). Bantam.

Giles Goat-Boy. John Barth. 1978. pap. 2.95 (ISBN 0-449-23524-6, Crest). Fawcett.

Giles Goat-Boy: Or, The Revised New Syllabus. John Barth. (P1052). 1967. pap., 1.25. Fawcett.

Giles Goat Boy or, the Revised New Syllabus. John Barth. LC 66-15666. Limited edition 25.00 (ISBN 0-385-07364-X). Doubleday.

Giles Ingilby: A Novel. William Edward Norris. LC 99-829. 1899. D. Biddle.

Gilian the Dreamer: His Youth, His Love, and Adventure. Neil Munro. LC 99-5444. 1899. Dodd, Mead and Company.

Gill and the Others. Muriel Herd. LC 27-19130. 1927. Longmans, Green and Co., Ltd.

Gill Netters. Jolie Paylin. LC 79-89031. 1979. 8.95 (ISBN 0-910726-82-5). Hillsdale Educational Publishers.

Gillespie. J Macdougall Hay. LC 14-17994. 1914. G. H. Doran Company.

Gilliam Unbuttoned. Alfred Gillespie. LC 77-5915. 8.95 (ISBN 0-316-31350-5). Little, Brown.

Gillian. Frank Yerby. LC 60-14688. 1960. Dial Press.

Gillian. Frank Yerby. 1976. 1.75. Dell Publishing Co.

Gilliane. Roberta Gellis. LC 78-20321. (Roselynde Chronicles: Bk. 4). 496p. 1979. pap. 2.95 (ISBN 0-86721-167-9). Playboy Pbks.

Gilligan's Last Elephant. 1st Ed. Gerald Hanley. 1962. World Pub. Co.

Gillyflower Kid: A Novel. Christine Bruckner. LC 82-13531. 14.95 (ISBN 0-88064-006-5). Fromm International Pub. Corp.

Gilman of Redford: A Story of Boston & Harvard College on the Eve of the Revolutionary War, 1770-1775. William Stearns Davis. LC 27-22488. 1927. The Macmillan Company.

Gilt Dragon Incident. James Harold Turner. LC 65-4443. (1 fold.). 1965. 6.00. Paterson Brokensha.

Gilt Edge see Suffer a Witch.

Gilt-Edge Tom: Conductor; or, The Pride of the Valley Route. A Railroad Story of to-Day. Erwin L Coolidge. LC 6-30196. (On cover: New York 10 cent library, no. 7). Katahdin Publishing Co.

Gilt Edged Bonds. Ian Fleming. Incl. Casino Royale; From Russia with Love; Doctor No. 1961. 6.95 o.p. (ISBN 0-02-538940-8, 53894). Macmillan.

Gilt-Edged Boy. Raymond Hitchcock. LC 76-582703. 1971. 1.50 (ISBN 0-491-00036-7). W. H. Allen.

Gilt-Edged Cockpit. James Douglas Rutherford McConnell. LC 75-131102. 1971. 4.50. Published for the Crime Club by Doubleday.

Gilt-Edged Cockpit. Douglas Rutherford. LC 75-131102. 1971. 1.95 o.p. (ISBN 0-385-08213-4). Doubleday.

Gilt Edged Guilt. Carolyn Wells. LC 38-11646. J. B. Lippincott Company.

Gilt-Edged Insecurity. Arthur Alan Hanbury-Sparrow. LC 35-1598. 1934. T. Nelson and Sons, Ltd.

Gilt-Edged Traitor. Matthew Eden. LC 73-157989. (Raven books). 1972. 5.95 (ISBN 0-200-71841-X). Abelard-Schuman.

Gilt Feather. Dora Polk. LC 78-20093. 1979. 7.95 (ISBN 0-385-13650-1). Doubleday.

Gilta: Or, The Czar and the Cantatrice. A Novel. Nadage Doree. LC 6-337224. Hurst & Company.

Gimmel Flask. Douglas Clark. (Murder Ink Ser.: No. 41). (Orig.). 1982. pap. 2.25 (ISBN 0-440-13160-X). Dell.

Gimpel the Fool. Isaac Bashevis Singer. 1980. pap. 2.50 (ISBN 0-449-24275-7, Crest). Fawcett.

Gimpel the Fool, and Other Stories. Isaac Bashevis Singer. LC 58-1234. Noonday Press.

Gin and Bitters. A. Riposte. LC 31-26702. Farrar & Rinehart, Incorporated.

Gin & Lime Street. Adam Aymes. (Orig.). 1969. pap. 1.75 o.s.i. (OPH140, Ophelia). Olympia.

Gin Palace. Emile Zola. LC 56-3603. (Avon, T-129). Avon Publications.

Gin Wife. Ann Lawrence. LC 33-1133. 1933. W. Godwin, Inc.

Gina. George Albert Glay. LC 48-100191. 1948. Pellegrini & Cudahy.

Ginerva. James David Horan. LC 79-12733. 12.95 (ISBN 0-517-53392-8). Crown Publishers.

Ginette's Happiness. Sibylle Gabrielle Marie Antoinette De Riquetti De Mirabeau Martel De Janville. Tr. by Derechef, Ralph. LC 7-24384. R. F. Fenno & Company.

Ginger. Herbert N Roe & Landers, William E., Joint Author. LC 30-261. Burton Publishing Company.

Ginger. Maria Sias. LC 29-10743. The Midwest Company.

Ginger and McGlusky. A. G. Hales. LC 17-29333. 1917. Hodder and Stoughton.

Ginger and Speed. Ethel Powelson Hueston. LC 29-898787. The Bobbs-Merrill Company.

Ginger Cat. Christopher Reeve. LC 29-19253. 1929. W. Morrow & Company.

Ginger Ella. Ethel Powelson Hueston. The Bobbs-Merrill Company.

Ginger Flower. Harry Lee Stuart. LC 48-521008. 1947. North River Press.

Ginger Griffin. Mary Dolling Sanders O'Malley. LC 34-12023. 1934. Little, Brown, and Company.

Ginger Hill. Sarah S Allen. LC 73-77901. 1973. 6.95 (ISBN 0-910244-72-3). J. F. Blair.

Ginger Lee: War Nurse. Dorothy Deming. LC 42-2417. (Career books). 1942. Dodd, Mead & Company.

Ginger Man. complete and unexpurgated ed. James Patrick Donleavy. LC 65-26495. 1965. Delacorte Press.

Ginger Man. a limited ed. James Patrick Donleavy. LC 78-108383. (Illus.). 1978. 45.00. Franklin Library.

Ginger Man. Complete, Unexpurgated Ed. James Patrick Donleavy. LC 65-26495. 5.75. Delacorte Dist. Dial.

Ginger Man. Complete. Unexpurgated Ed. James Patrick Donleavy. (Delta bk., 2886). 1966. pap., 1.95. Dell.

Ginger Star. Leigh Brackett. (Orig.). 1979. pap. 1.95 (ISBN 0-345-28514-X). Ballantine.

Ginger Star. Leigh Brackett. (Ballantine science fiction). 1974. (pbk.) 1.25 (ISBN 0-345-23963-6). Ballantine Books.

Ginger Tree. Oswald Wynd. LC 77-6892. 10.00 (ISBN 0-06-014729-6). Harper & Row.

Ginger, You're Barmy. 1st Ed. in the U.S. David Lodge. LC 65-139996. 1965. 4.50. Doubleday.

Gingerbread House. Eileen Bigland. LC 34-19485. 1934. D. Appleton-Century Company, Incorporated.

Gingerbread House. Alice Dwyer-Joyce. LC 76-28072. (O.s.i.). 1977. 7.95 o.s.i. (ISBN 0-312-32725-0). St Martin.

Gingerbread Man. Richard Parker. LC 54-8391. 1954. Scribner.

Gingertown. Claude McKay. LC 72-37554. (Short story index reprint series). 1972. (ISBN 0-8369-4113-6). Books for Libraries Press.

Gingertown. Claude McKay. LC 32-642734. 1932. Harper & Brothers.

Gingham and Silk. Anna V Culhane. LC 45-858773. 1945. The Society of the Divine Savior (Salvatorian Seminary) Publishing Dept.

Gingham Gunslinger. Barbra B Jackson. LC 75-12466. 1975. 1.50 (ISBN 0-915494-04-3). Fibonacci Corp.

Gingham Rose. Alice Woods Ullman. LC 4-10538. 1904. The Bobbs-Merrill Company.

Ginkgo. Felix Pollak. 1973. 16.00 (Pub. by Elizabeth Pr); pap. 8.00. SBD.

Ginkgo Tree. Sheelagh Burns. LC 57-10738. 1957. Rinehart.

Ginkgo Tree. Cora Hardy Jarrett. LC 35-16478. Farrar & Rienhart, Inc.

Ginny. Peggy O'More, pseud. LC 46-1784. 1946. Grammercy Publishing Company.

Ginsey Kreider. Sarah Endicott Ober. LC 5425. The Pilgrim Press.

Ginx's Baby: His Birth & Other Misfortunes. Edward Jenkins. LC 79-8142. Repr. of 1870 ed. 44.50 (ISBN 0-404-61944-4). AMS Pr.

Ginzburg Circle. Archie O'Neill. (Jeff Pride series, no. 4). 1974. (pbk.) 0.95. Bantam Books.

Giono Selections. Ed. by Maxwell A. Smith. Jean Giono. Ed. by Maxwell Austin Smith. LC 65-24037. pap., 2.80. Heath.

Giovanni's Room: A Novel. James B. Baldwin. LC 56-12125. 1956. Dial Press.

Gipsey's Daughter. Charlotte Mary Brame. (Smith's select series, no. 36). Street & Smith.

Gipsy: A Tale. George Payne Rainsford James. LC 22-16033. 1855. Harper & Brothers.

Gipsy Blair, the Western Detective. Judson R Taylor. LC 5593. (On cover: Magnet detective library, no. 148). 1900. Street & Smith.

Gipsy Count. Mabel Winifred Knowles. LC 9-10032. 1909. The John McBride Co.

Gipsy in the Parlour. 1st American Ed. Margery Sharp. LC 54-509816. 1954. Little, Brown.

Gipsy Patteran. Ed. by Joseph Ellner. LC 75-101807. (Short story index reprint series). 1969. (ISBN 0-8369-3195-5). Books for Libraries Press.

Gipsy Queen: Or, Brigand Captive. Hugh De Normand. (On cover: Lovell's library. no. 98). 1883. J. W. Lovell Company.

Gipsy Waggon: The Story of a Ploughman's Progress. Sheila Kaye-Smith. LC 33-27309. 1933. Harper & Brothers.

Gipsy's Baby, and Other Stories. Rosamond Lehmann. 1946. Reynal & Hitchcock.

Gipsy's Daughter. Bertha M. Clay. LC 44-11664. (Select series... no. 36). Street & Smith.

Gipsy's Prophecy: Or, The Bride of an Evening. Emma Dorothy Eliza Nevitte Southworth. LC 12-39191. T. B. Peterson & Brothers.

Gipsy's Warning. Eliza Ann Dupuy. LC 11-105263. T. B. Peterson & Brothers.

Girdle of the God: A Novel. Robert Shortz. (welcome series, no. 44). 1899. The Home Publishing Company.

Girdle of the Great: A Story of the New South. John Jordan Douglass. LC 8-809542. Broadway Publishing Co.

Giri. Marc Olden. LC 82-72061. 1982. 13.95 (ISBN 0-87795-422-4). Arbor Hse.

Girl. Catherine Cookson. 1978. pap. 2.25 (ISBN 0-553-14187-2). Bantam.

Girl. Gerald Green. LC 76-12051. 1977. 5.95 (ISBN 0-385-11650-0). Doubleday.

Girl. Katherine Keith. LC 17-3032. 1917. 1.35. H. Holt and Company.

Girl. Meridel Le Sueur. LC 77-93295. 1978. 3.50 (ISBN 0-931122-06-6). West End Press.

Girl, a Horse, and a Dog. Francis Lynde. LC 20-142901. 1920. C. Scribner's Sons.

Girl: A Novel. Catherine Cookson. LC 77-3676. 1977. 8.95 (ISBN 0-688-03218-4). Morrow.

Girl About Town. Frederic Chace. LC 38-22274. Phoenix Press.

Girl Adoring. Viola Meynell. LC 28-7952. E. P. Dutton & Company.

Girl Alone. Anne Austin. LC 30-19279. The White House.

Girl Alone. Davis Dreiser. LC 39-522423. Gramercy Publishing Co.

Girl Alone. Howel Evans. LC 19-5854. 1918. G. P. Putnam's Sons.

Girl Alone. Christa Winsloe & Scott, Agnes Neill, Tr. LC 36-1117. Farrar & Rinehart, Incorporated.

Girl and a Thousand Gobs. Joseph Shawn. LC 34-5597. 1934. W. Godwin, Inc.

Girl and the Bill. Bannister I. E. Henry Bannister Merwin. LC 9-9474. 1909. Dodd, Mead and Company.

Girl and the Deal. Karl Edwin Harriman. LC 5-175936. G. W. Jacobs & Co.

Girl and the Eagle. William Arthur Neubauer. LC 65-8382. 1965. Arcadia House.

Girl and the Ferryman. Ernst Emil Wiechert & Wilkins, Eithne, Tr. LC 47-339362. 1947. Pilot Press.

Girl and the Game: And Other College Stories. Jesse Lynch Williams. LC 76-152964. (Short story index reprint series). (Illus.). 1971. (ISBN 0-8369-3879-8). Books for Libraries Press.

Girl and the Game: And Other College Stories. Jesse Lynch Williams. LC 8-17249. 1908. C. Scribner's Sons.

Girl & the Game, & Other College Stories. facsimile ed. Jesse Lynch Williams. LC 76-152964. (Short Story Index Reprint Ser.). Repr. of 1908 ed. 18.00 (ISBN 0-8369-3879-8). Ayer Co.

Girl & the Godfather. Thomas H. Hilton. 192p. (Orig.). 1973. pap. 1.95 o.p. (ISBN 0-87056-307-6, 6307). Brandon.

Girl and the Governor. Charles Warren. LC 5851. 1900. C. Scribner's Sons.

Girl and the Guardsman. Alexander Black. LC 1-29999. 1900. C. Scribner's Sons.

Girl and the Kaiser. Pauline Bradford Mackie Cavendish. The Bobbs-Merrill Company.

Girl and the Kaiser. Pauline Bradford Mackie Hopkins. LC 4-32152. 1904. The Bobbs-Merrill Company.

Girl and the Ring. Rob Eden. LC 41-14047. Gramercy Publishing Co.

Girl at Big Loon Post. George Gray Van Schaick. LC 16-18023. Small, Maynard & Company.

Girl at Central. Geraldine Bonner. LC 15-8708. 1915. D. Appleton and Company.

Girl at Cobhurst. Frank Richard Stockton. LC 8-15664. 1898. C. Scribner's Sons.

Girl at the Crossroads. Jackson Gregory. LC 40-12656. 1940. Dodd, Mead & Company.

Girl at the Halfway House: A Story of the Plains. Emerson Hough. LC 4861. 1900. D. Appleton and Company.

Girl at the Teller's Window. Nell Marr Dean. LC 63-6866. 1963. Avalon Books.

Girl Beneath the Lion. Andre P. De Mandiargues. 1968. pap. 0.95 o.p. (B176, BC). Grove.

Girl Beneath the Lion. Translated by Richard Howard. Pieyre De Mandiargues, Andre. LC 58-138504. (Evergreen original, E-126). Grove Press.

Girl Between. Sheila Douglas. (Harlequin Romances). 192p. 1981. pap. 1.25 (ISBN 0-373-02392-8, Pub. by Harlequin). PB.

Girl Between. Vic Roman. pap. 1.25 o.p. (2071). Brandon.

Girl Bewitched. Marjorie Lewty. (Harlequin Romances Ser.). 192p. 1982. pap. 1.50 (ISBN 0-373-02498-3). Harlequin Bks.

Girl by the Roadside. Frederic Van Rensselaer Dey. LC 17-15974. 1917. 1.38. The Macaulay Company.

Girl by the Sea. Suzanne Ebel. (Cameo Romance#40). 1976. (pbk.) 0.95. Fawcett.

Girl Called Boots. Don Sted. (Orig.). pap. 0.60 o.p. (73-719). Lancer.

Girl Called Cricket. Colleen L. Reece. (Orig.). 1979. pap. 1.75 (ISBN 0-532-23202-X). Woodhill.

Girl Called Fay. Rob Eden. LC 50-8450. 1950. Gramercy Pub. Co.

Girl Died Laughing. Viola Isabel Paradise. LC 34-30882. 1934. Harper & Brothers.

Girl Died Singing. Nigel Morland. 206p. 1975. Repr. of 1956 ed. 5.75 o.s.i. (ISBN 0-86025-002-4). White Lion Pubs.

Girl Everybody Knew. James Thomas Farrell. LC 28-6520. 1928. Harper & Brothers.

Girl Explosion. Norman Singer. pap. 1.95 o.s.i. (OPH-238, Ophelia). Olympia.

Girl Factory. Robert F. Murphy. 1978. pap. 1.75 (ISBN 0-89083-389-3). Zebra.

Girl for Him: By Rebecca Marsh Pseud. William Arthur Neubauer. LC 54-131178. 1954. Arcadia House.

Girl Found Dead. John Michael Evelyn. LC 63-42526. 1963. Macdonald.

Girl from Abroad. Samuel Kahiga. LC 75-318611. (African writers series; 158). 1975. (ISBN 0-435-90158-3). Heinemann Educational.

Girl from Alsace: A Romance of the Great War; Originally Published Under the Title of Little Comrade. Burton Egbert Stevenson. LC 19-143628. 1915. Grosset & Dunlap.

Girl from Aquarius. Dani Lawrence. (Orig.). 1970. pap. 0.75 o.p. (ISBN 0-447-74596-4). Lancer.

Girl from Argentina. Laura Lavayen. 176p. 1976. 7.50 o.p. (ISBN 0-682-48463-6). Exposition.

Girl from Beyond the Coulee. Jim Clark. LC 45-3917. 1945. B. Humphries, Inc.

Girl from Farris's. authorized 1st ed. front. by frank frazetta. ed. Edgar Rice Burroughs. LC 66-1900. 1965. House of Greystoke.

Girl from Fort Wicked. Dee Alexander Brown. LC 64-22321. (Double D western). 1964. Doubleday.

Girl from Four Corners: A Romance of California to-Day. Rebecca Newman Porter. LC 20-6861. 1920. H. Holt and Company.

Girl from France. Vera Murdock Stuart Jervis. LC 47-200993. 1947. Hurst & Blackett, Ltd.

Girl from Frisco. William Heuman. LC 55-6374. 1955. Morrow.

Girl from Frozen Bend. Norma Bicknell Mansfield. LC 38-24738. Farrar & Rinehart., Incorporated.

Girl from Girton: And Other Stories About Schools. Charles William Bardeen. LC 14-22588. 1.00. C. W. Bardeen.

Girl from Glengarry. Charles William Gordon. LC 33-22223. 1933. Dodd, Mead & Company.

Girl from God's Mercie. William Byron Mowery. LC 29-22803. 1929. Doubleday, Doran & Cimpany, Inc.

Girl from Grand Pre. William Miller Bartlett. LC 27-2548. 1927. The Stratford Company.

Girl from Hampton Beach: An Adventure in Unconventional Living. Fred C Pillsbury. LC 37-16813. 1937. Meador Publishing Company.

Girl from Hell's Kitchen. Leslie Scott. LC 53-18609. 1952. Arco Pub. Co.

Girl from His Town. Marie Van Vorst. LC 10-8162. The Bobbs-Merrill Company.

Girl from Hollywood. Edgar Rice Burroughs. LC 23-11827. The Macaulay Company.

Girl from Home: A Story of Honolulu,Isobel Strong. Isobel Osbourne Field. LC 5-13028. 1905. McClure, Phillips & Co.

Girl from Hong-Kong: A Story of Adventure Under Five Suns. St. George Rathborne. LC 99-4453. (On cover: Eagle library, no. 126). Street & Smith.

Girl from Ipanema. Charles Edward Eaton. LC 72-183102. 1972. 5.95. Printed at Stinehour Press; Distributed by North Country Pub. Co.

Girl from Kankakee. Alexander Stuart Hunter. LC 26-5146. W. Neale.

Girl from Keller's. Harold Bindloss. LC 17-30278. Frederick A. Stokes Company.

Girl from Kurdistan. Jessie Douglas Kerruish. LC 19-7766. 1918. Hodder and Stoughton.

Girl from Lubeck. Bruce Marshall. LC 62-8171. 1962. Houghton Mifflin.

Girl from Macoupin: A Novel. Henry E Scott. LC 8-2920. (On cover: The pastime series, no. 128). Laird & Lee.

Girl from Malta. Fergus Hume. (On cover: Lovell's library. no. 1369). 1889. J. W. Lovell Company.

Girl from Mine Run. William Wilfrid Whalen. LC 26-21463. 1926. B. Herder Book Co.

Girl from Montana. Grace Livingston Hill. LC 75-32515. 1975. 9.95. American Reprint Co.

Girl from Montana. Grace Livingston Hill. LC 8-37189. 1908. The Golden Rule Company.

Girl from Montana. Grace Livingston Hill. LC 22-6613. J. B. Lippincott Company.

Girl from Montana. Grace Livingston Hill. LC 81-19274. (Hill, Grace Livingston, 1865-1947. Classics Ser.: 3). (ISBN 0-8007-1301-X). F.H. Revell Co.

Girl from Moscow, and Other Stories: Three Contemporary Russian Novelettes. Tr., Ed. by Lila Pargment. Ed. by Lila Pargment. Boris Nikolaevich Polevoi & Sholokhov, Mikhail Aleksandrovich. LC 67-28049. 1968. 5.50. Ungar.

Girl from New York. Elizabeth Charlton. LC 37-15196. 1937. Hillman-Curl, Inc.

Girl from No. 13. Reginald Heber Patterson. LC 15-163373. 1915. 1.25. The Macaulay Company.

Girl from Nowhere. Evelyn Bond. (Orig.). 1972. pap. 0.75 o.p. (94208). Beagle Bks.

Girl from Nowhere. Elinore Denniston. LC 49-8747. (Red badge mystery). 1949. Dodd, Mead.

Girl from Nowhere. Rae Foley. 1974. (pbk.) 0.95. Dell.

Girl from Nowhere. Maysie Greig. LC 42-10306. 1942. Doubleday, Doran & Co., Inc.

Girl from Nowhere. Charlotte Lamb, pseud. (Harlequin Presents Ser.). 192p. 1982. pap. 1.75 (ISBN 0-373-10478-2, Pub. by Harlequin). PB.

Girl from Nowhere. Paula Minton, pseud. LC 75-13439. 160p. (Orig.). 1975. pap. 1.25 (ISBN 0-89041-020-8, 3020). Major Bks.

Girl from Nowhere. Gertrude M. Robins Reynolds. LC 10-23627. Hodder & Stoughton, G. H. Doran Company.

Girl from Paris. Joan Aiken. LC 81-43422. 1982. 15.50 (ISBN 0-385-17979-0). Doubleday.

Girl from Paris. large print ed. Joan Aiken. LC 82-23201. 1983. 17.50 (ISBN 0-8161-3497-9). G.K. Hall.

Girl from Paris. A. R. Towner. 112p. 1975. 3.95 o.s.i. (ISBN 0-8181-0341-8). Pageant-Poseidon.

Girl from Paris: A Dramatic Novel. Roland Oswell Rankin. LC 11-16148. (On cover: Neely's continental library, no. 7). F. T. Neely.

Girl from Paris; or, The Scene Painter's Fancy. A Novel. Roland Oswell Rankin. LC 8-227. 1894. The Associated Authors.

Girl from Petrovka. George Feifer. 1973. (pbk) 0.95. Curtis Books.

Girl from Petrovka. George Feifer. LC 70-158413. 1972. 6.95 (ISBN 0-670-34161-4). Viking Press.

Girl from 'Peyton Place' A Biography of Grace Metalious, by George Metalious, June O'Shea. George Metalious. (2888). Dell.

Girl from Pike County. Bret Harte. Ed. by Walter Pauk & Raymond Harris. (Jamestown Classics Ser.). (Illus.). 43p. (gr. 5). 1976. pap. text ed. 2.00x (ISBN 0-89061-050-9, 521); tchrs. ed. 3.00 (523). Jamestown Pubs.

Girl from Pussycat. Ted Mark, pseud. 208p. 1976. pap. 1.50 o.p. (ISBN 0-532-15188-7, 532-19105). Woodhill.

Girl from Pussycat. Ted Mark, pseud. (Orig.). 1968. pap. 0.60 o.p. (73-446). Lancer.

Girl from Pussycat. Ted Mark, pseud. 208p. 1976. pap. 1.50 o.p. (ISBN 0-532-15188-7, 532-19105). Manor Bks.

Girl from Ruby's. Chester W Nichols. LC 51-13838. 1951. Vantage Press.

Girl from Scotland. Edgar Wallace. LC 29-30774. 1927. A. L. Burt Company.

Girl from Scotland Yard. Edgar Wallace. LC 27-54233. 1927. Doubleday, Page & Company.

Girl from Stokeyville. Frank Yerby. 1975. (pbk.) 1.75. Dell.

Girl from Storyville: A Victorian Novel. Frank Yerby. LC 72-4604. 1972. 8.95. Dial Press.

Girl from the Eastern Shore. William Arthur Neubauer. LC 44-47000. 1944. Grammercy Publishing Co.

Girl from the Farm. Gertrude Dix. LC 6-338716. (On cover: Keynotes series no. 14). 1895. Roberts Bros.

Girl from the Marsh Croft. Selma Ottiliana Lovisa Lagerlof. Tr. by Howard, Velma Swanston. LC 10-114723. 1910. Little, Brown, and Company.

Girl from the Mimosa Club: By Leslie Ford Pseud. Zenith Jones Brown. LC 57-7646. 1957. Scribner.

Girl from the Ranch: Or, The Western Girl's Rival Lovers. Edna Winfield, pseud. LC 2175. (On cover: Holly library. no. 155). 1900. The Mershon Co.

Girl from the Sea. Anne Weale. (Harlequin Presents Ser.). 192p. 1981. pap. 1.50 (ISBN 0-373-10408-1, Pub. by Harlequin). PB.

Girl from Tim's Place. Charles Clark Munn. 1906. Lothrop, Lee & Shepard Co.

Girl from Vermont: The Story of a Vacation School Teacher. Marshall Saunders. LC 10-6738. 1910. The Griffith & Rowland Press.

Girl from Woolworth's: Novelized. Karen Brown. LC 30-263. Efrus & Bennett, Inc.

Girl Going Nowhere. Darragh Aldrich. LC 30-840019. 1939. H. C. Kinsey & Company, Inc.

Girl Going Nowhere. Darragh Aldrich. LC 39-3400. 1939. H. C. Kinsey & Company, Inc.

Girl Gone Down. William G. Phillips. pap. 1.95 o.p. (8028). Cameo.

Girl Graduate. Celia Parker Woolley. LC 8-372373. 1889. Houghton, Mifflin and Company.

Girl Green As Elderflower. Randolph Stow. LC 81-40702. 1980. 9.95 (ISBN 0-670-34091-X). Viking Press.

Girl He Bought: Or, Bonny and Blue. Mary Edwards Bryan. (On cover: Library of American authors, no. 64). 1895. G. Munro's Sons.

Girl He Left Behind. Helen Beecher Long. LC 18-18334. G. Sully & Company.

Girl He Left Behind: Or, All Quiet in the Third Platoon. Marion Hargrove. LC 56-9124. 1956. Viking Press.

Girl: Helen Sawyer Stuart. Evelyn May. 1977. pap. 5.00 o.p. (ISBN 0-8283-1701-1). Branden.

Girl Hero: Or, The Plottings of Fate. Mary Grace Halpine. (On cover: Munro's library. v. 1. no. 401). 1885. N. L. Munro.

Girl Hunt. Laurence Dwight Smith. LC 37-5407. J. B. Lippincott Company.

Girl Hunters. Frank Morrison Spillane. LC 62-7806. 1962. Dutton.

Girl I Knew. 1st American Ed. Axel Jensen. LC 62-8672. 1962. Knopf.

Girl I Left Behind. Jane O'Reilly. 240p. 1982. pap. 3.50 (ISBN 0-553-20202-2). Bantam.

Girl I Left Behind Me. Weymer Jay Mills. LC 10-23671. 1910. Dodd, Mead & Company.

Girl in a Cage. Jack Angleman. pap. 1.95 o.p. (ISBN 0-87977-166-6, DBB166). Dansk Blue Bk.

Girl in a Mask. Helen K Maxwell. LC 73-135429. 1971. 5.95. Little, Brown.

Girl in a Shroud see Blonde.

Girl in a Swing. Richard George Adams. LC 79-3480. 1980. 11.95 (ISBN 0-394-51049-6). Knopf: Distributed by Random House.

Girl in a Trap. Renee Shann. (Orig.). 1971. pap. 0.75 o.p. (94153). Beagle Bks.

Girl in Black. Victor Bridges. LC 27-7727. 1927. J. B. Lippincott Company.

Girl in Black Velvet. Louis Leon De Jean. LC 37-3753. The Macaulay Company.

Girl in Blue. Pelham Grenville Wodehouse. LC 76-133098. 1971. 5.95 (ISBN 0-671-20802-0). Simon and Schuster.

Girl in Cabin B54. Lucille Fletcher, pseud. LC 68-14532. (A Random House mystery). 1968. Random House.

Girl in Checks: Or, The Mystery of the Mountain Cabin. James Walter Daniel. LC 6-33165. 1890. Printed for the Author.

Girl in Every Port. Charles Stanley Strong. LC 42-4718. 1942. Phoenix Press.

Girl in Fancy Dress. Annie Edith Foster Jameson. LC 21-260783. George H. Doran Company.

Girl in Golden Rags. Robert William Chambers. LC 36-3137. 1936. D. Appleton-Century Company, Incorporated.

Girl in His Garden. Marjorie Warby. 1972. pap. 0.75 o.p. (94242). Beagle Bks.

Girl in His House. Harold MacGrath. LC 18-10004. Harper & Brothers.

Girl in His Past. Georges Simenon. LC 77-357081. 1976. 2.95 (ISBN 0-241-89448-4). Hamilton.

Girl in His Past: A Novel. Georges Simenon. LC 52-8013. 1952. Prentice-Hall.

Girl in Jeopardy. Maysie Greig. (Candlelight Mystery). 1973. (pbk.) 0.75. Dell.

Girl in Khaki. Georgia Craig. 1944. Arcadia House, Inc.

Girl in Khaki. Peggy Gaddis, pseud. LC 44-1214. 1944. Arcadia House.

Girl in Love. Ann Gilmer, pseud. 1972. pap. 0.75 o.s.i. (01-353). Lancer.

Girl in Love: By Rebecca Marsh Pseud. William Arthur Neubauer. LC 56-134487. 1956. Arcadia House.

Girl in May. Bruce Marshall. LC 56-595662. 1956. Houghton Mifflin.

Girl in Melanie Klein. Ronald Harwood. LC 69-11797. 1969. 4.95. Holt, Rinehart and Winston.

Girl in Overalls: A Novel of Women in Defense Today. Ellen Ashley. LC 43-11958. 1943. Dodd, Mead & Company.

Girl in Question; a Story of Not So Long Ago. L. C. Violett Houk. LC 8-16715. 1908. J. Lane Company.

Girl in the Bar. Carter Sprague. 192p. (Orig.). 1973. pap. 1.95 o.p. (ISBN 0-87682-363-0, 7363). Barclay Hse.

Girl in the Blue Pinafore. Sara Ware Bassett. LC 57-7276. 1957. Doubleday.

Girl in the Brown Habit. A Sporting Novel. Mary E. Kennard. LC 7-11102. (Harper's Franklin square library, no. 560). Harper & Brothers.

Girl in the Cage. Cortland Fitzsimmons & Mulholland, John, 1898- Joint Author. LC 39-22043. 1939. Frederick A. Stokes Company.

Girl in the Cage: A Ralph Lindsey Mystery. Ben Benson. LC 54-5823. 1954. M. S. Mill Co. and W. Morrow.

Girl in the Cheongsam see Agency House, Malaya.

Girl in the Cockpit. Michael Avallone. (Orig.). 1972. pap. 0.75 o.p. (07261). Curtis.

Girl in the Cockpit. Michael Avallone. 1973. 0.75. Curtis Books.

Girl in the Diamond-Studded Bed. William R Bentley. 1975. (pbk.) 2.25 (ISBN 0-87056-429-3). Brandon Books.

Girl in the Family. Beatrice Burton Morgan. LC 33-27166. Farrar & Rinehart, Incorporated.

Girl in the Fog: A Mystery Novel. Joseph Gollomb. LC 23-127465. Boni and Liveright.

Girl in the Frame. William Hanscom Fuller. LC 57-700136. (Dell first edition, A133). 1957. Dell Pub. Co.

Girl in the Golden Atom. Ray Cummings. LC 73-13251. 1974. 9.95 (ISBN 0-88355-107-1) (ISBN 0-88355-107-1). Hyperion Press.

Girl in the Golden Atom. Ray Cummings. LC 24-5348. 1923. Harper & Brothers.

Girl in the Green Coat. Henry Leyford Gates. LC 30-24770. 1930. Barse & Co.

Girl in the Martian Moon. C. M. Alexander. (Orig.). 1979. pap. 1.95. Woodhill.

Girl in the Mirror. Peggy O'More, pseud. LC 64-9978. 1964. Arcadia House.

Girl in the Other Seat. Henry Kitchell Webster. LC 11-10637. 1911. D. Appleton and Company.

Girl in the Park: By Emily Noble Pseud. James Noble Gifford. LC 53-113071. 1953. Arcadia House.

Girl in the Photograph. Lygia F. Telles. 256p. 1982. pap. 3.95 (ISBN 0-380-80176-0, 80176-0, Bard). Avon.

Girl in the Plain Brown Wrapper. John Dann MacDonald. LC 72-8388. 1973. 5.95 (ISBN 0-397-00953-4). Lippincott.

Girl in the Plastic Cage. Marilyn Levy. 192p. (Orig.). 1982. pap. 1.95 (ISBN 0-449-70030-5, Juniper). Fawcett.

Girl in the Plywood Box. William R Bentley. 1974. (pbk.) 1.95 (ISBN 0-87056-362-9). Brandon Books.

Girl in the Red Velvet Swing: A Goldmedal Original. Charles Samuels. LC 53-27311. (Classic murder trial series). 1953. Fawcett Publications.

Girl in the River. Victor B Miller. 1975. (pbk.) 1.25 (ISBN 0-671-78817-5). Pocket Books.

Girl in the Shadows. Zoa Sherburne. (Cameo Gothic ser: No. 20). 1975. (pbk.) 0.95. Ace Books.

Girl in the Slumber-Boots. Adah Viola Rohrer Bienz. LC 12-24245. 1.00. Press of Jennings and Graham.

Girl in the Spike-Heeled Shoes. Martin Yoseloff. LC 49-109088. 1949. E. P. Dutton.

Girl in the Spike-Heeled Shoes see Dropout.

Girl in the Studio. Vivian Cory. LC 34-32757. The Macaulay Company.

Girl in the Telltale Bikini. Patrick Morgan. (Operation Hang Ten Ser). 1971. pap. 0.75 o.p. (75-394). Manor Bks.

Girl in the Tower. Jane Corby. 1978. pap. 1.50 o.s.i. (ISBN 0-8439-0538-7, Leisure Bks). Nordon Pubns.

Girl in the Trunk. Bruce Cassiday. (Ace mystery). 1973. (pbk.) 0.95. Ace.

Girl in the Turquoise Bikini. 1st Ed. Muriel Resnik. LC 61-766189. 1961. Doubleday.

Girl in the Valley. Peggy O'More, pseud. LC 47-12334. 1947. Gramercy Pub. Co.

Girl in the White Coat on the Delta Eagle. Gary Youree. LC 79-13087. 9.95 (ISBN 0-393-01278-6). Norton.

Girl in the White Ship. Peter Townsend. LC 82-3110. 224p. 1983. 15.95 (ISBN 0-03-057787-X). HR&W.

Girl in the Yellow Dress. Sonia Phillips. 1977. pap. 1.50 (ISBN 0-532-15282-4). Woodhill.

Girl in Waiting. Archibald Eyre. LC 6-6260. 1906. J. W. Luce and Company.

Girl in White. Julie Ellis. (O.s.i.). Date not set. pap. 1.75 o.s.i. WSP.

Girl in White. Julie Ellis (ISBN 0-671-80808-7). Pocket Books.

Girl in Winter. Philip Larkin. 1957. 4.50 o.p. St Martin.

Girl in Winter. Philip Larkin. LC 75-27291. 1978. 8.95 o.p.; pap. 4.95 o.p. (ISBN 0-87951-079-X). Overlook Pr.

Girl in Winter: A Novel. Philip Larkin. LC 78-15979. 1978. 8.95 (ISBN 0-87951-079-X). Overlook Press.

Girl in 304. Harold R Daniels. LC 56-10742. (Dell first edition, A112). 1956. Dell Pub. Co.

Girl in 906. Douglas Hall. LC 71-106427. 1970. 3.50. Zondervan Pub. House.

Girl Intern. Elizabeth Seifert. LC 73-79143. 1973. 5.95. Aeonian Press.

Girl Intern. Elizabeth Seifert. LC 48-2762. 1948. Triangle Books.

Girl Intern. Elizabeth Seifert. LC 44-341783. 1944. Dodd, Mead & Company.

Girl Like I. Rosemary McLeod. LC 77-357899. (Illus.). 1976. (ISBN 0-908565-13-5). J. McIndoe.

Girl Like Marilyn. Renee Shann. pap. 0.45 o.p. (56-992). Paperback Lib.

Girl Like Marilyn. Renee Shann. 1972. pap. 0.75 o.p. (94270). Beagle Bks.

Girl Like Me. Sandra Harmon. LC 74-31480. 1975. 7.95 (ISBN 0-525-11362-2). Dutton.

Girl Like Sylvia: A Love Story. Eleanor Elliott Carroll. LC 36-348473. Chelsea House.

Girl Meets Body. Jack Iams. LC 47-308624. 1947. W. Morrow.

Girl Missing. Sherry, Edna. LC 62-14128. (Red badge detective). 1962. Dodd, Mead.

Girl Model for Sale. Barbara Kenn. 192p. 1973. pap. 1.95 o.p. (ISBN 0-87977-185-2, DBB185). Dansk Blue Bk.

Girl Must Marry. Maysie Greig. LC 31-673710. 1931. L. MacVeagh, The Dial Press.

Girl Named Marcia. Margaretta Brucker. LC 52-8349. 1952. Arcadia House.

Girl Named Mary. Juliet Wilbor Tompkins. LC 18-14424. The Bobbs-Merrill Company.

Girl Named Sooner. Suzanne Clauser. LC 72-171283. 1975. (pbk.) 1.50 (ISBN 0-380-00216-7). Avon.

Girl Named Tamiko: A Novel. Ronald De Levington Kirkbride. LC 59-6492. 1959. F. Fell.

Girl Next Door. Anne Tedlock Brooks. LC 44-5956. 1944. Arcadia House, Inc.

Girl Next Door. Peggy Gaddis, pseud. LC 49-50405. 1949. Arcadia House.

Girl Next Door: Being the Crabbed Chronicle of a Misanthrope. Lee Wilson Dodd. LC 23-7998. E. P. Dutton & Company.

Girl Nobody Knows. Mark McShane. LC 65-11805. 3.50. Pub. for the Crime Club by Doubleday.

Girl O' the Mountains: A Story of the West and California in the Days of '49. George W Greene. LC 26-42529. 1926. Lewiston Journal Company.

Girl of Big Mountain. William Arthur Neubauer. LC 67-2438. 1967. Arcadia House.

Girl of Black Island. Christine Bennett, pseud. (Contemporary Teens Ser.). 224p. (Orig.). 1981. pap. 2.25 (ISBN 0-89531-141-0, 0146-96). Sharon Pubns.

Girl of Ghost Mountain. Joseph Allan Elphinstone Dunn. Small, Maynard & Company.

Girl of Grit: A Story of the Intelligence Department. Arthur George Frederick Griffiths. LC 99-1688. 1899. R. F. Fenno & Company.

Girl of Ideas. Annie Austin Flint. LC 3-8343. 1903. C. Scribner's Sons.

Girl of My Dreams. William Arthur Neubauer. LC 47-157924. 1947. Grammercy Publishing Co.

Girl of O. K. Valley: A Romance of the Okanagan. Robert Watson. LC 19-15568. George H. Doran Company.

Girl of the Blue Ridge. Payne Erskine. LC 15-8424. 1915. 1.35. Little, Brown, and Company.

Girl of the Commune. George Alfred Henty. LC 13-33879. 1895. R. F. Fenno & Company.

Girl of the Golden Gate. William Brown Meloney. LC 13-5416. 1.25. E. J. Clode.

Girl of the Golden West: A Novel. Julia Whedon. LC 72-95172. 1973. 5.95. Charterhouse.

Girl of the Golden West: Novelized from the Play. David Belasco. LC 11-27452. 1911. Dodd, Mead and Company.

Girl of the Guard Line. Charles Carey Waddel. LC 15-216252. 1915. Moffat, Yard and Company.

Girl of the Hills: A Novel. 1st Ed. Frances Jackson Thames. LC 54-10030. 1954. Pageant Press.

Girl of the Jungle Trail. 1951. Ethel Matson.

Girl of the Limberlost. Gene Stratton Porter. 1909. Doubleday, Page & Company.

Girl of the Limberlost. Gene Stratton Porter. LC 12-21236. 1911. Doubleday, Page & Company.

Girl of the Limberlost. Gene Stratton Porter. LC 21-13701. 1912. Grosset & Dunlap.

Girl of the Limberlost. Gene Stratton Porter. LC 15-20317. 1913. Doubleday, Page & Co.

Girl of the Limberlost. Gene Stratton Porter. LC 16-86977. 1916. 1.28. C. Scribner's Sons.

Girl of the Limberlost. George Stratton Porter. LC 26-1452. 1917. Grosset & Dunlap.

Girl of the Limberlost. Gene Stratton Porter. LC 44-7841. 1944. Triangle Books.

Girl of the Limberlost. Gene Stratton-Porter. 1974. Repr. of 1909 ed. lib. bdg. 30.00 (ISBN 0-8414-7977-1). Folcroft.

Girl of the Listening Heart. Bertha B. Moore McCurry. LC 38-7587. 1937. Wm. B. Eerdmans Publishing Co.

Girl of the Listening Heart. Bertha B Moore. LC 38-7587. 1937. Wm. B. Eerdmans Publishing Co.

Girl of the Ozarks. Cleo M. Stephens. (YA) 1973. 4.95 o.p. (Avalon). Bouregy.

Girl of the Ozarks. Elizabeth Montgomery Summers. LC 13-106625. The C. M. Clark Publishing Co.

Girl of the People. A Novel. Elizabeth Thomasina Meade Smith. LC 8-8647. (On cover: Lovell's international series, no. 52). F. F. Lovell and Company.

Girl of the Prairie. Margaret Shauers. 1975. 4.95. Avalon Books.

Girl of the Riverland. Stephen Morris Johnston. LC 35-545975. 1935. Benziger Brothers.

Girl of the Sea of Cortez. Peter Benchley. LC 81-43599. 1982. 13.95 (ISBN 0-385-17926-X). Doubleday.

Girl of the West. Bertha Bendele. LC 19-139702. Saulsbury Publishing Company.

Girl of the Woods. Grace Livingston Hill. LC 42-6833. 1942. J. B. Lippincott Company.

Girl of This Century: A Continution of "We Four Girls,". Mary Greenleaf Darling. LC 2-17858. 1902. Lee and Shepard.

Girl of Virginia. Lucy Meacham Kidd Thruston. 1902. Little, Brown, and Company.

Girl on a High Wire. Elinore Denniston. LC 79-91277. (Red badge mystery). 1969. 3.95. Dodd, Mead.

Girl on a High Wire. Rae Foley. LC 79-91277. 1983. pap. 2.95 (ISBN 0-396-08163-0). Dodd.

Girl on a High Wire. Rae Foley. (Red Badge Mystery Ser). 1969. 3.95 o.p. (ISBN 0-396-05989-9). Dodd.

Girl on First Base. Ralph Michaels. 1981. pap. 2.25 (ISBN 0-8439-0916-1, Leisure Bks). Nordon Pubns.

Girl on His Hands. Maysie Greig. LC 39-24726. 1939. Doubleday, Doran & Company, Inc.

Girl on the Beach. George Sumner Albee. LC 53-10780. (Dell first edition, 4). 1953. Dell Pub. Co.

Girl on the Beach: A Novel. Anne Holden. LC 73-12575. 1973. 5.95 (ISBN 0-440-03097-8). Delacorte Press.

Girl on the Boat. P. G. Wodehouse. 1956. 11.95 o.s.i. (ISBN 0-8277-0234-5). British Bk Ctr.

Girl on the Coca-Cola Tray. Nancy Winters. LC 76-21351. 1976. 7.95. Dial Press.

Girl on the Coca-Cola Tray. Nancy Winters. (Kangaroo Book). 1977. 1.75 (ISBN 0-671-81292-0). Pocket Books.

Girl on the Hilltop. Lorin Andrews Lathrop. LC 20-10304. 1.75. George H. Doran Company.

Girl on the Left Bank: By Joan Shepherd Pseud. B J Buchanan. LC 53-2443. 1953. I. Washburn.

Girl on the Make. Achmed Abdullah & Faith Cuthrell. LC 32-7122. 1932. R. Long & R. R. Smith, Inc.

Girl on the Run. Hillary Waugh. LC 65-23791. 1965. Published for the Crime Club by Doubleday.

Girl on the Run. Cover Painting by Lu Kimmel. Edward Sidney Aarons. LC 4-38659. (Gold medal books, 424). 1954. Fawcett Publications.

Girl on the Six O'clock News. Jessica Hyatt. 1978. pap. 1.95 o.s.i. (ISBN 0-8439-0592-1, Leisure Bks). Nordon Pubns.

Girl on the Stair. Eunice R Hart. LC 45-6557. 1945. Wm B. Eerdmans Publishing Company.

Girl on the Street. James Noble Gifford. LC 46-156856. 1946. Phoenix Press.

Girl on the Via Flaminia. Alfred Hayes. LC 49-7883. 1949. Harper.

Girl or Boy: A Satire and a Diversion. John North. LC 26-13796. Small, Maynard & Company.

Girl Ought to Work. Claude Binyon. LC 32-16257. 1932. H. Smith.

Girl Out There. Karl Edwin Harriman. LC 6-188416. 1906. G. W. Jacobs & Co.

Girl Outlaw. Robert Elmer Callahan. LC 53-3089. 1953. Christopher Pub. House.

Girl Outside. Anne Betteridge, pseud. 1973. pap. 0.75 o.p. (ISBN 0-345-20754-8). Beagle Bks.

Girl Philippa. Robert William Chambers. LC 16-14870. 1916. 1.40. D. Appleton and Company.

Girl Possessed. Peggy Swenson. 1973. (pbk.) 1.95 (ISBN 0-87056-326-2). Brandon Books.

Girl Possessed. Violet Winspear. (Harlequin Presents Ser.). 192p. 1981. pap. 1.50 (ISBN 0-373-10420-0, Pub. by Harlequin). PB.

Girl Proposition. George Ade. LC 74-96872. (Illus.). 1969. Literature House.

Girl Proposition: A Bunch of He and She Fables. George Ade. LC 26-3660. 1902. Harper & Brothers.

Girl Question: Founded on the Play of Will M. Hough and Frank R. Adams. John William Harding & Hough, Will M. G. W. Dillingham Company.

Girl Reporter. Carl Harry Claudy. LC 30-10085. 1930. Little, Brown, and Company.

Girl Rough Riders: A Romantic and Adventurous Trail of Fair Rough Riders Through the Wonderland of Mystery and Silence. Prentiss Ingraham. LC 3-12822. 1903. D. Estes & Company.

Girl Running: By Amam Knight Pseud. Lawrence Lariar. LC 56-13182. (Signet book, 1347). 1956. New American Library.

Girl Said No. Sarah Y Mason. LC 30-18312. World Wide Publishing Co., Inc.C.

Girl That He Marries. Rhoda Lerman. (Kangaroo Book). 1977. 1.95 (ISBN 0-671-80990-3). Pocket Books.

Girl That He Marries: A Novel. Rhoda Lerman. LC 75-29908. 6.95 (ISBN 0-03-015336-0). Holt, Rinehart and Winston.

Girl, the Gold Watch, & Everything. John Dann MacDonald. 1978. pap. 2.50 (ISBN 0-449-14296-5, GM). Fawcett.

Girl to Come Home to. Grace Livingston Hill. LC 75-35863. 1975. American Reprint Co.

Girl to Come Home to. Grace Livingston Hill. LC 45-922595. 1945. J. B. Lippincott Company.

Girl, Twenty. Kingsley Amis. LC 75-174504. 256p. 1972. 5.95 o.p. (ISBN 0-15-135690-4). HarBraceJ.

Girl Warriors: A Book for Girls. Adene Williams. LC 29-8261. 1901. D. C. Cook Publishing Company.

Girl Watcher. James Lawson. 1977. 1.95 (ISBN 0-446-89330-7). Warner Books.

Girl Watcher: A Novel. James Lawson. LC 76-10613. 7.95 (ISBN 0-399-11814-4). Putnam.

Girl Watcher's Funeral. Hugh Pentecost. (Red Badge Mystery Ser). 1969. 3.95 o.p. (ISBN 0-396-05983-X). Dodd.

Girl Watcher's Funeral: A Pierre Chambrun Mystery Novel. Judson Pentecost Philips. LC 73-80709. (Red badge mystery). 1969. 3.95. Dodd, Mead.

Girl Who Cast Out Fear. Dorothy Speare. LC 25-23219. George H. Doran Company.

Girl Who Cried Wolf. Hillary Waugh. LC 58-13910. 1958. Published for the Crime Club by Doubleday.

Girl Who Didn't Die. Ruby Jean Jensen. 1975. (pbk.) 1.25 (ISBN 0-446-76693-3). Warner Paperback Library.

Girl Who Fought. William Wilfrid Whalen. LC 27-7722. 1927. B. Herder Book Co.

Girl Who Got All the Breaks. Carol Eisen Rinzler. LC 79-24537. 9.95 (ISBN 0-399-12352-0). Putnam.

Girl Who Had Everything. Rae Foley. (Red Badge Novel of Suspence Ser.). 1977. 6.95 o.p. (ISBN 0-396-07492-8). Dodd.

Girl Who Had Everything: A Novel of Suspense. Elinore Denniston. LC 77-21529. 10.95 (ISBN 0-396-07492-8). Dodd, Mead.

Girl Who Had to Die. Elisabeth Sanxay Holding. LC 40-3032. 1940. Dodd, Mean & Company.

Girl Who Kept Knocking Them Dead. Hampton Stone, pseud. (Hampton Stone Mysteries Ser). 1971. pap. 0.75 o.p. (ISBN 0-446-64608-3, 64-608). Paperback Lib.

Girl Who Kept Knocking Them Dead: By Hampton Stone Pseud. Aaron Marc Stein. LC 57-3761. (Inner sanctum mystery). 1957. Simon and Schuster.

Girl Who Licked the World. Norman Singer. (Orig.). 1972. pap. 1.95 o.s.i. (TCP 2354). Olympia.

Girl Who Lived in the Woods. Marjorie Benton Cooke. LC 10-22062. 1910. 1.50. A. C. McClurg & Co.

Girl Who Loved the Land. Mai Rightor Mason. LC 17-9253. The Central Book Co.

Girl Who Never: A Novel in a Satirical Vein. 1st Ed. Ruth Khee. 1959. Greenwich Book Publishers.

Girl Who Passed for Normal. Hugh Fleetwood. LC 72-95909. 1973. 6.95 (ISBN 0-8128-1563-7). Stein and Day.

Girl Who Sang with the Beatles, and Other Stories. Robert Hemenway. LC 70-98664. 1970. 4.95. Knopf.

Girl Who Waited. Phyllis Yahnke. LC 48-1832. 1948. Gramercy Pub. Co.

Girl Who Walked Without Fear. Louise Guest Rice. LC 15-24549. Fleming H. Revell Company.

Girl Who Wanted a Say. Paul Zindel. 1982. pap. 2.25 (ISBN 0-553-22540-5). Bantam.

Girl Who Wanted Experience. Lee Shippey. LC 37-677. 1937. Houghton Mifflin Company.

Girl Who Wanted to Run to the Boston Marathon. Robert McKay. LC 79-20928. 7.95 (ISBN 0-525-66663-X). Elsevier/Nelson Books.

Girl Who Was Clairvoyant. Mignon Warner. LC 82-45549. 1982. 11.95 (ISBN 0-385-18362-3). Published for the Crime Club by Doubleday.

Girl Who Was Never Queen: A Biographical Novel of Princess Charlotte of Wales. 1st Ed. Mary Foster Main. LC 62-11311. 1962. Doubleday.

Girl Who Wasn't There. Thomas Blanchard Dewey. (O.S.I.). 1960. 2.95 o.s.i. (28645). S&S.

Girl Who Won. Elizabeth Ellis. LC 10-11473. 1910. 1.50. Dodd, Mead and Company.

Girl Who Wouldn't Talk. Cheryl Goldfeder & James Goldfeder. 1974. pap. 3.50 (ISBN 0-913072-17-6). Natl Assn Deaf.

Girl Who Wrote. Alfred J. Cohen. LC 2-20039. 1902. Quail & Warner.

Girl with a Golden Bar. Brenda Conrad. 1944. C. Scribner's Sons.

Girl with a Secret. Charlotte Armstrong. 1970. pap. 0.60 o.p. (R1370, Crest). Fawcett World.

Girl with a Squint. Georges Simenon. LC 77-84397. 7.95 (ISBN 0-15-135692-0). Harcourt Brace Jovanovich.

Girl with a Temper: A Romance of the Wills Act. H B Finlay Knight. LC 7-14180. (On cover: Harper's Franklin square library, no. 731). 1893. Harper & Brothers.

Girl with a Zebra. Perdita Buchan. LC 66-20344. 1966. bds., 4.50. Seribners.

Girl with Class. Dave Wallis. LC 59-7131. Coward-McCann.

Girl with Green Eyes. Edna O'Brien. 216p. 1975. pap. 1.95 o.p. (ISBN 0-14-002108-6). Penguin.

Girl with Jade Green Eyes. Boyd Upchurch. LC 78-10590. 1979. 1.95 (ISBN 0-14-004996-7). Penguin Books.

Girl with Red Hair. Rob Eden. LC 30-14874. Grosset & Dunlap.

Girl with Six Fingers. Hugh Pentecost. LC 69-15554. (Red Badge Mystery Ser). 1969. 3.95 o.p. (ISBN 0-396-05870-1). Dodd.

Girl with Six Fingers: A John Jericho Mystery Novel. Judson Pentecost Philips. LC 69-15554. (Red badge mystery). 1969. 3.95. Dodd, Mead.

Girl with Spunk. St. George, Judith. LC 75-4425. (Illus.). 1975. 6.95 (ISBN 0-399-20473-3). G. P. Putnam's Sons.

Girl with the Blue Sailor. Burton Egbert Stevenson. 1906. Dodd, Mead & Company.

Girl with the Dynamite Bangs. Lou Cameron. (Boomer Ser., No. 1). 1973. pap. 0.95 o.s.i. (75-462). Lancer.

Girl with the Dynamite Bangs. Lou Cameron. (Blaster #1). 1973. (pbk) 0.95. Lancer Books.

Girl with the Frightened Eyes... Lawrence Lariar. LC 45-8440. 1945. Dodd, Mead & Company.

Girl with the Glass Heart: A Novel. 1st Ed. Daniel Stern. LC 53-9866. 1953. Bobbs-Merrill.

Girl with the Glorious Genes. Albert H. Z Carbury. LC 68-19245. 1968. 0.75. Bantam Books.

Girl with the Golden Eyes. Honore De Balzac. Tr. by Ernest Christopher Dowson. LC 30-19718. 1930. Williams, Belasco & Meyers.

Girl with the Golden Eyes. Honore De Balzac. 1969. pap. 0.50 o.p. (62-059). McGraw.

Girl with the Golden Eyes. Honore De Balzac. 1969. pap. 0.50 o.p. (62-059). Paperback Lib.

Girl with the Golden Eyes: Translated by Ernest Dowson. Honore De Balzac. LC 50-14693. (Illustrated library). Halcyon House.

Girl with the Golden Eyes: Translated by Ernest Dowson. Honore De Balzac & Dowson, Ernest Christopher, 1867-1900, Tr. LC 31-33383. Illustrated Editions Company, Inc.

Girl with the Golden Key: And Other Stories. 1st Ed. Joseph Farrow. LC 54-617989. 1954. Exposition Press.

Girl with the Golden Yo-Yo. Edmund Schiddel. 160p. 1975. pap. 1.25 (ISBN 0-532-12262-3). Woodhill.

Girl with the Hole in Her Head. hampton stone pseud. ed. Aaron Marc Stein. LC 49-960682. (inner sanctum mysteery). 1949. Simon and Schuster.

Girl with the Hole in Her Head. Hampton Stone, pseud. (Hampton Stone Mystery Ser., No. 13). 1971. pap. 0.75 o.p. (ISBN 0-446-64704-7, 64-704-7). Paperback Lib.

Girl with the Hungry Eyes, and Other Stories. Leiber, Fritz. LC 49-4190. 1949. Avon Pub. Co.

Girl with the Jade Green Eyes. John Boyd. 1979. pap. 2.50 o.p. (ISBN 0-14-004996-7). Penguin.

Girl with the Jade Green Eyes. John Boyd. 1978. 8.95 o.p. (ISBN 0-670-34164-9). Viking Pr.

Girl with the Jade Green Eyes. Boyd Upchurch. LC 77-21954. 1978. 7.95 (ISBN 0-670-34164-9). Viking Press.

Girl with the Key. Mary Kay Simmons. 1974. (pbk.) 1.25. Dell.

Girl with the Peppermint Taste. Andre Launay. LC 72-86766. 1972. 5.95 (ISBN 0-8027-0402-6). Walker.

Girl with the Polka Dot Box. F. W. Paul. LC 74-591. (Man from S.T.U.D. Ser). (Orig.). 1969. pap. 0.75 o.p. Lancer.

Girl with the Rosewood Crutches. She Tells Some Chapters of Her Life. LC 12-225624. 1912. 1.20. McBride, Nast & Company.

Girl with Two Selves. Frederick Hankerson Costello. LC 13-9143. 1913. 1.00. A. C. McClurg & Co.

Girl Without Credit. Maysie Greig. LC 41-25256. 1941. Doubleday, Doran & Company, Inc.

Girl, 20. Kingsley Amis. 1973. 1.25 (ISBN 0-345-03044-3). Ballantine.

Girl, 20. Kingsley Amis. LC 75-174504. 1972. 5.95 (ISBN 0-15-135690-4). Harcourt Brace Jovanovich.
Girlfriends: A Novel. Dallas Miller. LC 76-55544. 1977. 1.75 (ISBN 0-380-00890-4). Avon.
Girlhood and Womanhood: Or, Sketches of My Schoolmates... A J Graves. LC 6-45437. 1844. T. H. Carter & Co. Etc.
Girlpower. Vida Hurst. LC 46-593. 1946. Grammercy Publishing Co.
Girls. Henry De Montherlant, pseud. Tr. by Terence Kilmartin. LC 68-28224. 1969. 8.95 o.p. (ISBN 0-06-011017-1, HarpT). Har-Row.
Girls. Edna Ferber. 1921. Doubleday, Page & Company.
Girls. Nicola Thorne, pseud. LC 67-22680. 1967. Random House.
Girls: A Tetralogy of Novels. Henry De Montherlant. LC 68-28224. 1968. 8.95. Harper & Row.
Girls Are Missing. Caroline Crane. LC 80-14784. 224p. 1980. 8.95 (ISBN 0-396-07877-X). Dodd.
Girls Are Missing. Caroline Crane. 1981. pap. 2.50 (ISBN 0-451-11018-8, AE1018, Sig). NAL.
Girls Are Missing: A Novel of Suspense. Caroline Crane. LC 80-14784. 8.95 (ISBN 0-396-07877-X). Dodd, Mead.
Girls at His Billet. Berta Ruck. LC 16-23626. 1916. Dodd, Mead and Company.
Girls at Play. Paul Theroux. LC 72-82944. 1969. 4.95. Houghton Mifflin.
Girls at War, and Other Stories. Chinua Achebe. LC 72-85361. 1973. 5.95 (ISBN 0-385-00852-X). Doubleday.
Girls Came C.O.D. J. J Montague. 1975. (pbk.) 2.25 (ISBN 0-87056-430-7). Brandon Books.
Girls Can Be Gallant. John Scott Douglas. LC 40-37522. Phoenix Press.
Girls' Dorm. Kim Savage. LC 52-1073. 1952. Vixen Press.
Girl's Farm. Jack Thomas. 1974. (pbk.) 1.25. Bantam Books.
Girls for Pleasure. Marshall Roberts. 192p. 1972. pap. 1.95 o.p. (ISBN 0-87977-150-X, DBB150). Dansk Blue Bk.
Girls from Esquire. Introd. by Frederic A. Birmingham. Esquire. LC 52-7523. 1952. Random House.
Girls from Orgy. Ted Mark, pseud. 224p. (Orig.). 1975. pap. 1.25 (ISBN 0-532-12299-2). Woodhill.
Girls from Planet 5. Richard Wilson. LC 55-11965. 1955. Ballantine Books.
Girls from the Five Great Valleys. Elizabeth Savage. LC 77-4512. 1977. 10.95 (ISBN 0-8161-6482-7). G. K. Hall.
Girls from the Five Great Valleys: A Novel. Elizabeth Savage. LC 76-44427. 7.95 (ISBN 0-316-77140-6). Little, Brown.
Girls, Gushers & Roughnecks. S. E. J. Cox. LC 78-182048. 1972. (ISBN 0-8111-0441-9). Naylor Co.
Girl's Heart. (On cover: Seaside library. Pocket ed. no. 954). 1887. G. Munro.
Girls in Advertising. Natalie West. 1974. (pbk.) 1.25. Ace Books.
Girls in Cosmetics. Florence Brown. 1975. (pbk.) 1.50. Ace Books.
Girls in Fashion. Natalie West. 1974. (pbk.) 1.25. Ace Books.
Girls in Publishing. Natalie West. 1974. (pbk.) 1.25. Ace Books.
Girls in Television. Michael Avallone. 1974. (pbk.) 1.25. Ace Books.
Girls in the Band. Isabel Bluefield. (O.s.i.). (Orig.). 1971. pap. 0.75 o.s.i. (B75-2148). Belmont-Tower.
Girls in the Newsroom. Marjorie Margolies. 1983. pap. 3.50 (ISBN 0-441-28929-0, Pub. by Charter Bks). Ace Bks.
Girls in Their Married Bliss. Edna O'Brien. LC 65-10455. 1968. bds., 4.95. S.&S.
Girls in 5J. Rita Samson Bernhard. LC 77-24205. 6.95 (ISBN 0-8037-2915-4). Dial Press.
Girls in 5J. Rita Samson Bernhard. 1978. 1.95 (ISBN 0-671-82112-1). Pocket Books.
Girl's Journey. Enid Bagnold. 1970. pap. 0.95 o.p. (0502-09039). Curtis.
Girl's Journey: The Happy Foreigner and The Squire. Enid Bagnold. LC 54-6789. 1954. Doubleday.
Girls of a Feather: A Novel. Amelia Edith Huddleston Barr. LC 6-7990. (choice series, no. 97). 1893. R. Bonner's Sons.
Girls of Feversham. Florence Marryat Church Lean. LC 7-13596. (On cover: Lovell's library, v. 19, no. 939). 1887. J. W. Lovell Company.
Girls of Gardenville. Carroll Watson Rankin. LC 6-67468. 1906. H. Holt and Company.
Girls of Huntington House. Blossom Elfman. LC 71-188992. 1972. 5.95 (ISBN 0-395-13951-1). Houghton Mifflin.
Girls of Ramrod Ranch. Cara Palmer. (O.s.i.). 1976. pap. 1.50 o.s.i. (BT50938). Belmont-Tower.
Girls of Silver Spur Ranch. Grace MacGowan Cooke & McQueen, Anne. LC 13-17997. 1.00. M. A. Donohue & Co.
Girls of Slender Means. Muriel Spark. LC 63-14614. 1963. Knopf.
Girls of Slender Means. Muriel Spark. LC 82-5236. 1982. 5.95 (ISBN 0-399-50659-4). Perigee Books.
Girls of '64. Emilie Benson Knipe & Knipe, Alden Arthur. LC 18-204759. 1918. The Macmillan Company.
Girls on the Jet Planes. Sheri Perrin. (O.s.i.). 224p. 1974. pap. 1.25 o.s.i. (AQ1150, Award). Univ Pub & Dist.
Girls on the Million-Dollar Mattress. William R Bentley. 1974. (pbk.) 2.25 (ISBN 0-87056-410-2). Brandon Books.
Girls on the Tenth Floor, & Other Stories. facs. ed. Steve Allen. LC 78-128718. (Short Story Index Reprint Ser). 1958. 12.00 (ISBN 0-8369-3608-6). Ayer Co.
Girls on the 10th Floor, and Other Stories. 1st Ed. Steve Allen. LC 58-76359. 1958. Holt.
Girls on the 10th Floor: And Other Stories. Steve Allen. LC 78-128718. (Short story index reprint series). 1970. Books for Libraries Press.
Girl's Ordeal. Lucy Cecil White Lillie. LC 7-19885. 1897. H. T. Coates & Co.
Girls' Rules. Beverley Gasner. LC 68-23957. 1968. 4.95. Knopf.
Girls, the Massage, and Everything. Bernhardt J Hurwood. (Fawcett Gold Medal Book). 1973. (pbk.) 1.25. Fawcett Publications, Inc.
Girls to Burn. James Lumpp. LC 41-23063. Phoenix Press.
Girls Turn Wives. Norma Klein. LC 75-35707. 8.95 (ISBN 0-671-22203-1). Simon and Schuster.
Girls Who Came to Murder. Kirby Carr. (Hitman#3). 1974. (pbk.) 1.50 (ISBN 0-89014-115-0). Canyon Books.
Girlwatcher's Funeral. Hugh Pentecost. 1972. pap. 0.75 o.p. (ISBN 0-515-02866-5, T2866). Pyramid Pubns.
Girondin... Hilaire Belloc. LC 11-12264. 1911. T. Nelson and Sons.
Girton Girl. Annie Edwards. (On cover: Seaside library. Pocket ed. no. 644). 1885. G. Munro.
Girton Girl. Annie Edwards. (On cover: Lovell's library. no. 681). 1885. J. B. Alden.
Girton Girl. A Novel. Annie Edwards. (Harper's Franklin square library. no. 510). 1886. Harper & Brothers.
Girty. Richard Taylor. LC 77-82790. (New World Writing Ser.). (Cloth ed. 10.50 o.p.). (Illus.). 1977. pap. 4.95 o.p. (ISBN 0-913666-18-1). Turtle Isl Foun.
Giselle. Geoffrey Bocca. LC 75-7981. 1975. 8.95 o.p. (ISBN 0-399-11527-7). Putnam.
Giselle. Brian Cooper. 1958. 3.50 o.p. (ISBN 0-8149-0487-4). Vanguard.
Giselle: A Novel. Geoffrey Bocca. LC 75-11745. 1975. 7.95. Putnam.
Gitana. Robert William Chambers. LC 31-103595. 1931. D. Appleton and Company.
Gitaway Box. Hilary H Milton. LC 68-21534. 1968. R. B. Luce.
Giuseppe, and Laughter Wins: Fairy Tales for Working-Men's Children, Containing the Hymn Cosmopolitan. Henry Thomas Schnittkind. LC 14-1909. 0.25. Stratford Publishing Company.
Give a Man a Gun. John Creasey. Orig. Title: Gun for Inspector West. 1972. pap. 0.95 o.p. (75-304). Lancer.
Give a Man a Gun. Leslie Charles Ernenwein. 1975. pap. 0.95 o.p. (LB239NK, Leisure Bks). Nordon Pubns.
Give a Man a Gun. Clay Turner, pseud. (Orig.). 1971. pap. 0.60 o.p. (ISBN 0-446-63508-1, 63-508). Paperback Lib.
Give a Man a Gun. 1st American Ed. John Creasey. 1954. Harper.
Give a Woman a House: An Inspiring Story of a Modern Family and How It Grew in Christian Love and Understanding. 1st Ed. Charles H Sanders. LC 57-14872. 1957. Greenwich Book Publishers.
Give and Take. Aaron Hoffman. LC 26-21777. (On cover: French's standard library edition). S. French.
Give Back Yesterday. Netta Muskett. 1974. pap. 0.75 o.p. (26580-7-075). Beagle Bks.
Give Beauty Back. Francis Xavier Connolly. LC 50-8560. 1950. Dutton.
Give 'em the Ax. Erle Stanley Gardner. 1944. W. Morrow.
Give Happiness a Chance. Phil Bosmans. LC 79-91535. (Illus.). 1980. 6.95. Rand McNally.
Give Him a Stone: A Novel. Gordon Weaver. LC 74-34055. 1975. 6.95 (ISBN 0-517-51897-X). Crown Publishers.
Give Him My Love: A Novel. Margaret Mackprang Mackay. LC 49-9598. 1949. J. Day Co.
Give Him the Earth. Rupert Croft-Cooke. LC 31-199087. 1931. A. A. Knopf.
Give It Back to the Indians. 1st Ed. Harlan Gerber. LC 55-12392. 1955. Pageant Press.
Give It Back to the Lemongrowers! A Novel. Temple, Willard. LC 61-10303. 1961. Crown Publishers.
Give Love the Air. Faith Baldwin. 286p. Repr. of 1947 ed. lib. bdg. 15.45x (ISBN 0-88411-626-3). Amereon Ltd.
Give Love the Air. Faith Baldwin Cuthrell. LC 47-3981. 1947. Rinehart & Company, Incorporated.
Give Love the Air: By Faith Baldwin. Faith Baldwin Cuthrell. 1973. 0.75. Warner Paperback Lib.
Give Me a Chance! A Novel. William Wilfrid Whalen. LC 29-14373. 1929. B. Herder Book Co.
Give Me Back My Heart. Denise Robins. 1.25 (ISBN 0-380-00796-7). Avon.
Give Me Back My Soul. Bebe Patten. 1973. pap. 1.25 o.p. (ISBN 0-8007-0645-5). Revell.
Give Me Back My Soul. Bebe. D. D Patten. 1973. (pbk.) 1.25 (ISBN 0-515-03255-7). Family Library.
Give Me Back Myself. Leslie Purnell Davies. LC 70-165385. 1971. 5.95. Doubleday.
Give Me Death. Isabel Briggs Myers. LC 34-34013. 1934. Frederick A. Stokes Company.
Give Me Liberty. Edward Bodin. LC 46-19868. 1946. Rockport Press, Inc.
Give Me Liberty: A Novel of Patrick Henry. Noel Bertram Gerson. LC 66-11732. 4.95. Doubleday.
Give Me Liberty: The Story of an Innocent Bystander. John Erskine. LC 40-34424. 1940. Frederick A. Stokes Company.
Give Me My Sin Again: A Novel. Naomi Gwladys Royde-Smith. LC 29-20111. 1929. Harper & Brothers.
Give Me Myself. 1st Ed. Sherman, Susan. LC 61-6647. 1961. World Pub. Co.
Give Me New Wings. Nina Bowyer. LC 45-6724. 1945. Arcadia House, Inc.
Give Me New Wings. Nina Conarain. LC 45-6724. 1945. Areadia House, Inc.
Give Me One Good Reason. Norma Klein. LC 73-82020. 1973. 6.95 (ISBN 0-399-11234-0). Putnam.
Give Me One Good Reason. Norma Klein. 1974. (pbk.) 1.50 (ISBN 0-380-00166-7). Avon.
Give Me One Summer. Emilie Baker Loring. LC 36-130470. The Penn Publishing Company.
Give Me Possession. Paul Horgan. LC 57-11225. 1957. Farrar, Straus and Cudahy.
Give Me Shelter. George E. Norris. 47p. 1973. 3.50 o.p. (ISBN 0-682-47849-0). Exposition.
Give Me the Daggers. Catherine Irvine Gavin. (Kangaroo Book). 1977. 1.95 (ISBN 0-671-81243-2). Pocket Books.
Give Me the Daggers. Catherine Irvine Gavin. LC 79-188182. (Illus.). 1972. 6.95. W. Morrow.
Give Me the Stars. Gladys Bagg Taber. LC 45-66776. 1945. Macrae-Smith-Company.
Give Me the Wind. Jan Jordan. LC 72-12587. 1973. 6.95 (ISBN 0-13-356824-5). Prentice-Hall.
Give Me Thine Heart. A Novel... Azel Stevens Rae. LC 7-39820. 1880. G. W. Carleton & Co.; Etc., Etc.
Give Me This Day. Maynah Lewis. 1974. pap. 0.75 o.p. (26569-075). Beagle Bks.
Give Me Thy Vineyard. Guy Howard. (Orig.). (YA) 1968. pap. 1.50 o.p. (ISBN 0-310-26272-0). Zondervan.
Give Me Thy Vineyard: A Novel of the Ozarks. Guy Howard. LC 49-10935. 1949. Zondervan Pub. House.
Give Me Tomorrow. William Farquhar Payson. LC 35-18077. 1935. Dodd, Mead & Company.
Give Me Tomorrow. J. A. Salvatore. 3.50 o.p. Carlton.
Give Me Your Golden Hand. Evelyn Sybil Mary Eaton. LC 51-9671. 1951. Farrar, Straus and Young.
Give Me Your Good Ear. Maureen Brady. LC 78-66097. 4.50 (ISBN 0-933216-00-9). Spinsters, Ink.
Give Me Your Love. Annette Eyre. (Signet book). 1975. (pbk.) 1.25. New American Library.
Give Me Your Love. Jerome Weidman. LC 53-164004. (Eton pocket-size books, E114). 1952. Eton Books.
Give My Love to Maria, and Other Stories. Florence Guertin Tuttle. LC 17-12390. The Abingdon Press.
Give Thanks to Death. Ruth Lenore Marting. LC 40-7859. 1940. Pub. for the Crime Club by Doubleday, Doran & Co., Inc.
Give the Boys a Great Big Hand: An Inner Sanctum 87th Precinct Mystery, by Ed McBain Pseud. Evan Hunter. LC 60-610331. 1960. Simon and Schuster.
Give the Boys a Great Big Hand: An 87th Precinct Mystery, by Ed McBain. Evan Hunter. (Signet book). 1975. (pbk.) 1.25. New American Library.
Give the Heart Rein. Sydney K. Russell. 1955. 2.75 o.p. Twayne.
Give the Little Corpse a Great Big Hand: By George Bagby Pseud. 1st Ed. Aaron Marc Stein. LC 53-6099. 1953. Published for the Crime Club by Doubleday.
Give Them a Tomorrow. Michael J. Carroll. 4.50 o.p. Vantage.
Give Them Their Dream. Norma Patterson. LC 38-33945. Farrar & Rinehart, Incorporated.
Give up the Body. Louis Trimble. LC 47-178. 1946. Superior Publishing Company.
Give up the Ghost. Margaret Erskine, pseud. 1977. 5.50 o.p. State Mutual Bk.
Give up the Ghost. Margaret Erskine. (Ace Gothic). 1974. (pbk.) 0.95. Ace Books.
Give up the Ghost. Wetherby Williams. LC 49-7270. 1949. Pub. for the Crime Club by Doubleday.
Give up Your Lovers. Louis Golding. LC 30-8171. 1930. Cosmopolitan Book Corporation.
Give Us Heroes. David Cort. LC 32-313045. Liveright, Inc.
Give Us Our Dream. Arthemise Goertz. LC 47-303364. 1947. Whittlesey House, McGraw-Hill Book Company, Inc.
Give Us Our Years. 1st Ed. Margaret Culkin Banning. LC 50-6622. 1950. Harper.
Give Us This Day. Ronald Frederick Delderfield. LC 73-10050. 1973. 9.95 (ISBN 0-671-21658-9). Simon and Schuster.
Give Us This Day. Gladys Bagg Taber. LC 44-4740. 1944. Macrae-Smith-Company.
Give Us This Day. Louis Zara. LC 36-10238. 1936. The Bobbs-Merrill Company.
Give Us This Day. 1st Ed. Richard Virgil Grace. LC 52-10761. 1952. Longmans, Green.
Give Us This Night. Ruth Lyons. LC 35-8669. The Macaulay Company.
Give Us This Night. Thelma Thompson. LC 39-320447. 1939. Arcadia House, Inc.
Give Us This Night. Thelma Thompson. LC 45-122167. 1945. Arcadia House, Inc.
Give Us This Valley. Tom Ham. LC 52-4193. 1952. Macmillan.
Give Warning to the World. John Brunner. 1974. (pbk.) 0.95. DAW Books.
Giveadamn Brown. Robert Deane Pharr. LC 73-79702. 1978. 7.95 (ISBN 0-385-05213-8). Doubleday.
Giveaway: A Novel. Stephen Gould Fisher. LC 54-7798. 1954. Random House.
Given His Way. David Harrop. 1973. 0.95. Curtis Books.
Given the Ammunition. Harriett Gilbert. LC 76-5535. 8.95 (ISBN 0-06-011514-9). Harper & Row.
Givers. Mary Eleanor Wilkins Freeman. LC 69-11896. (American short story series, v. 54). (Illus.). 1969. Garrett Press.
Givers. Mary Eleanor Wilkins Freeman. LC 72-8142. (American Short Story Series, V. 54). 1972. (ISBN 0-8422-8051-0). MSS Information Corp.
Givers and Takers. Megan Hughes & Orbach, Frank. (Leisure book). 1.95 (ISBN 0-8439-0623-5). Norden Pubns.
Givers: Short Stories. Mary Eleanor Wilkins Freeman. LC 4-14892. 1904. Harper & Brothers.
Giving & Receiving. facs. ed. Edward Verrall Lucas. LC 73-142657. (Essay Index Reprint Ser). 1922. 15.00 (ISBN 0-8369-2058-9). Ayer Co.
Giving Birth to Thunder, Sleeping with His Daughter. Barry Holstun Lopez. 208p. 1981. pap. 2.95 (ISBN 0-380-54551-9, 54551, Bard). Avon.
Giving the Bride Away. Neville, Margot. LC 30-7563. 1930. R. M. McBride & Company.
Glad & Sorry Seasons. Carol Evan. 1971. pap. 0.95 o.p. (ISBN 0-446-65606-2, 65-606). Paperback Lib.
Glad and Sorry Seasons. Cynthia Adele Kreke. LC 78-1409. 1978. 3.95 (ISBN 0-89293-073-X). Beta Book Co.
Glad and Sorry Seasons: A Novel. Carol Evan. LC 70-96019. 1970. 5.95. Harper's Magazine Press.
Glad Hand. Snoo Wilson. 72p. (Orig.). 1981. pap. 4.95 (ISBN 0-86104-212-3). Pluto Pr.
Glad Ray. Clara Palmer Goetzinger. Fisher Publishing Company.
Glad River. Will D Campbell. LC 81-6969. 13.95. Holt, Rinehart and Winston.
Glad Tidings. Lillian Stephenson De Waters. LC 9-32679. Mrs. Lillian De Waters.
Glad Tidings. Joyce Warren. LC 60-10448. 1960. Harper.
Glad to Be Here. Arthur Herzog. LC 79-7099. 1979. 12.45i (ISBN 0-690-01818-5). T Y Crowell.
Glade with Life-Giving Water. J. Aputis. 431p. 1981. 12.00 (ISBN 0-8285-2025-9, Pub. by Progress Pubs USSR). Imported Pubns.
Gladiator. William Earls. (Orig.). 1981. pap. 2.25 (ISBN 0-440-12995-8). Dell.
Gladiator. Thames Ross Williamson. LC 48-9050. 1948. Coward-McCann.
Gladiator. Philip Wylie. LC 73-13270. (Classics of science fiction.). 1974. 9.95 (ISBN 0-88355-124-1) (ISBN 0-88355-124-1). Hyperion Press.
Gladiator. Philip Wylie. LC 30-6546. 1930. A. A. Knopf.
Gladiator... Hill of the Dead. Andrew Quiller. 1975. (pbk.) 1.25 (ISBN 0-523-00765-5). Pinnacle Books.

Gladiator-at-Law: By Frederik Pohl and C. M. Kornbluth. Frederik Pohl & Cyril M. Kornbluth. LC 55-9559. 1955. Ballantine Books.
Gladiators. Arthur Koestler. Tr. by Simon, Edith. LC 39-16854. 1939. The Macmillan Company.
Gladiators: a Tale of Rome and Judea. new ed. George John Whyte-Melville. LC 7-18506. 1892. Longmans, Green, and Co.
Gladiators, a Tale of Rome and Judea. By G. J. Whyte Melville... George John Whyte-Melville. LC 7-18505. 1890. Longmans, Green, and Co.
Gladiators. Tr. by Edith Simon. New Postscript by the Author. Danube Ed. Arthur Koestler. LC 67-15780. 1967. 5.95. Macmillan.
Gladiola Murphy. Ruth Sawyer. LC 23-4292. 1923. Harper & Brothers.
Gladness in My Heart. Grace F Watkins. LC 68-10524. 1968. Zondervan Pub. House.
Gladys: A Romance. Mary Greenleaf Darling. LC 6-33067. (On cover: The round world series). D. Lothrop Company.
Gladys Fane. A Story of Two Lives. Wemyss Reid. (Harper's Franklin square library. no. 565). 1887. Harper & Brothers.
Gladys Greye. Bertha M. Clay. LC 44-116637. (Select series... no. 87). Street & Smith.
Gladys Lindsay. S. K Reeves. LC 99-4300. The Union Press.
Glamor" A Novel. Anna M Lucas. LC 38-178216. 1937. Buechler Publishing Co.
Glamor Girl. Sylvia Parker. LC 39-12731. Gramercy Publishing Company.
Glamour. William Babington Maxwell. LC 20-3060. The Bobbs-Merrill Company.
Glamour;" A Romance. Meta Orred. 1897. J. B. Lippincott Company.
Glamour Girl. Ann Gilmer, pseud. 1971. pap. 0.60 o.p. (60-469). Manor Bks.
Glamour Girl. Doris Lilly & Robin Moore. 1977. pap. 1.95 (ISBN 0-532-19135-8). Woodhill.
Glamour Incorporated. Peggy O'More, pseud. LC 45-7762.
Glamour Nurse. Adelaide Humphries. LC 50-8000. 1950. Arcadia House.
Glamourie: A Romance of Paris. William Samuel Johnson. LC 11-5188. 1911. 1.20. Harper & Brothers.
Glance Away. John Edgar Wideman. LC 67-19193. 1967. Harcourt, Brace & World.
Gland Stealers. Bertram Gayton. LC 22-17450. 1922. J.B. Lippincott Company.
Gland Time. Don J Townshend. LC 74-21093. 7.95. St. Martin's Press.
Glanmore: A Romance of the Revolution. Park Clinton. LC 6-21381. 1853. Stearns and Company.
Glass. Howard Stephenson. LC 34-217. C. Kendall.
Glass Alibi: A Case for Superintendent Slade. Leonard Reginald Gribble. LC 56-9517. Roy Publishers.
Glass & Gold: A Novel. James Oscar Greeley Duffy. LC 1-24499. 1901. J. B. Lippincott Company.
Glass and the Trumpet. Elizabeth Seifert. LC 73-79152. 1973. 6.95. Aeonian Press.
Glass and the Trumpet. Elizabeth Seifert. LC 48-1039. 1948. Dodd, Mead.
Glass Arcade. Adrian Brooks. 1980. pap. 2.75 (ISBN 0-671-82916-5). PB.
Glass Barracks: 1st Ed. Clarissa Fairchild Cushman. LC 50-6808. 1950. Little, Brown.
Glass Barrier. Joy Packer. 1961. 4.95 o.p. Lippincott.
Glass Barrier: A Novel. Joy Petersen Packer. LC 61-12254. 1961. Lippincott.
Glass Bead Game (Magister Ludi). Hermann Hesse. LC 78-80343. 1969. 7.95. Holt, Rinehart and Winston.
Glass Bed: A Novel. Norman Panama & Albert E. Lewin. LC 80-12804. 1980. 8.95 (ISBN 0-688-03676-7). Morrow.
Glass Bees. Translated from the German by Louise Bogan and Elizabeth Mayer. Ernst Junger. LC 60-100051. 1961. Noonday Press.
Glass-Blowers. Daphne Du Maurier. LC 63-8769. 1963. Doubleday.
Glass Cage. Edward Sidney Aarons. 1973. pap. 0.95 o.p. (ISBN 0-532-95264-2). Woodhill.
Glass Cage. Edward Sidney Aarons. 1973. pap. 0.95 o.p. (ISBN 0-532-95264-2). Manor Bks.
Glass Cage. Edward Sidney Aarons. 1973. (pbk.) 0.95. Manor Books.
Glass Cage. Kenneth W. Hassler. Ed. by Alice Sachs. 1969. lib. bdg. 3.50 o.p. Arcadia.
Glass Cage. Georges Simenon. LC 72-91840. 1973. 5.50 (ISBN 0-15-135800-1). Harcourt Brace Jovanovich.
Glass Cage: An Unconventional Detective Story. Colin Wilson. LC 67-12766. 1967. Random House.
Glass Canoe. David Ireland. LC 76-380681. 1976. (ISBN 0-333-21051-4). Macmillan.
Glass Castle. Violet Winspear. (Presents Ser.). 1974. pap. 1.25 (ISBN 0-373-70550-6, 70550, Pub by Harlequin). PB.
Glass Cell. Patricia Highsmith. (O.s.i.). 1968. pap. 0.75 o.s.i. (532-75199-075). Manor Bks.
Glass Cipher. Peter Winston. (Adjusters Ser, No. 4). (O.s.i.). (Orig.). 1968. pap. 0.60 o.s.i. (A359X, Award). Univ Pub & Dist.
Glass Crutch: The Biographical Novel of William Wynne Wister. James Alonzo Bishop. LC 45-114188. 1945. Doubleday, Doran & Co., Inc.
Glass Dove. 1st Ed. Sally Carrighar. LC 61-125012. 1962. Doubleday.
Glass Eyes by the Bottle. John Gould. 282p. 1979. pap. 3.95 (ISBN 0-89272-054-9, 198). Down East.
Glass Eyes by the Bottle: Some Conversations About Some Conversation Pieces. John Gould. LC 74-31108. 1975. 6.95 (ISBN 0-316-32181-8). Little, Brown.
Glass Flame. Phyllis A. Whitney. LC 78-1018. 1978. 8.95 (ISBN 0-385-14384-2). Doubleday.
Glass Flame. Phyllis A. Whitney. LC 78-27128. 1979. 14.95 (ISBN 0-8161-6653-6). G. K. Hall.
Glass Flowers. Donald Parson. 2.50 o.p. (ISBN 0-8283-1568-X). Branden.
Glass Heart... Marty Holland. LC 47-758. 1946. J. Messner, Inc.
Glass Heiress. Dwyer-Joyce, Alice. LC 81-14584. 1982. 9.95 (ISBN 0-312-32822-2). St. Martin's Press.
Glass Heiress. Dwyer-Joyce, Alice. LC 81-52364. 1981. 10.95 (ISBN 0-312-32822-2). St. Martin's Press.
Glass Highway. Loren D Estleman. LC 83-8387. (Amos Walker Mystery). 1983. 13.00 (ISBN 0-395-34636-3). Houghton Mifflin.
Glass House. Horace Marcus Coffey. LC 47-16342. 1946. The Business Bourse.
Glass House. Alice Lent Covert. LC 50-9229. 1950. Bouregy & Curl.
Glass House. Florence Morse Kingsley. 1909. Dodd, Mead and Company.
Glass House: A Novel. Horace Marcus Coffey. LC 47-16342. 1946. Business Bourse.
Glass House, a Novella and Stories. Laura Furman. LC 79-56282. 1980. 10.95 (ISBN 0-670-34179-7). Viking Press.
Glass House of Waldman. M. E. Cohane. 5.95 o.p. Vantage.
Glass Houses. Eleanor M. Patterson Gizycka. LC 26-8015. 1926. Minton, Balch & Company.
Glass Inferno. Thomas N. Scortia & Frank M. Robinson. LC 73-18909. 1974. 7.95 (ISBN 0-385-05147-6). Doubleday.
Glass Key. Dashiell Hammett. LC 66-7717. (B 66-12155). 1966. Penguin.
Glass Key. Dashiell Hammett. LC 31-10935. 1931. A. A. Knopf.
Glass Key. Dashiell Hammett. LC 81-17498. 1982. 13.95 (ISBN 0-89340-331-8). J. Curley.
Glass Knife. Lee Thayer. LC 32-107519. Sears Publishing Company, Inc.
Glass Knight: A Novel. David Helwig. LC 76-367714. (ISBN 0-88750-184-2) (ISBN 0-88750-185-0). Oberon Press.
Glass Ladder: A New Mystery Novel. Paul W Fairman. LC 50-31779. (Handi-book mystery, 110). 1950. Quinn Pub. Co.
Glass Man. Kenneth Robeson. (Avenger,#34). 1975. (pbk.) 0.95. Warner Paperback Library.
Glass Mask. Lenore Glen Offord. LC 44-51279. 1944. Duell, Sloan and Pearce.
Glass Mountain. Joseph Warren Beach. LC 30-28179. Macrae Smith Company.
Glass Mountain. Kenneth Robeson. (Avenger, #8). 1973. Warner Paperback Lib.
Glass Mountain: A Novel. Mary Frances Doner. LC 42-21648. 1942. Doubleday, Doran and Company, Inc.
Glass of Blessings. Barbara Pym. LC 79-56384. 1980. 10.95 (ISBN 0-525-11400-9). Dutton.
Glass of Dyskornis. Randall Garrett & Vicki A. Heydron. 144p. 1982. 2.50 (ISBN 0-553-20827-6). Bantam.
Glass of Stars. Robert F Young. LC 67-30930. 1968. Harris-Wolfe.
Glass on the Stairs. Margaret Scherf. LC 54-681863. 1954. Published for the Crime Club by Doubleday.
Glass Over Flower. Jean Temple. LC 29-15868. J. Cape and H. Smith.
Glass Palace. Mary Ann Gibbs, pseud. LC 75-43796. 1975. 6.95 (ISBN 0-88405-145-5). Mason/Charter.
Glass Palace. Mary Ann Gibbs. 1976. 1.50 (ISBN 0-449-23063-5). Fawcett Crest.
Glass Palace. Ethel Lewine. LC 68-29292. 1968. 5.95. Bobbs.
Glass People. Gail Godwin. LC 72-2238. 1972. 5.95 (ISBN 0-394-47288-8). Knopf.
Glass Playpen: The Story of a New York Call Girl. Edwin Fadiman. LC 56-10888. (Signet books, 1316). 1956. New American Library.
Glass Room... Edwin Rolfe & Fuller, Lester, 1908- Joint Author. LC 46-8243. 1946. Rinehart & Company, Inc.
Glass Room. Mary Towne, pseud. (gr. 5-7). 1972. pap. 0.75 o.p. (ISBN 0-671-29544-6). Archway.
Glass Rooster. 1st Ed. William McIlwain. LC 60-137415. 1960. Doubleday.
Glass Rose. Richard Bankowsky. LC 58-525900. 1958. Random House.
Glass-Sided Ants' Nest. Peter Dickinson. 1968. Harper & Row.
Glass-Sided Ants' Nest. Peter Dickinson. LC 80-28352. 1981. 2.95 (ISBN 0-14-005864-8). Penguin Books.
Glass Slipper. Mignon Good Eberhart. LC 38-27956. 1938. Doubleday, Doran & Co., Inc.
Glass Slipper. Mignon Good Eberhart. LC 40-34763. 1939. The Sun Dial Press, Inc.
Glass Slipper: By Allen Eppes Pseud. Watkins Eppes Wright. LC 48-10088. 1948. Gramercy Pub. Co.
Glass Spear. Sidney Hobson Courtier. LC 50-6306. 1950. Wyn.
Glass Teat. Harlan Ellison. 1983. pap. 2.95 (ISBN 0-441-28988-6, Pub. by Ace Science Fiction). Ace Bks.
Glass Totem. 1st Ed. David Chandler. LC 62-15461. 1962. Appleton-Century-Crofts.
Glass Tree. Keith Laumer. 1970. 4.50 o.p. Putnam.
Glass Triangle. George Harmon Coxe. LC 40-114900. 1940. A. A. Knopf.
Glass Village: A Novel. Ellery Queen, pseud. LC 54-8296. 1954. Little, Brown.
Glass Virgin. Catherine Cookson. LC 70-81283. 1969. 6.95. Bobbs-Merrill.
Glass Walls. Alden Hatch. LC 33-296383. 1933. Dial Press, Inc.
Glass Window: A Story of the Quare Women. Lucy Furman. LC 25-202569. 1925. Little, Brown, and Company.
Glass Zoo: A Novel. James McNeish. LC 75-29927. 1976. 10.95. St. Martin's Press.
Glassblower's Children. Maria Gripe. (Yearling book). (Illus.). 1974. (pbk.) 0.95. Dell.
Glasshouse. Allan Campbell McLean. LC 68-12583. 1968. Harcourt, Brace & World.
Glasshouse Gang. Gordon Landsborough. 1977. pap. 1.50 (ISBN 0-532-15255-7). Woodhill.
Glassy Pond. Frank Wright Moxley. LC 34-12181. Coward, McCann, Inc.
Glassy Sea. Marian Engel. LC 78-21405. 8.95 (ISBN 0-312-32832-X). St. Martin's Press.
Glastonbury Romance. John Cowper Powys. LC 56-18641. 1966. 6.95. Macdonald: Imprint Covered by Label: Colgate Univ. Pr., Hamilton, N. Y.
Glastonbury Romance. John Cowper Powys. LC 32-831087. 1932. Simon and Schuster.
Glaucia. A Story of Athens in the First Century. Emma Leslie. LC 7-14503. (Church history stories, v.1). Nelson & Phillips.
Glaucia. A Story of Athens in the First Century. Emma Leslie. LC 3-200643. (Church history stories. v. 1). 1891. Hunt & Eaton.
Glayds Greye. Charlotte Mary Brame. (Street & Smith's select series, no. 87). Street & Smith.
Gleam in the North: A Sequel to The Flight of the Heron. Dorothy Kathleen Broster. 1931. Coward-McCann, Inc.
Gleam O'dawn: A Novel. Arthur Frederick Goodrich. LC 8-17835. 1908. D. Appleton and Company.
Gleam of Bayonets. James Murfin. 3.98 o.p. (ISBN 0-498-06252-X, Encore). A S Barnes.
Gleam of Hate. Thomas Woodard. 4.00 o.p. (ISBN 0-8062-0531-8). Carlton.
Gleams of Scarlet: A Tale of the Canadian Rockies. Gertrude Amelia Proctor. LC 15-18829. 1915. 1.35. Sherman, French & Company.
Gleaners: A Novelette. Clara Elizabeth Laughlin. LC 12-687. 0.75. Fleming H. Revell Company.
Gleanings. Ora Pate Stewart. 2.95 o.p. (ISBN 0-87747-098-7). Deseret Bk.
Gleanings from Emmanuel's Land. Jerry Miles Humphrey. LC 11-32389. 1911. True Gospel Grain Pub. Co.
Gleanings from Real Life. M. M Gay. LC 6-44265. 1858. C. E. Felton, Printer.
Gleave Mystery. Louis Tracy. LC 26-11208. E. J. Clode, Inc.
Glen Ellyn: Paint Maker. Gordon Montagu. LC 10-17989. 1.50. Press of Little & Becker Printing Co.
Glen Elm: Or, Life in the West. A Novel. M. S. Robinson. 1873. H. N. McKinney & Co.
Glen Gablin and the Good Ethan. Asa Wilgus. LC 48-17884. 1948.
Glen Hazard. Maristan Chapman. LC 33-5478. 1933. A. A. Knopf.
Glen Mary. A Catholic Novel. Junius McGehee. LC 7-20006. 1887. J. Murphy & Co.
Glen of the Echoes: Or, Dan Mahony and Dora Sullivan. A Tale of Ireland. Harriet Martineau. (On cover: Lovell's library, v. 8, no. 400). 1884. J. W. Lovell Company.
Glen of the High North. Hiram Alfred Cody. LC 20-18933. 1.90. George H. Doran Company.
Glen O'weeping. Marjorie Bowen. 1971. pap. 1.25 o.p. (96164). Beagle Bks.
Glenanaar: A Story of Irish Life. Patrick Augustine Sheehan. LC 5-17592. 1905. Longmans, Green, and Co.
Glenarvon. 3d ed. Caroline Ponsonby Lamb. LC 70-37709. 1975. 50.00 (ISBN 0-404-56767-3). AMS Press.
Glenarvon (1816). Caroline Ponsonby Lamb. LC 71-161933. 1972. 20.00 (ISBN 0-8201-1093-0). Scholars' Facsimiles & Reprints.
Glencannon Afloat: Or, Golden Rule and Brass Knuckles on the S. S. Inchcliffe Castle. Guy Gilpatric. LC 41-4715. 1941. Dodd, Mead & Company.
Glencannon-Great Stories from the Saturday Evening Post. Guy Gilpatric. LC 77-23723. 320p. 1977. 5.95 (ISBN 0-89387-017-X, Co-Pub by Sat Eve Post). Curtis Pub Co.
Glencannon Omnibus: Including Scotch and Water, Half-Seas Over, Three Sheets in the Wind. Guy Gilpatric. 1938. Dodd, Mead & Company.
Glencoe Parsonage. Lydia Ann Emerson Porter. LC 7-37756. 1870. D. Lothrop & Co.
Glendora Route. Russell C. Collins. 3.95 o.p. Carlton.
Glendover. A Novel. Frederic B. Yates. LC 9-1458. The Authors' Publishing Company.
Glendower Country: A Novel. Martha Rofheart. LC 72-87625. 1973. 8.95 (ISBN 0-399-11075-5). Putnam.
Glendower Legacy. Thomas Gifford. 1979. pap. 2.50 (ISBN 0-671-82678-6). PB.
Glendower Legacy. Thomas Gifford. LC 78-9818. 1978. 10.00 o.p. (ISBN 0-399-12183-8). Putnam Pub Group.
Glendraco. Laura Black. LC 77-5017. 8.95 (ISBN 0-312-32917-2). St. Martin's Press.
Glendraco. Laura Black. LC 82-9203. 1982. 18.95 (ISBN 0-8161-3398-0). G.K. Hall.
Glendraco: A Novel of Scandal and Passion in 19th Century Scotland. Laura Black. 1978. 2.50 (ISBN 0-446-81528-4). Warner Books.
Glengarry School Days: A Story of Early Days in Glengarry. Charles William Gordon. LC 2-28287. 1902. F. H. Revell Company.
Glenlitten Murder. Edward Phillips Oppenheim. LC 29-16824. 1929. Little, Brown, and Company.
Glenmere. LC 6-43958. (On cover: Satchel ser. no. 15). 1879. The Author's Publishing Company.
Glenmornan. Patrick MacGill. LC 18-20937. George H. Doran Company.
Glennair: Or, Life in Scotland. Helen Hazlett. LC 7-3666. 1869. Claxton, Remsen & Haffelfinger.
Glenport, Illinois. Paul Darcy Boles. LC 55-13932. 1956. Macmillan.
Glenrannoch. Rona Randall. 224p. 1981. pap. 2.50 (ISBN 0-380-78311-8, 78311). Avon.
Glenrose Calling: A Novel. Amanda Wells West. LC 78-59477. 1978. 10.00 (ISBN 0-385-12642-5). Doubleday.
Glenwood. Anna Katharine Whiting. 1907. The C. M. Clark Publishing Co.
Glenwood of Shipbay. John Henry Walsh. LC 21-17194. 1921. The Macmillan Company.
Gli Duoi Fratelli Rivali: The Two Rival Brothers. Giambattista Della Porta. Tr. by Louise G. Clubb from Italian. LC 78-64458. 350p. 1980. 27.50x (ISBN 0-520-03786-3). U of Cal Pr.
Glibson. George Tichenor. LC 33-24085. Farrar & Rinehart, Incorporated.
Glide Path. Arthur Charles Clarke. LC 63-17768. 1963. Harcourt, Brace & World.
Glide Path. Arthur Charles Clarke. (Signet, Q5582). 1973. (pbk.) 0.95. New American Lib.
Glided Witch. Webb, Jack. LC 64-108. Regency Books.
Glider Gladiators (of World War II) A Historical Novel. Albert F. Perna. LC 70-91840. (Illus.). 1970. 6.95 (ISBN 0-9600302-0-4). Printed by Pine Hill Press.
Glimpse. Arnold Bennett. LC 74-5399. (Collected Works of Arnold Bennett: Vol. 23). 1976. Repr. of 1909 ed. 26.00 (ISBN 0-518-19040-4). Ayer Co.
Glimpse: An Adventure of the Soul. Arnold Bennett. LC 9-27998. 1909. D. Appleton and Company.
Glimpse into Terror. Clarissa Ross, pseud. 1971. pap. 0.75 o.p. (ISBN 0-447-74735-5). Lancer.
Glimpse of a Stranger. Joe David Brown. LC 68-14809. 1968. W. Morrow.
Glimpse of Canaan: By Robert P. Hansen. Robert P Hansen. LC 66-23352. 1966. bds., 4.95. Morrow.
Glimpse of Eden. Evelyn Ames. LC 67-11908. 1977. 12.95 (ISBN 0-910220-80-8). Berg.
Glimpse of Evil. T. Irving-James. 1981. 18.95x (Pub. by Remploy England). State Mutual Bk.
Glimpse of Glory: George Mason of Gunston Hall. Drawings by Elmo Jones. Marian Buckley Cox. LC 54-115368. 1954. Garrett & Massie.
Glimpse of Love: Or, The Doctor's Wooing. Flora Alice Lindsay. LC 10-11359. Lindsay Publishing Company.
Glimpse of Nothingness: Experiences in an American Zen Community. Janwillem Van de Wetering. 224p. 1981. pap. 2.50 (ISBN 0-671-41609-X). WSP.
Glimpse of Paradise. Arlene Hale. LC 74-19330. 1975. 6.95 (ISBN 0-316-33857-5). Little, Brown.

Glimpse of Paradise. Arlene Hale. LC 75-17974. 1975. 12.95 (ISBN 0-8161-6304-9). G. K. Hall.
Glimpse of Tiger. Herman Raucher. LC 72-158364. (Fawcett crest book). 1975. (pbk.) 1.50. Fawcett.
Glimpses. Cyril Guy. 3.95 o.p. Vantage.
Glimpses. Eric Partridge. LC 70-150194. 1971. (ISBN 0-8369-5707-5). Books for Libraries Press.
Glimpses from My Window. 1850. Massachusetts Sabbath School Society.
Glimpses of a Strange World. Henry Sande Stollnitz. 1908. Printed for the Author The University Press.
Glimpses of Pleasant Homes. A Few Tales for Youth. Mary Teresa Austin Carroll. 1869. The Catholic Publication Society.
Glimpses of the Moon. Edmund Crispin, pseud. 1979. pap. 2.50 (ISBN 0-380-45062-3, 58693-2). Avon.
Glimpses of the Moon. Edmund Crispin, pseud. 1978. 8.95 (ISBN 0-8027-5391-4). Walker & Co.
Glimpses of the Moon. Edith Newbold Jones Wharton. LC 22-14722. 1922. D. Appleton and Company.
Glimpses of the Moon: A Novel. Robert Bruce Montgomery. LC 78-51964. 1978. 8.95 (ISBN 0-8027-5391-4). Walker.
Glimpses of Truth. J. Biegeleisen. 1954. pap. 1.40 o.s.i. Eden.
Glinda of Oz. Lyman Frank Baum. 224p. 1981. pap. 2.25 (ISBN 0-345-28236-1, Del Rey). Ballantine.
Glint of Wings: The Story of a Modern Girl Who Wanted Her Liberty--and Got It. Cleveland Moffett & Hall, Virginia, Joint Author. LC 22-18473. The James A. McCann Company.
Glitter. Katharine Brush. LC 26-7902. 1926. Minton, Balch & Company.
Glitter. Katharine Brush. LC 33-28346. 1928. A. L. Burt Company.
Glitter and Ash. Dennis Smith. LC 79-20279. 9.95 (ISBN 0-525-11420-3). E. P. Dutton.
Glitter & the Gold. William D. Dubin. 3.75 o.p. Carlton.
Glitter Dome. Joseph Wambaugh. LC 80-26219. 1981. 12.95 (ISBN 0-688-00207-2). Morrow.
Glitter Dome. Joseph Wambaugh. LC 81-15095. 1982. 14.95 (ISBN 0-89340-376-8). J. Curley.
Glitter-Dust. Dwyer-Joyce, Alice. LC 77-25771. 1978. 7.95 (ISBN 0-312-32954-7). St. Martin's Press.
Glitter Girl. Joycelyn Day. (Second Chance at Love, Contemporary Ser.: No. 5). 192p. (Orig.). 1981. pap. 1.75 (ISBN 0-515-05878-5). Jove Pubns.
Glitter-Gold Mountain. De Forest C Steele. LC 51-8426. 1951. Christopher Pub. House.
Glitter Street. Tim D Sullivan. LC 78-72897. 8.95 (ISBN 0-89256-095-9). Rawson, Wade Publishers.
Glitterati. Charlotte Payne. LC 79-28638. 1980. 10.95 (ISBN 0-688-03632-5). Morrow.
Glitterburn. Heywood Gould. LC 76-62769. 1977. 7.95 (ISBN 0-312-32952-0). St. Martin's Press.
Glitterburn. Heywood Gould. LC 81-8752. 1981. 12.95 (ISBN 0-312-32952-0). St. Martin's Press.
Glittering Death. Joseph Peyre. Tr. by Whitall, James. LC 37-8147. Random House.
Glittering Girl: A Novel. May Christie. LC 34-991216. Grosset & Dunlap.
Glittering Hill. Clyde F Murphy. LC 44-7914. 1944. E. P. Dutton & Co., Inc.
Glittering Illusion. Ann Sumner. LC 32-20043. A. L. Burt Company.
Glittering Isle. Wilson Collison. LC 36-107572. Covici, Friede.
Glittering Lights. Barbara Cartland. (Barbara Cartland library no. 12). 1974. (pbk.) 1.25. Bantam Books.
Glittering Plain. new ed. William Morris. (Forgotten Fantasy Library: Vol. 1). Orig. Title: Story of the Glittering Plain. 192p. 1973. pap. 2.95 o.p. (ISBN 0-87877-100-X, F-100). Newcastle Pub.
Glittering Prizes. Frederic Raphael. LC 77-351582. 1976. 3.75 (ISBN 0-7139-1028-3). A. Lane.
Glittering Prizes. Frederic Raphael. LC 77-76651. 1977. 8.95 (ISBN 0-312-32957-1). St. Martin's Press.
Glittering Sham. Vida Hurst. LC 32-988604. 1932. Grosset & Dunlap.
Glittering Shores: A Novel. Catherine Hubbell. LC 51-11707. 1951. Norton.
Globe Hollow Mystery. Hannah Gartland. LC 23-4140. 1923. Dodd, Mead and Company.
Globes of Llarum. Gene Lancour. LC 78-20080. 1980. 7.95 (ISBN 0-385-14684-1). Doubleday.
Gloomy Egoist. Eleanor M. Sickels. LC 76-76008. 1969. Repr. of 1932 ed. lib. bdg. 24.00x (ISBN 0-374-97429-2). Octagon.
Gloria, 2 vols. in 1. Benito Perez Galdos. Tr. by C. Bell from Span. LC 73-21667. 692p. 1975. Repr. of 1882 ed. 27.50x (ISBN 0-86527-255-7). Fertig.
Gloria. Benito Perez Galdos. Ed. by Alexander H. Krappe & Lawrence M. Levin. (Sp., O.s.i.). text ed. 6.25 o.s.i. (ISBN 0-390-34348-X); pap. text ed. 2.60 o.s.i. (ISBN 0-390-70480-6). Appleton.
Gloria. George Frederic Turner. 1910. Dodd, Mead and Company.
Gloria: A Novel. Perez Galdos, Benito. LC 73-21667. 1974. H. Fertig.
Gloria: A Novel. Benito Perez Galdos. Tr. by Bell, Clara Courtenay (Poynte) LC 7-36350. 1882. W. S. Gottsberger.
Gloria. A Novel. Emma Dorothy Eliza Nevitte Southworth. LC 8-14247. (Ledger library, no. 48). 1891. R. Bonner's Sons.
Gloria, a Summer Rendezvous. Lincoln Hulley. LC 26-2355. E. O. Painter Printing Co.
Gloria and the Bullfighter: By Ethel Hamill Pseud. Jean Francis Webb. LC 54-12963. 1954. Avalon Books.
Gloria Gray: Love Pirate. Pearl Doles Bell. LC 14-620. 1.25. Roberts & Company.
Gloria Mundi. Harold Frederic. LC 42-26801. 1899. International Book and Publishing Company.
Gloria Mundi see Collected Works.
Gloria Mundi: A Novel. Eleanor Clark. LC 79-1874. 8.95 (ISBN 0-394-50536-0). Pantheon Books.
Gloria Victis. John Ames Mitchell. LC 7-81102. 1897. C. Scribner's Sons.
Gloria Victis!" A Romance. Lula Kirschner. Tr. by Maxwell, Mary. LC 1-19389. 1886. W. S. Gottaberger.
Gloria's Ghost. Christine Bennett, pseud. (Contemporary Teens Ser.). 224p. (Orig.). 1981. pap. 2.25 (ISBN 0-89531-140-2, 0146-96). Sharon Pubns.
Glories of Venus: A Novel of Modern Mexico. Susan Smith. LC 31-24068. 1931. Harper & Brothers.
Glorification of Al Toolum. Robert Alan Aurthur. LC 52-13574. 1953. Rinehart.
Glorified. Dorothy Wegman. LC 30-29258. 1930. Brentano's.
Glorinda. A Story. Anna Bowman Blake Dodd. LC 6-33863. 1888. Roberts Brothers.
Glorious Adventures of Tyl Ulenspiegl. Charles Theodore Henri De Coster & Eulenspiegel. LC 43-16193. 1943. Pantheon Books, Inc.
Glorious Apollo. Lily Moresby Adams Beck. LC 25-13520. 1925. Dodd, Mead and Company.
Glorious Betsy: Being the Romantic Story of the Dixie Belle Who Defied Napoleon. Arline De Haas & Young, Rida (Johnson) LC 28-11528. Grosset & Dunlap.
Glorious Dawn. Dorothy Garlock. 256p. (Orig.). 1982. pap. 2.50 (ISBN 0-449-14492-5, GM). Fawcett.
Glorious Flames. Elinor Sutherland Glyn. LC 33-771. The Macaulay Company.
Glorious Folly: A Novel of the Time of St. Paul. 1st Ed. Louis De Wohl. LC 57-10875. 1957. Lippincott.
Glorious Fortune. Walter Besant. (On cover: Seaside library. Pocket ed., no. 140). 1884. G. Munro.
Glorious Gallop. Mary E. Kennard. LC 7-11103. (On cover: Seaside library. Pocket ed. no. 1092). G. Munro.
Glorious Hope. Jane Burr. LC 23-8551. 1921. T. Seltzer.
Glorious Hope: A Novel. Jane Burr. LC 18-222487. 1918. Jane Burr.
Glorious in Another Day. Arthur Feff. LC 47-11055. 1947. J. B. Lippincott Co.
Glorious Life & Actions of St. Whigg see Perfidious P.
Glorious Morning. Julie Ellis. LC 82-72068. 14.95 (ISBN 0-87795-431-3). Arbor House.
Glorious Mornings. Paul Hyde Bonner. LC 67-29229. (Abercrombie & Fitch library). (Illus.). 1967. Arno Press.
Glorious Mornings: Stories of Shooting and Fishing. Paul Hyde Bonner. LC 54-5914. (Illus.). 1954. Scribner.
Glorious Nosebleed. Edward Gorey. (Illus.). 64p. 1982. pap. 5.95 (ISBN 0-312-92252-3). Congdon & Weed.
Glorious Obsession. Abraham Unger. (Belmont Tower Book.). 1978. 1.75 (ISBN 0-505-51253-X). Tower Pubns.
Glorious Ones. Francine Prose. LC 73-91627. 1974. 6.95 (ISBN 0-689-10599-1). Atheneum.
Glorious Passion. Stephanie Blake. 1983. pap. 3.50 (ISBN 0-515-07071-8). Jove Pubns.
Glorious Phantom: A Novel. Frederic Fadner. LC 44-43261. 1937. D. Ryerson, Inc.
Glorious Pool. Thorne Smith. LC 35-259. 1934. Doubleday, Doran & Company, Inc.
Glorious Pool. Thorne Smith. LC 36-900. 1935. Doubleday, Doran & Company, Inc.
Glorious Rascal (Pretty Maids All in a Row) Justin Huntly McCarthy. LC 15-205604. 1915. John Lane Company.
Glorious Thing. Christine Orr. LC 19-18377. 1919. 0.60. Hodder and Stoughton.
Glorious Third. Cynthia Propper Seton. LC 79-19604. 1980. 9.95 (ISBN 0-89340-230-3). J. Curley.
Glorious Third: A Novel. Cynthia Propper Seton. LC 78-14582. 8.95 (ISBN 0-393-08845-6). Norton.
Glorious Three. June Pat Wetherell. LC 51-12316. 1951. Dutton.
Glorious Thunder. Blanche Smith Ferguson. LC 35-2533. The Penn Publishing Company.
Glorious Triumph. Louise Harrison McCraw. LC 38-196183. Zondervan Publishing House.
Glory. Ronald S. Joseph. 528p. (Orig.). 1980. pap. 3.50 (ISBN 0-446-36175-5). Warner Bks.
Glory. Vladimir Vladimirovich Nabokov. (McGraw-Hill Paperback Ser.). 228p. 1980. pap. 4.95 (ISBN 0-07-045727-1). McGraw.
Glory. David Nemeroff. 2.50 (ISBN 0-671-82242-X). Pocket Books.
Glory. Nan Bagby Stephens. LC 32-4753. The John Day Company.
Glory. Francis Stuart. LC 33-31424. 1933. The Macmillan Company.
Glory: A Novel. Myra Baker Low, pseud. LC 36-33986. 1936. Meador Publishing Company.
Glory: A Novel. Vladimir Vladimirovich Nabokov. (Crest bk., M1788). 1972. Fawcett.
Glory and the Dream. Katharine Dunlap. LC 51-10601. (Illus.). 1951. Morrow.
Glory and the Dream. Frank Wilson Kenyon. LC 63-18375. 1963. Dodd, Mead.
Glory and the Dream. Anna Preston. LC 15-26776. 1915. 1.25. B. W. Huebsch.
Glory and the Dream. 1st Ed. Robert William Osmond. LC 56-127803. 1957. Vantage Press.
Glory and the Lightning. Taylor Caldwell. LC 74-6988. 1974. 6.95 (ISBN 0-385-06731-3). Doubleday.
Glory and the Lightning. Taylor Caldwell. (Fawcett crest book). 1975. (pbk.) 1.95. Fawcett.
Glory and the Parlour. Dorothy Walworth. LC 29-2816. 1929. Doubleday, Doran and Company, Inc.
Glory Bound. T. Whitecloud. 3.50 o.p. Carlton.
Glory Boys. Gerald Seymour. (Fawcett Crest Book). 1977. 1.95 (ISBN 0-449-23392-8). Fawcett Books.
Glory Boys: A Novel. Gerald Seymour. LC 76-10807. 8.95 (ISBN 0-394-40773-3). Random House.
Glory Circuit. Jess Gregg. LC 62-14161. 1962. St. Martin's Press.
Glory Day. Paul Darcy Boles. LC 78-57126. 9.95 (ISBN 0-394-50198-5). Random House.
Glory Gamblers. Lesley Forden. LC 64-5028. (Ballantine books, 528K). 1961. Ballantine Books.
Glory Game. Hunter Davies. 1973. 7.95 o.p. St Martin.
Glory Game. Keith Laumer. LC 72-84925. (Doubleday science fiction). 1973. 5.95 (ISBN 0-385-07380-1). Doubleday.
Glory Game. Keith Laumer. 1973. (pbk.) 1.25. Popular Library.
Glory Hand. Paul Boorstin & Sharon Boorstin. 320p. 1981. cancelled o.s.i. (ISBN 0-399-90100-0, Marek). Putnam Pub Group.
Glory Hole. Franz Kafka. LC 79-50835. pap. 2.25 o.s.i. (ISBN 0-89516-075-7). Condor Pub Co.
Glory Hole. George Brydges Rodney. E. J. Clode, Inc.
Glory Hole. Stewart Edward White. LC 24-29637. 1924. Doubleday, Page & Company.
Glory Hole: A Rousing Tale of Leadville in the Frontier Days. William MacLeod Raine. LC 52-9594. 1952. Houghton Mifflin.
Glory in Hell. Morris Hershman. pap. 0.60 o.p. Lancer.
Glory in the Midst". Faith Luce Hutcherson. LC 37-359013. The Author.
Glory in the Midst" Karmon and Jeneve Discover That a Holy Life Is Possible in a Troubled World. Faith Luce Hutcherson. LC 62-14843. 1962. Beacon Hill Press.
Glory Is Departed. LarnedHolenia, Alexader Maria & Harris, Alan, Tr. LC 37-105001. Harper & Brothers,
Glory Jam. Caroline Seaford. LC 34-248612. Minton, Balch & Company.
Glory Land. Dorothy Dowdell. 384p. (Orig.). 1981. pap. 2.75 (ISBN 0-449-14404-6, GM). Fawcett.
Glory O' the Dawn". Harold Trowbridge Pulsifer. LC 23-13731. 1923. Houghton Mifflin Company.
Glory of Clementina. William John Locke. LC 11-19661. 1911. John Lane Company.
Glory of Clementina Wing. William John Locke. LC 11-20592. 1911. John Lane.
Glory of Don Ramiro. Enrique Larreta. Tr. by L. B. Walton. 1977. pap. 59.95 (ISBN 0-8490-1891-9). Gordon Pr.
Glory of Don Ramiro: A Life in the Times of Philip II Enrique Rodriguez Larreta. Tr. by Walton, Leslie Bannister. LC 25-21495. 1924. J. M. Dent & Sons, Ltd.
Glory of Egypt. Lily Moresby Adams Beck. LC 26-20321. 1926. T. Nelson & Sons, Ltd.
Glory of Egypt: A Romance by Louis Moresby Pseud. Lily Moresby Adams Beck. LC 26-15276. George H. Doran Company.
Glory of Elsie Silver. Louis Golding. LC 46-25107. 1945. Dial Press.
Glory of Going on. John Owen. LC 24-15762. 1924. A. Melrose, Ltd.
Glory of Going on. Gertrude Pahlow. LC 19-13459. 1919. Duffield & Company.
Glory of Hera. Caroline Gordon. LC 70-157594. 1972. 7.95. Doubleday.
Glory of His Country: By Frederick Landis. Frederick Landis. LC 10-6492. 1910. C. Scribner's Sons.
Glory of Lois. Frank H. Shaw. LC 26-7122. 1925. Cassell and Company, Ltd.
Glory of the Conquered: The Story of a Great Love. Susan Glaspell. LC 9-62773. 1909. F. A. Stokes Company.
Glory of the Empire: A Novel, a History. Jean D' Ormesson. LC 74-7756. (Illus.). 1974. (ISBN 0-394-48121-6). Knopf; Distributed by Random House.
Glory of the Hawk. Leigh F. James. (Orig.). 1981. pap. 2.95 (ISBN 0-553-20096-8). Bantam.
Glory" of the Hills. Mary C McNamara. LC 30-9967. 1930. Mary C. McNamara.
Glory of the Hummingbird: A Novel. Peter De Vries. LC 74-9796. 1974. (ISBN 0-316-18199-4). Little, Brown.
Glory of the King's Daughter: Kvuda Bas Melech (the Laws of Modesty in Women's Dress) Moshe Wiener. 280p. (Orig., Hebrew & Eng.). 1980. 8.95 (ISBN 0-9605406-0-1); pap. 6.95 (ISBN 0-9605406-1-X). M Wiener.
Glory of the Pines: A Tale of the Onotonagon. William Chalmers Covert. LC 14-12211. 1914. 1.25. The Westminster Press.
Glory of the Seas. W. H Canaway. LC 74-21149. 1975. 5.95 (ISBN 0-672-52109-1). Bobbs-Merrill.
Glory of Youth. illustrated by henry hvtt & c. s. corson. ed. Temple Bailey. LC 13-19339. 1913. 1.25. The Penn Publishing Company.
Glory of Youth. Temple Bailey. LC 28-17927. 1924. The Penn Publishing Company.
Glory Place. Marian Bower. LC 30-24852. The Bobbs Merrill Company.
Glory Rides the Range. Ethel Arnold Smith Dorrance & Dorrance, James French, 1879-Joint Author. LC 20-55855. The Macaulay Company.
Glory Road. Alice Keenen Cripps. LC 41-22354. 1941. Wm. B. Eerdmans Publishing Company.
Glory Road. Robert Anson Heinlein. LC 79-13589. (Gregg Press science fiction series). (Illus.). 1979. 12.50 (ISBN 0-8398-2448-3). Gregg Press.
Glory Seeker. Louise MacKendrick. (Belmont Tower Book). (Illus.). 1.95 (ISBN 0-505-51230-0). Tower Pubns.
Glory Sharers. Victor Miller. (Orig.). 1979. write for info (ISBN 0-515-04890-9). Jove Pubns.
Glory Spent. Jean Woodman. LC 40-7108. Carrick & Evans, Inc.
Glory Tent. William Edmund Barrett. LC 67-15207. 1967. bds., 2.95. Doubleday.
Glory Tent. William Edmund Barrett. (60-2313). 1968. Popular Lib.
Glory That Was. Lyon Sprague De Camp. 1971. pap. 0.60 o.p. (63-542). Paperback Lib.
Glory Thrown in. Eric Lambert. 1981. 18.95x (Pub. by Remploy England). State Mutual Bk.
Glory Trail. Ray Hogan. LC 77-26526. 1978. 7.95 (ISBN 0-385-14280-3). Doubleday.
Glory Trail. Ray Hogan. LC 80-15156. 1980. 10.95 (ISBN 0-8161-3107-4). G. K. Hall.
Glory Trail. Meredith Reed. LC 31-9375. 1931. R. D. Henkle.
Glory Trail. 1st Ed. Virgil Reziah Walker. LC 56-5511. 1956. Vantage Press.
Glory Trap. Dan Sherman & Robin Williamson. (Orig.). 1981. pap. 2.25 (ISBN 0-505-51646-2). Tower Bks.
Glory Trap. Sherman Williamson. LC 77-79962. 1977. 6.95 (ISBN 0-8027-5370-1). Walker.
Glory Trap: By Dan Sherman and Robin Williamson. Dan Sherman & Williamson, Robin. 2.25 (ISBN 0-505-51646-2). Tower Publications.
Gloryhits. Bob Stickgold & Mark Noble. LC 77-6130. 1978. 1.95 (ISBN 0-345-27226-9). Ballantine Books.
Gloryland. Don Hall. 288p. (Orig.). 1981. pap. 2.95 (ISBN 0-523-41419-6). Pinnacle Bks.
Glory's Children. Hilton Brown. LC 36-19454. 1936. A.A. Knopf.
Glory's Net. 2nd. ed. William Tatem Tilden. LC 30-17941. 1930. Doubleday, Doran and Company, Inc.
Gloucester Branch. John Leggett. LC 64-18080. 1964. Harper & Row.
Gloucestermen, Stories of the Fishing Fleet. James Brendan Connolly. LC 30-8267. 1930. C. Scribner's Sons.
Gloved Hand: A Detective Story. Burton Egbert Stevenson. LC 13-5687. 1913. 1.30. Dodd, Mead and Company.
Gloved Hand: A New Mystery Novel. Nancy Rutledge. LC 47-23566. (Handi-book mysteries. No. 60). 1947. Quinn Publishing Company, Inc.

Glover: A Novel. Francis Pollini. LC 65-20686. bds., 5.95. Putnam.
Glover Undercover. Gary Blumberg. 1973. (pbk.) 1.25. Dell Pub. Co.
Glovers Illustrated Letters. Jack Glover. (Illus.). limited ed. 20.00; pap. 7.95. Cow Puddle.
Gloverson and His Silent Partners. Ralph Keeler. LC 7-11422. 1869. Lee and Shepard.
Glow. Brooks Stanwood, pseud. 320p. 1980. pap. 2.75 (ISBN 0-449-24333-8, Crest). Fawcett.
Glow: A Novel. Brooks Stanwood, pseud. LC 79-13502. 9.95 (ISBN 0-07-060879-2). McGraw-Hill.
Glow Job. Henry Kane. 1971. pap. 0.95 o.p. (ISBN 0-447-75158-1). Lancer.
Glow of Candles & Other Stories. Charles L. Grant. (Orig.). 1981. pap. 2.25 (ISBN 0-425-05145-5). Berkley Pub.
Glow of Morning. Irving A Greenfield. 1973. (pbk.) 1.50. Dell Pub. Co.
Glowering Gables. Luanna Churchill. 1974. 4.95 (ISBN 0-517-51562-8). Lenox Hill Press.
Glowing Emeralds. Francis I Bennett. LC 23-9749. 1923. H. R. Wohlers.
Glowing Stones. Zioneers. 1977. 1.50 o.p. (ISBN 0-8309-0177-9). Herald Hse.
Gloyne Murder. Carl Clausen. LC 90-10256. 1930. Dodd, Mead and Company.
Glue. Rev. ed. Benjamin Benedict. (Eggs Benedict Ser.). (Illus.). 144p. 1982. pap. 2.95 (ISBN 0-942764-01-3). Falcon Pub Venice.
Gluskap the Liar & Other Indian Tales. Horace P. Beck. (Illus.). 192p. 1966. 5.95 (ISBN 0-87027-083-4). Cumberland Pr.
Glynda: Susannah Leigh. 1979. New American Library.
Glyph Five: Textual Studies. LC 76-47370. 12.50x (ISBN 0-8018-2192-4); pap. 3.45x (ISBN 0-8018-2193-2). Johns Hopkins.
Gnaw-Wood: Or, New England Life in a Village. Henry W. B. Cher. 1938. The Chicago Law Institute.
Gnome There Was, and Other Tales of Science Fiction and Fantasy: By Lewis Padgett Pseud. Henry Kuttner. LC 50-11220. 1950. Simon and Schuster.
Gnomes of the Saline Mountains: A Fantastic Narrative. Anna Goldmark Gross. LC 13-39. 1912. 1.00. The Shakespeare Press.
Go. Clellon Holmes. LC 52-12794. 1952. Scribner.
Go. John Clellon Holmes. LC 76-39701. 1977. 10.00 (ISBN 0-911858-34-2). P. P. Appel.
Go. John Clellon Holmes. LC 80-82054. (Plume book). 1980. 4.95 (ISBN 0-452-25245-8). New American Library.
Go Ahead, Garrison!" A Story of News Broadcasting. Abel Alan Schechter. LC 41-531. 1940. Dodd, Mead & Company.
Go and Catch a Falling Star. Constance Noyes Robertson. LC 56-880855. 1957. Random House.
Go As You Please. Augustus George Greenwood. LC 29-801019. 1929. Frederick A. Stokes Company.
Go Ask the River. Evelyn Sybil Mary Eaton. LC 69-12033. 1969. Harcourt, Brace & World.
Go-Away Bird. Muriel Spark. 1961. 3.75 o.p. (ISBN 0-397-00129-0, Key). Lippincott.
Go-Away Bird, and Other Stories. Muriel Spark. LC 60-13586. 1960. Lippincott.
Go Away Thunder: A Novel. William F. Steuber. LC 72-83267. (Illus.). 1972. 6.95. Wisconsin House.
Go Away to Murder. John Creasey. 1972. pap. 0.95 o.p. (75-317). Lancer.
Go Back and Tell: A Mystic Novel. Saul Raskin. Whittier Books.
Go Back to Hell. John Thomas Edson. (Orig.). 1982. pap. 1.95 (ISBN 0-425-05618-X). Berkley Pub.
Go-Between. Therese Benson. LC 30-354182. 1930. Dodd, Mead and Company.
Go-Between. Leslie Poles Hartley. 1967. bds., 5.95. Stein & Day.
Go-Between. Leslie Poles Hartley. (Avon NS33). 1968. Avon.
Go-Between. Leslie Poles Hartley. LC 54-7196. 1954. Knopf.
Go Between. Leslie Poles Hartley. LC 54-7196. (Scarborough Book). 1.95 (ISBN 0-8128-6073-X)., C.
Go-Between. Arthur Maling. LC 79-105239. 1970. 4.95. Harper & Row.
Go-Between and Other Stories. Rinzo Shiina. LC 71-123475. 1970. 2.95 (ISBN 0-8170-0490-4). Judson Press.
Go-Devil. Marguerite Eyssen. LC 47-1747. 1947. Doubleday & Company, Inc.
Go Die in Afghanistan. Stuart Jason. (Butcher Ser.: No. 33). 208p. (Orig.). 1982. pap. 1.95 (ISBN 0-523-41664-4). Pinnacle Bks.
Go Down Dead. Shane Stevens. LC 66-26225. 1966-1967. Morrow.
Go Down, Death-- Sue Brown Hays. LC 46-4803. 1946. C. Scribner's Sons.
Go Down Girl. Michael Word. pap. 1.95 o.p. (8089). Cameo.
Go Down in the Valley. John Maggie. pap. 1.25 o.p. (2055). Brandon.
Go Down, Moses. William Faulkner. LC 72-8062. 1973. 1.95 (ISBN 0-394-71884-4). Vintage Books.
Go Down, Moses. William Faulkner. LC 55-6391. (Modern library of the world's best books 175). 1955. Modern Library.
Go Down, Moses, and Other Stories. William Faulkner. LC 42-16049. 1942. Random House.
Go Down, Moses: And Other Stories. William Faulkner. LC 42-17349. 1942. Random House.
Go Down Swinging. Thomas Shire. pap. 1.95 o.p. (ISBN 0-87682-256-1, 7256). Barclay Hse.
Go Fight City Hall. Ethel Rosenberg. LC 49-8950. 1949. Simon and Schuster.
Go for Broke. Rod Gray. (New Lady from L.U.S.T. Ser). (O.s.i.: No. 1). 1975. pap. 1.25 o.s.i. (BT50777). Belmont-Tower.
Go for Broke. John Welcome, pseud. LC 76-161117. 1972. 4.95 o.p. (ISBN 0-8027-5231-4). Walker & Co.
Go for Your Gan, a Western Novel: By Coe Williams Pseud. C. William Harrison. LC 55-33822. (.A Popular Library eagie book, EB39). 1955. Popular Library.
Go Forth and Find.". John R Jarboe. LC 7-10638. ("unknown" library no. 36). The Cassell Publishing Co.
Go Forth and Find. Edward Stewart Moffat. LC 16-160784. 1916. Moffat, Yard & Company.
Go Forth and Find. Hannah Daviess Pittman. LC 9-29778. 1910. R. G. Badger.
Go Get Buchanan. Jonas Ward. pap. price not set o.p. (GM). Fawcett World.
Go-Getter: A Story That Tells You How to Be One. Peter Bernard Kyne. LC 21-170799. 1921. Cosmopolitan Book Corporation.
Go-Getter Gray. Robert Ames Bennet. LC 26-19098. 1926. A. C. McClurg & Co.
Go Gospel. Manfred C. Gutzke. LC 68-8389. pap. 1.25 o.p. (ISBN 0-8307-0036-6, S222-1-08). Regal.
Go Home and Tell Your Mother. Max Wylie. LC 50-9572. 1950. Rinehart.
Go in Beauty. William Eastlake. LC 79-56815. (Zia book). 1980. 5.95 (ISBN 0-8263-0538-5). University of New Mexico Press.
Go in Beauty. 1st Ed. William Eastlake. LC 56-8779. 1956. Harper.
Go in Peace. Loyal Edward Davis. LC 54-10487. 1954. Putnam.
Go into Your Dance. Bradford Ropes. LC 34-20330. A. H. King.
Go, Lovely Rose. Jean Potts. 1954. Scribner.
Go, Man, Go. Frances Hunter. (Family Library). 1971. pap. 1.25 o.p. (FV2479). BJ Pub Group.
Go Marry. Brendan Williams. LC 31-18065. H. Liveright, Inc.
Go Naked in the World: Novel. Tom T Chamales. LC 59-12000. 1959. Scribner.
Go Naked to Eden. Marjorie Craft. (Berkley medallion book). 1975. (pbk.) 1.50 (ISBN 0-425-02773-2). Berkley Pub. Co.
Go, Said the Bird. Geoffrey Cotterell. 1967. 5.95 o.p. Little.
Go, Said the Bird. 1st Amer. Ed. Geoffrey Cotterell. LC 66-21985. 1966. 5.95. Little.
Go, Sam Sunday. Mullin Garr. pap. 1.95 o.s.i. (OPH-193). Olympia.
Go She Must! David Garnett. LC 27-1990. 1927. A. A. Knopf.
Go She Must. David Garnett. LC 42-477017. (Sun dial library). 1927. Garden City Publishing Company, Inc.
Go Slowly, Come Back Quickly. David Niven. LC 81-43241. 1981. 14.95 (ISBN 0-385-17561-2). Doubleday.
Go Slowly, Come Back Quickly. David Niven. LC 82-3082. 1982. 18.95 (ISBN 0-8161-3389-1). G.K. Hall.
Go Tell It on the Mountain. James B. Baldwin. LC 64-922. 1963. Dial Press.
Go the the Widow-Maker. James Jones. LC 67-171609. 1967. 7.50. Delacorte.
Go to It. George Vere Hobart. 1908. G. W. Dillingham Co.
Go to the Widow-Maker. James Jones. (2942). 1968. pap., 1.25. Dell.
Go to Thy Deathbed. Stanton Forbes, pseud. LC 68-27117. 1968. 3.95. Published for the Crime Club by Doubleday.
Go to Thy Deathbed see Labyrinth.
Go up for Glory. Bill Russel. 1980. pap. 2.25 (ISBN 0-425-04676-1). Berkley Pub.
Go West--Young Lady: A Sparkling Story Set in the Great American West. Inez Specking. LC 41-14058. Catholic Literary Guild.
Go West Ben Gold! Clay Turner. (Ben Gold western). 1974. (pbk.) 0.95. Warner Paperback Library.
Go West, Inspector Ghote. Henry Reymond Fitzwalter Keating. LC 80-3008. 1981. 9.95 (ISBN 0-385-17683-X). Published for the Crime Club by Doubleday.
Go West, Inspector Ghote. Henry Reymond Fitzwalter Keating. LC 82-3815. 1982. 2.95 (ISBN 0-14-006319-6). Penguin Books.
Go West, Young Maid. Allen Eppes. Arcadia House.
Go West, Young Maid. Watkins Eppes Wright. LC 35-2538. 1935. Arcadia House.
Go with Him Twain. Bertha B. Moore McCurry. LC 41-14665. 1941. Wm. B. Eerdmans Publishing Co.
Go with Him Twain. Bertha B Moore. LC 41-146653. 1941. Wm. B. Eerdmans Publishing Co.
Go Wrestle with the Wind. Robert Schaeffer. 1974. 7.50 o.p.; pap. 5.00 o.p. Wagon & Star.
Goad of Gold. H. Morgan Ruth. LC 30-9317. The Penn Publishing Company.
Goal. Phyllis Bottome. (Illus.). 1963. 6.00 o.p. (ISBN 0-8149-0057-7). Vanguard.
Goal Seekers. Ruby Wallace Walters. LC 48-187511. 1947. Story Book Press.
Goalie's Anxiety at the Penalty Kick. Peter Handke. LC 70-188957. 1972. 6.95 (ISBN 0-374-16376-6). Farrar, Straus and Giroux.
Goat-Foot God. Violet Mary Firth. LC 70-27597. 1971. 6.50 (ISBN 0-87728-111-4). S. Weiser.
Goat for Azazel: A Novel of Christian Origins. Vardis Fisher. LC 56-14254. (His Testament of man 9). 1956. A. Swallow.
Goat Island. William Hanscom Fuller. LC 54-8041. (Dell first edition, 28). 1954. Dell Pub. Co.
Goat Song: A Novel of Ancient Greece. Frank Yerby. LC 67-16540. 1967. 6.95. Dial.
Goat Song: A Novel of Ancient Greece. Frank Yerby. (Dell Book). 1977. 1.95 (ISBN 0-440-12911-7). Dell Pub. Co.
Goat Songs. John Weston. LC 76-162977. 1971. 6.95. Atheneum.
Goat Songs: Three Novellas. John Weston. 1971. 6.95 o.p. (ISBN 0-689-10471-5). Atheneum.
Goat, the Wolf, and the Crab. Gillian Martin. LC 76-49918. 7.95 (ISBN 0-684-14848-X). Scribner.
Goat Without Horns. Beale Davis. LC 25-181792. Brentano's.
Goatibex Constellation. Fazil Iskander. LC 75-307543. (Illus.). 1975. 9.95. (ISBN 0-88233-071-3) (ISBN 0-88233-072-1). Ardis Publishers.
Goat's Head. Seth Pfefferle. 1977. pap. 1.95. Woodhill.
Goat's Hoof. Algernon Crofton. LC 26-14555. 1928. P. Covici.
Gobbling Billy. Dynely James, pseud. LC 59-10774. 1959. Dutton.
Gobi or Shamo. Gilbert Murray. LC 77-84259. (Lost Race and Adult Fantasy Fiction). 1978. 23.00 (ISBN 0-405-11002-2). Arno Press.
Gobi or Shamo: A Story of Three Songs. Gilbert Murray. LC 41-30744. 1889. Longmans, Green, and Co.
Gobi, Prince of Moving Sand. James P Leynse. LC 73-175449. (One evening book). (Illus.). 1973. 2.95. Good News Publishers.
Goblin Gold. Maria Henrietta De La Cherois Crommelin. (Lovell's library. no. 1336). 1889. J. W. Lovell Company.
Goblin Gold: A Novel. Maria Henrietta De La Cherois Crommelin. LC 6-31976. (Harper's handy series. no. 36). 1885. Harper & Brothers.
Goblin Market. Helen McCloy. LC 43-16765. 1943. W. Morrow and Company.
Goblin Market: A Romance of to-Day Telling How Anthony Harrop, a Respectable Citizen, Met in with the Goblin Folk, How He Attended Their Market, What He Bought There and How It Served Him. Henry De Vere Stacpoole. LC 27-185554. George H. Doran Company.
Goblin Reservation. Clifford D. Simak. LC 68-25455. 1968. 4.95. Putnam.
Goblin Woman. Rose Cecil O'Neill. LC 30-32843. 1930. Doubleday, Doran & Company, Inc.
Goblins Go Barefoot. Max Steele. LC 66-130106. (Perennial lib., P84 D). 1966. Harper.
Goblins of Eros. Warren Eyster. LC 57-5361. 1957. Random House.
Goce Ahora, Pague Despues. Danilo Cesto. (Pimienta Collection Ser). (Sp.). 1977. pap. 1.00 (ISBN 0-88473-253-3). Fiesta Pub.
God Against the Gods. Allen Drury. LC 75-41673. (Illus.). 1976. 10.00 (ISBN 0-385-00199-1). Doubleday.
God Against the Gods. limited 1st ed. Allen Drury. LC 77-364864. (Illus.). 1976. Franklin Library.
God Ain't Even Sick. Frank D. Wiedeman. 5.95 o.p. Vantage.
God Ain't Even Sick: A Novel by Frank D. Wiedeman. Frank D Wiedeman. 1974. 5.95. (ISBN 0-533-01039-X). Vantage Press.
God and All His Angels. Graham Lord. LC 76-28181. 1977. 8.95 (ISBN 0-670-34280-7). Viking Press.
God & Harvey Grosbeck. Gilbert Millstein. LC 82-46015. (Illus.). 384p. 1983. 16.95 (ISBN 0-385-12450-3). Doubleday.
God & His Gifts. Ivy Compton-Burnett. 176p. 1983. pap. 3.95 (ISBN 0-14-006125-8). Penguin.
God and Lady Margaret. John Oxenham, pseud. LC 33-32271. 1933. Longmans, Green and Co.
God and Little Apples. John Desmond Sheridan. LC 62-11526. 1962. Farrar, Straus and Cudhay.
God and My Country. MacKinlay Kantor. LC 54-5543. 1954. World Pub. Co.
God and Sarah Pedlock. Stephen Longstreet. LC 75-37714. (Illus.). 8.95 (ISBN 0-679-50482-6). McKay.
God and Sarah Pedlock. Stephen Longstreet. (Illus.). 1977. 1.75 (ISBN 0-380-00919-6). Avon Books.
God and the General's Daughter. Anne Heagney. LC 53-104883. 1953. Bruce.
God and the Groceryman. Harold Bell Wright. LC 27-16098. 1927. D. Appleton and Company.
God and the Man. Robert Williams Buchanan. (Lovell's library, no. 1316). J. W. Lovell Company.
God and the Man. A Romance. Robert Williams Buchanan. (Harper's Franklin square library, no. 225). 1882. Harper & Brothers.
God and the Moon. Charles Samuel Poling. LC 42-18729. 1942. Kellaway-Ide Company.
God and the Others. M. M Costantin. LC 72-513. 1972. 6.95 (ISBN 0-395-13952-X). Houghton Mifflin.
God and Thirty. Stewart Lawrence Navarre. LC 47-189713. 1947. The Otterbein Press.
God and Woman (Dyrendal) Johan Bojer & Shelander, A. R., Tr. LC 21-21144. 1921. Moffat, Yard and Company.
God-Bearer. Benjamin Brooke Thomas Trege. LC 14-20112. The Gorham Press.
God Beyond Nature. R. E. Clark. LC 77-76108. (Redwood Ser.). 1978. pap. 3.95 o.p. (ISBN 0-8163-0002-X, 07345-2). Pacific Pr Pub Assn.
God Bless America. Stanley Johnson. LC 73-83642. 1974. 5.95 (ISBN 0-385-07207-4). Doubleday.
God Bless Love. Nanette Newman. (Illus.). 1973. 1.95 o.p. (ISBN 0-397-00975-5). Lippincott.
God Bless Our Aunts. Rachel Meisenhelder. LC 45-10148. 1945. Whittlesey House, McGraw-Hill Book Company, Inc.
God Bless Pawnbrokers. Peter Schwed. 192p. 1975. 7.95 o.p. (ISBN 0-396-07222-4). Dodd.
God Bless the Child. Kristin Hunter. LC 64-20054. 1964. Scribner.
God Bless the Devil! Liars' Bench Tales. Writers' Program. Tennessee & Aswell, James R. Ed. LC 40-32204. 1940. The University of North Carolina Press.
God Bless This Child. James Allen & Geneva Allen. 180p. 1975. 7.00 o.p. (ISBN 0-682-48163-7). Exposition.
God Bless You, Mr. Rosewater. Kurt Vonnegut, Jr. pap. 2.95 (ISBN 0-440-12929-X). Dell.
God Bless You, Mr. Rosewater. Kurt Vonnegut, Jr. LC 65-16434. 1974. pap. 8.95 (ISBN 0-440-52929-8, Delta). Dell.
God Bless You, Mr. Rosewater: Or, Pearls Before Swine. Kurt Vonnegut. (Delta 2929). 1968. pap., 1.75. Dell.
God Bless You, Mr. Rosewater: Or, Pearls Before Swine. Kurt Vonnegut. LC 65-16434. 1965. Holt, Rinehart and Winston.
God Bless You, Mr. Rosewater: Or, Pearls Before Swine. Kurt Jr Vonnegut. LC 65-16434. bds., 4.95. Holt.
God Boy. Ian Cross. 181p. 1972. pap. 5.40x (ISBN 0-7233-0356-8). Intl Pubns Serv.
God Cell. Wilbur Bradbury. LC 76-14786. 7.95. Putnam.
God Emperor of Dune. Frank Herbert. LC 80-25149. 12.95 (ISBN 0-399-12593-0). Berkley Pub. Corp.: Distributed by Putnam.
God Forbid: A Novel. 1st. ed. R. G Davis. 1974. 4.00 (ISBN 0-682-47964-0). Exposition Press.
God Forsaken: A Novel. Frederic Breton. LC 6-17388. G. P. Putnam's Sons.
God Game. Ralph Hayes. 320p. 1983. pap. 3.25 (ISBN 0-8439-2026-2, Leisure Bks). Dorchester Pub Co.
God Game. Karl A Olsson. LC 68-13699. 1968. World Pub. Co.
God, Gold & Gunman. Rebel M. Temple. 107p. (Orig.). 1981. pap. 2.25 (ISBN 0-89279-033-4). Graphic Pub.
God Had Seven Days. Henry Misrock. LC 50-5988. 1950. Doubleday.
God Has a Long Face. Robert Wilder. LC 40-33790. G. P. Putnam's Sons.
God Has a Sense of Humor. 1st Ed. Rubylea Hall. LC 60-544481. Duell, Sloan and Pearce.
God Have Mercy on Me! From the Diaries of a Lost Soul. Marjorie Erskine Smith. LC 31-15682. The Macaulay Company.
God Have Mercy on Us! A Story of 1918. William T Scanlon. LC 29-22118. 1929. Houghton Mifflin Company.
God Head. Leonard Cline. LC 25-20833. 1925. The Viking Press.
God Holds the Key. Aletha Caldwell Conner. LC 40-13011. Co-Operative Publishing Company.
God Hunters. William Kelley. LC 64-10625. 1964. Simon and Schuster.

God in Science Fiction. Ray Bradbury. Ed. by Norman E. Tanis. (Northridge Facsimile Ser.: Pt. XI). 1978. pap. 10.00 (ISBN 0-937048-10-0). CSUN.

God in the Car: A Novel. Anthony Hope Hawkins. LC 4-23570. (On cover: Appletons' town and country library, no. 154). 1894. D. Appleton and Company.

God in the Dock. Clive Staples Lewis. Ed. by Walter Hooper. 1970. pap. 6.95 (ISBN 0-8028-1456-5). Eerdmans.

God in the Mountain. Colin Thubron. 1978. 9.95 (ISBN 0-393-08785-9). Norton.

God in the Mountain: A Novel. Colin Thubron. LC 77-13906. 8.95 (ISBN 0-393-08785-9). Norton.

God in the Straw Pen: A Novel. John Porter Fort. LC 31-272073. 1931. Dodd, Mead & Company.

God Is an Englishman. Ronald Frederick Delderfield. LC 74-101871. (Illus.). 1970. 7.95. Simon and Schuster.

God Is Blue & Other Stories. Gerry Pratt. 150p. 1978. 8.50 (ISBN 0-917304-38-1); pap. 7.50. Timber.

God Is for White Folks. Will Thomas. LC 47-30938. 1947. Creative Age Press.

God Is Late. Christine Arnothy. LC 57-5319. 1957. E. P. Dutton.

God Keepers. E. Richard Johnson. LC 70-122890. 1970. 4.95. Harper & Row.

God Keepers: A Novel. E. Richard Johnson. 1973. (pbk.) 1.25. Dell.

God Loves a Dumbbell. Elisa Thomas. LC 33-2862. Pegasus Publishing Company.

God Machine. William Jon Watkins. LC 72-84952. (Doubleday science fiction). 1973. 5.95 (ISBN 0-385-05662-1). Doubleday.

God Machine: A Novel. Martin Caidin. LC 68-12450. 1968. Dutton.

God Made Little Apples. Sheridan, John Desmond. LC 62-6189. 1962. Dent.

God Made Little Apples. Sheridan, John Desmond. LC 62-11526. 1962. Farrar, Straus and Cudahy.

God Made Me Cry. Washington Irving Kilpatrick. LC 49-7156. 1948. Dorrance.

God Made Them Superstars. Barbara Anson. 1976. pap. 1.50 o.p. (LB405, Leisure Bks). Nordon Pubns.

God Makers. Frank Herbert. LC 74-186649. 1972. 5.95 (ISBN 0-399-11006-2). Putnam.

God Must Be Sad. Fannie Hurst. 1975. (pbk.) 1.50 (ISBN 0-515-03899-7). Pyramid Books.

God Must Be Sad. 1st Ed. Fannie Hurst. LC 61-13803. 1961. Doubleday.

God Novel. William Butler. LC 71-106549. 1969. 5.95. Scribner.

God of Channel 1. Donald Stacy. LC 56-8165. 1956. Ballantine Books.

God of Civilization. A Romance. M. A. Weeks Pittock. LC 7-38199. (On cover: Mid-ocean library, v. 1, no. 1). Eureka Publishing Company.

God of Clay. Henry Christopher Bailey. 1908. Brentano's.

God of Gotham. A Romance Front the Life of a Wellknown Actress. Lee Bascom. LC 6-9099. 1891. G. W. Dillingham.

God of His Fathers: And Other Stories. Jack London. LC 72-103523. (Short story index reprint series). 1969. Books for Libraries Press.

God of His Fathers: And Other Stories. Jack London. 1901. McClure, Phillips & Company.

God of His Fathers & Other Stories. Jack London. 1909. Doubleday, Page & Co.

God of Love. Justin Huntly McCarthy. LC 9-28000. 1909. Harper & Brothers.

God of Might. Elias Tobenkin. LC 25-7083. 1925. Minton, Balch & Company.

God of Planet 607. Edward Pohlman. LC 71-190503. 1972. (ISBN 0-664-20941-6) (ISBN 0-664-24962-0). Westminster Press.

God of Tarot. Piers Anthony, pseud. (Orig.). 1982. pap. 2.50 (ISBN 0-425-05719-4). Berkley Pub.

God of the Bees. Mary Chapin Smith. LC 13-18595. 1913. W. A. Butterfield.

God of the Forest. Francis Dorer & Nancy Dorer. 1978. pap. 1.50 (ISBN 0-532-15345-6). Woodhill.

God of the Labyrinth. Colin Wilson. 300p. 1982. pap. 5.95 (ISBN 0-914728-39-3). Wingbow Pr.

God of Things: A Novel of Modern Egypt. Florence Brooks Whitehouse. LC 2-13109. 1902. Little, Brown, and Company.

God of Wine. Jettie Irving Felps. LC 52-168. 1951. Book Craft.

God on the Rocks. Jane Gardam. LC 79-88614. 1979. 8.95 (ISBN 0-688-03531-0). Morrow.

God Only Knows. Floyd A. Hyatt. 1977. 4.50 o.p. (ISBN 0-533-02853-1). Vantage.

God Player. Eddie Constantine. LC 76-8282. 1976. 1.95 (ISBN 0-345-25409-0). Ballantine Books.

God Plucked a Violet. Goldie M Down. LC 68-24452. 1968. Southern Pub. Association.

God Rest Ye Merry, Gentlemen. Bertram Martin Adams. LC 66-29367. (Illus.). 1966. Heck & McMaster Publications.

God Rest Ye Merry, Gentlemen: By Bill Adams. Bertram Martin Adams. LC 66-29367. 1966. bxd. 2.50,. Heck & McMaster Pubns.

God Returns to the Vuelta Abajo: A Tale of the Cuban Vega by Melanie Earle Keiser; with Drawings by Josesph Low. Melanie Earle Keiser. LC 36-30934. W. R. Scott.

God Rides a Gale. James Robert Peery. LC 40-6733. Harper & Brothers.

God Save the Child. Robert B. Parker. LC 74-11454. (Midnight novel of suspense). 1974. 5.95 (ISBN 0-395-19955-7). Houghton Mifflin.

God Save the Child. Robert B Parker. (Berkley Medallion Book). 1976. (pbk.) 1.25 (ISBN 0-425-03037-7). Berkley Publishing Corp.

God Save the Duke. James Saxon Childers. LC 33-8149. 1933. D. Appleton and Company.

God Save the King: A Novel. Ronald MacDonald. LC 1-24842. 1901. The Century Co.

God Save the Mark. Donald E Westlake. LC 67-12765. 1967. Random House.

God Save the Mark: By Donald E. Westlake. Donald E Westlake. (Signet bk. T3625). 1968. New Amer. Lib.

God Save the Tsar. Susanna Hoe. LC 77-15924. 1978. 8.95 (ISBN 0-312-33032-4). St. Martin's Press.

God-Seeker. Sinclair Lewis. 1975. (pbk.) 1.95. Manor Books.

God-Seeker: A Novel. Sinclair Lewis. LC 49-418. 1949. Random House.

God Seeker: A Tale of Old Styria. Peter Rosegger. LC 1-27050. 1901. G. P. Putnam's Sons.

God Sends Sunday. Arna Wendell Bontemps. LC 74-148531. 1972. (ISBN 0-404-00137-8). AMS Press.

God Sends Sunday. Arna Wendell Bontemps. LC 31-6796. Harcourt, Brace and Company.

God Speed the Night. Dorothy Salisbury Davis & Jerome Ross. LC 68-17330. 1968. Scribner.

God Spigo. Anne Northgrave Tibble. LC 76-376899. 1976. 3.25 (ISBN 0-7156-1092-9). Duckworth.

God Stalk. P. C Hodgell. LC 82-1672. (Illus.). 1982. 10.95 (ISBN 0-689-30844-2). Atheneum.

God, the King, My Brother. Mary F Nixon Roulet. LC 3731. 1900. L. C. Page & Company.

God the Stonebreaker. Alvin Bennett. (Caribbean Writers Ser.). 1973. pap. text ed. 5.50x (ISBN 0-435-98100-5). Heinemann Ed.

God Was Here but He Left Early. Irwin Shaw. LC 72-87047. 1973. 7.95 (ISBN 0-87795-055-5). Arbor Hse.

God Was Here but He Left Early. Irwin Shaw. LC 72-87047. (Priam Ser.). 1980. pap. 5.95 (ISBN 0-87795-239-6). Arbor Hse.

God Was Here but He Left Early. Irwin Shaw. 1981. pap. 2.95 (ISBN 0-440-13303-3). Dell.

God Was Looking the Other Way. Jose L. Sanchez. 1973. 7.95 o.p. (ISBN 0-316-77005-1). Little.

God Wears a Bow Tie: A Novel of Show Business. Lyle Stuart. LC 49-11029. 1949. Greenberg.

God Who Didn't Laugh. Gleb Botkin. LC 29-23488. 1929. Payson & Clarke ltd.

God, Why Am I So Afraid. Donovan Marshall. 1982. pap. 2.95 (ISBN 0-570-03630-5, 39-1091). Concordia.

God Wills It!" A Tale of the First Crusade. William Stearns Davis. LC 1-26209. 1901. The Macmillan Company.

God...and Dr. Bannister. This War Can Be Stopped. Frank Bruce Robinson. LC 41-127227. 1941. "Psychiana," Inc.

Godd: A Novel. Ionel. LC 74-157685. 1972. 6.95. Macmillan.

Goddam Gypsy. Ronald Lee. LC 74-179639. (Illus.). 1972. 7.50 o.p. (ISBN 0-672-51642-X). Bobbs.

Goddam White Man. David Lytton. 1961. 3.50 o.p. (ISBN 0-671-28725-7). S&S.

Goddaughter: A Romance. Adrian Reid. LC 77-88194. 8.95 (ISBN 0-89256-041-X). Rawson Associates.

Godded & Codded. Julia O'Faolain. 1971. price not set o.p. Coward.

Goddess. Gouverneur Morris & Goddard, Charles W., Joint Author. LC 15-18575. 1915. Hearst's International Library Co.

Goddess. Miranda Seymour, pseud. LC 78-24536. (Illus.). 1979. 10.95 (ISBN 0-698-10972-4). Coward, McCann & Geoghegan.

Goddess. Miranda Seymour, pseud. LC 78-24536. 1981. 2.75 (ISBN 0-425-04494-7). Berkley Publishing Corporation.

Goddess Abides: A Novel. Pearl Sydenstricker Buck. LC 71-155012. 1973. (pbk) 1.50 (ISBN 0-671-78648-2). Pocket Books.

Goddess and Other Women. Joyce Carol Oates. LC 74-81808. 1974. 8.95 (ISBN 0-8149-0745-8). Vanguard Press.

Goddess and Other Women. Joyce Carol Oates. (Fawcett Crest Book). 1976. (pbk.) 1.95. Fawcett.

Goddess & the Gaiety Girl. Barbara Cartland. (Barbara Cartland Ser.: No. 130). 160p. (Orig.). 1980. pap. 1.75 (ISBN 0-553-14248-8). Bantam.

Goddess Game. Hugh Barron. Orig. Title: Love & Naked Light. 1969. pap. 0.95 o.p. (N2102). Pyramid Pubns.

Goddess Girl. Dorothea Deakin. LC 10-7926. 1910. Cassell and Company, Ltd.

Goddess Hangup. Joyce Elbert. LC 70-128484. 1970. 6.95. World Pub. Co.

Goddess in Exile: Or, The Spanish Plotters. A Tale of the Sunny South. Philip S Warne. (On cover: The select series, no. 81). 1891. Street & Smith.

Goddess Named Gold. Bhabani Bhattacharya. LC 60-8627. 1960. Crown Publishers.

Goddess of Atvatabar: Being the History of the Discovery of the Interior World, and Conquest of Atvatabar. William Richard Bradshaw. LC 74-15954. (Science Fiction). (Illus.). 1975. (ISBN 0-405-06279-6). Arno Press.

Goddess of Atvatabar: Being the History of the Discovery of the Interior World and Conquest of Atvatabar. William Richard Bradshaw. LC 6-15941. 1892. J. F. Douthitt.

Goddess of Atvatabar: History of the Discovery of the Interior World & Conquest of Atvatabar. William Richard Bradshaw. LC 74-15954. (Science Fiction Ser.). (Illus.). 318p. 1975. Repr. of 1892 ed. 19.00x (ISBN 0-405-06279-6). Ayer Co.

Goddess of Death. Michael Underwood. LC 81-23212. 1982. 10.95 (ISBN 0-312-33056-1). St. Martin's Press.

Goddess of Ganymede. Michael D Resnick. LC 68-683. (Illus.). 1967. D. M. Grant.

Goddess of Mercy: A Tale of Love and Turmoil in Modern China. James Livingstone Stewart. LC 27-19896. Fleming H. Revell Company.

Goddess of the Dawn: A Romance. Margaret Davies Sullivan. LC 14-247828. G. W. Dillingham Company.

Goddess Queen: A Novel Based on the Life of Nefertiti. Tr. from French by Johanna Harwood. 1st Amer. Ed. Nicole Vidal. LC 65-169065. bds., 4.50. McKay.

Goddess Stick. Aaron Flood. (Orig.). 1969. pap. 1.25 (ISBN 0-87067-174-X, BH174). Holloway.

Goddess to a God: An Historical Reconstruction. John Lloyd Balderston & Bolitho, Sybil. LC 48-9180. 1948. Macmillan Co.

Godfather. Nalbro Isadorah Bartley. LC 29-22691. Farrar & Rinehart Incorporated.

Godfather. Mario Puzo. LC 69-11465. 1969. 6.95. Putnam.

Godfather Must Live. Thayer Halstead. 1974. (pbk.) 1.25. Dell.

Godfather Papers & Other Confessions. Mario Puzo. LC 72-187892. 1972. 6.95. Putnam.

Godforgotten. Gladys Schmitt. LC 77-182333. 1972. 6.95 (ISBN 0-15-136065-0). Harcourt Brace Jovanovich.

Godforsaken. Chelsea Quinn Yarbo. 400p. (Orig.). 1983. pap. 3.95 (ISBN 0-446-30102-7). Warner Bks.

Godfrey Helstone. A Novel. Georgiana Marion Craik May. (Harper's Franklin square library, no. 382). 1884. Harper & Brothers.

Godfrey Helstone. A Novel. Georgiana Marion Craik May. (On cover: Seaside library. Pocket ed. no. 450). 1885. G. Munro.

Godfrey Morgan: A Californian Mystery. Jules Verne & Gordon, William John, Tr. 1884. C. Scribner's Sons.

Godhood of Man... His Religious, Political and Economic Development and the Sources of Social Inequality. Nicholas Michels. 1899. The Author.

Godiva Girl. Peggy Gaddis, pseud. LC 48-206932. 1948. Phoenix Press.

Godiva Marlow. Voltaire Lewis, pseud. LC 68-56290. (Illus.). 1968. 4.00 o.p. (ISBN 0-911736-01-8). Courthouse Pr.

Godless Breed. Gordon D. Shirreffs. (Orig.). 1968. pap. 0.50 o.p. (D1985, GM). Fawcett World.

Godmakers. Frank Herbert. (Berkley Book). 1978. 1.95 (ISBN 0-425-03919-6). Berkley Pub. Corp.

Godmakers see Worlds Beyond Dune: The Best of Frank Herbert.

Godmother. Janice Elliott. LC 67-11738. 1967. Holt, Rinehart and Winston.

Godmother. Hugh Fleetwood. 152p. 1980. 16.95 (ISBN 0-241-10126-3, Pub. by Hamish Hamilton England). David & Charles.

Godolphin. Edward George Earle Lytton Bulwer-Lytton Lytton. G. Routledge and Sons.

Godolphin. Edward George Earle Lytton Bulwer-Lytton Lytton. LC 7-8344. (On cover: Lovell's library, v. 5, no. 289). J. W. Lovell Company.

Godolphin. Edward George Earle Lytton Bulwer-Lytton Lytton. 1883. J. B. Lippincott & Co.

Godparents. Grace Sartwell Mason. LC 10-9264. 1910. Houghton Mifflin Company.

Godric. Frederick Buechner. LC 80-66014. 1980. 8.95 (ISBN 0-689-11086-3). Atheneum.

Gods. Shaw Desmond. LC 21-20440. 1921. C. Scribner's Sons.

Gods Abide. Thomas Burnett Swann. (Daw Science Fiction). 1976. pap. 1.25 o.p. (ISBN 0-87997-272-6, UY1272). DAW Bks.

Gods Abide. Thomas Burnett Swann. (Illus.) (ISBN 0-87997-272-6). Daw Books.

God's Acre Beautiful. William Robinson. 1882. Repr. 11.00 o.s.i. Finch Pr.

Gods & Fighting Men: The Story of the Tuatha de Danaan & of the Fianna of Ireland. Isabella A. Gregory. (Coole Edition of the Collected Works of Lady Gregory Ser.). (Illus.). 1970. text ed. 23.00x (ISBN 0-19-519478-0). Oxford U Pr.

Gods and Golems: Five Short Novels of Science Fiction. Lester Del Rey. 1973. 1.25 (ISBN 0-345-03087-7). Ballantine.

Gods and Heroes: Or, The Kingdom of Jupiter. Robert Edward Francillon. LC 15-19999. 1915. Ginn and Company.

Gods and Mr. Perrin: A Tragi-Comedy. Hugh Walpole. LC 11-28077. 1911. The Century Co.

Gods and One. Alberta Pierson Hannum. LC 41-51662. Duell, Sloan and Pearce.

Gods and Their Makers. Laurence Housman. LC 7-7134. 1897. John Lane.

God's Angry Man. Leonard Ehrlich. LC 32-31307. 1932. Simon and Schuster.

God's Angry Man. Leonard Ehrlich. LC 34-244937. 1934. Simon and Schuster.

God's Angry Man. Leonard Ehrlich. LC 41-12245. The Press of the Readers Club.

God's Anointed. Mary Katherine Finigan Maule. LC 21-152551. 1921. The Century Co.

Gods Are a-Thirst. The Authorised Translation from the French by Alfred Allinson with an Introd. by Andre Maurois and Illus. by Jean Oberle. Anatole France, pseud. 1957. Heritage Press.

Gods Are Angry. 1st Ed. Wilfrid Noyce. LC 58-5780. 1958. World Pub. Co.

Gods Are Athirst. Anatole France, pseud. LC 53-9773. 1953. Roy.

Gods Are Athirst. Anatole France, pseud. Tr. by Alfred Richard Allison. LC 66-43267. 1927. J. Lane, the Bodley Head; New York, Dodd, Mead.

Gods Are Athirst. Anatole France, pseud. Tr. by Allinson, Alfred Richard. LC 13-12345. John Lane.

Gods Are Athirst. Anatole France, pseud. Tr. by Allinson, Alfred Richard. LC 13-9205. (Half-title: The works of Anatole France in an English translation, ed. by F. Chapman). John Lane.

Gods Are Athirst. Anatole France & Jackson, Emilie, ". LC 26-28542. 1925. Dodd, Mead & Company.

Gods Are Athirst: Anatole France. Linda Frey et al. LC 78-31742. 1978. lib. bdg. 22.50 (ISBN 0-8482-0846-3). Norwood Edns.

Gods Are Not Mocked. Anna Taylor. LC 69-11429. 1968. 5.95. Morrow.

Gods Are Not to Blame. Ola Rotimi. (Three Crowns Bks.). 80p. 1971. pap. 1.50x o.p. (ISBN 0-19-911080-8). Oxford U Pr.

Gods Arrive. Annie E Holdsworth. LC 7-6124. 1897. Dodd, Mead and Company.

Gods Arrive. David John Walsh. LC 28-3963. The Avondale Press, Incorporated.

Gods Arrive. Edith Newbold Jones Wharton. LC 69-17050. 1969. 6.95. Scribner.

Gods Arrive. Edith Newbold Jones Wharton. 1932. D. Appleton and Company.

Gods Arrive: A Novel of American Life and American Business, 1928-1935. Grant Lewi. LC 37-3752. J. B. Lippincott Company.

Gods Arrive. Centennial Ed. Edith Newbold Jones Wharton. LC 62-5792. 1962. Appleton-Century-Crofts.

God's Bits of Wood. Sembene Ousmane. LC 75-133620. 1970. 1.95. Anchor Books.

God's Bits of Wood. Translated by Francis Price. 1st Ed. Sembene Ousmane. LC 62-11298. 1962. Doubleday.

God's Carnival. Norma Octavia Lorimer. LC 20-8451. 1916. Brentano's.

God's Child. Terrence S. Lake. 4.95 o.p. Vantage.

God's Counterpoint. John Davys Beresford. LC 15-13907. 1.50. George H. Doran Company.

God's Country--and the Woman. James Oliver Curwood. LC 15-169865. 1915. Doubleday, Page & Company.

God's Country and the Woman. James Oliver Curwood. LC 40-32554. 1940. Triangle Books.

God's Country: The Trail of Happiness. James O. Curwood. 1976. Repr. of 1921 ed. lib. bdg. 9.55 (ISBN 0-88411-853-3). Amereon Ltd.

Gods Cry. 1st Ed. Lara B Cluff. LC 54-13140. 1955. Vantage Press.

God's Defector. John Bingham. 1982. 15.00 (ISBN 0-333-19441-1, Pub. by Macmillan England). State Mutual Bk.

God's Defector: The Case of the Missing Priest. John Michael Ward Bingham Clanmorris. LC 77-352207. 1976. 3.25 (ISBN 0-333-19441-1). Macmillan.

God's Diary. James Price. LC 73-624. 1973. 2.00 (ISBN 0-9600646-1-3). Millet Books.

God's Earth: A Novel. Joseph Arthur Horne. LC 89-3612. Logan-Price Publishing Co.
God's Failures. Joseph Smith Fletcher. LC 7-3078. 1897. J. Lane.
God's Fool! Frederick Ellsworth Wolf. LC 46-18162. 1946. New Age Publications.
God's Fool: A Biographical Novel of Cagliostro. Andrew Susac. LC 72-76995. 1972. 4.50. Doubleday.
God's Fool: A Koopstad Story. Jozua Marius Willem Van Der Poorten Schwartz. LC 4-16870. 1892. D. Appleton and Company.
God's Fool: A Novel of Rome. Lawrence David Moon. LC 80-29113. 1981. 12.95 (ISBN 0-531-09946-6). Watts.
Gods for Tomorrow. Hans Santesson. (O.s.i.). (Orig.). pap. 0.60 o.s.i. (A240, Award). Univ Pub & Dist.
Gods for Tomorrow. Ed. by Hans S. Santesson. (Orig.). pap. 0.60 o.p. (A240X, Award). Univ Pub & Dist.
God's Foundling. Alec John Dawson. LC 6-32253. (Half-title: Appletons' town and country library, no. 228). 1897. D. Appleton and Company.
God's Front Porch: A Novel. Ketti Frings. LC 44-133616. 1944. W. Morrow & Company.
God's Frontier. Martin Descalzo, Jose Luis. LC 59-11746. 1959. Knopf.
God's Frontier. Translated from the Spanish by Harriet De Onis. 1st American Ed. Jose Luis Martin Descalzo. LC 59-117463. 1959. Knopf.
God's Gentleman. Garry August. LC 32-26338. 1932. A. A. Knopf.
Gods Give My Donkey Wings. James Barr. LC 6-6072. (Carnation series, v. 5). 1895. Stone & Kimball.
God's Good Man: A Simple Love-Story. Marie Corelli. LC 4-23713. 1904. Dodd, Mead & Company.
God's Good Man: A Simple Love-Story. Marie Corelli. LC 41-32203. 1907. Dodd, Mead & Company.
God's Good Man: A Simple Love-Story. Marie Corelli. LC 16-13108. 1912. Dodd, Mead & Company.
God's Grace. Bernard Malamud. LC 82-11880. 75.00 (ISBN 0-374-16466-5) (ISBN 0-374-16465-7). Farrar Straus Giroux.
God's Helicopter. Lee Gutkind. LC 82-19533. (Illus.). 9.50 (ISBN 0-918366-26-7). Slow Loris Press.
God's Helicopter. Lee Gutkind. LC 82-19533. (Slow Loris Press Fiction Ser.). (Illus.). 180p. 1983. pap. 9.50 (ISBN 0-918366-26-7). Slow Loris.
God's High Table: A Contemporary Adventure-Romance of the Pacific Northwest. Leland Frederick Cooley. LC 61-9497. 1962. Doubleday.
God's Hitchhiker: A Novel. 1st Ed. Edmund Kiernan. LC 54-13406. 1955. Exposition Press.
Gods in a Vortex. David Houston. 1979. pap. 1.75 (ISBN 0-8439-0699-5, Leisure Bks). Nordon Pubns.
Gods in Exile. Heinrich Heine. (Illus.). 1962. 8.00 o.p.; soft 5.00 o.p. Grant Dahlstrom.
Gods in Green. Willo Davis Roberts. 1973. (pbk.) 1.50. Lancer.
God's Junkie & the Addict Church see Once a Junkie.
God's Lap. Josiah Pitts Woolfolk. LC 36-192628. 1936. Godwin.
Gods Laughed. Poul Anderson. 320p. 1983. pap. 2.95 (ISBN 0-523-48550-6). Pinnacle Bks.
God's Law and Man's. Mayble E. B Hallion. LC 27-13653. Dorrance and Company.
God's Little Acre. Erskine Caldwell. LC 62-18188. (Illus.). 1962. Farrar, Straus and Cudahy.
God's Little Acre. Erskine Caldwell. LC 49-48226. (uniform edition of the works of Erskine Caldwell). 1949. Duell, Sloan and Pearce.
God's Little Acre. Erskine Caldwell. LC 33-3291. 1933. The Viking Press.
God's Little Acre. Erskine Caldwell. LC 34-103886. (Half-title: The modern library of the world's best books). 1934. The Modern Library.
God's Little Acre. Erskine Caldwell. LC 46-40167. 1940. Grosset & Dunlap.
God's Little Acre. large print ed. Erskine Caldwell. LC 81-21197. 1982. 10.95 (ISBN 0-89621-329-3). Thorndike Press.
God's Little Boy. Hannah Hirshfield Rentzer. LC 57-4896. 1957. Vantage Press.
Gods Look Down. Trevor Hoyle. (Q Ser.). 192p. 1982. pap. 2.50 (ISBN 0-441-29497-9). Ace Bks.
God's Madcap: Amy Carmichael. Nancy Robbins. 1974. pap. 1.95 (ISBN 0-87508-604-7). Chr Lit.
God's Man: A Novel. George Fitzalan Bronson Howard. LC 15-19075. 1915. The Bobbs Merrill Company.
God's Man: A Novel in Woodcuts. Lynd Ward. LC 77-91889. (Illus.). 1978. 7.95 o.p. (ISBN 0-312-33100-2); pap. 4.95 o.p. (ISBN 0-312-33101-0). St Martin.
God's Man: A Novel on the Life of John Calvin. Norton-Taylor, Duncan. LC 79-52951. 8.95 (ISBN 0-8010-6729-4). Baker Book House.
God's Men. Pearl Sydenstricker Buck. LC 51-1694. 1951. J. Day Co.
Gods, Men and Ghosts: The Best Supernatural Fiction of Lord Dunsany. Edward John Moreton Drax Plunkett Dunsany. LC 75-164735. (Illus.). 1972. 3.00 (ISBN 0-486-22808-8). Dover Publications.
Gods of Aquarius. Brad Steiger. 1981. pap. 2.50 (ISBN 0-425-04753-9). Berkley Pub.
Gods of Cerus Major. Gary Alan Ruse. LC 80-2626. (Doubleday Science Fiction). 1982. 10.95 (ISBN 0-385-17118-8). Doubleday.
Gods of Foxcroft. David Levy. LC 77-122640. 1970. 6.95. Arbor House.
Gods of Mars. Edgar Rice Burroughs. LC 62-21542. 1962. Canaveral Press.
Gods of Mars. Edgar Rice Burroughs. LC 18-185381. 1918. A. C. McClurg & Co.
Gods of Mars. Edgar Rice Burroughs. LC 24-285308. 1919. Grosset & Dunlap.
Gods of Our Time. Cothburn O'Neal. LC 60-8631. 1960. Crown Publishers.
Gods of Racing. Ray Sanchez. LC 81-81002. 1981. pap. 5.95 (ISBN 0-930208-13-7). Mangan Bks.
Gods of Soldier Mountain: A Story of Pioneer Life in Idaho. Katherine Burns Hanford. LC 54-13418. 1955. Exposition Press.
Gods of the North. Robert E. Howard. (Illus.). 1977. pap. 4.95. Necronomicon.
Gods of Wealth and War: A Tale of Modern China. James Livingstone Stewart. LC 31-134791. Fleming H. Revell Company.
Gods of Xuma. David J Lake. 1.50 (ISBN 0-87997-360-9). DAW Books.
Gods of Yesterday. James Warner Bellah. LC 28-2672. 1928. D. Appleton & Company.
Gods on Horseback. Samuel G Baggett. LC 52-13866. 1952. McBride Co.
God's Orchid: Translated from the Swedish of Hjalmar Bergman. Hjammar Fredrik Elgerus Bergman. Tr. by Classen, Ernest. LC 24-4263. 1924. A. A. Knopf.
God's Other Son. Vinton E Hickman. LC 66-129191. lim. ed. pap., 2.95,. Author, Norran Av.
God's Other Son: The Life and Times of the Rev. Billy Sol Hargus: a Novel. Don Imus. LC 81-5268. 12.95 (ISBN 0-671-22537-5) (ISBN 0-671-43167-6). Simon and Schuster.
God's Pay Day: A Novel. Edgar Clifton Bross. 1898. G. W. Dillingham Co.
God's Pulpit: A Story of Southern Mountains. Frank L Gale. LC 27-22996. 1927. Printed by Milburn & Scott Co.
God's Puppets. William Allen White. LC 16-628892. 1916. The Macillan Company.
God's Rebel. Hulbert Fuller. LC 133. 1900. L. C. Page and Company (Inc.
God's Rennants: Stories of Israel Among the Nations. Samuel Gordon. LC 16-8811. 1916. 1.35. E. P. Dutton & Company.
God's Scarlet Law. Francis Henry Wade. LC 25-8378. The Oxford Press.
God's Secret. Arthur Stanwood Pier. LC 35-422119. 1935. C. Scribner's Sons.
Gods Some Mortals, and Lord Wickenham. Pearl Mary Teresa Richards Craigie. LC 6-31098. 1895. D. Appleton and Company.
God's Stepchildren. Sarah Gertrude Liebson Millin. LC 24-22676. Boni and Liveright.
God's Sunlight... Lewis Worthington Smith. 1901. T. Y. Crowell & Co.
Gods' Temptress. Irving A Greenfield. 1978. 1.75 (ISBN 0-440-14275-X). Dell Pub. Co.
God's Tenth. Doreen Eileen Agnew Wallace. LC 34-17656. 1933. Harper & Brothers.
Gods Themselves. Isaac Asimov. LC 72-180055. 1972. 5.95 (ISBN 0-385-02701-X). Doubleday.
Gods Themselves. Isaac Asimov. (Crest Book, P1829). 1973. 1.25. Fawcett.
God's Thumb Down. Oscar De Liso. LC 49-26278. 1949. C. Scribner's Sons.
God's Trombones. James W. Johnson. (Illus.). 1927. 9.95 (ISBN 0-670-34340-4). Viking Pr.
God's Warrior. Frank Gill Slaughter. LC 67-10379. (Pathway of faith series 2). 1967. Doubleday.
God's Way: Man's Way: A Story of Bristol. Henrietta M. K Brownell. LC 6-17218. 1885. The Catholic Publication Society Co.; Etc., Etc.
God's Wayward Son: A Novel. Robert Joseph Schmitz. LC 54-312844. 1954. Morris Pub. Co.
Gods Were Promiscuous. John Held. LC 83-8343. 1937. The Vanguard Press.
God's Wilderness. Howard Reed & Irene Reed. 2.50 o.p. Carlton.
God's Will: And Other Stories. Ilse Akunian & Macdonnell, Helen A., Tr. LC 7-14376. ("unknown" library no. 28). The Cassell Publishing Co.
Gods Will Have Blood. Anatole France, pseud Tr. by Frederick Davies from Fr. (Classics Ser.). 1980. pap. 3.95 (ISBN 0-14-044352-5). Penguin.
God's World; an Anthology of Short Stories. Najib Mahfuz. LC 73-79201. (Studies in Middle Eastern Literatures, No. 2). (Illus.). 1973. (ISBN 0-88297-006-2). Bibliotheca Islamica.
God's World: An Anthology of Short Stories. Najib Mahfuz. Tr. by Akef Abadir & Roger Allen. LC 73-79201. (Studies in Middle Eastern Literatures: No. 2). 1973. pap. 9.00x (ISBN 0-88297-006-2). Bibliotheca.
Godsend. Bernard Taylor. 1977. (ISBN 0-380-00943-9). Avon Books.
Godsend. Bernard Taylor. LC 75-40808. 7.95. St. Martin's Press.
Godsfire. Cynthia Felice. 1978. 1.75 (ISBN 0-671-81472-9). Pocket Books.
Godsfire. 1975. pap. write for info. (ISBN 0-88074-601-7). Metagam.
Godson. Joseph Buonanno. pap. 1.95 o.p. (ISBN 0-87056-246-0, 6246). Brandon.
Godson see House of Lions.
Godson, a Fantasy. Winifred Ashton. LC 64-57227. 1964. Norton.
Godson of a Marquis. Andre Theurie. LC 12-15064. (Half-title: Collection of foreign authors, no. IX). 1878. D. Appleton and Company.
Godwhale. T. J Bass. 1974. (pbk.) 1.25. Ballantine Books.
Godwits Fly. Robin Hyde. Ed. by Gloria Rawlinson. (New Zealand Fiction Ser). 1970. 4.50x o.p. (ISBN 0-19-647584-8). Oxford U Pr.
Godwulf Manuscript. Robert B. Parker. LC 73-11404. (Midnight novel of suspense). 1974. 5.95. Houghton Mifflin.
Godwulf Manuscript. Robert B. Parker. LC 79-14983. 1979. 11.50 (ISBN 0-89340-218-4). J. Curley & Associates.
Goering Testament. George Markstein. LC 78-19628. 1979. 8.95 (ISBN 0-345-28095-4). Ballantine Books.
Goering Treasure. Gordon Davis, pseud. 288p. (Orig.). 1980. pap. 2.25 (ISBN 0-89083-692-2). Zebra.
Goethe and Schiller. Klara Muller Mundt. (On cover: Lovell's library, no. 1054). 1887. J. W. Lovell Company.
Goethe and Schiller. Klara Muller Mundt. Tr. by Coleman, Chapman. LC 16-1227. (historical romances of Louisa Muhlbach pseud.). D. Appleton and Company.
Goethe and Schiller. An Historical Romance. Klara Muller Mundt. Tr. by Coleman, Chapman. LC 7-25467. 1868. D. Appleton and Company.
Goethe and Scott. George Henry Needler. LC 51-1285. 1950. Oxford University Press.
Goethe's Novels. Hans Siegbert Reiss. LC 74-145426. 1971. 10.00 (ISBN 0-87024-198-2). University of Miami Press.
Goethe's Occasional Poetry. E. M. Oppenheimer. LC 73-81761. 1974. 25.00x (ISBN 0-8020-5293-2). U of Toronto Pr.
Gog: A Novel. Andrew Sinclair. LC 67-23623. (Illus.). 1967. Macmillan.
Gog and Magog. Vincent Sheean. LC 30-24247. Harcourt, Brace and Company.
Goggle-Eyed Pirates. Lee Falk. (Adventures of the Phantom). 1974. (pbk.) 0.95. Avon.
Gogglers: A Political Satire. Edward Raiden. LC 67-29388. (Illus.). 1967. Saturn Books.
Gogol's Wife & Other Stories. Landolfi, Tommaso. LC 63-21382. 1963. New Directions.
Goha the Fool. Albert Ades & Josipovici, Albert, 1892- Joint Author. LC 23-18066. 1923. Lieber & Lewis.
Goin' Jack M. Bickham. (Orig.). 1971. pap. 0.95 o.p. (ISBN 0-446-65628-3, 65-628). Paperback Lib.
Goin' on Fourteen, Being Cross-Sections Out of a Year in the Life of an Average Boy. Irvin Shrewsbury Cobb. 2.50. George H. Doran Company.
Going. Sumner Locke Elliott. LC 74-1882. 1975. 7.95 (ISBN 0-06-011242-5). Harper & Row.
Going. Sumner Locke Elliott. 1976. (pbk.) 1.75 (ISBN 0-671-80406-5). Pocket Books.
Going Abroad. Rose Macaulay. LC 34-24630. 1934. Harper & Brothers.
Going After Cacciato. Tim O'Brien. 1978. 8.95 o.p. (ISBN 0-440-02948-1, Sey Lawr). Delacorte.
Going After Cacciato: A Novel. Tim O'Brien. LC 77-11723. 8.95 (ISBN 0-440-02948-1). Delacorte Press/S. Lawrence.
Going All the Way. Dan Wakefield. LC 74-121870. ("A Seymour Lawrence book."). 1970. 6.95. Delacorte Press.
Going and Son: A Novel. Monk. LC 7-25454. 1869. American News Company.
Going Blind. Jonathan Penner. LC 76-29723. 7.95 (ISBN 0-671-22452-2). Simon and Schuster.
Going Blind. Jonathan Penner. LC 77-15532. 1977. 10.95 (ISBN 0-8161-6541-6). G. K. Hall.
Going Blind. Jonathan Penner. (Jove/HBJ Book). 1978. 1.75 (ISBN 0-515-04541-1). Jove Pubns.
Going Down. Oliver Cote. LC 78-70409. 1979. 9.95x o.p. (ISBN 0-917300-09-2); pap. 5.00 (ISBN 0-917300-08-4). Miles & Weir.
Going Down. David Markson. LC 79-103549. 1970. 5.95. Holt, Rinehart, Winston.
Going Down Fast. Marge Piercy. LC 78-79675. 1969. 6.95. Trident Press.
Going Down River Road. Meja Mwangi. LC 76-383416. (African writers series; 176). (H.E.B. paperback). 1976. 1.30 (ISBN 0-435-90176-1). Heinemann Educational.
Going for Mr. Big. Robert Gover. LC 72-12806. 1973. (pbk.) 1.50. Bantam Books.
Going for the Gold. Emma Lathen, pseud. LC 80-20835. 10.95 (ISBN 0-671-41407-0). Simon and Schuster.
Going for the Gold. large print ed. Emma Lathen, pseud. LC 81-4822. 1981. 12.95 (ISBN 0-8161-3200-3). G.K. Hall.
Going for the Rain. Simon J. Ortiz. LC 76-8707. 128p. 1976. 6.95i (ISBN 0-06-451511-7, HarpT); pap. 2.50 (ISBN 0-06-451512-5, HarpT). Har-Row.
Going Gently. Robert C. S Downs. LC 72-86551. 1973. 6.95. Bobbs-Merrill.
Going, Going, Gone: An Asey Mayo Mystery. Phoebe Atwood Taylor. 1943. W. W. Norton & Company, Inc.
Going, Going, Gone: An Asey Mayo Mystery. Phoebe Atwood Taylor. LC 45-13290. 1944. The Blakiston Company.
Going, Goingg, Gone: An Asey Mayo Mystery, by Phoebe Atwood Taylor. Phoebe Atwood Taylor. 1966. bds., 3.95. Norton.
Going Grand: A Novel. Jack MacLeod. LC 82-139224. 14.95 (ISBN 0-7710-5563-3). McClelland and Stewart.
Going Home. Edward Bernard. 1973. 4.95 o.p. (ISBN 0-8059-1796-9). Dorrance.
Going Home. Doris May Lessing. 256p. 1975. pap. 2.75 (ISBN 0-445-03089-5). Popular Lib.
Going Home. Danielle Steel. 1982. pap. 2.95 (ISBN 0-671-45764-0). PB.
Going Home. Danielle Steel. (General Ser.). 1982. lib. bdg. 13.95 (ISBN 0-8161-3378-6, Large Print Bks). G K Hall.
Going Home. Danielle Steel. 1973. (pbk.) 1.25 (ISBN 0-671-78332-7). Pocket Books.
Going Home. Danielle Steele. LC 82-12148. 1982. 13.95. G.K. Hall.
Going in Style. Robert Grossbach. (Orig.). 1979. 2.25 (ISBN 0-446-92485-7). Warner Bks.
Going It Alone. Michael Innes, pseud. 196p. 1980. 7.95 o.p. (ISBN 0-396-07819-2). Dodd.
Going It Alone. John Innes Mackintosh Stewart. LC 79-27521. 7.95 (ISBN 0-396-07819-2). Dodd, Mead.
Going Like Sixty. Richard Armour. (Adult Ser.). 178p. 1974. Repr. lib. bdg. 6.95 o.p. (ISBN 0-8161-6222-0, Large Print Bks). G K Hall.
Going Nowhere: A Novel. Alvin Greenberg. LC 71-154102. 1971. 4.95 (ISBN 0-671-20957-4). Simon and Schuster.
Going of the White Swan. Gilbert Parker. LC 12-27595. 1912. 0.75. D. Appleton and Company.
Going on Like This. John R. Gardiner. LC 82-73016. 224p. 1983. 12.95 (ISBN 0-689-11347-1). Atheneum.
Going Places. Candice Adams. (Love & Life Romance Ser.). (Orig.). 1982. pap. write for info. (ISBN 0-345-30525-6). Ballantine.
Going Places. Bertrand Blier. LC 74-13135. 1974. 7.95 (ISBN 0-397-01013-3) (ISBN 0-397-01013-3). Lippincott.
Going Places. Leonard Michaels. LC 69-13739. 1969. 4.95. Farrar, Straus & Giroux.
Going Places. William Stafford. 1976. pap. 2.50 o.p. (ISBN 0-915596-05-9). West Coast.
Going Public. Jack King. 1981. 5.95 (ISBN 0-917530-12-8); pap. fiction. Pig Iron Pr.
Going Public. David Westheimer. 1976. 1.50. Dell.
Going Snake Affair, No. 1. Joyce McKennon. (Orig.). 1979. pap. 1.95 (ISBN 0-532-23244-5). Woodhill.
Going Some: A Romance of Strenuous Affection. Rex Ellingwood Beach. LC 10-11140. 1910. 1.25. Harper & Brothers.
Going Somewhere. Max Ewing. LC 33-644. 1933. A. A. Knopf.
Going Their Own Ways: A Novel of Modern Marriage. Alec Waugh. LC 39-27012. Farrar & Rinehart, Incorporated.
Going Through the Motions: A Novel. Katherine Govier. LC 82-17041. 12.95 (ISBN 0-312-33135-5). St. Martin's Press.
Going to California. David Littlejohn. LC 80-16698. 11.95 (ISBN 0-698-11042-0). Coward, McCann & Geoghegan.
Going to Extreme's. Joe McGinniss. 1982. pap. 3.50 (ISBN 0-451-11819-7, AE1819, Sig). NAL.
Going to Jerusalem. Jerome Charyn. 1971. pap. 2.45 o.p. (ISBN 0-03-085489-X). HR&W.
Going to Jerusalem. Roger Dixon. LC 76-58023. 1977. 7.95 (ISBN 0-698-10813-2). Coward, McCann & Geoghegan.
Going to Jerusalem: A Novel. Judith Bruder. LC 79-12828. (Illus.). 9.95 (ISBN 0-671-24599-6). Simon and Schuster.

Going to Jerusalem: A Novel. Jerome Charyn. LC 67-21890. 1967. Viking Press.
Going to Jerusalem: A Novel. Roger Dixon. LC 76-58023. 224p. 1977. 7.95 o.p. (ISBN 0-698-10813-2, Coward). Putnam Pub Group.
Going to Meet the Man. James B. Baldwin. LC 65-15331. 1965. Dial Press.
Going to St. Ives. Anne Colver. LC 36-4200. 1936. Macrae Smith Company.
Going to the River. Fitz Gibbon, Constantine. LC 63-15869. 1963. W. W. Norton.
Going Under. Lidiia Korneevna Chukovskaia. LC 74-17403. 1975-1976. 6.95 (ISBN 0-8129-0510-5). Quadrangle/New York Times Book Co.
Going Under. Lidiia Koveneevna Chukovskaia. Tr. by Peter M. Weston from Rus. LC 75-36258. 144p. 1976. 6.95 o.p. (ISBN 0-8129-0510-5). Times Bks.
Going Under: Melville's Short Fiction and the American 1850s. Marvin Junior Fisher. LC 77-2986. 12.50 (ISBN 0-8071-0267-9). Louisiana State University Press.
Going West. Basil King. LC 19-13844. Harper & Brothers.
Golconda Bonanza. Jerome Alfred Hart. LC 23-17116. The Pioneer Press.
Gold. Clarence Budington Kelland. LC 31-7182. 1931. Harper & Brothers.
Gold. Wilbur A Smith. (Illus.). 1974. (pbk.) 1.50 (ISBN 0-515-02961-0). Pyramid Books.
Gold. Jakob Wassermann & Willcox, Mrs. Louise (Collier) 1865-1929, Tr. LC 24-11234. (Half-title: The European library, ed. by J. E. Spingarn). Harcourt, Brace and Company.
Gold. Stewart Edward White & Saxton, Eugene Francis, 1884- LC 13-212965. 1913. Doubleday, Page & Co.
Gold--and the Mounted. James Beardsley Hendryx. LC 28-231094. 1928. Doubleday, Doran & Company, Inc.
Gold" A Dutch-Indian Story. Annie Linden. LC 7-19014. 1896. The Century Co.
Gold: A Novel. Kenneth Perkins. LC 29-17279. 1929. Frederick A. Stokes Company.
Gold. A Novell. Laura Daintrey. 1893. G. W. Dillingham.
Gold and Dross: Or, The False Life and the True. S. A. Southworth. LC 8-10841. 1890. J. H. Earle.
Gold & Fish Signatures. Paul Reps. LC 68-29544. (Illus., Orig.). 1968. pap. 4.25 (ISBN 0-8048-0210-6). C E Tuttle.
Gold & Flesh. Benjamin Appel. Orig. Title: Four Roads to Death. 1972. pap. 0.95 o.p. (532-95185-095). Manor Bks.
Gold and Guilt: Or, The Mystery of Norwood. Edwin Sheppard. LC 8-5117. 1877. J. A. Moore.
Gold and Guns on Halfaday Creek. James Beardsley Hendryx. LC 42-147421. 1942. Carlton House.
Gold and Incense: A West Country Story. Mark Guy Pearse. LC 7-33501. 1895. Hunt & Eaton.
Gold and Iron. Joseph Hergesheimer. LC 18-14422. 1918. A. A. Knopf.
Gold and Name. Marie Sofle Birath Schwartz. Tr. by Borg, Selma & Shipley, Marie Adelaide (Brown) LC 8-2067. 1871. Lee and Shepard.
Gold and Silver Hooks. Ruth Moore. LC 69-11244. 1969. 5.95. Morrow.
Gold and the Glory. Chet Cunningham. 1977. 1.75. (ISBN 0-8439-0450-X). Leisure Books.
Gold Bag. Carolyn Wells. LC 11-2075. 1911. J. B. Lippincott Company.
Gold Bag. Carolyn Wells. LC 20-156046. 1917. A. L. Burt Company.
Gold Bait. Walter J. Sheldon. 1973. pap. 0.75 o.p. (T2691, GM). Fawcett World.
Gold Brick. George Timothy Bludworth. LC 33-10970. The Christopher Publishing House.
Gold Brick. Brand Whitlock. LC 10-23399. The Bobbs-Merrill Company.
Gold Brick Island. Alfred Walter Stewart. LC 33-10984. 1933. Little, Brown, and Company.
Gold-Bug. Edgar Allan Poe. LC 99-3403. (The young of heart series, 16). D. Estes & Company.
Gold Bug. Edgar Allan Poe. Ed. by Gildemeister, Theda. LC 2-10717. (Half-title: The Canterbury classicsw). Rand, McNally & Company.
Gold-Bug. Edgar Allan Poe. Ed. by Boyer, Philip Albert. LC 22-452910. 1921. Franklin Publishing and Supply Co., Inc.
Gold Bug. Edgar Allan Poe. Ed. by Hervey Allen. Mabbott, Thomas Ollive 1898- Ed. LC 28-192482. 1928. Rimington & Hooper.
Gold Bug see Murders in the Rue Morgue.
Gold Bug: And Other Selections from the Works of Edgar Allan Poe. Edgar Allan Poe. Ed. by Stewart, Robert Armistead. LC 12-8671. (Graded classic series). 0.25. B. F. Johnson Publishing Company.
Gold Bug: And Other Stories. Edgar Allan Poe. Ed. by William Kottmeyer. LC 47-19864. (The Everyreader library). 1947. Webster Publishing Company.
Gold Bug & Other Stories. Edgar Allan Poe. Ed. by William Kottmeyer et al. (Everyreader Ser). 1947. pap. 2.28 o.p. (ISBN 0-07-033735-7). McGraw.
Gold-Bug, and Other Tales. Edgar Allan Poe. LC 64-22334. (International pocket library, 22). 1965. International Pocket Library.
Gold Bug: And Other Tales and Poems. Edgar Allan Poe. LC 53-8488. (New children's classics). (Illus.). 1953. Macmillan.
Gold-Bug and Other Tales and Poems: By Edgar Allan Poe, Pictures by Carlos Sanchez, M. Edgar Allan Poe. LC 30-13873. (The Macmillan children's classics). 1930. The Macmillan Company.
Gold Bug: And The Black Cat. raven ed. Edgar Allan Poe. LC 384. R. E. Fenno & Company.
Gold Bug: The Purloined Letter, and Other Tales. Edgar Allan Poe. Ed. by Trent, William Peterfield. LC 14-21000. (Riverside literature series. no. 120). Houghton, Mifflin and Company.
Gold Bullets. Charles Gordon Booth. LC 29-1198. 1929. W. Morrow & Company.
Gold by Gemini. Jonathan Gash, pseud. LC 78-20205. 8.95 (ISBN 0-06-011463-0). Harper & Row.
Gold by Gold. Herbert S Gorman. LC 25-4605. 1925. Boni and Liveright.
Gold Cache. James Willard Schultz. LC 17-24276. 1917. 1.25. Houghton Mifflin Company.
Gold Chase. Robert William Chambers. LC 35-127725. 1935. D. Appleton-Century Company, Incorporated.
Gold Coast. Elmore Leonard. 224p. (Orig.). 1980. pap. 2.25 (ISBN 0-553-13321-7). Bantam.
Gold Coast Nocturne. Helen Nielsen. LC 51-12802. 1951. Washburn.
Gold Coin Robbery. Bob Wright. (Tom & Ricky Mystery Ser.: No. 2). (Illus.). 48p. 1983. pap. 2.00 (ISBN 0-87879-337-2). Acad Therapy.
Gold Comes in Bricks. A. A. Fair, pseud. LC 40-308823. 1940. W. Morrow & Company.
Gold Comes in Bricks. Erle Stanley Gardner. LC 40-30882. 1940. W. Morrow.
Gold Connection. Robin Moore & Julian Askin. 384p. 1980. pap. 2.50 (ISBN 0-441-29747-1, Pub. by Charter Bks). Ace Bks.
Gold Connection. Robin Moore & Julian Askin. LC 78-74946. 1979. pap. 2.50 o.s.i. (ISBN 0-89516-061-7). Condor Pub Co.
Gold Cord. Amy Carmichael. 1957. pap. 4.50 (ISBN 0-87508-068-5). Chr Lit.
Gold Country Nurse. Ethel E. Bangert. (YA) 1972. 4.50 o.p. (Avalon). Bouregy.
Gold Crew. Thomas N. Scortia & Frank M. Robinson. LC 79-23066. 1980. 12.50 (ISBN 0-446-60001-6). Warner Books.
Gold Crew. Thomas N. Scortia & Frank M. Robinson. 1981. 2.95 (ISBN 0-446-83522-6). Warner Books.
Gold Cure Curios. Harry W B Kantner. LC 7-11666. (Silver state series, v. 1, no. 1). The Silver State Engraving, Printing and Publishing Co.
Gold Diggers. Robert Creeley. 160p. 1980. pap. 6.95 (ISBN 0-7145-0256-1, Pub. by M Boyars). Merrimack Pub Cir.
Gold Diggers. Robert Creeley. 1972. pap. 2.45 o.p. (ISBN 0-684-12724-5, SL326). Scribner.
Gold Diggers. Andrew Magnus Fleming. LC 31-773. Meador Publishing Company.
Gold Diggers. Paul Monette. LC 78-67405. 4.95 (ISBN 0-380-43026-6). Avon.
Gold Diggers. And Other Stories. Robert Creeley. LC 65-23982. 3.95, 1.65 pap.,. Scribners.
Gold Diggers of Broadway. Eve Bernstein & Hopwood, Avery. LC 29-22417. Efrus & Bennett, Inc.
Gold Dollar: Studies in Nature and Life. Joseph M Duff. LC 26-91155. Fleming H. Revell Company.
Gold Door. Ardath Wise. 1972. 4.95. Lenox Hill Pr.
Gold Dust. Louise March. 1980. 10.00. Rochester Folk Art.
Gold Dust. Charlotte Mary Yonge. 1.50 o.p. (ISBN 0-448-01641-9). G&D.
Gold Dust: A Novel. Emeline Daggett Harvey. (On cover: The lotus library, v. l, no. 2). 1892. The Lotus Publishing Company.
Gold Dust & Ashes. Ion L. Idriess. 1967. Repr. pap. 1.25 o.s.i. Tri-Ocean.
Gold-Dust Darrell: Or, The Wizard of the Mines. Nathan D. Urner. (On cover: Secret service series, no. 30). 1890. Street & Smith.
Gold Earth. H. Kay Leung. 1982. 6.95 (ISBN 0-533-05382-X). Vantage.
Gold Elsie. Eugenie John. LC 7-99013. (On cover: Lovell's library. no. 1053). J. W. Lovell Company.
Gold Elsie. Eugenie John. Tr. by Wister, Annis Lee (Furness) LC 4-16862. 1896. J. B. Lippincott Company.
Gold Elsie: From the German of E. Marlitt Pseud.... Eugenie John. Tr. by Wister, Annis Lee (Furness) 1883. J. B. Lippincott & Co.
Gold Falcon: Or, The Haggard of Love, Being the Adventures of Manfred, Airman and Poet of the World War, and Later, Husband and Father, in Search of Freedom and Personal Sunrise, in the City of New York, and of the Consummationof His Life. LC 33-23676. 1933. H. Smith and R. Haas.
Gold Fever. David Case. 224p. (Orig.). 1982. pap. 2.25 (ISBN 0-505-51763-9). Tower Bks.
Gold Fever. David Norman. (Frontier Rakers Ser.: No. 3). 512p. (Orig.). 1980. pap. 2.50 (ISBN 0-89083-621-3). Zebra.
Gold Fish of Gran Chimu. Charles Fletcher Lummis. LC 7-14506. 1896. Lamson, Wolffe and Company.
Gold Fish of Gran Chimu. Charles Fletcher Lummis. LC 11-6443. 1911. A. C. McClurg & Co.
Gold for My Bride. Norman Collins. LC 40-13261. Harper & Brothers.
Gold for My Fair Lady. Sidney Hobson Courtier. LC 51-14547. 1951. A. A. Wyn.
Gold for Prince Charlie. Nigel G. Tranter. 1981. 18.95x (Pub. by Remploy England). State Mutual Bk.
Gold for the Caesars. Florence Augusta Seward. LC 61-5519. 1961. N.J., Prentice-Hall.
Gold for the Dead. Bradford Scott. LC 47-31456. 1947. Arcadia House.
Gold from Crete: Ten Stories. Cecil Scott Forester. LC 73-121441. 1970. 5.95. Little, Brown.
Gold Gap. Frank Gruber. LC 68-12454. 1968. Dutton.
Gold Gauze Veil. Opie Percival Read. LC 27-259248. 1927. The Canterbury Press.
Gold Girl. James Beardsley Hendryx. LC 20-6633. 1920. G. P. Putnam's Sons.
Gold Goes to the Mountain. Clay Turner. 1974. (pbk.) 0.95. Warner Paperback Library.
Gold, Gore & Gehenna. James Owen Hannay. LC 27-20082. The Bobs-Merrill Company.
Gold, Grace and Glory: A Story of Religious Life Among the Wealthy Classes of the West and South. W. H Mize. LC 7-25320. 1896. G. W. Dillingham.
Gold, Guns & Ghost Towns. W. A. Chalfant. 12.95 (ISBN 0-912494-33-6); pap. 7.95. Chalfant Pr.
Gold-Hatted Lover. Edmund Keeley. 1971. pap. 0.95 o.p. (09082). Curtis.
Gold-Hatted Lover: A Novel. 1st Ed. Edmund Keeley. LC 61-128071. 1961. Little, Brown.
Gold Hill Showdown. Charles E Wheeler. (YA) 1980. 6.95 (Avalon). Bouregy.
Gold Hungry. Glenhope Russell Stevens. LC 27-17411. Tribune Publishing Company.
Gold Hunters. James Oliver Curwood. LC 44-21220. 1944. Triangle Books.
Gold Hunters: A Story of Life & Adventure in the Hudson Bay Wilds. James Oliver Curwood. LC 9-22185. 1909. 1.50. The Bobbs-Merrill Company.
Gold Hunters' Adventures: Or, Life in Australia. William Henry Thomes. LC 8-20096. (Half-title: The gold-hunter's library). 1883. Donnelley, Loyd & Co.
Gold Hunters' Adventures: Or, Life in Australia. William Henry Thomes. (On cover: The detective and adventure library, no. 2). 1889. A. T. Loyd & Co.
Gold Hunter's Adventures: Or, Life in Australia. William Henry Thomes. (On cover: The library of choice fiction, no. 3). 1890. Laird & Lee.
Gold Hunters in Europe: Or, The Dead Alive. William Henry Thomes. LC 8-20095. (Half-title: The gold hunter's library). 1884. A. T. Loyd & Co.
Gold Hunters in Europe: Or, The Dead Alive. William Henry Thomes. (On cover: The detective and adventure library, no. 6). 1889. A. T. Loyd & Co.
Gold Hunters in Europe: Or, The Dead Alive. Thomes, William Henry. (On cover: The library of choice fiction, no. 43). 1892. Laird & Lee.
Gold in California! Willis Todhunter Ballard. LC 65-11058. 1965. Doubleday.
Gold in California! By Todhunter Ballard. Willis Todhunter Ballard. (Star bk., A-9). 1967. Ace.
Gold in Cumberland Valley-? Charles Tylsday. LC 76-26342. (His Sand's; 1). (Illus.). Tylsday.
Gold in Every Grave. Hugh Lawrence Nelson. LC 51-11617. (Murray Hill mystery). 1951. Rinehart.
Gold in Her Hair, No. 2. Anne Neville, pseud. (Starlight Romance Ser.). 144p. 1981. pap. 1.75 (ISBN 0-553-14364-6). Bantam.
Gold in Silver City. Frances E Hess. LC 39-4386. Chancery Row Printing House.
Gold in the Black Hills. Steve Mensing. (Orig.). 1981. pap. 1.75 (ISBN 0-505-51644-6). Tower Bks.
Gold in the Blue Ridge. Pauline B. Innis & Walter Dean Innis. 1982. 12.50 o.p. Caroline Hse.
Gold in the Blue Ridge: The True Story of the Beale Treasure. Pauline B Innis & Walter Dean Innis. LC 72-97710. (Illus.). 1973. 7.95. R. B. Luce.
Gold in the Glass. Virginia Chaquet. LC 75-10247. 1970. 6.95 o.p. (ISBN 0-03-084515-7). HR&W.
Gold in the Glass: A Novel. Virginia Chaquet. LC 75-102437. 1970. 6.95. Holt, Rinehart and Winston.
Gold in the Sea: Stories. 1st Ed. in the U. S. A. Brian Friel. LC 66-209698. 1966. 4.50. Doubleday.
Gold in the Sky. Max Catto. LC 57-104059. 1958. W. Morrow.
Gold in the Streets. Mary Vardoulakis. LC 45-9770. 1945. Dodd, Mead & Company.
Gold Is Where You Find It. James Beardsley Hendryx. LC 53-9995. (Double D western). 1953. Doubleday.
Gold Is Where You Find It. H. C. James. LC 49-10490. 1949. T. Y. Crowell Co.
Gold Is Where You Find It. Clements Ripley. LC 36-20444. 1936. D. Appleton-Century Company, Incorporated.
Gold Key. A Dramatic Story. LC 16-9351. 1869. J. B. Lippincott & Co.
Gold-Killer: A Mystery of the New Underworld. John Prosper. LC 22-7925. 1.75. George H. Doran Company.
Gold Lovers: Formerly Titled The Zolotov Affair. Robert H. Rimmer. LC 80-21894. 1980. 12.50 (ISBN 0-8290-0224-3). Irvington Publishers.
Gold Maker. Otto Boutin. (Orig.). 1981. pap. 1.95 (ISBN 0-8439-0923-4, Leisure Bks). Nordon Pubns.
Gold Medal. Rory Kashdan. 192p. (Orig.). 1973. pap. 1.95 o.p. (ISBN 0-87056-345-9, 6345). Brandon.
Gold, Men & Dogs. A. Allan. Repr. of 1931 ed. 14.00 o.s.i. Finch Pr.
Gold Mine. Betty Janson. LC 24-225219. The Covenant Book Concern.
Gold Mine. Wilbur A Smith. LC 74-116253. 1970. 5.95. Doubleday.
Gold-Mine Jail. Lester Wayne Merha. 1982. pap. 6.95 (Avalon). Bouregy.
Gold Mines of the Gila. A Sequel to Old Hicks the Guide. Charles Wilkins Webber. LC 8-36748. 1849. DeWitt & Davenport.
Gold Mountain. Charlotte Paul. LC 53-6907. 1953. Random House.
Gold Mountain. Charlotte Paul. 1977. 1.95 (ISBN 0-441-29802-8). Ace Books.
Gold Must Be Tried by Fire. Richard Aumerle Maher. LC 17-10983. 1917. The Macmillan Company.
Gold of Chickaree. Susan Warner & Warner, Anna Bartlett, 1820- Joint Author. LC 8-33706. 1876. G. P. Putnam's Sons.
Gold of Evening. Marjorie M Bitker. 1975. (pbk.) 1.25. Popular Library.
Gold of Fiddler's Gulch. Ernest Klette. LC 33-31757. 1933. Overlanoutwest Publications.
Gold of Freedom. Charles Edwin Winter. LC 44-10712. 1944. The Naylor Company.
Gold of Her Glory. Emmet Russell. LC 51-8667. 1951. Van Kampen Press.
Gold of Karinthy. Diana La Point. (Belmont Tower Books). 1978. 1.95 (ISBN 0-505-51261-0). Tower Pubns.
Gold of Malabar. Berkely Mather. LC 67-13422. 1967. bds., 4.95. Scribners.
Gold of Ophir. D. Howard Gwinn. LC 98-2172. F. T. Neely.
Gold of Ophir. D. Howard Gwinn. 1902. The Abbey Press.
Gold of Smoky Mess. Johnston McCulley. LC 42-203311. 1942. Gateway Books.
Gold of the Gods: The Mystery of the Incas Solved by Craig Kennedy--Scientific Detective. Arthur Benjamin Reeve. LC 15-24671. 1915. Hearst's International Library Co.
Gold of the River Sea. Charlton Ogburn. LC 65-113306. 6.95. Morrow.
Gold of Their Bodies: A Novel About Gauguin. Charles O Gorham. LC 55-709556. 1955. Dial Press.
Gold of Toulouse. Henry Bertram Law Webb. LC 36-9942. C. Kendall and W. Sharp, Inc.
Gold of Troy. Robert L Fish. LC 79-8560. 1980. 11.95 (ISBN 0-385-15260-4). Doubleday.
Gold on Her Shoulder. Caryl Hall. LC 64-17428. 1964. Funk & Wagnalls.
Gold on the Hoof. Walker A Tompkins. LC 52-140001. 1953. Macrae Smith Co.
Gold on Your Pillow. Angela Morgan, pseud. 3.00 o.p. (ISBN 0-87516-063-8). De Vorss.
Gold Out of Celebes. Aylward Edward Dingle. LC 20-8238. 1920. 1.75. Little, Brown and Company.
Gold Pencil. 1st Ed. Malcolm Stuart Boylan. LC 53-5258. 1953. Little, Brown.
Gold-Plated Hearse. Joseph Hedges. (Stark Ser.: No. 4). (Orig.). 1975. pap. 1.25 o.p. (ISBN 0-515-03708-7, V3708). Pyramid Pubns.
Gold-Plated Sin. Barry Devlin. LC 53-366888. 1953. Vixen Press.

TITLE INDEX GOLDEN COCKATRICE.

Gold Point: And Other Strange Stories. Charles Loring Jackson. LC 26-2810. 1926. The Stratford Company.
Gold-Rimmed Spectacles. Giorgio Bassani. 1960. 3.00 o.p. Atheneum.
Gold-Rimmed Spectacles. Translated from the Italian by Isabel Quigly. Giorgio Bassani. LC 60-11035. 3.00. Atheneum Publishers.
Gold Robbers. Celeste De Chabrillan. Orig. Title: Voleurs D'or. (Illus.). 1971. pap. 2.50 o.s.i. Tri-Ocean.
Gold Robbers. Moreton De Chabrillan, Elisabeth Celeste (Venard) De. LC 76-28515. (Illus.). 1970. 1.25 (ISBN 0-7251-0102-4). Sun Books.
Gold Seekers. A Tale of California. Gustave Aimard & St. John, Percy Bolingbroke, 1821-1889, Ed. LC 5-42203. (On cover: Lovell's library, no 1127). 1888. J. W. Lovell Company.
Gold Shield. Marie Castoire & Richard Posner. LC 82-7607. (est.) 15.95 (ISBN 0-399-12734-8). Putnam.
Gold Shield. Joseph Sorrentino. 1980. pap. 2.25 (ISBN 0-440-13097-2). Dell.
Gold Shod. Newton A Fuessle. LC 21-15187. Boni and Liveright.
Gold Shoe. Grace Livingston Hill. LC 30-29254. 1930. J. B. Lippincott Company.
Gold Shoe. Grace Livingston Hill. 1976. (pbk.) 1.25 (ISBN 0-553-02515-5). Bantam Books.
Gold Shoe. Grace Hill Livingston. 224p. 1976. pap. 1.75 (ISBN 0-553-12929-5). Bantam.
Gold Sickle: Or, Hena, the Virgin of the Isle of Sen. Eugene Sue & De Leon, Daniel, 1852-1914, Tr. LC 5-4548. 1904. New York Labor News Company.
Gold Skull Murders... Frank Lucius Packard. LC 31-33330. Pub. for the Crime Club, Inc., by Doubleday, Doran & Company, Inc.
Gold-Stealers: A Story of Waddy. Edward George Dyson. LC 1-27060. 1901. Longmans, Green.
Gold Strike. Peter McCurtin. (Sundance Ser.: No. 35). 1980. pap. 1.75 (ISBN 0-8439-0819-X, Leisure Bks). Nordon Pubns.
Gold Strike in Hell. Darwin Seymour Lambert. LC 64-13832. (Double D western). 1964. Doubleday.
Gold That Did Not Glitter. A Novel. Virginius Dabney. LC 6-32226. 1889. J. B. Lippincott Company.
Gold, Tinsel and Trash: Stories of Country and City. Erasmus W Jones. LC 7-11909. 1890. Hunt & Eaton.
Gold to Remember. Mary Wibberley. (Harlequin Presents Ser.). 192p. 1981. pap. 1.50 (ISBN 0-373-10432-4, Pub. by Harlequin). PB.
Gold Tooth. Eric Temple Bell. LC 27-22050. E. P. Dutton & Company.
Gold Torque: A Story of Galloway in Early Christian Times. Andrew McCormick. LC 52-16193. 1951. W. MacLellan.
Gold Town Gunman: A Western Novel. Ray Townsend. LC 54-31868. (Popular library, 590). 1954. Popular Library.
Gold Trackers. Hart-Davis, Duff. LC 73-103751. 1970. 5.95. Doubleday.
Gold Trail. Harold Bindloss. 1.30. Frederick A. Stokes Company.
Gold Trail: A Romance of the South Seas. Henry De Vere Stacpoole. LC 16-15154. 1916. 1.30. John Lane Company.
Gold Train. Chet Cunningham. (Jim Steel Ser.: No. 5). (Orig.). 1981. pap. 1.75 (ISBN 0-505-51615-2). Tower Bks.
Gold Train to San Miguil. Joseph A. Nyman. 111p. 1973. 3.95 o.p. (ISBN 0-533-00805-0). Vantage.
Gold Tried in the Fire: By C.M. Sic McConnell. 1st Ed. Charles W McConnell. LC 53-129126. 1953. Pageant Press.
Gold Under Skull Peak. O'Rourke, Frank. LC 52-5146. 1951. Random House.
Gold Wagon. Chet Cunningham. 1980. pap. 1.50 o.s.i. (ISBN 0-505-51460-5). Tower Bks.
Gold Was Our Grave: By Henry Wade Pseud. Harry Lancelot Aubrey-Fletcher. LC 54-12921. (Cock Robin mystery). 1954. Macmillan.
Gold Wolf. Robert Ames Bennet. LC 32-529426. 1932. G. H. Watt.
Gold Wolf. Max Pemberton. LC 3-6457. 1903. Dodd, Mead & Company.
Gold Worshipers. John Burland Harris-Burland. LC 6-42432. 1906. G. W. Dillingham Company.
Goldbug & Other Stories: The Black Cat, the Pit & the Pendulum. Edgar Allan Poe. (Illus.). 1962. pap. 2.50 (ISBN 0-8283-1437-3, 22, IPL). Branden.
Goldchester: More High Fantasy Adventures. Jeffrey Dillow. 1982. text ed. 15.95 o.p. (ISBN 0-8359-2568-4); pap. text ed. 13.95 (ISBN 0-8359-2567-6). Reston.
Golden Acre. Thyra Ferre Bjorn. LC 74-23893. 1975. 5.95 (ISBN 0-8007-0691-9). F. H. Revell Co.
Golden Acres: By Cynthia Millburn Pseud. Anne Tedlock Brooks. LC 50-11746. 1950. Arcadia House.
Golden Admiral. Francis Van Wyck Mason. LC 52-13559. 1953. Doubleday.
Golden Age. Constantine Fitz Gibbon. LC 75-4546. 1975. 6.95 (ISBN 0-393-08683-6). Norton.
Golden Age. Constantine Fitz Gibbon. (O.s.i.). 189p. 1975. 7.95 o.s.i. (ISBN 0-393-08683-6). Norton.
Golden Age. Kenneth Grahame. LC 4-23592. 1895. Stone & Kimball.
Golden Age. Kenneth Grahame. LC 4-16307. 1899. J. Lane.
Golden Age. Kenneth Grahame. LC 25-155046. 1900. John Lane.
Golden Age. Kenneth Grahame. LC 29-26906. 1929. Dodd, Mead & Co.
Golden Age. Kenneth Grahame. LC 45-25816. 1896. Stone & Kimball.
Golden Age. Kenneth Grahame. (Equinox edition). (Illus.). 1975. (pbk.) 4.95 (ISBN 0-380-00289-2). Avon.
Golden Age. Kenneth Grahame & Maxfield Parrish. LC 75-32198. (Classics of Children's Literature, 1621-1932). (Illus.). 1976. 27.00 (ISBN 0-8240-2308-0). Garland Pub.
Golden Age. Esther Jenkins. 1970. 4.95 o.p. Vantage.
Golden Age. Christine Whiting Parmenter. LC 42-235583. 1942. Thomas Y. Crowell Company.
Golden Age, and Dream Days. Foreword by Naomi Lewis, Illus. by Charles Keeping. Kenneth Grahame. LC 64-25458. 1965. 5.00. Dufour.
Golden Age in Transylvania. Mor Jokai. Tr. by Waite, S. L. LC 98-1403. 1898. R. F. Fenro & Company.
Golden Age of Science Fiction. bonanza 1980 ed. Ed. by Groff Conklin. LC 80-27208. 1980. 6.98 (ISBN 0-517-33486-0). Bonanza Books.
Golden Alaskan: By James French Dorrance... James French Dorrance. LC 31-3680. The Macaulay Company.
Golden Altar. Joan Sutherland. LC 29-11249. 1929. Harper & Brothers.
Golden Amber Shore. Kenneth Duncan. LC 54-6405. 1954. Tupper and Love.
Golden Angel: Papers on Proust. Elliott Coleman. LC 54-9610. 1954. C. Taylor.
Golden Answer. Sylvia Chatfield Bates. LC 21-7125. 1921. The Macmillan Company.
Golden Ape. Herbert Adams. LC 30-9490. 1930. J. B. Lippincott Company.
Golden Apple Tree. Virginia Stanton Sheard. LC 20-230249. The James A. McCann Company.
Golden Apples. Marjorie Kinnan Rawlings. LC 35-186882. 1935. C. Scribner's Sons.
Golden Apples. Eudora Welty. LC 56-58336. (Harvest books, 23). 1956. Harcourt, Brace.
Golden Apples. Eudora Welty. LC 49-10054. 1949. Harcourt, Brace.
Golden Apples of the Sun. Ray Bradbury. LC 76-135242. (Illus.). 1971. (ISBN 0-8371-5160-0). Greenwood Press.
Golden Apples of the Sun... Rosemary Obermeyer. LC 44-871. 1944. Books, Inc., Distributed by E. P. Dutton & Co., Inc.
Golden Apples of the Sun... Rosemary Obermeyer. LC 44-1704. 1944. The Blakiston Company, Distributed by E. P. Dutton & Co., Inc., New York.
Golden Apples of the Sun. Drawings by Joe Mugnaini. 1st Ed. Ray Bradbury. LC 52-13569. 1953. Doubleday.
Golden Archer: A Satirical Novel of 1975. Gregory Mason. LC 56-549. 1956. Twayne Publishers.
Golden Argosy: A Collection of the Most Celebrated Short Stories in the English Language, Edited by Van H. Cartmell & Charles Grayson. Rev. Ed. Ed. by Charles Grayson & Van Henry Cartmell. LC 55-206. Dial Press.
Golden Argosy: A Collection of the Most Celebrated Short Stories in the English Language. Ed. by Charles Grayson & Van Henry Cartmell. LC 47-115149. 1947. Dial Press.
Golden Arrow: A Story of Roger William's Day. Ruth Hall. 1901. Houghton, Mifflin and Company.
Golden Arrow & Other Stories. Frances I. Horner. 3.50 o.p. Carlton.
Golden Ashes. Freeman Wills Crofts. LC 40-6735. 1940. Dodd, Mead & Company.
Golden Ass. Apuleius. Tr. by Jack Lindsay. LC 62-1610. (Midland Bks.: No.36). 256p. 1962. pap. 4.95x (ISBN 0-253-20036-9). Ind U Pr.
Golden Ass. Apuleius. Tr. by Robert Graves. 1951. 5.95 o.p. (ISBN 0-374-16524-6). FS&G.
Golden Ass. Lucius Apuleius. Ed. by Harry C. Schnur. Tr. by William Adlington. (O.s.i.). 1962. pap. 0.95 o.s.i. (ISBN 0-02-048240-X, Collier). Macmillan.
Golden Ass: A Version. R. C. Kennedy. 1964. 6.00 o.p. Fernhill.
Golden Ass of Apuleius. Madaurensis Apuleius. Tr. by William Adlington. LC 78-158265. (Series: The Tudor Translations, 1st Ser., V. 4.). 1967. AMS Press.
Golden Autumn: A Novel. Annie French Hector. 1897. J. B. Lippincott Company.
Golden Axe. 1978. 1.50 (ISBN 0-8351-0612-8). China Bks.
Golden Balance. Arthur Dana Hall. LC 55-7228. 1955. Crown Publishers.
Golden Ball: And Other Stories. Agatha Miller Christie. LC 77-160861. 1971. 5.95. Dodd, Mead.
Golden Ball & Other Stories. Agatha Miller Christie. pap. 2.50 (ISBN 0-440-13272-X). Dell.
Golden Ball & Other Stories. Agatha Miller Christie. 1971. 5.95 o.p. (ISBN 0-396-06293-8). Dodd.
Golden Ballast. Henry De Vere Stacpoole. LC 24-21805. 1924. 2.00. Dodd, Mead and Company.
Golden Balls. Hero Haubold. 192p. (Orig.). 1971. pap. 1.95 o.s.i. (O*P*H261, Ophelia). Olympia.
Golden Barge. Michael Moorcock. (Science Fiction Ser.). 1980. pap. 1.75 (ISBN 0-87997-572-5, UE1572). DAW Bks.
Golden Barrier. Agnes Sweetman Castle & Castle, Egerton. LC 13-22867. 1913. 1.30. Doubleday, Page & Company.
Golden Barrier. Hallie Erminie Rives. LC 34-5599. 1934. Dodd, Mead & Company.
Golden Barrier. Mira Stables. (Coventry Romance Ser.: No. 187). 224p. 1982. pap. 1.50 (ISBN 0-449-50289-9, Coventry). Fawcett.
Golden Bauble. Genevieve Slear. LC 77-74312. 1977. 6.95 (ISBN 0-385-12829-0). Doubleday.
Golden Beast. Edward Phillips Oppenheim. 1926. Little, Brown, and Company.
Golden Bed. Wallace Irwin. LC 24-20149. 1924. G. P. Putnam's Sons.
Golden Bees: The Story of Betsy Patterson and the Bonapartes. Daniel MacIntyre Henderson. LC 28-6756. 1928. Frederick a Stokes Company.
Golden Bells: A Peal in Seven Changes. Robert Edward Francillon. LC 6-432663. (Harper's handy series, no. 106). 1886. Harper & Brothers.
Golden Bells: A Peal in Seven Changes. Robert Edward Francillon. LC 6-43267. (On cover: Lovell's library. v. 18. no. 856). J. W. Lovell Company.
Golden Bells. A Peal in Seven Changes. Robert Edward Francillon. (On cover: Seaside library. Pocket ed. no. 911). G. Munro.
Golden Bird. Maria Thompson Daviess. LC 18-17248. 1918. The Century Co.
Golden Bird, and Other Sketches. Dorothy Easton. LC 20-112254. 1920. A. A. Knopf.
Golden Blight. George Allan England. LC 74-15968. (Science Fiction). (Illus.). 1975. 19.00 (ISBN 0-405-06288-5). Arno Press.
Golden Blight. George Allan England. LC 17-2482. The H. K. Fly Company.
Golden Block. Sophie Kerr. LC 18-26172. (Illus.). 1918. Doubleday, Page & Compnay.
Golden Blood. rev. ed. Jack Williamson. (Illus.). 272p. 1980. Repr. of 1964 ed. 15.00 (ISBN 0-934438-19-6, Tamerlane). Underwood-Miller.
Golden Blood. Jack Williamson. (Orig.). pap. 0.60 o.p. (73-630). Lancer.
Golden Book of Cat Stories. Ed. by Era Zistel. 1946. Ziff-Davis Publishing Company.
Golden Book of Dog Stories. Ed. by Era Zistel. LC 47-12029. 1947. Ziff-Davis Pub. Co.
Golden Book of Love Stories: Selected by Charles Norman... Ed. by Charles Norman. LC 47-4041. 1947. Current Books, Inc., A. A. Wyn.
Golden Book of Venice: A Historical Romance of the 16th Century. Francese Hubbard Litchfield Turnbull. 1900. The Century Co.
Golden Bottle. Ignatius Donnelly. LC 68-28929. (Series in American Studies). 1968. Johnson Reprint Corp.
Golden Bottle: Or, The Story of Ephraim Benezet of Kansas. Ignatius Donnelly. LC 68-57523. (American novels of muckraking, propaganda, and social protest). (Illus.). 1968. Gregg Press.
Golden Bottle: Or, The Story of Ephraim Benezet of Kansas. Ignatius Donnelly. 1892. D. D. Merrill Company.
Golden Bough. George Fort Gibbs. LC 18-174107. 1918. D. Appleton and Company.
Golden Bowl. Feike Feikema, pseud. LC 44-891420. 1944. The Webb Publishing Company.
Golden Bowl. Henry James. LC 72-81107. 1972. (pbk) 3.95. World Pub.
Golden Bowl. Henry James. (Penguin modern classics). 1973. 1.95 (ISBN 0-14-002449-2). Penguin.
Golden Bowl. Henry James. LC 75-11552. (Apollo editions; A-386). 1975. 5.95 (ISBN 0-8152-0386-1). Crowell.
Golden Bowl. Henry James. LC 72-158802. (Scribner reprint editions). 1971. (ISBN 0-678-02823-0). A. M. Kelley.
Golden Bowl. Henry James. LC 4-32321. 1904. C. Scribner's Sons.
Golden Bowl. Archie Joscelyn. LC 31-9260. International Fiction Library.
Golden Bowl. Frederick Feikema Manfred. LC 75-40838. (Zia book). 1976. 3.45 (ISBN 0-8263-0407-9). University of New Mexico Press.
Golden Bowl. Frederick Feikema Manfred. LC 44-8914. 1944. Webb Pub. Co.
Golden Bowl see Bodley Head Henry James.
Golden Bowl: A Novel. Frederick Feikema Manfred. LC 70-92652. 1969. 4.00. Dakota Press.
Golden Bowl. Introd. by R. P. Blackmur. Henry James. LC 52-9331. 1952. Grove Press.
Golden Bowl 2 Vols. Henry James. 1909. 7.50 ea. o.p. Scribner.
Golden Box. Frances Kirkwood Crane. LC 42-120270. 1942. J. B. Lippincott Company.
Golden Bubble. Courtney Ryley Cooper. LC 28-5532. 1928. Little, Brown, and Company.
Golden Bull. Nick Carter. (Nick Carter Ser.). 224p. (Orig.). 1981. pap. 2.25 (ISBN 0-441-29782-X, Pub. by Charter Bks). Ace Bks.
Golden Butterfly. library ed. Walter Besant & Rice, James. LC 3-22387. 1888. Dodd, Mead & Company.
Golden Butterfly. Charlotte Grey. (Coventry Romance Ser.: No. 193). 192p. 1982. pap. 1.50 (ISBN 0-449-50291-0, Coventry). Fawcett.
Golden Butterfly. Alice Muriel Livingston Williamson. LC 26-13912. George H. Doran Company.
Golden Cage, a Novel. Tereska Torres. LC 59-13402. 1959. Dial Press.
Golden Cage. Translated from the French by Meyer Levin. Tereska Torres. (T-448). Avon.
Golden Calf. Adele Blackman. (O.S.I.). 1971. 5.95 o.s.i. (ISBN 0-8181-0213-6). Pageant-Poseidon.
Golden Calf. Ilia Arnoldovich Ilf & Evgenii Petrovich Petrov. LC 62-14440. 1962. Random House.
Golden Calf. Mary Elizabeth Braddon Maxwell. (On cover: Lovell's library. no. 88). 1883. J. W. Lovell Company.
Golden Calf. Mary Elizabeth Braddon Maxwell. (On cover: Seaside library. Pocket ed. no. 153). 1883. G. Munro.
Golden Calf. Louis Charles Vaczek. LC 56-5608. 1956. W. Sloane Associates.
Golden Carlotta. Lucy Poate Stebbins. LC 37-1396. The Penn Publishing Company.
Golden Casket: Chinese Novelias of Two Millennia. Wolfgang Bauer & Herbert Franke. LC 64-18278. 1964. Harcourt, Brace & World.
Golden Casket: Chinese Novellas of Two Millennia. Wolfgang Bauer & Herbert Franke. LC 71-391310. (Penguin classics L 189). (Illus.). 1967. Penguin.
Golden Casket: Chinese Novellas of Two Millenia. Wolfgang Bauer & Herbert Franke. (Helen & Kurt Wolff Book). 1964. 7.50 o.p. (ISBN 0-15-136290-4). HarBraceJ.
Golden Casket: Chinese Novellas of Two Millenia. Tr. by Christopher Levenson. LC 64-18278. (Classic Ser). Orig. Title: Goldenen Truhe. 1969. pap. 1.95 o.p. (ISBN 0-14-044189-1, L189). Penguin.
Golden Caskets: Chinese Novellas of Two Millennia. Wolfgang Bauer. Tr. by Christopher Levenson & Herbert Franke. LC 77-26034. Orig. Title: Die Goldeme Truhe. (Illus.). 1978. Repr. of 1964 ed. lib. bdg. 28.50 (ISBN 0-313-20091-2, BAGO). Greenwood.
Golden Centipede. Louise Gerard. LC 27-595827. 1927. E. P. Dutton & Company.
Golden Chain. Gwendolen Overton. (Half-title: Little novels by favourite authors). 1903. The Macmillan Company.
Golden Chair. Oren Arnold. LC 54-11379. Elsevier Press.
Golden Child. Penelope Fitzgerald. LC 77-93900. (Illus.). 1978. 7.95 (ISBN 0-684-15645-8). Scribner.
Golden Children. Bernard Brunner. LC 71-91102. 1970. 6.95. F. Fell.
Golden Chimney. Clifford MacClellan Sublette. LC 31-6377. 1931. Little, Brown, and Company.
Golden Christmas: A Chronicle of St. John's, Berkeley. William Gilmore Simms. LC 16-19168. (On cover: Walker, Richards & co's Series of popular southern books. no. 1). 1852. Walker, Richards and Co.
Golden Circle. Constance Noyes Robertson. LC 51-13569. 1951. Random House.
Golden City. Enver Carim. LC 70-82631. 1969. 4.95. Grove Press.
Golden City. Roy Clews. 1979. 14.95 (ISBN 0-575-02647-2, Pub. by Gollancz England). David & Charles.
Golden Cloud in Texas. Illus. by Pers Crowell. 1st Ed. Leland Silliman. LC 52-12898. 1953. Winston.
Golden Coast: A Novel. Philip Rooney. LC 49-7236. 1949. Duell, Sloan and Pearce.
Golden Cockatrice. Gavin Black. LC 73-14307. (Novel of Suspense). 224p. 1975. 6.95 o.p. (ISBN 0-06-010369-8, HarpT). Har-Row.

Golden Cockatrice. Oswald Wynd. LC 73-14307. 1975. 6.95 (ISBN 0-06-010369-8). Harper & Row.

Golden Cockerel: And Other Stories. Aleksandr Sergeevich Pushkin. Tr. by James Reeves. LC 68-16016. (Illus.). 1969. 4.95. F. Watts.

Golden Cocoon: A Novel. Ruth Cross. LC 24-5805. 1924. Harper & Brothers.

Golden Coin. Anor Lin. LC 46-2976. 1946. The John Day Company.

Golden Collar. Elizabeth Cadell. LC 69-11260. 1969. 4.95. Morrow.

Golden Cord. Warwick Deeping. LC 35-15324. 1935. A. A. Knopf.

Golden Creep. George Bagby, pseud. LC 81-43913. 1982. 10.95 (ISBN 0-385-18142-6). Published for the Crime Club by Doubleday.

Golden Crescent: A Collection of Stories. Bob Brister. LC 73-96908. (Illus.). Zephyr Press.

Golden Crocodile. F. Mortimer Trimmer. LC 8-29715. 1897. Roberts Brothers.

Golden Crucible. Jean Stubbs. LC 75-37713. 1976. 8.95 (ISBN 0-8128-1903-9). Stein and Day.

Golden Crucible. Jean Stubbs. LC 77-5513. 1977. 12.95 (ISBN 0-8161-6488-6). G. K. Hall.

Golden Crucible. Jean Stubbs. LC 76-383073. 1976. 3.95 (ISBN 0-333-17989-7). Macmillan.

Golden Crucible. Jean Stubbs. 1977. 1.95 (ISBN 0-380-01788-1). Avon Books.

Golden Dancer. Cyril Hume. LC 26-16085. George H. Doran Company.

Golden Dart. Selwyn Jepson. LC 49-101443. 1949. Pub. for the Crime Club by Doubleday.

Golden Dawn. Charlotte Mary Brame. LC 44-122553. (On cover: Lovell's library, v. 14, no. 738). J. W. Lovell Company.

Golden Dawn. Peter Bernard Kyne. LC 30-8164. 1930. Cosmopolitan Book Corporation.

Golden Dawn, and, Love for a Day. Charlotte Mary Brame. LC 44-122412. (On cover: Seaside library. Pocket ed. No. 306). G. Munro.

Golden Days. Robert Neill. LC 72-93986. 1973. 6.95. St. Martin's Press.

Golden Dead. Charles R. Pike, pseud. LC 80-69219. (Jubal Cade Westerns Ser.). 128p. 1981. pap. 2.95 (ISBN 0-87754-236-8). Chelsea Hse.

Golden Deed. Andrew Garve. pap. 0.60 o.p. (73-602). Lancer.

Golden Deed: By Andrew Garve Pseud. 1st Ed. Paul Winterton. LC 60-7553. 1960. Harper.

Golden Dishes. Rachel Swete Macnamara. LC 26-56273. Small, Maynard & Company.

Golden Dog: Le Chien D'or. William Kirby. (On cover: Lovell's library, v. 9, no. 454). 1884. J. W. Lovell Company.

Golden Dog: Le Chien D'or) A Romance of the Days of Louis Quinze in Quebec. William Kirby. LC 11-15072. 1896. J. Knight Company.

Golden Dog (le Chien D'or) A Romance of the Days of Louis Quinze in Quebec. William Kirby. LC 7-13210. (Red letter fiction series). 1897. L. C. Page and Company.

Golden Door. Evelyn Scott. LC 25-8264. 1925. F. Seltzer.

Golden Door. Bart Spicer. LC 51-982. 1951. Dodd, Mead.

Golden Dream. authorized ed. George Manville Fenn. LC 6-41105. (On cover: Lovell's international series, 172). J. W. Lovell Company.

Golden Dream. Ardath Mayhar. Date not set. pap. price not set (Pub. by Ace Science Fiction). Ace Bks.

Golden Dreams and Leaden Realities. George Payson. LC 75-104537. 1970. (ISBN 0-8398-1557-3). Literature House.

Golden Dress. Ione Montgomery. LC 44-6012. 1944. Select Publications, Inc.

Golden Dress: A Mystery Novel. Ione Montgomery. LC 40-29468. 1940. Pub. for the Crime Club by Doubleday, Doran & Co., Inc.

Golden Dynasty. Elizabeth Zachary. (Orig.). 1980. pap. 2.50 (ISBN 0-440-13184-7). Dell.

Golden Eagle. Robert William Murphy. LC 65-11408. 1965. E. P. Dutton.

Golden Eagle: A Novel Based on the Fabulous Life and Times of the Great Conquistador Hernando De Soto, 1500-1542. John Edward Jennings. LC 59-5677. Putnam.

Golden Eagle: Illus. by John Schoenherr. Robert William Murphy. LC 65-11408. 3.95. Dutton.

Golden Eagle Mystery. Ellery Queen, pseud. LC 42-25521. 1942. Frederick A. Stokes Company.

Golden Eagle: Or, The Privateer of 1776. A Tale of the Revolution. Sylvanus Cobb. (On cover: The sea and shore series, no. 15). 1890. Street & Smith.

Golden Eagle: Or, The Privateer of '76. A Tale of the Revolution. Sylvanus Cobb. LC 6-20722. 1850. F. Gleason.

Golden Eagle. 1st Ed. Noel Bertram Gerson. LC 53-5601. 1953. Doubleday.

Golden Earrings. Jolan Foldes. LC 46-2890. 1946. W. Morrow & Company.

Golden Egg. James S. Pollak. LC 76-52124. (Garland Classics of Film Literature; 25). 1978. 16.00 (ISBN 0-8240-2890-2). Garland Pub.

Golden Empire. A. E Maxwell. 1979. 2.50 (ISBN 0-449-14267-1). Fawcett Gold Medal.

Golden Empire: A Novel of the Northwest. Chalmer Orin Richardson. LC 38-22500. Greenberg.

Golden Evenings of Summer. Will Stanton. LC 74-122137. 1971. 4.95 (ISBN 0-8415-0085-1). McCall Pub. Co.

Golden Evenings of Summer: Movie Tie-in with Charley & the Angel. Will Stanton. 1972. pap. 0.95 o.s.i. (75-472). Lancer.

Golden Exile. Lawrence L Schoonover. LC 51-10226. 1951. Macmillan.

Golden Face: A Great "Crook" Romance. William Le Queux. LC 22-14900. 1922. Cassell and Company, Ltd.

Golden Face: A Great "Crook" Romance. William Le Queux. LC 22-19608. The Macaulay Company.

Golden Fancy. Jennifer Blake, pseud. 1980. pap. 2.75 (ISBN 0-449-14369-4, GM). Fawcett.

Golden Feather. Theda Kenyon. LC 43-78703. 1943. J. Messner, Inc.

Golden Fetich. Eden Phillpotts. 1903. Dodd, Mead & Company.

Golden Fever. Carole Mortimer. (Harlequin Presents Ser.). 192p. 1983. pap. 1.95 (ISBN 0-373-10579-7). Harlequin Bks.

Golden Fig. Nancy Smith. (Ace gothic). 1974. (pbk.) 0.95. Ace Books.

Golden Fire, Silver Ice. Marisa Zavala. (Candlelight Ecstasy Ser.: No. 27). (Orig.). 1981. pap. 1.75 (ISBN 0-440-13197-9). Dell.

Golden Fleece. Julian Hawthorne. LC 70-85684. (American fiction reprint series). (Illus.). 1969. Books for Libraries Press.

Golden Fleece. Norah Robinson Lofts. LC 43-18854. 1944. A. A. Knopf.

Golden Fleece. David G. Philips. Ed. by Abe C. Ravitz. (American Authors Ser). 1903. 20.75 o.s.i. (ISBN 0-512-00546-X). Garrett Pr.

Golden Fleece. David Graham Phillips. (American Author Ser.). 1981. Repr. lib. bdg. 29.00. Scholarly.

Golden Fleece. William Leete Stone. LC 41-23970. 1941. Falmouth Publishing House.

Golden Fleece. Frederick R. Warburton. 5.95 o.p. Vantage.

Golden Fleece: A Novel. John Gunther. LC 29-6661. 1929. Harper & Brothers.

Golden Fleece: A Romance. Julian Hawthorne. LC 12-24115. (On cover: The lotos library). 1896. J. B. Lippincott Company.

Golden Fleece: The American Adventures of a Fortune Hunting Earl. David Graham Phillips. LC 3-100359. 1903. McClure, Phillips & Co.

Golden Fleecing. Robert Upton. LC 79-16585. 1979. 9.95 (ISBN 0-312-33730-2). St. Martin's Press.

Golden Flood. Edwin Lefevre. LC 5-13023. 1905. McClure, Phillips & Co.

Golden Flood. A Cloud in Seven Colors. Robert Edward Francillon & Senior William. LC 6-43260. (On cover: Seaside library. Pocket ed. no. 656). G. Munro.

Golden Fool. Arthur Durham Divine. LC 54-7520. 1954. Macmillan.

Golden Footfall: A Tale of Duraid, the Shepherd Who Met Life with Love and Defeated Death with a High Dream. Lucy Embury. LC 49-153212.

Golden Fountain. William Schmidt. Tr. by Ireland, Mary Eliza (Haines) LC 18-574935. 1916.

Golden Frame. Cover Painting by James Meese. Joseph Chadwick. LC 55-38190. (Gold medal books, 493). 1955. Fawcett Publications.

Golden Fruits. Nathalie Sarraute. LC 64-12394. 1964. G. Braziller.

Golden Fury. Marian Castle. LC 49-7996. 1949. W. Morrow.

Golden Fury. Reprint Ed. Marian Castle. LC 50-3331. 1950. Sun Dial Press.

Golden Galleon. Mary St. Leger Kingsley Harrison. LC 10-22136. 1.20. Hodder and Stoughton, George H. Doran Company.

Golden Garden. Maysie Greig. 1972. pap. 0.75 o.p. (94230). Beagle Bks.

Golden Gate. James Noble Gifford. LC 39-7777. 1939. Gramercy Pub. Co.

Golden Gate. Carol Holliston. LC 39-7777. Gramercy Publishing Company.

Golden Gate. Alistair MacLean. LC 75-40734. 1976. 7.95 (ISBN 0-385-11647-0). Doubleday.

Golden Gate. Alistair MacLean. LC 77-1538. 1977. 11.95 (ISBN 0-8161-6477-0). G. K. Hall.

Golden Gate. Alistair MacLean. (Fawcett Crest Book). 1977. 1.95 (ISBN 0-449-23177-1). Fawcett Publications.

Golden Gate Caper. Mike Dolinsky. 1976. 1.50. Dell Publishing Co.

Golden Gates. Brame, Charlotte Mary, 1836-1884, Supposed Author. LC 44-11157. (On cover: Seaside library. Pocket ed. No. 1010). G. Munro.

Golden Geese. Everard Meade. LC 68-15411. 1968. Dodd, Mead.

Golden Gems" from "the Ozarks,". Sue Wilson Layton. LC 18-10159. 1917.

Golden Generation. Soterios De Pettas. LC 32-82016. 1932. Meador Publishing Company.

Golden Geyser. Wyatt Blassingame. LC 61-5959. (Mockingbird book). 1975. (pbk.) 1.75 (ISBN 0-345-24348-X). Ballantine Books.

Golden Geyser. 1st Ed. Wyatt Blassingame. LC 61-5959. 1961. Doubleday.

Golden Ghetto: A Novel. Noel Bertram Gerson. LC 69-20444. 1969. 6.95. M. Evans; Distributed in Association with Lippincott, Philadelphia.

Golden Girl. Frances Barney. pap. 0.75 o.p. (01-399). Lancer.

Golden Girl. Peter Lovesey. 1979. 2.25 (ISBN 0-345-27793-7). Ballantine Books.

Golden Girl. Juan Marse. LC 81-3762. 10.95 (ISBN 0-316-54677-1). Little, Brown.

Golden Girl. Agnes Louise Provost. LC 36-181351. 1936. Macrae-Smith Company.

Golden Girl. Harry Sylvester. LC 50-6735. 1950. Harcourt, Brace.

Golden Girl. Paulette Warren. 1979. pap. 1.95 (ISBN 0-532-19113-7). Woodhill.

Golden Girl. Paulette Warren. (Orig.). 1976. pap. 1.95 o.p. Woodhill.

Golden Girl. Paulette Warren. (Orig.). 1976. pap. 1.95 o.p. Manor Bks.

Golden Girl & All. Ralph Dennis. (Hardman,#3). (pbk.) 0.95. Popular Library.

Golden Girls: A Picture Gallery. Alan Muir. (On cover: Lovell's library, no. 312). 1883. J. W. Lovell Company.

Golden Girls." A Picture-Gallery. Alan Muir. (On cover: Seaside library. Pocket ed. no. 172). 1884. G. Munro.

Golden Gizmo. James Myers Thompson. LC 54-27800. (Lion book, 192). 1954. Lion Books by Arrangement with Classic Syndicate.

Golden Goat. Paul Auguste Arene & Huard, Mme. Frances (Wilson) Tr. LC 21-5077. George H. Doran Company.

Golden Goat. Paul Auguste Arene & Safford, Mary Joanne, Tr. (On cover: Harper's Franklin square library, no. 695). 1891. Harper & Brothers.

Golden Goat: The Parable of the Worthy Rich Man and the Unworthy Poor Man. English Version by Virgilia Peterson. Illus. by Richard Seewald. Raymond Leopold Bruckberger. LC 52-10029. 1952. Pantheon.

Golden God. Ralph Hayes. (Stoner: No. 1). 192p. (Orig.). 1976. pap. 1.25 o.p. (ISBN 0-532-12361-1). Woodhill.

Golden God. Ralph Hayes. (Stoner: No. 1). 192p. (Orig.). 1976. pap. 1.25 o.p. (ISBN 0-532-12361-1). Manor Bks.

Golden God see TaleSpinners I.

Golden Goddess. Rob Eden. LC 35-157300. J. H. Hopkins & Son.

Golden Gondola. Barbara Cartland. 1971. pap. 0.95 o.p. (N2409). Pyramid Pubns.

Golden Gondola. Barbara Cartland. 1975. pap. 1.25 o.p. (ISBN 0-515-03647-1, V3647). BJ Pub Group.

Golden Goose. Floyd Mahannah. LC 51-9614. (A Bloodhound mystery). Duell, Sloan and Pearce.

Golden Goose. Ellery Queen, pseud. LC 64-2286. 1964. Pocket Books.

Golden Goose. Ellery Queen. 1974. (pbk.) 0.95. New American Library.

Golden Goose Murders. Allan McRoyd. LC 38-320182. Greystone Press.

Golden Gospel: A Legend. Gabriel Scott & Worster, William W. LC 28-27588. 1928. Macy-Masius, The Vanguard Press.

Golden Gossip: Neighborhood Story Number Two. Adeline Dutton Train Whitney. 1892. Houghton, Mifflin and Company.

Golden Grain. Elizabeth Frances Corbett. LC 43-121171. 1943. D. Appleton-Century Company, Incorporated.

Golden Grain. Sara Lee Young. LC 16-12753. 1915. Monfort & Company.

Golden Grains from Life's Harvest Field. Timothy Shay Arthur. LC 6-2467. 1850. J. W. Bradley.

Golden Grasshopper. A Story of the Days of Sir Thomas Gresham, Knt., As Narrated in the Diary of Ernst Verner, Whilom His Page and Secretary, During the Reigns of Queens Mary and Elizabeth. William Henry Giles Kingston. LC 11-16140. I. Bradley & Co.

Golden Greek. Tute, Warren. LC 60-51241. 1960. Cassell.

Golden Greek. 1st American Ed. Tute, Warren. LC 61-10196. 1961. Knopf.

Golden Greyhound: A Novel. Dwight Tilton. LC 6-7723. Lothrop, Lee & Shepard Co.

Golden Gryphon Feather. Richard L. Purtill. (Science Fiction Ser.). (Illus., Orig.). 1979. pap. 1.75 o.p. (ISBN 0-87997-506-7, UE1506). Daw Bks.

Golden Guilt. Francis Gerard. LC 40-51884. 1940. E. P. Dutton & Co., Inc.

Golden Gypsy. Wanda Owen. (Orig.). 1983. pap. 3.75 (ISBN 0-8217-1188-1). Zebra.

Golden-Hair: A Tale of the Pilgrim Fathers. Frederick Charles Lascelles Wraxall. LC 8-37790. 1865. J. E. Tilton & Co.

Golden Hammock. Laetitia McDonald Irwin. LC 51-11496. 1951. Little, Brown.

Golden Hand. Edith Simon. LC 52-5272. 1952. Putnam.

Golden Harlot. Jeanne Wilson. LC 79-5331. 9.95 (ISBN 0-312-33737-X). St. Martin's Press.

Golden Hawk. Martha Edith Rickert. LC 7-15544. 1907. The Baker and Taylor Company.

Golden Hawk. Frank Yerby. LC 48-6428. 1948. Dial Press.

Golden Hawk of Zandraya. Mike Sirota. (Orig.). 1981. pap. 2.50 (ISBN 0-89083-876-3). Zebra.

Golden Heart. Ralph Henry Barbour. LC 10-22255. 1910. 2.00. J. B. Lippincott Company.

Golden Heart. Charlotte Mary Brame. LC 44-112588. (On cover: Seaside library. Pocket ed. No. 292). G. Munro.

Golden Heart. Charlotte Mary Brame. LC 3626. (Bertha M. Clay library, no. 3). 1900. Street & Smith.

Golden Heart. Charlotte Mary Brame. LC 42-261600. (On cover: Lovell's library, v. 17, no. 811). J. W. Lovell Company.

Golden Heart. Richard Strachey. LC 36-8970. Harcourt, Brace and Company.

Golden Heel. William Arthur Neubauer. LC 65-7722. 1965. Arcadia House.

Golden Height. Marguerite Mooers Marshall. LC 36-782358. 1936. Doubleday, Doran & Company, Inc.

Golden Helix. Theodore Sturgeon. (Orig.). 1980. pap. 1.95 (ISBN 0-440-12885-4). Dell.

Golden Herd. Robert Vernon Brown. LC 50-11182. 1950. Dorrance.

Golden Herd: A Novel. Curtis Kent Bishop. LC 50-9267. 1950. Morrow.

Golden Herd: A Novel. Curt Carroll. LC 50-9267. 1950. Morrow.

Golden Heritage. Francesca Falk Miller. LC 50-3384. 1950. Americana House.

Golden Heritage. William Leo Murphy. LC 29-21207. 1929. P. J. Kenedy & Sons.

Golden Highlander: Or, The Romantic Adventures of Alastair MacIver. Roberts Theodore Goodridge. LC 29-231188. L. C. Page & Company.

Golden Hills: A Novel of the German Vineyards. Clara Viebig Cohn & Rawson, Graham Stanhope, 1890-Tr. LC 30-26952. 1930. The Vanguard Press.

Golden Hoard. Edwin Balmer & Philip Wylie. LC 34-36558. 1934. Frederick A. Stokes Company.

Golden Hoard. Robert Morgan. 1975. (pbk.) 1.25 (ISBN 0-523-00553-9). Pinnacle Books.

Golden Hollow. Rena Cary Sheffield. LC 13-21258. 1913. John Lane Company; Etc., Etc.

Golden Honeycomb: A Novel. Kamala Markandaya, pseud. LC 76-27642. 9.95 (ISBN 0-690-01208-X). Crowell.

Golden Honeycomb: A Novel. Kamala Markandaya, pseud. (Signet Book). 1978. 2.50 (ISBN 0-451-07907-8). New American Library.

Golden Hope. Grace Sartwell Mason & John Northern Hilliard. LC 16-9547. 1916. D. Appleton and Company.

Golden Hope. William Clark Russell. LC 25-23766. (On cover: Lovell's library. v. 20, no. 997). 1887. John W. Lovell Company.

Golden Hope. A Romance of the Deep. William Clark Russell. (Harper's Franklin square library, no. 571). 1887. Harper & Brothers.

Golden Hope: A Story of the Time of King Alexander the Great. Robert Higginson Fuller. LC 5-834185. 1905. The Macmillan Company; Etc., Etc.

Golden Horde. La Selle Gilman. LC 42-22855. 1942. Smith and Durrell, Inc.

Golden Horizons. William Corcoran. LC 37-7992. 1937. Macrae-Smith Company.

Golden Horse: By Gay Rutherford Pseud. James Noble Gifford. LC 52-13501. 1952. Arcadia House.

Golden Horseshoe. Robert Aitken. LC 7-34306. 1907. The J. McBride Company.

Golden House. Charles Dudley Warner. LC 79-104589. (Illus.). 1970. Literature House.

Golden House. A Novel. Charles Dudley Warner. LC 4-15174. 1895. Harper & Brothers.

Golden Idol: A Tale of Adventures in Australia and New Zealand. M. C Walsh. (On cover: Dearborn series, no. 51). 1891. Donohue, Henneberry & Co.

Golden Illusion. Barbara Cartland. (Barbara Cartland Library#38). 1976. (pbk.) 1.25. Bantam Books.

Golden Inheritance. Reese Rockwell. 1884. Phillips & Hunt.

Golden Is the Wheat, a Novel. Moses, Eva E. LC 52-9822. 1952. Exposition Press.

Golden Journey. Agnes Sligh Turnbull. LC 55-10023. 1955. Houghton Mifflin.

Golden Journey. Agnes Sligh Turnbull. 1974. (pbk.) 1.25 (ISBN 0-380-00154-3). Avon.

Golden Journey of Mr. Paradyne. William John Locke. LC 24-25646. 1924. Dodd, Mead and Company.
Golden Jungle. Richard L Newhafer. LC 68-14671. 1968. New American Library.
Golden Jungle: A Novel. 1st Ed. William Howard Harris. LC 57-950557. 1957. Doubleday.
Golden Justice. William Henry Bishop. 1887. Houghton, Mifflin and Company.
Golden Kazoo. John G Schneider. LC 55-11020. 1956. Rinehart.
Golden Keel. Desmond Bagley. 1972. pap. 1.25 o.p. (V2647). Pyramid Pubns.
Golden Keel. Desmond Bagley. LC 64-14283. 1964. 4.95 o.p. (ISBN 0-385-00999-2). Doubleday.
Golden Keel. Desmond Bagley. 1974. pap. 1.50 o.p. (ISBN 0-515-03544-0, A3544). BJ Pub Group.
Golden Key. Helen R. Bamberger. LC 30-64350. 1930. L. MacVeagh, The Dial Press.
Golden Key. James Crawford McKinney Hamilton. LC 12-65613. 1911. The Cosmopolitan Press.
Golden Key & Other Fantasy Stories. George MacDonald. Ed. by Glenn G. Sadler. (Fantasy Stories of George MacDonald Ser.). 176p. 1980. pap. 2.95 (ISBN 0-8028-1859-5). Eerdmans.
Golden Key: Stories of Deliverance. Henry Van Dyke. 1926. C. Scribner's Sons.
Golden Kill. Marc Olden. (Black samurai,#2). 1974. (pbk.) 0.95. New American Library.
Golden Kingdom: Being an Account of the Quest for the Same As Described in the Remarkable Narrative of Doctor Henry Mortimer, Contained in the Manuscript Found Within the Boards of a Boer Bible During the Late War, and Ed. with a Prefatory Note. Andrew Balfour. LC 3-13821. 1903. L. C. Page & Company.
Golden Knight. George Challis. LC 37-28443. 1937. The Greystone Press.
Golden Knight. George Challis. LC 40-7854. 1940. The Greystone Press.
Golden Ladder. Rupert Hughes. LC 24-13016. Harper & Brothers.
Golden Ladder: A Novel. Margaret Horton Potter. LC 8-12224. 1908. Harper & Brothers.
Golden Ladder: Or, The Stolen Jewel. Sarah Ann Wright. LC 9-1476. 1871. American News Company.
Golden Ladies of Pampeluna. Philip Bertram Murray Allan. LC 35-892468. 1934. R. M. McBride & Company.
Golden Lady. Dorothy Gardiner. LC 36-7824. 1936. Doubleday, Doran & Company Inc.
Golden Lady. Dorothy Gardiner. LC 36-1828. 1936. The Literary Guild.
Golden Lamp. Phoebe Gray. LC 16-103067. 1.35. Small, Maynard & Company.
Golden Lane: A Novel. 1st Ed. James Madison Braden. LC 56-93343. 1956. Pageant Press.
Golden Lasso. Fern Michaels. 192p. (Orig.). 1980. pap. 1.50 (ISBN 0-671-57032-3, Pub. by Silhouette Bks). S&S.
Golden Legacy: A Story of Life's Phases. H. J. Moore. LC 7-19172. 1857. D. Appleton and Company.
Golden Legend. Jacobus De Voragine. 14.50 o.p. British Am Bks.
Golden Legend. Isabella Holt. LC 35-4047. The Bobbs-Merrill Company.
Golden Legend of Ethiopia: The Love-Story of Mageda, Virgin Queen of Axum & Sheba, & Solomon the Great King. Post Wheeler & Sheba, Queen of. Legend. LC 36-17995. 1936. D. Appleton-Century Company, Incorporated.
Golden Legend or Lives of the Saints, 7 vols in 4. Jacobus De Varagine. Ed. by F. S. Ellis. Tr. by William Caxton. LC 76-170839. Repr. of 1900 ed. Set. 127.50 (ISBN 0-404-06770-0). AMS Pr.
Golden Legends: Great Religious Stories from Ancient to Modern Times. Ed. by Samuel Cummings. LC 48-864486. 1948. Pellegrini & Cudahy.
Golden Lie. Thomas Hal Phillips. LC 51-10303. 1951. Rinehart.
Golden Lightning. Max Brand. LC 64-107785. 1975. (pbk.) 1.25. Warner Books.
Golden Lightning. Frederick Faust. LC 64-10778. (Silver star westerns). 1964. Dodd, Mead.
Golden Lily. Katharine Tynan Hinkson, pseud. LC 3-17528. 1902. Benziger Brothers.
Golden Link: A Novel Based on the Life of Mustafa Kemal. Mary Study Slater. LC 62-13680. (Exposition-Banner book). 1962. Exposition Press.
Golden Link: Or, The Shadow of Sin, a Story of Our Times. Ermina C Stray. LC 8-16889. 1891. Larger Hope Publishing Company.
Golden Lion and the Sun. Yoram Hamizrachi. LC 82-1393. 12.95. Dutton.
Golden Lion of Granpere. reprint ed. / introduction by david skilton. ed. Anthony Trollope. LC 80-1892. (Trollope, Anthony, 1815-1882. Selections. 1981). 1981. 39.00 (ISBN 0-405-14159-9). Arno Press.
Golden Lion of Granpere. A Novel. Anthony Trollope. LC 44-15603. 1872. Harper & Brothers.
Golden Lion of Granpers. Anthony Trollope. LC 38-168732. (Half-title: Everyman's library, ed. by Ernest Rhys. Fiction. no. 761). 1924. J. M Dent & Sons, Ltd.
Golden Lion of Granpers. Anthony Trollope. (Half-title: Everyman's library, ed. by Ernest Rhys. Fiction.). 1924. J. M. Dent & Sons, Ltd.
Golden Lion of Granpers. A Novel. Anthony Trollope. (In cover: The seaside library. Pocket ed. no. 667). 1886. G.G. Munro.
Golden Locket. Juliana Davison. (Berkley Medallion Book). 1.75 (ISBN 0-425-03769-X). Berkley Pub. Corp.
Golden Lode. Andrew Davidson. LC 57-99468. 1957. Abelard-Schuman.
Golden Lotus. Gladys Edson Locke. LC 27-2310. 1927. L. C. Page & Company.
Golden Lotus. Janet Louise Roberts. 464p. 1979. pap. 2.50 (ISBN 0-446-81997-2). Warner Bks.
Golden Lotus: A Translation from the Chinese Original by Clement Egerton. LC 54-4573. 1954. Grove Press.
Golden Lotus: A Translation, from the Chinese Original, of the Novel Chin Ping Mei. Tr. by Clement Egerton. LC 73-154469. 1972. (ISBN 0-7100-7349-6). Routledge & K. Paul.
Golden Love. Rochel Denore. (Americana Romance). 1978. 1.25 (ISBN 0-441-29730-7). Ace Books.
Golden Lure. Mark Denning. (Orig.). 1981. pap. 1.75 (ISBN 0-505-51664-0). Tower Bks.
Golden Lyre. Gerson, Noel Bertram. LC 63-8726. 1963. Doubleday.
Golden Magnet: Or, The Treasure Cave of the Incas. George Manville Fenn. LC 1708. (On cover: Medal library, no. 44). 1900. Street & Smith.
Golden Man. Philip K. Dick. 2.25 (ISBN 0-425-04288-X). Berkley Books.
Golden Man. Frances Louise Davis Lockridge & Richard Lockridge. 1961. 2.95 o.p. (ISBN 0-397-00130-4). Lippincott.
Golden Man: By Frances and Richard Lockridge. 1st Ed. Frances Louise Davis Lockridge & Richard Lockridge. LC 60-142162. (Main line mysteries). 1960. Lippincott.
Golden Marguerite. Ann Stanfield. 224p. 1981. pap. 1.95 (ISBN 0-449-50197-3, Coventry). Fawcett.
Golden Mask. Charlotte M. Stanley McKenna & Simpson, S. Palgrave. LC 8-28185. (On cover: Munro's library, v. 1, no. 116). 1884. N. L. Munro.
Golden Maze, the Fire of Life: The Impossible Dream. Hilary Wilde. (Harlequin Romances Ser.). 576p. 1982. pap. 3.50 (ISBN 0-373-20058-7). Harlequin Bks.
Golden Mean, 1913-1936. Charles Melville Barr. LC 36-12695. 1936.
Golden Mediocrity. A Novel. Eugenie Grindries Hamerton. LC 7-958. 1886. Roberts Brothers.
Golden Mile. 1st Ed. Anna M Engels. LC 56-12202. 1957. Vantage Press.
Golden Milestone. Bruce Beddow. LC 25-12987. 1925. Cassel and Company, Ltd.
Golden Millet Dream & Other Stories. Liu Lanyun. Tr. by Yu Fanqin & Wang Mingjie. (Chinese-English Readers). (Illus.). 296p. (Orig.). 1982. pap. 4.95 (ISBN 0-8351-1102-4). China Bks.
Golden Mirage: A Romance of the Great Southwest. Merton L Harris. Fleming H. Revell Company.
Golden Mirror. Claes Schaar. 1967. pap. 52.00 o.p. Adler.
Golden Mirror. Claes Schaar. 1967. pap. 52.00 o.p. Adler.
Golden Mistress. Basil Beyea. LC 74-34589. 1975. 9.95 (ISBN 0-671-21995-2). Simon and Schuster.
Golden Mistress. Basil Beyea. (Fawcett Crest Book). 1976. 1.95. Fawcett.
Golden Moment. Isabella Holt. LC 59-10841. 1959. Random House.
Golden Moment: the Novels of F. Scott Fitzgerald. Milton R Stern. LC 70-110422. 1970. 10.00 (ISBN 0-252-00107-9). University of Illinois Press.
Golden Moments. Henry Van Dyke. Ed. by Marianne Wilson & Peter Seymour. LC 71-127746. 1972. 2.50 o.p. (ISBN 0-87529-100-7). Hallmark.
Golden Naginata. Jessica A. Salmonson. 288p. 1982. pap. 2.75 (ISBN 0-441-29752-8). Ace Bks.
Golden Net. Ruby Virginia Redinger. LC 48-8991. 1948. Crown Publishers.
Golden Nightmare: A Mystery Novel. Walter Snow. LC 52-23911. 1952. Austin-Phelps.
Golden Notebook. Doris May Lessing. LC 62-12412. 1962. Simon and Schuster.
Golden Nymph. Roger Conway. (Orig.). 1968. pap. 0.75 o.p. (74-951). Lancer.
Golden Obsession. Georgia Cogswell. 1979. pap. 2.25 (ISBN 0-89083-467-9). Zebra.
Golden Olive. Cristabel, pseud. 1972. pap. 0.95 o.p. (09146). Curtis.
Golden Olive. Cristabel. 1972. 0.95. Curtis Books.
Golden One. Virginia Nielsen. LC 47-22936. 1947. Arcadia House.
Golden Ones: A Novel by C. V. Terry Pseud. 1st Ed. Frank Gill Slaughter. LC 57-8303. 1957. Hanover House.
Golden Orchid. Gerald Sparrow. LC 64-32174. 1963. Jarrolds.
Golden Oriole: Five Novellas. 1st Ed. Herbert Ernest Bates. LC 62-18365. 1962. Little, Brown.
Golden Oyster. Donald Gordon, pseud. LC 68-18584. 1968. 5.95 o.p. Morrow.
Golden Oyster. Donald Gordon Payne. LC 68-18584. 1968. Morrow.
Golden Page: A Biographical Novel. Alma M Myer. LC 77-71602. (Exposition-Lochinvar book). 10.00 (ISBN 0-682-48742-2). Exposition Press.
Golden Panther. Sylvia Thorpe. 1977. pap. 1.50 (ISBN 0-449-23006-6, Crest). Fawcett.
Golden Panther. Sylvia Thorpe. 1976. 1.50 (ISBN 0-449-23006-6). Fawcett Crest.
Golden Parrot. Frederic Abilgaard Fenger. LC 21-5174. 1921. 2.00. Houghton Mifflin Company.
Golden Passion. Ralph Hayes. 1979. 1.95 (ISBN 0-8439-0617-0). Nordon Pubns.
Golden Peacock. Gertrude Franklin Horn Atherton. LC 36-8052. 1936. Houghton Mifflin Company.
Golden Pharaoh. Philipp Vandenberg. (Illus.). 288p. 1981. 13.95 o.s.i. (ISBN 0-02-621580-2). Macmillan.
Golden Phoenix. Der Ling. LC 70-101799. (Short story index reprint series). (Illus.). 1969. Books for Libraries Press.
Golden Phoenix. Der Ling. LC 32-253293. 1932. Dodd, Mead & Company.
Golden Pilgrimage. Bayard Schindel. LC 29-177332. 1929. Doubleday, Doran & Company, Inc.
Golden Pilgrimage: A Novel. Clara Hammond Lanza. LC 7-14082. (library of choice fiction no. 48). 1892. Laird & Lee.
Golden Piper. Frederic Arnold Kummer. LC 33-968569. Sears Publishing Company.
Golden Plain. Translated by John and Doreen Weightman. Roger Bordier. LC 63-15958. 1963. Houghton Mifflin.
Golden Pleasures. Valerie Sherwood. 1977. 2.25 (ISBN 0-446-82416-X). Warner Books.
Golden Pomp. Arthur Thomas Quiller-Couch. Repr. of 1895 ed. 20.00. Scholars Ref Lib.
Golden Pool: A Story of a Forgotten Mine. Richard Austin Freeman. LC 15-6306. 1905. Cassell and Company, Limited.
Golden Poppy: A Novel. Jeffrey Deprend. LC 20-1697. 1920. 1.75. J. W. Wallace & Company.
Golden Porcupine. Muriel Roy Bolton. 1977. 1.95 (ISBN 0-380-01657-5). Avon.
Golden Porcupine. Muriel Roy Bolton. LC 47-312711. 1947. Doubleday.
Golden Portage. A Double D Western. Robert Ormond Case. LC 40-5183. 1940. Doubleday, Doran and Company, Inc.
Golden Princess. Alexander Baron. LC 54-13396. 1954. Washburn.
Golden Promise: A Novel of the Coming Era. 1st Ed. Stanley Zuber. LC 55-12525. Pageant Press.
Golden Quicksand: A Novel of Santa Fe. Anna Robeson Brown Burr. LC 36-3136. 1936. D. Appleton-Century Company, Incorporated.
Golden Quill: A Novel Based on the Life of Mozart. Bernard Grun. LC 56-10229. 1956. Putnam.
Golden Rain. Douglas Clark. (Murder Ink Ser.: No. 47). 224p. 1982. pap. 2.50 (ISBN 0-440-12932-X). Dell.
Golden Rain. Irene Roberts. (Inflation Fighter Ser.). 144p. 1982. pap. 1.50 (ISBN 0-8439-1083-6, Leisure Bks). Nordon Pubns.
Golden Rain. Irene Roberts. pap. 0.50 o.p. (B50-679). Belmont-Tower.
Golden Rain. Owen Rutter. LC 28-166232. 1928. Longmans, Green and Co.
Golden Rain. Margaret Widdemer. LC 33-31152. Farrar & Rinehart, Incorporated.
Golden Recovery: Revealing a Streamlined Cooperative Economic System Compiled from the Best Authorities of the World, Both Ancient and Modern. Werter Livingston Gross. LC 47-15852. 1946. Printed by Murray & Gee, Inc.
Golden Remedy. Rex Stout. LC 31-225823. 1931. The Vanguard Press.
Golden Rendezvous. Alistair MacLean. 1973. (pbk.) 0.75. Popular Lib.
Golden Rendezvous. Alistair Stuart MacLean. 1977. 1.75 (ISBN 0-449-23055-4). Fawcett Crest.
Golden Rendezvous. 1st Ed. Alistair MacLean. 1962. Doubleday.
Golden Ripple. Alec Waugh. LC 33-196948. Farrar & Rinehart, Incorporated.
Golden River. Archie Joscelyn. LC 66-2955. Arcadia House.
Golden Road. Frank Waller Allen. LC 10-27716. 1910. Wessels & Bissell Co.
Golden Road. Hao Ran. 1981. pap. 4.95 (ISBN 0-8351-0879-1). China Bks.
Golden Road. Lucy Maud Montgomery. LC 13-18473. 1913. L. C. Page & Company.
Golden Road: By Peter Bourne Pseud. Graham Montague Jeffries. LC 51-11423. 1951. Putnam.
Golden Road: Great Tales of Fantasy and the Supernatural. Ed. by Damon Francis Knight. LC 73-11541. 1974. 8.95 (ISBN 0-671-21554-X). Simon and Schuster.
Golden Road to Samarkand. Wilfrid Blunt. (Illus.). 1973. 16.95 o.p. (ISBN 0-670-34438-9, Studio). Viking Pr.
Golden Roads. Winifred Van Duzer. LC 27-8548. Grosset & Dunlap.
Golden Rock. Eleanor Louise Heckert. LC 70-103753. (Illus.). 1971. 5.95. Doubleday.
Golden-Rod: A Story of the West. Anna M. Saunders. Golden-Rod Publishing Company.
Golden-Rod: An Idyl of Mount Desert. Constance Cary Harrison. LC 7-7151. (Half-title: Harper's half-hour ser. no. 130). 1880. Harper & Brothers.
Golden Roof. Margaret Witter Fuller. LC 30-24249. 1930. W. Morrow & Co.
Golden Rooms. Vardis Fisher. LC 44-470413. 1944. The Vanguard Press.
Golden Rope. John William Brodie-Innes. LC 19-7081. 1919. John Lane.
Golden Rose. Pamela Hinkson. LC 44-751446. 1944. A. A. Knopf.
Golden Round. Frances Vinciguerra Grebanier. LC 28-20753. The Century Co.
Golden Round. Frances Winwar. LC 28-20753. 1928. The Century Co.
Golden Rubbish: A Novel. William Dudley Pelley. LC 29-19246. 1929. G. P. Putnam's Sons.
Golden Rule: A Tale of Texas. Robert Haskins Crozier. LC 1-299007. 1900. Whittet & Shepperson, Printers.
Golden Rule Dollivers. Margaret H. C. Cameron. LC 13-190742. 1913. Harper & Brothers.
Golden Runaways. Stephen Longstreet. LC 64-24930. 1964. Delacourt Press; Distributed by the Dial Press.
Golden Sabre. Jon Cleary. LC 80-26827. 1981. 12.95 (ISBN 0-688-03380-6). Morrow.
Golden Saddle. Archie Joscelyn. 1963. Arcadia House.
Golden Salamander. Victor Canning. LC 49-136. 1949. M. S. Mill Co. Distributed by W. Morrow.
Golden Sands of Mexico. A Meoral and Religious Tale: to Which Is Added True Riches; or, The Reward of Slef Sacrifice. Illus. by Croome, William H. LC 6-43742. 1850. Lindsay and Blakiston.
Golden Scalpel: A Novel. Seymour Kern. 1960. J. Day Co.
Golden Scarecrow. Hugh Walpole. LC 15-18911. George H. Doran Company.
Golden Scarecrow. Hugh Walpole. LC 42-47702. 1915. George H. Doran Company.
Golden Scorpio. Alan Burt Akers. (Science Fiction Ser.). (Orig.). 1978. pap. 1.50 o.p. (ISBN 0-87997-424-9, UW1424). DAW Bks.
Golden Scorpion. Sax Rohmer, pseud. 1976. Repr. of 1920 ed. lib. bdg. 16.30x (ISBN 0-89190-806-4). Am Repr-Rivercity Pr.
Golden Scorpion. Arthur Sarsfield Ward. LC 26-7492. 1920. A. L. Burt Company.
Golden Scorpion. Arthur Sarsfield Ward. LC 20-71379. 1920. R. M. McBride & Company.
Golden Sea. Joseph E. Brown. 1974. 16.95 o.p. (ISBN 0-87223-412-6, 16830K). Playboy.
Golden Season. Myra Kelly. LC 9-24016. 1909. 1.20. Doubleday, Page & Company.
Golden Season: A Romance of Early America. Oriana Torrey Atkinson. LC 52-14024. 1953. Bobbs-Merrill.
Golden Season: A Romance of Early America. Oriana Torrey Atkinson. 1974. (pbk.) 0.95. Popular Library.
Golden Sentinel: A Story. Emily Newlin Stearns. (Illus.). 1973. 4.00 (ISBN 0-682-47618-8). Exposition Pr.
Golden Sentinels. Ruth McCarthy Sears. 1974. 4.95. Lenox Hill Press.
Golden Sentinels. Ruth McCarthy Sears. 1975. (pbk.) 0.95. Leisure Books.
Golden Sequence. Martha Edith Almedingen. LC 49-11134. 1949. Westminster Press.
Golden Serpent. Ciro Alegria & Onis, Harriet De, Tr. LC 43-153517. 1943. Farrar & Rinehart, Incorporated.
Golden Shaft. Joseph Nazel. (Iceman#2). 1974. (pbk.) 1.50. Holloway House.
Golden Shaft. A Novel. Charles Gibbon. (Harper's Franklin square library, no. 287). 1882. Harper & Brothers.
Golden Shaft. By Charles Gibbon. Charles Gibbon. (Lovell's library. v. 2 no. 57). 1883. J. W. Lovell Company.
Golden Shames. Gershon Kranzler, pseud. saddle-stitched 3.00 (ISBN 0-87559-128-0). Shalom.
Golden Shoe. Justin Huntly McCarthy. LC 21-9517. 1921. John Lane Company.
Golden Shoes. 1982. 6.95; pap. 4.95 (ISBN 0-87306-267-1). Feldheim.

Golden Shoestring. Faith Baldwin Cuthrell. LC 49-8441. 1949. Rinehart.

Golden Shoestring. Faith Baldwin Cuthrell. 1974. (pbk.) 0.95. Warner Paperback Library.

Golden Shore. Harvey Aronson. 256p. 1982. 14.95 (ISBN 0-399-12731-3). Putnam Pub Group.

Golden Shore: A Novel of the Conquest of California. George Armin Shaftel. LC 43-8948. 1943. Coward-McCann, Inc.

Golden Shore: Great Short Stories Selected for Young Readers. Introd., by William Peden. Illus. by Karl Stucklen. Ed. by William Harwood Peden. LC 67-17176. 1967. 3.95. Platt & Munk.

Golden Sickle: A Tale. Davis Grubb. LC 68-28116. (Illus.). 1968. 4.95. World Pub. Co.

Golden Silence. Charles Norris Williamson & Alice Muriel Livingston Williamson. LC 10-16148. 1910. Doubleday, Page & Company.

Golden Skylark. Elizabeth Goudge. 337p. 1976. lib. bdg. 16.75x (ISBN 0-89966-103-3). Buccaneer Bks.

Golden Skylark: And Other Stories. Elizabeth Goudge. LC 41-51835. Coward-McCann, Inc.

Golden Slave. Poul Anderson. 256p. (Orig.). 1980. pap. 2.25 (ISBN 0-89083-651-5). Zebra.

Golden Sleep. Vivian Connell. LC 48-51460. 1948. Dial Press.

Golden Slipper: And Other Problems for Violet Strange. Anna Katharine Green Rohlfs. LC 15-23790. 1915. G. P. Putnam's Sons.

Golden Slippers. Peggy O'More. LC 50-6020. 1949. Arcadia House.

Golden Slippers. Lee Wyndham, pseud. 1953. 3.00 o.p. McKay.

Golden Snail: A Fantasy of London. Victor MacClure. LC 25-224512. The Bobbs-Merrill Company.

Golden Snare. James Oliver Curwood. LC 21-8027. Grosset & Dunlap.

Golden Soak. Hammond Innes. LC 72-11036. 1973. 6.95 (ISBN 0-394-48466-5). Knopf.

Golden Sorrow. Frances Sarah Johnston Cashel Hoey Hoey. (Seaside library. v. 25, no. 493). 1879. G. Munro.

Golden Sorrow. Maria Louise Pool. 1898. H. S. Stone & Company.

Golden Sovereigns. Jocelyn Carew, pseud. 408p. 1976. pap. 2.50 (ISBN 0-380-00845-9, 47381). Avon.

Golden Sovereigns. Jocelyn Carew, pseud. LC 76-47151 (ISBN 0-380-00845-9). Avon.

Golden Space. Pamela Sargent. LC 81-13591. 14.95 (ISBN 0-671-25314-X). Timescape Books: Distributed by Simon and Schuster.

Golden Spaniard. Rebecca Stratton. (Harlequin Romance Ser.). 192p. 1982. pap. 1.50 (ISBN 0-373-02489-4). Harlequin Bks.

Golden Spiders: A Nero Wolfe Novel. Rex Stout. LC 53-115834. 1953. Viking Press.

Golden Spike. Floyd Dell. LC 34-326706. Farrar & Rinehart, Incorporated.

Golden Spike: Fantasie in Prose. Edward King. LC 7-12163. 1886. Ticknor and Company.

Golden Spike. lNew York: Ballantine Books. Hal Ellson. LC 52-659274.

Golden Spur. Joseph Smith Fletcher. LC 28-11530. 1928. L. MacVeagh, The Dial Press.

Golden Spur: A Novel. Dawn Powell. LC 62-17933. 1962. Viking Press.

Golden Spy: Or, A Political Journal of the British Nights Entertainments of War and Peace, and Love and Politics. Charles Gildon. LC 77-170519. (Foundations of the Novel). 1972. (ISBN 0-8240-0526-0). Garland Pub.

Golden Squaw: Being the Story of Mary Jemison, the Irish Girl Stolen by the Indians from Buchanan Valley, Adams County, Pennsylvania, in 1758. A Story Too Strange and Grim Not to Be True. William Wilfrid Whalen. LC 26-8065. Dorrance and Company.

Golden Stairs. Cecilie Leslie. LC 67-15361. (Illus.). 1968. Doubleday.

Golden Stallion. (O.s.i.). 1.95 o.s.i. (ISBN 0-448-02252-4, G&D). Putnam Pub Group.

Golden Stallion. Mary Shannon. LC 52-14339. 1952. Bouregy & Curl.

Golden Stallion's Revenge: Illustrated by George Giguere. 1st Ed. Rutherford George Montgomery. LC 52-12630. 1953. Little, Brown.

Golden Star of Halich: A Tale of the Red Land in 1362. Eric Philbrook Kelly. LC 31-23969. 1931. The Macmillan Company.

Golden Steed. Jeffrey Lord. (Richard Blade, #13). 1975. (pbk.) 1.25 (ISBN 0-523-00559-8). Pinnacle Books.

Golden Stone. D. A. G Pearson. LC 30-4858. E. P. Dutton & Co., Inc.

Golden Story. Daisy Aldan. LC 79-114001. 14.50. Folder Editions.

Golden Story: Novella. Daisy Aldan. 1979. pap. 5.95 (ISBN 0-913152-49-8). Folder Edns.

Golden Strangers. Henry Treece. LC 56-8802. 1957. Random House.

Golden Strangers. Henry Treece. LC 57-18340. 1956. Bodley Head.

Golden Stream. Frances Roberta Sterrett. LC 31-103684. The Penn Publishing Company.

Golden Stud. Lance Horner. 1978. pap. 2.95 (ISBN 0-449-13666-3, GM). Fawcett.

Golden Stud. Lance Horner. (Fawcett gold medal book). 1975. (pbk.) 1.75. Fawcett.

Golden Summer. Iris Bromige. 1973. pap. 0.75 o.p. (94343). Beagle Bks.

Golden Summer. Anne Duffield. LC 55-101979. 1955. Arcadia House.

Golden Summer. Anne Duffield. (Berkley medallion book). 1974. (pbk.) 0.95 (ISBN 0-425-02500-4). Berkley Pub. Co.

Golden Summer: By Daniel Nathan Pseud. 1st Ed. Frederic Dannay. LC 52-12643. 1953. Little, Brown.

Golden Sunset. Ella Embery Tubbs. LC 16-17490. 1916. Kennedy-Morris Corporation.

Golden Swan. Nancy Springer. (Orig.). 1983. pap. 2.95 (ISBN 0-671-45253-3, Timescape). PB.

Golden Swan Murder. Dorothy Cameron Disney. LC 39-25151. Random House.

Golden Sword. Janet E. Morris. 384p. 1981. pap. 2.50 (ISBN 0-553-14846-X). Bantam.

Golden Tag: A Novel. Elliott Chaze. LC 50-7219. 1950. Simon and Schuster.

Golden Tales from Flaubert. Gustave Flaubert. LC 73-38720. (Short story index reprint series). 1972. (ISBN 0-8369-4133-0). Books for Libraries Press.

Golden Tales from Flaubert: With a Preface by George Saintsbury. Gustave Flaubert & Saintsbury, George Edward Bateman, 1845- Ed. LC 29-6678. 1928. Dodd, Mead and Company.

Golden Tales from Maupassant. Guy De Maupassant. LC 28-245775. 1928. Dodd, Mead and Company.

Golden Tales from Merimee. Prosper Merimee & Saintsbury, George Edward Bateman. Tr. by Waller, Emily Mary et al. LC 29-16820. 1929. Dodd, Mead and Company.

Golden Tales of Anatole France. Anatole France, pseud. LC 27-10647. 1926. Dodd, Mead & Company.

Golden Tales of Anatole France. Anatole France, pseud. LC 28-3427. 1927. Dodd, Mead & Company.

Golden Tales of Canada. Ed. by May Lamberton Becker. LC 75-37536. (Short story index reprint series). (Illus.). 1972. (ISBN 0-8369-4095-4). Books for Libraries Press.

Golden Tales of Canada. Ed. by May Lamberton Becker. LC 38-34550. 1938. Dodd, Mead & Company.

Golden Tales of New England. Ed. by May Lamberton Becker. LC 31-32637. 1931. Dodd, Mead & Company.

Golden Tales of Our America: Stories of Our Background and Tradition. Ed. by May Lamberton Becker. LC 29-9986. 1929. Dodd, Mead & Company.

Golden Tales of the Far West: Selected with an Introduction. Ed. by May Lamberton Becker. LC 35-20112. 1935. Dodd, Mead & Company.

Golden Tales of the Old South. Ed. by May Lamberton Becker. LC 30-30710. 1930. Dodd, Mead & Company.

Golden Tales of the Prairie States. Ed. by May Lamberton Becker. LC 32-32913. 1932. Dodd, Mead & Company.

Golden Tales of the Southwest. Ed. by May Lamberton Becker. LC 39-30337. 1939. Dodd, Mead & Company.

Golden Talisman. Hubert Phelps Whitmarsh. LC 99-4712. W. A. Wilde Company.

Golden Temple. Avin Harry Johnston. LC 63-9311. 1963. Zondervan Pub. House.

Golden Temptress. Original Title: The Broken Gate. lNew York. 1954, c1948 ed. Charles Grayson. LC 54-23523. (Ace double novel books, D-49).

Golden Thirteen. Ed. by Ellery Queen, pseud. 1970. 6.95 o.p. (A3264). World Pub.

Golden Thistle. Janet Louise Roberts. (Candlelight Regency, 117). 1973. (pbk.) 0.75. Dell.

Golden Thread. Mabel Anne McKee. LC 35-23923. Fleming H. Revell Company.

Golden Thread. Jean Nash. (Orig.). 1980. pap. 2.25 o.s.i. (ISBN 0-505-51483-4). Tower Bks.

Golden Thread. 1st Ed. Louis De Wohl. LC 52-9536. 1952. Lippincott.

Golden Three. William Le Queux. LC 32-13201. 1931. The Fiction League.

Golden Threshold. Harriette DeJarnette. 320p. (Orig.). 1981. pap. 2.50 (ISBN 0-8439-0946-3). Leisure Bks CT.

Golden Tide. Sondra Stanford. 192p. (Orig.). 1980. pap. 1.50 (ISBN 0-671-57006-4, Pub. by Silhouette Bks). S&S.

Golden Torc. Julian May. LC 81-4126. (May, Julian. Saga of Pliocene Exile: Vol. 2). (Illus.). 1982. 12.95 (ISBN 0-395-31261-2). Houghton Mifflin.

Golden Torrent. Jean Davison. LC 77-7012. 1978. 6.95 (ISBN 0-385-12856-8). Doubleday.

Golden Totem: A Novel of Modern Alaska. Florance Barrett Willoughby. 1945. Little, Brown and Company.

Golden Touch. Simone Hadary. 192p. 1982. pap. 1.75 (ISBN 0-515-06411-4). Jove Pubns.

Golden Touch. Stephen Longstreet. LC 41-4266. Random House.

Golden Touch: By Stephen Longstreet Pseud. Stephen Longstreet. LC 41-426683. Random House.

Golden Trap. Hugh Pentecost. 1972. pap. 0.75 o.p. (ISBN 0-515-02847-9). Pyramid Pubns.

Golden Trap: By Hugh Pentecost. Judson Pentecost Philips. LC 67-14306. (Red badge mystery). 1967. 3.95. Dodd.

Golden Treasures. Ethel Symonds Low. LC 50-11749. 1950. Zondervan Pub. House.

Golden Tress. Fortune Du Boisgobey. LC 6-34423. 1876. Claxton, Remsen & Haffelfinger.

Golden Triangle. Franklin M. Proud. LC 77-24120. 1977. 8.95 (ISBN 0-312-33785-X). St. Martin's Press.

Golden Triangle: The Return of Arsene Lupin. Maurice Leblanc. LC 19-16371. The Macaulay Company.

Golden Trollop. 1st Ed. Natalie Anderson Scott. 1961. Doubleday.

Golden Troubadour. Gordon B Bell. LC 79-21040. (Illus.). 10.95 (ISBN 0-07-004393-0). McGraw-Hill.

Golden Unicorn. Phyllis A. Whitney. LC 75-41676. 1976. 7.95 (ISBN 0-385-12088-5). Doubleday.

Golden Unicorn. Phyllis A. Whitney. LC 76-40947. 1976. 13.95 (ISBN 0-8161-6409-6). G. K. Hall.

Golden Unicorn: A Novel. Phyllis A Whitney. (Fawcett Crest Book). 1976. 1.95 (ISBN 0-449-23104-6). Fawcett Publications.

Golden Urge. Robert Kyle, pseud. LC 54-12978. (Dell first edition, 36). 1954. Dell Pub. Co.

Golden Valley. Daoma Winston. LC 75-28323. 8.95 (ISBN 0-671-22165-5). Simon and Schuster.

Golden Valley: A Novel of California. Frances Gragg & George Palmer Putnam. LC 50-42. 1950. Duell, Sloan and Pearce.

Golden Vanity. Isabel Bowler Paterson. LC 34-36041. 1934. W. Morrow and Company.

Golden Vase. Ludwig Lewisohn. LC 31-28151. 1931. Harper & Brothers.

Golden Veil. Paddy Kitchen. 320p. 1982. 14.95 o.p. (ISBN 0-241-10584-6, Pub. by Hamish Hamilton England). David & Charles.

Golden Venus. Martin Ryerson. (O.s.i.). (Orig.). 1968. pap. 0.75 o.s.i. (A368S, Award). Univ Pub & Dist.

Golden Venus. David Mynders Smythe. LC 60-8685. 1960. Doubleday.

Golden Village. Joseph Anthony. LC 24-24951. The Bobbs-Merrill Company.

Golden Violet: The Story of a Lady Novelist. Joseph Shearing. LC 41-18901. Smith & Durrell, Inc.

Golden Violet: The Story of a Lady Novelist. Joseph Shearing. LC 43-10910. 1943. The Press of the Readers Club.

Golden Virgin. Alan Dipper. LC 72-95757. 1973. 5.95 (ISBN 0-8027-5269-1). Walker.

Golden Voyage of Sinbad. Steve Hart. 1974. (pbk.) 0.95. Warner Paperback Lib.

Golden Wall. Jane Trumbull. Gramercy Publishing Co.

Golden Warrior. Hope Muntz. LC 76-107243. (Scribner library. Contemporary classics). 1970. 2.25. Scribner.

Golden Warrior: The Story of Harold and William. Hope Muntz. LC 49-7690. 1949. C. Scribner's Sons.

Golden Weather. Louis D. Rubin. 1961. 4.95 o.p. Atheneum.

Golden Weather. 1st Ed. Louis Decimus Rubin. LC 61-6740. 1961. Athencum.

Golden Web. Edward Phillips Oppenheim. LC 9-32369. 1910. 0.50. Little, Brown, and Company.

Golden Web. Edward Phillips Oppenheim. LC 11-774. 1911. 1.50. Little, Brown, and Company.

Golden Wedding. Jo Pagano. LC 74-17941. (Italian American Experience). 1975. 17.00 (ISBN 0-405-06412-8). Arno Press.

Golden Wedding. Jo Pagano. LC 43-5780. 1943. Random House.

Golden Wedding. Anne Parrish. LC 36-22622. 1936. Harper & Brothers.

Golden Wedding: And Other Tales. Ruth McEnery Stuart. LC 69-11919. (American short story series, v. 78). (Illus.). 1969. Garrett Press.

Golden Wedding, and Other Tales. Ruth McEnery Stuart. LC 72-8390. (American short story series, v. 78). 1972. (ISBN 0-8422-8113-4). MSS Information Corp.

Golden Wedding, and Other Tales. Ruth McEnery Stuart. LC 72-4416. (Short story index reprint series). (Illus.). 1972. (ISBN 0-8369-4190-X). Books for Libraries Press.

Golden Wedding: And Other Tales. Ruth McEnery Stuart. LC 8-16870. 1893. Harper & Brothers.

Golden West: Three Novels. Peter Bernard Kyne. LC 35-121932. Farrar & Rinehart, Incorporated.

Golden Whip. Abe Brouwer. Tr. by Hyma, Albert. LC 48-128700. 1947. Zondervan Pub. House.

Golden Widow. Floyd Mahannah. LC 56-10441. 1956. Macrae-Smith Co.

Golden Wildcat. 1st Ed. Margaret Widdemer. LC 54-107771. 1954. Doubleday.

Golden Wind. Lyon Sprague De Camp. LC 69-12205. (Illus.). 1969. 5.95. Doubleday.

Golden Wind. Takashi Ohta & Sperry, Margaret. LC 30-3650. (Paper books). 1929. C. Boni.

Golden Windmill: And Other Stories. Stacy Aumonier. LC 21-650034. 1921. The Macmillan Company.

Golden Windows: Being a More or Less Faithful Account of the Adversities and Wanderings of an Impoverished Family of Title. Andrew Soutar. LC 33-36954. 1932. Sears Publishing Company.

Golden Wings. Effie E. Sanders. 1969. 4.00 o.p. (ISBN 0-682-47021-X). Exposition.

Golden Wings: A Prose Romance and a Poem. William Morris. LC 4-22981. 1904. H. M. Caldwell Co.

Golden Wings, and Other Stories. William Morris. LC 76-374247. (Newcastle Forgotten Fantasy library; v. 8). (Newcastle Forgotten Fantasy classic). 1976. 2.95 (ISBN 0-87877-107-7). Newcastle Pub. Co.

Golden Wings, and Other Stories. William Morris. LC 80-19101. 1980. 9.95. Borgo Press.

Golden Witch. Zola Helen Ross. LC 55-10541. 1955. Bobbs-Merrill.

Golden Woman: The Story of a Western Mining Camp. Ridgwell Cullum. 1.25. G. W. Jacobs & Company.

Golden Years. Philip Hamilton Gibbs. LC 32-5025. 1932. Doubleday, Doran & Company, Inc.

Golden Years. Lee Trex Hill. LC 51-14482. 1951. Vantage Press.

Golden Years; a Novel Based on the Life and Loves of Percy Bysshe Shelley. Frank Wilson Kenyon. LC 59-113823. 1959. Crowell.

Golden Years Caper. Robert Carson. LC 72-117038. 1970. 5.95. Little, Brown.

Golden Youth: A Romantic Love Story. Claire Pomeroy. LC 32-13788. Grosset & Dunlap.

Golden Youth of Lee Prince: A Novel. Aubrey Goodman. LC 59-11195. 1959. Simon and Schuster.

Goldenen Truhe see Golden Casket: Chinese Novellas of Two Millenia.

Goldeneye. Malcolm Macdonald. 1932. pap. 3.95 (ISBN 0-451-11546-5, AE1546, Sig). NAL.

Goldeneye. Ross-Macdonald, Malcolm. LC 80-23235. 1981. 14.95. Knopf.

Goldengirl. Peter Lear, pseud. LC 76-56312. 1978. 8.95 o.p. (ISBN 0-385-12656-5). Doubleday.

Goldengirl. Peter Lovesey. LC 76-56312. 1978. 8.95 (ISBN 0-385-12656-5). Doubleday.

Goldengrove. Darryl Ponicsan. LC 78-163586. 1971. 5.95. Dial Press.

Goldengrove. Jill P. Walsh. 1973. pap. 1.50 (ISBN 0-380-01227-8, 50435). Avon.

Goldenrod. Herbert Harker. (Signet, Y5487). 1973. (pbk.) 1.25. New American Lib.

Goldenrod. Herbert Harker. LC 78-37045. 1972. 5.95 (ISBN 0-394-47890-8). Random House.

Goldenrod Farm. Jennie Maria Drinkwater Conklin. LC 6-30401. 1897. A. J. Rowland.

Goldfinger. Ian Fleming. pap. 4.50 fr. ed.; pap. 2.95 span. ed. French & Eur.

Goldfinger. Ian Fleming. 272p. 1982. pap. 2.75 (ISBN 0-425-05368-7). Berkley Pub.

Goldfinger: Reissue. Ian Fleming. LC 66-53. 1966. bds., 3.95. Macmillan.

Goldfish Bowl. Mary Caldwell McCall. LC 32-10531. 1932. Little, Brown, and Company.

Goldfish Murders. Will Mitchell. LC 50-36179. (Gold medal book, 118). 1950. Fawcett Publications.

Goldie. Kennilworth Bruce. LC 35-4009. 1933. W. Godwin, Inc.

Goldie Gets Along. Hawthorne Hurst. LC 31-14966. A. H. King, Inc.

Goldie Green. Samuel Merwin. LC 22-6605. The Bobbs-Merrill Company.

Goldie's Inheritance: A Story of the Siege of Atlanta. Louisa Maretta Bailey Whitney. LC 4-25363. 1903. Free Press Association.

Goldilocks. Evan Hunter. LC 77-80173. 1978. 8.95 (ISBN 0-87795-177-2). Arbor House.

Goldilocks. Ed McBain. LC 77-80173. 1978. 8.95 (ISBN 0-87795-177-2). Arbor Hse.

Goldilocks and the Three Bears. Lilian Obligado. LC 80-50141. (Golden storytime book). (Illus.). 1.50 (ISBN 0-307-11980-7). Golden Press.

Goldilocks & the Three Bears: A Rock Tragedy. Norty Cohen. (Illus.). 1980. 9.95 (ISBN 0-89554-019-3); pap. 5.95. Brasch & Brasch.

Golding's Lord of the Flies: A Critical Commentary. James B Scott. LC 66-30244. (Bar notes literature study and examination guides). Barrister Pub. Co.

Golding's Pincher Martin. Terence Dewsnap. LC 66-27286. (Monarch notes and study guides, 892-0). Distributed by Monarch Press.

Golding's Tale. Mark Rose. LC 74-183919. 1972. 5.95 (ISBN 0-8027-0367-4). Walker.

Goldman's, Translated from the Swedish. Sigfrid Siwertz & Nash, E. Gee, Tr. LC 30-9240. 1930. Cosmopolitan Book Corporation.
Goldpaw. William Stephenson. LC 76-363690. 1976. 4.95 (ISBN 0-7737-0024-2). Musson Book.
Goldseekers. William Riley Burnett. LC 62-8100. 1962. Doubleday.
Goldsmith: The Vicar of Wakefield. MacDonald Emslie. LC 63-18819. (Studies in Eng. lit., no. 9). 1963. Barrons.
Goldsmith's Row. Sheila Bishop. 1980. pap. 1.75 (ISBN 0-441-29813-3). Ace Bks.
Goldsmith's The Vicar of Wakefield. Oliver Goldsmith. Ed. by Hansen, Alexander Frederick. LC 11-107623. (Eclectic English classics). 0.20. American Book Company.
Goldsmith's The Vicar of Wakefield: And The Deserted Village. Oliver Goldsmith. Ed. by Tufts, James Arthur. (Half-title: The gateway series of English texts. General editor: Henry Van Dyke). American Book Company.
Goldsmith's Vicar of Wakefield: With Notes and Introduction, by William Henry Hudson... Oliver Goldsmith. Ed. by Hudson, William Henry. (Heath's English classics). 1898. D. C. Heath & Co.
Goldsmith's Wife. Eleanor Hibbert. 1976. 1.75 (ISBN 0-449-22891-6). Fawcett Crest.
Goldsmith's Wife. Eleanor Hibbert. LC 73-91717. 1974. 6.95. Putnam.
Goldsmith's Wife. Jean Plaidy. 272p. 1981. pap. 2.75 (ISBN 0-449-22891-6, Crest). Fawcett.
Goldsmith's Wife. Jean Plaidy. LC 73-91717. 320p. 1974. 6.95 o.p. (ISBN 0-399-11351-7). Putnam Pub Group.
Goldsmith's Wife. A Story. Henriette Etiennette Fanny Arnaud Reybaud. LC 7-30928. (Appletons' new handy-volume series v. 11). 1878. D. Appleton and Company.
Goldsmith's Wife: By Jean Plaidy Pseud. Eleanor Hibbert. LC 50-213. 1950. Appleton-Century-Crofts.
Goldspeed. L. Peter Rothschild. 1971. 6.00 o.p. (ISBN 0-682-47174-7). Exposition.
Golem. Barbara Anson. (Leisure Books). 1.75. Nordon Pubns.
Golem. Myles Eric Ludwig. LC 69-20129. 1969. 6.95 o.p. Weybright.
Golem. Gustav Meyrink. LC 75-38071. (Illus.). 1976. 4.50 (ISBN 0-486-23327-8). Dover Publications.
Golem, a Hero for Our Time. Myles Eric Ludwig. LC 69-20129. 1969. 6.95. Weybright and Talley.
Golem & "The Man Who Was Born Again" Two German Supernatural Novels. Gustav Meyrink & Paul Busson. Ed. by E. F. Bleiler. (Illus.). 479p. (Orig.). 1976. pap. 4.50 (ISBN 0-486-23327-8). Dover.
Golem Hundred. Alfred Bester. 432p. pap. 2.95 (ISBN 0-671-82047-8, Timescape). PB.
Golem: Mystical Tales of the Ghetto. Chayim Bloch. LC 75-183055. 288p. 1972. pap. 3.95 (ISBN 0-8334-1726-6, Steinbks). Garber Comm.
Golem One Hundred. Alfred Bester. (Illus.). 1980. 11.95 o.p. (ISBN 0-671-25321-2). S&S.
Golem 100. Alfred Bester. LC 79-23137. (Illus.). 10.95 (ISBN 0-671-25321-2). Simon and Schuster.
Golf Bum. Arthur E Pickens. LC 70-125040. 1970. 5.95. Crown Publishers.
Golf Club Murder. Oscar Jerome Friend. LC 29-12058. E. J. Clode, Inc.
Golf Course Mystery: Being a Somewhat Different Detective Story. Chester K Steele. LC 19-578631. 1.50. George Sully and Company.
Golf House Murder. Herbert Adams. LC 33-101552. J. B. Lippincott Company.
Golf Hustler. Denis J. Harrington. pap. cancelled o.s.i. (ISBN 0-89041-147-6, 3147). Major Bks.
Golf Is a Friendly Game. Paul Gallico. LC 42-20811. 1942. A. A. Knopf.
Golf Omnibus. Pelham Grenville Wodehouse. LC 73-6528. 1974. 7.95 (ISBN 0-671-21618-X). Simon and Schuster.
Golf Omnibus: Thirty-One Golfing Short Stories. P. G. Wodehouse. (O.s.i.). 1974. 7.95 o.s.i. (ISBN 0-671-21618-X). S&S.
Golf Widow. Barry Devlin. LC 53-31401. 1953. Vixen Press.
Golf Without Tears. Pelham Grenville Wodehouse. LC 24-13137. George H. Doran Company.
Golfer: A Novel. Wayne Greenhaw. LC 67-26610. 1967. Lippincott.
Golficide: And Other Tales of the Fair Green. William Gilbert Van Tassel Sutphen. LC 8-25651. 1898. Harper & Brothers.
Golgotha. Chayym Zeldis. 1974. (pbk.) 1.25. Avon.
Golgotha of the Heart: Des Herzens Golgotha. Hans Wachenhusen & Miller, Hettie E., Tr. LC 8-33099. (On cover: Globe library. no. 107). 1889. Rand, McNally & Company.
Goliath. J. Weatherby. 288p. (Orig.). 1981. pap. 2.75 (ISBN 0-553-14593-2). Bantam.
Goliath Head: A Novel About Caravaggio. Charles J Calitri & Bertram D. Brettschneider. LC 70-185096. 1972. 6.95. Crown.
Goliath Scheme. William Arden, pseud. (Red Badge Mystery Ser). 1971. 4.95 o.p. (ISBN 0-396-06287-3). Dodd.
Goliath Scheme. Dennis Lynds. LC 79-136501. (Red badge novel of suspense). 1971. 4.95 (ISBN 0-396-06287-3). Dodd, Mead.
Golightlys: Father & Son. Laurence North. 1.20. George H. Doran Company.
Golk. Richard G Stern. LC 60-6261. 1960. Criterion Books.
Golovlyov Family. Tr. by Nathalie Alexandrovna Ertel Duddington. Duddington, Mrs. Natalia Aleksandrovna (Ertel') Tr & Garnett, Edward, 1868- Ed. (Half-title: Everyman's library, ed. by Ernest Rhys. Fiction. no. 908). 1934. J. M. Dent & Sons, Ltd.
Golovlyov Family. Mikhail Evgrafovich Saltykov. LC 76-23897. (Classics of Russian literature). (Hyperion library of world literature). 1977. 12.50. (ISBN 0-88355-514-X) (ISBN 0-88355-515-8). Hyperion Press.
Golovlyov Family. Mikhail Evgrafovich Saltykov & Duddington, Mrs. Nathalie Alexandrovna (Ertel) Tr. LC 31-28489. 1931. The Macmillan Company.
Golovlyov Family. Mikhail Evgrafovich Saltykov & Samuel David Gioran. LC 76-57547. (Illus.). 14.95. (ISBN 0-88233-209-0). Ardis.
Gomery of Montgomery: a Family History. Charles Ames Washburn. LC 8-33480. 1865. Carleton.
Gomorrah. Marvin Karlins & Lewis M. Andrews. LC 74-1503. 1974. 4.95 (ISBN 0-385-02096-1). Doubleday.
Goncourt Brothers. Richard B Grant. LC 75-147186. (Twayne's world authors series, TWAS183. France). 1972. Twayne Publishers.
Gondolier. William Marchant. LC 61-7260. 1961. Random House.
Gondreville Mystery. Honore De Balzac. Tr. by Gerard Hopkins. 1958. 4.50 o.p. Dufour.
Gondreville Mystery: Une Tenebreuse Affaire) Tr. from French by Gerard Hopkins. Honore De Balzac. LC 64-57313. 1965. bds., 3.50. Elek Bks.
Gondreville Mystery: Une Tenebreuse Affaire. Un Episode Sous la Terreur. Honore De Balzac. Tr. by Ellen Marriage. LC 98-1722. (Half-title:... Comedie humaine...). J. M. Dent and Company.
Gone a Hundred Miles. Heather Ross Miller. LC 68-12586. 1968. Harcourt, Brace & World.
Gone: A Thread of Stories. Rumer Godden. LC 68-16632. (O.s.i.). 1968. 4.95 o.s.i. (ISBN 0-670-34536-9). Viking Pr.
Gone and Back. Nathaniel Benchley. LC 73-145998. 1971. 3.50 (ISBN 0-06-020469-9). Harper & Row.
Gone Are the Days. William Bruce Bell. LC 55-8970. 1955. Westminster Press.
Gone Are the Days. Emmy B. Self. 1970. 3.95 o.p. Vantage.
Gone Away! Edward Acheson. LC 35-172385. 1935. Macrae Smith Company.
Gone Away: A Novel. David H Brooks. LC 74-23466. 1975. 7.95 (ISBN 0-06-120475-7). Harper's Magazine Press.
Gone Beyond the Law. Joseph Eugene Matlock. LC 40-8387. Mathis, Van Nort & Company.
Gone from the Valley. John Vergara. 1979. pap. 2.25 (ISBN 0-532-22150-8). Woodhill.
Gone Haywire: Two Tenderfoots on the Montana Cattle Range in 1886. Philip Ashton Rollins. LC 40-2889. 1939. C. Scribner's Sons.
Gone in the Head: A Novel. Ian Cochrane. LC 75-300055. 1974. 8.75 (ISBN 0-7100-7974-5). Routledge & K. Paul.
Gone Man. Brad Solomon. LC 77-5992. 7.95 (ISBN 0-394-41274-5). Random House.
Gone Native. Archibald Charles Gardiner Hastings. LC 28-28958. 1928. G. P. Putnam's Sons.
Gone Native. Archibald Charles Gardiner Hastings. LC 29-7490. The Macaulay Company.
Gone Native: A Tale of the South Seas. Robert James Fletcher. LC 24-24694. Small, Maynard & Company.
Gone, No Forwarding. Joseph N Gores. LC 77-90265. (DKA file novel). 7.95 (ISBN 0-394-41191-9). Random House.
Gone North. Charles Alden Seltzer. LC 76-39979. 1976. 6.95 (ISBN 0-88411-117-2). Aeonian Press.
Gone North. Charles Alden Seltzer. LC 30-12988. 1930. Doubleday, Doran & Company, Inc.
Gone Out see Card Index & Other Plays.
Gone Sailing. Helen Adam. LC 80-10659. (Illus., Orig.). 1980. signed 20.00 (ISBN 0-915124-30-0, Bookslinger; Small Press Distribution); pap. 5.00 o.p. (ISBN 0-915124-29-7). Toothpaste.
Gone the Rainbow, Gone the Dove. Joan Bagnel. LC 73-82869. 1974. 8.95 (ISBN 0-671-27109-1). Trident Press.
Gone to Be Snakes Now: A Science Fiction Novel. Neal Bell. 1974. (pbk.) 0.95. Popular Library.
Gone to Earth. Mary Gladys Meredith Webb. LC 29-16990. 1929. E. P. Dutton & Co., Inc.
Gone to Earth. Mary Gladys Meredith Webb. LC 17-18165. E. P. Dutton & Co.
Gone to Earth. Mary Gladys Meredith Webb. LC 82-1441. (Virago Modern Classic). 1982. 8.95 (ISBN 0-385-27654-0). Dial Press.
Gone to Her Death. Pierre Audemars. LC 81-51981. 1981. 9.95 (ISBN 0-8027-5455-4). Walker.
Gone to Her Death. George Bellairs. 206p. 1981. 9.95 (ISBN 0-8027-5455-4). Walker & Co.
Gone to Texas. Forrest Carter. LC 74-23172. 1975. 6.95 (ISBN 0-440-04565-7). Delacorte Press.
Gone to Texas. John William Thomason. LC 37-25756. 1937. C. Scribner's Sons.
Gone to the Pictures. Hilda Winifred Lewis. LC 47-17301. 1946. Jarrolds Ltd.
Gone Tomorrow. Frederick Clyde Davis. LC 48-9611. 1948. Pub. for the Crime Club by Doubleday.
Gone Tomorrow: A Novel. Roger Burke Dooley. LC 61-9088. 1961. Bruce Pub. Co.
Gone with a Wang. (O.s.i.). 1980. 8.95 o.s.i. (ISBN 0-440-02790-X). Delacorte.
Gone with a Wang. Donna Zide. LC 80-12495. 7.95 (ISBN 0-440-02790-X). Delacorte Press.
Gone with the Old River. Evilena Filbeck. LC 73-169953. (Illus.). 1972. 4.00.
Gone with the Whip. Marcus Van Heller, pseud. (Orig.). 1969. pap. 1.95 o.s.i. (OPH164, Ophelia). Olympia.
Gone with the Wind. ed. is complete and unabridged ed. Margaret Mitchell. LC 67-6860. 1967. Macmillan.
Gone with the Wind. anniversary ed., with an introd. / by james a. michener. ed. Margaret Mitchell. LC 76-355793. 1975. 14.95. Macmillan.
Gone with the Wind. Margaret Mitchell. LC 77-364848. (Illus.). 1976. Franklin Library.
Gone with the Wind. Margaret Mitchell. LC 40-37533. 1937. The Macmillan Company.
Gone with the Wind. Margaret Mitchell. LC 40-37230. 1939. The Macmillan Company.
Gone with the Wind. Illustrated by Ben Stahl. Anniversary Ed. Margaret Mitchell. LC 61-8194. 1961. Micmillan.
Gone with the Wind. Motion Picture Ed. Margaret Mitchell. LC 39-33518. 1939. The Macmillan Company.
Gongs in the Night. Gordon H. Smith. (Illus.). 1943. pap. 0.75 o.p. (10817P). Zondervan.
Gongu-Hrolfs Saga. Tr. by Hermann Palsson. 144p. 1981. 15.00x (ISBN 0-8020-2392-4). U of Toronto Pr.
Gonji: Deathwind of Vedun. T. C. Rypel. (Gonji Ser.). 1982. pap. 2.95 (ISBN 0-8217-1006-0). Zebra.
Gonji, No. 3: Samurai Combat. T. C. Rypel. (Orig.). 1983. pap. 3.50 (ISBN 0-8217-1191-1). Zebra.
Gonji: Samurai Steel, No. 2. (Gonji Ser.). (Orig.). 1982. pap. 3.25 (ISBN 0-8217-1072-9). Zebra.
Goobersville Breakdown. Robert Lieberman. LC 78-74110. (Illus.). 4.95 (ISBN 0-933124-00-7). Gamma Books.
Good. C. P. Taylor. 1982. pap. 6.95 (ISBN 0-413-50250-3, NO. 2380). Methuen Inc.
Good Age. Alexander Comfort. (Illus.). 1978. pap. 5.95 (ISBN 0-671-24233-4, Fireside). S&S.
Good Americans. Constance Cary Harrison. LC 98-240. 1898. The Century Co.
Good and Bad Weather. Edmund Schiddel. LC 65-17103. bds., 5.95. S. & S.
Good & Dandy World. Kenneth Robbins. 1980. pap. 1.50. Eldridge Pub.
Good and the Bad. 1st Ed. Joan Margaret Fleming. 1953. Published for the Crime Club by Doubleday.
Good Angles Work Days. George V. Higgins. LC 81-18637. 1982. 12.95 (ISBN 0-394-51672-9). Knopf.
Good As Gold. Joseph Heller. LC 78-23894. 12.95 (ISBN 0-671-22923-0) (ISBN 0-671-23084-0). Simon and Schuster.
Good As Gold. Alfred Gerald Toombs. LC 55-9201. 1955. Crowell.
Good Bad Girl. Winifred Van Duzer. LC 26-155082. Grosset & Dunlap.
Good Behavior. Terry Fisher. (Orig.). 1979. pap. 2.25 (ISBN 0-446-82609-X). Warner Bks.
Good Behaviour. Mary Nesta Skrine Keane. LC 80-8792. 1981. 11.95 (ISBN 0-394-51818-7). Distributed by Random House.
Good Brother. Nelia Frayne. LC 41-270405. Gramercy Publishing Co.
Good-by to Gunsmoke. Ralph Catlin. LC 55-7458. 1955. Little, Brown.
Good-by to Love: A Love Story. Eleanor Elliott Carroll. LC 35-215716. Chelsea House.
Good-Bye. William H Manville. LC 77-1984. 8.95 (ISBN 0-671-22554-5). Simon and Schuster.
Good-Bye. authorized ed. Henrietta Eliza Vaughan Stannard. (On cover: Lovell's Westminster series. no. 28). United States Book Company.
Good-Bye and Amen. Francis Clifford. LC 74-12182. 1974. 6.95 (ISBN 0-15-136630-6). Harcourt Brace Jovanovich.
Good-Bye, Atlantis. Marianne Ross. LC 79-24535. 7.95 (ISBN 0-525-66670-2). Elsevier/Nelson Books.
Good Bye, Ava. 1st Ed. Richard Pike Bissell. LC 60-13972. 1960. Little, Brown.
Good-Bye Chicago. William Riley Burnett. 182p. 1981. 9.95 o.p. (ISBN 0-312-33851-1). St Martin.
Good-Bye Julie Scott. Alice Abbott. 1975. (pbk.) 0.95. Ace Books.
Good-Bye, Mr. Chips. a school ed., by salibelle royster. ed. James Hilton. LC 53-20688. (Illus.). 1953. Globe Book Co.
Good-Bye, Mr. Chips. James Hilton. LC 34-271746. 1934. Little, Brown, and Company.
Good-Bye, Mr. Chips. James Hilton. LC 36-4467. 1935. Little, Brown, and Company.
Good-Bye, Mr. Chips. Large Type Ed. James Hilton. (Keith Jennison bk.). 1966. 6.95. Watts.
Good-Bye, Mr. Shaft. Ernest Tidyman. LC 73-12799. 1973. 6.95. Dial Press.
Good-Bye, My Son. Marjorie Coryn. LC 43-2474. 1943. D. Appleton-Century Company, Incorporated.
Good-Bye, Proud World. Ellen Warner Olney Kirk. LC 3-21297. 1903. Houghton, Mifflin and Company.
Good-Bye Siberia. Nicholas F. Prychodko. LC 76-381255. 1976. 2.50 (ISBN 0-671-80367-0). Simon & Schuster of Canada.
Good-Bye, Son: And Other Stories. Janet Lewis, pseud. LC 46-2483. 1946. Doubleday & Company, Inc.
Good-Bye: Summer. Fannie Heaslip Lea. LC 31-281242. 1931. Dodd, Mead & Company.
Good-Bye Sweetheart. Rhoda Broughton. (On cover: Lovell's library, no. 1022). 1887. J. W. Lovell Company.
Good-Bye Sweetheart!" A Tale in Three Parts. Rhoda Broughton. (On cover: Seaside library. Pocket ed., no. 758). 1886. G. Munro.
Good-Bye to an Old Friend. 1st. american ed. Brian Freemantle. LC 72-95739. 1973. 6.95 (ISBN 0-399-11084-4). Putnam.
Good-Bye to Budapest. Jeannette Eyerly. 1980. pap. 1.75 (ISBN 0-425-04523-4). Berkley Pub.
Good-Bye, Union Square: A Writer's Memoir of the Thirties. Albert Halper. LC 76-124512. 1970. 6.95. Quadrangle Books.
Good-Bye, White Man: A Novel of A.D. 2711. With a Foreword by Charles E. Davis. 1st Ed. Frederic Vernon Bouic. LC 53-7364. 1953. Exposition Press.
Good-Bye, Wisconsin. Glenway Wescott. LC 70-140347. (Short story index reprint series). 1970. Books for Libraries Press.
Good-Bye, Wisconsin. Glenway Wescott. LC 28-21484. 1928. Harper & Brothers.
Good Cause. David Stone. LC 63-12522. 1963. Holt, Rinehart and Winston.
Good Chance. Hugh Fosburgh. LC 64-21959. 1964. W. Morrow.
Good Children Don't Kill. Louis C. Thomas. LC 68-21900. (Red badge mystery). 1968. Dodd, Mead.
Good Companions. John Boynton Priestley. LC 29-16857. 1929. Harper & Brothers.
Good Companions. John Boynton Priestley & Taft, Kendall Benard. (Harper's modern classics). Harper & Brothers.
Good Comrade. Una Lucy Silberrad. LC 7-30840. 1907. Doubleday, Page & Company.
Good Comrades. Felix Salten & Milton, Paul Robert, 1904- Tr. LC 42-36119. 1942. The Bobbs-Merrill Company.
Good Confession: A Novel. Elizabeth Savage. LC 74-23336. 1975. 6.95. (ISBN 0-316-77142-2). Little, Brown.
Good Conscience. Olav Duun. Tr. by Bjorkman, Edwin August. LC 28-24269. 1928. Harper & Brothers.
Good Conscience. Carlos Fuentes. LC 61-18829. 1961. I. Obolensky.
Good Crop. Elizabeth Holaday Emerson. LC 46-7970. 1946. Longmans, Green and Co.
Good Day to Die. Del Barton. LC 79-7794. 1980. 10.00 (ISBN 0-385-15667-7). Doubleday.
Good Day to Die. Del Barton. 320p. 1981. pap. 2.75 (ISBN 0-445-04646-5). Popular Lib.
Good Day to Die. Thomas Wakefield Blackburn. LC 67-12964. 1967. D. McKay Co.
Good Day to Die. James Harrison. 1981. pap. 4.95x (ISBN 0-440-53000-8, Delta). Dell.
Good Day to Die. James Harrison. LC 73-8224. 1973. 15.00 o.p. (ISBN 0-671-21574-4). Ultramarine Pub.
Good Day to Die. James Harrison. (O.s.i.). 160p. 1973. 5.95 o.s.i. (ISBN 0-671-21574-4). S&S.
Good Day to Die: A Novel. James Harrison. LC 73-8224. 1973. 5.95 (ISBN 0-671-21574-4). Simon and Schuster.
Good Day to Die: A Novel. James Harrison. (Delta / Seymour Lawrence Book.). 1982. 4.95 (ISBN 0-440-53000-8). Dell Publishing Co.

Good Deed: And Other Stories of Asia, Past and Present. Pearl Sydenstricker Buck. LC 69-10808. 1969. 5.95. John Day Co.
Good Deeds Must Be Punished. 1st Ed. Irving Shulman. LC 56-111655. 1956. Holt.
Good Die Poor. Henry W Clune. LC 37-28595. 1937. Longmans, Green and Co.
Good Doctor. Anne Stewart. LC 39-171056. Gramercy Publishing Co.
Good Earth. Pearl Sydenstricker Buck. 1961. Grosset & Dunlap.
Good Earth. Pearl Sydenstricker Buck. (Enriched classics series). (Illus.). 1973. 0.95 (ISBN 0-671-47897-4). Washington Sq. Pr.
Good Earth. Pearl Sydenstricker Buck. Ed. by Greene, Jay Elihu. LC 49-6831. 1949. Globe Book Co.
Good Earth. Pearl Sydenstricker Buck. LC 49-11632. 1949. J. Day Col.
Good Earth. Pearl Sydenstricker Buck. LC 31-26625. The John Day Company.
Good Earth. Pearl Sydenstricker Buck. LC 34-27027. (Half-title: The modern library of the world's best books). 1934. The Modern Library.
Good Earth. Large Type Ed. Pearl Sydenstricker Buck. (Keith Jennison bk.). 1967. 7.95. Watts.
Good Earth: With Illustrations. Pearl Sydenstricker Buck. LC 47-3919. (Half-title: The Living library). 1947. The World Publishing Company.
Good Enough for Nelson. John Winton. LC 78-301756. 1977-1978. 9.95 (ISBN 0-7181-1643-7). Joseph.
Good Enought for Grandpa. Curt Gerling. 237p. 1958. 5.95. Plaza Pubs.
Good Family. MacKinlay Kantor. LC 49-8913. 1949. Coward-McCann.
Good Family. Mabel Dana Lyon. LC 42-15696. 1942. Gramercy Publishing Co.
Good Feeling. Christopher. 1978. pap. 1.00 (ISBN 0-916940-03-9). World Light.
Good Fellow. Charles Paul De Kock. LC 7-14195. 1837. E. L. Carey & A. Hart.
Good Fight of Faith. Caroline J Freeland. LC 7-22750. T. Y. Crowell.
Good-for Nothing. A Novel. 1st Ed. James Yaffe. LC 53-7299. 1953. Little, Brown.
Good for Nothing: Or, All Down Hill. George John Whyte-Melville. (seaside library, v. 61, no. 1233). 1882. G. Munro.
Good for One More Ride. Walter I Frank. LC 55-116495. 1956. Vantage Press.
Good for the Soul. Margaret Wade Campbell Deland. LC 99-5621. (Little books by famous writers). 1899. Harper & Brothers.
Good Friday-1963: A Journey into the Heart of One Man-and into the Soul of America. Otis Carney. LC 61-112214. 1961. Morrow.
Good Gestes: Stories of Beau Geste, His Brothers, and Certain of Their Comrades in the French Foreign Legion. Percival Christopher Wren. LC 29-5708. 1929. Frederick A. Stokes Company.
Good Girl. Vincent O'Sullivan. LC 17-23647. 1917. 1.50. Small, Maynard & Company.
Good Girls Don't Get Murdered. Percy Spurlark Parker. LC 74-10944. 1974. (ISBN 0-684-13907-3). Scribner.
Good Goodies. Stan Dworkin & Floss Dworkin. 1979. pap. 2.50 (ISBN 0-449-23964-0, Crest). Fawcett.
Good Goods: A Novel. Phyllis Kluger & Richard Kluger. LC 82-8979. 15.75 (ISBN 0-02-527800-2). Macmillan.
Good Greenwood. Eric Rhodin. pap. 0.75 o.p. (ISBN 0-671-29563-2). Archway.
Good Guy. Lou Cameron. (Orig.). 1968. pap. 0.75 o.p. (74-960). Lancer.
Good-Guy Cake. Barbara Dillon. (Skylark Ser.). 64p. 1982. pap. 1.75 (ISBN 0-553-15156-8, Skylark). Bantam.
Good Guys & the Bad Guys. Joe Millard, pseud. 160p. 1971. pap. 0.60 o.p. (A577X, Award). Univ Pub & Dist.
Good Guys & the Bad Guys. Joe Millard, pseud. (O.s.i.). 1969. pap. 0.95 o.s.i. (AN1446, Award). Univ Pub & Dist.
Good Guys Wear Black. John M. Murray. Ed. by Alice Sachs. 1971. 3.95 o.p. Lenox Hill.
Good Hater. A Novel. Frederick Boyle. (Harper's Franklin square library, no. 438). 1885. Harper & Brothers.
Good Hater. A Novel. Frederick Boyle. (On cover: The seaside library. Pocket ed., no. 356). 1885. G. Munro.
Good Home with Nice People. Josephine Lawrence. LC 39-27002. 1939. Little, Brown and Company.
Good Hope. Henry Sydnor Harrison & Bryan, John Stewart. LC 31-5885. 1931. Houghton Mifflin Company.
Good Hunting. Norman Davey. LC 24-4508. George H. Doran Company.
Good Husband. Pamela Hansford Johnson. LC 78-27488. 8.95 (ISBN 0-684-16157-5). Scribner.
Good Husband. Pamela Hansford Johnson. LC 79-24980. 1980. 13.95. G. K. Hall.
Good Indian. Bertha Muzzy Sinclair. LC 12-21614. 1912. Little, Brown, and Company.
Good Indian: A Northwoods Mixup. E. J. Rath. LC 27-22051. 1927. G. H. Watt.
Good Intention Is Blue. Warja Honegger-Lavater. (Folded Story Ser: No. 8). (Illus., Eng., Fr. & Ger.). 1964. bds. 4.50 o.p. Wittenborn.
Good Investment. A Story of the Upper Ohio. William Joseph Flagg. (On cover: Library of select novels, no. 377). 1872. Harper & Brothers.
Good Is for Angels. 1st Ed. Christopher Clark. LC 50-9515. 1950. Harper.
Good Journey. Simon J. Ortiz. LC 77-82789. (New World Writing Ser.). (Illus.). 1977. 15.00 o.p. (ISBN 0-913666-21-1); pap. 6.95 o.p. (ISBN 0-913666-20-3). Turtle Isl Foun.
Good Keen Girl. Barry Crump. (Illus.). 1970. 3.50 o.p. (ISBN 0-589-00495-6). Reed.
Good Leadership. rev. abr. ed. Ralph Short. 170p. 1976. pap. 3.95 (ISBN 0-915800-02-0). Short Methods.
Good Leviathan. Pierre Boulle. LC 78-57255. 8.95 (ISBN 0-8149-0807-1). Vanguard Press.
Good Life. Douglass Wallop. LC 69-15504. 1969. 5.95. Atheneum.
Good Life Universal: Essence of All Religions and Other Faiths, Inspiration of World Government. Eugenia Winston Weller & Charles Frederick Weller. LC 51-432038. 1951. World Fellowship.
Good Light. Karl Bjarnhof. (YA) 1960. 5.95 o.p. (ISBN 0-394-42682-7). Knopf.
Good Listener. Pamela Hansford Johnson. LC 75-15326. 7.95 (ISBN 0-684-14369-0). Scribner.
Good Listener. Pamela Hansford Johnson. LC 75-44247. 1976. 11.95 (ISBN 0-8161-6349-9). G. K. Hall.
Good Looking. David A. Sohn. LC 75-27940. (Pap. ed. 5.95 o.p.). 1975. 8.95 o.p. (ISBN 0-912920-47-5). North Am Pub Co.
Good Looking Women. Ruth Park. 1981. 18.95x (Pub. by Remploy England). State Mutual Bk.
Good Lord, You're Upside Down! Clair Huffaker. LC 63-11459. 1963. Cornerstone Library.
Good Luck! Elisabeth Burstenbinder. LC 24-22223. A. L. Burt Company.
Good Luck!" (Gluck Auf.) Elisabeth Burstenbinder. Tr. by Shaw, Frances A. LC 6-19402. (Osgood's library of novels, no. 39). 1874. J. R. Osgood and Company.
Good Luck, Lieutenant! Russell Gordon Carter. LC 32-25318. 1932. Little, Brown, and Company.
Good Luck, Miss Wyckoff: A Novel. William Motter Inge. LC 75-110260. 1970. 4.95. Little, Brown.
Good Luck, Mister Cain. Brian Freeborn. LC 76-25504. 7.95. St. Martin's Press.
Good Luck, Mister Cain. Brian Freeborn. LC 76-376887. 1976. 2.90 (ISBN 0-436-41135-0). Secker and Warburg.
Good Luck" Or, Success and How He Won It. Elisabeth Burstenbinder. Tr. by Tyrrell, Christina. (On cover: Seaside library. Pocket ed., no. 2073). 1894. G. Munro.
Good Luck to the Corpse. Max Murray. LC 51-13729. 1951. Farrar, Straus and Young.
Good Man. George Frederick Hummel. LC 25-11483. 1925. Boni & Liveright.
Good Man. Jefferson Young. LC 52-13055. 1953. Bobbs-Merrill.
Good Man in Africa. William Boyd. LC 81-11041. 1981. (ISBN 0-688-00657-4). Morrow.
Good Man in Africa. William Boyd. LC 81-11041. 1981. (ISBN 0-688-00657-4). Morrow.
Good Man Is Hard to Find and Other Stories. Flannery O'Connor. LC 77-3306. (Harvest/HBJ book). 1977. 3.45 (ISBN 0-15-636465-4). Harcourt Brace Jovanovich.
Good Man Is Hard to Find, and Other Stories. Flannery O'Connor. LC 55-7423. 1955. Harcourt, Brace.
Good Man's Love. Edmee Elizabeth Monica De La Pasture. LC 32-20307. 1932. Harper & Brothers.
Good Marriage. Mary Jayne. LC 29-3483. London.
Good Men and Bad. James Beardsley Hendryx. LC 54-7324. (Double D western). 1954. Doubleday.
Good Men and Ture. Eugene Manlove Rhodes. LC 10-18654. 1910. H. Holt and Company.
Good Men Do Nothing. John Brunner. (Orig.). 1971. pap. 0.75 o.p. (T2443). Pyramid Pubns.
Good Mr. Satan. Georgina Houldsworth Parks. LC 51-19148. 1950. Columbia Press.
Good Morning Judge. Nicholas Albano. (Illus.). 1977. 9.95 o.s.i. (ISBN 0-8181-0410-4). Pageant-Poseidon.
Good Morning, Midnight. Jean Rhys. LC 73-16280. 1974. (pbk.) 1.95 (ISBN 0-394-71042-8). Vintage Books.
Good Morning, Midnight. Jean Rhys. LC 78-96002. 4.95. Harper & Row.
Good Morning, Miss Dove. Frances Gray Patton. LC 54-11240. (Illus.). 1954. Dodd, Mead.
Good Morning, Please: A Novel. Teddy Sullivan. LC 80-15670. 1980. 11.95 (ISBN 0-87460-354-4). Lion Books.
Good-Morning, Rosamond!". Constance Lindsay Skinner. LC 17-117911. 1917. Doubleday, Page & Company.
Good Morning, Young Lady. Ardyth Kennelly. LC 52-10909. 1953. Houghton Mifflin.
Good Mrs. Hypocrite: A Study in Self-Righteousness. Eliza M. J. Humphreys. LC 99-2662. 1899. F. M. Buckles & Company.
Good Mrs. Shephard. Florence Bonime. LC 50-14251. 1950. Crown Publishers.
Good Mrs. Shephard. Florence Cummings, pseud. LC 50-14251. 1950. Crown Publishers.
Good-Natur'd Man. Oliver Goldsmith. Repr. of 1921 ed. 7.00 o.p. (ISBN 0-403-04086-8). Somerset Pub.
Good Natur'd Man & She Stoops to Conquer. Oliver Goldsmith. Ed. by George P. Baker. 1979. Repr. of 1905 ed. lib. bdg. 25.00 (ISBN 0-8495-2003-7). Arden Lib.
Good Neighbor Murder. Eleanor Pierson. LC 41-14545. Howell, Soskin.
Good Neighbor Sam. Jack Finney. LC 63-15365. 1963. Simon and Schuster.
Good Neighbors and Other Strangers. Edgar Pangborn. 1973. (pbk.) 1.50. Collier Books.
Good Neighbors, and Other Strangers. Edgar Pangborn. LC 75-182023. 1972. 5.95. Macmillan.
Good News. Edward Abbey. LC 80-12815. 10.95. Dutton.
Good News: Formerly "Bubbles". Eloise Greenfield & Pat Cummings. 1977. 5.95 (ISBN 0-698-30651-1). Coward, McCann & Geoghegan.
Good Night and Good-Bye. Timothy Harris. LC 79-12066. 8.95 (ISBN 0-440-03234-2). Delacorte Press.
Good Night at San Garbriel. Susana Clayton Ott. LC 47-12065. 1947. Harper.
Good Night Irene. James Michael Ullman. LC 65-22263. (Inner sanctum mystery). 1965. Simon and Schuster.
Good Night, Jupiter. Raymond A Kennedy. LC 71-103827. 1970. 5.95. Atheneum.
Good Night, Ladies. Hilda Van Siller. LC 43-13682. 1943. Pub. for the Crime Club by Doubleday, Doran and Company, Inc.
Good Night, Sailor. J Inchardi. LC 56-13183. (Signet book, 1344). 1956. New American Library.
Good Night, Sheriff. Harrison Ross Steeves. Random House.
Good Night, Sweet Prince. Gene Fowler, pseud. 1978. Repr. of 1944 ed. 19.95x (ISBN 0-89966-095-9). Buccaneer Bks.
Good Night Willie Lee, I'll See You in the Morning. Alice Walker. 1979. 5.95 (ISBN 0-8037-2940-5); pap. 3.95 (ISBN 0-8037-3052-7). Dial.
Good of the Wicked: And The Party Sketches. Owen Frawley Kildare. LC 4-23764. 1904. The Baker & Taylor Co.
Good Old Anna. Marie Adelaide Belloc Lowndes. LC 17-12865. 1916. George H. Doran Company.
Good Old Boys. William L. Heath. LC 78-144813. 1971. 5.95 (ISBN 0-8415-0096-7). McCall Pub. Co.
Good Old Boys. Paul Hemphill. (O.s.i.). 1974. 7.95 o.s.i. (ISBN 0-671-21771-2). S&S.
Good Old Boys. Elmer Kelton. LC 77-78880. 1978. 8.95 (ISBN 0-385-13315-4). Doubleday.
Good Old Charlie. John Bingham. LC 78-84117. (O.S.I.). 1969. 4.95 o.s.i. (ISBN 0-671-20328-2). S&S.
Good Old Ernie. Bartch-Mallett. 6.95 (ISBN 0-8062-0932-1). Carlton.
Good Old Jack. Eric Hatch. LC 37-4460. 1937. Little, Brown, and Company.
Good Old Stuff: 13 Early Stories. John D MacDonald & Martin Harry Greenberg. LC 82-47540. 14.37 (ISBN 0-06-015038-6). Harper & Row.
Good Old Yesterday. Charles Hanson Towne. LC 35-4046. 1935. D. Appleton-Century Company, Incorporated.
Good Peace. Troy Conway, pseud. (Coxeman Ser). 1969. pap. 0.60 o.p. (63-141). Paperback Lib.
Good Pit Man. Keith Alldritt. LC 76-5367. 1976. 8.95. St. Martin's Press.
Good Place for Murder: A Tony Lantz and Eddie Wright Mystery. Clarence Mullen. LC 49-13593. 1948. Phoenix Press.
Good Place to Work and Die. Winfred Van Atta. LC 75-89095. 1970. 4.50. Published for the Crime Club by Doubleday.
Good Rector. Mary P Nichols. LC 56-8423. 1956. Comet Press Books.
Good Red Brick. Mary Synon. LC 29-9240. 1929. Little, Brown, and Company.
Good Red Earth a Novel. Eden Phillpotts. LC 1-6323. 1901. Doubleday, Page & Co.
Good References. E. J. Rath. LC 21-3812. W. J. Watt & Company.
Good Riddance. Barbara Abercrombie. LC 78-20197. 8.95 (ISBN 0-06-010021-4). Harper & Row.
Good Samaritan. Pat N. Dana. 1976. 5.95 o.p. (ISBN 0-8059-2325-X). Dorrance.
Good Samaritan. Pat N. Dana. 1976. 5.95 o.p. (ISBN 0-8059-2325-X). Dorrance.
Good Samaritan: A Novel. by pat n. dana. ed. Pat N Dana. 1976. 5.95 (ISBN 0-8059-2325-X). Dorrance.
Good Samaritan: A Novel. John Paul Pettavel. LC 51-35732. 1951. Kent, Hand and Flower Press.
Good Samaritan, and Other Stories. John O'Hara. LC 74-1483. 1974. 7.95 (ISBN 0-394-49070-3). Random House.
Good School. Richard Yates. 1979. 2.25 (ISBN 0-440-13000-X). Dell Publishing Co.
Good School: A Novel. Richard Yates. LC 78-17805. 8.95 (ISBN 0-440-03246-6). Delacorte Press/S. Lawrence.
Good Shepherd. Cecil Scott Forester. LC 55-7474. 1955. Little, Brown.
Good Shepherd. Gunnar Gunnarsson. Tr. by Kaufman, Kenneth Carlyle. LC 40-32078. The Bobbs-Merrill Company.
Good Shepherd. John Rathbone Oliver. 1915. Frederick A. Stokes Company.
Good Shepherd: A Novel. Thomas J Fleming. LC 73-82246. 1974. 7.95 (ISBN 0-385-03746-5). Doubleday.
Good Shepherd: A Novel of Tyrol. John Rathbone Oliver. LC 32-17672. 1932. Frederick A. Stokes Company.
Good Shepherdess: By Joan Sargent Pseud. Sara Lucile Jenkins. LC 50-9235. 1950. Bouregy & Curl.
Good Ship Mohock. William Clark Russell. LC 8-1802. 1895. D. Appleton and Company.
Good Sir John. Phoebe Fenwick Gaye. LC 30-25152. H. Liveright.
Good Sisters. FitzGerald, Kathleen. LC 81-66079. 11.95 (ISBN 0-02-924950-3). Contemporary Books.
Good Soldier. Ford Madox Ford. 256p. 1980. Repr. of 1951 ed. lib. bdg. 21.50x (ISBN 0-374-92773-1). Octagon.
Good Soldier: A Tale of Passion. Ford Madox Ford. LC 15-4803. 1915. John Lane Company.
Good Soldier: A Tale of Passion. Ford Madox Ford. LC 27-7734. 1927. A. & C. Boni.
Good Soldier: A Tale of Passion. Ford Madox Ford. LC 81-4805. 1981. 21.50 (ISBN 0-374-92773-1). Octagon Books.
Good Soldier; a Tale of Passion. With an Interpretation by Mark Schorer. Ford Madox Ford. LC 51-11066. 1951. Knopf.
Good Soldier; Schweik. Jaroslav Hasek. Tr. by Selver, Paul. LC 30-5693. 1930. Doubleday, Doran and Company, Inc.
Good Soldier Svejk. Jaroslav Hasek. Tr. by Cecil Parrott. 752p. 1973. 10.00 o.p. (ISBN 0-690-00123-1); pap. 5.95 o.p. (ISBN 0-690-00466-4). T Y Crowell.
Good Soldier Svejk and His Fortunes in the World War. Jaroslav Hasek. LC 73-13703. (Illus.). 1974. 10.00 (ISBN 0-690-00123-1). Crowell.
Good Son: A Novel. Craig Nova. LC 82-2478. 14.95 (ISBN 0-440-02916-3). Delacorte Press/S. Lawrence.
Good Spirit of Laurel Ridge. Jesse Stuart. LC 53-10630. 1953. McGraw-Hill.
Good Sport. Maysie Greig. LC 35-4394. 1934. Doubleday, Doran & Co., Inc.
Good Sport. Julia Whedon. LC 79-7670. 1981. 10.95 (ISBN 0-385-15528-X). Doubleday.
Good Sports. Olive Higgins Prouty. LC 19-5137. Frederick A. Stokes Company.
Good Stories... Kipling, Rudyard. LC 8-30015. 1908. Doubleday, Page & Company.
Good Stories. Frank Mott. Repr. of 1936 ed. 20.00 (ISBN 0-89987-155-0). Darby Bks.
Good Stories. Charles Reade. LC 41-332492. 1884. Harper & Brothers.
Good Stories: A Collection Adapted to the Study of the Various Phases of the Short Story. Ed. by Frank Luther Mott. 1936. The Macmillan Company.
Good Stories for Anniversaries. Frances Jenkins Olcott. Repr. of 1937 ed. 15.00 o.p. Folcroft.
Good Stories for Great Holidays. Frances Jenkins Olcott. Repr. of 1914 ed. 15.00 o.p. Folcroft.
Good Stories from Oxford & Cambridge. T. Selbey Henrey. 1928. 15.00. Havertown Bks.
Good Stories of Man and Other Animals. Charles Reade. (Harper's Franklin square library, no. 374). 1884. Harper & Brothers.
Good Stories... Parts 1-4. Hawthorne, Nathaniel et al. 1867-68. Ticknor and Fields.
Good Sword Belgarde: Or, How De Burgh Held Dover. Albert Charles Curtis. LC 8-31683. 1908. Dodd, Mead and Company.
Good, the Bad, & the Deadly. J. D. Hardin. LC 79-84822. (J.D. Hardin Ser.: No. 1). 224p. (Orig.). 1979. pap. 1.95 (ISBN 0-87216-844-1). Playboy Pbks.
Good, the Bad &The Ugly. Joe Millard, pseud. (O.s.i.). 160p. 1975. pap. 1.25 o.s.i. (AQ1495, Award). Univ Pub & Dist.
Good Thief. Robert J Rosenblum. LC 73-20528. 1974. 5.95 (ISBN 0-385-06326-1). Doubleday.
Good Thief. George W Sprenger. LC 41-12280. Fortuny's Publishers, Inc.

Good Things of Earth. For Any Man Under the Sun. Ed. by Arthur Gray. 1897. A. Gray & Co.
Good Tidings. William Dieterle. LC 50-8688. 1950. Farrar, Straus.
Good Tidings According to Matthias. Joseph MacNaughton Waterman. LC 38-2262. 1937. Lambeth Press.
Good Time! James Wodgwood Drawbell. LC 32-94343. 1932. L. MacVeagh, Dial Press, Inc.
Good-Time Charlie. Mullin Garr. LC 72-7613. 1969. 1.95. Ophelia Press.
Good Time Coming: A Novel. Edmund Schiddel. LC 73-79639. 1969. 6.95. Simon and Schuster.
Good-Time Girl: A Modern Novel. Conrad Maine. (Popular library, 679). 1955. Popular Library.
Good Time Girls. Charles Stanley Strong. LC 42-14117. 1942. Phoenix Press.
Good Time Man. Eva Pearl Murphy Keating. LC 32-175025. The Macaulay Company.
Good Times. Ethel Powelson Hueston. LC 32-34187. The Bobbs-Merrill Company.
Good Times, Bad Times. James Kirkwood. 1978. pap. 2.95 (ISBN 0-449-23975-6, Crest). Fawcett.
Good Times Coming. Robert H Wunder. LC 32-31732. Wonder Publishing Co.
Good Vibes. Jay Cronley. LC 78-22756. 1979. 7.95 (ISBN 0-385-14452-0). Doubleday.
Good Wife. Aurelia Levi. LC 59-6521. 1959. Rinehart.
Good Wife, Good Wife. Louise Dickerson & Ronald Himler. LC 77-23397. 1977. 5.95. (ISBN 0-07-044837-X) (ISBN 0-07-044838-8). McGraw-Hill.
Good Wife: Gramercy Publishing Company. James Noble Gifford. LC 44-5936.
Good Woman. Louis Bromfield. LC 27-15971. 1927. Frederick A. Stokes Company.
Good Work. Mary Dwinell Chellis. LC 6-23413. 1873. D. Lothrop & Co.
Good Yeomen. Jay Williams. LC 48-6708. 1948. Appleton-Century-Crofts.
Goodby Earth. Neil Goble. LC 75-27578. 3.50. Yarnspinners.
Goodby People. Gavin Lambert. LC 70-139636. 1971. 5.95 (ISBN 0-671-20820-9). Simon and Schuster.
Goodbye. William Sansom. LC 67-12428. 1967. New American Library.
Goodbye and Tomorrow. Leane Zugsmith. LC 31-57019. H. Liveright.
Goodbye, Aunt Elva. Elizabeth Fenwick. LC 68-27669. 1968. 4.95. Atheneum.
Goodbye, Bobby Thomson! Goodbye, John Wayne! Alan S Foster. LC 72-90390. 1973. 6.95 (ISBN 0-671-21357-1). Simon and Schuster.
Goodbye, Boys. Boris Balter. LC 67-20549. 1967. Dutton.
Goodbye California. Alistair MacLean. LC 77-80897. 1978. 8.95 (ISBN 0-385-12853-3). Doubleday.
Goodbye California. Alistair MacLean. LC 78-16526. 1978. 13.95 (ISBN 0-8161-6605-6). G. K. Hall.
Goodbye Chairman Mao. Christopher New. LC 78-13650. 8.95 (ISBN 0-698-10918-X). Coward, McCann & Geoghegan.
Goodbye Chicago: 1928, End of an Era. William Riley Burnett. LC 80-27564. 9.95 (ISBN 0-312-33851-1). St. Martin's Press.
Goodbye Columbus. Philip Roth. (gr. 8 up). 1970. pap. 2.95 (ISBN 0-553-20467-X). Bantam.
Goodbye, Columbus, and Five Short Stories. Philip Roth. LC 60-6744. (Meridian fiction. MF5). 1963. World Pub. Co.
Goodbye, Columbus: And Five Short Stories. Philip Roth. LC 59-7579. 1959. Houghton Mifflin.
Goodbye Darling, Be Happy. Mary Astor. (2992). 1967. Dell.
Goodbye Darling, Be Happy. Mary Astor. LC 65-22581. 1965. Doubleday.
Goodbye Europe. Richard De Combray. LC 82-45122. 1983. 13.95 (ISBN 0-385-18097-7). Doubleday.
Goodbye Friend. Sebastien Japrisot. (O.S.I.). 1969. 4.50 o.s.i. (ISBN 0-671-20287-1). S&S.
Goodbye, Friend. Jean Baptiste Rossi. LC 74-84203. (Inner sanctum mystery). 1969. 4.50. Simon and Schuster.
Goodbye, Gillian. Jonathan Burke. (Ace gothic). 1975. (pbk.) 0.95. Ace Books.
Goodbye Goliath. Elliot Chaze. 192p. 1983. 11.95 (ISBN 0-684-17844-3, ScribT). Scribner.
Goodbye, I Guess. Michael Blankfort. LC 62-7545. 1962. Simon and Schuster.
Goodbye, Indiana. Jan Reiss. 304p. (Orig.). 1982. pap. 3.25 (ISBN 0-8439-1056-9, Leisure Bks). Nordon Pubns.
Goodbye Is Just the Beginning. Gail Kimberly. (Orig.). 1979. pap. 2.50 (ISBN 0-89083-442-3). Zebra.
Goodbye, Janette. Harold Robbins. 1982. pap. 3.95 (ISBN 0-671-82481-3). PB.
Goodbye, Janette: A Novel. Harold Robbins. LC 81-4774. 12.95 (ISBN 0-671-22593-6). Simon and Schuster.
Goodbye, Jimmy, Goodbye. 1st Ed. in the U. S. A. Kate Christie. LC 61-9189. 1961. Doubleday.
Goodbye Look. Ross MacDonald. 1972. lib. bdg. 8.95 o.p. (ISBN 0-8161-6016-3, Large Print Bks). G K Hall.
Goodbye Look. Ross Macdonald. 1969. 4.95 o.p. (ISBN 0-394-41220-6). Knopf.
Goodbye Look. Kenneth Millar. LC 69-14735. 1969. 4.95. Knopf.
Goodbye Look. Kenneth Millar. LC 70-38828. 1972. (ISBN 0-8161-6016-3). G. K. Hall.
Goodbye, Mickey Mouse. Len Deighton. LC 82-47813. 1982. 13.95 (ISBN 0-394-51259-6). Knopf: Distributed by Random House.
Goodbye, Mr. Chips. Ed., Introd., Reading Aids by Lou E. Burmeister, Sch. Ed. James Hilton. (Reverside Reading Ser., G2). pap., 1.12. Houghton.
Goodbye: My Heart. Peggy Gaddis, pseud. LC 42-256748. 1941. Arcadia House, Inc.
Goodbye, Old Dry. Dan Cushman. LC 59-6988. (Illus.). 1959. Doubleday.
Goodbye Paper Doll. Anne Snyder. (Orig.). 1980. pap. 1.95 (ISBN 0-451-09826-9, E9826, Sig). NAL.
Goodbye People. Herb Gardner. 167p. 1974. 8.95 o.p. (ISBN 0-374-16560-2). FS&G.
Goodbye Piccadilly, Farewell Leicester Square. Arthur J La Bern. LC 67-15757. 1967. Stein and Day.
Goodbye Rosie. James Lowell McPherson. LC 65-11106. 5.95. Knopf.
Goodbye Rudolph. Floyd Brown. 3.00 o.p. Carlton.
Goodbye, Stranger. Stella Benson. LC 26-20320. 1926. The Macmillan Company.
Goodbye: Summer; a Novel. Allis McKay. LC 53-125353. 1953. Macmillan.
Goodbye to Berlin. Christopher Isherwood. LC 39-16412. 1939. Random House.
Goodbye to Earth. Leo P. Kelley. LC 78-68226. (Galaxy 5 Ser.: Bk. 1). 1979. pap. 4.24 (ISBN 0-8224-3201-3). Pitman Learning.
Goodbye to Love. Joanne Coleman. 1982. 7.95 (ISBN 0-533-04895-8). Vantage.
Goodbye to Some. Gordon Forbes. (War Library). 272p. 1982. pap. 2.50 (ISBN 0-345-30641-4). Ballantine.
Goodbye to the Hill: 1st Amer. Ed. Lee Dunne. LC 66-120674. 1966. 3.95. Houghton.
Goodbye to the Past: Scenes from the Life of William Meadows... William Riley Burnett. LC 34-28777. 1934. Harper & Brothers.
Goodbye to Yesterday. Arlene Hale. LC 73-4307. 1973. 6.95 (ISBN 0-316-33875-3). Little, Brown.
Goodbye to Yesterday. Arlene Hale. LC 73-11021. 1973. 9.95 (ISBN 0-8161-6141-0). G. K. Hall.
Goodbye un-America: A Novel. James Aldridge. LC 79-1029. 8.95 (ISBN 0-316-03114-3). Little, Brown.
Goodey's Last Stand. Charles E Alverson. LC 75-11871. (Midnight novel of suspense). 1975. 7.95 (ISBN 0-395-20672-3). Houghton Mifflin.
Goodhearts. Schoolteacher's Mary, a Delineation of Rural Romance. A Translation and Compilation from the Swiss-German Language; Two Books in One. Felix Ludwig Sophus Dahn & John, Eugenie. Tr. by Benjamin, Joseph. LC 36-935. 1935. The Standard Printing Co., Incorporated.
Goodhues of Sinking Creek. William Riley Burnett & Lankes, Julius J., 1884- Illus. LC 34-379825. 1934. Harper & Brothers.
Goodly Babe. Arturo Vivante. LC 66-10976. bds., 3.95. Little.
Goodly Fellowship. Rachel Capen Schauffler. LC 12-10135. 1912. The Macmillan Company.
Goodly Seed. 1st American Ed. John Wyllie. LC 55-507752. 1955. Dutton.
Goodman Beaver. Harvey Kurtzman & Will Elder. Ed. by Denis Kitchen. (Illus.). 98p. (Orig.). 1983. 17.95 (ISBN 0-87816-009-4); pap. 9.95 (ISBN 0-87816-008-6). Kitchen Sink.
Goodness Girl. Louise Elizabeth Dutton. LC 15-220662. 1915. 1.25. Mofat, Yard and Company.
Goodness Had Nothing to Do with It. Mae West. 1976. pap. 1.95 (ISBN 0-532-19109-9). Woodhill.
Goodness of St. Rocque and Other Stories. Alice Ruth Moore Dunbar Nelson. LC 73-18594. 1975. 12.50 (ISBN 0-404-11405-9). AMS Press.
Goodness of St. Rocque, and Other Stories. Alice Ruth Moore Dunbar Nelson. LC 76-76103. 1969. McGrath Pub. Co.
Goodness of St. Rocque, and Other Stories. Alice Ruth Moore Dunbar Nelson. LC 77-161258. (Black heritage library collection). 1971. (ISBN 0-8369-8817-5). Books for Libraries Press.
Goodness of St. Rocque: And Other Stories. Alice Ruth Moore Dunbar Nelson. LC 99-5827. 1899. Dodd, Mead and Company.
Goodnight Ladies: A Novel. Babs H Deal. LC 77-76229. 1978. 7.95 (ISBN 0-385-00831-7). Doubleday.
Goodnight Pelican. Diana Julia Marr-Johnson. LC 58-10055. 1958. St. Martin's Press.
Goods and Chattels. Laura Benet. LC 74-142258. (Short story index reprint series). 1970. (ISBN 0-8369-3742-2). Books for Libraries Press.
Goods and Chattels. Laura Benet. LC 30-11848. 1930. Doubleday, Doran & Company, Inc.
Goody Two Shoes. Intro. by C. Welsh. 1970. Repr. of 1766 ed. 6.00 o.p. Singing Tree.
Goody Two-Shoes: A Facsimile Reproduction of the Edition of 1766. LC 68-31083. (Illus.). 1970. Repr. of 1881 ed. 30.00x o.p. (ISBN 0-8103-3516-6). Gale.
Gooney Bird. William C. Anderson. 1969. pap. 0.75 o.p. (ISBN 0-446-64099-9, 64-099). Paperback Lib.
Gooney Bird: A Novel. William C Anderson. LC 68-20458. 1968. Crown Publishers.
Gooney Bird Squadron. J. H Reinburg. LC 65-29098. 1966. 3.50. Vantage.
Gooood Boy: A Novel 1st Ed. Ian Cross. LC 57-100636. 1957. Harcourt, Brace.
Goose Creek Folks: A Story of the Kentucky Mountains. Isabel Graham Bush & Bush, Florence, Lilian, Joint Author. LC 13-318. 1.00. Fleming H. Revell Company.
Goose Fair: A Novel. Cecil Roberts. LC 29-1671. 1929. Frederick A. Stokes Company.
Goose-Feather Bed. Ernest Temple Thurston. LC 27-6439. 1926. G. P. Putnam's Sons.
Goose-Feather Bed. Ernest Temple Thurston. LC 27-8461. 1927. George H. Doran Company.
Goose Girl. Harold MacGrath. LC 9-221818. The Bobbs-Merrill Company.
Goose Is Cooked. Emmett Hogarth, pseud. LC 40-31524. 1940. Simon and Schuster.
Goose Man. Jakob Wassermann & Porterfield, Allen Wilson, 1877- Tr. LC 43-27914. Grosset & Dunlap.
Goose Man. Jakob Wassermann & Porterfield, Allen Wilson, 1877- Tr. LC 22-21210. (Half-title: The European library, ed. by J. E. Spingarn). Harcourt, Brace and Company.
Goose on the Grave. John Hawkes. Bd. with Owl. LC 54-10040. 1953. 5.50 o.p. (ISBN 0-8112-0287-9). New Directions.
Goose with a Rose in Her Mouth, and Other Stories. Max Ehrmann. LC 25-17734. (On cover: Scarlet women series). Indiana Publishing Company.
Goose Woman: And Other Stories. Rex Ellingwood Beach. LC 25-13868. 1925. Harper & Brothers.
Gooseberry Fool. James McClure. LC 73-14317. 1974. 5.95 (ISBN 0-06-012898-4). Harper & Row.
Goosefoot: A Novel with Murder. Patrick McGinley. 280p. 1982. 13.95 (ISBN 0-525-24142-6, 01354-410, Joan Kahn Bk). Dutton.
Goosegirl's Love Story: And Other Stories. Caroline Dorothea Jensen Larsen. Tr. by Larsen, Alfred Ferdinand Olaf. LC 25-235153. The Tuttle Company.
Gooseneck Tidings. Nathan A. Ballbach. LC 75-28578. 1977. 4.50 (ISBN 0-918808-01-4). Northlands MI.
Goosepocket. A Collection of Yarns Illustrated by Hubert Harper. Luther Patrick. LC 55-7209. 1955. Vulcan Press.
Goose's Tale. Herbert Silvette. LC 47-4529. 1947. E. P. Dutton.
Gopher Dick: The Story of a Northern Cow-Puncher. Lee Sage. LC 32-17907. 1932. W. Morrow & Company.
Gopher Gold. 1st Ed. Willis Todhunter Ballard. LC 62-8958. (Double D western). 1962. Doubleday.
Gor Promotion. John Norman. Incl. Tarnsman of Gor. pap. 1.75 o. p. (ISBN 0-345-27135-1); Outlaw of Gor. pap. 1.75 o. p. (ISBN 0-345-27136-X); Priest Kings of Gor. pap. 1.75 o. p. (ISBN 0-345-27199-8); Nomad of Gor. pap. 1.75 o. p. (ISBN 0-345-27346-X); Assassin of Gor. pap. 1.75 o. p. (ISBN 0-345-27347-8); Raiders of Gor. pap. 1.75 o. p. (ISBN 0-345-27200-5); Captive of Gor. pap. 2.50 (ISBN 0-345-29414-9). 1973. pap. 2.50. Ballantine.
Gor Saga. Maureen Duffy. LC 81-69974. 1982. 13.95 (ISBN 0-670-34655-1). Viking Press.
Gora. Rabindranath Tagore. pap. 3.75 o.p. Verry.
Gordon see Demon's Feast.
Gordon Baldwin, and The Philosopher's Pendulum. Rudolf Lindau. (Appletons' new handy-volume series v.4). 1878. D. Appleton and Company.
Gordon Craig, Soldier of Fortune. Randall Parrish. LC 12-24816. 1912. 1.35. A. C. McClurg & Co.
Gordon Elopement: The Story of a Short Vacation. Carolyn Wells & Taber, Harry Persons, 1865- Joint Author. LC 4-5922. 1904. Doubleday, Page & Company.
Gordon Keith. Thomas Nelson Page. LC 3-13056. 1903. C. Scribner's Sons.
Gordon Keith. Thomas Nelson Page. LC 15-21855. 1909. C. Scribner's Sons.
Gordon Keith. Thomas Nelson Page. LC 15-17403. 1912. C. Scribner's Sons.
Gordon of the Lost Lagoon: A Romance of the Pacific Coast. Robert Watson. LC 24-221181. 1924. Minton, Balch & Company.
Gordon Reed: A Novel. J. P Bryan. LC 72-10818. 1968. Pemberton Press.
Gordon Reed, a Novel. J. P. Bryan, Sr. 6.95 o.p. Jenkins.
Gordons. Anna Johnson. LC 12-21948. 0.50. American Tract Society.
Gordo's Critters. Gus Arriola. (Illus.). 132p. (Orig.). Date not set. pap. 6.95 (ISBN 0-86679-001-2). Oak Tree Pubns.
Gore and Igor: An Extravaganza. Meyer Levin. LC 68-11013. 1968. Simon and Schuster.
Gorey Festival, 4 Bks. Edward Gorey. (O.s.i.). 1968. Set. slipcase 12.50 o.s.i. (ISBN 0-8392-1176-7). Astor-Honor.
Gorf. Michael McClure. LC 76-14932. (Illus.). 1976. 8.50 (ISBN 0-8112-0630-0); pap. 1.95 (ISBN 0-8112-0612-2, NDP416). New Directions.
Gorgeous. Laura Lou Brookman. LC 36-22612. J. H. Hopkins & Son, Inc.
Gorgeous Borgia: A Romance. Justin Huntly McCarthy. LC 9-5203. 1909. Harper & Brothers.
Gorgeous Ghoul Murder Case. Dwight Vincent Babcock. LC 44-7465. 1943. New Avon Library.
Gorgeous Girl. Nalbro Isadorah Bartley. LC 20-6713. 1920. Doubleday, Page & Company.
Gorgeous Hussy. Samuel Hopkins Adams. LC 34-615. 1934. Houghton Mifflin Company.
Gorgeous Isle. Gertrude Franklin Horn Atherton. LC 8-289953. 1908. Doubleday, Page & Company.
Gorgeous Towers. Lucy Poate Stebbins. LC 34-1294. The Penn Publishing Company.
Gorgo: A Romance of Old Athens. Charles Kelsey Gaines. LC 76-3311. 7.95 (ISBN 0-8265-1203-8). Vanderbilt University.
Gorgo: A Romance of Old Athens. Charles Kelsey Gaines. LC 3-20897. 1903. Lothrop Publishing Company.
Gorgon Festival. John Boyd. LC 73-185141. 192p. 1972. 4.95 o.p. McKay.
Gorgon Festival. Boyd Upchurch. 1974. (pbk.) 0.95. Bantam Books.
Gorgon Festival. Boyd Upchurch. LC 73-185141. 1972. 4.95. Weybright and Talley.
Gorgon's Head. Florence Hurd. (O.s.i.). 1971. pap. 0.75 o.s.i. (532-75441-075). Manor Bks.
Gorgon's Head. Florence Hurd. 1973. (pbk.) 0.95. Manor Books.
Gorgonzola, Won't You Please Come Home. Clyde Ames. pap. 0.60 o.p. Lancer.
Gorham's Gold. Louise Edna Dearborn Keesing. LC 15-25504. 1915. 1.35. R.G. Badger; Etc, Etc.
Gorilla. Colin D Willock. LC 77-10372. 8.95 (ISBN 0-312-34035-4). St. Martin's Press.
Gorilla, My Love. Toni Cade Bambara. LC 72-4091. 1972. 5.95 (ISBN 0-394-48201-8). Random House.
Gorilla, My Love. Toni Cade Bambara. LC 81-3013. 1981. 3.95 (ISBN 0-394-75049-7). Vintage Books.
Gorky Park. Martin Cruz Smith. LC 80-6022. (Illus.). 13.95 (ISBN 0-394-51748-2). Random House.
Gorky Park. large print ed. Martin Cruz Smith. LC 81-6833. 18.95 (ISBN 0-8161-6423-1). G.K. Hall.
Gorlin Clinic. Barbara Harrison. 1975. (pbk.) 1.75 (ISBN 0-380-00446-1). Avon.
Gormenghast. rev. ed. Mervyn Laurence Peake. LC 74-2446. (Illus.). 1968. 0.95. Ballantine Books.
Gormenghast. Mervyn Laurence Peake. LC 81-18902. (Illus.). 1982. 18.95 (ISBN 0-87951-144-3). Overlook Press.
Gormenghast Trilogy. rev. ed. Mervyn Laurence Peake. LC 67-26053. (Illus.). 1967. Weybright and Talley.
Gormenghast Trilogy, Vol. I: Titus Groan. Mervyn Laurence Peake. LC 81-18909. (Illus.). 512p. 1982. 18.95 (ISBN 0-87951-143-5). Overlook Pr.
Gormenghast Trilogy, Vol. III: Titus Alone. Mervyn Laurence Peake. LC 81-18908. (Illus.). 264p. 1982. 18.95 (ISBN 0-87951-145-1). Overlook Pr.
Gorodok. N. A. Teffi. LC 81-51328. 220p. (Rus.). 1982. 13.00 (ISBN 0-89830-061-4); pap. 7.95 (ISBN 0-89830-044-4). Russica Pubs.
Gosbeck: And Other Stories. Honore De Balzac. Tr. by Katharine Prescott Wormeley. LC 3-23181. (Half-title: The comedy of human life... Scenes from Parisian life). 1896. Roberts Brothers.
Goshawk. T. H. White. 1979. pap. 3.95 (ISBN 0-14-001931-6). Penguin.
Goshawk Squadron. Derek Robinson. LC 72-158419. 1972. 6.95 (ISBN 0-670-34672-1). Viking Press.
Goshen Street: A Novel. Wayland Wells Williams. LC 20-17177. Frederick A. Stokes Company.

Gospel. Jack Ansell. LC 72-82169. 1973. 7.95 (ISBN 0-87795-038-5). Arbor Hse.
Gospel According to Gamaliel. Gerald Heard. LC 45-9986. 1945. Harper & Brothers.
Gospel According to Joe: A Novel. Albert Ramsdell Gurney. LC 73-18689. 1974. 5.95 (ISBN 0-06-063526-6). Harper & Row.
Gospel According to Mother Goose. Edmund E. Wells. (O.s.i.). 1973. pap. 0.75 o.s.i. (ISBN 0-515-03008-2, FT3008). Pyramid Pubns.
Gospel According to Norton. Grady Nutt. LC 73-91610. (Illus.). 1974. (pbk.) 1.95 (ISBN 0-8054-5322-9). Broadman Press.
Gospel According to Pontius Pilate. James R. Mills. LC 77-4576. 1977. 6.95 (ISBN 0-913374-77-6). San Francisco Book Co.
Gospel According to St. Luke's: A Novel. Philip Stevenson. LC 31-6268. 1931. Longmans, Green and Co.
Gospel: An American Success Story. Jack Ansell. 1974. pap. 1.50 o.p. (ISBN 0-515-03363-4, A3363). Pyramid Pubns.
Gospel; an American Success Story. A Novel. Jack Ansell. LC 72-82169. 1973. 7.95 (ISBN 0-87795-038-5). Arbor House.
Gospel; an American Success Story: A Novel. Jack Ansell. 1974. (pbk.) 1.50 (ISBN 0-515-03363-4). Pyramid Books.
Gospel Fever. Frank Gill Slaughter. 1981. pap. write for Info. (ISBN 0-671-43488-8). PB.
Gospel Fever: A Novel About America's Most Beloved TV Evangelist. Frank Gill Slaughter. LC 79-6094. 1980. 12.50 (ISBN 0-385-15308-2). Doubleday.
Gospel Fever: A Novel About America's Most Beloved TV Evangelist. Frank Gill Slaughter. LC 80-25615. 12.95 (ISBN 0-89621-256-4). Thorndike Press.
Gospel Four Corners. Frances Gilchrist Wood. LC 30-23201. 1930. D. Appleton and Company.
Gospel Lamb. Jack S Scott, pseud. LC 80-7609. 9.95 (ISBN 0-06-014029-1). Harper & Row.
Gospel of Freedom. Robert Herrick. LC 7-4306. 1898. The Macmillan Company.
Gospel of Freedom see Collected Works.
Gospel of Judas Iscariot. Aaron Dwight Baldwin. 1902. Jamieson-Higgins Co.
Gospel Singer. Harry Crews. 1973. (pbk.) 0.95 (ISBN 0-671-77572-3). Pocket Books.
Gospel Singer. Harry Crews. LC 68-11425. 1968. Morrow.
Gospel Sound: Good News & Bad Times. Tony Heilbut. LC 76-156151. (O.s.i.). 1971. 8.95 o.s.i. (ISBN 0-671-20983-3). S&S.
Gospel Writ in Steel: A Story of the American Civil War. Arthur Henry Paterson. LC 98-392. (Half-title: Appletons' town and country library, bo. 249). 1898. D. Appleton and Company.
Goss Women. Robert Verlin Cassill. LC 73-83619. 1974. 8.95 (ISBN 0-385-07553-7). Doubleday.
Gossamer. James Owen Hannay. LC 15-225429. George H. Doran Company.
Gossamer Thread. Anne Lowing. 1977. pap. 1.25 o.p. (ISBN 0-515-04249-8). BJ Pub Group.
Gossamerfly. Meira Chand. LC 79-27033. 1980. 8.95 (ISBN 0-89919-002-2). Ticknor & Fields.
Gossip. Marc Olden. 1979. pap. 2.50 (ISBN 0-449-14260-4, GM). Fawcett.
Gossip from the Forest. Thomas Keneally. LC 75-34484. 8.95 (ISBN 0-15-136705-1). Harcourt Brace Jovanovich.
Gossip from the Sixteenth Century. William Bowen. LC 39-5254. 1938. The Zamorano Club.
Gossip from Thrush Green. LC 82-11718. (Illus.). 1982. 15.95 (ISBN 0-395-32215-4). Houghton Mifflin.
Gossip from Thrush Green. Miss Read. 1982. 18.50 (ISBN 0-395-32215-4). HM.
Gossip Shop. Annie Edith Foster Jameson. LC 17-253792. 1.35. George H. Doran Company.
Gossip Shop. Annie Edith Foster Jameson. LC 17-24288. 1917. Hodder and Stoughton.
Gossip Truth. John Frederick Burke. LC 68-11789. 1968. Published for the Crime Club by Doubleday.
Gossip Wars. Milt Machlin. (Orig.). 1981. pap. 2.75 (ISBN 0-505-51677-2). Tower Bks.
Gossips of Rivertown: With Sketches in Prose and Verse. Alice Bradley Haven. LC 7-2605. 1850. Hazard and Mitchell.
Gossip's Story, and a Legendary Tale. Jane West. LC 73-22192. (Feminist Controversy in England, 1788-1810). 1974. (ISBN 0-8240-0884-7). Garland Pub.
Gosta Berling's Saga. Selma Ottiliana Lovisa Lagerlof. Tr. by Tudeer, Lillie. LC 19-3215. (Half-title: Scandinavian classics, vol. x-xi). 1918. 3.00. The American-Scandinavian Foundation; Etc., Etc.
Got to Stop Draggin' That Little Red Wagon Around. Robert Paul Smith. LC 69-15264. 1969. 4.50. Harper & Row.
Gothic Ghosts. Hans Holzer. LC 72-98287. (Illus.). 1970. 6.00 o.p. (ISBN 0-672-50944-X, 50944). Bobbs.
Gothic Horror and Other Weird Tales: Fiction. George Wetzel. LC 78-102815. (Illus.). 1978. pbk. 4.00. Weirdbook.
Gothic Novels, 10 Bks. Ed. by Devendra P. Varma. 1972. Repr. Set. 250.00 (ISBN 0-405-00800-7). Ayer Co.
Gothic Novels, Series 2, 32 vols. in 10. facsimile ed. Ed. by Devendra P. Varma. 1974. Set. 400.00 (ISBN 0-405-06011-4). Ayer Co.
Gothic Tales of Terror. Ed. by Peter Haining. (pbk.) 2.50 (ISBN 0-14-003688-1). Penguin Books.
Gothic Tales of Terror: Classic Horror Stories from Great Britain, Europe, and the United States, 1765-1840. Ed. by Peter Haining. LC 78-158841. 1972. 11.95 (ISBN 0-8008-3590-5). Taplinger Pub. Co.
Gothic Tales of Terror, Vol. 1: Classic Horror Stories from Great Britain 1765-1840. Ed. by Peter Haining. 1973. pap. 3.25 o.p. (ISBN 0-14-003688-1). Penguin.
Gothic Tales of Terror, Vol. 2: Classical Horror Stories from Europe & the United States. Ed. by Peter Haining. 1973. pap. 2.95 o.p. (ISBN 0-14-003766-7). Penguin.
Gotland Deal. N. J Crisp. LC 76-17885. 1976. 7.95 (ISBN 0-670-34690-X). Viking Press.
Gotland Deal. N. J Crisp. LC 77-10066. (Penguin crime fiction). 1977-1976. 1.95. Penguin Books.
Gotobedde Lane. Marian Bower. LC 28-23663. The Bobbs Merrill Company.
Gouffe Case. Translated from the German by Michael Bullock. 1st American Ed. Joachim Maass. LC 61-6032. 1960. Harper.
Gourmet. Jim Nisbet. 160p. (Orig.). 1981. pap. 1.95 (ISBN 0-523-41523-0). Pinnacle Bks.
Governess. Elsie Cromwell, pseud. 1971. pap. 0.75 o.p. (64-697). Paperback Lib.
Governess: Or, The Effects of Good Example. An Original Tale, Being a Leaf from Every-Day Life. George Henry Miles. LC 49-39799. (Catholic reward library). 1895. T. B. Noonan.
Governess, or, The Effects of Good Example. An Original Tale. Being a Leaf from Every-Day Life. George Henry Miles. LC 7-18501. Hedian & O'Brien.
Governess's Strange Desires. Dennis Lord. pap. 2.25 o.s.i. (Venus). Grove.
Government. B Traven. LC 78-116873. 1971. 5.95 (ISBN 0-8090-5078-1). Hill and Wang.
Government Countess: A Novel of Departmental Life in Washington. Martha Lemon Schneider. LC 5-42427. 1905. The Neale Publishing Company.
Government House. Alice Robinson Perrin. LC 25-11595. 1925.
Government Nurse. Felicia Bryce. 1976. 4.95. Avalon Books.
Governor. Peter S Jennison. LC 63-17690. 1963. Morrow.
Governor. Karin Michaelis. Tr. by Skovgaard-Pedersen, Amy. LC 13-6767. 1.20. John Lane Company.
Governor. Robert Van Riper. LC 71-118974. 1970. 6.95. Lippincott.
Governor: And Other Stories. George Abiah Hibbard. LC 78-110198. (Short story index reprint series). 1970. Books for Libraries Press.
Governor, and Other Stories. George Abiah Hibbard. LC 7-4755. 1892. C. Scribner's Sons.
Governor: Being an Embittered and Bemused Account of the Life & Times of the Brother of the Irish Christ. Edward R. F Sheehan. LC 73-128485. 1970. 6.95. World Pub. Co.
Governor-General. Christopher Forsyth. LC 76-381804. 1976. (ISBN 0-86932-011-4). Widescope.
Governor Jane: A Story of "the New Woman,". Frank Marcellus Boyce. LC 13-18001. 1913. 1.00. M. S. Boyce.
Governor of Chi-Foo and Other Detective Stories. Edgar Wallace. LC 33-256801. The World Syndicate Publishing Company.
Governor of Massachusetts: A Novel in Three Parts. Elliot Harold Paul. LC 30-23893. H. Liveright.
Governor Ramage, R. N. A Novel. Dudley Pope. LC 73-1183. (Illus.). 1973. 8.95 (ISBN 0-671-21582-5). Simon and Schuster.
Governors. Edward Phillips Oppenheim. LC 9-14415. 1909. 1.50. Little, Brown and Company.
Governor's Boss. James S Barcus. LC 14-6797. 1914. 1.50. The Boss Publishing Co.
Governor's Choice: An Historical Romance. Charles Elmo Robinson. Zondervan Publishing House.
Governor's Daughter. Denton Whitson. LC 52-14023. 1953. Bobbs-Merrill.
Governor's Garden: A Relation of Some Passages in the Life of His Excellency Thomas Hutchinson, Sometime Captain General and Governor-in-Chief of His Majesty's Province of Massachusetts Bay. George Robert Russell Rivers. LC 7-41016. 1896. J. Knight Company.
Governor's Lady. Norman Collins. LC 79-79627. 1969. 6.95. Simon and Schuster.
Governor's Lady. 1st Ed. Thomas Head Raddall. LC 59-12641. 1960. Doubleday.
Governor's Mercy. A Story of the Tennessee Mountains. George Absalom Ross. LC 8-678. 1896. Ogden Bros. & Co., Printers.
Governor's Reverie, and Other Stories. Frank Seymour Sullivan. LC 16-25098. 1916. Crane & Company.
Governor's Wife. David Storr Unwin. LC 55-5346. 1955. Dutton.
Governor's Wife Madame Junot: Pictures from the Imperial Court of France, 1806-1807. Mathilda Kruse Malling & St. John, Henriette Langan, Tr. LC 4-10536. 1904. T. M. St. John.
Gov't Inspected Meat and Other Fun Summer Things. Dotson Rader. LC 73-120172. 1970. 5.95. D. McKay Co.
Gowanusiaus. Humorous Sketches of Every-Day Life Among Plain People. Maurice Edmund McLoughlin. LC 7-20431. 1894. Edmunds Publishing Company.
Gower Court Manor. Elizabeth Deare Bennett. 1976. (pbk.) 1.25. Dell Books.
Gower Street. Claire Rayner. LC 73-3782. 1973. 7.95 (ISBN 0-671-21550-7). Simon and Schuster.
Gower Street. Claire Rayner. (Fawcett crest book). 1974. (pbk.) 1.50. Fawcett.
Gown of Glory. Agnes Sligh Turnbull. LC 52-967. 1952. Houghton Mifflin.
Gowns by Roberta. Alice Duer Miller. LC 33-25373. 1933. Dodd, Mead & Company.
Goy. Mark Harris. LC 79-120467. 1970. 5.95. Dial Press.
Goya: Rebellious Genius. Marion Chapman. LC 40-951738. Egmont Press.
Gozame Y...Matalo. Rolando Reyes. (Pimienta Collection Ser). (Orig., Span.). 1977. pap. 1.00 (ISBN 0-88473-270-3). Fiesta Pub.
Grab. Maria Katzenbach. LC 77-3722. 1978. 8.95 (ISBN 0-688-03216-8). Morrow.
Grab. Maria Katzenbach. 1979. 2.25 (ISBN 0-671-82147-4). Pocket Books.
Grab. Zeno. LC 79-127224. 1970. 5.95 (ISBN 0-8128-1310-3). Stein and Day.
Grab Bag. William Daniel Trausch. Pegasus Publishing Company.
Grabbers. Tony James. 1977. pap. 1.50 o.p. (ISBN 0-8439-0498-4, Leisure Bks). Nordon Pubns.
Grabhorn Bounty. Clifton Adams. LC 65-12659. (Double D western).
Grace Abounding. Maureen Howard. LC 82-14056. 12.95 (ISBN 0-316-37462-8). Little, Brown.
Grace Allen's Minister: Or, How a Fine Young Man Was Constrained by Charming Christian Companions to Become a Minister. John William Richards. LC 24-13733. 1923. The Lutheran Literary Board.
Grace Baldwin: Or, Schnell's Place. Thomas Curry Bronson. Franklin Printing and Publishing Company.
Grace Divorce. Frank Arthur Swinnerton. LC 60-13560. 3.95. Doubleday.
Grace Dudley; or, Arnold at Saratoga. An Historical Novel. Charles Jacobs Peterson. T. B. Peterson.
Grace I Give You. Morton Gill Clark. LC 39-115741. 1939. W. Morrow & Company.
Grace Lealand: Or, Life-Scenes in a Christmas Family. Henriettas M Coon. LC 6-30190. American Baptist Publication Society.
Grace Lorraine: A Romance. Douglas Brooke Wheelton Sladen. LC 18-7297. 1917. Brentano's.
Grace of Lambs: Stories by Manuel Komroff. Manuel Komroff. LC 25-21066. 1925. Boni & Liveright.
Grace O'Malley: Princess and Pirate, Told by Ruari Macdonald, Redshank and Rebel; the Same Set Forth in the Tongue of the English. Robert Machray. LC 7-19996. F. A. Stokes Company.
Grace Porter: A Jewel Lost and Found. Joseph Patterson Dysart. LC 99-2902. The Author.
Grace Truman: Or, Love and Principle. Sallie Rochester Ford. LC 6-41389. 1857. Sheldon, Blakeman & Company.
Grace Weldon, or Frederica, the Bonnet-Girl: A Tale of Boston and Its Bay. Joseph Holt Ingraham. LC 6-243754. 1845. H. L. Williams.
Grace Winslow: Or, Gold and Dross. John W Spear. LC 8-15518. 1883. N. Tibbals & Sons.
Gracechurch. 4th impression. ed. Francis Browning Drew Bickerstaffe-Drew. LC 19-14020. 1918. Longmans, Green and Co.
Graces of Ballykeen. Una Troy. LC 59-7796. 1960. Dutton.
Gracie Allen Murder Case: A Philo Vance Story. Willard Huntington Wright. LC 38-34146. 1938. C. Scriber's Sons.
Gracie & Uncle Alex: Or, Pleasures Regulated by the Laws of Health. Agnes H. Carll. LC 6-24234. 1886. M. Hill Publishing Company.
Gracious Lady. Arthur Somers Roche. LC 32-22537. Sears Publishing Company, Inc.
Gracious Lady. Arthur Somers Roche. LC 36-21010. A. L. Burt Company.
Gracious Lily Affair. 1st Ed. Francis Van Wyck Mason. LC 57-11432. 1957. Doubleday.
Graded German Short Stories. Ed. by Curtis Churchill Doughty Vail. LC 41-129525. Oxford University Press.
Gradiva: A Pompeiian Fancy. Wilhelm Jensen. Tr. by Downey, Helen M. LC 18-8161. 1918. Moffat, Yard and Company.
Gradual Joy. Alma Routsong. LC 52-12766. 1953. Houghton Mifflin.
Graduate. Charles Richard Webb. LC 63-21804. 1963. New American Library.
Graduate Mistress. Kenneth Gunnell. pap. 1.95 o.p. (V1050T, Venus). Grove.
Graduate Nurse. Joseph Calvitt Clarke. LC 39-5223. Gramercy Pub. Co.
Graduate Nurse. Joseph Calvitt Clarke. LC 39-52234. 1938. Gramercy Publishing Co.
Graduate of Paris. Henry Thompson Stanton. LC 8-134531. W. H. Morrison.
Graduate Wife. Frederic Raphael. 1978. 15.00 o.p. (ISBN 0-86025-094-6). State Mutual Bk.
Grady Barr. Jack Donahue & Michel T. Halbouty. LC 81-66961. 352p. 1981. 12.95 (ISBN 0-87795-329-5). Arbor Hse.
Grafenbury People: Fiction but Fact. Reuen Thomas. LC 8-30877. (On cover: The round world series). D. Lothrop & Company.
Graffiti for the Johns of Heaven. James Broughton. LC 82-60091. (Illus.). 80p. 1982. pap. 6.00 (ISBN 0-9608372-1-3). Syzygy Pr.
Graffiti Gambit: A Novel. Alan Wingard. 1974. (pbk.) 1.25. Warner Paperback Library.
Grafted Twig. Allistene Starkey. LC 40-314576. 1940. Arcadia House, Inc.
Grafters. Francis Lynde. LC 4-926892. 1904. The Bobbs-Merrill Company.
Grafters. Illus. by Arthur I. Keller. Francis Lynde. LC 68-20017. (Americans in fic.). 1968. 10.00. Gregg Pr.
Graftons: A Novel. Archibald Marshall. LC 21-17629. 1919. Dodd, Mead and Company.
Graftons: Novel, by Archibald Marshall. Archibald Marshall. LC 18-105824. 1918. Dodd, Mead and Company.
Graftons; Or, Looking Forward. A Story of Pioneer Life. John Rankin Rogers. LC 7-40734. 1893. M. George Publishing House.
Gragas Efter Det Arnamagnaeanske Haandskriftnr. Three Hundred & Thirty-Four Fol. Stratharholsbok. Ed. by Vilhjalmur Finsen. LC 80-1992. Repr. of 1879 ed. 64.50 (ISBN 0-404-18670-X). AMS Pr.
Gragas: Islaendernes Lovbog I Fristatens Tid, 4 vol. set. Ed. by Vilhjalmur Finsen. LC 80-1991. 140.00 (ISBN 0-404-18680-7). AMS Pr.
Gragas: Stykkner, Som Findes I Det Arnamagnaeanske Haandskrift Nr 351 Fol., Skalholtsbok. Ed. by Vilhjalmur Finsen. LC 80-1966. Repr. of 1883 ed. 82.00 (ISBN 0-404-18671-8). AMS Pr.
Graham Greene. John Alfred Atkins. LC 58-12105. 1957. Roy Publishers.
Graham Hamilton... Caroline Ponsonby Melbourne. LC 7-15441. 1822. H. C. Carey and I. Lea.
Graham of Claverhouse. Constance Woodbury Dodge. LC 37-546. Covici-Friede.
Graham of Claverhouse. John Watson. McLeod & Allen.
Grahame: or Youth and Manhood. A Romance. By the Author of "Talbot and Vernon"... John Ludlum McConnell. LC 7-15426. 1850. Baker and Scribner.
Grail. Philip Michaels. 336p. 1982. pap. 2.95 (ISBN 0-380-79921-9, 79921). Avon.
Grail: A Novel. Babs H Deal. LC 63-19342. 1963. D. McKay.
Grail Brothers: Or, Was It an Accident? Sarah Helen Gale. LC 99-7941. (Neely's universal library, no. 54). 1899. F. T. Neely.
Grail Fire. Zephine Humphrey. LC 17-8347. E. P. Dutton & Co.
Grail Tree. Jonathan Gash, pseud. LC 79-2647. 8.95 (ISBN 0-06-011462-2). Harper & Row.
Grail War. Richard Monaco. LC 79-5270. (Illus.). 5.95 (ISBN 0-671-25182-1). Pocket Books: Distributed by Simon and Schuster.
Grain. Robert James Campbell Stead. LC 26-23684. George H. Doran Company.
Grain of Dust. David G. Phillips. Ed. by Abe C. Ravitz. (American Authors Ser). 1911. 23.00 o.s.i. (ISBN 0-512-00561-3). Garrett Pr.
Grain of Dust: A Novel. David Graham Phillips. LC 71-105359. (Series in American Studies). (Illus.). 1970. Johnson Reprint Corp.
Grain of Dust: A Novel. David Graham Phillips. LC 72-84638. 1974. (ISBN 0-403-02957-0). Scholarly Press.
Grain of Dust: A Novel. Illustrated by A. B. Wenzell. David Graham Phillips. LC 11-7868. 1911. 1.30. D. Appleton and Company.
Grain of Dust: A Novel. Illustrated by A. B. Wenzell. David Graham Phillips & Cooper, Frederic Taber. LC 15-20298. 1912. D. Appleton and Company.
Grain of Madness: A Romance. Lida Abbie Churchill. LC 2-26767. 1902. The Abbey Press.

Grain of Salt. Grigory Vinokur, pseud. LC 80-17406. 9.95. F. Fell Publishers.
Grain of the Wood. Michael Home, pseud. LC 51-9737. 1951. Macmillan.
Grain of the Wood: By Michael Home Pseud. Christopher Bush. LC 51-9737. 1951. Macmillan.
Grain of Truth. Nina Bawden. LC 68-28222. 1968. Harper & Row.
Grain of Wheat. Toyohiko Kagawa. Tr. by Draper, Marion Romer. Ed. by Clark, Glenn. LC 36-1534. 1936. Harper & Brothers.
Grain of Wheat. James Ngugi. LC 67-92814. 1967. 4.00, 1.25 pap.,. Heinemann.
Grains of Rice from a Chinese Bowl. Ida Belle Lewis. LC 26-14757. Fleming H. Revell Company.
Grains of Sand. Alfred Martin Harris. LC 70-373266. 1968. 3.75. Cassell Australia.
Gramercy Park: A Story of New York. John Seymour Wood. LC 13-9371. 1892. D. Appleton and Company.
Gramma," The Autobiography of a Cat, with Eight Half-Tone Illustrations... John S Owen. LC 2557. American Publishing Company.
Grammar of Love. Ivan Alekseevich Bunin. LC 76-23876. (Classics of Russian literature). (Hyperion library of world literature). 1977. 10.50. (ISBN 0-88355-481-X) (ISBN 0-88355-482-8). Hyperion Press.
Grammar of Love. Ivan Alekseevich Bunin & Cournos, John, 1881- Tr. LC 34-25157. 1934. H. Smith and R. Haas.
Grammar of Love. Ivan Alekseevich Bunin & Cournos, John, 1881- Tr. LC 34-25157. 1934. H. Smith and R. Haas.
Grammarian's Funeral. Acheson, Edward. LC 35-604717. 1935. Macrae Smith Company.
Gran Gatsby. Scott Fitzgerald. (Portico Ser.). pap. 1.25 o.p. (ISBN 0-671-08077-6). Monarch Pr.
Granby: A Novel, 3 vols. in 2. Thomas Henry Lister. LC 79-8156. Date not set. Repr. of 1826 ed. Set. 84.50 (ISBN 0-404-61983-5); Vol. 1. (ISBN 0-404-61984-3); Vol. 2. (ISBN 0-404-61985-1). AMS Pr.
Grand and the Glorious. Dan Cushman. LC 63-13155. 1963. McGraw-Hill.
Grand Army Man. Harvey Jerrold O'Higgins & David Belasco. LC 8-24451. 1908. The Century Co.
Grand Army Man. Harvey Jerrold O'Higgins & David Belasco. LC 8-24451. 1908. The Century Co.
Grand Babylon Hote: A Fantasia on Modern Themes. Arnold Bennett. LC 41-6790. (On cover: Penguin books. 1760). 1939. Penguin Books Limited.
Grand Babylon Hotel. Arnold Bennett. LC 74-5400. (collected works of Arnold Bennett). 1974. (ISBN 0-518-19105-2). Books for Libraries Press.
Grand Babylon Hotel. Arnold Bennett. LC 78-7940. Scholarly Press.
Grand Babylon Hotel: A Fantasia on Modern Themes. Arnold Bennett. 224p. 1976. pap. 1.95 o.p. (ISBN 0-14-000176-X). Penguin.
Grand Babylon Hotel, a Fantasia on Modern Themes. Arnold Bennett. 1904. 20.00 (ISBN 0-403-00004-1). Scholarly.
Grand Bouquet. Charles Gilbert Stahls. LC 51-20337. 1951. Watling.
Grand Canary. Archibald Joseph Cronin. 1933. 14.95 (ISBN 0-575-01607-8, Pub. by Gollancz England). David & Charles.
Grand Canary. Archibald Joseph Cronin. 1981. 20.00x (ISBN 0-575-01607-8, Pub. by Gollancz England). State Mutual Bk.
Grand Canary. Archibald Joseph Cronin. 1974. pap. 1.25 o.p. (V3447). BJ Pub Group.
Grand Canary: A Novel by A. J. Cronin. Archibald Joseph Cronin. LC 33-12037. 1933. Little, Brown, and Company.
Grand Canyon: A Novel. Victoria Mary Sackville-West. LC 42-363493. 1942. Doubleday, Doran and Company, Inc.
Grand Cayman Slam. Randy Striker. (Dusky MacMorgan Ser.: No. 7). 1982. pap. 2.25 (ISBN 0-451-11512-0, AE1512, Sig). NAL.
Grand Caynon of Arizona Romance. William Lee Popham. LC 13-26181. 1.00. The World Supply Company.
Grand Central Murder. Sue MacVeigh. LC 39-24447. 1939. Houghton Mifflin Company.
Grand Chaco. George Manville Frenn. LC 6-39374. United States Book Company.
Grand Chase. 1st Ed. Mark Venafro, pseud. LC 56-12551. 1956. Pageant Press.
Grand Circus Park, U. S. W. Harold Charles Le Baron Jackson. LC 39-53673. 1938. Arnold-Powers, Inc.
Grand Concourse: A Novel. 1st Ed. Eliot Wagner. LC 54-9493. 1954. Bobbs-Merrill.
Grand Crevasse, a Novel: Translated from the French by Janet Adam Smith. 1st American Ed. Frison-Roche, Roger. LC 51-14882. 1951. Prentice-Hall.
Grand Crossing. Alexander Plaisted Saxton. LC 43-11956. 1943. Harper & Brothers.
Grand Defiance. Bernard Frizell. 1973. 1.50. Dell.
Grand Defiance: A Novel. Bernard Frizell. LC 76-181593. 1972. 6.95. Morrow.
Grand Design. John Dos Passos. (District of Columbia Ser.). 1977. Repr. of 1949 ed. lib. bdg. 18.95x (ISBN 0-89244-036-8). Queens Hse.
Grand Design. John Dos Passos. 1966. 7.95 o.p. (ISBN 0-395-07619-6). HM.
Grand Design. David Pilgrim, pseud. LC 43-14648. 1943. Harper & Brothers.
Grand Dragon. Irma Kurtz. 1979. 9.95 o.p. (ISBN 0-525-11603-6, Thomas Congdon Book). Dutton.
Grand-Duc. Rene de Goscinny. (Lucky Luke Series). (French.). 1976. 5.95x (ISBN 2-205-00693-2). Intl Learn Syst.
Grand Duchess. Anne Duffield. LC 54-114715. 1954. Arcadia House.
Grand Duke and Mr. Pimm. 1st Ed. Lindsay Hardy. LC 59-106147. 1959. Harper.
Grand Duke's Finances. Gunnar Serner & Lee, Robert Emmons, Tr. LC 24-23178. Thomas Y. Crowell Company.
Grand Ecart. Jean Cocteau. LC 74-22403. 1975. 10.00. H. Fertig.
Grand Gennaro. Garibaldi Marto Lapolla. LC 74-17937. (Italian American Experience). 1975. 21.00 (ISBN 0-405-06408-X). Arno Press.
Grand Gennaro: A Novel. Garibaldi Marto Lapolla. LC 35-142356. 1935. The Vanguard Press.
Grand Hills for Sheep. Georgina McDonald. 1976. 11.40x o.p. (ISBN 0-7233-0447-5). Intl Pubns Serv.
Grand Hotel. Vicki Baum. Tr. by Creighton, Basil. LC 31-26356. 1931. Doublesday Doran & Company, Inc.
Grand Hotel... Vicki Baum. LC 46-22362. 1946.
Grand Hotel. Vicki Baum. 1974. (pbk.) 1.75. Manor Books.
Grand Inquisitor. Donald Douglas. LC 25-4609. Boni and Liveright.
Grand Jubilee. Suzette Haden Elgin. LC 81-43001. (Elgin, Suzette Haden. Ozark Fantasy Trilogy: Bk. 2). 1981. 9.95 (ISBN 0-385-15877-7). Doubleday.
Grand Jury. Elizabeth Rose. 1974. (pbk.) 1.50. Avon.
Grand Mademoiselle: From the Memoirs of Charles Alexander, Comte De Lannoy, Premier Ecuyer to the King, Louis Xiv. James Eugene Farmer. LC 45. 1899. Dodd, Mead & Company.
Grand Man. Catherine Cookson. LC 55-131995. 1955. Macmillan.
Grand Man. Catherine Cookson. LC 74-16916. 1975. 5.95 (ISBN 0-688-00343-5). Morrow.
Grand Man. Catherine Cookson. 1976. (pbk.) 1.50. Bantam Books.
Grand Manner. Louis Kronenberger. LC 29-6177. 1929. H. Liveright.
Grand Mesa. 1st Ed. Allan Vaughan Elston. 1957. Lippincott.
Grand Miracle. Clive Staples Lewis. (Epiphany Ser.). 176p. 1983. pap. 2.95 (ISBN 0-345-30539-6). Ballantine.
Grand Modena Murder: An Inspector Slade Detective Story... Leonard Reginald Gribble. LC 31-853425. Pub. for the Crime Club, Inc., by Doubleday, Doran & Company, Inc.
Grand Motel: By William and Milarde Brent. William Brent & Milarde Brent. LC 54-13195. Greenberg.
Grand National. John Brennan. LC 76-41682. 8.95 (ISBN 0-671-22452-2). Simon and Schuster.
Grand National. John Brennan. 1978. 1.95 (ISBN 0-449-23578-5). Fawcett Crest Books.
Grand National. John Welcome, pseud. LC 76-377656. 1976. 3.95 (ISBN 0-241-89338-0). Hamilton.
Grand Obese. Cesar J Rotondi. LC 78-66405. 8.95. (ISBN 0-312-34249-7). St. Martin's Press.
Grand Old Man. Baldwyn Dyke Acland. LC 31-35227. 1931. R.M. McBride & Company.
Grand Ole Opry Murders. Marvin Kaye. LC 73-18190. 1974. 5.95. Saturday Review Press.
Grand Opening: A Novel. Bernard Glemser. LC 75-45141. 8.95 (ISBN 0-316-31621-0). Little, Brown.
Grand Opening: A Novel. Bernard Glemser. 1977. 1.75 (ISBN 0-380-00954-4). Avon Books.
Grand Parade. Edith J. Lyttleton. LC 43-17032. 1943. Reynal & Hitchcock.
Grand Parade. Julian Mayfield. LC 61-5233. 1961. Vanguard Press.
Grand Parade see Nowhere Street.
Grand Piano; or: The Almanac of Alienation. Paul Goodman. LC 42-191642. 1942. The Colt Press.
Grand Portage: A Novel. Walter O'Meara. LC 51-9839. 1951. Bobbs-Merrill.
Grand Prix Monaco. Roderic Jeffries. LC 68-24499. (Illus.). 1968. 3.29. Putnam.
Grand Right and Left: A Novel. Louis Kronenberger. LC 52-7513. 1952. Viking Press.
Grand Rounds. Harrison Hopkins. LC 74-8924. 1974. 7.95 (ISBN 0-316-37271-4). Little, Brown.
Grand Scam. Richard Lipez & Stein, Peter. 1980. 1.95 (ISBN 0-445-04551-5). Fawcett Popular Library.
Grand Scam: A Novel. Richard Lipez & Peter Stein. LC 79-554. 8.95 (ISBN 0-8037-3089-6). Dial Press.
Grand Slam. Ritchie Perry. LC 80-7722. 8.95 (ISBN 0-394-51271-5). Pantheon Books.
Grand Slam. Ray Puechner. (O.S.I.). (Orig.). 1973. pap. 0.95 o.s.i. (ISBN 0-446-75215-0). Paperback Lib.
Grand Slam. Ray Puechner. 1973. (pbk) 0.95. Warner Paperback Lib.
Grand Slam: The Rise and Fall of a Bridge Wizard. Benjamin Russell Herts. LC 32-336996. 1932. J. L. Pratt.
Grand Slam: 13 Great Short Stories About Bridge. Eugene Roger Cole & James Edwards. LC 75-7673. (Illus.). 1975. 7.95. Putnam.
Grand Sophy. Georgette Heyer. LC 50-9908. 1950. Putnam.
Grand Street Collector. Joseph Arleo. LC 73-103857. (Berkley medallion book). 1975. (pbk.) 1.25 (ISBN 0-425-02839-9). Berkley Pub. Co.
Grand Tour: By Carol Holliston Pseud. James Noble Gifford. 1955. Arcadia House.
Grand Tour of Alphonse Marichaud. Florence Roma Muir O'Brien. LC 23-13318. 1923. A. A. Knopf.
Grand Tour of Alphonse Marichaud. Florence Roma Muir Wilson O'Brien. LC 23-13318. 1923. A. A. Knopf.
Grand Troupeau see Oeuvres Romanesques.
Grand Wheel. Barrington J Bayley. (Illus.). 1.50 (ISBN 0-87997-318-8). DAW Books.
Grand Wide Way. James Reynolds. LC 51-9234. 1951. Creative Age Press.
Grandborough's Filly: A Novel. Audrey Blanshard. (Fawcett Crest Book). 1977. 1.50 (ISBN 0-449-23210-7). Fawcett Pubns.
Granddaddy Longwheels. William W. McDowell. LC 81-85706. 80p. 1983. pap. 3.95 (ISBN 0-86666-055-0). GWP.
Granddaughter. Lois Wyse. LC 81-5800. 1981. 12.95 (ISBN 0-312-34259-4). St Martin's Press.
Grande Dames of Detection: Two Centuries of Sleuthing Stories by the Gentle Sex. Ed. by Seon Manley. LC 73-4947. (Illus.). 1973. 4.95 (ISBN 0-688-41551-2) (ISBN 0-688-41551-2). Lothrop, Lee & Shepard Co.
Grandee Jim. Thomas H. Uzzell. LC 72-97156. 200p. 1973. 6.95 o.p. (ISBN 0-8283-1494-2). Branden.
Grandest Guy in the World. C. Tennant Copeland. LC 51-4334. 1951. Christopher Pub. House.
Grandfather. V. A Mora-Rodriguez. LC 73-89452. 1974. 3.95. Libra Publishers.
Grandfather and the Globe. Dell B Wilson. LC 74-10166. (Illus.). 1969. 5.00. Pudding Stone Press.
Grandfather Lickshingle. R. W Criswell. (On cover: Lovell's library v. 7. no. 350). 1884. J. W. Lovell Company.
Grandfather Objects. Walter Beebe Wilder & Price, George, 1901- Illus. 1946. Doubleday & Company, Inc.
Grandfather Stories. Samuel Hopkins Adams. LC 55-6657. 1955. Random House.
Grandfathers. Conrad Richter. LC 64-13445. 1964. Knopf.
Grandfather's Love Pie. Miriam Gaines. LC 13-21361. 1913. 0.50. J. P. Morton & Company.
Grandfather's Steps. Joan Haslip. LC 32-23132. 1932. Minton, Balch & Company.
Grandfather's Strange Shepherd's Crook. Marjorie Rebert Dilcer. (Illus.). 1975. 4.00 (ISBN 0-682-48173-4). Exposition Press.
Grandfather's Treat:: a Story. 1st. ed. Walter D Green & Patricia Hauge. 1974. 3.50 (ISBN 0-682-47946-2). Exposition Press.
Grandison Mather. Henry Harland. LC 76-24391. (Decadent Consciousness). 1977. 26.00 (ISBN 0-8240-2768-X). Garland Pub.
Grandison Mather: Or, An Account of the Fortunes of Mr. and Mrs. Thomas Gardiner. Henry Harland. LC 7-1643. 1889. Cassell & Company, Limited.
Grandissimes. George Washington Cable. LC 72-84525. 1974. (lib. ed.) 18.50 (ISBN 0-403-02979-1). Scholarly Press.
Grandissimes. George Washington Cable. LC 8-15328. 1908. C. Scribner's Sons.
Grandissimes. George Washington Cable. LC 16-16158. 1916. C. Scribner's Sons.
Grandissimes see Collected Works.
Grandissimes: A Story of Creole Life. George Washington Cable. LC 6-6974. 1884. C. Scribner's Sons.
Grandissimes: A Story of Creole Life. by george w. cable... ed. George Washington Cable. LC 41-423891. 1886. C. Scribner's Sons.
Grandissimes; a Story of Creole Life. Introd. by Newton Arvin. George Washington Cable. LC 57-124451. (American century series, S-25). 1957. Sagamore Press.
Grandissimes... With Illustrations. George Washington Cable. LC 99-5045. 1899. C. Scribner's Sons.
Grandma. Elizabeth Lincoln Gould. LC 11-28434. 1911. 1.00. The Penn Publishing Company.
Grandma & the Buck Deer. Joel Vance. (Illus.). 176p. 1980. 12.95 (ISBN 0-87691-322-2). Winchester Pr.
Grandma Bates Sees the World. Eva Thomas Nettleton. LC 36-37298. Dorrance and Company.
Grandma Cigar see Willis & His Friends Series.
Grandma Strikes Back. Edwina Sherudi. 1980. pap. 1.95 (ISBN 0-8439-0810-6). Nordon Pubns.
Grandma, Why Don't You Try Zen? Beatrice C. Schuman. 1974. 6.00 o.p. (ISBN 0-682-47806-7). Exposition.
Grandma, Why Don't You Try Zen? first ed. Beatrice Chernuchin Schuman. 1974. 6.00 (ISBN 0-682-47806-7). Exposition Press.
Grandma's Letter to Her Grandchildren. Dena Rosenbohn. 3.50 o.p. Vantage.
Grandmere. Vina Delmar. LC 67-10759. 1967. Harcourt, Brace & World.
Grandmont: Stories of an Old Monastery. Walter T Griffin. LC 6-45432. Hunt & Eaton.
Grandmother. Georges Simenon. LC 80-14918. 8.95 (ISBN 0-15-136738-8). Harcourt Brace Jovanovich.
Grandmother: A Story of Country Life in Bohemia. Bozena Rakusana Nemcova. LC 76-48446. (Classics of European Literature). (Hyperion library of world literature). 1977. 12.95. (ISBN 0-88355-588-3) (ISBN 0-88355-589-1). Hyperion Press.
Grandmother: A Story of Country Life in Bohemia. Bozena Rakusana Nemcova. Tr. by Gregor, Frantiska. LC 7-25782. 1891. A. C. McClurg and Company.
Grandmother: A Story of Country Life in Bohemia. Bozena Rakusana Nemcova & Gregor, Frantiska, Tr. LC 7-25782. 1891. A. C. McClurg and Company.
Grandmother: A Tale of Old Kentucky. Sue Froman Matthews. LC 11-23504. J. S. Ogilvie Publishing Company.
Grandmother and the Comet: An Insubstantial Pageant. Victoria Lincoln. LC 44-540661. 1944. Farrar & Rinehart, Inc.
Grandmother and the Priests. Taylor Caldwell. LC 62-15874. 1963. Doubleday.
Grandmother in Cellophane. Frances Best. LC 54-12501. 1954. Meador Pub. Co.
Grandmother Martin Is Murdered. John Cournos. LC 30-4859. Farrar & Rinehart, Inc.
Grandmother Normandy. Mary Andrews Denison. LC 6-33994. (On cover: V. I. F. ser.). D. Lothrop and Company.
Grandmother Normandy. Mary Andrews Denison. LC 6-33993. (On cover: Household library. no. 5). 1886. D. Lothrop and Company.
Grandmother O Kyo. Etsu Inagaki Sugimoto. LC 40-7860. 1940. Doubleday, Doran & Co., Inc.
Grandmother S House: Farmor S House) by Soya. Tr. by Agnes Camilla Hansen. Eng. Tr. Rev., Ed. by Alan Moray Williams. Carl Erik Soya. Ed. by Alan Moray Williams. LC 65-26941. 1966. 4.50. Taplinger.
Grandmother Stories. Ida Hamilton Munsell. LC 15-88222. 1915. 0.25. Munsell Publishing Co.
Grandmother: The Story of a Life That Never Was Lived. Laura Elizabeth Howe Richards. LC 7-24770. (On verso of half-title: Handy volume editions of copyrighted fiction). D. Estes & Company.
Grandmothers. Kathleen Coburn. LC 50-9775. 1949. Oxford University Press.
Grandmothers. Glenway Wescott. LC 50-6732. 1962. pap. 1.45 o.p. (ISBN 0-689-70205-1, 11). Atheneum.
Grandmothers: A Family Portrait. Glenway Wescott. LC 27-268661. 1927. Harper & Brothers.
Grandmothers, a Family Portrait: With an Introd. by Fred B. Millett. Glenway Wescott. LC 50-6732. (Harper's modern classics). 1950. Harper.
Grandmother's House. J. B. Herman. (Orig.). 1980. pap. 1.75 (ISBN 0-532-23136-8). Woodhill.
Grandmother's House. rev ed. Soya. Ed. by A. M. Williams. Tr. by A. C. Hansen. 1966. 4.50 o.p. (ISBN 0-8008-3600-6). Taplinger.
Grandmother's Money. A Novel. Frederick William Robinson. (seaside library. v. 39, no. 810). 1880. G. Munro.
Grandmother's Pictures. Sam Cornish. LC 75-33566. (Illus.). 1976. 4.95. (ISBN 0-87888-092-5). Bradbury Press.
Grandon of Sierra. Charles Edwin Winter. LC 7-24285. Broadway Publishing Co.
Grandon of Sierra. Charles Edwin Winter. LC 26-7528. 1907. Printed by J. J. Little & Ives Co.

Grandpa and Frank. Janet Majerus. LC 75-33776. 7.95 (ISBN 0-397-01130-X). Lippincott.
Grandpa and Frank. Janet Majerus. (Kangaroo Book.). 1977. 1.75 (ISBN 0-671-80928-8). Pocket Books.
Grandpa and Frank. Janet Majerus. LC 77-18231. 1978. 8.95 (ISBN 0-89340-129-3). J. Curley.
Grandpa and the Girls. Louis M Heyward. LC 60-5540. 1960. Random House.
Grandpa Mazai & the Hares. N. Nekrasov. 15p. 1981. pap. 1.50 (ISBN 0-8285-2201-4, Pub. by Progress Pubs USSR). Imported Pubns.
Grandpa Weatherby. Lewis Guy Rohrbaugh. LC 37-183. Fleming H. Revell Company.
Grandparents Ideals. (Ideals Ser.). (Illus.). 80p. (Orig.). 1980. pap. 2.95 (ISBN 0-89542-334-0). Ideals.
Grandpaw's Epistle. E. J. Miller. 4.75 o.p. Carlton.
Grandson: A Sequel to "The Son". Hildur Dixelius. LC 28-23277. E. P. Dutton & Co., Inc.
Grandsons. Louis Adamic. LC 74-26092. 1982. 37.50 (ISBN 0-404-58401-2). AMS Press.
Grandstand Rookie. Irwin Zacharia. 1976. pap. 1.75 (ISBN 0-89041-133-6, 3133). Major Bks.
Granduca. Max Brand. (O.S.I.). 224p. (Orig.). 1973. pap. 0.95 o.s.i. (ISBN 0-446-75080-8). Paperback Lib.
Granduca. Frederick Faust. 1973. 0.95 (ISBN 0-446-75080-8). Warner Paperback Library.
Grangerfjord Monks. Ruth McCarthy Sears. 1974. 4.95. Lenox Hill Press.
Grania: The Story of an Island. Emily Lawless. LC 7-13622. 1892. Macmillan and Co.
Grania, the Story of an Island. Emily Lawless. LC 79-10896. (Ireland, from the Act of Union, 1800, to the Death of Parnell, 1891; 73). (Illus.). 1979. 64.00 (ISBN 0-8240-3522-4). Garland Pub.
Granite. Thomas Quinn. LC 26-12141. 1926. H. Vinal.
Granite and Clay. Sara Ware Bassett. 1922. 1.90. Little, Brown, and Company.
Granite & Rainbow. Virginia Stephen Woolf. LC 58-10898. 1958. 5.75 o.p. (ISBN 0-15-136779-5). HarBraceJ.
Granite Folly see Witch's Hammer.
Grannie. Mary C. E. Wemyss. LC 14-5424. 1914. The Macmillan Company.
Granny: Scenes from Country Life. Bozena Rakusana Nemcova. LC 76-48902. 1976. 19.75 (ISBN 0-8371-9355-9). Greenwood Press.
Granny's Wonderful Chair: Its Tales of Fairy Times. Frances Browne & Holmes, Mable Dodge; 1883- LC 32-22198. The John C. Winston Company.
Grant of Kingdom. Harvey Fergusson. LC 75-17378. (Zia book). 1975. 3.45 (ISBN 0-8263-0396-X). University of New Mexico Press.
Grant of Kingdom: A Novel. Harvey Fergusson. LC 50-7498. 1950. Morrow.
Grant Vernon: A Boston Boy's Adventures in Louisiana. E. Brandon Stanton. LC 9-10041. Roxburgh Publishing Company, Incorporated.
Grantley Manor: A Tale, 1847. Georgiana Charlotte Leveson-Gower Fullerton. Ed. by Robert L. Wolff. LC 75-451. (Victorian Fiction Ser.). 1975. lib. bdg. 66.00 (ISBN 0-8240-1531-2). Garland Pub.
Granville Crypt Murders. Lois Bull. LC 36-89783. 1936. The Macaulay Company.
Granville De Vigne: Or, Held in Bondage. A Tale of the Day. a new ed.... ed. Louise De La Ramee. LC 7-1639. 1876. J. B. Lippincott & Co.
Granville De Vigne: Or, Held in Bondage. A Tale of the Day. a new ed.... ed. Louise De La Ramee. LC 6-33325. 1881. J. B. Lippincott & Co.
Granville De Vigne: Or, Held in Bondage. A Tale of the Day. a new ed., complete in one volume... ed. Louise De La Ramee. LC 7-748. 1900. J. B. Lippincott Company.
Granville Hypothesis. Ted Mancuso. (Orig.). 1979. pap. 1.95 (ISBN 0-532-23102-3). Woodhill.
Grape for Benny. Kenneth Alberts. 3.75 o.p. Vantage.
Grape from a Thorn. James Payn. (Seaside library. v. 56, no. 1149). 1881. G. Munro.
Grape from a Thorn. A Novel. James Payn. (Harper's Franklin square library, no. 216). 1881. Harper & Brothers.
Grapefruit Gussie. Della Reneau. LC 49-16728. 1949.
Grapes. Steven C. Lake. 3.50 o.p. Vantage.
Grapes and Thorns: Or, A Priest's Sacrifice. Mary Agnes Tincker. LC 10-13529. 1909. Christian Press Association Publishing Co.
Grapes of Canaan: A Novel. Elma C. Ehrlich Levinger. LC 31-207473. The Stratford Company.
Grapes of Paradise: Eight Novellas. Herbert Ernest Bates. LC 75-310638. 1974. 0.60 (ISBN 0-14-003820-5). Penguin.
Grapes of Paradise: Four Short Novels. 1st American Ed. Herbert Ernest Bates. LC 60-12206. 1960. Little, Brown.
Grapes of Thorns: A Novel. Mary Teresa Waggaman. LC 17-10861. 1917. Benziger Brothers.
Grapes of Wrath. Ernest Andrew Ewart. LC 17-184461. E. P. Dutton & Co.
Grapes of Wrath. John Steinbeck. LC 76-176406. (Viking critical library). 1972. 2.95 (ISBN 0-670-34792-2) (ISBN 0-670-01808-2). Viking Press.
Grapes of Wrath. John Steinbeck. LC 39-27282. The Viking Press.
Grapes of Wrath. John Steinbeck. LC 41-727. The Heritage Press.
Grapes of Wrath. John Steinbeck. 1940. The Viking Press.
Grapes of Wrath. John Steinbeck. LC 41-51968. (Half-title: The Modern library of the world's best books). 1941. The Modern Library.
Grapes of Wrath. John Steinbeck. LC 47-26866. (Living Library). 1947. World Pub. Co.
Grapes of Wrath; and, The Moon Is Down; and, Cannery Row; and, East of Eden; and, Of Mice and Men. John Steinbeck. LC 77-369377. 1976. 3.95 (ISBN 0-7064-0569-2). Heinemann: Octopus.
Grapes of Wrath: A Tale of North and South. Mary Harriott Norris. 1901. Small, Maynard & Company.
Grapes of Wrath: Text and Criticism. John Steinbeck. LC 76-30628. (Viking critical library). 1977-1976. 2.25 (ISBN 0-14-015508-2). Penguin Books.
Grapes of Wrath (The) By John Steinbeck; Notes, Including Chapter Summaries and Commentaries, Selected Review Questions, Character Sketches, by Gary Carey. Gary Carey. pap., 1.00. Cliff's Notes.
Grapes of Wrath: With an Introd. by Charles Poore. John Steinbeck. LC 51-6233. (Harper's modern classics). 1951. Harper.
Grapevine. Jonathan Starr. LC 30-151044. H. Liveright.
Graphics. Harris Merton Lyon. LC 72-4458. (Short story index reprint series). 1972. (ISBN 0-8369-4182-9). Books for Libraries Press.
Graphics. Harris Merton Lyon. LC 14-500. 1913. W. M. Reedy.
Graphite. Varlam Tikhonovich. Shalamov. LC 81-3918. 14.95 (ISBN 0-393-01476-2). Norton.
Grapple. Grace MacGowan Cooke. LC 74-22775. (Labor Movement in Fiction and Non-Fiction). (Illus.). 1966. 24.50 (ISBN 0-404-58415-2). AMS Press.
Grappling with the World. James D. Salts. LC 28-30703. The Christopher Publishing House.
Grasp at Straws: A Sergeant Cass Harty Detective Story. Joseph Francis Delany. LC 38-13190. 1938. Pub. for the Crime Club, Inc., by Doubleday, Doran & Co., Inc.
Grasp of the Sultan. Demetra Vaka Brown. LC 16-14869. 1916. Houghton Mifflin Company.
Grass and Gold. 1st Ed. Allan Vaughan Elston. LC 51-11182. 1951. Lippincott.
Grass Creek Chronicle. Pat M. Carr. LC 75-39422. (Woodwind book). (Illus.). 1976. 4.00. Endeavors in Humanity Press.
Grass Eater, & Other Stories. Elena Calderon. 3.50 o.p. Vantage.
Grass Grows Green. Hortense Lion. LC 35-4912. 1935. Houghton Mifflin Company.
Grass Harp. Truman Capote. LC 51-13101. 1951. Random House.
Grass Harp, & A Tree of Night & Other Short Stories. Truman Capote. pap. 2.75 (ISBN 0-451-12043-4, AE2043, Sig). NAL.
Grass Is Always Greener. George Malcolm-Smith. LC 47-114166. 1947. Doubleday.
Grass Is Always Greener Over the Septic Tank. Erma Bombeck. LC 76-20645. (Illus.). 6.95 (ISBN 0-07-006450-4). McGraw-Hill.
Grass Is Greener. Amy Paul. (Illus.). 96p. (Orig.). 1981. pap. 1.95 (ISBN 0-380-78576-5, 78576, Flare). Avon.
Grass Is Singing. Doris May Lessing. LC 50-9419. 1950. Crowell.
Grass Is Singing. Doris May Lessing. 1975. 7.95 (ISBN 0-690-00747-7). Thomas Y. Crowell Company.
Grass Means Fight. Harry Sinclair Drago. LC 38-329951. The Macaulay Company.
Grass Money; Lawton's Own Story. Robert S. Sprague. LC 73-155074. (Illus.). 1972. 5.95.
Grass on the Mountain. Henry Lieferant & Sylvia Saltzberg Lieferant. LC 38-5293. 1938. E. P. Dutton & Company, Inc.
Grass on the Wayside. Natsume Soseki. Ed. by Edwin McClellan. LC 70-81224. (O.S.I.). 1969. 7.00x o.s.i. (ISBN 0-226-76831-7). U of Chicago Pr.
Grass on the Wayside: Michikusa: a Novel. Soseki Natsume. LC 74-184814. (UNESCO Collection of Representative Works: Japanese Series). (Phoenix book; P620). 1969. 2.95 (ISBN 0-226-76831-7) (ISBN 0-226-76832-5). University of Chicago Press.
Grass Roots. Jane Barry. LC 68-10589. 1968. Doubleday.
Grass Roots. Albert Goldman. (Orig.). 1980. pap. 2.75 (ISBN 0-446-85465-4). Warner Bks.
Grass Roots: A Novel of American Politics. Earl Schenck Miers. LC 44-40098. 1944. The Westminster Press.
Grass Roots Nurse see Future Nurse & Student Nurse.
Grass Roots Nurse see Student Nurse.
Grass. Translated from the French by Richard Howard. Claude Simon. LC 60-6241. 1960. 3.75. G. Braziller.
Grass War. Harley Hess. (Orig.). 1979. pap. 1.75 (ISBN 0-532-23180-5). Woodhill.
Grass Widow. Richard Edward Boyns. LC 19-8739. 1919. Harr Wagner Publishing Company.
Grass Widow. William Minto. LC 7-31112. (Mayfair series no. 2). E. Brandus & Co.
Grass Widows. Mary Orr, pseud. 72p. 1976. pap. 2.95x. Dramatists Play.
Grass Widow's Tale. Ellis Peters. 1979. 15.00x o.p. (ISBN 0-86025-085-7, Pub. by Ian Henry Pubns England). State Mutual Bk.
Grass-Widow's Tale. Ellis Peters. LC 68-19033. 1968. 4.50 o.p. Morrow.
Grasse: March 23, 1966. Nicholas Delbanco. LC 67-20286. 1968. 4.50 o.p. Lippincott.
Grasshopper. Su Walton. (Crest Book, M1772). 1973. 0.95. Fawcett.
Grasshopper. Su Walton. LC 75-96299. 1970. 5.95. Morrow.
Grasshopper, and Other Stories. Anton Pavlovich Chekhov. LC 72-37538. (Short story index reprint series). (Illus.). 1972. (ISBN 0-8369-4097-0). Books for Libraries Press.
Grasshopper: And Other Stories. Anton Pavlovich Chekhov. Tr. by Chamot, Alfred Edward. LC 26-26501. (The international library). 1926. 1.25. S. Paul & Co., Ltd.
Grasshopper Heart: By P. B. Abercrombie Pseud. 1st Ed. Patricia Abercrombie Barnes. LC 61-9477. 1961. Doubleday.
Grasshopper King: A Story of Two Confederate Exiles in Mexico During the Reign of Maximilian and Carlota. Elizabeth Boatwright Coker. LC 80-24974. (Illus.). 13.95 (ISBN 0-525-10716-9). Dutton.
Grasshopper Summer. Jamie Lee Cooper. LC 74-17682. 1975. 6.95 (ISBN 0-672-52040-0). Bobbs-Merrill.
Grasshoppers. Cecily Sidgwick. LC 8-7314. (On cover: West end series). F. A. Stokes Company.
Grasshoppers. Cecily Sidgwick. LC 8-7315. F. A. Stokes Company.
Grasshoppers Come. David Garnett. LC 31-14333. Brewer, Warren & Putnam.
Grasslands. Clyde M. Brundy. 496p. 1980. pap. 2.50 (ISBN 0-380-75499-1, 75499). Avon.
Grassleyes Mystery. Edward Phillips Oppenheim. LC 40-11558. 1940. Little, Brown and Company.
Grassman: A Novel. Len Fulton. LC 74-8581. (Illus.). 1974. 7.95 (ISBN 0-914476-26-2) (ISBN 0-914476-27-0). Thorp Springs Press.
Grassroots Senator. Anna Matilda Carlson. LC 52-11896. 1952. Vantage Press.
Grasville Abbey: A Romance. George Moore. LC 73-22769. (Gothic Novels II). 1974. (ISBN 0-405-06019-X). Arno Press.
Grateful Korean & Other Stories. Ty Pak. (Orig.). 1983. pap. write for info. (ISBN 0-910043-01-9). Bamboo Ridge Pr.
Grateful to Life& Death. R. K. Narayan. LC 53-3348. 1953. Michigan State College Press.
Gratia's Trials: Or, Making Her Own Way. Lucy Randall Comfort. LC 6-30663. (Street & Smith's select series, no. 7). 1888. Street & Smith.
Graustark, the Story of a Love Behind a Throne. 1971. Repr. of 1917 ed. 19.00 o.p. Scholarly.
Graustark: The Story of a Love Behind a Throne. George Barr McCutcheon. LC 72-145159. 1971. (ISBN 0-403-01087-X). Scholarly Press.
Graustark: The Story of a Love Behind a Throne. George Barr McCutcheon. LC 1-31640. 1901. H. S. Stone and Company.
Graustark: The Story of a Love Behind a Throne. George Barr McCutcheon. LC 16-3401. Grosset & Dunlap.
Graustark: The Story of a Love Behind a Throne. George Barr McCutcheon. LC 10-3724. 1903. Grosset & Dunlap.
Graustark: The Story of a Love Behind a Throne. George Barr McCutcheon. LC 20-188117. 1917. Dodd, Mead & Company.
Grave. Charles L. Grant. 224p. 1981. pap. 2.50 (ISBN 0-445-04664-3). Popular Lib.
Grave Affair. Nancy Bodington. LC 72-92244. 1973. 4.95 (ISBN 0-385-00592-X). Published for the Crime Club by Doubleday.
Grave Affair. Shelley Smith. LC 72-92244. 192p. 1973. 4.95 o.p. (ISBN 0-385-00592-X). Doubleday.
Grave Between Them. Clarence Boutelle. LC 6-14917. (On cover: American series, no. 257)). 1891. M. J. Ivers & Co.
Grave Business. Ed. by Alfred Joseph Hitchcock. 1975. (pbk.) 0.95. Dell.
Grave Case of Murder. Paul Winterton. LC 51-25450. 1951. Hutchinson.
Grave Case of Murder. Paul Winterton. LC 51-11884. 1951. Harper.
Grave Consequences. 1st Ed. Marten Cumberland. LC 52-5110. 1952. Published for the Crime Club by Doubleday.
Grave Danger. Kelley Pseud Roos. LC 65-27811. (Red badge detective). 1965. Dodd, Mead.
Grave Danger. Kelly Pseud Roos. LC 65-27811. (Red badge detective). bds., 3.50. Dodd.
Grave Danger: A Johnny Liddell Mystery. Frank Kane. LC 54-9098. 1954. I. Washburn.
Grave Descend. John Lange. 1975. (pbk.) 1.50. Bantam.
Grave Doubt. Ivon Baker. LC 72-87233. (MW suspense). 1972. 4.95. D. McKay Co.
Grave Doubt. Ivon Baker. 1975. (pbk.) 1.25. Dell.
Grave Error. Stephen Greenleaf. LC 79-826. 9.95 (ISBN 0-8037-2442-X). Dial Press.
Grave in the Forest. Harry C Lauer. LC 55-11735. 1955. Comet Press Books.
Grave Is Waiting. Andrew MacKenzie. LC 57-2040. (British bloodhound, bloodhound, no. 132). 1957. T. V. Boardman.
Grave Journey. John Harris. LC 73-95864. 1970. Harcourt, Brace & World.
Grave Journey. Mark Hebden, pseud. 1970. 5.95 o.p. (ISBN 0-15-136789-2). HarBraceJ.
Grave Lady Jane. Florence Alice Price James. LC 7-7418. (On cover: Mayflower library, no. 11). 1892. J. A. Taylor and Company.
Grave Matter. Leslie Purnell Davies. LC 68-22620. 1968. 3.95. Published for the Crime Club by Doubleday.
Grave Matters: By John Rhode Pseud. Cecil John Charles Street. LC 55-910391. (Red badge detective). 1955. Dodd, Mead.
Grave Mistake. Ngaio Marsh. LC 78-16910. 8.95 (ISBN 0-316-54671-2). Little, Brown.
Grave Mistake. Ngaio Marsh. LC 78-26793. 1979. 13.95 (ISBN 0-8161-6667-6). G. K. Hall.
Grave of Green Water. Jan Roffman. LC 68-10581. 1968. Published for the Crime Club by Doubleday.
Grave of the Twin Hills: A Novel. 1st Ed. Bowen Hosford. LC 60-7576. 1960. W.W. Norton.
Grave Undertaking. Lloyd Gold. 65p. 1976. pap. 2.95x. Dramatists Play.
Grave Undertaking. 1st Ed. Lionel White. LC 61-12486. 1961. Cutton.
Grave Without Grass: An Abelard Voss Mystery. Donald Clough Cameron. H. Holt and Company.
Gravedigger. Joseph Hansen. LC 81-6381. (Rinehart suspense novel). 11.95. Holt, Rinehart, and Winston.
Gravediggers. Phyllis Schlafly & Chester Ward. 1964. 0.75. Pere Marquette.
Gravedigger's Funeral. Arthur Arent. LC 67-212321. 1967. 5.00. Grossman.
Graven Image. Jean Dewitt Fitz. 1975. pap. 1.25 o.p. Pyramid Pubns.
Graven Image. Margaret Widdemer. LC 23-14562. Harcourt, Brace and Company.
Graven Images: Three Original Novellas of Science Fiction. Ed. by Edward L. Ferman. LC 77-24591. 6.95 (ISBN 0-8407-6557-6). T. Nelson.
Graven Images: Three Original Novellas of Science Fiction. Richard Frede et al. Ed. by Barry Malzberg & Ed Ferman. LC 77-24591. (Nelson Science Fiction Ser.). 1977. 7.95 (ISBN 0-525-66557-9). Elsevier-Nelson.
Graves at Kilmorna: A Story of '67. Patrick Augustine Sheehan. LC 15-4587. 1915. Longmans, Green, and Co.
Grave's Company. Sarah Nichols. (Queen-size gothic). 1975. (pbk.) 1.25. Popular Library.
Grave's in the Meadow. Manning Lee Stokes. 1973. pap. 0.95 o.p. (ISBN 0-532-95243-X). Woodhill.
Grave's in the Meadow. Manning Lee Stokes. 1973. pap. 0.95 o.p. (ISBN 0-532-95243-X). Manor Bks.
Gravetide. Carolyn McKnight. LC 78-3979. 1978. 8.95 (ISBN 0-312-34454-6). St. Martin's Press.
Graveyard. Marek Hasko. LC 74-27463. 1975. (ISBN 0-8371-7897-5). Greenwood Press.
Graveyard. Marek Hlasko. Tr. by Norbert Guterman from Pol. LC 74-27463. 126p. 1975. Repr. of 1959 ed. lib. bdg. 15.00 (ISBN 0-8371-7897-5, HLGR). Greenwood.
Graveyard. Philip Maitland Hubbard. LC 74-20354. 1975. 5.95 (ISBN 0-689-10654-8). Atheneum.
Graveyard Companion: Twenty Stories of Fantasy and Terror. Gray Usher & Shaun Usher. LC 80-11680. 7.95 (ISBN 0-525-66686-9). Elsevier/Nelson Books.
Graveyard Flower. Wilhelmine Birch Von Hillern & Bell, Mrs. Clara Courtenay (Poynter) 1834- Tr. LC 7-4748. 1884. W. S Gottsberger.
Graveyard Never Closes. Frederick Clyde Davis. LC 40-294648. 1940. Pub. for the Crime Club by Doubleday, Doran and Co., Inc.
Graveyard Nurse. Florence Stonebraker. LC 68-234. 1967. Arcadia House.

Graveyard Plot: By Margaret Erskine Pseud. 1st Ed. Wetherby Williams. LC 59-10694. 1959. Published for the Crime Club by Doubleday.
Graveyard Rolls. Maurice Procter. LC 63-20312. Harper & Row.
Graveyard to Let. Carter Dickson, pseud. 1978. pap. 1.50 o.s.i. (ISBN 0-505-51222-X). Tower Bks.
Graveyard to Let: Another Adventure of Sir Henry Merrivale. John Dickson Carr. LC 49-11468. 1949. W. Morrow.
Graveyard. Translated from the Polish by Norbert Guterman. 1st Ed. Marek Hlasko. LC 59-10775. 1959. Dutton.
Graveyard Watch. Samuel Shellabarger. LC 38-6692. Modern Age Books, Inc.
Gravity, and Other Stories. Catherine Petroski. LC 81-71003. 6.95 (ISBN 0-931362-05-9). Fiction International.
Gravity's Rainbow. Thomas Pynchon. LC 72-83804. 1973. 15.00 (ISBN 0-670-34832-5) (ISBN 0-670-34832-5). Viking Press.
Gravity's Rainbow. Thomas Pynchon. 1974. (pbk.) 2.50. Bantam Books.
Gravy Train. Whit Masterson, pseud. LC 74-145398. (Red badge novel of suspense). 1971. 4.95 (ISBN 0-396-06320-9). Dodd, Mead.
Gray and the Blue. A Story Founded on Incidents Connected with the War for the Union. Edward Reynolds Roe. LC 7-40248. 1884. Rand, McNally & Co.
Gray Angels. Nalbro Isadorah Bartley. LC 20-17174. 1.90. Small, Maynard & Company.
Gray Beginning. Edward Shenton. LC 24-10840. 1924. The Penn Publishing Company.
Gray Canaan. David Garth. LC 47-1676. 1947. G. P. Putnam's Sons.
Gray Captain. Jere Hungerford Wheelwright. LC 54-8693. 1954. Scribner.
Gray Charteris. Robert Simpson. LC 22-25804. The James A. McCann Company.
Gray Dawn. Stewart Edward White. LC 15-22540. Doubleday, Page & Co.
Gray Dream, & Other Stories of New England Life: Two Volumes in One. facsimile ed. Laura Wolcott. LC 70-169569. (Short Story Index Reprint Ser.). Repr. of 1918 ed. 16.00 (ISBN 0-8369-4032-6). Ayer Co.
Gray Dream and Other Stories of New England Life. Laura Wolcott. LC 70-169569. (Short story index reprint series). 1971. (ISBN 0-8369-4032-6). Books for Libraries Press.
Gray Dusk. Octavus Roy Cohen. LC 20-2646. 1920. 1.75. Dodd, Mead and Company.
Gray Eyes. Stuart Friedman. LC 55-112922. 1955. Abelard-Schuman.
Gray Fist. Maxwell Grant, pseud. (Shadow Ser.). 1977. pap. 1.25 o.p. (ISBN 0-515-04207-2). BJ Pub Group.
Gray Flannel Shroud. Henry Slesar. LC 59-5703. (Random House mystery). 1959. Random House.
Gray Gull. Henry Francis Granger. LC 24-7530. (Famous authors series. no. 48). 1924. Garden City Publishing Co., Inc.
Gray Gull Feathers. George Hoyt Smith. LC 24-155014. 1924. The State Company.
Gray House of the Quarries. Mary Harriott Norris. 1898. Lamson, Wolffe and Company.
Gray Itch: The Male Metapause Syndrome. Edmond C. Hallberg. 1980. pap. 3.95 (ISBN 0-446-30833-1). Warner Bks.
Gray Lensman. Edward Elmer Smith. LC 51-8198. 1951. Fantasy Press.
Gray Magic: A 'Gray Phantom' Mystery. Herman Landon. LC 25-4774. 1925. G. H. Watt.
Gray Man: A Novel. Samuel Rutherford Crockett. 1896. Harper & Brothers.
Gray Man Walks. Henry Bellamann. LC 36-8977. 1936. Pub. for the Crime Club, Inc., by Doubleday, Doran & Company, Inc.
Gray Mask. Charles Wadsworth Camp. 1920. Doubleday, Page & Company.
Gray Matters: A Novel. William Hjortsberg. LC 73-156153. 1971. 4.95 (ISBN 0-671-20976-0). Simon and Schuster.
Gray Mist: A Novel. Marguerite De Godart Cunliffe-Owen. LC 6-36179. 1906. Harper & Brothers.
Gray Mist: A Novel by the Author of The Martyrdom of an Empress. Illustrated with Water-Color Drawings by the Author. Marguerite De Godart Cunliffe-Owen. LC 6-36179. 1906. Harper.
Gray Moss. Edith Ogden Harrison. LC 30-6536. 1929. R. F. Seymour.
Gray Phantom. Herman Landon. LC 21-147998. W. J. Watt & Company.
Gray Phantom's Return. Herman Landon. LC 22-12630. W. J. Watt & Company.
Gray Powder: The Story of the Discovery and the Development of Cement. Charles Aloysius Fuschino. LC 50-2054. 1949.
Gray Prince. Jack Vance, pseud. LC 74-1902. 240p. 1974. 6.95 o.p. (ISBN 0-672-51994-1). Bobbs.
Gray Prince. Jack Vance, pseud. 1983. pap. 2.25 (ISBN 0-87997-716-7, UE1716). DAW Bks.
Gray Prince: A Science Fiction Novel. John Holbrook Vance. LC 74-1902. 1974. 6.95 (ISBN 0-672-51994-1). Bobbs-Merrill.
Gray Rocks: A Tale of the Middle-West. Willis George Emerson. (On cover: Library of choice fiction, serial no. 1). Laird & Lee.
Gray Roses. Henry Harland. LC 4-16827. (On cover: Keynotes series, 10). 1895. Roberts Bros.
Gray Sage. Francis W Hilton. LC 38-6697. 1938. H. C. Kinsey & Company, Inc.
Gray Sheep. Dillwyn Parrish. LC 27-15518. 1927. Harper & Brothers.
Gray Terror: A 'Gray Phantom' Detective Story. Herman Landon. LC 23-115187. 1923. G. H. Watt.
Gray Wolf & Other Fantasy Stories. George MacDonald. Ed. by Glenn G. Sadler. (Fantasy Stories of George MacDonald Ser.). 200p. 1980. pap. 2.95 (ISBN 0-8028-1862-5). Eerdmans.
Gray Wolf's Daughter. Gertrude Warden. LC 8-34844. The International News Company.
Gray Youth: The Story of a Very Modern Courtship and a Very Modern Marriage, by Oliver Onions... Oliver Onions. 1914. George H. Doran Company, Publishers in America for Hodder & Stoughton.
Graydon of the Windermere. Evah McKowan. LC 20-21188. George H. Doran Company.
Graymantle. John Morressy. LC 81-47266. 256p. (Orig.). 1981. pap. 2.50 (ISBN 0-87216-900-6). Playboy Pbks.
Grays. Charlotte Bacon. LC 23-6290. 1923. 2.00. G. P. Putnam's Son.
Grays Harbor: 1885-1913. Robert A. Weinstein. (Large Format Ser.). (Illus.). 1978. pap. 7.95 o.p. (ISBN 0-14-004890-1). Penguin.
Graysons. Edward Eggleston. Ed. by Donald Pizer. LC 78-96534. (American Authors Ser). 1970. lib. bdg. 20.25 o.s.i. (ISBN 0-512-00165-0). Garrett Pr.
Graysons: A Story of Illinois. Edward Eggleston. LC 70-129335. (Illus.). 1970. (ISBN 0-404-02267-7). AMS Press.
Graysons: A Story of Illinois. Edward Eggleston. 1888. The Century Co.
Grayspace Beast. Gordon Eklund. LC 75-36591. (Doubleday science fiction). 1976. 5.95 (ISBN 0-385-11547-4). Doubleday.
Grayspace Beast. Gordon Eklund. (Kangaroo Book). 1977. 1.50 (ISBN 0-671-81390-0). Pocket Books.
Graystone: A Novel. William Jasper Nicolls. LC 2-73012. 1902. J. B. Lippincott Company.
Graziella. Alphonse Marie Louis De Lamartine. Tr. by Barney, Samuel Chase. LC 1-13911. 1872. J. B. Lippincott & Co.
Graziella. A Story of Italian Love. Alphonse Marie Louis De Lamartine. Tr. by Runnion, James B. LC 1-13912. 1876. Jansen, McClurg & Co.
Grease. Ron De Christoforo. (Illus.). 1978. pap. 2.75 (ISBN 0-671-78278-9). PB.
Grease. Ed. by Fotonovel Publications Staff. (Illus.). 1979. pap. 2.75. Fotonovel.
Greased Lightning: A Novel. Kenneth Vose & DuKore, Lawrence. 1977. 1.50 (ISBN 0-446-88399-9). Warner Books.
Greased Samba: And Other Stories. John N Deck. LC 77-117571. 1970. 5.95. Harcourt Brace Jovanovich.
Greasy Luck. Gordon Grant. (Illus.). 1970. Repr. of 1932 ed. 17.50 (ISBN 0-917368-02-9). Caravan-Maritime.
Great Abduction. Arthur Somers Roche. LC 33-8540. Sears Publishing Company, Inc.
Great Accident. Ben Ames Williams. LC 20-5226. 1920. The Macmillan Company.
Great Adam: A Novel. George Dixon Snell. LC 34-16712. 1934. The Caxton Printers, Ltd.
Great Adventure. Arnold Bennett. LC 74-5329. (Collected Works of Arnold Bennett: Vol. 25). 1976. Repr. of 1913 ed. 16.75 (ISBN 0-518-19106-0). Ayer Co.
Great Adventure. Peter Stuyvesant. LC 18-12852. The Standard Publishing Company.
Great Adventure: A Novel. Janice Holt Giles. LC 66-12068. (Illus.). 1966. Houghton Mifflin.
Great Adventure Stories of Jack London. Jack London. LC 67-19750. (Bantam pathfinder editions). 1967. Bantam Books.
Great Adventurer. Robert Shackleton. LC 4-5921. 1904. Doubleday, Page and Co.
Great Adventures of Sherlock Holmes. new ed. Arthur Conan Doyle. Ed. by Kin Platt. (Now Age Illustrated Ser., No. 2). (Illus.). 64p. (gr. 5-10). 1974. 5.00 (ISBN 0-88301-205-7); pap. text ed. 1.95 (ISBN 0-88301-137-9). Pendulum Pr.
Great Adventures of the Old West. Ed. by Alvin M. Josephy, Jr. (Illus.). 1969. 8.95 o.p. (ISBN 0-07-001241-5). Am Her Pr.
Great Affair. Victor Canning. LC 78-142389. 1971. 6.95. Morrow.
Great Alphonse: A Novel. 1st Ed. Lawrence Levine. LC 59-11244. Norton.
Great Ambitions: A Story of the Early Years of Charles Dickens. Agnes Mary Robertson Dunlop & Elizabeth Kyle. 1968. Holt, Rinehart and Winston.
Great American Belly Dance. Daniela Gioseffi. LC 77-72413. 1977. 6.95 (ISBN 0-385-13060-0). Doubleday.
Great American Belly Dance. Daniela Gioseffi. (Dell book). 1979. 1.95 (ISBN 0-440-13068-9). Dell Pub. Co.
Great American Con Machine. Barry M. Riemer. Ed. by Sylvia Ashton. LC 74-76644. 1975. 10.95 (ISBN 0-87949-025-X). Ashley Bks.
Great American Detective. William Kittredge & Steven M Krauzer. LC 78-60035. (Mentor book; MEI689). 2.25 (ISBN 0-451-61689-8). New American Library.
Great American Detective Stories. William Anthony Parker White. LC 45-5985. 1945. The World Publishing Company.
Great American Empire. Stanley Berne. LC 82-3114. (Archives of Post-Modern Literature Series Publication; No. 105). (Illus.). 1982. 14.95 (ISBN 0-8180-0635-8) (ISBN 0-8180-0633-1). Horizon Press.
Great American Family. Lee Shippey. LC 38-2499. 1938. Houghton Mifflin Company.
Great American Family: A Comedy Adapted from the Novel. Aurania Ellerbeck Rouverol & Shippey, Lee. LC 47-12273. 1947. S. French.
Great American Jackpot. Herbert Gold. LC 71-85612. 1969. 6.95. Random House.
Great American Novel. Richard H. Clinton. 210p. (Orig.). 1981. pap. 3.95x (ISBN 0-9605338-1-8). Blue Lagoon.
Great American Novel". Clyde Brion Davis. LC 38-27458. Farrar & Rinehart, Incorporated.
Great American Novel. Philip Roth. LC 72-91577. 1973. 8.95 (ISBN 0-03-004516-9). Holt, Rinehart and Winston.
Great American Novel. Philip Roth. 1974. (pbk.) 1.95. Bantam Books.
Great American Novel. William Carlos Williams. LC 73-2637. 1973. Folcroft Library Editions.
Great American Pie Company. Ellis Parker Butler. LC 7-16376. 1907. McClure, Phillips & Co.
Great American Short Novels. Ed. by William Phillips. LC 46-25132. 1946. Dial Press.
Great American Short Stories. Stephen Graham. 1979. Repr. of 1931 ed. lib. bdg. 22.50 (ISBN 0-8495-2019-3). Arden Lib.
Great American Short Stories. LC 76-10933. 10.98. Reader's Digest Association.
Great American Short Stories. Reader's Digest Editors. LC 76-10933. 640p. 1977. 13.98 (ISBN 0-89577-033-4). RD Assn.
Great American Short Stories. Ed. by Wallace Earle Stegner & Stegner, Mary. LC 57-11102. (Laurel edition, LC 103). 1957. Dell Pub. Co.
Great American Short Stories: O. Henry Memorial Prize Winning Stories 1919-1932. Williams, Blanche Colton. LC 33-27047. 1933. Doubleday, Doran & Company, Inc.
Great American Stories. Edward Ames Richards. LC 42-31041. (Home service booklets. 148). Reader Mail, Inc.
Great Amherst Mystery: A True Narrative of the Supernatural. Walter Hubbell. LC 7-5656. 1888. Brentano's.
Great Amherst Mystery: A True Narrative of the Supernatural. Walter Hubbell. LC 7-56551. (On cover: Lovell's library. no. 1195). 1888. J. W. Lovell Company.
Great Amulet. Katherine Helen Maud Marshall Diver. LC 11-4108. 1910. 1.50. John Lane Company.
Great Amulet. rev. ed. Katherine Helen Maud Marshall Diver. LC 14-13580. 1914. 1.35. G. P. Putnam's Sons.
Great Appointment. Myra Goodwin Plantz. 1895. Hunt & Eaton.
Great April. James Kern Feibleman. LC 71-151013. 1971. 5.95 (ISBN 0-8180-0610-2). Horizon Press.
Great Argument... Philip Hamilton Gibbs. LC 38-8110. 1938. Doubleday, Doran & Company, Inc.
Great Assassins. Gerald Sparrow. LC 69-16270. 1969. 3.95 o.p. (ISBN 0-668-01897-6). Arco.
Great Atlantic Adventures. Edward R. Snow. (Illus.). 1970. 5.95 o.p. (ISBN 0-396-06256-3). Dodd.
Great Atomic Disaster: Blueprint for Survival. Bernard Mayne. LC 57-3086. College Pub. Co.
Great Auk: A Novel. Allan W Eckert. LC 63-18215. 1963. Little, Brown.
Great-Aunt Lavinia. Joseph Crosby Lincoln. LC 36-243982. 1936. D. Appleton-Century Company, Incorporated.
Great Australian Lover, and Other Stories. Frank Hardy. LC 73-163270. (Illus.). 1972. 3.95 (ISBN 0-17-001976-4). Thomas Nelson (Australia)
Great Awakening: By Blanche A. Draper Pseud. Blanche A Webb. LC 53-6468. 1953. Vantage Press.
Great Awakening: The Story of the Twenty-Second Century. Albert Adams Merrill. LC 99-3608. 1899. George Book Publishing Co.
Great Balls of Fire. Richard Ferry. pap. 1.95 o.s.i. (OPH-230, Ophelia). Olympia.
Great Balls of Fire. Harry Harrison. Ed. by Grace Shaw. (Illus.). 1977. 14.95 o.p. (ISBN 0-448-14377-1, G&D); pap. 6.95 o.p. (ISBN 0-448-14378-X, Today Press). Putnam Pub Group.
Great Balsamo: World-Renowned Magician and King of Escape Artists. Maurice Zolotow. LC 46-7544. 1946. Random House.
Great Bank Mystery: A Thrilling Story of Modern Events. E. O. Tilburn. LC 33-28355. (On cover: Pinkerton detective series. no. 75). 1901. Laird & Lee.
Great Bank Robbery: From the Diary of Inspector Byrnes. Julian Hawthorne & Byrnes, Thomas F., 1847?- LC 9-2213. Cassell & Company Limited.
Great Bear. Lester Cohen. LC 27-23449. 1927. Boni & Liveright.
Great Berwyck Bank Burglary. Howard Sylvester Ellis. (On cover: Once a week library, v. 11, no. 6). 1893. P. F. Collier.
Great Betrayal. Dorothy Gardiner. LC 49-739094. 1949. Doubleday.
Great Betrayal. Farley Mowat. 1977. pap. 5.95 (ISBN 0-316-58694-3, Pub. by Atlantic Monthly Pr.). Little.
Great Big Doorstep: A Delta Comedy. Edwin P O'Donnell. LC 41-20730. 1941. Houghton Mifflin Company.
Great Big Doorstep: A Delta Comedy. Edwin P O'Donnell. LC 41-20730. 1941. Houghton Mifflin Company.
Great Big Doorstep: A Delta Comedy. Edwin P. O'Donnell. LC 78-11516. (Lost American fiction). 1979. 11.95 (ISBN 0-8093-0888-6). Southern Illinois University Press.
Great Big Grown-up Love: A Tale of Texas. Baker B. Hoskins. LC 8-2607. Broadway Publishing Company.
Great Black Kanba. Constance Little & Gwenyth Little. LC 44-47947. 1944. Pub. for the Crime Club by Doubleday, Doran and Co., Inc.
Great Black Magic Stories. Michel Parry. LC 77-76574. 1977. 8.95 (ISBN 0-8008-3618-9). Taplinger Pub. Co.
Great Blizzard. Albert Edward Idell. LC 48-5878. 1948. H. Holt.
Great Bonacker Whiskey War: An Entertainment. Ralph Maloney. LC 67-11216. 1967. Little, Brown.
Great Boo-Boo. Henry S. Wilcox. LC 8-37028. 1892. J. B. Swinburne.
Great Books Retold As Short Stories. Anthony Praga. 223p. 1981. Repr. of 1932 ed. lib. bdg. 45.00 (ISBN 0-89987-663-3). Darby Bks.
Great Books Retold As Short Stories. Anthony Prga. Repr. of 1932 ed. 20.00 (ISBN 0-8414-9272-7). Folcroft.
Great Brain Robbery. James P. Fisher. (Orig.). 1970. pap. 0.75 o.p. (B75-2072). Belmont-Tower.
Great Bridge Conspiracy. Terry Quinn. LC 79-16603. 1979. 9.95 (ISBN 0-312-34496-1). St. Martin's Press.
Great Brighton Mystery. Joseph Smith Fletcher. LC 26-143472. 1926. A. A. Knopf.
Great British Detective. Ron Goulart. LC 82-81665. 3.95 (ISBN 0-451-62089-5). New American Library.
Great British Ghost Hunt. Hans Holzer. (Adult Ser.). Repr. lib. bdg. 9.95 o.p. (ISBN 0-8161-6307-3, Large Print Bks). G K Hall.
Great British Short Stories. Ed. by Edward Huberman. LC 68-19248. (Bantam classic). 1968. Bantam Books.
Great British Tales of Terror: Gothic Stories of Horror and Romance, 1765-1840. Ed. by Peter Haining. LC 74-162255. (Illus.). 1973. (ISBN 0-14-003589-3). Penguin.
Great Buffalo Hotel: A Novel. Gordon Webber. LC 78-26146. 8.95 (ISBN 0-316-92730-9). Little, Brown.
Great Buxton Mystery. A Story. William Thomas Standen. LC 8-13883. 1889.
Great Canadian Novel. Harry J Boyle. LC 72-180063. 1972. 6.95. Doubleday.
Great Canadian Short Stories: An Anthology. Ed. by Alec Lucas. 1971. pap. 2.25 (ISBN 0-440-33077-7, LE). Dell.
Great Captain: A Story of the Days of Sir Walter Raleigh. Katharine Tynan Hinkson, pseud. 1902. Benzinger Brothers.
Great Captain: The Lincoln Trilogy of Forever Free, With Malice Toward None, The Last Full Measure. Honore McCue Willsie Morrow. LC 35-27376. 1935. W. Morrow & Company.
Great Captains. Henry Treece. LC 55-8146. 1956. Random House.
Great Capture: Or, New Tactics in Detective Strategy. The Story of an Intricate Shadow. Harlan Page Halsey. (Old Sleuth's own, no. 89). 1897. Parlor Car Publishing Company.
Great Cases of the Thinking Machine. Jacques Futrelle. LC 76-9182. (Illus.). 1976. Dover Publications.

Great Chili Confrontation: A Dramatic History of the Decade's Most Impassioned Culinary Embroilment, with Recipes. Harry Allen Smith. LC 69-13008. 1969. 4.95. Trident Press.

Great Chin Episode. Roland Alexander Wood-Says. LC 9-1482. 1893. Macmillan and Co.

Great Christmas Strike. Robyn Harrison. 1983. pap. 2.50. Eldridge Pub.

Great Circle. Robert Carse. LC 56-5660. 1956. Scribner.

Great Circle: By Conrad Aiken. Conrad Potter Aiken. LC 33-12047. 1933. C. Scribner's Sons.

Great Circle. 1st Ed. Frank Rooney. LC 62-16738. 1962. Harcourt, Brace & World.

Great Circus Mystery: Or, Nat Ridley on a Crooked Trail. Nat Jr Ridley. LC 26-14125. (His Nat Ridley series-8). 1926. Garden City Publishing Co., Inc.

Great Conflict. Ethel Barrett. LC 75-100980. (Orig.). 1970. 5.95 o.p. (ISBN 0-8307-0071-4, 5102006). Regal.

Great Controversy. Ellen G. White. (Newsprint Ser.). 420p. 1982. pap. 1.25 (ISBN 0-8163-0511-0). Pacific Pr Pub Assn.

Great Controversy. Ellen G. White. 1970. pap. 0.95 o.p. (N2399). BJ Pub Group.

Great Crimes of San Francisco. Ed. by Dean W. Dickensheet. 192p. (Orig.). 1974. pap. 2.50 (ISBN 0-89174-033-3). Comstock Edns.

Great Cronin Mystery: Or, the Irish Patriot's Fate. (On cover: The Pinkerton detective series, v. 28). 1889. Laird & Lee.

Great Crooner. Clarence Budington Kelland. LC 33-794929. 1933. Harper & Brothers.

Great Crusade: A Chronicle of the Late War. Jennings Cropper Wise. LC 30-8777. 1930. L. MacVeagh, The Dial Press.

Great Cycle. Det Store Spelet. Tarjei Vesaas. LC 67-26629. (Nordic translation series). 1967. University of Wisconsin Press.

Great Dandelion. Jamie Lee Cooper. LC 79-190111. 1972. 5.95. Bobbs-Merrill.

Great Day. Georgette Carneal. LC 32-9556. Liveright, Inc.

Great Day. Elizabeth Seifert. LC 73-79135. 1973. 5.95. Aeonian Press.

Great Day. Elizabeth Seifert. 1939. Dodd, Mead & Company.

Great Day for a Ballgame. Fielding Dawson. LC 72-9880. 1973. 6.95 o.p. (ISBN 0-672-51794-9). Bobbs.

Great Day for a Ballgame: A Conscious Love Story. Fielding Dawson. LC 72-9880. 1973. 6.95 (ISBN 0-672-51794-9). Bobbs-Merrill.

Great Day for Dying. Jack Dillon. (Orig.). 1967. pap. 0.50 o.p. (D1877, GM). Fawcett World.

Great Day in the Morning: A Novel. Robert Douglas Andrews, pseud. LC 50-6445. 1950. Coward-McCann.

Great Days. Donald Barthelme. LC 78-10706. 7.95 (ISBN 0-374-16628-5). Farrar, Straus, Giroux.

Great Days. John Dos Passos. 1958. 6.00. Sagamore Pr.

Great Days: A Novel. Frank Harris. LC 14-13259. 1914. 1.35. M. Kennerley.

Great Debureau. Frantisek Kozik. Tr. by Round, Dora. LC 40-27273. Farrar & Rinehart, Inc.

Great Deception. Douglass Elliot. LC 81-68646. (American Patriot Series; Book 2). (Illus.). 1982. 2.95 (ISBN 0-345-29823-3). Ballantine Books.

Great Deception & Other Stories. Letitia West. 1967. 4.50 o.p. (ISBN 0-682-45728-0). Exposition.

Great Demonstration. Katharine Metcalf Roof. LC 20-19435. 1920. D. Appleton and Company.

Great Desire. Alexander Black. LC 19-149442. Harper & Brothers.

Great Destroyer. Hermann Brandau. LC 33-14411. 1932. The Carl Schirz Publishing Co.

Great Detective Stories: A Chronological Anthology. Ed. by Willard Huntington Wright. LC 27-236041. 1927. C. Scribner's Sons.

Great Detective Stories About Doctors. Groff Conklin & N. D. Fabricant. 1965. pap. 0.95 o.p. (01897, Collier). Macmillan.

Great Detective Stories from Costello to Stevenson. Ed. by Joseph Lewis French. LC 25-1966. (The Dial detective library). 1924. L. MacVeagh, The Dial Press.

Great Detective Stories from Dickens to Gaboriau. Ed. by Joseph Lewis French. LC 24-277509. (The Dial detective library). 1924. L. MacVeagh, The Dial Press.

Great Detective Stories from Voltaire to Poe. Ed. by Joseph Lewis French. LC 24-236036. (The Dial detective library). 1924. L. MacVeagh, The Dial Press.

Great Detective Stories of the World. Ed. by Joseph Lewis French. LC 29-27526. 1929. L. MacVeagh, The Dial Press.

Great Dethriffe. Courtlandt Dixon Barnes Bryan. LC 75-122791. 1970. 6.50. Dutton.

Great Diamond Pipe. John Buchan. LC 10-232033. 1910. 1.50. Dodd, Mead and Company.

Great Disciple, and Other Stories. William Bernard Ready. LC 51-11244. 1951. Bruce.

Great Divide. Frank M Robinson & John Levin. LC 80-5991. 11.95 (ISBN 0-89256-165-3). Rawson, Wade.

Great Divide. James J Tynan. LC 25-5547. Grosset & Dunlap.

Great Divide: A Novel. Frank M. Robinson & John Levin. 1982. 11.95 (ISBN 0-89256-165-3). Rawson Wade.

Great Divorce Case. Mary Grace Halpine. LC 7-1206. (On cover: Munro's library. v. 1. no. 408). N. L. Munro.

Great Drake. Mario Cappelli. LC 77-7840. (Illus.). 5.95 (ISBN 0-06-061303-3). Harper & Row.

Great Dream from Heaven. John Rolfe Gardiner. LC 74-2046. 1974. 7.95. Dutton.

Great Elephant. Alan Scholefield. LC 67-227503. 1968. bds., 4.95. Morrow.

Great Emergency & a Very Ill-Tempered Family. Juliana Horatia Gatty Ewing. LC 69-14799. (Illus.). 1969. 4.50x (ISBN 0-8052-3087-4); pap. 1.75 (ISBN 0-8052-0225-0). Schocken.

Great Empress. A Portrait. Maximilian Schele De Vere. LC 6-33878. 1870. J. B. Lippincott & Co.

Great Enchantment. Harriet Fleischmann. LC 67-14084. 1967. Chilton Books.

Great English Short Stories. Ed. by Lewis Saul Benjamin & Hargreaves, Reginald. LC 30-30771. 1930. The Viking Press.

Great English Short Stories. Ed. by Lewis Saul Benjamin & Hargreaves, Reginald. 1933. Blue Ribbon Books, Inc.

Great English Short Stories: Edited, and with a Foreword and Introd. Ed. by Christopher Isherwood. LC 57-8264. (Laurel edition, LC102). 1957. Dell Pub. Co.

Great English Short-Story Writers. Ed. by William James Dawson. LC 10-5056. (Their The reader's library). 1910. Harper Aand Brothers.

Great English Stories. Ed. by Lewis Melville & Reginald Hargreaves. 1979. Repr. of 1931 ed. lib. bdg. 30.00 (ISBN 0-8495-3789-4). Arden Lib.

Great Enigma: Or, Nick Carter's Triple Puzzle. John Russell Coryell. (On cover: Secret service series, no. 61). 1892. Street & Smith.

Great Eric Ackroyd Disaster. Bill Tidy. LC 77-356088. (Illus.). 1976. 2.50 (ISBN 0-09-127920-8). Hutchinson.

Great European Short Novels. Ed. by Anthony Winner. LC 77-352. (Perennial classic, P3082). Harper & Row.

Great Expectations. Charles Dickens. LC 62-125138. (Chandler ser. of Eng. novels). 1963. pap., 1.25. Chandler.

Great Expectations. Charles Dickens. LC 64-55610. (Harper's modern classics). 1963. Harper & Row.

Great Expectations. Charles Dickens. LC 62-21261. (Library of literature, 2). 1964. Bobbs-Merrill.

Great Expectations. Charles Dickens. LC 65-29850. (Penguin English library, EL3). 1965. Penguin Books.

Great Expectations. Charles Dickens. LC 65-6520. (Perennial classic). 1965. Harper & Row.

Great Expectations. Charles Dickens. (Washington Square Press Enriched Classics). 1973. (pbk.) 0.95. Pocket Books.

Great Expectations. 2d ed. Charles Dickens. LC 72-177918. (Rinehart editions, 20). 1972. (ISBN 0-03-077900-6). Holt, Rinehart, Winston.

Great Expectations. peterson's uniform ed.... ed. Charles Dickens. LC 6-37053. T. B. Peterson & Brothers.

Great Expectations... Charles Dickens. LC 6-26452. 1869. Hurd and Houghton.

Great Expectations. Charles Dickens. (Half-title: Everyman's library, ed. by Ernest Rhys. Fiction. no. 234). 1907. J. M. Dent & Co.

Great Expectations. Charles Dickens. (Half-title: The centenary edition of the works of Charles Dickens in 36 volumes). 1911. Chapman & Hall, Ltd.

Great Expectations. Charles Dickens. LC 26-26991. (Rittenhouse classics). 1926. G. W. Jacobs & Company.

Great Expectations. Charles Dickens. LC 36-37119. (Half-title: Everyman's library, ed. by Ernest Rhys. Fiction. no. 234). 1932. J. M. Dent & Sons, Ltd.

Great Expectations. Charles Dickens. LC 39-11441. For the Members of the Heritage Club.

Great Expectations. Charles Dickens. LC 49-2998. (Great Illustrated Classics). 1948. Dodd, Mead.

Great Expectations. Charles Dickens. LC 49-30758. (Rinehart editions. 20). 1949. Rinehart.

Great Expectations. Charles Dickens & Clark, Evert Mordecal. LC 31-10173. (modern readers' series). 1931. The Macmillan Company.

Great Expectations. Charles Dickens & Francis Arthur Fraser. LC 76-6693. (Illus.). 9.95 (ISBN 0-8055-1198-9) (ISBN 0-8055-0283-1). Hart Pub. Co.

Great Expectations. Charles Dickens & Whipple, Edwin Percy. LC 6-37245. (Half-title: Works... New illustrated library ed. vol. xxiii). 1877. Hurd and Houghton.

Great Expectations: Abridged Ed. with Introd. and Notes by Blanche Jennings Thompson. Charles Dickens. Ed. by Blanche Jennings Thompson. LC 50-678117. 1950. Harcourt, Brace.

Great Expectations: Adapted by Lou P. Bunce. Charles Dickens & Lou P Bunce. LC 51-13574. 1951. Globe Book Co.

Great Expectations: Ed. by Louise Stevens. Unabridged School Ed. Charles Dickens. Ed. by Louise Stevens. LC 66-4249. (Lit. heritage). 1966. 1.32, .95 pap.,. Macmillan.

Great Expectations. Ed. by R. D. McMaster. Charles Dickens. LC 65-20261. (Coll. classics in Eng.) Bibl.). pap., 1.35. Macmillan of Canada.

Great Expectations. Introd. by Clark Cory Livensparger. Charles Dickens. LC 53-119118. 1952. Fine Editions Press.

Great Expectations. Introd. by G. K. Chesterton. Charles Dickens. LC 50-11221. (Everyman's library, 234 A. Fiction). 1950. Dutton.

Great Expectations. Pictures from Italy. Master Humphrey's Clock. No Thoroughfare. Charles Dickens. LC 9-821. Aldine Book Publishing Co.

Great Expectations: With an Introd. by Edward Wagenknecht. Complete and Unabridged. Charles Dickens. LC 56-44037. (Pocket library, PL 50). 1956. Pocket Books.

Great Expectations: With 21 Illus. by F. W. Pailthorpe and an Introd. by Frederick Page. Charles Dickens. LC 53-9269. (New Oxford illustrated Dickens). 1953. Oxford University Press.

Great Explosion. Eric Frank Russell. LC 62-17824. (Torquil book). 1962. Distributed by Dodd, Mead.

Great Extinction. Michael Allaby & James Lovelock. LC 81-43613. 192p. 1983. 13.95 (ISBN 0-385-18011-X). Doubleday.

Great Fall. Mildred Savage. (O.s.i.). 1970. 7.95 o.s.i. (ISBN 0-671-20219-7). S&S.

Great Fetish. Lyon Sprague De Camp. LC 78-1239. 1978. 7.95 (ISBN 0-385-13139-9). Doubleday.

Great Fishing Stores. Ed. by Edwin Valentine Mitchell. 1946. Doubleday & Company, Inc.

Great Fishing Stories. Ed. by Edwin Valentine Mitchell. LC 48-65499. 1948. Garden City Pub. Co.

Great Fog, and Other Weird Tales. Gerald Heard. LC 44-78371. 1944. The Vanguard Press.

Great Fog: Weird Tales of Terror and Detection. Gerald Heard. LC 46-20545. 1946. The Sun Dial Press.

Great Forgery: A Novel. Edith Simon. LC 61-12816. 1961. Little, Brown.

Great Fortune. Gilbert Wolf Gabriel. LC 33-31429. 1933. Doubleday, Doran and Company, Inc.

Great Free Enterprise Gambit. James Baar. LC 79-25889. 1980. 8.95 (ISBN 0-395-29115-1). Houghton Mifflin.

Great French Romance, Selected, with an Introd., by Richard Aldington. Ed. by Richard Aldington. LC 49-1790. 1946. Pilot Press.

Great French Short Novels. Ed. by Frederick Wilcox Dupee. LC 52-10095. (Series: The Permanent Library Series). 1952. Dial Press.

Great French Short Stories. Ed. by Lewis Melivlle & Reginald Hargreaves. 1979. Repr. of 1928 ed. lib. bdg. 25.00 o.p. (ISBN 0-8492-5326-8). R West.

Great French Short Stories. Ed. by Lewis Melville & Reginald Hargreaves. 1066p. 1982. Repr. of 1928 ed. lib. bdg. 25.00 (ISBN 0-89760-583-7). Telegraph Bks.

Great French Short Stories. Ed. by Morris Edmund Speare. Repr. of 1943 ed. 10.00 o.p. Folcroft.

Great French Short Stories: 24 Masterpieces by the Outstanding Modern French Story-Tellers. Ed. by Morris Edmund Speare. LC 44-4615. 1943. The World Publishing Company.

Great Friends. David Garnett. LC 79-55596. (Illus.). 1980. 16.95 (ISBN 0-689-11039-1). Atheneum.

Great Fright: Onesiphore, Our Neighbor. Madge Hamilton Lyons Macbeth & Conway, A. B., Joint Author. LC 30-33263. 1929. L. Carrier & Co.

Great Game. Henry Christopher Bailey. LC 39-4661. 1939. Pub. for the Crime Club, Inc., by Doubleday, Doran & Co., Inc.

Great Game. Henry Christopher Bailey. LC 40-9072. 1940. The Sun Dial Press.

Great Game. Charles Platt Brown. LC 15-402. 1914. Broadway Publishing Company.

Great Game for a Girl. Tristram P. Coffin. 1980. 7.00 (ISBN 0-682-49566-2). Exposition.

Great Gatsby. Francis Scott Key Fitzgerald. LC 63-3885. (Scribner library. Fiction, SL1). 1961. Scribner.

Great Gatsby. Francis Scott Key Fitzgerald. LC 58-14791. 1958. Scribner.

Great Gatsby. limited ed. Francis Scott Key Fitzgerald. LC 75-323309. (Illus.). 1974. Franklin Library.

Great Gatsby. Francis Scott Key Fitzgerald. LC 25-10468. 1925. C. Scribner's Sons.

Great Gatsby. Francis Scott Key Fitzgerald. LC 34-312963. (Half-title: The modern library of the world's best books). 1934. The Modern Library.

Great Gatsby. Francis Scott Key Fitzgerald. LC 46-19679. (On cover: A Bantam book. 8). 1946. Bantam Books.

Great Gatsby see Three Great American Novels.

Great Gatsby a Facsimile of the Manuscript. Ed. by Matthew J. Bruccoli. 1973. deluxe ed. 100.00 boxed (ISBN 0-89723-032-9). Bruccoli.

Great Gatsby: A Facsimile of the Manuscript. Francis Scott Key Fitzgerald. LC 72-93657. 1973. (ISBN 0-910972-32-X). Microcard Editions Books.

Great Gatsby. Foreword and Study Guide by Albert K. Ridout. Francis Scott Key Fitzgerald. 1968. Scribners.

Great German Short Novels and Stories. Ed. by Bennett Alfred Cerf. LC 33-10806. (Half-title: The modern library of the world's best books). B. A. Cerf, D. S. Klopfer, The Modern Library.

Great German Short Novels and Stories. Ed. by Victor Lange & Bennett Alfred Cerf. LC 52-9773. (Modern library of the world's best books). 1952. Modern Library.

Great German Short Stories. Ed. by Lewis Saul Benjamin & Reginald Hargreaves. LC 72-169540. (Short story index reprint series). 1971. (ISBN 0-8369-4001-6). Books for Libraries Press.

Great Ghost Stories. Ed. by Joseph Lewis French. LC 70-37268. (Short story index reprint series). 1971. (ISBN 0-8369-4079-2). Books for Libraries Press.

Great Ghost Stories. Ed. by Joseph Lewis French. LC 18-10839. 1918. Dodd, Mead and Company.

Great Ghost Stories. Ed. by Philip Van Doren Stern. (Great American Thinkers Ser). (Orig.). (YA) (gr. 9-12). pap. 0.60 o.p. (W0592). WSP.

Great Ghost Stories of the Old West. Ed. by Betty Baker. Western Writers of America. LC 68-27268. (Illus.). 1968. 3.50. Four Winds Press.

Great Ghost Stories of the World. Ed. by Alexander Kinnan Laing. LC 39-17426. 1939. The Garden City Publishing Co., Inc.

Great Ghost Stories of the World. Ed. by Alexander Kinnan Laing. LC 42-13735. 1941. Blue Ribbon Books.

Great Ghost Towns of the American West. Ed. by Robert Silverberg. (Illus.). 1973. pap. 1.65 o.p. (ISBN 0-345-23273-9). Comstock Edns.

Great Gift. George Sidney Paternoster. LC 17-28803. 1917. John Lane.

Great Gittin' up Morning. John Oliver Killens. LC 75-171301. 1972. 3.95. Doubleday.

Great God Gold. William Le Queux. LC 10-23400. 1910. R. G. Badger.

Great God Now. Edward S. Hanlon. (Orig.). 1968. pap. 0.60 o.p. (53-657). Paperback Lib.

Great God Pan. Arthur Machen. LC 79-128737. (Short story index reprint series). 1970. Books for Libraries Press.

Great God Pan, and: The Inmost Light. Arthur Machen. LC 7-19998. (On cover: Keynotes series no. 5). 1894. Roberts Bros.; Etc., Etc.

Great God Success. David Graham Phillips. LC 67-29277. (Americans in Fiction Ser.). lib. bdg. 16.00 (ISBN 0-8398-1564-6); pap. text ed. 5.95x (ISBN 0-89197-777-5). Irvington.

Great God Success. David Graham Phillips. (American Authors Ser). 1901. lib. bdg. 17.25 o.s.i. (ISBN 0-512-00543-5). Garrett Pr.

Great God Success: A Novel. David Graham Phillips. LC 67-29277. (Americans in Fiction). 1967. Gregg Press.

Great God Success: A Novel. 3d ed. David Graham Phillips. LC 16-9355. Frederick A. Stokes Company.

Great Gold Mountain. James P. McCague. LC 58-832511. 1958. Crown Publishers.

Great Good Place see Author of Beltraffio.

Great Gorme. Colleen Cairns. LC 75-23087. 1975. 8.95 (ISBN 0-679-40125-3). Weybright and Talley.

Great Grandmother. James Owen Hannay. LC 23-732182. The Bobbs-Merrill Company.

Great-Grandmother Stories. Bonnie V. McGee. 1975. 4.95 o.p. (ISBN 0-8059-2209-1). Dorrance.

Great-Grandmother Stories. Bonnie V. McGee. 1975. 4.95 o.p. (ISBN 0-8059-2209-1). Dorrance.

TITLE INDEX GREAT PONDS.

Great-Grandmother's Secret. Louise Diard. Tr. by Murphy, Blanche Elizabeth Mary Anounciata (Noel) LC 6-34206. 1875. Benziger Brothers.
Great Grandpapa Billie: A Down Easter's Adventures North and South from Square Rig to Steam. Written and Illustrated by May Randlette Beck. May Randlette Beck. LC 59-25928. 1958. Rapier House.
Great Granny Webster. Caroline Blackwood. LC 78-54596. 1978. 7.95 (ISBN 0-684-15648-2). Scribner.
Great Granny Webster. Caroline Blackwood. LC 79-10514. 1979. 9.95 (ISBN 0-8161-6713-3). G. K. Hall.
Great Green: A Loose Memoir of Merchant Marine Life in the Middle of the Twentieth Century with Examples of True Experience Being Turned into Fiction. Calvin Kentfield. LC 73-10245. 1974. 8.95. Dial Press.
Great Gretzky. Stan Fischler. (Illus.). 160p. (Orig.). 1982. pap. 8.95 (ISBN 0-688-01695-2). Quill NY.
Great Gulf. Erich Ebermayer & Fisher, Morgan, Tr. LC 32-229890. 1932. D. Appleton & Company.
Great Haddon. Aryan Lewis Kelton. LC 33-14020. Hart Publishing Company.
Great Haddon. Aryan Lewis Kelton. LC 33-14020. 1933. Har Publishing Company.
Great Heads. Kenneth Tindall. LC 70-84888. 1969. 6.50. Grove Press.
Great Heiress: A Fortune in Seven Checks. Robert Edward Francillon. LC 6-43263. (On cover: Seaside library. Pocket ed. no. 135). G. Munro.
Great Highway. August Strindberg. 1954. 4.95 o.p. Liveright.
Great Highway: A Story of the World's Struggles. 3d ed. Stephen Watson Fullon. 1854. G. Routledge & Co.
Great Hijack. Alfred Tack. LC 77-111184. 1970. 4.50. Published for the Crime Club by Doubleday.
Great Hoggarty Diamond. William Makepeace Thackeray. LC 8-28201. (Lovell's library, v. 6, no. 316). 1883. J. W. Lovell Company.
Great Hold-up Mystery. Wilfrid Usher. LC 29-20114. International Fiction Library.
Great Horse Race. Fred Grove. LC 76-30338. 1977. 5.95 (ISBN 0-385-12101-6). Doubleday.
Great Horse Race. Fred Grove. 1978. 1.75 (ISBN 0-441-30259-9). Ace Books.
Great Horse Stories. Ed. by Page Cooper. Brown, Paul, 1893- Illus. LC 46-4128. 1946. Doubleday & Company, Inc.
Great Hotel Murder. Vincent Starrett. LC 35-73141. 1935. Pub. for the Crime Club, Inc., by Doubleday, Doran & Company, Inc.
Great Hotel Murder. Vincent Starrett. LC 37-10655. 1937. The Sun Dial Press, Inc.
Great Hotel Robbery, A Novel. John Minahan. 1982. 12.95 (ISBN 0-393-01604-8). Norton.
Great House. Kate Thompson. LC 55-5300. 1955. Houghton Mifflin.
Great House: A Story of Quiet Times. Stanley John Weyman. LC 19-14195. 1919. Longmans, Green and Co.
Great House in the Park: By the Author of "The House on Charles Street" and "The House on Smith Square". Anna Robeson Brown Burr. LC 24-12521. 1924. Duffield & Company.
Great Hunger. Johan Bojer. Tr. by W. J. Alexander Worster. Archer, Charles, 1803-Joint Tr. LC 36-293443. 1925. The Century Co.
Great Hunger. Johan Bojer & Worster, W. J. Alexander, Tr. LC 18-22828. 1918. Hodder and Stoghton.
Great Hunger. Johan Bojer & Worster, W. J. Alexander, Tr. LC 19-177518. 1919. Moffat, Yard and Company.
Great Hunger: By Johan Bojer; Tr. from the Norwegian by W. J. Alexander Worster and C. Archer. Johan Bojer. Tr. by W. J. Alexander Worster. Archer, Charles, 1863-Joint Tr. LC 22-10826. 1921. Moffat, Yard and Company.
Great I Am. Lewis Graham. LC 33-116264. The Macaulay Company.
Great Idea. Henry Hazlitt. LC 51-9833. 1951. Appleton-Century-Crofts.
Great Impersonation. Edward Phillips Oppenheim. LC 21-8171. 1921. Little, Brown and Company.
Great Impersonation. Edward Phillips Oppenheim. LC 20-629. 1920. Little, Brown, & Company.
Great Impersonation. Edward Phillips Oppenheim. LC 77-20546. 3.00 (ISBN 0-486-23607-2). Dover Publications.
Great Impersonation - Illustrated. Edward Phillips Oppenheim. 1976. Repr. of 1920 ed. lib. bdg. 11.15x (ISBN 0-89190-412-3). Am Repr-Rivercity Pr.
Great Infidel: A Biographical Novel. Joseph Jay Deiss. LC 63-7123. 1963. Random House.
Great Insurance Murders. Milton Morris Propper. LC 37-21537. 1937. Harper & Brothers.
Great International Novel Formula, or, The Ultimate Conspiracy. Keith Warren Jennison. LC 81-9727. 10.95 (ISBN 0-914378-74-0). Countryman Press.
Great Irish Short Stories. Ed. by Vivian Mercier. LC 64-4630. (Laurel edition). 1964. Dell Publ. Co.
Great Issue: Or, The Undertow. Eugene Walter. LC 8-13952. C. H. Doscher & Co.
Great Italian Short Stories. Ed. by P M Pasinetti. LC 59-4098. (Laurel edition, LC127). 1959. Dell Pub. Co.
Great Italian Short Stories. Decio Pettoello. Repr. of 1930 ed. 40.00 (ISBN 0-8414-9251-4). Folcroft.
Great Jasper. Fulton Oursler. LC 30-24236. 1930. Covici, Friede.
Great Jehosaphat and Gully Dirt! Jewell Ellen Smith. LC 75-33778. 7.95 (ISBN 0-910244-86-3). J. F. Blair.
Great Jewish Short Stories. Ed. by Saul Bellow. LC 63-3635. (Laurel edition, 3122). 1963. Dell Pub. Co.
Great John L. A Novelization of the Screen Play. James Edward Grant. LC 45-3730. 1945. The World Publishing Company.
Great Jones Street. Don DeLillo. LC 72-9076. 1973. 5.95 (ISBN 0-395-15566-5). Houghton Mifflin.
Great Jones Street. Don Delillo. (Pocket books, 78366). 1974. (pbk.) 1.25 (ISBN 0-671-78366-1). Pocket Books.
Great K. & A. Train Roberry: A Novel. Paul Leicester Ford. LC 6-41398. 1897. Dodd, Mead and Company.
Great Keinplatz Experiment: And Other Stories. Arthur Conan Doyle. LC 43-42360. Rand, McNally & Company.
Great Keinplatz Experiment: And Other Tales of Twilight and the Unseen. Arthur Conan Doyle. LC 26-8500. 1925. George H. Doran Company.
Great Kenton Feud: A Novel. Frederick Whittaker. (On cover: The popular series, no. 6). 1891. R. Bonner's Sons.
Great Kipling Stories: Together with a Life of Rudyard Kipling. Rudyard Kipling & Thomas, Lowell Jackson, 1892- LC 33-31571. The John C. Winston Company.
Great Lady. Ruth Reid. LC 1-29560. 1900. The Saalfield Publishing Company.
Great Lady: A Novel. Margaret Mackprang Mackay. LC 46-4756. 1946. The John Day Company.
Great Lady. A Romance. From the German of Van Dewall Pseud. August Kuhne. LC 7-14172. 1874. J. B. Lippincott & Co.
Great Laughter. Fannie Hurst. LC 36-23255. 1936. Harper & Brothers.
Great Leviathan. Dalgairns Arundel Barker. LC 20-22040. 1920. John Lane.
Great Light. Larry Barretto. LC 47-311321. 1947. Farrar, Straus.
Great Lion of God. Taylor Caldwell. LC 78-97653. 1970. 7.95. Doubleday.
Great Liquidator. John V. Grombach. 1981. pap. 2.95 (ISBN 0-89083-749-X). Zebra.
Great Locomotive Chase. MacLennan Roberts, pseud. LC 56-899816. (Dell first edition, 96). 1956. Dell Pub. Co.
Great Lord. Paul Frischauer. Tr. by Blewitt, Phyllis. LC 37-39117. Random House.
Great Los Angeles Blizzard: A Novel. Thom Racina. LC 77-4156. 1977. 8.95. Putnam.
Great Los Angeles Fire. Gordon Lish. LC 80-13550. 11.95 (ISBN 0-671-25135-X). Simon and Schuster.
Great Los Angeles Fire. Edward Stewart. 1980. 11.95 (ISBN 0-671-25135-X). S&S.
Great Los Angeles Fire. Edward Stewart. 288p. 1982. pap. 2.95 (ISBN 0-449-24526-8, Crest). Fawcett.
Great Love. Clara Louise Root Burnham. LC 16-25054. Houghton Mifflin Company.
Great Love. Clara Louise Root Burnham. LC 98-119. 1898. Houghton, Mifflin and Company.
Great Love. Aleksandra Mikhailovna Kollontai. LC 75-167457. (Short story index reprint series). 1971. (ISBN 0-8369-3983-2). Books for Libraries Press.
Great Love. Aleksandra Mikhailovna Kollontai. Tr. by Lore, Lily. LC 29-28945. The Vanguard Press.
Great Love. Aleksandra Mikhailovna Kollontai. LC 81-18696. 1982. 12.95 (ISBN 0-393-30028-5). W.W. Norton.
Great Love Scenes from Famous Novels, Selected by Carl P. Mason. Ed. by Carl P. Mason. LC 42-19445. 1942. The New Home Library.
Great Love Stories. Ed. by John R. Colter. LC 40-13736. 1940. Halcyon House.
Great Love Stories. Ed. by John J Maloney. LC 52-10276. 1952. Bobbs-Merrill.
Great Love Stories from The Saturday Evening Post. Ed. by Julie Eisenhower. LC 76-41559. 5.95 (ISBN 0-89387-003-X). Curtis Pub. Co.
Great Lover. Ross Sloane. LC 34-8576. 1934. W. Godwin, Inc.
Great Madness: Authorized Translation from the Hebrew Original by Jacob Freedman. Avigdor Hameiri. LC 52-207496. 1952. Vantage Press.
Great Magor Diamond: The Creaking Door. Herman Cyril McNeile. LC 31-14345. Doubleday, Doran & Company Inc.
Great Mail Robbery. 1st Ed. Clarence Budington Kelland. LC 51-11463. 1951. Harper.
Great Man. Arnold Bennett. LC 74-5321. (Collected Works of Arnold Bennett: Vol. 26). 1976. Repr. of 1911 ed. 20.75 (ISBN 0-518-19107-9). Ayer Co.
Great Man. Arnold Bennett. 1981. 18.95x (Pub. by Remploy England). State Mutual Bk.
Great Man. Walter Vogdes. LC 29-4754. 1929. Longmans, Green and Co.
Great Man: A Frolic. Arnold Bennett. LC 74-5321. (collected works of Arnold Bennett). 1974. (ISBN 0-518-19107-9). Books for Libraries Press.
Great Man: A Frolic. Arnold Bennett. 1910. Hodder & Stoughton Etc.
Great Man. Novel. Albert Morgan. LC 55-5345. 1955. Dutton.
Great Man of the Provinces in Paris. Honore De Balzac. Tr. by Katharine Prescott Wormeley. (Half-title: The comedy of human life... Scenes from provincial life). 1893. Roberts Brothers.
Great Man's Life, 1925 to 2000 A.C. Albert Archer Van Aetten. LC 59-6541. 1959. Utopian Publishers.
Great Maria. Cecelia Holland. LC 74-8551. 1974. 8.95 (ISBN 0-394-48509-2). Knopf; Distributed by Random House.
Great Match: And Other Matches. John Trawbridge. LC 12-37818. (No name series. 1st ser.). 1877. Roberts Brothers.
Great Meadow. Elizabeth Madox Roberts. LC 30-7676. 1930. The Viking Press.
Great Meadow. Elizabeth Madox Roberts. LC 76-12120. 1980. 27.50 (ISBN 0-404-15235-X). AMS Press.
Great Meadow. Elizabeth Madox Roberts. (Mockingbird book). 1975. (pbk.) 1.50 (ISBN 0-345-24446-X). Ballantine Books.
Great Merlini, 5 bks. Clayton Rawson. 45.00 (Gregg). G K Hall.
Great Merlini: The Complete Stories of the Magician Detective. Clayton Rawson. LC 79-10517. (Gregg Press Mystery Fiction Series). 1979. 9.95 (ISBN 0-8398-2546-3). Gregg Press.
Great Midland. Alexander Plaisted Saxton. LC 48-8993. 1948. Appleton-Century-Crofts.
Great Mildew Creek Harlot Massacre. Gilt Lamont. 1972. pap. 1.95 o.s.i. (OPH-4231, Ophelia). Olympia.
Great Mill Street Mystery: A Novel, by Adeline Sergeant !... Adeline Sergeant. LC 8-6850. (On cover: Lovell's international series, no. 124). 1890. J. W. Lovell Company.
Great Mirage: A Novel of the City Underneath It. James Lauren Ford. LC 15-1629. 1915. Harper & Brothers.
Great Mischief. Josephine Pinckney. LC 48-6015. 1948. Viking Press.
Great Miss Driver. Anthony Hope Hawkins. LC 8-25366. 1908. The McClure Company.
Great Mistake... Sophy Beckett. LC 6-9771. (On cover: The seaside library. Pocket edition, no. 244). 1884. G. Munro.
Great Mistake. Mary Roberts Rinehart. LC 40-33219. Farrar & Rinehart Incorporated.
Great Mistake. Mary Roberts Rinehart. LC 46-7672. 1946. Triangle Books, the Blakiston Company.
Great Mistake: And Other Stories. (On cover: Cassell's "rainbow" series, no. 28). 1888. Cassell & Company, Limited.
Great Mr. Knight. Dorothy Whipple. LC 34-353057. Farrar & Rinehart, Incorporated.
Great Modern American Stories: An Anthology. William Dean Howells. 1920. 30.00 (ISBN 0-8274-2444-2). R West.
Great Modern American Stories, an Anthology. by william dean howells. ed. Ed. by William Dean Howells. (On verso of half title: The great modern stories series). 1920. Boni and Liveright.
Great Modern American Stories: An Anthology. Ed. by William Dean Howells. 1972. Repr. of 1920 ed. 19.50 (ISBN 0-8422-8077-4). Irvington.
Great Modern American Stories: An Anthology. Ed. by William Dean Howells. LC 20-11148. (Important Literary Anthologies Ser). 1969. Repr. of 1902 ed. lib. bdg. 21.50 o.s.i. (ISBN 0-512-00769-1). Garrett Pr.
Great Modern Catholic Short Stories... Ed. by Mariella Gable. LC 42-24233. 1942. Shed & Ward.
Great Modern English Stories: An Anthology, Comp. & Ed., with an Introduction. Ed. by Edward Joseph Harrington O'Brien. LC 19-9538. (On verso of half-title: The great modern stories series). 1919. Boni and Liveright.
Great Modern English Stories: An Anthology. Ed. by Edward Joseph Harrington O'Brien. 1979. Repr. of 1919 ed. lib. bdg. 25.00 (ISBN 0-8495-4207-3). Arden Lib.
Great Modern European Short Stories. Ed. by Douglas Angus. LC 67-7941. (Fawcett premier book, m351). 1967. Fawcett Publications.
Great Modern French Stories. Ed. by Willard H. Wright. 1978. Repr. of 1917 ed. lib. bdg. 35.00 (ISBN 0-8495-5624-4). Arden Lib.
Great Modern Short Novels. Hilton, James. LC 66-5649. 1966. N. Doubleday.
Great Modern Short Stories. Ed. by Bennett Alfred Cerf. 2.95 o.p. (168). Modern Lib.
Great Modern Short Stories. Ed. by Grant Martin Overton. LC 30-261937. (Half-title: The modern library of the world's best books). The Modern Library.
Great Modern Short Stories: An Anthology of Twelve Famous Stories and Novelettes. Ed. by Bennett Alfred Cerf. LC 42-25441. (Half-title: The Modern library of the world's best books). 1942. The Modern Library.
Great Mogul. Louis Tracy. LC 5-14449. 1905. E. J. Clode.
Great Moment. Elinor Sutherland Glyn. LC 24-16420. 1923. J. B. Lippincott Company.
Great Moment. Elinor Sutherland Glyn & Barbara Cartland. LC 81-100867. (Barbara Cartland's Library of love; 14). ((Series: Cartland, Barbara, 1902-). (Library of love; 14.). 1980. 6.95 (ISBN 0-7156-1474-6). Duckworth.
Great Moments from Great Stories. edited with notes and an introduction by thomas l. doyle... ed. Ed. by Thomas L. Doyle. LC 28-10792. Globe Book Company.
Great Moments: In a Woman's Life. Emily Calvin Blake. LC 10-26918. 1910. Forbes & Company.
Great Monster Hunt. D. C. Cooke. 3.95 o.p. (21362). G&D.
Great Mother of Pearl. (Stanyan Bks.). 1973. 3.00 o.p. (ISBN 0-394-48597-1). Random.
Great Mutiny: India, Eighteen Fifty-Seven. Christopher Hibbert. 472p. 1980. pap. 7.95 (ISBN 0-14-004752-2). Penguin.
Great Myth. John Couchois Wright. LC 22-11290. The Michigan Education Company.
Great Natural Healer. Charles Heber Clark. LC 10-10774. 0.50. G. W. Jacobs & Co.
Great Novelists & Their Novels see World's Ten Greatest Novels.
Great Oakdale Mystery. Morgan Scott. LC 12-13192. 0.60. Hurst & Company.
Great Oaks. Ben Ames Williams. LC 30-30576. E. P. Dutton & Co., Inc.
Great One: A Novel. Nicholas Roland, pseud. LC 68-11925. 1968. Houghton Mifflin.
Great One: A Novel of American Life. Henry Hart. LC 34-12697. The John Day Company.
Great Ones: The Love Story of Two Very Important People. Ralph McAllister Ingersoll. LC 48-5232. 1948. Harcourt, Brace.
Great Oriental and Trans-Continental Railroad. A Political Novel... Filled with Wit, Humor, Satire and Philosophy. Charles Z Cash. LC 6-22795. 1896. The Commercial Herald Printing and Publishing House.
Great Original and Entrancing Romance: The Fireman's Bride, or, Beautiful Myria, the Mad Actress. The History of Myria Blakely, and Ringgold, Though Clothed in the Illusive Language and Plot of a Novellet, Yet Brings to Light Facts Most Startling and Strange... W. D Ritner. LC 6-24371. 1858. M. A. Milliette.
Great Pandolfo. William John Locke. LC 25-17123. 1925. Dodd, Mead and Company.
Great Pearl Secret. Charles Norris Williamson & Alice Muriel Livingston Williamson. LC 21-1282. 1921. Doubleday, Page & Company.
Great Pebble Affair. Brit Shelby. LC 75-40335. 7.95. Putnam.
Great Performance. Mullin Garr. pap. 1.95 o.s.i. (OPH-219, Ophelia). Olympia.
Great Permanence. Graham Sutton. LC 29-102991. 1929. R. M. McBride & Company.
Great Pike's Peak Rush: Or, Terry in the New Gold Fields. Edwin Legrand Sabin. LC 17-24099. Thomas Y. Crowell Company.
Great Pirate Stories, 2 vols. in one. Ed. by Joseph Lewis French. 1978. Repr. of 1943 ed. lib. bdg. 25.00 (ISBN 0-8495-1611-0). Arden Lib.
Great Pirate Stories. Ed. by Joseph Lewis French. 1969. Repr. of 1923 ed. price not set o.p. Singing Tree.
Great Place to Visit: A Political Novel of the 70s. Irving Schiffer. LC 72-77643. 1972. 7.95 (ISBN 0-87000-168-X). Arlington House.
Great Plan. Edith Huntington Mason. LC 13-25053. 1913. A. C. McClurg & Co.
Great Ponds. Elechi Amadi. (African Writers Ser.). 1970. pap. text ed. 3.00x (ISBN 0-435-90044-7). Heinemann Ed.
Great Ponds. Elechi Amadi. (African Writers Ser.: No. 44). 1970. pap. text ed. 1.50x o.p. (ISBN 0-435-90044-7). Humanities.

Great Ponds: A Novel. Elechi Amadi. LC 72-11582. 1973. 6.95 (ISBN 0-381-98235-1). John Day Co.
Great Porter Square. A Mystery. Benjamin Leopold Farjeon. (Harper's Franklin square library. no. 452). 1885. Harper & Brothers.
Great Possessions. Josephine Mary Ward. LC 9-27448. 1909. G. P. Putnam's Sons.
Great Possessions: A New Series of Adventures. Ray Stannard Baker. LC 17-28078. 1917. Doubleday, Page & Company.
Great Pretender. Jim Deane. (Decoy). (Signet book: Vol. 1). 1974. (pbk.) 1.25. New American Library.
Great Prevaricators: By Laurence E. Groat and May I. Groat. Laurence E Groat & Groat, May I. LC 63-21533. 1964. Dorrance.
Great Prince Died: A Novel. Bernard Wolfe. LC 59-7198. 1959. Scribner.
Great Prince Shan. Edward Phillips Oppenheim. LC 22-4981. 1922. Little, Brown and Company.
Great Prince Shan. Edward Phillips Oppenheim. LC 35-33396. A. L. Burt Company.
Great Promise. Noel Houston. 1973. (pbk) 1.25. Curtis Books.
Great Promise: A Novel. Noel Houston. LC 46-3136. 1946. Reynal & Hitchcock.
Great Pursuit. Tom Sharpe. LC 78-2073. 9.95. (ISBN 0-06-014011-9). Harper & Row.
Great Quest: A Romance of 1826, Wherein Are Recorded the Experiences Fo Josiah Woods of Topham, and of Those Others with Whom He Sailed for Cuba and the Gulf of Guinea. Charles Boardman Hawes. LC 21-17013. The Atlantic Monthly Press.
Great Question. Will Elmer Montgomery. LC 52-6226. Pageant Press.
Great Quill. Paul Garson. LC 73-80014. (Doubleday science fiction). 1973. 5.95 (ISBN 0-385-04910-2). Doubleday.
Great Railroad Stories of the World. Introd. by Freeman H. Hubbarb. Ed. by Samuel Moskowitz. LC 54-12968. 1954. McBride Co.
Great Railroad War. Giles A Lutz. LC 80-1851. 1981. 8.95 (ISBN 0-385-17348-2). Doubleday.
Great Rascal: By Estelle Latta and Arthur J. Burks. Estelle Cothran Latta. LC 55-30996. 1955. State Pub. Co.
Great Red Border. Jesse Edward Grinstead. LC 40-345969. Dodge Publishing Company.
Great Refusal. Henry Pine. LC 33-17938. 1933. Block Publishing Company.
Great Refusal. Mary Gleed Tuttiett. LC 6-1906. 1906. D. Appleton and Company.
Great Riches. Mateel Howe Farnham. LC 34-34437. 1934. Dodd, Mead & Company.
Great Road. Kummer, Frederic Arnold. LC 38-27597. The John C. Winston Company.
Great Romantic: Being an Interpretation of Mr. Sam. Pepys and Elizabeth His Wife. Lily Moresby Adams Beck. LC 33-7090. 1933. Doubleday, Doran & Company, Inc.
Great Rope. 2nd ed. Rosemary S. Nesbitt. 1980. lib. bdg. 7.95x. Mathom.
Great Roxhythe. Georgette Heyer. LC 77-78036. 1977. Buccaneer Books.
Great Roxhythe. Georgette Heyer. LC 23-8988. 1923. Small, Maynard and Company.
Great Russian Short Novels. Ed. by Philip Rahv. LC 51-13886. (Permanent library book). 1951. Dial Press.
Great Russian Short Stories. Ed. by Stephen Graham. LC 75-25530. 1975-1976. 15.95 (ISBN 0-87140-105-3) (ISBN 0-87140-615-2). Liveright Pub. Corp.
Great Russian Short Stories. Edited and Introduced by Norris Houghton. Ed. by Norris Houghton. LC 58-3282. (Laurel edition, LC110). 1958. Dell Pub. Co.
Great Russian Stories. Ed. by Isai Kamen. LC 59-16074. (Modern library paperbacks, P50). 1959. Random House.
Great Sale. John Bascom. LC 33-7851. 1933. A. H. King.
Great Santini. Pat Conroy. LC 76-911. 1976. 10.00 (ISBN 0-395-24297-5). Houghton Mifflin.
Great Santini. Pat Conroy. 1977. 1.95 (ISBN 0-380-00991-9). Avon Books.
Great Scenes from Great Novels: Edited by Robert Terrall. Introd. by Malcolm Cowley. Ed. by Robert Terrall. LC 57-5948. (Dell first edition, C105). Dell Pub. Co.
Great Science Fiction About Doctors. Groff Conklin & N. D. Fabricant. 1966. pap. 0.95 o.p. (01895, Collier). Macmillan.
Great Science Fiction Adventures. easy eye ed. Ed. by Larry T. Shaw. pap. 0.75 o.p. (74-944). Lancer.
Great Science Fiction by Scientists. Ed. by Groff Conklin. (Orig.). 1962. pap. 2.95 (ISBN 0-02-019030-1, Collier). Macmillan.
Great Science Fiction Series: Stories from the Best of the Series from 1944 to 1980 by Twenty All-Time Favorite Writers. Frederik Pohl & Martin Harry Greenberg. LC 79-1705. 16.95 (ISBN 0-06-013382-1). Harper & Row.
Great Science Fiction Series: Stories from the Best of the Science Fiction Series from 1944 to 1980 by 20 All-Time Favorite Writers. Frederik Pohl et al. Ed. by Martin H. Greenberg & Joseph Olander. LC 79-1705. 416p. 1980. 16.95i (ISBN 0-06-013383-X, HarpT). Har-Row.
Great Science Fiction Stories About Mars. Ed. by T. E. Dikty. LC 65-24057. 1965. bds., 3.95. Fell.
Great Science-Fiction Stories About the Moon. Ed. by T. E. Dikty. LC 67-12665. 1967. F. Fell.
Great Scoop. Molly Elliot Seawell. LC 3-16374. 1903. L. C. Page & Company.
Great Scott. Horace Atkisson Wade. LC 32-5039. 1932. L. MacVeagh, Dial Press, Inc.
Great Scout and Cathouse Thursday. Richard Shapiro. Popular Library.
Great Sea Stories. Ed. by Joseph Lewis French. LC 21-15818. Brentano's.
Great Sea Stories. Ed. by Joseph Lewis French. LC 38-25699. Tudor Publishing Co.
Great Sea Stories. Ed. by Joseph Lewis French. LC 43-513158. 1943. Tudor Publishing Co.
Great Sea Stories of All Nations. Henry Major Tomlinson. LC 30-26626. 1930. Doubleday, Doran & Company, Inc.
Great Sea Stories of All Nations. Henry Major Tomlinson. LC 37-10653. 1937. Garden City Publishing Co.,Inc.
Great Sea Stories: Second Series. Ed. by Joseph Lewis French. LC 75-122708. (Short story index reprint series). (Illus.). 1970. Books for Libraries Press.
Great Sea Stories: Second Series. Ed. by Joseph Lewis French. LC 25-8417. Brentano's.
Great Secret. Edward Phillips Oppenheim. LC 7-40278. 1908. Little, Brown, and Company.
Great Secret: And Other Stories. Jesse Charles Fremont Grumbine. LC 52-50332. Order of the White Rose.
Great Secret: Or, How to Be Happy. Emily Chubbuck Judson. LC 33-307949. 1942. Dayton & Newman.
Great Security. Lewis Anselin da Costa Ricci. LC 26-8621. 1925. Cassell and Company, Ltd.
Great Security. Lewis Anselin da Costa Ricci. LC 26-8621. 1925. Cassell and Company, Ltd.
Great Seven--the Greater Nine: A Story for the People. John Heber Flood. LC 6-41667. W.B. Conkey Company.
Great Shadow: A Novel. Arthur Conan Doyle. LC 6-34240. 1893. Harper & Brothers.
Great Shadow: A Novel. Arthur Conan Doyle. LC 25-15487. Harper & Brothers.
Great Shark Hunt. Hunter S. Thompson. 1980. pap. 3.95 (ISBN 0-445-04596-5). Popular Lib.
Great Short Novels: An Anthology. Ed. by Edward Weeks. LC 41-15018. 1941. Doubleday, Doran & Co., Inc.
Great Short Novels of Henry James. Henry James & Rahv, Philip, Ed. LC 44-47807. 1944. Dial Press Inc.
Great Short Novels of the American West. Ed. by Don Ward. (Collier books, AS299. Original). 1962. Collier Books.
Great Short Novels of the World: A Collection of Complete Tales Chosen from the Literatures of All Periods and Countries. Ed. by Barrett Harper Clark. LC 27-242666. 1927. R. M. McBride & Company.
Great Short-Stories. Ed. by William James Dawson. D & Dawson Coningsby William. LC 23-14411. 1923. Harper & Brothers.
Great Short Stories. Grace Bechtold Gans. (Sunrise library). (Illus.). 1962. Hart Pub. Co.
Great Short Stories. Ed. by William Patten. P. F. Collier & Son.
Great Short Stories. Ed. by Wilbur Lang Schramm. LC 50-8357. 1950. Harcourt, Brace.
Great Short Stories for Discussion & Delight. Bruce B. Clark & Quida R. Clark. (Illus.). 1979. text ed. 9.95 o.p. (ISBN 0-89260-126-4). Hwong Pub.
Great Short Stories from the World's Literature. Ed. by Charles Neider. LC 50-5394. 1950. Rinehart.
Great Short Stories from the World's Literature. enl. ed. Ed. by Charles Neider. LC 77-152908. 1972. (ISBN 0-03-083051-6). Holt, Rinehart and Winston.
Great Short Stories of Anatole France. Anatole France, pseud. Ed. by Shanks, Lewis Piaget & Parker, Richard Alexander. LC 36-15140. H. Holt and Company.
Great Short Stories of Guy De Maupassant. Guy De Maupassant. Tr. by Wallace Brockway. LC 39-23750. 1939. Pocket Books, Inc.
Great Short Stories of Guy De Maupassant. Guy De Maupassant. Tr. by Wallace Brockway. LC 44-51322. 1944. Pocket Books Inc.
Great Short Stories of Henry David Thoreau. Ed. by Wendell Glick. LC 82-47560. (Great Short Works Ser.). 352p. (Orig.). 1982. pap. 3.80i (ISBN 0-06-080598-6, P 598, PL). Har-Row.
Great Short Stories of John O'Hara. John O'Hara. 1973. (pbk) 1.25. Popular Library.
Great Short Stories of Robert Louis Stevenson. Robert Louis Stevenson. (Great Histories Ser). (YA) (gr. 9-12). pap. 0.45 o.p. (W0214). WSP.
Great Short Stories of the War. Edmund Blunden. Repr. of 1933 ed. 40.00 (ISBN 0-89987-158-5). Darby Bks.
Great Short Stories of the World. Barrett Harper Clark. Ed. by Maxim Lieber. 1978. Repr. of 1926 ed. lib. bdg. 50.00 (ISBN 0-8482-3520-7). Norwood Edns.
Great Short Stories of the World. Barrett Harper Clark. Ed. by Maxim Lieber. 1947. 9.95 o.p. (ISBN 0-529-03417-4, 1223). World Pub.
Great Short Stories of the World. LC 72-81158. 1972. Reader's Digest Association.
Great Short Stories of the World. 1972. 11.95 o.p. (ISBN 0-393-21409-5). Norton.
Great Short Stories of the World. Reader's Digest Editors. LC 72-81158. 800p. 1972. 13.98 (ISBN 0-89577-008-3). RD Assn.
Great Short Stories of the World: A Collection of Complete Short Stories Chosen from the Literatures of All Periods and Countries. de luxe ed. Ed. by Barrett Harper Clark. Lieber, Maxim, Joint Comp. LC 38-27457. 1938. Garden City Publishing Co., Inc.
Great Short Stories of the World: An Anthology Selected from the Literatures of All Periods and Countries. Ed. by Barrett Harper Clark. Lieber, Maxim, Joint Comp. LC 26-790. 1925. R. M. McBride & Company.
Great Short Tales of Mystery and Terror. LC 80-52212. (Illus.). 14.98 (ISBN 0-89577-091-1). Reader's Digest Association.
Great Short Tales of Mystery & Terror. Reader's Digest Editors. LC 80-52212. (Illus.). 640p. 1982. 14.98 (ISBN 0-89577-091-1). RD Assn.
Great Short Works. Joseph Conrad. LC 66-1155. (Perennial classic, P3039D). Harper.
Great Short Works. Stephen Crane. LC 65-6647. (Perennial classic). 1.50. Harper.
Great Short Works. Stephen Crane. LC 65-6647. (Perennial classic). 1965. Harper & Row.
Great Short Works. Fedor Mikhailovich Dostoevskii. LC 70-54. (Perennial classic P3081). 1968. 1.95. Harper & Row.
Great Short Works. Nathaniel Hawthorne. Ed. by Crews, Frederick C. LC 67-5113. (Perennial classic, P 3074). 1967. Harper & Row.
Great Short Works of Aldous Huxley. Aldous Leonard Huxley. LC 70-8177. (Perennial classic, P3088). 1969. 1.95. Harper & Row.
Great Short Works of Jack London: Call of the Wild, White Fang & Six Stories. Jack London. Ed. by Earle Labor. pap. 2.84i (ISBN 0-06-083041-7, P3041, PL). Har-Row.
Great Short Works of Jack London. Ed. with Introd. by Earle Labor. Jack London. Ed. by Earle Labor. LC 65-8470. (Perennial classic). 1.75. Harper.
Great Short Works of Leo Tolstoy. Lev Nikolaevich Tolstoi. Tr. by Louise Shanks Maude. LC 67-5426. (Perennial classic, P3071). 1967. Harper & Row.
Great Short Works of Nathaniel Hawthorne. Nathaniel Hawthorne. Ed. by Frederick C. Crews. pap. 3.50i (ISBN 0-06-083074-3, P3074, PL). Har-Row.
Great Short Works of Thomas Hardy. Ed., Introd. by Samuel Hynes. Thomas Hardy. (Perennial classic, P3076). 1967. pap., 1.25. Harper.
Great Short Works: The Lagoon, the Nigger of Narcissus, Youth, Heart of Darkness, Typhoon, the Secret Sharer. Joseph Conrad. 8.50 (ISBN 0-8446-0068-7). Peter Smith.
Great Short Works. With an Introd. by Jerry Allen. Herman Melville. LC 66-31640. (Perennial classic). 1966. Harper & Row.
Great Silver Bonanza. Don Martin. 1979. pap. 1.95 (ISBN 0-449-14202-7, GM). Fawcett.
Great Sky and the Silence. James S Rand, pseud. LC 77-8341. 1977. 8.95 (ISBN 0-07-051175-6). McGraw-Hill.
Great Sleepy Gun Animal Hunt. Oren Arnold. (YA) 1969. 4.95 o.p. (ISBN 0-8119-0070-3). Fell.
Great Smith. Edison Marshall. LC 43-472925. 1943. Farrar & Rinehart, Inc.
Great Snow: A Novel. Henry Morton Robinson. LC 47-1996. 1947. Simon and Schuster.
Great Son. Edna Ferber. LC 45-1874. 1945. Doubleday, Doran & Company, Inc.
Great Son. Edna Ferber. (Fawcett crest book). 1974. (pbk.) 0.95. Fawcett.
Great Soul Trial. John G. Fuller. 1969. 7.95 o.p. (54184). Macmillan.
Great Soviet Short Stories. Franklin D. Reeve. LC 62-5213. (Laurel edition, 3166). 1962. Dell Pub. Co.
Great Spanish Short Stories. Ed. by Angel Flores. LC 62-53613. (Laurel edition, 3170). 1962. Dell Pub. Co.
Great Spanish Short Stories Representing the Work of the Leading Spanish Writers of the Day. Tr. by Wells, Warre Bradley. 1932. The Houghton Mifflin Company.
Great Spanish Stories. 2.95 o.p. (129). Modern Lib.
Great Speckled Bird: And Other Stories. Illus. by Paula Gerard. Perrin Holmes Lowerey. LC 64-22332. 1964. 4.95. Regnery.
Great Speckled Bird & Other Stories. P. H. Lowrey. (Illus.). 1964. 4.95 o.p. Regnery.
Great Sports Detective Stories: Sporting Blood. Ed. by Ellery Queen, pseud. LC 46-7625. 1946. Blue Ribbon Books.
Great Spy Pictures. James R. Parish & Michael R. Pitts. LC 73-19509. (Illus.). 1974. 23.00 (ISBN 0-8108-0655-X). Scarecrow.
Great Spy Race. Adam Diment. LC 68-12459. 1968. Dutton.
Great Spy Stories from Fiction. Ed. by Allen Welsh Dulles. LC 69-15272. 1969. 6.95. Harper & Row.
Great Steamboat Race. John Brunner. LC 82-90222. 1983. (7.95, 10.25 can.) (ISBN 0-345-25853-3). Ballantine Books.
Great Stone Face: And Other Stories. Nathaniel Hawthorne & McCarter, Mrs. Margaret (Hill) 1860- Ed. LC 5-14965. (On cover: The Crane classics, no. 29). 1905. Crane & Company.
Great Stone Face: & Two Other Stories. Illus. by Leonard Everett Fisher. Nathaniel Hawthorne. LC 67-17804. 1967. 2.95, 2.21 lib. ed.,. Watts.
Great Stone of Sardis. biographical ed. Frank Richard Stockton. LC 99-5005. 1899. Harper & Brothers.
Great Stone of Sardis. Frank Richard Stockton. Belmont Tower Books.
Great Stone of Sardis: A Novel. Frank Richard Stockton. LC 8-15663. 1898. Harper & Brothers.
Great Stories. Arthur Conan Doyle. Ed. by John D. Carr. 1959. 9.95 o.s.i. (ISBN 0-8277-0023-7). British Bk Ctr.
Great Stories About Show Business. Ed. by Jerry D Lewis. LC 57-12201. 1957. Coward-McCann.
Great Stories by Nobel Prize Winners. Edited by Leo Hamalian and Edmond L. Volpe. Ed. by Leo Hamalian & Edmond Loris Volpe. LC 59-9450. Noonday Press.
Great Stories from the Saturday Evening Post, 1947. The Saturday Evening Post. Ed. by Hibbs, Ben. LC 48-11680. (Bantam book, 555). 1948. Bantam Books.
Great Stories from World Literature. Ed. by Doris Heitkotter. Richard Whittingham. LC 73-180342. (Home Adventure Library, 4). (Illus.). 1973. Southwestern Co.
Great Stories of All Nations: One Hundred Sixty Complete Short Stories from the Literatures of All Periods and Countries. Ed. by Maxim Lieber & Williams, Blanche Colton. LC 27-19408. 1927. Brentano's.
Great Stories of All Nations: One Hundred Sixty Complete Short Stories from the Literatures of All Periods and Countries. Ed. by Maxim Lieber & Williams, Blanche Colton. LC 38-9840. 1934. Tudor Publishing Co.
Great Stories of De Maupassant. Guy de Maupassant. pap. 0.45 o.p. (W0229). WSP.
Great Stories of Heroism and Adventure. Stephen Crane. Ed. by David Halberstam. 1967. Platt & Munk.
Great Stories of Love & Romances. Katherine Helen Maud Marshall Diver. Repr. lib. bdg. 8.50 o.p. Folcroft.
Great Stories of Mystery and Suspense. Reader's Digest Association (Canada) LC 73-76284. (Illus.). 1974. 11.95. Reader's Digest Association.
Great Stories of Mystery and Suspense. Reader's Digest Association (Canada) LC 73-76284. (Illus.). 1974. Reader's Digest Association.
Great Stories of Mystery & Suspense, 2 Vols. Reader's Digest Editors. LC 73-76284. (Open-ended Ser.). 1294p. 1981. Set. 15.99 (ISBN 0-89577-083-0). RD Assn.
Great Stories of Mystery & Suspense, 2 vols. Reader's Digest Editors. LC 73-76284. (Open-Ended Ser.). 1290p. 1977. 15.99 (ISBN 0-89577-136-5). RD Assn.
Great Stories of Science Fiction. William Fitzgerald Jenkins. LC 51-403313. 1951. Random House.
Great Stories of Sherlock Holmes. Arthur Conan Doyle. 1962. pap. 1.95 (ISBN 0-440-93190-8, LFL). Dell.
Great Stories of Suspense. Ed. by Ross Macdonald. LC 74-7743. 1974. (ISBN 0-394-49292-7). Knopf; Distributed by Random House.
Great Stories of the Sea & Ships. Ed. by N. C. Wyeth. 1980. pap. 8.95 (ISBN 0-679-51054-0). McKay.
Great Stories of the Sea & Ships. Ed. by N. C. Wyeth. (Nautical Ser.). (Illus.). 1977. 12.50 o.p. (ISBN 0-679-50773-6). McKay.
Great Stories of the West. Ed. by Edmund Collier. LC 79-89096. 1971. 5.95. Doubleday.
Great Struggle. Daniel Lyman. 185p. Date not set. 3.25 o.s.i. (ISBN 0-913390-11-9). Pathmark Bks.
Great Success. Mary Augusta Arnold Humphry Ward Ward. LC 16-6820. 1916. Hearst's International Library Co.

Great Succession: Henry James and the Legacy of Hawthorne. Robert Emmet Long. LC 79-922. (Critical essays in modern literature). (ISBN 0-8229-3398-5). University of Pittsburgh Press.

Great Sunflower. Clifford Stone. LC 76-10020. 192p. 1976. 8.95 (ISBN 0-8149-0775-X). Vanguard.

Great Sunflower: A Novel. Clifford Stone. LC 76-10020. 7.95 (ISBN 0-8149-0775-X). Vanguard Press.

Great Sunflower: A Novel. Clifford Stone. 1977. 1.50 (ISBN 0-380-01809-8). Avon Books.

Great Suspense Stories. Illustrated by Raymond Burns. Ed. by Rosamund Morris. LC 61-5152. (Sunrise library). 1962. Hart Pub. Co.

Great Sweet Days of Old Shibui. Harry Dallas Miller. LC 64-13829. 1964. Doubleday.

Great Sweet Days of Old Shibui see I Love Thee, Beast.

Great Sword. Cecil A. Gray. 3.00 o.p. Carlton.

Great Taboo. Grant Allen. LC 6-74. (On cover: Harper's Franklin square library, no. 691)). 1891. Harper & Brothers.

Great Taboo: By Grant Allen... Grant Allen. LC 6-753. (On cover: The advance library, no. 2)). 1891. Springfield Publishing Co.

Great Tales of City Dwellers. Ed. by Alex Austin. LC 56-26473. (Lion library edition, 53). 1955. Lion Library Editions.

Great Tales of Horror. Edgar Allan Poe. LC 64-12781. (Bantam pathfinder editions, FP58). 1964. Bantam Books.

Great Tales of Mystery. Ed. by Randolph Cecil Bull. LC 60-14784. (Illus.). 1960. Hill and Wang.

Great Tales of Mystery and Adventure... Robert Louis Stevenson. (Platt & Munk great writers collection). 1965. Platt & Munk.

Great Tales of Terror and the Supernatural. Ed. by Herbert Alvin Wise. Fraser, Phyllis Maurine, 1915- Joint Ed. LC 44-4879. 1944. Random House.

Great Tales of Terror and the Supernatural. Ed. by Herbert Alvin Wise & Fraser, Phyllis Maurine. LC 48-5552. (Modern library of the world's best books G 72). 1947. Modern Library.

Great Tales of the American West. Ed. by Harry Edward Maule. LC 45-4772. (Half-title: The Modern library of the world's best books). 1945. The Modern Library.

Great Tales of the Deep South. Ed. by Malcolm Cowley. LC 55-58949. (Lion Library edition, LL30. A Lion Library anthology). 1955. Lion Library Editions.

Great Tales of the Sea. Reader's Digest Editors. LC 77-81738. (Illus.). 640p. 1978. 14.98 (ISBN 0-89577-016-4). RD Assn.

Great Tales of the Supernatural. Ed. by Stephanie Dowrick. 1978. pap. 1.95x (ISBN 0-460-01266-5, Evman). Biblio Dist.

Great Taxicab Robbery. James H. Collins. Repr. of 1912 ed. 11.00 o.s.i. Finch Pr.

Great Test: Or, The Struggles and Triumph of Lorna Selover. Herman Devillo Clarke. LC 16-23626. 1916. 0.75. The American Sabbath Tract Society.

Great Tide. Rubylea Hall. LC 47-307549. 1947. Duell, Sloan and Pearce.

Great Time Machine Hoax. Keith Laumer. (O.s.i.). 176p. 1973. pap. 0.95 o.s.i. (AN1171, Award). Univ Pub & Dist.

Great Tomorrow. Ursula Bloom. 1978. pap. 1.95 (ISBN 0-89083-361-3). Zebra.

Great Tontine. A Novel. Hawley Smart. (Seaside library, v. 83, no. 1679). 1884. G. Munro.

Great Trace: A Novel. Vingie Eve Roe. LC 48-1982. 1948. Macrae-Smith-Co.

Great Tradition. Frances Parkinson Wheeler Keyes. LC 39-31789. J. Messner, Inc.

Great Tradition. Frances Parkinson Wheeler Keyes. 1974. 1.50 (ISBN 0-671-78728-4). Pocket Books.

Great Tradition. Frank Raymond Leavis. LC 54-4517. (Doubleday anchor books, A 40). 1954. Doubleday.

Great Tradition: And Other Stories. Katharine Fullerton Gerould. LC 15-6334. 1915. 1.35. C. Scribner's Sons.

Great Tradition: George Eliot, Henry James, Joseph Conrad. Frank Raymond Leavis. LC 63-6651. 1963. New York University Press.

Great Tradition: George Eliot, Henry James, Joseph Conrad. Frank Raymond Leavis. LC 49-557987. G. W. Stewart.

Great Train Hijack. Whit Masterson, pseud. 1976. (pbk.) 1.25 (ISBN 0-523-00791-4). Pinnacle Books.

Great Train Robbery. Michael Crichton. LC 75-26861. 1975. 12.95 (ISBN 0-8161-6228-X). G. K. Hall.

Great Train Robbery. Michael Crichton. 1976. 1.95 (ISBN 0-553-02424-8). Bantam Books.

Great Train Robbery. Michael Crichton. LC 74-25422. 1975. (ISBN 0-394-49401-6). Knopf: Distributed by Randon House.

Great Transfer. Basile S. Yanovsky. LC 73-15995. 1974. 6.50. Harcourt Brace Jovanovich.

Great Travel Stories of All Nations. Elizabeth D'Oyley. 1932. 35.00 (ISBN 0-932062-44-X). Sharon Hill.

Great Travers Case. A Wonderful Story of a Most Remarkable Mystery. St. George Rathborne. (secret service series, no. 36). 1890. Street & Smith.

Great Treason. A Story of the War of Independence. Mary A. M. Hoppus Marks. LC 7-25602. (On cover: Seaside library. Pocket ed. no. 170). G. Munro.

Great Treasure Hunt. Jim Spillman. 80p. (Orig.). 1981. pap. 2.95 (ISBN 0-86694-029-4). Omega Pubns OR.

Great True Detective Stories. pap. 0.75 o.p. (ISBN 0-448-05324-1, Tempo). G&D.

Great True Spy Stories. Allen Dulles. 1982. pap. 3.50 (ISBN 0-345-30181-1). Ballantine.

Great True Stories of the Wild West. Ed. by Phil Hirsch. (Orig.). 1971. pap. 0.75 o.p. (T2507). Pyramid Pubns.

Great Unrest. Florence Ethel Mills Young. LC 15-17134. 1915. John Lane.

Great Unsolved Mysteries. Jim Purvis. 1978. 8.95 o.p. (ISBN 0-448-14630-4); pap. 4.95 o.p. (ISBN 0-448-14631-2, Today Press). G&D.

Great Untold Stories of Fantasy & Horror. Ed. by Alden H. Norton & Sam Moskowitz. 1969. pap. 0.75 o.p. (T2093, T2093). Pyramid Pubns.

Great Urge. 1st Ed. Ann W Dunham. LC 51-16240. 1950. De Vorss.

Great Valley. Mary Johnston. LC 26-8947. 1926. Little, Brown, and Company.

Great Van Suttart Mystery. George Agnew Chamberlain. LC 25-156343. 1925. G. P. Putnam's Sons.

Great Victorian Collection. Brian Moore. LC 75-5553. 1975. 7.95. Farrar, Straus, Giroux.

Great Villains. Janet Pate. LC 75-10956. 1976. 8.95 o.p. (ISBN 0-672-52153-9). Bobbs.

Great Waldo Pepper. William Goldman. 1975. (pbk.) 1.50. Dell.

Great Wall of China: Stories and Reflections. Franz Kafka. Tr. by Willa Muir. Muir, Edwin,1887- Joint Tr. LC 46-810921. 1946. Schocken Books.

Great Waltz. Abraham Rothberg. LC 77-9576. 1978. 8.95 o.p. (ISBN 0-399-12076-9). Putnam Pub Group.

Great Waltz: A Novel. Abraham Rothberg. LC 77-9576. 8.95. Putnam.

Great War of 189- A Forecast. P. Colomb et al. LC 74-16390. (Science Fiction Ser). (Illus.). 320p. 1975. Repr. of 1893 ed. 20.00x. Ayer Co.

Great War Syndicate. Frank Richard Stockton. LC 72-104571. 1970. Literature House.

Great War Syndicate. Frank Richard Stockton. LC 31-342. 1902. Dodd, Mead & Company.

Great War Syndicate: By Frank R. Stockton... Frank Richard Stockton. LC 41-30746. Dodd, Mead & Company.

Great War Syndicate, Etc. Frank Richard Stockton. LC 12-39187. (novels and stories of Frank R. Stockton. VI). 1900. C. Scribner's Sons.

Great Waters. Vere Hutchinson. LC 24-7114. 2.00. The Century Co.

Great Wave, and Other Stories. Mary Lavin. 1961. Macmillan.

Great Way: A Story of the Joyful, the Sorrowful, the Glorious. Horace Fish. LC 21-10608. 1921. Cassell and Company, ltd.

Great Way: A Story of the Joyful, the Sorrowful, the Glorious. Horace Fish. LC 21-14439. 1921. M. Kennerley.

Great Weird Stories. Ed. by Arthur Neale. LC 72-3669. (Short story index reprint series). 1972. 14.00 (ISBN 0-8369-4156-X). Books for Libraries Press.

Great Weird Stories. Ed. by Arthur Neale. LC 29-26784. 1929. Duffield & Company.

Great Western Short Stories. Ed. by J. Golden Taylor. LC 67-26254. 1967. American West Pub. Co.

Great Western Stories: A Western Story Omnibus. Ed. by William Targ. LC 48-2860. (Penguin books, 654). 1947. Penguin Books.

Great Westerns from the Saturday Evening Post. Julie Nixon Eisenhower. LC 76-41560. 5.95 (ISBN 0-89387-004-8). Curtis Pub. Co.

Great White Gods: An Epic of the Spanish Invasion of Mexico and the Conquest of the Barbaric Aztec Culture of the New World. Edward Stucken & Martens, Frederick Herman, 1874-1932, Tr. LC 34-34744. Farrar & Rinehart, Inc.

Great White Pacer & Other Stories. Donald Schnell. 1970. 4.50 o.p. Vantage.

Great White Queen: A Tale of Treasure and Treason. William Le Queux. LC 74-16505. (Science Fiction). (Illus.). 1975. 18.00 (ISBN 0-405-06303-2). Arno Press.

Great White Silence. Louis Frederic Rouquette. Tr. by Allen, O. W. LC 30-8601. 1930. The Macmillan Company.

Great White Space. Basil Copper. LC 74-83573. 1975. 6.95 (ISBN 0-7091-4868-2). St. Martin's Press.

Great White Way: A Record of an Unusual Voyage of Discovery, and Some Romantic Love Affairs Amid Strange Surroundings. Albert Bigelow Paine. LC 74-16514. (Science Fiction). (Illus.). 1975. (ISBN 0-405-06309-1). Arno Press.

Great White Way: A Record of an Unusual Voyage of Discovery, and Some Romantic Love Affairs Amid Strange Surroundings. The Whole Recounted by One Nicholas Chase, Promoter of the Expedition, Whose Reports Have Been Arranged for Publication. Albert Bigelow Paine. LC 1-27446. 1901. J. F. Taylor Company.

Great Winds. Ernest Poole. LC 33-124222. 1933. The Macmillan Company.

Great Women Detectives and Criminals: The Female of the Species. Ed. by Ellery Queen, pseud. LC 46-3684. 1946. Blue Ribbon Books.

Great World. A Novel. Being the Confessions and Strange Experiences of the Hon. Eric Yorke. Joseph Hatton. (Harper's Franklin square library, no. 600). 1887. Harper & Brothers.

Great World and Timothy Colt. Louis Auchincloss. LC 56-9384. 1956. Houghton Mifflin.

Great World: By a Gentleman with a Duster. Harold Begbie. LC 25-23727. George H. Doran Company.

Great Yant Mystery. Albert Benjamin Cunningham. LC 43-9100. 1943. E. P. Dutton & Company, Inc.

Great Year: A Novel. Dilys Bennett Laing. 1948. Duell, Sloan and Pearce.

Great Yellowstone Steamboat Race. Robert J Steelman. LC 79-7675. 1980. 7.95 (ISBN 0-385-15026-1). Doubleday.

Greater Courage. Margaret Bass Pedler. LC 33-31887. 1933. Doubleday, Doran & Company, Inc.

Greater Glory. William Dudley Pelley. LC 19-15223. 1919. 1.75. Little, Brown, and Company.

Greater Glory: A Story of High Life. Jozua Marius Willem Van Der Poorten Schwartz. LC 4-16871.

Greater Glory: A Story of High Life. Jozua Marius Willem Van Der Poorten Schwartz. LC 4-16871. 1894. D. Appleton and Company.

Greater Hunger. Barbara Dodge Borland. LC 62-8493. 1962. Appleton-Century-Crofts.

Greater Inclination. Edith Newbold Jones Wharton. LC 70-8769. 1969. Scholarly Press.

Greater Inclination. Edith Newbold Jones Wharton. LC 72-86375. 1969. AMS Press.

Greater Inclination. Edith Newbold Jones Wharton. LC 99-1383. 1899. Charles Scribner's Sons.

Greater Infinity. Michael McCollum. 208p. (Orig.). 1982. pap. 2.50 (ISBN 0-345-30167-6, Del Rey). Ballantine.

Greater Joy: A Romance. Lida Clara Schem. G. W. Dillingham Company.

Greater Love. Frances Mocatta. LC 29-7498. 1929. G. H. Watt.

Greater Love. John Rathbone Oliver. LC 36-5934. 1936. The Macmillan Company.

Greater Love. Anna McClure Sholl. LC 8-17252. 1908. The Outing Publishing Company.

Greater Love Hath No Man. David P Allison. LC 38-8104. 1937. Wm. B. Eerdmans Publishing Co.

Greater Love Hath No Man. Frank Lucius Packard. LC 13-8906. George H. Doran Company.

Greater Love Hath No Woman. Howard Rockey. LC 32-33055. The Macaulay Company.

Greater Mischief: A Novel. Margaret Westrup. LC 7-33589. 1907. Harper & Brothers.

Greater Mischief: A Novel. Margaret Westrup. LC 8-5583. 1908. Harper & Brothers.

Greater Mystery. Edna De Fremery. LC 21-1278. 1920. Sunset Press.

Greater Need Below. O'Wendell Shaw. LC 73-144686. 1972. 10.00 (ISBN 0-404-00212-9). AMS Press.

Greater Power. Harold Bindloss. LC 9-23728. 1909. F. A. Stokes and Company.

Greater Punishment. Stephen Chalmers. LC 20-11075. 1920. Doubleday, Page & Company.

Greater Sin. Ivers McCrary. LC 51-21213. 1951. Vantage Press.

Greater Than All: Prize Winning Historical Novel. Rachael Borne. LC 51-14730. (Baptist General Conference of America. Centenaryseries). 1951. Baptist Conference Press.

Greater Than the Greatest. Hamilton Drummond. LC 18-7606. 1917. E. P. Dutton & Company.

Greater Trumps. Charles Williams. LC 50-6710. 1950. Pellegrini & Cudahy.

Greater Trumps. Charles Williams. LC 76-18873. 1976. 2.95 (ISBN 0-8028-1649-5). Eerdmans.

Greatest Adventure. Eric Temple Bell. LC 29-4213. E. P. Dutton & Company, Inc.

Greatest Adventure see Three Science-Fiction Novels.

Greatest Adventure see Time Stream.

Greatest Adventures of Sherlock Holmes. Arthur Conan Doyle. 2.50 o.p.; special ed. 3.50 o.p.; deluxe ed. 4.50 o.p. G&D.

Greatest American Short Stories. Ed. by Arthur Grove Day & William F. Bauer. LC 52-115079. 1953. McGraw-Hill.

Greatest American Short Stories: Twenty Classics of Our Heritage. Ed. by Arthur Grove Day. (Illus.). 1953. 7.95 o.p. (ISBN 0-07-016170-4). McGraw.

Greatest Breakthrough Since Lunchtime. Colin Douglas. LC 78-27167. 1979. 8.95 (ISBN 0-8008-3649-9). Taplinger Pub. Co.

Greatest Crime. Sloan Wilson. (Adventure & Suspense Ser.). 11.50 (ISBN 0-87795-296-5). Arbor Hse.

Greatest Crime. Sloan Wilson. 1981. pap. 3.50 (ISBN 0-89083-888-7). Zebra.

Greatest Crime in the World... William Albert Lewis. 1895. The American Job Printing Office.

Greatest Enemy. Douglas Reeman. LC 73-135260. 1971. 5.95. Putnam.

Greatest Fox of Them All. Allvine. 5.95 (ISBN 0-8184-0035-8). Lyle Stuart.

Greatest Gamble. Per Hansson. (Illus.). 1967. 4.50 o.p. (ISBN 0-393-08412-4). Norton.

Greatest Gift. Arthur Williams Marchmont. LC 1623. 1900. F. M. Buckles & Company.

Greatest Good. Belle Willey Gue. LC 26-13535. 1926. The Stratford Company.

Greatest Heiress in England. A Novel. Margaret Oliphant Wilson Oliphant. (Franklin square library, no. 102). 1880.

Greatest Heiress in England. A Novel. Margaret Oliphant Wilson Oliphant. (On cover: Seaside library. Pocket ed., no. 710). 1886. G. Munro.

Greatest Indian Stories. Zane Grey. 1982. 18.00x (ISBN 0-86025-169-1, Pub. by Ian Henry Pubns England). State Mutual Bk.

Greatest Indian Stories. Zane Grey. 1978. pap. 1.50 o.s.i. (ISBN 0-505-51303-X). Tower Bks.

Greatest Lover in the World. Alex Austin. LC 56-10683. 1956. Rinehart.

Greatest Man on Earth. Thomas Mack. LC 25-13869. 1925. B. Herder Book Co.

Greatest Men's Party on Earth: Inside the Bohemian Grove. John Van der Zee. LC 73-20143. 1974. 5.95 o.p. (ISBN 0-15-136905-4). HarBraceJ.

Greatest Need: A Novel. Olive C Meredith Brown. LC 50-14490. 1950. William-Frederick Press.

Greatest of All. John Mosedale. 256p. 1983. pap. 9.95 (ISBN 0-385-27805-5). Dial.

Greatest of These. Francis MacManus. LC 76-47358. 1977. 1.95 (ISBN 0-87973-201-6). Our Sunday Visitor.

Greatest of These. Archibald Marshall. LC 14-9280. 1914. 1.35. Dodd, Mead and Company.

Greatest of These. Archibald Marshall. LC 24-279650. 1919. Dodd, Mead and Company.

Greatest Plague of Life: Or, The Adventures of a Lady in Search of a Good Servant. Augustus Septimus Mayhew & Mayhew, Henry, 1812-1887, Joint Author. LC 42-34434. 1859. G. Routledge & Co.

Greatest Rebel. Robert Melvyn Spector. LC 69-16475. (Illus.). 1969. 4.50. H. Z. Walck.

Greatest Short Stories. LC 53-4129. 1953. P. F. Collier.

Greatest Short Stories. LC 15-15610. P. F. Collier & Son.

Greatest Short Stories ... LC 40-4879. P. F. Collier & Son Corporation.

Greatest Stories, and How They Were Written: Selected by W. E. Henley. With a Series of Introductions on the Art of Short Story Writing, by Sherwin Cody. Re-Edited Ed. Ed. by Sherwin Cody. LC 50-11919. 1950. Sherwin Cody Associates.

Greatest Stories of All Times: Tellers of Tales. Ed. by William Somerset Maugham. LC 44-8488. 1943. Garden City Publishing Company, Inc.

Greatest Story Ever Told: A Transformation. Fielding Dawson. LC 72-13804. 1973. (ISBN 0-87685-158-8) (ISBN 0-87685-157-X). Black Sparrow Press.

Greatest Success in the World. Og Mandino. 1982. pap. 2.75 (ISBN 0-553-22771-8). Bantam.

Greatest Thing Since Sliced Bread: A Novel. Don Robertson. LC 65-22223. 1965. Putnam.

Greatest Thing That Almost Happened. Robertson, Don. 1977. 1.95 (ISBN 0-446-89660-8). Warner Books.

Greatest Thing That Almost Happened: A Novel. Don Robertson. LC 70-132611. 1970. 5.95. Putnam.

Greatest Victory: And Other Baseball Stories. O'Rourke, Frank. LC 50-6235. 1950. Barnes.

Greatest Wish in the World. Ernest Temple Thurston. LC 10-111347. M. Kennerley.

Greatheart. Ethel May Dell. LC 18-8491. 1918. G. P. Putnam's Sons.

Greatheart. Ethel May Dell. LC 21-137133. 1921. Grosset & Dunlap.

Greatheart. Ethel May Dell & Barbara Cartland. LC 80-153864. (Barbara Cartland's Library of love; 15). ((Series: Cartland, Barbara, 1902-). (Library of love; 15.). 1980. 12.95 (ISBN 0-7156-1475-4). Duckworth.

Greatheart Silver. Philip Jose Farmer. 288p. (Orig.). 1982. pap. 2.75 (ISBN 0-523-48535-2). Pinnacle Bks.

Greathouse. Edward Eyre Hunt. LC 37-23920. Harcourt, Brace and Company.

Greatness and Decline of Cesar Birotteau. From the French of Honore De Balzac. Tr. by O. W. Wight and F. B. Goodrich. Honore De Balzac. Tr. by Orlando Williams Wight. Goodrich, Frank Boott, 1826-1894, Tr. (Half-title: Novels of M. Honore de Balzac. Library ed., v. 1). 1860. Rudd & Carleton.

Greatness in Little Things: Or, Way-Side Violets. Stopford James Ram. LC 8-29987. 1854. Dayton & Wentwroth et.C.

Greatness Revisited. Friderike M. Zweig. 1972. 12.50 o.p. (ISBN 0-8283-1297-4). Branden.

Gred of Nuremberg. A Romance of the 15th Century. Georg Moritz Ebers & Conder, E. V., Tr. (On cover: Seaside library. Pocket ed., no. 1193). 1889. G. Munro.

Greed for Power. David Blumenfeld. LC 56-9416. 1956. Comet Press Books.

Greed's Grip Broken: Or, The Right to Live. Joseph Weber Savage. LC 28-9995. The Avondale Press, Incorporated.

Greedy Young Swappers. O. R. Bassett. 192p. (Orig.). 1972. pap. 1.95 o.p. (ISBN 0-87682-272-3, 7272). Barclay Hse.

Greek. Tiffany Thayer. LC 32-2229. 1931. A. & C. Boni.

Greek: A Novel. Pierre Rey. LC 73-93742. 1974. 8.95 (ISBN 0-399-11347-9). Putnam.

Greek Affair. Frank Gruber. LC 64-19531. 1964. Dutton.

Greek Coffin Mystery. Ellery Queen. 370p. 1976. lib. bdg. 16.95x (ISBN 0-89966-151-3). Buccaneer Bks.

Greek Coffin Mystery: A Problem in Deduction. Ellery Queen, pseud. LC 32-10748. 1932. Frederick A. Stokes Company.

Greek Coffin Mystery: A Problem in Deduction. Ellery Queen, pseud. LC 42-50853. 1942. The Sun Dial Press.

Greek Fire. Chase, Glen, pseud. (Leisure Books). 1977. 1.50 (ISBN 0-8439-0462-3). Nordon Pubns.

Greek Fire: The Fabulous Secret Weapon That Saved Europe. W. H Spears. LC 69-19967. 1969. 4.95. Adams Press.

Greek Madonna: A Novel. Charles Wilbur De Lyon Nicholls. LC 7-32300. 1894. G. W. Dillingham.

Greek Night. Pitts Sanborn. LC 33-6481. 1933. L. MacVeagh, Dial Press, Inc.

Greek of Toledo: A Romantic Narrative About El Greco. Elizabeth Borton Trevino. LC 59-12507. 1959. Crowell.

Greek Passion. Nikos Kazantzakis. LC 53-10810. 1954. Simon and Schuster.

Greek Passion: Transalted by Jonathan Griffin. Nikos Kazantzakis. LC 53-10810. 1954. Simon and Schuster.

Greek Position: A Novel. Robert Roderick. LC 80-17850. 14.95 (ISBN 0-671-61015-5). Wyndham Books.

Greek Tragedy. George Douglas Howard Cole & Margaret Isabel Postgate Cole. LC 40-27169. 1940. The Macmillan Company.

Greek Treasure. Irving Stone. 1976. pap. 3.50 (ISBN 0-451-11684-4, AE1684, Sig). NAL.

Greek Treasure: A Biographical Novel of Henry and Sophia Schliemann. Irving Stone. LC 74-33740. (Illus.). 1975. 12.50. (ISBN 0-385-07309-7) (ISBN 0-385-11170-3). Doubleday.

Greek Treasure: A Biographical Novel of Henry and Sophia Schliemann. Irving Stone. (Signet book). 1976. 2.25 (ISBN 0-451-07211-1). New American Library.

Greek Tycoon: A Novel by Eileen Lottman; Based on a Screenplay by Mort Fine from a Story by Nico Mastorakis & Win Wells and Mort Fine. Eileen Lottman. (Illus.). 1978. 2.25 (ISBN 0-446-82712-6). Warner Books.

Greek Vase. Ed. by Stephen L. Hyatt. LC 81-83963. (Illus.). 186p. 25.00. Hudson-Mohawk.

Greek Wedding. Jane Aiken Hodge. LC 79-116214. 1970. 5.95. Doubleday.

Greeks Bring Gifts. Murray Leinster, pseud. 144p. 1975. pap. 0.95 (ISBN 0-532-95400-9). Woodhill.

Greeks Bring Gifts. Murray Leinster, pseud. 1964. pap. 0.50 o.p. (50-418). Manor Bks.

Green: A Novella and Eight Stories. Norma Stahl Rosen. LC 67-11974. 1967. Harcourt, Brace & World.

Green: A Novella and Eight Stories. Norma Stahl Rosen. LC 67-11974. 1967. Harcourt, Brace & World.

Green Ace: A Hildegarde Withers Mystery. Stuart Palmer. LC 50-10204. 1950. M. S. Mill and Morrow.

Green Alleys: A Comedy. Eden Phillpotts. 1916. The Macmillan Company.

Green and Gay. Lee Holt. LC 18-8991. 1918. John Lane.

Green and Golden. Alix Taylor. LC 61-9560. 1961. Doubleday.

Green Apple Harvest. Sheila Kaye-Smith. LC 21-874. 1920. Cassell and Company, Ltd.

Green Apple Harvest. Sheila Kaye-Smith. LC 21-80284. E. P. Dutton & Company.

Green Apples and Salt; Growing up on a Canadian Farm: A Novel. first ed. Margo Wilson Larsson. (Illus.). 1973. 6.50 (ISBN 0-682-47800-8). Exposition Press.

Green Arch. Claude Carlos Washburn. LC 25-23113. 1925. A. & C. Boni.

Green Archer. Edgar Wallace. LC 24-11553. Small, Maynard & Company.

Green Archer. New Introd. by Vincent Starrett. Rev. Ed. Edgar Wallace. LC 65-9591. (Seagull lib. of mystery and suspense). 3.95. Norton.

Green Are These Memories! An Edited and Revised Version of Breezie Langton (a Novel of 1855. Hawley Smart & Flood, Milford, Ed. 1944. Wetzel Publishing Co., Inc.

Green As Grass. Edmund Downey. LC 6-321731. Lovell, Coryell & Company.

Green Balloon. Jan Pallister. 1974. 7.95 o.p. (ISBN 0-89002-031-0); pap. 2.00 o.p. (ISBN 0-89002-028-0). Northwoods Pr.

Green Bay Tree: A Novel. Louis Bromfield. LC 24-7113. 1924. Frederick A. Stokes Company.

Green Bay Tree: A Novel. Louis Bromfield. LC 27-12670. 1926. Grosset & Dunlap.

Green Bay Tree: A Novel. Louis Bromfield. LC 30-12345. 1927. Grosset & Dunlap.

Green Bay Tree; a Tale of to-Day. William Henry Wilkins & Vivian, Herbert, 1865- LC 8-37786. 1894. J. S. Tait & Sons.

Green Bench. William Arthur Neubauer. LC 65-7066. Arcadia House.

Green Berets. Robin Moore, pseud. LC 65-15849. 1965. Crown Publishers.

Green Blot. Sinclair Gluck. LC 25-18353. 1925. Dodd, Mead & Company.

Green Bond. Adrian Bell. 124p. 1976. 10.00x (ISBN 0-8476-1421-2). Rowman.

Green Bondage. Frances Ogilvie. LC 31-7078. Farrar & Rinehart Incorporated.

Green Book: Or, Freedom Under the Snow, a Novel; Tr. Mor Jokai. Tr. by Waugh, Ellen. LC 7-12836. 1897. Harper & Brothers.

Green Bough. Ann Katherine Gilliland Ritner. LC 50-6576. 1950. Lippincott.

Green Bough. Ernest Temple Thurston. LC 21-547946. 1921. D. Appleton and Company.

Green Bough: A Tale of the Resurrection. Mary Hunter Austin. LC 13-506939. 1913. 0.50. Doubleday, Page & Co.

Green Boundary: A Novel. Boris Ilyin. LC 49-5057. 1949. Houghton Mifflin Co.

Green Brain. Frank Herbert. LC 80-25045. (Series: Gregg Press Science Fiction Series.). 1981. 13.95 (ISBN 0-8398-2667-2). Gregg Press.

Green Brain. Frank Herbert. 1974. (pbk.) 1.25. Ace Books.

Green Branch. Edith Pargeter. 1974. (pbk.) 1.25. Bantam Books.

Green Bush: With Nine Drawings. John Towner Frederick. LC 25-174201. 1925. A. A. Knopf.

Green Cape. Susanne Richardson. 1973. 4.95 (ISBN 0-517-51450-8). Lenox Hill Press.

Green Carnation. Robert Smythe Hichens. LC 69-18207. 1970. 1.50 (ISBN 0-486-22223-3). Dover Publications.

Green Carnation. Robert Smythe Hichens. Ed. by Stanley Weintraub. LC 74-93105. 1970. 1.95 (ISBN 0-8032-5703-1). University of Nebraska Press.

Green Carnation. Robert Smythe Hichens. LC 21-4126. 1895. D. Appleton and Company.

Green Carnation a Novel. Robert Smythe Hichens. LC 7-4700. 1894. D. Appleton and Company.

Green Carpet. Edith Austin Holton. LC 48-5708. 1948. G. P. Putnam's Sons.

Green Centuries. Caroline Gordon. LC 76-164529. 1971. (ISBN 0-8154-0398-4). Cooper Square Publishers.

Green Centuries. Caroline Gordon. LC 41-22068. 1941. C. Scribner's Sons.

Green Chain. Everett Whealdon. 80p. 1979. 2.50. Samisdat.

Green Chalk. Doris Somerville. LC 13-22876. 1913. John Lane.

Green Child. Herbert Edward Read. LC 48-95958. 1948. New Directions.

Green Circle. Chris Massie. LC 43-510589. 1943. Random House.

Green Clinic. Earl Jones. 1972. 1.75 (ISBN 0-87067-508-7). Holloway House.

Green Cloak. Yorke Davis. LC 10-10319. 1910. 1.50. Sturgis & Walton Company.

Green Complex. Harold MacGrath. LC 30-10078. 1930. Doubleday, Doran and Company, Inc.

Green Corn Moon. George Lanning. LC 68-29054. 1968. 5.95 (ISBN 0-670-35399-X). Viking Press.

Green Corn Rebellion: A Novel. William Cunningham. LC 35-154771. The Vanguard Press.

Green Country. 1st Ed. Gene Austin. LC 53-5971. (Double D western). 1953. Doubleday.

Green Darkness. Anya Seton. LC 70-177542. 1973. 8.95 (ISBN 0-395-13937-6). Houghton Mifflin.

Green Darkness. Anya Seton. (Crest Book, X2030). 1974. (pbk.) 1.75. Fawcett.

Green Days by the River. Michael Anthony. LC 67-20148. 1967. Houghton Mifflin.

Green Days by the River. Michael Anthony. LC 67-20148. 1967. Houghton Mifflin.

Green Death: And Other Stories. Brett Hutton. LC 41-11911. (On cover: Bantam books. 22). Bantam Publications, Inc.

Green December Fills the Graveyard. Maureen Sarsfield. LC 47-84. 1946. Coward-McCann Inc.

Green Desire. Anton Myrer. 528p. 1982. 14.95 (ISBN 0-399-12630-9). Putnam Pub Group.

Green Desire. Anton Myrer. 720p. 1983. pap. 3.95 (ISBN 0-380-61580-0, 61580-0). Avon.

Green Desire: A Novel. Anton Myrer. LC 81-15690. 14.95 (ISBN 0-399-12630-9). Putnam.

Green Devil: A Romance of Thornton Abbey in the Days of John Wyclif. Arthur Metcalf. LC 12-253218. 1912. 1.20. The Pilgrim Press.

Green Diamond: By Arthur Morrison...Illustrated by F. H. Townsend. Arthur Morrison. LC 4-21720. 1904. L. C. Page & Company.

Green Diary. Anna J Brush. LC 34-8052. The Christopher Publishing House.

Green Dolphin. Sara Ware Bassett. LC 26-19673. 1926. The Penn Publishing Company.

Green Dolphin Street. Elizabeth Goudge. LC 44-40169. 1944. Coward-McCann, Inc.

Green Dolphin Street. Elizabeth Goudge. LC 47-1743. 1946. The Sun Dial Press.

Green Domino: A Comedy. Anthony Dyllington. LC 9-13041. 1909. J. Lane.

Green Door. Mary Eleanor Wilkins Freeman. LC 10-25067. 1910. Moffat, Yard and Company.

Green Doors,. Ethel Cook Eliot. LC 39-3228. 1933. Little, Brown, and Company.

Green Dragon. Joseph Jefferson Farjeon. LC 26-10567. L. MacVeagh, The Dial Press.

Green Earth: A Novel. Frederick Feikema Manfred. LC 77-5707. 15.00 (ISBN 0-517-52985-8). Crown Pub.

Green Englishman. Arthur Birkett. 1970. 2.95 o.p. Vantage.

Green Entry. Florence Ruth Howard. LC 40-27759. 1940. W. Morrow & Company.

Green-Eyed Monster. Patrick Quentin. LC 60-12140. (Random House mystery). 1960. Random House.

Green Eyed One. Florence Roney Weir. LC 23-13323. Small, Maynard & Company.

Green Eyes. Ben Cunningham (ISBN 0-345-25465-1). Ballantine.

Green Eyes. Maxwell Grant, pseud. (Shadow Ser.: No. 13). 1977. pap. 1.25 o.p. (ISBN 0-515-04205-6). BJ Pub Group.

Green Eyes of Bast. Sax Rohmer, pseud. (O.S.I.). 1971. pap. 0.75 o.s.i. (T2414). Pyramid Pubns.

Green Eyes of Bast. Arthur Sarsfield Ward. LC 20-182562. 1920. R. M. McBride & Co.

Green Eyes of Bast. Arthur Sarsfield Ward. LC 26-24700. (Lettered on cover: Masterpieces of Oriental mystery). McKinlay, Stone & Mackenzie.

Green Fancy. George Barr McCutcheon. LC 17-23981. 1917. Dodd, Mead and Company.

Green Fields of Eden. Francis Clifford. (YA) 1963. 3.95 o.p. Coward.

Green Fields of Eden. Arthur Leonard Bell Thompson. LC 63-10149. 1963. Coward-McCann.

Green Fig Tree. Michael Parr. 1965. 3.95 o.p. St Martin.

Green Fire. large print ed. Anne Maybury. LC 81-23195. 1982. 9.95 (ISBN 0-89621-339-0). Thorndike Press.

Green Fire: A Romance. William Sharp. LC 8-4797. 1896. Harper & Brothers.

Green Fire: By John Taine Pseud. Eric Temple Bell. LC 52-37331. 1952. Fantasy Pub. Co.

Green Fire: The Story of the Terrible Days in the Summer of 1990. Now Told in Full for the First Time. Eric Temple Bell. LC 26-11529. E. P. Dutton & Company.

Green Flag and Other Stories of War and Sport. Arthur Conan Doyle. LC 70-101468. (Short story index reprint series). 1969. Books for Libraries Press.

Green Flag: And Other Stories of War and Sport. Arthur Conan Doyle. LC 2225. 1900. The S. S. McClure Co.

Green Flag & Other Stories of War & Sport. facsimile ed. Arthur Conan Doyle. LC 70-101468. (Short Story Index Reprint Ser.). 1900. 17.00 (ISBN 0-8369-3201-3). Ayer Co.

Green Fool. Patrick Kavanagh. 264p. 1975. pap. 3.50 (ISBN 0-14-004005-6, Pub. by Penguin England). Irish Bk Ctr.

Green for Danger. Christianna Brand, pseud. LC 81-47091. 256p. 1981. pap. 2.50i (ISBN 0-06-080551-X, P 551, PL). Har-Row.

Green for Danger. Mary Christina Lewis. LC 44-7194. 1944. Dodd, Mead & Company.

Green for Danger, Vol. 9. Christianna Brand, pseud. LC 78-69778. (Mystery Library). (Illus.). 1978. Repr. of 1944 ed. 10.95 o.p. (ISBN 0-89163-046-5). Pubs Inc.

Green Forest. Nathalie Sedgwick Colby. LC 27-2318. Harcourt, Brace and Company.

Green from the States: A Novel. 1st Ed. Elsie Hazeltine Griffin. LC 54-13172. 1955. Exposition Press.

Green Frontier. John Buxton Hilton. LC 81-14620. 7.95. St. Martin's Press.

Green Fuse: A Novel. 1st Ed. Maurice Albert Unger. LC 54-12357. 1954. Pageant Press.

Green Gate. A Romance. Ernst Wichert & Wister, Mrs. Annie Lee (Furness) 1830-1908, Tr. LC 3-8339. 1903. J. B. Lippincott Company.

Green Gates: An Analysis of Foolishness. Katharine Mary Cheever Meredith. LC 7-28230. 1896. D. Appleton and Company.

Green Gauntlet. Ronald Frederick Delderfield. LC 68-28910. 1975. (pbk.) 1.95 (ISBN 0-671-78869-8). Pocket Books.

Green Gauntlet: By R. F. Delderfield. Ronald Frederick Delderfield. LC 68-28910. 1968. 5.95. S.&S.

Green Gene. Peter Dickinson. LC 72-12857. 1973. 5.95 (ISBN 0-394-48542-4). Pantheon Books.

Green Gene. Peter Dickinson. (DAW Science Fiction Books, no. 174). 1975. (pbk.) 1.25. DAW Books.

Green Ginger. Arthur Morrison. LC 9-248948. 1909. F. A. Stokes Company.

Green Girl. Jack Williamson. LC 50-34022. (Avon fantasy novels, 2). 1950. Avon.

Green Girls. Donewell. 1971. pap. 1.45 o.p. (Z1062Q, Zebra). Grove.

Green God. David Dvorkin. 1.95 (ISBN 0-671-82080-X). Pocket Books.

Green God. Frederic Arnold Kummer. LC 11-25557. W. J. Watt & Company.

Green Goddess. Paul Edwards. LC 75-15080. (His John Eagle-expeditor; 12). 1975. 1.25 (ISBN 0-515-03913-6). Pyramid Books.

Green Goddess. Louise Jordan Miln. LC 22-17390. Frederick A. Stokes Compnay.

Green Gods. Nathalie Henneberg & Henneberg, Charles. (Illus.). 1980. 1.75 (ISBN 0-87997-538-5). DAW Books Inc.

Green God's Pavilion: A Novel of the Philippines. Mabel Wood Martin. LC 20-146011. Frederick A. Stokes Company.

Green Gold of Yucatan. Gregory Mason. LC 26-15397. 1926. Duffield and Company.

Green Grape. Simonne Ratel. Tr. by Sneyd, Marie. LC 37-24110. 1937. The Macmillan Company.

Green Grass, Blue Sky, White House. Wright Morris. LC 70-18557. (Illus.). 1970. Black Sparrow Press.

Green Grass of Wyoming. Mary Sture-Vasa. LC 46-6228. 1946. J. B. Lippincott Company.

Green Gravel. Dora Aydelotte. LC 37-3821. 1937. D. Appleton-Century Company, Incorporated.

Green, Green, My Valley Now. Richard Llewellyn. LC 74-18816. 1975. 6.95 (ISBN 0-385-03374-5). Doubleday.

Green Grow the Dollars. Emma Lathen, pseud. LC 81-18395. 13.95 (ISBN 0-671-44130-2). Simon and Schuster.

Green Grow the Dollars. Emma Lathen, pseud. LC 82-9166. 1982. 14.95 (ISBN 0-8161-3397-2). G.K. Hall.

Green Grow the Graves. M. E. Chaber, pseud. (Milo March Mystery Ser). 1971. pap. 0.60 o.p. (ISBN 0-446-63568-5, 63-568). Paperback Lib.

Green Grow the Graves. Kendell Foster Crossen. LC 77-87857. (Rinehart suspense novel). 1970. 4.50. Holt, Rinehart and Winston.

Green Grow the Rushes. Nelson Wolford & Shirley Wolford. LC 54-11241. 1954. Dodd, Mead.

Green Grow the Tresses-O: By Stanley Hyland. Henry Stanley Hyland. LC 66-29899. 1967. 3.95. Bobbs.

Green Half-Moon. James Francis Dwyer. LC 15-205621. 1915. A. C. McClurg & Co.

Green Hand. Lillian Beckwith. 1967. 5.95 (ISBN 0-09-082090-8, Pub. by Hutchinson). Merrimack Pub Cir.

"Green Hand." A "Short" Yarn. George Cupples. (Franklin square library. no. 68). 1879. Harper & Brothers.

Green Hand: A Story of the F. F. A. Paul Wilbur Chapman. LC 32-11380. J. B. Lippincott Company.

Green Hand: Adventures of a Naval Lieutenant. George Cupples. LC 99-4894. (Famous novels of the sea). 1899. C. Scribner's Sons.

Green Hat. Michael Arlen. LC 24-22007. George H. Doran Company.

Green Hazard. Manning Coles, pseud. LC 45-1736. 1945. Pub. for the Crime Club by Doubleday, Doran and Company, Inc.

Green Hazard. Manning Coles, pseud. LC 46-6602. 1946. Triangle Books, the Blakiston Company.

Green Heart. Vian Smith. LC 64-10024. 1964. Doubleday.
Green Hell Treasure. Robert L Fish. LC 70-136803. (Red mask mystery). 1971. 4.95. Putnam.
Green Helmet: A Novel. Jon Cleary. LC 58-536685. 1958. Morrow.
Green Henry. Translated from the German by A. M. Holt. Gottfried Keller. LC 59-117491. 6.50. Grove Press.
Green Hill Far Away. Peter Upton. LC 76-18246. 10.95 (ISBN 0-671-22344-5). Simon and Schuster.
Green Hill Far Away. Peter Upton. LC 76-378975. 1976. 4.50 (ISBN 0-85140-249-6). Arlington Books.
Green Hills: And Other Stories. Walter Macken. LC 56-42901. 1956. Macmillan.
Green Hills of Earth. Robert Anson Heinlein. LC 76-44408. 1976. 6.95 (ISBN 0-88411-881-9). Aeonian Press.
Green Hills of Earth: Rhysling and the Adventure of the Entire Solar System! Robert Anson Heinlein. LC 51-8740. (His Future history series). 1951. Shasta Pub.
Green Holly. Sue Kaufman. 1971. pap. 0.95 o.p. (ISBN 0-446-66779-X, 65-769). Paperback Lib.
Green House. Mario V. Llosa. 1973. pap. 4.95 (ISBN 0-380-01233-2, 60533, Bard). Avon.
Green House. Vargas Llosa, Mario. LC 68-28227. 1968. 6.95. Harper & Row.
Green House. Mario Vargas Llosa. LC 68-28227. 1969. 7.95 o.p. (ISBN 0-06-014503-X, HarpT). Har-Row.
Green Ice. Gerald A. Brown. 1978. 9.95 o.p. (ISBN 0-440-03034-X). Delacorte.
Green Ice. Gerald A Browne. LC 77-26242. 9.95 (ISBN 0-440-03034-X). Delacorte Press.
Green Ice. Gerald A Browne. 1979. 2.50 (ISBN 0-440-13224-X). Dell Pub. Co.
Green Ice. Raoul Whitfield. 1930. A. A. Knopf.
Green Ice. Raoul Whitfield. LC 80-17978. (Gregg Press mystery fiction series). 1980. 13.95 (ISBN 0-8398-2720-2). Gregg Press.
Green Ice Murders. Raoul Whitfield. LC 48-15384. (Murder mystery monthly no. 46). 1947. Avon Book Co.
Green in Between. 1st Ed. Robert V Doak. LC 53-387. 1952. Pageant Press.
Green Ink. and Other Stories. Joseph Smith Fletcher. Small,Maynard & Company.
Green Is the Golden Tree: A Novel. Rhoda Truax. LC 43-49773. 1943. The Bobbs-Merril Company.
Green Island. V. Datskevich. 59p. 1980. 3.60 (ISBN 0-8285-2015-1, Pub. by Progress Pubs USSR). Imported Pubns.
Green Island. Michael Schmidt. LC 82-205257. 10.95 (ISBN 0-8149-0862-4). Vanguard Press.
Green Isle. Alice Duer Miller. LC 30-24838. 1930. Dodd, Mead, & Co.
Green Jacket. Jennette Barbour Perry Lee. 1917. C. Scribner's Sons.
Green Jade Hand: In Which a New and Quite Different Type of Detective Unravels a Mystery Staged in Chicago, Bagdad on the Lakes, London of the West. Harry Stephen Keeler. LC 30-203539. E. P. Dutton & Co., Inc.
Green Julia. Paul Ableman. LC 66-276465. 1973. pap. 1.95 o.p. (ISBN 0-394-17803-3, E619). Grove.
Green Kangaroo. Fabian Worsham. pap. 3.00 o.s.i. Anhinga Pr.
Green Killer. Kenneth Robeson. (avenger, #20). 1974. (pbk.) 0.95. Warner Paperback Library.
Green Kingdom: A Novel. Rachel Maddux. LC 56-9918. 1957. Simon and Schuster.
Green Kingdom: A Novel. Rachel Maddux. 1977. 2.25 (ISBN 0-380-01705-9). Avon Books.
Green Knife. Robert McNair Wilson. LC 32-20733. 1932. J. B. Lippincott Company.
Green Knight. Vera Chapman. LC 77-93527. 1978. 1.50 (ISBN 0-380-01704-0). Avon.
Green Knight & Red Mourning. Richard E. Ogden. (Orig.). 1980. pap. 1.95 (ISBN 0-532-23218-6). Woodhill.
Green Lacquer Pavilion. Helen Beauclerk. LC 26-165331. George H. Doran Company.
Green Ladies: By W. Douglas Newton... Wilfrid Douglas Newton. LC 19-155708. 1919. D. Appleton and Company.
Green Lama: An Amazing Exploit Taken Right Out of the Case-Book of the Green Lama, in Which His Unusual Powers Are Put to the Test. Kendell Foster Crossen. LC 76-150891. (Pulp classics; no. 14). (Illus.). R. Weinberg.
Green Lama Mystery. Josephine Kains, pseud. (Mystery Puzzlers Ser.: No. 20). (Illus., Orig.). 1979. pap. 1.95 (ISBN 0-89083-455-5). Zebra.
Green Land. Zola Helen Ross. LC 52-10280. 1952. Bobbs-Merrill.
Green Lantern No. 1. (Green Lantern Ser). 160p. 1972. pap. 0.75 o.p. (ISBN 0-446-64729-2). Paperback Lib.
Green Leaf. Robert Nathan. 1950. 5.95 o.p. (ISBN 0-394-40354-1, 40354). Knopf.
Green Leaf in Drought. Isobel Kuhn. 1981. pap. 3.00 (ISBN 0-85363-021-6). OMF Bks.
Green Leaves of Summer. Auriel Rosemary Malet Vaughan. LC 51-10288. 1951. Little, Brown.
Green Light. Lloyd Cassel Douglas. LC 62-51. 1961. Grosset & Dunlap.
Green Light. Lloyd Cassel Douglas. LC 35-1935. 1935. Houghton Mifflin Company.
Green Light. Louise Platt Hauck. LC 31-75607. The Penn Publishing Company.
Green Light, Red Catch. Francis Ryck. LC 72-94863. 1973. 5.95 (ISBN 0-8128-1542-4). Stein and Day.
Green Lights Are Blue: A Pornosophic Novel. Ursule Molinaro. LC 67-14730. 1967. 4.50. New Amer. Lib.
Green Line. Tom Molloy. LC 82-1166. 12.95 (ISBN 0-89182-052-3). Charles River Books.
Green Lion. Francis Hackett. LC 36-8451. 1936. Doubleday, Doran & Company, Inc.
Green Madonna. C. E. L'Ami. LC 52-6522. 1952. Westminster Press.
Green Magic. Jack Vance, pseud. (Illus.). 272p. 1979. lib. bdg. 15.00 (ISBN 0-934438-13-7). Underwood-Miller.
Green Man. Kingsley Amis. LC 76-95862. 1970. Harcourt, Brace & World.
Green Man. Margaret Storm Jameson. LC 52-7784. 1953. Harper.
Green Man. Henry Treece. 1968. pap. 0.95 o.p. (ISBN 0-446-55752-8, 55-752). Paperback Lib.
Green Man: A Novel. Henry Treece & Saxo Grammaticus. LC 66-15592. 1966. Putnam.
Green Man & His Return. Harold Sherman. (Illus.). 1979. pap. 7.95 (ISBN 0-910122-57-1). Amherst Pr.
Green Man of Graypec. rev. and enl. ed. Festus Pragnell. LC 50-10205. 1950. Greenberg.
Green Mansion: A Romance of the Tropical Forest. William Henry Hudson. LC 16-68218. 1916. A. A. Knopf.
Green Mansion: A Romance of the Tropical Forest. William Henry Hudson. LC 23-15892. (Half-title: The collected works of W. H. Hudson). 1923. J. M. Dent & Sons, Ltd.
Green Mansion Mystery. Lawrence J. Joos. 2.50 o.p. Carlton.
Green Mansions. William Henry Hudson. LC 49-11310. (Great Illustrated Classics). 1949. Dodd, Mead.
Green Mansions. William Henry Hudson. LC 36-10533. (Universal library). 1931. Grosset & Dunlap.
Green Mansions. William Henry Hudson & Henderson, Keith, 1883- Illus. LC 32-21905. 1931. Illustrated Editions Company.
Green Mansions. William Henry Hudson & Kauffer, Edward McKnight, 1890- Illus. LC 44-41887. (Illustrated modern library). 1944. A. C. Barnes & Co., Inc.
Green Mansions: A Romance of the Tropical Forest. Paintings & Drawings by Horacio Butler. William Henry Hudson. LC 59-7997. 1959. Knopf.
Green Mansions: A Romance of the Tropical Forest. William Henry Hudson. LC 72-181624. (collected works of W. H. Hudson). (Illus.). 1968. AMS Press.
Green Mansions: A Romance of the Tropical Forest. William Henry Hudson. LC 5-4148. 1904. G. P. Putnam's Sons.
Green Mansions: A Romance of the Tropical Forest. William Henry Hudson. LC 33-28341. (Half-title: The modern library of the world's best books). 1920. The Modern Library.
Green Mansions: A Romance of the Tropical Forest. William Henry Hudson. LC 36-326426. The Heritage Press.
Green Mansions: A Romance of the Tropical Forest. William Henry Hudson & Butler, Horacio, 1897- Illus. LC 43-15360. 1943. A. A. Knopf.
Green Mansions: A Romance of the Tropical Forest. William Henry Hudson & Covarrubias, Miguel, 1902- Illus. LC 44-2501. (Heritage reprints). 1944. The Heritage Press.
Green Mansions: A Romance of the Tropical Forest. William Henry Hudson & Galsworthy, John, 1867-1938. LC 38-32636. 1938. The Sun Dial Press, Inc.
Green Mansions: A Romance of the Tropical Forest. William Henry Hudson & Kauffer, Edward McKnight, 1890- Illus. LC 45-35094. 1945. Random House.
Green Mansions: A Romance of the Tropical Forest. William Henry Hudson & Wilson, Edward Arthur, 1886- Illus. LC 35-11903. The Limited Editions Club.
Green Mansions. Introd. by Charles Dwoskin. William Henry Hudson. LC 57-4895. 1957. Fine Editions Press.
Green Mansions, with an Introd. By Louise Bogan. William Henry Hudson. LC 51-6235. (Harper's modern classics). 1951. Harper.
Green Mare. Marcel Ayme. Tr. by Norman Denny. LC 55-8038. 1963. pap. 1.45 (ISBN 0-689-70006-7, 42). Atheneum.
Green Mare. Translated from the French by Norman Denny. Marcel Ayme. LC 55-8038. Harper.
Green Margins. Edwin P O'Donnell. LC 36-21350. 1936. Houghton Mifflin Company.
Green Mariner: A Landsman's Account of a Deep-Sea Voyage. Howard Ireland. 1900. J. B. Lippincott Company.
Green Millenium. Fritz Leiber. LC 80-22108. (Gregg Press Science Fiction Series). 1980. 14.95 (ISBN 0-8398-2641-9). Gregg Press.
Green Millennium. Fritz Leiber. LC 53-106378. 1953. Abelard Press.
Green Millennium. Fritz Leiber. 1976. (pbk.) 1.25. Ace Books.
Green Mirror: A Quiet Story. Hugh Walpole. LC 17-30042. (His The rising city: II). George H. Doran Company.
Green Monday. Michael M Thomas. LC 80-10537. 12.95 (ISBN 0-671-61002-3). Wyndham Books.
Green Money. new ed. Dorothy Emily Stevenson. LC 74-15486. 1975. 7.95 (ISBN 0-03-013861-2). Holt, Rinehart and Winston.
Green Money. Dorothy Emily Stevenson. 1977. 1.50 (ISBN 0-441-30309-9). Ace Books.
Green Money. Dorothy Emily Stevenson. LC 39-23743. Farrar & Rinehart, Inc.
Green Money. Dorothy Emily Stevenson. LC 39-23743. Farrar & Rinehart, Inc.
Green Mountain Annals, a Tale of Truth. Gerritt Van Husen Forbes. LC 6-41407. 1832. Burnett & Smith.
Green Mountain Boys. Daniel Pierce Thompson. (Lovell's library, v. 1, no. 21). 1882. J. W. Lovell Company.
Green Mountain Boys: A Historical Tale of the Early Settlement of Vermont. Daniel Pierce Thompson. LC 8-28261. 1839. E. P. Walton and Sons.
Green Mountain Boys: A Historical Tale of the Early Settlement of Vermont. rev. ed. Daniel Pierce Thompson. LC 8-28260. 1857. Sanborn, Carter, Bazin & Co.
Green Mountain Boys. A Historical Tale of the Early Settlement of Vermont. Daniel Pierce Thompson. LC 4-16471. A. L. Burt Company.
Green Mountain Boys: A Historical Tale of the Early Settlement of Vermont. Daniel Pierce Thompson. LC 27-277875. T. Nelson & Sons.
Green Mountain Boys Ride. illustrations by frank dobias. ed. Gilbert Smith. LC 32-29190. The Century Co.
Green Mountain Farm. Elliott Merrick. 1978. 3.95 (ISBN 0-9603324-0-5). Sherry Urie.
Green Mountain Travellers' Entertainment. Josiah Barnes. LC 41-40967. (On cover: Library of travels and adventure). 1858. Derby & Jackson.
Green Mouse. Robert William Chambers. LC 10-9851. 1910. 1.50. D. Appleton and Company.
Green Moustache: A Fantasy of Modernism. Francis Warrington Dawson. LC 26-2805. 1925. The Bernard Publishing Co.
Green Mummy. Fergus Hume. LC 8-20710. 1908. G. W. Dillingham Company.
Green Murder Case. S. S. Van Dine, pseud. (YA) Repr. lib. bdg. 19.10x (ISBN 0-89190-514-6). Am Repr-Rivercity Pr.
Green Needles. Mae Foster Jay. LC 33-138. W. A. Wilde Company.
Green Odyssey. Philip Jose Farmer. LC 78-1324. (Gregg Press science fiction series). (Illus.). 1978. 9.00 (ISBN 0-8398-2414-9). Gregg Press.
Green Olive Tree. Irene Murray, pseud. LC 63-1132. Zondervan Pub. House.
Green Orange Purple Red. Chris Torrance. 1968. 12.50, signed ed o.p. (Pub. by Ferry Pr); 9.00 o.p.; pap. 5.00 o.p. SBD.
Green Oranges: Translated from the French by Norman Denny. 1st American Ed. Rene Masson. LC 52-12178. 1953. Knopf.
Green Orchard. Andrew Soutar. LC 16-8815. 1916. Cassell and Company, Ltd.
Green Overcoat. Hilaire Belloc. LC 70-165614. 1971. (ISBN 0-8369-5921-3). Books for Libraries Press.
Green Overcoat. Hilaire Belloc. LC 12-29131. 1912. McBride, Nast & Company.
Green Pack. Edgar Wallace. LC 34-2591. 1933. Pub. for the Crime Club, Inc., by Doubleday, Doran & Company, Inc.
Green Paradise. Heather Hill. 192p. 1981. pap. 1.50 (ISBN 0-671-57060-9). S&S.
Green Parrot. Marthe Lucie Lahovary Bibesco. Tr. by Cowley, Malcolm. LC 29-114386. Harcourt, Brace and Company.
Green Pastures. Ed. by Thomas Cripps & Tino Balio. LC 79-3959. (Wisconsin-Warner Bros. Screenplay Ser.). (Illus.). 1979. 17.50 (ISBN 0-299-07920-1); pap. 6.95 (ISBN 0-299-07924-4). U of Wis Pr.
Green Pastures: And Piccadilly. by william black... in conjunction with an american writer. ed. William Black. 1878. Harper & Brothers.
Green Pastures: And Piccadilly. William Black. LC 6-12932. (On cover: Lovell's library, v. 4, no. 184). J. W. Lovell Company.
Green Pastures: And Piccadilly. William Black. LC 6-12931. (Seaside library. Pocket ed. no. 138). G. Munro.
Green Patch. Betsey Riddle Hutton Zum Stolzenberg. LC 10-229331. 1.50. Frederick A. Stokes Company.
Green Path to the Moon. Davis Dresser. LC 38-3418. 1938. Hillman-Curl, Inc.
Green Pavilions. Helen E. Muse. 4.75 o.p. (ISBN 0-8062-0639-X). Carlton.
Green-Pea Pirates. Peter Bernard Kyne. LC 19-17748. 1919. Doubleday, Page & Company.
Green Peas: Picked from the Patch of Invisible Green, Esq.... William G Crippen. LC 9-3862. Livermore and Rudd.
Green Phoenix. Thomas Burnett Swann. (Orig.). 1972. pap. 0.95 o.p. (UQ1027). Daw Bks.
Green Place: A Novel. Keith Warren Jennison. LC 54-635944. 1954. Funk & Wagnalls.
Green Plaid Pants. Margaret Scherf. LC 51-11444. 1951. Published for the Crime Club by Doubleday.
Green Pond. Evan Brandon. LC 55-10478. 1955. Vanguard Press.
Green Pope. Miguel Angel Asturias. LC 75-129331. 1971. 8.95. Delacorte Press.
Green Rain. Paul Tabori. 1969. pap. 0.60 o.p. (X1941). Pyramid Pubns.
Green Ray. Vance Thompson. LC 24-24946. The Bobbs-Merrill Company.
Green Ray. Jules Verne. 3.95. Assoc Bk.
Green Ribbon... Edgar Wallace. LC 30-17709. 1930. Pub. for The Crime Club, Inc., by Doubleday, Doran & Company, Inc.
Green Ripper. John Dann MacDonald. LC 79-12063. 9.95 (ISBN 0-397-01362-0). Lippincott.
Green Ripper. John Dann MacDonald. LC 79-25960. 1980. 12.95 (ISBN 0-8161-3023-X). G. K. Hall.
Green River High. Duncan Kyle. LC 79-22860. 1979. 10.00 (ISBN 0-312-35012-0). St. Martin's Press.
Green Rope. Joseph Smith Fletcher. LC 27-14952. 1927. A. A. Knopf.
Green Rose: A Novel. Warren A Silver. LC 77-8700. 8.95 (ISBN 0-8037-3236-8). Dial Press.
Green Rose of Furley. Helen Corse Barney. LC 53-9968. 1953. Crown Publishers.
Green Rushes: A Novel. Maurice Walsh. LC 35-16896. 1935. Frederick A. Stokes Company.
Green Rust. Edgar Wallace. LC 20-4011. Small, Maynard & Company.
Green Salamander. Pamela Hill. 1978. 1.95 (ISBN 0-449-23642-0). Fawcett Books.
Green Salamander: A Historical Novel. Pamela Hill. LC 76-41856. 10.00 (ISBN 0-312-35017-1). St. Martin's Press.
Green Scamander. Maude Meagher. LC 33-7960. 1933. Houghton Mifflin Company.
Green Scarf: A Business Romance Having to Do with a Man Who Is Determined to Win Success Without the Help of Wealth or Family Prestige. Howard Vincent O'Brien. LC 24-4698. 1924. A. C. McClurg & Co.
Green Seal. Charles Edmonds Walk. LC 14-5423. 1914. A. C. McClurg & Co.
Green Seaweed & Salted Eggs. Lin Hai-Ying. 125p. 1980. 5.95 (ISBN 0-89955-160-2, Pub. by Mei Ya China). Intl Schol Bk Serv.
Green Shade. Robin Maugham. (Signet bk., T3214). 1967. New Amer. Lib.
Green Shaded Lamps. Cornelia Veenendaal. LC 76-55615. 64p. 1977. pap. 4.95 (ISBN 0-914086-16-2). Alicejamesbooks.
Green Shadow. James Edward Grant. LC 35-688210. 1935. The Hartney Press.
Green Shadow. Herman Landon. LC 28-11537. 1928. L. MacVeagh, The Dial Press.
Green Shadows. Lucile V. Stevens. 192p. (YA) 1973. 6.50 (Avalon). Bouregy.
Green Shiver: A Theocritus Lucius Westborough Story. Clyde B Clason. 1941. Pub. for the Crime Club by Doubleday, Doran & Company, Inc.
Green Shoots. Paul Morand. LC 70-150553. (Short story index reprint series). 1971. (ISBN 0-8369-3850-X). Books for Libraries Press.
Green Shoots. Paul Morand. Tr. by Woolf, H. I. LC 24-8045. 1924. T. Seltzer.
Green Stone. Suzanne Blanc. 1969. pap. 0.75 o.p. (74-578). Lancer.
Green Stone. Harold MacGrath. LC 24-21398. 1924. Doubleday, Page & Company.
Green Talons. Charles Rodda. LC 31-20524. The Bobbs-Merrill Company.
Green Tea; a Love Story. Vesta S. Simmons. LC 8-8993. (Half-title: The "unknown" library no. 17). Cassell Publishing Company.
Green Tea: And Other Ghost Stories. Joseph Sheridan Le Fanu. LC 46-51357. 1945. Arkham House.
Green Thumb & Silver Tongue. Peter Kanto. (Orig.). 1970. pap. 1.95 o.s.i. (OPH-176, Ophelia). Olympia.
Green Timber. Harold Bindloss. LC 24-5500. 1924. Frederick A. Stokes Company.
Green Timber. James Oliver Curwood & Bryant, Dorothes A. LC 30-109834. 1930. Doubleday, Doran and Company, Inc.
Green Timber. Ester Gerberding Hunt. LC 39-611. (John Rung prize series). The United Lutheran Church in America.

Green Timber Thoroughbreds. Roberts Theodore Goodridge. LC 24-7118. 1924. Garden City Publishing Co., Inc.
Green Toad. Walter S Masterman. LC 29-9793. E. P. Dutton & Co., Inc.
Green Tree and a Dry Tree. Carter Wilson. LC 79-184534. (Illus.). 1972. Macmillan.
Green Tree in Gedde. Alan Sharp. LC 65-17935. (NAL-World book). 1965. New American Library.
Green Tree Mystery. Lily Augusta Long. LC 17-24164. 1917. 1.40. D. Appleton and Company.
Green Valley. Thomas Patrick Buffington. LC 1-29450. The Abbey Press.
Green Valley. Katharine Reynolds. LC 19-4852. 1919. Little, Brown, and Company.
Green Valley School: A Pedagogical Story. Cornelius Willet Gillam Hyde. LC 7-190383. 1907. North-Western School Supply Co.
Green Vase. William Richards Castle. LC 12-6861. 1912. 1.30. Dodd, Mead and Company.
Green Vineyards. Helena Leigh. 352p. (Orig.). 1982. pap. 3.50 (ISBN 0-515-06068-2). Jove Pubns.
Green Water for a Granite Valley. William V. Sieller. 1970. 4.00 (ISBN 0-8233-0144-3). Golden Quill.
Green Willow. Barbara Bonham. LC 82-80212. 400p. (Orig.). 1982. pap. 3.50 (ISBN 0-86721-143-1). Playboy Pbks.
Green Willow. Ethel Edith Mannin. LC 76-381828. 1976. 3.50 (ISBN 0-7278-0136-8). Severn House: Distributed by Hutchinson.
Green Willow. Ethel Edith Mannin. LC 28-19242. 1928. Doubleday, Doran & Company, Inc.
Green Willows. Jan Alexander, pseud. (Kangaroo Book). 1977. 1.25 (ISBN 0-671-81037-5). Pocket Books.
Green Willows. Renee Shann. 1971. pap. 0.75 o.p. (94180). Beagle Bks.
Green Wine. Augustus George Greenwood. LC 31-19092. 1931. W. Morrow & Company.
Green Wings: Or, Under Italian Skies. Jane Frazer. LC 40-8384. Frazer Publishing Co.
Green Winter: A Novel. Jan Carew. LC 65-14394. 1965. Stein and Day.
Green Wolf Connection. Nick Carter. (Nick Carter Ser.). (O.s.i.). 176p. (Orig.). 1976. pap. 1.50 o.s.i. (ISBN 0-441-30328-5, Award). Univ Pub & Dist.
Green Wood Burns Slow. Monica Brice. LC 33-8697. 1938. Lothrop, Lee & Shepard Company.
Green Wound Contract. Philip Atlee. (Joe Gall Contract Ser). 1969. pap. 0.60 o.p. (R2552, GM). Fawcett World.
Green Years. Archibald Joseph Cronin. LC 44-741047. 1944. Little, Brown and Company.
Greenage Summer. Rumer Godden. 1974. (pbk.) 1.25. Avon.
Greenbanks. Dorothy Whipple. LC 32-32269. Farrar & Rinehart, Inc.
Greenbones. Vinnie Williams. LC 67-11263. 1967. Viking Press.
Greencomber. Peter Tate. LC 78-68370. 1979. 7.95 (ISBN 0-385-13637-4). Doubleday.
Greene Arbors. Mary Arleville Lobdell Palmer. 1959. Bruce Humphries.
Greene Murder Case. S. S. Van Dine, pseud. 1980. lib. bdg. 10.95 (ISBN 0-8398-2555-2, Gregg). G K Hall.
Greene Murder Case. S. S. Van Dine, pseud. 1981. 18.95x (Pub. by Remploy England). State Mutual Bk.
Greene Murder Case. Willard Huntington Wright. LC 45-13594. 1944.
Greene Murder Case. Willard Huntington Wright. LC 79-23029. (Series: Gregg Press Mystery Series.). (Illus.). 1980. 10.95 (ISBN 0-8398-2555-2). Gregg Press.
Greene Murder Case: A Philo Vance Story. Willard Huntington Wright. LC 28-9658. 1928. C. Scribner's Sons.
Greener Field. Russell P. Askue. 4.00 o.p. (ISBN 0-8283-1274-5). Branden.
Greener Than You Think. Ward Moore. LC 47-31071. 1947. W. Sloane Associates.
Greenery Street. Denis George Mackail. LC 25-15761. 1925. Houghton Mifflin Company.
Greenflames of Aries. Robert Lory. (Horrorscope,#1). 1974. (pbk.) 0.95 (ISBN 0-523-00310-2). Pinnacle Books.
Greengage Summer. Rumer Godden. LC 81-47096. 218p. 1981. pap. 2.95i (ISBN 0-06-080561-7, P 561, PL). Har-Row.
Greengage Summer: A Novel. Rumer Godden. LC 58-7066. 1958. Viking Press.
Greengates. Robert Cedric Sherriff. LC 36-10522. 1936. Frederick A. Stokes Company.
Greengroundtown. Christopher Fahy. Ed. by Constance Hunting. 1978. pap. 3.50 (ISBN 0-913006-13-0). Puckerbrush.
Greengroundtown: Stories. Christopher Fahy. LC 78-107103. 3.50 (ISBN 0-913006-13-0). Puckerbrush Press.
Greenhorn. Victor K. Johnson. 3.75 o.p. Vantage.
Greenhorn: A Novel. Paul King. LC 32-21898. The Macaulay Company.
Greenhorn: A Novel. Pal Kiralyhegyi. LC 32-21898. 1932. Macauley Co.
Greenhorn Marshal. Wayne D. Overholser. LC 74-8338. 1974. (pbk.) 0.95 (ISBN 0-345-24061-8). Ballantine Books.
Greenhorn Stampede. Kit Prate. (Orig.). 1981. pap. 1.75 (ISBN 0-505-51641-1). Tower Bks.
Greenhorn's Hunt. Clifford MacClellan Sublette. LC 34-30243. The Bobbs-Merrill Company.
Greenhouse. Antonia Lamb. 1971. pap. 0.75 o.p. (T2579). Pyramid Pubns.
Greenhouse. Antonia Lamb. 1974. pap. 0.95 o.p. (ISBN 0-515-03477-0, N3477). Pyramid Pubns.
Greenish Man. Snoo Wilson. 32p. (Orig.). 1981. pap. 3.95 (ISBN 0-86104-213-1). Pluto Pr.
Greenland Passage. Richard Harper. 224p. (Orig.). 1981. pap. 2.25 (ISBN 0-8439-1008-9, Leisure Bks). Nordon Pubns.
Greenlander: A Novel. Mark Adlard. LC 78-17069. 9.95 (ISBN 0-671-24044-7). Summit Books.
Greenleaf Fires. John A. Gould. LC 77-17824. (Illus.). 8.95 (ISBN 0-684-15478-1). Scribner.
Greenlow. Florence Roma Muir Wilson O'Brien. LC 27-21016. 1927. A. A. Knopf.
Greenmantle. John Buchan. LC 16-22977. 1.25. George H. Doran Company.
Greenmantle. John Buchan. LC 16-236283. 1916. Hodder and Stoughton.
Greenmantle. John Buchan. LC 17-20424. 1916. G. H. Doran Company.
Greenmantle. John Buchan. LC 36-17407. Houghton Mifflin Company.
Greenmask. Joseph Jefferson Farjeon. LC 44-4617. 1944. The Bobbs-Merrill Company.
Greenroom. Hamilton Basso. LC 49-10214. 1949. Doubleday.
Greensea Island: A Mystery of the Essex Coast. Victor Bridges. LC 22-6163. 1922. G. P. Putnam's Sons.
Greenstone. Ashton-Warner, Sylvia. LC 66-11061. 1966. Simon and Schuster.
Greenstone. Yvonne Kalman. LC 80-2862. (Illus.). 17.95 (ISBN 0-385-17510-8). Doubleday.
Greenvoe. George Mackay Brown. LC 72-78449. 1972. 5.95 (ISBN 0-15-137060-5). Harcourt Brace Jovanovich.
Greenwater - Death Valley's Greatest Copper Camp. Harold O. Weight. LC 78-83290. 1969. pap. 1.00 o.p. (ISBN 0-912714-02-6). Calico Pr.
Greenway. Leslie Moore. LC 21-146311. 1919. P. J. Kenedy & Sons.
Greenwillow. Drawings by Erik Blegvad. 1st Ed. Beatrice Joy Chute. LC 56-63103. 1956. Dutton.
Greenwood. Jean Phillips. 1970. pap. 0.75 o.p. (ISBN 0-447-74714-2). Lancer.
Greenwoods,". Lucile Grinnan Lyon. LC 15-158649. 1915. The Neal Publishing Company.
Greenyards. Joan Lingard. LC 80-19022. 12.95 (ISBN 0-399-12513-2). Putnam.
Greg Sheridan, Reporter. John Ernest Bechdolt. LC 49-10284. 1949. E. P. Dutton.
Gregg: A Novel. Fleta Campbell Springer. LC 19-3007. 1919. Harper & Brothers.
Gregg Barratt's Woman. Lilian Peake. (Harlequin Presents Ser.). 192p. 1981. pap. 1.50 (ISBN 0-373-10424-3, Pub. by Harlequin). PB.
Gregory Girls. Marjorie Warby. 1971. pap. 0.75 o.p. (94104). Beagle Bks.
Gregory Hill. W Craig Thomas. LC 57-6635. 1957. Appleton-Century-Crofts.
Gregory the Armenian: A Son of the King. Helen R Robb. The Pilgrim Press.
Gregory the Great. Gertrud Schmirger. LC 63-17769. 1963. Harcourt, Brace & World.
Greifenstein. Francis Marion Crawford. LC 6-30894. 1889. Macmillan and Co.
Greifenstein. Francis Marion Crawford. LC 23-174949. 1898. Macmillan and Co.
Greifenstein. Francis Marion Crawford. LC 16-19150. (Lettered on cover: Works of F. Marion Crawford). 1910. The Macmillan Company.
Grell Mystery. Frank Froest. LC 14-19690. 1.25. E. J. Clode.
Gremlins Go Home. Gordon R. Dickson & Ben Bova. (Illus.). 1974. 6.50 o.p. (ISBN 0-312-35035-X). St Martin.
Gremlin's Grampa. Robert L. Pike, pseud. LC 76-171312. 1972. 5.95 o.p. (ISBN 0-385-02166-6). Doubleday.
Gremlin's Grampa: A Police Procedural Novel. Robert L Fish. LC 76-171312. 1972. 5.95. Doubleday.
Grenadier: A Story of the Empire. James Eugene Farmer. LC 98-67. 1898. Dodd, Mead and Company.
Grenadine Etching: Her Life and Loves. Robert Chester Ruark. LC 47-31236. 1947. Doubleday.
Grenadine's Spawn. Robert Chester Ruark. LC 52-8748. 1952. Doubleday.
Grendel. John Champlin Gardner. LC 70-154911. (Illus.). 1971. 5.95 (ISBN 0-394-47143-1). Knopf.
Grendel. John Champlin Gardner. LC 77-38827. (Illus.). 1972. (ISBN 0-8161-6015-5). G. K. Hall.
Grenelle: A Novel of Suspense. Isabelle Holland. LC 76-15069. 8.95 (ISBN 0-89256-006-1). Rawson Associates Publishers.
Grenelle: A Novel of Suspense. Isabelle Holland. LC 80-24329. 1980. 9.95 (ISBN 0-89621-252-1). Thorndike Press.
Grenencourt. Iona Charles. (Queen-size gothic). 1975. (pbk.) 1.25. Popular Library.
Grenfell Legacy. Marjorie McEvoy. 1971. pap. 0.75 o.p. (T2394). Pyramid Pubns.
Greselda: A Story. Marian E Grey. LC 4-35073. 1904. H. B. Turner & Co.
Gresham Ghost. Willo Davis Roberts. (black Pearl Series-VIII). 1.95 (ISBN 0-445-04516-7). Fawcett Popular Libralry.
Gresham's War. William Crawford. (Orig.). 1968. pap. 0.60 o.p. (R1936, GM). Fawcett World.
Gret, the Story of a Pagan. Beatrice Mantle. 1907. The Century Co.
Greta. Maurice Mallin. LC 70-86902. 1969. 6.95. Delacorte Press.
Gretta. Erskine Caldwell. LC 55-74694. 1955. Little, Brown.
Gretta Alone: Or, The Environments of Life. Elvira Smith. LC 8-8657. Mrs. J. Smith.
Grettir the Outlaw: A Story of Iceland. Sabine Baring-Gould. LC 41-31411. Scribner and Welford.
Grettir's Saga. Tr. by Denton Fox & Herman Palsson. LC 72-90746. (Illus.). 1974. 20.00x (ISBN 0-8020-1925-0); pap. 6.95 (ISBN 0-8020-6165-6). U of Toronto Pr.
Greville Fane see Author of Beltraffio.
Grey Brethren, & Other Fragments in Prose & Verse. facs. ed. Margaret Fairless Barber. LC 75-125202. (Short Story Index Reprint Ser). 1905. 10.00 (ISBN 0-8369-3569-1). Ayer Co.
Grey Buffalo. by chuck stanley. ed. Charles Stanley Strong. LC 64-9158. (Arcadia westerns4). 1963. Arcadia House.
Grey Cloak. Harold MacGrath. LC 3-12290. 1903. The Bobbs-Merrill Company.
Grey Coast. Neil Miller Gunn. LC 77-352709. 1976. 3.50. (ISBN 0-285-62248-X) (ISBN 0-285-62253-6). Souvenir Press.
Grey Coast. Neil Miller Gunn. LC 26-15711. 1926. Little, Brown, and Company.
Grey Cottage. Gertrude McPherson. LC 33-23363. 1933. The Macmillan Company.
Grey Dawn--Red Night. James Lansdale Hodson. LC 30-449120. 1930. Doubleday, Doran and Company, Inc.
Grey Eyes: A Mystery of the Riviera. Katharine Adams. LC 34-5290. 1934. The Macmillan Company.
Grey Face. Arthur Sarsfield Ward. LC 75-46313. (Supernatural and Occult Fiction). 1976. 19.00 (ISBN 0-405-08175-8). Arno Press.
Grey Face. Arthur Sarsfield Ward. LC 24-24142. 1924. Doubleday, Page & Company.
Grey Fish. W. Victor Cook. LC 21-4554. 1920. Frederick A. Stokes Company.
Grey Gander. John Jones Sharon. LC 25-173432. 1925. Duffield & Company.
Grey Ghyll. Anne Rundle. LC 78-19392. 1979. 8.95 (ISBN 0-312-35047-3). St. Martin's Press.
Grey Goose of Arnheim. Leo Heaps. (Illus.). 1976. 8.95 o.p. (ISBN 0-688-03033-5). Morrow.
Grey Granite. James Leslie Mitchell. LC 35-51923. 1935. Doubleday, Doran & Company, Inc.
Grey Guest Chamber... Ella Taylor Disosway. LC 7-36325. Advance Printing House.
Grey Horse Legacy. John Clinton Hunt. LC 68-14884. 1968. Knopf.
Grey Knight. Elizabeth Bonham De La Pasture. LC 8-15880. 1908. E. P. Dutton & Company.
Grey Lady. Hugh Stowell Scott. LC 8-2916. 1895. Macmillan and Co.
Grey Lensman. Edward Elmer Smith. 306p. 1951. 22.50 o.p. (ISBN 0-89366-120-1). Ultramarine Pub.
Grey Maiden. Arthur D. Smith. (Time-Lost). 160p. 1975. pap. 1.25 o.p. (ISBN 0-87818-011-7). Centaur.
Grey Mane of Morning. Joy Chant. 1977. 12.50 (ISBN 0-04-823137-1). Allen Unwin.
Grey Mane of Morning. Joy Chant, pseud. 352p. 1982. pap. 3.50 (ISBN 0-553-22666-5). Bantam.
Grey Mask. Patricia Wentworth. LC 29-707787. 1929. J. B. Lippincott Company.
Grey Mist Murders. Constance Little & Little, Gwenyth. LC 38-11472. 1938. Pub. for the Crime Club, Inc., by Doubleday, Doran & Co., Inc.
Grey Morning" And Other Stories. Frank R Robinson. LC 32-35792. F. R. Robinson.
Grey Ones. John Lymington, pseud. 1970. pap. 0.60 o.p. (60-461). Manor Bks.
Grey Ones-a Sword Above the Night. John Lymington, pseud. 1978. pap. 1.95 (ISBN 0-532-19180-3). Woodhill.
Grey Prince. Jack Vance. LC 74-1902. 1975. (pbk.) 1.25. Avon.
Grey Room. Eden Phillpotts. LC 21-3630. 1931. The Macmillan Company.
Grey Roses. Henry Harland. LC 70-103517. (Short story index reprint series). 1969. Books for Libraries Press.
Grey Seas of Jutland. W. H. Canaway. 1981. 15.00x (Pub. by Ian Henry Pubns England). State Mutual Bk.
Grey Sentinels. Bill Knox. LC 63-8727. 1963. Published for the Crime Club By Doubleday.
Grey Shapes. Jack Mann. 1970. 5.00. Bookfinger.
Grey Sombrero: By Pete Fry Pseud. Clifford King. LC 59-5293. 1958. Roy Publishers.
Grey Studio. Antoinette Quinby Scudder. LC 34-31290. Ruth Hill.
Grey Tower. Donald F. Drummond. 1966. 3.00 o.p. Swallow.
Grey Towers: A Campus Novel. LC 23-11823. 1923. Covici-McGee Co.
Grey Weather: Moorland Tales. of My Own People. John Buchan. 1899. J. Lane.
Grey Wethers: A Romantic Novel. Victoria Mary Sackville-West. LC 23-12117. George H. Doran Company.
Grey Wig. facs. ed. Israel Zangwill. LC 74-85696. (Short Story Index Reprint Ser.). 1903. 24.00 (ISBN 0-8369-3039-8). Ayer Co.
Grey Wig: Stories and Novelettes. Israel Zangwill. LC 3-594046. 1903. The Macmillan Company.
Grey Wolf, Grey Sea. E. B. Gasaway. (War Library). 256p. 1983. pap. 2.75 (ISBN 0-345-30859-X). Ballantine.
Grey Woman, and Other Tales. Elizabeth Cleghorn Stevenson Gaskell. LC 70-163028. (Short story index reprint series). (Illus.). 1971. (ISBN 0-8369-3942-5). Books for Libraries Press.
Greybeard. Brian Wilson Aldiss. 1981. 18.95x (Pub. by Remploy England). State Mutual Bk.
Greyfax Grimwald: Circle of Light, No. 1. Niel Hancock. 1981. pap. 2.95 (ISBN 0-445-08595-9). Fawcett.
Greyflax Grimwald. Niel Hancock. (Circle of Light-1.). (Illus.). 1977. 1.95 (ISBN 0-445-08595-9). Popular Library.
Greyfriars Characters. John Wernham & Mary Cadogan. LC 77-361938. (Charles Hamilton Companion; V. 2). (Illus.). 1976. 3.00 (ISBN 0-905575-00-8). Museum Press.
Greygallows. Barbara Mertz. LC 72-11583. 1973. 10.95 (ISBN 0-8161-6065-1). G. K. Hall.
Greygallows. Barbara Mertz. LC 72-3149. 1972. 6.95 (ISBN 0-396-06635-6). Dodd, Mead.
Greygallows. Barbara Michaels. LC 72-3149. 320p. 1972. 6.95 o.p. (ISBN 0-396-06635-6). Dodd.
Greygallows. Barbara Michaels. 1973. lib. bdg. 10.95 o.p. (ISBN 0-8161-6065-1, Large Print Bks). G K Hall.
Greygallows. Barbara Michaels. 288p. 1974. pap. 1.25 o.p. (P1986, Crest). Fawcett World.
Greyhound in the Leash. Joyce Mary Horner. LC 49-7875. 1949. Doubleday.
Greylake of Mallerby. William Llanwarne Cribb. LC 14-14916. 1914. 1.35. H. Holt and Company.
Greyland. Dave Van Arnam. 1978. pap. 1.50 o.s.i. (ISBN 0-8439-0553-0, Leisure Bks). Nordon Pubns.
Greyling. Daphne Rooke. LC 63-8793. 1963. Reynal.
Greymarsh. Arthur John Rees. LC 27-13597. 1927. Dodd, Mead & Company.
Greymist: A Story Founded on an Actual Episode in Field Trials. by albert f. hochwalt. ed. Albert Frederick Hochwalt. LC 25-17579. C.
Greyslaer, a Romance of Mohawk, 2 Vols. in 1. Charles Fenno Hoffman. Ed. by J. V. Ridgely. LC 77-93627. (American Fiction Ser). 1970. lib. bdg. 23.50 o.s.i. (ISBN 0-512-00336-X). Garrett Pr.
Greyslaer: A Romance of the Mohawk. Charles Fenno Hoffman. LC 73-6209. 1968. Scholarly Press.
Greyslaer: A Romance of the Mohawk. Charles Fenno Hoffman. LC 1-116313. 1840. Harper & Brothers.
Greyslaer: A Romance of the Mohawk. 4th ed. Charles Fenno Hoffman. LC 1-1164. 1849. Baker & Scribner.
Greystone Heritage. Louisa Bronte. LC 76-11803. 1976. 1.50 (ISBN 0-345-25161-X). Ballantine Books.
Greystone Heritage. Louisa Bronte. LC 76-20764. (Greystone Tavern series). 1976. 9.95 (ISBN 0-89340-005-X). J. Curley.
Greystone Tavern. Louisa Bronte. LC 75-23073. 1975. 1.50 (ISBN 0-345-24642-X). Ballantine Books.
Greystone Tavern. Louisa Bronte. LC 76-17613. (Greyston Tavern series). 1976. 9.95 (ISBN 0-89340-000-9). J. Curley.
Greystones. Antonia Lamb. 1974. pap. 0.95 o.p. (ISBN 0-515-03520-3, N3520). Pyramid Pubns.
Greythorn Woman. J. H Brennan. LC 77-82616. 1979. 10.00 (ISBN 0-385-13020-1). Doubleday.

Grid Star. Ralph Cannon. LC 33-305623. 1933. The Reilly & Lee Co.
Gridiron Gambler. David Jackson. 1943. Dorrance and Company.
Grief Before Night. Peter Loring. LC 38-12294. 1938. Macrae-Smith Company.
Grief of the Smiling Irish. Owen Hernan. (Juniper Bks: No. 26). 1978. pap. 3.00. Juniper Pr Wi.
Grierson's Raid. D. Brown. 1972. pap. 1.25 o.p. (01024). Curtis.
Grieselda. Basil King. LC 1-29517. 1900. H. S. Stone and Company.
Grif. Benjamin Leopold Farjeon. LC 6-38637. (Lovell's library. no. 1342). 1889. J. W. Lovell Company.
Griff. Robert Weverka & Larry Cohen. 1973. (pbk.) 0.95. Bantam Books.
Griffins: A Colonial Tale. Mary Stuart Young. LC 4-32151. 1904. The Neale Publishing Company.
Griffin's Way. Frank Yerby. 1976. 1.75. Dell.
Griffith Gaunt. Charles Reade. (On cover: Lovell's library. v. 19, no. 913). 1887. J. W. Lovell Company.
Griffith Gaunt. Charles Reade. LC 42-32086. (Works. Library edition). 1895. Metropolitan Publishing Company.
Griffith Gaunt: Or, Jealousy. Charles Reade. LC 7-39661. 1866. Ticknor and Fields.
Griffith Gaunt: Or, Jealousy. Charles Reade. (On cover: Seaside library. Pocket ed., no. 231). 1884. G. Munro.
Griffith Gaunt: Or, Jealousy. Charles Reade. LC 45-42475. 1869. Fields, Osgood & Co.
Griffon. Stephen Dobyns. LC 76-10213. 96p. 1976. pap. 4.95 (ISBN 0-689-10736-6). Atheneum.
Grifters. James Myers Thompson. LC 64-1203. Regency Books.
Grille Gate. Robert Sproul Carroll. LC 22-12750. R. G. Badger.
Grim Fairy Tales for Adults. Joel Wells. LC 67-19683. (Illus.). 1967. Macmillan.
Grim Game. Sydney Horler. LC 37-1448. 1936. Little, Brown, and Company.
Grim Grow the Lilacs. Marie Freid Rodell. LC 41-22669. H. Holt and Company.
Grim Grow the Lilacs: By Marion Randolph Pseud. Marie Freid Rodell. LC 55-1793. (Murder revisited mystery novel, no. 12). 1955. Macmillan.
Grim Journey. Hoffman Birney. 1934. lib. bdg. 11.95 o.s.i. (ISBN 0-512-00821-3). Garrett Pr.
Grim Journey: The Story of the Adventures of the Emigrating Company Known As the Donner Party, Which in the Year 1846, Crossed the Plains from Independence, Missouri, to California. Wtih an Account of Their Sufferings Upon the Desert of the Great Salt Lake and Their Final Tragic Fate When Many Suffered Death on the Headwaters of the Truckee River in the Sierra Nevada Mountains. The Narrative from the Lips of a Survivor, Mr. Eddy, Late of Illinois, Who Lost Wife and Children by a Horrible Fate, and Who Participated in the Rescue of His Companions of the Migration. Hoffman Birney. LC 34-34549. 1934. Minton, Balch & Co.
Grim Rehearsal. 1st Ed. Ruth Fenisong. LC 50-10572. 1950. Published for the Crime Club by Doubleday.
Grim Smile of the Five Towns. Arnold Bennett. LC 74-5401. (Collected works of Arnold Bennett). 1974. (ISBN 0-518-19108-7). Books for Libraries Press.
Grim Thirteen: Short Stories. Ed. by Frederick Stuart Greene. LC 17-23978. 1917. Dodd, Mead and Company.
Grim Vengeance. Alfred Walter Stewart. LC 29-141054. 1929. Little, Brown, and Company.
Grim Youth. John Held. LC 30-11850. The Vanguard Press.
Grimble and Grimble at Christmas. Clement Freud. (Illus.). 1974. (ISBN 0-14-030673-0). Puffin Books.
Grime & Punishment. Harvey C. Gordon. (Orig.). 1981. pap. 1.95 (ISBN 0-446-90026-5). Warner Bks.
Grimm Death. Dorothy Foster Brown. LC 46-3692. 1946. Smith and Durrell.
Grimm Tales Made Gay. Guy Wetmore Carryl. LC 73-104428. (Illus.). Repr. of 1902 ed. lib. bdg. 14.50x (ISBN 0-8398-0253-6). Irvington.
Grimm's Fairy Tales. Complete Ed. Jakob Ludwig Karl Grimm & Wilhelm Karl Grimm. Tr. by Margaret Hunt & James Sterb. LC 44-40873. 1944. Pantheon Books.
Grimpy Letters: A Series of Letters Written by a Young Girl to Her Old Lady Chum. Mary Dyer Lemon. LC 17-24289. 1917. Indianapolis Book & Stationery Co.
Grimus: A Novel. Salman Rushdie. LC 78-65232. 1979. 10.00 (ISBN 0-87951-093-5). Overlook Press.
Grimus: A Novel. Salman Rushdie. LC 81-18969. 1982. 5.95 (ISBN 0-87951-138-9). Overlook Press.
Grinder Papers. Being the Adventures of Miss Charity Grinder, Wherein Are Detailed Her Numerous Hair-Breadth Escapes and Wonderful Adventures While on a Visit to New York from the Country. Mary Kyle Dallas. LC 6-33180. ("New York weekly" series. no. 7). 1877. G. W. Carleton & Co.
Grinder Papers. Being the Adventures of Miss Charity Grinder, Wherein Are Detailed Her Numerous Hair-Breadth Escapes and Wonderful Adventures While on a Visit to New York from the Country. Mary Kyle Dallas. LC 6-33179. (Street & Smith's select series, no. 74). Street & Smith.
Grinding: A Louisiana Story. Clara Goodyear Boise Bush. LC 21-12083. 1921. 2.00. H. Holt and Company.
Grindle Nightmare. Q. Patrick, pseud. LC 35-13180. 1935. The Hartney Press, Inc.
Gringo. Leonard London Foreman. 1969. pap. 0.50 o.p. (D2137, GM). Fawcett World.
Gringo. Charles G William Gordon. LC 30-257382. 1930. Doubleday, Doran & Company, Inc.
Gringo Bandit. William L Hopson. LC 47-4558. 1947. Phoenix Press.
Gringo Basin. Lewis Brant, pseud. 1973. 4.95. Lenox Hill Pr.
Gringo Cop. David L. Laughlin. 3.95 o.p. Carlton.
Gringo Gold. Dane Coolidge. LC 80-20495. (Series: Gregg Press Western Fiction Series.). 1980-1939. 12.95. Gregg Press.
Gringo Gold: A Story of Joaquin Murieta, the Bandit. Dane Coolidge. 1939. E. P. Dutton & Co., Inc.
Gringo Gun. easy eye ed. Eugene E. Halleran. 1968. pap. 0.60 o.p. (73-737). Lancer.
Gringo Gunfire. Harry Sinclair Drago. LC 42-24285. 1942. The Sun Dial Press.
Gringo Gunfire. A Double D Western. Harry Sinclair Drago. LC 40-33930. 1940. Doubleday, Doran & Co., Inc.
Gringo Guns. Peter Field. LC 35-186. 1935. W. Morrow & Co.
Gringo Killer. Harry Reed. 1971. pap. 0.60 o.p. (ISBN 0-447-73213-7). Lancer.
Gringo Privateer and Island of Desire. Peter Bernard Kyne. LC 31-971248. 1931. Cosmopolitan Book Corporation.
Gringo Yanqui. Hugh C. Stuntz. 192p. (Orig.). 1983. pap. 6.50 (ISBN 0-682-49933-1). Exposition.
Gringos: A Story of the Old California Days in 1849. Bertha Muzzy Sinclair. 1913. Little, Brown, and Company.
Gringos: A Story of the Old California Days in 1849. Bertha Muzzy Sinclair. LC 41-42438. 1913. Grosset & Dunlap.
Gringos: And Other Stories. Michael Rumaker. LC 67-19617. (Evergreen black cat bk., B168). 1968. pap., 1.25. Grove.
Grinmar: A Novel. Nathan Kussy. LC 7-14258. Broadway Publishing Co.
Grinning Ghoul. Luanna Churchill. 1974. 4.95. Lenox Hill Press.
Grinning Pig... Nap Lombard, pseud. 1943. Simon and Schuster.
Grip. Henrietta Eliza Vaughan Stannard. 1896. Stone & Kimball.
Grip of Fear. Maurice Level. LC 12-1800. 1911. M. Kennerley.
Grip of Fear. Rita Ritchie. 176p. (Orig.). 1976. pap. 1.25 (ISBN 0-89041-065-8, 3065). Major Bks.
Grip of Honor: A Story of Paul Jones and the American Revolution. Cyrus Townsend Brady. LC 2496. 1900. C. Scribner's Sons.
Grip of Iron. A Novel. (On cover: Drama series. no. 20). 1896. Street & Smith.
Grips: Or, Efforts to Revive the Host. Morton D Elevitch. LC 73-170613. 1972. 6.95 (ISBN 0-670-35539-9). Grossman Publishers.
Griselda. A Novel. Alice Mangold Diehl. LC 6-36826. (Harper's Franklin square library, no. 515). 1886. Harper & Brothers.
Grisette: A Tale of Paris and New York. Lewis Rosenthal. 1889. J. Delay.
Grishka & the Astronaut. A. Mityayev. 22p. 1981. pap. 1.60 (ISBN 0-8285-2218-9, Pub. by Progress Pubs USSR). Imported Pubns.
Grisly Grisell; or, The Laidly Lady of Whitburn: A Tale of the Wars of the Roses. Charlotte Mary Yonge. LC 9-2223. 1893. Macmillan and Co.
Grist. Edwin Carlile Litsey. Dorrance and Company.
Gristmill: A Novel. George S Caldwell. LC 75-12971. 1975. 6.95 (ISBN 0-8128-1846-6). Stein and Day.
Grit Lawless. Florence Ethel Mills Young. LC 12-22818. 1912. John Lane.
Grito: Or, From the Alamo to San Jacinto; a Novel. Moncure Lyne. 1904. The Neale Publishing Company.
Grizzly. Will Collins. 1976. (pbk.) 1.50. Pyramid Books.
Grizzly King: A Romance of the Wild. James Oliver Curwood. LC 21-20592. 1918. Grosset & Dunlap.
Grizzly Meadows. Frank Chester Robertson. LC 43-735818. 1943. E. P. Dutton & Co., Inc.
Groans and Grins of One Who Survived. Short Stories and Poems. Bruce Weston Munro. LC 7-32277. H. L. McQueen.
Grobo: Or, A Castle in Spain. Edward Harry William Meyerstein. LC 26-6810. George H. Doran Company.
Grocer & the Autumn (Siman wa Khareef) Arabic Novel. Najib Mahfuz. (Arabic.). 5.50x (ISBN 0-86685-162-3). Intl Bk Ctr.
Grooks Five. Piet Hein. 128p. 1973. Softbound 1.45 o.p. (ISBN 0-385-02985-3). Doubleday.
Grooks Four. Piet Hein. Softbound 1.45 o.p. (ISBN 0-385-00659-4). Doubleday.
Groom Lay Dead. George Harmon Coxe. LC 44-4727. 1944. A. A. Knopf.
Groote Park Murder. Freeman Wills Crofts. LC 25-8367. 1925. T. Seltzer.
Groove Bang & Jive Around. Steve Cannon. 1969. pap. 1.95 o.s.i. (OPH-168, Ophelia). Olympia.
Groovy Genius. Jack Siegel, pseud. (Orig.). 1971. pap. 0.95 o.p. (N2442). Pyramid Pubns.
Groovy Genius. Jack Siegel, pseud. 1971. pap. 0.95 o.p. (N2442). Pyramid Pubns.
Grope Carries on: Being the Further Adventures of Albert Grope. Francis Oscar Mann. LC 33-4501. Harcourt, Brace and Company.
Groper. Harold Hunter Armstrong. LC 19-13369. 1919. Boni and Liveright.
Gross Carriage of Justice. Robert L Fish. LC 78-22227. 1979. 7.95 (ISBN 0-385-11474-5). Doubleday.
Gross Intrusion & Other Stories. Steven Berkoff. 1980. 9.95 (ISBN 0-7145-3825-6); pap. 4.95 (ISBN 0-7145-3685-7). Riverrun NY.
Gross-Widow's Tale. Edith Pargeter. LC 68-19033. 1968. Morrow.
Grotesques. Gustave Leopold Van Roosbroeck. LC 30-116. 1929. Living Art.
Grotto. Grace Zaring Stone. LC 51-9445. 1951. Harper.
Grotto of the Formigans. Daniel Da Cruz. 1.95 (ISBN 0-345-29250-2). Ballantine Books, C.
Grotto. 1st Ed. David Wilton Charters. LC 55-12207. 1955. Pageant Press.
Grouch Pills. Ira R Blunk. LC 66-26941. 1967. Dorrance.
Ground Arms!" "Die Waffen Nieder!" A Romance of European War. 7th ed. Bertha Felicie Sophie Kinsky Suttner & Abbott, Alice Asbury, Tr. LC 6-17003. 1906. A. C. McClurg & Co.
Ground Arms!" The Story of a Life. Bertha Felicie Sophie Kinsky Suttner & Abbott, Alice Asbury, Tr. LC 8-25649. 1892. A. C. McClurg & Company.
Ground Mist. Elsie Frances Wilson Mack. LC 46-1781. 1946. Arcadia House, Inc.
Ground Mist. Frances Sarah Moore. LC 46-1781. 1946. Arcadia House, Inc.
Ground-Swell. Mary Hallock Foote. LC 19-15558. 1919. Houghton Mifflin Company.
Ground Swell. Alfred Boller Stanford. LC 23-288022. 1923. D. Appleton and Company.
Grounded. Belle Willey Gue. LC 22-18236. Dorance.
Grounding of Group Six. Julian Thompson. 304p. 1983. pap. 2.50 (ISBN 0-380-83386-7, Flare). Avon.
Groundrush. Greg Barron. LC 81-48277. 13.50 (ISBN 0-394-52214-1). Random House.
Grounds for Indecency. Milton Herbert Gropper & Sherry, Edna. LC 31-14327. The Macaulay Company.
Grounds for Murder. Thomas D. Carroll. pap. 0.60 o.p. Lancer.
Group. Mary Therese McCarthy. LC 63-15316. 1963. Harcourt, Brace & World.
Group Feast. Josephine Saxton. LC 74-171270. (Doubleday science fiction). 1971. 4.95. Doubleday.
Group of Noble Dames. Thomas Hardy. LC 1-20923. 1891. Harper and Brothers.
Group of Noble Dames. Thomas Hardy. LC 24-249885. Harper and Brothers.
Group Portrait with Lady. Heinrich Boll. LC 72-8835. 1973. 7.95 (ISBN 0-07-006423-7). McGraw-Hill.
Group Therapy M.D. Susanne Jaffe. 1975. (pbk.) 1.50. Ace Books.
Grouse Foolish & Other Stories. Harry Vanderweide. (Illus.). 144p. 1979. 7.95 (ISBN 0-89933-006-1). DeLorme Pub.
Grouse Moor Murder. John Alexander Ferguson. LC 34-34430. 1934. Dodd, Mead & Company.
Grove. Burton Bernstein. LC 61-11647. 1961. McGraw-Hill.
Grove of Doom. Walter Brown Gibson. LC 74-86705. (Tempo books, 5320). 1969. 0.60. Grosset & Dunlap.
Grove of Eagles. Winston Graham. 1968. 6.95 o.p. Doubleday.
Grove of Fever Trees. Daphne Rooke. LC 50-6036. 1950. Houghton Mifflin.
Grove of Night. Sara G. Harrell. 192p. 1981. pap. 2.25 (ISBN 0-380-77693-6, 77693). Avon.
Groves of Academe. Mary Therese McCarthy. LC 52-7255. 1952. Harcourt, Brace.
Groves of Academe. Mary Therese McCarthy. (Plume book). 1974. (pbk) 3.95. New American Library.
Groves of Academe. Mary Therese McCarthy. 1981. 2.95 (ISBN 0-380-52522-4). Avon Books.
Groves of Academe. 1st Ed. Mary Therese McCarthy. LC 52-7255. 1952. Harcourt, Brace.
Grow Toward the Sun: By Jeanne Bowman Pseud. Peggy O'More, pseud. LC 56-897417. 1956. Arcadia House.
Grow Young and Die. William O'Farrell. LC 52-6364. 1952. Published for the Crime Club by Doubleday.
Growing Anyway Up. Florence P. Heide. 128p. 1981. pap. 1.50 (ISBN 0-553-20504-8). Bantam.
Growing Pains. Anne Travis Keating. LC 38-9513. The Pyramid Press.
Growing Pains. John Peter Toohey. LC 29-13372. 1929. L. MacVeagh, The Dial Press.
Growing Pains. Paul Villiard. (Illus.). 1970. 6.95 o.p. (711120). Funk & W.
Growing Roots. Cornelia Jessey. LC 47-3709. 1947. Crown Publishers.
Growing Roots. Sussman, Cornelia (Silver) LC 47-3709. 1947. Crown Publishers.
Growing Season. Joy Cowley. LC 77-81785. 1978. 7.95 (ISBN 0-385-04449-6). Doubleday.
Growing Season. Jan Cox Speas. LC 63-16093. 1963. Morrow.
Growing Season. Jan Cox Speas. 1979. 2.25 (ISBN 0-380-44131-4). Avon Books.
Growing Terror. Bertil Martensson. Tr. by Steven T. Murray from Swedish. (Jan Erelius Police Mystery Ser.). Orig. Title: Vaexande Hot. 192p. (Orig.). 1983. pap. cancelled (ISBN 0-940242-02-8). Fjord Pr.
Growing Trees. Ruth Manning-Sanders. LC 31-30609. 1931. W. Morrow & Company.
Growing Up. Catherine Storr. 1975. pap. 2.95 (ISBN 0-09-910640-X, Pub. by Hutchinson). Merrimack Pub Cir.
Growing up. Angela Mackail Thirkell. LC 44-790. 1944. A. A. Knopf.
Growing up. Mary Marvin Heaton Vorse. LC 20-123789. Boni & Liveright.
Growing up At Gold Creek. Melody Zager. 1982. pap. 2.50 (ISBN 0-448-16925-8, Pub. by Tempo). Ace Bks.
Growing up in a Hurry. Winifred Madison. LC 72-11957. (Archway book). 1975. (pbk.) 0.95 (ISBN 0-671-29704-X). Pocket Books.
Growing up in the West. 1st Ed. Elbridge Wilkes Gillenwater. LC 53-11185. 1953. Pageant Press.
Growing up in Tier 3000. Felix C Gotschalk. (Ace Science Fiction Special#5). 1975. (pbk.) 1.25. Ace Books.
Growing up Rich. Anne Bernays. LC 75-11843. 1975. 7.95. Little, Brown.
Growing up Rich. Anne Bernays. 1.95. Ballantine.
Growing up Underground. Jane Alpert. LC 82-62184. 372p. 1983. Repr. pap. 6.95 (ISBN 0-688-01396-1). Quill NY.
Growing Wonder. Hildegarde Dolson. LC 57-5368. 1957. Random House.
Grown-Ups. Catherine Whitcomb. LC 37-3295. 1937. Random House.
Grownups and Lovers. Terrence Lore Smith. LC 77-180111. 1974. 6.95 (ISBN 0-385-00059-6). Doubleday.
Growth. Booth Tarkington. LC 27-27696. 1927. Doubleday, Page & Company.
Growth: A Novel. Margaret Georgina Todd. LC 7-17048. 1907. H. Holt and Company.
Growth of a Man. Mazo De La Roche. LC 38-277024. 1938. Little, Brown and Company.
Growth of the Soil. Knut Hamsun & Worster, William John Alexander, 1882-1929, Tr. LC 21-3287. 1921. A. A. Knopf.
Growth of the Soil. Knut Hamsun & Worster, William John Alexander, 1887-1929, Tr. LC 35-27139. (Half-title: The modern library of the world's best books. 12). 1935. The Modern Library.
Grub-and-Stakers Move a Mountain. large print ed. Alisa Craig. LC 81-5804. 9.95 (ISBN 0-89621-288-2). Thorndike Press.
Grub-and-Stakes Move a Mountain. Alisa Craig. LC 80-2074. 1981. 9.95 (ISBN 0-385-17411-X). Published for the Crime Club by Doubleday.
Grub Street Nights Entertainments. John Collings Squire. LC 24-310973. George H. Doran Company.
Grubstake. E. Hoffmann Price. (Orig.). 1980. pap. 1.95 (ISBN 0-89083-577-2). Zebra.
Grubstake: A Story of Early Mining Days in Nevada, Time--1874. Mark Lawrence Requa. LC 33-5486. 1933. C. Scribner's Sons.
Grubstake Gold. James Beardsley Hendryx. LC 36-181293. 1936. Doubleday, Doran & Company, Inc.
Grubstake Gold. James Beardsley Hendryx. LC 37-20209. 1937. The Sun Dial Press, Inc.
Grudge. Paul Chevalier. LC 80-51901. 13.95 (ISBN 0-312-35190-9). St. Martin's Press.

Grudge. Hubert Hitchens & Dolores Birk Hitchens. LC 63-20952. 1963. Published for the Crime Club by Doubleday.
Grudge. Giles A Lutz. LC 73-17769. 1974. 4.95 (ISBN 0-385-01386-8). Doubleday.
Grudge Fight. John Hale. LC 67-19947. 1967. Prentice-Hall.
Grudge Mountain. Albert Payson Terhune. LC 39-84801. 1939. Harper & Brothers.
Grue of Ice: A Novel. Geoffrey Jenkins. LC 61-137261. 1962. Viking Press.
Grugan's God. Frank Emerson Andrews. LC 54-114737. Muhlenberg Press.
Grummett's Log. Leaves from My Log Book. Flexible Grummett. LC 15-124709. 1835. Carey, Lea & Blanchard.
Gruntos. O. Robert Straumsnes. LC 78-95458. 1971. 3.95 (ISBN 0-8059-1400-5). Dorrance.
Grunty Grunts and Smiley Smile Indoors. Bertha E Feist. LC 20-20552. Henry Altemus Company.
Grushenka. Paul J. Gillette. (Orig.). 1966. pap. 1.95 (ISBN 0-87067-610-5, BH610). Holloway.
Grushenka. pap. 1.95 o.p. (ISBN 0-87056-222-3). Brandon.
Grushenka: Three Times a Woman. rev. ed. Ed. by Brian Kirby. (Illus.). pap. 1.25 o.p. (2007). Brandon.
Gryll Grange. Thomas Love Peacock. LC 7-33753. 1896. Macmillan and Co., Ltd.
Gryphon in Glory. Andre Norton, pseud. 224p. 1983. pap. 2.50 (ISBN 0-345-30950-2, Del Rey). Ballantine.
Guadalcanal. Edwin P. Hoyt. 320p. 1983. pap. 3.25 (ISBN 0-515-07103-X). Jove Pubns.
Guadalupe(or the Strange Shape of Love. Alexander Smith. pap. 1.25 o.p. Brandon.
Guaimi. Genaro Marin. LC 80-67818. 8.95 (ISBN 0-89729-263-4). Ediciones Universal.
Guam Interlude. Albert A Arnhym. LC 71-242. (Illus.). 1968. 5.00. Pageant Press.
Guant Gurley: Or, The Trappers of Umbagog. A Tale of Border Life. 4th thousand. ed. Daniel Pierce Thompson. LC 8-28262. 1860. J. W. Bradley.
Guaranteed to Fade. Aaron Marc Stein. LC 78-6360. 1978. 7.95 (ISBN 0-385-14499-7). Published for the Crime Club by Doubleday.
Guard of Honor. James Gould Cozzens. LC 48-8544. 1948. Harcourt, Brace.
Guard of Timberline. George Washington Ogden. LC 34-2566. 1934. Dodd, Mead & Company.
Guard, Son of Cop. Reginald M Cleveland. 1931. Milton Bradley Company.
Guard Your Daughters: A Novel. Diana Tutton. LC 54-7190. 1954. Macmillan.
Guarded Flame. William Babington Maxwell. LC 6-27707. 1906. D. Appleton and Company.
Guarded Halo. Margaret Bass Pedler. LC 29-10180. 1929. Doubleday, Doran & Company, Inc.
Guarded Heights. Charles Wadsworth Camp. LC 21-7336. 1921. Doubleday, Page & Company.
Guarded Moments. Lynn Fairfax. (Second Chance at Love Ser.: No. 96). 192p. 1983. pap. 1.75 (ISBN 0-515-06860-8). Jove Pubns.
Guarded Room. Joseph Smith Fletcher. LC 32-2878. 1931. E. J. Clode, Inc.
Guarded Room. G. I Whitham. 1921. John Lane.
Guarded Secret: Or, The Hidden Name. by william giles pseud.... ed. Guy Kenneth Whiteside. LC 44-128745. (Red-edge series). 1943. Old Homestead Book Shop.
Guardian. Frederick Orin Bartlett. LC 12-4140. 1.35. Small, Maynard and Company.
Guardian. Mary Ann Gibbs, pseud. 1974. pap. 0.95 o.p. (26578-5-095). Beagle Bks.
Guardian. John T Hough. LC 74-19075. 1975. 6.95 (ISBN 0-316-37393-1). Little, Brown.
Guardian. Thomas F Monteleone. LC 78-20087. (Illus.). 1980. 8.95 (ISBN 0-385-13694-3). Doubleday.
Guardian: A Novel. Sacha Carnegie, pseud. LC 66-24264. 1966. Dodd, Mead.
Guardian Angel. Oliver Wendell Holmes. LC 70-104486. 1970. Literature House.
Guardian Angel. Oliver Wendell Holmes. 1883. Houghton, Mifflin and Company.
Guardian Angel and Other Stories. Margery Latimer. LC 75-157783. (Short story index reprint series). 1971. (ISBN 0-8369-3895-X). Books for Libraries Press.
Guardian Angel and Other Stories. Margery Latimer. LC 32-25733. 1932. H. Smith & R. Haas.
Guardian Angels. Marcel Prevost. LC 14-3900. 1914. 1.25. The Macaulay Company.
Guardian Devil. Monette Cummings. (Orig.). 1981. pap. 1.75 (ISBN 0-8439-8020-6, Tiara Bks). Nordon Pubns.
Guardian of Innocence. Judy Boynton. (Orig.). 1980. pap. 1.25 (ISBN 0-440-11862-X). Dell.
Guardian of the Heart. Caroline Courtney. LC 80-19516. 1980. 11.95 (ISBN 0-8161-3095-7). G. K. Hall.
Guardian of Willow House. Dorothy Daniels. LC 77-3720. 1977. 7.95 (ISBN 0-89340-078-5). J. Curley.
Guardian of Willow House. Dorothy Daniels. 1975. (pbk.) 0.95 (ISBN 0-671-68008-0). Pocket Books.
Guardian Specter. Marc Lovell, pseud. 1977. pap. 1.75 (ISBN 0-532-17166-7). Woodhill.
Guardians. Lynn Abbey. 1982. pap. 2.95 (ISBN 0-441-30589-X, Pub. by Ace Science Fiction). Ace Bks.
Guardians. John Christopher. LC 78-99118. 1970. Macmillan.
Guardians. Kurt Mahr. (Perry Rhodan # 58). (Illus.). 1974. (pbk.) 0.95. Ace.
Guardians. Roger Parkes. LC 73-91143. 1974. 6.95. St. Martin's Press.
Guardians. Harriet Waters Preston & Dodge, Louise. LC 7-30117. 1888. Houghton, Mifflin and Company.
Guardians: A Novel. John Innes Mackintosh Stewart. LC 57-5500. 1957. Norton.
Guardians of the Coral Throne. Jeffrey Lord. (Blade series, 20) (ISBN 0-523-00881-3). Pinnacle Books.
Guardians of the Desert. Tom Gill. LC 33-4731. Farrar & Rinehart, Incorporated.
Guardians of the Sage. Harry Sinclair Drago. LC 32-30638. The Macaulay Company.
Guardians of the Singreale. Calvin Miller. LC 81-47852. (Illus.). 6.95 (ISBN 0-06-250573-4). Harper & Row.
Guardians of the Trail. Jackson Gregory. LC 41-12246. 1941. Dodd, Mead & Company.
Guardians of the Treasure... Herman Cyril McNeile. LC 31-18736. Pub. for the Crime Club, Inc., by Doubleday, Doran & Company, Inc.
Guardians of Time. rev. ed. Poul Anderson. 256p. 1981. pap. 2.95 (ISBN 0-523-48579-4). Pinnacle Bks.
Guardians on the Range. Jesse Edward Grinstead. Dodge Publishing Company.
Guardian's Trust. Mary Andrews Denison. LC 2-19106. 1902. Street & Smith.
Guards. A Novel ... LC 7-154. 1827. Collins and Hannay Etc.
Guardsman of Gor. John Norman. 1981. pap. 2.95 (ISBN 0-87997-664-0, UE 1664). DAW Bks.
Gudrid the Fair: A Tale of the Discovery of America. Maurice Henry Hewlett. LC 18-3837. 1918. 1.25. Dodd, Mead and Company.
Gudrid's Saga: The Norse Settlement in America, a Documentary Novel. Constance H. Frick Irwin. LC 73-89041. (Illus.). 1974. 8.95. St. Martin's Press.
Guelda: A Novel. (On cover: Seaside library. Pocket ed, no. 1186). 1889. G. Munro.
Guenn; a Wave on the Breton Coast. Blanche Willis Howard Von Teuffel. LC 4-151672. 1884. J. R. Osgood and Company.
Guenn: A Wave on the Breton Coast. Blanche Willis Howard Von Teuffel. LC 42-31603. 1887. Ticknor and Company.
Guerilla. Peter McCurtin. (Orig.). 1972. pap. 0.75 o.p. (BT 50248). Belmont-Tower.
Guerilla. Jack Slade, pseud. (Lassiter Ser). 1976. pap. 1.25 (ISBN 0-505-51105-3). Tower Bks.
Guerilla Attack. Jon Hart. LC 80-71035. (Mercenaries Ser.). 128p. 1981. pap. 2.95 (ISBN 0-87754-243-0). Chelsea Hse.
Guerillas. Vidiadhar Surajprasad Naipaul. LC 80-10925. 256p. 1980. pap. 3.95 (ISBN 0-394-74492-6, Vin). Random.
Guermantes Way. Marcel Proust. LC 76-22049. (His Remembrance of things past). 1970. 2.45 (ISBN 0-394-70596-3). Vintage Books.
Guermantes Way. Marcel Proust. Tr. by Scott-Moncrieff, Charles Kenneth. LC 25-9635. (His Remembrance of things past. iii-iv). 1925. T. Seltzer.
Guermantes Way. Marcel Proust. Tr. by Scott-Moncrieff, Charles Kenneth. LC 34-27028. (Half-title: The modern library of the world's best books). 1933. The Modern Library.
Guerndale; an Old Story. Frederic Jesup Stimson. LC 8-15679. 1882. C. Scribner's Sons.
Guernica Night: A Science Fiction Masterwork. Barry N Malzberg. LC 73-22672. 6.95 (ISBN 0-672-51991-7). Bobbs-Merrill.
Guerra. Alfred Neumann. Tr. by Paterson, Huntley. LC 30-9242. 1930. A. A. Knopf.
Guerra En la Cama. new ed. Juan Castellanos. (Pimienta Collection Ser). 160p. (Span.). 1974. pap. 1.00 o.p. (ISBN 0-88473-214-2). Fiesta Pub.
Guerre, Yes Sir! Roch Carrier. Tr. by Sheila Fischman from Fr. (Anansi Fiction Ser.: No. 10). 113p. 1970. 9.95 (ISBN 0-88784-410-3, Pub. by Hse Anansi Pr Canada); pap. 4.95 (ISBN 0-88784-310-7); study guide by Peter Carver 1.00x (ISBN 0-88784-068-X). U of Toronto Pr.
Guerrilla: A Novel. Edward John Moreton Drax Plunkett Dunsany. LC 44-7508. 1944. The Bobbs-Merrill Company.
Guerrilla Chief: Or, A. Romance of War... James Grant. LC 6-448473. H. Long & Brothers.
Guerrilla in the Kitchen. Linda Grimsley. LC 73-82428. 1974. 6.95 (ISBN 0-87140-573-3). Liveright.
Guerrillas. Vidiadhar Surajprasad Naipaul. LC 75-8236. 1975. 7.95 (ISBN 0-394-49898-4). Knopf.
Guerrillas. Vidiadhar Surajprasad Naipaul. LC 80-10925. 1980. 2.95 (ISBN 0-394-74492-6). Vintage Books.
Guess Who's Coming to Kill You. Ellery Queen, pseud. (Orig.). 1968. pap. 0.60 o.p. (73-802). Lancer.
Guess Who's Coming to the White House? Photos. by U.P.I. & Wide World. Jack Douglas. (No. 1). 1968. Fawcett.
Guest and His Going. Percy Howard Newby. 1960. 3.75 o.p. Knopf.
Guest at the Ludlow. Edgar Wilson Nye & James Whitcomb Riley. LC 73-91088. (American humorists series). (Illus.). 1969. Literature House.
Guest at the Ludlow: And Other Stories. Edgar Wilson Nye. LC 7-332757. 1897. The Bowen-Merrill Company.
Guest for the Night. Samuel Joseph Agnon. LC 68-13723. 1968. Schocken Books.
Guest in Paradise. Peggy Gaddis, pseud. LC 54-9907. 1954. Arcadia House.
Guest in the House. 1st Ed. Philip MacDonald. LC 55-5789. 1955. Published for the Crime Club by Doubleday.
Guest of Honor. William Hodge. LC 11-27103. 1911. 1.25. Chapple Publishing Company, Ltd.
Guest of Honour. Nadine Gordimer. LC 78-124317. 1970. 8.95. Viking Press.
Guest of Life. Nelle Margaret Scanlan. LC 39-9825. 1938. Arcadia House.
Guest of Quesnay. Booth Tarkington. 1908. The McClure Company.
Guest of Quesnay. Booth Tarkington. LC 22-14553. 1916. C. Scribner's Sons.
Guest the One-Eyed. Gunnar Gunnarsson. LC 22-4433. 1922. A. A. Knopf.
Guests Arrive. Cecil Roberts. LC 35-4456. 1935. D. Appleton-Century Company, Incorporated.
Guests at the Villa. Alice W. Hesse. 1977. 5.00 o.p. (ISBN 0-682-48691-4, Banner). Exposition.
Guests of Don Lorenzo: A Novel. Robert Pick. LC 50-5639. 1950. Lippincott.
Guests of Fame. Daniel Stern. LC 55-11646. 1955. Ballantine Books.
Guests of Hercules. Charles Norris Williamson & Alice Muriel Livingston Williamson. LC 12-9563. 1912. Doubleday, Page & Company.
Guests of Summer. Paul Milton Fulcher. LC 30-9248. 1930. The Macmillan Company.
Guests of Summer: A Novel. Hilde Abel. LC 51-11014. 1951. Dobbs-Merrill.
Guests of the Nation. Frank O'Connor, pseud. LC 31-23195. 1931. The Macmillan Company.
Guestward Ho. Patrick Dennis & Barbara Hooton. LC 56-5034. 1955. 8.95 o.s.i. (ISBN 0-8149-0086-0). Vanguard.
Guestward Ho! By Barbara C. Hooton, As Indiscreetly Confided to Patrick Dennis Pseud. Barbara C Hooton & Edward Everett Tanner. LC 56-5034. 1956. Vanguard Press.
Guetteur Melancolique. Guillaume Apollinaire. 7.95. French & Eur.
Guid Auld Jock. Albert Glenthorn Mackinnon. LC 19-18839. Frederick A. Stokes Company.
Guide: A Novel. R. K. Narayan. LC 58-783614. 1958. Viking Press.
Guide: A Novel. R. K. Narayan. LC 79-24521. 1980. 3.95 (ISBN 0-14-005453-7). Penguin Books.
Guide of the Desert. Gustave Aimard & St. John, Percy Bolingbroke, 1821-1889, Ed. LC 5-42202. (On cover: Lovell's library, no. 1071). 1887. J. W. Lovell Company.
Guided and Guarded: Or, Some Incidents in the Life of a Minister-Soldier. Joseph S Malone. LC 2-62040. 1901. The Abbey Press.
Guided Hearts. Charles Elmo Robinson. LC 38-1969. Zondervan Publishing House.
Guideroy. Louise De La Ramee. (On cover: Lovell's library, no. 1358). 1889. J. W. Lovell Company.
Guiding Light. John Ruthledge. LC 39-1741. Guiding Light Publishing Co.
Guiding Thread. Beatrice Harraden. LC 16-26775. 1.35. Frederick A. Stokes Company.
Guild Court. A London Story. George Macdonald. (Seaside library. v. 46, no. 938). 1881. G. Munro.
Guild Court: A London Story. George Macdonald. LC 12-18282. 1911. D. McKay.
Guilderoy. A Novel. Louise De La Ramee. LC 6-33326. 1894. The F. M. Lupton Publishing Company.
Guillaume: Alcools. Ed. by Appollinaire & A. E. Pilkington. (French Texts Ser.). 162p. 1970. pap. text ed. 10.00x (ISBN 0-631-00710-5, Pub. by Basil Blackwell). Biblio Dist.
Guillaume D'Orange: Four Twelfth-Century Epics. Tr. by Joan M. Ferrante from Fr. LC 74-4421. (Records of Civilization Ser). 311p. 1974. 22.50x (ISBN 0-231-03809-7). Columbia U Pr.
Guillible's Travels, Etc. Ring Wilmer Lardner. LC 25-10466. 1925. G. Scribner's Sons.
Guillotine. Mark Logan. LC 76-5376. 1977. 10.00 o.p. (ISBN 0-312-35315-4). St Martin.
Guillotine. Christopher Nicole. LC 76-5376. (Illus.). 10.00 (ISBN 0-312-35315-4). St. Martin's Press.
Guillotine. Christopher Nicole. LC 77-352711. (Illus.). 1976. 3.95 (ISBN 0-333-18767-9). Macmillan.
Guillotine Club: And Other Stories. Silas Weir Mitchell. LC 10-24303. 1910. The Century Co.
Guillotine Party and Other Stories. James Thomas Farrell. LC 35-25834. The Vanguard Press.
Guilt. Laszlo Nemeth. 1966. 13.95 (ISBN 0-7206-3845-3). Dufour.
Guilt: A Mystery Story. Henry James Forman. LC 24-7314. Boni & Liveright.
Guilt and Innocence. Marie Sofle Birath Schwartz. Tr. by Borg, Selma & Shipley, Marie Adeliade (Brown) LC 8-206698. 1871. Lee and Shepard.
Guilt Edged. William John Burley. LC 77-180694. 1972. 4.95 (ISBN 0-8027-5247-0). Walker.
Guilt Edged. Lee Thayer. LC 51-13637. (Red badge detective). 1951. Dodd, Mead.
Guilt Is Where You Find It. Lee Thayer. LC 57-5872. (Red badge detective). Dodd, Mead.
Guilt Makers. David Weiss. LC 52-13575. 1953. Rinehart.
Guilt Merchants. Ronald Harwood. LC 70-80333. 1969. 4.95. Holt, Rinehart and Winston.
Guilt of a Killer Town & Massacre Ridge. Lewis B Patten. (Signet Book). 1977. 1.75 (ISBN 0-451-07751-2). New American Library.
Guilt of August Fielding. Helen Tucker. LC 70-149823. 1971. 6.95 (ISBN 0-8128-1379-0). Stein and Day.
Guilt of Michael Pagett. George Hipp, pseud. 224p. (Orig.). 1973. pap. 1.25 o.p. (ISBN 0-532-12193-7). Woodhill.
Guilt of Michael Pagett. George Hipp, pseud. 224p. (Orig.). 1973. pap. 1.25 o.p. (ISBN 0-532-12193-7). Manor Bks.
Guilt with Honor. Jeffrey Ashford, pseud. LC 82-60142. 11.95 (ISBN 0-8027-5476-7). Walker.
Guilt Without Proof. Peter Alding. LC 74-149397. (A McCall suspense novel). 1971. 4.95 (ISBN 0-8415-0100-9). McCall Pub. Co.
Guiltless. Hermann Broch. LC 73-13704. 1974. 8.95 (ISBN 0-316-10894-4). Little, Brown.
Guilty. John William Aretander. LC 16-7139. 1910. Cochrane Publishing Company.
Guilty! Lee Thayer. LC 40-135573. 1940. Dodd, Mead & Company.
Guilty As Charged. Elizabeth Hanley, pseud. (Belmont Tower book). 1.75 (ISBN 0-505-51373-0). Tower Pubns.
Guilty As Hell. Brett Halliday, pseud. 1977. pap. 1.25 (ISBN 0-440-13291-6). Dell.
Guilty As Hell. Brett Halliday. (Mike Shayne mystery). 1975. (pbk.) 0.95 (ISBN 0-440-03291-1). Dell.
Guilty As Hell. John Hopkins. 68p. 1979. 4.95 (ISBN 0-8059-2615-1). Dorrance.
Guilty Bonds. William Le Queux. LC 7-12853. R. F. Fenno & Company.
Guilty Bystander. Wade Miller, pseud. LC 47-2409. 1947. Farrar, Straus and Company.
Guilty; Forgiven-Reclaimed: A Canadian Story from Real Life. Lance Bilton. LC 74-168851. (Toronto reprint library of Canadian prose and poetry). (ISBN 0-8020-7503-7). University of Toronto Press.
Guilty Guns. Lewis B Patten. (Signet book). 1979. 1.50 (ISBN 0-451-08471-3). New American Library.
Guilty Guns. Lewis B Patten. LC 80-27296. 1981. 10.50 (ISBN 0-89340-308-3). J. Curley.
Guilty Head. Romain Gary, pseud. LC 78-92535. 1969. 5.95. World Pub. Co.
Guilty House. Charles Kingston. LC 29-5963. E. P. Dutton & Company, Inc.
Guilty in the Tropics. Edmund S Whitman. LC 37-16367. Sheridan House.
Guilty Lips. Laura Lou Brookman. Grosset & Dunlap.
Guilty Man: Le Coupable. Francois Coppee. Tr. by Davis, Ruth Helen. LC 11-4601. 1.50. G. W. Dillingham Company.
Guilty Ones. George G. Gilman, pseud. (Edge Ser.: No. 31). 1979. pap. 1.95 (ISBN 0-523-42037-4). Pinnacle Bks.
Guilty Ones: A Novel. Dariel Telfer. LC 61-9598. 1961. Simon and Schuster.
Guilty or Not Guilty. A Novel. Amanda Minnie Douglas. (On cover: The idle hour series, no. 2). 1892. The F. M. Lupton Publishing Company.
Guilty: Or, Not Guilty. A Novel. Harriet Maria Gordon Smythies. LC 8-101948. W. B. Cordier & Co.
Guilty or Not Guilty: Or, Dora Elmyr's Worst Enemy. Metta Victoria Fuller Victor. LC 8-32798. (select series. no. 49). 1890. Street & Smith.
Guilty or Not Guilty? Or, Nat Ridley's Great Race Trawck Case. Nat Jr Ridley. LC 26-12838. (His Nat Ridley series--1). 1926. Garden City Publishing Co., Inc.

Guilty Pleasures. Donald Barthelme. LC 74-13193. (Illus.). 1974. 7.95 (ISBN 0-374-16737-0). Farrar, Straus and Giroux.
Guilty River: A Novel. Wilkie Collins. LC 6-26947. (Harper's handy series, no. 105). 1886. Harper & Brothers.
Guilty River: A Novel. Wilkie Collins. LC 6-26946. (On cover: Lovell's library. v. 17, no. 839). 1887. John W. Lovell Company.
Guilty Secret. Margaret Pemberton. LC 78-71180. 1979. 8.95 (ISBN 0-312-35317-0). St. Martin's Press.
Guilty: The Magazine-Gun Tragedy. Roy Norton & Hallowell, William C. LC 4-10077. 1904. Laird & Lee.
Guilty Thing Surprised. Ruth Rendell. LC 79-123706. 1970. 4.50. Published for the Crime Club by Doubleday.
Guilty Thing Surprised. Ruth Rendell. LC 80-25295. 1981. 12.50 (ISBN 0-89340-316-4). J. Curley.
Guilty Tongue. Illus. by Anderson, Alexander. LC 21-175923. The Gen Protestant Epiccopal Sunday School Union.
Guilty Witness. Morris Hershman. (O.s.i.). 1977. pap. 1.50 o.s.i. (AD1654, Award). Univ Pub & Dist.
Guimo. Walter Elwood. LC 15-2843. 1.35. The Reilly & Britton Co.
Guinea Girl: A Melodrama in Three Acts, Together with the Incidental Misuc, Here Presented for the Entertainment of the Curious. Norman Davey. LC 22-8712. George H. Doran Company.
Guinea Gold. Beatrice Ethel Grimshaw. LC 12-28406. 1912. 1.25. Moffat, Yard and Company.
Guinea Pig Turns. Lewis Graham. LC 34-1684. The Macaulay Company.
Guinea Pigs. Ludvik Vaculik. (Writers from the other Europe). 1975. (pbk.) 3.50 (ISBN 0-14-004043-9). Penguin Books.
Guinea Stamp: A Tale of Modern Glasgow. Annie S Swan Smith. 1892. Cranston & Curts.
Guinevere. Sharan Newman. LC 80-21753. 1981. 10.95 (ISBN 0-312-35318-9). St. Martin's Press.
Guinevere. large print ed. Sharan Newman. LC 81-6243. 1981. 14.95 (ISBN 0-8161-3254-2). G.K. Hall.
Guinevere's Lover. Elinor Sutherland Glyn. LC 13-8904. 1913. 1.30. D. Appleton and Company.
Guinever's Gift. Norma Johnston. LC 77-6008. 8.95 (ISBN 0-394-41167-6). Random House.
Guitar Against the Wall. David Gitin. 1972. 4.00 o.p. (ISBN 0-915572-08-7). Panjandrum.
Guity Lover: Or, The Amours of a Southerner. Adolphe Belot. (On cover: Richard K. Fox's sensational series, no. 6). 1892. R. K. Fox.
Gujarati Short Stories. Ed. by Sarala J. Mohan. (Vikas Library of Modern Indian Writing: No. 26). 147p. 1982. text ed. 20.00x (ISBN 0-7069-1962-9, Pub. by Vikas India). Advent NY.
Gulf Between: A Novel. Anna Miller Constantin. LC 12-18015. 1912. The John C. Winston Company.
Gulf Coast Goods. D. Thomas. 1981. pap. 2.25 (ISBN 0-8439-0936-6). Nordon Pubns.
Gulf Coast Run. D. Thomas. 1980. pap. 1.95 (ISBN 0-8439-0828-9). Nordon Pubns.
Gulf Coast Stories. 1st Ed. Erskine Caldwell. LC 56-106344. 1956. Little, Brown.
Gulf. Illus. by Will Mahony. Wellington. A. H. & A. W. Reed. Barry Crump. LC 65-959010. 1965. bds., 2.95. Tri-Ocean.
Gulf of Time. Digby George Gerahty. LC 48-2397. 1948. Macmillan Co.
Gulf Star Forty-Five. Kim Bartlett. 1979. 9.95 (ISBN 0-393-01265-4). Norton.
Gulf Stream. Marie Stanley. LC 30-23440. Coward-McCann, Inc.
Gulf Stream North. 1st ed. garden city. ed. Earl Conrad. LC 54-6787. 1954.
Gulfweed Voices. Michael G. Stevens. LC 78-111030. 1970. price not set o.p. (GP632). Grove.
Gull Against the Wind. J J Gonzalez. LC 76-55682. 1977. 6.95 (ISBN 0-385-12640-9). Doubleday.
Gull Cove Murders. Eli Colter. LC 44-3666. 1944. M. S. Mill Co., Inc.
Gull Number 737. Jean Craighead George. LC 64-16531. 1964. Crowell.
Gullibles Travels. Jill Johnston. (Illus.). 11.95 (ISBN 0-8256-3036-3, Quick Fox); pap. 4.95 (ISBN 0-8256-3025-8). Putnam Pub Group.
Gullibles Travels. Jill Johnston. LC 73-89674. 1974. 11.95 o.p. (ISBN 0-8256-3036-3, 030036, Pub. by Links Bks); pap. 4.95 o.p. (ISBN 0-8256-3025-8, 030025). Quick Fox.
Gullible's Travels, Etc. Ring W Lardner. LC 17-5401. 1.25. The Bobbs-Merrill Company.
Gullible's Travels, Etc. Ring Wilmer Lardner. LC 65-24435. (Chicago in fiction). 1965. University of Chicago Press.
Gullible's Travels: Etc. Introd. by Josephine Herbst. Ring Wilmer Lardner. (Phoenix bk., P252; Chicago in fic). 1967. pap., 1.95. Univ. of Chicago Pr.
Gulliver House. John Leggett. LC 79-827. 1979. 10.95 (ISBN 0-395-27759-0). Houghton Mifflin.
Gulliver Joi: His Three Voyages: Being an Account of His Marvelous Adventures in Kailoo, Hydrogenia and Ejario. Elbert Perce. LC 7-36361. 1851. C. Scribner.
Gulliver of Mars. Edwin Lester Linden Arnold. 1976. lib. bdg. 12.95x (ISBN 0-89968-173-5). Lightyear.
Gulliver Revived see Gulliveriana, No. 4.
Gulliver the Great, and Other Dog Stories. Walter Alden Dyer. LC 72-5906. (Short story index reprint series). (Illus.). 1972. (ISBN 0-8369-4214-0). Books for Libraries Press.
Gulliver the Great: And Other Dog Stories. Walter Alden Dyer. LC 16-176507. 1916. The Century Co.
Gulliveriana. Ed. by Jeanne K. Welcher & George E. Bush. Jonathan Swift. LC 70-18975. (ISBN 0-8201-1131-7). Scholars' Facsimiles & Reprints.
Gulliveriana, No. 1. Incl. Trip to the Moon. Murtagh McDermot. Repr. of 1728 ed; Trip to the Moon. Humphrey Lunatic. Repr. of 1764 ed. LC 73-133329. 220p. 1970. 30.00x (ISBN 0-8201-1084-1). Schol Facsimiles.
Gulliveriana, No. 3: Including Memoirs of the Court of Lilliput (1727) & Travels into Several Remote Nations of the World (1727). LC 72-4431. 480p. Repr. of 1727 ed. 53.00x (ISBN 0-8201-1101-5). Schol Facsimiles.
Gulliveriana, No. 4. Incl. Voyage to Cacklogallinia. Samuel Brunt. Repr. of 1727 ed; Journey to the World Underground. Ludwig Holberg. Repr. of 1742 ed; Kanor. Repr. of 1750 ed; Gulliver Revived. Rudolph E. Raspe. Repr. of 1787 ed; Mammuth, 2 vols. William Thomson. Repr. of 1789 ed. LC 70-18975. 1973. 47.00x (ISBN 0-8201-1122-8). Schol Facsimiles.
Gulliveriana, No. 5: Shorter Imitations of Gulliver's Travels. LC 74-7139. 1974. 47.00x (ISBN 0-8201-1131-7). Schol Facsimiles.
Gulliveriana, No. 6, 3 vols. LC 70-18975. 1104p. 1976. lib. bdg. 130.00x set (ISBN 0-8201-1168-6). Schol Facsimiles.
Gulliver's Secret. Pierre Henrion. LC 75-30764. (Illus.). 1975. 20.00 (ISBN 0-88305-289-X). Norwood Editions.
Gulliver's Travels. Ed. by Robert Bechtold Heilman. 1969. pap. 1.15 o.p. (ISBN 0-394-30922-7). Random.
Gulliver's Travels. Jonathan Swift. LC 65-6528. (Perennial classic). 1965. Harper & Row.
Gulliver's Travels. Jonathan Swift. Ed. by Robert Bechtold Heilman. LC 70-4100. (Modern Library college editions). 1969. (pbk) 1.15. Modern Library.
Gulliver's Travels. Jonathan Swift. Ed. by Paul Digby Lowry Turner. LC 72-21801. (Illus.). 1971. (u.s.) 2.50 (ISBN 0-19-911007-7). Oxford University Press.
Gulliver's Travels. ed., with an introd., by may lamberton becker. ed. Jonathan Swift. Ed. by Becker, May (Lamberton) LC 48-112581. (Rainbow classics). 1948. World Pub. Co.
Gulliver's Travels. Jonathan Swift. (Lowell's library, no. 68). 1883. J. W. Lovell Company.
Gulliver's Travels. Jonathan Swift. LC 3-17905. (Added t.-p.: Library for young people. vol. VI). 1903. P. F. Collier & Son.
Gulliver's Travels. Jonathan Swift. (Everyman's library, ed. by Ernest Rhys. Fiction, no. 60). 1906. J. M. Dent & Co.
Gulliver's Travels. Jonathan Swift. LC 13-2380. Rand, McNally & Company.
Gulliver's Travels. Jonathan Swift. LC 25-21914. 1925. A. A. Knopf.
Gulliver's Travels. Jonathan Swift. LC 33-7684. (The companion classics). W. J. Black, Inc.
Gulliver's Travels. Jonathan Swift. LC 41-13236. (Half-title: Everyman's library, ed. by Ernest Rhys. Fiction. no. 60). 1940. J. M. Dent & Sons, Ltd.
Gulliver's Travels. Jonathan Swift & Bernbaum, Ernest, 1873- Ed. LC 21-929. 1920. Harcourt, Brace and Howe.
Gulliver's Travels. Jonathan Swift & Case, Arthur Ellicott, 1834- Ed. LC 39-1109. 1938. T. Nelson and Sons.
Gulliver's Travels. Jonathan Swift & Warren Chappell. LC 77-2750. 1977. 14.95 (ISBN 0-19-519978-2). Oxford University Press.
Gulliver's Travels. Jonathan Swift & Cole, Herbert, Illus. LC 32-27283. 1931. John Lane.
Gulliver's Travels. Jonathan Swift & Colum, Padraic, Ed. LC 17-30040. 1917. The Macmillan Company.
Gulliver's Travels. Jonathan Swift & Jean Ignace Isidore Gerard Grandville. LC 80-22845. 1980. 37.50 (ISBN 0-915556-06-5). Great Ocean Publishers.
Gulliver's Travels. reconstructed text ed.. ed. Jonathan Swift & Colin McKelvie. LC 77-367008. (Illus.). 1976. 5.25. (ISBN 0-904651-09-6) (ISBN 0-904651-17-7). Appletree Press.
Gulliver's Travels. Jonathan Swift & Price, Martin, 1920- LC 62-21262. (Library of literature, 3). Bobbs-Merrill.
Gulliver's Travels. illustrated by warren hunter. ed. Jonathan Swift & Pulliam, Roy Avron. (Treasure book). 1949. Steck Co.
Gulliver's Travels. Jonathan Swift & Rackham, Arthur, 1867- Illus. (Half-title: Tales for children from many lands, ed. by F. C. Tilney). 1913. J. M. Dent & Sons, Limited.
Gulliver's Travels. Jonathan Swift & Rich, Edwin Gile, 1879- LC 23-2471. Small, Maynard & Company.
Gulliver's Travels. Jonathan Swift & Rich, Edwin Gile, 1870- LC 31-29811. 1931. Houghton Mifflin Company.
Gulliver's Travels. Jonathan Swift & Ross, John Frederic. LC 48-9820. (Rinehart editions, 10). 1948. Rinehart.
Gulliver's Travels. Jonathan Swift & Smith, Wuanita, 1896- Illus. LC 23-27443. (On cover: The Washington square classics). 1923. G. W. Jacobs and Company.
Gulliver's Travels. Jonathan Swift & Taylor, Rupert, 1883- Ed. LC 27-215640. (The modern readers' series). 1927. The Macmillan Company.
Gulliver's Travels. Jonathan Swift & Tweed, Anna, Ed. LC 12-22814. (Half-title: Golden books for children, ed. by C. Johnson) $1.20.). 1912. Doubleday, Page & Company.
Gulliver's Travels. Jonathan Swift & Winter, Milo Kendall, 1888- Illus. (The Windermere series). 1936. Rand McNally & Company.
Gulliver's Travels: A Facsimile Reproduction of a Large-Paper Copy of the First Edition, 1726, Containing the Author's Annotations. Jonathan Swift. LC 76-25231. (Illus.). 1976. 50.00 (ISBN 0-8201-1274-7). Scholars' Facsimiles & Reprints.
Gulliver's Travels: A Tale of a Tub and The Battle of the Books. Jonathan Swift. LC 50-12195. (Modern Library college editions, T32). 1950. Modern Library.
Gulliver's Travels: A Voyage to Lilliput and A Voyage to Brobdingnag. Jonathan Swift. LC 14-19282. Ginn and Company.
Gulliver's Travels: A Voyage to Lilliput, a Voyage to Brobdingnag. Jonathan Swift. LC 30-29338. (stories all children love series). J. B. Lippincott Company.
Gulliver's Travels: A Voyage to Lilliput, a Voyage to Brobdingnag. Jonathan Swift & Kirk, Maria Louise, 1895- Illus. LC 18-19140. (On verso of half-title: "Stories all children love"). 1918. J. B. Lippincott Company.
Gulliver's Travels Among the Little People of Lilliput. Jonathan Swift & Stead, William Thomas, 1849- Ed. LC 8-23523. 1908. The Penn Publishing Company.
Gulliver's Travels: An Account of the Four Voyages into Several Remote Nations of the World. Jonathan Swift & Eichenberg, Fritz, 1901- Illus. LC 40-6732. The Heritage Press.
Gulliver's Travels: An Account of the Four Voyages into Several Remote Regions of the World. Jonathan Swift & Quintanilla, Luis, 1895- Illus. LC 47-11890. 1947. Crown Publishers.
Gulliver's Travels: And Other Works. Jonathan Swift & Morley, Henry, 1822-1894. LC 24-11847. (Library of early novelists. v. 8). 1906. G. Routledge and Sons, Limited.
Gulliver's Travels: Designed and Illustrated by Gobin Stair. Jonathan Swift. LC 57-9951. 1957. Beacon Press.
Gulliver's Travels. Ed. by M. W. & G. Thomas. Illus. by Malvina Cheek. Jonathan Swift. Ed. by Maurice Walton Thomas & Gladys Thomas. (Shorter classics). 1966. bds., 2.50. Ginn.
Gulliver's Travels. I. A Voyage to Lilliput. II. A Voyage to Brobdingnag. Jonathan Swift. LC 8-25635. (On cover: Classics for children). 1886. Ginn & Company.
Gulliver's Travels into Lilliput and Brobdingnag. Jonathan Swift. Dodd, Mead & Company.
Gulliver's Travels into Several Remote Nations of the World. Jonathan Swift. LC 13-225132. 1913. Harper & Brothers.
Gulliver's Travels into Several Remote Nations of the World. Jonathan Swift. LC 40-3036. Pocket Books, Inc.
Gulliver's Travels into Several Remote Nations of the World. Jonathan Swift & Johnson, Clifton, 1865- Ed. (Macmillan's pocket American and English classics). 1904. The Macmillan Company.
Gulliver's Travels into Several Remote Nations of the World... Jonathan Swift & Mitford, John, 1781-1859. LC 8-25638. (Half-title: The works of Dean Swift). 1864. J. B. Lippincott & Co.
Gulliver's Travels into Several Remote Nations of the World. Jonathan Swift & Rackham, Arthur, 1867- Illus. LC 38-194107. 1909. J. M. Dent & Co.
Gulliver's Travels into Several Remote Nations of the World. a new ed. with explanatory notes and a life of the author by john francis waller... ed. Jonathan Swift & Waller, John Francis, 1810-1894, Ed. LC 43-39498. G. Routledge and Sons.
Gulliver's Travels into Several Remote Regions of the World. Jonathan Swift & Balliet, Thomas Minard, 1852- Ed. LC 6324. (On cover: Heath's home and school classics. The Young reader's series, no. 9-19). 1900. D. C. Heath & Co.
Gulliver's Travels into Several Remote Regions of the World. Jonathan Swift & Morten, Thomas, 1836-1866, Illus. LC 43-21295. Cassell & Company, Limited.
Gulliver's Travels into Some Regions of Thw World. Jonathan Swift. LC 8-25632. (Altemus' young people's library). 1896. H. Altemus.
Gulliver's Travels, One see Swiftiana.
Gulliver's Travels (Parts I-IV) Jonathan Swift. Ed. by N. L. Clay. (Guide Novel Ser.). pap. text ed. 4.50x (ISBN 0-435-16871-1). Heinemann Ed.
Gulliver's Travels. The Voyage to Lilliput. Jonathan Swift & Blaisdell, Albert Franklin, 1847- Ed. LC 8-25636. (English classic series, no. 60). Clark & Maynard.
Gulliver's Travels: The Voyages to Lilliput and Brobdingnag. Jonathan Swift. LC 8-25633. (The Riverside literature series. no. 89-90). Houghton, Mifflin and Company.
Gulliver's Travels: The Voyages to Lilliput and Brobdingnag. Jonathan Swift & Gaston, Charles Robert, 1874- Ed. LC 14-16763. (Eclectic English classics). American Book Company.
Gulliver's Travels, Three see Swiftiana.
Gulliver's Travels to Lilliput and Brobdingnag. Jonathan Swift & Mossa, R. G., Illus. LC 32-21206. 1930. Garden City Publishing Co., Inc.
Gulliver's Travels, Two see Swiftiana.
Gulliver's Travels: Voyages to Lilliput and Brobdignag ! Jonathan Swift. LC 8-25634. (Standard literature series no. 13). 1896. University Publishing Company.
Gulliver's Travels: With an Introd. by George Sherburn. Jonathan Swift. LC 50-6160. (Harper's modern classics). 1950. Harper.
Gulliver's Travels: With an Introd. by Maxwell Geismar. Jonathan Swift. LC 57-20930. (Pocket library, PL51). 1957. Pocket Books.
Gulliver's Travels. With an Introd. by Thomas Yoseloff. Jonathan Swift. LC 57-319699. 1957. Fine Editions Press.
Gulliver's Travels. With an Introd. by Thomas Yoseloff. Jonathan Swift. LC 57-3196. 1957. Fine Editions Press.
Gulliver's Travels with the Illustrations of J. J. Grandville. Jonathan Swift. LC 80-22845. (Illus.). 544p. 1981. 25.00 (ISBN 0-915556-09-X); ltd ed. 37.50x (ISBN 0-915556-06-5). Great Ocean.
Gulls Fly Inland. Sylvia Thompson. LC 41-5441. 1941. Little, Brown and Company.
Gulls on the Golf Course. Bob Jones. 64p. 1975. 3.95 o.p. (ISBN 0-8059-2172-9). Dorrance.
Gumbo. George Barlow. LC 80-2557. 96p. 1981. 9.95 (ISBN 0-385-17529-9); pap. 6.95 (ISBN 0-385-17530-2). Doubleday.
Gumbo. Mack Thomas. LC 65-141975. 3.50. Grove.
Gumdrop, Gumdrop, Let Down Your Hair. Jeannie Sakol. LC 77-80769. 1969. 5.95 (ISBN 0-13-371641-4). Prentice-Hall.
Gumption Island, a Fantasy of Coexistence. Felix Morley. LC 56-9761. 1956. Caxton Printers.
Gumption: The Progressions of Newson New. Nathaniel Clark Fowler. LC 5-35794. 1905. Small, Maynard and Company.
Gun. Cecil Scott Forester. 190p. 1978. 6.95 o.p. (ISBN 0-370-00681-X, Pub. by Chatto Bodley Jonathan). Merrimack Pub Cir.
Gun. Cecil Scott Forester. 1962. 4.50 o.p. (ISBN 0-370-00681-X). Dufour.
Gun. Michael T. Kaufman. (O.s.i.). 160p. (Orig.). 1974. pap. 1.25 o.s.i. (AQ1419, Award). Univ Pub & Dist.
Gun. O'Rourke, Frank. LC 51-3965. 1951. Random House.
Gun, a Novel. Cecil Scott Forester. LC 38-21272. 1933. Little, Brown and Company.
Gun and Glory of Granite Hendley. Ned Conquest. LC 70-84367. (DD western). 1969. 4.50. Doubleday.
Gun-Bearer. A Novel. Edward A Robinson & Wall, George A., Joint Author. (choice series, no. 107). (Ledger library, no. 107). 1894. R. Bonner's Sons.
Gun Blast. Steven C Lawrence, pseud. (Belmont Tower Books). 1977. 1.25 (ISBN 0-505-51208-4). Tower Pubns.
Gun-Blaze: A Jim Hatfield Western by Jackson Cole Pseud. Leslie Scott. LC 55-58523. (Pyramid books, 162). 1955. Pyramid Books.

Gun-Boss Reynolds. Charles Morris Martin. LC 39-15598. Greenberg.
Gun Brand. James Beardsley Hendryx. LC 28-368788. 1917. A. L. Burt Company.
Gun-Brand. James Beardsley Hendryx. LC 17-13183. 1917. G. P. Putnam's Sons.
Gun Bulldogger. Eugene Cunningham. LC 39-4285. 1939. Houghton Mifflin Company.
Gun Business. Victor B Miller. (Kojak#8). 1975. (pbk.) 1.25 (ISBN 0-671-78998-8). Pocket Books.
Gun Chore. Lee Floren. 1979. pap. 1.25 (ISBN 0-532-12590-8). Woodhill.
Gun Fanner. Kenneth Perkins. LC 25-7667. The Macaulay Company.
Gun Feud. Edward Beverly Mann. LC 39-27344. 1939. W. Morrow and Company.
Gun Feud at Stampede Valley. Samuel Anthony Peeples. LC 54-37047. (Avon, 596). 1954. Avon Publications.
Gun Feud at Tiedown: Rogues Rendezvous. Nelson Nye. 160p. (Orig.). 1976. pap. 2.25 (ISBN 0-441-30798-1). Ace Bks.
Gun Fighter. Robert Ames Bennett. LC 38-7462. I. Washburn, Inc.
Gun for Billy Hardin. John L. Shelley. 1970. pap. 0.60 o.p. (ISBN 0-446-63335-6, 63-335). Paperback Lib.
Gun for Billy Reo. Charles Hall Thompson. LC 54-8032. (Dell first edition 49). 1955. Dell Pub. Co.
Gun for Billy Reo. Charles Hall Thompson. (3314). 1964. Dell.
Gun for Dinosaur. L. Sprague de Camp. 1969. pap. 0.95 o.p. (0502-09018-095). Curtis.
Gun for Dinosaur, and Other Imaginative Tales. Lyon Sprague De Camp. LC 63-7693. (Doubleday science fiction). 1963. Doubleday.
Gun for Hire. Graham Greene. (pbk.) 1.75 (ISBN 0-671-78965-1). Pocket Books.
Gun for Hire. Jory Sherman. 1978. pap. 1.50 (ISBN 0-89041-212-X, 3212). Major Bks.
Gun for Hire. Jory Sherman. LC 75-21349. 176p. (Orig.). 1975. pap. 1.50 o.p. (ISBN 0-89041-218-9, 3218). Major Bks.
Gun for Inspector West see Give a Man a Gun.
Gun for Johnny Deere. Wayne D Overholser. LC 63-15692. 1963. Macmillan.
Gun for Silver Rose. Roy Hogan. (Shawn Starbuck Western). (Signet Book). 1.50 (ISBN 0-451-07696-6). New American Library.
Gun for Tom Fallon. William MacLeod Raine. 1974. (pbk.) 0.75. Popular Library.
Gun from Migrate Ridge. Chet W. Goodfellow. 1979. 7.95 (ISBN 0-89185-189-5); pap. 2.95 (ISBN 0-89185-190-9). Anthelion Pr.
Gun Gamble. Christian Kassel. (Orig.). 1981. pap. 1.95 (ISBN 0-505-51701-9). Tower Bks.
Gun Garden. Paul Stanton. (50505). 1967. Pocket Bks.
Gun Garden. Paul Stanton. LC 65-18513. (Illus.). 1965. M. S. Mill Co., Distributed by W. Morrow.
Gun Girl. John Weld. LC 32-6430. 1932. R. M. McBride & Company.
Gun Gospel. W. D Hoffman. LC 26-902276. 1926. A. C. McClurg & Co.
Gun Grudge. easy eye ed. Walt Coburn. pap. 0.60 o.p. Lancer.
Gun Hand. Frank O'Rourke. LC 53-9112. 1953. Ballantine Books.
Gun Hand. Frank O'Rourke. LC 53-9112. (Signet brand western). 1974. (pbk.) 0.95. New American Library.
Gun-Handy. Norman A Fox. LC 41-16487. Phoenix Press.
Gun Harvest. Oscar J Friend. LC 27-19190. 1927. A. C. McClurg & Co.
Gun Hawk. Leslie Charles Ernenwein. 1979. pap. 1.50 o.s.i. (ISBN 0-8439-0621-9, Leisure Bks). Nordon Pubns.
Gun Hawk. Edward Earl Repp. LC 36-35992. 1936. Godwin.
Gun-Hawk Valley. easy eye ed. Philip Ketchum. Orig. Title: Desperation Valley. 1969. pap. 0.60 o.p. (73-827). Lancer.
Gun in Daniel Webster's Bust. Margaret Scherf. LC 49-10571. 1949. Pub. for the Crime Club by Doubleday.
Gun in His Hand. Wayne C Lee. LC 64-7394. 1964. Arcadia House.
Gun in His Hand. Victor Rosen. LC 51-25627. (Gold medal book, 154). 1951. Fawcett Publications.
Gun-Johnnies of Texas. W. D. Hoffman. LC 45-121267. 1945. Phoenix Press.
Gun Junction. Barry Cord. (Leisure book). 1979. 1.25 (ISBN 0-8439-0612-X). Nordon Pubns.
Gun Justice. William Hobson. 1974. 4.50. Avalon Books.
Gun Justice. Oscar Schisgall. LC 34-42178. 1933. G. H. Watt.
Gun King of Melted Rocks. Randolph Hale. LC 41-5494. Dodge Publishing Company.
Gun Law at Vermillion. Llewellyn Perry Holmes. 1972. pap. 0.95 o.s.i. (75-347). Lancer.
Gun Law at Vermillion: By Matt Stuart Pseud. 1st Ed. Llewellyn Perry Holmes. LC 51-10941. 1951. Lippincott.
Gun Law in Toledo. Wes Harding. 1977. pap. 1.25 (ISBN 0-532-12516-9). Woodhill.
Gun Legion. C. William Harrison. 1972. pap. 0.60 o.p. (06156). Curtis.
Gun Lobos: By Wade Hamilton Pseud. Lee Floren. LC 52-14400. 1952. Arcadia House.
Gun Lords of Stirrup Basin. Lee Floren. 1977. pap. 1.25 (ISBN 0-532-12526-6). Woodhill.
Gun Luck. Lee Floren. 176p. 1975. pap. 0.95 o.p. (ISBN 0-532-95404-1). Woodhill.
Gun Luck. Lee Floren. 176p. 1975. pap. 0.95 o.p. (ISBN 0-532-95404-1). Manor Bks.
Gun Luck: By Wade Hamilton Pseud. Lee Floren. LC 54-114621. 1954. Arcadia House.
Gun Lust. W. L. Fieldhouse. 208p. (Orig.). 1982. pap. 2.25 (ISBN 0-505-51778-7). Tower Bks.
Gun Magic. George M Johnson. LC 34-65994. E. J. Clode, Inc.
Gun-Maker of Moscow: Or, Vladimir, the Monk; a Tale of the Empire Under Peter, the Great. Sylvanus Cobb. LC 6-20720. (On cover: Cassell's sunshine series, v. 1, no. 15). 1888. Cassell & Company.
Gun Quick. Drake C Denver, pseud. LC 42-141241. 1942. Phoenix Press.
Gun Quick. Drake C. Denver. LC 42-14124. 1942. Phoenix Press.
Gun Quick & the Desert Desperadoes. Nelson Nye. 1978. pap. 1.95 (ISBN 0-89083-399-0). Zebra.
Gun Quick & the Desert Desperados. Nelson Nye. 1981. pap. 2.50 (ISBN 0-89083-798-8). Zebra.
Gun Ranch: By Lynn Westland Pseud. Archie Joscelyn. LC 62-5642. 1962. Arcadia House.
Gun Rich. Giles A Lutz. (Ace Western). 1973. (pbk.) 0.75. Ace.
Gun Run. George G Gilman. (Adam Steele Series#5). 1976. (pbk.) 1.25 (ISBN 0-523-00871-6). Pinnacle Books.
Gun Runner. Arthur John Arbuthnott Stringer. LC 23-7544. The Bobbs-Merrill Company.
Gun-Runner: A Novel. Arthur John Arbuthnott Stringer. LC 9-92521. 1909. B. W. Dodge & Company.
Gun Shy Kid. Barry Cord. 1979. pap. 1.25 o.s.i. (ISBN 0-505-51379-X). Tower Bks.
Gun-Slammer. Lee Floren. 1945. Phoenix Press.
Gun Slinger. Galen C. Colin. LC 47-185924. 1947. Phoenix Press.
Gun-Slinger. George M Johnson. LC 27-20257. 1927. I. Washburn.
Gun Slinger: By Arthur Herbert Pseud. Herbert Arthur, pseud. LC 51-840. 1951. Rinehart.
Gun-Smoke. Dane Coolidge. LC 28-7332. E. P. Dutton & Company.
Gun Smoke. Al P Nelson. LC 35-8473. Phoenix Press.
Gun-Smoke. Nelson Coral Nye. LC 38-9620. Greenberg.
Gun Smoke at Clarion. Amos Moore. LC 37-427220. I. Washburn.
Gun-Smoke Cure. Thomas Ernest Mount. LC 35-381493. 1935. W. Morrow & Company.
Gun-Smoke Cure: By Stone Cody Pseud. Selected, and with an Introd., by Erle Stanley Gardner. Thomas Ernest Mount. LC 58-13136. (Triple-A western classic). 1958. Jefferson House.
Gun-Smoke in Sunset Valley. James Denson Sayers. LC 35-7020. Godwin.
Gun Smoke on the Mesa. Davis Dresser. LC 41-51068. Carlton House.
Gun Smoke Showdown: By Matt Stuart Pseud. 1st Ed. Llewellyn Perry Holmes. LC 50-7697. 1950. Lippincott.
Gun Smoke Yarns. Gene Autry. LC 48-3948. (Dell book). 1948. Dell Pub. Co.
Gun Talk: And Other Stories. Ernest Haycox. LC 56-26712. (Popular library, 728). 1956. Popular Library.
Gun Tamer. Max Brand. LC 29-927002. 1929. Dodd, Mead & Company.
Gun the Man Down. Dudley Dean. (Orig.). 1971. pap. 0.60 o.p. (R2388, GM). Fawcett World.
Gun-Thrower. William L Hopson. LC 40-11752. Phoenix Press.
Gun-Throwers. Steve Frazee. LC 54-44833. (Lion book, 217). 1954. Lion Books.
Gun Thunder on the Rio. James Denson Sayers. LC 35-9292. Godwin.
Gun to Gun. Lee Floren. 1977. pap. 1.25 (ISBN 0-532-12521-5). Woodhill.
Gun-Toter: And Other Stories of the Missouri Hills. MacKinlay Kantor. LC 64-2177. (Signet book). 1963. New American Library.
Gun Trap at Anabella. Ray Hogan. (Signet Book). 1978. 1.50 (ISBN 0-451-07930-2). New American Library.
Gun Trouble. William Frederick Bragg. LC 51-9291. 1950. Phoenix Press.
Gun Trouble. Claude Rister. LC 35-18081. E. J. Clode, Inc.
Gun Trouble in Tonto Basin. Romer Grey. LC 80-20644. 1981. 12.50. J. Curley.
Gun Vote at Valdoro. Richard Poole. 1979. pap. 1.50 o.s.i. (ISBN 0-505-51440-0). Tower Bks.
Gun Vote at Valdoro. Lee E Wells. LC 73-82955. (DD western). 1969. 4.50. Doubleday.
Gun-Whipped. Paul Evan Lehman. 1979. pap. 1.25 o.s.i. (ISBN 0-505-51369-2). Tower Bks.
Gun with the Waiting Notch. Thomas Ernest Mount. LC 33-25369. 1933. W. Morrow & Company.
Gun with the Waiting Notch: By Stone Cody Pseud. Selected and with an Introd. by Erle Stanley Gardner. Thomas Ernest Mount. LC 58-6223. (Triple-A western classic). 1958. Jefferson House.
Gun Wolf. Nelson Nye. 1980. pap. 1.95 (ISBN 0-89083-589-6). Zebra.
Gun Wolves of Lobo Basin. Lee Floren. 1978. pap. 1.25 (ISBN 0-532-12568-1). Woodhill.
Gunbelt. John Benteen. (Leisure Books). 1977. 1.50 (ISBN 0-8439-0494-1). Nordon Pubns.
Gunbelt. Peter McCurtin. (Sundance Ser.: No. 23). 176p. 1982. pap. 2.25 (ISBN 0-8439-1105-0, Leisure Bks). Nordon Pubns.
Gunblaze. Lee Bishop. (Leisure Book). 1978. 1.75. Norton Publications, Inc.
Gundown at Blood Camp. easy eye ed. Jack Riddle. (Orig.). 1968. pap. 0.60 o.p. (73-790). Lancer.
Gunfight at Laramie. Lee Hoffman. 1979. pap. 1.75 (ISBN 0-441-30785-X). Ace Bks.
Gunfight at Laramie. Lee Hoffman. (Ace western). 1974. (pbk.) 0.75. Ace Books.
Gunfight at Powder River. Lawrence Cortesi, pseud. (Orig.). 1980. pap. text ed. 1.95 o.s.i. (ISBN 0-505-51585-7). Tower Bks.
Gunfight at Razor Edge. William Robert Cox. (Orig.). 1970. pap. 0.60 o.p. (63-465). Paperback Lib.
Gunfight at Ringo Junction. Jack Slaoe. 1970. pap. 0.60 o.p. (B60-2011). Belmont-Tower.
Gunfight at the O.K. Corral. Nelson Coral Nye. (Leisure books). 1978. 1.50 (ISBN 0-8439-0548-4). Nordon Pubns.
Gunfight at the O.K. Corral. Nelson Coral Nye. LC 82-14840. (Atlantic large print). 1983. 11.95 (ISBN 0-89340-466-7). J. Curley.
Gunfighter. Martin Ryerson. (O.s.i.). 16p. 1974. pap. 0.95 o.s.i. (AN1286, Award). Univ Pub & Dist.
Gunfighter Breed. Nelson Coral Nye. LC 42-7962. 1942. The Macmillan Company.
Gunfighter Breed & Renegade Cowboy. Nelson Nye. 1978. pap. 1.95 (ISBN 0-89083-403-2). Zebra.
Gunfighter's Choice. Dumas, F. M. 1976. 4.95. Avalon Books.
Gunfighters Pay. William L Hopson. LC 52-14742. 1952. Bouregy & Curl.
Gunfighters Pay. William L Hopson. LC 52-14742. (Avalon Western). 1973. 4.50. Avalon Books.
Gunfighter's Pay. William L. Hopson. (Leisure book). 1978. 1.25 (ISBN 0-8439-0540-9). Nordon Pubns.
Gunfighter's Return. Max Brand. 1979. 7.95 o.p. (ISBN 0-396-07659-9). Dodd.
Gunfighter's Return. Max Brand. (General Ser.). 1980. lib. bdg. 11.95 (ISBN 0-8161-3055-8, Large Print Bks). G K Hall.
Gunfighter's Return. Leslie Charles Ernenwein. LC 51-17380. (Gold medal book, 140). 1950. Fawcett Publications.
Gunfighter's Return. Frederick Faust. LC 79-9814. (Silver star westerns). 1979. 7.95 (ISBN 0-396-07659-9). Dodd, Mead.
Gunfighter's Return. Frederick Faust. LC 79-28628. 1980. 11.95 (ISBN 0-8161-3055-8). G. K. Hall.
Gunfire & Flame. Scott Siegel. (Orig.). 1980. pap. 1.75 (ISBN 0-532-23137-6). Woodhill.
Gunfire at Flintlock. Terrell L. Bowers. (YA) 1981. 6.95 (Avalon). Bouregy.
Gunfire at Purgatory Gate. Martin Ryerson. 1978. pap. 1.50 (ISBN 0-89041-210-3, 3210). Major Bks.
Gunfire at Salt Fork. William L. Hopson. 1978. pap. 1.25 o.s.i. (ISBN 0-8439-0556-5, Leisure Bks). Nordon Pubns.
Gunfire at Salt Fork. William L. Hopson. 1970. pap. 0.60 o.p. (R2287, GM). Fawcett World.
Gunfire at Spanish Rock. J. D. Hardin. LC 81-82968. (J. D. Hardin Western Ser.). 224p. (Orig.). 1982. pap. 1.95 (ISBN 0-86721-002-8). Playboy Pbks.
Gunfire at Timberline. C. E. Parker. 208p. 1982. pap. 2.25 o.s.i. (ISBN 0-8439-1078-X, Leisure Bks). Nordon Pubns.
Gunfire at Wagon Wheel. Ray Humphreys. LC 64-9169. Arcadia House.
Gunflame. Wayne D Overholser. LC 52-10938. 1952. Lippincott.
Gunga Sahib. Talbot Mundy. LC 34-2644. 1934. D. Appleton Company, Incorporated.
Gunhand. Al Cody, pseud. 1967. pap. 0.50 o.p. (50-379). Manor Bks.
Gunhand. Al Cody, pseud. 128p. 1972. pap. 0.60 o.p. (60-496). Manor Bks.
Gunhand. Al Cody, pseud. Incl. Renegade. 256p. 1972. pap. 0.95 o.p. (532-95219-095). Manor Bks.
Gunhand and The Renegade. Archie Joseclyn. (MB double volume). 1972. 0.95. Manor Books.
Gunhandler. John Ringo. 1978. pap. 1.25 (ISBN 0-532-12581-9). Woodhill.
Gunhawk Harvest. 1st Ed. Leslie Charles Ernenwein. LC 50-11161. (Dutton Diamond D western). 1951. Dutton.
Gunhild, a Norwegian-American Episode. Dorothea Frances Canfield Fisher. LC 7-33199. 1907. H. Holt and Company.
Gunlock. Wayne D Overholser. LC 56-9243. 1956. Macmillan.
Gunlock. Wayne D Overholser. 1974. (pbk.) 0.95. Dell.
Gunlock Ranch: A Novel. Frank Hamilton Spearman. LC 35-4420. 1935. Doubleday, Doran & Company, Inc.
Gunmaker of Moscow: A Novel. Sylvanus Cobb. (On cover: The popular series, no. 28). 1892. R. Bonner's Sons.
Gunmaker of Moscow: A Novel. Sylvanus Cobb. 1898. G. W. Dillingham Co.
Gunmaker of Moscow: Or, Vladimir, the Monk. Sylvanus Cobb. LC 6-20721. 1888. R. Bonner's Sons.
Gunman. Archie Joscelyn. LC 53-11883. 1953. Avalon Books.
Gunman Brand. Thomas Thompson. LC 51-13967. (Double D western). 1951. Doubleday.
Gunman, Gunman. Nelson Coral Nye. LC 50-31782. (Western brand books, brand Bar D). Sage Books.
Gunman Rode North. William L Hopson. LC 55-14012. 1954. Avalon Books.
Gunman's Bluff. Edgar Wallace. LC 29-19450. 1929. Pub. for The Crime Club, Inc., by Doubleday, Doran & Company, Inc.
Gunman's Chance. A Double D Western Selection. Frederick Dilley Glidden. LC 41-13942. 1941. Doubleday, Doran & Company, Inc.
Gunman's Chance. A Double D Western Selection. Luke Short. LC 41-13942. 1941. Doubleday, Doran & Company, Inc.
Gunman's Gold. Max Brand. LC 39-232936. 1939. Dodd, Mead & Company.
Gunman's Gold. Max Brand. 1974. (pbk.) 0.95. Warner Paperback Library.
Gunman's Gold. E. R. Slade. (Orig.). 1979. pap. 1.50 (ISBN 0-532-15397-9). Woodhill.
Gunman's Justice. P. A Bechko. LC 73-17768. 1974. 4.95 (ISBN 0-385-01312-4). Doubleday.
Gunman's Legacy. Evan Evans, pseud. 257p. 1976. Repr. of 1949 ed. lib. bdg. 14.65x (ISBN 0-89190-202-3). Am Repr-Rivercity Pr.
Gunman's Legacy. Frederick Faust. LC 76-6898. 1976. 9.95 (ISBN 0-89190-202-3). American Reprint Co.
Gunman's Reckoning. Max Brand. 192p. 1976. 5.95 o.p. (ISBN 0-396-07297-6). Dodd.
Gunman's Reckoning. Frederick Faust. LC 76-8886. (Silver star westerns). 1976. 5.95. Dodd, Mead.
Gunman's Reckoning. Frederick Faust. LC 76-40912. 1976. 11.95 (ISBN 0-8161-6407-X). G. K. Hall.
Gunman's Reckoning. Frederick Faust. (Kangaroo Book). 1978. 1.50. Pocket Books.
Gunmaster: By Ford Pendleton Pseud. Gifford Paul Cheshire. LC 56-38433. (Graphic western, 133). 1956. Graphic Books.
Gunmaster of Saddleback. Dwight Bennett Newton. LC 48-4477. 1948. Phoenix Press.
Gunmen's Feud. Max Brand. LC 81-22042. 1982. 8.95 (ISBN 0-396-08053-7). Dodd, Mead.
Gunmen's Graveyard. Scott Siegel. (Warhunter Ser.: No. 3). 1981. pap. 2.25 (ISBN 0-89083-743-0). Zebra.
Gunn, No. 1: Dawn of Revenge. Jory Sherman. 224p. (Orig.). 1980. pap. 1.95 (ISBN 0-89083-594-2). Zebra.
Gunn, No. 1: Dawn of Revenge. Jory Sherman. (Orig.). pap. 2.25 (ISBN 0-89083-590-X). Zebra.
Gunn, No. 10: Hard Bullets. Jory Sherman. (Orig.). 1981. pap. 2.25 (ISBN 0-89083-896-8). Zebra.
Gunn, No. 11: Trial by Sixgun. Jory Sherman. (Orig.). 1982. pap. 2.25 (ISBN 0-89083-918-2). Zebra.
Gunn, No. 12: The Widowmaker. Jory Sherman. 1982. pap. 2.25 (ISBN 0-89083-987-5). Zebra.
Gunn, No. 13: Arizona Hardcase. Jory Sherman. (Orig.). 1982. pap. 2.25 (ISBN 0-8217-1039-7). Zebra.
Gunn, No. 14: The Buff Runners. Jory Sherman. 1982. pap. 2.25 (ISBN 0-8217-1093-1). Zebra.
Gunn, No. 15: Drygulched. Jory Sherman. 1983. pap. 2.25 (ISBN 0-8217-1142-3). Zebra.
Gunn, No. 16: Wyoming Wanton. Jory Sherman. (Orig.). 1983. pap. 2.25 (ISBN 0-8217-1196-2). Zebra.
Gunn, No. 2: Mexican Showdown. Jory Sherman. 224p. (Orig.). 1980. pap. 1.95 (ISBN 0-89083-628-0). Zebra.
Gunn, No. 3: Death's-Head Trail. Jory Sherman. 240p. (Orig.). 1980. pap. 1.95 (ISBN 0-89083-648-5). Zebra.
Gunn, No. 4: Blood Justice. Jory Sherman. 256p. (Orig.). 1980. pap. 1.95 (ISBN 0-89083-670-1). Zebra.

Gunn, No. 5: Winter Hell. Jory Sherman. 256p. (Orig.). 1981. pap. 1.95 (ISBN 0-89083-708-2). Zebra.
Gunn, No. 6: Duel in Purgatory. Jory Sherman. 1981. pap. 1.95 (ISBN 0-89083-739-2). Zebra.
Gunn, No. 7: Law of the Rope. Jory Sherman. (Orig.). 1981. pap. 2.25 (ISBN 0-89083-766-X). Zebra.
Gunn, No. 8: Apache Arrows. Jory Sherman. 1981. pap. 2.25 (ISBN 0-89083-791-0). Zebra.
Gunn, No. 9: Boothill Bounty. Jory Sherman. (Orig.). 1981. pap. 2.25. Zebra.
Gunnar: A Tale of Norse Life. Hjalmar Hjorth Boyesen. 1874. J. R. Osgood and Company.
Gunnar: A Tale of Norse Life. 10th ed. Hjalmar Hjorth Boyesen. 1908. C. Scribner's Sons.
Gunnar's Daughter. Sigrid Undset & Chater, Arthur G., Tr. LC 36-17119. 1936. A. A. Knopf.
Gunner. William Stevens. LC 68-12547. 1968. Atheneum.
Gunner Cade. Cyril Judd, pseud. LC 52-3697. 1952. Simon and Schuster.
Gunner Cade. Cyril Judd, pseud. LC 67-75170. (Penguin science fiction). 1966. Penguin.
Gunning for Trouble. 1st Ed. Leonard London Foreman. LC 53-6061. (Dutton Diamond D western). 1953. Dutton.
Gunnison. Jim Wilmeht. (Orig.). 1980. pap. text ed. 1.75 (ISBN 0-505-51561-X). Tower Bks.
Gunnysack Castle. Julian Silva. 285p. 1983. 15.95 (ISBN 0-8214-0743-0, 82-85124); pap. 6.95 (ISBN 0-8214-0744-9, 82-85132). Ohio U Pr.
Gunpowder Grass. Lee Floren. 1978. pap. 1.25 (ISBN 0-532-12572-X). Woodhill.
Gunpowder Heritage. George Brydges Rodney. LC 39-31195. 1939. Arcadia House, Inc.
Gunpowder Lightning. Bertrand William Sinclair. LC 30-17509. 1930. Little, Brown, and Company.
Gunpowder Mesa. Lee Floren. 1978. pap. 1.25 (ISBN 0-532-12588-6). Woodhill.
Gunrunners. George Garland. (O.s.i.). Orig. Title: Slow Wind in the West. 1975. pap. 0.95 o.s.i. (BT50852). Belmont-Tower.
Gunrunners. John Murphy. LC 66-195779. 5.95. Macmillan.
Gunrunners. John Murphy. (V2205). 1968. Avon.
Guns. Ed McBain. 1976. 7.95 o.p. (ISBN 0-394-40679-6). Random.
Guns. Ed McBain. 1976. 7.95 o.p. (ISBN 0-394-40679-6). Random.
Guns: A Novel. Evan Hunter. LC 76-12435. 6.95 (ISBN 0-394-40679-6). Random House.
Guns Along the Border. Charles Horace Snow. LC 39-3184. 1939. Macrae-Smith Company.
Guns Along the Pecos. Lee Floren. 1976. 0.95. Belmont Tower.
Guns Along the River. Donald B. Hobart. (Orig.). 1971. pap. 0.60 o.p. (06130). Curtis.
Guns Along the Yellowstone. Harry Sinclair Drago. LC 52-7333. (Silver star westerns). 1952. Dodd, Mead.
Guns at Broken Bow. William Heuman. LC 51-16293. (Gold medal book, 131). 1950. Frwcett Publications.
Guns at Genesis. Wayne C Lee. LC 81-15190. 1982. 11.95 (ISBN 0-89340-405-5). J. Curley.
Guns at Goliad. Roe Richmond. (Lashtrow Ser.: No. 4). 1980. pap. 1.75 (ISBN 0-8439-0796-7). Nordon Pubns.
Guns at Gray Butte. Lewis B Patten. LC 63-11215. (Double D western). 1963. Doubleday.
Guns at Lazy River. Stewart Adams. LC 35-12676. Godwin.
Guns at Twilight. Jonathan Scofield, pseud. (Freedom Fighters Ser.: No. 4). (Orig.). 1981. pap. 2.75 (ISBN 0-440-02919-8). Dell.
Guns for Fort Garryowen. Al Cody. 1975. 4.95. Avalon Books.
Guns for Grizzly Flat: A Powder Valley Western. Peter Field. 1957. Jefferson House.
Guns for Rebellion. Francis Van Wyck Mason. LC 76-42373. 1977. 8.95 (ISBN 0-385-01330-2). Doubleday.
Guns Forever Echo. Kenneth M Ellis. LC 41-17036. J. Messner, Inc.
Guns from Powder Valley. Peter Field. LC 41-425982. 1941. W. Morrow & Company.
Guns from the East. Dick Taylor. 224p. (Orig.). 1982. pap. 2.25 (ISBN 0-505-51824-4). Tower Bks.
Guns from Thunder Mountain. Clair Huffaker. 1975. (pbk.) 1.25 (ISBN 0-671-80083-3). Pocket Books.
Guns in the Forest. Bruce Lancaster. LC 52-5514. (Illus.). 1952. Little, Brown.
Guns in the Saddle: A Powder Valley Western. Peter Field. LC 52-10291. 1952. Jefferson House.
Guns in the Squawtooth. Forrest Raymond Brown. LC 35-215709. Dodge Publishing Company.
Guns of Arizona. Charles N Heckelmann. LC 49-105654. (Double D western). 1949. Doubleday.
Guns of Arrest. Philip McCutchan. LC 76-26654. 1976. 7.95. St. Martin's Press.
Guns of Autumn. Lauran Paine. LC 67-6688. 1967. Arcadia House.
Guns of Avalon. Roger Zelazny. LC 72-76223. (Doubleday science fiction). 1972. 5.95 (ISBN 0-385-08506-0). Doubleday.
Guns of Black Mesa. Claude Rister. LC 33-16355. E. J. Clode, Inc.
Guns of Buck Elder. Jack Ketchum. LC 68-551. 1967. Arcadia House.
Guns of Bull Run. Joseph Alexander Altsheler. 1976. Repr. of 1914 ed. lib. bdg. 17.70x (ISBN 0-88411-942-4). Amereon Ltd.
Guns of Burgoyne. Bruce Lancaster. LC 75-31620. 1975. 9.95 (ISBN 0-89190-881-1). Rivercity Press.
Guns of Burgoyne. Bruce Lancaster. LC 39-272530. 1939. Frederick A. Stokes Company.
Guns of Burgoyne. Bruce Lancaster. 1.95 (ISBN 0-523-00986-0). Pinnacle Books.
Guns of Chickamauga. 1st Ed. Richard O'Connor. LC 55-9238. 1955. Doubleday.
Guns of Darkness. Carter Travis Young. LC 74-9147. 1974. 4.95 (ISBN 0-385-00320-X). Doubleday.
Guns of Dodge City. Thomas Albert Curry. 1972. pap. 0.60 o.p. (06160). Curtis.
Guns of Dorking Hollow: By Max Brand Pseud. Frederick Faust. LC 65-24460. 1965. bds., 3.50. Dodd.
Guns of Dragonard. Rupert Gilchrist. 1982. pap. 2.95 (ISBN 0-553-22612-6). Bantam.
Guns of Ellsworth. Dwight Bennett. LC 72-92234. 192p. 1973. 4.95 o.p. (ISBN 0-385-08352-1). Doubleday.
Guns of Ellsworth. Dwight Bennett Newton. LC 72-92234. 1973. 4.95 (ISBN 0-385-08352-1). Doubleday.
Guns of Europe. Joseph Alexander Altsheler. LC 15-2850. (His World war series). 1915. D. Appleton and Company.
Guns of Folly. Orlando Rigoni. Ed. by Alice Sachs. (OSI). 1971. 3.95 o.s.i. Lenox Hill.
Guns of Fury. Ernest Haycox. 1972. pap. 0.75 o.p. (BT40118). Belmont-Tower.
Guns of Fury. Ernest Haycox. (O.s.i.). 1977. pap. 1.25 o.s.i. (BT51115). Belmont-Tower.
Guns of Galt. Denison Halley Clift. LC 27-43835. E. J. Clode, Inc.
Guns of Ghost Valley. Claude Rister. LC 42-12609. 1942. Dodge Publishing Company.
Guns of Hammer. Barry Cord. 1979. pap. 1.25 o.s.i. (ISBN 0-505-51338-2). Tower Bks.
Guns of Hammer: By Barry Cord Pseud. Peter Germano. LC 56-897282. 1956. Arcadia House.
Guns of Happy Valley. Lee E. Wells. 1973. pap. 0.75 o.p. (07339). Curtis.
Guns of Horse Prairie. Nelson Coral Nye. LC 43-8535. 1943. Phoenix Press.
Guns of Judgment Day. Cliff Farrell. (3338). 1968. Dell.
Guns of Judgment Day. Cliff Farrell. LC 67-21847. (Double D western). 1967. Doubleday.
Guns of Lost Valley. Archie Joscelyn. LC 40-33785. Phoenix Press.
Guns of MacCameron. William L. Hopson. 1971. pap. 0.60 o.p. (60-480). Manor Bks.
Guns of Mazatlan. Lee Parker. (Donovan's Devils Ser.). (O.s.i.). (Orig.). 1975. pap. 1.25 o.s.i. (AQ1398, Award). Univ Pub & Dist.
Guns of Mazatlan. Lee Parker. (Donovan's Devils). (Award adventure novel). 1975. (pbk.) 1.25. Award Books.
Guns of Montana. Lee Floren. 192p. 1981. pap. 1.95 (ISBN 0-8439-0965-X, Leisure Bks). Nordon Pubns.
Guns of Montana: By Brett Austin Pseud. Lee Floren. LC 52-7403. 1952. Arcadia House.
Guns of Morgette. Glenn G Boyer. LC 81-71192. 1982. 11.95 (ISBN 0-8027-4007-3). Walker.
Guns of Navarone. Alistair MacLean. LC 57-5527. 1957. Doubleday.
Guns of Navarrone. Alister MacLean. pap. 0.60 o.p. (105, RE). WSP.
Guns of Palembang. Peter McCurtin. (O.s.i.). 1977. pap. 1.25 o.s.i. (BT51113). Belmont-Tower.
Guns of Pelembang. Peter McCurtin. (Soldier of Fortune Ser.: No. 4). 208p. (Orig.). 1982. pap. 1.95 (ISBN 0-505-51786-8). Tower Bks.
Guns of Powder River. Lee Floren. LC 27-25008. 1947. Phoenix Press.
Guns of Redemption. James Wesley. (YA) 1978. 6.95 (Avalon). Bouregy.
Guns of Rio Conchos. Clair Huffaker. 1975. (pbk.) 1.25 (ISBN 0-671-78896-5). Pocket Books.
Guns of Roaring Fork. William Frederick Bragg. LC 54-7488. 1954. Arcadia House.
Guns of Salvation Valley. Grant Taylor. LC 34-244844. J. B. Lippincott Company.
Guns of Shiloh. Joseph Alexander Altsheler. 1976. Repr. of 1914 ed. lib. bdg. 17.15x (ISBN 0-88411-943-2). Amereon Ltd.
Guns of Silas Jennings. E. R Slade. (Avalon Books). 4.95. Thomas Bouregy.
Guns of Silver Valley. Bradford Scott. LC 37-19456. Dodge Publishing Company.
Guns of Smoky Fork. George Brydges Rodney. LC 39-11566. Phoenix Press.
Guns of Stingaree. Ray Hogan. (Shawn Storbuck Western). 1973. 0.75. New American Library.
Guns of Stingaree see Devil's Gunhand.
Guns of the Big Hills. Donald B. Hobart. 1973. pap. 0.60 o.p. (06109). Curtis.
Guns of the Clan. William L. Hopson. (Orig.). 1971. pap. 0.60 o.p. (06138). Curtis.
Guns of the Gods: A Story of Yasmini's Youth. Talbot Mundy. LC 21-10018. The Bobbs-Merrill Company.
Guns of the Gunfighters. Ed. by Garry James. (Petersen Books Sports & Hobbies Ser.). (Illus.). 1975. pap. 4.95 o.p. (ISBN 0-8227-0095-6). Petersen Pub.
Guns of the Oregon Trail. Eli Albert Chappe. LC 45-8634. 1945. Phoenix Press.
Guns of the Regressive Right: The Only Reconstruction of the Kennedy Assassination That Makes Sense. Morris Allison Bealle. LC 65-484. 1425. pap., 1.00. Columbia Pub. Co.
Guns of the Rimrock. Dwight Bennett Newton. LC 46-1842. 1946. Phoenix Press.
Guns of the Rimrock. Dwight Bennett Newton. LC 46-184265. 1946. Phoenix Press.
Guns of the Round Stone Valley. Vingie Eve Roe. LC 38-249099. M. S. Mill Co., Inc.
Guns of the Sioux. Thomas Albert Curry. (Orig.). 1971. pap. 0.60 o.p. (06143). Curtis.
Guns of the Timberlands. Louis L'Amour. LC 75-26862. 1975. (ISBN 0-8161-6327-8). G. K. Hall.
Guns of Tombstone. John Earl Lewis. (YA) 1981. 6.95 (Avalon). Bouregy.
Guns of Witchwater. Colby Wolford. LC 56-6869. 1956. Dodd, Mead.
Guns of Wyoming. Lee Floren. LC 52-3396. 1952. Arcadia House.
Guns of Wyoming. Lee Floren. 1975. (pbk.) 0.95. Leisure Books.
Guns off Gloucester. Joseph E. Garland. LC 75-21650. (Illus.). 1975. pap. 3.95 (ISBN 0-930352-06-8). Nelson B Robinson.
Guns on the Bitterroot. Archie Joscelyn. LC 55-13568. 1955. Avalon Books.
Guns on the Cimarron. Allan Vaughan Elston. LC 43-9393. 1943. Macrae-Smith-Company.
Guns on the High Mesa. Arthur Henry Gooden. LC 43-51107. 1943. Houghton Mifflin Company.
Guns on the Rio Grande. Robert Ames Bennet. LC 34-434826. 1934. I. Washbun.
Guns Roaring West: A Powder Valley Western. Peter Field. LC 53-101691. 1953. Jefferson House.
Guns to the Far East. V. A Stuart. (Hazard Saga, 7). 1975. (pbk.) 1.25 (ISBN 0-523-00674-8). Pinnacle Books.
Guns up. Ernest Haycox. 1972. pap. 0.75 o.p. (BT40117). Belmont-Tower.
Guns up. Ernest Haycox. (Belmont Tower Books). 1977. 1.25. Tower Publications.
Guns Wanted. John Keith Stanford. LC 50-215. 1949. Scribner.
Gunsharp. William Robert Cox. 160p. 1973. pap. 0.75 o.p. (T2811, GM). Fawcett World.
Gunships, No. 2: Fire Force. Jack H. Teed. 1983. pap. 2.50 (ISBN 0-8217-1159-8). Zebra.
Gunships: The Killing Zone. Jack H. Teed. 1983. pap. 2.50 (ISBN 0-8217-1130-X). Zebra.
Gunshot. Frank Gruber. 1976. (pbk.) 0.95. Avon.
Gunshy Kid: By Barry Cord Pseud. Peter Germano. LC 57-3669. 1957. Arcadia House.
Gunsight. Frank Gruber. LC 42-19433. 1942. Dodd, Mead & Company.
Gunsight Kid. Norman A Fox. LC 41-4549. Phoenix Press.
Gunsight Pass: How Oil Came to the Cattle Country and Brought the West. William MacLeod Raine. LC 21-5078. 1921. 2.00. Houghton Mifflin Company.
Gunsight Ranch. a double d western. ed. Frank Ramsay Adams. LC 39-27572. 1939. Doubleday, Doran & Co., Inc.
Gunsight Ranch. Archie Joscelyn. 1943. Phoenix Press.
Gunsight Range. William Colt MacDonald. LC 49-11282. (Double D Western). 1949. Doubleday.
Gunsight Trail. Alan Le May. LC 31-14412. Farrar & Rinehart, Incorporated.
Gunslammer. Lee Floren. 1976. 0.95. Belmont Tower.
Gunslammer. Alex Hawk, pseud. (Orig.). 1970. pap. 0.60 o.p. (63-331). Paperback Lib.
Gunslammer. Ralph Hayes. (Buffalo Hunter: No. 3). 144p. 1982. pap. 1.75 (ISBN 0-8439-1043-7, Leisure Bks). Nordon Pubns.
Gunslick. Alex Hawk, pseud. (Orig.). 1970. pap. 0.60 o.p. (63-381). Paperback Lib.
Gunslick Mountain. Coral Nye. LC 45-6157. 1945. Arcadia House, Inc.
Gunslinger. Edward Dorn. LC 74-80868. (Cloth ed. 15.00 o.p.). 1975. pap. 5.00 (ISBN 0-914728-05-9). Wingbow Pr.
Gunslinger Justice. Dean W. Ballenger. LC 75-28776. 176p. (Orig.). 1976. pap. 1.50 (ISBN 0-89041-197-2, 3197). Major Bks.
Gunslinger One & Two. Edward Dorn. 1970. 6.50 (ISBN 0-89760-134-3). Telegraph Bks.
Gunsmith No. 1: Macklin's Women. J. R. Roberts. 1982. pap. 1.95 (ISBN 0-441-30856-2). Ace Bks.
Gunsmith, No. 11: One-Handed Gun. J. R. Roberts. 224p. 1982. pap. 2.25 (ISBN 0-441-30866-X, Pub. by Charter Bks). Ace Bks.
Gunsmith, No. 3: The Woman Hunt. J. R. Roberts. (Gunsmith Ser.). (Illus.). 224p. 1982. pap. 2.25 (ISBN 0-441-30858-9, Pub. by Charter Bks). Ace Bks.
Gunsmith, No. 4: The Guns of Abilene. J. R. Roberts. 224p. 1982. pap. 2.25 (ISBN 0-441-30859-7, Pub. by Charter Bks). Ace Bks.
Gunsmith. No. 5: Three Guns for Glory. J. R. Roberts. 224p. 1982. pap. 2.25 (ISBN 0-441-30860-0, Pub. by Charter Bks). Ace Bks.
Gunsmith, No. 6: Leadtown. J. R. Roberts. 208p. (Orig.). 1982. pap. 2.25 (ISBN 0-441-30861-9, Pub. by Charter Bks). Ace Bks.
Gunsmith, No. 7: The Longhorn War. J. R. Roberts. 224p. (Orig.). 1982. pap. 2.25 (ISBN 0-441-30862-7, Pub. by Charter Bks). Ace Bks.
Gunsmith: The Chinese Gunmen. J. R. Roberts. 240p. 1982. pap. 2.25 (ISBN 0-441-30857-0, Pub. by Charter Bks). Ace Bks.
Gunsmoke. Wade Hamilton, pseud. (Leisure Books). 1977. 1.50. Nordon Pubns.
Gunsmoke. Charles Wesley Sanders. LC 32-32420. A. H. King, Inc.
Gunsmoke Bonanza. T. W. Ford. LC 49-636320. 1949. Phoenix Press.
Gunsmoke Bonanza. Charles Morris Martin. LC 53-8571. 1953. Arcadia House.
Gunsmoke Country. Donald B. Hobart. 1970. pap. 0.60 o.p. (06088). Curtis.
Gunsmoke Creek. abr. ed. Jack Bassett. Ed. by Alice Sachs. 1971. Repr. of 1967 ed. 3.95 o.p. Lenox Hill.
Gunsmoke Empire. Jackson Cole. 1973. 0.60. Popular Library.
Gunsmoke for McAllister. Matt Chisholm, pseud. 1971. pap. 0.75 o.p. (94096). Beagle Bks.
Gunsmoke from the Sagebrush. Olivia F. Young. LC 36-30325. Alliance Press.
Gunsmoke Gambler. Wade Hamilton, pseud. 160p. 1981. pap. 1.75 (ISBN 0-8439-1020-8, Leisure Bks). Nordon Pubns.
Gunsmoke Gold: By Tom West Pseud. 1st Ed. Fred East. LC 52-5287. (Dutton Diamond D western). 1952. Dutton.
Gunsmoke Graze. Peter Dawson. 224p. 1980. pap. 1.75 (ISBN 0-553-14179-1). Bantam.
Gunsmoke Graze. Jonathan H Glidden. LC 42-4609. 1942. Dodd, Mead & Company.
Gunsmoke Hacienda: A Novel. Grant Taylor. LC 36-923721. J. B. Lippincott Company.
Gunsmoke Holiday. Lee Floren. 1970. pap. 0.60 o.p. (ISBN 0-447-73892-5). Lancer.
Gunsmoke Holiday. Archie Joscelyn. LC 74-31243. 1975. 4.95 (ISBN 0-517-52117-2). Lenox Hill.
Gunsmoke in Nevada. Burt Arthur, pseud. 1976. pap. 1.25 (ISBN 0-532-12390-5). Woodhill.
Gunsmoke in Nevada: By Burt Arthur. Herbert Arthur, pseud. LC 57-12140. (Signet book, 1443). 1957. New American Library.
Gunsmoke in Paradise. Burt Arthur. 1978. pap. 1.25 o.s.i. (ISBN 0-505-51246-7). Tower Bks.
Gunsmoke in the Hills. Ray Palmer Tracy. LC 40-4507. 1939. Doubleday, Doran & Company, Inc.
Gunsmoke Justice: A Western Novel. Louis Trimble. LC 50-8410. 1950. Macrae Smith.
Gunsmoke Mesa. Dan James. 256p. (YA) 1974. 6.95 (Avalon). Bouregy.
Gunsmoke Mesa. Dan James. (Avalon westerns). 1974. 4.50. Avalon Books.
Gunsmoke Mesa. James D. Sayers. LC 55-14331. 1955. Avalon Books.
Gunsmoke Over Big Muddy. O'Rourke, Frank. LC 52-7151. 1952. Random House.
Gunsmoke Over Sabado. Paul Evan. 256p. (YA) 1974. 6.95 (Avalon). Bouregy.
Gunsmoke Over Sabado. Paul Evan Lehman. LC 55-14128. 1955. Avalon Books.
Gunsmoke Over Utah. Herbert Arthur, pseud. LC 45-3093. 1945. Phoenix Press.
Gunsmoke Over Utah. Herbert Shappiro. LC 45-309342. 1945. Phoenix Press.
Gunsmoke Payoff. T. W. Ford. LC 47-20364. 1946. Phoenix Press.
Gunsmoke Reckoning. Joseph Chadwick. LC 51-22484. (Gold medal book, 149). 1951. Gold Medal Books.
Gunsmoke Trail. Edward Beverly Mann. LC 42-9582. 1942. W. Morrow and Company.
Gunsmoke Trail. Margaret Ogan & George Ogan. 1979. pap. 1.75 (ISBN 0-89041-241-3, 3241). Major Bks.
Gunsmoke Trail. William MacLeod Raine. (pbk.) 0.75. Popular Library.
Gunsmoke Trail: By Barry Cord Pseud. Peter Germano. LC 51-12911. 1951. Phoenix Press.
Gunsmoke: 10 Short Stories Based on the CBS TV Program. Don Ward. LC 57-14674. (Ballantine books, 236). 1957. Ballantine Books.
Gunsong at Twilight. Al Cody, pseud. 192p. 1974. pap. 0.95 (ISBN 0-532-12388-3). Woodhill.
Gunsong at Twilight. Al Cody, pseud. 3.95 o.p. Lenox Hill.

Gunsong at Twilight. Al Cody. 1974. (pbk.) 0.95. Manor Books.

Gunston Cotton: A Romance of Secret Service. Rupert Grayson. LC 36-21650. 1936. E. P. Dutton & Co., Inc.

Gunston Cotton: Adventure. Rupert Grayson. LC 37-740. E. P. Dutton & Co., Inc.

Gunston Cotton in Mexico. Rupert Grayson. 1940. E. P. Dutton & Co., Inc.

Gunston Cotton: Secret Ariman. Rupert Grayson. LC 39-32379. 1939. E. P. Dutton & Co., Inc.

Gunswift. Jack Byrne. LC 41-6689. 1941. Doubleday, Doran & Company, Inc.

Gunswift. Stewart Gordon, pseud. LC 56-13293. 1956. Avalon Books.

Gunswift. Theodore V. Olsen. 1970. pap. 0.60 o.p. (R2286, GM). Fawcett World.

Gunther Heritage. Louisa Bronte. 384p. (Orig.). 1981. pap. 2.75 (ISBN 0-515-04311-7). Jove Pubns.

Guntown. Dan Carew. LC 43-5580. 1943. Phoenix Press.

Gunvote at Valdoro. Richard Poole. 1970. pap. 0.75 o.p. (B75-2067). Belmont-Tower.

Gurnet's Garden: And The New Boy at Southcott. Mary Ruth Baldwin. LC 6-63329. 1887. Phillips & Hunt.

Gurney Married: A Sequel to Gilbert Gurney. Theodore Edward Hook. LC 42-26807. G. Routledge and Sons.

Guru & the Policemen: A Novel. E. S. Modak. 150p. 1982. pap. text ed. 8.95 (Pub. by Vikas India). Advent NY.

Gus Harvey: The Boy Skipper of Cape Ann. Charlton Lyman Smith. LC 20-147064. 1920. Marshall Jones Company.

Gus in Bronze. Alexandra Marshall. LC 77-75017. 1977. 8.95 (ISBN 0-394-41156-0). Knopf.

Gus the Bus and Evelyn: The Exquisite Checker. Jack Lait. LC 17-28075. 1917. Doubleday, Page & Company.

Gus the Great: A Novel. Thomas William Duncan. 1947. J. B. Lippincott Co.

Gus Tomlins. Frank Sheldon Anthony. Ed. by Terry Sturm. (New Zealand Fiction Ser.). 1978. 14.50 o.p. (ISBN 0-19-647951-7). Oxford U Pr.

Gus Tomlins, Together with the Original Stories of "Me and Gus". Frank Sheldon Anthony & Terry Sturm. LC 78-315985. (New Zealand fiction; 11). 1977. 14.50. Auckland University Press.

Gush. Keith Abbott. LC 75-9878. 140p. (Orig.). 1975. 8.95 (ISBN 0-912652-16-0, DynaMite Books); pap. 3.95 (ISBN 0-912652-17-9). Blue Wind.

Gushing. R. W. Rhodes. 1970. 4.50 o.p. Vantage.

Gusliar Wonders. Kirill Vsevolodovich Bulychev. Tr. by Roger DeGaris. 320p. 1983. 16.95 (ISBN 0-02-518010-X). Macmillan.

Gustave Adolf, and the Thirty Years' War. An Historical Novel. Zakarias Topelius & Borg, Selma, Tr. LC 8-29978. (surgeon's stories (cycle 1)). 1872. G. W. Carleton & Co.; Etc., Etc.

Gustave Christian Hanson: Wealthy Swedish Adventurer and Magician. Carl E Hoffman. LC 56-43889. 1956.

Gustave Flaubert: An Introduction by Frank Thomas Marzials, the Translation by George Burnham Ives. Gustave Flaubert & Ives, George Burnham, 1856- Tr. LC 3-26367. 1903. G. P. Putnam's Sons.

Gustave Flaubert: An Introduction by Frank Thomas Marzials; the Translation by George Burnham Ives. Gustave Flaubert & Ives, George Burnham, 1856-1900, Tr. LC 41-27429. (Little French Masterpieces ed. by Alexander Jessup ii). 1909. G. P. Putnam's Sons.

Gustave Flaubert's Madame Bovary: And Three Tales. Arthur Rozen. LC 66-1789. (Monarch notes and study guides, 560-3). 1966. 2.50. Monarch Pr.

Gustavus Lindorm: Or, "Lead Us Not into Temptation.". Emilia Smith Flygare Carlen. Tr. by Perce, Elbert. LC 6-20146. 1853. C. Scribner.

Gutenberg Murders. Gwen Bristow & Manning, Bruce, Pseud., Joint Author. LC 31-137097. 1931. The Mystery League, Inc.

Gutenheim Way: By B. A. Henry Pseud. Henry B Abrahams. LC 57-7691. 1957. T. Yoseloff.

Guthrie of the Times: A Story of Success. Joseph Alexander Altsheler. LC 4-30147. 1904. Doubleday, Page & Company.

Gutter & the Ghetto. Donald Wilkerson & Herm Weiskopf. 1969. 4.95 o.p. (ISBN 0-87680-128-9). Word Bks.

Gutter Gang: By Jay DeBekker Pseud. Prentice Winchell. LC 55-32181. (Beacon book original, no. 107 i. e. 108). 1954. Beacon Publications Corp.

Guttersnipe. Tom Pickard. LC 79-164499. 1971. pap. 2.50 (ISBN 0-87286-071-X). City Lights.

"Guv," a Tale of Midwest Law and Politics. Walter Myers. LC 47-408920. 1947. F. Fell, Inc.

Guy Averall: A Patriotic Sketch. LC 7-2172. 1881. E. Claxton & Company.

Guy De Maupassant. Guy De Maupassant. Tr. by George Burnham Ives. LC 3-26368. (Little French masterpieces... vi). 1903. G. P. Putnam's Sons.

Guy De Maupassant: A Complete Novel, Pierre and Jean, an Essay, and Eleven Short Stories Edited with an Introd. by Francis Steegmuller. Guy De Maupassant. LC 59-4320. (Laurel reader, LC135). 1959. Dell Pub. Co.

Guy Deverell. Joseph Sheridan Le Fanu. LC 76-6015. (Le Fanu, Joseph Sheridan, 1814-1873. Works. 1976). 1976. (3vols.) 54.00 (ISBN 0-405-09255-5). Arno Press.

Guy Fawkes: Or, The Gunpowder Treason. William Harrison Ainsworth. LC 5-426033. G. Routledge and Sons.

Guy Garrick; an Adventure with a Scientific Gunman. Arthur Benjamin Reeve. LC 14-17089. 1914. Hearst's International Library Co.

Guy Gilpatric's Flying Stories. Guy Gilpatric. LC 46-1436. 1946. E. P. Dutton & Company, Inc.

Guy Hamilton; a Story of Our Civil War. Joanna Hooe Mathews. LC 7-17930. The American News Company.

Guy Herndon: Or, A Tale of Gettysburg, A Novel. Helen Margaret Graham. LC 6-27650. 1891. Bankers' and Brokers' Publishing Association.

Guy Hunter: A Novel. William Weldon Stark. LC 8-22563. 1908. Cochrane Publishing Co.

Guy Kenmore's Wife: Or, Her Mother's Secret. Alexander McVeigh Miller. (On cover: Munro's library, v. 1, no. 10). N. L. Munro.

Guy Kenmore's Wife: Or, Her Mother's Secret. Alexander McVeigh Miller. LC 1-30610. (Eagle series, no. 198). 1901. Street & Smith.

Guy Life. Edmee Elizabeth Monica De La Pasture. LC 33-28738. 1933. Harper & Brothers.

Guy Livingstone: Or, "Thorough"... George Alfred Lawrence. 1857. Harper & Brothers.

Guy Livingstone: Or, 'Thorough' George Alfred Lawrence. LC 42-30332. 1867. G. Routledge and Sons.

Guy Mannering. Walter Scott. LC 63-23989. (Nelson classics). T. Nelson.

Guy Mannering. Walter Scott. Ed. by Yonge, Charlotte Mary. LC 8-2936. 1886. Ginn & Company.

Guy Mannering. Walter Scott. LC 17-174378. (Harvard classics shelf of fiction, selected by C. W. Ellot. 4). P. F. Collier & Son.

Guy Mannering. Walter Scott & Yonge, Charlotte Mary. LC 23-17925. Ginn and Company.

Guy Mannering: Or, The Asterologer. Walter Scott. (English Comedie bumaine 1st series, v. 6). 1902. The Century Co.

Guy Mannering: Or, The Astrologer. Walter Scott. (Seaside library. v. 35, no. 723). 1880. G. Munro.

Guy Mannering: Or, The Astrologer. Walter Scott. (On cover: Lovell's library, no. 620). 1885. J. W. Lovell Company.

Guy Mannering: Or, The Astrologer. Walter Scott. Ed. by Case, Eva Warner. LC 19-11153. (Macmillan's pocket American and English classics). 1919. The Macmillan Company.

Guy Mannering; or, The Astrologer... From the Last Rev. Ed., Containing the Author's Final Corrections, Notes, &C. parker's ed. Walter Scott. (Waverley novels: Library ed. v. 2). 1829. Bazin & Ellsworth.

Guy Mervyn. Florence Louisa Charlesworth Barclay. LC 32-342282. 1932. G. P. Putnam's Sons.

Guy Named Joe. Randall M White & Trumbo, Dalton, 1905- 1944. Grosset & Dunlap.

Guy Ormsby: A Romance. Marian Calvert Wilson. LC 8-37093. 1889. C. T. Dillingham.

Guy Renton: A London Story. Alec Waugh. LC 52-12480. 1952. Farrar, Straus and Young.

Guy Rivers: A Tale of Georgia. new and rev. ed. William Gilmore Simms. LC 71-116011. 1970. AMS Press.

Guy Rivers; a Tale of Georgia. new and rev. ed. William Gilmore Simms. LC 22-10825. (Half-title: Border novels and romances of the South). 1856. Redfield.

Guy Rivers: a Tale of Georgia. new and rev. ed. William Gilmore Simms. LC 1-1407. (On cover: Lovell's library, v. 12, no. 690). 1885. J. W. Lovell Company.

Guy Rivers, a Tale of Georgia. new and rev. ed. William Gilmore Simms. LC 44-22014. 1882. A. C. Armstrong & Son.

Guy Tresillian's Fate. A Sequel to "Tresillian Court.". Harriet Lewis. (On cover: The choice series, no. 87). 1893. R. Bonner's Sons.

Guyfford of Weare. Jeffery Farnol. LC 28-20929. 1928. Little, Brown, and Company.

Guys and Dolls. Damon Runyon. LC 50-9056. 1950. Lippincott.

Guys and Dolls. Damon Runyon. LC 31-22138. 1931. Frederick A. Stokes Company.

Guys & Dolls in Uniform. Carl Schubbe. 192p. (Orig.). 1973. pap. 1.95 o.p. (ISBN 0-87682-327-4, 7327). Barclay Hse.

Guys Like Us. Tom Lorenz. LC 80-16371. 1980. 10.95 (ISBN 0-670-35815-0). Viking Press.

Guzman, Go Home: And Other Stories. Alan Sillitoe. LC 71-78687. 1969. 4.95. Doubleday.

Gwen: An Idyll of the Canyon. Charles William Gordon. LC 4-22984. 1904. F. H. Revell Company.

Gwen, in Green. Hugh Zachary. (Fawcett gold medal). 1974. (pbk.) 0.95. Fawcett.

Gwen, the Last Usher, Mediterranean Estates. Charles Webb. 1971. 6.95 o.p. Lippincott.

Gwendeline. Jane Ashford. 1981. pap. 1.75 (ISBN 0-446-94247-2). Warner Bks.

Gwendolen. Clare Darcy. LC 78-58345. 1978. 8.95 (ISBN 0-8027-0605-3). Walker.

Gwendolen. Clare Darcy. LC 79-16505. 1979. 12.95 (ISBN 0-8161-6745-1). G. K. Hall.

Gwenyth. Robin Carol. (Orig.). 1969. pap. 0.60 o.p. (63-175). Paperback Lib.

Gynecologist. Sol Allen. 1969. pap. 0.75 o.p. (T2073). Pyramid Pubns.

Gynga Chief. Johan Carl Cristina Brosball & Jensen, Carl, Tr. LC 31-332183. Dorrance & Company.

Gypsies. Werner Cohn. LC 73-2350. 1973. pap. price not set o.p. (ISBN 0-201-11362-7). A-W.

Gypsies of the Danes' Dike. A Story of Hedge-Side Life in England, in the Year 1855. George Searle Phillips. LC 7-36060. 1864. Ticknor and Fields.

Gypsum Throne. Barbara R. Ely. (Shield Romance Ser.). 1983. pap. 6.95 (ISBN 0-932906-11-7). Pan-Am Publishing Co.

Gypsy. William Budd Trites. LC 28-5563. 1928. Frederick A. Stokes Company.

Gypsy. A Tale. George Payne Rainsford James. (Franklin square library, no. 70). 1879. Harper & Brothers.

Gypsy and Ginger. Eleanor Farjeon. LC 20-17962. E. P. Dutton & Company.

Gypsy, Blood. Margaret Norris. LC 39-24925. 1939. Hillman Curl, Inc.

Gypsy Christ, and Other Tales. William Sharp. LC 71-163047. (Short story index reprint series). 1971. (ISBN 0-8369-3961-1). Books for Libraries Press.

Gypsy Condesa. Goroon Laugliy Hall. LC 58-87236. 1958. Macrae Smith Co.

Gypsy Detective: Or, Always Just in Time. Harlan Page Halsey. (On cover: The calumet series, no. 11). G. Munro.

Gypsy Down the Lane. Thames Ross Williamson. LC 26-9568. Small, Maynard & Company.

Gypsy Earth. George W. Harper. LC 81-43267. (Doubleday Science Fiction.). 1982. 17.95 (ISBN 0-385-17332-6). Doubleday.

Gypsy Fires. Mary Williams & Marianne Harvey. (Orig.). 1981. pap. 2.95 (ISBN 0-440-12860-9). Dell.

Gypsy Flame. Ursula Bloom. 1979. pap. 2.25 (ISBN 0-89041-254-5). Major Bks.

Gypsy Fortune Teller & the Sucker. Frank Armstrong. LC 75-2860. 40p. (Orig.). 1975. pap. 2.75 o.p. (ISBN 0-914184-21-0). Crescent Pubns.

Gypsy Fortune Teller & the Sucker. Frank Armstrong. LC 75-2860. 40p. (Orig.). 1975. pap. 2.75 o.p. (ISBN 0-914184-21-0). Crescent Pubns.

Gypsy from Cadiz. Tamsin Hamilton. LC 77-7619. 8.95 (ISBN 0-698-10785-3). Coward, McCann & Geoghegan.

Gypsy from Cadiz. Tamsin Hamilton. 1978. 1.95 (ISBN 0-441-30876-7). Ace Books.

Gypsy Gift. Joanne Webster. 128p. 1982. 9.95 (ISBN 0-525-66763-6, 0966-290). Lodestar Bks.

Gypsy Girl. Peggy O'More, pseud. LC 53-8573. 1953. Arcadia House.

Gypsy Grove. Mary Kay Simmons. 1974. (pbk.) 1.25. Dell.

Gypsy, Gypsy. Rumer Godden. LC 40-127342. 1940. Little, Brown and Company.

Gypsy, Gypsy. Godden, Rumer. 1976. (pbk.) 1.50 (ISBN 0-380-00569-7). Avon.

Gypsy Heiress. Ed. by Laura London. (Orig.). 1981. pap. 1.50 (ISBN 0-440-12960-5). Dell.

Gypsy in Amber. Martin Cruz Smith. 1973. 1.25. Dell.

Gypsy in Amber. Martin Cruz Smith. LC 79-163416. (Red mask mystery). 1971. 4.95. Putnam.

Gypsy Lad: The Story of a Champion Setter. Sterner St. Paul Meek. LC 34-329363. 1934. W. Morrow & Co.

Gypsy Legacy. Mary Williams. (Orig.). 1982. pap. 2.95 (ISBN 0-440-12990-7). Dell.

Gypsy Lover. Denise Robins. 1972. pap. 0.75 o.p. (94193). Beagle Bks.

Gypsy Moth: A Novel. John F Martin. LC 11-777641. Broadway Publishing Company.

Gypsy Moths. James Drought. LC 64-22902. 1964. Skylight Press.

Gypsy Sixpence. Edison Marshall. LC 49-110821. 1949. Farrar, Straus.

Gypsy Sold Me Heather. Emily Harris. 1976. pap. 2.00 (Pub. by Twowindows Pr). SBD.

Gypsy, the Witch, Pepe, Farinacci and Me. Toni Howard. LC 70-134297. 1971. 5.95. Gambit.

Gypsy Tribe. Zaharia Stancu. LC 72-2147. 1973. 8.95 (ISBN 0-200-71909-2). Abelard-Schuman.

Gypsy Wagon. Armando R. Rodriguez. (Creative Ser: No. 2). 1974. pap. 3.50 (ISBN 0-89551-005-7). UCLA Chicano Stud.

Gypsy Weather. Margaret Bell Houston. LC 35-12765. 1935. D. Appleton-Century Company, Incorporated.

Gypsy's Curse. Robin Carol. (O.s.i.). Date not set. pap. 1.50 o.s.i. (AD1698, Award). Univ Pub & Dist.

Gypsy's Curse. Harry Crews. 1976. 1.75 (ISBN 0-671-80688-2). Pocket Books.

Gypsy's Curse: A Novel. Harry Crews. LC 73-20753. 1974. 5.95 (ISBN 0-394-49196-3). Knopf; Distributed by Random House.

Gyron le Courtois, C. 1501. LC 76-58346. (Arthurian Romances ; 4). 1977. 80.00 (ISBN 0-85967-353-7). Scolar Press.

Gyrth Chalice Mystery. Margery Allingham. 1966. pap. 0.60 o.p. (60-249). Manor Bks.

Gyrth Chalice Mystery. 2nd ed. Margery Allingham. 1974. pap. 0.95 o.p. Manor Bks.

Gyrth Chalice Mystery. Margery Allingham. 1973. (pbk) 0.95. Manor Books.

Gyrth Chalice Mystery: An Albert Campion Detective Story... Margery Allingham. LC 31-8805. Pub. for the Crime Club, Inc., by Doubleday, Doran & Company, Inc.

Gyspy Lady. Shirlee Busbee. 1977. pap. 3.50 (ISBN 0-380-01824-1, 82859-6). Avon.

H

H--Family. Fredrika Bremer. LC 6-17403. 1843. J. Munroe and Company.

H As in Hangman. Lawrence Treat. LC 42-22722. 1942. Duell, Sloan and Pearce.

H As in Hangman. Lawrence Treat. LC 44-4743. 1944. Cornell Publishing Corp.

H As in Hunted. Lawrence Treat. LC 46-6605. 1946. Duell, Sloan and Pearce.

H. C. Of A. A Novel. De Keller Staney. LC 23-1204. 1922. The Roxburgh Publishing Company, Inc.

H. M. Pulham, Esquire. John Phillips Marquand. LC 41-51574. 1941. Little, Brown and Company.

H. M. S. Ulysses. Alistair MacLean. LC 57-104154. (Permabooks, M-4067. Fiction, 7). 1957. Permabooks.

H. M. S. Ulysses. 1st American Ed. Alistair MacLean. LC 56-5441. 1956. Doubleday.

H. R. Edwin Lefevre. LC 15-217851. 1915. Harper & Brothers.

H. R. H. The Man Who Will Be King. Tim Heald & Mayo Mohs. 1980. pap. 2.95 (ISBN 0-425-05206-0). Berkley Pub.

H. Rider Haggard's King Solomon's Mines, the Tale of a Fabulous Treasure Hunt: The Story of the MGM Motion Picture... Jean Francis Webb & Henry Rider Haggard. LC 50-12086. (Dell book, 433). 1950. Dell Pub. Co.

Ha-Abot We-Ha-Banim. Shalom Jacob Abramowitz. (Heb). 10.00 o.p. AMS Pr.

Ha-Ha. Jennifer Dawson. LC 61-14544. 1961. Little, Brown.

Haakon. C. F. Griffin. 1979. pap. 2.50 (ISBN 0-380-43745-7, 43745). Avon.

Haakon: A Novel. C F Griffin. LC 77-26043. 9.95 (ISBN 0-690-01703-0). Crowell.

Haas Sisters of Franklin Street. Frances B. Rothmann. (Illus.). 83p. 1979. pap. 8.95. Magnes Mus.

Hab Theory. Allan W. Eckert. 1977. pap. 2.95 (ISBN 0-445-08597-5). Popular Lib.

HAB Theory: A Novel. Allan W Eckert. LC 75-30880. 9.95 (ISBN 0-316-20859-0). Little, Brown.

Habeas Corpus, and Other Stories. 1st Ed. Green, Peter, pseud. LC 63-7244. 1963. World Pub. Co.

Habermeister: A Tale of the Bavarian Mountains. Hermann Theodor Von Schmid. 1869. Leypoldt & Holt.

Habit: And Other Short Stories. Darryl Francis Zanuck. LC 23-7835. 1923. Times-Mirror Press.

Habit of Loving. Doris May Lessing. LC 58-9187. Crowell.

Habit of Loving. Doris May Lessing. 1973. (pbk.) 0.95. Popular Lib.

Habit of Loving. Doris May Lessing. 1976. 1.75. Popular Library.

Habit of Loving. June Thomson. LC 78-4792. 1979. 7.95 (ISBN 0-385-14302-8). Published for the Crime Club by Doubleday.

Habitant-Merchant. James Edward Le Rossignol. LC 70-167461. (Short story index reprint series). (Illus.). 1971. (ISBN 0-8369-3987-5). Books for Libraries Press.

Habitant of Dusk. August William Derleth. 1.00 o.p. Arkham.

Habitation Saint Ybars. Alfred Mercier. (Novels by Franco-Americans in New England 1850-1940 Ser.). 343p. (Fr.). (gr. 10 up). pap. text ed. 5.50 (ISBN 0-911409-22-X). Natl Mat Dev.
Habits of Command. Joseph Rosner. LC 74-22406. 1975. 7.95 (ISBN 0-15-138330-8). Harcourt Brace Jovanovich.
Hacey Miller: a Novel. James Sherburne. LC 72-135860. 1971. 6.95 (ISBN 0-395-12106-X). Houghton Mifflin.
Hacienda. Katherine Anne Porter. LC 35-1970. Harrison of Paris.
Hacienda on the Hill: A Novel. Richard Henry Savage. (On cover: The welcome series, no. 45). 1899. The Home Publishing Company.
Hacienda. Translated from the Spanish by Tita Caistor. Martinez Bilbao, Oscar. LC 60-3457. 1960. pap., 2.00. Meador Pub. Co.
Hack. Wilfrid Sheed. LC 63-16129. 1963. Macmillan.
Hack. Wilfrid Sheed. LC 80-11284. 1980. 2.95 (ISBN 0-394-74534-5). Vintage Books.
Hackberry Cavalier: Being a Chronicle of the More Outstanding Adventures in Love and Life of That Bucolic Lothario, That Robin Hood of the Post Oak Woods, That Elegant Gentleman and Great Spirit: Edgar Selfridge, et Cronies. George Sessions Perry. LC 44-1892. 1944. The Viking Press.
Hackenfeller's Ape. Brigid Brophy. LC 54-8221. 1954. Random House.
Hackney Jade & the War Horse. Fritz W. Faiss. LC 76-15322. (Illus.). 64p. 1977. ltd. ed. signed 18.50x (ISBN 0-916678-00-8); hand-colored, signed ltd. ed. 200.00x (ISBN 0-916678-01-6). Green Hut.
Haco the Dreamer. A Tale of Scotch University Life. William Sime. (On cover: Seaside library. Pocket ed. no. 597). 1885. G. Munro.
Had She Foreseen... Dora Delmar. (On cover: Laurel library. no. 14). 1893. G. Munro's Sons.
Hadassah: Or, Esther, Queen to Ahasuerus. Margaret S Black. LC 6-12420. Laird & Lee.
Hadasseh: Or, "From Captivity to the Persian Throne.". E. Leuty Collins. 1891. Cassell Publishing Company.
Hadden Sisters. Sydney Thompson. LC 53-8365. 1953. Abelard Press.
Hadidan Aharam. Mohammed Mrabet & Paul Frederic Bowles. LC 76-361125. (Sparrow; 37). 1975. 0.75. Black Sparrow Press.
Hadji & Coco. Baron De Graulchier. 3.75 o.p. Vantage.
Hadji Murad, and Other Stories. Lev Nikolaevich Tolstoi & Wright, Charles Theodore Hagberg, 1862- Ed. LC 12-180193. 1912. T. Nelson and Sons.
Hadji Murad, by Leo Tolstoy... Lev Nikolaevich Tolstoi & Maude, Aylmer, 1858- Tr. 1912. Dodd, Mead and Company.
Hadji Murat: A Tale of the Caucasus. Tr. by W. G. Carey. Lev Nikolaevich Tolstoi. LC 63-6092. 1965. 3.50. Heinemann.
Hadji Murat: A Tale of the Cucasus. Lev Nikolaevich Tolstoi. LC 65-25923. 1965. McGraw-Hill.
Hadley: The Story of the First Mrs. Hemingway. Alice H. Sokoloff. LC 72-11253. (Illus.). 208p. 1973. 6.95 o.p. (ISBN 0-396-06768-9). Dodd.
Hadon of Ancient Opar. Philip Jose Farmer. (Science Fiction Ser.). 1981. pap. 2.50 o.p. (ISBN 0-87997-637-3, UE 1637). DAW Bks.
Hadon of Ancient Opar. Philip Jose Farmer. 1974. (pbk.) 1.25. DAW Books.
Hadrian Ransom. Allan Duane. LC 78-24411. 9.95. Putnam.
Hadrian Seventh. Peter Luke. 1968. 4.95 o.p. Knopf.
Hadrian, the Seventh. Baron Corvo. 1977. pap. 4.00 (ISBN 0-486-22323-X). Dover.
Hadrian the Seventh. Frederick B. Corvo. LC 69-19728. 1969. pap. 3.00 o.p. (ISBN 0-486-22323-X). Dover.
Hadrian the Seventh. Frederick William Rolfe. LC 69-19728. (Illus.). 1969. 2.00. Dover Publications.
Hadrian the Seventh. Frederick William Rolfe. LC 25-187722. (Half-title: Blue jude library). 1925. A. A. Knopf.
Hadrian the Seventh: By Frederick Baron Corvo Pseud. With an Introd. by Herbert Weinstock. Frederick William Rolfe. LC 52-14791. 1953. Knopf.
Haelstrom Manor. easy eye ed. S. J. Treibick. pap. 0.60 o.p. Lancer.
Haexringarna see Witches' Circles.
Hafto. Neva M Hageman. LC 28-22664. The Democrat Publishing Co.
Hag of the Dribble: And Other True Ghosts from the Files of Elliott O'Donnell. Ed. by Bernhardt J. Hurwood. LC 71-107014. 1971. 7.50 o.p. (ISBN 0-8008-3810-6). Taplinger.
Hagar. Mary Johnston. LC 13-22753. 1913. Houghton Mifflin Company.
Hagar. Ben Pinchot. LC 52-11741. 1952. Farrar, Straus and Young.
Hagar: A Novel. Lois T Henderson. LC 77-90118. 7.95 (ISBN 0-915684-29-2). Christian Herald Books.
Hagar: A Novel. Lois T Henderson. LC 82-48398. 1983. 6.68 (ISBN 0-06-063861-3). Harper & Row.
Hagar: A Novel. James Arthur MacKnight. LC 7-19979. Belford, Clarke & Co.
Hagar, a Story of to-Day. Alice Cary. LC 41-34784. 1852. Redfield.
Hagar Lot: Or, The Fate of the Poor Girl. Pierce Egan. (Seaside library, v. 58, no. 1180). 1882. G. Munro.
Hagar of the Pawn-Shop. Fergus Hume. LC 99-5083. 1899. F. M. Buckles & Company; Etc., Etc.
Hagar Revelly. Daniel Carson Goodman. LC 13-105365. 1913. 1.35. M. Kennerley.
Hagar the Horrible. Dik Brown. 128p. 1983. pap. 1.75 (ISBN 0-523-49039-9). Pinnacle Bks.
Hagar the Martyr: Or, Passion and Reality, a Tale of the North and South. Harriet Marion Ward Stephens. LC 72-3200. (Black Heritage Library Collection). 1972. 16.00. (ISBN 0-8369-9079-X). Books for Libraries Press.
Hagar, the Singing Maiden, with Other Stories and Rhymes. T. T Purvis. LC 77-174289. 1975. 14.50 (ISBN 0-404-00100-9). AMS Press.
Hagarene: A Novel. George Alfred Lawrence. LC 51-54802. 1875. Harper.
Hagarene. A Novel. George Alfred Lawrence. (seaside library, v. 70. no. 1423). 1882. G. Munro.
Hagar's Child. Grace Naismith. LC 34-1049. The Macaulay Company.
Hagar's Hoard. George Kibbe Turner. LC 75-104762. (Novel as American social history). 1970. University Press of Kentucky.
Hagar's Hoard. George Kibbe Turner. LC 20-17178. 1920. A. A. Knopf.
Hagar's Hoard. George Kibbe Turner. LC 25-219184. (Borsoi pocket books). 1925. A. A. Knopf.
Haggard's Manor. Evelyne Hayworth. (Queen-size gothic; large easy-to-read type). 1973. 0.95. Popular Library.
Hag's Harvest. John Bingham Morton. LC 33-314216. 1933. Doubleday, Doran & Company, Inc.
Hag's Nook. John Dickson Carr. LC 68-92382. (B67-24873). 1967. Penguin.
Hag's Nook. John Dickson Carr. LC 33-795936. 1933. Harper & Brothers.
Haidee. F Horace Rose. LC 17-138196. 1917. Hodder and Stoughton.
Haigerloch Project. Ib Melchior. LC 76-26272. 9.95 (ISBN 0-06-012946-8). Harper & Row.
Haiku Garland. (Classics Ser.). slip case 4.95 o.p. (ISBN 0-442-82516-1). Peter Pauper.
Hail, Alma Pater. Harry Dubin. LC 54-6664. (Illus.). 1954. Hermitage House.
Hail and Farewell: Ave, Salve, Vale. George Moore. LC 77-361833. (Illus.). 1976. (ISBN 0-7705-1467-7). Macmillan of Canada.
Hail, Hail, the Gang's All Here! Evan Hunter. LC 78-39799. 1972. 7.95 (ISBN 0-8161-6025-2). G. K. Hall.
Hail, Hail, the Gang's All Here! Evan Hunter. LC 70-139044. 1971. 5.95. Doubleday.
Hail, Hail, the Gang's All Here. Ed McBain. LC 70-139044. 1971. 5.95 o.p. (ISBN 0-385-01597-6). Doubleday.
Hail, Hail, the Gang's All Here. Ed McBain. 1972. Repr. lib. bdg. 7.95 o.p. (ISBN 0-8161-6025-2, Large Print Bks). G K Hall.
Hail, Hero! John Weston. LC 68-10866. 1968. D. McKay Co.
Hail Hibbler. Ron Goulart. (Science Fiction Ser.). 1980. pap. 1.75 o.p. (ISBN 0-87997-557-1, UE1557). Daw Bks.
Hail the Conquering Hero; a Novel. Frank Yerby. LC 77-12530. 10.95 (ISBN 0-8037-3417-4). Dial Press.
Hail to the Chief. Ed McBain. LC 73-7464. 1973. 6.95 o.p. (ISBN 0-394-48581-5). Random.
Hail to the Chief. James Reichley. LC 59-8862. 1960. Houghton Mifflin.
Hail to the Chief: An 87th Precinct Mystery. Evan Hunter. LC 73-7464. 1973. 5.95 (ISBN 0-394-48581-5). Random House.
Hail to the Chief: An 87th Precinct Mystery. Evan Hunter. (Signet book). 1975. (pbk.) 1.25. New American Library.
Hail to the Chiefs: My Life & Time with Six Presidents. Ruth Montgomery. (YA) 1970. 6.95 o.p. (ISBN 0-698-10147-2). Coward.
Hair. Ed. by Fotonovel Publications Staff. (Illus., Orig.). 1979. pap. 2.75. Fotonovel.
Hair Divides. Claude Houghton Oldfield. LC 31-8533. 1931. Doubleday, Doran and Company, Inc.
Hair of Harold Roux. Thomas Williams. LC 73-20583. 1974. 7.95 (ISBN 0-394-48988-8). Random House.
Hair of Harold Roux. Thomas Williams. 1975. (pbk.) 1.95. Ballantine Books.
Hair of the Dog. Jean Leslie. LC 47-12398. 1947. Pub. for the Crime Club by Doubleday.
Hair on a Cue Ball: The Hair-Raising Adventures of a Holly-Wood Writer. 1st Ed. Negley Monett. LC 55-8686. (Banner book). 1955. Exposition Press.
Hair Shirt. A. C. McLean. 6.50 o.p. Carlton.
Hair-Trigger Brand. Reginald Charles Barker.
Hair-Trigger Brand. Reginald Charles Barker. LC 29-7501. 1929. L. C. Page & Company.
Hair-Trigger Hombre. Hamilton Craigie. LC 46-1847. 1946. Phoenix Press.
Hair-Trigger Realm. Nelson Coral Nye. LC 40-6535. Phoenix Press.
Haircut & a Shave. Philip Green. 5.95 o.p. Vantage.
Haircut & Other Stories. Ring Lardner. 1962. 7.95, Large type ed. o.p. (ISBN 0-684-10345-1). Scribner.
Haircut & Other Stories. Ring Lardner. (Contemporary Classics). 1962. pap. 2.95 o.p. (ISBN 0-684-71834-0, SL53). Scribner.
Hairdresser. Judith Piccone. (O.s.i.). (Orig.). 1976. pap. 1.50 o.s.i. (AD1626, Award). Univ Pub & Dist.
Hairpin Duchess. Alice Woods. LC 24-256454. 1924. Duffield and Company.
Hair's Breadth... Lee Thayer, pseud. LC 46-1511. 1946. Dodd, Mead & Company.
Hairy Arm. Edgar Wallace. LC 25-15849. Small, Maynard & Company.
Haitian Vendetta. Don Smith. (Secret Mission Ser.). (O.s.i.). (Orig.). 1973. pap. 0.95 o.s.i. (AN1129, Award). Univ Pub & Dist.
Hajji Baba of Ispahan. (Hart Illustrated Classics). (Illus.). 480p. 1976. 8.95 o.p. (ISBN 0-8055-1173-3); pap. 5.95 o.p. (ISBN 0-8055-0249-1). Hart.
Hal Gilman: Or, A Mississippi Story Substantially True. Robert Haskins Crozier. LC 6-31945. (Mississippi library, no. 1). 1883. W. H. Crockett & Co.
Hal O' the Ironsides: A Story of the Days of Cromwell. Samuel Rutherford Crockett. LC 15-205881. 1.25. Fleming H. Revell Company.
Hal Porter. Hal Porter & Mary Lord. LC 80-509181. (Portable Australian Authors). 1980. 30.25 (ISBN 0-7022-1465-5) (ISBN 0-7022-1466-3). University of Queensland Press.
Halamar. Gertrude Potter Daniels. LC 3445. 1900. G. M. Hill Company.
Halcyon Days in Port Townsend: Historical Novel. Cornelius Holgate Hanford. LC 25-19106. Apex Printing Co.
Halcyon Drift. Brian M. Stableford. (Science Fiction Ser.). (Orig.). 1972. pap. 0.95 o.p. (UQ1032). DAW Bks.
Halcyon Way. Mark McShane. (Orig.). 1980. pap. 1.95 (ISBN 0-532-23148-1). Woodhill.
Halcyone. Elinor Sutherland Glyn. LC 12-16964. 1912. 1.30. D. Appleton and Company.
Haldane Station. Florence Engel Randall. LC 73-5794. 1973. 6.95 (ISBN 0-15-138400-2). Harcourt Brace Jovanovich.
Haldane Station. Florence Engel Randall. (Fawcett crest book). 1974. (pbk.) 1.25. Fawcett.
Half. Jordan Park. LC 53-27783. (Lion books, 135). 1953. Lion Books.
Half a Brain: A Musical Satire with Sheet Music. William J. Oswald. (Illus.). 112p. 1972. 4.50 o.p. (ISBN 0-682-47355-3). Exposition.
Half a Brick. Anne Schmidt. LC 74-16782. 1975. 5.95. Dorrance.
Half a Cage. Jean G Howard, pseud. LC 78-62962. (Illus.). 1978. 8.50 (ISBN 0-930954-07-6) (ISBN 0-930954-08-4). Tidal Press.
Half a Century. Cyrena Harper. 1970. 3.50 o.p. Vantage.
Half a Chance. Frederic Stewart Isham. LC 9-25179. The Bobbs-Merrill Company.
Half a Clew. Richard Howells Watkins. LC 27-18962. E. J. Clode, Inc.
Half a Dollar Is Better Than None: Illustrated by R. Taylor. 1st Ed. Nicholas Di Minno. LC 52-12352. 1952. Doubleday.
Half a Hero: A Novel. Anthony Hope Hawkins. LC 7-218314. (On cover: Harper's Franklin square library, no. 738). 1893. Harper & Brothers.
Half-a-Hundred: Stories for Men, Great Tales by American Writers. Ed. by Charles Grayson. LC 46-3565. 1946. Garden City Publishing Co., Inc.
Half-a-Hundred: Tales by Great American Writers. Ed. by Charles Grayson. LC 45-5278. 1945. The Blakiston Company.
Half a Life. Kirill Vsevolodovich Bulychev. Tr. by Helen S. Jacobson. 1979. pap. 2.95 o.s.i. (ISBN 0-02-017850-6, Collier). Macmillan.
Half a Life, and Other Stories. Kirill Vsevolodovich Bulychev. LC 77-8403. 10.95 (ISBN 0-02-518030-4). Macmillan.
Half a Loaf. Grace Hegger Lewis. LC 31-252313. H. Liveright, Inc.
Half-a-Man. G. Margel Holst. LC 78-65862. 1979. 7.95 (ISBN 0-533-04118-X). Vantage.
Half a Marriage. Violet Weingarten. LC 75-36794. 1976. 7.95 (ISBN 0-394-49374-5). Knopf: Distributed by Random House.
Half a Marriage. Violet Weingarten. (Kangaroo Book.). 1977. 1.75 (ISBN 0-671-80866-4). Pocket Books.
Half a Million of Money. Amelia Ann Blandford Edwards. (Seaside library. v. 8, no. 145). 1877. G. Munro.
Half a Minute's Silence, and Other Stories: By Maurice Baring. Maurice Baring. LC 26-26223. 1925. Doubleday, Page & Company.
Half a Minute's Silence, and Other Stories. Maurice Baring. LC 71-113647. (Short story index reprint series). 1970. Books for Libraries Press.
Half a Rogue. Harold MacGrath. 1906. The Bobbs-Merrill Company.
Half a Sovereign: An Improbable Romance. John Hay Beith. LC 26-15578. 1926. Houghton Mifflin Company.
Half a Treasure. Mark J Bond. (Leisure book). 1978. 1.50. Norden Pubs.
Half a Winter to Go. Sheila Collins. LC 76-12003. (Sunburst Originals Ser.: No. 4). 52p. (Orig.). 1976. pap. 2.25 (ISBN 0-934648-04-2). Sunburst Pr.
Half a World Away. Gloria Bevan. (Harlequin Romances Ser.). 192p. (Orig.). 1981. pap. 1.25 (ISBN 0-373-02377-4, Pub. by Harlequin). PB.
Half Angel. Barbara Jefferis. LC 59-11711. 1959. Sloane.
Half Angel. Fannie Heaslip Lea. LC 32-29686. 1932. Dodd, Mead & Company.
Half-Angel. L. M. McQuarrie. LC 46-1197. 1946. Doubleday & Company, Inc.
Half-Breed. Mick Clumpner. (Orig.). 1982. pap. 1.95 (ISBN 0-451-11281-4, AJ1281, Sig). NAL.
Half-Breed. Maurice Constantin-Weyer. LC 30-7304. The Macaulay Company.
Half Breed. John Thomas Edson. 1981. 1.95 (ISBN 0-425-04736-9). Berkle Books.
Half-Breed. Alex Hawk, pseud. (Alex Hawk Westerns Ser). (Orig.). 1971. pap. 0.60 o.p. (ISBN 0-446-63591-X, 63-591). Paperback Lib.
Half-Breed, and Other Stories. Walt Whitman. LC 72-6638. (Illus.). 1972. (ISBN 0-8414-0166-7). Folcroft Library Editions.
Half Brothers. Hesba Stretton. LC 8-16884. Cassell Publishing Company.
Half-Crown House. Helen Ashton. LC 56-10468. 1956. Dodd, Mead.
Half-Crown House. LC 56-10468. 1956. Dodd, Mead.
Half Dark Moon. Royal Dixon. Manfred, Van Nort & Co.
Half Gods. Charles G Bell. LC 68-23028. 1968. 7.95. Houghton Mifflin.
Half Gods. Lynn Montross. LC 24-8791. 2.00. George H. Doran Company.
Half-Gods. Murray Sheehan. LC 27-773297. E. P. Dutton & Company.
Half-Haunted Saloon. Dora Richards Shattuck. LC 45-3733. 1945. Simon and Schuster.
Half-Haunted Saloon. Richard Shattuck. LC 45-3733. 1945. Simon and Schuster.
Half-Heart. Amanda Preble. (Orig.). 1981. pap. 1.50 (ISBN 0-440-13442-0). Dell.
Half-Hearted. John Buchan. LC 5063. 1900. Houghton, Mifflin and Company.
Half-Hearted. John Buchan. LC 28-264563. 1928. Houghton Mifflin Company.
Half-Holiday. Edith Everett Taylor. LC 38-4880. 1938. E. P. Dutton & Co., Inc.
Half Hour Stories. Dora Harvey Munyon. LC 1-29545. The Abbey Press.
Half-Hours with Jimmieboy. John Kendrick Bangs. LC 6-6289. 1893. R. H. Russell & Son.
Half-Hours with the Christ. Thomas Moses. LC 45-499498. 1898. American Baptist Publication Society.
Half Hours with the Idiot. John Kendrick Bangs. LC 17-141821. 1917. 1.25. Little, Brown, and Company.
Half-Hours with the Millionaires. B. B West. LC 8-36234. 1892. Longmans, Green and Co.
Half-Hunter. John Sherwood. 1982. 15.00x (ISBN 0-86025-106-3, Pub. by Ian Henry Pubns England). State Mutual Bk.
Half in Shadow. Mary Elizabeth Counselman. LC 77-78597. 1978. 8.95 (ISBN 0-87054-081-5). Arkham House.
Half Inch of Candle. Arthur Hamilton Gibbs. LC 39-328255. 1939. Little, Brown and Company.
Half Jew: A Novel. Robert Beauvais. LC 79-26039. 1980. 9.95 (ISBN 0-8008-3799-1). Taplinger Pub. Co.
Half Loaves. Margaret Culkin Banning. LC 21-6896. George H. Doran Company.
Half Loaves: A Story. Helen Gansevoort Edwards Mackay. LC 11-4597. 1911. 1.30. Duffield and Company.
Half Married. Agame Game. Annie Bliss McConnell. LC 7-15293. 1887. J. B. Lippincott Company.
Half-Mast Murder... Milward Rodon Kennedy Burge. LC 30-20591. 1930. Pub. for The Crime Club, Inc., by Doubleday, Doran & Company, Inc.
Half-Mile to Heaven. Gerald Foster. LC 37-151253. 1937. Hill-Man-Curl, Inc.

'Half Moon' A Romance of the Old World and the New. Ford Madox Ford. LC 9-35786. 1909. Doubleday, Page & Company.
Half Moon Bay. Vida Hurst. LC 45-6684. 1945. Gramercy Publishing Co.
Half Moon Haven. Martin Russ. LC 59-120763. 1959. Rinehart.
Half-Moon Ranch. Oscar Jerome Friend. LC 32-3493. 1931. G. H. Watt.
Half of Paradise: A Novel. James Lee Burke. LC 64-177206. 4.95. Houghton.
Half-Past Mortem. John A Saxon. LC 47-31056. 1947. M. S. Mill Co.
Half Past the Eleventh Hour. Anne Elizabeth. 3.95 o.p. Vantage.
Half-Past Yesterday. Robert Sturgis. LC 45-6051. 1945. M. S. Mill Co., Inc.
Half Pint Flask. Du Bose Heyward. LC 30-6438. 1929. Farrar & Rinehart, Inc.
Half Portions. Edna Ferber. LC 74-132115. (Short story index reprint series). 1970. Books for Libraries Press.
Half Portions. Edna Ferber. 1920. Doubleday, Page & Company.
Half Portions. Life Publishing Co. 1900. Life Publishing Company.
Half-Price. Constance Travers Sweatman. LC 27-218807. 1927. W. Morrow & Company.
Half-Seas Over. Guy Gilpatric. 1932. Dodd, Mead & Company.
Half-Seen Face. Dorothy Lee Richardson. LC 78-24600. 1978. 6.95 (ISBN 0-87233-047-8). W. L. Bauhan.
Half-Sisters. Cynthia Propper Seton. LC 73-16155. 1974. 6.95 (ISBN 0-393-08689-5). Norton.
Half-Sisters. Cynthia Propper Seton. LC 79-19760. 1980. 10.95 (ISBN 0-89340-228-1). John Curley & Associates.
Half-Sisters: A Romance of the Southside. Ross Fitzgerald. LC 6-41117. 1867. Intelligencer Printing House.
Half-Sisters: A Tale, 2 vols. in 1. Geraldine Endsor Jewsbury. LC 79-8143. Repr. of 1848 ed. 44.50 (ISBN 0-404-61945-2). AMS Pr.
Half-Smart Set: A Novel. LC 8-16519. 1908. F. A. Stokes Company.
Half That Glory. Stanley Edgar Gray. LC 41-7649. 1941. The Macmillan Company.
Half the Fun: A Novel. Bentz Plagemann. LC 61-5921. 1961. Viking Press.
Half the House. Herbert Kohl. 1974. 7.95 o.p. (ISBN 0-525-12030-0). Dutton.
Half-Time Gypsy. Joyce Varney. 4.50 o.p. Bobbs.
Half-Told Tales. Henry Van Dyke. LC 25-20413. 1925. C. Scribner's Sons.
Half-Way, an Anglo-French Romance... Matilda Barbara Bertram Edwards. LC 6-36589. (Harper's handy ser. no. 41). 1885. Harper & Brothers.
Half-Way. An Anglo-French Romance. Matilda Barbara Bertram Edwards. (On cover: Seaside library. Pocket ed. no. 668). 1886. G. Munro.
Half-Way to Timberline. Ward West, pseud. LC 35-29215. Greenberg.
Half World: A Novel. Buena Vista Stine. LC 44-10709. 1944. Wetzel Publishing Co., Inc.
Halfbreed Ambush. Jim Wilmeth. 192p. (Orig.). 1981. pap. 1.95 (ISBN 0-505-51760-4). Tower Bks.
Halfhyde and the Flag Captain. Philip McCutchan. LC 80-29075. 9.95 (ISBN 0-312-35684-6). St. Martin's Press.
Halfhyde for the Queen: A Novel. Philip McCutchan. LC 78-4317. 1978. 7.95 (ISBN 0-312-35687-0). St. Martin's Press.
Halfhyde on Zanatu. Philip McCutchan. LC 82-10760. 1982. 10.95 (ISBN 0-312-35688-9). St. Martin's Press.
Halfhyde Ordered South. Philip McCutchan. LC 79-66344. 1980. 10.00 (ISBN 0-312-35689-7). St. Martin's Press.
Halfhyde to the Narrows. Philip McCutchan. LC 77-72303. 1977. 7.95 (ISBN 0-312-35690-0). St. Martin's Press.
Halfhyde's Island. Philip McCutchan. LC 75-24699. 1976. 7.95. St. Martin's Press.
Halfling, and Other Stories. Leigh Brackett. 1973. (pbk.) 1.25. Ace.
Halfway Down the Stairs: Novel. Charles Thompson. LC 57-6156. 1957. Harper.
Halfway Home. Julia Coley Duncan, pseud. LC 78-19845. 8.95 (ISBN 0-312-35710-9). St. Martin's Press.
Halfway Home. Julia Coley Duncan, pseud. 1980. 1.95 (ISBN 0-445-04559-0). Fawcett Popular Library.
Halfway Home. Julia Coley Duncan, pseud. LC 79-25180. 1980. 10.95 (ISBN 0-89340-224-9). J. Curley.
Halfway House. Ellery Queen, pseud. LC 41-4552. 1940. Triangle Books.
Halfway House... Ellery Queen, pseud. LC 45-13596. 1944.
Halfway House: A Comedy of Degrees. Maurice Henry Hewlett. LC 8-19024. 1908. C. Scribner's Sons.
Halfway House: A Problem in Deduction. Ellery Queen, pseud. LC 36-15570. 1936. Frederick A. Stokes Company.
Halfway There, No. 67. Aimee Duvall. 1982. pap. 1.75 (ISBN 0-515-06678-8). Jove Pubns.
Halfway to Heaven. Flair, Terrance. LC 57-770954. (Ballantine books, 191). 1957. Ballantine Books.
Halfway to Paradise. Janet Doran. LC 40-305733. Gramercy Publishing Co.
Halic: The Story of a Gray Seal. Ewan Clarkson. LC 74-95465. 1970. 5.95 o.p. (ISBN 0-525-12039-4). Dutton.
Haliefa. George Kline Baker. LC 14-499. 1913. 1.00. The Neale Publishing Company.
Hall and the Grange: A Novel. Archibald Marshall. LC 21-554055. 1921. Dodd, Mead and Company.
Hall of Death. Tyre, Nedra. LC 60-6104. (Inner sanctum mystery). 1960. Simon and Schuster.
Hall of Mirrors. Lenore Guinzburg Marshall. LC 37-211437. 1937. The Macmillan Company.
Hall of Mirrors. Robert Stone. LC 67-11109. 1967. Houghton Mifflin.
Hall of Mirrors. Robert Stone. LC 67-11109. 1975. (pbk.) 1.95 (ISBN 0-345-24524-5). Ballantine Books.
Hall of Mirrors. John Rowan Wilson. (95-155). 1967. Popular Lib.
Hall of Mirrors: A Novel. 1st. ed. John Rowan Wilson. LC 66-13277. 1966. Doubleday.
Hallam Succession. A Tale of Methodist, Life in Two Countries. Amelia Edith Huddleston Barr. LC 13-93782. 1885. Phillips & Hunt.
Hallelujah. Fannie Hurst. LC 44-379. 1944. Harper & Brothers.
Hallelujah! Arthur J La Bern. LC 75-329443. 1973. 2.75 (ISBN 0-491-00834-1). W. H. Allen.
Hallelujah Chariot. Evelyn Hathaway. LC 72-79924. 1969. 4.95. John Knox Press.
Hallelujah Harvest. Walter E. Adams. 325p. (Orig.). 1981. pap. 4.50 (ISBN 0-937408-05-0). Gospel Pubns FL.
Hallelujah Jamboree: The Sister Mary Mummy Stories. Greg Hoffman. (Illus.). 192p. 1981. pap. 5.95 (ISBN 0-938128-01-9). Jorgensen Pub.
Hallelujah, Mississippi. 1st Ed. Louis Cochran. LC 55-553518. Duell, Sloan and Pearce.
Hallelujah Trail. Bill Gulick, pseud. 1965. 3.95 o.p. Doubleday.
Hallelujah Trail: By Bill Gulick. Grover C. Gulick. LC 65-12355. 1965. 3.95. Doubleday.
Hallelujah Train: By Bill Gulick. Grover C Gulick. LC 63-17457. 1963. Doubleday.
Hallie Marshall, a True Daughter of the South. Frank Purdy Williams. LC 1-31802. The Abbey Press.
Hallig: Or, The Sheepfold in the Waters. A Tale of Humble Life on the Coast of Schleswig. Translated from the German of Biermatzki. Johanna Christoph Blernatzki. Tr. by Marsh, Caroline (Crane) LC 42-28864. 1857. Gould and Lincoln.
Hallmark Piece or, the Suicide Book. Millie M. Wicklund. 48p. (Orig.). 1983. 8.00 (ISBN 0-930012-27-5). Mudborn.
Hallowed Hour: By A. H. Parr. Adolph Henry Parr. LC 46-18351. Dependable Publishing Co.
Hallowed Years. Nash Buckingham. LC 53-10565. 1953. Stackpole Co.
Hallowe'en. Leslie Burgess. LC 41-13495. G. P. Putnam's Sons.
Halloween. Ben Greer. LC 78-15065. 9.95 (ISBN 0-02-545510-9). Macmillan.
Halloween. Curtis Richards. 176p. (Orig.). 1981. pap. 2.50 (ISBN 0-553-14036-1). Bantam.
Halloween. Curtis Richards. 176p. 1982. pap. write for info. (ISBN 0-553-22740-8). Bantam.
Hallowe'en Homicide. Lee Thayer, pseud. LC 41-16493. 1941. Dodd, Mead & Company.
Hallowe'en Party. Agatha Miller Christie. 1973. (pbk.) 0.95 (ISBN 0-671-77705-X). Pocket Books.
Hallowe'en Party. Agatha Miller Christie. LC 75-102733. 1969. 5.95. Dodd, Mead.
Halloween Three: Season of the Witch. Jack Martin. 1982. pap. 2.95 (ISBN 0-515-06885-3). Jove Pubns.
Halloween Two. Jack Martin. (Orig.). 1981. pap. 2.95 (ISBN 0-89083-864-X). Zebra.
Hallowell Partnership. Katharine Holland Brown. LC 12-24921. 1912. C. Scribner's Sons.
Hallowing. Fran P. Yariv. (Orig.). pap. 2.50 (ISBN 0-515-05192-6). Jove Pubns.
Halls of Anger. (Orig.). 1970. pap. 0.60 o.p. (63-340). Paperback Lib.
Halls of Dishonor. Jack M. Bickham. 1.79. C.
Hallucination of Death. Jack Martin. LC 75-324198. (ISBN 0-87881-026-9). Mojave Books.
Hallucinations. Iris Penrose. Ed. by Barbara Wilcox. 110p. (Orig.). 1981. pap. 5.95. Roark Pubns.
Hallucinations: Being an Account of the Life and Adventures of Friar Servando Teresa De Mier. Renaldo Arenas. 1976. 1.95 (ISBN 0-14-003895-7). Penguin Books.
Halo. Betsey Riddle Hutten Zum Stolzenberg. LC 7-36982. 1907. Dodd, Mead and Company.
Halo for Doctor Michael. Dorothy Worley. LC 53-12797. 1953. Avalon Books.
Halo for Nobody. Henry Kane. LC 47-12704. 1947. Simon and Schuster.
Halo for Satan. Howard Browne. LC 48-769976. 1948. Bobbs-Merrill Co.
Halo for the Devil. Barbara Cartland. 1973. pap. 1.25 o.p. (ISBN 0-515-03239-5, V3239). Pyramid Pubns.
Halo for the Devil. Barbara Cartland. 1977. pap. 1.50 o.p. (ISBN 0-515-04383-4). BJ Pub Group.
Halo in Blook. Howard Browne. LC 47-292591. (Bantam books, 74). 1946.
Halo in Brass: A Paul Pine Mystery. Howard Browne. LC 49-10015. 1949. Bobbs-Merrill Co.
Halo of Sin. Moss Tadrack, pseud. (Orig.). pap. 0.95 o.p. (1101). Brandon.
Halo of Spears. 1st Ed. Wyatt Blassingame. LC 62-760459. 1962. Doubleday.
Halt During the Chase. Rosemary Tonks. LC 73-4162. 1973. 5.95. Harper & Row.
Halt! Who's There? Wilfrid Meynell. LC 16-12236. 1916. 0.75. G. P. Putnam's Sons.
Halted Between Two Opinions: Or, A Madman's Confession. A Novel. James Cary. 1892. Press of Dispatch Printing Co.
Halter-Broke. John Henry Reese. LC 76-55680. 1977. 6.95 (ISBN 0-385-12820-7). Doubleday.
Halves. Harriet Henry. LC 28-8139. 1928. Longmans, Green and Co.
Halvor: A Story of Pioneer Youth. Translated from the Norwegian and Adapted by Inga B. Norstog and David T. Nelson. Peer Olsen Stromme. LC 60-44502. 1960. Luther College Press.
Ham and the Porcupine. Rudyard Kipling. LC 35-24925. 1935. Doubleday, Doran & Company, Inc.
Ham Martin, Class of '17. Edward Streeter. LC 67-13698. 1969. 6.95. Harper & Row.
Ham on Rye. Charles Bukowski. 288p. 1982. 14.00 (ISBN 0-87685-558-3); pap. 8.50 (ISBN 0-87685-557-5). Black Sparrow.
Ham with Wry. J. K. Stoner. (Illus.). 156p. (Orig.). 1980. pap. 4.50x (ISBN 0-935648-03-8). Halldin Pub.
Hamamatsu Chunagon Monogatari: A Tale of Eleventh Century Japan. Sugawara Takasue No Musume & Thomas H. Rohlich. LC 82-61380. 1983. 30.00 (ISBN 0-691-05377-4). Princeton University Press.
Hambro's Itch. Howard Robens & Jack Wassermann. LC 78-19262. 1979. 8.95 (ISBN 0-385-14560-8). Doubleday.
Hamburg Switch. Angus Ross. LC 79-48051. 1980. 9.95 (ISBN 0-8027-5418-X). Walker.
Hamdaani: A Traditional Tale from Zanzibar. Charles Bible. LC 77-3958. 6.50 (ISBN 0-03-020846-7). Holt, Rinehart and Winston.
Hamilton Avenue. Ronald Byron. LC 57-13483. 1958. Macmillan.
Hamilton Club. Alexander Rose. LC 60-609760. 1960. Simon and Schuster.
Hamilton Stark: A Novel. Russell Banks. LC 78-4960. 1978. 8.95 (ISBN 0-395-26471-5). Houghton Mifflin.
Hamilton Terrace. Elizabeth Frances Corbett. 1972. pap. 0.95 o.p. (95285). Beagle Bks.
Hamiltons: Or, Sunshine in Storm. Cora Berkley. LC 49-30238. 1865. J. B. Kirker.
Hamiltons: Or, Sunshine in Storm. Cora Berkley. LC 6-11330. 1856. E. Dunigan & Brother.
Hamiltons: Or, Sunshine in Storm. Cora Berkley. LC 16-1252. P. J. Kenedy.
Hamlet. William Faulkner. LC 56-7062. (Modern library paperbacks, P18). 1956. Random House.
Hamlet. 3d ed. William Faulkner. LC 64-7972. 1964. Random House.
Hamlet. William Faulkner. LC 72-8035. 1973. (ISBN 0-394-70139-9). Vintage Books.
Hamlet. William Faulkner. LC 40-7705. 1940. Random House.
Hamlet see Snopes: A Trilogy.
Hamlet, Revenge! Michael Innes, pseud. (Crime Ser.). 288p. 1976. pap. 2.95 (ISBN 0-14-001640-6). Penguin.
Hamlet, Revenge. Michael Innes, pseud. 1962. pap. 0.95 o.p. (02135, Collier). Macmillan.
Hamlet, Revenge! John Innes Mackintosh Stewart. LC 62-19122. (Collier mystery classics). 1962. Collier Books.
Hamlet, Revenge! John Innes Mackintosh Stewart. LC 37-17499. 1937. Dodd, Mead & Company.
Hamlet, Revenge ! A Story in Four Parts. John Innes Mackintosh Stewart. LC 77-367106. (Penguin crime fiction). 1976. 1.95 (ISBN 0-14-001640-6). Penguin.
Hamlet Ultimatum. Leonard Sanders. LC 79-16080. 8.95 (ISBN 0-684-16380-2). Scribner's.
Hamlet Warning. Leonard Sanders. LC 76-15814. 7.95 (ISBN 0-684-14651-7). Scribner.
Hamlet Warning. Leonard Sanders. 1977. 1.95 (ISBN 0-446-89370-6). Warner Books.
Hamlet's Father. Richard Flatter. LC 49-11713. 1949. Yale University Press.
Hamlet's Twin. Hubert Aquin. LC 79-317366. 1979. 12.95 (ISBN 0-7710-0800-7). McClelland and Stewart.
Hammed," a Tale of the Crusades: Arranged from the Memoirs of a Warrior-Monk. Frank Stiles Le Fevre. LC 8-248754.
Hammer: A Story of the Maccabean Time. Alfred John Church & Seeley, Richmond. LC 49-40498. 1890. G. P. Putnam's Sons.
Hammer: A Story of the Maccabean Times. Alfred John Church & Seeley, Richmond. LC 12-31356. (On cover: The Knickerbocker series). 1912. G. P. Putnam's Sons.
Hammer and Rapier. John Esten Cooke. LC 6-27179. 1870. Carleton: Etc., Etc.
Hammer and Rapier. John Esten Cooke. LC 34-25481. 1871. Carleton.
Hammer and Rapier. John Esten Cooke. LC 16-755746. G. W. Dillingham Co.
Hammer and Rapier. John Esten Cooke. LC 98-715. (Dillingham's globe library, no. 25). 1898. G. W. Dillingham Co.
Hammer in His Hand. Whit Masterson, pseud. LC 60-6668. (Red badge detective). 1960. Dodd, Mead.
Hammer Marks: A Biographical Novel. Arthur Hougham. LC 25-5778. 1924. Houghton Mifflin Company.
Hammer Me Home. Richard R Werry. LC 55-6204. (Red badge detective). 1955. Dodd, Mead.
Hammer of Doom. Francis William Stokes. LC 29-5701. The Bobbs-Merrill Company.
Hammer of God. Bo Giertz. Tr. by Clifford A. Nelson from Swedish. LC 60-8902. 344p. 1973. pap. 6.50 (ISBN 0-8066-1310-6, 10-2940). Augsburg.
Hammer of God. James Hogg Hunter. LC 64-8843. bds., 2.95. Zondervan.
Hammer of God. Alan Scholefield. LC 73-540. (Illus.). 1973. 6.95 (ISBN 0-688-00161-0). Morrow.
Hammer of the Scots. Jean Plaidy. LC 81-13789. (Plaidy, Jean, 1906-. Plantagenet Saga). 1981. 11.95 (ISBN 0-399-12641-4). Putnam.
Hammer of Thor. Alan Geoffrey Yates. LC 66-276. (Carter Brown mystery series). 1965. New American Library.
Hammer on the Sea. Theodore Vrettos. LC 65-137109. bds., 4.95. Little.
Hammered Gold. William Oscar Johnson. (Orig.). 1982. pap. 3.50 (ISBN 0-671-41487-9). PB.
Hammerhead Range: By Brett Austin Pseud. Lee Floren. LC 55-7930. 1955. Arcadia House.
Hammers of Hell. William Ernst Trautmann & Hagboldt, Peter. Joint Author. LC 22-11513. The New World Pub. Co.
Hammersleigh. Rosemary Ellerbeck. LC 76-6108. 7.95 (ISBN 0-679-50605-5). D. McKay Co.
Hammersmith: His Harvard Days. Mark Sibley Severance. LC 8-6874. 1878. Houghton, Osgood and Company.
Hammersmith: His Harvard Days. 11th ed. Mark Sibley Severance. 1898. Houghton, Mifflin and Company.
Hammersmith: His Harvard Days. Mark Sibley Severance. LC 6-18352. Houghton, Mifflin and Company.
Hammersmith Murders... Zenith Jones Brown. LC 20-17702. 1930. Pub. for The Crime Club, Inc., by Doubleday, Doran & Company, Inc.
Hammerstrike. Walter Winward. LC 78-25746. (Illus.). 9.95 (ISBN 0-671-24668-2). Simon and Schuster.
Hammerword Technique. Mary Spouse. (Orig.). 1980. pap. 2.25 o.s.i. (ISBN 0-505-51496-6). Tower Bks.
Hammett: A Novel. Joseph N Gores. LC 75-16400. 1975. 7.95 (ISBN 0-399-11600-1). Putnam.
Hammett Homicides. Dashiell Hammett & Queen, Ellery, Pseud., Ed. LC 47-1202. (On cover: Bestseller mystery. B61). 1946. L. E. Spivak.
Hammond Innes: Three in One. Hammond Innes. LC 77-118710. 1970. 8.95 o.p. (ISBN 0-394-42773-4). Knopf.
Hampdenshire Wonder. John Davys Beresford. LC 74-15952. (Science Fiction). 1975. 17.00 (ISBN 0-405-06278-8). Arno Press.
Hampdenshire Wonder. John Davys Beresford. LC 75-395. (Garland Library of Science Fiction). 1975. 11.00 (ISBN 0-8240-1401-4). Garland Pub.
Hampstead Mystery. John Reay Watson & Arthur John Rees. LC 16-21060. 1916. John Lane Company.
Hampton Heights: Or, The Spinster's Ward. Caleb Starbuck. LC 8-13447. 1856. Mason Brothers.
Hampton Heritage. Julie Ellis. LC 78-17050. 10.95 (ISBN 0-671-23072-7). Simon and Schuster.
Hampton Women. Julie Ellis. LC 80-12733. 13.95 (ISBN 0-671-24138-9). Simon and Schuster.
Hamptons. Leonard Harris. 1982. pap. 3.50 (ISBN 0-440-13785-3). Dell.
Hamptons. Leonard Harris. 1981. 14.95 (ISBN 0-671-61000-7, Wyndham Bks). S&S.
Hamptons: A Novel. Leonard Harris. LC 80-27718. 14.95 (ISBN 0-671-61000-7). Wyndham Books.

TITLE INDEX HANG FOR TREASON.

Han of Iceland. Victor Marie Hugo. (sea and shore series, no. 33). 1891. Smith & Smith.
Han Solo & the Lost Legacy. Brian Daley. 192p. (Orig.). 1980. pap. 2.25 (ISBN 0-345-28710-X). Ballantine.
Han Solo at Star's End: From the Adventures of Luke Skywalker; Based on the Characters and Situations Created by George Lucas. Brian Daley. LC 78-21442. 1979. 8.95 (ISBN 0-345-28251-5). Ballantine Books.
Han Solo's Revenge. Brian Daley. LC 79-5021. 1979. 8.95 (ISBN 0-345-28475-5). Ballantine Books.
Hand- Picked for Murder. Robert Lee Martin. LC 57-8320. (Red badge detective). 1957. Dodd, Mead.
Hand and Ring. Anna Katharine Green Rohlfs. LC 15-6312. (On cover: Hudson library, no. 50). 1901. G. P. Putnam's Sons.
Hand and Ring. Anna Katharine Green Rohlfs. LC 27-417. 1926. Dodd, Meade and Company.
Hand & the Glove. Machado De Assis, Joaquim Maria. LC 74-111502. (Studies in Romance languages, 2). 1970. 4.95. University Press of Kentucky.
Hand but Not the Heart. Timothy Shay Arthur. LC 78-104405. 1970. Literature House.
Hand but Not the Heart: Or, The Life-Trials of Jessie Loring. Timothy Shay Arthur. LC 6-3398. 1858. Derby & Jackson.
Hand-Clasp of the East and West: A Story of Pioneer Life on the Western Slope of Colorado. Henry Ripley & Ripley, Martha (Pedley) LC 15-155. 1914. 1.50. Press of the Williamson-Haffner Engraving & Printing Co.
Hand in Glove. Ngaio Marsh. 1976. Repr. of 1962 ed. lib. bdg. 13.85x (ISBN 0-88411-486-4). Amereon Ltd.
Hand in Glove. Ngaio Marsh. 1978. pap. 2.25 (ISBN 0-515-06136-0). Jove Pubns.
Hand in Glove. Ngaio Marsh. 1973. pap. 1.25 o.p. (ISBN 0-515-03158-5, N3158). BJ Pub Group.
Hand in Glove. 1st Ed. Ngaio Marsh. LC 62-123712. 1962. Little, Brown.
Hand in Hand. Mary Lee. 1971. pap. 1.95 o.p. (507234). Crown.
Hand in the Cobbler's Safe: And Seven Other True Detective Mysteries. Seth Bailey. LC 44-4737. 1944. Bartholomew House, Inc.
Hand in the Dark. Arthur John Rees. LC 20-13345. 1920. John Lane Company.
Hand in the Dark: A Story of the Mountain People. Charles Edward Hewitt. LC 49-51112. 1947.
Hand in the Game. Henry Gardner Hunting. LC 11-27849. 1911. 1.25. H. Holt and Company.
Hand in the Glove. Rex Stout. 1973. pap. 0.95 o.p. (ISBN 0-515-03025-2, N3025). Pyramid Pubns.
Hand in the Glove: A Dol Benner Mystery. Rex Stout. LC 37-22501. Farrar & Rinehart, Inc.
Hand in the Picture: A Story of Poland. Eric Philbrook Kelly & Lorentowicz, Irena, 1908. LC 47-4735. 1947. J. B. Lippincott Co.
Hand-Made Fables. George Ade. LC 20-4894. 1920. Doubleday, Page & Company.
Hand-Made Gentleman: A Tale of the Battles of Peace. Irving Bacheller. LC 9-10497. 1909. Harper & Brothers.
Hand-Made Lady. Frank Owen. LC 34-30689. Carlyle House.
Hand Me a Crime. Charlotte Murray Russell, pseud. LC 49-10249. 1949. Pub. for the Crime Club by Doubleday.
Hand-Me-Downs. Rhea Kohan. LC 80-5285. 10.00 (ISBN 0-394-51257-X). Random House.
Hand of a Thousand Rings, and Other Chinese Stories. Robert Bachmann. LC 76-178435. (Short story index reprint series). 1971. (ISBN 0-8369-4035-0). Books for Libraries Press.
Hand of a Thousand Rings: And Other Chinese Stories. Robert Bachmann. LC 24-28645. 1924. Cosmopolis Press.
Hand of Alexander. George Peterson Cherakis. LC 50-6439. 1950. Farrar, Straus.
Hand of Bronze. Burris Atkins Jenkins. LC 34-136719. Willett, Clark & Company.
Hand of Cain. Martin Thomas. 1973. 1.25. Lancer Books.
Hand of Death. Margaret Yorke. LC 81-14523. 9.95 (ISBN 0-312-35731-1). St. Martin's Press.
Hand of Destiny. Lula Kirschner. Tr. by Robinson, Mary A. LC 7-12821. (On cover: The fair library, no. 2). 1892. Worthington Co.
Hand of Ethelberta. Thomas Hardy. LC 77-79924. (Hardy New Wessex Editions). 1978. pap. 2.95 (ISBN 0-312-35736-2). St Martin.
Hand of Ethelberta. Thomas Hardy. 1876. 8.25 o.p. (ISBN 0-312-35735-4). St Martin.
Hand of Ethelberta: A Comedy in Chapters. Thomas Hardy. LC 7-191437. (Leisure hour series no. 62). 1876. H. Holt and Company.
Hand of Ethelberta. A Comedy in Chapters. Thomas Hardy. (Seaside library. v. 46, no. 946). 1881. G. Munro.
Hand of Ethelberta: A Comedy in Chapters. Thomas Hardy. LC 16-131001. 1895. Harper & Brothers.
Hand of Ethelberta: A Comedy in Chapters. Thomas Hardy. 1896. Harper & Brothers.
Hand of Fate. Michael Underwood. LC 81-14541. 1982. 9.95 (ISBN 0-312-35740-0). St. Martin's Press.
Hand of Fate: A Romance of the Navy. Kate Lilly Blue. LC 6-14208. 1895. C. H. Kerr and Company.
Hand of Fate: Or, A Study of Destiny; a Novel. Louis Hamon. (On cover: Neely's choice library, no. 88). F. T. Neely; Etc., Etc.
Hand of Fatima. Raphael Rothstein. (Orig.). 1979. pap. 1.75 (ISBN 0-532-17242-6). Woodhill.
Hand of Fu Manchu. Sax Rohmer, pseud. 1976. Repr. of 1917 ed. lib. bdg. 16.30x (ISBN 0-89190-802-1). Am Repr-Rivercity Pr.
Hand of Fu Manchu. Sax Rohmer, pseud. (Adventure Ser). 1971. pap. 0.60 o.p. (X2342). Pyramid Pubns.
Hand of Fu Manchu. Sax Rohmer, pseud. 1976. pap. 1.25 o.p. (ISBN 0-515-03941-1). Pyramid Pubns.
Hand of Fu-Manchu: Being a New Phase in the Activities of Fu-Manchu, the Evil Doctor. Arthur Sarsfield Ward. LC 21-4914. 1917. A. L. Burt Company.
Hand of Fu-Manchu: Being a New Phase in the Activities of Fu-Manchu, the Devil Doctor. Arthur Sarsfield Ward. LC 17-141781. 1917. R. M. McBride & Company.
Hand of Fu-Manchu: Being a New Phase in the Activities of Fu-Manchu, the Evil Doctor. Arthur Sarsfield Ward. LC 31-35238. A. L. Burt Company.
Hand of Fu-Manchu: Being a New Phase in the Activities of Fu-Manchu, the Devil Doctor. Arthur Sarsfield Ward. (Stories of Chinatown). 1920. R. M. McBride & Company.
Hand of Glory. Glen Petrie. LC 80-51819. 11.95 (ISBN 0-312-35742-7). St. Martin's Press.
Hand of God: A Novel. Wenceslaus Aloisius Dostal. LC 34-38325. 1934. Benziger Brothers.
Hand of God: A Novel. Cora Bennett Stephenson. 1909. The Ball Publishing Co.
Hand of God in Ethiopia. Wesley Curtwright. 3.95 o.p. Vantage.
Hand of Horror. Oscar Jerome Friend. LC 27-16667. E. J. Clode, Inc.
Hand of Kane. Robert E. Howard. (Time-Lost Ser., Vol. 4). Orig. Title: Red Shadows. (Illus.). 1973. pap. 1.50 o.p. (ISBN 0-87818-003-6). Centaur.
Hand of Mary Constable. Paul Gallico. LC 64-13102. 1964. Doubleday.
Hand of Michaelangelo. Sidney Alexander. LC 77-154999. 693p. 1977. pap. 10.95x (ISBN 0-8214-0235-8, 82-82378). Ohio U Pr.
Hand of Michelangelo. Sidney Alexander. 6.00 o.p. Twayne.
Hand of Oberon. Roger Zelazny. LC 75-39124. 1976. 5.95. Doubleday.
Hand of Oberon. Roger Zelazny. 1977. 1.50. Avon Books.
Hand of Peril: A Novel of Adventure. Arthur John Arbuthnott Stringer. LC 15-80854. 1915. The Macmillan Company.
Hand of Petrarch, and Other Stories. Thomas Russell Sullivan. LC 13-14819. 1913. Houghton Mifflin Company.
Hand of Power. Edgar Wallace. LC 30-19826. 1930. The Mystery League, Inc.
Hand of Solange. Marion Rippon. LC 75-78688. 1969. 4.50. Published for the Crime Club by Doubleday.
Hand of the Chimpansee. Robert Hare Hutchinson. LC 34-357002. 1934. Longmans, Green and Co.
Hand of the Hunter. Jerome Weidman. LC 51-16. 1951. Harcourt, Brace.
Hand of the Mighty: And Other Stories. Vaughan Kester & Kester, Paul, 1869- LC 12-203518. The Bobbs-Merrill Company.
Hand of the Potter. Ruthel. LC 78-54154. 1978. 9.95 (ISBN 0-87949-121-3). Ashley Books.
Hand of Zei. Lyon Sprague De Camp. (Illus.). 200p. 1981. Repr. of 1963 ed. 20.50 (ISBN 0-913896-20-9). Owlswick Pr.
Hand on Her Shoulder. Margaret Widdemer. LC 38-199313. Farrar & Rinehart, Incorporated.
Hand on My Shoulder: By William H. Brown. William Howard Brown., Vantage Press.
Hand on the Latch. Mary Cholmondeley. LC 9-9254. 1909. Dodd, Mead & Company.
Hand Out. Julian Rathbone. LC 68-13986. 1968. Walker.
Hand Over Fist. Henry H Noyes. LC 80-51041. 6.00 (ISBN 0-89608-025-0) (ISBN 0-89608-026-9). South End Press.
Hand Over Mind. Marc Lovell, pseud. LC 79-7669. 1979. 7.95 (ISBN 0-385-15639-1). Published for the Crime Club by Doubleday.
Hand-Reared Boy. Brian Wilson Aldiss. LC 74-96308. 1970. 5.95. McCall Pub. Co.
Hand That Cradles the Rock. Rita Mae Brown. (Illus.). 1974. pap. 4.50. Diana Pr.
Hand That Cradles the Rock. Rita Mae Brown. 1971. 4.50 o.p. (ISBN 0-8147-0966-4). NYU Pr.
Hand to Back: A Collection of Masonic Stories. William M Stuart. LC 27-40. 1926. Macoy Publishing and Masonic Supply Company.
Handbook for Poisoners: A Collection of Famous Poison Stories; Selected, with an Introd. on Poisons. Ed. by Raymond Tostevin Bond. LC 51-14407. 1951. Rinehart.
Handbook for Poisoners: A Collection of Great Poison Stories. Ed. by Raymond Tostevin Bond. pap. 0.95 o.p. (01695, Collier). Macmillan.
Handful of Blackberries: Translated by Darina Silone. 1st Ed. Ignazio Silone. LC 52-54718. 1953. Harper.
Handful of Darkness. Philip K Dick. LC 78-8156. (Gregg Press science fiction series). 1978. 11.00 (ISBN 0-8398-2413-0). Gregg Press.
Handful of Dominoes. James Leonard Johnson. LC 78-91676. 1970. 4.95. Lippincott.
Handful of Dust. Evelyn Waugh. LC 34-31076. Farrar & Rinehart, Incorporated.
Handful of Dust. Evelyn Waugh. LC 77-88233. 1977. 8.95 (ISBN 0-316-92614-0). Little, Brown.
Handful of Ghosts: Thirteen Eerie Tales by Australian Authors. Barbara Ker Wilson. LC 77-358994. 1976. (ISBN 0-340-20696-9). Hodder & Stoughton.
Handful of Lightning. Ed Mack Miller. LC 63-12968. Orig. Title: Exile to the Stars. 1968. pap. 0.75 o.p. (54-716). Paperback Lib.
Handful of Men. Robert Wilder. 1970. pap. 0.75 o.p. (T2335, GM). Fawcett World.
Handful of Rainbow. Waldon Porterfield. LC 66-11853. 4.95. Lyle Stuart.
Handful of Rice: A Novel by Kamala Markandaya. Pseud. Kamala Purnaiya Taylor. LC 66-18782. 1966. 5.95. John Day.
Handful of Silver. Victor Canning. LC 54-10895. 1954. W. Sloane Associates.
Handful of Silver. Philip Shorter. 1978. pap. 1.50 (ISBN 0-532-15382-0). Woodhill.
Handful of Silver: Six Stories of Silversmiths. Horace Townsend. LC 3-4667. 1903. The Gorham Company.
Handful of Stars! Ray House. LC 79-147266. 1970. 5.95. Touchstone Pub. Co.
Handicap: A Novel of Pioneer Days. Robert Edward Knowles. LC 10-24901. 1.20. Fleming H. Revell Company.
Handicapped. Emery Bemsley Pottle. LC 8-177893. 1908. J. Lane Company; Etc., Etc.
Handicapped Among the Free. Emma Rayner. LC 72-14094. (Black Heritage Library Collection). 1973. (ISBN 0-8369-9252-0). Books for Libraries Press.
Handicapped: The Story of a White-Haired Boy. Homer Greene. LC 14-18077. 1914. Houghton Mifflin Company.
Handicapper. Robert Allen Kalich. LC 79-25879. 12.95 (ISBN 0-517-54024-X). Crown Publishers.
Handle with Care: A Novel. Margaret Turnbull. LC 16-1398. 1916. Harper & Brothers.
Handle with Fear: A Singer Batts Mystery. Thomas Blanchard Dewey. LC 51-1780. 1951. M. S. Mill Co. and W. Morrow.
Handley Cross: Or, Mr. Jorrocks's Hunt. Robert Smith Surtees & John Leech. LC 75-41268. 1979. 49.50 (ISBN 0-404-14614-7). AMS Press.
Handmade Rainbows. Anita Blackmon Smith. W. Goodwin, Inc.
Handmaid of the Lord. Margaret Culkin Banning. LC 24-22206. George H. Doran Company.
Handmaid to Fame. Berta Ruck. LC 39-2162.
Handmaid to MDAS. Jane Arbor. (Harlequin Romances Ser.). 192p. 1983. pap. 1.75 (ISBN 0-373-02545-9). Harlequin Bks.
Hands. Charles Gilman Norris. LC 35-19679. Farrar & Rinehart, Incorporated.
Hands Across the Sea. John Henry Newman. LC 74-17560. 1975. 4.95 (ISBN 0-8059-2096-X). Dorrance.
Hands Across the Water. Ralph Arnold. LC 47-3394. 1947. The Macmillan Company.
Hands: And Other Stories. Sherwood Anderson. (Little blue book, no. 865, ed. by E. Haldeman-Julius). 1925. Haldeman-Julius Company.
Hands As Bands. Clinton T Revere. LC 32-25723. 1932. R. Long & R. R. Smith, Inc.
Hands for Sale. Charlie William Rice. Ed. by Byrnes, Floyd. LC 31-3163. Paulson Press.
Hands Full of Living. Kathleen Thompson Norris. 312p. 1975. Repr. of 1931 ed. lib. bdg. 16.30x (ISBN 0-89190-303-8). Am Repr-Rivercity Pr.
Hands in the Dark. Maxwell Grant, pseud. (Shadow Ser.: No. 4). 1975. pap. 0.95 o.p. (ISBN 0-515-03557-2, N3557). BJ Pub Group.
Hands of Cantu. Tom Lea. LC 64-17481. 1964. Little, Brown.
Hands of Compulsion. Amelia Edith Huddleston Barr. LC 9-6847. 1909. Dodd, Mead & Company.
Hands of Cormac Joyce. Illus. by Lydia Rosier. Leonard Patrick O'Connor Wibberley. 1967. 3.75. Morrow.
Hands of Esau. Margaret Wade Campbell Deland. LC 14-18918. 1914. Harper & Brothers.
Hands of Esau. 1st Ed. Hirma Collins Hayon. 1962. Harper.
Hands of Fate. Ann Lorraine Thompson. 1975. (pbk.) 1.75 (ISBN 0-380-00503-4). Avon.
Hands of Glory. Jaan Kangilaski. 272p. (Orig.). 1981. pap. 2.25 (ISBN 0-345-28489-5, Del Rey). Ballantine.
Hands of Healing Murder. Barbara L'Amato. 288p. (Orig.). 1980. pap. 2.50 (ISBN 0-441-31618-2, Pub. by Charter Bks). Ace Bks.
Hands of Innocence. Jeffrey Ashford, pseud. 1966. large type ed. 7.50 o.p. (ISBN 0-8027-5105-9). Walker & Co.
Hands of Innocence: By Jeffrey Ashford Pseud. Roderic Jeffries. LC 66-12660. 1966. bds., 3.50. Walker.
Hands of Justice. A Novel. Frederick William Robinson. LC 7-41963. (Harper's Franklin square library, no. 304). 1883. Harper & Brothers.
Hands of Nara. Richard Washburn Child. LC 22-5073. E. P. Dutton & Company.
Hands of Orlac. Maurice Renard & Crewe-Jones, Florence, Tr. LC 29-27927. E. P. Dutton & Co., Inc.
Hands of Veronica: A Novel by Fannie Hurst. Fannie Hurst. LC 47-1462. 1947. Harper & Brothers.
Hands off! Beulah Marie Dix. 1919. The Macmillan Company.
Hands Unseen. Herman Landon. LC 24-19328. 1924. G. H. Watt.
Hands Up. Edward Dorn. Ed. by LeRoi Jones. 46p. (Orig.). 1964. pap. 1.50 (ISBN 0-87091-033-7). Corinth Bks.
Hands up! Frederick Niven. LC 13-6901. 1913. 1.30. The John Lane Company.
Hands up! Albert M Treynor. LC 28-5870. 1928. Dodd, Mead & Company.
Hands up!, or, Public Enemy No. 1: A Novel. Lev Ivanovich Davydychev. LC 81-182108. (Illus.). 5.00. Progress.
Hands up, or 35 Yrs. of Detective Life. David J. Cook. Repr. of 1897 ed. 20.00 o.s.i. Finch Pr.
Handsome, but Dead: A Novel. Alberta Elizabeth Hughes Wahl. LC 42-21090. 1942. Howell, Soskin, Inc.
Handsome Heart. Peter De Vries. LC 43-10423. 1943. Coward-Mc-Cann, Inc.
Handsome Humes: A Novel. William Black. 1894. Harper & Brothers.
Handsome Man. Susan Cheever. LC 80-27179. 11.95 (ISBN 0-671-42395-9). Simon and Schuster.
Handsome Man. Margaret Turnbull. LC 28-20927. The Reilly & Lee Company.
Handsome Road. Gwen Bristow. 1961. Grosset & Dunlap.
Handsome Road. Gwen Bristow. LC 68-1656. 1968. T. Y. Crowell Co.
Handsome Road. Gwen Bristow. 1973. (pbk.) 1.25. Pocket Books.
Handsome Sinner. Dora Delmar. (On cover: Library of American authors. no. 65). 1896. G. Munro's Sons.
Handwriting on the Wall. Milton Morris Propper. LC 41-21544. Harper & Brothers.
Handwriting on the Wall: An Exploit of the Shadowers, Inc. Isabel Egenton Ostrander. LC 24-13130. 1924. R. M. McBride & Company.
Handwrought Ancestors. Marion N. Rawson. 1936. Repr. price not set o.p. Finch Pr.
Handy Andy. Samuel Lover. (On cover: Lovell's library. v. 17, no. 849). 1887. J. W. Lovell Company.
Handy Andy. Samuel Lover. LC 4-16548. 1901. Little, Brown & Company.
Handy Andy. A Tale of Irish Life. Samuel Lover. LC 7-18767. (Seaside library, v. 2, no. 33). 1877. G. Munro.
Handy Andy. A Tale of Irish Life. Samuel Lover. (On cover: The Seaside library. Pocket ed. no. 663). 1885. G. Munro.
Handy Andy: A Tale of Irish Life. Samuel Lover. LC 6-12132. (Half-title: The English Comedie humaine. 2d series). 1906. The Century Co.
Handy Andy: A Tale of Irish Life. Samuel Lover. (Half-title: Everyman's library, ed. by Ernest Rhys. Fiction. no. 178). 1907. J. M. Dent & Co.
Handy Death. Robert L Fish & Henry B. Rothblatt. LC 73-10510. (Simon and Schuster novel of suspense). 1973. 6.95 (ISBN 0-671-21594-9). Simon and Schuster.
Handyman. Gus Stevens. pap. 1.95 o.s.i. (OPH-184, Ophelia). Olympia.
Hang - Up. Sam Ross. 1968. 4.95 o.p. (ISBN 0-698-10149-9). Coward.
Hang and Rattle. Allan R Bosworth. LC 47-1722. 1947. Doubleday & Co., Inc.
Hang by Your Neck. Henry Kane. LC 49-9611. (Inner sanctum mystery). 1949. Simon and Schuster.
Hang Dead Hawaiian Style. Patrick Morgan. (Operation Hang Ten Ser). 1969. pap. 0.75 o.p. (75-237). Manor Bks.
Hang for Treason. Robert Newton Peck. LC 75-14836. 1976. 6.95. (ISBN 0-385-07337-2). Doubleday.

Hang in There. Dale Armstrong. LC 73-6361. (O.s.i.). 192p. 1974. 7.95 o.s.i. (ISBN 0-670-36041-4). Grossman.

Hang in There. Robert O. Laaser. 4.95 o.s.i. Eden.

Hang Loose. Glen Chase, pseud. (Cherry Delight Ser.: No. 18). 1974. pap. 1.25 o.p. (LB233ZK, Leisure Bks). Nordon Pubns.

Hang McAllister. Matt Chisholm, pseud. 1970. pap. 0.75 o.p. (94005). Beagle Bks.

Hang Me in Hong Kong. Earl Norman. LC 76-383321. 1976. 6.95. Jade Orient.

Hang My Heart. Anne Brooks. LC 42-191369. 1942. W. Morrow and Company.

Hang My Wreath. Francis Van Wyck Mason. LC 41-5579. 1941. W. Funk, Inc.

Hang My Wreath. Francis Van Wyck Mason. LC 42-50856. 1942. The Sun Dial Press.

Hang on. Hobb Swetnam. LC 50-637408. 1949. Christopher Pub. House.

Hang the Hangman. Manning Lee Stokes. LC 56-7019. 1956. Arcadia House.

Hang the Little Man. John Creasey. LC 64-20517. Scribner.

Hang Town. Peter McCurtin. 1970. pap. 0.60 o.p. (B60-1097). Belmont-Tower.

Hang-Up. James Colton, pseud. (Orig.). 1969. pap. 1.25 o.p. (2095). Brandon.

Hang-up: A Novel. Sam Ross. LC 68-13243. 1968. Coward-McCann.

Hang up the Fiddle. Frederic Babcock. LC 54-9833. 1954. Doubleday.

Hang-Ups. Peter Marks, pseud. LC 72-11844. 1973. 5.95 (ISBN 0-394-48362-6). Random House.

Hanged for a Sheep. Rosemary Gatenby. LC 72-6883. (Red badge novel of suspense). 1973. 4.95 (ISBN 0-396-06712-3). Dodd, Mead.

Hanged for a Sheep. Rosemary Gatenby. LC 73-13678. 1973. 7.95 (ISBN 0-8161-6152-6). G. K. Hall.

Hanged for a Sheep: A Mr. and Mrs. North Mystery. Frances Louise Davis Lockridge & Richard Lockridge. LC 42-227253. 1942. J. B. Lippincott Company.

Hanged Man. Edmund Ward. LC 76-382527. 1976. 3.95 (ISBN 0-297-77117-5). Weidenfeld and Nicolson.

Hanged Man's House. E. X Ferrars, pseud. LC 73-14045. 1974. 4.95 (ISBN 0-385-09621-6). Published for the Crime Club by Doubleday.

Hanged Man's House. E. X Ferrars, pseud. LC 77-369652. (Penguin crime fiction). 1977. 1.95 (ISBN 0-14-004299-7). Penguin Books.

Hanged Men: A Novel of Suspense. David Harper. LC 76-25557. 7.95 (ISBN 0-396-07346-8). Dodd, Mead.

Hanger Eighteen. Robert Werevka, Jr. & Charles E. Seller. 176p. (Orig.). 1980. pap. 2.25 (ISBN 0-553-14473-1). Bantam.

Hanger Stout, Awake! Jack Matthews. LC 67-19192. 1967. Harcourt, Brace & World.

Hanging at Bahia Mar. Hal M. Caudle. 1975. 5.95 (ISBN 0-87482-077-4). Wake-Brook.

Hanging at Pulpit Rock. Lee Leighton, pseud. 160p. (Orig.). 1980. pap. 1.75 (ISBN 0-345-28853-X). Ballantine.

Hanging at Whiskey Smith. Eric Allen. 1975. (pbk.) 0.95. Ace Books.

Hanging Book. Bob Nilson. LC 70-103552. (Illus.). 64p. (Orig.). 1981. pap. 3.95 (ISBN 0-03-084412-6). HR&W.

Hanging by a Thread. Joan Kahn. LC 79-82943. 1969. 7.95. Houghton Mifflin.

Hanging Captain. Henry Lancelot Aubrey-Fletcher. LC 33-27074. Harcourt, Brace and Company.

Hanging Captain. Henry Wade. LC 80-8855. 301p. 1981. pap. 2.50i (ISBN 0-06-080548-X, P548, PL). Har-Row.

Hanging Garden. David Wagoner. LC 80-10301. 9.95 (ISBN 0-316-91705-2). Little, Brown.

Hanging Heiress. Richard Edward Wormser. LC 49-6394. 1949. M. S. Mill Co.

Hanging Hills. Samuel Anthony Peeples. LC 52-6648. (Dutton Diamond D western). 1952. Dutton.

Hanging in Sweetwater. Stephen Overholser. LC 73-17595. 1974. 4.95 (ISBN 0-385-00554-7). Doubleday.

Hanging in Sweetwater. Stephen Overholser. 1975. (pbk.) 1.25 (ISBN 0-523-00655-1). Pinnacle Books.

Hanging Johnny. Myrtle Johnston. LC 28-8369. 1928. D. Appleton and Company.

Hanging Judge. Bruce Hamilton. LC 48-548720. 1948. Harper.

Hanging Justice. Jake Logan. LC 75-14618. 1.25. Playboy Press.

Hanging Matter. Mary Hastings Bradley. LC 37-346703. 1937. D. Appleton-Century Company, Incorporated.

Hanging Moss. Paul Lindau. Tr. by Ayer, Winchester & Folger, Helen. LC 7-19022. (On cover: Appletons' town and country library. no. 107). 1892. D. Appleton and Company.

Hanging of Constance Hillier. Sydney Fowler Wright. LC 32-17270. 1932. The Macauley Company.

Hanging of the Angels. James McClure. 1969. pap. 0.95 o.p. (N2069). Pyramid Pubns.

Hanging of the Angels. James G. McClure. LC 68-14525. 1969. 5.95 o.p. (ISBN 0-394-42763-7). Random.

Hanging on. Dean Koontz. LC 73-80168. 1973. 6.95 (ISBN 0-87131-118-6). M. Evans Distributed by Lippincott, Philadelphia.

Hanging Stones. Manly Wade Wellman. LC 82-45463. 1982. 10.95 (ISBN 0-385-17672-4). Doubleday.

Hanging Trail. Jon Sharpe. (Trailsman Ser.: No. 2). (Orig.). 1980. pap. 2.25 (ISBN 0-451-11053-6, AE1053, Sig). NAL.

Hanging Tree. Dorothy M Johnson. LC 57-9141. 1957. Ballantine Books.

Hanging Tree and Other Stories. Dorothy M Johnson. LC 79-28702. (Series: Gregg Press Western Fiction Series.). 1980. 9.95 (ISBN 0-8398-2616-8). Gregg Press.

Hanging Waters: A Novel. Kenneth Westmacott Lane. LC 32-32766. G. P. Putnam's Sons.

Hanging Woman. Cecil John Charles Street. LC 31-19569. 1931. Dodd, Mead & Company.

Hanging Woman Creek. Louis L'Amour. 160p. (Orig.). 1981. pap. 2.25 (ISBN 0-553-14476-6). Bantam.

Hanging Woman Creek. Louis L'Amour. 1973. (pbk) 0.95. Bantam.

Hanging's Too Good. Lee Thayer, pseud. LC 43-18940. 1943. Dodd, Mead & Company.

Hangman. Paul Geddes. LC 77-76633. 1977. 7.95 (ISBN 0-312-35951-9). St. Martin's Press.

Hangman. Paul Geddes. LC 77-19207. 1978. 9.95 (ISBN 0-8161-6556-4). G. K. Hall.

Hangman. Jack Slade, pseud. (Belmont Tower Book). 1977. 1.25 (ISBN 0-505-51146-0). Tower Pubns.

Hangman for Paradise. Jack Canon. (Paradise Ser.). 256p. (Orig.). 1980. pap. 1.95 (ISBN 0-441-31634-4, Pub. by Charter Bks). Ace Bks.

Hangman's Beach. Thomas Head Raddall. LC 66-12211. 1966. Doubleday.

Hangman's Choice. Clifford Knight. LC 49-998017. (Guilt edged mystery). 1949. E. P. Dutton.

Hangman's Cliff. 1st Ed. Robert Neill. LC 56-10988. 1956. Doubleday.

Hangman's Coulee: By Al Cody Pseud. Archie Joscelyn. LC 51-1168. (Dodd Mead silver star westerns). 1951. Dodd, Mead.

Hangman's Crusade. James Barwick. 1983. pap. 2.95. Ballantine.

Hangman's Crusade. James Barwick. 320p. 1981. 12.95 (ISBN 0-698-11037-4, Coward). Putnam Pub Group.

Hangman's Crusade. Donald James & Tony Barwick. LC 80-18536. 1981. 11.95 (ISBN 0-698-11037-4). Coward, McCann & Geoghegan.

Hangman's Dozen. With a Foreword by Stanley Ellin. David Alexander. LC 61-11046. 1961. Roy Publishers.

Hangman's Guests. Stuart Martin. LC 31-11732. 1931. Harper & Brothers.

Hangman's Gulch. Eli Albert Chappe. LC 44-9906. 1944. Phoenix Press.

Hangman's Handyman. Henning Nelms. LC 42-21898. 1942. Simon and Schuster.

Hangman's Harvest. M. E. Chaber, pseud. (Milo March Ser). 1971. pap. 0.60 o.p. (ISBN 0-446-63507-3, 63-507). Paperback Lib.

Hangman's Harvest: By M. E. Chaber Pseud. 1st Ed. Kendell Foster Crossen. LC 52-724. (Holt mystery). 1952. Holt.

Hangman's Hat. Paul Ernst. LC 51-11731. 1951. M. S. Mill Co., and W. Morrow.

Hangman's Hill. Frank E. Pelligrin. LC 46-3566. 1946. Dodd, Mead & Company.

Hangman's Holiday. Dorothy Leigh Sayers. LC 33-25197. Harcourt, Brace and Company.

Hangman's Holiday. Dorothy Leigh Sayers. LC 79-19906. 1979. 12.95 (ISBN 0-8161-6783-4). G. K. Hall.

Hangman's House. Donn Byrne. LC 26-9264. 1926. The Century Co.

Hangman's House. Donn Byrne. LC 35-35053. Grosset & Dunlap.

Hangman's Knot. Dwight Bennett. LC 74-9476. 1975. 4.95 (ISBN 0-385-01867-3). Doubleday.

Hangman's Knot. Peter McCurtin. (Sundance Ser.: No. 33). 1980. pap. 1.75 (ISBN 0-8439-0764-9, Leisure Bks). Nordon Pubns.

Hangman's Knot for Christmas & Other Stories. Fremont Fullmer. 59p. 1974. 3.50 o.p. (ISBN 0-682-48052-5). Exposition.

Hangman's Range. Lee Floren. 1975. (pbk.) 0.95. Leisure Books.

Hangman's Row. Aaron Marc Stein. LC 81-43397. (Crime Club Ser.). 192p. 1982. 10.95 (ISBN 0-385-17945-6). Doubleday.

Hangman's Song: A Novel. Jess Shelton. LC 60-8175. 1960. Chilton Co., Book Division.

Hangman's Springs. John Henry Reese. LC 76-3930. 1976. 5.95 (ISBN 0-385-12150-4). Doubleday.

Hangman's Tide. John Buxton Hilton. LC 74-24574. 1975. 6.95. St. Martin's Press.

Hangman's Tie. Frances Moyer Ross Stevens. LC 43-181192. 1943. Pub. for the Crime Club by Doubleday, Doran and Company, Inc.

Hangman's Tie. Frances Moyer Ross Stevens. LC 46-21781. (On cover: A Bart house mystery, 32). 1946.

Hangman's Tree. Dorothy Cameron Disney. LC 49-7482. 1949. Random House.

Hangman's Valley. Joseph Chadwick. (Orig.). 1970. pap. 0.75 o.p. (ISBN 0-447-74625-1). Lancer.

Hangman's Valley. Joseph Chadwick. 1973. pap. 0.75 o.s.i. (74-800). Lancer.

Hangman's Whip. Mignon Good Eberhart. LC 40-8548. 1940. Doubleday, Doran & Company, Inc.

Hangman's Whip. Mignon Good Eberhart. LC 42-25900. 1942. Triangle Books.

Hangmen of Sleepy Valley. Davis Dresser. LC 49-50390. (Triple-A western classic). 1950. Jefferson House.

Hangmen of Sleepy Valley. Davis Dresser. LC 40-31520. 1940. W. Morrow and Company.

Hangmen's Territory. Jack M. Bickham. 1981. pap. 1.95 (ISBN 0-441-31632-8). Ace Bks.

Hangover. Max Lief. LC 29-228069. 1929. H. Liveright.

Hangover House. Arthur Sarsfield Ward. LC 49-5059. 1949. Random House.

Hangover Murders. Adam Hobhouse. LC 35-2180. 1935. A. A. Knopf.

Hangover Square. Patrick Hamilton. 1967. pap. 0.75 o.p. (54-522). Paperback Lib.

Hangover Square: Or, The Man with Two Minds; a Story of Darkest Earl's Court in the Year 1939. Patrick Hamilton. LC 49-5686. 1942. Random House.

Hangsaman. Shirley Jackson. LC 51-10525. 1951. Farrar, Straus and Young.

Hangtown. Les Savage. LC 56-12820. (Ballantine Books, 181). 1957. Ballantine Books.

Hangtree. Steve Sherman. 1977. pap. 1.50 (ISBN 0-89041-163-8, 3163). Major Bks.

Hangtree Range. William L. Hopson. 1978. pap. 1.25 o.s.i. (ISBN 0-505-51249-1). Tower Bks.

Hangtree Range. William L. Hopson. 1971. pap. 0.60 o.p. (60-485). Manor Bks.

Hangtree Range: By John Sims Pseud. William L Hopson. LC 52-9329. 1952. Arcadia House.

Hangwoman. Pavel Kohout. LC 80-22407. 12.95 (ISBN 0-399-12416-0). Putnam.

Hania. Henryk Sienkiewicz. LC 72-11936. (Short story index reprint series). 1973. (ISBN 0-8369-4241-8). Books for Libraries Press.

Hania. Henryk Sienkiewicz. Tr. by Jeremiah Curtin. LC 8-25953. 1897. Little, Brown, and Company.

Hania. Henryk Sienkiewicz & Gonski, Casimir, Tr. LC 98-1669. 1898. H. Altemus.

Hanit, the Enchantress. Garrett Chatfield Pier. LC 21-9368. E. P. Dutton & Company.

Hank Long's First Voyage. Daniel Whitford. LC 8-19569. Printed Under Supervision of J. J. Rafter.

Hank Miller. M. Herbert Wolf. LC 28-17645. Greenberg.

Hank of Hair. Geraldine Jay. LC 64-12695. 1964. Harper & Row.

Hank the Cowdog. John R. Erickson. (Illus.). 105p. (Orig.). 1983. pap. 5.95 (ISBN 0-9608612-2-X). Maverick Bks.

Hankow Return. Charles Stanley Archer. LC 41-18228. 1941. Houghton Mifflin Company.

Hanky Panky. Leslie Jarreau. 224p. (Orig.). 1982. pap. 2.50 (ISBN 0-523-41843-4). Pinnacle Bks.

Hannah. Dinah Maria Mulock Craik. Harper & Brothers.

Hannah. Dinah Maria Mulock Craik. LC 6-31088. 1872. Harper & Brothers.

Hannah. Dinah Maria Mulock Craik. LC 16-9370. Harper & Brothers.

Hannah. Betty Neels. (Harlequin Romances Ser.). 192p. 1981. pap. 1.25 (ISBN 0-373-02403-7, Pub. by Harlequin). PB.

Hannah and the Peacocks. Edward Caddick. LC 67-12209. 1967. Little, Brown.

Hannah Bye. Harrison Smith Morris. LC 20-7646. 1920. The Penn Publishing Company.

Hannah Fowler. Janice Holt Giles. LC 56-5606. 1956. Houghton Mifflin.

Hannah Fowler. Janice Holt Giles. 1977. 1.75 (ISBN 0-380-01740-7). Avon Books.

Hannah Fowler. Janice Holt Giles. LC 79-23764. 1980. 16.95 (ISBN 0-8161-3051-5). G. K. Hall.

Hannah Hereafter. Elizabeth Sutherland. LC 76-368155. 1976. 3.50 (ISBN 0-09-460860-1). Constable.

Hannah Hereafter. Elizabeth Sutherland. LC 77-85251. 1978. 7.95 (ISBN 0-15-138448-7). Harcourt Brace Jovanovich.

Hannah Herself: A Novel. Ruth Franchere. 1977. 1.25. Avon Books.

Hannah Jackson. Sherry Kafka. LC 66-23348. 1966. bds., 3.95. Morrow.

Hannah Massey. Catherine Cookson. (Signet Book). 1973. (pbk) 0.95. New American Lib.

Hannah: One of the Strong Women. Julia MacNair Wright. LC 9-913. National Temperance Society and Publication House.

Hannah; or, A Glimpse of Paradise. A Tale... Herman M Moos. (On cover: Library of select novels). Literary Eclectic Publishing House.

Hannah Says Foul Play. Dwight Vincent Babcock. LC 47-102. (Murder mystery monthly, no. 38). 1946. Avon Book Company.

Hannah Thurston. Bayard Taylor. LC 68-57552. (Muckrakers Ser.). Repr. of 1864 ed. lib. bdg. 15.00 (ISBN 0-8398-1952-8). Irvington.

Hannah Thurston: A Story of American Life. Bayard Taylor. LC 8-256542. 1864. G. P. Putnam.

Hannah Thurston: A Story of American Life. household ed. Bayard Taylor. LC 7-3065. (On cover: Hudson library, no. 36). 1899. G. P. Putnam's Sons.

Hannah's House. Shelby Hearon. LC 74-20496. 1975. 6.95 (ISBN 0-385-09648-8). Doubleday.

Hannah's House. Shelby Hearon. 1976. (pbk.) 1.50 (ISBN 0-671-80467-7). Pocket Books.

Hannibal Brooks. Lou Cameron. (Orig.). 1969. pap. 0.60 o.p. (73829). Lancer.

Hannibal Hooker: His Death and Adventures. William Harlan Hale. Random House.

Hannibal, Man of Destiny. Mirza Taleb. LC 72-97060. 1974. 7.95 (ISBN 0-8283-1501-9). Branden Press.

Hannibal of Carthage. Mary Dolan. LC 55-14619. 1955. Macmillan.

Hannibal of New York: Some Account of the Financial Loves of Hannibal St. Joseph and Paul Cradge. Thomas Isaac Wharton. LC 8-30658. (Leisure season series no. 2). 1886. H. Holt and Company.

Hannibal's Man, and Other Tales. The Argus Christmas Stories. Leonard Kip. 1878. The Argus Company, Printers.

Hanno's Doll: By Evelyn Piper Pseud. 1st Ed. Merriam Modell. LC 61-12785. 1961. Atheneum.

Hanoi. Nick Carter. (Nick Carter Ser.). (O.s.i.). (Orig.). 1968. pap. 0.60 o.s.i. (A312X, Award). Univ Pub & Dist.

Hanover. David Bryant Fulton. LC 72-92240. (American Negro, His History and Literature). 1969. Arno Press.

Hanover Heritage. Lynn Furstenberg-Forbes. 352p. 1983. pap. 2.95 (ISBN 0-523-41342-4). Pinnacle Bks.

Hanover: Or, The Persecution of the Lowly. A Story of the Wilmington Massacre. David Bryant Fulton. LC 42-357118. 1901. M. C. L. Hill.

Hanrahan's Colony. Jean Stubbs. LC 66-42904. 1964. Macmillan.

Hans Brinker: Or, The Silver Skates, a Story of Life in Holland. Mary Mapes Dodge. LC 3-27263. 1879. C. Scribner's Sons.

Hans Christian of Elsinore. Eva M Kristoffersen. LC 37-237791. 1937. A. Whitman & Co.

Hans Morganner. Oakley Seyeler. LC 74-80396. 1974. 7.95 (ISBN 0-8059-2036-6). Dorrance.

Hans of Iceland. library ed. Victor Marie Hugo. Tr. by George Burnham Ives. LC 7-5863. 1894. Little, Brown, and Company.

Hans of Iceland. Victor Marie Hugo & Smith, Huntington, 1857- Tr. LC 7-5864. T. Y. Crowell & Company.

Hans of Iceland: Or, The Demon of the North. A Romance. Victor Marie Hugo & Hudson, J. T., Tr. LC 7-429184. J. Winchester.

Hans of Iceland: Or, The Demon of the North. A Romance. Victor Marie Hugo & Hudson, J. T., Tr. 1862. J. Bradburn.

Hans Sees the World. Lisa Tetzner & Goldsmith, Margaret Leland, 1894- Tr. LC 34-31982. Covici, Friede.

Hans: The Story of a Motherless Boy. William Harvey Erb. LC 6-38404. J. S. Treichler & Bro.

Hans, Who Goes There? Florence Helitzer. LC 64-18077. 1964. Harper & Row.

Hansel and Gretel in Beverly Hills: A Novel. Sheila Weller. LC 77-27123. 1978. 8.95 (ISBN 0-688-03302-4). Morrow.

Hansford: A Tale of Bacon's Rebellion. St. George Tucker. LC 8-28274. 1857. G. M. West.

Hansi, The Girl Who Left the Swastika. Maria Ann Hirschmann. 1973. pap. 5.95 (ISBN 0-8423-1291-9). Tyndale.

Hansu's Journey: A Korean Story. Philip Jaisohn. LC 22-10460. 1922. P. Jaisohn & Co.

Hanta Yo. Ruth Beebe Hill. LC 77-74792. (Illus.). 1979. 14.95 (ISBN 0-385-13554-8). Doubleday.

Hanta Yo. Ruth Beebe Hill. 1980. 3.50 (ISBN 0-446-96298-8). Warner Books.

Hanta Yo. Ruth Beebe Hill. LC 80-28481. 1981. 9.95 (ISBN 0-446-97857-4) (ISBN 0-446-97857-4). Warner Books.

Hao in Blood. Howard Browne. LC 46-4253. 1946. The Bobbs-Merrill Company.

Hapless Child. Edward Gorey. 1961. pap. 4.75 (ISBN 0-8392-1044-2). Astor-Honor.

Hapless Child. Edward Gorey. LC 61-6959. (Illus.). 64p. 1980. 5.95 o.p. (ISBN 0-396-07817-6). Dodd.

Hapless Child. Edward Gorey. (Illus.). 64p. 1982. pap. 5.95 (ISBN 0-312-92282-5). Congdon & Weed.

Hapless Orphan: Or, Innocnet Victim of Revenge, As a Novel Founded on Incidents in Real Life in a Series of Letters from Caroline Francis to Maria B--... LC 12-23258. 1793. Printed at the Apollo Press, by Belknap and Hall.

Haploids. Jerry Sohl. LC 52-5571. 1952. Rinehart.

Happening. Walter S. J Swanson. LC 74-103616. 1970. 5.95. A. S. Barnes.

Happening: A Carol for All Seasons. John Wahtera. LC 74-10830. 1974. 4.95 (ISBN 0-316-91750-8). Little, Brown.

Happening at San Remo. Bruce Cassiday. (Orig.). pap. 0.75 o.p. (T1614). Pyramid Pubns.

Happening Handbook. Linda Millgate. LC 76-27408. (Illus.). 1977. pap. 5.95 o.p. HarBraceJ.

Happenstance. Carol Shields. 224p. 1980. 12.95 (ISBN 0-07-092377-9, GB). McGraw.

Happenthing in Travel on. Carole Spearin McCauley. LC 75-16508. 4.00 (ISBN 0-913780-08-1). Daughters, Inc.

Happier Eden. Beatrice Kean Stapleton Seymour. LC 37-162255. 1937. Little, Brown and Company.

Happiest Hooker. Terri Lincoln. 192p. (Orig.). 1973. pap. 1.95 o.p. (ISBN 0-87056-302-5, 6302). Brandon.

Happiest Time of Their Lives. Alice Duer Miller. LC 18-106983. 1918. The Century Co.

Happily Ever After. Felice Buckvar. 192p. (Orig.). 1980. pap. 2.25 (ISBN 0-89083-595-0). Zebra.

Happily Ever After. Adelaide Humphries. LC 42-8276. 1942. Arcadia House, Inc.

Happily Ever After. Hartzell Spence. LC 49-10961. 1949. Whittlesey House.

Happily Married. Corra May White Harris. LC 20-3192. 1.75. George H. Doran Company.

Happiness, and Other Stories. Mary Lavin. LC 72-108302. 1970. 4.95. Houghton Mifflin.

Happiness Bastard. Kirby Doyle. 1968. pap. 1.95 o.p. (0106). Essex Hse.

Happiness Hill. Grace Livingston Hill. LC 32-26745. 1932. J. B. Lippincott Company.

Happiness in a Warm Pussy. Keith Kerner. (Orig.). 1970. pap. 1.95 o.s.i. (OPH-182, Ophelia). Olympia.

Happiness in Cities: A Novel. Daniel Stern. LC 79-1712. 9.95 (ISBN 0-06-014096-8). Harper & Row.

Happiness Is. George H. Taggart. 1970. pap. 0.95 o.s.i. Review & Herald.

Happiness Is a Squeeze. John L. Donnelly. 4.50 o.p. Vantage.

Happiness Is a Star. Margaret Sleeper. 1970. 2.95 o.p. Vantage.

Happiness Is Too Much Trouble: A Novel. Sandra Hochman. LC 75-37115. 7.95 (ISBN 0-399-11638-9). Putnam.

Happiness of Being Rich. Hendrik Conscience. LC 6-28064. 1869. J. Murphy & Co.

Happiness of Father Happe. Cecily Rosemary Hallack. LC 39-27447. 1938. P. J. Kennedy & Sons.

Happiness Round the Corner. Winifred Mary Scott. LC 41-23271. 1941. H. C. Kinsey & Company, Inc.

Happy Acres. Edna Henry Lee Turpin. LC 13-19500. 1913. The Macmillan Company.

Happy Alienist: A Viennese Caprice. Wallace Smith. LC 36-510166. 1936. H. Smith and R. Haas.

Happy All the Time. Laurie Colwin. 1979. 2.25 (ISBN 0-671-82777-4). Pocket Books.

Happy All the Time. Laurie Colwin. LC 78-27164. 1979. 11.95 (ISBN 0-8161-6683-8). G. K. Hall.

Happy All the Time: A Novel. Laurie Colwin. LC 78-2425. 1978. 7.95 (ISBN 0-394-50190-X). Knopf: Distributed by Random House.

Happy & Hopeless. LC 79-17977. (In Great Decades Ser.: Vol. I). 1979. pap. 4.95 (ISBN 0-934160-01-5); Boxed Set Of In Great Decades. 30.00 (ISBN 0-934160-00-7). Devon Pr.

Happy and Hopeless: A Novel. Michael Whitney Straight. LC 79-17977. (Straight, Michael Whitney, In Great Decades). 1980. 30.00 (ISBN 0-934160-01-5). Devon Press.

Happy Animal Families: Poems. Ernestine Cobern Beyer. (Nursery treasure bk.). 1962. 1.00. Grosset.

Happy Anniversary, Harrison High. John Farris. 1973. (pbk) 0.95. Pocket Books.

Happy As Larry. Thomas Willes Chitty. LC 58-6723. 1958. Criterion Books.

Happy As the Grass Was Green. Merle Good. 1973. (pbk.) 0.95. Family Lib.

Happy As the Grass Was Green. Merle Good. LC 73-158174. 1971. 3.95 (ISBN 0-8361-1654-2). Herald Press.

Happy Average. Brand Whitlock. LC 4-26118. 1904. The Bobbs-Merrill Company.

Happy Birthday, Wanda June. Kurt Vonnegut, Jr. 1971. 7.95 (ISBN 0-440-03399-3, Sey Lawr). Delacorte.

Happy Birthday, Wanda June. Kurt Vonnegut, Jr. 1974. pap. 6.95 (ISBN 0-440-53422-4, Delta). Dell.

Happy Boy. author's ed. Bjornstjerne Bjornson & Anderson, Rasmus Bjorn, 1846- Tr. LC 4-16404. 1881. Houghton, Mifflin and Company.

Happy Boy. Bjornstjerne Bjornson & Archer, Mrs. William, Tr. LC 4-21184. 1896. Macmillan and Co.

Happy Boy. Bjornstjerne Bjornson & Archer, Mrs. William, Tr. LC 31-269629. (The Green and blue library). 1931. The Macmillan Company.

Happy Boy: A Tale of Norwegian Peasant Life. Bjornstjerne Bjornson. Tr. by Helen R. Allyn Gade. LC 6-13116. 1870. Sever, Francis, & Co.

Happy Boy. A Tale of Norwegian Peasant Life. Bjornstjerne Bjornson & Gade, Helen R. Allyn, Tr. LC 6-13118. (On cover: Lovell's library, v. 1, no. 3). 1882. J. W. Lovell Company.

Happy Childhood. Mary T Bauer. LC 30-479. B. Humphries, Inc.

Happy Christmas. Daphne Du Maurier. LC 40-34068. 1940. Doubleday, Doran and Co., Inc.

Happy Christmas Tree. Carlotta Belle. 2.50 o.p. Vantage.

Happy Days. Samuel Beckett. 1961. 10.00 (ISBN 0-394-47507-0, GP647). Grove.

Happy Days. Alan Alexander Milne. LC 15-21143. George H. Doran Company.

Happy Days. Margaret Moose. LC 74-946. 1974. 7.95 (ISBN 0-671-21784-4). Simon and Schuster.

Happy Days. Mabel Nelson Thor. LC 49-50438. 1949. Augustana Book Concern.

Happy Death. Albert Camus. LC 78-171141. (His Cahier 1). 1972. 5.95 (ISBN 0-394-47262-4). Knopf; Distributed by Random House.

Happy Death. Albert Camus. LC 72-8028. (His Cahier 1). 1973. (pbk.) 1.95 (ISBN 0-394-71865-8). Vintage Books.

Happy Deathday. Westbrook, Perry D. LC 47-24773. 1947. Phoenix Press.

Happy Dodd: Or, "She Hath Done What She Could,". Rose Terry Cooke. 1887. Ticknor and Company.

Happy Dodd: Or, "She Hath Done What She Could,". Rose Terry Cooke. LC 4-15083. Houghton, Mifflin and Company.

Happy Dream. John Boynoton Priestley. 1977. leather bound 180.00x o.s.i. (ISBN 0-8277-5029-3); 45.00x o.s.i. (ISBN 0-8277-5028-5). British Bk Ctr.

Happy End. Joseph Hergesheimer. LC 19-15540. 1919. A. A. Knopf.

Happy End. Ben Ames Williams. LC 39-11961. The Derrydale Press.

Happy Ending. Jean Detre. LC 67-22942. 1967. Simon and Schuster.

Happy Ending. Arlene Hale. (Candlelight Romance, 203). 0.95. Dell.

Happy Ending. Elizabeth Savage. 1973. 0.95. Popular Lib.

Happy Ending: A Novel. Elizabeth Savage. LC 76-175468. 1972. 6.95. Little, Brown.

Happy Ending: A Novel. Elizabeth Savage. LC 72-362. 1972. 8.95 (ISBN 0-8161-6028-7). G. K. Hall.

Happy Endings; 15 Stories by the Masters of the Macabre. Ed. by Damon Francis Knight. LC 73-11804. 1974. 8.95 (ISBN 0-672-51879-1). Bobbs-Merrill.

Happy Ever After... Beatrice Kean Stapleton Seymour. LC 42-568925. 1942. The Macmillan Company.

Happy Ever After. Herbert Russell Wakefield. LC 29-7961. 1929. D. Appleton and Company.

Happy Exiles. 1st Ed. Felicity Shaw. LC 56-6050. 1956. Harper.

Happy Failure. Solita Solano. LC 25-162077. 1925. G. P. Putnam's Sons.

Happy Familes Are All Alike: A Collection of Stories. Peter Hillsman Taylor. LC 59-15376. 1959. McDowell, Obolensky.

Happy Families. Saul Maloff. LC 68-17333. 1968. Scribner.

Happy Family. Violet Hummel Curtis. 1974. 4.50 (ISBN 0-682-47617-X). Exposition Press.

Happy Family. Bertha Muzzy Sinclair. LC 10-9821. G. W. Dillingham Company.

Happy Family. Frank Arthur Swinnerton. LC 12-24483. Hodder & Stoughton, George H. Doran Company.

Happy Family. Patricia Zelver. LC 75-175481. 1972. 6.95. Little Brown.

Happy Family. A Reading Book for Youth. Translated from the French. Claude Lezay-Marnezia. LC 42-31851. (Catholic tract, no. 14). 1840. E. Cummiskey.

Happy Find: Tr. from the French of Madame Gagnebin. Suzanne Gagnebin. Tr. by Lee, E. V. LC 6-44494. T. Y. Crowell & Co.

Happy Fool. John Leslie Palmer, pseud. LC 22-20173. 1922. Harcourt, Brace and Company.

Happy Foreigner. Enid Bagnold. LC 20-14213. 1920. 1.90. The Century Co.

Happy Ghost: And Other Stories. Henry Howarth Bashford. LC 27-23261. 1925. Harper and Brothers.

Happy-Go-Lucky. John Hay Beith. LC 13-19073. 1913. Houghton Mifflin Company.

Happy-Go-Lucky. Miriam Coles Harris. LC 9-10496. Houghton Mifflin Company.

Happy-Go-Lucky. Anita Blackmon Smith. LC 38-12586. 1938. Arcadia House.

Happy-Go-Lucky: Or, Leaves from the Life of a Good for Nothing; Tr. from the German of Joseph Freiherr Von Eichendorff. Joseph Karl Benedikt Eichendorff & Wister, Mrs. Annis Lee (Furness) 1830-1908, Tr. LC 6-31646. 1906. J. B. Lippincott Company.

Happy Halloween. Hoffman Phyllis. LC 82-6803. 1982. pap. 2.95 (A-133, Pub. by Aladdin). Atheneum.

Happy Harvest. Jane V. Barker & Sybil Downing. (Colorado Heritage Ser.: Bk. 2). (Illus.). 45p. (gr. 3-4). 1978. pap. text ed. 3.50x (ISBN 0-87108-213-6); tchr's ed. 3.00x (ISBN 0-87108-223-3). Pruett.

Happy Harvest: A Novel. Jeffery Farnol. LC 40-27074. 1940. Doubleday, Doran & Company, Inc.

Happy Harvest: A Novel. Jeffery Farnol. LC 41-5219. 1941. The Sun Dial Press.

Happy Hawkins. Robert Alexander Wason. LC 9-35792. Small, Maynard and Company.

Happy Hawkins in the Panhandle. Robert Alexander Wason. LC 14-18801. Small, Maynard and Company.

Happy Hearing. Rutger Bleecker Green. LC 99-3780. (Neely's universal library, no. 81). 1889. F. T. Neely.

Happy Highway. Francis Brett Young. LC 40-31640. Reynal & Hitchcock.

Happy Highwayman: Some Further Adventures of the Saint. Leslie Charteris. LC 39-20168. 1939. Pub. for the Crime Club, Inc., by Doubleday, Doran & Co., Inc.

Happy Highwayman: Some Further Adventures of the Saint. Leslie Charteris. LC 40-11333. 1940. The Sun Dial Press.

Happy Highwayman: Some Further Adventures of the Saint... Leslie Charteris. LC 45-8053. (Pocket book 272). 1945.

Happy Highways. Edith Inglesby. LC 82-25265. 1983. 11.95 (ISBN 0-89340-574-4). J. Curley.

Happy Highways. Margaret Storm Jameson. LC 20-17966. 1920. 2.00. The Century Co.

Happy Holiday. James Noble Gifford. 1946. Gramercy Publishing Co.

Happy Holiday! Thaddeus O'Finn, pseud. LC 50-10279. (Murray Hill mystery). 1950. Rinehart.

Happy Holiday! By Thaddeus O'Finn Pseud. Joseph T McGloin. LC 50-10279. (Murray Hill mystery). 1950. Rinehart.

Happy Holiday: Or, How Not to Travel in a Luxurious Land Yacht. Reine Eliasen. LC 71-121123. (Illus.). 1970. 1.95. San Bernardino Pub. Co.

Happy Hooker. Xaviera Hollander. 1982. pap. 3.50 (ISBN 0-440-13450-1). Dell.

Happy Hour: Or, Holiday Fancies and Every-Day Facts for Young People ... LC 17-4972. D. Appleton and Company.

Happy House. Betsey Riddle Hutton Zum Stolzenberg. LC 20-1214. George H. Doran Company.

Happy Hunting Grounds. new ed. Stanley Vestal. LC 73-5134. 1975. 5.95 (ISBN 0-8061-1141-0). University of Oklahoma Press.

Happy Hustler. Jason Forbes. 192p. (Orig.). 1974. pap. 2.25 o.s.i. (ISBN 0-89053-102-1, LB102). Lambda Pr.

Happy Hypocrite. Max Beerbohm. LC 19-25373. 1915. John Lane.

Happy Hypocrite: A Fairy Tale for Tired Men. Max Beerbohm. LC 41-32416. 1919. John Lane Company.

Happy Is the Man. Carrie E. Myers Gruhn. LC 63-5638. 1963. Moody Press.

Happy Island. Dawn Powell. LC 38-24557. Farrar & Rinehart, Incorporated.

Happy Island. Darwin Le Ora Teilhet. LC 50-10508. 1950. Sloane.

Happy Island: A New "Uncle William" Story. Jennette Barbour Perry Lee. LC 10-14906. 1910. The Century Co.

Happy Isle. Vivian Donald. (Signet Book, P5333). 1973. 0.60. New American Library.

Happy Isles. Basil King. LC 23-16817. 1923. Harper & Brothers.

Happy Jack. Max Brand. LC 36-787329. 1936. Dodd, Mead & Company.

Happy Jack. Frederick Faust. LC 80-10605. (His A Max Brand western). 1980. 10.95 (ISBN 0-89340-277-X). J. Curley.

Happy Killers. Kenneth Robeson. (Avenger,#21). 1974. (pbk.) 0.95. Warner Paperback Lib.

Happy Land. Evelyn Hawes. 1965. 4.50 o.p. (ISBN 0-15-138470-3). HarBraceJ.

Happy Land. MacKinlay Kantor. LC 42-36434. 1943. Coward-McCann, Inc.

Happy Land. Eric Mowbray Knight. LC 40-4886. Harper & Brothers.

Happy Land and Gentle Annie. MacKinlay Kantor. LC 45-9221. 1944. The Sun Dial Press.

Happy Landing! Peggy Gaddis, pseud. LC 43-139438. 1943. Arcadia House, Inc.

Happy Landings. Fannie Heaslip Lea. LC 30-122918. 1930. Dodd, Mead & Company.

Happy Man. Robert Olney Easton. LC 77-89435. (Zia book). 3.95 (ISBN 0-8263-0458-3). University of New Mexico Press.

Happy Man. Robert Olney Easton. LC 43-1682. 1943. The Viking Press.

Happy Man: A Novel. Hermann Kesten & Crankshaw, Edward, Tr. LC 47-2433. 1947. A. A. Wyn, Inc.

Happy Man, &C., &C. Founded Upon the Popular Drama. Samuel Lover. LC 7-15832. (On cover: Lovell's library. v. 4, no. 163). 1883. J. W. Lovell Company.

Happy Marriage: And Other Stories. Robert Verlin Cassill. LC 66-63480. 1966. Purdue University Studies.

Happy Marriage & Other Stories. Robert Verlin Cassill. LC 66-63480. 122p. 1966. 3.50 (ISBN 0-911198-11-3). Purdue.

Happy Medium. Lissa Charell. LC 60-9667. 1960. Coward-McCann.

Happy Medium. Vera Wheatley. LC 27-6548. E. P. Dutton & Company.

Happy Mountain. Maristan Chapman. LC 28-19621. 1928. The Viking Press.

Happy New Year: Herbie, and Other Stories. Evan Hunter. LC 63-8156. 1963. Simon and Schuster.

Happy New Year: Kamerades- 11 Stories. Drawings by the Author. 1st Ed. Robert James Collas Lowry. LC 54-6783. 1954. Doubleday.

Happy Night. William James Patmore Clarke. LC 8-33158. 1908. Cochrane Publishing Co.

Happy Nightmare. Prosper Buranelli. LC 51-12011. 1953. Crown Publishers.

Happy Parrot. Robert William Chambers. LC 29-14907. 1929. D. Appleton & Company.

Happy Parrot. Robert William Chambers. LC 31-284322. 1931. D. Appleton & Company.

Happy People. Sara Lucile Jenkins. LC 52-13118. 1953. Crowell.

Happy Pollyooly: The Rich Little Poor Girl. Edgar Jepson. LC 15-6451. 1.25. The Bobbs-Merrill Company.

Happy Prince. Oscar Wilde. (Illus.). 1975. 5.00 (ISBN 0-87482-069-3). Wake-Brook.

Happy Prince, and Other Tales. Oscar Wilde & Ruzicka, Rudolph, 1883- Illus. LC 38-131932. 1936. The Overbrook Press.

Happy Prince, and Other Tales. Oscar Wilde & Shinn, Everett, 1876- Illus. LC 40-35119. The John C. Winston Company.

Happy Princess: By Emily Noble Pseud. James Noble Gifford. LC 53-722207. 1953. Arcadia House.

Happy Prisoner. Monica Dickens. LC 47-3826. 1947. J. B. Lippincott Company.

Happy Prisoner. Lorna Rea. LC 32-8079. 1932. Harper & Brothers.

Happy Rascals. F. Morton Howard. LC 22-15204. E. P. Dutton & Company.

Happy Return. Angela Mackail Thirkell. LC 52-8510. 1952. Knopf.

Happy Return (Number Fifteen) Angela Mackail Thirkell. 1973. pap. 1.25 o.p. (ISBN 0-515-03021-X, V3021). Pyramid Pubns.

Happy Returns. 1st Ed. Manning Coles, pseud. LC 55-9229. 1955. Doubleday.

Happy Sadist. Drawings by Raymond Davidson. 1st Ed. Robert Newton Peck. LC 61-12568. 1962. Doubleday.

Happy Season. Illus. by Jocelyn Campbell. Mireille Burnand Cooper. LC 51-12761. 1952. Pellegrini & Cudahy.

Happy-Ship: Setting Forth the Adventures of Shorty and Patrick, U.S.S. Oklahoma. Stephen French Whitman. LC 14-4064. 1913. McBride, Nast & Company.

Happy Sinner. Elizabeth Hamilton Herbert. LC 31-117253. Farrar & Rinehart Incorporated.

Happy Summer Days. Sue Kaufman. LC 59-5788. 1959. Scribner.

Happy Thought Hall. Francis Cowley Burnand. LC 42-26416. 1872. Roberts Brothers.

Happy Thoughts. Francis Cowley Burnand. LC 10-41895. (Half-Title: Handy Volume Series. No. 1). 1872. Roberts Brothers.

Happy Thoughts. By F. C. Burnand. Francis Cowley Burnand. LC 31-19514. (Handy Volume Series. No. 1). 1869. Roberts Brothers.

Happy Time. Robert Louis Fontaine & Duvoisin, Roger Antoine, 1904- Illus. LC 45-5346. 1945. Simon and Schuster.

Happy to Be Here. Garrison Keillor. LC 81-66033. 1982. 11.95 (ISBN 0-689-11201-7). Atheneum.

Happy to Be Here: Stories & Comic Pieces. Garrison Keillor. 1983. pap. 4.95 (ISBN 0-14-006482-6). Penguin.

Happy Trails. Blanche Evans Dean. LC 68-57838. (Her Southern regional nature series). (Illus.). 1972. 2.95. Southern University Press.

Happy Tree. Sheila Kaye-Smith. LC 49-8932. 1949. Harper.

Happy Tree. Rosalind Murray. LC 27-2658. Harcourt, Brace & Company.

Happy Trio. James Noble Gifford. LC 45-3740. 1945. Gramercy Publishing Company.

Happy-Unfortunate: Or, The Female-Page. Elizabeth Boyd. LC 76-170583. (Foundations of the Novel). 1972. (ISBN 0-8240-0568-6). Garland Pub.

Happy Vacation & Other Stories. Nellie A. Lucas. 2.00 o.p. Carlton.

Happy Valley. Max Brand. LC 31-16330. 1931. Dodd, Mead & Company.

Happy Valley: A Novel. Patrick White. LC 40-8825. 1940. The Viking Press.

Happy Valley: A Story of Oregon. Anne Shannon Monroe. LC 16-11579. 1916. A. C. McClurg & Co.

Happy Warrior. Arthur Stuart-Menteth Hutchinson. LC 12-287023. 1913. Little, Brown, and Company.

Happy Warrior. Arthur Stuart-Menteth Hutchinson. LC 22-657. 1921. Little, Brown, and Company.

Happy Woman. Maurice Weyl. LC 20-6129. 1920. M. Kennerley.

Happy Years. Inez Haynes Irwin. LC 19-15484. 1919. H. Holt and Company.

Har Lampkins;" A Narrative of Mountain Life on the Borders of the Two Virginias. Abel Patton. 1901. The Abbey Press.

Harangue the Trees Said to the Bramble Come Reign Over Us. Garet Garrett. LC 27-35177. E. P. Dutton & Company.

Haraszthy at the Mint. Brian McGinty. (Famous California Trials: Vol. 10). (Illus.). 62p. 1975. 8.50 (ISBN 0-87093-092-3). Dawsons.

Harbinger. Michael T. Hinkemeyer. 2.50 (ISBN 0-671-82179-2). Pocket Books.

Harbinger. Aryan Kelton. LC 28-18810. American-India Publishing Company.

Harbinger. Aryan Lewis Kelton. LC 28-18810. 1923. American-India Publishing Company.

Harbin's Ridge. Henry E Giles. LC 51-5287. 1951. Houghton Mifflin.

Harbin's Ridge. 2d ed. Henry E Giles & Janice Holt Giles. LC 76-47638. 1977. 8.95 (ISBN 0-395-25020-X). Houghton Mifflin.

Harbor. Ernest Poole. LC 57-9755. (American century series, S-3). 1957. Sagamore Press.

Harbor. Ernest Poole. LC 15-284422. 1915. The Macmillan Company.

Harbor. Ernest Poole. Ed. by Richards, Edward Bradley. LC 25-793897. (On cover: The Macmillan pocket classics). 1925. The Macmillan Company.

Harbor Lights. Anne Duffield. LC 54-107231. 1954. Arcadia House.

Harbor Master. Roberts Theodore Goodridge. LC 13-2841. 1913. 1.25. L. C. Page & Company.

Harbor Mouse. Hannah Tillich. LC 77-15967. 1978. 7.95 (ISBN 0-8128-2457-1). Stein and Day.

Harbor of Doubt. Francis William Sullivan. LC 15-24883. W. J. Watt & Company.

Harbor of Love. Ralph Henry Barbour. LC 12-14244. 1912. 1.50. J. B. Lippincott Company.

Harbor of the Heart. Joan Thompson. 192p. 1981. pap. 2.25 (ISBN 0-345-28747-9). Ballantine.

Harbor of the Little Boats: A Novel of Suspense. William E Huntsberry. LC 58-10695. 1958. Rinehart.

Harbor of Whales & Other Short Stories. Erje Ayden. 48p. (Orig.). 1964. pap. 8.00 (ISBN 0-89366-003-5). Ultramarine Pub.

Harbor Road. Sara Ware Bassett. LC 19-15282. 1919. The Penn Publishing Company.

Harbor Tales Down North. Norman Duncan. LC 72-121536. (Short story index reprint series). (Illus.). 1970. Books for Libraries Press.

Harbor Tales Down North. Norman Duncan. LC 18-268243. Fleming H. Revell Company.

Harbour. Philip MacDonald. LC 32-21184. 1932. Doubleday, Doran & Company, Inc.

Harbourmaster: A Novel. William McFee. LC 32-999. 1931. Doubleday, Doran & Company, Inc.

Harbourmaster: A Novel. William McFee. LC 31-28601. 1932. Doubleday, Doran & Company, Inc.

Harbourmaster: A Novel. William McFee. LC 36-323403. The Sun Dial Press.

Harcourt: Or, A Soul Illu,Ined. Anne Somers Gilchrist. LC 6-44059. 1886. J. B. Lippincott Company.

Harcourts: Illustrating the Benefit of Retrenchment and Reform. 3d ed. (Added t.-p.: Stories from real life pt. 3). 1837. S. Colman.

Hard Act to Follow. Troy Conway, pseud. (Coxeman Ser). (Orig.). 1972. pap. 0.75 o.p. (ISBN 0-446-64761-6, 64-761). Paperback Lib.

Hard As Stone. Ezio Taddei. LC 75-169565. (Short story index reprint series). (Illus.). 1971. (ISBN 0-8369-4028-8). Books for Libraries Press.

Hard As Stone. Ezio Taddei & Keene, Frances, Tr. LC 42-3958. 1948. New Writers.

Hard Blue Sky. Shirley Ann Grau. LC 58-7562. 1958. Knopf.

Hard-Boiled Blonde. Watkins Eppes Wright. LC 48-2115. 1941. Arcadia House, Inc.

Hard-Boiled Detective: Stories from Black Mask Magazine, 1920-1951. Herbert Ruhm. LC 76-27646. 1977. 2.45 (ISBN 0-394-72156-X). Vintage Books.

Hard-Boiled Omnibus: Early Stories from Black Mask, Edited, and with an Introduction. Black Mask & Shaw, Joseph Thompson, 1874- Ed. LC 46-82932. 1946. Simon and Schuster.

Hard-Boiled Virgin. Frances Newman. LC 76-51674. (Recovered Fiction by American Women). 1977. 22.00 (ISBN 0-405-10052-3). Arno Press.

Hard-Boiled Virgin. Frances Newman. LC 26-21301. 1926. Boni & Liveright.

Hard-Boiled Virgin. Frances Newman. LC 80-16376. 1980. 5.95 (ISBN 0-8203-0526-X). University of Georgia Press.

Hard-Boiled Virgin. Josiah Pitts Woolfolk. LC 48-15379. (New Avon library, 138). 1947. Avon Book Co.

Hard Cain. James Mallahan Cain. LC 80-12377. (Gregg Press Mystery Fiction Series). 1980. 13.95 (ISBN 0-8398-2656-7). Gregg Press.

Hard Candy: A Book of Stories. Tennessee Williams. LC 54-4797. 1954. New Directions.

Hard Candy: Short Stories. Tennessee Williams. LC 59-16430. 1959. pap. 5.95 (ISBN 0-8112-0221-6, NDP225). New Directions.

Hard Case. David Bean. LC 77-359349. 1976. 3.50 (ISBN 0-436-03702-5). Secker and Warburg.

Hard Cash. A Matter-of-Fact Romance. household ed. Charles Reade. Fields, Osgood & Co.

Hard Cash. A Matter-of-Fact Romance. Charles Reade. (Seaside library, v. 6, no. 112). 1877. G. Munro.

Hard-Core Murder. Paul Kenyon. (Baroness,#4). 1974. (pbk.) 0.95 (ISBN 0-671-77918-4). Pocket Books.

Hard Country. Chad Merriam. 1976. (pbk.) 1.25. Ballantine.

Hard Country and Gold. Clement Yore. LC 35-3927. Macauley Company.

Hard Day at the Scaffold. Alfred Hitchcock. 176p. 1981. pap. 2.25 (ISBN 0-440-13434-X). Dell.

Hard Day's Knight. Ted Mark, pseud. (Orig.). pap. 0.60 o.p. (73-508). Lancer.

Hard Day's Knight. Ted Mark. (Man from O.R.G.Y.). 1973. (pbk.) 1.25. Dell.

Hard Edge. Anthony DeStefano. 1978. pap. 1.50 (ISBN 0-532-15329-4). Woodhill.

Hard Facts. Howard Spring. LC 44-7464. 1944. The Viking Press.

Hard Feelings. Don Bredes. LC 76-42213. 8.95 (ISBN 0-689-10745-5). Atheneum.

Hard Ground. Dominick R Corbo. LC 53-12131. 1954. Vantage Press.

Hard Guys. Marcus Van Heller, pseud. LC 78-7581. 1969. 1.75. Ophelia Press.

Hard Guys and Hostages. Robert Moore, pseud. LC 74-27153. 1970. 1.95. Ophelia Press.

Hard Hat Girl, Power Engineer: A Novel. McCulloch Byers. LC 76-29554. 1976. 5.95. Fairfield House.

Hard Heart. From the German of Golo Raimund Pseud. Bertha Heyn Frederich. Tr. by H., S. LC 6-42857. 1884. J. B. Lippincott & Co.

Hard Hearts Are for Cabbages: A Novel. Vii Putnam. LC 59-9167. 1959. Crown Publishers.

Hard Hit. John William Wainwright. LC 74-15223. 1975. 6.95. St. Martin's Press.

Hard Hit. John William Wainwright. (Berkley book). 1979. 1.75 (ISBN 0-425-04136-0). Berkley Pub. Corp.

Hard Knot: A Novel. Charles Gibbon. (Harper's handy series, no. 14). 1885. Harper & Brothers.

Hard Laughter. Anne Lamott. LC 80-14143. 1980. 12.95 (ISBN 0-670-36140-2). Viking Press.

Hard Lesson. Emily Sharp H. Carmeron. LC 6-21855. (On cover: Braodway series, no. 5). J. A. Taylor and Company.

Hard Liberty. Rosalind Murray. LC 29-183325. Harcourt, Brace and Company.

Hard Life. David Danziger. 1973. pap. 1.95 o.p. (Z110, Zebra). Grove.

Hard Life: A Novel. Flann O'Brien. 1977. pap. 3.50 (ISBN 0-14-004517-1). Penguin.

Hard Life: A Novel. Brian O'Nolan. LC 77-6454. 1977. 1.95 (ISBN 0-14-004517-1). Penguin Books.

Hard Line. Michael Z Lewin. LC 82-8094. 1982. 10.45 (ISBN 0-688-01335-X). Morrow.

Hard Living on Clay Street. Joseph T. Howell. LC 73-79736. 440p. 1973. pap. 6.50 (ISBN 0-385-05317-7, Anch). Doubleday.

Hard Luck Money. Giles Tippette. (Orig.). 1982. pap. 2.50 (ISBN 0-440-13868-X). Dell.

Hard Man. Leo Katcher. LC 57-6759. 1958. Schuster.

Hard Man. Leo Katcher. LC 57-6759. 1957. MacMillan.

Hard Man. Keith Rockwell. 192p. (Orig.). 1974. pap. text ed. 1.95 o.p. (ISBN 0-87056-391-2, 6391). Brandon.

Hard Man to Kill. Ritchie Perry. LC 73-6700. (Midnight novel of suspense). 1973. 5.95 (ISBN 0-395-17204-7). Houghton Mifflin.

Hard Man with a Gun. 1st Ed. Charles N Heckelmann. LC 54-8293. 1954. Little, Brown.

Hard Maple. Anna Bartlett Warner. LC 8-33470. (On cover: Ellen Montgomery's book shelf vol. V). 1859. Shepard, Clark & Brown.

Hard Men. Jon Burmeister. LC 77-9170. 1978. 8.95 (ISBN 0-312-36196-3). St. Martin's Press.

Hard Men. Theodore V. Olsen. 160p. 1982. pap. 2.25 (ISBN 0-449-14475-5, GM). Fawcett.

Hard Men: Short Stories. Frank O'Rourke. LC 56-9578. 1956. Ballantine Books.

Hard Money. Clarence Budington Kelland. LC 30-132329. 1930. Harper & Brothers.

Hard Money. Clarence Budington Kelland. LC 34-68393. 1932. A. L. Burt Company.

Hard Money. A Double D Western. Frederick Dilley Glidden. LC 40-5399. 1940. Doubleday, Doran & Company, Inc.

Hard Monry. A Double D Western. Luke Short. LC 40-5399. 1940. Doubleday, Doran & Company, Inc.

Hard on the Road. Barbara Moore. LC 73-13091. 1974. 6.95 (ISBN 0-385-08191-X). Doubleday.

Hard-Pan: A Story of Bonanza Fortunes. Geraldine Bonner. LC 5333. 1900. The Century Co.

Hard Rain. Dinitia Smith. LC 80-13638. 9.95 (ISBN 0-8037-3409-3). Dial Press.

Hard Rain Falling. Don Carpenter. LC 66-12358. 1966. Harcourt, Brace & World.

Hard Rider. Charley Barstow. (Orig.). 1981. pap. 1.95 (ISBN 0-505-51653-5). Tower Bks.

Hard Riders. Frank Anvic, pseud. 192p. 1973. pap. 1.95 o.p. (ISBN 0-87682-374-6, 7374). Barclay Hse.

Hard Riders. Lee Floren. 1978. pap. 1.25 o.s.i. (ISBN 0-8439-0522-0, Leisure Bks). Nordon Pubns.

Hard Riders. Lee Floren. pap. 0.50 o.p. (50-310). Manor Bks.

Hard Riders. Tom J Hopkins. LC 49-932274. (Double D western). 1949. Doubleday.

Hard Riding Slim Magee. Clement Yore. LC 29-948668. The Macaulay Company.

Hard Road to Klondike. Michael MacGowan. Tr. by Valentin Iremonger from Irish. 1973. pap. 6.95 (ISBN 0-7100-7686-X). Routledge & Kegan.

Hard Rock Man. James Beardsley Hendryx. LC 40-32079. Carlton House.

Hard Rock Showdown. Bradford Scott. 1968. pap. 0.50 o.p. (R1913). Pyramid Pubns.

Hard Sell. William Haggard. 1966. 3.75 o.p. Washburn.

Hard Sell. Charles Rubin. LC 76-51783. 7.95 (ISBN 0-517-52956-4). Crown Publishers.

Hard Sell: By William Haggard. Richard Clayton. (Signet bk., P3165). 1967. New Amer. Lib.

Hard Sell: By William Haggard Pseud. 1st Amer. Ed. Richard Clayton. LC 66-14234. 1966. bds., 3.75. Washburn.

Hard Summer. Stephen E. Fugate. 224p. (Orig.). 1981. pap. 1.95 (ISBN 0-449-14389-9, GM). Fawcett.

Hard Texas Winter. Preston Lewis. (Orig.). 1981. pap. 1.75 o.s.i. (ISBN 0-505-51658-6). Tower Bks.

Hard Time Bunch. Clifton Adams. LC 72-96222. 1973. 4.95 (ISBN 0-385-02182-8). Doubleday.

Hard Times. Charles Dickens. LC 65-6516. (Perennial classic). 1965. Harper & Row.

Hard Times. Charles Dickens. LC 6-26454. 1854. T. L. McElrath & Co.

Hard Times. Charles Dickens. LC 6-264493. (Lovell's library, v. 4, no. 170). 1883. J. W. Lovell Company.

Hard Times. Charles Dickens. (Half-title: Everyman's library, ed. by Ernest Rhys. Fiction. no. 292). 1907. J. M. Dent & Co.

Hard Times. Charles Dickens. LC 36-37143. (Half-title: Everyman's library, ed. by Ernest Rhys. no. 292). 1927. J. M. Dent & Sons, Ltd.

Hard Times. Gordon Newman. 1975. (pbk.) 1.50. Dell.

Hard Times: A Novel. Charles Dickens. LC 6-26450. (Harper's Franklin square library. Duodecimo ed.). 1883. Harper & Brothers.

Hard Times: An Authoritative Text, Backgrounds, Sources, and Contemporary Reactions, Criticism. Charles Dickens. Ed. by George Harry Ford & Sylvere Monod. LC 66-11307. (Norton critical edition). 1966. W. W. Norton.

Hard Times and Arnie Smith. Clifton Adams. LC 75-175351. (Doubleday western). 1972. 4.95. Doubleday.

Hard Times, and Reprinted Pieces. Charles Dickens. LC 41-38119. (Half-title: Works of Charles Dickens... xvi). 1874. G. W. Carleton & Co.

Hard Times for These Times. Charles Dickens. Ed. by David Craig. LC 70-417894. (Penguin English library, EL42). 1969. Penguin.

Hard Times for These Times. Charles Dickens. LC 55-13926. (New Oxford illustrated Dickens). (Illus.). 1955. Oxford University Press.

Hard Times for These Times and Reprinted Pieces. Charles Dickens. 1867. Hurd and Houghton.

Hard Times for These Times and Reprinted Pieces... Charles Dickens. LC 6-26430. 1868. Hurd and Houghton.

Hard Times for These Times, Hunted Down, Holiday Romance, and George Silverman's Explanation. Charles Dickens. (Half-title: The centenary edition of the works of Charles Dickens in 36 volumes). 1911. Chapman & Hall, Ltd.

Hard to Be a God. Arkadii Natanovich Strugatskii. 1973. 6.66 o.p. (ISBN 0-07-073756-8). McGraw.

Hard to Be a God. Arkadii Natanovich Strugatskii & Boris Natanovich Strugatskii. 228p. 1973. 6.95 o.p. (ISBN 0-8164-9121-6, Continuum Bks). Seabury.

Hard to Be a God. Arkadii Natanovich Strugatskii & Boris Natanovich Strugatskii. (Science Fiction Ser). 1974. pap. 1.25 o.p. (UY1141). DAW Bks.

Hard to Get. Arthur Somers Roche. LC 37-16071. 1937. Dodd, Mead & Company.

Hard to Kill. Lewis Brant, pseud. 192p. (OSI). 1972. Repr. of 1965 ed. 3.95 o.s.i. Lenox Hill.

Hard to Kill. James Marcott. (Fawcett gold medal book). 1975. (pbk.) 0.95. Fawcett.

Hard Trade. Arthur Lyons. LC 80-19679. (Rinehart suspense novel). 10.95 (ISBN 0-03-053621-9). Holt, Rinehart, and Winston.

Hard Trail to Santa Fe. Tom West. 205p. (Orig.). 1980. pap. 1.95 (ISBN 0-89083-676-0). Zebra.

Hard-Up. Mark Henry. pap. 1.95 o.p. (8016). Cameo.

Hard Way. George G. Gilman, pseud. (Steele Ser.: No. 18). 160p. 1980. pap. 1.50 (ISBN 0-523-40528-6). Pinnacle Bks.

Hard Way. Robert V Williams. LC 52-9851. 1952. Putnam.

Hard Winners. John E Quirk. LC 65-11284. 5.95. Random.

Hard Winners. John E Quirk. LC 65-11284. (N133). 1966. Avon.

Hard Woman: A Story in Scenes. Violet Hunt. 1895. D. Appleton and Company.

Hard-Won Victory. Grace Denio Litchfield. LC 7-19001. 1888. G. P. Putman's Sons.

Hard Wood. Arthur Olney Friel. LC 25-15390. 1925. The Penn Publishing Company.

Hardacre. Clement Lister Skelton. LC 76-19039. 1976. 8.95 (ISBN 0-8037-3431-X). Dial Press.

Hardacre. Clement Lister Skelton. 1977. 2.25. Popular Library.

Hardboiled Dicks: An Anthology and Study of Pulp Detective Fiction. Ed. by Ron Goulart. LC 65-26328. 4.95. Sherbourne.

Hardboiled Dicks: An Anthology and Study of Pulp Detective Fiction, Ed. by Ron Goulart. Ed. by Ron Goulart. (50560). 1967. Pocket Bks.

Hardboiled Tenderfoot. John Ulrich Giesy. LC 39-15605. Dodge Publishing Company.

Hardcase. Frederick Dilley Glidden. LC 42-7369. 1942. Doubleday, Doran & Co., Inc.

Hardcase. Luke Short. LC 42-7369. 1942. Doubleday, Doran & Co., Inc.

Hardcastle. John Yount. LC 79-21977. 10.95 (ISBN 0-399-90076-4). R. Marek Publishers.

Harder They Come. Michael Thelwell. LC 79-2321. 1980. 12.50 (ISBN 0-394-50652-9, GP832). Grove.

Harder They Come: A Novel. Michael Thelwell & Perry Henzell. LC 79-2321. 1979. 10.00 (ISBN 0-394-50862-9). Grove Press: Distributed by Random House.

Harder They Fall: A Novel. Budd Schulberg. LC 47-30396. 1947. Random House.

Harder You Try, the Harder It Gets. Troy Conway, pseud. (Coxeman Ser). (Orig.). 1971. pap. 0.75 o.p. (ISBN 0-446-64768-3, 64-768-3). Paperback Lib.

Hardest Man in the Sierras. L P Holmes. 1975. (pbk.) 0.95. Ace Books.

Hardhats. Helen Marie Newell. LC 56-5057. 1956. Houghton Mifflin.

Hardican's Hollow. Joseph Smith Fletcher. LC 27-207571. George H. Doran Company.

Harding of Allenwood. Harold Bindloss. LC 15-128832. 1915. 1.30. Frederick A. Stokes Company.

Harditts in Sawna. Robert Nichols. LC 78-10765. (His Daily lives in Nghsi-Altai; book 3). 1979. 3.95 (ISBN 0-8112-0684-X). New Directions.

Hardliners. Richard Clayton. LC 77-123262. 1970. 4.95 (ISBN 0-8027-5209-8). Walker.

Hardliners. William Haggard. 4.95 o.p. (ISBN 0-8027-5209-8). Walker & Co.

Hardly a Man Is Now Alive. Herbert Brean. pap. 0.95 o.p. (01775, Collier). Macmillan.

Hardly a Man Is Now Alive: A Mystery Novel. Herbert Brean. LC 50-10463. 1950. Morrow.

Hardman: The Charleton Knife's Back in Town, No. 1. Ralph Dennis. 192p. (Orig.). 1982. pap. 2.25 (ISBN 0-523-41825-6). Pinnacle Bks.
Hardon. Ira Brukner. LC 80-18377. (Illus.). 1980. cloth 13.00 (ISBN 0-916906-30-2); pap. 7.50. Konglomerati.
Hardrock. Frank Bonham. LC 58-11401. (Ballantine westerns, 269K). 1958. Ballantine Books.
Hardrock and Silver Sage. Ross Santee. LC 51-12538. 1951. Scribner.
Hardrock Romeo. Peter Keyes. (Orig.). pap. 0.95 o.p. (1123). Brandon.
Hardware. Edward L McKenna. LC 29-10301. 1929. R. M. McBride & Company.
Hardwater Country. Frederick Busch. LC 78-23745. 1979. 8.95 o.p. (ISBN 0-394-50560-3). Knopf.
Hardwater: Stories. Frederick Busch. LC 78-23745. 1979. 8.95 (ISBN 0-394-50560-3). Knopf.
Hardway Diamonds Mystery. Miles Burton. LC 30-31592. 1930. The Mystery League, Inc.
Hardwicke: A Novel. Henry Edward Rood. 1902. Harper & Brothers.
Hardwood County Rescue Squad. James O. Page. 132p. (Orig.). (gr. 8-12). 1980. pap. 5.75 (ISBN 0-936174-01-3). Backdraft.
Hardy Breed: By Giles A. Lutz. 1st Ed. Giles A Lutz. LC 66-11722. (Double D western). 1966. Doubleday.
Hardy Norseman. Ada Ellen Bayly. LC 6-10295. (On cover: Seaside library. Pocket ed., no. 1196.). G. Munroe.
Hardy Perennial: By Helen Hull. Helen Rose Hull. LC 33-270641. Coward-McCann, Inc.
Hardy Rye. Daniel Chase. LC 26-19679. The Bobbs-Merrill Company.
Hardy: The Tragic Novels. Ed. by R. P. Draper. 1981. pap. 20.00x (ISBN 0-333-15502-5, Pub. by Macmillan England). State Mutual Bk.
Hardy's Poetic Vision in The Dynasts: The Diorama of a Dream. Susan Dean. LC 76-45895. 16.50 (ISBN 0-691-06324-9). Princeton University Press.
Hardy's Vision of Man. Frank Rodney Southerington. LC 77-25847. (Illus.). 1971. 10.00 (ISBN 0-389-04080-0). Barnes & Noble.
Hardy's Wessex Novels. Randall Williams. 1974. 20.00 o.p. Porter.
Hare. Ernest James Oldmeadow. 1921. 2.00. The Century Co.
Hare & the Hornbill. Okot P'Bitek. (African Writers Ser.). 1978. pap. text ed. 3.00x (ISBN 0-435-90193-1). Heinemann Ed.
Hare Sitting Up. Michael Innes, pseud. LC 82-47565. 224p. 1982. pap. 2.84i (ISBN 0-06-080590-0, P 590, PL). Har-Row.
Hare Sitting up. John Innes Mackintosh Stewart. LC 59-13634. 1959. Dodd, Mead.
Harem. Louis Charles Royer. LC 32-24978. Greenberg.
Harem Cross, a Novel of the Near East. 1st Ed. Gourgen Yanikian. LC 53-6721. 1953. Exposition Press.
Hare's Blanket & Other Tales. George Orwell. 1967. pap. 0.50 o.p. Northwestern U Pr.
Hargo: Or, The Age of Fire. Francis Marion Yates. 1898. G. S. Bowen.
Hargrave Deception. Howard Hunt. LC 79-3889. 1980. 10.95 (ISBN 0-8128-2714-7). Stein and Day.
Harilek: A Romance. Martin Louis Alan Gompertz. LC 23-15475. 1923. Houghton Mifflin Company.
Hariyana: Part One,"the Yoga of Dejection". Harvey Meyers. LC 79-84779. (Illus.). 256p. (Orig.). 1979. pap. 6.00 (ISBN 0-934094-01-2). Omkara Pr.
Hark, Hark, the Watchdogs Bark. Stanton Forbes, pseud. LC 74-33694. 1975. 5.95 (ISBN 0-385-07266-X). Published for the Crime Club by Doubleday.
Hark, Hark, the Watchdogs Bark. Tobias Wells. LC 74-33694. (Crime Club Ser). 144p. 1975. 5.95 o.p. (ISBN 0-385-07266-X). Doubleday.
Harker File. Marc Olden. (Signet Book). 1976. (pbk.) 1.50. New American Library.
Harkfast. Hugh C. Rae. LC 75-26196. 1976. 7.95 o.p. (ISBN 0-312-36295-1). St Martin.
Harkfast: The Making of the King. Hugh C Rae. LC 75-26196. 1976. 7.95. St. Martin's Press.
Harkfast: The Making of the King. Hugh C Rae. LC 77-350042. 1976. 3.25 (ISBN 0-09-461180-7). Constable.
Harking Back. Laurence Mell Glenn. LC 9-6100. 1908. Furman University.
Harkriders: A Novel. Opie Percival Read. LC 3-17532. Laird & Lee.
Harlan Symthe Grossfeld. Henry Edwards. LC 78-100631. 1970. 5.95. Prentice-Hall.
Harlem. Ed. by John Henrik Clarke. LC 72-20689. (Signet book). 1970. 0.95. New American Library.
Harlem Go-Getters & Other Short Stories. Elizabeth G. Conley. 1963. 2.50 o.p. (ISBN 0-682-41081-0). Exposition.
Harlem Hit. Roosevelt Mallory. (Radcliff, no. 10). 1973. (pbk.) 1.50 (ISBN 0-87067-435-8). Holloway House.
Harlem Showdown. Mike Barry. (Lone Wolf). (Berkley medallion book: Vol. 10). 1975. (pbk.) 0.95 (ISBN 0-425-02761-9). Berkley Pub. Co.
Harlem Story. John Henry Hewlett. LC 48-10998. 1948. Prentice-Hall.
Harlem todos los dias. Emilio Diaz. 232p. 1978. pap. 4.30 (ISBN 0-940238-17-9). Ediciones Huracan.
Harlem Underground. Ed Lacy. 1969. pap. 0.75 o.p. (T2075). Pyramid Pubns.
Harlequin. Morris L. West. LC 75-8638. 1975. 13.95 (ISBN 0-8161-6291-3). G. K. Hall.
Harlequin: A Novel. Morris L. West. LC 74-8822. 1974. 7.95 (ISBN 0-688-00309-5). Morrow.
Harlequin and Columbine. Booth Tarkington. LC 21-22104. 1921. Doubleday, Page & Company.
Harlequin and Columbine: And Other Stories... Booth I. E. Newton Booth Tarkington. LC 21-8687. (works of Booth Tarkington. vol. VIII). 1918. Doubleday, Page and Company.
Harlequin House. Margery Sharp. LC 30-272781. 1939. Little, Brown and Company.
Harlequin of Death. Sydney Horler. LC 33-21278. 1933. Little, Brown, and Company.
Harlequin Opal. Rosalie Wells. 1978. pap. 1.95 (ISBN 0-532-19200-1). Woodhill.
Harlequin Set. Dion Clayton Calthrop. LC 12-11858. 1911. 1.00. John Lane Company.
Harlequinade: A Novel. Holloway Horn. LC 21-4501. 1921. Frederick A. Stokes Company.
Harlette. Marion Polk Angellotti. LC 13-14822. 1913. The Century Co.
Harley. T. S Briley. LC 76-39754. 2.95. ETC.
Harling College. Mark Kirby, pseud. 1970. pap. 0.75 o.p. (75-339). Manor Bks.
Harliquin Opal: A Romance. Fergus Hume. LC 7-5840. (On cover: Rialto series. no. 52). 1893. Rand, McNally & Company.
Harlot High and Low: Splendeurs et Miseres Des Courtisanes) Honore De Balzac. LC 70-22523. (Penguin classics, L232). 1970 (ISBN 0-14-044232-4). Penguin.
Harlot of Jericho. James L Dial. LC 74-33071. 6.95. Commonwealth Press.
Harlot Queen. Hilda Winifred Lewis. LC 76-108713. 1970. 6.95. D. McKay Co.
Harlot's Progress: The Hated Son, and Other Stories. saintsbury ed. Honore De Balzac. Tr. by James Waring. Rudd, John, Joint Tr. LC 8-7000.
Harlot's Return. Peggy Gaddis, pseud. LC 37-3264. 1937. Godwin.
Harm in Trying. Michel Dedina. LC 67-20196. 1967. A. S. Barnes.
Harm in Trying. Michel Dedina. LC 67-20196. 1967. A. S. Barnes.
Harm Intended. Richard Parker. LC 56-9472. 1956. Scribner.
Harm Wulf, a Peasant Chronicle. Hermann Lons. Tr. by Saunders, Marion. LC 31-26802. 1931. Minton, Balch & Company.
Harmattan: A Novel of Suspense. Thomas Klop. LC 75-8824. 1975. 7.95. Bobbs-Merrill.
Harmen Pols. Jozua Marius Willen Van Der Poorten Schwartz. LC 10-233984. 1910. 1.35. John Lane Company.
Harmen Pols: By Maarten Maartens Pseud.... Jozua Marius Willem Van Der Poorten Schwartz. LC 10-23398. 1910. John Lane Company.
Harmless Poisons, Blameless Sins. Mohammed Mrabet & Paul Frederic Bowles. LC 76-27353. (Illus.). 1976. 10.00. (ISBN 0-87685-273-8) (ISBN 0-87685-274-6) (ISBN 0-87685-272-X). Black Sparrow Press.
Harmonetics Investigation. Gladys Heldman. LC 79-14285. 10.95 (ISBN 0-517-53926-8). Crown Publishers.
Harmonie: A Novella. Edited by Wayne Wonderley. Eduard Heinrich Nikolaus Graf Von Keyserling. LC 64-19398. 1964. Odyssey Press.
Harmons: A Story of Jewish Home Life. Addie Richman Altman. LC 17-24689. 1917. Bloch Publishing Company.
Harmony Farm. Jamie Mandelkau. 1975. (pbk.) 1.50 (ISBN 0-446-78283-1). Warner Paperback Library.
Harmony Hall. Jane Meredith. (Signet Book). 1978. 1.75 (ISBN 0-451-08082-3). New American Library.
Harmony Hall: A Romantic Historical Novel of the American Revolution. Jane Meredith. LC 70-28027. 1971. 6.95 (ISBN 0-911292-01-2). Rydal Press.
Harmony Hospital. Peggy O'More, pseud. LC 67-8666. 1967. Arcadia House.
Harmony of Hearts. Renee Shann. (Orig.). 1971. pap. 0.75 o.p. (94154). Beagle Bks.
Harm's Way. Roberta Tapley. LC 30-7792. 1930. A. A. Knopf.
Harness. Arthur Hamilton Gibbs. LC 28-23111. 1928. Little, Brown, and Company.
Harness Bull. Leslie Turner White. LC 37-4765. Harcourt, Brace and Company.
Harness of Death. William Stanley Sykes. LC 32-96681. 1932. Dodd, Mead and Company.
Harold and Maude. Colin Higgins. LC 70-168714. 1971. 4.95. Lippincott.
Harold Godwin. A Social Satire. Daniel Elliott Huger Wilkinson. LC 3394. J. S. Ogilvie Publishing Company.
Harold in Heavenland. H. A. Stokes. 5.95 o.p. Vantage.
Harold the Klansman. George Alfred Brown. LC 23-171150. 1923. The Western Baptist Publishing Company.
Harold, the Last of the Saxon Kings. Edward George Earle Lytton Bulwer-Lytton Lytton. LC 7-8339. 1838. Harper & Brothers Pref.
Harold, the Last of the Saxon Kings. the lord lytton ed. Edward George Earle Lytton Bulwer-Lytton Lytton. LC 6-6892. 1878. J. B. Lippincott & Co.
Harold, the Last of the Saxon Kings. Edward George Earle Lytton Bulwer-Lytton Lytton. LC 8-26643. G. Routledge and Sons.
Harold, the Last of the Saxon Kings. Edward George Earle Lytton Bulwer-Lytton Lytton. LC 7-8340. (On cover: Lovell's library, v. 5, no. 276). J. W. Lovell Company.
Harold. The Last of the Saxon Kings. Edward George Earle Lytton Bulwer-Lytton Lytton. LC 7-8341. (Half-title: Novels of Sir Edward Bulwer Lytton. Library ed. Historical romances, vol. IX). 1893. Little, Brown, and Company.
Harold, the Last of the Saxon Kings. Edward George Earle Lytton Bulwer-Lytton Lytton. LC 4-16550. (Half-title: Novels of Sir Edward Bulwer Lytton. Library edition. Historical romances, vol. IX-X). 1896. Little, Brown, and Company.
Harold, the Last of the Saxon Kings. Edward George Earle Lytton Bulwer-Lytton Lytton. LC 7-8342. (Standard literature series no. 12). 1896. University Publishing Company.
Harold, the Last of the Saxon Kings. Edward George Earle Lytton Bulwer-Lytton Lytton & Gomme, Sir George Laurence, 1853-1916, Ed. (Half-title: Library of historical novels and romances. 1). 1897. Longmans, Green, and Co.; Etc., Etc.
Harold, the Last of the Saxon Kings. Edward George Earle Lytton Bulwer-Lytton Lytton. LC 2-20036. 1902. C. Scribner's Sons.
Harold, the Last of the Saxon Kings. Edward George Earle Lytton Bulwer-Lytton Lytton. (Half-title: Everyman's library, ed. by Ernest Rhys. Fiction. no. 15). 1908. J. M. Dent & Co.
Harold, the Last of the Saxon Kings, Falkland, Calderon, the Courtier. Edward George Earle Lytton Bulwer-Lytton Lytton. LC 31-32284. (The novels and romances of Edward Bulwer Lytton. v. 4). Aldine Book Publishing Co.
Harold Was My King. H. Lewis. 1970. 4.95 o.p. (ISBN 0-679-50256-4). McKay.
Harp. Ethelreda Lewis. LC 25-12985. George H. Doran Company.
Harp and the Blade. John Myers Myers. LC 41-10681. 1941. E. P. Dutton & Co., Inc.
Harp and the Blade. John Myers Myers. LC 82-5014. 5.95 (ISBN 0-89865-193-X). Donning Co.
Harp into Battle. Cecil Maiden. LC 59-11170. 1959. Crowell.
Harp of a Thousand Strings. Harold Lenoir Davis. LC 47-6457. 1947. W. Morrow.
Harp of Burma. Tr. from Japanese by Howard Hibbett. Michio Takeyama. LC 66-205701. (Unesco Collection of Contemp. Works). 3.50. Tuttle.
Harp of Many Chords. Mary F Nixon Roulet. LC 5-33025. B. Herder.
Harp on the Willow. Winifred Waddell. LC 41-6552. 1941. Arcadia House, Inc.
Harper Prize Short Stories: The Twelve Prize-Winning Short Stories in the 1924-25 Short Story Contest Conducted by Harper's Magazine ... LC 25-183543. 1925. Harper & Brothers.
Harper's Bazaar The Uncommon Reader: Ed. by Alice S. Morris. Introd. Essay by V. S. Pritchett. Ed. by Alice S. Morris. LC 65-5623. (NS4). Avon.
Harpe's Head: A Legend of Kentucky. James Hall. LC 7-319448. 1833. Key & Biddle.
Harpoon. Francois Ponthier. LC 76-107069. 1970. 4.95. McKay.
Harpoon. Olaf Ruhen. 1975. pap. 1.25 o.p. (LB316, Leisure Bks). Nordon Pubns.
Harpoon Gun. Vassilis Vassilikos. LC 72-79925. 1973. 6.95 (ISBN 0-15-138800-8). Harcourt Brace Jovanovich.
Harpoon in Eden. Francis Van Wyck Mason. LC 69-12206. 1969. 6.95. Doubleday.
Harpoon of the Hunter. Markoosie. (Ltd. coll. ed. 40.00 o.p.). (Illus.). 1970. 9.95 (ISBN 0-7735-0102-9); pap. 4.95 (ISBN 0-7735-0232-7). McGill-Queens U Pr.
Harrad Experience. Robert H. Rimmer. 4.95 o.s.i. (ISBN 0-8202-0165-0). Sherbourne.
Harrad Experiment. Robert H. Rimmer. 1967. Bantam.
Harrad Experiment: A Novel. Robert H Rimmer. LC 66-17213. 1966. 4.95. Sherbourne.
Harriet. Jilly Cooper. LC 77-363641. 1976. 2.95 (ISBN 0-85140-241-0). Arlington Books.
Harriet. Elizabeth Jenkins. LC 34-60504. 1934. Doubleday, Doran & Company, Inc.
Harriet. Elizabeth Jenkins. LC 43-4978. 1943. Triangle Books.
Harriet. Elizabeth Jenkins. LC 80-218. 1980. 2.50 (ISBN 0-14-005582-7). Penguin Books.
Harriet. Joan Mellows. (Fawcett Crest Book). 1977. 1.50 (ISBN 0-449-23209-3). Fawcett Pubns.
Harriet. Joan Mellows. LC 79-10919. (Regency romance). 1979. 10.50 (ISBN 0-89340-208-7). J. Curley.
Harriet and the Piper. Kathleen Thompson Norris. LC 20-13977. 1920. Doubleday, Page & Company.
Harriet Dark: Branwell Bronte's Lost Novel. Barbara Rees & Patrick Branwell Bronte. LC 78-40405. 12.95 (ISBN 0-86033-075-3). Gordon & Cremonesi.
Harriet, Farewell. Margaret Erskine, pseud. LC 74-25103. 1975. 5.95 (ISBN 0-385-01822-3). Published for the Crime Club by Doubleday.
Harriet Hume, a London Fantasy. Rebecca West. LC 29-24736. 1929. Doubleday, Doran & Company, Inc.
Harriet Hume: A London Fantasy. rev. ed. Rebecca West. LC 81-15299. (Virago Modern Classic). 1982. 7.95 (ISBN 0-385-27410-6). Dial Press.
Harriet Marwood, Governess. John Glassco. LC 76-380109. (Trendsetter edition). 1976. 5.95 (ISBN 0-7736-0051-5). General Pub. Co.
Harriet, Marwood, Governess. LC 67-184116. (Black circle bk. Z-1025). 1968. pap., 1.50. Grove.
Harriet Marwood, Governess. (Black Circle Ser). 1967. 5.00 o.p. (GP382). Grove.
Harriet Marwood, Governess. pap. 1.95 o.p. (V1046T, Venus). Grove.
Harriet Said. Beryl Bainbridge. LC 73-76970. 1973. 5.95 (ISBN 0-8076-0687-1). G. Braziller.
Harriet Said. Beryl Bainbridge. (Signet book). 1974. (pbk.) 1.50. New American Library.
Harriet, the Haunted. Katheryn Kimbrough, pseud. (Saga of the Phenwick Women: Bk. 10). 256p. 1976. pap. 1.75 (ISBN 0-445-00382-0). Popular Lib.
Harriet the Spy. Louise Fitzhugh. 1978. pap. 2.25 (ISBN 0-440-93447-8, LFL). Dell.
Harrigan. Max Brand. 1971. 4.50 o.p. (ISBN 0-396-06328-4). Dodd.
Harrigan. Frederick Faust. 1973. (pbk.) 0.75 (ISBN 0-671-75752-0). Pocket Books.
Harrigan. Frederick Faust. LC 75-147135. 1971. 4.50 (ISBN 0-396-06328-4). Dodd, Mead.
Harrigan's File. August William Derleth. LC 75-2522. 1975. 6.50 (ISBN 0-87054-070-X). Arkham House.
Harrington. Maria Edgeworth. LC 25-237761. (Half-title: The novels of Maria Edgeworth, vol. ix). 1893. J. M. Dent & Co.
Harrington: A Story True Love. William Douglas O'Connor. LC 75-107851. (Series in American Studies). 1970. Johnson Reprint Corp.
Harringtons of Highcroft Farm. Joseph Smith Fletcher. LC 8-8308. 1907. B. W. Dodge and Company.
Harris-Ingram Experiment. Charles Edward Bolton. LC 5-572. 1905. The Burrows Brothers Company.
Harrison Affair. Gerald Seymour. 1981. pap. 2.95 (ISBN 0-440-13566-4). Dell.
Harrison Affair: Novel. Gerald Seymour. LC 79-20834. 10.95 (ISBN 0-671-44745-9). Summit Books.
Harrison High. John Farris. 1982. pap. 3.95 (ISBN 0-440-13448-X). Dell.
Harrowing. Ainslie Skinner. LC 80-5980. 13.95 (ISBN 0-89256-153-X). Rawson, Wade.
Harrowvale. Graham King. 324p. 1974. 7.95 o.p. (ISBN 0-440-03476-0). Delacorte.
Harrowvale: A Novel. Graham King. LC 74-6392. 1974. 6.95 (ISBN 0-440-03476-0). Delacorte Press.
Harry. rev. ed. Charles Brandon Rimmer. LC 73-82974. 1973. 4.95 (ISBN 0-88419-063-3). Creation House.
Harry Ambler and How He Saved the Homestead. Paschal Heston Coggins. LC 11-20581. 1893. The Penn Publishing Company.
Harry Ambler: Or The Stolen Deed. Paschal Heston Coggins. LC 11-179690. 1890. The Penn Publishing Company.
Harry and I. Helen C Andrews. LC 71-165356. 1971. 3.95 (ISBN 0-8158-0264-1). Christopher Pub. House.
Harry & the Bikini Bandits. Basil Heatter. (Orig.). 1970. pap. 0.75 o.p. (T2372, GM). Fawcett World.
Harry and Tonto. Josh Greenfeld & Paul Mazursky. LC 73-20422. 1974. 5.95. Saturday Review Press; Distributed by E. P. Dutton.
Harry and Tonto. Josh Greenfeld & Paul Mazursky. LC 74-16271. 1974. (ISBN 0-8161-6236-0). G. K. Hall.
Harry & Tonto. Josh Greenfeld & Paul Mazursky. 1974. (pbk.) 1.25. Popular Library.

Harry & Tonto. Josh Greenfield & Paul Mazursky. 232p. 1974. Repr. lib. bdg. 7.95 o.p. (ISBN 0-8161-6236-0, Large Print Bks). G K Hall.
Harry & Tonto. Josh Greenfield & Paul Mazursky. 1974. 6.95 o.p. (ISBN 0-8415-0306-0). Dutton.
Harry and Walter Go to New York. Sam Stewart. 1976. 1.50. Dell Publishing Co.
Harry Belten and the Mendelssohn Violin Concerto. Barry Targan. LC 75-17705. 1975. 5.95 (ISBN 0-87745-061-7) (ISBN 0-87745-060-9). University of Iowa Press.
Harry Black. David Harry Walker. LC 55-10022. 1956. Houghton Mifflin.
Harry Bleachbaker: A Novel. Norman Frederick Simpson. LC 76-359919. (Illus.). 1976. 2.95 (ISBN 0-245-52647-1). Harrap.
Harry Blount, the Detective: Or, The Martin Mystery Solved. T. J Flanagan. 1891. J. S. Ogilvie.
Harry Burnham, the Young Continental: Or, Memoirs of an American Officer During the Campaigns of the Revolution, and Sometime a Member of Washington's Staff. Henry A Buckingham. 1852. Burgess & Garrett.
Harry Coverdale's Courtship and All That Came of It. Francis Edward Smedley. LC 42-28898. G. Routledge and Sons.
Harry Coverdale's Courtship and All That Came of It. Francis Edward Smedley & Browne, Hablot Knight, 1815-1882, Illus. G. Routledge & Sons, Limited.
Harry Delaware. Or, An American in Germany. Mathilde Estvan. LC 6-38143. 1872. G. P. Putnam & Sons.
Harry Furniss Dickens: Containing Five Hundred Original Illustrations... Charles Dickens & Furniss, Harry. LC 10-10579. 30.00. J. T. Gleason.
Harry Heathcote of Gangoil. A Tale of Australian Bush-Life. Anthony Trollope & Fox-Hjnting. (On cover: The seaside library. Pocket ed. no. 622). 1885. G. Munro.
Harry Holbrooke of Holbrooke Hall. Randal Howland Roberts. (On cover: Lovell's library, v. 3, no. 101). 1883. J. W. Lovell Company.
Harry Idaho. Hugh Pendexter. LC 26-63370. The Bobbs-Merrill Company.
Harry Joscelyn. A Novel. Margaret Oliphant Wilson Oliphant. (Franklin square library, no. 183). 1881. Harper & Brothers.
Harry Joscelyn. A Novel. Margaret Oliphant Wilson Oliphant. (Seaside library, v. 48, no. 1004). 1881. G. Munro.
Harry Lorrequer. alta ed. Charles James Lever. LC 7-14383. 1872. Porter & Coates.
Harry Lorrequer. Charles James Lever. (On cover: Lovell's library, v. 6, no. 327). 1883. J. W. Lovell Company.
Harry Lorrequer. Charles James Lever. LC 4-165443. Little, Brown, & Company.
Harry Lorrequer. Charles James Lever. LC 26-26896. (On cover: The Home library). 1925. A. L. Burt Company.
Harry Lorrequer. Charles James Lever. LC 36-37233. (Half-title: Everyman's library, ed. by Ernest Rhys. Fiction. no. 177). 1926. J. M. Dent & Sons, Ltd.
Harry Lorrequer: With His Confessions. Charles James Lever. (Seaside library, v. 5, no. 98). 1877. G. Munro.
Harry Lorrequer: With His Confessions. Charles James Lever. (On cover: Seaside library. Pocket ed., no. 191). 1884. G. Munro.
Harry Martin's Wife. Elizabeth Frances Corbett. LC 67-20851. 1967. Meredith Press.
Harry Muir. A Story of Scottish Life. Margaret Oliphant Wilson Oliphant. (On cover: Seaside library. Pocket ed., no. 569). 1885. G. Munro.
Harry Muir: A Story of Scottish Life. Margaret Oliphant Wilson Oliphant. LC 7-32615. 1853. D. Appleton & Company.
Harry of Monmouth. A. M. Maugham. LC 56-53923. 1956. W. Sloane Associates.
Harry Ogilvie: Or, The Black Dragoons. James Grant. LC 44-31627. G. Routledge and Sons.
Harry Pickering. Robert E McClure. LC 38-14877. Harcourt, Brace and Company.
Harry Russell: A Rockland College Boy. John Edwin Copus. 1903. Benziger Brothers.
Harry Sharpe: The New York Detective. Ernest A. Young. (sunnyside series, no. 74). 1893. J. S. Ogilvie.
Harry, She's Laughing Again. Marilyn Ayars. 1980. pap. 2.95 (ISBN 0-89293-068-3). Beta Bk.
Harry the Newsboy & Other Stories. Isabel Byrum. 32p. 1982. pap. 0.35. Faith Pub Hse.
Harry: The Rat with Women, a Novel. Jules Feiffer. LC 63-15020. 1963. McGraw-Hill.
Harry Vernon at Prep. Franc Smith. LC 59-5527. 1959. Houghton Mifflin.
Harry Williams, the New York Detective. F. Lusk Broughton. (champion detective series, no. 18). J. S. Ogilvie and Company.
Harry Williams, the New York Detective. F. Lusk Broughton. LC 1-29448. (On cover: Magnet detective library. no. 160). Street & Smith.
Harry's Child. Suzanne Holly Jones. 1965. 2.80. Jacaranda Pr.
Harry's Game. gerald seymour. ed. Gerald Seymour. 1976. 1.95 (ISBN 0-449-23019-8). Fawcett Crest.
Harry's Game: A Novel. Gerald Seymour. LC 75-14048. 1975. 7.95 (ISBN 0-394-49902-6). Random House.
Harry's Work: Or, The Need of the Age. Morton Pennypacker. LC 99-5094. F. T. Neely.
Harsacarita of Banabhatta. 3rd ed. Tr. by P. V. Kane. 1973. pap. 4.95 (ISBN 0-89684-211-8). Orient Bk Dist.
Harsh Evidence. Pamela Fry. Roy Publishers.
Harsh Voice: Four Short Novels. Rebecca West. LC 35-27063. 1935. Doubleday, Doran & Company, Inc.
Hart. Lee Veillon. LC 73-4164. 1974. 5.95 (ISBN 0-06-014508-0). Harper & Row.
Hart Five: Blood on the Border. John B. Harvey. 1982. pap. 10.00x (ISBN 0-330-26313-7, Pub. by Pan Bks). State Mutual Bk.
Hart Four: The Silver Life. John B. Harvey. 1982. pap. 10.00x (ISBN 0-330-26087-1, Pub. by Pan Bks). State Mutual Bk.
Hart One: Cherokee Outlet. John B. Harvey. 1982. pap. 10.00x (Pub. by Pan Bks). State Mutual Bk.
Hart Six: Ride the Wide Country. John B. Harvey. 1982. pap. 10.00 (ISBN 0-330-26314-5, Pub. by Pan Bks). State Mutual Bk.
Hart Three: Tago. John B. Harvey. 1982. pap. 10.00x (ISBN 0-330-25994-6, Pub. by Pan Bks). State Mutual Bk.
Hart Two: Blood Trail. John B. Harvey. 1982. pap. 10.00x (ISBN 0-330-25993-8, Pub. by Pan Bks). State Mutual Bk.
Hartas Maturin: A Novel. Horace Frank Lester. LC 7-14377. (Lovell's international series, no. 2). F. F. Lovell & Company.
Harting's Hints on Hawks. James E. Harting. 12.95 o.p. (ISBN 0-8231-2019-8). Branford.
Hartmann, the Anarchist: Or, The Doom of the Great City. Edward Douglas Fawcett. LC 74-15970. (Science Fiction). (Illus.). 1975. 12.00 (ISBN 0-405-06290-7). Arno Press.
Hart's Hope. Orson Scott Card. 272p. 1983. pap. 2.75 (ISBN 0-425-05819-0). Berkley Pub.
Hartspring Blows His Mind. Ernest Lockridge. LC 68-15218. 1968. New American Library.
Hartwell Farm. Elizabeth Barker Comins. LC 6-30218. Loring.
Harum Scarum. The Story of a Wild Girl. Amelie Claire Leroy. LC 8-20122. The International News Company.
Harvard Episodes. Charles Macomb Flandrau. LC 76-94719. (Short story index reprint series). 1969. Books for Libraries Press.
Harvard Episodes. Charles Macomb Flandrau. LC 6-39544. 1897. Copeland and Day.
Harvard Has a Homicide. Timothy Fuller. LC 36-27378. 1936. Little, Brown, and Company.
Harvard Has a Homicide. Timothy Fuller. LC 42-50415. 1942. Triangle Books.
Harvard Stories: Sketches of the Undergraduate. Waldron Kintzing Post. LC 77-90589. (Short story index reprint series). 1969. Books for Libraries Press.
Harvard Stories: Sketches of the Undergraduate. Waldron Kintzing Post. LC 8-29650. 1893. G. P. Putnam's Sons.
Harvard Tree. Alma Stone. LC 54-10083. 1954. Houghton Mifflin.
Harvest. Jean Giono. Tr. by Fluchere, Henri. Tr. by Graux, Louis William. 1939. The Viking Press.
Harvest. Meyer Levin. 1979. 2.75 (ISBN 0-553-12265-7). Bantam Books.
Harvest. Henrietta Eliza Vaughan Stannard. LC 8-13861. (On cover: Lovell's international series, no. 21). 1889. F. F. Lovell & Company.
Harvest. Henrietta Eliza Vaughan Stannard. (On cover: Seaside library. Pocket ed. no. 1202). 1889. G. Munro.
Harvest. Mary Augusta Arnold Humphry Ward Ward. LC 20-628815. 1920. Dodd, Mead and Company.
Harvest: A Novel. Meyer Levin. LC 77-13076. 11.95 (ISBN 0-671-22550-2). Simon and Schuster.
Harvest & Song For My Time. Meridel Le Sueur. LC 77-14856. (Illus.). 1982. pap. 4.50 (ISBN 0-931122-27-9). West End.
Harvest Burns. Helga Moray. 1973. (pbk) 1.25 (ISBN 0-671-78345-9). Pocket Books.
Harvest: Collected Stories. Meridel Le Sueur. LC 77-155984. 1977. 2.50. West End Press.
Harvest Comedy: A Dramatic Chronicle. Frank Arthur Swinnerton. LC 38-27171. 1938. Doubleday, Doran & Company, Inc.
Harvest Home. David Toulmin. 1978. text ed. 14.95x (ISBN 0-8464-0472-9). Beekman Pubs.
Harvest Home. Thomas Tryon. LC 72-11047. 1973. 7.95 (ISBN 0-394-48528-9). Knopf; Distributed by Random House.
Harvest Home. Thomas Tryon. (Fawcett crest book). 1974. (pbk.) 1.75. Fawcett.
Harvest in Poland. Geoffery Pomeroy Dennis. LC 25-8314. 1925. A.A.Knopf.
Harvest in the Hills: A Dr. Merry Story. Peggy Gaddis, pseud. LC 47-1387. 1946. Arcadia House, Inc.
Harvest in the North. James Lansdale Hodson. LC 34-30247. 1934. A. A. Knopf.
Harvest Is Late. John Hyatt Downing. LC 44-738939. 1944. The Hampton Publishing Co., Distributed by W. Morrow & Company.
Harvest. Moon. Rupert Croft-Cooke. LC 53-12412. 1953. St. Martin's Press.
Harvest Moon. Joseph Smith Fletcher. LC 27-15200. George H. Doran Company.
Harvest Murder: A Dr. Priestley Detective Story. Cecil John Charles Street. LC 37-64569. 1937. Dodd, Mead & Company.
Harvest of Desire. Rochelle Larkin. (Signet Book). 1977. 1.95 (ISBN 0-451-07277-4). New American Library.
Harvest of Dreams. Anne Compton. pap. 0.50 o.p. (52-885). Paperback Lib.
Harvest of Fear. Ed. by Charles M. Collins. 1975. (pbk.) 1.25 (ISBN 0-380-00412-7). Avon.
Harvest of Fury. Jeanne Williams. (Orig.). 1981. pap. 2.95 (ISBN 0-671-83285-9). PB.
Harvest of Gold. Compiled by Ernest R. Miller. LC 72-92720. (Illus.). 96p. 1973. boxed 5.50 (ISBN 0-8378-1760-9). Gibson.
Harvest of Hope. Faith Baldwin. 1962. 3.50 o.p. (ISBN 0-03-031085-7). HR&W.
Harvest of Horrors. Eric Protter. LC 79-56028. (Illus.). 12.50 (ISBN 0-8149-0755-5). Vanguard Press.
Harvest of Horrors: Classic Tales of the Macabre. Ed. by Eric Protter. LC 79-56028. (Illus.). 286p. 1980. 12.50 (ISBN 0-8149-0755-5). Vanguard.
Harvest of Javelins: A Tale Out of the East. Bertram Atkey. LC 23-130038. Brentano's.
Harvest of Short Shorts: Selected Stories Published Over Three Decades. Marie De Nervaud Dun. LC 68-25851. 1968. 3.95. Silvermine Publishers.
Harvest of Stories: From a Half Century of Writing. Dorothy Canfield. LC 56-11298. 8.50 o.p. (ISBN 0-15-138987-X). HarBraceJ.
Harvest of Stories: From a Half Century of Writing. Dorothy Canfield. LC 56-11298. 8.50 o.p. (ISBN 0-15-138987-X). HarBraceJ.
Harvest of Stories, from a Half Century of Writing. Dorothea Frances Canfield Fisher. LC 56-11298. 1956. Harcourt, Brace.
Harvest of Terror. Adela Gale. 1978. pap. 1.50 o.s.i. (ISBN 0-8439-0529-8, Leisure Bks). Nordon Pubns.
Harvest of the Bitter Seed. Gordon F Morkel. LC 59-5696. 1959. Dorrance.
Harvest of the Heart: A Novel. May Mellinger. LC 54-12935. 1954. D. McKay Co.
Harvest of the Sea: A Tale of Both Sides of the Atlantic. Wilfred Thomason Grenfell. LC 5-8380. 1905. F. H. Revell Company.
Harvest of the Sun. Ernest Victor Thompson. LC 78-14992. 1979. 9.95 (ISBN 0-698-10931-7). Coward, McCann & Geoghegan.
Harvest of the Wind. Sarah Louisa Banning Sweeny. 1935. The Caxton Printers, Ltd.
Harvest of Thorns. H. C. Hoffman. (On cover: Munro's library, popular novels. v. 1. no. 393). 1885. N. L. Munro.
Harvest of Thorns. H. C. Hoffman. (On cover: Clover ser. no. 125). Street & Smith.
Harvest of Thorns. H. C. Hoffman. LC 1-30762. (On cover: Eagle series. no. 191). 1900. Street & Smith.
Harvest of Wild Oats. Florence Marryat Church Lean. (On cover: Lovell's library, v. 19, no. 946). 1887. J. W. Lovell Company.
Harvest of Years. Mary Forker Ford. (Candlelight romance,#165). 1975. (pbk.) 0.75. Dell.
Harvest of Years. Martha Lewis Beckwith Ewell Lewis. LC 6-38132. 1880. G. P. Putnam's Sons.
Harvest of Yesterdays. Gladys Bagg Taber. LC 75-44003. 1976. 7.95 o.p. (ISBN 0-397-01133-4). Har-Row.
Harvest on the Don. Mikhail Aleksandrovich Sholokhov. 1961. 8.95 o.p. (ISBN 0-394-42789-0). Knopf.
Harvest on the Shore. Grace Carstens. LC 56-7679. 1956. Macmillan.
Harvest Street. Kathalyn Krause. (Orig.). 1980. pap. text ed. 2.50 o.s.i. (ISBN 0-505-51581-4). Tower Bks.
Harvest Time: By Joan Garrison Pseud. William Arthur Neubauer. LC 56-702287. 1956. Arcadia House.
Harvest Time. 1st Ed. Edward M Scott. LC 54-12512. 1954. Pageant Press.
Harvest Waits: A Novel. Lorene Pearson. LC 41-15450. The Bobbs-Merrill Company.
Harvester. Gene Stratton Porter. LC 11-22758. 1911. Doubleday, Page & Company.
Harvester. Gene Stratton Porter. LC 12-16323. 1912. Doubleday, Page & Company.
Harvester. Gene Stratton Porter. LC 16-21934. 1916. 0.50. C. Scribner's Sons.
Harvester. Gene Stratton Porter. LC 21-16879. 1920. Grosset & Dunlap.
Harvester. Gene Stratton-Porter. 1977. Repr. of 1911 ed. lib. bdg. 25.00 (ISBN 0-8414-7937-2). Folcroft.
Harvesters. Lorraine Kettlewell. 192p. 1972. 6.00 o.p. (ISBN 0-682-47488-6). Exposition.
Harvesters. Aubrey Lanston. LC 3-24827. 1903. R. H. Russell.
Harvesting. Irving Bacheller. LC 34-22756. 1934. Frederick A. Stokes Company.
Harvesting of Green Fields. Edward Young Chapin. LC 50-5096. 1949. Exposition Press.
Harvey Fergusson. James K Folsom. LC 69-18408. (Southwest Writers Series, No. 20). 1969. 1.00. Steck-Vaughn.
Harvey Garrard's Crime. Edward Phillips Oppenheim. LC 26-17975. 1926. Little, Brown, and Company.
Harvey Garrard's Crime. Edward Phillips Oppenheim. LC 40-9078. 1940. Triangle Books.
Harvey Girls. Samuel Hopkins Adams. LC 42-25509. 1942. Random House.
Harvey Girls. Samuel Hopkins Adams. LC 47-237731. (Forum books. F-58). 1945. The World Publishing Company.
Harvey Landrum: A Novel, by Ridley Wills. Ridley Wills. LC 24-298253. 1924. Simon and Schuster.
Harwood. A Novel. George James Atkinson Coulson. LC 6-28999. (The "Odd trump" series of novels). 1875. E. J. Hale & Son.
Has Anybody Seen My Father? Harrison Kinney. LC 60-109778. 1960. Simon and Schuster.
Hasan. Piers Anthony, pseud. LC 77-24589. (Illus.). 1977. lib. bdg. 10.95x (ISBN 0-89370-115-7); pap. 4.95x (ISBN 0-89370-215-3). Borgo Pr.
Haschisch: A Novel. by thorold king pseud. ed. Charles Gatchell. LC 7-1244. 1886. A.C. McClurg & Company.
Haschisch: A Novel. Charles Gatchell. LC 6-442743. 1888. Brentano's.
Hasen. Reuben Bercovitch. LC 77-21165. 1978. 6.95. Knopf.
Hash Knife Outfit. Zane Grey. LC 33-30457. 1933. Harper & Brothers.
Hash-Knife Outfit. Zane Grey. 1975. (pbk.) 1.25 (ISBN 0-671-80085-X). Pocket Books.
Hasheesh Eater. Fitz Hugh Ludlow. LC 76-104521. 1970. Literature House.
Hasheesh Eater: Being Passages from the Life of a Pythagorean... Fitz Hugh Ludlow. LC 7-14501. 1857. Harper & Brothers.
Hashknife of Stormy River. Wilbur C Tuttle. LC 35-27235. 1935. Houghton Mifflin Company.
Hashknife of the Double Bar Eight. Wilbur C. Tuttle. 244p. 1980. Repr. of 1936 ed. lib. bdg. 12.95x (ISBN 0-89968-133-6). Lightyear.
Hashknife of the Double Bar 8. Wilbur C Tuttle. LC 37-270871. 1936. Houghton Mifflin Company.
Hasington. Eric Fyhrlund. (Orig.). 1979. pap. 1.95 (ISBN 0-532-23249-6). Woodhill.
Hassan; a Fellah: A Romance of Palestine. Henry Gillman. LC 6-44040. 1898. Little, Brown and Company.
Hassle and the Medicine Man. Clifton Adams. LC 72-89289. 1973. 4.95 (ISBN 0-385-02889-X). Doubleday.
Haste to Succeed: By Jason Striker Pseud. George William Howard. LC 61-15943. 1961. Appleton-Century-Crofts.
Hastening Wind. 1st American Ed. Edward Grierson. LC 53-6843. 1953. Knopf.
Hastings Conspiracy. Alfred Coppel. LC 80-12384. 12.95 (ISBN 0-03-056058-6). Holt, Rinehart and Winston.
Hasty Bunch: Short Stories. Robert McAlmon. LC 76-21290. (Lost American fiction series). 1977. 8.95 (ISBN 0-8093-0798-7). Southern Illinois University Press.
Hasty Heiress. Paul Miller. LC 68-8329. 1969. 3.95 o.p. Roy.
Hasty Heiress. Paul Muller. LC 68-8329. 1968. 3.95. Roy Publishers.
Hasty Marriage. Renee Shann. 1972. pap. 0.75 o.p. (94259). Beagle Bks.
Hasty Wedding. Mignon Good Eberhart. LC 38-27412. 1938. Doubleday, Doran & Company, Inc.
Hasty Wedding. Mignon Good Eberhart. 1942. The Sun Dial Press.
Hasty Wedding. Mignon Good Eberhart. LC 46-4569. 1946. Triangle Books, The Blakiston Company.
Hasty Wedding. Mignon Good Eberhart. LC 80-36836. 1980. 15.95 (ISBN 0-88411-761-8). Aeonian Press.
Hat and the Man: An Allegorical Tale. Henry Irving Dodge. LC 6-36044. 1906. G. W. Dillingham Company.
Hat-Check Girl. Rian James. LC 32-6316. A. H. King.
Hat Check Girl. Charles Stanley Strong. LC 42-253533. 1942. Phoenix Press.
Hat of Destiny. Elizabeth Paschal O'Connor. LC 23-10697. 1923. Lieber & Lewis.
Hat on the Bed. John O'Hara. (N2889). 1965. Bantam.

Hat on the Bed. John O'Hara. LC 63-20247. 1963. Random House.

Hat on the Bed. John O'Hara. LC 63-20247. 1975. (pbk.) 1.50. Popular Library.

Hat on the Hall Table. Jean Reynolds Davis. LC 67-21546. (Illus.). 1967. Harper & Row.

Hat Shop. Dorothy C. Bayliff Peel. LC 14-2302. 1914. 1.25. John Lane.

Hatch War: A Rapid-Transit Omnibus. Eric Hatch. LC 36-21008. 1936. Little, Brown, and Company.

Hatcher. Ted Kooser. LC 77-84789. (Illus.). 4.95 (ISBN 0-931534-07-0). Windflower Press.

Hatchet. Heno Magee. signed 7.50 (ISBN 0-912262-47-8); pap. 2.95x (ISBN 0-912262-48-6). Proscenium.

Hatchet in the Sky: A Novel. Margaret Cooper Gay. LC 54-9813. 1954. Simon and Schuster.

Hatchet Man. San Antonio. Tr. by Hugh Campbell. (San Antonio Ser). 1970. pap. 0.60 o.p. (ISBN 0-446-63394-1, 63-394). Paperback Lib.

Hatchet Man. Mel Arrighi. LC 75-12584. 1975. 6.95 (ISBN 0-15-139232-3). Harcourt Brace Jovanovich.

Hatchet Man. Winfred Van Atta. LC 62-16746. 1962. Published for the Crime Club by Doubleday.

Hatchet Man: A Yellowthread Street Mystery. William Leonard Marshall. LC 77-361856. 1976. 3.50 (ISBN 0-241-89335-6). Hamilton.

Hatchet Rides High. Virgil Earp, pseud. Ed. by Alice Sachs. 1969. lib. bdg. 3.50 o.p. Arcadia.

Hatchet. Tr. from Rumanian by Eugenia Farca. Mihail Sadoveanu. LC 65-8843. (Unesco Collection of Representative Works: European Ser.). bds., 4.50. Allen & Unwin.

Hatchett. Lee McGraw. LC 76-13843. 1.50 (ISBN 0-345-25303-5). Ballantine Books.

Hatchie, the Guardian Slave: Or, The Heiress of Bellevue. William Taylor Adams. LC 72-539. (Black Heritage Library Collection). (Illus.). 1972. (ISBN 0-8369-8976-7). Books for Libraries Press.

Hatching the American Eagle: A Narrative of the American Revolution. John Finch Barnhill. LC 37-37801. 1937. Margent Press.

Hatchways. Ethel Sidgwick. LC 16-228967. Small, Maynard & Company.

Hate. Arthur Douglas Howden Smith. LC 28-25184. 1928. J. B. Lippincott Company.

Hate Along the Rio. Thomas Albert Curry. LC 38-528688. The Dodge Publishing Company.

Hate Along the Rio. Thomas Albert Curry. LC 38-5286. The Dodge Publishing Company.

Hate Factory. W. G. Stone. As told to G. Hirliman. 272p. 1982. pap. 2.95 (ISBN 0-440-03686-0). Dell.

Hate Is for the Hunted. Stephen Frances. (John Gail Espionage Series). (O.s.i.). 160p. 1973. pap. 0.95 o.s.i. (AN1195, Award). Univ Pub & Dist.

Hate Merchant: A Novel. Niven Busch. LC 53-5934. 1953. Simon and Schuster.

Hate Ship. Graham Montague Jeffries. LC 28-13912. 1928. Dodd, Mead & Company.

Hate Thy Neighbor. Miriam Lynch. 1973. (pbk.) 0.95 (ISBN 0-671-77664-9). Pocket Books.

Hate Will Find a Way. Marten Cumberland. LC 47-524828. 1947. Pub. for the Crime Club by Doubleday.

Hated. George G. Gilman, pseud. (Edge Ser.: No. 13). 160p. 1975. pap. 1.50 (ISBN 0-523-40462-X). Pinnacle Bks.

Hated. George G Gilman. (Edge,#13). 1975. (pbk.) 1.25 (ISBN 0-523-00560-1). Pinnacle Books.

Hated One. Don Tracy. LC 63-8789. 1963. Simon and Schuster.

Hatfield - McCoy Feud Reader. Shirley Donnelly. 1971. pap. 3.50 (ISBN 0-87012-115-4). McClain.

Hath Not the Potter: Translated. Maxence Van Der Meersch. Tr. by Hopkins, Gerard. LC 37-284919. 1937. The Viking Press.

Hathaway House. Nelia Gardner White. LC 31-27240. 1931. Frederick A. Stokes Company.

Hathercourt. Mary Louisa Stewart Molesworth. LC 7-19176. (Seaside library, v. 21, no. 478). 1878. G. Munro.

Hathoo of the Elephants. Post Wheeler. LC 43-147825. 1943. The Viking Press.

Hatred's Web. Poppy Nottingham. (Ace gothic). 1974. (pbk.) 0.95. Ace Books.

Hats off! Arthur Henry Veysey. (Dillingham's metropolitan library, no. 52). 1899. G. W. Dillingham Co.

Hatter Fox. Marilyn Harris. LC 73-5057. 1973. 5.95 (ISBN 0-394-48514-9). Random House.

Hatter Fox. Marilyn Harris. 1974. (pbk.) 1.50. Bantam Books.

Hatter's Castle. Archibald Joseph Cronin. LC 31-187383. 1931. Little, Brown, and Company.

Hatter's Phantoms. Georges Simenon. LC 76-18254. 6.95. Harcourt Brace Jovanovich.

Hatzkel: The Water-Carrier and His Daughter. A Duvdevon. LC 63-2505. 1963. Pageant Press.

Haulin' A Novel. Phillip Finch. LC 74-22838. 1975. 6.95 (ISBN 0-385-01313-2). Doubleday.

Haunch, Paunch and Jowl: An Anonymous Autobiography. Samuel Badisch Ornitz. LC 23-17685. Boni and Liveright.

Haunted. Janice N Bennett. (Ace gothic). 1974. (pbk.) 0.95. Ace Books.

Haunted. Judith St. George. pap. 1.95. Bantam.

Haunted Adjutant: And Other Stories. Edmund Quincy. Ed. by Quincy, Edmund, D. LC 7-42418. 1885. Ticknor and Company.

Haunted Attic. Margaret Sutton. (Judy Bolton Mysteries). 1976. Repr. of 1932 ed. lib. bdg. 10.85x (ISBN 0-88411-715-4). Amereon Ltd.

Haunted Bookshop. Christopher Darlington Morley. LC 55-7993. (Illus.). 1955. Lippincott.

Haunted Bookshop. Christopher Darlington Morley. LC 23-14270. 1923. Doubleday, Page & Company.

Haunted Bookshop. Christopher Darlington Morley. LC 34-11260. 1934. Doubleday, Doran & Company, Inc.

Haunted Bridal Chamber: A Romance of Old-Time New Orleans. George Augustin. LC 2-14605. 1902. The Author.

Haunted Chair. Gaston Leroux. LC 32-329. E. P. Dutton & Co., Inc.

Haunted Chamber: A Novel. Margaret Wolfe Hamilton Hungerford. LC 7-9364. (On cover: Lovell's library. v. 14, no. 737). 1886. J. W. Lovell Company.

Haunted Dancers. Charles Birkin. pap. 0.50 o.p. (52-472). Paperback Lib.

Haunted Dusk: American Supernatural Fiction, 1820-1920. Howard Kerr & John William Crowley. LC 82-7011. 18.00 (ISBN 0-8203-0630-4). University of Georgia Press.

Haunted Earth. Dean Koontz. 1973. pap. 0.95 o.s.i. (75-445). Lancer.

Haunted Fountain. A Novel. Also, Hetty's Revenge. Katharine Sarah Gadsden Macquoid. LC 7-202864. (On cover: Lovell's international series, no. 71). J. W. Lovell Company.

Haunted Hacienda. 1st Ed. Madison A Cooper. LC 55-9329. 1955. Houghton Mifflin.

Haunted Hammock. Ethel Lockwood. 1973. 4.95. Lenox Hill Pr.

Haunted Harbor. Dayle Douglas. LC 43-8952. 1943. Mystery House.

Haunted Hat: A Detective Mystery. Knight, Richard. LC 99-710. 1898. The Bell Publishing Company.

Haunted Heart. Agnes Sweetman Castle & Castle, Egerton. LC 15-284888. 1915. 1.35. D. Appleton and Company.

Haunted Heart. Claudette Nicole. (Orig.). 1972. pap. 0.95 o.p. (ISBN 0-515-02798-7). Pyramid Pubns.

Haunted Heart. Claudette Nicole. 1975. pap. 0.95 o.p. (ISBN 0-515-03566-1, N3566). BJ Pub Group.

Haunted Hearts. John Palgrave Simpson. (On cover: Lovell's library, v. 3, no. 125). 1883. J. W. Lovell Company.

Haunted Heirloom. Marjorie Eatock. (queen-size gothic). 1975. (pbk.) 1.25. Popular Library.

Haunted Highways: The Ghost Towns of New Mexico. Ralph Looney. (Illus.). 1979. pap. 9.95 (ISBN 0-8263-0506-7). U of NM Pr.

Haunted Highways: The Ghost Towns of New Mexico. Ralph Looney. (Illus.). 1968. 12.95 o.p. (ISBN 0-8038-2967-1). Hastings.

Haunted Hills. Bertha Muzzy Sinclair. LC 34-33668. 1934. Little, Brown, and Company.

Haunted Hills. Bertha Muzzy Sinclair. LC 42-51488. 1942. Triangle Books.

Haunted Homestead: And Other Nouvellettes. With an Autobiography of the Author. Emma Dorothy Eliza Nevitte Southworth. LC 12-38908. T. B. Peterson & Brothers.

Haunted Honeymoon & Other Ozark Ghost Stories. Lida Pyles. (Illus.). 1982. pap. Cancelled. August Hse.

Haunted Hotel. Wilkie Collins. (Mystery Ser.). 127p. 1982. pap. 3.00 (ISBN 0-486-24333-8). Dover.

Haunted Hotel: A Mystery of Modern Venice. Wilkie Collins. LC 6-26945. (On cover: Lovell's library. no. 1003). 1887. J. W. Lovell Company.

Haunted Hotel: A Mystery of Modern Venice. Wilkie Collins. LC 82-1577. 1982. 3.00 (ISBN 0-486-24333-8). Dover Publications.

Haunted House. Hilaire Belloc. LC 28-561. 1928. Harper & Brothers.

Haunted House. Joan Williams. LC 78-19149. 4.95 (ISBN 0-89127-002-7). Omni.

Haunted House, and Other Short Stories: By Virginia Woolf. Virginia Stephen Woolf & Woolf, Leonard Sidney. LC 44-400700. 1944. Harcourt, Brace and Company.

Haunted House & Other Short Stories. Virginia Stephen Woolf. 1966. pap. 2.95 (ISBN 0-15-639401-4, Harv). HarBraceJ.

Haunted House, and Other Stories. Virginia Stephen Woolf. LC 74-160046. (Penguin modern classics). 1973. 0.30. Penguin.

Haunted House B Handbook. D. Scott Rogo. 1978. pap. 1.95 (ISBN 0-448-14668-1, Pub. bvy Tempo). Ace Bks.

Haunted House of Marley (Merely Michael) Mark Somers. LC 23-4988. 1923. Moffat, Yard & Company.

Haunted House on Hawthorne St. Ted Berndt. 3.95 o.p. Vantage.

Haunted Houses. Richard Winer & Nancy Osborn. 1979. pap. 2.50 (ISBN 0-553-14680-7). Bantam.

Haunted Husband. A Novel. Harriet Lewis. (On cover: The choice series, no. 76). 1893. R. Bonner's Sons.

Haunted Inheritance. Lucy B. Robe. LC 79-56903. (Illus., Orig.). 1980. pap. 5.95 (ISBN 0-89638-042-4). Compcare.

Haunted Island. Hester Bourne. 1971. pap. 0.75 o.p. (T2595). Pyramid Pubns.

Haunted Island. Hester Bourne. 1976. pap. 1.25 o.p. (ISBN 0-515-04124-6). BJ Pub Group.

Haunted Jester. Donald Corley. LC 79-106279. (Short story index reprint series). (Illus.). 1970. Books for Libraries Press.

Haunted Jester. Donald Corley. LC 31-25222. 1931. R. M. McBride & Company.

Haunted King. Thomas Emmet Moore. LC 10-20178. 1910. C. M. Clark Publishing Co. (Inc.

Haunted Lady. Mary Roberts Rinehart. LC 42-10686. 1942. Farrar & Rinehart, Inc.

Haunted Lady. Mary Roberts Rinehart. LC 49-26249. 1949. Sun Dial Press.

Haunted Land. Randolph Stow. LC 57-8268. 1957. Macmillan.

Haunted Life. Charlotte Mary Brame. LC 44-38280. (On cover: Lovell's library, v. 19, no. 933). John W. Lovell Company.

Haunted Life. Josephine R Fuller. LC 6-44573. (On cover: Temperance library. no. 1. Supplement). 1885. Funk & Wagnalls.

Haunted Life: Or, Her Terrible Sin. Charlotte Mary Brame. LC 44-12254. (On cover: Seaside library. Pocket ed. No. 958). G. Munro.

Haunted Life: Or, Her Terrible Sin. Charlotte Mary Brame. LC 4408. (Bertha Clay library, no. 14). 1900. Street & Smith.

Haunted Lives: A Novel. Joseph Sheridan Le Fanu. LC 76-5268. (Le Fanu, Joseph Sheridan, 1814-1873. Works. 1976). 1976. 54.00 (ISBN 0-405-09208-3). Arno Press.

Haunted Major. Robert Marshall. LC 60-9631. (Illus.). 1960. I. Washburn.

Haunted Man. Cleveland Huffman. LC 50-893. 1949. Ranno.

Haunted Man: The Haunted House and Going into Society. Charles Dickens. LC 6-26447. (On cover: Lovell's library, v. 5, no. 267). 1883. J. W. Lovell Company.

Haunted Mesa. Donald B. Hobart. (Orig.). 1971. pap. 0.60 o.p. (06142). Curtis.

Haunted Millionaire of Montecito. Marion P Earl. LC 18-1361. 1917. The Uplift Association.

Haunted Mirror: Stories. Elizabeth Madox Roberts. LC 76-12121. 1978. 23.50 (ISBN 0-404-15236-8). AMS Press.

Haunted Mirror: Stories by Elizabeth Madox Roberts. Elizabeth Madox Roberts. 1932. The Viking Press.

Haunted Monastery. Robert Van Gulik. 1969. 3.95 o.p. (ISBN 0-684-10614-0). Scribner.

Haunted Monastery. Robert Van Gulik. (Judge Dee Ser.). (O.s.i.). 160p. 1974. pap. 0.95 o.s.i. (ISBN 0-446-75454-4). Paperback Lib.

Haunted Monastery: A Chinese Dectective Story. Robert Hans Van Gulik, pseud. (Illus.). 1974. (pbk.) 0.95. Warner Paperback Library.

Haunted Monastery: A Chinese Detective Story. Robert Hans Van Gulik, pseud. LC 68-57074. (Illus.). 1969. 3.95. Scribner.

Haunted Monastery and The Chinese Maze Murders: Two Chinese Detective Novels, with 27 Illustrations by the Author. Robert Hans Van Gulik, pseud. LC 77-73303. 1977. 5.00 (ISBN 0-486-23502-5). Dover Publications.

Haunted Monastery & the Chinese Maze Murders. Robert Van Gulik. LC 77-73303. (Illus.). 1978. 5.00 (ISBN 0-486-23502-5). Dover.

Haunted Omnibus. Ed. by Alexander Kinnan Laing. LC 37-1268. Farrar & Rinehart, Inc.

Haunted Pajamas. Francis Perry Elliott. LC 11-12502. 1.25. The Bobbs-Merrill Company.

Haunted Photograph. facs. ed. Ruth McEnery Stuart. LC 79-132127. (Short Story Index Reprint Ser). 1911. 12.00 (ISBN 0-8369-3684-1). Ayer Co.

Haunted Photograph. Whence and Whither. A Case in Diplomacy. The Afterglow. Ruth McEnery Stuart. LC 79-132127. (Short story index reprint series). (Illus.). 1970. (ISBN 0-8369-3684-1). Books for Libraries Press.

Haunted Photograph, Whence and Whither. A Case in Diplomacy. The Afterglow. Ruth McEnery Stuart. LC 11-28078. 1911. The Century Co.

Haunted Place. Virginia Coffman. (Signet Book). 1978. 1.50. New American Library.

Haunted Pool. La Mare Au Diable). From the French of George Sand. George Sand & Potter, Frank Hunter, Tr. Dodd, Mead & Company.

Haunted Portrait. Ann Ashton, pseud. LC 75-21204. 262p. 1976. 5.95 o.p. (ISBN 0-385-11363-3). Doubleday.

Haunted Portrait. Ann Ashton, pseud. 1977. 1.25 (ISBN 0-380-00962-5). Avon Books.

Haunted Portrait. John M. Kimbro. LC 75-21204. 1976. 5.95 (ISBN 0-385-11363-3). Doubleday.

Haunted Sisters. Eleanor Hibbert. LC 77-23757. 1977. 8.95. Putnam.

Haunted Sisters. Jean Plaidy. LC 77-23757. (o.s.i.). 1977. 8.95 o.s.i. (ISBN 0-399-12073-4). Putnam Pub Group.

Haunted Spring. Manning Lee Stokes. LC 56-8987. 1956. Arcadia House.

Haunted Stars. Edmond Hamilton. LC 59-157213. (Torqull book). 1960. Distributed by Dodd, Mead.

Haunted Student. A Romance of the Fourteenth Century. Harriette Fanning Read. LC 7-36626. 1860. The Author.

Haunted Summer. Anne Edwards. (Bantam gothic novel). 1974. (pbk.) 1.25. Bantam Books.

Haunted Summer. Anne Edwards. LC 72-76663. 1972. 6.95 (ISBN 0-698-10446-3). Coward, McCann & Geoghegan.

Haunted Summer. Jeanne Judson. (YA) 1973. 4.95 o.p. (Avalon). Bouregy.

Haunted Summer. Jeanne Judson. (Avalon romances). 1973. 4.50. Avalon Books.

Haunted Valley & More Folk Tales. James Gay Jones. 1979. 4.95 (ISBN 0-87012-341-6). McClain.

Haunted Valley: By Jackson Cole. Jackson Cole, pseud. LC 45-6723. 1945. Arcadia House, Inc.

Haunted Woman. Sanford Friedman. LC 68-25765. 1968. Dutton.

Haunted Woman. David Lindsay. LC 74-30384. (Newcastle Forgotten Fantasy classic; F-103). 1975. 2.95 (ISBN 0-87877-103-4). Newcastle Pub. Co.

Haunted Woman. David Lindsay. LC 80-19459. 1980. 9.95. Borgo Press.

Haunted Wood. V. Marchenko. 189p. 1981. 8.00 (ISBN 0-8285-2041-0, Pub. by Progress Pubs USSR). Imported Pubns.

Haunted Yorkshireman. Joseph P. Whelan. 3.75 o.p. Vantage.

Hauntin Fear. Ethel E. Bangert. 1981. pap. 6.95 (Avalon). Bouregy.

Haunting. Catharine Amy Dawson Scott. LC 23-7525. 1922. A. A. Knopf.

Haunting at Lost Lake. Eleana Oliphant. 224p. (Orig.). Date not set. pap. price not set o.p. (ISBN 0-505-51721-3). Tower Bks.

Haunting Compulsion. Anne Mather. (Harlequin Presents Ser.). 192p. 1981. pap. 1.50 (ISBN 0-373-10429-4, Pub. by Harlequin). PB.

Haunting Hand. Walter Adolphe Roberts. LC 26-647224. The Macaulay Company.

Haunting Me. Paula Allardyce, pseud. 1979. 8.95 o.p. (ISBN 0-312-36420-2). St Martin.

Haunting Me. Ursula Torday. LC 79-2294. 8.95 (ISBN 0-312-36420-2). St. Martin's Press.

Haunting of Bally Moran. Helen Nuelle. 224p. 1976. pap. 1.25 (ISBN 0-532-12397-2). Woodhill.

Haunting of Cliffside. Jennette Dowling Letton. LC 74-7668. 1975. 7.95 (ISBN 0-8027-5326-4). Walker.

Haunting of Cliffside. Jennette Dowling Letton. (Berkley Medallion Book). 1977. 1.25 (ISBN 0-425-03391-0). Berkley Pub. Corp.

Haunting of Drumroe. Claudette Nicole. (Orig.). 1971. pap. 0.60 o.p. (R2393, GM). Fawcett World.

Haunting of Drumroe. Claudette Nicole. 144p. 1973. pap. 0.75 o.p. (T2717, GM). Fawcett World.

Haunting of Fog Island. Marilyn Ross. (Orig.). 1973. pap. 0.95 o.p. (09200). Curtis.

Haunting of Gad's Hall. Norah Robinson Lofts. LC 78-62603. 1979. 8.95 (ISBN 0-385-14386-9). Doubleday.

Haunting of Helen Wren. Jan Alexander, pseud. 1975. (pbk.) 1.25 (ISBN 0-671-78445-5). Pocket Books.

Haunting of Hill House. Shirley Jackson. LC 59-13414. 1959. Viking Press.

Haunting of Sara Lessingham. Pamela Bennetts. LC 78-16786. 1978. 11.50 (ISBN 0-8161-6602-1). G. K. Hall.

Haunting of Sara Lessingham. Margaret James. LC 77-9168. 1977. 7.95 o.p. (ISBN 0-312-36424-5). St Martin.

Haunting of Sarah Lessingham. Pamela Bennetts. LC 77-9168. 1978. 7.95 (ISBN 0-312-36424-5). St. Martin's Press.

Haunting of Sarah Lessingham. Pamela Bennetts. 1979. 1.25 (ISBN 0-440-13466-8). Dell Publishing Co.

Haunting of Toby Jugg. Dennis Yates Wheatley. 1976. 9.95 (ISBN 0-09-126890-7, Pub. by Hutchinson). Merrimack Pub Cir.

Haunting of Toby Jugg. Dennis Yates Wheatley. (Black magic ser.). 1972. 1.50. Ballantine.

Haunting of Villa Gabriel. Clarissa Ross, pseud. 1971. pap. 0.75 o.p. (ISBN 0-447-74770-3). Lancer.

Haunting Tales. Ed. by Barbara Ireson. LC 74-7222. 1974. 4.50 (ISBN 0-525-31533-0). Dutton.

Haunting Tales of Nathaniel Hawthorne. Ed. by Michael Hayes. 1981. 10.95 (ISBN 0-7145-3809-4). Riverrun NY.

Hauntings; Fantastic Stories. Violet Paget. LC 75-37280. (Series: Lovell's International Series, No. 73). (Short story index reprint series). 1971. (ISBN 0-8369-4093-8). Books for Libraries Press.

Hauntings. Fantastic Stories. Violet Paget. LC 7-33487. (On cover: Lovell's international series, no. 73). F. F. Lovell & Company.

Hauntings: Fantastic Stories. 2d ed. Violet Paget. 1906. New York, Lane.

Hauntings: Fantastic Stories. facsimile ed. Violet Paget. LC 75-37280. (Short Story Index Reprint Ser.). Repr. of 1890 ed. 15.00 (ISBN 0-8369-4093-8). Ayer Co.

Hauntings: Is There Anybody There? Norah Robinson Lofts. LC 74-25115. 1975. 6.95 (ISBN 0-385-03560-8). Doubleday.

Hauntings: Is There Anybody There? Norah Robinson Lofts. LC 75-31962. 1975. 9.95 (ISBN 0-8161-6336-7). G. K. Hall.

Hauntings: Is There Anybody There? North Robinson Lofts. (Fawcett Crest Book). 1977. 1.75 (ISBN 0-449-23393-6). Fawcett Books.

Hauntings: Tales of the Supernatural. Ed. by Henry Mazzeo. LC 68-17795. (Illus.). 1968. 4.50. Doubleday.

Haunts of Ancient Peace. Alfred Austin. LC 2-24240. 1902. The Macmillan Company.

Haunts of Men. Robert William Chambers. LC 78-103503. (Short story index reprint series). 1969. Books for Libraries Press.

Haunts of Men. Robert William Chambers. Frederick A. Stokes Company.

Hausa Tales & Traditions, Vol. 1. Ed. by Neil Skinner. LC 74-89679. Orig. Title: Tatsuniyoyi Na Hausa. 1970. lib. bdg. 17.50 o.p. (ISBN 0-8419-0021-3, Africana). Holmes & Meier.

Hauser's Memory. Curt Siodmak. LC 68-12111. 1968. Putnam.

Hausfrau Rampant. Julius Ernst Wilhelm Stinde & Lucas, Edward Verrall, 1868- LC 16-16388. George H. Doran Company.

Haute Noblesse: A Novel. George Manville Fenn. LC 11-8218. (On cover: Lovell's international series, no. 41). F. F. Lovell & Company.

Havana Bound. Cecil Roberts. LC 30-24246. 1930. D. Appleton and Company.

Havana Hit. Mike Barry. (Lone Wolf). (Berkley medallion book: Vol. 5). 1974. (pbk.) 0.95 (ISBN 0-425-02527-6). Berkley Pub. Co.

Havana Hotel Murders. Frank Dudley. LC 36-593732. 1936. Houghton Mifflin Company.

Havana Journal. Andrew Salkey. 1971. pap. 1.65 o.p. (ISBN 0-14-021303-1, A1303, Pelican). Penguin.

Havana X. Shelly Gross. 1980. pap. 2.25 (ISBN 0-440-14160-5). Dell.

Havana X: A Novel. Shelly Gross. LC 77-90665. 8.95 (ISBN 0-87795-182-9). Arbor House.

Have a Lovely Funeral: By A. T. Hopkins Pseud. Annette Turngren. LC 54-5650. (Murraru Hill mystery). 1954. Rinehart.

Have a Snort. Rod Gray. (New Lady from L.U.S.T. Ser). (O.s.i.: No. 2). 1975. pap. 1.25 o.s.i. (BT50794). Belmont-Tower.

Have a Snort! Red Grey. (Lady from L.U.S.T.,#2). 1975. (pbk.) 1.25. Belmont Tower Books.

Have and Give: And Other Parables. Annis Ford Eastman. LC 6-36817.

Have Gat: Will Travel. Richard S. Prather. (Shell Scott Series). 1968. pap. 0.50 o.p. (D1917, GM). Fawcett World.

Have His Carcase. Dorothy Leigh Sayers. LC 59-10623. 1959. Harper.

Have His Carcase. Dorothy Leigh Sayers. LC 32-13340. 1932. Brewer, Warren & Putnam.

Have His Carcase. Dorothy Leigh Sayers. LC 80-20876. 1980. 17.95 (ISBN 0-8161-3043-4). G. K. Hall.

Have His Carcase see Wimsey Set II.

Have His Carcase: A Lord Peter Wimsey Mystery... Dorothy Leigh Sayers. LC 45-167998. 1942.

Have I Got a Girl for You. Playboy Editors. LC 72-93812. 128p. 1974. pap. 0.95 o.p. (ISBN 0-87216-227-3, A16227). Playboy Pr Pbks.

Have Jump Shot Will Travel: A Novel. Charles Rosen. LC 75-304955. 1975. 6.95 (ISBN 0-87795-106-3). Arbor House.

Have Mercy Upon Us. Stanton Forbes, pseud. LC 74-7638. 1974. (ISBN 0-385-07327-5). Published for the Crime Club by Doubleday.

Have Mercy Upon Us. Tobias Wells. LC 74-7638. 168p. 1974. 4.95 o.p. (ISBN 0-385-07327-5). Doubleday.

Have with You to Saffron-Walden; or, Gabriell Harveys Hunt Is Up-Containing a Full Anser to the Eldest Sonne of the Halter Maker Or, Nashe His Confutation of the Sinful Doctor. Thomas Nash. 1975. Repr. of 1596 ed. text ed. 12.00x o.s.i. (ISBN 0-8277-3927-3). British Bk Ctr.

Have You Anything to Declare? Maurice Baring. 1936. 25.00 (ISBN 0-8274-2472-8). R West.

Have You Been to the River? A Novel. Chancellor Williams. LC 52-10988.

Have You Heard the Cricket Song? autographed gift ed. 4.95 (ISBN 0-918114-02-0). Inspiration Conn.

Have You Lived on Other Worlds Before, 2 vols. Ruth E. Norman. (Illus.). 1980. Vol. 1. pap. 7.95 (ISBN 0-932642-59-4); Vol. 2. pap. 6.95 (ISBN 0-932642-60-8). Unarius.

Have You Seen This Man? By Gene Hurley. Gene Hurley. LC 44-8333. 1944. The Bobbs-Merrill Company.

Haven. Dale Collins. LC 25-16605. 1925. A. A. Knopf.

Haven. first ed. Graham Diamond. LC 77-73437. 1.95. Playboy Press.

Haven. Eden Phillpotts. LC 9-27991. 1909. 1.50. J. Lane Company.

Haven for Jenny. Virginia K Smiley. (Fawcett gold medal book). 1974. (pbk.) 0.75. Fawcett.

Haven for the Gallant. Daniel Joseph Clinton. LC 36-27080. 1936. A. A. Knopf.

Haven of Darkness. E. C Tubb. (Dumarest of Terra; no. 16). 1977. 1.50 (ISBN 0-87997-299-8). DAW Books.

Haven of Fear. Patricia Ponder. 1977. pap. 1.75 (ISBN 0-532-17165-9). Woodhill.

Haven of Unrest. A Novel. Lewis Strange Wingfield. (seaside library, v. 54, no. 1095). 1881. G. Munro.

Haven. 1st Ed. Carmen R Waid. LC 53-372. 1952. Pageant Press.

Havenhurst. Sharon Wagner. 1975. (pbk.) 0.95 (ISBN 0-345-26695-1). Ballantine Books.

Haven's End. John Phillips Marquand. LC 77-130064. (Short story index reprint series). (Illus.). 1970. Books for Libraries Press.

Haven's End. John Phillips Marquand. LC 33-27263. 1933. Little, Brown, and Company.

Haverhill: Or, Memoirs of an Officer in the Army of Wolfe. James Athearn Jones. 1831. J. & J. Harper.

Havering Plot. Clifford James Wheeler Hosken. LC 29-3428. 1929. Harper & Brothers.

Haversham Legacy. Daoma Winston. LC 74-2792. 1974. 9.95 (ISBN 0-671-21754-2). Simon and Schuster.

Haversham Legacy. Daoma Winston. LC 74-2792. 1975. 1.95 (ISBN 0-671-80037-X). Pocket Books.

Haveth Childers Everywhere. James Augustine Aloysius Joyce. LC 76-47607. 1976. 17.50 (ISBN 0-8414-5315-2). Folcroft Library Editions.

Having a Wonderful Crime. Ed. by Alfred Hitchcock. (Dell Book). 1977. 1.25 (ISBN 0-440-10677-X). Dell Pub. Co.

Having Been There. Allan Luks. LC 79-84843. 8.95 (ISBN 0-684-16170-2). Scribner.

Having Wonderful Crime. Craig Rice. LC 43-5778. 1943. Simon and Schuster.

Having Wonderful Crime... Craig Rice. LC 46-4463. 1945.

Havoc. Tom Kristensen. Tr. by Carl Malmberg from Danish. (Nordic Translation Ser). 446p. 1968. 17.50 (ISBN 0-299-04711-3); pap. 6.00 (ISBN 0-299-04714-8). U of Wis Pr.

Havoc. Edward Phillips Oppenheim. LC 11-25678. 1911. Little, Brown, and Company.

Havoc... Frederic Franklyn Van De Water. LC 31-5754. Pub. for the Crime Club, Inc., by Doubleday, Doran & Company, Inc.

Havoc by Accident. Georges Simenon & Gilbert, Stuart, Tr. LC 43-13577. 1943. Harcourt, Brace and Company.

Havoc in Heaven, Adventures of the Monkey King. 1979. 1.95 (ISBN 0-8351-0667-5). China Bks.

Havoc in Islandia. Mark Saxton. LC 81-20139. (Illus.). 1982. 12.95 (ISBN 0-395-31833-5). Houghton Mifflin Co.

Havoc of a Smile. authorized ed. Lucy Bethia Colquhoun Walford. LC 8-32815. (On cover: Lovell's Westminister series, no. 13). 1890. J. W. Lovell Company.

Hawaii. James Albert Michener. (Crest bk., C1776). (Illus.). 1973. 1.95. Fawcett.

Hawaii. James Albert Michener. LC 59-10815. 1959. Random House.

Hawaiian Folk Tales. Thomas G. Thrum. LC 76-8499. 1976. Repr. lib. bdg. 25.00 (ISBN 0-8414-8543-7). Folcroft.

Hawaiian Harvest. Armine Von Tempski. LC 33-6473. 1933. Frederick A. Stokes Company.

Hawaiian Hellground. Don Pendleton. (Executioner#22). 1975. (pbk.) 1.25 (ISBN 0-523-00625-X). Pinnacle Books.

Hawaiian Hellground: Executioner Ser., No. 22. Don Pendleton. 192p. (Orig.). 1975. pap. 1.95 (ISBN 0-523-41086-7). Pinnacle Bks.

Hawaiian Idylls of Love and Death. Herbert Henry Gowen. LC 8-22540. 1908. Cochrane Publishing Co.

Hawaiian Interlude. Mary Ann Taylor. (Orig.). 1980. pap. 1.75 (ISBN 0-451-09031-4, E9031, Sig). NAL.

Hawaiian Lover. Joseph Harrington. LC 32-101073. The Macaulay Company.

Hawaiian Takeover. Dan Streib. (Hawk Ser.: No. 13). 192p. (Orig.). 1981. pap. 1.95 (ISBN 0-515-06028-3). Jove Pubns.

Hawaiian Tales. Allan Beekman. LC 76-21731. 3.95. Harlo Press.

Hawbucks. John Masefield. LC 29-22433. 1929. The Macmillan Company.

Hawk. Bret Sanders. (Hawk Ser.). (O.s.i.). 160p. (Orig.). 1973. pap. 0.95 o.s.i. (AN1186, Award). Univ Pub & Dist.

Hawk. Milton J Shapiro. 1975. (pbk.) 1.50. Ace Books.

Hawk. Roy Vickers. LC 30-10977. 1930. L. MacVeagh, The Dial Press.

Hawk, a Story of Aerial War. Ronald Legge. LC 9-12618. 1909. The J. McBride Co.

Hawk Alone. Jack Bennett. LC 65-20739. 1965. Little, Brown.

Hawk Among the Sparrows. Desmond Hawkins. LC 39-10520. 1939. A. A. Knopf.

Hawk Among the Sparrows: Three Science Fiction Novellas. Dean McLaughlin. LC 76-38. 7.95 (ISBN 0-684-14577-4). Scribner.

Hawk & the Dove. Leigh F. James. (American Southwest Ser.). 448p. (Orig.). 1980. pap. 2.95 (ISBN 0-553-20087-9). Bantam.

Hawk and the Sun. Byron Herbert Reece. LC 55-8881. 1955. Dutton.

Hawk and the Tree, a Novel. Patrick Carleton. LC 34-214756. E. P. Dutton & Co., Inc.

Hawk & Whippoorwill: 1960-63. Ed. by August William Derleth. 1972. 10.00 o.s.i. (ISBN 0-88451-009-3). Edco-Vis Assoc.

Hawk: California Shakedown. Don Streib. (Hawk Ser.: No. 5). 192p. (Orig.). 1981. pap. 1.95 (ISBN 0-515-05300-7). Jove Pubns.

Hawk Chief: A Tale of the Indian Country. John Treat Irving. LC 45-302349. Carey, Lea and Blanchard.

Hawk Gumbo and Other Stories. Jack Butler. LC 82-70167. (Illus.). 1982. 14.95 (ISBN 0-935304-35-5). August House.

Hawk in an Eagle's Nest. Almon Benson Richmond. LC 7-41229. 1881.

Hawk in the Wind. Helen Topping Miller. LC 38-5366. 1938. D. Appleton-Century Company, Incorporated.

Hawk Is Dying. Harry Crews. LC 72-8979. 1973. 5.95 (ISBN 0-394-48305-7). Knopf.

Hawk Is Dying. Harry Crews. 1974. (pbk.) 1.25 (ISBN 0-671-78405-6). Pocket Books.

Hawk Is Humming: A Novel. George Mendoza. LC 63-13534. 1964. Bobbs-Merrill.

Hawk Mission. Pat Nobel. (Orig.). 1979. pap. 1.95. Woodhill.

Hawk Moon. Sam Shepard. 120p. (Orig.). 1973. 15.00 o.p. (ISBN 0-87685-144-8). Black Sparrow.

Hawk Moon: A Book of Short Stories, Poems, and Monologues. Sam Shepard. LC 72-13808. 1973. 15.00 (ISBN 0-87685-145-6) (ISBN 0-87685-145-6). Black Sparrow Press.

Hawk of Como. John Oxenham, pseud. LC 28-147076. 1928. Longmans, Green and Co. Ltd.

Hawk of Detroit: A Novel. Arthur Pound. LC 39-279387. Reynal & Hitchcock.

Hawk of Egypt. Joan Conquest. LC 22-17063. The Macaulay Company.

Hawk of May. Gillian Bradshaw. LC 79-27135. 10.95 (ISBN 0-671-25093-0). Simon and Schuster.

Hawk of the Desert. Albert M Treynor. LC 30-277575. 1930. Dodd, Mead & Company.

Hawk of the Wilderness. William L. Chester. LC 36-430721. 1936. Harper & Brothers.

Hawk Over Whirlpools. Ruth Murray Underhill. LC 40-34749. J. J. Augustin.

Hawk Shadow. Monica Heath. 1.95 (ISBN 0-87216-656-2). Playboy Press Paperbacks.

Hawk That Dare Not Hunt. Scott O'Dell. 1978. pap. 1.50 (ISBN 0-440-93677-2, LFL). Dell.

Hawk: The Cargo Gods. Dan Streib. (Hawk Ser.: No. 10). 192p. (Orig.). 1981. pap. 1.95 (ISBN 0-515-05875-0). Jove Pubns.

Hawk: The Deadly Crusader. Dan Streib. (Hawk Ser.: No. 1). (Orig.). pap. 1.95 (ISBN 0-515-05234-5). Jove Pubns.

Hawk: The Death Riders. Dan Streib. (Hawk Ser.: No. 7). 208p. (Orig.). 1981. pap. 1.95 (ISBN 0-515-05872-6). Jove Pubns.

Hawk: The Enemy Within. Dan Streib. (Hawk Ser.: No. 8). 192p. (Orig.). 1981. pap. 1.95 (ISBN 0-515-05873-4). Jove Pubns.

Hawk: The Mind Twisters. Dan Streib. (Hawk Ser.: No. 2). pap. 1.95 (ISBN 0-515-05235-3). Jove Pubns.

Hawk: The Predators. Dan Streib. (Hawk Ser.: No. 4). (Orig.). pap. 1.95 (ISBN 0-515-05299-X). Jove Pubns.

Hawk: The Seeds of Evil. Dan Streib. (Hawk Ser.: No. 6). 224p. (Orig.). 1981. pap. 1.95 (ISBN 0-515-05301-5). Jove Pubns.

Hawk: The Treasure Divers. Dan Streib. (Hawk Ser.: No. 14). (Orig.). 1981. pap. 1.95 (ISBN 0-515-06029-1). Jove Pubns.

Hawk: The Young Osage; a Story of Indian Life and Adventures in the Early Times. Charles Henry Robinson. LC 13-20584. 1913. L. C. Page & Company.

Hawk Watch. Brandon Bird. LC 54-682254. (Red badge detective). 1954. Dodd, Mead.

Hawkeland Cache. Eugene Fitzmaurice. LC 80-162. 12.95 (ISBN 0-671-25345-X). Wyndham Books.

Hawkeland Cache. Eugene FitzMawia. 1982. pap. 2.95 (ISBN 0-425-05166-8). Berkley Pub.

Hawke's Indians. P. A Bechko. LC 78-22610. 1979. 7.95 (ISBN 0-385-14963-8). Doubleday.

Hawkes Nest. Jean Hayward. 1979. pap. 2.25 o.s.i. (ISBN 0-505-51443-5). Tower Bks.

Hawkeye. Herbert Quick. LC 23-119779. The Bobbs-Merrill Company.

Hawkfall, & Other Stories. George Mackay Brown. 220p. 1979. 8.95 o.p. (ISBN 0-7012-0391-9, Pub. by Chatto Bodley Jonathan). Merrimack Pub Cir.

Hawkland Cache. Eugene Fitzmaurice. 1980. 12.95 o.s.i. (ISBN 0-671-25345-X, Wyndam Bks). S&S.

Hawkline Monster. Richard Brautigan. LC 74-6204. (O.s.i.). 216p. 1975. pap. 2.95 o.s.i. (ISBN 0-671-22156-6, Touchstone Bks). S&S.

Hawkline Monster: A Gothic Western. Richard Brautigan. LC 74-6204. 1974. 3.95 (ISBN 0-671-21809-3). Simon and Schuster.

Hawkline Monster: /Richard Brautigan. Richard Brautigan. 1976. 1.75 (ISBN 0-671-80747-1). Pocket Books.

Hawkmistress! Marion Zimmer Bradley. 336p. 1982. pap. 2.95 (ISBN 0-87997-762-0). DAW Bks.

Hawkridge. Jane Blackmore. 1976. pap. 1.95 (ISBN 0-441-31930-0). Ace Bks.

Hawks. Joseph Amiel. LC 79-10989. 9.95 (ISBN 0-399-12312-1). Putnam.

Hawks. Joseph Amiel. 1980. 2.95 (ISBN 0-445-04620-1). Fawcett Popular Library.

Hawks & Harriers. Page Stegner. LC 75-163588. 1972. 6.95. Dial Press.

Hawk's Done Gone: And Other Stories. Mildred Haun. LC 68-20546. (Illus.). 1968. 7.95. Vanderbilt University Press.

Hawk's Done Gone & Other Stories. Mildred Haun. Ed. by Herschel Gower. LC 68-20546. (Illus.). 1968. 7.95 o.p. (ISBN 0-8265-1119-8). Vanderbilt U Pr.

Hawk's Done Gone: By Mildred Haun. Indianapolis. Mildred Haun. LC 40-32617. The Bobbs-Merril Company.

Hawk's Flight. Helen Rose Hull. LC 46-250996. 1946. Coward-McCann, Inc.

Hawk's Nest. Hubert Skidmore. LC 41-4553. 1941. Doubleday, Doran and Company, Inc.

Hawk's Nest: A Throbbing Tale of the Underworld, Based on the Motion Picture Story. Wid Gunning. LC 23-16160. Jacobsen-Hodgkinson-Corporation.

Hawks of Arcturus. Cecil Snyder. 1974. (pbk.) 0.95. DAW Books.

Hawks of Glenaerie. Ruth MacLeod. (1974 ed. o.p.). 192p. (Orig.). 1977. pap. 1.25 o.p. (ISBN 0-532-12469-3). Woodhill.

Hawks of Glenaerie. Ruth MacLeod. (1974 ed. o.p.). 192p. (Orig.). 1977. pap. 1.25 o.p. (ISBN 0-532-12469-3). Manor Bks.

Hawks of Glenaerie. Ruth MacLeod. 1974. (pbk.) 0.95. Manor Books.

Hawks of Hawk-Hollow: A Tale of Pennsylvania, 2 vols. Robert Montgomery Bird. LC 78-64062. Repr. of 1835 ed. 75.00 set (ISBN 0-404-17390-X). AMS Pr.

Hawks of Hawk-Hollow. A Tradition of Pennsylvania. Robert Montgomery Bird. LC 6-12726. 1835. Carey, Lea & Blanchard.

Hawks of Noon. John C Champion. (75-1273). 1968. Popular Lib.

Hawks of Noon. John C Champion. LC 65-22563. 1965. D. McKay Co.

Hawks of Outremer. Robert E. Howard. 15.00 (ISBN 0-937986-11-9). D M Grant.

Hawks View: A Family History of Our Own Times. Harriet Parr. LC 7-34723. 1860. W. A. Townsend and Company.

Hawksbill Manor. Alicia Grace. 1976. pap. 1.25 (ISBN 0-532-12431-6). Woodhill.

Hawksbill Station. Robert Silverberg. LC 68-22612. (Doubleday science fiction). 1968. 3.95. Doubleday.

Hawkshaw. Ron Goulart. LC 71-175377. 1972. 4.95. Doubleday.

Hawkshead. Janis Flores. LC 75-17071. 1976. 5.95 (ISBN 0-385-11364-1). Doubleday.

Hawkstone. William Sewell. LC 75-446. (Victorian Fiction: Novels of Faith and Doubt). 1976. 35.00 (ISBN 0-8240-1526-6). Garland Pub.

Hawkstone: A Tale of and for England in 184-... from the 2d london ed. William Sewell. LC 8-11251. 1848. Stanford & Swords.

Hawkstone: A Tale of & for England in 184-, 1845. William Sewell. Ed. by Robert L. Wolff. LC 75-446. (Victorian Fiction Ser.). 1975. lib. bdg. 66.00 (ISBN 0-8240-1526-6). Garland Pub.

Haworth Harvest: The Story of the Brontes. Nancy Brysson Morrison. LC 78-89661. (Illus.). 1969. 6.95. Vanguard Press.

Haworth's. Frances Hodgson Burnett. 1879. C. Scribner's Sons.

Haworth's. Frances Hodgson Burnett. LC 7-25664. 1907. C. Scribner's Sons.

Hawser Pirates. Oswald Wynd. LC 76-124827. 1970. Harcourt Brace Jovanovich.

Hawksmoor Heritage. Catherine Moreland. (Orig.). 1981. pap. 2.50 (ISBN 0-89083-898-4). Zebra.

Hawthorn Hill. Doris Shannon. LC 75-40806. 8.95. St. Martin's Press.

Hawthorn Wood. Jane Fleming. 1975. (pbk.) 0.95 (ISBN 0-425-02912-3). Berkley Publishing Corp.

Hawthorndean: Or, Philip Benton's Family. A Story of Every Day Life. Clara M. Thompson. LC 8-19971. 1873. P. F. Cunningham.

Hawthorne. Ruth Wolff. (Gothic Ser). Orig. Title: I, Keturah. 1969. pap. 0.60 o.p. (ISBN 0-446-63150-7, 63-150). Paperback Lib.

Hawthorne Dale, and Miscellaneous Sketches, Chiefly Masonic. William H Tucker & Tucker, William H. LC 8-28273. 1869. Chicago Printers' Co-Operative Association.

Hawthorne: Selections. Nathaniel Hawthorne. LC 7-3777. (On cover: American classics for schools). 1882. Houghton, Mifflin and Company.

Hawthorne: Short Stories. Nathaniel Hawthorne. Ed. by Newton Arvin. 1955. pap. 3.95 (ISBN 0-394-70015-5, V-15, Vin). Random.

Hawthorne: Tales of His Native Land. Ed. by Neal Frank Doubleday. Nathaniel Hawthorne. LC 62-51684. (Selected source materials for coll. res. papers). 1962. 2.00. Heath.

Hawthorne's House of the Seven Gables. Nathaniel Hawthorne & Opdycke, John Baker, 1878- Ed. LC 17-6330. (Half-title: English readings for schools, general editor, W. L. Cross). 0.52. H. Holt and Company.

Hawthorne's Mosses from an Old Manse. Nathaniel Hawthorne & Burbank, Charles Elroy, Ed. LC 8-25363. (Macmillan's pocket American and English classics). 1908. The Macmillan Company.

Hawthorne's Short Stories. Nathaniel Hawthorne. Ed. by Newton Arvin. (O.s.i.). (YA) 1946. 10.00 o.s.i. (ISBN 0-394-44528-7). Knopf.

Hawthorne's Short Stories: Edited, and with an Introduction. Nathaniel Hawthorne & Arvin, Newton, 1900- Ed. LC 46-391119. 1946. A. A. Knopf.

Hawthorne's Tanglewood Tales. Nathaniel Hawthorne & Beggs, Robert Henry, Ed. LC 7-13437. (Macmillan's pocket American and English classics). 1907. The Macmillan Company.

Hawthorne's The House of the Seven Gables. Nathaniel Hawthorne & Green, Ward Hamilton, Ed. LC 31-17598. (Golden key series). D. C. Heath and Company.

Hay-Wire. Bertha Muzzy Sinclair. LC 28-17203. 1928. Little, Brown, and Company.

Hayburn Family. Guy McCrone. LC 52-5795. 1952. Farrar, Straus and Young.

Haycott Album: A Novel. 1st Ed. William E Henning. LC 56-6415. 1956. Lippincott.

Hayden's Heritage. Bob Haning, pseud. LC 74-34108. 1975. 4.95 (ISBN 0-517-52160-1). Lenox Hill Press.

Haydocks' Testimony. Lydia Cope Wood. LC 9-3428. 1890. Christian Arbitration and Peace Society.

Haydocks' Testimony: A Tale of the American Civil War. new ed. Lydia Cope Wood. LC 7-27631. Headley Brothers.

Haym Salomon: Immigrant and Financier of the American Revolution. Haym Salomon Baron & Salomon, Haym. LC 28-10624. 1929. Bloch Publishing Co.

Haymarket. Claire Rayner. LC 74-5137. 1974. (ISBN 0-671-21812-3). Simon and Schuster.

Haymarket: A Novel. Claire Rayner. (Fawcett crest book). 1975. (pbk.) 1.50. Fawcett.

Haymon's Crowd. Robert Greenfield. 1979. 2.50 (ISBN 0-425-04193-X). Berkley Pub. Corp.

Haymon's Crowd: A Novel. Robert Greenfield. LC 78-3743. 1978. 9.95 (ISBN 0-671-40012-6). Summit Books.

Haystacks and Smokestacks. William Feather. LC 24-5339. 1923. The William Feather Company.

Hayvens of Demaret. Katherine Jones Bellamann. LC 51-3177. 1951. Simon and Schuster.

Haywire Town. Robert J McCaig. LC 54-708659. (Silver star westerns). 1954. Dodd, Mead.

Hazanda. Colin D Willock. LC 68-25468. 1968. 5.95. Putnam.

Hazard. Nancy Barr Mavity. LC 24-4870. 1924. Harper & Brothers.

Hazard: A Novel. Gerald A Browne. LC 72-82171. 1973. 7.95 (ISBN 0-87795-040-7). Arbor House.

Hazard: A Novel. Gerald A Browne. 1974. (pbk.) 1.50 (ISBN 0-671-78725-X). Pocket Books.

Hazard, a Novel. Roy Chanslor. LC 47-30573. 1947. Simon and Schuster.

Hazard in the Blue. John Oxenham, pseud. LC 23-13268. 1923. Hodder and Stoughton Ltd.

Hazard of Hearts. Barbara Cartland. (Historical Romance Ser. No. 2). 1972. pap. 0.95 o.p. (N2706). Pyramid Pubns.

Hazard of Hearts. Barbara Cartland. 1975. pap. 1.25 o.p. (ISBN 0-515-03648-X, V3648). BJ Pub Group.

Hazard of New Fortunes. William Dean Howells. LC 65-3229. 1965. New American Library.

Hazard of New Fortunes. William Dean Howells. LC 73-75402. (selected edition of W. D. Howells; v. 16). 1975. 20.00 (ISBN 0-253-32708-3). Indiana University Press.

Hazard of New Fortunes. William Dean Howells. LC 19-9539. (Half-title; The modern library of the world's best books). 1917. Boni and Liveright, Inc.

Hazard of New Fortunes: A Novel. William Dean Howells. LC 4-15121. 1890. Harper & Brothers.

Hazard of New Fortunes: A Novel. William Dean Howells. LC 7-5774. (On cover: Harper's Franklin square library. new ser., no. 698). 1891. Harper & Brothers.

Hazard of New Fortunes. New Introd. by George Warren Arms. William Dean Howells. LC 52-5309. (Everyman's library). 1952. Dutton.

Hazard of New Fortunes. With an Introd. by Van Wyck Brooks. William Dean Howells. LC 60-2062. (Bantam classic, SC59). 1960. Bantam Books.

Hazard of the Hills. Charles Neville Buck. LC 32-21422. The Macaulay Company.

Hazards of Belinda. Sophia Cleugh. LC 33-94003. 1933. Houghton Mifflin Company.

Hazards of Distance: A Novel. Linda Ty-Casper. 111p. 1982. pap. 6.50 (Pub. by New Day Philippines). Cellar.

Hazards of the Oregon. Trail: A Novel of the Northwest Pioneers in the 1850's. 1st Ed. Luna B Fisk. LC 55-10293. 1955. Exposition Press.

Haze of Evil: By Kenneth Lowe Pseud. 1st Ed. Elma K Lobaugh. LC 53-8348. 1953. Published for the Crime Club by Doubleday.

Hazel. John Sjoberg. LC 75-30923. (Cloth ed. 15.00 o.p.). 1976. pap. 4.00 o.p. (ISBN 0-915124-09-2). Toothpaste.

Hazel Kirke. Marie Walsh. (On cover: Seaside library. Pocket ed. no. 533). 1885. G. Munro.

Hazel Kirke. Marie Walsh. (On cover: The library of American authors, no. 24). 1890. G. Munro.

Hazel of Heatherland. Mabel Sarah Barnes Grundy. LC 6-10643. 1906. The Baker & Taylor Co.

Hazell and the Three Card Trick. P. B Yuill. LC 76-13828. 1976. 7.95 (ISBN 0-8027-5352-3). Walker.

Hazell Plays Solomon. P. B Yuill. LC 75-17481. 1975. 6.95 (ISBN 0-8027-5329-9). Walker.

He. Henrietta Eliza Vaughan Stannard. (On cover: Seaside library. Pocket ed. no. 966). 1887. G. Munro.

He: A Companion to She. Being a History of the Adventures of J. Theodosius Aristophano on the Island of Rapa Nai in Search of His Immortal Ancestor... John De Morgan. LC 7-25990. (Munro's library, v. 50, no. 721). 1887. N. L. Munro.

He, a Companion to She. Being a History of the Adventures of J. Theodosius Aristophano on the Island of Rapa Nui in Search of His Immortal Ancestor... Andrew Lang & Pollock, Walter Herries, 1850-1926, Supposed Author. LC 7-25990. (Munro's library, v. 50, no. 721). 1887. N. L. Munro.

He Ain't No Bum. O. A. Phillips & Ray Buck. 1980. pap. 1.95 (ISBN 0-451-09540-5, J9450, Sig). NAL.

He and I: Or, Was It He? Sarah Bridges Stebbins. LC 8-13440. 1877. G. W. Carleton & Co.; Etc., Etc.

He and She: A Novel. Edward Semple Le Comte. LC 60-13089. 1960. McDowell, Obolensky.

He" and "She" Or, A Point of Honor. Annie Edwards. 1887. G. W. Dillingham, Successor to G. W. Carleton & Co.; Etc. Etc.

He Arrived at Dusk. Rubie Constance Ashby. LC 33-163530. 1933. The Macmillan Company.

He Brings Great News: A Novel. Winifred Ashton. LC 45-8221. 1945. Random House.

He Called My Name. Frank Vandenberg. LC 44-5097. 1944. Wm. B. Eerdmans Publishing Company.

He Comes up Smiling. Charles Sherman. LC 12-1000. The Bobbs-Merrill Company.

He Conquered the Kaiser. H. A Mason. LC 15-737148. 1915. The Macaulay Company.

He Could Not Have Slipped! Francis Beeding. LC 39-27265. 1939. Harper & Brothers.

He Dared Not Look Behind. Cledwyn Hughes. LC 47-184428. 1947. A. A. Wyn, Inc.

He Didn't Mind Danger. Michael Francis Gilbert. LC 49-94501. Harper.

He Died Laughing. Lawrence Lariar. LC 43-10415. 1943. Phoenix Press.

He Died of Murder. Nancy Bodington. LC 48-5857. 1948. Harper.

He Done Her Wrong: A Toby Peters Mystery. Stuart M Kaminsky. LC 82-16912. 1983. 10.95 (ISBN 0-312-36491-1). St. Martin's Press.

He Dwelt Among Us. Charles William Gordon. LC 36-33985. Fleming H. Revell Company.

He Feeds the Birds. Terence Ford. LC 50-9210. 1950. Dial Press.

He Fell Among Thieves. authorized ed. David Christie Murray & Herman, Henry. LC 7-31829. (On cover: Lovell's international series, no. 166). 1891. J. W. Lovell Company.

He Fell Down Dead. Virginia Perdue. LC 43-44283. 1943. Pub. for the Crime Club by Doubleday, Doran & Co., Inc.

He Fought for His Queen: The Story Sir Philip Sidney. Barbara Willard, pseud. LC 56-136767. 1954. F. Warne.

He Had It Made: A Novel. Sidney Offit. LC 59-14018. 1959. Crown Publishers.

He Is Here. Charles Monroe Sheldon. LC 31-32748. 1931. Harper & Brothers.

He Knew He Was Right. Anthony Trollope. (World's Classics Ser: No. 507). 1975. 13.95 o.p. (ISBN 0-19-250507-6). Oxford U Pr.

He Knew He Was Right. Anthony Trollope. Ed. by P. D. Edwards. 1974. 15.00x (ISBN 0-7022-0848-5); pap. 9.95 (ISBN 0-7022-0842-6). U of Queensland Pr.

He Knew Women. Peggy Whitehouse. LC 27-20591. 1927. Boni and Liveright.

He Laughed at Murder. Clifford James Wheeler Hosken. LC 35-4042. H. Holt and Company.

He Leadeth Me & Other Stories. Naomi Strubhar. Ed. by Rosalyn B. Strubhar. 1959. pap. 2.50x o.s.i. (ISBN 0-87813-202-3). Park View.

He Learned About Women...". Berta Ruck. LC 40-333666. 1940. Dodd, Mead & Company.

He Looked for a City. Arthur Stuart-Menteth Hutchinson. LC 41-51510. Duell, Sloan and Pearce.

He Married a Doctor. Faith Baldwin Cuthrell. LC 43-18239. 1944. Farrar & Rinehart, Incorporated.

He Married a Doctor. Faith Baldwin Cuthrell. 1975. (pbk.) 0.95 (ISBN 0-446-75785-3). Warner Paperback Library.

He Never Came Back. Paul Tabor. LC 47-24308. 1947. E. P. Dutton.

He Never Came Back: A Novel. Paul Tabori. LC 47-24308. 1947. Dutton.

He of Samaria. William James Hiller. LC 72-97811. 1973. 4.95 (ISBN 0-8059-1831-0). Dorrance.

He Ought to Be Shot. 1st Ed. Joan Margaret Fleming. LC 55-765606. 1955. Published for the Crime Club by Doubleday.

He Passion Artist. John Hawkes. (Harper Colophon book). 1981. 3.95 (ISBN 0-06-090837-8). Harper & Row.

He Ran All the Way: A Novel. Sam Ross. LC 47-883. 1947. Farrar, Straus and Company.

He Rather Enjoyed It. Pelham Grenville Wodehouse. LC 25-14665. George H. Doran Company.

He Rather Enjoyed It. Pelham Grenville Wodehouse. LC 35-285906. 1927. A. L. Burt Company.

He Road Alone. Steve Frazee. 160p. 1981. pap. 1.75 (ISBN 0-449-14103-9, Crest). Fawcett.

He Rode Alone. Steve Frazee. 1969. pap. 0.60 o.p. (R2103, GM). Fawcett World.

He Sent Forth a Raven. Elizabeth Madox Roberts. LC 35-27098. 1935. The Viking Press.

He Stooped to Conquer. Jane Lane. LC 74-558590. 1968. 6.25x (ISBN 0-584-31042-0). Intl Pubns Serv.

He Swung and He Missed: A Novel. Eugene O'Brien. LC 37-19155. Reynal & Hitchcock.

He That Eateth Bread with Me. Hersilia A Mitchell Copp Keays. LC 4-8277. 1904. McClure, Phillips & Co.

He That Is Without Sin. Herman Arthur Haubold. LC 12-621. 1911. The Cosmopolitan Press.

He That Will Not When He May. A Novel. Margaret Oliphant Wilson Oliphant. (Franklin square library, no. 149). 1880. Harper & Brothers.

He, the Father. Frank Mlakar. LC 50-8544. 1950. Harper.

He Touched Me: My Pilgrimage of Prayer. John Powell. 1974. pap. 2.75 (ISBN 0-913592-47-1). Argus Comm.

He Walks in a Dark Shadow. John F. Rando. 2.00 o.p. Carlton.

He Was a Man. Rose Wilder Lane. LC 25-6944. 1925. Harper & Brothers.

He Went Away for a While. Max Miller. LC 33-6648. 1933. E. P. Dutton and Company, Inc.

He Went for a Soldier. authorized ed. Henrietta Eliza Vaughan Stannard. LC 8-3374. (On cover: Lovell's Westminster series, no. 19). 1890. United States Book Company.

He Went for a Soldier: Also Houp-la, and In Quarters with the 25th (The Black Horse) Dragoons. Henrietta Eliza Vaughan Stannard. G. Munro's Sons.

He Went for a Walk. Dorothy Evelyn Smith. LC 54-8851. 1954. Dutton.

He-Who-Always-Wins: And Other Navajo Campfire Stories. Richard Hettema Pousma & Ickes, Anna (Wilmarth) LC 34-24139. 1934. W. B. Eerdmans Publishing Company.

He Who Breaks. Inna Demens. LC 18-90752. 1918. Dodd, Mead and Company.

He-Who-Came! Constance Holme. (Oxford bookshelf). 1939. Oxford University Press.

He Who Digs a Grave. David Delman. LC 73-75163. 1973. 4.95 (ISBN 0-385-03738-4). Published for the Crime Club by Doubleday.

He Who Flees the Lion. Translated from the German by Richard and Clara Winston. 1st Ed. Klein-Haparash, Jacob. LC 63-17859. 1963. Atheneum.

He Who Gets Slapped: A Novel Adapted from Leonid Andreyev's Drama and the Victor Seastrom Photoplay. George A Carlin & Andreev, Leonid Nikolaevich. LC 26-134. Grosset & Dunlap.

He Who Hates God, a Comedy of Symbols. Farley O'Brien. LC 51-1932. 1951. Exposition Press.

He Who Hesitates. Ed McBain. 160p. 1982. pap. 2.25 (ISBN 0-345-29291-X). Ballantine.

He Who Hesitates. Ed McBain. 3.50 o.p. Delacorte.

He Who Hesitates: An 87th Precinct Novel, by Ed McBain Pseud. Evan Hunter. LC 65-15434. 3.50. Delacorte Dist. Dial.

He Who Rides a Tiger. Bhabani Bhattacharya. LC 54-11175. 1954. Crown Publishers.

He Who Whispers. John Dickson Carr. (O.s.i.). 240p. 1975. pap. 1.50 o.s.i. (AD1518, Award). Univ Pub & Dist.

He Who Whispers. John Dickson Carr. 1976. (pbk.) 1.50. Award Books.

He Who Whispers: A Dr. Fell Mystery Story. John Dickson Carr. LC 46-2640. 1946. Harper & Brothers.

He Will Return. Helen Campbell Dickson Reynolds. LC 60-1666. T. Bouregy.

He Will Stay till You Come: The Rise and Fall of Skinny Walker. Burr McCloskey. LC 78-59114. 10.95 (ISBN 0-87716-090-2). Moore Pub. Co.

He Would Be a Gentleman: Or, Treasure Trove. Being Accounts of Irish Heirs. Samuel Lover. (Seaside library. v. 8, no. 158). 1877. G. Munro.

He Would Have Me Be Brave. A Story Taken from Life. Frances I Katzenberger. LC 7-116741. 1895. Press of the Groneweg Printing Company.

He Would Provoke Death. Clodagh Gibson-Jarnice. LC 59-8443. 1959. Roy Publishers.

He Wouldn't Kill Patience. John Dickson Carr. LC 44-953. 1944. The Hampton Publishing Company, Distributed by W. Morrow & Company.

He Wouldn't Stay Dead. Frederick Clyde Davis. LC 39-29317. 1939. Pub. for the Crime Club, Inc., by Doubleday, Doran and Co., Inc.

Head. William D Fezler. LC 80-84391. 9.95 (ISBN 0-934810-02-8). Laurida Books Pub. Co.

Head Against the Wall: Translated from the French by W. J. Strachan. 1st American Ed. Herve Bazin. LC 52-859505. 1952. Prentice-Hall.

Head Against the Wall: Translated from the French by W. J. Strachan. Herve-Bazin, Jean Pierre Marie. LC 52-8595. 1952. Prentice-Hall.

Head Coach, Ralph Delahaye Paine. LC 10-8339. 1910. 1.50. C. Scribner's Sons.

Head Crusher. Bruno Rossi, pseud. (Sharps Shooter Ser., No. 7). 1974. pap. 0.95 o.p. (LB176NK). Leisure Bks.

Head for the Hills: A Novel of the Tennessee Mountains. Katherine Sherman. LC 65-4373. 1962. Exposition Press.

Head Girl. Peter Kevin. pap. 1.95 o.p. (ISBN 0-87682-244-8, 7244). Barclay Hse.

Head Hunter. Thomas H. Hilton. 192p. (Orig.). 1972. pap. 1.95 o.p. (ISBN 0-87682-270-7, 7270). Barclay Hse.

Head Hunters. James Lucano. 320p. 1980. pap. 2.25 (ISBN 0-345-28529-8). Ballantine.

Head-Hunter's Bride. Benjamin Harold Pearson. LC 51-14739. 1951. Cowman Publications.

Head in Green Bronze: And Other Stories. Hugh Walpole. LC 38-27284. 1938. Doubleday, Doran & Co., Inc.

Head in the Clouds. Sara Lucile Jenkins. LC 54-14469. 1954. Avalon Books.

Head in the Clouds. Sara Lucile Jenkins. (Red rose romance, no. 143). 1974. (pbk.) 0.75. Bantam Books.

Head in the Clouds. Joan Sargent. 1974. (pbk.) 0.75. Bantam Books.

Head in the Wind. Mabel Margaret Clark. LC 28-220614. 1928. Harper & Brothers.

Head Men: Destroyer No. 31. Warren Murphy. (Destroyer Ser.). 1977. pap. 1.75 (ISBN 0-523-40907-9). Pinnacle Bks.

Head Nurse. Ruth Dorset, pseud. pap. 0.75 o.s.i. (01-400). Lancer.

Head O' W-Hollow. Jesse Stuart. LC 36-8773. E. P. Dutton & Co., Inc.

Head of a Hundred: Being an Account of Certain Passages in the Life of Humphrey Hunton, Esq., Sometyme an Officer in the Colony of Virginia. Maud Wilder Goodwin. LC 6-27481. 1895. Little, Brown & Comp'y.

Head of a Hundred in the Colony of Virginia: 1622. Maud Wilder Goodwin. LC 6223. 1900. Little, Brown and Company.

Head of a Traveler. Nicholas Blake. 1976. pap. 2.25i (ISBN 0-06-080398-3, P398, PL). Har-Row.

Head of a Traveler. Cecil Day-Lewis. (Perennial Library). 1976. 1.75 (ISBN 0-06-080398-3). Harper & Row.

Head of a Traveler. Cecil Day-Lewis. LC 49-892493. 1949. Harper.

Head of Alvise. Lina Wertmuller. LC 82-3528. 1982. 12.00 (ISBN 0-688-01124-1). Morrow.

Head of Appollo. 1st Ed. Elizabeth Frances Corbett. LC 56-11680. 1956. Lippincott.

Head of Gold. Dalton Alexander. 1982. 10.00 (ISBN 0-533-05089-8). Vantage.

Head of Iron" A Romance of Colonial Pennsylvania. Burd Shippen Patterson. LC 8-25365. 1908. T. M. Walker.

Head of Medusa. Julia Constance Fletcher. LC 6-416851. 1880. Roberts Brothers.

Head of Medusa. Alicia Grace. 1978. pap. 1.25 (ISBN 0-532-12547-9). Woodhill.

Head of Pasht. Willis Boyd Allen. LC 3161. 1900. E. P. Dutton & Co.

Head of the Family. Alphonse Daudet. Tr. by Carnac, Levin. LC 6-33054. 1898. G. P. Putnam's Sons.

Head of the Family. Josephine Lawrence. LC 32-11121. Aventine Press.

Head of the Family. A Novel. Dinah Maria Mulock Craik. LC 6-31089. 1859. Harper & Brothers.

Head of the Firm: A Novel. Charlotte Eliza Lawson Cowan Riddell. LC 7-41419. J. W. Lovell Company.

Head of the Force. James Barnett. LC 78-19614. 1979. 8.95 (ISBN 0-312-36499-7). St. Martin's Press.

Head of the House. Grace Livingston Hill. 1962. Grosset & Dunlap.

Head of the House. Grace Livingston Hill. LC 40-23345. J. B. Lippincott Company.

Head of the House. Al Zuckerman. (Dell Book). 1978. 1.50 (ISBN 0-451-08298-2). Dell Pub. Co., Inc.

Head of the House of Coombe. Frances Hodgson Burnett. LC 22-301898. Frederick A. Stokes Company.

Head of the Line, a Collection of Short Stories. Gladys Hasty Carroll. LC 42-68302. 1942. The Macmillan Company.

Head of the Mountain. Ernest Haycox. LC 77-15535. 1978. 8.95 (ISBN 0-8161-6534-3). G. K. Hall.

Head Over Heels in Murder. Ione Sandberg Shriber. LC 40-8318. Farrar and Rinehart, Inc.

Head O'W-Hollow. Jesse Stuart. LC 70-178463. (Short story index reprint series). 1971. (ISBN 0-8369-4065-2). Books for Libraries Press.

Head O'W-Hollow. Jesse Stuart. LC 79-11240. 17.00 (ISBN 0-8131-0142-5). University Press of Kentucky.

Head Piece: By Ralph Temple Pseud. Robert William Alexander. LC 53-28914. 1953. S. Paul.

Head Station. Rosa Caroline Murray-Prior Praed. (Lovell's library, no. 1340). 1889. J. W. Lovell Company.

Head Station. A Novel of Australian Life. Rosa Caroline Murray-Prior Praed. (On cover: Seaside library. Pocket ed. no. 811). 1886. G. Munro.

Head Tide. Joseph Crosby Lincoln. LC 32-19271. 1932. D. Appleton and Company.

Head Virgin. Kip Cameron. 192p. (Orig.). 1973. pap. 1.95 o.p. (ISBN 0-87682-290-1, 7290). Barclay Hse.

Head Winds. Sara Ware Bassett. LC 47-4645. 1947. Doubleday.

Head Winds. James Brendan Connolly. LC 10-176548. 1916. C. Scribner's Sons.

Head Winds. A. M. Sinclair Wilt. LC 23-17478. 1923. Duffield and Company.

Headbirths, or, The Germans Are Dying Out. Gunter Grass. LC 81-48012. 9.95 (ISBN 0-15-139600-0). Harcourt Brace Jovanovich.

Headed for a Hearse. Jonathan Latimer. LC 35-13547. 1935. Pub. for the Crime Club, Inc., by Doubleday, Doran & Company, Inc.

Headed for a Hearse. Jonathan Latimer. LC 80-12148. (Gregg Press Mystery Fiction Series). 1980. 12.95 (ISBN 0-8398-2652-4). Gregg Press.

Headed for Hollywood. Homer Croy. 1932. Harper & Brothers.

Headhunters' Secret. Victor Dugas. LC 24-8573. South-West Press.

Heading West. Doris Betts. LC 81-47493. 320p. 1981. 13.50 (ISBN 0-394-51798-9). Knopf.

Heading West. Doris Betts. 1982. pap. 3.50 (ISBN 0-451-11913-4, AE1913, Sig). NAL.

Headland. George Troy. LC 52-10274. 1952. Bobbs-Merrill.

Headland: A Novel. Carol Ryrie Brink. LC 55-3387. 1955. Macmillan.

Headless Angel. Vicki Baum. LC 48-5904. 1948. Doubleday.

Headless Beings. Margaret Malcolm, pseud. LC 73-79693. 1973. 4.95 (ISBN 0-385-03802-X). Published for the Crime Club by Doubleday.

Headless Lady. Clayton Rawson. LC 40-32092. G. P. Putnam's Sons.

Headless Lady. Clayton Rawson. LC 79-11659. (Gregg Press Mystery Fiction Series). 1979. 9.95 (ISBN 0-8398-2544-7). Gregg Press.

Headless Victory: A Suspense Novel. David S Lifson. LC 77-89645. 7.95 (ISBN 0-498-02144-0). A. S. Barnes.

Headlights & Markers. Frank Donovan & Robert Henry. (Illus.). 1967. 7.95 o.p. (ISBN 0-87095-006-1). Golden West.

Headlights and Markers: An Anthology of Railroad Stories. Ed. by Frank Pierce Donovan. Henry, Robert Selph, 1889- Joint Ed. LC 46-806025. 1946. Creative Age Press, Inc.

Headlights and Markers: An Anthology of Railroad Stories. Ed. by Frank Pierce Donovan & Robert Selph Henry. LC 68-8776. (Illus.). 1968. 6.95. Golden West Books.

Headline, Romance! Florence Kerigan. (YA) 1978. 6.95 (Avalon). Bouregy.

Headlines. Rosalea Mary Campbell. LC 32-7119. 1932. Harper & Brothers.

Headlines. Mildred Evans Gilman. LC 28-23466. H. Liveright.

Headlong. Genevieve Parkhurst. LC 31-29014. H. Holt and Company.

Headlong. Emlyn Williams. LC 80-51775. 1981. 11.95 (ISBN 0-670-36439-8). Viking Press.

Headlong for Murder. Merlda Mace. LC 43-54301. 1943. J. Messner, Inc.

Headlong from Heaven: A Novel. Michael Valbeck. LC 47-30405. 1947. M. S. Mill Co.

Headlong Hall. Thomas Love Peacock. 1816. Pub. by M. Carey.

Headlong Hall and Nightmare Abbey. Thomas Love Peacock. LC 9-8362. (On cover: Knickerbocker nuggets. 2). G. P. Putnam's Sons, the Knickerbocker Press.

Headlong Hall and Nightmare Abbey. Thomas Love Peacock. (Half-title: Everyman's library, ed. by Ernest Rhys. Fiction). 1908. J. M. Dent & Co.

Headlong Hall and Nightmare Abbey. Thomas Love Peacock. LC 7-33750. 1896. Macmillan and Co.

Headlong Hall, Melincourt, Nightmare Abbey, Maid Marian. Thomas Love Peacock. (Half-title: The new universal library. The works of Thomas LovePeacock. i). G. Routledge & Sons, Ltd.

Headmaster. John Angus McPhee. 1966. pap. 1.45 o.p. (1081, Four Winds). Schol Bk Serv.

Headmistress. Angela Mackail Thirkell. (Barsetshire Romance Ser., No. 7). (O.S.I.). 1972. pap. 1.25 o.s.i. (ISBN 0-515-02771-5, V2771). Pyramid Pubns.

Headmistress: A Novel. Angela Mackail Thirkell. LC 44-406745. 1945. A. A. Knopf.

Headquarter Recruit: And Other Stories. Clotilde Inez Mary Graves. LC 13-17413. 1913. 1.25. Frederick A. Stokes Company.

Headquarter Recruit & Other Stories. facsimile ed. Clotilde Inez Mary Graves. LC 77-150544. (Short Story Index Reprint Ser.). Repr. of 1913 ed. 18.00 (ISBN 0-8369-3841-0). Ayer Co.

Heads. Edward Stewart. LC 69-10641. 1969. 4.95 o.p. (ISBN 0-02-614760-2). Macmillan.

Heads: A Metafictional History of Western Civilization, 1762-1975. Alan Goldfein. LC 73-9296. 1973. 5.95 (ISBN 0-688-00177-7). W. Morrow.

Heads I Win: A Tale of Murder and Detection, by Quentin Downes Pseud. Michael Harrison. LC 55-9305. Roy Publishers.

Heads of Cerberus. Gertrude Barrows Bennett. LC 77-84269. (Lost Race and Adult Fantasy Fiction). (Illus.). 1978. 15.00 (ISBN 0-405-11009-X). Arno Press.

Heads of Cerberus: By Francis Stevens Pseud. Illustratedby Ric Binkley, with an Introd. by Lloyd Arthur Eshbach. 1st Ed. Gertrude Barrows Bennett. LC 52-27268. (Polaris fantasy library, v. 1). 1952. Polaris Press.

Heads off at Midnight. Francis Beeding. LC 38-33409. 1938. Harper & Brothers.

Heads You Lose. Christianna Brand, pseud. LC 42-7949. 1942. Dodd, Mead & Company.

Heads You Lose. Mary Christianna Milne Lewis. LC 42-7949. 1942. Dodd, Mead & Company.

Heads You Lose. Mary Christina Lewis. LC 42-7949. 1942. Dodd, Mead & Company.

Heads You Lose. Jimmy Starr. LC 50-7679. 1950. Fell.

Heads, You Lose, and Other Apocryphal Tales. Francis Greig. LC 81-15144. 11.95 (ISBN 0-517-54490-3). Crown.

Heads You Lose: By Brett Halliday Pseud. Davis Dresser. LC 56-9465. (Torquil book). 1956. Distributed by Dodd, Mead.

Heads You Win, Tails I Lose. Isabelle Holland. (YA) 1977. 1.95 (ISBN 0-440-96547-0, LFL). Dell.

Headshrinker's Test. Sue Kaufman. LC 77-85580. 1969. 5.95. Random House.

Headshrinker's Test. Sue Kaufman. (Berkley medallion book). 1974. (pbk.) 1.25 (ISBN 0-425-02540-3). Berkley Pub. Co.

Headshrinker's Test. Sue Kaufmann. Ed. by J. M. Fox. LC 77-85580. (O.S.I.). 1969. 5.95 o.s.i. (ISBN 0-394-42800-5). Random.

Headsman: Or, The Abbaye Des Vignerons. A Tale. James Fenimore Cooper. 1833. Carey, Lea & Blanchard.

Headsman: Or, The Abbaye Des Vignerons. A Tale. new ed. James Fenimore Cooper. LC 6-29899. 1852. Stringer & Townsend.

Headsman: Or, The Abbaye Des Vignerons; a Tale. James Fenimore Cooper. (On cover: Lovell's library. no. 519). 1885. J. W. Lovell Company.

Headsman: Or, The Abbaye Des Vignerons. A Tale. James Fenimore Cooper. (On cover: Seaside library. Pocket ed. no. 385). 1885. G. Munro.

Headsman: Or, The Abbaye Des Vignerons. A Tale. James Fenimore Cooper. LC 4-19561. 1889. D. Appleton and Company.

Headsman: Or, The Abbaye Des Vignerons. A By J. Fenimore Copper... With the Latest Revision and Corrections of the Author. James Fenimore Cooper. LC 26-24691. (Half-title: The choice works of Cooper revised and corrected series. v. 13). 1856. Stringer & Townsend.

Headsman's Holiday: A Pharaoh Pharr Mystery. Dean Hawkins. LC 46-174261. 1946. Mystery House.

Headstrong Houseboat: Or, Barnacles Are Better Than Blowouts, but Beware of a Leaky Basement. William C Anderson. LC 70-185080. 1972. 5.95. Crown Publishers.

Headwaters: A Novel. 1st Ed. Archie Binns. LC 57-756642. 1957. Duell, Sloan and Pearce.

Headwind House. Sylvia Leonora Brett Brooke. LC 53-31408. 1953. Boardman.

Healer. Robert Herrick. LC 72-84659. 1976. (ISBN 0-403-03193-1). Scholarly Press.

Healer. Robert Herrick. LC 11-283554. 1911. The Macmillan Company.

Healer. Leonard Levitt. 240p. 1981. pap. 2.95 (ISBN 0-380-56531-5, 56531). Avon.

Healer. Daniel Pratt Mannix. 1973. 0.95. Avon.

Healer. Daniel Pratt Mannix. LC 70-108895. 1971. 5.95 (ISBN 0-525-12235-4). E. P. Dutton.

Healer. David Meltzer. pap. 1.95 o.p. (0122). Essex Hse.

Healer. Francis Paul Wilson. LC 75-40751. 1976. 5.95 (ISBN 0-385-11548-2). Doubleday.

Healer see Collected Works.

Healer: A Novel of the LaNague Federation. Francis Paul Wilson. (Dell Book). 1977. 1.50 (ISBN 0-440-13569-9). Dell Pub. Co.

Healer of All Flesh, a Novel. Abram Stilman. LC 59-16465. 1959. Whittier Books.

Healer. 1st Ed. Frank Gill Slaughter. LC 55-525922. 1955. Doubleday.

Healers. Gerald Green. LC 78-24534. 10.95 (ISBN 0-399-12119-6). Putnam.

Healers. Gerald Greene. LC 78-24534. 1979. 10.95 o.p. (ISBN 0-399-12119-6). Putnam Pub Group.

Healers. Benzion Liber. LC 28-10098. 1928. Rational Living.

Healers. Jozua Marius Willen Van Der Poorten Schwartz. LC 6-626620. 1906. D. Appleton and Company.

Healers: A Novel. Henry Denker. LC 82-20374. 13.45 (ISBN 0-688-01585-9). Morrow.

Healey. Jessie Fothergill. LC 6-40014. (On cover: The seaside library. Pocket ed. no. 572). 1885. G. Munro.

Healing Hands of Death. Pierre Audemars. 1977. 7.95 (ISBN 0-09-128780-4, Pub. by Hutchinson). Merrimack Pub Cir.

Healing Hills. Bertha B. Moore McCurry. LC 43-2002. 1941. Fundamental Truth Publishers.

Healing Light. Agnes Mary White Sandford. 5.95 (ISBN 0-910924-36-8); pap. 4.50 (ISBN 0-910924-37-6); pocketsize 2.50 (ISBN 0-910924-52-X). Macalester.

Healing Oath: Translated by Oliver Coburn. Andre Soubiran. LC 54-871047. 1954. Putnam.

Healing of the Hawaiian: A Story of the Hawaiian Islands. Evelyn Whitell. LC 23-106981. The Master Press.

Healing Time. Anthony Owen Colby. LC 78-653. 8.95 (ISBN 0-87223-482-7). Seaview Books: Trade Distribution by Simon and Schuster.

Healing Time. Anthony Owen Colby. 1980. 2.25 (ISBN 0-87216-523-X). Playboy Press Paperbacks.

Health Unto His Majesty. Eleanor Hibbert. LC 72-12846. 1973. 11.95 (ISBN 0-8161-6072-4). G. K. Hall.

Health Unto His Majesty. Eleanor Hibbert. (Crest Book, P2019). 1973. (pbk.) 1.25. Fawcett.

Health Unto His Majesty. Justin Huntly McCarthy. LC 12-15143. Hodder & Stoughton, George H. Doran Company.

Health Unto His Majesty. Jean Plaidy. 253p. Repr. of 1956 ed. lib. bdg. 12.45x (ISBN 0-88411-894-0). Amereon Ltd.

Health Unto His Majesty. Jean Plaidy. 288p. 1972. 6.95 o.p. (ISBN 0-399-10982-X). Putnam Pub Group.

Health Unto His Majesty. Jean Plaidy. 1973. lib. bdg. 11.95 o.p. (ISBN 0-8161-6072-4, Large Print Bks). G K Hall.

Healthy Season. Anne Steinhardt. 1971. 1.50 o.p. (Z1088D). Grove.

Healthy Way to Die. Lionel Black. 1979. pap. 1.95 (ISBN 0-380-43661-2, 43661). Avon.

Heaps of Money. A Novel. William Edward Norris. (Seaside library. v. 34, no. 707). 1880. G. Munro.

Hear and Forgive. Emyr Humphreys. 1953. Putnam.

Hear Me, Pilate! 1st Ed. Le Gette Blythe. LC 61-11599. 1961. Holt, Rinehart and Winston.

Hear My Heart Speak. Charlotte Paul. LC 50-6984. 1950. Messner.

Hear No Evil. Nan Bowen. LC 68-15263. (Cock Robin mystery). 1968. Macmillan.

Hear No Evil: By Stephen Ransome Pseud. 1st Ed. Frederick Clyde Davis. LC 53-106515. 1953. Published for the Crime Club by Doubleday.

Hear Not My Steps. Lloyd S Thompson. LC 53-6813. 1953. Abelard Press.

Hear That Train Blow. Kelly Covin. 1970. 6.95 o.p. (3530-6). Delacorte.

Hear That Train Blow: A Novel About the Scottsboro Case. Kelly Covin. LC 70-122467. 1970. 6.95. Delacorte Press.

Hear the Children Cry. Ruby Jean Jensen. 288p. 1981. pap. 2.50 (ISBN 0-8439-0968-4, Leisure Bks). Nordon Pubns.

Hear the Cook Crow. Barbara Dennis Avirett. LC 49-10963. 1949. Dodd, Mead.

Hear the Word: A Novel About Elijah and Elisha. Henry Bela Zador. LC 62-10798. 1962. McGraw-Hill.

Hear Them Grow. Maria T. Zeiser. 4.50 o.p. Vantage.

Hear This Woman! Ben Pinchot & Pinchot, Ann, Joint Author. LC 49-507443. 1949. Farrar, Straus.

Hear Us O Lord from Heaven Thy Dwelling Place. 1st Ed. Malcolm Lowry. LC 61-8688. 1961. Lippincott.

Hear, Ye Sons: A Novel. Irving Fineman. LC 74-27980. (Modern Jewish Experience). 1975. 19.00 (ISBN 0-405-06709-7). Arno Press.

Hear, Ye Sons: A Novel. Irving Fineman. LC 33-23926. 1933. Longmans, Green and Co.

Hear, Ye Sons: A Novel. Irving Fineman. LC 39-27955. (Half-title: The Modern library of the world's best books). 1939. The Modern Library.

Heard at the Nineteenth. Anderson & Grant. (Illus.). 13.50x (ISBN 0-392-03209-0, SpS). Sportshelf.

Hearing. Easton, Robert Olney. LC 64-23725. 1964. McNally and Loftin.

Hearing His Voice. John P. Grace. LC 79-54696. (Illus.). 160p. (Orig.). 1979. pap. 3.50 (ISBN 0-87793-187-9). Ave Maria.

Hearing Secret Harmonies: A Novel. Anthony Dymoke Powell. LC 75-25552. (His A dance to the music of time). 7.95 (ISBN 0-316-71592-1). Little, Brown.

Hearing Trumpet. Leonora Carrington. LC 76-6532. (Illus.). 7.95. St. Martin's Press.

Hearing Trumpet. Leonora Carrington. (Kangaroo Book). (Illus.). 1977. 1.75 (ISBN 0-671-81837-6). Pocket Books.

Hearken to the Evidence. Herbert Russell Wakefield. LC 34-340169. 1934. Doubleday, Doran & Company, Inc.

Hearken Unto the Voice. Franz V. Werfel. Tr. by William Rose. LC 38-27145. 1938. The Viking Press.

Hearn's Valley. Wayne D Overholser. LC 58-8158. 1958. Macmillan.

Hearsay: The Story of a Lie... Henry Wynans Jessup. LC 29-1673. 1928. W. Neale.

Hearse Horse Snickered: By Carolyn Thomas Pseud. 1st Ed. Actea Duncan. (Mainllne mysteries). 1954. Lippincott.

Hearse of a Different Color. Merle Constiner. LC 52-9474. 1952. Phoenix Press.

Hearse of a Different Color. Alfred Hitchcock. 1980. pap. 1.95 (ISBN 0-440-13550-8). Dell.

Hearse of Another Color. M. E. Chaber, pseud. (Milo March Ser). 1970. pap. 0.60 o.p. (ISBN 0-446-63486-7, 63-486). Paperback Lib.

Hearses Don't Hurry. Frederick Clyde Davis. LC 41-4409. 1941. Published for the Crime Club by Doubleday, Doran & Co., Inc.

Heart: A Social Novel. Martin Farquhar Tupper. LC 42-35209. (Wiley and Putnam's library of choice reading). 1845. Wiley & Putnam.

Heart Alone. George Locke Howe. LC 52-13642. 1953. Putnam.
Heart Alone. Nina Kaye. LC 40-14422. Phoenix Press.
Heart and Chart. Margarita Spalding Gerry. LC 11-26605. 1911. Harper & Brother.
Heart and Cross. Margaret Oliphant Wilson Oliphant. (Seaside library, v. 24, no. 475). 1879. G. Munro.
Heart and Science: A Story of the Present Time. Wilkie Collins. LC 6-269446. (On cover: Lovell's library. v. 2, no. 87). 1883. J. W. Lovell Co.
Heart and Soul: A Novel. Henrietta Channing Dana Skinner. LC 1-11761. 1901. Harper & Brothers.
Heart and Soul," By Norma Newcomb... William Arthur Neubauer. LC 45-950779. 1945. Grammercy Publishing Company.
Heart Appeal. Maysie Greig. LC 35-15733. 1935. Doubleday, Doran & Co., Inc.
Heart Appeal. Maysie Greig. LC 37-2758. 1937. The Sun Dial Press, Inc.
Heart Awakens. Janette Radcliffe. (Regency Romance). 1977. 1.50 (ISBN 0-440-13525-7). Dell Pub. Co.
Heart Awakes. Mervyn Brian Kennicott. LC 37-1451. 1936. Houghton Mifflin Company.
Heart Bandit. Laura Lou Brookman. LC 28-125509. Grosset & Dunlap.
Heart, Be Still. Isabel Wilder. LC 34-24865. Coward, McCann Inc.
Heart Beat. Carolyn Cassady. (gr. 11-12). 1980. pap. 1.95 (ISBN 0-671-83163-1). PB.
Heart Breaker. Charlotte Lamb, pseud. (Harlequin Presents Ser.). 192p. 1981. pap. 1.75 (ISBN 0-373-10460-X). Harlequin Bks.
Heart Burial. Charles A. Bradford. Repr. of 1933 ed. 14.00 o.s.i. Finch Pr.
Heart Change. Lynn Freed. 1982. pap. 2.95 (ISBN 0-451-11916-9, AE1916, Sig). NAL.
Heart Divided. Elsie Frances Wilson Mack. LC 47-17947. 1946. Arcadia House, Inc.
Heart Divided. Frances Sarah Moore. LC 47-17947. 1946. Arcadia House, Inc.
Heart Does Not Forget. Alice Mary Ross Colver. LC 42-22826. 1942. Macrae-Smith-Company.
Heart E Horsemen. Archie Joscelyn. LC 39-31415. Phoenix Press.
Heart Failures. Ursula Perrin. LC 78-52111. 1978. 7.95 (ISBN 0-385-14170-X). Doubleday.
Heart Failures. Ursula Perrin. 1980. 1.95 (ISBN 0-380-47589-8). Avon Books.
Heart Flights. Translated from the French by David Hughes and Marie-Jacqueline Mason. Felicien Marceau, pseud. LC 58-8629. 1958. Abelard-Schuman.
Heart for Elaine. William Arthur Neubauer. LC 52-3393. 1952. Arcadia House.
Heart for the Gods of Mexico. Conrad Potter Aiken. LC 73-11309. 1973. (ISBN 0-8414-2885-9). Folcroft Library Editions.
Heart Full of Horses. Florence Fenley. LC 75-25709. (Illus.). 1975. 8.95 (ISBN 0-8111-0575-X). Naylor Co.
Heart Has April Too. Gladys Bagg Taber. LC 44-962667. 1944. Macrae-Smith-Company.
Heart Has Reasons. Nona Coxhead. LC 46-5904. 1946. C. Scribner's Sons.
Heart Has Reasons. Stephanie Kincaid. (Candlelight Romance). 1.25 (ISBN 0-440-13455-2). Dell Pub. Co.
Heart Has Reasons. Marion Sturges-Jones. LC 48-478717. 1948. G. P. Putnam's Sons.
Heart Has Wings. Faith Baldwin. 317p. Repr. of 1930 ed. lib. bdg. 16.60x (ISBN 0-88411-627-1). Amereon Ltd.
Heart Has Wings. Faith Baldwin Cuthrell. LC 37-71303. Farrar & Rinehart, Incorporated.
Heart Has Wings. Faith Baldwin Cuthrell. 1974. (pbk.) 1.25 (ISBN 0-446-76683-6). Warner Paperback Library.
Heart-Histoires and Life-Pictures. Timothy Shay Arthur. LC 6-3399. 1853. C. Scribner.
Heart Hungry. Laura Lou Brookman. LC 30-329099. Grosset & Dunlap.
Heart-Hungry: A Novel. Maria Elizabeth Jourdan Westmoreland. LC 12-19557. 1872. G. W. Carleton & Co.
Heart in a Hurricane. Charles Green Shaw. LC 27-6052. Brentano's.
Heart in Darkness. Julia Grice. LC 47-20371. 1947. Arcadia House.
Heart in Exile. 1st American Ed. Rodney Garland. LC 54-10145. 1954. Coward-McCann.
Heart in Pilgrimage. Evelyn Sybil Mary Eaton & Moore, Edward Roberts, 1894- Joint Author. LC 48-635646. 1948. Harper.
Heart in the Desert: A Novel. Gilbert Phelps. LC 54-5886. 1954. J. Day Co.
Heart in the Highlands. Nancy Macdougall Kennedy. 1978. pap. 1.95 (ISBN 0-532-19192-7). Woodhill.
Heart in the Highlands. Jane Oliver, pseud. (O.S.I.). Orig. Title: Blue Heaven Bends All Over. 1973. pap. 1.50 o.s.i. (ISBN 0-515-03075-9). Pyramid Pubns.
Heart Is a Lonely Hunter. Carson Smith McCullers. LC 40-10298. 1940. Houghton Mifflin Company.
Heart Is a Lonely Hunter. Carson Smith McCullers. LC 46-20590. (On cover: Penguin books. 596). 1946. Penguin Books, Inc.
Heart Is a Stranger. Paul Cooper Murray. LC 49-8985. 1949. Harper.
Heart Is Broken. Barbara Cartland. (Romance Ser.: No. 20). 288p. 1983. pap. 2.25 (ISBN 0-515-06392-4). Jove Pubns.
Heart Is Broken. Barbara Cartland. 1974. pap. 1.25 o.p. (ISBN 0-515-03358-8, V3358). BJ Pub Group.
Heart Is Half a Prophet. Ruth Tessler Goldstein. LC 76-10720. 8.95 (ISBN 0-02-544590-1). Macmillan.
Heart Is Where the Hurt Is. Harry Marks. 1969. Repr. of 1966 ed. pap. 1.95 o.s.i. Tri-Ocean.
Heart Is Wiser. Jeanne Judson. LC 53-7474. 1953. Bouregy & Curl.
Heart-Keeper. Francoise Quoirez. LC 68-25788. 1968. 3.95. Dutton.
Heart-Keeper. Francoise Sagan, pseud. Tr. by Robert Westoff. LC 68-25788. 1968. 3.95 o.p. (ISBN 0-525-12260-5). Dutton.
Heart Knows Why: By Norma Newcomb Pseud. William Arthur Neubauer. LC 54-13354. 1954. Arcadia House.
Heart Line: A Drama of San Francisco. Gelett Burgess. LC 7-32840. 1907. The Bobbs-Merrill Company.
Heart Listens. Helen Van Slyke. LC 73-80736. 1973. 8.95 (ISBN 0-385-06011-4). Doubleday.
Heart Merchants. Lawrence L. Goldman. (Orig.). 1970. pap. 0.95 o.p. (65-250). Paperback Lib.
Heart Must Choose. Justine Sommers. (Americana Romance.). 1978. 1.25 (ISBN 0-441-29728-5). Ace Books.
Heart Never Fits Its Wanting. Lee K. Abbott, Jr. 1980. 9.95 (ISBN 0-915996-05-7); pap. 5.95 (ISBN 0-915996-06-5). North Am Rev.
Heart Never Forgets. Carolyn Thornton. 192p. (Orig.). 1980. pap. 1.50 (ISBN 0-671-57019-6). S&S.
Heart of a Child. Phyllis Bottome. LC 58-12191. 1958. Vanguard Press.
Heart of a Child. Phyllis Bottome. LC 40-33212. G. P. Putnam's Sons.
Heart of a Child: Being Passages from the Early Life of Sally Snape, Lady Kidderminster. Julia Davis Frankau. LC 8-11080. 1908. The Macmillan Company.
Heart of a Child: Being Passages from the Early Life of Sally Snape, Lady Kidderminster. Julia Davis Frankau. LC 16-7553. 1910. The Macmillan Company.
Heart of a Dog. Mikhail Afanasevich Bulgakov. LC 68-31233. 1968. Harcourt, Brace & Wolff.
Heart of a Dog. Mikhail Afanasevich Bulgakov. LC 68-54002. 1968. 3.95. Grove Press.
Heart of a Geisha. Mary Crawford Fraser. LC 8-31464. 2.00. G. P. Putnam's Sons.
Heart of a Goof. Pelham Grenville Wodehouse. LC 73-161899. (Penguin books). 1972. 0.30 (ISBN 0-14-002048-9). Penguin.
Heart of a Lark. Catherine Clark. LC 25-19621. 1925. T. Seltzer.
Heart of a Man. Richard Aumerle Maher. LC 15-18284. 1915. Banziger Brothers.
Heart of a Man. Georges Simenon. LC 51-11547. 1951. Prentice-Hall.
Heart of a Mystery: A Novel. Thomas Wilkinson Speight. LC 8-15510. R. F. Fenno & Company.
Heart of a Nurse. Helen Murray. (Orig.). 1980. pap. 1.75 (ISBN 0-8439-8001-X, Tiara Bks). Nordon Pubns.
Heart of a Queen. Delves-Broughton, Josephine. LC 50-6562. 1950. Whittlesey House.
Heart of a Rose: A Narrative Drama. William Mara Bell. LC 6-13099. The Klebold Press.
Heart of a Stranger. Lon Riley Woodrum. LC 62-53017. 1962. Zondervan Pub. House.
Heart of a Woman. Maya Angelou. 1983. pap. 3.50 (ISBN 0-553-22839-0). Bantam.
Heart of a Woman. Emmuska Orczy. LC 11-15193. Hodder & Stoughton, George H. Doran Company.
Heart of Alsace. Rene Schickele & Waller, Hannah, Tr. LC 29-5694. 1929. A. A. Knopf.
Heart of Alsace. Benjamin Vallotton. LC 18-133134. 1918. Dodd, Mead and Company.
Heart of an Indian: A Gripping Story Based Upon a Great American Truth. Robert Elmer Callahan. LC 28-2811. F. H. Hitchcock.
Heart of an Orphan. Amanda Mathews Chase. LC 12-24630. D. FitzGerald, Inc.
Heart of Another. Martha Gellhorn. LC 41-21540. 1941. C. Scribner's Sons.
Heart of Arethusa. Frances Barton Fox. LC 18-9496. 1.35. Small, Maynard and Company.
Heart of Canyon Pass. Thomas K Holmes. LC 21-18944. G. Sully & Company.
Heart of Cherry McBain: A Novel. Douglas Leader Durkin. LC 21-7413. 1920. Harper & Brothers.
Heart of Childhood... Ed. by William Dean Howells. Alden, Henry Mills, 1836-1919, Joint Ed. LC 6-45047. (Harper's novelettes). 1906. Harper & Brothers.
Heart of Darkness. Joseph Conrad. (Collateral classic, CC516). 1967. Washington Sq.
Heart of Darkness. Joseph Conrad. Limited Editions Club, Inc., New York. LC 71-5711. (Illus.). 1969. Arr. by Richard Ellis for the Members of the Limited Editions Club.
Heart of Darkness. Joseph Conrad. Ed. by Leonard Fellows Dean. LC 60-12243. (Illus.). 1960. Prentice-Hall.
Heart of Darkness. Joseph Conrad. LC 81-38511. 1981. 10.00 (ISBN 0-8376-0458-3). R. Bentley.
Heart of Darkness: An Authoritative Text, Backgrounds and Sources, Criticism. rev. ed. Joseph Conrad. Ed. by Robert Kimbrough. LC 78-152308. (Norton critical edition). (Illus.). 1972. (pbk.) 1.75 (ISBN 0-393-04347-9) (ISBN 0-393-09773-0). Norton.
Heart of Darkness: An Authoritative Text, Backgrounds and Sources, Essays in Criticism. Joseph Conrad. Ed. by Robert Kimbrough. LC 63-8031. (Norton critical editions, N307). (Illus.). 1963. Norton.
Heart of Darkness: And Other Stories. Joseph Conrad. LC 77-125650. (Riverside literature series, R39). (Illus.). 1970. Houghton Mifflin.
Heart of Darkness, and the Critics. Joseph Conrad. Ed. by Bruce Harkness. LC 60-9979. (Wadsworth guides to literary study). (Illus.). 1960. Wadsworth Pub. Co.
Heart of Darkness: And The Secret Sharer, by Joseph Conrad; Notes, Including Plot Summary, Synopsis of Sections with Critical Comments, Critical Analysis. Joseph Conrad. pap., 1.00. Cliff's Notes.
Heart of Darkness & the Secret Sharer. Joseph Conrad. 1978. Repr. of 1910 ed. lib. bdg. 13.95x (ISBN 0-89966-054-1). Buccaneer Bks.
Heart of Darkness & the Secret Sharer. Joseph Conrad. 1971. pap. 1.50 (ISBN 0-451-51668-0, CW1668, Sig Classics). NAL.
Heart of Darkness, and The Secret Sharer: With an Introd. by Albert J. Guerard. Joseph Conrad. LC 51-11. (Signet book). 1950. New American Library.
Heart of Darkness & Typhoon. Joseph Conrad. 1982. pap. 10.00x (ISBN 0-330-24796-4, Pub. by Pan Bks). State Mutual Bk.
Heart of Darkness: Conrad. M. L. Sutton. Bd. with Secret Sharer: Conrad. 88p. (gr. 9-12). 1968. pap. text ed. 1.00 o.p. (BN). B&N.
Heart of Darkness, Nigger of the Narcissus & the Secret Sharer. Joseph Conrad. 1970. pap. 0.75 o.p. (ISBN 0-671-46551-1). WSP.
Heart of Denise: And Other Tales. Sidney Kilner Levett-Yeats. LC 99-227. 1899. Longmans, Green, and Co.
Heart of Desire. Elizabeth Dejeans. LC 10-853754. 1910. 1.50. J. B. Lippincott Company.
Heart of Fame. Giles Playfair. LC 51-10462. 1951. Little, Brown.
Heart of Fire. Jean Corey. (On cover: Library of American authors, no. 60). 1894. G. Munro's Sons.
Heart of George Washington: A Simple Story of Great Love. Bernie Smade Babcock. LC 32-6892. 1932. J. B. Lippincott Company.
Heart of Gold. Russell H Greenan. LC 74-23865. 1975. 6.95 (ISBN 0-394-49495-4). Random House.
Heart of Gold. Paul Williams. 1982. pap. cancelled (ISBN 0-9601428-8-6); cancelled (ISBN 0-934558-10-8). Entwhistle Bks.
Heart of Happy Hollow. Paul Laurence Dunbar. LC 77-81112. (Illus.). 1969. Mnemosyne Pub. Inc.
Heart of Happy Hollow. Paul Laurence Dunbar. LC 77-110597. (Short story index reprint series). (Illus.). 1970. Books for Libraries Press.
Heart of Happy Hollow. Paul Laurence Dunbar. LC 79-88407. (Illus.). 1969. Negro Universities Press.
Heart of Happy Hollow. Paul Laurence Dunbar. LC 4-32322. 1904. Dodd, Mead and Company.
Heart of Hemlock. Clair Willard Perry. LC 20-15534. The Bobbs-Merrill Company.
Heart of Her Highness. Clara Elizabeth Laughlin. LC 17-25586. 1917. 1.50. G. P. Putnam's Sons.
Heart of Honor. large print ed. Caroline Courtney. LC 81-6284. 1981. 12.95 (ISBN 0-8161-3242-9). G.K. Hall.
Heart of Honor. Caroline Courtney. 1980. 1.75 (ISBN 0-446-94294-4). Warner Communications Company.
Heart of Hyacinth. Winnifred Eaton Babcock. 1903. Harper & Brothers.
Heart of It: A Romance of East and West. William Osborn Stoddard. (On cover: Knickerbocker novels). 1880. G. P. Putnam's Sons.
Heart of Jacqueline. Margaret Peterson. LC 31-5219. Sears Publishing Company, Inc.
Heart of Jade. Salvador De Madariaga. LC 44-2502. 1944. Creative Age Press.
Heart of Jade. Doris Irene Thompson. LC 33-150. 1932. G. H. Watt.
Heart of Jane Warner. Florence Marryat Church Lean. LC 7-13598. (On cover: Lovell's library. v. 19. no. 951). 1887. J. W. Lovell Company.
Heart of Jessy Laurie. Amelia Edith Huddleston Barr. LC 7-31283. 1907. Mead & Company.
Heart of Katie O'Doone. Leroy Scott. LC 25-21773. 1925. Houghton Mifflin Company.
Heart of Kentucky. Hannah Daviess Pittman. LC 8-30537. 1908. The Neale Publishing Company.
Heart of Lady Anne. Agnes Sweetman Castle & Castle, Egerton. 1905. F. A. Stokes Company.
Heart of Life. William Hurrell Mallock. LC 75-1538. (Victorian Fiction: Novels of Faith and Doubt; V. 86). 1975. 35.00 (ISBN 0-8240-1610-6). Garland Pub.
Heart of Life. William Hurrell Mallock. LC 7-24368. 1895. G. P. Putnam's Sons.
Heart of Life: From the French of Pierre De Coulevain Pseud. Helene Faure De Convelain & Ward, Alice Hall, Tr. E. P. Dutton & Company.
Heart of Little Shikara: And Other Stories. Edison Marshall. LC 22-20051. 1922. 1.90. Little, Brown, and Company.
Heart of Lynn. Mary Stewart Doubleday Cutting. LC 4-5419. 1904. J. B. Lippincott Company.
Heart of Mable Ware. A Romance. LC 17-50441. 1856. J. C. Derby.
Heart of Mid-Lothian. Walter Scott. LC 66-4882. (Riverside editions). 1966. Houghton Mifflin Co.
Heart of Mid-Lothian. Walter Scott. (On cover: Seaside library. Pocket ed. no. 391). 1885. G. Munro.
Heart of Mid-Lothian... From the Last Rev. Ed., Containing the Author's Final Corrections, Notes, &C. parker's ed. Walter Scott. LC 8-5770. (Waverley novels: Library ed. v. 6). 1855. Sanborn, Carter and Bazin.
Heart of Midlothian. Walter Scott. LC 63-6787. (Everyman's library, 134. Fiction). 1961. J. M. Dent.
Heart of Midlothian. Walter Scott. (Seaside library. v. 10, no. 196). 1878. G. Munro.
Heart of Midlothian. Walter Scott. (On cover: Lovell's library, no. 499). 1885. J. W. Lovell Company.
Heart of Midlothian. Walter Scott. Ed. by Lang, Andrew. LC 15-23130. (On cover: Waverley novels). D. Estes & Company.
Heart of Midlothian. Walter Scott. (Half-title: Everyman's library, ed. by Ernest Rhys. Fiction. no. 134). 1908. J. M. Dent & Co.
Heart of Midlothian. Walter Scott. Ed. by Trent, William Peterfield. LC 18-21378. (Half-title: The modern student's library, ed. by W. D. Howe). C. Scribner's Sons.
Heart of Midlothian. Walter Scott. Ed. by Paterson, Archibald. LC 27-259577. (modern readers' series). 1926. The Macmillan Company.
Heart of Midlothian. Walter Scott. LC 36-37005. (Half-title: Everyman's library, ed. by Ernest Rhys. Fiction. no. 134). 1932. J. M. Dent & Sons, Ltd.
Heart of Midlothian. Walter Scott & David Daiches. LC 69-17649. (Rinehart editions, 14). Holt, Rinehart and Winston.
Heart of Midlothian. Ed., Introd. by John Henry Raleigh. Walter Scott. (Riverside eds., B83). pap., 1.75. Houghton.
Heart of My Heart: Mother and Child. Ellis Meredith. LC 13-5413. 1.00. D. Fitzgerald, Inc.
Heart of Myrrha Lake: Or, Into the Light of Catholicity. Julia Amanda Sargent Wood. LC 8-375486. 1872. The Catholic Publication Society.
Heart of Nami-San (Hototogisu) a Story of War, Intrigue and Love. Kenjiro Tokutomi & Goldberg, Isaac, 1887- Tr. LC 18-18332. 1918. The Stratford Company.
Heart of Nashville. Robert Vaughan. 1975. (pbk.) 1.50 (ISBN 0-671-80099-X). Pocket Books.
Heart of Night Wind: A Story of the Great North West. Vingie Eve Roe. LC 13-10500. 1913. Dodd, Mead and Company.
Heart of O. Henry. Dale Kramer. LC 54-9346. 1954. Rinehart.
Heart of O Sono San. Elizabeth Cooper. LC 17-28073. Frederick A. Stokes Company.
Heart of Oak. Adelbert Gilroy Clark. LC 16-14278. 1916.
Heart of Old Hickory: And Other Stories of Tennessee. William Allen Dromgoole. LC 3-3614. 1895. The Arena Publishing Co.
Heart of Old Hickory & Other Stories of Tennessee. William Allen Dromgoole. LC 72-113658. (Short Story Index Reprint Ser.). 1895. 15.00 (ISBN 0-8369-3387-7). Ayer Co.
Heart of Philura. Florence Morse Kingsley. LC 15-187298. 1914. Dodd, Mead and Company.
Heart of Princess Osra. Anthony Hope Hawkins. LC 4-15313. F. A. Stokes Company.

Heart of Princess Osra. buckingham ed. Anthony Hope Hawkins. LC 7-218496. F. A. Stokes Company.

Heart of Princess Osra. Anthony Hope Hawkins. LC 3-24936. (Half-title: Author's edition. Works of Anthony Hope...). D. Appleton and Company.

Heart of Rachael. Kathleen Thompson Norris. 1916. Doubleday, Page & Company.

Heart of Rome: A Tale of the "Lost Water,". Francis Marion Crawford. LC 3-25549. 1903. The Macmillan Company.

Heart of Rome: A Tale of the "Lost Water". Francis Marion Crawford. LC 8-26624. 1904. The Macmillan Company.

Heart of Sally Temple. Rupert Sargent Holland. LC 13-23197. 1913. McBridge, Nast & Company.

Heart of Salome. Allen Raymond. LC 25-16485. Small, Marynard & Company.

Heart of Silence. Walter Samuel Cramp. LC 9-191715. 1909. The C. M. Clark Publishing Company.

Heart of Silence: A Novel. Bentz Plagemann. LC 67-11632. 1967. Morrow.

Heart of Sindhra. A Novel. Frederick Houk Law. LC 98-1577. (On cover: Neely's universal library. no. 38). 1898. F. T. Neely.

Heart of Standing Is You Cannot Fly. Raji Narasimhan. (Writers Workshop Greenbird Book Ser.). 131p. 1975. 14.00 (ISBN 0-88253-558-7); pap. text ed. 6.75 (ISBN 0-88253-557-9). Ind-US Inc.

Heart of Standing Is You Cannot Fly: A Novel. Raji Narasimhan. LC 76-904242. (Writers Workshop greenbird book). 1975. (ISBN 0-88253-558-7). Writers Workshop.

Heart of Stone. Nino Modica. LC 66-13383. 1966. Doubleday.

Heart of Texas. Al Cody, pseud. 1981. pap. 1.95 (ISBN 0-8439-0861-0, Leisure Bks). Nordon Pubns.

Heart of the Ancient Wood. Charles George Douglas Roberts. LC 6697. Silver, Burdett and Company.

Heart of the Blue Ridge. Waldron Baily. LC 15-11450. 1.25. W. J. Watt & Company.

Heart of the Bush. Edith Searle Grossmann. LC 11-4102. 1911. 1.50. John Lane Company.

Heart of the Clan. Barbara Cartland. (Barbara Cartland Ser.: No. 13). 192p. (Orig.). 1981. pap. 1.75 (ISBN 0-515-05929-3). Jove Pubns.

Heart of the Country. Bland Simpson. LC 82-19236. 17.95 (ISBN 0-399-31007-X). Seaview/Putnam.

Heart of the Country see Indian Maiden's Captivity.

Heart of the Crimson Cross. Jerry Maurice Henry. LC 30-123402. The Stratford Company.

Heart of the Desert (Kut-le of the Desert) Honore McCue Willsie Morrow. LC 18-16556. 1913. A. L. Burt Company.

Heart of the Desert (Kut-le of the Desert) Honore McCue Willsie Morrow. LC 13-19325. 1913. Frederick A. Stokes Company.

Heart of the Doctor: A Story of the Italian Quarter. Mable G Foster. LC 2-219801. 1902. Houghton, Mifflin and Company.

Heart of the Dog. Thomas A. Roberts. LC 72-4409. 1972. 5.95 (ISBN 0-394-47978-5). Random House.

Heart of the Faithful. Kathryn K Ecenbarger. LC 65-25949. bds., 3.50. Zondervan.

Heart of the Family. Elizabeth Goudge. LC 53-5302. 1953. Coward-McCann.

Heart of the Flame. Araby Scott. 304p. 1982. pap. 2.95 (ISBN 0-380-79459-4, 79459). Avon.

Heart of the Furnace. Lambert Williams. LC 37-219593. 1937. D. Appleton-Century Company, Incorporated.

Heart of the Game. Robert Ray. 1975. (pbk.) 1.50 (ISBN 0-425-02909-3). Berkley Publishing Corp.

Heart of the Harbor. Katrinka Blickle. LC 78-22755. 1979. 8.95 (ISBN 0-385-15181-0). Doubleday.

Heart of the Hills. John Fox. LC 28-23053. 1913. A. L. Burt Company.

Heart of the Hills. John Fox. LC 13-461485. 1913. C. Scribner's Sons.

Heart of the House. Naomi Ellington Jacob. LC 51-5404. 1951. Hutchinson.

Heart of the Hunter. Laurens Van Der Post. LC 80-15539. 1980. pap. 4.95 (ISBN 0-15-640003-0, Harv). HarBraceJ.

Heart of the Lion. Eleanor Hibbert. LC 80-13826. (Illus.). 1980. 10.95 (ISBN 0-399-12538-8). Putnam.

Heart of the Lion. Jean Pliady. 320p. 1982. pap. 2.95 (ISBN 0-449-24490-3, Crest). Fawcett.

Heart of the Matter. Graham Greene. LC 51-3441. 1951. Garden City Books.

Heart of the North. William Byron Mowery. LC 30-17705. 1930. Doubleday, Doran & Company, Inc.

Heart of the People: A Picture of Life As It Is to-Day. Jacob Ralph Abarbanell. LC 8-31463. 1908. The C.M. Clark Publishing Company.

Heart of the Range. William Patterson White. LC 21-10024. 1921. Doubleday, Page & Company.

Heart of the Red Firs: A Story of the Pacific Northwest. Ada Woodruff Anderson. LC 8-98156. 1908. Little, Brown, and Company.

Heart of the River. Carolyn Slaughter. LC 82-17055. 1983. 11.95 (ISBN 0-312-36600-0). St. Martin's Press.

Heart of the River. Carolyn Slaughter. 288p. 1983. 11.95 (ISBN 0-312-36600-0). St Martin.

Heart of the Skyloo. Ottis Bedney Sperlin. LC 34-33470. 1934. Metropolitan Press.

Heart of the South. Archibald Hamilton Rutledge. LC 24-29074. 1924. The State Company.

Heart of the Storm. Patricia Wright. LC 78-22775. 1980. 8.95 (ISBN 0-385-14232-3). Doubleday.

Heart of the Stranger: A Story of Little Italy. Christian McLeod. LC 8-31466. F. H. Revell Company.

Heart of the Stranger: A Story of Little Italy. Anna Christian Ruddy. LC 74-17947. (Italian American Experience). 1975. 13.00 (ISBN 0-405-06417-9). Arno Press.

Heart of the Sunset. Rex Ellingwood Beach. LC 15-18727. 1915. Harper & Brothers.

Heart of the West. William Sydney Porter. 1907. The McClure Company.

Heart of the West. William Sydney Porter. LC 15-174141. 1913. Doubleday, Page & Company.

Heart of the West. William Sydney Porter. LC 19-135221. 1918. Doubleday, Page & Company.

Heart of the West. William Sydney Porter. LC 22-16016. 1919. Doubleday, Page & Company, for Review of Reviews Co.

Heart of the West. William Sydney Porter. LC 20-12370. 1920. Doubleday, Page & Company.

Heart of the West: An American Story. LC 7-50452. 1871. Steam Printing House of Hand & Hart.

Heart of the Woods. Isabel Adams. LC 28-299593. The Century Co.

Heart of the World. Henry Rider Haggard. LC 6-46137. 1895. Longmans, Green, and Co.

Heart of the World. Henry Rider Haggard. LC 80-19175. (Newcastle Forgotten Fantasy library; v. 10). 1980. 10.95 (ISBN 0-87877-509-9). Borgo Press.

Heart of the World. Illus. by Hookway Cowles. Henry Rider Haggard. LC 66-5435. 1966. bds., 2.95. Macdonald.

Heart of Thunder Mountain. Edfrid A Bingham. 1916. 1.35. Little, Brown, and Company.

Heart of Toil. Alice French. LC 70-98569. (Short story index reprint series). 1969. Books for Libraries Press.

Heart of Toil. Alice French. LC 98-866. 1898. C. Scribner's Sons.

Heart of Unaga. Ridgwell Cullum. LC 20-183017. 1920. G. P. Putnam's Sons.

Heart of Uncle Terry. Charles Clark Munn. LC 15-7113. 1915. 1.25. Lothrop, Lee & Shepard Co.

Heart of Us: A Novel. Thomas Russell Sullivan. LC 12-3381. 1912. Houghton Mifflin Company.

Heart of Virginia. J. Perkins Tracy. (Added t.-p.: The flag series, no. 9). Street & Smith.

Heart of War. John Masters. LC 80-12491. (Loss of Eden Ser.). 608p. 1980. 13.95 (ISBN 0-07-040782-7). McGraw.

Heart of Washington... Dorothea Heness Knox. 1909. 1.25. The Neale Publishing Company.

Heart of Washington... Dorothea Knox Martin. LC 9-22003. 1909. The Neale Publishing Company.

Heart on Her Sleeve. Clarence Budington Kelland. LC 44-5856. Harper & Brothers.

Heart or Purse: A Story of to-Day. Adelaide D. Kingsley. 1887. S. P. Rounds, Jr. & Co.

Heart Payments. Gerald Jay Goldberg. LC 81-65285. 1982. 13.95 (ISBN 0-670-36466-5). Viking Press.

Heart Possessed. Elizabeth Borton Trevino. LC 79-14429. 6.95 (ISBN 0-89340-212-5). J. Curley & Associates.

Heart Possessed: A Love Story. Elizabeth Borton Trevino. LC 77-26523. 1978. 7.95 (ISBN 0-385-03536-5). Doubleday.

Heart Regained, a Novel. Elisabeth & Mitchell, Mrs. Mary A., Tr. LC 6-37254. 1888. Cupples and Hurd.

Heart Remembers. Faith Cutherell Baldwin. 1973. (pbk.) 0.95 (ISBN 0-446-75234-7). Warner Paperback Library.

Heart Remembers. Nina Bowyer. LC 46-20740. 1946. Arcadia House, Inc.

Heart Remembers. Nina Conarain. LC 46-20740. 1946. Arcadia House, Inc.

Heart Remembers. Ruth Rosemary Corby. LC 37-191570. Arcadia House.

Heart Remembers. Faith Baldwin Cuthrell. Farrar and Rinehart, Inc.

Heart Remembers. Peggy Gaddis, pseud. 1976. (pbk.) 0.95. Belmont Tower.

Heart Remembers. Peggy Gaddis, pseud. LC 48-3509. 1948. Gramercy Pub. Co.

Heart Remembers. Arlene Hale. (Signet Book). 1975. (pbk.) 0.95. New American Library.

Heart Returneth. Vera Lebedeff. LC 43-43105. 1943. J. B. Lippincott Company.

Heart Returns. Peggy O'More, pseud. LC 46-8065. 1946. Grammercy Publishing Co.

Heart Sings. Georgiana L. Lahr. 3.50 o.p. Vantage.

Heart Song: Love's Pilgrimage. Kristin Michaels. 352p. pap. 2.95 (ISBN 0-451-12078-7, Sig). NAL.

Heart Songs. Lucy Hannah Heath. LC 26-24149. The Cornhill Publishing Company.

Heart Speaks. Hertha Koorn. 3.95 o.p. Vantage.

Heart Speaks Many Ways. Madeleine A. Polland. 374p. 1982. 15.95 (ISBN 0-440-03598-8). Delacorte.

Heart Specialist. Graeme Lorimer & Lorimer, Sarah. LC 36-27016. 1935. Little, Brown, and Company.

Heart Stories. Theodore Bartlett. Ed. by Bridgman, Helen (Bartlett) LC 6-9401. 1889. G. P. Putnam's Sons.

Heart Story. William Arthur Neubauer. 1947. Grammercy Pub. Co.

Heart Surrendered. Kay Richardson. (YA) 1978. 6.95 (Avalon). Bouregy.

Heart That Knows. Charles George Douglas Roberts. LC 6-30929. 1906. L. C. Page & Company.

Heart to Artemis. Winifred Bryher. (Helen & Kurt Wolff Book). 1962. 5.95 o.p. (ISBN 0-15-139816-X). HarBraceJ.

Heart to Find. Hazel Heidergott. LC 45-2139. 1945. Macrae-Smith-Company.

Heart Too Full. Carole Bolton. 1978. pap. 1.50 o.s.i. Dale Books Inc.

Heart Too Proud. Laura London. (Candlelight regency special). 1978. 1.50 (ISBN 0-440-13498-6). Dell Pub. Co.

Heart Troubles: Short Stories. Stephen Birmingham. LC 68-28223. 1968. Harper & Row.

Heart Twice Won: Or, Second Love. Elizabeth Van Loon. LC 8-30220. T. B. Peterson & Brothers.

Heart Unafraid: By Helen St. Bernard... St. Bernard, Helen. LC 41-6549.

Heart under Siege. Joy St. Clair. (Harlequin Romances Ser.). 192p. 1982. pap. 1.50 (ISBN 0-373-02472-X). Harlequin Bks.

Heart Upon the Rock. Joseph Gaer. LC 50-9812. 1950. Dodd, Mead.

Heartache of Love. Kay Winslow. 144p. 1982. pap. 1.75 (ISBN 0-523-41809-4). Pinnacle Bks.

Heartache: Published Serially Under the Title The Melody Girl. Ruth Dewey Groves. LC 32-3607. Grosset & Dunlap.

Heartbeat. Stacy Aumonier. LC 22-15851. Boni and Liveright.

Heartbeat. Eugene Dong & Spyros Andreopoulos. LC 77-10720. 8.95. Coward, McCann & Geoghegan.

Heartbeat. Clara Miller. LC 51-5516. 1951. Vantage Press.

Heartbreak. Mabel Dana Lyon. LC 35-11489. Godwin.

Heartbreak for Two. Maysie Greig. LC 42-23553. 1942. Doubleday, Doran & Company, Inc.

Heartbreak Girl. Rob Eden. LC 31-29423. Barse & Co.

Heartbreak Hill: A Comedy Romance. Herman Knickerbocker Viele. 1908. Duffield & Company.

Heartbreak Honeymoon. Watkins Eppes Wright. LC 41-7082. 1941. Arcadia House,Inc.

Heartbreak Hotel. Anne Rivers Siddons. LC 76-10735. 7.95 (ISBN 0-671-22315-1). Simon and Schuster.

Heartbreak Tango: A Serial. Manuel Puig. LC 73-79562. 1973. 6.95. Dutton.

Heartbreak Tango: A Serial. Manuel Puig. LC 80-6124. 1981. 3.50 (ISBN 0-394-74660-0). Vintage Books.

Heartbreak Triangle. Nora Hampton. 1979. pap. 1.75 (ISBN 0-449-50001-2, Coventry). Fawcett.

Heartbreak. 1st Ed. Lillian Ann Escoffier. LC 54-4941. 1954.

Heartbreaker. John Meyer. LC 82-45600. 288p. 1983. 14.95 (ISBN 0-385-18421-2). Doubleday.

Heartbreaker, and Other Short Stories. 1st Ed. William Howard Harris. LC 53-8093. 1953. Pageant Press.

Heartbroken Melody. Kathleen Thompson Norris. LC 38-275543. 1938. Doubleday, Doran & Company, Inc.

Hearth and Eagle. Anya Seton. LC 48-9296. 1948. Houghton Mifflin Co.

Hearth and the Strangeness. Beatrice Ann Wright. LC 55-12705. 1956. Macmillan.

Hearth of Midlothian. Walter Scott. (Rinehart editions, 14). 1948. Rinehart.

Hearthstones. Elisabeth Stancy Payne. LC 27-20432. 1927. The Penn Publishing Company.

Hearthstones: A Novel of the Roanoke River Country in North Carolina. Bernice Kelly Harris. LC 48-8327. 1948. Doubleday.

Heartthrob. Margarett McKean. (Second Chance at Love Ser.: No. 32). 1982. pap. 1.75 (ISBN 0-515-06305-3). Jove Pubns.

Heartland. Lynn Fairfax. (Second Chance at Love Ser.: No. 37). 192p. (Orig.). 1982. pap. 1.75 (ISBN 0-515-06282-0). Jove Pubns.

Heartland. David Hagberg. 416p. (Orig.). 1983. pap. 3.50 (ISBN 0-523-48051-2). Pinnacle Bks.

Heartland. Stuart Legg. 1970. 8.95 o.p. (ISBN 0-374-16866-0). FS&G.

Heartland: A Novel. Saul Maloff. LC 76-85249. 1973. 6.95 (ISBN 0-684-13410-1). Scribner.

Heartland: Stories of the Southwest. Ruben Dario Salaz. LC 78-112650. 4.95 (ISBN 0-932482-01-5). Blue Feather Press.

Heartland Stories of the Southwest. Ruben Dario Salaz. 1978. pap. 4.95 (ISBN 0-932482-01-5). Blue Feather.

Heartless Hussy. James Noble Gifford. LC 45-5486. 1945. Phoenix Press.

Heartless Light. Gerald Green. LC 61-7205. 1961. Scribner.

Heartless Love. Patricia Lake. (Harlequin Presents Ser.). 192p. 1982. pap. 1.75 (ISBN 0-373-10538-X). Harlequin Bks.

Hearts. Hilma Wolitzer. LC 80-18556. 1980. 10.95 (ISBN 0-374-16870-9). Farrar, Straus, and Giroux.

Hearts. A Novel. David Christie Murray. (Harper's Franklin square library, no. 339). 1883. Harper & Brothers.

Hearts Afire: A Novel. rev. ed. May Christie. LC 26-103226. Grosset & Dunlap.

Hearts Aglow. Marlene Daehlin. 3.95 o.p. (ISBN 0-8111-0343-9). Naylor.

Hearts and Coronets: A Story for Young People. Alice Wilson-Fox. LC 10-21018. 1910. The Macmillan Company.

Hearts and Coronets: Or, Who's the Noble? A Novel. Jane G Fuller. LC 6-44575. (choice series, no. 85). 1893. R. Bonner's Sons.

Hearts and Creeds. Anna Chapin Ray. LC 6-6489. 1906. Little, Brown and Company.

Hearts & Faces. John Murray Gibbon. LC 16-107239. 1916. 1.35. John Lane Company.

Hearts and Gold. Charlotte M. Stanley McKenna. LC 8-28184. (On cover: Munro's library, v. 1, no. 119). 1884. N. L. Munro.

Hearts and Hands. A Story in Sixteen Chapters. Frances Christine Tiernan. LC 8-19813. (On cover: Appletons' library of American fiction no. 13). 1875. D. Appleton and Company.

Hearts and Heads. 1st American Ed. Christopher Veiel. LC 55-746095. 1955. Little, Brown.

Hearts and Homes: A Story of American Life. Francis Brelsford. LC 3812. 1900. Germantown Telegraph.

Hearts and Lives. Florence Blackburn White Schoeffel. (On cover: The laurel library, no. 2). 1892. G. Munro.

Hearts and Masks. Harold MacGrath. LC 5-37161. 1905. The Bobbs-Merrill Company.

Hearts and the Cross. Harold Morton Kramer. LC 6-19778. 1906. Lothrop, Lee & Shepard Co.

Hearts and the Diamond. Gerald Beaumont. LC 21-17196. 1921. Dodd, Mead and Company.

Hearts and the Highway: A Romance of the Road, First Set Forth by Lady Katharine Clanranald and Sir Hugh Richmond, and Now Transcribed by Cyrus Townsend Brady... Cyrus Townsend Brady. LC 11-7743. 1911. 1.25. Dodd, Mead and Company.

Hearts Are Trumps. Alexander Otis. LC 9-10042. 1909. The J. McBride Co.

Hearts at Sea. James Noble Gifford. LC 39-1104. 1938. Gramercy Publishing Co.

Hearts at Sea. Gay Rutherford. LC 39-110414. Gramercy Publishing Co.

Heart's Awakening. Rose Marie Ferris. (Candelight Romance Ser.). (Orig.). 1981. pap. 1.75 (ISBN 0-440-13519-2). Dell.

Heart's Bitterness. Charlotte Mary Brame. (On cover: Far and near series. no. 2). Street & Smith.

Heart's Bitterness. Bertha M. Clay. LC 44-11674. (On cover: Far and near series, no. 2). Street & Smith.

Heart's Blood. Ethel May Kelley. LC 23-11808. 1923. A. A. Knopf.

Hearts Come Home: And Other Stories. Pearl Sydenstricker Buck. LC 62-59622. (Cardinal edition, GC-151). 1962. Pocket Books.

Hearts Contending: A Novel. Katharine Riegel Loose. LC 10-926229. 1910. 1.50. Harper & Brothers.

Heart's Content. Ralph Henry Barbour. LC 15-209122. 1915. J. B. Lippincott Company.

Heart's Country. Mary Marvin Heaton Vorse. LC 14-86973. 1914. Houghton Mifflin Company.

Hearts Courageous. Hallie Erminie Rives. LC 2-14853. The Bowen-Merrill Company.

Heart's Delight. A Novel. Elizabeth Winslow Allderdice. LC 6-477468. 1879. G.W. Carleton & Co.; Etc., Etc.

Heart's Delight. A Story. Charles Gibbon. (Harper's Franklin square library, no. 473). 1885. Harper & Brothers.

Heart's Desire. Alice Lent Covert. LC 51-14012. 1951. Bouregy & Curl.
Heart's Desire. Alice Lent Covert. (Candlelight romance, 121). 1973. (pbk.) 0.75. Dell.
Heart's Desire. Cecilia Metz Elser. LC 69-20024. 1969. 5.95. C. M. Elser Pub. Co.
Heart's Desire. Emerson Hough. 1976. lib. bdg. 16.25x (ISBN 0-89968-045-3). Lightyear.
Heart's Desire. Rita Perker. LC 38-7801. The Dodge Publishing Co.
Heart's Desire: A Novel Fo Three American Generations and of a Brave and Noble Woman. Winifred Victoria Talbot. LC 58-9101. 1958. Greenwich Book Publishers.
Heart's Desire: The Story of a Contented Town, Certain Peculiar Citizens, and Two Fortunate Lovers; a Novel. Emerson Hough. LC 5-32735. 1905. The Macmillan Company.
Heart's Desire: The Story of a Contented Town, Certain Peculiar Citizens, and Two Fortunate Lovers. Emerson Hough. LC 81-3380. 1981. 22.50 (ISBN 0-8032-2315-3) (ISBN 0-8032-7209-X). University of Nebraska Press.
Hearts Divided. Paula Moore. (Dell / Bryans Book). 2.50 (ISBN 0-440-03917-7). Dell Publishing.
Hearts Do Not Break. Josephine Lawrence. pap. 0.50 o.p. (52-482). Paperback Lib.
Hearts Do Not Break. 1st Ed. Josephine Lawrence. LC 60-10915. 1960. Harcourt, Brace.
Heart's Ease in Death. James Fraser, pseud. LC 76-50766. 1977. 6.95 o.p. (ISBN 0-385-12659-X). Doubleday.
Heart's Ease in Death. Alan White. LC 76-50766. 1977. 5.95 (ISBN 0-385-12659-X). Published for the Crime Club by Doubleday.
Heart's Fury. Lucy Lee. (Superromances Ser.). 384p. 1982. pap. 2.50 (ISBN 0-373-70010-5, Pub. by Worldwide). Harlequin Bks.
Heart's Garrison. Desemea Wilson. LC 31-9678. 1931. E. P. Dutton & Co., Inc.
Heart's Grown Brutal. David Brewster. LC 72-76670. 1972. 6.95 (ISBN 0-698-10452-8). Coward, McCann & Geoghegan.
Heart's Haven. Sara Ware Bassett. 1944. Doubleday, Doran and Co., Inc.
Heart's Haven. Katharine Evans Blake. LC 5-32731. 1905. The Bobbs-Merrill Company.
Heart's Haven. Ruth Rosemary Corby. LC 40-102923. 1939. Arcadia House, Inc.
Hearts' Haven: A Novel. Clara Louise Root Burnham. LC 18-204762. 1918. 1.50. Houghton Mifflin Company.
Heart's Heritage. Joseph McCord. LC 35-17095. 1935. Macrae-Smith Company.
Heart's Highest Hurdle: A Novel of the Olympics. Dorothy Clark Haskin. LC 60-3395. 1960. Zondervan Pub. House.
Heart's Highway: A Romance of Virginia in the Seventeenth Century. Mary Eleanor Wilkins Freeman. LC 3396. 1900. Doubleday, Page & Co.
Heart's Home. Peggy Gaddis, pseud. LC 46-2680. 1946. Arcadia House, Inc.
Heart's Idol. Brame, Charlotte Mary, 1836-1884, Supposed Author. LC 44-11665. (On cover: Seaside library.--Pocket ed. No. 1171). G. Munro.
Hearts in Conflict. Adel Pryor, pseud. LC 64-11961. 1964. Zondervan Pub. House.
Hearts in Jeopardy. Florence Kerigan. 1974. 4.50. Avalon.
Hearts in Jeopardy. Florence Kerigan. (Fawcett Gold Medal Book). 1976. (pbk.) 1.25. Fawcett.
Hearts in Swing Time. Vida Hurst. LC 39-204407. Gramercy Publishing Co.
Hearts in the Highlands. Lynna Cooper, pseud. 1980. pap. 2.50 (ISBN 0-451-11568-6, AE1568, Sig). NAL.
Hearts in Unity: A Fictional Melodrama. Mary Foy Scharstein. 1946. The Hobson Book Press.
Heart's Journey. New Catechism. 5.95 o.p. (ISBN 0-07-073778-9). McGraw.
Heart's Justice. Amanda Benjamin Hall. LC 23-205353. George H. Doran Company.
Heart's Kindred. Zona Gale. LC 15-19624. 1915. 1.35. The Macmillan Company.
Heart's Kingdom. Maria Thompson Daviess. LC 17-254321. 1.35. The Reilly & Britton Co.
Hearts of Gold. I Edhor. LC 3-310173. 1903. Benziger Brothers.
Hearts of Grace. Philip Verrill Mighels. LC 13-5067. D. FitzGerald, Inc.
Hearts of Hickory: A Story of Andrew Jackson and the War of 1812. John Trotwood Moore. LC 26-494508. 1926. Cokesbury Press.
Hearts of Steel. A Novel. Frances Christine Tiernan. LC 12-39596. 1883. D. Appleton and Company.
Hearts of Steel. An Irish Historical Tale of the Last Century. James McHenry. 1825. A. R. Poole.
Hearts of the West. Jordan Crittenden. 1975. (pbk.) 1.25. Bantam Books.
Hearts of the West. Thomas Francis Murphy. LC 28-24697. The Christopher Publishing House.
Hearts of Three. Jack London. LC 20-17822. 1920. The Macmillan Company.
Hearts of Three. Jack London. LC 77-84251. 1978. (Lost Race and Adult Fantasy Fiction). 1978. 24.00 (ISBN 0-405-10997-0). Arno Press.
Hearts on Holiday. William Arthur Neubauer. LC 47-250315. 1947. Grammercy Pub. Co.
Hearts: Queen, Knave, and Deuce. David Christie Murray. (On cover: Seaside library. Pocket ed., no. 695). 1886. G. Munro.
Heart's Retreat. Peggy Gaddis, pseud. LC 37-15197. 1937. Arcadia House.
Heart's Shadow. Prudence Martin. (Candlelight Ecstasy Ser.: No. 119). (Orig.). 1983. pap. 1.95 (ISBN 0-440-13694-6). Dell.
Hearts Steadfast. Edward Stewart Moffat. LC 15-19972. 1915. Moffat, Yard & Company.
Hearts That Understand. Louise Harrison McCraw. LC 36-9697. The Moody Press.
Hearts Triumphant. Edith Sessions Tupper. LC 6-34075. 1906. D. Appleton and Company.
Hearts Triumphant: A Modern Romance. Flavel Woodruff Sullivan. LC 14-22141. The Roxburgh Publishing Company, Incorporated.
Hearts Undaunted: A Romance of Four Frontiers. Eleanor Stackhouse Atkinson. LC 17-31031. 1917. Harper & Brothers.
Hearts Unveiled: Or, "I Know You Would Like Him.". Sarah Emery Saymore. LC 8-2020. 1852. D. Appleton & Company.
Hearts up. Juliet Cox Coleman. LC 36-4929. Broadman Press.
Hearts Walking. Anita Blackmon Smith. LC 36-204422. 1936. Arcadia House.
Heartsblood: A Novel. Paul Marttin. LC 73-100051. 1970. 5.95. Delacorte Press.
Heartsease: Or, The Brother's Wife. 11th thousand. ed. Charlotte Mary Yonge. LC 4-22083. 1861. D. Appleton and Company.
Heartsease: Or, The Brother's Wife. Charlotte Mary Yonge. 1902. Macmillan and Co., Limited.
Heartwood. Anne Miller Downes. LC 45-7613. 1945. J. B. Lippincott Company.
Heartwood. Tom Gill. LC 37-186550. Farrar & Rinehart, Inc.
Heat. Isa Glenn. LC 26-744486. 1926. A. A. Knopf.
Heat. Arthur Herzog. (Signet Book). 1978. 1.95 (ISBN 0-451-08115-3). New American Library.
Heat. Ed McBain. LC 81-65263. 288p. 1981. 12.95 (ISBN 0-670-36479-7). Viking Pr.
Heat. Ed McBain. 208p. 1983. pap. 2.50 (ISBN 0-345-30673-2). Ballantine.
Heat. John O'Mara. (Orig.). 1969. pap. 0.60 o.p. (B60-1009). Belmont-Tower.
Heat: An 87th Precinct Novel. Ed McBain. LC 81-65263. 12.95 (ISBN 0-670-36479-7). Viking Press.
Heat: An 87th Precinct Novel. Ed McBain. LC 82-1032. 1982. 12.95 (ISBN 0-8161-3336-0). Hall.
Heat and Dust. Ruth Prawer Jhabvala. LC 72-25088. 1976. 7.95 (ISBN 0-06-012197-1). Harper & Row.
Heat and Dust. Ruth Prawer Jhabvala. (Perennial Library). 1977. 1.95 (ISBN 0-06-080431-9). Harper & Row.
Heat Lightaing: By Wilene Shaw Pseud. Virginia M Harrison. LC 54-40763. (Ace Books, S-74). 1954. Ace Books.
Heat Lightning. Hildegarde Dolson. LC 78-85114. 1970. 4.95. Lippincott.
Heat Lightning. Helen Rose Hull. LC 32-262887. Coward-McCann, Inc.
Heat of the Day. Elizabeth Bowen. LC 49-420. 1949. A. A. Knopf.
Heat of the Sun: Stories and Tales 1st Ed. Sean O'Faolain. LC 66-21560. 1966. bds., 5.95. Little.
Heat Wave. Denise Robins & Pertwee, Roland. LC 31-8326. 1930. L. MacVeagh, The Dial Press.
Heat Wave. Caesar Smith. LC 58-8567. 1958. Ballantine Books.
Heat Wave. Elleston Trevor. LC 58-8567. 1958. Ballantine Books.
Heat Wave: A Novel/Y Timothy Harris; Based on a Screenplay by Herschel Weingrad. Timothy Harris. 2.25 (ISBN 0-440-13103-0). Dell Publishing Co.
Heath Introduction to Fiction. John Jacob Clayton. LC 77-77435. 5.95 (ISBN 0-669-99986-5). Heath.
Heath Ten Short Novels. Ed. by Thomas L. Ashton. 704p. 1978. pap. text ed. 13.95 (ISBN 0-669-01029-4). Heath.
Heathcliff. Jeffrey Caine. LC 77-8031. 1978. 7.95 (ISBN 0-394-41879-4). Knopf.
Heathcliff. Jeffrey Caine. LC 78-16208. 1978. 12.95. G. K. Hall.
Heather and Peat. A. D Stewart. 1.20. Fleming H. Revell Company.
Heather and Snow a Story. George Macdonald. 1893. Harper & Brothers.
Heather from the Brae, Scottish Character Sketches: By David Lyall Pseud. Helen Buckingham Mathers Reeves. LC 7-15435. 1896. F. H. Revell Company.
Heather Heretics. Marshall N Goold. LC 26-6147. 1926. Houghton Mifflin Company.
Heather Heritage. John Brown Duncan. LC 43-371146. 1943. Liveright Publishing Corporation.
Heather Mary. 1st Ed. James Maurice Scott. LC 52-123362. 1953. Dutton.
Heather Moon. Charles Norris Williamson & Alice Muriel Livingston Williamson. LC 12-24818. 1912. Doubleday, Page & Co.
Heather of the High Hand: A Novel of the North. Arthur John Arbuthnott Stringer. LC 37-12723. The Bobbs-Merrill Company.
Heather Wild. Phyllis Taylor Pianka. (Candlelight Regency Ser.: No. 696). (Orig.). 1982. pap. 1.75 (ISBN 0-440-13537-0). Dell.
Heathercotes. Matt Crim. LC 6-316063. (Morning news library. no. 5). J. H. Estill.
Heatherton Heritage: A Novel. Pamela Hill. LC 74-83577. 1976. 8.95. St. Martin's Press.
Heath's Ten Short Novels. Ed. by Thomas L. Ashton. 1978. pap. text ed. 9.95x o.p. (ISBN 0-669-01029-4). Heath.
Heat's on. Chester B Himes. LC 66-10469. bds., 4.95. Putnam.
Heaven--Kissed Hill. Joseph Smith Fletcher. LC 22-16328. Hodder and Stoughton, Ltd.
Heaven--Kissed Hill. Joseph Smith Fletcher. LC 24-205492. 2.00. George H. Doran Company.
Heaven--Sent Witness and Other Stories. Joseph Smith Fletcher. LC 30-14880. 1930. Doubleday, Doran and Company, Inc.
Heaven and Earth of Dona Elena. Grace Zaring Stone. LC 29-9718. The Bobbs-Merrill Company.
Heaven and Earth: Translated from the Italian by Frances Frenaye. 1st American Ed. Carlo Coccioli. LC 52-1989. 1952. Prentice-Hall.
Heaven and Hardpan Farm. Nancy Hale. LC 57-6470. 1957. Scribner.
Heaven & Hell. Aldous Leonard Huxley. 1971. pap. 1.25 o.p. (ISBN 0-06-080219-7, P219, PL). Har-Row.
Heaven and Hell and the Megas Factor. Robert Nathan. LC 75-4820. 1975. 5.95 (ISBN 0-440-04328-X). Delacorte Press.
Heaven and Hell and the Megas Factor. Robert Nathan. LC 75-33136. 1975. 7.95 (ISBN 0-8161-6337-5). G. K. Hall.
Heaven & Hell & the Megus Factor. Robert Nathan. 128p. 1975. 6.95 o.p. (ISBN 0-440-04328-X). Delacorte.
Heaven and Vice Versa. Ethel Powelson Hueston. LC 47-30602. 1947. Bobbs-Merrill Co.
Heaven Below. Albert Quandt. LC 50-12837.
Heaven by the Hems. Marina De Berg. 1961. 3.00 o.p. (ISBN 0-8362-0238-4, Pub. by Sheed). Guild Bks.
Heaven by the Hems: From Stage to Cloister. Translated from the French by Joanna Richardson. Marina De Berg. LC 61-7295. 1961. Sheed and Ward.
Heaven Came So Near. Hubert Skidmore. LC 38-13188. 1938. Doubleday, Doran & Co., Inc.
Heaven Can Wait. Ed. by Fotonovel Publications Staff. (Illus., Orig.). 1978. pap. 2.50 (ISBN 0-89752-001-7). Fotonovel.
Heaven Can Wait. Elizabeth L Langman. LC 39-25560. Gramercy Publishing Co.
Heaven Faces West. Miriam Burt Young. LC 48-4965. 1948. Appleton-Century-Crofts.
Heaven for Two. Joyce Penrose. LC 32-127591. The Macaulay Company.
Heaven Has No Favorites. Erich Maria Remarque. 1968. pap. 0.75 o.p. (T1191, Crest). Fawcett World.
Heaven Has No Favorites. Translated by Richard and Clara Winston. 1st Ed. Erich Maria Remarque. LC 61-897810. 1961. Harcourt, Brace & World.
Heaven Help Us! Herbert Tarr. LC 66-21485. 1968. Random House.
Heaven in My Hand. Alice Lee Humphreys. LC 50-3332. 1950. John Knox Press.
Heaven in My Heart. Ronda Rivers. LC 56-10543. 1956. Vantage Press.
Heaven in the Ozarks: By James L. Hill and Henry W. Hill. 1st Ed. James L Hill & Henry W. Hill. 1957. Pageant Press.
Heaven in Your Hand. Norah Robinson Lofts. (Fawcett Crest book). 1975. (pbk.) 1.25. Fawcett.
Heaven in Your Hand. 1st Ed. Norah Robinson Lofts. LC 58-13284. 1958. Doubleday.
Heaven Is a Hat. Morgan Cunnington. LC 32-32905. The Vanguard Press.
Heaven Is a Sunswept Hill. Earl Guy. LC 43-8949. 1943. The Macmillan Company.
Heaven Is for the Angels. Estelle Schrott. LC 44-734. D. Appleton-Century Company, Incorporated.
Heaven Is So High. 1st Ed. Rosalie Lieberman. LC 50-5520. 1950. Bobbs-Merrill.
Heaven Is Too High. Mildred Masterson McNeilly. LC 44-2025. 1944. The Hampton Publishing Co., Distributed by W. Morrow & Company.
Heaven Is Where You Find It. Esther Ward Freeman. 1974. 5.95. (ISBN 0-533-00928-6). Vantage Press.
Heaven Isn't Here. Maysie Greig. LC 41-5298. 1941. Doubleday, Doran and Company, Inc.
Heaven-Kissing Hill. Julia Magruder. LC 99-1155. 1899. H. S. Stone and Company.
Heaven Knows: Mr. Allison. Charles Shaw. LC 52-10767. 1952. Crown Publishers.
Heaven Knows Where. Moira Gaskin. LC 52-7372. Crowell.
Heaven Knows Why. Samuel Woolley Taylor. LC 48-2720. 1948. A. A. Wyn.
Heaven Knows Why. 2d ed. Samuel Woolley Taylor. LC 79-84300. 1979. 3.95 (ISBN 0-9602626-0-1). Millennial Productions.
Heaven Lies Ahead: By Sara Sloane Pseud. Ursula Bloom. LC 51-4919. 1951. Arcadia House.
Heaven Makers. Frank Herbert. 192p. 1982. pap. 2.25 (ISBN 0-345-30290-7, Del Rey). Ballantine.
Heaven on Earth: A Novel. 1st Ed. Esther Allen Hirsch. LC 56-12762. 1957. Pageant Press.
Heaven Pays No Dividends, a Novel: Translated from the German by Eric Mosbacher. Richard Kaufmann. LC 52-11380. 1952. Viking Press.
Heaven Ran Last. William P McGivern. LC 49-9954. (Red badge mystery.). 1949. Dodd, Mead.
Heaven to Betsy. Maud Hart Lovelace & Neville, Vera. 1980. 2.95 (ISBN 0-06-440110-3). Harper & Row.
Heaven Tree. Edith Pargeter. LC 60-8680. 1960. Doubleday.
Heaven Trees. Stark Young. LC 26-19105. 1926. C. Scribner's Sons.
Heavenly Discourse. Charles E. Wood. (O.s.i.). 1927. 4.50 o.s.i. (ISBN 0-8149-0218-9). Vanguard.
Heavenly Foreigner. Denis Devlin. Ed. by Brian Coffey. LC 68-2569. (Illus.). 1967. 12.50 o.p. (ISBN 0-85105-120-0). Dufour.
Heavenly Harmony. Henry Lieferant & Sylvia Saltzberg Lieferant. LC 42-21518. 1942. The Dial Press.
Heavenly Ladder. Compton Mackenzie. LC 24-168851. 1924. Cassell & Company, Ltd.
Heavenly Ladder. Compton Mackenzie. LC 24-286728. 2.50. George H. Doran Company.
Heavenly Pomegranate. Lanhei Kim Park. (Illus.). 1973. (pbk.) 3.00. Simpson Pub. Co.
Heavenly Sinner: The Life and Loves of Lola Montez. Thomas Everett Harre. LC 35-19874. The Macaulay Company.
Heavenly Twins. Sarah Grand. LC 6-27660. Cassell Publishing Company.
Heavenly Twins. Sarah Grand. LC 1-5806. 1901. Street & Smith.
Heavenly World Series: And Other Baseball Stories. O'Rourke, Frank. LC 52-8981. 1952. A. S. Barnes.
Heavens Above! A Novel. Oliver Claxton. LC 33-31154. The John Day Company.
Heavens Blaze Forth. Amanda Hart Douglass. (Belmont Tower Book.). 1978. 1.75 (ISBN 0-505-51252-1). Tower Pubns.
Heaven's Command: An Imperial Progress. James Morris. LC 79-24327. (Illus.). 554p. 1980. pap. 7.95 (ISBN 0-15-640006-5, Harv). HarBraceJ.
Heaven's Dooryard. Marguerite Pearman McIntire. LC 40-305771. Farrar & Rinehart, Inc.
Heaven's Horizon. Lydia Lancaster. 464p. 1983. pap. 3.50 (ISBN 0-446-90581-X). Warner Bks.
Heaven's My Destination. Thornton Niven Wilder. LC 35-323. (Bard book). 1975. (pbk.) 1.65 (ISBN 0-380-00331-7). Avon.
Heaven's My Destination. Thornton Niven Wilder. LC 35-4227. 1934. Longmans, Green and Co.
Heaven's My Destination... Thornton Niven Wilder. 1935. Harper & Brothers.
Heaven's My Destination. Thornton Niven Wilder. LC 45-4721. (New Avon library. 59). 1945.
Heaven's My Destination. With an Introd. by John Henry Raleigh. Thornton Niven Wilder. LC 60-8693. (Anchor books, A205). 1960. Doubleday.
Heaven's Not Far Away. Katherine Ursula Parrott. LC 42-22451. 1942. Dodd, Mead & Company.
Heaven's Price. Sandra Brown. (Loveswept Ser.: No. 1). 1983. pap. 1.95. Bantam.
Heaviest Pipe: A Story of Mystery and Adventure. Arthur Willis Patterson. LC 21-7124. G. W. Jacobs & Company.
Heavy Feather. A. L. Barker. LC 78-26479. 234p. 1979. Repr. of 1978 ed. 8.95 (ISBN 0-8076-0911-0). Braziller.
Heavy Feather: A Novel. A. L. Barker. LC 78-26479. 1979. 8.95 (ISBN 0-8076-0911-0). G. Braziller.
Heavy Heavy Hangs. Doris Miles Disney. 1976. (pbk.) 1.50. Ace Books.
Heavy, Heavy Hangs. 1st Ed. Doris Miles Disney. LC 52-6354. 1952. Published for the Crime Club by Doubleday.
Heavy Laden. Philip Wylie. LC 28-9741. 1928. A. A. Knopf.
Heavy Number. Jack W. Thomas. 176p. (Orig.). 1976. pap. 2.25 (ISBN 0-553-14967-9). Bantam.

Heavy Number. Jack W Thomas. 1976. (pbk.) 1.50. Bantam Books.
Heavy Sand. Anatolii Naumovich Rybakov. LC 80-51773. 13.95 (ISBN 0-670-36499-1). Viking Press.
Heavy Sand. Anatolii Naumovich Rybakov. LC 82-226953. 1982. 4.95 (ISBN 0-14-005535-5). Penguin.
Heavy Water Raid. John Drummond. (O.s.i.). 224p. 1962. pap. 1.25 o.s.i. (AQ1223, Award). Univ Pub & Dist.
Heavy Weather. Michael E Knerr. (belmont tower book). 1.75 (ISBN 0-505-51426-5). Tower Publications, Inc.
Heavy Weather. P. G Wodehouse. LC 82-125995. 1966. 2.95 (ISBN 0-14-002569-3). Penguin Books.
Heavy Weather. Pelham Grenville Wodehouse. LC 33-193971. 1933. Little, Brown, and Company.
Hebrew Deluge Story. Albert T. Clay. (Yale Oriental Researches Ser.: No. V, Pt. III). 1922. 19.50x. Elliots Bks.
Hec Ramsey. Dean Owen. (Hec Ramsey Ser.). (O.s.i.). 160p. (Orig.). 1973. pap. 0.95 o.s.i. (AN1169, Award). Univ Pub & Dist.
Hecate's Cauldron. Ed. by Susan Shwartz. 256p. 1982. pap. 2.95 (ISBN 0-87997-705-1, UE1705). DAW Bks.
Hecatomb: A Novel. Bruce Palmer. LC 65-17102. 7.50. S. & S.
Heck. Morris Renek. LC 73-138794. 1971. 6.50 o.p. (ISBN 0-06-127000-8). Harper Mag Pr.
Heck: A Novel. Morris Renek. LC 73-138794. 1972. Popular Lib.
Heckler. Ed McBain. 1982. pap. 2.25 (ISBN 0-451-11421-3, AE1421, Sig). NAL.
Heckler: An Inner Sanctum 87th Precinct Mystery, by Ed McBain Pseud. Evan Hunter. LC 60-10983. 1960. Simon and Schuster.
Heckletooth 3: A Novel. David Shetzline. LC 69-16453. (Illus.). 1969. 5.95. Random House.
Hecla Sandwith. Edward Abram Uffington Valentine. LC 5-7382. 1905. The Bobbs-Merrill Company.
Hector Among the Doctors: Or, A Search for the True Church. A Volume of Thoughts for Thinkers. Daniel Sommer. LC 8-10213. D. Sommer.
Hector Graeme. Evelyn Brentwood. LC 12-6707. 1912. 1.25. John Lane.
Hector, My Dog: His Autobiography. Egerton Ryerson Young. LC 5-33972. W. A. Wilde Company.
Hector Servadac. uniform ed. Jules Verne. LC 4-17511. 1903. C. Scribner's Sons.
Hedayat: An Anthology of Short Stories. Ed. by Ehsan Yarshater. (Bibliotheca Persica: Modern Persian Literature Ser.: No. 2). 1979. lib. bdg. 20.00 o.s.i. (ISBN 0-89158-386-6). Westview.
Hedge Against the Sun. Barbara Bentley. LC 43-15368. 1943. Dodd, Mead & Company.
Hedge of Thorns. Helen Ashton. LC 58-107826. Dodd, Mead.
Hedged in. Elizabeth Stuart Phelps Ward. LC 8-33111. 1870. Fields, Osgood, & Co.
Hedged in. 28th ed. Elizabeth Stuart Phelps Ward. LC 8-33110. 1898. Houghton, Mifflin and Company.
Hedgehog & the Fox. Isaiah Berlin. pap. 2.50 o.p. (ISBN 0-671-20709-1, Touchstone Bks). S&S.
Hedgerow. Florence Engel Randall. LC 67-10768. 1967. Harcourt, Brace & World.
Hedgerow. Ilka Rezette. LC 67-10768. 1967. Harcourt, Brace & World.
Hedges. Elisabeth Stancy Payne. LC 29-24381. The Penn Publishing Company.
Hedonists. James Malcolm. (Orig.). 1969. pap. 1.75 o.p. (3059). Brandon.
Hedri: Or, Blind Justice. Helen Buckingham Mathers Reeves. LC 7-30680. (On cover: Lovell's international series. no. 50). 1889. F. F. Lovell & Company.
Hedwig: A Novel. Vance Randolph. LC 35-8374. The Vanguard Press.
Hedylus. rev. ed. Hilda Doolittle. LC 79-22495. (Imagist Ser). (Illus.). 160p. 1980. 17.50x (ISBN 0-933806-00-0). Black Swan CT.
Heed the Thunder: A Novel. James Myers Thompson. LC 46-2077. 1946. Greenberg.
Heel Is Born. Carl Driver. (Orig.). pap. 0.95 o.p. (1146). Brandon.
Heel of Achilles. Edmee Elizabeth Monica De La Pasture. LC 21-11026. 1921. The Macmillan Company.
Heel of Spring. Frank Rooney. LC 56-7886. 1956. Vanguard Press.
Heels of a Gale. George Hook Grant. LC 37-2566. 1937. Little, Brown and Company.
Hegerty, M.D. Elizabeth Seifert. LC 66-18346. 3.75. Dodd.
Hegira. Gregory Bear. 1979. pap. 1.75 (ISBN 0-440-13473-0). Dell.
Heidenmaer: Or, The Benedictines. A Legend of the Rhine. James Fenimore Cooper. LC 4-19572. 1888. D. Appleton and Company.
Heidenmauer: Or, The Benedictines. A Legend of the Rhine. new ed. James Fenimore Cooper. LC 6-29894. 1852. Stringer & Townsend.
Heidenmauer: Or, The Benedictines, a Legend of the Rhine. James Fenimore Cooper. (On cover: Lovell's library. no. 517). 1885. J. W. Lovell Company.
Heidenmaur: Or, The Benedictines. A Legend of the Rhine. a new ed. James Fenimore Cooper. LC 42-47065. 1836. Carey, Lea, & Blanchard.
Heidenmauer: Or, The Benedictines. A Legend of the Rhine. people's ed. James Fenimore Cooper. LC 6-26803. 1860. W. A. Townsend & Co.
Heidenmaver: Or, The Benedictines. A Legend of the Rhine. James Fenimore Cooper. LC 6-29896. 1832. Carey & Lea.
Heidi. Johanna Heusser Spyri & Edwardes, Marian, Tr. LC 36-37317. (Half-title: Everyman's library, ed. by Ernest Rhys. For young people. no. 431). 1932. J. M. Dent & Sons, Ltd.
Heidi. Johanna Heusser Spyri & Heal, Edith, 1903- LC 31-154170. 1931. T. S. Rockwell Company.
Heidi. Johanna Heusser Spyri & Petersham, Mrs. Maud, Illus. Garden City Publishing Company, Inc.
Heidi: A Story for Girls. Johanna Heusser Spyri & Melcon, H. A., Tr. A. L. Burt.
Heidi: Edited, with Introduction, Notes, Questions and Themes, and Vocabulary. Johanna Heusser Spyri & Hins, Stella M., Ed. LC 33-117350. 1933. Prentice-Hall, Inc.
Height of the Scream. J. Ramsey Campbell. LC 75-44849. 1976. 7.50 (ISBN 0-87054-075-0). Arkham House.
Heights: A Story of Vision. Marguerite Bryant. LC 24-197284. 1924. 2.00. Duffield & Company.
Heights of Eidelberg. Helen Hazlett. LC 7-3667. 1871. Claxton, Remsen & Haffelfinger.
Heights of Havenrest. Valerie Subond, pseud. (Orig.). 1972. pap. 0.75 o.p. (94313). Beagle Bks.
Heights of Rimring. Hart-Davis, Duff. LC 80-69379. 1981. 12.95 (ISBN 0-689-11148-7). Atheneum.
Heights of Zervos. Raymond H. Sawkins. LC 71-146827. (Illus.). 1971. 5.95 (ISBN 0-525-12272-9). E. P. Dutton.
Heike Story. Translated from the Japanese by Fuki Wooyenaka Uramatsu. 1st Ed. Eiji Yoshikawa. LC 56-5778. 1956. A. A. Knopf.
Heil! Hollywood. John Preston Buschlen. LC 39-7772. 1939. Reilly & Lee.
Heil! Hollywood. John Preston Buschlen. LC 76-52095. (Garland Classics of Film Literature). 1978. 14.00 (ISBN 0-8240-2869-4). Garland Pub.
Heilige: Novelle. Conrad Ferdinand Meyer. Ed. by W. A. Coupe. (Blackwell's German Texts Ser.). 1965. pap. 4.50x o.p. (ISBN 0-631-01700-3, Pub. by Basil Blackwell). Biblio Dist.
Heimsljos see World Light.
Heintz. Alan Lake Chidsey. LC 45-5189. 1945. Southern Publishers, Inc.
Heir. Roger Burlingame. LC 30-10979. 1930. C. Scribner's Sons.
Heir. Christopher Keane. LC 77-1888. 1977. 8.95 (ISBN 0-688-03202-8). Morrow.
Heir. facs. ed. Victoria M. Sackville-West. LC 70-140339. (Short Story Index Reprint Ser). 1922. 10.00 (ISBN 0-8369-3731-7). Ayer Co.
Heir. Roger Lichtenberg Simon. LC 68-14719. 1968. Macmillan.
Heir: A Love Story. Sackville-West, Victoria Mary. LC 70-140339. (Short story index reprint series). 1970. Books for Libraries Press.
Heir: A Love Story. Victoria Mary Sackville-West. LC 24-26193. 1922. George H. Doran Company.
Heir Apparent. 1st Ed. E. L. Withers, pseud. LC 61-9571. 1961. Published for the Crime Club by Doubleday.
Heir at Large. John Tinney McCutcheon. LC 23-6145. The Bobbs-Merrill Company.
Heir, Cet Inconnu. Jean S. MacLeod. (Harlequin Romantique Ser.). 192p. 1983. pap. 1.95 (ISBN 0-373-41179-0). Harlequin Bks.
Heir Expectant. Isabella Harwood. LC 43-27335. (With Robinson, F. W. A bridge of glass. New York, 1872). 1870. Harper & Brothers.
Heir Hunters: By Bill S. Ballinger. William Sanborn Ballinger. LC 66-13933. bds., 4.50. Harper.
Heir of Barachah. Jean Katherine Baird. LC 11-23501. 1911. 1.00. Monfort & Company.
Heir of Buckingham. Paul Feval & M. Lassez. LC 29-3430. (His The years between; adventures of D'Artagnan and Cyrano de Bergerac. IV). 1929. Longmans, Green and Co.
Heir of Charlton: A Story of Shaddeck Light As Published in the New York Weekly, Volume XXXII, No. 49. May Agnes Early Fleming. LC 5-20440. G. W. Dillingham Company.
Heir of Duncarron. Amy McLaren. LC 16-5896. 1916. G. P. Putnam's Sons.
Heir of Gaymouth: A Novel. John Esten Cooke. LC 6-27194. 1870. Van Evrie, Horton & Co.
Heir of Glenville. A Novel. Francis Alexander Durivage. (On cover: The idle hour series, no. 13). 1892. The F. M. Lupton Publishing Company.
Heir of Grangerfjord Castle. Ruth McCarthy Sears. (Orig.). 1975. pap. 0.95 o.p. (LB273NK, Leisure Bks). Nordon Pubns.
Heir of Grangerfjord Castle. Ruth McCarthy Sears. 1974. 4.95. Lenox Hill Press.
Heir of Linne. Robert Williams Buchanan. (On cover: Seaside library. Pocket ed., no. 1104). 1888. G. Munro.
Heir of Radclyffe. Charlotte Mary Yonge. 1971. Repr. of 1924 ed. 39.00 o.p. (ISBN 0-403-00818-2). Scholarly.
Heir of Redclyffe. Charlotte Mary Yonge. LC 52-44807. 1952. W. B. Eerdmans Pub. Co.
Heir of Redclyffe. Charlotte Mary Yonge. LC 74-476. (Victorian Fiction: Novels of Faith and Doubt; V. 30). 1975. 35.00 (ISBN 0-8240-1554-1). Garland Pub.
Heir of Redclyffe. 13th thousand. ed. Charlotte Mary Yonge. LC 9-1215. 1861. D. Appleton & Company.
Heir of Redclyffe. Charlotte Mary Yonge. 1891. Macmillan and Co.
Heir of Redclyffe. Charlotte Mary Yonge. (Half-title: Everyman's libraby,ed. by Ernest Rhys. Fiction. no 362). 1909. J. M. Dent & Co.
Heir of Redclyffe. Charlotte Mary Yonge. LC 36-37173. (Half-title: Everyman's library, ed. by Ernest Rhys. Fiction. no. 302). 1924. J. M. Dent & Sons, Ltd.
Heir of Sea & Fire. Tr. by McKillip, Patricia A. 1978. pap. 2.25 (ISBN 0-345-28882-3, Del Rey Bks). Ballantine.
Heir of Sherburne. Amanda Minnie Douglas. (The Sherburne series). Dodd, Mead & Company.
Heir of Starvelings. Evelyn Berckman. (O.s.i.). 1977. Repr. of 1967 ed. lib. bdg. 8.95 o.s.i. (ISBN 0-89244-029-5). Queens Hse.
Heir of Starvelings. Evelyn Berckman. 4.50 o.p. Doubleday.
Heir of Starvelings: A Novel of Innocence and Evil. 1st Ed. Evelyn Berckman. LC 67-16900. 1967. 4.50. Doubleday.
Heir of Starvelings. A Novel of Innocence and Evil. Evelyn Berckman. (3567). 1968. Dell.
Heir of the Ages. James Payn. (On cover: Seaside library. Pocket ed. no. 823). 1886. G. Munro.
Heir of the Ages. A Novel. James Payn. (Harper's Franklin square library, no. 531). 1886. Harper & Brothers.
Heir Presumptive. Florence Marryat Church Lean. (On cover: Lovell's library. v. 19. no. 949). 1887. J. W. Lovell Company.
Heir Presumptive. Henry Wade. 1981. 18.95x (Pub. by Remploy England). State Mutual Bk.
Heir Presumptive; a Murder Story: By Henry Wade Pseud. Harry Lancelot Aubrey-Fletcher. LC 53-12531. 1953. Macmillan.
Heir Presumptive and the Heir Apparent. authorized ed. Margaret Oliphant Wilson Oliphant. LC 7-32506. (On cover: Lovell's international series, no. 156). 1891. J. W. Lovell Company.
Heir to a Pair of Boots. Mary Jane Moore. LC 76-18795. 4.95 (ISBN 0-8111-0615-2). Naylor Co.
Heir to Ashley: And The Red-Court Farm. Ellen Price Henry Wood Wood. (On cover: Seaside library. Pocket ed. no. 1021). 1887. G. Munro.
Heir to Empire. Walter Samuel Cramp. LC 13-20573. 1.25. R. G. Badger.
Heir to Falconhurst. Lance Horner. LC 68-5811. (Fawcett gold medal book). 1968. 0.95. Fawcett Publications.
Heir to Kings. Winifred Duke. LC 27-406899. 1926. F. A. Stokes.
Heir to Kuragin. Constance Heaven. LC 78-14442. 1979. 8.95 (ISBN 0-698-10943-0). Coward, McCann & Geoghegan.
Heir to Kuragin. Constance Heaven. LC 79-10649. 1979. 14.95 (ISBN 0-8161-6703-6). G. K. Hall.
Heir to Millions. Edgar Fawcett. LC 6-38796. (On cover: The Ariel library. no. 19)). 1892. F.J. Schulte & Company.
Heir to Pendarrow. Constance Fecher, pseud. LC 77-85363. 1969. 3.75. Farrar, Straus & Giroux.
Heir to Polvention. Marjorie Watson. 1974. 6.95 o.p. (ISBN 0-8415-0292-7). Dutton.
Heir to Polventon. Marjorie Watson. LC 73-18755. 1974. 6.95 (ISBN 0-8415-0292-7). Saturday Review Press.
Heir to Rowanlea. Sally James. 224p. 1981. pap. 1.95 (ISBN 0-449-50175-2, Coventry). Fawcett.
Heiress. Alice Marie Celeste Durand. Tr. by Hewitt, Emma C. & Colmar, Julien. LC 6-35692. 1892. Worthington Company.
Heiress. Kristina Roy. LC 79-56301. 3.95 (ISBN 0-89107-176-8). Good News Publishers.
Heiress. Sally M Singer. LC 75-34218. 1976. 1.75 (ISBN 0-345-24881-3). Ballantine Books.
Heiress. An Autobiography. Ann Sophia Winterbotham Stephens. LC 8-14272. T. B. Peterson and Brothers.
Heiress Apparent. Dorothy Phoebe Ansle. LC 77-122119. 1970. 5.95 (ISBN 0-8415-0035-5). McCall Pub. Co.
Heiress Apparent. Laura Conway. 1970. 5.95 o.p. (ISBN 0-8415-0035-5). Sat Rev Pr.
Heiress Companion, No. 155. Madeleine Robins. 224p. 1981. pap. 1.50 (ISBN 0-449-50228-7, Coventry). Fawcett.
Heiress in Name Only: Or, The Adventures of Gwendolyn. Amelia M A Roth. LC 19-163676. Saulsbury Publishing Company.
Heiress Nurse. Peggy Gaddis, pseud. 1968. pap. 0.60 o.p. (73-747). Lancer.
Heiress of Bellefont. Emerson Bennett. LC 7-34428. T. B. Peterson.
Heiress of Cameron Hall. Laura Jean Libbey. (On cover: The library of American authors, no. 5). 1889. G. Munro.
Heiress of Carrigmona. Anna Hanson McKenney Dorsey. LC 6-33713. 1887. J. Murphy & Co.
Heiress of Carrigmona. Anna Hanson McKenney Dorsey. LC 43-20452. John Murphy Company.
Heiress of Castle Vale: Or, A Fair Plebeian. Mary E. Stone Bassett. LC 6-9096. (On cover: The pastime series, no. 84). 1892. Laird & Lee.
Heiress of Cranham Hall. Meredith, Junior, Pseud. LC 11-10759. Broadway Publishing Co.
Heiress of Cronenstein. Ida Marie Luise Sophie Friederike Gustava Hahn-Hahn & Allies, Mary H., Tr. LC 25246. 1900. Benziger Brothers.
Heiress of Egremont. Harriet Lewis. (On cover: The select series, no. 29). 1889. Street & Smith.
Heiress of Glen Gower: Or, The Hidden Crime. May Agnes Early Fleming. LC 6-41676. (On cover: The laurel library. no. 7). 1892. G. Munro.
Heiress of Hendee Hall: A Novel. Etta W Pierce. LC 59-48520. (Leisure hour library, v. 8, no 321). 1891. F. M. Lupton.
Heiress of Hendee Hall. A Novel. Etta W Pierce. (On cover: The idle hour series, no. 5). The F. M. Lupton Publishing Company.
Heiress of Hilldrop: Or, The Romance of a Young Girl. Charlotte Mary Brame. LC 44-11259. (On cover: Seaside library. Pocket ed. No. 741). G. Munro.
Heiress of Kilorgan: Or, Evenings with the Old Geraldines. Mary Anne Madden Sadlier. LC 8-165149. 1867. D. & J. Sadlier & Co.
Heiress of the Forest: A Romance of Old Anjou. Eleanor C Price. LC 7-735. 1901. T. Y. Crowell & Co.
Heiress to Craig Castle. Minerva Rossetti. 1973. 4.95. Lenox Hill Pr.
Heiress to the Mafia. Denti Di Pirajno, Alberto. LC 64-13838. 1974. (pbk.) 1.50. Manor Books.
Heiress to the Mafia. Alberto D. Di Pirajno. 304p. 1974. pap. 1.50 o.p. (ISBN 0-532-15135-6). Woodhill.
Heiress to the Mafia. Alberto D. Di Pirajno. 304p. 1974. pap. 1.50 o.p. (ISBN 0-532-15135-6). Manor Bks.
Heiresses of Fotheringay. A Tale Founded on Fact. Augustin Kennerly. 1856. E. K. Woodward.
Heirloom. Eleanora Brownleigh. 1983. pap. 3.95 (ISBN 0-8217-1200-4). Zebra.
Heirloom. Thomas Luke. (Orig.). 1982. pap. 2.75 (ISBN 0-671-43303-2). PB.
Heirlooms. Carole Morgan. 288p. 1981. pap. 2.75 (ISBN 0-523-41594-X). Pinnacle Bks.
Heirlooms: A Novel. Carole Morgan. LC 80-14586. (ISBN 0-02-586940-X). Macmillan.
Heirs. Cornelia James Cannon. LC 30-4846. 1930. Little, Brown, and Company.
Heirs: A Novel About a Great European Family. G. Y Dryansky. LC 78-5222. 12.50 (ISBN 0-399-11976-0). Putnam.
Heirs Apparent. Judy Bloodworth & Dennis Bloodworth. 1973. 7.95 o.p. (ISBN 0-374-16898-9). FS&G.
Heirs Apparent. Philip Hamilton Gibbs. LC 24-5831. 2.00. George H. Doran Company.
Heirs of a Promise. new ed. Allen C. Deeter. 48p. 1972. pap. 1.95 (ISBN 0-87178-359-2). Brethren.
Heirs of Bradley House. Amanda Minnie Douglas. LC 6-33484. 1892. Lee and Shepard.
Heirs of Cain. Abraham Rothberg. 1966. 5.95 o.p. (ISBN 0-399-10393-7). Putnam.
Heirs of Cain. Abraham Rothbergh. (3564). 1967. Dell.
Heirs of Cain: A Novel. Abraham Rothberg. LC 66-278263. 1966. bds., 5.95. Putnam.
Heirs of Darkness. Zilpha Keatley Snyder. LC 78-53799. 1978. 8.95 (ISBN 0-689-10913-X). Atheneum.
Heirs of Love. Barbara Ferry Johnson. 1980. 2.95 (ISBN 0-380-75739-7, 75739). Avon.
Heirs of Mrs. Willingden, a Novel. Mathilde Eiker. LC 34-236614. 1934. Doubleday, Doran & Co., Inc.
Heirs of the Kingdom. Kennedy Hudner. LC 80-39503. 11.95 (ISBN 0-03-049831-7). Holt, Rinehart and Winston.

Heirs of the Kingdom. Zoe Oldenbourg. LC 70-147805. 1976. (pbk.) 1.95 (ISBN 0-380-00578-6). Avon.

Heirs of the Kingdom. Zoe Oldenbourg. Tr. by Anne Carter from Fr. LC 70-147805. 1971. Repr. 8.95 o.p. (ISBN 0-394-46835-X). Pantheon.

Heirs of Truth. James A. Madison. 217p. 1975. 7.50 o.p. (ISBN 0-682-48109-2). Exposition.

Heirs of Yesterday. Emma Wolf. LC 1-29612. 1900. A. C. McClurg & Co.

Heirs to the Past. Driss Chraibi. (African Writers Ser.). 1972. pap. text ed. 4.00x (ISBN 0-435-90079-X). Heinemann Ed.

Heiteres und Ernstes: Eine Auswahl Deutscher Geschichten Des Jahrhunderts, Ed. by James B. Hepworth and Heinz F. Rahde. 2d Ed. Ed. by James B. Hepworth. LC 67-166409. 1967. pap., 3.95. Macmillan.

Helbeck of Bannisdale. Mary Augusta Arnold Humphry Ward Ward. LC 75-465. (Victorian Fiction: Novels of Faith and Doubt). 1975. 35.00 (ISBN 0-8240-1543-6). Garland Pub.

Helbeck of Bannisdale. Mary Augusta Arnold Humphry Ward Ward. LC 4-153393. 1898. The Macmillan Company.

Held by the Heights: Poems. Dolly Ann Morgan. LC 49-8580. 1949. Exposition Press.

Held for Orders: Being Stories of Railroad Life. Frank Hamilton Spearman. LC 1-25661. 1901. McClure, Phillips & Company.

Held for Orders, Being Stories of Railroad Life. 3d impression ed. Frank Hamilton Spearman. LC 4-16108. 1902. McClure, Phillips & Company.

Held for Ransom. Ruth Peterman. 1975. pap. 1.75 (ISBN 0-8423-1414-8). Tyndale.

Held for Trial. John Russell Coryell. LC 1-30260. (On cover: Magnet detective library. no. 165). 1900. Street & Smith.

Held in Bondage: Or, Granville De Vigne. A Tale of the Day. Louise De La Ramee. 1864. J. B. Lippincott & Co.

Held to Answer: A Novel. Peter Clark Macfarlane. LC 16-261408. 1916. 1.35. Little, Brown, and Company.

Heldenplatz; Roman. Ernst Lothar. LC 46-3073. 1945. Schoenhof.

Held's Angels: By John Held, Jr. and Frank B. Gilbreth, Jr. Frank Bunker Gilbreth. LC 52-8847. 1952. Crowell.

Helen. E. V. Cunningham, pseud. 1969. pap. 0.60 o.p. (0502-06008-060). Curtis.

Helen. Maria Edgeworth. LC 6-26303. G. Routledge and Sons.

Helen. Maria Edgeworth. LC 25-237740. (Half-title: The novels of Maria Edgeworth, vol. xi, xii). 1893. J. M. Dent & Co.

Helen. Maria Edgeworth & Ritchie, Anne Isabella (Thackeray) Lady, 1837-1919, Ed. LC 4-16522. 1896. Macmillan and Co., Ltd.

Helen. Arthur Sherburne Hardy. LC 16-22403. 1916. Houghton Mifflin Company.

Helen. Georgette Heyer. LC 28-15632. 1928. Longmans, Green and Co.

Helen. Oswald Sickert. LC 8-34867. (Half-title: The incognito library, no. 5). 1894. G. P. Putnam's Sons.

Helen: A Novel. Howard Melvin Fast. LC 66-12212. 1966. Doubleday.

Helen: A Story of Things to Be. Lu Wheat. LC 8-16472. The Grafton Press.

Helen Adair. Louis Becke. LC 17-6116. 1903. T. F. Unwin.

Helen Adair. Louis Becke. LC 27-1857. 1924. J. B. Lippincott Company.

Helen All Alone. William James De L'Aigle Buchan. LC 61-13552. 1961. Morrow.

Helen & All. Frances Weissman. (Orig.). 1980. pap. 3.95 o.p. (ISBN 0-89260-192-2). Hwong Pub.

Helen & Desire. Alexander Trocchi. 208p. pap. 1.95 o.p. (ISBN 0-87056-247-9, 6247). Brandon.

Helen Ayr: A Story of the Square Deal. Francis Sidney Hayward. LC 8-37183. 1908. Cochrane Publishing Co.

Helen Blair: A Novel. Nina Miller Elliott. LC 16-555. Thos. W. Jackson Publishing Co.

Helen Brent, M. D. A Social Study. Annie Nathan Meyer. LC 7-411241. Cassell Publishing Company.

Helen Comes Home. Watkins Eppes Wright. LC 43-11145. 1943. Arcadia House.

Helen Dale: Christian Science Story. Ephie Gladys Virtue. LC 12-269009. 1912. Virtue Printing Co.

Helen Duval: A French Romance. James L Young. LC 9-1200. 1891. The Bancroft Company.

Helen Erskine. Martha Harrison Robinson. LC 74-164574. (American fiction reprint series). 1971. (ISBN 0-8369-7051-9). Books for Libraries Press.

Helen Erskine. Martha Harrison Robinson. 1870. J. B. Lippincott & Co.

Helen Ethinger: Or, Not Exactly Right. Elsie Leigh Whittlesey. LC 8-36533. 1872. Claxton, Remsen & Haffelfinger.

Helen Gardner's Wedding-Day: Or, Colonel Floyd's Wards. A Battle Summer. Mary Virginia Terhune. LC 8-260513. 1870. Carleton; Etc., Etc.

Helen Harlow's Vow. Lois Nichols Waisbrooker. 1870. W. White and Company.

Helen Howard: Or The Bankrupt and Broker. A Mysterious Tale of Boston. Ashby. LC 5-4156. 1845. F. Gleason.

Helen in Exile: A Novel. Ian McLachlan. LC 80-15837. 10.95 (ISBN 0-8037-3561-8). Dial Press.

Helen Kennedy--Christian. Wynema Atherton. LC 38-23544. Zondervan Publishing House.

Helen Leeson: A Peep at New York Society... 1855. Parry & McMillan.

Helen Lincoln: A Tale. Carrie Capron. LC 6-22820. 1856. Harper & Brothers.

Helen of Four Gates. Ethel Holdsworth. LC 17-16318. E. P. Dutton & Co.

Helen of London. Sidney Floyd Gowing. LC 23-7996. 1923. G. P. Putnam's Sons.

Helen of the Old House. Harold Bell Wright. LC 21-146246. 1921. D. Appleton and Company.

Helen of Troy and Rose. Phyllis Bottome. LC 18-18533. 1918. The Century Co.

Helen; or, Will She Save Him? Sarah Maria Clinton Perkins. LC 7-36345. 1886. Funk & Wagnalls.

Helen Polska's Lover: Or, The Merchant Prince. Adolphe Danziger De Castro. LC 9-9409. A. Danziger.

Helen Templeton's Daughter. 1st Ed. Louise Eskrigge Crump. LC 52-8171. 1952. Longmans, Green.

Helen Treveryan: Or, The Ruling Race. Henry Mortimer Durand. LC 6-36563. 1892. Macmillan and Co.

Helen Walks Alone. Jeanne Judson. 1975. 4.95. Avalon Books.

Helen Walks Alone. Jeanne Judson. (Cameo Romance#39). 1976. (pbk.) 0.95. Fawcett.

Helen Whitney's Wedding, and Other Tales. Ellen Price Henry Wood Wood. (On cover: Seaside library. Pocket ed. no. 513). 1885. G.Munro.

Helen with the High Hand. Arnold Bennett. LC 74-5402. (Collected works of Arnold Bennett). 1974. (ISBN 0-518-19109-5). Books for Libraries Press.

Helen with the High Hand: An Idyllic Diversion. Arnold Bennett. 1910. George H. Doran Company.

Helen Young: A Story. by Paul Lindau. Paul Lindau & McFadden, P. Jr., Tr. LC 7-19021. (On cover: Globe library. v. 1, no. 168). 1892. Rand, McNally & Company.

Helena. Mary Augusta Arnold Humphry Ward Ward. LC 19-18643. 1919. Dodd, Mead and Company.

Helena. Evelyn Waugh. LC 57-3391. (Doubleday image book, D57). 1957. Image Books.

Helena, a Novel. Evelyn Waugh. LC 50-10054. 1950. Little, Brown.

Helena's Boys. Ida Lublenski Ehrlich. LC 27-23180. (On cover: French's standard library edition). S. French.

Helena's Path. Anthony Hope Hawkins. LC 7-29569. 1907. The McClure Company.

Helene. Vicki Baum. Tr. by Zeitlin, Ida. LC 33-9684. 1933. Doubleday, Doran & Company, Inc.

Helene. Leonora Blythe. 1979. pap. 1.75 (ISBN 0-449-50004-7, Coventry). Fawcett.

Helene. John Bowers. LC 76-11804. 1976. 1.50 (ISBN 0-345-24906-2). Ballantine Books.

Helene. A Love Episode. Emile Zola & Sherwood, Mrs. Mary (Neal) Tr. LC 9-1325. T. B. Peterson & Brothers.

Helene." A Novel. Ernest H Heinrichs. LC 7-4110. Nicholson Print.

Helene. A Tale of Love and Passion. Emile Zola & Sherwood, Mrs. Mary (Neal) Tr. LC 9-1324. T. B. Peterson & Brothers.

Helene Buderoff: Or, A Strange Duel. Martha Morton. (On cover: American authors' series, no. 5). J. W. Lovell Company.

Helene of the Yukon. Elden Pollock. LC 41-1982. Argus Press.

Helene Sainte Maur. Secrets of a Boudoir). Luman Allen. LC 6-46. (On cover: Dearborn series, no. 53). Donohue, Henneberry & Co.

Helene's Sweetheart (The Marriage of Gerard) Andre Theuriet & Watkins, Mary Linsay, Tr. (On cover: The pastime series, no. 76). 1899. Laird & Lee.

Helen's Babies. John Habberton. LC 4-356627. Hurst & Company.

Helen's Babies. John Habberton. LC 8-18407. Grosset and Dunlap.

Helen's Babies. John Habberton. 1915. F. A. Stokes Company.

Helen's Babies. John Habberton. LC 34-40506. Whitman Publishing Company.

Helen's Babies. With Some Account of Their Ways Innocent, Crafty, Angelic, Impish, Witching, and Repulsive. Also, a Partial Record of Their Actions During Ten Days of Their Existence. John Habberton. (On cover: Loring's tale of the day). Loring.

Helen's Babies: With Some Account of Their Ways, Innocent, Crafty, Angelic, Impish, Witching, and Repulsive. Also, a Partial Record of Their Actions During Ten Days of Their Existence. John Habberton. LC 18-10677. Hurst & Company.

Helen's Babies. With Some Account of Their Ways Innocent, Crafty, Angelic, Impish, Witching and Repulsive. Also, a Partial Record of Their Actions During Ten Days of Their Existence... John Habberton. LC 12-24113. T. B. Peterson & Brothers.

Helen's Babies: With Some Account of Their Ways, Innocent, Crafty, Angelic, Impish, Witching, and Repulsive, Also a Partial Record of Their Actions During Ten Days of Their Existence. the author's ed. John Habberton. 1907. Moffat, Yard & Company.

Helen's Babies. With Some Account of Their Ways, Innocent, Crafty, Angleic, Impish, Witching and Repulsive. Also, a Partial Record of Their Actions During Ten Days of Their Existence. John Habberton. LC 8-33779. H. Altemus Company.

Helen's Babies: With Some Account of Their Ways, Innocent, Crafty, Angelic, Impish, Witching and Repulsive. Also a Partial Record of Their Actions During Ten Days of Their Existence. John Habberton. LC 21-15107. Frederick A. Stokes Company.

Helen's Choice: A Tale of Long Island. Metta Horton Cook. LC 13-20754. J. S. Ogilvie Publishing Co.

Helga's Web. Jon Cleary. LC 70-102188. 1970. 6.50. Morrow.

Helianthus. Louise De La Ramee. LC 8-26831. 1908. The Macmillan Company.

Helicopter Pilot. William E Butterworth. 1967. Norton.

Helionde: Or, Adventures in the Sun. Sydney Whiting. LC 75-46314. (Supernatural and Occult Fiction). 1976. 24.00 (ISBN 0-405-08176-6). Arno Press.

Heliotrope: Or, The Soldier's Legacy. A Novel. Aimee Carey. LC 6-22817. 1884.

Helix. David Culberson Loughlin. LC 47-3824. 1947. Harper & Brothers.

Helix. Desmond Ryan & Joel N. Shurkin. LC 79-16814. 9.95 (ISBN 0-393-01250-6). Norton.

Helix File. William D Blankenship. LC 78-186185. 1972. 4.95 (ISBN 0-8027-5252-7). Walker.

Hell Above Water. Harry P. McKeever. 1981. pap. 2.25 (ISBN 0-8439-0856-4). Nordon Pubns.

Hell and Hallelujah! Norton S Parker. LC 31-686880. 1931. L. MacVeagh, The Dial Press.

Hell at White Pass. Cy Martin. 208p. 1982. pap. 2.25 (ISBN 0-505-51832-5). Tower Bks.

Hell at Yuma. Jack Slade. (Lassiter,#15). 1974. (pbk.) 0.95. Belmont Tower Books.

Hell Bay. Samuel Llewellyn. 1981. pap. 2.50 (ISBN 0-345-29642-7). Ballantine.

Hell-Bent. Hedi Bried. LC 53-172752. 1952. Woodford Press.

Hell Bent for Blitzkrieg: A Novel of World War Two. 1st Ed. Alton M Olson. LC 61-15773. Greenwich Book Publishers.

Hell-Bent for Danger. Walt Grove. LC 51-16234. (Gold medal book, 134). 1950. Fawcett Publications.

Hell Bent for Heaven. Shannon O'Cork. 224p. 1983. 12.95 (ISBN 0-312-36698-1). St Martin.

Hell-Bent for Heaven: The Diary of a Baby Sitter in 'Heaven Haven.' 1st Ed. Albert M Paschall. LC 58-37379. 1958. Exposition Press.

Hell Bent Kid: A Novel, 1st Ed. Charles O Locke. LC 57-6556. 1957. Norton.

Hell-Black Night. Stephen Gould Fisher. 192p. 1970. 4.50 o.p. (ISBN 0-8202-0062-X). Sherbourne.

Hell Canyon. Ray Corey. (O.s.i.). 160p. (Orig.). 1973. pap. 0.75 o.s.i. (AS1136, Award). Univ Pub & Dist.

Hell Cat. John Taintor Foote. LC 36-17943. 1936. D. Appleton-Century Company, Incorporated.

Hell-Cat and the King. Barbara Cartland. LC 77-15531. 1977. 6.95 (ISBN 0-87272-030-6). Duron Books.

Hell Catholic: By Father X. Robert C Hilkert. LC 52-10610. 1952. Sheed and Ward.

Hell-Crazy Range. Francis W Hilton. LC 34-29904. 1934. H. C. Kinsey & Company, Inc.

Hell Creek Cabin. Frank Roderus. LC 79-7054. 1979. 7.95 (ISBN 0-385-15177-2). Doubleday.

Hell Fer Sartain" and Other Stories. John Fox. LC 68-55674. (American short story series, v. 14). 1969. Garrett Press.

Hell Fer Sartain", and Other Stories. John Fox. LC 72-8173. (American short story series, v. 14). 1972. (ISBN 0-8422-8048-0). MSS Information Corp.

Hell Fer Sartain" And Other Stories. John Fox. 1897. Harper & Brothers.

Hell-Fire Harrison. Wallace Delois Wattles. LC 10-25577. 1910. L. C. Page & Company.

Hell Fire Ranch. H. P Blackburn. (Leisure book). 1.50 (ISBN 0-8439-0546-8). Nordon Pubns.

Hell for Leather. Archie Joscelyn. LC 51-6761. (Western novel classic, 111). 1951. Novel Selections.

Hell for McAllister. Matt Chisholm, pseud. 1970. pap. 0.75 o.p. (94006). Beagle Bks.

Hell Gate. James Dawson. LC 67-21633. 1967. D. McKay Co.

Hell-Gate Tides. Lee Thayer, pseud. LC 33-856. Sears Publishing Company.

Hell Harbor. Gordon Davis, pseud. (Sergeant Ser.: No. 2). 272p. (Orig.). 1980. pap. 2.25 (ISBN 0-89083-623-X). Zebra.

Hell Has No Exit. J. Lance Gilmer. (Orig.). 1976. pap. 1.50 (ISBN 0-87067-814-0, BH043). Holloway.

Hell Hath Fury. George Hay. 1963. 3.95 o.p. Wehman.

Hell Hath No Fury. Lois Christine Eby & Fleming, John Chester, 1906- Joint Author. LC 47-1268. 1947. E. P. Dutton & Company, Inc.

Hell Hath No Fury. Charles Williams. (Gold medal book, 286). 1953. Fawcett Publications.

Hell, Heaven or Hoboken. James Kline McVey. LC 35-5963. Langille Publishing Co.

Hell House. Richard Matheson. (288p). 1971. 6.50 o.p. (ISBN 0-670-36585-8). Viking Pr.

Hell in Georgia. John D Odom. LC 60-876. 1960. Corlies, Macy.

Hell in Hindu Land. Joseph Rosenberger. (Death Merchant, 20). 1.25 (ISBN 0-523-00994-1). Pinnacle Books.

Hell in His Holsters. Charles N Heckelmann. LC 52-5236. (Double D western). 1952. Doubleday.

Hell in Paradise Valley. Barry Cord. 1978. pap. 1.25 o.s.i. (ISBN 0-505-51316-1). Tower Bks.

Hell in the Palo Duro. John Thomas Edson. (Orig.). 1982. pap. 1.95 (ISBN 0-425-05294-X). Berkley Pub.

Hell in the Saddle. Edward Earl Repp. LC 36-8691. 1936. Godwin.

Hell Is a City. William Ard. LC 55-7729. (Timothy Dane mystery). 1955. Rinehart.

Hell Is Forever. J. Lance Gilmer. (Orig.). 1977. pap. 1.50 (ISBN 0-87067-817-5, BH039). Holloway.

Hell Is My Heaven. Jeneth Murrey. (Harlequin Romances Ser.). 192p. 1982. pap. 1.50 (ISBN 0-373-02483-5). Harlequin Bks.

Hell Is Not Anywhere. 1st Ed. Richard Gordon Moores. LC 59-10206. 1959. Bobbs-Merrill.

Hell Is Relative. 1st Ed. Virginia Rose. LC 57-79292. 1958. Pageant Press.

Hell Is Too Crowded. Jack Higgins, pseud. 160p. 1977. pap. 1.95 (ISBN 0-449-14274-4, GM). Fawcett.

Hell Is Too Crowded. Jack Higgins. (Gold Medal Book). 1.50 (ISBN 0-449-13568-3). Fawcett.

Hell Let Loose. Francis Beeding. LC 37-39114.

Hell Masters. Keith Spore. 1977. pap. 1.75 (ISBN 0-89041-175-1, 3175). Major Bks.

Hell of a Good Time: And Other Stories. James Thomas Farrell. LC 48-10591. (Avon modern short story monthly, 41). 1948. Avon Book Co.

Hell of a Way to Die. Jack Slade, pseud. 1972. pap. 0.75 o.p. (BT40142). Belmont-Tower.

Hell of a Woman. James Myers Thompson. LC 55-16142. (Lion original, 218). 1954. Lion Books.

Hell of Loneliness. Henry Von Rhau. 47p. Repr. of 1929 ed. pap. 2.00 o.s.i. Guild Pr Ltd.

Hell on a Holiday. Roe Richmond. (Lashtrow Ser.: No. 3). 1980. pap. 1.95 (ISBN 0-8439-0781-9). Nordon Pubns.

Hell on Friday. William Bogart. LC 42-8140. J. Swift.

Hell on Horseback. Johanas L. Bouma. 1981. pap. 1.75 (ISBN 0-8439-0893-9, Leisure Bks). Nordon Pubns.

Hell on Legg's Hill. Robert Trimnell. 1976. pap. 1.25 (ISBN 0-532-12426-X). Woodhill.

Hell on the Pecos. Edward Earl Repp. LC 35-9854. 1935. Godwin.

Hell on Wheels. John Benteen. (Fargo Western Adventure Series). 1976. (pbk.) 1.25. Belmont Tower Books.

Hell on Wheels. Thornton Martin. LC 39-32488. The Penn Publishing Company.

Hell Raiser. Ray Hogan. 1980. pap. 1.75 (ISBN 0-451-09489-1, E9489, Sig). NAL.

Hell Riders. Steve Mensing. (Orig.). 1980. pap. text ed. 1.75 o.s.i. (ISBN 0-505-51588-1). Tower Bks.

Hell-Roarin' Texas Trail. Robert Denver. LC 32-689633. The Macaulay Company.

Hell! Said the Duchess: A Bedtime Story. Michael Arlen. LC 34-35466. 1934. Doubleday, Doran & Company, Inc.

Hell Screen & Other Stories. Ryunosuke Akutagawa. Tr. by W. H. Norman. LC 78-98800. Repr. of 1948 ed. lib. bdg. 19.25x (ISBN 0-8371-3017-4, AKHS). Greenwood.

Hell Screen ("Jigoku Hen") and Other Stories. Ryunosuke Akutagawa. LC 78-98800. (Illus.). 1971. (ISBN 0-8371-3017-4). Greenwood Press.

Hell Seed. Colin D Peel. LC 78-19654. 1979. 8.95 (ISBN 0-312-36726-0). St. Martin's Press.

Hell Ship to Kuma. Cover Painting by James Meese. Calvin Clements. LC 54-43098. (Gold medal books, 412). 1954. Fawcett Publications.

Hell Street: By Max Franklin Pseud. Richard Deming. LC 54-11109. (Murray Hill mystery). 1954. Rinehart.

Hell Strip: By Lee Richards Pseud. Cover Painting by Lu Kimmel. Lee E Wells. LC 55-38183. (Gold medal books, 495). 1955. Fawcett Publications.

Hell Was Her Destiny. James E. Lewis. 1982. 6.95 (ISBN 0-533-05011-1). Vantage.

Hell with Elaine. Van Siller. LC 73-10978. (Crime Club Ser.). 192p. 1974. 4.95 o.p. (ISBN 0-385-08900-7). Doubleday.

Hell with Elaine. Hilda Van Siller. LC 73-10978. 1974. (pbk.). 4.95 (ISBN 0-385-08900-7). Published for the Crime Club by Doubleday.

Hell with Red Hair. Macy West. (Orig.). pap. 0.95 o.p. (1104). Brandon.

Hellbane. Anthony Esler. LC 75-4818. 1975. 8.95 (ISBN 0-688-02928-0). Morrow.

Hellbane. Anthony Esler. (Fawcett Crest Book). 1977. 1.95. Fawcett Pubns.

Hellbent for a Hangrope: By Clement Hardin Pseud. Dwight Bennett Newton. LC 54-332270. 1954. Ace Books.

Hellbent Kid. McLean. LC 73-86950. 1973. pap. 1.25 o.p. (ISBN 0-88419-065-X). Creation Hse.

Hellbent Kid. McLean. LC 73-86950. 1973. pap. 1.25 o.p. (ISBN 0-88419-065-X). Creation Hse.

Hellbirds. Austin Mitchelson & Nicholas Utechin. (O.s.i.). 1976. pap. 1.50 o.s.i. (BT50980). Belmont-Tower.

Hellbomb Flight. Lionel Derrick. (penetrator series, 10). 1975. (pbk.) 1.25 (ISBN 0-523-00690-X). Pinnacle Books.

Hellborn. Gary Brandner. 224p. (Orig.). 1981. pap. 2.50 (ISBN 0-449-14414-3, GM). Fawcett.

Hellbound for Ballarat: Trouble at Quinn's Crossing. Nelson Nye. 160p. (Orig.). 1976. pap. 2.25 (ISBN 0-441-32727-3). Ace Bks.

Hellbox. John O'Hara. LC 47-30414. 1947. Random House.

Hellcat of Sabrehill. Raymond Giles. 384p. (Orig.). 1983. pap. 3.50 (ISBN 0-449-12382-0, GM). Fawcett.

Hellcopter. Jonathan F. Kass. LC 81-81946. 144p. 1983. 9.95 (ISBN 0-86666-041-0). GWP.

Hellcrest. Leo Leaston Spears. LC 29-14869. Smith-Brooks.

Helldorados, Ghosts & Camps of the Old Southwest. Norman D. Weis. LC 73-83117. (Illus.). 1977. 9.95 (ISBN 0-87004-243-2). Caxton.

Heller. William E. Henning. LC 47-6380. 1947. C. Scribner's Sons.

Heller from Texas. William Heuman. (Orig.). 1968. pap. 0.50 o.p. (D2537, GM). Fawcett World.

Heller with a Gun. Louis L'Amour. LC 80-24989. (Series: Gregg Press Western Fiction Series.). 1981. 11.95 (ISBN 0-8398-2696-6). Gregg Press.

Heller With a Gun see Complete L'Amour.

Heller With a Gun see L'Amour Westerns.

Heller's Leap. Ian Wallace. 1979. 2.25 (ISBN 0-87997-475-3). DAW Books.

Hellfire. Jake Logan. LC 80-83591. (Jake Logan Ser.). 256p. (Orig.). 1981. pap. 1.95 (ISBN 0-87216-795-X). Playboy Pbks.

Hellfire at Brimstone. Jim Wilmeth. (Orig.). 1981. pap. 1.95 (ISBN 0-505-51656-X). Tower Bks.

Hellfire Heritage. Willo Davis Roberts. (Black Pearl Ser.: No. 6). 1979. pap. 1.75 (ISBN 0-445-04453-5). Popular Lib.

Hellfire in Tripoli. Edwin Palmer Hoyt. 1974. (pbk.) 1.25 (ISBN 0-523-00349-8). Pinnacle Books.

Hellfire Jackson. Garland Roark & Charles Thomas. LC 66-17433. 1966. Doubleday.

Hellfire Jackson: By Garland Roark, Charles Thomas. Garland Roark. (75-1276). 1968. Popular Lib.

Hellfire Range. Jesse Edward Grinstead. LC 42-13274. 1942. Dodge Publishing Company.

Hellfire Trail. Jory Sherman. (Leisure books). 1979. 1.50 (ISBN 0-8439-0652-9). Nordon Pubns.

Hellflower. George Oliver Smith. 1969. pap. 0.60 o.p. (X1957). Pyramid Pubns.

Hellflower: A Science-Fiction Novel. George Oliver Smith. LC 53-8686. 1953. Abelard Press.

Hellgate. William C. MacDonald. 1982. 18.00x (Pub. by Ian Henry Pubns England). State Mutual Bk.

Hellgate. William C. MacDonald. 1978. pap. 1.25 o.s.i. (ISBN 0-505-51298-X). Tower Bks.

Hellgate. William C. MacDonald. Orig. Title: Devil's Drum. 1969. pap. 0.60 o.p. (B60-1021). Belmont-Tower.

Hellgate. William C. MacDonald. 1972. pap. 0.75 o.p. (BT40130). Belmont-Tower.

Hellgate Canyon. 1st Ed. Fred Delano. LC 52-6219. (Holt western). Holt.

Hellhole. Ralph Hayes. (Buffalo Hunter Ser.: No. 1). 160p. 1982. pap. 1.75 (ISBN 0-8439-1031-3, Leisure Bks). Nordon Pubns.

Hellhound Project. Ron Goulart. LC 74-27582. 1975. 5.95 (ISBN 0-385-06275-3). Doubleday.

Helliconia Spring. Brian Wilson Aldiss. LC 81-66036. 1982. 15.95 (ISBN 0-689-11196-7). Atheneum.

Hellion. Kim Savage. LC 51-8197. 1951. Vixen Press.

Hellions. Rick Walters, pseud. LC 60-1062. 1969. Repr. pap. 0.60 o.p. (B60-1062). Belmont-Tower.

Hellions' Hostage. Abe Canuck. 1974. 4.95 (ISBN 0-517-51558-X). Lenox Hill Press.

Hello, Anna. Renee Shann. 1973. pap. 0.75 o.p. (94319). Beagle Bks.

Hello Carol. B. Johnson. 160p. 1982. pap. 3.95 (ISBN 0-441-32731-1). Ace Bks.

Hello, Good-Bye. Lynn Klamkin. LC 72-12438. 1973. 5.95 (ISBN 0-396-06782-4). Dodd, Mead.

Hello, Grandma? Bil Keane. (Family Circus Ser.). (Illus.). 1978. pap. 1.50 (ISBN 0-449-14169-1, GM). Fawcett.

Hello, I Love You! Voices from Within the Sexual Revolution. Ed. by Jeanne Pasle-Green & Jim Haynes. LC 77-77389. (Orig.). 1977. pap. 4.50 (ISBN 0-87810-032-6). Times Change.

Hello, Lemuria, Hello. Ron Goulart. 1979. 1.50 (ISBN 0-87997-451-6). DAW Books.

Hello, Mr. Henderson.". William Hazlett Upson. LC 49-6773. 1949. Rinehart.

Hello, My Love. Daisy H. Thomson. 1974. pap. 0.95 o.p. (ISBN 0-515-03291-3, N3291). BJ Pub Group.

Hello, Wisconsin! John Paul Cullen. LC 31-32077. 1931. Meador Publishing Company.

Hell's Acres. Jesse Edward Grinstead. LC 41-231097. 1941. Dodge Publishing Company.

Hell's Acres: A Historical Novel of the Wild East in the '50's. Clair Willard Perry & Pell, John Leggett Everitt. LC 26-5861. L. Furman, Inc.

Hell's Belle. Joan Margaret Fleming. LC 73-93677. 1969. 3.95. I. Washburn.

Hell's Belle. Bernard Molohon. LC 33-33269. Deseret Book Company.

Hell's Bells: A Comedy of the Underworld. Marmaduke Dixey. LC 37-9923. E. P. Dutton & Co., Inc.

Hell's Desert: A Novel. Frank Hamilton Spearman. LC 33-31426. 1933. Doubleday, Doran and Company, Inc.

Hell's Edge. John R. Townsend. 1974. pap. 0.95 o.p. (ISBN 0-14-030342-1, Puffin). Penguin.

Hell's Full. William Harrison. 1977. pap. 1.75 (ISBN 0-532-17169-1). Woodhill.

Hell's Gate. Dean R. Koontz. (Orig.). 1970. pap. 0.75 o.p. (ISBN 0-447-74656-1). Lancer.

Hell's Halfacre. Brick Killerman. 224p. (Orig.). 1981. pap. 2.25 (ISBN 0-505-51744-2). Tower Bks.

Hell's Harvest. Joseph Nathaniel Publicover Wilson. LC 40-69164. 1940. Meador Publishing Company.

Hell's Hatches. Lewis R Freeman. LC 21-409127. 1921. Dodd, Mead and Company.

Hell's Highroad. Ernest Pascal. LC 25-18356. Grosset & Dunlap.

Hell's Hip Pocket. Dane Coolidge. LC 38-29549. 1938. E. P. Dutton & Co., Inc.

Hell's Horseman. William L Hopson. LC 46-4251. 1946. Phoenix Press.

Hell's Junction. George G Gilman. (Adam Steele series#3). 1976. (pbk.) 1.25 (ISBN 0-523-00814-7). Pinnacle Books.

Hell's Kitchen: A Novel. Benjamin Appel. LC 76-44014. (YA) 1977. 7.95 (ISBN 0-394-83236-1). Pantheon.

Hell's Loose. Roland Pertwee. LC 29-772015. 1929. Houghton Mifflin Company.

Hell's Odyssey (Coal Boat Cargo) Amy Josephine Baker. LC 42-21767. 1942. Hutchinson & Co. Ltd.

Hell's Paradise. Hjalmar Rutzebeck. LC 47-6349. 1947. B. Humphries.

Hell's Paradise. Hjalmar Rutzebeck. LC 47-6349. 1946. B. Humphries.

Hell's Pavement. Damon Francis Knight. 192p. 1980. pap. 1.95 (ISBN 0-380-52381-7, 52381). Avon.

Hell's Playground. Ida Vera Simonton. LC 13-134936. 1912. Moffat, Yard and Company.

Hell's Playground. Ida Vera Simonton. LC 36-29473. 1914. The Macaulay Company.

Hell's Playground. Ida Vera Simonton. LC 25-767235. Brentano's.

Hell's Ransom. Karl Meyer. (Orig.). 1980. pap. 2.25 (ISBN 0-532-23183-X). Woodhill.

Hell's Seven. George G. Gilman, pseud. (Edge Ser.: No. 8). 160p. 1973. pap. 1.75 (ISBN 0-523-41286-X). Pinnacle Bks.

Hell's Stamping Ground. Westmoreland Gray. LC 35-933028. J. B. Lippincott Company.

Hellsgrin. Steve Frazee. LC 60-5229. 1960. Rinehart.

Hellspout. Bill Knox. LC 76-2788. 1976. 5.95 (ISBN 0-385-11546-6). Published for the Crime Club by Doubleday.

Helltank. 1981. pap. write for info. (ISBN 0-88074-019-1). Metagam.

Helluva War. Arthur Guy Empey. LC 27-15389. 1927. D. Appleton and Company.

Helmet and Wasps: A Novel. Michael Mott. LC 66-10714. 1966. Houghton Mifflin.

Helmet of Navarre. Bertha Runkle. LC 1-312263. 1901. The Century Co.

Heloise & Abelard, 2 Vols. in One. George Moore. (Black & Gold Lib). 1945. 7.95 o.p. (ISBN 0-87140-871-6). Liveright.

Heloise: Or The Unrevealed Secret. A Tale. Therese Albertine Louise Robinson. LC 7-42185. 1850. D. Appleton & Company.

Helon Wheels. Mark Crane. LC 42-17238. 1943. B. Humphries, Inc.

Helon's Pilgrimage to Jerusalem: A Picture of Judaism, in the Century Which Preceded the Advent of Our Saviour. from the german frederick strauss by john kenrick rev. and abr. by baron stow... ed. Gerhard Friedrich Abraham Strauss & Stow, Baron, 1801-1869, Ed. LC 8-16892. 1835. W. D. Ticknor.

Help from the Baron. John Creasey. (O.s.i.). 1977. 6.95 o.s.i. (ISBN 0-8027-5368-X). Walker & Co.

Help from the Baron. John Creasey. 188p. 1983. pap. 2.95 (ISBN 0-8027-3000-0). Walker & Co.

Help, I Am Being Held Prisoner. Donald E Westlake. LC 73-92922. 1974. 6.95 (ISBN 0-87131-149-6). M. Evans.

Help is on the Way. A. Roy Hahn. LC 82-90075. 231p. (Orig.). 1982. pap. 4.50 (ISBN 0-942822-00-5). Sundance OR.

Help, Please. Edith-Jane Bahr. LC 74-9474. 1975. 5.95 (ISBN 0-385-09776-X). Published for the Crime Club by Doubleday.

Help to the Family. Anne Tyler. 1972. 6.95 o.p. Knopf.

Help Wanted -- for Murder. William L Rohde. LC 50-35209. (Gold medal book,115). 1950. Fawcett Publications.

Help Wanted: A Novel of Today Done from Jack Lait's Great Play. Webster Denison & Lait, Jack. LC 31-19516. 1916. The Macaulay Company.

Help Wanted, Female. LC 37-182533. The Macaulay Company.

Help Yourself to Happiness. Frank Ramsay Adams. LC 29-16851. The Macaulay Company.

Help Yourself to Love. Peggy Gaddis, pseud. LC 41-154408. 1941. Arcadia House, Inc.

Helpers. Francis Lynde. LC 99-4672. 1899. Houghton, Mifflin and Company.

Helpers. Francis Lynde. LC 4-15468. 1901. Houghton, Mifflin and Company.

Helpers. Francis Lynde. LC 18-7786. 1917. Houghton Mifflin Company.

Helpers. Stanley Winchester. LC 79-105578. 1970. 6.95. Putnam.

Helping Hand. Celia Dale. LC 66-22500. bds., 3.95. Walker.

Helping Hand. Celia Dale. (U6122). 1968. Ballantine.

Helping Hersey. Betsey Riddle Hutton Zum Stolzenberg. LC 20-26758. 1920. George H. Doran Company.

Helping Muriel Make It Through the Night: Stories. Lee Zacharias. LC 75-18047. 1975. 7.95 (ISBN 0-8071-0166-4) (ISBN 0-8071-0177-X). Louisiana State University Press.

Helping the Alcoholic & His Family. Thomas J. Shipp. 1966. pap. 1.75 o.p. (ISBN 0-8006-5002-6). Fortress.

Helpless. Fraizer W Stallings. LC 75-99101. 1970. 6.95. Dorrance.

Helpmate. May Sinclair. LC 7-25509. 1907. H. Holt and Company.

Helsinki Affair. Mauri Sariola. 1973. Curtis Bks.

Helsinki Affair. Mauri Sariola. LC 70-147793. 1971. 4.95 (ISBN 0-8027-5230-6). Walker.

Helter Skelter. Patricia Moyes. 1979. 15.00x (ISBN 0-86025-145-4, Pub. by Ian Henry Pubns England). State Mutual Bk.

Hem of His Garment: A Novel. Argye M Briggs. LC 51-7929. 1951. Eerdmans.

Hembra Caliente. Danilo Cesto. (Pimienta Collection Ser.). 1977. pap. 1.00 (ISBN 0-88473-266-5). Fiesta Pub.

Hembra Insaciable. Eustaquio Ramirez. (Pimienta Collection Ser). (Span.). 1977. pap. 1.00 o.p. (ISBN 0-88473-258-4). Fiesta Pub.

Hembra Perversa. Roberto Ramirez. (Pimienta Collection Ser.). (Orig., Span.). 1977. pap. 1.00 (ISBN 0-88473-272-X). Fiesta Pub.

Hembras a Granel. new ed. Lino Martel. (Pimienta Collection Ser). 160p. (Span.). 1974. pap. 1.00 o.p. (ISBN 0-88473-215-0). Fiesta Pub.

Hemingway. Ernest Hemingway & Cowley, Malcom, 1898- Ed. LC 44-8271. (Viking portable library). 1944. The Viking Press.

Hemingway & The Sun Set. Bertram D. Sarason. LC 72-76990. (O.s.i.). (Illus.). 270p. 1972. 16.00 o.s.i. (ISBN 0-910972-06-0). IHS-PDS.

Hemingway Gift Edition No. 2: 3 Vols., in Our Time, Sun Also Rises, Farewell to Arms. Ernest Hemingway. pap. 4.85, boxed set o.p. Scribner.

Hemingway: High on the Wild. Lloyd R Arnold. LC 77-71746. (Illus.). 1977. 17.95 (ISBN 0-448-14290-2). Grosset & Dunlap.

Hemingway's African Stories: The Stories, Their Sources, Their Critics. Ed. by John M. Howell. LC 69-14263. (Scribner research anthologies). 1969. Scribner.

Hemingway's Spanish Tragedy. Lawrence R Broer. LC 73-13011. (Illus.). 1973. 7.50 (ISBN 0-8173-7103-6). University of Alabama Press.

Hemlock and After: A Novel. Angus Wilson. LC 52-12465. 1952. Viking Press.

Hemlock Avenue Mystery. Lily Augusta Long. LC 8-6663. 1908. Little, Brown, and Company.

Hemlock Swamp: And a Season at the White Sulphur Springs. Elsie Leigh Whittlesey. LC 8-36532. 1873. Claxton, Remsen & Haffelfinger.

Hemlock Tree. Eileen Lottman. (queen-size gothic). 1975. (pbk.) 1.25. Popular Library.

Hemming: The Adventurer. Roberts Theodore Goodridge. LC 4-2988. 1904. L. C. Page & Company.

Hempfield: A Novel. Ray Stannard Baker. LC 15-21426. 1915. Doubleday, Page & Company.

Hemps of Agrimony. Lionel Evelyn Oswald Charlton. LC 36-183. 1935. T. Nelson & Sons, Ltd.

Hen Lays Murder, and Other Stories. Laurelle Miller. LC 44-28977. 1944. Jupiter Publishing Co., Ltd.

Henchman. Mark Lee Luther. LC 2-24322. 1902. The Macmillan Company.

Henderson Equation. Warren Adler. LC 76-13040. 8.95 (ISBN 0-399-11755-5). Putnam.

Henderson Equation. Warren Adler. 1979. 2.25 (ISBN 0-671-81735-3). Pocket Books.

Henderson the Rain King. Saul Bellow. 1976. pap. 4.95 (ISBN 0-14-004229-6). Penguin.

Henderson the Rain King. Saul Bellow. 1959. 12.95 (ISBN 0-670-36655-2). Viking Pr.

Henderson, the Rain King: A Novel. Saul Bellow. 1965. pap., 1.65. Viking.

Henderson's Head: A Novel. Peter Cookson. LC 73-78613. 1973. 7.95 (ISBN 0-399-11165-4). Putnam.

Hendon Inheritance. Clara Mathis. pap. 0.75 o.s.i. (01-403). Lancer.

Hendon's First Case: The First Great Crime Solved by the New Police College at Hendon. Cecil John Charles Street. LC 35-31029. Dodd, Mead & Company.

Hendricks the Hunter: Or, The Border Farm: a Tale of Zululand. William Henry Giles Kingston. LC 72-5609. (Black Heritage Library Collection). (Series: Romances and adventures afloat and ashore.). (Illus.). 1972. (ISBN 0-8369-9143-5). Books for Libraries Press.

Hendricks the Hunter: Or, The Border Farm: a Tale of Zululand. William Henry Giles Kingston. LC 49-444532. (Romances and Adventures Afloat and Ashore). A. C. Armstrong.

Henley on the Battle Line. Frank Ernest Channon. LC 13-21058. (His The Henley schoolboys series). 1913. 1.50. Little, Brown, and Company.

Henrietta. Charlotte Ramsay Lennox. LC 74-17305. (Flowering of the Novel). 1974. (ISBN 0-8240-1149-X). Garland Pub.

Henrietta: A Novel. Harriet Scott. LC 8-2922. 1892.

Henrietta Temple: A Love Story. Benjamin Disraeli Beaconsfield. LC 76-12447. (Works of Benjamin Disraeli, Earl of Beaconsfield; v. 8-9). (Illus.). 1976. 16.50 (ISBN 0-404-08800-7). AMS Press.

Henrietta Temple: A Love Story. new ed. Benjamin Disraeli Beaconsfield. LC 6-28839. G. Routledge and Sons.

Henrietta Temple: A Love Story. Benjamin Disraeli Beaconsfield. (Seaside library. v. 21, no. 405). G. Munro.

Henrietta Temple: A Love Story. Benjamin Disraeli Beaconsfield. (In his The Bradenham edition of the novels and tales. New York, 1934? vol. VI). Alfred A. Knopf.

Henrietta Who? Catherine Aird. 1968. Published for the Crime Club by Doubleday.

Henrietta's Wish; or: Domineering. by charlotte m. yonge. ed. Charlotte Mary Yonge. (On cover: Seaside library. Pocket ed. no. 535). 1885. G. Munro.

Henriette: Or, A Corsican Mother. Francois Coppee. Tr. by Wakefield, Edward. LC 41-35132. 1889. Worthington Co.

Henry. Elizabeth Eliot. LC 51-9612. 1951. Duell, Sloan and Pearce.

Henry and Cato. Iris Murdoch. LC 77-8044. 1977. 2.95 (ISBN 0-14-004569-4). Penguin Books.

Henry and Cato. Iris Murdoch. LC 76-380698. 1976. 4.00 (ISBN 0-7011-2195-5). Chatto & Windus.

Henry and Cato. Iris Murdoch. LC 76-27653. 1977. 10.00 (ISBN 0-670-36697-8). Viking Press.

Henry and the Great Society. Herbert L. Roush. LC 77-12822. 1977. 2.95 (ISBN 0-89293-048-9). Beta Books.

Henry Ashton: A Thrilling Story and How the Famous Cooperative Commonwealth Was Established in Zanland. Robert Addison Dague. LC 4-37017. 1903. The Author.

Henry Belk-Son of Sweet Union. Moses Rountree. LC 75-4487. 1975. 10.95 (ISBN 0-87716-058-9, Pub. by Moore Pub Co). F Apple.

Henry Bourland: The Passing of the Cavalier. Albert Elmer Hancock. LC 1-7299. 1901. The Macmillan Company.

Henry Brocken: His Travels and Adventures in the Rich, Strange, Scarce-Imaginable Regions of Romance. Walter John De La Mare. LC 24-4621. 1924. A. A. Knopf.

Henry Courtland; or: What a Farmer Can Do. A J Cline. LC 6-207355. 1870. J. B. Lippincott & Co.

Henry Dunbar: Or, The Outcast. Mary Elizabeth Braddon Maxwell. (Seaside library. v. 10, no. 190). 1877. G. Munro.

Henry Elizabeth. Justin Huntly McCarthy. LC 20-13543. 1920. John Lane Company.

Henry Elwood: A Theological Novel. Milton Robinson Scott. LC 8-2908. 1892. Newark American Print.

Henry Esmond. William Makepeace Thackeray. LC 36-37083. (Everyman's library, ed. by Ernest Rhys. Fiction. no. 73). 1931. J. M. Dent & Sons, Ltd.

Henry Esmond. William Makepeace Thackeray & Henneman, John Bell, 1864-1908, Ed. LC 30-14666. (Half-title: New pocket classics). The Macmillan Company.

Henry Esmond and Lovel the Widower. household ed. William Makepeace Thackeray. 1869. Fields, Osgood & Co.

Henry Esmond and Lovel the Widower. William Makepeace Thackeray. LC 41-418467. (Thackeray's novels. Illustrated library edition). 1874. J. R. Osgood and Company.

Henry Esmond; Catherine; Denis Duval and Lovel the Widower. William Makepeace Thackeray. LC 31-258. Caxton Publishing Co.

Henry Fielding: Mask and Feast, by, Andrew Wright. Andrew H Wright. LC 65-196874. (Call28). 1966. pap., 1.50. Univ. of Calif. Pr.

Henry Fielding: Tom Jones. Ed. by Neil Compton. 1981. pap. 20.00 (ISBN 0-333-07739-3, Pub. by Macmillan England). State Mutual Bk.

Henry Fielding's Tom Jones and the Romance Tradition. Henry Knight Miller. LC 77-352735. (English Literary Studies: ELS Monograph Ser.: No. 6). 1976. English Literary Studies, University of Victoria.

Henry for Hugh: A Novel. Ford Madox Ford. LC 34-32947. 1934. J. B. Lippincott.

Henry Hippo. Barbara Carlson Travaglini. (Illus.). 1973. 3.75 (ISBN 0-533-00524-8). Vantage.

Henry in a Silver Frame. James Eastwood. LC 70-190000. 1972. 4.95. D. McKay Co.

Henry in a Silver Frame. James Eastwood. 1973. (pbk) 0.95 (ISBN 0-671-77691-6). Pocket Books.

Henry Is Twenty: A Further Episodic History of Henry Claverly, 3rd. Samuel Merwin. LC 18-192943. 1.50. The Bobbs-Merrill Company.

Henry James in Northampton: Visions and Revisions. Dean Flower. LC 74-31209. (Illus.). 1971. Friends of the Smith College Library.

Henry James Reader. Selected with a Foreword, Headnotes by Leon Edel. Henry James. Ed. by Leon Edel. LC 65-22875. bds. 7.50. Scribners.

Henry James: Selected Fiction. Henry James. Ed. by Leon Edel. pap. 2.45 o.p. (ISBN 0-525-47140-5). Dutton.

Henry James: Seven Stories Anc Studies. Edward Stone, Editor. Henry James. Ed. by Edward Stone. LC 61-669043. (Gomentree books). 1961. Appleton-Century-Crofts.

Henry James: Seven Stories & Studies. Henry James. Ed. by Edward Stone. (Orig.). pap. text ed. 2.95 o.p. (ISBN 0-390-47990-X). Appleton.

Henry James: Stories of the Supernatural. Henry James. Ed. by Leon Edel. LC 78-125479. 1980. pap. 9.95 (ISBN 0-8008-3829-7). Taplinger.

Henry Kempton. Evelyn Brentwood. LC 13-9721. 1913. John Lane.

Henry, King of France. Heinrich Mann & Sutton, Eric, Tr. LC 39-119981. 1939. A. A. Knopf.

Henry Lawson's Best Stories: Chosen by Cecil Mann. Henry Archibald Hertzberg Lawson. Ed. by Cecil Mann. LC 66-28938. 1966. 5.95. Angus & Robertson.

Henry Lovell: A Temperance Story, for Old and Young. Alexander Streeter Arnold. LC 6-2067. 1878. A. S. Arnold.

Henry Lyle: Or, Life and Existence. Emilia Marryat. LC 44-14010. Garrett & Co.

Henry Lyle: Or, Life and Existence. Emilia Marryat. LC 43-36300. 1857. Garrett, Dick & Fitzgerald.

Henry Maynard's Adventures in the Arctic Regions. A J Petersen. LC 7-36171. The Gazette Print.

Henry Miller: Between Heaven and Hell; a Symposium. Ed. by Emil White. LC 61-15269. 1962. pap., 2.25. Big Sur Guide Bks.

Henry Miller: Colossus of One by Kenneth C. Dick. Kenneth C Dick. LC 67-25831. 1967. 6.00. Alberts.

Henry Miller Dinner Chats. Henry Miller & Twinka Thiebaud. LC 80-26138. 1981. 6.95 (ISBN 0-88496-166-4). Capra Press.

Henry Miller Trilogy. Henry Miller. Incl. Tropic of Cancer; Tropic of Capricorn; Black Spring. 1963. boxed set 15.00 o.p. (GBI). Grove.

Henry Miller's Thanksgiving Prayer. Brad Binau. (Orig.). 1980. pap. 1.75 (ISBN 0-937172-06-5). JLJ Pubs.

Henry Northcote. John Collis Snaith. 1906. H. B. Turner & Co.

Henry of Navarre: A Romance of August, 1572. Mabel Winifred Knowles. LC 8-30614. 1908. G. P. Putnam's Sons.

Henry of Navarre, Ohio. Harold Everett Porter. LC 14-110441. 1914. 1.00. The Century Co.

Henry of Ofterdingen: A Romance. Friedrich Leopold Hardenberg & Tieck, Johann Ludwig, 1773-1858. LC 7-1922. 1842. J. Owen.

Henry of Ofterdingen: A Romance. Friedrich Leopold Hardenberg & Tieck, Johann Ludwig, 1773-1853. 1853. H. H. Moore.

Henry Rand's Family. Ida May Linkins Broughton. LC 38-31048. Chapman & Grimes, Inc.

Henry St. John, Gentleman. John Esten Cooke. (American Historical Novel Ser). 1859. 13.95 o.s.i. (ISBN 0-512-00828-0). Garrett Pr.

Henry St. John: Gentleman, of "Flower of Hundreds," in the County of Prince George, Virginia. A Tale of 1774-75... John Esten Cooke. LC 41-32422. 1859. Harper & Brothers.

Henry Smeaton: A Jacobite Story of the Reign of George the First. George Payne Rainsford James. LC 7-8000. Harper & Brothers.

Henry the Eight and His Court. Klara Muller Mundt. Tr. by Pierce, Henry Niles. LC 16-1240. (historical romances of Louisa Muhlbach pseud.). D. Appleton and Company.

Henry the Sheriff. Wilbur C Tuttle. LC 36-5938. 1936. Houghton Mifflin Company.

Henry Viii. and His Court: Or Catharine Parr. An Historical Novel. Klara Muller Mundt. Tr. by Pierce, Henry Niles. LC 7-25468. 1867. D. Appleton and Company.

Henry VIII and His Six Wives. Maureen Peters. LC 72-78434. 1972. 5.50. St. Martin's Press.

Henry Wallace: Or The Victim of Lottery Gambling. A Moral Tale. J. R. McDowell. LC 7-16281. 1832. Wilson & Swain.

Henry Worthington, Idealist. Margaret Pollock Sherwood. LC 99-3677. 1899. The Macmillan Company.

Henry's War. Jeremy Brooks. pap. 0.95 o.p. (ISBN 0-14-002140-X). Penguin.

Hen's House: A Novel. Peter Israel. LC 66-20285. 1967. Putnam.

Hepburn. Jan Vlachos Westcott. LC 50-6477. 1950. Crown Publishers.

Hephaestus Plague. Thomas Page. LC 73-78646. 1973. 5.95 (ISBN 0-399-11184-0). Putnam.

Hephaestus Plague. Thomas Page. 1975. (pbk.) 1.75. Bantam Books.

Hephzibah Guinness. facsimile ed. Silas Weir Mitchell. LC 74-178448. (Short Story Index Reprint Ser.). Repr. of 1880 ed. 12.50 (ISBN 0-8369-4049-0). Ayer Co.

Hephzibah Guinness; Thee and You: And A Draft on the Bank of Spain. Silas Weir Mitchell. LC 74-178448. (Short story index reprint series). 1971. (ISBN 0-8369-4049-0). Books for Libraries Press.

Hephzibah Guinness: Thee and You; and A Draft on the Bank of Spain. Silas Weir Mitchell. LC 7-31095. 1880. J. B. Lippincott & Co.

Hephzibah Guinness: Thee and You; and A Draft on the Bank of Spain. Silas Weir Mitchell. 1899. The Century Co.

Hepplestall's. Harold Brighouse. LC 22-741192. 1922. R. M. McBride & Company.

Hepsey Burke. Frank Noyes Westcott. LC 15-17804. The H. K. Fly Company.

Heptameron of Margaret: Queen of Navarre. flameng ed. Marguerite d'Angouleme. LC 7-16593. 1876. Gebbie and Barrie, Importers.

Heptameron of the Tales of Margaret: Queen of Navarre (Newly Tr. into English) from the Authentic Text, Based on the Mss. in the Possession of the Societe Des Bibliophiles Francais. Marguerite d'Angouleme. Ed. by Le Roux De Lincy, Antoine Jean Victor. Vizetelly, Ernest Alfred. LC 2-29621. Printed for the Bibliophilist Library.

Heptameron: Or, Tales and Novels of Marguerite, Queen of Navarre; Tr. Marguerite d'Angouleme. Tr. by Machen, Arthur. (On cover: Early novelists; ed. by E. A. Baker). 1905. G. Routledge & Sons, Limited.

Heptameron: Tales and Novels of Marguerite, Queen of Navarre. Marguerite D'Angouleme. LC 74-48439. (Classics of European Literature). (Series: Borzoi classics.). (Hyperion Library of world literature). 1977. 14.50. (ISBN 0-88355-574-3) (ISBN 0-88355-575-1). Hyperion Press.

Her. Anonymous. LC 77-125827. 1970. 6.00. L. Stuart.

Her. Lawrence Ferlinghetti. LC 60-9221. (New Directions paperbook no. 88). 1960. New Directions.

Her American Daughter. Annie T Colcock. LC 6-36. 1905. The Neale Publishing Company.

Her Anal Lovers. Sterling Harkins. 192p. pap. 1.95 o.p. (6172). Brandon.

Her Back to the Wall. Andrew Laird. pap. 1.95 o.s.i. (OPH-197, Ophelia). Olympia.

Her-Bak, "Chick-Pea" The Living Face of Ancient Egypt. Schwaller De Lubicz, Isha. LC 72-194873. (Penguin metaphysical library). 3.95 (ISBN 0-14-003448-X). Penguin Books.

Her-Bak, "Chick-Pea" The Living Face of Ancient Egypt. Schwaller De Lubicz, Isha & Lucie Lamy. LC 78-7459. 1978. 6.95 (ISBN 0-89281-003-3). Inner Traditions International.

Her-Bak: Egyptian Initiate. Isha Schwaller De Lubicz. Tr. by Ronald Fraser. LC 68-119197. 1967. 7.00 o.p. Verry.

Her-Bak, Egyptian Initiate. Schwaller De Lubicz, Isha & Lucie Lamy. LC 77-28467. (Illus.). 1978. 6.95 (ISBN 0-89281-002-5). Inner Traditions International.

Her-Bak, the Living Face of Ancient Egypt. Isha Schwaller De Lubicz. Tr. by Charles E. Spague from Fr. (Illus.). 368p. 1980. pap. 8.95 (ISBN 0-89281-003-3). Inner Tradit.

Her Beautiful Hands: A Romantic Novel of Milwaukee Life. Paul Goadby Gregory. LC 50-5572. 1950. Inter-Ocean Book Co.

Her Best Friend's Husband. Betty Wright. (Orig.). 1981. pap. 2.95 (ISBN 0-89083-868-2). Zebra.

Her Black Body. Sallie Wear Laing. LC 22-408899. 1921. The Essex Press.

Her Blind Folly. Henry M Ross. LC 6-6971. 1906. Benziger Brothers.

Her Body Speaks. Aaron Marc Stein. LC 31-196818. 1931. Covici, Friede.

Her Boston Experiences: A Picture of Modern Boston Society and People. Anna Farquhar Bergengren. LC 3938. 1960. L. C. Page & Co.

Her Boy Friend. Joy Wheeler Dow. LC 34-41968. 1934. Imprinted by Y' Meador Press.

Her Bridge to Happiness. Sallie Lee Bell. LC 61-16196. 1961. Zondervan Pub. House.

Her Bright Future... Eva Katherine Clapp Gibson. LC 6-25375. 1880. H. A. Summer and Company.

Her Bright Future... Eva Katherine Clapp Gibson. LC 11-10518. G. W. Ogilvie.

Her Brother Donnard. Emily Elizabeth Ferris Veeder. LC 8-30206. 1890. J. B. Lippincott Company.

Her Brother's Letters: Wherein Miss Christine Carson, of Cincinnati, Is Shown How the Affairs of Girls and Women Are Regarded by Men in General and, in Particular, by Her Brother, Lent Carson, Lawyer, of New York City. Anonymous. Drawings by F. Vaux Wilson and C. M. Relyea. LC 6-34373. 1906. Moffat, Yard & Company.

Her Bungalow: An Atlantian Memory. Nancy McKay Gordon, pseud. LC 98-2265. 1898. Hermetic Publishing Co.

Her Christmas at the Hermitage: A Tale About Rachel and Andrew Jackson. 1st Ed. Helen Topping Miller. LC 55-9896. 1955. Longmans, Green.

Her Closed Hands. Bertram Lenox Simpson. LC 27-193176. 1927. The Macmillan Company.

Her Country. Mary Raymond Shipman Andrews. LC 13-10963. 1918. C. Scribner's Sons.

Her Crime ... LC 7-4277. (No name series. 3d series, v. 13). 1882. Roberts Brothers.

Her Day in Court. Peggy Dern, pseud. 2.95. Arcadia House.

Her Dearest Foe. Annie French Hector. (Seaside library, v. 2 no. 30). 1877. G. Munro.

Her Dearest Foe. Annie French Hector. (On cover: The home library). A. L. Burt Company.

Her Dearest Foe: A Novel. Annie French Hector. LC 7-516634. (Leisure hour series no. 56). 1876. H. Holt and Company.

Her Dearest Foe. A Novel. Annie French Hector. (On cover: Seaside library. Pocket ed., no. 806). 1886. G. Munro.

Her Death of Cold: A Father Dowling Mystery. Ralph M McInerny. LC 76-39728. 7.95 (ISBN 0-8149-0781-4). Vanguard Press.

Her Death of Cold: A Father Dowling Mystery. Ralph M McInerny. LC 79-4266. 1979. 9.95 (ISBN 0-89340-196-X). J. Curley.

Her Decision. Irma Walker. LC 81-22922. (Love & Life; 3). 1982. 1.75 (ISBN 0-345-29875-6). Ballantine Books.

Her Demon Lover. Wendy Perriam. LC 80-1865. 1981. 11.95 (ISBN 0-385-17374-1). Doubleday.

Her Demon Lover. Janet Louise Roberts. (Kangaroo Book). 1.75 (ISBN 0-671-81307-2). Pocket Books.

Her Desert Lover. Florence Stonebreaker. LC 43-12153. 1943. Phoenix Press.

Her Double Life. Harriet Lewis. (ledger library, no. 1). R. Bonner's Sons.

Her Dream Prince. Rob Eden. LC 50-13584. 1949. Gramercy Pub. Co.

Her Elephant Man: A Story of the Sawdust Ring. Pearl Doles Bell. LC 19-155634. 1919. R. M. McBride & Company.

Her Fair Fame: A Novel. Edgar Fawcett. LC 6-38795. 1894. Merrill & Baker.

Her Fairy Prince. Gertrude Warden. LC 8-34843. (On cover: Lippincott's select novels, no. 174). 1895. J. B. Lippincott Company.

Her Faithful Knight. Gertrude Warden. LC 1065. Street & Smith.

Her Faithful Knight: A Novel. Maria Henrietta De La Cherois Crommelin. (Manhattan library of new copyright fiction). 1902. A. L. Burt Company.

Her Father's Daughter. Gene Stratton Porter. LC 21-14286. 1921. Doubleday, Page & Company.

Her Father's Daughter. Gene Stratton-Porter. 1974. Repr. of 1921 ed. lib. bdg. 25.00 (ISBN 0-8414-7978-X). Folcroft.

Her Father's Daughter. A Novel. Katharine Tynan Hinkson, pseud. LC 1-25826. 1901. Benzinger Brothers.

Her Father's House. Leonard Lloyde Burns. LC 55-136126. 1955. Bruce Humphries.

Her Father's House: Here Is Eleanor, Daughter of Gethin Tretower, Gentleman of the Hafod, in the County of Radnor; Wife of Evan Harris; Shepherdess, Maidservant, Exile, and Wayfarer. She Loved Her Father's House. Hilda Vaughan. LC 30-13094. 1930. Harper & Brothers.

Her Father's Name. Florence Marryat Church Lean. (On cover: Seaside library. Pocket ed. no. 1251). 1889. G. Munro.

Her Father's Right Hand, and Nannie's Heroism. E Delauney De Melville. LC 6-34199. (On cover: The Catholic home library). 1892. Benziger Brothers.

Her Father's Share: A Novel. Edith Mary Power. LC 16-23627. 1916. Benziger Brothers.

Her Father's Voice. Elsie Goerner Friedlander. LC 24-8656. Lincoln Printing Company.

Her Fiance. facs. ed. Josephine Dodge Daskam Bacon. LC 73-121520. (Short Story Index Reprint Ser). 1904. 12.00 (ISBN 0-8369-3476-8). Ayer Co.

Her Fiance: Four Stories of College Life. Josephine Dodge Daskam Bacon. LC 73-121520. (Short story index reprint series). (Illus.). 1970. Books for Libraries Press.

Her Fiance: Four Stories of College Life. Josephine Dodge Daskam Bacon. LC 4-22966. 1904. H. Altemus Company.

Her First Adventure: A Metaphysical Narrative. Egbert G Roe. LC 7-40251. (On cover: Vanity fair series, no. 2). 1891. E. Brandus & Co.

Her First Appearance. Richard Harding Davis. LC 1-27441. 1901. Harper & Brothers.

Her First Hot Summer. Crown Maricot. pap. 1.95 o.p. (8003). Cameo.

Her First Sin: By Jack Woodford Pseud.... Josiah Pitts Woolfolk. LC 44-4119. 1944. Phoenix Press.

Her Fondest Hope. Rob Eden. LC 49-11954. 1949. Gramercy Pub. Co.

Her Foreign Conquest: A Novel. Richard Henry Savage. LC 8-2003. The Home Publishing Co.

Her French Husband. Phyllis Hastings. LC 56-5007. 1956. Dutton.

Her Gentle Deeds. Henrietta Keddie. LC 7-11416. (On cover: Seaside library. Pocket ed. no. 160). G. Munro.

Her Girlhood's Lover. Bertha N Clay. (On cover: The Melbourne ser., no. 8). 1893. Melbourne Publishing Co.

Her Golden Hours: The Confidences of a Modern Girl. LC 16-23588. 1916. Moffat, Yard & Company.

Her Good Name. Vida Hurst. Gramercy Publishing Co.

Her Grace Presents... By March Cost Pseud. Peggy Morrison, pseud. LC 57-6830. 1957. Lippincott.

Her Great Surprise. Harlan Page Halsey. LC 7-1188. (On cover: Parlor car series, no. 4). The Parlor Car Publishing Co.

Her Guiding Voice. John Edward Ambrose. LC 23-11446. The Christopher Publishing House.

Her Heart in Her Throat. Ethel Lina White. LC 42-20280. 1942. Harper & Brothers.

Her Heart Was True: A Story of the Peninsular War Founded on Fact. E. M. Cuttim. LC 6-32235. ("Unknown" library, v. 21). Cassell Publishing Company.

Her Heart's Captain. Elizabeth Mansfield, pseud. 192p. 1983. pap. 2.25 (ISBN 0-425-05501-9). Berkley Pub.
Her Hearts Desire. Lynna Cooper, pseud. Bd. with Offer of Marriage. 1980. pap. 1.75 (ISBN 0-451-09081-0, E9081, Sig). NAL.
Her Heart's Desire. Lynna Cooper. (Signet Book). 1976. (pbk.) 0.95. New American Library.
Her Heart's Desire. Henriette Eugenie Delamare. LC 15-7363. 0.75. H. L. Kilner & Co.
Her Heart's Desire. Charles Garvice. (On cover: Munro's library of popular novels. no. 267). 1898. G. Munro's Sons.
Her Heart's Desire: An Offer of Marriage. Lynna Cooper. 1983. pap. 2.95 (ISBN 0-451-12017-5, Sig). NAL.
Her Heart's Gift. Oliver Kent. LC 13-18224. 1.25. G. W. Dillingham Company.
Her Highness: An Adirondack Romance. LC 10-15397. 1910. R. G. Badger.
Her Home. Victor Briggs. 416p. 1982. pap. 2.75 (ISBN 0-441-32788-5). Ace Bks.
Her Husband: The Mystery of a Man. Julia Magruder. LC 11-283584. Small, Maynard and Company.
Her Husband's Country. Sybil Swendolen Spottiswoode. LC 11-16889. 1911. Duffield and Company.
Her Husband's Friend. Linn Boyd Porter. LC 7-37771. (On cover: The albatross novels). 1891. G. W. Dillingham.
Her Husband's House. Catherine Pomeroy Stewart. LC 46-1913. 1946. C. Scribner's Sons.
Her Husband's Purse. Helen Reimensnyder Martin. LC 16-6759. 1916. 1.35. Doubleday, Page & Company.
Her Husband's Wife. Herman Alfred Kasen. LC 35-3116. 1934. G. H. Watt.
Her Infinite Variety. Brand Whitlock. LC 4-3396. 1904. The Bobbs-Merrill Company.
Her Johnnie. Henrietta Eliza Vaughan Stannard. LC 8-13459. (On cover: Lovell's library. v. 20, no. 963). 1887. J. W. Lovell Company.
Her Johnnie. By Violet Whyte Pseud. Henrietta Eliza Vaughan Stannard. (On cover: Seaside library. Pocket ed. no. 956). 1887. G. Munro.
Her Journey's End. Frances Cooke. LC 11-6713. 1911. 1.25. Benziger Brothers.
Her Knight Comes Riding. John Van Alstyne Weaver. LC 28-185001. 1928. London, A. A. Knopf.
Her Knight on a Barge. Margaret SeBastian, pseud. 1979. 1.75 (ISBN 0-445-04399-7). Popular Library.
Her Ladyship... Thomas C. Minor. LC 7-19690. 1880. P. G. Thomson.
Her Ladyship's Companion. Joanna W. Bourne. (Regency Romance Ser.). 224p. 1983. pap. 2.75 (ISBN 0-380-81596-6, 81596-6). Avon.
Her Ladyship's Conscience. Ellen Thorneycroft Fowler. LC 13-24833. Hodder and Stoughton.
Her Ladyship's Elephant. David Dwight Wells. LC 5-2443. 1898. H. Holt and Company.
Her Last Performance. Wade S Gray. LC 44-521616. 1944. Rapid Printing & Publishing Co.
Her Last Throw. A Novel. Margaret Wolfe Hungerford. LC 7-93630. (On cover: Lovell's Westminster series. no. 1). 1890. J. W. Lovell Company.
Her Little Highness. A Novel. Nataly Von Eschstruth & Lathrop, Elise L, Tr. LC 6-38156. (choice ser. no. 109). 1894. R. Bonner's Sons.
Her Little Highness. A Novel. Nataly Von Eschstruth & Lathrop, Elise L., Tr. LC 6-38155. (ledger library. no 109). 1894. R. Bonner's Sons.
Her Little World. Sarah E Chester. LC 11-17968. American Tract Society.
Her Little Young Ladyship. Myra Kelly. LC 11-22134. 1911. 1.25. C. Scribner's Sons.
Her Lord and Master. Florence Marryat Church Lean. LC 7-13600. (On cover: Lovell's library. v. 19. no. 905). 1887. J. W. Lovell Company.
Her Lord and Master. Martha Morton & Morton, Victoria. LC 3-4671. 1902. D. Biddle.
Her Love and His Life: A Novel. Frederick William Robinson. LC 7-41983. (On cover: Harper's Franklin square library, no. 689). 1891. Harper & Brothers.
Her Love, Her Ruin: Or, The Deadly Love. Adolphe Belot. (On cover: Richard K. Fox's sensational series, no. 3). 1892. R. K. Fox.
Her Love Problem. Laura Lou Brookman. LC 28-235399. Grosset & Dunlap.
Her Magic Island. Helen E. Yates. Ed. by Alice Sachs. 1971. 3.95 o.p. Lenox Hill.
Her Majesty; a Romance of to-Day. Elizabeth Knight Tompkins. (The Hudson library, no. 6). 1895. G. P. Putnam's Sons.
Her Majesty the King: A Romance of the Harem; Done into American from the Arabic. James Jeffrey Roche. LC 98-1654. 1899. R. G. Badger & Co.
Her Majesty the Queen. A Novel. John Esten Cooke. LC 1-31527. 1901. G. W. Dillingham Co.
Her Majesty's Captain: Being the Manuscript of Robert Dudley, Duke of Northumberland, Earl of Warwick, and Earl of Leicester in the Holy Roman Empire, from His Own Hand: a Novel. Derek A Wilson. LC 78-24309. 9.95 (ISBN 0-316-94497-1). Little, Brown.
Her Majesty's Mice. Norman Ward. LC 77-369938. (Illus.). 10.00 (ISBN 0-7710-8824-8). McClelland and Stewart.
Her Majesty's Rebels. Sidney Royse Lysaght. LC 7-35217. 1907. Macmillan and Co., Limited.
Her Man. Beatrice Burton Morgan. LC 26-13536. Grosset & Dunlap.
Her Man of Affairs. Elizabeth Mansfield, pseud. (Orig.). 1980. pap. 2.25 (ISBN 0-425-04595-1). Berkley Pub.
Her Martyrdom. Charlotte Mary Brame. (On cover: Lovell's library. v. 13. no. 680). John W. Lovell Company.
Her Martyrdom. Charlotte Mary Brame. LC 44-12253. (On cover: Seaside library. Pocket ed. No. 576). G. Munro.
Her Mash Letters. LC 7-4281. (Dillingham's American authors library, no. 20). 1896. G. W. Dillingham Co.
Her Master. Marcel Prevost. Tr. by Terry, Jane. LC 31-22657. Sears Publishing Company, Inc.
Her Memory. Jozua Marius Willem Van Der Poorten Schwartz. LC 98-645. 1898. D. Appleton and Company.
Her Mothers. E. M Broner. LC 75-938. 1975. 7.95 (ISBN 0-03-014721-2). Holt, Rinehart and Winston.
Her Mothers. E. M Broner. (Berkley medallion book). 1976. 1.75 (ISBN 0-425-03206-X). Berkely.
Her Mother's Darling. A Novel. Charlotte Eliza Lawson Cowan Riddell. (Seaside library, v. 41, no. 847). 1880. G. Munro.
Her Mother's Daughter. Nalbro Isadorah Bartley. LC 26-15400. George H. Doran Company.
Her Mother's Daughter. Vida Hurst. LC 42-25438. 1942. Gramercy Publishing Company.
Her Mother's Sin. Charlotte Mary Brame. (On cover: Lovell's library. v. 4. no. 183). John W. Lovell Company.
Her Mother's Sin. Charlotte Mary Brame. LC 44-38165. (On cover: Seaside library. Pocket ed. No. 19). G. Munro.
Her Mother's Sin. Charlotte Mary Brame. (On cover: The Charlotte M. Braeme series, no. 1). G. Munro.
Her Mother's Sin: Or, A Bright Wedding Day. Charlotte Mary Brame. LC 4263. (Bertha Clay library, no. 9). 1900. Street & Smith.
Her Mountain Lover. Hamlin Garland. LC 1-31298. 1901. The Century Co.
Her Mountain Lover see Collected Works.
Her Naked Soul. Anna Spanuth Webb. LC 7-13434. Broadway Publishing Company.
Her Name Was Tokio. Charles Lloyd-Jones. LC 34-28968. Farrar & Rinehart, Incorporated.
Her Nurse's Vengeance: A Novel. George H Masson. (On cover: American novelists' series, no. 36). 1890. J. W. Lovell Company.
Her Object in Life. Isabella Fyvie Mayo. (seaside library. v. 75, no. 1527). 1883. G. Munro.
Her Only Brother. Bertha Behrens & Wylie, Jean W., Tr. LC 6-9746. T. Y. Crowell & Co.
Her Only Sin and His Broken Promise. Bertha M. Clay. LC 1-5237. (With Brame, Charlotte M. On her wedding morn. New York 1900)). 1900. Street & Smith.
Her Own Devices. C G Compton. LC 6-30381. (Pioneer series). 1896. E. Arnold.
Her Own Doing: A Novel. William Edward Norris. LC 7-33181. (Harper's handy series, no. 80). 1886. Harper & Brothers.
Her Own Doing. A Novel. William Edward Norris. (On cover: Seaside library. Pocket ed. no. 824). 1886. G. Munro.
Her Own Life. Alice Marie Dodge. LC 39-254421. Phoenix Press.
Her Own Person. Carole N. Douglas. (Love & Life Romance Ser.). 176p. (Orig.). 1982. pap. 1.75 (ISBN 0-345-30733-X). Ballantine.
Her Own Sister. Emma Sara Williamson. (On cover: Seaside library. Pocket ed. no. 984). 1887. G. Munro.
Her Own Sort, and Others. Charles Belmont Davis. LC 17-7925. 1917. 1.35. C. Scribner's Sons.
Her Pauper Knight. Shirley Brander. LC 31-8682. E. J. Clode, Inc.
Her Picture. Philip Gilbert Hammerton. LC 7-957. (No name series. 2d series, v. 11). 1882. Roberts Brothers.
Her Pirate Partner. Berta Ruck. LC 27-3939. 1927. Dodd, Mead & Company.
Her Place Assigned. A Story for Older Sunday-School Scholars. Walter Erwin Schuette. LC 8-2049. (On cover: The John Rung prize series). Lutheran Publication Society.
Her Place in the World. Amanda Minnie Douglas. LC 6-33483. Lee and Shepard.
Her Playthings: Men. A Novel. Mabel Esmonde Cahill. LC 6-218743. 1890. Russell Bros., Printers.
Her Prairie Knight, and Rowdy of the "Cross L,". Bertha Muzzy Sinclair. LC 7-23641. 1907. G. W. Dillingham Company.
Her Price. May Walsh. LC 37-13707. King Bros., Inc.
Her Private Devil. Anita Blackmon Smith. LC 34-12033. 1934. W. Goodwin, Inc.
Her Private Lover. James Noble Gifford. LC 43-6906. 1943. Phoenix Press.
Her Private Passions. Marty Holland. LC 49-1756. (New Avon library181). 1948. Avon Pub. Co.
Her Privates, We. Frederic Manning & Private 19022. LC 30-15624. 1930. G. P. Putnam's Sons.
Her Promise True. Dora Russell. LC 12-384201. (On cover: Globe library, vol. ii. no. 282). Rand, McNally & Company.
Her Provincial Cousin: A Story of Brittany. Edith Elmer Wood. LC 9-508. (On cover: The "unknown" library no. 20.). The Cassell Publishing Co.
Her Ready-Made Family. Julia MacNair Wright. LC 9-9123. The National Temperance Society and Publication House.
Her Reason. Anonymous. LC 12-20200. 1912. The Macaulay Company.
Her Reputation. Talbot Mundy. LC 38-3171. A. L. Burt Company.
Her Reputation. Talbot Mundy & King, Bradley. LC 23-12711. The Bobbs-Merrill Company.
Her Rescue from the Turks: A Novel. St. George Rathborne. (On cover: Neely's library of choice literature, no. 59). 1896. F. T. Neely.
Her Rescue from the Turks: A Novel. St. George Rathborne. LC 954. (On cover: Eagle library, no. 142). 1899. Street & Smith.
Her Right Divine. Oliver Kent. LC 13-633582. 1.25. G. W. Dillingham Company.
Her Roman Lover. Eugenia Brooks Frothingham. LC 11-250142. 1911. 1.25. Houghton Mifflin Company.
Her Sacrifice. Zelda Edloe Davies. LC 13-24117. 1913. 1.25. Broadway Publishing Company.
Her Sailor: A Love Story. Marshall Saunders. LC 183. 1900. L. C. Page and Company.
Her Sailor Love. Katharine Sarah Gadsden Macquoid. (Seaside library, v. 83, no. 1684). 1883. G. Munro.
Her Second Choice. Charlotte M. Stanley McKenna. LC 8-28183. (On cover: The library of American authors. no. 27). 1890. G. Munro.
Her Second Love. Bertha M. Clay. LC 1-30007. 1900. Street & Smith.
Her Second Love... Annie Ogle. LC 7-324977. T. B. Peterson & Brothers.
Her Secret Fear. Adel Pryor, pseud. LC 72-146566. 1971. 3.50. Zondervan Pub. House.
Her Secret Self. Rhondi Villot. (Sweet Dreams Ser.: No. 25). 1982. pap. 1.95 (ISBN 0-553-22543-X). Bantam.
Her Secret Star. Bennie Caroline Hall. LC 47-31423. 1947. Gramercy Pub. Co.
Her Secret World. Stanley Lawton. 1947. William-Frederick Press.
Her Senator: A Novel. Archibald Clavering Gunter. LC 6-46702. The Home Publishing Co.
Her Serence Highness. Collin Brooks. LC 29-5695. J. H. Sears & Company, Inc.
Her Serene Highness. David Graham Phillips. (American Author Ser.). 1981. Repr. lib. bdg. 19.00. Scholarly.
Her Serene Highness. David Graham Phillips. Ed. by Donald Pizer. LC 76-96669. (American Authors Ser). 1970. lib. bdg. 14.00 o.s.i. (ISBN 0-512-00544-3). Garrett Pr.
Her Serene Highness: A Novel. David Graham Phillips. LC 2-13256. 1902. Harper & Brothers.
Her Shadowed Life: A Romance of St. Augustine. Beatrice Marean. LC 7-204433. (On cover: The Lucile series, no. 3). E. A. Weeks and Company.
Her Shattered Idol, by. Belle V Logan. LC 7-14800. (On cover: The Midland series. v. 1, no. 38). 1893. Morrill, Higgins & Co.
Her Shining Splendor. Valerie Sherwood. 576p. (Orig.). 1980. pap. 3.95 (ISBN 0-446-30536-7). Warner Bks.
Her Side of It. Thomas Savage. LC 80-25755. 12.50 (ISBN 0-316-77157-0). Little, Brown.
Her Sin. Harry Whittington. LC 47-17703. 1947. Phoenix Press.
Her Sister's Rival. Albert Delpit. Tr. by Loranger, Alexina. LC 6-34174. (library of choice fiction. no. 25). 1891. Laird & Lee.
Her Son: A Chronicle of Love. Horace Annesley Vachell. LC 7-31481. 1907. Dodd, Mead & Company.
Her Son: A Chronicle of Youth. Margaret Witter Fuller. LC 29-4420. 1929. W. Morrow & Company.
Her Son's Wife. Dorothea Frances Canfield Fisher. LC 26-15178. Harcourt, Brace and Company.
Her Son's Wife. Dorothea Frances Canfield Fisher. LC 42-236418. (National home library, 17). 1936. National Home Library Foundation.
Her Son's Wife. M. V. B. Smith. (On cover: Munro's library, no. 672). 1886. N. L. Munro.
Her Soul and Her Body. Louise Hale. 1912. Moffat, Yard and Company.
Her Soul to Keep. Marguerite Mooers Marshall. LC 40-335932. 1940. Macrae Smith Company.
Her Stepfather's House. June Wetherell. (Orig.). 1972. pap. 0.95 o.s.i. (75-367). Lancer.
Her Strange Amour: Or, More Than Satisfied. LC 7-4278. (On cover: Minerva series, no. 57). 1891. The Minerva Publishing Company.
Her Strange Fate: A Novel. Celia Logan Connelly. LC 7-18771. (On cover: The household library, no. 20, v. 4). 1888. Belford, Clarke and Company.
Her Strange Sweet Agony. Laura Grimes. pap. 1.95 o.p. (8015). Cameo.
Her Tragic Fate. Henryk Sienkiewicz & Bay, Jens Christian, 1871- Tr. LC 42-35040. Hurst & Company.
Her Two Husbands: And Other Novelettes. Emile Zola & Cox, George D., Tr. LC 9-13238. T. B. Peterson & Brothers.
Her Two Millions. The Story of a Fortune. William Westall. LC 15-23104. (Harper's Franklin square library. no. 609). 1887. Harper & Brothers.
Her Unborn Child. Grace Hayward & Hatton, Frederic, 1879- LC 30-7198. World Wide Publishing Co., Inc.
Her Unwelcome Husband. Walter Lionel George. LC 22-18090. Harper & Brothers.
Her Victory. Alan Sillitoe. LC 82-215199. 1982. 16.95 (ISBN 0-531-09884-2). F. Watts.
Her Waiting Heart. Henrietta Hardy Hammond. LC 7-563. 1875. The Authors' Publishing Company.
Her Wall of Sophistication. 1st Ed. Ingeborg Iversen Duffy. LC 56-125994. 1957. Pageant Press.
Her Wanton Majesty. Gleb Botkin. LC 33-28938. The Maculay Company.
Her Washington Experiences: As Related by a Cabinet Minister's Wife in a Series of Letters to Her Sister. Anna Farquhar Bergengren. LC 1-18547. 1902. L. C. Page & Company.
Her Washington Season. Jeanie Thomas Gould Lincoln. 1884. J. R. Osgood and Company.
Her Ways Are Death. Jack Mann. 287p. 1981. 6.50. Bookfinger.
Her Wedding Night: A Story. Guy Kenneth Whiteside. 1909. Printed by G. K. Whiteside.
Her Week's Amusement. Margaret Wolfe Hungerford. LC 7-9362. (On cover: Lovell's library. v. 16, no. 792). 1886. J. W. Lovell Company.
Her Weight in Gold. George Barr McCutcheon. LC 12-9958. 1912. Dodd, Mead and Company.
Her Weight in Gold. George Barr McCutcheon. LC 14-6236. 1914. Dodd, Mead and Company.
Her Wild Oat. Earl Marion Seel. LC 21-18243. Dorrance & Company.
Her Wings. Francis Newton Symmes Allen. LC 14-16471. 1914. Houghton Mifflin Company.
Her Word of Honor. Edith Macvane. 1912. Little, Brown, and Company.
Her Work: Stories by Texas Women. Ed. by Lou H. Rodenberger. LC 82-60562. 347p. 1982. 16.95 (ISBN 0-940672-05-7); pap. 8.95 (ISBN 0-940672-04-9). Shearer Pub.
Her World Against a Lie: By Florence Marryat... Florence Marryat Church Lean. (On cover: Lovell's library. v. 20. no. 979). 1887. J. W. Lovell Company.
Her World of Men. Maysie Greig. LC 38-12836. 1938. Doubleday, Doran & Company, Inc.
Her Young Lover. Jim Layne. LC 63-21020. Universal Pub. and Distributing Corp.
Herald. Michael Shaara. LC 80-27495. 11.95. McGraw-Hill.
Herald of Doom. John Creasey. LC 74-4457. (Rinehart suspense novel). 1975. (ISBN 0-03-012226-0). Holt, Rinehart and Winston.
Herald of the West: An American Story of 1811-1815. Joseph Alexander Altsheler. LC 98-686. 1898. D. Appleton and Company.
Herald Personal: The Secret Agents of Brazil, Nick Carter's Vacation; Three Complete Stories of the Exploits of Nicholas Carter Pseud. America's Greatest Detective. John Russell Coryell. LC 1584. (On cover: Magnet detective library, no. 117). 1900. Street & Smith.
Herald to Chaos: The Novels of Elizabeth Madox Roberts. Earl H Rovit. LC 60-13722. 5.00. University of Kentucky Press.
Heralds of Empire: Being the Story of One Ramsay Stanhope, Lieutenant to Pierre Radisson in the Northern Fur Trade. Agnes Christina Laut. LC 2-12480. 1902. D. Appleton and Company.
Herapath Property. Joseph Smith Fletcher. LC 21-201965. 1921. A. A. Knopf.
Herb-Moon: A Fantasia. Pearl Mary Teresa Richards Craigie. LC 6-31096. 1896. Frederick A. Stokes Company.
Herb of Grace. Rosa Nouchette Carey. 1901. J. B. Lippincott Company.

Herbert Gardenell's Children. Susanna Rebecca Graham Clark. (On cover: Yensie Walton books). D. Lothrop Company.
Herbert Lacy. Thomas Henry Lister. 1828. Carey, Lea & Carey.
Herbert Severance. A Novel. Mary French Sheldon. LC 8-5099. (On cover: The Rialto series, no. 15). 1889. Rand, McNally & Company.
Herbert Vanlennert. Charles Francis Keary. 1895. J. B. Lippincott Company.
Herbert Wendall: A Tale of the Revolution ... LC 5-18456. 1835. Harper & Brothers.
Herbs and Apples. Helen Hooven Santmyer. 1925. Houghton Mifflin Company.
Hercule and the Gods. Pierre Audemars. LC 46-493276. 1946. Rinehart & Company, Inc.
Hercule Poirot: Master Detective... Agatha Miller Christie. LC 36-15687. 1936. Dodd, Mead & Company.
Hercule Poirot's Christmas. Agatha Miller Christie. (Greenway Ed.). 8.95 (ISBN 0-396-06963-0). Dodd.
Hercule Poirot's Christmas see Death in the Clouds.
Hercule Poirot's Early Cases. Agatha Miller Christie. LC 74-11501. 1974. 6.95 (ISBN 0-396-07021-3). Dodd, Mead.
Hercule Poirot's Early Cases. Agatha Miller Christie. LC 74-32271. 1975. 12.95 (ISBN 0-8161-6265-4). G. K. Hall.
Herculean: Or, From the Ferris Wheel to the Sun. Richard S Johnson. LC 10-4194. 1894.
Hercules Brand. Arthur M. Cummings. LC 6-32171. 1885. National Temperance Society and Publication House.
Hercules, My Shipmate. Robert Graves. 464p. 1945. pap. 8.95 (ISBN 0-374-51677-4). FS&G.
Hercules, My Shipmate: A Novel. Robert Graves. LC 45-8179. 1945. Creative Age Press, Inc.
Hercules, My Shipmate: A Novel. Robert Graves. LC 79-9879. 1979. 29.75 (ISBN 0-313-20991-X). Greenwood Press.
Hercules, the Big Greek Story. George Kirgo. LC 58-6755. 1958. Abelard-Schuman.
Herd: A Story. Jane Olive Patricia Ward. 1908. Cochrane Publishing Co.
Herd Boy and His Hermit. Charlotte Mary Yonge. LC 5-9279. 1889. T. Whittaker.
Herdsman. Dorothy Clarke Wilson. LC 46-215753. 1946. The Westminster Press.
Herdsman & the Linden Tree. Vincas Kreve. Tr. by Baranauskas et al. 1964. 3.95 (ISBN 0-87141-010-9). Manyland.
Herdsman and the Linden Tree. Vincas Kreve-Mickervicius. LC 64-23673. 1964. Manyland Books.
Here. Maryann Forrest. LC 74-96777. 1970. 4.95. Coward-McCann.
Here. Charles Francis Stocking. LC 31-10518. 1931. The Maestro Co.
Here and Beyond. Edith Newbold Jones Wharton. LC 26-95749. 1926. D. Appleton & Company.
Here & Hereafter. Ruth Montgomery. 176p. 1982. pap. 2.50 (ISBN 0-449-24166-1, Crest). Fawcett.
Here and There a Man. Robert Emmet Barrett. LC 19-15225. The Roxburgh Publishing Company, Inc.
Here Are Ladies. James Stephens. LC 13-22511. 1913. 1.25. The Macmillan Company.
Here Are Lovers. Hilda Vaughan. LC 26-17972. 1926. Harper & Brothers.
Here Are My Children. Mona Goodwyn Williams. The Mohawk Press.
Here Are My People. Arthur J. Burks. LC 34-4065. 1934. Funk & Wagnalls Company.
Here at Kennebunkport. Lois Lowry. (Illus., Orig.). 1978. pap. 4.95 (ISBN 0-911764-20-8). Durrell.
Here Be Daemons. Basil Copper. LC 77-99120. 1978. 7.95 (ISBN 0-312-36984-0). St. Martin's Press.
Here Be Dragons. Stella Gibbons. LC 73-154739. 1972. 5.95. White Lion.
Here Before Kilroy. Su Walton. LC 69-10921. 1969. 5.95. Morrow.
Here Come Joe Mungin: A Novel. Chalmers Swinton Murray. LC 42-3382. 1942. G.P. Putnam's Sons.
Here Come Swords! Coutts Brisbane. LC 27-11622. 1926. Dodd, Mead & Company.
Here Come the Brides. Geraldine Napier. (60-2184). 1967. Popular Lib.
Here Come the Brides: A Novel. Bernard Glemser. LC 66-15112. 1966. Crown Publishers.
Here Come the Brides: A Novel. Geraldine Napier. LC 66-15112. 4.50. Crown.
Here Come the Dead. Robert Portner Koehler. LC 42-51189. 1942. Phoenix Press.
Here Come the Hippies. William C. Spatari. (Orig.). pap. 0.95 o.p. (1117). Brandon.
Here Comes a Candle. Jane Aiken Hodge. LC 67-12860. 1967. Doubleday.
Here Comes a Candle... Margaret Storm Jameson. LC 39-27001. 1939. The Macmillan Company.
Here Comes a Candle: A Novel. Fredric Brown. LC 50-8824. 1950. Dutton.
Here Comes a Sailor. Robert Bachmann. LC 32-4451. R. G. Badger.
Here Comes an Old Sailor. Alfred Tresidder Sheppard. LC 28-13164. 1928. Doubleday, Doran & Company, Inc.
Here Comes Charlie. Janice H. Lollis. 150p. 1981. pap. 4.95. Crossroads Prods.
Here Comes Charlie M. Brian Freemantle. LC 77-27701. 1978. 7.95 (ISBN 0-385-13022-8). Doubleday.
Here Comes Charlie M. Brian Freemantle. LC 80-26791. 1981. 11.50 (ISBN 0-89340-313-X). J. Curley.
Here Comes Daredevil. (Super Hero Collection). (Illus., Orig.). 1968. pap. 0.50 o.p. (72-170). Lancer.
Here Comes Jamie: A Novel. William Wetmore. LC 73-105354. 1970. 5.95. Little, Brown.
Here Comes Pete Now. Thomas Anderson. LC 61-6848. 1961. Random House.
Here Comes the Bandwagon. Henry Leyford Gates. LC 28-226630. 1928. Dodd, Mead & Company.
Here Comes the Bride: There Goes Mother. Irene Kampen. LC 67-12899. (Illus.). 1967. World Pub. Co.
Here Comes the Corpse. George A Bagby, pseud. LC 41-5976. 1941. Pub. for the Crime Club by Doubleday, Doran and Company, Inc.
Here Comes the Corpse. Aaron Marc Stein. LC 41-5976. 1941. Pub. for the Crime Club by Doubleday, Doran and Company, Inc.
Here Comes the Judge. Kelly L. Segraves. 1980. pap. 2.95 (ISBN 0-89293-053-5). Beta Bk.
Here Comes the King. Philip Lindsay. LC 33-21273. 1933. Little, Brown, and Company.
Here Comes the Sun! Emilie Baker Loring. LC 24-5101. 1924. The Penn Publishing Company.
Here Comes the Toff. John Creasey. LC 67-23646. 1967. 3.95. Walker.
Here Dwells Enchantment. Winifred Wadell. LC 40-316373. 1940. Arcadia House, Inc.
Here Goes Kitten. Robert Gover. LC 64-13784. 1964. Grove Press.
Here I Stay. Elizabeth Jane Coatsworth. LC 38-275831. 1938. Coward McCann.
Here in This Island. Susanne McConnaughey. LC 55-11351. Appleton-Century-Crofts.
Here Is Einbaum. Wright Morris. LC 73-11149. 1973. (pbk.) 3.00 (ISBN 0-87685-164-2) (ISBN 0-87685-163-4) (ISBN 0-87685-165-0). Black Sparrow Press.
Here Is Joy: By Carol Holliston Pseud. James Noble Gifford. LC 56-898172. 1956. Arcadia House.
Here Is My Body. Josiah Pitts Woolfolk. LC 32-5302. 1931. W. Godwin, Inc.
Here Is My Heart, a Love Story. Ellen Hogue. LC 32-25725. Chelsea House.
Here Is My Home. Robert Gessner. LC 41-277180. Alliance Book Corporation.
Here Lies. Doris Miles Disney. 1967. Repr. pap. 0.60 o.p. (60-296). Manor Bks.
Here Lies a Most Beautiful Lady. Richard Blaker. LC 36-5510. The Bobbs-Merrill Company.
Here Lies Blood. M. M. Mannon. LC 42-13733. 1942. The Bobbs-Merrill Company.
Here Lies Georgia Linz. Paul Mason. LC 68-13700. 1968. World Pub. Co.
Here Lies Gloria Mundy. Gladys Mitchell. 192p. 1983. 9.95 (ISBN 0-312-36986-7). St Martin.
Here Lies Love. Guy Mainwaring Morton. LC 34-5601. 1934. Dodd, Mead & Company.
Here Lies Margot. Pamela Hill. LC 58-5470. 1958. Putnam.
Here Lies Nancy Frail. Jonathan Ross. LC 70-171986. 1972. 5.95 o.p. (ISBN 0-8415-0139-4). Sat Rev Pr.
Here Lies Nancy Frail. John Rossiter. LC 70-171986. 1972. 5.95 (ISBN 0-8415-0139-4). Saturday Review Press.
Here Lies Our Sovereign Lord. Eleanor Hibbert. LC 72-97307. 1973. 6.95 (ISBN 0-399-11137-9). Putnam.
Here Lies Our Sovereign Lord. Jean Plaidy. 320p. 1973. 6.95 o.p. (ISBN 0-399-11137-9). Putnam Pub Group.
Here Lies the Body. Richard Burke. LC 41-26738. G. P. Putnam's Sons.
Here Lies. The Collected Stories of Dorothy Parker. Dorothy Rothschild Parker. LC 39-273963. 1939. The Viking Press.
Here, Now, Always. Edwin Brock. LC 76-54314. 1977. 8.50 (ISBN 0-8112-0638-6) (ISBN 0-8112-0639-4). New Directions Pub. Corp.
Here O'Hara: Three Novels and Twenty Short Stories. John O'Hara. LC 46-4951. 1946. Duell, Sloan and Pearce.
Here There Be Dragons. Robert Bentley. 256p. 1973. 7.95 o.s.i. (ISBN 0-913254-01-0). Ontario Pr.
Here to Die. Mark Sadler, pseud. LC 70-140725. 1971. 4.95 (ISBN 0-394-46763-9). Random House.
Here to Get My Baby Out of Jail. Louise Shivers. LC 82-18536. 11.95 (ISBN 0-394-52388-1). Random House.
Here Today: A Novel. John Coates. LC 50-13189. C.
Here Today and Gone Tomorrow: Four Short Novels. Louis Bromfield. LC 34-741878. 1934. Harper & Brothers.
Here Was a Man. 3rd ed. Norah Robinson Lofts. 1975. pap. 1.25 (ISBN 0-532-12329-8). Woodhill.
Here Was a Man. Norah Robinson Lofts. 1971. pap. 1.25 o.p. (125-112). Manor Bks.
Here Was a Man. 2nd ed. Norah Robinson Lofts. 224p. 1973. pap. 1.25 o.p. (532-12176-125). Manor Bks.
Here Was a Man: A Romantic History of Sir Walter Raleigh, His Voyages His Discoveries, and His Queen. Norah Robinson Lofts. LC 36-25287. 1936. A. A. Knopf.
Here We Go Round the Mulberry Bush. 1st Amer. Ed. Hunter Davies. LC 66-10978. 1966. bds., 4.95. Little.
Heredity and Environment: A Novel of Alaska and the North. Walter S Smith. LC 30-8269. Meador Publishing Company.
Heredity: Or, Harry Harwood's Inheritance. Mary C Woodbury. LC 8-37542. 1892. The McDonald & Gill Co.
Hereford: A Story. Maria Dunton Sparrow. LC 10-5879. 1910. R. G. Badger.
Heremakhonon. Maryse Conde. Tr. by Richard Philcox. LC 81-51667. 188p. 1982. 15.00 (ISBN 0-89410-232-X); pap. 7.00 (ISBN 0-89410-233-8). Three Continents.
Here's Alfred. Robert Shure, pseud. LC 76-55495. (Illus.). 4.95 (ISBN 0-914690-08-6). Rampage.
Here's Blood in Your Eye. Manning Long. LC 41-17614. Duell, Sloan and Pearce.
Here's Luck!". Hugh Wiley. LC 28-20342. J. H. Sears & Company, Inc.
Here's Luck: A Social Footnote. Stephen French Whitman. LC 31-9380. 1931. D. Appleton and Company.
Here's My Heart. Joye Hoekzema. LC 47-23055. 1947. Zondervan Publishing House.
Here's to the Day!". Charles Agnew MacLean & Blighton, Frank Harris, 1874- Joint Author. LC 15-421118. George H. Doran Company.
Here's to the Gods. Austin Parker. LC 23-14266. Harper & Brothers.
Here's to Togetherness: A Modern Fable. Herbert Faulkner West. LC 62-52021. 1961. Westholm Publications.
Here's to Your Health, Comrade Shifrin! Ilia Petrovich Suslov. LC 76-26422. 8.95 (ISBN 0-253-13710-1). Indiana University Press.
Heresiarch and Co. Tr. from French by Remy Inglis Hall. Guillaume Apollinaire. LC 65-21524. 3.95. Doubleday.
Heresiarque et Cie. Guillaume Apollinaire. 8.95. French & Eur.
Heresy. Laurence Snelling. LC 73-8927. 1973. 6.95 (ISBN 0-393-08373-X). Norton.
Heresy of Jacob Hobbs: A Novel. Raymond Durbin Miller. LC 51-10914. 1951. Exposition Press.
Heresy of Yesterday. Cyrenus M Lane. LC 13-23887. Davis & Bond.
Heresy: Or Led to the Light. Hudson Tuttle. LC 37-18314. 1895. The Author.
Heretic. Daniel Alfred Poling. LC 28-24276. 1928. Doubleday, Doran and Company, Inc.
Heretic: A Novel. 1st Amer. Ed. Alison Macleod. LC 66-11222. 1966. 4.50. Houghton.
Heretic of Soana. Gerhart Johann Robert Hauptmann & Morgan, Bayard Quincy, 1883- Tr. LC 24-3457. 1923. B. W.Huebsch, Inc.
Heretic of Soana. Gerhart Johann Robert Hauptmann & Salpeter, Harry. LC 28-23923. (Half-title: The Modern library of the world's best books). The Modern Library.
Heretic of Soana. Introd. by Harold Von Hofe. Tr. from German by Bayard Quincy Morgan. Gerhart Johann Robert Hauptmann. (Ungar paperback, 2121). 1961. pap., 1.25. Ungar.
Heretic of Soana. With an Introd. by Harold Von Hofe. Translated from the German by Bayard Quincy Morgan. Gerhart Johann Robert Hauptmann. LC 58-59868. 1958. F. Ungar Pub. Co.
Heretical Songs. Curtis White. LC 79-3848. 1981. 9.95 (ISBN 0-914590-62-6); pap. 4.95 (ISBN 0-914590-63-4). Fiction Coll.
Heretics: A Novel. Humphrey Slater. LC 47-30884. 1947. Harcourt, Brace.
Hereward, the Last of the English. Charles Kingsley. LC 7-12162. 1866. Ticknor and Fields.
Hereward, the Last of the English. new ed. Charles Kingsley. LC 4-16536. 1883. Macmillan and Co.
Hereward the Wake. Charles Kingsley. 1909. 5.00x o.p. (ISBN 0-460-00296-1, Evman). Dutton.
Hereward the Wake, "Last of the English,". luxenbourg ed. Charles Kingsley. 1908. T. Y. Crowell & Company.
Hereward the Wake, "Last of the English". Charles Kingsley. (Half-title: Everyman's library, ed. by Ernest Rhys. Fiction. no. 293). 1909. J. M. Dent & Co.
Hereward the Wake, 'last of the English' Charles Kingsley & Raymond, Charles Harlow, Ed. LC 23-17187. (Macmillan's pocket American and English classics). 1923. The Macmillan Company.
Herione of Charity and Other Stories. A Catholic Story Book. Mary Rowena Cotter. LC 6-29017. 1893. Press of the Catholic Journal Printing and Publishing Co.
Heritage. Peter Driscoll. LC 81-43409. 1982. 17.95 (ISBN 0-385-17884-0). Doubleday.
Heritage. Rose Caroline Feld. LC 28-217366. 1928. A. A. Knopf.
Heritage. George Frederick Hummel. LC 35-5815. 1935. Frederick A. Stokes Company.
Heritage. Ralph A Janson. LC 48-1364. 1947. Brentwood Press.
Heritage. Frances Parkinson Wheeler Keyes. LC 68-20992. (Illus.). 1968. McGraw-Hill.
Heritage. Siegfried Lenz. LC 80-84608. 16.95 (ISBN 0-8090-5466-3). Hill and Wang.
Heritage. Guy De Maupassant. Tr. by Arthur Kent. LC 7-25598. H. Murray & Co.
Heritage. Lewis Orde. 1982. pap. 3.75 (ISBN 0-8217-1100-8). Zebra.
Heritage. Victoria Mary Sackville-West. George H. Doran.
Heritage. Sheila Tagliavia. LC 76-9210. 8.95 (ISBN 0-06-014206-5). Harper & Row.
Heritage. Anthony P. West. LC 54-5966. 1955. Random House.
Heritage. Anthony P. West. LC 57-108292. (Cardinal edition, G-235. Fiction, 5). 1957. Pocket Books.
Heritage: A Story of Defeat and Victory. Burton Egbert Stevenson. LC 2-21990. 1902. Houghton, Mifflin and Company.
Heritage, and Other Stories. Viola Brothers Shore. LC 21-17815. George H. Doran Company.
Heritage De Ran-Tan-Plan. Rene de Goscinny. (Lucky Luke Series). (French.). 1976. 5.95x (ISBN 2-205-00747-5). Intl Learn Syst.
Heritage in Powdersmoke. Archie Joscelyn. LC 67-5284. 1967. Arcadia House.
Heritage of Blackoaks. Ashley Carter, pseud. 1981. pap. 2.95 (ISBN 0-449-14424-0, GM). Fawcett.
Heritage of Bob Hardwick. Rev. Ed.) A Personal Narrative of Colorful Events and Human Experiences. Henry Howard Harper. LC 34-1045. 1933. Printed by the Torch Press.
Heritage of Buddha: The Story of Siddhartha Gautama. Celina LuZanne Boozer. LC 53-7900. 1953. Philosophical Library.
Heritage of Cain. Isabel Egenton Ostrander. LC 16-165244. 1916. 1.25. W. J. Watt & Company.
Heritage of Dedlow Marsh and Other Tales. Bret Harte. LC 76-121561. (Short story index reprint series). 1970. Books for Libraries Press.
Heritage of Dedlow Marsh: And Other Tales. Bret I. E. Francis Bret Harte. LC 13-7675. 1889. Macmillan and Co.
Heritage of Folly. Katie McMullen. (Red rose romance,#144). 1974. (pbk.) 0.75. Bantam Books.
Heritage of Folly. Catherine Marchant, pseud. pap. 0.50 o.p. (72-796). Lancer.
Heritage of Hastier. Marion Zimmer Bradley. (Darkover novel). 1975. (pbk.) 1.50. DAW Books.
Heritage of Hastur. Marion Zimmer Bradley. LC 77-4365. (Gregg Press science fiction series; III). 1977. 14.00 (ISBN 0-8398-2363-0). Gregg Press.
Heritage of Hatcher Ide. Booth Tarkington. LC 41-2817. 1941. Doubleday, Doran and Company, Inc.
Heritage of Honor: A Novel. Tabitha Ann Mauldin. LC 74-187035. 1972. 7.95 (ISBN 0-87667-072-9). Droke House/Hallux.
Heritage of Honor: By Alan Hudson; Illustrated by Roy Ives Conklin. Alan Bedford Hudson. LC 13-4424. R. G. Badger.
Heritage of Murder. G. V. Kulkarni. 303p. 1974. 4.50 o.p. (ISBN 0-88253-467-X). InterCulture.
Heritage of Nurse O'Hara. Colleen L Reece. (Avalon Books). 4.95. Thomas Bouregy.
Heritage of Peril. Arthur Williams Marchmont. LC 1-15316. 1901. New Amsterdam Book Company.
Heritage of Quincas Borba. Joaquim M. Assis. 1977. lib. bdg. 59.95 (ISBN 0-8490-1946-X). Gordon Pr.
Heritage of Stars. Clifford D. Simak. LC 76-53742. 7.95. Berkley Pub. Corp.: Distributed by Putnam.
Heritage of Stars. Clifford D Simak. 1978. 1.75 (ISBN 0-425-03773-8). Berkley Pub. Corp.
Heritage of Strangers. Pamela D'Arcy, pseud. (Berkley Medallion Book). 1978. 1.75 (ISBN 0-425-03668-5). Berkley Pub. Corp.
Heritage of Strangers. Mary Linn Roby. 1978. pap. 1.75 (ISBN 0-425-03668-5, Medallion). Berkley Pub.
Heritage of the Bluestem, a Romance of the Prairies. Anna Matilda Carlson. LC 32-327. Burton Publishing Company.

Heritage of the Desert. Zane Grey. LC 80-14211. 1980. 10.95 (ISBN 0-89340-282-6). J. Curley.
Heritage of the Desert: A Novel. Zane Grey. LC 10-19618. 1910. 1.50. Harper & Brothers.
Heritage of the Dessert: A Novel. Zane Grey. LC 21-13693. 1920. Grosset & Dunlap.
Heritage of the Heart. Pamela D'Arcy, pseud. 176p. (Orig.). 1980. pap. 1.75 (ISBN 0-515-05201-9). Jove Pubns.
Heritage of the Heart. Nina Pykare. (Candlelight Ecstasy Ser.: No. 65). (Orig.). 1982. pap. 1.95 (ISBN 0-440-13576-1). Dell.
Heritage of the Hills. Arthur Preston Hanksin. LC 22-5604. 1922. Dodd, Mead and Company.
Heritage of the Quest. Gertrude Venetta Cope. LC 36-4943. 1936. Marshall Jones Company.
Heritage of the River. Muriel Elwood. 1976. pap. 1.75 (ISBN 0-532-17136-5). Woodhill.
Heritage of the River: An Historical Novel of Early Montreal. Muriel Elwood. LC 45-35149. 1945. C. Scribner's Sons.
Heritage of the Sioux. Bertha Muzzy Sinclair. LC 16-18915. 1916. Little, Brown, and Company.
Heritage of Tomorrow. Lisa De Orleans. LC 64-66252. 3.95, lim. ed. Dominion Pub. Co., P.O. Box.
Heritage of Unrest. Gwendolen Overton. LC 68-57544. 1969. Literature House.
Heritage of Unrest: A Novel. Gwendolen Overton. LC 1-31040. 1901. The Macmillan Company.
Heritage Perilous. Jeffery Farnol. LC 47-11681. 1947. R.M. McBride.
Heritage Perilous. Jeffery Farnol. LC 47-11681. 1917. R. M. McBride.
Herk: Hero of the Skies. Joseph Dabney. pap. 8.95 (ISBN 0-932298-16-8). Copple Hse.
Herland. Charlotte Perkins Stetson Gilman. LC 78-20418. 8.95 (ISBN 0-394-50388-0) (ISBN 0-394-73665-6). Pantheon Books.
Herma. MacDonald Harris. LC 81-66005. 1981. 16.95 (ISBN 0-689-11179-7). Atheneum.
Herman Had Two Daughters. Zelda Popkin. LC 68-17500. 1968. Lippincott.
Herman Melville; Cycle and Epicycle. Ed. by Eleanor Melville Metcalf. LC 75-104230. (Illus.). 1970. Greenwood Press.
Herman Melville: Voyages. Herman Melville. Ed. by Stanley Hendricks. LC 72-122359. (Illus.). 1970. 2.50 (ISBN 0-87529-109-0). Hallmark Editions.
Herman Melville: Voyages. Herman Melville. Ed. by Stanley Hendricks. LC 72-122359. 1970. 2.50 o.p. (ISBN 0-87529-109-0). Hallmark.
Herman: Or, Young Knighthood. Sara Hammond Palfrey. LC 7-35799. 1866. Lee and Shepard.
Hermana Sam. Paul King. LC 76-25601. 8.95 (ISBN 0-698-10795-0). Coward, McCann & Geoghegan.
Hermann Agha: An Eastern Narrative. William Gifford Palgrave. LC 7-35780. (Leisure hour series. no. 6). 1872. Holt & Williams.
Hermann Hesse's "Glasperlenspiel.". Joseph Mileck. LC 52-9762. (California. University of California Publications in Modern Philology: Voll 36, No. 9). 1952. University of California Press.
Hermanos! William Herrick. 1974. (pbk.) 1.50. Bantam Books.
Hermes. James Price. 1974. pap. 2.50 o.p. L Olds.
Hermes: A Novel. James Price. LC 74-82255. 1974. 2.50 (ISBN 0-9600646-3-X). Millet Books.
Hermes Fall. John Baxter. LC 77-28894. 7.95 (ISBN 0-671-24055-2). Simon and Schuster.
Hermes Fall. John Baxter. 1979. 2.25 (ISBN 0-345-28081-4). Ballantine Books.
Hermes Stone. Robert Eilers. (Orig.). 1980. pap. 1.95 (ISBN 0-532-23264-X). Woodhill.
Hermes to His Son Thoth: Being Joyce's Use of Giordano Bruno in Finnegans Wake. Frances Motz Boldereff. LC 68-21486. (Illus.). 1968. Classic Non-Fiction Library.
Hermes 3000. William Kotzwinkle. LC 76-175642. 1972. 5.95 (ISBN 0-394-47621-2). Pantheon Books.
Hermetic Whore: Fictions. Peter Spielberg. LC 77-70900. 8.95. (ISBN 0-914590-40-5) (ISBN 0-914590-41-3). Fiction Collective: Distributed by G. Braziller.
Hermia Suydam. Gertrude Franklin Horn Atherton. LC 6-4518. The Current Literature Publishing Co.
Hermione. H. D, pseud. LC 81-9518. 15.00 (ISBN 0-8112-0816-8) (ISBN 0-8112-0817-6). New Directions Pub. Corp.
Hermit. Eugene Ionesco. LC 73-20944. 1974. 6.95 (ISBN 0-670-36891-1). Viking Press.
Hermit. Peter Longueville. LC 75-170572. (Foundations of the Novel Ser.: Vol. 51). lib. bdg. 50.00 (ISBN 0-8240-0563-5). Garland Pub.
Hermit: A Story of the Wilderness. Charles Clark Munn. 1903. Lee and Shepard.
Hermit and the Good People of Harlington Town. A Novel. Guy Kenneth Whiteside. LC 43-16592. (Red-edge series). Old Homestead Book Shop.
Hermit and the Wild Woman: And Other Stories. Edith Newbold Jones Wharton. LC 8-27101. 1908. C. Scribner's Sons.
Hermit Doctor of Gaya: A Love Story of Modern India. Ida Alexa Ross Wylie. LC 16-5895. 1916. G. P. Putnam's Sons.
Hermit in London: Or Sketches of English Manners... Felix McDonough. LC 7-16466. 1820. E. Duyckinck.
Hermit in the Country: Or, Sketches of English Manners. By the Author of "The Hermit in London"... Felix McDonough. LC 7-16464. 1820. Published by L. and F. Lockwood, No. Broadway.
Hermit in Van Diemen's Land. Henry Savery. Ed. by Cecil Hadgraft & Margriet Roe. 1964. 15.00x (ISBN 0-7022-0393-9). U of Queensland Pr.
Hermit Island. Katharine Lee Bates. LC 13-9389. 1890. D. Lothrop Company.
Hermit of Far End. Margaret Bass Pedler. LC 20-5408. 1920. George H. Doran Company.
Hermit of Far End. Margaret Bass Pedler. LC 33-17509. 1922. Grosset & Dunlap.
Hermit of Holcombe. Mary Dwinell Chellis. LC 23411. (Added t.-p: The standard series of temperance tales v. 4). H. A. Young & Co.
Hermit of Livry. A Story of the 16th Century. M. R. Housekeeper. LC 7-7136. (Pilgrim price series. v. 3). Congregational Sunday School and Publishing Society.
Hermit of Nottingham. A Novel. Charles Conrad Abbott. 1898. J.B. Lippincott Company.
Hermit of the Adirondacks. Della Trombly. LC 15-27930. 1915. Sherman, French & Company.
Hermit of the Cavern: A Novel of the Early Sixties Abounding in Dramatic Situations--the Struggle of Those Early German Settlers in Southwest Texas to Maintain Their Neutrality in a Nation Torn Asunder by Internal Strife. A Siemering & Francis, May E., 1880- Tr. LC 32-322661. 1932. Naylor Printing Company.
Hermit of the Chesapeake: Or, Lessons of a Lifetime. Barclay & Co.
Hermit of the Culebra Mountains: Or, the Adventures of Two Schoolboys in the Far West. Everett McNeil. LC 4-21658. 1904. E. P. Dutton & Company.
Hermit of the Nonquon. Charles Nelson Johnson. LC 7-10537. (On cover: Rialto series, no. 55). 1893. Rand, McNally & Co.
Hermit of the Rock. A Tale of Cashel. Mary Anne Madden Sadlier. LC 8-1652. (On cover: Cottage and parlor library). D. & J. Sadlier & Co.
Hermit of Thunder King. Jackson Gregory. LC 45-1818. 1945. Dodd, Mead & Company.
Hermit of Turkey Hollow: The Story of an Alibi, Being an Exploit of Ephraim Tutt, Attorney & Counselor at Law. Arthur Cheney Train. LC 21-16801. 1921. C. Scribner's Sons.
Hermit: Or, The Unparalleled Sufferings and Surprising Adventures of Mr. Philip Quarll, an Englishman. Peter Longueville & Alexander Bicknell. LC 75-170572. (Foundations of the Novel). (Illus.). 1972. (ISBN 0-8240-0563-5). Garland Pub.
Hermitage. Mary Kay Simmons. 1975. (pbk.) 0.95. Dell.
Hermitage Hill: By Dorothy Daniels. Dorothy Daniels. (Signet Book). 1978. 1.50 (ISBN 0-451-08092-0). New American Library.
Hermitage Island. Gertrude Pahlow. LC 34-962134. The Penn Publishing Company.
Hermsprong: Or, Man As He Is Not. Robert Bage. LC 78-60853. (Novel, 1720-1805: 13). 1979. 84.00 (ISBN 0-8240-3662-X). Garland Pub.
Hermsprong; or, Man As He Is Not, 3 vols. Robert Bage. LC 78-60853. (Novel 1720-1805 Ser.: Vol. 13). 1980. Set. lib. bdg. 93.00 (ISBN 0-8240-3662-X). Garland Pub.
Hermsprong: Or, Man As He Is Not. A Novel... Robert Bage. LC 41-26877. 1803. Printed by W. Duane,, High Street.
Hermsprong: Or, Man As He Is Not. Edited by Vaughan Wilkins. Robert Bage. LC 52-6511. 1951. Library Publishers.
Hernani the Jew: A Story of Russian Oppression. A N Homer. LC 12-34453. (Illus.). Rand, McNally & Company.
Hero. W. Arby. 4.75 o.p. Carlton.
Hero. William Somerset Maugham. LC 75-30390. (Maugham, William Somerset, 1874-1965. Works. 1976). 1976. 16.00 (ISBN 0-405-07811-0). Arno Press.
Hero. David Meltzer. (Orig.). 1973. pap. 4.00 o.p. (ISBN 0-87685-124-3). Black Sparrow.
Hero, and Other Tales. Dinah Maria Mulock Craik. LC 42-33232. 1853. Harper & Brothers.
Hero and the Man. L. Curry Morton. LC 12-95704. 1912. A. C. McClurg & Co.
Hero and the Terror. Michael Blodgett. LC 82-6212. 13.95 (ISBN 0-517-54692-2). Harmony Books.
Hero at Home. Elizabeth Alexander. LC 40-11016. 1940. Doubleday, Doran and Company, Inc.
Hero Azriel. Thomas Friedmann. LC 79-87896. 4.00 (ISBN 0-916288-07-2). Micah Publications.
Hero, Bread Upon the Waters, Alice Learmont. new ed. (originally published in 1853.) ed. Dinah Maria Mulock Craik. LC 41-34797. 1859. Harper & Brothers.
Hero Breed: A Novel. Pat Mullen. LC 37-272652. R. M. McBride & Company.
Hero by Proxy: A Kaleidoscopic Misadventure. Hildegarde Tolman. LC 42-16137. 1942. Little, Brown and Company.
Hero Carthew: Or, The Prescotts of Pamphillon. Louisa Taylor Parr. LC 7-347169. (Leisure hour series no. 16). 1873. H. Holt and Company.
Hero Continues: A Novel. Donald Windham. LC 60-12542. 1960. Crowell.
Hero Driver. Alfred Coppel. LC 54-6629. 1954. Crown Publishers.
Hero for Henry. Herbert R Purdum. LC 68-15600. 1968. Doubleday.
Hero for Jamaica: A Novel of the Living Legend of Marcus Garvey. Gershom Antonio Williams. LC 73-82094. 1973. 5.00 (ISBN 0-682-47730-3). Exposition Press.
Hero for Leanda. Andrew Garve. 1978. pap. 1.50i (ISBN 0-06-080429-7, P 429, PL). Har-Row.
Hero for Leanda: By Andrew Garve Pseud. 1st Ed. Paul Winterton. LC 59-10620. 1959. Harper.
Hero for Regis. Jack Hoffenberg. 1963. 5.95 o.p. Dutton.
Hero for Regis: A Novel. Jack Hoffenberg. LC 63-7258. 1963. Dutton.
Hero from Otherwhere. Jay Williams. (Laurel Leaf Library). 1973. (pbk) 0.95. Dell.
Hero in His Time: A Novel. Arthur Allen Cohen. LC 75-10303. 7.95. Random House.
Hero in Homespun: A Tale of the Loyal South. new ed. William Eleazar Barton. LC 1-30230. (Half-title: Appleton's town and country library, no. 295). 1901. D. Appleton and Company.
Hero in Homespun. A Tale of the Loyal South. William Eleazar Barton. LC 6-9414. 1897. Lamson, Wolffe and Company.
Hero in the Tower. Hans Hellmut Kirst. LC 70-187145. 1972. 6.95. Coward, McCann & Geoghegan.
Hero Jesse. Lawrence Millman. LC 81-14582. 10.95 (ISBN 0-312-37004-0). St. Martin's Press.
Hero Like Me: A Hero Like You. Robert Rossner. LC 75-182476. 1972. 6.95 (ISBN 0-8415-0145-9). Saturday Review Press.
Hero Machine. Howard Berk. LC 67-21803. 1967. 5.50. New Amer. Lib.
Hero of Antietam: By Eulalie Beffel. Eulalie Beffel. LC 43-11548. 1943. E. P. Dutton & Company, Inc.
Hero of Carillon, or, Fort Ticonderoga in 1777. Ella J. H Sellingham. 1897. W. T. Bryan.
Hero of Downways. Michael G. Coney. (Science Fiction Ser.). (Orig.). 1973. pap. 0.95 o.p. (UQ1070). DAW Bks.
Hero of Herat: A Frontier Romance. Katherine Helen Maud Marshall Diver. LC 24-24992. 1913. G. P. Putnam's Sons.
Hero of Our Own Times. Mikhail IUrevich Lermontov. (World Classics, No. 563). 1959. 1.75 o.p. (ISBN 0-19-250563-7). Oxford U Pr.
Hero of Our Time. Mikhail IUrevich Lermontov. LC 66-7240. (Penguin classics). 1975. (pbk.) 1.95. Penguin Books.
Hero of Our Time. Mikhail IUrevich Lermontov & Wisdom, J. H., Tr. LC 24-15763. (Borzol pocket books). A. A. Knopf.
Hero of Our Time: A Novel. Vasco Pratolini. LC 51-6316. 1951. Prentice-Hall.
Hero of Our Time; a Novel. Translated from the Russian by Vladimir Nabokov in Collaboration with Dmitri Nabokov. 1st Ed. Mikhail IUrevich Lermontov. LC 58-6583. (Doubleday anchor books, A133). 1958. Doubleday.
Hero of Our Time: By M. Y. Lermontov. Mikhail IUrevich Lermontov. Tr. by Wisdom, J. H. & Murray, Marr. LC 24-15763. (Borzol pocket books). A. A. Knopf.
Hero of Our Time. Tr. from the Russian of M. Y. Lermontov. Mikhail IUrevich Lermontov & Wisdom, J. H., Tr. LC 17-1334. 1916. A. A. Knopf.
Hero of Our Time. Tr., Introd. by Paul Foote. Mikhail IUrevich Lermontov. LC 66-72403. (Penguin classics, L176). 1966. Penguin.
Hero of Our Time. Translated from the Russian by Martin Parker. With a New Introd. by George Reavey. Mikhail IUrevich Lermontov. LC 62-11016. (Classic Collier books, AS181V). 1962. Collier Books.
Hero of Saint Roger. 1st Ed. Jerrard Tickell. LC 54-12016. 1954. St Ed.
Hero of the Ages: A Story of the Nazarene. Catherine Robertson McCartney. LC 7-15175. F. H. Revell Company.
Hero of the Town: A Novel. David Lozell Martin. LC 65-22621. 1965. Morrow.
Hero of the West: A Romance of the Valley, the Prairie and the Mountain. Forrest G Byloff. LC 20-6131. Hassler-De Atley Pub. Co.
Hero of Ticonderoga. Rowland Evans Robinson. 1898. H. J. Shanley & Co.
Hero of Trent: Or, Saved from the Jaws of Hell. E. M Isaac. LC 10-18655. The Christian Witness Co.
Hero on a Donkey. Miodrag Bulatovic. LC 69-18520. (NAL book.). 1969. 6.95. World Pub. Co.
Hero Rat. Wally Charleston. 1975. (pbk.) 1.25 (ISBN 0-446-76596-1). Warner Paperback Library.
Hero Ship. Henry Hunt Searls. LC 69-10750. 1969. 5.95. World Pub. Co.
Hero Tales Told in School. James A. Baldwin. LC 4-10921. (On verso of half-title: Scribner's series of school reading). 1904. C. Scribner's Sons.
Hero: The Tale of a Political Murder... Alfred Neumann. Tr. by Paterson, Huntley. LC 31-21756. 1931. A. A. Knopf.
Hero Without Honor. Arthur George Joseph Whitehouse. LC 70-186050. 1972. 6.95 (ISBN 0-385-02725-7). Doubleday.
Hero-Worship Nymphets. 1973. (pbk.) 1.95 (ISBN 0-87056-335-1). Brandon Books.
Herod. H. E. Nightingale. 4.50 o.p. Vantage.
Herod and Mariamne. Par Lagerkvist. LC 81-16200. 1982. 2.95 (ISBN 0-394-70818-0). Vintage Books.
Herod and Mariamne. Par Fabian Lagerkvist. LC 68-23949. 1968. 4.95. Knopf.
Herod Conspiracy. Russell L Rhodes. LC 80-15323. 11.95 (ISBN 0-396-07865-6). Dodd, Mead.
Herodotus: The Persian War. William Shepherd. LC 81-38532. (Translations from Greek & Roman Authors Ser.). (Illus.). 112p. 1982. pap. text ed. 4.95 (ISBN 0-521-28194-6). Cambridge U Pr.
Herod's Children. Ilse Aichinger. 1963. 4.50 o.p. (ISBN 0-689-10001-9). Atheneum.
Heroes. Millen Brand. 1939. Simon and Schuster.
Heroes. James Carabatsos. (Berkley Medallion Book). 1977. 1.75 (ISBN 0-425-03718-5). Berkley Pub. Corp.
Heroes. McKie. pap. 1.60 o.s.i. Tri-Ocean.
Heroes & Horrors. Fritz Leiber. Ed. by Stuart D. Schiff. 1980. pap. 2.25 (ISBN 0-671-83225-5, Timescape). PB.
Heroes and Orators. Robert Phelps. LC 58-125781. 1958. McDowell, Obolensky.
Heroes Die Young. Rick Sandford. (Belmont Tower Book). 1.75 (ISBN 0-505-51361-7). Tower Publications.
Heroes of Peace: A Story of the Twentieth Century Revolution. William Victor Holley. 1900. The Commercial Publishing Co.
Heroes of the Empty View. 1st American Ed. James Aldridge. LC 54-7193. 1954. Knopf.
Heroes of the Jazz Age. Jose Reyes Martin. LC 36-17730. 1936. The Author.
Heroes of the Teton Mythos. new ed. Sam Hamill. LC 73-89673. (Illus.). 65p. 1973. pap. 2.50 (ISBN 0-914742-00-0). Copper Canyon.
Heroic Adventures: Selections from the Youth's Companion. LC 6-20853. (Companion series). 1906. P. Mason Company.
Heroic Dust. Theodora Dehon. LC 40-2121. 1940. The Macmillan Company.
Heroic Epic of the Khalkha Mongols. 2nd, rev. ed. N. Poppe. (Occasional Papers: No. 11). 1979. pap. 8.00x (ISBN 0-910980-51-9). Mongolia.
Heroic Fantasy. Ed. by Page & Reinhardt. (Science Fiction Ser). 1979. pap. 1.95 o.p. (ISBN 0-87997-455-9, UJ1455). DAW Bks.
Heroic Garrison. V. A Stuart. (Adventures of Alexander Sheridan # 5). (Illus.). 1975. (pbk.) 1.25 (ISBN 0-523-00628-4). Pinnacle.
Heroic Happenings Told in Verse and Story. Elbridge Streeter Brooks. LC 12-30970. 1893. G. P. Putnam's Sons.
Heroic Love. 1st Ed. Edward Loomis. LC 60-9989. 1960. Knopf.
Heroic Sinner and the Pilgrim Spinster. A Romance. Elizabeth Lawrence. LC 7-13625. 1893. The Granite Publishing Company.
Heroics. George Alec Effinger. LC 78-22733. 1979. 7.95 (ISBN 0-385-12723-5). Doubleday.
Heroides and Amores: With an English Translation. Publius Ovidius Naso. Tr. by Showerman, Grant. LC 15-2791. (Half-title: The Loch classical library). 1914. W. Heinemann.
Heroin Triple Cross. John Weisman & Brian Boyer. (Headhunters, # 1). 1974. (pbk.) 1.25 (ISBN 0-523-00312-9). Pinnacle Books.
Heroine. Eaton Stannard Barrett. LC 30-654909. (Half-title: The rescue series). 1928. Frederick A. Stokes Company.
Heroine in Bronze. James Lane Allen. Repr. of 1912 ed. lib. bdg. 20.00 (ISBN 0-8414-3064-0). Folcroft.
Heroine in Bronze: Or, A Portrait of a Girl; a Pastoral of the City. James Lane Allen. LC 12-24622. 1912. The Macmillan Company.

Heroine of Santiago De Cuba (a Sequel) Or, What Followed the Sinking of the Merrimac. Antoinette Sheppard. The Abbey Press.

Heroine of Tampico: Or, Wildfire the Wanderer. A Tale of the Mexican War. Harry Halyard. 1848. F. Gleason.

Heroine of Tampico: Or Wildfire the Wanderer. A Tale of the Mexican War. Harry Halyard. 1852. F. Gleason's Publishing Hall.

Heroine of the Prairies: A Romance of the Oregon Trail. Sheba Hargreaves. LC 30-23198. 1930. Harper & Brothers.

Heroine of the Strait: A Romance of Detroit in the Time of Pontiac. Mary Catherine Crowley. LC 2-11135. 1902. Little, Brown, and Company.

Heroine of '49: A Story of the Pacific Coast. Mary P. Sawtelle. LC 8-2019.

Heroine; or, Adventures of a Fair Romance Reader, 3 vols. in 1. Eaton Stannard Barrett. LC 79-8233. Repr. of 1813 ed. 44.50 (ISBN 0-404-61775-1). AMS Pr.

Heroine: Or Adventures of Cherubina. the 1st american, from the 2d london ed.... ed. Eaton Stannard Barrett. LC 16-13092. 1815. Published for M. Carey.. Chesnut St.

Heroines of George Meredith. Herbert Bedford. LC 78-160742. (Illus.). 1972. (ISBN 0-8046-1555-1). Kennikat Press.

Heroines of Petosega. Frederic Alva Dean. LC 6-32900. 1889. The Hawthorne Publishing Company.

Heroine's Sister. Frances Murray. LC 74-21088. 1975. 7.95. St. Martin's Press.

Heron. Giorgio Bassani. LC 70-95855. 1970. Harcourt, Brace & World.

Heron Dancer. John Solensten. LC 81-83878. (Minnesota Voices Project Ser.: No. 3). (Illus.). 155p. 1981. pap. 5.00 (ISBN 0-89823-026-8). New Rivers Pr.

Heronbrook. Anne Rundle. 1974. (pbk.) 1.25. Bantam Books.

Heronford. Samuel Robert Keightley. LC 99-5429. 1899. Dodd, Mead & Company.

Herons. Helen Shipton. LC 8-7338. 1895. Macmillan and Co.

Heronsmill: A Country Story of Little England Beyond Wales. Roscoe Howells. LC 79-27178. (Illus.). 11.95 (ISBN 0-312-37181-0). St. Martin's Press.

Hero's Great Great Great Great Great Grandson: A Novel. George Cuomo. LC 70-139305. 1971. 6.95. Atheneum.

Hero's Last Days: Or, Nepenthe. Mary A Fowles. LC 6-43282. 1883. W. J. Duffie.

Hero's Oak: A Novel. William Richards Castle. LC 45-37861. 1945. The Readers Press.

Hero's Walk: By Robert Crane Pseud. Bernard Glemser. LC 54-7559. 1954. Ballantine Books.

Hero's Welcome. M. J. Naparsteck. 288p. (Orig.). 1982. pap. 2.25 (ISBN 0-8439-0947-1). Leisure Bks CT.

Herovit's World. Barry N Malzberg. LC 72-11447. 1973. 4.95 (ISBN 0-394-48141-0). Random House.

Herovit's World. Barry N Malzberg. 1974. (pbk.) 0.95 (ISBN 0-671-77753-X). Pocket Books.

Herr Biedermann und Die Brandstifter: Rip Van Winkle, Zwei Hoerspiele. Max Frisch. (Suhrkamp Taschenbucher: No. 599). 128p. 1980. pap. text ed. 3.25 (ISBN 3-518-37099-5, Pub. by Suhrkamp Verlag Germany). Suhrkamp.

Herr Doctor. Robert MacDonald. LC 2-22847. (The hour-glass stories, no. 4). 1902. Funk & Wagnalls Company.

Herr Nightingale and the Satin Woman. William Kotzwinkle. LC 78-54911. 1978. 8.45 (ISBN 0-394-50106-3). Knopf: Distributed by Random House.

Herr Paulus: His Greatness, and His Fall. Walter Besant. (On cover: Seaside library. Pocket ed., no. 1065). 1888. G. Munro.

Herr Paulus: His Rise, His Greatness, and His Fall. Walter Besant. (On cover: Harper's Franklin square library. no. 618). 1888. Harper & Brothers.

Hers. Alfred Alvarez. 1976. 1.75. Dell.

Hers. Alfred Alvarez. LC 74-29613. 1975. 7.95 (ISBN 0-394-48702-8). Random House.

Hers the Kingdom. Shirley Streshinsky. LC 81-13763. 14.95 (ISBN 0-399-12576-0). Putnam.

Herself. Hortense Calisher. LC 72-82174. 1972. 10.00 (ISBN 0-87795-042-3). Arbor House.

Herself. Elizabeth Garver Jordan. LC 43-3875. 1943. D. Appleton-Century Company, Incorporated.

Herself. Ethel Sidgwick. LC 12-120091. Small, Maynard & Company.

Herself, Himself & Myself: A Romance. Ruth Sawyer. LC 17-25083. 1917. Harper & Brothers.

Herself: Mrs. Patrick Crowley: A Romantical Tale. Doran Hurley. LC 39-271912. 1939. Longmans, Green and Co.

Herself Surprised. Joyce Cary. 275p. 1976. Repr. of 1948 ed. lib. bdg. 16.95x (ISBN 0-89244-070-8). Queens Hse.

Herself Surprised. Joyce Cary. 1980. pap. 4.95 (ISBN 0-7145-0270-7). Riverrun NY.

Herself Surprised: A Novel. Joyce Cary. LC 48-8103. 1948. Harper.

Herself Surprised: A Novel. Joyce Cary. LC 77-21373. 1977. 9.95 (ISBN 0-89244-070-8). Queens House.

Hertha. authorized american ed.... ed. Fredrika Bremer. Tr. by Mary Botham Howitt. LC 6-17400. 1856. G.P. Putnam & Co.

Hertha: A Romance. authorized ed. Ernst Eckstein & Bell, Mrs. Edward Hamilton, Tr. LC 6-263212. 1892. G. G. Peck.

Herzl, the King. Norman Kotker. LC 76-38280. 1972. 6.95 (ISBN 0-684-12832-2). Scribner.

Herzog. Saul Bellow. (Crest bk., m868). 1965. Fawcett.

Herzog. Saul Bellow. Ed. by Irving Howe. LC 75-42290. (Viking critical library). 1976. 8.95 (ISBN 0-670-36913-6) (ISBN 0-670-01810-4). Viking Press.

Herzog. Saul Bellow. 1.95 (ISBN 0-380-00869-6). Avon.

Herzog. Saul Bellow. LC 64-19794. 1964. Viking Press.

Herzog Legacy. (Illus.). 1977 (ISBN 0-380-00960-9). Avon Books.

Herzog Legacy. (Illus.). 1977 (ISBN 0-380-00960-9). Avon Books.

Herzog Legacy. Gertrude Schweitzer. LC 75-21245. (Illus.). 1976. 10.00 (ISBN 0-385-03897-6). Doubleday.

He's Late This Morning. Frances Moyer Ross Stevens. LC 49-8224. 1949. Pub. for the Crime Club by Doubleday.

He's My Baby, Now. Jeannette Eyerly. (Kangaroo Book). 1978. 1.50 (ISBN 0-671-82072-9). Pocket Books.

Hesitant Heart. Anne Edwards. LC 73-5010. 1974. 5.95 (ISBN 0-394-48484-3). Random House.

Hesitant Heart. Anne Edwards. LC 74-9992. 1974. (lib. bdg.) 10.95. G. K. Hall.

Hesitant Heir: A Novel. by georgina grey. ed. Georgina Grey, pseud. 1978. 1.50 (ISBN 0-449-23582-3). Fawcett Crest Books.

Hesitant Wolf & Scrupulous Fox: Fables Selected from World Literature. Ed. by Karen Kennerly. LC 82-3328. (Illus.). 352p. 1983. pap. 9.95 (ISBN 0-8052-0717-1). Schocken.

Hesper see Collected Works.

Hesper: A Novel. Hamlin Garland. LC 72-84707. 1974. 18.00 (ISBN 0-403-02951-1). Scholarly Press.

Hesper: A Novel. Hamlin Garland. LC 3-24946. 1903. Harper & Brothers.

Hess Cross. James Stewart Thayer. LC 77-9017. 8.95. Putnam.

Hesse, Goethe, Jung, You, & Me: A Story. Carole F. Cox. pap. 2.95 o.p. Star Pub Fla.

Hessian. Howard Melvin Fast. 1980. pap. 2.25 (ISBN 0-440-13536-2). Dell.

Hessian. Howard Melvin Fast. 192p. 1972. 6.95 o.p. (ISBN 0-688-00053-3). Morrow.

Hessian: A Novel. Howard Melvin Fast. LC 76-170236. 1972. 5.95. Morrow.

Hester. Norma Lee Clark. 1978. 1.75 (ISBN 0-449-23753-2). Fawcett Pubns.

Hester. Brian Talbot Cleeve. LC 79-660. (Illus.). 1980. 10.95 (ISBN 0-698-10987-2). Coward, McCann & Geoghegan.

Hester and Her Family: A Romance. Harold Webber Freeman. LC 35-253831. H. Holt and Company.

Hester: And Other New England Stories. Harriet Mulford Stone Lothrop. LC 7-14768. D. Lothrop and Company.

Hester Blair: The Romance of a Country Girl. William Henry Carson. LC 2-5871. 1902. C. M. Clark Publishing Company.

Hester Craddock. Alyse Gregory. LC 31-291951. 1931. Longmans, Green and Company.

Hester Hyde: A Colonial Romance. Mary Caroline Hyde. 1902. The Abbey Press.

Hester Kirton. Katharine Sarah Gadsden Macquoid. (Seaside library, v. 41. no 833). 1880. G. Munro.

Hester Lilly, and Twelve Short Stories. Elizabeth Taylor. LC 78-38724. (Short story index reprint series). 1972. (ISBN 0-8369-4137-3). Books for Libraries Press.

Hester Lilly, and Twelve Short Stories. Elizabeth Taylor. LC 54-9595. 1954. Viking Press.

Hester Morley's Promise. Hesba Stretton. (Seaside library, v. 38, no. 779). 1880. G. Munro.

Hester of the Grants: A Romance of Old Bennington. Theodora Agnes Peck. LC 5-13201. 1905. Fox, Duffield & Co.

Hester of the Grants: A Romance of Old Bennington. Theodora Agnes Peck. LC 7-23717. 1907. Duffield & Company.

Hester of the Hills: A Romance of the Ozark Mountains. Grover Clay. LC 7-31284. 1907. L. C. Page & Company.

Hester Roon. Norah Robinson Lofts. LC 40-30576. 1940. A. A. Knopf.

Hester Strong's Life Work: Or, The Mystery Solved. S. A. Southworth. LC 8-32298. 1870. Lee and Shepard.

Hester Strong's Life Work: Or, The Mystery Solved. S. A. Southworth. (On cover: American girls series v. 28). 1900. Lee and Shepard.

Hestia. C. J. Cherryh. (Daw Science Fiction Ser.). (Orig.). 1979. pap. 2.25 (ISBN 0-87997-680-2, UE1680). Daw Bks.

Heston House Horror. Veronica Leigh. 1977. pap. 1.25 (ISBN 0-532-12524-X). Woodhill.

Hetaira. Cornelia Dodd Brown. LC 33-36226. R. F. Seymour.

Heterodox Marriage of a New Woman. Mary Van Lennup Ives Todd. LC 8-26755. R. L. Weed Company.

Hetty. Henry Kingsley. LC 25-23758. 1869. Harper & Brothers.

Hetty Geybert. Georg Hermann Borchart & Barwell, Anna, Tr. LC 24-25749. 1924. George H. Doran Company.

Hetty or The Old Grudge: A Novel Also Working the Oracle. James H Connelly. LC 6-30689. (choise series. no. 96). 1893. R. Bonner's Sons.

Hetty, or The Old Grudge: A Novel Also Working the Oracle. James H Connelly. LC 6-30688. (Ledger library, no. 96). 1893. R. Bonner's Sons.

Hetty Wesley. Arthur Thomas Quiller-Couch. LC 3-24819. 1903. The Macmillan Company.

Hetty Wesley. Arthur Thomas Quiller-Couch. (Half-title: Everyman's library, ed. by Ernest Rhys. Fiction. no. 864). 1931. J. M. Dent & Sons, Ltd.

Hetty's Strange History. Helen Maria Fiske Hunt Jackson. LC 12-37885. (No name series. 1st ser.). 1877. Roberts Brothers.

Heu-Heu: Or, The Monster. Henry Rider Haggard. LC 24-79458. 1924. Doubleday, Page & Company.

Hewers of Wood: A Story of the Michigan Pine Forests. William George Puddefoot & Rankin, Isaac Ogden. LC 3-28843. 1903. The Pilgrim Press.

Hewn to Shape. George G. Haydu. 4.00 o.p. (ISBN 0-8283-1269-9). Branden.

Hex. Robert Curry Ford. LC 79-92145. 288p. (Orig.). 1980. pap. 2.25 (ISBN 0-87216-651-1). Playboy Pbks.

Hex Murder. Forrester Hazard. LC 35-19149. 1936. J. B. Lippincott Company.

Hex Woman. Raube Walters. The Macaulay Company.

Hexandria... Alice Weldon Wasserback Darton. LC 29-30768. 1894. Pathfinder Publishing Company.

Hey, Big Spender! Frank Bonham. LC 72-179056. 1972. 4.95 (ISBN 0-525-31855-0). Dutton.

Hey Diddle Diddle. Tamar Lane. LC 38-8991. 1932. The Adelphi Press.

Hey Doc. Louis Barron. 1980. pap. 4.00 (ISBN 0-89502-045-9). FEB.

Hey Dummy. Kin Platt. 1973. pap. 1.75 (ISBN 0-440-93548-2, LFL). Dell.

Hey, Jewboy. Sam Siegel. LC 67-9562. (Illus.). 1967. S & G Releasing Co.

Hey Lenny, Hey Jack. Alan Brody. LC 77-24389. 1978. 8.95 (ISBN 0-688-03249-4). Morrow.

Hey Teacher: Days of the Little Red Schoolhouse. Ethel Miller. 4.95 o.p. (ISBN 0-8062-0701-9). Carlton.

Hey, White Girl. Susan Gregory. 1970. pap. 0.95 o.p. (ISBN 0-447-75141-7). Lancer.

Hey, White Girl. Susan Gregory. (Contempora Ser.). (Orig.). 1972. pap. 1.25 o.p. (33-010). Lancer.

Heyday. Jane Ludlow Drake Abbott. LC 28-207645. 1928. J. B. Lippincott Company.

Heyday. Linda Dubreuil. 1978. pap. 1.95 (ISBN 0-532-19212-5). Woodhill.

Heyday. Bamber Gascoigne. LC 73-3505. 1974. 6.95 (ISBN 0-670-36954-3). Viking Press.

Heyday. Anthony Gibbs. LC 31-120208. 1931. Doubleday, Doran & Company, Inc.

Heyday. William Mode Spackman. LC 52-14047. 1953. Ballantine Books.

Hezekiah's Kortship: By Hezekiah Jones' Wife. Frank Augustus Van Denburg. LC 4-10535. 1904. R. G. Badger.

Hi Hattie, I'm in the Navy Now" The Salty Letters of a Sailor to His Girl Friend. Johnny Viney. LC 42-109. M. S. Mill Co., Inc.

Hi-Ho Silver, Away. Bill Stokes. (Illus.). 227p. 1979. pap. 3.95. Milwaukee Journal.

Hi-Li, the Moon-Man: Or, Free-Silver in America: Being a Diverting Contribution to the McKinley-Bryan Presidential Campaign. John Lockwood. LC 7-34696. J. Lockwood.

Hi Lo Country. Max Evans. 1975. (pbk.) 0.95. Dell.

Hi Lo Country. Max Evans. LC 80-410. (Series: Gregg Press Western Fiction Series.). 1980. 10.95 (ISBN 0-8398-2685-0). Gregg Press.

Hi Lo Country. Max Evans. LC 83-6992. 1983. 4.95 (ISBN 0-8263-0697-7). University of New Mexico Press.

Hi, Mr. Stu! Bill Appenzeller. 1977. 4.95 o.p. (ISBN 0-533-02619-9). Vantage.

Hi, the Story of a Giraffe. Illustrated by Elinor Armer. Alberta Armer & Armer, Elinor, Illus. LC 64-8301. 1964. Simmons Pub. Co.

Hialdo. A Novel. Sequel to Senorita Margarita. F. K. Irvine. 1892. Olympic Publishing Co.

Hibiscus Lagoon. Dorothy Dowdell. LC 82-10336. 1982. 9.95 (ISBN 0-89621-379-X). Thorndike Press.

Hibiscus Lagoon. Dorothy Dowdell. (O.s.i.). (Orig.). 1981. pap. 1.50 (ISBN 0-440-14494-9). Dell.

Hibiscus Lagoon. large type ed. Dorothy Dowdell. LC 82-10336. 267p. 1982. Repr. of 1981 ed. 9.95 (ISBN 0-89621-379-X). Thorndike Pr.

Hic et Hec. LC 68-20637. (Black Circle Ser). (Fr). 1968. 4.50 o.p. (GP456). Grove.

Hickey and Boggs. Phillip Rock. 1972. Popular Library.

Hickory: Dickory, Death. Agatha Miller Christie. LC 55-10662. (Red badge detective). 1955. Dodd, Mead.

Hickory Dickory Death. Agatha Miller Christie. 1976. pap. 2.50 (ISBN 0-671-41594-8). PB.

Hickory Dickory Dock see Nursery Rhyme Murders: An Anthology.

Hickory Grew Tall: A Story of Appalachia. Ralph V. Cutlip. 1970. 6.00 o.p. (ISBN 0-682-47191-7). Exposition.

Hickory Hall. Emma Dorothy Eliza Nevitte Southworth. (arm chair library. no. 42). 1893. F. M. Lupton.

Hickory Hall: Or, The Outcast. A Romance of the Blue Ridge. Emma Dorothy Eliza Nevitte Southworth. LC 8-10821. T. B. Peterson and Brothers.

Hickory Limb. Parker Hoysted Fillmore. LC 10-25576. 1910. 0.50. John Lane Company; Etc., Etc.

Hickory Shirt: A Novel of Death Valley in 1850. George Palmer Putnam. LC 49-3219. 1949. Duell, Sloan and Pearce.

Hickory Stick: A Novel. Virgil Joseph Scott. LC 48-8553. 1948. Swallow Press.

Hicks Jarou. Effie Woodward Merriman. LC 27-2814. R. G. Badger.

Hidalgo, Liberator of Mexico: And Other Stories. Cora Walker. LC 36-861846. The Christopher Publishing House.

Hidalgo's Beard: A California Fantasy. Conger Beasley. 1979. 9.95 o.p. (ISBN 0-8362-6103-8); pap. 5.95 o.p. (ISBN 0-8362-6100-3). Andrews & McMeel.

Hidalso's Beard: A California Fantasy. William Conger Beasley, pseud. LC 79-447. 9.95 (ISBN 0-8362-6103-8) (ISBN 0-8362-6100-3). Andrews and McMeel.

Hidden and the Hunted. Howard Swiggett. LC 50-6161. 1950. Morrow.

Hidden Assets. C. Peterson. 1981. pap. 2.95 (ISBN 0-380-78535-8, 78535). Avon.

Hidden Away: Or, The Specter of Desmond Hall. Etta W Pierce. (American series no. 278). 1892. M. J. Ivers & Co.

Hidden Blood. Wilbur C Tuttle. LC 43-10688. 1943. Houghton Mifflin Company.

Hidden Book. Mary Linn Roby. 1977. pap. 1.25 (ISBN 0-425-03364-3, Medallion). Berkley Pub.

Hidden Book. Mary Linn Roby. (Berkley Medallion Book). 1977. 1.25 (ISBN 0-425-03364-3). Berkley Pub. Corp.

Hidden Boundary. Elsie Frances Wilson Mack. LC 52-9997. 1952. Bouregy & Curl.

Hidden Chain. Dora Russell. (On cover: Globe library, v. 1, no. 238). 1896. Rand, McNally & Company.

Hidden Chains, from the German. Tr. by Benze, Charles Theodore. LC 10-13852. 1.50. The Erie Printing Co.

Hidden Chapel. William Edward Daniel Ross. LC 67-5891. 1967. Arcadia House.

Hidden Children. Robert William Chambers. LC 14-14920. 1914. D. Appleton and Company.

Hidden City. Philip Hamilton Gibbs. LC 30-38753. 1930. Doubleday, Doran & Company, Inc.

Hidden City. Walter Hugh McDougall. LC 7-20103. Cassell Publsihing Company.

Hidden Creek. Katharine Newlin Burt. LC 20-15343. 1920. 2.00. Houghton Mifflin Company.

Hidden Creek. Katharine Newlin Burt. 1974. (pbk.) 0.75. New American Library.

Hidden Departures: And Other Stories. Bernhardt E Schubert. LC 73-153103. 1970. 3.00 (ISBN 0-909470-00-6). National Press.

Hidden Depths see Use & Abuse.

Hidden Depths: A Tale for the Times. Felicia Mary Frances Skene. LC 8-9016. (On cover: Rialto series, no. 66). 1894. Rand, McNally & Company.

Hidden Door. Arthur Gask. LC 35-7026. The Macaulay Company.

Hidden Door... Frank Lucius Packard. LC 33-5931. 1933. Pub. for the Crime Club, Inc., by Doubleday, Doran & Company, Inc.

Hidden Dream. Sallie Lee Bell. LC 67-22688. 1967. Zondervan Pub. House.

Hidden Empire: A Tale of True Deeds and Great Ones Which the Tropic Sun Witnessed. Robert Willson Fenn. LC 11-24398. 1911. 1.30. Dodd, Mead and Company.
Hidden Empires. Oreon Marie Jackson McKee. LC 54-489693. 1954. College Pub. Co.
Hidden Evil. Barbara Cartland. 1971. pap. 0.95 o.p. (N2539). Pyramid Pubns.
Hidden Evil. Barbara Cartland. 1976. pap. 1.25 o.p. (ISBN 0-515-04064-9). BJ Pub Group.
Hidden Eyes. Eric Levison. LC 20-16929. The Bobbs-Merrill Company.
Hidden Face. Marie Baumer. LC 53-2042. 1953. Scribner.
Hidden Faces. Salvador Dali. LC 73-15250. (Illus.). 1974. 7.95 (ISBN 0-688-00237-4). Morrow.
Hidden Faces... Salvador Dali & Chevalier, Haakon Maurice, 1902- Tr. LC 44-5688. 1944. The Dial Press.
Hidden Faith: An Occult Story of the Period. Alwyn M Thurber. LC 8-19944. F. M. Harley Publishing Co.
Hidden Fire. 1st Ed. Sherman Baker. LC 55-7457. 1955. Little, Brown.
Hidden Fires. Janette Radcliffe. 400p. 1982. pap. 3.50 (ISBN 0-440-10657-5). Dell.
Hidden Flames. Ethel Winifred Savi. LC 34-424134. 1933. G. H. Watt.
Hidden Flower. Pearl Sydenstricker Buck. LC 52-6174. 1952. J. Day Co.
Hidden Force: A Story of Modern Java. Louis Marie Anne Couperus. Tr. by Teixeira De Mattos, Alexander Louis. LC 21-20659. 1921. Dodd, Mead and Company.
Hidden from View: & other Stories. William Gellin. LC 82-62517. 1983. 10.00 (ISBN 0-88400-092-3). Shengold.
Hidden Gold. Wilder Anthony. LC 22-8709. The Macaulay Company.
Hidden Gold. Mary Elizabeth Baldy. LC 40-8740. Fortuny's.
Hidden Grave: By Peter Hardin Pseud. 1st Ed. Louis Charles Vaczek. LC 55-659823. 1955. Harper.
Hidden Hand. Carroll John Daly. LC 29-12057. E. J. Clode, Inc.
Hidden Hand: A Novel. Emma Dorothy Eliza Nevitte Southworth. LC 22-22222. A. L. Burt Company.
Hidden Harbor. Kathrene Pinkerton. LC 51-13350. 1966. pap. 0.75 o.p. (ISBN 0-15-640185-1, AVB46, VoyB). HarBraceJ.
Hidden Heart. Dorothy Black. LC 48-105978. 1948. Triangle Books.
Hidden Heart. Dorothy Black. LC 47-1596. 1947. Macrae-Smith Company.
Hidden Heart. Barbara Cartland. 1977. pap. 1.25 o.p. (ISBN 0-515-03538-6, V3538). BJ Pub Group.
Hidden Heritage. Kathleen Pieper. (YA) 1979. 6.95 (Avalon). Bouregy.
Hidden Hills. Alex Hawk, pseud. (Orig.). 1970. pap. 0.60 o.p. (63-399). Paperback Lib.
Hidden Hills. Peggy O'More, pseud. LC 46-203656. 1946. Grammercy Publishing Co.
Hidden Hour: By Stephen Ransome Pseud. Frederick Clyde Davis. LC 66-11895. (Red badge detective). bds., 3.50. Dodd.
Hidden Hunger. K. B. Raul. (Orig.). 1968. pap. 0.95 o.p. (55-724). Paperback Lib.
Hidden Island. Elizabeth Frances Corbett. 1972. pap. 0.95 o.p. (95286). Beagle Bks.
Hidden Key. George Harmon Coxe. 1963. 3.50 o.p. Knopf.
Hidden Kingdom. Francis Beeding. LC 27-948. 1927. Little, Brown, and Company.
Hidden Life. Waldomiro Autran Dourado. LC 69-10679. 1969. 4.50. Knopf.
Hidden Lives. Marvin H. Albert. 1982. pap. 3.95 (ISBN 0-440-13500-1). Dell.
Hidden Lives. Margaret Leonora Pitcairn Eyles. LC 23-12747. Boni and Liveright.
Hidden Lives: A Novel. Marvin H Albert. LC 80-21362. 12.95. Delacorte Press.
Hidden Love. Carole Mortimer. (Harlequin Presents Ser.). 192p. 1983. pap. 1.95 (ISBN 0-373-10587-8). Harlequin Bks.
Hidden Malice. Evelyn Berckman. 1976. (pbk.) 1.25. Belmont Tower.
Hidden Man: A Novel. Charles Felton Pidgin. LC 6-34810. (Half-title: The "love and laughter" library). 1906. Mayhew Publishing Company.
Hidden Manna. Alec John Dawson. LC 2-29264. 1902. A. S. Barnes & Company.
Hidden Meanings. Charlotte Vale Allen. 1976. 1.50. Warner Books.
Hidden Mine. Joseph Alexander Altsheler. 1898. Continental Pub. Co.
Hidden Mine: By Joseph Altsheler... Joseph Alexander Altsheler. LC 6-62. (On cover: Western life series, no 2). J. S. Tait & Sons.
Hidden Mountain. Translated from the French by Harry Binsse. 1st Ed. Gabrielle Carbotte Roy. LC 62-19589. 1962. Harcourt, Brace & World.
Hidden Part. Stan Barstow. LC 69-16524. 1969. 6.95. Coward-McCann.
Hidden Path. Mary Virginia Terhune. LC 8-26052. (On cover: Marion Harland's novels). 1898. G. W. Dillingham Co.
Hidden Pearls. LC 67-26978. 1967. 3.50. Macrae.
Hidden Pearls. Virginia Frances Voight. LC 67-26978. 1967. Macrae Smith Co.
Hidden Perils. Mary Cecil Hay. (On cover: Lovell's library, v. 20, no. 977). 1887. J. W. Lovell Company.
Hidden Places. Bertrand William Sinclair. LC 22-655. 1922. Little, Brown, and Company.
Hidden Planet: Science-Fiction Adventures on Venus. Ed. by Donald A. Wollheim. LC 59-8650. (Ace book, D-354). 1959. Ace Books.
Hidden Player. Alfred Noyes. LC 24-25644. 1924. Frederick A. Stokes Company.
Hidden Portal. Garnett Weston. 1946. Pub. for the Crime Club by Doubleday & Company, Inc.
Hidden Power. John G Willacy. LC 17-176183. Passing Show Printing Co.
Hidden Power. A Secret History of the Indian Ring, Its Operations, Intrigues and Machinations. Revealing the Manner in Which It Controls Three Important Departments of the United States Government. A Defense of the U.S. Army, and a Solution of the Indian Problem. Thomas Henry Tibbles. LC 8-28258. 1881. G. W. Carleton & Co.; Etc., Etc.
Hidden Princess. Chad Calhoun, pseud. (Brad Spear Ser.: No. 6). (Orig.). 1982. pap. 2.95 (ISBN 0-440-03727-1, Banbury). Dell.
Hidden Princess: A Modern Romance. Frederick Jackson. LC 10-206043. 1910. 1.30. G. W. Jacobs & Co.
Hidden Rainbow. Christmas Carol Miller Kauffman. 1963. pap. 3.95 (ISBN 0-8024-3807-5). Moody.
Hidden Rainbow. Christmas Carol Miller Kauffman. LC 57-13005. (Illus.). 1957. 3.95 o.p. (ISBN 0-8361-1373-X). Herald Pr.
Hidden Rainbow: Illustrated by Allan Eitzen. Chrimas Carol Miller Kauffman. LC 57-13005. 1957. Herald Press.
Hidden Rainbow. Illustrated by Allan Eitzen. Christmas Carol Miller Kauffman. LC 57-13005. 1957. Herald Press.
Hidden Record: Or, The Old Sea Mystery. Elijah Whittier Blaisdell. LC 6-13852. T.B. Peterson & Brothers.
Hidden River. Margaret Storm Jameson. 1981. 18.95x (Pub. by Remploy England). State Mutual Bk.
Hidden River: 1st Ed. Margaret Storm Jameson. LC 54-12186. 1955. Harper.
Hidden Road. frontispiece by c. allen gilbert. ed. Charles Wadsworth Camp. LC 22-10546. 1922. Doubleday, Page Company.
Hidden Road. Elsie Singmaster. LC 23-89910. 1923. Houghton Mifflin Company.
Hidden Room. Elva D. Codrington. 1980. 4.50 (ISBN 0-8062-1415-5). Carlton.
Hidden Season... Robert Sturgis. LC 46-21573. 1946. M. S. Mill Co., Inc.
Hidden Seed. G. E. Schiavone. 5.00 o.p. Carlton.
Hidden Shoals. Sara Ware Bassett. LC 35-12773. 1935. Doubleday, Doran & Company, Inc.
Hidden Sin. A Novel. Frances Brown. (On cover: The seaside library. Pocket ed., no. 518). 1885. G. Munro.
Hidden Sin. A Sequel to "The Dethroned Heiress,". Eliza Ann Dupuy. T. B. Peterson & Brothers.
Hidden Spring: A Novel. Clarence Budington Kelland. 1916. Harper & Brothers.
Hidden Target. Helen MacInnes. LC 80-7953. 12.95 (ISBN 0-15-140198-5). Harcourt Brace Jovanovich.
Hidden Target. Helen MacInnes. LC 81-173. 1981. 15.95 (ISBN 0-8161-3153-8). G.K. Hall.
Hidden Terror. Mary Albert. LC 5-42178. (On cover: Seaside library. Pocket ed., no. 933). 1887. G. Munro.
Hidden Things. Harry Sinclair Drago. LC 15-26980. 1915. The Macaulay Company.
Hidden Trails. William Patterson White. LC 20-120582. 1920. Doubleday, Page & Company.
Hidden Trails. William Patterson White. LC 33-7795. 1922. A. L. Burt Company.
Hidden Treasure: A Tale of Troublous Times. Lucy Ellen Guernsey. LC 7-149. 1890. T. Whittaker.
Hidden Treasure of Mokoloho: This Story Is Written from the Time When Dr. Livingston and H. Stanly Explored North Africa... Jeanette Wheeler- Cooper. LC 20-163. J. Cremer.
Hidden Treasures. Beatrice Levin. LC 79-87530. 232p. 1981. 5.95 (ISBN 0-89896-049-5, Pub. by the Lindahl Press). Larksdale.
Hidden Treasures of Egypt: A Romance. Eustace Rawlins. LC 26-13991. Stratford Press.
Hidden Universe. Farley. 4.00 o.p.; pap. 2.00 o.p. Fantasy Pub Co.
Hidden Valley. Muriel Hine Coxon. LC 20-1287. 1919. John Lane.
Hidden Valley. Douglas Cecil Percy. (Orig.). (YA) 1968. pap. 0.95 o.p. (10506P). Zondervan.
Hidden Valley: An African Mystery Novel. Douglas Cecil Percy. LC 51-14630. 1951. Zondervan Pub. House.
Hidden Variables. Charles Sheffield. 384p. (Orig.). 1981. pap. 2.50 (ISBN 0-441-32991-8). Ace Bks.
Hidden Voice: Or The Ghost of the Old Genesee. An Interesting Story of Rochester, N.Y. A Novel. Edward P Schaefer. LC 8-2025. 1887. Press of H. H. Smith.
Hidden Water. Dane Coolidge. LC 10-25064. 1910. 1.35. A. C. McClurg & Co.
Hidden Ways. Frederic Franklyn Van De Water. LC 35-22397. The Bobbs-Merrill Company.
Hidden Wings & Other Stories. facs. ed. Timothy S. Arthur. LC 72-137719. (American Fiction Reprint Ser.). Repr. of 1864 ed. 15.00 (ISBN 0-8369-7018-7). Ayer Co.
Hidden Wings: And Other Stories. Timothy Shay Arthur. LC 72-137719. (His Arthur's home stories, 1). (American fiction reprint series). (Illus.). 1970. Books for Libraries Press.
Hidden Woman. James Hay. 1929. Dodd, Mead & Company.
Hidden World. Stanton Arthur Coblentz. LC 57-12666. (Science fiction). 1957. Avalon Books.
Hidden Worlds of Zandra. William Rotsler. (Science Fiction Ser.). 192p. 1983. 11.95 (ISBN 0-385-14614-0). Doubleday.
Hidden Wrath. Stella Phillips. 200p. 1982. 11.95 (ISBN 0-8027-5481-3). Walker & Co.
Hidden Years. John Oxenham. LC 58-2330. 1955. Longmans, Green.
Hidden Years. John Oxenham, pseud. LC 25-20709. 1925. Longmans, Green and Co.
Hide and Go Seek. Anne Colver. LC 33-7850. 1933. Minton, Batch & Company.
Hide and Go Seek: By Andrew Garve Pseud. Paul Winterton. LC 66-11481. bds., 3.95. Harper.
Hide-&-Seek. Lindsay Maracotta. 288p. 1982. pap. 2.95 (ISBN 0-671-83622-6). PB.
Hide and Seek. Renee Shann. LC 47-17765. 1947. Arcadia House, Inc.
Hide & Seek. Jessamyn West. LC 72-88797. 1973. 7.50 (ISBN 0-15-140215-9). HarBraceJ.
Hide and Seek. Jacqueline Wilson. LC 73-78965. 1973. 4.95 (ISBN 0-385-06031-9). Published for the Crime Club by Doubleday.
Hide and Seek in Forest-Land. Robert William Chambers. LC 9-16424. 1909. D. Appleton and Company.
Hide and Seek, or, The Mystery of Mary Grice. dover ed. Wilkie Collins. LC 81-66300. (Illus.). 5.00 (ISBN 0-486-24211-0). Dover Publications.
Hide-and-Seek: Or, The Mystery of Mary Grice. A Novel. Wilkie Collins. LC 3-27266. 1874. Harper & Brothers.
Hide & Seek: The Mystery of Mary Grice. Wilkie Collins. (Illus.). 384p. 1982. pap. 5.00 (ISBN 0-486-24211-0). Dover.
Hide and Sex. C. S Vanek. LC 73-9897. (Traveller's companion series, TC-453). 1969. 1.95. Olympia Press.
Hide & Tallow Men. John Thomas Edson. 1978. pap. 1.95 (ISBN 0-425-05069-6). Berkley Pub.
Hide-Away Island. Barry Fox. LC 34-509817. Greenberg.
Hide Fox, and After All. Rafael Yglesias. 1974. (pbk.) 1.50. Dell.
Hide Fox, and All After. Rafael Yglesias. LC 73-171330. 1972. 5.95. Doubleday.
Hide Her from Every Eye: A John Jericho Mystery Novel, by Hugh Pentecost Pseud. Judson Pentecost Philips. LC 65-259103. (Red badge detective). bds., 3.50. Dodd.
Hide Hunters. Lewis B Patten. (Signet brand Western, T5533). 1973. (pbk.) 0.75. New American Lib.
Hide in Plain Sight. Leslie Waller. 1980. pap. 2.25 (ISBN 0-440-13603-2). Dell.
Hide in the Dark. Frances Noyes Hart. LC 29-173899. Doubleday, Doran & Company, Inc.
Hide of a Rhinoceros. Marjorie P. Kaiser. 4.95 o.p. Vantage.
Hide Rustlers. Trev Roberts, pseud. LC 67-3555. 1967. Arcadia House.
Hide Rustlers. Les Savage. LC 50-8213. (A Double D western). 1950. Doubleday.
Hide the Baron. John Creasey. LC 77-91362. 1978. 6.95 (ISBN 0-8027-5383-3). Walker.
Hide the Body? Milton Morris Propper. LC 39-297206. 1939. Harper & Brothers.
Hideaway. Maurice Procter. LC 68-28233. 1968. 4.95. Harper &Row.
Hideaway. Joan Sherman. 1970. pap. 0.60 o.p. (60-455). Manor Bks.
Hideaway House. James Noble Gifford. LC 39-12730. 1937. Gramercy Publishing Co.
Hideaway House. Gay Rutherford. LC 39-127301. Gramercy Publishing Co.
Hideous Strength: A Modern Fairy-Tale for Grown-Ups. Clive Staples Lewis. LC 68-7663. 1968. 5.95. Macmillan.
Hideout. Egon Hostovsky & Long, Fern, Tr. LC 45-1694. 1945. Random House.
Hider. Loren D Estleman. LC 77-81786. 1978. 6.95 (ISBN 0-385-13627-7). Doubleday.
Hider. Loren D Estleman. 1980. 1.75 (ISBN 0-671-83273-5). Pocket Books.
Hiding. Norma Klein. LC 76-17592. 5.95 (ISBN 0-590-07435-0). Four Winds Press.
Hiding. Norma Klein. (Kangaroo Book). 1977. 1.50 (ISBN 0-671-81688-8). Pocket Books.
Hiding Place. Lane Johnstone. LC 58-13661. 1958. Sagamore Press.
Hiding Place. Carlton Keith, pseud. 1969. pap. 0.60 o.p. (0502-06028-060). Curtis.
Hiding Place. Keith Robertson. LC 65-13704. 1965. Published for the Crime Club by Doubleday.
Hiding Place. Collin Wilcox. LC 72-7487. 1973. 4.95 (ISBN 0-394-48234-4). Random House.
Hiding-Places: A Novel. Allen French. LC 17-8201. 1917. 1.35. C. Scribner's Sons.
Hiding Wall. Michael Arve. 1970. 2.95 o.p. Vantage.
Hie to the Hunters. high school ed. Stuart, Jesse. LC 51-6676. 1951. Harcourt, Brace.
Hie to the Hunters. Jesse Stuart. LC 50-7330. 1950. Whittlesey House.
Hiero-Salem: The Vision of Peace. A Fiction Founded in Ideals... 2d ed.... ed. Eveleen Laura Mason. LC 9-12622. The Author, E. L. Mason.
Hiero-Salem: The Vision of Peace. A Fiction Founded on Ideals... Eveleen Laura Mason. LC 7-25573. J. G. Cupples Company.
Hieroglyphic Tales. Horace Walpole. LC 74-16031. 1974. (ISBN 0-8414-9564-5). Folcroft Library Editions.
Hieroglyphics of Love. Stories of Sonoratown and Old Mexico. Amanda Mathews Chase. LC 6-46348. 1906. The Artemisia Bindery.
Hieros Gamos of Sam and An Smith. Josephine Saxton. LC 69-20071. (Doubleday science fiction). 1969. 4.50. Doubleday.
Hiero's Journey. Sterling E. Lanier. 1974. (pbk.) 1.25. Bantam Books.
Hiero's Journey: A Romance of the Future. Sterling E Lanier. LC 73-4999. 1973. 6.50 (ISBN 0-8019-5834-2). Chilton Book Co.
Higgler. Alfred Edgar Coppard. LC 44-49690. 1930. The Chocorua Press.
High. Thomas Willes Chitty. LC 69-16050. 1969. 5.95. Walker.
High. Thomas Hinde. 1970. pap. 0.95 o.p. (N2187). Pyramid Pubns.
High Adventure. Jeffery Farnol. LC 26-61469. 1926. Little, Brown, and Company.
High Adventure. Fjeril Hess. 8.00 o.p. R & E Res Assoc.
High Adventure. John Oxenham, pseud. LC 11-30783. 1911. Duffield & Company.
High Altar. Agnes Edwards Rothery. LC 24-211477. 1924. Doubleday, Page & Company.
High & Dry. Dick Selvig & Don Riley. 368p. 1983. pap. 3.50 (ISBN 0-523-41921-X). Pinnacle Bks.
High and Outside. Linnea A Due. LC 79-3406. 8.95 (ISBN 0-06-011102-X). Harper & Row.
High and the Mighty. Ernest Kellogg Gann. (Kangaroo Book). 1977. 1.95 (ISBN 0-671-81196-7). Pocket Books.
High and the Mighty. Ernest Kellogg Gann. LC 53-5252. 1953. Sloane.
High Anxiety. Robert H. Pilpel & Mel Brooks. LC 77-87790. (Illus.). 12.95 (ISBN 0-448-14575-8) (ISBN 0-448-14576-6). Grosset & Dunlap.
High Are the Mountains. Hannah Priebsch Closs. (Tarn Trilogy; 1). 1978. 1.95 (ISBN 0-445-04219-2). Popular Library.
High Are the Mountains: A Novel. Hannah Priebsch Closs. LC 59-5091. 1959. Vanguard Press.
High Barbaree. Charles Bernard Nordhoff & James Norman Hall. LC 45-84509. 1945. Little, Brown and Company.
High Bid for Murder. Archie O'Neill, pseud. LC 74-8089. (Jeff Pride series,#3). 1974. (pbk.) 0.95. Bantam Books.
High Bonnet. Idwal Jones. LC 45-9821. 1945. Prentice-Hall, Inc.
High Book of the Grail: A Translation of the Thirteenth Century Romance of Perlesvaus. Tr. by Nigel Bryant. LC 78-319632. 1978. 23.50 (ISBN 0-85991-039-3). Brewer.
High Book of the Grail: A Translation of the 13th Century Romance of "Perlesvaus". Tr. by Nigel Bryant. 265p. 1978. 26.75x (ISBN 0-8476-6042-7). Rowman.
High Border Riders. Lee Floren. (Orig.). 1979. pap. 1.50 (ISBN 0-532-15391-X). Woodhill.
High Bradford. Mary Rogers Bangs. LC 12-10139. 1912. Houghton Mifflin Company.
High Bridge. Ethel Powelson Hueston. LC 38-157303. The Bobbs-Merrill Company.
High Bright Buggy Wheels. Luella Sanders Bruce Creighton. LC 52-10157. Dodd, Mead.
High Cage. Steve Frazee. LC 57-5626. 1957. Macmillan.
High Calling. Charles Monroe Sheldon. LC 11-254379. Hodder & Stoughton, George H. Doran Company.
High Calling. Street, James Howell. LC 51-11225. 1951. Doubleday.

High Card: Faro Blake, No. 18. Zeke Masters, pseud. 1982. pap. 1.95 (ISBN 0-671-44082-9). PB.

High Cards. Bernard Gunther & Corita Kent. 4.95 o.p. (ISBN 0-06-061585-0, HarpR). Har-Row.

High Carnival. 1st Ed. John J Pugh. LC 59-5932. 1959. Little, Brown.

High Church. Frederick William Robinson. LC 75-498. (Victorian Fiction: Novels of Faith and Doubt). 1975. 35.00 (ISBN 0-8240-1573-8). Garland Pub.

High Citadel. Desmond Bagley. LC 65-11059. 1965. Doubleday.

High Class. Peter Engel. 1980. Berkley Books.

High Command Murder. Joseph Rosenberger. (Death Merchant Ser.: No. 42). 192p. (Orig.). 1980. pap. 1.95 (ISBN 0-523-41020-4). Pinnacle Bks.

High Commission. A Story of the Spanish-American War. Fredericka Spangler Cantwell. LC 99-1656. F.T. Neely.

High Commissioner. Jon Cleary. (75-8067). 1968. Popular Lib.

High Commissioner: A Novel. Jon Cleary. LC 66-23351. 1966. bds., 4.50. Morrow.

High Cost of Living. Marge Piercy. LC 77-6149. 10.00 (ISBN 0-06-013339-2). Harper & Row.

High Cost of Living: A Novel. Marge Piercy. 2.25 (ISBN 0-449-23812-1). Fawcett Crest.

High Couch of Silistra. Janet Morris. 256p. (Orig.). 1981. pap. 2.50 (ISBN 0-553-14532-0). Bantam.

High Country. Peter Dawson. 144p. 1981. pap. 1.75 (ISBN 0-553-14537-1). Bantam.

High Country. Peter Dawson. 1974. (pbk.) 0.95. Bantam.

High Country. Jonathan H. Glidden. LC 47-35956. 1947. Dodd, Mead & Company.

High Country. Harold Channing Wire. LC 47-177675. 1947. The Westminster Press.

High Country: By Chuck Stanley Pseud. Charles Stanley Strong. LC 53-855812. 1953. Arcadia House.

High Country Dreamer. William Arthur Neubauer. LC 65-7330. 1965. Arcadia House.

High Country Illuminator. Daniel Ford. LC 79-131075. 1971. 5.95. Doubleday.

High Country Pride. Lynn Erickson. (Tapestry Romance Ser.). 320p. (Orig.). 1982. pap. 2.50 (ISBN 0-671-46137-0). PB.

High Country Showdown. Ray Gaulden. 1979. pap. 1.50 o.s.i. (ISBN 0-505-51438-9). Tower Bks.

High Courage. Jackson Gregory. LC 34-4679. 1934. Dodd, Mead & Company.

High Courts of Heaven: A Story of the R. A. F. John Vernon Hewes. LC 43-2268. 1943. Doubleday, Doran and Co., Inc.

High Crimes. William Deverell. LC 81-21409. 1982. 15.95 (ISBN 0-312-37221-3). St Martin's Press.

High Crimes and Misdemeanors. Joanne Greenberg. LC 79-11111. 8.95 (ISBN 0-03-044946-4). Holt, Rinehart and Winston.

High Crusade. Poul Anderson. 1975. (pbk.) 0.95. Manor Books.

High Crusade. Poul Anderson. (Berkley Medallion Book). 1978. 1.50 (ISBN 0-425-03670-7). Berkley Pub. Corp.

High Crusade. 1st Ed. Poul Anderson. LC 60-13499. 1960. Doubleday.

High Crystal. Martin Caidin. LC 73-91500. 1974. 6.95 (ISBN 0-87795-079-2). Arbor House.

High Deeds of Finn & Other Bardic Romances of Ancient Ireland. Thomas W. Rolleston. (Illus.). 214p. 1973. Repr. of 1910 ed. 15.00 o.s.i. (ISBN 0-87696-053-0). Lemma.

High Deryni. Katherine Kurtz. 1976. pap. 2.25 (ISBN 0-345-28614-6). Ballantine.

High Deryni. Katherine Kurtz. (Adult Fantasy Original). 1973. (pbk.) 1.25. Ballantine Books.

High Desire. Leslie Simon. 80p. 1983. pap. 4.95 (ISBN 0-914728-41-5). Wingbow Pr.

High Dive. Frank O'Rourke. LC 54-538511. 1954. Random House.

High Empire. Clyde M. Brundy. 432p. 1980. pap. 2.50 (ISBN 0-380-00040-7, 76166). Avon.

High Empire. Clyde M Brundy. 1974. (pbk.) 1.75 (ISBN 0-380-00040-7). Avon.

High Encounter. Burton Wohl. 1975. (pbk.) 1.25. Bantam Books.

High Explosive. Gordon Phillips. LC 26-26230. 1926. Dodd, Mead and Company.

High Fantasy Boxed Set. Jeffrey Dillow. 1981. pap. text ed. 21.95 (ISBN 0-8359-2830-6). Reston.

High Fences. Grace Louise Smith Richmond. LC 30-17708. 1930. Doubleday, Doran & Company, Inc.

High Fever: A Novel of the Sales Promotion Decade, the New Economic Era with Its Brittle Pageantry of Klannishness, Florida Gold Rush, Rum Rackets, and Saffron Journalism. Melvin Lostutter. LC 35-10587. 1935. Harper & Brothers.

High Fires. Marjorie Barkeley McClure. 1924. Little, Brown and Company.

High Flame of Courage. Ethel Foresman. LC 56-119880. 1956. Meador Pub. Co.

High Flight. Ruth Dewey Groves. LC 29-5697. Grosset & Dunlap.

High-Flying Hookers. Lydia Wilkinson. 192p. (Orig.). 1973. pap. 1.95 o.p. (ISBN 0-87682-355-X, 7355). Barclay Hse.

High Forfeit: A Novel. Basil King. LC 25-18058. 1925. Harper & Brothers.

High Frontier. Leland Shattuck Jamieson. LC 40-316300. 1940. W. Morrow & Company.

High Game. Paul Geddes. LC 68-28266. 1968. 5.50. Weybright and Talley.

High Garth. Mira Stables. 224p. 1980. pap. 1.75 (ISBN 0-449-50032-2, Coventry). Fawcett.

High Gear. Great Stories About Fast Cars and Their Drivers. 1st Ed. Ed. by Evan Jones. LC 55-25861. (Bantam books, 1313). 1955. Bantam Books.

High Gloss. Peter H Engel. LC 78-21359. 10.00 (ISBN 0-312-37232-9). St. Martin's Press.

High Goal: A Novel. Elizabeth Harding Daly. LC 34-103291. Macrae Smith Company.

High Graders. Louis L'Amour. 176p. 1975. pap. 1.95 (ISBN 0-553-13770-0, Y13770-0). Bantam.

High Grass Valley. William MacLeod Raine & Wayne D. Overholser. LC 55-7795. 1955. Houghton Mifflin.

High Green Gun. Ray Hogan. (Shawn Starbuck Western). (Signet Book: Vol. 21). 1976. (pbk.) 0.95. New American Library.

High Ground. Esther Loewen Vogt. LC 75-84683. 1970. 3.95. Herald Press.

High Ground. Odella Phelps Wood. LC 47-18972. 1946. The Exposition Press.

High Ground: A Novel. John Calvin Mellett. The Bobbs-Merrill Company.

High Gun. Lee Floren. (Orig.). 1979. pap. 1.50 (ISBN 0-532-23110-4). Woodhill.

High Gun, a Gold Medal Original. Cover Painting by Frank McCarthy. Leslie Charles Ernenwein. LC 57-20959. (Gold medal books, no. 620). 1956. Fawcett Publications.

High Hand. Jacques Futrelle. LC 11-103402. 1.25. The Bobbs-Merrill Company.

High Hat: A Radio Romance. Alma Sioux Scarberry. LC 30-19831. Grosset & Dunlap.

High Hazard. Richard Martin Stern. LC 60-7344. 1960. Scribner.

High Hazard. Sam Victor. (Kilburn Series). (Berkley medallion book: Vol. 3). 1975. (pbk.) 0.95 (ISBN 0-425-02788-0). Berkley Pub. Co.

High Hazard: A Romance of the Far Arctic. Robert Watson. LC 30-10473. 1929. L. Carrier & Co.

High Heart. Basil King. LC 22-4734. 1917. Grosset & Dunlap.

High Heart. Basil King. LC 17-24285. 1917. 1.50. Harper & Brothers.

High Heaven. Peter Harmon. 192p. 1972. pap. 0.95 o.p. (532-00202-075). Manor Bks.

High Heels. Miles Tripp. 1982. 15.00x (ISBN 0-333-27409-1, Pub. by Macmillan England). State Mutual Bk.

High Heroic. Constantine Fitz Gibbon. LC 69-14697. 1969. 4.95 o.p. (ISBN 0-393-08585-6). Norton.

High Heroic: A Novel. Fitz Gibbon, Constantine. LC 69-14697. 1969. 4.95. Norton.

High Hills. John Lawson. LC 80-53537. (Illus.). 220p. (Orig.). 1981. pap. 4.95 (ISBN 0-938658-01-8). West SW Pub Co.

High Hills Calling. Anne Miller Downes. LC 51-9989. 1951. Lippincott.

High History of the Holy Graal. Tr. by Sebastian Evans. LC 74-171444. 1969 (ISBN 0-227-67727-7). James Clarke.

High History of the Holy Graal. Perlesvaus. Tr. by Evans, Sebastian. LC 8-2165. 1903. J. M. Dent & Co.

High History of the Holy Graal. Perlesvaus & Perceval (Romances, Etc.) Tr. by Evans, Sebastian. LC 37-5580. (Half-title: Everyman's library, ed. by Ernest Rhys. Romance. no. 445). 1929. J. M. Dent & Sons, Ltd.

High Holiday. Kathleen Thompson Norris. LC 75-31899. 1975. 9.95 (ISBN 0-89190-304-6). American Reprint Co.

High Holiday. Kathleen Thompson Norris. LC 49-7405. 1949. N. Y., Doubleday.

High Hunt. David Eddings. LC 72-87613. 1973. 7.95 (ISBN 0-399-11055-0). Putnam.

High Hunt. David Eddings. (Fawcett Crest Book). 1976. (pbk.) 1.75. Fawcett.

High Hurdles. Joseph Husband. LC 23-8989. 1923. Houghton Mifflin Company.

High Ideals? James Harris. LC 77-13737. (Harvest/HBJ book). 1978. 8.95 (ISBN 0-15-140221-3) (ISBN 0-15-640195-9). Harcourt Brace Jovanovich.

High Iron. Willis Todhunter Ballard. LC 52-11828. 1953. Houghton Mifflin.

High Is the Wall. Ruth Muirhead Berry. LC 55-11315. 1955. Muhlenberg Press.

High John, the Conqueror. John Walter Wilson. LC 48-10609. 1948. Macmillan Co.

High Justice. Jerry Pournelle. (Orig.). 1977. pap. 2.25 (ISBN 0-671-83266-2). PB.

High Life. Edouard I. E. Victor Edouard Cadol. Tr. by Cooke, H. O. (On cover: Idle moments series, no. 4). 1891. The Price-McGill Publishing Company.

High Life: And Other Stories. Harrison Garfield Rhodes. LC 20-17527. 1920. R. M. McBridg & Co.

High Life in New York. Ann Sophia Winterbotham Stephens. LC 30-12314. (Lettered on cover: Peterson's illustrated uniform edition of humorous American works). T. B. Peterson and Brothers.

High-Lights... Caroline Leslie Field. LC 6-41190. 1886. Houghton, Mifflin and Company.

High Lonesome. Al Cody, pseud. 1978. pap. 1.25 (ISBN 0-532-12585-1). Woodhill.

High Lonesome. Louis L'Amour. 160p. 1980. pap. 2.25 (ISBN 0-553-20257-X). Bantam.

High Lonesome World: The Death and Life of a Country Music Singer. Babs H Deal. LC 73-78690. 1969. 5.95. Doubleday.

High, Low and Wide Open. James Francis Rabbitt. LC 35-37770. The Macaulay Company.

High Marks: Stories That Make Good Reading. Annette Sloan & Albert Capaccio. (Orig.). (gr. 9). 1981. pap. text ed. 5.17 (ISBN 0-87720-393-8). AMSCO Sch.

High Mesa. Jack Webb. LC 52-7789. (A Dutton Diamond D western). 1952. Dutton.

High Mettled Racer: Being the Story of "Revenge", Racehorse and Hunter. Ernest Blakeman Vesey. LC 35-511708. 1935. E. P. Dutton & Co., Inc.

High Midnight. Stuart M. Kaminsky. 160p. 1981. 9.95 o.p. (ISBN 0-312-37234-5). St Martin.

High Midnight: A Toby Peters Mystery. Stuart M Maminsky. LC 80-29121. 1981. 9.95 (ISBN 0-312-37234-5). St. Martin's Press.

High Morning Fog: A Novel. 1st Ed. Markham Harris. LC 52-5097. 1952. Lippincott.

High Mountain. 2nd ed. LC 65-26326. 1978. 7.50 (ISBN 0-935490-03-5). Euclid Pub.

High New House. Thomas Williams. LC 63-10558. 1963. Dial Press.

High Noon. Ruby Mildred Ayres. LC 37-1864. 1937. Doubleday Doran & Company, Inc.

High Noon. Ruby Mildred Ayres. LC 38-6352. 1938. The Sun Dial Press, Inc.

High Noon. Alice Brown. LC 75-121526. (Short story index reprint series). 1970. Books for Libraries Press.

High Noon. Alice Brown. LC 4-311. 1904. Houghton, Mifflin and Company.

High Noon. Crosbie Garstin. LC 25-8543. 1925. Frederick A. Stokes Company.

High Noon. Clarence Pendleton Lee. LC 43-16385. 1943. The Macmillan Company.

High Noon: A New Sequel to "Three Weeks.". LC 11-17625. 1911. 1.50. The Macaulay Company.

High of Heart. Emilie Baker Loring. LC 38-333948. 1938. Little, Brown and Company.

High on a Hill. Lucy Daniels. LC 61-13753. McGraw-Hill.

High on a Hill. Mae Foster Jay. LC 35-1206. W. A. Wilde Company.

High on a Hill. Frances Y McHugh. LC 68-212. 1967. Arcadia House.

High on Gold. Lee Richmond. LC 72-84213. 1972. 7.95. Charter House.

High on Gold. Lee Richmond. 1974. (pbk.) 1.50. Avon.

High on the Energy Bridge. Eric K. Goodman. LC 79-1930. 264p. 1980. 11.95 (ISBN 0-03-047166-4); pap. 6.95 (ISBN 0-03-056841-2). HR&W.

High Passes. 1st Ed. John Henry Reese. LC 55-5327. Little, Brown.

High-Pitched Hum. George William McArthur Reynolds. LC 77-150348. 5.00 (ISBN 0-8059-2375-6). Dorrance.

High-Pitched Laugh of a Painted Lady: Stories. Lewis W. Green. LC 80-16382. 10.00 (ISBN 0-89587-017-7) (ISBN 0-89587-020-7). J. F. Blair.

High Place. Geoffrey Household. LC 50-7611. 1950. Little, Brown.

High Place. Margaret Jessup Van Briggle. LC 64-11945. 1964. Zondervan Pub. House.

High Place: A Comedy of Disenchantment. James Branch Cabell. LC 24-3793. 1923. R. M. McBride & Company.

High Place: A Comedy of Disenchantment. James Branch Cabell. LC 31-30269. (Bonibooks). 1931. A. & C. Boni.

High Place: A Comedy of Disenchantment. James Branch Cabell. LC 78-52155. (Illus.). 1978. 4.00 (ISBN 0-486-23670-6). Dover Publications.

High Places. Paul Ferris. LC 76-42202. 1977. 8.95 (ISBN 0-698-10799-3). Coward, McCann & Geoghegan.

High Places: A Novel. Helen Todd. LC 47-1741. 1947. J. B. Lippincott Company.

High Places: A Novel. 1st Ed. Edward Branch. LC 55-11113. 1957. Exposition Press.

High-Plains Drifter. Ernest Tidyman. LC 73-2950. 1973. (pbk.) 0.75. Bantam Books.

High Plains Temptress. Dirk Fletcher. (Spur Ser.: No. 1). 224p. 1982. pap. 2.25 (ISBN 0-8439-1123-9, Leisure Bks). Nordon Pubns.

High Pockets. Herbert Arthur, pseud. LC 46-7727. 1946. R. M. McBride.

High Pockets. Herbert Shappiro. LC 46-7727. 1946. R. M. McBride & Company.

High Prairie. Caleb A. Fuqua. 3.50 o.p. Carlton.

High Prairie. Eugene E Halleran. LC 50-14986. 1950. Macrae Smith.

High Prairie. Archie Joscelyn. LC 58-12505. 1958. Avalon Books.

High Pressure Center. Gerry Courtney. LC 80-13351. 1980. 8.95 (ISBN 0-87949-127-2). Ashley Books.

High Price of Gratitude. Janice Peters. (Orig.). 1980. pap. 1.95 (ISBN 0-87067-674-1, BH674). Holloway.

High Priestess. Robert Grant. LC 15-178031. 1915. C. Scribner's Sons.

High Red for Dead. William L Rohde. LC 51-20412. (Gold medal book, 145). 1951. Fawcett Publications.

High Rendezvous. 1st Ed. Kathleen Moore Knight. LC 54-6245. 1954. Published for the Crime Club by Doubleday.

High Requiem. Desmond Cory, pseud. (Johnny Fedora Ser., No. 6). 1969. pap. 0.60 o.p. (A377, Award). Univ Pub & Dist.

High Rider. Vance Donovan. (Orig.). 1969. pap. 0.75 o.p. (ISBN 0-446-64232-0, 64-232). Paperback Lib.

High-Rise. J. G. Ballard. LC 76-29899. 1977. 6.95 (ISBN 0-03-020651-0). Holt, Rinehart and Winston.

High-Rise. J. G. Ballard. 1978. 1.95 (ISBN 0-445-04181-1). Popular Library.

High Rise. Leo Heaps. LC 72-189228. 1972. 2.50 (ISBN 0-491-00502-4). W. H. Allen.

High Rising. Angela Mackail Thirkell. LC 51-13139. 1951. Knopf.

High Risk. Irene Stiles. LC 26-17627. 1926. Cassell and Company, Ltd.

High Road. Emma Sarah Gage Allen. LC 17-259733. The Meridian Press.

High Road. Faith Baldwin. 1976. Repr. of 1939 ed. lib. bdg. 15.45x (ISBN 0-88411-608-5). Amereon Ltd.

High Road. Faith Baldwin Cuthrell. LC 74-82148. 1974. Aeonian Press.

High Road. Faith Baldwin Cuthrell. LC 38-290919. Farra & Rinehart, Inc.

High Road. Grace Wallace Doonan. LC 30-28843. P. J. Kenedy & Sons.

High Road. Frances Grinstead. LC 45-1559. 1945. Doubleday, Doran & Company, Inc.

High Road. Janet Ramsay. LC 24-623285. 2.00. The Century Co.

High Road. Faith Shannon. LC 66-18942. 1966. Zondervan Pub. House.

High Road: By Mary Douglas Watren Pseud. Maysie Greig. LC 54-133529. 1954. Arcadia House.

High Road to China. Jon Cleary. 320p. 1983. pap. 2.95 (ISBN 0-446-31178-2). Warner Bks.

High Road to China. Jon Cleary. LC 76-54823. 1977. 8.95 o.p. Morrow.

High Road to China: A Novel. Jon Cleary. LC 76-54823. 1977. 8.95 (ISBN 0-688-03143-9). Morrow.

High Road to China: A Novel. Jon Cleary. 1979. 1.95. Popular Library.

High Road to Hell. Henry Leyford Gates. LC 38-7796. 1938. Godwin.

High Road to Honor. Julia Green Scott Vrooman. LC 24-22268. 1924. Minton, Balch & Company.

High Rocks. Loren D Estleman. LC 78-62646. 1979. 7.95 (ISBN 0-385-14696-5). Doubleday.

High Rocks. Loren D Estleman. 1980. 1.95 (ISBN 0-671-83267-0). Pocket Books.

High Roller; or, Plunging and Honeyfugling on the Race-Track. A Sporting Romance. Fortune Du Boisgobey & Williams, Henry Llewellyn, Jr., Tr. LC 6-33867. (On cover: Pollard's popular publications, no. 5). 1891. The Pollard Publishing Company.

High Rollers. D. Y. Cohn. (Orig.). 1975. pap. 1.50 o.p. (ISBN 0-515-03790-7). Pyramid Pubns.

High Roof. 1st Ed. Joy Petersen Packer. LC 59-130732. 1959. Lippincott.

High Saddle. William L Hopson. LC 56-16712. (Ace double novel books, D-128). 1955. Ace Books.

High Saddle. William L Hopson. LC 52-8360. 1952. Arcadia House.

High School Gent. Miriam Khamadi Were. LC 72-983376. (Series: New Fiction from Africa Series.). 1972. 12.00. Oxford University Press.

High School Girls & Their Teachers. Warren. pap. 1.95 o.p. (ISBN 0-87682-196-4, 7196). Barclay Hse.

High School Hookers. Ruth Miller, pseud. 1979. pap. 1.75 o.s.i. (ISBN 0-505-51417-6). Tower Bks.

High School Hookers. Ruth Miller, pseud. (O.s.i.). pap. 1.50 o.s.i. (LB390, Leisure Bks). Nordon Pubns.

High School Hookers. Ruth Miller. Leisure Books.

High School Hotbed. Jan Cheux. pap. 1.95 o.p. (8017). Cameo.

High Seas. Cyril Abraham. (Onedin Line). (Signet Book). 1977. 1.50 (ISBN 0-451-07426-2). New American Library.

High Sierra. Ed. by Tino Balio & Douglas Gomery. LC 79-3961. (Wisconsin-Warner Bros. Screenplay Ser.). (Illus.). 200p. 1979. 17.50 (ISBN 0-299-07930-9); pap. 6.95t (ISBN 0-299-07934-1). U of Wis Pr.

High Sierra. William Riley Burnett. LC 40-5663. 1940. A. A. Knopf.

High Sierra. William Riley Burnett. LC 47-20842. (Murder mystery monthly, no. 40). 1946.

High Silver. Anthony Richardson. LC 26-19020. 1926. Dodd, Mead and Company.

High Slaughter. Jon Hart. LC 80-71037. (Mercenaries Ser.). 128p. 1981. pap. 2.95 (ISBN 0-87754-229-5). Chelsea Hse.

High Snow. Martin Louis Alan Gompertz. George H. Doran Company.

High Sorcery. Andre Norton, pseud. 1982. pap. 2.25 (ISBN 0-441-33709-0, Pub. by Ace Science Fiction). Ace Bks.

High Speed. Clinton Holland Stagg. LC 16-21392. W. J. Watt & Company.

High Speed Girl: A Novel. May Christie. LC 31-120212. Grosset & Dunlap.

High Spirits. William Robertson Davies. LC 83-113063. 1982. 6.95 (ISBN 0-14-006505-9). Penguin Books.

High Spirits: Being Certain Stories Written in Them. James Payn. (Franklin square library, no. 88). 1879. Harper & Brothers.

High Stakes. Dick Francis. LC 75-25082. 7.95 (ISBN 0-06-011307-3). Harper & Row.

High Stakes. Dick Francis. (Kangaroo Book). 1977. 1.75 (ISBN 0-671-81109-6). Pocket Books.

High Stakes. Emma Murdoch Van Deventer. LC 792. (On cover: Pinkerton detective series, no. 42). Laird & Lee.

High Stakes: A Story of Strange People and Happenings. Curt Riess. LC 42-18467. 1942. G. P. Putnam's Sons.

High Stakes and Desperate Men: Classics of Espionage. Reader's Digest Association. LC 74-3808. (Illus.). 1974. Reader's Digest Association.

High Starlight. Llewellyn Perry Holmes. LC 52-11007. (Double D western). 1952. Doubleday.

High Storm. Brian Wynne Garfield. 1970. pap. 0.60 o.p. (ISBN 0-447-73204-8). Lancer.

High Street. Andre Ernotte & Elliot Tiber. 1977. 1.50 (ISBN 0-380-00927-7). Avon Books.

High Summer. Richard Church. LC 32-4106. 1932. R. Long & R. R. Smith, Inc.

High Table. Joanna Cannan, pseud. LC 31-213314. 1931. Doubleday, Doran & Company, Inc.

High Tension. William Wister Haines. LC 38-10963. 1938. Little, Brown and Company.

High Tension. Dean Ing. 256p. (Orig.). 1982. pap. 2.50 (ISBN 0-441-33712-0). Ace Bks.

High Tension. 1st Ed. Theodora McCormick Du Bois. LC 50-8638. 1950. Published for the Crime Club by Doubleday.

High Terrace. Virginia Coffman. pap. 1.50 (ISBN 0-451-08228-1, W8228, Sig). NAL.

High Terrace. Virginia Coffman. (Signet Book). 1975. (pbk.) 1.25. New American Library.

High Terrace see Curse of the Island Pool.

High Terror. Irving A Greenfield. 1978. 1.95 (ISBN 0-445-04244-3). Popular Library.

High Threshold: A Novel. Nicoline Kildahl Allen. LC 53-5693. 1953. Vantage Press.

High Thrust. Renee Auden, pseud. pap. 1.95 o.s.i. (OPS-42). Olympia.

High Thursday. Roger Burlingame. LC 28-3171. 1928. C. Scribner's Sons.

High Tide. Philip Maitland Hubbard. LC 75-111493. 1970. 4.95. Atheneum.

High Tide. Philip Maitland Hubbard. LC 81-47379. (Fifty Classics of Crime Fiction, 1950-1975). 1982. 14.95 (ISBN 0-8240-4982-9). Garland.

High Tide and Other Stories. George Hoyt Smith. LC 29-4756. The Christopher Publishing House.

High Tide at Midnight. Sara Craven. (Harlequin Presents Ser.). 1979. pap. 1.50 (ISBN 0-373-70791-6, Pub by Harlequin). PB.

High Tide at Noon. Elisabeth Ogilvie. LC 75-34483. 1975. 6.95 (ISBN 0-88411-183-0). Aeonian Press.

High Tide at Noon. Elisabeth Ogilvie. LC 44-40069. 1944. Thomas Y. Crowell Company.

High Tide at Noon. Elisabeth Ogilvie. 1975. (pbk.) 1.75 (ISBN 0-380-00537-9). Avon.

High Tide: By Frances Hanna... Frances Nichols Hanna. LC 39-23754. 1939. Arcadia House, Inc.

High Tide Talker, and Other Stories. Elspeth Davie. LC 77-357253. 1976. 3.75 (ISBN 0-241-89446-8). Hamilton.

High Time. Mary Lasswell. LC 44-8654. 1944. Houghton Mifflin Company.

High Times and Hard Times: Sketches and Tales. George Washington Harris. Ed. by M. Thomas Inge. LC 67-21655. 1967. Vanderbilt University Press.

High Tower. Bill Poth. 192p. 1975. 7.50 o.p. (ISBN 0-682-48422-9). Exposition.

High Towers. Thomas Bertram Costain. LC 48-9680. 1949. Doubleday.

High Towers. Reprint Ed. Thomas Bertram Costain. LC 50-3330. 1950. Sun Dial Press.

High Trail. Elers Koch. LC 52-11876. (Illus.). 1953. Caxton Printers.

High Trail. Marian Templeton Place. LC 57-874410. 1957. Avalon Books.

High Trail to Rawhide. Lee Thomas. 1978. pap. 1.25 (ISBN 0-532-12577-0). Woodhill.

High Trial. Vivian Gurney Breckenfeld. LC 48-8742. 1948. Doubleday.

High Twelve: A Sequel to Low Twelve. "By Their Deeds Ye Shall Know Them"; a Series of Striking and Truthful Incidents Illustrative of the Fidelity of Free Masons to One Another in Times of Distress and Danger. Edward Sylvester Ellis. LC 12-23759. 1912. 1.50. Macoy Publishing & Masonic Supply Co.

High Vacuum: By Charles Eric Maine Pseud. David McIlwain. LC 57-12239. (Ballantine books, 218). 1957. Ballantine Books.

High Valley. Jessica Nelson North MacDonald. LC 72-12848. 1973. 5.95 (ISBN 0-394-48103-8). Random House.

High Valley. Jessica North. LC 72-11460. 1973. 5.95 (ISBN 0-394-48103-8). Random House.

High Valley. Jessica North. LC 73-17028. 1973. 8.95 (ISBN 0-8161-6166-6). G. K. Hall.

High Valley. Jessica North. (Signet book). 1974. (pbk.) 1.50. New American Library.

High Valley: By Charmian Clift and George Johnston. Charmian Clift. LC 50-7494. 1950. Bobbs-Merrill.

High Valley River. Zane Grey. 1982. 18.00x (ISBN 0-86025-181-0, Pub. by Ian Henry Pubns England). State Mutual Bk.

High Vengeance. Frank O'Rourke. LC 54-35671. (Ballantine books, 82). 1954. Ballantine Books.

High Vermilion. Frederick Dilley Glidden. LC 48-596710. 1948. Houghton, Mifflin Co.

High Voltage. Thomas Chastain. LC 79-6977. 1979. 8.95 (ISBN 0-385-14437-7). Doubleday.

High Voltage. Thomas Chastain. 1981. 2.50 (ISBN 0-425-04831-4). Berkley Publishing Corporation.

High Wall. Alan R Clark. LC 36-778914. 1936. H. Smith & R. Haas.

High Walls. Arthur Tuckerman. LC 29-129143. 1929. Doubleday, Doran and Company, Inc.

High Water: A Novel. Bettie Johnson Sutcliffe. LC 29-1958. The Grafton Press.

High Water at Catfish Bend. Ben L. Burman. 2.95. Taplinger.

High Water at Catfish Bend. Ben Lucien Burman. (Puffin book). (Illus.). 1974. (ISBN 0-14-030711-7). Penguin.

High Water at Four. 1st Ed. in U. S. A. Jerrard Tickell. LC 65-10635. 1966. 4.50. Doubleday.

High-Water-Mark. A Novel. Ferris Jerome. 1879. J. B. Lippincott & Co.

High Water: 1st Ed. Richard Pike Bissell. 1954. Little, Brown.

High Way. Caroline Atwater Mason. LC 24-317141. Fleming H. Revell Company.

High-Ways and by-Ways: Or, Tales of the Roadside, Picked up in the French Provinces. Thomas Colley Grattan. LC 6-45435. 1825. H. C. Carey & I. Lea.

High Weeds. Edith Ann Ulmer. LC 32-33157. 1932. W. K. Stewart Co.

High White Forest. Ralph Allen. LC 64-19264. 1964. Doubleday.

High, Wide and Handsome: By Curt Brandon Pseud. 1st Ed. Curtis Kent Bishop. LC 50-12230. (Dutton Diamond D western). 1950. Dutton.

High, Wide & Lonesome. Hal Glen Borland. Incl. Country Editor's Boy. 1970. boxed set 12.90 o.p. (ISBN 0-397-00646-2). Lippincott.

High, Wide and Ransom. Don Tracy. (Giff). 1976. (pbk.) 1.25 (ISBN 0-671-80254-2). Pocket Books.

High Wind in Jamaica. Richard Arthur Warren Hughes. LC 65-2620. 1965. Harper & Row.

High Wind in Jamaica: The Innocent Voyage. Richard Arthur Warren Hughes & Peterson, Mrs. Isabel (Bowler) LC 32-16967. (Half-title: The modern library of the world's best books). 1932. The Modern Library.

High Wind Rising: A Novel. Elsie Singmaster. LC 42-24105. 1942. Houghton Mifflin Company.

High Window. Raymond - Chandler. LC 76-11807. 1976. 1.95 (ISBN 0-394-72141-1). Vintage Books.

High Window. Raymond Chandler. LC 42-17988. 1942. A. A. Knopf.

High Windows: By Helen St. Bernard... Helen St. Bernard. LC 33-32226. Grosset & Dunlap.

High Winds. Arthur Cheney Train. LC 27-8780. 1927. C. Scribner's Sons.

High Wire. Richard Clayton. LC 63-18128. 1963. I. Washburn.

High Wire & Hot Lead. C. William Harrison. 1972. pap. 0.60 o.p. (06158). Curtis.

High Wynne, Free Quaker: Sometime Brevet Lieutenant-Colonel on the Staff of His Excellency General Washington. continental ed... ed. Silas Weir Mitchell. LC 99-4677. 1899. The Century Co.

High Yield in Death. Nick Carter. (Nick Carter Ser.). (O.s.i.). (Orig.). 1976. pap. 1.25 o.s.i. (AQ1609, Award). Univ Pub & Dist.

Highbinders. Oliver Bleeck. (O.s.i.). 1976. pap. 1.50 o.s.i. (ISBN 0-671-80803-6). WSP.

Highbinders. Oliver Bleeck. 1974. 5.95 o.p. (ISBN 0-688-00210-2). Morrow.

Highbinders. Ross Thomas. LC 73-10102. 1974. 5.95 (ISBN 0-688-00210-2). Morrow.

Highboy Rings Down the Curtain. George Agnew Chamberlain. LC 24-137422. 1923. Evening News Company.

Higher Animals. H. E. F. Donohue. 1965. 4.95 o.p. (ISBN 0-670-37166-1). Viking Pr.

Higher Animals: A Romance. H. E. F Donohue. LC 64-18483. 4.95. Viking.

Higher Command. Edlef Koppen. LC 31-322368. 1931. J. Cape & H. Smith.

Higher Court. Mary Stewart Daggett. LC 11-30392. 1.25. R. G. Badger.

Higher Ground. Meredith Sue Willis. LC 81-8912. 1981. 12.95 (ISBN 0-684-17225-9). Scribner.

Higher Ground. large print ed. Meredith Sue Willis. LC 82-5184. 1982. 14.95 (ISBN 0-89340-517-5). J. Curley & Associates.

Higher Law: A Romance, 3 vols. in 2. Edward Maitland. LC 79-8165. Date not set. Repr. of 1869 ed. Set. 84.50 (ISBN 0-404-62184-8). AMS Pr.

Higher Than the Arrow. Judy Van Der Veer. LC 68-22393. (Illus.). 1975. (pbk.) 0.95 (ISBN 0-380-00194-2). Avon.

Higher Than the Church. Wilhelmine Birch Von Hillern & Lyon, Vivian Elsie, Tr. LC 17-83. (students' literal translations). 0.50. Translation Publishing Company, Inc.

Higher Than the Church: An Art Legend of Ancient Times. Wilhelmina Birch Von Hillern & Safford, Mary Joanna, Tr. LC 7-46733. 1881. W. S. Gottsberger.

Higher They Fly. Christopher Hodder-Williams. (YA) 1964. 4.95 o.p. (ISBN 0-399-10399-6). Putnam.

Highest Dream. Phyllis A Whitney. LC 56-859948. 1956. D. McKay Co.

Highest Dream. Phyllis A Whitney. (Signet book). 1975. (pbk.) 1.25. New American Library.

Highest Good. Oswald Chambers. 1965. pap. 2.50 (ISBN 0-87508-112-6). Chr Lit.

Highest References: A Novel. Florence Alice Price James. (On cover: Lovell's Westminister series, no. 42). 1891. J. W. Lovell Company.

Highest Virtue. Alan Stang. LC 74-14602. 1974. 10.95. Western Islands.

Highflyers. Clarence Budington Kelland. LC 19-3995. 1919. Harper & Brothers.

Highgrader. Hal George Evarts. 1973 (ISBN 0-671-55132-9). Pocket Bks.

Highgrader. William MacLeod Raine. LC 15-118740. 1.25. G. W. Dillingham Company.

Highland Annals. Olive Tilford Dargan. LC 72-6081. (Short story index reprint series). 1972. (ISBN 0-8369-4207-8). Books for Libraries Press.

Highland Brooch. Rebecca Danton, pseud. (Orig.). 1980. pap. 1.75 (ISBN 0-449-50022-5, Coventry). Fawcett.

Highland Chronicle. Samuel Bayard Dod. LC 6-33866. 1892. Dodd, Mead & Company.

Highland Cousins: A Novel. William Black. 1894. Harper & Brothers.

Highland Fling. May Mackintosh. LC 74-23319. 1975. 7.95 (ISBN 0-440-04564-9). Delacorte Press.

Highland Fling. Nancy Mitford. 1974. pap. 0.95 o.p. (09261). Curtis.

Highland Hawk. Leslie Turner White. LC 52-5674. 1952. Crown Publishers.

Highland Lover. Allison Lawrence. (Candlelight Regency Ser.: No. 702). (Orig.). 1982. pap. 1.75 (ISBN 0-440-13587-7). Dell.

Highland Lovesong. Stephanie Kincaid. 1979. 1.25 (ISBN 0-440-13469-2). Dell Pub. Co.

Highland Marauder. Maurice Clark Turner. LC 50-11498. 1950. Christopher Pub. House.

Highland Mary: The Romance of a Poet. Clayton Mackenzie Legge. LC 7-6768. 1906. C. M. Clark Publishing Co.

Highland Masquerade. Mary Elgin, pseud. (Bantam gothic novel). 1973. (pbk.) 0.95. Bantam Books.

Highland Masquerade. Mary Elgin, pseud. LC 66-11663. 1966. M. S. Mill Co., Distributed by W. Morrow.

Highland Mills. Clarence B. Kearfott. 1970. 10.00 o.p. Vantage.

Highland Mistress. Chloe Gartner. 1981. pap. 2.95 (ISBN 0-89083-811-9). Zebra.

Highland Night. Neil Miller Gunn. LC 35-2720. Harcourt, Brace and Company.

Highland Nurse. A Tale. George Douglas Campbell Argyll. LC 6-21859. J. W. Lovell Company.

Highland River. Neil Miller Gunn. LC 37-16650. J. B. Lippincott Company.

Highland Rogue, Anonymous: Love Upon Tick, Anonymous; The Matchless Rogue, Anonymous. LC 78-170554. (Foundations of the Novel). 1973. (ISBN 0-8240-0552-X). Garland Pub.

Highland Rogue: The Memorable Actions of the Celebrated Robert Mac-Gregor, Commonly Called Rob-Roy. Bd. with Love Upon Tick: Implicit Gallantry. LC 75-170556; Matchless Rogue; or, an Account of the Contrivances, Cheats, Stratagems & Amours of Tom Merryman, Commonly Called Newgate Tom. LC 78-170554. LC 71-170555. (Foundations of the Novel Ser.: Vol. 40). lib. bdg. 50.00 o.s.i. (ISBN 0-8240-0552-X). Garland Pub.

Highland Twilight. Ishbel Ross. LC 34-28618. 1934. Harper & Brothers.

Highland Velvet. Jude Deveraux, pseud. (Montgomery Annals: No. 2). (Orig.). 1982. pap. 2.95 (ISBN 0-671-45034-4). PB.

Highlander. Paul Allan Curtis. LC 37-38047. 1937. Lothrop, Lee & Shepard Co.

Highlanders: A Tale. Felix McDonough. 1824. E. Duyckinck Etc.

Highlights & Shadows. Winnie W. Childre. 1970. 3.00 o.p. Carlton.

Highliners. William B. McCloskey. LC 78-13717. 1978. 9.95 (ISBN 0-07-044856-6). McGraw-Hill.

Highly Colored. Octavus Roy Cohen. LC 21-18806. 1921. 2.00. Dodd, Mead and Company.

Highly Inflammable. Max Saltmarsh. LC 36-11953. 1936. Little, Brown, and Company.

Highly Ramified Tree. Robert Canzoneri. LC 76-28363. 224p. 1976. 8.95 o.p. (ISBN 0-670-37205-6). Viking Pr.

Highly Respectable Marriage. Sheila Walsh. 1982. pap. 2.25 (ISBN 0-451-11830-8, AE1830, Sig). NAL.

Highroad: Being the Autobiography of an Ambitious Mother. LC 4-12772. 1904. H. S. Stone & Company.

Highroad to Happiness. Janet Doran. LC 39-157058. Gramercy Publishing Co.

Highroads of Peril: Being the Adventures of Franklin Darlington, American, Among the Secret Agents of the Exiled Louis Xviii, King of France... Alfred Hoyt Bill. LC 26-15795. 1926. Little, Brown, and Company.

Highroller's Man. Ray Hogan. (Shawn Starbuck Western,#14). 1973. (pbk.) 0.75. New American Lib.

Highville: A Girl Scout and Prohibition Story. Hamilton Fay Northrop. LC 30-28741. The Evangelical Press.

Highway Nurse. Florence Stonebraker. LC 65-29981. 1965. Arcadia House.

Highway of Fate. Rosa Nouchette Carey. LC 2-221789. 1902. J. B. Lippincott Company.

Highway of Sorrow: A Novel. Hesba Stretton & Kravchinskii, Sergrei Mikhailovich, 1853-1895, Joint Author. LC 8-16883. 1894. Dodd, Mead & Company.

Highway to Happiness. Ruby Lorraine Radford. LC 47-17971. 1947. Arcadia House.

Highway to Heaven. Cecile Hulse Matschat. LC 42-10939. 1942. Farrar & Rinehart.

Highway to Hell. Heinz Gunther. LC 77-367330. 1976. 4.25 (ISBN 0-85628-034-8). A. Ellis.

Highway to Romance. Eleanor Browne. LC 37-540684. Arcadia House.

Highwayman. Frank Gruber. LC 55-508102. Rinehart.

Highwayman. Guy Rawlence. LC 11-25672. 1.25. W. J. Watt & Company.

Highwayman. Sylvia Thorpe. 1979. pap. 1.75 (ISBN 0-449-23695-1, Crest). Fawcett.

Highwayman. 1st Ed. Noel Bertram Gerson. LC 55-10506. 1955. Doubleday.

Highwayman's Bride: Or, The Capture of Claude Duval, in Which Are Related the Remarkable Adventures in Hornsey Church-Yard, and the Fight of the Mohocks. LC 10-2863. 1862. R. M. De Witt.

Highwayman's Daughter. Kathleen A Shoesmith. 1977. 1.50 (ISBN 0-441-33706-6). Ace Books.

Highwayman's Lady. Rose Somerset. (Berkley Book). 1978. 1.75 (ISBN 0-425-03814-9). Berkley Pub. Corp.

Highways. Elsie Aultman Ballou. LC 32-9804. 1931. R. G. Badger.

Highway's Edge. Grace Cash. LC 65-8673. bds., 2.95. Moody.

Highways in Hiding. George Oliver Smith. pap. 0.60 o.p. (73-636). Lancer.

Highways in Hiding. 1st Ed. George Oliver Smith. LC 56-10475. Gnome Press.

Highways to Happiness. Richard Le Gallienne. 1913. Repr. lib. bdg. 20.00 (ISBN 0-8414-5794-8). Folcroft.

Highways to Nowhere. Richard Hebert. LC 72-76928. 1972. 7.95 o.p. (ISBN 0-672-51635-7). Bobbs.

TITLE INDEX
HIMSELF AGAIN: A NOVEL.

Hijack. Edward Wellen. (Orig.). 1971. pap. 0.95 o.p. (95070). Beagle Bks.
Hijack. Lionel White. 224p. 1975. pap. 1.25 (ISBN 0-532-12347-6). Woodhill.
Hijack. Lionel White. 1969. pap. 0.75 o.p. (532-75248-075). Manor Bks.
Hijacked. David Harper. LC 78-123502. 1970. 5.95. Dodd, Mead.
Hijacked. J. M. Marks. (Alpha Books). (Illus., Orig.). 1979. pap. 2.95x (ISBN 0-19-424212-9). Oxford U Pr.
Hijacking Manhattan. Lionel Derrick. (Penetrator,#4). 1974. (pbk.) 0.95 (ISBN 0-523-00338-2). Pinnacle Books.
Hiker Joy. James Brendan Connolly. LC 20-8795. 1920. C. Scribner's Sons.
Hilary. Jerry B Jenkins. LC 80-20256. 1980. 2.50 (ISBN 0-8024-4313-3). Moody Press.
Hilary on Her Own. Mabel Sarah Barnes Grundy. LC 8-24457. 1908. The Baker & Taylor Co.
Hilary Thornton. Hubert Wales. LC 9-4486. D. Estes & Co.; Etc., Etc.
Hilary's Folly. Charlotte Mary Brame. (On cover: Seaside library. Pocket ed. no. 297). G. Munro.
Hilary's Folly. Charlotte Mary Brame. LC 44-39941. (On cover: Seaside library. Pocket ed. No. 297). G. Munro.
Hilary's Folly: Or, Her Marriage Vow. Charlotte Mary Brame. LC 1-29446. (Bertha Clay library, no. 42). 1900. Street & Smith.
Hilary's Folly: Or, Her Marriage Vow. Charlotte Mary Brame. LC 44-38166. (On cover: Seaside library. Pocket ed. No. 953). G. Munro.
Hilda. Charlotte Mary Brame. (On cover: Seaside library. Pocket ed. no. 294). G. Munro.
Hilda. Bertha M. Clay. LC 44-38094. (On cover: Seaside library. Pocket ed. No. 294). G. Munro.
Hilda. Howard A Farrens. LC 41-1973. The Story Book Press.
Hilda, a Novel. 1st Ed. Essie Braboy Kennedy. LC 57-101596. 1957. Pageant Press.
Hilda, a Romance of the Revolution: With a Historical Preface. Francis C Koehler. LC 33-135. Krone Brothers.
Hilda: A Story of Calcutta. Sara Jeannette Duncan Cotes. LC 98-1802. Frederick A. Stokes Company.
Hilda Against the World. Vivian Cory. LC 14-14365. 1914. 1.25. The Macaulay Company.
Hilda Alive,". Sammy Lillibridge. LC 43-138367. 1943. Coryell County News.
Hilda and I. A Story of Three Loves. Elizabeth Dundas Bedell Benjamin. LC 7-34444. 1880. G. W. Carleton & Co.; Etc., Etc.
Hilda Lessways. Arnold Bennett. LC 74-5331. (collected works of Arnold Bennett). 1974. (ISBN 0-518-19110-9). Books for Libraries Press.
Hilda Lessways. Arnold Bennett. LC 11-24362. 1911. E. P. Dutton & Company.
Hilda Lessways. Arnold Bennett. LC 76-372219. 1976. 1.95 (ISBN 0-14-003887-6). Penguin.
Hilda Manning, a Novel. Allan Seager. LC 56-9910. 1956. Simon and Schuster.
Hilda: Or, The False Vow. Charlotte Mary Brame. (On cover: Seaside library, Pocket ed. no. 928). G. Munro.
Hilda; or, The False Vow. Bertha M. Clay. LC 44-38095. (On cover: Seaside library. Pocket ed. No. 928). G. Munro.
Hilda Stafford: A California Story. Beatrice Harraden. LC 7-2859. 1897. Dodd Mead and Company.
Hilda, Take Heed: By Jeremy York Pseud. John Creasey. 1957. Scribner.
Hilda Wade: A Woman with Tenacity of Purpose. Grant Allen. 1900. G. P. Putnam's Sons.
Hilda Ware. Lizzie Allen Harker. LC 26-14679. 1926. H. Holt and Company.
Hilda's Lover: Or, The False Vow. Charlotte Mary Brame. LC 4264. (Bertha Clay library, no. 8). 1900. Street & Smith.
Hilda's Mascot: A Tale of "Maryland, My Maryland,". Mary Eliza Haines Ireland. LC 10-152359. The Saalfield Publishing Co.
Hilda's Miracle. Ellenia Bates Crowe. LC 55-7607. Dorrance.
Hildegarde. Kathleen Thompson Norris. LC 26-19256. 1926. Doubleday, Page & Company.
Hildegarde Withers Makes the Scene. Stuart Palmer & Fletcher Flora. LC 73-85634. 1969. 4.50. Random House.
Hildegarde's Campaign. M. E Torrance. (On cover: The crescent library, no. 3). 1892. The Price-McGill Company.
Hildreth. Harlow Estes. LC 40-34191. 1940. Dodd, Mead & Company.
Hill. Eleanor Green. LC 36-748217. 1936. Doubleday, Doran & Co., Inc.
Hill. David Greenhood. LC 43-51115. 1943. Duell, Sloan and Pearce.
Hill. Charles Mohler. LC 74-113759. 1970. 6.95. Prentice-Hall.
Hill: A Novel. Ray Rigby. LC 65-20729. 4.50. John Day.
Hill: A Romance of Friendship. Horace Annesley Vachell. LC 6-4634. 1906. Dodd, Mead & Company.
Hill and Valley: Or, Hands and Machinery. Harriet Martineau. (On cover: Lovell's library, v. 7, no. 372). 1884. J. W. Lovell Company.
Hill Around Havana. Carl Huntington Bottume. LC 48-56271. 1948. Appleton-Century-Crofts.
Hill Beyond. Daisy Fisher. LC 33-245326. 1933. Doubleday Doran & Company, Inc.
Hill Billies. Joseph Medley Rowland. LC 24-15193. 1924. Cokesbury Press.
Hill-Billy. Rose Wilder Lane. LC 26-7764. 1926. Harper & Brothers.
Hill Billy Kid. Frank Edwin Wilson. LC 27-15521. 1927. Rand, McNally & Company.
Hill Country North. John W. Andrews. 3.75 o.s.i. (ISBN 0-8283-1226-5). Branden.
Hill Country: The Story of J. J. Hill and the Awakening West. Ramsey Benson. LC 28-192843. 1928. Frederick A. Stokes Company.
Hill-Crest. Julia Colliton Flewellyn. LC 6-41674. 1895. Arena Publishing Company.
Hill Fox. Ernest Blakeman Vesey. LC 37-25343. 1937. Coward-McCann, Inc.
Hill Girl. Charles Williams. LC 51-22493. (Gold medal book, 141). 1951. Fawcett Publication.
Hill Grows Steeper. Fannie Cook. LC 38-239204. 1938. G.P. Putnam's Sons.
Hill Is Level. Lenore Guinzburg Marshall. LC 59-571445. 1959. Random House.
Hill Is Mine. Maurice Walsh. LC 40-32628. 1940. Frederick A. Stokes Company.
Hill of Ashes. Leslie Ames, pseud. LC 68-3407. 1968. Arcadia House.
Hill of Destiny. Jean Giono. Tr. by Le Clercq, Jacques Georges Clemenceau. LC 29-23129. 1929. Brentano's.
Hill of Devi & Other Indian Writings. Edward Morgan Forster. Ed. by Oliver Stalybrass. (Abinger Edition of E. M. Forster Ser.). 400p. 1983. text ed. 55.00 (ISBN 0-8419-5828-9). Holmes & Meier.
Hill of Devl. Edward Morgan Forster. LC 53-9224. (Illus.). 1971. pap. 3.95 (ISBN 0-15-640265-3, HB204, Harv). HarBraceJ.
Hill of Doves. Stuart Cloete. LC 41-212741. 1941. Houghton Mifflin Company.
Hill of Dreams. Arthur Machen. LC 23-2810. 1923. A. A. Knopf.
Hill of Evil Counsel. Amos Oz. 1982. pap. 2.95 (ISBN 0-553-22921-4). Bantam.
Hill of Evil Counsel: Three Stories Translated from the Hebrew by Nicholas De Lange in Collaboration with the Author. Amos Oz. LC 77-92543. 7.95 (ISBN 0-15-140234-5). Harcourt Brace Jovanovich.
Hill of Fools. r. l. peteni ed. R. L Peteni. (African Writers Series). 2.00 (ISBN 0-435-90178-8). Heinemann.
Hill of Fools: A Novel of the Ciskei. R. L. Peteni. LC 77-365486. 1976. 4.00 (ISBN 0-949968-61-7). Philip (David) Publisher.
Hill of Fortune. Robert Wernick. LC 51-9917. 1951. Scribner.
Hill of Glass. Catharine Whitcomb. LC 50-8612. 1950. Random House.
Hill of Happiness. George Nauman Shuster. LC 77-178462. (Short story index reprint series). 1971. (ISBN 0-8369-4063-6). Books for Libraries Press.
Hill of Happiness. George Nauman Shuster. LC 26-17108. 1926. D. Appleton and Company.
Hill of Lies. Heinrich Mann & Muir, Edwin, 1887- Tr. LC 35-7030. E. P. Dutton & Company, Inc.
Hill of Many Dreams. Richard Llewellyn. LC 73-10547. 1974. 6.95. Doubleday.
Hill of Pains. Gilbert Parker. LC 99-1180. R. G. Badger & Co.
Hill of Summer. Allen Drury. LC 80-1849. 504p. 1981. 15.95 (ISBN 0-385-00234-3). Doubleday.
Hill of Summer. Allen Drury. 576p. 1982. pap. 3.95 (ISBN 0-523-41806-X). Pinnacle Bks.
Hill of Summer: A Novel of the Soviet Conquest. Allen Drury. LC 80-1849. 1981. 13.95 (ISBN 0-385-00234-3). Doubleday.
Hill of the Dead. Andrew Quiller. LC 80-71033. (Gladiators Ser.). Orig. Title: Eagles: the Hill of the Dead. 128p. 1981. pap. 2.95 (ISBN 0-87754-226-0). Chelsea Hse.
Hill of the Hawk. Scott O'Dell. LC 47-31207. 1947. Bobbs-Merrill Co.
Hill of the Rooster. 1st Ed. Curry Holden. LC 56-7057. 1956. Holt.
Hill of the Terrified Monk. Daniel Mainwaring. LC 43-9683. 1943. W. Morrow and Company.
Hill of Triumph: A Story of Jerusalem in the Time of Christ. William Leo Murphy. LC 28-10100. P. J. Kenedy & Sons.
Hill of Venus. Nathan Gallizier. LC 13-6543. 1913. 1.35. L. C. Page & Company.
Hill People: Chronicles of an Insular Community. Helen Moriarty. LC 25-20022. 1925. B. Herder Book Co.
Hill Rest. Susan W Moulton. D. Lothrop and Company.
Hill Rise. William Babington Maxwell. LC 7-36409. Empire Book Company.
Hill Rise. William Babington Maxwell. LC 8-271. Empire Book Company.
Hill Smoke. Llewellyn Perry Holmes. LC 59-6875. (Silver star western). 1959. Dodd, Mead.
Hill Smoke. Llewellyn Perry Holmes. 1979. 1.75 (ISBN 0-445-04435-7). Pocket Books.
Hill Station & Other Stories. Nirmal Varma. (Writers Workshop greenbird book). (Illus.). 1975. (ISBN 0-88253-560-9). Writers Workshop.
Hill Top. Jennette Dowling Letton. 160p. 1972. pap. 0.75 o.p. Paperback Lib.
Hill Top House: By Rebecca Marsh Pseud. William Arthur Neubauer. LC 56-701873. 1956. Arcadia House.
Hill-Top Nurse. Peggy Gaddis, pseud. 1970. pap. 0.50 o.p. (50-501). Manor Bks.
Hillbilly Doctor. Elizabeth Seifert. LC 73-79137. 1973. 5.95. Aeonian Press.
Hillbilly Doctor. Elizabeth Seifert. LC 40-311907. 1940. Dodd, Mead & Company.
Hillbilly Doctor. Elizabeth Seifert. LC 44-7713. 1944. Triangle Books.
Hillbilly Heritage. Rea Walker. 3.50 o.p. Carlton.
Hillikin. Rollo Walter Brown. LC 35-336120. Coward-McCann.
Hillman. Edward Phillips Oppenheim. LC 17-6983. 1917. 1.35. Little, Brown, and Company.
Hills & Valleys. Lois L. Carver & Kathryn C. Matheidas. 3.95 o.p. Vantage.
Hills Beyond. Thomas Wolfe. 1941. 12.50 o.p. (ISBN 0-06-014700-8, HarpT). Har-Row.
Hills Beyond Manhattan. Guido D'Agostino. LC 42-206. 1942. Doubleday, Doran and Company, Inc.
Hills Beyond: With a Note on Thomas Wolfe. Thomas Wolfe & Aswell, Edward C. LC 41-21548. Harper & Brothers.
Hills Beyond: With a Note on Thomas Wolfe. Thomas Wolfe & Aswell, Edward C. LC 45-162391. (New Avon library. 57).
Hills, Hollers and Hickory Flats. Jack Hester. LC 42-51489.
Hills Look Down. Allan Eugene Updegraff. W. Funk, Inc.
Hills O' Hampshire. Will Martin Cressy & Harvey, James Clarence. LC 13-24112. 1.25. D. Estes & Company.
Hills of Beverly. 1st Ed. Libbie Block. LC 57-5780. 1957. Doubleday.
Hills of Desire. Richard Aumerle Maher. LC 19-7043. 1919. The Macmillan Company.
Hills of Destiny. Agnes Louise Provost. LC 35-5189. 1935. Macrae-Smith Company.
Hills of Fear. Frederick Ritchie Bechdolt. LC 43-7517. 1943. Doubleday, Doran & Company, Inc.
Hills of Fire. Dorothy Daniels. (Warner Paperback Library Gothic). 1973. (pbk) 0.95. Warner Paperback Lib.
Hills of Freedom. Joseph William Sharts. LC 4-27123. 1904. Doubleday, Page & Company.
Hills of Han: A Romantic Incident. Samuel Merwin. LC 20-6286. The Bobbs-Merrill Company.
Hills of Hebron: A Jamaican Novel. Sylvia Wynter. LC 62-14285. 1962. Simon and Schuster.
Hills of Home. Juliet Mann. 1970. 3.95 o.p. B Franklin.
Hills of Home. Curtis Martin. LC 43-15959. 1943. Houghton Mifflin Company.
Hills of Home: The Rural Ozarks of Arkansas. Roger Minick. LC 74-14226. (Illus.). 164p. 1975. 12.95 o.p. (ISBN 0-912020-48-2). Scrimshaw Calif.
Hills of Refuge: A Novel. William Nathaniel Harben. LC 18-203278. 1918. Harper & Brothers.
Hills of Rest. John Michael Cooney. LC 26-5827. The Abbey Press.
Hills of Ruel: And Other Stories, Illustrated in Colour and Black and White. William Sharp. LC 25-9559. 1921. Duffield and Company.
Hills of Sickness. Graham Harris. 1981. 15.00 (ISBN 0-533-04945-8). Vantage.
Hills of the Shatemuc. Susan Warner. LC 8-33705. 1856. D. Appleton and Company.
Hills on the Highway, a Novel. David Goldknopf. 1948. Harper.
Hills Stand Watch. August William Derleth. 6.95 o.p. (ISBN 0-88361-052-3). Stanton & Lee.
Hills Step Lightly. Alberta Pierson Hannum. LC 34-27268. 1934. W. Morrow & Co.
Hills Were Higher Then. Hugh MacNair Kahler. LC 31-324146. Farrar & Rinehart, Incorporated.
Hills Were Joyful Together. Roger Mais. (Caribbean Writers Ser.). 1981. pap. text ed. 6.50x (ISBN 0-435-98586-8). Heinemann Ed.
Hills Were Liars: A Novel. Riley Hughes. LC 55-7862. 1955. Bruce Pub. Co.
Hillsboro People. Dorothea Frances Canfield Fisher. LC 15-26257. 1915. H. Holt and Company.
Hillsborough's Haunted House & Aunt Mary's Adoption. E. J. Craig. 3.50 o.p. Carlton.
Hillside: A Tale of New England Country Life. Henry H Berry. 1904. Will County Printing Co.
Hillside Parish. Samuel Bayard Dod. LC 6-33865. 1893. Dodd, Mead & Company.
Hillside Strangler. Neville Romain. LC 78-71411. 1978. pap. 2.25 o.s.i. (ISBN 0-89516-073-0). Condor Pub Co.
Hillside Strangler. Ted Schwarz. 1982. pap. 2.75 (ISBN 0-451-11452-3, AE1452, Sig). NAL.
Hilltop. Evelyn Miller Pierce Crowell. LC 31-8680. A. H. King.
Hilltop. James Noble Gifford. LC 39-17655. 1939. Arcadia House.
Hilltop. Warren Howard. LC 39-176552. 1939. Arcadia House.
Hilltop. Jennette Dowling Letton. LC 63-12443. (O.S.I.). Orig. Title: Jenny & I. 1968. pap. 0.75 o.s.i. (64-953). Paperback Lib.
Hilltop Farm: A Novel. Harrie Victor Schieren. LC 30-31800. R. G. Badger.
Hilltop House. Alice Mary Ross Colver. LC 30-27758. 1930. Dodd, Mead & Company.
Hilltop House. Albert Quandt. LC 49-9532. 1949. Arcadia House.
Hilltop in Hazard. Anne Rider. LC 68-12596. 1968. Harcourt, Brace & World.
Hilltop in the Rain. James Saxon Childers. LC 28-178138. 1928. D. Appleton & Company.
Hilltop of the Gods. Ethel M Sampson. bds. 3.95. Vantage.
Hilltop Summer. Eugenia Laura Morris. LC 7-109513. Lee and Shepard.
Hilltops Clear. Emilie Baker Loring. LC 33-20280. The Penn Publishing Company.
Hilltops Have Sunshine. Nelle Davis. LC 45-437645. House of Field-Doubleday, Inc.
Hillview House: By Nancy Paschal Peud. Grace Trotter. LC 63-16199. 1963. Westminster Press.
Hillyars & the Burtons. Henry Kingsley. (Australian Literary Reprints Ser.). 464p. 1973. 12.50x (ISBN 0-424-06490-1, Pub. by Sydney U Pr); pap. 7.50x (ISBN 0-424-06500-2). Intl Schol Bk Serv.
Hillyars and the Burtons: A Story of Two Families. Henry Kingsley. 1865. Ticknor and Fields.
Hillyars and the Burtons: A Story of Two Families. Henry Kingsley. LC 34-377801. 1866. Ticknor and Fields.
Hillyars and the Burtons: A Story of Two Families. Henry Kingsley. (On cover: Lovell's library, v. 14, no. 728). 1886. J. W. Lovell Company.
Hillyars and the Burtons: A Story of Two Families. new ed.--6th thousand. with a note on old chelsea church by clement shorter, illustrated by herbert railton. ed. Henry Kingsley & Shorter, Clement King, 1857-1926. LC 4-16539. 1899. Longmans, Green & Co.
Hillyars and the Burtons, a Story of Two Families. new ed.-4th thousand. with a note on old chelsea church by clement shorter. illustrated by herbert railton. ed. Henry Kingsley & Shorter, Clement King, 1857-1926. LC 47-35490. (Half-title: Henry Kingsley's novels. New ed.). 1895. Ward, Lock and Bowden, Limited.
Hilma. William Tillinghast Eldridge. 1907. Dodd, Mead and Company.
Hilo Legends. Charlotte Hapai. (Illus.). 1966. pap. 2.25 o.p. (ISBN 0-912180-03-X). Petroglyph.
Hilo Legends. Charlotte Hapai. (Illus.). 1966. pap. 2.25 o.p. (ISBN 0-912180-03-X). Petroglyph.
Hilt to Hilt. From the Mss. of Colonel Surrey of Eagle's Nest. John Esten Cooke. LC 16-3403. G. W. Dillingham Co.
Hilt to Hilt. From the Mss. of Colonel Surrey of Eagles Neat. John Esten Cooke. LC 6-271933. 1893. G. W. Dillingham.
Hilt to Hilt: Or, Days and Nights on the Banks of the Shenandosh in the Autumn of 1864. From the Mss. of Colonel Surry of Eagle's Nest. John Esten Cooke. LC 42-26097. 1871. Carleton.
Hilton Bedside Book: A Treasury of Entertaining Reading, Selected Exclusively for the Guests of the Hilton Hotels. Hilton Hotels Corporation. LC 52-3786. 1952. Hilton Hotels Corp.
Hilton Hall: Or, A Thorn in the Flesh. A Novel. Louise Dubois. LC 6-34211. 1898. G. Q. Cannon & Sons Co., Printers.
Hilton Head. Josephine Pinckney. LC 41-1359. Farrar & Rinehart, Inc.
Him. E. E. Cummings. 1972. pap. 2.25 (ISBN 0-553-14468-5). Bantam.
Himalayan Assignment: A Colonel North Novel. Francis Van Wyck Mason. LC 52-5116. 1952. Doubleday.
Himalayan Concerto. John Masters. LC 76-2805. 1976. 8.95 (ISBN 0-385-00161-4). Doubleday.
Himalayan Concerto: A Novel of Adventure. John Masters. LC 76-372632. (Illus.). 1976. 4.25 (ISBN 0-7181-1461-2). Joseph.
Himmo, King of Jerusalem. Yoram Kaniuk. LC 68-9824. 1969. 5.75. Atheneum.
Himself Again: A Novel. J. C Goldsmith. LC 6-43739. (On cover: Standard library. no. 118). 1884. Funk & Wagnalls.

Himself His Worst Enemy: Or, Philip, Duke of Wharton's Career... Alfred Paxton Brotherhead. LC 6-18962. 1871. J. P. Lippincott & Co.

Hind Let Loose. Charles Edward Montague. LC 24-4264. 1924. Doubleday, Page & Company.

Hindenburg's March into London. Paul Georg Munch. Ed. by Marshall, Logan. Redmond-Howard, Louis G. LC 16-8809. 1916. The John C. Winston Company.

Hindered Hand: Or, The Reign of the Repressionist. Sutton Elbert Griggs. LC 72-79025. 1969. Mnemosyne Pub.

Hindered Hand: Or, The Reign of the Repressionist. 3d ed. rev. ed. Sutton Elbert Griggs. LC 77-100533. (Illus.). 1969. AMS Press.

Hindered Hand: Or, The Reign of the Repressionist. Sutton Elbert Griggs. LC 5-280024. 1905. The Orion Publishing Company.

Hinderers: A Novel. Richard Thrift. LC 78-51481. (Illus.). 1978. 10.95. Thrift.

Hinderers: A Story of the Present Time. Ada Ellen Bayly. LC 2-146075. 1902. Longmans, Green, and Co.

Hindi Short Stories. Ed. by Shrawan Kumar & Prabhar Machwe. Tr. by Shrawan Kumar & Prabhar Machwe. 175p. 1970. pap. 1.80 (ISBN 0-88253-053-4). Ind-US Inc.

Hindi Short Stories-an Anthology. Ed. by Rajendra Awasthy. 175p. 1981. text ed. 17.95x (ISBN 0-7069-1312-4, Pub. by Vikas India). Advent NY.

Hindi Short Stories: An Anthology. Ed. by Rajendra Awasthy. 192p. 1982. 35.00x (ISBN 0-7069-1312-4, Pub. by Garlandfold England). State Mutual Bk.

Hindle Wakes. Stanley Houghton. 2.50 o.p. (ISBN 0-8283-1140-4). Branden.

Hindred Hand. Sutton Elbert Griggs. pap. 3.25 (N273P). Mnemosyne.

Hind's Kidnap: A Pastoral on Familiar Airs. Joseph McElroy. LC 69-15280. 1969. 8.95. Harper & Row.

Hindu Heaven. Max Wylie. LC 33-5775. Farrar & Rinehart, Incorporated.

Hinge of Heaven. Stephena Cockrell. LC 28-21057. 1928. W. Morrow & Company.

Hinges of Custom. Ednah Robinson Aiken. LC 23-413992. 1923. Dodd, Mead and Company.

Hinges of Hell: A Marshal Pedley Mystery, by Stewart Sterling Pseud. Prentice Winchell. LC 55-3000. 1955. I. Washburn.

Hip Shot Forest. Elizabeth Beachley. LC 27-25773. 1927. The Canterbury Company.

Hippocratic Oath. Edgar Leon Dittler. LC 38-11068. Liveright Publishing Corporation.

Hippocritic Oath. John Eros. 3.00 o.p. Carlton.

Hippocritic Oath. John Eros. 1974. 5.50 o.p. (ISBN 0-682-47910-1). Exposition.

Hippodrome. Rosa Chambers. LC 13-6075. 1.25. George H. Doran Company.

Hippodrome. Cyrus Colter. 1976. (pbk.) 1.50. Popular Library.

Hippodrome: A Novel. Cyrus Colter. LC 72-96164. 1973. 5.95 (ISBN 0-8040-0625-3). Swallow Press.

Hippolyte and Golden-Beak. Two Stories. George Bassett. LC 6-9098. 1895. Harper & Brothers.

Hippy Buchan. Ethel Mary Young Boileau. LC 25-8155. George H. Doran Company.

Hippy Cult Murders. Ray Stanley. (Orig.). 1970. pap. 0.95 o.p. (95-137). Manor Bks.

Hira Singh: When India Came to Fight in Flanders. Talbot Mundy. LC 18-17761. The Bobbs-Merrill Company.

Hiram Abif, Jubelum & King Solomon's Temple: A Solar Allegory. Edward Clark. (Illus.). 61p. wrappers 5.00 o.p. Cramer Bkstore.

Hiram Blair. Drew Tufts. LC 12-9513. 1912. A. C. McClurg & Co.

Hiram Golf's Religion: Or, The "Shoemaker by the Grace of God,". 43d thousand. ed. George Hughes Hepworth. LC 41-332417. 1904. E. P. Dutton & Company.

Hiram Golf's Religion: Or, The "Shoemaker by the Grace of God,". George Hughes Hepworth. LC 10-206129. 1910. E. P. Dutton & Company.

Hiram Golf's Religion; or, the "Shoemaker. George Hughes Hepworth. LC 7-4275. 1893. E. P. Dutton & Company.

Hiram Harding of Hardscrabble. Samuel Leslie Bradbury. LC 36-235214. The Tuttle Publishing Co., Inc.

Hiram und Solomon. Albert Steffen. Tr. by Virginia Brett from Ger. 96p. 1971. 6.00x (ISBN 0-913152-06-4); bds. 5.95x (ISBN 0-913152-05-6). Folder Edns.

Hiran Gray: The Rebel Christian. Jonathan Wood. LC 15-10286. Printed by W. B. Conkey Co.

Hired Baby. Marie Corelli & Doyle, Sir Arthur Conan. (On cover: Seaside library. Pocket ed., no. 2089). 1895. G. Munro's Sons.

Hired Girl. Amos Hatter. 1971. pap. 0.75 o.p. (75-421). Manor Bks.

Hired Guns. Frederick Faust. LC 48-776458. (Silver star westerns). 1948. Dodd, Mead.

Hired Guns. Frederick Faust. LC 77-14011. 1978. 9.95 (ISBN 0-89340-118-8). J. Curley.

Hired Hand. Nelson Coral Nye. (Silver star westerns). 1954. Dodd, Mead.

Hired Hand & Lonely Grass. Nelson Nye. 1978. pap. 1.95 (ISBN 0-89083-373-7). Zebra.

Hired Husband. Watkins Eppes Wright. LC 49-628. Phoenix Press,

Hired Lover. Tony Trelos, pseud. (Orig.). pap. 0.95 o.p. (1167). Brandon.

Hired Man. Melvyn Bragg. LC 76-98647. 1970. 5.95. Knopf.

Hired Men of Laureldale: A New England Saga. Hazel Andrews. LC 79-165307. 1971. 5.95. Douglas-West Publishers.

Hired Nose. Ronald Koertge. 1975. 2.50 (ISBN 0-917554-15-9). Maelstrom.

Hired Wife. Lynna Cooper, pseud. (Signet Book). 1978. 1.50 (ISBN 0-451-08230-3). New American Library.

Hireling. Leslie Poles Hartley. LC 58-62536. 1958. Rinehart.

Hireling. Alison Macleod. LC 68-16271. 1968. 4.95. Houghton Mifflin.

Hirondelle. Henry Cottrell Rowland. LC 22-18300. 1922. Harper & Brothers.

Hiroshima Mon Amour. Ed. by Marguerite Duras. (Illus.). 5.00 o.p. (ISBN 0-8446-2014-9). Peter Smith.

Hiroshima Reef. Eric Lambert. LC 67-17682. 1967. Norton.

His Affair. Jo Fleming. LC 76-15245. 204p. 1976. 6.95 (ISBN 0-87131-216-6). M Evans.

His Angel. A Romance of the Far West. Henry Herman. LC 7-4312. 1891. Ward, Look, Bowden & Co.

His Baltimore Madonna: And Other Stories. Charles Weathers Bump. LC 6-36175. 1906. Nunn & Company.

His Baptism of War Among Spaniards and Cuban Insurgents. A History of the Perilous Ventures and Hairbreadth Escapes of Murry Marguart on the Island of Cuba. Edgar R Hoadley. LC 98-1832. (On cover: Neely's popular library, no. 128). F. T. Neely.

His Baptism of Was Among Spaniards and Cuban Insurgents. A History of the Perilous Ventures and Hairbreadth Escapes of Murray Marquart on the Island of Cuba, As Told by Himself and Here Set Forth. Edgar R Hoadley. LC 98-217787. F. T. Neely.

His Battalion; and, Live Until Dawn. Vasilii Uladzimiravich Bykau. LC 82-131543. (Contemporary Russian Writing). 14.95. University of Queensland Press.

His Beard Grew on Only One Cheek. Mauro Senesi. LC 68-12491. 1968. Scribner.

His Beautiful Life. Guy H Wilson. LC 11-7263. 1910. Johnston Printing Co.

His Beautiful Wife, and Other Stories. Max Ehrmann. LC 25-17735. (On cover: Scarlet women series). Indiana Publishing Company.

His Best Friend. Jessie Wright Whitcomb. The Pilgrim Press.

His Better Self: A Novel. Thomas J. Hughes. LC 10-11144. The Saalfield Publishing Company.

His Black Adonis. Dick Garfield. pap. 1.95 o.p. (8039). Cameo.

His Bright Designs. Eileen Mitson. LC 68-22831. 1968. (ISBN 0-7208-2005-7). Zondervan Pub. House.

His Broken Sword. Winnie Louise Taylor. LC 8-25670. 1888. A. C. McClurg and Company.

His Brother, the Bear. 1st Ed. Jack Ansell. LC 60-11372. 1960. Doubleday.

His Brother's Crime. John Roy Musick. LC 98-1607. (On cover: Neely's universial library. no. 41). 1898. F. T. Neely.

His Brother's Keeper. Homer Van Meter. 1973. 4.95 (ISBN 0-533-00823-9). Vantage Press.

His Brother's Keeper. Homer Van Meter. 4.95 o.p. Vantage.

His Brother's Keeper: Or, Christian Stewardship. Charles Monroe Sheldon. LC 8-5093. Congregational Sunday-School and Publishing Society.

His Brother's Sin. Pasquale Lancio. LC 29-476108. The Christopher Publishing House.

His Brother's Widow. Mary Grace Halpine. LC 7-120506. (On cover: Munro's library. v. 1. no. 405). N. L. Munro.

His Brother's Wife. Howard Buck. LC 35-19147. The Macaulay Company.

His Burial Too. Catherine Aird, pseud. LC 73-79638. 1973. 4.95 (ISBN 0-385-06016-5). Published for the Crime Club by Doubleday.

His Celestial Highness; a Collection of Short Stories. Edwin Samuel. LC 67-15240. 1968. Abelard-Schuman.

His Celestial Marriage: Or, The Bar-Sinister, a Social Study. Jeannette Ritchie Hadermann Walworth. (On cover: Holly library, no. 153). The Mershon Company.

His Children's Children. Bette J. Hardy. 1982. pap. 4.95 (ISBN 0-87397-212-0). Strode.

His Children's Children. Arthur Cheney Train. LC 23-4808. 1923. C. Scribner's Sons.

His Chinese Doll. Louis Chadman. LC 38-5474. The Stratford Company.

His Chinese Idol. Carroll Prescott Lunt. LC 52-56517. 1921. Lane.

His Comrades' Verdict: And Other Stories. Emma C Street. LC 8-16888. (On cover: Catholic library, v. 27). 1898. C. Wildermann.

His Country Cousin: Or, Mercy Craven's Lovers. A Story of Hearts and Homes. Charlotte M. Stanley McKenna. LC 8-281823. (On cover: The library of American authors. no. 29). 1891. G. Munro.

His Courtship. Helen Reimensnyder Martin. LC 7-15920. 1907. McClure, Phillips & Co.

His Cousin, the Doctor. A Story. Minnie Willis Baines Miller. LC 6-8628. 1891. Cranston & Stowe.

His Cuban Sweetheart: A Novel. Richard Henry Savage & Gunter, Esther Lisbeth (Burns) "Mrs. A. C. Gunter," Joint Author. LC 8-2010. The Home Publishing Company.

His Cuban Wife, a Romantic Novel. Mariana Beeching De Prieto. LC 54-146484. 1954. College Pub. Co.

His Darling Sin: A Novel. Mary Elizabeth Braddon Maxwell. LC 99-2950. Harper & Brothers Pub. for the Author.

His Daughter First. Arthur Sherburne Hardy. LC 3-11495. 1903. Houghton, Mifflin and Company.

His Days Are As Grass. Charles Henry Mergendahl. LC 46-2896. 1946. Little, Brown and Company.

His Dear Unintended. John Breckenridge Ellis. LC 17-23551. 1917. Th Macaulay Company.

His Defense: And Other Stoires. Harry Stillwell Edwards. LC 128. 1899. The Century Co.

His Defense: And Other Stories. Harry Stillwell Edwards. LC 69-11890. (American short story series, v. 48). (Illus.). 1969. Garrett Press.

His Defense, and Other Stories. Harry Stillwell Edwards. LC 72-8539. (American short story series, v. 48). 1972. MSS Information Corp.

His Duaghter. Gouverneur Morris. LC 18-3838. 1918. C. Scribner's Sons.

His Egyptian Wife: An Anglo-Egyptian Romance. Hilton Hill. (On cover: Premium library. no. 79). 1895. Home Book Company.

His Elizabeth: A Novel. Elswyth Thane. LC 28-7494. 1928. Frederick A. Stokes Company.

His Eminence, Death. Simon Quinn. (Inquisitor,#4). 1974. (pbk.) 0.95. Dell.

His End Was His Beginning. Henrietta Henkle. LC 36-10351. The Henkle-Yewdale House, Inc.

His Evil Eye: Or, Sybil's Trials. Harrie Irving Hancock. LC 7-552. (Sunnyside series, no. 28). 1891. J. S. Ogilvie.

His Excellency. Emile Zola. 1958. 9.95 (ISBN 0-236-30883-1, Pub. by Paul Elek). Merrimack Pub Cir.

His Excellency, the Ambassador. Erico Verissimo. LC 67-11628. 1967. MacMillan.

His Excellency the Minister. Ten Etchings. Jules Claretie & Roberts, Henri, Tr. LC 3834. (Half-title:... Roman contemporain. Romancists v. 3). G. Barrie & Son.

His Family. Ernest Poole. LC 74-180358. 1974. 10.95. N. S. Berg.

His Family. Ernest Poole. LC 17-13623. 1917. The Macmillan Company.

His Fatal Success: Being the Strange Adventure of John Stuart, with a Prologue by the Editor, Malcolm Bell. Malcolm Bell. LC 7158. (On cover: The household library, no. 15, v. 4). Belford, Clarke & Co.; Etc., Etc.

His Father's Ghost: By Stratford Davis Pseud. Bolton, Maisie (Sharman) LC 63-13999. 1963. Abelard-Schuman.

His Father's Son: A Novel of New York. Brander Matthews. LC 7-25564. 1895. Harper & Brothers.

His Father's Way: A Novel. Cornelius Francis Donovan. LC 26-21900. J. H. Meier.

His Father's Wife. Day Keene. 1970. pap. 0.75 o.p. (75-372). Manor Bks.

His Father's Wife. John Edward Patterson. LC 13-20345. 1913. 1.35. The Macmillan Company.

His Fifty Years of Exile: Israel Potter. Herman Melville. LC 57-976529. (American century series, S-13). 1957. Sagamore Press.

His First and Only Love. May Brannan. LC 32-17519. The Christopher Publishing House.

His First Leave. Lizzie Allen Harker. 1908. C. Scribner's Sons; Etc., Etc.

His First Love: Or, Poynsett of Poynsett Hall. Lucy Randall Comfort. LC 26-24716. (Seaside library. v. 50, no. 1910). 1881. G. Munro.

His First Million Women. George Weston. Farrar & Rinehart, Incorporated.

His First Minute After Noon. Sally Daniels. LC 66-15019. 1966. Harcourt, Brace & World.

His Fleeting Ideal. A Romance of Baffled Hypnotism. Barnum, Phineas Taylor, 1810-1891 & Sullivan, John Langdon, 1777-1865. LC 33-28345. (red cover series. no. 87). J. S. Ogilvie.

His Fortunate Grace. Gertrude Franklin Horn Atherton. LC 4-16428. (Half-title: Canvas-back library of popular fiction, vol. II). 1904 J. Lane.

His Foster Sister. Linn Boyd Porter. LC 7-37770. (Dillingham's American authors library, no. 22). 1896. G. W. Dillingham Co.

His Four Women. 1st Ed. Edythe Tate Perlman. LC 56-12837. 1957. Vantage Press.

His Friend and His Wife: A Novel of the Quaker Hill Colony. Cosmo Hamilton. LC 20-6492. 1920. 1.75. Little, Brown, and Company.

His Friend Miss McFarlane: A Novel. Kate Lee Langley Bosher. 1919. Harper & Brothers.

His Golden Girl. Margaret Agnes Smith. LC 30-11854. R. G. Badger.

His Good Angel. William Arthur Neubauer. LC 48-165531. 1948. Gramercy Pub. Co.

His Grace. William Edward Norris. LC 7-33293. United States Book Company.

His Grace Gives Notice. Laura Gurney Troubridge. LC 22-9196. 1922. Duffield & Company.

His Grace, of Grub Street. Gertrude Violet McFadden. LC 18-22032. 1918. John Lane.

His Grace of Osmonde: Being the Portions of That Nobleman's Life Omitted in the Relation of His Lady's Story Presented to the World of Fashion Under the Title of A Lady of Quality. Frances Hodgson Burnett. LC 6-16427. 1897. C. Scribner's Sons.

His Grace of Osmonde: Being the Portions of That Nobleman's Life Omitted in the Relation of His Lady's Story Presented to the World of Fashion Under the Title of A Lady of Quality. Frances Hodgson Burnett. LC 16-6320. 1913. C. Scribner's Sons.

His Grandmothers; a Summer Salad. Helen Campbell. LC 6-21491. 1877. G. P. Putnam's Sons.

His Great Adventure. Robert Herrick. LC 13-18718. 1913. 1.35. The Macmillan Company.

His Great Adventure see Collected Works.

His Great Revenge. Fortune Du Boisgobey. Tr. by Caroline A. Merighi. (Seaside library, v. 71, no. 1432). 1882. G. Munro.

His Great Self. Mary Virginia Terhune. LC 10-22488. 1892. J. B. Lippincott Company.

His Hand Against Every Man. 1st Ed. Mary Alice Siddall. LC 53-12700. 1953. Pageant Press.

His Heart's Delight. A Novel. Maude Rutledge. LC 8-1350. T. B. Peterson & Brothers.

His Heart's Desire. A Novel... Ellen Warner Olney Kirk. 1878. J. B. Lippincott & Co.

His Highness Commands Pendragon. 192p. 1976. 7.95 o.p. (ISBN 0-8415-0421-0). Dutton.

His Highness Commands Pendragon: Another Swashbuckling Adventure for Victoria's Special Agent. Forrest-Webb, Robert. LC 75-32665. 7.95 (ISBN 0-8415-0421-0). Saturday Review Press.

His Holiness Gives an Example: Dialogues. Paul Tate & Richard Turner. LC 73-177639. 1973. 0.50. Kite Books.

His Honor: Or, Fate's Mysteries. A Thrilling Realistic Story of the United States Army. Cynthia Eloise Cleveland. LC 6-20992. 1889. The American News Company.

His Honor, the Mayor and Other Tales. John Talbot Smith. 1891. The Vatican Library Co.

His Honour, and a Lady. Sara Jeannette Duncan Cotes. LC 6-29020. 1896. D. Appleton and Company.

His Hour. Elinor Sutherland Glyn. 1910. 1.50. D. Appleton and Company.

His Hour. Elinor Sutherland Glyn. LC 33-175131. 1912. D. Appleton and Company.

His Human Majesty. Kay Boyle. LC 49-8270. 1949. Whittlesey House.

His Ideas of Honor. A Study. Harold W Ridgeway. LC 7-41643. 1890. Metropolitan Publishing Company.

His Idol. A Novel... Richard Burleigh Kimball. LC 11-150885. G. W. Carleton & Co.; Etc., Etc.

His Inheritance. Adeline Trafton Knox. LC 8-30859. 1878. Lee and Shepard.

His Island Castle: By Helga Marietta Pseud. Hilda Marietta Matson. 1953. Wetzel Pub. Co.

His Jewels; or, A Story of New England in War Time. Founded on Facts... Written for the Congregational Sabbath-School and Publishing Society, and Approved by the Committee of Publication. Congregational Sabbath-School and Publishing Society. Committee of Publication. LC 7-4687. 1868. Cong. Sabbath-School and Publishing Society.

His Job. Horace William Bleackley. LC 18-8992. 1918. John Lane.

His Kingdom for a Horse. facs. ed. Wyatt Blassingame. LC 75-81263. (Short Story Index Reprint Ser). 1957. 15.00 (ISBN 0-8369-3015-0). Ayer Co.

His Last Bow. Arthur Conan Doyle. LC 37-144078. 1937. The Sun Dial Press, Inc.

His Last Bow: A Reminiscence of Sherlock Holmes. Arthur Conan Doyle. LC 17-28606. George H. Doran Company.

His Last Bow: A Reminiscence of Sherlock Holmes. Arthur Conan Doyle. LC 21-13710. 1920. A. L. Burt Company.

His Last Passion: A Sensational and Realistic Story of English Modern Life. 15th thousand ed. Telemachus Thomas Timayenis. (On cover: Minerva series, no. 41). The Minerva Publishing Company.

His Legal Wife. Mary Edwards Bryan. LC 11-10534. (On cover: Library of American authors. no. 62). 1894. G. Munro's Sons.

His Lesbian Love. Wayne Wallace. (Orig.). pap. 0.95 o.p. (1150). Brandon.

His Letters. Julie Grinnell Storrow Cruger. LC 6-31585. Cassell Publishing Company.

His Level Best: And Other Stories. Edward Everett Hale. LC 13-17739. 1872. Roberts Brothers.

His Level Best: And Other Stories. Edward Everett Hale. 1873. J. R. Osgood and Company.

His Level Best & Other Stories. Edward Everett Hale. 1972. Repr. of 1872 ed. 19.50 (ISBN 0-8422-8065-0). Irvington.

His Level Best & Other Stories. Edward Everett Hale. Ed. by Clarence Gohdes. (American Short Story Ser., Vol. 18). 1969. Repr. of 1872 ed. lib. bdg. 14.75 o.s.i. (ISBN 0-512-00287-8). Garrett Pr.

His Little Mother. Dinah Maria Mulock Craik. LC 6-31087. ("Cosy corner series"). 1896. J. Knight Company.

His Little World: The Story of Hunch Badeau. Samuel Merwin. LC 3-22506. 1903. A. S. Barnes & Company.

His Lordship's Leopard: A Truthful Narration of Some Impossible Facts. David Dwight Wells. 1900. H. Holt and Company.

His Lordship's Mistress. Joan Wolf. 1982. pap. 2.25 (ISBN 0-451-11459-0, AE1459, Sig). NAL.

His Love for Helen.". J. B. H Janeway. LC 7-10329. 1893. G. W. Dillingham.

His Love So True: Or, She Trusted Him. Charles Garvice. (On cover: Laurel library. no 25). 1896. G. Munro's Sons.

His Love Story. illustrations by howard chandler christy. ed. Marie Van Vorst. LC 13-10991. The Bobbs-Merrill Company.

His Majesty, Ben Suva. Ione A Green. LC 55-9799. 1955. Comet Press Books.

His Majesty, Myself... William Mumford Baker. LC 6-6863. (Half-title: No name series. 2d series, v. 3). 1880. Roberts Brothers.

His Majesty, Myself... William Mumford Baker. LC 6-6864. (Half-title: No name series 2d series, v. 3). 1884. Roberts Brothers.

His Majesty the King: Being the Chronicle of Certain Hours, in the Ill-Starred Life of Charles the Second of England, During the Period of His Exile in Flanders with Those of the Faithful That Fled from the Despot, Oliver Cromwell, the Which Have Received of on Account in the History of His Time. Cosmo Hamilton. LC 26-12321. 1926. Printed by Doubleday, Page & Company.

His Majesty's Agent. David Shahar. Tr. by Dalya Bilu. LC 80-7940. (Helen & Kurt Wolff Bk). 416p. 1980. 14.95 (ISBN 0-15-140356-2). HarBraceJ.

His Majesty's Agent: A Novel. David Shahar. LC 80-7940. 1980. 14.95 (ISBN 0-15-140198-5). Harcourt Brace Jovanovich.

His Majesty's Frigate. Simon White. LC 78-20672. 1979. 7.95 o.p. (ISBN 0-312-37325-2). St Martin.

His Majesty's Guest. Charles E Stubbs. LC 23-18069. 1923. Moffat, Yard and Company.

His Majesty's Highlanders. Leslie Turner White. LC 64-23795. 1964. Crown Publishers.

His Majesty's Highwayman. Donald Barr Chidsey. LC 58-8323. 1958. Crown Publishers.

His Majesty's Pyjamas. Gene Markey. LC 34-31984. Covici, Friede.

His Majesty's U-Boat. Douglas Reeman. LC 73-78604. 1973. 6.95 (ISBN 0-399-11195-6). Putnam.

His Majesty's Well-Beloved: An Episode in the Life of Mr. Thomas Betterton As Told by His Friend John Honeywood. Emmuska Orczy. LC 19-17888. 1919. Hodder and Stoughton.

His Majesty's Well-Beloved: An Episode in the Life of Mr. Thomas Betterton As Told by His Friend John Honeywood. Emmuska Orczy. LC 19-190541. 1.75. George H. Doran Company.

His Majesty's Yankees. Thomas Head Raddall. LC 42-25187. 1942. Doubleday, Doran and Company, Inc.

His Male Lover. Kym Allyson, pseud. Orig. Title: Queer Letters. 192p. 1974. pap. 2.25 o.s.i. (ISBN 0-89053-108-0, LB-108). Lambda Pr.

His Marriage Vow. Caroline Elizabeth Fairfield Corbin. LC 6-30695. 1874. Lee and Shepard.

His Marriage Vow. new ed. Caroline Elizabeth Fairfield Corbin. LC 6-30694. 1891. Lee and Shepard.

His Master's Voice. Stanislaw Lem. LC 82-15765. 1983. 12.95 (ISBN 0-15-140360-0). Harcourt Brace Jovanovich.

His Mistress and I. Marcel Prevost. Tr. by Fleming, Noel. LC 27-114897. George H. Doran Company.

His Monkey Wife: Or, Married to a Chimp. John Collier. LC 57-5636. 1957. Doubleday.

His Monkey Wife: Or, Married to a Chimp. John Collier. LC 31-7175. 1931. D. Appleton & Company.

His Mortgaged Wife. Bonnie Melbourne Busch. LC 23-11264. Dorrance.

His Mother's Arms. Frank Anvic, pseud. 192p. (Orig.). 1973. pap. 1.95 o.p. (ISBN 0-87682-296-0, 7296). Barclay Hse.

His Mother's Sinful Sister. Frank Anvic, pseud. 192p. (Orig.). 1973. pap. 1.95 o.p. (ISBN 0-87682-318-5, 7318). Barclay Hse.

His Name Was Death. Fredric Brown. LC 54-6828. (Guilt edged mystery). 1954. Dutton.

His Nameless Love. V. Tyayanov. 357p. 1974. 7.95 (ISBN 0-8285-1081-4, Pub. by Progress Pubs USSR). Imported Pubns.

His Native Coast. Edith L. Tiempo. 1979. pap. 7.75x. Cellar.

His Native Soil. Lettie Duncan Cooke. LC 45-1207. 1944. The Wartburg Press.

His Native Wife. Louis Becke. LC 6-9777. (On cover: The lotos library). 1897. J. B. Lippincott Company.

His Native Wife. Louis Becke. LC 5-41008. (With his By reef and palm. Philadelphia, 1900). 1900. J. B. Lippincott Company.

His Natural Life. Marcus Andrew Hislop Clarke & New York Tribune. LC 19-2891. (Library of Tribune extras, v. 1, no. 3)). 1889. The Tribune Association.

His Natural Life. A Novel. Marcus Andrew Hislop Clarke. (Harper's library of select novels. no. 458.). 1876. Harper & Brothers.

His Neigbor's Wife. Gilson Willets. LC 12-10684. (On cover: Neely's continental library, no. 16). 1898. F. T. Neely.

His One Desire: Being an Account of the Growth of the Greatest Wish of His Heart, and How He Secured the Attainment Thereof. Milton Nella. LC 7-25786. (peerless series, no. 57). 1892. J. S. Ogilvie.

His Only Son. Leopoldo Alas. LC 80-20837. 22.50 (ISBN 0-8071-0759-X). Louisiana State University Press.

His Opportunity. Henry Clemens Pearson. 1886. J. H. Earle.

His Other Wife. A Novel. Rose Ashleigh. LC 6-452849. (select series, no. 70). 1890. Street & Smith.

His Own Appointed Day. Dominic Devine. LC 66-13602. 1966. bds., 3.50. Walker.

His Own Country. Paul Kester. LC 17-17972. 1917. The Bobbs-Merrill Company.

His Own Estate. Lemira Frederick. LC 11-14718. 1911. 1.00. Cochrane Publishing Company.

His Own Image. A Novel. Alfred J. Cohen. LC 6-26738. 1899. G. W. Dillingham Co.

His Own Interpreted: A Novel of Faith. 1st Ed. Mary Celestia Pearson. LC 56-12376. 1956. Exposition Press.

His Own Man. Harry Paul Jeffers. (Orig.). pap. 1.25 o.p. (2058). Brandon.

His Own People. Cliff Knoble. LC 40-35540. Reilly & Lee.

His Own People. Leon W Rogers. LC 29-247351. Laidlaw Brothers.

His Own People. Booth Tarkington. LC 7-30869. 1907. Doubleday, Page & Co.

His Own Place. Harold Webber Freeman. LC 41-10772. 1941. W. Morrow & Company.

His Own Rooftree. Louise Platt Hauck. LC 33-756756. The Penn Publishing Company.

His Own Where. June Jordan. LC 71-146283. 1971. 3.95 (ISBN 0-690-38133-6). Crowell.

His Own Wife. Peggy O'More, pseud. LC 44-9908. 1944. Grammercy Publishing Co.

His Perpetual Adoration: Or, The Captain's Old Diary. Joseph Frederick Flint. LC 6-41671. 1895. Arena Publishing Company.

His Prison Bars: And the Way of Escape. Alphonso Alva Hopkins. LC 7-5251. 1875. Rural Home Publishing Co.

His Private Character. Linn Boyd Porter. LC 11-15085. (On cover: The Albatross novels). 1889. G. W. Dillingham.

His Private Honour. Rudyard Kipling. LC 7-12587. 1891. Macmillan and Co.

His Rise to Power. Henry Russell Miller. LC 11-269512. The Bobbs-Merrill Company.

His Robe of Honor. Ethel Arnold Smith Dorrance & Dorrance, James French, 1879-Joint Author. LC 16-20435. 1916. Moffat, Yard & Company.

His Royal Happiness. Sara Jeannette Duncan Cotes. LC 14-167562. 1914. 1.35. D. Appleton and Company.

His Royal Highness. An International Episode. George Hastings. (On cover: Vanity fair series, no. 3). 1891. E. Brandus & Co.

His Royal Nibs. Winnifred Eaton Babcock. LC 25-20259. 1925. W. J. Watt & Co.

His Royal Nibs. Winifred Eaton Reeve. LC 25-20259. W. J. Watt & Co.

His Second Campaign... Maurice Thompson. LC 8-19966. (On cover: Round-robin series). 1883. J. R. Osgood and Company.

His Second Love. A Novel. Emma May Buckingham. (Dillingham's American authors library, no. 15). 1896. G. W. Dillingham.

His Second Venture. Gertrude M. Robins Reynolds. LC 24-22566. George H. Doran Company.

His Second Wife. Ernest Poole. LC 18-10003. 1918. The Macmillan Company.

His Secretary. Margaretta Brucker. LC 44-6547. 1944. Gramercy Publishing Co.

His Serene Highness. Henry Christopher Bailey. LC 22-693852. E. P. Dutton & Company.

His Sombre Rivals. Edward Payson Roe. LC 7-40231. (On cover: Dodd, Mead & company's library of fiction, no. 10). Dodd, Mead & Company.

His Sombre Rivals. Edward Payson Roe. LC 7-40232. (On cover: Roe's works). Dodd, Mead and Company.

His Soul Goes Marching on. Mary Raymond Shipman Andrews. LC 22-6934. 1922. C. Scribner's Sons.

His Struggle Magnificent. William Sidney Bond. LC 10-186525. 1910. Cochrane Publishing Company.

His Sweetheart. Adelheid MacKenxie. LC 7-19983. 1877. J. A. Moore.

His Sword: A Tale of the Vikings. Alfred C Muller. LC 42-13730. 1942. Meador Publishing Company.

His Terrible Secret: Or, The Man Monkey. A Novel Founded Upon the Romantic Melodrama of the Same Title. Charles E Blaney & Turner, William H., Dramatist. His Terrible Secret. LC 48-35764. (Play book series, no. 106). J. S. Ogilvie Pub. Co.

His Three Wives: Or, The Bar-Sinister, a Mormon Study. Jeannette Ritchie Hadermann Walworth. LC 2581. The Mershon Company.

His Tribute. Florence Martin Eastland. LC 9-281491. Jennings and Graham.

His Triumph. Mary Andrews Denison. LC 6-33992. 1883. Lee & Shepard.

His Two Loves. Albert Delpit. Tr. by Merriam, R. H. LC 6-34173. The Price-McGill Publishing Co.

His Two Wives. Mary Clemmer Ames. LC 6-25302. 1875. Hurd and Houghton.

His Uncle's Wife. Ruth Felicia Adams Neuberger. LC 12-203068. 1.00. The Alice Harriman Company.

His Unknown Wife. Louis Tracy. LC 16-20556. E. J. Clode.

His Version of It. Paul Leicester Ford. LC 5-30570. 1905. Dodd, Mead & Company.

His Ward. Blanche Alice Bray. LC 12-44. 1911. 1.50. The Cosmopolitan Press.

His Was the Fire. Showell Styles. LC 57-7679. 1957. Vanguard Press.

His Way and Her Will: A Novel. Frances Aymar Mathews. LC 7-25568. 1888. Belford, Clark & Co.

His Way and Her Will: A Novel. Frances Aymar Mathews. LC 3055. (On cover: Eagle library, no. 160). 1900. Street & Smith.

His Way and Hers. W. A Robinson. LC 7-42187. 1895. Cranston & Curts.

His Way to Greatness. LC 7-4686. 1881. E. Claxton & Company.

His Wedded Wife. Sophy Beckett. LC 6-9741. (On cover: The seaside library. Pocket edition, no. 461). 1885. G. Munro.

His Weight in Gold. Maurice Procter. LC 66-13937. bds., 4.50. Harper.

His Wife. Warren Cheney. LC 7-31211. 1907. The Bobbs-Merrill Company.

His Wife-in-Law. Marie Oemler. LC 25-5617. The Century Co.

His Wife-in-Law. Marie Conway Oemler. LC 25-5617. 2.00. The Century Co.

His Wife or Widow? A Novel. Marie Walsh. 1889. G. W. Dillingham.

His Wife, the Doctor. Joseph McCord. LC 41-35376. 1941. Macrae-Smith Company.

His Wife, the Doctor. Joseph McCord. LC 42-20795. 1942. Triangle Books.

His Wife's Job. Grace Sartwell Mason. LC 19-7041. D. Appleton & Company.

His Wife's Judgment. Charlotte Mary Brame. LC 44-14382. (On cover: Seaside library. Pocket ed. No. 1006). G. Munro.

His Wife's Judgment: A Novel. Charlotte Mary Brame. LC 4665. (Bertha Clay library, no. 16). 1900. Street & Smith.

His Wife's Romance. Clara De Longworth Chambrun. LC 29-172205. 1929. D. Appleton & Company.

His Will and Hers. Dora Russell. LC 8-133612. (On cover: Rialto series, no. 63). 1894. Rand, McNally & Company.

His Wisdom, the Defender. Simon Newcomb. LC 74-16513. (Science Fiction Ser). (Illus.). 338p. 1975. Repr. 19.00x (ISBN 0-405-06308-3). Ayer Co.

His Wisdom, the Defender: A Story. Simon Newcomb. LC 74-16513. (Science Fiction). (Illus.). 1975. 19.00 (ISBN 0-405-06308-3). Arno Press.

His Wisdom, the Defender: A Story. Simon Newcomb. LC 5788. 1900. Harper & Brothers.

His Word of Honor: Flammenzeichen. Elisabeth Burstenbinder. (Primrose edition, no. 7). 1890. Street & Smith.

His Worldly Goods. Margaretta Muhlenberg Perkins Tuttle. LC 12-12865. The Bobbs-Merrill Company.

His Worshipful Majesty. T. MofOlorynso Aluko. (African Writers Ser.). 1973. pap. text ed. 4.00x (ISBN 0-435-90130-3). Heinemann Ed.

His Young Wife. A Novel. Julie P. Smith. LC 8-81792. 1877. G. W. Carleton & Co.; Etc., Etc.

Hispanics in the United States: An Anthology of Creative Literature. Ed. by Gary D. Keller & Francisco Jimenez. LC 80-66273. 176p. 1980. pap. 10.00x (ISBN 0-916950-19-0). Bilingual Pr.

Hispaniola Plate: 1683-1893. John Edward Bloundelle-Burton. LC 6-22256. 1895. The Cassell Publishing Co.

Hissing Tales. Romain Gary, pseud. LC 64-12685. 1964. Harper & Row.

Histoire. Claude Simon. LC 68-16109. 1968. G. Braziller.

Historia de una Escalera. A. Buero Vallejo. Bd. with Tejedora de Suenos; Irene o el Tesoro; Sonador Para un Pueblo. (Span.). pap. 2.50 o.s.i. French & Eur.

Historical and Humorous Sketches of the Donkey, Horse and Bicycle. The Bicycle Viewed from Four Standpoints: Anatomical, Phisiological !, Sociological, and Financially. Also an Allegory on the Bicycle Road to Hell... Charles Edward Nash. LC 7-25797. 1896. Press of Tunnah & Pittard.

Historical Fiction. Alfred Leo Duggan. 1957. lib. bdg. 8.50 (ISBN 0-8414-3868-4). Folcroft.

Historical Fiction. James R. Kaye. 1920. Repr. 45.00 (ISBN 0-8274-2497-3). R West.

Historical Miniatures, Vol. 1. August Strindberg. Tr. by Claude Field. LC 72-3469. (Short Story Index Reprint Ser.). Repr. of 1913 ed. 21.00 (ISBN 0-8369-4163-2). Ayer Co.

Historical Mystery. Honore De Balzac. LC 3-23190. (Half-title: The comedy of human life... Scenes from political life). 1891. Roberts Brothers.

Historical Nights' Entertainment. First Series. Rafael Sabatini. LC 71-150485. (Short story index reprint series). (Illus.). 1971. (ISBN 0-8369-3826-7). Books for Libraries Press.

Historical Nights' Entertainment, First Series. facsimile ed. Rafael Sabatini. LC 71-150485. (Short Story Index Reprint Ser.). Repr. of 1917 ed. 19.00 (ISBN 0-8369-3826-7). Ayer Co.

Historical Nights' Entertainment. Second Series. Rafael Sabatini. LC 75-150486. (Short story index reprint series). 1971. (ISBN 0-8369-3827-5). Books for Libraries Press.

Historical Nights' Entertainment, Second Series. facsimile ed. Rafael Sabatini. LC 75-150486. (Short Story Index Reprint Ser.). Repr. of 1919 ed. 19.00 (ISBN 0-8369-3827-5). Ayer Co.

Historical Romances... Stanley John Weyman. LC 32-28185. 1933. Longmans, Green and Co.

Historical Romances of Louisa Muhlbach Pseud. brandenburg ed. Klara Muller Mundt. LC 98-513. D. Appleton and Company.

Historical Vignettes. Bernard Edward Joseph Capes. LC 64-22038. (IPL, 30). 1965. Intl. Pocket Lib.

Histories and Dynasties. Arlene Zekowski. LC 81-85002. (Archives of Post-Modern Literature Series Publication; No. 106). (Illus.). 1982. 14.95 (ISBN 0-8180-0634-X) (ISBN 0-8180-0632-3). Horizon Press.

History: A Novel. Elsa Morante. LC 76-45755. 1977. 10.95 (ISBN 0-394-49802-X). Knopf.

History: A Novel. Elsa Morante. (Bard book). 1979. 2.95 (ISBN 0-380-41889-4). Avon Books.

History and Adventures of Gil Blas of Santillane. Alain Rene Le Sage. LC 74-170537. (Foundations of the Novel). (ISBN 0-8240-0539-2). Garland Pub.

History and Remarkable Life of the Truly Honourable Col. Jacque, Commonly Call'd Col. Jack. Ed., Introd. by Samuel Holt Monk. Daniel Defoe. LC 65-29730. (Oxford Eng. novels). 5.75. Oxford.

History and Remarkable Life of the Truly Honourable Colonel Jacque, Commonly Called Colonel Jack. Daniel Defoe. LC 74-13450. (Illus.). 1974. (ISBN 0-404-07920-2). AMS Press.

History Man: A Novel. Malcolm Bradbury. LC 75-33236. 1976. 7.95 (ISBN 0-395-24085-9). Houghton Mifflin.

History of a Nation of One. Jecon Gregory. 1969. 5.95 o.p. HarBraceJ.

History of a Parisienne. Histoire D'une Parisienne). Being the Story of a Parisian Woman of Fashion. Octave Feuillet & Ripley, Charles, Tr. LC 6-395231. T. B. Peterson & Brothers.

History of a Peasant. Emile Erckmann & Chatrian, Alexandre, 1826-1890, Joint Author. (Half-title: Everyman's library, ed. by Ernest Rhys. Fiction. no. 706-707). J. M. Dent & Sons, Ltd.

History of a Pocket Prayer Book. Written by Itself... Benjamin Dorr. LC 6-33720. 1839. G. W. Donohue.

History of a Pocket Prayer Book. Written by Itself... new ed. Benjamin Dorr. LC 6-33719. 1844. R. S. H. George.

History of a Pocket Prayer Book: Written by Itself. ... 3d ed., rev. and enl. ed. Benjamin Dorr. LC 6-337180. 1850. B. E. Peterson.

History of a Reprobate: Or, The Very Interesting and Suprising Adventures of David Doubtful. 2d american ed. Henry Brooke. LC 6-19394. 1795. Printed for the Rev. M. L. Weems, by Jacob Johnson & Co., Marketstreet.

History of a Slave. Harry Hamilton Johnston. (On cover: Seaside library. Pocket ed., no. 1212). 1889. G. Munro.

History of a Town: Or, The Chronicle of Foolov. Mikhail Evgrafovich Saltykov & Susan Brownsberger. LC 81-20666. (Illus.). 18.50 (ISBN 0-88233-610-X) (ISBN 0-88233-611-8). Ardis.

History of a Week. Lucy Bethia Colquhoun Walford. (On cover: Lovell's library. no. 1056). 1887. J. W. Lovell Company.

History of Amelia. Henry Fielding. LC 1-18357. 1852. Stringer & Townsend.

History of Anthony Waring. May Sinclair. LC 27-19630. 1927. The Macmillan Company.

History of Arsaces. Charles Johnstone. LC 74-17038. (Flowering of the Novel). 1974. (ISBN 0-8240-1205-4). Garland Pub.

History of Aythan Waring. Violet Jacob. LC 8-36755. 1908. E. P. Dutton & Company.

History of Betty Barnes. Sarah Fielding. LC 74-16028. (Flowering of the Novel). 1974. (ISBN 0-8240-1137-6). Garland Publishing.

History of Button Hill. Gordon Stowell. LC 30-26996. 1930. R. R. Smith, Inc.

History of Charles Wentworth, Esq. Edward Bancroft. LC 74-26666. (Flowering of the Novel). 1975. (ISBN 0-8240-1192-9). Garland Pub.

History of Charlotte Temple. A Tale of Truth. Susanna Haswell Rowson. LC 1-15063. 1808. N. Elliot, Printer, Catskill..

History of Constantius and Pulchera: Or, Virtue Rewarded ... LC 6-8351. 1821. A. B. Parker.

History of Cornelia. Sarah Robinson Scott. LC 74-16062. (Flowering of the Novel). 1974. (ISBN 0-8240-1128-7). Garland Pub.

History of David Grieve. Mary Augusta Arnold Humphry Ward Ward. LC 8-36028. 1892. Macmillan and Co.

History of Don Quixote of the Mancha. Miguel de Cervantes de Saavedra. Tr. by Thomas Shelton. LC 73-159347. (Series: The Tudor Translations, 1st Ser., V. 13-16.). 1967. AMS Press.

History of Dungeon Rock. Completed Sept. 17th, 1858. Nannette Snow Emerson. LC 43-46672. 1865. Bela Marsh.

History of Dungeon Rock. Completed Sept. 7th, 1856. 2d ed. Nannette Snow Emerson. LC 6-37832. 1859. B. Marsh.

History of Egg Panderville: A Pure Fiction. Gerald William Bullett. LC 29-6672. 1929. A. A. Knopf.

History of Emily Montague. Frances Moore Brooke. LC 74-16303. (Flowering of the Novel). 1974. (ISBN 0-8240-1184-8). Garland Pub.

History of England from the Accession of James the Second. Thomas Babington Macaulay Macaulay. LC 2-25541. (Seaside library, v. 48, no. 976).

History of Henry Esmond. Thackeray, William Makepeace. LC 50-14749. 1950. Literary Guild of America.

History of Henry Esmond, Esq. Thackeray, William Makepeace. LC 50-6162. (Harper's modern classics). 1950. Harper.

History of Henry Esmond, Esq. William Makepeace Thackeray. (Half-title: Everyman's library, ed. by Ernest Rhys. Fiction. no. 73). 1909. J. M. Dent & Co.

History of Henry Esmond, Esq. William Makepeace Thackeray. LC 37-270150. (Half-title: The modern library of the world's best books). 1936. The Modern Library.

History of Henry Esmond, Esq. William Makepeace Thackeray & Phelps, William Lyon, 1865- Ed. LC 2-22846. (lake English classics). 1902. Scott, Foresman and Company.

History of Henry Esmond, Esq. William Makepeace Thackeray & Phelps, William Lyon, 1865- Ed. LC 20-9276. (Lake English classics). Scott, Foresman and Company.

History of Henry Esmond, Esq. William Makepeace Thackery & Du Maurier, George Louis Pahnella Busson, 1834-1898, Illus. LC 12-31097. (Half-title: The biographical edition. The works of... Thackeray... vol. VII). 1899. Harper & Brothers.

History of Henry Esmond, Esq. A Colonel in the Service of Her Majesty Q. Anne, Written by Himself. With a New Introd. by Laura Benet and Illus. by Edward Ardizzone. William Makepeace Thackeray. LC 56-142581. 1956. Heritage Press.

History of Henry Esmond, Esq. A Colonel in the Service of Her Majesty Q. Anne, Written by Himself. With a New Introd. by Laura Benet and Illus. by Edward Ardizzone. William Makepeace Thackeray. LC 56-59103. 1956. Printed for the Members of the Limited Editions Club.

History of Henry Esmond, Esq. A Colonel in the Service of Her Majesty Q. Anne. Thackeray, William Makepeace. LC 56-59103. 1956. Printed for the Members of the Limited Editions Club.

History of Henry Esmond, Esq. A Colonel in the Service of Her Majesty Queen Anne. William Makepeace Thackeray. LC 2348. (Riverside literature series, no. 140). Houghton, Mifflin and Company.

History of Henry Esmond, Esq. A Colonel in the Service of Her Majesty Queen Anne. William Makepeace Thackeray & Graham, Walter James, 1885- Ed. LC 26-103209. (modern readers' series). 1926. The Macmillan Company.

History of Henry Esmond, Esq. A Colonel in the Service of Her Majesty Queen Anne. William Makepeace Thackeray & Lester, John Ashby, 1873- LC 14-22560. (Riverside literature series) $0.75.). Houghton, Mifflin Company.

History of Henry Esmond, Esq. A Colonel in the Service of Her Majesty Queen Anne. William Makepeace Thackeray & Moore, Hamilton Byron, Ed. LC 5-32337. (On cover: Standard English classics). Ginn & Company.

History of Henry Esmond, Esq. A Colonel in the Service of Her Majesty Queen Anne. William Makepeace Thackeray & Moore, Hamilton Byron, Ed. LC 24-10643. Ginn and Company.

History of Henry Esmond, Esq. A Colonel in the Service of Her Majesty Queen Anne. William Makepeace Thackery. LC 42-27104. (Half-title: Illustrated romances). 1898. Frederick A. Stokes Company.

History of Henry Esmond, Esq. Colonel in the Service of Her Majesty Queen Anne. William Makepeace Thackeray. LC 8-28200. (Franklin square library, no. 65). 1879. Harper & Brothers.

History of Henry Esmond, Esq. Colonel in the Service of Her Majesty Queen Anne. William Makepeace Thackeray & Henneman, John Bell, 1864- Ed. LC 6-34638. (Macmillan's pocket American and English classics). 1906. The Macmillan Company.

History of Henry Esmond, Esq. Introd. by Edward R. Easton. William Makepeace Thackeray. (Collateral classic, CC508). 1966. Washington Sq.

History of Henry Esmond, Esq. Introd. by G. Robert Stange. William Makepeace Thackeray. LC 62-11871. (Rinehart editions, 116). 1962. Holt, Rinehart and Winston.

History of Henry Esmond, Esquire. William Makepeace Thackeray. LC 50-12194. (Modern Library college editions, T34). 1950. Modern Library.

History of Henry Esmond, Esquire. William Makepeace Thackeray. LC 66-1388. 1963. Washington Square Press.

History of James Lovegrove, Esq. James Ridley. LC 74-20930. (Flowering of the Novel). 1974. 25.00. (ISBN 0-8240-1157-0). Garland Pub.

History of Jemmy and Jenny Jessamy. Eliza Fowler Haywood. LC 74-17292. (Flowering of the Novel). 1974. (ISBN 0-8240-1138-4). Garland Pub.

History of Lorenzo and Virginia: Or Virtue Rewarded. An Address to the Young Ladies of Columbia, Calculated to Inspire the Bosom with Pleasing Sensations and Arm the Virtuous with Fortitude Under the Most Forlorn Circumstances... T H Cauldwell. LC 6-15446. 1834. Eastman & Chadwick, Printers.

History of Lucy Temple: Daughter of Charlotte Temple; an Account of Her Pathetic Young Life's Trials, Her Love and Its Consequences... John Barnitz Bacon. LC 8-948. Barclay & Co.

History of Margaret Catchpole, a Suffolk Girl. Richard Cobbold. (Half title: The world's classics. cxix). 1923. H. Milford, Oxford University Press.

History of Maria Kittle. Ann Eliza Schuyler Bleecker. LC 77-10813. (Garland Library of Narratives of North American Indian Captivities; V. 20). 1978. 29.50 (ISBN 0-8240-1644-0). Garland Pub.

History of Michael Kemp: The Happy Farmer's Lad: a Tale of Rustic Life, Illustrative of the Spiritual Blessings and Temporal Advantages of Early Piety. from the 6th london ed. Anne Cox Woodrooffe. LC 8-37540. 1841. R. Carter.

History of Miss Betsy Thoughtless. Eliza Fowler Haywood. LC 78-60837. (Novel, 1720-1805; 4). 1979. 112.00 (ISBN 0-8240-3653-0). Garland Pub.

History of Mr. Polly. Herbert George Wells. LC 10-737. 1909. Duffield and Company.

History of Mr. Polly. Herbert George Wells. LC 41-15202. 1941. The Press of the Readers Club.

History of Mister Polly. Herbert George Wells. Ed. by Gordon N. Ray. LC 61-169. 1961. pap. 4.50 (ISBN 0-395-05149-5, B52, RivEd, 3-47686). HM.

History of Mr. Polly. Edited with an Introd. by Gordon N. Ray. Herbert George Wells. LC 61-169. (Riverside editions, B52). 1960. Houghton Mifflin.

History of Nora Beckham: A Museum of Home Life. Joseph Stanley Pennell. LC 48-8382. 1948. C. Scribner's Sons.

History of Ophelia. Sarah Fielding. LC 74-16024. (Flowering of the Novel). 1974. (ISBN 0-8240-1154-6). Garland Pub.

History of Pamela: Or, Virtue Rewarded. Samuel Richardson. LC 35-161288. 1797. Printed and Sold by S. Hall, in Cornhill.

History of Pendennis. William Makepeace Thackeray. LC 72-192881. (Penguin English library). (Illus.). 1972. (0.75, 3.95) (ISBN 0-14-043076-8). Penguin.

History of Pendennis. His Fortunes and Misfortunes, His Friends and His Greatest Enemy. William Makepeace Thackeray. LC 31-263. Caxton Publishing Co.

History of Pendennis. His Fortunes and Misfortunes, His Friends and His Greatest Enemy. William Makepeace Thackeray. LC 8-27762. 1850. Harper & Brothers.

History of Pendennis: His Fortunes and Misfortunes, His Friends and His Greatest Enemy. household ed. William Makepeace Thackeray. 1869. Fields, Osgood & Co.

History of Pendennis: His Fortunes and Misfortunes, His Friends and His Greatest Enemy. William Makepeace Thackeray. LC 8-2126. (Added t.-p.: The works of William Makepeace Thackeray... v. 3, 4). 1879. Smith, Elder, & Co.

History of Pendennis. His Fortunes and Misfortunes, His Friends and His Greatest Enemy. William Makepeace Thackeray. LC 8-28204. (On cover: Lovell's library, v. 4, no. 193). 1883. J. W. Lovell Company.

History of Pendennis. His Fortunes and Misfortunes, His Friends and His Greatest Enemy. William Makepeace Thackeray. LC 43-39495. 1873. Harper & Brothers.

History of Pendennis: His Fortunes and Misfortunes, His Friends and His Greatest Enemy. William Makepeace Thackeray & Lovett, Robert Morss, 1870- Ed. LC 17-116982. (Half-title: The modern student's library, ed. by W. D. Howe). C. Scribner's Sons.

History of Pompey the Little. Francis Coventry. LC 74-16199. (Flowering of the Novel). (Illus.). 1974. (lib. bdg.) 25.00 (ISBN 0-8240-1131-7). Garland Pub.

History of Pompey the Little: Or, The Life and Adventures of a Lap-Dog. Francis Coventry. LC 75-300058. (Oxford English novels). (Illus.). 1974. 13.00 (ISBN 0-19-255354-2). Oxford University Press.

History of Rasselas, Prince of Abissinia. A Tale. The Vision of Theodore. The Fountains. A Fairy Tale. Samuel Johnson. LC 7-19659. 1850. Hogan and Thompson.

History of Rasselas, Prince of Abissinia: By Johnson; Ed., Introd. Notes by J.P. Hardy. Samuel Johnson. Ed. by John P Hardy. LC 68-134393. 1968. pap., 1.25. Oxford Univ. Pr.

History of Rasselas, Prince of Abissinia. Samuel Johnson. Ed. by Geoffrey Tillotson & Brian Jenkins. LC 76-562416. (Oxford English novels). 1971. 1.50 (ISBN 0-19-255342-9). Oxford University Press.

History of Rasselas, Prince of Abissinia. Samuel Johnson. LC 3-1773. 1902. Van Vechten & Ellis.

History of Rasselas, Prince of Abissinia: A Tale. Samuel Johnson. Ed. by Chapman, Robert William. LC 29-5000. 1927. The Clarendon Press.

History of Rasselas, Prince of Abissinia. Samuel Johnson & Dennis Joseph Enright. LC 77-359474. (Penguin English library). 1976-1977. 1.95 (ISBN 0-14-043108-X). Penguin.

History of Rasselas: Prince of Abyssinia. Edited by Gwin J. Kolb. Samuel Johnson. Ed. by Gwin J. Kolb. LC 62-17553. (Crofts classics). 1962. Appleton-Century-Crofts.

History of Rasselas: Prince of Abyssinia. Edited, with an Introd. by Warren Fleischauer. Samuel Johnson. Ed. by Warren Fleischaler. LC 61-182086. (Barron's educational series). 1962. Barron's Educational Series, Inc.

History of Rasselas, Prince of Abyssinia. A Tale. Samuel Johnson. (Lovell's library, v 2, no. 44). 1882. J. W. Lovell Company.

History of Rasselas, Prince of Abyssinia. A Tale. Samuel Johnson. LC 41-38135. (With Saint-Pierre, J. H. B. de. Paul and Virginia. Chicago, New York etc. 1888). 1888. Belford, Clarke & Co.

History of Rasselas, Prince of Abyssinia. Samuel Johnson. Ed. by Emerson, Oliver Farrar. LC 4-31656. (On cover: English readings). 1895. H. Holt and Company.

History of Rhedi. William Duff. LC 74-16061. (Flowering of the Novel). 1974. (ISBN 0-8240-1200-3). Garland Pub.

History of Rhedi, the Hermit of Mount Ararat: An Oriental Tale, 1773. William Duff. (Flowering of the Novel, 1740-1775 Ser: Vol. 101). 1974. lib. bdg. 50.00 (ISBN 0-8240-1200-3). Garland Pub.

History of Rome Hanks and Kindred Matters. Joseph Stanley Pennell. LC 44-6553. 1944. C. Scribner's Sons.

History of Russelas, Prince of Abyssinia. Samuel Johnson. LC 7-10550. (On cover: English readings.). 1894. H. Holt and Company.

History of St. Giles and St. James. Douglas William Jerrold. LC 7-3524. 1847. Burgess, Stringer and Company.

History of Samuel Titmarsh and the Great Hoggarty Diamond. A Little Dinner at Timmins's, and Notes of a Journey from Cornhill to Grand Cairo. William Makepeace Thackeray. LC 8-7697. (Added t.-p.: The works of William Makepeace Thackeray... v. 12). 1879. Smith, Elder, & Co.

History of Shadows. Robert C. Reinhart. 320p. (Orig.). 1982. pap. 2.95 (ISBN 0-380-79616-3, 79616). Avon.

History of Sir Charles Grandison. Samuel Richardson. LC 73-152832. (Oxford English novels). 1972. (set) 48.00 (ISBN 0-19-255358-5). Oxford University Press.

History of Sir Charles Grandison. from the 10th london ed. Samuel Richardson. LC 15-12473. 1798. Printed by Havila & Oliver Farnsworth, for Oliver D. & I. Cooke, Book-Sellers, Hartford.

History of Sir Richard Calmady: A Romance. Mary St. Leger Kingsley Harrison. LC 10-3725. A.L. Burt Company.

History of Sir Richard Calmady: A Romance. Mary St. Leger Kingsley Harrison. LC 1-256865. 1901. Dodd, Mead & Company.

History of Sir Richard Calmady: A Romance, 2 vols. in 1. Lucas Malet. LC 79-8424. Date not set. Repr. of 1901 ed. 44.50 (ISBN 0-404-62015-9). AMS Pr.

History of the Adventures of George Whigham & His Friend Mr. Claney Hobson: Illustrated by Carl Rose. Kyle Samuel Crichton. LC 51-10003. 1951. Crown Publishers.

History of the Adventures of Joseph Andrews and His Friend Mr. Abraham Adams. Wood-Engravings by Derrick Harris. Henry Fielding. LC 53-11091. 1953. Folio Society.

History of the Adventures of Joseph Andrews and His Friend Mr. Abraham Adams. Henry Fielding. LC 59-1083. (Norton library, N2). 1958. Norton.

History of the Adventures of Joseph Andrews and His Friend Mr. Abraham Adams. Henry Fielding. (English Comedie humaine. 1st series. v. 3). 1902. The Century Co.

History of the Adventures of Joseph Andrews & His Friend Mr. Abraham Adams. Henry Fielding. (Half-title: Everyman's library, ed. by Ernest Rhys. Fiction no.467). 1910. J. M. Dent & Sons, Ltd.

History of the Adventures of Joseph Andrews and of His Friend Mr. Abraham Adams: Written in Imitation of the Manner of Cervantes, Author of Don Quixote. With an Introd. by Howard Mumford Jones. Henry Fielding. LC 50-12242. (Modern Library college editions, T16). 1950. Modern Library.

History of the Adventures of Joseph Andrews, and of His Friend Mr. Abraham Adams: And, An Apology for the Life of Mrs. Shamela Andrews. Henry Fielding. Ed. by Douglas Brooks. LC 78-548668. (Oxford English novels). 1970 (ISBN 0-19-255323-2). Oxford U.P.

History of the Adventures of Joseph Andrews: And of His Friend Mr. Abraham Adams, Written in Imitation of the Manner of Cervantes, Author of Don Quixote. Henry Fielding. Ed. by Mack, Maynard. LC 49-1642. (Rinehart editions, 15). 1949. Rinehart.

History of the American Film. Christopher Durang. LC 78-53965. (Bard Book). 1978. 1.95 (ISBN 0-380-39271-2). Avon.

History of the Caliph Vathek. 8th ed. William Beckford. Ed. by Samuel Henley. J. W. Lovell Company.

History of the Caliph Vathek. 8th ed. William Beckford & Henley, Samuel, 1740-1815, Ed. W. L. Allison.

History of the Caliph Vathek, Including The Episodes of Vathek: An Arabian Tale. William Beckford. LC 71-26229. (Adult fantasy). 1971. 0.95. Ballantine Books.

History of the Chevalier Des Grieux and of Manon Lescaut. Antoine Francois Prevost. Tr. by Waddell, Helen Jane. Saintsbury, George Edward Bateman. LC 31-28156. 1931. R. R. Smith, Inc.

History of the Countess of Dellwyn. Sarah Fielding. LC 74-17444. (Flowering of the Novel). 1974. 25.00 (ISBN 0-8240-1152-X). Garland Pub.

History of the Excellence and Decline of the Constitution, Religion, Laws, Manners, and Genius of the Sumatrans. John Shebbeare. LC 74-26592. (Flowering of the Novel). 1975. (ISBN 0-8240-1165-1). Garland Pub.

History of the Human Heart: Or, The Adventures of a Young Gentleman. LC 74-17441. (Flowering of the Novel). 1974. (ISBN 0-8240-1125-2). Garland Pub.

History of the Lady Betty Stair: A Novel. Molly Elliot Seawell. 1897. C. Scribner's Sons.

History of the Life and Adventures of Mr. Anderson. Edward Kimber. LC 75-7026. (Garland Library of Narratives of North American Indian Captivities; V. 7). 1975. 21.00 (ISBN 0-8240-1631-9). Garland Pub.

History of the Life of the Late Mr. Jonathan Wild, the Great: And A Journey from This World to the Next. Henry Fielding. LC 1-18378. 1853. Stringer & Townsend.

History of the Life of the Late Mr. Jonathan Wild, the Great. Henry Fielding. LC 26-9674. (On cover: The rogues' bookshelf). Greenberg.

History of the Life of the Late Mr. Jonathan Wild the Great. of jonathan wild, by daniel defoe, with an introduction by wilson follett. ed. Henry Fielding & Defoe, Daniel, 1661?-1731. LC 26-17965. 1926. A. A. Knopf.

History of the Long Captivity and Adventures of Thomas Pellow, in South Barbary. Thomas Pellow. LC 75-170600. (Foundations of the Novel). 1973. 22.00 ea. (ISBN 0-8240-0583-X). Garland Pub.

History of the Loves of Antiochus and Stratonice. Lewis Theobald. LC 76-170540. (Foundations of the Novel). 1973. 22.00 (ISBN 0-8240-0541-4). Garland Pub.

History of the Proceedings of the Mandarins & Proatins of the Britomartian Empire see Impartial Secret History of Arlus, Fortunatus, & Odolphus, Ministers of State to the Empress Ofgrand-Insula.

History of the Thirteen. Honore De Balzac. LC 74-195973. (Penguin classics). 1974. 2.50 (ISBN 0-14-044301-0). Penguin Books.

History of Tom Jones. Henry Fielding. LC 6-11549. (Half-title: The English Comedie humaine. 2d series). 1906. The Century Co.

History of Tom Jones. Henry Fielding. (Half-title: Everyman's library, ed. by Ernest Rhys. Fiction). 1909. J. M. Dent & Co.

History of Tom Jones. Henry Fielding. LC 17-17519. (Harvard classics shelf of fiction, selected by C. W. Ellot. 1-2). P. F. Collier & Son.

History of Tom Jones. Henry Fielding. LC 25-261180. 1924. A. A. Knopf.

History of Tom Jones. Henry Fielding. LC 31-26756. (Half-title: The modern library of the world's best books). 1931. The Modern Library.

History of Tom Jones. Henry Fielding. LC 40-27705. (Half-title: The modern library of the world's best books). 1940. The Modern Library.

History of Tom Jones. Henry Fielding & Stevenson, Burton Egbert, 1872- Ed. LC 4-31010. (Condensed classics). 1904. H. Holt and Company.

History of Tom Jones. Henry Fielding & Townsend, George Henry, D. 1869. LC 41-42393. G. Routeledge and Sons, Limited.

History of Tom Jones: A Foundling. Henry Fielding. LC 66-5490. (Macdonald illus. classics, 26). 1966. 3.50. Macdonald.

History of Tom Jones, a Foundling. Henry Fielding. LC 63-5691. 1963. Washington Square Press.

History of Tom Jones: A Foundling. Henry Fielding. LC 67-12291. (Great illustrated classics: Titan editions). (Illus.). 1967. Dodd, Mead.

History of Tom Jones: A Foundling. Henry Fielding. Ed. by Maugham, William Somerset. LC 48-8368. (Ten Greatest Novels of the World). 1948. J. C. Winston.

History of Tom Jones: A Foundling... illustrated sterling ed. Henry Fielding. LC 43-36865. D. Estes & Company.

History of Tom Jones, a Foundling. Henry Fielding & Fredson Thayer Bowers. LC 73-15009. (Wesleyan edition of the works of Henry Fielding). (Illus.). 1975. 44.00 (ISBN 0-8195-4068-4). Wesleyan University Press.

History of Tom Jones, a Foundling. wesleyan ed. / the text edited by fredson bowers; with an introduction and commentary by martin c. battestin. ed. Henry Fielding & Fredson Thayer Bowers. LC 75-316777. (Illus.). 1974. 20.00 (ISBN 0-19-812472-4). Clarendon Press.

History of Tom Jones: A Foundling. Henry Fielding & Chappell, Warren, 1904- Illus. LC 43-51332. 1943. The Modern Library.

History of Tom Jones: A Foundling. Henry Fielding & Tom Jones. LC 64-7276. 1964. Random House.

History of Tom Jones, a Foundling by Henry Fielding... Henry Fielding. LC 1-18373. G. Routledge and Sons, Limited.

History of Tom Jones: A Foundling. With Eight Pages of Illus. and an Introd. by Arthur Sherbo. Henry Fielding. LC 67-12291. (Great illus. classics: Titan eds.). 1967. 4.95. Dodd.

History of Tom Jones, a Foundling: With Illus. by T. M. Cleland, and an Introd. by Louis Kronenberger. Henry Fielding. LC 52-8568. 1952. Limited Editions Club.

History of Tom Jones: Ed. by R. P. C. Mutter. Henry Fielding. LC 66-3336. (Penguin Eng. lib., EL9). 1966. pap., 1.65. Penguin.

History of Tom Jones, the Foundling, in His Married State. LC 74-16071. (Flowering of the Novel). 1974. (ISBN 0-8240-1127-9). Garland Pub.

Hit. Brian Wynne Garfield. 1973. 0.75. Popular Lib.

Hit. Brian Wynne Garfield. LC 75-93719. (Cock Robin mystery). 1970. Macmillan.

Hit. Julian Mayfield. 1970. pap. 0.95 o.p. (B95-2048). Belmont-Tower.

Hit! Arthur Stackman & Arthur R Trustman. 1973. (pbk.) 0.95. Bantam Books.

Hit: A Novel. Julian Mayfield. LC 57-12251. 1957. Vanguard Press.

Hit and Miss: A Story of Real Life. Angie Stewart Manly. 1883. J. L. Regan & Co.

Hit & Run. L. Atkinson. 1981. 8.90 (ISBN 0-531-04265-0). Watts.

Hit and Run. Alice Duer Miller. LC 43-1144. 1943. Dodd, Mead & Company.

Hit Man. Robert J. Flood. 336p. 1972. pap. 1.25 o.p. (ISBN 0-532-12190-2). Woodhill.

Hit Man. Robert J. Flood. 336p. 1972. pap. 1.25 o.p. (ISBN 0-532-12190-2). Manor Bks.

Hit Me with a Rainbow. James Kirkwood. (O.s.i.). 1980. 9.95 o.s.i. (ISBN 0-440-03397-7). Delacorte.

Hit Me with a Rainbow. James Kirkwood. 1981. pap. 3.25 (ISBN 0-440-13622-9). Dell.

Hit Me with a Rainbow: A Novel. James Kirkwood. LC 79-19469. 9.95 (ISBN 0-440-03397-7). Delacorte Press.

Hit Team. David Tinnin & Dag Christensen. 1976. 7.95 o.p. (ISBN 0-316-84590-6). Little.

Hit the Rivet, Sister. Mary Beatty Trask. LC 43-163345. 1943. Howell, Soskin.

Hit the Saddle: A Western Novel. Allan Vaughan Elston. LC 48-18940. Triangle Books.

Hit the Saddle: A Western Novel. Allen Vaughan Elston. LC 47-31011. 1947. Macrae-Smith Co.

Hit Woman. Gary Blumberg. 1975. (pbk.) 1.25. Dell.

Hitch Hike. Weldon Matthews. LC 35-229624. Godwin.

Hitch in Hell. Andy Bakjian. LC 74-18340. 1974. 6.95 (ISBN 0-8111-0542-3). Oliver Co.

Hitchcock Edition of David Gray... David Gray. LC 30-4021. 1929. The Derrydale Press.

Hitchhiker. H. R. Kaye, pseud. pap. 1.95 o.p. (6007). Brandon.

Hitchhiker's Guide to the Galaxy. Douglas Adams. LC 80-14572. 1980. 6.95 (ISBN 0-517-54209-9). Harmony Books.

Hitherto: A Story of Yesterdays. Adeline Dutton Train Whitney. Loring.

Hitherto: A Story of Yesterdays. Adeline Dutton Train Whitney. LC 8-36545. 1893. Houghton, Mifflin and Company.

Hitler Diamonds. Desmond Cory, pseud. (Johnny Fedora Ser. No. 7). 1969. pap. 0.60 o.p. (A516X, Award). Univ Pub & Dist.

Hitler Diaries. Richard F Hugo. LC 82-14350. 1983. 12.95 (ISBN 0-688-01546-8). Morrow.

Hitler Has Won: A Novel. Frederic Mullally. LC 75-11846. 1975. 8.95 (ISBN 0-671-22074-8). Simon and Schuster.

Hitler Was My Friend. Ed. by Heinrich Hoffmann. Tr. by R. H. Stevens from Ger. 1978. pap. 4.50x (ISBN 0-911038-36-1). Noontide.

Hitler's Daughter. Gary Goss. 1973. 7.95 (ISBN 0-8184-0157-5). Lyle Stuart.

Hitler's Treasure. Michael Makris. 240p. 1982. 12.95 (ISBN 0-8059-2829-4). Dorrance.

Hitler's War. 1981. pap. text ed. write for info. (ISBN 0-88074-250-X). Metagam.

Hitler's Werewolves. Charles Whiting. (War Bks.). 240p. 1983. pap. 2.95 (ISBN 0-86721-197-0). Jove Pubns.

Hitler's Wife. Antoni Gronowicz & Rockwell, Donald Shumway, 1895- Tr. LC 43-5349. 1942. Paramount Publishing Company.

Hittite. Noel Bertram Gerson. LC 61-5968. 1961. Doubleday.

Hittite Must Die. Moshe Shamir. Tr. by Margaret Benaya from Hebrew. (Illus.). 1978. Repr. of 1964 ed. pap. 3.95 (ISBN 0-85222-231-9, East & West Lib). Hebrew Pub.

Hive. Camilo Jose Cela. LC 82-11540. (Neglected Books of the Twentieth Century). 1983. 6.95 (ISBN 0-88001-004-5). Ecco Press.

Hive. Camilo Jose Cela. LC 81-11540. (Neglected Books of the 20th Century Ser.). 257p. 1983. pap. 6.95. Ecco Pr.

Hive. Camilo Jose Cela. 1953. 13.50x o.p. M McCosh Bkslr.

Hive of Busy Bees. Effie M Williams. LC 31-34929. The Warner Press.

Hive of Glass. Philip Maitland Hubbard. LC 65-21707. 1965. Atheneum.

Hive of Glass: 1st Amer. Ed. Philip Maitland Hubbard. LC 65-217075. bds., 3.95. Atheneum.

Hive. Tr. from Spanish by J.M. Cohen with Arturo Barea. Introd. by Arturo Barea. Camilo Jose Cela. LC 53-10415. (Masters of mod. lit., Noonday 276). 1965. pap., 1.95. Farrar.

Hive: Translated by J. M. Cohen in Consultation with Arturo Barea. With an Introd. by Arturo Barea. Camilo Jose Cela. LC 53-10415. 1953. Farrar, Straus and Young.

Hiwa: A Tale of Ancient Hawaii. Edmund Pearson Dole. LC 2697. 1900. Harper & Brothers.

Hiwa, a Tale of Ancient Hawaii. Edmund Pearson Dole. (Illus.). 1977. pap. 2.75 (ISBN 0-912180-31-5). Petroglyph.

Hizzoner the Mayor: A Novel. Joel Sayre. LC 33-6056. The John Day Company.

Hjalmar: Or, The Immigrant's Son. James A Peterson. LC 22-23907. 1922. K. C. Holter Publishing Company.

Hjalmar's Christmas Story. George Ollman. 2.75 o.p. Vantage.

H.M.S. Hood vs. Bismarck: The Battleship Battle. Theodore Taylor. 144p. 1982. pap. 2.25 (ISBN 0-380-81174-X, 81174-X, Flare). Avon.

HMS Leviathan. John Winton. LC 67-21512. 1967. Coward-McCann.

H.M.S. Saracen: 1st Amer. Ed. Douglas Reeman. LC 66-104776. 1966. 5.95. Putnam.

H.M.S. Surprise. Patrick O'Brian. LC 73-5938. 1973. 7.95 (ISBN 0-397-00998-4). Lippincott.

Ho, the Fair Wind: A Novel. Ida Alexa Ross Wylie. LC 45-10241. 1945. Random House.

Hoarding. John Owen. LC 23-98572. 1923. Hodder and Stoughton, Ltd.

Hoarding. John Owen. E. P. Dutton & Company.

Hoaxer's. Morris Kominsky. 12.50 o.p. (ISBN 0-8283-1288-5). Branden.

Hobbit. John Ronald Reuel Tolkien. LC 77-78707. (Illus.). 1977. 35.00 (ISBN 0-8109-1060-8). Abrams.

Hobbit. John Ronald Reuel Tolkien. (Illus.). 1938. 8.95 (ISBN 0-395-07122-4). HM.

Hobbit. collector's ed. John Ronald Reuel Tolkien. (Illus.). 320p. 1973. slip cased 18.95 (ISBN 0-395-17711-1). HM.

Hobbit & the Lord of the Rings, 4 vols. John Ronald Reuel Tolkien. 1979. Set. pap. 18.95 (ISBN 0-395-28263-2). HM.

Hobbits Journal: Being a Blank Book with Some Curious Illustrations of Friends & Foes of the Nine Companions. Illus. by Michael Green. LC 79-20203. (Illus.). 1979. lib. bdg. 12.90 (ISBN 0-89471-089-3); pap. 4.95 (ISBN 0-89471-090-7). Running Pr.

Hobbledehoy's Hero. Curtis L Johnson. LC 59-10076. 1959. Pennington Press.

Hobby House. Russell Neale. LC 29-4759. 1929. Harper & Brothers.

Hobby Shop. Morton Grosser. 1967. 4.95 o.p. HM.

Hobby Shop: A Novel. Morton Grosser. LC 67-19894. 1967. 4.95. Houghton.

Hobgoblin. John Coyne. LC 81-12055. 11.95 (ISBN 0-399-12643-0). Putnam.

Hobgoblin Murder. Kay Cleaver Strahan. LC 34-186903. The Bobbs-Merrill Company.

Hobo. Richard Dillon. (Orig.). 1981. pap. text ed. 1.95 o.s.i. (ISBN 0-505-51632-2). Tower Bks.

Hobo & the Fairy. Jack London. Repr. lib. bdg. 14.85x (ISBN 0-89190-653-3). Am Repr-Rivercity Pr.

Hoboken: A Romance of New York. Theodore Sedgwick Fay. LC 6-38773. 1843. Harper & Brothers.

Hobomok, a Tale of Early Times. Lydia Maria Francis Child. LC 71-93604. (American fiction series). 1970. (ISBN 0-512-00095-6). Garrett Press.

Hobomok: A Tale of Early Times. Lydia Maria Francis Child. LC 6-20980. 1824. Cummings, Hilliard & Co.

Hobomok: A Tale of Early Times. Lydia Maria Francis Child. 1972. Repr. of 1824 ed. 16.50 (ISBN 0-8422-8185-1). Irvington.

Hobomok: A Tale of Early Times. Ed. by Edward Foster. LC 71-93604. (American Fiction Ser). 1970. lib. bdg. 7.95 o.s.i. (ISBN 0-512-00095-6). Garrett Pr.

Hochmann Miniatures: By Robert L. Fish. Robert L Fish. LC 67-169439. 1967. 4.50. New Amer. Lib.

Hockey Sweater & Other Stories. Roch Carrier. Tr. by Sheila Fischman from Fr. (Anansi Fiction Ser.: No. 40). 160p. (Orig.). 1979. pap. 6.95 (ISBN 0-88784-078-7, Pub. by Hse Anansi Pr Canada). U of Toronto Pr.

Hodak. Tom Pendleton. 1969. 5.95 o.p. (ISBN 0-07-049256-5). McGraw.

Hodak. Edmund Van Zandt. LC 68-55423. 1969. McGraw-Hill.

Hoenaje a Carlos Fuentes. Variaciones Interpretativas En Torno a Su Obra. Fuad Giacoman, Helmy & Carlos Fuentes. (Coleccion homenajes). (Illus.). 1972. 10.00. Las Americas.

Hoffman. Ernest Gebler. LC 69-10963. 1969. 4.95. Doubleday.

Hoffman's Row: A Novel. Walter H Carnahan. LC 63-18293. 1963. Bobbs-Merrill.

Hofmannsthal's Novel, Andreas: Memory and Self. David H Miles. LC 70-155001. (Princeton essays in European and comparative literature). 1972. 8.50 (ISBN 0-691-06208-0). Princeton University Press.

Hog Butcher. Ronald L. Fair. 1973. 0.95. Bantam.

Hog Butcher. Ronald L Fair. LC 66-19486. 1966. Harcourt, Brace & World.

Hog Murders. William L DeAndrea. LC 79-52460. 1979. 1.95 (ISBN 0-380-47548-0). Avon.

Hogan, M. P. May Laffan Hartley. LC 79-10777. (Ireland, from the Act of Union, 1800, to the Death of Parnell, 1891). 1979. 42.00 (ISBN 0-8240-3515-1). Garland Pub.

Hogan, M. P. A Novel. M. P. Hogan. (Seaside library, v. 58, no. 1175). 1882. G. Munro.

Hohensteins: A Novel. author's ed. Friedrich Spielhagen. Tr. by Maximilian Schele De Vere. LC 8-14065. 1870. Leypoldt & Holt.

Hohenzollern: A Story of the Time of Frederick Barbarossa. Cyrus Townsend Brady. LC 2-9132. 1902. The Century Co.

Hokey. Donald Stahl. LC 68-18763. 1968. 4.95. L. Stuart.

Holcha-an and Other Poems: Tales of the Mayas. Charles Edward Lee. LC 41-2155.

Holcombes. A Story of Virginia Home-Life. Mary Tucker Magill. LC 11-821112. 1871. J. B. Lippincott & Co.

Holcroft Covenant. Robert Ludlum. LC 77-95295. 10.95 (ISBN 0-399-90001-2). R. Marek Publishers.

Hold a Candle to the Sun. Ellen Newman & Kane, Mrs. Alline (Ellis) Joint Author. LC 38-36500. Mathis, Van Nort & Co.

Hold Autumn in Your Hand. George Sessions Perry. LC 50-5369. 1950. Whittlesey House.

Hold Autumn in Your Hand. George Sessions Perry. LC 75-7473. (Zia book). 1975. 2.95 (ISBN 0-8263-0377-3). University of New Mexico Press.

Hold Autumn in Your Hand. George Sessions Perry. LC 41-51540. 1941. The Viking Press.

Hold Back the Dawn. Ketti Frings. LC 40-27692. Duell, Sloan and Pearce.

Hold Back the Heart: By Sheila Burns Pseud. Ursula Bloom. LC 51-2267. 1951. Arcadia House.

Hold Back the Night. Abra Taylor. (Orig.). 1983. pap. 2.95 (ISBN 0-671-45863-9). PB.

Hold Back the Night. 1st Ed. Pat Frank. LC 51-11197. 1952. Lippincott.

Hold Back the Sun. June L. Shiplett. 1981. pap. 2.95 (ISBN 0-451-11015-3, AE1015, Sig). NAL.

Hold Back the Sun: By John Vail Pseud. Cover Painting by Frank McCarthy. Robert Carse. LC 56-1212. (Gold medal books, 556). 1956. Fawcett Publications.

Hold Bright the Star. Sue McConkey. 1963. 5.00 o.p. (ISBN 0-87482-024-3). Wake-Brook.

Hold Close the Day. Isabel Black. LC 54-6628. 1954. Crown Publishers.

Hold Fast 'Til Morning. Beth Brookes. (Second Chance at Love Ser.: No. 36). 192p. (Orig.). 1982. pap. 1.75 (ISBN 0-515-06304-5). Jove Pubns.

Hold Fast to Love. Jo Ann Simon. 288p. 1982. pap. 3.50 (ISBN 0-380-80945-1, 80945-1). Avon.

Hold High the Lamp. Alice Jennings Darrow. LC 71-75023. 1969. 6.95. Dorrance.

Hold Me Fast. Cecile Gilmore. LC 50-5836. 1950. Avalon Books.

Hold My Hand I'm Dying. John G. Davis. 1968. 6.95 o.p. (ISBN 0-07-023800-6). McGraw.

Hold My Hand, I'm Dying. John G. Davis. 1971. pap. 1.25 o.p. (P1565, Crest). Fawcett World.

Hold My Hand: I'm Dying. John Gordon Davis. LC 68-20719. 1968. McGraw-Hill.

Hold on to Love. Barry Caldwell. LC 37-15198. 1937. Hillman Curl, Inc.

Hold Saipan. William Herber. (Leisure book). 1979. 2.25 (ISBN 0-8439-0614-6). Nordon Pubns.

Hold with the Hares. Len Zinberg. LC 48-8533. 1948. Doubleday.

Holden with Cords: Or, The Power of the Secret Empire. A Faithful Representation in Story of the Evil Influence of Freemasonry. Elizabeth E Flagg. LC 6-41129. 1883. E. A. Cook.

Holden with the Cords. Elizabeth E. Flagg. 1874. E. P. Dutton & Company.

Holdenhurst Hall: A Novel. Walter Bloomfield. (Choice Series, No. 126). (ledger library, no. 126). 1895. R. Bonner's Sons.

Holdfast Games. Odell Shepard & Shepard, Willard Odell, Joint Author. LC 46-11985. 1946. The Macmillan Company.

Holding of Recapture Valley. Raymond A Berry. LC 34-5971. 1934. Macrae Smith Company.

Holding onto Nothing. Gordon Bishop. LC 78-84038. 1969. 1.25. Pound Press.

Holding Patterns: A Novel. Ellen Roddick. LC 80-22079. 10.95 (ISBN 0-312-38833-0). St. Martin's Press.

Holding Wonder. Zenna Henderson. LC 75-144271. (Doubleday science fiction). 1971. 5.95. Doubleday.

Holding Your Eight Hands: An Anthology of Science Fiction Verse. Ed. by Edward Lucie-Smith. 120p. 1970. 14.00 o.p. (ISBN 0-85391-162-2). Ultramarine Pub.

Holding Your Eight Hands: An Anthology of Science Fiction Verse. Ed. by Edward Lucie-Smith. LC 69-15580. 1969. pap. 1.95 o.p. Doubleday.

Holdouts. William Decker. 1981. pap. 1.95 (ISBN 0-671-42081-X). PB.

Holdouts: A Novel. William Decker. LC 79-13348. 8.95 (ISBN 0-316-17917-5). Little, Brown.

Hole and Corner. Patricia Wentworth. LC 36-18154. J. B. Lippincott Company.

Hole in Space. Larry Niven. (Science fiction original). 1974. (pbk.) 1.25 (ISBN 0-345-24011-1). Ballantine.

Hole in the Ground. Andrew Garve. pap. 0.50 o.p. (72-730). Lancer.

Hole in the Ground. Paul Winterton. LC 52-11698. 1952. Harper.

Hole in the Head. Francis Stuart. LC 77-84433. (Illus.). 1977. 9.95 (ISBN 0-917712-02-1). Longship Press.

Hole in the Hill. Earl T. English. 4.98 o.p. Vantage.

Hole in the Lead Apron, and Six Other Stories. Jesse Bier. LC 64-19941. 1964. Harcourt, Brace & World.

Hole in the Wall. Frederick John MacIsaac. LC 27-11212. 1927. Henry Waterson Company.

Hole in the Wall. Arthur Morrison. LC 2-21578. 1902. McClure, Phillips & Co.

Hole in the Zero. M. K Joseph. LC 68-15661. 1968. Dutton.

Holes in the Wall: A Novel of the Cold War. Jerome Bahr. LC 70-110764. (His All good Americans, v. 6). 1970. 4.95. R. B. Luce.

Holiday. Waldo David Frank. LC 23-127483. Boni and Liveright.

Holiday. C Lenanton. LC 28-14547. 1928. D. Appleton and Company.

Holiday. Stanley Middleton. 1974. 8.95 (ISBN 0-09-119910-7, Pub. by Hutchinson). Merrimack Pub Cir.

Holiday. Stevie Smith. 192p. 1982. pap. 2.75 (ISBN 0-523-41684-9). Pinnacle Bks.

Holiday: A Novel. Constantine Fitz Gibbon. LC 53-10811. 1953. Simon and Schuster.

Holiday Book: Sketches of Men, Women and Things, Founded on Truth and from the Actual Observation and Experiences of the Author. Elizabeth S Roberts. LC 7-41034. 1890. E. Scott, Printer.

Holiday by the Sea. Gerald Brenan. 1962. 3.95 o.p. FS&G.

Holiday Cruise for Swappers. Thomas H. Hilton. 192p. (Orig.). 1973. pap. 1.95 o.p. (ISBN 0-87682-304-5, 7304). Barclay Hse.

Holiday for Hearts. Elinor Brown. LC 40-29641. 1940. Arcadia House, Inc.

Holiday for Inspector West. John Creasey. 1971. pap. 0.75 o.p. (ISBN 0-447-74720-7). Lancer.

Holiday for Love. Glenna Finley, pseud. 1976. pap. 1.95 (ISBN 0-451-09951-6, J9951, Sig). NAL.

Holiday for Murder... Agatha Miller Christie. LC 47-23571. (New Avon library, no. 124). 1947.

Holiday for Tears. Yeghishe Avedissian. LC 50-14369. 1950. Exposition Press.

Holiday Friend. Pamela Hansford Johnson. LC 72-11128. 1973. 6.95 (ISBN 0-684-13281-8). Scribner.

Holiday from God: A Novel. 1st Ed. Richard Mealand. LC 59-13982. 1959. Doubleday.

Holiday Homicide. Rufus King. LC 40-7918. 1940. Pub. for the Crime Club by Doubleday, Doran & Co., Inc.

Holiday Husband. Kathleen Shepard. LC 33-772. A. H. King, Inc.

Holiday Husband. Dolf Wyllarde. LC 19-84688. 1919. John Lane Company.

Holiday in Bed, and Other Sketches. With a Short Biographical Sketch of the Author. James Matthew Barrie. LC 70-160930. (Short story index reprint series). (Illus.). 1971. (ISBN 0-8369-3909-3). Books for Libraries Press.

Holiday Interlude. 1st Ed. Bernard F D'Aleo. LC 55-8622. 1955. Vantage Press.

Holiday Madness. Alan Williams. LC 34-12879. 1934. W. Godwin, Inc.

Holiday Nurse. Peggy Gaddis, pseud. LC 63-6671. 1963. Arcadia House.

Holiday Stories. Stephen Fiske. LC 6-41110. 1891. B. R. Tucker.

Holiday Tales: Christmas in the Adirondacks. William Henry Harrison Murray. LC 98-1606. Springfield Printing and Binding Company.

Holiday Touch, and Other Tales of Undaunted Americans. Charles Battell Loomis. LC 8-29333. 1908. H. Holt and Company.

Holiday with a Vengeance. Ritchie Perry. LC 75-6650. (Midnight novel of suspense). 1975. 6.95 (ISBN 0-395-20717-7). Houghton Mifflin.

Holidays at Roselands: A Sequel to Elsie Dinsmore. Martha Finley. Dodd, Mead & Company.

Holidays in Kyoto. Noboru Asakura. 1978. 10.00 o.p. (ISBN 0-533-03235-0). Vantage.

Holladay Case: A Tale. Burton Egbert Stevenson. LC 3-28963. 1903. H. Holt and Company.

Holland Suggestions: A Novel of Suspense. John Dunning. LC 75-8696. 1975. 7.95 (ISBN 0-672-52110-5). Bobbs-Merrill.

Holland-Tide; or, Munster Popular Tales. Gerald Griffin. (Nineteenth Century Fiction Ser.: Ireland: Vol. 26). 382p. 1979. lib. bdg. 46.00 (ISBN 0-8240-3475-9). Garland Pub.

Holland Wolves. John Breckenridge Ellis. LC 2-22857. 1902. A. C. McClurg & Company.

Hollow: A Hercule Poirot Mystery. Agatha Miller Christie. LC 46-7098. 1946. Dodd, Mead & Company.

Hollow Bracken: A Novel. Hanson Penn Diltz. 1899. G. W. Dillingham Co.

Hollow Chest: A Leonidas Witherall Mystery. Phoebe Atwood Taylor. LC 41-13507. W. W. Norton & Company Inc.

Hollow Field. Marcel Ayme. 1933. Dodd, Mead & Company.

Hollow Folk. Mandel Sherman & Thomas E. Henry. (Illus.). 215p. Repr. of 1933 ed. pap. 3.50; 7.50. Va Bk.

Hollow Hills. Mary Stewart. LC 72-102. (Illus.). 1973. 7.95 (ISBN 0-688-00179-3). Morrow.

Hollow Hills. Mary Stewart. (Fawcett crest book). 1974. (pbk.) 1.75. Fawcett.

Hollow Hills. Mary Stewart. LC 82-11929. 1982. 19.95 (ISBN 0-8161-3339-5). G.K. Hall.

Hollow Lands. Michael Moorcock. 1977. 1.50 (ISBN 0-380-01794-6). Avon Books.

Hollow Lands. Michael Moorcock. LC 74-10770. (His The dancers at the end of time, v. 2). 1974. 6.95 (ISBN 0-06-013002-4). Harper & Row.

Hollow Man. John Roeburt. LC 54-5467. (Inner sanctum mystery). 1954. Simon and Schuster.

Hollow Men. Sean Flannery, pseud. 388p. 1982. pap. 3.25 (ISBN 0-441-34231-0, Pub. by Charter Bks). Ace Bks.

Hollow Men. Bruce Hutchinson. LC 44-8825. 1944. Coward-McCann, Inc.

Hollow Mountains. Oliver B. Patton. 384p. 1981. pap. 2.75 (ISBN 0-445-08462-6). Popular Lib.

Hollow Mountains. Patton, Oliver B. 1976. (pbk.) 1.95. Popular Library.

Hollow Needle. George Harmon Coxe. LC 48-8142. 1948. A. A. Knoof.

Hollow Needle: Further Adventures of Arsene Lupin. Maurice Leblanc. Tr. by Teixeira De Mattos, Alexander Louis. LC 19-726. 1910. Doubleday, Page & Company.

Hollow Needle: Further Adventures of Arsene Lupin. Maurice Leblanc. Tr. by Teixeira De Mattos, Alexander Louis. LC 21-8691. Grosset & Dunlap.

Hollow of Her Hand. George Barr McCutcheon. LC 12-151483. 1912. Dodd, Mead and Company.

Hollow of the Wave. Edward Newhouse. LC 49-7021. 1949. W. Sloane Associates.

Hollow Queen. Frank Ely Gaebelein. LC 33-5932. The Christopher Publishing House.

Hollow Rock. Alice Moody. 252p. 1971. 7.00 o.p. (ISBN 0-682-47353-7). Exposition.

Hollow Sea. Geoffrey Jenkins. LC 79-186799. 1972. 5.95. Putnam.

Hollow Silver. Helen Topping Miller. LC 53-10209. 1953. Appleton-Century-Crofts.

Hollow Skin. Virginia Swain. LC 38-442925. Farrar & Rinehart, Incorporated.

Hollow Target. Paul Bryers. LC 77-359481. (Illus.). 1976. 3.75 (ISBN 0-233-96756-7). Deutsch.

Hollow Triumph. Murray Forbes. LC 46-4663. 1946. Ziff-Davis Publishing Company.

Hollow Vengeance. Anne Morice. LC 81-21420. 10.95 (ISBN 0-312-38834-9). St. Martin's Press.

Holly and Pizen: And Other Stories. Ruth McEnery Stuart. LC 78-98598. (Short story index reprint series). (Illus.). 1969. Books for Libraries Press.

Holly and Pizen: And Other Stories. Ruth McEnery Stuart. LC 195. 1899. The Century Co.

Holly & Pizen & Other Stories. Ruth McEnery Stuart. LC 78-98598. (Short Story Index Reprint Ser.). 1899. 15.00 (ISBN 0-8369-3173-4). Ayer Co.

Holly Andrews: Nurse in Alaska. Suzanne Roberts. (Candlelight romance). 1974. (pbk.) 0.75. Dell.

Holly Hathaway, Physical Therapist. Marilyn Austin. 1976. 4.95. Avalon Books.

Holly Hedge: And Other Christmas Stories. Temple Bailey. LC 25-19004. 1925. The Penn Publishing Company.

Holly: The Romance of a Southern Girl. Ralph Henry Barbour. LC 7-33207. 1907. J. B. Lippincott Company.

Holly-Tree. Charles Dickens. 1904. H. Altemus Company.

Holly-Tree and Other Christmas Stories. Charles Dickens. 1926. Charles Scribner's Sons.

Holly Tree Inn, and A Christmas Tree: As Writtten in the Christmas Stories by Charles Dickens. Charles Dickens. LC 7-37549. 1907. The Baker & Taylor Company.

Hollywood Agent. James Lee. LC 38-12299. The Macaulay Company.

Hollywood and LeVine. Andrew Bergman. LC 74-15472. 1975. 6.95 (ISBN 0-03-013816-7). Holt, Rinehart and Winston.

Hollywood Assassin. Stuart Jason. (Butcher series, 20) (ISBN 0-523-00893-7). Pinnacle Books.

Hollywood Detective: The Wolf. Jeff Rovin. (Hollywood Detective: No. 2). 192p. 1975. pap. 1.25 o.p. (ISBN 0-532-12337-9). Woodhill.

Hollywood Detective: The Wolf. Jeff Rovin. (Hollywood Detective: No. 2). 192p. 1975. pap. 1.25 o.p. (ISBN 0-532-12337-9). Manor Bks.

Hollywood Doctor. Seth Young. (Orig.). 1969. pap. 0.75 o.p. (64-038). Paperback Lib.

Hollywood Episode. Henry H Rabbes. LC 47-580. 1946. Dorrance & Company.

Hollywood Extra: Roman. Jules Raucourt. LC 38-18715. 1938. Hollycrofters.

Hollywood Girl. Beatrice Burton Morgan. LC 27-12296. Grosset & Dunlap.

Hollywood Gold. Phyllis Gordon Demarest. 1930. The Macaulay Company.

Hollywood Gothic. Thomas Gifford. LC 79-15618. 10.95 (ISBN 0-399-12411-X). Putnam.

Hollywood Haunted House: And Other Stories. Eave Nightingale. LC 53-7354. 1954. Wetzel Pub. Co.

Hollywood Murder Mystery. Herbert Crooker. LC 32-14534. 1930. The Macaulay Company.

Hollywood Murders. Ellery Queen, pseud. LC 57-10876. 1957. Lippincott.

Hollywood Mystery. Ben Hecht. LC 46-184832. (On cover: Bart house mystery, 25). 1946. Bartholomew House, Inc.

Hollywood Nightmare: Tales of Fantasy and Horror from the Film World. Ed. by Peter Haining. LC 76-145543. 1971. 5.95 (ISBN 0-8008-3921-8). Taplinger Pub. Co.

Hollywood Shorts: Compiled from Incidents in the Everyday Life of Men and Women Who Entertain in Pictures. Charles Ray. LC 36-5815. 1935. California Graphic Press.

Hollywood Siren. Keane McGrath. LC 32-35782. 1932. W. Godwin, Inc.

Hollywood Star Dust: A Love Story. Margaret Gibbons MacGill. LC 36-214550. Chelsea House.

Hollywood Star: Roman. Jules Raucourt. LC 35-8790. 1935. Hollycrofters.

Hollywood Starlet. Don James. 1969. pap. 0.60 o.p. (60-409). Manor Bks.

Hollywood Unreel: Fantasies About Hollywood and the Movies. Martin Harry Greenberg & Charles Waugh. LC 81-16742. 1982. 12.95 (ISBN 0-8008-3197-7). Taplinger Pub. Co.

Hollywood Zoo. Jackie Collins. 1975. (pbk.) 1.75 (ISBN 0-523-00579-2). Pinnacle Books.

Hollywood's Bad Boy. John Gorman. Eugene V. Brewster Co.

Hollywood's Irish Rose. Nora Bernard. LC 78-67801. 1979. 1.95 (ISBN 0-380-41061-3). Avon Books.

Holm Oaks: 1st Amer. Ed. Philip Maitland Hubbard. LC 66-113971. 1966. bds., 3.95. Atheneum.

Holmby House: a Tale of Old Northamptonshire. author's ed. George John Whyte-Melville. LC 7-19686. (On cover: Library of standard fiction, no. 2). 1859. Ticknor and Fields.

Holmby House: a Tale of Old Northamptonshire. new ed. George John Whyte-Melville. LC 41-42360. 1890. Longmans, Green, and Co.

Holmby House, a Tale of Old Northamptonshire. George John Whyte-Melville. 1899. Longmans, Green & Co.

Holocaust. Gerald Green. LC 78-17502. 9.95 (ISBN 0-87272-041-1). Duron Books.

Holocaust. Henry Kane. LC 67-23589. 1967. Trident Press.

Holocaust. Charles Reznikoff. 112p. (Orig.). 1977. 10.00 (ISBN 0-87685-232-0); pap. 4.00 (ISBN 0-87685-231-2). Black Sparrow.

Holocaust: A Novel of Survival & Triumph. Gerald Green. 1978. pap. 2.50 (ISBN 0-553-13564-3). Bantam.

Holocaust Auction. Paul Edwards. (John Eagle Expeditor Ser.: No. 10). (Orig.). 1975. pap. 1.25 o.p. (ISBN 0-515-03705-2, V3705). BJ Pub Group.

Holocaust for Hire. Joseph Silva. (Marvel Novel Series; #4). 1979. 1.95 (ISBN 0-671-82086-9). Pocket Books.

Holroyd Papers. Chandler W. Sterling. LC 72-96136. 1969. 5.95. Bartholomew House; Distributed by Delacorte Press.

Holsters and Heroes: Stories from the Western Writers of America. With a Pref. by Noel M. Loomis. Western Writers of America. LC 54-13316. 1954. Macmillan.

Holton of the Navy: A Story of the Freeing of Cuba. Lawrence Perry. LC 13-7082. 1913. 1.35. A. C. McClurg & Co.

Holy Blood, Holy Grail. Michael Baigent et al. 1983. pap. 3.95 (ISBN 0-440-13648-2). Dell.

Holy City. Paris Matthew. LC 79-828. 1979. pap. 5.95x (ISBN 0-914140-05-1). Carpenter Pr.

Holy City: A Novel. Matthew Paris. LC 79-828. 5.00 (ISBN 0-914140-08-6). Carpenter Press.

Holy City: Jerusalem II, from the Swedish of Selma Lagerlof. Selma Ottiliana Lovisa Lagerlof. Tr. by Howard, Velma (Swanston) LC 18-7989. 1918. Doubleday, Page & Company.

Holy Cross: And Other Tales. Eugene Field. LC 72-94718. (Short story index reprint series). (Illus.). 1969. Books for Libraries Press.

Holy Cross: And Other Tales. Eugene Field. LC 6-41192. 1893. Stone & Kimball.

Holy Cross & Other Tales. Eugene Field. LC 72-94718. (Short Story Index Reprint Ser.). 1893. 16.00 (ISBN 0-8369-3097-5). Ayer Co.

Holy Days & Holidays: Prayer Celebrations with Children. Gaynell B. Cronin. 1979. pap. 6.95 (ISBN 0-03-042761-4). Winston Pr.

Holy Deadlock... Alan Patrick Herbert. LC 34-27217. 1934. Doubleday, Doran & Company, Inc.

Holy Disorders. Edmund Crispin, pseud. 240p. 1980. pap. 2.25 (ISBN 0-380-51508-3, 51508). Avon.

Holy Disorders. Edmund Crispin, pseud. (General Ser.). 1980. lib. bdg. 13.95 (ISBN 0-8161-3111-2, Large Print Bks). G K Hall.

Holy Disorders. Edmund Crispin, pseud. LC 79-64814. (Walker Mystery Ser.). (O.s.i.). 254p. 1979. 9.95 o.s.i. (ISBN 0-8027-5411-2). Walker & Co.

Holy Disorders. Robert Bruce Montgomery. LC 46-188374. 1946. J. B. Lippincott Company.

Holy Disorders. Robert Bruce Montgomery. LC 79-64814. 1979. 9.95 (ISBN 0-8027-5411-2). Walker.

Holy Experiment: A Novel About the Harmonist Society. Lois T Henderson. LC 74-195112. 1974. 7.50 (ISBN 0-682-48115-7). Exposition Press.

Holy Fire, and Other Stories. Ida Alexa Ross Wylie. LC 71-144175. (Short story index reprint series). 1971. (ISBN 0-8369-3790-2). Books for Libraries Press.

Holy Fire: And Other Stories. Ida Alexa Ross Wylie. LC 20-8791. 1920. John Lane Company.

Holy Fool. Harold L. Fickett. 360p. 1983. pap. 7.95 (ISBN 0-89107-227-6, Crossway Bks). Good News.

Holy Fools in Moscow. IUrii Kuper. LC 73-93829. 1974. 7.95 (ISBN 0-8129-0450-8). Quadrangle.

Holy Foot. 1st American Ed. Robert Romanis. LC 54-5059. 1954. Dutton.

Holy Ireland. Norah Hoult. LC 36-5251. Reynal & Hitchcock.

Holy Land. Par Lagerkvist. LC 81-16147. (Illus.). 1982. 2.95 (ISBN 0-394-70819-9). Vintage Books.

Holy Land. Tr. from Swedish by Naomi Walford. Illus. by Emil. Antonucci. 1st Amer. Ed. Par Fabian Lagerkvist. LC 66-12001. 3.95. Random.

Holy Lover. Marie Conway Oemler. LC 27-10735. 1927. Boni & Liveright.

Holy Masquerade. Olov Hartman. Tr. by Karl A. Olsson. 1964. pap. 1.95 o.p. (ISBN 0-8028-6006-0). Eerdmans.

Holy Masquerade. Olov Hartman. 1964. pap. 1.95 o.p. (ISBN 0-8028-6006-0). Eerdmans.

Holy Masquerade. Translated by Karl A. Olsson. Olov Hartman. LC 63-22532. 1963. Eerdmans.

Holy Nativity. Harvey B. Hatcher. LC 57-10298. (Orig.). 1957. pap. 1.25 (ISBN 0-8054-9702-1). Broadman.

Holy of Holies. Alan Williams. LC 80-51255. 12.95 (ISBN 0-89256-147-5). Rawson, Wade Publishers.

Holy Orders: The Tragedy of a Quiet Life. Marie Corelli. LC 8-23928. 1908. Frederick A. Stokes Company.

Holy Place. Carlos Fuentes. Tr. by Suzanne J. Levine. 1978. pap. 3.95 o.p. (ISBN 0-525-47528-1). Dutton.

Holy Rose. Walter Besant. (On cover: Seaside library.Pocket ed., on 904). 1886. G. Munro.

Holy Rose. Walter Besant. (On cover: Lovell's library, no 847). 1887. J. W. Lovell Company.

Holy Secrets. Richard Rhodes. LC 76-56329. 1978. 8.95 (ISBN 0-385-02565-3). Doubleday.

Holy Sinner. Thomas Mann. LC 51-11092. 1951. Knopf.

Holy Smoke. Fanny Howe. LC 78-68130. (Illus.). 8.95 (ISBN 0-914590-54-5). Fiction Collective.

Holy Suburb. Elizabeth Atkins. LC 41-1123. 1941. E. P. Dutton & Co., Inc.

Holy Terror. Leslie Charteris. LC 72-106261. (Short story index reprint series). 1970. Books for Libraries Press.

Holy Terror. Richard Sapir & Warren Murphy. (Destroyer#19). 1975. (pbk.) 1.25 (ISBN 0-523-00640-3). Pinnacle Books.

Holy Terror. Herbert George Wells. LC 39-11398. 1939. Simon and Schuster.

Holy Terrors. Illus. by the Author. Tr. from French by Rosamond Lehmann. New Directions. Jean Cocteau. LC 56-13357. 1966. pap., 1.95. Lippincott.

Holy Terrors: With Illus. by the Author. Translated by Rosamond Lehmann. Jean Cocteau. LC 56-13357. 1957. New Directions.

Holy the Firm. Annie Dillard. LC 77-6883. 1977. 7.95i (ISBN 0-06-011061-9, HarpT). Har-Row.

Holy Tree. Gerald O'Doncvan. LC 23-498214. Boni and Liveright.

Holy War. John Bunyan. (Wycliffe Classic Ser.). 1978. pap. 8.95 (ISBN 0-8024-3567-X). Moody.

Holy War. John Bunyan. Ed. by Roger Sharrock & James F. Forrest. (Oxford English Texts Ser.). 1980. 72.00x (ISBN 0-19-811887-2). Oxford U Pr.

Holy War. 1979. pap. text ed. write for info. (ISBN 0-88074-013-2). Metagam.

Holy War in Modern English. John Bunyan. pap. 1.95 o.p. (ISBN 0-8254-2251-5, RBDH). Kregel.

Holy War of Jacob Lavin. Michael Kaufman. LC 75-33137. Saturday Review Press.

Holy Wars. James Brady. 1983. 14.95 (ISBN 0-671-42589-7). S&S.

Holy Wednesday. Manuel Galvez & Wells, Warre Bradley, 1892- Tr. LC 34-19487. 1934. D. Appleton-Century Company, Incorporated.

Holy Week: A Novel. Translated by Haakon Chevalier. Louis Aragon. LC 61-5679. 1961. Putnam.

Holy Well: By Valentin Katayev. Tr. from Russian by Max Hayward, Harold Shukman. Valentin Petrovich Kataev. LC 67-132263. 1967. 4.95. Walker.

Holyland: Exclusive Authorized Translation of "Hilligenlei", by Gustav Frenssen... Gustav Frenssen. Tr. by Hamilton, Mary Agnes (Adamson) LC 6-32857. 1906. D. Estes & Company; Etc., Etc.

Homage to Blenholt. Daniel Fuchs. LC 36-5256. The Vanguard Press.

Homage to Sherwood Anderson. Ed. by Paul P. Appel. LC 77-105304. 1970. lib. bdg. 12.00x (ISBN 0-911858-02-4). Appel.

Hombomuk, a Tale of Early Times. Lydia Maria Francis Child. 1977. Repr. 21.00 o.p. (ISBN 0-403-07452-5). Scholarly.

Hombre. Elmore Leonard. 1974. pap. 1.75 (ISBN 0-345-28850-5). Ballantine.

Hombre from Sonora. Will Charles, pseud. Ed. by Alice Sachs. 1971. 3.95 o.p. Lenox Hill.

Hombre Que No Sudaba. Jaime Carrero. LC 81-68070. 200p. (Span.). 1981. pap. 7.50 (ISBN 0-934770-14-X). Arte Publico.

Hombre Tigre De Terrahpur. new ed. Errol Lecale, pseud. Tr. by John A. Reed from Eng. (Artifice Ser: No. 2). Orig. Title: Tigerman of Terrahpur. 160p. (Span.). 1974. pap. 0.85 (ISBN 0-88473-622-9). Fiesta Pub.

Homburg Story. Charles Walston. LC 13-17736. (Half-title: The ethics of the surface series, no. II). 1897. M. Manges.

Home. Anna Leland. LC 7-13152. J.C. Derby.

Home. Penelope Mortimer. 1973. pap. 0.95 o.p. (09248). Curtis.

Home: A Novel. George Agnew Chamberlain. LC 14-2135. 1914. 1.30. The Century Co.

Home Again. George Macdonald. LC 41-42389. 1888. D. Appleton and Company.

Home Again. George Macdonald. (On cover: Seaside library. Pocket ed., no. 1041). 1888. G. Munro.

Home Again. George Macdonald. LC 12-182792. 1911. G. Routledge and Sons, Limited.

Home Again. Margaret Mary Olsen Scott. LC 44-3270. The Westminster Press.

Home Again, Home Again. Elaine Markson. LC 78-7008. 1978. 8.95 (ISBN 0-688-03360-1). Morrow.

Home Again, Home Again. Anthony Robinson. LC 69-11291. 1969. 5.95. Morrow.

Home Again. 1st Ed. James Edmiston. LC 55-526566. 1955. Doubleday.

Home and Freedom. Paul Bruno Steinke. LC 42-40212. Union-Star Press.

Home and Murder. Aaron Marc Stein. LC 62-11447. 1962. Published for the Crime Club by Doubleday.

Home and Other Moments. Elroy Bode. LC 75-2744. (Illus.). 8.00 (ISBN 0-87404-052-3). Texas Western Press.

Home and the World. 1857. D. Appleton and Company.

Home As Found. James Fenimore Cooper. 1838. Lea & Blanchard, Successors to Carey & Co.

Home As Found. Sequel to "Homeward Bound". new ed. James Fenimore Cooper. LC 6-29892. 1852. Stringer and Townsend.

Home As Found. Sequel to "Homeward Bound.". James Fenimore Cooper. LC 26-246939. (Half-title: The choice works of Cooper. Revised and corrected series. v. 15). 1856. Stringer & Townsend.

Home As Found: Sequel to Homeward Bound. James Fenimore Cooper. (On cover: Lovell's library. no. 441). 1884. J. W. Lovell Company.

Home As Found. Sequel to "Homeward Bound". James Fenimore Cooper. (On cover: Seaside library. Pocket ed. no. 379). 1885. G. Munro.

Home at Last. Ernst Ludwig Harthern Jackson. Tr. by Kaufman, Kenneth Carlyle. LC 39-8611. The Bobbs-Merrill Company.

Home at Sundown. Lucy Walker, pseud. 1971. pap. 0.75 o.p. (94039-075). Beagle Bks.

Home Before Dark. Eileen Bassing. LC 56-8796. 1957. Random House.

Home Before Dark. Sue Ellen Bridgers. (gr. 8-12). 1977. pap. 1.75 (ISBN 0-553-13691-7, X13691-7). Bantam.

Home by the Lake. Peggy O'More, pseud. LC 51-14980. 1951. Arcadia House.

Home by the River. Archibald Rutledge. (Illus.). 1970. Repr. of 1941 ed. 10.00 o.p. (ISBN 0-87844-003-8). Sandlapper Pr.

Home-Comers. Winifred Margaretta Kirkland. LC 10-22060. 1910. 1.20. Houghton Mifflin Company.

Home Coming... Constance Holme. LC 16-10725. 1916. R. M. McBride & Company.

Home-Coming in the Ozarks. Laura Johnson. LC 23-48973. Glad Tidings Publishing Company.

Home-Coming of Jessica... by Mary E. Wilkins An Idyl of a Soul... by Roberts Grant. Mary Eleanor Wilkins Freeman & Matthews, Brander. LC 2-1094. 1901. The Crowell & Kirkpatrick Co.

Home Fires. David Long. LC 82-4927. (Illinois Short Fiction Ser.). 136p. 1982. 11.95 (ISBN 0-252-00991-6); pap. 4.95 (ISBN 0-252-00992-4). U of Ill Pr.

Home Fires Burning. Dale Harris. LC 68-19023. 1968. Macmillan.

Home Fires Burning. Robert David Quixano Henriques. LC 45-7502. 1945. The Viking Press.

Home Fires in France. Dorothea Frances Canfield Fisher. LC 18-26756. 1918. H. Holt and Company.

Home for Christmas. Lloyd Cassel Douglas. LC 37-38603. 1937. Houghton Mifflin Company.

Home for Him. Peggy O'More, pseud. LC 44-5935. 1944. Grammercy Publishing Company.

Home for Mary. William Arthur Neubauer. LC 52-7406. 1952. Arcadia House.

Home for the Heart. Hope Goodwin. (Orig.). 1980. pap. 1.95 (ISBN 0-532-23135-X). Woodhill.

Home for the Wedding. Elizabeth Cadell. LC 73-14868. 1973. 9.95 (ISBN 0-8161-6159-3). G. K. Hall.

Home for the Wedding. Elizabeth Cadell. LC 73-165134. 1972. 5.95. Morrow.

Home Free. Dan Wakefield. LC 76-30636. (ISBN 0-440-03748-4). Delacorte Press.

Home from Sea. Joy Petersen Packer. (Illus.). 1964. 4.95 o.p. (ISBN 0-525-12617-1). Dutton.

Home from Sea. George Savary Wasson. LC 70-142281. (Short story index reprint series). (Illus.). 1970. Books for Libraries Press.

Home from Sea. George Savary Wasson. 1908. Houghton, Mifflin and Company.

Home from the Hill. William Humphrey. pap. 1.95 o.p. (ISBN 0-394-70305-7, V305, Vin). Random.

Home from the Hill. 1st Ed. William Humphrey. LC 57-12069. 1958. Knopf.

Home from the Shore. Gordon R. Dickson. 1979. pap. 2.25 (ISBN 0-441-34256-6). Ace Bks.

Home Front. Margaret Craven. 1982. pap. 3.95 (ISBN 0-440-13517-6). Dell.

Home Front. Margaret Craven. 252p. 1981. 11.95 (ISBN 0-399-12568-X). Putnam Pub Group.

Home Front: Collected Stories. Margaret Craven. LC 81-6282. 1981. 17.95 (ISBN 0-8161-3267-4). G.K. Hall.

Home Front: Collected Stories by Margaret Craven. Margaret Craven. LC 80-25717. 11.95 (ISBN 0-399-12568-X). Putnam.

Home Front Nurse. Adelaide Humphries. LC 52-6992. 1952. Bouregy & Curl.

Home Girl. James Noble Gifford. LC 48-189445. 1948. Gramercy Pub. Co.

Home Girls. Olga Masters. (Paperback prose). 14.50 (ISBN 0-7022-1811-1) (ISBN 0-7022-1821-9). University of Queensland Press.

Home Ground. Albert Haley. LC 78-25834. 9.95 (ISBN 0-525-12625-2). Dutton.

Home Ground. Cecelia Holland. LC 80-2710. 1981. 12.95 (ISBN 0-394-50405-4). Knopf.

Home-Heroes, Saints, and Martyrs. Timothy Shay Arthur. LC 6-3401. 1865. J. B. Lippincott & Co.

Home in the Dark. Will Perry. (Orig.). 1976. pap. 1.50 o.p. (ISBN 0-515-03686-2). BJ Pub Group.

Home in the Hills. Loren Scott Noblitt. LC 68-554. 1967. Mitchell-Fleming Print. Co.

Home Influencd. A Tale for Mothers and Daughters. Grace Aguilar. LC 3-4646. (Harper's Franklin square library. no. 479). 1885. Harper & Brothers.

Home Influence: A Tale for Mothers and Daughters. new ed. Grace Aguilar. LC 3-4647. 1857. Hickling, Swan, & Brewer.

Home Influence: A Tale for Mothers and Daughters. new ed. Grace Aguilar. LC 26-23550. 1870. D. Appleton & Co.

Home Influence: A Tale for Mothers and Daughters. new ed. Grace Aguilar. 1904. D. Appleton and Company.

Home Is a One-Way Street. William Heyliger. LC 45-919419. 1945. The Westminster Press.

Home Is an Island. Alfred Lewis. LC 51-9287. 1951. Random House.

Home Is If You Find It. Harry Nye. LC 47-3819. 1947. Doubleday & Company, Inc.

Home Is Not a Home. G. Janet Tulloch. LC 75-28220. (Continuum book). 6.95 (ISBN 0-8164-9269-7). Seabury Press.

Home Is on Top of a Dog House. Charles M Schulz. LC 77-8413. (Illus.). Determined Productions.

Home Is the Heart. Lucy Beatrice Malleson. LC 42-360979. 1942. Howell, Soskin.

Home Is the Heart. William Arthur Neubauer. LC 46-1782. 1946. Grammercy Publishing Co.

Home Is the Hotel. Jean Nicol. LC 76-380326. 1976. 3.50 (ISBN 0-7181-1492-2). Joseph.

Home Is the Hunted, a Novel. Abraham Bernstein. LC 47-31402. 1947. Dial Press.

Home Is the Hunter. Gontran De Montaigne Poncins & Chevalier, Haakon Maurice, 1902- Tr. LC 43-18431. 1943. Reynal & Hitchcock.

Home Is the Hunter & the Big Kayo. John William Wainwright. 1982. 15.00x (ISBN 0-333-26294-8, Pub. by Macmillan England). State Mutual Bk.

Home Is the Place. 1st Ed. Stefanie Lauer. LC 57-8912. 1957. Knopf.

Home Is the Prisoner. Jean Potts. LC 60-12596. 1960. Scribner.

Home Is the Sailor. Jorge Amado. (Bard Book). 1979. 2.75 (ISBN 0-380-45187-5). Avon Books.

Home Is the Sailor. Ruth Blodgett. LC 32-19190. Harcourt, Brace and Company.

Home Is the Sailor. Day Keene. pap. 0.60 o.p. (60-336). Manor Bks.

Home Is the Sailor: The Whole Truth Concerning the Redoubtful Adventures of Captain Vasco Moscoso De Aragao, Master Mariner. Jorge Amado. LC 64-12295. 1964. Knopf.

Home Is Upriver. Brian Harwin. LC 52-12875. 1952. Macmillan.

Home Is Where the Heart Is. Rosemary Frances Rees. LC 35-22387. Arcadia House.

Home Is Where You Hang Your Childhood: And Other Stories. Leane Zugsmith. LC 37-14925. Random House.

Home Is Where You Start from! Eugene Horowitz. (752140). 1967. Pocket Bks.

Home Is Where You Start from! A Novel. Eugene Horowitz. LC 65-24923. bds., 4.50. Norton.

Home, James. Ethel May Kelley. LC 27-104633. 1927. A. A. Knopf.

Home Late. Joseph Arleo. 1974. (pbk.) 1.25. Warner Paperback Library.

Home Lights and Shadows. Timothy Shay Arthur. LC 6-3403. 1853. C. Scribner.

Home-Made Dragon & Other Incredible Stories. Norman Hunter. 1974. pap. 0.95 o.p. (ISBN 0-14-030679-X, Puffin). Penguin.

Home-Made Dragon and Other Incredible Stories. Norman Hunter. (Puffin book). (Illus.). 1974. (pbk.) 0.95 (ISBN 0-14-030679-X). Penguin.

Home Made Happy: Or, Pictures of Every Day Life for the Family Circle... LC 7-12827. 1858. H. C. Peck & T. Bliss.

Home-Made Heaven. Peggy Gaddis, pseud. LC 43-7866. 1943. Arcadia House, Inc.

Home-Makers. Dorothea Frances Canfield Fisher. LC 24-263829. Harcourt, Brace and Company.

Home Makers: A Novel. Ivy Strick. LC 78-20706. 1979. 8.95 (ISBN 0-8008-3923-4). Taplinger Pub. Co.

Home Memories. Eli Barber. 1908. R.G. Badger.

Home Movies. Don Meredith. 176p. 1982. pap. 2.25 (ISBN 0-380-79855-7, 79855). Avon.

Home Nook: Or, The Crown of Duty. Amanda Minnie Douglas. LC 6-33482. 1874. Lee and Shepard.

Home Nook: Or, The Crown of Duty. Amanda Minnie Douglas. LC 2-11142. 1901. Lee and Shepard.

Home of the Brave. Joel Gross. LC 81-84529. 448p. 1982. 14.95 (ISBN 0-87223-771-0, Seaview Bks). Putnam Pub Group.

Home of the Gentry. Ivan Sergeevich Turgenev. LC 73-14852. (Penguin classics). 1970. 1.65. Penguin Books.

Home of the Inquisitor. Maxine Reynolds. (Orig.). 1972. pap. 0.75 o.p. (94312). Beagle Bks.

Home of the Seven Devils. Horace W. C Newte. LC 13-23732. 1913. John Lane Company.

Home of Their Own. Besse Sprague. LC 40-654476. Gramercy Publishing Co.

Home on the Moon. Peggy O'More, pseud. LC 48-151434. 1948. Gramercy Pub. Co.

Home on the Mountain. Mattie Doherty Feldsmith. LC 6-38973. 1897. Press of the Evening Wisconsin Co.

Home: Or, Family Cares and Family Joys. Fredrika Bremer. LC 76-28470. 1976. 22.50. H. Fertig.

Home: Or, Family Cares and Family Joys. tr. from the swedish, by mary howitt. ed. Fredrika Bremer. Tr. by Mary Botham Howitt. LC 6-17399. 1843. Harper & Brothers.

Home: Or, Life in Sweden. And Strife and Peace. Fredrika Bremer. Tr. by Mary Botham Howitt. LC 13-2065. (On cover; Bohn's libraries). 1892. G. Bell & Sons.

Home, Peace & Plenty. Leon Burns. 3.95 o.p. Vantage.

Home Pictures. Mary Andrews Denison. LC 6-33991. 1853. Harper & Brothers.

Home Place. Wright Morris. LC 48-7192. 1948. C. Scribner's Sons.

Home Place. Wright Morris & Wright Morris. (Bison bk., BB386). 1968. pap., 1.95. Univ. of Neb. Pr.

Home Place. Dorothy Thomas. LC 36-169259. 1936. A. A. Knopf.

Home Place: A Story of the People. George Washington Ogden. LC 12-237085. 1912. Harper & Brothers.

Home Place. Illus. by Ruth Gannett. Dorothy Thomas & Ruth Chrisman Illus Gannett. (Bisoa bk. BB 346). 1966. pap., 1.70. Univ. of Neb Pr.

Home Place. 1st Ed. Frederick Benjamin Gipson. LC 50-9635. 1950. Harper.

Home Port. Olive Higgins Prouty. LC 47-3618. 1947. Houghton Mifflin Company.

Home Ranch. Will James. LC 35-27364. 1935. C. Scribner's Sons.

Home Ranch. Ralph Moody. 1962. 7.95 o.p. (ISBN 0-393-08509-0). Norton.

Home Range. Archie Joscelyn. LC 48-11362. 1948. Phoenix Press.

Home Rule of Eliza. Frederick W Becker. LC 13-9145. The Platt & Peck Co.

Home Scenes and Heart Studies. Grace Aguilar. LC 5-42962. 1873. D. Appleton and Company.

Home Scenes and Heart Studies. By Grace Aguilar. Grace Aguilar. LC 41-312952. 1878. D. Appleton and Co.

Home Scenes: And Home Influence. Timothy Shay Arthur. LC 6-3400. (On cover: Lovell's library, v. 10, no. 545). J. W. Lovell Company.

Home Scenes and Home Sounds: Or, The World from My Window. Short Stories and Poems. Harriet Marion Ward Stephens. LC 8-12403. 1854. Fetridge and Company.

Home Scenes During the Rebellion. Maggie Roberts. LC 7-41037. 1875. J. F. Trow & Son, Printers.

Home Sounds. A Novel. Elisabeth Burstenbinder. Tr. by Conduit, E. W. (On cover: Seaside library. Pocket ed., no. 1089). 1888. G. Munro.

Home Spread. Galen C Colin. LC 51-1597. 1951. Phoenix Press.

Home Stories. By Mrs. Alice B. Haven ("Cousin Alice". Alice Bradley Haven. LC 7-26069. 1869. D. Appleton and Company.

Home, Sweet Home. Barrie Stavis. LC 49-7969. 1949. Sheridan House.

Home Sweet Home Has Wheels; or Please Don't Tailgate the Real Estate. William C. Anderson. 1979. 9.95 o.p. (ISBN 0-517-53830-X). Crown.

Home Sweet Homicide. Craig Rice. LC 44-134157. 1944. Simon and Schuster.

Home Talent. Louise Hale. LC 26-5892. H. Holt and Company.

Home Through the Dark. Anthea Fraser. LC 76-55795. 1977. 9.95 (ISBN 0-8161-6442-8). G. K. Hall.

Home Through the Dark: A Novel of Suspense. Anthea Fraser. LC 76-6873. 1976. (ISBN 0-396-07286-0). Dodd, Mead.

Home-to-Avalon. Arthur H. Landis. 1982. pap. 2.50 (ISBN 0-87997-778-7, UE1778). Daw Bks.
Home to Cypresswood. Lucile V. Stevens. pap. 0.75 o.s.i. (01-346). Lancer.
Home to Harlem. Claude McKay. LC 28-6523. 1928. Harper & Brothers.
Home to Kentucky: A Novel of Henry Clay. 1st Ed. Alfred Leland Crabb. 1953. Bobbs-Merrill Co.
Home to Morning Star. Margaret Way. (Harlequin Romance Ser.). 192p. 1982. pap. 1.50 (ISBN 0-373-02490-8). Harlequin Bks.
Home to My Love. Mair Unsworth. 224p. 1981. pap. 1.95 (ISBN 0-441-34261-2). Ace Bks.
Home to Roost. Andrew Garve. (Crime Ser). 1978. pap. 2.95 (ISBN 0-14-004741-7). Penguin.
Home to Roost. Andrew Garve. LC 76-3521. 172p. 1976. 6.95 o.p. (ISBN 0-690-01141-5). T Y Crowell.
Home to Roost. Paul Winterton. LC 76-3521. 7.95 (ISBN 0-690-01141-5). Crowell.
Home to Roost. Paul Winterton. LC 77-23756. 1978. 1.95 (ISBN 0-14-004741-7). Penguin Books.
Home to Tennessee: A Tale of Soldiers Returning. Alfred Leland Crabb. LC 52-6804. 1952. Bobbs-Merrill.
Home to Texas. Willis Todhunter Ballard. LC 74-2502. (Double D western). 1974. 4.95 (ISBN 0-385-09595-3). Doubleday.
Home to Texas. Frank Roderus. 1.75 (ISBN 0-441-34265-5). Ace Books.
Home to Texas: Double D Western. Willis Todhunter Ballard. LC 74-2502. 168p. 1974. 4.95 o.p. Doubleday.
Home to the Hermitage: A Novel of Andrew and Rachel Jackson. Alfred Leland Crabb. LC 48-1555. 1948. Bobbs-Merrill Co.
Home to the Hills. Watkins Eppes Wright. LC 44-7573. 1944. Arcadia House, Inc.
Home to the Mountain. Brenda Brown Canary. LC 74-82167. 1975. 7.95 (ISBN 0-8027-0474-3). Walker.
Home to the Mountains. Brenda Canary. LC 74-82167. 192p. 1975. 11.95 o.p. (ISBN 0-8027-0578-2); pap. 7.95 (ISBN 0-8027-0474-3). Walker & Co.
Home to the Night. Julia Thatcher, pseud. LC 76-17862. (Zodiac gothic: Capricorn). 1976. 8.95 (ISBN 0-89340-006-8). J. Curley & Associates.
Home to the Night: An Astrological Gothic Novel, Capricorn. Julia Thatcher. LC 75-30976. 1.25 (ISBN 0-345-24770-1). Ballantine Books.
Home to the Valley. Arlene Hale. LC 74-5057. 1974. 6.95 (ISBN 0-316-33872-9). Little, Brown.
Home to the Valley. Arlene Hale. LC 74-18276. 1974. 10.95 (ISBN 0-8161-6242-5). G. K. Hall.
Home-Town Doctor. Elizabeth Seifert. LC 59-6198. 1959. Dodd, Mead.
Home-Town Doctor. Elizabeth Seifert. LC 73-791763. 1974. 5.95. Aeonian Press.
Home with a View. Peggy O'More, pseud. LC 47-4815. 1947. Grammercy Pub. Co.
Home with Hazel, and Other Stories. Mark Van Doren. LC 57-5301. 1957. Harcourt, Brace.
Homebase. Shawn Wong. LC 79-63331. (Orig.). 1979. 10.00 (ISBN 0-918408-15-6); pap. 5.95 (ISBN 0-918408-14-8). Reed & Cannon.
Homebase: A Novel. Shawn Wong. LC 79-63331. 10.00 (ISBN 0-918408-14-8). I. Reed Books.
Homebuilders. Karl Edwin Harriman. LC 70-81267. (Short story index reprint series). 1969. Books for Libraries Press.
Homebuilders. Karl Edwin Harriman. LC 3-31025. 1903. G. W. Jacobs and Company.
Homeburg Memories. with illustrations by irma deremeaux. ed. George Helgeson Fitch. LC 15-3970. 1915. Little, Brown, and Company.
Homecoming. Nicholas Brady, pseud. (Belmont Tower Book). 1.50 (ISBN 0-505-51216-5). Tower Pubns.
Homecoming. Alice Mary Ross Colver. LC 45-656442. 1945. Macrae-Smith-Company.
Homecoming. Paul Eldridge. 1966. 4.50 o.p. (ISBN 0-498-06171-X). A S Barnes.
Homecoming. Earl Hamner, Jr. 1970. 5.95 (ISBN 0-394-41929-4). Random.
Homecoming. Norah Robinson Lofts. LC 75-14829. 1976. 7.95 (ISBN 0-385-00957-7)., C.
Homecoming. Adeline McElfresh. LC 53-8568. 1953. Arcadia House.
Homecoming. Russell O'Neil. (Orig.). 1980. pap. 2.25 (ISBN 0-440-13389-0). Dell.
Homecoming. Jiro Osaragi, pseud. LC 76-54833. 1977. 18.00 (ISBN 0-8371-9369-9). Greenwood Press.
Homecoming. Seifert, Elizabeth. LC 50-6185. 1950. Dodd, Mead.
Homecoming. Elizabeth Seifert. LC 73-79155. 1973. 6.95. Aeonian Press.
Homecoming. Charles Percy Snow. (His Strangers and brothers 7). 1965. pap., 1.65. Scribners.
Homecoming. Charles Percy Snow. LC 56-10199. (His Strangers and brothers 7). 1956. Scribner.
Homecoming. Cynthia Voigt. 320p. 1982. pap. 2.25 (ISBN 0-449-70024-0, Juniper). Fawcett.
Homecoming: A Chronicle of a Refugee Family. Paul Eldridge. LC 64-17411. 4.50. A. S. Barnes.
Homecoming: A Novel. Lofts, Norah Robinson. (Fawcett Crest Book). 1977. 1.95 (ISBN 0-449-23166-6). Fawcett Pubns.
Homecoming: A Novel About Spencer's Mountain. Earl Hamner. LC 78-19844. 1970. 4.95. Random House.
Homecoming Game: A Novel. Howard Nemerov. LC 57-5679. 1957. Simon and Schuster.
Homecoming. Illus. by Rita Parsons. 1st Amer. Ed. Marlena Frick. LC 65-18710. 1965. 3.75. McKay.
Homecoming Nurse. Rose Dana, pseud. 1970. pap. 0.60 o.p. (ISBN 0-447-73875-5). Lancer.
Homecoming. Translated from the Japanese by Brewster Horwitz, with an Introd. by Strauss. 1st Ed. Jiro Osaragi, pseud. LC 54-12040. 1955. Knopf.
Homecoming. 1st Ed. Borghild Margarethe Dahl. LC 53-103397. 1953. Dutton.
Homecooming, by Jiro Osaragi Pseud. Translated from the Japanese by Brewster Horwitz, with an Introd. by Harold Strauss. 1st Ed. Kiyohiko Nojiri. LC 54-12040. 1955. Knopf.
Homefront: A Novel. Winston M. Estes. LC 76-17579. 8.95 (ISBN 0-397-01147-4). Lippincott.
Homefront: A Novel. Winston M. Estes. 1977. 1.95 (ISBN 0-380-01768-7). Avon.
Homegrown. George R. Nevin, Jr. (Orig.). 1980. pap. 2.50 (ISBN 0-532-23140-6). Woodhill.
Homeland. Georges Surdez. LC 46-4609. 1946. Doubleday & Company, Inc.
Homeland: A Present-Day Love Story. Margaret Hill McCarter. LC 22-9665. Harper & Brothers.
Homely Lilla. Robert Herrick. LC 72-84664. 1974. (lib. ed.) 11.50 (ISBN 0-403-03050-1). Scholarly Press.
Homely Lilla. Robert Herrick. LC 23-3437. Harcourt, Brace and Company.
Homely Lilla see Collected Works.
Homenaje a Fernando Alegria: Variaciones Interpretativas En Torno a Su Obra. Helmy Fuad Giacoman. (Coleccion homenajes). 1972. 8.50. Las Americas.
Homeplace. Maristan Chapman. LC 29-168272. 1929. The Viking Press.
Homer: An Introduction to the Hiad and the Odyssey. new ed. Richard Claverhouse Jebb. LC 32-16287. 1889. Ginn and Company.
Homer in the Sagebrush. James Stevens. LC 28-202210. 1928. A. A. Knopf.
Homer Wasn't Blind. Andrew K Dutch. LC 51-16243. W. C. Hunt.
Homer's Daughter. Robert Graves. LC 55-5256. (Illus.). 1955. Doubleday.
Homer's Daughter. Robert Graves. LC 82-16383. 1982. 14.95 (ISBN 0-89733-058-7) (ISBN 0-89733-059-5). Academy Chicago.
Homer's Hill. Marjorie Hayes. LC 44-960. 1944. J. B. Lippincott Company.
Homes Abroad. Harriet Martineau. (On cover: Lovell's library, v. 7, no. 356). 1884. J. W. Lovell Company.
Homes in Schafhausen: Stories from the Seven Petitions of the Lord's Prayer. tr. from the 10th ed of the german of pastor fries, by mary e. ireland. ed. Nikolaus Fries. Tr. by Ireland, Mary Eliza (Haines) LC 13-21127. 1913. The German Literary Board.
Homesick Heart. Peggy Gaddis, pseud. (O.s.i.). 1976. pap. 1.25 o.s.i. (AQ1650, Award). Univ Pub & Dist.
Homesickness for Big Men. Gena Ford. 1972. 16.00 o.p. (Pub. by Elizabeth Pr); pap. 8.00 o.p. SBD.
Homespun. Rosaline Lena Herman Guingrich. LC 71-162023. 1971. 3.95 (ISBN 0-8059-1581-8). Dorrance.
Homespun. Emmet Russell. LC 54-33273. 1954. Zondervan Pub. House.
Homespun: A Story of Some New England Folk. Lottie Blair Parker. LC 9-148246. 1909. 1.50. H. Holt and Company.
Homespun and Gold. Alice Brown. LC 20-195048. 1920. The Macmillan Company.
Homespun of Oatmeal Gray. Paul Goodman. 1970. 5.00 o.p. (ISBN 0-394-40362-2). Random.
Homespun Tales: Rose O' the River, The Old Peabody Pew, and Susanna and Sue. Kate Douglas Smith Wiggin. LC 21-4136. Houghton Mifflin Company.
Homespun Yarns of Maine. Mabel Crankshaw. LC 42-25682. 1942. Dorrance and Company.
Homestead. Dale Eunson. LC 35-249442. Farrar & Rinehart, Incorporated.
Homestead. Zephine Humphrey. LC 19-108352. E. P. Dutton & Company.
Homestead Grays. James Wylie. LC 77-3641. 10.00 (ISBN 0-399-12003-3). Putnam.
Homestead Grays. James Wylie. 1978. 1.95 (ISBN 0-380-38604-6). Avon Books.
Homestead Justice. Don P. Jenison. (Orig.). 1980. pap. 1.95 (ISBN 0-89083-566-7). Zebra.
Homestead on the Hillside, and Other Tales. Mary Jane Hawes Holmes. LC 7-8480.
Homestead on the Hillside, and Other Tales. Mary Jane Hawes Holmes. LC 7-848180. G. W. Carleton & Co.
Homestead on the Hillside, and Other Tales. Mary Jane Hawes Holmes. LC 3476. (On cover: Madison square library, no. 105). 1897. G. W. Dillingham Co.
Homestead Ranch. Elizabeth G Young. LC 22-4921. 1922. D. Appleton and Company.
Homestead Range. Al Cody, pseud. pap. 0.50 o.p. (50-339). Manor Bks.
Homesteader. Ben Smith. LC 63-6871. 1963. Avalon Books.
Homesteader: A Novel. Oscar Micheaux. LC 71-76118. (Illus.). 1969. McGrath Pub. Co.
Homesteaders. Kate Boyles Bingham & Boyles, Virgil Dillin. LC 9-24261. 1909. 1.50. A. C. McClurg & Co.
Homesteaders. Robert James Campbell Stead. LC 73-82583. (Literature of Canada; poetry and prose in reprint). 1973. 12.50 (ISBN 0-8020-2067-4) (ISBN 0-8020-2067-4). University of Toronto Press.
Homesteaders. Lee D. Willougby, pseud. (Making of America Ser.). (Orig.). 1981. pap. 2.75 (ISBN 0-440-03628-3). Dell.
Homesteader's Daughter: A Story of the Times (Founded on Fact. Jennes Bryasen. LC 5662. 1900.
Hometown. Cleveland Amory. LC 50-5049. 1950. Harper.
Hometown. Marijane Meaker. LC 66-12228. 1967. Doubleday.
Hometown Angel. Reita Lambert. LC 40-4501. 1940. Macrae-Smith-Company.
Hometown Angel. Reita Lambert. LC 42-206531. 1942. Triangle Books.
Hometown Visions of the Bluejean Outlaw Kid. Jamie Mendelkau. LC 74-178151. 1973. 2.00. W. H. Allen.
Homeward and Beyond. Poul Anderson. LC 74-24483. (Doubleday science fiction). 1975. 6.95 (ISBN 0-385-05540-4). Doubleday.
Homeward and Beyond. Poul Anderson. (Berkley Medallion Book). 1976. 1.50 (ISBN 0-671-80695-5). Berkley.
Homeward Borne: A Novel. Ruth Chatterton. LC 50-6936. 1950. Simon and Schuster.
Homeward Bound. Thomas Bradbury Chetwood. LC 41-1826. J. F. Wagner, Inc.
Homeward Bound. Jacob Glatstein. LC 68-10640. 1969. 4.95 (ISBN 0-498-06656-8). T. Yoseloff.
Homeward Bound. Jules Verne. 3.95. Assoc Bk.
Homeward Bound: Or, The Chase. A Tale of the Sea. James Fenimore Cooper. LC 6-29890. 1838. Carey, Lea & Blanchard.
Homeward Bound: Or, The Chase. A Tale of the Sea. James Fenimore Cooper. LC 26-240927. (Half-title: The choice works of Cooper. Revised and corrected series. v. 14). 1856. Stringer & Townsend.
Homeward Bound: Or, The Chase. A Tale of the Sea... James Fenimore Cooper. (On cover: Lovell's library, no. 378). 1884. J. W. Lovell Company.
Homeward the Heart: A Novel. Margaret Mackprang Mackay. LC 44-36881. 1944. The John Day Company.
Homeward to Ithaca. Leonard Patrick O'Connor Wibberley. LC 77-11984. 1978. 7.95 (ISBN 0-688-03266-4). Morrow.
Homeward to Ithaka. Leonard Wibberley. LC 77-11984. 1978. 7.95 o.p. (ISBN 0-688-03266-4). Morrow.
Homeward Trail. Waldron Baily. LC 16-228491. 1.35. W. J. Watt & Company.
Homeward Trail. Joyce Berggren. LC 52-31747. 1952. Zondervan Pub House.
Homeward Winds the River. Barbara Ferry Johnson. LC 78-62041. 1979. 2.50 (ISBN 0-380-42952-7). Avon Books.
Homeworld. Harry Harrison. 208p. (Orig.). 1980. pap. 1.95 (ISBN 0-553-13917-7). Bantam.
Homicidal Horse. Hugh Pentecost. (Julian Quist Mystery Novel & Red Badge Novel of Suspense). 1979. 7.95 o.p. (ISBN 0-396-07724-2). Dodd.
Homicidal Horse. Judson Pentecost Philips. LC 79-20185. (Red badge novel of suspense). 1979. 7.95 (ISBN 0-396-07724-2). Dodd, Mead.
Homicidal Lady. Day Keene. LC 54-376228. (Graphic mystery, 87). 1954. Graphic Books.
Homicide. Leslie Turner White. LC 37-23923. Harcourt, Brace and Company.
Homicide Blonde. LC 65-14669. 3.95. Harper.
Homicide Call: A Lieutenant Abe Larson Mystery Novel. Samuel A Krasney. LC 62-118961. 1962. Morrow.
Homicide Club. Gwyn Evans. LC 32-13347. 1932. L. MacVeagh, Dial Press, Inc.
Homicide for Hannah. Dwight Vincent Babcock. LC 41-1049. 1941. A. A. Knopf.
Homicide for Hannah. Dwight Vincent Babcock. LC 44-14237. (Murder mystery monthly. No. 10). 1943. Avon Book Company.
Homicide Haven. John Victor Turner. LC 36-5814. 1936. D. Appleton-Century Company, Incorpoated.
Homicide House: Mr. Pinkerton Returns, by David Frome Pseud. Zenith Jones Brown. LC 50-6413. (Murray Hill mystery). 1950. Rinehart.
Homicide Hussy. Cover Painting by James Meese. Atha McGuire. LC 55-42201. (Gold medal books, 502). 1955. Fawcett Publications.
Homicide Trinity: A Nero Wolfe Threesome. Rex Stout. LC 62-11671. 1962. Viking Press.
Homicide West. Samuel A Krasney. LC 61-112227. 1961. Morrow.
Homicide Zone Four. Nick Christian. 1978. 1.95 (ISBN 0-451-08285-0). New American Library.
Homing. Jeffrey Campbell, pseud. LC 79-17477. 9.95 (ISBN 0-399-12441-1). Putnam.
Homing. Grace Livingston Hill. LC 38-13397. J. B. Lippincott Company.
Homing. Lilyan Stratton. LC 23-15478. Colyer Printing Co.
Homing. Elswyth Thane. LC 80-25636. 1981. 15.95 (ISBN 0-8161-3164-3). G. K. Hall.
Homing Pigeon. Emily Coddington Williams. LC 27-18971. The Macaulay Company.
Homing. 1st Ed. Elswyth Thane. LC 57-5012. 1957. Duell, Sloan and Pearce.
Homme Au Masque De Fer. Alexandre Dumas. Ed. by E. A. Robertson. text ed. 0.90 o.p. Cambridge U Pr.
Homo Faber. Max Frisch. Tr. by Michael Bullock from Ger. LC 60-5123. 1971. pap. 3.95 (ISBN 0-15-642135-6, Harv). HarBraceJ.
Homo Farm. Victor Jay. (Orig.). pap. 1.25 o.p. (2059). Brandon.
Homo Hunt. Gene Evans. pap. 1.95 o.p. (8004). Cameo.
Homo in the Guest House. Jack Michaels. ('rig). 1968. pap. 1.25 o.p. (2081). Brandon.
Homo Playboy. Meredith Gorman. (Orig.). 1969. pap. 1.75 o.p. (3063). Brandon.
Homo Sapiens: A Novel in Three Parts. Stanislaw Przybyszewski. LC 72-127895. 1970. (ISBN 0-404-05147-2). AMS Press.
Homo Sum. popular uniform ed. Georg Moritz Ebers. Tr. by Bell, Clara Courtenay (Poynter) LC 16-157141. (historical romances of Georg Ebers. vol. vii). 1915. D. Appleton and Company.
Homo Sum: A Novel. authorized ed. Georg Moritz Ebers. Tr. by Clara Courtenay Bell. 1880. W. S. Gottsberger.
Homo Sum. A Novel. Georg Moritz Ebers. Tr. by Clara Courtenay Bell. (On cover: Seaside library. Pocket ed., no. 1094). 1888. G. Munro.
Homo Sum: A Novel. Georg Moritz Ebers. Tr. by Clara Courtenay Bell. LC 4-168606. 1900. D. Appleton and Company.
Homocide Johnny. Stephen Gould Fisher. LC 40-296456. 1940. Mystery House.
Homos Don't Cry. George Anthony. (Orig.). 1968. pap. 1.75 o.p. (3049). Brandon.
Homoselle... Mary Spear Nicholas Tiernan. LC 8-19798. (On cover: Round-robin series). 1881. J. R. Osgood and Company.
Homunculus. David Henry Keller. LC 49-11754. 1949. Prime Press.
Homunculus: A Magic Tale. Sven Delblanc. LC 69-13116. 1969. 4.95. Prentice-Hall.
Homzas' Son. Mark A. Anderson. 1983. 8.95 (ISBN 0-533-05187-8). Vantage.
Hon. Rocky Slade. 1st Ed. William Wister Haines. LC 57-6444. 1957. Little Brown.
Hon. Stanbury: And Others. (On cover: The incognito library no. 2). 1894. G. P. Putnam's Sons.
Honcho. Jack Slade, pseud. (Sundance Ser.: No. 13). 1978. pap. 1.50 o.s.i. (ISBN 0-8439-0587-5, Leisure Bks). Nordon Pubns.
Honcho. Jack Slade. (Sundance,#13). 1974. (pbk.) 0.95. Leisure Books.
Honda the Samurai: A Story of Modern Japan. William Elliot Griffis. Congregational Sunday-School and Publishing Society.
Hondo. Louis L'Amour. LC 78-14555. (Gregg Press Western Fiction Series). 1978. 7.95 (ISBN 0-8398-2452-1). Gregg Press.
Hondo see Complete L'Amour.
Honest Dealer. Frank Gruber. LC 47-2063. 1947. Rinehart & Company, Inc.
Honest Effort. William Crawford. LC 77-80452. Date not set. 9.95 (ISBN 0-916546-06-3). Racz Pub.
Honest John Vane. A Story. John William De Forest. LC 6-33392. 1875. Richmond & Patten.
Honest Lawyer. Gertrude Violet McFadden. LC 17-6331. 1916. John Lane.
Honest Lawyer: A Novel. Alvah Milton Kerr. LC 7-10819. (On cover: The Ariel library, no. 10). F. J. Schulte & Company.
Honest Reliable Corpse. George Babby. 1970. pap. 0.60 o.p. (0502-06111). Curtis.
Honest Reliable Corpse. George Bagby, pseud. LC 69-12180. (Crime Ser). 1969. 3.95 o.p. Doubleday.

Honest, Reliable Corpse. Aaron Marc Stein. LC 69-12180. 1969. 3.95. Published for the Crime Club by Doubleday.

Honest Thief: And Other Stories. Fedor Mikhailovich Dostoevskii. Tr. by Constance Black Garnett. LC 20-26192. (Half-title: The novels of Fyodor Dostoevsky. Vol. XI). 1919. The Macmillan Company.

Honest Thief, & Other Stories. Fedor Mikhailovich Dostoevskii. Tr. by Constance Garnett. LC 74-15163. 404p. 1975. Repr. of 1919 ed. lib. bdg. 29.75x (ISBN 0-8371-7807-X, DOHT). Greenwood.

Honest Thief, and Other Stories. Fedor Mikhailovich Dostoevskii & Constance Black Garnett. LC 74-15163. 1975. 19.50 (ISBN 0-8371-7807-X). Greenwood Press.

Honest Thief: And Other Stories by Fyodor Dostoevsky; from the Russian by Constance Garnett. Fedor Mikhailovich Dostoevskii. Tr. by Constance Black Garnett. LC 32-32580. (Half-title: The novels of Fyodor Dostoevsky. vol. XI). 1923. The Macmillan Company.

Honest Try. Bob Scriver. LC 74-32526. (Illus.). 1975. 25.00 (ISBN 0-913504-22-X). Lowell Pr.

Honest Woman. Jack Dunphy. LC 70-159339. (Illus.). 1971. 6.95 (ISBN 0-394-46570-8). Random House.

Honesty. Linda Lauren. LC 81-14581. 9.95 (ISBN 0-312-38946-9). St. Martin's Press.

Honesty's Garden. Paul Creswick. LC 10-359859. 1910. G. P. Putnam's Sons.

Honey. Elizabeth Jenkins. LC 68-57376. 1968. 4.95. Coward-McCann.

Honey. Josiah Pitts Woolfolk & John Burton Thompson. LC 51-11480. 1951. Arco Pub. Co.

Honey Badger. Robert Chester Ruark. LC 65-23822. bds., 6.95. McGraw.

Honey Badger. Robert Chester Rurark. LC 65-23822. 1965. McGraw -- Hill.

Honey Bear on Lasqueti Island, British Columbia: Poems, Photographs, Recipes, Prints. Robert Sward. (Illus.). 1978. pap. 3.50 o.s.i. (ISBN 0-919590-27-6). Soft Pr.

Honey Bee: A Story of a Woman in Revolt. Samuel Merwin. LC 15-102835. 1.35. The Bobbs-Merrill Company.

Honey Bird. Stuart Cloete. 1981. 18.95x (Pub. by Remploy England). State Mutual Bk.

Honey Boy. John Maggie. 192p. 1974. pap. 2.25 o.s.i. (ISBN 0-89053-109-9, LB-109). Lambda Pr.

Honey Bunch: A Novel. Patricia Zelver. LC 78-97909. 1970. 5.95. Little, Brown.

Honey-Colored Moon. Winifred Mary Scott. LC 40-14538. 1940. H. C. Kinsey & Company, Inc.

Honey, Don't Blame Me! Ian Kay. LC 37-50269. 1937. Godwin.

Honey Dwarf. Gene Detro LC 75-321158. 5.95. (ISBN 0-913218-23-5) (ISBN 0-913218-24-3). Dustbooks.

Honey Dwarf. Gene Detro. 1974. 5.95 (ISBN 0-913218-23-5). Dustbooks.

Honey Flow. Kylie Tennant, pseud. LC 56-37160. 1956. Macmillan.

Honey for Tea. Elizabeth Cadell. LC 62-7715. 1962. Morrow.

Honey for the Bears. Anthony Burgess. 1978. pap. 3.95 (ISBN 0-393-00905-X, N905, Norton Lib). Norton.

Honey for the Bears. Anthony Burgess. 1964. 3.95 o.p. (ISBN 0-393-08481-7). Norton.

Honey for the Bears. John Anthony Burgess Wilson. LC 64-10565. 1964. W. W. Norton.

Honey for the Bears see Clockwork Orange.

Honey for the Ghost. Louis Golding. LC 49-10824. 1949. Dial Press.

Honey for Tomorrow. Robert Lait. LC 61-6239. 1961. Random House.

Honey from a Dark Hive. Bernice Kavinoky. LC 56-52894. 1956. Rinehart.

Honey Guides. Hunter North. LC 73-13286. 1973. Touchstone-International Associates.

Honey Horn. John Maggie. (Orig.). 1969. pap. 1.95 o.p. (7054). Barclay Hse.

Honey in the Horn. Harold Lenoir Davis. LC 35-167872. 1935. Harper & Brothers.

Honey Lou: The Love Wrecker. Beatrice Burton Morgan. LC 27-5601. Grosset & Dunlap.

Honey Makers. Hendry Van Dieman. 176p. pap. 1.95 o.p. (6110). Brandon.

Honey Man. Mike Panos. (Orig.). 1968. pap. 1.75 (ISBN 0-87067-158-8, BH158). Holloway.

Honey Man: A Novel. Burette Stinson Tillinghast. LC 75-40390. 7.95. E. P. Dutton.

Honey of Danger: An Adventure Story. Frank Lillie Pollock. LC 42-10427. Chelsea House.

Honey on Her Tail. G. G. Fickling, pseud. (Orig.). 1971. pap. 0.75 o.p. (T2410). Pyramid Pubns.

Honey on the Hill. Selig Jacob Seligman. LC 53-5410. 1953. Sloane.

Honey on the Moon. Maude Phelps McVeigh Hutchins. LC 64-10734. 1964. Morrow.

Honey Out of Stone. Gary Adelman. LC 72-89097. 1970. 5.95. Doubleday.

Honey-Pot. Marguerite Florence Helene Evans. LC 16-4389. 1916. E. P. Dutton & Company.

Honey Pot. Mira Stables. 1979. 1.75 (ISBN 0-449-23915-2). Fawcett Crest Books.

Honey Pot: Or: In the Garden of Lelita. Norval Richardson. LC 12-22312. 1912. L. C. Page & Company.

Honey Seems Bitter. 1st Ed. Benedict Kiely. LC 52-10438. 1952. Dutton.

Honey Shops. Jack Kaye. LC 49-98353. 1949. Dorrance.

Honey Spike. Bryan MacMahon. LC 67-10066. 1967. Dutton.

Honey, You've Been Dealt a Winning Hand. Marilyn Krysl. LC 80-17285. 1980. 5.95 (ISBN 0-88496-154-0). Capra Press.

Honeyball Farm. Ethel May Dell. LC 37-28333. 1937. G. P. Putnam's Sons.

Honeybath's Haven. Michael Innes, pseud. 1978. 6.95 o.p. (ISBN 0-396-07555-X). Dodd.

Honeybath's Haven. Michael Innes, pseud. (Crime Monthly Ser). 1979. pap. 2.95 (ISBN 0-14-004885-5). Penguin.

Honeybath's Haven. John Innes Mackintosh Stewart. LC 78-1751. (Red badge novel of suspense). 1978. 6.95 (ISBN 0-396-07555-X). Dodd, Mead.

Honeybath's Haven. John Innes Mackintosh Stewart. LC 79-16662. (Penguin crime fiction.). 1979. 1.95 (ISBN 0-14-004885-5). Penguin Books.

Honeybuzzard. Angela Carter. (71001). 1968. Ballantine.

Honeybuzzard. LC 67-10525. 1967. Simon and Schuster.

Honeycomb. Dorothy Miller Richardson. 286p. 1977. Repr. of 1919 ed. lib. bdg. 13.95x (ISBN 0-89966-155-6). Buccaneer Bks.

Honeycomb: Ballad of a North Beach Cabaret. Don Asher. LC 78-75155. (Illus.). 3.95 (ISBN 0-89395-021-1). California Living Books.

Honeyed Peace: Stories. Martha Gellhorn. LC 70-130057. (Short story index reprint series). 1970. Books for Libraries Press.

Honeyed Peace: Stories. Martha Gellhorn. LC 53-7982. 1953. Doubleday.

Honeyflow. Ben Ames Williams. LC 32-766. 1932. E. P. Dutton & Co., Inc.

Honeyfogling Time. Virginia Dale. LC 46-2497. 1946. Harper & Brothers.

Honeymaid: The Story of Silver Dollar Tabor. new ed. Martha G. Roberts. 1977. pap. 3.95x (ISBN 0-87315-064-3). Golden Bell.

Honeymaker's Son. Ray Hogan. LC 74-12857. 1975. 4.95 (ISBN 0-385-03124-6). Doubleday.

Honeymaker's Son. Ray Hogan. (Signet Book). 1976. (pbk.) 0.95. New American Library.

Honeyman Festival: A Novel. Marian Engel. LC 70-184561. 1972. 5.95. St. Martin's Press.

Honeymoon. Arnold Bennett. LC 74-5328. (Collected Works of Arnold Bennett: Vol. 30). 1976. Repr. of 1910 ed. 16.75 (ISBN 0-518-19111-7). Ayer Co.

Honeymoon. Elisabeth Ogilvie & Kanin, Michael. LC 47-4657. (Bart House film hit of the month. 103). 1947. Bartholomew House.

Honeymoon; Mom. Hugh Fox. LC 78-73822. (Illus.). 1978. 5.00 (ISBN 0-913204-10-2). December Press.

Honeymoon Alone. Maysie Greig. LC 41-8170. 1941. Doubleday, Doran and Company, Inc.

Honeymoon Alone. Maysie Greig. LC 42-24740. 1942. The Sun Dial Press.

Honeymoon Arranged. Maysie Greig. LC 38-20125. 1938. Doubleday, Doran and Co., Inc.

Honeymoon, Bittermoon. Perez De Ayala, Ramon. LC 79-116667. 1972. 8.95 (ISBN 0-520-01727-7). University of California Press.

Honeymoon Confidences. LC 9-25640. The Hudson Press.

Honeymoon Delayed. Rob Eden. LC 37-2023. M. S. Mill Co., Inc.

Honeymoon Delayed. Josiah Pitts Woolfolk. LC 37-99303. 1937. Godwin.

Honeymoon Dialogues. Arthur Henry Adams. LC 22-191. E. P. Dutton & Company.

Honeymoon Diary. James Alonzo Bishop. LC 63-17710. 1963. Harper & Row.

Honeymoon Diary see This Man & This Woman.

Honeymoon for Three. Gwendolyn Ross Mandell. LC 30-343135. 1929. Authors & Publishers Corporation.

Honeymoon House: Romantic Comedy. Gladys Mary Attenborough. 1934. Frederick A. Stokes Company.

Honeymoon in a Tackle Box. Romaine Fundarek. 2.95 o.p. Vantage.

Honeymoon in a Taxicab. H. G Vartanian. LC 70-126960. 1970. 3.50. Harlo Press.

Honeymoon in Hell. Fredric Brown. LC 58-9474. (Bantam book, A18122). 1958. Bantam Books.

Honeymoon in Hell. Gail Elton Mayo. LC 44-3160. 1944. Doubleday, Doran and Co., Inc.

Honeymoon in Honolulu. Jean Francis Webb. LC 50-58104. 1950. Avalon Books.

Honeymoon in Space. George Chetwynd Griffith. LC 74-15978. (Science Fiction). (Illus.). 1975. 17.00 (ISBN 0-405-06295-8). Arno Press.

Honeymoon in the Sky. Nell Marr Dean. LC 53-722787. 1953. Arcadia House.

Honeymoon Killers. Paul Buck. 160p. 1980. pap. 1.95 (ISBN 0-441-34269-8, Pub. by Charter Bks). Ace Bks.

Honeymoon Killers. Paul Buck. (O.s.i.). 1970. pap. 0.75 o.s.i. (A705S, Award). Univ Pub & Dist.

Honeymoon Limited. Vida Hurst. LC 32-468984. Grosset & Dunlap.

Honeymoon Millions. Steuart M Emery. LC 28-13169. E. P. Dutton & Company.

Honeymoon Mountain. Frances Shelley Wees. LC 34-5902. 1934. Macrae Smith Company.

Honeymoon Path. Kathleen Rollins. LC 35-100497. Arcadia House.

Honeymoon Perversion. Defence Eakens. pap. 1.95 o.s.i. (TCP-004). Olympia.

Honeymoon. Remembrance of a Bridal Tour Through Scotland. Medina Pomar, De. LC 7-18509. 1874. J. B. Lippincott & Co.

Honeymoon Trail. Gertrude Pahlow. LC 31-4962. The Penn Publishing Company.

Honeymoon Wife. Agnes Louise Provost. LC 32-7613. 1932. Macrae Smith Company.

Honeymoon with Death. Hugh Pentecost. (Red Badge Novel of Suspense). 188p. 1975. 5.95 o.p. (ISBN 0-396-07212-7). Dodd.

Honeymoon with Death. Judson Pentecost Philips. LC 75-29192. (Red badge novel of suspense). 1975. 5.95 (ISBN 0-396-07212-7). Dodd, Mead.

Honeymoons Arranged. Maysie Greig. LC 40-830642. 1940. Triangle Books.

Honeymoon's End. Howard Rockey. LC 26-13140. The Macaulay Company.

Honeymoonshine. James Oliver. LC 36-156924. Longmans, Green and Co.

Honeypot Girls. Sterling Harkins. 192p. (Orig.). 1973. pap. 1.95 o.p. (ISBN 0-87682-322-3, 7322). Barclay Hse.

Honeypot High. Peter Bronson. pap. 1.95 o.p. (ISBN 0-87682-254-5, 7254). Barclay Hse.

Honey's Money. James Gerald Dunton. LC 33-6574. Sears Publishing Company.

Honfleur Decision. Alan Hunter. LC 80-54824. 1981. 9.95 (ISBN 0-8027-5437-6). Walker.

Hong Kong. Clayton Matthews. 1976. (pbk.) 1.95. Pocket Books.

Hong Kong Detective. Kenneth Andrew. (Illus.). 15.00 (ISBN 0-392-03260-0, LTB). Sportshelf.

Hong Kong Kill. Peter Bryan George. LC 59-6697. (Chantecler mystery novel). 1959. Washburn.

Hong Kong Kill. Bryan Peters. LC 59-51426. (British bloodhound, no. 210). 1958. T. V. Boardman.

Hong Kong Kill. Bryan Peters. LC 59-6697. (Chantecler mystery novel). 1959. Washburn.

Hong Kong Missey. Rosalie Hamric Smith. LC 67-24834. 1967. 4.00. Dorrance.

Hongkong Airbase Murders... Francis Van Wyck Mason. 1937. Pub. for the Crime Club, Inc., by Doubleday, Doran & Co., Inc.

Hongkong Airbase Murders... Francis Van Wyck Mason. LC 39-724. The Sun Dial Press, Inc.

Honk! A Motor Romance. Doris F Halman. LC 26-10310. 1926. Frederick A. Stokes Company.

Honk & Horace: Or, Trimming the Tropics. Emmet Forrest Harte. LC 13-237305. 1.00. The Reilly & Britton Co.

Honk If You Love Boise Hafter: A Chronicle. John Wallace. LC 72-89698. 1973. 7.95 (ISBN 0-672-51786-8). Bobbs-Merrill.

Honk If You've Found Jesus. Don Tracy. LC 73-93749. 1974. 6.95 (ISBN 0-399-11334-7). G. P. Putnam.

Honkers. Thomas Chastain. 160p. (Orig.). 1973. pap. 0.75 o.p. (A953*S, Award Hse). Univ Pub & Dist.

Honking Geese see White Crane Has No Mourners.

Honkytonk Man. Clancy Carlile. LC 80-19024. 12.95 (ISBN 0-671-41212-4). Simon and Schuster.

Honolulu. Arthur Moore. 1976. (pbk.) 1.95 (ISBN 0-671-80411-1). Pocket Books.

Honolulu Hayride! Sanford Rollins. LC 52-167. 1951. Murray & Gee.

Honolulu Madam. Lolana Mitsuko. (Orig.). 1969. pap. 1.95 (ISBN 0-87067-620-2, BH620). Holloway.

Honolulu, Port of Call: A Selection of South Sea Tales. Ed. by Joseph N. Gores. LC 74-195962. 1974. 1.95 (ISBN 0-345-24296-3). Ballantine Books.

Honolulu Story. Zenith Jones Brown. LC 46-25200. 1946. C. Scribner's Sons.

Honor: A Novel. Maud Elliott. LC 6-37783. The Price-McGill Company.

Honor Among Women. George Fort Gibbs. LC 33-20822. 1933. D. Appleton-Century Company, Incorporated.

Honor Among Women. Peggy O'More, pseud. LC 36-19558. Phoenix Press.

Honor Bound. Jack Bethea. LC 27-643739. 1927. Houghton Mifflin Company.

Honor Bound. Theresa Conway. 352p. (Orig.). 1980. pap. 2.50 (ISBN 0-449-14340-6, GM). Fawcett.

Honor Bound. Faith Baldwin Cuthrell. LC 34-24632. Farrar & Rinehart, Incorporated.

Honor Bound. Colleen L Reece. LC 82-20873. 3.95 (ISBN 0-8024-0153-8). Moody Press.

Honor Bright. Honor Bright. 1975. (pbk.) 1.50 (ISBN 0-671-78762-4). Pocket Books.

Honor Bright. Frances Parkinson Wheeler Keyes. LC 36-25557. J. Messner, Inc.

Honor Bright. A Romance. Sue Chesnutwood Perkins. LC 7-36191. 1883. P. Paul & Bro.

Honor Dalton: A Novel. Frances Campbell Sparhawk. LC 3-21016. 1903. F. H. Revell Company.

Honor Divided. Grace Darling Hall & Merlanti, Ernesto Giuseppe, 1895- Joint Author. LC 35-173855. Gleming H. Revell Company.

Honor Edgeworth: Or, Ottawa's Present Tense. Vera. LC 74-168875. (Toronto reprint library of Canadian prose and poetry). (ISBN 0-8020-7505-3). University of Toronto Press.

Honor Girl. Grace Livingston Hill. 256p. 1975. Repr. of 1927 ed. lib. bdg. 14.40 (ISBN 0-89190-012-8). Am Repr-Rivercity Pr.

Honor Girl. Grace Livingston Hill. 1927. 2.95 o.p. (ISBN 0-448-05231-8). G&D.

Honor Girl, No. 57. Grace Livingston Hill. 1980. pap. 1.95 (ISBN 0-553-14015-9). Bantam.

Honor May: A Story. Mary Bartol. LC 6-9390. 1866. Ticknor and Fields.

Honor of a Heart: A Novel. Emil Mario Vacano & Bergsoe, Vilhelm I.E, Jorgen Vilhelm, 1835-1911. (On cover: The choice series, no. 83). 1893. R. Bonner's Sons.

Honor of a Lee. Libbie Miller Travers. LC 8-27104. 1908. Cochrane Publishing Co.

Honor of Dr. Shelton. Elizabeth Seifert. LC 62-973233. 1962. Dodd, Mead.

Honor of Dr. Shelton. Elizabeth Seifert. LC 73-79183. 1974. 6.95. Aeonian Press.

Honor of Gaston Le Torche: A Novel. Translated from the French by Anne Cliff & Fernand G. Renier. Jacques Perret. LC 54-13521. 1955. Norton.

Honor of His House. Andrew Soutar. LC 15-541932. G. W. Dillingham Company.

Honor of Preston Reed. Louise Harrison McCraw. LC 52-4316. 1952. Moody Press.

Honor of the Big Snows. James Oliver Curwood. LC 11-394410. The Bobbs-Merrill Company.

Honor of the Braxtons: A Novel. James William Fosdick. LC 2-11133. 1902. J. F. Taylor & Company.

Honor of the Name: Tr. from the French of Emile Gaboriau. Emile Gaboriau. LC 2820. 1900. C. Scribner's Sons.

Honor of the Name: Translated from the French of Emile Gaboriau. Emile Gaboriau. LC 26-3670. 1903. C. Scribner's Sons.

Honor of the Name: Translated from the French of Emile Gaboriau. Emile Gaboriau. LC 25-221193. 1921. C. Scribner's Sons.

Honor: Or, The Slave-Dealer's Daughter. Stephen Greenleaf Bulfinch. LC 72-8577. (Black Heritage Library Collection). 1972. (ISBN 0-8369-9185-0). Books for Libraries Press.

Honor Ormthwaite: A Novel. LC 7-5188. 1896. Harper & Brothers.

Honor, Power, Riches, Fame, and the Love of Women. Ward S Just. LC 79-10123. 8.95. Dutton.

Honor Sherburne. Amanda Minnie Douglas. LC 4-24506. (Her The Sherburne series). 1904. Dodd, Mead & Company.

Honor System. Dick Dabney. LC 75-25078. 7.95 (ISBN 0-06-010951-3). Harper & Row.

Honor Them, Then. Eve Walters. LC 36-8266. 1936. Doubleday, Doran & Company, Inc.

Honor Thy Father. Robert A Roripaugh. LC 63-16380. (Illus.). 1963. Morrow.

Honor Thy Godfather. Thomas P Mulkeen. LC 72-83415. 1973. 5.95. Stein and Day.

Honor Thy Mother. Thomas H. Hilton. pap. 1.95 o.p. (ISBN 0-87056-234-7). Brandon.

Honor to the Bride Like the Pigeon That Guards Its Grain Under the Clove Tree. Jane Kramer. LC 78-122828. 1970. 5.95. Farrar, Straus & Giroux.

Honorable Ancestor. Hannah Gibson. 192p. (Orig.). 1981. pap. 1.95 (ISBN 0-8439-0975-7, Leisure Bks). Nordon Pubns.

Honorable Beggars. Hagop Baronian. Tr. by Jack Antreassian from Armenian. LC 79-24482. (Illus.). 132p. (Orig.). 1980. pap. 4.95 (ISBN 0-935102-03-5). Ashod Pr.

Honorable Estate. Lane Kauffmann. LC 64-11854. 1964. Lippincott.

Honorable Estate: A Novel. Rosamond Neal Du Jardin. LC 43-15503. 1943. Macrae-Smith-Company.

Honorable John Hale: A Comedy of American Politics. Clifford Samuel Raymond. LC 46-8061. 1946. The Bobbs-Merrill Company.

Honorable Miss: A Story of an Old-Fashioned Town. authorized ed. Elizabeth Thomasina Meade Smith. LC 8-8648. (Lovell's international series, no. 139). United States Book Company, Successors to J. W. Lovell Company.

Honorable Miss Cherry Blossom: A Novel. Luellen Teters Bussenius. LC 25-9141. 1924. N. L. Brown.
Honorable Miss Clarendon. A. Gladstone. (Orig.). 1975. pap. 1.25 o.p. (ISBN 0-515-03712-5). Pyramid Pubns.
Honorable Miss Moonlight. Winnifred Eaton Babcock. LC 12-22135. 1912. 1.00. Harper & Brothers.
Honorable Mrs. Vereker. Margaret Wolfe Hungerford. (On cover: Seaside library. Pocket ed., no. 1103). 1888. G. Munro.
Honorable Offer. Catherine Coulter. (Orig.). 1981. pap. 2.25 (ISBN 0-451-11209-1, AE 1209, Sig). NAL.
Honorable Percival. Alice Caldwell Hegan Rice. LC 14-18879. 1914. The Century Co.
Honorable Peter Sterling. Paul Leicester Ford. LC 68-20013. 1977. lib. bdg. 13.50 (ISBN 0-8398-0560-8); pap. text ed. 4.95x (ISBN 0-89197-791-0). Irvington.
Honorable Peter Stirling. Paul Leicester Ford. LC 73-79655. (Series in American Studies). 1969. Johnson Reprint Corp.
Honorable Peter Stirling: And What People Thought of Him. Paul Leicester Ford. LC 68-20013. (Americans in fiction). 1968. Gregg Press.
Honorable Peter Stirling: And What People Thought of Him. Paul Leicester Ford. LC 20-18819. H. Holt and Company.
Honorable Peter Stirling: And What People Thought of Him. Paul Leicester Ford. LC 1-2011. (On cover: The international paper novels, no. 1). International Book and Publishing Company.
Honorable Peter Stirling: And What People Thought of Him. 35th ed. Paul Leicester Ford. LC 1-2428. 1899. H. Holt and Company.
Honorable Peter Stirling: And What People Thought of Him. 53rd ed. Paul Leicester Ford. LC 16-93768. 1910. H. Holt and Company.
Honorable Peter Stirling: And What People Thought of Him. Paul Leicester Ford. LC 21-168567. Stitt Publishing Company.
Honorable Peter Stirling: And What People Thought of Him. Paul Leicester Ford. LC 32-19504. 1930. Grosset & Dunlap.
Honorable Picnic. Thomas Raucat. Tr. by Cline, Leonard. LC 27-13797. 1927. The Viking Press.
Honorable Senator Sage-Brush. Francis Lynde. LC 13-19335. 1913. C. Scribner's Sons.
Honorable Surrender. Mary Adams. LC 5-42968. 1883. C. Scribner's Sons.
Honorable Uncle Lancy. Ethel Powelson Hueston. LC 39-3180. The Bobbs-Merrill Company.
Honorary Consul. Graham Greene. LC 73-5254. 1973. 7.95 (ISBN 0-671-21569-8). Simon and Schuster.
Honorary Consul. Graham Greene. LC 73-21919. 1974. (lib. bdg.). 11.95 (ISBN 0-8161-6182-8). G. K. Hall.
Honorary Counsel. Graham Greene. 1983. pap. 3.95. PB.
Honore De Balzac: An Introduction by Ferdinand Brunetiere. Balzac, Honore De. Tr. by George Burnham Ives. LC 3-26300. 1903. G. P. Putnam's Sons.
Honore De Balzac: An Introduction by Ferdinand Brunetiere. Honore De Balzac. Tr. by George Burnham Ives. LC 41-20073. (Little French masterpieces, ed. by Alexander Jessup iv). 1909. G. P. Putnam's Sons.
Honored Guest. Sara Elizabeth Gosselink. LC 47-169521. 1947. Wm. B. Eerdmans Publishing Company.
Honoria: Or, The Gospel of a Life. Rose Porter. LC 7-37748. A. D. F. Randolph & Company.
Honor's Price. Ursula Bloom. 1979. pap. 2.25 (ISBN 0-89041-259-6). Major Bks.
Honor's Worth; or, The Cost of a Vow. A Novel. Meta Orred. (Franklin square library, no. 9). Harper & Brother.
Honour Among Thieves. Henry Christopher Bailey. LC 47-30904. 1947. Pub. for the Crime Club by Doubleday.
Honour & Other People's Children. Helen Garner. LC 81-82837. 176p. 1982. 10.50 (ISBN 0-87223-742-7, Seaview Bks). Putnam Pub Group.
Honour Come Back--". Naomi Ellington Jacob. LC 35-10857. 1935. The Macmillan Company.
Honour of Ravensholme. Caroline Stafford, pseud. LC 79-272. 8.95 (ISBN 0-671-24801-4). Simon and Schuster.
Honour of Ravensholme. Caroline Watjeu. 1979. 10.00 o.p. (ISBN 0-671-24801-4). S&S.
Honour of Savelli: A Romance. Sidney Kilner Levett-Yeats. LC 4-16594. 1895. D. Appleton and Company.
Honour of the Clinton. Archibald Marshall. LC 13-166511. 1913. Dodd, Mead and Company.
Honour of the Flag. William Clark Russell. LC 70-103528. (Short story index reprint series). 1969. Books for Libraries Press.
Honour of the Flag. William Clark Russell. LC 8-1803. (On cover: The Autonym library no. 4). 1895. G. P. Putnam's Sons.
Honour of the Flag & Other Stories. William C. Russell. LC 70-103528. (Short Story Index Reprint Ser.). 1895. 12.00 (ISBN 0-8369-3270-6). Ayer Co.
Honour of the House. Mary Crawford Fraser & Stahlmann, J. I. LC 13-22278. 1913. 1.30. Dodd, Mead and Company.
Honourable Ancestor. Robert Standish. 1981. 18.95x (Pub. by Remploy England). State Mutual Bk.
Honourable Estate: A Novel of Transition. Vera Mary Brittain. LC 36-29004. 1936. The Macmillan Company.
Honourable Gentleman and Others. Achmed Abdullah. LC 74-140324. (Short story index reprint series). 1970. Books for Libraries Press.
Honourable Gentleman and Others. Achmed Abdullah. LC 19-159689. 1919. 1.50. G. P. Putnam's Sons.
Honourable Jane. Annie Hall Thomas Cudlip. LC 6-31171. J. W. Lovell Company.
Honourable Jim. Emmuska Orczy. LC 24-6737. 2.00. George H. Doran Company.
Honourable Mr. Tawnish. Jeffery Farnol. LC 13-22290. 1913. Little, Brown, and Company.
Honourable Mrs. Garry. Elizabeth Bonham De La Pasture. LC 12-34918. E. P. Dutton & Company.
Honourable Schoolboy. John Le Carre. LC 77-75001. 1977. 10.95 (ISBN 0-394-41645-7). Knopf.
Honourable Schoolboy. John Le Carre. LC 77-15484. 1977. 18.95 (ISBN 0-8161-6539-4). G. K. Hall.
Honours Board. Pamela Hansford Johnson. LC 73-123821. 1970. 6.95. Scribner.
Honours of War and Peace. Warren Tute. LC 76-375633. 1976. 3.25 (ISBN 0-09-460980-2). Constable.
Honyocker. giles a. lutz. ed. Giles A Lutz. 1976. 1.50. Ace Books.
Honyocker. 1st Ed. Giles A Lutz. LC 61-12550. (Double D western). 1961. Doubleday.
Honyok. Lucy Hester Thurston Abbott. LC 29-186972. Barse & Co.
Hooch! Charles Francis Coe. LC 29-8650. 1929. Pub. for The Crime Club, Inc., by Doubleday, Doran & Company, Inc.
Hood of Death. Nick Carter. (Nick Carter Ser.). (O.s.i.). 160p. (Orig.). 1968. pap. 0.95 o.s.i. (AN1228, Award). Univ Pub & Dist.
Hood of Stars. Winifred Wadell. LC 40-104510. 1940. Arcadia House, Inc.
Hood River Nurse. Beatrice Warren. 1983. 6.95 (Avalon). Bouregy.
Hood, Thomas. (On cover: Seaside library. Pocket ed., no. 407). 1885. G. Munro.
Hooded Asp. Jesse Allen McManis. LC 28-73349. Wetzel Publishing Company.
Hooded Falcon. Archie Joscelyn. 1978. pap. 2.25 (ISBN 0-532-22141-9). Woodhill.
Hooded Vulture Murders. Robert Portner Koehler. LC 47-21836. 1947. Phoenix Press.
Hoodoo Horror. Stuart Jason. (Butcher Ser.: No. 32). 192p. (Orig.). 1981. pap. 1.95 (ISBN 0-523-41262-2). Pinnacle Bks.
Hoods: By Harry Grey Pseud. Harry Goldberg. LC 52-5671. 1952. Crown Publishers.
Hoods of Manor Grove. Otis Dunbar Richardson. 1976. 10.00 o.p. (ISBN 0-682-48492-X). Exposition.
Hoods of Manor Grove. Otis Dunbar Richardson. 1976. 10.00 o.p. (ISBN 0-682-48492-X). Exposition.
Hoodwink: A "Nameless Detective" Mystery. Bill Pronzini. LC 80-29346. 1981. 10.95 (ISBN 0-312-38969-8). St. Martin's Press.
Hoof Beats. Philip Hichborn. 1.00. R. G. Badger.
Hoof Trails and Wagon Tracks. Western Writers of America. Ed. by Don Ward. LC 75-167473. (Short story index reprint series). 1971. (ISBN 0-8369-3999-9). Books for Libraries Press.
Hoof Trails and Wagon Tracks: Stories of the Western Trails by Members of Western Writers of America. Edited with an Introd. by Don Ward. Western Writers of America. Ed. by Don Ward. LC 57-13063. 1957. Dodd, Mead.
Hoofbeats. William Surrey Hart. LC 33-13637. 1933. The Dial Press, Inc.
Hoofbeats. William Surrey Hart. LC 44-472039. 1944. Times-Mirror.
Hoofbeats Along the Llano. 1st Ed. Edwin Robert Bogusch. LC 55-14272. 1955. Naylor Co.
Hoofbeats on the Trail. Vivian Gurney Breckenfeld. LC 50-10014. (Illus.). 1950. Doubleday.
Hoofbeats, the Great Horse Stories of John Taintor Foote. John Taintor Foote. LC 50-7357. (Illus.). 1950. Appleton-Century-Crofts.
Hook. C118p. Illus. 19cm. Vahe Katcha. LC 58-131696. (French's standard library edition).
Hook, No. 1: Gilded Canary. Brad Latham. (Men of Action Ser.). 176p. (Orig.). 1981. pap. 1.95 (ISBN 0-446-90882-7). Warner Bks.
Hook, No. 2: Sight Unseen. Brad Latham. (Men of Action Ser.). 192p. (Orig.). 1981. pap. 1.95 (ISBN 0-446-90841-X). Warner Bks.
Hook, No. 5: Corpses in the Cellar. Brad Latham. (Men of Action Ser.). (Orig.). 1982. pap. 1.95 (ISBN 0-446-90985-8). Warner Bks.
Hooker-Smash Operation. Joseph Rosenberger. (Murder Master Ser.: No. 3). 192p. 1974. pap. 1.25 o.p. (ISBN 0-532-12243-7). Woodhill.
Hooker-Smash Operation. Joseph Rosenberger. (Murder Master Ser.: No. 3). 192p. 1974. pap. 1.25 o.p. (ISBN 0-532-12243-7). Manor Bks.
Hookers. Richard F Mann. LC 32-13062. House of Bourbon.
Hookmen. Antoni Gronowicz. LC 72-12017. 1973. 6.95 (ISBN 0-396-06748-4). Dodd, Mead.
Hooks for the Darkness. Russell L. Hamm. 4.95 o.p. (ISBN 0-8111-0430-3). Naylor.
Hooky & the Villainous Chauffeur. Laurence Walter Meynell. 1982. 15.00x (ISBN 0-333-25590-9, Pub. by Macmillan England). State Mutual Bk.
Hooky Cop. James Gabrielson. LC 72-96712. 1970. 6.95. Hewitt House.
Hooky Gets the Wooden Spoon. Laurence Walter Meynell. LC 77-21168. 1977. 7.95 (ISBN 0-8128-2424-5). Stein and Day.
Hooligan. David Dodge. 1970. pap. 0.75 o.p. (T2320). Pyramid Pubns.
Hooligan. David Dodge. LC 69-10464. 1969. 5.95 o.p. (53197). Macmillan.
Hooligan Nights: Being the Life and Opinions of a Young and Unrepentant Criminal, Recounted by Himself. LC 99-2837. 1899. Holt.
Hoop. John Collis Snaith. LC 27-142104. 1927. D. Appleton & Company.
Hoop la! Crosbie Garstin. LC 29-15584. 1929. Frederick A. Stokes Company.
Hooper Dooper! Frank Fitzhugh Buckner Houston. LC 30-12694. Barse & Co.
Hooper Haller. Dean Hughes. LC 81-176432. (Illus.). 1981 (ISBN 0-87747-867-8). Deseret Book Co.
Hoopoe. Christine Goutiere Weston. LC 72-96006. 1970. 8.95. Harper & Row.
Hoosier Chronicle. Meredith Nicholson. LC 12-62223. 1912. Houghton Mifflin Company.
Hoosier Editor. A Tale of Indiana Life. George L Perrow. 1877. Tilford & Carlon.
Hoosier Mosaics. Maurice Thompson. LC 69-11922. (American short story series, v. 81). 1969. Garrett Press.
Hoosier Mosaics. Maurice Thompson. LC 72-8149. (American short story series, v. 81). 1972. (ISBN 0-8422-8118-5). MSS Information Corp.
Hoosier Mosaics. Maurice Thompson. LC 8-19965. 1875. E. J. Hale & Son.
Hoosier Mosaics: 1875; a Facsimile Reproduction. With an Introd. by John T. Flanagan. Maurice Thompson. LC 56-9144. 1956. Scholars' Facsimiles& Reprints.
Hoosier Odd Fellows: A Story of Indiana. James H Kinkead. LC 7-12532. 1877. J. H. Kinkead & Company.
Hoosier Practitioner: Or, Medicine on the Wabash. Ellis Horton. LC 7-7158. T. A. Randall & Co., Printers.
Hoosier School-Boy. edition specially arranged by the author for use as a reader in schools, and with the addition of definitions and occasional notes and questions. ed. Edward Eggleston. 1890. C. Scribner's Sons.
Hoosier School-Master: A Novel. Edward Eggleston. LC 75-36059. (Illus.). 2.95 (ISBN 0-8055-0254-8). Hart Pub. Co.
Hoosier School-Master: A Novel. Edward Eggleston. LC 57-9753. (American century series, S-1). 1957. Sagamore Press.
Hoosier School-Master. A Novel. Edward Eggleston. LC 8-30418. 1883. C. Scribner's Sons.
Hoosier School-Master: A Novel. new and rev. ed. Edward Eggleston. LC 3-19546. 1893. Orange Judd Company.
Hoosier School-Master: A Story of Backwoods Life in Indiana. rev., with an introd. and notes on the district, by the author. ed. Edward Eggleston. LC 72-84564. 1974. 8.95 (ISBN 0-403-03052-8). Scholarly Press.
Hoosier Schoolmaster. Edward Eggleston & Robert James Dixson. LC 54-55679. (American Classics Simplified and Adapted for Greater Reading Pleasure, Book 6). (Illus.). 1973. (pbk.) 1.25. Regents Pub. Co.
Hoosier Schoolmaster: A Novel. new and rev. ed. Edward Eggleston. LC 3-19545. 1892. Orange Judd Company.
Hoosier Schoolmaster. A Novel. Edward Eggleston. LC 3-19544. Orange Judd and Company.
Hoosier Schoolmaster: A Story of Backwoods Life in Indiana. Edward Eggleston & Holloway, Emory, 1885- Ed. LC 28-25351. (modern readers' series). 1928. The Macmillan Company.
Hoosier Schoolmaster: A Story of Backwoods Life in Indiana. Revised with an Introduction and Notes on the District. Edward Eggleston. Grosset & Dunlap.
Hoosier Schoolmaster: Simplified and Adapted by Robert J. Dixson. Drawings by Syd Browne. With Exercises for Study and Vocabulary Drill. Edward Eggleston & Robert James Dixson. LC 54-556731. (American classics, book 6). 1954. Regents Pub. Co.
Hoosier Volunteer. Kate Boyles Bingham & Boyles, Virgil Dillin. LC 14-5816. 1914. 1.35. A. C. McClurg & Co.
Hoosier Widow. Thomas Sawyer Spivey. LC 8-5225. 1908. The Neale Publishing Company.
Hoot Owl Canyon. Archie Joscelyn. LC 38-31058. Phoenix Press.
Hopalong Cassidy. Clarence Edward Mulford. LC 73-89638. (Illus.). 1974. 6.95. Aeonian Press.
Hopalong Cassidy. 2d ed. Clarence Edward Mulford. LC 10-7304. 1910. 1.50. A. C. McClurg & Co.
Hopalong Cassidy. Clarence Edward Mulford. LC 25-15484. 1912. A. L. Burt Company.
Hopalong Cassidy and the Eagle's Brood. abridged ed. Clarence Edward Mulford. LC 50-6601. (His Hopalong Cassidy series). 1950. Garden City Pub. Co.
Hopalong Cassidy and the Eagle's Brood. Clarence Edward Mulford. LC 73-89653. 1973. 6.95. Aeonian Press.
Hopalong Cassidy and the Eagle's Brood. Clarence Edward Mulford. LC 31-6863. Doubleday, Doran & Company, Inc.
Hopalong Cassidy & the Riders of High Rock. Tex Burns, pseud. 320p. 1974. Repr. of 1951 ed. lib. bdg. 12.05x (ISBN 0-88411-207-1). Amereon Ltd.
Hopalong Cassidy and the Riders of High Rock. Louis L'Amour. LC 73-89654. 1973. 6.95. Aeonian Press.
Hopalong Cassidy and the Riders of High Rock: By Tex Burns Pseud. 1st Ed. Louis L'Amour. LC 51-13671. (Double D western). 1951. Doubleday.
Hopalong Cassidy & the Rustlers of West Fork. Tex Burns, pseud. 1976. Repr. of 1950 ed. lib. bdg. 11.40 (ISBN 0-88411-242-X). Amereon Ltd.
Hopalong Cassidy and the Rustlers of West Fork. Louis L'Amour. LC 76-40931. 1976. 5.95. Aeonian Press.
Hopalong Cassidy and the Rustlers of West Fork: By Tex Burns Pseud. 1st Ed. Louis L'Amour. LC 51-9214. (Double D western). 1951. Doubleday.
Hopalong Cassidy and the Trail to Seven Pines: By Tex Burns Pseud. 1st Ed. Louis L'Amour. LC 51-4765. (Double D western). 1951. Doubleday.
Hopalong Cassidy & the Trail to Seven Pines. Tex Burns, pseud. 1976. Repr. of 1950 ed. lib. bdg. 12.05x (ISBN 0-88411-243-8). Amereon Ltd.
Hopalong Cassidy and the Trail to Seven Pines. Louis L'Amour. LC 76-40930. 1976. 5.95. Aeonian Press.
Hopalong Cassidy Big Three. Clarence Edward Mulford. LC 40-91403. 1940. The Sun Dial Press.
Hopalong Cassidy Returns. abridged ed. Clarence Edward Mulford. LC 50-6602. (His Hopalong Cassidy series). 1950. Garden City Pub. Co.
Hopalong Cassidy Returns. Clarence Edward Mulford. LC 73-89639. 1974. 6.95. Aeonian Press.
Hopalong Cassidy Returns. Clarence Edward Mulford. LC 24-21144. 1924. Doubleday, Page & Company.
Hopalong Cassidy Returns. Clarence Edward Mulford. LC 43-4986. 1943. Triangle Books.
Hopalong Cassidy Serves a Writ. Clarence Edward Mulford. LC 73-89642. 1974. 6.95. Aeonian Press.
Hopalong Cassidy Serves a Writ. Clarence Edward Mulford. LC 42-50433. 1942. The Sun Dial Press.
Hopalong Cassidy Serves a Writ. A Double D Western. Clarence Edward Mulford. LC 41-19195. 1941. Doubleday, Doran and Co., Inc.
Hopalong Cassidy Takes Cards. Clarence Edward Mulford. LC 73-89643. 1974. 6.95. Aeonian Press.
Hopalong Cassidy Takes Cards. Clarence Edward Mulford. LC 50-479918. (His Hopalong Cassidy series). 1937. Garden City Pub. Co.
Hopalong Cassidy Takes Cards. Clarence Edward Mulford. LC 38-3722. 1937. Doubleday, Doran & Company, Inc.
Hopalong Cassidy Takes Cards. Clarence Edward Mulford. LC 39-256. 1938. The Sun Dial Press, Inc.
Hopalong Cassidy Takes Cards. Clarence Edward Mulford. LC 42-979396. 1942. Triangle Books.
Hopalong Cassidy: Trouble Shooter. Tex Burns, pseud. 1976. Repr. of 1952 ed. lib. bdg. 12.05x (ISBN 0-88411-241-1, 241). Amereon Ltd.
Hopalong Cassidy, Trouble Shooter. Louis L'Amour. LC 80-18368. 1980. 9.60 (ISBN 0-88411-241-1). Aeonian Press.
Hopalong Cassidy, Trouble Shooter: By Tex Burns Pseud. 1st Ed. Louis L'Amour. LC 52-5122. 1952. Doubleday.

Hopalong Cassidy with the Trail Herd. Clarence Edward Mulford. LC 50-6604. (His Hopalong Cassidy series). 1950. Garden City Pub. Co.

Hopalong Cassidy's Bar 20 Rides Again. Clarence Edward Mulford. LC 50-6605. (His Hopalong Cassidy series). 1950. Garden City Pub. Co.

Hopalong Cassidy's Protege. Clarence Edward Mulford. LC 73-89640. 1974. 6.95. Aeonian Press.

Hopalong Cassidy's Protege. Clarence Edward Mulford. LC 26-4941. 1926. Doubleday, Page & Company.

Hope & Glory. Leslie Arlen. (Borodins Ser.: Bk. 4). (Orig.). 1982. pap. 3.25 (ISBN 0-515-06041-0). Jove Pubns.

Hope Benham. A Story for Girls. Nora Perry. LC 4-18935. 1903. Little, Brown, and Company.

Hope Chest. Mark Lee Luther. LC 18-4156. 1918. Little, Brown, and Company.

Hope Deferred. Jeanette Seletz. LC 43-6459. 1943. The Macmillan Company.

Hope for the Flowers. Trina Paulus. LC 74-179985. (Illus.). 1972. (pbk.) 4.95. Newman Press.

Hope Hathaway: A Story of Western Ranch Life. Frances Parker. 1904. C. M. Clark Publishing Co. (Inc.

Hope Leslie: Or, Early Times in the Massachusetts. Catharine Maria Sedgwick. LC 72-8150. 1972. (ISBN 0-8422-8107-X). MSS Information Corp.

Hope Leslie: Or, Early Times in the Massachusetts. Catharine Maria Sedgwick. LC 16-7005. 1827. White, Gallaher, and White.

Hope Leslie: Or, Early Times in the Massachusetts. Catharine Maria Sedgwick. LC 8-11241. 1842. Harper & Brothers.

Hope Loring. Lilian Lida Bell. LC 2-25045. 1903. L. C. Page & Company.

Hope Meredith. A Novel. Eliza Tabor Stephenson. (Seaside Library, v. 32, no. 652). 1879. G. Munro.

Hope Mills: Or, Between Friend and Sweetheart. Amanda Minnie Douglas. Lothrop, Lee & Shepard Co.

Hope of Earth. Margaret Lee Runbeck. LC 47-30361. 1947. Houghton Mifflin Co.

Hope of Glory: Being Part of a Correspondence Written in the Roman Empire Between the Years 52 and 66 A. D. William Schuyler. Ed. by Fisher, Mary. LC 16-21062. 1915. The Four Seas Company.

Hope of Happiness. Meredith Nicholson. LC 23-13882. 1923. C. Scribner's Sons.

Hope of Heaven. John O'Hara. LC 38-6976. Harcourt, Brace and Company.

Hope of Heaven. John O'Hara. 1973. (pbk.) 1.25. Popular Lib.

Hope of Living. John Hyatt Downing. LC 39-6114. 1939. G. P. Putnam's Sons.

Hope of Living. John Hyatt Downing. LC 39-6114. 1939. G. P. Putnam's Sons.

Hope of Refuge. 1st Ed. Sikes Johnson. LC 56-5929. 1956. Little, Brown.

Hope of the House. Agnes Sweetman Castle & Castle, Egerton. LC 15-19415. 1915. Cassell and Company, Ltd.

Hope of the House. Agnes Sweetman Castle & Castle, Egerton. LC 15-19969. 1915. 1.35. D. Appleton and Company.

Hope Should Always: Stories. Ann Jones. LC 72-93763. (Breakthrough Bks). 124p. 1973. 8.95 (ISBN 0-8262-0139-3); pap. 5.95 (ISBN 0-8262-0138-5). U of Mo Pr.

Hope, the Hermit. Ada Ellen Bayly. LC 90-235. 1898. Longmans, Green, & Co.

Hope to Die. Hillary Waugh. LC 48-6729. (Gargoyle mystery). 1948. Coward-McCann.

Hope Trueblood. Patience Worth. Curran, Mrs. Pearl Lenore (Pollard) 1888- & Yost, Casper Salathiel, 1864- Ed. LC 18-10176. 1918. H. Holt and Company.

Hopedale Tavern and What It Wrought. J. William Van Namee. LC 71-137732. (American fiction reprint series). (Illus.). 1970. Books for Libraries Press.

Hopeful Heart. Philip Hamilton Gibbs. 1948. Ziff-Davis Pub. Co.

Hopeful Heart. Philip Hamilton Gibbs. LC 47-94091. Hutchinson & Co. Ltd.

Hopeful Journey. Beatrice Kean Stapleton Seymour. LC 23-14269. 1923. T. Seltzer.

Hopeless Case. Edgar Fawcett. LC 76-85683. (American fiction reprint series). 1969. Books for Libraries Press.

Hopeless Case. Fawcett, Edgar. LC 6-38794. 1880. Houghton, Mifflin and Company.

Hopeless Case: The Remarkable Experience of an Unromantic Individual with a Romantic Name. Luther H Bickford. LC 6-12907. 1889. C. H. Kerr & Company.

Hopes and Fears: Or, Scenes from the Life of a Spinster. Charlotte Mary Yonge. LC 9-12144. 1861. D. Appleton and Company.

Hopes and Fears: Or, Scenes from the Life of a Spinster. Charlotte Mary Yonge. (On cover: Seaside library. Pocket ed. no 800). 1886. G. Munro.

Hopes & Promises. Dusty Sang. 384p. (Orig.). 1981. pap. 2.95 (ISBN 0-932844-03-0). R H Sang & Son.

Hope's Heart Bells. A Romance. Sara Louisa Vickers Oberholtzer. LC 7-331873. 1884. J. B. Lippincott & Co.

Hope's Heart Bells. A Romance. Sara Louisa Vickers Oberholtzer. LC 7-33187. 1884. J. B. Lippincott & Co.

Hope's Highway: A Novel. Sarah Lee Fleming. LC 79-144607. 1973. 10.00 (ISBN 0-404-00158-0). AMS Press.

Hope's Highway: A Novel. Sarah Lee Fleming. LC 18-21534. 1918. The Neale Publishing Company.

Hopi Girl. Dama Margaret Smith. LC 31-32059. 1931. Stanford University Press.

Hopi: The Cliff-Dweller. Martha Jewett. LC 10-35147. Educational Publishing Co.

Hopie & the Los Homes Gang. Hilary McGuire. (Illus.). 1978. pap. 1.95 o.p. (ISBN 0-8189-1150-6). Alba.

Hopjoy Was Here. Colin Watson. (Scene of the Crime Ser.: No. 53). 1982. pap. 2.50 (ISBN 0-440-13625-3). Dell.

Hopkins Manuscript. Robert Cedric Sherriff. LC 63-16131. (Macmillan's library of science fiction classics). 1963. Macmillan.

Hoppy's Adventure. Vincent A. Kelly. 3.75 o.p. Vantage.

Hopscotch. Julio Cortazar. LC 66-10409. (Bard book). 1975. (pbk.) 2.65 (ISBN 0-380-00372-4). Avon.

Hopscotch. Brian Wynne Garfield. LC 74-14536. 1975. 7.95 (ISBN 0-87131-164-X). M. Evans; Distributed by Lippincott, Philadelphia.

Hopscotch. Brian Wynne Garfield. 1976. (pbk.) 1.75. Fawcett.

Hopscotch: Tr. from Spanish by Gregory Rabassa. Julio Cortazar. LC 66-104092. 6.95. Pantheon.

Hopscotch. Tr. from Spanish by Gregory Rabassa. Julio Cortazar. (Signet bk., Q3329). 1967. New Amer. Lib.

Horace Blake. Josephine Mary Hope-Scott W. P. Ward Ward. LC 13-22813. 1913. G. P. Putnam's Sons.

Horace Chase. Constance Fenimore Woolson. LC 77-104603. 1970. (ISBN 0-8398-2177-8). Literature House.

Horace Chase: A Novel. Constance Fenimore Woolson. LC 8-37230. 1894. Harper & Brothers.

Horace McLean: A Story of a Search in a Strange Place. Alice O'Hanlon. (Franklin square library, no. 147). 1880. Harper & Brothers.

Horace Sippog and the Sirens' Song. Su Walton. LC 68-12149. 1968. W. Morrow.

Horace Vernon: Or, Fashionable Life ... LC 7-5235. 1839. Lea and Blanchard.

Horacio, a Tale of Brazil. Robert Willson Fenn. LC 11-17623. 1911. The Author.

Horacio; a Tale of Brazil. Robert Willson Fenn. LC 13-26687. 1.00. American Tract Society.

Horan: The Story of the World's First Cure for Sex. Philip C Lewis. LC 74-13438. 1974. (ISBN 0-06-012604-3). Harper & Row.

Horatia. Mary Ann Gibbs. 1973. pap. 0.95 o.p. (345-26502-5-095). Beagle Bks.

Horatio and Anna: A Tale of Recent Occurrences in the West. In Chief Founded on Facts. Presenting Their Correspondence While Resident in the City of Cincinnati, in Original Poetry... To Which Are Added: the Beauties of the Mind Preferable to All Personal Attractions: and Two Elegies, Written on the Death of Two Individuals in the Said City, in the Years 1840 and 1841. H. Burgoyne Bowen. LC 20-171362. 1842. R. C. Langdon, Printer.

Horatio Plodgers: A Story of to-Day. S. H Church. W. B. Smith & Co.

Horatio's Story. Gordon Congdon King. LC 23-14115. Boni and Liveright.

Hordes of the Red Butcher. Grant Stockbridge. (Spider#2). 1975. (pbk.) 0.95 (ISBN 0-671-77944-3). Pocket Books.

Horizon. Robert Carse. LC 27-7189. 1927. Dodd, Mead and Company.

Horizon. Lee Head. LC 81-8561. 13.95 (ISBN 0-399-12638-4). Putnam.

Horizon. Helen MacInnes Highet. 1946. Little, Brown and Company.

Horizon. Helen MacInnes. 192p. 1981. pap. 2.50 (ISBN 0-449-24012-6, Crest). Fawcett.

Horizon. Helen MacInnes. LC 46-3853. 1971. 6.95 (ISBN 0-15-142171-4). HarBraceJ.

Horizon Book of Lost Worlds see Lost Worlds.

Horizon Fever... Robert Dunn. LC 32-33986. 1932. A. and C. Boni.

Horizon Home: By Jeanne Bowman Pseud. Peggy O'More, pseud. Arcadia House.

Horizon Stories. Cyril Connolly. LC 46-2867. 1946. The Vanguard Press.

Horizons. Dorothy Fletcher. (Orig.). 1981. pap. 2.95 (ISBN 0-89083-808-9). Zebra.

Horizons. Janet Thomas Van Osdel. LC 30-31797. The Christopher Publishing House.

Horizons of Love. Barbara Cartland. (Barbara Cartland Ser.). (Orig.). pap. 1.75 (ISBN 0-515-05569-7). Jove Pubns.

Horizons of the Mind, a New Odyssey. Ramon Fernandez-Marina & Eckardt, Ursula Maria Von. LC 64-20428. 1964. Philosophical Library.

Horizons of the Mind: A New Odyssey, by Ramon Fernandez-Marina, Ursula Maria Von Eckardt. Ramon Fernandez-Marina & Ursula Maria Von Eckardt. LC 64-20428. 1965. 7.00. Philosophical.

Horizontal Hold. R. R Irvine. 1978. 1.75 (ISBN 0-445-04321-0). Popular Library.

Horizontal Hour. Robert Marks. LC 57-11074. 1957. D. McKay Co.

Horizontal Man. Helen Eustis. LC 75-44970. (Fifty Classics of Crime Fiction, 1900-1950; 16). 1976. 12.00 (ISBN 0-8240-2365-X). Garland Pub.

Horizontal Man. Helen Eustis. LC 46-2671. 1946. Harper & Brothers.

Horizontal Man. Helen Eustis. LC 81-17933. 1982. 3.50 (ISBN 0-14-000718-0). Penguin Books.

Horizontal Woman see Social Worker.

Hormone Holocaust. L. Thomas Reineke. 1974. 8.50 o.p. (ISBN 0-682-47893-8). Exposition.

Hormone Holocaust: A Novel. 1st. ed. L. Thomas Reineke. 1974. 8.50 (ISBN 0-682-47893-8). Exposition Press.

Horn. John Clellon Holmes. LC 58-8763. 1958. Random House.

Horn. D. Keith Mano. LC 69-11730. 1969. 5.95. Houghton Mifflin.

Horn & the Forest. Jamie Lee Cooper. 1963. 4.00 o.p. Bobbs.

Horn and the Roses: A Novel Based on the Life of Peter-Paul Rubens. Ira Jan Wallach. LC 47-466071. 1947. Boni and Gaer.

Horn Book. 1971. pap. 1.75 o.p. (Z1070K, Zebra). Grove.

Horn Crown. Andre Norton, pseud. (Science Fiction Ser.). 1981. pap. 2.95 (ISBN 0-87997-635-7, UE1635). DAW Bks.

Horn of Africa. Philip Caputo. 544p. 1981. pap. 3.95 (ISBN 0-440-13675-X). Dell.

Horn of Africa: A Novel. Philip Caputo. LC 79-27513. 12.95 (ISBN 0-03-042136-5). Holt, Rinehart and Winston.

Horn of Life. Gertrude Franklin Horn Atherton. LC 42-22141. 1942. D. Appleton-Century Company, Incorporated.

Horn of Plenty. Valma Clark. LC 45-8603. 1945. Duell, Sloan and Pearce.

Horn of Roland. Edith Pargeter. LC 74-3801. 1974. 5.95 (ISBN 0-688-00320-6). Morrow.

Horn of Roland. Ellis Peters. 224p. 1974. 5.95 o.p. (ISBN 0-688-00320-6). Morrow.

Horn of the Hunter. Robert Chester Ruark. 1970. pap. 0.95 o.p. (M1488, Crest). Fawcett World.

Horn of the Ram. Gloria Howe Bremkamp. LC 81-68640. 1981. 7.95 (ISBN 0-915684-98-5). Christian Herald Books.

Horn of Time. Poul Anderson. LC 78-147. (Anderson, Paul, 1926-. The World's of Paul Anderson). 1978. 8.50 (ISBN 0-8398-2428-9). Gregg Press.

Hornbeam Tree: A Novel. 1st Ed. Cid Ricketts Sumner. LC 53-107651. 1953. Bobbs-Merrill.

Hornblower & the Atropos. Cecil Scott Forester. 1953. 9.95 (ISBN 0-316-28911-6). Little.

Hornblower & the Atropos. Cecil Scott Forester. (Hornblower Saga Ser.: No. 4). 1980. pap. 2.50 (ISBN 0-523-41389-0). Pinnacle Bks.

Hornblower and the Atropos. 1st Ed. Cecil Scott Forester. LC 52-9090. 1953. Little, Brown.

Hornblower & the Hotspur. Cecil Scott Forester. 1962. 9.95 (ISBN 0-316-28899-3). Little.

Hornblower & the Hotspur. Cecil Scott Forester. (Hornblower Saga Ser.: No. 3). 352p. 1980. pap. 2.75 (ISBN 0-523-41790-X). Pinnacle Bks.

Hornblower During the Crisis. Cecil Scott Forester. (Hornblower#11). 1975. (pbk.) 1.25 (ISBN 0-523-00391-9). Pinnacle Books.

Hornblower During the Crisis, and Two Stories: Hornblower's Temptation and The Last Encounter. Cecil Scott Forester. LC 67-21100. 1967. Little, Brown.

Hornblower Goes to Sea. Selected by G. P. Griggs. Illus. by Geoffrey Whittam 1st Amer. Ed. Cecil Scott Forester. LC 65-17322. (Cadet ed. of Hornblower, v.1). 1965. 2.95. Little.

Hornblower in Captivity. Selected by G. P. Griggs. Illus. by Geoffrey Whittam 1st Amer. Ed. Cecil Scott Forester. LC 65-17323. (Cadet ed. of Hornblower, v.3). 1965. 2.95. Little.

Hornblower Takes Command. Selected by G. P. Griggs. Illus. by Geoffrey Whittam 1st Amer. Ed. Cecil Scott Forester. LC 65-17324. (Cadet ed. of Hornblower, v.2). 1965. 2.95. Little.

Hornblower's Triumph. Selected by G. P. Griggs. Illus. by Geoffrey Whittam 1st Amer. Ed. Cecil Scott Forester. LC 65-173257. (Cadet ed. of Hornblower, v.4). 1965. 2.95. Little.

Hornbook for the Double Damned: An American Satiricon. Samuel Milton Elam. (Meridian books, MG47). 1962. World Pub. Co.

Horncasters. Victor Hugo Johnson. LC 47-310174. 1947. Greenberg.

Horned Cat. authorized ed. James Maclaren Cobban. LC 6-26765. (On cover: Lovell's international series, no. 175). 1891. J. W. Lovell Company.

Horned Shepherd. Edgar Jepson. LC 27-24497. 1927. Macy-Masius.

Horned Snake. Louis Oliver. Ed. by Stanley H. Barken. (Cross-Cultural Chapbook: No. 15). 16p. 1981. pap. 2.00 (ISBN 0-89304-814-3). Cross Cult.

Hornehurst Rectory. Mary Frances Cusack. LC 6-32244. 1872. D. & J. Sadlier & Company.

Hornet's Longboat. William Roos. LC 40-335969. 1940. Houghton Mifflin Company.

Hornets' Nest. Helen Ashton. LC 35-1210. 1935. The Macmillan Company.

Hornets' Nest. Bruno Fischer. LC 44-17053. 1944. Books Inc., Distributed by W. Morrow & Company.

Hornet's Nest. Nancy Mann Waddel Wilson Woodrow Woodrow. LC 17-925201. 1917. Little, Brown, and Company.

Hornet's Nest: A Story of Love and War. Edward Payson Roe. LC 13-177226. Dodd, Mead and Company.

Horns for Our Adornment. Aksel Sandemose & Gay-Tifft, Eugene, Tr. LC 38-25349. 1938. A. A. Knopf.

Horns for the Devil. Louis Malley. LC 51-5188. 1951. Appleton-Century-Crofts.

Horn's Fort. Ernest C. Miller. 208p. 1975. 5.95 o.p. (ISBN 0-8059-2173-7). Dorrance.

Horns of Capricorn. Helen Topping Miller. LC 50-9494. 1950. Appleton-Century-Crofts.

Horns of Fear. Translated from the Spanish by Ilsa Barea. 1st American Ed. Angel Maria De Lera. LC 61-565095. 1961. Dutton.

Horns of Glass. Paul Eldridge. LC 43-3425. 1943. Harbinger House.

Horns of Ramadan. Arthur Cheney Train. LC 28-236612. 1928. C. Scribner's Sons.

Horns on Their Heads. R. A Lafferty. LC 76-41034. (Illus.). 1976. (ISBN 0-914010-01-8). Pendragon Press.

Hornstein's Boy. John Donaldson Voelker. LC 62-11104. 1962. St. Martin's Press.

Horoscope. A Romance of the Reign of Francois Ii. Alexandre Dumas. LC 6-43607. (Half-title: The romances of Alexandre Dumas. New series). 1897. Little, Brown, and Company.

Horoscope Cannot Lie & Other Stories. G. D. Khosla. 4.50x o.p. (ISBN 0-210-33991-8). Asia.

Horowitz & Mrs. Washington. Henry Denker. LC 79-1114. 10.95 (ISBN 0-399-12341-5). Putnam.

Horrible Man. Michael Avallone. 1972. pap. 0.75 o.p. (07220). Curtis.

Horrible Picnic. Daniel Caro. 3.00 o.p. Carlton.

Horrid Mysteries: A Story Tr. from the German of the Marquis of Grosse by Peter Will. Karl Friedrich August Grosse. LC 68-98586. (Northanger Set of Jane Austen Horrid Novels). 1968. Folio Pr.

Horror. William Voltz. (Perry Rhodan#66). (Illus.). 1975. (pbk.) 1.25. Ace Books.

Horror & Supernatural. Playboy Press Editors. pap. 0.95 o.p. (BA119). Playboy.

Horror at Fontenay. Alexandre Dumas. LC 75-26180. 192p. 1976. 7.95 o.p. (ISBN 0-312-39095-5). St Martin.

Horror at Fontenay. Alan Hull Walton & Alexandre Dumas. LC 75-26180. (Dennis Wheatley library of the occult; v. 25). 1976. 7.95. St. Martin's Press.

Horror at Henning House. Evelyn Wray. (YA) 1980. 6.95 (Avalon). Bouregy.

Horror at Oakdeene and Others. Brian Lumley. LC 76-17994. 1977. 7.50 (ISBN 0-87054-078-5). Arkham House.

Horror from the Hills. LC 63-3144. 1963. Arkham House.

Horror from the Tombs. Florence Stevenson. (O.s.i.). 1977. pap. 1.50 o.s.i. (AD1658, Award). Univ Pub & Dist.

Horror House. 1976. pap. 1.50 (ISBN 0-532-15212-3). Woodhill.

Horror House. Paulette Warren. (Orig.). 1973. pap. 0.95 o.s.i. (75-427). Lancer.

Horror House. Carolyn Wells. LC 31-12129. 1931. J. B. Lippincott Company.

Horror House. J. N. Williamson. LC 80-85113. 304p. (Orig.). 1981. pap. 2.95 (ISBN 0-87216-832-8). Playboy Pbks.

Horror Hunters. Ed. by Roger Elwood & Vic Ghidalia. 1971. pap. 0.75 o.p. (532-75416-075). Manor Bks.

Horror Hunters. Ed. by Roger Elwood & Vic Ghidalia. (Horror Anthology Ser). 192p. 1975. pap. 0.95 o.p. (532-95406-095). Manor Bks.

Horror in the Museum. Howard Phillips Lovecraft et al. 1971. pap. 0.95 o.p. (95159). Beagle Bks.

Horror in the Museum, and Other Revisions. Howard Phillips Lovecraft. LC 70-121893. 1970. 7.50. Arkham House.

Horror Mansion. J. N. Williamson. (Orig.). 1982. pap. 2.95 (ISBN 0-8217-1051-6). Zebra.

Horror of Cabrini-Green. Bruce C. Conn. 224p. (Orig.). 1975. pap. 1.95 (ISBN 0-87067-658-X, BH023). Holloway.

Horror of Cabrini-Green. Bruce C Conn. 1975. (pbk.) 1.50 (ISBN 0-87067-470-6). Holloway House.

Horror of Montauk Cave. Karen Liberatore. (Perspectives I Novel Ser.). 48p. 1982. 2.50 (ISBN 0-87879-294-5). Acad Therapy.

Horror on the Asteroid: And Other Tales of Planetary Horror. Edmond Hamilton. LC 75-5745. (Gregg Press science fiction series). 1975. 12.50 (ISBN 0-8398-2304-5). Gregg Press.

Horror on the Asteroid & Other Tales of Planetary Horror. Edmond Hamilton. (Science Fiction Ser). 272p. 1975. Repr. of 1936 ed. lib. bdg. 12.50 o.p. (ISBN 0-8398-2304-5, Gregg). G K Hall.

Horror on the Ruby X. Frances Kirkwood Crane. 1956. Random House.

Horror Range. Cliff Austin. LC 40-3775. Greenberg.

Horror Story. Oliver McNab. LC 79-14990. 1979. 8.95 (ISBN 0-395-27765-5). Houghton Mifflin.

Horror Trek. R. W. Levering. 6.50 o.p. (ISBN 0-8062-1036-2). Carlton.

Horrors. Charles L. Grant. LC 81-47255. 224p. (Orig.). 1981. pap. 2.25 (ISBN 0-87216-905-7). Playboy Pbks.

Horrors! Ferdinand Charles Valentine. LC 8-308713. S. W. Green's Son.

Horrors, Horrors, Horrors. Ed. by Helen Hoke. LC 78-2350. (Terrific Triple Titles Ser.). (Illus.). 1978. lib. bdg. 8.90 s&l (ISBN 0-531-02211-0). Watts.

Horrors of Love. Jean Dutourd. LC 75-3991. 1976. 30.00 (ISBN 0-8371-7481-3). Greenwood Press.

Horrors of Love. Jean Dutourd. LC 67-12873. 1967. Doubleday.

Horrors of Oakendale Abbey: A Romance. LC 7-7155. 1812. J. F. Gilbert.

Horrors of Paris. A Sequel to "The Mohicans of Paris.". Alexandre Dumas. LC 6-42335. 1875. T. B. Peterson & Brothers.

Horrors Unknown. Ed. by Sam Maskowitz. 1970. 5.95 o.p. (ISBN 0-8027-5534-8). Walker & Co.

Horrors Unknown. Ed. by Samuel Moscowitz. (Berkley Medallion Book). 1976. (pbk.) 0.95 (ISBN 0-425-03063-6). Berkley Publishing Corp.

Horrors Unknown: Newly Discovered Masterpieces by Great Names in Fantastic Terror. Ed. by Samuel Moskowitz. LC 70-155734. 1971. 5.95 (ISBN 0-8027-5534-8). Walker.

Horrors Unseen. Ed. by Samuel Moskowitz. (Berkley medallion book). 1974. (pbk.) 0.75 (ISBN 0-425-02583-7). Berkley Pub. Co.

Horse. Siegfried Stander. LC 69-15701. (Illus.). 1969. 4.50. World Pub. Co.

Horse and Buggy. Bellamy Partridge. LC 37-5390. Arcadia House.

Horse and Buggy Memories: The Story of a Life That Was Full of Romance and Interesting Incidents. Thomas White Stewart. LC 39-16408. Times-Mirror.

Horse and His Shadow: A Novel. Enrique Amorim. Tr. by O'Connell, Richard L. LC 43-121462. 1943. C. Scribner's Sons.

Horse & Two Goats. R. K. Narayan. LC 70-83229. (Illus.). 1970. 5.75 o.p. (ISBN 0-670-37885-2, Studio). Viking Pr.

Horse Called Ringo. Anthony Licata. 1981. 4.75 (ISBN 0-8062-1758-8). Carlton.

Horse Called September. Anne Digby. 128p. 1982. 8.95 (ISBN 0-312-39143-9). St Martin.

Horse Crazy. Jesse Lilienthal. J. Messner, Inc.

Horse Fair. James A. Baldwin. LC 76-9890. (Illus.). 1976. 19.75 (ISBN 0-8486-0201-3). Core Collection Books.

Horse Fair. James A. Baldwin. LC 6-6886. 1895. The Century Co.

Horse for Christmas Morning & Other Stories. Gordon Grand. (Illus.). 1970. 12.50 o.p. (ISBN 0-87691-019-3). Winchester Pr.

Horse Goddess. Morgan Llywelyn. LC 82-6234. (Illus.). 1982. 15.95 (ISBN 0-395-32514-5). Houghton Mifflin.

Horse Heaven: By Chuck Stanley Pseud. Charles Stanley Strong. LC 54-133582. 1954. Arcadia House.

Horse Heaven Hill. Zane Grey. LC 61-4902. (Great western edition 58). Grosset & Dunlap.

Horse Heaven Hill. 1st Ed. Zane Grey. LC 59-12465. 1959. Harper.

Horse in Arizona. Louis Paul. LC 36-15258. 1936. Doubleday, Doran & Co., Inc.

Horse in the Gray Flannel Suit. Eric Hatch. (Laurel-leaf lib., 3727). 1968. Dell.

Horse in the Moon: Twelve Short Stories. Luigi Pirandello & Putnam, Samuel, Tr. LC 32-2348. E. P. Dutton & Co., Inc.

Horse in the Sky. Margerie Bonner. LC 47-11090. 1947. C. Scribner's Sons.

Horse Is Dead. Robert Klane. LC 68-14493. 1968. Random House.

Horse Is Dead. Robert Klane. 1976. (pbk.) 1.50. Ballantine.

Horse-Ketchum. Dane Coolidge. LC 30-10814. 1930. E. P. Dutton & Company, Inc.

Horse Knows the Way. John O'Hara. LC 64-7751. 1964. Random House.

Horse-Leech's Daughters. Margaret Doyle Jackson. 1904. Houghton, Mifflin and Company.

Horse-Lovers Anthology. Shirley Faulkner-Horne. 1980. 11.00x (ISBN 0-85493-090-6, Pub. by Witherby). State Mutual Bk.

Horse Lover's Treasury. Ed. by Genevieve Murphy. (Illus.). 1964. 4.95 o.p. Doubleday.

Horse Marines. Rudyard Kipling. LC 10-22792. 1910. Doubleday, Page & Company.

Horse Mistress. Justine Paris. pap. 1.95 o.s.i. (OPH-249, Ophelia). Olympia.

Horse of Another Color. Carolyn Osborn. LC 77-21724. (Illinois short fiction). 7.50. (ISBN 0-252-00671-2) (ISBN 0-252-00672-0). University of Illinois Press.

Horse of Darius. Justin Cartwright. LC 79-27025. 9.95 (ISBN 0-02-521500-0). Macmillan.

Horse of Her Own: A Novel. Barbara Webster. LC 51-13011. 1951. Longmans, Green.

Horse of Selene. Juanita Casey. LC 72-184715. 1971. (ISBN 0-85105-187-1). Dolmen Press.

Horse of Selene. Juanita Casey. LC 77-184476. 1972. 6.95 (ISBN 0-670-37913-1). Grossman Publishers.

Horse of Thunder. Leigh Nichols. (Orig.). 1982. pap. write for info. (ISBN 0-671-43266-4). PB.

Horse Shoe Bottoms. Thomas Tippett. LC 35-15729. 1935. Harper & Brothers.

Horse Shoe Robinson... John Pendleton Kennedy. (Lovell's library, v. 2, no. 67). 1883. J. W. Lovell Company.

Horse-Shoe Robinson. John Pendleton Kennedy. LC 9-2676. (Standard literature series. v. 10). 1897. University Publishing Company.

Horse-Shoe Robinson. John Pendleton Kennedy. Ed. by Leisy, Ernest Erwin. LC 37-4088. (Half-title: American fiction series; general editor, H. H. Clark). American Book Company.

Horse Shoe Robinson: A Tale of the Tory Ascendency. John Pendleton Kennedy. LC 3-16071. 1835. Carey, Lea & Blanchard.

Horse Shoe Robinson: A Tale of the Tory Accendency. rev. ed. John Pendleton Kennedy. LC 3-19517. 1852. G. P. Putnam.

Horse Shoe Robinson. A Tale of the Tory Ascendency. rev. ed. John Pendleton Kennedy. 1865. J. B. Lippincott & Co.

Horse-Shoe Robinson. Edited with Introd., Chronology, and Bibliography by Ernest E. Leisy. Kennedy, John Pendleton. Ed. by Leisy, Ernest E. LC 62-17003. (American fiction series). 1962. Hafner Pub. Co.

Horse Soldiers. Harold Sinclair. LC 55-11296. Harper.

Horse-Stealers: And Other Stories. Anton Pavlovich Chekhov. Tr. by Garnett, Constance (Black) LC 21-12357. (Half-title: The tales of Chekhov, vol. x). 1921. The Macmillan Company.

Horse That Could Whistle "Dixie" And Other Stories. Jerome Weidman. LC 39-13611. 1939. Simon and Schuster.

Horse That Played the Outfield. William Heuman. pap. 0.95 o.p. (ISBN 0-396-06301-2). Dodd.

Horse Thief Canyon. George Nutting. LC 40-85995. 1941. W. Morrow and Company.

Horse-Thief Gulch. Samuel Harkness. LC 28-6413. J. H. Sears & Company, Inc.

Horse Thief Masquerade. William L Hopson. LC 49-9527. 1949. Phoenix Press.

Horse Thief: Or, The Maiden and Negro, A Tale of the Prairies. H. A Harris. LC 7-2625. 1845. Gleason's Publishing Hall.

Horse Thief Trail. J. D. Harkleroad. 1980. pap. 1.75 o.s.i. (ISBN 0-8439-0716-9, Leisure Bks). Nordon Pubns.

Horse Thieves of Ballysaggert: And Other Stories. Brian Talbot Cleeve. LC 67-356. 1966. Mercier Press.

Horse Tradin' Ben K. Green. (Illus.). (YA) 1967. 13.95 (ISBN 0-394-42929-X). Knopf.

Horse Under Water. Len Deighton. 1980. pap. 2.50 (ISBN 0-425-05475-6). Berkley Pub.

Horse Under Water: A Novel. 1st Amer. Ed. Len Deighton. LC 67-10088. 1968. 4.95. Putnam.

Horse with Eight Hands. Joan Phipson. LC 74-76280. 1974. 7.50 (ISBN 0-689-50013-0). Atheneum.

Horseback Government; Ad Interim Administration, Republic of Texas, 1836. Ruth Juby Carnes. LC 74-3188. (Illus.). 1974. 4.95 (ISBN 0-8111-0521-0). Naylor Co.

Horseclan, No. 9: The Witch Goddess. Robert Adams. 1982. pap. 2.75 (ISBN 0-451-11792-1, AE1792, Sig). NAL.

Horseclans, No. 1: The Coming of the Horseclans. Robert Adams. 1982. pap. 2.50 (ISBN 0-451-11652-6, AE1652, Sig). NAL.

Horseclans Odyssey. Robert Adams. (Orig.). 1981. pap. 2.75 (ISBN 0-451-09744-0, E9744, Sig). NAL.

Horsehead Crossing. Elmer Kelton. 144p. 1982. pap. 1.95 (ISBN 0-553-20845-4). Bantam.

Horseless Buggy. Katrine MacGlashan. LC 42-244342. 1942. Little, Brown and Co.

Horseman of Death. Robert McNair Wilson. LC 26-6760. 1928. J. B. Lippincott Company.

Horseman of the King (John Wesley) Cyril Davey. 1964. pap. 1.95 (ISBN 0-87508-605-5). Chr Lit.

Horseman of the Plains. Joseph Alexander Altsheler. 1976. Repr. of 1910 ed. lib. bdg. 19.10x (ISBN 0-88411-946-7). Amereon Ltd.

Horseman on Foot. Mary Nicholson. LC 38-931. 1937. Longmans, Green and Co.

Horseman on the Roof: Translated from the French by Jonathan Griffin. 1st American Ed. Jean Giono. LC 52-12177. 1954. Knopf.

Horseman, Pass by. Larry McMurtry. LC 79-4119. 1979. 1.95 (ISBN 0-14-004691-7). Penguin Books.

Horseman, Pass By. Larry McMurty. 1979. pap. 2.95 (ISBN 0-14-004691-7). Penguin.

Horseman: Pass by. 1st Ed. Larry McMurtry. 1961. Harper.

Horseman Riding by. Ronald Frederick Delderfield. LC 67-20800. 1967. Simon and Schuster.

Horsemaster. Thomas Broughton. LC 81-876. 13.50. Dutton.

Horsemen. Joseph Kessel. LC 68-17292. 1968. Farrar, Straus & Giroux.

Horsemen from Hell. Cover Painting by Frank McCarthy. Homer Hatten. LC 56-230673. (Gold medal books, 541). 1955. Fawcett Publications.

Horsemen of the Law. Frederic Franklyn Van De Water. LC 26-16148. 1926. D. Appleton and Company.

Horsemen of the Plains: A Story of the Great Cheyenne War. Joseph Alexander Altsheler. LC 10-22794. 1910. The Macmillan Company.

Horses and Men: Tales, Long and Short, from Our American Life. Sherwood Anderson. LC 24-3399. 1923. B. W. Huebsch, Inc.

Horse's Head. Evan Hunter. 1967. 4.95 o.p. Delacorte.

Horse's Head: A Novel. Evan Hunter. LC 67-14996. 1967. 4.95. Delacorte.

Horse's Head: A Novel. Evan Hunter. (3726). 1968. Dell.

Horses, Honor, and Women. John Henry Reese. LC 75-94330. 1970. 4.95. Doubleday.

Horses in the Kitchen: True Tales of Outback Australia. Illus. by John Raird. R. H Conquest. LC 65-23904. 1966. bds., 3.95. Tri-Ocean.

Horses in the Sky. Larry Barretto. LC 29-19782. The John Day Company.

Horse's Mouth. Joyce Cary. LC 58-4556. (Universal library, UL-48). Grosset & Dunlap.

Horse's Mouth: A Novel. 1st American Ed. Joyce Cary. LC 50-5264. 1950. Harper.

Horse's Mouth. With an Introd. by Andrew Wright. Joyce Cary. LC 58-14385. (Harper's modern classics). 1959. Harper.

Horses Nine: Stories of Harness and Saddle. Sewell Ford. LC 70-122701. (Short story index reprint series). (Illus.). 1970. Books for Libraries Press.

Horses Nine: Stories of Harness and Saddle. Sewell Ford. LC 3-6870. 1903. C. Scribner's Sons.

Horses of Instruction. Hazard Adams. LC 68-20059. 1968. Harcourt, Brace & World.

Horses of the Sun. Kathryn Marion Whitten. LC 42-7973. 1942. Meador Publishing Company.

Horses of the Sun: By Oriel Malet Pseud. 1st American Ed. Auriel Rosemary Malet Vaughan. LC 60-5272. 1960. Putnam.

Horses of Winter. A. A. T Davies. LC 68-14519. 1968. 4.95. Random House.

Horse's Tale. Samuel Langhorne Clemens. LC 7-34780. 1907. Harper & Brothers.

Horses, Women & Guns. Nelson Nye. 160p. 1975. pap. 0.95 (ISBN 0-532-15428-2). Woodhill.

Horseshoe Bend: By Bruce Palmer and John Clifford Giles. Bruce Palmer & John Clifford Giles. LC 62-9599. 1962. Simon and Schuster.

Horseshoe Combine. Leslie Charles Ernenwein. LC 49-9978. (Dutton Diamond D western). 1949. E. P. Dutton.

Horseshoe Kid. T. W. Ford. LC 48-28174. 1948. Phoenix Press.

Horseshoe Nails. George Weston. 1927. Dodd, Mead & Company.

Horseshoe Range. Michael Crowley. LC 36-22616. R. M. McBride & Company.

Horseshoe Robinson: A Tale of the Tory Ascendency in South Carolina, in 1780. John Pendleton Kennedy. LC 36-16941. 1928. A. L. Burt Company.

Horseshoe Trail. Donald Bayne Hobart. LC 52-11393. 1952. Arcadia House.

Horsethief Canyon. Jerry Brucker. 1981. pap. 1.95 (ISBN 0-8439-0911-0, Leisure Bks). Nordon Pubns.

Horsethief Creek. Harry Sinclair Drago. LC 44-7327. 1944. Doubleday, Doran and Co., Inc.

Horsethief Crossing. 1st Ed. Tom J Hopkins. LC 53-559699. (Double D western). 1953. Doubleday.

Horsethief Hole. Robert Ames Bennet. LC 36-5102. 1936. I. Washburn, Inc.

Horsethief Pass. Charles Horace Snow. LC 44-25088. 1944. Macrae-Smith-Company.

Horsy Set: A Novel. Pamela Moore. LC 63-7625. 1963. Simon and Schuster.

Hortense. Bertha Behrens. Tr. by Mary E. Almy. LC 6-9745. (On cover: Globe library. v. 1. no. 148). 1891. Rand, McNally & Company.

Hortensius: Friend of Nero. Edith Pargeter. LC 37-12719. 1937. The Greystone Press.

Horton Twins. Fannie Kilbourne. LC 74-142266. (Short story index reprint series). 1970. (ISBN 0-8369-3750-3). Books for Libraries Press.

Horton Twins. Fannie Kilbourne. LC 26-161935. 1926. Dodd, Mead and Company.

Hortons: Or, American Life at Home. Davis B Casseday. LC 6-22794. 1866. J. S. Claxton.

Hosannah Tree. Margaret Cochran Shedd. LC 67-10382. (Illus.). 1967. Doubleday.

Hosea Jackson. John K. Shannon. 1979. pap. 3.00 (ISBN 0-932282-43-1). Caledonia Pr.

Hospital. Frederick Boyden. LC 51-3690. 1951. Farrar, Straus and Young.

Hospital. Kenneth Fearing. LC 39-21567. Random House.

Hospital. Rhoda Truax. LC 32-456119. 1932. E. P. Dutton & Co., Inc.

Hospital. Agnes Brooks Young. LC 75-130349. 1970. 6.50. Simon and Schuster.

Hospital--Quiet Please. Henry Lieferant & Sylvia Saltzberg Lieferant. LC 41-11498. 1941. E. P. Dutton & Co., Inc.

Hospital Bums. Frank Dell' Isola. LC 40-358129. House of Field, Inc.

Hospital Cap: A Story. Oliver Perry Manlove. Broadway Publishing Co.

Hospital Homicides. Edward Spence De Puy. LC 38-776. Phoenix Press.

Hospital Horror. Otto O Binder. (Frankenstein horror series). 1973. (pbk) 0.75. Popular Library.

Hospital Makers. Irwin Philip Sobel. LC 72-79426. 1973. 7.95 (ISBN 0-385-00567-9). Doubleday.

Hospital Makers. Irwin Philip Sobel. (Crest Book, P2033). 1974. (pbk.) 1.25. Fawcett Pubns.

Hospital Murders. Means Davis. LC 34-1942. 1934. H. Smith and R. Hass.

Hospital Nocturne: A Novel. Alice Elinor Lambert. LC 32-314577. 1932. The Vanguard Press.

Hospital Ship. Martin Bax. LC 76-16033. 7.95 (ISBN 0-8112-0584-3) (ISBN 0-8112-0585-1). New Directions.

Hospital Ship. Martin Bax. LC 76-375601. 1976. 3.95 (ISBN 0-224-01255-X). Cape.

Hospital Sketches: And Camp and Fireside Stories. Louisa May Alcott. LC 9-2003. 1872. Roberts Brothers.

Hospital Sketches and Camp and Fireside Stories. Louisa May Alcott. LC 4-15057. 1892. Roberts Brothers.

Hospital Sketches. Introd. by Earl Schenck Miers. Louisa May Alcott. LC 57-12435. (American century series, S-15). 1957. Sagamore Press.

Hospital Station. James White. 1979. pap. 2.25 (ISBN 0-345-29613-3). Ballantine.

Hospital War. Charles H Knickerbocker. (3736). 1967. Dell.

Hospital War: By Charles H. Knickerbocker. 1st Ed. Charles H Knickerbocker. LC 66-11741. 1966. Doubleday.

Hospital Wife. Howard Warren. LC 40-6546. Phoenix Press.

Hospital Zone. Elizabeth Seifert. LC 73-79153. 1973. 6.95. Aeonian Press.

Hospital Zone. Elizabeth Seifert. LC 48-8223. 1948. Dodd, Mead.

Hospitality of the House. Doris Miles Disney. 1967. pap. 0.60 o.p. (60-276). Manor Bks.

Hospitality Route. Alfred Bertram Guthrie. LC 76-43383. 1.95. Harlo.

Host for Dying. Pierre Audemars. 1972. pap. 0.75 o.p. (07219). Curtis.

Host Rock. Mary Frances Doner. LC 52-6358. 1952. Doubleday.

Hostage. Robert C Crissman. 1974. 4.95 (ISBN 0-533-01055-1). Vantage Press.

Hostage. Charles Henry. LC 59-108094. (Random House mystery). 1959. Random House.

Hostage. Archie Joscelyn. LC 52-10654. 1952. Bouregy & Curl.

Hostage. Colin Mason. 221p. 1973. 5.95 o.p. (ISBN 0-8027-5289-6). Walker & Co.

Hostage. L. Jay Perry. 192p. 1972. pap. 1.95 o.p. (ISBN 0-87056-224-X, 6224). Brandon.

Hostage Bride. Janet Dailey. LC 81-20128. 1982. 11.95 (ISBN 0-8161-3313-1). G.K. Hall.

Hostage for Hinterland. Arsen Darnay. LC 76-13584. 1976. 1.50 (ISBN 0-345-25306-X). Ballantine Books.

Hostage Game. Mark McShane. (Orig.). 1979. pap. 2.25 (ISBN 0-89083-458-X). Zebra.

Hostage Heart. Gerald Green. 1976. 8.95 o.p. (ISBN 0-87223-430-4, Dist. by S&S). Playboy.
Hostage Heart. Renee Roszel. (Harlequin American Romance Ser.). 256p. 1983. pap. 2.50 (ISBN 0-373-16010-0). Harlequin Bks.
Hostage Heart: A Novel. Gerald Green. LC 74-33555. 8.95 (ISBN 0-87223-430-4). Playboy Press.
Hostage Heart: A Novel. Gerald Green. 1977. 1.95 (ISBN 0-380-00944-7). Avon Books.
Hostage in Illyria. Constance Leonard. (Red Badge Novel of Suspense Ser.). 1976. 5.95 o.p. (ISBN 0-396-07323-9). Dodd.
Hostage in Illyria: A Novel of Suspense. Constance Leonard. LC 76-7979. 5.95 (ISBN 0-396-07323-9). Dodd, Mead.
Hostage in Peking. Anthony Grey. Orig. Title: Room in Peking. 1971. 7.95 o.p. (ISBN 0-385-05118-2). Doubleday.
Hostage in Tokyo. Gerard De Villiers. (Malko Series#11). 1976. (pbk.) 1.25 (ISBN 0-523-00781-7). Pinnacle Books.
Hostage-London: The Diary of Julian Despard. Geoffrey Household. LC 76-53841. 8.95 (ISBN 0-316-37437-7). Little, Brown.
Hostage London: The Diary of Julian Despard. Geoffrey Household. LC 77-26948. 1978. 1.95 (ISBN 0-14-004835-9). Penguin Books.
Hostage Nurse. Jane Converse. (Signet Book). 1973. (pbk) 0.75. New American Library.
Hostage of War. Mary Greene Bonesteel. LC 2059. 1900. Benziger Brothers.
Hostage of Zir. Lyon Sprague De Camp. LC 77-10137. 7.95. Berkley Pub. Corp.: Distributed by Putnam.
Hostage of Zir. Lyon Sprague De Camp. (Berkley book). 1978. 1.75 (ISBN 0-425-03870-X). Berkley Pub. Corp.
Hostage of Zir. L. Sprague de Camp. 1978. pap. 1.75 (ISBN 0-425-03870-X, Dist. by Putnam). Berkley Pub.
Hostage to Death. Roderic Jeffries. LC 77-80204. 1977. 6.95 (ISBN 0-8027-5376-0). Walker.
Hostage to Heaven. Barbara Underwood & Betty Underwood. 1979. 10.95 o.p. (ISBN 0-517-53875-X, C N Potter Bks). Crown.
Hostaged Island. Don Pendleton & Dick Stivers. (Able Team Ser.). 192p. 1982. pap. 1.95 (ISBN 0-373-61202-8, Pub. by Worldwide). Harlequin Bks.
Hostages. Charles E Israel. LC 66-21815. 1966. Simon and Schuster.
Hostages. Geoffrey R. Lomas. 1979. 8.95 o.p. (ISBN 0-684-16072-2, ScribT). Scribner.
Hostages. Chris Stratton. (Adam-12 Ser.). (O.s.i.). 160p. (Orig.). 1974. pap. 0.95 o.s.i. (AN1174, Award). Univ Pub & Dist.
Hostages, a Novel. Stefan Heym. LC 42-23672. 1942. G. P. Putnam's Sons.
Hostages: A Novel. Geoffrey R Lomas. LC 78-26743. 8.95 (ISBN 0-684-16072-2). Scribner.
Hostages of Fate. Botho Kohlweck. 4.50 o.p. Carlton.
Hostages of Hell. Ralph Hayes. (Orig.). 1979. pap. 2.25 (ISBN 0-89083-441-5). Zebra.
Hostages to Fortune. Edward R. Eastman. 1958. text ed. 3.95 o.p. Interstate.
Hostages to Fortune. Barbara K. Hodges. LC 33-20281. 1933. G. P. Putnam's Sons.
Hostages to Fortune. Mary Elizabeth Braddon Maxwell. (On cover: Seaside library. Pocket ed. no. 552). 1885. G. Munro.
Hostages to Fortune. Mary Elizabeth Braddon Maxwell. (On cover: Lovell's library. no. 892). 1887. J. W. Lovell Company.
Hostages to Fortune. Caroline Moorehead. LC 79-51398. 1980. 12.95 (ISBN 0-689-11005-7). Atheneum.
Hoster: a Story of Contemporary Life. A Story of Contemporary Life. Margaret Oliphant Wilson Oliphant. (Harper's Franklin square library, no. 359). 1884. Harper & Brothers.
Hostile Engagement. Jessica Steele. (Harlequin Romance Ser.). (Orig.). 1979. pap. 1.25 (ISBN 0-373-02302-2, Pub. by Harlequin). PB.
Hostile Hills. Eugene E Halleran. LC 57-9140. (Ballantine books, 205). 1957. Ballantine Books.
Hostile Plains. Jack Scott. LC 34-33274. 1934. The Dial Press, Inc.
Hostile Valley. Ben Ames Williams. LC 34-103753. E. P. Dutton & Co., Inc.
Hosts of the Air: The Story of a Quest in the Great War. Joseph Alexander Altsheler. LC 15-18968. (His World war series). 1915. D. Appleton and Company.
Hosts of the Lord. Flora Annie Webster Steel. LC 5151. 1900. The Macmillan Company.
Hosts of the Lord. Flora Annie Webster Steel. LC 425. 1899. The Macmillan Company.
Hot. Joe Johnson. LC 77-9988. (Illus.). 1977. pap. 1.50 (ISBN 0-916382-16-8). Telephone Bks.
Hot and Copper Sky. Bruce Stewart. LC 81-16529. 1982. 14.95 (ISBN 0-312-39239-7). St. Martin's Press.
Hot and the Cool: A Novel. Edwin Gilbert. LC 53-9127. 1953. Doubleday.
Hot As a Pistol. Gene Curry. (Saddler Ser.: No. 4). (Orig.). 1980. pap. text ed. 1.75 o.s.i. (ISBN 0-505-51552-0). Tower Bks.
Hot Blue Sea: A Novel. Richard Jessup. LC 73-83641. 1974. 5.95 (ISBN 0-385-07132-9). Doubleday.
Hot Body. Michael Avallone. (Ed Noon Ser.). 1973. pap. 0.75 o.p. (07340). Curtis.
Hot Boys and Cold Girls. Charles Tekeyan. LC 54-770178. 1954. Beekman.
Hot Breath of Heaven. Mona Goodwyn Williams. LC 61-5824. 1961. Putnam.
Hot Bullets. Brick Killerman. (Orig.). 1981. pap. 2.25 (ISBN 0-505-51728-0). Tower Bks.
Hot Cargo. Brad Collins. (Perspectives II Ser.). (Illus.). 48p. (gr. 7-12). 1982. pap. 2.50 (ISBN 0-87879-313-5). Acad Therapy.
Hot Coals: A Story of to-Day. Edgar La Verne Vincent. LC 11-1850. The C. M. Clark Publishing Company.
Hot Corn Ike. James Lauren Ford. LC 23-38961. E. P. Dutton & Company.
Hot Corn: Life Scenes in New York Illustrated. Including the Story of Little Katy, Madalina, the Rag-Picker's Daughter, Wild Maggie, &C. With Original Designs, Engraved by N. Orr. Solon Robinson. LC 7-42181. 1854. De Witt and Davenport.
Hot Corner. Robert Sidney Bowen. LC 51-10196. 1951. Lothrop, Lee & Shepard.
Hot Country. Waldon Porterfield. LC 68-18760. 1968. L. Stuart.
Hot Day, Hot Night. Chester B Himes. (Signet Book). (Coffin Ed Johnson and Grove Digger Jones series). 1975. (pbk.) 1.25. New American Library.
Hot Day in Heaven. S. J Turidu. LC 73-76981. 1974. 6.75 (ISBN 0-8181-0314-0). Pageant-Poseidon.
Hot for Certainties. Robin Douglas-Home. LC 64-23214. 1964. Dutton.
Hot for the Pastor a Novel. W. T Hacker. LC 6-45966. 1896. Christian Publishing Company.
Hot Freeze. Martin Brett. LC 53-852402. (Red badge detective). 1954. Dodd, Mead.
Hot Gates & Other Occasional Pieces. Gerald Jay Goldberg. LC 66-12363. pap. 1.35 (ISBN 0-15-642180-1, Harv). HarBraceJ.
Hot Gold. Frederick Ritchie Bechdolt. LC 42-50861. 1942. The Sun Dial Press.
Hot Ice. Robert Joseph Casey. LC 33-3744. The Bobbs-Merrill Company.
Hot Iron. Elmer Kelton. LC 56-7233. 1956. Ballantine Books.
Hot Kids & Their Older Lovers. Peggy Swenson, pseud. pap. 1.95 o.p. (ISBN 0-87056-190-1). Brandon.
Hot Land, Cold Season. Pedro Juan Soto. (Laurel-leaf library, 3749). 1973. (pbk) 0.75. Dell.
Hot Lead. Robert Ames Bennet. LC 37-2319. I. Washburn.
Hot Lead. Dwight Bruckner. (Belmont Tower Book). 1.25. Tower Pubns.
Hot Lead. Jesse Edward Grinstead. LC 41-20162. Dodge Publishing Company.
Hot Lead & Cold Nerve. Bradford Scott. 1973. pap. 0.75 o.p. (ISBN 0-515-03059-7, T3059). Pyramid Pubns.
Hot Line. Joy Van Allen. (Orig.). 1982. pap. 2.75 (ISBN 0-515-05580-8). Jove Pubns.
Hot Lips. James Noble Gifford. LC 39-12729. Phoenix Press.
Hot Lips. John Saxon. LC 39-12729. Phoenix Press.
Hot Mahatma. Rod Gray. (The Lady from L.U.S.T. Ser.). (O.s.i.). 1973. pap. 0.95 o.s.i. (BT50617). Belmont-Tower.
Hot Men: An Erotic Coloring Book. John Harris. (Illus.). 32p. 1982. pap. 7.95 (ISBN 0-312-39240-0). St Martin.
Hot Month. Clifford Hanley. LC 66-12069. 1967. Houghton Mifflin.
Hot Mouth Daughters. Geoffrey Kyle. pap. 1.95 o.p. (ISBN 0-87056-188-X). Brandon.
Hot Mouth People. William G. Phillips. 224p. pap. 1.95 o.p. (7130). Barclay Hse.
Hot Mouth Sinners. Sterling Harkins. 192p. pap. 1.95 o.p. (6157). Brandon.
Hot Mouth Sisters. Peter Kevin. pap. 1.95 o.p. (ISBN 0-87056-183-9). Brandon.
Hot News. Emile Henry Gauvreau. LC 31-15681. The Macaulay Company.
Hot Night in Purgatory. Steve Travis. (Orig.). 1981. pap. 2.25 (ISBN 0-505-51713-2). Tower Bks.
Hot Nights. pap. 1.95 o.s.i. (Venus). Grove.
Hot Number. James Noble Gifford. LC 46-18354. 1946. Phoenix Press.
Hot Oil. Mitchell Carlton. (Orig.). 1980. pap. 1.75 o.s.i. (ISBN 0-505-51477-X). Tower Bks.
Hot Oil. George Palmer Putnam & Shipman, Helen (Barham) LC 35-15903. Greenberg.
Hot on the Trail. Antony James, pseud. 224p. (Orig.). 1981. pap. 2.25 (ISBN 0-505-51759-0). Tower Bks.
Hot Pants. Richard F. Kirby. 3.00 o.p. Carlton.
Hot Places. Alan Pryce-Jones. LC 33-1134. 1933. A. A. Knopf.
Hot Plowshares. Albion Winegar Tourgee. LC 77-104583. (Illus.). 1970. Literature House.
Hot Plowshares. A Novel. Albion Winegar Tourgee. LC 1-2777. 1883. Fords, Howard & Hulbert.
Hot Property. Judy Feiffer. LC 72-10930. 1973. 5.95 (ISBN 0-394-48376-6). Random House.
Hot Property. Judy Feiffer. 1974. (pbk.) 1.25. Bantam Books.
Hot Pursuit. Leo Katcher. LC 70-145631. 1971. 5.95. Atheneum.
Hot Pursuit. Gavin Scott. LC 77-99121. 7.95 (ISBN 0-312-39241-9). St. Martin's Press.
Hot Rain. Howard N Portnoy. LC 77-6369. 8.95 (ISBN 0-399-11920-5). Putnam.
Hot Red Money. Baynard Hardwick Kendrick. LC 59-11696. (Red badge detective). 1959. Dodd, Mead.
Hot Rock. Gloria Bell. pap. 1.95 o.p. (8019). Cameo.
Hot Rock. Donald E Westlake. LC 70-107263. 1970. 5.95. Simon and Schuster.
Hot Rocks. Glen Chase, pseud. 1974. pap. 1.25 o.p. (LB143ZK). Leisure Bks.
Hot Rocks see Gemas Fatales.
Hot Rod. Henry Gregor Felsen. (Literature Ser). (gr. 9-12). 1950. pap. text ed. 4.25 (ISBN 0-87720-754-2). AMSCO Sch.
Hot Saturday. Harvey Fergusson. LC 26-153963. 1926. A. A. Knopf.
Hot Season. Gordon Merrick. LC 58-6671. 1958. Morrow.
Hot Sleep. Orson Scott Card. (Analog Book). 1979. pap. 5.95 (ISBN 0-89437-054-5). Baronet.
Hot Sleep: The Worthing Chronicle. Orson Scott Card. 1979. pap. 2.25 (ISBN 0-441-34345-7). Ace Bks.
Hot Snow. Iurii Vasilevich Bondarev. 399p. 1976. 12.00 (ISBN 0-8285-1663-4, Pub. by Progress Pubs USSR). Imported Pubns.
Hot Spot. Muriel Davidson. LC 79-23690. 10.95 (ISBN 0-399-90072-1). R. Marek Publishers.
Hot Spot. 1979. pap. write for info. (ISBN 0-88074-015-9). Metagam.
Hot Springs. Shirley Parenteau. (Love & Life Romance Ser.). 176p. 1983. pap. 1.75 (ISBN 0-345-30963-4). Ballantine.
Hot Springs Doctor. Seven Storiettes... John Mortimer Harrell. LC 99-4739. W. M. Conkey Co.
Hot Star. Robert W. Tracy. LC 52-13293. 1952. Arco.
Hot Star: By Robert W. Tracy Pseud. James Matthews. LC 52-13293. 1952. Arco.
Hot Stuff. Sam Koperwas. 1978. 8.95 o.p. (ISBN 0-525-12795-X, Henry Robbins Book). Dutton.
Hot Summer. Oscar Graeve. LC 33-28727. Farrar & Rinehart, Inc.
Hot Summer Killing. Judson Pentecost Philips. 1970. pap. 0.60 o.p. (ISBN 0-446-63379-8, 63-379). Paperback Lib.
Hot Summer Killing: A Peter Styles Suspense Novel. Judson Pentecost Philips. LC 68-29805. (Red Badge Mystery Ser). 1969. 3.95 o.p. (ISBN 0-396-05852-3). Dodd.
Hot Summer Night. Elston Barrett. 1980. pap. 1.95 o.s.i. (ISBN 0-8439-0711-8, Leisure Bks). Nordon Pubns.
Hot Swamp: A Romance of Old Albion. Robert Michael Ballantyne. LC 11-10558. 1892. T. Nelson and Sons; Etc., Etc.
Hot Swappers. Charles Richards. pap. 1.95 o.p. (ISBN 0-87056-176-6). Brandon.
Hot, Sweet, and Blue. Cover Painting by Mitchell Hooks. John Baird. LC 56-178827. (Gold medal books, 557). 1956. Fawcett Publications.
Hot Thirty. Jeannie Sakol. (O.s.i.). 1980. 9.95 o.s.i. (ISBN 0-440-03394-2). Delacorte.
Hot Thirty. Jeannie Sakol. 1981. pap. 3.75 (ISBN 0-440-13429-3). Dell.
Hot Times. William R Cox. (Fawcett Gold Medal Book). 1973. (pbk.) 1.25. Fawcett.
Hot Tip... 1st Ed. Jack Dolph. LC 51-1101. 1951. Published for the Crime Club by Doubleday.
Hot to Trot. John Lahr. LC 74-7742. 1974. 6.95 (ISBN 0-394-49352-4). Knopf; Distributed by Random House.
Hot to Trot. John Lahr. (Fawcett Crest Book). 1975. (pbk.) 1.50. Fawcett.
Hot Town. Frank Malachy. LC 56-10590. (Permabooks, 3059. Western, 9). 1956. Permabooks.
Hot Triggers. Paul Evan Lehman. 1979. pap. 1.75 o.s.i. (ISBN 0-8439-0661-8, Leisure Bks). Nordon Pubns.
Hot Triggers. Paul Evan Lehman. Orig. Title: Passion in the Dust. pap. 0.50 o.p. (50-440). Manor Bks.
Hot Type. Marjorie Lipsyte. LC 79-8502. 1980. 10.00 (ISBN 0-385-15798-3). Doubleday.
Hot Water. Pelham Grenville Wodehouse. 1932. Doubleday, Doran & Company, Inc.
Hot Water. Pelham Grenville Wodehouse. LC 33-18743. 1933. Doubleday, Doran & Company, Inc.
Hot Water Man. Deborah Moggach. LC 81-18838. 1982. 11.50 (ISBN 0-688-00812-7). Morrow.
Hot 30. Jeannie Sakol. 8.95 (ISBN 0-440-03394-2). Delacorte Press.
Hotel. Elizabeth Bowen. LC 73-141416. 1972. 12.25 (ISBN 0-8371-4685-2). Greenwood Press.
Hotel. Elizabeth Bowen. LC 28-4075. 1928. L. MacVeagh, The Dial Press.
Hotel. Arthur Hailey. LC 65-10622. 1965. Doubleday.
Hotel Belvedere. Elizabeth Frances Corbett. 1970. 5.95 o.p. Hawthorn.
Hotel Belvedere: A Novel. Elizabeth Frances Corbett. LC 79-115907. 1970. 5.95. Hawthorn Books.
Hotel Berlin '43. Vicki Baum. LC 44-3663. 1944. Doubleday, Doran & Company, Inc.
Hotel Berlin '43. Vicki Baum. LC 47-23770. 1945. The Sun Dial Press.
Hotel D'Angleterre: And Other Stories. Mary Elizabeth Hawker. LC 7-2618. (On cover: The "unknown" library, v. 6). Cassell Publishing Company.
Hotel De Dream. Emma Tennant. LC 76-383477. 1976. 3.95 (ISBN 0-575-02128-4). Gollancz.
Hotel De la Liberte. Arthur Kaplan. LC 64-11071. 1964. Dutton.
Hotel Durascamas y Otras Historietas. George Delgado & Ron Christensen. (Historietas Graficas Bilingues: No. 1). (Illus.). 120p. (Spa.). 1982. pap. 3.95 (ISBN 0-940038-02-1). Andante Pub.
Hotel Dwellers. Ed Lacy. LC 66-106465. 4.50. Harper.
Hotel Fever. Arnold Gifford. LC 55-7229. 1955. Crown Publishers.
Hotel Hostess. Faith Baldwin. 1976. Repr. of 1938 ed. lib. bdg. 15.15x (ISBN 0-88411-609-3). Amereon Ltd.
Hotel Hostess. Faith Baldwin Cuthrell. LC 74-82149. 1974. Aeonian Press.
Hotel Hostess. Faith Baldwin Cuthrell. LC 38-25347. Farrar & Rinehart, Inc.
Hotel Jacarandas. Katrina Britt. 192p. 1982. pap. 1.50 (ISBN 0-373-02449-5, Pub. by Harlequin). PB.
Hotel Lobby. Sally Chayes. LC 40-37519. Phoenix Press.
Hotel Mamie Stover. William Bradford Huie. LC 63-18754. 1963. C. N. Potter.
Hotel New Hampshire. John Irving. LC 81-2610. 15.50 (ISBN 0-525-12800-X). Dutton.
Hotel New Hampshire. John Irving. 1982. 3.95 (ISBN 0-671-44027-6). Pocket Books.
Hotel Nurse. Ruth Dorset, pseud. LC 68-613. 1967. Arcadia House.
Hotel Nurse. easy eye ed. Lorraine Paulson. pap. 0.60 o.p. Lancer.
Hotel Nurse. William Edward Daniel Ross. LC 68-613. 1967. Arcadia House.
Hotel on the Lake. Robert Miller Smith. LC 43-173173. 1943. Farrar & Rinehart, Inc.
Hotel Room: A Novel. Agnar Mykle. LC 63-8602. 1963. Dutton.
Hotel Room: By Cornell Woolrich Pseud. Cornell George Hopley-Woolrich. LC 58-10947. 1958. Random House.
Hotel Room 30: By J. Johnstone Pseud. 1st Ed. John S. Johnston. LC 55-7870. 1955. Greenwich Book Publishers.
Hotel Splendide. Ludwig Bemelmans. (Compass bk., C-129). 1963. pap., 1.35. Viking.
Hotel Splendide. Ludwig Bemelmans. LC 47-8358. (Penguin books, 637). 1947.
Hotel Talleyrand. Paul Hyde Bonner. 1970. pap. 0.75 o.p. (75-354). Manor Bks.
Hotel Talleyrand: A Novel. Paul Hyde Bonner. LC 53-8035. 1953. Scribner.
Hotel Transylvania: A Horror Novel. Chelsea Quinn Yarbro. (Signet book). 1979. 1.95 (ISBN 0-451-08461-6). New American Library.
Hotel Transylvania: A Novel of Forbidden Love. Chelsea Quinn Yarbro. LC 77-21535. 8.95 (ISBN 0-312-39248-6). St. Martin's Press.
Hotel Vesuvius: A Gay Novel of Grapes, Wine and Sunshine. Johan Wigmore Fabricius & Stephens, M. S., Tr. LC 47-163483. 1947. Rinehart & Company, Incorporated.
Hotel Wife. Ruth Lyons. LC 33-2631. The Macaulay Company.
Hotel Wife. Wright Williams. LC 43-164410. 1943. Phoenix Press.
Hotel Wife. Watkins Eppes Wright. LC 43-16441. 1943. Phoenix Press.
Hotel 61. Elizabeth Bowen. 1980. 2.25 (ISBN 0-380-48546-X). Avon Books.
Hotelman. Jerry Seelbach. LC 75-5296. 1.95 (ISBN 0-914242-07-5). Bookworld Communications Corp.
Hotels with Empty Rooms. Harriett Gilbert. LC 72-9768. 1973. 5.95 (ISBN 0-06-011519-X). Harper & Row.
Hotep: A Dream of the Nile. William Wilshire Myers. LC 5-38486. 1905. The R. Clarke Company.
Hothouse. Brian Wilson Aldiss. LC 76-10744. (Gregg Press science fiction series). 1976. 12.50 (ISBN 0-8398-2325-8). Gregg Press.
Hothouse. Joyce Thompson. 1981. pap. 2.95 (ISBN 0-380-78212-X, 78212). Avon.

Hothouse by the East River. Muriel Spark. LC 72-90671. 1973. 5.95 (ISBN 0-670-37960-3). Viking Press.

Hotspur. A Tale of the Old Dutch Manor. Mansfield Tracy Walworth. LC 8-331243. 1864. Carleton.

Hotspur. A Tale of the Old Dutch Manor. Mansfield Tracy Walworth. LC 28-179043. 1865. Carleton.

Hound. Frederic Morton. LC 47-11493. (Intercollegiate literary fellowship prize novels). 1947. Dodd, Mead.

Hound and the Fox and the Harper. Shaun Herron. LC 76-117710. 1970. 4.95. Random House.

Hound & Unicorn. George Brandon Saul. 1977. 12.50 o.p. Porter.

Hound-Dog Man. Frederick Benjamin Gipson. LC 49-7116. 1949. Harper.

Hound-Dog Man. Frederick Benjamin Gipson. LC 80-10995. 1980. 4.95 (ISBN 0-8032-7005-4). University of Nebraska Press.

Hound-Dog Man: Reissue. Frederick Benjamin Gipson. LC 49-7116. 1966. lib. ed., 4.11. Harper.

Hound from the North. Ridgwell Cullum. 1904. L. C. Page & Company.

Hound of Earth. Vance Nye Bourjaily. LC 54-13161. 1955. Scribner.

Hound of Florence: A Novel. Felix Salten & Paterson, Huntley, Tr. LC 30-15343. 1930. Simon and Schuster.

Hound of Heaven. Sarah Addington. LC 35-14233. 1935. D. Appleton-Century Company, Incorporated.

Hound of Heaven. Thompson. 3.95 (ISBN 0-88088-296-4). Peter Pauper.

Hound of Ireland: And Other Stories. Donn Byrne. LC 70-116942. (Short story index reprint series). 1970. Books for Libraries Press.

Hound of Ireland and Other Stories: By Donn Byrne. Donn Byrne. LC 35-5383. 1935. D. Appleton-Century Company Incorporated.

Hound of the Baskervilles. Arthur Conan Doyle. (Classics ser. CL42). 1965. Airmont.

Hound of the Baskervilles. Arthur Conan Doyle. LC 75-44969. (Fifty Classics of Crime Fiction, 1900-1950; 15). (Illus.). 1976. 12.00 (ISBN 0-8240-2364-1). Garland Pub.

Hound of the Baskervilles. Arthur Conan Doyle. LC 76-27103. 1977. 7.95 (ISBN 0-385-12282-9). Doubleday.

Hound of the Baskervilles. Arthur Conan Doyle. LC 61-13199. (Looking glass library, 26). (Illus.). 1961. Looking Glass Library; Distributed by Random House.

Hound of the Baskervilles. Arthur Conan Doyle. LC 27-3411. (The Lambskin library. no 53). 1926. Doubleday, Page & Company.

Hound of the Baskervilles. Arthur Conan Doyle. 1959. pap. 1.95 (ISBN 0-440-93758-2, LFL). Dell.

Hound of the Baskervilles. Arthur Conan Doyle. 1981. pap. 2.50 (ISBN 0-14-000111-5). Penguin.

Hound of the Baskervilles. Arthur Conan Doyle. 1962. pap. 0.65 o.p. (01967, Collier). Macmillan.

Hound of the Baskervilles. Arthur Conan Doyle. 1959. pap. 0.95 o.p. (ISBN 0-8092-6050-6). Regnery.

Hound of the Baskervilles. new ed. Arthur Conan Doyle. Ed. by Joseph W. Nash. (O.s.i.). 1976. pap. 0.95 o.s.i. (ISBN 0-89319-000-4). Andor Pub.

Hound of the Baskervilles. Arthur Conan Doyle Doyle. 1976. 1.25. Belmont Tower Books.

Hound of the Baskervilles. Sir Arthur Conan Doyle. 1975. (pbk.) 1.25 (ISBN 0-345-24718-3). Ballantine Books.

Hound of the Baskervilles: Another Adventure of Sherlock Holmes: a Facsimile of the Adventure As It Was First Published in the Strand Magazine, London. Arthur Conan Doyle. LC 75-24568. (Illus.). 1975. 4.95 (ISBN 0-8052-3602-3) (ISBN 0-8052-0505-5). Schocken Books.

Hound of the Baskervilles: Another Adventure of Sherlock Holmes. Arthur Conan Doyle. LC 68-9765. (Great illustrated classics). (Illus.). 1968. Dodd, Mead.

Hound of the Baskervilles: Another Adventure of Sherlock Holmes. Arthur Conan Doyle. LC 12-22658. Doubleday, Page & Company.

Hound of the Baskervilles: Another Adventure of Sherlock Holmes. Arthur Conan Doyle. 1902. McClure, Phillips & Co.

Hound of the Baskervilles: Another Adventure of Sherlock Holmes. Arthur Conan Doyle. LC 22-8518. Grosset & Dunlap.

Hound of the Baskervilles: Facsimile of the First Publication with All the Original Sidney Paget Illustrations. Arthur Conan Doyle. LC 75-24568. (Illus.). 1975. 4.95 o.p. (ISBN 0-8052-3602-3); pap. 2.95 o.p. (ISBN 0-8052-0505-5). Schocken.

Hound-Tuner of Callaway. Raymond Weeks. LC 71-167472. (Short story index reprint series). 1971. (ISBN 0-8369-3998-0). Books for Libraries Press.

Hounded Man. Francis Carco. Tr. by Jorand, Alex. LC 25-1545. 1924. T. Seltzer.

Hounds and Jackals. Barbara Wood. LC 77-12888. 1978. 7.95 (ISBN 0-385-12972-6). Doubleday.

Hounds of Banba. Daniel Corkery. LC 75-128728. (Short story index reprint series). 1970. Books for Libraries Press.

Hounds of Cloneen. Vivian Connell. LC 51-9665. 1951. Dial Press.

Hounds of Dracula: A Novel. Ken Johnson. (Signet Book). 1977. 1.75 (ISBN 0-451-07739-3). New American Library.

Hounds of God: A Romance. Rafael Sabatini. LC 28-24060. 1928. Houghton, Mifflin Company.

Hounds of Hell. Virginia Coffman. 1975. (pbk.) 1.25. Ace Books.

Hounds of Hell: Stories of Canine Horror and Fantasy. Michel Parry. LC 73-16635. 1974. 6.95 (ISBN 0-8008-3945-5). Taplinger Pub. Co.

Hounds of Hell. Tr. from French by Xan Fielding. 1st. Amer. Ed. Jean Larteguy. LC 66-12258. 5.95. Dutton.

Hounds of Spring. Sylvia Thompson. LC 26-4585. 1926. Little, Brown, and Company.

Hounds of Spring, and Other Stories. Julian Fane. LC 77-353749. 1976. Hamilton: St George's Press.

Hounds of Summer and Other Stories: Mary McCarthy's Short Fiction. Mary Therese McCarthy. LC 80-69929. (Bard book). 1981. 3.50 (ISBN 0-380-78196-4). Avon Books.

Hounds of the Moon. Elisabeth Offutt Allen. (Queen-size gothic). 1974. (pbk.) 0.95. Popular Library.

Hounds of Tindalos. Frank Belknap Long. LC 46-1779. 1946. Arkham House.

Hound's Tooth. Robert Emmett McDowell. LC 65-24826. bds., 3.50. Mill, Dist. Morrow.

Houndstooth. Gary A. Ruse. LC 74-23829. 288p. 1975. 7.95 o.p. (ISBN 0-13-394957-5). P-H.

Houndstooth: A Novel. Gary Alan Ruse. LC 74-23829. 1975. 7.95 (ISBN 0-13-394957-5). Prentice-Hall.

Houp-La: A Novelette. Henrietta Eliza Vaughan Stannard. (Harper's handy series, no. 26). 1885. Harper & Brothers.

Houp-La: A Novelette. Henrietta Eliza Vaughan Stannard. (On cover: The seaside library. Pocket ed. no. 600). 1885. G. Munro.

Hour. Bernard De Voto. 1951. 3.00 o.p. (ISBN 0-395-07606-4). HM.

Hour After Requiem: And Other Stories. 1st Ed. Lawrence O'Sullivan. LC 66-20957. 1966. 4.50. Doubleday.

Hour After Westerly: And Ohter Stories. Robert Myron Coates. LC 57-5293. 1957. Harcourt, Brace.

Hour & the Man, 3 vols. in 1. Harriet Martineau. LC 75-148341. Repr. of 1841 ed. 40.00 (ISBN 0-404-08890-2). AMS Pr.

Hour Awaits: By March Cost Pseud. 1st American Ed. Peggy Morrison, pseud. LC 52-137275. 1953. Lippincott.

Hour Before Midnight. Velda Johnston. 1978. 7.95 o.p. (ISBN 0-396-07565-7). Dodd.

Hour Before Midnight. John Salisbury. 1980. pap. 2.50 (ISBN 0-440-13421-8). Dell.

Hour Before the Dawn. William Somerset Maugham. LC 75-25354. (Works of W. Somerset Maugham Ser.). 1977. Repr. of 1942 ed. 15.00x (ISBN 0-405-07812-9). Ayer Co.

Hour Before the Dawn: A Novel. William Somerset Maugham. LC 75-25354. (Maugham, William Somerset, 1874-1965. Works. 1976). 1977. 15.00 (ISBN 0-405-07812-9). Arno Press.

Hour Before the Dawn: A Novel. William Somerset Maugham. LC 42-164564. 1942. Doubleday, Doran and Company, Inc.

Hour Is Forever. Ethel Blackledge. LC 77-79631. 1977. 1.50 (ISBN 0-380-01682-6). Avon Books.

Hour of Barabbas. Otto Joseph Michael Knab. LC 43-8399. 1943. Sheed & Ward.

Hour of Conflict. Arthur Hamilton Gibbs. LC 14-449525. 1.25. George H. Doran Company.

Hour of Death. Lillian Morningstar. LC 50-13851. 1950. Phoenix Press.

Hour of Giving. Luis Zalamea. LC 65-166097. 4.95. Houghton.

Hour of Glory. Robert Lund. LC 50-9714. 1950. J. Day Co.

Hour of Gold, Hour of Lead. Anne Morrow Lindbergh. LC 72-88792. 1973. 7.95 (ISBN 0-15-142176-5). HarBraceJ.

Hour of Last Things: And Other Stories. George P. Elliott. LC 68-16310. 1968. Harper & Row.

Hour of Nightfall. Myron Brinig. LC 47-5466. 1947. Rinehart.

Hour of Redemption. F. B. Johnson. 395p. 1978. pap. 2.50 (ISBN 0-532-25000-1). F B Johnson.

Hour of Redemption. F. B. Johnson. 1978. pap. 2.50 (ISBN 0-532-25000-1). Woodhill.

Hour of Splendor. Esther Penny Boutcher. LC 59-7399. 1959. Morrow.

Hour of Spring. Mary Deasy. LC 76-6334. (Irish-Americans). 1977. 22.00 (ISBN 0-405-09330-6). Arno Press.

Hour of Spring. Mary Deasy. LC 47-125341. 1948. Little, Brown.

Hour of the Bell: A Novel of the 1821 Greek War of Independence Against the Turks. Harry Mark Petrakis. LC 75-40738. 1976. 10.00 (ISBN 0-385-04877-7). Doubleday.

Hour of the Blue Fox. Jeffrey Bocco. (Orig.). 1975. pap. 1.75 o.p. (ISBN 0-515-03964-0). BJ Pub Group.

Hour of the Blue Fox. Hugh C McDonald. LC 75-27007. 1975. (pbk.) 1.75 (ISBN 0-515-03964-0). Pyramid Books.

Hour of the Cat. Gene DeWeese. LC 79-7194. 1980. 7.95 (ISBN 0-385-12098-2). Doubleday.

Hour of the Clown. Amos Aricha. (Orig.). 1981. pap. 2.95 (ISBN 0-451-09717-3, E9717, Sig). NAL.

Hour of the Dog. Berkely Mather. LC 82-16799. (Illus.). 14.95 (ISBN 0-312-39251-6). St. Martin's Press.

Hour of the Dragon. Robert E. Howard. LC 77-13159. (CIP). (YA) 1977. 2.25 (ISBN 0-425-05043-2, Dist. by Putnam). Berkley Pub.

Hour of the Dragon. Robert E. Howard. 1977. pap. 1.95 (ISBN 0-425-03608-1, Medallion). Berkley Pub.

Hour of the Dragon: Conan. authorized ed. Robert E. Howard. LC 77-13159. (Illus.). 1.95 (ISBN 0-399-12096-3). Putnam.

Hour of the Harp. Lynna Cooper, pseud. LC 75-6511. 1975. 7.95 (ISBN 0-8415-0388-5). Saturday Review Press.

Hour of the Horde. Gordon R Dickson. 1978. 1.50 (ISBN 0-87997-397-8). DAW Books.

Hour of the Hyenas. John Sherwood. 1982. 15.00x (ISBN 0-333-27047-9, Pub. by Macmillan England). State Mutual Bk.

Hour of the Oxrun Dead. Charles L. Grant. LC 77-75386. 1977. 6.95 (ISBN 0-385-13173-9). Doubleday.

Hour of the Oxrun Dead. Charles L. Grant. 1979. 1.75 (ISBN 0-445-04363-6). Popular Library.

Hour of the Scorpion. Anthony Taylor. (Orig.). 1982. pap. 2.95 (ISBN 0-515-05393-7). Jove Pubns.

Hour of the Sunshine Now: Short Stories. Norbert Blei. LC 78-51456. (Illinois Writers; No. 1). (Illus.). 12.50. (ISBN 0-931704-01-4) (ISBN 0-931704-00-6). Story Press.

Hour of the Wolf. Nick Carter. (Nick Carter Ser.). (O.s.i.). 192p. 1975. pap. 1.25 o.s.i. (AQ1387, Award). Univ Pub & Dist.

Hour of the Wolf. Robert Charles, pseud. 1975. (pbk.) 1.25 (ISBN 0-523-00638-1). Pinnacle Books.

Hour of Truth: A Novel. David Albert Davidson. LC 49-599. 1949. Random House.

Hour Upon the Stage. Ann Pinchot. LC 29-18424. 1929. Dodd, Mead & Company.

Hour Will Come: A Tale of the Alpine Cloister. Wilhelmina Birch Von Hillern & Bell, Mrs. Clara Courtenay (Poynter) 1834-1927, Tr. LC 7-467450. 1880. W. S. Gottsberger.

Hourglass. David Alman. LC 47-1998. 1947. Simon and Schuster.

Hourglass. Edwin Gilbert. pap. 0.75 o.p. (74-851). Lancer.

Hourglass Man: A Novel About a Psychiatrist's Breakdown. Carl Tiktin. LC 76-48785. 7.95 (ISBN 0-87795-161-6). Arbor House.

Hourney up: A Novel. Robert Smythe Hichens. LC 38-36265. 1938. Doubleday, Doran & Co., Inc.

Hours. Lon Albert. (O.s.i.). (Orig.). 1969. pap. 0.75 o.s.i. (A507S, Award). Univ Pub & Dist.

Hours of Light. Janet Tanner. LC 80-29074. 1981. 13.95 (ISBN 0-312-39252-4). St. Martin's Press.

Hour's Promise. Annie Eliot Trumbull. (On cover: Cassell's sunshine series of choice fiction. v. 1, no. 23). 1889. Cassell & Company, Limited.

Hours Together: A Novel. 1st Ed. Clara Winston. LC 61-12250. 1961. Lippincott.

Hourse After Midnight. Joseph Arnold Hayes. LC 58-986518. 1958. Random House.

House. Henry Bordeaux & Houghton, Mrs. Louise (Seymour) 1838- Tr. LC 14-14800. 1914. Duffield & Company.

House. Barbara Villy Cormack. LC 56-35660. 1956. Bouregy & Curl.

House: A Novel. Grace Kellogg Griffith. LC 26-7336. 1926. The Penn Publishing Company.

House Above Cuzco. August William Derleth. LC 75-76502. 1969. 6.00. Candlelight Press.

House Above Hollywood. Velda Johnston. LC 68-13599. (Red badge mystery). 1968. Dodd, Mead.

House Above the River. Michael Foster. LC 46-67082. 1946. Little, Brown and Company.

House Across the River. Margaret Bonham. LC 51-9237. 1951. Macmillan.

House Across the River. Elizabeth Frances Corbett. LC 34-6607. 1934. Reynal & Hitchcock.

House Across the Way. Foxhall Daingerfield. LC 28-2517. 1928. D. Appleton and Company.

House & Its Head. Ivy Compton-Burnett. 280p. 1983. pap. 4.95 (ISBN 0-14-001317-2). Penguin.

House & Its Head. Ivy Compton-Burnett. 1966. 9.00 o.p. (ISBN 0-575-01579-9). Intl Pubns Serv.

House and the Sea. Johan Bojer & Ager, Trygve Martinus, Tr. LC 34-29906. 1934. D. Appleton-Century Company, Incorporated.

House and the Tower. Fredrika Shumway Smith. LC 52-6047. 1951. Christopher Pub. House.

House at Adampur: A Story of Modern India. 1st Ed. Anand Lall. LC 56-6649. 1956. Knopf.

House at Akiya. William Butler. LC 72-85264. 1969. 4.95. Scribner.

House at Balnesmoor. Hugh C Rae. LC 69-18915. 1969. 4.95. Coward-McCann.

House at Bell Orchard. Sylvia Thorpe. 1979. pap. 1.75 (ISBN 0-449-50006-3, Coventry). Fawcett.

House at Canterbury. Fortune Kent. 1975. (pbk.) 1.25 (ISBN 0-671-80196-1). Pocket Books.

House at Crague: Or, Her Own Way. Mary Breck Sleight. LC 8-9602. T. Y. Crowell & Co.

House at Fern Canyon. Willo Davis Roberts. (Orig.). 1970. pap. 0.75 o.p. (ISBN 0-447-74631-6). Lancer.

House at Gray Eagle. Elisabeth Macdonald. LC 75-37542. 6.95 (ISBN 0-684-14556-1). Scribner.

House at Haunted Inlet. Valerie Subond. (YA) 1978. 6.95 (Avalon). Bouregy.

House at Hawk's End. Claudette Nicole. (Orig.). 1971. pap. 0.60 o.p. (R2418, GM). Fawcett World.

House at Hawk's End. Claudette Nicole. 144p. 1973. pap. 0.75 o.p. (T2707, GM). Fawcett World.

House at High Bridge: A Novel. Edgar Fawcett. 1887. Ticknor and Company.

House at Kilgallen. Mary Linn Roby. (Signet Book, T5671). 1973. (pbk.) 0.75. New American Library.

House at Luxor. Florence Stevenson. (Signet book). New American Library.

House at Old Vine. Norah Robinson Lofts. Repr. lib. bdg. 19.70x (ISBN 0-89190-226-0). Am Repr-Rivercity Pr.

House at Old Vine. Norah Robinson Lofts. 1978. pap. 1.95 (ISBN 0-449-23792-3, Crest). Fawcett.

House at Old Vine. Norah Robinson Lofts. 1977. Repr. of 1961 ed. lib. bdg. 16.95x (ISBN 0-89244-049-X). Queens Hse.

House at Old Vine: 1st Ed. Norah Robinson Lofts. LC 61-9532. 1961. Doubleday.

House at Rivers Bend. Ruby Jean Jensen. (Candlelight Gothic). 1975. (pbk.) 0.75. Dell.

House at Sandalwood. Coffman, Virginia. LC 73-90734. 1974. 7.95 (ISBN 0-87795-075-X). Arbor House.

House at Sandalwood. Virginia Coffman. (Fawcett crest book). 1975. (pbk.) 1.25. Fawcett.

House at Satan's Elbow. John Dickson Carr. bds., 3.95. Harper.

House at Sunset. Norah Robinson Lofts. Repr. lib. bdg. 18.55x (ISBN 0-89190-227-9). Am Repr-Rivercity Pr.

House at Sunset. Norah Robinson Lofts. 1977. Repr. of 1962 ed. lib. bdg. 16.95x (ISBN 0-89244-050-3). Queens Hse.

House at Sunset: 1st Ed. Norah Robinson Lofts. 1962. Doubleday.

House at Swansea. Alicia Grace. 1976. pap. 1.25 (ISBN 0-532-12387-5). Woodhill.

House at Windridge. Ellouise A. Rife. 1981. pap. 2.25 (ISBN 0-89083-740-6). Zebra.

House Behind the Cedars. Charles Waddell Chesnutt. LC 68-25716. 1968. 10.00. Gregg Pr.

House Behind the Cedars. Charles Waddell Chesnutt. LC 6369. 1900. Houghton, Mifflin and Company.

House Behind the Mint. Laurie Huffman. LC 68-22516. 1969. 5.95. Doubleday.

House Between the Trees: A Novel. John Russell Lane. LC 9-6842. 1909. The C. M. Clark Publishing Company.

House Between the Worlds. Marion Zimmer Bradley. LC 79-7800. 1980. 10.00 (ISBN 0-385-12936-X). Doubleday.

House-Boat Enigma. Ralf Ridgway Hillman. LC 38-5144. Dorrance and Company.

House-Boat on the Styx. biographical ed. John Kendrick Bangs. LC 71-112788. (Illus.). 1970. AMS Press.

House-Boat on the Styx. John Kendrick Bangs. LC 99-5164. 1899. Harper & Brothers.

House-Boat on the Styx: Being Some Account of the Divers Doings of the Associated Shades. John Kendrick Bangs. 1896. Harper & Brothers.

House-Boat on the Styx: Being Some Account of the Divers Doings of the Associated Shades. John Kendrick Bangs. LC 20-16470. Harper & Brothers.

House-Boat on the Styx: Being Some Account of the Divers Doings of the Associated Shades. John Kendrick Bangs. LC 3-19540. 1896. Harper & Brothers.

House by an African Path. Evelyn Evans. LC 78-67998. (Illus.). 5.95 (ISBN 0-8054-6316-X). Broadman Press.

House by Exmoor. Caroline Stafford, pseud. LC 75-9737. 1975. 7.95 (ISBN 0-671-22077-2). Simon and Schuster.

House by Exmoor. Caroline Stafford, pseud. 1977. 1.50 (ISBN 0-449-23058-9). Fawcett Crest.

House by the Church-Yard. Joseph Sheridan Le Fanu. LC 76-5270. (Le Fanu, Joseph Sheridan, 1814-1873. Works. 1976). 1976. (3 vols.) 60.00 (ISBN 0-405-09212-1). Arno Press.

House by the Church-Yard: A Novel. Joseph Sheridan Le Fanu. LC 74-148811. 1975. 30.00 (ISBN 0-404-08877-5). AMS Press.

House by the Churchyard. Joseph Sheridan Le Fanu. LC 79-18495. (Ireland, from the Act of Union, 1800, to the Death of Parnell, 1891). 1979. 42.00 (ISBN 0-8240-3509-7). Garland Pub.

House by the Medlar Tree. Giovanni Verga. LC 75-11490. 1975. 15.00 (ISBN 0-8371-8205-0). Greenwood Press.

House by the Medlar Tree. Giovanni Verga. LC 74-17480. 1975. (ISBN 0-374-17300-1) (ISBN 0-374-51188-8). Farrar, Straus and Giroux.

House by the Medlar Tree. A New Translation with a Foreword by Raymond Rosenthal. Giovanni Verga. LC 64-4816. (Signet classic). 1964. New American Library.

House by the Medlar-Tree: The Translation by Mary A. Craig; an Introduction by W. D. Howells. Giovanni Verga. LC 8-30008. 1890. Harper & Brothers.

House by the Medlar Tree. Translated from the Italian by Eric Mosbacher. Giovanni Verga. LC 55-702750. (Doubleday anchor book A 47). 1955. Doubleday.

House by the Medlar Tree: Translated from the Italian by Eric Mosbacher. Giovanni Verga. LC 53-8070. 1953. Grove Press.

House by the River. August William Derleth. 1965. 3.50 o.p. (ISBN 0-696-64986-1). Hawthorn.

House by the River. Alan Patrick Herbert. LC 21-3815. 1921. A. A. Knopf.

House by the River. Alan Patrick Herbert. LC 35-2263. 1935. Doubleday, Doran & Company, Inc.

House by the River. Florence Alice Price James. LC 5-35792. J. S. Ogilvie Publishing Company.

House by the River, a Novel. By Barbara Kent. With Illustrations by Warren B. Davis. Also, The Children's Crusade. By F. Whittier. Barbara Kent & Whittaker, Frederick. (choice series. no. 123). (Ledger library. no. 123). 1895. R. Bonner's Sons.

House by the Road. Charles Judson Dutton. LC 24-6683. 1924. Dodd, Mead and Company.

House by the Road. Anna M Lucas. LC 34-134244. 1934. Buechler Publishing Co.

House by the Sea. Kofi Awoonor. 1978. perfect bdg. 3.00 (ISBN 0-912678-33-X). Greenfld Rev Pr.

House by the Sea & Timothy. Harriet E. Gowey. 1975. 4.95 o.p. (ISBN 0-8059-2220-2). Dorrance.

House by the Side of the Road. E. V. Austin. LC 75-31566. (Illus.). 4.00 (ISBN 0-916078-01-9). Iris Press.

House by the Side of the Road. Willie Williamson Rogers. LC 13-2843. Printed by Von Boeckmann-Jones Company.

House by the Watch Tower. Denise Robins. LC 68-2871. 1968. Arcadia House.

House by the Windmill. Agnes Edwards Rothery. LC 23-9232. 1923. Doubleday, Page & Company.

House Called Bellevigne. Jacqueline Gilbert. (Harlequin Presents). 192p. 1983. pap. 1.95 (ISBN 0-373-10600-9). Harlequin Bks.

House Called Edenhyde. Nancy Buckingham. 1973. (pbk) 0.75. Dell.

House Called Edenhythe. Nancy Buckingham. LC 77-158010. 1972. 5.95. Hawthorn Books.

House Called Memory. Richard Collier. 1961. 5.00 o.p. Dutton.

House Called Pleasance. Dorothy Phoebe Ansle. LC 78-61706. 1978. 7.95 (ISBN 0-525-12802-6). Dutton.

House Called Pleasance. Laura Conway. 1978. 7.95 o.p. (ISBN 0-525-12802-6). Dutton.

House Cried Murder. Frank Nash. LC 52-8535. 1952. Phoenix Press.

House Divided. Pearl Sydenstricker Buck. 1975. (pbk.) 1.50 (ISBN 0-671-78797-7). Pocket Books.

House Divided. Pearl Sydenstricker Buck. LC 35-1591. Reynal & Hitchcock.

House Divided. Sydney Horler. LC 29-19027. 1929. The Macaulay Company.

House Divided. Ben Ames Williams. LC 47-4896. 1947. Houghton Mifflin Co.

House Divided. Ben Ames Williams. LC 47-6587. 1947. Houghton Mifflin Co.

House Divided: A Novel. Henry Brereton Marriott Watson. LC 1-24653. 1901. Harper & Brothers.

House Divided: A Novella, and Other Stories. Sally Mirliss Blake. LC 68-18554. 1968. McGraw-Hill.

House Divided: A Novella & Other Stories. Sara, pseud. 1968. 5.95 o.p. (ISBN 0-07-054736-X). McGraw.

House Divided Against Itself. Margaret Oliphant Wilson Oliphant. (On cover: Seaside library. Pocket ed., no. 703). 1886. G. Munro.

House Divided Against Itself. A Novel. Margaret Oliphant Wilson Oliphant. (Harper's Franklin square library, no. 511). 1886. Harper & Brothers.

House for Emily. Elizabeth Bishop Reeves. Farrar & Rinehart, Inc.

House for Jonnie O. Blossom Elfman. LC 76-41689. 1977. 6.95 (ISBN 0-395-24901-5). Houghton Mifflin.

House for Jonnie O. Blossom Elfman. 1978. 1.95 (ISBN 0-553-11091-8). Bantam Books.

House for Mr. Biswas. Vidiadhar Surajprasad Naipaul. 592p. 1976. pap. 4.95 (ISBN 0-14-003025-5). Penguin.

House for Sale: A Novel. Elissa Landi. LC 32-26359. 1932. Doubleday, Doran & Compay, Inc.

House for the Sparrow. Julia Truitt Yenni. LC 42-2432. 1942. Reynal and Hitchcock.

House Full of Angels. Richard A Duprey. LC 64-14462.

House Full of Brothers. Jon Palmer. 352p. (Orig.). 1973. pap. 1.50 (ISBN 0-87067-429-3, BH429). Holloway.

House Full of People. Carel Theodorus Scharten & Scharten, Margo Sybranda Everdina (Antink) 1869- Joint Author. LC 24-4265. Small, Maynard & Company.

House Full of Strangers: A Contemporary Novel. Eileen Mitson. LC 71-133358. 1971. 3.50. Zondervan Pub. House.

House Full of Women. Philip James McFarland. LC 60-10978. 1960. Simon and Schuster.

House Guest. Mary Dupuy Bickel. LC 36-5928. Coward-McCann.

House Happy. Muriel Resnik. LC 58-10447. 1958. Crowell.

House in Balfour-Street. A Novel. Charles Patton Dimitry. LC 20-19325. 1868. G. S. Wilcox.

House in Bloomsbury: A Novel. Margaret Oliphant Wilson Oliphant. LC 7-32507. 1894. Dodd, Mead & Company.

House in Clewe Street. Mary Lavin. LC 45-401734. 1945. Little, Brown and Company.

House in Demetrius Road. John Davys Beresford. LC 14-161989. 1.30. George H. Doran Company.

House in Disorder. Charles U Becker. LC 34-6272. Dorrance & Company, Inc.

House in Dormer Forest. Mary Gladys Meredith Webb. LC 21-6904. 1921. George H. Doran Company.

House in Dormer Forest. Mary Gladys Meredith Webb. LC 29-16859. 1929. E. P. Dutton & Co., Inc.

House in Dormer Forest. Mary Gladys Meredith Webb. LC 39-23195. 1937. F. P. Dutton and Company, Inc.

House in Half Moon Street and Other Stories. Hector Bolitho. LC 36-232733. 1936. D. Appleton-Century Company, Incorporated.

House in Holly Walk. Dorothy Wakely. 1980. pap. 1.75 (ISBN 0-441-34375-9). Ace Bks.

House in Hook Street. Margaret Erskine, pseud. LC 77-74301. 1977. 6.95 (ISBN 0-385-13137-2). Published for the Crime Club by Doubleday.

House in Lodz. Akbar Del Piombo. (Orig.). 1969. pap. 1.95 o.s.i. (TC462, Travellers Comp). Olympia.

House in Lordship Lane... Alfred Edward Woodley Mason. LC 46-3351. 1946. Dodd, Mead & Company.

House in Milan. Translated by Sidney Alexander. 1st American Ed. Giovanni Testori. LC 62-19593. 1962. Harcourt, Brace & World.

House in Munich. Dorothy Dowdell. 1975. (pbk.) 0.95 (ISBN 0-380-00337-6). Avon.

House in November. Keith Laumer. 1970. 4.95 o.p. (ISBN 0-399-10420-8). Putnam.

House in November: A Science Fiction Novel. Keith Laumer. LC 70-124173. 1970. 4.95. Putnam.

House in Order: By Nigel Dennis. Nigel Forbes Dennis. LC 66-288870. 1966. bds., 4.95. Vanguard.

House in Paris. Elizabeth Bowen. LC 36-4991. 1936. A. A. Knopf.

House in Paris. Elizabeth Bowen. LC 79-65445. 1979. 2.50 (ISBN 0-380-44602-2). Avon Books.

House in Paris. 1st Vintage Ed. Elizabeth Bowen. (Vintage book, K-48). 1957. Vintage Books.

House in Peking. 1st Ed. Pierre Stephen Robert Payne. LC 56-6538. 1956. Doubleday.

House in Quenn Anne Square. William Darling Lyell. LC 21-7338. 1921. G. P. Putnam's Sons.

House in Ralston Place. Alan B Moody. LC 26-33782. Gem Publishing Company.

House in Ruins. Robert S Weekley. LC 58-5277. 1958. Random House.

House in St. Cloud. Beatrix Demarest Lloyd. LC 35-57003. R. M. McBride & Company.

House in the Dust. Doris Oppenheim Leslie, pseud. LC 42-5126. 1942. The MacMillan Company.

House in the Fog. Lois Geumlek. 1974. (pbk.) 0.95. Avon.

House in the Forest. 1st. Ed. Marten Cumberland. LC 50-8626. 1950. Published for the Crime Club by Doubleday.

House in the Hills. Simonne Ratel. Tr. by Sutton, Eric. 1934. The Macmillan Company.

House in the Hills: A Novel of Romantic Adventure. Laurence Walter Meynell. LC 38-27138. 1938. Harper & Brothers.

House in the Hills & Other Short Stories. Sujatha B. Subramanian. (Indian Short Stories Ser.). 123p. 1974. 6.85 (ISBN 0-88253-464-5). Ind-US Inc.

House in the Hollow. Ethel Lockwood. 1972. 4.95. Lenox Hill Press.

House in the Hoo. Esther Wood & Kalab, Theresa, Illus. LC 41-19433. Longmans Green and Co.

House in the Kasbah. Maxine Reynolds. 1972. pap. 0.75 o.p. (94283). Beagle Bks.

House in the Mist. Anna Katharine Green Rohlfs. LC 5-13025. (On cover: The pocket books). 1905. The Bobbs-Merrill Company.

House in the Road: A Fantasy of Truth. Hervey White. LC 13-25944. 1913. The Maverick Press.

House in the Shadows. Carolyn McKnight. LC 79-16367. 1979. 8.95 (ISBN 0-312-39255-9). St. Martin's Press.

House in the Sun. Dane Chandos. LC 49-116338. 1949. Putman's Sons.

House in the Uplands. Erskine Caldwell. LC 49-48374. (Uniform edition of the works of Erskine Caldwell). 1949. Duell, Sloan and Pearce.

House in the Uplands. Erskine Caldwell. LC 46-395216. 1946. Duell, Sloan and Pearce.

House in the Woods. Arthur Henry. LC 4-10884. 1904. A. S. Barnes & Company.

House in Tuesday Market. Joseph Smith Fletcher. LC 29-1083. 1929. A. A. Knopf.

House in Vienna. Edith De Born. 1960. 4.95 o.p. Knopf.

House in Vienna. Marianne Philips. Tr. by Clephane, Irene. LC 36-115512. Harcourt, Brace and Company.

House Is Dark. Rebecca Salsbury James. 1977. 1.95 (ISBN 0-445-04014-9). Popular Library.

House Is Dark. Rebecca Salsbury James. LC 75-21230. 1976. 7.95 (ISBN 0-385-03135-1). Doubleday.

House Keepers. Linda Grover. LC 70-95961. 1970. 5.95. Harper & Row.

House Made of Dawn. Natachee Scott Momaday. LC 67-28820. 1968. Harper & Row.

House Made with Hands. Adelaide Champneys. LC 27-23356. 1927. The Bobbs-Merrill Company.

House Made with Hands. Miss Triverton Goes Out, Author of. LC 27-23356. The Bobbs-Merrill Company.

House Malign. easy eye ed. Julie Wellsley. pap. 0.95 o.s.i. (75-271). Lancer.

House-Mates. John Davys Beresford. LC 17-12391. 1.35. George H. Doran Company.

House Mother. Fran Owen. LC 29-17528. 1929. The Lantern Press, Inc.

House Next Door. Jane Corley. (Alouette Romance Ser.). 128p. (Orig.). 1981. pap. 2.25 (ISBN 0-89531-136-4, 0198-96). Sharon Pubns.

House Next Door. Anne Rivers Siddons. LC 78-18431. 9.95 (ISBN 0-671-24018-8). Simon and Schuster.

House Next Door. Lionel White. LC 58-4002. (Signet book, 1442). 1957. New American Library.

House Next Door: A Detective Story. Burton Egbert Stevenson. LC 32-57460. 1932. Dodd, Mead & Company.

House Next Door: A Novel. Galen B Finch. LC 45-7241. 1945. The Bartlett Publishing Co.

House Next Door. 1st Ed. Lionel White. LC 56-52634. (Guilt edged mystery). 1956. Dutton.

House of a Merchant Prince: A Novel of New York. William Henry Bishop. LC 6-127129. 1883. New York, Houghton, Mifflin and Company.

House of a Stranger. Gerald Earl Bailey. LC 77-90591. 6.95 (ISBN 0-87141-065-6). Manyland Books.

House of a Thousand Candles. Meredith Nicholson. 1905. The Bobbs-Merrill Company.

House of a Thousand Candles. Meredith Nicholson. LC 9-322930. 1907. A. Wessels Company.

House of a Thousand Candles. Meredith Nicholson. LC 24-14939. Grosset & Dunlap.

House of a Thousand Lanterns. Eleanor Hibbert. LC 73-20514. 1974. 6.95 (ISBN 0-385-00817-1). Doubleday.

House of a Thousand Lanterns. Eleanor Hibbert. LC 75-8856. 1975. 14.95 (ISBN 0-8161-6272-7). G. K. Hall.

House of a Thousand Lanterns. Victoria Holt, pseud. 384p. 1978. pap. 2.95 (ISBN 0-449-23685-4, Crest). Fawcett.

House of a Thousand Lanterns. Victoria Holt, pseud. (Adult Ser.). 1975. lib. bdg. 14.95 o.p. (ISBN 0-8161-6272-7, Large Print Bks). G K Hall.

House of a Thousand Lanterns. Victoria Holt. (Fawcett crest book). 1975. (pbk.) 1.75. Fawcett.

House of a Thousand Welcomes: "Cead Mille Fail-the". Edward Raphael Lipsett. LC 12-16431. 1912. 1.30. John Lane Company.

House of Adventure. Warwick Deeping. LC 22-474. 1921. Cassell and Company, Ltd.

House of Adventure. Warwick Deeping. LC 22-129872. 1922. The Macmillan Company.

House of Alarcon. Joseph Dispenza. LC 78-3598. 9.95 (ISBN 0-698-10928-7). Coward, McCann & Geoghegan.

House of All Nations. Christina Stead. 1974. (pbk.) 2.45. Bard Books Published by Avon.

House of All Nations. Christina Stead. LC 72-80210. 1972. 10.00 (ISBN 0-03-001946-X). Holt, Rinehart and Winston.

House of All Nations: A Novel. Christina Stead. LC 38-14591. Simon and Schuster.

House of America. Richard Dodge La Guardia. LC 25-17941. The Christopher Publishing House.

House of Another Kind. William Fritts. (Orig.). 1981. pap. 2.25 (ISBN 0-505-51669-1). Tower Bks.

House of Armour: A Novel. Marshall Saunder. LC 8-1833. 1897. A. J. Rowland.

House of Baltazar. William John Locke. LC 20-26105. 1920. John Lane Company.

House of Bethlehem. Wallace Winchell. LC 70-186602. (Living Poets' Library Ser). pap. 2.50. Dragons Teeth.

House of Bisque & Sawdust. Connie Kidwell. (Orig.). 1980. pap. 1.95 (ISBN 0-532-23205-4). Woodhill.

House of Bondage. Reginald Wright Kauffman. LC 68-58271. 1968. Gregg Press.

House of Bondage. Reginald Wright Kauffman. LC 10-18881. 1910. Moffat, Yard and Company.

House of Bondage. Reginald Wright Kauffman. LC 21-14442. 1921. Grosset & Dunlap.

House of Borgia. rev. ed. Marcus Van Heller, pseud. pap. 1.25 o.p. (2035). Brandon.

House of Brass. Ellery Queen, pseud. LC 68-13406. 1968. New American Library.

House of Brass. Ellery Queen, pseud. LC 77-14546. (Ellery Queen mystery). 1978. 8.95 (ISBN 0-89340-109-9). J. Curley.

House of Brass see Face to Face.

House of Breath. William Goyen. LC 74-23987. 1975. 6.95. (ISBN 0-394-49699-X) (ISBN 0-394-73053-4). Random House.

House of Breath. William Goyen. LC 50-944. 1950. Random House.

House of Broken Dreams. Christine Jope-Slade. LC 24-23286. 2.00. George H. Doran Company.

House of Cain. Suzanne Roberts. (Candlelight gothic,#163). 1975. (pbk.) 0.75. Dell.

House of Cain. Arthur William Upfield. LC 29-20644. Dorrance and Company.

House of Candles. Patty Brisco, pseud. (1973 ed. o.p.). 192p. (Orig.). 1976. pap. 1.25 (ISBN 0-532-12434-0). Woodhill.

House of Candles. Patty Brisco. (gothic novel.). 1973. (pbk.) 0.95. Manor Books.

House of Cards". Alice Curtayne. (Half-title: Science and culture series: J. Husslein... general editor). The Bruce Publishing Company.

House of Cards. Stanley Ellin. (3792). 1968. Dell.

House of Cards. Stanley Ellin. LC 66-21502. 1967. Random House.

House of Cards. Leon Garfield. 304p. 1983. 12.95 (ISBN 0-312-39259-1). St Martin.

House of Cards. Hannah Gartland. LC 22-853979. 1922. Dodd, Mead and Company.

House of Cards. Alice S Wolf. LC 8-37124. (Half-title: The peacock library). 1896. Stone & Kimball.

House of Cards: A Record. John Heigh. 1905. The Macmillan Company.

House of Care. William John Burley. 192p. 1982. 10.95 (ISBN 0-8027-5464-3). Walker & Co.

House of Certain Death. Albert Cossery. LC 49-11979. (Direction, 11). 1949. New Directions.

House of Chance. Gertie De S Wentworth-James. LC 12-814341. 1912. W. Rickey & Company.

House of Children: A Novel. Joyce Cary. LC 55-11282. Harper.

House of Christina. Ben Haas. 1981. pap. 2.95 (ISBN 0-440-13793-4). Dell.

House of Christina: A Novel. Ben Haas. LC 76-30373. 9.95 (ISBN 0-671-22526-X). Simon and Schuster.

House of Clay. Carolyn Bell. Ed. by Alice Sachs. 1971. 3.95 o.p. Lenox Hill.

House of Clay: A Novel. Ruth Beeghly Statler. LC 51-28012.

House of Cobwebs. George Robert Gissing & Seccombe, Thomas. (wayfarer's library). 1915. E. P. Dutton & Co.

House of Cobwebs. Mary Reisner. LC 44-3418. 1944. Dodd, Mead & Company.

House of Cobwebs & Other Stories. George Robert Gissing. Repr. of 1906 ed. 11.00 o.p. (ISBN 0-404-08822-8). AMS Pr.

House of Cobwebs: And Other Stories. 2d impression. ed. George Robert Gissing & Seccombe, Thomas. 1906. E. P. Dutton & Company.

House of Cobwebs, and Other Stories. To Which Is Prefixed The Work of George Gissing. George Robert Gissing. LC 77-160932. (Short story index reprint series). 1971. (ISBN 0-8369-3911-5). Books for Libraries Press.

House of Conrad. Elias Tobenkin. LC 76-104580. 1970. (ISBN 0-8398-1960-9). Literature House.

House of Conrad. Elias Tobenkin. LC 18-5214. Frederick A. Stokes Company.

House of Courage. Jessie Louisa Moore Rickard. LC 19-13460. 1919. Dodd, Mead.

House of Courage. Jessie Louisa Moore Rickard. LC 19-13460. 1919. Dodd, Mead and Company.

House of Cray. Pamela Hill. LC 81-21533. 12.95 (ISBN 0-312-39260-5). St. Martin's Press.

House of Creeping Horror. George Frank Worts. LC 34-12965. A. H. King.

House of Dark Illusions. Carolina Farr. Incl. Secret of the Chateau. 1977. pap. 2.50 (ISBN 0-451-11691-7, AE1691, Sig). NAL.

House of Dark Illusions. Caroline Farr. (Signet, T5579). 1973. (pbk.) 0.75. New American Lib.

House of Dark Illusions & The Secret of the Chateau. Caroline Farr. (Signet Book). 1977. 1.75 (ISBN 0-451-07662-1). New American Library.

House of Dark Shadows. Marilyn Ross. (Dark Shadows Ser). (Illus., Orig.). 1970. pap. 0.75 o.p. (ISBN 0-446-64537-0, 64-537). Paperback Lib.

House of Darkness. Allan MacKinnon. LC 47-1197. 1947. Pub. for the Crime Club by Doubleday & Company, Inc.

House of Darkness. Charles Elbert Scoggins. LC 31-522220. The Bobbs-Merrill Company.

House of David. Jerry Landay. 1974. 14.95 o.p. (ISBN 0-8415-0290-0). Dutton.

House of Dawn. Charles Elbert Scoggins. LC 35-108502. 1935. D. Appleton-Century Company, Incorporated.

House of De Mailly: A Romance. Margaret Horton Potter. LC 1-16621. 1901. Harper & Brothers.

House of Deadly Night. Iris Barry. (Orig.). 1970. pap. 0.75 o.p. (B75-2060). Belmont-Tower.

House of Deadly Night. Iris Barry. (O.s.i.). 1972. pap. 0.75 o.s.i. (BT50253). Belmont-Tower.

House of Death. Kenneth Robeson. (Avenger, no. 15). 1973. (pbk.) 0.75. Warner Paperback Lib.

House of Deceit... LC 14-176213. 1914. H. Holt and Company.

House of Deceit. Rae Loomis, pseud. 1970. pap. 0.75 o.p. (75-318). Manor Bks.

House of Defence. Edward Frederic Benson. LC 6-29529. McLeod & Allen.

House of Delusion. Rupert Sargent Holland. LC 22-221561. G. W. Jacobs & Company.

House of Desdemona or the Laurels & Limitations of Historical Fiction. Lion Feuchtwanger. Tr. by Harold A. Basilius. LC 63-8063. (Waynebooks Ser: No. 12). (Orig.). 1963. pap. 3.95x o.p. (ISBN 0-8143-1218-7). Wayne St U Pr.

House of Dies Drear. Virginia Hamilton. (YA) 1978. pap. 1.75 (ISBN 0-440-93679-9, LFL). Dell.

House of Discord. Virginia Lee Ward. LC 47-24296. 1947. Dorrance.

House of Dr. Edwardes. Francis Beeding. LC 28-676. 1928. Little, Brown, and Company.

House of Dolls. Karol Cetynski. LC 54-12363. 1955. Simon and Schuster.

House of Dolls. Ka-Tzetnik. 1969. pap. 0.75 o.p. (T2119). Pyramid Pubns.

House of Dolls. Ka-Tzetnik. 1977. pap. 1.50 o.p. (ISBN 0-515-04201-3). BJ Pub Group.

House of Doom, House of Desire. Sharon Wagner. 224p. (Orig.). 1980. pap. 1.95 (ISBN 0-89083-602-7). Zebra.

House of Dread. Ray Dorain. 1968. pap. 0.60 o.p. (53-720). Paperback Lib.

House of Dreams. William James Dawson. LC 6-32249. 1897. Dodd, Mead and Company.

House of Dreams-Come-True. Margaret Bass Pedler. LC 19-17179. 1.75. George H. Doran Company.

House of Dreams-Come-True. Margaret Bass Pedler. LC 28-4853. Grosset & Dunlap.

House of Earth: A Novel. Dorothy Clarke Wilson. LC 52-10040. 1952. Westminster Press.

House of Earth: The Good Earth; Sons; A House Divided... Pearl Sydenstricker Buck. LC 35-27091. 1935. Reynal & Hitchcock.

House of Egremont: A Novel. Molly Elliot Seawell. LC 6704. 1900. C. Scribner's Sons.

House of Elnora Garland. Wanda Lutrell. (Orig.). 1971. pap. 0.75 o.p. (B75-2165). Belmont-Tower.

House of Evil. John Trinian. 1970. pap. 0.75 o.p. (75-379). Manor Bks.

House of Evil: By Clayre and Michel Lipman. Clayre Lipman & Michel Lipman. LC 55-21029. (Lion book, 231). 1954. Lion Books.

House of False Faces. Helen Weston. (Orig.). 1970. pap. 0.60 o.p. (63-272). Paperback Lib.

House of Fancy. Julie Connor. (Orig.). 1969. pap. 0.75 o.p. (B75-230). Belmont-Tower.

House of Fear. Charles Wadsworth Camp. LC 16-17418. 1916. 1.35. Doubleday, Page & Company.

House of Fear. by robert w. service... ed. Robert William Service. 1927. Dodd, Mead & Company.

House of Fear: A Novel. Robert William Service. LC 28-17931. 1928. Dodd, Mead & Company.

House of Fiction: An Anthology of the Short Story, with Commentary, by Caroline Gordon and Allen Tate. Ed. by Caroline Gordon & Allen Tate. LC 50-7725. 1950. Scribner.

House of Fiction: An Anthology of the Short Story, with Commentary. 2d ed. Ed. by Caroline Gordon & Allen Tate. LC 60-6360. (Illus.). 1960. Scribner.

House of Five Gables. Mary Johnson Holmes. LC 7-12588. (On cover: Columbian series. no. 4). 1892. Hurst and Company.

House of Five Swords: A Romance. Tristram Tupper. LC 22-22703. George H. Doran Company.

House of Five Talents. Louis Auchincloss. LC 60-8761. 1960. Houghton Mifflin.

House of Flesh. Bruno Fischer. LC 50-39709. (Gold medal book, 123). 1950. Fawcett Publications.

House of Flesh: A Novel. William Wetmore. LC 68-14743. 1968. Little, Brown.

House of Fools. Jan Alexander, pseud. 1971. pap. 0.75 o.p. (ISBN 0-447-74745-2). Lancer.

House of Four Widows. S. J. Treibick. pap. 0.60 o.p. Lancer.

House of Four Windows. Delphine C. Lyons. 1972. pap. 0.95 o.s.i. (75-354). Lancer.

House of Fulfillment: The Romance of a Soul. Lily Moresby Adams Beck. LC 27-191141. 1927. Cosmopolitan Book Corporation.

House of Fulfilment. George Madden Martin. LC 4-25102. 1904. McClure, Phillips & Co.

House of Fury. Jo Anne Creighton. (Orig.). 1973. pap. 0.95 o.p. Curtis.

House of Fury. Felice Swados. LC 41-280688. 1941. Doubleday, Doran & Co., Inc.

House of Gair: A Novel. 1st American Ed. Eric Robert Russell Linklater. LC 54-52514. 1954. Harcourt, Brace.

House of Gentlefolk; a Novel. Ivan Sergeevich Turgenev. LC 71-10350. (His Novels, v. 2). 1970. AMS Press.

House of Gentlefolk, and Fathers and Children. Ivan Sergieevich Turgenev. Tr. by Constance Garnett. LC 17-17425. (Harvard classics shelf of fiction, selected by C. W. Eliot. 19). P. F. Collier & Son.

House of Gladness. Emma Sarah Gage Allen. LC 15-160069. 1915. G.W. Jacobs & Company.

House of Glass. Georgina Ferrand. LC 75-22345. 1975. 1.25 (ISBN 0-345-24639-X). Ballantine Books.

House of Glass. J. Harvey Howells. LC 65-16271. 1965. Appleton-Century.

House of Glass. Peggy V. M. Wrightson. LC 51-9017. 1951. Morrow.

House of God. Samuel Shem. 1980. pap. 3.50 (ISBN 0-440-13368-8). Dell.

House of God: A Novel. Samuel Shem. LC 78-18368. (Illus.). 9.95 (ISBN 0-399-90023-3). R. Marek Publishers.

House of God and Minnie May. Hilary H Milton. LC 70-87996. 1969. 4.95. Robert B. Luce.

House of Gold. Ann Anderson. 1974. (pbk.) 0.95. Dell.

House of Gold. Elizabeth Cullinan. LC 70-86625. 1970. Houghton Mifflin.

House of Gold. Liam O'Flaherty. LC 29-20012. Harcourt, Brace and Company.

House of Good Repute. Cara Palmer. (O.s.i.). 1976. pap. 1.50 o.s.i. (BT50895). Belmont-Tower.

House of Granite. Elizabeth Renier. 221p. 1981. pap. 1.95 (ISBN 0-441-34411-9). Ace Bks.

House of Graydon. A Novel. W P Needham. LC 7-25789. 1888. M. Cullaton & Co., Printers.

House of Green Dragons. Rosa Hill. LC 83-2930. 224p. 1983. 12.95 (ISBN 0-312-39261-3). St Martin.

House of Green Turf. Edith Pargeter. LC 69-16862. 1969. 5.50. Morrow.

House of Green Turf. Ellis Peters. 1969. 5.50 o.p. Morrow.

House of Green Turf. Ellis Peters. 1970. pap. 0.60 o.p. (X2227). Pyramid Pubns.

House of Halliwell. authorized ed. Ellen Price Henry Wood Wood. LC 8-37880. (On cover: Lovell's international series, 130). 1890. United States Book Company.

House of Happiness. Kate Lee Langley Bosher. LC 13-220962. 1913. Harper & Brothers.

House of Happiness, and Other Stories. Ethel May Dell. LC 72-5866. (Short story index reprint series). 1972. (ISBN 0-8369-4209-4). Books for Libraries Press.

House of Happiness: And Other Stories. Ethel May Dell. LC 27-75093. 1927. G. P. Putnam's Sons.

House of Hate. Jean Erskine Ferris. 1974. 4.95 (ISBN 0-517-51569-5). Lenox Hill Press.

House of Hate: A Novel. Rita Wellman. LC 24-29075. 1924. R. M. McBride & Company.

House of Hearts in Eighty-Second St. A Novel. G. Allen Mason. LC 13-1641. Broadway Publishing Company.

House of Helen. Corra May White Harris. George H. Doran Company.

House of Her Own. Robert F Mirvish. LC 52-138332. 1953. Sloane.

House of Hidden Treasure. 1898. D. Appleton & Co.

House of Hidden Treasure. Mary Gleed Tuttiett. LC 98-418. 1898. D. Appleton and Company.

House of Hope. Lynne Reid Banks. LC 62-16388. 1962. Simon and Schuster.

House of Hostile Women. Florence Faulkner. (YA) 1978. 6.95 (Avalon). Bouregy.

House of Hunger. Dambudzo Marechera. (African Writers Ser.: No.207). 160p. 1978. pap. text ed. 4.50x (ISBN 0-435-90207-5). Heinemann Ed.

House of Hunger: A Novella & Short Stories. Dambudzo Marechera. LC 79-2284. 1979. 7.95 (ISBN 0-394-50832-7). Pantheon Books.

House of Hunger: Short Stories. Dambudzo Marechera. LC 79-306669. (African writers series; 207). 1978. 7.95 (ISBN 0-435-90207-5). Heinemann Educational.

House of Ibuki. Clayton Eshleman. 1969. pap. 2.45 (ISBN 0-912090-02-2). Sumac Mich.

House of Incest. Anais Nin. LC 82-70910. 72p. 1958. pap. 3.95 (ISBN 0-8040-0148-0). Swallow.

House of Incest. Photomontages by Val Telberg. Anais Nin. LC 59-32839. 1958.

House of Intrigue. Arthur John Arbuthnott Stringer. LC 18-6516. The Bobbs-Merrill Company.

House of Inver. E. E. Somerville & Martin Ross. 1973. pap. 0.95 o.p. (09243). Curtis.

House of Iron Men. Jack Steele. LC 11-22006. 1.20. D. Fitzgerald Inc.

House of Islam. Marmaduke William Pickthall. LC 6-31647. 1906. D. Appleton and Company.

House of Jackdaws. Dwyer-Joyce, Alice. LC 79-3459. 1980. 8.95 (ISBN 0-312-39262-1). St. Martin's Press.

House of Joy. Laurence Housman. LC 73-81268. (Short story index reprint series). (Illus.). 1969. Books for Libraries Press.

House of Joy: A Story of Stage-Life in Holland. Jo Van Ammers-Kuller. Tr. by Wyhe, H. Van. LC 20-268984. E. P. Dutton & Co., Inc.

House of Judah. Charles Edward Hewitt. LC 19-321713. The Abingdon Press.

House of Kingsley Merrick. Deborah Hill. LC 78-2192. 1978. 10.95 (ISBN 0-698-10866-3). Coward, McCann & Geoghegan.

House of Kingsley Merrick. Deborah Hill. (Signet Book). 1979. 2.50 (ISBN 0-451-08918-9). New American Library.

House of Krupp. Peter Batty. LC 67-14093. 1969. pap. 4.95 (ISBN 0-8128-1232-8). Stein & Day.

House of Kuragin. Constance Heaven. LC 73-15827. 1973. 10.95 (ISBN 0-8161-6158-5). G. K. Hall.

House of Landell: Or, Follow and Find. Gertrude Capen Whitney. LC 17-20422. R. F. Fenno & Company.

House of Landsdown. Caroline Farr. (Signet Book). 1977. 1.50 (ISBN 0-451-07700-8). New American Library.

House of Lee. Gertrude Franklin Horn Atherton. LC 40-30878. 1940. D. Appleton-Century Company, Incorporated.

House of Liars. Elsa Morante. LC 51-12849. 1951. Harcourt, Brace.

House of Lies... Austin Moore. LC 32-18612. Pub. for the Crime Club, Inc., by Doubleday, Doran & Company, Inc.

House of Lies. Translated from the French by Herma Briffault. Francoise Mallet-Joris. LC 57-12156. 1957. Farrar, Straus.

House of Lions. Gloria V. Basile. Orig. Title: Godson. 1978. pap. 2.25 (ISBN 0-523-40191-4). Pinnacle Bks.

House of Lost Identity: Tales & Drawings. facsimile ed. Donald Corley. LC 73-106280. (Short Story Index Reprint Ser.). Repr. of 1927 ed. 19.00 (ISBN 0-8369-4007-5). Ayer Co.

House of Lost Indentity. Donald Corley. LC 27-17118. 1927. R. M. McBride & Company.

House of Love. Elizabeth Cheney. LC 14-16216. 1.25. The Abingdon Press.

House of Love. Ka-Tzetnik. LC 72-177263. 1971. 1.75 (ISBN 0-491-00057-X). W. M. Allen.

House of Luck. Harris Dickson. LC 16-229399. 1.35. Small, Maynard & Company.

House of Lust. Alex Ayers. 192p. pap. 1.95 o.p. (6095). Brandon.

House of Lynch. Leonard Merrick. LC 34-8657. (Half-title: The works of Leonard Merrick). 1923. Hodder & Stoughton.

House of Madam Lindy: A Novel. 1st Ed. Frank B Felton. LC 56-12673. 1957. Exposition Press.

House of Madelaine. Elaine Kraf. LC 78-150283. 1971. 5.95. Doubleday.

House of Many Doors. Dorothy Daniels. (Orig.). 1971. pap. 0.60 o.p. (ISBN 0-446-63545-6, 63-545). Paperback Lib.

House of Many Rooms. Rodello Hunter, pseud. LC 65-18753. 240p. 1981. Repr. 9.95 (ISBN 0-914740-22-9). Western Epics.

House of Many Rooms. 1st Ed. Robin White. LC 58-8871. 1958. Harper.

House of Many Shadows. Barbara Mertz. LC 74-10006. 1974. 6.95 (ISBN 0-396-07016-7). Dodd, Mead.

House of Many Shadows. Barbara Michaels. LC 74-10006. 288p. 1974. 6.95 o.p. (ISBN 0-396-07016-7). Dodd.

House of Many Worlds. Sam Merwin. LC 51-12481. (Doubleday science fiction). 1951. Doubleday.

House of Martha. Frank Richard Stockton. LC 4-15158. 1891. Houghton, Mifflin and Company.

House of Martha at Bethany. Herman Joseph Heuser. LC 27-18486. 1927. Longmans, Green and Co.

House of Men. easy eye ed. Catherine Marchant, pseud. 1969. pap. 0.75 o.p. (74-995). Lancer.

House of Mendoza: A Romance of Modern Spain. Condes Neve. LC 25-15760. 1925. Dorrance and Company.

House of Merrilees. Archibald Marshall. LC 22-108371. 1919. Dodd, Mead and Company.

House of Mirror Images. Daoma Winston. Bd. with House of Mirror Images; Trificante Treasure; Shadow on Mercer Mountain. 1972. pap. 1.65 o.s.i. (70-404). Lancer.

House of Mirror. 1st Ed. Nona Coxhead. LC 50-12119. 1950. Dutton.

House of Mirrors. Yvonne Whittal. (Harlequin Romances Ser.). 192p. 1983. pap. 1.75 (ISBN 0-373-02538-6). Harlequin Bks.

House of Mirth. Edith Newbold Jones Wharton. 1905. C. Scribner's Sons.

House of Mirth. Edith Newbold Jones Wharton. LC 21-16883. 1908. C. Scribner's Sons.

House of Mirth. Edith Newbold Jones Wharton. LC 24-204840. 1922. C. Scribner's Sons.

House of Mirth. Edith Newbold Jones Wharton. LC 44-44937. 1905. Macmillan and Co., Limited.

House of Mirth. Edith Newbold Jones Wharton. (Half-title: The World's classics. CDXXXVII). 1936. Oxford University Press, Humphrey Milford.

House of Mirth. Edith Newbold Jones Wharton. 1981. 2.95 (ISBN 0-425-04611-7). Berkley Publishing Corp.

House of Mirth. Edith Newbold Jones Wharton & Lily Harmon. LC 75-322678. (Illus.). 1975. Limited Editions Club.

House of Mirth. Introd. by Irving Howe. Edith Newbold Jones Wharton. LC 62-9521. (Rinehart editions, 113). 1962. Holt, Rinehart and Winston.

House of Mirth: With a Foreword by Marcia Davenport. Edith Newbold Jones Wharton. LC 51-14301. 1951. Scribner.

House of Mist. Maria Luisa Bombal. LC 47-2411. 1947. Farrar, Straus and Company.

House of Mohun. George Fort Gibbs. LC 22-12893. 1922. D. Appleton and Company.

House of Moonlight. August William Derieth. LC 53-13412. 1953. Prairie Press.

House of Moonlight. August William Derleth. 10.00 (ISBN 0-88361-054-X). Stanton & Lee.

House of Moonlight. August William Derleth. 4.95 o.s.i. (ISBN 0-88451-011-5). Edco-Vis Assoc.

House of Moreys. phyllis bentley. ed. Eleanor Phyllis. 1976. 1.50. Ace Books.

House of Moreys: A Romance. Phyllis Eleanor Bentley. LC 53-10421. 1953. Macmillan.

House of Mrs. Caroline: A Novel. Charles Marie Franzero, pseud. LC 43-15960. 1943. Howell, Soskin.

House of Murder. Henry Leyford Gates. LC 31-1516. 1930. The Fiction League.

House of Mystery. Lida Lavinia Coghlan. 1926. B. Herder Book Co.

House of Mystery: An Episode in the Career of Rosalie Le Grange, Clairvoyant. William Henry Irwin. LC 10-893387. 1910. The Sentury Co.

House of Nations. R. Stanton. 1972. 10.00 o.p. (ISBN 0-03-001946-X). HR&W.

House of Night. Leslie Howard Gordon. LC 21-9370. Small, Maynard & Company.

TITLE INDEX

HOUSE OF THE SEVEN

House of Numbers. Jack Finney. LC 57-7752. (Dell first edition, A139). 1957. Dell Pub. Co.
House of Orchids: A Novel. 1st Ed. Hazel Ai Chun Lin. LC 60-12350. 1960. Citadel Press.
House of Peril. Louis Tracy. LC 22-107750. E. J. Clode.
House of Pleasure. Joe Greene. 1968. pap. 0.75 o.p. (ISBN 0-446-54669-0, 54-669). Paperback Lib.
House of Pomegranates. Oscar Wilde. LC 41-38918. (Half-title: Old world series). 1906. T. B. Mosher.
House of Power. Sami Bindari. LC 79-24665. 1980. 7.95 (ISBN 0-395-28540-2). Houghton Mifflin.
House of Pride: And Other Tales of Hawaii. Jack London. LC 12-6553. 1912. The Macmillan Company.
House of Pride: And Other Tales of Hawaii. Jack London. LC 18-20839. 1914. The Macmillan Company.
House of Prophecy. Gilbert Cannan. LC 24-216687. 1924. T. Seltzer.
House of Quai Notre Dame. Georges Simenon. LC 75-9682. 1975. 6.95 (ISBN 0-15-142181-1). Harcourt Brace Jovanovich.
House of Quiet: An Autobiography. Arthur Christopher Benson. LC 43-36623. 1906. E. P. Dutton and Company.
House of Quite: An Autobiography. Arthur Christopher Benson. LC 7-21535. 1907. E. P. Dutton & Company.
House of Rancour. Sarah Nichols. 1974. (pbk.) 0.95. Popular Library.
House of Ravensbourne. Mary Ann Gibbs. 1973. pap. 0.95 o.p. (ISBN 0-515-03192-5, N3192). BJ Pub Group.
House of Refuge. Grace Sothcote Leake. LC 32-253265. 1932. W. F. Payson.
House of Rimmon. Mary Stanbery Watts. LC 22-4677. 1922. The Macmillan Company.
House of Romance: Certain Stories, Including La Bella and Others. Agnes Sweetman Castle & Castle, Egerton. LC 1-17004. 1901. F. A. Stokes Company.
House of Ross: And Other Tales. Albert Gallatin Riddle. LC 7-41433. 1881. Hall and Whiting.
House of Scorpio. Pat Wallace. 1975. (pbk.) 1.95 (ISBN 0-380-00532-8). Avon.
House of Seclusion. Marion Harvey. LC 25-101472. 1925. Small, Maynard & Company.
House of Secrets. Edna Ames. LC 75-28777. 176p. (Orig.). 1976. pap. 1.25 (ISBN 0-89041-043-7, 3043). Major Bks.
House of Secrets. Caroline Farr. (Signet gothic, T5368). 1973. (pbk) 0.75. New American Library.
House of Secrets. Sydney Horler. LC 27-2557. George H. Doran Company.
House of Secrets. Harriet Lewis. (On cover: The select series, no. 17). 1888. Street & Smith.
House of Serravalle. Richard Bagot. LC 11-5226. 1911. 1.50. John Lane Company.
House of Seven Gables. Nathaniel Hawthorne. LC 4580. W. B. Conkey Company.
House of Seventy Mats. Lincoln Haynes. LC 72-90677. 1973. 3.95 (ISBN 0-8059-1776-4). Dorrance.
House of Shade. Michael Home, pseud. LC 42-21689. 1942. W. Morrow & Co.
House of Shade. 1st American Ed. Mary Margaret Kaye. LC 59-110023. 1959. Coward-McCann.
House of Shadows. Evelyn Bond. 256p. 1975. pap. 1.25 (ISBN 0-532-12284-4). Woodhill.
House of Shadows. easy eye ed. Evelyn Bond. pap. 0.75 o.p. Lancer.
House of Shadows. Renate Chapman. 1982. pap. 6.95 (Avalon). Bouregy.
House of Shadows. Florence Hurd. 176p. (Orig.). 1973. pap. 0.75 o.p. (T2745, GM). Fawcett World.
House of Shadows. Sharon Wagner. (Orig.). 1972. pap. 0.75 o.p. (94302). Beagle Bks.
House of Shame: A Novel... Charles Felton Pidgin. LC 13-116. 1912. 1.25. The Cosmopolitan Press.
House of Shanahan. 1st Ed. Roger Burke Dooley. LC 52-5768. 1952. Doubleday.
House of Silence. Louis Tracy. LC 11-1312. E. J. Clode.
House of Silence. A Tale of New Orleans. John Hovey Robinson. LC 7-42158. (sea and shore series, no. 20). 1890. Street & Smith.
House of Sin. Allen Upward. LC 27-3409. 1927. J. B. Lippincott Company.
House of Sinners. Peggy Gaddis, pseud. (O.s.i.). 1971. pap. 0.75 o.s.i. (532-75435-075). Manor Bks.
House of Slammers: A Novel. Nathan C. Heard. 256p. 1983. 9.95 o.p. Macmillan.
House of Sleep. Helen Woods Edmonds. LC 47-5147. 1947. Doubleday.
House of Soldiers: By Andrew Garve Pseud. 1st Ed. Paul Winterton. LC 61-14833. 1961. Harper.
House of Sorcery. Alan Geoffrey Yates. LC 68-1671. (Carter Brown mystery series). 1967. New American Library.
House of Souls. Arthur Machen. LC 72-152947. (Short story index reprint series). 1971. (ISBN 0-8369-3806-2). Books for Libraries Press.
House of Souls. Arthur Machen. LC 22-15673. 1922. A. A. Knopf.
House of Spies. Warwick Deeping. LC 13-7525. 1913. 1.35. Cassell & Company, Limited.
House of Spies. Warwick Deeping. LC 38-17826. 1938. R. M. McBride and Company.
House of Stolen Memories. Dorothy Daniels. Orig. Title: Mansion of Lost Memories. 1969. pap. 0.75 o.p. (74-575). Lancer.
House of Storm. Mignon Good Eberhart. LC 49-8744. 1949. Random House.
House of Strange Guests. John Victor Turner. LC 32-30524. H. Holt and Company.
House of Strange Secrets: A Detective Story. A. Eric Bayly. LC 99-4361. 1899. E.P. Dutton & Company.
House of Strange Victims. Bertram Atkey. LC 30-182028. 1930. D. Appleton and Company.
House of Strangers. J. Hale. pap. 0.95 o.s.i. (75-280). Lancer.
House of Strangers. Edith Simon. LC 52-13643. 1953. Putnam.
House of Strength. Edwin Brown. LC 22-15476. 1922. The Four Seas Company.
House of Sudden Sleep. John Hawk. LC 30-22209. 1930. The Mystery League, Inc.
House of Sun-Goes-Down. Bernard Augustine De Voto. LC 28-124302. 1928. The Macmillan Company.
House of Swappers. Karl Rockwood. pap. 1.95 o.p. (ISBN 0-87056-186-3). Brandon.
House of Tara. Lucille Lilienthal. 1977. 5.95 o.p. (ISBN 0-533-02643-1). Vantage.
House of Tarot. Rachel Cosgrove Payes. (Berkley medallion book). 1975. (pbk.) 0.95 (ISBN 0-425-02740-6). Berkley Pub. Co.
House of Tavelinck. Jo Van Ammers-Kuller. Tr. by Duym, Alfred Van Ameyden Van. LC 38-29965. Farrar & Rinehart, Inc.
House of Tears. Edmund Downey. (On cover: Lovell's library, no. 1126). J. W. Lovell Company.
House of Terror. Edward Woodward. LC 31-2169. 1930. The Mystery League, Inc.
House of Thane. Elizabeth Dejeans. LC 13-124985. 1913. 1.25. J. B. Lippincott Company.
House of the Angel. Translated from the Spanish by Joan Coyne MacLean. Beatriz Guido. LC 57-7232. 1957. McGraw-Hill.
House of the Arrow. Alfred Edward Woodley Mason. LC 24-23087. George H. Doran Company.
House of the Arrow. Alfred Edward Woodley Mason. LC 28-24486. (S. S. Van Dine detective library). 1928. C. Scribner's Sons.
House of the Bears. John Creasey. LC 75-7517. (His A Doctor Palfrey thriller). 1975. 5.95 (ISBN 0-8027-5325-6). Walker.
House of the Beautiful Hope. Robert Stuart Christie. LC 23-4295. 1923. T. Seltzer.
House of the Bittern. Pamela Ropner. (Illus.). 1967. Coward-McCann.
House of the Black Ring. Fred Lewis Pattee. LC 5-9719. 1905. H. Holt and Company.
House of the Brandersons: A Novel of Possession. Raymond Rudorff. LC 73-82187. 1973. 7.95 (ISBN 0-87795-067-9). Arbor House.
House of the Burgesses. M. R. Burgess. LC 80-10759. (Borgo Family Histories Ser.: No. 1). 168p. 1983. lib. bdg. 14.95x (ISBN 0-89370-801-1); pap. 6.95x (ISBN 0-89370-901-8). Borgo Pr.
House of the Cat. Alexandra Roudybush. LC 79-116249. 1970. 4.50. Published for the Crime Club by Doubleday.
House of the Damned. Anthony M Rud. LC 34-387208. The Macaulay Company C.
House of the Dancing Dead. Aola Vandergriff. (Warner gothic). 1974. (pbk.) 1.25. Warner Paperback Library.
House of the Darkest Death. Alicia Grace. 1976. pap. 1.25 (ISBN 0-532-12428-6). Woodhill.
House of the Dawn. Marah Ellis Martin Ryan. LC 14-18881. 1914. A. C. McClurg & Co.
House of the Dead. Fedor Mikhailovich Dostoevskii. LC 63-885. Dent; New York, Dutton.
House of the Dead. Fedor Mikhailovich Dostoevskii. 1975. 9.95x (ISBN 0-460-00533-2, Evman); pap. 3.95x (ISBN 0-460-01533-8, Evman). Biblio Dist.
House of the Dead. Fedor Mikhailovich Dostoevskii. 1979. 7.00x o.p. (ISBN 0-460-00533-2, Evman); pap. 3.95 o.p. (ISBN 0-460-01533-8). Biblio Dist.
House of the Dead: A Novel in Two Parts. Fedor Mikhailovich Dostoevskii. LC 15-8156. (Half-title: The novels of Fyodor Dostoevsky. vol. V). 1915. The Macmillan Company.
House of the Dead: Or, Prison Life in Siberia. Fedor Mikhailovich Dostoevskii. (Half-title: Everyman's library, ed. by Ernest Rhys. Fiction. no. 533). 1911. J. M. Dent & Sons, Ltd.
House of the Deer. Dorothy Emily Stevenson. LC 78-117278. 1971. 5.95 o.p. (ISBN 0-03-066560-4). HR&W.
House of the Dey: A Story of Algiers. Florence Riddell. LC 30-878029. 1930. J. B. Lippincott Company.
House of the Evening Star. Louise Bergstrom. 1976. 4.95. Avalon Books.
House of the Evil Winds. Millie J. Ragosta. 1973. 4.50 o.p. (Avalon). Bouregy.
House of the Falcon. Harold Lamb. LC 21-4165. 1921. D. Appleton and Company.
House of the Fiery Cauldron. Alice Brennan. (Berkley Large Type Gothic). (Berkley medallion book). 1975. (pbk.) 0.95 (ISBN 0-425-02827-5). Berkley Pub. Co.
House of the Fighting-Cocks. Henry Philip Bernard Baerlein. LC 23-9947. 1923. Harcourt, Brace and Company.
House of the Four Winds. John Buchan. LC 35-10859. 1935. Houghton Mifflin Company.
House of the Haunted Child. Mildred Ames. 1975. 4.95. Avalon Books.
House of the Lost Count. Alice Muriel Livingston Williamson. LC 8-8102. 1908. The McClure Company.
House of the Lost Woman. Louise O'Flaherty. 1974. pap. 1.25 o.p. (ISBN 0-515-03456-8, V3456). BJ Pub Group.
House of the Lost Woman. Louise O'Flaherty. LC 74-1578. 1974. (pbk.) 1.25 (ISBN 0-515-03456-8). Pyramid Books.
House of the Missing. Sinclair Gluck. LC 24-15987. 1924. Dodd, Mead and Company.
House of the Misty Star: A Romance of Youth and Hope and Love in Old Japan. Fannie Macaulay. LC 15-8430. 1915. The Century Co.
House of the Musician. Virginia Wales Johnson. (On cover: Ticknor's paper series of choice reading, no. 8). 1887. Ticknor and Company.
House of the Nightmare: And Other Eerie Tales. Ed. by Kathleen Lines. LC 68-237491. 1968. 3.95. Farrar.
House of the Opal. Jackson Gregory. LC 32-154332. 1932. C. Scribner's Sons.
House of the Prophet. Louis Auchincloss. LC 79-21382. 1980. 10.95 (ISBN 0-395-29084-8). Houghton Mifflin.
House of the Prophet. Louis Auchincloss. LC 80-23761. 1980. 14.95 (ISBN 0-8161-3133-3). G. K. Hall.
House of the Rancher. May Neatherlin. LC 55-14270. 1955. Naylor Co.
House of the Roses. Charlotte Baker. 1942. E. P. Dutton & Co., Inc.
House of the Secret: La Maison Des Hommes Vivants. Claude Farrere. Tr. by Livingston, Arthur. LC 23-6379. E. P. Dutton & Company.
House of the Seven Courts. Dorothy Daniels. (Orig.). pap. 0.60 o.p. (73-638). Lancer.
House of the Seven Flies. Victor Canning. LC 52-9697. 1952. M. S. Mill Co. and W. Morrow.
House of the Seven Gabblers. Nina Larrey Smith Duryea. LC 11-16259. 1911. 1.25. D. Appleton and Company.
House of the Seven Gables. Nathaniel Hawthorne. (Magnum easy eye ed., 14-606). Lancer.
House of the Seven Gables. Nathaniel Hawthorne. Ed. by Waggoner, Hyatt Howe. LC 64-55765. (Riverside editions, A89). 1964. Houghton Mifflin.
House of the Seven Gables. salem ed. Nathaniel Hawthorne. LC 41-32220. 1894. Houghton, Mifflin and Company.
House of the Seven Gables. Nathaniel Hawthorne. LC 7-3876. (On cover: Riverside literature series, no. 91). Houghton, Mifflin and Company.
House of the Seven Gables. Nathaniel Hawthorne. Ed. by Robert Herrick. LC 98-598. (On cover: The Lake English classics). 1898. Scott, Foresman and Company.
House of the Seven Gables. Nathaniel Hawthorne. LC 13-19080. 1913. Houghton Mifflin Company.
House of the Seven Gables. Nathaniel Hawthorne. Ed. by Robert Herrick. LC 19-18166. (Half-title: The Lake English classics, general editor, L. T. Damon...). Scott, Foresman and Company.
House of the Seven Gables. Nathaniel Hawthorne. Ed. by Clyde Bowman Furst. Moffett, Harold Young. LC 30-10970. (Half-title: New pocket classics). The Macmillan Company.
House of the Seven Gables. Nathaniel Hawthorne. LC 37-5398. (Immortal masterpieces of literature. vol. vii). The Spencer Press.
House of the Seven Gables. Nathaniel Hawthorne & Castleman, Josiah Hamilton, 1873- Ed. LC 7-29571. (Merrill's English texts). C. E. Merrill Co.
House of the Seven Gables. Nathaniel Hawthorne & Cowles, Maude Alice, 1871-1905, Illus. LC 98-1538. 1899. Houghton, Mifflin & Company.
House of the Seven Gables. Nathaniel Hawthorne & Davidson, Mrs. Hannah Amelia (Noyes) 1852-1932, Ed. (On cover: Riverside literature series. no. 91). Houghton, Mifflin and Company.
House of the Seven Gables. Nathaniel Hawthorne & Robert James Dixson. LC 52-118062. (American Classics Simplified and Adapted for Greater Reading Pleasure, Book 1). (Illus.). 1973. (pbk.) 1.25. Regents Pub. Co.
House of the Seven Gables. Nathaniel Hawthorne & Ferber, Edna, 1887- So Big. LC 42-3994. (Prose and poetry individualized program. The novel). 1942. The L. W. Singer Company.
House of the Seven Gables. Nathaniel Hawthorne & Neville, Mark Anthony, 1899- LC 49-8420. 1949. Globe Book Co.
House of the Seven Gables. Nathaniel Hawthorne & Milton R Stern. LC 81-2828. (Penguin American Library). 1981. 2.95 (ISBN 0-14-039005-7). Penguin.
House of the Seven Gables see Best Known Works.
House of the Seven Gables: A Romance. Nathaniel Hawthorne. LC 65-6645. (Harper perennial classic). 1965. Harper & Row.
House of the Seven Gables: A Romance. Nathaniel Hawthorne. Ed. by Philip Young. LC 70-126912. (Rinehart editions, no. 89). 1970. (ISBN 0-03-084420-7). Holt, Rinehart and Winston.
House of the Seven Gables: A Romance. Nathaniel Hawthorne. LC 7-3868. 1851. Ticknor, Reed, and Fields.
House of the Seven Gables: A Romance. Nathaniel Hawthorne. LC 41-32428. (The Altemus library, no. 21). 1893. H. Altemus.
House of the Seven Gables: A Romance. Nathaniel Hawthorne. LC 99-393889. T. Y. Crowell & Company.
House of the Seven Gables: A Romance. Nathaniel Hawthorne. Ed. by Clyde Bowman Furst. LC 5-16122. (Macmillan's pocket American and English classics). 1905. The Macmillan Company.
House of the Seven Gables: A Romance. Nathaniel Hawthorne. LC 29-30785. (Lettered on cover: The home library). A. L. Burt Company.
House of the Seven Gables: A Romance. Nathaniel Hawthorne. LC 25-26579. (Half-title: The world's classics. CCLXIII). 1924. H. Milford.
House of the Seven Gables: A Romance. Nathaniel Hawthorne & Grosse, Helen Mason, Illus. LC 24-24806. 1924. Houghton Mifflin Company.
House of the Seven Gables: A Romance. Nathaniel Hawthorne & Angelo Valenti. LC 35-11909. 1935. The Limited Editions Club.
House of the Seven Gables: A Romance. With an Introd. by Philip Young. Nathaniel Hawthorne. LC 57-774167. (Rinehart editions, 89). 1957. Rinehart.
House of the Seven Gables, a Romance. With an Introd. by Philip Young. Nathaniel Hawthorne. LC 57-7741. (Rinehart editions, 89). 1957. Rinehart.
House of the Seven Gables: And The Snow Image, and Other Twice-Told Tales. Nathaniel Hawthorne. LC 4-15452. (Half-title: Riverside ed. The complete works of Nathaniel Hawthorne. vol. iii). Houghton, Mifflin and Company.
House of the Seven Gables: By Nathaniel Hawthorne. Nathaniel Hawthorne. LC 36-37232. (Half-title: Everyman's library, ed. by Ernest Rhys. Fiction. no. 176). 1930. J. M. Dent & Sons, Ltd.
House of the Seven Gables. Ed. by Seymour L. Gross. 1st Ed. Nathaniel Hawthorne. Ed. by Seymour Lee Gross. LC 67-110809. (Norton crit. eds.). 1967. 4.97, 1.95 pap.,. Norton.
House of the Seven Gables: Edited, with a Life of Hawthorne, Notes, and Other Aids to the Study of the Book. Nathaniel Hawthorne & Merrill, A. Marion, Ed. LC 23-6560. (academy classics). Allyn and Bacon.
House of the Seven Gables. Introd. by Charles Angoff. Nathaniel Hawthorne. LC 57-952. Fine Editions Press.
House of the Seven Gables. Introd., Newly Ed. Text by Hyatt H. Waggoner. Nathaniel Hawthorne. Ed. by Hyatt Howe Waggoner. LC 64-55765. (Riverside eds., A89). pap., 1.35. Houghton.
House of the Seven Gables: Simplified and Adapted by Robert J. Dixson. Drawings by Syd Browne. With Exercise I. E. Exercises for Study and Vocabulary Drill. Nathaniel Hawthorne & Robert James Dixson. LC 53-118069. (American classics, book 1). Regents Pub. Co.
House of the Seven Gables (The) and The Marble Faun: Notes by Charles Leavitt. Ed. by Edward T. Byrnes. Edit. Bd. of Consultants: Stanley Cooperman, Charles Leavitt, Unicio J. Violi. (Monarch notes and study guides, 670-0). pap., 1.00. Monarch Pr.

House of the Seven Gables (The) By Nathaniel Hawthorne; Notes, Including Chapter Summaries, Complete Synopsis of Book, Character Sketches, Selected Examination Questions, by Bruce Nicoll. pap., 1.00. Cliff's Notes.

House of the Seven Gables. With a New Introd. by Richard Harter Fogle. Nathaniel Hawthorne. LC 62-19120. 1962. Collier Books.

House of the Seven Gables. With Illus. Reproducing Drawings for Early Editions and Photos. of Contemporary Scenes Together with an Introductory Biographical Sketch of the Author and Anecdotal Captions by Basil Davenport. Nathaniel Hawthorne. LC 50-6979. (Great Illustrated Classics). 1950. Dodd, Mead.

House of the Seventh Cross. Denise Robins. 1973. pap. 0.75 o.p. (26549-1-075). Beagle Bks.

House of the Sleeping Beauties and Other Stories. Yasunari Kawabata. LC 69-19272. 1969. 4.50. Kodansha International.

House of the Solitary Maggot. James Purdy. LC 74-4866. 1974. 7.95 (ISBN 0-385-04413-5). Doubleday.

House of the Sorcerer: Being an Account of Certain Things That Chanced Therein. Haldane Macfall. LC 99-4822. 1900. R. G. Badger & Co.

House of the Spaniard. Arthur Behrend. LC 36-1296. 1936. Doubleday, Doran & Company, Inc.

House of the Sphinx. Louise Bergstrom. (candlelight romance). 1975. (pbk.) 0.75. Dell.

House of the Sphinx: A Novel. Henry Ridgely Evans. LC 7-42015. 1907. The Neale Publishing Company.

House of the Strange Woman. Monica Heath. (Signet Book). 1977. 1.50 (ISBN 0-451-07469-6). New American Library.

House of the Three Ganders. Irving Bacheller. LC 29-26042. The Bobbs-Merrill Company.

House of the Twelve Caesars. Phyllis Hastings. (Berkely Medallion Book). 1976. (pbk.) 1.25. Berkley Publishing Corp.

House of the Two Barbels. Andre Theuriet. LC 8-27743. (Appletons' new handy-volume series v. 8). 1878. D. Appleton and Company.

House of the Two Green Eyes. Stephen Chalmers. LC 26-29076. 1928. Pub. for the Crime Club, Inc., by Doubleday, Doran & Company, Inc.

House of the Vampire. George Sylvester Viereck. LC 75-46309. (Supernatural and Occult Fiction). 1976. 12.00 (ISBN 0-405-08171-5). Arno Press.

House of the Vampire. George Sylvester Viereck. LC 7-289699. 1907. Moffat, Yard & Company.

House of the Vanishing Goblets. Arlo C Edington & Edington, Mrs. Carmen Ballen, 1894- Joint Author. LC 30-931620. The Century Co.

House of the Whispering Pines. Anna Katharine Green Rohlfs. LC 10-7026. 1910. G. P. Putnam's Sons.

House of the Whispering Pines. Anna Katharine Green Rohlfs. LC 21-12956. G. P. Putnam's Sons.

House of the Whispering Pines. Anna Katharine Green Rohlfs. LC 19-181705. 1919. A. L. Burt Company.

House of the White Shadows. Benjamin Leopold Farjeon. 1903. New Amsterdam Book Company.

House of the Wizard. Mary Imlay Taylor. LC 99-4843. 1899. A. C. McClurg and Company.

House of the Wolf. Basil Copper. LC 83-3747. 14.95 (ISBN 0-87054-095-5). Arkham House Publishers.

House of the Wolf. Stanley John Weyman. LC 48-44538. (Marguerite Series, No. 120). Henneberry Co.

House of the Wolf. Stanley John Weyman. (On cover: Seaside library. Pocket ed. no. 2086). 1895. G. Munro's Sons.

House of the Wolf. Stanley John Weyman. LC 11-17966. H. Altemus.

House of the Wolf. M. K. Wren, pseud. 288p. (Orig.). 1981. pap. 2.75 (ISBN 0-425-05058-0). Berkley Pub.

House of the Wolf. A Romance. Stanley John Weyman. 1890. Longmans, Green, and Co.

House of the Wolf. A Romance. new ed. Stanley John Weyman. LC 4-16850. 1894. Longmans, Green and Co.

House of the Wolf. A Romance. new american ed.... ed. Stanley John Weyman. LC 45-45008. (Peerless series, no. 80). 1894. J. S. Ogilvie Publishing Company.

House of the Wolfings. William Morris. (Forgotten Fantasy Library: Vol. 16). 1978. pap. 4.95 (ISBN 0-87877-115-8). Newcastle Pub.

House of the Worm. Gary Myers. LC 75-2523. (Illus.). 1975. 5.50 (ISBN 0-87054-071-8). Arkham House.

House of Three Eagles. Charles Miron. 1978. pap. 1.50 (ISBN 0-532-15343-X). Woodhill.

House of Torchy. Sewell Ford. LC 18-19981. E. J. Clode.

House of Tragedy. Arlene J. Fitzgerald. 192p. (Orig.). 1973. pap. 0.95 o.p. (532-65223-095). Manor Bks.

House of Treachery. Caroline Farr. (Signet Book). 1977. 1.25 (ISBN 0-451-07366-5). New American Library in Association with Horwitz Publications.

House of Treason. Elinore Denniston. LC 36-32335. 1936. The Greystone Press.

House of Treason: By Dennis Allan. Dennis Allan. LC 36-323354. 1936. The Greystone Press.

House of Troy (La Casa De la Troya) Perez Lugin, Alejandro. Tr. by Crocker, Marion A. LC 22-14996. R. G. Badger.

House of Trujillo. Anne Cameron. 1935. D. Appleton-Century Company, Incorporated.

House of Two Wives. William D. Fissell. pap. 0.60 o.p. Lancer.

House of Two Wives see Death Lives in the Mansion.

House of Vanished Splendor. William James McNally. LC 32-182452. 1932. G. P. Putnam's Sons.

House of Vengeance. Annie Laurie McAlister. (Berkley Medallion Book). 1976. (pbk.) 0.95 (ISBN 0-425-03058-X). Berkley Publishing Corp.

House of Violence. Felicia Gizycka. LC 32-8433. 1932. C. Scribner's Sons.

House of War. Catherine Irvine Gavin. LC 75-121053. (Illus.). 1970. 6.95. Morrow.

House of War. Marmaduke William Pickthall. LC 16-86921. 1916. Duffield and Company.

House of Water. Elizabeth Renier. 192p. 1981. pap. 1.75 (ISBN 0-441-34414-3). Ace Bks.

House of Whispers. Jill Baer. (Orig.). 1971. pap. 0.75 o.p. (ISBN 0-446-64717-9, 64-700-4). Paperback Lib.

House of Whispers. William Andrew Johnston. LC 18-6647. 1918. 1.40. Little, Brown, and Company.

House of Wives. Elizabeth Hamilton Herbert. LC 32-5861. Farrar & Rinehart, Incorporated.

House of Women. Herbert Ernest Bates. LC 36-285533. 1936. H. Holt and Company.

House of Women. Chaim I. Bermant. LC 83-2925. 1983. 12.95 (ISBN 0-312-39306-7). St. Martin's Press.

House of Women. Eric Lawson Malpass. LC 74-33907. 1975. 7.95. St. Martin's Press.

House of Wraith. Edward J Millward. LC 36-791. 1935. Houghton Mifflin Company.

House of Yesterday. Concordia Merrel. LC 32-30515. 1932. Doubleday, Doran & Company, Inc.

House of Yorkes. Mary Agnes Tincker. LC 8-27020. 1872. The Catholic Publication Society.

House of Yost. Katharine Riegel Loose. LC 23-48980. Boni & Liveright.

House of Young. Alice B. Greenwell. 272p. 1982. 11.00 (ISBN 0-682-49835-1); pap. 5.95 (ISBN 0-682-49836-X). Exposition.

House of Youth. Maude Lavinia Radford Warren. LC 23-141236. The Bobbs-Merrill Company.

House of Zeor. Jacqueline Lichtenberg. LC 73-13278. (Doubleday science fiction). 1974. 5.95 (ISBN 0-385-09650-X). Doubleday.

House of Zeor. Jacqueline Lichtenberg. (Kangaroo Book). 1977. 1.75 (ISBN 0-671-80937-7). Pocket Books.

House of Zeor. Jacqueline Lichtenberg. 1981. 2.25 (ISBN 0-87216-801-8). Playboy Paperbacks.

House on a Street. Dale Curran. LC 35-2338. Covici, Friede.

House on Bitterness Street. Elizabeth B. De Trevino. 1970. 5.95 o.p. Doubleday.

House on Bitterness Street. Elizabeth Borton Trevino. LC 69-20073. 1970. 5.95. Doubleday.

House on Black Bayou. Mary Sellers. 1975. (pbk.) 1.25. Warner Paperback Library.

House on Charles Street. Anna Robeson Brown Burr. LC 21-21547. 1921. Duffield & Company.

House on Cherry Street. Amelia Edith Huddleston Barr. LC 9-28120. 1909. 1.50. Dodd, Mead & Company.

House on Cheyne Walk. Perry Organ. LC 74-30606. 1975. 7.95 (ISBN 0-698-10665-2). Coward, McCann & Geoghegan.

House on Coliseum Street. Shirley Ann Grau. (O.s.i.). 1961. 4.95 o.s.i. (ISBN 0-394-42940-0). Knopf.

House on Corbett Street: A Black Novel. William Matthews Johnson. 1975. pap. 5.50 (ISBN 0-87164-026-0). William-F.

House on Corbett Street: A Novel of Negro Stirrings Amid Discontent. William Matthews Johnson. LC 67-24641. 1967. William-Frederick Press.

House on Curtin Street. Millie J Ragosta. LC 78-22539. 1979. 7.95 (ISBN 0-385-12255-1). Doubleday.

House on E Street. Karen Moore. 1979. pap. 1.75 o.s.i. (ISBN 0-505-51446-X). Tower Bks.

House on Esplanade. William Biery. LC 73-84875. 1973. 6.95 (ISBN 0-88405-001-7). Mason & Lipscomb.

House on Fire. Arch Oboler. 1969. 6.95 o.p. Bartholomew.

House on Fire. Arch Oboler. 6.95 o.p. Delacorte.

House on Fire: A Novel. Arch Oboler. LC 75-79433. 1969. 5.95. Bartholomew House.

House on Gannet's Point. Cynthia Van Hazinga. (Queen-size Gothic). 1974. (pbk.) 0.95. Popular Library.

House on Greenapple Road. Harold R Daniels. LC 66-12020. 1966. Random House.

House on Hay Hill. Dorothy Eden. 224p. 1978. pap. 2.25 (ISBN 0-449-23789-3, Crest). Fawcett.

House on Hay Hill. Dorothy Eden. (Fawcett Crest Book). 1976. (pbk.) 1.75. Fawcett.

House on Hibiscus Hill. Juanita Tyree Osborne. (Avalon Books). (Illus.). 4.95. Thomas Bouregy.

House on K Street. Lionel White. LC 65-16292. 3.75. Dutton.

House on Lark Street. Jessie Douglas Fox. LC 39-11268. 1939. Macrae Smith Company.

House on Line Street. William Edward Daniel Ross. 1976. 4.95. Avalon Books.

House on Little Finger. Thomas Meekin. LC 29-693. The Grafton Press.

House on Malador Street. Phyllis Hastings. LC 77-97090. 1970. 4.95. Putnam.

House on Ninth Street. John S. Strange. LC 75-32720. 192p. 1976. 6.95 o.p. (ISBN 0-385-11603-9). Doubleday.

House on Prague Street. Hanna Demetz. LC 79-27312. 1980. 8.95 (ISBN 0-312-39322-9). St. Martin's Press.

House on Prague Street. Hanna Demetz. LC 80-22593. 1980. 12.95 (ISBN 0-8161-3143-0). G. K. Hall.

House on Rainbow Leap. Rena M Vale. (Ravenswood Gothic). 1973. (pbk) 1.25 (ISBN 0-671-78331-9). Pocket Books.

House on Russian Hill. Florence Hurd. (Signet Book.). 1977. 1.25 (ISBN 0-451-07294-4). New American Library.

House on Sky High Road. Isabel S. Way. 1970. pap. 0.75 o.p. (B75-1096). Belmont-Tower.

House on Sky High Road. Isabel S. Way. (O.s.i.). 1972. pap. 0.75 o.s.i. (BT50252). Belmont-Tower.

House on Smith Square. Anna Robeson Brown Burr. LC 23-6150. 1923. Duffield & Company.

House on Somber Lake. easy eye ed. Alix De Marquand. (Orig.). 1968. pap. 0.60 o.p. (73-751). Lancer.

House on Stilts: A Novel. R. H Hazard. LC 10-19615. G. W. Dillingham Company.

House on the Beach. E L Withers, pseud. LC 57-109468. 1957. Rinehart.

House on the Beach. Julia MacNair Wright. LC 9-911. Congregational Sunday-School and Publishing Society.

House on the Beach. A Realistic Tale. George Meredith. LC 1-20261. (On cover: Harper's half-hour series. v. 22). 1877. Harper & Brothers.

House on the Black Moor. Dora Polk. (Orig.). 1972. pap. 0.75 o.p. (94293). Beagle Bks.

House on the Bluff. A Western Flood Story. Julia MacNair Wright & Whitcomb, Mrs. Jessie (Wright) LC 9-220865. 1896. American Tract Society.

House on the Borderland... William Hope Hodgson. LC 75-28857. (Classics of science fiction). 1976. 12.95. (ISBN 0-88355-371-6) (ISBN 0-88355-456-9). Hyperion Press.

House on the Borderland: And Other Novels. William Hope Hodgson. LC 46-7118. 1946. Arkham House.

House on the Canal: Bibliotheca Neerlandica Ser. Frans Coenen. Incl. Alienation. J. Van Oudshoorn. 1965. 10.00x o.s.i. (ISBN 0-8277-0020-2). British Bk Ctr.

House on the Canal: Bibliotheca Neerlandica Ser. Frans Coenen. Incl. Alienation. J. Van Oudshoorn. 1965. 10.00x o.s.i. (ISBN 0-8277-0020-2). British Bk Ctr.

House on the Canal: By Frans Coenen Tr. FromDutch by James Brockway Alienation by J. Van Oudshoorn Pseud. Tr. from Dutch by N. C. Clegg Levden. Sythoff. Frans Coenen & J. K. Feylbrief. (Bibliotheca Neerlandica, 7). 1966. 5.95. London House.

House on the Cliff. Laurence Walter Meynell. LC 32-186118. 1932. J. B. Lippincott Company.

House on the Cliff. Dorothy Emily Stevenson. LC 66-23225. 1966. Holt, Rinehart and Winston.

House on the Cliff. Dorothy Emily Stevenson. 1978. 1.95 (ISBN 0-441-34395-3). Ace Books.

House on the Cliffs. Caroline Farr. (Signet book). 1974. (pbk.) 0.95. New American Library.

House on the Downs. Gladys Edson Locke. 1925. L. C. Page & Company.

House on the Drive. Bettina Kingsley. 1975. (pbk.) 1.25. Dell.

House on the Dunes. Ruth McCarthy Sears. (Avalon romances). 1974. 4.50. Avalon Books.

House on the Fens. easy eye ed. Catherine Marchant, pseud. Orig. Title: Fen Tiger. pap. 0.75 o.p. (74-904). Lancer.

House on the Heath. Maureen Stephenson. 1982. pap. 2.50 (ISBN 0-8217-1026-5). Zebra.

House on the Hill. Jonathan Black. (Berkley Medallion Book). 1977. 1.95 (ISBN 0-425-03648-0). Berkley Pub. Corp.

House on the Hill. 1968. pap. 2.25 o.p. (ISBN 0-448-00212-4, G&D). Putnam Pub Group.

House on the Hill. Heli Ludwig. 1878. 8.95 (ISBN 0-533-03551-1). Vantage.

House on the Hill. Cesare Pavese. Tr. by W. J. Strachan. 1961. 4.95 o.p. Walker & Co.

House on the Hill. Anne Putnam. LC 30-8606. 1930. Dodd, Mead & Company.

House on the Left Bank: A Novel of Suspense. Velda Johnston. LC 74-30255. 1975. 6.95 (ISBN 0-396-07061-2). Dodd, Mead.

House on the Leftbank. Velda Johnston. (Signet Book). 1977. 1.50 (ISBN 0-451-07279-0). New American Library.

House on the Mall. Edgar Jepson. LC 11-25746. 1.25. G. W. Dillingham Company.

House on the Marsh. Joseph Jefferson Farjeon. LC 33-213842. 1933. L. MacVeagh, Dial Press Inc.

House on the Marsh. Florence Alice Price James. (On cover: Seaside library. Pocket ed., no. 248). 1884. G. Munro.

House on the Marsh. Florence Alice Price James. (On cover: Lovell's library. v. 20, no. 931). 1887. J. W. Lovell Company.

House on the Marsh: A Novel. Helen Reimensnyder Martin. LC 36-1121. 1936. Dodd, Mead & Company.

House on the Moat. Virginia Coffman. (Signet Book). 1977. 1.50 (ISBN 0-451-07661-3). New American Library.

House on the Moor. Margaret Oliphant Wilson Oliphant. (On cover: Seaside library. Pocket ed., no. 351). 1885. G. Munro.

House on the Mound. August William Derleth. LC 74-166393. 1973. E.V.A.

House on the North Shore. Marion Foster Washburne. LC 9-24263. 1909. A. C. McClurg & Co.

House on the Park. Marjorie Muir Worthington. LC 46-6909. 1946. Doubleday & Company, Inc.

House on the Prairie. Sandra Dark. (Orig.). 1979. pap. 2.25 (ISBN 0-532-23318-2). Woodhill.

House on the Quay. Lesley Wilson. LC 66-5986. 1966. Arcadia House.

House on the Rhine. Frances Faviell. LC 56-7815. 1956. Farrar, Straus and Cudahy.

House on the Rock. Matilda Anne Mackarness. LC 7-16439. 1852. J. Munroe and Company.

House on the Rocks. Theresa Charles, pseud. pap. 0.50 o.p. (52-924). Paperback Lib.

House on the Roof. Mignon Good Eberhart. LC 35-7806. 1935. Doubleday, Doran & Company, Inc.

House on the Sands. Charles Marriott. LC 3-20901. 1903. J. Lane.

House on the Sands. 1st Ed. John Louis Bonn. LC 50-9845. 1950. Doubleday.

House on the Scar. Bertha Thomas. LC 8-28190. (On cover: Lovell's international series, no. 101). 1890. J. W. Lovell Company.

House on the Sound: 1st Amer. Ed. Kathrin Perutz. LC 64-24262. 1965. bds., 3.95. Coward.

House on the Strand. Daphne Du Maurier. LC 74-78693. (Illus.). 1969. 5.95. Doubleday.

House on Thunder Hill. Suzanne Somers, pseud. (Orig.). 1973. pap. 0.95 o.p. (09201). Curtis.

House on Tollard Ridge. Cecil John Charles Street. LC 29-4214. 1929. Dodd, Mead & Company.

House on Trevor Street. Florence Hurd. 176p. (Orig.). 1972. pap. 0.75 o.p. (532-00484-075). Manor Bks.

House on Twyford Street. Constance Gluyas. LC 75-41320. 8.95 (ISBN 0-679-50588-1). D. McKay Co.

House on Vickers' Island. Jeananne St. Clair. 1974. 4.95 (ISBN 0-517-51806-6). Lenox Hill Press.

House on Wath Moor. Maureen Stephenson. (Illus., Orig.). 1979. pap. 1.95 (ISBN 0-89083-461-X). Zebra.

House on Wheels: Or, Far from Home. Fanny Begon & Bell, Nancy R. E. (Meugens) "Mrs. A. G. Bell," Tr. LC 7-1625. 1874. Scribner, Welford & Armstrong.

House on Wolf Trail. Lanora Miller. 1.50. Ace Books.

House on 9th Street. Dorothy Stockbridge Tillet. LC 75-32720. 1976. 6.95 (ISBN 0-385-11603-9). Doubleday.

House Opposite. Joseph Jefferson Farjeon. LC 31-821026. 1931. L. Mac Vaugh, The Dial Press.

House Opposite, a Mystery. Elizabeth Kent. LC 2-21410. 1902. G. P. Putman's Sons.

House Out of Order. Richard Bolling. 5.50 o.p. (ISBN 0-525-12804-2). Dutton.

House Party. Edmee Elizabeth Monica De La Pasture. LC 31-3500. Harper & Brothers.

TITLE INDEX

HOW HE MADE HIS

House Party. Louise De La Ramee. LC 6-33323. (On cover: Lovell's library. v. 18 (i. e. 17) no. 805). 1886. J. W. Lovell Company.
House Party: An Account of Stories Told at a Gathering of Famous American Authors, the Story Tellers Being Introduced by Paul Leicester Ford. Roberts, Charles George Douglas, 1800- et al. LC 1-27444. 1901. Small, Maynard & Company.
House Party: By Virginia Rowans Pseud. Edward Everett Tanner. LC 54-6893. 1954. Crowell.
House Party Murder. Colin Ward. LC 34-15787. 1934. W. Morrow & Company.
House Party Murders. Edgar Allan Poe. LC 40-3965. J. B. Lippincott Company.
House Possessed. Charity Blackstock. 222p. 1976. Repr. of 1962 ed. lib. bdg. 16.95x (ISBN 0-89244-077-5). Queens Hse.
House Possessed. Leslie Paige. 1974. (pbk.) 0.95. Belmont Tower Books.
House Possessed. Ursula Torday. LC 62-16857. 1962. Lippincott.
House-Room. Ida Wild. 1916. John Lane.
House 'round the Corner. Louis Tracy. LC 19-4443. E. J. Clode.
House Terrible. Ausburn Towner. (Once a week library, no. 26). 1893. P. F. Collier.
House That Berry Built. Cecil William Mercer. LC 45-9780. 1945. G. P. Putnam's Sons.
House That Died. Josephine Eckert Gill. LC 55-7653. 1955. Published for the Crime Club by Doubleday.
House That Died: La Maison Morte. Henry Bordeaux & Harper, Harold, Tr. LC 22-207353. 1922. Duffield & Company.
House That Hate Built. Sara Elizabeth Mason. LC 44-620243. 1944. Pub. for the Crime Club by Doubleday, Doran & Co., Inc.
House That Jack Built. Alison. (On cover: Seaside library. Pocket ed., no. 481). G. Munro.
House That Jack Built. James Wesley Johnston. LC 5-8675. Eaton & Mains.
House That Jack Built: A Story. Amy Ella Blanchard. LC 26-2452. W. A. Wilde Company.
House That Moved. Marguerite H. Lapp. 3.75 o.p. Stewart.
House That Samuel Built. Ruby Jean Jensen. (Warner paperback library gothic). 1974. (pbk.) 1.25. Warner Paperback Library.
House That Shadows Built. Will Irwin. LC 75-124012. (Literature of Cinema, Ser. 1). Repr. of 1928 ed. 10.00 (ISBN 0-405-01618-2). Ayer Co.
House That Stood Still. Alfred Elton Van Vogt. LC 50-10531. (Corwin book). 1950. Greenberg.
House That Tai Ming Built. Virginia Chin-Lan Lee. LC 63-15688. 1963. Macmillan.
House That Was Never Finished,". Lillian Escoffier. LC 47-17770. Arrow Press.
House That Whispered. Samuel Emery. LC 29-3964. 1929. E. P. Dutton & Co. Inc.
House Too Old: A Novel. Mark Schorer. LC 35-15150. Roynal & Hitchcock.
House Under the Sea: A Romance. Max Pemberton. LC 2-210981. 1902. D. Appleton and Company.
House Under the Water. Francis Brett Young. 1932. Harper & Brothers.
House Undivided. K. C. Panigrahi. Tr. by Lila Ray from Oriya. (Orient Paperbacks Ser.). Orig. Title: Matira Manisha. 148p. 1973. pap. 2.40 o.p. (ISBN 0-88253-247-2). InterCulture.
House Upon the Sand. Jurgis Gliauda. LC 63-17248. 1963. Manyland Books.
House Upon the Sand. Jurgis Gliauda. 3.95 o.p. Twayne.
House with a Bad Name. Perley Poore Sheehan. LC 21-5269. Boni and Liveright.
House with Green Shudders. Amelia Reynolds Long. LC 50-7997. 1950. Phoenix Press.
House with No Address. Edith Nesbit Bland. LC 9-6278. 1909. Doubleday, Page & Company.
House with Stairs. Marie Campbell. LC 50-10213. 1950. Rinehart.
House with the Blue Door. Hulbert Footner. LC 42-22142. 1942. Harper & Brothers.
House with the Golden Door. Philip Van Rensselaer. LC 65-15047. bds., 4.95. Trident.
House with the Golden Door. Philip Van Rensselaer. (75161). 1966. Pocket Bks.
House with the Golden Windows. Annie Edith Foster Jameson. LC 21-103996. 1.90. George H. Doran Company.
House with the Green Shutters. George Douglas Brown. LC 75-115232. 1970. Scholarly Press.
House with the Green Shutters. George Douglas Brown. LC 1-230083. 1901. McClure, Phillips & Co.
House with the Green Shutters. 6th impression ed. George Douglas Brown. LC 3-26196. 1902. McClure, Phillips & Co.
House with the Green Shutters. George Douglas Brown. LC 24-27747. 1924. T. Seltzer.
House with the Green Shutters. George Douglas Brown. LC 27-107338. (Half-title: The modern library of the world's best books). The Modern Library.
House with the Green Shutters. George Douglas Brown. LC 39-27703. (Half-title: The World's classics, 466). 1938. Oxford University Press, H. Milford.
House with the Green Tree. Kelvin Lindemann & Alexander, Henry, 1890- LC 44-5522. 1944. L. B. Fischer.
House with the Magnolias. Ralph Arnold. LC 31-221410. 1931. L. MacVeagh, The Dial Press.
House with the Mezzanine: And Other Stories. Anton Pavlovich Chekhov. Tr. by Koteliansky, Samuel Solomonovitch. LC 17-22089. 1917. C. Scribner's Sons.
House with Two Doors: And Other Stories. Alice Eddy Curtiss. LC 6-31704. Congregational Sunday-School and Publishing Society.
House Without a Door. Thomas L. Sterling. LC 50-5177. (An Inner sanctum mystery). 1950. Simon and Schuster.
House Without a Key. Earl Derr Biggers. LC 25-7069. The Bobbs-Merrill Company.
House Without a Key. Earl Derr Biggers. LC 40-14071. 1940. Triangle Books.
House Without a Key... Earl Derr Biggers. 1943.
House Without a Key. Earl Derr Biggers. pap. 0.75 o.p. (T2004). Pyramid Pubns.
House Without a Key. Earl Derr Biggers. (Charlie Chan mystery #1). 1974. (pbk.) 0.95. Bantam Books.
House Without a Roof. Joel Sayre. LC 48-8889. 1948. Farrar, Straus.
House Without Love. Iris Bromige. 1973. pap. 0.75 o.p. (ISBN 0-345-20717-3). Beagle Bks.
House Without the Door. Elizabeth Daly. LC 42-179913. 1942. Farrar & Rinehart, Inc.
Houseboat on the Nile (Saraarah Fouk el Nil) Arabic Novel. Najib Mahfuz. (Arabic.). 5.50x (ISBN 0-86685-160-7). Intl Bk Ctr.
Houseboy. Ferdinand Oyono. Tr. by John Reed from Fr. (African Writers Ser.). (Orig.). 1966. pap. text ed. 3.00x (ISBN 0-435-90029-3). Heinemann Ed.
Housebreaker of Shady Hill. pap. 0.60 o.p. (60-430). Manor Bks.
Housebreaker of Shady Hill. And Other Stories. 1st Ed. John Cheever. LC 58-11397. 1958. Harper.
Houseful of Love. Marjorie Housepian. LC 57-5386. 1957. Random House.
Household Ghosts. 1st American Ed. James Kennaway. LC 61-12782. 1961. Atheneum.
Household of Bouverie: Or, The Elixir of Gold. Catherine Ann Ware Warfield. LC 12-19554. T. B. Peterson & Brothers.
Household of Bouverie: Or, The Elixir of Gold. A Romance. Catherine Ann Ware Warfield. LC 8-34836. 1860. Derby & Jackson.
Household of Peter; a Novel. Rosa Nouchette Carey. LC 5-31871. 1905. J. B. Lippincott Compnay.
Household of Sir Tho. More. new edition, with an appendix. ed. Anne Manning. Dodd & Mead, Publishers.
Household of Sir Thomas More. Anne Manning & Lodge, Edmund, 1756-1839. LC 7-16794. 1852. C. Scribner.
Household of Sir Thomas More. Anne Manning & William Roper. (Half-title: Everyman's library, ed. by Ernest Rhys. Fiction. no. 19). 1908. J. M. Dent & Co.
Household of Sir Thomas More. Anne Manning & William Roper. LC 36-37051. (Half-title: Everyman's library, ed. by Ernest Rhys. Fiction. no. 19). 1932. J. M. Dent & Sons, Ltd.
Household Saints. Francine Prose. LC 80-29116. 10.95 (ISBN 0-312-39341-5). St. Martins's Press.
Household Tales. Job Puritan. LC 7-42396. 1861. J. Munroe and Company.
Household Tales of Moon & Water. Nancy Willard. LC 82-4804. 96p. 1982. 9.95 (ISBN 0-15-142184-6). HarBraceJ.
Household Words. Joan Silber. LC 79-14742. 1980. 9.95 (ISBN 0-670-38037-7). Viking Press.
Householder. Ruth Prawer Jhabvala. LC 60-7578. 1960. Norton.
Householder. Ruth Prawer Jhabvala. LC 76-48892. (Norton library). 1977. 2.95 (ISBN 0-393-00851-7). Norton.
Housekeeper's Daughter. Donald Henderson Clarke. LC 36-81060. The Vanguard Press.
Housemaid: A Novel in Three Parts. Naomi Gwladys Royde-Smith. LC 26-9829. 1926. A. A. Knopf.
Houseman's Tale. Colin Douglas. LC 78-57603. 1978. 8.95 (ISBN 0-8008-3952-8). Taplinger Pub. Co.
Housemaster: A Novel. John Hay Beith. LC 37-2352. 1937. Houghton Mifflin Company.
Houseparty. Henry Leyford Gates. LC 32-194941. 1932. Grosset & Dunlap.
Houses in Between: A Novel. Howard Spring. LC 51-11956. 1952. Harper.
Houses of Belgrade. Borislav Pekic. LC 78-7988. 9.95 (ISBN 0-15-142183-8). Harcourt Brace Jovanovich.
Houses of Glass. A Philosophical Romance. Wallace Lloyd. 1898. G. W. Dillingham Co.
Houses of Glass: Stories of Paris. Helen Gansevoort Edwards Mackay. LC 9-9473. Duffield & Company.
Houses of Horror. Hans Holzer. 192p. 1982. pap. 2.25 (ISBN 0-8439-1143-3, Leisure Bks). Dorchester Pub Co.
Houses of Rising Sin. Ray Kainen. (Orig.). 1969. pap. 1.95 o.s.i. (TC458, Travellers Comp). Olympia.
Houses That Kill. Roger De Lafforest. (Berkley medallion book). 1974. (pbk.) 1.25 (ISBN 0-425-02620-5). Berkley Pub. Co.
Housesitter. Lee Karr. 1980. pap. 2.25 (ISBN 0-380-76364-8, 76364). Avon.
Housewarming. George Sklar. LC 53-5244. 1953. Crown Publishers.
Housewife and the Assassin. Susan Trott. LC 78-69745. 8.95 (ISBN 0-312-39346-6). St. Martin's Press.
Housewife and the Assassin. Susan Trott. 1980. 1.95 (ISBN 0-380-49551-1). Avon Books.
Housewife & the Boys. Roscoe Sherman. 192p. (Orig.). 1973. pap. 1.95 o.p. (ISBN 0-87682-336-3, 7336). Barclay Hse.
Housewife and the Handyman. Anne Saddens. 1974. (pbk.) 1.95 (ISBN 0-87056-388-2). Brandon Books.
Housewife for Blackmail. Marshall Roberts. 192p. 1973. pap. 1.95 o.p. (ISBN 0-87977-188-7, DBB188). Dansk Blue Bk.
Housewife for Rent. L. Jay Perry. 192p. (Orig.). 1972. pap. 1.95 o.p. (ISBN 0-87977-174-7, DBB-174). Dansk Blue Bk.
Housewife Hustlers. Linda DuBreiul. (Orig.). 1976. pap. 1.50 o.p. (LB334DK, Leisure Bks). Nordon Pubns.
Housewife's Diary. Marsha Alexander. (Original Brandon Book). 1973. (pbk.) 1.95 (ISBN 0-87056-341-6). Brandon Books.
Housewives & the Salesman. Thomas Eastwood. 192p. (Orig.). 1973. pap. 1.95 o.p. (ISBN 0-87682-325-8, 7325). Barclay Hse.
Houston. Louise Horton. 181p. (Orig.). 1982. 15.95x (ISBN 0-918186-05-6); pap. 7.95x (ISBN 0-918186-04-8). White Cross.
Houston Heat. Jaye Wilson. 1979. pap. 2.50 (ISBN 0-449-14213-2, GM). Fawcett.
Hove up by the Tide. Gertrude Gould Pickard. LC 17-23762. 1917. 0.50. Smith & Sale.
Hovenden, V. C. The Destiny of a Man of Action. Frances Mabel Robinson. LC 8-1641. (On cover: Lovell's international series, 182). 1891. J. W. Lovell Company.
Hovering Darkness. Evelyn Berckman. LC 57-11386. (Read badge detective). 1957. Dodd, Mead.
Hovering Darkness. Evelyn Berckman. (Signet book). 1974. (pbk.) 0.95. New American Library.
How a Bride Was Won: Or, A Chase Across the Pampas. Friedrich Wilhelm Christian Gerstacker. Tr. by Jordan, Francis. LC 6-442353. 1869. D. Appleton and Company.
How a Husband Forgave: A Novel. Edgar Fawcett. LC 6-38792. (On cover: The Belford American novel series. v. 2. no. 10)). 1890. Belford Company.
How About Tomorrow Morning? Helen Liebman Haberman. LC 45-3924. 1945. Prentice-Hall, Inc.
How Amelia Secured the Tie That Binds with a Very Loose Knot. Lorna Novak. LC 66-12213. 4.50. Doubleday.
How Amusing! And a Lot of Other Fables. Denis George Mackail. LC 76-144160. (Short story index reprint series). 1971. (ISBN 0-8369-3775-9). Books for Libraries Press.
How Amusing! And a Lot of Other Fables. Denis George Mackail. LC 30-947455. 1929. Houghton Mifflin Company.
How and Why Wonder Book of Building. Donald Barr. (How and why wonder books, 5051). 1964. Wonder Books.
How and Why Wonder Book of Famous Scientists. Jean Bethell. LC 64-9598. (How and why wonder books, 5049). 1964. Wonder Books.
How and Why Wonder Book of Time. deluxe ed. Gene Liberty. LC 63-163173. (Illus.). 1963. Grosset & Dunlap.
How Are the Mighty Fallen. (Science Fiction Ser.). 1974. pap. 0.95 o.p. (UQ1100). DAW Bks.
How Are the Mighty Fallen. Polly A. Hutchison. (Orig.). 1980. pap. 2.95 (ISBN 0-89293-026-8). Beta Bk.
How Are the Mighty Fallen. Thomas Burnett Swann. 1974. (pbk.) 0.95. DAW Books.
How Awful About Allan. Henry Farrell. LC 63-12830. 1963. Holt, Rinehart and Winston.
How Baldy Won the County Seat. 2d ed. Charles Josiah Adams. LC 13-938033. J. S. Ogilvie Publishing Company.
How Beautiful Are Thy Feet. Alan Marshall. LC 73-177197. 1972. 1.95 (ISBN 0-7260-0089-2). Gold Star Publications.
How Bessie Became Famous. L. Vance & R. Sondag. 4.50 o.p. (ISBN 0-8062-0795-7). Carlton.
How Big Is Big? Zev Wanderer & David Radell. (Orig.). 1982. pap. 2.95 (ISBN 0-446-90621-2). Warner Bks.
How Bob and I Kept House. A Story of Chicago Hard Times. Bessie Albert. LC 6-496326. (On cover: Satchel series, no. 28). The Authors' Publishiny Company.
How Brave We Live. Paul Monash. LC 50-5613. 1950. Scribner.
How Came He Dead? Joseph Fitzgerald Molloy. (On cover: Lovell's international series, no. 105.). J. W. Lovell Company.
How Can I Get Married! A Woman Bares Her Soul. Macfadden, Bernarr Adolphus, 1868- LC 27-4648. 1927. Macfadden Publications, Inc.
How Can the Heart Forget. Emilie Loring. 1974. (pbk.) 0.75. Bantam Books.
How Can the Heart Forget. Emilie Baker Loring. Grosset & Dunlap.
How Can the Heart Forget. Emilie Baker Loring. LC 77-6772. 1977. 9.95 (ISBN 0-89340-089-0). J. Curley.
How Can the Heart Forget. 1st Ed. Emilie Baker Loring. LC 60-11634. 1960. Little, Brown.
How Come Christmas: A Modern Morality. Roark Bradford. LC 48-9848. 1948. Harper.
How Could He Escape? A Temperance Tale. Julia MacNair Wright. LC 9-910. 1870. The National Temperance Society and Publication House.
How Could He Help It? Or, The Heart Triumphant. Azel Stevens Roe. LC 7-39821. 1860. Derby & Jackson.
How Dare You, Sir! Noel Godber. LC 38-29168. 1938. M. S. Mill Co., Inc.
How Darkness Fell! R. A. Ellsworth. 5.95 o.p. Vantage.
How Deacon Tubman and Parson Whitney Kept New Year's: And Otherr Stories. William Henry Harrison Murray. LC 7-17253. 1887. Caledonia County Publishing Company.
How Dear to My Heart. 1970. 1.95 o.p. (ISBN 0-442-82259-6). Peter Pauper.
How Deep Is Love? Frankie Lee. LC 62-10613. 1962. Adams Press.
How Deep the Cup. Jessyca R. Gaver. (Orig.). 1975. pap. 1.50 o.p. (LB280DK, Leisure Bks). Nordon Pubns.
How Deep the Cup. Jessyca Russell Gaver. 1975. (pbk.) 1.50. Leisure Books.
How Deep Was the Valley. Robert E McLeod. LC 55-141161. 1955. Meador Pub. Co.
How Did You Get Where You Are. Beatrice Bliss. 1978. 7.95 (ISBN 0-914558-07-2); pap. 3.95 (ISBN 0-914558-08-0). Georgetown Pr.
How Do I Change My Man? Earnest Larsen. LC 74-80939. 1974. pap. 1.95 o.p. (ISBN 0-89243-010-9, 46400). Liguori Pubns.
How Do I Change My Man? Earnest Larsen. LC 74-80939. 1974. pap. 1.95 o.p. (ISBN 0-89243-010-9, 46400). Liguori Pubns.
How Do I Love Thee. Lucille Iremonger. LC 75-34315. 1976. 9.95 (ISBN 0-688-03013-0). W. Morrow.
How Do They Build It? Tim Hildebrandt & Greg Hildebrandt. LC 73-19371. (Illus.). 1974. 3.95 (ISBN 0-8228-7610-8). Platt & Munk.
How Do You Say Goodby. Margaret Burman. 1982. pap. 1.95 (ISBN 0-553-22517-0). Bantam.
How Doth the Simple Spelling Bee. Owen Wister. LC 7-8533. 1907. The Macmillan Company.
How Evil the Word. Helen Graham Farrar. (Avon gothic). 1974. (pbk.) 0.95 (ISBN 0-380-00155-1). Avon.
How False My Laughter: By George and Nora Jorgenson. 1st Ed. George Ellington Jorgenson & Nora Jorgenson. LC 53-8096. 1953. Pageant Press.
How Far to Bethlehem? A Novel. Norah Robinson Lofts. LC 65-15092. 1965. Doubleday.
How Firm a Foundation. Edward Everett Tanner. LC 68-8363. 1968. 5.95. Morrow.
How George Edwards Scrapped Religion. Simon FitzSimons. LC 23-8189. 1923. The Stratford Company.
How German Is It. Walter Abish. LC 80-20838. 1980. 5.95 (ISBN 0-8112-0776-5). New Directions.
How Great Is That Darkness: A Novel. Kurt Kurdi. LC 59-10350. Bridgeway Press.
How Great Will Be Your Joy! Gary J. Coleman. 1977. 3.95 (ISBN 0-89036-086-3). Hawkes Pub Inc.
How Green Was My Valley. Richard Llewellyn. LC 40-27043. 1940. The Macmillan Company.
How Hard to Kill. Thomas Blanchard Dewey. (O.s.i.). 1962. 3.50 o.s.i. (ISBN 0-671-32305-9). S&S.
How He Got the Mule. Doug Odom. 1979. pap. 1.00 o.p. Samisdat.
How He Made His Fortune. Julia A W De Witt. LC 6-33395. (Pilgrim prize series v. 6). Congregational Sunday School and Publishing Society.

How He Reached the White House; or, A Famous Victory... E. Goodman Holden. (On cover: Lovell's library. no. 402). J. W. Lovell Company.
How He Won Her. A Sequel to "Fair Play.". Emma Dorothy Eliza Nevitte Southworth. 1869. T. B. Peterson & Brothers.
How He Won Her: And A False Friend. Geraldine Fleming. LC 6-39925. (On cover: Munro's library, v. 1, no. 150). 1885. N. L. Munro.
How He Won Her, and A False Friend. John Russell Coryell. LC 6-39925. (On cover: Munro's library, v. 1, no. 150). 1885. N. L. Munro.
How High Are the Stars! Can Man Live a Year of His Life Entirely Within the Will of God? William S Cannon. LC 70-117301. 1970. 4.50. Broadman Press.
How High the Stars: A Novel. 1st Ed. H L Bouchon. 1956. Exposition Press.
How I Became a Holy Mother, and Other Stories. Ruth Prawer Jhabvala. LC 76-9206. 8.95 (ISBN 0-06-012198-X). Harper & Row.
How I Became a Holy Mother and Other Stories. Ruth Prawer Jhabvala. LC 76-373945. 1976. 3.95 (ISBN 0-7195-3309-0). J. Murray.
How I Became a Holy Mother: And Other Short Stories. Ruth Prawer Jhabvala. LC 76-9206. (Orig.). 1979. pap. 2.50i (ISBN 0-06-080474-2, P 474, PL). Har-Row.
How I Became a Preacher. A Sequel to "How I Became a Sailor". A Novel. Omer T Gillett. LC 6-44048. 1893. Cranston & Curtis.
How I Became a Sailor: And Other Sketches. Omer T Gillett. LC 6-44047. 1891. Cranston & Stowe.
How I Escaped: A Novel. W. H Parkins. Ed. by Gunter, Archibald Clavering. LC 7-34731. 1889. The Home Publishing Company.
How I Grow. LC 70-408653. (Petals). (Illus.). 1968. 1.95. Paul Flesch.
How I Spent My Million: A Christmas Story. John Edgar Park. LC 13-22098. 0.75. The Pilgrim Press.
How I Wanted to Pour Salt on a Rabbit's Tail: & Other Stories by Vitali Bianki. Tr. from Russian by Anne Terry White. Vitalii Valentinovich Bianki. LC 67-198733. (Venture bk.). 1967. 3.95. Braziller.
How I Won the War. Patrick Ryan. LC 64-7885. (Illus.). 1964-1965. Morrow.
How I Won the War: By Lieutenant Ernest Goodbody, As Told to Patrick Ryan. Patrick Ryan. (U6110). 1967. Ballantine.
How I Wrote Jubilee. Margaret Walker. LC 72-80786. (Series: Black Paper (Atlanta). 1972. 1.00. Third World Press.
How Is Your Man? Or, The Sharks of Sharksville. Realities of the Graveyard Insurance System. LC 7-7129. 1882. Lee & Shepard.
How It All Began: The Greensboro Sit-Ins. Miles Wolff, Jr. LC 75-104632. 1971. pap. 1.95 (ISBN 0-8128-1445-2). Stein & Day.
How It All Came Round. Elizabeth Thomasina Meade Smith. (On cover: Lovell's library. v. 6, no. 328). 1883. J. W. Lovell Company.
How It Ended. Marie Flaacke. LC 6-41125. (On cover: Satchel series no. 17). The Authors' Publishing Company.
How It Happened. Kate Lee Langley Bosher. LC 14-162152. 1914. Harper & Brothers.
How It Happened: Being a Story in Three Books and Several Manners. Josephine Winfield Brake. LC 3810. The American News Company.
How It Is. Samuel Beckett. LC 63-16998. 1964. Grove Press.
How Jerem Came Home. Paul Kaser. LC 80-13548. 10.00 (ISBN 0-684-16623-2). Scribner.
How John Norton the Trapper Kept His Christmas. William Henry Harrison Murray. LC 7-17254. 1891. De Wolfe, Fiske & Co.
How John Norton the Trapper Kept His Christmas. William Henry Harrison Murray. LC 11-18192. 1.00. The Platt & Peck Co.
How Joy Was Found: A Fantasy. Isobel W Hutchison. LC 17-24237. Frederick A. Stokes Company.
How Leslie Loved. Anne Warner French. LC 11-2077. 1911. 1.50. Little, Brown, and Company.
How Like a God. Rex Stout. LC 29-201132. 1929. The Vanguard Press.
How Like a Woman. Florence Marryat Church Lean. LC 7-13602. Lovell, Coryell & Company.
How Like an Angel. Archibald Gordon Macdonnell. LC 35-327. 1935. The Macmillan Company.
How Like an Angel. Margaret Millar. LC 62-8457. 1962. Random House.
How Long the Heart Remembers: A Novel. Mary H Hollingsworth. LC 76-43275. 1977. 7.95 (ISBN 0-395-25021-8). Houghton Mifflin.
How Luke Discovered Christmas. Anita Trueman Pickett. LC 51-14773. 1951. Beacon Press.
How Many Blocks in the Pile. David Meltzer. pap. 1.95 o.p. (0107). Essex Hse.
How Many Cards? Isabel Egenton Ostrander. LC 20-19916. 1920. R. M. McBride & Co.
How Many Diamond Rings. Linda N. Rye. 62p. 1972. 3.95 (ISBN 0-913976-01-6). Discovery Bks.
How Many Miles to Babylon? Ann Borowik. LC 63-7348. 1963. Pantheon Books.
How Many Miles to Babylon? A Novel. Jennifer Johnston. LC 74-1502. 1974. 5.95 (ISBN 0-385-05690-7). Doubleday.
How Many More Must Die? John W. Raymond. 5.95 o.p. Vantage.
How Mean Can You Get? John W Corlis. 1974. 4.95 (ISBN 0-533-00930-8). Vantage Press.
How Mickey Made It. Jayne Anne Phillips. LC 81-10131. 35.00 (ISBN 0-939778-02-5) (ISBN 0-939778-01-7) (ISBN 0-939778-03-3). Bookslinger Editions.
How Mr. Rhodda Broke the Spell. Mark Guy Pearse. LC 99-2828. T. Y. Crowell & Company.
How Much. Burt Blechman. 1961. 7.95 (ISBN 0-8392-1050-7). Astor-Honor.
How Much? A Novel by B. Halpern As Told to Burt Blechman. Burt Blechman. LC 61-13185. 1961. Il Obolensky.
How Murder Speaks. Rupert Sargent Holland. LC 33-657522. Sears Publishing Company, Inc.
How My Brother Leon Brought Home a Wife, and Other Stories. Manuel Estabillo Arguilla. LC 70-98743. 1970. Greenwood Press.
How Not to Be a Success in Business. Martin M Keener. LC 66-9543. (Illus.). 1966. New Voices Pub. Co.
How Our Grandfathers Lived. Albert B. Hart & Annie B. Chapman. LC 78-164331. 1971. Repr. of 1921 ed. 37.00x (ISBN 0-8103-3795-9). Gale.
How Phoebe Found Herself. Helen Dawes Brown. LC 12-22128. 1912. 1.15. Houghton Mifflin Company.
How Private Geo. W. Peck Put Down the Rebellion. George Wilbur Peck. LC 71-91090. (American humorist series). (Illus.). 1969. (ISBN 0-8398-1559-X). Literature House.
How Private Geo. W. Peck Put Down the Rebellion: Or, The Funny Experience of a Raw Recruit... George Wilbur Peck. LC 7-30327. 1887. Belford, Clarke & Co.
How Private George W. Peck Put Down the Rebellion. George Wilbur Peck. LC 71-91090. (American Humorists Ser.). 1979. Repr. of 1887 ed. lib. bdg. 17.50x (ISBN 0-8398-1559-X). Irvington.
How Red This Dust. 1st Ed. John Alexander Hayes. LC 55-8802. 1955. Pageant Press.
How Right You Are, Jeeves. P. G. Wodehouse. Repr. lib. bdg. 11.75x (ISBN 0-89190-293-7). Am Repr-Rivercity Pr.
How Right You Are, Jeeves. P. G. Wodehouse. 1960. 3.50 o.p. (ISBN 0-671-32460-8). S&S.
How Right You Are: Jeeves. Pelham Grenville Wodehouse. LC 60-6106. 1960. Simon and Schuster.
How Rough Can It Get? A Novel. Joe Weiss. LC 52-16440. 1951. Woodford Press.
How She Came into Her Kingdom: A Romance... Charlotte Clark. LC 6-25357. 1878. Jansen, McClurg & Co.
How She Did It. Mary Cruger. 1888. D. Appleton and Company.
How She Died. Helen Yglesias. (Paperback Lib., 76093). 1973. 1.25. Warner Paperback Lib.
How She Died. Helen Yglesias. LC 76-173778. 1972. 6.95 (ISBN 0-395-13529-X). Houghton Mifflin.
How She Helped Him. Mary Andrews Denison. 1889. I. Bradley & Co.
How She Married Him, and Other Stories. Alexander Hamilton Jr. Laidlaw. LC 7-19405. 1892. Dickson & Laidlaw.
How She Won Him: Or, The Bride of Charming Valley. David Albert Moore. LC 28-4872. T. B. Peterson & Brothers.
How Sherlock Holmes Solved the Mystery of Edwin Drood. Harry Bache Smith. LC 34-41089. 1934. W. Klinefelter.
How Simon & I Escaped from the Hospital. John Tedman & Alison Tedman. (New Oxford Supplementary Readers Ser). (Illus.). 64p. 1966. pap. text ed. 0.70x o.p. (ISBN 0-19-422411-2). Oxford U Pr.
How Six Girls Made Money: And Occupations for Women. Marion Edmonds Roe. LC 7-40253. (Fowler & Wells library, no. 21). 1892. Fowler & Wells Co.
How Sleep the Brave. Catherine Irvine Gavin. LC 79-28414. 10.95 (ISBN 0-312-39534-5). St. Martin's Press.
How Sleep the Brave! A Novel of 17th Century Scotland. James Hogg Hunter. LC 56-19037. 1955. Zondervan Pub. House.
How Sleeps the Beast. Don Tracy. LC 38-5863. M. S. Mill Co., Inc.
How Still My Love. Doris Siegel. LC 57-10401. 1957. M. S. Mill Co., and W. Morrow.
How Thankful Was Bewitched. James Kendall Hosmer. LC 7-7154. (The Hudson library, no. 3). 1894. G. P. Putnam's Sons.
How the Fishes Live. Joel Lieber. LC 67-12311. 1967. McKay Co.
How the Gods Wove in Kyrannon. Ardath Mayhar. LC 78-22759. 1979. 7.95 (ISBN 0-385-13636-6). Doubleday.
How the Irish Built the Erie. Harvey Chalmers. LC 64-250618. 1965. 3.50. Bkman.
How the Old Woman Got Home. Matthew Phipps Shiel. LC 28-27813. 1928. Macy-Masius, The Vanguard Press.
How the Totem Pole Was Made, & Other Tales. Ladie Fonville Penick. 2.75 o.p. Vantage.
How the Victory Was Won. A Story. Walter W Brown. LC 6-172393. 1892. Printed for the Author.
How the West Was One. Bernard Gunther. 1971. 4.95 o.p. Macmillan.
How the West Was Won. Lou Cameron & Calvin Clements. LC 77-25159. 1978. 1.95 (ISBN 0-345-27401-6). Ballantine Books.
How the West Was Won. Louis L'Amour. (gr. 7-12). pap. 1.95 (ISBN 0-553-14411-1). Bantam.
How the West Was Won. Louis L. L'Amour. 256p. 1981. pap. 2.25 (ISBN 0-553-20003-8). Bantam.
How the West Was Won: A Novel. Louis L'Amour & James R Webb. LC 63-8935. 1963. Bantam Books.
How They Chose the Dead. Hollis Spurgeon Summers. LC 72-94153. 1973. 7.50 (ISBN 0-8071-0221-0). Louisiana State University Press.
How They Chose the Dead: Short Stories by Hollis Summers. Hollis Summers. LC 72-94153. 192p. 1973. 11.95 (ISBN 0-8071-0221-0). La State U Pr.
How They Kept the Faith: A Tale of the Huguenots of Languedoc. Annie Raymond Stillman. LC 42-26183. 1889. T. Nelson and Sons.
How They Kept the Faith. A Tale of the Huguenots of Languedoc. Annie Raymond Stillman. LC 4-33148. 1889. A. D. F. Randolph & Company.
How They Kept the Faith. A Tale of the Hugenots of Lanquedoc. Annie Raymond Stillman. Presbyterian Committee of Publication.
How They Lived in Hampton: A Study of Practical Christianity Applied in the Manufacture of Woolens. Edward Everett Hale. LC 79-154443. (Utopian Literature Ser). 1971. Repr. of 1888 ed. 16.00 (ISBN 0-405-03526-8). Ayer Co.
How They Loved Him. Florence Marryat Church Lean. (On cover: Seaside library. Pocket ed. no. 1250). 1889. G. Munro.
How to Be a Man-About-Town. Illus. by John Jensen. Vivian Ellis. LC 66-466. 1966. bds., 4.25. F. Muller.
How to Build a Life. Kay M. Gold. 3.50 o.p. Carlton.
How to Burn Your Candle. George E. Vandeman. LC 77-94240. (Stories That Win Ser.). 1978. pap. 0.95 (ISBN 0-8163-0003-8, 08831-0). Pacific Pr Pub Assn.
How to Catch and Tame a Husband: An Instructive Romance. Robert Torrington Furman. LC 50-3445. 1949. Distributed by Manufacturers Service Co.
How to Communicate in Sobriety. Luther Lord & Eileen Lord. LC 77-94793. (Illus., Orig.). 1978. pap. 5.95 (ISBN 0-89486-046-1). Hazelden.
How to Cook Husbands. Elizabeth Strong Worthington. LC 99-2863. 1899. The Dodge Publishing Company.
How to Execute an Agency. E. Waterhouse Allen. LC 79-53977. (Illus., Orig.). 1980. pap. 3.95 (ISBN 0-9603338-1-9). Bark-Back.
How to Get Balled in Berkeley: A Historical Romance of the Sixties. Anne Steinhardt. LC 75-30990. 7.95 (ISBN 0-670-38335-X). Viking Press.
How to Get Out from Under. Richard Burger & Jan J. Slavicek. 256p. 1970. pap. 5.95 o.s.i. (ISBN 0-8202-0065-4). Sherbourne.
How to Get Rid of a Woman: Being an Intimate Record of the Remarkable Love-Affairs of Wilton Olmstedd, Esq., Man of the World and Student of Life, Together with His Revealing Impressions of Women and His Amazing Discoveries Concerning the Sex. Edward Anthony. LC 28-18756. The Bobbs-Merrill Company.
How to Kill a Man. Stanton Forbes, pseud. LC 71-175405. 1972. 4.95. Published for the Crime Club by Doubleday.
How to Kill a Man. Tobias Wells. LC 71-175405. (Crime Club Ser). 1972. 4.95 o.p. (ISBN 0-385-02203-4). Doubleday.
How to Light a Water Heater & Other War Stories. Donald Kaul. LC 75-106602. (Illus.). 1970. 5.95x o.p. (ISBN 0-8138-0860-X). Iowa St U Pr.
How to Live Dangerously. Joan Margaret Fleming. LC 74-16595. (Red mask mystery). 1975. 5.95 (ISBN 0-399-11435-1). Putnam.
How to Live Dangerously. Joan Margaret Fleming. LC 75-11573. 1975. 10.95 (ISBN 0-8161-6294-8). G. K. Hall.
How to Live with a Tiger. George E. Vandeman. LC 77-94242. (Stories That Win Ser.). 1978. pap. 0.95 (ISBN 0-8163-0004-6, 08873-2). Pacific Pr Pub Assn.
How to Make It to Friday. Larry Jones. LC 79-67429. 3.95 (ISBN 0-89081-210-1). Harvest House Publishers.
How to Save Your Own Life. Erica Jong. 1978. pap. 2.50 (ISBN 0-451-07959-0, E7959, Sig). NAL.
How to Save Your Own Life: A Novel. Erica Jong. LC 76-29905. 8.95 (ISBN 0-03-017726-X). Holt, Rinehart and Winston.
How to Stay Married. George Fort Gibbs. LC 25-707489. 1925. D. Appleton and Company.
How to Steal a Pennant. Maury Wills & Don Freeman. LC 75-34442. (Illus.). 1976. 8.95 o.p. (ISBN 0-399-11699-0). Putnam Pub Group.
How to Study "The Best Short Stories" An Analysis of Edward J. O'Brien's Annual Volumes of the Best Short Stories of the Year. Blanche Colton Williams. LC 19-26577. Small, Maynard & Company.
How to Succeed at Business Spying by Trying: A Novel About Industrial Espionage. Shepherd Mead. LC 68-14841. 1968. Simon and Schuster.
How to Succeed in Bed Without Really Trying. Evan Marcus. LC 75-1049. (Orig.). 1969. pap. price not set o.p. (B75-1049). Belmont-Tower.
How to Travel with Parents. Eloise Barrangen. LC 56-8116. 1956. Dial Press.
How to Write Short Stories (with Samples) Ring Wilmer Lardner. LC 75-145130. 1971. (ISBN 0-403-01063-2). Scholarly Press.
How to Write Short Stories: With Samples. Ring Wilmer Lardner. LC 24-10848. 1924. C. Scribner's Sons.
How to Write Short Stories: With Samples. Ring Wilmer Lardner. LC 35-28592. 1925. C. Scribner's Sons.
How Tom and Dorothy Made and Kept a Christian Home. Harriet Mulford Stone Lothrop. LC 7-14769. D. Lothrop Company.
How We Live: Contemporary Life in Contemporary Fiction; an Anthology. Ed. by Penney Chapin Hills. LC 68-11266. 1968. Macmillan.
How Wide the Heart. Elisabeth Ogilvie. Repr. lib. bdg. 12.05x (ISBN 0-88411-332-9). Amereon Ltd.
How Will It End! A Romance. Joseph Converse Heywood. LC 7-4750. 1872. J. B. Lippincott & Co.
How Women Love: And Other Tales (Soul Analysis. Max Simon Nordau. 1896. F. T. Neely.
How Young They Die: A Novel About the First World War. Stuart Cloete. LC 73-80654. 1969. 6.95 (ISBN 0-671-27041-9). Trident Press.
How Zach Came to College. Clinkscales, John George. LC 5-600. 1904. W. F. Barnes.
How 007 Got His Name. Mary Wickham Bond. LC 66-71321. 1966. bds., 2.50. Collins.
Howard Ashton, and the World He Lived in. Virginia Miller. United Presbyterian Board of Publication.
Howard Chase, Red Hill, Kansas. Charles Monroe Sheldon. LC 18-2602. George H. Doran Company.
Howard Hughes Affair. Stuart M Kaminsky. LC 79-5032. 8.95 (ISBN 0-312-39617-1). St. Martin's Press.
Howard Phillips Lovecraft: Dreamer on the Nightside. Frank Belknap Long. LC 74-18652. (Illus.). 1975. 8.50 (ISBN 0-87054-068-8). Arkham House.
Howard Pinckney. A Novel. Frederick William Thomas. LC 8-27048. 1840. Lea and Blanchard.
Howard Street. Nathan C. Heard. 256p. 1973. pap. 2.50 (ISBN 0-451-09542-1, E9542, Sig). NAL.
Howard Street: A Novel. Nathan C Heard. LC 68-9459. 1968. 4.95. Dial Press.
Howard's Bag: A Novel. Douglass Wallop. LC 72-11777. 1973. 6.95 (ISBN 0-393-08674-7). Norton.
Howards End. Edward Morgan Forster. LC 54-12051. (Vintage book, K7). 1954. Vintage Books.
Howards End. Edward Morgan Forster. LC 10-30577. 1910. G. P. Putnam's Sons.
Howards End. Edward Morgan Forster. LC 21-17626. 1921. A. A. Knopf.
Howards of Caxley. Miss Read. (Illus.). 1968. 4.00 o.p. (ISBN 0-395-08114-9). HM.
Howards of Caxley. Dora Jessie Saint. LC 68-16272. (Illus.). 1968. Houghton Mifflin.
Howbah Indians. Simon J. Ortiz. (Fiction Ser.). (Orig.). 1977. pap. 4.95 (ISBN 0-933188-06-4). Blue Moon Pr.
Howdoyoudo: The Story of a Dog. Neve Conklin. 1974. 4.50 (ISBN 0-682-47896-2). Exposition Press.

Howdy, Honey, Howdy. Paul Laurence Dunbar. LC 73-164799. (Illus.). Repr. of 1905 ed. 12.50 (ISBN 0-404-00035-5). AMS Pr.

Howdy Honey Howdy. facs. ed. Paul Laurence Dunbar. LC 79-78993. (Black Heritage Library Collection Ser). (Illus.). 1905. 10.00 (ISBN 0-8369-8556-7). Ayer Co.

Howell's The Rise of Silas Lapham. Randall Keenan. LC 66-1764. (Monarch notes and study guides, 675-9). 1966. 2.50. Monarch Pr.

Howl at the Moon. Robert J. Hogan. (O.s.i.). pap. 0.60 o.s.i. (A148X, Award). Univ Pub & Dist.

Howling. Gary Brandner. (Fawcett Gold Medal Book). 1.75 (ISBN 0-449-13824-0). Fawcett Pubns.

Howling in the Woods. Velda Johnston. LC 68-24024. (Red badge mystery). 1968. 3.95. Dodd, Mead.

Howling: Mad. Ed.: Albert B. Feldstein. William M Gaines. (Signet bk., D3268). 1967. New Amer. Lib.

Howling Two. Gary Brandner. 1979. pap. 2.50 (ISBN 0-449-14091-1, GM). Fawcett.

Hoy Es Fiesta see En la Ardiente Obscuridad.

Hoyden. A Novel. Margaret Wolfe Hungerford. (Lippincott's select novels, no. 147). 1893. J. B. Lippincott Company.

Hoyden Bride. Margaret Rau. LC 80-922. 1980. 8.95 (ISBN 0-385-17163-3). Doubleday.

Hoyo Secreto. span. ed. Jim Kelly. (Small Star Stories). (Illus.). 1975. 5.95 o.p. (ISBN 0-02-645760-1, 64576). Glencoe.

Hoyt's Child. Robert Verlin Cassill. LC 75-21218. 1976. 7.95 (ISBN 0-385-09675-5). Doubleday.

Hte Shining Light. Ralph Webster Neighbour. LC 60-51882. 1960. Zondervan Pub. House.

Huasipungo. The Villagers, a Novel. Jorge Icaza. LC 64-10478. (Contemporary Latin American classics). 1964. Southern Illinois University Press.

Huasipungo. The Villagers: a Novel. Jorge Icaza. LC 73-9551. (Arcturus books, AB 118). 1973. 2.85 (ISBN 0-8093-0653-0). Southern Illinois University Press.

Hubbard's Trail. Alfred Hubbard Holt. LC 52-4432. 1952. Erle Press.

Hubble-Bubble. Margaret Bell. LC 27-21340. 1927. Dodd, Mead and Company.

Hubbub. A Story. Emma C Currier. LC 6-31182. The Authors' Publishing Company.

Hubert's Arthur. Frederick William Rolfe & Pirie-Gordon, Charles Harry Clinton. LC 77-92409. (Lost Race and Adult Fantasy Fiction). 1978. 27.00. Arno Press.

Hubert's Wife: A Story for You. Julia Amanda Sargent Wood. LC 49-40825. (Library of Catholic Novels). 1890. Excelsior Catholic Pub. House.

Hubert's Wife: A Story for You. Julia Amanda Sargent Wood. LC 8-37547. 1875. Kelley, Piet & Co.

Hubertus: A Novel. 1st American Ed. Edgar Mittelholzer. LC 54-104611. 1955. J. Day Co.

Hubschmann Effect. Thomas Patrick McMahon. LC 72-86985. (Simon and Schuster novel of suspense). 1973. 5.95 (ISBN 0-671-21453-5). Simon and Schuster.

Hubschmann Effect. Thomas Patrick McMahon. 1974. (pbk.) 1.25 (ISBN 0-671-78403-X). Pocket Books.

Huck Finn and His Critics. Samuel Langhorne Clemens. Ed. by Richard Lettis. LC 62-14372. 1962. Macmillan.

Huckle, Buckle Beanstalk. M. William Herbst. 3.50 o.p. Vantage.

Huckleberries Gathered from New England Hills. Rose Terry Cooke. LC 69-11885. (American short story series, v. 43). 1969. Garrett Press.

Huckleberries Gathered from New England Hills. Rose Terry Cooke. LC 72-8089. (American short story series, v. 43). 1972. (ISBN 0-8422-8029-4). MSS Information Corp.

Huckleberries Gathered from New England Hills. Rose Terry Cooke. LC 6-27181. 1891. Houghton, Mifflin and Company.

Huckleberry Finn. Mark Twain. Ed. by Corbin S. Carnell. (Graded Readers for Students of English Ser.). (Illus.). 1979. pap. text ed. 3.50 o.p. (ISBN 0-89285-151-1). English Lang.

Huckleberry Finn. Mark Twain. (Regents Illustrated Classics Ser.). (Illus.). 62p. (gr. 7-12). 1981. pap. text ed. 2.25 (ISBN 0-88345-464-5). Regents Pub.

Huckleberry Finn. Mark Twain. (Nelson Classics). 1.75 o.p. Nelson.

Huckleberry Finn. Mark Twain. Ed. by C. S. Porter. (Classics Ser). (Illus.). (gr. 7-12). 1967. text ed. 2.95 o.p. (H78295). St Martin.

Huckleberry Finn. Mark Twain. (Illus.). 318p. (gr. 7-12). 1970. pap. text ed. 0.75 o.p. (ISBN 0-88301-049-6). Pendulum Pr.

Huckleberry Finn see Tom Sawyer.

Huckleberry Finn; Text, Sources, and Criticism. Samuel Langhorne Clemens. Ed. by Kenneth Schuyler Lynn. LC 61-9261. (Harbrace sourcebooks). 1961. Harcourt, Brace & World.

Huckleberry Hill: By Ann Carter Pseud. Anne Tedlock Brooks. LC 50-14609. 1950. Arcadia House.

Hucksters. Frederic Wakeman. LC 46-3141. 1946. Rinehart & Company, Incorporated.

Huddle! Francis Wallace. LC 30-32846. Farrar & Rhinehart Incorporated.

Huddle: A Fleming Stone Detective Novel. Carolyn Wells. LC 36-185604. J. B. Lippincott Company.

Hudson! Helen L. Poole. (Whitewater Dynasty Ser.). 400p. (Orig.). 1980. pap. 2.50 (ISBN 0-89083-607-8). Zebra.

Hudson Crossroads: A Documentary Narrative of Three Centuries in Upper New York. 1st Ed. Mary Hun Sears. LC 54-10343. 1955. Exposition Press.

Hudson Rejoins the Herd. Claude Houghton Oldfield. LC 39-25701. 1939. The Macmillan Company.

Hudson River Bracketed. Edith Newbold Jones Wharton. LC 69-17049. 1969. 7.95. Scribner.

Hudson River Bracketed. Edith Newbold Jones Wharton. LC 29-24077. 1929. D. Appleton and Company.

Hudson River Bracketed. Centennial Ed. Edith Newbold Jones Wharton. LC 62-5223. 1962. Appleton-Century-Crofts.

Hudson's Last Voyage. Edward Oliver. LC 62-18658. Greenwich Book Publishers.

Hue and Cry. Thomas Blanchard Dewey. LC 44-909271. 1944. Jefferson House.

Hue & Cry. James Alan McPherson. 1979. pap. 2.25 (ISBN 0-449-24192-0, Crest). Fawcett.

Hue and Cry. Patricia Wentworth. LC 27-18379. 1927. J. B. Lippincott Company.

Hue and Cry. Elizabeth Yates. LC 53-8893. 1953. Corward-McCann.

Hue and Cry: Short Stories. James Alan McPherson. LC 69-16969. 1969. 5.95. Little, Brown.

Huelga! A Novel. David Chandler. LC 79-116502. 1970. 6.95. Simon and Schuster.

Huellas-Footprints. Emilio Bejel & Marie J. Panico. LC 82-71933. 122p. (Span. & Eng.). 1982. pap. 6.50 (ISBN 0-935318-07-0). Edins Hispamerica.

Huey, the Engineer. Wood Engravings by Mallette Dean. Jesse Stuart. LC 61-26932. 1960. J. E. Beard.

Huff Case. May Stranathan. LC 12-554895. R. G. Badger.

Huffley Fair. 1st Ed. Dorothy Evelyn Smith. LC 55-8320. 1955. Dutton.

Huge Season. Wright Morris. LC 54-10858. viii, 306p. 1975. pap. 5.50 (ISBN 0-8032-5805-4, BB 590, Bison). U of Nebr Pr.

Huge Season. Wright Morris. 1969. pap. 0.75 o.p. (T1983). Pyramid Pubns.

Huge Season: A Novel. Wright Morris. LC 75-310315. 1975. 2.95 (ISBN 0-8032-5805-4). University of Nebraska Press.

Huge Season: A Novel. Wright Morris. LC 54-10858. 1954. Viking Press.

Hugger-Mugger in the Louvre: A Homer Evans Murder Mystery. Elliot Harold Paul. LC 40-3665. Random House.

Hugging to Music. A Story from Life. R. B. Smith. 1890. University Publishing Company.

Hugh Campbell. Charles William Macfarlane. LC 31-17248. 1930. The Penn Publishing Company.

Hugh Carlin: Or, Truth's Triumph. James Hiram Stark. LC 8-13454. 1896. Christian Publishing Company.

Hugh Darnaby: A Story of Kentucky. Garrett Morrow Davis. LC 6611. 1900. Gibson Bros.

Hugh Graham: A Tale of the Pioneers. Frank Sumner Townsend. LC 16-6644. The Abingdon Press.

Hugh Gwyeth: A Roundhead Cavalier. Beulah Marie Dix. LC 99-1238. 1899. The Macmillan Company.

Hugh Lane. Isabella A. Gregory. (Coole Edition of the Collected Works of Lady Gregory Ser.). (Illus.). 1973. text ed. 19.95x (ISBN 0-19-519725-9). Oxford U Pr.

Hugh Laval: A Romance of the Up Country. Thomas Rose Elliott. LC 27-19412. 1927. The Macmillan Company.

Hugh Worthington... A Novel. Mary Jane Hawes Holmes. LC 7-8483. 1865. Carleton.

Hugh Worthington. A Novel. Mary Jane Hawes Holmes. LC 7-8482. G. W. Dillingham.

Hugh Wynne, Free Quaker. Silas W. Mitchell. LC 67-29274. (Americans in Fiction Ser: No. 16). 1967. Repr. of 1896 ed. lib. bdg. 11.50x o.p. (ISBN 0-8398-1265-5). Gregg.

Hugh Wynne, Free Quaker. Silas Weir Mitchell. LC 67-29274. (Americans in Fiction Ser.). Repr. of 1896 ed. lib. bdg. 16.50 (ISBN 0-8398-1265-5). Irvington.

Hugh Wynne, Free Quaker: Some Time Brevet Lieutenant-Colonel on the Staff of His Excellency General Washington. Silas Weir Mitchell. Ed. by Vincent Bean Bretcht. LC 23-1749. 1922. The Century Co.

Hugh Wynne, Free Quaker: Sometime Brevet Lieutenant-Colonel on the Staff of His Excellency General Washington. Silas Weir Mitchell. LC 67-29274. 1967. Gregg Pr.

Hugh Wynne, Free Quaker: Sometime Brevet Lieutenant-Colonel on the Staff of His Excellency General Washington. Silas Weir Mitchell. LC 75-3261. (Illus.). 1968. Scholarly Press.

Hugh Wynne, Free Quaker: Sometime Brevet Lieutenant-Colonel on the Staff of His Excellency General Washington. Silas Weir Mitchell. LC 7-25780. 1896. The Century Co.

Hugh Wynne, Free Quaker, Sometime Brevet Lieutenant-Colonel on the Staff of His Excellency General Washington. Mitchell, Silas Weir. 1897. The Century Co.

Hugh Wynne, Free Quaker, Sometime Brevet Lieutenant-Colonel on the Staff of His Excellency General Washington. Silas Weir Mitchell. 1898. The Century Co.

Hugh Wynne, Free Quaker: Sometime Brevet Lieutenant-Colonel on the Staff of His Excellency, General Washington. Silas Weir Mitchell. LC 8-34332. 1900. The Century Co.

Hugh Wynne, Free Quaker, Sometime Brevet Lieutenant-Colonel on the Staff of His Excellency General Washington. Silas Weir Mitchell. Ed. by Vincent Bean Bretcht. 1922. The Century Co.

Hughe Wynne: Free Quaker, Sometime Brevet Lieutenant-Colonel on the Staff of His Excellency General Washington. Silas Weir Mitchell. LC 17-490. 1897. The Century Co.

Hughie Roddis. Gerald Savory. LC 42-7966. 1942. Alliance Book Corporation.

Hugo. Arnold Bennett. LC 74-5403. (Collected Works of Arnold Bennett: Vol. 34). 1976. Repr. of 1906 ed. 20.75 (ISBN 0-518-19115-X). Ayer Co.

Hugo: A Fantasia on Modern Themes. Arnold Bennett. LC 74-5403. (collected works of Arnold Bennett). 1974. (ISBN 0-518-19115-X). Books for Libraries Press.

Hugo: A Fantasia on Modern Themes. Arnold Bennett. LC 6-41708. 1906. F. M. Buckles and Company.

Hugo: A Fantasia on Modern Themes. Arnold Bennett. LC 24-279772. George H. Doran Company.

Hugo: A Legend of Rockland Lake. Found Amongst the Papers of the Late Ernest Helfenstein Pseud.... 2d ed. Elizabeth Oakes Prince Smith. LC 8-8638. 1851. J. S. Taylor.

Hugo Blanc, the Artist. A Tale of Practical and Ideal Life. V. M Griswold. LC 7-161. 1867. Hilton & Co.

Hugo of the Blade. Julius Frederick Seebach. LC 38-29972. (John Rung prize series). The Board of Publication of the United Lutheran Church in America.

Hugo, the Deformed. Horatio Alger, Jr. (Illus.). 84p. 1978. 19.50. G K Westgard.

Hugo Winners, Vol. III, Bk. I. Ed. by Isaac Asimov. 1979. pap. 2.25 (ISBN 0-449-23841-5, Crest). Fawcett.

Hugo Winners, Vol. 1. Isaac Asimov. 320p. 1977. pap. 2.25 (ISBN 0-449-23917-9, Crest). Fawcett.

Hugo Winners, Vol. 2. Ed. by Isaac Asimov. LC 62-14132. 1971. 9.95 o.p. (ISBN 0-385-05803-9). Doubleday.

Hugo Winners, Vol. 3. Ed. by Isaac Asimov. LC 73-180538. 1977. 14.95 (ISBN 0-385-12218-7). Doubleday.

Hugo Winners. 1st Ed. Ed. by Isaac Asimov. LC 62-14132. 1962. Doubleday.

Huguenot Exiles: Or, The Times of Louis Xiv A Historical Novel... Eliza Ann Dupuy. LC 6-3585. 1856. Harper & Brothers.

Huguenot Lovers. A Tale of the Old Dominion. Collinson Pierrepont Edwards Burgwyn. LC 6-18657. 1889. Pub. by the Author.

Huguenot Sword: The History of the Adventures of the Chevalier De Marquette, Special Courier to Gaspard De Cologny, Admiral of France. Jean Baptiste Thill. F. T. Neely.

Hula: A Romance of Hawaii. Armine Von Tempski. LC 27-31763. 1927. Frederick A. Stokes Company.

Hula-Hula. Amos Tyree. LC 31-34141. National Capital Press, Inc.

Hulda. A Romance of the West: David of Juniper Gulch). Lillian Hinman Shuey. LC 8-7321. (On cover: Library of choice fiction, no. 70). 1894. Laird & Lee.

Hulda: Or, The Deliverer; a Romance After the German of F. Lewald. Fanny Lewald-Stahr & Wister, Mrs. Annie Lee (Furness) 1830-1908, Tr. LC 8-28111. 1874. J. B. Lippincott & Co.

Huldah. Juliet Alves. LC 42-19940. 1942. C. Scribner's Sons.

Huldah: Proprietor of the Wagon-Tire House and Genial Philosopher of the Cattle Country. Grace MacGowan Cooke & MacGowan, Alice. LC 4-10933. 1904. The Bobbs-Merrill Company.

Huling's Quest. McCready Huston. LC 25-173419. 1925. C. Scribner's Sons.

Hull Down, Sea Lore, Sea Legends & the Days of the Sailing Ships. P. A. Eaddy. 1977. lib. bdg. 69.95 (ISBN 0-8490-2026-3). Gordon Pr.

Human? Ed. by Judith Merril. LC 54-356725. (Lion book, 205). 1954. Lion Books By Arrangement with Postal Publications.

Human: A Sequence. Alexander Baron. LC 53-7548. Washburn.

Human & Inhuman Stories. 2nd ed. Dorothy Leigh Sayers. (1974 ed. o.p.). 176p. 1977. pap. 1.25 (ISBN 0-532-12482-0). Woodhill.

Human & Inhuman Stories. Dorothy Leigh Sayers. 1967. pap. 0.60 o.p. (60-298). Manor Bks.

Human and Other Beings. Ed. by Albert P Blaustein. LC 63-10209. (Collier science fiction). 1963. Collier Books.

Human and Other Beings. Ed. by Allen De Graeff, pseud. LC 63-10209. (Collier science fiction). 1963. Collier Books.

Human Angle: By William Tenn Pseud. Philip Klass. LC 56-11224. 1956. Ballantine Books.

Human Bail. Prentiss Payson. LC 32-295003. 1932. Meador Publishing Company.

Human Beast. Emile Zola & Coleman, Louis, Tr. LC 32-5895. 1832. Julian Press.

Human Being: A Story. Christopher Darlington Morley. LC 32-28154. 1932. Doubleday, Doran & Company, Inc.

Human Being: A Story. Christopher Darlington Morley. LC 40-27704. (Half-title: The modern library of the world's best books). 1940. Modern Library.

Human Being, a Story: By Christopher Morley. Christopher Darlington Morley. LC 36-35240. The Sun Dial Press.

Human Beings Vs. Things. Asenath Carver Coolidge. LC 9-30118. 1910. 1.00. Hungerford-Holbrook Company.

Human Boy. Eden Phillpotts. LC 70-170592. (Short story index reprint series). 1971. (ISBN 0-8369-4021-0). Books for Libraries Press.

Human Boy. Eden Phillpotts. LC 7-73650. 1900. Harper & Brothers.

Human Boy. Eden Phillpotts. LC 5-56. 1904. Harper & Brothers.

Human Boy and the War. Eden Phillpotts. LC 70-128748. (Short story index reprint series). 1970. Books for Libraries Press.

Human Boy and the War. Eden Phillpotts. LC 16-140906. 1916. 1.25. The Macmillan Company.

Human Boy's Diary. Eden Phillpotts. LC 24-7952. 1924. The Macmillan Company.

Human Brutes: La Bete Humaine) a Realistic Novel. Emile Zola & Valcourt-Vermont, Edgar De, Tr. LC 9-1322. (pastime series. v. 38). 1890. Laird & Lee.

Human Chips. Boris V Monomack. LC 33-339505. 1933. Overland-Outwest Publications.

Human Cobweb: A Romance of Peking. Bertram Lenox Simpson. LC 10-4639. 1910. Dodd, Mead & Company.

Human Comedy. William Saroyan & Freeman, Don, Illus. LC 43-51036. 1943. Harcourt, Brace and Company.

Human Comedy. William Saroyan & Sheridan, Marion C., Ed. LC 44-4340. 1944. Harcourt, Brace and Company.

Human Commitment: An Anthology of Contemporary Short Fiction. Ed. by Don Gold. LC 67-25869. 1967. Chilton Book Co.

Human Crowd: New Fiction from the Minnesota Review. Ed. by Scott Sanders & Roger Mitchell. LC 81-81271. 151p. (Orig.). 1981. pap. 3.00 (ISBN 0-936484-01-2). Minn Rev Pr.

Human Desire. Violet Mary Irwin. LC 13-23019. 1.35. Small, Maynard and Company.

Human Document. new ed. William Hurrell Mallock. LC 7-24367. (On cover: Cassell's sunshine series. no. 103). 1892. Cassell Publishing Company.

Human Document: A Novel. William Hurrell Mallock. LC 75-1537. (Victorian Fiction: Novels of Faith and Doubt; V. 85). (Series: Cassell's sunshine series; no. 103.). 1975. 35.00 (ISBN 0-8240-1609-2). Garland Pub.

Human Equation. Clell Edgar Bowman. 1976. 8.00 o.p. (ISBN 0-682-48437-7). Exposition.

Human Equation. William F. Nolan. 1978. pap. 4.95 o.s.i. (ISBN 0-8202-5029-5). Sherbourne.

Human Equation. William F. Nolan. 254p. 1971. 7.50 o.p. Sherbourne.

Human Exile. Bela Fischer. LC 74-75081. 1974. 6.00 (ISBN 0-8022-2139-4). Philos Lib.

Human Factor. Graham Greene. LC 77-17169. 9.95 (ISBN 0-671-24085-4). Simon and Schuster.

Human Factor. Graham Greene. LC 78-16119. 1978. 13.95 (ISBN 0-8161-6598-X). G. K. Hall.

Human Factor. Graham Greene. 1979. 2.75 (ISBN 0-380-50302-6). Avon Books.

Human Factor. Simon Quinn. 1975. (pbk.) 1.25. Dell.

Human Follies. La Betise Humaine. Claude Antoine Jules Cairon. Tr. by Marlow, George. (On cover: Foreign library, no. 5). 1863. F. Leypoldt.

Human Harvest. Anthony Francis Raspono. LC 44-2185. Times-Mirror Press, Distributed by Interstate Book Company.
Human Hearts: A Romantic Story, Based Upon the Play of the Same Name. Grace Miller White. LC 48-34208. (Play book series, no. 36). J. S. Ogilvie Pub. Co.
Human Image. Robert Miller Smith. 1945. Harper & Brothers.
Human Interest: A Study in Incompatibilities. Violet Hunt. LC 99-4658. 1899. H. S. Stone and Company.
Human Machine. Arnold Bennett. LC 74-5290. (Collected Works of Arnold Bennett: Vol. 35). 1976. Repr. of 1908 ed. 14.75 (ISBN 0-518-19116-8) Ayer Co.
Human Machine. Loretta Shaw. LC 82-73479. 140p. (Orig.). 1982. pap. 6.95 (ISBN 0-931494-33-8). Brunswick Pub.
Human Machines: An Anthology of Stories About Cyborgs. Thomas N. Scortia & George Zebrowski. LC 75-13382. 1975. 2.95 (ISBN 0-394-71607-8). Vintage Books.
Human Natur'. William Andrew Peters. LC 7-36173. 1885. Knickerbocker Book Co.
Human Nature. Edith Newbold Jones Wharton. LC 33-6573. 1933. D. Appleton and Company.
Human Odds and Ends: Stories and Sketches. George Robert Gissing. LC 76-20076. (Decadent Consciousness). 1977-1978. 26.00 (ISBN 0-8240-2759-0). Garland Pub.
Human Revolution. Daisaku Ikeda. LC 72-79121. (Illus.). (v. 1) 7.50 (ISBN 0-8348-0074-8). Weatherhill.
Human Season. Edward Lewis Wallant. (Harbrace paperbound lib., HPL 58). 1973. 1.65 (ISBN 0-15-642330-8). Harcourt.
Human Season. 1st Ed. Edward Lewis Wallant. LC 60-10923. 1960. Harcourt, Brace.
Human Senses. Jeanne Bendick. LC 76-451548. (Science experiences). (Illus.) 1968 (ISBN 0-85166-095-9). Franklin Watts Ltd.
Human Sexual Inability. Mas Turzan. (Orig.). 1972. pap. 0.75 o.p. (A884S, Award). Univ Pub & Dist.
Human Shore. 1st Ed. Harvena Richter. LC 59-7634. 1959. Little, Brown.
Human Time Bomb. Nick Carter. (Nick Carter Ser.). 160p. 1981. pap. 2.25 (ISBN 0-441-34909-9). Ace Bks.
Human Time Bomb. Nick Carter. (Nick Carter Ser.). (O.s.i.). 192p. 1975. pap. 1.25 o.s.i (AQ1474, Award). Univ Pub & Dist.
Human Touch. Herman Cyril McNeile. LC 19-580. 1918. Hodder and Stoughton.
Human Touch. Herman Cyril McNeile. LC 18-22827. George H. Doran Company.
Human Touch: A Tale of the Great Southwest. Edith M Nicholl Bowyer. 1905. Lothrop Publishing Company.
Human Warmth & Other Stories. Daniel Curzon. LC 80-23270. 10.00 (ISBN 0-912516-53-4) (ISBN 0-912516-54-2). Grey Fox Press.
Human Whirlpool: A Story of Wanderlust and Adventure. Robert E Callahan. LC 47-17758. 1946. Murray & Gee, Inc.
Human Zero: The Science Fiction Stories of Erle Stanley Gardner. Erle Stanley Gardner & Martin Harry Greenberg. LC 80-22494. 1981. 12.95 (ISBN 0-688-00122-X). Morrow.
Human Zero: The Science Fiction Stories of Erle Stanley Gardner. Ed. by Martin Harry Greenberg & Charles G. Waugh. LC 80-22494. 432p. 1981. 12.95 (ISBN 0-688-00122-X). Morrow.
Humanity. A Sporting and Military Story from the... Arthur D Hall & Vane, Sutton Humanity. (On cover: Drama series, no. 27). 1897. Street & Smith.
Humanization of Eddie Cement. George Deaux. LC 64-12476. 1964. Simon and Schuster.
Humanoid Touch. Jack Williamson. LC 80-13817. 9.95 (ISBN 0-03-056052-7). Holt, Rinehart, and Winston.
Humanoids. Ed. by Charles Bowen. 256p. 1975. pap. 3.95 o.p. (ISBN 0-8092-8231-3). Contemp Bks.
Humanoids. Jack Williamson. LC 49-100193. 1949. Simon and Schuster.
Humanoids. Jack Williamson. LC 79-18576. (Gregg Press science fiction series). (Illus.). 1980. 13.50 (ISBN 0-8398-2549-8). Gregg Press.
Humble Enterprise. Ada Cambridge Cross. LC 6-31959. (Half-title: Appleton's town and country library, no. 196). 1896. D. Appleton and Company.
Humble Lear. Lorna Doone Beers. LC 29-12768. E. P. Dutton & Co., Inc.
Humble Powers. Paul Horgan. LC 56-13663. (Doubleday image book, D35). 1956. Image Books.
Humble Romance: And Other Stories. Mary Eleanor Wilkins Freeman. LC 69-11894. (American short story series, v. 52). 1969. Garrett Press.
Humble Romance, and Other Stories. Mary Eleanor Wilkins Freeman. LC 71-130991. 1970. (ISBN 0-404-02574-9). AMS Press.

Humble Romance, and Other Stories. Mary Eleanor Wilkins Freeman. LC 72-8163. (American short story series, v. 52). 1972. (ISBN 0-8422-8052-9). MSS Information Corp.
Humble Romance: And Other Stories. Mary Eleanor Wilkins Freeman. LC 1-2478. 1887. Harper & Brothers.
Humble Romance: And Other Stories. Mary Eleanor Wilkins Freeman. LC 1-2479. 1899. Harper & Brothers.
Humbled Pride: A Story of the Mexican War. John Roy Musick. LC 7-33329. (On cover: Columbian historical novels. v. 11). 1893. Funk & Wagnalls Company.
Humboldt's Gift. Saul Bellow. LC 75-12595. 1975. 10.00 (ISBN 0-670-38655-3). Viking Press.
Humbug: A Study in Education. Edmee Elizabeth Monica De La Pasture. LC 22-4087. 1922. The Macmillan Company.
Humbug Coulee: The Diary of a Census Enumerator: Fiction Based on Facts of the Federal Decennial Census and Rural Life in the Coulee Region of Wisconsin in 1950. Estella Bryhn. LC 76-152134. (Illus.). St. Mary's College Press.
Humdrum. Harold Marie Mitchell Acton. LC 29-82633. Harcourt, Brace and Company.
Humdrum House? Maximilian Foster. LC 24-18765. 1924. D. Appleton and Company.
Humdrum House. Jeannette Clarke Phillips Gibbs. LC 29-3184. 1929. Little, Brown, and Company.
Humility. Andrew Murray. 1974. pap. 2.50 (ISBN 0-87508-383-8). Chr Lit.
Hummer's Lucky Day. Educational Challenges, Inc. (Turning Point I Ser.). (gr. 7-12). pap. text ed. 3.00 (ISBN 0-8009-1889-4). McCormick-Mathers.
Humming Bird: A Novel. Eleanor Farjeon. LC 37-27103. 1937. Frederick A. Stokes Company.
Humming-Bird Tree. Ian McDonald. (Caribbean Writers Ser.). (Orig.). 1974. pap. text ed. 4.50x (ISBN 0-435-98575-2). Heinemann Ed.
Humming Precipice. Mary Sheppard. 1973. pap. 0.75 o.s.i. (01-374). Lancer.
Humming Top. Dorothy Gladys Spicer. LC 68-31176. 1968. 4.95. S. G. Phillips.
Hummingbird. LaVyrle Spencer. 416p. 1983. pap. 3.50 (ISBN 0-515-07108-0). Jove Pubns.
Humoresque: A Laugh on Life with a Tear Behind It. Fannie Hurst. LC 19-4096. 1919. Harper & Brothers.
Humoresque: A Laugh on Life with a Tear Behind It. Fannie Hurst. LC 22-516109. A. L. Burt Company.
Humoresque: A Laugh on Life with a Tear Behind It. Fannie Hurst. LC 34-27236. 1934. P. Smith.
Humorous Ghost Stories. Dorothy Scarborough. Repr. 12.50 o.p. Folcroft.
Humorous Ghost Stories: Selected. Ed. by Dorothy Scarborough. LC 21-8834. 1921. G. P. Putnam's Sons.
Humorous Mr. Bowser. Charles Bertrand Lewis. LC 11-23705. J. S. Ogilvie Publishing Company.
Humorous Short Stories. Ed. by Greta A Clark. LC 60-8086. Hart Pub. Co.
Humorous Side of Erskine Caldwell: An Anthology, Edited with an Introd. by Robert Cantwell. Erskine Caldwell. LC 51-9609. 1951. Duell, Sloan and Pearce.
Humorous Stories. John Brougham. 1859. Derby & Jackson.
Humorous Stories. Barry Eric Odell Pain. LC 79-37281. (Short story index reprint series). (Illus.). 1971. (ISBN 0-8369-4091-1). Books for Libraries Press.
Humorous Tales of Rudyard Kipling. Rudyard Kipling. LC 31-28150. 1931. Doubleday, Doran & Company, Inc.
Humorous Tales of Rudyard Kipling. Rudyard Kipling. LC 41-13231. 1941. Triangle Books.
Humors of the Fair. Julian Hawthorne. (Marguerite series, no. 12). 1893. F. A. Weeks & Company.
Humour & Fantasy. Thomas Anstey Guthrie. LC 78-3255. (Lost Race and Adult Fantasy Fiction). 1978. 68.00 (ISBN 0-405-10953-9). Arno Press.
Humour & Fantasy: Vice Versa, the Tinted Venus, a Fallen Idol, the Talking Horse, Salted Almonds, the Brass Bottle. Henry Rider Haggard. Ed. by R. Reginald & Douglas Melville. LC 77-84195. (Lost Race & Adult Fantasy Ser.). 1978. Repr. of 1931 ed. lib. bdg. 68.00x (ISBN 0-405-10953-9). Ayer Co.
Humour of Russia. Ed. by Ethel Lillian Boole Voynich. Frenzeny, Paul, Illus. LC 1-22381. (On cover: International humour). 1895. W. Scott, Ltd.
Humours of Eutopia: A Tale of Colonial Times. Ezekiel Sanford. LC 6-31727. 1828. Carey, Lea & Carey.

Humphrey Bold: A Story of the Time of Benbow. Herbert Strang & Benbow, John, 1653-1702-Fiction. LC 9-28461. 1909. The Bobbs-Merrill Company.
Humphrey Clinker. Tobias George Smollett. pap. 2.95 (ISBN 0-451-51557-9, CE1557, Sig Classics). NAL.
Humphrey Clinker. Tobias George Smollett. 3.00 o.p. (ISBN 0-00-422632-1). Collins-World.
Humphry Clinker. Tobias George Smollett. LC 44-27432. (Routledge's railway library). G. Routledge and Sons.
Humument: A Treated Victorian Novel. Tom Phillips, pseud. (Illus.). 1983. pap. 12.95 (ISBN 0-500-27284-0). Thames Hudson.
Hunch. Ray Humphreys. LC 34-356910. Loring & Mussey.
Hunchback. John T Yates. LC 31-3873. The Christopher Publishing House.
Hunchback House. Donald Bayne Hobart. LC 30-851651. Whitman Publishing Co.
Hunchback of Notre-Dame. Victor Marie Hugo. (C1162). 1968. Airmont.
Hunchback of Notre Dame. Victor Marie Hugo. LC 57-13607. 1957. Grosset & Dunlap.
Hunchback of Notre Dame. Victor Marie Hugo. LC 47-12434. (Great Illustrated Classics). 1947. Dodd, Mead.
Hunchback of Notre-Dame. Victor Marie Hugo. LC 7-586675. 1834. Carey, Lea and Blanchard.
Hunchback of Notre Dame. Victor Marie Hugo. (Seaside library, v. 29, no. 597). 1879. G. Munro.
Hunchback of Notre Dame. Victor Marie Hugo. (On cover: The sea and shore series, no. 38). 1891. Street & Smith.
Hunchback of Notre Dame. Victor Marie Hugo. (On cover: Seaside library. Pocket ed., no. 2135). 1895. G. Munro's Sons.
Hunchback of Notre Dame. Victor Marie Hugo. LC 26-26998. (Rittenhouse classics). 1926. G. W. Jacobs & Company.
Hunchback of Notre Dame. Victor Marie Hugo. LC 37-8146. (Classic romances of literature. vol. v). The Spencer Press.
Hunchback of Notre-Dame. Victor Marie Hugo. 1939. Dodd, Mead and Company.
Hunchback of Notre Dame. Victor Marie Hugo. LC 40-5532. 1940. Triangle Books.
Hunchback of Notre Dame. Victor Marie Hugo. LC 41-51535. (Half-title: The Modern library of the world's best books). 1941. The Modern Library.
Hunchback of Notre Dame. Victor Marie Hugo & Cobb, Walter J., Tr. LC 65-6369. (Signet classic, CT295). 1965. New American Library.
Hunchback of Notre Dame: Or, Notre Dame De Paris... Victor Marie Hugo. LC 45-26344. (Pocket books. 31). 1939. Pocket Books, Inc.
Hundred Altars. Juliet Bredon. LC 34-344384. 1934. Dodd, Mead and Company.
Hundred & One Dalmatians. Dodie Smith. 1981. Repr. lib. bdg. 15.95x (ISBN 0-89966-420-2). Buccaneer Bks.
Hundred and Other Stories. Gertrude Hall Brownell. LC 147. 1898. Harper & Brothers.
Hundred Bridges to Go. Agnes Danforth Hewes. LC 50-10682. 1950. Dodd, Mead.
Hundred Camels in the Courtyard. Paul Frederic Bowles. LC 62-515138. 1962. City Lights Books.
Hundred Cuirassiers: Or, Arthur Blane. James Grant. (Seaside library, v. 18, no. 347). G. Munro.
Hundred Days. Max Pemberton. LC 5-6944. 1905. D. Appleton and Company.
Hundred Days and The Woman Ayisha. Talbot Mundy. LC 31-28470. 1931. The Century Co.
Hundred-Fold: Or, Mrs. Belmont's Harvest. Susan M Griffith. Presbyterian Committee of Publication.
Hundred Headless Woman. bi-lingual ed. Max Ernst. Tr. by Dorothea Tanning from Fr. LC 81-67737. Orig. Title: La Femme 100 Tetes. (Illus.). 325p. 1981. 30.00 (ISBN 0-8076-1023-2); pap. 14.95 (ISBN 0-8076-1024-0). Braziller.
Hundred Hills. Howard Breslin. LC 60-8250. 1960. Crowell.
Hundred Islands. Mavis Thorpe Clark. LC 77-361854. (Illus.). 1976. (ISBN 0-340-20715-9). Hodder & Stoughton.
Hundred Maples. Elaine Goodale Eastman. LC 35-6657. 1935. Stephen Daye Press.
Hundred Merry Tales & Other English Jestbooks of the Fifteenth & Sixteenth Centuries. Ed. by P. M. Zall. LC 63-14692. (Landmark Edition). (Illus.). 1963. 24.50x (ISBN 0-8032-0947-9). U of Nebr Pr.
Hundred Percent Black Steinway Grand: 15 Stories. Laurel Speer. LC 79-55766. (Gusto Press short story discovery series). 5.00. Gusto Press.
Hundred Stories: Les Cent Nouvelles Nouvelles Tr. from French by Robert B. Douglas. Cent Nouvelles Nouvelles. English. LC 61-2372. (Ace star, A-130). 1961. Ace Books.

Hundred Stories (Lescentnouvelles Nouvelles) Translated by Robert B. Douglas. Tr. by Robert Bruce Douglas. LC 61-2372. (Ace star, A-130). Ace Books.
Hundred Tales: Les Cent Nouvelles Nouvelles. Tr. by Rossell Hope Robbins. LC 60-15389. (Illus.). 1960. Crown Publishers.
Hundred Thousand Dollars in Gold. How to Make It. A Practical Narrative, Suggesting How to Use, and Not Abuse It; How to Gain, and How to Lend It... A Novel. George P Burnham. LC 6-19668. 1875. W. J. Holland.
Hundred Wagons: A Novel. William Daniel Gale. LC 47-16491. 1946. J. Long, Limited.
Hundred-Yard War. Gary Cartwright. LC 68-22523. 1968. 5.95. Doubleday.
Hundred Years of Education. Alexander D. Peterson. 1962. pap. 0.95 o.p. (Collier). Macmillan.
Hundredth Acre. John Camden. LC 5-16522. 1905. H. B. Turner & Co.
Hundredth Chance. Ethel May Dell. LC 17-10669. 1917. 1.50. G. P. Putnam's Sons.
Hundredth Chance. Ethel May Dell. LC 21-13704. 1920. Grossett & Dunlap.
Hundredth Door: By Rae Foley Pseud. Elinore Denniston. LC 50-8781. (Red badge detective). 1950. Dodd, Mead.
Hundredth Sheep. Emma Marr Grace. LC 18-12230. 1918. Printed by Advent Christian Pub. Society.
Hundredth Sheep, a Story, a Life... Press of the Chauncey Holt Co.
Hundreth Man. Frank Richard Stockton. LC 8-15543. The Century Co.
Hung. Leonard Chris. pap. 1.95 o.p. (8063). Cameo.
Hung for a Song: A Novel of the Lives and Adventures of Major Stede Bonnet and Blackbeard the Pirate. Dillwyn Parrish. LC 35-2342. Farrar & Rinehart.
Hung Until Dead. Philip Johnson. LC 40-318770. Phoenix Press.
Hungarian Brothers... Anna Maria Porter. LC 1-2084. 1825. J. & B. Williams.
Hungarian Exiles. Benjamin Cowell. 1900. The Young Churchman Co.
Hungarian Game. Roy Hayes. LC 72-90395. 1973. 8.95 (ISBN 0-671-21476-4). Simon and Schuster.
Hungarian Girl: A Novel. Marie Hrussoczy & Boggs, Mrs. Sara Elisabeth (Siegrist) 1843- LC 8-26040. (On cover: The choice series, no. 66). 1892. R. Bonner's Sons.
Hungarian Heroes and Legends. Joseph Domjan. LC 63-20487. 1963. Van Nostrand.
Hungarian Nabob. Mor Jokai. Tr. by Bain, Robert Nisbet. LC 99-1305. 1899. Doubleday & McClure Co.
Hungarian Short Stories. Ed. by A. Alvarez. 1967. 6.00 o.p. (ISBN 0-19-250609-9). Oxford U Pr.
Hunger. Knut Hamsun. LC 67-21525. 1967. Farrar, Straus and Gireux.
Hunger. Knut Hamsun. LC 67-21525. (Bard Book). 1975. (pbk). 1.75 (ISBN 0-380-00556-5). Avon.
Hunger. Knut Hamsun. LC 77-356935. (Picador). (Illus.). 1976. 0.75 (ISBN 0-330-24629-1). Pan Books.
Hunger. Knut Hamsun & Bright, Mary Chavelita (Dunne) "Mrs. R. G. Bright", Tr. LC 20-21963. 1920. A. A. Knopf.
Hunger. Knut Hamsun & Bright, Mary Chavelita (Dunne) "Mrs. R. G. Bright", Tr. LC 24-28525. 1921. A. A. Knopf.
Hunger. Whitley Strieber. LC 80-21355. 1981. 10.95 (ISBN 0-688-03757-7). Morrow.
Hunger and Love. Lionel Britton. LC 31-7559. 1931. Harper & Brothers.
Hunger: And Others Stories. Charles Beaumont. LC 57-6720. 1957. Putnam.
Hunger and the Hate. Cover Painting by James Meese. Harry Vernor Dixon. LC 55-258586. (Gold medal books, 8454). 1955. Fawcett Publications.
Hunger & Thirst & Other Plays. Eugene Ionesco. Tr. by Donald Watson from Fr. Incl. Picture; Anger; Salutations. 1969. pap. 3.95 (ISBN 0-394-17316-3, E506, Ever). Grove.
Hunger in Her Flesh. Z. L. Darryl. pap. 1.95 o.s.i. (Venus). Grove.
Hunger Mountain. William Ralph Scott. LC 55-107701. (Dell first edition, 63). 1955. Dell Pub. Co.
Hunger of Memory: The Education of Richard Rodriguez. 1982. pap. 3.95. Bantam.
Hunger of Souls. Margaret Ellison. LC 22-11791. Printed by J. A. Alles Co.
Hunger Range. Orlando Rigoni. Ed. by Alice Sachs. 1970. 3.95 o.p. Lenox Hill.
Hunger Trace. Adrienne Poy Clarkson. LC 70-102788. 1970. 5.95. W. Morrow.
Hunger Was Their Heritage. 1st Ed. Ludwig Grein. LC 53-5831. 1952. Pageant Press.
Hunger Wears Many Faces. Olga Del Glorno. 2.75 o.p. Vantage.
Hungered One: Early Writings. Ed Bullins. LC 72-142390. 1971. Morrow.

Hungry As the Sea. Wilbur A Smith. LC 78-22368. 10.95 (ISBN 0-385-13605-6). Doubleday.
Hungry As the Sea. Wilbur A. Smith. (Signet Book). 3.50 (ISBN 0-451-09599-5).
Hungry Debutante. Cory Randolph. 1.95 o.p. (DBB102). Dansk Blue Bk.
Hungry Dog. Frank Gruber. LC 41-9965. Farrar & Rinehart, Inc.
Hungry Dog Murders. Frank Gruber. LC 44-856143. (Murder mystery monthly. No. 12). 1943. Avon Book Company.
Hungry Ghosts: Seven Allusive Comedies. Joyce Carol Oates. LC 74-2272. 1974. 7.95 (ISBN 0-87685-204-5) (ISBN 0-87685-204-5). Black Sparrow Press.
Hungry Goblin: A Victorian Detective Novel. John Dickson Carr. LC 70-181668. 1972. 6.95 (ISBN 0-06-010616-6). Harper & Row.
Hungry Grass. LC 76-76966. 1969. 5.95. Dial Press.
Hungry Grass. Richard Power. 1969. 5.95 o.p. Dial.
Hungry Heart. Arlene Hale. 1977. pap. 1.25 (ISBN 0-440-13798-5). Dell.
Hungry Heart. David Graham Phillips. Ed. by Abe C. Ravitz. LC 72-96684. (American Authors Ser). 1970. lib. bdg. 25.25 o.s.i. (ISBN 0-512-00559-1). Garrett Pr.
Hungry Heart: A Novel. David Graham Phillips. LC 9-22750. 1909. D. Appleton and Company.
Hungry Heart: A Novel. David Graham Phillips. LC 16-9361. 1911. D. Appleton and Company.
Hungry Hearts. Francine Prose. 210p. 1983. 12.95. Pacific Search.
Hungry Hearts. Francine Prose. 1983. 12.95 (ISBN 0-394-52767-4). Pantheon.
Hungry Hearts. Anzia Yezierska. LC 74-29530. (Modern Jewish Experience). 1975. 18.00 (ISBN 0-405-06754-2). Arno Press.
Hungry Hearts. Anzia Yezierska. LC 20-18936. 1920. Houghton Mifflin Company.
Hungry Hill. Daphne Du Maurier. LC 78-184732. 1971. 8.50 (ISBN 0-8376-0414-1). R. Bentley.
Hungry Hill. Daphne Du Maurier. LC 43-51190. 1943. Doubleday, Doran and Co., Inc.
Hungry Hill. Daphne Du Maurier. LC 44-402678. 1944. Doubleday, Doran and Co., Inc.
Hungry Hills. William Robinson Calvert. LC 34-1285. 1933. Putnam.
Hungry Hollow. Benjamin Birch Milnes. LC 32-1272. Dorrance & Company, Inc.
Hungry House. Lilian Lauferty. LC 43-9538. 1943. Simon and Schuster.
Hungry Husband. Norman Singer. pap. 2.25 o.s.i. (OPH-133, Ophelia). Olympia.
Hungry Journey. Gordon Allred. 160p. 1973. pap. 2.50 (ISBN 0-89036-000-6). Hawkes Pub Inc.
Hungry Land. Bill Gulick, pseud. Orig. Title: Land Beyond. 1970. pap. 0.60 o.p. (63-311). Paperback Lib.
Hungry Leopard: A Novel. 1st Ed. Mary Borden. LC 56-120777. 1956. Longmans, Green.
Hungry Man Dreams. Margaret Lee Runbeck. LC 52-6084. 1952. Houghton Mifflin.
Hungry Men. Edward Anderson. 1935. Doubleday, Doran & Co., Inc.
Hungry People. Kenneth Anderson. LC 48-289220. 1947. Zondervan Pub. House.
Hungry Sea. Leslie Ames. 1973. (pbk) 0.95. Manor Books.
Hungry Sea. William Edward Daniel Ross. LC 67-9485. 1967. Arcadia House.
Hungry Spider. Selwyn Jepson. LC 50-9122. 1950. Published for the Crime Club by Doubleday.
Hungry Stones & Other Stories. Rabindranath Tagore. LC 70-120774. Repr. of 1916 ed. 14.50 (ISBN 0-404-06332-2). AMS Pr.
Hungry Years. Jessyca R. Gaver. 1978. pap. 1.75 (ISBN 0-532-17197-7). Woodhill.
Hungry Young Lady. Marian Spitzer. LC 30-35351. 1930. H. Liveright.
Hunkins. Samuel George Blythe. LC 19-15576. 1.75. George H. Doran Company.
Hunky. Thames Ross Williamson. LC 29-14908. 1929. Coward McCann Inc.
Hunry Shakespeare: An American Novel, by Dox and John Crow Pseud. 1st Ed. Dox Crow & John Crow. LC 55-9398. 1955. Exposition Press.
Hunt. Alfred Alvarez. LC 78-16201. 8.95 (ISBN 0-671-24421-3). Simon and Schuster.
Hunt. Warren Pendleton Carrier. LC 52-12092. New Directions.
Hunt. James Powell. LC 81-43450. 1982. 10.95 (ISBN 0-385-17994-4). Doubleday.
Hunt. Maurice Sachs. 172p. 1982. pap. 6.95 (ISBN 0-8128-6155-8). Stein & Day.
Hunt Angel. Frederick H Christian. (Angel series, 7). 1975. (pbk.) 0.95 (ISBN 0-523-00643-8). Pinnacle Books.
Hunt Ball Mystery. William Magnay. LC 18-5506. 1918. Brentano's.
Hunt for Heaven. Elsie Marion Oakes Barber. LC 50-8908. 1950. Macmillan.
Hunt for Richard Thorpe. Jerrard Tickell. LC 60-8686. 1960. Doubleday.
Hunt for the Meteor. Jules Verne. 3.95. Assoc Bk.
Hunt the Beast Down. Logan Winters. (Spectros Ser.: No. 2). (Orig.). 1981. pap. 1.75 (ISBN 0-505-51613-6). Tower Bks.
Hunt the Man Down. Lewis B Patten. LC 76-53414. 1977. 6.95 (ISBN 0-385-12890-8). Doubleday.
Hunt the Man Down. Lewis B Patten. (Signet Book). 1978. 1.50 (ISBN 0-451-08051-3). New American Library.
Hunt the Man Down. William Pearson. LC 56-13812. (Inner sanctum mystery). 1956. Simon and Schuster.
Hunt the Slipper: A Novel. Oliver Madox Hueffer. LC 14-11361. 1914. John Lane Company.
Hunt the Toff. John Creasey. LC 69-16135. 1969. 4.50. Walker.
Hunt the Tortoise: By E. X. Ferrars Pseud. Morna Doris MacTaggart Brown. LC 50-7847. 1950. Published for the Crime Club by Doubleday.
Hunt the Witch Down. Margaret Ronan. 1976. pap. 0.85 o.p. (ISBN 0-590-10246-X). Schol Bk Serv.
Hunt with the Hounds. Mignon Good Eberhart. LC 50-8527. 1950. Random House.
Hunted. Albert Joseph Guerard. LC 44-788. 1944. A. A. Knopf.
Hunted. Michael Hartmann. LC 79-2131. 8.95 (ISBN 0-312-40155-8). St. Martin's Press.
Hunted. Elmore Leonard. 1977. 1.75 (ISBN 0-440-13425-0). Dell Pub. Co.
Hunted. Joe Millard, pseud. (Hec Ramsey Ser). (O.s.i.). 160p. (Orig.). 1974. pap. 0.95 o.s.i. (AN1232, Award). Univ Pub & Dist.
Hunted: By George Gibbs. George Fort Gibbs. LC 37-172409. 1937. D. Appleton-Century Company. Incorporated.
Hunted Chief: Or, The Female Rancher. A Tale of the Mexican War. Newton Mallory Curtis. 1847. Williams Brothers.
Hunted Down. A Mystery Solved. Max Hillary. LC 7-4742. 1885. A. N. Marquis & Company.
Hunted Man. Walter S Masterman. LC 38-186052. 1938. E. P. Dutton & Co., Inc.
Hunted Piccaninnies. W. M Fleming. LC 28-30779. 1928. E. P. Dutton & Co.
Hunted Riders. Max Brand. LC 35-12786. 1935. Dodd, Mead & Company.
Hunted Riders. Frederick Faust. LC 35-12786. 1935. Dodd, Mead & Company.
Hunted Riders. Frederick Faust. 1974. (pbk.) 0.75 (ISBN 0-671-75815-2). Pocket Books.
Hunted Wolf. Robert Ames Bennet. LC 33-6701. 1933. I. Washburn.
Hunted Woman. James Oliver Curwood. LC 16-558394. 1916. Doubleday, Page & Company.
Hunted Woman. James Oliver Curwood. LC 30-12344. 1918. Grosset & Dunlap.
Hunted Woman. Heidi Huberta Freybe Loewengard. LC 52-7132. 1952. Random House.
Hunter. Dorothy Lockwood Aitken. Ed. by Max Phillips. (Daybreak). 128p. 1982. pap. 4.95 (ISBN 0-8163-0469-6). Pacific Pr Pub Assn.
Hunter. James Aldridge. 272p. (O.S.I). 1973. Repr. of 1951 ed. lib. bdg. 5.95 o.s.i. White Lion Pubs.
Hunter. Nick Carter. 208p. (Orig.). 1982. pap. 2.50 (ISBN 0-441-34999-4, Pub. by Charter Bks). Ace Bks.
Hunter. Watson Dyke. LC 18-6521. 1918. G. P. Putnam's Sons.
Hunter. Hugh Fosburgh. LC 50-5349. 1950. Scribner.
Hunter. Hugh Fosburgh. (Belmont Tower Books). 1977. 1.50 (ISBN 0-505-51182-7). Tower Pubns.
Hunter. Robert Holland. LC 73-160355. 1971. 5.95. Stein and Day.
Hunter. Richard Stark. 1981. lib. bdg. 10.95 (ISBN 0-8398-2706-7, Gregg). G K Hall.
Hunter, a Novel. 1st American Ed. James Aldridge. LC 51-10713. 1951. Little, Brown.
Hunter: A Story of Bushman Life. Ernest Glanville. LC 26-15274. Harcourt, Brace and Company.
Hunter and The Trap: By Howard Fast. Howard Melvin Fast. LC 67-16536. 1967. bds., 4.50. Dial.
Hunter and the Whale: A Tale of Africa. Laurens Van Der Post. LC 67-8170. 1967. W. Morrow.
Hunter at Large. Thomas Blanchard Dewey. (O.S.I.). 1961. bds. 3.50 o.s.i. (36235). S&S.
Hunter Deep in Summer: A Novel. Edward Loomis. LC 61-10442. 1961. Viking Press.
Hunter Equation. Harry Gibbons. (Orig.). 1981. pap. 2.25 (ISBN 0-440-13931-7). Dell.
Hunter in the Dark. Estelle Thompson. LC 78-67178. 1979. 7.95 (ISBN 0-8027-5393-0). Walker.
Hunter in the Shadows. Jennie Melville, pseud. LC 75-113822. (MW Suspense). 1970. 4.95. McKay.
Hunter Is the Hunted. Albert Benjamin Cunningham. LC 49-50403. (Guilt edged mysteries). 1950. Dutton.
Hunter-Killer. Geoffrey Jenkins. (YA) 1967. 5.95 o.p. (ISBN 0-399-10429-1). Putnam.
Hunter-Killer. J. D. Macdonnell. (WWII Men in Action Ser.). 1979. pap. cancelled o.s.i. (ISBN 0-8439-0684-7, Leisure Bks). Nordon Pubns.
Hunter-Killer. 1st Amer. Ed. Geoffrey Jenkins. LC 67-15123. 1967. 4.95. Putnam.
Hunter of East. Anne Hampson. (Presents Ser.). 1974. pap. 1.25 (ISBN 0-373-70551-4, 705551, Pub by Harlequin). PB.
Hunter of Men. C. H Guenter. (Max Galan,#1). 1975. (pbk.) 1.25 (ISBN 0-523-00677-2). Pinnacle Books.
Hunter of the Alps. Raffaelle Ballerini & Curtin, J. C., Tr. LC 6-6102. 1879. D. & J. Sadlier & Co.
Hunter of the Blood: A Novel of Suspense. Whit Masterson, pseud. LC 76-58518. 6.95 (ISBN 0-396-07417-0). Dodd, Mead.
Hunter of Worlds. C. J Cherryh. 1977. 1.75 (ISBN 0-87997-314-5). DAW Books.
Hunter of Worlds: Dumarest No. 18. C. J. Cherryh. (Science Fiction Ser). (Orig.). 1977. pap. 2.25 (ISBN 0-87997-559-8, UE1559). DAW Bks.
Hunter Tick & Gumberoo. cancelled o.p. (ISBN 0-8092-8700-5). Regnery.
Hunters. Peter Hill. LC 76-21299. 6.95 (ISBN 0-684-14807-2). Scribner.
Hunters. Peter Hill. LC 76-370252. 1976. 3.50 (ISBN 0-432-06735-3). P. Davies.
Hunters. Clark Howard. LC 76-13852. 1976. 7.95 (ISBN 0-8037-3939-7). Dial Press.
Hunters. Jack Lovejoy. 256p. (Orig.). 1982. pap. 2.75 (ISBN 0-523-48523-9). Pinnacle Bks.
Hunters. Peter McCurtin. (Sundance Ser.: No. 40). 208p. (Orig.). 1981. pap. 1.95 (ISBN 0-8439-1010-0, Leisure Bks). Nordon Pubns.
Hunters. Burt Wetanson & Thomas Hoobler. LC 77-92233. (Doubleday science fiction.). 1978. 7.95 (ISBN 0-385-12935-1). Doubleday.
Hunters. Burt Wetanson & Hoobler, Thomas. 1979. 1.50 (ISBN 0-87216-559-0). Playboy Press.
Hunters. Phillip Whitfield. (O.s.i.). (Illus.). 1978. 14.95 o.s.i. (ISBN 0-671-24398-5). S&S.
Hunters and the Fox. Victor H De Chellis. LC 74-78666. 4.95 (ISBN 0-8059-2017-X). Dorrance.
Hunters and the Hunted. Ivan Bahrianyi. LC 55-9819. 1956. Macmillan.
Hunters & the Hunted. Lesley Egan, pseud. LC 78-22810. (Crime Club Ser.). 1979. 9.95 o.p. (ISBN 0-385-15265-5). Doubleday.
Hunters and the Hunted. Elizabeth Linington. LC 78-22810. 1979. 7.95 (ISBN 0-385-15265-5). Published for the Crime Club by Doubleday.
Hunters Blood. Jere Cunningham. (Fawcett Gold Medal Book.). 1977. 1.75 (ISBN 0-449-13794-5). Fawcett Publications.
Hunter's Cabin: An Episode of the Early Settlements of Southern Ohio. Edward Sylvester Ellis. LC 11-13613. 0.50. Hurst & Company.
Hunter's Folly. Lee E. Caster. (Orig.). 1979. pap. 1.95 (ISBN 0-532-23288-7). Woodhill.
Hunter's Green. Phyllis A. Whitney. LC 81-6846. 1981. 13.95 (ISBN 0-8161-3296-8). G.K. Hall.
Hunter's Green: By Phyllis A. Whitney. 1st Ed. Phyllis A. Whitney. LC 68-14185. 1968. 4.95. Doubleday.
Hunter's Hill. Mary Bishop. (Dell book). 1973. (pbk) 0.95. Dell Publishing Co.
Hunter's Horn. Harriette Louisa Simpson Arnow. LC 49-8978. 1949. Macmillan Co.
Hunter's Horn. Harriette Louisa Simpson Arnow. LC 78-67251. 1979. 2.50 (ISBN 0-380-42283-2). Avon.
Hunter's Horn. Peirson Ricks. LC 47-11037. 1947. C. Scribner's Sons.
Hunters in the Snow: A Collection of Short Stories. David Kranes. LC 78-70705. 1979. 7.00 (ISBN 0-87480-128-1). University of Utah Press.
Hunter's Moon. Nathaniel Benchley. LC 72-2899. 1973. (pbk.) 1.25. Ballantine.
Hunter's Moon. Ralph Hayes. 192p. (O.s.i.). 1972. 3.95 o.s.i. Lenox Hill.
Hunter's Moon. Norah Hess. LC 76-43403. Playboy Press.
Hunter's Moon. Helen Topping Miller. LC 43-11851. 1943. D. Appleton-Century Company, Incorporated.
Hunter's Moon. Ernest Poole. LC 25-172733. 1925. The Macmillan Company.
Hunter's Moon. Margaret Way. (Harlequin Romances Ser.). 192p. 1983. pap. 1.75 (ISBN 0-373-02556-4). Harlequin Bks.
Hunters of Euboia see Three Greek Romances.
Hunters of Gor. John Norman. (Science Fiction Ser.). 1974. pap. 2.75 (ISBN 0-87997-678-0, UE1678). DAW Bks.
Hunters of Karinball. Carl-Henning Wijkmark (ISBN 0-380-00612-X). Avon.
Hunters of the Plains, 1870's: A Historical Novel. Fred S. Kaufman. LC 76-616. (Illus.). North Plains Press.
Hunters of the Red Moon. Marion Zimmer Bradley. (Science Fiction Ser). pap. 1.95 (ISBN 0-87997-713-2, UE1713). DAW Bks.
Hunters of the Red Moon. Marion Zimmer Bradley. (Orig.). 1973. pap. 0.95 o.p. (UQ1071). Daw Bks.
Hunter's Orange. William Dieter. LC 82-73280. 256p. 1983. 12.95 (ISBN 0-689-11379-X). Atheneum.
Hunters Point. George Sims. (Crime Ser.). 1977. pap. 1.95 o.p. (ISBN 0-14-004142-7). Penguin.
Hunters. 1st Ed. James Salter. LC 55-9690. Harper.
Hunterstone Outrage. Seldon Truss, pseud. LC 31-25217. 1931. The Mystery League, Inc.
Hunting Animal. Norman Bogner. LC 73-15832. 1974. 7.95 (ISBN 0-688-00187-4). Morrow.
Hunting Animal. Norman Bogner. 1975. (pbk.) 1.75. Bantam Books.
Hunting-Ground, a Novel. Arthur Leonard Bell Thompson. LC 64-13064. 1964. Coward-McCann.
Hunting-Ground: A Novel by Francis Clifford Pseud. 1st American Ed. Arthur Leonard Bill Thompson. LC 64-13064. 3.95. Coward.
Hunting Gun. Yasushi Inoue. LC 61-8740. 1977. pap. 3.95 (ISBN 0-8048-0257-2). C E Tuttle.
Hunting Gun. Translated by Sadamichi Yokoo and Sanford Goldstein. 1st Ed. Yasushi Inoue. LC 61-8740. (Library of Japanese literature). 1961. C. E. Tuttle Co.
Hunting Horn, and Other Dog Stories. Paul Annixter, pseud. LC 57-5844. 1957. Hill and Wang.
Hunting Horn: And Other Dog Stories by Paul Annixter Pseud. Jane Annixter, pseud. LC 57-5844. 1957. Hill and Wang.
Hunting of Cain: A True Story of Money, Greed & Fratricide. Dan E. Moldea. LC 82-73032. 320p. 1983. 12.95 (ISBN 0-689-11357-9). Atheneum.
Hunting on Kunderer. William Barton & John T Phillifent. (Ace double SF). 1973. Ace.
Hunting Party. Joe Millard, pseud. (Orig.). 1971. pap. 0.75 o.p. (A867S, Award). Univ Pub & Dist.
Hunting Party. Joe Millard, pseud. (O.s.i.). (Orig.). pap. 0.95 o.s.i. (AN1444, Award). Univ Pub & Dist.
Hunting Shack. Gunnard Landers. LC 78-72918. 8.95 (ISBN 0-87795-207-8). Arbor House.
Hunting Shirt. Mary Johnston. LC 31-25772. 1931. Little, Brown, and Company.
Hunting Sketches. Ivan Sergeevich Turgenev. LC 62-6687. (Signet classic, CT135). 1962. New American Library.
Hunting Stories. Franklin Welles Calkins. LC 8-13318. (With his Indian tales. Chicago 1893). 1893. M. A. Donohue & Co.
Hunting the Romantic: Or, The Adventures of a Novel Reader. Jules Sandeau. LC 8-4772. 1852. Stringer & Townsend.
Hunting Variety. Richard Flanagan. LC 73-78645. 1973. 5.95 (ISBN 0-399-11218-9). Putnam.
Hunting Without a Gun: And Other Papers. Rowland Evans Robinson. LC 5-13280. 1905. Forest and Stream Publishing Company.
Huntington, Jr. A Romance of to-Day. Edward Clary Root. LC 6-16646. 1906. F. A. Stokes Company.
Huntington: Or, Scenes of Real Life, a Story. Theresa J Freeman. LC 17-23018. 1890. Continental Printing Co.
Huntingtower. John Buchan. LC 73-106682. 1972. (ISBN 0-8371-3353-X). Greenwood Press.
Huntingtower. John Buchan. LC 22-23567. George H. Doran Company.
Huntingtower. John Buchan. LC 32-26473. 1932. Hougton Mifflin Company.
Huntress. Hulbert Footner. LC 22-18854. The James A. McCann Company.
Huntress. Mitchell A Wilson. LC 66-174344. 5.95. Doubleday.
Huntress: By Mitchell Wilson. Mitchell A Wilson. (T1138). 1968. Fawcett.
Huntress Is Dead: A Wade Paris Mystery. Ben Benson. LC 60-14495. 1960. M. S. Mill Co. and W. Morrow.
Huntsford Fortune. A Love Story. Charlotte M. Stanley McKenna & Wood, Ellen (Price) "Mrs. Henry Wood," 1814-1887. (On cover: Munro's library, v. 1, no. 113). 1884. N. L. Munro.
Huntsman at the Gate. Almet Jenks. LC 52-7468. (Illus.). 1952. Lippincott.
Huntsman in the Sky. Granville Toogood. LC 30-7573. 1930. Brewer and Warren Inc., Payson & Clarke Ltd.
Hurcotts. Muriel Hine Coxon. LC 27-5419. 1927. Dodd, Mead and Company.
Hurdcott. Francis Browning Drew Bickerstaffe-Drew. LC 11-22331. 1911. B. Herder.
Hurdy-Gurdy: A Novel. Margaret Bell Houston. LC 32-200456. 1932. D. Appleton and Company.

Hurdy-Gurdy on Olympus. Berton Braley. LC 27-10650. 1927. D. Appleton and Company.
Hurok of the Stone Age. Lin Carter. 1981. 1.75 (ISBN 0-87997-597-0). DAW Books.
Hurrah! The Flag. 1st American Ed. Philip Mackie. LC 58-5097. 1958. Norton.
Hurray for Me: A Novel. S. J. Wilson. LC 63-21122. 1964. Crown Publishers.
Hurricane. Gardner F. Fox. 1976. pap. 1.50 o.p. (LB375DK, Leisure Bks). Nordon Pubns.
Hurricane. Gardner F Fox. Leisure Books.
Hurricane. Charles Bernard Nordhoff & Hall, James Norman. LC 36-40316. 1936. Little, Brown, and Company.
Hurricane. Charles Bernard Nordhoff & Hall, James Norman. 1941. The Sun Dial Press.
Hurricane. Nahum Sabsay. LC 31-29197. 1931. C. Scribner's Sons.
Hurricane: A Thrilling Romantic, Adventurous Drama of the Seven Seas. Norman Springer. LC 30-15213. Jacobsen Publishing Company, Inc.
Hurricane Alert. Walter T. Donovan. 1970. 5.00 o.p. (ISBN 0-682-47062-7). Exposition.
Hurricane Caye: A Novel of the Tropics. Margaret Cochran Shedd. LC 42-147440. 1942. Harper & Brothers.
Hurricane Coming! Thomas Monroe Helm. LC 64-24705. 1964. Dodd, Mead.
Hurricane Fighters: Pauline B. Innis and Joseph Archibald. Pauline B Innis & Joseph Archibald. LC 62-13204. 1962. D. McKay Co.
Hurricane Haven. Charles W Knight. LC 62-131058. 1961. Moody Press.
Hurricane Heart. Cateau De Leeuw. LC 43-228607. 1943. Arcadia House, Inc.
Hurricane Hunters: A Novel. William C Anderson. LC 72-84286. 1972. 5.95 (ISBN 0-517-50050-7). Crown.
Hurricane Hurry: Or, The Adventures of a Naval Officer Afloat and on Shore. 8th thousand. ed. William Henry Giles Kingston. LC 44-20552. 1873. Griffith and Farran.
Hurricane Hush. Laurie Havron. LC 41-19718. The Greystone Press.
Hurricane Island. Henry Brereton Marriott Watson. LC 5-4546. 1905. Doubleday, Page & Company.
Hurricane Man. Omar Fletcher. (Orig.). 1976. pap. 1.50 (ISBN 0-87067-815-9, BH815). Holloway.
Hurricane Man. Omar Fletcher. 1977. 1.50 (ISBN 0-87067-815-9). Hollaway House.
Hurricane of Ice. LC 76-43402. 1976. 1.95. Playboy Press.
Hurricane of Ice. H. L. Perry. LC 76-43402. 1976. pap. 1.95 o.p. (ISBN 0-87216-358-X, E16358). Playboy Pr Pbks.
Hurricane Road: A Novel of a Railroad That Went to Sea by Nora K. Smiley and Louise V. White. 1st Ed. Nora K Smiley & Louise V White. LC 54-999775. 1954. Exposition Press.
Hurricane Season. Ralph Winnett. LC 57-8324. 1957. Reynal.
Hurricane Season: A Novel with Murder. Mickey Friedman. 1983. 14.95 (ISBN 0-525-24175-2, 01354-410). Dutton.
Hurricane Wake. Rosalind Ashe. LC 77-71366. 7.95 (ISBN 0-03-021366-5). Holt, Rinehart, and Winston.
Hurricane Williams. Gordon Ray Young. LC 22-7883. The Bobbs-Merrill Comany.
Hurricane Years. Cameron Hawley. LC 68-24244. 1968. Little, Brown.
Hurrish: A Study. Emily Lawless. LC 7-13622. (Harper's handy series. no. 61). 1886. Harper & Brothers.
Hurry, Gringo: A Novel. Kenneth Grahame Farrar. LC 78-31374. 8.95 (ISBN 0-87949-143-4). Ashley Books.
Hurry Home. John Edgar Wideman. LC 70-95871. 1970. Harcourt, Brace & World.
Hurry Home to My Heart. Sam Byrd. LC 45-9672. 1945. Houghton Mifflin Company.
Hurry, Hurry Home. John Klempner. LC 48-8381. 1948. C. Scribner's Sons.
Hurry Sundown. K. B. Gilden. 8.95 o.p. Doubleday.
Hurry the Darkness. Maurice Procter. LC 51-5560. 1951. Harper.
Hurry up and Wait. Margaret Applegate Buell Wilder. LC 46-807. 1946. Whittlesey House, McGraw-Hill Book Company, Inc.
Hurrying Fate and Geraldine. Florence Morse Kingsley. LC 13-19505. Franklin Bigelow Corporation.
Hurrying Feet. Frederic Franklyn Van De Water. LC 28-17215. 1928. D. Appleton and Company.
Hurt in the Heart. Urie A Bender. LC 65-182313. (HP150). pap., 1.50. Herald.
Hurt Me No More. Israel B. Oliveri. 3.75 o.p. Vantage.
Hurt Runner. John Symonds. LC 78-89306. 1969. 5.95. John Day Co.
Husband. Catherine Cookson. (Signet Book). 1976. (pbk.) 1.50. New American Library.
Husband. Natalie Anderson Scott. LC 49-8577. 1949. E. P. Dutton.
Husband. Eileen Harriet Anstruther Wilkinson Squire. LC 20-8450. 1919. John Lane.
Husband. Sol Stein. 1969. 5.95 o.p. (ISBN 0-698-10170-7). Coward.
Husband: A Novel. Sol Stein. LC 69-10927. 1968. 5.95. Coward-McCann.
Husband and Foe. Effie Adelaide Maria Albanesi. (On cover: Eagle library, no 154). 1900. Street & Smith.
Husband by Proxy. Jack Steele. LC 9-14450. D. FitzGerald, Inc.
Husband Campaign. Anne Gardner, pseud. LC 32-30519. Grosset & Dunlap.
Husband for Gail. Barbara Corcoran. 1981. pap. 1.95 (ISBN 0-345-29733-4). Ballantine.
Husband for Helen. Ethel Lockwood. Ed. by Alice Sachs. 1970. 3.95 o.p. Lenox Hill.
Husband for Hiliary. Joseph McCord. LC 39-7580. 1939. Macrae Smith Company.
Husband for Jennie: By Georgia Craig Pseud. Peggy Gaddis, pseud. LC 51-14494. 1951. Arcadia House.
Husband for Kutani. Fran Owen. LC 38-30008. L. Furman, Inc.
Husband for Mama. Louis Paul. LC 50-14254. 1950. Crown Publishers.
Husband Hunter. Ruth Dewey Groves. LC 32-7126. Grosset & Dunlap.
Husband-Hunter: Or, "Das Schiksal". William Joseph O'Neill Daunt. LC 7-18738. 1839. Lea and Blanchard.
Husband Hunters. Barbara Cartland. (Barbara Cartland Library#39). 1976. (pbk.) 1.25. Bantam.
Husband Hunters. Peter Keyes. 192p. 1972. pap. 1.95 o.p. (ISBN 0-87056-226-6, 6226). Brandon.
Husband Hunting: Or, The Mother and Daughters. A Tale of Fashionable Life... J--N, S--I. LC 7-11678. 1825. Wells and Lilly.
Husband in Boarding School. Giovanni Guareschi. LC 67-22432. 1967. Farrar, Straus and Giroux.
Husband in Texas. Ella Harley. LC 13-24980. 1913. 1.00. The Neale Publishing Company.
Husband in the House. Stuart David Engstrand. LC 52-5796. 1952. Farrar, Straus and Young.
Husband Isn't Everything. Jeanette Kamins. LC 66-21869. 1966. St. Martin's Press.
Husband Isn't Everything. Jeanette Kemins. (3939). 1967. Dell.
Husband of Delilah: A Novel. Eric Robert Russell Linklater. LC 63-8080. 1963. Harcourt, Brace & World.
Husband of Mary. Elizabeth Dillingham Hart. LC 35-203003. J. B. Lippincott Company.
Husband of No Importance. Eliza Margaret J. Humphrey. LC 7-5790. (Half-title: The incognito library. no. 4). 1894. G. P. Putnam's Sons.
Husband of One Wife. Venn. LC 8-30205. (On cover: Harper's Franklin square library, no. 748). 1894. Harper & Brothers.
Husband Test. Mary Carolyn Davies. LC 21-6032. 1921. The Penn Publishing Company.
Husband to Anna. Barbara Hedworth. LC 35-31021. 1935. E. P. Dutton & Co., Inc.
Husband to Keep. Peggy O'More, pseud. LC 43-601. 1943. Grammercy Publishing Co.
Husband Who Ran Away. Hildegarde Dolson. LC 48-8234. 1948. Random House.
Husband. 1st American Ed. Vera Caspary. LC 58-6168. Harper.
Husbands and Lovers. Leslie J Swabacker. LC 32-21901. 1932. The Vanguard Press.
Husband's Notes About Her. Eve Merriam. LC 75-25973. (O.s.i.). 96p. 1976. 9.95 o.s.i. (ISBN 0-02-584350-8, 58435). Macmillan.
Husband's Notes About Her. Eve Merriam. LC 75-25970. (O.s.i.). 104p. 1976. pap. 2.95 o.s.i. (ISBN 0-02-070120-9, Collier). Macmillan.
Husbands of Edith. George Barr McCutcheon. LC 8-13724. 1908. Dodd, Mead & Company.
Husband's Story. Norman Collins. LC 78-3594. 1978. 10.95 (ISBN 0-689-10898-2). Atheneum.
Husband's Story. David G. Philips. Ed. by Abe C. Ravitz. (American Authors Ser). 1910. 27.00 o.s.i. (ISBN 0-512-00560-5). Garrett Pr.
Husband's Story. A Novel. (On cover: The seaside library. Pocket ed. no. 198). 1884. G. Munro.
Husband's Story: A Novel. David Graham Phillips. LC 10-20846. 1910. D. Appleton and Company.
Husband's Story: A Novel. David Graham Phillips. LC 16-9360. 1912. D. Appleton and Company.
Husband's Story: A Novel. David Graham Phillips. LC 21-16857. 1912. Grosset & Dunlap.
Husbands Who Swap. Jim Stacey. 192p. pap. 1.95 o.p. (7161). Barclay Hse.
Hush-a-Bye Murder. David Alexander. LC 57-5391. (His A Bart Hardin mystery novel). 1957. Random House.
Hush Bush Johnson. Natalie Gates. LC 67-12581. (Rinehart suspense novel). 1967. Holt, Rinehart and Winston.
Hush, Gabriel! Veronica Parker Johns. LC 40-337021. Duell, Sloan and Pearce.
Hush, Gabriel!... Veronica Parker Johns. LC 45-273. 1944.
Hush-Hush Murders. Margaret Tayler Yates. LC 37-170329. 1937. The Macmillan Company.
Hush, Little Baby. Judi Miller. (Orig.). 1983. pap. 2.95 (ISBN 0-671-43182-X). PB.
Hush Money. Max Collins. (Nolan Ser.: No.4). 192p. (Orig.). 1981. pap. 1.95 (ISBN 0-523-41162-6). Pinnacle Bks.
Hush Money. Peter Israel. LC 74-8992. 1974. 5.95 (ISBN 0-690-00547-4). Crowell.
Hush Puppies & Other Stories. P. L. Barton. 4.50 o.p. Carlton.
Hushed Were the Hills. Millie McWhirter. LC 69-19741. 1969. 3.95. Abingdon Press.
Hush,Winifred Is Dead. Audrey P Johnson. 1976. 4.95. Avalon Books.
Husk of Enmity. Eloise Turner. 3.50 o.p. Carlton.
Husks. Colonel Floyd's Wards. Mary Virginia Terhune. LC 8-26053. 1863. Sheldon & Company.
Husky, Co-Pilot of the Pilgrim. Rutherford George Montgomery. LC 42-20565. 1942. H. Holt and Company.
Hussar. George Robert Gleig. LC 44-24882. 1838. U. P. James.
Hussar. A Romance of the Franco-Prussian War. August Kuhne. Tr. by Miller, Hettie E. LC 7-14174. (On cover: Dearborn series, no. 48). 1891. Donohue, Henneberry & Co.
Hussar Honeymoon. Jerrard Tickell. LC 63-11204. 1963. Doubleday.
Hussein: An Entertainment. Richard Patrick Russ. LC 39-726. 1938. Oxford University Press.
Hussy. Peggy Gaddis, pseud. LC 38-13185. 1938. Godwin.
Hussy. Boyne Grainger. LC 24-5107. 1924. Boni and Liveright.
Hustle. Steve Shagan. LC 74-16618. (Signet Book). 1975. (pbk.) 1.75. New American Library.
Hustle into Death. Santana Arroyo. 1977. pap. 1.50 (ISBN 0-532-15289-1). Woodhill.
Hustler. Walter S Tevis. 1.50 (ISBN 0-380-00860-2). Avon.
Hustler Joe: And Other Stories. Eleanor Hodgman Porter. LC 78-128750. (Short story index reprint series). 1970. Books for Libraries Press.
Hustler Joe: And Other Stories. Eleanor Hodgman Porter. LC 24-206111. 2.00. George H. Doran Company.
Hustler. 1st Ed. Walter S Tevis. LC 58-13814. 1959. Harper.
Hutoka: Or, The Maid of the Forest: a Tale of the Indian Wars. LC 7-9026. 1846. Gleason's Publishing Hall.
Huxley: A Biographical Introduction. Philip Malcolm Waller Thody. LC 72-12155. (Leaders of modern thought). (Scribner library. Lyceum editions: biography). 1973. 5.95 (ISBN 0-684-13053-X) (ISBN 0-684-13053-X). Scribner.
Hvis Det Virkelig Var en Film see If It Really Were a Film.
Hyacinth: An Excursion. Dion Clayton Calthrop. LC 27-236097. 1927. Duffield & Company.
Hyacinth from Limbo, and Other Stories. Jean Rogers Smith. LC 58-14951. 1958. Philosophical Library.
Hyacinth from Limbo: And Other Stories. Jean Rogers Smith. LC 76-81274. (Short story index reprint series). 1969. Books for Libraries Press.
Hyacinthe. Paul Simonsen. LC 82-82726. 352p. 1983. 11.95 (ISBN 0-86666-113-1). GWP.
Hyacinths. Chelsea Q. Yarbo. LC 80-720. (Science Fiction Ser.). 192p. 1983. 11.95 (ISBN 0-385-15453-4). Doubleday.
Hyacinths. Chelsea Quinn Yarbro. LC 80-720. (Doubleday Science Fiction). 1983. 11.95 (ISBN 0-385-15453-4). Doubleday.
Hybrid. Steve Vance. 224p. (Orig.). 1981. pap. 2.25 (ISBN 0-505-51736-1). Tower Bks.
Hybrid: A Novel. Diane Cilento. LC 77-124732. 1971. 5.95. Delacorte Press.
Hyde Place. Virginia Coffman. (Fawcett crest book). 1975. (pbk.) 1.25. Fawcett.
Hyde Place: A Novel. Coffman, Virginia. LC 74-80704. 1974. 7.95 (ISBN 0-87795-086-5). Arbor House.
Hyde Place: A Novel. large print ed. Virginia Coffman. LC 81-6242. 1981. 14.95 (ISBN 0-8161-3256-9). G.K. Hall.
Hydra. James A. Grazier. LC 74-77645. 1969. 3.95 o.p. (ISBN 0-87426-017-5). Whitmore.
Hydra Conspiracy. Philip Kirk. (Butler Ser.: No. 1). 1979. pap. 1.75 o.s.i. (ISBN 0-8439-0655-3, Leisure Bks). Nordon Pubns.
Hydra Head. Carlos Fuentes. LC 78-12603. 8.95 (ISBN 0-374-17397-4). Farrar, Straus, Giroux.
Hydra Pit. Jay Barbree. LC 77-70423. (Illus.). 8.95 (ISBN 0-87949-084-5). Ashley Books.
Hydra with Six Heads. Josephine Bell. LC 77-21249. 1977. 7.95 (ISBN 0-8128-2407-5). Stein and Day.
Hydrabyss Red. William Tedford. (Timequest Ser.: No. 2). 1981. pap. 2.25 (ISBN 0-8439-0887-4, Leisure Bks). Nordon Pubns.
Hydrosphere. A. J Merak. LC 68-211. 1967. Arcadia House.
Hymn to Life. James Schuyler. 1974. 6.95 o.p. (ISBN 0-394-48887-3); pap. 1.95 o.p. (ISBN 0-394-70681-1). Random.
Hymn to the Sun. Malcolm Harrison Ross. LC 30-6154. 1930. C. Scribner's Sons.
Hymn to the Sun. Wesley Tanner. 1972. wrappers 0.75. Arif.
Hymn Tune Mystery. LC 31-659652. The Bobbs-Merrill Company.
Hymns. Christopher Smart. 1975. text ed. 11.95x o.s.i. (ISBN 0-8277-3979-6); pap. text ed. 6.95x o.s.i. (ISBN 0-8277-2368-7). British Bk Ctr.
Hymns of Zarathustra. Ed. by Jacques Duchesne-Guillemin & M. Henning. (Orig.). 1963. pap. 1.65 o.p. (ISBN 0-8070-5789-4, LR19). Beacon Pr.
Hypatia. Charles Kingsley. LC 1-25690. (Century classics). 1901. The Century Co.
Hypatia: Introduction by Ernest Rhys. Everyman's Ed. Reprinted. Charles Kingsley. LC 68-131614. (Everyman's lib. no. 230). 1968. 3.50. Dent.
Hypatia: Or, New Foes with an Old Face. Charles Kingsley. LC 75-496. (Victorian Fiction: Novels of Faith and Doubt; V. 47). 1975. 35.00 (ISBN 0-8240-1571-1). Garland Pub.
Hypatia: Or, New Foes with an Old Face. 2d ed. Charles Kingsley. LC 15-20282. 1854. Crosby, Nichols, and Company.
Hypatia: Or, New Foes with an Old Face. 5th ed. Charles Kingsley. LC 7-12146. 1856. Crosby, Nichols and Company.
Hypatia: Or, New Foes with an Old Face. 7th ed. Charles Kingsley. LC 7-121472. 1858. Crosby, Nichols and Company.
Hypatia: Or, New Foes with an Old Face. 9th ed. Charles Kingsley. LC 25-15519. 1862. Crosby, and Nichols.
Hypatia: Or, New Foes with an Old Face. 13th ed. Charles Kingsley. 1880. Macmillan and Co.
Hypatia: Or, New Foes with an Old Face. Charles Kingsley. LC 7-12148. 1895. Harper & Brothers.
Hypatia: Or, New Foes with an Old Face. Charles Kingsley. LC 4-16537. 1897. T. Y. Crowell & Company.
Hypatia: Or, New Foes with an Old Face. Charles Kingsley. LC 4-21181. 1902. Macmillan and Co., Limited.
Hypatia: Or, New Foes with an Old Face. Charles Kingsley. (Half-title: Everyman's library; edited by Ernest Rhys. Fiction. no. 230). 1906. J. M. Dent Co.
Hypatia: Or, New Foes with an Old Face. Charles Kingsley. LC 42-85047. 1902. Hurst & Co.
Hypatia or New Foes with an Old Face. Charles Kingsley. 1968. Repr. of 1906 ed. 8.95x (ISBN 0-460-00230-9, Evman). Biblio Dist.
Hypatia: Or, New Foes with an Old Face. Charles Kingsley & Goddard, Mabel, Ed. LC 29-296806. (modern readers' series). 1929. The Macmillan Company.
Hypatia: Or, New Foes with an Old Face. A Novel. Charles Kingsley. (Franklin square library. no. 130). 1880. Harper & Brothers.
Hypatia; or, New Foes with an Old Face: 1853. Charles Kingsley. Ed. by Robert L. Wolff. (Victorian Fiction Ser.). 1975. lib. bdg. 66.00 (ISBN 0-8240-1571-1). Garland Pub.
Hype! Leonard Jordan. (Fawcett Gold Medal Book). 1.75 (ISBN 0-449-13792-9). Fawcett Pubns.
Hyperaesthesia. A Novel. Mary Cruger. LC 6-31176. 1886. Fords, Howard & Hulbert.
Hyperion: A Romance. Henry Wadsworth Longfellow. LC 7-3043. 1839. S. Colman.
Hyperion: A Romance. 2d ed. Henry Wadsworth Longfellow. LC 7-14786. 1845. J. Owen.
Hyperion: A Romance. 11th ed. Henry Wadsworth Longfellow. LC 7-14785. 1852. Ticknor, Reed, and Fields.
Hyperion: A Romance. 13th ed. Henry Wadsworth Longfellow. LC 22-513686.
Hyperion: A Romance. 15th ed. Henry Wadsworth Longfellow. 1855. Ticknor and Fields.
Hyperion: A Romance. rev. ed.... ed. Henry Wadsworth Longfellow. LC 9-3027. 1876. J. R. Osgood and Company.
Hyperion: A Romance. 42d ed., rev.... ed. Henry Wadsworth Longfellow. 1882. Houghton, Mifflin and Company.
Hyperion: A Romance. rev. ed.... ed. Henry Wadsworth Longfellow. LC 4-15466. Houghton, Mifflin and Company.
Hyperion: Or, The Hermit in Greece. Friedrich Holderlin. LC 66-532. 1965. New American Library.
Hyperion: Or, The Hermit in Greece. Tr. from German by Willard R. Trask. Foreword by Alexander Gode-Von Aesch. Friedrich Holderlin. LC 65-28263. 5.00. Ungar.
Hyphen. Lida Clara Schem. LC 20-17964. E. P. Dutton & Company.

Hypnerotomachia, the Strife of Love in a Dream: London 1592. Francesco Colonna & Robert Dallington. LC 75-27858. (Renaissance and the Gods; No. 15). 1976. 40.00 (ISBN 0-8240-2064-2). Garland Pub.

Hypnotic Crime: And Other Like True Tales. Being a Free Adaptation from the Minutes of the Society for Psychical Research. Willard Douglas Coxey. LC 6-28855. 1896.

Hypnotic Experiment of Dr. Reeves and Other Stories. Charlotte Rosalys Jones. LC 1-21249. 1894. Bliss, Sands and Foster.

Hypnotic Tales and Other Tales. James Lauren Ford. LC 33-283586. 1891. Keppler & Schwarzmann.

Hypnotic Tales, and Other Tales. new ed. James Lauren Ford. LC 6-41400. 1894. G. H. Richmond & Co.

Hypnotist. Brad Steiger. (Dell / Quick silver Book). 1979. 2.50 (ISBN 0-440-13771-3). Dell Pub. Co.

Hypocritical Romance, and Other Stories. Caroline Ticknor. LC 8-19939. 1896. J. Knight Company.

Hypolitus Earl of Douglas. The Island of Content. Marie Catherine Jumelle De Berneville Aulnoy & Author Of The Pleasures Of A Single Life. LC 76-170516. (Foundations of the Novel). 1973. 22.00 ea. (ISBN 0-8240-0524-4). Garland Pub.

Hysterical Fugue. Susan Lawton. 66p. (Orig.). 1982. pap. 5.00 (ISBN 0-937998-07-9). Cumberland.

I. 192p. (Orig.). 1980. pap. 2.75 (ISBN 0-553-14241-0). Bantam.

I

I, a Groupie. Michael Gross. 1975. (pbk.) 1.50 (ISBN 0-523-00787-6). Finnacle Books.

I, a Stranger. Ruth Peabody Harnden. LC 50-5362. 1950. Whittlesey House.

I Accuse. Mette Ejlersen. (O.s.i.). (Orig.). pap. 0.95 o.s.i. (A471N, Award). Univ Pub & Dist.

I Ain't Much Baby, but I'm All I've Got. Jess Lair. 1978. pap. 2.50 (ISBN 0-449-23585-8, Crest). Fawcett.

I Ain't Well, but I Sure Am Better: Mutual Need Therapy. Jess Lair. 1976. pap. 2.50 (ISBN 0-449-24193-9, Crest). Fawcett.

I Always Wanted to Be Somebody. Althea Gibson. (Illus.). pap. 0.75 o.p. (ISBN 0-06-080029-1, PL). Har-Row.

I Am. Henry Gutowski. 6.95 o.p. Vantage.

I Am a Barbarian. Edgar Rice Burroughs. LC 67-28547. (Illus.). 1967. E. R. Burroughs, Inc.

I Am a Barbarian. Edgar Rice Burroughs. 1975. (pbk.) 1.50. Ace Books.

I Am a Billboard: A Novel. Evelyn Keyes. LC 79-156890. 1971. 5.95. L. Stuart.

I Am a Cat. Soseki Natsume. LC 78-182064. 1972. 5.00 (ISBN 0-8048-1034-6). C. E. Tuttle Co.

I Am a Cat. Soseki Natsume. LC 81-17271. (UNESCO Collection of Representative Works. Japanese Series). 1982. 14.95 (ISBN 0-698-11144-3). Coward, McCann & Geoghegan.

I Am a Cat. Natsume Soseki. Tr. by Katsue Shibata & Motonari Kai. LC 81-17271. (UNESCO Collection of Representative Works, Japanese Ser.). 431p. 1982. 15.95 (ISBN 0-698-11144-3, Coward); pap. 8.95. Putnam Pub Group.

I am a Cat, Bk. II. Natsume Soseki. Tr. by Aiko Ito & Graeme Wilson. LC 78-182064. 286p. 1979. pap. 9.95 (ISBN 0-8048-1280-2). C E Tuttle.

I Am a Cat: A Novel. Soseki Natsume. LC 81-15391. (Illus.). 1982. 7.95 (ISBN 0-399-50609-8). Putnam.

I Am: A Novel of Psychotherapy. Florence Edythe Blake- Hedges. LC 10-24181. The Roxburgh Publishing Company (Incorporated.

I Am a Village. Arthur Conte. Tr. by F. Frenaye. 1960. 3.50x o.p. Verry.

I Am a Village. Tr. from French by Frances Frenaye. Arthur Conte. 1966 bds., 3.00. Hutchinson.

I Am a Woman. Ann Bannon. LC 75-13750. (Homosexuality). 1975. 9.00 (ISBN 0-405-07406-9). Arno Press.

I Am a Woman. facsimile ed. Ann Dannon. Ed. by Jonathan Katz. LC 75-13750. (Homosexuality Ser.). 1975. Repr. of 1959 ed. 12.00x (ISBN 0-405-07406-9). Ayer Co.

I Am Adam. 1st Ed. Kaufman, Maxine. LC 56-8909. 1956. Knopf.

I Am Afraid. Elma K Lobaugh. LC 40-1525. 1949. Pub. for the Crime Club by Doubleday.

I Am Anthony. Peg Stokes. LC 61-8516. 1961. Prentice-Hall.

I Am Clarence. Elaine Kraf. LC 75-78696. 1969. 4.95. Doubleday.

I Am Elijah Thrush. James Purdy. LC 76-180099. 1972. 4.95. Doubleday.

I Am Fa-Ying. Maud Linker. LC 60-32776. 1960. Katydid Pub. Co.

I Am Gabriella! Anne Maybury. 1977. 1.75. Ace.

I Am Heaven. Jinsie K S Chun. LC 72-11101. 1973. 7.95 (ISBN 0-8255-2410-5). Macrae Smith Co.

I Am Here" Lagardere: Or, The Hunchback of Paris. Paul Henri Corentin Fevel & Williams, Henry Llewellyn, Jr. Tr. LC 6-39536. Pollard & Moss.

I Am Here!" The Duke's Motto: Or, The Little Parisian. Paul Henri Corentin Fevel & Williams, Henry Llewellyn Jr., Tr. LC 6-39535. R. M. DeWitt.

I Am in Urgent Need of Advice. 1st Ed. Josephine Lawrence. LC 62-14466. 1962. Harcourt, Brace & World.

I Am Joe's Body. J. D. Ratcliff. 1980. pap. 2.50 (ISBN 0-425-04550-1). Berkley Pub.

I Am Jonathan Scrivener. Claude Houghton Oldfield. LC 30-20079. 1930. Simon and Schuster.

I Am Jonathan Scrivener. Claude Houghton Oldfield. LC 35-256. 1934. Doubleday, Doran & Company, Inc.

I Am Jonathan Scrivener. Claude Houghton Oldfield. LC 37-20892. 1935. Doubleday, Doran & Company, Inc.

I Am Julie. Mary Kathleen Harris. LC 56-9695. 1956. Crowell.

I Am Legend. Richard Matheson. LC 71-123266. 1970. 4.95 (ISBN 0-8027-5524-0). Walker.

I Am Legend. Richard Matheson. (Berkley book). 1979. 1.75 (ISBN 0-425-04053-4). Berkley Pub. Corp.

I Am Legend. Cover Painting by Stan Meltzoff. Richard Matheson. LC 54-430954. (Gold Medal books, 417). 1954. Fawcett Publications.

I Am Lidian. Naomi Lane Babson. LC 51-10510. 1951. Harcourt, Brace.

I Am Loving, Strangely. Dwayne Simpson. 1971. pap. 1.75 o.p. (ISBN 0-447-79308-X). Lancer.

I Am Lucifer: Confessions of the Devil As Dictated to Clude B. Clason. Clyde B Clason. LC 60-6185. 1960. Muhlenberg Press.

I Am Mary Dunne. Brian Moore. 1977. pap. 1.95 (ISBN 0-14-003634-2). Penguin.

I Am Mary Dunne: A Novel. Brian Moore. LC 68-19771. 1968. Viking Press.

I Am Mary Shelley. Barbara L. Devlin. LC 77-80309. 1977. pap. 1.95 o.s.i. (ISBN 0-89516-007-2). Condor Pub Co.

I Am Mary Tudor. Hilda Winifred Lewis. (Illus.). 1973. 1.50. Warner Paperback Lib.

I Am Mary Tudor. Hilda Winifred Lewis. LC 70-185132. 1972. 6.95. McKay.

I Am Not the Other Houdini. Michael Conner. LC 77-11794. (Perennial Library). 1979. 1.95 (ISBN 0-06-080470-X). Harper & Row.

I Am the Beautiful Stranger. Rosalyn Drexler. LC 65-16854. bds., 4.50. Grossman.

I Am the Beautiful Stranger. Rosalyn Drexler. (Signet Books Q5282). 1972. 0.95. New American Library.

I Am the Cat. Rosemary Kutak. LC 48-5812. 1948. Farrar, Straus.

I Am the Cheese. Robert Cormier. 1978. pap. 2.25 (ISBN 0-440-94060-5, LFL). Dell.

I Am the Daughter. Elizabeth Zelvin. (Illus.). 88p. 1981. pap. 3.00 (ISBN 0-89823-025-X). New Rivers Pr.

I Am the Fox. Winifred Mayne Van Etten. LC 36-18551. 1936. Little, Brown, and Company.

I Am the King: Being the Account of Some Happenings in the Life of Godfrey De Bersac, Crusader-Knight. Sheppard Stevens. LC 98-1268. 1898. Little, Brown and Company.

I Am the Withered Man. John Creasey. LC 72-96618. 1973. 4.95. McKay.

I Am Thinking of Kelda. Evelyn Wells. LC 72-89357. 1974. 7.95 (ISBN 0-385-00825-2). Doubleday.

I Am Thinking of My Darling. Vincent McHugh. LC 43-10625. 1943. Simon and Schuster.

I Am Thinking of My Darling. Vincent McHugh. LC 77-84254. (Lost Race and Adult Fantasy Fiction). 1978. 19.00 (ISBN 0-405-10998-9). Arno Press.

I Am Thinking of My Darling: An Adventure Story. Vincent McHugh. Ed. by R. Reginald & Douglas Melville. LC 77-84254. (Lost Race & Adult Fantasy Ser.). 1978. Repr. of 1943 ed. lib. bdg. 19.00x (ISBN 0-405-10998-9). Ayer Co.

I Am Two Men. Margaret McEathron. LC 80-15442. 12.95 (ISBN 0-87949-190-6). Ashley Books.

I Am Your Brother. Gabriel Marlowe. LC 35-272224. Harcourt, Brace and Company.

I and Claudie. 1st Ed. Dillon Anderson. LC 51-12708. 1951. Little, Brown.

I and My True Love. Hersilia A Mitchell Copp Keays. LC 8-28998. 1908. Small, Maynard and Company.

I & My True Love. Helen MacInnes. 1978. pap. 2.75 (ISBN 0-449-23798-2, Crest). Fawcett.

I & My True Love. Helen MacInnes. LC 52-13765. 6.95 o.p. (ISBN 0-15-143403-4). HarBraceJ.

I & Tex. Royal B. Hassrick. 4.50 o.p. Vantage.

I and Tex. first ed. Royal B. Hassrick. 1972. 4.50 (ISBN 0-533-00155-2). Vantage.

I Asked No Other Thing. Cora Hardy Jarrett. LC 37-27365. Farrar & Rinehart, Inc.

I, B. I. T. C. H. (Orig.). 1970. pap. 0.95 o.p. (ISBN 0-447-75132-8). Lancer.

I, Barbarian. new revised, and enlarged edition ed. John Jakes. 1.50 (ISBN 0-523-00971-2). Pinnacle Books.

I Been There. Carol Hall & Sammis McLean. 6.95 (ISBN 0-385-13083-X). Doubleday.

I Believe. T. Rampa. pap. 2.95. Weiser.

I Belong to You. Denison Halley Clift. LC 33-25195. The Macaulay Company.

I Call This History: And Other Stories. Alfred Gold. LC 45-20318. 1945. The William-Frederick Press.

I Came to a Castle. Velda Johnston. LC 76-81625. (Red badge mystery). 1969. 4.50. Dodd, Mead.

I Came to Kill: A Gold Medal Original, by Gordon Davis Pseud. Howard Hunt. LC 54-407. (Gold medal books, 349). 1953. Fawcett Publications.

I Came to Love You Late. Joyce Landorf. LC 77-21366. 8.95 (ISBN 0-8007-0884-9). F. H. Revell Co.

I Came to the Highlands. Velda Johnston. LC 74-32420. 1975. 10.95 (ISBN 0-8161-6264-6). G. K. Hall.

I Came to the Highlands. Velda Johnston. (Signet Book). 1978. 1.95 (ISBN 0-451-08218-4). New American Library.

I Came to the Highlands: A Novel of Suspense. Velda Johnston. LC 74-96. 1974. 5.95 (ISBN 0-396-06950-9). Dodd, Mead.

I Can Get It for You Wholesale. Jerome Weidman. LC 59-5909. (Modern library of the world's best books 225). 1959. Modern Library.

I Can Get It for You Wholesale. Jerome Weidman. LC 37-708221. 1937. Simon and Schuster.

I Can Handle This Town. Rene Rothchild. (Orig.). 1970. pap. 0.95 (ISBN 0-87067-203-7, BH203). Holloway.

I Can Lick Seven. Robert W Richards. LC 42-178001. 1942. Little, Brown and Company.

I Can Only Touch You Now. R. Levy. 1973. ref. ed. 14.95 o.p. (ISBN 0-13-448746-X); pap. text ed. 9.95 o.p. (ISBN 0-13-448738-9). P-H.

I Can See You but You Can't See Me. Paul Chevalier. LC 67-11306. 1967. Lippincott.

I Can Stop Any Time I Want. James Trivers. (YA) 1977. pap. 1.75 (ISBN 0-440-94111-3, LFL). Dell.

I Can Take It All. Anthony Geoffrey Leo Simon Glyn. LC 60-7428. 1960. Harcourt, Brace.

I Can Wait. Adelaide Champneys. LC 33-12239. 1933. The Bobbs-Merrill Company.

I Can Wait. Adelaide Champneys. LC 33-12239. The Bobbs-Merrill Company.

I Can Wait. Patricia Linn. (Orig.). 1980. pap. 2.25 o.s.i. (ISBN 0-505-51526-1). Tower Bks.

I Can't Die Here,". Jeannette Covert Nolan. LC 45-7610. 1945. J. Messner, Inc.

I Can't Stand Cindy, Lord! Barbara Bush. LC 76-40991. 4.95. Zondervan Pub. House.

I Can't Stop Running: By Edward Ronns Pseud. Edward Sidney Aarons. LC 51-31788. (Gold medal books, 166). 1951. Fawcett Publications.

I Capture the Castle. Dorothy Gladys Smith. LC 48-4880. 1948. Little, Brown.

I, Chaser. Grant Elliott. pap. 1.95 o.p. (8007). Cameo.

I Choose. Gertrude Capen Whitney. LC 10-9268. 1910. Sherman, French & Company.

I Choose. Gertrude Capen Whitney. LC 19-18606. 1919. The Four Seas Company.

I, Claudius. Robert Graves. 448p. 8.95 (ISBN 0-394-60811-9). Modern Lib.

I, Claudius: From the Autobiography of Tiberius Claudius, Born B. C. 10, Murdered and Deified A. D. 54... Robert Graves. LC 34-27150. 1934. H. Smith and R. Haas.

I, Claudius: From the Autobiography of Tiberius Caludius, Born B. C. 10, Murdered and Deified A. D. 54. Robert Graves. LC 37-27271. (Half-title: The modern library of the world's best books). 1937. The Modern Library.

I, Claudius: From the Autobiography of Tiberius Claudius, Emperor of the Romans, Born BC 10, Murdered and Deified AD 54. Robert Graves. LC 77-373884. (Illus.). 1976. 3.95 (ISBN 0-413-37070-4). Eyre Methuen.

I, Cleopatra. William Bostock, pseud. 1977. 2.50 (ISBN 0-446-81379-6). Warner Books.

I Come As a Thief. Louis Auchincloss. LC 72-8756. 1972. 8.95 (ISBN 0-8161-6055-4). G. K. Hall.

I Come As a Thief. Louis Auchincloss. LC 77-190053. 1972. 6.95 (ISBN 0-395-13939-2). Houghton Mifflin.

I Confess. Johannes Mario Simmel. 1977. 1.95 (ISBN 0-445-04121-8). Popular Library.

I Conquered,". Harold Titus. LC 16-6822. Rand, McNally & Company.

I Could a Tale Unfold. David Whitelaw. LC 59-8449. Roy Publishers.

I Could Be Good to You. Charlotte Keppel. LC 79-26841. 10.00 (ISBN 0-312-40171-X). St. Martin's Press.

I Could Have Died. Aaron Marc Stein. LC 78-20005. 1979. 7.95 (ISBN 0-385-14987-5). Published for the Crime Club by Doubleday.

I Could Murder Her. Edith Caroline Rivett. LC 51-13070. 1951. Published for the Crime Club by Doubleday.

I Counted Only April. Simon Perchik. 1964. pap. 4.00 (Pub. by Elizabeth Pr). SBD.

I Cover the Waterfront. Max Miller. LC 32-266584. E. P. Dutton and Company, Inc.

I Cover the Waterfront. Max Miller. LC 38-33037. (A Mercury book, no. 12). The American Mercury, Inc.

I Cried All Night. Field Williamson. LC 42-16023. 1942. J. Swift.

I Detest All My Sins. Jack Weeks. LC 54-804304. (Dell first edition, D20). 1954. Dell Pub. Co.

I Did Not Kill Osborne: An Adventure in the Essex Marshes. Victor Bridges. LC 34-528116. The Penn Publishing Company.

I Didn't Know I Would Live So Long. Michael Blankfort. LC 72-1188. 1973. 6.95 (ISBN 0-684-13008-4). Scribner.

I Didn't Know You Cared. J. M. Raso. 4.50 o.p. Vantage.

I Die Possessed. James Brendan O'Sullivan. LC 53-9198. 1953. M. S. Mill Co., and W. Morrow.

I Don't Know Why. 1st Ed. William S Kibler. LC 52-4940. 1852. Pageant Press.

I Don't Like Cats. Lindsay Anson. LC 40-13622. 1940. Pub. for the Crime Club by Doubleday, Doran & Co., Inc.

I Don't Need You Anv More: Stories. Arthur Miller. (N3707). 1968. Bantam.

I Don't Need You Any More: Stories. Arthur Miller. LC 67-11269. 1967. Viking Press.

I Don't Own a Pornograph: Fiction and Fantasy. Colin Jameson. LC 67-9613. 1967. Exposition Press.

I Don't Scare Easy. Bernard Dougall. LC 41-17320. 1941. Dodd Mead & Company.

I Doubted Flying Saucers. Stan Layne. LC 58-826854. 1958. Meador Pub. Co.

I Drank the Water Everywhere. Charles N. Barnard. (Illus.). 1976. 7.95 o.p. (ISBN 0-396-07211-9). Dodd.

I Dream in Irish. Oliver Robinson. LC 67-23442. 1967. 5.00. Branden Pr.

I Dream Now of the Sun. Toni Ortner-Zimmerman. (Illus.). 1977. 10.00 (ISBN 0-916906-09-4); pap. 4.00 (ISBN 0-916906-08-6). Konglomerati.

I Dreamt I Was a Nymphomaniac! Imagining. Kathy Acker. (Illus.). 116p. 1980. 4.00 (ISBN 0-936578-00-9). Travelers Digest Edns.

I (EE), Bk. 3, Bell's Book. 2nd ed. Helen Luster. (Illus.). 7.00 o.p. (ISBN 0-912662-15-8); pap. 3.00 o.p. Fur Line Pr.

I (EE), Bk. 7, Crystal. Helen Luster. (Illus.). 1979. 7.00 o.p. (ISBN 0-912662-22-0); pap. 5.00 o.p. (ISBN 0-912662-21-2). Fur Line Pr.

I Elieve in Man. Scott Brobston. LC 66-18792. 1966. 3.00. Bronston.

I, Etcetera. Susan Sontag. LC 79-10994. 1979. 2.95 (ISBN 0-394-72944-7). Vintage Books.

I, Etcetera: Stories. Susan Sontag. LC 78-123. 7.95 (ISBN 0-374-17402-4). Farrar, Straus and Giroux.

I Fasten a Bracelet. David Potter. LC 11-24972. 1911. 1.25. J. B. Lippincott Company.

I Fear the Greeks. Aaron Marc Stein. LC 66-17070. 3.50. Pub. for the Crime Club by Doubleday.

I Followed Gold! Adventures Hunting Gold. E. C. Trelawney-Ansell. cancelled o.p. (ISBN 0-87380-102-4). Rio Grande.

I Forbid the Banns!" The Story of a Comedy Which Was Played Seriously. Frank Frankfort Moore. LC 7-25303. Cassell Publishing Company.

I Fought You from the Skies. Willi Heilman. (O.s.i.). (Orig.). pap. 0.60 o.s.i. (A176, Award). Univ Pub & Dist.

I Found Cleopatra. Thomas P Kelley. LC 80-20507. 1980. 11.95. Borgo Press.

I Found Him Dead. Gale Gallagher, pseud. LC 47-114878. (gargoyle mystery). 1947. Coward-McCann.

I Found It at the Movies. Atlantis. pap. 1.95 o.s.i. (TC-496, Travellers Comp). Olympia.

I Gave at the Office. Donald E Westlake. LC 71-139666. 1971. 5.95 (ISBN 0-671-20839-X). Simon and Schuster.

I Give My Heart. M. Lindsey. 4.95 o.p. Vantage.

I Give Thee Back. Kenneth O'Donnell Horan. LC 42-1105. 1942. E. P. Dutton & Company, Inc.

I Give You Oscar Wilde: A Biographical Novel. Desmond Hall. LC 65-125711. (NAL-World bk.). 5.95. New Amer. Lib.

I Got a Country: A Novel of Alaska. Gilbert Wolf Gabriel. LC 44-7328. 1944. Doubleday, Doran & Co., Inc.

I Guess: Or, Jess and Aramintha. E. H. Burling. LC 6-16394. W. B. Conkey Company.

I Had Wild Jack for a Lover. Meredith Marsh. LC 77-7473. 8.95 (ISBN 0-698-10847-7). Coward, McCann & Geoghegan.

I Hardly Knew You. Edna O'Brien. LC 77-76261. 1978. 7.95 (ISBN 0-385-13239-5). Doubleday.

I Hate Actors! Ben Hecht. LC 44-7255. 1944. Crown Publishers.

I Hate Blondes. Wolfe Kaufman. LC 46-3140. 1946. Simon and Schuster.

I Hate Good-Byes. Ethel V Skinner Higginson. LC 49-71557. 1948. Dorrance.

I Have a Ghetto in My Heart. James Steele. 1973. pap. 2.35 (ISBN 0-87148-428-5). Pathway Pr.

I Have a Great Desire: A Novel. Jan Stephen. LC 61-5124. 1961. Houghton Mifflin.

I Have Been Little Too Long. Alice Mary Ross Colver. LC 35-16582. 1935. Dodd, Mead & Company.

I Have Been Young. Elizabeth Lomond. LC 33-6059. Harcourt, Brace and Company.

I Have Come Here to Be Alone. Ingrid Bengis. LC 76-22610. 7.95 (ISBN 0-671-22330-5). Simon and Schuster.

I Have Feet of Clay. H. Morton Lieberman. 3.95 o.p. Vantage.

I Have Fought the Good Fight. Carter Wilson. LC 67-20289. 1967. Lippincott.

I Have Friends in Heaven. 1st Amer. Ed. Max Catto. LC 66-148992. 1966. bds., 4.95. Little.

I Have Killed a Man! Cecil Freeman Gregg. LC 31-3308. 1931. L. MacVeagh, The Dial Press.

I Have Lived and Loved. By Mrs. Forrester Pseud.... Mrs. Bridges. (On cover: Lovell's library, v. 17, no. 845). 1887. J. W. Lovell Company.

I Have No Mouth & I Must Scream. Harlan Ellison. 1972. pap. 0.75 o.p. (T2638). Pyramid Pubns.

I Have No Mouth & I Must Scream. Harlan Ellison. 1974. pap. 1.25 o.p. (ISBN 0-515-03521-1, N3521). BJ Pub Group.

I Have Only Myself to Blame. Elizabeth Asquith Bibescu. LC 21-20192. 2.00. George H. Doran Company.

I Have Touched the Earth. Sylvia Chatfield Bates. LC 34-55937. The Bobbs-Merrill Company.

I Have What You Want. Chris Harrison. 1969. pap. 1.25 o.p. (88-707). Lancer.

I Hear Adventure Calling. Emilie Baker Loring. LC 48-9218. 1948. Little, Brown.

I Hear America Swinging. Peter De Uries. LC 75-44099. 7.95 (ISBN 0-316-18200-1). Little, Brown.

I Hear America Swinging. Peter De Vries. 1976. 7.95 (ISBN 0-316-18200-1). Little.

I Hear Thunder. Samuel Selvon & Full Name: Samuel Dickson Selvon. LC 63-17260. 1963. St Martin's Press.

I Heard My Sister Speak My Name. Thomas Savage. LC 77-8473. 8.95 (ISBN 0-316-77139-2). Little, Brown.

I Heard My Sister Speak My Name. Thomas Savage. LC 78-7489. 1978. 11.95 (ISBN 0-8161-6582-3). G. K. Hall.

I Heard of a River: The Story of the Germans in Pennsylvania. 1s ed. Elsie Singmaster. LC 48-9347. (Land of the Free Series). 1948. J. C. Winston Co.

I Heard the Death Bell: A Jane Amanda Edwards Story. Charlotte Murray Russell, pseud. LC 40-13555. 1940. Pub. for the Crime Club by Doubleday, Doran and Co., Inc.

I Heard the Owl Call My Name. Margaret Craven. LC 73-10801. 1973. 4.95 (ISBN 0-385-02586-6). Doubleday.

I Heard the Owl Call My Name. Margaret Craven. LC 74-5018. 1974. 7.95 (ISBN 0-8161-6203-4). G. K. Hall.

I Heard Them Sing. Ferdinand Reyher. LC 46-2897. 1946. Little, Brown and Company.

I Hide, We Seek. Richard Martin Stern. LC 65-22813. 1965. Scribner.

I in You. Darlene Bridge. 1973. pap. 4.95 (ISBN 0-915358-01-8). Bridgeberg.

I, Jack Swilling: Founder of Phoenix, Arizona. John Myers Myers. LC 61-7202. 1961. Hastings House.

I, James Blunt. Henry Canova Vollam Morton. LC 42-16453. 1942. Dodd, Mead & Company.

I: James Lewis. Gilbert Wolf Gabriel. LC 32-264432. 1932. Doubleday, Doran & Company, Inc.

I, James McNeill Whistler: An Autobiography. Lawrence Williams. LC 76-185769. (Illus.). 1972. 7.95 (ISBN 0-671-21168-4). Simon and Schuster.

I, Jan Cremer: 1st Amer. Ed. Introd by Seymour Krim. Jan Cremer. LC 65-23716. pap., 4.95. Shorecrest Dist. Shorewood.

I, Jerry, Take Thee, Joan. Cleo Lucas. LC 31-290189. 1931. Doubleday, Doran and Company, Incorporated.

I, John. Benn E. Lewis. 1977. pap. 2.00x (ISBN 0-682-47154-2). Arlin J Brown.

I, John Mordaunt. Virgil Scott. LC 64-14634. 1964. Harcourt, Brace & World.

I, Judas. Taylor Caldwell. (Signet Book). 1978. 2.50 (ISBN 0-451-08212-5). New American Library.

I, Judas. Taylor Caldwell & Jess Stearn. LC 77-5518. 1977. 10.95 (ISBN 0-689-10806-0). Atheneum.

I Just Wanted Someone to Know. Bette Craig & Joyce Kornbluh. LC 81-85377. 1981. pap. 3.95 (ISBN 0-918266-16-5). Smyrna.

I Kept My Knees Crossed: The Sex Life of a State Capitol; an Expose. Gloria Robbins. LC 48-9674. 1948. William-Frederick Press.

I, Keturah see Hawthorne.

I. Keturah: A Novel. Ruth Wolff. LC 63-15904. 1963. John Day Co.

I Killed Stalin. Sterling Novel. LC 51-12054. 1951. Farrar, Straus and Young.

I Killed to Live. limited ed. George C. Cowles. LC 68-4840. (Illus.). 1968. Haywood Pub. Co.

I Killed Winky Adams. (Stories That Win Ser.). 55p. 1968. pap. 0.95 o.p. (ISBN 0-8163-0055-0, 09045-6). Pacific Pr Pub Assn.

I Knew Daisy Smuten. Hunter Davies. LC 78-135264. 1970. 5.95. Coward-McCann.

I Knew MacBean. Wetherby Williams. LC 48-5143. 1948. Pub. for the Crime Club by Doubleday.

I Know a Little Milliner: A Novel. Fannie Ferber Fox. LC 41-22958. 1941. Hale, Cushman & Flint.

I Know a Place: Three Stories. William Mills. LC 75-46397. (Illus.). (ISBN 0-912960-08-6). Press of the Nightowl.

I Know a Secret. Mabel Goode Frantz. LC 45-11428. 1945. Dorrance & Company.

I Know My Love. Fan Nichols. 1971. pap. 0.75 o.p. (75-411). Manor Bks.

I Know What I'd Do. Alice Beal Parsons. LC 46-2495. 1946. E. P. Dutton & Co., Inc.

I Know What I'm Doing. Hans Koning. 1964. 3.95 o.p. (ISBN 0-671-36560-6). S&S.

I Know What I'm Doing: A Novel. Hans Koningsberger. LC 64-19935. 1964. Simon and Schuster.

I Know What the Small Girl Knew. Anya Achtenberg. LC 82-81350. 72p. 1983. pap. 4.00 (ISBN 0-930100-11-5). Holy Cow.

I Know Where I've Been. Harriett Gilbert. LC 72-79709. 1972. 6.95 (ISBN 0-06-011522-X). Harper & Row.

I Know Who God Is. Edwin B. Hodshire. 5.95 o.p. Vantage.

I Know Your Heart, Marco Polo: Stories. Henry Bromell. LC 78-3580. 1979. 7.95 (ISBN 0-394-50116-0). Knopf.

I, Krupskaya: My Life with Lenin. A Novel. Jane Barnes Casey. LC 74-1353. 1974. 6.95. Houghton Mifflin.

I, Leo: A Novel. Lew Welch. LC 76-54941. 5.00. (ISBN 0-912516-23-2) (ISBN 0-912516-24-0). Grey Fox Press.

I, Libertine. Frederick R Ewing, pseud. LC 56-11536. Ballantine Books.

I Lift My Lamp. Anna Balmer Myers. LC 67-30440. 1968. Dorrance.

I Like a Good Murder. Brian Hill. 1930. J. B. Lippincott Company.

I Like Bears. Thomas Burnett Swann. (Illus.). 1960. 2.50 o.p. (ISBN 0-8233-0105-2). Golden Quill.

I Like It Here. 1st American Ed. Kingsley Amis. LC 58-5925. 1958. Harcourt, Brace.

I Like It Tough: A Novel of Suspense. James A Howard. LC 55-43393. (Popular Library eagle book, EB46). 1955. Popular Library.

I Like You So Much. Helen Marion Edginton. LC 33-211317. The Macaulay Company.

I Liked This Story. Betty White. 1930. Doubleday, Doran & Company, Inc.

I Live Again. Warwick Deeping. LC 92-200934. 1942. A. A. Knopf.

I Live in the Watchmakers Town. Ruth Roston. LC 81-83880. (Minnesota Voices Project Ser.: No. 4). (Illus.). 76p. 1981. pap. 3.00 (ISBN 0-89823-028-4). New Rivers Pr.

I Live Under a Black Sun: A Novel. Edith Sitwell. LC 70-171419. 1973. 13.25 (ISBN 0-8371-6260-2). Greenwood Press.

I Live Under a Black Sun: A Novel. Edith Sitwell. LC 38-5862. 1938. Doubleday, Doran & Co., Inc.

I Look at Me! Mari Evans. LC 74-75591. (pre-school reader). (Illus.). 1974. 2.50 (pbk.) 4.95, (ISBN 0-88378-038-0). Third World Press.

I Looked Over Jordan, and Other Stories. Ernie Brill. LC 80-51042. 15.00 (ISBN 0-89608-118-4). South End Press.

I Looked Right. 1st American Ed. Elizabeth Denham. LC 56-765556. 1956. Doubleday.

I Lost It All in Montreal. Donna Steinberg. 272p. 1983. pap. 2.95 (ISBN 0-380-81836-1, 81836-1). Avon.

I Lost My Girlish Laughter. Jane Allen. LC 38-27404. 1938. Random House.

I Lost My Heart. Maysie Greig. LC 36-893717. 1936. Doubleday, Doran & Company, Inc.

I Lost My Heart. Maysie Greig. LC 37-16227. 1937. The Sun Dial Press, Inc.

I Love a Lass. Elizabeth Cadell. LC 56-11221. 1956. Morrow.

I Love Abe Lee. Brenda Brown. 1970. 3.50 o.p. Vantage.

I Love Miss Tilli Bean. Ilka Chase. LC 47-1748. 1946. Doubleday & Company, Inc.

I Love Myself When I Am Laughing... and Then Again When I Am Looking Mean and Impressive: A Zora Neale Hurston Reader. Zora Neale Hurston & Alice Walker. LC 79-17582. 1979. 14.95 (ISBN 0-912670-56-8). Feminist Press.

I Love the King!" A Romantic Novel. Lou Wedemar. LC 37-16383. 1937. Hillman-Curl, Inc.

I Love Thee, Beast. Harry Dallas Miller. Orig. Title: Great Sweet Days of Old Shibui. 1966. pap. 0.75 o.p. (532-75173-075). Manor Bks.

I Love to Travel with My Wife. Herman G. Wallenfels. 2.95 o.p. Vantage.

I Love You. Remy Charlip. 1981. pap. 1.50 (ISBN 0-380-53090-2, 53090). Avon.

I Love You Again. Octavus Roy Cohen. LC 37-145760. 1937. D. Appleton Century Company, Incorporated.

I Love You, Alice B. Toklas! Bill Friday. LC 70-12939. 1968. 0.75. Bantam Books.

I Love You Better Now. Lois Wyse. LC 72-115802. 1970. 7.64i (ISBN 0-690-00350-1). T Y Crowell.

I Love You Honey, but the Season's Over. C. Clausen. 1972. pap. 0.95 o.p. (09123). Curtis.

I Love You, I Hate You, Drop Dead! Variations on a Theme. Artie Shaw. LC 65-16311. 4.50. Fleet.

I Love You, I Hate You, Drop Dead! Variations on a Theme. Artie Shaw. (Signet bk., P2804). 1966. New Amer. Lib.

I Love You, Irene. MacKinlay Kantor. LC 72-76176. 1972. 7.95. Doubleday.

I Love You, Mom. Mary L. Elchert. 3.50 o.p. Carlton.

I Love You, Ruby Compton. Florence Stuart. (Alouette Romance Ser.). 128p. (Orig.). 1981. pap. 2.25 (ISBN 0-89531-126-7, 0198-96). Sharon Pubns.

I Love You, Stupid! Harry Mazer. 192p. 1983. pap. 2.50 (ISBN 0-380-61432-4, 61432-4, Flare). Avon.

I Love You Truly. Constance Bannister. 1970. pap. 1.00 (ISBN 0-671-10439-X, Fireside). S&S.

I Loved Rose Ann. Lee Bennett Hopkins & Ingrid Fetz. (Illus.). 4.95 (ISBN 0-394-83100-4) (ISBN 0-394-93100-9). Knopf.

I Loved Tiberius. Elisabeth Dored. LC 62-14258. 1963. Pantheon Books.

I Loved You Wednesday: A Novel. David Marlow. LC 74-30564. 1975. 7.95 (ISBN 0-399-11497-1). Putnam.

I, Lucifer. Peter O'Donnell. LC 67-22464. Doubleday.

I, Madame Tussaud: 1st Ed. Sylvia Pass Martin. LC 56-6027. Harper.

I Married a Dead Man. Cornell George Hopley-Woolrich. LC 48-7768. 1948. J. B. Lippincott Co.

I Married a Prince: A Cinderella Story from Hawaii. Myrtle King Kaapu. LC 76-40773. 1977. 10.00 o.p. (ISBN 0-682-48649-3). Exposition.

I Married a Wife: A Novel. Henrietta Eliza Vaughan Stannard. (On verso of half-title: Twentieth century series). F. A. Stokes Company.

I Married a Witch's Love. Margaret Lindhares. 4.50 o.p. Vantage.

I Married Four Children. 1st Ed. Elsa Marvel Lothrop. LC 54-673553. 1954. Pageant Press.

I Married My Sister. Madge I. Enos. 3.00 o.p. Carlton.

I Married Them: A Novel. Janet H. Dunning Van Duyn. LC 45-35074. 1945. Howell, Soskin.

I, Mary Magdalen. Juliet Thompson. LC 40-138092. Delphic Studios.

I May Not Be Totally Perfect, but Parts of Me Are Excellent. Ashleigh Brilliant. LC 79-10052. (Illus.). 1979. 9.95 (ISBN 0-912800-66-6); pap. 4.95 (ISBN 0-912800-67-4). Woodbridge Pr.

I Met a Gypsy. Norah Robinson Lofts. LC 35-38584. 1935. A. A. Knopf.

I Met a Man. Michael Blankfort. LC 37-35186. The Bobbs-Merrill Company.

I Met a Man with Seven Wives: A Novel. Liz Holloway. LC 77-155942. 1972. 6.95 (ISBN 0-200-71837-1). Abelard-Schuman.

I Met Murder. Selwyn Jepson. LC 30-22431. 1930. Harper & Brothers.

I Met Murder on the Way. Margaret Echard. LC 65-17613. 1965. Published for the Crime Club by Doubleday.

I Miss You When You're Here. Lee Leonard. LC 75-35958. 1976. 8.95 (ISBN 0-8128-1905-5). Stein and Day.

I Must Not Rock. Linda Marie. LC 77-80960. (Orig.). 1977. pap. 5.00 (ISBN 0-913780-19-7). Daughters.

I Must Ride Alone. Jackson Gregory. LC 40-384932. 1940. Dodd, Mead & Company.

I, My Ancestor. Nancy Wilson Ross. LC 49-50368. 1950. Random House.

I. N. R. I. A Prisoner's Story of the Cross. Peter Rosegger. Tr. by Lee, Elizabeth. LC 5-35298. 1905. McClure, Phillips & Co.

I Name Thee Mara. Edmund Gilligan. LC 46-11951. 1946. C. Scribner's Sons.

I Need the Money. George Vere Hobart. LC 4-3736. G. W. Dillingham Co.

I Never Promised You a Rose Garden. Joanne Greenberg. LC 64-11018. 1964. Holt, Rinehart and Winston.

I Never Promised You a Rose Garden: A Novel by Hannah Green. Joanne Greenberg. (Signet bk., T2592). 1965. New Amer. Lib.

I Never Saw an Arab Like Him. James A Maxwell. LC 48-6250. 1948. Houghton Mifflin Co.

I Object. Leah Weiss. LC 23-18620. Printed for the Author by the Caxton Press.

I-Opener. R. Platt. 1976. pap. 12.50 (ISBN 0-13-448779-6). P-H.

I, Paul: An Autobiograpghy of the Prince Among Missionaries. Lester A Wolf. LC 49-417. 1948. Concordia Pub. House.

I, Paul: An "Autobiography" of the Apostle to the Gentiles. Rex Miller. LC 40-29541. Duell, Sloan and Pearce.

I Pose. Stella Benson. LC 16-127320. 1916. The Macmillan Company.

I Promessi Sposi. Alessandro Manzoni. Ed. by J. Geddes, Jr. & E. H. Wilkins. 1911. pap. text ed. 2.75x o.p. (30320). Heath.

I Promessi Sposi. Commento Critico Di Luigi Russo. Alessandro Manzoni. LC 64-9079. (Scrittori italiani). 1964. pap., 4.00. Nuova Italia Dist. Philadelphia. Chilton.

I Promessi Sposi: or: The Betrothed Lovers. A Milanese Story of the Seventeenth Century. Alessandro Manzoni. LC 7-19679. 1834. D. Green.

I Pronounce Them: A Story of Man and Wife. Geoffrey Anketell Studdert-Kennedy. LC 27-19776. George H. Doran Company.

I Put My Right Foot in. 1st Ed. Harry J Essex. LC 54-6883. 1954. Little, Brown.

I. Q. Merchant. John Boyd. LC 72-87330. 1972. 5.95 o.p. (ISBN 0-679-40051-6). Weybright.

I Quit: The Dead Issue Fable. Duane Thorin. pap. 1.50 o.p. (ISBN 0-8407-5575-9). Nelson.

I, Rachel: A Biographical Novel, by March Cost Pseud. Peggy Morrison, pseud. LC 57-12255. 1957. Vanguard Press.

I Reckon As How.". John Henry Woerner. LC 48-11766. B. & W. Pub. Co.

I, Rembrandt: A Novel. David Weiss. LC 78-21352. 10.95 (ISBN 0-312-40261-9). St. Martin's Press.

I Remember Babylon & Other Stories. Arthur C. Clarke. 240p. Repr. lib. bdg. 13.85x (ISBN 0-89190-955-9). Am Repr-Rivercity Pr.

I Remember Christine. Oscar Lewis. LC 42-512754. 1942. A. A. Knopf.

I Remember Love. Mollie Hardwick. LC 82-17069. 1983. 11.95 (ISBN 0-312-40265-1). St. Martin's Press.

I Remember. 1st Ed. Tyyne Eleanor Konga. LC 55-10847. 1956. Vantage Press.

I Resign You, Stallion: A Novel. Vinnie Williams. LC 64-20857. bds., 4.95. Viking.

I Ride in My Coach. Hughes Mearns. LC 23-10553. 1923. The Penn Publishing Company.

I, Roberta. Elizabeth Gray Vining. (Signet bk. T 3620). 1968. New Amer. Lib.

I, Roberta. Elizabeth Gray Vining. LC 67-26611. 1967. Lippincott.

I, Robot. Isaac Asimov. 1978. pap. 2.25 (ISBN 0-449-23949-7, Crest). Fawcett.

I, Robot. 1st Ed. Isaac Asimov. LC 51-9134. 1950. Gnome Press.

I Rode the Rods Through Naval Intelligence. George Dewey Weeden. 1954. Vantage Press.

I Rode with Stonewall. Henry K. Douglas. 1979. pap. 2.50 (ISBN 0-89176-027-X). Mockingbird Bks.

I. S. Turgenev: Dvoryanskoye Gnezdo. Ed. by P. Waddington. 1969. 24.00 (ISBN 0-08-012923-4); pap. 10.75 (ISBN 0-08-012922-6). Pergamon.

I!" Said the Demon. George Baxt. LC 68-28571. 1969. 4.50. Random House.

I, Said the Fly. Morna Doris MacTaggart Brown. LC 45-7301. 1945. Published for the Crime Club by Doubleday, Doran.

I, Said the Fly. Elizabeth Ferrars, pseud. LC 45-7301. 1945. Pub. for the Crime Club by Doubleday, Doran and Co., Inc.

I, Sappho of Lesbos: The Autobiography of a Strange Woman. Translated from the Medieval Latin; Edited by Michel Darius. Ed. by Michel Darius. LC 61-955. Castle Books.

I Sat at the Gate Beautiful (Being the Record of Jacob of Nazareth, Who Was Thrown to the Lions in the Roman Arena in the Year 91 A.D.) Carl Holliday. 1925. Cokesbury Press.

I Saw Gooley Fly. Joseph Bayly. (YA) 1968. 3.50 o.p. (ISBN 0-8007-0146-1). Revell.

I Saw Three Ships: And Other Winter Tales. Arthur Thomas Quiller-Couch. (On cover: Cassell's sunshine series, no. 109. Extra). 1892. Cassell Publishing Company.

I Saw Three Ships: And Other Winter Tales. Arthur Thomas Quiller-Couch. LC 6-29008. 1898. C. Scribner's Sons.

I Saw Three Ships and Other Winter's Tales. Quiller-Couch, Arthur Thomas. LC 77-169560. (Short story index reprint series). (Illus.). 1971. (ISBN 0-8369-4023-7). Books for Libraries Press.

I Saw Tokyo Burning. Robert Guillain. LC 82-81999. 320p. 1982. pap. 2.95 (ISBN 0-86721-223-3). Playboy Pbks.

I Say No" Or, The Love-Letter Answered; and Other Stories. Wilkie Collins. LC 3-27273. 1886. Harper & Brothers.

I Say No" Or, The Love Letter Answered, and Other Stories. Wilkie Collins. LC 16-7569. Harper & Brothers.

I Say No; or, the Loveletter Answered; and Other Stories, 2 vols in 1. Wilkie Collins. LC 72-5864. (Short Story Index Reprint Ser). Repr. of 1886 ed. 24.00 o.p. (ISBN 0-8369-4205-1). Ayer Co.

I Screwed My Sister. Adam Slade. 192p. pap. 1.95 o.p. (2043). Intimate Lib.

I See a Wondrous Land: A Novel. Gudmunder Kamban. LC 38-810. 1938. G. P. Putnam's Sons.

I See Red. Sterling Noel. LC 55-37186. (Ace double novel books, D-109). 1955. Ace Books.

I See You. Charlotte Armstrong. LC 66-13114. 1966. bds., 4.50. Coward.

I Seek a City. Gilbert Rees. LC 50-9424. 1950. Dutton.

I Sent a Letter to My Love. Bernice Rubens. LC 77-15925. 1978. 7.95 (ISBN 0-312-40267-8). St. Martin' Press.

I, Sex Master. Gene North. 192p. pap. 1.95 o.p. (6137). Brandon.

I Shall Dwell: The Youthful Years of David, King of Israel. Ruby Evans Grimes. LC 47-198674. 1947. Wm. B. Eardmans Publishing Company.

I Shall Not Hear the Nightingale. Khushwant Singh. LC 68-56043. 1968. Greenwood Press.

I Shall Nothear the Nightingale. Khushwant Singh. LC 59-12219. 1959. Grove Press.

I, Sherlock Holmes: Memoirs of Mr. Sherlock Holmes, OM, Late Consulting Private Detective-in-Ordinary to Their Majesties Queen Victoria, King Edward VII, and King George V. Michael Harrison. LC 76-11874. (Illus.). 8.95 (ISBN 0-525-13085-3). Dutton.

I, Sherlock Holmes: The Memoirs of Sherlock Holmes, OM, Sometime Consulting Detective-in-Ordinary to Her Majesty the Queen. Michael Harrison. LC 76-11874. 1977. 12.50 o.p. (ISBN 0-525-13085-3). Dutton.

I, Sherlock Holmes: The Memoirs of Sherlock Holmes, OM, Sometime Consulting Detective-in-Ordinary to Her Majesty the Queen. Michael Harrison LC 76-11874. 1977. 12.50 o.p. (ISBN 0-525-13085-3). Dutton.

I Should Have Known. Denise Robins. 1970. pap. 0.75 o.p. (T2296, GM). Fawcett World.

I Should Have Known. Denise Robins. 192p. 1973. pap. 0.75 o.p. (T2754, GM). Fawcett World.

I Should Have Stayed Home. Horace McCoy. LC 38-5606. 1938. A. A. Knopf.

I Should Have Stayed Home. Horace McCoy. LC 76-52112. (Garland Classics of Film Literature). 1978. 13.00 (ISBN 0-8240-2883-X). Garland Pub.

I Shoulda Been Home Yesterday. David Harris. (O.s.i.). 1976. 7.95 o.s.i. (ISBN 0-440-04156-2, Sey Lawr). Delacorte.

I Shouldn't Be Telling You This. Mary Breasted. LC 82-48141. 15.95 (ISBN 0-06-015092-0). Harper & Row.

I Sing the Body Electric. Ray Bradbury. 1976. pap. 2.25 (ISBN 0-553-14102-3). Bantam.

I Sing the Body Electric! Stories. Ray Bradbury. LC 75-88745. 1969. 6.95. Knopf.

I Sit Alone-- Waldemar Theodor Ager & Stork, Charles Wharton, 1881- Tr. LC 31-6077. 1931. London, Harper & Brothers.

I Sleep Around: A Novel. Nadya Bernard. LC 79-108473. (Illus.). 8.00. Literati Press.

I Slept with Ten Million Soldiers. John F. Beall, Sr. 4.95 o.p. Vantage.

I Smell Esther Williams & Other Stories. Mark Leyner. LC 82-83107. 1983. 11.95 (ISBN 0-914590-76-6); pap. 5.95 (ISBN 0-914590-77-4). Fiction Coll.

I Smell the Devil. Carey Magoon. LC 43-15970. 1943. Farrar & Rinehart, Inc.

I Speak for the Dead. John J. Maloney. LC 82-16316. 12.95 (ISBN 0-8362-6118-6). Andrews and McMeel.

I Spy. Natalie Sumner Lincoln. LC 16-115882. 1916. D. Appleton and Company.

I Start Counting. 1st Ed. Audrey Erskine Lindop. LC 66-20971. 1966. 4.95. Doubleday.

I Still Dream About Columbus: A Novel. Jack M Bickham. LC 82-5742. 13.95 (ISBN 0-312-40276-7). St Martin's Press.

I Swear. Frank H Powers. LC 7-30307. (On cover: The Vires library, no. 1). 1891. Vires Publishing Company.

I Swear and Vow. Translated by Helen Sebbs. 1st Ed. Stefan Olivier. LC 60-13743. Doubleday.

I Swear by Apollo. Agnes Brooks Young. LC 68-22975. 1968. 6.95. Simon and Schuster.

I Take Thee, Serenity. Daisy Newman. LC 75-8984. 1975. (ISBN 0-395-20551-4). Houghton Mifflin.

I Take Thee, Serenity. Daisy Newman. 1.95 (ISBN 0-345-25222-5). Ballantine.

I Take This Land. Richard Powell. 1982. pap. 2.95 (ISBN 0-89176-038-5, 6038). Mockingbird Bks.

I Take This Man. Anne Brooks. LC 46-223601. 1946. Gramercy Publishing Co.

I Take This Man. Emilie Baker Loring. LC 77-6769. 1977. 8.95 (ISBN 0-89340-087-4). J. Curley.

I Take This Man. 1st Ed. Emilie Baker Loring. LC 55-5527. 1954. Little, Brown.

I Take This Squaw. Rosa Fulghum Biggs. LC 42-155532. 1942. Dorrance and Company.

I Take This Stranger. Paulette Warren. (Berkley Medallion Book.). (Illus.). 1977. 1.25. (ISBN 0-425-03342-2). Berkley Pub. Corp.

I Take This Woman. Rajinder S. Bedi. Tr. by Khushwant Singh. 103p. 1967. pap. 2.25 (ISBN 0-88253-014-3). Ind-US Inc.

I Tell of Greenland: An Edited Translation of the Sauarkrokur Manuscripts. Francis Berry. LC 78-302452. (Illus.). 1977. 10.95 (ISBN 0-7100-8591-5). Routledge & Kegan Paul.

I, the Criminal. David Sharp. LC 33-27049. 1933. Houghton Mifflin Company.

I, the Jury. Frank Morrison Spillane. LC 47-5468. 1947. E. P. Dutton.

I, the King. Howard Clewes. LC 79-51249. (Illus.). 1979. 9.95 (ISBN 0-688-03382-2). Morrow.

I, the King: By Frances Parkinson Keyes. Frances Parkinson Wheeler Keyes. LC 66-17870. 1966. McGraw-Hill.

I, the King: The Story of a Rich Young Man. Wayland Wells Williams. LC 24-5828. 1924. Frederick A. Stokes Company.

I, the King: Translated from the German. Hermann Kesten & Dunlop, Geoffrey, 1894- Tr. LC 41-4922. 1940. Alliance Book Corporation Etc.

I, the Machine. easy eye ed. Paul W. Fairman. (Orig.). pap. 0.60 o.p. (73-735). Lancer.

I, the Sun. Janet Morris. Date not set. pap. 2.25 (ISBN 0-553-13309-8). Bantam.

I, the Tiger. Manuel Komroff. LC 33-32225. 1933. Coward-McCann, Inc.

I Thee Wed. Gilbert Wolf Gabriel. LC 48-1782. 1948. Macmillan Co.

I Think I May Paint the House in August: Fiction. Vicky Draham. LC 75-18086. 7.95. Draham.

I Think I Remember: Being the Random Recollections of Sir Wickham Woolicomb, an Ordinary English Snob and Gentleman. Magdalen King-Hall. LC 27-12724. 1927. D. Appleton and Company.

I Think I'm Having a Baby. Caryl Hansen. 112p. 1982. pap. 1.95 (ISBN 0-380-80564-2, 80564, Flare). Avon.

I Think of Warri. Robert J Attaway. LC 73-14305. 1974. 5.95 (ISBN 0-06-010169-5). Harper & Row.

I, Thou and the Other One: A Love Story. Amelia Edith Huddleston Barr. LC 99-764. 1898. Dodd, Mead and Company.

I, Thou, and the Other One: A Love Story. Amelia Edith Huddleston Barr. LC 26-24702. 1901. International Association of Newspapers and Authors.

I Thought of Daisy. Edmund Wilson. LC 53-6726. 1953. Farrar, Straus and Young.

I Thought of Daisy. Edmund Wilson. LC 29-18421. 1929. C. Scribner's Sons.

I Thought of Daisy see Galahad.

I, Tom Horn. Henry Wilson Allen. LC 74-23407. 1975. 7.95 (ISBN 0-397-01073-7). Lippincott.

I, Tom Horn. Will Henry, pseud. LC 74-23407. (O.s.i.). 1975. 7.95 o.s.i. (ISBN 0-397-01073-7). Lippincott.

I, Too, Have Loved. Denise Robins. 1979. 1.95 (ISBN 0-380-42432-0). Avon Books.

I Took My Love to the Country. 1st Ed. Margaret Culkin Banning. LC 66-20749. 1966. 4.95. Harper.

I, Victoria Strange. Ruth Willock. LC 73-21317. 1975. 7.95 (ISBN 0-8015-0148-2). Hawthorn Books.

I Wait for Miracles. Thomas Theodor Heine & Stillman, Clara (Gruening) Tr. LC 47-31285. 1947. Greenberg.

I Wake up Screaming. Stephen Gould Fisher. LC 41-3327. 1941. Dodd, Mead & Company.

I Walk Alone. Kathleen Wallace. LC 31-8638. 1931. Doubleday, Doran & Company, Inc.

I Walked in Arden. Jack Randall Crawford. LC 22-105495. 1922. A. A. Knopf.

I Wanna Be a Lady Plumber. Reinold Shubert. (Illus.). 1968. 2.50 o.p. Vantage.

I Want a Black Doll. Frank Hercules. LC 67-19819. 1967. Simon and Schuster.

I Want It Now. Kingsley Amis. LC 69-12024. 1969. Harcourt, Brace & World.

I Want More. Greg Dorian. pap. 1.95 o.p. (ISBN 0-87977-168-2, DBB168). Dansk Blue Bk.

I Want to Be a Lady. Maximilian Foster. LC 27-15795. 1926. J. B. Lippincott Company.

I Want to Be in Love Again. Barbara Rex. LC 77-1632. 8.95 (ISBN 0-393-08767-0). Norton.

I Want to Go Home: A Captain Heimrich Mystery. Richard Lockridge & Frances Louise Davis Lockridge. LC 48-141911. (Main line mysteries). 1948. J. B. Lippincott Co.

I Want to Keep My Baby. Joanna Lee. (Signet Book). 1977. 1.50 (ISBN 0-451-07649-4). New American Library.

I Want to Know. Gordon W Hanson. LC 55-27086. Story Book Press.

I Want to Live. Vasilii Makarovich Shukshin. 257p. 1973. pap. 3.95 (ISBN 0-8285-1044-X, Pub. by Progress Pubs USSR). Imported Pubns.

I Want to Live Again. 1st Ed. Alice Lighter Stockwell. LC 57-8455. 1957. Vantage Press.

I Want What I Want. Geoff Brown. LC 67-14262. 1967. Putnam.

I Want You Myself... Anna Brand. LC 38-19066. 1938. Doubleday, Doran & Company, Inc.

I Want You Only. Ann Bigelow. LC 37-29656. 1937. Hillman-Curl, Inc.

I Wanted to Die. Rose Chapman. LC 54-3781. 1954. Comet Press Books.

I Wanted to Murder... Clarissa Fairchild Cushman. LC 40-31111. Farrar and Rinehart, Inc.

I Was a Male War Bride: By Henri Rochard Pseud. Roger Henri Charlier. LC 54-44384. Montgrove Press.

I Was a Probationer. Corinne Johnson Kern. 1937. E. P. Dutton & Co., Inc.

I Was a Spy for Hitler: A Novel. 1st Ed. Theodore Alexander Kaucher. LC 58-59460. 1958. Vantage Press.

I Was a Stranger. Statler, Ruth Beeghly. LC 60-59. 1959. Brethren Press.

I Was a Teen-Age Dwarf: Introd. by Art Linkletter. N.P. B. Geis Associates; Districuted by Random House New York,1959. Shulman, Max. LC 59-13752.

I Was Dancing. Edwin O'Connor. LC 64-12013. 1964. Little, Brown.

I Was Eleanor Summers. Sarah Drew. LC 40-7856. 1940. Longmans, Green and Co.

I Was Following This Girl. Desmond Skirrow. LC 68-11380. 1968. Doubleday.

I Was Going Anyway. Robert Switzer. LC 61-7053. (Cock Robin mystery). 1961. Macmillan.

I Was Never the Princess: A Novel. Jeannie Sakol. LC 79-155030. 1971. 6.95. World Pub.

I Was Seduced by the Paper-Bulls. Edward H Geissler. LC 73-94387. 1974. 10.95 (ISBN 0-8059-1993-7). Dorrance.

I Was the Man". Pamela Frankau. LC 32-30635. Sears Publishing Company.

I Wasn't Born Yesterday: An Anonymous Autobiography. Allen Rivkin & Spigelgass, Leonard. LC 35-2728. The Macaulay Company.

I Watch Lois. Laurence Klavan. 192p. (Orig.). 1981. pap. 1.95 (ISBN 0-523-41318-1). Pinnacle Bks.

I, Weapon. Charles W. Runyon. LC 73-22537. 1974. 4.95 (ISBN 0-385-06491-8). Doubleday.

I Will Arise: A Novel. Blanche Marie Peters. LC 56-13211. (Nobel book). Comet Press Books.

I Will Be Faithful. Kathleen Shepard. LC 34-434172. A. H. King.

I Will Be Good. Hester W Chapman. LC 46-1519. 1946. Houghton Mifflin Company.

I Will Fear No Evil. Robert Anson Heinlein. LC 75-126443. 1970. 6.95. Putnam.

I Will Fear No Evil. Robert Anson Heinlein. LC 78-23878. (Gregg Press Science Fiction Series). 1978. 15.00 (ISBN 0-8398-2449-1). Gregg Press.

I Will Go Barefoot All Summer for You. Katie L. Lyle. 1974. pap. 1.75 (ISBN 0-440-94327-2, LFL). Dell.

I Will, I Will...for Now. Al Friedman. 1976. (pbk.) 1.25. Warner Books.

I Will Lift up Mine Eyes. Edgar Zavitz Palmer & Opal Y. Palmer. LC 77-88272. 4.50 (ISBN 0-918626-02-1). Word Services.

I Will Lift up Mine Eyes. Hubert Skidmore. LC 36-10520. 1936. Doubleday, Doran & Company, Inc.

I Will Ne'er Consent: A Novel. Mary Schell Hoke Bacon. LC 7-3190. (On cover: The Belford American novel series, no. 1). R. Belford.

I Will Not Serve. Eveline Mahyere. LC 59-107818. 1960. Dutton.

I Will Repay: A Romance. Emmuska Orczy. LC 6-41710. 1906. J. B. Lippincott Company.

I Wish He Would Not Die. 1st Ed. James Aldridge. LC 58-10018. 1958. Doubleday.

I Wonder. N. Morrison. 1973. pap. 0.95 o.p. (ISBN 0-07-073922-6). McGraw.

I Won't Be Home for Christmas & Other Short Stories. Carrie W. Foster. 57p. 1980. 4.00x (ISBN 0-682-49662-6). Exposition.

I Would Be Private. Rose Macaulay. LC 37-4764. 1937. Harper & Brothers.

I Would Have Saved Them If I Could. Leonard Michaels. LC 75-6899. 1975. 7.95 (ISBN 0-374-17411-3). Farrar, Straus & Giroux.

I Would Rather Stay Poor. James Hadley Chase. 1974. (pbk.) 0.95 (ISBN 0-671-77773-4). Pocket Books.

I Wouldn't Be in Your Shoes. Cornell George Hopley-Woolrich. LC 43-4643. 1943. J. B. Lippincott Company.

I, Yahweh: A Novel in the Form of an Autobiography. Robert Munson Grey. LC 38-8696. 1937. Willett, Clark & Company.

I, Zombie. Curt Selby. 160p. 1982. pap. 2.25 (ISBN 0-87997-763-9). DAW Bks.

Iaia Garcia. Machado De Assis, Joaquim Maria. LC 76-24338. (Studies in Romance Languages; 17). 12.50 (ISBN 0-8131-1353-9). University Press of Kentucky.

Ian Fleming: the Fantastic 007 Man. Richard Gant. (73-500). Lancer.

Ian Fleming: the Spy Who Came in with the Gold. Henry A Zeiger. (60-2131). 1966. Popular Lib.

Ian Fleming, the Spy Who Came in with the Gold. Henry A Zeiger. LC 65-26809. 1965. Duell, Sloan and Pearce.

Ian of the Orcades: or, The Armourer of Girnigoe. William Wilfred Campbell. LC 8-15730. 1907. Fleming H. Revell Company.

Iba, the Dawn. Margaret J Campbell. LC 63-14333. 1963. Christopher Pub. House.

Ibe of Atlan. Ira Albert Cole. 1947. Johnson Pub. Co.

Ibiza Syndicate. Bill Reade. LC 76-10565. 7.95. St. Martin's Press.

Iblis in Paradise: A Story of the Temptation. George Roe. LC 8-33778. H. Altemus Company.

Ibrahim the Writer. Ibrahim Abd Al-Qadir Al-Mazini & Marsden Jones. LC 77-960312. 1976. 1.20 (ISBN 9-7720-1099-2). General Egyptian Book Organization.

Icarus. Peter Way. LC 79-25792. 1980. 9.95 (ISBN 0-698-11030-7). Coward, McCann & Geoghegan.

ICARUS Complex. Jack H Bailey. LC 72-3917. 1972. 6.95 (ISBN 0-396-06539-2). Dodd, Mead.

Icarus Seal. Christopher Hyde. LC 82-11805. 1982. 13.95 (ISBN 0-395-32044-5). Houghton Mifflin.

Icarus to Be and Other Observations. Fausto Sax. LC 72-153404. 1971. 4.95 (ISBN 0-912282-01-0). Pulse-Finger Press.

Ice. Helen Woods Edmonds. LC 70-126384. (Doubleday science fiction). 1970. 4.50. Doubleday.

Ice! Arnold Federbush. 1978. pap. 2.50 (ISBN 0-553-14033-7). Bantam.

Ice. James Follett. LC 78-56947. 1978. 8.95 (ISBN 0-8128-2528-4). Stein and Day.

Ice. Anna Kavan. LC 70-126384. 1970. 4.50 o.p. (ISBN 0-385-02503-3). Doubleday.

Ice. Anna Kavan. LC 70-126384. 1974. (pbk.) 0.95. Popular Library.

Ice. Ed McBain. 305p. 1983. 15.50 (ISBN 0-87795-468-2). Arbor Hse.

Ice: A Major New Novel About the World of the 87th Precinct. Ed McBain. LC 82-74061. 15.50 (ISBN 0-87795-468-2). Arbor House.

Ice Age. Margaret Drabble. LC 77-3319. 1977. 8.95 (ISBN 0-394-41790-9). Knopf.

Ice Age: A Novel. Translated by John Simon and Others. Tamas Aczel. LC 65-17105. 1965. Simon and Schuster.

Ice and Iron. Wilson Tucker. LC 74-9146. 1974. 4.95 (ISBN 0-385-00485-0). Doubleday.

Ice & Iron. Wilson Tucker. LC 75-22399. 1975. 1.50. Ballantine Books.

Ice & Swizzle Sticks. Carl Rouch. 3.75 o.p. Vantage.

Ice Before Killing. Marion Strobel. LC 43-147783. 1943. C. Scribner's Sons.

Ice Bomb Zero. Nick Carter. (Nick Carter Ser). (O.s.i.). (Orig.). 1971. pap. 0.95 o.s.i. (AN1088, Award). Univ Pub & Dist.

Ice Brothers. Sloan Wilson. LC 79-52252. 1979. 11.95 (ISBN 0-87795-232-9). Arbor Hse.

Ice Castle. Elizabeth Wolfe. 256p. (Orig.). 1982. pap. 2.50 (ISBN 0-8439-1040-2, Leisure Bks). Nordon Pubns.

Ice Castles. Ed. by Fotonovel Publications Staff. (Illus., Orig.). 1979. pap. 2.50. Fotonovel.

Ice Cold in Alex. Christopher Landon. LC 57-54285. 1957. W. Sloane Associates.

Ice Cold Marriage. Christine Jope-Slade. LC 32-7350. The Bobbs-Merrill Company.

Ice-Cream Alley: A Novel. Henry Albert Collins. LC 18-21821. 1918. 1.35. J. W. Franks & Sons.

Ice-Cream Headache & Other Stories. James Jones. 1968. 5.00 o.p. (ISBN 0-440-03947-9). Delacorte.

Ice-Cream War. William Boyd. LC 82-20813. (Illus.). 1983. 13.95 (ISBN 0-688-01904-8). Morrow.

Ice Crown. Andre Norton, pseud. 224p. 1981. pap. 2.25 (ISBN 0-441-35843-8). Ace Bks.

Ice Dragon. Jeffrey Lord. (Blade Ser., No. 10). (Orig.). 1974. pap. 1.50 (ISBN 0-523-40440-9). Pinnacle Bks.

Ice Dragon. Jeffrey Lord. (Richard Blade series,#10). 1974. (pbk.) 0.95 (ISBN 0-523-00355-2). Pinnacle Books.

Ice Falcon. R. Richie. 3.95 o.p. (21110). G&D.

Ice from Space. David Houston. (Tales of Tomorrow Ser.: No. 4). 208p. (Orig.). 1982. pap. 2.25 o.s.i. (ISBN 0-8439-1132-8, Leisure Bks). Nordon Pubns.

Ice Goddess. Paul Edwards. LC 74-9345. 1974. (pbk.) 0.95 (ISBN 0-515-03336-7). Pyramid Books.

Ice Harvest. Orvel L. Trainer. LC 72-161830. 1971. 5.95 (ISBN 0-87108-046-X). Pruett Pub. Co.

Ice in Egypt. A. M MacCrindle. LC 31-32957. 1931. W. Morrow & Co.

Ice in His Veins. Carole Mortimer. (Harlequin Presents Ser.). 192p. 1981. pap. 1.50 (ISBN 0-373-10437-5, Pub. by Harlequin). PB.

Ice in the Bedroom. Pelham Grenville Wodehouse. LC 61-5849. 1961. Simon and Schuster.

Ice Is Breaking. Leonard Stromberg & Alexis, Joseph Emanuel Alexander, Tr. LC 26-2180. Midwest Book Company.

Ice Is Coming. Patricia Wrightson. Date not set. pap. 2.25 (ISBN 0-345-29485-8, Del Rey). Ballantine.

Ice King. Daniel Casolaro. LC 81-52154. 168p. 1981. 8.95 (ISBN 0-87426-052-3). Whitmore.

Ice-King: Or, The Fate of the Lost Steamer. A Fanciful Tale of the Far North. Also Not in Despair, for I've a Friden. A Lesson of Life. Edward Zane Carroll Judson. LC 7-11447. 1848. G. H. Williams.

Ice Maiden. Sally Wentworth. (Harlequin Romances Ser.). (Orig.). 1980. pap. 1.25 (ISBN 0-373-02310-3, Pub. by Harlequin). PB.

Ice Man. Wynn L Morgan. (Dell book). 1979. 1.95 (ISBN 0-440-14043-9). Dell Pub. Co.

Ice Mirror. Charles MacHardy. LC 72-79633. 1972. 6.50. St. Martin's Press.

Ice Never F. Gil Orlovitz. LC 70-494994. 360p. 1979. 15.00 (ISBN 0-7145-0281-2, Pub. by M Boyars). Merrimack Pub Cir.

Ice Palace. Edna Ferber. LC 58-5936. 1958. Doubleday.

Ice People. Rene Barjavel. LC 78-135150. 1973. 1.25. New York.

Ice People. Rene Barjavel. LC 78-135150. 1971. 5.95. Morrow.

Ice Pick. John Baldwin. LC 82-14369. 1983. 12.50 (ISBN 0-688-00679-5). Morrow.

Ice Pilot. Henry Leverage. LC 21-2388. 1921. Doubleday, Page & Company.

Ice Saints. Frank Tuohy. LC 64-20616. 1964. Scribner.

Ice Schooner: A Tale. Michael Moorcock. LC 76-47249. 1977. 7.95 (ISBN 0-06-013006-7). Harper & Row.

Ice Station Zebra. Alistair MacLean. LC 63-17272. 1963. Doubleday.

Ice Towers. Duncan McGeary. 208p. (Orig.). 1982. pap. 2.25 (ISBN 0-505-51774-4). Tower Bks.

Ice War. 1978. pap. write for info. (ISBN 0-88074-009-4). Metagam.

Iceberg. Clive Cussler. LC 75-11859. 1975. 6.95 (ISBN 0-396-07185-6). Dodd, Mead.

Iceberg. Robyn Donald. (Harlequin Romances Ser.). 192p. 1981. pap. 1.50 (ISBN 0-373-02437-1). Harlequin Bks.

Icebound. W. F. Roscoe. LC 53-12153. (Illus.). 1954. Vantage Press.

Icebreaker. John Gardner. 304p. 1983. 10.95 (ISBN 0-399-12811-5, Putnam). Putnam Pub Group.

Icebreaker. John E Gardner. LC 82-21614. 10.95 (ISBN 0-399-12811-5). Putnam.

Iceland Fisherman. Julien Viaud & De Koven, Anna (Farwell) "Mrs. Reginald De Koven," 1860- Tr. (Half-title: Laurel crowned tales). 1899. A. C. McClurg and Company.

Iceland Fisherman. Julien Viaud & Endore, S. Guy, 1901- Tr. LC 46-7451. (Borzoi books for young people). 1946. A. A. Knopf.

Iceland Fisherman: Tr. from the French by Pierre Loti Pseud... 159th ed. Julien Viaud. Tr. by Dole, Mrs. Helen James (Bennett) LC 8-29996. 1896. T. Y. Crowell & Company.

Iceland Fisherman: Tr. from the French of Pierre Loti Pseud. with a Critical Introduction. Julien Viaud. LC 3-8442. (Half-title: A century of French romance. Parisian ed. vol. xx). 1902. D. Appleton & Co.

Iceland Fisherman: Tr. from the French of Pierre Loti Pseud. Julien Viaud & Melcon, H. A., Tr. LC 1-14003. (On cover: The Home library). 1901. A. L. Burt.

Icelandic Short Stories. Ed. by Evelyn Scherabon Firchow. LC 74-8735. (Library of Scandinavian Literature, V. 26). 1975. (ISBN 0-8057-3314-0). Twayne Publishers.

Iceman: A Novel. Weldon Hill, pseud. LC 76-15607. 1976. 8.95 (ISBN 0-688-03071-8). Morrow.

Iceman, No. Five: Spinning Target. Joseph Nazel. (Orig.). 1974. pap. 1.50 (ISBN 0-87067-457-9, BH457). Holloway.

Iceman, No. Four: Sunday Fix. Joseph Nazel. (Orig.). 1974. pap. 1.50 (ISBN 0-87067-454-4, BH454). Holloway.

Iceman, No. One: Billion Dollar Death. Joseph Nazel. (Orig.). pap. 1.50 (ISBN 0-87067-440-4, BH440). Holloway.

Iceman, No. Seven: The Shakedown. Joseph Nazel. (Orig.). 1975. pap. 1.50 (ISBN 0-87067-475-7, BH475). Holloway.

Iceman, No. Six: Canadian Kill. Joseph Nazel. (Orig.). 1974. pap. 1.50 (ISBN 0-87067-462-5, BH462). Holloway.

Iceman, No. Three: Slick Revenge. Joseph Nazel. (Orig.). pap. 1.50 (ISBN 0-87067-452-8, BH452). Holloway.

Iceman, No. Two: The Golden Shaft. Joseph Nazel. (Orig.). pap. 1.50 (ISBN 0-87067-442-0, BH442). Holloway.

Icepick. Aaron Fletcher. 208p. 1982. pap. 2.25 (ISBN 0-8439-1026-7, Leisure Bks). Nordon Pubns.

Icepick: A Novel About Life and Death in a Maximum Security Prison. Bruce Dobler. LC 74-10885. 1974. 7.95 (ISBN 0-316-18915-4). Little, Brown.

Icequake. Richard Moran. LC 82-6398. 1982. 12.00 (ISBN 0-688-01147-0). Morrow.

Icerigger. Alan Dean Foster. 1978. pap. 2.25 (ISBN 0-345-29454-8, Del Rey Bks). Ballantine.

Icerigger. Alan Dean Foster. 1974. (pbk.) 1.25. Ballantine Books.

Iceworld. Hal Clement. 1970. pap. 0.95 o.p. (ISBN 0-447-75128-X). Lancer.

Iceworld. Hal Clement. 1973. pap. 0.95 o.s.i. (75-422). Lancer.

Iceworld: By Hal Clement Pseud. 1st Ed. Harry C Stubbs. LC 53-95472. 1953. Gnome Press.

Ich Ohne Gewaehr: Gegenwartsautoren Aus der Schweiz. Gerda Zeltner. (Ger.). 1980. pap. 13.00 (ISBN 3-288-04743-8, Pub. by Suhrkamp Verlag Germany). Suhrkamp.

Icicle Heart. Jessica Steele. (Harlequin Romance). 1979. pap. 1.25 (ISBN 0-373-02297-2, Pub. by Harlequin). PB.

I'd Do It Again. Frank Tilsley. LC 36-18204. 1936. Dodd, Mead & Company.

Id of the Squid. Arch E. Benthic, pseud. LC 79-129864. 120p. 4.95. Compass Va.

I'd Rather Fight Than Swish. Troy Conway, pseud. (Coxeman Ser). (Orig.). 1969. pap. 0.75 o.p. (ISBN 0-446-64671-7, 64-671). Paperback Lib.

Ida. Ardelle Allen. LC 79-17461. 96p. (Orig.). 1979. pap. 3.95 (ISBN 0-89621-040-5). Thorndike Pr.

Ida: A Novel. Gertrude Stein. LC 72-692. 1972. 1.65 (ISBN 0-394-71797-X). Vintage Books.

Ida: A Novel. Gertrude Stein. LC 41-4374. Random House.

Ida, a Novel. Gertrude Stein. LC 77-147315. 1971. Repr. of 1941 ed. 20.00x (ISBN 0-8154-0378-X). Cooper Sq.

Ida; an Adventure in Morocco. A Novel. Mabel Collins Cook. LC 6-8660. (On cover: Lovell's international series, no. 74). J. W. Lovell Company.

Ida Brandt. Herman Joachim Bang. Tr. by Arthur G. Chater. LC 28-25957. 1928. A. A. Knopf.

Ida Chaloner's Heart: Or, The Husband's Trial. Lucy Randall Comfort. LC 6-30662. (On cover: The library of American authors, no. 12). 1889. G. Munro.

Ida Elisabeth. Sigrid Undset & Chater, Arthur G., Tr. LC 33-25685. 1933. A. A. Knopf.

Ida Goldwin: Or, The Perils of Fortune. Aleck Derby. LC 6-33973. 1876. R. M. De Witt.

Ida May: A Story of Things Actual and Possible. Mary Hayden Green Pike. LC 72-6534. (Black Heritage Library Collection). 1972. (ISBN 0-8369-9171-0). Books for Libraries Press.

Ida May: A Story of Things Actual and Possible. Mary Hayden Green Pike. LC 7-35894. 1855. Phillips, Sampson and Company.

Ida Norman: Or, Trials and Their Uses. Almira Hart Lincoln Phelps. LC 7-36083. 1848. Cushing & Brother.

Ida Norman: Or, Trials and Their Uses. Almira Hart Lincoln Phelps. LC 7-36082. 1854. Sheldon, Lamport & Blakeman.

Ida Norton: Or, Life at Chautauqua. H. H Moore. LC 14-19354. 1878. M. Bailey.

Ida Throws a Whing Ding: Illustrated by Bob Buckingham and Arthur Ingalls. Ada L Clendenen. LC 53-103432. 1953. Crosing Pub. Co.

Ida Vane. A Tale of the Restoration. Andrew B. A Reed. (Seaside library, v. 48, no. 980). 1881. G. Munro.

Ida Wears the Britches. Ada L Clendenen. LC 52-9683. 1952. Vantage Press.

Idaho. Paul Evan Lehman. LC 33-14288. The Macaulay Company.

Idaho & Only the Brave. Paul Evan Lehman. 1979. pap. 2.25 o.s.i. (ISBN 0-505-51429-X). Tower Bks.

Idaho Raiders. Thomas Albert Curry. 1973. pap. 0.75 o.p. Curtis.

Idalia: A Novel. Louise De La Ramee. LC 6-33322. 1867. J. B. Lippincott & Co.

Idalia: A Novel. Louise De La Ramee. LC 6-33321. 1881. J. B. Lippincott & Co.

I.D.B. in South Africa. Louise Vescelius-Sheldon. LC 8-509795. J. W. Lovell Company.

Iddo: An Historical Sketch, Illustrating Jewish History, During the Times of the Maccabees. B. C. 167-150. LC 7-88492. America Sunday-School Union.

Idea of the Canterbury Tales. Donald R. Howard. LC 74-81433. 400p. 1976. 30.00x (ISBN 0-520-02816-3); pap. 5.95 (ISBN 0-520-03492-9). U of Cal Pr.

Ideal Age. Noel Bertram Gerson. LC 58-6232. 1958. Beacon Press.

Ideal Age. Cynthia Ann Vautier. LC 58-6232. 1958. Beacon Press.

Ideal Attained: Being the Story of Two Steadfast Souls, and How They Won Their Happiness and Lost It Not. Eliza Woodson Burhans Farnham. LC 6-38665. 1865. C. M. Plumb & Co.

Ideal Christian Life. William Harrison Norton. LC 10-2507. 1909. 1.00. The Index Printing Company.

Ideal City. Cosimo Noto. LC 70-154454. (Utopian Literature Ser). 1971. Repr. of 1903 ed. 22.00 (ISBN 0-405-03536-5). Ayer Co.

Ideal Fanatic. Hester Edwards Porch. LC 7-37784. 1883. H. A. Sumner & Company.

Ideal Love: A Novel. Charlotte Mary Brame. (On cover: Eagle library. no. 119). Street & Smith.

Ideal Love: A Novel. Bertha M. Clay. LC 44-38096. (On cover: Eagle library, no. 119). Street & Smith.

Ideal Republic: Or, Way Out of the Fog. Corwin Phelps. LC 7-36081. (American politics. no. 10). 1896. W. L. Raynolds.

Ideala. Sarah Grand. LC 35-33414. Optimus Printing Company.

Idealia, a Utopia Dream: Or, Resthaven. Harriet Alfarata Thompson. LC 23-3216. Printed by J. B. Lyon Company.

Idealist. Heber Sensenig. LC 40-11105. Dorrance and Company.

Ideals: A Book of Farce & Comedy. Evelyn Scott. LC 27-24572. 1927. A. & C. Boni.

Idelette: A Novel Based on the Life of Madame John Calvin. Edna Gerstner. LC 63-9313. 1963. Zondervan Pub. House.

Identical Strangers. Violet Hawthorne. 1975. (pbk.) 0.95 (ISBN 0-345-26709-5). Ballantine Books.

Identity Card. Fereidoun M. Esfandiary. 1968. pap. 1.25 o.p. (B182). Grove.

Identity Card: A Novel, by F. M. Esfandiary. Fereidoun M Esfandiary. LC 66-231856. (Evergreen black cat ed., B-182). 1968. pap., 1.25. Grove Pr.

Identity Crisis. Lorraine Latham. LC 74-32414. 1975. 6.95 (ISBN 0-688-02906-X). Morrow.

Identity Matrix. Jack L. Chalker. (Orig.). 1982. pap. 2.95 (ISBN 0-671-44481-6). PB.

Identity of Dr. Frazier. George Skiar. LC 61-13491. 1961. Knopf.

Identity of Douglas Bain. Charles Francis Stocking. LC 28-172073. 1928. The Maestro Co.

Identity Seven. Robert Lory. 1974. (pbk.) 0.95. DAW Books.

Identity; Stories for This Generation. Ed. by Katherine Hondius. LC 66-10821. 1966. 2.95. Scott, Foresman.

Identity Unknown. Newman, Robert. LC 45-4852. 1945. Ziff-Davis Publishing Company.

Ides of August: A Novel. William Converse Haygood. LC 56-9254. 1956. World Pub. Co.

Ides of March. Florence Willingham Pickard. LC 99-2588. (On cover: Neely's popular library. no. 138). 1899. F. T. Neely.

Ides of March. Florence Willingham Pickard. LC 4-2540. Broadway Publishing Company.

Ides of March. Gertrude M. Robins Reynolds. LC 7-39613. J. W. Lovell Company.

Ides of March. Thornton Niven Wilder. (Bard book). 1975. (pbk.) 1.75. Avon.

Ides of March. Thornton Niven Wilder. LC 48-647. 1948. Harper.

Ides of March Conspiracy. Clyde Matthews. LC 80-83593. 320p. 1981. pap. 2.75 (ISBN 0-87216-789-5). Playboy Pbks.

Ides of March Conspiracy: The IRS Got What It Deserves. Clyde Matthews. 1981. 2.75 (ISBN 0-87216-789-5). Playbook Paperbacks.

Ides of March Conspiracy: The Year the IRS Got What It Deserves. Clyde Matthews. LC 78-57331. 9.95 (ISBN 0-87795-201-9). Arbor House.

Ides of November. Florence Stevenson. 1975. (pbk.) 0.95. New American Library.

Ides of Tomorrow: Original Science Fiction Tales of Horror. Ed. by Terry Carr. LC 76-24866. 6.95 (ISBN 0-316-12970-4). Little, Brown.

Idess of March. Thornton Niven Wilder. LC 57-13644. (Grosset's universal library, UL 13). 1957. Grosset & Dunlap.

Idiot. John Kendrick Bangs. LC 6-6127. 1895. Harper & Brothers.

Idiot. Fedor Mikhailovich Dostoevskii. LC 65-6640. 1965. Washington Square Press.

Idiot. Fedor Mikhailovich Dostoevskii. LC 79-75218. (Signet books, CQ442). 1969. 0.95. New American Library.

Idiot. Fedor Mikhailovich Dostoevskii. Tr. by Constance Black Garnett. LC 49-784. 1948. Macmillan.

Idiot. Fedor Mikhailovich Dostoevskii. Tr. by Eva M. Martin. 1953. 5.00x o.p. (ISBN 0-460-00682-7, E682, Evman); pap. 2.50 o.p. (ISBN 0-460-01682-2, Evman). Biblio Dist.

Idiot, 2 vols. Fedor Mikhailovich Dostoevskii. 709p. 8.45 (ISBN 0-8285-0955-7, Pub. by Progress Pubs USSR). Imported Pubns.

Idiot. Fedor Mikhailovich Dostoevskii. (Classic Ser.). 1969. pap. 2.50 (ISBN 0-451-51618-4, CE1618, Sig Classics). NAL.

Idiot. Fedor Mikhailovich Dostoevskii. Tr. by David Magarshack. (Classics Ser.). (Orig.). pap. 4.95 (ISBN 0-14-044054-2). Penguin.

Idiot. Fedor Mikhailovich Dostoevskii. Tr. by John W. Strahan. (O.s.i.). (Orig.). (YA) (gr. 9-12). pap. 1.25 o.s.i. (ISBN 0-671-48122-3). WSP.

Idiot. Fedor Mikhailovich Dostoevskii. Tr. by Constance Garnett. LC 82-42864. 10.95 (ISBN 0-394-60434-2). Modern Lib.

Idiot. Fedor Mikhailovich Dostoevskii & Martin, Eva M., Ed. (Half-title: Everyman's library, ed. by Ernest Rhys. Fiction. no. 682). 1914. J. M. Dent & Sons, Ltd.

Idiot. Fyodor Mikhailovich Dostoevskii & Robinson, Boardman, 1876- Illus. (Half-title: The Modern library of the world's best books. Modern library giants). 1942. The Modern Library.

Idiot. Fedor Dostoyevsky. (Modern Library Giants). 4.95 o.p. (ISBN 0-394-60760-0, G60). Modern Lib.

Idiot: A Novel in Four Parts. Fedor Mikhailovich Dostoevskii. Tr. by Constance Black Garnett. LC 13-17100. (Half-title: The novels of Fyodor Dostoevsky. vol. II). 1913. The Macmillan Company.

Idiot: A Novel in Four Parts. Fedor Mikhailovich Dostoevskii. Tr. by Constance Black Garnett. Robinson, Boardman, 1876- Illus. LC 35-19677. 1935. Random House.

Idiot: A Novel in Four Parts. The Translation by Constance Garnett Rev. & Edited for This Ed., with an Introd., by Avrahm Yarmolinsky and Illustrated with Wood-Engravings by Fritz Eichenberg. Fedor Mikhailovich Dostoevskii. LC 56-4466. 1956. Heritage Press.

Idiot: A Novel in Four Parts. The Translation by Constance Garnett Rev. & Edited for This Ed., with an Introd., by Avrahm Yakolre-Kh&- Illustrated with Wood-Engravings by Fritz Eichenberg; for the Members of the Limited Editions Club. Fedor Mikhailovich Dostoevskii. Tr. by Constance Black Garnett. LC 56-14084. 1956.

Idiot at Home. John Kendrick Bangs. LC 5649. 1900. Harper & Brothers.

Idiots First. Bernard Malamud. (Delta bk. 3946). 1965. pap., 1.45. Dell.

Idiots First. Bernard Malamud. LC 63-19562. 1975. (pbk.) 1.75 (ISBN 0-671-78810-8). Pocket Books.

Idle Born: A Comedy of Manners. Hobart Chatfield Chatfield-Taylor & De Koven, Reginald I. E. Henry Louis Reginald. LC 2-21099. 1900. H. S. Stone and Company.

Idle Dreams of an Idle Day. Henry Elliot Harman. LC 18-10308. 1.00. The State Company.

Idle Hands. Edward Charles. LC 36-6316. 1936. Lothrop, Lee and Shepard Company.

Idle Hands. Janet Ayer Fairbank. LC 27-10464. The Bobbs-Merrill Company.

Idle Hands. William O'Rourke. (O.s.i.). 1981. 12.95 o.s.i. (ISBN 0-440-04064-7). Delacorte.

Idle Hands. William O'Rourke. 1982. pap. 2.95 (ISBN 0-440-13945-7). Dell.

Idle Hands: A Novel. William O'Rourke. LC 80-21918. 10.95 (ISBN 0-440-04064-7). Delacorte Press.

Idle Hours of a Busy Lawyer. Robert Mandiville Peadro. LC 10-4641. 1.00. The Shelby County Leader.

Idle Husband. Mary Alden Hopkins. LC 33-6787. 1933. R. M. McBride & Company.

Idle Island. Ethel Powelson Hueston. LC 27-5082. The Bobbs-Merrill Company.

Idle Moments in Florida. George Vere Hobart. LC 21-5483. George H. Doran Company.

Idle Pleasures. George Alec Effinger. 208p. 1983. pap. 2.25 (ISBN 0-425-05744-5). Berkley Pub.

Idle Rainbow. Helen Partridge. LC 36-19022. Arcadia House.

Idle Thoughts of an Idle Fellow. Jerome Klapka Jerome. 144p. 1982. pap. text ed. 4.25x (ISBN 0-86299-009-2, Pub. by Sutton England). Humanities.
Idle Time Tales... Tr. by Oscar Albert Bierstadt. Balzac, Honore De et al. LC 7-11680. (Globe Library 013.Vol. 1, No. 150). (On cover: Globe library. v. 1, no. 150). 1891. Rand, McNally & Company.
Idle Wives. James Oppenheim. LC 14-756150. 1914. 1.30. The Century Co.
Idle Women. Dorothy Black. LC 28-25632. 1928. J. B. Lippincott Company.
Idlers. Morley Roberts. LC 6-7397. 1906. L. C. Page & Company.
Idlers' Gate: La Porte Des Faineants. John Winch. LC 32-29094. 1932. W. Morrow & Company.
Idol. David Benjamin. LC 78-12844. 10.95 (ISBN 0-399-12287-7). Putnam.
Idol. Pauline Cassin Caro. LC 17-6108. (With Haggard, H. Rider. Nada the lily. New York, 1894). 1894. P. F. Collier.
Idol for Others. Gordon Merrick. 1977. pap. 2.95 (ISBN 0-380-00971-4, 78667). Avon.
Idol from Passa. Kurt Mahr. (Perry Rhodan # 98). 1976. 1.25. Ace Books.
Idol Hunter. Barry Unsworth. LC 80-14989. 10.95 (ISBN 0-671-25357-3). Simon and Schuster.
Idol Hunter. large print ed. Barry Unsworth. LC 81-5341. 10.95 (ISBN 0-89621-284-X). Thorndike Press.
Idol-Maker: A Novel. Emily Frances Adeline Sergeant. LC 8-6851. (Appleton's Town & Country Library: No. 202). 1896. D. Appleton and Company.
Idol of Paris: A Romance. Sarah Bernhardt. Tr. by Tongue, Mary. LC 22-5071. 1922. 1.75. The Macaulay Company.
Idol of the Blind: A Novel. Tom Gallon. LC 99-5227. 1899. D. Appleton and Company.
Idolaters: A Novel. William Hegner. LC 72-96816. 1973. 8.95 (ISBN 0-671-27105-9). Trident Press.
Idolaters: A Novel by Dale Collins. Dale Collins. LC 29-16855. 1929. Little, Brown, and Company.
Idolatry. Alice Robinson Perrin. 1909. Duffield & Company.
Idolatry: A Romance. Julian Hawthorne. LC 7-3893. 1874. J. R. Sogood and Company.
Idols. Dennis Cooper. LC 79-66660. 1979. pap. 4.95. Sea Horse.
Idols. 3d ed. William John Locke. LC 5-9718. (Half-title: Canvasback library of popular fiction, vol. xx). 1904. J. Lane.
Idols. William John Locke. LC 20-15617. 1911. John Lane Company.
Idols and Axle Grease. Francis Irby Gwaltney. LC 74-32305. (Illus.). 1975. 8.95 (ISBN 0-8161-6268-9). G. K. Hall.
Idols and Axle Grease. Francis Irby Gwaltney. LC 73-22658. (Illus.). 1974. 5.95. Bobbs-Merrill.
Idols and the Prey. 1st Ed. John B L Goodwin. LC 53-536954. 1953. Harper.
Idols of the Cave. Frederic Prokosch. LC 78-178788. 1973. 14.75 (ISBN 0-8371-6289-0). Greenwood Press.
Idols of the Cave. Frederic Prokosch. LC 46-754545. 1946. Doubleday & Company, Inc.
Idols: Or, The Secret of the Rue Chausee D'Antin. Tr. from the French of Raoul De Navery Pseud. Marie De Saffron David & Sadlier, Anna Theresa. LC 22-4748. 1882. Benziger Brothers.
Idomen: Or, The Vale of Yumuri,. Maria Gowen Brooks. LC 6-19383. 1843. S. Colman.
Idonea. Anne Beale. (On cover: Seaside library. Pocket ed., no. 188). G. Munro.
Idonia: A Romance of Old London. Arthur Frederick Wallis. LC 13-24827. 1914. Little, Brown, and Company.
Idu. Flora Nwapa. (African Writers Ser.). 1970. pap. text ed. 3.00x (ISBN 0-435-90056-0). Heinemann Ed.
Iduna, and Other Stories. George Abiah Hibbard. LC 72-4472. (Short story index reprint series). 1972. (ISBN 0-8369-4178-0). Books for Libraries Press.
Iduna, and Other Stories. George Abiah Hibbard. LC 7-4753. (Half-title: Harper's Franklin square library. no. 706. Extra.). 1891. Harper & Brothers.
Iduna: And Other Stories. George Abiah Hibbard. LC 72-4472. (Short Story Index Reprint Ser). Repr. of 1891 ed. 18.00 (ISBN 0-8369-4178-0). Ayer Co.
Iduna's Universe: Dumarest of Terra. E. C. Tubb. (Science Fiction Ser.). (Orig.). 1979. pap. 1.75 o.p. (ISBN 0-87997-500-8, UE1500). Daw Bks.
Idwymon: A Story of Napoleonic Complications, Orleans and Bourbonic Entanglements... Frederick Alanson Randle. LC 8-222. 1895. G. W. Dillingham.
Idyl of the Wabash: And Other Stories. Anna Nicholas. LC 98-1057. 1899. The Bowen-Merrill Company.
Idyl of Twin Fires. Walter Prichard Eaton. LC 15-7366. 1915. 1.35. Doubleday, Page & Company.
Idyl of Twin Fires. Walter Prichard Eaton. LC 24-25741. W. A. Wilde Company.
Idyl of War-Times. William Chambers Bartlett. LC 6-9413. 1890. L. Vanderpoole Publishing Company.
Idyll in the Desert. William Faulkner. LC 32-1098. 1931. Random House.
Idyll of All Fools' Day. Josephine Dodge Daskam Bacon. 1908. Dodd, Mead and Company.
Idyll of the White Lotus. Mabel Collins. LC 74-7341. 128p. 1974. pap. 1.25 (ISBN 0-8356-0301-6, Quest). Theos Pub Hse.
Idyll of the White Lotus. Mabel Collins. 1974. pap. 1.25 o.p. (ISBN 0-515-03504-1, V3504). BJ Pub Group.
Idyll of the White Lotus. Mabel Collins. LC 74-7341. 1974. (pbk.) 1.25 (ISBN 0-515-03504-1). Pyramid Books.
Idyll of the White Lotus. Mabel Collins Cook. LC 74-7341. (Re-quest books). 1974. 1.25 (ISBN 0-8356-0301-6). Published by Pyramid Publications for the Theosophical Pub. House.
Idyll of the White Lotus. Mabel Collins Cook. LC 6-28082. J. W. Lovell Company.
Idyll of the White Lotus. Mabel Collins Cook. LC 1-29458. 1900. The Metaphysical Publishing Company.
Idyll of the White Lotus. Mabel Collins Cook. LC 7-32157. 1907. Theosophical Publishing Co.
Idyll's End. Jean Schopfer. LC 30-259093. 1930. Dodd, Mead & Company.
Idylls of the King. Alfred L. Tennyson. (gr. 10-12). pap. 0.95 o.p. (TR708). WSP.
Idylls of the King: Selections. Ed. by Allan Knee. Bd. with Camelot. 1967. pap. 2.50 (ISBN 0-440-93948-8, LE). Dell.
Idylls of the Queen. Phyllis Ann Karr. 352p. (Orig.). 1982. pap. 2.95 (ISBN 0-441-35848-9). Ace Bks.
Idylls of the Sea. Frank Thomas Bullen. LC 71-98564. (Short story index reprint series). 1969. Books for Libraries Press.
Idylls of the Sea. Frank Thomas Bullen. LC 2-28409. 1899. D. Appleton and Company.
Idyls of the Gass. Martha Wolfenstein. LC 74-94748. (Short story index reprint series). 1969. (ISBN 0-8369-3128-9). Books for Libraries Press.
Idyls of the Gass. Martha Wolfenstein. LC 1-27069. 1901. The Jewish Publication Society of American.
Iermola. Jozef Ignacy Kraszewski. Tr. by Carey, M. LC 7-14165. Dodd, Mead and Company.
Iesat Nassar: The Story of the Life of Jesus the Nazarene, by Peter F. Mamreov, Anna F. Mamreov and B. A. F. Mamreov. Peter Von Finkelstein B Mamreov. LC 57-9480. 1957. Meador Pub. Co.
Iesht Nassar: The Story of the Life of Jesus the Nazarene. Peter Von Finkelstein Mamreov & Mamreov, Anna F., Joint Author. LC 7-24358. 1895. Sunrise Publishing Company.
If?--the Pen! Ruth Clifford Young. LC 48-8833. 1948. Exposition Press.
If a Body. George Worthing Yates. LC 41-2819. 1941. W. Morrow & Company.
If a Body. George Worthing Yates. LC 42-25899. 1942. Triangle Books.
If a Body Kill a Body. Peter Mortimer, pseud. LC 46-598. 1946. Mystery House.
If a Body Meet a Body. George Malcolm-Smith. LC 59-7968. 1959. Published for the Crime Club by Doubleday.
If a Lion Could Talk. Mildred Walker, pseud. LC 75-124832. 1970. Harcourt Brace Jovanovich.
If a Man Answers; a Novel. 1st Ed. Winifred Wolfe. LC 61-9207. 1961. Doubleday.
If a Man Be Born. H L Swanson. LC 51-10070. 1951. Vantage Press.
If After Every Tempest... Paul Eldridge. LC 41-10771. Harbinger House.
If All Else Fails... Craig Strete. LC 79-7117. 1980. 8.95 (ISBN 0-385-15237-X). Doubleday.
If All the Rebels Die. Samuel B Southwell. LC 66-122145. 5.95. Doubleday.
If Any Man Sin. Hiram Alfred Cody. LC 15-16443. 1.25. George H. Doran Company.
If Anything. Martha Swearingen. LC 79-25965. 8.95. Elsevier/Nelson Books.
If Anything Should Happen to Me. Albert Baker. (Orig.). 1973. pap. 0.95 o.p. Curtis.
If Beale Street Could Talk. James B. Baldwin. LC 74-1161. 1974. 6.95 (ISBN 0-8037-4169-3). Dial Press.
If Beale Street Could Talk. James B. Baldwin. LC 74-1161. (Signet book). 1975. (pbk.) 1.95. New American Library.
If Birds Are Free. Evelyn Wilde Mayerson. LC 80-7864. 10.95 (ISBN 0-690-01890-8). Lippincott & Crowell.
If Chance a Stranger. Charles Fullerton. LC 57-12520. 1958. W. Sloane Associates.
If Cows Could Talk. May Neatherlin. LC 58-594572. 1958. Naylor Co.
If David Knew: A Novel. Frances Aymar Mathews. LC 10-228002. 1.50. G. W. Dillingham Company.
If Death Ever Slept: A Nero Wolfe Novel. Rex Stout. LC 57-12614. 1957. Viking Press.
If Dreams Came True. (Illus.). 4.95 (ISBN 0-910550-39-5). Centurion Pr.
If Dreams Come True. Alice Mary Ross Colver. LC 25-6196. 1925. The Penn Publishing Company.
If He Can Make Her So. Haniel Long. (Illus.). 85p. 1968. 6.00; pap. 3.00. Frontier Press Calif.
If He Hollers Let Him Go. Chester B Himes. LC 45-10120. 1945. Doubleday, Doran & Company, Inc.
If I Come Home: A Novel. Nellise Child. LC 74-29041. (Labor Movement in Fiction and Non-Fiction). 1977. 21.50 (ISBN 0-404-58522-1). AMS Press.
If I Come Home: A Novel. Nellise Child. LC 43-15967. 1943. Doubleday, Doran and Co., Inc.
If I Could Sleep Deeply Enough. Vassar Miller. 1974. 6.95 (ISBN 0-87140-607-1); pap. 2.50 (ISBN 0-87140-291-2). Liveright.
If I Die Before I Wake. Raymond Sherwood King. LC 38-7789. 1938. Simon and Schuster.
If I Die in a Combat Zone, Box Me up & Send Me Home. Tim O'Brien. (O.s.i.). 1973. 8.95 o.s.i. (ISBN 0-440-03853-7). Delacorte.
If I Don't Find Pleasure I Will Die. Roger W. Langton. 1977. pap. 2.00 (ISBN 0-916296-04-0). Poor Souls Pr.
If I Don't Tell: A Novel. Donald Olson. LC 75-43768. 6.95 (ISBN 0-399-11722-9). Putnam.
If I Forget Thee. Robert S DeRopp. LC 56-10008. 1956. St. Martin's Press.
If I Found a Wistful Unicorn. Ann Ashford. LC 78-59094. (Illus.). 1978. 8.95 (ISBN 0-931948-00-2). Peachtree Pubs.
If I Had a Million. Robert Douglas Andrews, pseud. LC 40-14070. 1940. Triangle Books.
If I Have Four Apples. Josephine Lawrence. LC 36-213. 1935. Frederick A. Stokes Company.
If I Knew What I Was Doing... Arthur D Goldstein. LC 74-6321. 1974. 5.95 (ISBN 0-394-49092-4). Random House.
If I Knew What I Was Doing... Albert Ross. LC 74-6321. 1974. 5.95 o.p. (ISBN 0-394-49092-4). Random.
If I Know What I Mean. Elsie Janis. LC 25-21519. 1925. G. P. Putnam's Sons.
If I Loved You Less. Vivien Grey. LC 46-500394. 1946. Arcadia House, Inc.
If I Make My Bed in Hell. John B Porter. LC 69-20234. 1969. 4.95. Word Books.
If I Should Die Before I Wake. Jerry Allen Potter. 256p. 1981. pap. 2.50 (ISBN 0-445-04691-0). Popular Lib.
If I Should Murder. Amelia Reynolds Long. LC 45-1390. 1945. Phoenix Press.
If I Were a Cricket... Kazue Mizumura. (Illus.). 1973. 4.50. T. Y. Crowell.
If I Were a Man" The Story of a New-Southerner. Harrison Robertson. LC 99-1059. (The ivory series). 1899. C. Scribner's Sons.
If I Were King. Justin Huntly McCarthy. 1901. R. H. Russell.
If I Were King. Justin Huntly McCarthy. LC 21-102601. Harper & Brothers.
If I Were You. Julien Green. Tr. by McEwen, John Hellas F. LC 49-7294. 1949. Harper.
If I Were You. Pelham Grenville Wodehouse. LC 31-28055. 1931. Doubleday, Doran & Company, Inc.
If I Were You. Pelham Grenville Wodehouse. LC 35-28586. 1932. A. L. Burt Company.
If Israel Lost the War. Richard Z. Chesnoff & Edward Klein. LC 68-23376. (Illus.). 1969. 5.95. Coward-McCann.
If It Could Be. 1st Ed. Thelma Faulkner. LC 36-550119. 1956. Vantage Press.
If It Moves, Salute It. Bob Duncan. 1969. pap. 0.75 o.p. (ISBN 0-446-64218-5, 64-218). Paperback Lib.
If It Prove Fair Weather. Isabel Bowler Paterson. LC 40-12035. G. P. Putnam's Sons.
If It Really Were a Film. Dorrit Willumsen. Tr. by Anne M. Rasmussen. Orig. Title: Hvis Det Virkelig Var en Film. 126p. (Orig.). 1982. pap. 6.00 (ISBN 0-915306-35-2). Curbstone.
If It Returns with Scars... Arthur Raymond Macdougall. LC 42-21651. 1942. A. R. Macdougall, Jr.
If It Returns with Scars: Dud Dean Stories. Arthur Raymond Macdougall. LC 81-9293. 1981. 5.95 (ISBN 0-89621-065-0). Thorndike Press.
If It Takes All Summer" The Life Story of Ulysses Grant. Elizabeth Frances Corbett. LC 30-5696. 1930. Frederick A. Stokes Company.
If It's God Yer Tryin T' Understand. Steve Welp. 43p. 1978. pap. 2.25 o.p. Hse of One Pub.
If It's Raining This Must Be the Weekend. Nancy Stahl. 1980. pap. 2.25 (ISBN 0-425-04460-2). Berkley Pub.
If Laurel Shot Hardy the World Would End. Stanton Forbes, pseud. LC 70-103745. 1970. 4.50. Published for the Crime Club by Doubleday.
If Life Is a Bowl of Cherries, What Am I Doing in the Pits? Erma Bombeck. 1979. pap. 2.50 (ISBN 0-449-23894-6, Crest). Fawcett.
If Love Be Love: A Forest Idyl. D. Cecil Gibbs. (Harper's handy series, no. 74). 1886. Harper & Brothers.
If Love Be Love. A Forest Idyl. D Cecil Gibbs. (On cover: Seaside library. Pocket ed., no. 807). 1886. G. Munro.
If Love Be Love, the Cave of the White Rose: The Taming of Lisa. Flora Kidd. (Harlequin Romances Ser.). 576p. 1982. pap. 3.50 (ISBN 0-373-20059-5). Harlequin Bks.
If Love Comes. Gladys Malvern. LC 32-12125. C. Kendall.
If Love I Must... Katharine Newlin Burt. LC 39-33000. 1939. Macrae-Smith Company.
If Love Means This. Maude Williamson. LC 39-6846. Farrar & Rinehart, Inc.
If Morning Ever Comes. Anne Tyler. LC 64-19103. 1964. Knopf; Distributed by Randon House.
If Morning Ever Comes. Anne Tyler. 1977. 1.95 (ISBN 0-445-04091-2). Popular Library.
If Morning Ever Comes. Anne Tyler. LC 81-933. 1981. 10.95. J. Curley.
If My Arms Could Hold: A Vivid and Colorful Romance of Bath in the Time of Beau Nash, by Doris Ponsonby. Doris Almon Ponsonby. LC 47-18600. 1947. Liveright Publishing Corporation.
If My Love Leaves Me. Robert Rushmore. LC 74-17671. 1975. 8.95 (ISBN 0-672-52041-9). Bobbs-Merrill.
If My Love Leaves Me. Robert Rushmore. 1.75 (ISBN 0-671-80802-8). Pocket Books.
If Not for Love. Carol Franz. (Orig.). 1981. pap. text ed. 2.50 o.s.i. (ISBN 0-505-51603-9). Tower Bks.
If Not Victory. Frank Olney Hough. LC 39-30531. Carrick & Evans, Inc.
If Nothin' Don't Happen. David McCheyne Newell. LC 74-7745. (Illus.). 1975. Knopf.
If on a Winter's Night a Traveler. Italo Calvino. LC 80-8741. 12.95 (ISBN 0-15-143689-4). Harcourt Brace Jovanovich.
If Only the Fuehrer Knew see Twilight Men.
If Passion Flies. Bowen Ingram. LC 45-8643. 1945. Dodd, Mead & Company.
If Reader of Science Fiction: Ed. by Frederik Pohl. If. Ed. by Frederik Pohl. LC 66-12247. 1966. 4.50. Doubleday.
If She Be Fair. Vivien Grey. LC 49-11845. 1949. Arcadia House.
If She Should Die. Forbes Ryddel. LC 61-5979. (Crime Club selection). 2.95. Published for the Crime Club by Doubleday.
If She Should Die. Forbes Rydell, pseud. LC 61-5979. 1961. Published for the Crime Club by Doubleday.
If She Will She Will. Mary Andrews Denison. LC 6-339895. (On cover: Good company ser. no. 8). Lee and Shepard.
If Sugar Burns: A Novel on Man's Fight Against Diabetes. John Christian Krantz. 1942. John D. Lucas Company.
If the Bough Breaks. Lois Seyster Montross. LC 38-10195. 1938. D. Appleton-Century Company, Incorporated.
If the Cap Fits. Humphrey Fry. LC 58-13321. 1959. Day.
If the Gods Laugh. Rosita Torr Forbes. LC 26-789. The Macaulay Company.
If the Heart Be Hasty: A Novel. Alexandra Jane Benchly. LC 67-31275. 1969. 5.95. Chekhov Productions.
If The If Reader of Science Fiction: Ed. by Frederik Pohl. Ed. by Frederik Pohl. (H19). 1967. Ace.
If the Mirrow Break. Vaclav Rezac. LC 59-5768. 1959. Chilton Co.
If the Reaper Ride. Elizabeth Norman. LC 78-50881. 1.95 (ISBN 0-380-01886-1). Avon Books.
If the Shoe Fits: By Lee Roberts Pseud. Robert Lee Martin. LC 59-6194. (Red Badge detective). 1959. Dodd, Mead.
If the Shroud Fits. Paul Kruger. LC 75-84127. (Inner sanctum mystery). 1969. 4.95. Simon and Schuster.
If the Shroud Fits. Kelley Roos. LC 41-18115. 1941. Dodd, Mead & Company.
If the Shroud Fits. Kelley Roos. LC 44-8485. (Murder mystery monthly. no. 13). 1943. Avon Book Company.
If the Sky Fall. Helen Partridge. LC 34-41287. Arcadia House.
If the South Had Won the Civil War. MacKinlay Kantor. LC 65-2513. (Pathfinder ed., EP102). 1965. Bantam.
If the Stars Are Gods. Gregory Benford & Gordon Eklund. LC 76-28692. 7.95 (ISBN 0-399-11942-6). Berkley Pub. Corp.: Distributed by Putnam.

If There Be Thorns. Virginia C. Andrews. LC 81-5317. 14.95 (ISBN 0-671-43122-6). Simon and Schuster.

If There Be Thorns. large print ed. Virginia C. Andrews. LC 82-23314. 1983. 18.95 (ISBN 0-8161-3429-4). G.K. Hall.

If They Come in the Morning. Angela Davis. pap. 1.25 (ISBN 0-451-04999-3, Y4999, Sig). NAL.

If This Be Error. Zoe Girling. LC 34-41610. 1934. Harper & Brothers.

If This Be Forgetting. Earl Reed Silvers. LC 44-3449. The Westminster Press.

If This Be Love. Elizabeth Charlton. LC 38-19072. 1938. Hillman-Curl, Inc.

If This Be Murder. Ruth Darby. LC 41-6172. 1941. Pub. for the Crime Club by Doubleday, Doran and Co., Inc.

If This Be My Harvest. Lee Atkins. LC 48-89870. Crown Publishers.

If This Be Treason. Margaret Echard. LC 44-8967. 1944. Pub. for the Crime Club by Doubleday, Doran and Co., Inc.

If This Be Virtue. 1st American Ed. Paula Batchelor. LC 56-646420. 1956. Holt.

If Thou Hadst Known. Stanley W. Paher. (Illus.). 1978. 5.95 (ISBN 0-913814-21-0). Nevada Pubns.

If Today Be Sweet: By Ednah Aiken... Ednah Robinson Aiken. LC 23-15160. 1923. Dodd, Mead and Company.

If Today Have No Tomorrow. Olive Gilbreath. LC 26-8617. E. P. Dutton & Company.

If Tomorrow Comes. Louis Aaron Reitmeister. LC 74-154458. (Utopian Literature). (Illus.). 1971. (ISBN 0-405-03540-3). Arno Press.

If Tomorrow Comes. Louis Aaron Reitmeister. LC 34-38719. 1934. The Walden Press.

If Tomorrow Were Today: A Novel. Bernard Sacks. LC 31-22653. R. Field, Inc.

If Two of Them Are Dead. Stanton Forbes, pseud. LC 68-14187. 1968. Published for the Crime Club by Doubleday.

If Two of Them Are Dead. Mason Gregory. LC 53-856339. 1953. Arcadia House.

If We Dream Too Long. Goh Poh Seng. (Writing in Asia Ser.). 1972. text ed. 5.50x (00225). Heinemann Ed.

If We Must Die. Junius Edwards. LC 63-12971. 1963. Doubleday.

If We Only Had Money. Lee Shippey. LC 39-207743. 1939. Houghton Mifflin Company.

If We Should Fail. Marion White. LC 42-509175. 1942. M. S. Mill Co., Inc.

If Winter Comes. Arthur Stuart-Menteth Hutchinson. LC 21-15552. 1921. Little, Brown, and Company.

If Winter Comes. Arthur Stuart-Menteth Hutchinson. LC 42-28977. 1923. Grosset & Dunlap.

If Winter Don't: A. B. C. D. E. F. Notsomuchinson. Barry Eric Odell Pain. LC 22-20425. Frederick A. Stokes Company.

If Wishes Were Hearses: By Guy Cullingford Pseud. 1st American Ed. Constance Lindsay Taylor. LC 52-13729. (Main line mysteries). 1953. Lippincott.

If Wishes Were Horses. Marguerite Florence Helene Evans. LC 17-9812. E. P. Dutton & Co.

If with All Your Heart: A Novel. Winifred Turner Sarre. LC 69-18870. 1969. Herald Pub. House.

If with All Your Hearts. Louise Platt Hauck. The Penn Publishing Company.

If, Yes and Perhaps. Edward Everett Hale. LC 68-55676. (American short story series, v. 17). 1969. Garrett Press.

If, Yes, and Perhaps. Edward Everett Hale. LC 72-8084. (American short story series, v. 17). 1972. (ISBN 0-8422-8068-5). MSS Information Corp.

If, Yes, and Perhaps. Four Possibilities and Six Exagerations, with Some Bits of Fact. Edward Everett Hale. 1868. Ticknor and Fields.

If, Yes, and Perhaps. Four Possibilities and Six Exagerations, with Some Bits of Fact. Edward Everett Hale. LC 9-38707. 1874. J. R. Osgood and Company.

If You Believe the Soldiers. Alexander Cordell, pseud. LC 73-13277. 1974. 5.95 (ISBN 0-385-09612-7). Doubleday.

If You Can Wait-- Gloria Goddard. LC 33-9097. J. B. Lippincott Company.

If You Can't Be Good. Ross Thomas. LC 73-4226. 1973. 6.95 (ISBN 0-688-00169-6). Morrow.

If You Could See Me Now. Peter Straub. LC 76-57730. 1977. 8.95 (ISBN 0-698-10817-5). Coward, McCann & Geoghegan.

If You Could See Me Now. Peter Straub. 1979. 2.50 (ISBN 0-671-81844-9). Pocket Books.

If You Don't Like Me You Can Leave Me Alone. James Koller. 1977. pap. 3.00 (ISBN 0-942396-26-X). Blackberry ME.

If You Don't Watch Out: 1st Amer. Ed. Alex Hamilton. LC 65-24267. 1966. bds., 4.50. McKay.

If You Face the Sun. Fannie Harper. Rogers. LC 39-5850. Dorrance and Company.

If You Have Tears. Howard Browne. LC 47-5874. 1947. Mystery House.

If You Hear a Song. Lon Riley Woodrum. LC 52-687141. 1952. Zondervan Pub. House.

If You Lived Here. Edward Harris Heth. LC 49-80859. 1949. Harper.

If You Touch Them They Vanish. Gouverneur Morris. LC 13-21259. 1913. C. Scribner's Sons.

If You Want a Murder Well Done. Margaret Scherf. LC 74-5537. 1974. (ISBN 0-385-05588-9). Published for the Crime Club by Doubleday.

If You Want to See Your Wife Again... A Novel of Suspense. John Craig. LC 73-172409. 1971. 5.95. Putnam.

If Young Hearts. Portia Maxwell. LC 37-203172. Gramercy Publishing Company.

If You're Ready, Here's the Car. Ray Brock. (O.s.i.). (Illus.). 24p. (Orig.). 1974. lib. bdg. 4.58 o.s.i. (ISBN 0-8037-4395-5); pap. 1.50 o.s.i. (ISBN 0-8037-4363-7). Dial.

If Youth but Knew!". Agnes Sweetman Castle & Castle, Egerton. LC 6-11310. 1906. The Macmillan Company.

IFO Report. Thierry J. Sagnier. 336p. 1983. pap. 3.50 (ISBN 0-380-83337-9, 83337-9). Avon.

Ignorance Is the Enemy of Love: A Novel. Farrax M. Cawl. Tr. by Andrzejewski from Somali. 128p. 1982. pap. 9.95 (ISBN 0-905762-86-X, Pub. by Zed Pr England, Pub. by Zed Pr England). Lawrence Hill.

Ignorant Armies. E. M. Halliday. (O.s.i.). (Orig.). pap. 0.60 o.s.i. (A108, Award). Univ Pub & Dist.

Igor's Summer: A Story of Our Russian Friends. Lorraine Levey Beim & Jerrold Beim. LC 44-703. 1943. Russian War Relief, Inc.

II, a Dus. James Drought. LC 64-887643. 5.00, 2.50 pap.,. Skylight.

Ikael Torass. N. D Williams. LC 77-553089. 1976. Casa De las Americas.

Ike Glidden in Maine: A Story of Rural Life in a Yankee District. Alexander D. McFaul. LC 3-138253. 1903. Dickerman Publishing Co.

Ikey's Letters to His Father. George Vere Hobart. LC 7-17359. 1907. G. W. Dillingham Company.

Ikon, a Novel. Clayton C Barbeau. LC 61-6838. 1961. Coward-MaCcnn.

Ikon Maker. Desmond Hogan. LC 79-13542. 1979. 8.95 (ISBN 0-8076-0929-3). G. Braziller.

Ikon Maker: A Novel. Desmond Hogan. LC 76-377978. 1976. 0.90 (ISBN 0-905441-00-1). Co-Op Books.

Il Boom. Katharine Topkins & Richard Topkins. LC 73-20574. 1974. 5.95 (ISBN 0-394-48791-5). Random House.

Il Boom. Richard Topkins & Katherine Topkins. LC 73-21830. 1974. (ISBN 0-394-48791-5). Random House.

Il Filostrato: The Story of the Love of Troilo As It Was Sung in Italian. Giovanni Boccaccio & Cummings, Hubertis Maurice, 1884- Tr. LC 25-7392. 1924. Princeton University Press.

Il Ne Faut Jurer De Rien. Alfred De Musset. 1965. pap. 2.95. French & Eur.

Il Novellino: The Hundred Old Tales. Il Novellino. Ed. by Storer, Edward. LC 26-6552. (Broadway translations). 1925. G. Routledge & Sons Ltd.

Il Novellino: The Hundred Old Tales. Il Novellino & Storer, Edward, 1882- Ed. and Tr. LC 26-6552. (Broadway translations). 1925. G. Routledge & Sons Ltd.

Il NY a Pas De Pays Sans Grand-Pere see No Country Without Grandfathers.

Ilbarana. Donald Stuart. LC 72-183967. 1971. 3.50 (ISBN 0-85585-484-7) (ISBN 0-85585-485-5). Georgian House.

Ile Mysterieuse, 2 vols. Jules Verne. Set. pap. 9.90. French & Eur.

Ilex Avenue. 1st Ed. Janet Payne Whitney. LC 56-5931. 1956. Little, Brown.

Ili Frosh! Edgar Samuel Bacon. LC 67-2861. 1967. Equinox Press.

Iliad. Wilson Daugherty & Barnes & Noble, Inc. New York. LC 66-30580. (Barnes & Noble book notes, 824). 1967. Barnes & Noble.

Iliad. Homer. LC 74-3528. 600p. 1975. pap. 5.95 (ISBN 0-385-05941-8, Anch). Doubleday.

Iliad. Homer. Tr. by Robert Fitzgerald. LC 74-3528. 600p. 1974. 15.00 (ISBN 0-385-05940-X, Anchor Pr). Doubleday.

Iliad, 2 Vols. Homer. (Loeb Classical Library: No. 170-171). 12.00x ea. Vol. 1, Bks. 1-12 (ISBN 0-674-99188-5). Vol. 2, Bks. 13-24 (ISBN 0-674-99189-3). Harvard U Pr.

Iliad. Homer. Ed. by S. H. Butcher & A. Lang. (O.s.i.). 1947. 4.50g o.s.i. (ISBN 0-02-553540-4). Macmillan.

Iliad. Homer. Tr. by Andrew Lang et al. 1961. text ed. 5.95 o.p. (ISBN 0-312-40565-0). St Martin.

Iliad. Homerus. Tr. by Butler, Samuel. Ed. by Willcock, Malcolm M. LC 64-6688. (Washington Square Press classics). 1964. Washington Square Press.

Iliad. Homerus. Tr. by Robert Fitzgerald. LC 74-3528. 1974. 15.00 (ISBN 0-385-05940-X). Anchor Press.

Iliad. Homerus. Ed. by Richmond Alexander Lattimore. LC 62-19604. (Illus.). 1962. University of Chicago Press.

Iliad. Homerus & Robert Fitzgerald. LC 76-383509. (100 greatest books of all time). (Illus.). 1976. Franklin Library.

Iliad. Homerus & Rees. Ennis, Tr. LC 63-11620. 1963. Random House.

Iliad and the Odyssey. Homerus. Tr. by Samuel Butler. LC 55-10314. (Great books of the Western World, v. 4). 1955. Encyclopdia Britannica.

Iliad and the Odyssey: The Heroic Story of the Trojan War, the Fabulous Adventures of Odysseus. Jane Werner Watson & Homerus, Paraphrases, Tales, Etc. LC 65-7140. 1964. Golden Press.

Iliad of Homer. Homerus. LC 76-56428. (Library of liberal arts; 228). 5.95 (ISBN 0-672-61414-6). Bobbs-Merrill Educational Pub.

Iliad of Homer. Homerus. Tr. by Samuel Butler. LC 72-186947. (Shrewsbury edition of the works of Samuel Butler, v. 13). (Illus.). 1968. AMS Press.

Iliad of Homer. Homerus & Butler, Samuel, 1835-1902, Tr. LC 43-1663. (On cover: Classics club library). 1942. Published for the Classics Club by W. J. Black.

Iliad of Homer: Tr., Introd. by Richmond Lattimore. Homerus. Ed. by Richmond Alexander Lattimore. (Phoenix bk. P63). 1961. pap., 1.95. Univ. of Chic. Pr.

Iliad: The Story of Achilles. Translated by W. H. D. Rouse. Homerus. Tr. by William Henry Denham Rouse. LC 54-2687. (Mentor books, Ms 110). 1954. New American Library.

Iliad. Tr. by Ennis Rees. Homerus. LC 64-55728. (Mod. lib., 166). 1964. 2.45. Random.

Ilian: Or, The Curse of the Old South Church of Boston. A Psychological Tale of the Late Civil War. James Johnson Kane. LC 7-11664. 1888. J. B. Lippincott Company.

Iliana: Stories of a Wandering Race. Konrad Bercovici. LC 24-21818. 1924. Boni and Liveright.

Ilka on the Hill-Top. facs. ed. Hjalmar Hjorth Boyesen. LC 78-142259. (Short Story Index Reprint Ser). 1881. 15.00 (ISBN 0-8369-3743-0). Ayer Co.

Ilka on the Hill-Top, and Other Stories. Hjalmar Hjorth Boyesen. LC 78-142259. (Short story index reprint series). 1970. (ISBN 0-8369-3743-0). Books for Libraries Press.

Ilka on the Hill-Top: And Other Stories. Hjalmar Hjorth Boyesen. LC 6-15221. 1881. C. Scribner's Sons.

I'll Always Be with You. Frederick Ehrenfried Baume. 1946. Dodd, Mead & Company.

I'll Be Damned. Harry Kimball. 2.95 o.p. Vantage.

I'll Be Right Home, Ma. Henry Denker. LC 49-761601. T. Y. Crowell Co.

I'll Be Sad for Nobody. Ione Griffith. 1937. Arcadia House.

I'll Be Seeing You. Larry Fagin. LC 77-28219. 1978. 17.95 (ISBN 0-916190-10-2); pap. 6.00 (ISBN 0-916190-11-0). Full Court NY.

I'll Bow Sadly: A Story of Giuseppe Verdi. Illus. by Brother Harold Ruplinger. Roy Nash. LC 56-15677. 1955. Dujarie Press.

I'll Bury My Dead: By James Hadley Chase Pseud. 1st American Ed. Rene Raymond. LC 53-10847. (Guilt edged mystery). 1954. Dutton.

I'll Cry Tomorrow. L. S. Bogart. 4.50 o.p. (ISBN 0-8062-1045-1). Carlton.

Ill-Earth War: The Chronicles of Thomas Covenant, the Unbeliever, Vol. 2. Stephen R. Donaldson. (Del Rey Bk.). 1979. pap. 2.50 (ISBN 0-345-25717-0). Ballantine.

I'll Eat You Last... Henry C Branson. LC 41-11891. 1941. Simon and Schuster.

I'll Find You. Richard Himmel. LC 50-4412. (Gold medal book, 104). 1950. Fawcett Publications.

I'll Get By. Elizabeth Byrd. 224p. 1982. pap. 1.95 (ISBN 0-449-70020-8, Juniper). Fawcett.

I'll Get Over It. Maysie Greig. LC 36-4914. 1936. Doubleday Doran and Co., Inc.

I'll Get Over It. Maysie Greig. LC 36-32345. 1936. The Sun Dial Press.

I'll Get Over It. Maysie Greig. LC 42-50859. 1942. The Sun Dial Press.

I'll Get You for This. Rene Raymond. LC 47-3980. 1947. Jarrolds, Ltd.

I'll Get You for This: By James Hadley Chase. Rene Raymond. LC 51-3373. (Avon monthly novel, no. 18). 1951. Avon Novels.

I'll Get You Yet: A Novel of Suspense. James A Howard. LC 55-20864. (Popular Library eagle book, EB30). 1954. Popular Library.

I'll Grind Their Bones. Theodore Roscoe. LC 36-9223. Dodge Publishing Company.

I'll Hate Myself in the Morning and Summer in December. Elliot Harold Paul. LC 45-57747. 1945. Random House.

I'll Have a Fine Funeral. Pierre La Maziere. Tr. by Le Clerq, Jacques Georges Clemenceau. LC 27-4633. 1927. Brentano.

I'll Kill You Next! By Adam Knight Pseud. Lawrence Lariar. LC 54-6682. 1954. Appleton-Century- Crofts.

I'll Know My Love. Pearl Bucklen Bentel. LC 55-6726. 1955. Longmans, Green.

I'll Live. Stephen Manes. 160p. 1982. pap. 2.25 (ISBN 0-380-81737-3, 81737-3, Flare). Avon.

I'll Love You When You're More Like Me. M. E. Kerr. 1979. pap. 1.95 (ISBN 0-440-94405-8, LE). Dell.

Ill-Made Knight. Terence Hanbury White. LC 40-332212. 1940. G. P. Putnam's Sons.

I'll Marry Tomorrow. Louise Marks Clancy. LC 36-14927. Greenberg.

Ill Met by a Fish Shop on George Street. Mark McShane. LC 68-10676. 1968. Published for the Crime Club by Doubleday.

Ill Met by by Moonlight. Zenith Jones Brown. LC 37-2027. Farrar & Rinehart, Incorporated.

Ill Met in Mexico. Charlotte Murray Russell, pseud. LC 48-2900. 1948. Pub. for the Crime Club by Doubleday.

I'll Mourn You Later. Catharine Whitcomb. LC 36-2210. 1936. Houghton Mifflin Company.

I'll Never Be Young Again. Daphne Du Maurier. LC 32-17261. 1932. Doubleday, Doran & Company, Inc.

I'll Never Forget You. Renee Shann. LC 45-877032. 1945. Random House.

I'll Never Forget You. Renee Shann. LC 47-20009. 1946. Triangle Books, the Blakiston Company.

I'll Never Forgive You. Margaret Mackprang Mackay. LC 51-22488. (Hutchinson's new romance series, no. 69). 1951. Hutchinson.

I'll Never Go There Any More. Jerome Weidman. LC 41-164962. 1941. Simon and Schuster.

I'll Never Let You Go. Isabel Moore. LC 42-18663. 1942. Farrar & Rinehart, Inc.

I'll Never Love Again. Peggy O'More, pseud. LC 38-4946. 1938. Hillman-Curl, Inc.

I'll Never Move Again. Fitzhugh Green. LC 26-8491. E. P. Dutton & Company.

I'll Never Smile Again,". Ethel Le Vane & Lowe, Ruth. I'll Never Smile Again. LC 45-7758. 1945. Gramercy Publishing Company.

I'll Remember in April. Angela Lorden. LC 39-21859. 1939. Arcadia House.

I'll Say She Does!... Peter Cheyney. LC 46-188243. 1946. Dodd, Mead & Company.

Ill Seen Ill Said. Samuel Beckett. LC 81-47695. 1981. 8.95 (ISBN 0-394-52233-8). Grove Press.

I'll Show You the Morning Sun. (Stanyan Books Ser.). 1971. 3.00 o.p. (ISBN 0-394-47126-1). Random.

I'll Show You the Town. Elmer Holmes Davis. LC 24-8166. 1924. R. M. McBride & Company.

I'll Sing at Your Funeral. Hugh Pentecost. LC 42-7963. 1942. Dodd, Mead & Company.

I'll Sing at Your Funeral. Judson Pentecost Philips. LC 42-7963. 1942. Dodd, Mead & Company.

I'll Sing No More. Winifred Comstock. LC 56-8466. Roy Publishers.

I'll Sing You the Death of Bill Brown. Bruce Dexter. LC 63-11850. 1963. McGraw-Hill.

Ill-Starred Babbie. William Wilfrid Whalen. LC 12-23518. Mayhew Pub. Co.

I'll Storm Hell: A Biographical Novel of "Mad Anthony" Wayne. Noel Bertram Gerson. LC 67-19090. 1967. Doubleday.

I'll Take What's Mine. Cover Painting by Saul Tepper. Nard Jones. LC 54-27005. (Gold medal books, 388). 1954. Fawcett Publications.

I'll Tell My Big Brother. Edward Dean Sullivan. LC 30-21865. The Vanguard Press.

I'll Tell Them I Remember You. William Peter Blatty. LC 73-5561. 1973. 5.95 (ISBN 0-393-07479-X). Norton.

I'll Tell You Everything. John Boynton Priestley & Bullett, Gerald William. LC 32-15197. 1933. The Macmillan Company.

I'll Wait for You. Barbara Hedworth. LC 44-5301. 1944. Arcadia House, Inc.

I'll Wait for You. Margaret Gorman Nichols. LC 42-2910. 1941. Arcadia House, Inc.

Ill Wind. William L. Heath. LC 56-8783. 1957. Harper.

Ill Wind. James Hilton. LC 32-32017. 1932. W. Morrow & Co.

Ill Wind Contract. Philip Atlee. (Joe Gall Contract Ser). (Orig.). 1971. pap. 0.75 o.p. (T2270, GM). Fawcett World.

Ill Wind: Nine Stories with a Single Thread. James Hilton. LC 44-7257. (Avon modern short story monthly. No. 5). Avon Book Company.

Ill Wind. 1st Ed. Ruth Fenisong. LC 50-5985. 1950. Published for the Crime Club by Doubleday.

Illan Yenrutt. A Romance. Thomas P May. 1880. Printed at the New Orleans Democrat Office.

Illearth War. Stephen R Donaldson. LC 77-73868. (Donaldson, Stephen R. The Chronicles of Thomas Covenant, the Unbeliever: Bk. 2). 1977. 10.00 (ISBN 0-03-022776-3). Holt, Rinehart and Winston.

Illegal Assembly. Karen Brodine. 1980. pap. 3.00 (ISBN 0-914610-17-1). Hanging Loose.

Illegal Doctor. Karl Ashton. LC 33-28596. 1933. W. Godwin, Inc.

Illegal Entry. Robert Bernard Martin. LC 75-169041. 1971. 5.95 (ISBN 0-393-08662-3). Norton.

Illegal Man. Patrick Dearen. 1981. pap. 2.25 (ISBN 0-8439-0872-6, Leisure Bks). Nordon Pubns.

Illegal Marriage: Or, Cecy Morgan's Trial. Evelyn Ashby. LC 6-4526. (select series, no. 61). 1890. Street & Smith.

Illegal Nurse. Karl Ashton. LC 36-14933. Godwin.

Illegal Tender. Dominic Devine. LC 70-120400. 1970. 4.95 (ISBN 0-8027-5210-1). Walker.

Illegitimate. Josiah Pitts Woolfolk. LC 33-21930. 1933. W. Godwin, Inc.

Illegitimate Doctor. Ann Burkhart. LC 41-3533. The Pyramid Press.

Illegitimates. Raymond Aitchison. LC 65-1410. 1965. bds., 3.30. Rigby.

Illini, a Story of the Prairies. Clark Ezra Carr. LC 4-35332. 1904. A. C. McClurg & Co.

Illinois Reader. Ed. by Clyde C. Walton. LC 70-105676. 468p. 1970. pap. 7.50 (ISBN 0-87580-516-7). N Ill U Pr.

Illinois River Hokeypokey. Charles Gerard. LC 69-12210. 1969. 4.50. Doubleday.

Illma: Or, Which Was Wife? A, M L. 1881. Cornwell & Johnson.

Illuminations: A Novel. Tamas Aczel. LC 81-47485. 1981. 15.50 (ISBN 0-394-51260-X). Pantheon Books.

Illuminoids. Neal Wilgus. 1978. pap. 2.25 (ISBN 0-671-81949-6, Timescape). PB.

Illusion. Frances Keinzley. LC 78-122426. 1970. 5.95. Stein and Day.

Illusion. Charlotte Lamb, pseud. (Harlequin Presents Ser.). 192p. 1981. pap. 1.50 (ISBN 0-373-10448-0, Pub. by Harlequin). PB.

Illusion. Arthur Cheney Train. LC 29-116508. 1929. C. Scribner's Sons.

Illusion at Haven's Edge. Dorothy Daniels. LC 77-3179. 1977. 9.95 (ISBN 0-89340-080-7). J. Curley.

Illusion at Haven's Edge. Dorothy Daniels. 1975. (pbk.) 0.95 (ISBN 0-671-77994-X). Pocket Books.

Illusion (Dansons la Trompeuse) Raymond Escholier. LC 22-5892. 1922. G. P. Putnam's Sons.

Illusion in Java. Gene Fowler, pseud. LC 39-30877. Random House.

Illusionist. Francoise Mallet-Joris. LC 52-122770. 1952. Farrar, Straus and Young.

Illusionist. Mallet-Joris, Francoise. LC 75-12335. (Homosexuality). 1975. 10.00 (ISBN 0-405-07383-6). Arno Press.

Illusionists. Wolf Peter Rilla. LC 76-56822. 1977. 9.50 (ISBN 0-312-40670-3). St. Martin's Press.

Illusionless Man: Fantasies and Mediations. 1st Ed. Allen Wheelis. LC 66-18081. 1966. bds., 4.50. Norton.

Illusions. Richard Bach. 1978. gift ed. 12.95 o.p. (ISBN 0-440-04105-8, E Friede). Delacorte.

Illusions. Donald Honig. LC 73-10859. 1974. 8.95 (ISBN 0-385-08912-0). Doubleday.

Illusion's End. Clay Mobley. LC 38-7802. Bucklee Publishing Company, Inc.

Illusions of Mr. and Mrs. Bressingham. Gerard Bendall. LC 13-44. 1912. 1.25. John Lane.

Illusions: The Adventures of a Reluctant Messiah. Richard Bach. LC 76-30788. 5.95 (ISBN 0-440-04318-2). Delacorte Press.

Illusions: The Adventures of a Reluctant Messiah. Richard Bach. LC 77-12838. 1977. 10.95 (ISBN 0-8161-6520-3). G. K. Hall.

Illusory Flame. Tr. by Howard S. Levy. (Illus.). 1962. 4.50x o.p. Paragon.

Illusory Flame: Chinese Love Stories. Tr. by Howard S. Levy. (Illus.). 1962. 10.00 (Pub. by Levy). Oriental Bk Store.

Illustrated Ben-Hur. Lewis Wallace. LC 78-17956. (Illus.). 1978. 5.98 (ISBN 0-517-25948-6). Bonanza Books.

Illustrated Cloudy Sky: Or, the Unfortunate Children; a True Tale. with Thirteen Illustrations. 3d ed. Narcissa Smith Springer. LC 8-14043. 1884.

Illustrated Dracula: Original Text. Bram Stoker. LC 74-22562. (Illus.). 1975. 12.95 (ISBN 0-87749-809-1). Drake Publishers.

Illustrated Dune. Frank Herbert. 1978. pap. 7.95 (ISBN 0-425-03891-2, Windhover). Berkley Pub.

Illustrated Emmanuelle: Based on the Novel by Emmanuelle Arsan. Emmanuelle Arsan. LC 80-999. 144p. 1980. 25.00 o.p. (ISBN 0-8021-0206-9, GP837). Grove.

Illustrated Faerie Queene. Douglas Arthur Hill & Edmund Spenser. LC 80-392. 16.95 (ISBN 0-88225-297-6). Newsweek Books.

Illustrated Life & Adventures of Nicholas Nickleby. Charles Dickens. LC 82-7793. 1982. 19.95. Macmillan.

Illustrated Man. Ray Bradbury. LC 51-1140. 1951. Doubleday.

Illustrated Roger Zelazny. Roger Zelazny. Ed. by Byron Preiss. (Illus.). 1978. 14.95 (ISBN 0-89437-020-0); pap. 8.95 (ISBN 0-89437-014-6). Baronet.

Illustrated Tarzan Books... Picturized from the Novel "Tarzan of the Apes". Edgar Rice Burroughs & Foster, Harold, Illus. LC 29-195273. Grosset & Dunlap.

Illustrated Temperance Tales. Timothy Shay Arthur. LC 6-3402. 1850. J. W. Bradley.

Illustrated Works of Mark Twain. avenel 1979 ed. Samuel Langhorne Clemens & Michael Patrick Hearn. LC 79-14393. (Illus.). 1979. 5.98 (ISBN 0-517-27912-6). Avenel Books: Distributed by Crown Publishers.

Illustrations of Medieval Romance on Tiles from Chertsey Abbey. Roger Sherman Loomis. LC 16-16085. (Added to t.-p.: University of Illinois studies in language and literature. vol. ii, no. 2). 1916. University of Illinois.

Illustrious Corpse. Tiffany Thayer. LC 30-25309. 1930. The Fiction League.

Illustrious Emperor. Hope Danby. LC 47-1264. 1946. Ziff-Davis Publishing Company.

Illustrious House of Ramires. Eca De Queiroz, Jose Maria De. LC 68-29766. 1968. 5.00. Ohio University Press.

Illustrious O'Hagan. Justin Huntly McCarthy. LC 6-39729. 1906. Harper & Brothers.

Illustrious Prince. Edward Phillips Oppenheim. LC 10-11367. 1910. 1.50. Little, Brown, and Company.

Illyria, Lady. Constance Butler. LC 35-56950. 1935. Houghton Mifflin Company.

Illyrian Spring. Anne Bridge. pap. 1.25 o.p. (09166). Curtis.

Illyrian Spring. Mary Dolling Sanders O'Malley. LC 35-11492. 1935. Little, Brown, and Company.

Ilona. Hans Habe. LC 61-13352. 1961. Harcourt, Brace & World.

Ilona: By Hans Habe Pseud. Translated from TheGerman by Michael Bullock. Adapted for the American Ed. by Catherine Hutter. 1st American Ed. Jean Bekessy, pseud. LC 61-13352. 1961. Harcourt, Brace & World.

Ilsa. Madeleine L'Engle. LC 46-25101. 1946. The Vanguard Press.

Ilyitch Slept Here. Henry C. Carlisle. LC 64-22178. 1965. 4.95. Lippincott.

I'm Afraid I'll Live! Katharine S Cole. 1936. Houghton Mifflin Company.

I'm All Right Jack. 1st Ed. Alan Hackney. LC 59-5685. 1959. Norton.

Im Anderen Deutschland: Reader 3. Rita M. Walbruck. LC 80-22199. (Auf Heisser Spur Ser.). (gr. 9-12). 1981. pap. 1.95 (ISBN 0-88436-852-1). EMC.

I'm Cherry, Fly Me. Glen Chase, pseud. 1976. pap. 1.25 o.p. (LB368ZK, Leisure Bks). Nordon Pubns.

I'm Cherry, Fly Me. Glen Chase, pseud. (Cherry Delight Ser., No. 6). 1974. pap. 1.25 o.p. (LB129ZK). Leisure Bks.

I'm Expecting to Live Quite Soon. Paul West. LC 69-15286. 1970. 6.95. Harper & Row.

I'm Free. Hildreth Scott. (Uplook Ser.). 31p. 1973. pap. 0.75 o.p. (ISBN 0-8163-0073-9, 09340-1). Pacific Pr Pub Assn.

I'm from Missouri (They Had to Show Me) George Vere Hobart. LC 4-18493. 1904. G. W. Dillingham Co.

Im Geist der Gegenwart. Ed. by Daniel Catlin McCluney. LC 59-6033. 1959. Oxford University Press.

I'm Getting Married. Halasz, George, Tr & Halasz, George, Tr. LC 38-1047. Farrar & Rinehart, Incorporated.

I'm Here for an Education...Really, I Am. A. David Shane. 72p. (Orig.). 1980. pap. 2.50 (ISBN 0-9604862-0-8). Westlake.

I'm in Bed with the President, and Mao Tse Tung Is Knocking at the Door: The American Dream of an American Girl) Amram M Ducovny. LC 77-167724. 1971. 5.95. Ashley Books.

I'm Looking for Baby K. Franz T Hansell. LC 74-7599. (Traveller's companion series, TC-439). 1969. 1.75. Olympia Press.

I'm Lucky at That. David Betts. LC 30-4853. 1930. Doubleday, Doran and Company, Inc.

I'm No Hero. Alfred Kreymborg. LC 33-5476. 1933. W. Morrow & Company.

I'm Nobody's Child. Kenneth J. Herrmann. LC 82-2002. 10.00 (ISBN 0-87426-054-X). Whitmore Pub. Co.

I'm Not Complaining. Ruth Adam. LC 36-27900. 1938. Liveright Publishing Corporation.

I'm Not Stiller. Max Frisch. 1958. pap. 2.95 (ISBN 0-394-70219-0, V-219, Vin). Random.

I'm off! Sense and Nonsence for Summer Reading, 1884. 2d ed. LC 7-8843. 1884. The American News Company.

I'm Owen Harrison Harding. James Whitfield Ellison. LC 55-5576. 1955. Doubleday.

I'm Really Dragged but Nothing Gets Me Down. Nat Hentoff. 1969. pap. 1.50 (ISBN 0-440-93988-7, LFL). Dell.

Im Schnenschein; Ein Grunes Blatt, Von Theodor Storm. Theodor Storm & Swiggett, Glen Lavin, 1867- Ed. LC 6-10497. American Book Company.

I'm the Happiest Girl in the World. John Held. LC 35-431. The Vanguard Press.

I'm the King of the Castle. Susan Hill. LC 75-119771. 1970. 5.95. Viking Press.

I'm Trying to Give It up. Desmond Skirrow. LC 77-77091. 1969. 5.95. Doubleday.

I'm Waiting. Sammy Reese, pseud. LC 73-10816. 1974. 5.95 (ISBN 0-385-08527-3). Doubleday.

Im Western Nichts Neues. Prepared with Introduction, Notes, and Vocabulary. Erich Maria Remarque. Tr. by Waldo Cutler Peebles. LC 38-6946. 1938. Harper & Brothers.

Image. Jean De Berg. Tr. by Patsy Southgate. 1966. 5.00 o.p. (GP378). Grove.

Image. William Wister Haines. LC 68-16138. 1968. Simon and Schuster.

Image. Jean Le Berg. Tr. by Patsy Southgate. 1966. pap. 0.95 o.p. (ISBN 0-394-17400-3, B307, Dist by Dell). Grove.

Image. Charlotte Paul. (Orig.). 1980. pap. 2.75 (ISBN 0-446-95145-5). Warner Bks.

Image. Pamela Townley. 360p. (Orig.). 1981. pap. 2.75 (ISBN 0-345-29115-8). Ballantine.

Image and the Flesh. Richard Posner. (Fawcett gold medal). 1975. (pbk.) 1.50. Fawcett.

Image and the Search: A Novel. 1st American Ed. Walter Baxter. LC 54-5481.

Image Breakers. Gertrude Dix. LC 3447. F. A. Stokes Company.

Image for the Future. Jesse W. Stapp. 4.95 o.p. Vantage.

Image Impact. Jacqueline Thompson. 288p. 1982. pap. 6.95 (ISBN 0-441-36691-0). Ace Bks.

Image in a Golden Circle. Becky L. Weyrich. 1978. pap. 1.25 (ISBN 0-532-12566-5). Woodhill.

Image in the Path. Grenville Vernon. LC 27-20262. 1927. L. MacVeagh, The Dial Press.

Image Killer. William Maner. LC 68-27130. 1968. 3.95. Published for the Crime Club by Doubleday.

Image Makers. Raymond Dreyfack. 192p. (Orig.). 1976. pap. 1.50 (ISBN 0-89041-092-5, 3092). Major Bks.

Image Men. John Boynton Priestley. LC 69-15075. 1969. Little, Brown.

Image Men. John Boynton Priestley. LC 75-875628 (ISBN 0-14-003013-1). Penguin.

Image of a Drawn Sword. 1st American Ed. Jocelyn Brooke. LC 51-9200. 1951. Knopf.

Image of a Ghost. Dorothy Daniels. 1973. (pbk.) 0.95. Warner Paperback Library.

Image of a Lover. Elisabeth Ogilvie. LC 74-5016. 1974. 7.95 (ISBN 0-07-047648-9). McGraw-Hill.

Image of a Lover. Elisabeth Ogilvie. (Illus.). 1976. (ISBN 0-380-00656-1). Avon.

Image of America in Mazzini's Writings. Joseph Rossi. 1974. 3.50 o.p. Brown Bk.

Image of an Angel. Marcia Marcoux. (Orig.). pap. 0.95 o.p. (1128). Brandon.

Image of Chekhov: Forty Stories in the Order in Which They Were Written. Anton Pavlovich Chekhov. LC 62-15559. (Illus.). 1963. Knopf.

Image of Eve: A Romance with Alleviations. Margaret Sutton Briscoe Hopkins. LC 9-28152. 1909. Harper & Brothers.

Image of Josephine. Booth Tarkington. LC 45-2270. 1945. Doubleday, Doran and Company, Inc.

Image of Kate. 1st Ed. Mary Astor. LC 62-8396. 1962. Doubleday.

Image of Tallie. Elick Moll. LC 64-22408. 1964. Simon and Schuster.

Image of the Beast. Philip Jose Farmer. pap. 1.95 o.p. (0108). Essex Hse.

Image of the Beast & Blown. Philip Jose Farmer. LC 79-53029. 336p. 1979. pap. 2.50 (ISBN 0-87216-845-X). Playboy Pbks.

Image Seller. Kate Ostrander. (Queen-size gothic). 1974. (pbk.) 0.95. Popular Library.

Image. Tr. from French by Patsy Southgate. Pref. by Pauline Reage. Jean De Berg. LC 66-29270. (Evergreen black cat bk., BC139). 1966-1967. Grove.

Imagen De Tu Huella see Rayo Que No Cesa.

Images. Paul Young. LC 76-95381. 1969. 6.95. Nash Pub. Corp.

Images in a Mirror. Sigrid Undset & Chater, Arthur G., Tr. LC 38-276798. 1938. A. A. Knopf.

Images of Evil. Marianne Joyce Maglich. 1974. (pbk.) 1.50 (ISBN 0-89014-111-8). Canyon Books.

Images of Love. Anne Mather. (Harlequin Presents Ser.). 192p. 1980. pap. 1.50 (ISBN 0-373-10402-2, Pub. by Harlequin). PB.

Images of Mary. Duane Hutchinson. (Illus.). pap. 6.95 (ISBN 0-934988-03-X). Foun Bks.

Images of Rose. Anna Gilbert. LC 73-17103. 1974. 6.95. Delacorte Press.

Images of Rose. Anna Gilbert. 1975. (pbk.) 1.25. Dell.

Imaginacion y Fantasia: Cuentos De las Americas. rev. ed. Donald A. Yates & J. Dalbor. (4th-6th semesters). (gr. 10-12). 1968. text ed. 4.80 o.p. (ISBN 0-03-069110-9, HoltC); pap. text ed. 3.90 o.p. (ISBN 0-03-074475-X); tapes. 12 reels 7.5 ips dbl. track s.p. 120.00 o.p. HR&W.

Imaginary Crimes. Sheila Ballantyne. LC 81-65259. 1982. 13.95 (ISBN 0-670-48022-3). Viking Press.

Imaginary Crimes. Sheila Ballantyne. LC 82-19078. (Penguin Contemporary American Fiction Series). 1983. 4.95 (ISBN 0-14-006540-7). Penguin Books.

Imaginary Friends. Alison Lurie. LC 67-21510. 1967. Coward-McCann.

Imaginary Interviews. William Dean Howells. LC 69-13938. (Illus.). 1969. Greenwood Press.

Imaginary Life: A Novel. David Malouf. LC 77-18601. 1978. 7.95 (ISBN 0-8076-0884-X). G. Braziller.

Imaginary Speeches for a Brazen Head: A Novel. Philip Whalen. LC 72-179394. 1972. (ISBN 0-87685-097-2) (ISBN 0-87685-096-4). Black Sparrow Press.

Imagination Unlimited: Science-Fiction a Nd Science, Edited. by Everett F. Bleiler and T. E. Dikty. Ed. by Everett Franklin Bleiler. LC 52-1555. Farrar, Straus and Young.

Imaginative Man. Robert Smythe Hichens. LC 76-24387. (Decadent Consciousness). 1977. 26.00 (ISBN 0-8240-2763-9). Garland Pub.

Imaginative Man. Robert Smythe Hichens. LC 7-4761. 1895. D. Appleton and Company.

Imaginative Qualities of Actual Things. Gilbert Sorrentino. LC 72-155772. 1971. 6.95 (ISBN 0-394-47108-3). Pantheon Books.

Imagine a Man in a Box. Herbert Russell Wakefield. LC 31-302671. 1931. D. Appleton and Company.

Imagined Corners: A Novel. Willa Muir. LC 32-330. 2.50. The Century Co.

Imagined World: A Story of Scientific Discovery. June Goodfield. 1982. pap. 5.95 (ISBN 0-14-006204-1). Penguin.

Imaginocrats. George Constable. LC 68-12569. 1968. Harcourt, Brace & World.

Imaro. Charles R. Saunders. 1981. pap. 2.50 (ISBN 0-87997-667-5, UE 1667). DAW Bks.

Imbroglio. Richard Colin. LC 80-14394. 1980. 12.95 (ISBN 0-312-40938-9). St. Martin's Press.

Imgar: A Story of India. Frederick Alanson Randle. LC 8-223. 1889.

Imgar: A Story of India. 2d ed. Frederick Alanson Randle. LC 8-224. 1890. J. B. Alden.

Imitation of Life. Fannie Hurst. 1974. (pbk.) 1.50 (ISBN 0-515-03423-1). Pyramid Books.

Imitation of Life: A Novel. Fannie Hurst. LC 33-2858. 1933. Harper & Brothers.

Imitation Sin. Albert Quandt. LC 49-8618. 1949. Phoenix Press.

Imitation Thieves. Marc Lovell, pseud. LC 77-139043. 1971. 4.50. Published for the Crime Club by Doubleday.

Imitator: A Novel. Percival Pollard. LC 2-2772. 1901. W. M. Reedy.

Immaculate. Allen Katzmann. 1970. 4.50 o.p. Doubleday.

Immaculate Murders. Kate Brooks. (Orig.). 1979. pap. 1.95 (ISBN 0-532-23268-2). Woodhill.

Immaterial Murder Case. Julian Symons. LC 57-12223. (Murder revisited mystery novel, no. 19). 1957. Macmillan.

Immediate Action. Richard Neebel. 304p. (Orig.). 1982. pap. 2.50 (ISBN 0-441-36868-9, Pub. by Charter Bks). Ace Bks.

Immediate Family. Nalbro Isadorah Bartley. LC 30-16607. 1930. Farrar & Rinehart Incorporated.

Immediate Jewel of His Soul. Herman Dreer. LC 72-144596. Repr. of 1919 ed. 23.50 (ISBN 0-404-00149-1). AMS Pr.

Immediate Jewel of His Soul: A Romance. Herman Dreer. LC 72-144596. (Illus.). 1975. 15.00 (ISBN 0-404-00149-1). AMS Press.

Immediate Jewel of His Soul: A Romance. Herman Dreer. LC 79-76101. (Illus.). 1969. McGrath Pub. Co.

Immediate Jewel of His Soul: A Romance. Herman Dreer. LC 20-225911. 1919. The St. Louis Argus Publishing Company.

Immediate Release. William Mathewson. LC 81-14623. 13.50 (ISBN 0-671-43036-X). Simon and Schuster.

Immen-See. From the German of Th. Storm. Theodor Storm & Clark, H. LC 8-16290. 1863. F. Leypoldt.

Immensee. Theodor Storm & Schimmelfennig, Bertha M., Tr. LC 2-18604. 1902. T. Y. Crowell & Co.

Immensee. Theodor Storm & Upton, George Putnam, 1834-1919, Tr. LC 7-33212. 1907. A. C. McClurg & Co.

Immensee. Theodor I. E. Hans Theodor Woldsen Storm & Lyon, Vivian Elsie, Tr. LC 17-82. (students' literal translations). Translation Publishing Company, Inc.

Immigrant. Carl M Nielsen. LC 42-2425. 1942. Meador Publishing Company.

Immigrants. Howard Melvin Fast. LC 77-9317. 1977. 9.95 (ISBN 0-395-25699-2). Houghton Mifflin.

Immigrants. Howard Melvin Fast. LC 77-27940. 1978. 17.95 (ISBN 0-8161-6546-7). G. K. Hall.

Immigrants. Reginald Massey & Jamila Massey. (Orient Paperbacks Ser.). 172p. (Orig.). 1973. pap. 2.50 (ISBN 0-88253-243-X). Ind-US Inc.

Immodest Proposal. Dena Rhee. (Candlelight Regency Ser.: No. 694). (Orig.). 1982. pap. 1.75 (ISBN 0-440-13980-5). Dell.

Immolation. Goh Poh Seng. (Writing in Asia Ser.). 1977. pap. text ed. 5.50x (00226). Heinemann Ed.

Immoral Marriage. Wright Williams. LC 39-17424. 1939. Phoenix Press.

Immoral Marriage. Wright Williams. LC 39-174240. Phoenix Press.

Immoralist. Andre Paul Guillaume Gide. Tr. by Richard Howard. LC 70-98648. 1970. 5.00. Knopf.

Immoralist. Andre Paul Guillaume Gide. Tr. by Bussy, Dorothy (Strachey) LC 49-2770. 1948. A. A. Knopf.

Immoralist. Andre Paul Guillaume Gide. Tr. by Bussy, Dorothy (Strachey) 1930. A. A. Knopf.

Immoralist: Translated from the French by Dorothy Bussy. Andre Paul Guillaume Gide. LC 54-12052. (Vintage book, K-8). 1954. Vintage Books.

Immoraliste. Andre Paul Guillaume Gide. 1958. 9.50. French & Eur.

Immorality. T. Hayes Hunter. LC 27-5951.

Immortal. Alphonse Daudet. Tr. by Safford, Mary Joanna. 1889. J. B. Alden.

Immortal. Walter Ross. LC 58-7510. 1958. Simon and Schuster.

Immortal. Walter Sanford Ross. LC 58-7510. 1958. Simon and Schuster.

Immortal Athalia. Harry Franklin Haley. LC 22-10548. C.

Immortal Ease. Kathleen Coyle. LC 39-14384. 1939. E. P. Dutton & Co., Inc.

Immortal Flame. Marie Bjelke Petersen. LC 19-15551. Harper & Brothers.

Immortal Garland: A Story of American Life. Anna Robeson Brown Burr. (Half-title: Appleton's town and country library, no. 232). 1900. D. Appleton and Company.

Immortal Gymnasts. Marie Scherr. LC 15-25505. George H. Doran Company.

Immortal Helen: A Novel. Elizabeth Frances Corbett. LC 48-504153. 1948. Doubleday.

Immortal Hero. 1st Ed. Verner Meurice Whitney. LC 52-18387. 1952. C.P. Hoagland Co.

Immortal Longings. Ben Ames Williams. LC 27-10322. E. P. Dutton & Company.

Immortal Lover: A Burns Romance. John Alexander Steuart. LC 29-23487. J. B. Lippincott Company.

Immortal Marriage. Gertrude Franklin Horn Atherton. LC 27-10319. 1927. Boni and Liveright.

Immortal Moment; the Story of Kitty Tailleur. May Sinclair. 1908. Doubleday, Page & Co.

Immortal of World's End. Lin Carter. (Science Fiction Ser.). 1976. pap. 1.25 o.p. (ISBN 0-87997-254-8, UY1254). DAW Bks.

Immortal: Or, One of the "Forth." (L'immortel). Alphonse Daudet. Tr. by Verrall, Arthur Wooligar. LC 42-26573. (On cover: Rialto series, no. 4. Dec. 1888). 1892. Rand, McNally & Company.

Immortal Queen. Elizabeth Byrd. LC 56-10189. 1956. Ballantine Books.

Immortal Rendezvous. Verna S. Turner. 2.75 o.p. Carlton.

Immortal Sergeant. John Brophy. LC 42-13381. 1942. Harper & Brothers.

Immortal: Short Novels of the Transhuman Future. Jack Dann. LC 76-26264. 9.95 (ISBN 0-06-010962-9). Harper & Row.

Immortal Sinner. Mabel Wagnalls. LC 33-4500. 1933. Funk & Wagnalls Company.

Immortal Soul: A Novel. William Hurrell Mallock. LC 8-31158. 1908. Harper & Brothers.

Immortal Soul of Edwin Carlysle. Blanche Howard. LC 77-366987. 8.95 (ISBN 0-7710-4245-0). McClelland and Stewart.

Immortal Storm. Ed. by Samuel Moskowitz. LC 73-15069. (Classics of Science Fiction Ser.). (Illus.). 269p. 1974. 12.00 o.p. (ISBN 0-88355-131-4); pap. 3.50 o.p. (ISBN 0-88355-160-8). Hyperion Conn.

Immortal Tales of Joe Shaun: An Enchanting Artist Makes the Five Immortal Hopes and Dreams of Mankind Come True. Delightful Catnip for the Mind. John Joseph Meyer. LC 44-7469. 1944. The Caryldale Library.

Immortal Wheat: A Personal Interpretation, Mainly in Fictional Form, of the Life and Works of the Brontes. Kathleen Wallace. LC 52-5282. 1952. Putnam.

Immortal Wife. Irving Stone. 504p. 1972. pap. 3.95 (ISBN 0-451-11172-9, AE1172, Sig). NAL.

Immortal Wife: The Biographical Novel of Jessie Benton Fremont. Irving Stone. LC 44-8140. 1944. Doubleday, Doran & Company, Inc.

Immortal Wife: The Biographical Novel of Jessie Benton Freemont. Irving Stone. LC 46-21218. 1946. The Sun Dial Press.

Immortal Woman. Gleb Botkin. LC 33-3985. The Maculay Company.

Immortalist. Heathcote Williams. 1980. pap. 3.95 (ISBN 0-7145-3714-4). Riverrun NY.

Immortality: A Novel. Aleksei Kuzmich Iugov. LC 52-21552. 1945. Hutchinson.

Immortality, As Much As Can Be Managed. Franklin Edward Powell. LC 76-79732. 1969. 4.95. Libra Publishers.

Immortals. Rene Barjavel. LC 74-6234. 1974. 6.95 (ISBN 0-688-00269-2). Morrow.

Immortals. Rene Barjavel. 1975. (pbk.) 1.50. Ballantine Books.

Immortals. Nancy Mars Freedman. LC 75-40787. 10.95. St. Martin's Press.

Immortals. Nancy Mars Freedman. 1977. 2.25. Warner Books.

Immortals. James Edward Gunn. LC 62-20940. (Bantam book). 1962. Bantam Books.

Immortals. Harold E Scarborough. LC 24-7950. 1924. D. Appleton and Company.

Immortals: A Novel of Shanghai. Natasha Peters. 1983. pap. 6.95 (ISBN 0-449-90088-6, Columbine). Fawcett.

Immortals of the Mountain. Constantin Virgil Gheorghiu. LC 73-88853. 1969. 5.95. H. Regnery Co.

Immutable Law. Laura Cooke Barker. 1921. The Roycrofters.

Imogen. Jilly Cooper. 224p. 1982. pap. 2.25 (ISBN 0-449-24491-1, Crest). Fawcett.

Imogen: A Pastoal Romance from the Ancient British. Reprinted from the 1784 Ed. Introd. by Jack W. Marken. Critical Discussion by Martha Winburn England, Burton R. Pollin, Irwin Primer. William Godwin. LC 63-18142. 1963. pap., 2.50. N.Y. Pub. Lib.

Imogene: And Other Stories. Betty Bigg. LC 56-12340. 1956. Comet Press Books.

Imp & the Angel. facs. ed. Josephine Dodge Daskam Bacon. LC 74-81260. (Short Story Index Reprint Ser.). 1901. 13.00 (ISBN 0-8369-3012-6). Ayer Co.

Impact! R. V Fodor & Taylor, G.J. (Leisure books). 1979. 1.95 (ISBN 0-8439-0648-0). Nordon Pubns.

Impact. Harry Olesker. LC 61-6237. (Random House mystery). INew York.

Impact of Evidence. Edith Caroline Rivett. LC 54-12014. 1954. Published for the Crime Club by Doubleday.

Impact: Short Stories for Pleasure. Ed. by Donald L. Stansbury. LC 77-148493. 1971. 4.95 (ISBN 0-13-451724-5). Prentice-Hall.

Impartial Secret History of Arlus, Fortunatus, and Odolphus. Robert Harley Oxford & Daniel Defoe. LC 75-170521. (Foundations of the Novel). 1972. (ISBN 0-8240-0528-7). Garland Pub.

Impartial Secret History of Arlus, Fortunatus, & Odolphus, Ministers of State to the Empress Ofgrand-Insula. Bd. with History of the Proceedings of the Mandarins & Proatins of the Britomartian Empire. LC 79-170522; Adventures of Five Englishmen from Pub Condoro, a Factory of the New Company in the East-Indies Who Were Shipwreckt Upon the Little Kingdom of Jehore. Walter Vaughan. LC 75-170521. (Foundations of the Novel Ser.: Vol. 16). lib. bdg. 50.00 o.s.i. (ISBN 0-8240-0528-7). Garland Pub.

Impassioned Foothills. Kathleen Rollins. LC 37-5064. 1937. Arcadia House.

Impassioned Pygmies. John Keith Winter. LC 36-7477. Doubleday, Doran & Company, Inc.

Impatient Griselda. Dorothy Scarborough. LC 27-16972. 1927. Harper & Brothers.

Impatient Lovers. Peggy Gaddis, pseud. LC 50-537648. 1949. Phoenix Press.

Impatient Virgin. Donald Henderson Clarke. LC 49-238054. (Avon, 198). 1949. Avon Pub. Co.

Impatient Virgin. Donald Henderson Clarke. LC 31-718439. The Vanguard Press.

Impeachment of President Israels. Frank Barkley Copley. LC 13-2574. 1913. The Macmillan Company.

"Impenetrable Mystery" of Zora Burns. author's copyright ed. Will Bone. LC 6-10672. 1888.

Imperative Duty see Shadow of a Dream.

Imperative Duty. A Novel. William Dean Howells. LC 7-5772. (On cover: Harper's Franklin square library. new ser. no 732). 1893. Harper & Brothers.

Imperator Plot. Steven G. Spruill. LC 79-6606. (Science Fiction Ser.). 192p. 1983. 11.95 (ISBN 0-385-15037-7). Doubleday.

Imperfect Crime. Graham Montague Jeffries. LC 33-3859. J. B. Lippincott Company.

Imperfect Imposter. Norman Venner. LC 25-27462. 1925. Frederick A. Stokes Company.

Imperfect Joy. Jean Stubbs. LC 81-8970. 1981. 13.95 (ISBN 0-312-40981-8). St. Martin's Press.

Imperfect Lover. Andrew Soutar. LC 19-15980. 1919. Hodder and Stoughton.

Imperfect Lover: A London Novel. Robert Gore-Browne. LC 29-11015. Doubleday, Doran & Company.

Imperfect Mother. John Davys Beresford. LC 20-823717. 1920. The Macmillan Company.

Imperia: A Story from the Court of Austria. Mary Alice Ives Seymour. LC 8-6880. 1892. C. W. Moulton.

Imperial Affair. Gretchen Haskin. LC 79-20731. 10.95 (ISBN 0-8037-1953-1). Dial Press.

Imperial Blue. Evelyn Bond. (Orig.). 1973. pap. 0.95 o.p. (26542-4-095). Beagle Bks.

Imperial Caesar. Rex Warner. LC 60-6532. 1960. Little, Brown.

Imperial City. Elmer L. Rice. LC 37-28493. 1937. Coward-McCann, Inc.

Imperial Courtesan. Frank Wilson Kenyon. LC 67-12948. 1967. Dodd, Mead.

Imperial Dragon. Judith Gautier & Bourchier, M. H., Tr. LC 28-16046. 1928. Brentano's.

Imperial Earth. Arthur Charles Clarke. LC 75-30595. 7.95 (ISBN 0-15-144233-9). Harcourt Brace Jovanovich.

Imperial Earth. Arthur Charles Clarke. LC 80-17642. 1980. 16.95 (ISBN 0-8161-3037-X). G. K. Hall.

Imperial Express. James Bellah. 320p. (Orig.). 1982. pap. 2.95 (ISBN 0-515-05449-6). Jove Pubns.

Imperial Governor. George Shipway. LC 67-16797. (Illus.). 1968. Doubleday.

Imperial Lover. Mary Imlay Taylor. LC 8-25974. 1897. A. C. McClurg and Company.

Imperial Marriage. Arthur Williams Marchmont. LC 9-29257. Dodge Publishing Company.

Imperial Messages: One Hundred Modern Parables. Ed. by Howard Schwartz. LC 76-29195. (Bard Book) (ISBN 0-380-00682-0). Avon.

Imperial Mission. Reinhold Schneider. Tr. by Oden, Walter. 1948. Gresham Press.

Imperial Nights. Olivia O'Neill. (Orig.). 1979. pap. text ed. 2.50 (ISBN 0-425-04233-2). Berkley Pub.

Imperial Palace. Arnold Bennett. LC 74-5409. (collected works of Arnold Bennett). 1974. (ISBN 0-518-19117-6). Books for Libraries Press.

Imperial Palace. Arnold Bennett. LC 31-26102. 1930. Doubleday, Doran and Company, Inc.

Imperial Palace. Arnold Bennett. LC 33-142973. 1933. Garden City Publishing Company, Inc.

Imperial Pawn. Rose Meadows. 1974. (pbk.) 0.95 (ISBN 0-671-77732-7). Pocket Books.

Imperial Renegade. Louis De Wohl. 1950. Lippincott.

Imperial Self. Quentin Anderson. pap. 2.45 o.p. (ISBN 0-394-71824-0, V824, Vin). Random.

Imperial Splendor. Barbara Cartland. 1979. 8.95 o.p. (ISBN 0-525-13198-1). Dutton.

Imperial Splendour. Barbara Cartland. LC 78-31315. 8.95. Dutton.

Imperial Stars. E. E. Smith & Stephen Goldin. (Family d'Alembert Ser.: No. 1). 240p. 1982. pap. 2.50 (ISBN 0-425-05592-2). Berkley Pub.

Imperial Treasure: A Novel. Val Henry Gielgud. LC 31-16913. 1931. Houghton Mifflin Company.

Imperial Venus: A Novel of Napoleon's Favorite Sister. Edgar Maass. LC 46-2718. 1946. The Bobbs-Merrill Company.

Imperial Waltz. William Miller Abrahams. LC 54-7125. 1954. Dial Press.

Imperial Winds. Priscilla Hayter Napier. LC 81-5448. 16.95 (ISBN 0-698-11108-7). Coward, McCann & Geoghegan.

Imperial Woman: A Novel. Pearl Sydenstricker Buck. LC 55-11370. J. Day Co.

Imperialist. Sara Jeannette Duncan Cotes. LC 6-13098. 1904. D. Appleton and Company.

Imperium in Imperio. Sutton Elbert Griggs. LC 76-79026. 1969. Mnemosyne Pub.

Impermanence of Heroes: By C. F. Griffin Pseud. Eunice Cleland Fikso. LC 65-22546. 3.95. Chilton.

Impersonation Game. George E. Vandeman. LC 78-51271. (Stories That Win Ser.). 1978. pap. 0.95 (ISBN 0-8163-0005-4, 09370-8). Pacific Pr Pub Assn.

Impersonation of a Lady. Maude Parker. LC 34-25920. 1934. Houghton Mifflin Company.

Impersonator. Mary Imlay Taylor. LC 6-37607. 1906. Little, Brown, and Company.

Imperturbe: A Novel of Peace Without Victory. Elliot Harold Paul. LC 24-10702. 1924. A. A. Knopf.

Impervious to Pain. David Malcolm. 1972. pap. 1.95 o.s.i. (V1070T, Venus). Grove.

Impetuous Duchess. Barbara Cartland. 1975. (pbk.) 1.25. Bantam Books.

Impetuous Heart. William Arthur Neubauer. LC 56-117053. 1956. Arcadia House.

Impetuous Masquerade. Anne Mather. (Harlequin Presents Ser.). 192p. pap. 1.75 (Harlequin). PB.

Impetuous Surrogate. Alice Morgan. (Candlelight Ecstasy Ser.: No. 67). (Orig.). 1982. pap. 1.95 (ISBN 0-440-14169-9). Dell.

Implacable Colonel Corby. Charles Rodda. 1981. 4.95 (ISBN 0-8062-1639-5). Carlton.

Implements in Their Places. W. S. Graham. 1978. pap. 4.95 o.p. (ISBN 0-571-10955-1). Faber & Faber.

Implosion. Dennis Feltham Jones. LC 68-15509. 1968. Putnam.

Importance of Being Murdered: A Fleming Stone Detective Novel. Carolyn Wells. LC 39-1743. J. B. Lippincott Company.

Important Family. Dorothy Eden. LC 81-19026. 1982. 14.00 (ISBN 0-688-01148-9). Morrow.

Important People: A Novel. Robert Van Gelder. LC 48-7626. 1948. Doubleday.

Imported Bridegroom: And Other Stories of the New York Ghetto. Abraham Cahan. LC 68-55667. (American short story series, v. 7). 1968. Garrett Press.

Imported Bridegroom: And Other Stories of the New York Ghetto. Abraham Cahan. LC 72-8212. (American short story series, v. 7). 1972. (ISBN 0-8422-8021-9). MSS Information Corp.

Imported Bridegroom: And Other Stories of the New York Ghetto. Abraham Cahan. LC 6-21876. 1898. Houghton, Mifflin and Company.

Imported Bridegroom & Other Stories of the New York Ghetto. Abraham Cahan. 1898. 25.00 o.p. (ISBN 0-403-04110-4). Somerset Pub.

Imported Bridegroom & Other Stories of the New York Ghetto. Abraham Cahan. Ed. by Clarence Gohdes. (American Short Story Ser., Vol. 7). 1968. Repr. of 1898 ed. 14.25 o.s.i. (ISBN 0-512-00084-0). Garrett Pr.

Imported Bridegroom & Other Stories of the New York Ghetto see Yekl.

Impossible. Laurence M. Janifer. (Orig.). pap. 0.50 o.p. (B50-810). Belmont-Tower.

Impossible Apollo. Thomas Cobb. LC 21-4553. 1920. John Lane.

Impossible Appetites: Nine Stories. James Fetler. LC 80-17200. (Iowa School of Letters award for short fiction). (Series: Iowa. University. School of Letters.). (Iowa School of Letters award for short fiction.). 1980. 9.95 (ISBN 0-87745-101-X) (ISBN 0-87745-102-8). University of Iowa Press.

Impossible Boy. Nina Wilcox Putnam. LC 13-6544. 1.35. The Bobbs-Merrill Company.

Impossible Buildings. Judith Johnson Sherwin. LC 72-94759. 144p. 1973. pap. 2.50 o.p. (ISBN 0-385-01862-2). Doubleday.

Impossible Doctor Butch. limited autographed ed. Morris Marsh. LC 52-64698. 1952. Harbinger House.

Impossible Dream. Dorothy Dowdell. LC 82-16751. 286p. 1982. Repr. of 1981 ed. 9.95 (ISBN 0-89621-390-0). Thorndike Pr.

Impossible Dreams: A Novel. Patricia Hill. LC 76-4419. (Illus.). 4.50 (ISBN 0-914086-13-8). Alice James Poetry Cooperative.

Impossible Evensen: A Novel. Anthon Bernhard Elias Nilsen. Tr. by Hagen, E. F. LC 34-145464. 1933. Coward-McCann, Inc.

Impossible Marriage. Pamela Hansford Johnson. LC 55-5321. 1955. Harcourt, Brace.

Impossible Mrs. Bellew. David Lisle. LC 16-86941. 1.30. Frederick A. Stokes Company.

Impossible Object. Nicholas Mosley. LC 68-23379. 1969. 4.95. Coward-McCann.

Impossible People. Mary C. E. Wemyss. LC 18-4155. 1918. Houghton Mifflin Company.

Impossible Possibility: Or, Can Such Things Be? A Novel. Charles Edgar Lewis Wingate. LC 8-37046. (On cover: The household library. no. 8, v. 4). 1888. Belford, Clarke & Co.

Impossible Proof. Hans Erich Nossack. LC 68-14912. 1968. Farrar, Straus & Giroux.

Impossible Shore. Robert Kee. LC 50-10373. 1950. McGraw-Hill.

Impossible Spy. Kirby Carr. LC 75-21346. 176p. (Orig.). 1976. pap. 1.25 (ISBN 0-89041-041-0, 3041). Major Bks.

Impossible Tree. Mary F. Lamport. 4.50 o.p. Vantage.

Impossible Virgin. Peter O'Donnell. LC 77-160888. 1971. 5.95. Doubleday.

Impossible Ward. Dorothy Mack. (Candlelight Regency special). 1978. 1.50 (ISBN 0-440-13994-5). Dell Pub. Co.

Impossible World. Eando Binder, pseud. (Orig.). 1970. pap. 0.75 o.p. (0502-07113). Curtis.

Imposter. Joan Brady. LC 78-24642. 214p. 1979. 7.95 (ISBN 0-8076-0915-3). Braziller.

Imposter. Jean Cocteau. 1966. pap. 1.50 o.p. (ISBN 0-8065-0116-2, 223). Citadel Pr.

Imposter, a Tale of Old Annapolis. John Reed Scott. LC 10-21157. 1910. J. B. Lippincott Company.

Impostor. Noel Bertram Gerson. LC 54-5299. 1954. Doubleday.

Impostor. John W Jakes. LC 59-1499. (Mystery house). 1959. T. Bouregy.

Impostor. Rudolf Kagey. LC 42-17987. 1942. Harcourt, Brace and Company.

Impostor. Edmund Keeley. LC 77-89102. 1970. 5.95. Doubleday.

TITLE INDEX IN BISCAYNE BAY.

Impostor; A Novel of Suspense: A Novel of Suspense. Helen McCloy. LC 77-7460. 6.95 (ISBN 0-396-07441-3). Dodd, Mead.
Impostor. Translated from the French by Dorothy Williams. Jean Cocteau. LC 60-35483. 1957. Noonday Press.
Impotent General. Charles Pettit. Tr. by Troubridge, Una Elena (Taylor) LC 31-10977. H. Liveright.
Impounded Waters: A Novel of John McDonogh. Marion Murdoch Laird. LC 51-5020. 1951.
Impoverished Heiress. Diana Burke. (Candlelight Regency Special Ser.: No. 681). (Orig.). 1981. pap. 1.75 (ISBN 0-440-13842-6). Dell.
Impregnable City: A Romance. Max Pemberton. LC 7-36380. 1895. Dodd, Mead & Company.
Impregnable Women. Eric Robert Russell Linklater. LC 38-19254. Farrar & Rinehart, Incorporated.
Impress of a Gentlewoman. Fannie E Newberry. LC 7-17285. Bradley & Woodruff.
Impression Club: A Novel. John Henton Carter. LC 99-5197. 1899. Carter & Bro.
Impressions. Wesley Apker. 3.75 o.p. Vantage.
Impressions of Africa: A Novel. Raymond Roussel. LC 67-13139. 1967. University of California Press.
Impressions of Theophrastus Such. George Eliot. LC 7-301. 1879. Harper & Brothers.
Impressions of Theophrastus Such. George Eliot. LC 8-30416. Harper & Brothers.
Impressions of Theophrastus Such. George Eliot. J. W. Lovell Company.
Impressions of Theophrastus Such. George Eliot. LC 42-27098. (On cover: Munro's library, popular novels...v. 1, no 28). 1883. N. L. Munro.
Impressions of Theophrastus Such. George Eliot. (On cover:Seaside library- Pocket ed. no. 762). 1886. G. Munro.
Impressive Rhymer. F. D. Fuller. 3.95 o.p. Carlton.
Imprisoned Freeman. Helen Smith Woodruff. 1918. G. Sully & Company.
Imprisoned Heart. Jasmine Craig. (Second Chance at Love Ser.: No. 118). 1983. pap. 1.75 (ISBN 0-515-07206-0). Jove Pubns.
Imprisoned Splendor. Angela Morgan, pseud. LC 16-97. 1915. The Baker & Taylor Company.
Improbable Fiction. Sara Woods, pseud. 1973. 0.75. Dell.
Improbable Fiction. Sara Woods, pseud. LC 70-138880. (Rinehart suspense novel). 1971. 4.95 (ISBN 0-03-085088-6). Holt, Rinehart and Winston.
Improbable Tables. Clinton Ross. LC 8-671. 1892. G. P. Putnam's Sons.
Impromptu: A Novel in Four Movements. Elliot Harold Paul. 1923. A. A. Knopf.
Impromptu Impostor. Victor Vicas & Victor Haim. LC 72-141673. (Raven books). 1971. 5.95 (ISBN 0-200-71783-9). Abelard-Schuman.
Improper Betrothment, No. 75. Henrietta Houston. 1982. pap. 1.75 (ISBN 0-515-06686-9). Jove Pubns.
Improper Bostonian. Camden Wells. LC 70-100661. 1971. 6.95 (ISBN 0-8283-1270-2). Branden Press.
Improper Companion. April Kihlstrom. 224p. 1983. pap. text ed. 2.25 (ISBN 0-451-12066-3, Sig). NAL.
Improper Prue. Gloria Manning. 1909. B. W. Dodge & Company.
Improvisation, or The Shepherd's Chameleon see Killer & Other Plays.
Improvisatore. author's ed. Hans Christian Andersen. Tr. by Howitt, Mary (Botham) LC 43-36154. 1869. Hurd and Houghton.
Improvisatore. author's ed. Hans Christian Andersen. Tr. by Howitt, Mary (Botham) LC 42-27493. (On cover: Andersen's works). 1879. Houghton, Osgood and Company.
Improvisatore. author's ed. Hans Christian Andersen. Tr. by Howitt, Mary (Botham) LC 4-16836. (On cover: Andersen's works). Houghton, Mifflin and Company.
Improvisatore. Hans Christian Andersen. Tr. by Howitt, Mary (Botham) LC 6-24454. (choice series, no. 38). 1891. R. Bonner's Sons.
Improvisatore. From the Danish of Hans Christian Andersen. Hans Christian Andersen. Tr. by Howitt, Mary (Botham) LC 7-1645. (On cover: Library of select novels. no. 49). 1863. Harper & Brothers.
Imprudence of Prue. Sophie Fisher. LC 11-5374. The Bobbs Merrill Company.
Imprudent Lady. Joan Smith. 1.75 (ISBN 0-449-23663-3). Fawcett Crest.
Imprudent Lady. Joan Smith. LC 79-10899. (Series: Regency Romance.). 1979. 10.95 (ISBN 0-89340-205-2). J. Curley.
Imprudent Lady. Joan Smith. LC 79-16571. 1979. 13.95 (ISBN 0-8161-6746-X). G. K. Hall.
Impudence of Youth. Warwick Deeping. 1946. The Dial Press.
Impudent Comedian & Others. Frank Frankfort Moore. LC 1-20943. 1897. H. S. Stone and Co.
Impudent Rifle. Dick Pearce, pseud. LC 51-1423. 1951. Lippincott.
Impudent Widow. Maggie Gladstone, pseud. LC 78-20322. (Lacebridge Ladies). 192p. (Orig.). 1979. pap. 1.75 (ISBN 0-87216-508-6). Playboy Pbks.
Impulses: Stories Touching the Life of Sandy, in the City of Saint Francis. Harriet Holmes Haslett. LC 20-11500. The Cornhill Company.
Impy. Vernette Landers. 3.50 o.p. Vantage.
Imram: Vol. II of the Blessing Trilogy. William Barnwell. 272p. (Orig.). 1981. pap. 2.75 (ISBN 0-671-41272-8, Timescape). PB.
Imre: A Memorandum. Edward Irenaeus Prime-Stevenson. LC 75-12337. (Homosexuality). 1975. 9.00 (ISBN 0-405-07388-7). Arno Press.
In a Beautiful Pea Green Boat. James Maurice Scott. LC 72-90002. 1969. Chilton Book Co.
In a Bind. Glen Chase, pseud. (Cherry Delight Ser: No. 19). (Orig.). 1975. pap. 1.25 o.p. (LB242ZK, Leisure Bks). Nordon Pubns.
In a Bind. Glen Chase, pseud. (Cherry Delight#19). 1975. (pbk.) 1.25. Leisure Books.
In a Bluebird's Eye. Anita Clay Kornfeld. LC 74-18867. 1975. 6.95 (ISBN 0-03-013921-X). Holt, Rinehart and Winston.
In a Bluebird's Eye. Anita Clay Kornfeld. 1976. 1.50 (ISBN 0-380-00672-3). Avon Books.
In a Brazilian Jungle: Being a Story of Adventure, with an Insight into Brazilian Life and Industries. Claude Hazeltine Wetmore. LC 3-22810. W. A. Wilde Company.
In a Class by Herself. Linda Crawford. 288p. 1976. 7.95 o.p. (ISBN 0-684-14759-9). Scribner.
In a Class by Herself: A Novel. Linda Crawford. 1978. 1.95 (ISBN 0-445-04218-4). Popular Library.
In a Cloud of Dust. Nellie Morris. LC 40-2117. Mathis, Van Nort & Company.
In a Cold Country. Michael Rubin. 1971. 7.95 o.p. (ISBN 0-07-054188-4). McGraw.
In a Corner of Asia: Being Tales and Impressions of Men and Things in the Malay Peninsula. Hugh Charles Clifford. LC 77-106265. (Short story index reprint series). 1970. (ISBN 0-8369-3302-8). Books for Libraries Press.
In a Corsican Village. Shirley Deane. (O.s.i.). 5.95 o.s.i. (ISBN 0-8149-0080-1). Vanguard.
In a Crucible: A Novel. Eliza Lofton Phillips Pugh. LC 7-42193. 1872. Claxton, Remsen & Haffelfinger.
In a Cup of the Hills: A Story of the Ozarks. Fenetta Sargent Haskell. LC 30-19827. The Christopher Publishing House.
In a Dark Garden. Joanne Gille Aldrich. 1975. 4.95. Avalon Books.
In a Dark Garden. Frank Gill Slaughter. LC 76-2360. 1976. 9.95. Rivercity Press.
In a Dark Garden. Frank Gill Slaughter. LC 48-8266. 1947. Sun Dial Press.
In a Dark Time. Lawrence Watson. LC 79-9165. 1979. 8.95 (ISBN 0-684-16285-7). Scribner.
In a Dark Wood. Marina Warner. LC 77-4366. 1977. 8.95 (ISBN 0-394-41144-7). Knopf.
In a Dark Wood. Marina Warner. LC 77-75013. 1977. 8.95 (ISBN 0-394-41144-7). Knopf.
In a Desert Land. Valentina Hawtrey. LC 16-26138. 1915. Duffield and Company.
In a Dike Shanty. Maria Louise Pool. LC 7-38179. 1896. Stone & Kimball.
In a Far Country. Adam Kennedy. 464p. 1983. 16.95 (ISBN 0-440-04217-8). Delacorte.
In a Far Distant Land: Selected Stories. Ivan Alekseevich Bunin. LC 82-21296. 1983. 8.50 (ISBN 0-938920-27-8). Hermitage.
In a Farther Country: A Romance. William Goyen. LC 55-8143. 1955. Random House.
In a Free State. Vidiadhar Surajprasad Naipaul. LC 79-154916. 1971. 5.95 (ISBN 0-394-47185-7). Knopf.
In a Free State. Vidiadhar Surajprasad Naipaul. LC 78-310863. 1977. 1.95 (ISBN 0-14-003711-X). Penguin.
In a German Pension. Katherine Mansfield. LC 75-328068. (Penguin modern classics). 1975. 0.50 (ISBN 0-14-002181-7). Penguin.
In a German Pension. Katherine Mansfield. Ed. by John Middleton Murry. LC 26-26286. 1926. A. A. Knopf.
In a Glass Darkly. Janet Caird. LC 66-24560. 1966. bds., 3.95. Morrow.
In a Glass Darkly. E. V. Dillon. LC 74-82216. 216p. 1974. 7.95 o.p. (ISBN 0-8059-2054-4). Dorrance.
In a Glass Darkly. Joseph Sheridan Le Fanu. LC 76-5271. (Le Fanu, Joseph Sheridan, 1814-1873. Works. 1976). 1976. (3 vols.) 54.00 (ISBN 0-405-09216-4). Arno Press.
In a Green Shade. facs. ed. Maurice Henry Hewlett. LC 70-86760. (Essay Index Reprint Ser). 1920. 13.00 (ISBN 0-8369-1169-5). Ayer Co.
In a Harbour Green. 1st Ed. Benedict Kiely. LC 50-9315. 1950. Dutton.
In a Hawaiian Valley. Kathleen Dickenson Mellen. LC 47-11606. 1947. Hastings House.
In a High Place: A Novel. Joanne Meschery. LC 81-9028. 14.95 (ISBN 0-671-43024-6). Simon and Schuster.
In a Hollow of the Hills. Bret Harte. LC 79-96884. 1969. Literature House.
In a Hollow of the Hills. Bret Harte. LC 41-38124. 1895. Houghton Mifflin Company.
In a House Unknown. Dolores Birk Hitchens. LC 72-92221. 1973. 4.95 (ISBN 0-385-03265-X). Published for the Crime Club by Doubleday.
In a House Unknown. Dolores Birk Hitchens. LC 74-4123. 1974. (lib. bdg.) 8.95 (ISBN 0-8161-6199-2). G. K. Hall.
In a Lady's Service. Tom Ardies. LC 76-1697. 1976. 6.95 (ISBN 0-385-04583-2). Doubleday.
In a Large Room: A Novel of Christian Dedication in Everyday Life. With the Collaboration of Arthur C. Peabody. 1st Ed. Gladys Barry Peabody. 1960. Greenwich Book Publishers.
In a Little Town. Rupert Hughes. 1917. Harper & Brothers.
In a Lonely Place. Dorothy Belle Flanagan Hughes. LC 47-31459. 1947. Duell, Sloan and Pearce.
In a Lonely Place. Dorothy Belle Flanagan Hughes. LC 79-21743. 1980. 11.95 (ISBN 0-89340-236-2). J. Curley & Associates.
In a Lonely Place. Karl Edward Wagner. 288p. 1983. pap. 2.95 (ISBN 0-446-30534-0). Warner Bks.
In a Man's Time. Peter Marin. LC 73-18929. 1974. 7.95 (ISBN 0-671-21708-9). Simon and Schuster.
In a Monk's Cassock. Pearl Van Antwerp Moran. LC 10-263713. 1.00. W. B. Conkey Company.
In a Murderous Time. R. D. Skillings. 180p. 1983. signed ltd. ed. 17.95 (ISBN 0-918222-35-4); pap. 5.95 (ISBN 0-918222-34-6). Apple Wood.
In a Mysterious Way. Anne Warner French. 1909. 1.50. Little, Brown, and Company.
In a Narrow Grave. Larry McMurtry. 1974. Repr. 7.50 (ISBN 0-88426-041-0). Encino Pr.
In a Narrow Grave. Larry McMurtry. 1971. pap. 3.95 o.p. (ISBN 0-671-20475-0, Touchstone Bks). S&S.
In a Nazi Garden. Lona Mosk. LC 34-11259. The Vanguard Press.
In a North Country Village. Mary E. Sweetman Blundell. LC 7-3082. 1893. Little, Brown & Company; Etc. Etc.
In a Pig's Eye. Viggiani. LC 81-67765. 12.95 (ISBN 0-88008-000-0). Epimetheus Press.
In a Promised Land: A Novel. M A Bengough. LC 7-34446. (On cover: Harper's Franklin square library. no. 733). 1893. Harper & Brothers.
In a Province. Laurens Van Der Post. LC 35-7318. 1934. Coward-McCann, Inc.
In a Province: Reissue. Laurens Van Der Post. 1965. 4.50. Morrow.
In a Shallow Grave. James Purdy. LC 75-30399. 7.50 (ISBN 0-87795-124-1). Arbor House.
In a Shantung Garden. Louise Jordan Miln. LC 24-17123. 1924. Frederick A. Stokes Company.
In a Silent World: The Love Story of a Deaf Mute. LC 7-883912. 1896. Dodd Mead and Company.
In a Small Town a Kid Went to Schul. Ben Deutschman. LC 76-148013. 1971. 4.50 (ISBN 0-87695-139-6). Aurora Pubs.
In a Spasm of Enthusiam. Wanda G. Cunningham. 1964. 3.00 o.p. (ISBN 0-8233-0156-7). Golden Quill.
In a State of Decay. Ralph Raymon Jump. 176p. 1975. 6.00 o.p. (ISBN 0-682-48097-5). Exposition.
In a State of Decay:: a Novel. 1st. ed. Ralph Raymon Jump. 1975. 6.00 (ISBN 0-682-48097-5). Exposition Press.
In a Steamer Chair and Other Shipboard Stories. Robert Barr. LC 74-116935. (Short story index reprint series). 1970. Books for Libraries Press.
In a Steamer Chair and Other Shipboard Stories. Robert Barr. LC 6-8634. (On cover: Cassell's sunshine series, no. 107). 1892. Cassell Publishing Company.
In a Steamer Chair, and Other Shipboard Stories. Robert Barr. LC 13-12917. F. A. Stokes Company.
In a Strange Land. Vladimir Galaktionovich Korolenko. LC 74-14354. 1975. 13.00 (ISBN 0-8371-7801-0). Greenwood Press.
In a Strange Land. Vladimir Galaktionovich Korolenko. Tr. by Zilboorg, Gregory. LC 25-8124. 1925. Bernard G. Richards Co., Inc.
In a Summer Season: A Novel. Ludwig Lewisohn. LC 55-5748. 1955. Farrar, Straus.
In a Summer Season: A Novel. Elizabeth Taylor. LC 61-5920. 1961. Viking Press.
In a U-Haul North of Damascus. David Bottoms. 59p. 1983. pap. 3.95 (ISBN 0-688-01743-6). Quill NY.
In a Valley of This Restless Mind. Malcolm Muggeridge. LC 77-19367. (Illus.). 8.95 (ISBN 0-529-05489-2). Collins.
In a Wild Sanctuary. William Harrison. LC 71-83693. 1975. (pbk.) 1.50 (ISBN 0-446-78956-9). Warner Books.
In a Year of Grace. Honor Lilbush Wingfield Tracy. LC 74-29595. 1975. 6.95 (ISBN 0-394-49506-3). Random House.
In a Yellow Wood. Gore Vidal. LC 47-1967. 1947. E. P. Dutton & Company, Inc.
In a Yun-Nan Courtyard. Louise Jordan Miln. LC 27-20762. 1927. Frederick A. Stokes Compnay.
In Accordance with the Evidence. Oliver Onions. LC 75-44996. (Fifty Classics of Crime Fiction, 1900-1950; No. 39). 1976. 12.00 (ISBN 0-8240-2388-9). Garland Pub.
In Accordance with the Evidence. Oliver Onions. 1.25. George H. Doran Company, Publishers in America for Hodder & Stoughton.
In Adam's Fall: A Novel. Constance Woodbury Dodge. LC 46-7122. 1946. Macrae-Smith-Company.
In Adullam's Lair. Charles Olson. LC 76-353742. (Archetype; 1). (Illus.). To the Lighthouse Press.
In After Years. John Singleton Thomas. LC 13-16341. 1913. The Foley Railway Printing Company.
In All Its Fury: Story of January 12th, 1888 Blizzard. W. H. O'Gara. 1975. pap. 5.00. D Jenkins.
In All Its Glory. Edith Warren Huggins. LC 45-5353. 1945. Dorrance & Company.
In All Walks of Life. Josephine Lawrence. LC 68-20070. 1968. Harcourt, Brace & World.
In Amazon Land: Adaptations from Brazilian Writers. Martha F Sesselberg. 1893. G. P. Putnam's Sons.
In Ambush. Marie Van Vorst. LC 9-28121. 1909. J. B. Lippincott Company.
In an Alpine Valley. Isabel Constance Clarke. LC 39-4598. 1938. Longmans, Green & Co.
In an Evil Hour, and Other Stories. Margaret Wolfe Hungerford. (On cover: Seaside library. Pocket ed., no. 1009). 1887. G. Munro.
In & Around the Stable Stories. Maud Lines. 3.50 o.p. Vantage.
In and Out. Edgar Franklin Stearns. LC 17-17078. 1.35. W. J. Watt & Company.
In and Out. Ann Taylor. LC 71-7610. 1969. 1.75. Ophelia Press.
In and Out of a French Country-House. Anna Bowman Blake Dodd. LC 10-23743. 1910. Dodd, Mead & Company.
In and Out of Never-Never Land: 22 Stories. Maeve Brennan. LC 68-12488. 1969. 5.95. Scribner.
In Another Country. John Bayley, pseud. LC 55-100764. 1955. Coward-McCann.
In Another Country: A Novel. David Albert Davidson. LC 50-10019. 1950. Random House.
In Another Girl's Shoes. Berta Ruck. LC 16-167166. 1916. 1.35. Dodd, Mead and Company.
In Another Moments. Charles Belmont Davis. LC 13-9791. 1.25. The Bobbs-Merrill Company.
In Any Case: A Novel. Richard G Stern. LC 62-17648. 1962. McGraw-Hill.
In Apple-Blossom Time: A Fairy-Tale to Date. Clara Louise Root Burnham. LC 19-15316. 1919. Houghton Mifflin Company.
In Araby Orion. Edward John Thompson. LC 30-28405. Farrar & Rinehart, Incorporated.
In at the Death. Zenith Jones Brown. LC 30-8608. 1930. Longmans, Green and Co.
In at the Kill. E. X Ferrars, pseud. LC 78-20025. 1979. 7.95 (ISBN 0-385-14913-1). Published for the Crime Club by Doubleday.
In at the Kill. E. X Ferrars, pseud. LC 80-18148. 1980. 2.50 (ISBN 0-14-005644-0). Penguin Books.
In Bad Hands: And Other Stories. Frederick William Robinson. LC 7-41964. (Harper's Franklin square library, no. 595). 1887. Harper & Brothers.
In Bad with Sinbad. Arthur John Arbuthnott Stringer. LC 26-8386. The Bobbs-Merrill Company.
In Beauty Like the Night. David Evans. LC 49-10014. Bobbs-Merrill Co.
In Beaver Cove and Elsewhere. Matt Crim. LC 6-316053. 1892. C. L. Webster & Co.
In Bed One Night and Other Brief Encounters. Robert Coover. LC 83-3721. 15.00 (ISBN 0-930901-16-9) (ISBN 0-930901-17-7). Burning Deck.
In Bed We Cry. abridged ed. Ilka Chase. LC 48-1895. (New Avon library, 140). 1947. Avon Book Co.
In Bed We Cry. Ilka Chase. LC 43-16719. 1943. Doubleday, Doran & Company, Inc.
In Bethany House: A Story of Social Service. Mary Elizabeth Smith. LC 12-11152. Fleming H. Revell Company.
In Between the Sheets, and Other Stories. Ian McEwan. LC 79-1034. 7.95 (ISBN 0-671-24290-3). Simon and Schuster.
In Between the Sheets and Other Stories. Ian McEwan. (Berkley book). 1985. 2.25 (ISBN 0-425-04719-9). Berkley Pub. Corp.
In Biscayne Bay. Caroline Washburn Rockwood. 1891. Dodd, Mead and Company.

In Black and Gold: A Story of Twin Dragons. Julia MacNair Wright. LC 9-909. Congregational Sunday-School and Publishing Society.

In Black and White. Rudyard Kipling. LC 9-3019. The Lovell Company.

In Black and White. Rudyard Kipling. LC 42-27367. 1899. R. F. Fenno & Company.

In Black & Whitey. 2nd ed. Ed Lacy. (Orig.). 1969. pap. 0.75 o.p. (74-521). Lancer.

In Blessed Cyrus. Laura Elizabeth Howe Richards. LC 21-18583. 1921. D.Appleton and Company.

In Blue Uniform: An Army Novel. George Israel Putnam. LC 19-2892. 1893. C. Scribner's Sons.

In Bonds. A Novel. Louise Palmer Heaven. LC 7-5042. 1867. A. Roman & Company.

In Brighter Climes: Or Life in Socioland. Albert Chavannes. LC 6-23429. (On cover: The new thought library, no. 1). 1897. Chavannes and Co.

In Buff and Blue: Being Certain Portions from the Diary of Richard Hilton, Gentleman, of Haslet's Regiment of Delaware Foot, in Our Ever Glorious War of Independence. George Brydges Rodney. LC 7-39807. 1897. Little, Brown and Company.

In Buncombe County. Maria Louise Pool. LC 7-38178. 1896. H. S. Stone & Company.

In Caesar's Shadow. Mary Machado. 376p. 1975. pap. 3.95 o.p. (ISBN 0-8059-2203-2). Dorrance.

In Calvert's Valley. Margaret Prescott Montague. LC 8-31465. 1908. 1.50. The Baker & Taylor Company.

In Camp with a Tin Soldier. John Kendrick Bangs. LC 6-6126. 1892. R. H. Russell & Son.

In Case. James Sherry. (Contemporary Literature Ser.: No. 11). 54p. (Orig.). 1981. pap. 5.00 (ISBN 0-940650-11-8). Sun & Moon MD.

In Case of Emergency. Georges Simenon. LC 58-9371. 1958. Doubleday.

In Castle and Colony. Emma Rayner. LC 99-2966. 1899. H. S. Stone and Company.

In Caverns Below. Stanton Arthur Coblentz. LC 75-399. (Garland Library of Science Fiction). 1975. 11.00 (ISBN 0-8240-1405-7). Garland Pub.

In Chancery. John Galsworthy. LC 20-18920. 1920. C. Scribner's Sons.

In Chancery: And Awakening. John Galsworthy. LC 71-8102. (His The Forsyte chronicles, v. 2). (Scribner library. Contemporary classics.). 1969. 1.95. Scribner.

In Charge of the Consul. Ella Florence Padon. LC 8-1404. 1907. R. G. Badger.

In Circling Camps; a Romance of the Civil War. Joseph Alexander Altsheler. LC 3399. 1900. D. Appleton and Company.

In Circling Camps; a Romance of the Civil War. Joseph Alexander Altsheler. LC 24-28537. 1921. D. Appleton and Company.

In Clay and in Bronze: A Study in Personality. Brinsley MacNamara. LC 21-9709. Brentano's.

In Clay and in Bronze: A Study in Personality. A. E. Weldon. LC 21-9709. 1920. Brentano's.

In Cold Blood. Armstrong Livingston. LC 31-23468. The Bobbs-Merrill Company.

In Cold Pursuit. Ursula Reilly Curtiss. 1979. pap. 1.95 (ISBN 0-345-28443-7). Ballantine.

In Cold Pursuit. Ursula Reilly Curtiss. 1982. 15.00x (ISBN 0-333-23387-5, Pub. by Macmillan England). State Mutual Bk.

In Cold Pursuit: A Novel of Suspense. Ursula Reilly Curtiss. LC 77-22447. 6.95 (ISBN 0-396-07466-9). Dodd, Mead.

In Colonial Days. Nathaniel Hawthorne. LC 6-29091. 1906. L. C. Page & Company.

In Colonial Days: A Tale of Rhode Island and Providence Plantations. L. M. N & N., L. M. LC 8-34325. American Baptist Publication Society.

In Colonial Times: The Adventures of Ann, the Bound Girl of Samuel Wales, of Braintree, in the Province of Massachusetts Bay. Mary Eleanor Wilkins Freeman. LC 99-2626. Lothrop Publishing Company.

In Comes Death. 1st Ed. Paul Whelton. LC 51-3967. (Main line mysteries). 1951. Lippincott.

In Connection with Kilshaw. Peter Driscoll. LC 73-20288. 1974. 7.95 (ISBN 0-397-00985-2). Lippincott.

In Connection with the De Willoughby Claim. Frances Hodgson Burnett. LC 4-15419. 1899. C. Scribner's Sons.

In Connection with the De Willoughby Claim. Frances Hodgson Burnett. LC 41-347824. 1907. C. Scribner's Sons.

In Constant Flight: Stories. Elizabeth Tallent. LC 82-48722. 1983. 11.95 (ISBN 0-394-52816-6). Knopf: Distributed by Random House.

In Corner B. Ezekiel Mphahlele. 1967. pap. 2.00 o.p. (Pub. by East African Publ Hse). Northwestern U Pr.

In Cotton Wool. William Babington Maxwell. LC 12-13893. 1912. D. Appleton and Company.

In Council Rooms Apart. John Craig. LC 77-136802. 1971. 5.95. Putnam.

In Crossfire of Hate. Martha Wall. 1970. 4.95 o.p. Moody.

In Crowd. Cecil R. Guiles. 1976. pap. 3.50 (ISBN 0-87148-627-X). Pathway Pr.

In Cupid's Chains. A Novel of Incident. Charles Garvice. (On cover: Laurel library. no. 26). 1896. G. Munro's Sons.

In Cupid's Net. Charlotte Mary Brame. (On cover: Seaside library. Pocket ed. no. 304). G. Munro.

In Cupid's Net. Charlotte Mary Brame. (On cover: Lovell's library. v. 14. no. 700). J. W. Lovell Company.

In Cure of Her Soul. Frederic Jesup Stimson. 1906. D. Appleton and Company.

In Daddy's Bed. Stephen A. Jones. pap. 1.95 o.p. (ISBN 0-87056-191-X). Brandon.

In Dark Places. John Russell. LC 23-8944. 1923. A. A. Knopf.

In Darkest Childhood. Richard Gibson Hubler. LC 54-6537. 1954. Coward-McCann.

In Darkness. Roger Bourgeon. LC 70-103316. 1969. 5.50. Morrow.

In Days of Old When Knights Were Bold. Mabel Cronise Jones. LC 11-318546. 1.50. Broadway Publishing Co.

In Days That Are Dead. Hugh Charles Clifford. LC 77-113651. (Short story index reprint series). 1970. Books for Libraries Press.

In Days That Are Dead. Hugh Charles Clifford. LC 26-21461. 1926. Doubleday, Page & Company.

In Days to Come. Ashtar. (Illus.). 1975. pap. 3.95 o.p. Sauцerian.

In Deacon's Orders. Walter Besant. LC 75-1541. (Victorian Fiction: Novels of Faith and Doubt). 1976. 35.00 (ISBN 0-8240-1612-2). Garland Pub.

In Deacon's Orders: And Other Stories. Walter Besant. LC 76-128720. (Short story index reprint series). 1970. Books for Libraries Press.

In Deacon's Orders, and Other Stories. Walter Besant. LC 6-12391. 1895. Harper & Brothers.

In Dead Earnest. Julia Breckinridge. LC 6-17939. The Authors' Publishing Company.

In Deep. Patricia Cooper. LC 67-19970. 1967. Delacorte Press.

In Deep. Damon Francis Knight. 176p. 1972. pap. 0.75 o.p. (532-00444-075). Manor Bks.

In Deep Abyss: A Novel. Georges Ohnet. Tr. by Rothwell, Fred. LC 1-7310. 1901. Funk & Wagnalls Company.

In Deep. 1st Ed. Bernard Wolfe. LC 56-577723. 1957. Knopf.

In Defense of Mrs. Maxon: A Novel. George Agnew Chamberlain. LC 38-211681. The Bobbs-Merrill Company.

In Defiance of the King: A Romance of the American Revolution. Chauncey Crafts Hotchkiss. LC 7-71443. (Appletons' town and country library, no. 178). 1895. D. Appleton and Companh.

In Desert and Wilderness. Henryk Sienkiewicz. Tr. by Max Anthony Drezmal. LC 12-3599. 1912. Little, Brown, and Company.

In Desert and Wilderness. Henryk Sienkiewicz. Tr. by Max Anthony Drezmal. LC 23-13013. 1923. Little, Brown, and Company.

In Desert Arizona. Sullivan Calvin Richardson. LC 38-18908. Zion's Printing and Publishing Company.

In Desperation. Ethel Winifred Savi. LC 33-11791. 1932. G. H. Watt.

In Direst Peril: A Novel. David Christie Murray. LC 7-31828. 1894. Harper & Brothers.

In Divers Paths. Stories. Sarah Perot Brooks. 1896. The Student Publishing Company.

In Dixie Land: Stories of the Reconstruction Era. Henrietta Raymer Palmer. LC 27-5603. 1926. The Purdy Press.

In Dixie Land; Stories of the Reconstruction Era. Ed. by Henrietta Raymer Palmer. LC 73-267. (Short story index reprint series). 1973. 12.50 (ISBN 0-8369-4250-7). Books for Libraries Press.

In Dreamland: A Story of Living and Giving. Hannah Daviess Pittman. LC 15-220671. R. G. Badger; Etc., Etc.

In Dreams Begin Responsibilities. Delmore Schwartz. Ed. by James Atlas. LC 77-15989. (Cloth ed. 10.95 o.p.). 1978. pap. 5.95 (ISBN 0-8112-0680-7, NDP454). New Directions.

In Dreams Begin Responsibilities and Other Stories. Delmore Schwartz & James Atlas. LC 77-15989. 1978. 10.95 (ISBN 0-8112-0679-3) (ISBN 0-8112-0680-7). New Directions Pub. Corp.

In Dubious Battle. John Steinbeck. LC 36-2209. 1963. Viking.

In Dubious Battle. John Steinbeck. LC 36-2209. Covici-Friede.

In Dubious Battle. John Steinbeck. LC 39-27817. (Half-title: Modern library of the world's best books). 1939. The Modern Library.

In Dubious Battle. John Steinbeck. LC 78-1530. 1978. 1.95 (ISBN 0-14-004888-X). Penguin Books.

In Durance Vile, and Other Stories. Margaret Wolfe Hungerford. LC 7-9361. (On cover: Lovell's library. v. 10, no. 530). 1885. J. W. Lovell Company.

In Durance Vile, and Other Stories. Margaret Wolfe Hungerford. LC 24-14928. 1903. J. B. Lippincott Company.

In Durance Vile & Other Stories. facsimile ed. Margaret Wolfe Hungerford. LC 73-103518. (Short Story Index Reprint Ser.). 1903. 17.00 (ISBN 0-8369-3260-9). Ayer Co.

In Durance Vile: And Other Stories. Margaret Wolfe Hamilton Hungerford. LC 73-103518. (Short story index reprint series). 1969. Books for Libraries Press.

In Editha's Days. A Tale of Religious Liberty. Mary Ellen Bamford. LC 6-6296. (On cover: The crown series). 1894. American Baptist Publication Society.

In Empty Rooms: Tales of Love. Henry H Roth. LC 79-50422. (Illus.). 5.00 (ISBN 0-913204-11-0). December Press.

In Enemy Hands. Richard Sapir & Warren Murphy. (Destroyer, 26). 1.25 (ISBN 0-523-00992-5). Pinnacle Books.

In Enemy Hands: The Destroyer No. 26. Warren Murphy. (Destroyer Ser.). 1977. pap. 1.75 (ISBN 0-523-40902-8). Pinnacle Bks.

In England, Once. Hugh Chesterman. LC 27-184782. 1926. D. Appleton and Company.

In Evil Hour. Garcia Marquez, Gabriel. LC 81-5049. 8.95 (ISBN 0-06-011414-2). Harper & Row.

In Evil Hour. Gabriel Garcia Marquez. 1980. pap. 2.75 (ISBN 0-380-52167-9, 52167, Bard). Avon.

In Exchange for a Soul. Mary Linskill. LC 11-8213. F. F. Lovell & Company.

In Exchange for a Soul. A Novel. Mary Linskill. (Harper's Franklin square library. no. 611). 1887. Harper & Brothers.

In Exile. LC 8-33272. 1871. J. B. Lippincott & Co.

In Exile: And Other Stories. Mary Hallock Foote. LC 69-11891. (American short story series, v. 49). 1969. Garrett Press.

In Exile, and Other Stories. Mary Hallock Foote. LC 72-8174. (American short story series, v. 49). 1972. (ISBN 0-8422-8045-6). MSS Information Corp.

In Exile: And Other Stories. Mary Hallock Foote. LC 6-41411. 1894. Houghton, Mifflin and Company.

In Extremis. A Novelette. Sarah Dana Loring Greenough. LC 6-44861. 1872. Roberts Brothers.

In Far Lochaber. William Black. LC 6-12935. (Seaside library. Pocket ed., no. 1132). 1888. G. Munro.

In Far Lochaber: A Novel. William Black. LC 41-42325. 1888. Harper & Brothers.

In Fear of Silence. John Slimming. LC 61-6206. 1959. Harper.

In Fetters: the Man or the Priest? Thomas Kirwan. LC 7-14284. 1893. De Wolfe, Fiske & Co.

In Flagrant Delight. Brian McNaughton. pap. 1.95 o.s.i. (OPS-46). Olympia.

In Florida's Dawn: A Romance of History. Pleasant Daniel Gold. LC 26-625918. 1926. H. & W. B. Drew Company.

In for a Penny. Sophie Kerr. LC 31-23577. Farrar & Rinehart, Incorporated.

In for a Penny: With Illus. by John Mackey. Oliver Anderson. LC 50-9842. 1950. Morrow.

In Freedom's Dawn. Alice Shelbourne. LC 55-11948. 1957. B. Humphries.

In Freshman Year: The Story of a Real Boy and His Dad. John Gaylord Coulter. LC 24-295398. 1934. W. H. Wise & Company.

In Friends We Trust. Marjorie Bayley. LC 38-30609. 1938. Coward-McCann, Inc.

In Gallant. Alexander Kent. 1978. 1.95 (ISBN 0-425-03987-0). Berkley Pub. Corp.

In Gallant Company. Alexander Kent. LC 77-3988. 1977. 8.95 (ISBN 0-399-11987-6). Putnam.

In Garde We Trust. Jerry LaPlante. (Chameleon Ser.: No. 2). (Orig.). 1979. pap. 1.95 (ISBN 0-89083-513-6). Zebra.

In God We Trust: All Others Pay Cash. Jean Shepherd. pap. 5.95 (ISBN 0-385-02174-7, Dolp). Doubleday.

In God We Trust: All Others Pay Cash. 1st Ed. Jean Shepherd. LC 64-19321. 1966. 4.50. Doubleday.

In "God's Country" A Novel. Dora Higbee Geppert. LC 6-44246. (On cover: The Belford American novel series, no. 218). 1890. Belford Company.

In "God's Country," A Southern Romance. Dora Higbee Geppert. LC 6-44245. (On cover: Fornightly series, no. 39). American Publishers Corporation.

In God's Good Time: A Novel. Henry M Ross. LC 7-11206. 1907. Benziger Brothers.

In God's Land. Martin Andersen Nexo. LC 33-8302. 1933. P. Smith.

In God's Way: A Novel. Bjornstjerne Bjornson. LC 77-14542. (Bjrnson, Bjrnstjerne, 1832-1910. The Novels of Bjrnstjerne Bjrnson: Vols. 9-10). 1978. 18.00. H. Fertig.

In God's Way, a Novel. Bjornstjerne Bjornson & Carmichael, Elizabeth, Tr. LC 11-10563. (On cover: Lovell's series of foreign literatures, no. 3). J. W. Lovell Company.

In Gold and Silver... George Herman Ellwanger. LC 6-37837. 1892. D. Appleton and Company.

In Golden Shackles. Louie Alien Baker. LC 6-6877. 1896. Dodd, Mead & Company.

In Grape Time. Juanita Tobin. LC 82-507. 64p. 10.00 (ISBN 0-942190-02-5); pap. 95.00 (ISBN 0-942190-01-7). Pubn Arts.

In Great Waters. Thomas Allibone Janvier. LC 70-98577. (Short Story Index Reprint Ser.). 1901. 15.00 (ISBN 0-8369-3151-3). Ayer Co.

In Great Waters: Four Stories. Thomas Allibone Janvier. LC 70-98577. (Short story index reprint series). (Illus.). 1969. Books for Libraries Press.

In Great Waters: Four Stories. Thomas Allibone Janvier. LC 1-25441. 1901. Harper & Brothers.

In Guiana Wilds: A Study of Two Women. James Rodway. LC 99-4106. 1899. L. C. Page and Company (Incorporated).

In Guilt and in Glory: Novel. David Hanly. LC 78-12474. 1979. 10.95 (ISBN 0-688-03421-7). W. Morrow.

In Hampton Roads: A Dramatic Romance. Charles Eugene Banks & Cook, George Cram, 1873-1924, Joint Author. LC 90-5165. 1899. Rand, McNally & Company.

In Happy Hollow. Charles Heber Clark. LC 3-128202. 1903. H.T. Coates & Co.

In Happy Valley. John Fox. 1917. C. Scribner's Sons.

In Hazard. Richard Arthur Warren Hughes. LC 71-5561. 1969. P. Smith.

In Hazard. Richard Arthur Warren Hughes. LC 38-27865. 1938. Harper & Brothers.

In Her Day. Rita Mae Brown. LC 76-7817. 4.50 (ISBN 0-913780-14-6). Daughters, Inc.

In Her Earliest Youth. Jessie Catherine Huybers Couvreur. (On cover: Lovell's international series, no. 66). F. F. Lovell & Company.

In Her Earliest Youth: A Novel. Jessie Catherine Huybers Couvreur. LC 6-28870. (On cover: Harper's Frauklin square library no. 670). 1890. Harper & Brothers.

In Her Garden. Jon Godden. LC 80-19849. 1981. 9.95 (ISBN 0-394-51361-4). Knopf: Distributed by Random House.

In Her Garden. large print ed. Jon Godden. LC 81-9087. (Illus.). 10.95 (ISBN 0-89621-308-0). Thorndike Press.

In Her Own Hands. Helen Albee Monsell. LC 43-14492. 1943. The Bobbs-Merrill Company.

In Her Own Right. John Reed Scott. LC 11-135211. 1911. 1.25. J. B. Lippincott Company.

In Her Own Words. George Sand & Joseph Amber Barry. LC 78-55845. 1979. 4.95 (ISBN 0-385-13346-4). Anchor Books.

In Her Prime. Carole N. Douglas. (Love & Life Romance Ser.). 160p. (Orig.). 1982. pap. 1.75 (ISBN 0-345-30523-X). Ballantine.

In High Places. Mary Schell Hoke Bacon. LC 7-312120. 1907. Doubleday, Page & Company.

In High Places. Arthur Hailey. 1970. pap. 2.95 (ISBN 0-553-14529-0). Bantam.

In High Places. Arthur Hailey. LC 61-9513. 1961. 10.95 (ISBN 0-385-04159-4). Doubleday.

In High Places. William Brown Meloney. LC 39-25704. 1939. A. A. Knopf.

In High Places: A Novel. 1st Ed. Arthur Hailey. LC 61-9513. 1962. Doubleday.

In Him Was Life. Caroline Glyn. LC 76-26492. 5.95 (ISBN 0-664-24118-2). Westminster Press.

In His Blood: An Original Novel. Harold R Daniels. LC 55-12028. (Dell first edition, 73). 1955. Dell Pub. Co.

In His Garden: The Anatomy of a Murderer. Leo Damore. LC 79-54008. (Illus.). 1981. 14.95 (ISBN 0-87795-250-7). Arbor Hse.

In His Hands, a Novel. 1st Ed. Edwin Balmer. LC 4-6665. 1954. Longmans, Green.

In His Name: A Christmas Story. Edward Everett Hale. LC 6-461793. (Old and new series; no. 2). 1873. Published by the Proprietors of Old and New.

In His Name. A Story of the Waldenses Seven Hundred Years Ago. Edward Everett Hale. 1882. Fairbanks, Palmer & Co.

In His Name. A Story of the Waldenses, Seven Hundred Years Ago. Edward Everett Hale. LC 6-46181. 1888. Roberts Brothers.

In His Name. A Story of the Waldenses, Seven Hundred Years Ago. Edward Everett Hale. LC 1-270521. 1901. Little, Brown, and Co.

In His Name. A Story of the Waldenses, Seven Hundred Years Ago. Edward Everett Hale. LC 42-477061. 1877. Roberts Brothers.

In His Name, and Christmas Stories. Edward Everett Hale. LC 4-15397. (Half-title: The works of E. E. Hale. Library ed. vol. II). 1899. Little, Brown, and Company.

In His Own Country: A Novel. John Gill. LC 35-5461. 1935. E. P. Dutton & Co., Inc.

In His Own Image. Mary Briarly. LC 21-7411. 1921. The Macmillan Company.

In His Own Image. new ed. Frederick William Rolfe. LC 70-157795. (Short story index reprint series). 1971. (ISBN 0-8369-3907-7). Books for Libraries Press.

In His Own Image. Frederick William Rolfe. LC 26-6027. 1925. A. A. Knopf.

In His Own Image. Frederick William Serafino Austin Lewis Mary D. Rolfe. LC 8-3366. 1901. J. Lane.

In His Steps. Charles Monroe Sheldon. LC 67-17245. (Great religious bks.). 1967. bds., 2.95. Zondervan.

In His Steps. authorized ed. Charles Monroe Sheldon. LC 48-12869. 1947. Universal Book and Bible House.

In His Steps. Charles Monroe Sheldon. LC 99-304199. H. Altemus.

In His Steps. Charles Monroe Sheldon. LC 20-10056. The Christian Herald Bible House.

In His Steps. authorized ed. Charles Monroe Sheldon. LC 35-29211. Grosset & Dunlap.

In His Steps. authorized ed., with an appreciation by daniel a. poling... ed. Charles Monroe Sheldon. LC 37-5029. The John C. Winston Company.

In His Steps. large type ed. Charles Monroe Sheldon. LC 82-165576. (Large Type Christian Classics). 1982. 14.95 (ISBN 0-87983-291-6). Keats Pub.

In His Steps see En Sus Pasos.

In His Steps: By Charles M. Sheldon, And, The Christian's Secret of a Happy Life, by Hannah Whitall Smith. Charles Monroe Sheldon & Hanna Whitall - The Christian'S Secret Of A Happy Life Smith. LC 62-2538. Guideposts Associates.

In His Steps Today. Marti Hefley. LC 75-42375. 4.95 (ISBN 0-8024-4057-6). Moody Press.

In His Steps Today. Charles Monroe Sheldon. LC 29-13682. 1928. David C. Cook Publishing Company.

In His Steps. "What Would Jesus Do?". Charles Monroe Sheldon. LC 51-28791. (Permabooks, P 29). 1949. Permabooks.

In His Steps: "What Would Jesus Do?". Charles Monroe Sheldon. LC 8-5798. 1897. Advance Publishing Co.

In His Steps: "What Would Jesus Do?". author's revised ed., with illustrations by j. w. kennedy. also a biographical sketch of the author by f. w. blackmar. ed. Charles Monroe Sheldon. 1899. H. M. Caldwell Company.

In His Steps: "What Would Jesus Do?". Charles Monroe Sheldon. LC 99-4840. (On cover: Alliance library, no. 1). 1899. Street & Smith.

In His Steps: "What Would Jesus Do?". authorized ed.--rev. ed. Charles Monroe Sheldon. LC 1654. Laird & Lee.

In Honor Bound. By Charles Gibbon ... (Seaside library, v. 37, no. 75). 1880. G. Munro.

In Honour's Cause. A Tale of the Days of George the First. George Manville Fenn. LC 6-39375. 1896. Dodd, Mead and Company.

In Hostile Red. Joseph Alexander Altsheler. 1976. lib. bdg. 15.80x (ISBN 0-89968-003-8). Lightyear.

In Hostile Red; a Romance of the Manmouth Campaign. Joseph Alexander Altsheler. 1902. Doubleday, Page and Company.

In Hostile Red; a Romance of the Monmouth Campaign. Joseph Alexander Altsheler. LC 6152. 1900. Doubleday, Page and Company.

In Hostile Red, a Romance of the Monmouth Campaign. Joseph Alexander Altsheler. LC 19-18906. 1901. International Association of Newspapers and Authors.

In Hot Blood. J. J Savage. LC 77-6478. 1968. 1.75. Ophelia Press.

In Hot Pursuit. Karl Flinders. pap. 1.95 o.s.i. (OPH-253, Ophelia). Olympia.

In Iron Years. Gordon R Dickson. LC 80-664. 1980. 8.95 (ISBN 0-385-01555-0). Doubleday.

In Jeopardy. William Gilbert Van Tassel Sutphen. LC 22-18297. Harper & Brothers.

In Joy & in Sorrow. Joan Joseph. (Orig.). 1982. pap. 3.50 (ISBN 0-440-14367-5). Dell.

In Kali's Country: Tales from Sunny India. Emily Churchill Thompson Sheets. Fleming H. Revell Company.

In Kedar's Tents. Hugh Stowell Scott. LC 5-2457. 1897. Dodd, Mead and Company.

In Kentucky with Daniel Boone. John Thomas McIntyre. LC 13-238822. (His The buckskin books). 1913. 0.75. The Penn Publishing Company.

In Kings' Byways. Stanley John Weyman. 1902. Longmans, Green, and Co.

In King's Houses: A Romance of the Days of Queen Anne. Julia Caroline Ripley Dorr. LC 6-33717. 1898. L. C. Page and Company.

In Krusack's House. Thames Ross Williamson. LC 31-23675. Harcourt, Brace and Company.

In Lawless Lands. Charles Joseph Finger. LC 79-157776. (Short story index reprint series). 1971. (ISBN 0-8369-3888-7). Books for Libraries Press.

In Lawless Lands. Charles Joseph Finger. LC 24-8163. 1924. M. Kennerley.

In League with Israel: A Tale of the Chattanooga Conference. Annie Fellows Johnston. LC 7-10795. 1896. Curts & Jennings.

In Lilac Time. Louise Platt Hauck. LC 36-8768. 1936. Macrae-Smith-Company.

In Lilac Time. Jean Randall. LC 36-8768. 1936. Macrae Smith Company.

In Line of Duty. Richmond Pearson Hobson. LC 10-20900. 1910. D. Appleton and Company.

In Line of Duty: A Novel. Francis P Scannell. LC 46-2486. 1946. Harper & Brothers.

In Little Place, a Novel. Grace Lillian Irwin. 1959. Eerdmans.

In Live with a T-Man. Rob Eden. LC 37-9862. M. S. Mill Co., Inc.

In London: The Story of Adam and Marriage. Conal O'Connell O'Riordan. LC 22-23915. Harcourt, Brace and Company.

In Love. Alfred Hayes. LC 53-8750. 1953. Harper.

In Love & Trouble: Stories of Black Women. Alice Walker. LC 73-15987. (Harvest book, HB277). 1974. 6.50. Harcourt Brace Jovanovich.

In Love and Truth: Or, The Downfall of Samuel Seele, Healer. Anita Clay Munoz. LC 1-31649. The Abbey Press.

In Love & War. Lorinda Hagen. (Leisure Book). 1980. 2.25 (ISBN 0-8439-0719-3). Nordon Publications, Inc.

In Love with Love: Four Life-Studies. James Harcourt West. (On cover: Life series, v. 2). 1894. J. H. West.

In Love with Time. Laura Benet. 1959. 5.00 (ISBN 0-87482-010-3). Wake-Brook.

In Loveless Clarity, and Other Stories. Norval Rindfleisch. LC 72-185526. 1972. 3.95 (ISBN 0-87886-017-7). Ithaca House.

In Love's Crucible. Charlotte Mary Brame. (Street & Smith's select series, no. 37). Street & Smith.

In Love's Crucible. Bertha M. Clay. LC 44-38279. (Select series... no. 37). Street & Smith.

In Love's Domains. A Trilogy. Marah Ellis Martin Ryan. LC 8-1355. (On cover: The Rialto series. v. 1, no. 26). 1890. Rand, McNally & Company.

In Love's Own Fashion. Arlene Hale. LC 80-20883. (Arlene Hale Romance). 1981. 11.50 (ISBN 0-89340-293-1). J. Curley.

In Love's Own Fashion. Arlene Hale. (Signet Book). 1976. (pbk.) 1.25. New American Library.

In Luck at Last. Walter Besant. (On cover: Seaside library. Pocket ed., no. 324). 1885. G. Munro.

In Luck at Last. Walter Besant. (On cover: Lovell's library, no. 1159). 1888. J. W. Lovell Company.

In Luck's Way. Henritta Eliza Vaughan Stannard & Baring-Gould, Sabine, 1834-1924. (On cover: Lovell's international series, no. 173). J. W. Lovell Company.

In Maiden Meditation. Eva Trezevant. LC 8-29717. 1894. A. C. McClurg and Company.

In Maine. John Cole. 1974. 6.95 o.p. (ISBN 0-525-13217-1). Dutton.

In Maremma. Louise De La Ramee. (On cover: Lovell's library. v. 18, no. 851). 1887. J. W. Lovell Company.

In Maremma. A Story. Louise De La Ramee. LC 6-33319. 1882. J. B. Lippincott & Co.

In Market Overt. A Novel. James Payn. LC 7-33774. (On cover: Lippincott's series of select novels). 1895. J. B. Lippincott Company.

In Mary's Reign. Emmuska Orczy. LC 8-14959. The Cupples & Leon Co.

In Memoriam; Mexican Short Stories. Martinez Caceres, Arturo. LC 67-9192. 1967. Vantage Press.

In Memory of Murder... Dean Hawkins. LC 37-5304. 1937. Pub. for the Crime Club, Inc., by Doubleday, Doran & Co., Inc.

In Midsummer Days, and Other Tales. August Strindberg. LC 72-3286. (Short story index reprint series). 1972. (ISBN 0-8369-4164-0). Books for Libraries Press.

In Midsummer Days: And Other Tales, Vol. 1. August Strindberg. Tr. by Ellie Schleussner. LC 72-3286. (Short Story Index Reprint Ser). Repr. of 1913 ed. 16.00 (ISBN 0-8369-4164-0). Ayer Co.

In Miners' Mirage-Land. Idah Meacham Strobridge. LC 4-22979. 1904. Printed by the Baumgardt Publishing Company.

In Miss Armstrong's Room. Elizabeth Frances Corbett. 1973. pap. 0.95 o.p. (345-26514-4-095). Beagle Bks.

In Miss Armstrong's Room. 1st Ed. Elizabeth Frances Corbett. LC 53-891753. 1953. Lippincott.

In Mr. Knox's Country. Edith Anna CEnone Somerville & Violet Florence Martin. 1915. Longmans, Green and Co.

In Mr. Knox's Country. Edith Anna CEnone Somerville & Violet Florence Martin. LC 36-10830. (Half-title: The Longman stories of laughter. no. 6). 1935. Longmans, Green and Co.

In Mountain Shadow: A Tale of the Pennsylvania-Dutch Country. George Brandon Saul. LC 74-27957. Walton Press.

In My End Is My Beginning. Maurice Baring. 1931. 25.00 (ISBN 0-8274-2562-7). R West.

In My Enemy's Arms. R. T. Stevens. 400p. 1980. pap. 2.75 (ISBN 0-446-85662-2). Warner Bks.

In My Father's Court. Isaac Bashevis Singer. 1979. pap. 2.50 (ISBN 0-449-24074-6, Crest). Fawcett.

In My Father's Court. Isaac Bashevis Singer. pap. 1.95 o.p. (ISBN 0-374-50592-6, N320, Noonday). FS&G.

In My Father's House. Charlotte Culbertson. LC 39-2160. 1939. Bookhaven Press, Kellaway-Ide Company.

In My Father's House. Ernest J. Gaines. LC 77-20357. 1978. 7.95 (ISBN 0-394-47938-6). Knopf: Distributed by Random.

In My Father's House. Ernest J. Gaines. LC 78-21565. 1979. 12.50 (ISBN 0-8161-6648-X). G. K. Hall.

In My Father's House. Mabel W. Mullett. (Illus.). 1977. 5.95 o.p. (ISBN 0-533-02403-X). Vantage.

In My Father's House. James Howell Street. LC 41-56794. 1941. The Dial Press.

In My Father's Pastures. Soma Morgenstern & Lewisohn, Ludwig, 1882- Tr. LC 47-7164. Jewish Publication Society of America.

In My Father's Time. Eamon Kelly. LC 76-376202. 1.10 (ISBN 0-85342-457-8). Mercier Press.

In My Garden. Letha Witten Ledbetter. LC 68-3358.

In My Lady's Chamber. John Hawkesworth. LC 79-20187. 1980. 11.95 (ISBN 0-8161-6795-8). G. K. Hall.

In My Lady's Chamber. Elizabeth N. Walker. 224p. 1981. pap. 1.50 (ISBN 0-449-50214-7, Crest). Fawcett.

In My Lady's Chamber: A Novel. Juliet Rolleston. LC 63-1377. 1962. Angus and Robertson.

In My Lady's Garden: Pages from the Diary of Sir John Elwynne. Kate Nichols Trask. LC 7-67669. 1907. J. Lane.

In My Own Good Time. Anthony Gibbs. LC 77-107404. 1970. 6.95. Gambit.

In My Parent's Bedroom. Barry N. Malzberg. pap. 1.25 o.s.i. (OPS-17). Olympia.

In My Time. John D. Lurvey. 1978. 4.95 o.p. (ISBN 0-533-03548-1). Vantage.

In Naaman's House. Marian MacLean Finney. LC 22-186532. The Abingdon Press.

In Noah's Wake. Allan Block. 80p. 1972. 3.95 o.s.i. (ISBN 0-87233-025-7). Bauhan.

In Nueva York. Nicholasa Mohr. LC 76-42931. 7.95 (ISBN 0-8037-4044-1). Dial Press.

In Nueva York. Nicholasa Mohr. ("Laurel Leaf Library"). 1979. 1.75 (ISBN 0-440-94092-3). Dell Pub. Co. Inc.

In Office: A Story of Washington Life and Society. Lewis Vital Bogy. (On cover: The Ariel library. extra no.). 1891. F. J. Schulte & Company.

In Old Alabama: Being the Chronicles of Miss Mouse, the Little Black Merchant. Anne Hobson. LC 73-253. (Short story index reprint series). 1973. (ISBN 0-8369-4246-9). Books for Libraries Press.

In Old Alabama: Being the Chronicles of Miss Mouse, the Little Black Merchant. Anne Hobson. LC 3-213011. 1903. Doubleday, Page & Company.

In Old Bellaire. Mary C Johnson Dillon. 1906. The Century Co.

In Old France and New. William McLennan. LC 161. 1899. Harper & Brothers.

In Old Kentucky: A Story of the Bluegrass and the Mountains Founded on Charles T. Dazey's Play. Edward Marshall & Dazey, Charles Turner. LC 10-8421. 1.50. G. W. Dillingham Company.

In Old Narragansett: Romances and Realities. Alice Morse Earle. (The ivory series). 1898. C. Scribner's Sons.

In Old New York: A Romance. Wilson Barrett. 1900. L. C. Page and Company.

In Old Plantation Days. Paul Laurence Dunbar. LC 70-88429. (Illus.). 1969. Negro Universities Press.

In Old Plantation Days. Paul Laurence Dunbar. LC 3-23486. 1903. Dodd, Mead and Company.

In Old Quivira. Margaret Hill McCarter. LC 8-37709. 1908. Crane & Company.

In Old St. Stephen's: A Novel. Jeanie Drake. LC 6-34229. (On cover: Appletons' town and country library, no. 102). 1892. D. Appleton and Company.

In Old Vintage Days. Frona Eunice Wait Smith Colburn. LC 37-4541. 1937. Printed by J. H. Nash.

In Olden Days Beyond the Sea: From the German. Rebecca H Schively & Blaul, Freidrich, 1800-1863. 1890. Reformed Church Publicaiton House.

In Ole Virginia. Thomas Nelson Page. LC 4-15145. 1896. C. Scribner's Sons.

In Ole Virginia: Or, Marse Chan, and Other Stories. Thomas Nelson Page. LC 68-23723. (Illus.). 1968. Gregg Press.

In Ole Virginia: Or, Marse Chan and Other Stories. Thomas Nelson Page. LC 71-77316. (Southern literary classics series). (Chapel Hill books, chb-40.). 1969. 2.95. University of North Carolina Press.

In Ole Virginia: Or, Marse Chan, and Other Stories. Thomas Nelson Page. LC 12-31300. 1910. C. Scribner's Sons.

In Ole Virginia or Marse Chan & Other Stories. Thomas Nelson Page. 1977. Repr. of 1913 ed. lib. bdg. 20.00 (ISBN 0-8482-2154-0). Norwood Edns.

In One Era & Out the Other. Sam Levenson. (Adult Ser.). 350p. 1974. Repr. lib. bdg. 9.95 o.p. (ISBN 0-8161-6194-1, Large Print Bks). G K Hall.

In One Girl's Experience. Mary Hubbard Howell. LC 7-661995. The American Sunday-School Union.

In One Town. Edmund Downey. (Lovell's library, no. 1216). 1888. J. W. Lovell Company.

In Orbit. Wright Morris. LC 67-117929. (Signet bk., P3291). 1968. New Amer. Lib.

In Orbit. Wright Morris. LC 75-14359. 8.50 (ISBN 0-8032-0882-0) (ISBN 0-8032-5830-5). University of Nebraska Press.

In Orchard Glen. Mary Esther MacGregor. LC 19-5045. 1.50. George H. Doran Company.

In Other Beds. Ed. by Chandler Brossard. (Orig.). pap. 0.75 o.p. (B75-214). Belmont-Tower.

In Other Days: 15 Stories. Prepared Under the Direction of Betty Russell. Designed and Illustrated by Catherine Hinkle. Ed. by Frances Humphreville. LC 56-3673. 1956. Scott, Foresman.

In Oudemon: Reminiseenes of an Unknown People, by an Occasional Traveler, Ed. Henry Shipman Drayton. LC 1-31167. 1901. The Grafton Press.

In Our Convent Days. Agnes Repplier. LC 73-93188. 1969. AMS Press.

In Our Convent Days. Agnes Repplier. LC 78-131817. 1970. (ISBN 0-403-00704-6). Scholarly Press.

In Our Convent Days. Agnes Repplier. LC 5-33973. 1905. Houghton, Mifflin and Company.

In Our County: Stories of Old Virginia Life. Mary Virginia Terhune. LC 1-23092. 1901. G. P. Putnam's Sons.

In Our Time. Ernest Hemingway. LC 25-20973. 1925. Boni & Liveright.

In Our Time. Ernest Hemingway & Wilson, Edmund, 1895- LC 31-26125. 1930. C. Scribner's Sons.

In Our Time, Stories. Ernest Hemingway. LC 62-1045. (Scribner library, SL56). Scribner.

In Our Town. Damon Runyon & Williams, Garth, Illus. LC 46-3771. 1946. Creative Age Press.

In Our Town. William Allen White. LC 72-150567. (Short story index reprint series). (Illus.). 1971. (ISBN 0-8369-3865-8). Books for Libraries Press.

In Our Town. William Allen White. LC 6-12564. 1906. McClure, Philips & Co.

In Palace and Faubourg. A Story of the French Revolution. Caroline J Freeland. LC 6-43128. 1889. T. Nelson and Sons.

In Paradise: A Novel. Paul Johann Ludwig Von Heyse. LC 7-6610. (Half-title: Collection of foreign authors. No. 12). 1878. D. Appleton and Company.

In Passion's Dragnet: A Novel. Hattie Horner Louthan. LC 3-29834. 1903. R. G. Badger.

In Passion's Tempest. Cassandra Dorth. (Orig.). 1981. pap. 2.25 (ISBN 0-505-51634-9). Tower Bks.

In Pastures New. George Ade. LC 74-91072. (American humorists series). (Illus.). 1969. Literature House.

In Pawn. Ellis Parker Butler. LC 21-18166. 1921. 1.90. Houghton Mifflin Company.

In Pawn to a Throne. Demetra Vaka Brown & Brown, Kenneth, 1868- Joint Author. LC 19-15673. 1919. John Lane Company.

In People. Julian Paull. (Orig.). pap. 0.60 o.p. (A213X, Award). Univ Pub & Dist.

In Peril and Privation: Stories of Marine Disaster Retold. James Payn. LC 7-33772. (Harper's handy series, no. 23). 1885. Harper & Brothers.

In Peril and Privation. Stories of Marine Disaster Retold. James Payn. (On cover: Seaside library. Pocket ed. no. 577). 1885. G. Munro.

In Peril of His Life. Emile Gaboriau. LC 6-44551. (Lovell's library. v. 3. no. 120). 1883. J. W. Lovell Company.

In Peril of His Life. Emile Gaboriau. LC 20-12339. (On cover: The Astor prose series). 1902. T. Y. Crowell & Company.

In Peril on the Sea. Montague Thomas Hainsselin. LC 19-12168. 1919. Hodder and Stoughton.

In Piccadilly. William Romaine Paterson. 1903. G. P. Putnam's Sons.

In Pious Memory. Margery Sharp. LC 67-12210. 1967. Little, Brown.

In Place of Love. Aviva Hellman. LC 77-10098. 8.95. Putnam.

In Plain Air. Elizabeth Lyman Cabot. LC 6-21883. 1897. H. Holt and Company.

In Plain Russian: Stories. Vladimir Voinovich. LC 79-11980. 1979. 10.00 (ISBN 0-374-17580-2). Farrar, Straus and Giroux.

In Polish Woods. Joseph Opatoshu. Tr. by Goldberg, Isaac. LC 39-2386. 1938. The Jewish Publication Society of America.

In Praise of Babies. Ed. by James B. Adler. LC 68-14049. (Illus.). 1968. 1.49 o.p. Doubleday.

In Praise of Darkness. Jorge Luis Borges. LC 73-79553. 1974. 8.95 (ISBN 0-525-13225-2). Dutton.

In Praise of Older Women: The Amorous Recollections of Andras Vajda. Stephen Vizinczey. (U7008). 1966. Ballantine.

In Praise of Older Women: The Amorous Recollections of Andras Vajda. Stephen Vizinczey. LC 66-1173. 1966. Trident Press.

In Praise of Swift see Swiftiana.

In Primo: A Story of Facts and Factors. Sarah M De Line. LC 99-1672. 1899. Fleming H. Revell Company.

In Princeton Town. Day Edgar. LC 29-212142. 1929. C. Scribner's Sons.

In Prison and Out. Hesba Stretton. (On cover: Lovell's library, v. 14, no. 729). 1886. J. W. Lovell Company.

In Pursuit of Death. Rupert H. Davis. (Orig.). pap. 1.25x o.p. (LTB). Soccer.

In Pursuit of Evil. Hugh Mills. LC 67-13305. 1967. Lippincott.

In Pursuit of Happiness. Lev Nikolaevich Tolstoi & Delano, Mrs. Arline P. (Kuzmistchev) 1845- Tr. LC 1-19458. D. Lothrop Company.

In Pursuit of Laughter. Agnes Repplier. 230p. 1981. Repr. of 1936 ed. lib. bdg. 25.00 (ISBN 0-8495-4645-1). Arden Lib.

In Pursuit of Priscilla: A Chronicle of the Man Willing and the Woman Wilful. Edward Salisbury Field. LC 7-36088. H. Altemus Company.

In Pursuit of the Awa Maru. W. Jonis & Bill Bunton. 288p. (Orig.). 1981. pap. 2.50 (ISBN 0-553-12624-5). Bantam.

In Quarters with the 25th Dragoons: The Black Horse. Henrietta Eliza Vaughan Stannard. (On cover: Lovell's library, no. 1169). 1888. J. W. Lovell Company.

In Quarters with the 25th: The Black Horse) Dragoons. Henrietta Eliza Vaughan Stannard. LC 8-13859. (Harper's handy series, no. 35). 1885. Harper & Brothers.

In Quest of a Kingdom. Weatherhead. 1.25 o.p. Abingdon.

In Quest of Adventure. Mary Ellen Mannix. LC 14-534932. 1914. Benziger Brothers.

In Quest of Aztec Treasure. Arthur Howard Noll & Wilson, Bourdon. 1911. 1.50. The Neale Publishing Company.

In Quest of Candlelighters. Kenneth Patchen. LC 71-183393. 1972. 6.95 (ISBN 0-8112-0344-1); pap. 1.95 (ISBN 0-8112-0141-4, NDP334). New Directions.

In Quest of Eden. Louis Arthur Cunningham. LC 53-85726. 1953. Arcadia House.

In Quest of Eden: A Novel. Bernard Lewis. LC 79-16347. 8.95 (ISBN 0-87949-131-0). Ashley Books.

In Quest of Gold: Being a Romance Dealing with the Remarkable Expedition of Ferdinand De Soto and His Cavaliers to Florida in the Year 1839. Charles Edward Knowles. LC 12-5156. 1912. 1.00. John Lane Company.

In Quest of Qalara. (Spaceways Ser.: No. 9). 224p. 1983. pap. 2.95 (ISBN 0-86721-236-5). Playboy Pbks.

In Quest of Splendor: Translated by Harry Lorin Binsee. Roger Lemelin. LC 56-18913. 1955. McClelland & Stewart.

In Quest of the Golden Chest: A Story of Adventure. George Barton. LC 13-22281. 1913. 1.15. Benziger Brothers.

In Quest of Truth: Glimpses of Roman Scenes During the Reign of the Emperor Domitian. Robert Muenchgesang. LC 6-1022. 1905. B. Herder.

In Quire. Doug Palmer. 1973. pap. 2.50 (Pub. by Oyez). SBD.

In Rank and File: What It Cost; or, Debtor and Creditor) F Sullivan & Sullivan, I. E. Joint Author. (On cover: Library of choice fiction, no. 36). Laird & Lee.

In Re: Sherlock Holmes: Adventures of Solar Pons. August William Derleth. 3.00 o.p. Arkham.

In Re: Sherlock Holmes" The Adventures of Solar Pons. August William Derleth. LC 45-11429. 1945. Mycroft and Moran.

In Realms Unknown: A Story of Adventure, Invention and Romance. Robert Bell. LC 34-214215. 1934. Bell Publishing Company.

In Realms Unknown: A Story of Adventure, Invention, and Romance. Robert Bell. LC 54-7402. 1954. Vantage Press.

In Red and Gold. Samuel Merwin. LC 21-4502. The Bobbs-Merrill Company.

In Red Weather. Robert S Taylor. LC 61-11726. 1961. Holt, Rinehart and Winston.

In Remembrance of Me. Frank W. Lemons. 1975. 4.25 (ISBN 0-87148-430-7); pap. 3.25 (ISBN 0-87148-431-5). Pathway Pr.

In Rooms of Falling Rain. Sheila B. Nickerson. LC 76-28466. (Orig.). 1976. lib. bdg. 8.00 (ISBN 0-914476-56-4); pap. 4.00 (ISBN 0-914476-59-9). Thorp Springs.

In Safe Hands. Mary Hubbard Howell. LC 7-6618. The American Sunday-School Union.

In Sagrasso." Missing: A Romance; Narrative of Capt. Austin Clarke, of the Tramp Steamer "Carribas," Who, for Two Years Was a Captive Among the Savage People of the Seaweed Sea. Julius Chambers. 1897. Continental Publishing Co.

In Samson's Eye. Betty Littleton. 4.50. Atheneum.

In Samson's Eye. 1st Ed. Littleton, Betty. LC 65-22830. 1965. Atheneum.

In Sancho Panza's Pit. B. Sim Cunningham. LC 6-31729. 1883. J. B. Lippincott & Co.

In Sargasso." Missing: A Romance; Narrative of Capt. Austin Clark, of the Tramp Steamer "Caribas," Who, for Two Years, Was a Captive Among the Savage People of the Seaweed Sea. Julius Chambers. LC 6-32169. 1896. The Transatlantic Publishing Company.

In Scarlet and Grey. Florence Ellen Hungerford Milnes Henniker. LC 76-20067. (Decadent Consciousness). (Series: Keynotes series; 25.). 1977. 26.00 (ISBN 0-8240-2762-0). Garland Pub.

In Scarlet and Grey: Stories of Soldiers and Others. Florence Ellen Hungerford Milnes Henniker. (On cover: Keynotes series. 25). Roberts Bros.

In Scorn of Consequence: Or, My Brother's Keeper. Theodora Corrie. LC 6-28726. (Harper's handy series, no. 100). 1886. Harper & Brothers.

In Search of a Character. Graham Greene. 112p. 1981. pap. 3.95 (ISBN 0-14-002822-6). Penguin.

In Search of a Herd. William Bayer. 4.95. World.

In Search of a Hero. William Bayer. LC 66-15079. 1966. World Pub. Co.

In Search of a Home. Belle V Chisholm. LC 6-20972. 1890. Presbyterian Publishing Company.

In Search of a Husband. Corra May White Harris. LC 13-21295. 1913. 1.35. Doubleday, Page & Company.

In Search of a Name. Norah Whittle. (Rainbow Romance Edition). 1973. (pbk) 0.60. New American Lib.

In Search of a Religion. Dennis Hird. 1897. G. P. Putnam's Sons.

In Search of a Stranger. Warren E. Siegmond. Ed. by Irene Zola et al. LC 80-69803. 472p. (Orig.). 1981. pap. 5.95 (ISBN 0-937868-01-9). Cameo Pr.

In Search of a Villain: A Story of Detection. Robert Gore-Browne. LC 28-9738. 1928. Pub. for the Crime Club, Inc., by Doubleday, Doran & Company, Inc.

In Search of Arcady. Nina Wilcox Putnam. LC 12-4462. 1912. 1.20. Doubleday, Page & Company.

In Search of Dr. Thorndyke. Norman Donaldson. 300p. 1971. 8.95 (ISBN 0-87972-013-1); pap. 3.95x (ISBN 0-87972-014-X). Bowling Green Univ.

In Search of Dr. Thorndyke. Norman Donaldson. LC 72-147819. (Illus.). 1971. 7.95x o.p.; pap. 3.00x o.p. Beacon Pr.

In Search of Eagles. Christopher Sloan. (Orig.). 1982. pap. 2.50. Zebra.

In Search of Ghosts. Hans Holzer. (Orig.). 1979. pap. 2.25 (ISBN 0-532-23272-0). Woodhill.

In Search of Gold: The Story of a Liberal Life. John E Wheelock. LC 72-164579. (American fiction reprint series). 1971. (ISBN 0-8369-7056-X). Books for Libraries Press.

In Search of Gold: The Story of a Liberal Life. John E Wheelock. LC 8-360491. 1884. H. W. Thompson.

In Search of Gold: The Story of a Liberal Life. facsimile ed. John E. Whellcock. LC 72-164579. (American Fiction Reprint Ser). Repr. of 1884 ed. 25.00 (ISBN 0-8369-7056-X). Ayer Co.

In Search of Gregory. Bonnie Golightly. (O.s.i.). (Orig.). 1970. pap. 0.75 o.s.i. (A556S, Award). Univ Pub & Dist.

In Search of Love. Francis Stuart. LC 35-165854. 1935. The Macmillan Company.

In Search of Love: A Collection of Stories. Bernard Rothman. LC 67-17187. 1967. William-Frederick Press.

In Search of Love and Beauty. Ruth Prawer Jhabvala. LC 82-24906. 1983. 12.95 (ISBN 0-688-02035-6). Morrow.

In Search of Love: Stories of Unbridled Sex. Bernard Rothman. pap. 1.00 (ISBN 0-87164-081-3). William-F.

In Search of Mademoiselle. George Fort Gibbs. LC 1-31734. 1901. H. T. Coates & Co.

In Search of Mihailo. Dolores Pala. LC 75-105238. 1969. 4.95. Harper & Row.

In Search of My Beloved. Thorbergur Thordarson. Tr. by Kenneth G. Chapman from Icelandic. (Library of Scandinavian Literature: Vol. 1). 1967. 5.00x (ISBN 0-89067-013-7). Am Scandinavian.

In Search of My Beloved. Thorbergur Thordarson. Tr. by Kenneth G. Chapman from Icelandic. (Library of Scandinavian Literature). 1967. lib. bdg. 4.75x (ISBN 0-8057-3316-7). Irvington.

In Search of My Beloved. Tr. from the Icelandic by Kenneth G. Chapman. Introd. by Kristjan Karlsson. Thorbergur Thordarson. LC 66-30536. (Lib. of Scandinavian Lit., V.1). 1967. bds., 3.00. Twayne.

In Search of Quiet: A Country Journal, May-July a Novel. Walter Frith. LC 6-44720. 1896. Harper & Brothers.

In Search of the Castaways: Screenplay by Lowell S. Hawley. Hettie Jones. (Kangaroo Book). 1.50 (ISBN 0-671-81936-4). Pocket Books.

In Search of the Unknown. Robert William Chambers. LC 73-13249. (Classics of science fiction). (Illus.). 1974. (ISBN 0-88355-105-5) (ISBN 0-88355-134-9). Hyperion Press.

In Search of Twilight. Colleen L Reece. (Avalon Books). 4.95. Thomas Bouregy.

In Search of Wonder. rev. & enl. ed. Damon Knight. LC 67-4260. 1967. 10.00 (ISBN 0-911682-07-4); pap. 5.50 (ISBN 0-911682-15-5). Advent.

In Season & Out. Bruce Clanton. LC 80-54272. 80p. 1981. pap. 6.95 (ISBN 0-89390-025-7). Resource Pubns.

In Secret. Robert William Chambers. LC 19-10146. 1.50. George H. Doran Company.

In Secret. Robert William Chambers. LC 22-4744. 1919. Grosset & Dunlap.

In Secret Battle. Lawrence Lipton. LC 44-8715. 1944. D. Appleton-Century Company, Incorporated.

In Secret Places. Seldon Truss, pseud. LC 58-8112. 1958. Published for the Crime Club of Doubleday.

In Shallow Waters. A Novel. Annie Armitt. (Harper's handy series, no. 64). 1886. Harper & Brothers.

In Sheep's Clothing. A Novel. Adelaide Day Rollston. LC 7-40759. (On cover: Once a week library. v. 9, no. 6). 1892. P. F. Collier.

In Shelly's Leg: A Novel. Sara Vogan. LC 80-20390. 1981. 10.95 (ISBN 0-394-51451-3). Knopf.

In Sickness and in Health. Ruth Rendell. LC 76-24850. 1976. 7.95 (ISBN 0-89340-023-8). J. Curley.

In Sickness and in Health. 1st Ed. Ruth Rendell. LC 66-20970. 1966. 3.50. Pub. for the Crime Club by Doubleday.

In Sight of Eden: Translated from the French. Roger Vercel & Bessie, Alvah C. Tr. LC 34-5829. Harcourt, Brace and Company.

In Sight of St. Paul's. Sutton Vane. (On cover: Drama series, no. 18). Street & Smith.

In Silk Attire. William Black. (Lovell's library, v. 4, no. 188). J. W. Lovell Company.

In Silk Attire. William Black. (Seaside library. Pocket ed. no. 39). 1883. G. Munro.

In Silk Attire: A Novel. library ed. William Black. LC 4-16497. 1900. Harper & Brothers.

In Simpkinsville: A Character Tales. Ruth McEnery Stuart. LC 4-15165. 1897. Harper & Brothers.

In Simpkinsville: Character Tales. Ruth McEnery Stuart. LC 71-98599. (Short story index reprint series). (Illus.). 1969. Books for Libraries Press.

In Sin and Splendor. Joseph Francis Dinneen. LC 32-14019. R. M. McBride & Company.

In Single Strictness. George Moore. LC 73-37557. (Short story index reprint series). (Illus.). 1972. 11.50 (ISBN 0-8369-4116-0). Books for Libraries Press.

In Six Months: Or, The Two Friends. Mary Miller Meline. LC 7-25852. 1874. Kelly, Piet and Company.

In Spacious Times. Justin Huntly McCarthy. LC 16-228523. 1916. John Lane Company.

In Spite of All: A Novel. Ada Ellen Bayly. LC 1-25418. 1901. Longmans, Green, and Co.

In Spite of All: A Novel. Edith Staniforth. LC 17-29024. 1917. Benziger Brothers.

In Spite of Foes: Or, Ten Years' Trial. Charles King. LC 1-31010. 1901. J. B. Lippincott Company.

In Spite of Himself. From the French of Dubut De Laforest. Jean Louis Dubut De Laforest & Howe, Frank Howard, Tr. (On cover: Belford American novel series. 17). 1891. Belford Company.

In Spite of Integrity: Would You Under These Circumstances Have Stolen One Hundred Thousand. Samuel E. Wells. LC 8-36638. 1889. The American News Company.

In Spite of Thunder: A Dr. Fell Detective Novel. 1st Ed. John Dickson Carr. LC 59-13305. 1960. Harper.

In Stella's Shadow. Linn Boyd Porter. LC 7-37769. (On cover: The albatross novels). 1890. G. W. Dillingham.

In Story-Land. Ruth Irma Low. LC 14-22590. 1914. Athens Publishing Co.

In Such a Night. Babette Deutsch. LC 27-7506. 1927. The John Day Company.

In Such Dark Places. Joseph Caldwell. LC 77-8782. 1978. 10.00 (ISBN 0-374-17648-5). Farrar, Straus, Giroux.

In Summer Shade: A Novel. Mary E. Rackham Mann. LC 7-20457. (On cover: Harper's Franklin square library. no. 729). 1892. Harper & Brothers.

In Sunflower Land: Stories by God's Own Country. Roswell Martin Field. LC 6-41696. 1892. F. J. Schulte & Company.

In Sunshine and Shadow: Pages from Poe. Edgar Allan Poe. Ed. by Lou P. Bunce. Holmes, Mabel Dodge, 1883- Ed. LC 46-19194. (CEBCO classics for enjoyment). 1946. College Entrance Book Company.

In Suspicion's Shadow: Ro, Nick Carter's Costly Error. Nick Carter & Dey, Frederic Van Rensselaer. LC 34-38271. (On cover: New magnet library. no. 838). Street & Smith.

In Tent and Bungalow. E M Cuttim. LC 6-32234. ("Unknown" library, v. 13). Cassell Publishing Company.

In Texas with Davy Crocket. John Thomas McIntyre. LC 14-142608. (His The buckskin books). 1914. 0.75. The Penn Publishing Company.

In the Absence of Angels: Stories. Hortense Calisher. LC 51-14079. 1951. Little, Brown.

In the Absence of Magic. Ernst Pawel. LC 60-6166. 1960. Macmillan.

In the Absence of Mrs. Petersen. Nigel Balchin. LC 66-24031. 1966. 4.50. S.&S.

In the Alamo. Opie Percival Read. LC 1-29107. Rand, McNally & Company.

In the Animal Kingdom. Warren Fine. LC 77-142954. 1971. 3.50 (ISBN 0-394-46969-0). Knopf.

In the Arena: Stories of Political Life. Booth Tarkington. LC 68-55687. (American short story series, v. 27). (Illus.). 1969. Garrett Press.

In the Arena: Stories of Political Life. Booth Tarkington. LC 5-3791. 1905. McClure, Phillips & Co.

In the Arena: Stories of Political Life. Booth Tarkington. LC 22-16011. 1920. Doubleday, Page & Company.

In the Arms of a Stranger. Deborah Joyce. (Second Chance at Love Ser.: No. 109). 1.75 (ISBN 0-515-06873-X). Jove Pubns.

In the Arms of Love. Barbara Cartland. (Barbara Cartland Ser.: No. 91). 1981. pap. 1.75 (ISBN 0-515-05958-7). Jove Pubns.

In the Arms of Love. Alexis Hill. (Candlelight Ecstasy Ser.: No. 115). (Orig.). 1983. pap. 1.95 (ISBN 0-440-14203-2). Dell.

In the Arms of Love. Abi S Jackman. (On cover: Pollard's popular publications, no. 14). 1891. Pollard Publishing Co.

In the Balance. Patricia Wentworth. LC 41-170384. J. B. Lippincott Company.

In the Balance. M. E White. LC 67-28822. 1968. Harper & Row.

In the Bank...or up the Chimney? 1976. pap. 3.95 o.p. (ISBN 0-8019-6501-2). Chilton.

In the Beginning. Norman Douglas. LC 76-144980. 1971. (ISBN 0-403-00946-4). Scholarly Press.

In the Beginning. Norman Douglas. LC 28-14705. The John Day Company.

In the Beginning. Chaim Potok. LC 75-8238. 1975. 8.95 (ISBN 0-394-49960-3). Knopf: Distributed by Random House.

In the Beginning. Alan Sullivan. LC 27-18546. E. P. Dutton & Company.

In the Beginning & Hereafter. Robert YoHody. 1967. 3.50 o.p. (ISBN 0-682-45707-8). Exposition.

In the Beginning Was the Myth. Allan Dowling. 1968. 2.95 o.p. Vantage.

In the Bishop's Carriage. Miriam Michelson. LC 4-9457. 1904. The Bobbs-Merrill Company.

In the Blazing Light. Charles William White. LC 46-606. 1946. Duell, Sloan and Pearce.

In the Blue Pike: A Romance of German Civilization at the Commencement of the Sixteenth Century. Georg Moritz Ebers & Safford, Mary Joanne, Tr. LC 6-437243. 1896. D. Appleton and Company.

In the Border Country. Josephine Dodge Daskam Bacon. LC 79-106244. (Short story index reprint series). (Illus.). 1970. (ISBN 0-8369-3280-3). Books for Libraries Press.
In the Border Country. Josephine Dodge Daskam Bacon. LC 9-27445. 1909. 1.00. Doubleday, Page & Company.
In the Brave Days of Old: A Story of Adventure in the Time of King James the First. Ruth Hall. LC 98-7350. 1898. Houghton, Mifflin and Company.
In the Breath of Night. Michael Mastroyannis. 1979. 7.50 o.p. (ISBN 0-533-03809-X). Vantage.
In the Briar Patch: A Book of Stories. George Palmer Garrett. (Illus.). 1961. 5.00 o.p. (ISBN 0-292-73276-7). U of Tex Pr.
In the Bride's Mirror. Margaret Turnbull. LC 34-597549. 1934. J. B. Lippincott Company.
In the Bright April Weather. Susanna Valentine Mitchell. LC 59-5801. 1952. Farrar, Straus and Young.
In the Bronx: And Other Stories. Jack Micheline. LC 66-48763. 1965. S. Hooker Press.
In the Brooding Wild. Ridgwell Cullum. 1905. L. C. Page & Company.
In the Bundle of Time. Arlo Bates. LC 71-116937. (Short story index reprint series). 1970. Books for Libraries Press.
In the Bundle of Time. Arlo Bates. LC 6-9087. 1893. Roberts Brothers.
In the Bunker: A Novel. Fitz Gibbon, Constantine. LC 73-2718. 1973. 5.95 (ISBN 0-393-08378-0). Norton.
In the Bunker: A Novel. Constantine Fitz Gibbon. 256p. 1973. 6.95 o.p. (ISBN 0-393-08378-0). Norton.
In the Cage. Henry James. LC 98-23. 1898. H. S. Stone & Company.
In the Cage and Other Stories. Henry James. Ed. by Samuel Gorley Putt. LC 74-185847. (Penguin modern classics). 1974. (0.40, 1.50 u.s.) (ISBN 0-14-003500-1). Penguin.
In the Cage & Other Tales. Henry James. Ed. by Morton D. Zabel. Orig. Title: Fourteen Stories. 1958. 4.50 o.p. Dufour.
In the Cage & Other Tales. Edited, and with an Introd. by Morton Dauwen Zabel. 1st Ed. Henry James. LC 58-6356. (Doubleday anchor books, A131). 1958. Doubleday.
In the Camargue. Emily Bowles. LC 22-10833. 1877. Loring.
In the Carbon Hills: A Romance of the Land of Coal. William Hampton Reynolds. LC 17-24290. The Ziegler Publishing Co.
In the Carquinez Woods. Bret Harte. LC 7-3644. 1884. Houghton, Mifflin and Company.
In the Catskills. John Burroughs. LC 10-21755. (Illus.). 263p. (Orig.). 1974. pap. 10.95 o.p. (ISBN 0-910220-58-1). Berg.
In the Cause of Freedom. Arthur Williams Marchmont. LC 7-16375. 1907. F. A. Stokes Company.
In the Cheering-up Business. Mary Catherine Jenkins Lee. 1891. Houghton, Mifflin and Company.
In the China Sea. A Novel, by Seward W. Hopkins. With Illustrations by Pruett Share and H. M. Eaton. Seward W Hopkins. (choice series, no. 110). 1894. R. Bonner's Sons.
In the City of Under. Evelyne Elise Rynd. LC 15-26258. 1914. Longmans, Green & Co.
In the Clap Shack and the Long March. William Styron. (Plume book). 1975. (pbk.) 3.50. New American Library.
In the Claws of the Dragon. Charles Georges Soulie. LC 21-15953. 1921. A. A. Knopf.
In the Closed Room. Frances Hodgson Burnett. LC 4-27871. 1904. McClure, Philips & Co.
In the Clouds: A Story. Mary Noailles Murfree. LC 7-318383. 1887. Houghton, Mifflin and Company.
In the Clutches of Homo and Sapience: A Dissident Intellectual's View of the Modern Scene in Its Bedlam and Progress. Mark Aaron Graubard. LC 67-20907. 1967. T. S. Denison.
In the Coils: Or, The Coming Conflict. Edwin Brown Graham. LC 7-8833. 1882. A. T. McDill.
In the Company of Eagles. Ernest Kellogg Gann. 240p. (Orig.). 1981. pap. 2.50 (ISBN 0-515-05484-4). Jove Pubns.
In the Company of Eagles. Ernest Kellogg Gann. (O.s.i.). 1966. 7.50 o.s.i. (ISBN 0-671-37085-5). S&S.
In the Company of Eagles: By Ernest K. Gann. Ernest Kellogg Gann. LC 66-26934. 1966. 5.95. S. & S.
In the Company of Spies. Stephen Barlay. LC 81-4674. 13.95 (ISBN 0-671-43050-5). Summit Books.
In the Confessional and The Following. Adolphe Danziger De Castro. LC 6-33160. (On cover: Western authors' series, no. 2). 1893. Western Authors' Publishing Association.
In the Cool of the Evening. Elliott White Springs. LC 29-18558. E. Springs and Company.
In the Counselor's House. Eugenie John. Tr. by Wood, Annie. (Seaside library. v. 43, no. 878). 1880. G. Munro.
In the Counselor's House. Eugenie John. Tr. by Wood, Annie. LC 7-9902. (On cover: Seaside library. Pocket ed. no. 1111). G. Munro.
In the Country God Forgot: A Story of Today. Frances Asa Charles. LC 2-13112. 1902. Little, Brown, & Company.
In the Country of the Walking Dead. Walter O'Meara. (O.s.i.). 1972. pap. 1.50 o.s.i. (AD1586, Award). Univ Pub & Dist.
In the Court Circle: A Tale of Washington Life. James Alexander Edwards. 1895. The Columbian Publishing Company.
In the Courtyards of Jerusalem: Short Stories. Tr. from Hebrew by Hillel Halkin. Illus. by Joan Drescher. 1st Ed. Hayim Brandwein. LC 67-16185. 1967. 4.50. Jewish Pubn. Soc. of Amer.
In the Crescent's Dark Shadow. John H Crabb. LC 52-13706. 1952. Dorrance.
In the Crucible: A Novel. Grace Denio Litchfield. LC 7-19000. (The Hudson library. no. 18). 1897. G. P. Putnam's Sons.
In the Crucible: Tales from Real Life. Isabel Cecilia Williams. LC 9-14822. P. J. Kenedy & Sons.
In the Current. William Bullock. LC 11-31747. 1911. 1.25. W. Rickey & Company.
In the Dark. Donald Randall Richberg. LC 12-20307. 1912. Forbes & Company.
In the Dark. Elias Tobenkin. LC 31-28916. 1931. Doubleday, Doran & Company, Inc.
In the Dark, Move Slowly. Tuomas Anhava. Tr. by Anselm Hollo from Finn. LC 71-93576. (Cape Goliard Ser). 1970. pap. 2.50 o.p. (ISBN 0-670-39681-8, Grossman). Penguin.
In the Dark Night. Margaret Page Hood. LC 57-7016. 1957. Coward-McCann.
In the Dark of the Moon. Adrienne D. McGillicuddy. 1980. 4.95 (ISBN 0-533-04418-9). Vantage.
In the Day of Adversity: A Romance. John Edward Bloundelle-Burton. LC 6-16696. (Half-title: Appletons' town and country library, no. 176 187). 1895. D. Appleton and Company.
In the Day of Adversity. A Romance. John Edward Bloundelle-Burton. LC 6-16695. (Half-title: Appletons' town and country library, no. 187). 1896. D. Appleton and Company.
In the Day of Battle: A Romance. John Alexander Steuart. LC 8-12390. (On cover: Neely's international library). 1894. F. T. Neely.
In the Day's March. Ruby Mildred Ayres. LC 30-20590. 1930. Doubleday, Doran & Company, Inc.
In the Days of Alfred the Great. Eva March Tappan. LC 5164. 1900. Lee and Shepard.
In the Days of Brigham Young. Arthur Thomas Hannett. LC 15-12988. Broadway Publishing Co.
In the Days of Drake a Novel. Joseph Smith Fletcher. 1897. Rand, McNally & Company.
In the Days of My Youth. A Novel. Amelia Ann Blanford Edwards. LC 22-14542. (On cover: International series). 1874. Porter & Coates.
In the Days of Poor Richard. Irving Bacheller. LC 22-14188. The Bobbs-Merrill Company.
In the Days of Poor Richard. Irving Bacheller. LC 26-19823. The Bobbs-Merrill Company.
In the Days of Queen Elizabeth. Eva March Tappan. (Makers of England series). 1902. Lee and Shepard.
In the Days of Queen Victoria. Eva March Tappan. LC 3-14845. (Makers of England series). 1903. Lee and Shepard.
In the Days of St. Clair: A Romance of the Muskingum Valley. James Ball Naylor. LC 2-19994. 1902. The Saalfield Publishing Co.
In the Days of Simon Stern: A Novel. Arthur Allen Cohen. LC 72-11429. 1973. 8.95 (ISBN 0-394-48303-0). Random House.
In the Days of Simon Stern: A Novel. Arthur Allen Cohen. (Laurel edition). 1974. (pbk.) 1.75. Dell.
In the Days of the Comet. Herbert George Wells. 1906. The Century Co.
In the Days of the Comet. Herbert George Wells. LC 24-27742. 1924. C. Scribner's Sons.
In the Days of the Councillor. Tryggve Andersen. LC 71-99537. (Library of Scandinavian Literature, V. 4). 1969. 5.00. Twayne.
In the Days of the Mutiny: A Military Novel. George Alfred Henty. LC 3-21930. (On cover: Broadway series, no. 21). J. A. Taylor and Company.
In the Days of Thy Youth. Mary Britton Miller. LC 43-12462. 1943. C. Scribner's Sons.
In the Days of William the Conqueror. Eva March Tappan. LC 1-16502. 1901. Lee and Shepard.
In the Days When the World Was Wide. Henry Lawson. 1967. Repr. pap. 1.60 o.s.i. Tri-Ocean.
In the Dead of Night. John Thomas McIntyre. LC 8-125585. 1908. J. B. Lippincott Company.
In the Dead of Night: An Anthology of Horror Stories. Ed. by Michael Sissons. LC 62-1581. 1961. Canterbury Press.
In the Death of a Man. Lesley Egan, pseud. LC 71-96011. (Novel of Suspense Ser). 1970. 4.95 o.p. (ISBN 0-06-012639-6, HarpT). Har-Row.
In the Death of a Man. Elizabeth Linington. LC 71-96011. 1970. 5.95. Harper & Row.
In the Deep of the Snow. Charles George Douglas Roberts. LC 7-21228. T. Y. Crowell & Co.
In the Depths of the First Degree: A Romance of the Battle of Bull Run. James Of San Francisco Doran. LC 6-33724. 1898. The Peter Paul Book Company.
In the Depths. The Godmother. Ursula. Our Mannie. Bertha Behrens. Tr. by Kate Dykers. (On cover: The Marguerite series. 20). E. A. Weeks & Company.
In the Desert. Georg Moritz Ebers & Safford, Mary Joanne, Tr. LC 5030. 1900. Dodd, Mead and Company.
In the Desert. LC 77-13037. (Collected works of Karl May ; ser. 3, v. 1). 1977. 12.95 (ISBN 0-8164-9290-5). Seabury Press.
In the Desert. Karl May. Tr. by Michael Shaw from Ger. LC 77-13037. 1977. 10.95 (ISBN 0-8264-0116-3). Continuum.
In the Distance: A Novel. George Parsons Lathrop. LC 7-13851. 1882. J. R. Osgood and Company.
In the Ditch. Buchi Emecheta. 128p. 1980. pap. 4.95 (ISBN 0-8052-8010-3, Pub. by Allison & Busby England). Schocken.
In the Dog House: A Collection of Short Stories. Lola F. Minear. LC 80-53774. 47p. 1981. 6.95 (ISBN 0-533-04878-8). Vantage.
In the Dwellings of Silence, a Romance of Russia. Walker Kennedy. LC 7-10957. 1893. Dodd, Mead & Company.
In the Dwellings of the Wilderness. C. Bryson Taylor. LC 4-11528. 1904. H. Holt and Company.
In the Eagle's Talon: A Romance of the Louisiana Purchase. Sheppard Stevens. 1902. Little, Brown, and Company.
In the Early Days: Philippine Sketches. Charles Elliott Currier. LC 15-2391. 1914. 1.00. Broadway Publishing Company.
In the End: Being the Romance of Two Worlds. Frederick Rogers. The Editor Publishing Company.
In the Event of My Death. Hester Bourne. LC 64-11403. 1964. Published for the Crime Club by Doubleday.
In the Eye of the Beholder: Tales of Egyptian Life from the Writings of Yusuf Idris; Edited by Roger Allen. Yusuf Idris & Roger M. A Allen. LC 78-50505. 18.00 (ISBN 0-88297-019-4). Bibliotheca Islamica.
In the Eye of the Beholder: Tales of Egyptian Life from the Writings of Yusuf Idris. LC 78-50505. (Studies in Middle Eastern Literatures: No. 10). 1978. 18.00x (ISBN 0-88297-019-4); pap. 11.50x (ISBN 0-88297-020-8). Bibliotheca.
In the Eye of the Law. Lorinda Hagen. (Belmont Tower Book). 1979. 1.75 (ISBN 0-505-51392-7). Tower Publications.
In the Face of the Sun. Birdsall Briscoe. LC 34-1474. E.J. Clode, Inc.
In the Face of the Verdict: A Dr. Priestley Story. Cecil John Charles Street. 1940. Dodd, Mead & Company.
In the Favour of the King. Hawthorne Daniel. LC 22-8239. 1922. Doubleday, Page & Company.
In the Fine Summer Weather. Catharine Whitcomb. LC 38-8901. Random House.
In the Fire. Lee Lozowick. LC 78-54139. (Illus.). 1978. pap. 5.95 (ISBN 0-89556-002-X). IDHHB.
In the Fire of the Forge: A Romance of Old Nuremberg. Georg Moritz Ebers & Safford, Mary Joanne, Tr. LC 6-36804. 1895. D. Appleton and Company.
In the First Degree. Margret Holmes Ernsperger Bates. LC 7-37267. 1907. R. G. Cooke, Inc.
In the First Degree: An Inspector Kane Mystery... Roger Scarlett. LC 33-31427. 1933. Pub. for the Crime Club, Inc., by Doubleday, Doran & Company, Inc.
In the First Person: A Novel. Maria Louise Pool. LC 7-38177. 1896. Harper & Brothers.
In the Flesh. Roger Bowdler. 1974. (pbk.) 1.25. Dell.
In the Flesh. Hilma Wolitzer. LC 77-1704. 1977. 8.95 (ISBN 0-688-03204-4). Morrow.
In the Fog. Richard Harding Davis. LC 1-27442. 1901. R. H. Russell.
In the Fog. Richard Harding Davis. Harper & Brothers.
In the Fog. Edmund W Nash. LC 65-19898. 1967. Doubleday.
In the Fog of the Season's End. Alex La Guma. (African Writers Ser.). 1972. pap. text ed. 5.00x (ISBN 0-435-90110-9). Heinemann Ed.
In the Fog of the Season's End. Alex La Guma. LC 72-93381. 1973. 8.95 o.p. (ISBN 0-89388-058-2). Okpaku Communications.
In the Fog of the Seasons' End: A Novel. Alex La Guma. LC 72-93381. 1973. 6.95 (ISBN 0-89388-058-2). Third Press.
In the Footsteps of Sherlock Holmes. Michael Harrison. LC 75-178081. (Illus.). 1972. 6.95 (ISBN 0-87749-156-9). Drake Publishers.
In the Footsteps of Sherlock Holmes. Michael Harrison. LC 60-16149. (Illus.). 1960. F. Fell.
In the Footsteps of the Master. Ed. by James A. Kuse. (Illus.). 1979. pap. 3.95 (ISBN 0-89542-064-3). Ideals.
In the Forest of Arden. Hamilton Wright Mabie & Low, Will Hicok, 1853- Illus. LC 98-1850. 1898. Dodd, Mead and Company.
In the Forests of the Night. Kenneth Sydney Davis. LC 42-7194. 1942. Houghton Mifflin Company.
In the Frame. Dick Francis. LC 77-361822. (Illus.). 1976. 3.25 (ISBN 0-7181-1527-9). Joseph.
In the Frame. Dick Francis. LC 76-47255. 8.95 (ISBN 0-06-011341-3). Harper & Row.
In the Fullness of Time. Charles Brandon Rimmer. LC 49-252549. 1948. Berne Witness Co.
In the Fulness of Time. Gertrude Capen Whitney. LC 39-847168. 1936. B. Humphries, Inc.
In the Future. LC 74-15946. (Science Fiction). 1975. 8.00 (ISBN 0-405-06299-0). Arno Press.
In the Future. LC 74-15946. (Science Fiction Ser). 1975. Repr. of 1875 ed. 8.00x (ISBN 0-405-06299-0). Ayer Co.
In the Future Perfect. Walter Abish. LC 77-9443. 10.75 (ISBN 0-8112-0659-9) (ISBN 0-8112-0660-2). New Directions.
In the Game of Gold. Annie Walton Bruce. LC 36-15929. The Christopher Publishing House.
In the Garden of Delight. Lily Hardy Hammond. LC 16-17728. Thomas Y. Crowell Company.
In the Garden of the Heart. Ernest Leaverton. LC 19-12878. J. F. Tapley Co.
In the Garden of the North American Martyrs. Tobias Wolff. LC 80-880. 151p. 1981. 10.95 (ISBN 0-912946-82-2). Ecco Pr.
In the Garden of the North American Martyrs. Tobias Wolff. LC 81-880. 151p. 1982. pap. 6.95 (ISBN 0-912946-83-0). Ecco Pr.
In the Gates of Israel: Stories of the Jews. Herman Bernstein. LC 2-20988. 1902. J. F. Taylor & Company.
In the Gloaming. Marie Cecelia Chamberlain. LC 1-29018. 1900. Scroll Publishing Company.
In the Golden City. Dora Delmar. (On cover: Library of American authors. no. 66). 1896. G. Munro's Sons.
In the Golden Days. Ada Ellen Bayly. LC 42-315952. 1887. D. Appleton and Cmopany.
In the Golden Days. Ada Ellen Bayly. LC 4-86118. Donohue, Henneberry & Co.
In the Golden Days: A Novel. Ada Ellen Bayly. LC 4-16402. 1900. D. Appleton and Company.
In the Green Star's Glow. Lin Carter. (Science Fiction Ser.). pap. 1.50 (ISBN 0-87997-399-4, UW1399). DAW Bks.
In the Green Star's Glow. Lin Carter. (Green Star Sage). (DAW science fiction books, no. 180: Vol. 5). 1976. (pbk.) 1.25. DAW Books.
In the Green Star's Glow. (Science Fiction Ser.). 1976. pap. 1.50 o.p. (UW1399). DAW Bks.
In the Grip of Terror. Ed. by Groff Conklin. LC 51-35745. (Permsbooks, 117). 1951. Permabooks.
In the Grip of the Mullah: A Tale of Adventure in Somaliland. Frederick Sadleir Brereton. LC 3-25399. 1903. C. Scribner's Sons.
In the Guardianship of God Stories. Flora Annie Webster Steel. LC 3-129693. 1903. The Macmillan Company.
In the Hall of the Dragon King. Steve Lawhead. LC 82-71942. (Illus.). 7.95 (ISBN 0-89107-257-8). Crossway Books.
In the Halls of Evil. T. A. Waters. (Orig.). pap. 0.60 o.p. (73-623). Lancer.
In the Hands of Glory. Phyllis Eisenstein. 1981. pap. 2.75 (ISBN 0-671-83335-9, Timescape). PB.
In the Hands of Our Enemies: Stories. Daniel Curley. LC 78-135473. 1971. 5.95 (ISBN 0-252-00141-9). University of Illinois Press.
In the Hands of the Senecas. Walter Dumaux Edmonds. LC 47-30040. 1947. Little, Brown and Company.
In the Heart of a Fool. William Allen White. LC 18-20938. 1918. The Macmillan Company.
In the Heart of a Fool. William Allen White. LC 19-2897. 1919. The Macmillan Company.
In the Heart of Hoosierland: A Story of the Pioneers, Based on Many Actual Experiences. Louis Ludlow. LC 25-8156. Pioneer Book Company.
In the Heart of the Christmas Pines. Leona Dalrymple. LC 13-24832. 1913. 0.50. McBride Nast & Company.
In the Heart of the Christmas Pines. Leona Dalrymple. LC 14-18308. 1914. 1.00. McBride, Nast & Company.
In the Heart of the Country. J. M. Coetzee. LC 82-7493. 1982. 4.95 (ISBN 0-14-006228-9). Penguin Books.

In the Heart of the Heart of the Country: And Other Stories. William H. Gass. 1.95 (ISBN 0-671-80827-3). Pocket Books.

In the Heart of the Heart of the Country, and Other Stories. William H. Gass. LC 68-11820. 1968. Harper & Row.

In the Heart of the Heart of the Country and Other Stories. William H. Gass. LC 80-83962. (Series: Nonpareil Books; No. 21.). 1981. 7.95 (ISBN 0-87923-374-5). D. R. Godine.

In the Heart of the Heart of the Country. William H. Gass. LC 80-83962. 1981. pap. 7.95 (ISBN 0-87923-374-5). Godine.

In the Heart of the Heart of the Country. William H. Gass. LC 68-11820. (O.s.i). 1968. 10.00i (ISBN 0-06-011468-1, HarpT). Har-Row.

In the Heart of the Seas. Samuel Joseph Agnon. Tr. by Lask, Israel Meir. LC 48-5223. (Schocken library, 9). 1948. Schocken Books.

In the Heart of the Seas: A Story of a Journey to the Land of Israel. Tr. from the Hebrew by I. M. Lask. Drawings by T. Herzl Rome. Samuel Joseph Agnon. Tr. by Israel Meir Lask. LC 66-30349. 1967. bds., 3.95. Schocken.

In the Heart of the Seas: A Story of a Journey to the Land of Israel. Samuel Joseph Agnon. LC 66-30349. (Illus.). 1966. 3.95x o.p. (ISBN 0-8052-3110-2). Schocken.

In the Heart of the Storm: A Tale of Modern Chivalry. authorized ed. Mary Gleed Tuttiett. LC 8-32316. (On cover: Lovell's international series, no. 157). 1891. United States Book Company.

In the Heat of the Night. John Dudley Ball. (F3355). 1967. Bantam.

In the Heat of the Night. John Dudley Ball. LC 65-14667. 1965. Harper & Row.

In the Heat of the Summer. John Katzenbach. LC 81-69158. 1982. 12.95 (ISBN 0-689-11269-6). Atheneum.

In the Highest Tradition. Edward F Droge. LC 74-81454. 1974. 8.95 (ISBN 0-689-10641-6). Atheneum.

In the Highlands Since Time Immemorial. Joanna Ostrow. LC 73-98649. 1970. 5.95. Knopf.

In the Hour Before Midnight. Jack Higgins, pseud. 1978. pap. 2.25 (ISBN 0-449-13954-9, GM). Fawcett.

In the Hour Before Midnight. Jack Higgins, pseud. 1982. pap. 2.95 (ISBN 0-440-14350-0). Dell.

In the Hour Before Midnight. Jack Higgins, pseud. 1971. pap. 0.75 o.p. (ISBN 0-447-74730-4). Lancer.

In the Hour Before Midnight. Jack Higgins, pseud. 1969. 4.50 o.p. Doubleday.

In the Hour Before Midnight. Jack Higgins. (Fawcett Gold Medal Book). 1975. (pbk.) 1.25. Fawcett.

In the Hour Before Midnight. Henry Patterson. LC 79-92625. 1969. 4.50. Published for the Crime Club by Doubleday.

In the Hours of Night: A Novel. William Bradford Huie. LC 75-12640. 1975. 7.95 (ISBN 0-440-04367-0). Delacorte Press.

In the house Before Midnight see Sicilian Heritage.

In the House of Another. Beatrice Mantle. LC 20-17410. 1920. The Century Co.

In the House of Dark Music. Frances Lynch. 352p. 1983. pap. 2.75 (ISBN 0-446-30544-8). Warner Bks.

In the House of Her Friends. 1906. R. G. Cooke, Incorporated.

In the House of the Lord. Robert Flynn. LC 68-23961. 1969. 5.95. Knopf.

In the King's Country. Gisela Dittrick Britt. LC 19-16150. The Christian Endeavor World.

In the King's Country. Amanda Minnie Douglas. LC 6-33480. 1894. Lee and Shepard.

In the Labor Pool. Charles N. Aronson. LC 77-78227. (Illus.). 12.00 (ISBN 0-915736-13-6). C. N. Aronson.

In the Labyrinth. (Fantasy Trip Ser.). 1980. pap. write for info. (ISBN 0-88074-450-2). Metagam.

In the Labyrinth: A Novel. Robbe-Grillet, Alain. LC 77-92785. (Black cat book; B-408). 3.95 (ISBN 0-394-17032-6). Grove Press Distributed by Random House.

In the Labyrinth. A Novel. Translated by Richard Howard. Alain Robbe-Grillet. LC 60-11099. (Evergreen original novel, E-262). 1960. Grove Press.

In the Lamb White Days. F. H. Hall. LC 75-6388. 1975. 6.95 (ISBN 0-672-52165-2). Bobbs-Merrill.

In the Lamb White Days. F. H. Hall. (Kangaroo Book). 1977. 1.50 (ISBN 0-671-80948-2). Pocket Books.

In the Land of Cockaigne. Heinrich Mann & Clark, Axton D. B., Tr. LC 29-9290. (Transatlantic library). 1929. The Macaulay Company.

In the Land of Cotton. Dorothy Scarborough. LC 23-7285. 1923. The Macmillan Company.

In the Land of Cotton. Dorothy Scarborough. LC 28-18122. 1925. The Macmillan Company.

In the Land of Dreamy Dreams. Ellen Gilchrist. LC 81-3067. 1981. text ed. 14.95 (ISBN 0-938626-02-7); pap. text ed. 5.95 (ISBN 0-938626-03-5). U of Ark Pr.

In the Land of Extremes. M. R Harlan. LC 9-15399. 1909. Cochrane Publishing Company.

In the Land of Jay-Jaybooboo. Kit Lawrence. (O.s.i.). (Orig.). pap. 0.60 o.s.i. (A242X, Award). Univ Pub & Dist.

In the Land of Morning: A Novel. Harry Mark Petrakis. LC 72-92648. 1973. 6.95. D. McKay Co.

In the Land of the Chippewa: A True Blue Story of the Last Indian Outbreak in America. Eddy E Billberg. LC 27-14347. Syndicate Printing Company.

In the Land of the Gods: Some Stories of Japan, by Alice Mabel Bacon. Alice Mabel Bacon. LC 5-32692. 1905. Houghton, Mifflin and Company.

In the Land of the Head-Hunters. Edward S. Curtis. LC 76-358249. (Series: Indian Life and Indian Lore.). (Illus.). 3.95 (ISBN 0-913668-47-8) (ISBN 0-913668-48-6). Tamarack Press.

In the Land of the Living Dead: An Occult Story. Prentiss Tucker. LC 21-7334. 1921. The Rosicrucian Fellowship, Etc., Etc.

In the Land of the Loon. Frank Kimball Scribner & Mayo, Earl Williams. LC 99-2974. F. T. Neely.

In the Land of the Romburg; a Society Story. Benjamin Clark Warren. LC 7-445. Broadway Publishing Co.

In the Land of to-Morrow. J P Cranke. LC 10-15482. 1910. 1.50. Broadway Publishing Co.

In the Land of Youth. James Stephens. LC 24-24943. 1924. The Macmillan Company.

In the Lap of Atlas: Stories of Morocco. Richard Arthur Warren Hughes. LC 79-322120. 1979. 13.95 (ISBN 0-7011-2430-X). Chatto & Windus.

In the Last Analysis. Amanda Cross, pseud. LC 64-11757. (Cock Robin mystery). 1964. Macmillan.

In the Last Analysis. large print ed.. ed. Amanda Cross, pseud. LC 81-18426. 1982. 10.95 (ISBN 0-89621-335-8). Thorndike Press.

In the Last Analysis. Amanda Cross, pseud. LC 81-47350. (Fifty Classics of Crime Fiction, 1950-1975). 1982. 14.95 (ISBN 0-8240-4960-8). Garland Pub.

In the Last Degree. Edwin Arnold Brenholtz. LC 6-26480. The Ariel Press.

In the Levant, 2 vols. Charles Dudley Warner. 1973. Repr. of 1893 ed. 25.00 set (ISBN 0-8274-0812-9). R West.

In the Limestone Valley: Pen Pictures of Early Days in Western Wisconsin. Stirling Wilson Brown. LC 6178. 1900.

In the Lion's Mouth: The Story of Two English Children in France. Eleanor Catherine Price. LC 7-30105. 1894. Macmillan and Co.

In the Lives of Men. Alan Hart. LC 37-65183. W. W. Norton & Company, Inc.

In the Looking Glass: Twenty-One Modern Short Stories by Women. Nancy Dean & Myra Stark. LC 76-29075. 8.95. Putnam.

In the Louisiana Lowlands: A Sketch of Plantation Life, Fishing and Camping Just After the Civil War, and Other Tales. Fred Mather. LC 4212. 1900. Forest and Stream Publishing Co.

In the Market Places: A Few Chapters Concerning Carolyn Anselm's Journalistic Career. Rosa Hudspeth. LC 5433. 1900. Douglas Printing Co.

In the Maze: Or, The Marvels That Befell Belenor. Edward Ingle. The Sun Printing Office.

In the Meadows of Memory. James Stanley Durkee. LC 21-4505. 1.50. The Christopher Publishing House.

In the Meantime. Mary Mayer Abbott. LC 41-11498. Fortuny's.

In the Middle Distance: A Novel. Nicholas Delbanco. LC 72-151915. 1971. 6.95. Morrow.

In the Middle of a Life: A Novel. Richard Bruce Wright. LC 73-81056. 1973. 7.95 (ISBN 0-374-17653-1). Farrar, Straus and Giroux.

In the Middle of the Fields, and Other Stories. Mary Lavin. LC 67-30579. 1969. Macmillan.

In the Middle of the Night. A Novel. Walter E McCann. LC 7-15276. 1895. Gallery & McCann.

In the Middle Watch: Sea Stories. William Clark Russell. LC 8-1804. (Harper's handy series, no. 45). 1885. Harper & Brothers.

In the Middle Watch. Sea Stories. William Clark Russell. (On cover: Seaside library. Pocket ed., no. 682). 1886. G. Munro.

In the Midst of Alarms. Robert Barr. LC 74-170528. (Toronto reprint library of Canadian prose and poetry). (Original ed. issued in series: Twentieth century series.). (Illus.). 1973. University of Toronto Press.

In the Midst of Alarms. Robert Barr. LC 7146. 1893. J. B. Lippincott Company.

In the Midst of Alarms. Robert Barr. LC 7147. (Twentieth century series). Frederick A. Stokes Company.

In the Midst of Alarms: A Novel. 9th ed. Robert Barr. LC 5651. 1900. Frederick A Stokes Company.

In the Midst of Death. Lawrence Block. 192p. 1982. pap. 2.75 (ISBN 0-515-06731-8). Jove Pubns.

In the Midst of Death. Helen Luce. 1982. 15.00x (ISBN 0-333-27756-2, Pub. by Macmillan England). State Mutual Bk.

In the Midst of Earth. Marilyn Harris. LC 69-12211. 1969. 5.95. Doubleday.

In the Midst of Life. Ambrose Bierce. LC 76-6981. 1976. 5.95 (ISBN 0-89190-181-7). American Reprint Co.

In the Midst of Life: And Other Tales. Afterword by Marcus Cunliffe. Ambrose Bierce. (Signet classic CP60). New Amer. Lib.

In the Midst of Life, and Other Tales. With an Afterword by Marcus Cunliffe. Ambrose Gwinnett Bierce. LC 61-59613. (Signet classic, CP60). 1961. New American Library.

In the Midst of Life: Tales of Soldiers and Civilians. Ambrose Gwinnett Bierce. LC 6-13102. 1898. G. P. Putnam's Sons.

In the Midst of Life: Tales of Soldiers and Civilians. Ambrose Gwinnett Bierce. LC 35-33432. 1918. Boni & Liveright.

In the Midst of Life: Tales of Soldiers and Civilians. Ambrose Gwinnett Bierce. LC 27-191968. (Half-title: The modern library of the world's best books). The Modern Library.

In the Midst of Lions. Smith Hempstone. LC 68-17548. (Illus.). 1968. Harper & Row.

In the Mikado's Service: A Story of Two Battle Summers in China. William Elliot Griffis. LC 1-24972. W. A. Wilde Company.

In the Mink. Scott-James, Anne. LC 53-5210. 1953. Dutton.

In the Miro District and Other Stories. Peter Hillsman Taylor. LC 76-28760. 1977. 7.95. Knopf.

In the Mist, and Other Uncanny Encounters. Elizabeth Walter. LC 78-58752. (Illus.). 1979. 8.95 (ISBN 0-87054-083-1). Arkham House.

In the Mist of a Dream. Bill Stevens, II. LC 72-81642. 1972. 2.50 o.p. (ISBN 0-8059-1725-X). Dorrance.

In the Money. Arthur Somers Roche. LC 36-161943. 1936. Dodd, Mead and Company.

In the Money. William Carlos Williams. LC 40-351706. (NDP 240). 1967. 2.75 pap., 4.95. New Directions.

In the Morning Glow. Roy Rolfe Gilson. LC 72-94726. (Short Story Index Reprint Ser.). 1902. 15.00 (ISBN 0-8369-3105-X). Ayer Co.

In the Morning Glow: Short Stories. Roy Rolfe Gilson. LC 2-241000. 1902. Harper & Brothers.

In the Morning Light. Charles Angoff. LC 52-14848. 1953. Beechhurst Press.

In the Morning of Time. Charles George Douglas Roberts. LC 22-7099. Frederick A. Stokes Company.

In the Morning of Time: The Story of the Norse God Balder. Cynthia King. LC 79-81702. (Illus.). 1970. 5.38. Four Winds Press.

In the Mountains. LC 20-19505. 1920. Doubleday, Page & Company.

In the Name of a Woman. Arthur Williams Marchmont. (Illus.). 363p. 1981. pap. write for info. (ISBN 0-86649-037-X). Twentieth Century.

In the Name of a Woman: A Romance. Arthur Williams Marchmont. LC 1-29535. F. A. Stokes Company.

In the Name of Liberty: A Story of the Terror. by owen johnson... ed. Owen McMahon Johnson. LC 5-1182. 1905. The Century Co.

In the Name of Love. Bruce Cassiday. (General Hospital Ser). (O.s.i.). 160p. (Orig.). 1974. pap. 0.95 o.s.i. (AN1238, Award). Univ Pub & Dist.

In the Name of Love. Allene Soule Corliss. LC 44-736. 1944. Farrar & Rinehart, Inc.

In the Name of Love. large print ed. Arlene Hale. LC 82-10666. 1982. 10.95 (ISBN 0-89621-388-9). Thorndike Press.

In the Name of Love. Josephine Lawrence. LC 63-13498. 1963. Harcourt, Brace & World.

In the Name of My Friends see Bird.

In the Name of the People: A Novel. James M Galbraith. LC 76-21048. 8.95 (ISBN 0-913264-25-3). Douglas-West Publishers.

In the Name of the Son: A Novel. Herve-Bazin, Jean Pierre Marie. LC 62-9595. 1962. Simon and Schuster.

In The Nantahalas: A Novel. Metta Folger Townsend. LC 11-844. 1910. Broadway Pub. Co.

In the National Interest. Marvin L Kalb & Ted Koppel. LC 77-22828. 9.95 (ISBN 0-671-22656-8). Simon and Schuster.

In the National Interest: A Novel. Marvin L. Kalb & Koppel, Ted. 1978. 2.50 (ISBN 0-671-22656-8). Fawcett Crest.

In the New Town Together. Tr. from Bulgarian by Peter Tempest. Kamen Kalchev. LC 66-1132. 1965. bds., 1.90. Foreign Langs Pr.

In the Nick of Time: Or, Nat Ridley Saving a Life. Nat Jr Ridley. LC 26-12982. (His Nat Ridley series--3). 1926. Garden City Publishing Co., Inc.

In the Night. 3d impression. ed. Ronald Gorell Barnes Gorell. LC 17-29538. 1917. Longmans, Green and Co.

In the Night: A Story. Denise Levertov. LC 70-2442. (Albondocani Press publication no. 1). 1968. Albondocani Press.

In the Night All Cats Are Grey. Gavin Lambert. LC 76-365780. 1976. 3.50 (ISBN 0-491-01656-5). W. H. Allen.

In the Night Did I Sing. Joseph O'Kane Foster. LC 42-4607. 1942. C. Scribner's Sons.

In the Night Season. Christiaan Neethling Barnard. 1979. 2.25 (ISBN 0-445-04379-2). Popular Library.

In the Night Season: A Novel. Christiaan Neethling Barnard & Siegfried Stander. LC 78-51825. 8.95 (ISBN 0-13-453654-1). Prentice-Hall.

In the Ocean of Night. Gregory Benford. 1978. pap. 1.95 (ISBN 0-440-13999-6). Dell.

In the Ocean of Night: A Novel. Gregory Benford. LC 77-87161. 8.95 (ISBN 0-8037-4218-5). Dial Press/James Wade.

In the Oceans of Night. Gregory Benford. (Quantum Science Fiction Ser.). (O.s.i.). 1977. 8.95 o.s.i. (ISBN 0-8037-4218-5, J Wade). Dial.

In the Old Chateau: A Story of Russian Poland. Richard Henry Savage. (On cover: Neely's library of choice literature, no. 45). 1895. F. T. Neely.

In the Old Palazzo. A Novel. Gertrude Forde. LC 6-40383. (Harper's Franklin square library, no. 529)). 1886. Harper & Brothers.

In the Old South with Brer Rabbit & His Neighbors. F. Roy Johnson. 1977. 4.95 (ISBN 0-930230-35-3). Johnson NC.

In the Olden Time. Margaret Roberts. LC 7-41039. (On cover: Leisure hour series. no. 151). 1883. H. Holt and Company.

In the Onyx Lobby. Carolyn Wells. LC 20-15956. George H. Doran Company.

In the Palace of the King. Francis Marion Crawford. LC 25-15506. (works of F. Marion Crawford). 1914. McKinlay, Stone & Mackenzie.

In the Palace of the King: A Love Story of Old Madrid. Francis Marion Crawford. LC 6375. 1900. The Macmillan Company.

In the Palace of the King: A Love Story of Old Madrid. Francis Marion Crawford. LC 844. 1900. The Macmillan Co.

In the Palace of the King: A Love Story of Old Madrid. Francis Marion Crawford. LC 2-3525. 1901. The Macmillan Company.

In the Palace of the King: A Love Story of Old Madrid. Francis Marion Crawford. LC 25-155074. 1924. Grosset & Dunlap.

In the Pale: Stories and Legends of the Russian Jews. Henry Iliowizi. LC 7-8844. 1897. The Jewish Publication Society of America.

In the Pale: Stories and Legends of the Russian Jews. Henry Iliowizi. LC 1-29061. 1900. H. T. Coates & Co.

In the Palomar Arms. Hilma Wolitzer. LC 83-1632. 1983. 13.95 (ISBN 0-374-17656-6). Farrar/Straus/Giroux.

In the Parish of St. John. Raymond Joseph Martinez. LC 25-22758. 1925. G. A. Martin & Co.

In the Path of Eagles. Elizabeth Mayhew. 1.50 (ISBN 0-671-80582-7). Pocket Books.

In the Path of the Beast. Angelos Pappas. LC 52-38414. 1952.

In the Path of the Storm. James Rutherford Franklin. LC 27-147051. E. P. Dutton & Company.

In the Path of the Winds: The Case of the New Patriot. 1st Ed. Victor Rine. LC 55-7637. 1955. Pageant Press.

In the Permanent Way. Flora Annie Webster Steel. LC 8-13433. 1897. The Macmillan Company.

In the Pine Woods. Thomas L Baily. LC 6-5008. American Tract Society.

In the Pocket: My Life As a Quarterback. Earl Morrall. LC 74-86669. 1969. 5.95 o.p. (ISBN 0-448-01788-1). G&D.

In the Potter's House. George Dyre Eldridge. LC 8-4438. 1908. Doubleday, Page & Company.

In the Problem Pit. Frederik Pohl. 1976. (pbk.) 1.50 (ISBN 0-553-08857-2). Bantam Books.

In the Purely Pagan Sense: A Novel by. John Lehmann. LC 77-358969. 1976. 3.95 (ISBN 0-85634-054-5). Blond and Briggs.

In the Quarter,". Robert William Chambers. LC 6-23335. (Neely's library of choice literature, no. 34). 1894. F. T. Neely.

In the Rapids. A Romance. Thomas J. Irving. LC 21-12968. 1871. J. B. Lippincott & Co.

TITLE INDEX IN THOSE DAYS: AN

In the Realm of Terror: 8 Haunting Tales. Algernon Blackwood. LC 57-6599. 1957. Pantheon.
In the Red: A Novel. Roy Milton Iliff. LC 30-19626. 1930. Frederick A. Stokes Company.
In the Reign of Peace. Hugh Nissenson. 1973. pap. 0.95 o.p. (09245). Curtis.
In the Reign of Peace: Stories. Hugh Nissenson. LC 71-179794. 1972. 5.95 (ISBN 0-374-17657-4). Farrar, Straus & Giroux.
In the Roar of the Sea. Sabine Baring-Gould. LC 6-7233. Lovell, Coryell & Company.
In the Roar of the Sea. Sabine Baring-Gould. LC 2-12295. (Sea shore & mountain series). 1902. Street & Smith.
In the Rockies with Kit Carson. John Thomas McIntyre. LC 13-237288. (His The bucksin books). 1913. 0.75. The Penn Publishing Company.
In the Saddle with Gomez. Mario Carrillo. LC 98-568. F. T. Neely.
In the Sanctuary. Sequel to On the Heights of Himalay. Albert Van Der Naillen. LC 8-30229. (On cover: California authors' series, no. 1). 1896. W. Doxey.
In the Sanctuary: Sequel to On the Heights of Himalay. Albert Van Der Naillen. LC 30-12326. 1908. D. Fitzgerald, Inc.
In the Sargasso Sea: A Novel. Thomas Allibone Janvier. 1898. Harper & Brothers.
In the Schillingscourt. Eugenie John. Tr. by Steinestel, Emily R. LC 8-7698. (The royal series, v. 14). G. Munro's Sons.
In the Schillingscourt. Eugenie John. Tr. by Steinstel, Emily R. LC 7-990461. (On cover: Seaside library. Pocket ed. no. 1993). G. Munro.
In the Schillingscourt. Eugenie John. Tr. by Miller, Hettie E. LC 7-9905. (On cover: The enterprise series, no. 52). E. A. Weeks & Company.
In the Schillingscourt. A Romance. From the German of E. Marlitt Pseud.... Eugenie John. Tr. by Wister, Annis Lee (Furness) LC 7-990361. 1879. J. B. Lippincott & Co.
In the Schillingscourt: A Romance from the German of E. Marlitt Pseud.... Eugenie John. Tr. by Wister, Annis Lee (Furness) 1901. J. B. Lippincott Company.
In the Sealed Cave: Being a Modern Commentary on a Strange Discovery Made by Captain Lemuel Gulliver in the Year 1721 and Now Published from Manuscript Notes Recently Come to Light; a Scientific Fantasy. Louis Herrman. LC 35-9077. 1935. D. Appleton-Century Company, Incorporated.
In the Second Year. Margaret Storm Jameson. LC 36-271173. 1936. The Macmillan Company.
In the Secret State. Robert McCrum. LC 79-20770. 10.95 (ISBN 0-671-25282-8). Simon and Schuster.
In the Service of the Princess. Henry Cottrell Rowland. LC 10-853697. 1910. 1.50. Dodd, Mead and Company.
In the Seven Mountains: Legends Collected in Central Pennsylvania. Henry Wharton Shoemaker. LC 14-507. 1913. The Bright Printing Company.
In the Shadow. Henry Cottrell Rowland. LC 6-13934. 1906. D. Appleton and Company.
In the Shadow of Black Rock. Anna May Wright. LC 56-11210. 1956. Vantage Press.
In the Shadow of Freedom. Egils Kalme. (Orig.). 1979. pap. 1.95 (ISBN 0-532-19264-8). Woodhill.
In the Shadow of God. Guy Arthur Jamieson. LC 10-7829. 1.00. R. F. Fenno & Company.
In the Shadow of Gold. Paul Studer. LC 37-3296. 1935. Greenberg.
In the Shadow of Islam. Demetra Vaka Brown. LC 11-257448. 1911. Houghton Mifflin Company.
In the Shadow of Lantern Street. Herbert G Woodworth. LC 20-3065. Small, Maynard & Company.
In the Shadow of Omizantrim. Robert E. Vardeman & Victor Milan. LC 81-82972. (War of Powers Ser.: Bk. 5). 224p. (Orig.). 1982. pap. 2.50 (ISBN 0-87216-999-5). Playboy Pbks.
In the Shadow of San Juan. Maurice McNeill Armstrong. LC 10-13851. 1910. Pueblo Publishing Co.
In the Shadow of the Alamo. Clara Driscoll. LC 6-18591. 1906. G. P. Putnam's Sons.
In the Shadow of the Cat. Wendy England. 1980. pap. 2.25 (ISBN 0-8439-0803-3). Nordon Pubns.
In the Shadow of the Cheka. John De Navarre Kennedy. LC 35-13194. The Macaulay Company.
In the Shadow of the Falcon. Ewan Clarkson. 1973. 6.95 o.p. (ISBN 0-525-13270-8). Dutton.
In the Shadow of the Hills. George Clifford Shedd. LC 19-159753. The Macaulay Company.
In the Shadow of the Lord: A Romance of the Washingtons. Mary Crawford Fraser. 1906. H. Holt and Company.
In the Shadow of the Pines: A Tale of Tidewater Virginia. John Hamilton Howard. LC 6-13100. Eaton & Mains.
In the Shadow of the Pyramids: The Last Days of Ismail Khedive. 1879. Richard Henry Savage. (On cover: Rialto series, no. 81). 1898. Rand, McNally & Co.
In the Shadow of the Tower. Ruth McCarthy Sears. 1975. pap. 0.95 o.p. (LB251NK, Leisure Bks). Nordon Pubns.
In the Shadow of the Tower. Ruth McCarthy Sears. 1972. 4.95. Lenox Hill Pr.
In the Shadow of the Tower. Ruth McCarthy Sears. (Large print gothic). 1975. (pbk.) 0.95. Leisure Books.
In the Shadow of Tyranny. Peter Vlcko. 8.95 o.p. Vantage.
In the Shadows. Dorothy Daniels. 1978. 1.75 (ISBN 0-451-08265-6). New American Library.
In the Shadows of Thy Wings. Aundrae Morgan. LC 58-48170. 1958. Great Western Pub. Co.
In the Sherburne Line. Amanda Minnie Douglas. LC 7-32889. 1907. Dodd, Mead and Company.
In the Shoe String Country: A True Picture of Southern Life. Frederick Carleton Chamberlin. LC 6-10302. 1906. C. M. Clark Publishing Co., Inc.
In the Sixties. Harold Frederic. LC 74-144611. 1971. (ISBN 0-404-02573-0). AMS Press.
In the Sixties. Harold Frederic. 1897. C. Scribner's Sons.
In the Slipstream: Stories. David Zane Mairowitz. LC 76-52777. 1977. 7.95 (ISBN 0-914090-27-5). Chicago Review Press: Distributed by Swallow Press.
In the Smoke of War: A Story of Civil Strife. Walter Raymond. LC 7-36632. 1895. Macmillan and Co.
In the Soft Night. Phyllis Yahnke. LC 45-5453. 1945. Gramercy Publishing Company.
In the Soul's Riptide. Anne Bailie. LC 82-4442. (Orig.). 1982. pap. 5.00 (ISBN 0-941608-02-6). Chantry Pr.
In the Southland. Susanna Shulrick Hayne Pinckney. 1906. The Neale Publishing Company.
In the Spring the War Ended: A Novel. Steven Linakis. LC 65-206780. bds., 5.95. Putnam.
In the Springtime of the Year. Susan Hill. LC 73-21329. 192p. 1974. 5.95 o.p. (ISBN 0-8415-0304-4). Dutton.
In the Springtime of the Year: A Novel. Susan Hill. LC 73-21329. 1974. 5.95 (ISBN 0-8415-0298-6). Saturday Review Press.
In the "Stranger People's" Country: A Novel. Mary Noailles Murfree. LC 4-151413. 1891. Harper & Brothers.
In the Suicide Mountains. John Champlin Gardner. LC 77-74993. 1977. 8.95 (ISBN 0-394-41880-8). Knopf.
In the Suicide Mountains. John Champlin Gardner & Joe Servello. LC 80-12156. (Illus.). 1980. 5.95 (ISBN 0-395-29468-1). Houghton Mifflin.
In the Sun. Jon Godden. 1965. 5.95 o.p. (ISBN 0-394-43033-6). Knopf.
In the Sun: 1st Amer. Ed. Jon Godden. LC 65-11102. 4.95. Knopf.
In the Sun's Angry Clutch see Everything Else.
In the Suntime of Her Youth. Beatrice Whitby. LC 8-36037. (On cover: Appletons' town and country library, no. 109). 1893. D. Appleton and Company.
In the Swim: A Story of Currents and Under-Currents in Gayest New York. Richard Henry Savage. LC 8-2005. (On cover: Rialto series, no. 82). 1898. Rand, McNally & Company.
In the Teeth of the Evidence. Dorothy Leigh Sayers. pap. 2.95 (ISBN 0-380-01280-4, 62943-7). Avon.
In the Teeth of the Evidence: And Other Stories. Dorothy Leigh Sayers. LC 40-27171. Harcourt, Brace and Company.
In the Teeth of the Evidence: And Other Stories. Dorothy Leigh Sayers. LC 44-7529. New Avon Library.
In the Tennessee Mountains. Mary Noailles Murfree. LC 68-20019. (Americans in Fiction). 1968. Gregg Press.
In the Tennessee Mountains. Mary Noailles Murfree. 1884. Houghton, Mifflin and Company.
In the Tennessee Mountains. Mary Noailles Murfree. LC 34-37791. 1886. Houghton, Mifflin and Company.
In the Tenth Moon. Sidney Clark Williams. LC 23-9851. 1923. The Penn Publishing Company.
In the Thicket. Solomon Simon. LC 63-13256. 1963. Jewish Publication Society of America.
In the Thirties. Edward Upward. LC 79-496382. 1969. Penguin.
In the Three Zones. Frederic Jesup Stimson. LC 79-37561. (Short story index reprint series). 1972. 8.00 (ISBN 0-8369-4120-9). Books for Libraries Press.
In the Three Zones. Frederic Jesup Stimson. LC 8-15678. 1893. C. Scribner's Sons.
In the Tideways. Flora Annie Webster Steel. LC 8-13434. 1897. The Macmillan Company.
In the Tiger's Cage. Carolyn Wells. LC 34-168659. 1934. J. B. Lippincott Company.
In the Time of Attila. Francis William Rolt-Wheeler. LC 28-22063. Lothrop, Lee & Shepard Co.
In the Time of Greenbloom. Gabriel Fielding, pseud. (YA) (gr. 9-12). pap. 1.95 o.p. (A87). Apollo Eds.
In the Time of Greenbloom. Gabriel Fielding, pseud. 1957. 5.95 o.p. Morrow.
In the Time of Greenbloom. Gabriel Fielding, pseud. pap. 1.95 o.p. (A87). Apollo Eds.
In the Time of Greenbloom: By Gabriel Fielding Pseud. Alan Gabriel Barnsley. LC 57-9382. 1957. Morrow.
In the Time of Surveys & Other Stories of Americans Abroad. Albert Drake. LC 78-53998. 1978. 3.00 (ISBN 0-917976-02-9). White Ewe Press.
In the Time of the Cherry Viewing: An Episode in Japan. Margaret Peale. 1889. G. P. Putnam's Sons.
In the Toils. Thomas Ring. (On cover: Neely's choice library, no. 79). 1898. F. T. Neely.
In the Toils of Slavery. Ivy Chambers Blackburn. LC 6-32350. The American Baptist Publication Society.
In the Toils of the Charmer. Mary E. Kennard. LC 12-36159. 1898. Rand, McNally & Company.
In the Toils: Or, Martyrs of the Latter Days. Cornelia Paddock. LC 7-34703. 1879. Dixon & Shepard.
In the Toils: Or, Martyrs of the Latter Days. Cornelia Paddock. (On cover: American novelists' series, no. 20). 1890. J. W. Lovell Company.
In the Trail of the Wind. Ed. by John Bierhorst. 1972. pap. 4.95 o.p. (ISBN 0-374-50901-8, N400). FS&G.
In the Turkish Camp and Other Stories. Konrad Kummel. Tr. by Gray, Mary Richards. 1899. B. Herder.
In the Twelfth Year of the War: A Novel. Philip Appleman. LC 71-127711. 1970. 5.95. Putnam.
In the Twilight Zone. Roger Carey Craven. LC 9-29258. 1909. 1.50. The C. M. Clark Publishing Company.
In the Twinkling of an Eye. Sydney Watson. LC 33-32920. Fleming H. Revell Company.
In the Valley. Harold Frederic. LC 72-84573. 1974. (lib. ed.) 17.95 (ISBN 0-403-02976-7). Scholarly Press.
In the Valley. Harold Frederic. LC 4-15106. 1890. C. Scribner's Sons.
In the Valley see Collected Works.
In the Valley of the Damned. Young S. Rhee. 3.95 o.p. G&D.
In the Valley of the Shadows. Thomas Lee Woolwine. LC 9-4961. 1909. Doubleday, Page & Company.
In the Valley of Tophet. Henry Woodd Nevinson. 1896. H. Holt and Company.
In the Van. S. Marshak. 12p. 1982. pap. 1.25 (ISBN 0-8285-2289-8, Pub. by Progress Pubs USSR). Imported Pubns.
In the Vestibule Limited. Brander Matthews. LC 7-24701. (Lettered on cover: Harper's black and white series). 1892. Harper and Brothers.
In the Village of the Man. Loyd Little. LC 77-27285. 1978. 8.95 (ISBN 0-670-12204-1). Viking Press.
In the Village of Viger. Duncan Campbell Scott. LC 8-2923. 1896. Copeland and Day.
In the Vultures' Nest: Or, The Huguenots at the Court of France in 1572. Mildred Fairfax. LC 6-38429. Congregational Sunday-School and Publishing Society.
In the Wake of a Stranger. Ian Stuart Black. 1981. 18.95x (Pub. by Remploy England). State Mutual Bk.
In the Wake of Man: A Science Fiction Triad. R. A Lafferty & Gene Wolfe. LC 74-21146. 7.95 (ISBN 0-672-52090-7). Bobbs-Merrill.
In the Wake of the Green Banner. Eugene Paul Metour. LC 9-12620. 1909. C. Scribner's Sons.
In the Wake of War: A Tale of the South Under Carpet-Bagger Administration. Verne Seth Pease. 1900. G. M. Hill Company.
In the Wallowas: A Novel in Two Parts. Caroline Wasson Thomason. LC 54-6186. 1954. Exposition Press.
In the Way. Grace Livingston Hill. LC 7-4698. 1897. A. J. Rowland.
In the Weaving. Wallace Jerome Chambers. LC 42-256832. 1942. Meador Publishing Company.
In the Web of Life. Virginia Belle Terhune Van De Water. LC 14-19284. Hearst's International Library Co.
In the West Countrie. A Novel. Maria Henrietta De La Cherois Crommelin. LC 6-31974. (Harper's Franklin square library. no. 380). 1884. Harper & Brothers.
In the West Countrie. A Novel. Maria Henrietta De La Cherois Crommelin. (On cover: The seaside library. Pocket ed. no. 452). 1885. G. Munro.
In the Wet. Nevil Shute. 1982. 14.95 (ISBN 0-434-69913-6, Pub. by Heinemann). David & Charles.
In the Wet: By Nevil Shute Pseud. Nevil Shute Norway. LC 53-5216. 1953. Morrow.
In the Whirlpool: La Curee. Emile Zola & Sherwood, Mrs. Mary (Neal) Tr. LC 9-1321. T. B. Peterson & Brothers.
In the Wilderness. Sigrid Undset & Chater, Arthur G., Tr. LC 29-20430. 1929. A. A. Knopf.
In the Wilderness. Charles Dudley Warner. 1973. Repr. of 1878 ed. 10.00 o.p. (ISBN 0-8274-0813-7). R West.
In the Wilderness: A Novel. Robert Smythe Hichens. LC 17-5984. Frederick A. Stokes Company.
In the Wilds of New Mexico. George Manville Fenn. LC 6-39376. (Munsey's popular series, no. 12). 1888. F. A. Munsey.
In the Wink of an Eye: A Novel. Kelly Cherry. LC 82-18737. 1983. 15.95 (ISBN 0-15-144656-3). Harcourt Brace Jovanovich.
In the Wire-Grass: A Novel. Louis Beauregard Pendleton. LC 7-36364. (On cover: Appleton's town and country library. no. 29). 1889. D. Appleton and Company.
In the Wood: A Novel in Three Parts. Naomi Gwladys Royde-Smith. LC 28-13166. 1928. Harper & Brothers.
In the Workshop of St. Joseph. Herman Joseph Heuser. LC 35-34801. 1925. Benziger Brothers.
In the World: A Novel, by George P. Elliott. George P Elliott. LC 65-19267. 1965. Viking Press.
In the World Celestial,". 2d ed. Thomas Augustus Bland. LC 4-8626. 1902. T. A. Bland & Co.
In the World Celestial" by T. A. Bland... With an Introduction. 4th ed. Thomas Augustus Bland. LC 32-19532. 1905. T. A. Bland & Co.
In the Wrong Rain. 1st Ed. Robert R Kirsch. LC 59-76376. 1959. Little, Brown.
In the Year of Jubilee. George Robert Gissing. LC 75-29849. (Society and the Victorians). 1976. 18.50 (ISBN 0-8386-1886-3). Fairleigh Dickinson University Press.
In the Year of Jubilee. George Robert Gissing. LC 75-80633. 1969. AMS Press.
In the Year of Jubilee. George Robert Gissing. LC 77-354710. (Society and the Victorians; No. 27). 1976-1977. 21.00 (ISBN 0-85527-064-0). Harvester Press.
In the Year of Jubilee: A Novel. George Robert Gissing. LC 6-43980. 1895. D. Appleton and Company.
In the Year '13: A Tale of Macklenburg Life. Fritz Reuter & Lewes, Charles Lee, 1843-1891, Tr. LC 7-30646. (Half-title: Collection of German authors. v. 4). 1867. Leypoldt & Holt; Etc., Etc.
In the Years of Our Lord. Manuel Komroff. LC 42-10310. 1942. Harper & Brothers.
In Their Own Image. Hamilton Basso. LC 35-4225. 1935. C. Scribner's Sons.
In Their Wisdom. Charles Percy Snow. LC 74-12273. 1974. 7.95 (ISBN 0-684-13941-3). Scribner.
In These Times. Verlie Forsyth. LC 57-3027. Vantage Press.
In This Corner! Peter Heller. (O.s.i.). 1973. 10.00 o.s.i. (ISBN 0-671-21568-X). S&S.
In This House of Brede. Rumer Godden. LC 78-83231. 1969. 6.95. Viking Press.
In This Our Life. Ellen Anderson Gholson Glasgow. LC 77-460446. (Illus.). 1976. Franklin Library.
In This Our Life. Ellen Anderson Gholson Glasgow. LC 41-516290. Harcourt, Brace and Company.
In This Sign. Joanne Greenberg. LC 75-117261. 1970. 5.95 (ISBN 0-03-085066-5). Holt, Rinehart and Winston.
In This Thy Day. Michael McLaverty. LC 47-1621. 1947. The Macmillan Company.
In This Transparent Forest. Jonathan Griffin. LC 76-58108. 1977. 12.00 (ISBN 0-940580-03-9); pap. 6.00 (ISBN 0-940580-04-7). Green River.
In This Valley. Michael Home, pseud. LC 34-27269. 1934. W. Morrow and Company.
In This World: And Other Stories. Eugene Ziller. LC 60-6278. 1960. Braziller.
In This World and the Next: Selected Writings. Translated from the Yiddish by Moshe Spiegel. Isaac Loeb Peretz. LC 57-13111. 1958. T. Yoseloff.
In This World of Ours. Minnie Milbank Dodds. LC 12-11154. 1912. 1.50. The Shakespeare Press.
In Those Days: An Impression of Change. Harvey Fergusson. LC 29-5600. 1929. A. A. Knopf.

In Those Days: An Impression of Change. Harvey Fergusson. LC 78-13366. (Gregg Press Western Fiction Series). 1978. 9.95 (ISBN 0-8398-2472-6). Gregg Press.

In Those Days: The Story of an Old Man, by Jehudah Steinberg. Tr. from Hebrew by George Jeshurun. Illus. by Ezekiel Schloss. Judah Steinberg. LC 67-8417. (Keter lib.). 1967. 4.50. Jewish Educ. Comm. Pr.

In Those Days: The Story of an Old Man. Judah Steinberg. Tr. by Jeshurun, George. LC 15-7362. 1915. 1.00. The Jewish Publication Society of America.

In Thraldom: A Psychological Romance. Leon Mead. LC 7-25868. (Fireside series, no. 33). 1887. J. S. Ogilvie & Company.

In Three Cities and a State or Two: Or, The Holcomb Family and Fortune, and Other Tales. George S Fraser. LC 6-431562. 1889. G. P. Putman's Sons.

In Time. Robert Kelly. 70p. 1971. pap. 3.00. Frontier Press Calif.

In Time for Murder: Another Investigation by the Curious Mr. Tolefree. Robert Alfred John Walling. 1933. W. Morrow & Company.

In Time of Harvest. John L Sinclair. LC 43-12124. 1943. The Macmillan Company.

In Time of Harvest. John L. Sinclair. LC 78-21434. (Zia book). 1979. 4.50 (ISBN 0-8263-0505-9). University of New Mexico Press.

In Time of Peace. Thomas Alexander Boyd. LC 35-4003. Minton, Balch & Company.

In Times Like These. Emilie Baker Loring. LC 76-41713. 1976. 6.95 (ISBN 0-88411-356-6). Aeonian Press.

In Times Like These. Emilie Baker Loring. LC 68-25901. 1968. 4.75. Little, Brown.

In Times Like This. Emilie Baker Loring. 1976. Repr. of 1968 ed. lib. bdg. 14.10x (ISBN 0-88411-356-6). Amereon Ltd.

In Times Likes These. Emilie Baker Loring. LC 79-11703. 1979. 12.50 (ISBN 0-8161-6731-1). G. K. Hall.

In Touch. Marco Vassi. 192p. (Orig.). 1975. pap. 1.50 (ISBN 0-532-15158-5). Woodhill.

In Tragic Life. Vardis Fisher. LC 32-35789. 1932. The Caxton Printers, Ltd.

In Tragic Life. Vardis Fisher. 1933. Doubleday, Doran & Company, Inc., and Caldwell, Id., The Caxton Printers, Ltd.

In Transit. Brigid Brophy. 1970. 5.95 o.p. (ISBN 0-399-10449-6). Putnam.

In Transit: An Heroi-Cyclic Novel. Brigid Brophy. LC 70-97075. 1970. 5.95. Putnam.

In Treaty with Honor: A Romance of Old Quebec. Mary Catherine Crowley. LC 6-32678. 1906. Little, Brown, and Company.

In Trust: Or, Dr. Bertrand's Household. Amanda Minnie Douglas. 1891. Lee & Shepard.

In Trust; or Dr. Bertrand's Household. Armanda Minnie Douglas. 1977. Repr. 38.00 o.p. (ISBN 0-403-08366-4). Scholarly.

In Trust. The Story of a Lady and Her Lover. Margaret Oliphant Wilson Oliphant. (Seaside library, v. 51, no. 1049). 1881. G. Munro.

In Tune with Wedding Bells. Grace Livingston Hill. LC 41-9966. J. B. Lippincott Company.

In Two Moods. Also, In Bad Society. Vladimir Galaktionovich Korolenko. Tr. by Kravchinskii, Sergiei Mikhailovich & Westall, William. LC 7-14116. (On cover: Lovell's International series, no. 178). J. W. Lovell Company.

In Vain. Henryk Sienkiewicz. Tr. by Jeremiah Curtin. LC 99-2690. 1899. Little, Brown, and Company.

In Vain: An Original Novel. Richard Daniel. LC 82-1425. 1981. 3.95 (ISBN 0-942086-00-7). Custom House Publications.

In Varying Moods. american copyright ed. Beatrice Harraden. LC 77-110195. (Short story index reprint series). 1970. Books for Libraries Press.

In Varying Moods. american copyright ed. Beatrice Harraden. LC 7-2860. 1894. G. P. Putnam's Sons.

In Walked Anny: A Novel. Lucile Selk Edgerton. LC 40-3847. The Penn Publishing Company.

In War Time. Silas Weir Mitchell. LC 34-25498. 1885. Houghton, Mifflin and Company.

In War Times at La Rose Blanche. Mary Evelyn Moore Davis. LC 6-32866. D. Lothrop Company.

In Watermelon Sugar. Richard Brautigan. (Laurel edition). 1973. (pbk.) 0.95. Dell.

In Watermelon Sugar. Richard Brautigan. LC 68-20130. (Writing 21). 1968. 1.95. Four Seasons Foundation.

In Watermelon Sugar see Trout Fishing in America.

In Wedlock Wake: A Novel. Marion Sturges-Jones. LC 46-207951. 1946. G. P. Putnam's Sons.

In Whaling Days. Howland Tripp. LC 9-15087. 1909. Little, Brown, and Company.

In What Torn Ship. Evelyn Sybil Mary Eaton. LC 44-5662. 1944. Harper & Brothers.

In White and Black: A Story. William Washington Pinson. LC 72-1560. (Black Heritage Library Collection). 1972. 14.50 (ISBN 0-8369-9047-1). Books for Libraries Press.

In White and Black: A Story. William Washington Pinson. LC 2-6280. The Saalfield Publishing Company.

In Wild Rose Time. Amanda Minnie Douglas. LC 6-33478. 1895. Lee & Shepard.

In, Wilma. Will Chambliss. LC 80-68881. (Illus., Orig.). 1981. pap. 3.95 (ISBN 0-938108-00-X). Crystal Pr.

In Winter Light. Edwin Corle. LC 49-1507. 1949. Duell, Sloan and Pearce.

In-World. Lionel Roberts, pseud. LC 68-2937. 1968. Arcadia House.

In Youth Is Pleasure. Denton Welch. LC 46-3295. 1946. L. B. Fischer.

In Zanzibar. Ralph Delahaye Paine. LC 25-11002. 1925. Houghton Mifflin Company.

Ina: A Novel. Katharine Sedgwick Washburn. LC 8-33479. 1871. J. R. Osgood and Company.

Inanna: Queen of Heaven & Earth. Diane Wolkstein & Samuel N. Kramer. LC 80-8690. (Illus.). 224p. 12.95i (ISBN 0-06-014713-X, HarpT); pap. 4.95i (ISBN 0-06-090854-8). Har-Row.

Inca Death Squad. Nick Carter. (Nick Carter Ser.). (Illus.). 176p. 1982. pap. 2.25 (ISBN 0-441-35868-3, Pub. by Charter Bks). Ace Bks.

Inca Death Squad. Nick Carter. (Nick Carter Ser.). (O.s.i.). 1972. pap. 0.95 o.s.i. (AN1016, Award). Univ Pub & Dist.

Incaland: A Story of Adventure in the Interior of Peru and the Closing Chapters of the War with Chile. Claude Hazeltine Wetmore. 1902. W. A. Wilde Company.

Incandescence. Craig Nova. LC 77-3801. 10.95 (ISBN 0-06-013196-9). Harper & Row.

Incandescent Lily, and Other Stories. Gouverneur Morris. LC 73-142271. (Short story index reprint series). 1970. (ISBN 0-8369-3755-4). Books for Libraries Press.

Incandescent Lily: And Other Stories. Gouverneur Morris. LC 14-9083. 1914. C. Scribner's Sons.

Incandescent Ones. Fred Hoyle & Geoffrey Hoyle. LC 76-47254. 7.95 (ISBN 0-06-011956-X). Harper & Row.

Incandescent Ones. Fred Hoyle & Geoffrey Hoyle. (Signet Book). 1978. 1.75 (ISBN 0-451-08062-9). New American Library.

Incarnation of Krishna Mulvaney. Rudyard Kipling. 1899. Doubleday and McClure Company.

Ince Affair: A Novel. Joe Morella & Epstein, Edward Z. (Signet Book). 1978. 1.75 (ISBN 0-451-08177-3). New American Library.

Incese to Idols. Sylvia Ashton-Warner. LC 60-10988. 1960. Simon and Schuster.

Incest Among the Rich. Hal Edwards. 224p. pap. 1.95 o.p. (7133). Barclay Hse.

Incest Clan. Sterling Harkins. 192p. (Orig.). 1972. pap. 1.95 o.p. (ISBN 0-87682-226-X, 7226). Barclay Hse.

Incest Contest. Hal Edwards. 192p. (Orig.). 1972. pap. 1.95 o.p. (ISBN 0-87682-220-0, 7220). Barclay Hse.

Incest Diary. Hans Melcher. 192p. pap. 1.95 o.p. (6098). Brandon.

Incest Game. Thomas Shire. 192p. pap. 1.95 o.p. (6168). Brandon.

Incest Jigsaw:: Fathers, Daughters, Mothers and Sons. S. P Blake. 1974. (pbk.) 1.95 (ISBN 0-87056-405-6). Brandon Books.

Incest Kid. William Horton. pap. 1.95 o.p. (8088). Cameo.

Incest Lovers. Paul DeKock. 192p. pap. 1.95 o.p. (7139). Barclay Hse.

Incest Lovers. Thomas Shire. pap. 1.95 o.p. (ISBN 0-87056-180-4, 6180). Brandon.

Incest Swingers. S. C. Carew, pseud. pap. 1.95 o.p. (ISBN 0-87056-192-8, 6192). Brandon.

Incest Twins. Carter Sprague. 192p. pap. 1.95 o.p. (6171). Brandon.

Incestuous Daughters. Carter Sprague. pap. 1.95 o.p. (ISBN 0-87056-181-2, 6181). Brandon.

Incestuous Summer. Karl Rockwood. pap. 1.95 o.p. (ISBN 0-87056-194-4, 6194). Brandon.

Inch by Inch. Ed Martin. (Orig.). 1968. pap. 1.95 o.s.i. (TC502, Travellers Comp). Olympia.

Inch of Snow. William Edward Cobb. LC 64-14723. 1964. J. F. Blair.

Inch of Taper: By Hugh Talbot Pseud. Argentine Francis Alington. LC 51-17395. 1950. Wingate.

Inch of Time... James Norman Schmidt. LC 44-382. 1944. Books Inc., W. Morrow & Co.

Inchin' Along. Welbourn Kelley. LC 32-23137. 1932. W. Morrow & Company.

Incident: And Other Happenings. Sarah Barnwell Elliott. LC 79-94717. (Short story index reprint series). (Illus.). 1969. Books for Libraries Press.

Incident, and Other Happenings. Sarah Barnwell Elliott. LC 99-792. 1899. Harper & Brothers.

Incident at Ashton. Jay Milner. LC 61-14642. 1961. Appleton-Century-Crofts.

Incident at Bloody Axe. Glenn R. Vernam. 1979. pap. 1.50 o.s.i. (ISBN 0-505-51451-6). Tower Bks.

Incident at Caprock. Sally Tyree Smith. 1981. pap. 6.95 (Avalon). Bouregy.

Incident at Hawk's Hill. Allan W. Eckert. 1972. pap. 1.95 (ISBN 0-440-94020-6, LFL). Dell.

Incident at Hendon. Jennette Dowling Letton. LC 67-26973. 1967. Macrae Smith.

Incident at Horado City. William C. MacDonald. 1978. pap. 1.25 o.s.i. (ISBN 0-505-51288-2). Tower Bks.

Incident at La Junta. Oliver Lange. LC 72-96961. 1973. 6.95 (ISBN 0-8128-1535-1). Stein and Day.

Incident at Muc Wa. Daniel Ford. (T-1780). 1968. Pyramid.

Incident at Muc Wa. Daniel Ford. LC 67-12876. 1967. Doubleday.

Incident at Naha. Malcolm J. Bosse. LC 72-179588. (Inner sanctum mystery). 1972. 5.95 (ISBN 0-671-21159-5). Simon and Schuster.

Incident at One Hundred Twenty Fifth Street. J. E. Brown. (O.s.i.). 192p. 1972. pap. 0.95 o.s.i. Woodhill.

Incident at One Hundred Twenty-Fifth Street. J. E. Brown. LC 70-89103. 1970. 4.95 o.p. (ISBN 0-385-02825-3). Doubleday.

Incident at One Hundred Twenty Fifth Street. J. E. Brown. (O.s.i.). 192p. 1972. pap. 0.95 o.s.i. Manor Bks.

Incident at Sakai & Other Stories. Mori Ogai. Ed. by David Dilworth & J. Thomas Rimer. Tr. by David Dilworth & J. Thomas Rimer. LC 76-58462. 1977. text ed. 12.95x (ISBN 0-8248-0453-8). UH Pr.

Incident at Sun Mountain. Willis Todhunter Ballard. LC 52-5255. 1952. Houghton Mifflin.

Incident at Villa Rahmana. Lois Dwight Cole. 1973. (pbk.) 0.75. Dell.

Incident at Villa Rahmana. Anne Eliot, pseud. 1972. 5.95 o.p. Hawthorn.

Incident at 125th Street. John Edward Brown. LC 70-89103. 1970. 4.95. Doubleday.

Incident in a Texas Town. Mitchell Dana. 1975. (pbk.) 0.95 (ISBN 0-380-00211-6). Avon.

Incident in Iceland. Bill Knox. LC 79-7513. 1979. 7.95 (ISBN 0-385-15478-X). Published for the Crime Club by Doubleday.

Incident in Iceland. Noah Webster. (Crime Club Ser.). 1979. 7.95 o.p. (ISBN 0-385-15478-X). Doubleday.

Incident on Ath: Dumarest, No. 18. E. C. Tubb. (Science Fiction Ser). (Orig.). 1978. pap. 2.50 (UE1668). DAW Bks.

Incident on the Way to a Killing. Michael Hammonds. LC 76-42332. 1977. 6.95 (ISBN 0-385-12569-0). Doubleday.

Incident Over the Pacific. 1st Ed. James Murdoch Macgregor. LC 60-13543. 1960. Doubleday.

Incident. Translated by Charlotte Haldane. 1st Ed. Anne Rives. LC 62-782183. 1962. Dutton.

Incident. 1st Ed. Marc Rivette. LC 57-10933. 1957. World Pub. Co.

Incidental Bishop. A Novel. Grant Allen. LC 6-76. 1898. D. Appleton and Company.

Incidental Bishop: A Novel by Grant Allen. Grant Allen. LC 6-77. (Added t.-p.: Appleton's town and country library, no 238)). 1898. D. Appleton and Company.

Incidents in Montana: Old Vintage. 1st Ed. William J Stratton. LC 54-13215. Pageant Press.

Incidents of Social Life Amid the European Alps. From the German of J. Heinrich D. Zschokke. Zschokke, Heinrich & Strack, Louis, Tr. LC 8-37801. 1844. D. Appleton & Co.

Inclinations see Three More Novels.

Incognita, or Love & Duty Reconcil'd: A Novel. William Congreve. 1974. text ed. 10.50x o.s.i. (ISBN 0-8277-3780-7); pap. text ed. 4.95x o.s.i. (ISBN 0-8277-2175-7). British Bk Ctr.

Incognito. Petru Dumitriu. 1964. 8.50 o.p. M McCosh Bkslr.

Incognito: A Novel. Robert Smythe Hichens. LC 48-8767. 1948. R.M. McBride.

Incognito: A Novel. LC 64-22599.

Incomparable Bellairs. Agnes Sweetman Castle & Castle, Egerton. LC 3-28589. 1963. F. A. Stokes Company.

Incomparable Max. Jerome Lawrence & Robert E. Lee. 1972. pap. 2.45 o.p. (ISBN 0-8090-1227-8, Mermaid). Hill & Wang.

Incomparable Miss Brady. Sheila Walsh. (Signet Regency Romance). 1980. 1.75 (ISBN 0-451-09245-7). New American Library.

Incompetents... Robin Edgerton Spencer. LC 35-12235. 1933. A. A. Knopf.

Incomplete Adventurer: And The Boom in Belltopps. Tighe Hopkins. G. Munro.

Incomplete Amorist. Edith Nesbit Bland. LC 6-26195. 1906. Doubleday, Page & Company.

Incomplete Enchanter. Lyon Sprague De Camp & Pratt, Fletcher. LC 41-16597. H. Holt and Company.

Incomplete Mariner. Leonard Hastings Nason. LC 29-22804. 1929. Doubleday, Doran & Company, Inc.

Incongruous Spy. John Le Carre. (O.s.i.). 5.95 o.s.i. (ISBN 0-8027-5113-X). Walker & Co.

Inconsequent Lives. Joseph Henry Pearce. LC 7-33508. J. W. Lovell Company.

Inconsistent Villains. Neville Aldridge Holdaway. LC 29-12767. E. P. Dutton & Co., Inc.

Inconsolable Memories. Edmundo Desnoes. LC 67-19163. 1967. New American Library.

Inconstant Flame. Harlow Wilson Estes. LC 43-13939. 1943. Dodd, Mead & Company.

Inconstant Lady. Nigel Heseltine. LC 54-6117. 1954. Lippincott.

Inconstant Season. Sally Daniels. (YA) 1962. 4.50 o.p. Atheneum.

Inconstant Star. Adelaide Humphries. LC 40-294662. 1940. Arcadia House, Inc.

Inconvenience of Living, and Other Stories. Marvin Cohen. LC 77-11990. 1977. 8.95. (ISBN 0-916354-46-6) (ISBN 0-916354-47-4). Urizen Books.

Inconvenient Bride. James W. Knipscheer. LC 48-8787. (Gargoyle mystery)). 1948. Coward-McCann.

Inconvenient Corpse. E. P Fenwick. 1943. Farrar & Rinehart, Inc.

Incorrigible: A Novel. Karl Brown. LC 47-114755. 1947. Duell, Sloan and Pearce.

Incorrigible Dukane. George Clifford Shedd. LC 11-25675. Small, Maynard and Company.

Incorrigibles. Harold McGowan. 1978. 10.00 (ISBN 0-682-48980-8). Exposition.

Incorruptible. Marjorie Coryn. LC 43-121477. 1943. D. Appleton-Century Company, Incorporated.

Incorruptible. Helma De Bois, pseud. 1972. pap. 1.25 o.p. (01030). Curtis.

Incorruptible: A Tale of Revolution and Royalty. Helma De Bois. LC 64-238228. 5.95. Crown.

Incredible Adventures. Algernon Blackwood. LC 14-191678. 1914. 1.35. The Macmillan Company.

Incredible Adventures of Dennis Dorgan. Robert E. Howard. LC 74-83075. 1974. 11.95 o.p. (ISBN 0-913960-06-3). Fax Collect.

Incredible Borgias. Alfred Henschke & Brink, Louise, 1876- Tr. LC 29-212202. 1929. H. Liveright, Inc.

Incredible Brazilian. Zulfikar Ghose. LC 72-80208. 6.95 (ISBN 0-03-001951-6). Holt, Rinehart and Winston.

Incredible Charlie Carewe. Mary Astor. LC 60-11373. 1960. Doubleday.

Incredible Crimes. Linda Atkinson. (Hi Lo Ser.). 96p. 1981. pap. 1.50 (ISBN 0-553-14938-5). Bantam.

Incredible Honeymoon. Edith Nesbit Bland. LC 16-225965. 1916. Harper & Brothers.

Incredible Honeymoon. Barbara Cartland (ISBN 0-553-02806-5). Bantam.

Incredible Hulk. (Super Hero Collection). (Illus., Orig.). 1968. pap. 0.50 o.p. (72-124). Lancer.

Incredible Interlude at Tahoe. Arthur R. Roberts. 1977. pap. 1.95 (ISBN 0-87881-066-8). Mojave Bks.

Incredible Journey. Sheila Every Burnford. 1977. pap. 1.95 (ISBN 0-553-10220-6, 13075-7). Bantam.

Incredible Journey. Sheila Every Burnford. (Winner of the Lewis Carroll Shelf Award 1971). (Illus.). 1961. 10.95 (ISBN 0-316-11714-5, Pub. by Atlantic Monthly Pr). Little.

Incredible Journey. Sheila Every Burnford. (Keith Jennison Large Type Bks). 7.95 o.p. Watts.

Incredible Mysteries & Legends of the Sea. Edward R. Snow. (Illus.). 1967. 5.00 o.p. (ISBN 0-396-05627-X). Dodd.

Incredible Planet. John Wood Campbell. LC 49-11571. 1949. Fantasy Press.

Incredible Radio Exploits of Doc Savage, Vol. 1. Kenneth Robeson, pseud. (Illus.). pap. 9.95x (ISBN 0-933752-24-5). Odyssey MA.

Incredible Schlock Holmes. Robert L Fish. (Equinox Book). 1976. (pbk.) 2.95 (ISBN 0-380-00636-7). Avon Books.

Incredible Schlock Homes. Introd. by Anthony Boucher. Robert L Fish. LC 66-16159. 3.95. S. & S.

Incredible Truth. Chris Massie. LC 58-5280. 1958. Random House.

Incredible Umbrella. Marvin Kaye. LC 78-3259. 1979. 7.95 (ISBN 0-385-14321-4). Doubleday.

Incredible Voyage. Tristan Jones. 1980. pap. 2.95 (ISBN 0-380-49999-1, 49999). Avon.

Incredible Voyage. Keith Knoche. (Uplook Ser.). 1975. pap. 0.75 (ISBN 0-8163-0184-0, 09446-6). Pacific Pr Pub Assn.

Incredible William Bowles. Joseph Millard. LC 66-14672. Chilton Books.

Incredible Year. Faith Cutherell Baldwin. 1976. 1.25 (ISBN 0-446-86266-5). Warner Books.

Incredible Year. Faith Baldwin Cuthrell. LC 29-18412. 1929. Dodd Mead & Company.

Incredulity of Father Brown. Gilbert Keith Chesterton. LC 75-317516. (Penguin crime fiction). 1974. 1.50 (ISBN 0-14-001069-6). Penguin.

Incredulity of Father Brown. Gilbert Keith Chesterton. LC 26-20061. 1925. Cassell and Company, Ltd.

TITLE INDEX INEZ: A TALE OF

Incredulity of Father Brown. Gilbert Keith Chesterton. LC 26-137974. 1928. Dodd, Mead and Company.
Incubator Baby. Ellis Parker Butler. 1906. Funk & Wagnalls Company.
Incubus. Cameron Michaelis. LC 81-86424. 192p. 1983. pap. 6.95 (ISBN 0-86666-118-2). GWP.
Incubus. Ray Russell. LC 75-25619. 1976. 7.95 (ISBN 0-688-02981-7). Morrow.
Incubus. Tr. from Italian by William Weaver. 1st Amer. Ed. Giuseppe Berto. LC 66-10028. 1966. 5.95. Knopf.
Incunabular Sherlock Holmes. Ed. by Edgar Wadsworth Smith. LC 58-2897. 1958. Baker Street Irregulars.
Incurable. Nell Dunn, pseud. LC 76-132504. 1971. 4.95. Doubleday.
Incurable Romantic. Roderick Peattie. 1941. Repr. 14.00 o.s.i. Finch Pr.
Indecent? Josiah Pitts Woolfolk. LC 34-223. 1934. W. Godwin, Inc.
Indecent Exposure. Susan Quist. LC 73-90378. 1974. 6.95 (ISBN 0-8027-0441-7). Walker.
Indecent Obsession. Colleen McCullough. LC 81-20333. 15.95 (ISBN 0-8161-3373-5). G.K. Hall.
Indecent Relations. Kenneth R. McKay. LC 81-82365. 288p. (Orig.). 1982. pap. 2.95 (ISBN 0-87216-949-9). Playboy Pbks.
Indecision. Claire M. Stieff. LC 27-15196. The Christopher Publishing House.
Indeed This Flesh. Grace C. Hodgson Flandrau. LC 34-13508. 1934. H. Smith and R. Haas.
Indefinite River. Preston Schoyer. LC 47-11499. 1947. Dodd, Mead.
Indelible. Elliot Harold Paul. LC 39-612748. (A Mercury book, no. 15). The American Mercury, Inc.
Indelible: A Story of Life, Love, and Music, in Five Movements. Elliot Harold Paul. LC 22-12391. 1922. 1.75. Houghton Mifflin Company.
Indemnity Only. Sara Paretsky. (Nightingale Ser.). 1982. pap. 8.95 (ISBN 0-8161-3439-1, Large Print Bks). G K Hall.
Indemnity Only. Sara Paretsky. 224p. 1983. pap. 2.50 (ISBN 0-345-30684-8). Ballantine.
Indemnity Only: A Novel. Sara Paretsky. LC 81-5452. 12.95 (ISBN 0-385-27213-8). Dial Press.
Indemnity Only: A Novel. Sara Paretsky. LC 82-11918. 1982. 8.95. G.K. Hall.
Independence! large print ed.. ed. Dana Fuller Ross. LC 81-13448. (Ross, Dana Fuller. Wagons West: Vol. 1). 1982. 16.95 (ISBN 0-8161-3315-8). G.K. Hall & Co.
Independence: A Story of the Revolution. John Roy Musick. LC 7-333284. (On cover: Columbian historical novels v. 9). 1893. Funk & Wagnalls Company.
Independent Heart. Ann Pinchot. 1976. pap. 1.25 o.p. (ISBN 0-515-03936-5). BJ Pub Group.
Independent Means: A Novel. Frank Singleton. LC 48-1833. 1948. Macmillan Co.
Independent People. Halldor Kiljan Laxness & Thompson, J. Anderson, Tr. LC 46-4757. 1946. A. A. Knopf.
Independent People: An Epic. Halldor Laxness, pseud. Tr. by J. A. Thompson from Icelandic. LC 76-7973. 1976. Repr. of 1946 ed. lib. bdg. 31.50x (ISBN 0-8371-8872-5, LAIP). Greenwood.
Independent People, an Epic. Halldor Kiljan Laxness & J. Anderson Thompson. LC 76-7973. 1976. 25.00 (ISBN 0-8371-8872-5). Greenwood Press.
Independent Witness. Henry Cecil. 1974. 5.95 o.s.i. (ISBN 0-8277-3344-5). British Bk Ctr.
Index Finger a Story. Tulis Atrojal. 1898. R. F. Fenno & Company.
Index to Sybil: A Novel. Sturm, Justin. LC 51-11536. 1951. Dorrance.
India Allan. Elizabeth Boatwright Coker. LC 53-10340. 1953. Dutton.
India & Her Miracle Feast-Come & Enjoy Yourself, 5 pts. Chinmoy. Incl. Pt. 1. Traditional Indian Stories About Troilanga Swami. (ISBN 0-88497-354-9); Pt. 2. Traditional Indian Stories About Shayama Charan Lahiri. (ISBN 0-88497-355-7); Pt. 3. Traditional Indian Stories About Shayama Charan Lahiri. (ISBN 0-88497-356-5); Pt. 4. Traditional Indian Stories About Bhaskarananda. (ISBN 0-88497-357-3); Pt. 5. Traditional Indian Stories About Devadas Maharaj. (ISBN 0-88497-358-1). (Orig.). 1977. pap. 1.00 ea. Aum Pubns.
India Rubber Men. Edgar Wallace. LC 30-13235. 1930. Pub. for the Crime Club, Inc., by Doubleday, Doran & Company, Inc.
India, the Hungry. Irmgard Muske. LC 71-111693. 1970. Concordia.
India: The Pearl of Pearl River. Emma Dorothy Eliza Nevitte Southworth. LC 4-35877. 1856. T. B. Peterson.
Indian Beef. Harold Channing Wire. LC 40-304092. 1940. Doubleday, Doran and Company, Inc.
Indian Chief: A Tale of the Desert. Gustave Aimard & St. John, Percy Bolingbroke, 1821-1889, Ed. LC 5-42587. (On cover: Lovell's library, no 1133). 1888. J. W. Lovell Company.
Indian Cottage: A Unitarian Story... Charles Constantine Pise. LC 7-38201. F. Lucas, Jun.
Indian Country. Dorothy M Johnson. LC 79-16722. (Series: Gregg Press Western Fiction Series.). (Illus.). 1979. 7.95 (ISBN 0-8398-2586-2). Gregg Press.
Indian Country. Stories. Dorothy M Johnson. LC 53-8871. 1953. Ballantine Books.
Indian Day. Edward John Thompson. LC 27-9305. 1927. A. A. Knopf.
Indian Drum. William Briggs MacHarg. LC 17-25511. 1917. Little, Brown, and Company.
Indian Drums & Broken Arrows. Craig Massey. 1970. pap. 0.95 o.p. Moody.
Indian Dust: Studies of the Orient Including a Biographical Appreciation of Lawrence Hope. 2d ed. Otto Rothfield. LC 10-22416. 1910. John Lane Company.
Indian Hater. Glenn R Vernam. LC 69-20074. 1969. 4.95. Doubleday.
Indian Heritage, Indian Pride: Stories That Touched My Life. Jimalee Burton. LC 73-7426. (Illus.). 1981. pap. 11.95 (ISBN 0-8061-1707-9). U of Okla Pr.
Indian Idyls. E M Cuttim. LC 6-32233. Cassell Publishing Company.
Indian Killer. Harold Calin. 1981. pap. 1.95 (ISBN 0-505-51726-4). Tower Bks.
Indian Killer. Harold Calin. (O.s.i.). (Orig.). 1973. pap. 0.75 o.s.i. (BT50519). Belmont-Tower.
Indian Killer. Harold Calin. 1976. 1.25. Leisure Books.
Indian Killer. Harold Kalin. 1976. pap. 1.25 o.p. (LB425ZK, Leisure Bks). Nordon Pubns.
Indian Lily: And Other Stories. Hermann Sudermann. LC 71-134982. 1970. Books for Libraries Press.
Indian Lily, and Other Stories. Hermann Sudermann & Lewisohn, Ludwig, 1882- Tr. LC 12-285. 1911. B. W. Huebsch.
Indian Love Letters. Marah Ellis Martin Ryan. LC 72-8453. (Illus.). 1972. (ISBN 0-87380-094-X). Rio Grande Press.
Indian Love Letters. Marah Ellis Martin Ryan. LC 7-10045. 1907. A. C. McClurg & Co.
Indian-Lover. Lewis Owen. 1975. (pbk.) 1.95. Bantam Books.
Indian Maiden's Captivity. E. R. Zietlow. Bd. with Heart of the Country. LC 78-61093. 1979. 9.95 (ISBN 0-917624-10-6). Lame Johnny.
Indian Maiden's Dream." A Novel. Kate Burmeister. LC 6-18652. 1895. Pub. by the Author.
Indian Outpost. Thomas Albert Curry. (Orig.). 1973. pap. 0.75 o.p. (07308). Curtis.
Indian Paul. John Eugene Moore. LC 45-8894. 1945. Harcourt, Brace and Company.
Indian Pipe Dream. Enid Irwin. 2.50 o.p. Vantage.
Indian Point Conspiracy. Ron Felber. 1977. pap. 1.50 (ISBN 0-532-15267-0). Woodhill.
Indian Ribaldry. Randor Guy. LC 77-113907. (Illus.). 1970. C. E. Tuttle Co.
Indian Saddle-up. Glenn Balch. (Illus.). 4.00 o.p. (ISBN 0-8446-0018-0). Peter Smith.
Indian Scene: Collected Short Stories. facsimile ed. Flora Annie Webster Steel. LC 72-37282. (Short Story Index Reprint Ser.). Repr. of 1934 ed. 30.00 (ISBN 0-8369-4092-X). Ayer Co.
Indian Scene: Collected Short Stories of Flora Annie Steel. Flora Annie Webster Steel. LC 72-37282. (Short story index reprint series). 1971. (ISBN 0-8369-4092-X). Books for Libraries Press.
Indian Scout: A Story. Gustave Aimard & St. John, Percy Bolingbroke, 1821-1889, Ed. LC 5-42586. (On cover: Lovell's library, no 1098). 1887. J. W. Lovell Company.
Indian Sign. John Gunther. 1971. pap. 0.95 o.p. (ISBN 0-06-087013-3, HW). Har-Row.
Indian Sign: A Novel. John Gunther. LC 71-108945. 1970. 5.00. Harper & Row.
Indian Special. Estelle Aubrey Armstrong. LC 12-22862. H. Lechner.
Indian States & Ruling Princes. Sidney Low. 1929. 15.00 (ISBN 0-8482-4857-0). Norwood Edns.
Indian Steps, and Other Pennsylvania Mountain Stories. Henry Wharton Shoemaker. LC 12-20308. 1912. The Bright Printing Company.
Indian Summer. William Dean Howells. Ed. by Scott Bennett. LC 79-165051. (Selected edition of W. D. Howells, v. 11). 1971. 10.50. Indiana University Press.
Indian Summer. William Dean Howells. LC 7-5771. 1886. Ticknor and Company.
Indian Summer. William Dean Howells. LC 4-15457. Houghton, Mifflin and Company.
Indian Summer. Emily Grant Hutchings. LC 22-15474. 1922. A. A. Knopf.
Indian Summer. John Knowles. LC 66-12280. 4.95. Random.
Indian Summer. John Collis Snaith. LC 31-164486. 1931. D. Appleton and Company.
Indian Summer: A Novel. Robert Sylvester. LC 52-5142. 1952. Random House.
Indian Summer. New Introd. by William M. Gibson. William Dean Howells. LC 51-7375. (Everyman's library, 643A. Fiction). 1951. Dutton.
Indian Summer of Gabriel Murray. Hugo Charteris. LC 77-78876. 1970. Harcourt, Brace & World.
Indian Tales. Franklin Welles Calkins. LC 8-13320. 1893. M. A. Donohue & Co.
Indian Tales. Rudyard Kipling. ("First issued in Bonibook series, February 1963."--Verse of t.-p.). 1933. Albert & Charles Boni.
Indian Tales. original ed. Rudyard Kipling. LC 99-424979. H. M. Caldwell Company.
Indian Tales and Others. John Gneisenau Neihardt. LC 26-16707. 1926. The Macmillan Company.
Indian Tales: By Elizabeth Sharpe. Phoebe Elizabeth Sharpe. LC 40-12187. 1965. 3.00. Luzac.
Indian Territory. David Everitt. 208p. (Orig.). 1982. pap. 2.25 (ISBN 0-8439-1041-0, Leisure Bks). Nordon Pubns.
Indiana. George Sand & George Burnham Ives. LC 75-25896. 1975. 14.00. H. Fertig.
Indiana. George Sand & George Burnham Ives. LC 77-27987. (Illus.). 1978. 12.95 (ISBN 0-915864-58-4) (ISBN 0-915864-57-6). Cassandra Editions.
Indiana. A Love Story. George Sand. LC 6-34608. T. B. Peterson & Brothers.
Indiana Jane. Cecil Roberts. LC 29-178585. 1930. D. Appleton and Company.
Indiana Man. Le Roy Armstrong. LC 43-468713. (On cover: The Ariel library series. No. 7). 1895. The Schulte Publishing Company.
Indiana Man. Le Roy Armstrong. LC 6-2434. 1890.
Indians. John Rothfork. LC 79-92931. 1980. 13.50 (ISBN 0-89002-126-0); pap. 3.50 (ISBN 0-89002-125-2). Northwoods Pr.
Indians, Finns, and Their Thunderbirds. Walter Mattila. LC 74-160851. (Illus.). 1973. 5.00.
Indians of the Oaks. rev. ed. Melicent H. Lee. (Illus.). 1978. pap. 6.95 (ISBN 0-916552-17-9). Acoma Bks.
Indians' Summer. Nasnaga. LC 74-20816. (Native American Publishing Program Ser.). 224p. (YA) 1975. 6.95i (ISBN 0-06-451510-9, HarpT). Har-Row.
Indians Won. Martin Cruz Smith. 224p. 1981. pap. 2.50 (ISBN 0-8439-1012-7, Leisure Bks). Nordon Pubns.
Indians Won. Martin Cruz Smith. (Orig.). 1970. pap. 0.95 o.p. (B95-2045). Belmont-Tower.
Indictment: A Novel from Behind the Iron Curtain. 1960. Augsburg Pub. House.
Indifference. Peter De Polnay. LC 74-171232. 1974. 2.25 (ISBN 0-491-01452-X). W. H. Allen.
Indifference of Juliet. Grace Louise Smith Richmond. LC 5-12161. 1905. Doubleday, Page & Company.
Indifferent Blade. Lilian Van Ness. LC 47-4399. 1947. Doubleday.
Indifferent Children. Louis Auchincloss. LC 64-57393. 1964.
Indifferent Children. Louis Auchincloss. LC 47-413765. 1947. Prentice-Hall Inc.
Indifferent Heart. large print ed. Alexandra Sellers. LC 82-11923. 1982. 7.95 (ISBN 0-8161-3441-3). G.K. Hall.
Indifferent Ones. Alberto Pincherle & Mastrangelo, Aida, Tr. LC 32-20041. E. P. Dutton & Co., Inc.
Indignations of E.W. Howe see Collected Works.
Indigo. Christine Goutiere Weston. LC 43-156480. 1943. C. Scribner's Sons.
Indigo Bend. 1st Ed. Alice Walworth Graham. LC 54-5218. 1954. Doubleday.
Indigo Necklace. Frances Kirkwood Crane. LC 45-283843. 1945. Random House.
Indigo Nights. Olivia O'Neill. (Berkley Medallion Book). 1977. 1.95 (ISBN 0-425-03629-4). Berkley Pub. Corp.
Indigoes. Jon C. Randall. 1975. 2.00. Broadside.
Indiscreet Confessions of a Nice Girl. LC 35-47256. W. Godwin, Inc.
Indiscreet Girl. Bernard Sobel. LC 35-153923. Farrar & Rinehart, Incorporated.
Indiscreet Letter. Eleanor Hallowell Abbott. LC 15-14445. 1915. 0.50. The Century Co.
Indiscreet Year. Larry Barretto. LC 31-6600. Farrar & Rinehart, Incorporated.
Indiscretion in the Life of an Heiress, Hardy's Lost Novel. Thomas Hardy. Ed. by Carl J. Weber. (Illus.). 1965. Repr. of 1935 ed. 7.00 o.p. Russell.
Indiscretion in the Life of an Heiress. Hardy's 'lost Novel,' Ed., Introd., Notes by Carl J. Weber. Thomas Hardy. Ed. by Carl Jefferson Weber. LC 65-13931. 1965. 6.00. Russell & Russell.
Indiscretion in the Life of an Heiress. Thomas Hardy. LC 77-352529. 1976. 2.95 (ISBN 0-09-126010-8). Hutchinson.
Indiscretion in the Life of an Heiress. Thomas Hardy. Ed. by Weber, Carl Jefferson. LC 35-425083. 1935. The Johns Hopkins Press.
Indiscretion in the Life of an Heiress. Thomas Hardy. LC 78-19335. (Johns Hopkins University Press reprints). (Illus.). 1979. 14.00 (ISBN 0-405-10604-1). Arno Press.
Indiscretion of Lady Usher. Diary of My Honeymoon, Author of. LC 13-2377. 1913. 1.25. The Macaulay Company.
Indiscretion of the Duchess and Mr. Witt's Widow. Anthony Hope Hawkins. LC 3-24938. (Half-title: Author's edition. Works of Anthony Hope...). D. Appleton and Company.
Indiscretion of the Duchess: Being a Story Concerning Two Ladies, a Nobleman, and a Necklace. Anthony Hope Hawkins. LC 4-16532. 1894. H. Holt and Company.
Indiscretions. Evelyn Konrad. LC 78-13199. 8.95 (ISBN 0-8037-3684-3). Dial Press.
Indiscretions of a French Model see Black Satin Jungle.
Indiscretions of Archie. Pelham Grenville Wodehouse. LC 21-267376. George H. Doran Company.
Indiscretions of Archie. Pelham Grenville Wodehouse. LC 35-334092. 1923. A. L Burt Company.
Indiscretions of Maister Redhorn. John Joy Bell. LC 11-26600. 0.60. Fleming H. Revell Company.
Individual. Muriel Hine Coxon. LC 16-10451. 1916. John Lane Company.
Individualist. Philip Hamilton Gibbs. LC 25-7200. 1925. E. J. Clode, Inc.
Individualist: Or, A Tale of the Canadian Northland. Frank Howard Collins. LC 40-12429. 1940. Meador Publishing Company.
Indoctrinaire. Christopher Priest. LC 76-123984. 1970. 5.95. Harper & Row.
Indomitable Hornblower. C. S. Forester. Bd. with Commodore Hornblower; Lord Hornblower; Admiral Hornblower in the West Indies. 13.95. (Illus.). 1963. 13.95 (ISBN 0-316-28904-3). Little.
Indomitable Hornblower: Commodore Hornblower, Lord Hornblower and Admiral Hornblower in the West Indies, Complete Novels. Cecil Scott Forester. LC 63-17970. 1963. Little, Brown.
Indoor Gardens. Ware Budlong. (O.s.i.). 1975. pap. text ed. 1.25 o.s.i. (BT50833). Belmont-Tower.
Indulge the Lady: By James Noble Gifford. James Noble Gifford. LC 32-28970. 1932. A. H. King.
Indulgent Husband. Sidonie Gabrielle Colette & Henry Gauthier-Villars. Tr. by Blossom, Frederick Augustus. LC 35-5122. Farrar & Rinehart, Inc.
Industrial Crisis: Or, Giant Labor and Giant Capital Face to Face. A Story of the "Toiling Masses" and the "Thrifty Rich.". Frederick Charles Lange. LC 3-14850. 1903.
Industrial Turmoil: A Story of New England. Frederic Burnham Jacobs. LC 29-29426. Burton Publishing Company.
Ineluctable Sea. Edna Meudt. 1975. 5.95 (ISBN 0-87482-040-5). Wake-Brook.
Inevitable. Louis Marie Anne Couperus. Tr. by Teixeira De Mattos, Alexander Louis. LC 20-18761. 1920. Dodd, Mead and Company.
Inevitable: A Novel by Philip Verrill Mighels; with a Frontispiece by John Wolcott Adams. Philip Verrill Mighels. LC 2-25047. 1902. J. B. Lippincott Company.
Inevitable Book. Lynn Harold Hough. The Abingdon Press.
Inevitable Dawn. Arthur Charles Baldwin. LC 39-9062. Harper & Brothers.
Inevitable Hour. Martyn Boggon. (O.s.i.). 1969. pap. 0.75 o.s.i. (A398S, Award). Univ Pub & Dist.
Inevitable Hour. Hilda Sylvaine. LC 31-22583. Sears Publishing Company, Inc.
Inevitable Hour: A Novel of Martinique. Edison Marshall. LC 57-107181. 1957. Putnam.
Inevitable Millionaires. Edward Phillips Oppenheim. LC 25-891. 1925. Little, Brown, and Company.
Inexhaustible Cup. Ivan Sergieevich Shmelev & France, Mrs. Tatiana (Deechtereva) Tr. LC 28-21378. E. P. Dutton & Company.
Inexistences: Constructivist Fictions. Richard Kostelanetz. LC 78-61087. 1978. pap. text ed. 50.00 (ISBN 0-932360-26-2). RK Edns.
Inexorable: Or, The Wages of Sin. LC 6-20491. Hurst & Co.
Inexpensive Love. Daniel Tupper. 2.75 o.p. Carlton.
Inexperienced Ghost: And Nine Other Stories. Herbert George Wells. Ed. by Leavitt, Hart Day. LC 65-1387. (Bantam pathfinder editions, FP81). Bantam Books,
Inez: A Tale of the Alamo. Augusta Jane Evans Wilson. LC 13-9381. 1855. Harper & Brothers.
Inez: A Tale of the Alamo. Augusta Jane Evans Wilson. LC 4-866. 1882. G. W. Carleton & Co.

Inez and Trilby May. Sewell Ford. LC 21-20437. 1921. Harper & Brothers.

Infallibles. G. T. Vitale. 10.00 o.p. Carlton.

Infamous Army. Georgette Heyer. LC 65-11396. 1965. 4.95. Dutton.

Infamous Army. Georgette Heyer. (Fawcett Crest Book). 1977. 1.75. Fawcett Pubns.

Infamous Army. Georgette Heyer. LC 38-128480. 1938. Doubleday, Doran & Co., Inc.

Infamous Attachment. Helen Tucker. 224p. (Orig.). 1980. pap. 1.75 (ISBN 0-449-50072-1, Coventry). Fawcett.

Infamous John Friend. Martha Roscoe Garnett. LC 9-20137. 1909. H. Holt and Company.

Infamous Woman. Doris Knight. LC 34-9623. 1934. W. Godwin, Inc.

Infans Amoris: The Tale of a Once Sorrowful Soul, a Romance. Thomas Everett Harry. LC 2-12944. 1902. The Abbey Press.

Infant & Child Care for the Indian Mother. Subhash C. Srya. 195p. 1972. 9.50x (ISBN 0-8002-1566-4). Intl Pubns Serv.

Infant with the Globe. From the Spanish by Robert Graves. Pedro Antonio De Pedro Antonio De Alarcon Y Ariza. Alarcon. LC 59-12180. 1959-1960. 3.50. T. Yoseloff.

Infant with the Globe. From the Spanish by Robert Graves. 1st American Ed. Pedro Antonio De Alarcon. LC 59-12180. 1959. T. Yoseloff.

Infants of the Spring. Wallace Thurman. LC 72-4615. (Black Heritage Library Collection). 1972. 12.75 (ISBN 0-8369-9129-X). Books for Libraries Press.

Infants of the Spring. Wallace Thurman. LC 73-18608. 1975. 12.50 (ISBN 0-404-11418-0). AMS Press.

Infants of the Spring. Wallace Thurman. LC 32-7659. The Macaulay Company.

Infants of the Spring: A Novel. Wallace Thurman. LC 78-16906. (Lost American fiction). 1979. 10.95 (ISBN 0-8093-0864-9). Southern Illinois University Press.

Infant's Skull: Or, The End of the World, a Tale of the Millennium. Eugene Sue & De Leon, Daniel, 1852-1914, Tr. LC 5-4547. 1904. New York Labor News Company.

Infatuation. Sibylle Gabrielle Marie Antoinette De Riquette De Mirabeau Martel De Janville. Tr. by Paul, Elise. R. F. Fenno & Company.

Infatuation. Lloyd Osbourne. LC 9-73350. 1909. 1.50. The Bobbs-Merrill Company.

Infatuation. Lloyd Osbourne. LC 14-10505. 1909. Grosset & Dunlap.

Infatuation. Denise Robins. 1972. pap. 0.75 o.p. (94268). Beagle Bks.

Infatuation: Or, Maria's Misfortunes. Bithia Mary Sheppard Croker. LC 98-466. 1899. J. B. Lippincott Company.

Infelice: A Novel. Augusta Jane Evans Wilson. LC 3-175339. 1903. G. W. Dillingham Co.

Infernal Grove. Malcom Muggeridge. (Chronicles of Wasted Time, Chronicle 2). 1974. 7.50 (ISBN 0-688-00953-0). Morrow.

Infernal Machine. Archibald Fleming MacLiesh & De San Marzano, Robert A., Joint Author. 1947. Houghton Mifflin Co.

Infernal Revenue. Constance Bannister. (O.s.i.). pap. 1.00 o.s.i. (ISBN 0-671-10264-8, Fireside). S&S.

Infernal Revenue Rackets and Tales. Earl C Crouter. LC 64-12017. Dorance.

Inferno. Henri Barbusse. Tr. by Edward Joseph Harrington O'Brien. LC 19-2828. 1918. Boni and Liveright.

Inferno. John Creasey. LC 66-225013. 1966. bds., 3.95. Walker.

Inferno. John Creasey. (Medallion, X1627). 1968. Berkley.

Inferno. Fred Hoyle & Geoffrey Hoyle. LC 73-4151. 1973. 5.95 (ISBN 0-06-011987-X). Harper & Row.

Inferno. Larry Niven & J. E. Pournelle. LC 79-14258. (Gregg Press science fiction series). 1979. 12.95 (ISBN 0-8398-2450-5). Gregg Press.

Inferno. Larry Niven & Jerry Pournelle. 1976. (pbk.) 1.75 (ISBN 0-671-80490-1). Pocket Books.

Inferno: Alone & Other Writings. August Strindberg. Ed. & tr. by Evert Sprinchorn. 8.50 (ISBN 0-8446-3026-8). Peter Smith.

Infidel. Georgia Elizabeth Taylor. LC 78-4002. 10.95 (ISBN 0-312-41598-2). St. Martin's Press.

Infidel: A Romance. Mary Elizabeth Braddon Maxwell. LC 5244. 1900. Harper & Brothers.

Infidel Doctor of Salem. Effie M. Williams. 52p. pap. 0.40; pap. 1.00 3 copies. Faith Pub Hse.

Infidel of Love. June Casey. (Superromances Ser.). 384p. 1982. pap. 2.50 (ISBN 0-373-70025-3, Pub. by Worldwide). Harlequin Bks.

Infidel: Or, The Fall of Mexico. A Romance. Robert Montgomery Bird. LC 6-13128. 1835. Carey, Lea & Blanchard.

Infidel; or the Fall of Mexico: A Romance, 2 vols. Robert Montgomery Bird. LC 78-64064. Repr. of 1835 ed. Set. 75.00 (ISBN 0-404-17150-8). AMS Pr.

Infidelities. Angela Huth. LC 79-14400. 8.95 (ISBN 0-517-53874-1). C. N. Potter: Distributed by Crown Publishers.

Infidelities. Richard Posner. (Orig.). 1982. pap. 3.50 (ISBN 0-440-14022-6). Dell.

Infidelity. Peggy Gaddis, pseud. LC 38-12696. 1938. Godwin.

Infidelity: Being a Veracious Account of the Somewhat Farcical "Pennyworth Affair". Arthur Edward Pearse Brome Weigall. LC 28-12075. 1928. Brentano's.

Infiltrator. Christopher Nicole. LC 70-157641. 1971. 5.95. Doubleday.

Infiltrator. Martin Walker. LC 78-19042. 7.95 (ISBN 0-8037-4004-2). Dial Press/James Wade.

Infiltrator. Andrew York. LC 70-157641. 1971. 5.95 o.p. (ISBN 0-385-03278-1). Doubleday.

Infinite Arena: Seven Science Fiction Stories About Sports. Ed. by Terry Carr. LC 76-30758. 6.95 (ISBN 0-8407-6538-X). T. Nelson.

Infinite Brain. Charles Russell Long. LC 57-8740. 1957. Avalon Books.

Infinite Cage. Keith Laumer. (Berkley medallion book). 1974. (pbk.) 0.95. Berkley Pub. Co.

Infinite Cage. Keith Laumer. LC 70-186648. 1972. 5.95. Putnam.

Infinite Dreams. Joe W Haldeman. LC 78-3959. 1978. 8.95 (ISBN 0-312-41605-9). St. Martin's Press.

Infinite Dreams. Joe W Haldeman. 1979. 2.25 (ISBN 0-380-47605-3). Avon Books.

Infinite Jests: The Lighter Side of Science Fiction. Ed. by Robert Silverberg. LC 74-2106. 1974. 5.95 (ISBN 0-8019-5931-4). Chilton Book Co.

Infinite Longing. Marie Schmitz. LC 32-22988. Harcourt, Brace.

Infinite Longing. Marie Verhoeven Schmitz. Tr. by Renier, Gustaaf Johannes. LC 32-22988. Harcourt, Brace and Company.

Infinite Man. Daniel F Galouye. LC 73-957. (Illus.). 1973. (pbk.) 0.95. Bantam Books.

Infinite Passion of Expectation: Twenty-Five Stories. Gina Berriault. LC 82-81480. 288p. 1982. pap. 12.50 (ISBN 0-86547-082-0). N Point Pr.

Infinite Summer. Christopher Priest. LC 79-53957. 1979. 8.95 (ISBN 0-684-16274-1). Scribner.

Infinite Web: Eight Stories of Science Fiction. Ed. by Robert Silverberg. LC 76-42928. (gr. 7 up). 1977. 7.95 o.s.i. (ISBN 0-8037-4135-9). Dial.

Infinite Woman. Edison Marshall. LC 50-10337. 1950. Farrar, Straus.

Infinite Woman: Garden City Books Reprint Ed. Edison Marshall. LC 52-25494. 1951. Garden City Books.

Infiniteness of Great Artistry. Alma Groninger. 3.50 o.p. Carlton.

Infinity Box: A Collection of Speculative Fiction. Kate Wilhelm. LC 74-15894. 1975. 8.95 (ISBN 0-06-014653-2). Harper & Row.

Infinity Box: A Collection of Speculative Fiction. Kate Wilhelm. (Kangaroo Book). 1977. 1.75 (ISBN 0-671-80955-5). Pocket Books.

Infinity Five. Ed. by Bob Hoskins. 1973. pap. 0.95 o.s.i. (75-477). Lancer.

Infinity Four. Ed. by Robert Hoskins. 1972. pap. 0.95 o.s.i. (75-387). Lancer.

Infinity I. Ed. by Robert Hoskins. (Orig.). 1970. pap. 0.95 o.p. (ISBN 0-447-75108-5). Lancer.

Infinity of Mirrors. Richard Condon. 1974. (pbk.) 1.50. Dell.

Infinity of Mirrors. Richard Condon. LC 64-17935. 1964. Random.

Infinity of Questions. Cecil John Eustace. 1946. Repr. 8.50 o.p. (ISBN 0-8274-2570-8). R West.

Infinity Three. Ed. by Robert Hoskins. (Orig.). 1972. pap. 0.95 o.s.i. (75-320). Lancer.

Infinity Two. Ed. by Robert Hoskins. 1971. pap. 0.95 o.p. (ISBN 0-447-75166-2). Lancer.

Inflation Fighters. Barbara Anson. 192p. 1982. pap. 1.50 (ISBN 0-8439-1095-X). Leisure Bks CT.

Influence of a Single Life. James Walter Tinley. LC 2-18606. 1902. The Franklin Printing and Publishing Co.

Informant. Mildred Gordon & Gordon Gordon. LC 72-89414. 1973. 6.95 (ISBN 0-385-01433-3). Doubleday.

Information Girl. Charles Stanley Strong. LC 40-10306. Phoenix Press.

Information Received. Ernest Robertson Punshon. LC 34-14229. 1934. Houghton Mifflin Company.

Informed Consent. Neil Ravin. LC 82-18095. 15.95 (ISBN 0-399-12800-X). Putnam.

Informed Sources: A Novel. Lawrence Kamarck. LC 79-11049. 7.95 (ISBN 0-8037-4110-3). Dial Press.

Informed Sources: Day East Received. Willard S Bain. LC 69-10946. 1969. 2.95. Doubleday.

Informer. Liam O'Flaherty. LC 25-183553. 1925. A. A. Knopf.

Informer. Liam O'Flaherty. LC 25-183554. 1925. A. A. Knopf.

Informer. Liam O'Flaherty. LC 79-26156. (Harvest/HBJ book). 1980. 2.95. Harcourt Brace Jovanovich.

Informer. Afterword by Donagh MacDonagh. Liam O'Flaherty. (Signet classics, CP80). 1961. New Amer. Lib.

Infra Blood. Perry D. Westbrook & Nathanael Howard - Engle. LC 51-38396. 1950. Phoenix Press.

Inga. Roger Bowen. LC 79-52903. 1979. 9.95 (ISBN 0-9602986-1-4). Normandie Pub. Co.

Inga. Karen Lustig. (O.s.i.). (Orig.). pap. 0.75 o.s.i. (A466S, Award). Univ Pub & Dist.

Ingagi & Other Stories. James Reight. 3.75 o.p. (ISBN 0-8062-0687-X). Carlton.

Ingemisco a Novel. Marian Calhoun Legare Reeves. LC 7-30668. 1867. Blelock & Co.

Ingenious Gentleman Don Quixote De la Mancha. Miguel de Cervantes de Saavedra. Ed. by Putnam, Samuel. LC 49-10215. 1949. Viking Press.

Ingenious Mr. Stone... Robert Player. LC 46-312919. 1946. Rinehart & Company, Inc.

Ingenue: An Original Novel. Millicent Brower. (Ballantine books, 286K). 1959. Ballantine Books.

Ingenue: Or, The First Days of Blood. Alexandre Dumas. Tr. by Marguerittes, Julie (Granville) Comtessee De. LC 6-42334. 1855. Lippincott, Grambo, & Co.

Ingham Papers. Edward Everett Hale. 1869. 25.00 (ISBN 0-932062-70-9). Sharon Hill.

Ingham Papers: Some Memorials of the Life of Capt. Frederic Ingham, U.S.N., Sometime Pastor of the First Sandemanian Church in Naguadavick, and Major General by Brevet in the Patriot Service in Italy. Edward Everett Hale. LC 9-2509. 1869. Fields, Osgood, & Co.

Ingledew House: And, More Bitter Than Death. Charlotte Mary Brame. (On cover: Seaside library. Pocket ed. no. 303). G. Munro.

Ingo: The First Novel of a Series Entitled Our Forefathers. Gustav Freytag. Tr. by Malcolm, Georgiana. LC 6-44736. (Leisure hour series. v. 22). 1873. Holt & Williams.

Ingo: Tr. from the German. Gustav Freytag & Schierbrand, Wolf Von. LC 48-366883. P. F. Collier.

Ingoldsby Legends. Richard Harris Barham. 1972. pap. 1.95 o.p. (ISBN 0-460-01185-5, Evman). Dutton.

Ingomar: Or, The Triumph of Love. Founded on the Romantic Drama of "Ingomar", As Performed by Mary Anderson. Nathan D Urner. (On cover: The select series, no. 20). 1889. Street & Smith.

Ingraban: The Second Novel of a Series Entitled Our Forefathers. Gustav Freytag. Tr. by Malcolm, Georgiana. LC 6-44737. (Leisure hour series. v. 25). 1873. H. Holt & Company.

Ingrate. Magnus Bredenbek. LC 15-13840. 1915. 1.35. The Cheston Publishing Co.

Inhabitant of the Lake and Less Welcome Tenants. J. Ramsey Campbell. LC 64-2840. 1964. Arkham House.

Inhabitants. Wright Morris. 1972. 12.95 o.p. Amphoto.

Inhabitants of Mars: Their Manners and Advancement in Civilization and Their Opinion of Us. Willis Mitchell. LC 7-31088. 1895. C. E. Spofford & Co.

Inhabitants. 1st Ed. Julius Horwitz. LC 60-11451. 1960. World Pub. Co.

Inhale & Exhale. William Saroyan. LC 72-4430. (Short story index reprint series). 1972. 15.00 (ISBN 0-8369-4187-X). Books for Libraries Press.

Inhale & Exhale. William Saroyan. LC 36-5256. Random House.

Inherit the Darkness. Willo Davis Roberts. Repr. lib. bdg. 13.25x (ISBN 0-89190-865-X). Am Repr-Rivercity Pr.

Inherit the Earth. Margaret Shaw. LC 40-6915. The Bobbs-Merrill Company.

Inherit the Earth. Margaret Cochran Shedd. LC 44-86841. 1944. Harper & Brothers.

Inherit the Earth. Lon Riley Woodrum. LC 53-339314. 1953. Zondervan Pub. House.

Inherit the Earth: Stories from Mexican Ranch Life. Alvin J Gordon. LC 63-11977. (Illus.). 1963. University of Arizona Press.

Inherit the Mirage. Julia Thatcher, pseud. LC 76-44853. (Zodiac gothic: Libra). 1977. 1.25 (ISBN 0-89340-015-7). J. Curley & Associates.

Inherit the Mirage: An Astrological Gothic Novel, Libra. Julia Thatcher, pseud. LC 76-20579. (Zodiac gothic series). 1.25 (ISBN 0-345-25209-8). Ballantine Books.

Inherit the Night. Robert Christie. LC 49-970248. 1949. Farrar, Straus.

Inherit the Stars. James P Hogan. LC 76-56444. 1977. 1.50. Ballantine Books.

Inherit the Sun. Maxwell Grant, pseud. LC 80-25172. 13.95 (ISBN 0-698-11074-9). Coward, McCann & Geoghegan.

Inherit the Wind... Maxeda Ferguson Von Hense. LC 43-15651. 1943. W. Morrow & Company.

Inheritance. Josephine Dodge Daskam Bacon. LC 12-21327. 1912. D. Appleton and Company.

Inheritance. Phyllis Eleanor Bentley. LC 32-23133. 1932. The Macmillan Company.

Inheritance. Owen Brookes. LC 79-9359. 10.95 (ISBN 0-03-047626-7). Holt, Rinehart and Winston.

Inheritance. Owen Brookes. 1981. 2.75 (ISBN 0-671-41398-8). Pocket Books.

Inheritance. Owen Brooks. 1981. pap. 2.75 (ISBN 0-671-41398-8). PB.

Inheritance... Susan Edmonstone Ferrier. LC 6-39267. 1893. Roberts Brothers.

Inheritance. Whitfield G Howell. LC 20-13733. The Roxburgh Publishing Company, Inc.

Inheritance. Harriet Elizabeth Prescott Spofford. LC 4-8632. (The ivory series). 1897. C. Scribner's Sons.

Inheritance: A Novel. Allan Seager. LC 4-6058. 1948. Simon and Schuster.

Inheritance of Jean Trouve. Nevil Gratiot Henshaw. LC 22-3893. The Bobbs Merrill Company.

Inherited Barriers. Julia M Walter. LC 58-14515. 1958. Vantage Press.

Inherited Bride. Rebecca Stratton. (Harlequin Romances). 192p. 1981. pap. 1.25 (ISBN 0-373-02399-5, Pub. by Harlequin). PB.

Inherited Deception. Gail MacMillan. 1976. 4.95. Avalon Books.

Inherited Freedom: Dedicated to the Daughters of the Revolution in America, the D. R. and the D. A. R. Annie Fields Vila. LC 5-30268. W. B. Clarke Company.

Inherited Husband. Cecile Gilmore. LC 46-4758. 1946. D. Curl, Inc.

Inheritor. Edward Frederic Benson. LC 30-3361. 1930. Doubleday, Doran & Company, Inc.

Inheritors. Joseph Conrad & Ford Madox Ford. LC 76-11814. (Gregg Press science fiction series). 1976. 15.00 (ISBN 0-8398-2350-9). Gregg Press.

Inheritors. William Gerald Golding. LC 62-16724. 1962. Harcourt, Brace & World.

Inheritors. Michael Hardwick. 1978. 9.95 o.p. (ISBN 0-86025-048-2). State Mutual Bk.

Inheritors. Harold Robbins. 1977. pap. 3.95 (ISBN 0-671-41712-6). PB.

Inheritors. Harold Robbins. 1969. 6.95 o.s.i. (ISBN 0-671-27044-3). Trident.

Inheritors. Harold Rubin. LC 76-97039. 1969. 6.95. Trident Press.

Inheritors: A Novel. Philip Atlee. LC 49-34593. 1940. The Dial Press.

Inheritors: An Extravagant Story. Joseph Conrad & Ford Madox Ford. LC 1-10008. 1901. McClure, Phillips & Co.

Inheritors: Gateway to Never. A. Bertram Chandler. 384p. 1981. pap. 2.50 (ISBN 0-441-37064-0). Ace Bks.

Inheritors of Earth. P. Anderson & G. Eklund. 1976. pap. 1.25 o.p. (ISBN 0-515-04068-1). BJ Pub Group.

Inheritors of Earth. Gordon Eklund & Poul Anderson. LC 74-10553. 1974. 6.50 (ISBN 0-8019-6071-1). Chilton Book Co.

Inheritors of the Storm. Victor Sondheim. LC 81-215742. (7.95, 8.95 can.) (ISBN 0-440-54066-6). Dell Pub. Co.

Inheritors. 1st Ed. Jane Ludlow Drake Abbott. LC 53-8930. 1953. Lippincott.

Inhibited Madam. Jeanne F. Weinreb. 177p. 1971. 5.50 o.p. (ISBN 0-682-47391-X). Exposition.

Inigo Sandys. Emily Beatrix Coursolles Jones. LC 24-26489. 1924. H. Holt and Company.

Inimitable Jeeves. P. G. Wodehouse. 1956. 4.95 o.p. (ISBN 0-8277-0213-2). British Bk Ctr.

Inish: By Bernard Share. 1st Amer. Ed. Bernard Share. LC 67-16157. 1967. 3.95. Knopf.

Inishairlach. A Tale. LC 4-883. (On cover: The Franklin library of modern literature. pt. xxv). 1835. Wallis & Newell.

Initial Experience: And Other Stories. Ed. by Charles King. LC 41-313742. 1896. J. B. Lippincott Company.

Initials. A Novel. Jemima Montgomery Tautphoeus. (Seaside library, v. 25, no. 528). 1879. G. Munro.

Initials. A Story of Modern Life. Jemima Montgomery Tautphoeus. LC 8-25555. 1879. T. B. Peterson & Brothers.

Initials: A Story of Modern Life. Jemima Montgomery Tautphoeus. LC 4-16584. 1892. G. P. Putnam's Sons.

Initials Only. Anna Katharine Green Rohlfs. LC 11-24678. 1911. Dodd, Mead & Company.

Initiates. Paul Virdell. LC 80-70225. 12.50 (ISBN 0-87795-314-7). Arbor House.

Initiation. Robert Hugh Benson. LC 14-426373. 1914. Dodd, Mead and Company.

Initiation. Elisabeth Haich. Tr. by John Robertson from Ger. 380p. (Orig.). 1974. pap. 8.00 (ISBN 0-916108-04-X). Seed Center.

Initiation. William W. Johnstone. (Orig.). 1982. pap. 2.95 (ISBN 0-89083-967-0). Zebra.

Initiation. George Shively. LC 25-4205. Harcourt, Brace and Company.

Initiation Dream. Pauline Oliveros & Becky Cohen. (Illus.). 35p. (Orig.). 1981. pap. 4.00 (ISBN 0-937122-07-6). Astro Artz.

Initiation of Aurora Trill. Richard Ruddy. 1972. pap. 1.75 o.s.i. (V1076K, Venus). Grove.

Initiation Rites. T. Phillip Stone. 1972. pap. 1.75 o.s.i. (V1067K, Venus). Grove.

Initiation: Stories and Short Novels on Three Themes. 2d ed. Ed. by David Thorburn. LC 75-32644. 5.95 (ISBN 0-15-541512-3). Harcourt Brace Jovanovich.

Initiation; Stories and Short Novels on Three Themes. Ed. by David Thorburn. LC 75-155561. 1971. 3.95 (ISBN 0-15-541511-5). Harcourt, Brace, Jovanovich.

Initiations of Suzon see Arlette & Her Friends.

Initimate Affairs of a Good Girl. The Indiscreet Confessions of a Nice Girl, Author of. LC 37-142836. 1936. Godwin.

Injun Blood: A Novel. Bert Cloos. LC 63-426. 1963. Macmillan.

Injury Time: A Comedy of Middle-Aged Passion. Beryl Bainbridge. LC 77-21051. 1978. 7.95 (ISBN 0-8076-0881-5). Braziller.

Injury Time: A Novel. Beryl Bainbridge. LC 77-21127. 1977. 7.95 (ISBN 0-8076-0881-5). G. Braziller.

Injustice Collectors. Louis Auchincloss. LC 50-14014. 1950. Houghton Mifflin.

Injustice Collectors. Louis Auchincloss. 1974. (pbk.) 1.25 (ISBN 0-380-00039-3). Avon.

Ink. A Novel. John Calvin Mellett. LC 30-7423. The Bobbs-Merrill Company.

Ink Truck. William Kennedy. LC 76-91114. 1969. 5.95. Dial Press.

Inkling. Fred Chappel. 1965. 3.95 o.p. (ISBN 0-15-144400-5). HarBraceJ.

Inkling. Fred Chappell. LC 65-19053. 3.95. Harcourt.

Inkling. Fred Chappell. LC 67-81329. (Illus.). 1966. Chapman & Hall.

Inklings. Geoffrey Wolff. LC 77-5988. 7.95 (ISBN 0-394-49349-4). Random House.

Inland Island. Josephine Winslow Johnson. LC 69-12090. (Illus.). 1969. 5.00. Simon and Schuster.

Inland Passage. George Harmon Coxe. LC 49-108202. 1949. A. A. Knopf.

Inland Whale: Nine Stories Retold from California Indian Legends. Theodora Kroeber. (£1.20). (Illus.). (YA) 1959. pap. 3.95 (ISBN 0-520-00676-3, CAL88). U of Cal Pr.

Inland Whale: Nine Stories Retold from California Indian Legends. Theodora Kroeber. (Illus.). 6.50 o.p. (ISBN 0-8446-2407-1). Peter Smith.

Inlander: A Novel. Harrison Robertson. 1901. C. Scribner's Sons.

Inmates. John Cowper Powys. LC 52-14518. 1952. Philosophical Library.

Inn. Julian Stryjkowski. LC 78-184121. 1971. (ISBN 0-15-144415-3). Harcourt Brace Jovanovich.

Inn at the Red Oak. Latta Griswold. LC 17-24857. R. J. Shores.

Inn by the Sea. Charlotte Elvira Gray. LC 14-3563. 1.25. Jennings and Graham.

Inn of Disenchantment. Lisa Ysaye. LC 17-24509. 1917. Houghton Mifflin Company.

Inn of Evil. JoAnne Greighton. 1974. (pbk.) 1.25. Popular Library.

Inn of Five Lovers: Translated from the French by Coburn Gilman. Illus. by Ernest Fiere. Jacques Laurent. LC 53-9640. 1953. Fiction Library.

Inn of That Journey. Emerson Price. LC 77-23199. (Lost American fiction). 1977. 7.95 (ISBN 0-8093-0812-6). Southern Illinois University Press.

Inn of That Journey. Emerson Price. LC 39-1207. 1939. The Caxton Printers. Ltd.

Inn of That Journey: A Novel. Emerson Price. LC 77-23199. (Lost American Fiction Ser.). (Lost American fiction (er)). 276p. 1977. 7.95 (ISBN 0-8093-0812-6). S Ill U Pr.

Inn of the Cats. Gustavo Adolfo Becquer. Tr. by J. R. Carey from Span. (Harrap's Bilingual Ser.). 110p. 1945. 5.00 (ISBN 0-911268-49-9). Rogers Bk.

Inn of the Clowns. Paula G Paul. 1976. 4.95. Avalon Books.

Inn of the Hawk and Raven: A Tale of Old Graustark. George Barr McCutcheon. LC 27-16582. 1927. Dodd, Mead and Company.

Inn of the Silver Moon. Herman Knickerbocker Viele. LC 1-29244. 1900. H. S. Stone & Company.

Inn of the Silver Moon. Herman Knickerbocker Viele. LC 33-3746. 1932. Duffield & Green.

Inner Circle. Jonathan Fast. LC 78-24579. 8.95 (ISBN 0-440-04031-0). Delacorte Press.

Inner Circle. Jerzy Pietrkiewicz. LC 67-72959. (B66-17468). Macmillan.

Inner City Hoodlum. Donald Goines. 224p. (Orig.). 1975. pap. 1.95 (ISBN 0-87067-639-3, BH033). Holloway.

Inner City Hoodlum. Donald Goines. 1975. (pbk.) 1.50 (ISBN 0-87067-457-6). Holloway House.

Inner City Mother Goose. Eve Merriam. pap. 3.95 o.p. (ISBN 0-671-20290-1, Touchstone Bks). S&S.

Inner City Sunshine Blues. Richard J. Todd. 1970. 3.50 o.p. Carlton.

Inner Darkness. Ethelda Daggett Hesser. LC 24-4010. 1924. Harper & Brothers.

Inner Door. Nergis Dalal. 144p. 1975. pap. 1.85 (ISBN 0-89253-028-6). Ind-US Inc.

Inner Door. Alan Sullivan. LC 17-20669. 1917. The Century Co.

Inner Flame: A Novel. Clara Louise Root Burnham. LC 12-22127. 1912. Houghton Mifflin Company.

Inner Harbor. Frederick Wright. LC 49-2902. 1949. Little, Brown.

Inner House. Walter Besant. (On cover: Seaside library. pocket ed., no. 1143). 1888. G. Munro.

Inner House. Walter Besant. LC 6-123909. (On cover: Harper's Franklin square library, no. 630). 1888. Harper & Brother.

Inner House. Walter Besant. (On cover: Lovell's library, no. 1307). J. W. Lovell Company.

Inner Joy. Harold H. Bloomfield & Robert B. Kory. LC 81-83487. 320p. 1982. pap. 3.50 (ISBN 0-86721-034-6). Playboy Pbks.

Inner Landscape. Peake et al. 1971. pap. 0.75 o.p. (ISBN 0-446-64614-8, 64-614). Paperback Lib.

Inner Law: A Novel. William Nathaniel Harben. Harper & Brothers.

Inner Light. Leona Rothgeb. 1958. 2.50 o.p. (ISBN 0-682-47162-3). Exposition.

Inner Man: Adapted from the French of Michel Corday and Andre Courveur ! jones... ed. Michel Corday & Couvreur, Andre. Tr. by Crewe-Jones, Florence. LC 13-22095. 1.25. G. W. Dillingham Company.

Inner Number. Frank Chenhalls Williams. LC 27-1640. 1927. Longmans, Green and Co., Ltd.

Inner Room. Vera Randal. LC 64-17700. 1964. Knopf.

Inner Sanctum Edition of War & Peace. Lev Nikolaevich Tolstoi. 1941. 24.95 (ISBN 0-671-79700-X, 79700). S&S.

Inner Secret. Ghristobel Gallup. LC 23-17769. W. W. Walter.

Inner Shrine. Cecily Ullmann Sidgwick. LC 15-8943. (Hodder & Stoughton's sevenpenny library). 1912. Hodder and Stoughton.

Inner Shrine: A Novel of Today... Basil King. LC 9-12616. 1901. Harper & Brothers.

Inner Steps. Sara Cardiff. LC 72-10356. 1973. 5.95 (ISBN 0-394-48423-1). Random House.

Inner Steps. Sara Cardiff. (Fawcett crest book). 1975. (pbk.) 1.25. Fawcett.

Inner Street. Fred B. Holmberg. LC 78-59256. (Illus., Orig.). 1978. pap. 3.25 (ISBN 0-932006-05-1). Durrell.

Inner Voice. Jennie Sworn Duryea. LC 33-179403. God's Bible School and Missionary Training Home.

Inner Voice. Nina Wilcox Putnam. LC 40-35996. Sheridan House.

Inner Weather. Robert S. Phillips. 1966. 3.00 (ISBN 0-8233-0082-X). Golden Quill.

Inner Wheel. Keith Roberts. LC 75-116248. (Doubleday science fiction). 1970. 4.95. Doubleday.

Innermost Cage: A Novel, by Kathrine Talbot Pseud. Ilse Eva Louise Gross Barker. LC 55-5668. 1955. Putnam.

Innerspace Nomads. James W Pope & Gerard A. Dougherty. LC 66-31234. 1966. San Diego Herald.

Innkeeper's Tale. David De Forest Burrell. LC 44-28604. Brant & Borden.

Innocence. Harriet Daimler. 1968. pap. 1.95 o.s.i. (OPS6, Travellers Comp). Olympia.

Innocence & a Broad. G. Leonard Gordon. 190p. 1975. 7.00 o.p. (ISBN 0-682-48261-7). Exposition.

Innocence and Experience. Phyllis Bottome. LC 34-378291. 1934. Houghton Mifflin Company.

Innocence Has Gone, Daddy. Andre Launay. 1976. (pbk.) 1.75. Ballantine.

Innocence of Father Brown. Gilbert Keith Chesterton. LC 75-44963. (Fifty Classics of Crime Fiction, 1900-1950; 10). 1976. 12.00 (ISBN 0-8240-2359-5). Garland Pub.

Innocence of Father Brown. Gilbert Keith Chesterton. LC 11-21590. 1911. Cassell and Company, Ltd.

Innocence of Father Brown. Gilbert Keith Chesterton. LC 11-25052. 1911. John Lane Company.

Innocence of G. K. Chesterton. Gerald Bullett. 1973. Repr. of 1923 ed. 17.50 (ISBN 0-8274-1799-3). R West.

Innocence of Prairie. Robert Edward Gard. 1978. 10.00 (ISBN 0-913370-05-3). Wisconsin Bks.

Innocent. Marie Corelli. pap. 4.95 (ISBN 0-910122-37-7). Amherst Pr.

Innocent. Marie Corelli. 3.50 o.p. Wehman.

Innocent. Richard E. Kim. LC 68-31587. 1968. 6.95. Houghton Mifflin.

Innocent. Evelyn Piper. pap. 0.95 o.p. (02359, Collier). Macmillan.

Innocent. A Novel of Suspense. LC 49-7784. (Inner sanctum suspense special). 1949. Simon and Schuster.

Innocent: a Tale of Modern Life. Margaret Oliphant Wilson Oliphant. (On cover: Seaside library. Pocket ed., no. 604). 1885. G. Munro.

Innocent Abroad. Ronald De Levington Kirkbride. LC 61-776019. 1961. Prentice-Hall.

Innocent Abroad. Jessica Steele. (Harlequin Romances Ser.). 192p. 1981. pap. 1.50 (ISBN 0-373-02446-0, Pub. by Harlequin). PB.

Innocent Accomplice. Gertrude M. Robins Reynolds. LC 28-29727. 1928. Pub. for the Crime Club, Inc., by Doubleday, Doran & Company, Inc.

Innocent Adulteress. Dee Stuart. (Candlelight Regency Special Ser.: No. 686). 256p. (Orig.). 1981. pap. 1.75 (ISBN 0-440-14045-5). Dell.

Innocent Adultery & Other Short Novels. Paul Scarron. LC 67-29562. 1968. B. Blom.

Innocent Adventuress. Mary Hastings Bradley. LC 21-977. 1921. D. Appleton and Company.

Innocent and the Guilty: Stories. Sylvia Townsend Warner. LC 76-104138. 1971. 5.95 (ISBN 0-670-39837-3). Viking Press.

Innocent Bigamy & Other Stories. Olive Tilford Dargan. LC 62-17310. 1962. 3.75 (ISBN 0-910244-30-8). Blair.

Innocent Birds. Theodore Francis Powys. LC 26-11207. 1926. A. A. Knopf.

Innocent Blood. P. D James. LC 79-28699. 8.95 (ISBN 0-684-16591-0). Scribner.

Innocent Blood. P. D James. LC 81-874. 1981. 14.95 (ISBN 0-8161-3180-5). G.K. Hall.

Innocent Blood. P. D James. 1981. 3.50 (ISBN 0-445-04630-9). Popular Library.

Innocent Bottle: An Arthur Crook Mystery. Lucy Beatrice Malleson. LC 49-751393. 1949. A. S. Barnes.

Innocent Bystander. George Bagby, pseud. LC 76-24046. (Crime Club Ser.). 1977. 5.95 o.p. (ISBN 0-385-12626-3). Doubleday.

Innocent Bystander. Faith Baldwin Cuthrell. LC 34-8067. Farrar & Rinehart, Incorporated.

Innocent Bystander. Faith Baldwin Cuthrell. 1973. (pbk.) 0.95. Warner Paperback Lib.

Innocent Bystander. Barbara Frost. LC 55-100802. 1955. Coward-McCann.

Innocent Bystander. Craig Rice. LC 49-1570. (Inner sanctum mystery). 1949. Simon and Schuster.

Innocent Bystander. Aaron Marc Stein. LC 76-24146. 1977. 5.95 (ISBN 0-385-12626-3). Published for the Crime Club by Doubleday.

Innocent Bystanders. James Mitchell. LC 74-79335. 1970. 5.95. Knopf.

Innocent Bystanders. James Munro. (Illus.). 256p. 1982. pap. 2.50 (ISBN 0-441-37076-4, Pub. by Charter Bks). Ace Bks.

Innocent Bystanders. James Munro. LC 74-79335. 1970. 5.95 o.p. (ISBN 0-394-43063-8). Knopf.

Innocent Bystanders. Sandra Scoppettone. 1982. 13.95 (ISBN 0-453-00422-9, H422). NAL.

Innocent Cause. Josephine Gibson Knowlton. LC 48-8066. 1948. Pub. by Caslon Press.

Innocent Cheat. Ruth Dewey Groves. LC 32-19493. Grosset & Dunlap.

Innocent Cheat: Or, Episodes of the Everlasting Comedy. Thomas Cooper De Leon. LC 6-34188. F. T. Neely.

Innocent Criminal. John Davys Beresford. LC 31-211966. E. P. Dutton & Co., Inc.

Innocent Curate. Paris Leary. LC 63-18224. 1963. Doubleday.

Innocent Dark. James Fritzhand. (Orig.). 1983. pap. 3.75 (ISBN 0-440-03852-9). Dell.

Innocent Daughter. Sterling Harkins. pap. 1.95 o.p. (ISBN 0-87977-126-7, DBB126). Dansk Blue Bk.

Innocent Desires. Grant Watson, Elliot Lovegood. LC 76-121553. (Short story index reprint series). 1970. Books for Libraries Press.

Innocent Desires. facsimile ed. Elliot Lovegood Grant Watson. LC 76-121553. (Short Story Index Reprint Ser.). Repr. of 1924 ed. 17.00 (ISBN 0-8369-3509-8). Ayer Co.

Innocent Dreamers. Alice Tisdale Nourse Hobart. LC 63-18984. 1963. Bobss-Merrill.

Innocent Erendira, and Other Stories. Garcia Marquez, Gabriel. LC 74-15873. 9.95 (ISBN 0-06-011416-9). Harper & Row.

Innocent Erendira and Other Stories. Garcia Marquez, Gabriel. (Harper Colophon Books). 3.95 (ISBN 0-06-090701-0)., C.

Innocent Eve. Robert Nathan. LC 51-10299. 1951. Knopf.

Innocent Fire. Brooke Hastings. 192p. (Orig.). 1980. pap. 1.50 (ISBN 0-671-57026-9). S&S.

Innocent Flower. Carman Armstrong. 1965. pap. 0.95 o.s.i. (ISBN 0-02-016280-4, Collier). Macmillan.

Innocent Flower: A MacDougal Duff Mystery. Charlotte Armstrong. LC 45-3289. 1945. Coward-McCann, Inc.

Innocent Girl. Charles Garvice. LC 11-16144. (On cover: Laurel library, no. 31). G. Munro's Sons.

Innocent Greed. Robert Troop. LC 68-29120. 1968. Dutton.

Innocent Heart. Rochel DeNore. (Americana Romance Series 1). 1977. 1.25 (ISBN 0-441-37075-6). Ace Books.

Innocent Heiress. Barbara Cartland. (Historical Romance Ser., No. 15). 1972. pap. 1.25 o.p. (V2636). BJ Pub Group.

Innocent, Her Fancy and His Fact: A Novel. Marie Corelli. LC 14-18339. 1.35. Hodder & Stoughton, George H. Doran Company.

Innocent House: By Frances and Richard Lockridge. Frances Louise Davis Lockridge & Richard Lockridge. LC 59-5404. (Main line mysteries). 1959. Lippincott.

Innocent Impostor, and Other Stories. Mary Gleed Tuttiett. LC 8-32315. (On cover: Appletons' town and country library, no. 122). 1893. D. Appleton and Company.

Innocent in Mayfair. Barbara Cartland. (Orig.). 1976. pap. 1.25 o.p. (ISBN 0-515-03985-3). BJ Pub Group.

Innocent in Paris. Barbara Cartland. 1971. pap. 0.95 o.p. (N2490). Pyramid Pubns.

Innocent in Paris. Barbara Cartland. 1975. pap. 1.25 o.p. (ISBN 0-515-03564-5, V3564). BJ Pub Group.

Innocent in Russia, No. 148. Barbara Cartland. (Orig.). 1981. pap. 1.95 (ISBN 0-553-20126-3). Bantam.

Innocent Knights: Translated from the French by Geoffrey Sainsbury. Gil Buhet. LC 53-8820. 1953. Viking Press.

Innocent Libertine. Sidonie Gabrielle Colette. LC 78-105063. 1978. 3.95 (ISBN 0-374-51456-9). Farrar Straus Giroux.

Innocent Madame: The Novel of a Lovely Lady Who Turned to Sin. Eleanore Browne. LC 30-25104. Newark, N.J., Barse & Co.

Innocent Mrs. Duff: A Novel of Suspense. Elisabeth Sanxay Holding. LC 46-107847. 1946. Simon and Schuster.

Innocent Murderers. William Andrew Johnston & West, Paul Clarendon. LC 10-9849. 1910. 1.50. Duffield and Company.

Innocent Obsession. Anne Mather. (Harlequin Presents Ser.). 192p. 1981. pap. 1.75 (ISBN 0-373-10468-5, Pub. by Harlequin). PB.

Innocent One. Lisa March. (O.s.i.). (Orig.). 1969. pap. 0.75 o.s.i. (A498, Award). Univ Pub & Dist.

Innocent One. James Reach. LC 53-8890. 1953. Coward-McCann.

Innocent Ones. Jean Cornu. LC 78-110967. 1970. 3.50. Dorrance.

Innocent Outcast; or, "Chemically Pure;" A Tale of South Carolina During Her Most Trying Ordeal--Namely; the Foisting Upon Her of the Iniquitous Dispensary Law. May Agnes Early Fleming. F. T. Neely.

Innocent Party. Celia Dale. LC 73-83196. 1973. 6.95 (ISBN 0-8027-0433-6). Walker.

Innocent Sailor. Translated from the French by Mervyn Savill. Anne De Tourville. LC 54-9371. 1955. Farrar, Straus and Young.

Innocent Schoolteacher. Waleman. pap. 1.95 o.p. (ISBN 0-87977-113-5). Dansk Blue Bk.

Innocent Sinner. Selma Adler Gruber. LC 27-1842. 1926. Gruber and Gruber.

Innocent Summer. Frances Mary Frost. Farrar & Rinehart, Incorporated.

Innocent Summer. Frances Mary Frost. LC 36-1852. 1936. Farrar & Rinehart, Incorporated.

Innocent Surrender. Susan Berencsi. LC 82-45346. (Starlight Romance Ser.). (Illus.). 192p. 1983. 11.95 (ISBN 0-385-18258-9). Doubleday.

Innocent Villa, a Novel. Barnaby Conrad. LC 48-1823. 1948. Random House.

Innocent Voyage. Richard Arthur Warren Hughes. LC 29-666887. 1929. Harper & Brothers.

Innocent Voyage. Richard Arthur Warren Hughes & Ward, Lynd Kendall, 1905- Illus. LC 45-2891. 1944. The Limited Editions Club.

Innocent Voyage: A High Wind in Jamaica. Richard Arthur Warren Hughes. LC 58-14384. (Harper's modern classics). 1959. Harper.

Innocent Wanton. Kirk Westley. 1969. pap. 0.75 o.p. (75-276). Manor Bks.

Innocent Wanton: By Gail Jordan Pseud. Peggy Gaddis, pseud. LC 50-11864. 1950. Phoenix Press.

Innocent Wife. Sidonie Gabrielle Colette & Henry Gauthier-Villars. Tr. by Blossom, Frederick Augustus. LC 36-17718. Farrar & Rinehart, Incorporated.

Innocent Without Cause. Edouard Sandoz. LC 58-3516. 1958. Vantage Press.

Innocent. 1st Ed. Madison Jones. LC 57-530060. 1957. Harcourt, Brace.

Innocente Victime. Adelard Lambert. (Novels by Franco-Americans in New England 1850-1940 Ser.). 82p. (Fr.). (gr. 10 up). 1980. pap. 4.50x (ISBN 0-911409-16-5). Natl Mat Dev.

Innocents. Richard Savage. LC 59-9056. 1959. Washburn.

Innocents. Margery Sharp. LC 72-12606. 1973. 6.95 (ISBN 0-8161-6070-8). G. K. Hall.

Innocents. Margery Sharp. LC 75-175473. 1972. 5.95. Little, Brown.

Innocents. Georges Simenon. LC 73-16004. 1974. 6.50 (ISBN 0-15-144430-7). Harcourt Brace Jovanovich.

Innocents. Clyde Ware. LC 69-14711. 1969. 4.95. Norton.

Innocents: A Legend of War-Time. Alfred Machard & Stawell, Maud Margaret (Key) LC 19-6346. 1918. Hodder and Stoughton.

Innocents: A Story for Lovers. Sinclair Lewis. LC 17-24286. 1917. Harper & Brothers.

Innocents Abroad: Or, The New Pilgrim's Progress by Mark Twain. Introd. by Francis R. Gemme. Samuel Langhorne Clemens. (Classics ser., CL151). 1967. Airmont.

Innocents at Ten Acres. Louise Grether. LC 40-35538. Pegasus Publishing Co.

Innocents of Paris. Gilbert Cesbron & Waldman, Marguerite, Tr. LC 46-5000. 1946. Houghton Mifflin Company.

Innocents: Variations on a Theme. A. L. Barker. LC 48-5360. 1948. C. Scribner's Sons.

Innovator. John Brett Robey. LC 45-1829. 1945. Doubleday, Doran and Company, Inc.

Inocencia. Escragnolle Taunay, Alfredo De & Chamberlain, Henriqueta, Tr. 1945. The Macmillan Company.

Inoculate! Neil Bayne. 1979. pap. 2.25 o.s.i. (ISBN 0-8439-0664-2, Leisure Bks). Nordon Pubns.

Inquest. Robert Neumann. LC 45-4304. 1945. E. P. Dutton & Co., Inc.

Inquest. Percival Wilde. LC 40-65489. Random House.

Inquirendo Island. William James Roe. LC 7-40731. 1886. G. P. Putnam's Sons.

Inquiring Mind. Edmund Brown. LC 72-95571. 1973. 4.50 (ISBN 0-8059-1803-5). Dorrance.

Inquiry into Life. 3rd ed. Henry E. Childs, Jr. & I. Louise Cramer. 1968. pap. 3.95 o.p. (ISBN 0-697-04525-0). Wm C Brown.

Inquisition. Marc Olden. (Black Samurai). (Signet book: Vol. 5). 1974. (pbk.) 1.25. New American Library.

Inquisitor: A Novel. Hugh Walpole. LC 35-273238. 1935. Doubleday, Doran & Company, Inc.

Inquisitors. Jerzy Andrzejewski. LC 76-6896. 1976. 11.25 (ISBN 0-8371-8868-7). Greenwood Press.

Inquisitor's House. Robert Somerlott. LC 68-29712. 1968. 5.95 (ISBN 0-670-39861-6). Viking Press.

Inquisitors. Translated from the Polixh by Konrad Syrop. Jerzy Andrzejewski. LC 60-365650. Knopf,

Inquisitory. Tr. by Donald Watson. Robert Pinget. LC 66-29524. 1967. 6.50. Grove.

Insane City. Kenneth Bulmer. (Orig.). 1971. pap. 0.75 o.p. (07122). Curtis.

Insanity Runs in Our Family. Hal Z. Bennett. LC 76-48600. 1977. 7.95 (ISBN 0-385-06664-3). Doubleday.

Insatiability: A Novel in Two Parts. Stanisaw Ignacy Witkiewicz. LC 76-10760. 18.95 (ISBN 0-252-00572-4). University of Illinois Press.

Insatiable Claudette. Andrew MacInnes. 1968. pap. 1.95 o.p. (6016). Brandon.

Insatiable Co-Eds. Thomas Eastwood. 192p. (Orig.). 1973. pap. 1.95 o.p. (ISBN 0-87682-349-5, 7349). Barclay Hse.

Insatiable Sensualists. Gerda Mundinger. 1972. pap. 1.75 o.s.i. (V1105K, Venus). Grove.

Inscrutable: A Story. Amelie Claire Leroy. (On cover: Broadway series, no. 18). 1892. J. A. Taylor and Company.

Inscrutable Charlie Muffin. Brian Freemantle. LC 78-20027. 1979. 8.95 (ISBN 0-385-14391-5). Doubleday.

Inscrutable Charlie Muffin. Brian Freemantle. LC 80-29339. 1981. 11.50 (ISBN 0-89340-314-8). J. Curley.

Insect Colony: A Novel. Charles R Larson. LC 78-4701. 8.95 (ISBN 0-03-041896-8). Holt, Rinehart and Winston.

Insect Parables. Robert J. Baker. LC 76-21398. 1976. pap. 1.95 (ISBN 0-8361-1337-3). Herald Pr.

Inseparables. Margaret Pirie. LC 55-42035. 1955. Light and Life Press.

Inseparables. 1st Ed. Mary Bancroft. LC 58-10065. 1958. Little, Brown.

Inserat Grotesk I: Special Issue 10. pap. 1.00 o.p. The Smith.

Inshore Squadron. Alexander Kent. LC 78-15222. 1978. 8.95 (ISBN 0-399-12303-2). Putnam.

Inside. Dan Morgan. (Berkley medallion book). 1974. (pbk.) 0.95 (ISBN 0-425-02734-1). Berkley Pub Co.

Inside: A Chronicle of Secession. William Mumford Baker. LC 6-86316. 1866. Harper & Brothers.

Inside Daisy Clover. Gavin Lambert. 1963. 4.50 o.p. (ISBN 0-670-39920-5). Viking Pr.

Inside Guzman De Alfarache. Carroll B Johnson. LC 76-55569. (California. University. University of California Publications in Modern Philology). (University of California publications in modern philology; v. 111.: Vol. 111). 1978. 10.00 (ISBN 0-520-09569-3). University of California Press.

Inside Information. Nicolas Bentley. LC 78-302778. (Penguin crime fiction). 1978. 1.95 (ISBN 0-14-004277-6). Penguin.

Inside Job. Stella Allan. LC 77-29096. 7.95 (ISBN 0-684-15587-7). Scribner.

Inside Job. Nicholas Brady, pseud. 1978. 1.95 (ISBN 0-8439-0571-9). Nordon Pubns.

Inside Job: By Stella Allan. Stella Allan. LC 77-29096. 1980. 2.25 (ISBN 0-380-50237-2). Avon Publishers.

Inside Kasrilevke. Sholom Aleichem. LC 65-14829. (Illus.). 1968. 9.95x (ISBN 0-8052-3113-7); pap. 4.95 (ISBN 0-8052-0173-4). Schocken.

Inside Kasrilevke. Shalom Rabinowitz. Tr. by Goldstick, Isidore. LC 48-6108. (Schocken library, 11). 1948. Schocken Books.

Inside Kasrilevke: By Shalom Aleichem Pseud. Tr. from Yiddish by Isidore Goldstick Drawings by Ben Shahn. Shalom Rabinowitz. Tr. by Isidore Goldstick. LC 65-14289. (SB173). 1968. pap., 1.95. Schocken.

Inside Kasrilevke: By Sholom Aleichem Pseud. Tr. from Yiddish by Isidore Goldstick Drawings by Ben Shahn. Shalom Rabinowitz. Tr. by Isidore Goldstick. Ben Shahn. LC 65-14289. 4.95. Schocken.

Inside, Looking Out. Harding Lemay. 320p. (Orig.). 1982. pap. 3.25 (ISBN 0-8439-1086-0, Leisure Bks). Nordon Pubns.

Inside Man. George Harmon Coxe. LC 73-21699. 1974. 5.95 (ISBN 0-394-49096-7). Knopf; Distributed by Random House.

Inside Man. E. Richard Johnson. LC 79-81875. (Joan Kahn-Harper novel of suspense). 1969. 4.95. Harper & Row.

Inside Mover. Todd Walton. Date not set. pap. 2.50 (ISBN 0-451-09661-4, E9661, Sig). NAL.

Inside Moves. Todd Walton. LC 77-12893. 1978. 6.95 (ISBN 0-385-13553-X). Doubleday.

Inside Moves. Todd Walton. (Signet book). 1979. 2.25 (ISBN 0-451-08596-5). New American Library.

Inside My Own Skin. Hoffman Reynolds Hays. 1975. pap. 2.00 (ISBN 0-87711-054-9). Kayak.

Inside No. Ten. Marcia Williams. LC 72-76686. (YA) 1972. 7.95 o.p. (ISBN 0-698-10484-6). Coward.

Inside of the Cup. Winston Churchill. LC 13-11391. 1913. The Macmillan Company.

Inside of the Cup. Winston Churchill. LC 24-204824. 1922. Grosset & Dunlap.

Inside of the Cup. Winston Churchill. LC 28-17939. 1927. The Macmillan Company.

Inside Our Gate. Christine Chaplin Brush. LC 6-16414. 1889. Roberts Brothers.

Inside Out. Judd Bernard. (O.s.i.). 208p. 1976. pap. 1.50 o.s.i. (AD1553, Award). Univ Pub & Dist.

Inside Out. Judd Bernard. 1976. (pbk.) 1.50. Award Books.

Inside Out. Gertrude Ethel Mallette. LC 42-21969. 1942. Doubleday, Doran & Co., Inc.

Inside Out: A Curious Book. Samuel Ward Francis. LC 6-43165. 1862. Miller, Mathews & Clasback.

Inside-Out Heist. Thomas B Reagan. LC 78-135256. (Red mask mystery). 1970. 4.95. Putnam.

Inside, Outside. Philip Jose Farmer. LC 80-19038. (Series: Gregg Press Science Fiction Series.). 1980. 11.95 (ISBN 0-8398-2622-2). Gregg Press.

Inside Straight. Zeke Masters, pseud. (Zeke Masters Western Ser.: No. 20). (Orig.). 1982. pap. 1.95 (ISBN 0-671-45179-0). PB.

Inside the Cults. Tracy Cabot. pap. 1.50 o.p. (BH406). Holloway.

Inside the Easter Egg. Marian Engel. (Anansi Fiction Ser.: No. 33). 172p. 1975. 16.95 o.p. (ISBN 0-88784-436-7, Pub. by Hse Anansi Pr Canada). U of Toronto Pr.

Inside the Golden Gate: A Story of Old San Francisco. William Thomas Sebelle. LC 54-8375. 1954. Vantage Press.

Inside the Lines. Earl Derr Biggers & Ritchie, Robert Welles. LC 15-198098. 1.25. The Bobbs-Merrill Company.

Inside the Ropes. Charles Emmett Van Loan. LC 13-673766. Small, Maynard and Company.

Inside the Wardrobe. Morris Lurie. LC 77-82656. 1978. pap. 3.95 (ISBN 0-8180-0625-0). Horizon.

Insider. Alice Beal Parsons. LC 29-7489. E. P. Dutton & Co., Inc.

Insider. 1st Ed. James Kelly. LC 58-12806. 1958. Holt.

Insiders. Susan Morrow. LC 67-14124. 1967. Published for the Crime Club by Doubleday.

Insiders. Rosemary Rogers. 1978. pap. 2.95 (ISBN 0-380-40576-8, 81885). Avon.

Insidious Dr. Fu Manchu. Sax Rohmer, pseud. 1976. lib. bdg. 13.95x (ISBN 0-89968-143-3). Lightyear.

Insidious Dr. Fu Manchu. Sax Rohmer, pseud. 1970. pap. 0.60 o.p. (X2166). Pyramid Pubns.

Insidious Dr. Fu Manchu. Sax Rohmer, pseud. 1975. pap. 1.25 o.p. (ISBN 0-515-03945-4). BJ Pub Group.

Insidious Dr. Fu-Manchu. Arthur Sarsfield Ward. LC 13-22449. 1913. McBride, Nast & Company.

Insidious Dr. Fu-Manchu: Being a Somewhat Detailed Account of the Amazing Adventures of Nayland Smith in His Trailing of the Sinister Chinaman. Arthur Sarsfield Ward. LC 21-3418. 1917. A. L. Burt Company.

Insidious Dr. Fu-Manchu: Being a Somewhat Detailed Account of the Amazing Adventures of Nayland Smith in His Trailing of the Sinister Chinaman. Arthur Sarsfield Ward. LC 22-5151. 1920. A. L. Burt Company.

Insight: English Literature. Ed. by Erwin R. Steinberg & Robert C. Slack. Incl. Insight: English Literature. 6.60 o.p. (ISBN 0-8107-0067-0); tchrs. guide 3.60 o.p. (ISBN 0-8107-0068-9); Satire. pap. 3.20 o.p. (ISBN 0-8107-0069-7); Social Comedy. pap. 4.00 o.p. (ISBN 0-8107-0070-0); Two Novels. pap. 4.00 o.p. (ISBN 0-8107-0071-9); tchrs. guide 3.60 o.p. (ISBN 0-8107-0072-7). (Insight Ser.). (gr. 9-12). 1968-69. Bowmar-Noble.

Insight: English Literature see Insight: English Literature.

Insights & Poems. Huey P. Newton & Ericka Huggins. LC 74-31259. 88p. (Orig.). 1975. pap. 2.00 (ISBN 0-87286-079-5). City Lights.

Insignificant Woman. A Story of Artist Life. Bertha Behrens & Smith, Mrs. Mary Stuart (Harrison) 1834- (Ledger library. no. 42). R. Bonner's Sons.

Insomniacs' Cabaret: A Novel. Voltaire Lewis, pseud. LC 71-112867. 1970. 3.95. Courthouse Square Enterprises.

Inspector. Enzo Bettiza. Tr. by F. Frenaye. 1966. 4.00 (ISBN 0-8184-0108-7). Lyle Stuart.

Inspector. Jan De Hartog. 1960. 4.00 o.p. Atheneum.

Inspector. Steinberg. (Illus.). 1976. pap. 6.95 (ISBN 0-14-004285-7). Penguin.

Inspector Burmann's Busiest Day. Belton Cobb. LC 39-132143. 1939. Longmans, Green and Co.

Inspector French and the Cheyne Mystery. Freeman Wills Crofts. LC 65-5024. (Penguin crime, 917). 1965. Penquin Books.

Inspector French's Greatest Case. Freeman Wills Crofts. LC 65-6774. 1965. Penquin Books.

Inspector French's Greatest Case. Freeman Wills Crofts. LC 25-176601. 1925. T. Seltzer.

Inspector Frost in Crevenna Cove. Herbert Maynard Smith. LC 33-29200. 1933. Minton, Balch Co.

Inspector Frost in the City... Herbert Maynard Smith. LC 30-18560. 1930. Pub. for The Crime Club, Inc., by Doubleday, Doran & Company, Inc.

Inspector Frost's Jigsaw. Herbert Maynard Smith. LC 29-17856. 1929. Pub. for The Crime Club, Inc., by Doubleday, Doran & Company, Inc.

Inspector Ghote Breaks an Egg. Henry Reymond Fitzwalter Keating. LC 74-195243. (Penguin crime fiction). 1974. (u.s.) 1.25 (ISBN 0-14-003839-6). Penguin Books.

Inspector Ghote Breaks an Egg. Henry Reymond Fitzwalter Keating. LC 77-144277. 1971. 4.95. Published for the Crime Club by Doubleday.

Inspector Ghote Caught in Meshes: By H. R. F. Keating. 1st Ed. Henry Reymond Fitzwalter Keating. LC 67-20554. 1968. 4.50. Dutton.

Inspector Ghote Draws a Line. Henry Reymond Fitzwalter Keating. LC 78-14683. 1979. 7.95 (ISBN 0-385-14873-9). Published for the Crime Club by Doubleday.

Inspector Ghote Goes by Train. Henry Reymond Fitzwalter Keating. LC 77-180083. 1972. 4.95. Published for the Crime Club by Doubleday.

Inspector Ghote Hunts the Peacock. Henry Reymond Fitzwalter Keating. LC 68-25767. 1968. Dutton.

Inspector Ghote Plays a Joker. Henry Reymond Fitzwalter Keating. LC 69-13341. 1969. 4.50. Dutton.

Inspector Ghote Trusts the Heart. Henry Reymond Fitzwalter Keating. LC 72-89321. 1973. 4.95 (ISBN 0-385-01810-X). Published for the Crime Club by Doubleday.

Inspector Ghote's Good Crusade. Henry Reymond Fitzwalter Keating. LC 66-14688. 3.95. Dutton.

Inspector Ghote's Good Crusade. Henry Reymond Fitzwalter Keating. LC 66-14688. 1966. Dutton.

Inspector Higgins Hurries: Being a Day in His Life. Cecil Freeman Gregg. LC 22-34034. 1932. L. MacVeagh, Dial Press Inc.

Inspector Higgins Sees It Through. Cecil Freeman Gregg. LC 34-21808. (Tired business man's library of adventure, detective, and mystery novels). 1934. D. Appleton-Century Company, Incorporated.

Inspector McLean's Casebook. George Goodchild. LC 73-153758. 1972. (ISBN 0-85617-701-6). White Lion Publishers Ltd.

Inspector Maigret and the Burglar's Wife. Maigret et la Grande Perche. Translated from the French by J. Maclaren-Ross. 1st American Ed. Georges Simenon. LC 56-5966. 1956. Published for the Crime Club by Doubleday.

Inspector Maigret and the Dead Girl. Maigret et la Jeune Morte. Translated from the French by Daphne Woodward. 1st Ed. Georges Simenon. LC 55-105182. 1955. Published for the Crime Club by Doubleday.

Inspector Maigret and the Killers. Georges Simenon. LC 54-11161. 1954. Published for the Crime Club by Doubleday.

Inspector Maigret and the Strangled Stripper. Translated from the French Maigret Au 'Picratt's' by Cornelia Schaeffer. 1st Ed. Georges Simenon. LC 54-9143. 1954. Published for the Crime Club by Doubleday.

Inspector Maigret & the Strangled Stripper. Georges Simenon. 1973. pap. 0.95 o.p. (09195). Curtis.

Inspector Maigret in New York's Underworld: Maigret New York) Translated from the French by Adrienne Foulke. Georges Simenon. LC 56-58087. (Signet book, 1338). 1956. New American Library.

Inspector Morgan's Dilemma. John Michael Ward Bingham. LC 56-6817. (Red badge detective). 1956. Dodd, Mead.

Inspector Morgan's Dilemma. John Michael Ward Bingham Clanmorris. LC 56-6817. (Red badge detective). 1956. Dodd, Mead.

Inspector of Ruins. Translated from the French by Norman Cameron. Elsa Triolet. LC 53-744972. 1953. Roy Publishers.

Inspector Queen's Own Case. Ellery Queen, pseud. LC 77-13999. (Ellery Queen mystery). 1978. 8.95 (ISBN 0-89340-104-8). J. Curley.

Inspector Queen's Own Case: November Song. Ellery Queen, pseud. LC 66-20546. 1966. Bantam Books.

Inspector Queen's Own Case: November Song. Ellery Queen, pseud. LC 56-14123. (Inner sanctum mystery). 1956. Simon and Schuster.

Inspector Rusby's Finale. Virgil Markham. LC 33-16997. Farrar & Rinehart, Incorporated.

Inspector. Tr. from Italian by Frances Frenaye. Enzo Bettiza. LC 67-15885. 1967. 4.00. Lyle Stuart.

Inspector West Alone. John Creasey. LC 75-7519. 1975. 6.95 (ISBN 0-684-14354-2). Scribner.

Inspector West at Home. John Creasey. LC 73-1114. 1973. 5.95 (ISBN 0-684-13396-2). Scribner.

Inspector West Regrets. John Creasey. 1971. pap. 0.75 o.p. (ISBN 0-447-74709-6). Lancer.

Inspector West Takes Charge. John Creasey. LC 72-1189. 1972. 5.95 (ISBN 0-684-13007-6). Scribner.

Inspector: 1st Ed. Jan De Hartog. LC 60-7777. 1960. Atheneum.

Inspector's Holiday: An Inspector Heimrich Mystery. Richard Lockridge. LC 79-134933. 1971. 4.95. Lippincott.

Inspector's Opinion: The Chappaquiddick Incident. Malcolm Reybold. LC 75-15731. 1975. 7.95 (ISBN 0-8415-0399-0). Saturday Review Press.

Inspector's Opinion: The Chappaquiddick Incident. Malcolm Reybold. 1976. 1.95 (ISBN 0-446-79917-3). Warner Books.

Inspector's Puzzle: Or, Trapped at the Last Turn. Charles Matthew. LC 99-2570. (On cover: Magnet detective library, no. 84). 1899. Street & Smith.

Inspiration: A Story of Today. Caroline A. Gattie. LC 14-13685. 1914. G.W. Dillingham Company.

Inspiration Ideal. Ed. by Maryjane H. Tonn. 80p. 1976. pap. 2.50 o.p. (ISBN 0-89542-305-7, 1131569). Ideals.

Inspiration of Youth: With Introduction and Notes... Sears, Joseph Hamblen. LC 26-200717. (Lettered on cover: The royal collection). J. H. Sears & Company, Inc.

Inspiration Valley. Coningsby William Dawson. LC 35-139062. 1935. A. A. Knopf.

Instant Enemy. Ross Macdonald. LC 81-172. 1981. 12.95 (ISBN 0-89340-333-4). J. Curley.

Instant Enemy. Kenneth Millar. LC 68-12667. 1968. Knopf.

Instant Gold. Frank O'Rourke. LC 64-17879. 1964. W. Morrow.

Instant in the Wind. Andre Philippus Brink. LC 77-357959. 1976. 3.95 (ISBN 0-491-01617-4). W. H. Allen.

Instant Lives. Howard Moss. LC 73-18495. (Illus.). 1974. 5.95. Saturday Review Press; Distributed by E. P. Dutton.

Instant Lives. howard moss; drawings by edward gorey. ed. Howard Moss. (Illus.). 1.95 (ISBN 0-380-00812-2). Avon Books.

Instant Parent. Suzy Kalter. 1980. pap. 2.50 (ISBN 0-425-04737-7). Berkley Pub.

Instant Saint. John Sherlock. LC 65-22972. 4.95. Morrow.

Instar. Ryder Brady. LC 75-30458. 240p. 1976. 6.95 o.p. (ISBN 0-385-11508-3). Doubleday.

Instead of Him. Peggy O'More, pseud. 1944. Grammercy Publishing Co.

Instead of the Thorn. Georgette Heyer. LC 24-7673. Small, Maynard & Company.

Instead of the Thorn. Bastian Kruithof. LC 41-949829. The Half Moon Press.

Instead of the Thorn: A Novel. Clara Louise Root Burnham. LC 16-822731. 1916. 1.25. Houghton Mifflin Company.

Instinct of Step-Fatherhood. Lilian Lida Bell. LC 98-836. 1898. Harper & Brothers.

Institute. James Mallahan Cain. 272p. 1982. pap. 2.95 (ISBN 0-8439-1034-8, Leisure Bks). Nordon Pubns.

Institute. Robert Petyo. 1978. pap. 1.50 (ISBN 0-532-15335-9). Woodhill.

Institute: A Novel. James Mallahan Cain. LC 76-17573. 1976. 7.95 (ISBN 0-88405-351-2). Mason/Charter.

Institution: A Novel. Walter Adamson. LC 77-361282. 1976. (ISBN 0-86888-038-8) (ISBN 0-86888-039-6). Outback Press.

Instruct My Sorrows. Clare Jaynes, pseud. LC 42-360921. 1942. Random House.

Instructive Rambles in London, and the Adjacent Villages. Designed to Amuse the Mind, and Improve the Understanding of Youth. Elizabeth Helme. 1814.

Instrument. John O'Hara. LC 67-12717. 1967. 14.95 (ISBN 0-394-43093-X). Random.

Instrument of Destiny: A Detective Story. John Davys Beresford. LC 28-225772. The Bobbs-Merrill Company.

Instrument of the Gods, and Other Stories of the Sea. Lincoln Colcord. LC 72-5863. (Short story index reprint series). 1972. (ISBN 0-8369-4202-7). Books for Libraries Press.

Instrument of the Gods: And Other Stories of the Sea. Lincoln Colcord. LC 22-17615. 1922. The Macmillan Company.

Instrumentos De Placer. Luis Andrade. (Pimienta Collection Ser). 1976. pap. 1.25 (ISBN 0-88473-252-5). Fiesta Pub.

Instruments of Darkness: And Other Stories. by alice duer miller... ed. Alice Duer Miller. LC 26-910806. 1926. Dodd, Mead and Company.

Insubordination: Or, The Shoemaker's Daughters: an American Story of Real Life. Timothy Shay Arthur. LC 6-3404. 1848. T. B. Peterson.

Insulators. John Creasey. LC 72-95773. 1973. 5.95 (ISBN 0-8027-5274-8). Walker.

Insulted and Injured. Fedor Mikhailovich Dostoevskii. LC 75-19182. 1975. 17.25 (ISBN 0-8371-8248-4). Greenwood Press.

Insulted and Injured: A Novel in Four Parts and an Epilogue. Fedor Mikhailovich Dostoevskii. Tr. by Constance Black Garnett. LC 15-266542. (Half-title: The novels of Fyodor Dostoevsky. Vol. VI). 1915. The Macmillan Co.

Insulted and Injured. Translated from the Russian by Constance Garnett. Evergreen Ed. Fedor Mikhailovich Dostoevskii. LC 57-2694. (Evergreen book, E-22). 1955. Grove Press.

Insulted & the Humiliated. Fedor Mikhailovich Dostoevskii. 406p. 1976. 6.95 (ISBN 0-8285-0958-1, Pub. by Progress Pubs USSR). Imported Pubns.

Insurance Thrillers: Sinister Mysteries Centering About Insurance Frauds, Originally Published in the Weekly Underwriter During 1932. Weekly Underwriter. LC 32-33839. The Underwriter Printing and Publishing Company.

Insurgent Chief. Gustave Aimard & St. John, Percy Bolingbroke, 1821-1889, Ed. LC 5-42588. (On cover: Lovell's library, no. 1075). 1887. J. W. Lovell Company.

Insurgent of St. Mary's. Henry Spencer Booth. 1911. 1.50. The King Printing Co.

Insurgent Summer. Charlotte Aiken Yarborough. LC 44-461476. 1944. Harper & Brothers.

Insurgents. Jean Bruller. LC 78-22223. (Aging and Old Age). 1979. 20.00 (ISBN 0-405-11836-8). Arno Press.

Insurgents: An Historical Novel... Ralph Ingersoll Lockwood. LC 7-15846. 1835. Carey, Lea & Blanchard.

Insurgents: By Vercors Pseud. Translated from the French by Rita Barisse. 1st Ed. Jean Bruller. LC 56-11960. 1956. Harcourt, Brace.

Insurrection. Dan Brennan. (O.s.i.). (Orig.). 1970. pap. 0.95 o.s.i. (B95-2054). Belmont-Tower.

Insurrection. Liam O'Flaherty. 1951. Little, Brown.

Insurrection. Antonio Skarmeta. 240p. 1983. pap. 7.50. Ediciones Norte.

Insurrection of Hippolytus Brandenberg. Roy Friedman. LC 68-29025. 1968. Stein and Day.

Insurrectionist (L'insurge) Jules Louis Joseph Valles. LC 70-140689. 1971. 7.95 (ISBN 0-13-468884-8). Prentice-Hall.

Integregated Man. Michael Berlyn. (Orig.). 1980. pap. 1.95 (ISBN 0-553-13999-1). Bantam.

Intellect Is a Brute: A Novel. Samuel Hanson Ordway. LC 29-838619. 1929. Duffield and Company.

Intellectual Graveyard. Josephine Moikobu. 4.50 o.p. Vantage.

Intellectual Graveyard. Josephine Moraa Moikobu. 1974. 4.50 (ISBN 0-533-00963-4). Vantage Press.

Intellectual Lover: And Other Stories. David Freedman. LC 40-35319. Harper & Brothers.

Intellectual Miss Lamb. Florence Morse Kingsley. LC 6-15735. 1906. The Century Co.

Intellectuals: An Experiement in Irish Club-Life. Patrick Augustine Sheehan. LC 11-4598. 1911. Longmans, Green, and Co.

Intemperate Season. Blythe Morley. LC 48-6735. 1948. Farrar, Straus.

Intensive Care: A Novel. Janet Frame, pseud. LC 78-110305. 1970. 6.95. G. Braziller.

Intent to Kill. Michael Bryan. LC 56-6758. (Dell first edition, 88). Dell Pub. Co.

Inter Ice Age Four. Kobo Abe. Tr. by E. Dale Saunders from Jap. (Perigee Japanese Library). 240p. 1981. pap. 4.95 (ISBN 0-399-50519-9, Perige). Putnam Pub Group.

Inter Ice Age 4. Kobo Abe. LC 70-111245. (Illus.). 1970. 5.95. Knopf.

Intercept. Ken Bernstein. 1974. (pbk.) 0.95 (ISBN 0-523-00327-7). Pinnacle Books.

Intercept: A Novel of Suspense. Ken Bernstein. LC 74-136437. 1971. 6.95. Coward, McCann & Geoghegan.

Intercept & Board. Emery Huntoon. LC 75-20724. (Illus.). 1975. 6.95 (ISBN 0-8323-0251-1); pap. 4.95 (ISBN 0-8323-0252-X). Binford.

Intercept-but Don't Shoot. Renato Vesco. pap. 1.95 o.p. (Z1081T, Zebra). Grove.

Interceptor Pilot. Kenneth Gangemi. LC 79-56849. 1980. 13.95 (ISBN 0-7145-2699-1). M. Boyars.

Interceptor Pilot. Kenneth Gangemi. 160p. 1981. 11.50 (ISBN 0-7145-2699-1, Pub. by M. Boyars). Merrimack Pub Cir.

Interceptor Pilot. Kenneth Gangemi. LC 79-56849. 160p. 1982. pap. 7.95 (ISBN 0-7145-2765-3, Pub. by M Boyars). Merrimack Pub Cir.

Intercessor, and Other Stories. May Sinclair. LC 71-140342. (Short story index reprint series). 1970. Books for Libraries Press.

Intercessor and Other Stories. May Sinclair. LC 32-45605. 1932. The Macmillan Company.

Interchange. 1st Ed. Judith Shatnoff. LC 62-8679. 1962. Knopf.

Intercom Conspiracy. Eric Ambler. LC 70-90827. 1969. 5.95. Atheneum.

Interesting Case. A Novel. Elizabeth Winslow Allerdice. LC 6-476. (On cover: Lovell's library, v. 7, no. 346). 1884. J. W. Lovell Company.

Interesting Memoirs of Four German Gentlemen, Particularly Distinguished by Their Adventures ! Among the Fair Sex: With an Appropriate Appendix. John Kortz. LC 7-14173. 1819. Printed by S. Marks.

Interesting Times. Joan Thompson. LC 80-52100. (Illus.). 13.95 (ISBN 0-312-41914-7). St. Martin's Press.

Interface. Mark Adlard. 1977. 1.50 (ISBN 0-441-37090-X). Ace Books.

Interface. Joseph N Gores. LC 73-91882. 1974. 5.95 (ISBN 0-87131-146-1). M. Evans.

Interface Assignment. William Rayner. LC 77-4493. 1977. 6.95 (ISBN 0-689-10804-4). Atheneum.

Interfaces. Ursula K Le Guin & Virginia Kidd. LC 80-110007. 5.95 (ISBN 0-441-37092-6). Ace Books.

Interference: A Mystery Story. Roland Pertwee. LC 27-24494. 1927. Houghton Mifflin Company.

Interference of Patricia. Lilian Lida Bell. 1903. L. C. Page & Company.

Intergalac Agent. Kenneth W. Hassler. Ed. by Alice Sachs. 1971. 3.95 o.p. Lenox Hill.

Intergalactic Polish: We Wax the Cars of the Stars. Bruce Braunstein. (Orig.). 1980. pap. 10.00. Tetragrammaton.

Interim. Ray Coryton Hutchinson. LC 45-3707. 1945. Farrar & Rinehart, Inc.

Interim. Dorothy Miller Richardson. LC 20-9715. (Her Pilgrimage. pt. V). 1920. A. A. Knopf.

Interior Castle: Including Boston Adventure, The Mountain Lion, and a New Collection of Short Stories, Children Are Bored on Sunday. Jean Stafford. LC 54-2132. 1953. Harcourt, Brace.

Interior Exile. Miguel De Salabert. 1963. 4.50 o.p. (ISBN 0-671-37670-5). S&S.

Interlocking Lives. Alex Katz & Kenneth Koch. LC 76-111331. (Illus.). 1970. Kulchur Press; Distributed by Citadel Press.

Interloper. Robyn Donald. (Harlequin Presents Ser.). 192p. 1981. pap. 1.50 (ISBN 0-373-10441-3, Pub. by Harlequin). PB.

Interloper. Violet Jacob. LC 4-19643. 1904. Doubleday, Page & Company.

Interloper. Frank Milburn. LC 82-45837. 216p. 1983. 13.95 (ISBN 0-385-19008-5). Doubleday.

Interloper. Edward Phillips Oppenheim. LC 26-2813. 1926. Little, Brown, and Company.

Interloper. Edward Phillips Oppenheim. LC 42-11120. 1941. Triangle Books.

Interloper: A Novel. Frances Mary Peard. LC 7-33506. 1894. Harper & Brothers.

Interlopers. Donald Hamilton. (Matt Helm Ser.). 1978. pap. 1.95 (ISBN 0-449-13994-8, GM). Fawcett.

Interlopers. Julie Mathilde Lippmann. LC 17-30720. 1917. The Penn Publishing Company.

Interlopers: A Novel. Griffing Bancroft. LC 17-20421. 1917. The Bancroft Company.

Interlude. Margaret Gayle. (Superromances Ser.). 384p. 1983. pap. 2.95 (ISBN 0-373-70080-6, Pub. by Worldwide). Harlequin Bks.

Interlude at Pelican Bend. Stewart Vanderveer. LC 47-21838. 1947. Phoenix Press.

Interlude for Sally: Being Some Further Chapters in the Life of Sally Dunn. Beatrice Kean Stapleton Seymour. LC 34-35697. 1934. A. A. Knopf.

Interlude (Frauenraub) Frank Thiess & Fredrick, Caroline, Tr. LC 29-7297. 1929. A. A. Knopf.

Interlude in Venice. Florence Bowes. LC 80-2555. (Starlight Romances). 1981. 9.95 (ISBN 0-385-17316-4). Doubleday.

Interlude of Gold. James F Gordon. LC 35-4044. Fleming H. Revell Company.

Interlude on Siliko 5. Kurt Brand. (Perry Rhodan, 59). 1974. (pbk.) 0.95. Ace Books.

Intermere. William A. Taylor. LC 70-154465. (Utopian Literature Ser). (Illus.). 1971. Repr. of 1901 ed. 12.00 (ISBN 0-405-03547-0). Ayer Co.

Intermezzo. Jean Giraudoux & Reilly, John H., Ed. LC 67-14570. 1967. Appleton Century-Crofts.

Intermezzo, No.14. Eleanor A. Cox. 224p. 1981. pap. 1.50 (ISBN 0-449-50219-8, Coventry). Fawcett.

Intermission: A Novel. Calvin Tomkins. LC 51-11772. 1951. Viking Press.

International. Alfred Maund. LC 61-13430. 1961. McGraw-Hill.

International Creek League: Or, The Band That Had a Flaw. Nick Carter & Dey, Frederic Van Rensselaer. LC 34-382723. (On cover: New magnet library. no. 826). Street & Smith.

International Episode. Henry James. LC 7-7444. (On cover: Harper's half-hour series. no. 91). 1879. Harper & Brothers.

International Episode. Henry James. LC 4-15462. 1902. Harper & Brothers.

International Episode. Henry James. LC 6-32115. 1906. Harper & Brothers.

International Episode see Four Selected Novels of Henry James.

International Episode see Lady Barbarina.

International Living - Education & Training. Campbell & King. price not set o.p. Beatty.

International Relations Through Science Fiction. Martin Harry Greenberg & Joseph D Olander. LC 77-15486. 1978. 12.95 (ISBN 0-531-05401-2). New Viewpoints.

International Science Fiction Yearbook. Ed. by Colin Lester. (Illus.). 1978. pap. 7.95 o.p. (ISBN 0-8256-3121-1, Quick Fox). Putnam Pub Group.

International Science Fiction Yearbook. Ed. by Colin Lester. (Illus.). 1978. pap. 7.95 o.p. (ISBN 0-8256-3121-1, Quick Fox). Music Sales.

International Short Novels: A Contemporary Anthology. Ed. by Leo Hamalian. LC 73-18251. 1974. (pbk.) 6.95 (ISBN 0-471-34621-7). Wiley.

International Short Stories. Ed. by Virginia Woodson Frame Church. LC 72-5902. (Short story index reprint series). 1972. (ISBN 0-8369-4199-3). Books for Libraries Press.

International Short Stories. Ed. by Virginia Woodson Frame Church. LC 34-9018. Lyons & Carnahan.

International Short Stories. Frank Victor Higgins. LC 65-20279. 1965. Varsity Pr.

International Short Stories. Ed. by William Patten. LC 10-7933. 2.10. P. F. Collier & Son.

International Short Stories: American. William Patten. 1978. Repr. of 1910 ed. lib. bdg. 20.00 (ISBN 0-8492-2098-X). R West.

International Symposium: The Nucleolus, Its Structure and Function Proceedings. Hugh Travers Mills. LC 67-23282. 1967. Harper & Row.

International Ties. Mary McArthur Thompson Tuttle. LC 16-60600. The Crane Press.

Interne. Wallace Thurman & Furman, Abraham L., Joint Author. LC 32-115593. The Macaulay Company.

Interns. Richard Frede. LC 60-5539. 1960. Random House.

Intern's Tale. Colin Douglas. LC 82-47995. 192p. 1982. pap. 7.95 (ISBN 0-394-17996-X, E831, Ever). Grove.

Interplanetary Adventurers. Jack Bertin. Ed. by Alice Sachs. 1970. 3.95 o.p. Lenox Hill.

Interplanetary Hunter. 1st Ed. Arthur K Barnes. LC 56-784497. 1956. Gnome Press.

Interplay. Beatrice Harraden. LC 8-297396. 1908. F. A. Stokes Company.

Interpreter: A Novel... Philip Hamilton Gibbs. LC 43-13338. 1943. Doubleday, Doran and Company, Inc.

Interpreter: A Novel. 54th thousand. ed. Philip Hamilton Gibbs. LC 43-9543. 1943. Hutchinson & Co. Ltd.

Interpreter: A Novel. Gertrude Capen Whitney. LC 28-732819. The Four Seas Company.

Interpreter: A Novel by March Cost Pseud. 1st Ed. Peggy Morrison, pseud. LC 60-135836. 1960. Lippincott.

Interpreters. Wole Soyinka. LC 71-101727. (American Library). 1970. 1.50. Collier Books.

Interpreter's House. Maxwell Struthers Burt. LC 24-3919. 1924. C. Scribner's Sons.

Interrogation. Jean Marie Gustave Le Clezio. LC 64-22098. 1964. Atheneum.

Interrogators. Allan Prior. LC 65-12592. 1965. Simon and Schuster.

Interrupted. Isabella Macdonald Alden. LC 52-50338. D. Lothrop.

Interrupted Act see Card Index & Other Plays.

Interrupted Courtship: An American Saga, 1904-1915. Henry Goddard Leach. LC 63-3597. 1963. Exposition Press.

Interrupted Honeymoon. Jane Grosvenor Cooke. LC 7-347743. 1907. A. S. Barnes & Company.

Interrupted Honeymoon. Pauline Benedict Fischer. LC 35-22657. The Penn Publishing Company.

Interrupted Journey. Ivy Preston. 1971. pap. 0.75 o.p. (94182). Beagle Bks.

Interrupted Melody. Sallie Lee Bell. LC 64-11949. 1964. Zondervan Pub. House.

Interrupted Night. Isabella Macdonald Alden & Lutz, Mrs. Grace (Livingston) Hill, 1865- LC 29-23492. 1929. J. B. Lippincott Company.

Interrupted Passage. Terje Stigen. LC 73-3957. (Library of Scandinavian Literature, V. 24). 1974. 7.50 (ISBN 0-8057-3322-1). Twayne Publishers.

Interstate. Borden Deal. LC 72-103740. 1970. 7.95. Doubleday.

Interstellar Empire. John Brunner. (Science Fiction Ser.). 1978. pap. 2.50 (ISBN 0-87997-668-3, UE1668). DAW Bks.

Interstellar Empire. John Brunner. (Science Fiction Ser.). 1976. pap. 1.50 o.p. (UW1252). DAW Bks.

Interval Ashore. Horton Giddy. LC 36-30931. 1936. C. Scribner's Sons.

Interval in Carolina. William Miller Abrahams. 1945. Simon and Schuster.

Interval in Eden. Elizabeth Hall Yates. LC 34-19029. R. D. Henkle.

Intervening Lady. Edgar Jepson. LC 14-9879. 1.25. The Bobbs-Merrill Company.

Interventions. Georgia Wood Pangborn. LC 11-26023. 1911. C. Scribner's Sons.

Interventions: A Cold War Novel of Love & Death. Patrick Breslin. LC 79-6091. 264p. 1980. 10.95 (ISBN 0-385-15816-5). Doubleday.

Interview: A Novel. Hugh C Rae. LC 71-96212. 1969. Coward-McCann.

Interview with the Vampire. Anne Rice. 1979. pap. 2.25 (ISBN 0-345-28126-8). Ballantine.

Interview with the Vampire: A Novel. Anne Rice. LC 75-36792. 1976. 8.95 (ISBN 0-394-49821-6). Knopf.

Interworld. Isidore Haiblum. 1977. 1.50 (ISBN 0-440-12285-6). Dell Pub. Co.

Interworld: A Novel. John W Whitham. LC 33-643. Film Row Press.

Intimacy: A Novel. August F Coppola. LC 78-52981. 1978. 8.95 (ISBN 0-394-50121-7). Grove Press: Distributed by Random House.

Intimate Acrobatics. Donald Stites Fairchild. LC 27-8777. 1927. R. M. McBride & Company.

Intimate & Agonizing Diary of a Man Who Fell Madly in Love with a Catholic Nun. (New Psychology Library Book). (Illus.). 1979. deluxe ed. 27.85 (ISBN 0-930582-25-X). Gloucester Art.

Intimate Apparel. Terry Stokes. LC 79-55712. (Illus.). 3.00 (ISBN 0-913722-19-7). Release Press.

Intimate Behaviour. Desmond Morris. (YA) 1972. 8.95 o.p. (ISBN 0-394-47919-X). Random.

Intimate Enemies. Jessica Steele. (Harlequin Presents Ser.). 192p. 1983. pap. 1.95 (ISBN 0-373-10605-X). Harlequin Bks.

Intimate Friends. Charlotte Vale Allen. LC 82-12964. 300p. 1983. 14.95 (ISBN 0-525-24161-2, 01451-440). Dutton.

Intimate Illusion. Sarah Litsey. LC 55-5438. 1955. Appleton-Century-Crofts.

Intimate Journal of Rudolph Valentino. LC 41-34804. 1931. W. Faro, Inc.

Intimate Journal of Warren Winslow. 1st Ed. Jean Leslie. LC 52-10998. 1952. Published for the Crime Club by Doubleday.

Intimate Story. Rose Franken. LC 55-9980. 1955. Doubleday.

Intimate Stranger. Eugene Thomas. LC 32-13341. Sears Publishing Company, Inc.

Intimate Strangers. Chelsea Farraday. (Leisure book). 1979. 1.95 (ISBN 0-8439-0608-1). Nordon Pubns.

Intimate Strangers. Dorothy Herzog. LC 33-13757. The Macaulay Company.

Intimate Strangers. Julie Logan. 1974. (pbk.) 1.25. Dell.

Intimate Strangers. Denise Mathews. (Candlelight Ecstacy Ser.: No. 106). (Orig.). 1983. pap. 1.95 (ISBN 0-440-14048-X). Dell.

Intimate Victims. Vin Packer. 192p. 1972. pap. 0.95 o.p. Woodhill.

Intimate Victims. Vin Packer. 192p. 1972. pap. 0.95 o.p. Manor Bks.

Intimations. J. G. Bennett. 1976. pap. 3.95 (ISBN 0-87728-327-3). Weiser.

Intimations of Eve. Vardis Fisher. LC 46-2410. 1946. The Vanguard Press.

Intimidators. Donald Hamilton. (Matt Helm Ser.). 1978. pap. 1.95 (ISBN 0-449-14110-1, GM). Fawcett.

Intimidators. Donald Hamilton. (Matt Helm series). 1974. (pbk.) 1.25. Fawcett.

Intinerant House: And Other Stories. Emma Frances Dawson. LC 3-32251. 1897. W. Doxey.

Into a Black Sun. first ed. Takeshi Kaiko. LC 80-50500. 1980. 9.95 (ISBN 0-87011-428-X). Kodansha International.

Into a Neutral Country. Hugo Wolfram. LC 69-16825. 1969. 5.95. Hill and Wang.

Into an Unknown World. Henrietta Eliza Vaughan Stannard. LC 8-13858. (On cover: Lippincott's series of select novels). 1897. J. B. Lippincott Company.

Into Another Dawn. Chaman Lal Nahal. 1977. text ed. 10.50x o.p. (ISBN 0-8426-1007-3). Verry.

Into Darkness. Milton Krims. The Macaulay Company.

Into Deeper Waters. Harry Brewster. LC 68-17329. 1968. Scribner.

Into Deepest Space. Fred Hoyle & Geoffrey Hoyle. LC 74-4859. 1974. 6.95 (ISBN 0-06-011984-5). Harper & Row.

Into It. Edward Pomerantz. LC 71-37448. 1972. 5.95. Dial Press.

Into Man. Charles N. Aronson. LC 76-44030. (Eagle Series; 3). (Illus.). 15.00. (ISBN 0-915736-11-X) (ISBN 0-915736-12-8). Aronson.

Into Passion's Dawn. Michele DuBarry. (Loves of Angela Carlyle Ser.: No. 1). 1981. pap. 2.50 (ISBN 0-8439-0902-1, Leisure Bks). Nordon Pubns.

Into the Abyss. John Knittel. LC 28-15789. 1928. Doubleday, Doran & Company, Inc.

Into the Abyss. John Knittel. LC 36-290127. 1936. Frederick A. Stokes Company.

Into the Abyss. Jules Verne. 1964. 3.95. Assoc Bk.

Into the Aether. Richard A Lupoff. 1974. (pbk.) 0.95. Dell.

Into the Alternate Universe: Contraband from Outer Space. A. Bertram Chandler. 320p. 1981. pap. 2.75 (ISBN 0-441-37109-4). Ace Bks.

Into the Arena. Emma Darby. LC 76-183291. 1972. 5.95. St. Martin's Press.

Into the Arena. Emma Darby. (Signet Books, T5433). 1973. 0.75. New American Library.

Into the Back Country. Maurice L'Heureux. 160p. 1983. pap. 2.75 (ISBN 0-380-81588-5). Avon.

Into the Crack. Colin Lavage. 192p. (Orig.). 1971. pap. 1.95 o.s.i. (O*P*H259, Ophelia). Olympia.

Into the Dangerous World: A Novel. 1st Ed. Richard McLaughlin. LC 67-16294. 1967. pap., 2.95. A. Howard Pr.

Into the Dawn. Gaile Churchill McElhiney. LC 45-5351. 1945. De Vorss & Co.

Into the Day. J. H. Prynne. 1972. pap. 3.00 o.p. Ferry Pr.

Into the Forest. Roderick Thorp. LC 61-12149. 1961. Random House.

Into the Harem. Akbar Del Piombo. LC 78-28561. (Traveller's companion series, TC-491). 1.95. Traveller's Companion, Inc.

Into the Labyrinth see Sin Underneath.

Into the Light: Or, The Jewess. C. A. Ogden. LC 7-23681. 1868. Loring.

Into the Mist. Ben Harrison Subin. LC 48-798171. 1948. Meador Pub. Co.

Into the Niger Bend. Jules Verne. 1969. 3.95. Assoc Bk.

Into the Night: A Story of New Orleans. Frances Nimmo Greene. LC 9-242565. 1909. T. Y. Crowell & Co.

Into the Noonday Sun. D. R Sherman. LC 66-11628. 1966. Little, Brown.

Into the Playhouse. Scott. pap. 1.95 o.s.i. (TC-481, Travellers Comp). Olympia.

Into the Primitive. Robert Ames Bennet. LC 8-12557. 1908. A. C. McClurg & Co.

Into the Shade: And Other Stories. Mary Cecil Hay. (Franklin square library, no. 170). 1881. Harper & Brothers.

Into the Slave Nebula. John Brunner. (Orig.). 1968. pap. 0.60 o.p. (73-797). Lancer.

Into the Strong City. Patrick O'Connor. 1979. 16.95 (ISBN 0-241-10065-8, Pub. by Hamish Hamilton England). David & Charles.

Into the Sunset. Jackson Gregory. LC 36-19986. 1936. Dodd, Mead & Company.

Into the Twilight Zone. Rod Serling. Repr. lib. bdg. 16.85x (ISBN 0-89190-446-8). Am Repr-Rivercity Pr.

Into the Unknown: Eleven Tales of Imagination. Ed. by Terry Carr. LC 73-7826. 192p. 1973. 7.95 o.p. (ISBN 0-525-66342-8). Elsevier-Nelson.

Into the Void: A Bookshop Myster. Florence Converse. LC 26-156071. 1926. Little, Pbrown, and Company.

Into the Wind. Richard Warren Hatch. LC 29-772538. 1929. The Macmillan Company.

Into the Wind. Robert Henderson. LC 81-3024. (Illinois Short Fiction Ser.). 150p. 1981. 11.95 (ISBN 0-252-00899-5); pap. 4.95 (ISBN 0-252-00924-X). U of Ill Pr.

Into Thin Air. Jack Iams. LC 52-9704. 1952. Morrow.

Into Thin Air. Horatio Gates Winslow & Quirk, Leslie W., 1882- Joint Author. LC 29-7300. 1929. Pub. for The Crime Club, Inc., by Doubleday, Doran & Company, Inc.

Into Thin Air: By Harry Carmichael Pseud. 1st Ed. Leopold Horace Ognall. LC 58-557958. 1958. Published for the Crime Club by Doubleday.

Into Thin Air. 1st Ed. Warren Beck. LC 51-428. 1951. Knopf.

Into What Port? Agnes Edwards Rothery. LC 31-25230. Coward-McCann, Inc.

Into Your Tent I'll Creep. Peter De Vries. LC 70-161422. 1975. (pbk.) 1.50. Popular Library.

Intoxicated Ghost, and Other Stories. Arlo Bates. LC 72-4419. (Short story index reprint series). 1972. 12.00 (ISBN 0-8369-4170-5). Books for Libraries Press.

Intra Muros; or, Within the Walls. A Dream of Heaven. Rebecca Ruter Springer. (New Sabbath library. vol. 1, no. 10). 1899. David C. Cook Publishing Co.

Intrepid Encounter. Rebecca Ashley. (Candlelight Regency Ser.: No. 707). (Orig.). 1982. pap. 1.75 (ISBN 0-440-14233-4). Dell.

Intrepid Visions. Jacques Carrie. LC 81-67260. (Illus.). 138p. (Orig.). 1982. pap. 4.95 (ISBN 0-937578-01-0). Fablewaves.

Intricate Land. John Knoepfle. 1970. 5.00 (Pub. by New Rivers Pr); signed ltd ed 10.00. SBD.

Intrigue. Clive Desmond. LC 19-6333. Hodder and Stoughton.

Intrigue for Empire: An Adventure-Mystery. Kathleen Moore Knight. LC 44-62038. 1944. Pub. for the Crime Club by Doubleday, Doran and Co., Inc.

Intrigue: Four Complete Novels, 4 vols. in 1. Eric Oler. Incl. Journey into Fear; Coffin for Dimitrios; Cause for Alarm; Background to Danger. 1960. 7.95 o.p. (41234). Knopf.

Intrigue in Baltimore. 1st Ed. Janet Payne Whitney. LC 51-13639. 1951. Little, Brown.

Intrigue in Rome. Ellen Morley. 1978. pap. 1.25 (ISBN 0-532-12530-4). Woodhill.

Intrigue in the High Court. Thomas D. Parks. pap. 0.95 o.p. (ISBN 0-89107-115-6). Good News.

Intrigue on Halfaday Creek. James Beardsley Hendryx. LC 52-13567. (Double D western). 1953. Doubleday.

Intrigue on the Upper Level. Thomas Temple Hoyne. LC 34-7407. 1934. Reilly & Lee Co.

Intrigue, the Great Spy Novels of Eric Ambler. Eric Ambler. LC 43-293341. 1943. A. A. Knopf.

Intriguer. Maude Parker. LC 51-14908. (Murray Hill mystery). 1952. Rinehart.

Intriguers. Horol Bindloss. LC 14-390210. 1914. Frederick A. Stokes Company.

Intriguers. Donald Hamilton. (Matt Helm Ser.). 208p. 1978. pap. 2.25 (ISBN 0-449-13999-9, GM). Fawcett.

Intriguers. William Le Queux. LC 21-40896. The Macaulay Company.

Intriguers. A Novel. John Daniel Barry. LC 6-9408. (Half-title: Appletons' town and country library, no. 203). 1896. D. Appleton and Company.

Intriguers: A Second Omnibus of Novels, 4 vols. in 1. Eric Ambler. Incl. Passage of Arms; State of Siege; Schirmer Inheritance; Judgement on Deltchev. 1965. 5.95 o.p. (43071). Knopf.

Intriguers: Four Superb Novels of Suspense. Eric Ambler. LC 65-101439. 1965. 5.95. Knopf.

Intriguing for a Princess. An Adventure with Mexican Banditti. Emerson Bennett. LC 7-34427. (Bradley's library no. 3). 1859. J. W. Bradley.

Intriguing Lady. Daphne Woodward. (Second Chance at Love Ser.: No. 45). (Orig.). 1982. pap. 1.75 (ISBN 0-515-05818-1). Jove Pubns.

Intro Eight - the Liar's Craft. George Palmer Garrett. 1977. pap. 3.95 o.p. (ISBN 0-385-12375-2, Anch). Doubleday.

Introducing C. B. Greenfield. Lucille Kallen. LC 78-22100. 7.95 (ISBN 0-517-53666-8). Crown Publishers.

Introducing Mr. Sherlock Holmes. Ed. by Edgar Wadsworth Smith. LC 59-16404. 1959. Baker Street Irregulars.

Introducing Shirley Braverman. Hilma Wolitzer. 1978. pap. 1.25 (ISBN 0-440-94112-1, LFL). Dell.

Introducing Terry Sloane. Concordia Merrel. LC 34-11034. 1934. Doubleday, Doran & Company, Inc.

Introduction Five: Stories by New Writers. 240p. 1974. 8.95 o.p. (ISBN 0-571-10478-9). Faber & Faber.

Introduction Four: Stories by New Writers. 230p. 1971. 8.95 o.p. (ISBN 0-571-09535-6). Faber & Faber.

Introduction of Islandia: Its History, Customs, Laws, Language, and Geography. Basil Davenport & Wright, Austin Tappan. LC 42-14079. 1942. Farrar & Rinehart, Inc.

Introduction of Literature: Stories. 2d ed. Ed. by Lynn Altenbernd & Leslie Lisle Lewis. LC 69-10891. 1969. Macmillan.

Introduction to Fiction. Ed. by Paul J. Dolan. LC 73-18250. 1974. (pbk.). 5.95 (ISBN 0-471-21751-4). Wiley.

Introduction to Fiction. X. J Kennedy. LC 75-20735. 5.95. Little, Brown.

Introduction to Fiction. 2d ed. X. J Kennedy. LC 78-19247. 6.95 (ISBN 0-316-48871-2). Little, Brown.

Introduction to Literature: Fiction: Ed. by Theodore Gross, Norman Kelvin. Ed. by Theodore L. Gross. LC 67-12366. 1967. pap., 2.50. Random.

Introduction to Literature, Stories. 3d ed. Ed. by Lynn Altenbernd & Leslie Lisle Lewis. LC 79-9780. 8.95 (ISBN 0-02-302070-9). Macmillan.

Introduction to Modern Bulgarian Literature: An Anthology of Short Stories. Ed. by Nikolai Kirilov. LC 72-91322. (Twayne's introductions to world literature series). 1969. Twayne Publishers.

Introduction to Sally. Mary Annette Beauchamp Russell Russell. LC 26-27598. 1926. Doubleday, Page & Company.

Intrude No More. Virginia Creed. LC 40-14074. Duell, Sloan and Pearce.

Intruder. Gabriele D' Annunzio. Tr. by Arthur Hornblower. LC 9-3453. (His The romances of the rose). 1898. G. H. Richmond.

Intruder. Louis Charbonneau. 304p. 1982. pap. 2.95 (ISBN 0-425-05594-9). Berkley Pub.

Intruder. Helen Marjorie Fowler. LC 52-138280. 1953. Morrow.

Intruder. Margaret Storm Jameson. LC 56-14596. 1956. Macmillan.

Intruder. Maurice Maeterlinck. Ed. by Edmund R. Brown. (International Pocket Library). pap. 3.00. Branden.

Intruder. Anton Myrer. 1980. pap. 2.95 (ISBN 0-425-05505-1). Berkley Pub.

Intruder. Carter Travis Young. LC 77-25582. 1979. 8.95 (ISBN 0-385-13019-8). Doubleday.

Intruder: A Novel. Charles Beaumont. Putnam.

Intruder: A Novel of Boston. Anton Myrer. LC 65-10692. 1965. Little, Brown.

Intruder at Maison Benedict. Susan Richard. 1970. pap. 0.60 o.p. (ISBN 0-446-63495-6, 63-495). Paperback Lib.

Intruder: El Intruso. Vicente Blasco Ibanez & Gillespie, Mrs. W. A., Tr. LC 26-30268. E. P. Dutton & Co., Inc.

Intruder from the Sea. Gordon McDonell. LC 53-10227. 1953. Little, Brown.

Intruder in the Dust. William Faulkner. LC 48-8519. (Modern Library coll. eds., T88). 1967. pap., 1.45. Random.

Intruder in the Dust. William Faulkner. LC 48-8519. 1948. Random House.

Intruder Marriage. Berta Ruck. LC 44-7190. 1944. Dodd, Mead & Company.

Intruder. Translated from the Dutch by James S. Holmes and Hans Van Marle. Adriaan Van Der Veen. LC 58-6791. 1958. Abelard-Schuman.

Intruders. Robert Bright. LC 46-250713. 1946. Doubleday & Company, Inc.

Intruders in Eden. Peggy Gaddis, pseud. pap. 0.50 o.p. (B50-711). Belmont-Tower.

Intrusion. David Combs. 224p. 1981. pap. 2.25 (ISBN 0-380-77883-1, 77883). Avon.

Intrusion. Beatrice Kean Stapleton Seymour. 1922. T. Selzer.

Intrusion of Jimmy. Pelham Grenville Wodehouse. LC 10-11365. 1910. W. J. Watt & Company.

Intrusion of Jimmy. Pelham Grenville Wodehouse. 1929. G. H. Watt.

Intrusions. Robert Aickman. 216p. 1980. 17.50 (ISBN 0-575-02854-8, Pub. by Gollancz England). David & Charles.

Intrusions. Ursula Hegi. LC 80-25568. 1981. 12.95 (ISBN 0-670-40065-3). Viking Press.

Intrusions of Peggy: A Novel. Anthony Hope Hawkins. LC 2-239951. 1902. Harper & Brotehrs.

Intrusive Tourist. Gertrude M. Robins Reynolds. LC 35-885724. 1935. Pub. for the Crime Club, Inc., by Doubleday, Doran & Company, Inc.

Invader. Albert F. Hill & David C. Hill. 304p. (Orig.). 1981. pap. 2.75 (ISBN 0-515-05415-1). Jove Pubns.

Invader. Marjorie Kaplan. 1972. pap. 2.25 o.p. (ISBN 0-913006-03-3). Puckerbrush.

Invader. Emma N. Papert & Ethne Marenco. (Orig.). 1974. pap. 1.25 o.p. (V3169). Pyramid Pubns.

Invader: A Novel. Margaret Louisa Bradley Woods. LC 7-17049. 1907. Harper & Brothers.

Invader: A Tale of Adventure and Passion. Hilda Vaughan. LC 28-17647. 1928. Harper & Brothers.

Invaders. Francis Newton Symmes Allen. LC 13-5065. 1913. Houghton Mifflin Company.

Invaders. 256p. 1976. write for info. o.p. (ISBN 0-8415-0393-1). Dutton.

Invaders. Walter Kempley. LC 75-38704. 8.95 (ISBN 0-8415-0343-5). Saturday Review Press.

Invaders. Keith Laumer. (Orig.). pap. 0.50 o.p. (R1664). Pyramid Pubns.

Invaders, a Novel. Waldo David Frank. LC 48-681294. 1948. Duell, Sloan and Pearce.

Invaders: A Story of Fantastic Adventures in Anticommunism. Roland Roggenbrod. LC 54-41575. 1954. Story Book Press.

Invaders: A Story of the "Hole-in-the-Wall" Country. Jacque Lloyd Morgan. LC 10-28163. R. F. Fenno & Company.

Invaders, and Other Stories. Lev Nikolaevich Tolstoi & Dole, Nathan Haskell, 1852- Tr. LC 8-26746. T. Y. Crowell & Co.

Invaders at Ground Zero. David Houston. (Tales of Tomorrow Ser.: No. 1). 1981. pap. 2.25 (ISBN 0-8439-0928-5, Leisure Bks). Nordon Pubns.

Invaders from Space: Ten Stories of Science Fiction. Ed. by Robert Silverberg. LC 75-179117. 1972. 6.95. Hawthorn Books.

Invaders from the Dark. Greye La Spina. LC 60-51680. 1960. Arkham House.

Invaders from the Dark see Shadow of Evil.

Invaders from the Infinite. 1st Ed. John Wood Campbell. LC 60-53080. Gnome Press.

Invaders, No see Army of the Undead.

Invaders of Earth. Ed. by Groff Conklin. LC 52-6778. 1952. Vanguard Press.

Invaders on the Moon. Kris Neville. 1970. pap. 0.75 o.p. (B75-1085). Belmont-Tower.

Invader's Son. William Antony Kennedy. LC 19-13457. G. Sully and Company.

Invahoe. Walter Scott. LC 8-2933. (Standard literature series no. 24). 1897. University Publishing Company.

Invahoe: A Romance. Walter Scott. LC 8-3031. (English classics for schools). 1892. American Book Company.

Invasion! Elwyn Whitman Chambers. LC 43-535725. 1943. E. P. Dutton & Co., Inc.

Invasion. Maxence Van Der Meersch. Tr. by Hopkins, Gerard. LC 37-1015. 1937. The Viking Press.

Invasion: A Narrative of Events Concerning the Johnston Family of St. Mary's. Janet Lewis, pseud. LC 51-9163. (American Fiction Library). (Illus.). University of Denver Press.

Invasion: A Narrative of Events Concerning the Johnston Family of St. Mary's. Janet Lewis, pseud. LC 32-25848. Harcourt, Brace and Company.

Invasion-Earth. Harry Harrison. LC 82-153745. (Ace science fiction). (Illus.). 5.95 (ISBN 0-441-37153-1). Ace Books.

Invasion from Mars: Interplanetary Stories; Thrilling Adventures in Space. Ed. by Orson Welles. LC 49-5999. (Dell book, 305). 1949. Dell Pub. Co.

Invasion of France in 1814. Emile Erckmann & Chatrian, Alexandre, 1826-1890, Joint Author. LC 98-1210. 1898. C. Scribner's Sons.

Invasion of France in 1814: Comprising the Night-March of the Russian Army Past Phalsbourg. Emile Erckmann & Chatrian, Alexandre, 1826-1890, Joint Author. LC 41-26683. 1871. C. Scribner & Co.

Invasion of New York: Or, How Hawaii Was Annexed. John Henry Palmer. LC 7-35777. F. T. Neely.

Invasion of Privacy. Harry Kurnitz. LC 55-5796. 1955. Random House.

Invasion of the Air Eaters. 1979. pap. write for info. (ISBN 0-88074-012-4). Metagam.

Invasion of the Body Snatchers. Jack Finney. 1978. pap. 2.25 (ISBN 0-440-14317-9). Dell.

Invasion of the Body Snatchers. Jack Finney. (O.s.i.). 1973. pap. 1.50 o.s.i. (AD1594, Award). Univ Pub & Dist.

Invasion of the Body Snatchers. Ed. by Fotonovel Publications Staff. (Illus., Orig.). 1979. pap. 2.50. Fotonovel.

Invasion of the Clones. Joseph Rosenberger. (Death Merchant#16). 1976. (pbk.) 1.25 (ISBN 0-523-00857-0). Pinnacle Books.

Invasion of the Klingon Empire. John DuMaurier. (Illus.). 1978. pap. 4.00 (ISBN 0-89502-015-7). FEB.

Invasion of the Robots. Ed. by Roger Elwood. 1969. pap. 0.60 o.p. (63-078). Paperback Lib.

Invasion of the Space Invaders. Martin Amis. 128p. 1982. pap. 9.95 (ISBN 0-89087-351-8). Celestial Arts.

Invective & Abuse: An Anthology. Hugh Kingsmill. 224p. 1982. Repr. of 1944 ed. lib. bdg. 25.00 (ISBN 0-8495-3133-0). Arden Lib.

Invention of Morel: And Other Stories from La Trama Celeste. Adolfo Bioy-Casares. LC 64-10312. 1964. University of Texas Press.
Invention of Morel & Other Stories: From la Trama Celeste. Adolfo Bioy-Casares. Tr. by Ruth L. Simms. (Illus.). 1964. 7.95 o.p. (ISBN 0-292-73280-5). U of Tex Pr.
Invention of the West. Alvin Greenberg. LC 76-14552. (Equinox book). 2.95 (ISBN 0-380-00596-4). Avon Books.
Invention of the World: A Novel. Jack Hodgins. LC 77-11195. 8.95 (ISBN 0-15-145281-4). Harcourt Brace Jovanovich.
Inventions of the Idiot. John Kendrick Bangs. LC 4-9629. 1904. Harper & Brothers.
Inverted Pyramid. Bertrand William Sinclair. LC 24-8648. 1924. Little, Brown, and Company.
Inverted World: A Novel. Christopher Priest. LC 73-18671. (Illus.). 1974. 6.95 (ISBN 0-06-013421-6). Harper & Row.
Investigating Officer. Frederick L Keefe. LC 66-13650. 5.95. Delacorte Dist. Dial.
Investigation. stanislaw lem; translated by adele milch. ed. Stanislaw Lem. 1.50 (ISBN 0-380-00665-0). Avon Books.
Investigation. Dorothy Uhnak. (Kangaroo Book). 1978. 2.50 (ISBN 0-671-81806-6). Pocket Books.
Investigation: A Novel. Dorothy Uhnak. LC 77-7981. 9.95 (ISBN 0-671-22617-7). Simon and Schuster.
Investigations and Experience of M. Shawtinbach: At Saar Soong, Sumatra. A Ret or Sequel to "The Manatitlans". Elton R. Smilie. LC 15-630038. 1879. J. Winterburn & Company, Printers.
Investigators. Joseph Smith Fletcher. LC 31-9392. 1930. E. J. Clode, Inc.
Invincible. Stanislaw Lem. LC 72-10574. (Continuum book). 1973. 6.95 (ISBN 0-8164-9123-2). Seabury Press.
Invincible Adam. George Sylvester Viereck & Eldridge, Paul, 1888- Joint Author. LC 32-6655. Liveright, Inc.
Invincible Adam. George Sylvester Viereck & Eldridge, Paul, 1888- Joint Author. LC 39-4171. 1938. Gold Label Books, Inc.
Invincible Minnie. Elisabeth Sanxay Holding. LC 20-522930. George H. Doran Company.
Invincible Surmise. Granville Paul Smith. LC 36-9079. 1936. Houghton Mifflin Company.
Invincibles. Noel Bertram Gerson. LC 58-5958. 1958. Doubleday.
Invincibles. Carter A Vaughan, pseud. LC 58-5958. 1958. Doubleday.
Inviolable: A Novel. Helen M Bulger. LC 32-17257. 1932. Benziger Brothers.
Inviolable Sanctuary. James Owen Hannay. LC 12-118571. T. Nelson and Sons.
Invisble Book: Epilogue) Sergei Dovlatov. LC 78-74200. 9.00 (ISBN 0-88233-285-6). Ardis.
Invisible Assassins. (Executioner Ser.). 192p. 1983. pap. 1.95 (ISBN 0-373-61053-X, Pub. by Worldwide). Harlequin Bks.
Invisible Balance Sheet. Kate Nichols Trask. LC 16-22851. 1916. John Lane Company.
Invisible Barriers. David Osborne, pseud. LC 58-9122. (Science fiction). 1958. Avalon Books.
Invisible Boarder. Mildred Davis. (Dell Book). 1977. 1.50 (ISBN 0-440-13938-4). Dell Pub. Co.
Invisible Boarder. Mildred B Davis. LC 74-4316. 1974. 5.95 (ISBN 0-394-49022-3). Random House.
Invisible Bond. Eleanor Talbot Kinkead. LC 6-14545. 1906. Moffat, Yard & Company.
Invisible Brand. Charles Horace Snow. LC 33-124248. Macrae Smith Company.
Invisible Bridge. Francis K Allan. LC 47-11749. 1947. Reynal & Hitchcock.
Invisible Chimes. Margaret Sutton. (Judy Bolton Mysteries Ser.). 1976. Repr. of 1932 ed. lib. bdg. 10.85x (ISBN 0-88411-716-2). Amereon Ltd.
Invisible Cities. Italo Calvino. LC 74-8836. 1974. 6.50 (ISBN 0-15-145290-3). Harcourt Brace Jovanovich.
Invisible Cities. Italo Calvino. LC 77-16002. (Harvest/HBJ book). 1978. 2.45 (ISBN 0-15-645380-0). Harcourt Brace Jovanovich.
Invisible City: A New York Sketchbook. Pete Hamil. LC 80-5276. 9.95 (ISBN 0-394-50377-5). Random House.
Invisible Cord. Catherine Cookson. LC 75-812. 1975. 7.95 (ISBN 0-525-13475-1). Dutton.
Invisible Cord. Catherine Cookson. 1976. (pbk.) 1.75. Bantam.
Invisible Death. Lin Carter. LC 75-9219. 173p. 1975. 12.50 o.p. (ISBN 0-385-08768-3). Ultramarine Pub.
Invisible Death. Lin Carter. LC 75-9219. (Science Fiction Ser). 168p. 1975. 5.95 o.p. (ISBN 0-385-08768-3). Doubleday.
Invisible Empire. Albion Winegar Tourgee. LC 68-20023. (Americans in Fiction Ser.). (Illus.). Repr. of 1883 ed. lib. bdg. 13.50x (ISBN 0-8398-1966-8). Irvington.
Invisible Enemy. George Clifford Shedd. LC 18-108373. 1918. The Macaulay Company.
Invisible Event. John Davys Beresford. LC 15-9312. 1.35. George H. Doran Company.
Invisible Evil. Robert Gaines. LC 63-19197. 1963. Walker.
Invisible Fire. Pat Graversen. 224p. 1981. pap. 2.25 (ISBN 0-449-14422-4, GM). Fawcett.
Invisible Fore: A Story Adapted from the Play by Walter Hackett. Louise Jordan Miln. LC 20-11300. Frederick A. Stokes Company.
Invisible Gate. Constance Beresford-Howe. LC 49-11668. Dodd, Mead.
Invisible Gentleman. Dalton. LC 6-39305. 1833. E. L. Carey & A. Hart.
Invisible Glass. Loren Wahl. 1965. 3.95 o.s.i. Guild Pr Ltd.
Invisible Gods: A Novel. Edith Franklin Wyatt. LC 23-42944. 1923. Harper & Brothers.
Invisible Green. John Thomas Sladek. 186p. 1983. pap. 2.95 (ISBN 0-8027-3020-5). Walker & Co.
Invisible Green: A Thackeray Phin Mystery. John Thomas Sladek. LC 78-68541. 1979. 7.95 (ISBN 0-8027-5404-X). Walker.
Invisible Hand. A Tale ... LC 7-9715. 1815. D. Longworth.
Invisible Hands. A Novel. After the German of F. Von Zobeltitz. Fedor Karl Maria Hermann August Von Zobeltitz & Boggs, Mrs. Sara Elisabeth (Siegrist) 1843-Tr. LC 9-2202. (Ledger library. no. 111). 1894. R. Bonner's Sons.
Invisible Host. Gwen Bristow. LC 30-30571. 1930. The Mystery League, Inc.
Invisible Island: A Novel. Irwin Stark. LC 48-74612. 1948. Viking Press.
Invisible Links. Selma Ottiliana Lovisa Lagerlof. Tr. by Flach, Pauline Bancroft. 1899. Little, Brown and Company.
Invisible Man. Ralph Ellison. LC 52-5159. 1952. Random House.
Invisible Man. Ralph Ellison. LC 72-10419. 1973. (ISBN 0-394-71715-5). Vintage Books.
Invisible Man. Michael Jahn. 1975. (pbk.) 1.25. Fawcett.
Invisible Man. Herbert George Wells. LC 57-1081. (Pocket book, 1140. Science fiction, O). 1957. Pocket Books.
Invisible Man. Herbert George Wells. LC 64-6750. (Airmont classics). 1964. Airmont Pub. Co.
Invisible Man: A Grotesque Romance. Herbert George Wells. 1897. E. Arnold.
Invisible Man: A Grotesque Romance. Herbert George Wells. LC 20-16469. Harper & Brothers.
Invisible Man: A Grotesque Romance. Herbert George Wells. LC 41-6696. (On cover: Penguin books. 151). 1939. Penguin Books Limited.
Invisible Man & War of the Worlds. Herbert George Wells. 1983. pap. 3.95 (ISBN 0-671-47113-9). WSP.
Invisible Man Murders: A Chin Kham Mystery. Richard Foster, pseud. LC 46-869924. (On cover: Five star mystery). 1945. Green Publishing Co.
Invisible Man: Thirtieth Anniversary Edition. Ralph Ellison. 1982. 15.95 (ISBN 0-394-52549-3). Random.
Invisible Might. Robert Bowman. LC 15-122510. 1915. 1.10. McBride, Nast & Company.
Invisible Outlaw. Frederick Faust. (First published in 1932.). 1974. (pbk.) 0.95. Warner Paperback Library.
Invisible Parade: The Fiction of Flannery O'Connor. Miles Orvell. LC 72-91132. 1972. 9.00 (ISBN 0-87722-023-9). Temple University Press.
Invisible Plague. Jack M. Bickham. 1975. pap. 1.25 o.p. (ISBN 0-515-03532-7). BJ Pub Group.
Invisible Police: A Novel. Louis Beauregard Pendleton. LC 32-32769. The New-Church Press.
Invisible Red. Maude Parker. LC 52-12103. 1953. Rinehart.
Invisible Sun. Mildred Lee, pseud. LC 46-4003. 1946. The Westminster Press.
Invisible Swords. James Thomas Farrell. 1973. 1.50. Manor Books.
Invisible Swords. James Thomas Farrell. LC 77-103744. 1971. 6.95. Doubleday.
Invisible Tides. Beatrice Kean Stapleton Seymour. 1921. T. Seltzer.
Invisible Victory. Gordon Ostlere. LC 77-21368. 1978. 8.95 (ISBN 0-689-10836-2). Atheneum.
Invisible Voices. Matthew Phipps Shiel. LC 74-160950. (Short story index reprint series). 1971. (ISBN 0-8369-3929-8). Books for Libraries Press.
Invisible Weapons. Cecil John Charles Street. LC 38-14880. 1938. Dodd, Mead & Company.
Invisible Wife. Jane Arbor. 192p. 1982. pap. 1.50 (ISBN 0-373-02467-3). Harlequin Bks.
Invisible Wings. Mary Geary Grant. LC 23-11039. Moffat, Yard & Company.
Invisible Woman. Herbert Quick. LC 24-27436. The Bobbs-Merrill Company.
Invisible Worm. Rosamond Campion. 96p. 1972. 4.95 o.s.i. (ISBN 0-02-521080-7). Macmillan.
Invisible Worm. Margaret Millar. LC 41-11800. 1941. Pub. for the Crime Club by Doubleday, Doran and Company, Inc.
Invisible Worm. Gordon Sager. LC 50-10266. 1950. Vanguard Press.
Invisible Wounds. Frederick Palmer. LC 25-707085. 1925. 2.00. Dodd, Mead and Company.
Invisibles see Novella Box.
Invisibles: A Novel. Edgar Earl Christopher. 1903. The Saalfield Publishing Company.
Invitation. Catherine Cookson. 256p. 1974. pap. 1.50 (ISBN 0-451-06429-1, W6429, Sig). NAL.
Invitation from Minervey March Cost: Pseud. 1st Ed. Peggy Morrison, pseud. 1954. Lippincott.
Invitation to a Beheading. Vladimir Vladimirovich Nabokov. LC 59-11024. 1959. Putnam.
Invitation to a Dynamite Party. Peter Lovesey. 1981. pap. 2.95 (ISBN 0-14-004029-3). Penguin.
Invitation to a Hanging. Walt Coburn. (Belmont Tower Books). 1977. 1.25 (ISBN 0-505-51196-7). Tower Pubns.
Invitation to a Strangling. R. L. Brent. (Liquidator Ser.). 176p. (Orig.). 1980. pap. 1.95 o.p. (ISBN 0-441-37205-8). Charter Bks.
Invitation to a Strangling. R. L. Brent. (Liquidator Ser). (O.s.i.). 176p. 1975. pap. 1.25 o.s.i. (AQ1459, Award). Univ Pub & Dist.
Invitation to a Strangling. R. L Brent. 1975. (pbk.) 1.25. Award Books.
Invitation to a Waltz. Beverly C Warren. LC 82-45563. 1983. 11.95 (ISBN 0-385-18398-4). Doubleday.
Invitation to a Waltz. Beverly C. Warren. LC 82-45563. (Starlight Romance Ser.). 168p. 1983. 11.95 (ISBN 0-385-18398-4). Doubleday.
Invitation to Danger. Pat Phillips. 1976. 4.95. Avalon Books.
Invitation to Danger. Alfred Boller Stanford. LC 29-195280. 1929. W. Morrow & Company.
Invitation to Death. Amelia Reynolds Long. LC 40-8386. Phoenix Press.
Invitation to Evil. Willo Davis Roberts. 1970. pap. 0.75 o.p. (ISBN 0-447-74717-7). Lancer.
Invitation to Evil. Willo Davis Roberts. 1973. pap. 0.95 o.s.i. (75-434). Lancer.
Invitation to Folly. Susan Ertz. LC 53-5366. 1953. Harper.
Invitation to Kill. Gardner Low. LC 37-22822. 1937. G. P. Putnam's Sons.
Invitation to Life. Eric Mowbray Knight. LC 47-34766. Greenberg.
Invitation to Live. Lloyd Cassel Douglas. LC 62-52. 1961. Grosset & Dunlap.
Invitation to Live. Lloyd Cassel Douglas. LC 40-330621. 1940. Houghton Mifflin Company.
Invitation to Murder. Ione Sandberg Shriber. LC 43-15957. 1943. Farrar & Rinehart, Inc.
Invitation to Murder: By Leslie Ford Pseud. Zenith Jones Brown. LC 54-8689. 1954. Scribner.
Invitation to Nonsense: The Satirical Meditations of Beelzebub. Essa G. Hannoush. LC 74-75411. (Illus.). 160p. 1974. 6.95 o.p. (ISBN 0-8059-2001-3). Dorrance.
Invitation to Paradise. Lesley Howard. LC 73-87595. 1974. 6.95 (ISBN 0-698-10576-1). Coward, McCann & Geoghegan.
Invitation to the Dance. Madge Jenison. LC 29-22147. 1929. Doubleday, Doran & Company, Inc.
Invitation to the Waltz. Rosamond Lehmann. LC 75-5990. (Harvest book; HB 316). 1975. 2.95 (ISBN 0-15-645384-3). Harcourt Brace Jovanovich.
Invitation to the Waltz. Rosamond Lehmann. LC 32-30640. H. Holt and Company.
Invitation to the Waltz. Rosamond Lehmann. LC 47-4734. 1947. Reynal & Hitchcock.
Invitation to the Wedding. Patricia Hagan. LC 73-6940. 1973. (pbk.) 0.75. Bantam Books.
Invitation to Vengeance: A Novel of Suspense. 1st Ed. Kathleen Moore Knight. LC 60-15179. 1960. Published for the Crime Club by Doubleday.
Invitation to Violence. 1st Ed. Lionel White. LC 58-5231. 1958. Cutton.
Involuntary Chaperon. Margaret H. C. Carmeron. LC 9-26953. 1909. 1.50. Harper & Brothers.
Involvement: Choice in Christian Vocations. Pierre Babin & Frank McMahon. (gr. 10-12). 1970. text ed. 1.95 o.p. (ISBN 0-8164-6082-5, Crossroad Bks); tchrs' manual 2.95 o.p. (ISBN 0-8164-6083-3). Seabury.
Involvement of Arnold Wechsler. John Alexander Graham. LC 77-149474. 1971. 5.95. Little, Brown.
Inward Eye. Peggy Bacon. LC 52-7365. 1952. Scribner.
Inward Voyage. Peter Packer. LC 48-6936. 1948. Whitlesey House.
Inyo-Sierra Passage: A Novel. Jack Rowe. LC 79-24077. 1980. 9.95 (ISBN 0-07-054085-3). McGraw-Hill.
Inzorbital. Bill Pearlman. 1974. pap. 3.00 (Pub. by Duende). SBD.
Io: A Tale of the Olden Fane. K Barton. LC 6-9101. 1851. D. Appleton & Company.
I.O. U. for Emily. Lu Gene Weldon. LC 67-259936. 1967. 5.00. Arlington House.
Iola, the Senator's Daughter: A Story of Ancient Rome (About 24 B. C. Mansfield Lovell Hillhouse. LC 7-4677. 1894. G. P. Putnam's Sons.
Iolanthe's Wedding. Hermann Sudermann. LC 72-132128. (Short story index reprint series). 1970. Books for Libraries Press.
Iolanthe's Wedding. Hermann Sudermann & Seltzer, Mrs. Adele Szold, 1876- Tr. 1918. Boni and Liveright.
Iole. Robert William Chambers. LC 5-16890. 1905. D. Appleton & Co.
Iole. Robert William Chambers. LC 12-20340. 1910. D. Appleton & Co.
Ion. Liviu. Rebreanu. Ed. by Ralph M. Aderman. LC 67-25190. 1967. 18.95x (ISBN 0-8057-5695-7). Irvington.
Ion War. Colin Kapp. 1978. 1.95 (ISBN 0-441-37217-1). Ace Books.
Iona. Fiona MacLeod. 1982. pap. 7.25 (ISBN 0-86315-500-6, Pub. by Floris Books). St George Bk Serv.
Ione, a Broken Love Dream: A Novel. Laura Jean Libbey. (On cover: The choice series, no. 17). 1890. R. Bonner's Sons.
Ione, a Novel. Laura Jean Libbey. (On cover: The popular series, no. 30). 1893. R. Bonner's Sons.
Ione. A Sequel to "Vashti.". Charlotte Crisman Cox. 1900. Eastern Publishing Company.
Ione March. Samuel Rutherford Crockett. LC 99-4179. 1899. Dodd, Mead and Company.
Ione Stewart. Elizabeth Lynn Linton. (On cover: Lovell's library. no. 275). 1883. J.W. Lovell Company.
Ione Stewart. A Novel. Elizabeth Lynn Linton. (Harper's Franklin square library. no. 346.). 1883. Harper & Brothers.
Ione Stewart. A Novel. Elizabeth Lynn Linton. (On cover: Seaside library. Pocket ed. no. 122). 1883. G. Munro.
Ionia: Land of Wise Men & Fair Women. Alexander Craig. LC 76-154437. (Utopian Literature Ser). (Illus.). 1971. Repr. of 1898 ed. 17.00 (ISBN 0-405-03520-9). Ayer Co.
IOU Blues. Shirley Gaultney. LC 73-83921. 1974. 7.95 (ISBN 0-87949-017-9). Ashley Books.
Iowa Crackerbarrel. Wood Cowan. (Illus.). 1969. text ed. 3.95 o.p.; pap. 1.95 o.p. Silvermine.
Iowa Interiors. Ruth Suckow. LC 26-274424. 1926. A. A. Knopf.
Iowa Interiors. Ruth Suckow. LC 76-51679. (Rediscovered Fiction by American Women). 1977. 22.00 (ISBN 0-405-10057-4). Arno Press.
Iowa, O Iowa see Collected Works.
Iowa Pioneers. Andrew Magnus Fleming. LC 33-37448. 1933. Meador Publishing Company.
Ipane. Robert Bontine Cunninghame Graham. LC 70-169553. (Short story index reprint series). 1971. (ISBN 0-8369-4015-6). Books for Libraries Press.
Ipane. Robert Bontine Cunninghame Graham. LC 26-12981. 1925. A. & C. Boni.
Ipcress File. Len Deighton. LC 63-15370. 1963. Simon and Schuster.
Ippolita. Denti Di Pirajno, Alberto. LC 61-9576. 1961. Doubleday.
Ipsis: A Fairy Tale by Ali. Alexander Homics. LC 77-70961. 1977. pap. 4.95 o.p. (ISBN 0-912760-39-7). Valkyrie Pr.
IQ Eighty-Three. Arthur Herzog. 1980. pap. 2.50 (ISBN 0-425-04433-5). Berkley Pub.
IQ 83. Arthur Herzog. LC 78-2485. 8.95. Simon and Schuster.
IQ 83. Arthur Herzog. 1980. 2.50 (ISBN 0-425-04433-5). Berkley Publishing Corp.
Ira and Isabella: Or, The Natural Children. A Novel, Founded in Fiction. A Posthumous Work. William Hill Brown. LC 5-2557. 1807. Published by Belcher and Armstrong..
Iracema, the Honey-Lips: A Legend of Brazil. Jose Martiniano De Alencar. LC 75-44268. 1976. 10.00. H. Fertig.
Iracema, the Honey-Lips: A Legend of Brazil. Jose M. De Alencar. LC 75-44268. 1977. Repr. of 1886 ed. 16.50x (ISBN 0-86527-263-8). Fertig.
Iran Diary. Martie Sterling & Robin Sterling. 1980. pap. 2.50 (ISBN 0-425-04467-X). Berkley Pub.
Iranian. Elizabeth Patton Moss. LC 52-14137. 1952. Muhlenberg Press.
Iran's Men of Destiny. Jamal Kashani. 1983. 12.50 (ISBN 0-533-05375-7). Vantage.
Iras: A Mystery. H. D. Everett. LC 3-3615. 1896. Harper & Brothers.
Ireland. Harriet Martineau. LC 79-11106. (Ireland, from the Act of Union, 1800, to the Death of Parnell, 1891; No. 45). 1979. 42.00 (ISBN 0-8240-3494-5). Garland Pub.
Irena. Kathryn Kilby Borland & Helen Ross Speicher. LC 78-68357. 1979. 7.95 (ISBN 0-385-12971-8). Doubleday.

Irena. Jane Land. LC 78-68357. (Romantic Suspense Ser.). 1979. 7.95 (ISBN 0-385-12971-8). Doubleday.

Irene. Albert De Routesie. Tr. by Lowell Bair. 1969. pap. 0.95 o.p. (ISBN 0-394-17404-6, B237, Bc). Grove.

Irene. Albert De Routisie. LC 75-84884. (Evergreen black cat book, B-237). 1970. 0.95. Grove Press.

Irene: A Novel. Ronald James Marsh. LC 49-859430. 1949. Houghton Mifflin Co.

Irene Iddesleigh. Edward Gorey. 1970. 3.95 o.p. (20396). S&S.

Irene Iddesleigh: A Novel. Amanda M'Kittrick Ros & Beer, Thomas. LC 27-21349. 1927. Boni & Liveright.

Irene Liscomb: A Story of the Old South. Mary Elizabeth Jordan Lamb. LC 9-286. Broadway Publishing Co.

Irene o el Tesoro see Historia de una Escalera.

Irene of Corinth: An Historic Romance of the First Century. P. J Harold. 1884. Index Publishing Company.

Irene of the Mountains: A Romance of Old Virginia. George Cary Eggleston. LC 9-13427. 1909. Lothrop, Lee & Shepard Co.

Irene of Tundra Towers. Elizabeth Burrows. LC 28-166176. 1928. Doubleday, Doran & Company, Inc.

Irene: Or, A Young Man's Folly. Annie A Gibbs. (On cover: American novelists' series, no. 53). 1890. J. W. Lovell Company.

Irene: Or, Beach-Broken Billows. Benjamin F Baer. LC 6-5019. (On cover: Authors' international prize series). 1875. Authors' Publishing Company.

Irene: Or, The Autobiography of an Artist's Daughter. And Other Tales. Gertrude Vingut & Fairfield, Genevieve Genevra, 1832- LC 8-32702. 1853. Damrell and Moore.

Irene, or: The Lonely Manor. Klara Bauer. (Lovell's library. v. 1 no. 29). 1882. J. W. Lovell Company.

Irene: Or, The Road to Freedom. A Novel. Sada Bailey Fowler. LC 11-7168. 1886. H. N. Fowler & Company.

Irene the Missionary. John William De Forest. LC 6-33389. 1879. Roberts Brothers.

Irene Viesca: A Tale of the Magee Expedition in the Gauchipin War in Texas, A. D. 1812-13. Hiram H McLane. LC 7-24375. 1886. San Antonio Printing Company, Printers.

Irene's Vow. Charlotte Mary Brame. LC 44-12249. (On cover: Seaside library. Pocket ed. No. 1031). G. Munro.

Iridescent Chain of Short Stories. Matilda Ackerman. 1970. 4.50 o.p. Vantage.

Iridion. Zygmunt Krasinski. LC 74-30841. 1975. (ISBN 0-8371-7937-8). Greenwood Press.

Irina: A Love Stronger Than Terror. Hermann Hartfield. LC 81-65724. 320p. 1981. pap. 6.95 (ISBN 0-915684-90-X). Christian Herald.

Iris in Winter. Elizabeth Cadell. LC 49-9859. 1949. W. Morrow.

Iris, the Bewitched. Katheryn Kimbrough, pseud. (Saga of the Phenwick Women: No. 39). 224p. 1982. pap. 2.50 (ISBN 0-445-04714-3). Popular Lib.

Irish. Doris F. Ladd. 640p. (Orig.). 1983. pap. 3.95 (ISBN 0-440-04845-1, Banbury). Dell.

Irish Beauties. Lily Moresby Adams Beck. LC 31-27211. 1931. Doubleday, Doran & Company, Inc.

Irish Captain. Patrick Joseph Gregory Kavanagh. LC 77-25599. 1979. 8.95 (ISBN 0-385-13684-6). Doubleday.

Irish Cousin. new and rev. ed. Edith Anna CEnone Somerville & Violet Florence Martin. LC 26-223036. 1903. Longmans, Green, and Co.

Irish Detective: Or, On His Track. Harlan Page Halsey. LC 7-1187. (On cover: The calumet series, no. 8). G. Munro.

Irish Dream. Margaret Bassett. LC 56-8088. 1956. Vantage Press.

Irish Emigrant. An Historical Tale Founded on Fact. Douglass, Adam, Supposed Author & An Hibernian, Pseud. LC 10-224896. 1817. J. T. Sharrocks.

Irish Faustus. Lawrence Durrell. 3.95 o.p. (ISBN 0-525-05511-8). Dutton.

Irish Fireside Tales. Robert Dwyer Joyce. 1871. P. Donahoe.

Irish Flats: A Ghost of San Antonio's Past. Marie Fitzhugh. LC 72-4250. 1972. 6.95 (ISBN 0-8111-0456-7). Naylor Co.

Irish Folk Stories & Fairy Tales. Ed. by William Butler Yeats. 1957. pap. 2.25 o.p. (ISBN 0-448-00021-0, UL). G&D.

Irish Folk Tales & Fairy Tales. Ed. by Sean Kelly. 364p. 1982. 13.95 (ISBN 0-8317-5001-4). Smith Pubs.

Irish Game: A Novel. J. R Lowell. LC 67-19948. 1967. Prentice-Hall.

Irish Ghost Stories. Ed. by Patrick Byrne. 1969. pap. 3.95 (ISBN 0-85342-037-8). Irish Bk Ctr.

Irish Ghost Stories. Ed. by Joseph Hone. 1978. 17.95 (ISBN 0-241-89680-0, Pub. by Hamish Hamilton England). David & Charles.

Irish Ghost Stories of LeFanu. Ed. by Patrick Byrne. 1973. pap. 3.95 (ISBN 0-85342-375-X). Irish Bk Ctr.

Irish Ghost Stories, 2nd Book. 1971. pap. 3.95 (ISBN 0-85342-264-8). Irish Bk Ctr.

Irish Gypsy. Virginia Henley. 304p. 1982. pap. 2.75 (ISBN 0-380-80598-7, 80598). Avon.

Irish Heirs. Samuel Lover. 1862. Dick & Fitzgerald.

Irish Idylls. Jane Barlow. LC 77-94703. (Short story index reprint series). 1969. Books for Libraries Press.

Irish Idylls. Jane Barlow. LC 6-72248. 1893. Dodd, Mead & Company.

Irish Idylls. Jane Barlow. LC 4-15276. 1897. Dodd, Mead, & Co.

Irish in Her. Peggy O'More, pseud. LC 42-18285. 1942. Gramercy Publishing Co.

Irish Lad and Other Stories: By J. C. Bendrodt. Foreword by Frank Clune. James Charles Bendrodt. LC 66-75256. 1966. bds., 4.75. Angus & Robertson.

Irish Legend; or, M'Donnell, and the Norman De Borgos: A Biographical Tale. By Archibald M'Sparran... Archibald McSparran. LC 7-16611. 1846. A. Gross.

Irish Lullaby. Frederick Hazlitt Brennan. LC 50-7105. 1950. Rinehart.

Irish Monte Cristo Abroad: Or, The Secrets of the Catacombs. Alexander Robertson. (sea and shore series, no. 13). 1889. Street & Smith.

Irish Monte Cristo: Or, The Treasure of the Lake. A Tale of Strage Adventure. John Sherman. (sea and more series, no. 1). 1888. Street & Smith.

Irish Monte Cristo's Search: Or, The Bonanza King in New York. Alexander Robertson. (sea and shore series, no. 11). 1889. Street & Smith.

Irish Monte Cristo's Trail: Or, Hunted from the Pyramids to Berlin. Alexander Robertson. (sea and shore series, no. 19). 1890. Street & Smith.

Irish Pastorals. Shan F Bullock. LC 1-25674. 1901. McClure, Phillips & Co.

Irish Patriot. Walter Fortescue. LC 98-23357. (Neeley's continental library. no. 14). F. T. Neeley.

Irish Short Stories. Seumas O'Kelly. 91p. 1969. pap. 3.95 (ISBN 0-85342-141-2). Irish Bk Ctr.

Irish Stories and Tales. Ed. by Devin A. Garrity. LC 56-59153. (Pocket library, PL 48). 1956. Pocket Books.

Irish Tales. William Carleton & Yeats, William Butler, 1865-1939. LC 43-27403. (Ariel booklets, 77). G. P. Putnam's Sons.

Irish Ways. Jane Barlow. LC 77-121521. (Short story index reprint series). (Illus.). 1970. Books for Libraries Press.

Irkutsk Story. Alexis Arbuzov. Ed. by Spencer Roberts. (Orig., Rus.,.). pap. 3.25x o.p. (388). Pitman.

Irlich, the Stalin Assassination: A Novel. Tom Costopoulos. LC 78-70359. (Illus.). 11.95 (ISBN 0-932634-00-1). NPC Pub. Co.

Irma: A Franco-Russian Story. Lawrence Gordon. LC 6-27484. (American series no. 256). M. J. Ivers & Co.

Irma & Jerry. George Selden. 1982. pap. 2.50 (ISBN 0-380-80978-8, 80978-8, Camelot). Avon.

Iroka: Tales of Japan. Kinnosuke' Adachi. 1900. Doubleday & McClure Co.

Iron and Smoke. Sheila Kaye-Smith. LC 28-25134. E. P. Dutton & Co.

Iron and the Anger. Francis G Rayer. LC 67-6689. 1967. Arcadia House.

Iron Arrow Head: Or, The Buckler Maiden, a Tale of the Northman Invasion. Eugene Sue & De Leon Daniel, 1852-1914, Tr. LC 9-10030. 1909. New York Labor News Company.

Iron Baby Angel: A Novel. 1st Ed. Charles R McDowell. LC 54-5455. 1954. Holt.

Iron Brigade: A Story of the Army of the Potomac. Charles King. G. W. Dillingham Company.

Iron Bronc. Harry Sinclair Drago. LC 44-7588. 1944. Jefferson House.

Iron Bronc: By Will Ermine Pseud. Harry Sinclair Drago. LC 53-5673. (Triple-A western classic.). 1953. Jefferson House.

Iron Burgess: The Government Detective. Harlan Page Halsey. (On cover: The calument series, no. 16). G. Munro.

Iron Butterflies. Andre Norton, pseud. (Orig.). 1980. pap. 2.25 (ISBN 0-449-24309-5, Crest). Fawcett.

Iron Cage. Andre Norton, pseud. 288p. 1981. pap. 2.25 (ISBN 0-441-37292-9). Ace Bks.

Iron Candlestick: By Dimiter Talev. Tr. by Marguerite Alexieva. Dimitur Talev. LC 66-230870. 1964. 3.00. Foreign Langs. Pr.

Iron Cayuse. Charles Stanley Strong. LC 45-1208. 1945. Phoenix Press.

Iron Chain. Edward Newhouse. LC 46-7725. 1946. Harcourt, Brace and Company.

Iron Chalice. Octavus Roy Cohen. LC 25-16898. 1925. 2.00. Little, Brown, and Company.

Iron City. Marion Hawthorne Hedges. LC 74-26114. (Labor Movement in Fiction and Non-Fiction). 1977. 21.50 (ISBN 0-404-58439-X). AMS Press.

Iron City. Marion Hawthorne Hedges. LC 19-15320. 1919. Boni and Liveright.

Iron City: A Novel. Lloyd Louis Brown. LC 51-4920. 1951. Masses & Mainstream.

Iron Clew. Phoebe Atwood Taylor. 1970. Repr. of 1947 ed. 4.95 o.p. (ISBN 0-393-08594-5). Norton.

Iron Clew: A Leonidas Witherall Mystery. Phoebe Atwood Taylor. LC 47-23767. 1947. Farrar, Straus.

Iron Cobweb. Ursula Reilly Curtiss. LC 52-141141. (Red badge detective). 1953. Dodd, Mead.

Iron Cobweb. Ursula Reilly Curtiss. (Kangaroo Book). 1977. 1.50 (ISBN 0-671-81066-9). Pocket Books.

Iron Collar: A Novel from the Days of the Counter Reformation. Translated by Andrew S. Berky. 1st English Ed. Fedor Sommer. LC 56-12562. 1956. Schwenkfelder Library.

Iron Collar: Or, Faustina and Syomara; a Tale of Slavery Under the Romans. Eugene Sue & De Leon, Daniel, 1852-1914, Tr. LC 9-12278. 1909. New York Labor News Company.

Iron Country: A Novel. Mary Patterson. LC 65-22213. 1966. Houghton Mifflin.

Iron Cousins. Cecily Ullmann Sidgwick. LC 20-1283. W. J. Watt & Company.

Iron Crown. Clare Barroll. LC 74-13376. (Illus.). 1975. 7.95 (ISBN 0-684-13951-0). Scribner.

Iron Crown: A Novel of the Vikings & Byzantium. Clare Barroll. 400p. 1975. 10.00 o.p. (ISBN 0-684-13951-0). Scribner.

Iron Crown: A Tale of the Great Republic... Thomas Stewart Denison. LC 6-339773. 1885. T. S. Denison.

Iron Doctor: A Story of Deep-Water Diving. Agnes Danforth Hewes. LC 40-30574. 1940. Houghton Mifflin Company.

Iron Dream. Norman Spinrad. LC 77-5016. (Gregg Press science fiction series). 1977. 13.00 (ISBN 0-8398-2361-4). Gregg Press.

Iron Facade. Catherine Cookson. LC 79-27604. 1980. 8.95 (ISBN 0-688-03624-4). Morrow.

Iron Facade. Catherine Marchant, pseud. 224p. 1981. pap. 2.50 (ISBN 0-440-14059-5). Dell.

Iron Facade. Catherine Marchant, pseud. LC 79-27604. 183p. 1980. 8.95 (ISBN 0-688-03624-4). Morrow.

Iron Flood. 3d ed. Aleksandr Serafimovich Popov. LC 72-90311. (Library of selected Soviet literature). (Illus.). 1973. (ISBN 0-88355-021-0). Hyperion Press.

Iron Flood. Aleksandr Serafimovich Popov. LC 36-17483. 1935. International Publishers.

Iron Flood. A. Serafimovich. 175p. 1974. 4.45 (ISBN 0-8285-1034-2, Pub. by Progress Pubs USSR). Imported Pubns.

Iron Furrow. George Clifford Shedd. LC 20-742225. 1920. Doubleday, Page & Company.

Iron Game: A Tale of War. Henry Francis Keenan. LC 7-12838. (On cover: Appletons' town and country library, no. 70). 1891. D. Appleton and Company.

Iron Garden. Simon Blumenfeld. LC 36-783. 1936. Doubleday, Doran & Company, Inc.

Iron Gates. Margaret Millar. 1974. (pbk.) 0.95 (ISBN 0-380-00015-6). Avon.

Iron Gates: A Psychological Novel. Margaret Millar. LC 45-2399. 1945. Random House.

Iron Hand. Lee Floren. 1970. pap. 0.60 o.p. (B60-2013). Belmont-Tower.

Iron Hand: A Story of the Times. Howard Dean. The Abbey Press.

Iron Hand: Or, Deldee, the Ward of Waringham. Florence Alice Price James. (On cover: Seaside library. Pocket ed., no. 286). 1884. G. Munro.

Iron Hand: Or, The Knight of Mauleon. Alexandre Dumas. LC 24-28546. T. B. Peterson & Brothers.

Iron Heel. Jack London. LC 7-3084. 1907. The Macmillan Company.

Iron Heel. Jack London. LC 8-6034. 1908. The Macmillan Company.

Iron Heel. Jack London. LC 24-22815. 1924. The Macmillan Company.

Iron Heel. Introd. by Max Lerner. Jack London. LC 57-12443. (American century series, S-28). 1957. Sagamore Press.

Iron Hoop. Constantine Fitz Gibbon. LC 49-10556. 1949. A. A. Knopf.

Iron Horse. Allen Ginsberg. LC 73-93941. 1974. pap. 3.00 (ISBN 0-87286-077-9). City Lights.

Iron Horse Country. Al Cody, pseud. (1974 ed. o.p.). 192p. 1976. pap. 1.25 (ISBN 0-532-12448-0). Woodhill.

Iron Horse Country. Al Cody. (Manor western). 1974. (pbk.) 0.95. Manor Books.

Iron Horse Gunsmoke. Donald B. Hobart. 1970. pap. 0.60 o.p. (0502-06069). Curtis.

Iron Horse: Novelized. Edwin Conger Hill & Kenyon, Charles, 1889- LC 24-28335. Grossett & Dunlap.

Iron Horse Town. Johnston McCulley. LC 52-12733. 1952. Arcadia House.

Iron Jehu. Ray Hogan. LC 76-10518. 1976. 5.95 (ISBN 0-385-12409-0). Doubleday.

Iron Jehu. Ray Hogan. (Signet Book). 1977. 1.50 (ISBN 0-451-07752-0). New American Library.

Iron King. Maurice Druon. 1956. 4.50 o.p. (ISBN 0-684-10133-5). Scribner.

Iron King: A Novel. Translated from the French by Humphrey Hare. Maurice Druch. LC 56-10197. 1956. Scribner.

Iron Lace. Lorena Dureau. (Tapestry Romance Ser.). (Orig.). 1983. pap. 2.50 (ISBN 0-671-46052-8). PB.

Iron Land. Dorothy Cleland Ogley. LC 46-5744. 1946. Doubleday & Company, Inc.

Iron Lion. Peter Dickinson. 1973. 3.50 o.p. (ISBN 0-04-823108-8). Allen Unwin.

Iron Lord. Samuel Rutherford Crockett. LC 8-274. Empire Book Company.

Iron Maiden. Carter Brown, pseud. (Signet book). 1975. (pbk.) 0.95. New American Library.

Iron Maiden. 1st Ed. Edwin Moultrie Lanham. LC 54-6387. 1954. Harcourt, Brace.

Iron Man. William Riley Burnett. LC 30-842. L. MacVeagh, The Dial Press.

Iron Man. Robert E. Howard. 7.00 (ISBN 0-937986-12-7). D M Grant.

Iron Man. Kay Thorpe. (Presents Ser.). 1975. pap. 1.25 (ISBN 0-373-70581-6, 70581, Pub by Harlequin). PB.

Iron Man and Gold. A. Leslie. LC 47-234442. 1946. Arcadia House, Inc.

Iron Marshal. Louis L'Amour. 1980. pap. 8.95 o.p. (ISBN 0-8161-3101-5, Large Print Bks). G K Hall.

Iron Marshall. Louis L'Amour. LC 79-23118. 1979. 12.95 (ISBN 0-8161-3015-9). G. K. Hall.

Iron Marshall. Louis L'Amour. 1.75 (ISBN 0-553-13065-X). Bantam Books Inc.

Iron Mask. Les Deux Merles De Monsieur De Saint-Mars). Fortune Du Boisgobey. Tr. by Caroline A. Merighi. (Seaside library. v. 91. no. 1842). G. Munro.

Iron Mask: Or, The Feats and Adventures of Raoul De Bragelonne. Being the Final Conclusion of "The Three Guardsmen": "Twenty Years After": and "Bragelonne, the Son of Athos". Alexandre Dumas & Maquet, Auguste. Tr. by Williams, Thomas. LC 6-42299. 1850. T. B. Peterson.

Iron Men. Peter McCurtin. (Sundance: No. 37). 192p. 1981. pap. 1.95 (ISBN 0-8439-0977-3, Leisure Bks). Nordon Pubns.

Iron Men & Silver Stars. Donald Hamilton. 192p. 1973. pap. 0.75 o.p. (T2701, GM). Fawcett World.

Iron Mistress. Paul Iselin Wellman. LC 51-11485. 1951. Doubleday.

Iron Mistress: Condensed and Simplified for Quick Reading by James L. Summers. Paul Iselin Wellman. LC 54-6845. (Hanover House headliners). 1954.

Iron Mother. Charles Maurice Braibant. LC 35-27028. 1935. Harper & Brothers.

Iron Mountain. Philip Duffield Stong. LC 42-213. Farrar & Rinehart, Inc.

Iron Mustang. Jake Logan. LC 78-54989. (Jake Logan Western Ser.). 176p. 1982. pap. 2.95 (ISBN 0-86721-102-4). Playboy Pbks.

Iron Noose. Michael Bonner. LC 61-8875. (Double D western). 1961. Doubleday.

Iron Noose. Anne Bonner Glasscock. LC 61-8875. (Double D western). 1961. Doubleday.

Iron Orchard. Edmund Van Zandt. LC 67-11210. 1966. McGraw-Hill.

Iron Pineers: Or, Mylio and Karvel, a Tale of the Albigensian Crusades. Eugene Sue & De Leon, Daniel, 1852-1914, Tr. LC 9-29775. 1909. New York Labor News Company.

Iron Pirate: A Plain Tale of Strange Happenings on the Sea. Max Pemberton. LC 7-36379. Rand, McNally & Company.

Iron Rainbow. Gordon Ray Young. LC 42-19559. 1942. Doubleday, Doran and Co., Inc.

Iron Roads. Forbes Bramble. LC 81-8725. 1981. 13.95 (ISBN 0-312-43638-6). St. Martin's Press.

Iron Rule: Or, Tyranny in the Household. Timothy Shay Arthur. LC 6-340524. T. B. Peterson.

Iron Sanctuary. Robert Macleod, pseud. (Rinehart Suspense Novel). 1968. 3.95 o.p. (ISBN 0-03-065575-7). HR&W.

Iron Sanctuary: By Robert MacLeod. 1st Ed. Bill. Knox. LC 68-10055. (Rinehart suspense novel). 1968. 3.95. Holt.

Iron Skillet Bill. Thomas Monroe Helm. LC 75-3642. 1975. 5.95 (ISBN 0-385-11060-X). Doubleday.

Iron Skull. Kenneth Robeson. (avenger#35). 1975. (pbk.) 0.95 (ISBN 0-446-75848-5). Warner Paperback Library.

Iron Spiders. Baynard Hardwick Kendrick. LC 36-7114. 1936. Greenberg.

Iron Stair: A Romance of Dartmoor. Eliza M. J. Humphreys. 1916. G. P. Putnam's Sons.

Iron Stair Case. Georges Simenon. LC 80-25624. (Harvest/HBJ book). 1981. 11.95 (ISBN 0-15-251699-9) (ISBN 0-15-251698-0). Harcourt Brace Jovanovich.
Iron Staircase. Georges Simenon. LC 77-73061. 1977. 7.95 (ISBN 0-15-145630-5). Harcourt Brace Jovanovich.
Iron Staircase. Georges Simenon. LC 67-90003. 1967. Penguin in Association with Hamish Hamilton.
Iron Stallions. Max Hennessy, pseud. LC 81-69132. (Illus.). 320p. 1982. 10.95 (ISBN 0-689-11245-9). Atheneum.
Iron Star. Eric Temple Bell. LC 75-10670. (Classics of science fiction). 1976. 12.95. (ISBN 0-88355-355-4) (ISBN 0-88355-463-1). Hyperion Press.
Iron Star. Eric Temple Bell. LC 30-4843. E. P. Dutton & Co., Inc.
Iron Star. John Taine, pseud. LC 75-10670. (Classics of Science Fiction Ser.). vii, 357p. 1976. 13.95 (ISBN 0-88355-355-4); pap. 4.95 (ISBN 0-88355-463-1). Hyperion Conn.
Iron Star: By John Taine Pseud. Eric Temple Bell. LC 51-13975. 1951. Fantasy Pub. Co.
Iron Swastika Plot. Joseph Rosenberger. (Death Merchant series#15). 1976. (pbk.) 1.25 (ISBN 0-523-00823-6). Pinnacle Books.
Iron Tiger. Jack Higgins, pseud. 1979. pap. 2.25 (ISBN 0-449-14225-6, GM). Fawcett.
Iron Tomb. Hendrik Conscience. LC 6-28063.
Iron Tomb: Or The Mock Count of New York. A Local Tale, Written in Scenes, with a Free Hand, Especially for the Readers of the 'Uncle Sam'... Charley Bowline. G. H. Williams.
Iron Trail. Rex Ellingwood Beach. 1977. pap. 2.25 (ISBN 0-89174-022-8). Comstock Edns.
Iron Trail. Max Brand. LC 38-3239. 1938. Dodd, Mead & Company.
Iron Trail. Frederick Faust. LC 38-3239. 1938. Dodd, Mead & Company.
Iron Trail. Frederick Faust. (Kangaroo Book). 1978. 1.50 (ISBN 0-671-81755-8). Pocket Books.
Iron Trail: An Alaskan Romance. Rex Ellingwood Beach. LC 65-278503. (Dolphin bks.). 1965. pap., 1.25. Doubleday.
Iron Trail: An Alaskan Romance. Rex Ellingwood Beach. LC 13-18006. 1913. Harper & Brothers.
Iron Trail to Stirrup. Lynn Westland. 1975. 4.95. Avalon Books.
Iron Trevet: Or, Jocelyn the Champion; a Tale of the Jacquerie. Sue, Eugene & De Leon, Daniel, 1852-1914, Tr. LC 6-23154. 1906. New York Labor News Company.
Iron Virgin: By James M. Fox Pseud. 1st Ed. James M. W. Knipscheer. LC 51-14224. 1951. Little, Brown.
Iron Way: A Tale of the Builders of the West. Sarah Pratt Carr. LC 7-12974. 1907. A. C. McClurg & Co.
Iron Widow. Harry Hervey. LC 31-36927. H. Liveright.
Iron Will. Margaret Culkin Banning. LC 36-736732. 1936. Harper & Brothers.
Iron Will. Charles Neville Buck. LC 27-19216. 1927. Doubleday. Page & Company.
Iron Woman. Margaret Wade Campbell Deland. LC 19-14358. 1911. A. L. Burt Company.
Iron Woman. Margaret Wade Campbell Deland. LC 11-35751. 1911. Harper & Brothers.
Irona: Or, Life on the Southwest Border. Edward Sylvester Ellis. LC 11-13614. 0.50. Hurst & Company.
Ironbrand. John Morressy. LC 80-80999. 320p. (Orig.). 1980. pap. 2.25 (ISBN 0-87216-689-9). Playboy Pbks.
Ironcastle. Philip Jose Farmer & J. H. Rosny. (Science Fiction Ser.). 1976. pap. 1.25 o.p. (UY1225). DAW Bks.
Ironcastle. J. H Rosny. (Daw Science Fiction#187). 1976. (pbk.) 1.25. Daw Books.
Ironclad Pledge: A Story of Christian Endeavor. Jessie Hunter Brown. LC 6-18940. 1890. Standard Publishing Company.
Ironclad Pledges, a Story of Christian Endeavor. Jessie Hunter Brown Pounds. LC 6-18940. 1890. Standard Publishing Company.
Ironhand. John L. Shelley. (Orig.). 1970. pap. 0.60 o.p. (63-398). Paperback Lib.
Ironheart. William MacLeod Raine. LC 23-9859. 1923. Houghton Mifflin Company.
Ironica: A Romance of the Rockies. Mary Kroh Colvin. LC 12-323. 1911. 1.50. H. Lechner.
Ironies. Richard Edward Connell. LC 30-22757. 1930. Minton, Balch & Company.
Ironmaster. Anne Powers, pseud. LC 51-9841. 1951. Bobbs-Merrill.
Ironmaster of Crimson Furnace: A Historical Novel. 1st Ed. Clifford T Stafford. LC 53-67196. 1953. Exposition Press.
Ironmaster: Or, Love and Pride. Georges Ohnet. LC 4-1688. 1890. Rand, McNally & Company.
Ironmaster: Or, Love and Pride (Le Maitre De Forges. Georges Ohnet. LC 16-17186. 1916. Rand, McNally & Company.
Ironwood. Jennie Melville, pseud. LC 72-81686. 1972. 4.95. McKay.
Ironwood: A Novel. Jennie Melville, pseud. (Crest Book, M1882). 1973. (pbk.) 0.95. Fawcett.
Irralie's Bushranger: A Story of Australian Adventure. Ernest William Hornung. 1896. C. Scribner's Sons.
Irrational Knot. George Bernard Shaw. LC 5-32700. 1905. Brentano's.
Irrational Numbers. George Alec Effinger. LC 75-14818. (Doubleday science fiction.). 1976. 5.95 (ISBN 0-385-11189-4). Doubleday.
Irreconcilable Differences. Carol J. Bangs. 1979. pap. 3.00 (ISBN 0-917652-18-5). Confluence Pr.
Irregardless: Or, Seminal Official Lifestyle Control Manual. U S Weiter. LC 70-146202. 1971. 1.50. April Dawn Pub. Co.
Irregulars Strike Again. August William Derleth. LC 64-12443. 5.95 (ISBN 0-88361-056-6). Stanton & Lee.
Irregulars Strike Again. August William Derleth. 1964. 3.50 o.p. (ISBN 0-696-66494-1). Hawthorn.
Irregulars Strike Again. August William Derleth. 4.95 o.s.i. (ISBN 0-88451-033-6). Edco-Vis Assoc.
Irrelevant Saint: By Reuben L I.E. H. Lewis. Reuben H. Lewis. LC 66-28739. 1966. bds., 5.95. Morrow.
Irresistible Buck. Barbara Cartland. 1975. pap. 1.25 o.p. (ISBN 0-515-03829-6, V3829). BJ Pub Group.
Irresistible Current. I Lowenberg. Broadway Publishing Co.
Irresistible Intruder. William Caine. LC 14-2276. 1914. 1.25. John Lane.
Irresistible Mrs. Ferrers. Arabella Kenealy. LC 12-25070. 1.25. G. W. Dillingham Company.
Irresistible Tramp. Selma Bell. 192p. (Orig.). 1974. pap. 1.95 o.p. (ISBN 0-87682-380-0, 7380). Barclay Hse.
Irresistible Tramp. Selma Bell. 1973. (pbk.) 1.95 (ISBN 0-87682-380-0). Barclay House.
Irresponsible. Henry Leyford Gates. LC 38-19070. 1938. Godwin.
Irrestible Force. Barbara Cartland. LC 78-13320. 1978. 6.95 (ISBN 0-87272-046-2, Duron Bks). Brodart.
Irsud. Jo Clayton. (Science Fiction Ser.). (Orig.). 1981. pap. 2.50 (ISBN 0-87997-839-2, UE 1839). DAW Bks.
Irsud. Jo Clayton. (Science Fiction Ser.). (Orig.). 1978. pap. 1.75 o.p. (ISBN 0-87997-403-6, UE1403). DAW Bks.
Irving Solution. Leonard Simon. LC 76-39719. 7.95 (ISBN 0-87795-158-6). Arbor House.
Irving Solution. Leonard Simon. 1978. 1.75 (ISBN 0-380-01928-0). Avon.
Irving Stone, Three Complete Novels. 1981 ed. Irving Stone. LC 81-15068. 6.98 (ISBN 0-517-35061-0). Avenel Books: Distributed by Crown Publishers.
Irving Tales; Being Good Short Stories, Original and Selected. LC 15-231120. (On cover: The Irving library. vol. ii, no. 126). 1885. J. B. Alden.
Irving's Delight. art buchwald; illustrations by reynolds ruffins. ed. Art Buchwald. (Illus.). 1.50 (ISBN 0-380-00678-2). Avon Books.
Irving's Delight: At Last! A Cat Story for the Whole Family! Art Buchwald. LC 75-16236. (Illus.). 1975. 6.95 (ISBN 0-679-50569-5). D. McKay.
Irwin Shaw Short Stories: Five Decades. Irwin Shaw. (gr. 7-12). 1983. pap. 6.95 (ISBN 0-440-34075-6, LE). Dell.
Is a Ship Burning? Richard Sale. LC 38-302298. 1938. Dodd, Mead & Company.
Is Anybody Driving. George E. Vandeman. LC 75-11469. (Stories That Win Ser.). 1975. pap. 0.95 o.p. (ISBN 0-8163-0175-1, 12523-7). Pacific Pr Pub Assn.
Is Anything All Right. Percy Seitlin. LC 69-16541. 1969. 4.95 o.p. (ISBN 0-670-40186-2). Grossman.
Is He Popenjoy! Anthony Trollope. LC 45-35010. (Half-title: The World's classics, CDXCII-CDXCIII). 1944. H. Milford, Oxford University Press.
Is He Popenjoy? A Novel. Anthony Trollope. (Franklin square library. no. 1). Harper & Brothers.
Is It Legal to Barbecue an Eagle? Max Noble Mack. LC 74-77516. (Illus.). 1974. (ISBN 0-914892-00-2). Noble Prentiss Pub. Co.
Is It Really in Your Head? Albert Michael Barrett. LC 63-18654. 1963. Dorrance.
Is It the Sun, Philibert? Roch Carrier. Tr. by Sheila Fischman from Fr. LC 75-190705. (Anansi Fiction Ser.: No. 20). 100p. 1972. pap. 4.95 (ISBN 0-88784-321-2, Pub. by Hse Anansi Pr Canada). U of Toronto Pr.
Is Love a Curse? Franchette Romaine. LC 54-9138. 1954. Vantage Press.
Is Marriage a Failure? A Novel... Hana Jean. LC 7-10187. 1898. American Book Publishing Co.
Is Marriage a Lottery? 16547. Evelyn Adams. 1891. E. Adams.
Is My Flesh of Brass. Pincus Jacob Wolfson. LC 34-18187. 1934. The Vanguard Press.
Is No One Innocent? Milton Herbert Gropper & Sherry, Edna. LC 30-211713. 1930. Cosmopolitan Book Corporation.
Is She Not a Woman? Or, Vengeance Is Mine. Ernest S. Hanson. (On cover: Cassell's Union square library, no. 2). 1895. The Cassell Publishing Co.
Is Skin-Deep, Is Fatal. Henry Reymond Fitzwalter Keating. (Signet bk., P3074). 1967. New Amer. Lib.
Is Skin-Deep, Is Fatal. Henry Reymond Fitzwalter Keating. LC 65-24119. 1965. Dutton.
Is That All! Harriet Waters Preston. LC 7-30941. (No name series). 1876. Roberts Brothers.
Is That All There Is? E. May Acton. 1977. pap. 2.00 (ISBN 0-89502-017-3). FEB.
Is That You Out There? Tony Clark & Doug Bock. LC 72-93650. 1973. pap. text ed. 9.95 o.p. (ISBN 0-675-09020-2). Merrill.
Is That Your Best Offer? Arnold Malcolm Auerbach. LC 71-160865. 1971. 6.95. Doubleday.
Is the Devil a Gentleman? The Best Fiction of Seabury Quinn. Seabury Quinn. LC 75-94775. (Voyager series). (Illus.). 1970. 5.95. Mirage.
Is the United States Ready for Self-Government? A Novel. Robert Saffron. LC 65-25699. 1965. Trident Press.
Is There a Doctor in the Zoo? David Taylor. 1979. pap. 2.50 (ISBN 0-553-13891-X). Bantam.
Is There a Hole in Your Head? Written, Illus. by Neil Applebaum. Neil Applebaum. LC 63-12382. (Astor bk). 1963. 2.50. Obolensky.
Is There Life After Advertising? Donald Gilmore Calhoun. LC 73-91860. 1974. 6.95 (ISBN 0-8128-1695-1). Stein and Day.
Is There Sex After Death. Alan Abel & Jeanne Abel. (Illus.). 1976. (pbk.) 1.95. Bantam Books.
Is This Coffin Taken? Jean F. Webb. (Mystery Puzzler Ser.: No. 4). (Illus., Orig.). 1978. pap. 1.95 (ISBN 0-89083-398-2). Zebra.
Is This Naomi & Other Stories: A Cycle of Rural Life. L. D. Clark. (Fiction Ser.). (Illus., Orig.). 1980. pap. 4.95 (ISBN 0-933188-11-0). Blue Moon Pr.
Is This the End? William Ross Elliott. LC 45-71969. 1945. Southwestern Publishers.
Is This True? Louise Battles Cooper. (On cover: An antithesis to the Kreutzer someta). 1893. The Author.
Is This Your Son, My Lord? A Novel. Helen Hamilton Chenoweth Gardener. LC 7-1521. 1890. Arena Publishing Company.
Isa: A Pilgrimage. Chesebro', Caroline. LC 6-249153. 1852. Redfield.
Isaac Asimov Presents the Best Horror and Supernatural of the 19th Century. Isaac Asimov & Charles Waugh. LC 82-20794. 16.95 (ISBN 0-8253-0128-9). Beaufort Books.
Isaac Asimov Presents the Best Science Fiction of the 19th Century. Isaac Asimov & Charles Waugh. LC 80-27721. 12.95 (ISBN 0-8253-0038-X). Beaufort Books.
Isaac Asimov Presents the Great Science Fiction Stories. Ed. by Isaac Asimov & Greenberg, Martin H. 1979. 2.25 (ISBN 0-87997-454-0). DAW Books.
Isaac Asimov Presents the Great SF Stories, No. 1. Ed. by Isaac Asimov & Martin H. Greenberg. (Science Fiction Ser.). 1979. pap. 2.95 (ISBN 0-87997-700-0, UE1700). DAW Bks.
Isaac Asimov Presents the Great SF Stories, No. 2. Ed. by Isaac Asimov & Martin H. Greenberg. (Daw Science Fiction Ser.). (Orig.). 1979. pap. 2.25 (ISBN 0-87997-483-4, UE1483). Daw Bks.
Isaac Asimov Presents the Great SF Stories, No. 3. Ed. by Isaac Asimov & Martin H. Greenberg. 1980. pap. 2.25 o.p. (ISBN 0-87997-523-7, UE1523). Daw Bks.
Isaac Asimov Presents the Great SF Stories, No. 5. Ed. by Isaac Asimov & Martin H. Greenberg. 1981. pap. 2.75 (ISBN 0-87997-604-7, UE1604). Daw Bks.
Isaac Asimov Presents the Great SF Stories, No. 6. Ed. by Isaac Asimov & Martin H. Greenberg. (Science Fiction Ser.). 1981. pap. 2.95 (ISBN 0-87997-670-5, U E 1670). DAW Bks.
Isaac Asimov Presents the Great SF Stories, No. 7. Ed. by Isaac Asimov & Martin H. Greenberg. 368p. 1982. pap. 3.50 (ISBN 0-87997-746-9, UE1746). DAW Bks.
Isaac Asimov Presents the Great SF Stories, No. 8. Ed. by Isaac Asimov & Martin H. Greenberg. 1982. pap. 3.50 (ISBN 0-87997-780-9, UE1780). DAW Bks.
Isaac Asimov's Adventures of Science Fiction. George H. Scithers. LC 80-131220. 9.95 (ISBN 0-8037-3533-2). Dial Press: Davis Publications.
Isaac Asimov's Aliens & Outworlders. Ed. by Shawna McCarthy. 288p. 1983. 12.95 (ISBN 0-385-27912-4). Davis Pubns.
Isaac Asimov's Marvels of Science Fiction. Ed. by George H. Scithers. 1979. 9.95 o.s.i. (ISBN 0-8037-3773-4). Davis Pubns.
Isaac Asimov's Masters of Science Fiction. George H. Scithers. LC 78-60795. (Illus.). 8.95 (ISBN 0-8037-3697-5). Davis Publications.
Isaac Asimov's Near Futures & Far. Ed. by George H. Scithers. 288p. 1981. 10.95 (ISBN 0-385-27205-7). Davis Pubns.
Isaac Asimov's Wonders of the World. Kathleen Moloney & Shawna McCarthy. LC 82-227983. (Illus.). 12.95 (ISBN 0-385-27776-8). Dial Press.
Isaac Bashevis Singer Reader. Isaac Bashevis Singer. LC 79-164543. 1971. 10.95 (ISBN 0-374-17747-3). Farrar, Straus and Giroux.
Isaac Bashevis Singer, Three Complete Novels. Isaac Bashevis Singer. LC 82-11346. 1982. 6.98. Avenel Books.
Isaac Cheek: The 'Man of Wax.' Douglas William Jerrold. LC 7-12788. (On cover: Men of characters). 1851. Bunce & Brother.
Isaac Draque, the Buckeye. Thomas Mathew. LC 13-17734. (On cover: Franklin series v. 5, no. 3). 1898. W. B. Conkey Company.
Isabel. Gerald Gould. LC 32-169630. 1932. Brewer, Warren & Putnam, Inc.
Isabel Graham: Or, Charity's Reward. by henry william herbert... ed. Henry William Herbert. LC 7-4289. 1848. Williams Brothers.
Isabel Rawsthorne Standing in a Street in Soho. Alexandra Grilikhes. 72p. 1972. 6.00x (ISBN 0-913152-08-0); pap. 3.25x (ISBN 0-913152-07-2). Folder Edns.
Isabel Stirling. Evelyn Schuyler Schaeffer. LC 20-17965. 1920. C. Scribner's Sons.
Isabel the Fair. Margaret Campbell Barnes. (Signet Books, Y5386). 1973. 1.25. New American Library.
Isabel the Fair. Margaret Campbell Barnes. LC 57-12007. 1957. Macrae Smith.
Isabella Gray. A Novel. LC 7-947952. 1858. C. Desilver.
Isabella Stockton: A Tale of the French and Indian War. Willis Fryatt Evans. LC 30-8234. The Christopher Publishing House.
Isabelle. Jean Freustie. LC 73-153839. 1972. 2.50 (ISBN 0-491-00622-5). W. H. Allen.
Isabelle: Or, The Emigrant's Daughter. A Tale of Boston and the West. By Osgood Bradbury, Esq. Also, The Rescued Maiden. Osgood Bradbury & Nelson, S. LC 6-15206. 1848. F. Gleason.
Isabelle: Roman. Andre Paul Guillaume Gide. (Fr). 1960. pap. 3.95. French & Eur.
Isabelle, the Frantic. Katheryn Kimbrough, pseud. (Kathryn Kimbrough's Saga of the Phenwick Women). 1978. 1.75 (ISBN 0-445-04238-9). Popular Library.
Isabelle. Translated from the French by David Hughes. Jean Forton. LC 60-6259. half cloth, 3.95. Criterion Books.
Isadore Merton, or, The Reverses of Fortune. A Story of Real Life. Frank Mauren. LC 24-25015. 1847. F. Gleason, at the Flag of Our Union Office.
Isadra. Willis Steell. LC 13-17735. (Neely's library of choice literature. no. 73). 1897. F. T. Neely.
Iscariot. Walter Farnham. LC 28-10791. The Christopher Publishing House.
Ish-Noo-Ju-Lut-Sche, or, the Eagle of the Mohawks, 2 Vols. facs. ed. John Linnaeus Edward Whitridge Shecut. LC 78-137731. (American Fiction Reprint Ser.). 1841. Set. 33.00 (ISBN 0-8369-7030-6). Ayer Co.
Ish-Noo-Ju-Lut-Sche: Or, The Eagle of the Mohawks, a Tale of the Seventeenth Century. John Linnaeus Edward Whitridge Shecut. LC 78-137731. (American fiction reprint series). 1970. Books for Libraries Press.
Ish-Noo-Ju-Lut-Sche: Or, The Eagle of the Mohawks. A Tale of the Seventeenth Century... John Linnaeus Edward Whitridge Shecut. LC 8-5088. 1841. P. Price.
Ish River. Robert Sund. LC 82-73721. 80p. (Orig.). 1983. pap. 7.50 (ISBN 0-86547-102-9). N Point Pr.
Isha, the Magic Doll. Tina Jordan. 3.50 o.p. Vantage.
Isha the Magic Doll & Other Stories. 1981. 2.25 (ISBN 0-938574-04-3). Cherubim.
Ishmael. A Novel. Mary Elizabeth Braddon Maxwell. (Harper's Franklin square library, no. 467). 1885. Harper & Brothers.
Ishmael, a Self-Portrait. Christopher Davis. LC 75-86909. 1969. 5.95. Harper & Row.
Ishmael: Or, In the Depths. Emma Dorothy Eliza Nevitte Southworth. LC 33-7773. (Lettered on cover: The home library). A. L. Burt Company.
Ishmael: Or, In the Depths. Emma Dorothy Eliza Nevitte Southworth. LC 4-19034. 1904. R. F. Fenno & Company.
Ishmaelite. Mary Elizabeth Braddon Maxwell. (On cover: Seaside library. Pocket ed. no. 263). 1884. G. Munro.
Ishmaelite: A Novel. Mary Elizabeth Braddon Maxwell. (On cover: Lovell's library. no. 444). 1884. J. W. Lovell Company.

Ishmael's White World: A Phenomenological Reading of Moby Dick. Paul Brodtkorb. LC 65-11176. (Yale Publications in American Studies, 9). 1965. Yale University Press.
Isidra: A Novel. Willis Steell. LC 8-16316. 1883. Ticknor and Company.
Isidro. Mary Hunter Austin. LC 79-104408. (Illus.). 1970. Literature House.
Isidro. Mary Hunter Austin. LC 5-10051. 1905. Houghton, Mifflin and Company.
Iskandarnamah: A Persian Medieval Alexander-Romance. Tr. by Minoo S. Southgate. LC 77-27047. 1978. 22.50x (ISBN 0-231-04416-X). Columbia U Pr.
Iskander: A Romance of the Court of Philip of Macedon and Alexander the Great. Marshall Monroe Kirkman. LC 3-14987. 1903. The World Railway Publishing Company.
Isla De Pasiones. new ed. Evelio Rojas. (Pimienta Collection Ser). (Illus.). 160p. (Span.). 1975. pap. 1.25 (ISBN 0-88473-242-8). Fiesta Pub.
Island. Peter Benchley. LC 78-19658. 1979. 8.95 (ISBN 0-385-13172-0). Doubleday.
Island. Robert Creeley. 192p. 1980. pap. 6.95 (ISBN 0-7145-0305-3, Pub. by M Boyars). Merrimack Pub Cir.
Island. Robert Creeley. (Orig.). 1963. pap. 2.45 First Editions o.p. (ISBN 0-684-71739-5, SL177). Scribner.
Island. Aldous Leonard Huxley. LC 77-359300. 1976. 0.75 (ISBN 0-586-04439-6). Triad/Panther.
Island. Robert Merle. LC 64-7561. 1964. St. Martin's Press.
Island. Mildred Nelson. 1973. (pbk.) 0.95. Pocket Books.
Island. Bertha Runkle. LC 21-16432. 1921. 1.75. The Century Co.
Island. Claire Spencer. LC 35-272020. 1935. H. Smith and R. Haas.
Island: A Love Story. Naomi Gwladys Royde-Smith. 1930. Harper & Brothers.
Island: A Novel. Aldous Leonard Huxley. 1973. (lib. ed.) 6.48. Harper.
Island: A Novel. Aldous Leonard Huxley. LC 62-7923. 1962. Harper.
Island: A Novel. Nard Jones. LC 48-9337. 1948. W. Sloane.
Island Affair. Hettie Grimstead. (Fawcett gold medal). 1975. (pbk.) 0.95. Fawcett.
Island at the End of the World. Translated from the French by Lowell Bair. Henri Crouzat. (Berkley Medallion G437). 1960. Berkley Pub. Corp.
Island at the Top of the World. Ian Cameron, pseud. 1974. (pbk.) 1.25 (ISBN 0-380-00151-9). Avon.
Island Autumn. Cathryn Ladd. (Adventures in Love Ser.: No. 30). 1982. pap. 1.75 (ISBN 0-451-11747-6, AE1747, Sig). NAL.
Island Between. Margaret E Murie. LC 76-62991. (Illus.). 1977. 9.95 (ISBN 0-912006-04-8). University of Alaska Press.
Island Born. Sterner St. Paul Meek. LC 37-5982. 1937. Godwin.
Island by the Keys. Ethel Lockwood. 1973. pap. 0.75 o.s.i. (01-382). Lancer.
Island Cabin. Arthur Henry. 1902. McClure, Phillips & Co.
Island Cabin. Arthur Henry. LC 4-11537. 1904. A. S. Barnes & Company.
Island Called Moreau. Brian Wilson Aldiss. 1981. pap. 2.25 (Timescape). PB.
Island Called Moreau. Brian Wilson Aldiss. 1981. 12.95 o.s.i. (ISBN 0-671-25453-7). S&S.
Island Called Moreau: A Novel. Brian Wilson Aldiss. LC 80-24124. 10.95 (ISBN 0-671-25453-7). Simon and Schuster.
Island Chronicle. William G Cummings. LC 24-108419. 1924. A. A. Knopf.
Island Conquest. Brooke Hastings. 192p. 1981. pap. 1.50 (ISBN 0-671-57067-6). S&S.
Island Cure. Grace Blanchard. LC 22-6525. 1922. Lothrop, Lee & Shepard Co.
Island Death. Sol Yurick. LC 74-15898. 1975. 6.95 (ISBN 0-06-014784-9). Harper & Row.
Island Ecstasy. Karen Harper. (Orig.). 1982. pap. 3.50 (ISBN 0-89083-964-6). Zebra.
Island Farm. Hildegarde Hawthorne. LC 26-151371. 1926. D. Appleton and Company.
Island Fiesta. Jane Corrie. (Harlequin Romances Ser.). 192p. (Orig.). 1981. pap. 1.25 (ISBN 0-373-02384-7). Harlequin Bks.
Island Flame. Karen Robards. 352p. (Orig.). 1982. pap. 3.25 (ISBN 0-8439-1511-0, Leisure Bks). Nordon Pubns.
Island Flower. Vivien Grey. LC 40-33104. 1940. Arcadia House, Inc.
Island for Dreams. Katrina Britt. (Harlequin Romances Ser.). 192p. 1980. pap. 1.25 (ISBN 0-373-02371-5). Harlequin Bks.
Island for Two. Ludek Pesek. LC 75-11116. 1975. 6.95 (ISBN 0-87888-088-7). Bradbury Press.
Island God: A Tale of the Kamehameha. Gurdon S Mumford. LC 7-33321. 1897. Printed for the Author.
Island God Forgot. Charles B Stilson & Beahan, Charles, Joint Author. LC 22-16743. 1922. H. Holt and Company.
Island Gold. Valentine Williams. LC 23-6837. 1923. Houghton Mifflin Company.
Island Heirs. Jeanne Judson. LC 58-9131. 1958. Avalon Books.
Island in Harlem: A Novel. Manuel Manrique. LC 65-207279. 1966. 4.50. John Day.
Island in the Air: A Story of Singular Adventures in the Mesa Country. Ernest Ingersoll. LC 5-32682. 1905. The Macmillan Company.
Island in the Atlantic. Waldo David Frank. LC 46-6710. 1946. Duell, Sloan and Pearce.
Island in the Atlantic: A Novel. Waldo David Frank. LC 73-104243. 1970. Greenwood Press.
Island in the Atlantic, a Novel. Waldo David Frank. Repr. of 1946 ed. lib. bdg. 19.75x (ISBN 0-8371-3925-2, FRIA). Greenwood.
Island in the Corn. John Selby. LC 41-12279. Farrar & Rinehart, Inc.
Island in the Sky. Ernest Kellogg Gann. LC 44-6034. 1944. The Viking Press.
Island in the Sky. Manly Wade Wellman. Avalon Books.
Island in the Square: A Novel. William Edward Burghardt Du Bois. LC 47-66773. 1947. Farrar, Straus.
Island in the Sun: A Story of the 1950's Set in the West Indies. Alec Waugh. LC 56-5065. 1955. Farrar, Straus and Cudahy.
Island in the Wind. Noel Bertram Gerson. LC 79-150897. 1972. Popular Library.
Island in the Wind: A Novel. Noel Bertram Gerson. LC 79-150897. 1971. 6.95. Doubleday.
Island-in-Waiting. Anthea Fraser. LC 78-21202. 1979. 8.95 (ISBN 0-312-43741-2). St. Martin's Press.
Island Interlude. Jane Edwards. (Candlelight Mystery). 1973. (pbk.) 0.75. Dell.
Island Light. 1st Ed. Alexander Key. LC 50-5853. 1950. Bobbs-Merrill.
Island-Lovers. Ruth Lyons. LC 69-10964. 1969. 4.95. Doubleday.
Island Lovesong. large print ed. Louise Bergstrom. LC 81-5338. 9.95. Thorndike Press.
Island Loving. Jan MacLean. (Harlequin Presents Ser.). 192p. 1982. pap. 1.75 (ISBN 0-373-10529-0). Harlequin Bks.
Island Magic. Elizabeth Goudge. LC 36-27091. 1936. Coward-McCann, Inc.
Island Magic. Anne Lynch. (Orig.). 1979. pap. 1.95 (ISBN 0-532-23171-6). Woodhill.
Island-Maker. Roy Marz. LC 82-17282. 100p. (Orig.). 1982. pap. 6.00 (ISBN 0-87886-120-3). Ithaca Hse.
Island Mystery. James Owen Hannay. LC 18-180001. George H. Doran Company.
Island Neighbor. Anne Tedlock Brooks. LC 56-124601. 1956. Arcadia House.
Island Neighbors. A Novel of American Life. Antionette Louisa Brown Blackwell. LC 3-26206. 1871. Harper & Brothers.
Island Nights' Entertainments. Robert Louis Stevenson. LC 74-31328. (Pacific classics, 6). (Illus.). 1975. 3.95 (ISBN 0-8248-0286-1). University Press of Hawaii.
Island Nights' Entertainments... Robert Louis Stevenson. LC 78-131841. (Illus.). 1970. Scholarly Press.
Island Nights' Entertainments. Robert Louis Stevenson. LC 8-15702. 1893. C. Scribner's Sons.
Island Nights' Entertainments. Robert Louis Stevenson. LC 5-20451. (Half-title: The biographical edition of the works of Robert Louis Stevenson). 1905. C. Scribner's Sons.
Island Nights' Entertainments. Robert Louis Stevenson. LC 20-12369. (Half-title: The biographical edition of the works of Robert Louis Stevenson). 1917. C. Scribner's Sons.
Island Nights' Entertainments. Robert Louis Stevenson. LC 24-20491. (Half-title: The biographical edition of the works of Robert Louis Stevenson). 1921. C. Scribner's Sons.
Island Noon. Mabel Louise Robinson. LC 42-7964. 1942. Random House.
Island of Allure: A Romance of the South Seas. Jackson Gregory. LC 34-20788. 1934. Dodd, Mead & Company.
Island of Apples: A Novel. Glyn Jones. LC 65-137443. bds., 4.50. Day.
Island of Apples: A Novel. Glyn Jones. LC 65-13744. 1965. John Day Co.
Island of Beautiful Things: A Romance of the South. William Allen Dromgoole. LC 12-22588. 1912. L. C. Page & Company.
Island of Bitter Memories. Dorothy Daniels. 1974. (pbk.) 0.95. Warner Paperback Lib.
Island of Captain Sparrow. Sydney Fowler Wright. LC 28-178179. 1928. Cosmopolitan Book Corporation.
Island of Desire. Helen Murray. (Orig.). 1981. pap. 1.75 (ISBN 0-8439-8032-X, Tiara Bks). Nordon Pubns.
Island of Destiny. Arthur John Rees. LC 23-128759. 1923. Dodd, Mead and Company.
Island of Doctor Death and Other Stories. Gene Wolfe. 2.95 (ISBN 0-671-82824-X). Pocket Books.
Island of Doctor Moreau. Herbert George Wells. LC 33-45055. Duffield and Green.
Island of Doctor Moreau. Herbert George Wells. LC 80-110. 1981. 10.00 (ISBN 0-8376-0431-1). R. Bentley.
Island of Dr. Moreau. Herbert George Wells. (Magnum Easy Eye Classic Ser). 1968. pap. 0.60 o.p. (13-435). Lancer.
Island of Doctor Moreau: A Possibility. Herbert George Wells. LC 8-36644. 1896. Stone & Kimball.
Island of Dr. Moreau: Novelization. Joseph Silva. (Illus.). 1977. 1.95 (ISBN 0-441-37421-2). Ace Books.
Island of Eden. Leona Morrison. LC 76-41021. 1977. 8.95 (ISBN 0-688-03151-X). Morrow.
Island of Eleadar: A Pilgrimage to Novel-Land. Icarus De Plume. LC 21-5272. Marshall Jones Company.
Island of Enchantment: By Justus Miles Forman; Illustrated by Howard Pyle. Justus Miles Forman. LC 5-32396. 1905. Harper & Brothers.
Island of Evil. Caroline Farr. (Signet book). 1979. 1.50 (ISBN 0-451-08476-4). New American Library.
Island of Faith. Margaret Elizabeth Sangster. LC 21-12085. Fleming H. Revell Company.
Island of Fantasy: A Romance. Fergus Hume. LC 7-5841. Lovell, Coryell & Company.
Island of Fear. Hulbert Footner. LC 36-14924. 1936. Harper & Brothers.
Island of Fear. Katherine Ursula Parrott. LC 43-14783. 1943. Dodd, Mead & Company.
Island of Flowers. Denise Robins. LC 76-55920. 1977. 1.25 (ISBN 0-380-00891-2). Avon Books.
Island of Fu Manchu. Sax Rohmer, pseud. 1971. pap. 0.60 o.p. (X2481). Pyramid Pubns.
Island of Fu Manchu. Sax Rohmer, pseud. 1976. pap. 1.25 o.p. (ISBN 0-515-04055-X). BJ Pub Group.
Island of Fu Manchu. Arthur Sarsfield Ward. LC 41-243929. 1941. Pub. for the Crime Club by Doubleday, Doran and Co., Inc.
Island of Fu Manchu... Arthur Sarsfield Ward. LC 42-25557. 1942. The Sun Dial Press.
Island of Gold. Bruce Crowther. LC 78-62355. 1978. 7.95. Walker.
Island of Green Myrtles. Shirley Watkins. LC 37-2176. Macrae Smith Company.
Island of Intrigue. Isabel Egenton Ostrander. LC 18-21824. 1918. R. M. McBride & Co.
Island of Life: An Allegory. Frederic Gardiner. LC 7-9384. 1851. J. Munroe & Company.
Island of Life: An Allegory. ... new ed. Frederic Gardiner. LC 7-9385. 1853. J. Munroe & Company.
Island of Lost Women. Henry De Vere Stacpoole. LC 30-166111. Sears Publishing Company, Inc.
Island of Love. Julia Alcott. (Signet Book). 1977. 1.25 (ISBN 0-451-07369-X). New American Library.
Island of Mystery. Arlene Hale. LC 77-24161. 7.95 (ISBN 0-316-33853-2). Little, Brown.
Island of Mystery. Arlene Hale. LC 77-27943. 1978. 10.95 (ISBN 0-8161-6552-1). G. K. Hall.
Island of Not-Me: A True Chronicle of the Life of Geoghan Willbe on the Island of Not-Me, Preceded by an Account of His Person Before His Arrival Upon That Famous Isle. Ezra Gerson Gotthelf. LC 36-8550. 1935. The Galleon Press.
Island of Regeneration: A Story of What Ought to Be. Cyrus Townsend Brady. LC 9-27083. 1909. Dodd, Mead and Company.
Island of Regeneration: A Story of What Ought to Be. Cyrus Townsend Brady. LC 17-31655. 1910. A. L. Burt Company.
Island of Salvation. Wiodzimierz Odojewski. LC 65-14712. 1965. Harcourt, Brace & World.
Island of Shadows. Elisabeth Beresford. 1979. pap. text ed. 1.50 o.s.i. (ISBN 0-89559-153-7). Dale Books Inc.
Island of Sheep. Cadmus & Harmonia. LC 20-7649. 1920. 1.50. Houghton Mifflin Company.
Island of Silence. rev. ed. Carolyn B. Norris. (Illus.). 1978. 5.95x o.p. (ISBN 0-933076-00-2); pap. 2.50x o. p. o.p. (ISBN 0-933076-01-0). Alinda Pr.
Island of Surprise. Cyrus Townsend Brady. LC 15-19074. 1915. 1.35. A. C. McClurg & Co.
Island of Terror. Elsie W Strother. 1976. 4.95. Avalon Books.
Island of the Accursed. easy eye ed. Wilma Winthrop. pap. 0.75 o.p. Lancer.
Island of the Angels. Leonard Patrick O'Connor Wibberley. LC 65-13578. bds., 3.50. Morrow.
Island of the Blue Dolphins. Scott O'Dell. 1978. pap. 2.25 (ISBN 0-440-94000-1, LFL). Dell.
Island of the Blue Macaws: And Sixteen Other Stories. James Ramsey Ullman. LC 52-13740. 1953. Lippincott.
Island of the Great Mother: Or, The Miracle of Ille Des Dames; a Story from the Utopian Archipelago. Gerhart Johann Robert Hauptmann & Muir, Willa, Tr. LC 25-214926. 1925. B. W. Heubsch and the Viking Press.
Island of the Innocent. Vardis Fisher. pap. 1.95 o.p. (14). Swallow.
Island of the Innocent. Madeleine Kent. LC 45-7348. 1945. Harper & Brothers.
Island of the Innocent. Grant Martin Overton. LC 23-5522. 2.00. George H. Doran Company.
Island of the Innocent: A Novel of Greek and Jew in the Time of the Maccabees. 1st Ed. Vardis Fisher. LC 52-8909. 1952. Abelard Press.
Island of the Pit: By Vincent James Pseud. James Gribben. LC 56-6799. 1956. Messner.
Island of the Seven Hills. Zoe Cass. LC 73-20576. 1974. 6.95 (ISBN 0-394-49063-0). Random House.
Island of the Stairs: Being a True Account of Certain Strange and Wonderful Adventures of Master John Hampdon, Seaman, and Teller of the Tale, and Mistress Lucy Wilberforce, Gentlewoman, in the Great South Seas. Cyrus Townsend Brady. LC 13-24793. 1913. A. C. McClurg & Co.
Island of the Winds. Marian Jonson. 1970. incl. anthology 4.50x (ISBN 0-85343-509-X). Coach Hse.
Island of the Winds: A Historical Novel. Athena G. Dallas-Damis. LC 76-370950. (Illus.). 1976. 8.95 (ISBN 0-89241-022-1). Caratzas Bros.
Island of the Winds: A Historical Novel. Athena G Dallas-Damis. (Signet Book). 1978. 1.95 (ISBN 0-451-07905-1). New American Library.
Island of Truth, & Other Stories. English Language Services. (Collier-Macmillan English Readers Ser.). pap. 1.40 (ISBN 0-02-971380-3). Macmillan.
Island of Youth: And Other Stories. Donn Byrne. LC 74-116943. (Short story index reprint series). 1970. Books for Libraries Press.
Island of Youth and Other Stories. Donn Byrne. LC 33-27393. 1933. The Century Co.
Island on Fire: A True Saga. Joseph Arnold Hayes. LC 74-857. 12.95 (ISBN 0-448-11607-3). Grosset & Dunlap.
Island: Or, The Adventures of a Person of Quality. 2d ed. Richard Whiteing. 1899. The Century Co.
Island Paradise. Patricia Bird. 1974. 4.50. Avalon.
Island People. Stanton Arthur Coblentz. (Orig.). 1971. pap. 0.75 o.p. (75-2180). Belmont-Tower.
Island People. Coleman Dowell. LC 75-34150. (New Directions book). 1976. 12.50 (ISBN 0-8112-0604-1). New Directions Pub. Corp.
Island Pharisees. rev. ed. John Galsworthy. LC 8-27808. 1908. G. P. Putnam's Sons.
Island Plant: A Nantucket Story. Mary Catherine Jenkins Lee. LC 7-12593. 1896. Goldenrod Literary and Debating Society.
Island Players. Ilka Chase. 1970. pap. 0.75 o.p. (07124). Curtis.
Island Players. 1st Ed. Ilka Chase. LC 56-558318. 1956. Doubleday.
Island Priest. Henri Queffelec. LC 52-8257. 1952. Dutton.
Island Princess: A Story of Six Weeks--and Afterwards. Theodora Havers Boulger. LC 6-15012. (On cover: The Hudson library no. 7)). 1895. G. P. Putnam's Sons.
Island Prisoner. Vivian D. Gunderson. 1974. pap. 1.25 (12-9). Rapids Christian.
Island Promise. W. Ware Lynch. 336p. (Orig.). 1981. pap. 2.75 (ISBN 0-440-04139-2, Banbury). Dell.
Island Rescue (Appointment with Venus) Tickell, Jerrard. LC 52-5232. 1952. Doubleday.
Island Snatchers. George H Smith. 1978. DAW Books.
Island Stories: Tales & Legends from the West. Ed. by Paul O'Sullivan. (World of Stone Ser.: Bk. 3). (Illus.). 1977. pap. 4.95 (ISBN 0-905140-22-2). Irish Bk Ctr.
Island Summers. Mary Hochstadter. LC 40-11751. The Boothbay Register Press.
Island; Three Tales. Tr. by Ronald Strom. Gustaw Herling. LC 67-11435. 1967. 4.95. WOrld.
Island Voices: Stories from the West Indies. new ed. Vidiadhar Surajprasad Naipaul et al. Ed. by Andrew Salkey. 1970. pap. 4.95 o.p. Liveright.
Island Voices: Stories from the West Indies. Ed. by Andrew Salkey. LC 73-114386. 1970. 4.95 (ISBN 0-87140-504-0). Liveright.
Island Winds Blow Deep. Gay Burk. (Orig.). 1979. pap. 1.95 (ISBN 0-532-19233-8). Woodhill.
Island Within. Ludwig Lewisohn. LC 74-29503. (Modern Jewish Experience). 1975. 22.00 (ISBN 0-405-06730-5). Arno Press.
Island Within. Ludwig Lewisohn. LC 68-15790. (JPS library of contemporary American Jewish fiction). 1968. Jewish Publication Society of America.
Island Within. Ludwig Lewisohn. LC 28-677059. 1928. Harper & Brothers.

Island Within. Ludwig Lewisohn. LC 40-273423. (Half-title: The Modern library of the world's best books. 123). 1940. The Modern Library.
Island Within. Ludwig Lewisohn. LC 79-14091. (Jewish legacy book). (Reprint of the 1968 ed. published by the Jewish Publication Society of America, Philadelphia, in series: The JPS library of contemporary American Jewish fiction.). 1979. 5.95 (ISBN 0-87441-318-4). Behrman House.
Island 49. Merle Miller. LC 45-4538. 1945. Thomas Y. Crowell Company.
Islanders. Helen Rose Hull. LC 27-654678. 1927. The Macmillan Company.
Islanders: A Novel. Peadar O'Donnell. 1963. pap. 4.50 (ISBN 0-85342-392-X). Irish Bk Ctr.
Islanders, a Romance of Martha's Vineyard. Evelyn Woodford Ware. LC 8-34840. 1892. Press of A. Mudge & Son.
Islanders-Armored Train. Evgeny Zamiatin & Ivanov Vsevolod. LC 78-58278. 1978. 12.95 (ISBN 0-931558-01-8); pap. 3.95 (ISBN 0-931558-00-X). Trilogy Pubs.
Islanders: By Joseph Auslander and Audrey Wurdemann. 1st Ed. Joseph Auslander & Audrey Wurdemann. LC 51-9417. 1951. Longmans, Green.
Islandia. Austin Tappan Wright. LC 58-12225. 1958. Rinehart.
Islandia. Austin Tappan Wright. (Plume book). 1975. (pbk.) 5.95. New American Library.
Islandia. Austin Tappan Wright. LC 42-720816. 1942. Farrar & Rinehart, Inc.
Islands. Gerald Warner Brace. LC 36-27262. G. P. Putman's Sons.
Islands. Marta Randall. (Orig.). 1980. pap. 1.95 (ISBN 0-671-83411-8, Timescape). PB.
Islands. Marta Randall. (Orig.). 1976. pap. 1.25 o.p. (ISBN 0-515-03664-1). BJ Pub Group.
Islands in the Sky. Arthur Charles Clarke. LC 79-72. (Gregg Press science fiction series). (Illus.). 1979. 9.50 (ISBN 0-8398-2516-1). Gregg Press.
Islands in the Stream. Ernest Hemingway. LC 71-123834. (Illus.). 1970. 10.00. Scribner.
Islands of Adventure. Roberts Theodore Goodridge. LC 19-1588. 1918. Hodder and Stoughton.
Islands of Desire: A Novel. Desemea Wilson. LC 21-5656. E. P. Dutton & Company.
Islands of E Cono & My: A Fable of a World Beset by Economic Problems from Which It Almost Escapes. Simon Ramo. 192p. 1973. 5.95 o.p. (504081). Crown.
Islands of Space. 1st Ed. John Wood Campbell. LC 57-24574. Fantasy Press.
Islands of the Florida Coast: Stories of Adventure, Histories of the Pirates, and True Tales-of Buried Treasure, Including the 'Gasparilla' Story, a Life of Jose Gs. ar, the famous pirate of florida. illus. by the author. ed. Jack Beater. LC 56-9817.
Islands of Unwisdom. Robert Graves. LC 49-11053. 1949. Doubleday.
Islar: A Narrative of Lang III. Mark Saxton & Austin Tappan Wright. LC 74-88367. (Illus.). 1969. 5.95. Houghton Mifflin.
Islar: A Narrative of Lang Third. Mark Saxton. 1969. 5.95 o.p. (ISBN 0-395-08151-3). HM.
Isle for a Stranger. Dorothy Mackie Low. (Ace Gothic). 1973. (pbk.) 0.95. Ace Books.
Isle in the Water. Katharine Tynan Hinkson, pseud. 1896. A. & C. Black.
Isle O' Dreams. Frederick Ferdinand Moore. LC 20-5120. 1920. Doubleday, Page & Company.
Isle of Dead Ships. Crittenden Marriott. LC 9-25978. 1909. 1.00. J. B. Lippincott Company.
Isle of Dead Ships: A Tale of the Sargasso Sea. Crittenden Marriott. LC 25-9694. 1925. J. B. Lippincott Company.
Isle of Demons. John Clarke Bowman. LC 53-512917. 1953. Dial Press.
Isle of Devils: A Historical Tale, Founded on an Anecdote in the Annals of Portugal. a faithful reprint of the rare ed. of 1827. ed. Matthew Gregory Lewis. LC 74-23891 1974. (ISBN 0-8414-5686-0). Folcroft Library Editions.
Isle of Dreams. Myra Kelly. LC 7-14256. 1907. D. Appleton & Co.
Isle of Eden: A Story of Porto Rico. Janie Prichard Duggan. LC 13-118. 1912. 1.25. The Griffith & Rowland Press.
Isle of Enchantment: Stories and People of Puerto Rico. Clement Manly Morton. LC 75-105053. 1970. 1.95. Bethany Press.
Isle of Escape. Ishbel Ross. LC 42-212357. 1942. Harper & Brothers.
Isle of Feminine. Charles Elliot Niswonger. 1893. Brown Printing Company.
Isle of Gladness. Eliot Randall. (Orig.). 1969. pap. 1.75 o.s.i. (TC445, Travellers Comp). Olympia.
Isle of Glory. Jane Oliver, pseud. LC 64-20729. 1964. Putnam.
Isle of Hope. James Noble Gifford. LC 38-38334. 1938. Gramercy Publishing Co.
Isle of Hope. Emily Noble. Gramercy Publishing Co.
Isle of Illusion. George Fort Gibbs. LC 29-23876. J. H. Sears & Company, Inc.
Isle of Life: A Romance. Stephen French Whitman. 1913. C. Scribner's Sons.
Isle of Lost and Found. Florence Rook MacConnell. LC 28-21180. The Stratford Company.
Isle of Palms: Adventures While Wrecking for Gold, Encounter with a Mad Whale, Battle with a Devil-Fish, and Capture of a Mermaid. Charles Martin Newell. LC 7-17281. (Fleetwing series. v. 2). 1888. De Wolfe, Fiske & Co.
Isle of Peril. Alan Wade. LC 57-8745. 1957. Mystery House.
Isle of Princes. Hasan Ozbekhan. LC 57-6230. 1957. Simon and Schuster.
Isle of Retribution. Edison Marshall. LC 23-355256. 1923. Little, Brown and Company.
Isle of Seven Moons: A Romance of Uncharted Seas and Untrodden Shores. Robert Gordon Anderson. LC 22-8047. 1922. 1.90. G. P. Putnam's Sons.
Isle of Shadows. Ellen Jane MacLeod. 1974. 4.95. Lenox Hill Press.
Isle of Strife. George Clifford Shedd. LC 12-13894. Small, Maynard and Company.
Isle of Temptation. Arthur Stanley Colleton. LC 9-15519. 1909. The Stuyvesant Press.
Isle of the Damned. George J. Seaton. 1970. pap. 0.95 o.p. (N2318). Pyramid Pubns.
Isle of the Dead. Roger Zelazny. LC 76-10757. (Gregg Press science fiction series). 1976. (ISBN 0-8398-2346-0). Gregg Press.
Isle of the Dead. Roger Zelazny. 1974. (pbk.) 0.95. Ace Books.
Isle of the Dolphins. Janet Louise Roberts. (Kangaroo Book). 1978. 1.75 (ISBN 0-671-81381-1). Pocket Books.
Isle of the Rainbows, the Rebel Bride: The Plantation Boss. Anne Hampson. (Harlequin Romances Ser.). 576p. 1981. pap. 3.50 (ISBN 0-373-20053-6). Harlequin Bks.
Isle of the Seventh Sentry. Fortune Kent. (Ravenswood gothic). 1974. (pbk.) 0.95. Pocket Books.
Isle of the Snakes. Robert L Fish. LC 63-9267. (Inner sanctum mystery). 1963. Simon and Schuster.
Isle of the Undead. Virginia Coffman. (Signet Book). 1978. 1.50 (ISBN 0-451-08032-7). New American Library.
Isle of the Virgins: A Romance. Matthew J Royal. 1899. The Wenborne-Sumner Co.
Isle of the Winds: An Adventrous Romance. Samuel Rutherford Crockett. LC 2958. 1900. Doubleday & McClure Co.
Isle of the Winds: An Adventurous Romance. Samuel Rutherford Crockett. LC 24-20483. 1904. Doubleday, Page & Co.
Isle of Thorns. Sheila Kaye-Smith. LC 24-17836. 1924. E. P. Dutton & Company.
Isle of Unrest. Hugh Stowell Scott. LC 6-5827. 1900. Dodd, Mead & Company.
Isle of Whims. Carol Hoyt Powers. LC 13-26607. 1.00. R. G. Badger.
Isle of Whispers: A Tale of the New England Seas. Edward Laurence Dudley. LC 10-6736. 1910. 1.50. H. Holt and Company.
Islensdzk Aeventyri: Islandische Legenden, Novellen & Marchen, 2 vol. Ed. by Hugo Gering. LC 80-1967. 100.00 (ISBN 0-404-18667-X). AMS Pr.
Isles of Desire. Basil Carey. LC 31-25920. E. J. Clode, Inc.
Isles of the Blest. Wilbur Daniel Steele. LC 24-25743. 1924. Harper & Brothers.
Ismay's Children. May Hartley. LC 44-22838. 1887. Macmillan and Co.
Isobel: A Romance of the Northern Trail. James Oliver Curwood. LC 13-97200. 1913. Harper & Brothers.
Isobel: A Romance of the Northern Trail. James Oliver Curwood. LC 21-136959. 1916. Grosset & Dunlap.
Isobel's Between Times. Jennie Maria Drinkwater Conklin. LC 6-30402. 1887. R. Carter and Brothers.
Isolated: A Novel. first ed. Robert G. Waldvogel. 1973. 3.50 (ISBN 0-682-47816-4). Exposition Press.
Isolation of Lupe. Daisy R. Binkley. LC 74-32197. 1974. 4.95 (ISBN 0-8111-0556-3). Naylor Co.
Isora's Bridal Vow. A Novel. Mary O'Francis. (On cover: The idle hour series, no. 8). 1892. The F. M. Lupton Publishing Company.
Isotope Man: By Charles Eric Maine Pseud. David McIlwain. LC 57-8943. 1957. Lippincott.
Israel Mort, Overman. A Story of the Mine. John Saunders. (Seaside library, v. 37, no. 764). 1880. G. Munro.
Israel Potter. Herman Melville. Ed. by Harrison Hayford et al. LC 82-81178. (Writings of Herman Melville Ser.). 405p. 1982. 29.95 (ISBN 0-8101-0552-7). Northwestern U Pr.
Israel Potter: His Fifty Years of Exile. Herman Melville. Ed. by Raymond Melbourne Weaver. LC 24-23604. (Half-title: The printed edition of Herman Melville's collection works). 1921. A. & C. Boni.
Israel Potter. His Fifty Years of Exile. Herman Melville. LC 25-3551. 1925. The St. Botolph Society.
Israeli Connection. Nick Carter. (Nick Carter Ser.). (Illus.). 192p. 1982. pap. 2.50 (ISBN 0-441-35881-0, Pub. by Charter Bks). Ace Bks.
Israeli Love Story. Zola Levitt. LC 77-27611. 2.50 (ISBN 0-8024-4181-5). Moody Press.
Israeli Stories: A Selection of the Best Contemporary Hebrew Writing. Introd. by Robert Alter. Ed. by Joel Blocker. LC 61-14918. 1962. Schocken Books.
Issue. George Morgan. LC 4-8584. 1904. J. B. Lippincott Company.
Issue: A Story of the River Thames. Edward Noble. 1900. Doubleday, Page & Company.
Issue at Hand. William Atheling, Jr. LC 65-2533. 1964. 8.00 (ISBN 0-911682-09-0); pap. 4.00 (ISBN 0-911682-17-1). Advent.
Issue of the Bishop's Blood. Thomas Patrick McMahon. LC 70-175390. 1972. 4.95. Published for the Crime Club by Doubleday.
Istanbul Nights. Clarissa Ross, pseud. LC 78-63427. (Jove/ HBJ Book.). 1978. 2.25 (ISBN 0-515-04631-0). Jove Publications, Inc.
Istar of Babylon. Margaret Horton Potter. LC 77-84263. (Lost Race and Adult Fantasy Fiction). 1978. 30.00 (ISBN 0-405-11004-9). Arno Press.
Istar of Babylon: A Phantasy. Margaret Horton Potter. LC 2-23294. 1902. Harper & Brothers.
Isthmus of Samuel Greenberg. Jeremy Reed. 1975. pap. 2.50 (Pub. by Trigram Pr). SBD.
Istoriia Moei Golubiatni. Isaak Emmanuilovich Babel. (Rus.). 1978. pap. 3.00 (ISBN 0-933884-03-6). Berkeley Slavic.
It. Chris Aulich. LC 78-312394. 1977. 10.95 (ISBN 0-909331-33-2) (ISBN 0-909331-31-6). Wild & Woolley.
It". Elinor Sutherland Glyn. LC 27-23634. The Macaulay Company.
It" A Wild, Weird History of Marvelous, Miraculous, Phantasmagorial Adventures in Search of He, She, and Jess, and Leading to the Finding of "It" A Haggard Conclusion... John De Morgan. LC 7-25989. (Munro's library. v. 50, no. 726). 1887. N. L. Munro.
It." A Wild, Weird History of Marvelous, Miraculous, Phantasmagorial Adventures in Search of He, She, and Jess, and Leading to the Finding of "It." A Haggard Conclusion... Andrew Lang & Pollock, Walter Herries, 1850-1926, Supposed Author. LC 7-25989. (Munro's library, v. 50, no. 728). 1887. N. L. Munro.
It Ain't Hay. David Dodge. LC 47-7632. 1946. Simon and Schuster.
It: And Other Stories. Gouverneur Morris. LC 12-68633. 1912. C. Scribner's Sons.
It Beats the Shakers: Or, A New Tune. Anna D Evans. LC 6-26072. Anglo-American Corporation.
It Began in Eden. Frances Shelley Wees. LC 36-1740. 1936. Macrae Smith Company.
It: Being Our Individual Magneto. Elizabeth Snowden Nichols Watrous. LC 10-26919. 1910. Cochrane Publishing Company.
It: Being Our Individual Magnets. Elizabeth Snowden Nichols Watrous. LC 11-25049. 1911. The Shakespeare Press.
It Boil Down to Murder. Perry D Westbrook. LC 53-7224. 1953. Arcadia House.
It Came to Pass. Mary Farley Sanborn Sanborn. LC 8-3754. (On cover: Good company series. no. 19). 1892. Lee and Shepard.
It Can't Always Be Caviar: The Fabulously Daring Adventures and Exquisite Cooking Recipes of the Involuntary Secret Agent Thomas Lieve Lieven..., Told by Johannes Mario Simmel. Tr. from German by James Cleugh 1st Ed. in U.S.A. Johannes Mario Simmel. LC 65-10626. 5.95. Doubleday.
It Can't Happen Here. Sinclair Lewis. pap. 1.95 (ISBN 0-451-09386-0, J9386, Sig). NAL.
It Can't Happen Here: A Novel. Sinclair Lewis. LC 35-19689. 1935. Doubleday, Doran & Company, Inc.
It Can't Happen Here: A Novel. Sinclair Lewis. LC 36-17330. 1936. Doubleday, Doran & Company, Inc.
It Can't Happen Here: A Novel. Sinclair Lewis. LC 36-352393. The Sun Dial Press.
It Can't Happen Here: A Novel. Sinclair Lewis. LC 40-3250. 1939. Triangle Books.
It Comes by Night. Clarissa Ross, pseud. (Orig.). 1972. pap. 0.95 o.s.i. (75-418). Lancer.
It Couldn't Be Murder... Hugh Austin. LC 35-10316. 1935. Pub. for the Crime Club, Inc., by Doubleday, Doran & Company, Inc.
It Couldn't Be Murder... Hugh Austin. LC 37-5414. 1937. The Sun Dial Press, Inc.
It Couldn't Be Murder. Robert B Sinclair. LC 54-9210. 1954. M. S. Mill Co.
It Couldn't Matter Less. Peter Cheyney. (Boxer Ser). 1971. pap. 0.95 o.p. (95110). Beagle Bks.
It Doesn't Happen Every Day. Robin Moore & Peter Dane. 1977. pap. 1.95 (ISBN 0-532-19134-X). Woodhill.
It Ends in Marriage. Bela Zsolt & Rittenberg, Louis, Tr. LC 31-3687. H. Liveright.
It Ends with Revelations. Dodie Smith. 1967. 5.95 o.p. (ISBN 0-316-79957-2, Pub. by Atlantic Monthly Pr). Little.
It Ends with Revelations: A Novel. Dorothy Gladys Smith. LC 67-22614. 1967. Little, Brown.
It Fell Upon a Day. Ruth Hunter. LC 47-1204. 1946. C. Scribner's Sons.
It Had Been a Mild, Delicate Night. Barrington Kaye. LC 60-8961. 1960. Abelard-Schuman.
It Had Been a Mild, Delicate Night. 1st English Ed. Tom Kaye. LC 60-8961. 1960. Abelard-Schuman.
It Had to Be a Woman. Paul Newlin. LC 79-65120. 1979. 9.95 (ISBN 0-8128-2688-4). Stein and Day.
It Had to Be You. Hilda Van Siller. LC 76-97690. 1970. 4.50. Published for the Crime Club by Doubleday.
It Happened at Andover: Well, Most of It Did, Anyway. James Chandler Graham. LC 20-159541. 1920. 1.90. Houghton Mifflin Company.
It Happened at the Lake. Joseph Thompson Shaw. LC 37-1267. 1937. Dodd, Mead & Company.
It Happened Gently. Joan Cathey. 1970. 2.95 o.p. Vantage.
It Happened in a Rooming House. Tania Toplitsky. 1970. 4.50 o.p. Vantage.
It Happened in Atlantic City. Thomas B Senger. LC 15-8823. R. G. Badger; Etc., Etc.
It Happened in Boston? Russell H Greenan. LC 68-28574. 1969. 5.95. Random House.
It Happened in Egypt. Charles Norris Williamson. LC 14-506. 1914. Doubleday, Page & Co.
It Happened in Peking. Louise Jordan Miln. LC 26-17802. 1926. Frederick A. Stokes Company.
It Happened in PRK. Harry Summerfield Hoff. LC 34-31291. Coward-McCann.
It Happened in Rome: A Novel. Isabel Constance Clarke. LC 25-229909. 1925. Benziger Brothers.
It Happened in Spain. condensed for modern readers ed. Ivy Valdes. (Signet bk., P5332). 1973. 0.60. New American Lib.
It Happened on Halfaday Creek. James Beardsley Hendryx. LC 44-3444. 1944. Doubelday, Doran and Co., Inc.
It Happened on Rush Street. Walter Schwimmer. 1971. 5.95 o.p. (ISBN 0-8119-0205-6). Fell.
It Happened on Rush Street. A Group of Short Stories and Vignettes. Walter Schwimmer. LC 70-162867. 1971. 5.95 (ISBN 0-8119-0205-6). F. Fell.
It Happened One Day: A Novel. Majorie Bartholomew Paradis. LC 32-8081. 1932. Harper & Brothers.
It Happened "Over There,". Burris Atkins Jenkins. LC 19-140625. Fleming H. Revell Company.
It Happened the Day the Sun Rose: And Other Stories. Tennessee Williams. 1982. cancelled (ISBN 0-671-43626-0). S&S.
It Happened This Way. Rose Eytinge & Fisher, S. Ada. LC 6-381284. (On cover: American authors ser. 27). 1890. United States Book Company, Successors to J. W. Lovell Company.
It Happened to Didymus. Upton Beall Sinclair. LC 58-10384. 1958. Sagamore Press.
It Happened to Susan. Jane Blackmore. 1973. (pbk) 0.95. Dell.
It Happened Tomorrow, a Novel. Francis Williams. LC 52-11944. 1952. Abelard Press.
It Happened Tomorrow: A Novel by Francis Williams. Edward Francis Williams Francis-Williams. LC 52-11944. 1952. Abelard Press.
It Happened up in Maine. Benjamin Cole. (Illus.). 1980. pap. 7.95 o.s.i. (ISBN 0-941238-02-4). Penobscot Bay.
It Happens Every Spring. Valentine Davies. LC 49-9348. 1949. Farrar, Straus.
It Is a Dream. 1st Ed. John Manson. LC 57-6190. 1957. Holt.
It Is Always Summer: A Novel. David Helwig. LC 82-4256. 208p. 1982. 12.95 (ISBN 0-8253-0097-5). Beaufort Bks NY.
It Is Enough! A Romance of Musical Life. Harriette Russell Campbell. LC 13-128684. 1913. 1.00. Harper & Brothers.
It Is Morning. Jennie Harris Oliver. LC 38-15833. Burton Publishing Company.
It Is Never Too Late to Mend. Charles Reade. LC 48-44540. (works of Charles Reade. Library ed.). 1895. Metropolitan Pub. Co.
It Is Never Too Late to Mend. Charles Reade. (On cover: Lovell's library, v. 19, no. 916). 1887. J. W. Lovell Company.
It Is Never Too Late to Mend." A Matter-of-Fact Romance. Charles Reade. (Seaside library, v. 2, no. 24). 1877. G. Munro.
It Is Never Too Late to Mend: A Matter-of-Fact Romance. by charles reade. ed. Charles Reade. LC 4-16312. Rand, McNally & Company.

It Is Never Too Late to Mend: A Matter-of-Fact Romance. Charles Reade. (On cover: The English Comedie humaine. 1st series, v. 10). 1902. The Century Co.

It Is Not Lawful. Arthur Hamilton De Long. LC 13-19075. 1.25. Eaton & Mains.

It Is Not Safe to Know... Gertrude M. Robins Reynolds. LC 39-30069. 1939. Doublday, Doran & Company, Inc.

It Is Possible. A Story of Life. Helen Van Metre Van-Anderson Gordon. LC 8-30237. 1891. New Era Publishing Co.

It Is Still the Morning. Louis Danz. LC 43-13714. 1943. W. Morrow & Co.

It Is the Fashion. From the German of Adelheid Von Auer Pseud. Charlotte Von Cosel. LC 7-39785. 1872. J. B. Lippincott & Co.

It, Is the Fashion. From the German of Adelheid Von Auer Pseud. Charlotte Von Cosel. LC 14-22437. 1879. J. B. Lippincott & Co.

It Is the Law. A Story of Marriage and Divorce in New York. Thomas Edgar Willson. Belford, Clarke & Company.

It Is They Who Hate Us: Or, The War on Washington's Race. Walter Marion Raymond. LC 26-4416.

It Is Time, Lord. Fred Chappell. LC 63-17848. 1963. Atheneum.

It Just Is. Ed. by Paul Hodges. LC 80-80784. 1980. 9.95 o.p. (ISBN 0-89002-144-9); pap. 2.95 o.p. (ISBN 0-89002-143-0). Northwoods Pr.

It Lives Again. James Dixon. 1978. 1.95 (ISBN 0-345-27693-0). Ballantine Books.

It Looked Like for Ever. Mark Harris. LC 79-14423. 8.95 (ISBN 0-07-026720-0). McGraw-Hill.

It Looks Alive to Me! Tom Baum. 5.50 (ISBN 0-06-020403-6) (ISBN 0-06-020404-4). Harper & Row.

It May Never Happen: And Other Stories. Victor Sawdon Pritchett. LC 47-2727. 1947. Reynal & Hitchcock.

It Might Be. A Story of the Future Progress of the Sciences, the Wonderful Advancement in the Methods of Government and the Happy State of the People. Herbert E Swan. 1896. H. E. Swan.

It Might Have Been: Or Mrs. Leslie and Mrs. Lennox, a Novel. LC 5409. (Princess series. no. 21). 1900. Street & Smith.

It Might Have Been: the Story of the Gunpowder Plot. Emily Sarah Holt. LC 7-5184. 1889. R. Carter & Brothers.

It Might Lead Anywhere. Ernest Robertson Punshon. LC 47-9568. 1947. The Macmillan Company.

It Must Be Love, 'Cause I Feel So Dumb! Arthur Barron. (Orig.). 1976. pap. 1.25 o.p. (ISBN 0-515-04178-5). Pyramid Pubns.

It Must Be Music. Marian Woodruff. (Sweet Dreams Ser.: No. 26). 176p. 1982. pap. 1.95 (ISBN 0-553-22692-4). Bantam.

It Must Be Now the Kingdom Coming: An Historical Romance. Perry Lentz. LC 72-96656. 1973. 6.95 (ISBN 0-517-50421-9). Crown.

It Must Be the Climate. Leo Vaughan, pseud. LC 68-18278. 1968. H. Regnery Co.

It Must Have Been an Angel. Marjorie L. Lloyd. (Redwood Ser.). 1980. pap. 3.95 (ISBN 0-8163-0363-0). Pacific Pr Pub Assn.

It Never Can Happen Again. William Frend De Morgan. LC 9-28954. 1909. H. Holt and Company.

It Never Could Happen: Or, The Second American Revolution. Shaemas O'Sheel. LC 33-31156. 1932. Coventry House.

It Never Did Run Smooth. A Novel. Jane Goodwin Austin. (On cover: The Idle hour series, no. 20). The F. M. Lupton Publishing Company.

It Never Rains in Los Angeles. Charles F. Flowers. LC 74-135263. 1970. 5.95. Coward-McCann.

It Only Hurts a Minute: A Novel. Don M. Mankiewicz. LC 66-104741. 5.95. Putnam.

It Pays to Advertise. Samuel Field & Megrue, Roi Cooper, 1883- LC 15-4801. 1915. 1.25. Duffield & Company.

It Pays to Smile. Nina Wilcox Putnam. LC 20-19578. 1.90. George H. Doran Company.

It Shall Be Conquered. Ja Leslee. LC 62-20693. 1962. Christopher Pub. House.

It Shall Be Forever. Louise Harrison McCraw. LC 65-10557. bds., 2.95. Revell.

It Shouldn't Happen to a Dog. Colin Watson. LC 76-45534. 7.95 (ISBN 0-399-11881-0). Putnam.

It Started in Ravenswood. Vincent Crimi. LC 48-1825. 1947. Capra Pub. Co.

It Takes a Man to Cry. Steve Whalen. LC 80-12998. 12.95 (ISBN 0-531-09554-1). D. Elliott Publisher: Distributed by F. Watts.

It Takes a Thief. Dan Billany. LC 41-4370. Harper & Brothers.

It Takes a Thief. Dan Billany. LC 44-59520. (Black cat detective series). 1944. Crestwood Publishing Co., Inc.

It Takes All Kinds. Louis Bromfield. LC 39-27847. 1939. Harper & Brothers.

It Was. Louis Zukofsky. LC 61-15165. 1961. Origin Press.

It Was see Ferdinand.

It Was a Lover and His Lass. A Novel. Margaret Oliphant Wilson Oliphant. (Harper's Franklin square library, no. 294). 1883. Harper & Brothers.

It Was a Wonderful Summer for Running Away. Charles N Barnard. LC 78-17282. 8.95 (ISBN 0-396-07574-6). Dodd, Mead.

It Was Forever. Daisy Hendley Gold. LC 41-527. Dorrance and Company.

It Was Left to Peter. Berta Ruck. LC 40-4504. 1940. Dodd, Mead & Company.

It Was Like This. Anne Goodwin Winslow. LC 49-10840. 1949. A. A. Knopf.

It Was Locked. John Hawk. LC 30-593031. Farrar & Rinehart, Incorporated.

It Was Mary. Eleanor Arnett Nash. LC 47-31372. 1947. D. Appleton-Century Co.

It Was Not My World. Deaderick Franklin Jenkins. LC 42-24098. 1942. The Author.

It Was Only a Dream. William Arthur Neubauer. LC 45-8588. 1945. Grammercy Publishing Co.

It Was the Lark. Catherine MacArthur. LC 78-19835. 1978. 7.95 (ISBN 0-312-43914-8). St. Martin's Press.

It Wasn't a Nightmare. Lindsay Fitzgerald Hay. LC 37-3595. 1937. The Macmillan Company.

It Won't Be Flowers. Judith Kelly. LC 36-8201. 1936. Harper & Brothers.

It Won't Be Flowers: A Novel. Elizabeth Berridge. LC 49-85911. 1949. Simon and Schuster.

It Won't Get You Anywhere. Desmond Skirrow. LC 66-232481. 1966. 4.95. Lippincott.

Italian. Ann Ward Radcliffe. Ed. by Frederick Garber. (World's Classics Ser.). 1982. pap. 6.95 (ISBN 0-19-281572-5). Oxford U Pr.

Italian Campaign: A Novel. Tr. from French by Patrick O'Brian. Michel Mohrt. 1967. bds., 4.75. Viking.

Italian Child Life: Or, Marietta's Good Times. Marietta Ambrosi. D. Lothrop Company.

Italian Connection. Robin Moore & Al Dempsey. (Pulsar,#2). 1975. (pbk.) 1.25 (ISBN 0-523-00393-5). Pinnacle Books.

Italian Connection see Conexion Italiana.

Italian Fables. Italo Calvino. 1961. pap. 0.95 o.p. (04944, Collier). Macmillan.

Italian for Love. D. H Thomson. 1973. (pbk) 0.75 (ISBN 0-671-75771-7). Pocket Books.

Italian Girl. Iris Murdoch. (S193). 1965. Avon.

Italian Girl, a Novel. Iris Murdoch. LC 64-18481. 1964. Viking Press.

Italian Girl: A Novel. Katharine Sedgwick Washburn. LC 8-33477. 1874. Lee and Shepard.

Italian Letters: Or, The History of the Count De St. Julian. Ed., Introd. by Burton R. Pollin. William Godwin. Ed. by Burton Ralph Pollin. LC 65-132606. 4.50. Univ. of Neb. Pr.

Italian or the Confessional of the Black Penitents. Ann Ward Radcliffe. Ed. by Frederick Garber. (Oxford Paperbacks Ser: No. 262). 1971. pap. 5.75x o.p. (ISBN 0-19-281105-3). Oxford U Pr.

Italian; or, The Confessional of the Black Penitents: A Romance. Ann Ward Radcliffe. LC 68-10942. 1968. Russell & Russell.

Italian: Or, The Confessional of the Black Penitents, A Romance. Ann Ward Radcliffe. 1797. Printed by W. Durell, for R. Magill, S. Cambell ! E. Duyckinck & Co., Gain & Teneyck, N. Judah, P. P. Mesier, J. Harrisson, T. Greenleaf, & Thomas, Andrews & Penniman.

Italian: Or, The Confessional of the Black Penitents: a Romance by Ann Radcliffe; Ed., Introd. by Frederick Garber. Ann Ward Radcliffe. Ed. by Frederick Garber. LC 68-84437. (Oxford English novels). 1968. 5.60. Oxford Univ. Pr.

Italian Portraits in Engadine Frames, G. E. X. Lydia Ethel Painter. LC 5-10182. The Philosopher Press, Van Vechten & Ellis.

Italian Regional Tales of the Nineteenth Century. Ed. by Archibald Colquhoun & Neville Rogers. Tr. by Bernard Wall. 1961. 2.60x o.p. (ISBN 0-19-255103-5). Oxford U Pr.

Italian Renaissance Tales. Tr. by Janet Levarie Smarr from Ital. (Illus.). 284p. 1983. pap. 13.95 (ISBN 0-933760-03-5). Solaris Pr.

Italian Short Stories. Ed. by Raleigh Trevelyan. (Orig., Bilingual). (YA) (gr. 9 up). 1965. pap. 2.50 o.p. (ISBN 0-14-002196-5). Penguin.

Italian Short Stories. Ed. by Ernest Hatch Wilkins. Altrocchi, Rudolph, 1882- Joint Ed. LC 13-109. (Heath's modern language series). D. C. Heath & Co.

Italian Short Stories. Racconti Italiani. Ed. by Raleigh Trevelyan. LC 65-2418. (Penguin parallel texts, 2196). Penguin.

Italian Short Stories 2. Ed. by Dimitri Vittorini. LC 73-166559. (Penguin parallel texts). 1972. 0.35. Penguin.

Italian Stories. Novelle Italiane. Stories in the Original Italian. With Translations, Critical Introductions, Notes and Vocabulary by the Editor. Ed. by Robert Anderson Hall. (Bantam dual-language book, S2189). 1961. Bantam Books.

Italian Stories of Today. John Lehmann. 1959. 15.00. Havertown Bks.

Italian Tragedy: The Story of a Humble People. Nicola V Curinga. LC 45-5193. 1945. Liveright Publishing Corporation.

Italian Wife. Emyr Humphreys. LC 58-8845. 1958. McGraw-Hill.

Italian Woman. Eleanor Hibbert. LC 75-22749. 1975. 7.95 (ISBN 0-399-11685-0). Putnam.

Italian Woman. Eleanor Hibbert. (Berkley Medallion). 1.50 (ISBN 0-425-03262-0). Berkley.

Italian Woman. Jean Plaidy. 304p. 1975. 7.95 o.p. (ISBN 0-399-11685-0). Putnam Pub Group.

Italian Writers of Today: An Anthology of Short Stories, with Introd., Notes, Exercises and Vocabulary. Ed. by Howard Rosario Marraro. LC 55-2361. 1955. S. F. Vanni.

Itching Parrot: El Periquillo Sarniento. Jose Joaquin Fernandez De Lizardi & Porter, Katherine Anne, 1894- LC 42-11448. 1942. Doubleday, Doran and Co., Inc.

Item 7. Alan Nixon. LC 72-155425. (Inner sanctum mystery). 1971. 5.95 (ISBN 0-671-21028-9). Simon and Schuster.

Iter Lunare. David Russen. LC 76-14908. (Gregg Press science fiction series). 1976. 10.00 (ISBN 0-8398-2343-6). Gregg Press.

Iter-Lunare: A Voyage to the Moon see Female Critick: Letters in Drollery from Ladies to Their Humble Servants.

Ithuriel's Hour. Joanna Cannan, pseud. LC 32-8073. 1932. Doubleday, Doran & Company, Inc.

Itinerant. William Herrick. LC 67-11603. 1967. McGraw-Hill.

Itinerant Ivory Tower: Scientific & Literary Essays. G. E. Hutchinson. 1953. Repr. 30.00 (ISBN 0-8274-2592-9). R West.

Itinerant Side: Or, Pictures of Life in the Itinerancy. 3d Thousand. Lucius Daniel Davis. Carlton & Porter.

Itinerant's Daughter. James Leslie Roberts. LC 28-174906. The Christopher Publishing House.

Itinerary of Beggars. Herbert Edward Francis. LC 73-80957. 1973. 7.95 (ISBN 0-87745-039-0). University of Iowa Press.

Itoma: A Forest Romance. Taylor Alexander. LC 10-587782. The Kuyahorn Press, Inc.

It's a Battlefield. Graham Greene. LC 62-19606. 1962. Viking Press.

It's a Battlefield. Graham Greene. LC 34-714283. 1934. Doubleday, Doran & Company, Inc.

It's a Boy's World. August William Derleth. 4.95 (ISBN 0-88361-057-4). Stanton & Lee.

It's a Crime. Richard Ellington. LC 48-85211. 1948. W. Morrow.

It's a Deal. William Allen. LC 41-7690. J. W. McDermott.

It's a Free Country. Ben Ames Williams. LC 45-62202. 1945. Houghton Mifflin Company.

It's a Free Country. Ben Ames Williams. LC 47-19998. 1947. The Sun Dial Press.

It's a Gay Life: A Novel. Bertha Bement. LC 51-10006. 1951. Exposition Press.

It's a Great War! ' Mary Lee. LC 29-22421. 1929. Houghton Mifflin Company.

It's a Great World! Emilie Baker Loring. LC 35-10321. The Penn Publishing Company.

It's a Kids' World. Ed. by Paula B. Rehr. (Illus.). 110p. (Orig.). 1980. pap. 4.00 (ISBN 0-936920-00-9). Ridgeview Jr High Pr.

It's a Picnic. Nancy McIntyre. (William Cole Bks). 1969. 5.95 o.p. (ISBN 0-670-40451-9). Viking Pr.

It's a Way Love Has. A Novel. William Featherstone. LC 6-38976. 1887. G. W. Dillingham; Etc., Etc.

It's a Wise Child: A Disorderly Comedy of Fatherhood. Anne Benson Fisher. LC 49-10918. 1949. Bobbs-Merrill Co.

It's a Wise Child: A Novel. Thomas Curley. LC 60-11430. 1960. New Authors Guild.

It's a Woman's World, a Collection of Stories from Harper's Bazaar. Harper's Bazaar & Aswell, Mary Louise (White) 1902- Ed. LC 44-2899. 1944. Whittlesey House, McGraw-Hill Book Company, Inc.

It's About Crime. MacKinlay Kantor. LC 61-1194. (Signet book, S1871). 1960. New American Library.

It's All in the Family. Margaret Millar. LC 48-1255. 1948. Random House.

It's All in the Game, and Other Tennis Tales. 2nd, illustrated by arthur scwieder. ed. William Tatem Tilden. LC 22-5372. 1922. Doubleday, Page and Company.

It's All in Your Mind. Robert Bloch. 1971. pap. 0.75 o.p. (07147). Curtis.

It's All Right: A Novel. Inez Specking. LC 29-130688. 1929. B. Herder Book Co.

It's All Right, Ma, I'm Only Sighing. Joanne Joyce. LC 74-367938. 1968. 0.55. Horwitz.

It's All Zoo. Gerald A Browne. LC 68-24829. 1968. 4.95. Doubleday.

It's Always Four O'clock: A Novel. James Updyke. LC 56-98438. 1956. Random House.

It's Always Tomorrow. St. John, Robert. LC 44-479483. 1944. Doubleday, Doran and Company, Inc.

It's an Ill Will. Dorothy Mayor. LC 47-20645. 1947. M. S. Mill Co., Inc.

It's an Old Country. John Boynton Priestley. LC 67-78006. 1967. Heinemann.

It's an Old Country: A Novel, by J. B. Priestley. 1st Amer. Ed. John Boynton Priestley. LC 67-14448. 1967. 5.95. Little.

It's April... Remember! A Novel of Hollywood. 1st Ed. Kathleen Clifford. LC 55-11116. 1955. Exposition Press.

It's Been Fun. Vern Tucker. 1970. 3.50 o.p. Vantage.

It's Cold in Pongo-Ni. Edward Herbert Franklin. LC 65-17368. 3.95. Vanguard.

It's Cold Out There. Malcolm Braly. 1971. pap. 0.75 o.p. (B75-2121). Belmont-Tower.

Its Cold Out There. Malcolm Braly. 1976. pap. 1.50 o.p. WSP.

It's Cold Out There. Malcolm Braly. 1.50 (ISBN 0-671-80801-X). Pocket Books.

It's Different Abroad. Henry Calvin, pseud. LC 82-48241. 192p. 1983. pap. 2.84i (ISBN 0-06-080640-0, P 640, PL). Har-Row.

It's Different Abroad. Henry Calvin, pseud. 1974. (pbk.) 0.95. Dell.

It's Different Abroad. Clifford Hanley. LC 63-10615. 1963. Harper & Row.

It's Different for a Woman. Mary Jane Ward. LC 52-10091. 1952. Random House.

It's Elementary: Great Detectives Greatest Cases. Paul Janeczko. 256p. (Orig.). 1981. pap. cancelled (ISBN 0-553-02830-8). Bantam.

It's Getting Harder All the Time. Troy Conway, pseud. (Coxeman Ser). (Orig.). 1968. pap. 0.75 o.p. (ISBN 0-446-64995-3, 53-725). Paperback Lib.

It's Hard to Leave While the Music's Playing. Irving Spencer Cooper. LC 76-26930. (Illus.). 7.95 (ISBN 0-393-08756-5). Norton.

It's Hard to Leave While the Music's Playing. Irving Spencer Cooper. 1978. 1.95 (ISBN 0-445-04267-2). Popular Library.

It's Hard to Sin. Jack Kahane. LC 35-4007. Greenberg.

It's Hell to Be a Ranger. Caddo Cameron. LC 37-22641. 1937. Doubleday, Doran & Company, Inc.

It's Hell to Be Ranger. Caddo Cameron. LC 39-476. 1938. The Sun Dial Press, Inc.

It's Her Own Funeral. Edith Caroline Rivett. LC 52-9064. 1952. Published for the Crime Club by Doubleday.

It's Later Than You Think. Kenneth O'Donnell Horan. LC 34-4671. R. O. Ballou.

It's Love I'm After. Florence Eberhard. LC 37-34668. The Dodge Publishing Company.

It's Love I'm After... Florence Eberhard. LC 47-21436. (On cover: A Golden willow romance. No. 56). 1947.

It's Mating Time. Estelle Davenport Ezell. LC 51-9748. 1951. Dorrance.

It's Me & I'm Here: From West Point to Esalen: How a Rigid Overachiever Revolutionized His Life. Harold C. Lyon, Jr. 224p. 1974. 6.95 o.p. (ISBN 0-440-04355-7). Delacorte.

It's Mighty Strange: Or, "The Older, the Newer,". Arthur March Clark. LC 18-3018. 1918. The Stratford Company.

It's Moments Like These. Frank J Hardy. LC 73-162917. 1972. 1.95 (ISBN 0-7260-0008-6). Gold Star Publications.

It's Murder with Dover: A Novel. Joyce Porter. LC 73-84056. (MW suspense). 1973. 4.95. D. McKay Co.

It's My Attic. Gayle A. Hayes. 1975. 4.95 o.p. (ISBN 0-8059-2221-0). Dorrance.

It's My Own Funeral. Dana Lyon. LC 44-2814. 1944. Farrar & Rinehart, Inc.

It's My Own Funeral. Mabel Dana Lyon. LC 44-2814. 1944. Farrar & Rinehart, Inc.

It's Never Over. Morley Callaghan. LC 30-654134. 1930. C. Scribner's Sons.

It's Never Too Late. Larry B. Mathes & Harold W. Epling. 1970. 4.50 o.p. Vantage.

It's Not Done. William Christian Bullitt. LC 26-744064. Harcourt, Brace and Company.

It's Not Done. William Christian Bullitt. LC 34-382702. 1929. Grosset & Dunlap.

It's Not Easy to Marry an Elephant: And Other Fables. Beatrice C. Schuman. LC 81-68909. (Illus.). 192p. 1982. 10.95 (ISBN 0-8119-0436-9). Fell.

It's Not Easy to Marry an Elephant: And Other Fables. Beatrice Chernuchin Schuman & Roland Wolff. LC 81-68909. (Illus.). 10.95 (ISBN 0-8119-0436-9). F. Fell Publishers.

It's Not Far but I Don't Know the Way. Hoke Norris. LC 70-81965. 1969. 5.00. Swallow Press.

It's Not My Problem. Kenneth O'Donnell Horan. LC 38-28956. 1938. Doubleday, Doran & Company, Inc.
It's Not That Easy. Winifred Halsted. LC 41-549532. 1941. Dodd Mead & Company.
It's Not What You'd Expect. Norma Klein. 128p. 1982. pap. 1.95 (ISBN 0-380-00011-3, 59253-3, Flare). Avon.
It's OK If You Don't Love Me. Norma Klein. LC 76-42926. 6.95 (ISBN 0-8037-4053-0). Dial Press.
It's Okay If You Don't Love Me. Norma Klein. 256p. 1982. pap. 2.25 (ISBN 0-449-23526-2, Crest). Fawcett.
It's Only Temporary. Charles Henry Mergendahl. LC 50-11190. 1950. Doubleday.
It's Raining Violence. Theodora McCormick Du Bois. LC 49-11672. 1949. Published for the Crime Club by Doubleday.
It's Raining Violence see Money, Murder & the McNeills.
It's Spring Again: By Gay Rutherford Pseud. James Noble Gifford. LC 51-12253. 1951. Arcadia House.
It's the Climate: Stories of the Caribbean. Charles Horace Rathbone. LC 71-134974. (Short story index reprint series). (Illus.). 1970. Books for Libraries Press.
It's the Climate: Stories of the Caribbean. Charles Horace Rathbone. LC 36-19562. 1936. R. R. Smith.
It's the Last Time! A Novel. 1st Ed. Jessie M Beard. LC 52-12340. 1953. Exposition Press.
It's Time, My Love, It's Time. Vasilii Pavlovich Aksenov. LC 71-114774. 1969. 4.95. Aurora Publishers.
It's Time, My Love, It's Time. Vasiliy Aksyonov. LC 77-108294. (O.s.i.). 226p. 1974. 3.95 o.s.i. (ISBN 0-87695-026-8). Aurora Pubs.
It's Time to Say Goodbye. Isabel Moore. LC 44-735663. 1944. Farrar & Rinehart, Inc.
Its Ugly Head. Derek Monsey. (O.S.I.). 1960. 3.50 o.s.i. (ISBN 0-671-39005-8). S&S.
It's up to You: A Story of Domestic Bliss. George Vere Hobart. LC 3-169253. 1902. G. W. Dillingham Co.
It's What You Are. Mark Lee Luther. LC 31-10356. The Bobbs-Merrill Company.
It's You I Want. Allene Soule Corliss. LC 36-962280. Farrar & Rinehart Inc.
Ivalu, the Eskimo Wife. Peter Freuchen. LC 74-5834. 1975. 27.50 (ISBN 0-404-11639-6). AMS Press.
Ivalu: The Eskimo Wife. Peter Freuchen. Tr. by Jusztis, Janos. LC 35-38104. L. Furman, Inc.
Ivan and Artemis. 1st Ed. Panos Demetrios Bardis. LC 57-8219. Pageant Press.
Ivan De Biron: Or, The Russian Court in the Middle of Last Century. Arthur Helps. LC 7-38270. 1874. Roberts Brothers.
Ivan Ilych and Hadji Murad. Lev Nikolaevich Tolstoi & Maude, Mrs. Louise (Shanks) 1855- Tr. (Half-title: The world's classics. 432). 1935. H. Milford, Oxford University Press.
Ivan Ilyitch, and Other Stories. Lev Nikolaevich Tolstoi & Dole, Nathan Haskell, 1852-1935, Tr. LC 9-3811. T. Y. Crowell & Co.
Ivan Moscow. Boris Andreevich Vogau. LC 72-90305. 1973. 7.50. Hyperion Press.
Ivan Moscow. Boris Andreevich Vogau & Schwartzman, Aaron S., 1900- Tr. LC 35-186893. The Christopher Publishing House.
Ivan the Fool, and Other Tales. Lev Nikolaevich Tolstoi. Tr. by Gay Daniels. LC 66-10285. 1966. Macmillan.
Ivan the Fool and Other Tales. Lev Nikolaevich Tolstoi & Maude, Aylmer, 1858-1938, Tr. LC 31-28498. 1931. Oxford University Press.
Ivan the Fool: Or, The Old Devil and the Three Small Devils, Also A Lost Opportunity, and Polikushka. Lev Nikolaevich Tolstoi & Norraikow, Adolphus, Graf, Tr. 1891. C. L. Webster and Company.
Ivan, the Serf. Sylvanus Cobb. LC 2799. (On cover: Columbia library, v. 2, no. 26). Street & Smith.
Ivan the Serf. A Novel. Sylvanus Cobb. (On cover: The idle hour series, no. 9). 1892. The F. M. Luton Publishing Company.
Ivan Vasileff. Edmond Darcourt. LC 46-21819. 1946. Meador Publishing Company.
Ivanhoe. Walter Scott. LC 51-3933. 1951. Limited Editions Club.
Ivanhoe. the american illuminated abbotsford ed. of the waverley novels ed. Walter Scott. LC 8-5772. 1850. Hewet, Tillotson & Co.
Ivanhoe. Walter Scott. (Seaside library. v. 2, no. 39). 1877. G. Munro.
Ivanhoe. Walter Scott. (On cover: Lovell's library. no. 145). 1883. J. W. Lovell Company.
Ivanhoe. Walter Scott. (On cover: Seaside library. Pocket ed., no. 28). 1883. G. Munro.
Ivanhoe. Walter Scott. Ed. by Simonds, Willam Edward. LC 99-4598. (Lake English classics ed. by L. T. Damon). 1899. Scott, Foresman and Company.
Ivanhoe. Walter Scott. Ed. by Stoddard, Francis Hovey. LC 5-2433. (Half-title: The gateway series of English texts). 1904. American Book Company.
Ivanhoe. Walter Scott. LC 5-20920. (On cover: Maynard's English classics series). Maynard, Merrill, & Co.
Ivanhoe. Walter Scott. (Half-title: The "prairie" classics). 1907. A. C. McClurg & Co.
Ivanhoe. Walter Scott. LC 8-371816. (Standard literature series v. 68). Newson & Company.
Ivanhoe. Walter Scott. Ed. by Blakely, Gilbert Sykes. LC 11-324451. (Merrill's English texts). Charles E. Merrill Company.
Ivanhoe. Walter Scott. LC 13-766018. (On cover: Maynard's English classics series). C. E. Merrill Co.
Ivanhoe. Walter Scott. Ed. by Simonds, William Edward. LC 19-170712. (Lake English classics). Scott, Foresman and Company.
Ivanhoe. Walter Scott. Ed. by Cavenagh, Francis Alexander. LC 22-16602. 1921. The Clarendon Press.
Ivanhoe. Walter Scott. LC 23-12782. 1922. Harper & Brothers.
Ivanhoe. Walter Scott. Ed. by Gordon, Elizabeth Hope & Hawley, Hattie L. LC 24-13703. (Lettered on cover: The modern readers' series). 1924. The Macmillan Company.
Ivanhoe. Walter Scott. Ed. by Harrison, Marion Clifford. (Half-title: University classics for high schools--colleges--universities). 1925. The University Publishing Company.
Ivanhoe. Walter Scott. Ed. by Tressler, Jacob Cloyd. LC 26-17967. (Academy classics for junior high schools). Allyn and Bacon.
Ivanhoe. Walter Scott. LC 29-1563. (father and son library). J. H. Sears & Company, Inc.
Ivanhoe. Walter Scott. Ed. by McGraw, Hiram Ward. LC 28-22579. (Merrill's English texts). Charles E. Merrill Company.
Ivanhoe. Walter Scott. Ed. by Hitchcock, Alfred Marshall. Moffett, Harold Young. LC 29-20591. (Half-title: New pocket classics). The Macmillan Company.
Ivanhoe. abridged ed. Walter Scott. Ed. by McGraw, Hiram Ward. LC 29-7736. (Merrill's English texts). Charles E. Merrill Company.
Ivanhoe. Walter Scott. Ed. by Waldo, Lucile & Waldo, Hal. LC 36-19839. 1936. Harcourt, Brace and Company.
Ivanhoe. Walter Scott & Dana, Richard Henry. LC 42-3998. (Prose and poetry individualised program. The novel). 1942. The L. W. Singer Company.
Ivanhoe. Walter Scott & Adolphe Lalauze. LC 76-20911. (Illus.). 9.95. (ISBN 0-8055-1197-0) (ISBN 0-8055-0284-X). Hart Pub. Co.
Ivanhoe. new impression. ed. Walter Scott & West, Michael Philip. (On cover: New method readers... First supplementary reader 6). 1934. Longmans, Green and Co.
Ivanhoe: A Historical Romance. Walter Scott. 1943. Globe Book Company.
Ivanhoe: A Romance. Walter Scott. LC 65-6644. (Harper perennial classic). 1965. Harper & Row.
Ivanhoe: A Romance. with 17 original illus. by edward augustiny. ed. Walter Scott. LC 50-5582. (World's greatest literature). 1949. Foundation Press.
Ivanhoe: A Romance. Walter Scott. Ed. by Yonge, Charlotte Mary. LC 8-3030. (Classics for children). 1886. Ginn and Company.
Ivanhoe: A Romance. Walter Scott. LC 8-3032. T. Y. Crowell & Company.
Ivanhoe: A Romance. Walter Scott. LC 8-3033. (Riverside literature series no. 86). Houghton, Mifflin and Company.
Ivanhoe: A Romance. Walter Scott. Ed. by Hitchcock, Alfred Marshall. LC 513543. (Half-title: Macmillan's pocket English classics). 1900. The Macmillan Company.
Ivanhoe: A Romance. Walter Scott. Ed. by Maxcy, Carroll Lewis. LC 3103. (English classics--Star series). Globe School Book Company.
Ivanhoe: A Romance. Walter Scott. Ed. by Dracass, Carrie E. Tucker. (Twentieth century text-books). 1904. D. Appleton and Company.
Ivanhoe: A Romance. Walter Scott. Ed. by Eaton, Margaret A. 0.50. Educational Publishing Company.
Ivanhoe: A Romance. Walter Scott. 1913. Hougton Mifflin Company.
Ivanhoe: A Romance. Walter Scott. Ed. by Miller, Edwin Lillie. LC 17-163194. (Lettered on cover: Atlas series). 0.50. Lyons & Carnahan.
Ivanhoe: A Romance. Walter Scott. LC 18-13908. Rand, McNally & Company.
Ivanhoe; a Romance. Walter Scott.
Ivanhoe: A Romance... new ed., edited by elizabeth w. baker... ed. Walter Scott. Ed. by Baker, Elizabeth Whitemore. (Riverside literature series). Houghton Mifflin Company.
Ivanhoe: A Romance. Walter Scott. LC 36-37048. (Half-title: Everyman's library, ed. by Ernest Rhys. Fiction. no. 16). 1931. J. M. Dent & Sons, Ltd.
Ivanhoe: A Romance. Walter Scott & MacClintock, Porter Lander. (Heath's English classics). 1900. D. C. Heath & Co.
Ivanhoe: A Romance. Walter Scott & Schreiber, Mae E. LC 1-31130. (Eclectic English classics). American Book Company.
Ivanhoe: A Romance by Sir Walter Scott. National Home Library Edition, Complete and Unabridged. Walter Scott. LC 43-27397. (On cover: National home library). 1935. National Home Library Foundation.
Ivanhoe: A Romance by Sir Walter Scott; with a Preface by the Hon. Mrs. Maxwell Scott of Abbotsford. Illustrated with Maurice Grieffenhagen. Walter Scott. J. B. Lippincott Company.
Ivanhoe; a Romance... From the Last Rev. Ed., Containing the Author's Final Corrections, Notes. &C. parker's ed. Walter Scott. (Waverley novels: Library ed. v. 8). 1830. Bazin & Ellsworth.
Ivanhoe. Ed. by M. W. and G. Thomas. Illus. by Faith Jagues. Walter Scott. LC 66-6653. (Shorter classics). 1966. bds., 2.50. Ginn.
Ivanhoe for Pleasure Reading. Edward William Dolch & Walter Scott. LC 61-4981. (Their Pleasure reading series 1B). (Illus.). 1961. Garrard Press.
Ivanhoe Keeler. Philip Duffield Stong. LC 39-294237. Farrar & Rinehart, Incorporated.
Ivar; or, The Skjuts-Boy. A Romance. Emilia Smith Flygare Carlen. Tr. by Krause, Alex. L. LC 6-20145. 1852. Harper & Brothers.
Ivdas: A Life of Judas Iscariot. Elliott Krefetz. LC 77-78042. 8.95 (ISBN 0-918976-01-4). Minmor Pub. Co.
I've Always Loved You. Maysie Greig. LC 43-8275. 1943. Doubleday, Doran & Company, Inc.
I've Been Thinking. Charles Battell Loomis. LC 5-32466. 1905. J. Pott & Company.
I've Been to London. Temple Bailey. LC 37-162152. The Penn Publishing Company.
I've Come to Stay: A Love Comedy of Bohemia. Mary Marvin Heaton Vorse. LC 19-6568. 1918. The Century Co.
I've Got Mine... Richard Gibson Hubler. LC 46-2498. 1946. G. P. Putnam's Sons.
I've Got Viktor Schalkenburg. William Mulvihill. (Berkley medallion book). 1974. (pbk.) 0.95. Berkley Pub. Co.
I've Had It see Presumed Dead.
I've Married Marjorie. Margaret Widdemer. LC 20-136997. 1920. Harcourt, Brace and Howe.
I've Never Known a Happily Married Couple: A Novel. Robert K Carey. LC 77-11705. 1969. 1.25. Hogarth Press.
Ivorstone Manor. Elsie Cromwell, pseud. 1972. pap. 0.75 o.p. (ISBN 0-446-64717-9, 64-717-9). Paperback Lib.
Ivory. Geoffrey Wills. 1.98 o.p. (ISBN 0-498-06866-8, Encore). A S Barnes.
Ivory Ball. Chauncey Crafts Hotchkiss. LC 20-6863. W. J. Watt & Company.
Ivory Balls & Other Stories. Nancy C. Ing. 120p. 1980. 4.95 (ISBN 0-89955-154-8, Pub. by Mei Ya China); pap. 3.95 (ISBN 0-89955-187-4). Intl Schol Bk Serv.
Ivory Child. with four illustrations by a. c. michael. ed. Henry Rider Haggard. LC 16-8072. 1916. 1.35. Longmans, Green, and Co.
Ivory Child. Illus. by Hookway Cowles. Henry Rider Haggard. 1966. bds., 2.95. Macdonld.
Ivory Cup. Louise Boggan. LC 76-4739. 1976. 4.95 o.p. (ISBN 0-87397-095-0). Strode.
Ivory Dagger. Patricia Wentworth. 1976. Repr. of 1951 ed. lib. bdg. 14.65x (ISBN 0-88411-735-9). Amereon Ltd.
Ivory Dagger. Patricia Wentworth. 240p. 1980. pap. 2.25 (ISBN 0-553-20415-7). Bantam.
Ivory Dagger. Patricia Wentworth. 1973. pap. 0.95 o.p. (ISBN 0-515-02924-6, N2924). Pyramid Pubns.
Ivory Dagger. 1st Ed. Patricia Wentworth. LC 51-9805. (Her A Miss Silver mystery). 1951. Lippincott.
Ivory Disc. Percy James Brebner. LC 20-103662. 1920. 1.75. Duffield and Company.
Ivory Fan. Valerie Bradstreet. 160p. (Orig.). 1982. pap. 2.25 (ISBN 0-380-79244-3, 79244). Avon.
Ivory Fan. Adrian Heard. LC 20-19434. 1921. G. P. Putnam's Sons.
Ivory Gate: A Novel. Walter Besant. 1892. Harper & Brothers.
Ivory Graves: A Novel. Hector Livingstone Duff. LC 26-124667. 1926. Doubleday, Page & Company.
Ivory Graves: A Novel. Hector Livingstone Duff. 1926. T. Nelson & Sons, Ltd.
Ivory Grin. Ross Macdonald. LC 81-4764. 1981. 13.95 (ISBN 0-89340-335-0). J. Curley.
Ivory Grin. Kenneth Millar. LC 51-13221. 1952. Knopf.
Ivory Legend. James P. McCague. (Orig.). 1979. pap. 2.25 (ISBN 0-89083-459-8). Zebra.
Ivory Mischief... Arthur Meeker. LC 41-23967. 1941. Houghton Mifflin Company.
Ivory Mischief... Arthur Meeker. LC 42-7201. 1942. Houghton Mifflin Company.
Ivory Snuff Box. Frederic Arnold Kummer. LC 12-24202. 1.25. W. J. Watt & Company.
Ivory Swing. Jeanette T Hospital. LC 82-20946. 1983. 14.95 (ISBN 0-525-24170-1). Dutton.
Ivory Tower. Marjorie Eatock. (Orig.). 1972. pap. 0.95 o.p. (09128). Curtis.
Ivory Tower. Henry James. Ed. by Lubbock, Percy. LC 17-29022. 1917. C. Scribner's Sons.
Ivory Trail. Talbot Mundy. LC 19-11151. The Bobbs-Merrill Company.
Ivy: Cousin and Bride. A Novel. Percy Greg. (Franklin square library, no. 209). 1881. Harper & Brothers.
Ivy Fennhaven: Or, Womanhood in Christ. A Story of Processes ... LC 7-9478. 1872. D. Lothrop & Co.
Ivy Gripped the Steps: And Other Stories. Elizabeth Bowen. LC 46-31346. 1946. A. A. Knopf.
Ivy Hedge. Maurice Francis Egan. LC 14-20502. 1914. Benziger Brothers.
Ivy Trap. 1st Ed. Douglas Angus. LC 59-14076. 1959. Bobbs-Merrill.
Ivy Tree. Mary Stewart. LC 61-13513. 1961-1962. M. S. Mill.
Ixion in Heaven, and Endymion: Disraeli's Skit and Aytoun's Burlesque. Benjamin Disraeli Beaconsfield. Ed. by Eric Partridge. LC 76-117903. 1970. Books for Libraries Press.
Ixion's Wheel. Gerry Max. 120p. 1979. pap. 4.95 (102). William of Orange.
Iz Evreskikh Poetov. Vladislav Khodasevich. (Rus.). 1982. 10.50 (ISBN 0-88233-412-3); pap. 3.50. Ardis Pubs.
Izamal. Joseph F Wynne. LC 11-16478. The Angelus Publishing Company.
Izamal. Joseph F. Wynne. LC 11-1647. 1911. The Angelus Publishing Company.
Izbrannoe: Selected Stories. Mikhail Zoshchenko. Ed. by Marc Slonim. LC 61-13499. (Rus.). 1960. 6.00 o.p. (ISBN 0-472-99915-X). U of Mich Pr.
Izma: Or, Sunshine and Shadow. A Novel. M. Ozella Shields. LC 8-73163. (Fireside series. no. 80). J. S. Ogilvie.
Izu Dancer and Other Stories. Yasushi Inoue. LC 74-78150. (Tut books. L). 1974. 3.75 (ISBN 0-8048-1141-5). C. E. Tuttle Co.
Izu Dancer & Other Stories. Incl. The Izu Dancer. Yasunari Kawabata. Tr. by Edward Seidensticker; The Counterfeiter, Obasute & the Full Moon. Yasushi Inoue. Tr. by Leon Picon. LC 74-78150. 1974. pap. 4.25 (ISBN 0-8048-1141-5). C E Tuttle.
Izu Dancer and Other Stories. Yasunari Kawabata. lib. bdg. 5.00 o.p. Gannon.
Izumi Shikibu Diary: A Romance of the Heian Court. Edwin A. Cranston. Ed. by Izumi Shikibu. LC 69-13766. (Harvard-Yenching Institute Monograph Ser.: No. 19). 1969. 16.50x (ISBN 0-674-46985-2). Harvard U Pr.

J

J. Archibald McKackney: Collector of Whiskers) Being Certain Episodes Taken from the Diary and Notes of That Estimable Gentleman-Student and Now for the First Time Set Forth. Ralph Delahaye Paine. LC 7-38263. 1907. The Outing Publishing Company.
J. B.'s Daughter. John Sherlock. 408p. (Orig.). 1982. pap. 3.25 (ISBN 0-441-37996-6). Ace Bks.
J C Saves. Robert Gover. LC 68-26707. 1968. 4.50. Trident Press.
J. Cole. Emma Gellibrand. LC 7-1611. H. Altemus Company.
J. Cole. Emma Gellibrand. LC 7-14257. 1907. E. J. Clode.
J. Cole. Emma Gellibrand. LC 17-101651. (On verse of half-title: The children's classics). 1917. 0.50. J. B. Lippincott Company.
J. Cole: The Story of a Boy. Emma Gellibrand. Dodge Publishing Company.
J. Devlin--Boss: A Romance of American Politics. Francis Churchill Williams. LC 1-18548. Lothrop Publishing Company.
J. F. K. Conspiracy. J. W. Dees. 1978. 7.95 (ISBN 0-89185-151-8); pap. 2.95 (ISBN 0-89185-150-X). Anthelion Pr.
J. G. the Upright Ape: Being a Novel About the Way Things Are As Discovered in the Adventures of an Innocent Hero and Illuminated by His Forthright Reaction to Women, Men, Progress, and Other Contemporary Phenomena. 1st Ed. Roger Price. LC 59-13602. 1960. L. Stuart.
J. Hamilton Rose. Robert L. Merriam. 29p. (Orig.). 1979. pap. 2.00. R L Merriam.
J. Hardin & Son. Brand Whitlock & Paul William Miller. LC 82-2240. (Illus.). 1982. 18.95 (ISBN 0-8214-0640-X) (ISBN 0-8214-0641-8). Ohio University Press.
J. Hardin & Son: A Novel. Brand Whitlock. LC 23-14564. 1923. D. Appleton and Company.
J. Johnson: Or, "The Unknown Man"; an Answer to Mr. Thos. Dixon's "Sins of the Fathers.". Thomas Hamilton B. Walker & Dixon, Thomas, 1864- The Sins of the Father. LC 15-16777. The E. O. Painter Printing Co.

J-Jones--Christian. George Shepard Southworth. LC 33-8632. Fleming H. Revell Company.
J. P. Dunbar: A Story of Wall Street. William Cadwalader Hudson. 1906. B. W. Dodge and Company.
J. P. Miller's Days of Wine and Roses: A Novel. David Westheimer & James Pinckney Miller. LC 62-21014. 1963. Bantam Books.
J. Poindexter, Colored. Irvin Shrewsbury Cobb. LC 22-26758. 1.75. George H. Doran Company.
J R. William Gaddis. LC 75-8230. 1975. 10.95 (ISBN 0-394-49550-0) (ISBN 0-394-73142-5). Knopf: Distributed by Random House.
J. W. Thinks Black: Volume Number Two in the John Wesley, Jr., Series. Jay Samuel Stowell. LC 22-12390. The Methodist Book Concern.
J. W. Thinks Black: Volume Number Two in the John Wesley, Jr., Series. Jay Samuel Stowell & Dan Brearley Brummit. LC 78-38026. (Black Heritage Library Collection). (Illus.). 1972. (ISBN 0-8369-8992-9). Books For Libraries Press.
Jaakobs Traum see Jacob's Dream.
Jac and Gill: Or, A Sister's Fidelity; a Novel. Hortense Gardner Gregg. 1898. Advertiser Book Print.
Jacaranda Tree. st ed.. ed. Herbert Bates. LC 48-966002. 1949. Little, Brown.
Jaccardin. William Ryer. G. W. Dillingham Company.
J'accuse: Nice, the Dark Side. Graham Greene. 48p. (Eng. & Fr.). 1982. pap. 3.95 (ISBN 0-370-30930-8, Pub. by Chatto-Bodley-Jonathan). Merrimack Pub Cir.
Jacel. Joseph D Bell. 1929. Willatts Printing Company.
Jacintha. Sara Hylton. LC 81-14583. 10.95 (ISBN 0-312-43938-5). St. Martin's Press.
Jacintha. Sara Hylton. LC 82-12153. 1982. 14.95 (ISBN 0-8161-3419-7). G.K. Hall.
Jacintha Point. Elizabeth Graham, pseud. (Harlequin Romances Ser.). 192p. 1980. pap. 1.25 (ISBN 0-373-02374-X). Harlequin Bks.
Jack. Alphonse Daudet. Tr. by Ensor, Laura. LC 9-3006. 1890. G. Routledge and Sons.
Jack. Alphonse Daudet. LC 6-33052. (primrose series, no. 23). 1891. Street & Smith.
Jack. Alphonse Daudet. (On cover: Seaside library. Pocket ed. no. 534). G. Munro.
Jack. Frank Walker. LC 76-13471. (Illus.). 1976. 7.95 (ISBN 0-698-10752-7). Coward, McCann & Geoghegan.
Jack-- One of Us; a Novel in Verse. Gilbert Frankau. LC 12-16110. 1.20. George H. Doran Company.
Jack Adams: Or, The Mutiny of the Bounty. Frederick Chamier. LC 45-42398. (On cover: Captain Chamier's novels). G. Routledge & Sons.
Jack & Ari: For Love or Money. George Carpozi. pap. 0.75 o.p. Lancer.
Jack and Gil: Or, The Wonderful Adventures of Two Acrobats. Harlan Page Halsey. (Old Sleuth's own; no. 106). 1898. The Parlor Car Publishing Co.
Jack and I in Lotus Land. Fannie Macaulay. LC 22-202815. 1922. Harper & Brothers.
Jack & Jill: Two Novellas and a Short Story. Rick De Marinis. LC 78-17727. 9.95 (ISBN 0-525-12795-X). Dutton.
Jack and the Flying Saucer: And Other Children's Stories. Margaret Ricaud Kelly. (Illus.). 1973. 3.75 (ISBN 0-533-00565-5). Vantage.
Jack and Three Jills. Francis Charles Philips. (On cover: Lovell's library, no. 1097). 1887. J. W. Lovell Company.
Jack and Three Jills. A Novel. Francis Charles Philips. (On cover: Seaside library. Pocket ed. no. 1048). 1887. G. Munro.
Jack Ashore. Edward Howard. LC 7-7145. 1840. Carey and Hart.
Jack Ballington, Forester. John Trotwood Moore. LC 11-9896. The John C. Winston Co.
Jack Be Nimble. George Cuomo. 3.95 o.p. Doubleday.
Jack Be Quick. Richard B Koiner. LC 66-11852. 1966. L. Stuart.
Jack Betrayed His Buddy. Sam Mumford. 2.75 o.p. Vantage.
Jack Brag. new ed. Theodore Edward Hook. LC 42-26360. 1872. G. Routledge and Sons.
Jack Brainard: A Romance of the Cherokee Hills. John Wesley Yoes. LC 5-4089. 1904. Eastern Publishing Company.
Jack Brereton's Three Months' Service. Maria McIntosh Cox. LC 11-105313. D. Lothrop Company.
Jack Carter and the Law. Ted Lewis. LC 75-8246. 1975. 6.95 (ISBN 0-394-49539-X). Knopf: Distributed by Random House.
Jack Carter & the Mafia Pigeon. Ted Lewis. 220p. 1978. 10.95 (ISBN 0-7181-1372-1, Pub. by Michael Joseph). Merrimack Pub Cir.
Jack Casey and Molly O'Dea. John Joseph Mullins. LC 30-12528. Printed by The Wyoming State Journal.
Jack Chaloner: Or, The Fighting Forty-Third. James Grant. LC 43-28886. 1883. G. Routledge and Sons.
Jack Chanty: A Story of Athabasca. Hulbert Footner. LC 13-20126. 1913. Doubleday, Page & Co.
Jack Crews. Martha Frye Boggs. LC 96. 1899. G. W. Dillingham Co.
Jack Datchett, the Clerk: An Old Man's Tale... John Donaldson. LC 6-39370. 1846. H. Colburn.
Jack Doyle's Daughter. Robert Edward Francillon. (Seaside library, v. 65, no. 1327). G. Munro.
Jack. From the French of Alphonse Daudet... Alphonse Daudet. Tr. by Sherwood, Mary Neal. LC 6-33053. (Cobweb series of choice fiction). 1877. Estes and Lauriat.
Jack. From the French of Alphonse Daudet... Alphonse Daudet. Tr. by Sherwood, Mrs Mary Neal. (On cover: Lovell's library. v. 12. no. 613). J. W. Lovell Company.
Jack Gordon, Knight Errant: Gotham, 1883. William Cadwalader Hudson. LC 7-5647. (On cover: Cassell's sunshine series of choice fiction. v. 1, no. 41). 1890. Cassell Publishing Company.
Jack Hardin's Rendering of the Arabian Nights: Being a New Translation in up-to-Date English, with Wise Comments, Explanations, &C., by This Eminent Linquist. James Winfield Scott. LC 2-11813. 1903. H. B. Turner & Co.
Jack Hartnett. A Story of Naples. Gilbert Lee Lyon. LC 21-20583. (Dillingham's globe library, no. 10). 1896. G. W. Dillingham.
Jack Hinton, the Guardsman. Charles James Lever. (Seaside library, v. 7, no. 132). 1877. G. Munro.
Jack Hinton, the Guardsman. Charles James Lever. LC 3-14811. (On cover: Seaside library. Pocket edition. no. 2070). 1894. G. Munro.
Jack Hinton, the Guardsman. Charles James Lever. LC 4-16545. 1902. Little, Brown, & Company.
Jack Hopeton: Or, The Adventures of a Georgian. William Wilberforce Turner. LC 72-2929. (Black Heritage Library Collection). 1972. 15.00 (ISBN 0-8369-9085-4). Books for Libraries Press.
Jack Hopeton: Or, The Adventures of a Georgian. William Wilberforce Turner. LC 9-2505. 1860. Derby & Jackson.
Jack Horner: a Novel. Mary Spear Nicholas Tiernan. LC 8-19823. 1890. Houghton, Mifflin and Company.
Jack Horner's Pie: A Book of Nursery Rhymes. Ed. by Lois Lenski. LC 27-24307. 1927. Harper & Brothers.
Jack-in-the-Box. Alfred Walter Steward. LC 43-188523. 1944. Little, Brown and Company.
Jack in the Jungle: A Tale of Land and Sea. Being Perilous Adventures Among Wild Men, and the Capturing of Wild Beasts; Showing How Menageries Are Made. Phineas Taylor Barnum. LC 8-24460. G. W. Dillingham Co.
Jack Is a King. Norman Keifetz. LC 62-17687. 1962. Dial Press.
Jack-Knife Man. Ellis Parker Butler. LC 13-195022. 1913. The Century Co.
Jack London: Short Stories. Jack London. Ed. by Maxwell Geismar. (Orig.). 1960. pap. 1.95 o.p. (ISBN 0-8090-0033-4, AmCen). Hill & Wang.
Jack London: Twelve Short Stories. Jack London. Ed. by Jeffery Tillet. (Illus.). (gr. 9-12). 1970. pap. text ed. 1.60 o.p. St Martin.
Jack London's Klondike Tales. Jack London. 224p. (Orig.). Date not set. pap. price not set o.p. (ISBN 0-505-51797-3). Tower Bks.
Jack London's Tales of Adventure. Jack London. LC 56-5714. 1956. 10.00 o.p. (ISBN 0-385-01496-1). Doubleday.
Jack London's Tales of Hawaii. Jack London. LC 81-23492. 1982. 4.95. Press Pacifica.
Jack London's Tales of Hawaii. Jack London. LC 81-23492. 80p. 1982. pap. 4.95 o.p. (ISBN 0-916630-25-0). Pr Pacifica.
Jack London's Yukon Women. Jack London. 224p. Date not set. pap. price not set o.p. (ISBN 0-505-51807-4). Tower Bks.
Jack Manly. His Adventures by Sea and Land. James Grant. LC 6-276746. (Seaside library, v. 13, no. 245). G. Munro.
Jack Morning's Treasure. Bailey Millard. LC 9-25390. E. J. Clode.
Jack Norton. Ernst Hofer. LC 13-3755. 1.25. R. G. Badger.
Jack-O'-Chance: A Novel. Grosvenor Sadler. LC 31-34493. The Four Seas Company, Incorporated.
Jack O' Judgment. Edgar Wallace. LC 21-19847. Small, Maynard & Company.
Jack O' Lantern. George Goodchild. LC 31-417719. 1930. The Mystery League, Inc.
Jack O'Doon: A Novel. Marie Taylor Beale. LC 6-10274. (On cover: Buckram series). 1894. H. Holt and Company.
Jack of Deer Creek. Joseph Elgon Norvell. LC 16-14635. 1916. 1.00. The Christian Witness Co.
Jack of Eagles. James Blish. LC 52-5618. 1952. Greenberg.
Jack of Hearts. Don Von Elsner. (Jake Winkman Ser., No. 3). (O.s.i.). (Orig.). 1968. pap. 0.60 o.s.i. (A370X, Award). Univ Pub & Dist.
Jack of Hearts. A Story Of Bohemia. H T Johnson. (On cover: Seaside library. Pocket ed., no. 1183). 1889. G. Munro.
Jack of Shadows. Roger Zelazny. LC 70-142849. 1971. 5.95 (ISBN 0-8027-5535-6). Walker.
Jack of Swords. E. C. Tubb. (Dumarest Ser.: N0. 14). 1976. pap. 1.25 o.p. (ISBN 0-87997-239-4, UY1239). DAW Bks.
Jack of Swords. E. C Tubb. (Dumarest of Terra). (Dumarest of terra #14: Vol. 14). 1976. 1.25. Daw Books.
Jack O'Lantern. Kathleen A Shoesmith. 1973. (pbk.) 0.75. Ace.
Jack on the Gallows Tree. Leo Bruce, pseud. LC 83-3746. 1983. 14.95 (ISBN 0-89733-071-4) (ISBN 0-89733-072-2). Academy Chicago.
Jack on the Gallows Tree. Leo Bruce, pseud. 1982. 15.00x (ISBN 0-86025-158-6, Pub. by Ian Henry Pubns England). State Mutual Bk.
Jack Payton and His Friends. A Book in Four Parts. May Anderson Hawkins. LC 7-2190. 1896. Presbyterian Committee of Publication.
Jack Racer. Mary Gay Humphreys. LC 1-21949. 1901. McClure, Phillips & Co.
Jack Raymond. Ethel Lillian Boole Voynich. LC 1-8326. 1901. J. B. Lippincott Company.
Jack Runnymede: The Man of Many Thanks. Douglas William Jerrold. (Men of character). Bunce & Brother.
Jack Shelby: A Story of the Indiana Backwoods. George Cary Eggleston. LC 6-20455. 1906. Lothrop, Lee & Shepard Co.
Jack Sheppard: A Romance, 3 vols. in 2. William Harrison Ainsworth. LC 79-8224. (Illus.). Repr. of 1839 ed. Set. 84.50 (ISBN 0-404-61751-4). AMS Pr.
Jack Sprat. Isabel Campbell. LC 29-19779. 1929. Coward-McCann, Inc.
Jack Spurlock--Prodigal. George Horace Lorimer. LC 8-16951. 1908. Doubleday, Page & Company.
Jack Sutherland: A Tale of Bloody Marsh. Theodore E. Oertel. LC 74-2401. (Illus.). 346p. 1974. Repr. of 1926 ed. 16.50 (ISBN 0-87152-183-0). Reprint.
Jack the Bear. Dan McCall. LC 73-10809. 1974. 5.95 (ISBN 0-385-02545-9). Doubleday.
Jack the Bear. Dan McCall. (Fawcett Crest Book). 1976. (pbk.) 1.50. Fawcett.
Jack the Fisherman. Elizabeth Stuart Phelps H. D. Ward Ward. LC 8-33109. 1887. Houghton, Mifflin and Company.
Jack the Giant-Killer. Anne Isabella Thackeray Ritchie. LC 7-41664. (On cover: Loring's tales of the day). 1867. Loring.
Jack the Ripper: A Novel of Suspense Based on the Original Screen Play by Jimmy Sangster; Plus a True-to-Life Account of the Actual 'Ripper' Murders--the Most Infamous Series of Unsolved Crimes in the History of Scotland Yard--by Bill Doll. Stuart James. (143). Monarch Books.
Jack the Ripper: A Novel of Suspense. Based on the Original Screen Play by Jimmy Sangster. Plus Bill Doll's Factual Account of the Actual 'Ripper' Murders... James, Stuart. LC 60-875. 1960. F. Fell.
Jack Tier: Or, The Florida Reef. James Fenimore Cooper. LC 6-29887. 1848. Burgess, Stringer & Co.
Jack Tier: Or, The Florida Reef. new ed. James Fenimore Cooper. LC 6-29886. 1852. Stringer and Townsend.
Jack Tier: Or, The Florida Reef. James Fenimore Cooper. LC 26-24684. (Half-title: The choice works of Cooper. Revised and corrected series v. 19). 1856. Stringer & Townsend.
Jack Tier: Or, The Florida Reef. household ed. James Fenimore Cooper. Ed. by Cooper, Susan Fenimore. LC 6-29885. 1884. Houghton, Mifflin and Company.
Jack Tier: Or, The Florida Reef. James Fenimore Cooper. (On cover: Lovell's library, no. 611). 1885. J. W. Lovell Company.
Jack Tier: Or, The Florida Reef. James Fenimore Cooper. (On cover: Seaside library. Pocket ed. no 416). 1885. G. Munro.
Jack Tier: Or, The Florida Reef. new ed. James Fenimore Cooper. LC 48-41607. 1856. Stringer and Townsend.
Jack Urquhart's Daughter. A Novel. Pamela Sneyd. LC 22-173647. (Seaside library, v. 64, no. 1302). 1882. G. Munro.
Jack Wheeler: A Western Story. John Murphy. LC 2126. (Medal library, no. 45). 1900. Street & Smith.
Jack Winthrop of Old 15. A Story of School-Life in a New-York City Public School. Abram W Moynihan. 1887. The Author.
Jackals' Gold. Kenneth Fowler. LC 79-7797. 1980. 8.95 (ISBN 0-385-15683-9). Doubleday.
Jackal's Head. Elizabeth Peters, pseud. LC 68-19028. 1968. Meredith Press.
Jackal's Head: By Elizabeth Peters. 1st Ed. Barbara Mertz. LC 68-19028. 1968. 4.95. Meredith.
Jackanapes & Other Stories. Juliana Horatia Gatty Ewing. (Legacy Library Ser). 1966. Repr. of 1884 ed. 4.95 o.p. (LL01007). Univ Microfilms.
Jackdaw. Christopher Hill. LC 75-21460. (Rinehart suspense novel). 1976. 6.95. Holt, Rinehart and Winston.
Jackdaw. Henry H Roth. LC 76-151179. (Beyond Baroque Newbook). (Beyond Baroque Foundation publications; v. 7, no. 4). Beyond Baroque Foundation.
Jackdaws Strut. Harriet Henry, pseud. LC 30-137053. 1930. W. Morrow & Co.
Jacket. Jack London. LC 69-12446. (Horizon edition of the works of Jack London). 1969. 3.95. Horizon Press.
Jackie. Marguerite Florence Helene Evans. LC 21-5175. 1921. Houghton Mifflin Company.
Jackie, with Love: We, the People of Camelot. Hy Farnum. LC 74-82899. 92p. 1975. 6.95 (ISBN 0-915790-01-7); padded cover 2.95 (ISBN 0-915790-02-5); pap. 1.50 (ISBN 0-915790-03-3). Farnum Films.
Jackknife John. Frank Borden Hanes. LC 64-25243. 1964. Naylor.
Jacklighting. Ann Beattie. (Metacom Limited Edition Ser.: No. 3). 24p. 1981. ltd. 25.00x (ISBN 0-911381-02-3). Metacom Pr.
Jacklove Affair: A Novel. Peter Menegas. LC 68-54159. 1968. 4.95. Coward-McCann.
Jackman's Wolf. Ray Hogan. LC 76-123696. (Double D western). 1970. 4.50. Doubleday.
Jackpine Savage. Art Lee. 1981. 5.95 (ISBN 0-934860-15-7). Adventure Pubns.
Jackpot: The Short Stories of Erskine Caldwell. Erskine Caldwell. LC 40-31621. Duell, Sloan and Pearce.
Jack's Afire," Or, The Burton Torch. Florence M Campbell. LC 6-21495. J. L. Regan.
Jack's Courtship. William Clark Russell. (On cover: Lovell's library. v. 17, no. 834). 1886. J. W. Lovell Company.
Jack's Courtship. A Sailor's Yarn of Love and Shipwreck. William Clark Russell. (On cover: Seaside library. Pocket ed., no. 743). 1886. G. Munro.
Jack's Father and Other Stories. William Edward Norris. LC 7-33292. J. W. Lovell Company.
Jack's Return Home. Ted Lewis. LC 71-97670. 1970. 4.95. Doubleday.
Jackson County Jail. Sam Stewart. (Dell Book). 1977. 1.50 (ISBN 0-440-14254-7). Dell Pub. Co.
Jackson Gregory's Golden West Omnibus Containing Three Complete Novels: Wolf Breed, Redwood and Gold, Sentinel of the Desert. Jackson Gregory. LC 37-17799. 1936. Grosset & Dunlap.
Jackson Hole Trouble. Jake Logan. 224p. (Orig.). 1983. pap. 2.25 (ISBN 0-425-06139-6). Berkley Pub.
Jackson Mahaffey: A Novel. Fred E Ross. LC 50-11539. Houghton Mifflin.
Jackson Street. Anne Austin. LC 27-228407. Greenberg.
Jackson Trail. Max Brand. LC 32-30784. 1932. Dodd, Mead & Company.
Jackson Trail. Frederick Faust. LC 32-30784. 1932. Dodd, Mead & Company.
Jackson Trail. Frederick Faust. LC 79-1294. 1981. 11.50 (ISBN 0-89340-199-4). J. Curley.
Jackson's Hole Story: An Historical Novel Set in the Grand Teton Mountains of Wyoming. Josephine C Fabian. LC 63-4594. 1963. Desert Book Co.
Jackson's War: A Novel. Ray Rigby. LC 67-20173. 1967. Lippincott.
Jackson's Way. Gerard Herzog. LC 77-17773. 1978. 9.95 (ISBN 0-374-17855-0). Farrar, Straus, Giroux.
Jackstraws. Leslie Curtis. LC 32-32020. The Mitchell Company.
Jacob: An Autobiographical Novel... Irving Fineman. LC 41-21279. Random House.
Jacob and His Wives. Sarah Clifford. LC 68-21573. 1968. M. W. Lads Pub. Co.
Jacob and the Angel. Maurits Ignatius Boas. LC 61-9264. 1961. F. Fell.
Jacob and the Lion. Virginia Sarah Thatcher. LC 51-941. 1950. Humphries.
Jacob and the Lion: By Shelby G. Wooster Pseud. Virginia Sarah Thatcher. LC 51-941. 1950. Humphries.
Jacob Atabet: A Speculative Fiction. Michael Murphy. LC 77-79875. 4.95 (ISBN 0-89087-207-4). Celestial Arts.
Jacob Faithful. Frederick Marryat. LC 42-268173. G. Routledge and Sons.
Jacob Faithful. Frederick Marryat. LC 4-16564. 1895. Macmillan and Co.
Jacob Faithful. Frederick Marryat. LC 36-37608. (Half-title: Everyman's library, ed. by Ernest Rhys. Fiction. no. 618). 1931. J. M. Dent & Sons, Ltd.

Jacob Faithful. Frederick Marryat. LC 36-27340. (Half-title: The world's classics. 439). 1936. H. Milford, Oxford University Press.
Jacob Faithful: Or, The Adventures of a Waterman. Frederick Marryat. (Seaside library, v. 14, no. 266). 1878. G. Munro.
Jacob Faithful: Or, The Adventures of a Waterman. Frederick Marryat. LC 7-24686. (Seaside library. Pocket ed. no. 2107). 1895. G. Munro's Sons.
Jacob Have I Loved. Jean A Rees. LC 63-25833. 1963. Eerdmans.
Jacob Schuyler's Millions. A Novel. Thomas Dunn English. LC 6-38406. 1886. A. Appleton and Company.
Jacob the Liar. Jurek Becker. LC 75-19184. 1975. 7.95 (ISBN 0-15-145975-4). Harcourt Brace Jovanovich.
Jacob. Translated from the French by Gerard Hopkins. 1st Ed. Jean Cabries. LC 58-10819. 1958. Dutton.
Jacob Two Two Meets the Hooded Fang. Mordecai Richler. 1981. pap. 2.50. Bantam.
Jacob Valmont, Manager. George A Wall & Heckel, George B., Joint Author. LC 8-33287. 1889. Rand, McNally & Company.
Jacobean & Restoration Shorter Novels. Ed. by Philip Henderson. 3.25x o.p. (ISBN 0-460-00841-2, Evman). Dutton.
Jacobi's Wife. A Novel. Adeline Sergeant. (Harper's Franklin square library, no. 591). 1887. Harper & Brothers.
Jacob's Dream. Richard Beer-Hofmann. Tr. by Ida B. Wynn from Ger. Orig. Title: Jaakobs Traum. 1946. text ed. 8.50x. M S Rosenberg.
Jacob's Ladder. Elizabeth Carfrae, pseud. LC 40-113321. G. P. Putnam's Sons.
Jacob's Ladder. Bradford Kempton Daniels. LC 49-8510. 1949. B. Humphries.
Jacob's Ladder. LC 65-17699. 5.00. Bobbs.
Jacob's Ladder. Kathryn Johnston Noyes. LC 65-17699. 1965. Bobbs-Merrill.
Jacob's Ladder. Edward Phillips Oppenheim. LC 21-4320. 1921. Little, Brown, and Company.
Jacob's Ladder. Arthur Cheney Train. 1935. C. Scribner's Sons.
Jacob's Ladder: Illustrated by Jessie Ayers. Marjorie Kinnan Rawlings. LC 50-10988. 1950. University of Miami Press.
Jacobs Park Killings: A Police-Procedural Mystery. William Camp. LC 78-57257. 8.95 (ISBN 0-8149-0803-9). Vanguard Press.
Jacob's Room. Virginia Stephen Woolf. LC 77-358943. 1976. 0.90 (ISBN 0-586-04445-0). Triad.
Jacob's Room. Virginia Stephen Woolf. LC 23-389221. Harcourt, Brace and Company.
Jacob's Room. Virginia Stephen Woolf. LC 77-92141. (Harvest/HBJ book). 1978. 2.95 (ISBN 0-15-645742-3). Harcourt Brace Jovanovich.
Jacob's Room & the Waves. Virginia Stephen Woolf. 383p. 1960. pap. 2.95 o.p. (ISBN 0-15-645750-4, HB37, Harv). HarBraceJ.
Jacob's Son. Ben Field. LC 71-147327. 1971. 6.95 o.p. Crown.
Jacoby's First Case. J. C. S Smith. LC 79-55604. 1980. 8.95 (ISBN 0-689-11057-X). Atheneum.
Jacomo, the Bandit Chief: Translated from the French. Adelbert Von Chamisso & Manning, George, Tr. LC 44-14014. C. Hagan & Co.
Jaconetta Stories. Fannie Heaslip Lea. LC 12-8411. 1912. 1.00. Sturgis & Walton Company.
Jaconetta Stories. Fanny Heaslip Lea. LC 76-130061. (Short story index reprint series). (Illus.). 1970. Books for Libraries Press.
Jacquelien of the Carrier-Pigeons. Augusta Huiell Seaman. LC 10-7830. 1910. Sturgis and Walton Company.
Jacqueline. Francis Browning Drew Bickerstaffe-Drew. 1918. P. J. Kenedy & Sons.
Jacqueline. ed. de luxe ed. Marie Therese Blanc. (Added t.-p.: The Immortals; masterpiece of fiction...). Maison Mazarin.
Jacqueline. Marie Therese Blanc. LC 42-1410. 1910. Current Literature Publishing Company.
Jacqueline: And Four Other Stories from the French by Henri Duvernois. Pierre Mille, J. Joseph-Renaud, Andre Warnod, Maurice Level. Henri Duvernois et al. LC 25-24590. 1925. Minton, Balch & Company.
Jacqueline and the Japanese. Heinrich Eduard Jacob & Cross, Samuel Hazzard. LC 30-9243. 1930. Little, Brown and Company.
Jacqueline of Golden River. H. M Egbert. LC 21-757. 1920. Doubleday, Page & Company.
Jacqueline Susann's Dolores. Jacqueline Susann. LC 76-3584. 1976. 6.95 (ISBN 0-688-03057-2). Morrow.
Jacqueminot see Deadly Rose.
Jacqueminot: The Romance of a Rose. by may howell beecher... ed. May Howell Beecher. LC 1-22981. (On cover: Neely's popular library, no. 6.). 1901. F. T. Neely Co.
Jacques. 2d ed. George Sand & Blackwell, Anna, Tr. LC 6-34602. 1847. J. S. Redfield.
Jacques le Fataliste, I. Denis Diderot. (Classiques Larousse). (Fr). pap. 0.95 o.p. Larousse.
Jacques the Fatalist & His Master. Denis Diderot. Tr. by J. Robert Loy. 1979. pap. 5.95 (ISBN 0-393-00903-3, N895, Norton Lib). Norton.
Jacques the Fatalist & His Master. Denis Diderot. Tr. by J. Robert Loy. 1959. 7.95x o.p. (ISBN 0-8147-0122-1). NYU Pr.
Jacques the Fatalist & His Master. Denis Diderot. Ed. by J. Robert Loy. 1962. pap. 1.50 o.p. (05048, Collier). Macmillan.
Jacquine of the Hut: A Romance of the Channel Islands. E. Gallienne Robin. LC 11-28740. 1912. 1.35. G. P. Putnam's Sons.
Jacquou the Rebel: Jacquou le Croquant. Eugene Le Roy & Brooks, Mrs. Eleanor Kenyon (Stimson) Tr. LC 19-2017. (Half-title: The library of French fiction, ed. by B. J. Reyer). E. P. Dutton & Company.
Jade: A Novel. Lynn Devon. (Fawcett Gold Medal Book). 1.75 (ISBN 0-449-13941-7). Fawcett Books.
Jade: A Novel of China. Pat Barr. LC 82-5658. (Illus.). 14.95 (ISBN 0-312-43943-1). St. Martin's Press.
Jade Alliance. Elizabeth Darrell. LC 79-14342. 10.95 (ISBN 0-399-12342-3). Putnam.
Jade; and Other Stories. Hugh Wiley. LC 21-20188. 1921. A. A. Knopf.
Jade Bough, White Shadows. Sue McConkey. 1967. 5.00 o.p. (ISBN 0-87482-050-2). Wake-Brook.
Jade Box. Nancy Faulkner. (queen-size gothic). (Illus.). 1974. (pbk.) 0.95. Popular Library.
Jade Cat. George Mair. (Lou Brick Ser.: No. 1). (Orig.). 1974. pap. 0.95 o.p. (ISBN 0-515-03515-7, N3515). BJ Pub Group.
Jade Dragon. Nancy Buckingham. LC 74-7886. 7.95 (ISBN 0-8015-8312-8). Hawthorn Books.
Jade Eagle. Elizabeth Baldwin Hazelton. LC 72-123837. 1970. 4.95. Scribner.
Jade Earrings. Berta Ruck. 1941. Dodd, Mead & Company.
Jade Ecstasy. Celia G. Richards. 1981. pap. 2.95 (ISBN 0-89083-790-2). Zebra.
Jade Elephant: A Novel by Elsie Sic Fraser. Elise Fraser. LC 52-68717. 1952. Van Kampen Press.
Jade Enchantress. E. Hoffman Price. 1982. pap. 2.75 (ISBN 0-345-29835-7, Del Rey). Ballantine.
Jade, Fact and Fable: With Lists of Reported Finds of Jadestone and of Prehistoric Objects of Worked Jade. Charles Hardinge & George Hardinge. LC 67-11730. 1961. Published for the Bulbenkian Museum, School of Oriental Studies, University of Durham, by Luzac.
Jade Figurine. Jack Foxx. LC 72-80802. (Black bat mystery). 1972. 4.95. Bobbs-Merrill.
Jade Figurines. Jan Alexander, pseud. (Orig.). 1973. pap. 0.95 o.p. (09170). Curtis.
Jade for a Lady. M. E. Chaber, pseud. (Milo March Mystery Ser). 1970. pap. 0.60 o.p. (63-204). Paperback Lib.
Jade God. Alan Sullivan. LC 25-2347. The Century Co.
Jade Green. Dorothy Daniels. 1973. 0.95. Warner Paperback Library.
Jade Green Cats. Eleanor Blake Atkinson Pratt. LC 31-7177. 1931. R. M. McBride & Company.
Jade in Aries. Tucker Coe. LC 79-101335. 1971. 4.95 o.p. (ISBN 0-394-43100-6). Random.
Jade in Aries. Donald E Westlake. LC 77-127533. 1971. 4.95. Random House.
Jade Is Green. Guat-Hoon Khaw. LC 60-13890. 1960. Pageant Press.
Jade Lotus. Dorothy Cunynghame. LC 34-13423. C. Kendall.
Jade Mountain. Witter Bynner. pap. 1.45 o.p. (A411, Anch). Doubleday.
Jade of Destiny. Jeffery Farnol. LC 31-30602. 1931. Little, Brown, and Company.
Jade Pagoda. Betty Hale Hyatt. LC 79-8433. 1980. 8.95 (ISBN 0-385-15746-0). Doubleday.
Jade Piccolo. C. L Shipley. LC 69-20012. 1969. 5.95. Atheneum.
Jade Rabbit. Adele Blood & Marrioett, Tam, Joint Author. LC 27-7886. 1927. L. McVeagh, The Dial Press.
Jade Star. Manuel Komroff. LC 51-14944. Sloane.
Jade Tiger. Craig Thomas. LC 82-70235. 1982. 14.95 (ISBN 0-670-40469-1). Viking Press.
Jade Unicorn. Jay Halpern. LC 79-18773. 9.95 (ISBN 0-02-547560-6). Macmillan.
Jade Vendetta. Janet Louise Roberts. 1976. (pbk.) 1.75 (ISBN 0-671-80312-3). Pocket Books.
Jade Venus. George Harmon Coxe. LC 45-156072. 1945. A. A. Knopf.
Jade Warrior. Jeffrey Lord. (Richard Blade Ser). (Orig.). 1969. pap. 0.75 o.p. (75-246). Manor Bks.
Jade Wind. John Harris. LC 71-78707. 1969. 5.95. Doubleday.
Jaded Vengeance. Murray Painter. 5.95 o.p. Vantage.
Jades and Dragons. Der Ling. LC 32-14949. The Mohawk Press.
Jadie Greenway: A Novel. Isador S Young. LC 47-30843. 1947. Crown Publishers.
Jaffery. William John Locke. LC 15-26351. 1915. 1.35. John Lane Company.
Jagged Edge. Wendy Westervelt. (Orig.). 1981. pap. 2.25 (ISBN 0-505-51620-9). Tower Bks.
Jagua Nana. Cyprian Ekwensi. (African Writers Ser.). 1975. pap. text ed. 4.00x (ISBN 0-435-90146-X). Heinemann Ed.
Jagua Nana. Cyprian Ekwensi. 1969. pap. 0.75 o.p. (T454, Prem). Fawcett World.
Jaguar and the Golden Stag: A Novel. Dexter Allen. LC 54-6047. (Illus.). 1954. Coward-McCann.
Jail Bait. Sally Chayes. LC 33-285996. 1933. W. Godwin, Inc.
Jail Bait. Albert Harry Martin. LC 32-176737. D. G. Fischer.
Jail Gates Are Open. John Victor Turner. LC 35-23331. D. Appleton-Century Company, Incorporated.
Jailbait & the Stud. Geoffrey Kyle. 192p. pap. 1.95 o.p. (6159). Brandon.
Jailbird. Kurt Vonnegut. 1979. 9.95 (ISBN 0-440-05449-4, Sey Lawr). Delacorte.
Jailbird. Kurt Vonnegut. 1980. pap. 3.50 (ISBN 0-440-15447-2). Dell.
Jailbird. Kurt Vonnegut. (General Ser.). 1980. pap. 8.95 (ISBN 0-8161-3103-1, Large Print Bks). G K Hall.
Jailbird: A Novel. Kurt Vonnegut. 1979. Delacorte Press/Seymour Lawrence.
Jailbird: A Novel. Kurt Vonnegut. LC 79-24919. 1980. 13.95 (ISBN 0-8161-3022-1). G. K. Hall.
Jailbird: By Susan Vincent Pseud. Lillie Morgan. LC 54-8339. 1954. Vantage Press.
Jailbirds in the Backseat. pap. 1.95 o.s.i. (OPH-177, Ophelia). Olympia.
Jailbirds in the Backseat. Marcus Van Heller, pseud. LC 70-5672. 1.75. Ophelia Press.
Jailer, My Jailer. Marian Gavin. 1964. Doubleday.
Jailhouse Harem. Garry Seneca. pap. 1.95 o.p. (8069). Cameo.
Jaime De Angulo Reader. Jaime De Angulo. Ed. by Bob Callahan. LC 78-59741. (New World Writing Ser.). (Illus.). 1979. pap. 8.95 (ISBN 0-913666-30-0). Turtle Isl Foun.
Jaimie. John Leonard Becker. LC 80-65424. 1980. 10.00 (ISBN 0-87923-340-0). D. R. Godine.
Jake. Phyllis Hegland. 1979. pap. 2.95 (ISBN 0-89185-199-2). Anthelion Pr.
Jake. Eunice Hammond Tietjens. LC 21-6498. Boni and Liveright.
Jake: A Novel. Naomi Gwladys Royde-Smith. LC 35-13903. 1935. The Macmillan Company.
Jake & Katie. Brad Solomon. LC 78-23926. 9.95 (ISBN 0-8037-4163-4). Dial Press.
Jake Bell: Range Rider. Upton Barnard. LC 54-1589. 1954. Naylor Co.
Jake Home. Ruth McKenney. LC 43-36646. 1943. Harcourt, Brace and Company.
Jake of Diamonds. Don Von Elsner. (O.s.i.). 1967. pap. 0.60 o.s.i. (A262X, Award). Univ Pub & Dist.
Jake; or, The Young Dragoon. A Story of the Revolutionary Struggle. Edwards Keeler Olmstead. (Owl library, no. 1). 1892. G. W. Studley.
Jake's Thing. Kingsley Amis. LC 78-24127. 1979. 10.00 (ISBN 0-670-40471-3). Viking Press.
Jake's Thing. Kingsley Amis. LC 80-13178. 1980. 2.95 (ISBN 0-14-005096-5). Penguin Books.
Jakob von Gunten. Robert Walser. Tr. by Christopher Middleton from Ger. 154p. 1969. 10.95x (ISBN 0-292-70015-6); pap. 0.00 o.p. U of Tex Pr.
Jakob Von Gunten: A Novel. Robert Walser. LC 75-108962. 1969. 5.50. University of Texas Press.
Jalna. Mazo De La Roche. LC 27-20980. 1927. Little, Brown, and Company.
Jalna. Mazo De La Roche. LC 36-29636. 1928. Grosset & Dunlap.
Jalna... Mazo De La Roche. LC 45-20697. 1945.
Jalna. Mazo De La Roche. 1979. pap. 1.95 (ISBN 0-449-24118-1, Crest). Fawcett.
Jam for Breakfast. Winifred Halsted. LC 40-7593. 1940. H. C. Kinsey & Company, Inc.
Jam Girl. Frances Roberta Sterrett. LC 14-2352. 1914. 1.25. D. Appleton and Company.
Jamaic Inn. Daphne Du Maurier. 1979. Repr. lib. bdg. 17.95x (ISBN 0-89966-432-6). Buccaneer Bks.
Jamaica. Amanda Hart Douglass. (Leisure Books). 1.75 (ISBN 0-8439-0492-5). Nordon Pubns.
Jamaica Inn. Daphne Du Maurier. LC 36-8941. 1936. Doubleday, Doran & Company, Inc.
Jamaica Inn. Daphne Du Maurier. 1943. Triangle Books.
Jamaica Inn: By Daphne Du Maurier, and The Thirty-Nine Steps, by John Buchan. Edited and Abridged by Jay E. Greene. Daphne Du Maurier & John Buchan. LC 51-7131. 1951. Globe Book Co.
Jamaica Lady, or the Life of Baria see Four Before Richardson: Selected English Novels, 1720-1727.
Jamaica Passage. Rupert Challoner. 1982. pap. 2.95 (ISBN 0-671-44308-9). PB.
Jamaica White. Hal Underhill. LC 68-12076. 1967. Macmillan.
Jamaican American. Bob Cox. LC 76-14564. 1976. 10.00 (ISBN 0-89307-003-3). Quail Street Pub. Co.
Jamaican Exchange. Nick Carter. (Nick Carter Ser.). 192p. (Orig.). 1979. pap. 1.95 o.p. (ISBN 0-441-51633-5). Charter Bks.
Jamais Plus de Secrets. Sandra Field. (Collection Harlequin). 192p. 1983. pap. 1.95 (ISBN 0-373-49322-3). Harlequin Bks.
Jamba. Wilfrid Dyson Hambly. LC 47-113723. 1947. Pellegrini & Cudahy.
Jambeaux. Laurence Gonzales. LC 79-1824. 9.95 (ISBN 0-15-146038-8). Harcourt Brace Jovanovich.
Jamboree. Michael Upchurch. LC 80-18489. 1981. 9.95 (ISBN 0-394-51150-6). Knopf: Distributed by Random House.
James and Joan. Anne Jackson Fremantle. LC 48-5472. 1948. H. Holt.
James and Macarthur: A Novel About Two Cats. Jenny Laird. LC 51-12748. (Illus.). 1951. Longmans, Green.
James at 15. April Smith & Dan Wakefield. (Dell Book). 1977. 1.50 (ISBN 0-440-14389-6). Dell Pub., Co.
James Bevanwood: Baronet. Henry St. John Cooper. LC 21-50884. George H. Doran Company.
James Bond. John Pearson. (Illus.). 1973. 7.95 o.p. (ISBN 0-688-00216-1). Morrow.
James Bond & Moonraker. Christopher Wood. (Orig.). 1979. pap. 2.25 (ISBN 0-515-05344-9). Jove Pubns.
James Bond: the Authorized Biography of 007: A Fictional Biography. John Pearson. LC 73-16584. 1973. 7.95 (ISBN 0-688-00216-1). Morrow.
James Boys. A Complete and Accurate Recital of the Dare-Devil Criminal Career of the Famous Bandit Brothers Frank and Jesse James and Their Noted Band of Bank Plunderers, Train Robbers and Murderers, Specially Comp. for the Publishers... Edward Thomas Roe. (On cover: The Melbourne series, no. 6). E. A. Weeks & Company.
James, by the Grace of God. Ross Williamson, Hugh. LC 56-14171. 1956. H. Regnery Co.
James Clavell's King Rat. James Clavell. LC 82-19790. 1983. 15.95 (ISBN 0-440-04392-1). Delacorte Press.
James Clavell's Shogun. James Clavell. LC 82-19788. 1983. 21.95 (ISBN 0-440-08721-X). Delacorte Press.
James Clavell's Tai-Pan. James Clavell. LC 82-18339. 1983. 19.95 (ISBN 0-440-08724-4). Delacorte Press.
James Fenimore Cooper: Short Stories Excerpted from His Novels. Ed. by Sidney Finkelstein. (Orig.). 1970. pap. 1.50 o.p. (ISBN 0-7178-0111-X). Intl Pub Co.
James Fenimore Cooper's The Last of the Mohicans. James Fenimore Cooper. Ed. by Richardson, Charles Francis. LC 6-29879. (Longmans' English classics). 1897. Longmans, Green and Co.
James Gordon's Wife. A Novel... Frances Elizabeth Georgia Brock. (On cover: Seaside library. Pocket ed., no. 519). 1885. G. Munro.
James Hurd: A Novel. Richard Orton Prowse. LC 13-17333. 1913. J. B. Lippincott Company; Etc., Etc.
James Joyce Murder. Amanda Cross, pseud. LC 67-11566. (Cock robin mystery). bds., 3.95. Macmillan.
James Joyce Murder. Amanda Cross, pseud. LC 82-6027. 9.95 (ISBN 0-89621-373-0). Thorndike Press.
James Joyce, the Citizen and the Artist. Charles Peake. LC 76-47985. 1977. 16.95 (ISBN 0-8047-0914-9). Stanford University Press.
James Latrew. Rosa Wyatt. 1890. J. B. Alden.
James Lee. William Fuller Conners. LC 6-45046. The Clinic Publishing Company.
James Murray: Or, Merit Exalted. An Irish Story. Mary Anna Moffitt. LC 7-19178. 1866. J. Craft, Printer.
James Norris,". copyright ed. Albert Pyrmont. LC 16-5898. 1915. 1.00. C. Regenhardt.
James Russian, a Novel. Roger Beard Siddall. LC 51-7231. 1951. Beard, Francis.
James Shore's Daughter. Stephen Vincent Benet. LC 73-131620. 1972. (ISBN 0-403-00507-8). Scholarly Press.
James the Second: Or The Revolution of 1688. William Harrison Ainsworth. LC 5-42989. 1848. Carey and Hart.
James Vansittart's Vengeance: A Novel. Mary Anna Lupton Needell. LC 7-25794. 1895. D. Appleton and Company.
James Wallace. Robert Bage. LC 78-60847. (Series: Novel, 1720-1805.). 1979. 28.00 (ISBN 0-8240-3660-3). Garland Pub.
Jamesie. Ethel Sidgwick. LC 18-163729. Small, Maynard & Company.
Jameson Girls: By Jan Hilliard Pseud. Hilda Kay Grant. LC 56-5915. 1956. Abelard -Schuman.

Jamesons. Mary Eleanor Wilkins Freeman. LC 99-2182. 1899. Doubleday & McClure Company.

Jamey: Novel of a Period, 1967-1968. Edwin Gilbert. LC 69-15861. 1969. 5.95. Trident Press.

Jamie. Jack Bennett. LC 63-15144. 1963. Little, Brown.

Jamie Is My Heart's Desire. Alfred Chester. LC 57-12253. (O.s.i.). 3.50 o.s.i. (ISBN 0-8149-0465-3). Vanguard.

Jamie on His Own. Elizabeth Batt. (YA) 1972. pap. 0.95 o.p. (ISBN 0-87508-680-2). Chr Lit.

Jamie Parker, the Fugitive. Emily Catharine Pierson. LC 7-35901. 1851. Brockett, Fuller and Co.

Jamie Reid. Gordon Ogilvie. 448p. 1981. pap. 2.75 (ISBN 0-380-76737-6, 76737). Avon.

Jamie, The Adventures of. Tom Bowie. LC 78-62815. (Illus.). 1978. 12.50 (ISBN 0-932508-00-6); pap. 3.95 (ISBN 0-932508-01-4). Seven Oaks.

Jamie the Red. Gordon R. Dickson & Roland Green. Date not set. pap. price not set (Pub. by Ace Science Fiction). Ace Bks.

Jamintha. Beatrice Parker. 1975. (pbk.) 1.25. Dell.

Jan. Muriel Morgan Gibbon. LC 21-2588. 1920. Doubleday, Page & Company.

Jan a Dog and a Romance. Alec John Dawson. LC 15-19862. 1915. 1.25. Harper & Brothers.

Jan and Her Job. Lizzie Allen Harker. LC 17-10199. 1917. 1.50. C. Scribner's Sons.

Jan Compagie see John Company.

Jan in India. Otis Adelbert Kline. LC 73-94035. (Illus.). 1974. 3.50 (ISBN 0-87707-131-4). Fictioneer Books.

Jan Le Witt. Herbert Read & Jean Cassou. 172p. 1972. 42.00 o.p. (ISBN 0-912050-17-9, Library Pr). Open Court.

Jan the Romantic: A Story of France. Albert Bigelow Paine. LC 30-448. 1929. Harper & Brothers.

Jan the Romantic: A Story of France. 2d ed....drawings by ralph b. wilkins. ed. Albert Bigelow Paine. LC 33-27372. 1933. The Penn Publishing Company.

Jan Vedder's Wife. Amelia Edith Huddleston Barr. LC 4-15067. 1885. Dodd, Mead & Company.

Jana. Nellie Herbison. LC 80-126030. 1980. 9.95 (ISBN 0-934444-06-4). Aazunna Pub. Co.

Jandar of Callisto. Lin Carter. (Illus.). 1972. 0.95. Dell.

Jane. Phyllis Bottome. LC 57-7681. 1957. Vanguard Press.

Jane. Anna Alice Chapin. LC 20-7764. 1920. 1.75. G. P. Putnam's Sons.

Jane. Dee Wells. LC 73-7087. 1974. 6.95 (ISBN 0-670-40539-6). Viking Press.

Jane. Dee Wells. 1977. 1.95 (ISBN 0-380-00222-1). Avon Books.

Jane--Our Stranger: A Novel. Mary Borden. LC 23-13337. 1923. A.A. Knopf.

Jane: A Social Incident. Marie Corelli. LC 6-28744. (On cover: The lotos library). 1897. J. B. Lippincott Company.

Jane, a Social Incident. Marie Corelli. LC 43-84445. (On cover: The Lotos library). 1897. J. B. Lippincott Company.

Jane and Prudence. Barbara Pym. LC 81-68399. 1981. 11.50 (ISBN 0-525-13640-1). E.P. Dutton.

Jane Arden, Registered Nurse: By Kathleen Harris Pseud. Adelaide Humphries. LC 56-3009. 1956. Avalon Books.

Jane Arden, Staff Nurse: By Kathleen Harris Pseud. Adelaide Humphries. LC 57-8741. 1957. Avalon Books.

Jane Arden, Student Nurse: By Kathleen Harris Pseud. Adelaide Humphries. LC 55-146307.

Jane Arden, Surgery Nurse: By Kathleen Harris Pseud. Adelaide Humphries. LC 58-912930. 1958. Avalon Books.

Jane Austen. Brian Wilks. LC 79-300977. (Illus.). 1978. 9.75 (ISBN 0-600-30356-X). Hamlyn.

Jane Austen: Emma. Ed. by David Lodge. 1981. pap. 20.00x (ISBN 0-333-01954-7, Pub. by Macmillan England). State Mutual Bk.

Jane Avril of the Moulin Rouge. Jose Shercliff. LC 52-44335. 1952. Jarrolds.

Jane Avril of the Moulin Rouge. Jose Shercliff. LC 54-12147. (Illus.). 1954. Macrae Smith Co.

Jane Cable. George Barr McCutcheon. LC 6-27704. 1906. Dodd, Mead & Company.

Jane Cable. George Barr McCutcheon. LC 26-7516. A. L. Burt Company.

Jane Cable. George Barr McCutcheon. LC 16-25049. 1914. Dodd, Mead & Company.

Jane Cable. George Barr McCutcheon. LC 21-86824. 1918. Dodd, Mead & Company.

Jane Carroll. Ernest Temple Thurston. LC 28-9063. 1927. G. P. Putnam's Sons.

Jane Carroll. Ernest Temple Thurston. LC 28-9465. 1928. Doubleday, Doran & Company, Inc.

Jane Castle Manuscript. Philip L. Greene. (Dell bk., 4183). 1972. 1.25. Dell.

Jane Castle Manuscript: A Novel. Philip L. Greene. LC 77-153676. 1971. 5.95. Delacorte Press.

Jane Dawson: A Novel. William Nathaniel Harben. LC 11-246822. 1911. Harper & Brothers.

Jane Eyre. Charlotte Bronte. LC 65-6521. (Perennial classic). 1965. Harper & Row.

Jane Eyre. Charlotte Bronte. LC 66-77630. (Penguin English library, EL11) 5/-(B 66-10560). 1966. Penguin.

Jane Eyre. Charlotte Bronte. LC 73-3125. (Bronte, Charlotte, 1816-1855. Life & Works of the Sisters Bronte: Vol. 1). (Illus.). 1973. 25.00 (ISBN 0-404-08831-7). AMS Press.

Jane Eyre. Charlotte Bronte. Ed. by Margaret Smith. LC 73-168716. (Oxford English novels). (Illus.). 1972. (ISBN 0-19-255346-1). Oxford University Press.

Jane Eyre. Charlotte Bronte. (Enriched classics series). (Illus.). 1973. 0.95 (ISBN 0-671-47898-2). Pocket Books.

Jane Eyre. Charlotte Bronte. (Signet Classic). 1973. (pbk.) 0.60. New American Lib.

Jane Eyre. Charlotte Bronte. (Harcourt library of English and American classics). 1962. Harcourt, Brace & World.

Jane Eyre. Charlotte Bronte. LC 49-495442. (World's greatest literature). 1949. Fountain Press.

Jane Eyre. 6th ed. Charlotte Bronte. (Seaside library, v. 1, no. 3). 1877. G. Munro.

Jane Eyre. Charlotte Bronte. (Seaside library v. 20. no. 396). 1878. G. Munro.

Jane Eyre. Charlotte Bronte. (On cover: Seaside library. Pocket ed., no. 15). 1883. G. Munro.

Jane Eyre. Charlotte Bronte. (Lovell's library, v. 2, no. 74). 1883. J. W. Lovell Company.

Jane Eyre. Charlotte Bronte. LC 41-381151. The F. M. Lupton Publishing Company.

Jane Eyre. Charlotte Bronte. LC 6-179540. T. Y. Crowell and Co.

Jane Eyre. Charlotte Bronte. Ed. by Harriet Elizabeth Prescott Spofford. LC 6-17953. (Half-title: The world's great books... Aldine ed.). 1898. D. Appleton and Company.

Jane Eyre. Charlotte Bronte. LC 26-26543. (modern readers' series). 1926. The Macmillan Company.

Jane Eyre. Charlotte Bronte. LC 33-273873. (Half-title: The modern library of the world's best books). 1933. The Modern Library.

Jane Eyre. Charlotte Bronte. LC 36-37140. (Half-title: Everyman's library, ed. by Ernest Rhys. Fiction. no. 287). 1934. J. M. Dent & Sons, Ltd.

Jane Eyre. Charlotte Bronte. (English Comedie humaine 1st series, v. 9). 1937. Grosset & Dunlap.

Jane Eyre. Charlotte Bronte. LC 37-6523. (Classic romances of literature. vol. II). The Spencer Press.

Jane Eyre. Charlotte Bronte. Ed. by Helen Sewell. LC 38-27625. 1938. Oxford University Press.

Jane Eyre. Charlotte Bronte. LC 42-17248. 1942. The Heritage Press.

Jane Eyre. Charlotte Bronte. LC 43-42714. (On cover: Gladstone series). Syndicate Trading Company.

Jane Eyre. Charlotte Bronte. LC 45-40836. (Half-title: The novels of Charlotte, Emily, & Anne Bronte). 1922. J. M. Dent & Sons Ltd.

Jane Eyre. Charlotte Bronte. LC 43-726. (On cover: Great illustrated classics). 1942. Dodd, Mead & Company.

Jane Eyre. Charlotte Bronte. LC 43-18004. 1943. Random House.

Jane Eyre. illustrated by edward a. wilson... ed. Charlotte Bronte. LC 44-40198. (Illustrated modern library). 1944. A. S. Barnes & Co., Inc.

Jane Eyre. Charlotte Bronte. LC 46-5532. (Half-title: Rainbow classics. General editor: May L. Becker). 1946. The World Publishing Company.

Jane Eyre. Charlotte Bronte. Ed. by Lou P. Bunce. Benscoter, Grace A., Ed. LC 47-221792. (CEBCO classics for enjoyment). 1947. College Entrance Book Company.

Jane Eyre. Charlotte Bronte. LC 2-29428. (E,glish Comedie humaine 1st series, v. 9). 1902. The Century Co.

Jane Eyre. Charlotte Bronte. (Half-title: Everyman's library, ed. by Ernest Rhys. Fiction no. 287). 1908. J. M. Dent & Co.

Jane Eyre. Charlotte Bronte. Ed. by Margaret Smith. LC 79-41333. (World's classics). 1980. 2.95 (ISBN 0-19-251017-7). Oxford University Press.

Jane Eyre. A Novel. Charlotte Bronte. (Franklin square library, no. 86). 1879. Harper & Brothers.

Jane Eyre. An Autobiography. Charlotte Bronte. LC 6-17956. (On cover: Library of select novels, no. 109). 1848. Harper & Brothers.

Jane Eyre. Ed. by M. W. and G. Thomas. Illus. by Robert Hunt. Charlotte Bronte. Ed. by Maurice Walton Thomas & Gladys Thomas. LC 66-6652. (Shorter classics). 1963. bds., 2.50. Ginn.

Jane Eyre. Ed. by Q. D. Leavis. Charlotte Bronte. LC 66-765063. (Penguin Eng. lib., EL11). 1966. Penguin.

Jane Eyre. Edited with an Introd. by Mark Schorer. Charlotte Bronte. LC 59-2292. (Riverside editions, B35). 1959. Houghton Mifflin.

Jane Eyre. Illustrated by Ati Forberg. Afterword by Clifton Fadiman. Charlotte Bronte. LC 62-18387. (Macmillan classics, 6). 1962. Macmillan.

Jane Eyre: Illustrated by John Huehnergarth. Charlotte Bronte. LC 54-5013. 1954. International Collectors Library, American Headquarters.

Jane Eyre. Introd. by Joe Lee Davis. Charlotte Bronte. LC 50-6935. (Rinehart editions, 24). 1950. Rinehart.

Jane Eyre. Introd. by William Peden. Charlotte Bronte. LC 50-12236. (Modern Library college editions, T3). 1950. Modern Library.

Jane Eyre. With a New Introd. by William H. Marshall. Charlotte Bronte. LC 62-17576. (Collier books, HS35. Classic). 1962. Collier Books.

Jane Eyre. With an Introd. by Alice Green Fredman. Charlotte Bronte. LC 56-126431. (Harper's modern classics). 1957. Harper.

Jane Eyre. With an Introd. by Phyllis Bentley. Suggestions for Reading and Discussion by Robert J. Lumsden. Charlotte Bronte. LC 65-5768. (RLS: Riverside literature series, R30). 1965. Houghton Mifflin.

Jane Eyre. With Lithographs by Barnett Freedman. Charlotte Bronte. LC 57-28107. 1955. Collins, by Arrangement with Heritage Press, New York.

Jane Field. Mary Eleanor Wilkins Freeman. LC 78-104456. (Illus.). 1970. Literature House.

Jane Field: A Novel. Mary Eleanor Wilkins Freeman. LC 6-40019. 1893. Harper & Brothers.

Jane Hadden. Rosamond Van Der Zee Marshall. LC 52-215. 1952. Prentice-Hall.

Jane Jansen: A Story of a Woman's Heritage in the Heart of Appalachia. Involving Adventures in Hawaii, Japan, and Korea ... and Relating the Incidents of a ... Life in Southwestern Pennsylvania, Including an Escape from the Johnstown Flood ... LC 9-2240. 1895. The Oliver Publishing House.

Jane Journeys on. Ruth Comfort Mitchell. LC 22-42109. 1922. D. Appleton and Company.

Jane of Lantern Hill. Lucy Maud Montgomery. LC 37-169370. 1937. Frederick A. Stokes Company.

Jane Oglander. Marie Adelaide Belloc Lowndes. LC 11-9156. 1911. 1.25. C. Scribner's Sons.

Jane Seton: Or, The King's Advocate. James Grant. LC 44-286006. 1892. G. Routledge and Sons.

Jane Seymour. Frances Clark. 1972. pap. 0.95 o.p. (95247). Beagle Bks.

Jane Street of Gopher Prairie. James Stetson Metcalfe. LC 21-12360. 1921. The Probono Publishing Company.

Jane Stuart at Rivercroft. Grace May Remick. LC 15-16341. 1915. The Penn Publishing Company.

Jane Stuart's Chum. Grace May Remick. 1914. The Penn Publishing Company.

Jane Takes a Chance. Emilie Keltie. LC 35-233278. Godwin.

Jane Talbot. Charles Brockden Brown. LC 63-24273. (His Novels, v. 5). 1963. Kennikat Press.

Jane Talbot. Charles Brockden Brown. LC 41-38116. 1827. S. G. Goodrich.

Jane Talbot. Charles Brockden Brown. LC 6-18971. 1857. M. Polock.

Jane Talbot. Charles Brockden Brown. LC 17-13042. (Half-title: Charles Brockden Brown's novels, vol. v). 1887. D. McKay.

Jane Talbot, a Novel. Charles Brockden Brown. LC 25-6585. 1801.

Jane, the Courageous. Katheryn Kimbrough, pseud. (Saga of the Phenwick Women Ser.: Bk. 2). 256p. (Orig.). 1975. pap. 1.75 (ISBN 0-445-00278-6). Popular Lib.

Jane's Career. Herbert G. De Lisser. (Caribbean Writers Ser.). 1972. pap. text ed. 4.00x (ISBN 0-435-98540-X). Heinemann Ed.

Jane's Career. Herbert G. De Lisser. LC 78-162467. (Colonial Novel Ser). 207p. 1971. text ed. 27.50x (ISBN 0-8419-0078-7, Africana). Holmes & Meier.

Jane's House. Robert Kimmel Smith. LC 82-2277. 1982. 13.95 (ISBN 0-688-01255-8). Morrow.

Janet. A Character Study. Cuyler Reynolds. LC 7-30925. 1889. J. B. Lyon.

Janet and Her Father. Mary Ellen Bamford. LC 6-6890. Congregational Sunday-School and Publishing Society.

Janet Goes Abroad. Jeanne Judson. (Fawcett gold medal book). 1975. (pbk.) 0.75. Fawcett.

Janet Goes Abroad. Jeanne Judson. 3.25. Avalon Dist. Bouregy.

Janet March. rev. ed. Floyd Dell. LC 27-20819. George H. Doran Company.

Janet March: A Novel. Floyd Dell. LC 23-14114. 1923. A. A. Knopf.

Janet of Kootenay: Life, Love and Laughter in an Arcady of the West. Evah McKowan. LC 19-13299. George H. Doran Company.

Janet of the Dunes. by carle michel boog. ed. Harriet Theresa Smith Comstock. 1908. Little, Brown, and Company.

Janet Strong. Virginia Frances Townsend. LC 8-29817. 1865. J. B. Lippincott & Co.

Janet Thurso: A Simple Chronicle. Alexander Moray. LC 26-16531. Harcourt, Brace and Company.

Janet Vardoff. Susanna Rebecca Graham Clark. LC 10-262252. 1910. 1.50. The Griffith & Rowland Press.

Janet Ward, a Daughter of the Manse. Margaret Elizabeth Munson Sangster. LC 2-21407. Fleming H. Revell Company.

Janet's Home. Annie Keary. LC 7-11129. (Seaside library, v. 74, no. 1493). G. Munro.

Janet's Repentance. George Eliot. LC 6-40738. (On cover: Harper's half-hour series, v. 31). 1877. Harper & Brothers.

Janet's Repentance. George Eliot. (On cover: Seaside library. Pocket ed., no. 728). 1886. G. Munro.

Janey: Being the Record of a Short Interval in the Journey Through Life and the Struggle with Society of a Little Girl of Nine... Inez Haynes Irwin. LC 11-27848. 1911. H. Holt and Company.

Janey Jeems. Bernice Kelly Harris. LC 46-5987. 1946. Doubleday & Company, Inc.

Janey Wilpot Journal. Ramona Kleff. 1973. pap. 1.50 o.s.i. (71-354). Lancer.

Janice. Junie Candler Garrett. LC 13-10666. 1913. 1.25. Broadway Publishing Co.

Janice Meredith: A Story of the American Revolution. Paul Leicester Ford. LC 2-13610. 1899. Dodd, Mead and Company.

Janice Meredith: A Story of the American Revolution. Paul Leicester Ford. LC 3-12293. Grosset & Dunlap.

Janice Meredith: A Story of the American Revolution. Paul Leicester Ford. LC 20-55885. 1919. Dodd, Mead and Company.

Janie. Josephine Bentham. LC 40-35315. Dial Press.

Janis Hall, Nurse Instructor. Lucy Bowdler. (Avalon Books). 4.95. Thomas Bouregy.

Janissa. Robert Thomas Newcomb. LC 43-11144. 1943. Destiny Publishers.

Janissaries. Jerry Pournelle & Bermejo. LC 80-118076. (Illus.). 1979. 6.95 (ISBN 0-441-38285-1). Ace Books.

Janissaries: Clan & Crown. Jerry Pournelle & Roland Green. (Illus.). 437p. 1982. pap. 5.95 (ISBN 0-441-38288-6, Pub. by Ace Science Fiction). Ace Bks.

Janissary. Alan Gelb. 1980. pap. 2.25 (ISBN 0-440-14173-7). Dell.

Janissary: A Novel of Obsession. Alan Gelb. LC 78-54039. 9.95 (ISBN 0-89256-062-2). Rawson, Wade Publishers.

Janse Douw's Descendants. Ida F Humphreys. LC 23-12996. Dorrance.

January. Katharine Pleydell-Bouverie. LC 24-30085. 1924. Boni and Liveright.

January Thaw. Bellamy Partridge. LC 45-7501. 1945. Whittlesey House, McGraw-Hill Book Company, Inc.

January Thirty-First. Albert Goldbarth. LC 73-22534. 120p. 1974. pap. 5.95 o.p. (ISBN 0-385-05955-8). Doubleday.

Janus. Robert Leigh James. LC 72-12018. 1973. 6.95 (ISBN 0-396-06749-2). Dodd, Mead.

Janus: A Novel. Edward Irenaeus Prime-Stevenson. LC 8-16092. Belford, Clarke & Company.

Janus Imperative. Evelyn Anthony. LC 79-20768. 9.95 (ISBN 0-698-11016-1). Coward, McCann & Geoghegan.

Janus Island. Sloan Wilson. 1967. 6.95 o.p. Little.

Janus Island. Sloan Wilson. 1971. pap. 0.95 o.p. (M1422, Crest). Fawcett World.

Janus Island: A Novel. Sloan Wilson. LC 67-23838. 1967. Little, Brown.

Janus Lovers: A Novel. Miggs Pomeroy. LC 66-12801. 1966. Norton.

Janus Murder. John Nichols Datesh. (Leisure Book). 1.75 (ISBN 0-8439-0649-9). Nordon Publications.

Janus Syndrome. Steven E. McDonald. 288p. (Orig.). 1981. pap. text ed. 2.95 (ISBN 0-553-14993-8). Bantam.

Jap Herron: A Novel Written from the Ouija Board; with an Introduction, The Coming of Jap Herron. Emily Grant Hutchings & Hays, Lola V. LC 17-28757. 1917. M. Kennerley.

Japan Sinks. Sakyo Komatsu. LC 74-15876. (Illus.). 7.95 (ISBN 0-06-012449-0). Harper & Row.

Japanese Blossom. Winnifred Eaton Babcock. LC 6-36037. 1906. Harper & Brothers.

Japanese Bride. Naomi Tamura. LC 13-12918. (On cover: Harper's black and white series). 1893. Harper & Brothers.

Japanese Corpse. Janwillem Van De Wetering. LC 77-5027. 1977. 7.95 (ISBN 0-395-25777-8). HM.

Japanese Corpse. Janwillem Van De Wetering. 1978. pap. 2.95 (ISBN 0-671-81922-4). PB.

Japanese Corpse. Janwillem Van De Wetering. (Kangaroo Book). 1978. 1.95 (ISBN 0-671-81922-4). Pocket Books.

Japanese Corpse: A Novel. Wetering, Janwillem Van De. LC 77-5027. 1977. 7.95 (ISBN 0-395-25777-8). Houghton Mifflin.

Japanese Fairy Tales. William Elliot Griffis. LC 23-11104. T. Y. Crowell Co.

Japanese Family Storehouse: Or, The Millionaire's Gospel Modernised. Nippon Eitai-Gura, or Daifuku Skin Choja Kyo (1688) Translated from the Japanese with Introd. and Commentary by G. W. Sargent. With the Original Illus. and Decorations. Saikaku Ibara. LC 59-1893. (Cambridge. University. Oriental Publications: No. 3). 1959. University Press.

Japanese Girl. Winston Graham. LC 70-171293. 1972. 6.95. Doubleday.

Japanese Grandmother. Emma Gerberding Lippard. LC 34-11656. Fleming H. Revell Company.

Japanese Marriage. Douglas Brooke Wheelton Sladen. LC 49-39691. 1895. A. and C. Black.

Japanese Mistress. Richard Neely. 1973. (pbk) 0.95. Popular Library.

Japanese Mistress. Richard Neely. LC 78-182482. 1972. 5.95 (ISBN 0-8415-0158-0). Saturday Review Press.

Japanese Nightingale. Winnifred Eaton Babcock. 1901. Harper & Bros.

Japanese Notebook Ox. Gregory Corso. 1974. pap. 4.95x (ISBN 0-934450-05-6). Unmuzzled Ox.

Japanese Revenge. Tracy, Louis. LC 44-25791. (On cover: Adventure series, 114). The Arthur Westbrook Company.

Japanese Romance. Clive Holland. LC 4-31324. 1904. F. A. Stokes Company.

Japanese Short Stories. Ryunosuke Akutagawa. LC 75-92703. (Liveright paperbound edition). (Illus.). 1970. 2.45. Liveright.

Japanese Short Stories. Translated by TakashiKojima. Introd. by John McVittie. With Very Unusual Illus. by Masakazu Kuwata. Ryunosuke Akutagawa. 1961. Vwliveight Pub. Corp.

Japanese Tales of Mystery & Imagination. Rampo Edogawa. LC 56-6809. 1956. C. E. Tuttle Co.

Japanese Tales of Mystery & Imagination: By Edogawa Rampo Pseud. Translated by James B. Harris; Jacket Design & Illus. by M. Kuwada. Taro Hirai. LC 56-6809. 1956. C. E. Tuttle Co.

Japan's First Modern Novel: Ukigumo of Futabatei Shimei. Marleigh Grayer Ryan. LC 67-15896. (Columbia University. East Asian Institute. East Asian Institute Studies). 1967. Columbia University Press.

Japan's First Modern Novel: Ukigumo of Futabatei Shimei. Tr. and Critical Commentary by Marleigh Grayer Ryan. Marleigh Grayer Ryan. LC 67-158963. (Columbia University. East Asian Institute. East Asian Institute Studies). 1967. 10.00. Columbia.

Japhet in Search of a Father. Frederick Marryat. LC 25-15499. 1870. D. Appleton & Company.

Japhet in Search of a Father. Frederick Marryat. LC 7-17581. 1878. D. Appleton and Company.

Japhet in Search of a Father. Frederick Marryat. LC 9-3852. G. Routledge and Sons, Limited.

Japhet in Search of a Father. Frederick Marryat. LC 7-24685. (On cover: Seaside library. Pocket ed. no. 2106). G. Munro's Sons.

Japhet in Search of a Father. Frederick Marryat. LC 42-536. H. M. Caldwell Co.

Japhet in Search of a Father. Frederick Marryat & Hannay, David. LC 4-15325. 1895. Macmillan and Co.

Japonette. Robert William Chambers. LC 12-7621. 1912. D. Appleton and Company.

Japonette. Robert William Chambers. LC 20-15596. 1914. A. L. Burt Company.

Japonica Grove. Mary Barrow Linfield. LC 35-459748. 1935. Doubleday, Doran & Company, Inc.

Jaquelina: Or, The Outlaws Bride. Alexander McVeigh Miller. (On cover: Munro's library, v. 1, no. 5). N. L. Munro.

Jaquelle's Shadow. Sharon Wagner. (Adventures in Love Ser.: No. 28). 1982. pap. 1.75 (ISBN 0-451-11707-7, AE1707, Sig). NAL.

Jardinier De Tir Glyn. Jane Donnelly. (Harlequin Romantique Ser.). 192p. 1983. pap. 1.95 (ISBN 0-373-41191-X). Harlequin Bks.

Jargal: A Novel. Victor Marie Hugo & Wilbour, Charles Edwin, 1833-1896, Tr. 1866. Carleton; Etc., Etc.

Jargoon Pard. Andre Norton, pseud. LC 74-76279. 1974. 6.95 (ISBN 0-689-50011-4). Atheneum.

Jargoon Pard. Andre Norton, pseud. LC 74-762796. (Fawcett Crest Book). 1975. (pbk.) 1.25. Fawcett.

Jarl's Daughter & Other Novelettes. facsimile ed. Frances Burnett. LC 75-94708. (Short Story Index Reprint Ser). 1883. 12.00 (ISBN 0-8369-3087-8). Ayer Co.

Jarl's Daughter: And Other Novelettes. Frances Hodgson Burnett. LC 75-94708. (Short story index reprint series). 1969. Books for Libraries Press.

Jarl's Daughter: And Other Novelettes. Frances Hodgson Burnett. T. B. Peterson & Brothers.

Jarl's Daughter: And Other Stories. Frances Hodgson Burnett. T. B. Peterson & Brothers.

Jarnegan. Jim Tully. LC 26-15787. 1926. A. & C. Boni.

Jarrah Tree. Mary Kistler. LC 76-23771. 1977. 5.95 (ISBN 0-385-12598-4). Doubleday.

Jarrah Tree. Mary Kistler. 1979. 1.75 (ISBN 0-445-04372-5). Popular Library.

Jarrett's Jade. Yerby, Frank. 1976. (pbk.) 1.75. Dell Books.

Jarrett's Jade, a Novel. Frank Yerby. LC 59-15486. 1959. Dial Press.

Jarvis. Reginald Wright Kauffman. LC 23-8607. 1923. The St. Botolph Society.

Jarvis of Harvard. Reginald Wright Kauffman. LC 1-24834. 1901. L. C. Page & Company.

Jasius Pursuit. Douglas Orgill. LC 72-93929. 1973. 5.95. St. Martin's.

Jasmine. Jennifer Mandy. 1973. 4.95 (ISBN 0-517-51394-3). Lenox Hill Press.

Jasmine Farm. Elizabeth. 1973. pap. price not set o.p. Curtis.

Jasmine Farm. Mary Annette Beauchamp Russell Russell. LC 34-41609. 1934. Doubleday, Doran & Company, Inc.

Jasmine Moon. Frances Patton Statham. 1.95 (ISBN 0-449-13988-3). Fawcett Gold Medal Books.

Jasmine Paradise. Penelope Neri. 1983. pap. 3.75 (ISBN 0-8217-1170-9). Zebra.

Jasmine Passion. Paula Fairman. 288p. (Orig.). 1981. pap. 2.95 (ISBN 0-523-41783-7). Pinnacle Bks.

Jasmine Splendour. Margo Bode. 1981. 2.75 (ISBN 0-671-42431-9). Pockeet Books.

Jasmine Street. Clifford Dowdey. LC 52-5237. 1952. Doubleday.

Jasmine Trail. Harry J Hagerty. LC 36-994097. 1936. Lothrop, Lee & Shepard Company.

Jasmine Veil. Gimone Hall. 1982. pap. 2.95 (ISBN 0-451-11451-5, AE1451, Sig). NAL.

Jason. Henry Treece. LC 61-6265. 1961. Random House.

Jason, a Romance. Justus Miles Forman. LC 9-13923. 1909. Harper & Brothers.

Jason Burr's First Case. Hoffman Birney. LC 41-9781. 1941. Random House.

Jason Burr's First Case. David Kent. LC 41-9781. Random House.

Jason Edwards, an Average Man. Hamlin Garland. 1897. D. Appleton and Company.

Jason Evers, His Own Story. Frank Roderus. LC 79-6888. 1980. 8.95 (ISBN 0-385-15755-X). Doubleday.

Jason Goose. Robert Luther Duffus. 1969. 5.50 o.p. (ISBN 0-393-08413-2). Norton.

Jason Jones: The Life Story of an American Politician; an-Autobiographical Sketch Found Among the Papers of a Capitalist and Political Boss, Recently Deceased. James Martin. LC 10-2503. 1909. The Chronicle Publishing Co.

Jason Kilkenny's Gun. Kit Prate. (Orig.). 1981. pap. 1.95 (ISBN 0-505-51700-0). Tower Bks.

Jason McGee. Robert H Fowler. LC 78-20203. 10.00 (ISBN 0-06-011382-0). Harper & Row.

Jason Potter's Space Walk: A Novel. Robert Luther Duffus. LC 71-116097. 1970. 4.95. Norton.

Jason's Quest. Margaret Laurence. 144p. 1981. pap. 2.95. Bantam.

Jason's Song. Michael Scott Cain. 1974. (pbk.) 1.25. Warner Paperback Library.

Jasper and the Love of Money. Robert E. Reardon. LC 66-10378. 1966. bds., 4.95. Morrow.

Jasper Fairfax. Margret Holmes Ernsperger Bates. LC 6-907721. R. F. Fenno & Company.

Jassy. Norah Robinson Lofts. LC 45-5092. 1945. A. A. Knopf.

Jataka Tales. Francis & Thomas. (Jaico Paperback Ser). pap. 2.75 o.p. (ISBN 0-87902-090-3). Orientalia.

Jaubert Ring. Willo Davis Roberts. LC 75-40742. 1976. 5.95 (ISBN 0-385-11591-1). Published for the Crime Club by Doubleday.

Jaufry the Knight & the Fair Brunissende: A Tale of the Times of King Arthur. Ed. by R. Reginald & Douglas Alver Menville. LC 80-19436. (Newcastle Forgotten Fantasy Library: Vol. 21). 156p. 1980. Repr. of 1979 ed. lib. bdg. 11.95x (ISBN 0-89370-520-9). Borgo Pr.

Jaufry the Knight & the Fair Brunissende. LC 79-15119. (Forgotten Fantasy Library: Vol. 21). 1979. pap. 4.95 (ISBN 0-87877-120-4). Newcastle Pub.

Jaunty in Charge. Mary C. E. Wemyss. LC 16-16522. 1916. E. P. Dutton & Company.

Java Edge. Joseph Emerson Newton. LC 55-3471. 1955. Bruce Humphries.

Java Girl. Schwartzenberg En Hohnlansberg, William Herman & Harrison, Mary Bennett. LC 31-6075. 1931. Brentano's.

Java Head. Joseph Hergesheimer. LC 19-579. 1919. A. A. Knopf.

Java Head. Joseph Hergesheimer. LC 46-7190. 1946. A. A. Knopf.

Java-Java. Francis Steegmuller. LC 28-17098. 1928. A. A. Knopf.

Java-Java. Francis Steegmuller. LC 28-17098. 1928. A. A. Knopf.

Javan Ben Seir, a Story of Olden Israel. Walker Kennedy. F. A. Stokes Company.

Javelin of Fate. Jeanie Thomas Gould Lincoln. LC 5-357976. 1905. Houghton, Mifflin and Company.

Jawbone of an Ass. Glena Wood. 1970. 6.50 o.p. Vantage.

Jaws. Peter Benchley. LC 73-80799. 1974. 6.95 (ISBN 0-385-04771-1). Doubleday.

Jaws of Circumstance: By Carl Clausen. Carl Clausen. LC 31-1816. 1931. Dodd, Mead & Company.

Jaws of Death. Richard Silver. (Captain Shark Series#2). 1975. (pbk.) 1.25 (ISBN 0-523-00783-3). Pinnacle Books.

Jaws of Death... Lee Thayer, pseud. LC 46-7636. 1946. Dodd, Mead & Company.

Jaws of Fear, and Other Stories. Grace A Baughman. LC 72-75514. 1972. Celestial Press.

Jaws of Menx. Ann Maxwell. 256p. (Orig.). 1981. pap. 2.75 (ISBN 0-451-11037-4, AE1037, Sig). NAL.

Jaws of the Watchdog. Ivor Drummond. LC 72-89593. 1973. 6.95. St. Martin's Press.

Jaws of the Watchdog. Ivor Drummond. 1974. (pbk.) 1.25 (ISBN 0-515-03367-7). Pyramid Books.

Jaws That Bite. Anthony Pollice. LC 76-92339. 1970. 5.95. Prentice-Hall.

Jaws That Bite, the Claws That Catch. Michael G Coney. 1975. (pbk.) 1.25. DAW Books.

Jay Bok, Esq. By A. Lewis O. Anthony Lewis Oswald. LC 55-13863. 1955. Christopher Pub.House.

Jay Gould Harmon: With Maine Folks. George Selwyn Kimball. 1905. C. M. Clark Publishing Co., Inc.

Jay-Hawkers: A Story of Free Soil and Border Ruffian Days. Adela Elizabeth Richards Orpen. LC 4096. 1900. D. Appleton and Company.

Jaybird. MacKinlay Kantor. LC 32-712824. Coward-McCann, Inc.

Jayhawk. Dorothy M. Keddington. LC 78-13429. 1978. 6.95 (ISBN 0-913420-80-8). Olympus Pub. Co.

Jayhawker. John Andrew Martin. LC 8-26823. 1908. The C. M. Clark Publishing Co.

Jayhawkers. Thompson B. Ferguson. LC 71-104449. 1970. (ISBN 0-8398-0554-3). Literature House.

Jayhawkers. A Tale of the Border War. Kansas in the Early Days. Thompson B Ferguson. LC 6-38984. 1892. State Capital Printing Company.

Jay's Journal. Beatrice Mathews Sparks. LC 78-19612. 7.95 (ISBN 0-8129-0801-5). Times Books.

Jazz Band. Wyatt Rundell. LC 35-8039. Greenberg.

Jazz Bum. William Gwinn. LC 54-424784. (Lion book, 225). 1954. Lion Books by Arrangement with Margood Pub. Corp.

Jazz Country. Nat Hentoff. (Perennial library). 1976. 1.25 (ISBN 0-06-080355-X). Harper and Row.

Jazz, Jazz, Jazz: A Novel. Patrick Skene Catling. LC 81-14530. 11.95 (ISBN 0-312-44073-1). St. Martin's Press.

Jazz Mad: A Stirring Romance of Genius and Love, Based on the Motion Picture Story. Svend Gade. LC 28-9844. Jacobsen-Hodgkinson-Corporation.

Jazz Singer. Richard Woodley. 192p. (Orig.). 1980. pap. 2.25 (ISBN 0-553-13236-9). Bantam.

Jazz Singer: A Story of Pathos and Laughter. Arline De Haas & Raphaelson, Samson. The Day of Atonement. LC 27-22654. Grosset & Dunlap.

Jazz Widow: A Novel. May Christie. LC 30-246242. Grosset & Dunlap.

Jazzy. Margaret Doerkson. LC 81-1156. 11.95 (ISBN 0-8253-0039-8). Beaufort Books.

Jeacrow. Mark Elder. (Gold medal books, P2911). 1973. (pbk) 1.25. Fawcett Publications.

Jealous Ear: A Novel. Robert Early. LC 73-4286. 1973. 5.95 (ISBN 0-395-17115-6). Houghton Mifflin.

Jealous Ghost. Leonard Alfred George Strong. LC 30-30567. 1930. A. A. Knopf.

Jealous God. John Braine. 1965. 4.95 o.p. (ISBN 0-395-07446-0). HM.

Jealous God: 1st Amer. Ed. John Braine. LC 65-15159. 1965. 4.95. Houghton.

Jealous Goddess. Madge Mears. LC 15-13475. 1915. John Lane.

Jealous Gods. Gertrude Franklin Horn Atherton. 1928. lib. bdg. 15.00 (ISBN 0-8414-3088-8). Folcroft.

Jealous Gods: A Processional Novel of the Fifth Century, B. C. (Concerning One Alcibiades. Gertrude Franklin Horn Atherton. LC 28-25179. 1928. H. Liverright.

Jealous House. Clarence Budington Kelland. LC 34-24631. 1934. Harper & Brothers.

Jealous Love. Daisy H. Thomson. 1974. pap. 0.95 o.p. (ISBN 0-515-03369-3, N3369). BJ Pub Group.

Jealous Mistress. Robert Traver. 1968. 4.95 o.p. Little.

Jealous Mistress: By Robert Traver. 1st Ed. John Donaldson Voelker. LC 67-28226. 1968. 4.95. Little, Brown.

Jealous Mistress: Translated from the German by Ruth Lachenbruch. Paul Elbogen. LC 53-5025. 1953. Random House.

Jealous Mrs. Simkins. Everard Roberts. LC 6-15733. The Knickerbocker Press.

Jealous One. Celia Fremlin, pseud. LC 65-17972. bds., 3.50. Lippincott.

Jealous One. Celia Fremlin, pseud. (S241). 1966. Avon.

Jealous Wife. Elizabeth Mitchell. LC 74-182585. 1973.

Jealous Wives. Ernest Lynn. LC 30-19273. The White House.

Jealous Woman. James Mallahan Cain. LC 50-39495. (Avon monthly novel, 17). 1950. Avon Novels.

Jealous Yesterdays. Marcia Miller. (Avalon romances). 1974. 4.50. Avalon Books.

Jealous Yesterdays. Marcia Miller. (Gold Medal Book). 1.25 (ISBN 0-449-13541-1). Fawcett.

Jealousies of a Country Town: The Thirteen, and Other Stories. saintsbury ed. Honore De Balzac. Tr. by Ellen Marriage. Rudd, John, Joint Tr. 1899. The Gebbie Publishing Co., Ltd.

Jealousy. Norah C James. LC 33-2634. 1933. Covici, Friede.

Jealousy: A Novel. Robbe-Grillet, Alain. LC 77-92783. 1978. 2.95 (ISBN 0-8021-4152-8) (ISBN 0-394-17031-8). Grove Press: Distributed by Random House.

Jealousy, a Novel. Translated by Richard Howard. Alain Robbe-Grillet. LC 59-138902. 1959. Grove Press.

Jealousy & Episode. William Faulkner. LC 77-903. 1977. lib. bdg. 12.50 (ISBN 0-8414-4173-1). Folcroft.

Jealousy and Episode: Two Stories. William Faulkner. LC 77-903. 1977. 12.50 (ISBN 0-8414-4173-1). Folcroft Library Editions.

Jealousy and Medicine. Michal Choromanski. LC 64-16825. (New Directions book). 1964. New Directions.

Jealousy: Or, Teverino. A Novel. Tr. by Oliver S. Leland. Leland, Oliver Shepard, 1833-1870, Tr. LC 6-34606. The F. M. Lupton Publishing Company.

Jealousy: Or, Teverino. A Novel. George Sand & Leland, Oliver S., Tr. LC 7-25673. T. B. Peterson & Brothers.

Jean. A Novel. Mary Wentworth Newman. (seaside library. v. 69, no. 1406). 1882. G. Munro.

Jean at Noon: Or, Summer's Treasure. Jane Duncan, pseud. LC 76-166479. 1972. 4.95. St. Martin's Press.

Jean Baptiste: A Story of French Canada. James Edward Le Rossignol. LC 75-301122. (Toronto reprint library of Canadian prose and poetry). (ISBN 0-8020-7525-8). University of Toronto Press.

Jean Barois. Martin Du Gard, Roger. LC 49-8550. 1949. Viking Press.

Jean Berny: Sailor. Julien Viaud & Robins, E. P., Tr. LC 8-29995. 1893. Cassell Publishing Company.

Jean Bradley. Florence Stonebraker. LC 48-17794. 1948. Gramercy Pub. Co.

Jean Carroll: A Tale of the Ozark Hills. John Homer Case. LC 11-278105. 1911. 1.50. Broadway Publishing Co.

Jean-Christophe. Romain Rolland. Tr. by Gilbert Canaan. LC 33-27190. (Half-title: Modern library of the world's best books. Modern library giants). 1938. The Modern Library.

Jean-Christophe: Dawn, Morning, Youth, Revolt. Romain Rolland. Tr. by Gilbert Canaan. LC 10-283331. 1910. H. Holt and Company.

Jean-Christophe: Dawn, Morning, Youth, Revolt. Romain Rolland. Tr. by Gilbert Canaan. LC 15-17400. 1915. H. Holt and Company.
Jean-Christophe in Paris: The Market-Place, Antoinette, The House. Romain Rolland. Tr. by Gilbert Canaan. LC 11-27915. 1911. H. Holt and Company.
Jean-Christophe. Journey's End; Love and Friendship, The Burning Bush, The New Dawn. Romain Rolland. Tr. by Gilbert Canaan. LC 13-35299. 1913. H. Holt and Company.
Jean Gilles. Andre Lafon. Tr. by Davidson, Theodore (Keppel) LC 14-15175. 1914. 1.50. G. P. Putnam's Sons,S.
Jean Grant: A Novel. Archibald M'Alpine Taylor. LC 8-25653. 1890. A Lovell & Co.
Jean Huguenot. Stephen Vincent Benet. LC 23-13372. 1923. H. Holt and Company.
Jean in the Morning. Janet Sandison. LC 76-86384. 1971. 4.95 o.p. (J20000). St Martin.
Jean in the Twilight. Janet Sandison, pseud. LC 72-87052. 256p. 1973. 6.50 o.p. St Martin.
Jean in the Twilight: Or, The Mists of Autumn. Jane Duncan, pseud. LC 72-87052. 1973. 6.50. St. Martin's Press.
Jean Lafitte: Gentleman Smuggler. Mitchell Vaughn Charnley. LC 34-22753. 1934. The Viking Press.
Jean le Bleu see Oeuvres Romanesques.
Jean le Bleu: Nouvelles. Jean Giono. (Coll. Soleil). 13.25. French & Eur.
Jean Mitchell's School: A Story. Angelina W Wray. LC 2-478. 1902. Public-School Publishing Company.
Jean Monteith. Margaret Greenway McClelland. (On cover: Leisure hour series. no. 204). 1887. H. Holt and Company.
Jean Monteith. Mary Greenway McClelland. LC 7-15266. (Leisure hour series. No. 204). 1887. H. Holt and Company.
Jean of the Lazy A. Bertha Muzzy Sinclair. LC 15-209112. 1915. 1.30. Little, Brown, and Company.
Jean Pauline: An Indian Tragedy. Maud Emery. LC 77-354559. (ISBN 0-919900-16-X). Nunaga.
Jean Santeuil. Translated by Gerard Hopkins. With a Pref. by Andre Maurois. Marcel Proust. LC 55-12297. 1956. Simon and Schuster.
Jean Towards Another Day. Janet Sandison, pseud. LC 74-21091. 1975. 7.95 o.p. (ISBN 0-312-44135-5). St Martin.
Jean Towards Another Day; or, Can Spring Be Far Away? Jane Duncan, pseud. LC 74-21091. 1975. 7.95. St. Martin's Press.
Jeanie. Wilma Ross Westphal. LC 60-941653. 1960. Review and Herald Pub. Association.
Jeanie Nairn's Wee Laddie. A Simple Story of the Old Town. Maria M Grant. (Seaside library, v. 77, no. 1560). G. Munro.
Jeanie's Quiet Life. A Novel. Eliza Tabor Stephenson. (Seaside library, v. 24, no. 477). 1879. G. Munro.
Jeanne. Theda Kenyon. LC 28-229546. 1928. I. Washburn.
Jeanne la Fileuse. Honore Beaugrand. (Novels by Franco-Americans in New England 1850-1940 Ser.). 188p. (Fr.). (gr. 10 up). 1980. pap. 4.50 (ISBN 0-911409-17-3). Natl Mat Dev.
Jeanne Margot. Sophia Cleugh. LC 27-205843. 1927. The Macmillan Company.
Jeanne-Marie's Triumph. Clara Elizabeth Laughlin. LC 22-27474. Fleming H. Revell Company.
Jeanne of the Marshes. Edward Phillips Oppenheim. LC 13-7655. 1908. Little, Brown, and Company.
Jeanne of the Marshes. Edward Phillips Oppenheim. LC 9-26148. 1909. Little, Brown, and Company.
Jeanne, Relapse et Sainte. Georges Bernanos. 6.50. French & Eur.
Jeanne: The Story of a Fresh Air Child. LC 6-44566. 1893. Press of Brandow Printing Company.
Jeannette's Cisterns. Mary Louise Parmelee Peebles. LC 7-30567. 1881. H. B. Nims & Co.
Jeannie. Katharine Howard. (Belmont Tower books). 1.95 (ISBN 0-505-51331-5). Tower Pubns.
Jeannie. Frances Mims. LC 74-76734. 1974. 7.95. Kells.
Jeannie Gerhardt: A Novel. Theodore Dreiser. LC 22-4767. Harper & Brothers.
Jean's Tragic Dilemma: A Novel. 1st Ed. Muriel Anscombe. LC 59-2839. 1959. Vantage Press.
Jeb. Jeffrey Lord. (Orig.). 1970. pap. 0.95 o.p. (65-157). Paperback Lib.
Jeb Hutton: The Story of a Georgia Boy. by james b. connolly; illustrated by m.j. burns. ed. James Brendan Connolly. LC 2-22177. 1902. C. Scribner's Sons.
Jed Blaine's Woman. Evelyn Wells. LC 47-30243. 1947. Doubleday & Company, Inc.
Jed Smith: Freedom River. Fred Lawrence. (American Explorers Ser.: No. 1). 368p. (Orig.). 1981. pap. 2.50 (ISBN 0-440-04214-3, Standish). Dell.
Jeeves. Cyril Northcote Parkinson. LC 80-29160. 1981. 8.95 (ISBN 0-312-44144-4). St. Martin's Press.
Jeeves. Pelham Grenville Wodehouse. LC 23-135757. George H. Doran Company.
Jeeves. Pelham Grenville Wodehouse. LC 30-12325. 1925. A. L. Burt Company.
Jeeves... Pelham Grenville Wodehouse. LC 45-8054. 1945.
Jeeves & the Feudal Spirit. P. G. Wodehouse. 1962. 11.95 o.s.i. (ISBN 0-8277-0214-0). British Bk Ctr.
Jeeves and the Tie That Binds. Pelham Grenville Wodehouse. LC 75-159142. 1971. 5.95 (ISBN 0-671-21038-6). Simon and Schuster.
Jeeves and the Tie That Binds. Pelham Grenville Wodehouse. LC 72-38097. 1971. 7.95 (ISBN 0-8161-6011-2). G. K. Hall.
Jeff Benton, M.D. Adeline McElfresh. 1976. 0.95. Belmont Tower.
Jeff White; Young Woodsman. Lew Dietz. LC 49-10188. 1949. Little, Brown.
Jefferson Boone-Handyman No. 6: The Inheritors. Jon Messman. 1975. pap. 1.25 o.p. (ISBN 0-515-03813-X). BJ Pub Group.
Jefferson Boone: Handyman: The Monetu Papers, a Novel. Jon Messman. 1973. (pbk) 0.95 (ISBN 0-515-02995-5). Pyramid.
Jefferson Boone, Handyman 1: The Moneta Papers. Jon Messman. (Orig.). 1973. pap. 0.95 o.p. (ISBN 0-515-02995-5, N2995). Pyramid Pubns.
Jefferson McGraw. Weldon Hill, pseud. 1972. 6.95 o.p. (ISBN 0-688-00109-2). Morrow.
Jefferson Secret: A Mystery with Love and Without a Murder. Richard Blaker. LC 29-147575. 1929. Doubleday, Doran & Company, Inc.
Jefferson Selleck. 1st Ed. Carl Jonas. LC 52-5171. 1952. Little, Brown.
Jefferson Square: A Novel. Noel Bertram Gerson. LC 68-14054. 1968. M. Evans; Distributed in Association with Lippincott, Philadelphia.
Jefferson Wildrider. Mary E Bennett. LC 98-1525. The Baker and Taylor Company.
Jefferson's Birthday & Postface. Dick Higgins, pseud. (Illus.). 1964. 35.00 o.p. (ISBN 0-89366-098-1). Ultramarine Pub.
Jeffy's Lookin' at Me! Bil Keane. (Family Circus Ser.). (Illus.). 128p. 1982. pap. 1.95 (ISBN 0-449-14096-2, GM). Fawcett.
Jefta und Seine Tochter; Roman. Lion Feuchtwanger. LC 57-2858. 1957. Putnam.
Jehenne Lefevre: Or, A Miner's Daughter. Daniel Sommer. D. Sommer.
Jehovah Blues (Phoenix Rising) 1st American Ed. Marguerite Steen. LC 52-8051. 1952. Doubleday.
Jehovah's Day. Mary Borden. LC 29-9096. 1929. Doubleday, Doran & Company, Inc.
Jelard: A Novel. S. E Henderson. LC 7-4123. 1892. Longwell & Cummings.
Jelly: A Novel. Jack Ansell. 1973. (pbk) 0.95 (ISBN 0-671-77648-7). Pocket Books.
Jelly: A Novel. Jack Ansell. LC 75-167745. 1971. 5.95 (ISBN 0-87795-018-0). Arbor House.
Jellybean. Robert Carson. LC 73-15653. 1974. 6.95 (ISBN 0-316-13026-5). Little, Brown.
Jellybean Society. Patrick Oliphant. 200p. 1981. pap. 6.95 (ISBN 0-8362-1250-9). Andrews & McMeel.
Jellyroll. David Mason. (Orig.). 1969. pap. 1.95 o.s.i. (OPH-173, Ophelia). Olympia.
Jem. Frederik Pohl. LC 78-3983. 10.00 (ISBN 0-312-44155-X). St. Martin's Press.
Jemima. Auriel Rosemary Malet Vaughan. LC 52-9782. 1952. Little, Brown.
Jemma. Beverly Byrne. 512p. 1981. pap. 2.75 (ISBN 0-449-14375-9, GM). Fawcett.
Jemmy Button: Translated from the Spanish by Mary and Fred Del Villar. Benjamin Subercaseaux. LC 54-85383. 1954. Macmillan.
Jemmy Daily: Or, The Little News Vender. A Tale of Youthful Struggles and the Triumph of Truth and Virtue Over Vice and Falsehood. Joseph Holt Ingraham. LC 52-46333. 1843. Brainard.
Jen of the Marshes: By John Frederic Herbin... John Frederic Herbin. LC 21-176254. The Cornhill Publishing Company.
Jena. Constance Bogen. (Orig.). 1970. pap. price not set o.p. (Award). Univ Pub & Dist.
Jenghiz-Khan: A Tale of the 13th Century. Vasilli G. Yan. Tr. by L. Britton from Rus. LC 75-39020. (Soviet Literature in English Translation Ser.). 272p. 1978. Repr. of 1945 ed. 18.50 (ISBN 0-88355-421-6). Hyperion-Conn.
Jenghiz-Khan: A Tale of 13th Century Asia. Vasilii Grigorevich Ian. LC 75-39020. (Early Soviet Literature in English Translation). 1978. 18.50 (ISBN 0-88355-421-6). Hyperion Press.
Jenifer. Lucy Meacham Kidd Thruston. LC 7-16941. 1907. Little, Brown, and Company.
Jenifer. A Novel. Annie Hall Thomas Cudlip. (Harper's Franklin square library. no. 349). 1883. G. Munro.
Jenifer. A Novel. Annie Hall Thomas Cudlip. (seaside library. v. 86, no. 1750). 1883. G. Munro.
Jenifer. A Novel. Annie Hall Thomas Cudlip. (On cover: Seaside library. Pocket ed. no. 142). 1884. G. Munro.
Jenkins' Ear. Odell Shepard & Shepard, Willard Odell. LC 51-9818. 1951. Macmillan.
Jenna Look. Diane Watson. (Orig.). 1981. pap. 2.50 (ISBN 0-505-51715-9). Tower Bks.
Jenner Guns. Ray Hogan. (Shawn Starbuck western). 1974. (pbk.) 0.95. New American Library.
Jennette Browning: Or A Hoosier Girl's Victory, a True History of a Remarkable Life. Jennie Brown Doremus. LC 6-33721. Pub. by the Author.
Jennie Gerhardt. Theodore Dreiser. 1973. 8.95 o.p. (ISBN 0-529-03410-7). World Pub.
Jennie Gerhardt: A Novel. Theodore Dreiser. 1911. Harper & Brothers.
Jennie Gerhardt: A Novel. Theodore Dreiser. LC 35-2265. 1934. Pub. in Cooperation with Simon & Schuster by the Garden City Publishing Co., Inc.
Jennie Gerhardt: A Novel. Theodore Dreiser. LC 81-84117. 1982. 8.95 (ISBN 0-8052-0692-2). Schocken Books.
Jennifer. Janet Payne Whitney. LC 40-36105. 1941. W. Morrow & Company.
Jennifer, Bk. 1. pap. 2.95. Dell.
Jennifer, Bk. 4. 176p. 1982. pap. 2.95 (ISBN 0-440-04246-1, Emerald). Dell.
Jennifer, Bk. 5. (Orig.). 1982. pap. 2.95 (ISBN 0-440-04158-9, Emerald). Dell.
Jennifer, Bk. 6. 192p. (Orig.). 1983. pap. 2.95 (ISBN 0-440-04280-1, Emerald). Dell.
Jennifer, Bk. 7. (Orig.). 1983. pap. 2.95 (ISBN 0-440-04183-X). Dell.
Jennifer, Bk. 8. 192p. (Orig.). 1983. pap. 2.95 (ISBN 0-440-04338-7, Emerald). Dell.
Jennifer, Bk. 9. (Orig.). 1983. pap. 2.95 (ISBN 0-440-04243-7). Dell.
Jennifer by Moonlight. William Edward Daniel Ross. LC 73-4750. (Red rose romance). 1973. 0.75. Bantam Books.
Jennifer Hale. Rob Eden. LC 34-36231. Grosset /& Dunlap.
Jennifer Lorn: A Sedate Extravaganza. Elinor Hoyt Wylie. LC 23-178453. 1923. George H. Doran Company.
Jennifer's House. Christine Noble Govan. LC 45-2275. 1945. Houghton Mifflin Company.
Jenny. Natalie Johnson. (Caprice Romance Ser.). (Illus.). 160p. 1982. pap. 1.95 (ISBN 0-448-16979-7, Pub. by Tempo). Ace Bks.
Jenny. Ada Cook Lewis. LC 56-6821. 1956. Rinehart.
Jenny. Ada Cook Lewis. (Berkley Medallion book). 1974. (pbk.) 1.50 (ISBN 0-425-02705-8). Berkley Pub. Co.
Jenny: A Novel. Sigrid Undset. LC 74-12378. 1975. H. Fertig.
Jenny: a Novel: Tr. from the Norwegian of Sigrid Undset. Sigrid Undset & Emme, W., Tr. LC 21-18947. 1921. A. A. Knopf.
Jenny and Barnum: A Novel of Love. Roderick Thorp. LC 81-43215. 14.95 (ISBN 0-385-15058-X). Doubleday.
Jenny & I see Hilltop.
Jenny and I: A Novel of Suspense. Jennette Dowling Letton. LC 63-12443. 1963. Macrae Smith.
Jenny Angel. Elsie Marion Oakes Barber. LC 54-12160. 1954. Macmillan.
Jenny Be Good. Wilbur Finley Fauley. LC 19-13458. Britton Publication Company.
Jenny by Nature. Erskine Caldwell. LC 61-840656. Farrar, Straus and Caudhy.
Jenny Cartwright. George Stevenson. LC 15-13360. 1914. 1.25. John Lane.
Jenny Devlin. Sophie Kerr. LC 43-13681. 1943. Farrar & Rinehart, Inc.
Jenny Doone, Office Nurse. Addie Adam. 1976. 4.95. Avalon Books.
Jenny Essenden. Agnes Russell Weekes. LC 21-979. 1921. R. M. McBride & Co.
Jenny Fowler. Margaret Weymouth Jackson. LC 30-231964. The Bobbs-Merrill Company.
Jenny Heysten's Career. Jo Van Ammers-Kuller. Tr. by Wyhe, H. Van. LC 30-22437. E. P. Dutton & Co. Inc.
Jenny Kissed Me. Ruth Fenisong. 1965. pap. 0.95 o.p. (01980, Collier). Macmillan.
Jenny Kissed Me: A Novel of Murder. Ruth Fenisong. LC 44-4099. 1944. Pub. for the Crime Club by Doubleday, Doran and Co., Inc.
Jenny, My Diary. Yorick Blumenfeld. LC 82-83282. (Illus.). 5.95 (ISBN 0-316-10032-3). Little, Brown.
Jenny Newstead. Marie Adelaide Belloc Lowndes. LC 32-206179. 1932. G. P. Putnam's Sons.
Jenny Rorke. Muriel Hine Coxon. LC 33-1847. 1933. D. Appleton and Company.
Jenny the Joyous. Cornelia Stratton Parker. LC 24-116566. Harcourt, Brace and Company.
Jenny: The Romance of a Nurse. Norma Patterson. Farrar & Rinehart, Inc.
Jenny, the Work Girl: Or, A Daughter's Love: a Tale of City Life. Paul Prichard. (On cover: Bunce's ten cent novels, no. 2). 1860. W. J. Bunce.
Jenny Treibel. Theodor Fontane. LC 76-15648. 8.50. (ISBN 0-8044-2209-5) (ISBN 0-8044-6154-6). F. Ungar Pub. Co.
Jenny Villiers: A Story of the Theatre. John Boynton Priestley. LC 47-11508. 1947. Harper.
Jenny W. R. E. N. Ursula Bloom. LC 45-2141. 1945. Arcadia House, Inc.
Jenny W. R. E. N. Sheila Burns, pseud. LC 45-214119. 1945. Arcadia House, Inc.
Jenny's Coat. Miska Miles, pseud. (Skylark Ser.). 48p. 1982. pap. 1.75 (ISBN 0-553-15125-8, Skylark). Bantam.
Jenny's Moonlight Adventure. Esther Averill. 1982. pap. write for info. Bantam.
Jeopardy. Manfred Conte. LC 56-5146. 1956. W. Sloane Associates.
Jerbo: The Jumper. Hal George Evarts. LC 30-23231. Whitman Publishing Company.
Jerd Cless. Myra Daley. LC 9-30114. 1909. 1.50. Cochrane Publishing Co.
Jeremiah. J. Challenor. 1969. pap. 0.75 o.p. (80126). Glencoe.
Jeremiah and the Princess. Edward Phillips Oppenheim. LC 33-17389. 1933. Little, Brown, and Company.
Jeremiah, Eight Twenty. Carol Hill. 1970. 8.95 o.p. (ISBN 0-394-43119-7). Random.
Jeremiah Painter. George Wolk. 1973. (pbk) 0.95. Dell.
Jeremiah Thunder. Harold Heifetz. LC 68-11791. 1968. Doubleday.
Jeremiah 8: 20: A Novel. Carol Hill. LC 71-102322. 1970. 6.95. Random House.
Jeremiah's Sammy. Charles Summer Gabriel. LC 12-6555. 1.50. The C. M. Clark Publishing Co.
Jeremy. Hugh Walpole. LC 58-833. (St. Martin's library). 1957. Macmillan.
Jeremy. Hugh Walpole. LC 19-19673. 1919. Cassell and Company, Limited.
Jeremy. Hugh Walpole. LC 19-15685. George H. Doran Company.
Jeremy & Hamlet. Hugh Walpole. 1923. 3.95 o.p. St Martin.
Jeremy at Crale. Hugh Walpole. 1927. 3.50 o.p. St Martin.
Jeremy at Crale: His Friends, His Ambitions and His One Great Enemy. Hugh Walpole. LC 27-22485. George H. Doran Company.
Jeremy Bell. Clyde Brion Davis. 1947. Rhinehart & Company, Inc.
Jeremy Hamlin. Alice Brown. LC 34-3727. 1934. D. Appleton-Century Company, Incorporated.
Jeremy Poldark, a Novel of Cornwall, 1790-1791. Winston Graham. LC 79-10051. 1979. 14.95 (ISBN 0-8161-6678-1). Hall.
Jeremy Takes a Hand. Cornelia Kane Rathbone. LC 27-369036. 1927. D. Appleton and Company.
Jeremy Todd: A Novel. Hamilton Maule. LC 59-7836. 1959. Random House.
Jeremy's Version. James Purdy. LC 78-116246. 1970. 5.95. Doubleday.
Jericho. Anthony Costello. LC 81-15048. 1982. 14.95 (ISBN 0-553-05009-5). Bantam Books.
Jericho. Anson Wright. LC 77-79285. 2.95 (ISBN 0-912874-13-9). Out of the Ashes Press.
Jericho Commandment. James Patterson. 1981. pap. 2.50 (ISBN 0-345-29241-3). Ballantine.
Jericho Commandment. James Patterson. 1979. 10.00 o.p. (ISBN 0-517-53626-9). Crown.
Jericho Commandment: A Novel. James Patterson. LC 78-21241. (Illus.). 10.00 (ISBN 0-517-53626-9). Crown.
Jericho Road. Charlotte Elvira Gray. LC 12-249225. 1.25. Jennings and Graham.
Jericho Road: A Story of Western Life... John Habberton. 1877. Jansen, McClurg & Co.
Jericho Sands: A Novel. Mary Borden. LC 26-1534. 1926. A. A. Knopf.
Jericho Sleep Alone. Berl Make Tea. Chaim I Bermant. LC 66-13199. 1966. Holt, Rinehart and Winston.
Jericho's Daughters: A Novel. 1st Ed. Paul Iselin Wellman. LC 56-10775. 1956. Doubleday.
Jerico Papers: A Quaint and Amusing Side of Early New England Life... Joseph Vahle. The Jerico Papers Stuyvesant Press.
Jeritan. Nor H. Mustafa. (Karyawan Malaysia Ser.). (Malay.). 1979. pap. text ed. 3.75x o.p. (00353). Heinemann Ed.
Jermiah Bacon. James A. Janke. (Orig.). 1980. pap. 1.95 (ISBN 0-440-15289-5). Dell.
Jerome, a Poor Man: A Novel. Mary Eleanor Wilkins Freeman. LC 6-40020. 1897. Harper & Brothers.
Jerome Leaster of Roderick, Leaster & Co. Lillian E Sommers. LC 8-10216. 1890. C. H. Sergel & Co.
Jerome: Or, The Latitude of Love. Maurice Bedel. Tr. by Lawrence Shackelford Morris. LC 28-18285. 1928. The Viking Press.
Jerry. Elenore Meherin. LC 28-14117. Grosset & Dunlap.
Jerry. Arthur Stanwood Pier. LC 17-431392. 1917. Houghton Mifflin Company.

Jerry: A Novel. Sarah Barnwell Elliott. LC 4-15101. 1891. H. Holt and Company.
Jerry Bleeker: Or, Is Marriage a Failure? Robert C Givins. (pastime ser., v. 30). 1889. Laird & Lee.
Jerry Dowd: Fraternity Man. Lawrence A Keating. LC 47-30934. (Teen-age library). 1947. Lantern Press.
Jerry Foster, Salesman. Elmer Ellsworth Ferris. LC 42-11042. 1942. Doubleday, Doran & Company, Inc.
Jerry Junior. Jean Webster. LC 24-14938. 1907. Grosset & Dunlap.
Jerry, Junior: By Jean Webster... with Illustrations by Orson Lowell. Jean Webster. LC 7-13435. 1907. The Century Co.
Jerry Rides the Range. George M Johnson. LC 32-33053. E. J. Clode, Inc.
Jerry the Dreamer: A Novel. Will Payne. LC 7-33764. 1896. Harper & Brothers.
Jerry the Put. Richard Cloke. LC 78-57812. 2.25 (ISBN 0-917458-06-0). Kent Publications.
Jersey Blue: An Irreverent Saga of the Making of the New World. Rebecca Singleton. LC 81-17807. 16.95 (ISBN 0-671-44584-7) (ISBN 0-671-44583-9). Poseidon Press.
Jersey Bounce. Glen Chase, pseud. (Cherry Delight,#9). 1974. (pbk.) 1.25. Leisure Books.
Jersey Bounce: Cherry Delight Ser., No. 9. Glen Chase, pseud. 1974. pap. 1.25 o.p. (LB151ZK). Leisure Bks.
Jersey Guns. Don Pendleton. (Executioner,#17). 1974. (pbk.) 1.25 (ISBN 0-523-00328-5). Pinnacle Books.
Jersey Luck. Tom De Haven. LC 80-7602. 10.00 (ISBN 0-06-011087-2). Harper & Row.
Jersey Street & Jersey Lane. facsimile ed. Henry Cuyer Bunner. LC 74-94705. (Short Story Index Reprint Ser.). 1896. 15.00 (ISBN 0-8369-3083-5). Ayer Co.
Jersey Street and Jersey Lane: Urban and Suburban Sketches. Henry Cuyler Bunner. LC 74-94705. (Short story index reprint series). (Illus.). 1969. Books for Libraries Press.
Jerusalem. Selma Ottiliana Lovisa Lagerlof. Tr. by Jessie Brochner. LC 75-98777. 1970. Greenwood Press.
Jerusalem: A Novel, from the Swedish of Selma Lagerlof. Selma Ottiliana Lovisa Lagerlof. Tr. by Howard, Velma (Swanston) LC 15-190705. 1915. 1.35. Doubleday, Page & Company.
Jerusalem Conspiracy. David Allen Riis. 2.50 (ISBN 0-440-14340-3). Dell Publishing.
Jerusalem Diamond. Noah Gordon. LC 78-23254. 10.95 (ISBN 0-394-50416-X). Random House.
Jerusalem File. Nick Carter. (Killmaster spy chiller). 1975. (pbk.) 1.25. Award Books.
Jerusalem Poker. Edward Whittemore. LC 77-13414. ((His). (Jerusalem quartet). 10.00 (ISBN 0-03-018516-5). Holt, Rinehart and Winston.
Jerusalem Poker. Edward Whittemore. 1979. 2.50 (ISBN 0-380-44305-8). Avon.
Jerusalem Rock: A Novel. Dina Mitosky. LC 79-16665. 1979. 10.95 (ISBN 0-87131-297-2). Evans.
Jerusalem the Golden. Margaret Drabble. LC 67-201866. 1967. bds., 3.95. Morrow.
Jerusalem the Golden: An Historical Novel of the Finger Lake Country of New York. St. John, Robert Porter. LC 26-23679. 1926. F. H. Hitchcock.
Jerusalem Vampire. Jos. M. Scovitch. 1979. pap. 2.95 (ISBN 0-89185-180-1). Anthelion Pr.
Jerusha's Jim. Mary E. Stone Bassett. LC 6-9095. (On cover: Satchet series, no. 32). W. B. Smith & Co.
Jerushy in Brooklyn. Anna Olcott Commelin. (Fowler & Wells library. no. 15). 1893. Fowler & Wells Co.
Jervaise Comedy. John Davys Beresford. LC 19-5693. 1919. The Macmillan Company.
Jess. James Matthew Barrie. LC 96-1107. (The young of heart series, v. 11). 1898. D. Estes & Company.
Jess. Henry Rider Haggard. LC 6-46139. (On cover: Lovell's library. v. 13, no. 900). 1887. J. W. Lovell Company.
Jess. A Novel. Henry Rider Haggard. LC 6-46138. (Harper's Franklin square library. no. 567). 1887. Harper & Brothers.
Jess: A Novel. Henry Rider Haggard. LC 17-499. 1908. Longmans, Green & Co.
Jess & Co. John Joy Bell. LC 4-22670. 1904. Harper & Brothers.
Jess Edwards Rides Again. Alice Ward Smith. LC 34-211544. The Christopher Publishing House.
Jess of Harbor Hill. Ramie A Sheridan. LC 11-861052. (His Harbor hill romances). Cupples & Leon Company.
Jess of the Rebel Trail. Hiram Alfred Cody. LC 21-17011. 1.90. George H. Doran Company.
Jess of the River. Roberts Theodore Goodridge. LC 14-13261. 1.25. G. W. Dillingham Company.
Jess Roundtree: Texas Ranger. Dane Coolidge. LC 33-1358. 1933. E. P. Dutton & Co., Inc.
Jessamine. A Novel. Mary Virginia Terhune. LC 8-26057. 1873. G. W. Carleton & Co.; Etc., Etc.
Jessamines: A New Story of the Old South. Sallie Hightower C. E. Broyles Broyles. LC 21-125523. 1921. The Stratford Company.
Jessamy Bride. 5th impression ed. Frank Frankfort Moore. LC 7-25307. 1899. H. S. Stone & Company.
Jessamy Bride. Frank Frankfort Moore. LC 26-744528. 1926. Duffield & Company.
Jessamy Court. Anne Maybury. LC 74-8673. 1974. 6.95 (ISBN 0-394-49372-9). Random House.
Jessamy Court. Anne Maybury. 1976. (pbk.) 1.75. Bantam Books.
Jessamy John. Philip Duffield Stong. LC 47-11845. 1947. Doubleday.
Jesse: A Story in the Time of Christ. Annette Lucile Noble. American Tract Society.
Jesse and Maria. Enrica Ludovica Maria Handel-Mazzetti & Shuster, George Nauman, 1894- Tr. LC 31-233481. H. Holt and Company.
Jesse Ben David, a Shepherd of Bethlehem. James Meeker Ludlow. LC 7-38030. F. H. Revell Company.
Jesse James. Rene de Goscinny. (Lucky Luke Ser.). (French.). 1976. 5.95x (ISBN 2-205-00393-3). Intl Learn Syst.
Jesse James' Bold Stroke: Or, The Double Bank Robbery. William Writer Of Adventure Stories Ward. LC 44-38241. (Adventure series. No. 31). The Arthur Westbrook Company.
Jesse Stuart Harvest. Jesse Stuart. 288p. (Orig.). 1974. pap. 1.50 o.p. (24298). Mockingbird Bks.
Jessica Fayer. John L'Heureux. LC 75-31970. 7.95 (ISBN 0-02-571650-6). McMillan.
Jessica Letters: An Editor's Romance. Paul Elmer More. LC 4-12091. 1904. G. P. Putnam's Sons.
Jessica, My Daughter: A Novel. Ari Ibu-Sahav & Meltzer, Julian Louis, 1904- Tr. LC 48-8782. 1948. Crown Publishers.
Jessica: Or, A Diamond with a Blemish. A Novel. W. H White. LC 8-36561. 1884. G. W. Carleton & Co.; Etc., Etc.
Jessica's First Prayer, Repr. Of 1867 Ed. Sarah Smith. Ed. by Robert L. Wolff. Bd. with Little Meg's Children; Alone in London. Repr. of 1869 ed; Pilgrim Street. Repr. of 1872 ed. (Victorian Fiction Ser.). 1975. lib. bdg. 60.00 o.s.i. (ISBN 0-8240-1569-X). Garland Pub.
Jessica's First Prayer; Little Meg's Children; Alone in London; Pilgrim Street. Hesba Stretton. LC 75-493. (Victorian Fiction: Novels of Faith and Doubt; 45). 1975. 35.00 (ISBN 0-8240-1569-X). Garland Pub.
Jessica's Mother. Hesba Stretton. LC 98-5349. H. Altemus.
Jessica's Wife. Hester Mundis. LC 74-79692. 1975. 6.95 (ISBN 0-698-10594-X). Coward, McCann & Geoghegan.
Jessica's Wife. Hester Mundis. 1976. (pbk.) 1.75 (ISBN 0-380-00587-5). Avon.
Jessie. Harriet Maria Gordon Smythies. LC 8-10195. (On cover: Seaside library. Pocket ed. no, 1046). G. Munro.
Jessie. A Novel. Harriet Maria Gordon Smythies. (On cover: Lovell's library. no. 1106). J. W. Lovell Co.
Jessie Allen: Or, The Power of Truth. Jonathan Gaines Bow. LC 16-21936. Baptist Book Concern.
Jessie Deane. Charlotte M. Stanley McKenna. LC 8-28181. (On cover: Munro's library, v. 1, no. 115). 1884. N. L. Munro.
Jessie's Flirtations. Curtis. (On cover: Library of select novels. no. 76). 1846. Harper & Brothers.
Jessie's Three Resolutions. Mary Ellen Bamford. LC 6-6295. American Baptist Publication Society.
Jessop Bequest. Anna Robeson Brown Burr. LC 7-34309. 1907. Houghton, Mifflin and Company.
Jessup. Newton A Fuessle. Boni and Liveright.
Jest of God. Margaret Laurence. LC 66-66458. (B 66-12619). 1966. Macmillan.
Jest of God. Margaret Laurence. LC 66-14920. (Illus.). 1966. Knopf.
Jester. Leslie Moore. LC 15-5745. 1915. 1.35. G. P. Putnam's Sons.
Jester Men. Chester Mann. LC 10-1141. 1909. Weed-Parsons Printing Co.
Jester's Prayer. Aimee Torriani & Connor, Helen. LC 43-51061. The Grail.
Jester's Reign. Boyne Grainger. LC 38-353618. Carrick & Evans, Inc.
Jester's Sword: How Aldebaran, the King's Son, Wore the Sheathed Sword of Conquest. Annie Fellows Johnston. LC 9-17658. 1909. L. C. Page & Company.
Jesting Army. Ernest Raymond. LC 31-2440. 1931. D. Appleton and Company.
Jesting Pilate: An Intellectual Holiday. Aldous Leonard Huxley. LC 74-11882. (Illus.). 326p. 1974. Repr. of 1926 ed. lib. bdg. 20.75x (ISBN 0-8371-7698-0, HUJP). Greenwood.
Jesuit. John Gallahue. LC 72-95911. 1973. 7.95 (ISBN 0-8128-1531-9). Stein and Day.
Jesuit a Story. Felicia Buttz Clark. LC 8-337874. Eaton & Mains.
Jesuit of to-Day. Orange McNeill. LC 7-20206. J. S. Tait & Sons.
Jesuit's Ring: A Romance of Mount Desert. Augustus Allen Hayes. LC 7-3751. 1887. C. Scribner's Sons.
Jesus As Others Saw Him. Joseph Jacobs. LC 73-2211. (Jewish People: History, Religion, Literature). 1973. 15.00 (ISBN 0-405-05275-8). Arno Press.
Jesus Bar-Abba, the Son of the Rabbi, a Story of the Crucifixion. Edmund Elmore Carter. LC 27-11620. The Hebron Journal.
Jesus Boy. Richard Laurence Gordon. LC 74-13898. 1975. 6.95 (ISBN 0-690-00548-2). Crowell.
Jesus Came Again: A Parable. Vardis Fisher. LC 56-13625. (His Testament of man). 1956. A. Swallow.
Jesus Christs. A. J. Langguth. LC 67-28818. 1968. Harper & Row.
Jesus Delaney: A Novel. Joseph Gordon Donnelly. LC 99-1821. 1899. The Macmillan Company.
Jesus Factor. Edwin Corley. LC 72-104642. 1970. 6.95. Stein and Day.
Jesus Gave Them to Me. Ercelle Moore. 1981. pap. 4.50 (ISBN 0-930024-14-1). Cedar Rock.
Jesus II. Frank Riley. 1978. pap. 4.95 o.s.i. (ISBN 0-8202-5027-9). Sherbourne.
Jesus Incident. Frank Herbert & Bill Ransom. LC 78-24581. (Illus.). 10.95. Berkley Pub. Co.: Distributed by Putnam.
Jesus Incident. Frank Herbert & Ransom, Bill. 1980. 2.50 (ISBN 0-425-04504-8). Berkley Pub. Corp.
Jesus Incident see Worlds Beyond Dune: The Best of Frank Herbert.
Jesus Is Here!" Continuing the Narrative of In His Steps (What Would Jesus Do? Charles Monroe Sheldon. LC 14-6234. Hodder & Stoughton, George H. Doran Company.
Jesus Man: A Novel. Robert Casey. LC 79-17451. 8.95 (ISBN 0-87131-301-4). M. Evans.
Jesus of Gramoven. Perez Esclarin, Antonio. LC 79-22085. 5.95 (ISBN 0-88344-228-0). Orbis Books.
Jesus of the Twentieth Century: By Herman J. Schick. Herman John Schick. LC 38-2817. Printed by Eden Publishing House.
Jesus on a Stick. Ian Cochrane. LC 75-320624. 1975. 10.50 (ISBN 0-7100-8206-1). Routledge & K. Paul.
Jesus on Horseback: The Mooney County Saga. John Henry Reese. LC 74-157618. 1971. 7.95. Doubleday.
Jesus on Mars. Philip Jose Farmer. 1979. pap. 1.95 (ISBN 0-523-40184-1). Pinnacle Bks.
Jesus Tales: A Novel. Romulus Linney. LC 80-18280. 1980. 10.00 (ISBN 0-86547-020-0). North Point Press.
Jesus Two. Frank Riley. 212p. 1972. 5.95 o.p. (ISBN 0-8202-0095-6). Sherbourne.
Jet. Frank Harvey. LC 55-11964. 1955. Ballantine Books.
Jet: Her Face or Fortune? A Novel. Annie Edwards. (Appletons' new handy volume series v. 1). 1878. D. Appleton and Company.
Jet: Her Face or Her Fortune? Annie Edwards. (On cover: Lovell's library. no. 1362). 1889. J. W. Lovell Company.
Jet: Her Face or Her Fortune? A Novel. Annie Edwards. (On cover: Seaside library. Pocket ed. no. 841). 1886. G. Munro.
Jet Plane Mystery. Roy Judson Snell. LC 45-6102. Wilcox & Follett Co.
Jet Race. James Broom Lynne. LC 77-25752. 9.95 (ISBN 0-399-11917-5). Putnam.
Jet Set. Burton Wohl. LC 64-11907. 1964. Dial Press.
Jet Stewardess. Jane Gerard. 1973. pap. 0.75 o.s.i. (01-381). Lancer.
Jet Stream: A Novel. Austin Ferguson. LC 73-13718. 1974. 6.95. Morrow.
Jet Stream: A Novel. Austin Ferguson. 1974. (pbk.) 1.50. Bantam Books.
Jethro Bacon of Sandwich: And The Weaker Sex. Frederic Jesup Stimson. LC 2-26348. 1902. C. Scribner's Sons.
Jethro Hammer: A Novel. Craig Rice. LC 44-7027. 1944. Coward-McCann, Inc.
Jethrow's Cabin. Thomas Starling, pseud. LC 80-53312. 237p. 1982. pap. 3.95 (ISBN 0-914864-02-5); pap. 5.95 autographed. Spindrift.
Jetta: A Story of the South. Lucy A Orrick. (On cover: Unity library, no. 34a). 1894. C. H. Kerr & Company.
Jeune Franco-Americaine. Alberte Gastonguay. (Novels by Franco-Americans in New England 1850-1940 Ser.). 65p. (Fr.). (gr. 10 up). 1980. pap. 4.50x (ISBN 0-911409-18-1). Natl Mat Dev.
Jew. Jozef Ignacy Kraszewski. Tr. by Da Kowalewska, Linda. LC 7-14166. Dodd, Mead & Company.
Jew, and Mumu. Ivan Sergeevich Turgenev. LC 24-27955. (On cover: Little leather library. no. 59). Little Leather Library Corporation.
Jew and Other Stories. Ivan Sergeevich Turgenev. LC 74-86153. (Short story index reprint series). 1969. Books for Libraries Press.
Jew: And Other Stories. Ivan Sergeevich Turgenev. LC 75-10272. (His Novels, v. 15). 1970. AMS Press.
Jew in Love. Ben Hecht. LC 31-2673. Covici, Friede.
Jew Is... Howard H Hirschhorn. LC 72-81303. 1972. 3.95. Christopher Pub. House.
Jew of Chamant: A Romance of Crime... George Hatfield Dingley Gossip. LC 99-4799. F. T. Neely.
Jew of Chamant: Or, The Modern Monte Cristo: a Roman of Crime. George Hatfield Dingley Gossip. LC 98-181702. 1898. Printed by G. M. Hausauer.
Jew of Rome. Lion Feuchtwanger. Tr. by Willa Muir. Muir, Edwin, 1887- Joint Tr. LC 36-558. 1936. The Viking Press.
Jewel. Claire Goll. Tr. by Loving Pierre. LC 31-15561. 1931. A. A. Knopf.
Jewel: A Chapter in Her Life. Clara Louise Root Burnham. LC 3-22519. 1903. Houghton, Mifflin and Company.
Jewel-Hinged Jaw. Samuel R. Delany. 1978. pap. 4.95 (ISBN 0-425-03852-1, Windhover). Berkley Pub.
Jewel in the Crown: A Novel. Paul Scott. LC 66-16404. bds., 5.95. Morrow.
Jewel in the Crown: A Novel. Paul Scott. 1979. 2.25 (ISBN 0-380-40410-9). Avon Books.
Jewel in the Lotos. A Novel. Mary Agnes Tincker. LC 8-27019. 1884. J. B. Lippincott & Co.
Jewel in the Lotus: A Novel. Rosita Torr Forbes. LC 22-13777. 1922. Cassell and Company, Ltd.
Jewel in the Sand. Alma Newton. LC 20-1890. 1919. Duffield and Company.
Jewel in the Skull. Michael Moorcock. (Science Fiction Ser.). 1977. pap. 1.95 (ISBN 0-87997-841-4, UE1841). DAW Bks.
Jewel in the Skull. Michael Moorcock. 1.25 (ISBN 0-87997-276-9). Daw.
Jewel Mysteries I Have Known: From a Dealer's Note Book. Max Pemberton. LC 75-32772. (Literature of Mystery & Detection). (Illus.). 1976. Repr. of 1894 ed. 16.00x (ISBN 0-405-07892-7). Ayer Co.
Jewel of Death. Evelyn Berekman. 1971. pap. 0.75 o.p. (T2547). Pyramid Pubns.
Jewel of Doom. Nick Carter. (Nick Carter Ser.). (O.s.i.). (Orig.). 1970. pap. 0.95 o.s.i. (AN1090, Award). Univ Pub & Dist.
Jewel of Jarhen. A "Cap Kennedy" Novel. Gregory Kern. 1974. (pbk.) 0.95. Daw Books.
Jewel of Mahabar. Edison Marshall. LC 38-6336. 1938. H. C. Kinsey & Company, Inc.
Jewel of Seven Stars. Bram Stoker. 1979. pap. 1.95 (ISBN 0-89083-416-4). Zebra.
Jewel of Tharn. Jeffrey Lord. (Richard Blade Ser). (Orig.). 1969. pap. 0.75 o.p. (75-272). Manor Bks.
Jewel of the Desert. Robert Nasif Sheban. LC 32-6107. 1932. The Central Publishing House.
Jewel of the Java Sea. Dan Cushman. LC 51-20415. (Gold medal book, 142). 1951. Fawcett Publications.
Jewel of the Seas. Ellen Argo. LC 77-3180. 8.95 (ISBN 0-399-11959-0). Putnam.
Jewel of the Seas. Ellen Argo. (Kangaroo Book). 1978. 2.25 (ISBN 0-671-81845-7). Pocket Books.
Jewel of the Seas. Jessie Kaufman. LC 12-23064. 1912. 1.25. J. B. Lippincott Company.
Jewel of Their Souls. Susan Taber. LC 14-18421. 1914. Duffield & Company.
Jewel of Ynys Galon. Owen Vaughan. LC 3-26216. 1895. Longmans, Green and Co.
Jewel of Ynys Galon: Being a Hitherto Unprinted Chapter in the History of the Sea Rovers. Owen Vaughan. LC 3-26217. 1895. Longmans, Green, and Co.
Jewel: Undercover Cop. Genia Fogelson. (Orig.). 1980. pap. 1.95 (ISBN 0-87067-665-2, BH665). Holloway.
Jewel Weed. Alice Ames Winter. LC 6-36042. 1906. The Bobbs-Merrill Company.
Jeweled Dagger. Julie Ellis. 1973. (pbk.) 0.75. Dell.
Jeweled Daughter. Anne Maybury. LC 75-40560. 7.95 (ISBN 0-394-40198-0). Random House.
Jeweled Herd. Ida M Evans. LC 27-20815. J. H. Sears & Company, Inc.
Jeweled Secret. Elizabeth St. Clair. (Signet Book). 1978. 1.50 (ISBN 0-451-08227-3). New American Library.
Jeweled Serpent. Katharine Treat Blackledge. LC 22-10637. The Cornhill Publishing Company.
Jeweled Sword. Ruth L. Hill, pseud. 1957. 2.95 o.p. (ISBN 0-448-05233-4). G&D.
Jeweled Sword. Ruth Livingston Hill Munce. LC 75-35723. 1975. 9.95 (ISBN 0-89190-252-X). American Reprint Co.
Jeweled Sword. 1st Ed. Ruth Livingston Hill Munce. LC 55-11320. Lippincott.

Jewelene. Claudette Williams. 1979. pap. 1.75 (ISBN 0-449-50060-8, Coventry). Fawcett.
Jewell in the Skull. Michael Moorcock. (Orig.). 1968. pap. 0.60 o.p. (73-691). Lancer.
Jewelled Path. Rosalind Laker. LC 82-45264. (Illus.). 384p. 1983. 15.95 (ISBN 0-385-18089-6). Doubleday.
Jewelled Snuff Box. Alice C. Ley. 1974. pap. 0.95 o.p. (26591-2-095). Beagle Bks.
Jewelled Sword. Ruth L. Hill, pseud. 253p. 1975. Repr. of 1955 ed. lib. bdg. 14.40x (ISBN 0-89190-252-X). Am Repr-Rivercity Pr.
Jeweller of Bagdad. Fritz Wittels & Martens, Frederick Herman, 1874- Tr. LC 27-19633. George H. Doran Company.
Jewels. Robert Perrin. LC 78-66252. 1979. 9.95 (ISBN 0-8128-2592-6). Stein and Day.
Jewels for a Shroud, a Mystery. Walter George De Steiguer. LC 50-14309. 1950. Morrow.
Jewels for His Crown. Anita Blackmon Smith. LC 36-1010. Arcadia House.
Jewels from a Temple. Stories. Mark Halpern. LC 50-57059. (Gusto classics). 1950. House-Warven.
Jewels of Aptor. Samuel R Delany. LC 76-10730. (Gregg Press science fiction series). 1976. 9.00. Gregg Press.
Jewels of Elsewhen. Ted White. LC 81-5435. 5.95 (ISBN 0-89865-061-5). Donning Co.
Jewels of Gwahlur. Robert E. Howard. 20.00 (ISBN 0-937986-13-5). D M Grant.
Jewels of Romance. Minna Bardon. LC 50-6856. 1950. Arcadia House.
Jewels of Terror. Janet Louise Roberts. 1970. pap. 0.75 o.p. Lancer.
Jewels That Got Away. Gary Madderom. (Orig.). 1973. pap. 0.75 o.p. (07311). Curtis.
Jewess, Leonora. A Novel. Franc Busch. LC 6-16683. 1896. W. P. Caruthers.
Jewish-American Stories. Irving Howe. LC 76-54127. (Mentor book; ME 1546). 2.50 (ISBN 0-451-61546-8). New American Library.
Jewish Caravan: Great Stories of Twenty-Five Centuries. rev. and enl. ed. Ed. by Leo Walder Schwarz. LC 75-37043. 1976. 9.95 (ISBN 0-8052-0514-4). Schocken Books.
Jewish Caravan: Great Stories of Twenty-Five Centuries. Ed. by Leo Walder Schwarz. LC 35-17518. Farrar & Rinehart, Incorporated.
Jewish Children. Shalom Rabinowitz. Tr. by Berman, Hannah. LC 20-26870. 1920. A. A. Knopf.
Jewish Children. Shalom Rabinowitz. Tr. by Berman, Hannah. LC 22-5455. 1922. A. A. Knopf.
Jewish Children. Shalom Rabinowitz. Tr. by Berman, Hannah. LC 26-6910. (Borsol pocket books). A. A. Knopf.
Jewish Gauchos of the Pampas. Alberto Gerchunoff. LC 55-5049. (Illus.). 1955. Abelard-Schuman.
Jewish Government and Other Stories. Lamed Shapiro. LC 77-120532. 1971. Twayne Publishers.
Jewish Greeting Cards. Ed. Sibbett, Jr. (Illus.). 32p. (Orig.). 1975. pap. 3.00 (ISBN 0-486-23225-5). Dover.
Jewish Short Stories. Ed. by Ludwig Lewisohn. LC 46-6427. 1945. Behrman House.
Jewish Tales. Leopold Von Sacher-Masoch & Cohen, Harriet Lieber, Tr. LC 8-1367. 1894. A. C. McClurg and Company.
Jews: A Fictional Venture into the Follies of Antisemitism. Roger Peyrefitte. LC 67-23034. 1967. Bobbs-Merrill.
Jews of Barnow. Karl Emil Franzos. Tr. by Macdowall, M. W. LC 6-43159. 1883. D. Appleton and Company.
Jews of Barnow: Stories. Karl Emil Franzos. LC 74-27985. (Modern Jewish Experience). 1975. 22.00 (ISBN 0-405-06712-7). Arno Press.
Jews of Silence. Elie Wiesel. pap. 1.95 (ISBN 0-452-25066-8, Z5066, Plume). NAL.
Jews Without Money. Michael Gold. pap. 2.50 (ISBN 0-380-01309-6, 29520, Bard). Avon.
Jezebel. Jefferson Cooper, pseud. (Orig.). 1968. pap. 0.75 o.p. (54-731). Paperback Lib.
Jezebel. J. L. Hair. LC 53-11626. Vantage Press.
Jezebel. Dorothy Clarke Wilson. LC 55-104179. 1955. McGraw-Hill.
Jezebel: A Romance in the Days When Ahab Was King of Israel. Lafayette McLaws. LC 2-17551. 1902. Lothrop Publishing Company.
Jezebel in Crinoline. Cover Painting by Barye Phillips. Homer Hatten. LC 54-430971. (Gold medal books, 416). 1954. Fawcett Publications.
Jezebel the Jeep. Fairfax Davis Downey & Brown, Paul, 1893- Illus. LC 44-4717. 1944. Dodd, Mead & Company.
Jezebel's Daughter. Alan Robert Craig. LC 35-6926. 1935. Doubleday, Doran & Company, Inc.
Jezebel's Husband & the Sleeping Beauty. Robert Nathan. 1953. 3.50 o.p. Knopf.
Jhereg. Steven Brust. 1983. pap. 2.50 (ISBN 0-441-38551-6, Pub. by Ace Science Fiction). Ace Bks.
Jig-Saw. Eden Phillpotts. LC 26-15270. 1926. The Macmillan Company.
Jig-Saw Puzzle Murder. Walter F Eberhardt. LC 33-3923. Grosset & Dunlap.
Jig-Time Murders. Charles G Givens. LC 36-12115. The Bobbs-Merrill Company.
Jigger Moran. John Roeburt. LC 44-549783. 1944. Greenberg.
Jigger Whitchet's War. Avery E Kolb. LC 59-11197. 1959. Simon and Schuster.
Jigsaw. Ed McBain. 1970. 4.95 o.p. Doubleday.
Jigsaw: A Novel. Judy Stewart. LC 81-8475. 11.95 (ISBN 0-02-614660-6). Macmillan.
Jigsaw: An 87th Precinct Mystery. Evan Hunter. LC 78-99264. (Illus.). 1970. 4.95. Doubleday.
Jigsaw John. al martinez. ed. Al Martinez. 1.50. Avon Books.
Jigsaw Man. Dorothea Bennett. LC 75-38926. 1976. 8.95 (ISBN 0-698-10729-2). Coward, McCann & Geoghegan.
Jigsaw Man. Dorothea Bennett. 1977. 1.95 (ISBN 0-446-89414-1). Warner Books.
Jihad. Geoffrey Clarkson. 320p. (Orig.). 1981. pap. 2.95 (ISBN 0-523-48011-3). Pinnacle Bks.
Jilkington Drama. Edgar Mittelholzer. LC 66-10125. bds.8 3.95. Abelard.
Jill. Edmee Elizabeth Monica De La Pasture. LC 27-265340. Harper & Brothers.
Jill. Philip Larkin. LC 75-27292. 256p. 1976. 8.95 (ISBN 0-87951-038-2). Overlook Pr.
Jill. Thomas St. Martin. 1979. pap. 2.25 (ISBN 0-440-14230-X). Dell.
Jill. St. Martin, Thomas. (Dell / Bernard Geis Associates Book). 2.25 (ISBN 0-440-14230-X). Dell.
Jill. Elizabeth Thomasina Meade Smith. LC 8-8649. United States Book Company.
Jill. Jean Wick. LC 28-12547. E. J. Clode, Inc.
Jill, a Novel. Philip Larkin. LC 64-17922. 1964. St. Martin's Press.
Jill Fell Down. Jerrard Tickell. LC 39-1206. 1939. W. Morrow and Company.
Jill For Jack: By Emily Noble Pseud. James Noble Gifford. LC 54-749572. 1954. Arcadia House.
Jill Nolan, R.N. Adeline McElfresh. (Inflation Fighters Ser.). 160p. 1982. pap. 1.25 (ISBN 0-8439-1069-0, Leisure Bks). Nordon Pubns.
Jill Nolan, R.N. Adeline McElfresh. (O.s.i.). 1976. pap. 0.95 o.s.i. (BT50981). Belmont-Tower.
Jill Somerset: By Alec Waugh. Alec Waugh. LC 36-34616. Farrar & Rinehart, Incorporated.
Jill the Reckless. P. G. Wodehouse. 1958. 11.95 o.s.i. (ISBN 0-8277-0215-9). British Bk Ctr.
Jill's Hollywood Assignment. Marguerite Nelson, pseud. LC 58-7593. 1958. Avalon Books.
Jilly's Canal. Jack M Bickham. LC 73-168282. 1971. 4.95. Doubleday.
Jilt. A Novel. Charles Reade. LC 7-39659. (On cover: Harper's half-hour series no. 20). 1877. Harper & Brothers.
Jilt. A Novel. "the marrying man," &c. ed. Harriet Maria Gordon Smythies. LC 8-10197. 1844. R. Bentley.
Jilted. Jennifer Ames. 1972. pap. 0.75 o.p. (94231). Beagle Bks.
Jilted... Laura Lou Brookman. LC 33-12421. Grosset & Dunlap.
Jilted Aardvark & Other Improbable Tales from the Wall Street Journal. Ed. by Michael Gartner. LC 75-123547. (Orig.). 1970. pap. 1.95 o.s.i. (ISBN 0-87128-459-6). Dow Jones.
Jilted Bridegroom: The London Coquet see Adventures of Lindamira, a Lady of Quality.
Jim. John Joy Bell. LC 11-14750. 0.60. Hodder & Stoughton, George H. Doran Company.
Jim. Reginald Wright Kauffman. LC 15-12882. 1915. 1.35. Moffat, Yard and Company.
Jim Bowie & Lost Mine. Herman Toepperwein. pap. text ed. 1.50 (ISBN 0-910722-08-0). Highland Pr.
Jim Crow. John Joy Bell. LC 11-14408. Hodder and Stoughton.
Jim Cummings: Or, The Crime of the 'Frisco Express. Francis Farrars. (Jesse James detective series). 1887. R. R. Publishing Co.
Jim Dawson Returns. rev. ed. Gene Hoopes. LC 63-22788. 1964. Naylor.
Jim Dawson Returns. Illus. by George Phippen. 1st Ed. Gene Hoopes. LC 52-13991. 1952. Exposition Press.
Jim for Sale. Peter Kortner. (Dell book, 4207). 1973. 1.25. Dell.
Jim for Sale. Peter Kortner. LC 74-155778. 1971. 5.95. D. McKay Co.
Jim Hands. Richard Washburn Child. LC 10-26170. 1910. The Macmillan Company.
Jim Hanvey, Detective. Octavus Roy Cohen. LC 23-136568. 1923. 2.00. Dodd, Mead and Company.
Jim Hickey: A Story of the One-Night Stands. George Vere Hobart. 1904. G. W. Dillingham Company.
Jim Hunter International Spy Stories. Butterworth & Stockdale. (gr. 6-12). 1975-82. pap. 44.00 boxed set of 16 bks. with tchrs. guide (ISBN 0-8224-3781-3). Pitman Learning.
Jim Kane. J. P. S Brown. LC 70-92734. 1970. 6.95. Dial Press.
Jim Kane see Pocket Money.
Jim Lofton, American. George Brydges Rodney. LC 20-22157. 1920. The James A. McCann Company.
Jim Maitland. Herman Cyril McNeile. LC 24-24811. George H. Doran Company.
Jim Miller's Girls. Lewis Erwin Finney. LC 14-20739. The Roxburgh Publishing Company, Inc.
Jim Morse: Gold-Hunter. Joseph Allan Elphinstone Dunn. LC 20-190434. Small, Maynard & Company.
Jim Mundy. Robert H Fowler. (Jove/HBJ Book). 1978. 2.95 (ISBN 0-515-04707-4). Jove Publications, Inc.
Jim Mundy: A Novel of the American Civil War. Robert H Fowler. LC 77-3789. 10.00 (ISBN 0-06-011303-0). Harper & Row.
Jim the Conqueror. Peter Bernard Kyne. LC 20-17527. 1929. Cosmopolitan Book Corporation.
Jim, the Parson. Elizabeth Dundas Bedell Benjamin. LC 7-34443. (On cover: Lovell's library. no. 1077). 1887. J. W. Lovell Company.
Jim the Penman. A Thrilling Detective Story. Welcho Gordon. LC 6-27486. (On cover: The Pinkerton detective series. no. 37). 1891. Laird & Lee.
Jim-Unclassified: A Romance. Robert J Kelly. LC 16-15150. 1916. 1.35. Dodd, Mead and Company.
Jimbo, a Fantasy. Algernon Blackwood. LC 9-70372. 1909. The Macmillan Company.
Jimgrim. Talbot Mundy. LC 31-7640. 2.00. The Century Co.
Jimgrim and Allah's Peace. Talbot Mundy. LC 36-24947. 1936. D. Appleton-Century Company, Incorporated.
Jiminy. Gilbert Wolf Gabriel. LC 22-26483. 2.00. George H. Doran Company.
Jimmie Allen in The Sky Parade. Wallace West. LC 36-9392. Lynn Publishing Co., Inc.
Jimmie Dale and the Blue Envelope Murder. Frank Lucius Packard. LC 30-22898. 1930. Doubleday, Doran & Company, Inc.
Jimmie Dale and the Missing Hour... Frank Lucius Packard. LC 35-7671. 1935. Pub. for the Crime Club, Inc., by Doubleday, Doran & Company, Inc.
Jimmie Dale and the Phantom Clue. Frank Lucius Packard. LC 22-20537. George H. Doran Company.
Jimmie Higgins: A Story. Upton Beall Sinclair. LC 70-104766. (Novel as American social history). 1970. University Press of Kentucky.
Jimmie Higgins; a Story. Upton Beall Sinclair. LC 19-8807. 1919. Boni and Liveright.
Jimmie Moore of Bucktown. Melvin Earnest Trotter. LC 77-107384. 1970. 1.50. Kregel Publications.
Jimmie Moore of Bucktown. Melvin Earnest Trotter. LC 4-22980. 1904. The Winona Publishing Company.
Jimmie the Sixth. Frances Roberta Sterrett. LC 8-20479. 1918. 1.50. D. Appleton and Company.
Jimmy Jones, the Autobiography of an Office Boy. Roy Larcom McCardell. LC 7-25052. D. Estes & Company.
Jimmy Riddle: A Novel. Ian Brook. LC 61-10334. 1961. Putnam.
Jimmy the Kid. Donald E Westlake. LC 73-80175. 1974. 6.95 (ISBN 0-87131-157-7). M. Evans.
Jimmy, the New Boy: By Archibald Marshall... with Frontispiece in Colour by Howard L. Hastings. Archibald Marshall. LC 23-17724. 1923. Frederick A. Stokes Company.
Jimmy Trilogy. Jacques Poulin. Tr. by Sheila Fischman from Fr. (Anansi Fiction Ser.: No. 39). 250p. (Orig.). 1979. pap. 8.95 (ISBN 0-88784-074-4, Pub. by Hse Anansi Pr Canada). U of Toronto Pr.
Jimmy Vandizer's Vacation. Charles Elbert Whelan. LC 28-20418. Modern Woodmen Press.
Jimmyjohn Boss and Other Stories. Owen Wister. LC 68-55692. (American short story series, v. 32). (Illus.). 1969. Garrett Press.
Jimmyjohn Boss, and Other Stories. Owen Wister. LC 72-8213. (American short story series, v. 32). 1972. (ISBN 0-8422-8127-4). MSS Information Corp.
Jimmyjohn Boss: And Other Stories. Owen Wister. LC 2583. 1900. Harper & Brothers.
Jimmy's Gentility. Henry Francis Dryden. LC 15-15609. 1915. Sherman, French & Company.
Jimmy's Place: A California Story by R. L. Duffus. 1st Ed. Robert Luther Duffus. LC 66-176911. 1966. bds., 4.95. Norton.
Jimmy's Wife. Jessie Champion. LC 17-248558. 1917. John Lane.
Jimsy: The Christmas Kid. Leona Dalrymple. LC 15-24006. 1915. 0.50. R. M. McBride & Company.
Jimty, and Others. Margaret Sutton Briscoe Hopkins. LC 73-101284. (Short story index reprint series). (Illus.). 1969. Books for Libraries Press.
Jimty, and Others. Margaret Sutton Briscoe Hopkins. LC 4-151191. 1898. Harper & Brothers.
Jincey. Celestine Sibley. LC 78-26168. 8.95 (ISBN 0-671-22603-7). Simon and Schuster.
Jing Affair. D. J Spencer. LC 65-15318. 1965. Funk & Wagnalls.
Jingala. Legson Kayira. LC 69-20077. 1969. 4.95. Doubleday.
Jinglebob. Philip Ashton Rollins & Wyeth, Newell Convers, 1882- Illus. LC 30-23552. 1930. C. Scribner's Sons.
Jinglebob: A True Story of a Real Cowboy. Philip Ashton Rollins. 1927. C. Scribner's Sons.
Jingling in the Wind. Elizabeth Madox Roberts. LC 28-223534. 1928. The Viking Press.
Jingling Spurs. William MacLeod Raine. LC 50-11858. 1951. Houghton Mifflin.
Jingo. George Randolph Chester. LC 12-21918. 1.35. The Bobbs-Merrill Company.
Jingo. George Randolph Chester. LC 77-84210. (Lost Race and Adult Fantasy Fiction). (Illus.). 1978. 26.00 (ISBN 0-405-10965-2). Arno Press.
Jink. Thomas Patrick McMahon. LC 70-161615. (Inner sanctum mystery). 1971. 4.95 (ISBN 0-671-20903-5). Simon and Schuster.
Jinker. Joseph Schull. LC 72-81624. 1969. 4.50. Dodd, Mead.
Jinks. Mary Carter Roberts. 3.50 o.p. Carlton.
Jinny the Carrier: A Folk-Comedy of Rural England. Israel Zangwill. LC 19-11564. 1919. The Macmillan Company.
Jinx Lady. Hayton Monteith. (Candlelight Ecstasy Ser.: No. 95). (Orig.). 1982. pap. 1.95 (ISBN 0-440-14191-5). Dell.
Jinx: Stories of the Diamond. Allen Sangree. LC 11-259918. G. W. Dillingham Company.
Jinx Theatre Murder. Alexander Hazard Williams. LC 33-5480. W. F. Payson.
Jirel of Joiry. Catherine L. Moore. 336p. 1982. pap. 2.75 (ISBN 0-441-38570-2, Pub. by Ace Science Fiction). Ace Bks.
Jirel of Joiry. Catherine L. Moore. (Orig.). 1969. pap. 0.60 o.p. (63-166). Paperback Lib.
Jitter Run. Robert F Germann. LC 44-365. 1944. The Hampton Publishing Company, Distributed by W. Morrow & Company.
Jiu San, No. 107. Kenneth Robeson, pseud. 208p. (The Black Witch no. 108). 1981. pap. text ed. 1.95 (ISBN 0-553-14901-6). Bantam.
Jive Jungle. 1st Ed. Ida Martucci. LC 56-5813. 1956. Vantage Press.
Jnbelonging. Alice M Robinson. LC 58-5121. 1958. Macmillan.
Jo: A Telegraphic Tale. Edward J Smith. 1885. E. J. Smith & Co.
Jo Anne & the Octopus. Laura Lupo. LC 81-90500. (Illus.). 49p. 1982. 4.95 (ISBN 0-533-05217-3). Vantage.
Jo Dunn: All-American. Clinton Ralza Morse. LC 41-24403. The Christopher Publishing House.
Jo Ellen. Alexander Black. LC 23-131023. Harper & Brothers.
Jo Stern. David R. Slavitt. LC 77-11548. 8.95 (ISBN 0-06-013994-3). Harper & Row.
Joachim a Des Ennuis. Rene de Goscinny. LC 67-7723. (His Les aventures du petit Nicolas). (Illus.). 1967. Harcourt, Brace & World.
Joan. Rhoda Broughton. (On cover: Lovell's library, no. 1027). 1887. J. W. Lobell Company.
Joan: A Romance of an English Mining Village. Amelia Edith Huddleston Barr. LC 17-3151. 1.50. D. Appleton and Company.
Joan: A Tale. Rhoda Broughton. LC 6-18954. (On cover: Library of choice novels, no. 55). 1877. D. Appleton and Company.
Joan: A Tale. Rhoda Broughton. (On cover: Seaside library. Pocket Ed., no. 757). 1886. G. Munro.
Joan: A Tale. Rhoda Broughton. LC 18-777479. (Macmillan's two shilling library. no. 5). 1899. Macmillan and Co., Limited.
Joan & Co. Frederick Orin Bartlett. LC 19-12170. 1919. Houghton Mifflin Company.
Joan and Peter: The Story of an Education. Herbert George Wells. 1918. The Macmillan Company.
Joan, Freelance Writer. Alice Mary Ross Colver. LC 48-1980. 1948. J. Messner.
Joan Haste: A Novel. Henry Rider Haggard. 1895. Longmans, Green, and Co.
Joan Kennedy. Henry Channon. LC 29-16168. E. P. Dutton & Co., Inc.
Joan of Arc of the North Woods. Holman Francis Day. LC 22-20646. Harper & Brothers.
Joan-of-Arc Replay. Pierre Barbet. 1978. 1.50 (ISBN 0-87997-374-9). DAW Books.
Joan of Garioch. Albert Kinross. LC 8-293375. 1908. The Macmillan Company.
Joan of Overbarrow. Alister McAllister. LC 22-6518. George H. Doran Company.
Joan of Rainbow Springs. Frances Marian Mitchell. LC 11-11897. 1911. Lothrop, Lee & Shepard Co.
Joan of the Island. Ralph Henry Barbour. LC 20-4709. 1.75. Small, Maynard & Company.

Joan of the Sword Hand. Samuel Rutherford Crockett. LC 1790. 1900. Dodd, Mead and Company.
Joan of the Tower. Warwick Deeping. LC 11-10054. 1911. 2.60. Cassell and Company, Ltd.
Joan Seaton. A Story of Percival Dion in the Yorkshire Dales. Mary Beaumont. LC 6-10263. F. A. Stokes Company.
Joan Strathmore. Marjorie Sinclair. LC 28-29965. Marjorie Sinclair.
Joan the Maid: Deliverer of England and France. A Story of the Fifteenth Century Done into Modern English. Elizabeth Rundle Charles. LC 41-321994. 1880. T. Nelson and Sons.
Joan the Maid, Deliverer of France and England: A Story of the Fifteenth Century, Done into Modern English. Elizabeth Rundle Charles. 1879. Dodd, Mead & Company.
Joan Thursday: A Novel. Louis Joseph Vance. LC 13-20209. 1913. Little, Brown, and Company.
Joan Wentworth. Katharine Sarah Gadsden Macquoid. (On cover: Lovell's library, no. 898). J. W. Lovell Company.
Joan Wentworth: A Novel. Katharine Sarah Gadsden Macquoid. LC 7-20285. (Harper's handy series, no. 98). 1886. Harper & Brothers.
Joan Wentworth. A Novel. Katharine Sarah Gadsden Macquoid. (On cover: Seaside library. Pocket ed. no. 914). 1887. G. Munro.
Joanie. G. B. Trudeau. (Illus.). 1979. pap. 1.50 (ISBN 0-553-10296-6). Bantam.
Joanna. Helen Ashton. LC 44-6988. 1944. S. Curl, Inc.
Joanna. Roberta Gellis. LC 78-59971. 560p. (Orig.). 1978. pap. 2.25 (ISBN 0-87216-490-X). Playboy Pbks.
Joanna. Michael Sarne. (Orig.). 1969. pap. 0.60 o.p. (X1996). Pyramid Pubns.
Joanna and Ulysses: A Tale. May Sarton. LC 64-10571. 1963. Norton.
Joanna Builds a Nest. Juliet Wilbor Tompkins. LC 20-18300. The Bobbs-Merrill Company.
Joanna Godden. Sheila Kaye-Smith. LC 22-273891. E. P. Dutton & Company.
Joanna Godden. by sheila kaye-smith... ed. Sheila Kaye-Smith. LC 36-280068. 1936. E. P. Dutton & Company, Inc.
Joanna Godden Married, and Other Stories. Kaye-Smith, Sheila. LC 77-163035. (Short story index reprint series). 1971. (ISBN 0-8369-3949-2). Books for Libraries Press.
Joanna Godden Married, and Other Stories. Sheila Kaye-Smith. LC 26-17286. 1926. Harper & Brothers.
Joanna Lord: A Novel. Mary Fassett Hunt. LC 54-10849. 1954. Bobbs-Merrill Co.
Joanna of Naples. Louisa Jane Hall. LC 7-28533. 1838. Hilliard, Gray and Company.
Joanna, of the Skirts Too Short and the Lips Too Red and the Tongue Too Pert. Henry Leyford Gates. LC 26-2450. 1926. Barse & Hopkins.
Joanna Reddinghood: A Novel. Elly Welt. LC 80-5297. 11.95 (ISBN 0-394-50915-3). Random House.
Joanna Traill, Spinster. Annie E Holdsworth. LC 7-6125. 1894. C. L. Webster & Company.
Joanna Traill, Spinster. Annie E Holdsworth. LC 7-6126. (On cover: Cassell's sunshine series, no. 163). The Cassell Publishing Co.
Joanna's Miracle. William H. Armstrong. LC 77-89708. 1977. 6.50 (ISBN 0-8054-6921-4). Broadman.
Joanna's People. Augusta Blinick. LC 82-61565. 260p. 1983. pap. 9.95 (ISBN 0-910873-00-3). Springtide.
Joanne. Scott Stone. 1955. Vixen Press.
Job Abroad. George Bartram. LC 74-30372. 1975. 7.95 (ISBN 0-02-521030-0). Macmillan.
Job: An American Novel. Sinclair Lewis. LC 17-6323. 1917. Harper & Brothers.
Job for Jenny. Faith Baldwin Cuthrell. LC 45-798014. 1945. Farrar & Rinehart, Inc.
Job for Jenny. Faith Baldwin Cuthrell. 1973. 0.75. Warner Paperback Lib.
Job Lot Sketches and Stories. John Pennington Marsden. LC 7-24674. 1892. Hallowell & Co.
Job Secretary; an Impression. Josephine Mary Hope-Scott W. P. Ward Ward. LC 11-12125. 1911. Longmans, Green, and Co.
Job, the Story of a Simple Man. Joseph Roth. Tr. by Thompson, Dorothy. LC 31-28313. 1931. The Viking Press.
Job, the Story of a Simple Man. Joseph Roth. LC 81-18935. 1982. 15.00 (ISBN 0-87951-149-4). Overlook Press.
Job: The Story of a Simple Man. Joseph Roth. Tr. by Dorothy Thompson from Ger. LC 81-18901. 252p. 1982. 15.00 (ISBN 0-87951-149-4). Overlook Pr.
Job's House. Caroline Beach Slade. LC 41-51679. The Vanguard Press.
Job's Niece. Grace Livingston Hill. 1962. Grosset & Dunlap.
Job's Niece. Grace Livingston Hill. LC 27-10052. J. B. Lippincott Company.
Job's Year. Joseph Hansen. LC 82-21290. 15.95 (ISBN 0-03-061689-1). Holt, Rinehart, and Winston.
Joby. Stan Barstow. LC 73-429552. 1968. Penguin.
Jocelyn. John Galsworthy. LC 77-145030. 1972. 14.50 (ISBN 0-403-00977-4). Scholarly Press.
Jocelyn. John Galsworthy. LC 76-29902. 1977. 6.95 (ISBN 0-03-020431-3). Holt, Rinehart and Winston.
Jocelyn. John Galsworthy. LC 77-362260. 1976. 3.95 (ISBN 0-283-98244-6). Duckworth: Sidgwick and Jackson.
Jocelyn. John Galsworthy. LC 71-98836. 1971. (ISBN 0-8371-3101-4). Greenwood Press.
Jocelyn West: A Tale of the Grand Canon. Katharine Sharp. LC 12-23763. The Goodhue Company.
Jodinareh. John Cleve, pseud. LC 78-23983. (Brandon House library edition, 6115). 1970. 1.95. Brandon House.
Joe; a Remarkable Case. Edward Reynolds Roe. LC 7-40249. (On cover: Globe library, no. 74). 1889. Rand, McNally & Company.
Joe and Jennie. Donald Henderson Clarke. LC 49-172412. 1949. Vanguard Press.
Joe and the Gladiator. (Signet Book). 1.25 (ISBN 0-451-07435-1). New American Library.
Joe and the Gladiator. (Signet Book). 1.25 (ISBN 0-451-07435-1). New American Library.
Joe Broderick's Woman. John H. Arbor. 1978. pap. 1.50 (ISBN 0-532-15323-5). Woodhill.
Joe Cummings: Or, The Story of the Son of a Squaw in Search of His Mother. C. W Wright. LC 8-372203. J. G. Cupples Co.
Joe Hill; a Biographical Novel. Wallace Earle Stegner. LC 69-15576. 1969. 6.95. Doubleday.
Joe Hill, a Biographical Novel. Wallace Earle Stegner. LC 80-10760. 1980. 19.50 (ISBN 0-8032-4116-X) (ISBN 0-8032-9115-9). University of Nebraska Press.
Joe Jacoby. Junius Watson. 1970. 4.95 o.p. (ISBN 0-8415-0030-4). Sat Rev Pr.
Joe Jason of Omaha: Or, His Story of Love As Told by Himself. Anson Doner Eby. LC 6-26328. 1897.
Joe Jenkins Detective. Paul Rosenhayn. Tr. by Head, June. LC 30-7565. 1930. Doubleday, Doran & Company, Inc.
Joe Leslie's Wife: Or, A Skeleton in the Closet. Alexander Robertson. LC 7-41677. (On cover: The silver series, v. 2, no. 2). 1892. H. J. Smith & Co.
Joe Muller: Detective; Being the Account of Some Adventures in the Professional Experience of a Member of the Imperial Austrian Police. Grace Isabel Colbron & Groner, Fran Auguste, 1850- Joint Author. 1910. Duffield and Company.
Joe Nichols: Or, Difficulties Overcome. Alfred Beach. LC 2923. (On cover: Medal library, no. 54). 1900. Street & Smith.
Joe Overstreet. David Henderson. (Illus.). 1972. pap. cancelled o.p. (ISBN 0-914412-03-5). Interbk Inc.
Joe Panther. Kelly R. Masters. LC 50-10209. (Illus.). 1950. Holiday House.
Joe Pepper. Lee McElroy. LC 74-18886. 1975. 4.95 (ISBN 0-385-09691-7). Doubleday.
Joe Pete. Florence E McClinchey. LC 29-28181. H. Holt and Company.
Joe Pine. Elbert A Smith. LC 16-21393. 1916. Herald Publishing House.
Joe Saxton in Japan. A Story of the East and the West. D. A Selden. 1897. The Deutsch Company, Printers.
Joe: The Book Farmer, Making Good on the Land. Garrard Harris. LC 13-19935. 1913. Harper & Brothers.
Joe, the Nasty Bus Driver. Joseph N. Leechak. 5.00 o.p. (ISBN 0-8181-0075-3). Pageant-Poseidon.
Joe Welch in the Shoemaker. A Powerful Picture of Nature Adapted from Hal Reid's Famous Drama of the Same Name. Helen Burrell D'Apery & Reid, James Halleck. LC 33-28365. (On cover: Play book series. no. 90). J. S. Ogilvie Publishing Company.
Joel 'n Jangles. Marilyn Huyett-Barding. 1981. 8.95 (ISBN 0-8062-1775-8). Carlton.
Joe's Women. Karl Rivers. pap. 1.95 o.s.i. (TCP-001). Olympia.
Joey, a Novel. David Lord. LC 49-5037. 1949. E. P. Dutton.
Joey & DeVon. James Bruce Eure. 1976. 8.00 o.p. (ISBN 0-682-48414-8). Exposition.
Joey Collects. Dave Fisher & Joey. 256p. (Orig.). 1980. pap. 2.50 (ISBN 0-441-40500-2, Pub. by Charter Bks). Ace Bks.
Joey Story. Rosanna P. Warren. (Illus.). 1964. 2.95 o.p. (ISBN 0-394-43135-9). Random.
Joffre Chaps and Some Others. Pierre Mille & Drillien, Berengere, Tr. LC 16-263. 1915. John Lane.
Jog Rummage. Grahame Wright. LC 74-9089. 1974. 5.95 (ISBN 0-394-49484-9). Random House.
Joggin'erlong. facs. ed. Paul Laurence Dunbar. LC 78-83921. (Black Heritage Library Collection Ser). (Illus.). 1906. 10.00 (ISBN 0-8369-8557-5). Ayer Co.
Jogging: A Love Story. Sandra Hochman. LC 78-21236. 8.95 (ISBN 0-399-12189-7). Putnam.
Johanna at Daybreak. Ray Coryton Hutchinson. LC 78-83633. 1969. 6.95. Harper & Row.
'Johanna Maria. Arthur Van Schendel & Downs, Brian Westerdale, Tr. LC 35-18567. 1935. Longmans, Green and Co.
Johannes, a Novel. Renate Christine Wolff. LC 58-9050. 1958. Simon and Schuster.
Johannesburg Friday. Albert Segal. LC 53-12881. 1954. McGraw-Hill.
Johannesburg Requiem: A Novel. Sheila Roberts. LC 79-25581. 1980. 8.95 (ISBN 0-8008-4405-X). Taplinger Pub. Co.
John. Irene Baird. LC 37-226361. J. B. Lippincott Company.
John-a-Dreams. A Tale... Julian Sturgis. LC 8-16860. (On cover: Appletons' new handy-volume series no. 18). 1878. D. Appleton and Company.
John, a Love Story. Margaret Oliphant Wilson Oliphant. (On cover: Seaside library. Pocket ed., no. 357). 1885. G. Munro.
John, a Love Story. Margaret Oliphant Wilson Oliphant. (On cover: Lovell's library, v. 19, no. 920). 1887. J. W. Lovell Company.
John A. Macdonald Album. Lena Newman. LC 74-83070. 25.00 (ISBN 0-912766-12-3); pap. 14.95. Tundra Bks.
John: A Tale of King Messiah. Katharine Pearson Woods. 1896. Dodd, Mead and Company.
John Adam-Samurai. Christopher Wood. 1974. (pbk.) 1.25. Dell.
John and I and the Church. Elizabeth Grinnell. LC 7-28821. 1897. F. H. Revell Company.
John and Mary. Mervyn Jones. LC 67-16063. 1967. Atheneum.
John and the Demijohn: A Temperance Tale. Julia MacNair Wright. LC 9-908. H. Hoyt.
John & the Missus: A Novel. Gordon Pinsent. LC 74-196945. 1974-1975. 7.95 (ISBN 0-07-082201-8). McGraw-Hill Ryerson.
John Anderson and I. Mary E Craigie. 1888. Wenborne and Company.
John Andrews, Boss: A Novel. John Philip Barnhart. LC 37-24566. The Stratford Company.
John Andross: A Novel. Rebecca Harding Davis. LC 6-32466. Orange Judd Company.
John Andross, a Novel. Rebecca Harding Davis. Repr. of 1874 ed. cancelled o.s.i. Johnson Repr.
John Applegate, Surgeon: A Novel. Mary Harriott Norris. LC 7-33303. (On cover: The Golden library, no. 6). The Price-McGill Company.
John Arrowsmith--Planter. Belle Johnston Bushnell. LC 9-293684. 1910. 1.50. The Torch Press.
John Ashton: A Story of the War Between the States. Capers Dickson. LC 6-37252. 1896. The Foote & Davies Company.
John Auburntop: Novelist. His Development in the Atmosphere of a Fresh-Water College. Anson Uriel Hancock. LC 7-554. 1891. C. H. Kerr & Company.
John Baring's House. Elsie Singmaster. LC 20-19433. 1920. Houghton Mifflin Company.
John Barleycorn. Jack London. (Illus.). 343p. 1981. pap. 7.95 (ISBN 0-934136-17-3). Western Tanager.
John Barry. Donald F. Bedford. LC 47-31391. 1947. Creative Age Press.
John Bartel, Jr. Donald Henderson Clarke. LC 48-3927. (New Avon library. 149). 1949. Avon Book Co.
John Bartel, Jr. Donald Henderson Clarke. LC 32-24988. The Vanguard Press.
John Bodewin's Testimony. Mary Hallock Foote. LC 4-151052. 1886. Ticknor and Company.
John Bogardus: A Novel. George Agnew Chamberlain. LC 16-5188. 1916. 1.35. The Century Co.
John Bonwell: A Novel of the Ohio River Valley, 1818-1862. Charles K Pulse. LC 52-6978. 1952. Farrar, Straus and Young.
John Bozeman: Mountain Journey. Greg Hunt. (American Explorers Ser.: No. 13). (Orig.). 1983. pap. 2.95 (ISBN 0-440-04340-9). Dell.
John Brandon: A Novel. Humphrey Pakington. LC 65-11002. bds., 3.95. Norton.
John Brent. Theodore Winthrop. LC 9-946. (Leisure hour series. 63). 1876. H. Holt and Company.
John Brent. Theodore Winthrop. LC 4-16115. Dodd, Mead and Company.
John Brody's Astral Body: And Other Stories About Schools. Charles William Bardeen. LC 9-841. 1908. C.W. Bardeen.
John Brown: The Magnificent Failure... Harry Dean Saddler. LC 51-4264. 1951. Dorrance.
John Brown's Body. Stephen Vincent Benet. 1982. Repr. lib. bdg. 18.95x (ISBN 0-89966-405-9). Buccaneer Bks.
John Brown's Cousin. Jane Hutchens. LC 40-30530. 1940. Doubleday, Doran and Company, Inc.
John Brown's Legs: Or, Leaves from a Journal in the Lowlands. Kenward Philp. LC 7-36050. (On cover: Munro's library, popular novels, no. 152). 1884. N. L. Munro.
John Brown's Soul: A Novel. Earl Jerome Ellison. LC 51-2442. 1951. Duell, Sloan and Pearce.
John Bull & the Papists; or, Passages in the Life of an Anglican Rector, 1846. A. H. Edgar. Ed. by Robert L. Wolff. (Victorian Fiction Ser.). 1975. lib. bdg. 66.00 (ISBN 0-8240-1527-4). Garland Pub.
John Bull in America. James Kirke Paulding. LC 71-104536. 1970. (ISBN 0-8398-1554-9). Literature House.
John Bull in America: Or, The New Munchausen. James Kirke Paulding. LC 7-34068. 1825. C. Wiley.
John Bull's Misfortunes. The Destruction of the Entire English Navy--the Blowing-up of the Woolwich Arsenal--the Capture of London and the Downfall of Great Britain in the Year 1887. Camille I. E. Jean Baptiste Camille Debans. Tr. by Abarbnell, Jacob Ralph. (On cover: Munro's library, popular novels, v. 1, no. 246). N. L. Munro.
John Bunyan. Gwilym O. Griffith. 1973. Repr. of 1927 ed. lib. bdg. 20.00 (ISBN 0-8414-4623-7). Folcroft.
John Bunyan. W. H. Hutton. 1973. Repr. of 1927 ed. 10.00 o.p. R West.
John Burnet of Barnes. John Buchan. 317p. 1982. Repr. of 1898 ed. 9.95 (ISBN 0-88289-321-1, 37-51-4, Pub. by Canongate Pub Scotland). Pelican.
John Burnet of Barns: A Romance. John Buchan. LC 70-144914. 1973. 19.50 (ISBN 0-403-00877-8). Scholarly Press.
John Burnet of Barns: A Romance. John Buchan. 1924. Dodd, Mead and Company.
John Burt. Frederick Upham Adams. LC 3-24538. 1903. D. Biddle.
John Caldigate. Anthony Trollope. LC 76-29421. Repr. of 1946 ed. 38.50 (ISBN 0-404-15327-5). AMS Pr.
John Caldigate. Anthony Trollope. (Zodiac Press Ser.). 472p. 1978. 10.95 (ISBN 0-7011-1715-X, Pub. by Chatto Bodley Jonathan). Merrimack Pub Cir.
John Caldigate. A Novel. Anthony Trollope. (Franklin square library. no. 68). 1879. Harper & Brothers.
John Carson. Robert L. Merriam. (Illus.). 23p. (Orig.). 1977. pap. 2.00. R L Merriam.
John Carter of Mars. Edgar Rice Burroughs. 1973. pap. 1.95 (ISBN 0-345-27844-5). Ballantine.
John Carter of Mars. Edgar Rice Burroughs. LC 64-15790. (Illus.). 10.00 (ISBN 0-940724-04-9). Canaveral.
John Cave. William Budd Trites. LC 13-6735. 1913. Duffield & Company.
John Charaxes: A Tale of the Civil War in America. George Ticknor Curtis. LC 6-31711. 1889. J. B. Lippincott Company.
John Charity. Horace Annesley Vachell. 1901. Dodd, Mead & Company.
John Collier Reader. John Collier. LC 71-154906. 1972. 10.00 (ISBN 0-394-46186-X). Knopf.
John Company. Arthur Van Schendel. Ed. by E. M. Beekman. Tr. by Frans Van Rosevelt from Dutch. LC 82-21877. (Library of the Indies). Orig. Title: Jan Compagie. 224p. 1983. lib. bdg. 16.00x (ISBN 0-87023-383-1). U of Mass Pr.
John Cornelius: His Life and Adventures. Hugh Walpole. LC 37-286475. 1937. Doubleday, Doran & Company, Inc.
John Creasey's Crime Collection 1982. Ed. by Herbert Harris. 192p. 1982. 12.95 (ISBN 0-312-44296-3). St Martin.
John Crews. Arthur Chapman. LC 26-4271. 1926. Houghton Mifflin Company.
John Crow: A Novel Founded on Facts. John W Ryder. LC 1741. 1900. P. Anstadt & Sons.
John Dawn. Robert Peter Tristram Coffin. LC 36-192491. 1936. The Macmillan Company.
John De Lancaster. A Novel. Richard Cumberland. LC 6-31153. 1809. Printed for E. Sargeant, Corner of Broadway and Wall-Street, Opposite Trinity Church, and M. & W. Ward, No. City Hotel, By D. & G. Bruce.
John Dean's Journey. Marjorie Barkeley McClure. LC 32-8807. 1932. Minton, Balch & Company.
John Delavoy: A Story. Henry James. LC 7-7443. 1897. The Macmillan Company.
John Dene of Toronto: A Comedy of Whitehall. Herbert George Jenkins. LC 19-15677. 1.50. George H. Doran Company.
John Dickson Carr Trio: Including The Three Coffins, The Crooked Hinge and The Case of the Constant Suicides. John Dickson Carr. LC 56-87771. 1957. Harper.
John Doe and Richard Roe: Or, Episodes of Life in New York. Edward Sherman Gould. LC 6-27641. 1862. Carleton.
John Doe, Murderer. William Dale. LC 42-20325. 1942. Gateway Books.
John Doe, Murderer. William Dale. LC 44-6604. (Black cat detective series. No. 11). 1944. Crestwood Publishing Co., Inc.

John Eagle, Expeditor, No. 11: Poppies of Death. Paul Edwards. (John Eagle Ser. No. 11). (Orig.). 1975. pap. 1.25 o.p. (ISBN 0-515-03788-5). Pyramid Pubns.

John Eagle Expeditor, No. 2: The Brain Scavengers. Lyle K. Engle. 1973. pap. 0.95 o.p. (ISBN 0-515-03018-X, N3018). BJ Pub Group.

John Eagle Expeditor, No. 3: The Laughing Death. Paul Edwards. (Orig.). 1973. pap. 0.95 o.p. (ISBN 0-515-03236-0, N3236). Pyramid Pubns.

John Eagle Expeditor, No. 4: Expeditor No. 4 - the Fist of Fatima. Paul Edwards. (Orig.). 1973. pap. 0.95 o.p. (ISBN 0-515-03157-7, N3157). Pyramid Pubns.

John Eagle Expeditor, No. 6: Glyphs of Gold. Paul Edwards. (Orig.). 1973. pap. 0.95 o.p. (ISBN 0-515-03264-6, N3264). Pyramid Pubns.

John Eagle, Expeditor No. 7: The Ice Goddess. Paul Edwards. (Orig.). 1974. pap. 0.95 o.p. (ISBN 0-515-03336-7, N3336). BJ Pub Group.

John Eagle, Expeditor No. 8: The Death Devils. Paul Edwards. (Orig.). 1974. pap. 0.95 o.p. (ISBN 0-515-03366-9, N3366). Pyramid Pubns.

John Eagle, Expeditor, No. 9: Deadly Cyborgs. Paul Edwards. (Orig.). 1975. pap. 0.95 o.p. (ISBN 0-515-03702-8, N3702). BJ Pub Group.

John Eagle, Expeditor: Operation Weatherkill. Paul Edwards. 1975. pap. 1.25 o.p. Pyramid Pubns.

John Eagle, Expeditor: Silverskull, No. 14. Paul Edwards. 1975. pap. price not set o.p. Pyramid Pubns.

John Eagle, Expeditor: The Green Goddess, No. 12. Paul Edwards. 1975. pap. 1.25 o.p. (ISBN 0-515-03913-6). Pyramid Pubns.

John Eax and Mamelon. Albion Winegar Tourgee. LC 70-104584. 1970. Literature House/Gregg Press.

John Eax and Mamelon: Or, The South Without the Shadow. Albion Winegar Tourgee. LC 8-34330. Fords, Howard, & Hulbert.

John Ermine of the Yellowstone. Frederic Remington. LC 68-20020. (Americans in Fiction). (Illus.). 1968. Gregg Press.

John Ermine of the Yellowstone. Frederic Remington. LC 2-26864. 1902. The Macmillan Company.

John Esten Cooke, Virginian. John Owen Beaty. LC 65-27110. 1965. 6.00. Kennikat.

John Faithful: Schoolmaster. Clarence Ellis Birch. LC 49-2203. 1949. Exposition Press.

John Forsyth's Aunts. Eliza Orne White. LC 1-26195. 1901. McClure, Phillips & Company.

John Franklin Bardin Omnibus. John Franklin Bardin. (Crime Ser.). 608p. 1976. pap. 2.95 o.p. (ISBN 0-14-004130-3). Penguin.

John Frensham, K.C. Alan Sullivan. LC 28-25818. 1928. E. P. Dutton & Co., Inc.

John Fury. Jack Dunphy. LC 76-6338. (Irish-Americans). 1976. 27.00 (ISBN 0-405-09351-9). Arno Press.

John Fury: A Novel in Four Parts. Jack Dunphy. LC 46-7497. 1946. Harper & Brothers.

John Gayther's Garden and the Stories Told Therein. Frank Richard Stockton. LC 76-116965. (Short story index reprint series). (Illus.). 1970. Books for Libraries Press.

John Gayther's Garden: And the Stories Told Therein. Frank Richard Stockton. LC 2-26865. 1902. C. Scribner's Sons.

John Glynn: A Novel of Social Work. Arthur Henry Paterson. LC 7-14252. 1907. H. Holt and Company.

John Godfrey's Fortunes: Related by Himself. A Story of American Life. Bayard Taylor. LC 6-39309. 1864. G. P. Putnam, Hurd and Houghton.

John Godfrey's Fortunes: Related by Himself. A Story of American Life. Bayard Taylor. LC 8-256552. 1865. G. P. Putnam Etc.

John Goldfarb, Please Come Home! William Peter Blatty. LC 63-12973. 1963. Doubleday.

John Golding's Vision. Carolyn Renfrew. LC 39-1034. Burton Publishing Company.

John Gordon: Invictus Georgia Love Story. Juliet Cox Coleman. 1980. 8.95 (ISBN 0-533-04441-3). Vantage.

John Gray. James Lane Allen. Repr. of 1893 ed. lib. bdg. 20.00 (ISBN 0-8414-3065-9). Folcroft.

John Greenleaf, Minister: Or, The Full Stature of a Man. Julia Warth Parsons. LC 7-34091. D. Lothrop Company.

John Gresham's Girl. Concordia Merrel. 1928. Doubleday, Doran & Company, Inc.

John Guilderstring's Sin. A Novel. C. French Richards. 1864. Carleton.

John Halifax: Gentleman. Dinah Maria Mulock Craik. LC 4-15293. 1877. Harper & Brothers.

John Halifax: Gentleman. Dinah Maria Mulock Craik. LC 6-31085. (Lovell's library, v. 1. no. 33). J. W. Lovell Company.

John Halifax: Gentleman. Dinah Maria Mulock Craik. LC 6-31083. 1897. L. C. Page & Company.

John Halifax: Gentleman. Dinah Maria Mulock Craik. LC 7-33373. T. Y. Crowell & Company.

John Halifax: Gentleman. Dinah Maria Mulock Craik. LC 5382. W. B. Conkey Company.

John Halifax: Gentleman. Dinah Maria Mulock Craik. (Half-title: Everyman's library, ed. by Ernest Rhys. Fiction). 1907. J. M. Dent & Co.

John Halifax: Gentleman. Dinah Maria Mulock Craik. Ed. by Brown, Eleanor M. LC 29-13781. (modern readers' series). 1929. The Macmillan Company.

John Halifax, Gentleman. Mulock. 1972. pap. 1.95 o.p. (ISBN 0-460-01123-5, EP1123, Evman). Dutton.

John Halifax, Gentleman. Dinah M. Mulock. 1976. 8.95x o.p. (ISBN 0-460-00123-X, Evman). Biblio Dist.

John Halifax, Gentleman. By Miss Mulock... Dinah Maria Mulock Craik. (On cover: Seaside library. Pocket ed. no. 11). G. Munro.

John Halifax, Gentlemen. A Novel. Dinah Maria Mulock Craik. LC 41-332325. (On cover: Burt's library of the world's best books). 1890. A. L. Burt.

John Halsey: The Anti-Monopolist. A Novel. pocket ed. Robert Upton Collins. LC 6-26959. G. F. Neal & Co.

John Harvey: A Tale of the Twentieth Century. James M Galloway. LC 7-41208. 1897. C. H. Kerr & Company.

John Henry. Roark Bradford. LC 77-116941. (Short story index reprint series). (Illus.). 1970. Books for Libraries Press.

John Henry. George Vere Hobart. LC 1-31543. G. W. Dilingham Co.

John Henry: And Other Stories... Charels Austin Hobbs. LC 26-749398. The Superior Printing Company.

John Henry Smith: A Humorous Romance of Outdoor Life. Frederick Upham Adams. 1905. Doubleday, Page & Company.

John Herring: A West of England Romance. Sabine Baring-Gould. LC 6-7958. (On cover: Lovell's international series, no. 19). F. F. Lovell & Company.

John Holden, Unionist: A Romance of the Days of Destruction and Reconstruction. Thomas Cooper De Leon & Ledyard, Erwin. The Price-McGill Company.

John Holdsworth, Chief Mate. A Novel. William Clark Russell. (Harper's Franklin square library, no. 379). 1884. Harper & Brothers.

John Holdsworth, Chief Mate: A Novel. William Clark Russell. (On cover: Lovell's library, v. 7, no. 399). 1884. J. W. Lovell Company.

John Holdsworth: Chief Mate. A Novel. William Clark Russell. (On cover: Seaside library. Pocket ed., no. 209). 1884. G. Munro.

John Howard Payne, Skywalker: A Biographical Novel of the Man Who Wrote Home, Sweet Home. Maude Barragan. LC 54-167912. 1953. Dietz Press.

John Ingerfield, and Other Stories. Jerome Klapka Jerome. LC 75-86148. (Short story index reprint series). (Illus.). 1969. Books for Libraries Press.

John Ingerfield: And Other Stories. Jerome Klapka Jerome. LC 7-9919. (On Cover: Buckram Series). 1894. H. Holt and Company.

John Inglesant. Joseph Henry Shorthouse. LC 75-480. (Victorian Fiction: Novels of Faith and Doubt; V. 33). 1975. 35.00 (ISBN 0-8240-1557-6). Garland Pub.

John Inglesant: A Romance... 4th ed. Joseph Henry Shorthouse. 1882. Macmillan and Co.

John Inglesant, a Romance... 6th ed. Joseph Henry Shorthouse. LC 9-3857. 1882. Macmillan and Co.

John Inglesant. A Romance. Joseph Henry Shorthouse. LC 3-15790. (Seaside library. v. 60, no. 1229). 1882. G. Munro.

John Inglesant, a Romance... Joseph Henry Shorthouse. LC 41-311383. 1889. Macmillan and Co.

John Inglesant; a Romance... 7th ed. Joseph Henry Shorthouse. LC 3-1577. 1897. The Macmillan Company.

John Inglesant; a Romance... 8th ed. Joseph Henry Shorthouse. LC 3-1578. 1900. The Macmillan Company.

John Inglesant: A Romance. Joseph Henry Shorthouse. LC 77-115270. 1970. Repr. of 1900 ed. 42.00 (ISBN 0-403-00298-2). Scholarly.

John Jasper's Secret: Sequel to Charles Dicken's Mystery of Edwin Drood, by Charles Dickens, Jr. and Wilkie Collins. Henry Morford & Collins, Wilkie, 1824-1889, Supposed Joint Author. LC 7-26202. 1898. R. F. Fenno & Company.

John Jenkin: Public Enemy. Graham Montague Jeffries. LC 35-3809. 1935. J. B. Lippincott Company.

John Jerome His Thoughts and Ways. A Book Without Beginning. Jean Ingelow. LC 7-8852. 1886. Roberts Brothers.

John, John, and His Son John: A Study in Motive. Gertrude Capen Whitney. LC 29-173914. The Four Seas Company.

John Keith, Intern. Jeanne Judson. 1963. Avalon Books.

John Kemp's Wager. Robert Graves. 1925. 10.00 o.s.i. Ridgeway Bks.

John Kenadie: Being the Story of His Perplexing Inheritance. Ripley Dunlap Saunders. LC 2-13395. 1902. Houghton, Mifflin and Company.

John Kendry's Idea. with frontispiece by c. d. williams. ed. Chester Bailey Fernald. LC 7-24157. 1907. The Outing Publishing Company.

John King, Manager. A Story of the Stage. Edmond Nolcini & Emmons, Grant. (Dillingham's American authors library, no. 27). 1897. G. W. Dillingham Co.

John Laurens, Envoy to Paris: Bayard of the American Revolution. Juliet Cox Coleman & Juliet Cox Coleman. LC 77-371711. (Illus.). 6.50 (ISBN 0-533-02494-3). Vantage Press.

John Leighton, Jr.; a Novel. Kate Nichols Trask. LC 8-29723. 1898. Harper & Brothers.

John Lillibud. Francis Gordon Hurrell. LC 35-3242. C. Kendall & W. Sharp, Inc.

John Littlejohn, of J. Being in Particular an Account of His Remarkable Entanglement with the King's Intrigues Against General Washington. George Morgan. LC 7-17264. 1897. J. B. Lippincott Company.

John Macnab. John Buchan. LC 25-17114. 1925. Houghton Mifflin Company.

John Maidment. Julian Sturgis. (On cover: Seaside library. Pocket ed., no. 694). 1886. G. Munro.

John Malcolm: A Novel. Edward Fuller. 1902. Snow & Farnham.

John March, Southerner. George Washington Cable. LC 72-83933. 1969. Mnemosyne Pub. Co.

John March, Southerner. George Washington Cable. LC 73-96494. (Works of George W. Cable). 1970. Garrett Press.

John March, Southerner. George Washington Cable. 1894. C. Scribner's Sons.

John March, Southerner see Collected Works.

John Marchamont's Legacy. Mary Elizabeth Braddon Maxwell. (On cover: Seaside library. Pocket ed. no. 570). 1885. G. Munro.

John Marchmont's Legacy. Mary Elizabeth Braddon Maxwell. (On cover: Lovell's library. no. 870). 1887. J. W. Lovell Company.

John Marchmont's Legacy: A Novel. Mary Elizabeth Braddon Maxwell. (On cover: Library of select novels. no. 238). 1864. Harper & Brothers.

John Maribel. A Novel. Maria Darrington Deslonde. LC 6-33882. 1877. G. W. Carleton & Co.

John Marmaduke. A Romance of the English Invasion of Ireland in 1649. Samuel Harden Church. LC 6-25397. 1897. G. P. Putnam's Sons.

John Marsh's Millions: A Novel by Charles Klein and Arthur Hornblow... Illustrations by Samuel Cahan. Charles Klein & Hornblow, Arthur. LC 10-17326. 1.50. G. W. Dillingham Company.

John Martin of Martin's Corner. Adelbert Gilroy Clark. LC 17-155471. 1917.

John Martin's Clerks: A Tale of the Store. Frank Farrington. LC 7-23462. 1907. Merchants' Helps Publishing Co.

John Marvel: Assistant. Thomas Nelson Page. LC 20-18810. 1919. C. Scribner's Sons.

John Maxwll's Marriage. Stephen Lucius Gwynn. 1903. The Macmillan Company.

John Medicinewolf. Michael E Moon. LC 78-16860. 6.95 (ISBN 0-8037-4220-7). Dial Press.

John Merrill's Pleasant Life: A Novel. Alice Beal Parsons. LC 30-5338. E. P. Dutton & Co. Inc.

John Milton and His Times: A Historical Novel in Three Parts. Max Ring. LC 76-23306. 1976. 45.00 (ISBN 0-8414-7231-9). Folcroft Library Editions.

John Milton and His Times. An Historical Novel. Max Ring. Tr. by Jordan, F. LC 7-41650. 1868. D. Appleton & Co.

John Milton: Paradise Lost a Prose Rendition. Robert Shepherd, Jr. (Illus.). 160p. (Orig.). 1983. 17.95 (ISBN 0-8164-0534-4); pap. 8.95 (ISBN 0-8164-2415-2). Seabury.

John Montcalm: Heretic; a Tale of the Maryland Hills. Frederick Augustine Rupp. LC 8-37062. 1908. I. M. Beaver.

John Needham's Double: A Novel. Joseph Hatton. LC 7-2199. (Harper's handy series, no. 9). 1885. Harper & Brothers.

John Nielson Had a Daughter. Ruth L. Hill, pseud. 1976. Repr. of 1950 ed. lib. bdg. 14.40x (ISBN 0-89190-255-4). Am Repr-Rivercity Pr.

John Nielson Had a Daughter. Ruth L. Hill, pseud. 2.95 o.p. G&D.

John Nielson Had a Daughter. Ruth Livingston Hill Munce. LC 50-9563. 1950. Lippincott.

John Nielson Had a Daughter. Ruth Livingston Hill Munce. LC 75-31750. 1975. 9.95 (ISBN 0-89190-255-4). American Reprint Co.

John-No-Brawn. George Looms. LC 23-160449. 1923. Doubleday, Page & Company.

John Norton, M.D., By Alvin Campbell. Alvin Campbell. LC 6-21496. (On cover: Satchel series, no. 38). W. B. Smith & Co.

John Norton's Thanksgiving Party: And Other Stories. William Henry Harrison Murray. LC 7-32490. De Wolfe, Fiske & Co.

John O' Jamestown. Vaughan Kester. LC 7-360982. 1901. The McClure Company.

John O' the Green: A Romance. Jeffery Farnol. 1935. Little, Brown, and Company.

John O'Brien: Or, The Orphan of Boston. A Tale of Real Life. John T Roddan. LC 7-39804. 1856. P. Donahoe.

John of America. David Loring MacKaye. 1947. Longmans, Green and Co.

John of Oregon. Daniel Alfred Poling. LC 26-16208. George H. Doran Company.

John of Strathbourne: A Romance of the Days of Francis I. R. D Chetwode. LC 3-12971. (Half-title: Appletons' town and country library, no. 243). 1898. D. Appleton and Company.

John O'May, and Other Stories. Maxwell Struthers Burt. LC 18-176092. 1918. 1.35. C. Scribner's Sons.

John O'Partletts' A Tale of Strife and Courage. Jean Edgerton Hovey. LC 13-21263. 1913. L. C. Page & Company.

John Paget: A Novel. Sarah Barnwell Elliott. LC 6-37575. 1893. H. Holt and Company.

John Parmalee's Curse. Julian Hawthorne. (On cover: Cassell's "rainbow" series, v. 1, no. 23). 1888. Cassell & Company, Limited.

John Parmelee's Curse. Julian Hawthorne. LC 7-3892. Cassell & Company, Limited.

John Parmelee's Curse. Julian Hawthorne. LC 45-539184. 1886. Cassell & Company, Limited.

John Paul's Rock. Frank Parker Day. LC 32-6105. 1932. Minton, Balch & Company.

John Percyfield, the Anatomy of Cheerfulness. Charles Hanford Henderson. 1903. Houghton, Mifflin and Company.

John Peters: A Novel. Aella Greene. LC 6-45554. 1890. C. W. Bryan & Co., Printers.

John Poverty: Tr. from the Spanish of Luis Coloma, S. J. Luis Coloma. Tr. by Brookes, E. M. LC 11-32253. 1.25. H. L. Kilner & Co.

John Punterick: A Novel of Life in the Old Dutch Fork. Orlando B. Mayer & James E Kibler. LC 81-11937. (South Caroliniana Series; 7). (Illus.). 1981. 20.00 (ISBN 0-87152-346-9). Reprint Co.

John Quixote. Charles Elbert Scoggins. LC 29-160833. The Bobbs-Merrill Company.

John Rantoul. Henry Loomis Nelson. 1885. J. R. Osgood and Company.

John Rawn: Prominent Citizen. Emerson Hough. LC 12-4768. The Bobbs-Merrill Company.

John Read, American. Edwin Chapin Washburn. LC 28-18114. The Grafton Press.

John St. John: A Story of Missouri and Illinois. Nephi Anderson. LC 18-7660. 1917. 0.85. Zion's Printing and Publishing Company.

John Seneschal's Margaret. Agnes Sweetman Castle & Castle, Egerton. LC 20-17318. 1920. D. Appleton and Company.

John Sherman & Dhoya. William Butler Yeats. Ed. by Richard J. Finneran. LC 69-14424. (Illus.). 1969. 5.95. Wayne State University Press.

John Sherman, and Dhoya. William Butler Yeats. LC 7-1523. (Half-title: The "unknown" library. no. 16). Cassell Publishing Company.

John Sherwood: Ironmaster. Silas Weir Mitchell. LC 11-120563. 1911. The Century Co.

John Ship, Mariner: Or, By Dint of Valor. Frank Mackenzie Savile. LC 8-2018. F. A. Stokes Company.

John Silence: Five Stories. Algernon Blackwood. 1965. bds., 4.00. Richards Pr.

John Silence: Physician Extraordinary. Algernon Blackwood. LC 41-38113. 1909. J. W. Luce & Company.

John Silence: Physician Extraordinary. Algernon Blackwood. 1910. Brentano's.

John Silence: Physician Extraordinary. Algernon Blackwood. LC 20-8737. 1920. E. P. Dutton & Company.

John Slaughter's Way. James Wyckoff. LC 63-8746. (Double D western). 1963. Doubleday.

John Smith. A Journey Along the High-Ways and by-Ways of Life. Sebastian Brown. LC 6-18685. 1893. The Monumental Publishing Company.

John Smith Hears Death Walking. Wyatt Blassingame. LC 44-9794. 1944. Bartholomew House, Inc.

John Smith's Funny Adventures on a Crutch: Or, The Remarkable Peregrinations of a One-Legged Soldier After the War. Alonzo F Hill. LC 7-4941. 1869. J. E. Potter and Company.

John, Son of Thunder. Ellen Gunderson Traylor. LC 77-93755. 5.95 (ISBN 0-8423-1902-6). Tyndale House Publishers.

John Splendid: The Tale of a Poor Gentleman and the Little Wars of Lorn. Neil Munro. LC 98-925444. 1898. Dodd, Mead and Company.

John Stevens' Courtship. A Story of the Echo Canyon War. Susa Young Gates. LC 9-25186. 1909. The Deseret News.

John Stuyvesant Ancestor and Other People. Alvin Saunders Johnson. LC 75-134967. (Short story index reprint series). 1970. Books for Libraries Press.

John Stuyvesant Ancestor and Other People. Alvin Saunders Johnson. LC 19-15744. 1919. Harcourt, Brace and Howe.

John Temple: Merchant Adventurer, Convict and Conqistador. Ralph Anthony Durand. LC 11-269501. 1911. 1.25. The Macmillan Company.

John the Fool: An American Romance. Charles Tenney Jackson. LC 15-6068. 1.25. The Bobbs-Merrill Company.

John: The Harbinger. Charles A. Modlin. LC 39-14611. Times-Mirror.

John Thisselton. Marian Bower. LC 6876. 1900. H. Holt and Company.

John Thomas and Lady Jane. David Herbert Lawrence. LC 70-185281. 1972. 8.95 (ISBN 0-670-40812-3). Viking Press.

John Thorndyke's Cases. Richard Austin Freeman. LC 74-10486. (Illus.). 1975. (ISBN 0-88355-201-9). Hyperion Press.

John Tom Alligator and Others. Robert Edward Stuart Chambers. LC 37-7991. 1937. E. P. Dutton & Company.

John Trevena: A Study with Special Reference to the Romantic Elements in His Work... Myrtle Catherine Henry. LC 35-972337. 1935.

John Vale's Guardian. David Christie Murray. LC 43-37377. 1890. Macmillan and Co.

John Van Buren, Politician: A Novel of to-Day. LC 4-32157. 1904. Harper & Brothers.

John Van Buren, Politician: A Novel of to-Day. 1905. Harper & Brothers.

John Varholm's Heir: Or, The Denwold Mills. Ellen Elizabeth Armes. LC 5-37784. 1905. Sentinel Printing Company.

John Verney. Horace Annesley Vachell. LC 11-12714. Hodder & Stoughton, George H. Doran Company.

John Vytal: A Tale of the Lost Colony. William Farquhar Payson. LC 1-3938. 1901. Harper & Brothers.

John W. Campbell Anthology. John Wood Campbell. LC 72-89301. (Doubleday science fiction). 1973. 9.95 (ISBN 0-385-06819-0). Doubleday.

John W. Campbell Anthology. Lester Del Rey. LC 72-89301. 540p. 1973. 9.95 o.p. (ISBN 0-385-06819-0). Doubleday.

John Ward, M.D. By Charles Vale Pseud. Arthur Hooley. LC 13-26555. 1913. 1.25. M. Kennerley.

John Ward, Preacher. Margaret Wade Campbell Deland. LC 67-29263. (Americans in fic.). 1967. Gregg Pr.

John Ward: Preacher. Margaret Wade Campbell Deland. LC 6-33381. 1888. Houghton, Mifflin and Company.

John Ward: Preacher. 27th thousand. ed. Margaret Wade Campbell Deland. LC 32-33586. 1889. Houghton, Mifflin and Company.

John Ward's Governess. Annie Lyndsay MacGregor. LC 7-200019. 1892. G. W. Dillingham.

John Ward's Governess. A Novel. Annie Lyndsay MacGregor. LC 7-16459. 1868. J. B. Lippincott & Co.

John Wesley, Jr. The Story of an Experiment. Dan Brearley Brummitt. LC 21-11100. Cincinnati, The Methodist Book Concern.

John Williamson of Hardscrabble... Moses Ayers McCoid. LC 3-1280. M. A. Donohue & Company.

John Winterbourne's Family. Alice Brown. LC 10-220598. 1910. Houghton Mifflin Company.

John Winthrop's Defeat: A Novel. Jean Kate Ludlum. (choice series, no. 46). 1891. R. Bonner's Sons.

John Worthington's Name. A Novel. Frank Lee Benedict. LC 7-34453. 1874. Harper & Brothers.

John Wyndham Omnibus. John Beynon Harris. LC 66-448. 1966. Simon and Schuster.

John X Sargent. Alfred W Denham. LC 39-5775. The Constitution Co.

Johnathan Livingston Pigeon: The Tale of a Gull. John T. Toppen. LC 75-35389. (Illus.). 216p. 1976. 6.95 o.p. (ISBN 0-89144-011-9). Crescent Pubns.

Johndover. Margaret H. C. Cameron. LC 24-8655. Harper & Brothers.

Johnnie. Dorothy Belle Flanagan Hughes. LC 44-7073. 1944. Duell, Sloan and Pearce.

Johnnie. Elmer Osborn Laughlin. LC 98-1040. 1899. The Bowen-Merrill Co.

Johnnie: A Memory of Boyhood. Elmer Osborn Laughlin. LC 3-26365. 1903. The Bobbs-Merrill Company.

Johnnie Death. William Schnurr. 1974. (pbk.) 1.50 (ISBN 0-671-78634-2). Pocket Books.

Johnnie Mountain. Lillian K Craig. LC 36-18148. 1936. Doubleday, Doran & Company, Inc.

Johnnie Panic & His Fantastic Circus of Fear. Jim Sorcic. 1975. pap. 2.50 (Pub. by New Rivers Pr); pap. 10.00 signed ed. SBD.

Johnnie Quickstep's Whaling Voyage. George Paul Goff. 1894.

Johnno. David Malouf. LC 78-60218. 1978. 7.95 (ISBN 0-8076-0905-6). G. Braziller.

Johnny & the Winged Horse. John Pagano. 1970. 2.50 o.p. (ISBN 0-8059-1479-X). Dorrance.

Johnny AppElessed: The Romance of the Sower. Eleanor Stackhouse Atkinson. LC 15-7116. 1915. Harper & Brothers.

Johnny Appleseed's Rhymes. Denton Jaques Snider. Sigma Publishing Co.

Johnny-Bingo. Browning Norton. (gr. 5-7). 1973. pap. 1.25 o.p. (ISBN 0-671-29777-5). Archway.

Johnny-Bingo. Browning Norton. (gr. 5-7). 1973. pap. 1.25 o.p. (ISBN 0-671-29777-5). Archway.

Johnny Bogan: A Novel. Leonora Baccante. LC 31-6599. The Vanguard Press.

Johnny Christmas: A Novel. Forrester Blake. LC 48-5629. 1948. W. Morrow.

Johnny Come Jingle-O: A Novel, by Richard B. Erno. Richard B Erno. LC 66-26159. 4.50. Crown.

Johnny Concho. Noel M Loomis. LC 56-4656. (Gold medal giant, S587). 1956. Fawcett Publications.

Johnny Counterfiet. Mary Yale Shapleigh. LC 38-36504. J. H. Hopkins, Inc.

Johnny Forsaken. Gladys Bronwyn Stern. LC 54-85376. 1954. Macmillan.

Johnny Get Your Gun: A Novel. John Dudley Ball. LC 71-79361. 1969. 5.95. Little, Brown.

Johnny Goes North see Swastika Hunt.

Johnny Goes West. Desmond Cory, pseud. (O.s.i.). 1968. pap. 0.60 o.s.i. (A324X, Award). Univ Pub & Dist.

Johnny Goes West: By Desmond Cory. Shaun McCarthy. LC 67-13223. 1967. bds., 3.95. Walker.

Johnny Got His Gun. Dalton Trumbo. LC 59-39624. 1959. L. Stuart.

Johnny Got His Gun. Dalton Trumbo. LC 71-115416. 1970. 5.95. L. Stuart.

Johnny Got His Gun. Dalton Trumbo. LC 39-176531. J. B. Lippincott Company.

Johnny Guitar: A Novel. Roy Chanslor. LC 53-9901. 1953. Simon and Schuster.

Johnny Liddell's Morgue. Frank Kane. LC 56-12165. (Dell first edition, A117). 1956. Dell Pub. Co.

Johnny Lost. Philip M. Jones. LC 66-131982. (Rinehart suspense novel). 1966. bds., 3.95. Holt.

Johnny Ludlow. Ellen Price Henry Wood Wood. LC 21-15371. (Seaside library, v. 45, no. 914). 1881. G. Munro.

Johnny Ludlow Short Stories. Ellen Price Henry Wood Wood. (Seaside library, v. 45, no. 914). 1881. G. Munro.

Johnny Nelson. Clarence Edward Mulford. 354p. 1974. Repr. of 1920 ed. lib. bdg. 18.30x (ISBN 0-88411-222-5). Amereon Ltd.

Johnny Nelson: How a One-Time Pupil of Hopalong Cassidy of the Famous Bar-20 Ranch in the Pecos Valley Performed an Act of Knight-Errantry and What Came of It. Clarence Edward Mulford. LC 73-89644. (Illus.). 1974. 6.95. Aeonian Press.

Johnny Nelson: How a One-Time Pupil of Hopalong Cassidy of the Famous Bar-20 Ranch in the Pecos Valley Performed an Act of Knight-Errantry and What Came of It. Clarence Edward Mulford. LC 20-92740. 1920. A. C. McClurg & Co.

Johnny Nelson: How a One-Time Pupil of Hopalong Cassidy of the Famous Bar-20 Ranch in the Pecos Valley Performed an Act of Knight-Erranty and What Came of It. Clarence Edward Mulford. LC 27-7327. 1920. A. L. Burt Company.

Johnny Noon. Frances Shine. LC 73-7491. 1973. 6.95 (ISBN 0-396-06839-1). Dodd, Mead.

Johnny on the Spot. Amen Dell. LC 43-5776. 1943. Mystery House.

Johnny Ortiz, Presidente de USA. Hugo Hanriot. Ed. by SLUSA. 100p. (Orig., Sp.). 1982. lib. bdg. 12.00 (ISBN 0-9606758-3-3); pap. 6.00. SLUSA.

Johnny Osage. Janice Holt Giles. 1977. 1.75 (ISBN 0-380-01810-1). Avon Books.

Johnny Osage. Janice Holt Giles. LC 79-28207. 1979. 15.95 (ISBN 0-8161-3053-1). G. K. Hall.

Johnny Painter. Anita Pettibone. LC 44-9396. 1944. Farrar & Rinehart, Inc.

Johnny Panic and the Bible of Dreams, and Other Prose Writings. Sylvia Plath. LC 77-181659. 10.00 (ISBN 0-06-013377-5). Harper & Row.

Johnny Pryde. John Joy Bell. LC 18-10584. Fleming H. Revell Company.

Johnny Purple. John Wyllie. LC 56-6311. 1956. Dutton.

Johnny Rapana. Charles Frances. LC 65-1805. 1965. 3.10. Whitcombe & Tombs.

Johnny Reb: A Story of South Carolina. Marie Conway Oemler. LC 29-19457. The Century Co.

Johnny Shiloh: A Novel of the Civil War by James A. Rhodes and Dean Jauchius. 1st Ed. James A Rhodes & Dean Jauchlus. LC 59-14298. 1959. Bobbs-Merrill.

Johnny Sundance. Samuel Anthony Peeples. LC 52-10431. (Dutton Diamond D western).

Johnny Tall Dog see TaleSpinners I.

Johnny Transplant. Orvill E. Ault. 3.75 o.p. Carlton.

Johnny Tremain. Esther Forbes. 305p. 1981. Repr. lib. bdg. 14.95x (ISBN 0-89966-306-0). Buccaneer Bks.

Johnny Under Ground. Patricia Moyes. LC 66-101210. (Rinehart suspense novel). 1966. bds., 3.95. Holt.

Johnny Under Ground. Patricia Moyes. LC 81-47339. (Fifty Classics of Crime Fiction, 1950-1975). 1982. 14.95 (ISBN 0-8240-4987-X). Garland Pub.

Johnny Vengeance. Frank Gruber. LC 54-63772. 1954. Rinehart.

Johnny Vengence. Frank Gruber. 128p. 1981. pap. text ed. 1.95. Bantam.

Johnny Vengeance. Frank Gruber. 1976. Repr. of 1954 ed. lib. bdg. 9.50 o.p. Buccaneer Bks.

Johnny's Headache from Ali Baba. John Puoplo. 1970. 3.50 o.p. Carlton.

Johnny's Sister, a Novel. Leigh Howard, pseud. LC 54-4224. 1954. Longmans, Green.

Johnny's Stolen Pet. Christine Wood. 1971. pap. 0.95 o.p. (ISBN 0-87508-694-2). Chr Lit.

Johns. Georgia E Bennett. LC 38-31614. The Christopher Publishing House.

John's Alive: Or, The Bridge of a Ghost, and Other Sketches. William Tappan Thompson & Wade, Mrs. May A. (Thompson) Ed. 1883. D. McKay.

John's Son John. Louis Paul Kirby. LC 36-356136. 1936. Meador Publishing Company.

Johnson Manor: A Tale of Olden Time in New York. James Kent. LC 7-10961. 1877. G. P. Putnam's Sons.

Johnson's History of Rasselas, Prince of Abyssinia: Ed. with an Introduction on Methods of Study. Samuel Johnson. Ed. by Scott, Fred Newton. LC 13-33859. (On cover: The students' series of English classics). 1891. Leach, Shewell, & Sanborn.

Johnstone of the Border. Harold Bindloss. LC 16-171831. 1916. 1.35. Federick A. Stokes Company.

Johnstown Stage, and Other Stories. Robert Howe Fletcher. LC 6-41691. (On cover: Appleton's town and country library. no 83). 1891. D. Appleton and Company.

Johnsville in the Olden Time: And Other Stories. Nathan J Bailey. LC 9-1846. 1884. Printed by E. O. Jenkins' Sons.

Join the Club. Nancy Bruff, pseud. 6.95 o.p. Bartholomew.

Join the Club. Nancy Bruff, pseud. 6.95 o.p. Delacorte.

Joiner. James Whitehead. LC 69-10687. 1971. 7.95 (ISBN 0-394-43143-X). Knopf.

Joining Charles and Other Stories. Elizabeth Bowen. LC 29-25349. 1929. L. MacVeagh, The Dial Press.

Joining Stone. Noelle B. McCue. (Loveswept Ser.: No. 3). 1983. pap. 1.95. Bantam.

Joint Guardians. Evelyn Everett Green. LC 6-45547. I. Bradley & Co.

Joint Venture: A Tale in Two Lands. E. A Fitzsimon. LC 6-41123. 1878. J. Sheehy.

Joke. Milan Kundera & Michael Henry Heim. LC 81-48055. 14.95 (ISBN 0-06-014987-6). Harper & Row.

Joke Goes a Long Way in the Country. Alannah Hopkin. LC 82-73014. 1983. 9.95 (ISBN 0-689-11353-6). Atheneum.

Joker. Helena Osborne. LC 78-26800. 1979. 8.95 (ISBN 0-698-10975-9). Coward, McCann & Geoghegan.

Joker see TaleSpinners I.

Joker, a Novel. Jean Malaquais. 1974. (pbk.) 1.50 (ISBN 0-446-78396-X). Warner Paperback Library.

Joker: A Novel Translated from the French by Herma Briffault. 1st Ed. Jean Malaquais. LC 54-517228. 1954. Doubleday.

Joker Take Queen. Bruce Munslow. LC 66-13104. (Rinehart suspense novel). 1966. Holt, Rinehart and Winston.

Joko's Anniversary. Roland Topor. LC 74-114949. 1970. 5.95. Orion Press.

Jolie Benoit, R.N. Ruth McCarthy Sears. (Candlelight romances, 102). 1972. Dell.

Joline. Harriet Theresa Smith Comstock. LC 25-23222. 1925. Doubleday, Page & Company.

Jolly. John Weston. LC 65-12265. 1965. D. McKay Co.

Jolly Corner. Henry James. LC 72-182362. 1971. Aquarius Press.

Jolly Corner see Altar of the Dead.

Jolly Corner: & The Real Thing. Henry James. LC 68-10282. (Illus.). 1968. F. Watts.

Jolly J's of Silver Creek. Bertha B. Moore McCurry. LC 50-8237. (Colportage library, 196.). 1949. Moddy Press.

Jolly Parisiennes: And Other Novelettes. Emile Zola & Cox, George D., Tr. T. B. Peterson & Brothers.

Jolly Raftsman on the Wisconsin. the knapsack ed. Georgenia Josephine Luke Koppke & The Knapsack. Mayer Printing Company.

Jolly Rogerson. Ralph M McInerny. LC 67-19092. 1967. Doubleday.

Jolly Time. Mary Dwinell Chellis. LC 6-23410. (On cover: Fife and drum series, no. 7). 1882. National Temperance Society and Publication House.

Jolts and Jars of Amanda Hunter and A Family Jar. Christine Crosby Whelen. LC 19-10460. Saulsbury Publishing Company.

Jonah. James Herbert. (Orig.). 1981. pap. 2.95 (ISBN 0-451-11066-8, AE1066, Sig). NAL.

Jonah. Robert Nathan. LC 25-4208. 1925. R. M. McBride & Company.

Jonah and Co. Cecil William Mercer. LC 77-354724. (Mercer, Cecil William, 1885-1960. Berry Books). (Illus.). 1976. 3.50 (ISBN 0-7063-1674-6). Ward Lock.

Jonah and Co. Cecil William Mercer. LC 27-6436. 1927. Minton, Balch & Company.

Jonah Game. Joel Abel. (Orig.). 1973. pap. 0.75 o.p. (07305). Curtis.

Jonah. Introd. by Ronald McCuaig. 3d. Australian Ed. Louis Stone. LC 66-5385. 1965. 4.50. Angus & Robertson.

Jonah Kit. Ian Watson. LC 75-40938. 6.95 (ISBN 0-684-14600-2). Scribner.

Jonah: Or, The Withering Vine. Robert Nathan. LC 34-33472. 1934. A. A. Knopf.

Jonah Watch. Jack Cady. 224p. 1983. pap. 2.75 (ISBN 0-380-62828-7, 62828-7). Avon.

Jonah Watch: A True-Life Ghost Story in the Form of a Novel. Jack Cady. LC 81-66973. 12.50 (ISBN 0-87795-342-2). Arbor House.

Jonah's Ark. Roland Barker. LC 40-11445. 1940. Caryle House.

Jonah's Gourd Vine. Zora Neale Hurston. LC 70-166496. 1971. 5.95. Lippincott.

Jonah's Gourd Vine. Zora Neale Hurston. 1934. J. B. Lippincott Company.

Jonas Hawley. William Wesley Pennell. LC 11-192738. 1.50. The C. M. Clark Publishing Company.

Jonathan. Dan Neidermyer. LC 72-10287. 1973. 5.95 (ISBN 0-8361-1705-0). Herald Press.

Jonathan: A Novel. Christina Catherine Fraser-Tytler Liddell. LC 8-31914. (On cover: Leisure hour series. no.: 58). 1876. H. Holt and Company.

Jonathan: A Tragedy. Thomas Ewing. LC 3-465. 1902. Funk & Wagnalls Company.

Jonathan. Based on an Idea by Ann Noyes Guettel. Russell O'Neil. LC 59-7323. 1959. Appleton-Century-Crofts.

Jonathan Bishop: A Novel. Herbert Sherman Gorman. LC 33-37021. Farrar & Rinehart, Incorporated.

Jonathan Blair: Bounty Lands Lawyer. William Donohue Ellis. (54-342). 1966. Paperback Lib.

Jonathan Blair: Bounty Lands Lawyer. William Donohue Ellis. LC 54-10451. (Illus.). 1954. World Pub. Co.

Jonathan Dearborn: A Novel of the War of 1812. Willard Mosher Wallace. LC 67-11225. 1967. Little, Brown.

Jonathan Draws the Long Bow: New England Popular Tales & Legends. Richard M. Dorson. LC 75-102488. (Illus.). 1970. Repr. of 1946 ed. 11.50x (ISBN 0-8462-1253-6). Russell.

Jonathan Eagle. Authorized Abridgment. Alexander Kinnan Laing. LC 57-11880. (Bantam books, F.)1643, #). 1957. Bantam-Books.

Jonathan Eagle. 1st Ed. Alexander Kinnan Laing. LC 54-5132. 1955. Duell, Sloan and Pearce.

Jonathan Fish and His Neighbors. Hu Maxwell. LC 2-15355. 1902. The Acme Publishing Company.

Jonathan Forge, Preacher in the Hills: A Lusty and Uninhibited Novel. Earl Delmer Zachman. LC 56-5846. 1956. William-Frederick Press.

Jonathan Found. Cecil Maiden. Crowell.

Jonathan Livingston Seagull. Richard Bach. (Keith Jennison Large Type Ser). 8.95 o.p. (ISBN 0-531-00320-5). Watts.

Jonathan Livingston Seagull: A Story. Richard Bach. 96p. 1975. slipcase 7.95 o.p. Macmillan.

Jonathan Scroll. Alfred M. Natali. 64p. 1973. 4.95 o.p. (ISBN 0-8059-1951-1). Dorrance.

Jonathan Segal Chicken. Sol Weinstein & Howard Albrecht. LC 73-166232. (Illus.). 1973. (pbk.) 1.25. Pinnacle Books.

Jonathan Troy. Edward Abbey. LC 54-5665. 1954. Dodd, Mead.

Jonathan Wild. Henry Fielding. LC 32-35922. (The companion classics). W. J. Black, Inc.

Jonathan Wild, and The Journal of a Voyage to Lisbon. Henry Fielding. (Half-title: Everyman's library, ed. by Ernest Rhys. Fiction. no.377). 1932. J. M. Dent & Sons, Ltd.

Jonathan's Daughter. Lida Larrimore Thomas. LC 33-31663. 1933. Macrae Smith Company.

Jonathan's New Boy. Pythias Damon. LC 4269. (On cover: Denison's series. vol. x, no. 60). 1900. T. S. Denison.
Jonce Smiley, the Yankee Boy Who Had No Friends. Horatio Hastings Weld. LC 8-367324. (On cover: Library of American novels, no. 3). 1845. E. Ferrett and Company.
Jondelle. E. C. Tubb. (Science Fiction Ser). pap. 0.95 o.p. (UQ1075). DAW Bks.
Jondelle. E. C Tubb. 1973. (pbk) 0.95. DAW Books.
Jonel Fortunat: A Roumanian Romance. Marco Brociner & Miller, Hettie E., Tr. LC 6-17967. (On cover: The optimus series, no. 5). 1891. Donohue, Henneberry & Co.
Jones: A Novel. James E Myers. LC 81-1810. 9.95 (ISBN 0-916392-77-5). Oak Tree Publications.
Jones Aboard. Robert C Givins. LC 11-14096. 1.25. The Jones Abroad Publishing Company.
Jones and Brown: Or, Value and Waste. A Novel. Charles Henry Allison. LC 6-54. Allison, Neff & Co.
Jones Girls. Dorothy Worley. LC 54-10326. 1954. Avalon Books.
Jones Men. Vern E Smith. LC 74-6910. 1974. 6.95 (ISBN 0-8092-8306-9). Regnery.
Jones Men. Vern E Smith. 1976. (pbk.) 1.75 (ISBN 0-446-59101-7). Warner Books.
Jones Unbound. Walter Lockwood. LC 72-12740. 1973. 5.95 (ISBN 0-13-510065-8). Prentice-Hall.
Joneses and the Asterisks: A Story in Monologue. Gerald Fitzgerald Campbell. LC 6-21494. 1895. J. Lane.
Jonesport Raffle. John Gould. (Illus.). 193p. 1979. pap. 3.95 (ISBN 0-89272-059-X). Down East.
Joni of Storm Hill. Lucile Vernon Stevens. 1976. 4.95. Avalon Books.
Jonie's Direct Line. Jo-An Ritchie. LC 75-44644. (Crown Ser.). 1976. pap. 4.50 (ISBN 0-8127-0110-0). Review & Herald.
Jono. Leonard B. Kaufman. (Orig.). 1970. pap. 0.60 o.p. (63-304). Paperback Lib.
Jono of Bali. 1st. ed. Terrie Miller. (Illus.). 1974. 4.50 (ISBN 0-533-01296-1). Vantage Press.
Jonoah and the Green Stone. Henry Dumas. LC 75-40563. 7.95 (ISBN 0-394-49791-0). Random House.
Joop's Dance. Stephen Geller. LC 73-81982. 1969. 5.95. Dutton.
Joppa Door. Hope Williams Sykes. LC 37-273201. G. P. Putnam's Sons.
Jordan Beachhead: A Novel of Biblical Times. Foreword by Charlton Heston. 1st Ed. James H Kepler. LC 56-109731. 1956. Exposition Press.
Jordan Country: A Landscape in Narrative. Shelby Foote. LC 54-712238. 1954. Dial Press.
Jordan Intercept. J. Alexander McKenzie. LC 80-68581. (Canaan Trilogy Ser.). 266p. (Orig.). 1980. pap. 2.95 (ISBN 0-87123-269-3, 200269). Bethany Hse.
Jordan Patrol. Yigal Lev. LC 70-84375. 1970. 4.95. Doubleday.
Jordan Saga. Ronald Kirkbridge. 1974. (pbk.) 1.75. New American Library.
Jordans. Sarah Gertrude Millin. LC 23-141222. Boni and Liveright.
Jordans by Sarah Gertrude Millin. Sarah Gertrude Liebson Millin. LC 23-14122. Boni and Liveright.
Jordanstown: A Novel. Josephine Winslow Johnson. LC 74-22790. (Labor Movement in Fiction and Non-Fiction). 1976. 16.50 (ISBN 0-404-58444-6). AMS Press.
Jordanstown: A Novel. Josephine Winslow Johnson. LC 37-4839. 1937. Simon and Schuster.
Jordi: A Composite Case History. Theodore Isaac Rubin. LC 60-11818. 1960. Macmillan.
Joretta: A Love Story. Edna Robb Webster. LC 32-15439. Grosset & Dunlap.
Jorgen Stein. Jacob Paludan. LC 66-22852. (Nordic translation series). 1966. University of Wisconsin Press.
Jorgensen. Tristram Tupper. LC 26-12139. 1926. J. B. Lippincott Company.
Joris of the Rock. Leslie Barringer. LC 29-6347. 1929. Doubleday, Doran & Company, Inc.
Joris of the Rock. Leslie Barringer. LC 80-19241. (His The Neustrian cycle; book 2). 1980. 10.95. Borgo Press.
Joris of the Rock: The Neustrian Cycle, Bk. 2. Leslie Barringer. (Forgotten Fantasy Library: Vol. 9). 318p. 1976. pap. 4.95 (ISBN 0-87877-108-5, F-108). Newcastle Pub.
Joris of the Rock: The Neustrian Cycle, Bk. 2. Leslie Barringer. Ed. by R. Reginald & Douglas Menville. LC 80-19241. (Newcastle Forgotten Fantasy Library: Vol. 9). 318p. 1980. Repr. of 1976 ed. lib. bdg. 11.95x (ISBN 0-89370-508-X). Borgo Pr.
Jorkens Remembers Africa. Edward John Moreton Drax Plunkett Dunsany. LC 72-4421. (Short story index reprint series). 1972. 12.00 (ISBN 0-8369-4174-8). Books for Libraries Press.
Jorkens Remembers Africa. Edward John Moreton Drax Plunkett Dunsany. LC 34-37434. 1934. Longmans, Green & Co.
Jornado. E. R. Slade. (Orig.). 1979. pap. 1.95 (ISBN 0-532-23270-4). Woodhill.
Jornads. Robert Luther Duffus. LC 35-3357. Covici, Friede.
Jorrocks, Jaunts & Jollities. Robert Smith Surtees. Ed. by Herbert Van Thal. (First Novel Library). 1969. pap. 2.50 o.p. Dufour.
Jory. Milton R. Bass. 1973. pap. 0.95 o.p. (M1794, Crest). Fawcett World.
Jory. Milton R. Bass. (YA) 1969. 6.95 o.p. (ISBN 0-399-10466-6). Putnam.
Jo's Boys, and How They Turned Out. A Sequel to "Little Men". Louisa May Alcott. LC 4-16116. 1886. Roberts Brothers.
Joscelyn. William Gilmore Simms. LC 76-10257. (Simms Revolutionary War novels; v. 1). 1976. 15.00 (ISBN 0-87152-235-7). Published for the Southern Studies Program, University of South Carolina by The Reprint Company.
Joscelyn Cheshire: A Story of Revolutionary Days in the Carolinas... Sara Beaumont Cannon Kennedy. LC 1-10011. 1901. Doubleday, Page & Co.
Joscelyn Cheshire: A Story of Revolutionary Days in the Carolinas. Sara Beaumont Cannon Kennedy. LC 4-35657. 1902. Doubleday, Page & Co.
Joscelyn Vernon. A Story of the Days of King Charles the First. Archibald Campbell Knowles. LC 98-1843. 1898. G. W. Jacobs & Co.
Jose. Otto Ruppius. Ed. by Myers, Lillie E. (On cover: Primrose edition, no. 6). 1890. Street & Smith.
Jose, a Story of Spanish Love: Translated from the Spanish of Armanda Palacio Valdes by Minna Caroline Smith, with a Brief Foreword by Alma Laird. Palacio Valdes, Armando & Smith, Minna Caroline, 1860- Tr. LC 31-14418. (students' literal translations). Translation Publishing Company, Inc.
Jose: A Tale from South America. Illus. by Hans Baltzer. Tr. by Stella Humphries. Gunther Feustel. LC 67-24092. 1968. 3.95. Delacorte.
Jose: Authorized Translation from the Original of A. Palacio Valdes... Palacio Valdes, Armando & Smith, Minna Caroline, 1860- Tr. LC 2-5583. 1901. Brentano's.
Jose Marti, Letras y Huellas Desconocidas. Carlos Ripoll. 1976. 10.95 (ISBN 0-88303-024-1); pap. 6.50. E Torres & Sons.
Joselin Takes a Hand. Andrew Cassels Brown. LC 27-18383. 1927. Dodd, Mead & Company.
Joseph. Mervyn Jones. LC 78-119615. 1970. 7.95. Atheneum.
Joseph. Joyce Landorf. 320p. 1980. 12.95 (ISBN 0-8007-1095-9). Revell.
Joseph: A Biographical Novella of the Carpenter of Nazareth. Annie Ellis Campdon. LC 65-17339. 1966. William-Frederick Press.
Joseph: A Novel. Joyce Landorf. LC 80-12686. 1980. 12.50 (ISBN 0-8007-6048-4). Revell.
Joseph and His Brethren. Harold Webber Freeman. LC 29-196831. H. Holt and Company.
Joseph and His Brothers. Thomas Mann. Tr. by Helen Tracy Lowe. LC 34-27154. (His Joseph and his brothers, I). 1934. A. A. Knopf.
Joseph and His Brothers. Thomas Mann. Tr. by Helen Tracy Lowe. LC 37-9261. (His Joseph and his brothers, I). 1936. A. A. Knopf.
Joseph and His Brothers: Translated from the German for the First Time. Thomas Mann. Tr. by Helen Tracy Lowe. LC 34-271546. 1934. A. A. Knopf.
Joseph and His Brothers: Translated from the German for the First Time. Thomas Mann. Tr. by Helen Tracy Lowe. LC 37-926131. 1936. A. A. Knopf.
Joseph and His Friend: A Story of Pennsylvania. Bayard Taylor. 1870. G. P. Putnam & Sons; Etc., Etc.
Joseph and Judith: Or, A Bundle of Old Love Letters. Edward Cary Bass. LC 7-13440. J. H. Earle & Company.
Joseph & Potiphar's Wife: An International Anthology of the Story of the Chaste Youth & the Lustful Stepmother. Ed. by John D. Yohannan. LC 68-25550. 1968. 8.50 o.p.; pap. 2.95 o.p. (NDP262). New Directions.
Joseph and the Sancta Sindone: A Novel of Jesus' Time. 1st Ed. Fletcher Shackelford. LC 56-9568. 1956. Exposition Press.
Joseph Andrews. Henry Fielding. LC 63-6970. (Everyman's library, 467). 1962. Dent; New York, Dutton.
Joseph Andrews. Fielding, Henry. LC 67-78009. (Wesleyan edition of the works of Henry Fielding) 63/-). 1967. Clarendon P.
Joseph Andrews. Henry Fielding. LC 36-37322. (Half-title: Everyman's library, ed. by Ernest Phys. Fiction no. 467). 1935. J. M. Dent & Sons, Ltd.
Joseph Andrews. Henry Fielding & R. F Brissenden. LC 78-309165. (Penguin English library). 1977. 1.95 (ISBN 0-14-043114-4). Penguin Books.
Joseph Andrews, and Shamela. Henry Fielding. Ed. by Sheridan Warner Baker. LC 75-165373. (Crowell critical library). 1972. (ISBN 0-690-46545-9). Crowell.
Joseph Andrews. Ed. by Martin C. Battestin. 1st Amer. Ed. Henry Fielding. Ed. by Martin C. Battestin. LC 66-23927. 1967. 10.00. Weseleyan Univ. Pr.
Joseph Andrews, Preceded by Shamela. Henry Fielding. Ed. by A. R Humphreys. (Everyman's University Library). 1975. (ISBN 0-460-10467-5). J. M. Dent & Sons Ltd.
Joseph Balsamo. Alexandre Dumas & Maquet, Auguste. LC 6-42331. (American series. no. 311). M. J. Ivers & Co.
Joseph Balsamo. Alexandre Dumas & Maquet, Auguste. LC 6-42332. (On cover: Seaside library. Pocket ed. no. 2118). G. Munro's Sons.
Joseph Balsamo. A Novel... Alexandre Dumas & Auguste Maquet. LC 45-49323. 1878. T. B. Peterson & Brothers.
Joseph Brant (Thayendanegea) Howard Thomas. LC 73-80132. 1973. 4.95 (ISBN 0-913710-04-0). Prospect Books.
Joseph File. Alfred Harris. 1976. (pbk.) 1.50 (ISBN 0-425-03118-7). Berkley Publishing Corp.
Joseph File: A Novel. Alfred Harris. LC 74-79649. 1974. 6.95 (ISBN 0-399-11316-9). Putnam.
Joseph Greer and His Daughter: A Novel. Henry Kitchell Webster. LC 22-221573. The Bobbs-Merrill Company.
Joseph Ii. and His Court. An Historical Novel. Klara Muller Mundt. Tr. by Chaudron, Adelaide De Vendel. LC 7-24118. 1884. D. Appleton and Company.
Joseph in Egypt... Translated from the German for the First Time. Thomas Mann. Tr. by Helen Tracy Lowe. LC 38-27135. 1938. A. A. Knopf.
Joseph in Jeopardy. Julia Davis Frankau. LC 12-4352. 1912. 1.35. The Macmillan Company.
Joseph in the Snow. A Tale. Berthold Auerbach. LC 6-4507.
Joseph Scroll. Clifford A. Wilson. LC 78-65633. 1979. pap. 3.95 (ISBN 0-89051-054-7). CLP Pubs.
Joseph, Slave of Mystery: A Novel. Grady Tyree Cantrell. LC 49-181373. Vulcan Books.
Joseph the Dreamer. Addison Leroy Phillips. LC 49-117242. 1949. W. A. Wilde Co.
Joseph: The Husband of Mary; a Novel. Hiram Graham. LC 34-38324. R. Freelander, The Yorktown Press.
Joseph the Provider. Thomas Mann. Tr. by Helen Tracy Lowe. LC 44-5709. (His Joseph and his brothers, IV). 1944. A. A. Knopf.
Joseph the Second and His Court. Klara Muller Mundt. Tr. by Chandron, Adelaide De Vendel. LC 16-1243. (The historical romances of Louisa Muhlbach pseud.). D. Appleton and Company.
Joseph Vance. William Frend De Morgan. LC 24-27968. Grosset & Dunlap.
Joseph Vance: An Ill-Written Autobiography. William Frend De Morgan. LC 6-25695. 1906. H. Holt and Company.
Joseph Vance: An Ill-Written Autobiography. William Frend De Morgan. LC 8-11006. 1907. H. Holt and Company.
Joseph Zalmonah. Edward King. LC 67-29271. (Americans in Fiction Ser.). lib. bdg. 16.00x (ISBN 0-8398-1054-7); pap. text ed. 5.95x (ISBN 0-89197-814-3). Irvington.
Joseph Zalmonah: A Novel. Edward King. LC 67-29271. (Americans in Fic.). 1968. 10.00. Gregg Pr.
Joseph Zalmonah: A Novel. Edward King. LC 3-3606. 1893. Lee and Shepard.
Josephine. Hubert Cole. (Belmont Tower book). 1979. 1.95 (ISBN 0-505-51351-X). Tower Pubns.
Josephine. Kathleen Coyle. LC 42-89042. 1942. Harper & Brothers.
Josephine Eloise: A Novel. Adelaide F. Hammond. 1872. Baltimore News Company.
Josephine, Empress of France. Barbara Cartland. 1974. pap. 1.25 o.p. (ISBN 0-515-03326-X, V3326). BJ Pub Group.
Josephine Joseph: Texas Sketches. Eugenie Mouton. 1900. The Editor Publishing Co.
Josephine: Or, The Romish Poison, a Romance of the Present. J Harrington. LC 7-2846. Burgess & Day.
Josephine's Heart: A Novel. Reinhold Ortmann. Tr. by Lowrey, D. M. (On cover: The popular series. no. 25). 1892. R. Bonner's Sons.
Joseph's Coat. A Story. David Christie Murray. (Seaside library, v. 57, no. 1156). 1881. G. Munro.
Josephus. Lion Feuchtwanger. Tr. by Willa Muir. Muir Edwin, 1887- Joint Tr. LC 32-28823. 1932. The Viking Press.
Josephus and the Emperor. Lion Feuchtwanger & Oram, Caroline, Tr. LC 42-7500. 1942. The Viking Press.
Josh. William Weber. LC 69-12412. 1969. McGraw-Hill.
Josh Canzy's Experience: What He Saw and What Use He Made of It. William A Morrison. LC 7-32485. 1897. The Barta Press.
Josh Lawton: A Novel. Melvyn Bragg. LC 75-171151. 1972. (ISBN 0-394-48031-7). Knopf; Distributed by Random House.
Joshua. Jan Hartman. 1977. pap. 1.75 (ISBN 0-445-02552-2). Popular Lib.
Joshua: A Biblical Picture. only authorized ed. Georg Moritz Ebers. LC 6-36803. (On cover: Lovell's series of foreign literature, no. 1). 1889. J. W. Lovell Company.
Joshua: A Story of Biblical Times. Georg Moritz Ebers. Tr. by Safford, Mary Joanna. LC 16-157101. (historical romances of Georg Ebers. vol. iii). 1915. D. Appleton and Company.
Joshua: A Story of Biblical Times. Georg Moritz Ebers & Safford, Mary Joanne, Tr. LC 6-36802. 1890. W. S. Gottsberger & Co.
Joshua Beene and God. Jewel Gibson. LC 46-71811. 1946. Random House.
Joshua Doan. Gladys Francis Lewis. LC 56-4503. 1956. Bouregy & Curl.
Joshua Haggard's Daughter. Mary Elizabeth Braddon Maxwell. (Seaside library. v. 25, no. 500). 1879. G. Munro.
Joshua Haggard's Daughter. Mary Elizabeth Braddon Maxwell. (On cover: Lovell's library. no. 871). 1887. J. W. Lovell Company.
Joshua Moore, American. George Frederick Hummel. LC 43-51156. 1943. Doubleday, Doran & Company, Inc.
Joshua, Son of None. Nancy Mars Freedman. LC 73-4014. 1973. 7.95. Delacorte Press.
Joshua Then & Now. Mordecai Richler. 384p. 1981. pap. 3.25 (ISBN 0-553-14583-5). Bantam.
Joshua Then and Now: A Novel. Mordecai Richler. LC 79-3489. 1980. 11.95 (ISBN 0-394-49351-6). A. A. Knopf: Distributed by Random House.
Joshua Todd. Fulton Oursler. LC 35-751. Farrar & Rinehart, Inc.
Joshua Tree. Robert Cabot. LC 78-103073. 1970. 6.95. Atheneum.
Joshua Wiggins & the Tough Challenge. Charles Beamer. (Joshua Wiggins Ser.: No. 2). 144p. (Orig.). 1983. pap. 3.95 (ISBN 0-87123-266-9). Bethany Hse.
Joshua Wray: A Novel. Hans Stevenson Beattie. LC 6-10265. United States Book Company.
Joshua's People. Alan Caillou, pseud. 384p. (Orig.). 1982. pap. 2.95 (ISBN 0-523-41622-9). Pinnacle Bks.
Joshua's Vision. William John Locke. LC 28-29080. 1928. Dodd, Mead and Company.
Josiah. DavidL. Kimball. (Illus.). 300p. 1982. 14.95 (ISBN 0-942698-01-0); pap. 6.95 (ISBN 0-942698-02-9). Trends & Events.
Josiah: A Story of the Old South. William H Emerson. LC 6-32348. 1906. Search Light Printing House.
Josiah Allen on the Woman Question. Marietta Holley. LC 14-19283. Fleming H. Revell Company.
Josie and Joe. Ruth Gipson Plowhead. LC 38-306076. 1938. The Caxton Printers, Ltd.
Josie, Con Amore. Milla Zenovich Logan. LC 65-25944. bds., 4.95. Norton.
Josie: The Little Madcap. Charles E Blaney & Williams, Lottie Josie, the Little Madcap. LC 48-35765. (Play book series, no. 117). J. S. Ogilvie Pub. C.
Josie's Way: A Novel. Winifred Wolfe. LC 79-56018. 10.00 (ISBN 0-87795-259-0). Arbor House.
Josselyn's Wife. Kathleen Thompson Norris. LC 18-184036. 1918. Doubleday, Page & Company.
Josslyn: The Story of an Incorrigible Dreamer. by henry justin smith... ed. Henry Justin Smith. LC 24-10843. 1924. Covici-McGee Co.
Jou Pu Tuan. Li Yu. (O.s.i.). 1967. pap. 1.95 o.s.i. (ISBN 0-394-17104-7, B106, BC). Grove.
Jou Pu Tuan: A Seventeenth Century Erotic Moral Novel. Li Yu. Tr. by Richard Martin. (Illus.). 1967. pap. 1.95 o.p. (ISBN 0-394-17104-7, B106, BC). Grove.
Jou Pu Tuan: A Seventeenth Century Erotic Moral Novel. Li Yu. (Illus.). 1963. 7.50 o.p. (GP418). Grove.
Jou Pu Tuan: The Prayer Mat of Flesh. Yu Li. LC 67-20503. (Illus.). 1967. Grove Press.
Journal d'une Poete see Oeuvres Completes.
Journal for the Protection of All Beings, No. 3. Ed. by Sandra Corrie & Laura Stine. (Illus.). 1969. pap. 1.50 o.p. (ISBN 0-87286-024-8). City Lights.
Journal from an Obscure Place. Judith Miles. LC 78-60279. 144p. 1978. pap. 2.95 (ISBN 0-87123-273-1, 200273). Bethany Hse.
Journal from Ellipsis. Calisher, Hortense. LC 65-21355. 1965. Little, Brown.
Journal-Nocturnal, and Seven Stories. E. M Broner. LC 68-20063. 1968. Harcourt, Brace & World.
Journal-Nocturnal: And Seven Stories by E. M. Broner. 1st Ed. E. M Broner. LC 68-20063. 1968. 5.95. Harcourt.

Journal of a Live Woman. Helen Van Metre Van-Anderson Gordon. LC 8-30236. 1895. G. H. Wright.
Journal of a Neglected Bull Dog: Being Impressions of His Master's Love Affairs. Barbara Blair. LC 11-19987. 1911. G. W. Jacobs & Co.
Journal of a Neglected Wife. Mabel Herbert Urner. LC 9-5215. 1909. B. W. Dodge & Company.
Journal of a Recluse: Tr. from the Original French. Mary Fisher. LC 9-25177. T. Y. Crowell & Co.
Journal of a Solitude. May Sarton. 1977. pap. 3.95 (ISBN 0-393-00853-3, N853, Norton Lib). Norton.
Journal of a Voyage to Nowhere. Charles Fenn. 194p. 1972. Repr. 5.95 o.p. (ISBN 0-393-07329-7). Norton.
Journal of a Young Man. Martin Delaney. LC 36-9698. The Vanguard Press.
Journal of Albion Moonlight. Kenneth Patchen. LC 68-28283. 1961. pap. 6.95 (ISBN 0-8112-0144-9, NDP99). New Directions.
Journal of Arthur Stirling: ". Upton Beall Sinclair. LC 3-2703. 1903. D. Appleton and Company.
Journal of Arthur Stirling. "The Valley of the Shadow.". Upton Beall Sinclair. 1906. Doubleday Page & Company.
Journal of Colonel De Lancey. James Warner Bellah. LC 67-19423. 1957. Chilton Books.
Journal of David Q. Little: By R. Daniel McMichael. R. Daniel McMichael. LC 67-149943. 1967. 6.95. Arlington House.
Journal of Edwin Carp. Richard Haydn. LC 54-9794. (Illus.). 1954. Simon and Schuster.
Journal of Henry Bulver: A Novel. Ethel Williamson. LC 21-8614. 1921. G. P. Putnam's Sons.
Journal of Madame Giovanni. Alexandre Dumas & Saint Mars, Gabrielle Anne Cisterne De Courtiras, Vicomtesse De, 1804-1872, Supposed Author. LC 44-1809. 1944. Liveright Publishing Corporation.
Journal of Mary Hervey Russell. Margaret Storm Jameson. LC 45-1695. 1945. The Macmillan Company.
Journal of My Other Self. Rainer Maria Rilke. Tr. by Linton, John. LC 30-30579. W. W. Norton & Company.
Journal of the Heart. Charlotte Campbell Bury. LC 6-16687. 1830. Carey and Lea.
Journal of the Lady Pamela Foxe: Being Her Account of Her Adventures, in England, in the Colony of Massachusetts and at Sea, Together with the Story of Her One True Love and Her Reflections Upon the Vicissitudes of Fortune, All the Events Narrated Having Occurred in the Year of Our Lord 17... Dorothea Malm. LC 47-3372. 1947. Prentice-Hall, Inc.
Journal of Wilfred T. Carroll: To Be Known As: The Decline and Fall of Daphne Finn. R. Bruce Moody. LC 66-20156. 5.95. Coward.
Journey. Anne Cameron. LC 82-11525. 5.95 (ISBN 0-380-79087-4). Avon.
Journey. Robert Heman. 1977. pap. 1.50 (ISBN 0-918406-02-1). Future Fr.
Journey. Fred B. Holmberg. (Illus., Orig.). 1971. pap. 2.95. Durrell.
Journey. Martha McKelvie. (Illus.). 1962. 3.50 o.p. (ISBN 0-8059-0189-2). Dorrance.
Journey. Jiro Osaragi, pseud. Tr. by Ivan Morris from Japanese. 350p. 1960. pap. 7.95 (ISBN 0-8048-1377-9). C E Tuttle.
Journey. Marta Randall. 1978. 1.95 (ISBN 0-671-81207-6). Pocket Books.
Journey. Robert Paul Smith. LC 43-13009. 1943. H. Holt and Company.
Journey. James Tucker. (Stone Ser.: No. 2). (Illus.). 1981. pap. 2.95 (ISBN 0-89083-849-6). Zebra.
Journey Across Three Worlds: Popular Soviet Science-Fiction Stories. M. Emtsev et al. (Illus.). 255p. 1975. 10.00 o.p. Beekman Pubs.
Journey at Dawn. Nancy Dorer & Frances Dorer. (Orig.). 1980. pap. 1.95 (ISBN 0-532-23179-1). Woodhill.
Journey Behind the Wind. Patricia Wrightson. 192p. 1982. pap. 2.25 (Del Rey). Ballantine.
Journey by the River. John Brewster Prescott. LC 54-7453. 1954. Random House.
Journey Down. Aline Frankau Bernstein. LC 32-688746. 1938. A. A. Knopf.
Journey Downstairs. Herbert Edmund Howard. LC 34-41603. 1934. Pub. for the Crime Club, Inc., by Doubleday, Doran & Company, Inc.
Journey for Joedel: A Novel. Guy Owen. LC 73-108076. 1970. 4.95. Crown.
Journey for Myself. Sidonie Gabrielle Colette. LC 72-80808. 1972. 6.95 o.p. (ISBN 0-672-51576-8). Bobbs.
Journey from Baghdad. David Roberts, pseud. LC 72-78718. 1969. 5.95. Doubleday.
Journey from Doubt, and Other Short Stories. Mary Jane Comstock. LC 74-77316. 1974. Adams Press.
Journey from This World to the Next. Henry Fielding. LC 75-46270. (Supernatural and Occult Fiction). 1976. 11.00 (ISBN 0-405-08127-8). Arno Press.
Journey Home. Zelda Popkin. LC 45-6108. 1945. J. B. Lippincott Company.
Journey Home. Harold Sinclair. LC 36-30067. 1936. Doubleday, Doran & Co., Inc.
Journey Homeward. 1st Ed. Gerald Hanley. LC 61-581457. 1961. World Pub. Co.
Journey in Other Worlds. A Romance of the Future. John Jacob Astor. LC 6-4533. 1894. D. Appleton and Company.
Journey in Search of Christmas. Owen Wister. LC 4-27872. 1904. Harper & Brothers.
Journey in the Dark. Martin Flavin. LC 78-104220. 1970. Greenwood Press.
Journey in the Dark. Martin Flavin. LC 43-15647. 1943. Harper & Brothers.
Journey into Christmas. Bess Streeter Aldrich. 265p. Repr. of 1949 ed. lib. bdg. 14.85x (ISBN 0-88411-262-4). Amereon Ltd.
Journey into Christmas, and Other Stories. Bess Streeter Aldrich. LC 63-16828. 1963. Appleton-Century.
Journey into Christmas, and Other Stories. Bess Streeter Aldrich. LC 49-6300. 1949. Appleton-Century-Crofts.
Journey into Fear. Eric Ambler. LC 40-81514. 1940. A.A. Knopf.
Journey into Fear. Marianne Ruuth. (Belmont Tower Book). 1.50 (ISBN 0-505-51193-2). Tower Pubns.
Journey into Fire. Patricia Wright. LC 76-42413. 1977. 8.95 (ISBN 0-385-12131-8). Doubleday.
Journey into Fire. Patricia Wright. 1978. 2.50 (ISBN 0-446-81525-X). Warner Books, Inc.
Journey into Freedom. Klaus Mann & Reil, Rita, Tr. LC 36-490163. 1936. A. A. Knopf.
Journey into Heaven: By Beth Lewis Pseud., and Perry Lewis Pseud. Beth Lipkin. LC 52-6124. 1951. Merlin Press.
Journey into Limbo. Scott Michel. 1962. 6.95 o.p. (ISBN 0-87140-801-5). Liveright.
Journey into Limbo. Scott Michel. 1968. pap. 0.75 o.p. (75-214). Manor Bks.
Journey into Limbo. Scott Michel. 1962. 6.95 o.p. (ISBN 0-87140-801-5). Liveright.
Journey into Limbo: A Novel of Intimate Adventure. Milton Scott Michel. LC 62-175306. 1962. Liveright Pub. Corp.
Journey into Love. Phyllis Waite. LC 40-32101. Carlton House.
Journey into Morning. Anne Maybury. LC 45-6101. 1945. Arcadia House, Inc.
Journey into Nowhere. Eddie H. Lee. 3.50 o.p. Carlton.
Journey into Spring. Winston David Armstrong Clewes. 1949. A. A. Knopf.
Journey into Stone. Audrey Erskine Lindop. LC 74-180085. 1972. 6.95 (ISBN 0-385-04151-9). Doubleday.
Journey into Terror. Dorothy Daniels. Orig. Title: Angrey Scar. 1970. pap. 0.60 o.p. (X2191). Pyramid Pubns.
Journey into Terror. Dorothy Daniels. (O.s.i.). 1974. pap. 0.95 o.s.i. (ISBN 0-515-03387-1, N3387). Pyramid Pubns.
Journey into Terror. George Alec Effinger. (Planet of the Apes#3). 1975. (pbk.) 0.95. Award Books.
Journey into the Light, Vol. 2. LC 58-5810. 1972. 6.50 o.p. Euclid Pub.
Journey into Twilight. Miriam Lynch. 1970. pap. 0.75 o.p. (ISBN 0-447-74689-8). Lancer.
Journey into Twilight see Doomsday Bells.
Journey into Violence. Douglas Orgill. 1963. 3.95 o.p. Morrow.
Journey Inward. Kurt Heuser & Muir, Willa. LC 32-20523. 1932. The Viking Press.
Journey Man Joiner: Or, The Companion of the Tour of France. George Sand & Shaw, Francis George, 1809-1882, Tr. LC 6-34605. 1847. W. H. Graham.
Journey Not to End. Paul Herr. LC 61-7829. 1961. B. Geis Associates; Distributed by Random House.
Journey of a Man. Thomas Wiseman. LC 67-19093. 1967. Doubleday.
Journey of August King. John Ehle. LC 71-160656. 1971. 6.95 (ISBN 0-06-011166-6). Harper & Row.
Journey of Simon McKeever. Albert Maltz. LC 49-2576. 1949. Little, Brown.
Journey of Tao Kim Nam. 1st Ed. Malcolm J Bosse. LC 59-6351. 1959. Doubleday.
Journey of Tapiola. Robert Nathan. LC 38-27957. 1938. A. A. Knopf.
Journey of the Flame. Walter Nordhoff. 1955. 4.95 o.p. (ISBN 0-395-08051-7). HM.
Journey of the Flame: Being an Account of One Year in the Life of Senor Don Juan Obrigon, Known During Past Years in the Three Californias As Juan Colorado, and to the Indiada of the Same As the Flame, Born at San Jose Del Arroyo, Lower California, Mexico, in 1798, and, Having Seen Three Centuries Change Customs and Manners, Died Alone in 1902 at the Great Cardon, Near Rosario, Mexico, with His Face Turned Toward the South. Antonio De Fierro Blanco & De Steiguer, Walter, Tr. LC 33-325905. 1933. Printed by The Riverside Press for Houghton Mifflin Company.
Journey of the Flame: Being an Account of One Year in the Life of Senor Don Juan Obrigon, Known During Past Years in the Three Californias As Juan Colorado, and to the Indiada of the Same As the Flame... Written Down by Antonio De Fierro Blanco, Who Is Now Revealed to Be Truly Walter Nordhoff. With Illus. by Alfredo Ramos Martinez and a Pref. to the 2d Ed. by Scott O'Dell. Walter Nordhoff. LC 55-14970. 1955. Houghton Mifflin.
Journey of the Flame: Being an Account of One Year in the Life of Senor Don Juan Obrigon, Known During Past Years in the Three Californias As Juan Colorado, and to the Indiada of the Same As the Flame, Born at San Jose Del Arroyo, Lower California, Mexico, in 1798, and, Having Seen Three Centuries Change Customs and Manners, Died Alone in 1902 at the Great Cardon, Near Rosario, Mexico, with His Face Turned Toward the South. Walter Nordhoff. LC 33-32590. 1933. Printed by the Riverside Press for Houghton Mifflin Company.
Journey of the Oceanauts. Louis Wolfe. 1970. pap. 0.75 o.p. (T2299). Pyramid Pubns.
Journey of the Oceanauts: Across the Bottom of the Atlantic Ocean on Foot. Louis Wolfe. (Illus.). 1968. Norton.
Journey of the Wolf. Douglas Day. LC 76-41224. 1977. 8.95 (ISBN 0-689-10771-4). Atheneum.
Journey of the Wolf. Douglas Day. (Kangaroo Book). 1978. 1.75 (ISBN 0-671-81801-5). Pocket Books.
Journey Proud. Thomasine Cobb McGehee. LC 39-27706. 1939. The Macmillan Company.
Journey: Reissue. Lillian Eugenia Smith. LC 65-7524. 1965. 4.50. Norton.
Journey Round My Room. Xavier Maistre & Attwell, Henry, Tr. LC 7-16602. 1871. Hurd and Houghton.
Journey Through the Light. Peter Goblen. 50p. 1973. pap. 1.95 o.s.i. (ISBN 0-913964-01-8). Koheleth Pub.
Journey Through Time. Larry Barretto. LC 40-80879. Farrar and Rinehart, Inc.
Journey to a High Mountain. James Howard Wellard. LC 50-5556. 1950. Dodd, Mead.
Journey to a Safe Place. Ian Stuart Black. LC 79-5334. 1979. 10.95 (ISBN 0-312-44510-5). St. Martin's Press.
Journey to a Star. C. O Lamp. LC 59-2260. Whittier Books.
Journey to a Woman. Ann Bannon. LC 75-13752. (Homosexuality). 1975. 9.00 (ISBN 0-405-07408-5). Arno Press.
Journey to a Woman. facsimile ed. Ann Dannon. Ed. by Jonathan Katz. LC 75-13752. (Homosexuality Ser.). 1975. Repr. of 1960 ed. 12.00x (ISBN 0-405-07408-5). Ayer Co.
Journey to Adventure. Lorena Ann Olmsted. (Avalon Books). 4.95. Thomas Bouregy.
Journey to Arcady. Rona Randall. LC 55-10196. 1955. Arcadia House.
Journey to Arzrum. Aleksandr Sergeevich Pushkin. Tr. by Birgitta Ingemanson. (Pap. ed. 2.50 o.p.). 1974. 7.95 (ISBN 0-88233-067-5). Ardis Pubs.
Journey to Boston. Mary Ellen Chase. 1973. 0.75. Curtis Books.
Journey to Boston: A Novel. Mary Ellen Chase. LC 64-23875. 1965. Norton.
Journey to Cuzco. Mary Ruth Myers. LC 77-22988. 7.95 (ISBN 0-698-10840-X). Coward, McCann & Geoghegan.
Journey to Delta Centaurus. Reginald Foxx. LC 81-86213. 112p. 1983. pap. 4.95 cancelled (ISBN 0-86666-044-5). GWP.
Journey to Freedom. William D. Sheehan. 1968. 4.50 o.p. Vantage.
Journey to Infinity. Introduced by Fletcher Pratt. 1st Ed. Ed. by Martin Greenberg. LC 51-9207. (Adventures in science fiction series). 1951. Gnome Press.
Journey to Love. Glenna Finley, pseud. 1971. pap. 1.95 (ISBN 0-451-11495-7, AJ1495, Sig). NAL.
Journey to Love. Daisy H. Thomson. 1974. pap. 0.95 o.p. (ISBN 0-515-03355-3, N3355). BJ Pub Group.
Journey to Mars. Gustavus W. Pope. LC 73-13262. (Classics of Science Fiction Ser). (Illus.). 55p. 1974. 16.50 (ISBN 0-88355-116-0); pap. 5.75 (ISBN 0-88355-145-4). Hyperion Conn.
Journey to Mars. The Wonderful World; Its Beauty and Splendor; Its Mighty Races and Kingdoms; Its Final Doom. Gustavus W Pope. LC 7-38164. (Romances of the planets. no. 1). 1894. G. W. Dillingham.
Journey to Matecumbe. With Illus. by Joseph Papin. Robert Lewis Taylor. LC 61-9774. 1961. McGraw-Hill.
Journey to Mesharra. Mike Sirota. (Ro-Lan Ser.: No. 3). (Orig.). (YA) 1981. pap. 2.25 (ISBN 0-89083-726-0). Zebra.
Journey to Nashville: A Story of the Founding. Alfred Leland Drabb. LC 57-9849. Bobbs Merrill.
Journey to Nature. Andrew Carpenter Wheeler. LC 1-31648. 1901. Doubleday, Page and Co.
Journey to Nature. Andrew Carpenter Wheeler. LC 2-26091. 1902. Doubleday, Page Ad Co.
Journey to Nowhere: A New World Tragedy. Shiva Naipaul. 1982. pap. 5.95 (ISBN 0-14-006189-4). Penguin.
Journey to Nowhere. 1st Ed. Nedra Tyre. LC 53-9483. 1954. Knopf.
Journey to Orassia: By Alan Caillou Pseud. Alan Lyle-Smythe. LC 65-10597. 4.50. Doubleday.
Journey to Paradise. Barbara Cartland. LC 78-61009. 1979. 7.95 (ISBN 0-525-13756-4). E. P. Dutton.
Journey to Paradise. Barbara Cartland. 1974. (pbk.) 0.95. Bantam Books.
Journey to Paradise. Sharon Wagner. (Adentures in Love Ser.: No. 34). 1982. pap. 1.95 (ISBN 0-451-11841-3, Sig). NAL.
Journey to Quiet Waters. William Lavender. 496p. 1980. pap. 2.75 (ISBN 0-515-05389-9). Jove Pubns.
Journey to Sahalin. James McConkey. LC 72-157489. 1971. 6.95. Coward, McCann & Geoghegan.
Journey to Shiloh: By Will Henry Pseud. Henry Allen. LC 60-12141. 1960. Random House.
Journey to Somewhere: A Novel. 1st Ed. Carroll Abbing, John Patrick. LC 55-8599. 1955. Longmans, Green.
Journey to the Center. Brian M. Stableford. 176p. 1982. pap. 2.50 (ISBN 0-87997-756-6, UE1756). DAW Bks.
Journey to the Center of the Earth. Jules Verne & Inc. New York Limited Editions Club. LC 67-2221. 1966. Printed for the Members of the Limited Editions Club.
Journey to the Center of the Earth. Voyage Au Centre De la Terre. Jules Verne. LC 57-3287. (Ace double-size books, D-155). Ace Books.
Journey to the Centre of the Earth. Jules Verne. LC 61-65314. (Fitzroy edition of Jules Verne). 1961. Associated Booksellers.
Journey to the Centre of the Earth. Jules Verne. LC 59-10646. (Great illustrated classics). (Illus.). 1959. Dodd, Mead.
Journey to the Centre of the Earth. Jules Verne. LC 1-9867. (In his Stories of adventure. ii). 1874. Scribner, Armstrong & Co.
Journey to the Centre of the Earth... Jules Verne & Riou, Edouard, 1833-1900, Illus. LC 1-9866. H. L. Shepard & Co.
Journey to the Dawn. Charles Angoff. LC 51-9402. 1951. Beechhurst Press.
Journey to the Earth's Interior. large type ed. Marshall B. Gardner. (Illus.). pap. 7.50 (ISBN 0-910122-48-2). Amherst Pr.
Journey to the East. Hermann Hesse. LC 68-2467. 1968. Farrar, Straus & Giroux.
Journey to the East. Translated by Hilda Rosner. Hermann Hesse. LC 57-8034. 1957. Noonday Press.
Journey to the End of the Night. Louis-Ferdinand Celine & Ralph Manheim. LC 82-7970. 1983. 19.95 (ISBN 0-8112-0846-X) (ISBN 0-8112-0847-8). New Directions.
Journey to the End of the Night. Louis Ferdinand Destouches. LC 49-8925. (Modern Readers Series). 1949. New Directions.
Journey to the Future. Clarence E. Foster. 1966. 5.00 o.p. (ISBN 0-682-44117-1). Exposition.
Journey to the Hangman. Arthur William Upfield. LC 59-6383. 1959. Published for the Crime Club by Doubleday.
Journey to the Interior. Percy Howard Newby. LC 46-7341. 1946. Doubleday.
Journey to the Interior. Percy Howard Newby. LC 46-7341. 1946. Doubleday & Company, Inc.
Journey to the Orient. Gerard De Nerval. Tr. & intro. by Norman Glass. LC 76-185604. (Illus.). 215p. 1972. 14.95x (ISBN 0-8147-5752-9). NYU Pr.
Journey to the Third World. David J. Gonzalez. LC 79-88887. (Orig.). 1979. pap. 3.00 o.s.i. (ISBN 0-9602972-1-9). Indigena.
Journey to the Underground World. Lin Carter. (Science Fiction Ser.). (Orig.). 1979. pap. 1.75 (ISBN 0-87997-499-0, UE1499). Daw Bks.
Journey to the West. Darwin Le Ora Teilhet. LC 38-8220. 1938. Doubleday, Doran & Co., Inc.
Journey to the World Underground see Gulliveriana, No. 4.

Journey to the World Underground, 1742. Ludwig Holberg. Ed. by Michael F. Shugrue. LC 74-18234. (Novel in England 1700-1775). 1974. lib. bdg. 50.00 (ISBN 0-8240-1105-8). Garland Pub.
Journey to Utah. Frank Roderus. LC 76-57867. 1977. 6.95 (ISBN 0-385-13003-1). Doubleday.
Journey to Utah. Frank Roderus. LC 82-13983. 1983. 11.95 (ISBN 0-89340-510-8). J. Curley.
Journey with Grandmother. Edith Unnerstad. LC 60-13231. 1960. Macmillan.
Journey with Jonah. Madeleine L'Engle. 1967. 9.95 (ISBN 0-374-33927-9); pap. 3.95 (ISBN 0-374-51462-3). FS&G.
Journey with Love. Denys Val Baker. 4.95 o.p. Wehman.
Journey with Strangers. Ray Coryton Hutchinson. LC 52-5563. 1952. Rinehart.
Journey Within. I. N. Aniebo. LC 79-304442. (African Writers Ser.). 1978. pap. text ed. 5.00x (ISBN 0-435-90206-7). Heinemann Ed.
Journey Without End. Victi Victuri Vincendi. Manes Sperber. LC 53-79877. 1954. Doubleday.
Journey. 1st Ed. Lillian Eugenia Smith. LC 53-664323. 1954. World Pub. Co.
Journeying Travels in Italy, Egypt, Sinai, Jerusalem & Cyprus. Nikos Kazantzakis. Tr. by Themi Vasils & Theodora Vasils. 1975. 7.50 o.p. (ISBN 0-316-48390-7); pap. 3.95 o.p. (ISBN 0-316-48391-5). Little.
Journeyman. Alan Brilliant. pap. 3.50 (ISBN 0-87775-014-9). Unicorn Pr.
Journeyman. Erskine Caldwell. LC 35-1721. The Viking Press, Inc.
Journeyman. Erskine Caldwell. LC 38-5280. 1938. The Viking Press.
Journeyman Joiner: Or, The Companion of the Tour of France. George Sand. LC 76-7364. 1976. 16.50. H. Fertig.
Journeyman Missionary by Jesse C. Fletcher. Jesse C Fletcher. LC 67-174261. 1967. bds., 1.50. Broadman.
Journeys. Gunter Eich. Tr. by Michael Hamburger from Ger. LC 70-121408. (Cape Editions Ser). 1970. pap. 1.50 o.p. (ISBN 0-670-40957-X, Grossman). Penguin.
Journey's End. Evelyn Berckman. LC 76-18334. 1977. 6.95 (ISBN 0-385-12415-5). Doubleday.
Journey's End. Evelyn Berckman. 1978. 1.50 (ISBN 0-380-37655-5). Avon Books.
Journey's End. Enda Adelaide Brown. LC 21-689576. Lothrop, Lee & Shepard Co.
Journey's End: A Novel. George William Marque Maier. LC 30-1702. The Christopher Publishing House.
Journey's End, a Novel. Robert Cedric Sherriff & Bartlett, Vernon, Joint Author. LC 30-8600. 1930. Frederick A. Stokes Company.
Journeys End: A Romance of to-Day. Justus Miles Forman. LC 3-3872. 1903. Doubleday, Page & Company.
Journeys in Science Fiction: Edited by Richard L. Loughlin and Lilian M. Popp. Ed. by Richard L Loughlin & Lilian M. Popp. LC 61-457. 1961. Globe Book Co.
Journeys in the Sun. Donald M Nelson. LC 55-12666. 1955. Story Book Press.
Jour...Une Autre Chance. Julia Carole. (Collection Colombine Ser.). 192p. 1983. pap. 1.95 (ISBN 0-373-48067-9). Harlequin Bks.
Joy. Georges Bernanos & Varese, Louise (McCutcheon) Tr. LC 46-6983. 1946. Pantheon Books.
Joy Bringer: A Tale of the Painted Desert. Grace MacGowan Cooke. LC 13-6255. 1913. 1.25. Doubleday, Page & Co.
Joy Comes Again to the Valley. Laura Hollon Henderson. LC 53-12140. Vantage Press.
Joy Delle. Lucena Belle Walker Mountain. LC 12-18796. 1.00. Press of Jennings and Graham.
Joy Forever. Joyce Lee. (Candlelight Regency Ser.: No. 698). (Orig.). pap. 1.75 (ISBN 0-440-14245-8). Dell.
Joy Girl. Helen Marion Edginton. LC 28-4066. The Penn Publishing Company.
Joy-Girl. John Van Alstyne Weaver. LC 32-14112. 1932. A. A. Knopf.
Joy House. Day Keene. LC 54-41717. (Lion book, 210). 1954. Lion Books by Arrangement with Classic Syndicate.
Joy House Girls. Hugo Rich. 192p. (Orig.). 1973. pap. 1.95 o.p. (ISBN 0-87682-381-9, 7381). Barclay Hse.
Joy in Our Cause: Short Stories. Carol Emshwiller. LC 73-14310. 1974. 6.95 (ISBN 0-06-011234-4). Harper & Row.
Joy in the Morning. Mary Raymond Shipman Andrews. LC 19-15565. 1919. C. Scribner's Sons.
Joy in the Morning. Betty Smith. LC 62-14560. 1963. Harper & Row.
Joy in the Morning. Betty Smith. LC 82-879. 1982. 15.95 (ISBN 0-8161-3300-X). G.K. Hall.
Joy in the Morning. Pelham Grenville Wodehouse. LC 46-6087. 1946. Doubleday & Company, Inc.
Joy in Work: Ten Short Stories of Today. Ed. by Mary Augusta Laselle. LC 20-20427. 1920. 0.92. H. Holt and Company.
Joy Is My Name. Coralie Hobson. LC 30-8904. Payson & Clarke Ltd.
Joy of Captain Ribot: Authorized Translation from the Original of A. Palacio Valdes. Palacio Valdes, Armando & Smith, Minna Caroline, 1860- Tr. LC 216231. 1900. Brentano's.
Joy of Christmas. 1st Ed. Ed. by Llewellyn Miller. LC 60-12630. 1960. Bobbs-Merrill.
Joy of Lex. Gyles Brandreth. 320p. 1983. pap. 6.95. Quill NY.
Joy of Life: A Novel. Emma Wolf. LC 8-37123. 1896. A. C. McClurg and Company.
Joy of Living. Sidney Floyd Gowing. LC 22-3494. 1922. G. P. Putnam's Sons.
Joy of Man's Desiring. Jean Giono. Tr. by Clarke, Katherine Allen. LC 40-9861. 1940. The Viking Press.
Joy of Man's Desiring. Jean Giono. LC 80-14932. 1980. 9.50 (ISBN 0-86547-015-4). North Point Press.
Joy of Reading: An LDS Family Anthology. Robert K Thomas. LC 78-60639. 1978. 4.95 (ISBN 0-88494-343-7). Bookcraft.
Joy of Spring. Ed. by James A. Kuse. (Illus.). 1979. pap. 4.95 (ISBN 0-89542-063-5). Ideals.
Joy of Youth. Eden Phillpotts. LC 13-16792. 1913. 1.30. Little, Brown, and Company.
Joy of Youth. Eden Phillpotts. LC 15-174213. 1914. Little, Brown, and Company.
Joy: Or, The Light of Cold-Home Ford, a Novel. Maria Henrietta De La Cherois Crommelin. (Harper's Franklin square library, no. 406). 1884. Harper & Brothers.
Joy Ride. John Gordon Brandon. LC 27-155197. 1927. L. MacVeagh, The Dial Press.
Joy-Ride! A Novel. Berta Ruck. LC 29-4211. 1929. Dodd, Mead and Company.
Joy Street. Clifton Cuthbert. LC 31-324039. 1931. W. Godwin, Inc.
Joy Street. Frances Parkinson Wheeler Keyes. LC 50-10755. 1950. Messner.
Joy Street. Frances Parkinson Wheeler Keyes. 1974. (pbk) 1.50 (ISBN 0-671-78709-8). Pocket Books.
Joy Street: A Love Story. Claire Pomeroy. LC 31-257738. N. Y., Chelsea House.
Joy Supplement One. Helen B. Lee. (Illus.). 1970. pap. 1.00 o.p. (ISBN 0-87106-011-6). Globe Pequot.
Joy the Deaconess. Elizabeth E Holding. LC 7-66003. 1893. Cranston & Curts.
Joy to Levine. Norma Gangel Rosen. 1972. pap. 0.75 o.p. (07238). Curtis.
Joy Train. Douglas Fairbairn. LC 57-10975. 1957. Simon and Schuster.
Joy Wagon. Arthur Twining Hadley. LC 58-5404. 1958. Viking Press.
Joy Way. Guy King. 1973. pap. 2.50 (ISBN 0-87508-280-7). Chr Lit.
Joy Wheel. Paul W Fairman. LC 54-27797. (Lion book, 190). 1954. Lion Books by Arrangement with Cornell Pub. Corp.
Joyce. Margaret Oliphant Wilson Oliphant. LC 41-31382. 1888. Macmillan and Co.
Joyce: A Novel. Louise Platt Hauck. LC 27-6814. 1927. The Penn Publishing Company.
Joyce Cary and the Novel of Africa. Michael J. C Echeruo. LC 72-76609. 1973. 10.00 (ISBN 0-8419-0131-7). Africana Pub. Co.
Joyce of the Jasmines. Ralph Henry Barbour. LC 11-27919. 1911. J. B. Lippincott Company.
Joyce of the North Woods. Harriet Theresa Smith Comstock. LC 11-5371. 1911. Doubleday, Page & Company.
Joyce, the Beloved. Katheryn Kimbrough, pseud. (Saga of the Phenwick Women Ser.: No. 27). 1979. pap. 1.75 (ISBN 0-445-04438-1). Popular Lib.
Joyce's Investments. Fannie E Newberry. LC 4221. 1899. A. I. Bradley & Co.
Joyful Condemned. Kylie Tennant, pseud. LC 53-858734. 1953. St. Martin's Press.
Joyful Delaneys: A Novel. Hugh Walpole. LC 38-27894. 1938. Doubleday, Doran & Company, Inc.
Joyful Heatherby. Payne Erskine. LC 13-626. 1913. 1.35. Little, Brown, and Company.
Joyful Journey. Berta Ruck. LC 50-6797. 1950. Dodd, Mead.
Joyful Years: A Novel. F. T Wawn. LC 17-195081. E. P. Dutton & Co.
Joykin. Michael Arabian. LC 27-6914. 1927. Boni & Liveright.
Joyleg. Avram Davidson & Ward Moore. LC 74-142850. 1971. 5.95 (ISBN 0-8027-5536-4). Walker.
Joyless Years: L'Age Ingrat. Jose Cabanis. LC 73-143027. (New library of French classics). 1971. 7.95 (ISBN 0-13-511634-1). Prentice-Hall.
Joyous Adventure. Emmuska Orczy. LC 32-22975. 1932. Doubleday, Doran and Company, Inc.
Joyous Adventures of Aristide Pujol. William John Locke. LC 12-228091. 1912. 1.30. John Lane Company.
Joyous Betrayal. Charles Pelton Jacobs. LC 30-25310. The John Day Company.
Joyous Conspirator. George Fort Gibbs. LC 27-818876. J. H. Sears & Company, Inc.
Joyous Friar: The Story of Fra Filippo Lippi. Arthur James Anderson. LC 27-18301. 1927. Frederick A. Stokes Company.
Joyous Heart. Viola Roseboro. LC 3-10201. 1903. McClure, Phillips & Company.
Joyous Hills. Peggy Gaddis, pseud. LC 55-793290. 1955. Arcadia House.
Joyous Judy. Bertha B. Moore McCurry. LC 36-14935. 1936. Wm. B. Eerdmans Publishing Co.
Joyous Judy. Bertha B. Moore. LC 36-14935. Wm. B. Eerdmans Publishing Co.
Joyous Miracle. Frank Norris. LC 6-18842. 1906. Doubleday, Page & Company.
Joyous Pretender. Louise Ayres Garnett. LC 28-25176. 1928. The Macmillan Company.
Joyous Season. Patrick Dennis, pseud. 1965. 4.75 o.p. (ISBN 0-15-146478-2). HarBraceJ.
Joyous Season: By Patrick Dennis. Edward Everett Tanner. (V2215). 1967. Avon.
Joyous Season: By Patrick Dennis Pseud. Edward Everett Tanner. LC 64-18284. 1965. 4.75. Harcourt.
Joyous Trouble Maker. Jackson Gregory. LC 18-8987. 1918. Dodd, Mead and Company.
Joyous Wayfarer. Humfrey Robertson Jordan. LC 11-31745. 1911. 1.35. G. P. Putnam's Sons.
Joyride. Gordon Chaplin. LC 82-5090. 12.95 (ISBN 0-698-11185-0). Coward, McCann & Geoghegan.
Joyride. Stephen Crye. 1983. pap. 2.95. Pinnacle Bks.
Joys of Motherhood. Buchi Emecheta. LC 78-24640. 1979. 8.95 (ISBN 0-8076-0914-5); pap. 4.95 (ISBN 0-8076-0950-1). Braziller.
Joys of Success: A Novel. James Lord. LC 58-56958. 1958. J.Day Co.
Joys She Chose. Matthew Peters. LC 54-8042. (Dell first edition, 24). 1954. Dell Pub. Co.
Joysprick. Anthony Burgess. 1973. 10.50 o.p. (ISBN 0-12-785081-3). Acad Pr.
Ju Ware of the Sung Dynasty. (Porcelain of the National Palace Museum, Vol. 1). 60.00x o.p. (ISBN 0-8188-2000-4). Paragon.
Juan & Lucy. Tana Reiff. LC 78-75219. (LifeTimes Ser.). 1979. pap. 3.32 (ISBN 0-8224-4317-1). Pitman Learning.
Juan in America. Eric Robert Russell Linklater. LC 31-763747. J. Cape & H. Smith.
Juan in China. Eric Robert Russell Linklater. LC 37-426563. Farrar & Rinehart, Inc.
Juan Ortiz, Gentleman of Seville: A Novel. Mary Bethell Alfriend. LC 41-7298. Chapman and Grimes, Inc.
Juan Pico. Will R Halpin. LC 99-197116. R. S. Weed Company.
Juan Pico. Will R Halpin. LC 99-1971. 1899. Robert Lewis Weed Company.
Juan the Landless. Juan Goytisolo. LC 76-55024. 1977. 10.00 (ISBN 0-670-41004-7). Viking Press.
Juan, the White Slave; and the Rebel Planter's Daughter. A Stirring Story of Slavery, Secession, Suffering and Revenge--Revealing the Deep Treachery of the Great Southern Rebellion. R. W. D. LC 7-4460. 1865. Barclay & Co.
Juana: And Other Stories. Honore De Balzac. Tr. by Katharine Prescott Wormeley. LC 3-231868. (Half-title: The comedy of human life... Philosophical studies). 1896. Roberts Brothers.
Juancho, the Bull-Fighter: Tr. from the French of Theophile Gautier. Theophile Gautier & Lewis, Mrs. Benjamin, Tr. Cassell Publishing Company.
Juanita: A Romance of Real Life in Cuba Fifty Years Ago. Mary Tyler Peabody Mann. D. Lothrop Company.
Jubal. Norman Daniels. (Orig.). 1970. pap. 0.95 o.p. (65-249). Paperback Lib.
Jubal Cade Westerns, 13 vols. Charles R. Pike, pseud. 1981. 2.95 ea.; Set. 33.95 (ISBN 0-87754-223-6). Chelsea Hse.
Jubal Troop. Paul Iselin Wellman. LC 39-81261. Carrick & Evans, Inc.
Jubel's Children. Lenard Kaufman. LC 50-9912. 1950. Random House.
Jubilee. Margaret Walker. LC 66-11218. (Illus.). 1966. Houghton Mifflin.
Jubilee Girl. Arthur Preston Hanksin. LC 21-17085. 1921. Dodd, Mead and Company.
Jubilee of a Ghost. March Cost, pseud. LC 68-8080. (O.s.i.). 1968. 7.95 o.s.i. (ISBN 0-8149-0048-8). Vanguard.
Jubilee of a Ghost. Peggy Morrison, pseud. LC 68-8080. 1968. 4.95. Vanguard Press.
Jubilee Trail. Gwen Bristow. LC 50-5268. 1950. Crowell.
Jubjub Bird. William M Hardy. LC 66-13122. 1966. Coward-McCann.
Jucklins: A Novel. Opie Percival Read. Laird & Lee.
Judah. Allan Appel. 1976. pap. 1.75 o.p. (LB418KK, Leisure Bks). Nordon Pubns.
Judah the Pious. Francine Prose. LC 72-90513. 1973. 6.95. Atheneum.
Judah Touro: A Biographical Romance. Moses Wassermann & Mayer, Harriet W., Tr. LC 24-12440. 1923. Bloch Publishing Company.
Judah's Lion. 10th ed. Charlotte Elizabeth Browne Tonna. LC 43-267147. 1848. M. W. Dodd.
Judah's Lion. 11th ed. Charlotte Elizabeth Browne Tonna. LC 42-270692. 1850. M. W. Dodd.
Judas. E. Richard Johnson. LC 74-135184. 1971. 4.95 (ISBN 0-06-012212-9). Harper & Row.
Judas. Eric Robert Russell Linklater. LC 39-20244. Farrar & Rinehart, Incorporated.
Judas: A Novel. Yigal Mossenson. LC 63-9412. 1963. St Martin's Press.
Judas Boy. Simon Raven. (Alms for Oblivion Ser.: No. 5). 1968. 8.50x o.p. (ISBN 0-85634-996-8). Intl Pubns Serv.
Judas: By Anton and Elly Van Heurn. Anton Van Heurn & Elly Van Heurn. LC 58-5747. 1958. Muhlenberg Press.
Judas Cat. Dorothy Salisbury Davis. LC 49-7029. 1949. C. Scribner's Sons.
Judas Conspiracy. John Bishop Ballem. LC 77-352126. 1976. 6.95. (ISBN 0-7737-0028-5) (ISBN 0-7737-7129-8). Musson Book Co.
Judas Country. Gavin Lyall. LC 75-1449. 1975. 7.95 (ISBN 0-670-41030-6). Viking Press.
Judas Cross. Jeffrey M Wallmann. LC 73-20601. 1974. 5.95 (ISBN 0-394-48843-1). Random House.
Judas Cross. Jeffrey M Wallmann. 1978. 1.50 (ISBN 0-380-01846-2). Avon Books.
Judas Diary. easy eye ed. W. Howard Baker. pap. 0.75 o.p. Lancer.
Judas Figures. Audrey Erskine Lindop. LC 56-7569. 1956. Appleton-Century-Crofts.
Judas Flowering. Jane Aiken Hodge. LC 76-9768. 1976. 9.95 (ISBN 0-698-10741-1). Coward, McCann & Geoghegan.
Judas Flowering: A Novel. Jane Aiken Hodge. (Fawcett Crest Book). 1977. 1.95 (ISBN 0-449-23221-2). Fawcett Pubns.
Judas Freak. Hugh Pentecost. LC 74-10009. (Juliet Quist Mystery Novel Ser.). 194p. 1974. 5.95 o.p. (ISBN 0-396-07001-9). Dodd.
Judas Freak. Judson Pentecost Philips. LC 74-10009. (Red badge novel of suspense). 1974. 5.95 (ISBN 0-396-07001-9). Dodd, Mead.
Judas Gene. Albert S. Klainer & Jo-Ann Klainer. 258p. 1981. pap. 2.95 (ISBN 0-441-39298-9, Pub. by Charter Bks). Ace Bks.
Judas Gene: A Novel. Jo-Ann Klainer & Albert S. Klainer. LC 79-18104. 12.50 (ISBN 0-399-90067-5). R. Marek.
Judas Goat. Robert B. Parker. LC 78-6594. 1978. 8.95 (ISBN 0-395-26682-3). Houghton Mifflin.
Judas Goat. Robert B Parker. (berkley Book). 1979. 1.95 (ISBN 0-425-04204-9). Berkley Pub. Corp.
Judas Goat. Robert B. Parker. LC 79-14926. 1981. 10.50 (ISBN 0-89340-220-6). J. Curley.
Judas Goat. 1st Ed. Leslie Edgley. LC 52-5858. 1952. Published for the Crime Club by Doubleday.
Judas Gospel. Peter Van Greenaway. 1973. (pbk.) 1.50. Dell Pub. Co.
Judas Gospel. Peter Van Greenaway. LC 72-84260. 1972. 6.95. Atheneum.
Judas Gun. Wayne D Overholser. LC 60-13229. 1960. Macmillan.
Judas, Incorporated: A Mystery Novel. Rudolf Kagey. LC 39-9207. 1939. Little, Brown and Company.
Judas Iscariot, an Imaginative Autobiography. 1st Ed. Albert Levitt. LC 61-15129. (Flagstones library, no. 2). 1961. Flagstone Publications.
Judas Journey: By Lee Roberts Pseud. Robert Lee Martin. LC 56-5739. (Red badge detective). Dodd, Mead.
Judas Judge, No. 27. Stuart Jason. (Butcher Ser.). (Orig.). 1979. pap. 1.75 (ISBN 0-523-40710-6). Pinnacle Bks.
Judas Kiss. Victoria Holt, pseud. LC 81-43291. 408p. 1982. 13.95 (ISBN 0-385-17786-0). Doubleday.
Judas Kiss. Victoria Holt, pseud. 336p. 1983. pap. 3.50 (ISBN 0-449-20055-8, Crest). Fawcett.
Judas Kiss. Jean Plaidy. LC 81-43291. 1982. 12.95 (ISBN 0-385-17786-0). Doubleday.
Judas Kiss. Sally Wentworth. 192p. 1982. pap. 1.75 (ISBN 0-373-10480-4, Pub. by Harlequin). PB.
Judas Kiss: A Novel. 1st Ed. Jay Dratler. LC 55-507691. Holt.
Judas Kissed? A Novel. Clare Grain. LC 54-12647. Vantage Press.
Judas Mandala. Damien Broderick. (Orig.). 1982. pap. 2.50 (ISBN 0-671-45032-8, Timescape). PB.
Judas Mandate. Clive Egleton. 1974. (pbk.) 1.25 (ISBN 0-523-00352-8). Pinnacle Books.
Judas Mandate. Clive Egleton. LC 78-183550. 1972. 6.95. Coward, McCann & Geoghegan.
Judas, My Brother. Frank Yerby. (O.s.i.). 1968. 6.95 o.s.i. (ISBN 0-8037-4289-4). Dial.

Judas, My Brother: The Story of the Thirteenth Disciple. Frank Yerby. 1975. (pbk.) 1.75. Dell.

Judas of Kerioth: A Romance of Old Judes 1st. Philip Robert Dillon. LC 53-8504. 1953. Exposition Press.

Judas Pair. Jonathan Gash, pseud. LC 77-6889. 1977. 8.95 (ISBN 0-06-011464-9). Harper & Row.

Judas Scrolls. Joseph Rosenberger. (Death Merchant Ser.: No. 53). 208p. (Orig.). 1983. pap. 2.25 (ISBN 0-523-41660-1). Pinnacle Bks.

Judas Seed. Anthony Gentile. 304p. (Orig.). 1982. pap. 2.95 (ISBN 0-440-14375-6). Dell.

Judas Sheep. Jan Roberts. LC 74-26958. 1975. 6.95 (ISBN 0-8415-0360-5). Saturday Review Press.

Judas Sheep. Jan Roberts. 1976. (pbk.) 1.75. Bantam Books.

Judas Ship. Brian Callison. LC 78-52330. 1978. 7.95 (ISBN 0-525-13780-7). Dutton.

Judas Spy. Nick Carter. (Nick Carter Ser). (O.s.i.). (Orig.). 1968. pap. 0.60 o.s.i. (A325X, Award). Univ Pub & Dist.

Judas Spy. Nick Carter. (Nick Carter Ser). (O.s.i.). 160p. 1975. pap. 1.25 o.s.i. (AQ1501, Award). Univ Pub & Dist.

Judas Spy. (Nick Carter Ser.). 1978. pap. 1.75 (ISBN 0-441-41295-5, Pub. by Charter Bks). Ace Bks.

Judas Squad. James N. Rowe. LC 77-24114. (Illus.). 8.95 (ISBN 0-316-75972-4). Little, Brown.

Judas Squad. James N. Rowe. (Berkley Book). 1979. 2.25 (ISBN 0-425-03937-4). Berkley Pub. Corp.

Judas Time. Isidor Schneider. LC 47-24163. 1946-1947. The Dial Press.

Judas Tree. Archibald Joseph Cronin. (A novel). 1961. 6.95 o.p. (ISBN 0-316-16162-4). Little.

Judas Tree. Neil Harmon Swanson. LC 33-144042. G. P. Putnam's Sons.

Judas Tree, No. 7. Matthew Braun. 1982. pap. 2.25 (ISBN 0-671-41994-3). PB.

Judas Window. John Dickson Carr. LC 38-2491. 1938. W. Morrow and Company.

Judd & Judd. Nalbro Isadorah Bartley. LC 24-450607. 1924. 2.00. G. P. Putnam's Sons.

Judd for the Defense. Lawrence L. Goldman. (Orig.). 1968. pap. 0.60 o.p. (53-625). Paperback Lib.

Judd Rankin's Daughter. Susan Glaspell. LC 45-85962. 1945. J. B. Lippincott Company.

Jude the Obscure. Thomas Hardy. (Papermac, P57). 1966. pap., 1.50. Macmillan & Co. Ltd.

Jude the Obscure. Thomas Hardy. Ed. by Robert C. Slack. LC 67-18704. (Modern library college editions, T90). 1967. Modern Library.

Jude the Obscure. Thomas Hardy. Ed. by Frank Rodney Southerington. LC 76-140800. (Library of literature). (Illus.). 1972. Bobbs-Merrill.

Jude the Obscure. Thomas Hardy. Ed. by Robert C. Slack. LC 67-18704. (Modern library college editions, T90). 1967. Modern Library.

Jude the Obscure. Thomas Hardy. LC 1-24732. Harper & Brothers.

Jude the Obscure. Thomas Hardy. LC 7-1915. 1896. Harper & Brothers.

Jude the Obscure. Thomas Hardy. LC 24-249909. Harper & Brothers.

Jude the Obscure. Thomas Hardy. LC 28-26468. (Half-title: The Modern library of the world's best books). 1927. The Modern Library.

Jude the Obscure. Thomas Hardy. LC 40-37525. (Half-title: The modern library of the world's best books). The Modern Library.

Jude the Obscure. Thomas Hardy & John Bayley. LC 71-7653. (Illus.). 1969. Limited Editions Club.

Jude the Obscure. the standard ed. of the wessex text of 1912 john paterson, general editor. ed. Thomas Hardy & Hellman, Robert Bechtold, 1906-Ed. LC 66-12790. (Perennial classic, P3062F). 1966. Harper & Row.

Jude the Obscure: An Authoritative Text, Backgrounds and Sources, Criticism. Thomas Hardy. LC 77-14056. (Norton critical edition). (Illus.). 17.50 (ISBN 0-393-04473-4). Norton.

Jude the Obscure. Ed., Introd. by Irving Howe. Thomas Hardy. (Riverside ed., B96). 3.00, 1.25 pap.,. Houghton.

Jude the Obscure. With an Introd. by Carl J. Weber. Thomas Hardy. LC 56-126454. (Harper's modern classics). 1957. Harper.

Jude the Obscure. With an Introd. by Morton Dauwen Zabel. Thomas Hardy. LC 62-17490. (Collier books HS12V). 1962. Collier Books.

Judge. Elia Wilkinson Peattie. (On cover: Globe library, no. 142). 1891. Rand, McNally & Company.

Judge. Rebecca West. LC 22-26985. George H. Doran Company.

Judge: A Novel. Rebecca West. LC 80-27260. (Virago Modern Classic). 6.95 (ISBN 0-8037-3996-6). Dial Press.

Judge and Fool. Vladimir Evgen'Evich Zhabotinskii & Brooks, Cyrus Harry, 1890- Tr. LC 30-376619. H. Liveright.

Judge & His Hangman see Quarry.

Judge and His Hangman; The Quarry: Two Hans Barlach Mysteries. Friedrich Durrenmatt, pseud. LC 82-81347. (Godine double detectives; no. 2). 1983. 7.95 (ISBN 0-87923-437-7). D.R. Godine.

Judge and His Hangman. Translated from the German by Therese Pol. 1st Ed. Friedrich Dürrenmatt. LC 55-80415. 1955. Harper.

Judge and Two Lizzies. Charles T Fullwood. LC 26-20527. Dorrance and Company.

Judge Colt. Archie Joscelyn. LC 47-1388. 1946. Arcadia House, Inc.

Judge Colt. Robert E. Mills. (Kansan Ser.: No. 4). 1981. pap. 1.95 (ISBN 0-8439-0937-4). Nordon Pubns.

Judge Colt... William MacLeod Raine. LC 27-9069. 1927. Doubleday, Page & Company.

Judge Dee at Work. Robert Van Gulik. LC 72-1210. 178p. 1973. 4.95 o.p. (ISBN 0-684-13027-0). Scribner.

Judge Dee at Work: Eight Chinese Detective Stories. Robert Hans Van Gulik, pseud. LC 72-1210. (Illus.). 1973. 4.95 (ISBN 0-684-13027-0). Scribner.

Judge Dee at Work: Eight Chinese Detective Stories. Robert Van Gulik. (Judge Dee Mysteries). 1979. pap. 1.95 (ISBN 0-684-16179-6, SL858, ScribT). Scribner.

Judge Elbridge. Opie Percival Read. LC 99-5537. 1899. Rand, McNally & Co.

Judge Everett's Decree. Jennie Clark Carver. LC 32-17787. Printed by G. H. Shornhorst Co.

Judge Fritznoodle: A Correct Chronicle of the Doings in the German-American Settlement of Prairiestadt, Cabbage Township, Richsoil County, "Out-West," During the Free Soil Period. Martyn W Strouse. LC 9-22745. 1909. The Roxburgh Publishing Company, Incorporated.

Judge Is Reversed. Frances Louise Davis Lockridge & Richard Lockridge. 1975. Repr. of 1960 ed. lib. bdg. 12.05x (ISBN 0-89190-910-9). Am Repr-Rivercity Pr.

Judge Is Reversed; a Mr. and Mrs. North Mystery, by Frances and Richard Lockridge. 1st Ed. Frances Louise Davis Lockridge & Richard Lockridge. LC 60-7854. (Main line mysteries). 1960. Lippincott.

Judge Is Reversed: A Mr. and Mrs. North Mystery. Frances Louise Davis Lockridge & Richard Lockridge. LC 76-214. 1976. (ISBN 0-89190-910-9). Rivercity Press.

Judge Ketchum's Romance. Horace Annesley Vachell. LC 8-319263. J. S. Tait & Sons.

Judge Ladd: A Novel. Noble Smithson. 1900. Ogden Bros. & Co., Printers.

Judge Lynch: A Romance of the California Vineyards. George Henry Jessop. LC 5-41068. Belford, Clarke & Co.; Etc., Etc.

Judge Me Not. John Dann MacDonald. 1978. pap. 2.25 (ISBN 0-449-14057-1, GM). Fawcett.

Judge Not" Or, Hester Powers' Girlhood. Edwin Sheppard. LC 8-5116. 1868. Loring.

Judge Priest Turns Dectective. Irvin Shrewsbury Cobb. LC 37-27212. The Bobbs-Merrill Company.

Judge Priest Turns Detective. Irvin Shrewsbury Cobb. LC 42-111162. 1942. Triangle Books.

Judge Robinson Murdered! Raymond Leslie Goldman. LC 36-1008. Coward-McCann.

Judge Sums up. Joseph Jefferson Farjeon. LC 42-18492. 1942. The Bobbs-Merrill Company.

Judge the Obscure. Thomas Hardy. LC 77-70258. 1977. 2.95 (ISBN 0-312-44661-6). St. Martin's Press.

Judgement: A Novel. Alice Brown. LC 3-23049. 1903. Harper & Brothers.

Judgement Books: A Story. Edward Frederic Benson. LC 3-21952. (Harper's little novels). 1895. Harper & Brothers.

Judgement Day. Nick Sharman. 1982. pap. 2.95 (ISBN 0-451-11450-7, AE1450, Sig). NAL.

Judgement Day at Cooper Globe: Nordon Publications. Keith Wright. (Leisure Book). 1.75 (ISBN 0-8439-0651-0).

Judgement House. Gilbert Parker. LC 24-22233. 1922. Harper & Brothers.

Judgement in St. Peters. Aaron Nathan Rotsstein. 256p. 1981. pap. 2.50 (ISBN 0-445-04651-1). Popular Lib.

Judgement in Stone. Ruth Rendell. LC 77-76961. 6.95 (ISBN 0-385-13223-9). Doubleday.

Judgement in Stone. Ruth Rendell. LC 78-16484. 1978. 10.95 (ISBN 0-8161-6604-8). G. K. Hall.

Judgement of Charis. Gertrude M. Robins Reynolds. LC 22-26761. George H. Doran Company.

Judgement of Deke Hunter. George V. Higgins. LC 76-10215. 8.95 (ISBN 0-316-36081-3). Little, Brown.

Judgement of God. A Romance. Elisabeth Burstenbinder. Tr. by Smith, Mary Stuart (Harrison) & Smith, Gessner Harrison. (On cover: Seaside library. Pocket ed., no. 1154). 1889. G. Munro.

Judgement of Jane. Robert Rudd Whiting. LC 15-19971. 1915. Moffat, Yard and Company.

Judgement of Love. Barbara Cartland. LC 78-13318. 1978. 6.95 (ISBN 0-87272-044-6). Duron Books.

Judgement of Paris. Carleton Kemp Allen. LC 25-6516. 1925. Dodd, Mead and Company.

Judgement of the Sea, Four Novellas. Introd. by Karl Stern. Translated by Isabel and Florence McHugh. Gertrud Von Le Fort. LC 62-9593. H. Regnery Co.

Judgement of the Sword: The Tale of the Kabul Tragedy, and of the Part Played Therein by Major Eldred Pottinger, the Hero of Herat. Katherine Helen Maud Marshall Diver. LC 13-26609. 1913. 1.35. G. P. Putnam's Sons.

Judgement on Deltchev. Eric Ambler. 229p. Repr. of 1951 ed. lib. bdg. 12.05x (ISBN 0-89190-463-8). Am Repr-Rivercity Pr.

Judges' Cave: Being a Romance of the New Haven Colony in the Days of the Regicides, 1661. Harriet Mulford Stone Lothrop. LC 1618. Lothrop Publishing Company.

Judges of Hades & Other Simon Ark Stories. Edward D. Hock. 1974. pap. 0.75 o.p. (LB335). Leisure Bks.

Judges of the Secret Court. David Stacton. LC 61-7451. 1961. Pantheon Books.

Judge's Story. Charles Morgan. LC 47-5859. 1947. Macmillan Co.

Judgment. Mary Rayner Hyman King. LC 11-12710. 1911. Cochrane Publishing Co.

Judgment. Mary Rayner Hyman King. LC 11-19410. 1.20. The Demille Publishing Co.

Judgment: A Novel. Tom Wicker. LC 61-686163. 1961. W. Sloane Association.

Judgment Day. Norman Davey. LC 28-23538. The Bobbs-Merrill Company.

Judgment Day. James Thomas Farrell. LC 35-6055. 1935. The Vanguard Press.

Judgment Day. Penelope Lively. LC 80-2749. 1981. 11.95 (ISBN 0-385-15814-9). Doubleday.

Judgment Day. Richard Sapir & Warren Murphy. (Destroyer, #14). 1974. (pbk.) 1.25 (ISBN 0-523-00303-X). Pinnacle Books.

Judgment Day: A Story of the Seven Years of Great Tribulation. Joshua Hill Foster. LC 10-13917. 1910. 0.75. Baptist World Publishing Company.

Judgment Day: With a New Introd. by the Author. James Thomas Farrell. LC 51-27098. (Signet book, 875. A Signet giant). 1951. New American Library.

Judgment Day. 1st Ed. Thomas Chastain. LC 62-7611. 1962. Doubleday.

Judgment House. Gilbert Parker. LC 13-5686. 1913. Harper & Brothers.

Judgment in St. Peter's. Aaron Nathan Rotsstein. LC 79-16951. 9.95 (ISBN 0-399-12444-6). Putnam.

Judgment Night. Donald Honig. (Orig.). 1971. pap. 0.95 o.p. (B95-2127). Belmont-Tower.

Judgment Night: A Selection of Science Fiction. Catherine L Moore. LC 53-1769. 1952. Gnome Press.

Judgment of Borso: A Little Novel of Ferrara. Maurice Henry Hewlett. LC 99-1848. 1899. The Macmillan Company.

Judgment of Dragons. Phyllis Bloom Gotlieb. LC 79-22295. 1980. 10.95 (ISBN 0-399-12469-1). Berkley Pub. Corp.: Distributed by Putnam.

Judgment of Eve. May Sinclair. LC 8-9176. 1908. Harper & Brothers.

Judgment of Eve: A Novel of Human Inquiry. Edgar Pangborn. LC 66-20255. 1966. Simon and Schuster.

Judgment of Helen. Thomas Cobb. LC 39. 1899. John Lane.

Judgment of Paris. Gore Vidal. LC 65-16900. 1965. 4.75. Little.

Judgment of Paris. Gore Vidal. LC 52-5296. 1952. Dutton.

Judgment of Peace: A Novel. Adolf Andreas Latzko. Tr. by Lewisohn, Ludwig. LC 20-1372. 1919. Boni and Liveright.

Judgment of the Storm. Roy Mason & Middleton, Ethel Styles. LC 24-1648. 1923. Doubleday, Page & Company.

Judgment on Deltchev. 1st Ed. Eric Ambler. LC 51-1927. 1951. Knopf.

Judgment on Janus. Alice Mary Norton. LC 63-16035. 1963. Harcourt, Brace & World.

Judgments of the Sea: And Other Stories. Ralph Delahaye Paine. LC 12-11153. 1912. Sturgis & Walton Company.

Judicial Body. 1st Ed. Margaret Scherf. LC 57-10464. 1957. Published for the Crime Club by Doubleday.

Judicial Committee of the Privy Council, 1833-1876, Its Origins, Structure, and Development. Peter Anthony Howell. LC 78-54326. (Cambridge Studies in English Legal History). 1979. 29.50 (ISBN 0-521-22146-3). Cambridge University Press.

Judith. Arnold Bennett. LC 74-5397. (Collected Works of Arnold Bennett: Vol. 42). 1976. Repr. of 1919 ed. 14.75 (ISBN 0-518-19123-0). Ayer Co.

Judith. Brian Talbot Cleeve. LC 78-5781. 9.95 (ISBN 0-698-10910-4). Coward, McCann & Geoghegan.

Judith. Brian Talbot Cleeve. (Berkley book). 1979. 2.25 (ISBN 0-425-04168-9). Berkley Pub. Corp.

Judith. James Thomas Farrell. 1978. pap. 2.25 (ISBN 0-532-22113-3). Woodhill.

Judith. Albert Kantof. (Dell book). 1978. 1.95 (ISBN 0-440-14465-5). Dell Pub. Co.

Judith. Betty Neels. (Harlequin Romances Ser.). 192p. 1982. pap. 1.50 (ISBN 0-373-02500-9). Harlequin Bks.

Judith. Aritha Van Herk. LC 78-60696. 8.95 (ISBN 0-316-89696-9). Little, Brown.

Judith. Janet Payne Whitney. LC 43-15355. 1943. W. Morrow & Company.

Judith. Stella Wilchek. LC 69-17287. (Illus.). 1969. 6.95. Harper & Row.

Judith: a Chronicle of Old Virginia. Mary Virginia Terhune. ("Our continent" library. v. 5). 1883. Our Continent Publishing Co.

Judith: A Novel. Emily Graham Butcher. LC 44-63123. 1944. Chapman & Grimes, Inc.

Judith, a Story of the Candle-Lit Fifties. Grace Alexander. LC 6-7399. 1906. The Bobbs-Merrill Company.

Judith, and Other Stories. James Thomas Farrell. LC 70-180073. 1973. 7.95 (ISBN 0-385-04819-X). Doubleday.

Judith Carson: Or, Which Was the Heiress? William Henry Platt. LC 41-31134. 1887. E. R. Andrews.

Judith: Dictated by Spirit Control Through Marie Corelli. Blanche A Draper & Marie Coreill. LC 50-2901. 1950. Christopher Pub. House.

Judith, Dictated by Spirit Control Through Marie Corelli: By Blanche A. Draper Pseud. Blanche A Webb & Marie Coreill. LC 50-2901. 1950. Christopher Pub. House.

Judith Duchesne: A Novel. Lynda Sargent. LC 79-14294. 8.95 (ISBN 0-517-53905-5). Crown Publishers.

Judith Mc Nair. Laeta Marion Ramage. LC 7-145852. 1907. Broadway Publishing Co.

Judith Madrier: A Novel. Henri Troyat & Whitall, James, 1888- Tr. LC 41-9279. I. Washburn, Inc.

Judith of Blue Lake Ranch. Jackson Gregory. LC 19-8467. 1919. C. Scribner's Sons.

Judith of the Cumberlands. Alice MacGowan. LC 8-283144. 1908. G. P. Putnam's Sons.

Judith of the Godless Valley. Honore McCue Willsie Morrow. LC 22-167603. Frederick A. Stokes Company.

Judith of the Plains: A Novel. Marie Manning. LC 3-26877. 1903. Harper & Brothers.

Judith Paris. Hugh Walpole. 1972. pap. 1.25 o.p. (01029). Curtis.

Judith Paris: A Novel. Hugh Walpole. LC 31-28166. 1931. Doubleday, Doran & Company, Inc.

Judith Shakespeare... William Black. (Seaside library. Pocket ed. no. 265). G. Munro.

Judith Shakespeare. by william black. ed. William Black. (Lovell's library. v. 9, no. 456). J. W. Lovell Company.

Judith Shakespeare: Her Love Affairs and Other Adventures. illustrated by e. a. abbey. ed. William Black. LC 4-15286. 1884. Harper & Brothers.

Judith Silver... Hector Bolitho. LC 29-7073. 1929. A. A. Knopf.

Judith, the Daughter of Judas. A Tale. Margaret E O'Brien. LC 7-33161. 1891. J. B. Lippincott Company.

Judith Trachtenberg: A Novel. Karl Emil Franzos. Tr. by Lewis, L. P. LC 6-43158. (On cover: Harper's Franklin square library, no. 707). 1891. Harper & Brothers.

Judith Triumphant. Thompson Buchanan. LC 5-10539. 1905. Harper & Brothers.

Judith Wynne. A Novel. Catharine Louisa Pirkis. (On cover: The seaside library. Pocket ed. no. 332). 1885. G. Munro.

Judith's Garden. Mary E. Stone Bassett. LC 2-15213. 1902. Lothrop Publishing Company.

Judith's Journal. Janie Prichard Duggan. LC 6-34631. 1895. American Baptist Publication Society.

Judson Murder Case. Earl Augustus Aldrich. LC 33-54812. E. J. Clode, Inc.

Judy. Elizabeth Carfrae, pseud. LC 41-1054. G. P. Putnam's Sons.

Judy. Lewis Nachod. LC 39-11750. Gramercy Publishing Co.

Judy: A Remembrance. David Melton. (Stanyan Books Ser). 1972. 3.00 o.p. (ISBN 0-394-48062-7). Random.

Judy: A Story of Divine Corners. Faith Baldwin. 1976. Repr. of 1930 ed. lib. bdg. 14.40x (ISBN 0-88411-619-0). Amereon Ltd.

Judy and the Angel. Edith L Gibson. LC 42-3379. 1942. Burton Publishing Company.

Judy George, Student Nurse. Pattie Wright Stone. pap. 0.50 o.p. (52-441). Paperback Lib.

Judy's Man. Helen R. Bamberger. LC 26-7342. 1926. The Enn Publishing Company.

Juell Demming: A Story. Albert Lathrop Lawrence. LC 1-23041. 1901. A. C. McClurg & Co.

Jug Night. Robert Malstrom & Michel Orceyre. LC 73-4862. 1973. 6.95 (ISBN 0-15-146500-2). Harcourt Brace Jovanovich.
Jug-or-Not. Julia MacNair Wright. LC 9-539. 1870. National Temperance Society and Publication House.
Jugger. Richard Stark. LC 66-3827. (Pocket books, 50149). 1965. Pocket Books.
Jugger, a Novel. Sterling Quinlan. LC 60-11697. 1960. McDowell, Obolensky.
Juggernaut. Alice Ormond Campbell. LC 28-234635. 1928. Pub. for the Crime Club, Inc., by Doubleday, Doran & Company, Inc.
Juggernaut. Heinrich Muller. (Orig.). 1981. pap. 2.75 (ISBN 0-89083-854-2). Zebra.
Juggernaut: A Veiled Record. George Cary Eggleston. LC 6-37561. 1891. Fords, Howard, & Hulbert.
Juggernaut: A Veiled Record. George Cary Eggleston & Bacon, Mrs. Mary Schell (Hoke) 1870- Joint Author. LC 3-8561. 1903. Lothrop Publishing Company.
Juggernaut of the Moderns: A Novel. Rosa Hudspeth. LC 7-5642. 1896. Arena Publishing Company.
Juggler: A Story. Mary Noailles Murfree. LC 7-31837. 1897. Houghton, Mifflin and Company.
Juggler. 1st Ed. Michael Blankfort. LC 52-5011. 1952. Little, Brown.
Jugglers. Ezra Selig Brudno. LC 20-214809. 1920. Moffat, Yard & Company.
Jugglers: A Story. Molly Elliot Seawell. LC 11-26411. 1911. 1.00. The Macmillan Company.
Juggler's Kiss. Manuel Komroff. LC 27-24348. 1927. Boni and Liveright.
Juice: A Novel. Stephen D Becker. LC 58-11809. 1958. Simon and Schuster.
Juice of the Lemon Is Sour. Mitzie Shodo. 1970. 3.75 o.p. Vantage.
Juice of the Pomegranate. Ethel May Dell. LC 38-94265. 1938.
Juices of Lust. Valorie Smyth-Jones. 192p. pap. 1.95 o.p. (6088). Brandon.
Juju-Man. Armstrong Livingston & Griffiths, Thomas H. LC 27-16677. 1926. Siebel Publishing Corporation.
Julanar the Lioness. John Cleve. (Crusader). (Dell-Grove book: Vol. 3). 1975. (pbk.) 1.50. Dell.
Jule. George Wylie Henderson. LC 46-6709. 1946. Creative Age Press, Inc.
Jule Maghee's Anarchy. Celia Anderson. LC 6-2449. 1892.
Juleps and Clover. M. Vaughan Wilde. LC 8-37025. R. F. Fenno & Company.
Jules & Jim. Henri-Pierre Roche. 240p. 1980. pap. 2.75 (ISBN 0-380-00024-5, 52399, Bard). Avon.
Jules & Jim. Henri-Pierre Roche. 240p. 1981. 12.95 (ISBN 0-7145-0322-3, Pub. by M Boyars). Merrimack Pub Cir.
Jules Verne, Master of Science Fiction. Jules Verne. Ed. by Idriayn Oliver Evans. LC 58-1092. Rinehart.
Jules Verne Omnibus: Twenty Thousand Leagues Under the Sea, Around the World in Eighty Days, The Blockade Runners, from the Earth to the Moon, 4 Vols in 1. Jules Verne. 1951. 7.95 o.p. (ISBN 0-397-00031-6). Lippincott.
Juletty: A Story of Old Kentucky. Lucy Cleaver McElroy. LC 1-31641. T. Y. Crowell & Co.
Julia.". Hornblower. LC 7-5197. 1859. R. Carter & Brothers.
Julia. Betsey Riddle Hutten Zum Stolzenberg. LC 24-30856. George H. Doran Company.
Julia. Barbara Riefe. LC 81-83496. (Shackleford Legacy Ser.). 352p. (Orig.). 1982. pap. 2.95 (ISBN 0-86721-029-X). Playboy Pbks.
Julia: A Novel. Helen Maria Williams. LC 73-22212. (Feminist Controversy in England, 1788-1810). 1974. (2 vols.) 44.00 (ISBN 0-8240-0887-1). Garland Pub.
Julia & the Bazooka. Anna Kavan. 1975. 6.95 o.p. (ISBN 0-394-49445-8). Knopf.
Julia and the Bazooka, and Other Stories. Helen Woods Edmonds. LC 74-21336. 1975. (ISBN 0-394-49445-8). Knopf: Distributed by Random House.
Julia & the Illuminated Baron. Sally S. Wood. LC 71-93671. (American Fiction Ser). 1970. lib. bdg. 14.75 o.s.i. (ISBN 0-512-00742-X). Garrett Pr.
Julia Bride. Henry James. LC 9-24962. 1909. Harper & Brothers.
Julia Bride see Altar of the Dead.
Julia Comes Home. Elizabeth Fair. LC 54-9732. 1954. Funk & Wagnalls.
Julia de Roubigigne, 2 vols. Henry MacKenzie. Ed. by Ronald Paulson. LC 78-60840. (Novel 1720-1805 Ser.). (O.s.i.: Vol. 7). 1979. Set. lib. bdg. write for info. o.s.i. (ISBN 0-8240-3656-5); lib. bdg. 50.00 ea. o.s.i. Garland Pub.
Julia De Roubigne. Henry Mackenzie. LC 76-25570. (Mackenzie, Henry, 1745-1831. The Novels of Henry Mackenzie). (novels of Henry Mackenzie). ((Series: Mackenzie, Henry, 1745-1831.). (novels of Henry Mckenzie.). (Illus.). 1976. 16.25(65.00 set) (ISBN 0-404-04094-2). AMS Press.
Julia De Roubigne. Henry Mackenzie. LC 78-60840. (Novel, 1720-1805: 7). 1979. 56.00 (ISBN 0-8240-3656-5). Garland Pub.
Julia de Roubigne see Novels of Henry Mackenzie.
Julia France and Her Times. Gertrude Franklin Horn Atherton. LC 12-9188. 1912. 1.35. The Macmillan Company.
Julia Gwynn: An American Gothic Tale. Robert K Marshall. LC 51-10424. 1952. Duell, Sloan and Pearce.
Julia Harrington. Richard Bissell. (A novel). 1969. 7.95 o.p. (ISBN 0-316-09673-3). Little.
Julia in Ireland. Ann Bridge, pseud. LC 72-13049. 264p. 1973. 7.95 o.p. (ISBN 0-07-007736-3). McGraw.
Julia in Ireland. Mary Dolling Sanders O'Malley. LC 72-13049. 1973. 7.95 (ISBN 0-07-007736-3). McGraw-Hill.
Julia Involved: Three Julia Probyn Novels: the Light-Hearted Quest, The Portuguese Escape and The Numbered Account. Mary Dolling Sanders O'Malley. LC 62-17639. 1962. McGraw-Hill.
Julia: Or, Sister Agnes. John W Vahey. LC 8-31922. 1875. Bray Bro's Western Catholic Publishing House.
Julia Ormond: Or, The New Settlement. Mary Hughs. LC 7-5413. (Half-title: Dunigan's home library. no. vii). 1846. E. Dunigan.
Julia Takes Her Chance. Concordia Merrel. LC 21-188929. 1921. T. Seltzer.
Julia Valeria, a Story of Ancient Rome: Illustrated by Bruno Frost. Elizabeth Gale. LC 51-10261. 1951. Putnam.
Julian. Gore Vidal. LC 64-15048. 1970. Repr. of 1964 ed. 3.95 o.s.i. (ISBN 0-394-60395-8, M395). Modern Lib.
Julian: A Novel. Gore Vidal. LC 76-10593. (Illus.). 1977. 1.95 (ISBN 0-394-72101-2). Vintage Books.
Julian: A Vovel. Gore Vidal. LC 64-15048. 1964. Little, Brown.
Julian Grant Loses His Way. Claude Houghton Oldfield. LC 33-24533. 1933. Doubleday, Doran & Company, Inc.
Julian Grenfell. Nicholas Mosley. LC 76-4720. 1976. 12.95 o.p. (ISBN 0-03-017596-8). HR&W.
Julian Home. A Tale of College Life. Frederic William Farrar. LC 6-38659. (On cover: The college library). W. L. Allison Co.
Julian Karslake's Secret. A Novel. Mary Anna Lupton Needell. (seaside library. v. 56, no. 1146). 1882. G. Munro.
Julian: Or Scenes in Judea. William Ware. LC 8-360246. 1841. C. S. Francis.
Julian: Or, Scenes in Judea. 2d ed. William Ware. LC 24-28539. 1865. J. Miller.
Julian: Or, Scenes in Judea. William Ware. 1870. J. Miller.
Julian: Or, Scenes in Judea. William Ware. LC 8-360239. 1874. J. Miller.
Julian: Or, Scenes in Judea. William Ware. LC 78-100318. (America and the Holy Land). 1977. 40.00 (ISBN 0-405-10220-8). Arno Press.
Julian: Or, Scenes in Judes. William Ware. LC 41-42132. T. R. Knox & Co.
Julian the Apostate. Dmitrii Sergieevich Merezhkovskil. Tr. by Johnston, Charles. LC 1-20283. H. Altemus.
Julian the Apostate: The Death of the Gods. Dmitril Sergieevich Merezhkovskil. Tr. by Guerney, Bernard Guilbert. LC 29-26505. (Half-title: The Modern library of the world's best books). The Modern Library.
Julie. Jane Kesner Morris Ardmore. LC 52-6011. 1952. McGraw-Hill.
Julie. Ruth Babcock. LC 47-30659. 1947. Coward-McCann.
Julie. John Benton. LC 80-20010. 2.50 (ISBN 0-8007-8399-9). F. H. Revell Co.
Julie. Jay Brothers. LC 73-13225. 1974. 6.95 (ISBN 0-672-51903-8). Bobbs-Merrill.
Julie. Bernard Frizell. 1960. 4.50 o.p. S&S.
Julie. Preston Harriman. pap. 1.95 o.p. (ISBN 0-87056-240-1, 6240). Brandon.
Julie. Jane Kesner Morris. LC 52-6011. 1952. McGraw-Hill.
Julie. Francis Stuart. LC 38-128333. 1938. A. A. Knopf.
Julie Cane. Harvey Jerrold O'Higgins. 1924. Harper & Brothers.
Julie Morrow. Sophia Belzer Engstrand. LC 42-500769. 1942. The Dial Press.
Julien Ware. Guthrie Wilson. LC 52-5273. 1952. Putnam.
Julie's Girl. Vivian Donald, pseud. (Signet Book). 1978. 1.50. New American Library.
Juliet Dies Twice. Lange Lewis. LC 43-2514. 1943. The Bobbs-Merrill Company.
Juliet in Mantua. Robert Nathan. 1966. 4.50 o.p. (ISBN 0-394-40605-2). Knopf.
Juliet, Inc. Louise Platt Hauck. LC 39-416627. The Penn Publishing Company.
Juliet Is Twenty. Jane Ludlow Drake Abbott. LC 26-121468. 1926. J. B. Lippincott Company.
Juliet Room. Gimone Hall. 1977. pap. 1.25 (ISBN 0-532-12510-X). Woodhill.
Juliet Room. Gimone Hall. (Manor gothic). 1974. (pbk.) 0.95. Manor Books.
Julietta. Louise De Vilmorin. LC 54-10597. 1954. J. Messner.
Juliette. Donatien Alphonse Francois Sade. Tr. by Austryn Wainhouse from Fr. 1968. pap. 14.95 (ISBN 0-394-17131-4, E676, Ever). Grove.
Juliette. Donatien Alphonse Francois Sade. 1969. pap. 1.25 o.p. (78-621). Lancer.
Juliette. Donatien Alphonse Francois Sade. Tr. by Austryn Wainhouse. 1968. 17.50 o.p. (ISBN 0-394-47510-0, GP444). Grove.
Juliette De Sade. Maude Poiret. (O.s.i.). (Orig.). 1970. pap. 0.75 o.s.i. (A618S, Award). Univ Pub & Dist.
Juliette Irving and the Jesuit: A Novel. Thomas Robinson Warren. LC 11-7149. 1895. J. Heidingsled.
Juliette: Or, Now and Forever. Harriette Newell Woods Baker. LC 6-6881. (Half-title: Home life series, v. 4). 1869. Lee and Shepard.
Juliette: Or, Sunstroke. Pierre Viallet. LC 76-56393. 1977. 1.75 (ISBN 0-345-25250-0). Ballantine Books.
Julio Jurenito. Ilia Grigorevich Ehrenburg. LC 76-9856. 1976. 17.25 (ISBN 0-8371-8889-X). Greenwood Press.
Julius: A Novel. Harold Begbie. LC 27-190270. George H. Doran Company.
Julius, and Other Tales from the German. Ed. by William Henry Furness. Toepffer, Rodolphe & Zschokke, Heinrich. LC 6-44567. 1856. Parry & McMillan.
Julius Caesar Is Alive & Well. Irving A. Greenfield. 1977. pap. 1.95 (ISBN 0-532-19160-9). Woodhill.
Julius Caesar Murder Case. Wallace Irwin. LC 35-3211. 1935. D. Appleton-Century Company, Incorporated.
Julius Le Vallon: An Episode. Algernon Blackwood. LC 16-14281. 1916. Cassell and Company, Ltd.
Julius Le Vallon: An Episode. Algernon Blackwood. LC 16-155071. 1916. E. P. Dutton & Company.
July Book. Theodore Enslin. (Illus.). 1976. pap. 3.50. Sand Dollar.
July's People. Nadine Gordimer. LC 80-24877. 1981. 10.95 (ISBN 0-670-41048-9). Viking Press.
July's People. Nadine Gordimer. LC 82-376. 1982. 3.95 (ISBN 0-14-006140-1). Penguin Books.
Jumbee and Other Uncanny Tales. Henry St. Clair Whitehead. LC 44-8799. 1944. Arkham House.
Jumble: That Scrambled Word Game, No. 19. Henri Arnold & Bob Lee. (Orig.). 1981. pap. 1.95 (ISBN 0-451-12170-8, AJ2170, Sig). NAL.
Jumbo, Giant Circus Elephant. Justin Denzel. LC 72-9349. (Famous animal stories). (Illus.). 1973. 2.98 (ISBN 0-8116-4850-8). Garrard Pub. Co.
Jumeau Doll. Margaret Whitton. LC 80-65737. (Illus.). 96p. (Orig.). 1981. pap. 6.00 (ISBN 0-486-23954-3). Dover.
Jument Verte. Marcel Ayme. (Illus.). deluxe ed. 61.25. French & Eur.
Jump. Richard Wheelwright. (Orig.). 1971. pap. 0.75 o.p. (ISBN 0-446-64728-4, 64-728). Paperback Lib.
Jump Cut: A Novel. R. R Irvine. 1974. (pbk.) 0.95. Popular Library.
Jump for Glory. Gordon McDonell. LC 37-1522. Green Circle Books.
Jumper Time. Kate Wilhem. 1980. pap. 2.75 (ISBN 0-671-83336-7, Timescape). PB.
Jumping Frog. Samuel Langhorne Clemens. (Classics Ser.). slip case 2.95 o.p. (ISBN 0-442-82511-0). Peter Pauper.
Jumping Frog. Mark Twain. (Illus.). 4.50 o.p. (ISBN 0-8446-0278-7). Peter Smith.
Jumping Frog in English: Then in French, Then Clawed Back into a Civilized Language Once More by Patient, Unremunerated Toil. Samuel Langhorne Clemens. LC 79-142286. (Illus.). 1971. 1.25 (ISBN 0-486-22686-7). Dover Publications.
Jumping Frog: In English, Then in French, Then Clawed Back into a Civilized Language Once More by Patient, Unremunerated Toil. Samuel Langhorne Clemens. LC 3-29612. 1903. Harper & Brothers.
Jumping Judas. Solon Doggett. (Solon Doggett's novels). 1896. B. B. Russell.
Jumping Jupiter. Ernestine Moller Gilbreth Carey. LC 52-6915. 1952. Crowell.
Jumping Meridians. Linton Wells & Jorgensen, Nels Leroy, Joint Author. LC 26-17287. 1926. Doubleday, Page & Company.
Jumping off Place. Garet Rogers. LC 61-155072. 1962. Dial Press.
Jumping-off Place. Ethel Shackelford. LC 13-10664. George H. Doran Company.
Jumping-off Place: Stories. Baine Kerr. LC 80-14023. (Breakthrough book; no. 33). 1981. 11.00 (ISBN 0-8262-0311-6). University of Missouri Press.
Junction. Jack Dann. (Orig.). 1981. pap. 2.50 (ISBN 0-440-14416-7). Dell.
June. Edith Barnard Delano. LC 16-183323. 1916. 1.25. Houghton Mifflin Company.
June: A Love Story. Mrs. Bridges. (On cover: Lovell's library, v. 18, no. 865). 1887. J. W. Lovell Company.
June Again. Thurman McCormick. 1970. 7.50 o.p. Vantage.
June Gold. Waldron Baily. LC 23-7010. W. J. Watt & Company.
June Jeopardy. Inez Haynes Irwin. LC 8-17784. 1908. B. W. Huebsch.
June, Moon, and Murder. Charlotte Murray Russell, pseud. LC 52-11621. 1952. Published for the Crime Club by Doubleday.
June of the Cabins. An Milford. LC 19-14015. Saulsbury Publishing Company.
June of the Hills: The Junaluska Prize Novel, a Story of the Southern Mountains with Lake Junaluska, N.C., As the Center of Action. David English Camak.
June Romance. Norman Rowland Gale. LC 45-26354. Stone & Kimball.
June Romance. Norman Rowland Gale. LC 99-2535. (Half-title: Blue cloth books). 1899. H. S. Stone & Company.
June Thirtieth, June Thirtieth. Richard Brautigan. (O.s.i.). 1977. 6.95 o.s.i. (ISBN 0-440-04295-X, Sey Lawr). Delacorte.
June Walters: By Gay Rutherford Pseud. James Noble Fifford. LC 56-124596. 1956. Arcadia House.
Jungle. Charity Blackstock. 1974. (pbk.) 1.25 (ISBN 0-380-00009-1). Avon.
Jungle. Michael Brett, pseud. 1976. 1.50. Dell.
Jungle. James Hiner. LC 68-56912. 4.95. Olivant Press.
Jungle. Upton Beall Sinclair. LC 65-29805. 1965. Printed for the Members of the Limited Editions Club, by the Garamond Press.
Jungle. Upton Beall Sinclair. LC 79-151835. 1971. (ISBN 0-8376-0400-1). R. Bentley.
Jungle. Upton Beall Sinclair. LC 6-6264. 1906. Doubleday Page & Company.
Jungle. Upton Beall Sinclair. LC 26-163656. 1926. Vanguard Press.
Jungle. Upton Beall Sinclair. LC 27-214082. 1927. Vanguard Press.
Jungle. Upton Beall Sinclair. LC 46-25296. 1946. The Viking Press.
Jungle. Ursula Torday. LC 70-172625. 1972. 6.95. Coward, McCann & Geoghegan.
Jungle. Robert Westerby. LC 77-95384. 1969. 4.95. Nash Pub. Corp.
Jungle & Backyard. M. Krishnan. (Illus.). 148p. 1961. bds. 1.85x o.p. (ISBN 0-88253-329-0). InterCulture.
Jungle Antagonist. Diana Gair. (Harlequin Romances Ser.). 192p. 1983. pap. 1.50 (ISBN 0-373-02530-0). Harlequin Bks.
Jungle Blitz. Lionel Derrick, pseud. (Penetrator Ser.: No. 48). 192p. (Orig.). 1983. pap. 2.25 (ISBN 0-523-41680-6). Pinnacle Bks.
Jungle Born. John Seymour Eyton. LC 25-6699. 2.00. The Century Co.
Jungle Captive. Edith Maude Hull. LC 39-17648. 1939. Dood, Mead & Company.
Jungle Fever. Marcus Van Heller, pseud. pap. 1.95 o.s.i. (OPH-251, Ophelia). Olympia.
Jungle Fire: A Novel, by Bruce Porterfield. Bruce E Porterfield. LC 67-17234. 1967. 2.50. Zondervan.
Jungle Girl. Edgar Rice Burroughs. LC 32-108363. E. R. Burroughs, Inc.
Jungle Girl. Gordon Casserly. LC 22-19056. E. J. Clode.
Jungle Gold. Rex Ellingwood Beach. LC 35-13166. Farrar & Rinehart, Incorporated.
Jungle Gold. Harold Bindloss. LC 32-29207. 1932. Frederick A. Stokes Company.
Jungle Harvest. Tom Gill. LC 43-4271. 1943. G. P. Putnam's Sons.
Jungle Holiday. Alice W. Hesse. 112p. 1983. 7.00 (ISBN 0-682-49979-X). Exposition.
Jungle. Illus. by Fletcher Martin. New Pref. by the Author. Upton Beall Sinclair. 1966. 6.95. Heritage Pr. Dist. Dial.
Jungle Jest. Talbot Mundy. LC 32-192696. 2.00. The Century Co.
Jungle John: A Book of the Big-Game Jungles. John Austin Budden. LC 27-18477. 1927. 2.50. Longmans, Green and Co., Ltd.
Jungle Kids: A Collection of Stories. Evan Hunter. (Pocket book 1126. Fiction 6). 1956. Pocket Books.
Jungle Love. Louise Gerard. LC 25-836414. The Macaulay Company.
Jungle Lovers. Paul Theroux. LC 70-144074. 1971. 5.95 (ISBN 0-395-12107-8). Houghton Mifflin.
Jungle Maid: A Story of Adventure. John H Warner. LC 52-5709. 1952. Exposition Press.
Jungle Menace: Starring Frank Buck. Noel Sainsbury. LC 38-380573. Cupples & Leon Company.
Jungle Nurse. Polly Mark, pseud. (YA) 1981. 6.95 (Avalon). Bouregy.

Jungle of Desire. Antoinette Beaudry. 352p. (Orig.). 1982. pap. 2.95 (ISBN 0-523-41401-3). Pinnacle Bks.
Jungle of Stars. Jack L Chalker. LC 76-15209. 1976. 1.50 (ISBN 0-345-25457-0). Ballantine Books.
Jungle Patrol. Erik A. Lindgren. 3.50 o.p. Vantage.
Jungle Seas. Arthur Ainsley Ageton. LC 54-5786. 1954. Random House.
Jungle Tales: Adventures in India. Howard Anderson Musser. LC 22-14720. 1.50. George H. Doran Company.
Jungle Tales of Tarzan. Edgar Rice Burroughs. LC 19-5696. 1919. 1.40. A. C. McClurg & Co.
Jungle Tales of Tarzan. Edgar Rice Burroughs. LC 21-13697. 1919. Grosset & Dunlap.
Jungle Tales of Tarzan, No. 6. Edgar Rice Burroughs. 192p. 1975. pap. 1.95 (ISBN 0-345-29478-5). Ballantine.
Jungle Terror. Harvey Wickham. LC 20-7289. 1920. Doubleday, Page & Company.
Jungle: With an Introd. by John Fischer. Upton Beall Sinclair. LC 51-6236. (Harper's modern classics). 1951. Harper.
Juniata Valley. Virginia Cassel. LC 80-25173. 1981. 13.95 (ISBN 0-670-41085-3). Viking Press.
Junie's Love-Test. Laura Jean Libbey. (On cover: The library of American authors, no. 11). 1889. G. Munro.
Junior Bachelor Society. John Alfred Williams. LC 75-32297. 1976. 7.95 (ISBN 0-385-09455-8). Doubleday.
Junior League Murders: By Claudia Canyon Pseud. Betty Anderson. LC 54-5840. 1954. Arcadia House.
Junior Miss. Sally Benson. LC 41-517721. Random House.
Junior Officer of the Watch: By Rufus Fairchild Zogbaum; Illustrated by the Author. Rufus Fairchild Zogbaum. LC 8-10434. 1908. D. Appleton and Company.
Junior Partners. Abel M Rawson. LC 8-596. 1891. J. Stuart & Company.
Junior Prom Girl. Georgia Craig. (Contemporary Teens Ser.). 224p. (Orig.). 1981. pap. 2.25 (ISBN 0-89531-138-0, 0146-96). Sharon Pubns.
Junior Science Book of Beavers. Alexander L Crosby. (Junior science books). 1962. Grosset & Dunlap.
Junior Trophy. Ralph Henry Barbour. LC 13-6769. 1913. D. Appleton and Company.
Juniper Green. John Keir Cross. LC 53-5125. 1953. Dial Press.
Juniper Hill. Dorothy Daniels. (O.s.i.). 1976. pap. 1.50 o.s.i. (ISBN 0-671-80807-9). WSP.
Juniper Hill. Dorothy Daniels (ISBN 0-671-80807-9). Pocket Books.
Juniper Hill. Marian Winnek. LC 32-288307. The Bobbs-Merrill Company.
Juniper Island. Charles H Knickerbocker. LC 58-9878. 1958. Random House.
Juniper Loa. Lin Yutang. LC 63-18745. 1963. World Pub. Co.
Juniper Loa. Lin Yutang. 251p. 1980. 4.95 (ISBN 0-89955-167-X, Pub. by Mei Ya China); pap. 3.95 (ISBN 0-89955-196-3). Intl Schol Bk Serv.
Juniper Time. Kate Wilhelm. 1980. 2.50 (ISBN 0-671-83336-7). Pocket Books.
Juniper Time: A Novel. Kate Wilhelm. LC 78-22447. 9.95 (ISBN 0-06-014657-5). Harper & Row.
Juniper Tree. Faith Baldwin Cuthrell. LC 52-8736. 1952. Rinehart.
Junipero Serra, Pioneer of the Cross. Bernice Scott. LC 75-27785. (Illus.). 1976. 8.95 (ISBN 0-913548-32-4). Valley Publishers.
Junk Pusher. Robert W Taylor. LC 54-331681. (Pyramid books, 126). 1954. Pyramid Books.
Junkers. Piers Paul Read. LC 69-10684. 1975. (pbk.) 1.75. Avon.
Junketeers. I. G Broat. (Kangaroo Book). 1978. 1.95 (ISBN 0-671-81802-3). Pocket Books.
Junky. William S. Burroughs. 1977. pap. 3.50 (ISBN 0-14-004351-9). Penguin.
Juno's Adventure: Antics of an Airedale; a Story. 1st. ed. Dorothy Green. (Illus.). 1974. 3.50 (ISBN 0-682-48005-3). Exposition.
Juny: Or, Only One Girl's Story. A Romance of the Society Crust--Upper and Under. Thomas Cooper De Leon. LC 6-34186. 1890. The Gossip Printing Company.
Jupiter. Carol Pohl. Ed. by Frederik Pohl. 1973. (pbk.) 1.25 (ISBN 0-345-23662-9). Ballantine Books.
Jupiter Crisis. William Harrington. LC 79-165086. 1971. 6.95. McKay.
Jupiter Experiment. Margaret Moon & Maurine. 250p. 1976. pap. 1.95 (ISBN 0-87542-498-8). Llewellyn Pubns.
Jupiter Lights: A Novel. Constance Fenimore Woolson. LC 72-137309. 1971. (ISBN 0-404-07037-X). AMS Press.
Jupiter Lights: A Novel. Constance Fenimore Woolson. LC 8-37229. 1889. Harper & Brothers.
Jupiter Lights, a Novel. Constance Fenimore Woolson. 1971. Repr. of 1889 ed. 17.00 o.p. Scholarly.
Jupiter Plague. Harry Harrison. 288p. (Orig.). 1982. pap. 2.95 (ISBN 0-523-48540-9). Pinnacle Bks.
Jupiter Project. Gregory Benford. LC 75-17913. 1975. 6.95 (ISBN 0-8407-6456-1). T. Nelson.
Jupiter Theft. Donald Moffitt. LC 77-6131. 1977. 1.95 (ISBN 0-345-25505-4). Ballantine Books.
Jupiter's Daughters: A Novel. Henrietta Camilla Jackson Jenkin. LC 28-1647. (Leisure hour series). 1874. H. Holt and Company.
Jupiter's Travels. Ted Simon. 360p. 1981. pap. 4.95 (ISBN 0-14-005410-3). Penguin.
Jurgen. James B. Cabell. (Xanadu Library). pap. 1.45 o.p. Crown.
Jurgen: A Comedy of Justice. James Branch Cabell. LC 19-14946. 1919. R. M. McBride & Co.
Jurgen: A Comedy of Justice. James Branch Cabell. LC 24-27962. 1922. R. M. McBride & Company.
Jurgen: A Comedy of Justice. James Branch Cabell. LC 34-23085. (Half-title: The modern library of the world's best books). The Modern Library.
Juror. John Michael Evelyn. LC 74-83585. 1975. 6.95. St. Martin's Press.
Juror. Michael Underwood. LC 74-83585. 1975. 6.95 o.p. (ISBN 0-312-44905-4). St Martin.
Juror: A Novel. Harvey Jacobs. LC 80-16261. 1980. 8.95 (ISBN 0-531-09932-6). F. Watts.
Juror No. 17. Charles Carey Waddel. LC 31-925516. A. H. King.
Jurors. Benjamin Siegel. 1974. (pbk.) 1.50. Dell.
Jurors: A Novel. Benjamin Siegel. LC 72-13688. 1973. 6.95. Delacorte Press.
Jursen with Wings. Adelaide Humphries. LC 53-12923. 1953. Arcadia House.
Jury. Gerald William Bullett. LC 75-44960. (Fifty Classics of Crime Fiction, 1900-1950; 7). 1976. 12.00 (ISBN 0-8240-2356-0). Garland Pub.
Jury. Gerald William Bullett. LC 35-9296. 1935. A. A. Knopf.
Jury. Eden Phillpotts. LC 27-21139. 1927. The Macmillan Company.
Jury Disagree: By George Goodchild and Bechhofer Roberts. George Goodchild & Carl Eric Bechhofer Roberts. LC 55-474054. (Murder revisited mystery novel, no. 14). 1955. Macmillan.
Jury of Death, Twelve Against the Underworld... Robert Collyer Washburn. LC 30-253813. 1930. Pub. for the Crime Club, Inc., by Doubleday, Doran & Company, Inc.
Jury of His Peers: A Novel. Jack Pearl, pseud. LC 75-15690. 1975. 8.95 (ISBN 0-13-513994-5). Prentice-Hall.
Jury of One. Mignon Good Eberhart. LC 77-14245. 1978. 7.95 (ISBN 0-89340-098-X). J. Curley.
Jury of One. Mignon Good Eberhart. LC 60-5543. 1973. (pbk.) 0.95. Popular Library.
Jury of Six. Matthew Braun. (Orig.). 1980. pap. 1.95 (ISBN 0-671-82032-X). PB.
Jury People. John William Wainwright. LC 77-90102. 1978. 8.95 o.p. (ISBN 0-312-44910-0). St Martin.
Juryman. Donald MacKenzie. LC 58-5339. 1958. Houghton Mifflin.
Jusitce of Gideon. Gates, Eleanor. LC 10-23323. 1910. The Macaulay Company.
Just a Corpse at Twilight. Robert Lee Martin. LC 55-9725. (Red badge detective). 1955. Dodd, Mead.
Just a Girl. Charles Garvice. (On cover: Laurel library, no. 27). 1896. G. Munro's Sons.
Just a Little Inconvenience. Joshua Brooke. (Dell Book). 1.50 (ISBN 0-440-15287-9). Dell Pub. Co.
Just a Little Love. James Noble Gifford. LC 48-165434. 1948. Gramercy Pub. Co.
Just a Missourian: The Story of a Missouri Pioneer. James Lee Martin. LC 15-15293. 1915. The News Publishing Co.
Just a Silly Millimeter Longer. Troy Conway, pseud. (Coxeman Ser). (Orig.). 1969. pap. 0.60 o.p. (ISBN 0-446-63201-5, 63-201). Paperback Lib.
Just a Summer Affair. Mary Adelaide Keeler. LC 7-11421. F. T. Neely.
Just a Woman. Richard Parker & Walter, Eugene. LC 16-18327. 1916. 1.25. The Macaulay Company.
Just Above My Head. James B. Baldwin. LC 79-53577. 12.95 (ISBN 0-8037-4777-2) (ISBN 0-8037-4867-1). Dial Press.
Just Among Friends: Observations and Experiences. Nathan Sulzberger. LC 26-16337. 1926.
Just an Old Sweet Song. Melvin Van Peebles (ISBN 0-345-25565-8). Ballantine Books.
Just and the Unjust. Richard Bagot. LC 1-30868. 1901. J. Lane.
Just and the Unjust. James Gould Cozzens. LC 42-179923. (Harvest bk., HB91). 1965. pap., 1.95. Harcourt.
Just and the Unjust. James Gould Cozzens. LC 42-17982. 1942. Harcourt, Brace and Company.
Just and the Unjust. Vaughan Kester. LC 12-134724. The Bobbs-Merrill Company.
Just Another Redskin. Edward G Ferris. LC 72-95806. 1973. 4.95 (ISBN 0-8059-1808-6). Dorrance.
Just Another Shade of Brown. Lorna Wright. LC 77-375909. (Illus.). 1976. (ISBN 0-85574-011-6). Australian Freedom from Hunger Campaign: E. J. Dwyer (Australia)
Just Another Sucker. James Hadley Chase. 1974. (pbk.) 0.95 (ISBN 0-671-77934-6). Pocket Books.
Just Anything. Carmen Buccola. 3.00 o.p. Carlton.
Just Around the Corner: Romance En Casserole. Fannie Hurst. LC 14-307934. 1914. 1.35. Harper & Brothers.
Just Around the Coroner. Louis Trimble. LC 48-1783. 1948. M. S. Mill Co.
Just As I Am. Mary Elizabeth Braddon Maxwell. (On cover: Lovell's library. no. 889). 1887. J. W. Lovell Company.
Just As I Am. A Novel. Mary Elizabeth Braddon Maxwell. (Franklin square library, no. 141). 1880. Harper & Brothers.
Just As I Am: Or, A Living Lie. Mary Elizabeth Braddon Maxwell. (On cover: Seaside library. Pocket ed. no. 531). 1885. G. Munro.
Just As I Feared. Damaria Arklow. LC 41-2802. The Bobbs-Merrill Company.
Just As of Old. Nellie Alice Mills. LC 34-202132. Dorrance & Company, Inc.
Just Away: A Story of Hope. Della Thompson Lutes. 1906. Crist, Scott & Parbhall I.E. Parshall.
Just Before Dawn. Anne Green. LC 43-4646. 1943. Harper & Brothers.
Just Between Themselves: A Book About Dichtenberg. Anne Warner French. LC 10-9920. 1910. 1.50. Little, Brown, and Company.
Just Between Women. Alice Lent Covert. LC 47-11771. 1867. S.Curl.
Just Between Women: By Maxine Dale Pseud. Alice Lent Covert. LC 47-11771. 1947. S. Curl.
Just Beyond. Marie Jensen. LC 32-9555. 1932. Meador Publishing Company.
Just Boys and Girls of Dear Old Chicago. Marie E. Taylor. LC 30-100914. The Christopher Publishing House.
Just Causes. Malcolm McConnell. LC 80-23692. (Illus.). 1981. 13.95 (ISBN 0-670-41092-6). Viking Press.
Just David. Eleanor Hodgman Porter. LC 16-6721. 1916. Houghton Mifflin Company.
Just David. Eleanor Hodgman Porter. LC 29-30749. Grosset & Dunlap.
Just Deserts. Roderic Jeffries. LC 80-53087. 1980. 9.95 (ISBN 0-312-44942-9). St. Martin's Press.
Just Desserts. Tim Heald. LC 78-10856. 7.95 (ISBN 0-684-16098-6). Scribner.
Just Desserts. Tim Heald. 1980. 1.95 (ISBN 0-345-28683-9). Ballantine Books.
Just Folks". Clara Elizabeth Laughlin. LC 10-23129. 1910. 1.50. The Macmillan Company.
Just for the Bride. 1st Ed. Dorothy Park Clark. LC 50-5153. 1950. Published for the Crime Club by Doubleday.
Just for Tonight: A New Novel. Mary Savage. LC 61-690643. (Torquil book). 1961. Distributed by Dodd, Mead.
Just for Two. Mary Stewart Doubleday Cutting. LC 9-25639. 1909. 1.00. Doubleday, Page & Company.
Just Friends. James Knudsen. 1982. pap. 2.25 (ISBN 0-380-80481-6, 80481-6, Flare). Avon.
Just Friends: A Common Sense Story. Mary Van Lennup Ives Todd. 1908. Calkins and Company.
Just Happy: The Story of a Dog-and Some Humans. Grace Wallace Doonan. LC 20-5124. The Devin-Adair Company.
Just Horses. Sewell Ford. LC 76-121545. (Short story index reprint series). (Illus.). 1970. Books for Libraries Press.
Just Horses. Sewell Ford. LC 10-11135. 1910. 1.00. M. Kennerley.
Just Jane. Kay Mann. LC 34-4563. The Christopher Publishing House.
Just Jemima. John Joy Bell. LC 19-27512. Fleming H. Revell Company.
Just Killing Time. Richard Ellington. LC 52-13825. 1953. Morrow.
Just Like a Girl. Louise Platt Hauck. LC 40-32091. 1940. Macrae-Smith-Company.
Just Like a Girl. Jean Randall. LC 40-32091. 1940. Macrae-Smith Company.
Just Like Humphrey Bogart. Adam Kennedy. LC 77-9062. 1977. 8.95 (ISBN 0-670-41100-0). Viking Press.
Just Lucky, I Guess. Mary Wood. 1967. 1.49 o.p. Doubleday.
Just Mother: And Other Stories. Eleanor Hodgman Porter. LC 27-19632. George H. Doran Company.
Just Murder, Darling. James Arnold Brussel. LC 59-11319. 1959. Scribner.
Just My Luck. LC 75-23639. 1.25. Playboy Press.
Just My Luck. Playboy Editors. LC 75-23639. 192p. 1976. pap. 1.25 o.p. (ISBN 0-87216-297-4, B16297). Playboy Pr Pbks.
Just off Fifth. Edith P Begner. LC 59-7260. 1959. Rinehart.
Just One Cat. Asa Wilgus. LC 50-12833. 1950.
Just One Cat. 1st Trade Ed. Asa Wilgus. LC 52-6923. 1952. A.A. Wyn.
Just One Day. John Habberton. LC 7-123362. 1879. G. R. Lockwood.
Just Outside. Stacy Aumonier. LC 17-29621. 1917. The Century Co.
Just Over the Border. Franklin D. Reeve. LC 75-89462. 1969. 5.95. Morrow.
Just Patty. Jean Webster. LC 11-27453. 1911. The Century Co.
Just Patty. Jean Webster. LC 24-222032. 1922. The Century Co.
Just Plain Folks: A Story of "Lost Opportunities,". E. Stillman Doubleday. LC 6-33493. 1894. Arena Publishing Company.
Just Plain Larnin' James M Shields. LC 34-2562. 1934. Coward-McCann, Inc.
Just Relations. Rodney Hall. LC 82-40369. 1983. 16.95 (ISBN 0-670-41114-0). Viking Press.
Just Sally. Frances D. Hancock. pap. 0.75 o.s.i. (01-398). Lancer.
Just Sally. Jeanne Judson. 1963. Avalon Books.
Just Sheaffer: Or, Storms in the Troubled Heir. Ian Mowatt. LC 72-91837. 1973. 5.95 (ISBN 0-15-146590-8). Harcourt Brace Jovanovich.
Just So Stories. Rudyard Kipling. 1976. Repr. of 1902 ed. lib. bdg. 9.55x (ISBN 0-88411-993-9). Amereon Ltd.
Just Steward. Clotilde Inez Mary Graves. LC 22-23722. George H. Doran Company.
Just Stories. Gertrude M O'Reilly. LC 14-22669. 1914. 1.25. The Devin-Adair Company.
Just Stories. John Meloy Stahl. LC 16-6823. M. A. Donohue & Co.
Just Sweethearts: A Christmas Love Story. Harry Stillwell Edwards. LC 19-19597. The J. W. Burke Company.
Just Tell Me What You Want. Jay Presson Allen. LC 75-12508. 1975. 8.95 (ISBN 0-525-13785-8). Dutton.
Just the Way It Is. Rene Raymond. LC 44-7193. 1944. Jarrolds Limited.
Just Under Heaven. Theodore Pauls. LC 45-3919. 1945. Chapman & Grimes, Inc.
Just What the Doctor Ordered. Colin Watson. LC 76-75847. (Red mask mystery). 1969. 4,50. Putnam.
Just What the Doctor Ordered. Colin Watson. LC 81-47345. (Fifty Classics of Crime Fiction, 1950-1975). 1982. 14.95 (ISBN 0-8240-4952-7). Garland Pub.
Just 25 Cents and Three Wheaties Boxtops. Lee Foster. LC 72-129814. (Illus.). 1970. 4.95. Pacific Coast Publishers.
Justice. Corra May White Harris. LC 15-20393. 1915. 0.50. Hearst's International Library Co.
Justice at Iritara. Lawrence Cortesi, pseud. 224p. (Orig.). 1982. pap. 2.25 (ISBN 0-505-51776-0). Tower Bks.
Justice Be Damned. Alec Rowley Hilliard. LC 41-9496. Farrar & Rinehart, Inc.
Justice Comes to Tomahawk. William MacLeod Raine. LC 52-415. 1952. Houghton Mifflin.
Justice Deferred. William MacLeod Raine. LC 42-5733. 1942. Houghton Mifflin Company.
Justice Ends at Home, and Other Stories. Rex Stout & John J McAleer. LC 76-53837. 1977. 8.95 (ISBN 0-670-41105-1). Viking Press.
Justice Has No Sword: A Mystery Thriller, by Max Franklin Pseud. Richard Deming. LC 53-8228. 1953. Rinehart.
Justice Hunger: A Short Novel and Nine Stories. Meyer Liben. LC 66-27389. 1967. Dial Press.
Justice in the Bye-Ways: A Tale of Life. Francis Colburn Adams. LC 5-42965. 1856. Livermore & Rudd; Etc., Etc.
Justice Is a Woman. Helen Liebman Haberman. LC 47-3424. 1947. Prentice-Hall, Inc.
Justice: My Brother! A Novel of Oklahoma in the Early Nineteen Hundreds by James Keene Pseud. Will Cook. LC 57-5394. 1957. Random House.
Justice of Allah. William Ransted Berry. LC 29-799. Hale, Cushman & Flint.
Justice of the Heart: By E. Arnot Robertson. Eileen Arbuthnot Robertson. LC 58-12440. 1958. Macmillan.
Justice of the King. Hamilton Drummond. LC 11-1963. 1911. The Macmillan Company.
Justice of the Peace. Frederick John Niven. LC 23-18070. Boni and Liveright.
Justice on Halfaday Creek. 1st. ed. James Beardsley Hendryx. LC 49-8048. (A Double D western). 1949. Doubleday.
Justice on the Rocks. Bill Knox. LC 67-20918. 1967. Published for the Crime Club by Doubleday.
Justice to All. Ruth Kirby Skipper. LC 38-5364. The Christopher Publishing House.
Justice to the Woman. Bernie Smade Babcock. LC 1-22974. 1901. A. C. McClurg & Co.

Justice to the Woman. Bernie Smade Babcock. LC 3-28838. 1903. Broadway Publishing Company.

Justice Will Win: Or, The Trials and Final Triumphs of Arthur Steele. F. V. B Madeira. LC 7-20275. 1883. Sherman & Co.

Justicer: By Thomas Fall Pseud. Donald Clifford Snow. LC 59-12302. 1959. Rinehart.

Justifiable Falsehood: A Story of Love and Mystery. Arthur Wellington Glass. LC 9-8419. 1909. Courier Publishing Company.

Justin Bayard. Jon Cleary. LC 56-9000. 1956. Morrow.

Justin Harley: A Romance of Old Virginia. John Esten Cooke. LC 44-24881. 1875. Claxton, Remsen & Haffelfinger.

Justin Moyan. David Weiss. LC 65-11331. 1965. W. Morrow.

Justin Wilson's Cajun Humor. Justin Wilson. 1974. pap. 2.50 o.p. (ISBN 0-88289-018-2). Pelican.

Justin Wingate, Ranchman. John Harvey Whitson. LC 5-11073. 1905. Little, Brown, and Company.

Justina: Or, The Will. A Domestic Story ... LC 7-11663. 1823. C. Wiley.

Justine. Lawrence Durrell. LC 57-11251. 1957. Dutton.

Justine. Donatien Alphonse Francois Sade. 1969. pap. 1.25 o.p. (78-614). Lancer.

Justine. Donatien Alphonse Francois Sade. 3.95 o.p. Wehman.

Justine: A Comic Strip. Donatien Alphonse Francois Sade. 1970. 7.50 o.p. (GP589); pap. 2.00 o.p. Grove.

Justine or the Misfortune of Virtue. Donatien Alphonse Francois Sade. Tr. by Helen Weaver. 1966. 5.00 o.p. (ISBN 0-399-10472-0). Putnam.

Justine: Or, The Misfortunes of Virtue. Donatien Alphonse Francois Sade. LC 66-19627. 1966. Putnam.

Justine: Or, The Misfortunes of Virtue. Donatien Alphonse Francois Sade & Berman, Harold, 1904- Ed. and Tr. LC 35-32804. 1935. The Risus Press.

Justine: Or, The Misfortunes of Virtue. Donatien Alphonse Francois Sade & Blaine, Mahlon, Illus. LC 32-12880. 1931. Printed for the Risus Press.

Justine's Lovers. John William De Forest. Ed. by Donald Pizer. LC 78-96518. (American Authors Ser). 1970. Repr. of 1878 ed. lib. bdg. 9.95 o.s.i. (ISBN 0-512-00136-7). Garrett Pr.

Justine's Lovers: A Novel. Jane L Howell. LC 8-30221. (On cover: Library of American fiction, no. 2). 1878. Harper & Brothers.

Justine's Lovers: A Novel. Jane L. Howell. (On cover: Library of American fiction. no. 2). 1878. Harper & Brothers.

Justly Dear: Charles and Mary Lamb. A Biographical Novel. Elsie Prentys Thornton-Cook. LC 30-270992. 1939. C. Scribner's Sons.

Justus. Arthur L Lapham. LC 73-79486. 1973. 5.95 (ISBN 0-570-03231-8). Concordia Pub. House.

Justus. Arthur L Lapham. 1974. (pbk.) 1.50 (ISBN 0-515-03408-8). Pyramid Books.

Jutland Cottage, No. 16. Angela Mackail Thirkell. 1973. pap. 1.25 o.p. (ISBN 0-515-03049-X, V3049). Pyramid Pubns.

Jutland Cottage. 1st American Ed. Angela Mackail Thirkell. LC 53-109250. 1953. Knopf.

Juve in the Dock. Marcel Allain & Allinson, Alfred Richard, Tr. LC 26-6644. (Famtomas detective novels). David McKay Company.

Juvenile Lead. Pearson Groves. pap. 1.75 o.p. (3029). Brandon.

Juxtaposition. Piers Anthony, pseud. LC 81-69507. (Illus.). 1982. 13.50 (ISBN 0-345-30196-X). Ballantine Books.

Juyungo: The First Black Ecuadorian Novel. Adalberto Ortiz. Tr. by Jonathan Tittler & Susan Hill. LC 81-51674. x, 234p. (Orig.). 1982. 20.00x (ISBN 0-89410-090-4); pap. 8.00x (ISBN 0-89410-091-2). Three Continents.

K

K. Kathleen Thompson Norris. Repr. lib. bdg. 16.30x (ISBN 0-89190-306-2). Am Repr-Rivercity Pr.

K. Mary Roberts Rinehart. LC 15-160093. 1915. Houghton Mifflin Company.

K. Mary Roberts Rinehart. LC 43-4975. 1943. The Sun Dial Press.

K: A Novel. William Wiser. LC 79-131111. 1971. 5.95. Doubleday.

K. K. K. Charles Waller Tyler. LC 2-14140. The Abbey Press.

K. Lamity's Texas Tales. John Sturgis Bonner. LC 5-755. 1904. Press of Von Boeckmannn ! Jones Company.

K-9 Guard. Alvin M. Bartett. (Penguin Ser.). 1971. 1.85 o.s.i. Review & Herald.

Ka of Gifford Hillary. Dennis Yates Wheatley. (Black magic series). 1973. 1.50. Ballantine.

Ka'a'awa: A Novel About Hawaii in the 1850's. O. A. Bushnell. LC 72-83490. 350p. 1972. 10.00 (ISBN 0-8248-0206-3). UH Pr.

Ka'a'awa: A Novel About Hawaii in the 1850s. O. A. Bushnell. LC 72-83490. (Pacific Classics Ser.: No. 7). 506p. 1980. pap. 6.95 (ISBN 0-8248-0729-4). UH Pr.

Kaaawa: A Novel About Hawaii in the 1850s. Oswald A Bushnell. LC 72-83490. 1972. 10.00 (ISBN 0-8248-0206-3). University Press of Hawaii for Friends of the Library of Hawaii.

Kabacosa: Or, The Warriors of the West. A Tale of the Last War. Anna L Snelling. LC 8-10202. 1842. Printed for the Publisher by D. Adee.

Kabbalah. David Scott Milton. LC 79-3360. 12.95 (ISBN 0-15-146608-4). Harcourt Brace Jovanovich.

Kadin. Bertrice Small. LC 77-99226. 1978. 1.95 (ISBN 0-380-01699-0). Avon Books.

Kady. Patience Stapleton. LC 8-13449. Belford, Clarke & Co.

Kafir Stories. William Charles Scully. LC 8-3389. (Added t.-p.: Buckram series). 1895. H. Holt and Company.

Kafka Gift Set: The Castle, Amerika, The Trial. Franz Kafka. 1974. pap. 9.85 (ISBN 0-8052-2905-1). Schocken.

Kafka's Castle. S. Y Baibi. 1973. 5.00 (ISBN 0-913054-07-0). Poet Gallery Press.

Kafka's the Trial. 6.95 o.p.; pap. text ed. 2.45 o.p. P-H.

Kagan's Superfecta & Other Stories. Allen Hoffman. 304p. 1982. 12.95 (ISBN 0-89659-234-0); special ltd. ed. 100.00 (ISBN 0-89659-271-5). Abbeville Pr.

Kahawa. Donald E Westlake. LC 81-51887. (Illus.). 14.95 (ISBN 0-670-41132-9). Viking Press.

Kahuna Killer. Juanita Sheridan. LC 51-10228. 1951. Published for the Crime Club by Doubleday.

Kai Lung Beneath the Mulberry-Tree. Ernest Bramah, pseud. Ed. by R. Reginald & Douglas Melville. LC 77-84202. (Lost Race & Adult Fantasy Ser.). 1978. Repr. of 1940 ed. lib. bdg. 19.00x (ISBN 0-405-10959-8). Ayer Co.

Kai Lung Beneath the Mulberry-Tree. Ernest Bramah, pseud. 1940. 3.00 o.p. Verry.

Kai Lung Beneath the Mulberry-Tree. Ernest Bramah Smith. LC 77-84202. (Lost Race and Adult Fantasy Fiction). 1978. 19.00 (ISBN 0-405-10959-8). Arno Press.

Kai Lung Beneath the Mulberry-Tree: By Ernest Bramah Pseud. Ernest Bramah Smith. LC 40-7599. 1965. 3.00. Richards.

Kai Lung: Six: Uncollected Stories from Punch. Ernest Bramah Smith. LC 74-184087. (Illus.). 1974. Non-Profit Press.

Kai Lung Unrolls His Mat. Ernest Bramah, pseud. 1928. 6.00 o.p. Verry.

Kai Lung Unrolls His Mat. Ernest Bramah, pseud. (Original Adult Fantasy). 1974. (pbk.) 1.25. Ballantine.

Kai Lung Unrolls His Mat. Ernest Bramah Smith. LC 28-14321. 1928. Doubleday, Doran & Company, Inc.

Kai Lung Unrolls His Mat: By Ernest Bramah Pseud. Ernest Bramah Smirth. 1965. 3.00. Richards.

Kai Lung's Golden Hours. Ernest Bramah, pseud. 1922. 6.00 o.p. Verry.

Kai Lung's Golden Hours. LC 23-712253. George H. Doran Company.

Kai Lung's Golden Hours. Ernest Bramah Smith. LC 72-185186. 1972. 1.25 (ISBN 0-345-02574-1). Ballantine Books.

Kai Lung's Golden Hours: By Ernest Bramah Pseud. Preface by Hilair Belloc. Ernest Bramah Smith. LC 23-1751. 1965. revised 3.00. G. Richards.

Kaiser Goes: The Generals Remain. Theodor Plivier & Wheen, Arthur Wesley, Tr. LC 33-225955. 1933. The Macmillan Company.

Kaiser, King and Pope. Richard Roth. Tr. by Ireland, Mary Eliza (Haines) LC 18-8993. 1917. Augsburg Publishing House.

Kaiser's Coolies: Translated from the German. Theodor Plivier & Green, Margaret Minns, 1886- Tr. LC 31-495898. 1931. A. A. Knopf.

Kaiuolani: A Princess of Hawaii. I. William Adams. LC 12-26288. 1912. The Mikilosch Press.

Kalahari. Henry Kolarz. Tr. by Joachim Neugroschel from Ger. 1979. pap. 2.50 (ISBN 0-445-04501-9). Popular Lib.

Kalani of Oahu. An Historical Romance of Hawaii. Charles Martin Newell. LC 7-172806. 1881. Pub. by the Author.

Kalasandra Revisted. Barbara Kimenye. LC 66-77085. (three crowns book). 1966. Oxford U.P.

Kalawao. Mary Alice McNarny. LC 54-740595. 1954. Vantage Press.

Kaleema. Marion McClelland. LC 21-1176. 1921. The Century Co.

Kaleidoscope. Eleanor Farjeon. (Illus.). 1963. H. Z. Walck.

Kaleidoscope. Eleanor Farjeon. LC 29-9369. 1929. Frederick A. Stokes Company.

Kaleidoscope. Carole A. Raboch. 1980. pap. 4.00 (ISBN 0-89502-079-3). FEB.

Kaleidoscope, a Novel in Four Parts. Gertrude McConnell Dick. LC 44-86582. 1944. Dorrance & Company.

Kaleidoscope: A Variety of Short Stories. Ed. by Ralph E. West. (gr. 9-11). 1970. pap. text ed. 4.50x (ISBN 0-88334-030-5). Ind Sch Pr.

Kaleidoscope: Thirteen Stories and Novelettes. Stefan Zweig. LC 34-7143. 1934. The Viking Press.

Kalevide. Lou Goble. 1982. pap. 3.95 (ISBN 0-553-22531-6). Bantam.

Kaligarh Fault. Paul Roadarmel. LC 78-13900. (Illus.). 9.95 (ISBN 0-06-013600-6). Harper & Row.

Kalin. E. C. Tubb. (Dumerest of Terra Ser.). 192p. 1982. pap. 2.25 (ISBN 0-441-42802-9). Ace Bks.

Kalki. Gore Vidal. 1978. 14.95 (ISBN 0-394-42053-5). Random.

Kallocain. Karin Boye. LC 66-13798. (Nordic translation series). 1966. University of Wisconsin Press.

Kaloolah. Adventures of Jonathan Romer, of Nantudket. William Starbuck Mayo. LC 18-173181. (Lettered on cover: Putnam's library of choice reading). 1878. G. P. Putnam's Sons.

Kaloolah: Or, Journeyings to the Djebel Kumri; an Autobiography of Jonathan Romer. William Starbuck Mayo. LC 72-2071. (Black Heritage Library Collection). 1972. 19.75 (ISBN 0-8369-9059-5). Books for Libraries Press.

Kaloolah: Or, Journeyings to the Djebel Kumri: an Atuobiography of Jonathan Romer. William Starbuck Mayo. LC 42-29446. G. P. Putnam.

Kaloolah, or, Journeyings to the Djebel Kumri: An Autobiography of Jonathan Romer. 2d ed. William Starbuck Mayo. LC 42-35044. 1849. G. P. Putnam.

Kama Sutra Tango. J. F. Burke. LC 76-47257. (Harper Novel of Suspense). 1977. 7.95 o.p. (ISBN 0-06-010569-0, HarpT). Har-Row.

Kama Sutra Tango. J. F. Burke. LC 76-47257. (Harper Novel of Suspense). 1977. 7.95 o.p. (ISBN 0-06-010569-0, HarpT). Har-Row.

Kamaiwea, the Coeur D'Alene: The Heart of an Awl. Alice Sutton McGeorge. LC 40-2310. Burton Publishing Company.

Kamal. D. W Arathorn. LC 81-47682. 13.94 (ISBN 0-06-014925-6). Harper & Row.

Kamehameha, the Conquering King: The Mystery of His Birth, Loves, and Conquests; a Romance of Hawaii. Charles Martin Newell. LC 7-17279. 1885. G. P. Putnam's Sons.

Kamera Obskura. Vladimir Vladimirovich Nabokov. (Rus.). 1979. 15.00 (ISBN 0-88233-391-7); pap. 7.00 (ISBN 0-88233-388-7). Ardis Pubs.

Kamikaze Assignment. Andrew Sugar. (Israeli Commandos Ser.: No. 3). 192p. (Orig.). 1975. pap. 1.25 o.p. (ISBN 0-532-12247-X). Woodhill.

Kamikaze Assignment. Andrew Sugar. (Israeli Commandos Ser.: No. 3). 192p. (Orig.). 1975. pap. 1.25 o.p. (ISBN 0-532-12247-X). Manor Bks.

Kamikaze Assignment. Andrew Sugar. (Israeli Commandos no. 3). 1975. (pbk.) 1.25. Manor Books.

Kamikaze Justice. Patrick Lee. (Six-Gun Samurai Ser.: No. 4). 192p. (Orig.). 1981. pap. 1.95 (ISBN 0-523-41416-1). Pinnacle Bks.

Kamiti: A Forester's Dream. Richard St. Barbe Baker. LC 60-5048. (Illus.). Duell, Sloan and Pearce.

Kamouraska: A Novel. Anne Hebert. LC 72-96657. 1973. 5.95. Crown Publishers.

Kampong. Ronald Hardy. LC 57-6710. 1958. Doubleday.

Kampoon Street. Tai-Yi Lin. LC 63-18590. 1964. World Pub. Co.

Kampuchea: From Tragedy to Rebirth. A. Usvatov et al. 184p. 1979. pap. 5.45 (ISBN 0-8285-1595-6, Pub. by Progress Pubs USSR). Imported Pubns.

Kanata. Dennis Adair & Janet Rosenstock. 1981. pap. 2.95 (ISBN 0-380-77826-2, 77826). Avon.

Kandar. Kenneth Bulmer. (Orig.). 1969. pap. 0.50 o.p. (62-120). Paperback Lib.

Kandi Man. McLane Birch. 1970. pap. 1.00 o.p. Broadside.

Kane & Abel. Jeffrey Archer. LC 79-23311. 11.95 (ISBN 0-671-25121-X). Simon and Schuster.

Kane and the Goldbar Killers. Lee Frank. (Paperback Library western). 1973. (pbk.) 0.95. Warner Paperback Library.

Kane and the Outlaw Double Cross. Lee Frank. 1975. (pbk.) 0.95. Warner Paperback Library.

Kane's World. Leonard Lamensdorf. LC 68-21309. (O.S.I.). 1968. 5.95 o.s.i. (ISBN 0-671-20020-8). S&S.

Kane's World: A Novel. Leonard Lamensdorf. LC 68-21309. 1968. 5.95. Simon and Schuster.

Kanesbrake. Jennifer Blair. (Candlelight romance). 1975. (pbk.) 0.75. Dell.

Kang--He Vase. Joseph Smith Fletcher. LC 26-663993. 1926. A. A. Knopf.

Kang--He Vase. Joseph Smith Fletcher. LC 34-37773. 1928. Grosset & Dunlap.

Kanga Creek. Havelock Ellis. LC 72-175517. (Nelson's Australasian paperbacks). (Illus.). 1970. (ISBN 0-17-004821-7). Thomas Nelson (Australia.

Kangaroo. David Herbert Lawrence. LC 23-13261. 1923. T. Seltzer.

Kanor see Gulliveriana, No. 4.

Kansan. Roe Richmond. LC 60-2554. 1960. Avalon Books.

Kansan: A Novel. Mack Cretcher. LC 23-16272. Dorrance.

Kansan. Complete and Unabridged. Richard Brister. LC 54-44360. (Avon, 606). 1954. Avon Publications.

Kansan's Woman. Robert E. Mills. (Kansan Ser: No. 10). 205p. pap. 2.50 (ISBN 0-8439-2020-3, Kable Bks). Dorchester Pub Co.

Kansas City Kit: A Story of Thought and Adventure. 1st Ed. John Thomas Reed. LC 53-10548. 1953. Exposition Press.

Kansas City Milkman. Reynolds Packard. LC 50-5952. 1950. Dutton.

Kansas City Rejects. 1st ed. Lou Temple et al. (Illus.). 56p. 1974. pap. 2.25 o.p. (ISBN 0-914024-15-9). Peace & Pieces.

Kansas Farmer in Politics. Nick T Hunt. LC 99-3562. 1899. Hudson-Kimberly Publishing Company.

Kansas Irish. Charles Benedict Driscoll. LC 43-7558. 1943. The Macmillan Company.

Kansas Marshal. Charles Stanley Strong. LC 46-22353. 1946. Phoenix Press.

Kansas Marshall. Thomas Albert Curry. (Orig.). 1972. pap. 0.75 o.p. (06166). Curtis.

Kansas Trail. Hascal Giles. LC 56-13476. Ballantine Books.

Kanthapura. LC 63-18637. (NDP224). 1967. pap., 1.95. New Directions.

Kanthapura. Rao Raja. LC 77-3040. 1977. Repr. of 1963 ed. lib. bdg. 18.00x (ISBN 0-8371-9573-X, RAKA). Greenwood.

Kao Yu Pao. 2nd, rev. ed. 1975. pap. 2.50 o.p. (ISBN 0-8351-0122-3). China Bks.

Kao Yu Pao. 2nd, rev. ed. 1975. pap. 2.50 o.p. (ISBN 0-8351-0122-3). China Bks.

Kappa. new ed., rev. translated from the japanese by seiichi shiojiri. ed. Ryunosuke Akutagawa. LC 71-98801. (Illus.). 1970. (ISBN 0-8371-3064-6). Greenwood Press.

Kappa; a Novel. Ryunosuke Akutagawa. LC 79-157260. (Tut L books). 1971. 1.95 (ISBN 0-8048-0994-1). C. E. Tuttle Co.

Kappillan of Malta. Nicholas Monsarrat. LC 73-17592. (Illus.). 1974. 8.95 (ISBN 0-688-00243-9). Morrow.

Kaputt. Curzio Malaparte & Foligno, Cesare, 1878- Tr. LC 46-7374. 1946. E. P. Dutton & Co., Inc.

Karadac, Count of Gersay: A Romance by K. & Hesketh Prichard... Kate O'Brien Hesketh Prichard & Hesketh Vernon Hesketh Prichard. LC 1-23691. Frederick A. Stokes Company.

Karamanov Equations: A Novel. Marshall Goldberg. LC 70-168379. 1972. 7.95 (ISBN 0-529-04516-8). World Pub.

Karamazov Brothers, 2 vols. Fedor Mikhailovich Dostoevskii. 1173p. 1980. Set. 15.95 (ISBN 0-8285-2244-8, Pub. by Progress Pubs USSR). Imported Pubns.

Karamour. Ariadne Pritchett. 160p. 1973. pap. 0.75 o.p. (T2812, GM). Fawcett World.

Karan Kringle's Journal. Being Comical Episodes in an "Old Maid's Life.". Emma Scarr Booth. LC 6-15037. T. B. Peterson & Brothers.

Karate Is a Thing of the Spirit. Harry Crews. 1971. 5.95 o.p. (ISBN 0-688-01933-1). Morrow.

Karate Is a Thing of the Spirit: A Novel. Harry Crews. LC 74-137521. 1971. 5.95. Morrow.

Karen. Marie Killilea. Ed. by Virginia F. Allen. (Falcon Books Ser). (YA) (gr. 10-12). 1967. Set Of 42 Copies Of 8 Pbks. pap. 37.50 o.p. Bowmar-Noble.

Karen Connors, Family Therapist. Marilyn Austin. (YA) 1978. 6.95 (Avalon). Bouregy.

Karen Evans, M.D. Number One: Shocktrauma. Kathryn Jessup. LC 82-80211. (Karen Evans, M.D. Ser.). 256p. (Orig.). 1982. pap. 2.50 (ISBN 0-86721-142-3). Playboy Pbks.

Karen Evans, M.D. Number Three: Space Medicine. Kathryn Jessup. LC 81-81383. (Karen Evans, M.D. Ser.). 256p. 1982. pap. 2.50 (ISBN 0-86721-199-7). Playboy Pbks.

Karen Evans, M.D. Number Two: Woman Surgeon. Kathryn Jessup. LC 82-81198. (Karen Evans, M.D. Ser.). 256p. (Orig.). 1982. pap. 2.50 (ISBN 0-86721-171-7). Playboy Pbks.

Karen's Destiny. Harriet Theresa Smith Comstock. LC 34-139031. 1934. Doubleday, Doran & Company, Inc.

Karen's Memory. Anne Duffield. 1939. Arcadia House, Inc.

Karin Ellis. Michael Jackson. LC 41-8357. The Penn Publishing Company.

Karin, From the German of Wilhelm Jensen. Wilhelm Jensen. LC 7-102158. 1882. H. T. Mercur.
Karin of Sweden. Wilhelm Jensen. Tr. by Waugh. LC 7-10320. (Once a week library. v. 11. no. 23). P. F. Collier.
Karine a Story of Swedish Love. Wilhelm Jensen. Tr. by Endlich, Emma A. LC 3-1779. (Lettered on cover: Tales from foreign lands. v. 7). 1896. A. C. McClurg and Company.
Karin's Mother: By Margaret Goldsmith. Margaret Leland Goldsmith. LC 28-9469. Payson & Clarke Limited.
Karl and Gretchen's Christmas. Louise W Tilden. LC 16-5302. 1878. R. Clarke & Co.
Karl and the Twentieth Century. Rudolf Brunngraber. Tr. by Paul, Eden. LC 33-32587. 1933. W. Morrow and Company.
Karl Grier: The Strange Story of a Man with a Sixth Sense. Louis Tracy. LC 6-300443. 1906. E. J. Clode.
Karl of Erbach: A Tale of Lichtenstein and Solgau. Henry Christopher Bailey. LC 2-27944. 1902. Longmans, Green, and Co.
Karl of Erbach: A Tale of Lichtenstein and Solgau. Henry Christopher Bailey. LC 17-23009. 1903. Longmans, Green, and Co.
Karl the Lion. A Novel. Sylvanus Cobb. (On cover: The popular series, no. 17). 1891. R. Bonner's Sons.
Karlamagnus Saga Ok Kappa Hans. Ed. by C. R. Unger. LC 80-1959. 74.50 (ISBN 0-404-18698-X). AMS Pr.
Karlene Hoy: Or, In Need of a Guide and Guard. Emma Young Prewitt. LC 7-30108. 1889. J. B. Lippincott Company.
Karls of Karltonville and Their New Thought: Or, The Life Beautiful. Anna Atwood Drew. LC 6-5141. 1905. J.H. Earle & Company.
Karlyn. Jerry B Jenkins. LC 80-18661. 2.50 (ISBN 0-8024-4312-5). Moody Press.
Karma. Arsen Darnay. LC 78-4404. 1978. 8.95 (ISBN 0-312-45085-0). St. Martin's Press.
Karma: A Novel. new ed. Alfred Percy Sinnett. LC 33-28349. 1886. Rand, McNally & Company.
Karma Machine. Michael Davidson. 288p. 1975. pap. 1.50 (ISBN 0-445-03202-2). Popular Lib.
Karma of Love. Barbara Cartland. (Barbara Cartland library, 14). 1975. (pbk.) 1.25. Bantam Books.
Karmel the Scout: Or, The Rebel of the Jerseys. A Story of the American Revolution. Sylvanus Cobb. LC 6-30991. Cassell & Company.
Karmel, the Scout: Or, The Rebel of the Jerseys. A Story of the American Revolution. Sylvanus Cobb. (On cover: Cassell's sunshine series, no. 14). The Cassell Publishing Co.
Karmel, the Scout; or, The Rebel of the Jerseys: A Story of the American Revolution. Sylvanus Cobb. LC 42-34426. (On cover: Cassell's universal library). The Cassell Publishing Co.
Karpov's Brain. Gerald Green. 384p. 1983. 15.95 (ISBN 0-688-01889-0). Morrow.
Kasamance: A Fantasy. Katherine Dunham. LC 73-92612. (Illus.). 5.95 (ISBN 0-89388-128-7). Odarkai Books.
Kashf 'an Masawi al Mutanabbi. Al Sahib. Tr. by Arthur Wormhoudt from Arabic. (Arab Translation Ser.: No. 9). 1974. pap. 6.50x (ISBN 0-916358-59-3). Wormhoudt.
Kashmiri Passions. Clarissa Ross, pseud. 1978. 2.25 (ISBN 0-446-82839-4). Warner Books.
Kasia and the Empress. Sacha Carnegie, pseud. LC 72-9937. 1973. 6.95 (ISBN 0-396-06764-6). Dodd, Mead.
Kasia and the Empress. Sacha Carnegie, pseud. 1974. (pbk.) 1.25. Bantam Books.
Kasriel the Watchman: And Other Stories. Israel Goldberg. LC 26-15267. 1925. The Jewish Publication Society of America.
Kassandra and the Wolf. Margarita Karapanou. LC 76-229. 6.95 (ISBN 0-15-142174-9). Harcourt Brace Jovanovich.
Kassia: A Romance of Byzantium. George Handrulis. LC 34-21157. Athenaeum Publishing Company, Inc.
Katana. George MacBeth. 240p. 1983. pap. 2.95 (ISBN 0-425-05823-9). Berkley Pub.
Katana. Marc Olden. (Black Samurai). (Signet book: Vol. 8). 1975. (pbk.) 1.25. New American Library.
Katana: A Novel. George MacBeth & John Beeby. LC 81-13550. 14.50 (ISBN 0-671-43245-1). Simon and Schuster.
Kate. Brian Talbot Cleeve. LC 76-57150. 1977. 9.95 (ISBN 0-698-10812-4). Coward, McCann & Geoghegan.
Kate. Veronica Heley. (Coventry Romance Ser.: No. 185). 224p. 1982. pap. 1.50 (ISBN 0-449-50287-2, Coventry). Fawcett.
Kate: A Comedy in Four Acts. Bronson Howard. 1906. Harper & Brothers.
Kate and Emma: 1st Amer. Ed. Monica Dickens. LC 65-10889. 1965. 4.95. Coward.
Kate Aylesford. A Story of the Refugees. Charles Jacobs Peterson. LC 7-36159. T. B. Peterson.
Kate Beaumont. John William De Forest. (On cover: Osgood's library of novels. no. 5). 1872. J. R. Osgood and Company.
Kate Bonnet: The Romance of a Pirate's Daughter. Frank Richard Stockton. 1902. D. Appleton and Company.
Kate Bouverie: And Other Tales and Sketches, in Prose and Verse. Caroline Elizabeth Sarah Sheridan Norton. LC 7-33179. 1835. E. L. Carey & A. Hart.
Kate Callender: Or, School-Girls of '54, and the Women of to-Day. Anna L White. LC 8-36627. 1870. The Author.
Kate Carnegie. John Watson. LC 4-15344. 1896. Dodd, Mead and Company.
Kate Clarendon: Or, Necromancy in the Wilderness. by emerson bennett... ed. Emerson Bennett. LC 7-34426. 1848. Stratton & Bernard.
Kate Clarendon: Or, Necromancy in the Wilderness. Emerson Bennett. T. B. Peterson.
Kate Comerford: Or, Sketches of Garrison Life. Anna Holloway. LC 8-29699. 1881. J. B. Lippincott & Co.
Kate Cronin's Dowry. Frances Sarah Johnston Cashel Hoey Hoey. LC 7-6144. (Half-title: Harper's half-hour ser. v. 23). 1877. Harper & Brothers.
Kate Daniels, TV Star. Jean Hart. (YA) 1979. 6.95 (Avalon). Bouregy.
Kate Danton: Or, Captain Danton's Daughters. by may agnes fleming... ed. May Agnes Early Fleming. LC 11-8222. 1876. G. W. Carleton & Co.; Etc., Etc.
Kate Danton: Or, Captain Danton's Daughters. by may agnes fleming... ed. May Agnes Early Fleming. 1888. G. W. Dillingham; Etc., Etc.
Kate Felton: Or, A Peep at Realities. Maria I Weston. 1859. E. P. Weston.
Kate Fennigate. Booth Tarkington. LC 43-511972. 1943. Doubleday, Doran & Co., Inc.
Kate Ford's Family. Susan Howard Jewett Howe. 1899. The Editor Publishing Co.
Kate Fuller, M.D. Dorothy Carle Pierce Walker. LC 50-5064. 1950. Macrae Smith Co.
Kate Greenway's Mother Goose. facsimile ed. Kate Greenaway. 1974. pap. 2.25 o.p. Huntington Lib.
Kate Hardy. Dorothy Emily Stevenson. LC 47-31386. 1947. Rinehart.
Kate Kennedy. A Novel. Emma Newby. LC 7-26118. (On cover: Turners' select novels, no. 2). Turner Brothers & Co.
Kate McDermott. Ruth Irma Low. LC 70-132426. 1971. 3.95. Dorrance.
Kate Marstone: Or, Happy Hearts Make Happy Homes. A Fireside Story ... LC 7-11668. 1866. Carleton.
Kate Meredith: Financier. complimentary ed. Charles John Cutcliffe Wright Hyne. LC 7-5068. 1906. The Authors and Newspapers Association.
Kate Meredith: Financier. Charles John Cutcliffe Wright Hyne. McLeod & Allen.
Kate Mulhall: A Romance of the Oregon Trail. Ezra Meeker. E. Meeker.
Kate O'Donoghue. Charles James Lever. (Seaside library, v. 9, no. 174). 1877. G. Munro.
Kate of Gotham. A Romance. Barbara Black. LC 6-124225. (On cover: Dillingham's metropolitan library, no. 2). 1895. G. W. Dillingham.
Kate of Kate Hall. Ellen Thorneycroft Fowler & Felkin, Alfred Laurence. LC 4-27982. 1904. D. Appleton and Company.
Kate Percival. Kate Percival. pap. 1.95 o.s.i. (Venus). Grove.
Kate Plus 10. Edgar Wallace. LC 17-23659. Small, Maynard & Company.
Kate Russell: Wartime Nurse. Elisabeth Carleton Hubbard Lansing. LC 42-97921. 1942. Thomas Y. Crowell Company.
Kate Stanton. A Page from Real Life ... 2d ed. LC 7-11669. 1856. J. French and Company.
Kate, the Curious. Katheryn Kimbrough, pseud. (Saga of the Phenwick Women: No. 13). 1976. pap. 1.50 (ISBN 0-445-00430-4). Popular Lib.
Kate Trimingham. Frances Mary Frost. LC 40-33216. Farrar & Rinehart, Inc.
Kate Trimingham. Frances Mary Frost. LC 40-33216. Farrar & Rinehart, Inc.
Kate Vaughan: or Polygamy Exposed. Marie A Walsh. LC 99-666. 1898. The Mascot Publishing Co.
Kate Walsingham. A Novel. Ellen Pickering. T. B. Peterson.
Kate Weathers; or, Scattered by the Tempest. A Novel. Frank Vaughan. LC 8-30209. 1878. J. B. Lippincott & Co.
Kate Wetherill: An Earth Comedy. Jennette Barbour Perry Lee. LC 1551. 1900. The Century Co.
Kate Wilder, R.N. Ann Gilmer, pseud. 1967. Repr. pap. 0.50 o.p. (50-386). Manor Bks.
Kate's Story. Christopher Leach. 1972. pap. 0.95 o.p. (ISBN 0-590-04534-2). Schol Bk Serv.
Kate's Way. Robert F Joseph. (Berkley Medallion Book). 1977. 1.50 (ISBN 0-425-03295-7). Berkley Pub. Corp.
Kathakoca or Treasury of Stories. C. H. Tawney. LC 75-903877. 1975. Repr. of 1895 ed. 11.00x (ISBN 0-88386-639-0). South Asia Bks.
Katharine Blythe: A Novel. Katharine Lee Rawlings Jenner. LC 7-23207. (Harper's handy series. no. 87). 1886. Harper & Brothers.
Katharine Conway. Margaret E Blackburn. LC 98-1295. 1899. C. W. Moulton.
Katharine Frensham. Beatrice Harraden. LC 3-26870. 1903. Dodd Mead and Company.
Katharine Kent. Mary Sewall Gardner. LC 46-5164. 1946. The Macmillan Company.
Katharine Lauderdale. Francis Marion Crawford. LC 78-5213. (Illus.). 1968. Scholarly Press.
Katharine Lauderdale. Francis Marion Crawford. LC 6-30895. 1894. Macmillan and Co.
Katharine North: A Novel. Maria Louise Pool. LC 5-2446. 1893. Harper & Brothers.
Katharine Regina. A Novel. Walter Besant. (On cover: Seaside library, Pocket ed., no. 1055). 1887. G. Munro.
Katharine Regina. A Novel. Walter Besant. (On cover: Lovell's library, no. 1109). 1887. J. W. Lovell Company.
Katharine Walton: Or, The Rebel of Dorchester. new and rev. ed. William Gilmore Simms. LC 76-8888. (Simms Revolutionary War novels; v. 4). 1976. 21.00 (ISBN 0-87152-238-1). Reprint Co. Publishers.
Katharine Walton: Or, The Rebel of Dorchester. new and rev. ed. William Gilmore Simms. 1882. A. C. Armstrong & Son.
Katharine Walton: Or, The Rebel of Dorchester. new and rev. ed. William Gilmore Simms. (On cover: Lovell's library, v. 12, no. 657). 1885. J. W. Lovell Company.
Katharine's Experiment. Felicia Buttz Clark. 1896. Eaton & Mains.
Katharine's Lover. Ronald Gorell Barnes Gorell. LC 32-21900. 1932. L. MacVeagh, Dial Press, Inc.
Katharine's Yesterday: And Other Christian Endeavor Stories. Grace Livingston Hill. LC 7-4694. 1895. Lothrop Publishing Company.
Katherine. Alexander Edwards. 1975. (pbk.) 1.25. Warner Books.
Katherine. Anya Seton. LC 57-4107. (Cardinal giant, GC752. Fiction, 2). 1957. Pocket Books.
Katherine. Anya Seton. LC 53-9260. 1954. Houghton Mifflin.
Katherine. Van-Loon, Antonia. LC 79-16365. 11.95 (ISBN 0-312-45091-5). St. Martin's Press.
Katherine: A Novel. Florence Lucinda Carpenter Dieudonne. LC 6-38433. W. J. Brewer.
Katherine: A Novel. Ernest Temple Thurston. 1907. Harper & Brothers.
Katherine. A Novel. Susa S Vance. LC 8-30233. 1885. J. B. Lippincott & Co.
Katherine and the Dark Angel. Mary Reisner. LC 48-10302. 1948. Dodd. Mead.
Katherine Barry. A Novel. Harry Hughes. LC 2093. 1900. G. W. Dillingham Co.
Katherine Christian. Hugh Walpole. 1973. pap. 1.25 o.p. (01040). Curtis.
Katherine Christian. Sir Hugh Walpole. (His The Herries saga, no. 6). 1973. (pbk) 1.25. Curtis Books.
Katherine Christian: A Novel. Hugh Walpole. LC 43-10912. 1943. Doubleday, Doran and Company, Inc.
Katherine Day. Anna Fuller. LC 1-12815. 1901. G. P. Putnam's Sons.
Katherine Earle. Adeline Trafton Knox. LC 2-22404. (Letered on cover: American girls' series. v. 34). 1902. Lee and Shepard.
Katherine Mansfield: Life & Stories. Anne Friis. 1973. Repr. of 1946 ed. 20.00 o.p. R West.
Katherine of Aragon. Julia Hamilton, pseud. Orig. Title: Princess of Aragon. 1972. pap. 0.95 o.p. (95244). Beagle Bks.
Katherine Parr. Jane Evans. Orig. Title: Royal Widow. 1972. pap. 0.95 o.p. (95249). Beagle Bks.
Katherine Somerville: Or, The Southland Before and After the Civil War. Annie Somers Gilchrist. LC 6-46350. 1906. Press of Marshall & Bruce Co.
Katherine Tree. Nan Morrison. pap. 0.75 o.s.i. (01-331). Lancer.
Katherine Trevalyan. Louise Maunsell Field. LC 8-10431. 1908. The McClure Company.
Katherine Walton. William Gilmore Simms. 1974. Repr. of 1882 ed. lib. bdg. 30.00 (ISBN 0-8414-8063-X). Folcroft.
Katherine Wentworth. Dorothy Emily Stevenson. LC 64-21921. 1964. Holt, Rinehart and Winston.
Katherine's Sheaves. Sarah Elizabeth Forbush G. S. Downs Downs. LC 4-12778. 1904. Street & Smith.
Katheryn the Wanton Queen. Maureen Peters. 1971. pap. 0.95 o.p. (95115). Beagle Bks.
Kathi" of Skenesborough. May Bell Curtis. LC 14-7565. 1.25. Champlain Publishing Company.
Kathie: A Novel. Anna Oldfield Wiggs. LC 8-37034. 1889. G. W. Dillingham.
Kathie the First. Rob Eden. LC 45-946046. 1945. Gramercy Publishing Co.
Kathie's Margaret. Lydia L. Rouse. LC 8-691. American Baptist Publication Society.
Kathleen. Amanda Hart Douglass. (Belmont Tower Book). 1977. 1.95 (ISBN 0-505-51201-7). Tower Pubns.
Kathleen. Barbara Hazard. 224p. 1980. pap. 1.75 (ISBN 0-449-50033-0, Coventry). Fawcett.
Kathleen. Christopher Darlington Morley. LC 20-5771. 1920. Doubleday, Page & Company.
Kathleen. Sigrid E Woodward. LC 29-11645. Dorrance and Company.
Kathleen. A Love Story. Frances Hodgson Burnett. LC 11-821787. T. B. Peterson & Brothers.
Kathleen Douglas. A Novel. Julia Truitt Bishop. LC 6-12720. (On cover: Primrose edition, no. 4). 1890. Street & Smith.
Kathleen Norris, 6 Vols. Kathleen Thompson Norris. pap. 4.50, boxed set o.p. (KN-B). Paperback Lib.
Kathleen Rhodora: A Novel. Oakley Prentice Hevener. LC 22-10171. Fairmont Printing Co.
Kathleen's Love: The Story of a Woman's Love. Anthony Gascoyne Young. LC 25-150518. 1925. C. W. Russell.
Kathleen's Surrender. Nancy H. Ryan. 1983. pap. 3.50 (ISBN 0-8217-1139-3). Zebra.
Kathrine: A Novel by Hans Habe Pseud. Jean Bekessy. Tr. by Harry Hansen. LC 43-15325. 1943. The Viking Press.
Kathy. Charles P. Conn & Barbara Miller. 1981. pap. 2.75 (ISBN 0-425-05766-6). Berkley Pub.
Kathy. 1st Ed. Florence Gildea. LC 55-10857. Vantage Press.
Kati in Italy. Illustrated by Daniel Dupuy. Astrid Ericsson Lindgren. LC 61-1135. 1961. Grosset & Dunlap.
Katia. Lev Nikolaevich Tolstoi. LC 8-26744. 1887. W. S. Gottsberger.
Katie. Michael McDowell. 1982. pap. 3.50 (ISBN 0-380-80184-1, 80184). Avon.
Katie. Clara Bernice Miller. LC 66-19606. 1966. Herald Press.
Katie: An Impertinent Fairy Tale. Beatrice Joy Chute. LC 77-11658. 7.95. Dutton.
Katie Jones Goes to Washington. Suzanne Roberts. pap. 0.75 o.s.i. (01-325). Lancer.
Katie, Kelly, and Heck. Jack M Bickham. LC 72-84890. (Double D western). 1973. 4.95 (ISBN 0-385-07501-4). Doubleday.
Katie Mulholland. Catherine Cookson. 512p. 1981. pap. 2.75 (ISBN 0-553-13935-5). Bantam.
Katie Mulholland. Catherine Cookson. LC 67-18656. 6.95 o.p. (ISBN 0-672-50727-7). Bobbs.
Katie Mulholland: A Novel. Catherine Cookson. LC 67-18656. 1967. Bobbs-Merrill.
Katie Stewart. A True Story. Margaret Oliphant Wilson Oliphant. (Seaside library, v. 7, no. 136). 1877. G. Munro.
Katie Von Walden: Or, Langenstein and Bobbingen. Marie Karoline Elisabeth Luise Scheele Von Nathusius. Tr. by Robinson, Mary A. LC 7-25795. The American Sunday-School Union.
Katie's Terror. David E. Fisher. LC 81-22299. 288p. 12.50 (ISBN 0-688-01114-4). Morrow.
Katie's Young Doctor. Elizabeth Seifert. LC 64-13692. 1964. Dodd, Mead.
Katika. Maria Molnar. LC 47-30229. 1947. Harper & Brothers.
Katinks. Irene Flemming Forbes-Mosse & Williams, Oakley, Tr. LC 31-26719. 1931. Dodd, Mead and Company.
Katka: A Novel. Maria Kanis Sinak. LC 46-1840. 1946. S. J. Bloch Publishing Co.
Katmandu. Gary Chafetz. 1974. (pbk.) 1.50. New American Library.
Katrin Becomes a Soldier. Adrienne Thomas & Goldsmith, Margaret Leland, 1894- Tr. LC 31-28318. 1931. Little, Brown, and Company.
Katrina. Jeramie Price. LC 55-8753. 1955. Farrar, Straus and Cudahy.
Katrina. Sally Salminen & Walford, Naomi, Tr. LC 37-285909. Farrar & Rinehart, Inc.
Katrina: A Story. Roy Rolfe Gilson. LC 6-35735. 1906. The Baker & Taylor Company.
Katrine: A Novel. Elinor Macartney Lane. LC 15-20283. Harper & Brothers.
Katrine: A Novel. Elinor Macartney Lane. LC 41-28062. 1909. Grosset & Dunlap.
Katrine, the Pride of Glen Aire: A Story of Love and Adventure in the Cascade Mountains. Alfred Rochefort Calhoun. (On cover: The laurel library, no. 16). 1894. G. Munro's Sons.
Katy and the Big Snow. Virginia Lee Burton. (Sandpiper book). 1974. (pbk.) 0.95 (ISBN 0-395-18562-9). Houghton, Mifflin.
Katy Gaumer. Elsie Singmaster. LC 15-458219. 1915. Houghton Mifflin Company.
Katy of Catoctin: Or, The Chain-Breakers; a National Romance. George Alfred Townsend. LC 4-896. 1886. D. Appleton and Company.
Katy of Catoctin: Or, The Chain-Breakers; a National Romance. George Alfred Townsend. LC 4-895. 1887. D. Appleton and Company.
Katy of Catoctin: Or, The Chain-Breakers, a National Romance by George Alfred Townsend, "Gath.". new ed., with an introd by harold b. manakee. ed. George Alfred Townsend. LC 59-15802. 1959. Tidewater Publishers.

Katya. Lucy Michaella Cores. LC 79-22919. 10.95 (ISBN 0-312-45096-6). St. Martin's Press.

Katz-Cohen: A Novel. Samuel Astrachan. LC 77-20128. 12.95 (ISBN 0-02-503950-4). Macmillan.

Katz und Maus. Gunter Grass. Ed. by H. F. Brookes & C. E. Fraenkel. 272p. (Orig.). 1971. pap. text ed. 9.00. Heinemann Ed.

Katz und Maus. Gunter Grass. LC 69-17077. 1969. text ed. 5.75x o.p. (ISBN 0-471-00211-9). Wiley.

Katzimo, Mysterious Mesa. Bobette Gugliotta. LC 73-19084. (Illus.). 1974. 4.50 (ISBN 0-396-06923-1). Dodd, Mead.

Kau-Bau-Gwas-Shee: A Flat River Story. Robertson M Augustine. LC 73-75470. (Illus.). 1973. 6.95.

Kaufman Snatch. Robin Moore. Manor Books.

Kaula. Robert L. Pruett. 1970. 3.75 o.p. Carlton.

Kavanagh: A Tale. Henry Wadsworth Longfellow. LC 7-14783. 1849. Ticknor, Reed, and Fields.

Kavanagh: A Tale. portland ed.... ed. Henry Wadsworth Longfellow. LC 28-17924. 1893. Houghton, Mifflin and Company.

Kavanagh: A Tale. Ed. for the Modern Reader by Jean Downey. Henry Wadsworth Longfellow. LC 65-256317. (Masterworks of lit. ser., M-10). pap., 1.65. Coll. & Univ. Pr.

Kavanagh: And Other Pieces. Henry Wadsworth Longfellow. LC 4-15467. Houghton, Mifflin and Company.

Kavin's World. David Mason. 1972. pap. 0.95 o.s.i. (75-372). Lancer.

Kawich's Gold Mine: An Historical Narrative of Mining in the Grand Canyon of the Colorado and of Love and Adventure Among the Polygamous Mormons of Southern Utah. by josiah f. gibbs... ed. Josiah Francis Gibbs. LC 13-3808. 1913. 1.25. Century Printing Company.

Kay Allen on Overseas Mission. Elisabeth Carleton Lansing. LC 45-4150. 1945. Thomas Y. Crowell Company.

Kay Allen on Overseas Mission. Elisabeth Carleton Hubbard Lansing. LC 45-4150. 1945. Thomas Y. Crowell Company.

Kay Danforth's Camp. Beulah Marie Dix. LC 17-25857. 1917. 1.25. Duffield and Company.

Kay Price & Stella Pajunas: Work for a Poetry Context 1967-1969. Vito Acconci. LC 77-77011. 1982. pap. text ed. 10.95 o.p. (ISBN 0-915570-08-4). Oolp Pr.

Kay Rogers: Copy Writer, by Jane Scott Pseud. Adeline McElfresh. LC 56-13297. 1956. Avalon Books.

Kay: The Left-Handed. Leslie Barringer. LC 35-19678. 1935. Doubleday, Doran & Company, Inc.

Kays. Margaret Wade Campbell Deland. LC 26-17995. 1926.

Kazan. James Oliver Curwood. LC 24-27981. Grosset & Dunlap.

Kazan: By James Oliver Curwood... with Illustrations by Gayle Hoskins. James Oliver Curwood. LC 14-516685. 1.25. The Bobbs-Merrill Company.

Kazan, the Wolf-Dog. James Oliver Curwood. LC 14-3973. 1914. 0.60. Cassell and Company, Ltd.

Kazohinia. Sandor Szathmari. 373p. 1975. 6.25x (ISBN 963-13-3518-6). Intl Pubns Serv.

Ke Whonkus People. A Story of the North Pole Country. John O Greene. LC 6-45559. 1893. Vincent Publishing Company.

Kean Land, and Other Stories. Jack Warner Schaefer. LC 59-609629. 1959. Houghton Mifflin.

Keats As Doctor & Patient. William Hale-White. 1972. lib. bdg. 13.00x (ISBN 0-374-93376-6). Octagon.

Kecksies and Other Twilight Tales. Marjorie Bowen. LC 76-17992. 7.50 (ISBN 0-87054-077-7). Arkham House.

Kedar Kross: A Tale of the North Country. Jacob Van Der Veer Shurts. LC 8-2378. 1907. R. G. Badger.

Keeban. Edwin Balmer. LC 23-7882. 1923. Little, Brown, and Company.

Keef: A Life-Story in Nine Phases. Timothy Wilfred Coakley. LC 6-20726. 1897. C. E. Brown & Co.

Keen Desire. Frank B Elser. LC 26-10203. 1926. Boni & Liveright.

Keener Love. Sally Thompson. LC 60-9039. 1960. McDowell,Obolensky.

Keenie's Tomorrow. Jennie Maria Drinkwater Conklin. LC 6-30403. D. Lothrop and Company.

Keep a Cool Head & a Warm Bosom. David Karli. LC 82-72722. 180p. (Orig.). 1982. pap. 4.00 (ISBN 0-931494-27-3). Brunswick Pub.

Keep Away from Water! Alice Ormond Campbell. LC 35-5968. Farrar & Rinehart, Incorporated.

Keep Cool: A Novel Written in Hot Weather, by Somebody, M.D.C. 2 Vols. John Neal. LC 79-93649. (American Fiction Ser). 1970. lib. bdg. 22.50 o.s.i. (ISBN 0-512-00530-3). Garrett Pr.

Keep Cool, a Novel. Written in Hot Weather. John Neal. LC 11-179627. 1817. J. Cushing.

Keep Cool: A Novel Written in Hot Weather, 2 vols. John Neal. LC 78-64084. Repr. of 1817 ed. 75.00 set (ISBN 0-404-17320-9). AMS Pr.

Keep Cool: A Novel Written in Hot Weather. John Neal. LC 72-78795. 1817. Repr. 16.00 o.p. (ISBN 0-403-01980-X). Somerset Pub.

Keep Cool, Mr. Jones. Timothy Fuller. LC 50-8759. 1950. Little, Brown.

Keep 'em Crawling: Earthworms at War. William Hazlett Upson. LC 43-986. 1943. Farrar & Rinehart, Inc.

Keep It Legal! Curtis W. Casewit. 1976. pap. 4.40 o.p. (ISBN 0-88409-037-X). Creative Bk Co.

Keep It Peaking. Hugh Fox. cancelled (ISBN 0-930012-17-8, 79-87598, Erasmus); pap. cancelled (ISBN 0-930012-16-X). Bandanna Bks.

Keep It Quiet. Richard Henry Sampson. LC 36-100619. G. P. Putnam's Sons.

Keep Love Flying. Charlotte Montgomery. LC 42-24969. 1942. Arcadia House, Inc.

Keep Murder Quiet. Selwyn Jepson. LC 41-2433. 1941. Pub. for the Crime Club, by Doubleday, Doran and Co., Inc.

Keep My Secret. A Novel. Gertrude M. Robins Reynolds. LC 7-39812. (Harper's Franklin square library, no. 536). 1886. Harper & Brothers.

Keep off My Ranch see Saddle Wolves.

Keep off the Grass. George Allan England. Small, Maynard & Company.

Keep off the Grass. Noel Godber. LC 51-38082. 1951. J. Long.

Keep the Aspidistra Flying. George Orwell. LC 56-5326. 1956. Harcourt, Brace.

Keep the Change." A Sketch of the Life of a News Agent with Details of Many Experiences on and off the Cars... R. R. Burke. LC 6-18655. 1895. Commercial Printing & Publishing Co.

Keep the Coffins Coming... Julius Long. LC 47-185954. 1947. J. Messner, Inc.

Keep the River on Your Right. Tobias Schneebaum. (Illus.). 1969. pap. 9.95 (ISBN 0-394-62438-6, E838, Ever). Grove.

Keep Up the Good Work, Charlie Brown. Charles M. Schulz. (Peanuts Ser.). (Illus.). 1979. pap. 1.75 (ISBN 0-449-23748-6, Crest). Fawcett.

Keep Your Quilt, Mary Ann. Maude Hill Beaton. LC 44-958343. 1944. Margent Press.

Keeper: A Novel. Audrey Louise Laski. LC 68-28251. 1968. 4.95. W. W. Norton.

Keeper for Lord Linford. Margaret Sebastian, pseud. (Coventry Romance Ser.: No. 170). 224p. 1982. pap. 1.50 (ISBN 0-449-50271-6, Coventry). Fawcett.

Keeper of Accounts. Irena Klepfisz. LC 82-18910. 108p. 1982. pap. 5.95 (ISBN 0-930436-17-2). Persephone.

Keeper of Antiquities: A Novel. IUrii Osipovich Dombrovskii. LC 69-16252. 1969. McGraw-Hill.

Keeper of Red Horse Pass. Wilbur C Tuttle. LC 38-1977. 1937. Houghton Mifflin Company.

Keeper of Secrets. Lester Goran. LC 77-139532. 1971. 5.95 (ISBN 0-8415-0093-2). McCall Pub. Co.

Keeper of the Bees. Gene Stratton Porter. LC 61-66510. 1961. Grosset & Dunlap.

Keeper of the Bees. Gene Stratton Porter. LC 25-16601. 1925. Doubleday, Page & Company.

Keeper of the Bees. Gene Stratton-Porter. 505p. 1981. Repr. of 1925 ed. lib. bdg. 35.00 (ISBN 0-89987-785-0). Darby Bks.

Keeper of the Children. William H Hallahan. LC 78-6578. 1978. 8.95 (ISBN 0-688-03291-5). Morrow.

Keeper of the Children. William H Hallahan. 1979. 2.50 (ISBN 0-688-03291-5). Avon Books.

Keeper of the Door. Ethel May Dell. LC 15-5818. 1915. G. P. Putnam's Sons.

Keeper of the Door. Ethel May Dell. LC 20-3266. 1919. A. L. Burt Company.

Keeper of the Faith, No. 20. Grace Livingston Hill. 192p. 1982. pap. 2.25 (ISBN 0-553-20829-2). Bantam.

Keeper of the Flame. Ida Alexa Ross Wylie. LC 42-140483. 1942. Random House.

Keeper of the Keys. Earl Derr Biggers. pap. 0.75 o.p. (T2003). Pyramid Pubns.

Keeper of the Keys. Frederick William Robinson. LC 7-41984. (On cover: Lovell's international series, 109). 1890. J. W. Lovell Company.

Keeper of the Vineyard: A Tale of the Ozarks. Caroline Abbot Stanley. LC 13-359697. Fleming H. Revell Company.

Keeper of the Wolves. Norma Bicknell Mansfield. LC 34-29905. Farrar & Rinehart, Incorporated.

Keepers. Russell H Greenan. LC 78-19410. 8.95 (ISBN 0-312-45106-7). St. Martin's Press.

Keepers of the Faith. Emilie Baker Loring. LC 76-29709. 1976. 6.95 (ISBN 0-88411-357-4). Aeonian Press.

Keepers of the Faith. Emilie Baker Loring. LC 44-8721. 1944. Little, Brown and Company.

Keepers of the Flesh. A. Degranamour. pap. 1.95 o.s.i. (Venus). Grove.

Keepers of the Gate. Steven G Spruill. LC 76-18367. 1977. 5.95 (ISBN 0-385-12420-1). Doubleday.

Keepers of the House. Shirley Ann Grau. LC 64-12306. 1964. Knopf.

Keepers of the House. Shirley Ann Grau. LC 77-154202. (Illus.). 1977. 1.50 (ISBN 0-449-23031-7). Franklin Library.

Keepers of the House. Harry Harrison Kroll. LC 40-27157. The Bobbs-Merrill Company.

Keepers of the Keys: A Charlie Chan Story. Earl Derr Biggers. LC 32-19192. The Bobbs-Merrill Company.

Keepers of the Kingdom. Glennita Miller. 1983. 18.95 (ISBN 0-671-42523-4). S&S.

Keepers of the Kingdom: A Novel. Glennita Miller. LC 82-16788. 1982. 12.95 (ISBN 0-671-42523-4). Simon and Schuster.

Keepers of the Obelisk: A Novel. Howard Shaw. LC 68-11337. 1968. Holt, Rinehart and Winston.

Keepers of the Secret. Barnaby Conrad & Nico Mastorakis. 256p. pap. 2.95 (ISBN 0-515-05544-1). Jove Pubns.

Keepers of the Trail: A Story of the Great Woods. Joseph Alexander Altsheler. LC 16-7496. (His The young trailers series). 1916. D. Appleton and Company.

Keepers of the Trail: A Story of the Great Woods. Joseph Alexander Altsheler. LC 24-28533. (His The young trailers series). 1922. D. Appleton and Company.

Keepers of the Walls. Helga Harrison. LC 56-8107. 1956. Dial Press.

Keeper's Price. Marion Zimmer Bradley. (Science Fiction Ser.). 1980. pap. 2.50 (ISBN 0-87997-837-6, UE1837). DAW Bks.

Keeping House for Jan. Maxine Hewson. LC 48-3930. 1948. Arcadia House.

Keeping Secrets: A Novel. Suzanne Morris. LC 78-22233. 1979. 12.50 (ISBN 0-385-11535-0). Doubleday.

Keeping the Church Year. H. Boone Porter. 1978. pap. 4.95 (ISBN 0-8164-2161-7). Seabury.

Keeping the Peace. Gouverneur Morris. LC 24-21148. 1924. C. Scribner's Sons.

Keeping Time. David Bear. LC 79-16368. 1979. 9.95 (ISBN 0-312-45110-5). St. Martin's Press.

Keeping up Appearances. Maximilian Foster. LC 14-7282. 1914. 1.25. D. Appleton and Company.

Keeping up with Jones. Dora Cox. 1979. pap. 4.00 (ISBN 0-89502-038-6). FEB.

Keeping up with Lizzie. Irving Bacheller. LC 11-3473. 1911. Harper & Brothers.

Keepsake. Paul Huson. 320p. (Orig.). 1981. pap. 2.95 (ISBN 0-446-90790-1). Warner Bks.

Keepsake. Ann Katherine Gilliland Ritner. LC 52-5100. 1952. Lippincott.

Keepsake Stories: "My Aunt Margaret's Mirror," "Death of the Laird's Jock," and "The Tapestried Chamber.". Walter Scott. (On cover: Lovell's library, no. 605). 1885. J. W. Lovell Company.

Keg and I. 1st Ed. Gertrude M Lockwood. LC 55-10673. 1955. Pageant Press.

Keith Deramore. Beatrice May Butt. LC 6-166744. 1892. Longmans, Green, and Co.

Keith of Kinnellan. Agnes Mure Mackenzie. LC 31-5762. 1930. R. R. Smith Inc.

Keith of the Border: A Tale of the Plains. Randall Parrish. LC 10-21301. 1910. 1.50. A. C. McClurg & Co.

Keith: Or, Righted at Last. Mary E Scott. 1881. J. B. Lippincott & Co.

Kek Huuygens, Smuggler. Robert L Fish. LC 76-7153. (Illus.). 1976. 10.00. (ISBN 0-89296-027-2). Mysterious Press.

Kela Bai: An Anglo-Indian Idyll. Charles Johnston. LC 2255. 1900. Doubleday & McClure Co.

Kelea: the Surf-Rider: A Romance of Pagan Hawaii. Alexander Stevenson Twombly. LC 6478. 1900. Fords, Howard & Hulbert.

Kell: A Novel. Jack Flannery. LC 77-10045. 8.95 (ISBN 0-316-28567-6). Little, Brown.

Keller's Anna Ruth. Elsie Singmaster. LC 26-733945. 1926. Houghton Mifflin Company.

Keller's Continental Revue. Winifred Bambrick. LC 46-11834. 1946. Houghton Mifflin Company.

Keller's Kleider Machen Leute. Keller. Ed. by Sidonie Cassirer. (German Literature Ser.). 96p. 1972. text ed. 6.95 o.p. (ISBN 0-07-010210-4); pap. text ed. 4.95 o.p. (ISBN 0-07-010209-0). McGraw.

Kelleway's Luck. Roe Richmond. 240p. (Orig.). 1981. pap. 2.25 (ISBN 0-8439-0969-2, Leisure Bks). Nordon Pubns.

Kellogg Junction. Bart Spicer. LC 69-15519. 1969. 7.95. Atheneum.

Kelly. David Chandler. LC 81-71684. 320p. 1982. 14.95 (ISBN 0-87795-395-3). Arbor Hse.

Kelly. Donald Henderson Clarke. LC 35-80406. The Vanguard Press.

Kelly. Donald Henderson Clarke. LC 47-24086. (New Avon library. 116). 1946. Avon Book Co.

Kelly: A Novel. Martin Jerome Scott. LC 24-21669. 1924. Benziger Brothers.

Kelly Among the Nightingales. J. F. Burke. LC 78-11394. 8.95. Dutton.

Kelly Blue. William W. Johnson. LC 78-21773. (Illus.). 194p. 1979. 14.95 (ISBN 0-89096-073-9). Tex A&M Univ Pr.

Kellys & the O'Kelleys. Anthony Trollope. (World's Classics Ser: No. 341). 1975. 13.95 o.p. (ISBN 0-19-250341-3). Oxford U Pr.

Kellys and the O'Kellys. Anthony Trollope. (seaside library, v. 71, no. 1436). 1882. G. Munro.

Kellys and the O'Kellys. Anthony Trollope. LC 30-15222. (Half-title: The World's classics, CCCXLI). 1929. H. Milford, Oxford University Press.

Kellys & the O'Kellys. Anthony Trollope. LC 37-27283. Random House.

Kellys & The O'Kellys. Anthony Trollope & Thorold, Algar Labouchere, Ed. LC 12-39447. (Half-title: The new pocket library). 1906. John Lane.

Kellys & the O'Kellys: Or Landlords & Tenants. Anthony Trollope. Ed. by W. J. McCormack. (World's Classics Ser.). 550p. 1982. pap. 6.95 (ISBN 0-19-281577-6). Oxford U Pr.

Kelly's Bar. Steven Farrell. 1980. pap. 4.00 (ISBN 0-89502-029-7). FEB.

Kelly's Heroes. Burt Hirschfeld. (Orig.). 1970. pap. 0.60 o.p. (ISBN 0-447-73888-7). Lancer.

Kelly's Man. Rosemary Carter. (Harlequin Presents Ser.). (Orig.). 1980. pap. text ed. 1.50 (ISBN 0-373-10362-X, Pub. by Harlequin). PB.

Kelpie Ledge. Ellen Jane MacLeod. 1972. 4.95. Lenox Hill Press.

Kelpie's Burn: A Novel. John Latimer. LC 76-372656. 1976. (ISBN 0-7737-0021-8). Musson Book.

Kelston Knoll. Catherine Dupre. LC 80-14196. 1980. 11.95 (ISBN 0-312-45137-7). St. Martin's Press.

Kelston Knoll. Catherine Dupre. ("A Signet Book.). 1981. 2.95 (ISBN 0-451-09895-1). New American Library.

Kelverdale. A Novel. William Ulick O'Connor Cuffe Desart. (Franklin square library, no. 40). 1879. Harper & Brothers.

Kelwin. Neal Barrett, Jr. (Orig.). 1970. pap. 0.95 o.p. (ISBN 0-447-75133-6). Lancer.

Kemmler: Or, The Fatal Chair. A Thrilling Dedective Story. John A Fraser. LC 6-43148. (Globe detective series. v. 1, no. 21). 1890. The Eagle Publishing Co.

Kempton-Wace Letters... Jack London & Strunsky, Anna. LC 3-12286. 1903. The Macmillan Company.

Kempton-Wace Letters. Jack London & Anna Strunsky Walling. LC 67-30817. Haskell House Publishers.

Ken, the Courageous. Robert Ames Bennet. LC 28-323. 1927. A. C. McClurg & Co.

Ken Ward in the Jungle. Zane Grey. 312p. Repr. of 1912 ed. lib. bdg. 16.30x (ISBN 0-89190-763-7). Am Repr-Rivercity Pr.

Kendall's Sister. Robert Swasey. LC 22-424097. 1922. Little, Brown, and Company.

Kenelm Chillingly: His Adventures and Opinions. the globe ed. Edward George Earle Lytton Bulwer-Lytton Lytton. LC 7-8465. 1873. J. B. Lippincott & Co.

Kenelm Chillingly, His Adventures and Opinions. library ed.... ed. Edward George Earle Lytton Bulwer-Lytton Lytton. LC 34-37783. 1873. J. B. Lippincott & Co.

Kenelm Chillingly: His Adventures and Opinions. Edward George Earle Lytton Bulwer-Lytton Lytton. LC 8-26644. G. Routledge and Sons.

Kenelm Chillingly, His Adventures and Opinions. Edward George Earle Lytton Bulwer-Lytton Lytton. LC 7-8464. J. W. Lovell Company.

Kenelm Chillingly: His Adventures and Opinions. Edward George Earle Lytton Bulwer-Lytton Lytton. LC 27-136899. (Seaside library. v. 59, no. 1205). 1882. G. Munro.

Kenelm Chillingly; His Adventures and Opinions. Edward George Earle Lytton Bulwer-Lytton Lytton. LC 7-8463. (Half-title: Novels of Sir Edward Bulwer Lytton. Library ed. Novels of life and manners, vol. XIII-XIV). 1893. Little, Brown, and Company.

Kenelm Chillingly: His Adventures and Opinions. Edward George Earle Lytton Bulwer-Lytton Lytton. LC 43-466664. 1873. Harper & Brothers.

Kenelm's Desire. Hughes Cornell. LC 6-106541. 1906. Little, Brown, and Company.

Kenguru. Yuz Aleshkovsky. 85p. (Rus.). 1980. 13.50 o.p. (ISBN 0-88233-566-9); pap. 6.00 (ISBN 0-88233-567-7). Ardis Pubs.

Kenilworth. Sir Walter Scott & Alice Cecilia Cooper. LC 50-6396. 1950. Globe Book Co.

Kenilworth. Walter Scott. LC 57-59453. (Great illustrated classics). (Illus.). 1956. Dodd, Mead.

TITLE INDEX KEY TO MY PRISON.

Kenilworth... Walter Scott. LC 8-5774. 1869. Fields, Osgood, & Co., Successors to Ticknor and Fields.
Kenilworth... Walter Scott. LC 8-30293. (Waverley novels. Household ed.). 1871. J. R. Osgood and Company (Late Ticknor & Fields, and Fields, Osgood, & Co.
Kenilworth. Walter Scott. (Seaside library. v. 10, no. 183). 1877. G. Munro.
Kenilworth. Walter Scott. (On cover: Lovell's library, no. 625). 1885. J. W. Lovell Company.
Kenilworth. Walter Scott. (On cover: Seaside library. Pocket ed., no. 1063). 1888. G. Munro.
Kenilworth. Walter Scott. LC 21-21460. (Manhattan library. no. 24). 1892. A. L. Burt.
Kenilworth. Walter Scott. Ed. by Lang, Andrew. LC 16-3381. (On cover: Waverley novels). Dana, Estes & Company.
Kenilworth. Walter Scott. LC 8-2930. (Standard literature series. no. 7). 1896. University Publishing Company.
Kenilworth. Walter Scott. Ed. by Norris, Mary Harriott. (Eclectic school readings). American Book Company.
Kenilworth. Walter Scott. (Half-title: The "prairie" classics). 1907. A. C. McClurg & Co.
Kenilworth. Walter Scott. (Half-title: Everyman's library, ed. by Ernest Rhys. Fiction. no. 135). 1907. J. M. Dent & Co.
Kenilworth. Walter Scott. Ed. by Castleman, Josiah Hamilton. LC 7-12271. (Macmillan's pocket American and English classics). 1907. The Macmillan Company.
Kenilworth. Walter Scott. LC 26-23566. Thomas Y. Crowell Company.
Kenilworth. Walter Scott. 1920. D. McKay Company.
Kenilworth. Walter Scott. LC 36-37006. (Half-title: Everyman's library, ed. by Ernest Rhys. Fiction. no. 135). 1929. J. M. Dent & Sons, Ltd.
Kenilworth. Walter Scott. Ed. by Stauffer, Ruth Matilda. LC 40-32369. (academy classics). Allyn and Bacon.
Kenilworth. Walter Scott. Ed. by Cleveland, Eunice Jeannette. LC 28-22775. (modern readers' series). 1928. The Macmillan Company.
Kennedy for the Defense. George V. Higgins. LC 79-18484. 1980. 9.95 (ISBN 0-394-42406-9). Knopf.
Kennedy Kids. Bill Adler. LC 76-9586. 1976. pap. 1.75 o.p. (ISBN 0-87216-326-1, K16326). Playboy.
Kennedy of Bar 77. Claude Rister. LC 37-18254. Phoenix Press.
Kennedy of Glenhaugh: Being a Faithful History of the Strange Happening That Befell Master John Kennedy...in the Year of Grace 1789, and Set Forth by Adam Gillicuddy... David Maclure. LC 1553. The Mershon Company.
Kennedy Square. Francis Hopkinson Smith. LC 11-22130. 1911. C. Scribner's Sons.
Kennedy's Gold. Michael Bonner. LC 60-7939. (Double D western). 1960. Doubleday.
Kennedy's Second Best: A Story of the Great North-West. John Dolliver Freeman. LC 26-146303. Fleming H. Revell Company.
Kennel Murder Case. S. S. Van Dine, pseud. 1980. lib. bdg. 10.95 (ISBN 0-8398-2558-7, Gregg). G K Hall.
Kennel Murder Case. Willard Huntington Wright. LC 79-22861. (Gregg Press Mystery Fiction Series). (Illus.). 1980. 10.95 (ISBN 0-8398-2558-7). Gregg Press.
Kennel Murder Case: A Philo Vance Story. Willard Huntington Wright. LC 33-18452. 1933. C. Scribner's Sons.
Kenneth Roberts Reader. Kenneth Roberts. 460p. 1976. Repr. of 1945 ed. lib. bdg. 9.95 (ISBN 0-89190-444-1). Am Repr-Rivercity Pr.
Kenny. Louis Bromfield. LC 47-4067. 1947. Harper & Brothers.
Kenny. Leona Dalrymple. LC 17-21645. 1.35. The Reilly & Britton Co.
Kenny's Stories. Kenny McGuire. 1981. 4.95 (ISBN 0-8062-1559-3). Carlton.
Ken's Bright Room. Dorothy Hamilton. (Illus.). 88p. (Orig.). 1982. 6.95 (ISBN 0-8361-3327-7); pap. 3.50 (ISBN 0-8361-3328-5). Herald Pr.
Kensho. Dennis Schmidt. 320p. 1981. pap. 2.50 (ISBN 0-441-43526-2). Ace Bks.
Kent Barstow, Special Agent. Rutherford George Montgomery. LC 58-10438. 1958. Duell, Sloan and Pearce.
Kent Dell's Warpath. Lester Wayne Merha. (YA) 1980. 6.95 (Avalon). Bouregy.
Kent Family Chronicles, No. 2. Incl. Titans; Warriors; Lawless; Americans. Date not set. pap. 13.45 boxed set (ISBN 0-515-06813-6). Jove Pubns.
Kent Fort Manor; a Novel. William Henry Babcock. LC 3-1575. 1902. H. T. Coates & Co.
Kent Heiress. Roberta Gellis. (Orig.). 1982. pap. 3.50 (ISBN 0-440-14537-6). Dell.
Kent Knowles: Quahaug. Joseph Crosby Lincoln. LC 14-18497. 1914. D. Appleton and Company.
Kent Squire: Being a Record of Certain Adventures of Ambrose Gwynett, Esquire of Thornhaugh. Frederick William Hayes. LC 2242. 1900. The F. M. Lupton Publishing Company.
Kentons. William Dean Howells. LC 72-165052. (Selected edition of W. D. Howells, v. 25). (Illus.). 1971. 10.00 (ISBN 0-253-33173-0). Indiana University Press.
Kentons. William Dean Howells. LC 76-98769. 1969. Greenwood Press.
Kentons: A Novel. William Dean Howells. LC 71-145085. 1970. Scholarly Press.
Kentons: A Novel. William Dean Howells. LC 2-11891. 1902. Harper & Brothers.
Kents. Le Grand Cannon. LC 33-34556. Farrar & Rinehart, Incorporated.
Kentuckian: A Thrilling Tale of Ohio Life in the Early Sixties. James Ball Naylor. LC 6-3125. 1905. C. M. Clark Publishing Co., Inc.
Kentuckian in New York. William Alexander Caruthers. LC 68-23714. (Americans in Fiction Ser.). lib. bdg. 15.00 (ISBN 0-8398-0255-2); pap. text ed. 5.50x (ISBN 0-89197-817-8). Irvington.
Kentuckian in New-York. Or, The Adventures of Three Southerns. William Alexander Caruthers. LC 6-24219. 1834. Harper Brothers.
Kentuckian in New-York: Or, the Adventures of Three Southerns. William Alexander Caruthers & A Virginian. LC 68-23714. (Americans in Fiction). 1968. Gregg Press.
Kentuckian" Or, "A Woman's Reaping,". Isaac Marshall Page. LC 17-4312. Billings Ptg. Co.
Kentuckians. Janice Holt Giles. LC 53-707447. 1953. Houghton Mifflin Co.
Kentuckians. Janice Holt Giles. 1976. (pbk.) 1.50 (ISBN 0-380-00496-8). Avon.
Kentuckians: A Knight of the Cumberland, by John Fox, Jr.; Illustrated by W. T. Smedley and F. C. Yohn. John Fox. LC 9-13915. 1909. C. Scribner's Sons.
Kentuckians: A Novel. John Fox. LC 76-164561. (American fiction reprint series). 1971. (ISBN 0-8369-7037-3). Books for Libraries Press.
Kentuckians: A Novel. John Fox. LC 5-2453. 1898. Harper & Brothers.
Kentucky Cardinal. new ed., rev. with a new preface; with illustrations by hugh thomason. ed. James Lane Allen. (Macmillan's modern Action library). 1913. The Macmillan Company.
Kentucky Cardinal: A Story. James Lane Allen. LC 68-20002. (Americans in Fic.). 1968. 10.00. Gregg Pr.
Kentucky Cardinal: A Story. James Lane Allen. LC 24-22220. (On cover: Harpers little novels). Harper & Brothers.
Kentucky Cardinal: A Story. James Lane Allen. LC 1-5114. (Lettered on cover: Harper's little novels). 1895. Harper & Brothers.
Kentucky Cardinal: A Story. James Lane Allen. LC 99-5564. (Lettered on cover: Harper's little novels). 1898. Harper & Brothers.
Kentucky Cardinal: A Story. James Lane Allen. LC 21-21464. 1920. The Macmillan Company.
Kentucky Cardinal: A Story. James Lane Allen. (Lettered on cover: Harper's little novels). 1898. Harper & Brothers.
Kentucky Cardinal, Aftermath, and Other Selected Works. James Lane Allen & William K. Bottorff. LC 67-17939. 1967. College & University Press.
Kentucky Cardinal, Aftermath: And Other Selected Works. Ed. for the Modern Reader by William K. Bottorff. James Lane Allen & William K. Bottorff. LC 67-179396. (Masterworks of lit. ser.). 1967. 4.50, 1.95 pap.,. Coll. & Univ.
Kentucky Cardinal: And Aftermath. new ed., rev., with a new preface and one hundred illustrations by hugh thompson. ed. James Lane Allen. LC 1-29256. 1900. The Macmillan Company.
Kentucky Cardinal & Aftermath. edited for school use by jane c. tunnell... ed. James Lane Allen & Tunnell, Jane C., Ed. LC 24-30860. 1924. The Macmillan Company.
Kentucky Chivalry. Lulie McLaughlin. 1932. L. M. C. Baxley.
Kentucky Chronicle. John Thompson Gray. 1906. The Neale Publishing Company.
Kentucky Colonel. Opie Percival Read. LC 7-36501. 1890. F. J. Schulte & Company.
Kentucky Folks and Some Others. Frankie Parker Davis. LC 2221. 1900. The Editor Publishing Co.
Kentucky Girl: Or, A Question Unanswered. Ann Searcy Jett. LC 9-29972. 1909. Printing Department, Berea College.
Kentucky Ham. William Burroughs. LC 72-94695. 1973. 5.95 (ISBN 0-525-13850-1). E. P. Dutton.
Kentucky Jane. Martha Griffis Marler. LC 62-13770. 1962. Printed by Naylor Co.
Kentucky Nurse. Florence Stonebraker. LC 63-22867. 1963. Arcadia House.
Kentucky of Kentucky: A Romance of the Blue Grass Region. Thomas Henderson Kniffin. LC 9-26665. 1909. 1.25. Cochrane Publishing Co.
Kentucky Pride. Gene Markey. LC 56-7736. 1956. Random House.
Kentucky Ranger. Edward T Curnick. LC 24-1647. 1923. The Christian Witness Co.
Kentucky Spitfire: Caitlyn McGregor. Kitt Brown. (Frontier Woman Saga Ser.: No. 1). 1982. pap. 2.95 (GM). Fawcett.
Kentucky Stand. Jere Hungerford Wheelwright. LC 51-978. 1951. Scribner.
Kentucky Story: A Collection of Short Stories. Ed. by Hollis Spurgeon Summers. LC 54-7480. 1954. University of Kentucky Press.
Kentucky Trace: A Novel of the American Revolution. Harriette Louisa Simpson Arnow. LC 73-20748. 1974. 6.95 (ISBN 0-394-48990-X). Knopf; Distributed by Random House.
Kentucky Warbler. James Lane Allen. LC 18-2605. 1918. Doubleday, Page & Company.
Kentucky's Love: Or, Roughing It Around Paris. Edward King. LC 7-12166. 1873. Lee and Shepard.
Kenworthys. Margaret Wilson. LC 25-159848. 1925. Harper & Brothers.
Kenya Mist. Florence Riddell. LC 24-234907. 1924. H. Holt and Company.
Kenyatta's Escape. Al C Clark. 1974. (pbk.) 1.50 (ISBN 0-87067-460-9). Holloway House.
Kenyatta's Escape. Donald Goines. (Orig.). 1974. pap. 1.95 (ISBN 0-87067-661-X, BH661). Holloway.
Kenyatta's Last Hit. Al C Clark. 1975. (pbk.) 1.50 (ISBN 0-87067-471-4). Holloway House.
Kenyatta's Last Hit. Donald Goines. 224p. (Orig.). 1975. pap. 1.95 (ISBN 0-87067-669-5, BH024). Holloway.
Keoni, My Brother. Virginia Nielsen, pseud. LC 65-22394. 1965. D. McKay Co.
Kepler. John Banville. LC 82-3142. 192p. 1983. 13.95 (ISBN 0-87923-438-5). Godine.
Kept: A Story of Post-War London. Alec Waugh. LC 25-19826. 1925. A. & C. Boni.
Kept in the Dark. Anthony Trollope. LC 77-20469. 1978. 2.50 (ISBN 0-486-23609-9). Dover Publications.
Kept Man. Rosalind Wade. LC 33-16581. 1933. E. P. Dutton & Co., Inc.
Kept Men. Linda DuBreuil. (Orig.). 1976. pap. 1.50 o.p. (LB341DK, Leisure Bks). Nordon Pubns.
Kept Woman. Vina Delmar. LC 29-20433. Harcourt, Brace and Company.
Kept Woman. Vina Delmar. LC 47-24083. (New Avon library. 121). 1947. Avon Book Co.
Keren of Lowbole. Una Lucy Silberrad. George H. Doran Company, Publishers in America for Hodder & Stoughton.
Kerkhoven's Third Existence. Jakob Wassermann & Paul, Eden, 1865- Tr. LC 34-28478. Liveright Publishing Corporation.
Kermanshah Transfer. Efrem Sigel. LC 72-11954. 1973. 6.95. Macmillan.
Kernel Corn of Kentucky. William Rufus Scott. LC 28-19549. Press of Byron S. Adams.
Kerrigan's Quality. Jane Barlow. LC 4-15277. 1894. Dodd, Mead & Company.
Kerry. Grace Livingston Hill. LC 31-30499. 1931. J. B. Lippincott Company.
Kesey. Ken Kesey & Michael Strelow. LC 77-936. (Illus.). 1977. 6.95. (ISBN 0-918402-01-8) (ISBN 0-918402-02-6). Northwest Review Books.
Kesey's Garage Sale. Ken Kesey. LC 77-186734. (Illus.). 1973. pap. 5.95 o.p. (ISBN 0-670-00346-8). Penguin.
Kesrick. Lin Carter. 1982. pap. 2.25 (ISBN 0-87997-779-5, UE1779). DAW Bks.
Kessler Alliance. Thomas Horstman. (Belmont Tower Book)). 2.25 (ISBN 0-505-51463-X). Tower Publications.
Kessler Legacy. Richard Martin Stern. LC 67-17297. 1967. 4.95. Scribners.
Kestell of Greystone: A Novel. Amelie Claire Leroy. (Added t.-p.: Lovell's international series, no. 75). 1890. F. F. Lovell & Co.
Kestle Mount. Joan Hunter, pseud. 1979. 1.95 (ISBN 0-671-82273-X). Pocket Books.
Kestrel House Mystery. T. C. H Jacobs, pseud. LC 36-10835. 1933. The Macaulay Company.
Kettel Mill Mystery. Inez Hildagard Oellrichs. LC 39-29480. 1939. Pub. for the Crime Club by Doubleday Doran & Co., Inc.
Kettel Mill Mystery. Inez Hildagard Oellrichs. LC 39-29480. 1939. Pub. for the Crime Club by Doubleday Doran & Co., Inc.
Ketti Shalom. James Murdock. LC 53-502653. 1953. Random House.
Kettle. Gustav Eckstein. LC 33-9094. 1933. Harper & Brothers.
Kettle Drums and Tom Toms. James Herman Craig. LC 29-2469. Burton Publishing Company.
Kettle of Fish. Ronald Frederick Henry Duncan. LC 74-881718. 1971. 2.00 (ISBN 0-491-00367-6). W. H. Allen.
Kevin. Wallace Hamilton. LC 79-26871. 10.95 (ISBN 0-312-45179-2). St. Martin's Press.
Kew Gardens. Virginia Stephen Woolf. LC 77-24759. 1977. 20.00 (ISBN 0-8414-9492-4). Folcroft Library Editions.
Key. John P. Cohane. LC 75-34509. (Illus.). 288p. 1976. pap. 5.95 o.p. (ISBN 0-8052-0527-6). Schocken.
Key. Jun'Ichiro Tanizaki. LC 80-39939. 1981. 4.95 (ISBN 0-399-50522-9). Perigee Books.
Key. Lee Thayer, pseud. LC 24-29640. 1924. Doubleday, Page & Company.
Key: A Miss Silver Mystery. Patricia Wentworth. LC 44-9911. 1944. J. B. Lippincott Company.
Key Above the Door: A Novel. Maurice Walsh. LC 26-142358. 1927. Frederick A. Stokes Company.
Key Exchange. Kevin Wade. 96p. 1982. pap. 2.50 (ISBN 0-380-61119-8, 61119-8, Discus). Avon.
Key Game. Don James. pap. 0.60 o.p. (60-387). Manor Bks.
Key Lock Man. Louis L'Amour. (Orig.). 1970. pap. 1.95 (ISBN 0-553-13881-2). Bantam.
Key Man. Valentine Williams. LC 26-17283. 1926. Houghton Mifflin Company.
Key Man. 1st Ed. Clarence Budington Kelland. LC 52-7288. 1952. Harper.
Key Next Door: A Novel. Mathilde Eiker. LC 37-27363. 1937. Doubleday, Doran & Company, Inc.
Key Note: A Novel. Clara Louise Root Burnham. LC 21-19849. 1921. Houghton Mifflin Company.
Key of Dreams: A Romance of the Orient. Lily Moresby Adams Beck. LC 22-22155. 1922. Dodd, Mead and Company.
Key of Eden: Adam and Eve: Or, The Garden of Nature... Cornelia Walker Currie. LC 6-34001. 1890. H. M. Mott's Councelor Print.
Key of Gold. Jan Hathaway. (Contemporary Teens Ser.). 224p. (Orig.). 1981. pap. 2.25 (ISBN 0-89531-145-3, 0146-96). Sharon Pubns.
Key of Gold: A Novel. Lawrence L Schoonover. LC 68-11533. 1968. Little, Brown.
Key of Life. Francis Brett Young. LC 28-106242. 1928. A. A. Knopf.
Key of Paradise: A Novel. Sidney Pickering. LC 3-12816. 1903. The Macmillan Company.
Key of the Chest. Neil Miller Gunn. LC 46-196861. 1946. G. W. Stewart, Inc.
Key of the Fields: And Boldero. Henry Milner Rideout. LC 18-3170. 1918. 1.35. Duffield and Company.
Key of the Holy House: A Romance of Old Antwerp. Albert Lee. LC 98-1236. (Half-title: Appletons' town and country library, no. 255). 1899. D. Appleton and Company.
Key of the Unknown. Rosa Nouchette Carey. 1909. 1.50. J. B. Lippincott Company.
Key Out of Time. Andre Norton, pseud. 224p. 1981. pap. 2.25 (ISBN 0-441-43675-7). Ace Bks.
Key Out of Time. Andre Norton, pseud. 1979. lib. bdg. 9.95 (ISBN 0-8398-2424-6, Gregg). G K Hall.
Key to Death. Frances Louise Davis Lockridge & Richard Lockridge. 224p. 1975. Repr. of 1954 ed. lib. bdg. 13.25x (ISBN 0-89190-906-0). Am Repr-Rivercity Pr.
Key to Death: A Mr. and Mrs. North Mystery. Frances Louise Davis Lockridge & Richard Lockridge. LC 76-212. 1976. 11.00 (ISBN 0-89190-906-0). Rivercity Press.
Key to Death, by Frances and Richard Lockridge. 1st Ed. Frances Louise Davis Lockridge & Richard Lockridge. LC 54-942739. (Their A. Mr. and Mrs. North mystery). 1954. Lippincott.
Key to Happiness. Albert Quandt. LC 49-868018. 1949. Arcadia House.
Key to Her Heart. Julia Alcott. (Signet Book). 1976. (pbk.) 1.25. New American Library.
Key to Laurels. March Cost, pseud. LC 72-90476. (O.s.i.). 7.95 o.s.i. (ISBN 0-8149-0723-7). Vanguard.
Key to Laurels. Peggy Morrison, pseud. LC 72-90476. 1973. 5.95 (ISBN 0-8149-0723-7). Vanguard Press.
Key to Love. Renee Shann. LC 47-23978. 1947. Random House.
Key to Many Doors. Emilie Baker Loring. LC 76-41708. 1977. 6.95 (ISBN 0-88411-358-2). Aeonian Press.
Key to Many Doors. Emilie Baker Loring. LC 67-23835. 1967. Little, Brown.
Key to Many Doors. large print ed. Emilie Baker Loring. LC 81-2814. 1981. 12.95 (ISBN 0-8161-3210-0). G.K. Hall.
Key to Midnight. Leigh Nichols. 1979. 2.50 (ISBN 0-671-80915-6). Pocket Books.
Key to Murder. Ralph Cross. (Orig.). 1980. pap. 1.95 o.s.i. (ISBN 0-505-51487-7). Tower Bks.
Key to My Heart. Victor Sawdon Pritchett. (O.s.i.). 1964. 7.95 o.s.i. (ISBN 0-394-43187-1). Random.
Key to My Prison. Harris Downey. LC 64-13652. 1965. bds., 3.95. Delacorte, Dist. Dial.

Key to Nicholas Street. Stanley Ellin. LC 52-8353. (Inner sanctum mystery). 1952. Simon and Schuster.

Key to Nicholas Street. Stanley Ellin. LC 81-47378. (Fifty Classics of Crime Fiction, 1950-1975). 1982. 14.95 (ISBN 0-8240-4981-0). Garland.

Key to Rebecca. Ken Follett. LC 80-16760. 1980. 12.95 (ISBN 0-688-03734-8). Morrow.

Key to Rebecca. Ken Follett. LC 80-27397. 1981. 16.95 (ISBN 0-8161-3151-1). G. K. Hall.

Key to Romance. Louis Arthur Cunningham. LC 54-107212. 1954. Arcadia House.

Key to St. Louis. Shirley Seifert. 1975. Repr. of 1963 ed. lib. bdg. 5.95 (ISBN 0-89190-136-1). Am Repr-Rivercity Pr.

Key to the Cage. Allan L Kolber. LC 57-9831. (Milestone book). 1957. Comet Press Books.

Key to the Casa. Maud Keck & Orbison, Olive. LC 29-90983. 1929. I. Washburn.

Key to the Complete Course of Exercises in Latin Syntex: Adapted to Zumpt's Grammar. John Kenrick. LC 11-11477. 1831. G. & C. & H. Carvill.

Key to the Copeland Crime. May Roberts Clark. LC 43-37793. 1938. The Rosicrucian Press, Ltd.

Key to the Disunion Conspiracy. The Partisan Leader. Nathaniel Beverley Tucker. LC 4-884. 1861. Reprinted by Rudd & Carleton.

Key to the Door. Alan Sillitoe. 1962. 5.95 o.p. Knopf.

Key to the Morgue. Robert Lee Martin. LC 59-121578. (Red badge detective). 1959. Dodd, Mead.

Key to the Other. Georgianne Sampson. LC 52-5119. 1952. Doubleday.

Key to the Other. Georgianne Sampson Trask. LC 52-5119. 1952. Doubleday.

Key to the Suite. John Dann MacDonald. 1978. pap. 1.95 (ISBN 0-449-13995-6, GM). Fawcett.

Key to Yesterday. Charles Neville Buck. LC 10-16976. 1910. 1.50. W. J. Watt & Company.

Key: Translated from the Japanese by Howard Hibbett. Jun'Ichiro Tanizaki. LC 60-53232. 1961. half cloth 3.50. Knopf.

Key West. Burt Hirschfeld. LC 78-12600. 1979. 9.95 (ISBN 0-688-03416-0). Morrow.

Key West Connection. Randy Striker. (Dusky MacMorgan Ser.: No. 1). (Orig.). 1981. pap. 1.95 (ISBN 0-451-09567-7, J9567, Sig). NAL.

Key Witness. Frank Kane. LC 57-5949. (Dell first edition, A126). 1956. Dell Pub. Co.

Key Witness. Willo Davis Roberts. LC 74-30580. (Red mask mystery). 1975. 5.95 (ISBN 0-399-11508-0). Putnam.

Keyhole Peeper: By Jay De Baker Pseud. Prentice Winchell. LC 57-25378. (Bedcon book original, no. 110). 1955. Beacon Publications Corps.

Keynote: Monsieur Des Lourdines. Alphonse De Chateaubriant. Tr. by Davidson, Theodora (Keppel) LC 12-22311. 1.20. Hodder & Stoughton, George H. Doran Company.

Keynotes. Mary Chavelita Bright. LC 6-253845. (On cover: Keynotes, ser. no. 1). 1893. Roberts Brothers.

Keys of England. W. Victor Cook. LC 29-104274. 1929. L. MacVeagh, The Dial Press.

Keys of Fate: A Novel. Herman Shores. 1895. Arena Publishing Co.

Keys of Heaven. Clara Elizabeth Laughlin. LC 18-260191. 1.50. George H. Doran Company.

Keys of Hell. Jack Higgins, pseud. 160p. 1976. pap. 1.95 (ISBN 0-449-14298-1, GM). Fawcett.

Keys of Hell: By Martin Fallon Pseud. Henry Patterson. LC 65-14276. (Raven bk.). bds., 3.50. Abelard.

Keys of My Prison. Frances Shelley Wees. LC 56-544660. 1956. Published for the Crime Club by Doubleday.

Keys of St. Peter, a Novel. Translated from the French by Edward Hyams. Roger Peyrefitte. LC 56-10194. Criterion Books.

Keys of the City. Elmer Holmes Davis. LC 25-42076. 1925. R. M. McBride & Company.

Keys of the City. Oscar Graeve. LC 16-176556. 1916. 1.35. The Century Co.

Keys of the Kingdom. Archibald Joseph Cronin. LC 41-123433. 1941. Little, Brown and Company.

Key's Secret. Rubye Kilgore Hancock. 1967. Zondervan Pub. House.

Keys to Love. Dorothy Brenner Frances. 1975. 4.95. Avalon Books.

Keys to the House. Elizabeth Marion. LC 44-3823. 1944. Thomas Y. Crowell Company.

Keystone Counselor: The Life and Times of Benjamin Sachariah Moyer, Lawyer, Teacher, and Naturalist. Isaac J Vanartsdalen. LC 59-44066. 1959. Exposition Press.

Keystone Kid. Frank Roderus. LC 77-27717. 1978. 7.95 (ISBN 0-385-14158-0). Doubleday.

Kezdodik-Elolrol. Leslie Konnyu. (Hungarian.). pap. 1.25 (ISBN 0-911862-12-9). Hungarian Rev.

Kezia and the Doctor: Or, The Infidel's School. Lydia L Rouse. LC 8-692. 1888. American Sunday-School Union.

Keziah Comr. Joseph Crosby Lincoln. LC 9-244509. 1909. D. Appleton and Company.

Keziah Dane. Sue Grafton. LC 67-22615. 1967. Macmillan.

KG Two Hundred. J. D. Gilman & John Clive. 1978. pap. 2.25 (ISBN 0-380-39115-5, 39115). Avon.

KG 200. J. D. Gilman & John Clive. LC 77-21716. 8.95 (ISBN 0-671-22890-0). Simon and Schuster.

KG 200. J. D. Gilman & John Clive. LC 78-7282. 1978. 14.95 (ISBN 0-8161-6591-2). G. K. Hall.

KGB Directive. Richard Hubert Francis Cox. LC 81-50684. 1981. 12.95 (ISBN 0-670-41280-5). Viking Press.

Khai of Ancient Khem. Brian Lumley. 1980. 2.25 (ISBN 0-425-04528-5). Berkley Books.

Khaki; How Tredick Got into the War. Freeman Tilden. LC 18-134501. 1918. The Macmillan Company.

Khaki Mafia: A Novel. Robin Moore & June Collins. LC 79-168317. 1971. 5.95. Crown Publishers.

Khaled: A Tale of Arabia. Francis Marion Crawford. LC 9-2503. 1891. Macmillan and Co.

Khamba and Thoibi: The Unscaled Height of Love. Tombi Singh, N. LC 76-904040. (Illus.). 1976. 50.00. Chitrebirentombichand Khorjeirup.

Khan: Phantom Emperor of 1940. Jerome Oliver. LC 34-295462. (On cover: Cosmopolitan publications). J. C. Reklar and Co.

Kharduni, a Mystery of the Secret Service. Andrew Soutar. LC 34-5592. The Macaulay Company.

Khi to Freedom. Ardath Mayhar. 1983. pap. 1.95 (Pub. by Ace Science Fiction). Ace Bks.

Khufra Run. James Graham, pseud. LC 72-92213. 192p. 1973. 5.95 o.p. (ISBN 0-385-01941-6). Doubleday.

Khufra Run. Henry Patterson. LC 72-92213. 1973. 5.95 (ISBN 0-385-01941-6). Doubleday.

Khufra Run. Henry Patterson. (Fawcett Crest Book). 1976. (pbk.) 1.25. Fawcett.

Kiai! Piers Anthony & Roberto Fuentes. (Berkley medallion book). 1974. (pbk) 0.95 (ISBN 0-425-02511-X). Berkley Pub. Co.

Kiamichi of the Choctaws. June Cullison Otjen. LC 40-30183. Burton Publishing Company.

Kiana: A Tradition of Hawaii. James Jackson Jarves. LC 7-10344. 1857. J. Munroe and Company.

Kibei: A Novel. Max Templeman. LC 79-12020. 1979. 10.95 (ISBN 0-916630-12-9). Daimax Pub. House.

Kiboko. 1st Ed. Daniel Pratt Mannix. LC 58-5849. 1958. Lippincott.

Kick Him Down Hill: Or, Ups and Downs in Business. M. M Smith. LC 8-9616. 1875. United States Publishing Company.

Kick-in: A Novelization of Willard Mack's Play. D Torbett. Mack, Willard. E. J. Clode.

Kick Me in the Traditions. Translated from the Danish by Carl Malmberg. Leif Panduro. LC 61-5174. Eriksson-Taplinger.

Kick Start. James Douglas Rutherford McConnell. LC 74-77299. 1974. 5.95. Walker.

Kick Start. Douglas Rutherford. LC 74-77299. 192p. 1974. 5.95 o.p. (ISBN 0-8027-5303-5). Walker & Co.

Kick the Dog Gently. Ozro Franklin Grant. LC 65-25168. 1965. Bobbs-Merrill.

Kicked to Death by a Camel. Richard W Bulliet. LC 73-4152. 1973. 5.95 (ISBN 0-06-012157-2). Harper & Row.

Kicked to Death by a Camel. Clarence J. Jackson, pseud. LC 73-4152. (Novel of Suspense Ser.). 168p. 1973. 5.95 o.p. (ISBN 0-06-012157-2, HarpT). Har-Row.

Kid. John Baxter. LC 80-25042. 1981. 13.95 (ISBN 0-670-41297-X). Viking Press.

Kid. John D Seelye. 1973. (pbk.) 0.95. Dell.

Kid. John D Seelye. LC 71-171891. 1972. (ISBN 0-670-41298-8). Viking Press.

Kid. John D Seelye. LC 82-6998. 1982. 4.95 (ISBN 0-8032-9131-0). University of Nebraska Press.

Kid Andrew Cody & Julie Sparrow: A Novel. Tony Curtis. LC 76-42321. 1977. 8.95 (ISBN 0-385-12405-8). Doubleday.

Kid Andrew Cody & Julie Sparrow: A Novel. Tony Curtis. (Signet Book). 1978. 2.25 (ISBN 0-451-08010-6). New American Library.

Kid Comes Home. Leo Mailman. 1976. 2.00 (ISBN 0-916918-01-7, Pub. by Duck Down Press). Maelstrom.

Kid Deputy. William Fitzgerald Jenkins. LC 35-4102. A. H. King.

Kid for Two Farthings: Illustrated by James Boswell. 1st American Ed. Wolf Mankowitz. LC 53-10861. 1954. Dutton.

Kid from Lincoln County. Nelson Nye. 128p. (Orig.). 1976. pap. 1.95 (ISBN 0-441-43740-0). Ace Bks.

Kid from Mars. Oscar Jerome Friend. LC 49-5792. (Fell's science-fictionlibrary). 1949. F. Fell.

Kid from Rincon. Arthur Moore. (Gold Medal Book) (ISBN 0-449-13612-4). Fawcett.

Kid from Sunset Bluffs. T. W. Ford. LC 50-8885. 1950. Phoenix Press.

Kid Galahad. Francis Wallace. LC 36-15573. 1936. Little, Brown, and Company.

Kid Glove Charlie: A Ballad of Charlie Peace (1832-1879) John Cashman, pseud. LC 77-3786. 10.00 (ISBN 0-06-010698-0). Harper & Row.

Kid Mallory. Hal D. White. (Orig.). 1981. pap. 1.95 (ISBN 0-505-51657-8). Tower Bks.

Kid Rodelo. Louis L'Amour. 1977. pap. 1.95 (ISBN 0-553-14227-5). Bantam.

Kid Scanlan. Harry Charles Witwer. LC 20-10733. Small, Maynard & Company.

Kid Scanlan. Harry Charles Witwer. 1925. Grosset & Dunlap.

Kid Tinsel. Octavus Roy Cohen. 1941. D. Appleton Century Company Incorporated.

Kid Was Last Seen Hanging Ten. Aaron Marc Stein. LC 66-21818. (Inner sanctum mystery). 1966. Simon and Schuster.

Kid Was Last Seen Hanging Ten. Hampton Stone, pseud. (Hampton Stone Mystery Ser.). 1971. pap. 0.75 o.p. (ISBN 0-446-64506-0, 64-506). Paperback Lib.

Kid Who Batted 1.000: By Bob Allison and Frank Ernest Hill; Illustrated by Paul Galdone. 1st Ed. Bob Allison. LC 51-13749. 1951. Doubleday.

Kid Who Came Home with a Corpse. Aaron Marc Stein. LC 70-189544. (Inner sanctum mystery). 1972. 4.95 (ISBN 0-671-21174-9). Simon and Schuster.

Kid Who Came Home with a Corpse. Hampton Stone, pseud. (Inner Sanctum Mystery Ser.). (O.s.i.). 1972. 4.95 o.s.i. (ISBN 0-671-21174-9). S&S.

Kiddush Ha-Shem: An Epic of 1648. Shalom Asch. LC 74-27960. (Modern Jewish Experience). 1975. 14.00 (ISBN 0-405-06691-0). Arno Press.

Kiddush Hashem: Cat in the Ghetto. new ed. Rachmil Bryks. Tr. by S. Morris Engel. LC 75-51976. (A Jewish Legacy Book). 164p. (Orig.). 1977. pap. text ed. 3.95x o.p. (ISBN 0-87441-240-4). Behrman.

Kidnap. Marcus Van Heller, pseud. pap. 1.25 o.p. (2029). Brandon.

Kidnap Club. Arthur Benjamin Reeve. LC 32-8806. The Macaulay Company.

Kidnap Murder Case: A Philo Vance Story. Willard Huntington Wright. LC 36-239144. 1936. C. Scribner's Sons.

Kidnaped Child. John Creasey. LC 72-21887. (Rinehart suspense novel). 1971. 4.50 (ISBN 0-03-085043-6). Holt, Rinehart and Winston.

Kidnaper. Robert Bloch. LC 54-30491. (Lion original, 185). 1954. Lion Books.

Kidnapped. Ed. by William A. Kottmeyer. 1972. text ed. 5.76 o.p. (ISBN 0-07-034021-8, W). McGraw.

Kidnapped. Curtis Bill Pepper. (Illus.). 1978. 7.95 o.p. (ISBN 0-517-53438-X, Dist. by Crown). Crown.

Kidnapped. Robert Louis Stevenson. LC 60-2935. (Children's illustrated classics). 1960. Dent.

Kidnapped. Robert Louis Stevenson. LC 68-56085. (Cambridge classics library). (Illus.). 1968. Cambridge Book Co.

Kidnapped. Robert Louis Stevenson. LC 48-118281. (Illustrated junior library). 1948. Grosset & Dunlap.

Kidnapped. Robert Louis Stevenson. LC 49-10611. (Great illustrated classics). 1949. Dodd, Mead.

Kidnapped. Robert Louis Stevenson. LC 98-411. H. Altemus.

Kidnapped. Robert Louis Stevenson. Ed. by Brown, John Thompson. LC 9-2263. (Macmillan's pocket American and English classics). 1909. The Macmillan Company.

Kidnapped. Robert Louis Stevenson. Ed. by Leonard, Arthur Willis. LC 14-6235. (Lake English classics). 0.35. Scott, Foresman and Company.

Kidnapped. Robert Louis Stevenson. LC 15-22680. (Lettered on cover: The Washington square classics). 1915. G. W. Jacobs and Company.

Kidnapped. Robert Louis Stevenson. (golden books for children). 1917. D. McKay.

Kidnapped. Robert Louis Stevenson. Ed. by Leonard, Arthur Willis. LC 20-5406. (Half-title: The Lake English classics, general editor, L. T. Damon...). Scott, Foresman and Company.

Kidnapped. Robert Louis Stevenson. Ed. by De Mille, Alban Bertram. LC 25-15981. (Lettered on cover: Academy classics). Allyn and Bacon.

Kidnapped. Robert Louis Stevenson. Ed. by Kaufmann, Myrtle L. LC 25-10694. (On cover: The Winston clear-type popular classics). The John C. Winston Company.

Kidnapped. Robert Louis Stevenson. LC 27-161. The Saalfield Publishing Company.

Kidnapped. Robert Louis Stevenson. Ed. by Brown, John Thompson. Moffett, Harold Young. LC 30-10972. (Half-title: New pocket classics). The Macmillan Company.

Kidnapped. Robert Louis Stevenson. LC 32-19276. Garden City Publishing Co., Inc.

Kidnapped. Robert Louis Stevenson. LC 43-5932. (Newberry classics). 1942. David McKay Company.

Kidnapped. Robert Louis Stevenson. LC 47-303582. (Rainbow Classics). 1947. World Pub. Co.

Kidnapped. Robert Louis Stevenson & Eaton, Margaret A. LC 12-23207. Educational Publishing Company.

Kidnapped. Robert Louis Stevenson & Ruth Thompson King. LC 50-8477. 1950. Globe Book Co.

Kidnapped. Robert Louis Stevenson & Sharp, William. LC 49-4122. 1949. Random House.

Kidnapped. A Novelette... Thaddeus Warsaw Williams. 1873.

Kidnapped, & Catriona. Robert Louis Stevenson. 3.00 o.p. (ISBN 0-00-422636-4); lea. 5.00 o.p. (ISBN 0-00-423636-X). Collins-World.

Kidnapped: Being Memoirs of the Adventures of David Balfour in the Year 1751... Robert Louis Stevenson. LC 65-6530. (Perennial classic). 1965. Harper & Row.

Kidnapped: Being Memoirs of the Adventures of David Balfour in the Year 1751. How He Was Kidnapped and Cast Away; His Sufferings in a Desert Isle; His Journey in the Wild Highlands; His Acquaintance with Alan Breck Stewart and Other Notorious Highland Jacobites; with All That He Suffered at the Hands of His Uncle, Ebenezer Balfour of Shaws, Falsely So-Called. Robert Louis Stevenson. LC 42-26501. The F. M. Lupton Publishing Company.

Kidnapped: Being Memoirs of the Adventures of David Balfour in the Year 1751... Robert Louis Stevenson. LC 4-31670. (Ivy series no. 26). 1899. G. Munro's Sons.

Kidnapped: Being Memoirs of the Adventures of David Balfour in the Year 1751... Robert Louis Stevenson. LC 4-16580. 1904. C. Scribner's Sons.

Kidnapped: Being Memoirs of the Adventages of David Balfour in the Year 1751... Robert Louis Stevenson. LC 5-13039. (Half-title: The biographical edition of the works of Robert Louis Stevenson). 1905. C. Scribner's Sons.

Kidnapped: Being Memoirs of the Adventures of David Balfour in the Year 1751... Robert Louis Stevenson. LC 13-22512. 1913. C. Scribner's Sons.

Kidnapped: Being Memoirs of the Adventures of David Balfour, in the Year 1751... Robert Louis Stevenson. LC 16-5899. (Ranally series). 1.00. Rand, McNally & Company.

Kidnapped: Being Memoirs of the Adventures of David Balfour in the Year 1751. Robert Louis Stevenson. LC 25-15674. (The Macmillan childrens classics). 1925. The Macmillan Company.

Kidnapped: Being Memoirs of the Adventures of David Balfour in the Year 1751; How He Was Kidnapped and Cast Away; His Sufferings in a Desert Isle; His Journey in the Wild Highlands; His Acquaintance with Alan Breck Stewart and Other Notorious Highland Jacobites; with All That He Suffered at the Hands of His Uncle, Ebenezer Balfour of Shaws, Falsely So-Called. Robert Louis Stevenson. LC 38-17710. (Windermere series). Rand, McNally & Company.

Kidnapped: Being Memoirs of the Adventures of David Baleourin the Year 1751. illustrated by tom o sullivan ed. Robert Louis Stevenson. LC 54-14467. 1954. Junior Deluxe Editions.

Kidnapped, Being the Memoirs of the Adventures of David Balfour in the Year MDCCLI. Robert Louis Stevenson. LC 75-312430. (Illus.). 1974. 1.95 (ISBN 0-19-274522-0). Oxford University Press.

Kidnapped: Being the Memoirs of the Adventures of David Balfour in the Year 1751 and The Strange Case of Dr. Jekyll and Mr. Hyde. Robert Louis Stevenson. LC 37-5396. (Immortal masterpieces of literature. vol. v). The Spencer Press.

Kidnapped Bride. Dan Bradley. 192p. (Orig.). 1973. pap. 1.95 o.p. (ISBN 0-87977-190-9, DBB-190). Dansk Blue Bk.

Kidnapped. Catriona. Robert Louis Stevenson & Maurice Roy Ridley. LC 62-51427. (Everyman's library, 762. Fiction). 1962. Dent.

Kidnapped Child. G. Ashe. 1971. 4.50 o.p. (ISBN 0-03-085043-6). HR&W.

Kidnapped Child. John Creasey. LC 76-117280. 1971. 4.50 o.p. (ISBN 0-03-085043-6). HR&W.

Kidnapped Colony. Mary Raymond Shipman Andrews. LC 3-24537. 1903. Harper & Brothers.

TITLE INDEX KILLER PLANTS OF BINAARK.

Kidnapped Damozel. The Oval Diamond, Alraschid in Petticoates. David Skaats Foster. LC 15-7731. 1.25. The Franklin Book Company.
Kidnapped. Ed. by M. W. and G. Thomas, Illus, by Excell. Robert Louis Stevenson. Ed. by Maurice Walton Thomas & Gladys Thomas. LC 66-6328. (Shorter classics). 1966. bds., 2.50. Ginn.
Kidnapped: Memoirs of the Adventures of David Balfour in the Year 1751. Robert Louis Stevenson. Whitman Publishing Company.
Kidnapped Saint & Other Stories. B Traven. LC 74-9349. 7.95 (ISBN 0-88208-049-0). L. Hill.
Kidnapped Saint & Other Stories by B. Traven. Ed. by Nina C. Klein & H. Arthur Klein. LC 74-9349. 1977. 8.95 (ISBN 0-88208-049-0); pap. 5.95 o.s.i. (ISBN 0-88208-074-1). Lawrence Hill.
Kidnapped. Strange Case of Dr. Jekyll and Mr. Hyde. Treasure Island... Robert Louis Stevenson. (Harper's Franklin square library, no. 570). 1887. Harper & Brothers.
Kidnapped Surgeon. Alexander Knox. LC 76-50032. 1977. 7.95. St. Martin's Press.
Kidnapped: The Adventures of David Balfour in the Year 1751. Robert Louis Stevenson. LC 8-195722. McLoughlin Brothers.
Kidnapped: The Adventures of David Balfour. Robert Louis Stevenson. LC 82-5562. (Illus.). 1982. 18.95 (ISBN 0-684-17634-3). Scribner.
Kidnappers. Warren Kiefer. LC 76-47251. 8.95 (ISBN 0-06-012368-0). Harper & Row.
Kidnappers. Albert Edward Ullman. LC 33-2071. Amour Press, Inc.
Kidnapping. Carmen P. Bergman. 72p. 1980. 4.50 (ISBN 0-8059-2634-8). Dorrance.
Kidnapping of President Lincoln: And Other War Detective Stories. Joel Chandler Harris. 1909. Doubleday, Page & Co.
Kidnapping of the President: A Novel. Charles Templeton. LC 74-23337. (Illus.). 1975. 7.95 (ISBN 0-380-00396-1). Simon and Schuster.
Kidneyed Caper. Allan Chase. LC 60-6087. 1960. Simon and Schuster.
Kierkegaard: A Fiction. Barbara Anderson. LC 74-7861. 1974. 8.75 (ISBN 0-8156-0100-X). Syracuse University Press.
Kiev Encounter. Serge G. Mironovitch. LC 77-78039. 12.50 (ISBN 0-8283-1693-7). Branden Press.
Kif: An Unvarnished History. Elizabeth Mackintosh. LC 29-7074. 1929. D. Appleton & Company.
Kiki. John Gill. LC 79-10404. 8.95 (ISBN 0-316-31341-6). Little, Brown.
Kilbourne Connection. Gaylord D. Larsen. LC 80-67904. 192p. (Orig.). 1980. pap. 2.95 (ISBN 0-87123-305-3, 200305). Bethany Hse.
Kilburn. Sam Victor. (Kilburn # 1). 1974. (pbk.) 0.95. Berkley Pub. Co.
Kilburns: A Novel. Annie Hall Thomas Cudlip. LC 6-31168. (On cover: Lovell's international ser. no. 64). F. F. Lovell & Company.
Kilcaraig. Annabel Carothers. LC 81-21506. 1982. 17.95 (ISBN 0-312-45284-5). St. Martin's Press.
Kildares of Storm. Eleanor Mercein Kelly. LC 16-21973. 1916. 1.40. The Century Co.
Kildee: Or, The Sphinx of the Red House. Mary Edwards Bryan. (On cover: Seaside library. Pocket ed., no. 857). 1886. G. Munro.
Kildee: Or, The Sphinx of the Red House. Mary Edwards Bryan. (On cover: Library of American authors. no. 58). 1894. G. Munro's Sons.
Kildhurm's Oak. Julian Hawthorne. (On cover: The Manhattan series, no. 9). 1889. A. L. Burt.
Kildhurm's Oak: Also, A Strange Friend. Julian Hawthorne. (On cover: The select series, no. 58). 1890. Street & Smith.
Kilgaren. Isabelle Holland. 1975. (pbk.) 1.25. Bantam Books.
Kilgaren. large print ed. Isabelle Holland. LC 81-14448. 1981. 10.95 (ISBN 0-89621-324-2). Thorndike Press.
Kilgaren: A Novel. Isabelle Holland. LC 74-9889. 1974. (ISBN 0-8161-6228-X). G. K. Hall.
Kilgroom; a Story of Ireland. John Alexander Steuart. LC 8-12389. (On cover: The Belford American novel series, v. 2, no. 3). 1890. Belford Company.
Kilkenny. Louis L'Amour. LC 55-16138. (Ace books, S-82). 1954. Ace Books.
Kilkenny. Louis L'Amour. LC 79-28245. (Series: Gregg Press Western Fiction Series.). 1980. 9.95 (ISBN 0-8398-2692-3). Gregg Press.
Kilkenny. Louis L'Amour. (Fawcett gold medal). 1974. (pbk.) 0.95. Fawcett.
Kilkenny see Complete L'Amour.
Kill. Alan Ryan. 320p. (Orig.). 1983. pap. 2.95 (ISBN 0-523-48055-5). Pinnacle Bks.
Kill. Emile Zola. 1957. 13.95 o.p. (ISBN 0-236-30899-8, Pub. by Paul Elek). Merrimack Pub Cir.
Kill a Wicked Man. Kyle Hunt, pseud. (O.s.i.). 1957. 2.95 o.s.i. (39830). S&S.
Kill and Tell. Howard Rigsby. LC 51-13616. 1951. Morrow.
Kill As Directed. Ellery Queen. (Signet Book, Q5665). 1973. (pbk.) 0.95. New American Library.
Kill-Box. Original Title: Run for Your Life! Michael Stark. LC 54-31820. (Ace double novel books, D-55). 1954. Ace Books.
Kill City. Andrew Sugar. (Enforcer Ser., No. 3). 1973. pap. 0.95 o.s.i. (75-473). Lancer.
Kill City. Andrew Sugar. (Enforcer # 3). 1973. (pbk.) 0.95. Lancer.
Kill Claudio. Philip Maitland Hubbard. LC 79-7076. 1979. 7.95 (ISBN 0-385-15359-7). Published for the Crime Club by Doubleday.
Kill Cultist. Charles Hansen. pap. 1.95 o.p. (8055). Cameo.
Kill Cure. Julian Rathbone. LC 74-83582. 1975. 7.95. St. Martin's Press.
Kill 'em with Kindness. Fred Dickenson. LC 50-8254. 1950. Bell Pub. Co.
Kill Factor. Richard Harper. 208p. (Orig.). 1983. pap. 2.50 (ISBN 0-449-12383-9, GM). Fawcett.
Kill for It. Robert Hawkes. (Narc). (Signet Book: Vol. 9). 1975. (pbk.) 1.25. New American Library.
Kill for the Millions. Henry Kane. (Peter Chambers Ser.). (Orig.). 1972. pap. 0.95 o.s.i. (75-412). Lancer.
Kill Her--You'll Like It. Michael Avallone. (Orig.). 1973. pap. 0.75 o.p. (07293). Curtis.
Kill Her with Love. Rod Gray. (New Lady from L.U.S.T. Ser). (O.s.i.). 1975. pap. 1.25 o.s.i. (BT50858). Belmont-Tower.
Kill Him, Again. W. R Garwood. LC 80-66355. (Diamond back westerns). 9.95 (ISBN 0-937618-00-4). Bath Street Press.
Kill Him Tonight. Jeremy Lane. LC 46-184864. 1946. Phoenix Press.
Kill Is a Four-Letter Word. Aaron Marc Stein. LC 68-17805. 1968. Published for the Crime Club by Doubleday.
Kill Joy. Elisabeth Sanxay Holding. LC 42-51485. 1942. Duell, Sloan and Pearce.
Kill McAllister. Matt Chisholm. 1972. pap. 0.75 o.p. (94211). Beagle Bks.
Kill Me Again! John Bentley. LC 47-29774. 1947. Dodd, Mead & Company.
Kill Me Gently, Darling. Barbara Faith. 1978. pap. 1.95 (ISBN 0-532-19208-7). Woodhill.
Kill Me, Please. William Johnston. (Medical Story). (Signet Book: Vol. 2). 1976. (pbk.) 1.50. New American Library.
Kill Me Quick. Meja Mwangi. (African writers series, 143). 1975. (ISBN 0-435-90143-5). Heinemann.
Kill My Love. John Creasey. 192p. 1973. Repr. of 1958 ed. lib. bdg. 5.95 o.s.i. White Lion Pubs.
Kill My Love. Kyle Hunt, pseud. (O.s.i.). 1958. 2.95 o.s.i. (39840). S&S.
Kill Now, Pay Later see Trio for Blunt Instruments: A Nero Woolfe Threesome.
Kill Once, Kill Twice. John Creasey. 1975. (pbk.) 1.25. Belmont Tower Books.
Kill Once, Kill Twice. Kyle Hunt, pseud. (O.s.i.). 1956. 2.75 o.s.i. (39850). S&S.
Kill One Kill Two. Walter Wadsley Anderson. LC 44-819440. 1944. Mohawk Publishing Corp.
Kill or Cure. Joan Margaret Fleming. LC 68-8724. 1968. 3.95. I. Washburn.
Kill or Cure. William Francis. LC 42-18053. 1942. W. Morrow & Company.
Kill or Cure: By E. X. Ferrars Pseud. 1st Ed. Morna Doris MacTaggart Brown. LC 56-13280. 1956. Published for the Crime Club by Doubleday.
Kill Price. Jose Yglesias. LC 75-29960. 1976. 6.95 (ISBN 0-672-52200-4). Bobbs-Merrill.
Kill Quick or Die. Stuart Jason. (Butcher Ser.: No. 1). 1979. pap. 1.75 (ISBN 0-523-40678-9). Pinnacle Bks.
Kill Squad. Walter Bond. (Orig.). 1968. pap. 0.60 o.p. (73-788). Lancer.
Kill Squad. 1976. pap. 1.25 o.p. Woodhill.
Kill Squad. 1976. pap. 1.25 o.p. Manor Bks.
Kill the Clown. Richard S. Prather. (Shell Scott Ser). (Orig.). 1969. pap. 0.60 o.p. (R2083, GM). Fawcett World.
Kill the Dead. Tanith Lee. (Science Fiction Ser.). 1980. pap. 1.75 (ISBN 0-87997-562-8, UE1562). Daw Bks.
Kill the Dragon. Robert Hawkes. (Narc). (Signet book: Vol. 5). 1974. (pbk.) 1.25. New American Library.
Kill the Toff. John Creasey. LC 66-24077. 1966. Walker.
Kill to Fit. Bruno Fischer. LC 46-22510. 1946. Five Star Mysteries, Inc.
Kill with Care. Hugh Lawrence Nelson. (Murray Hill mystery). 1953. Rinehart.
Kill. With Illus. by Peter Emmerich; Introd. by Angus Wilson. Translated from the French, La Curee, by A. Teixeira de Mattos. Emile Zola. LC 54-13243. (Illustrated novel library). 1954. Farrar, Straus & Young.
Kill with Kindness. Elizabeth Linington. LC 68-12150. 1968. W. Morrow.
Kill with Kindness. Dell Shannon. 1971. pap. 0.75 o.p. (T2408). Pyramid Pubns.
Kill with Style. Hal Gulliver. LC 73-19262. 1974. 6.95. Scribner.
Kill 3. Milton Shulman. LC 67-22679. 1967. Random House.
Killdeer. Dorothy Hamilton. LC 72-170199. 1972. 3.95 (ISBN 0-8361-1663-1). Herald Press.
Killdeer Mountain: A Novel. Dee Alexander Brown. LC 82-15460. 10.95 (ISBN 0-03-040691-9). Holt, Rinehart and Winston.
Killdog. Jonathan George, pseud. LC 76-111165. 1970. 4.50. Published for the Crime Club by Doubleday.
Killed by Scandal. Raymond Chapman. LC 81-47405. (Fifty Classics of Crime Fiction, 1950-1975). 1982. 14.95 (ISBN 0-8240-4965-9). Garland Pub.
Killed by Scandal. Simon Nash. Ed. by J. Barzun & W. h. Taylor. LC 81-47405. (Crime Fiction 1950-1975 Ser.). 223p. 1982. lib. bdg. 14.95 (ISBN 0-8240-4965-9). Garland Pub.
Killed in the Act. William L DeAndrea. LC 81-43259. 1981. 10.95 (ISBN 0-385-17824-7). Published for the Crime Club by Doubleday.
Killed in the Open. A Novel. Mary E. Kennard. LC 7-11104. (Harper's Franklin square library, no. 527). Harper & Brothers.
Killed in the Ratings. William L DeAndrea. LC 77-85185. 7.95 (ISBN 0-15-146963-6). Harcourt Brace Jovanovich.
Killed in the Ratings. William L Deandrea. 1979. 1.95 (ISBN 0-380-43612-4). Avon.
Killed with a Passion. William L. DeAndrea. LC 82-45353. (Crime Club Ser.). 192p. 1983. 11.95 (ISBN 0-385-18275-9). Doubleday.
Killer. Burt Arthur, pseud. 176p. 1975. pap. 0.95 o.p. Woodhill.
Killer. Burt Arthur, pseud. 176p. 1975. pap. 0.95 o.p. Manor Bks.
Killer. Steven Havill. LC 80-1987. 1981. 9.95 (ISBN 0-385-17287-7). Doubleday.
Killer. Wade Miller, pseud. LC 51-25332. (Gold medal book, 152). 1951. Fawcett Publications.
Killer. Robert Moore, pseud. (Orig.). 1970. pap. 1.95 o.s.i. (OPH-179, Ophelia). Olympia.
Killer. Richard Parker. LC 64-16223. 1964. Doubleday.
Killer. Peter Tomkin. (Signet Book.). 2.50 (ISBN 0-451-09241-4). New American Library.
Killer. Peter Tonkin. LC 79-1482. (Illus.). 1979. 9.95 (ISBN 0-698-10974-0). Coward, McCann & Geoghegan.
Killer. Carolyn Wells. LC 38-245583. J. B. Lippincott Company.
Killer. Stewart Edward White. LC 19-13047. 1919. Doubleday, Page & Company.
Killer. Stewart Edward White. LC 20-9477. 1920. Doubleday, Page & Company.
Killer Among Us. Robert Lee Martin. LC 58-130892. (Red badge detective). 1958. Dodd, Mead.
Killer & Other Plays. Eugene Ionesco. Tr. by Donald Watson from Fr. Incl. Improvisation, or The Shepherd's Chameleon; Maid to Marry. 1960. pap. 3.95 (ISBN 0-394-17218-3, E189, Ever). Grove.
Killer and the Slain: A Strange Story. Hugh Walpole. LC 42-13389. 1942. Doubleday, Doran & Company, Inc.
Killer Angels. Michael Shaara. LC 73-91120. 1980. pap. 2.75 (ISBN 0-345-28605-7). Ballantine.
Killer Angels: A Novel About the Four Days at Gettysburg. Michael Shaara. LC 73-91120. 374p. 1974. 12.95 (ISBN 0-679-50466-4). McKay.
Killer at Large. Don Bannon. 1975. (pbk.) 1.25 (ISBN 0-523-00663-2). Pinnacle Books.
Killer at Large. Maurice Procter. pap. 0.95 o.p. (02399, Collier). Macmillan.
Killer at Large: 1st Ed. Maurice Procter. 1959. Harper.
Killer Beware. Scott Corbett. 1972. 4.95 o.p. (15692-2R, Pub. by Atlantic Monthly Pr). Little.
Killer Blizzard! Dan Jorgensen. 176p. (Orig.). 1976. pap. 1.50 (ISBN 0-89041-102-6, 3102). Major Bks.
Killer Boy Was Here. George Bagby, pseud. (Crime Club Ser). 1970. 4.50 o.p. Doubleday.
Killer Boy Was Here. George Bagby, pseud. (O.s.i.). 1972. pap. 0.95 o.s.i. (BT50213). Belmont-Tower.
Killer Boy Was Here. Aaron Marc Stein. LC 75-116185. 1970. 4.50. Published for the Crime Club by Doubleday.
Killer Brand. William Colt MacDonald. LC 50-7194. (Double D western). 1950. Doubleday.
Killer Breath. John Wyllie. LC 78-22622. 1979. 7.95 (ISBN 0-385-15204-3). Published for the Crime Club by Doubleday.
Killer Chromosomes. Warren Murphy. (Destroyer Ser.: No. 32). 1978. pap. 1.75 (ISBN 0-523-40908-7). Pinnacle Bks.
Killer Colt. James W. Smith. 1971. pap. 0.75 o.p. (T2564). Pyramid Pubns.
Killer Come to Shiloh. C. H. Hasseloff. 176p. (Orig.). 1981. pap. 1.95 (ISBN 0-553-14742-0). Bantam.
Killer Comes Riding. Rod Patterson. LC 56-26168. (Ace double novel books, D-144). 1956. Ace Books.
Killer Cop. Dom Gober. 1975. (pbk.) 1.50 (ISBN 0-87067-485-4). Holloway House.
Killer Cops. Edwin D. Krell & Major J. Vasel. (Orig.). 1979. pap. 1.95 (ISBN 0-532-23265-8). Woodhill.
Killer Dolphin. Ngaio Marsh. 1976. Repr. of 1966 ed. lib. bdg. 17.70x (ISBN 0-88411-487-2). Amereon Ltd.
Killer Dolphin. large type ed. Ngaio Marsh. 1978. pap. cancelled (ISBN 0-425-03623-5, Medallion). Berkley Pub.
Killer Dolphin. Ngaio Marsh. (Ngaio Marsh Mystery Ser.). 256p. 1983. pap. 2.50 (ISBN 0-515-06820-9). Jove Pubns.
Killer Dolphin. Ngaio Marsh. write for info (ISBN 0-515-05435-6, Jove). Putnam Pub Group.
Killer Dolphin see Ngaio Marsh.
Killer Dolphin. 1st Ed. Ngaio Marsh. LC 66-21001. 1966. bds., 4.95. Little.
Killer Elite. Robert S Hopkins. LC 72-10640. 1973. 5.95. Delacorte Press.
Killer Elite. Robert S Hopkins. 1974. (pbk.) 1.50. Dell.
Killer for the Chairman. John Harris. LC 78-174510. 1972. (ISBN 0-15-146985-7). Harcourt Brace Jovanovich.
Killer for the Chairman. Mark Hebden, pseud. LC 58-174510. 1972. 5.95 o.p. (ISBN 0-15-146985-7). HarBraceJ.
Killer from Yuma. Lewis B Patten. (Signet Book). 1977. 1.50 (ISBN 0-451-07796-2). New American Library.
Killer Genesis. Axel Kilgore. (Orig.). 1980. pap. 2.25 (ISBN 0-89083-678-7). Zebra.
Killer Gray. Jason Manning. (Orig.). 1980. pap. 1.95 (ISBN 0-532-23212-7). Woodhill.
Killer in My Mind. Gary Blumberg. 1975. (pbk.) 1.25. Warner Paperback Library.
Killer in the House. Borden Deal. LC 57-9176. (Signet book, 1383). 1967. New American Library.
Killer in the Kitchen. Robert Godley. LC 47-24306. 1947. Lantern Press.
Killer in the Rain. Raymond Chandler. LC 64-17361. 1964. Houghton Mifflin.
Killer in the Street. Helen Nielsen. LC 67-15155. 1967. Morrow.
Killer Is Loose Among Us. Robert Terrall. LC 48-8934. (Bloodhound mystery). 1948. Duell, Sloan and Pearce.
Killer Is Loose. Cover Painting by Lu Kimmel. Gil Brewer. LC 54-249693. (Gold medal books, 380). 1954. Fawcett Publications.
Killer Loose! By Genevieve Holden Pseud. 1st Ed. Genevieve Long Pou. LC 53-5277. 1953. Published for the Crime Club by Doubleday.
Killer Marshal. Wayne D Overholser. LC 61-15187. 1961. Macmillan.
Killer Mice. Kit Reed, pseud. LC 77-361324. 1976. 3.75 (ISBN 0-575-02133-0). Gollancz.
Killer Mine. Ralph Hammond-Innes. LC 49-7471. 1947. Harper.
Killer Mine. Mickey Spillane, pseud. 1968. pap. 1.95 (ISBN 0-451-11797-2, AJ1797, Sig). NAL.
Killer Mountains. Curt Gentry. LC 68-21365. (Illus.). 1976. pap. 2.95 (ISBN 0-89174-020-1). Comstock Edns.
Killer Music. Lisa Eisenberg. LC 79-52657. (Laura Brewster Book.). (Pacemaker book). (Illus.). 1981. 4.42 (ISBN 0-8224-1085-0). Fearon Pitman Publishers.
Killer of Cibescue. Nelson Coral Nye. LC 36-29809. Greenberg.
Killer of Fort Norman: A Malloy of the Mounted Story. Charles Stanley Strong. LC 44-40375. 1944. Arcadia House.
Killer of Horseman's Flats. Rosemary Anne Sisson. LC 72-92243. 1973. 4.95 (ISBN 0-385-03301-X). Doubleday.
Killer of Kings. R. Wright Campbell. LC 78-11198. 1979. 8.95 o.p. (ISBN 0-672-52583-6). Bobbs.
Killer of Sheep River: A Malloy of the Royal Mounted Story. Charles Stoddard. LC 46-268245. 1946. Arcadia House, Inc.
Killer of Sheep River: A Malloy of the Royal Mounted Story. Charles Stanley Strong. LC 46-2682. 1946. Arcadia House.
Killer on the Catwalk. Judson Pentecost Philips. LC 59-12155. (Red badge detective). 1959. Dodd, Mead.
Killer on the Keys. Michael Avallone. (Orig.). 1973. pap. 0.75 o.p. (07312). Curtis.
Killer on the Prowl. Frank Scarpetta. (Marksman, # 17). 1975. (pbk) 1.25. Belmont Tower Books.
Killer Pack. Albert Herbert & Roger Myers. 1976. pap. 1.50 (ISBN 0-532-15211-5). Woodhill.
Killer Patrol see Patrulla Homicida.
Killer Pine. Lindsay Gutteridge. LC 72-97295. 1973. 5.95 (ISBN 0-399-11129-8). Putnam.
Killer Plants of Binaark. Jeffrey Lord. (Blade Ser.: No. 33). 192p. (Orig.). 1980. pap. 1.75 (ISBN 0-523-40852-8). Pinnacle Bks.

Killer Satellites. Philip Kirk. (Butler Ser.: No. 6). (Orig.). 1980. pap. 1.75 o.s.i. (ISBN 0-8439-0730-4, Leisure Bks). Nordon Pubns.

Killer See, Killer Do. Jonathan Wolfe. 1977. 1.50 (ISBN 0-8439-0505-0). Nordon Pubns.

Killer Silver. Charles R. Pike, pseud. LC 80-68163. (Jubal Cade Westerns Ser.). 144p. 1980. pap. 2.95 (ISBN 0-87754-233-3). Chelsea Hse.

Killer Spores. Richard Woodley. (Dell Book.). 1978. 1.50 (ISBN 0-440-15926-1). Dell Pub. Co.

Killer Tank. 2nd ed. Norman Daniels. Orig. Title: Strike Force. 1969. pap. 0.75 o.p. (74503). Lancer.

Killer That's Dead. Carl L. Brown. 1977. 3.95 o.p. (ISBN 0-533-01080-2). Vantage.

Killer Thing. Kate Wilhelm. LC 66-20972. (Doubleday science fiction). 1967. Doubleday.

Killer to Come. Sam Merwin. LC 53-10108. 1953. Abelard Press.

Killer Touch. Ellery Queen, pseud. LC 65-9773. Pocket Books,

Killer Touch. Ellery Queen, pseud. (Signet book). 1975. (pbk.) 0.95. New American Library.

Killer Trail. Joseph Chadwick. (Orig.). 1971. pap. 0.60 o.p. (R2422, GM). Fawcett World.

Killer Virus. Philip Kirk. (Butler Ser.: No. 9). 240p. (Orig.). 1983. pap. 2.50 (ISBN 0-8439-1130-1, Leisure Bks). Dorchester Pub Co.

Killer Warrior. Marc Olden. (Black samurai, # 3). 1974. (pbk.) 0.95. New American Library.

Killer Watches the Manhunt. Albert Benjamin Cunningham. LC 50-8882. (Guilt edged mystery). 1950. Dutton.

Killer. 1st Ed. Herbert Arthur. LC 52-8749. (Double D western). 1952. Doubleday.

Killerbowl. Gary K Wolf. LC 75-2857. (Doubleday science fiction). (Illus.). 1975. 5.95 (ISBN 0-385-04738-X). Doubleday.

Killers. George Owen Baxter. LC 31-14328. The Macaulay Company.

Killers. Ed. by Peter Dawson. 1974. (pbk.) 1.25. Bantam Books.

Killers. Frederick Faust. LC 31-14328. 1931. The Macaulay Company.

Killers. George C Henderson. LC 36-5817. Greenberg.

Killers. Ed. by Phil Hirsch. (Orig.). 1971. pap. 0.75 o.p. (T2540). Pyramid Pubns.

Killers. Peter McCurtin. (Carmody Ser., No. 2). 1974. pap. 0.95 o.p. (LB131NK). Leisure Bks.

Killers. Peter McCurtin. (Carmody Ser). (Orig., Osi). 1971. pap. 0.75 o.s.i. (B75-2130). Belmont-Tower.

Killers. Daniel Pratt Mannix. LC 68-25776. (Illus.). 1968. 5.95 o.p. (ISBN 0-525-13892-7). Dutton.

Killers at Sea. Jon Messman. (Logan Ser). (Orig.). 1970. pap. 0.60 o.p. (B60-2034). Belmont-Tower.

Killer's Bargain. Dean Owen. 144p. 1975. pap. 0.95 o.p. (ISBN 0-532-95415-7). Woodhill.

Killer's Bargain. Dean Owen. 144p. 1973. pap. 0.75 o.p. (532-75517-075). Manor Bks.

Killer's Bargain. Dean Owen. 144p. 1975. pap. 0.95 o.p. (ISBN 0-532-95415-7). Manor Bks.

Killer's Brand. easy eye ed. Henry A. De Rosso. (Orig.). 1968. pap. 0.60 o.p. (73-801). Lancer.

Killer's Breed. George G. Gilman, pseud. (Edge Ser., No. 4). 192p. 1972. pap. 1.95 (ISBN 0-523-42032-3). Pinnacle Bks.

Killers Cannot Live. Alvin Kinlay. (Orig.). pap. 1.25x o.p. (LTB). Soccer.

Killer's Canyon. Bill Knott. LC 76-51692. 1977. 6.95 (ISBN 0-385-12821-5). Doubleday.

Killer's Caress. Cary Moran. LC 36-8055. 1936. Valhalla Press.

Killers' Carnival. Temple Field. LC 32-186138. Farrar & Rinehart, Incorporated.

Killer's Choice - an 87th Precinct Mystery. Ed McBain. 1981. pap. 2.50 (ISBN 0-345-29288-X). Ballantine.

Killer's Choice: By Ed McBain Pseud. Evan Hunter. LC 58-20225. (Permabooks M-3108. Mystery, 8). 1958. Permabooks.

Killer's Code. Charles Wesley Sanders. LC 34-568832. A. H. King.

Killers Corral. Merle Constiner. 1978. pap. 1.25 o.s.i. (ISBN 0-505-51237-8). Tower Bks.

Killer's Council. Scott Siegel. (Warhunter Ser.: No. 1). (Orig.). 1981. pap. 1.95 (ISBN 0-89083-729-5). Zebra.

Killer's Crossing. Burt Arthur, pseud. 1969. pap. 0.50 o.p. (B50-859). Belmont-Tower.

Killers Five. William L. Hopson. (O.s.i.). 1976. pap. 1.25 o.s.i. (AQ1640, Award). Univ Pub & Dist.

Killer's Gun. Ray Hogan. 1974. (pbk.) 0.95. Ace Books.

Killers in Paradise. John Godwin. 1966. Hart.

Killer's Moon. John Benteen. Belmont Tower.

Killers of Eden. Tom Mead. 1967. Repr. pap. 1.60 o.s.i. Tri-Ocean.

Killers of Green's Cove. Jesse Edward Grinstead. LC 41-240773. Dodge Publishing Company.

Killers of Innocence: A Doctor Palfrey Thriller. John Creasey. LC 71-161113. 4.95 (ISBN 0-8027-5234-9). Walker.

Killers of Karawals. Edward Ernest Smith. LC 62-17598. 1962. Morrow.

Killers of Starfish. Jackson Gillis. LC 77-6231. 8.95 (ISBN 0-397-01201-2). Lippincott.

Killers of the City: A Novel of the Third Punic War. Elbert L Harris. LC 67-188. 1966.

Killers of the Diamond A. James D. Sayers. 1970. pap. 0.60 o.p. (ISBN 0-447-73896-8). Lancer.

Killers of the Dream. Lillian Eugenia Smith. LC 49-6772. 1949. W. W. Norton.

Killers of the Mind: A Collection of Stories by the Mystery Writers of America. Ed. by Lucy Freeman. Mystery Writers of America. LC 74-9092. 1974. 7.95 (ISBN 0-394-49306-0). Random House.

Killers on the Diamond A. James Denson Sayers. LC 35-35378. Godwin.

Killer's Payoff. Ed McBain. 1974. (pbk.) 0.95. New American Library.

Killer's Payoff: By Ed McBain Pseud. Evan Hunter. LC 58-31994. (Permabooks, M-3113. Mystery, 3). 1958. Permabooks.

Killers Play Rough. Blair Reed. LC 47-579. 1946. Crown Publishers.

"Killer's" Protege. Robert J Horton. LC 28-7493. 1928. A. C. McClurg & Co.

Killers' Range. Edward Beverly Mann. LC 49-132. (Triple-A western classic). 1949. Jefferson House.

Killers' Range. Edward Beverly Mann. LC 33-1736. 1933. W. Morrow & Co.

Killer's Ransom. Harley Hess. (Orig.). 1979. pap. 1.75 (ISBN 0-532-23230-5). Woodhill.

Killer's Trail. Robert J. Hogan. 1971. pap. 0.60 o.p. Lancer.

Killer's Trail. Giles A Lutz. LC 79-68339. 1980. 8.95 (ISBN 0-385-15783-5). Doubleday.

Killers Two. Allan K. Echols. 1972. pap. 0.60 o.p. (532-00500-060). Manor Bks.

Killers Two see Saddle Wolves.

Killer's Wedge. Evan Hunter. (Signet book). (87th precinct mystery). 1974. (pbk.) 0.95. New American Library.

Killer's Wedge. Ed McBain. 1974. pap. 1.75 (ISBN 0-451-09614-2, E9614, Sig). NAL.

Killer's Wedge: By Ed McBain Pseud. Evan Hunter. LC 59-636. (Inner sanctum mystery). 1959. Simon and Schuster.

Killgloom Park. Neil Boyton. LC 38-32631. 1938. Benziger Brothers.

Killing. Lawrence Swaim. LC 79-3436. 10.95 (ISBN 0-03-048336-0). Holt, Rinehart, and Winston.

Killing- Ground. Elleston Trevor. LC 57-5209. 1957. Macmillan.

Killing a Mouse on Sunday. 1st Ed. Emeric Pressburger. LC 61-13350. 1961. Harcourt, Brace & World.

Killing Affair. Peter Baker. LC 79-135677. (Midnight novel of suspense). 1971. 4.95 (ISBN 0-395-12039-X). Houghton Mifflin Co.

Killing at Ngo Tho. Gene D Moore. (T-1795). 1968. Pyramid.

Killing at Ngo Tho. Gene D Moore. LC 67-12445. 1967. Norton.

Killing at the Big Tree. David McCarthy. LC 60-5937. 1960. Published for the Crime Club by Doubleday.

Killing Billy. Joe Goldberg. 1975. (pbk.) 1.25. Dell.

Killing Bottle. Leslie Poles Hartley. LC 32-358071. 1932. Putnam.

Killing Circle. Chris Wiltz. LC 81-13648. 10.95 (ISBN 0-02-630150-4). Macmillan.

Killing Claim. George G. Gilman, pseud. (Edge Ser.: No. 41). 192p. 1983. pap. 2.25 (ISBN 0-523-41924-4). Pinnacle Bks.

Killing Comes Easy. Peter Chester, pseud. LC 59-84478. Roy Publishers.

Killing Cousins. Fletcher Flora. LC 60-12952. (Cock Robin mystery). 1960. Macmillan.

Killing Edge. Richard Forrest. (Orig.). 1980. pap. text ed. 1.75 o.s.i. (ISBN 0-505-51567-9). Tower Bks.

Killing Everybody. Mark Harris. (O.s.i.). 1973. 6.95 o.s.i. (ISBN 0-8037-4492-7). Dial.

Killing Everybody: A Novel. Mark Harris. LC 72-10635. (Illus.). 1973. 6.95. Dial Press.

Killing Floor. Ai. 7.95 o.s.i. (ISBN 0-395-27593-8); pap. 3.95 o.s.i. (ISBN 0-395-27590-3). HM.

Killing Floor. Arthur Lyons. 1982. pap. 3.95 (ISBN 0-03-060397-8, Owl BKs). HR&W.

Killing Floor: A Novel. Arthur Lyons. LC 76-44429. 1976. 7.95 (ISBN 0-88405-372-5). Mason/Charter.

Killing for Charity. Arthur Kaplan. LC 75-28050. 7.95 (ISBN 0-698-10720-9). Coward, McCann & Geoghegan.

Killing for Christ. Pete Hamill. LC 68-9044. (NAL book). 1968. 5.50. World Pub. Co.

Killing for the Hawks. Frederick Escreet. Smith. 1968. Ace.

Killing for the Hawks. Frederick Escreet Smith. LC 67-21218. 1967. D. McKay Co.

Killing Frost: A Novel. Sylvia Wilkinson. LC 67-20280. 1967. Houghton Mifflin.

Killing Frost: A Novel. Sylvia Wilkinson. (Kangaroo Book). 1978. 1.75 (ISBN 0-671-82020-6). Pocket Books.

Killing Game. 1st Ed. Bill Knox. LC 63-20508. 1963. Published for the Crime Club by Doubleday.

Killing Gift. Bari Wood. 1977. pap. 3.50 (ISBN 0-451-09885-4, E9885, Sig). NAL.

Killing Gift. Bari Wood. LC 75-18630. 320p. 1975. 8.95 (ISBN 0-399-11562-5). Putnam Pub Group.

Killing Ground! Dom Gober. (Black Cop Ser.: No. 4). (Orig.). 1976. pap. 1.95 (ISBN 0-87067-685-7, BH685). Holloway.

Killing Ground. John Hardesty. (Leisure Books). 1978. 1.50 (ISBN 0-8439-0535-2). Nordon Pubns.

Killing Ground. Steven Linakis. LC 71-113821. 1970. 4.95. McKay.

Killing Ground. Charles R. Pike, pseud. LC 80-70090. (Jubal Cade Westerns Ser.). 144p. 1981. pap. 2.95 (ISBN 0-87754-239-2). Chelsea Hse.

Killing Ground. Mary Lee Settle. LC 82-2477. 14.95 (ISBN 0-374-18107-1). Farrar, Straus, Giroux.

Killing in Antiques. Bill Knox. LC 80-2967. 1981. 9.95 (ISBN 0-385-17625-2). Published for the Crime Club by Doubleday.

Killing in Gold. Joe L. Hensley. LC 76-56300. 1978. 6.95 (ISBN 0-385-12854-1). Published for the Crime Club by Doubleday.

Killing in Kiowa: Feud at Chimney Rock. Lewis B. Patten. 1982. pap. 2.75 (ISBN 0-451-11425-6, AE1425, Sig). NAL.

Killing in Malta. Bill Knox. LC 75-186049. 1972. 4.95. Published for the Crime Club by Doubleday.

Killing in Malta. Noah Webster. LC 75-186049. 192p. 1972. 4.95 o.p. (ISBN 0-385-05638-9). Doubleday.

Killing in Rome. Robert S Hopkins. LC 76-26586. 7.95 (ISBN 0-440-04468-5). Delacorte Press.

Killing in Swords. Reginald Bretnor. (Kangaroo Book). 1978. 1.75 (ISBN 0-671-81313-7). Pocket Books.

Killing in the Market. John Dudley Ball & Bevan Smith. LC 77-82614. 1978. 6.95 (ISBN 0-385-13411-8). Published for the Crime Club by Doubleday.

Killing Jar. E. M. Beekman. LC 76-20542. 1976. 7.95 (ISBN 0-395-24763-2). Houghton Mifflin.

Killing Kin. Mona Naomi Anne Hocking Messer. LC 51-4766. 1951. Published for the Crime Club by Doubleday.

Killing Kind. Elliot West. LC 75-34111. 1976. 7.95 (ISBN 0-395-24078-6). Houghton Mifflin.

Killing Machine. Jack Vance, pseud. (Science Fiction Ser). 1978. pap. 1.75 (ISBN 0-87997-409-5, UE1409). DAW Bks.

Killing No Murder. C. Howard Shaw. LC 80-27273. 1981. 8.95 (ISBN 0-684-16884-7). Scribner's.

Killing of Billy Jowett. Clay Randall, pseud. (Orig.). 1981. pap. 1.95 (ISBN 0-505-51729-9). Tower Bks.

Killing of Judge MacFarlane. Mary Plum. LC 30-2367. 1930. Harper & Brothers.

Killing of Katie Steelstock. Michael Francis Gilbert. LC 79-3409. 12.95 (ISBN 0-06-011494-0). Harper & Row.

Killing of Katie Steelstock. Michael Francis Gilbert. LC 81-2054. 1981. 2.95. Penguin Books.

Killing of Katie Steelstock. large print ed. Michael Francis Gilbert. LC 82-8299. 1982. 13.95 (ISBN 0-89340-528-0). John Curley.

Killing of RFK. Donald Freed. 1975. (pbk.) 1.50. Dell.

Killing of Richard the Third. Robert Farrington. LC 70-162742. (Illus.). 1971. (ISBN 0-684-12567-6). Scribner.

Killing of the Golden Goose. Robert Jere Black. LC 34-5686. Loring & Murray.

Killing of the King. David R. Slavitt. LC 73-15370. 1974. 7.95 (ISBN 0-385-07899-4). Doubleday.

Killing Place. Tad Richards. Dell.

Killing Run. Mike Barry. (Lone Wolf; no. 13). 1975. (pbk.) 0.95 (ISBN 0-425-02920-4). Berkley Publishing Corp.

Killing Season. John Redgate. LC 67-16403. 1967. Trident Press.

Killing Spree. John Benteen. (O.s.i.). 1972. pap. 0.75 o.s.i. (BT50285). Belmont-Tower.

Killing the Goose. Frances Louise Davis Lockridge & Richard Lockridge. LC 48-10779. (Their A Mr. and Mrs. North mystery). 1948. Avon Pub. Co.

Killing the Goose. Frances Louise Davis Lockridge & Richard Lockridge. LC 44-121646. 1944. J. B. Lippincott Company.

Killing Time. Thomas Berger. 1981. pap. 7.95 (ISBN 0-440-54544-7, Delta). Dell.

Killing Time. Joe Steinmetz. Ed. by Barbara P. Norfleet. (Illus.). 64p. 1982. pap. 9.95 (ISBN 0-87923-453-9). Godine.

Killing Time. Donald E Westlake. LC 61-6245. (Random House mystery). 1961. Random House.

Killing Time: A Novel. Thomas Berger. LC 67-25306. 1967. Dial Press.

Killing Touch. William Murray. LC 73-16397. 1974. 6.95. Dutton.

Killing Trail. large print ed. Charles R Pike, pseud. LC 81-4739. 1981. 7.95 (ISBN 0-89621-279-3). Thorndike Press.

Killing with Kindness. Anne Morice. LC 74-14401. 1975. 6.95. St. Martin's Press.

Killing with Kindness. Anne Morice. LC 75-9839. 1975. 8.95 (ISBN 0-8161-6298-0). G. K. Hall.

Killing Wonder. Dorothy Bryant. LC 81-66995. 180p. 1981. 10.00 (ISBN 0-931688-06-X); pap. 6.00 (ISBN 0-931688-07-8). Ata Bks.

Killing Zone. William Howard Woods. LC 74-123989. 1970. 5.95 o.p. (ISBN 0-06-129710-0). Har-Row.

Killing Zone: A Novel. William Crawford Woods. LC 74-123989. 1970. 5.95. Harper's Magazine Press.

Killinger. P. K. Palmer. 256p. 1980. pap. 1.95 (ISBN 0-523-40968-0). Pinnacle Bks.

Killings. Clark Howard. LC 73-8701. 1973. 7.95. Dial Press.

Killings. Clark Howard. 1974. (pbk.) 1.75. Warner.

Killings at Coyote Springs. Lewis B Patten. LC 76-24213. 1977. 5.95 (ISBN 0-385-12668-9). Doubleday.

Killings at Coyote Springs. Lewis B Patten. (Signet Book). 1978. 1.50 (ISBN 0-451-07886-1). New American Library.

Killings in Carter Cave. Kenneth Whipple. LC 34-8581. A. H. King.

Killoe. Louis L'Amour. 160p. 1973. pap. 2.25 (ISBN 0-553-20083-6). Bantam.

Killraine. Thorne Douglas. 1979. pap. 1.50 (ISBN 0-449-14227-2, GM). Fawcett.

Killraine. Thorne Douglas. (Fawcett gold medal book). 1975. (pbk.) 0.95. Fawcett.

Killtest. Graham King. LC 77-15926. 1978. 7.95 (ISBN 0-312-45371-X). St. Martin's Press.

Killy. Westlake, Donald E. LC 63-8344. (Random House mystery). 1963. Random House.

Kilman's Landing: A Novel. William Judson, pseud. LC 76-71. 1975. 7.95 (ISBN 0-88405-138-2). Mason/Charter.

Kilmeny. William Black. (Lovell's library, v. 4, no. 180). J. W. Lovell Company.

Kilmeny. William Black. (Seaside library. Pocket ed. no. 126). G. Munro.

Kilmeny: A Novel. William Black. LC 42-27474. 1877. Harper & Brothers.

Kilmeny: A Novel. library ed. William Black. 1901. Harper & Brothers.

Kilmeny in the Dark Wood. Florence Stevenson. (Signet Book). 1973. (pbk.) 0.75. New American Library.

Kilmeny of the Orchard. Lucy Maud Montgomery. LC 10-10508. 1910. L. C. Page & Company.

Kilo: Being the Love Story of Eliph' Hewlitt, Book Agent. Ellis Parker Butler. LC 7-36094. 1907. The McClure Company.

Kilo Forty. Miles Tripp. LC 64-2231. 1963. Macmillan.

Kilometer 95: A Novel by Herbert Russcol and Margalit Banai. Herbert Russcol & Margalit Banai. LC 58-5112. 1958. Houghton Mifflin.

Kilraven. Mary Bishop. 1975. (pbk.) 0.95. Dell.

Kilrogan Cottage: A Novel, by Matilda Despart. Matilda Pratt Despard. (On cover:Harper's library of American fiction no. 6). 1878. Harper & Brothers.

Kilrone. Louis L'Amour. (Western Ser). 1970. pap. 2.25 (ISBN 0-553-14881-8). Bantam.

Kilroy Gambit. Irwin R Blacker. LC 60-5807. 1960. World Pub. Co.

Kilroy Hall. Monica Ewer. LC 50-7415. 1950. Arcadia House.

Kilt Beneath My Cassock. R. H. Falconer. 1978. 15.00x (ISBN 0-905312-02-3, Pub. by Scottish Academic Pr Scotland). Columbia U Pr.

Kilted Stranger. Margaret Pargeter. (Romances Ser.). (O.s.i.). pap. 0.95 (ISBN 0-373-01973-4, 51973, Pub by Harlequin). PB.

Kim. Robert Colby. 1970. pap. 0.75 o.p. (75-336). Manor Bks.

Kim. Rudyard Kipling. LC 1-25039. 1901. Doubleday, Page & Company.

Kim. Rudyard Kipling. LC 8-2109. 1901. Doubleday, Page & Company.

Kim. Rudyard Kipling. LC 24-20479. 1922. Doubleday, Page & Company.

Kim. Rudyard Kipling. LC 40-39679. The Sun Dial Press, Inc.

Kim & Ting. Miriam Dunn. 1981. pap. 1.95 (ISBN 0-85363-137-9). OMF Bks.

Kim Dawson. Alice M Fox. LC 50-7667. 1950. Doubleday.

Kim, "I Will Make Darkness Light". Hugh Steven & Kim Wickes. LC 75-18908. 1975. pap. 3.95 (ISBN 0-89081-013-3, 0133). Harvest Hse.

Kim Su Bang: And Other Stories of Korea. Ellasue Canter Wagner. LC 9-28698. Publishing House of the M. E. Church, South, Smith & Lamar, Agents.

TITLE INDEX

KING IN BABYLON.

Kim. The Naulahka, a Story of West and East (in Collaboration with Wolcott Balestier. Rudyard Kipling. LC 52-56510. (Mandalay edition of the works of Rudyard Kipling). 1925. Doubleday, Page.
Kim. With a New Introd. Rudyard Kipling. LC 62-19631. 1962. Collier Books.
Kim. With an Introd. by Charles Edmund Carrington and Illus. by Robin Jacques. Rudyard Kipling. LC 62-52840. 1962. For the Members of the Limited Editions Club.
Kim. With Biographical Illus. and Pictures from Early Editions of the Book, Together with an Introd. by J. I. M. Stewart (Michael Innes. Rudyard Kipling. LC 62-9720. (Great illustrated classics). 1962. Dodd, Mead.
Kimball Collection. Elizabeth Frances Corbett. 1972. pap. 0.95 o.p. (95311). Beagle Bks.
Kimball Collection. Elizabeth Frances Crobett. LC 42-3378. 1942. D. Appleton-Century Company, Incorporated.
Kimballs: A Novel. Mitchell A Wilson. LC 47-7001. 1947. Simon and Schuster.
Kimono. John Paris, pseud. LC 22-5524. Boni and Liveright.
Kin. Stephen Goodwin. LC 74-1886. 1975. 7.95 (ISBN 0-06-011608-0). Harper & Row.
Kin. Vahrah Von Klopp. LC 31-4183. 1931. Dodd, Mead & Company.
Kin. Gladys Malvern. LC 31-4183. 1931. Dodd, Mead & Company.
Kin-Da-Shon's Wife: An Alaskan Story. Caoline McCoy White Willard. F. H. Revell Company.
Kin of Ata Are Waiting for You. Dorothy Bryant. LC 76-8195. 1976. 4.95; pap. 2.95. Moon Bks.
Kin of Ata Are Waiting for You. Dorothy Bryant. 1976. 6.95 o.p. (ISBN 0-394-40729-6); pap. 4.95 (ISBN 0-394-73292-8). Random.
Kincaid of Red Butte. Leslie Charles Ernenwein. LC 42-10017. 1942. Phoenix Press.
Kincaids. Matthew Braun. LC 75-34224. 8.95 (ISBN 0-399-11620-6). Putnam.
Kincaid's Battery. George Washington Cable. LC 72-84535. 1974. (ISBN 0-403-02953-8). Scholarly Press.
Kincaid's Battery. George Washington Cable. 1908. 1.50. C. Scribner's Sons.
Kincaid's Battery. George Washington Cable. LC 28-1283. 1911. C. Scribner's Sons.
Kinch. Matthew Braun. LC 74-2506. 1975. 4.95 (ISBN 0-385-09599-6). Doubleday.
Kinch. Matthew Braun. 1978. 1.75 (ISBN 0-441-44464-4). Ace Books.
Kind Are Her Answers. Mary Renault, pseud. LC 40-7804. 1940. W. Morrow and Co.
Kind Are Her Answers. Mary Renault, pseud. LC 77-17345. 1978. 9.95 (ISBN 0-89244-078-3). Queens House.
Kind Are Her Answers. Mary Renault. 1974. (pbk.) 1.50 (ISBN 0-515-03368-5). Pyramid Books.
Kind Hearts and Coronets" By J. Harrison... J Harrison. LC 4-9461. 1904. Benziger Brothers.
Kind Man. Helen Nielsen. LC 51-9560. 1951. Washburn.
Kind of Anger. Eric Ambler. LC 64-23634. 1964. Atheneum.
Kind of Fighting: A Novel. Patrick Cruttwell. LC 60-6162. 1960. Macmillan.
Kind of Glory. Richard Shelton. 28p. (Orig.). 1982. pap. 28.00 (ISBN 0-914742-67-1). Copper Canyon.
Kind of Honor. large print ed. Joan Wolf. LC 81-17372. 1982. 12.95 (ISBN 0-89340-386-5). J. Curley & Associates.
Kind of Honor. Joan Wolf. 192p. (Orig.). 1980. pap. 1.75 (ISBN 0-451-09296-1, E9296, Sig). NAL.
Kind of Justice: By Edward Lindall Pseud. Edward Ernest Smith. LC 64-16444. 1964. Morrow.
Kind of Magic. Edna Ferber. 1963. 5.75 o.p. Doubleday.
Kind of Misfortune. Richard Parker. LC 54-13162. 1955. Scribner.
Kind of Prisoner. John Creasey. 1982. 15.00x (ISBN 0-86025-187-X, Pub. by Ian Henry Pubns England). State Mutual Bk.
Kind of Rape. Henry Kane. LC 73-91625. 1974. 7.95 (ISBN 0-689-10596-7). Atheneum.
Kind of Rape. Henry Kane. 1975. (pbk.) 1.75. Dell.
Kind of Treason. Robert S Elegant. LC 66-13099. (Rinehart suspense novel). 1966. Holt, Rinehart and Winston.
Kind of War. Pamela Haines. LC 76-363501. 1976. 3.50 (ISBN 0-434-31158-8). Heinemann.
Kindergarten. Elzbieta Ettinger. LC 70-86350. 1970. 5.95. Houghton Mifflin Co.
Kindergarten. Peter Rushforth. LC 79-3500. 1980. 8.95 (ISBN 0-394-50917-X). Knopf.
Kindergarten. Elzbieta Zettinger. 304p. 1972. pap. 1.25 o.p. (B12-2195). Belmont-Tower.
Kinderlied. Gunter Grass. (Illus.). 60p. 1983. 50.00 (ISBN 0-935716-18-1). Lord John.
Kindest Use a Knife. Louisa Revell. LC 52-13930. 1952. Macmillan.
Kindle the Trees. Tate McKenna. (Candlelight Ecstasy Ser.: No. 142). (Orig.). 1983. pap. 1.95 (ISBN 0-440-14506-6). Dell.
Kindled Flame. Margaret Bass Pedler. LC 31-21540. 1931. Doubleday, Doran & Company, Inc.
Kindling. Janice Elliott. LC 79-111234. 1970. 5.95. Knopf.
Kindling. easy eye ed. Nevil Shute. 1970. pap. 0.75 o.p. (6-74-88). Lancer.
Kindling. easy eye ed. Nevil Shute. 1968. pap. 0.75 o.p. (74-884). Lancer.
Kindling: A Novel. Nevil Shute Norway. LC 38-27422. 1938. W. Morrow & Company.
Kindling: A Novel. Large Type Ed., Complege and Unabridged. Nevil Shute Norway. LC 68-2000. 7.95. Watts.
Kindling: A Story of to-Day, from the Play of Charles Kenyon. Arthur Hornblow & Kenyon, Charles, 1880- LC 12-12864. G. W. Dillingham Company.
Kindling and Ashes: Or, The Heart of Barbara Wayne. George Barr McCutcheon. LC 26-16196. 1926. Dodd, Mead and Company.
Kindling and Ashes: Or, The Heart of Barbara Wayne. George Barr McCutcheon. LC 30-123225. 1928. A. L. Burt Company.
Kindling. 1st Ed. Frederick Stallknecht Wight. LC 51-10479. 1951. Little, Brown.
Kindly Contagion: Stories. Toman, Walter. LC 59-10207. 1959. Bobbs-Merrill.
Kindly Dig Your Grave and Other Wicked Stories. Stanley Ellin. LC 76-353090. (First book publication; no. 6). (Ellery Queen presents). 1975. 1.60. Davis Publications.
Kindly Ones. 1st American Ed. Anthony Dymoke Powell. (His The music of time). 1962. Little, Brown.
Kindness Cup. Thea Astley. LC 75-322060. 1974. 5.95 (ISBN 0-17-005015-7). Thomas Nelson (Australia)
Kindness in a Corner. Theodore Francis Powys. LC 30-125263. 1930. The Viking Press.
Kindness of Dr. Avicenna: A Novel. John Pearson. LC 81-20171. 15.50. Holt, Rinehart, and Winston.
Kindness of Strangers: 1st Ed. Stanley Wade Baron. LC 61-6573. 1961. Little, Brown.
Kindred. Octavia E Butler. LC 78-22597. 1979. 8.95 (ISBN 0-385-15059-8). Doubleday.
Kindred. Octavia E Butler. 1981. 2.75 (ISBN 0-671-83483-5). Pocket Books.
Kindred. Alice Prescott Smith. LC 25-145141. 1925. Houghton Mifflin Company.
Kindred by Choice. Johann Wolfgang Von Goethe. Tr. by H. M. Waidson. 1980. pap. 4.95 (ISBN 0-7145-0324-X). Riverrun NY.
Kindred of the Dust. Peter Bernard Kyne. LC 20-8274. 1920. Cosmopolitan Book Corporation.
Kindred of the Dust. Peter Bernard Kyne. LC 24-20458. 1922. Grosset & Dunlap.
Kindred Spirit. large print ed. Ginger Chambers. LC 81-21421. 9.95. Thorndike Press.
Kindred Spirit. Richard Sherman. LC 51-121. 1951. Little, Brown.
Kindred Spirits. DeAnn Patrick. (Tapestry Romance Ser.). 320p. (Orig.). 1982. pap. 2.50 (ISBN 0-671-46186-9). PB.
Kinds of Crime. Maxwell Grant, pseud. (Shadow Ser.: No. 11). 1976. pap. 0.95 o.p. (ISBN 0-515-03967-5). BJ Pub Group.
Kinds of Love. May Sarton. LC 70-125860. 1970. 12.95 o.p. (ISBN 0-393-08620-8). Norton.
Kinds of Love. May Sarton. 352p. 1980. pap. 4.95 (ISBN 0-393-00968-8). Norton.
Kinds of Love: A Novel. May Sarton. LC 70-125860. 1970. 6.95 (ISBN 0-393-08620-8). Norton.
Kinds of Love: A Novel. May Sarton. LC 79-27520. 1980. 3.95 (ISBN 0-393-00968-8). Norton.
Kinds of Love, Kinds of Death. Tucker Coe. 224p. 1979. pap. 1.95 o.p. (ISBN 0-441-44467-9). Charter Bks.
Kinds of Love, Kinds of Death. Tucker Coe. 224p. 1979. pap. 1.95 o.p. (ISBN 0-441-44467-9). Charter Bks.
Kinds of Love, Kinds of Death. Donald E. Westlake. LC 66-21501. 1966. Random House.
Kindy's Crossing: A Novel. Margaret Weymouth Jackson. LC 34-1685. The Bobbs-Merrill Company.
Kinflicks. Lisa Alther. 1977. pap. 3.95 (ISBN 0-451-11985-1, AE1985, Sig). NAL.
Kinflicks: A Novel. Lisa Alther. LC 75-36782. 1976. 10.00 (ISBN 0-394-49836-4). Knopf: Distributed by Random House.
Kinfolk. Pearl Sydenstricker Buck. LC 49-2037. 1949. J. Day Co.
Kinfolks: The Wilgus Stories. Gurney Norman. LC 77-82064. 6.50. (ISBN 0-917788-07-9) (ISBN 0-917788-10-9). Gnomon.
King. William Laurence Coleman. LC 67-24435. 1967. McGraw-Hill.
King. Morton Cooper. (Signet bk., Q3367). 1968. New Amer. Lib.
King. William Matthews Johnson. LC 77-16717. 1978. 7.95 o.p. (ISBN 0-312-45425-2). St Martin.
King. William Johnston & Abby Mann. LC 77-16717. 7.95 (ISBN 0-312-45425-2). St. Martin's Press.
King--of Kearsarge. Arthur Olney Friel. LC 21-15888. 1921. The Penn Publishing Company.
King--of the Khyber Rifles: A Romance of Adventure. Talbot Mundy. LC 16-23093. 1.35. The Bobbs-Merrill Company.
King: A Novel. Morton Cooper. LC 67-13096. 1967. Bernard Geis Associates; Distributed by New American Library.
King; a Romance of the Camp and Court of Alexander the Great. The Story of Theba, the Macedonian Captive. Marshall Monroe Kirkman. LC 13-222112. Cropley Phillips Company.
King Ahab's Feast. Enrique Lafourcade. LC 63-9411. 1963. St Martin's Press.
King Akhnaton: A Chronicle of Ancient Egypt. Simeon Strunsky. LC 28-20464. 1928. Longmans, Green and Co.
King Albert. Francis Bebey. LC 81-12799. 1981. 10.00 (ISBN 0-88208-138-1) (ISBN 0-88208-139-X). L. Hill.
King Alcohol: A Romance of the Keeley Institute. Harry Meredith. LC 7-26233. 1893.
King and a Few Dukes: A Romance. Robert William Chambers. LC 4-15290. 1896. G. P. Putnam's Sons.
King and Four Queens: An Original Western, by Theodore Sturgeon Pseud. Edward Hamilton Waldo, pseud. LC 56-12764. (Dell first edition, A128). 1956. Dell Pub. Co.
King and His Campaigners. Verner Von Heidenstam. Tr. by Axel Tegnier. LC 70-113676. 1970. Books for Libraries Press.
King and Joker. Peter Dickinson. LC 75-38119. 6.95 (ISBN 0-394-40603-6). Pantheon Books.
King and Joker. Peter Dickinson. LC 76-47633. 1976. 10.95 (ISBN 0-8161-6434-7). G. K. Hall.
King and Joker. Peter Dickinson. 1977. 1.50 (ISBN 0-380-01767-9). Avon.
King & Queen. 1968. pap. 2.45 o.p. (ISBN 0-448-00213-2, G&D). Putnam Pub Group.
King and Queen of Mollebusch: Or, The Indispensables. Georg Moritz Ebers & Safford, Mary Joanne, Tr. LC 99-419172. Brown and Company.
King & Queen of Moonlight Bay. Michael De Guzman. (Orig.). 1982. pap. 2.75 (ISBN 0-440-14578-3). Dell.
King and the Cat. Thomas Starling, pseud. LC 74-82405. 1975. 6.95 (ISBN 0-914864-00-9). Spindrift Press.
King and the Corpse. Max Murray. LC 48-7630. 1948. Farrar, Straus.
King and the Cross: A Tale of Old and New France. George Alfred Stringer & Stringer, Eliza C. Walker, Joint Author. LC 2-2768. 1901. Eastern Publishing Company.
King & the Queen. Ramon Jose Sender. pap. 2.45 o.p. (213, UL). G&D.
King Arthur and His Knights. Henry Frith. LC 36-901. (golden books for children). D. McKay.
King Arthur and His Knights: A Selection from What Has Been Known As Le Morte Darthur. Thomas Malory. Ed. by Reginald Thorne Davies. LC 67-6948. 1967. Barnes & Noble.
King Arthur and His Knights of the Round Table. Roger Lancelyn Green & Lotte Reiniger. LC 79-28131. (Illus.). 1980. 2.95 (ISBN 0-14-005589-4). Penguin Books.
King Arthur and His Knights: Selected Tales. Thomas Malory. Ed. by Eugene Vinaver. LC 74-33054. (Galaxy book; 434). (Illus.). 1975. 2.95 (ISBN 0-19-501905-9). Oxford University Press.
King Arthur and His Knights: Selected Tales. rev. and enl. ed. Thomas Malory. Ed. by Eugene Vinaver. LC 70-798. (Riverside editions, B8). 1968. 1.35. Houghton Mifflin.
King Arthur and His Knights: Selections from the Works of Sir Thomas Malory. Edited with an Introd. and Notes by Eugene Vinaver. Thomas Malory & Arthur, King (Romances, Etc.) Ed. by Eugene Vinaver. LC 56-14069. (Riverside editions,). 1956. Houghton Mifflin.
King Arthur & the Knights of the Round Table. Roger Lancelyn Green. 1980. pap. 2.95 o.p. (ISBN 0-14-030073-2). Penguin.
King Arthur and the Knights of the Round Table. Thomas Malory & Holland, Rupert Sargent, 1878- Ed. LC 19-15897. (On cover: The Washington square classics). G. W. Jacobs and Company.
King Arthur and the Round Table. Illustrated with 8 Colour Plates and 14 Black & White Drawings by Donald Seton Cammell. Alice Mary Hadfield. LC 53-10769. (Children's illustrated classics). 1953. Dent.
King Arthur: Not a Love Story. Dinah Maria Mulock Craik. LC 6-31082. (Harper's handy series, no. 76). 1886. Harper & Brothers.
King Arthur: Not a Love Story. Dinah Maria Mulock Craik. (On cover: Lovell's library. v. 15, no. 751). J. W. Lovell Company.
King Arthur. Not a Love Story. Dinah Maria Mulock Craik. LC 7-3511. (On cover: Seaside library. Pocket ed. no. 808). G. Munro.
King Arthur Today: The Arthurian Legend in English & American Literature. Nathan C. Starr. 1954. pap. 3.50 o.p. (ISBN 0-8130-0218-4). U of Fla Pr.
King Arthur's Daughter. Vera Chapman. 1978. 1.75 (ISBN 0-380-01958-2). Avon.
King Behind the King. Warwick Deeping. LC 15-9315. 1914. McBride, Nast & Company.
King Bird Rides. Max Brand. LC 36-14275. 1936. Dodd, Mead & Company.
King Bird Rides. Frederick Faust. LC 36-14275. 1936. Dodd, Mead & Company.
King, Bishop, Knight. Robert Emmett. (American Avenger Ser.: No. 4). 1982. pap. 2.50 (ISBN 0-451-11620-8, Sig). NAL.
King by Night. Edgar Wallace. LC 26-10073. 1926. Doubleday, Page & Company.
King Cayuse. Archie Joscelyn. LC 39-33515. Phoenix Press.
King Circumstance. Edwin William Pugh. LC 7-42191. 1898. H. Holt and Company.
King Coal; a Novel. Upton Beall Sinclair. LC 17-24400. 1917. The Macmillan Company.
King Coal: A Novel. Upton Beall Sinclair. LC 74-22813. (Series: Labor Movement in Fiction and Non-Fiction.). 1980. 24.00 (ISBN 0-404-58469-1). AMS Press.
King Cobra. Mark Channing. LC 34-188384. J. B. Lippincott Company.
King Cobra. Ward Greene. LC 40-27436. Carrick & Evans, Inc.
King Coffin. Conrad Potter Aiken. LC 85-184182. 1935. C. Scribner's Sons.
King Cole: A Novel. William Riley Burnett. LC 36-20997. 1936. Harper & Brothers.
King Colt. Luke Short. LC 80-16925. 1980. 11.95 (ISBN 0-8161-3110-4). G. K. Hall.
King Conan. Stories. Robert E. Howard. LC 53-8200. (His The Hyborean Age). 1953. Gnome Press.
King Coppersmith. Robert J. Griffin. (Orig.). 1971. pap. 0.95 o.p. (N2460). Pyramid Pubns.
King Corso: A Novel. William Hegner. 1973. (pbk) 1.25 (ISBN 0-671-78279-7). Pocket Books.
King Cotton. Evelyn K. Combs. 228p. (Orig.). 1982. pap. 6.95 (ISBN 0-933078-10-2). M Arman.
King Dan, the Factory Detective. A Rattling Story of the Spindle City. George W Goode. (On cover: New York 10 cent. library. no. 3). Katahdin Publishing Company.
King David Report: A Novel. Stefan Heym. LC 73-78603. 1973. 6.95 (ISBN 0-399-11197-2). Putnam.
King David. 1st Ed. Gwyn Jenkins. LC 61-9520. 1961. Doubleday.
King David's Spaceship. J. E. Pournelle. LC 80-21909. (Illus.). 11.95 (ISBN 0-671-25328-X). Simon and Schuster.
King Death. Nik Cohn. LC 75-14277. 1975. 5.95 (ISBN 0-15-147223-8). Harcourt Brace Jovanovich.
King Diaries. 1st Ed. Douglas Moon. LC 66-28833. 1967. bds., 4.95. McGraw.
King Disputed. Trygve Raubach De Lange. LC 30-27930. Democrat Printing Company.
King Dobbs. A Satirical Romance. a new ed. James Hannay. LC 7-35192. 1856. G. Routledge & Co.
King Edward Plot. Robert Lee Hall. LC 79-20435. 9.95 (ISBN 0-07-025609-8). McGraw-Hill.
King-Errant. Flora Annie Webster Steel. LC 12-252023. 1912. 1.30. Frederick A. Stokes Company.
King Fisher Lives. Julian Rathbone. LC 75-40803. 1976. 8.95. St. Martin's Press.
King Fisher Lives. Julian Rathbone. LC 77-368308. 1976. 3.50 (ISBN 0-7181-1471-X). Joseph.
King Fisher's Road. Shepard Rifkin. 160p. 1977. pap. 1.50 (ISBN 0-449-14236-1, GM). Fawcett.
King from Ashtabuls. Vern J Sneider. LC 60-8482. 1960. Putnam.
King Goshawk and the Birds. Eimar O'Duffy. LC 26-17279. 1926. The Macmillan Company.
King Haber, and Other Stories. Alfred Neumann. LC 71-128743. (Short story index reprint series). 1970. Books for Libraries Press.
King Haber and Other Stories. Alfred Neumann. Tr. by Busch, Marie & King, Alfred H. LC 30-8907. 1930. A. H. King.
King Hal's Fifth Wife. Samuel Travers Clover. LC 33-15942. 1933. Saturday Night Publishing Company.
King Harald & the Icelanders: Five Icelandic Stories. Tr. by Pardee Lowe, Jr. from Icelandic. (Illus.). 1979. 15.00 (ISBN 0-915778-21-1); deluxe ed. 40.00x deluxe ed (ISBN 0-915778-22-X). Penmaen Pr.
King Hereafter: A Novel. Dorothy Dunnett. LC 81-48112. (Illus.). 1982. 16.95 (ISBN 0-394-52378-4). Knopf: Distributed by Random House.
King in Babylon. Burton Egbert Stevenson. LC 17-24692. 1.50. Small, Maynard & Company.

King in Check. Talbot Mundy. LC 34-25913. (Tired business man's library of adventure, detective, and mystery novels). 1934. D. Appleton-Century Company, Incorporated.

King in Hell. Beverly Balin. 1973. 1.95 (ISBN 0-515-02958-0). Pyramid.

King in Khaki. Henry Kitchell Webster. 1909. D. Appleton and Company.

King in Love. Barbara Cartland. LC 81-22080. 10.95 (ISBN 0-89696-166-4). Everest House.

King in Prussia. Rafael Sabatini. LC 44-7467. 1944. Hutchinson Co. Ltd.

King in Rags. Cleveland Moffett. LC 7-36249. 1907. D. Appleton and Company.

King in Yellow. Robert William Chambers. LC 72-75775. (Short story index reprint series). (Illus.). 1969. Books for Libraries Press.

King in Yellow. Robert William Chambers. LC 24-222251. (Neely's prismatic library). F. T. Neely.

King in Yellow. Robert William Chambers. 1902. Harper & Brothers.

King in Yellow. memorial ed. Robert William Chambers & Hughes, Rupert. LC 38-15216. 1938. D. Appleton-Century Company, Incorporated.

King in Yellow: And Other Horror Stories. Robert William Chambers. LC 70-98301. 1970. 2.75 (ISBN 0-486-22500-3). Dover Publications.

King in Yellow & Other Horror Stories. Robert William Chambers. 5.00 o.p. (ISBN 0-8446-0056-3). Peter Smith.

King in Yellow & Other Tales of Supernatural Horror. Robert William Chambers. Ed. by E. F. Bleiler. LC 70-98301. 1970. pap. 3.50 (ISBN 0-486-22500-3). Dover.

King Is a Fink. Johnny Hart & Brant Parker. (Wizard of Id Ser.). (Illus.). 128p. 1982. pap. 1.95 (ISBN 0-449-13709-0, GM). Fawcett.

King Is a Witch. Evelyn Sybil Mary Eaton. LC 74-80846. 1974. 6.95. St. Martin's Press.

King Is Coming. 2nd ed. H. L. Willmington. 1981. pap. 5.95 (ISBN 0-8423-2086-5). Tyndale.

King Is Dead. Ellery Queen, pseud. LC 52-5529. 1952. Little Brown.

King Is Dead. Ellery Queen, pseud. LC 82-7296. 1982. 12.95 (ISBN 0-89340-524-8). J. Curley.

King Is Dead. Ellery Queen. (Signet mystery, Q5290). 1972. New American Lib.

King Is Dead on Queen Street. Audrey Walz. LC 45-8121. 1945. Duell Sloan and Pearce.

King Jaguar. Dan Sherman. LC 78-73867. 9.95 (ISBN 0-87795-221-3). Arbor House.

King James Version: A Novel. Stanley N Stewart. LC 76-14194. 8.95 (ISBN 0-394-40042-9). Random House.

King Jesus. Robert Graves. 1967. pap. 2.50 o.p. (ISBN 0-308-60004-5, M10, Minerva). Funk & W.

King Jesus: A Novel. Robert Graves. LC 81-12459. (Illus.). 1981. 17.95 (ISBN 0-374-18114-4) (ISBN 0-374-51664-2). Farrar, Straus, Giroux.

King John: A Tale of the South. George F Robertson. LC 27-14795. Lowell Publishing Co.

King John of Jingalo: The Story of a Monarch in Difficulties. Laurence Housman. LC 12-27190. 1912. H. Holt and Company.

King John of Jungalo: The Story of a Monarch in Difficulties. Laurence Housman. LC 37-16539. 1937. C. Scribner's Sons.

King John's Treasure. Millie J Ragosta. LC 75-36607. 1976. 5.95 (ISBN 0-385-11419-2). Doubleday.

King Joker, a King in Search of a Civilization. Clifford E. Dennis. 1970. 6.00. Willoughby.

King Jude. David Helton. LC 74-84124. (O.S.I.). 1969. 4.95 o.s.i. (ISBN 0-671-20327-4). S&S.

King Jude: A Novel. David Helton. LC 74-84124. 1969. 4.95. Simon and Schuster.

King Julian: A Novel. Tom Gatch. LC 54-833393. 1954. Vantage Press.

King-Killers. Thomas Blanchard Dewey. LC 68-19431. (Red mask mystery). 1968. Putnam.

King Kong. M. Cooper & E. Wallace. 1982. Repr. lib. bdg. 17.95x (ISBN 0-89966-440-7). Buccaneer Bks.

King Kong. Debs Wheeler Lovelace & Edgar Wallace. LC 76-27267. (Illus.). 1976. 2.95 (ISBN 0-448-12788-1) (ISBN 0-448-13410-1). Grosset & Dunlap.

King Kong. Delos W Lovelace. 1.95. Ace.

King Kong. Delos Wheeler Lovelace & Edgar Wallace. LC 33-140. Grosset & Dunlap.

King Kull. Robert E. Howard & Lin Carter. (Orig.). 1968. pap. 0.75 o.p. (73-650). Lancer.

King Kull. Robert E. Howard & Lin Carter. 1972. pap. 0.95 o.s.i. (75-371). Lancer.

King Kuriosity. George William Mitchell. LC 26-17111. Small, Maynard & Company.

King Lazarus. Mongo Beti. Tr. by Peter Green from Fr. (African Writers Ser.: No. 77). (Orig.). 1981. pap. text ed. 4.00x (ISBN 0-435-90077-3). Heinemann Ed.

King Lazarus: A Novel. Mongo Beti. LC 78-117968. (American Library). 1971. 1.50. Collier Books.

King Lethal. Norman Solomon. 70p. (Orig.). 1972. pap. 1.00 o.p. (ISBN 0-912874-04-X). Out of the Ashes.

King Liveth. Jeffery Farnol. LC 44-39454. 1944. Doubleday, Doran and Co., Inc.

King Maker. Kenneth Robeson. (Doc Savage no. 80). 1975. (pbk.) 0.95. Bantam.

King Midas: a Romance. Upton Beall Sinclair. LC 1-25225. 1901. Funk & Wagnalls Company.

King Murder: A Leighton Swift Detective Story. Charles Reed Jones. LC 29-8545. E. P. Dutton & Co., Inc.

King Must Die. Mary Renault, pseud. LC 58-7202. 1958. Pantheon.

King Must Die. Mary Renault. 1974. (pbk.) 1.75. Bantam Books.

King Noanett: A Story of Devon Settlers in Old Virginia and Massachusetts Bay. Frederic Jesup Stimson. LC 4-15156. 1897. J. Lane.

King Noanett: A Story of Old Virginia and the Massachusetts Bay. Frederic Jesup Stimson. LC 8-163132. 1896. Lamson, Wolffe and Company.

King Noanett: A Story of Old Virginia and the Massachusetts Bay. 2d ed. with map ed. Frederic Jesup Stimson. LC 8-16314. 1896. Lamson, Wolffe, and Company; Etc., Etc.

King of a Rainy Country. 1st American Ed. Brigid Brophy. LC 57-525235. 1957. Knopf.

King of Abilene. Thomas Thompson. LC 53-11938. 1953. Ballantine Books.

King of Alberia. A Romance of the Balkans. L D. LC 6-33195. 1895. G. W. Dillingham.

King of Andaman: A Saviour of Society. James Maclaren Cobban. LC 6-26764. (Half title: Appleton's town and country library, no. 180). 1895. D. Appleton and Company.

King of Andorra. Henry E Harris. LC 2-975. The Abbey Press.

King of Arcadia. Francis Lynde. LC 9-657335. 1909. C. Scribner's Sons.

King of Argent. John T. Phiillifent. (Science Fiction Ser). 1981. pap. 2.25 o.p. (ISBN 0-87997-649-7, UE1649). DAW Bks.

King of Argent. John T Phillifent. (Daw SF Books, no. 46). (Illus.). 1973. (pbk) 0.95. Daw Books.

King of Cimarron Crossing: By Chuck Stanley. Charles Stanley Strong. LC 59-1597. 1959. Arcadia House.

King of Clubs. Howard Goldberg. LC 81-85466. 12.95 (ISBN 0-942276-01-9). Parthenon Press.

King of Culla. Sally Wentworth. (Harlequin Presents Ser.). 192p. 1981. pap. 1.75 (ISBN 0-373-10462-6). Harlequin Bks.

King of Diamonds: A Tale of Mystery and Adventure. Louis Tracy. Grosset & Dunlap.

King of Dreams: A Romance of the Days of the Christ. Gertrude Roper Warmington. LC 26-14156. George H. Doran Company.

King of Fassarai: By David Divine Pseud. Arthur Durham Divine. LC 50-5877. 1950. Macmillan.

King of Flesh and Blood. Translated from the Hebrew by David Patterson. Moshe Shamir. LC 58-13902. 1958. Vanguard Press.

King of Folly Island: And Other People. Sarah Orne Jewett. LC 7-9935. 1888. Houghton, Mifflin and Company.

King of Folly Island & Other People. Sarah Orne Jewett. Ed. by Kenneth Lynn. LC 75-96658. (American Authors Ser., Collected Works of Sarah Orne Jewett). 1970. Repr. of 1888 ed. lib. bdg. 19.50 o.s.i. (ISBN 0-512-00375-0). Garrett Pr.

King of Folly Island & Other People see Collected Works.

King of Gold; the Mystery of the Lost Mine. A Story of Mistakes and Deception. E. O. Tilburn. (On cover: Globe detective series, no. 6). 1888. The Eagle Publishing Co.

King of Hearts. David R. Slavitt. LC 76-29228. 8.95 (ISBN 0-87795-153-5). Arbor House.

King of Heaven. Burt Hirschfeld. 320p. (Orig.). 1983. pap. 3.50 (ISBN 0-345-29864-0). Ballantine.

King of Honey Island. A Novel. Maurice Thompson. (On cover: Ledger library. no. 79). 1893. R. Bonner's Sons.

King of Hualpi Valley. Jesse Edward Grinstead. Dodge Publishing Company.

King of Kielder. Margaret Rome. (Harlequin Romance Ser.). 192p. 1982. pap. 1.50 (ISBN 0-373-02487-8). Harlequin Bks.

King of Kings. Henry MacMahon & MacPherson, Jeanie, Joint Author. LC 27-10729. Grosset & Dunlap.

King of Kings: A Novel. Malachi Martin. LC 80-23950. 15.95 (ISBN 0-671-24707-7). Simon and Schuster.

King of Kor: Or, She's Promise Kept. Sidney John Marshall. LC 77-84255. (Lost Race and Adult Fantasy Fiction). (Illus.). 1978. 16.00 (ISBN 0-405-10999-7). Arno Press.

King of Liberty Bend. Nancy C Wood. LC 75-25105. 8.95 (ISBN 0-06-014738-5). Harper & Row.

King of No Man's Land. Arthur Olney Friel. LC 24-7529. 1924. Harper & Brothers.

King of Nobody's Island. Thomas Enright. LC 9-19034. The Gibson Publishing Company.

King of Paris. Guy Endore. 1970. pap. 1.25 o.p. (ISBN 0-447-78644-X). Lancer.

King of Paris: A Novel. S. Guy Endore. LC 56-9908. 1956. Simon and Schuster.

King of Pirates, Being an Account of the Famous Enterprises of Captain Avery: With Lives of Other Pirates and Robbers. Daniel Defoe. LC 74-13451. (Illus.). 1974. (ISBN 0-404-07926-1). AMS Press.

King. of Proxy Street: A Story. Stanley Kauffmann. LC 41-16060. The John Day Company.

King of Rothenburg: A Historical Romance. Paul Schreckenbach. Tr. by Bookstaver, Mary Andrews Leonard. LC 14-6002. 1.25. R. G. Badger; Etc., Etc.

King of Schnorrers: Grotesques and Fantasies. Israel Zangwill. LC 8-37871. 1894. Macmillan and Co.

King of Schnorrers. To Which Is Added an Essay, On Jewish Humor, by Bernard N. Schilling. Israel Zangwill & Bernard Nicholas. On Jewish Humor Schilling. LC 53-13484. 1953. Shoe String Press.

King of Schnorrers. With a New Introd. by Maurice Wohlgelernter. Israel Zangwill. LC 65-15518. 1965. Dover Publications.

King of Scuffletoun: A Croatan Romance. John Paul Lucas & Groome, Bailey Troy. LC 40-81633. Garrett and Massie, Incorporated.

King of Shadows. Margaret Routledge Yeo. LC 29-19691. 1929. The Macmillan Company.

King of Silverhill. Archie Joscelyn. LC 64-7364. Arcadia House.

King of Spades. Frederick Feikema Manfred. (Manfred, Frederick Feikema, 1912-. The Buckskin Man Tales: 4). 1968 (75272). Pocket Bks.

King of Spades. Frederick Feikema Manfred. (Signet Book). 1973. (pbk) 1.25. New American Lib.

King of Spades. Frederick Feikema Manfred. LC 66-22121. (His The Buckskin man tales, 4). 1966. Trident Press.

King of Spades. Frederick Feikema Manfred. LC 79-26382. (Series: Gregg Press Western Fiction Series.). 1980. 14.95 (ISBN 0-8398-2592-7). Gregg Press.

King of Spain's Daughter. McCready Huston. The Bobbs-Merrill Company.

King of Terrors. John D Spooner. LC 74-23290. 1975. 7.95 (ISBN 0-316-80754-0). Little, Brown.

King of Terrors: Tales of Madness and Death. Robert Bloch. LC 76-16892. 1977. 10.00. (ISBN 0-89296-029-9) (ISBN 0-89296-030-2). Mysterious Press.

King of the Air: Or, To Monocco on an Airship. Herbert Strang. LC 9-2776. The Bobbs-Merril Company.

King of the Amazon. Peter Davis. LC 33-16727. The Macaulay Company.

King of the Archers. Rene Bazin. Tr. by Mary Russell. LC 34-22745. 1934. The Macmillan Company.

King of the Barbareens. Janet Hitchman. LC 66-70276. (Peacock Books, Pk59: B66-4350). 1966. Penguin.

King of the Bastards: A Novel. Sarah Gertrude Liebson Millin. LC 49-7707. 1949. Harper.

King of the Broncos: And Other Stories of New Mexico. Charles Fletcher Lummis. LC 73-125231. (Short story index reprint series). (Illus.). 1970. Books for Libraries Press.

King of the Broncos: And Other Stories of New Mexico. Charles Fletcher Lummis. LC 7-14507. 1897. C. Scribner's Son.

King of the Broncos, & Other Stories of New Mexico. Charles Fletcher Lummis. LC 73-125231. (Short Story Index Reprint Ser). 1897. 15.00 (ISBN 0-8369-3598-5). Ayer Co.

King of the Bush. William MacLeod Raine. LC 37-23926. 1937. Houghton Mifflin Company.

King of the Camorra: By E. Searo. E Serao. LC 12-25074. G. W. Dillingham Company.

King of the Castle. Eleanor Hibbert. LC 67-10974. 1967. Doubleday.

King of the Castle. Victoria Holt, pseud. LC 67-10974. 1967. 13.95 (ISBN 0-385-07672-X). Doubleday.

King of the Castle. Victoria Holt, pseud. 1978. pap. 2.75 (ISBN 0-449-23587-4, Crest). Fawcett.

King of the Castle. Eugene McCabe. signed 7.50 (ISBN 0-912262-49-4); pap. 2.95x (ISBN 0-912262-50-8). Proscenium.

King of the Castle. Peter C. Newman. 1980. pap. 2.75 (ISBN 0-671-83083-X). PB.

King of the Castle: A Novel. John Keble Bell. LC 23-3890. Small, Maynard & Company.

King of the Dead: A Weird Romance. Frank Atkins. Ed. by R. Reginald & Douglas Melville. LC 77-84197. (Lost Race & Adult Fantasy Ser.). 1978. Repr. of 1903 ed. lib. bdg. 20.00x (ISBN 0-405-10956-3). Ayer Co.

King of the Dead: A Weird Romance. Frank Aubrey. LC 77-84197. (Lost Race and Adult Fantasy Fiction). 1978. 20.00 (ISBN 0-405-10956-3). Arno Press.

King of the Detectives. Harlan Page Halsey. (On cover: The calumet series, no. 5). 1891. G. Munro.

King of the Gamblers. Adolphe Belot. Tr. by Lee, Miss S. (Seaside library, v, 52, no. 1057). G. Munro.

King of the Golden Gate. Peter Gentry, pseud. 320p. 1981. pap. 2.95 (ISBN 0-449-14429-1). Fawcett.

King of the Golden Mask & Other Stories. Marcel Schwob. Tr. by Iain White from French. 224p. 1982. text ed. 14.75x (ISBN 0-85635-403-1, 30268, Pub. by Carcanet New Pr England). Humanities.

King of the Golden River. John Ruskin. (Legacy Library Ser). 1966. Repr. of 1851 ed. 4.95 o.p. (LL02002). Univ Microfilms.

King of the Golden River. John Ruskin. 5.00 o.p. (ISBN 0-87482-056-1). Wake-Brook.

King of the Golden River: Or, The Black Brothers. John Ruskin. LC 30-25659. 1930. William Edwin Rudge.

King of the Hill. Thomas J Fleming. (NAL). 1966. 4.95. New Amer. Lib.

King of the Hill. William M. Green. LC 75-8639. 1975. Bobbs-Merrill.

King of the Hill. A. E Hotchner. LC 72-77751. 1972. 6.95 (ISBN 0-06-011964-0). Harper & Row.

King of the Hurons. Peter Hamilton Myers. LC 7-23122. 1850. G. P. Putnam; Etc., Etc.

King of the Jews. Mary Borden. LC 35-3433. 1935. Little, Brown, and Company.

King of the Jews. Leslie Epstein. LC 78-14558. 9.95 (ISBN 0-698-10955-4). Coward, McCann & Geoghegan.

King of the Jews. Leslie Epstein. 1980. 2.50 (ISBN 0-380-48074-3). Avon Books.

King-of the Khyber Rifles. Talbot Mundy. 15.00 (ISBN 0-937986-14-3). D M Grant.

King of the Mesa. Hoffman Birney. 1927. The Penn Publishing Company.

King of the Mesa. James Lyon Rubel. LC 38-22134. Phoenix Press.

King of the Money Kings. Lincoln Truax. LC 16-629110. 1916. The Money Kings Pub. Co.

King of the Mountain. George Cassidy. 1980. pap. 1.75 o.s.i. (ISBN 0-8439-0717-7, Leisure Bks). Nordon Pubns.

King of the Mountains. Edmond Francois Valentin About & Kingsbury, Mrs. Carlton A., Tr. LC 5-425998. 1897. Rand, McNally & Company.

King of the Mountains. Edmond Francois Valentine About & Booth, Mary Louise, 1831-1889, Tr. 1861. J. E. Tilton and Company.

King of the Mountains (Le Roi Des Montagnes) Edmond Francois Valentin About & Crewe-Jones, Florence, Tr. LC 24-14881. 1924. Cupples & Leon Company.

King of the Panhandle. Charles Stanley Strong. LC 49-412494. 1949. Phoenix Press.

King of the Plains: Stories of Ranch, Indian, and Mine. Tilden Tilford. LC 10-23204. 1910. Harper & Brothers.

King of the Rainy Country. Nicolas Freeling. (U 5112). 1968. Ballantine.

King of the Rainy Country. Nicolas Freeling. 1975. (pbk.) 1.25 (ISBN 0-14-002853-6). Penguin.

King of the Rainy Country. Nicolas Freeling. LC 67-10490. 1966. Harper & Row.

King of the Range. Frank Austin. LC 35-1090. 1935. Dodd, Mead & Company.

King of the Range. Ford Bowne, pseud. LC 68-2938. 1968. Arcadia House.

King of the Range. Max Brand. 1982. pap. 1.95 (ISBN 0-671-83374-X). PB.

King of the Range. Romer Grey. LC 81-3109. 1981. 13.95 (ISBN 0-89340-355-5). J. Curley & Associates.

King of the Rangeland. Jesse Edward Grinstead. Dodge Publishing Company.

King of the Road. Frank Clune, pseud. 1967. Repr. pap. 1.60 o.s.i. Tri-Ocean.

King of the Rodeo. Archie Joscelyn. LC 41-2812. 1941. Phoenix Press.

King of the Roses. V. S. Anderson. LC 83-3005. 384p. 1983. 14.95 (ISBN 0-312-45512-7). St Martin.

King of the Royal Mounted & the Great Jewel Mystery. Zane Grey. Repr. lib. bdg. 15.95x (ISBN 0-89190-758-0). Am Repr-Rivercity Pr.

King of the Sea. Derek Bickerton. LC 79-4787. 8.95 (ISBN 0-394-50516-6). Random House.

King of the Sea. Donald J. Campbell. 3.50 o.p. Carlton.

King of the Sea: A Tale of the Fearless and Free. Edward Zane Carroll Judson. LC 7-114496. 1847. Flag of Our Union Office.

King of the Stars. Leo P. Kelley. LC 78-68231. (Galaxy 5 Ser.: Bk. 6). 1979. pap. 4.24 (ISBN 0-8224-3206-4). Pitman Learning.

King of the Street. William Gill. (Dillingham's metropolitan library, no. 32). 1897. G. W. Dillingham Co.

King of the Town. Ellen Mackubin. LC 7-19978. 1898. Houghton, Mifflin, and Company.

King of the Two Lands: The Pharaoh Akhenaten. Jacquetta Hawkes. LC 66-21495. 1967. Random House.

King of the Two Sicilies. Andrzej Kusniewicz. LC 80-7935. 1980. 9.95 (ISBN 0-15-147271-8). Harcourt Brace Jovanovich.

King of the West Side. William Heuman. LC 60-129261. 1961. Eerdmans.

King of the Wilderness. Albert Cooper Allen. LC 26-19728. 1926. G.H. Watt.

King of the Wood. John Maddox Roberts. LC 82-45335. (Science Fiction Ser.). 192p. 1983. 11.95 (ISBN 0-385-17584-1). Doubleday.

King of This Hill. Nathaniel Meserve. LC 47-31148. 1947. Doubleday.

King of Thomond: A Story of Yesterday. Martin W Barr. LC 7-14249. 1907. H. B. Turner & Company.

King of Thunder Valley. Archie Joscelyn. LC 36-4985. Phoenix Press.

King of Tyre: A Tale of the Times of Ezra and Nehemiah. James Meeker Ludlow. LC 7-14502. 1891. Harper & Brothers.

King of Utah. Lee E. Wills. (Orig.). 1973. pap. 0.75 o.p. (07322). Curtis.

King of White Lady. R. Lance Hill. LC 75-14206. 1975. 7.95 (ISBN 0-399-11547-1). Putnam.

King of White Lady. R. Lance Hill. 1977. 1.50 (ISBN 0-449-23056-2). Fawcett Crest.

King of Zunga. Jeffrey Lord. (Richard Blade,#12). 1975. (pbk.) 1.25 (ISBN 0-523-00523-7). Pinnacle Books.

King Oil. Max Catto. LC 72-101868. 1970. 5.95. Simon and Schuster.

King on Queen. F. W. Paul. 1971. pap. 0.95 o.p. (ISBN 0-447-75168-9). Lancer.

King or Knave, Which Wins? An Old Tale of Hugenot Days. William Henry Johnson. LC 99-1563. 1899. Little, Brown and Company.

King Ottokar's Sceptre. Georges Remy. LC 73-21251. (Adventures of Tintin). (Atlantic Monthly Press book). (Illus.). 1974. (pbk.) 2.50 (ISBN 0-316-35831-2). Little Brown.

King Otto's Crown: Tr. from the German of Richard Roth. Richard Roth. Tr. by Ireland, Mary Eliza (Haines) LC 17-31884. 1917. Concordia Publishing House.

King Over the Water: Or, The Marriage of Mr. Melancholy. Justin Huntly McCarthy. LC 11-7302. 1911. Harper & Brothers.

King Pin. Helen Finnegan Wilson. 1939. The Macmillan Company.

King, Queen, Knave. Vladimir Vladimirovich Nabokov. (Rus). 1969. 6.95 (ISBN 0-07-045716-6, GB). McGraw.

King, Queen, Knave. Vladimir Vladimirovich Nabokov. 288p. 1980. pap. 5.95 (ISBN 0-07-045722-0, GB). McGraw.

King, Queen, Knave: A Novel. Vladimir Vladimirovich Nabokov. LC 68-22764. 1968. McGraw-Hill.

King Rat. James Clavell. 1982. pap. 3.95 (ISBN 0-440-14546-5). Dell.

King Rat. James Clavell. 384p. 1983. 17.95 (ISBN 0-440-04392-1). Delacorte.

King Rat. James Clavell. 1969. pap. 0.95 o.p. (M1246, Crest). Fawcett World.

King Rat. James Clavell. 1962. 6.95 o.p. Little.

King Rat: A Novel. 1st Ed. James Clavell. LC 62-123736. 1962. Little, Brown.

King Reluctant: A Novel. William Vaughan Wilkins. 1953. Macmillan.

King Sex for President. Tony Crechales, pseud. (Orig.). 1968. pap. 1.25 o.p. (2076). Brandon.

King Silky! Leo Calvin Rosten. LC 79-3413. 9.95 (ISBN 0-06-013684-7). Harper & Row.

King-Sized Murder. 1st Ed. William Herber. LC 54-5599. (Main line mysteries). 1954. Lippincott.

King Solomon's Children: Some Parodies of H. Rider Haggard. R. Reginald & Douglas Alver Menville. LC 77-84281. (Lost Race and Adult Fantasy Fiction). 1978. 37.00 (ISBN 0-405-11018-9). Arno Press.

King Solomons' Mines. Henry Rider Haggard. LC 64-7441. ((Nelson classics)). 1962. T. Nelson.

King Solomons' Mines. Haggard, Henry Rider. LC 62-19974. 1962. Collier Books.

King Solomon's Mines. Henry Rider Haggard. LC 6-46142. (On cover: Lovell's library. v. 18 i. e. 17 no. 813). 1886. J. W. Lovell Company.

King Solomon's Mines. Henry Rider Haggard. LC 6-46143. (On cover: Cassell's "Rainbow" series. v. 1, no. 13). 1888. Cassell & Company, Limited.

King Solomon's Mines. Henry Rider Haggard. LC 43-44543. (On cover: Cassell's Rainbow series of original novels). Cassell & Company, Limited.

King Solomon's Mines: A Novel. Henry Rider Haggard. LC 72-100485. (Illus.). 1970. (ISBN 0-87636-003-7). Imprint Society.

King Solomon's Mines. A Novel. Henry Rider Haggard. LC 6-46141. (Harper's Franklin square library. no. 552. Extra). 1886. Harper & Brothers.

King Solomon's Mines: A Novel. Henry Rider Haggard. LC 41-42423. 1887. Harper & Brothers.

King Solomon's Mines: A Novel. Henry Rider Haggard. LC 4-16530. 1901. Longmans, Green and Co.

King Solomon's Mines: A Novel. Henry Rider Haggard. LC 20-16459. 1920. Longmans, Green and Co.

King Solomon's Mines: A Novel. new impression. ed. Henry Rider Haggard. LC 27-793445. 1926. Longmans, Green and Co.

King Solomon's Mines: A Novel. Henry Rider Haggard & Walter Paget. LC 76-20910. (Illus.). 8.95 (ISBN 0-8055-1202-0) (ISBN 0-8055-0289-0). Hart Pub. Co.

King Solomon's Mines. Allan Quatermain. Henry Rider Haggard. LC 43-20451. P. F. Collier & Son.

King Solomon's Ring. Konrad Z. Lorenz. LC 52-7373. (Apollo Eds.). (YA) (gr. 9-12). pap. 3.95 o.p. (ISBN 0-8152-0016-1, A16, TYC-T). T y Crowell.

King Solomon's Treasures. John De Morgan. (Munro's library. v. 50, no. 737). 1887. N. L. Munro.

King Solomon's Treasures. Andrew Lang & Pollock, Walter Herries, 1850-1926, Joint Author. LC 44-15521. (Munro's library, v. 50, no. 737). 1887. N. L. Munro.

King Solomon's Wives. John De Morgan. (Munro's library. no. 736). 1887. N. L. Munro.

King Solomon's Wives: Or. The Phantom Mines. John De Morgan. (On cover: Seaside library. Pocket ed. no. 970). 1887. G. Munro.

King Spruce: A Novel. Holman Francis Day. LC 8-11702. 1908. Harper & Brothers.

King Stork of the Netherlands: A Romance of the Early Days of the Dutch Republic. Albert Lee. LC 5997. (Half-title: Appletons' town and country library, no. 292). 1900. D. Appleton and Company.

King Strut. Chuck Stone. LC 74-98282. 1970. 6.95. Bobbs-Merrill.

King There Was- Evelyn Charles H Vivian. LC 77-84273. (Lost Race and Adult Fantasy Fiction). 1978. 22.00. Arno Press.

King Tolstoy's Symphony: Or, An Adamless Eve; a Counterpart to the Kreutzer Sonata. 2d ed. H. B. Sanneborn. LC 8-10218. (pastime series, no. 43). 1890. Laird & Lee.

King Tommy. James Owen Hannay. LC 24-519780. The Bobbs-Merrill Company.

King Tree. Marie Therese Colette Boecop-Malye. LC 44-40000. 1944. Doubleday, Doran & Company, Inc.

King Tut-Ankh-Amen: His Romantic History, Relating How, As Prince of Hermonthis, He Won the Love of Senpa, Priestess of the Temple of Karnak, and Through Her Interest Achieved the Throne of the Pharaohs. Archie Bell. LC 23-9412. 1923. The St. Botolph Society.

King Versus Wargrave. Joseph Smith Fletcher. LC 24-628773. 1924. A. A. Knopf.

King Was in His Counting House: A Comedy of Commonsence. James Branch Cabell. LC 38-38072. Farrar & Rinehart, Inc.

King Washington: A Romance of the Hudson Highlands. Adelaide Skeel & Brearley, William Henry, 1846- Joint Author. LC 8-9012. 1898. J. B. Lippincott Company.

King Who Came: A Tale of the Great Revolt. Joseph William Sharts. LC 14-49341. 1913. Duffield & Company.

King Who Was a King: An Unconventional Novel. Herbert George Wells. LC 72-600. 1972. (ISBN 0-8371-6337-4). Greenwood Press.

King Who Was a King: An Unconventional Novel. Herbert George Wells. LC 29-12492. 1929. Doubleday, Doran & Company, Inc.

King Who Was a King, an Unconventional Novel. Herbert George Wells. LC 72-600. 272p. 1972. Repr. of 1929 ed. lib. bdg. 15.00m (ISBN 0-8371-6337-4, WEKK). Greenwood.

King Who Went on Strike. Pearson Choate. LC 24-6684. 1924. Dodd, Mead and Company.

King William the Wanderer: An Old British Saga, from Old French Versions. hyperion reprint ed. Chretien De Troyes. LC 76-48418. (Hyperion library of world literature). 1978. 13.50 (ISBN 0-88355-534-4). Hyperion Press.

King Windom. John Farris. LC 67-11247. 1967. Trident Press.

King with Two Faces: An Historical Romance. Mary Elizabeth Coleridge. LC 79-8255. Repr. of 1897 ed. 44.50 (ISBN 0-404-61831-6). AMS Pr.

Kingblood. Stuart Jason. (Orig.). 1969. pap. 0.95 o.p. (65-219). Paperback Lib.

Kingbreaker. 1st Ed. Elizabeth Linington. LC 58-8099. 1958. Doubleday.

Kingdom. Harold Elsdale Goad. LC 13-8757. 1913. 1.25. Frederick A. Stokes Company.

Kingdom. James Hanley. LC 77-93934. 1978. 9.95 (ISBN 0-8180-0627-7). Horizon.

Kingdom. L. W Henderson. 1974. (pbk.) 1.75 (ISBN 0-380-00000-8). Avon.

Kingdom. Ronald S Joseph. 1978. 2.50. Warner Books.

Kingdom. Robert Lacey. 656p. 1983. pap. 4.95 (ISBN 0-380-61762-5, 61762-5). Avon.

Kingdom at Hand. P. C. Hatch. 2.50 o.p. Vantage.

Kingdom Carver. Ernest G. Perrault. LC 68-14190. 1968. 6.95 o.p. Doubleday.

Kingdom Come. Melvyn Bragg. 1980. 16.50 (ISBN 0-436-06714-5, Pub. by Secker & Warburg). David & Charles.

Kingdom Come. Gwen Davis. LC 72-94259. 1973. 5.95 (ISBN 0-399-11106-9). Putnam.

Kingdom Come. Virginia Eggertsen Sorensen. LC 60-7427. 1960. Harcourt, Bruce.

Kingdom Comes. Helen R Eaton. LC 51-149354. Vantage Press.

Kingdom for a Song. Ira J Morris. LC 63-9850. 1963. Dutton.

Kingdom in the Cactus. Charles Alden Seltzer. LC 74-21534. 1974-1975. 5.95 (ISBN 0-88411-102-4). Aeonian Press.

Kingdom in the Cactus. Charles Alden Seltzer. LC 36-235268. 1936. Doubleday, Doran & Co., Inc.

Kingdom in the Cactus. Charles Alden Seltzer. LC 37-39263. 1937. The Sun Dial Press, Inc.

Kingdom in the Sage. Don P. Jenison. (Orig.). 1979. pap. 1.95 (ISBN 0-89083-501-2). Zebra.

Kingdom in the Sky. Alice Brown. LC 32-760519. 1932. The Macmillan Company.

Kingdom Lost. Patricia Wentworth. LC 30-8789. 1930. J. B. Lippincott Company.

Kingdom of Death: By Hugh Pentecost Pseud. Judson Pentecost Philips. LC 60-666700. (Red badge detective). 1960. Dodd, Mead.

Kingdom of Death: The Further Adventures of Albert Campion, Private Investigator... Margery Allingham. LC 33-17387. 1933. Pub. for the Crime Club, Inc., by Doubleday, Doran & Company, Inc.

Kingdom of Dreams. John Joy Bell. LC 11-11285. 1911. 1.20. Cassell and Company, Limited.

Kingdom of Dreams. Russell Ernest O'Hara. LC 26-155097. The Macaulay Company.

Kingdom of Earth. Edward Phillips Oppenheim. LC 9-13542. 1909. 1.50. Little, Brown, and Company.

Kingdom of Evil: A Continuation of the Journal of Fantazius Mallare. Ben Hecht. LC 76-25685. (Supernatural and Occult Fiction). 1976. 12.00 (ISBN 0-405-09665-8). Arno Press.

Kingdom of Evil: A Continuation of the Journal of Fantazius Mallare. Ben Hecht. LC 78-7288. (Harvest/HBJ book). 1978. 3.95 (ISBN 0-15-647123-X). Harcourt Brace Jovanovich.

Kingdom of Fukkian. A. Philo Mann. (Orig.). 1969. pap. 1.25 o.p. (B12-1037). Belmont-Tower.

Kingdom of Grass. Charles Field, pseud. 192p. 1971. Repr. of 1964 ed. 3.95 o.p. Lenox Hill.

Kingdom of Hate: A Romance. Tom Gallon. LC 99-2913. (Half-title: Appletons' town and country library. No. 267). 1899. D. Appleton and Company.

Kingdom of Heaven. Hester Ekhart & Opal Ekhart. LC 67-12674. 1967. Dorrance.

Kingdom of Illusion. Edward R F Sheehan. LC 64-11988. 1964. Random House.

Kingdom of Innocents. Mildred Cram. LC 40-328599. 1940. A. A. Knopf.

Kingdom of Joy. Delle Barotz. 1976. pap. 1.50 o.p. (ISBN 0-515-04025-8). BJ Pub Group.

Kingdom of Moltz. Irwin A. Schiff. LC 80-14628. 1980. pap. 2.50 (ISBN 0-930374-02-9). Freedom Bks.

Kingdom of Royth. Jeffrey Lord. (Blade Ser., No. 9). 192p. (Orig.). 1974. pap. 1.50 (ISBN 0-523-40439-5). Pinnacle Bks.

Kingdom of Royth. Jeffrey Lord. (Richard Blade series,#9). 1974. (pbk.) 0.95 (ISBN 0-523-00295-5). Pinnacle Books.

Kingdom of Slender Swords. Hallie Erminie Rives. LC 10-3289. The Bobbs-Merrill Company.

Kingdom of Summer. Gillian Bradshaw. 1982. pap. 2.75 (ISBN 0-451-11550-3, AE1550, Sig). NAL.

Kingdom of the Blind. Edward Phillips Oppenheim. LC 16-21059. 1916. 1.35. Little, Brown, and Company.

Kingdom of the Blind. Edward Phillips Oppenheim. LC 21-13719. 1918. A. L. Burt Company.

Kingdom of the Bulls. Paul Capon. 1962. 3.75 o.p. (21007). G&D.

Kingdom of the Earth. William Heinesen. LC 73-2711. (Library of Scandinavian Literature, V. 22). 1974. 6.50 (ISBN 0-8057-3324-8). Twayne Publishers.

Kingdom of the Heart. Lucy Walker, pseud. 1971. pap. 1.75 (ISBN 0-345-29276-6). Ballantine.

Kingdom of the Rose. Margaret Bacon. 530p. 1982. 27.00x o.p. (ISBN 0-86188-117-6, Pub. by Judy Piatkus). State Mutual Bk.

Kingdom of the Spiders: Novelization. Bernhardt J Hurwood. (Illus.). 1977. 1.95 (ISBN 0-441-44512-8). Ace Books.

Kingdom of the Spur. Gene Markey. LC 52-14048. 1953. Ballantine Books.

Kingdom of Theophilus. William John Locke. LC 27-19222. 1927. Dodd, Mead and Company.

Kingdom of This World. A. Carpentier. 1971. pap. 1.50 o.s.i. (ISBN 0-02-049600-1, Collier). Macmillan.

Kingdom of This World. Translated from the Spanish by Harriet De Onis. Alejo Carpentier. 1957. Knopf.

Kingdom on Earth. Anne Brooks. LC 41-665235. 1941. W. Morrow & Company.

Kingdom Round the Corner. Coningsby William Dawson. LC 29-30780. 1928. Grosset & Dunlap.

Kingdom Round the Corner-- A Novel. Coningsby William Dawson. LC 21-8836. 1921. Cosmopolitan Book Corporation.

Kingdom Under the Sea. Translated from the French by Len Ortzen. Henri Queffelec. LC 58-11775. 1959. Pantheon.

Kingdom Within: A Novel. Siebold Ulfers. LC 53-9736. 1953. Eerdmans.

Kingdoms: A Novel. Barry Targan. LC 80-154403. 9.95 (ISBN 0-87395-461-0). State University of New York Press.

Kingdom's Castle. Daoma Winston. (Berkley medallion book). 1975. (pbk.) 1.25. Berkley Pub. Co.

Kingdoms of Elfin. Sylvia Townsend Warner. LC 76-41753. (Illus.). 1977. 8.95 (ISBN 0-670-41350-X). Viking Press.

Kingdoms of Sorcery. Lin Carter. LC 75-14810. 1976. 6.95 (ISBN 0-385-09975-4). Doubleday.

Kingdoms of the World. Margaretta Muhlenberg Perkins Tuttle. LC 26-19678. 1926. G. P. Putnam's Sons.

Kingfisher. LC 22-9188. 2.00. George H. Doran Company.

Kingfisher. Gerald Seymour. 1979. 2.25 (ISBN 0-380-40592-X). Avon Books.

Kingfisher: A Novel. Gerald Seymour. LC 77-15584. 10.00. Summit Books.

Kingfisher Scream. Anthony Fox, pseud. LC 80-51769. 1981. 10.95 (ISBN 0-670-41352-6). Viking Press.

Kingfishers Catch Fire. Rumer Godden. LC 53-5609. 1975. (pbk.) 1.50 (ISBN 0-380-00512-3). Avon.

Kingfishers Catch Fire: A Novel. Rumer Godden. LC 53-5609. 1953. Viking Press.

Kingkill. Thomas Gavin. (Illus.). 1977. 10.00 o.p. (ISBN 0-394-49827-5). Random.

Kingkill: A Novel. Thomas Gavin. LC 76-53455. 10.00 (ISBN 0-394-49827-5). Random House.

Kingmaker. Henry Denker. (Dell Book). 1973. 1.75. Dell.

Kingmaker. Henry Denker. LC 75-185139. 1972. 6.95. D. McKay Co.

Kingmaker. Henry Denker. (Kangaroo Book). 1978. 2.50 (ISBN 0-671-81676-4). Pocket Books.

Kingmaker. Malcolm D. MacDougall. 1978. 8.95 o.p. (ISBN 0-517-53232-8, C N Potter Bks). Crown.

Kingmaker: A Novel. Malcolm D MacDougall. LC 77-18061. 8.95 (ISBN 0-517-53232-8). C. Potter: Distributed by Crown Publishers.

Kingmakers. Burton Egbert Stevenson. LC 22-20994. 1922. 1.90. Dodd, Mead and Company.

Kingpin. Tom Wicker. LC 53-8344. 1953. Sloane.

Kingpin. Tom Wicker. 1974. (pbk.) 1.50 (ISBN 0-380-00136-5). Avon.

King's Achievement. Edited, and with a Foreword, by Francis X. Connolly. Robert Hugh Benson. LC 57-6995. 1957. P. J. Kenedy.

King's Agent. Justus Kent Clark. LC 58-6216. 1958. Scribner.

King's Agent. Arthur Henry Paterson. LC 2-26871. 1902. D. Appleton and Company.

Kings and Numbers. Tiffany Thayer. LC 34-33126. 1934. W. Morrow & Co.

King's Arrow. Joseph Patrick Walsh. LC 51-11191. 1951. Lippincott.

King's Arrow: A Tale of the United Empire Loyalists. Hiram Alfred Cody. LC 22-19682. 2.00. George H. Doran Company.

King's Assegai. A Matabili Story. Bertram Mitford. LC 13-17730. (On cover: Seaside library. Pocket ed., no. 2168). 1897. G. Munro's Sons.

Kings-at-Arms. Marjorie Bowen. LC 19-15981. 1919. E. P. Dutton & Company.

Kings Back to Back. Whitey the Irrepressible Infests Europe. Carroll Graham & Graham, Garrett. LC 32-31308. 1932. The Vanguard Press.

King's Bed. Margaret Campbell Barnes. 258p. 1981. pap. 2.75 (ISBN 0-441-44518-7). Ace Bks.

King's Blacks. Leslie Gladson. (Orig.). 1969. pap. 0.95 o.p. (75-076). Lancer.

King's Blood Four. Sheri S. Tepper. 1983. pap. 2.50 (ISBN 0-441-44524-1, Pub. by Ace Science Fiction). Ace Bks.

King's Blue Riband. Elizabeth Ellis. LC 12-27601. Hodder and Stoughton.

King's Blue Riband. Elizabeth Ellis. LC 12-119. 1.25. Hodder & Stoughton, George H. Doran Company.
King's Bounty. Roy Clews. LC 76-370075. 1976. 3.90 (ISBN 0-434-13721-9). Heinemann.
King's Brat. Constance Gluyas. LC 72-4760. 1972. 8.95 (ISBN 0-13-516237-8). Prentice-Hall.
King's Brat. Constance Gluyas. 1979. 2.50 (ISBN 0-446-91125-9). Warner Books.
King's Bride. E. T. Hoffman. pap. 1.95 o.p. Transatlantic.
King's Bride. Ernst Theodor Amadeus Hoffman. 1959. pap. text ed. 1.75x o.p. Humanities.
King's Bride. Ernst Theodor Amadeus Hoffmann. 1980. pap. 3.95 (ISBN 0-7145-0326-6). Riverrun NY.
King's Cannon. Jonathan Scofield, pseud. 1981. pap. 2.75 (ISBN 0-440-04292-5). Dell.
King's Castle. Leslie Ames, pseud. 3.95 o.p. Lenox Hill.
King's Cavalier. Samuel Shellabarger. 1974. (pbk.) 1.50. Avon.
King's Champion. William Gilbert Van Tassel Sutphen. LC 27-20341. 1927. Harper & Brothers.
King's Coil. Conde Benoist Pallen. LC 28-30066. 1928. Manhattanville Press.
King's Coming: A Story of the Happy End. William De Carrick. LC 19-9657. 1919. The Sherwood Company.
King's Company. Drawings by Addison Burbank. Frank Ernest Hill. LC 50-10883. 1950. Dodd. Mead.
King's Constable. Shirley Niles Carr. LC 51-14680. 1951. Garrett & Massie.
King's Counselor: A Novel of the Time of King David. Annie Ellis Campdon. LC 67-1606. 1967. Exposition Press.
King's Crew. Frank Ramsay Adams. LC 32-107546. 1932. R. Long & R.R. Smith, Inc.
Kings Cross Commando. 1st Ed. Lloyd Martin Emery. LC 56-5512. 1956. Vantage Press.
King's Curse. Warren Murphy. (Destroyer Ser.: No. 24). 1976. pap. 1.95 (ISBN 0-523-41239-8). Pinnacle Bks.
King's Damosel. Vera Chapman. 1978. 1.50 (ISBN 0-380-01916-7). Avon.
King's Daughter. A Novel. G Cardella. LC 6-22819. (On cover: Once a week library, v. 9, no. 10-11). 1892. P. F. Collier.
King's Daughters. Molly Costain Haycraft. LC 76-154847. (Signet book). 1975. (pbk.) 1.25. New American Library.
King's Daughters. Molly Costain Haycraft. LC 72-1972. 1972. (ISBN 0-8161-6034-1). G. K. Hall.
King's Daughters: A Fascinating Romance. Ellen E Dickinson. LC 6-37082. 1888. Hubbard Brothers.
King's Daughters; or, The Heiress and the Outcast. Mary Jane Hoffman. 1889. N. L. Munro.
King's Day. T. E. Porter. LC 75-20728. (Haystack Ser). (Illus.). 64p. 1975. 6.00 (ISBN 0-913142-14-X, Pub. by Mulch Pr); pap. 3.50 (ISBN 0-913142-13-1). SBD.
King's Detective: Or, A New York Detective's Great Guest; an Amazing Detective Narrative. Harlan Page Halsey. (Old Sleuth's own, no. 107). 1898. The Parlor Car Publishing Co.
King's Diary: A Story. Percy White. (On cover: The "Unknown" library). The Cassell Publishing Co.
King's Divinity. Mary Schell Hoke Bacon. LC 6-343650. 1906. H. Holt and Company.
King's Ex. Marilyn Harris. LC 67-11175. 1967. Doubleday.
King's Fifth. Scott O'Dell. 1976. pap. 1.50 (ISBN 0-440-94538-0, LFL). Dell.
King's Fool. Margaret Campbell Barnes. (Signet book). 1974. (pbk.) 1.25. New American Library.
King's Fool. Margaret Campbell Barnes. LC 59-13261. 1959. Macrae Smith.
Kings Full of Aces: A Nero Wolfe Omnibus. Rex Stout. LC 67-20290. 1969. 4.50. Viking Press.
King's General. Daphne Du Maurier. LC 46-250041. 1946. Doubleday & Company, Inc.
King's General. Daphne Du Maurier. LC 47-20004. 1947. The Sun Dial Press.
King's General. Condensed and Simplified for Quick Reading by Lee Wyndham. Daphne Du Maurier. LC 54-6849. (Hanover House headliners). 1954.
Kings Go Forth. Joe David Brown. LC 56-6363. 1956. Morrow.
King's Gold: A Story. Elizabeth Cheney. LC 1-31096. Eaton & Mains.
King's Good Servant. Olive Bernardine White. LC 36-8195. 1936. The Macmillan Company.
King's Grey Mare. Rosemary Hawley Jarman. LC 73-7766. (Illus.). 1973. (ISBN 0-316-45781-7). Little, Brown.
King's Henchman: A Chronicle of the Sixteenth Century, Brought to Light and Ed. William Henry Johnson. 1898. Little, Brown and Company.
King's Highway. Amelia Edith Huddleston Barr. LC 6-7989. 1897. Dodd, Mead and Company.
King's Highway. Lucille Papin Borden. LC 41-24963. 1941. The Macmillan Company.
King's Highway. A Novel. George Payne Rainsford James. LC 7-7996. 1840. Harper & Brothers.
King's Highway. A Novel. George Payne Rainsford James. (Seaside library, v. 34, no. 692). 1880. G. Munro.
King's Highway: A Romance of the Franciscan Order in Alta California. Madeline Deaderick Willard. LC 14-501.
Kings in Exile. Alphonse Daudet. Tr. by Wormeley, Katharine Prescott. LC 4270. 1900. Little, Brown and Company.
Kings in Exile: A Novel of Parisian Life. Alphonse Daudet. Tr. by Lord, Grace Virginia. LC 6-33051. 1880. Lee and Shepard Etc.
Kings in Exile: A Novel of Parsian Life. Alphonse Daudet. Tr. by Lord, Grace Virginia. LC 6-33050. (On cover: The Rialto series, no. 16). 1889. Rand, McNally & Company.
Kings in the Counting House. Herbert Mitgang. LC 82-72062. 1983. 14.50 (ISBN 0-87795-424-0). Arbor Hse.
Kings in Winter. Cecelia Holland. LC 68-12541. (Illus.). 1968. Atheneum.
King's Indian: Stories and Tales. John Champlin Gardner. 1976. (pbk.) 2.25 (ISBN 0-345-24806-6). Ballantine.
King's Indian: Stories and Tales. John Champlin Gardner. LC 73-22489. (Illus.). 1974. (ISBN 0-394-49221-8). Knopf; Distributed by Random House.
King's Iron. Robert Newton Peck. LC 77-24572. 8.95 (ISBN 0-316-69655-2). Little, Brown.
King's Jackal. Richard Harding Davis. LC 6-26295. 1898. C. Scribner's Sons.
King's Jackal. Richard Harding Davis. LC 99-4897. 1899. C. Scribner's Sons.
King's Jackal. Richard Harding Davis. 1903. C. Scribner's Sons.
King's Jackal. Richard Harding Davis. 1910. C. Scribner's Sons.
King's Legacy. Constance Heaven. 1.50. Dell.
King's Man. C. M. Edmondston & Hyde, M. L. F., Joint Author. LC 48-5821. 1948. Longmans, Green.
King's Mark: A Story of Early Portlan. Gran Matthews Bangs. LC 8-30617. 1908. The C. M. Clark Publishing Co.
Kings' Masque. Evan John Simpson. LC 41-983. 1941. E. P. Dutton & Co., Inc.
King's Men. Johan Bojer & Mussey, June Barrows, 1910- Tr. LC 40-5843. 1940. D. Appleton-Century Company, Incorporated.
King's Men. John Leslie Palmer, pseud. LC 16-112273. 1916. G. P. Putnam's Sons.
King's Men: A Tale of to-Morrow. Robert Grant. LC 74-15973. (Science Fiction). 1975. 15.00 (ISBN 0-405-06292-3). Arno Press.
King's Men: A Tale of to-Morrow. Robert Grant & O'Reilly, John Boyle. LC 6-44750. 1884. C. Scribner's Sons.
King's Men: A Tale of Tomorrow. Robert Grant et al. LC 74-15973. (Science Fiction Ser). 276p. 1975. Repr. of 1884 ed. 15.00x (ISBN 0-405-06292-3). Ayer Co.
King's Messenger. Samuel Edwards, pseud. LC 56-6162. 1956. Farrar, Straus and Cudahy.
King's Messenger. Noel Bertram Gerson. LC 56-6162. 1956. Farrar, Straus and Cudahy.
King's Messenger: A Novel. Suzanne Antrobus A. A. Robinson Robinson. LC 1-24481. 1901. Harper & Brothers.
King's Minion: Being the Rise and Fall of Robert Carr of Ferniehurst, Earl of Somerset, Viscount Rochester, Baron Winwick, Baron Brancepeth, Knight of the Most Noble Order of the Garter, a Member of His Majesty's Most Honorable Privy Council, &C., &C., &C. Rafael Sabatini. LC 30-24774. 1930. Houghton Mifflin Company.
King's Mirror: A Novel. Anthony Hope Hawkins. LC 99-4548. 1899. D. Appleton and Company.
King's Mirror: A Novel. Anthony Hope Hawkins. LC 3-24942. (Half-title: Author's edition. Works of Anthony Hope...). D. Appleton and Company.
King's Mirror (Speculum Regale--Konungs Skuggsja) Tr. by Laurence M. Larson from Old Norse. LC 72-1542. 1917. lib. bdg. 8.25x (ISBN 0-8057-3328-0). Irvington.
King's Mistress. Jean Plaidy. 1971. pap. 0.95 o.p. (N2487). Pyramid Pubns.
King's Mistress. Jean Plaidy. 1974. pap. cancelled o.p. (ISBN 0-515-03514-9). Pyramid Pubns.
Kings Mountain. Florette Henri. LC 50-9855. 1950. Doubleday.
Kings of Beacon Hill. Christine Whiting Parmenter. LC 35-5191. Thomas Y. Crowell Company.
Kings of Capital and Knights of Labor. John McDowell Leavitt. LC 51-48707. 1886. Powers & Le Craw.
Kings of Infinite Space. Nigel Balchin. LC 68-11792. 1968. Doubleday.
Kings of the Missouri. Hugh Pendexter. LC 21-130652. The Bobbs-Merrill Company.
Kings of the Sea. Joan Van Every Frost. 640p. (Orig.). 1982. pap. 3.50 (Crest). Fawcett.
Kings of Vain Intent. Graham Shelby. LC 71-159823. (Illus.). 1971. 6.95. Weybright and Talley.
King's Orchard. Agnes Sligh Turnbull. LC 62-8131. 1963. Houghton Mifflin.
King's Orchard. Agnes Sligh Turnbull. LC 62-8131. (Fawcett crest book). 1975. (pbk.) 1.50. Fawcett.
King's Orchard. Agnes Sligh Turnbull. LC 83-204. 1983. 19.95 (ISBN 0-8161-3480-4). G.K. Hall.
King's Own. Frederick Marryat. LC 42-158236. G. Routledge & Sons.
King's Own. Frederick Marryat. 1896. Macmillan and Co., Ltd.
King's Own. Frederick Marryat. LC 36-37498. (Half-title: Everyman's library ed. by Ernest Rhys. Fiction. no. 580). 1924. J. M. Dent & Sons, Ltd.
King's Own Borderers: A Military Romance. James Grant. G. Routledge and Sons.
King's Page: A Legend of the Moorish Wars in Spain and Other Stories. Anna Theresa Sadlier. LC 8-16426. 1877. D. & J. Sadlier & Co.
King's Pardon. Henry Bedford-Jones. LC 33-11080. 1933. Covici, Friede.
King's Passenger. Nathan Schachner. LC 42-14078. 1942. J. B. Lippincott Company.
King's Passport. Henry Bedford-Jones. LC 28-423368. 1928. G.P. Putnma's Sons.
King's Pawn. Hamilton Drummond. LC 1-30670. 1901. Doubleday, Page & Co.
King's Pawn. Willo Davis Roberts. 1971. pap. 0.75 o.p. (ISBN 0-447-74734-7). Lancer.
King's Persons. Joanne Greenberg. LC 63-7271. 1963. Holt, Rinehart and Winston.
King's Pleasure. Eleanor Hibbert. LC 49-1013. 1949. Appleton-Century-Crofts.
King's Pleasure. Norah Robinson Lofts. LC 79-79966. 1969. 5.95. Doubleday.
King's Pleasure. Ellis Middleton. LC 27-202616. 1927. L. MacVeagh, The Dial Press.
King's Pleasure. Ida Zeitlin & Nadejen, Theodore, Illus. LC 29-25612. 1929. Harper & Brothers.
King's Point. Peter L. Sandberg. LC 78-8315. (Illus.). 8.95 (ISBN 0-87223-505-X). Playboy Press.
King's Rangers. 1st Ed. John Brick. 1954. Doubleday.
King's Ransom. Ralph Hayes. 1978. pap. 1.25 (ISBN 0-532-12535-5). Woodhill.
King's Ransom. Evan Hunter. (Signet book). (87th precinct mystery). 1975. (pbk.) 1.25. New American Library.
King's Ransom. Victor J. H Suthren. LC 81-14499. (Illus.). 9.95 (ISBN 0-312-45610-7). St. Martin's Press.
King's Ransom: By Ed. McBain Pseud. Evan Hunter. LC 59-13147. (Inner sanctum mystery). 1959. Simon and Schuster.
King's Rebel. James David Horan. LC 53-5674. 1953. Crown Publishers.
King's Reeve and How He Supped with His Master: An Old World Comedy. Edward Gilliat. LC 29-8248. 1928. E. P. Dutton and Company.
King's Revenge. Claude Bray. LC 6-17935. (Half-title: Appleton town and country library, no. 199). 1896. D. Appleton and Company.
King's Rhapsody: Based on the Play by Ivor Novello. Hester W Chapman & Ivor Novello. LC 51-6720. 1951. Houghton Mifflin.
King's Road. Mariella Novotny. 240p. 1972. pap. 1.25 (ISBN 0-532-12132-5). Woodhill.
King's Rogue. Dennis Max Cornelius Woodruffe-Peacock. LC 47-253683. 1947. Macrae-Smith-Company.
Kings Row. Henry Belamann. LC 4-7412. 1940. Simon and Schustr.
Kings Row. Henry Bellamann. LC 47-20001. 1946. The Sun Dial Press.
King's Royal. John Quigley. LC 74-79689. 1975. 9.95 (ISBN 0-698-10620-2). Coward, McCann & Geoghegan.
King's Stockbroker: The Sequel to "A Princess of Paris": a Novel. Archibald Clavering Gunter. LC 6-46700. 1894. The Home Publishing Co.
King's Stratagem, and Other Stories. Stanley John Weyman. LC 70-113695. (Short story index reprint series). (Illus.). 1970. Books for Libraries Press.
King's Strategem: And Other Stories. Stanley John Weyman. LC 8-36219. 1895. Platt & Bruce.
King's Talisman: Or, The Lion of Mount Hor. An Eastern Romance. Sylvanus Cobb. (On cover: The select series, no 25). 1889. Street & Smith.
King's Traitor. Doris Oppenheim Leslie. 1973. (pbk.) 0.95. Popular Lib.
King's Treasure House: A Romance of Ancient Egypt. Wilhelm Walloth & Safford, Mary Joanna, Tr. 1886. W. S. Gottsberger.
King's Valley. Gladis DePree. 1972. pap. 1.25 o.p. (9518P). Zondervan.
King's Vixen. Pamela Hill. LC 54-7867. 1954. Putnam.
King's Ward. Jessie Perry Van Zile Belden. LC 98-44. 1898. F. T. Neely.
King's Wench. Charlotte Denis. 1976. 1.50 (ISBN 0-671-80768-4). Pocket Books.
King's Widow. Gertrude M. Robins Reynolds. LC 19-6406. George H. Doran Company.
King's Wife. Ursula Bloom. 1979. pap. 2.25 (ISBN 0-89041-263-4, 3263). Major Bks.
Kings Will Be Tyrants. 1st Ed. Ward Hawkins. LC 59-14185. 1959. McGraw-Hill.
Kingsbane. John Morressy. LC 81-85181. 256p. (Orig.). 1982. pap. 2.50 (ISBN 0-86721-098-2). Playboy Pbks.
Kingsblood Royal. Sinclair Lewis. LC 47-2064. 1947. Random House.
Kingsblood Royal. Sinclair Lewis. 1974. (pbk.) 1.75. Manor Books.
Kingsford Mark. Victor Canning. LC 75-33326. 1976. 6.95 (ISBN 0-688-02999-X). Morrow.
Kingslayer. Hubbard, La Fayette Ronald. LC 49-49236. 1949. Fantasy Pub. Co.
Kingsley's Empire. Michael Jahn, pseud. (Orig.). 1980. pap. 2.50 (ISBN 0-449-14324-4, GM). Fawcett.
Kingsley's Fortune. Michael Jahn, pseud. 256p. 1982. pap. 2.75 (ISBN 0-449-14497-6). Fawcett.
Kingsmead: A Novel. Betsey Riddle Hutton Zum Stolzenberg. LC 9-5216. 1909. Dodd, Mead and Company.
Kingsridge. Alice Mary Ross Colver. Macrae-Smith Co.
Kingsroads Legacy. Dorinda Kamm. 1981. pap. 2.95 (ISBN 0-89083-780-5). Zebra.
Kings's Mirror: A Novel. popular ed. Anthony Hope Hawkins. LC 5-18475. 1904. D. Appleton and Company.
Kingston Fortune. Stephen Longstreet. 1975. (pbk.) 1.95 (ISBN 0-380-00366-X). Avon.
Kingston Papers. R. S. Silverman. 1978. pap. 1.50 (ISBN 0-532-15362-6). Woodhill.
Kink. Alister McAllister. LC 27-4635. Harper & Brothers.
Kinkaid. Lessie Charles Ernenwein. 1975. (pbk.) 0.95. Belmont Tower Books.
Kinkaid's Battery see Collected Works.
Kinks. Rolf Sinerker. pap. 1.95 o.s.i. (Venus). Grove.
Kinks, Meaning Love--Money--Mystery (Anonymous) Edward Michael Wickes. LC 27-5134. 1927. Adelaide Ambrose, Inc.
Kinley Hollow, a Novel. Gideon Hiram Hollister. LC 7-6042. (Leisure hour series. no. 138). 1882. H. Holt and Company.
Kinnakeet Adventure. Stanley E. Green. 1970. 4.50 o.p. Vantage.
Kinship of Souls: A Narrative. Reuen Thomas. 1899. Little, Brown, and Company.
Kinsman. Cecily Ullmann Sidgwick. LC 7-4161. 1907. The Macmillan Company.
Kinsman: A Novel. Benjamin Bova. LC 79-283. (Quantum novel). 8.95 (ISBN 0-8037-4569-9). Dial Press.
Kinsman & Foreman. T. MofOlorynso Aluko. (African Writers Ser.). 1968. pap. text ed. 3.00x (ISBN 0-435-90032-3). Heinemann Ed.
Kinsman and Foreman: By T. M. Aluko. T. MofOlorynso Aluko. LC 68-877540. (African writers ser., 32). 1967. 3.00, 1.25 pap, +011. Heinemann.
Kinsmen. Percival John Cooney. LC 16-22903. 1.50. Goerge H. Doran Company.
Kinsmen. William Haggard. LC 74-82171. 1974. 5.95 o.p. (ISBN 0-8027-5308-6). Walker & Co.
Kinsmen All. A Story for Youth and Age. Clara H. Morse Rennelson. LC 392. The Union Press.
Kinsmen of the Grail. Dorothy James Roberts. LC 63-8962. 1963. Little, Brown.
Kinsmen: Or, The Black Riders of Congaree. A Tale. William Gilmore Simms. LC 8-130612. 1841. Lea and Blanchard.
Kioga of the Wilderness. William L. Chester. (Science Fiction Ser.). 1976. pap. 1.50 o.p. (ISBN 0-87997-253-X, UW1253). DAW Bks.
Kioga of the Wilderness. William L Chester. 1.50. Daw Books.
Kiowa. Elgin Earl Groseclose. LC 78-55386. 6.95. (ISBN 0-89191-114-6). D. C. Cook Pub. Co.
Kiowa Blood. Will C Knott. (Berkley Medallion Book). 1977. 1.25 (ISBN 0-425-03547-6). Berkley Pub. Corp.
Kiowa Fires. Donald Porter. (American Indians Ser.: No. 11). (Orig.). 1983. pap. 3.50 (ISBN 0-440-04558-4). Dell.
Kiowa Flats Raiders. Patrick Andrews. (Orig.). 1980. pap. 1.75 (ISBN 0-532-23145-7). Woodhill.
Kiowa Pass. Archie Joscelyn. 1976. 4.95. Avalon Books.
Kiowa Plains. Frank Ketchum. LC 77-16734. 1978. 7.95 (ISBN 0-312-45624-7) (ISBN 0-312-45625-5). St. Martin's Press.
Kiowa Trail. Louis L'Amour. 160p. (Orig.). 1980. pap. 1.95 (ISBN 0-553-13882-0). Bantam.
Kip. Mark Dunster. (Rin: Part 33). 79p. (Orig.). 1975. pap. 4.00 (ISBN 0-89642-022-1). Linden Pubs.

Kipling Boy Stories. Rudyard Kipling. LC 16-60586. (Ranally series). Rand, McNally & Company.

Kipling Sampler. Rudyard Kipling. Ed. by Alexander Greendale. 1970. pap. 0.75 o.p. (Prem). Fawcett World.

Kipling: Short Stories, Vol. 1. Ed. by Andrew Rutherford. 1977. pap. 3.95 (ISBN 0-14-003281-9). Penguin.

Kipling: Short Stories, Vol. 2. Ed. by Andrew Rutherford. 1977. pap. 3.95 (ISBN 0-14-003282-7). Penguin.

Kipling: Short Stories Selected and Introduced by Edward Parone. Rudyard Kipling. LC 60-511087. (Laurel reader, LC146). 1960. Dell Pub. Co.

Kipling Stories: Twenty-Eight Exciting Tales. Rudyard Kipling. LC 60-124260. (Platt & Munk great writters collection). 1960. Platt & Munk.

Kipps. Herbert George Wells. 3.00 o.p. (ISBN 0-00-422681-X). Collins-World.

Kipps: The Story of a Simple Soul. Herbert George Wells. LC 5-32391. 1905. C. Scribner's Sons.

Kipps: The Story of a Simple Soul. Herbert George Wells. LC 24-27744. 1924. C. Scribner's Sons.

Kira Georgievna. Viktor Flatonovich Nekrasov. LC 62-11077. 1962. Pantheon Books.

Kira Georgievna. Viktor Flatonovich Nekrasov. LC 62-11077. 1962. Pantheon Books.

Kirbys. Margaret Whipple. LC 31-244921. 1931. G. P. Putnam's Sons.

Kiriov Tapes. Owen Sela. LC 73-4311. 1974. 5.95 (ISBN 0-394-48534-3). Pantheon Books.

Kirkland Revels. Eleanor Hibbert. LC 62-7646. 1962. Doubleday.

Kirkland Revels. Victoria Holt, pseud. 256p. 1982. pap. 2.95 (ISBN 0-449-23920-9, Crest). Fawcett.

Kirkland Revels. 1st Ed. Victoria Holt, pseud. LC 62-7646. 1962. Doubleday.

Kirkwood Fires. Deborah Lewis. (Orig.). 1978. pap. 1.95 (ISBN 0-89083-405-9). Zebra.

Kirlian Quest. Piers Anthony, pseud. 1978. pap. 2.50 (ISBN 0-380-01778-4, 79764). Avon.

Kirschen Der Freiheit & Selected Stories. Alfred Andersch. Ed. by C. A. H. Russ. 177p. (Orig., Ger.). pap. text ed. 7.00x (ISBN 0-435-38000-1). Heinemann Ed.

Kirsteen; the Story of a Scotch Family Seventy Years Ago. Margaret Oliphant Wilson Oliphant. (On cover: Harper's Franklin square library, no. 683). 1890. Harper & Brothers.

Kirstie. Mary Fisher. LC 12-20787. 1912. Thomas Y. Crowell Company.

Kirsty Affair. Douglas Hall. LC 79-187962. 1972. 3.95. Zondervan Pub. House.

Kisimusi: The Story of a Zulu Girl. Thomas M Calkins. LC 62-10341. 1962. Bruce Pub. Co.

Kismet. Julia Constance Fletcher. LC 72-164560. (American fiction reprint series). (Illus.). 1971. (ISBN 0-8369-7036-5). Books for Libraries Press.

Kismet. Julia Constance Fletcher. LC 6-41686. (No name series). 1877. Roberts Brothers.

Kismet in Kenya: By Florence Riddell. Florence Riddell. LC 32-32129. 1932. J. B. Lippincott Company.

Kiss. LC 76-5091. (Illus.). 96p. (Orig.). 1976. pap. 4.95 (ISBN 0-87663-947-3). Universe.

Kiss. Robert Lebeck. (Illus.). 176p. 1981. pap. 6.95 o.p. (ISBN 0-312-45687-5). St Martin.

Kiss. Marion Karl Wisehart. LC 28-586940. The Century Co.

Kiss a Stranger. Glenna Finley, pseud. 1972. pap. 1.95 (ISBN 0-451-11228-8, AJ1228, Sig). NAL.

Kiss, and Be Friends. A Novel. Julie P. Smith. LC 8-8180. 1899. G. W. Carleton & Co.; Etc., Etc.

Kiss and Kill. Marion Strobel. 1946. C. Scribner's Sons.

Kiss and Kill: By Adam Knight Pseud. Lawrence Lariar. LC 53-5676. 1953. Crown Publishers.

Kiss, and Other Stories. Anton Pavlovich Chekhov. LC 76-37539. (Short story index reprint series). 1972. 11.50 (ISBN 0-8369-4098-9). Books for Libraries Press.

Kiss: And Other Stories. Anton Pavlovich Chekhov. Tr. by Long, Robert Edward Crozier. LC 16-10125. 1916. Frederick A. Stokes Company.

Kiss and Tell. Lillian Day. LC 31-294241. Farrar & Rinehart Incorporation.

Kiss and the Queue: And Other Stories. Isabel Weld Perkins Anderson. LC 25-11320. The Four Seas Company.

Kiss Before Dying. Ira Levin. LC 53-2041. (Inner sanctum mystery). 1953. Simon and Schuster.

Kiss Daddy Goodbye. Thomas Altman. 320p. (Orig.). 1980. pap. 2.75 (ISBN 0-553-13738-7). Bantam.

Kiss Daddy Goodnight. Louise Armstrong. 1979. pap. 2.75 (ISBN 0-671-41656-1). PB.

Kiss for a Killer. Bruce Sanders. LC 56-9519. Roy Publishers.

Kiss for Caroline. Gloria Goddard. LC 35-30053. Phoenix Press.

Kiss for Christina. Blakely St. James. LC 80-83597. 256p. (Orig.). 1981. pap. 2.95 (ISBN 0-86721-082-6). Playboy Pbks.

Kiss for Corinna: A Novel. May Christie. LC 30-102521. Grosset & Dunlap.

Kiss for Elaine. Hilda Nickson. Orig. Title: Love Is the Anchor. pap. 0.50 o.p. (52-927). Paperback Lib.

Kiss for the King. Barbara Cartland. (Bantam Barbara Cartland Library # 33). 1976. (pbk.) 1.25. Bantam Books.

Kiss from France and Some Soldiers from Everywhere. Albert Michael Neil Lyons. LC 17-16548. 1916. Hodder and Stoughton.

Kiss in the Dark: By J. Jasmin Pseud. Translated from the Lithuanian by Milton Stark. Jonas Jasinskas. LC 54-2239. 1954. International Press.

Kiss in the Sunlight. Maysie Greig. LC 57-8749. 1957. Avalon Books.

Kiss, Inc. Lois Wyse. LC 76-42417. 1977. 7.95 (ISBN 0-385-12083-4). Doubleday.

Kiss, Inc. Lois Wyse. (Dell Book). 1978. 1.95 (ISBN 0-440-14487-6). Dell Pub. Co.

Kiss, Kiss. Roald Dahl. LC 60-5186. 1960. Knopf.

Kiss, Kiss, Kill, Kill. Henry Kane. 1970. pap. 0.75 o.p. (ISBN 0-447-74643-X). Lancer.

Kiss Love Goodbye. Peggy Gaddis, pseud. LC 42-24966. 1942. Arcadia House, Inc.

Kiss Me Again: Stranger a Collection of Eight Stories, Long and Short. Drawings by Margot Tomes. 1st American Ed. Daphne Du Maurier. LC 53-5038. 1953. Doubleday.

Kiss Me, Deadly. Spillane, Frank Morrison. LC 52-5311. 1952. Dutton.

Kiss Me Kill Me. Kate Cameron, pseud. 1979. pap. 1.50 o.s.i. (ISBN 0-505-51384-6). Tower Bks.

Kiss Michelle Goodbye. Carter Brown, pseud. 176p. (Orig.). 1981. pap. 1.95 (ISBN 0-505-51756-6). Tower Bks.

Kiss Mommy Goodbye. Joy Fielding. LC 80-1692. 312p. 1981. 11.95 (ISBN 0-385-17291-5). Doubleday.

Kiss Mommy Goodbye. Joy Fielding. 1982. pap. 3.50 (ISBN 0-451-11544-9, AE1544, Sig). NAL.

Kiss Mommy Goodbye: A Novel. Joy Fielding. LC 80-1692. 1981. 11.95 (ISBN 0-385-17291-5). Doubleday.

Kiss My Assasin. Rod Gray. (The Lady from L.U.S.T. Ser.). (O.s.i.). 1973. pap. 0.95 o.s.i. (BT50594). Belmont-Tower.

Kiss My Aztec. Richard Pierce. 1973. pap. 1.95 o.s.i. (76-328). Lancer.

Kiss My Firm but Pliant Lips. Dan Greenburg. LC 65-168550. 1965. 4.50. Grossman.

Kiss of a Tyrant. Margaret Pargeter. (Harlequin Romances Ser.). 192p. 1980. pap. 1.25 (ISBN 0-373-02375-8, Pub. by Harlequin). PB.

Kiss of Apollo. Martha Gilbert Dickinson Bianchi. 1915. 1.35. Duffield & Company.

Kiss of Death. Lawrence Paul Bachmann. LC 46-5867. 1946. A. A. Knopf.

Kiss of Death. Charles Birkin. (O.s.i.). (Illus.). 1969. pap. 0.75 o.s.i. (A438S, Award). Univ Pub & Dist.

Kiss of Death. A Crime Novel. Eleazar Lipsky. LC 47-31158. 1947. Penguin Books.

Kiss of Glory, by Grace Duffle Boylan. Grace Duffle Boylan. LC 2-24847. 1902. G. W. Dillingham Company.

Kiss of Kin. Mary Lee Settle. LC 55-107189. Harper.

Kiss of Life, No. 136. Barbara Cartland. 144p. 1981. pap. 1.75 (ISBN 0-553-14504-5). Bantam.

Kiss of Paris. Barbara Cartland. 224p. pap. 2.25 (ISBN 0-515-06391-6). Jove Pubns.

Kiss of Paris. Barbara Cartland. (Historical Romance Ser. No. 38). 1972. pap. 0.95 o.p. (ISBN 0-515-02751-0, N2751). Pyramid Pubns.

Kiss of Paris. Barbara Cartland. 1972. pap. 1.25 o.p. (ISBN 0-515-02751-0, V2751). BJ Pub Group.

Kiss of Paris. Barbara Cartland. 1976. pap. 1.25 o.p. (ISBN 0-515-04154-8). BJ Pub Group.

Kiss of Silk. Barbara Cartland. (Historical Romances Ser.: No. 32). 1974. pap. 1.25 o.p. (ISBN 0-515-03474-6, V3474). BJ Pub Group.

Kiss of the Cannibal. Lewis Carey. 1980. 8.95 (ISBN 0-533-04155-4). Vantage.

Kiss of the Devil. Barbara Cartland. 1975. pap. 1.25 o.p. (ISBN 0-515-03587-4, V3587). BJ Pub Group.

Kiss of the Raven. Jonathan Cox. 224p. (Orig.). 1981. pap. 2.25 (ISBN 0-449-14415-1, GM). Fawcett.

Kiss of the Spider Woman. Manuel Puig. LC 78-14307. 1979. 8.95 (ISBN 0-394-50366-X). Knopf: Distributed by Random House.

Kiss of the Spider Woman. Manuel Puig. LC 80-12179. 1980. 3.95 (ISBN 0-394-74475-6). Vintage Books.

Kiss of the Unborn & Other Stories. Fyodor Sologub. Tr. by Murl G. Barker. LC 76-27836. 1977. 12.50x (ISBN 0-87049-202-0). U of Tenn Pr.

Kiss of the Unborn, and Other Stories. Fedor Kuzmich Teternikov. LC 76-27836. 10.00 (ISBN 0-87049-202-0). University of Tennessee Press.

Kiss of Youth. Denise Robins. 1975. (pbk.) 0.95 (ISBN 0-380-00470-4). Avon.

Kiss-off. Douglas Heyes. LC 51-11261. (Inner sanctum mystery). 1951. Simon and Schuster.

Kiss on Each Cheek. Donald De Simone. 448p. (Orig.). 1981. pap. 2.95 (ISBN 0-523-40469-7). Pinnacle Bks.

Kiss Proof. Margot Neville. LC 29-8256. 1929. R. M. McBride & Company.

Kiss That Killed. Gaston Leroux. LC 34-18833. The Macaulay Company.

Kiss the Blood off My Hands. Gerald Alfred Butler. LC 46-1627. 1946. Farrar & Rinehart, Inc.

Kiss the Boss Good-Bye. Hugh C Rae. LC 70-145457. (Red mask mystery). 1971. 4.95. Putnam.

Kiss the Boys and Make Them Die. James Yardley. 1973. (pbk) 0.95. New American Library.

Kiss the Bride. James Noble Gifford. LC 44-4115. 1944. Gramercy Publishing Company.

Kiss the Killer. Joseph Shallit. LC 52-5634. (Main line mysteries). 1952. Lippincott.

Kiss the Tears Away. Anne Hudson. (Candlelight Ecstasy Ser.: No. 156). (Orig.). 1983. pap. 1.95 (ISBN 0-440-14525-2). Dell.

Kiss the Toff. John Creasey. 1970. pap. 0.75 o.p. (ISBN 0-447-74700-2). Lancer.

Kiss to Remember. Elsie W. Strother. (YA) 1980. 6.95 (Avalon). Bouregy.

Kiss Tomorrow Good-Bye: A Novel. Horace McCoy. LC 48-6632. 1948. Random House.

Kiss Your Elbow. Alan Handley. LC 48-8269. (armchair mystery). 1948. D. McKay Co.

Kissed by Moonlight. Dorothy Vernon. 192p. 1981. pap. 1.50 (ISBN 0-671-57059-5). S&S.

Kissed Corpse. Asa Baker, pseud. LC 39-33013. 1939. Carlyle House.

Kissed Grass. Mary L. Burkhalter. LC 23-138. (Orig.). 1979. pap. 3.50 (ISBN 0-934284-00-8). Jolean Pub Co.

Kissed the Girls and Made Them Cry. John Hale. LC 66-23657. 1966. Prentice-Hall.

Kisses. R. B. DeCarlos. 3.00 o.p. Carlton.

Kisses for Maxine. Octave Foerster Schully. LC 38-3530. 1938. Hillman-Curl, Inc.

Kisses Leave No Fingerprints. Mike Fredman. LC 79-26899. 8.95 (ISBN 0-312-45691-3). St. Martin's Press.

Kisses of Fate. A Study of Mere Human Nature. Edward Heron-Allen. LC 6-65. 1888. Belford, Clarke & Co.

Kissing Cousins. Per Dionne. 1.95 o.p. (DBB104). Dansk Blue Bk.

Kissing Cousins. Anna James. 224p. (Orig.). 1980. pap. 1.75 (ISBN 0-449-50122-1, Coventry). Fawcett.

Kissing Covens. Colin Watson. LC 75-188725. (Red mask mystery). 1972. 4.95. Putnam.

Kissing Covens. Colin Watson. LC 75-188725. (Berkley medallion book). 1974. (pbk.) 0.95 (ISBN 0-425-02675-2). Berkley Pub. Co.

Kissing Fish. Translated from the French by Richard Howard. Monique Lange. LC 60-977891. 2.75. Criterion Books.

Kissing Gate. Pamela Haines. LC 79-6581. 1981. 14.95 (ISBN 0-385-15309-0). Doubleday.

Kissing Gourami. Kin Platt. (Max Roper Ser.). 224p. 1980. pap. 1.95 (ISBN 0-441-44717-1, Pub. by Charter Bks). Ace Bks.

Kissing Gourami. Kin Platt. pap. 0.95 o.p. (N2820). Pyramid Pubns.

Kissing Kin. Elswyth Thane. LC 48-9235. 1948. Duell, Sloan and Pearce.

Kissing Kin. Elswyth Thane. LC 80-25641. 1981. 16.95 (ISBN 0-8161-3162-7). G. K. Hall.

Kissing Lesson. Joanna Burgess. 192p. (Orig.). 1981. pap. 1.95 (ISBN 0-515-05534-4). Jove Pubns.

Kissing the Rod. A Novel. Edmund Hodgson Yates. LC 31-20581. 1866. Harper & Brothers.

Kissinger Caper. Harold Von Steinbergh. Orig. Title: Kissinger Complex. (Illus.). 319p. Date not set. pap. 5.95 (ISBN 0-87754-266-X). Chelsea Hse.

Kissinger Complex see Kissinger Caper.

Kissinger Complex: A Novel. F. R LeDrew. LC 74-81718. 1975. 8.95 (ISBN 0-88373-016-2). Stonehill.

Kissinger Noodles... or Westward, Mr. Ho: A Novel. Max Wilk. 1976. 7.95 (ISBN 0-393-08728-X). Norton.

Kit: a Memory. A Novel. James Payn. (Harper's Franklin square library, no. 288). 1882. Harper & Brothers.

Kit and Kitty. Richard Doddridge Blackmore. LC 6-13859. (On cover: Seaside library. Pocket ed., no. 1267). 1890. G. Munro.

Kit & Kitty. Sarah Carlisle. 224p. 1981. pap. 1.95 (ISBN 0-449-50202-3, Crest). Fawcett.

Kit and Kitty: A Novel. Richard Doddridge Blackmore. LC 6-13860. (On cover: Harper's Franklin square library, no. 663). 1889. Harper & Brothers.

Kit Brandon: A Portrait. Sherwood Anderson. LC 36-29911. 1936. C. Scribner's Sons.

Kit Caffrey's Grit. A Story of Texas. George W Hamilton. LC 7-9510. The Standard Publishing Company.

Kit Carey's Protege: Or, The West Point Conspiracy. Lionel Lounsberry. LC 99-2556. (Medal library. no. 8). 1899. Street & Smith.

Kit Carson. Jacket by the Author. Claude Gentry. LC 56-14088. 1956. Magnolia Publishers.

Kit Carson, the Prince of the Gold Hunters: Or The Adventures of the Sacramento. A Tale of the New Eldorado, Founded on Actual Facts. Charles E Averill. LC 24-38548. 1849. G. H. Williams.

Kit Carson's Last Trail. Leon Lewis. (On cover: The popular series, no. 4). 1891. R. Bonner's Sons.

Kit Carson's Way. Thomas Albert Curry. 1972. pap. 0.60 o.p. (06159). Curtis.

Kit Kennedy: Country Boy. Samuel Rutherford Crockett. LC 99-4180. 1899. Harper & Brothers.

Kit Larkin. Ramona Stewart. LC 66-11723. 1966. Doubleday.

Kit Musgrave's Luck. Harold Bindloss. LC 21-14699. Frederick A. Stokes Company.

Kit O'Brien. Edgar Lee Masters. LC 27-9367. 1927. Boni & Liveright.

Kit Wyndham: Or, Fettered for Life. Frank Barrett. LC 6-8667. (On cover: Lovell's international series, no. 35). F. F. Lovell & Company.

Kitab al Badi' Ibn al Mu'Tazz. (Arab Trans. Ser.: No. 44). 1979. pap. 6.50x (ISBN 0-916358-94-1). Wormhoudt.

Kitchen Cake Murder. Christopher Bush. LC 34-333. 1934. W. Morrow & Company.

Kitchener Chaps. Albert Michael Neil Lyons. LC 15-18428. 1915. John Lane.

Kite in the Sea: A Novel. Claude F. Koch. LC 64-12362. 1964. Chilton Books.

Kite Trust (a Romance of Wealth) 3d ed. Lebbeus Harding Rogers. LC 1-29378. Kite Trust Publishing Company.

Kite Trust (a Romance of Wealth) 4th ed. Lebbeus Harding Rogers. LC 2-4955. 1902. Kite Trust Pub. Co.

Kites of War. Derek Lambert. LC 70-81007. 1969. 5.95. Coward-McCann.

Kites Will Fly: A Novel. Bhisham Sahni. 200p. 1982. text ed. 22.50x (ISBN 0-7069-1332-9, Pub. by Vikas India). Advent NY.

Kith. Percy Howard Newby. LC 77-5204. 7.95 (ISBN 0-316-60420-8). Little, Brown.

Kith and Kin. George Hyde Lee. LC 1-29072. 1900. The Neale Company.

Kith and Kin: Nine Tales of Family Life. Phyllis Eleanor Bentley. LC 60-129515. 1960. Macmillan.

Kittatinny: A Tale of Magic. Joanna Russ. LC 77-94981. (Illus.). 1978. pap. 5.00 (ISBN 0-913780-24-3). Daughters.

Kitty. Warwick Deeping. LC 27-22759. 1927. A. A. Knopf.

Kitty. Matilda Barbara Betham- Edwards, pseud. 1870. Harper & Brothers.

Kitty. Mary Ann Gibbs, pseud. (Coventry Romance Ser.: No. 198). 192p. 1982. pap. 1.50 (ISBN 0-449-50301-1, Coventry). Fawcett.

Kitty. Lena Kennedy. LC 81-20124. 1982. 14.95 (ISBN 0-8161-3345-X). G.K. Hall.

Kitty. Rosamond Van Der Zee Marshall. LC 43-18114. 1943. Distributed by Duell, Sloan & Pearce.

Kitty. Rosamond Van Der Zee Marshall. LC 47-23970. (Forum books. F-76). 1946. The World Publishing Company.

Kitty Alone. A Story of Three Fires. Sabine Baring-Gould. LC 6-7231. 1894. Dodd, Mead & Company.

Kitty Bell, the Orphan: Possibly an Earlier Version of Charlotte Bronte's "Jane Eyre.". Bronte, Charlotte & Sue, Eugene I. E. Marie Joseph Eugene. Ed. by Chadwick, Esther Alice. LC 14-9886. 1914. Sir Isaac Pitman & Sons, Ltd.

Kitty Canary: A Novel. Kate Lee Langley Bosher. LC 18-356096. 1918. Harper & Brothers.

Kitty Carstairs. John Joy Bell. LC 19-11945. 1918. Frederick A. Stokes Company.

Kitty Dixon, Bells of the South Anna: A Wee Bit of Love and War. Clarence Archibald Bryce. LC 7-23714. 1907. The "Southern Clinic" Press.

Kitty Foyle. Christopher Darlington Morley. LC 40-37535. 1940. J. B. Lippincott Company.

Kitty Frew. Jane Ludlow Drake Abbott. LC 31-161356. 1931. J. B. Lippincott Company.

Kitty, I Hardly Knew You. 1st Ed. Edward McSorley. LC 59-10678. 1959. Doubleday.

Kitty Knight. Richard Beverley Eggleston. LC 13-12871. 1913. Whittet & Shepperson.

Kitty of the Roses. Ralph Henry Barbour. LC 4-32158. 1904. J. B Lippincott Company.

Kitty the Rag. Eliza M. J. Humphreys. LC 7-57911. R. F. Fenno & Company; Etc., Etc.

Kitty Torture. D. S. Phantom. (How-to Ser.: No. 1). 1979. pap. 2.14 (ISBN 0-934646-01-5). S & S Pr TX.

Kitty's Class Day. Louisa May Alcott. 1976. Repr. of 1868 ed. 25.00 o.p. (ISBN 0-403-05870-8, Regency). Scholarly.

Kitty's Conquest. Charles King. LC 7-12231. 1884. J. B. Lippincott & Co.

Kitty's Conquest. Charles King. LC 16-131151. 1912. J. B. Lippincott Company.

Kitty's Engagement: A Novel. Florence Alice Price James. LC 7-7416. 1895. D. Appleton and Company.

Kitty's Father. Frank Barrett. LC 6-8666. United States Book Company.

Kitwyk Stories. Anna Eichberg Lane. LC 6-15451. 1895. The Century Co.

Kitwyk Stories. Anna Eichberg Lane. LC 4-14369. (Half-title: Canvasback library of popular fiction. vol. vi). 1904. J. Lane.

Kiver up the Still, Ma -- Thar's a Stranger Comin'. Fun in the Ozarks with Forrest Brown. Forrest Raymond Brown. LC 65-2137. 1965. Exposition Press.

KKK. Bill Meilen. Orig. Title: Bull Pen. 1969. pap. 0.75 o.p. (64-144). Paperback Lib.

K.K.K. Charles Waller Tyler. LC 72-2063. (Black Heritage Library Collection). 1972. 14.50 (ISBN 0-8369-9072-2). Books for Libraries Press.

Klan Killer. R. L. Mack. 80p. 1982. 5.50 (ISBN 0-682-49770-3). Exposition.

Klansman. William Bradford Huie. (4590). 1968. Dell.

Klansman. William Bradford Huie. 1974. (pbk.) 1.50. Dell.

Klaus Bewer's Wife: From the German of Paul Lindau. Paul Lindau. Tr. by Fleishman, Clara S. LC 7-19020. (Leisure season series. no. 5). 1886. H. Holt and Company.

Klaw. W. L. Fieldhouse. (Klaw Ser.: No. 1). (Orig.). 1980. pap. 1.95 (ISBN 0-505-51586-5). Tower Bks.

Kleath. Madge Hamilton Lyons Macbeth. LC 17-24097. Small, Maynard & Company.

Kleber Flight. Hans Koning. LC 81-66025. 1981. 12.95 (ISBN 0-689-11221-1). Atheneum.

Kleber's Convoy. Antony Trew. LC 73-87281. (Illus.). 1973. 6.95. St. Martin's Press.

Kleber's Convoy. Antony Trew. 1975. (pbk.) 1.50. Popular Library.

Kleinzeit. Russell Hoban. LC 74-4533. 1974. (ISBN 0-670-41458-1). Viking Press.

Klingon Gambit. Robert E. Vardeman. 1981. pap. 2.50 (ISBN 0-671-83276-X, Timescape). PB.

Klingsor's Last Summer. Hermann Hesse. 1974. (pbk.) 1.50. Bantam Books.

Klingsor's Last Summer. Hermann Hesse. LC 77-122825. 1970. 6.50. Farrar, Straus and Giroux.

Klondike Clan: A Tale of the Great Stampede. Samuel Hall Young. LC 17-85. Fleming H. Revell Company.

Klondike Picnic: The Story of a Day. Eleanor Cecilia Donnelly. LC 98-1497. 1898. Benziger Brothers.

Klondike Widow. Alice McGill Erspamer. LC 53-12319. 1953. Pageant Press.

Kloochman: A Novel. Jack Curtis. LC 66-11312. 1966. Simon and Schuster.

Klosterheim; or, The Masque. Thomas De Quincey. Ed. by MacKenzie, Robert Shelton. LC 6-33974. 1855. Whittemore, Niles, and Hall.

Klosterheim, or, The Masque. Thomas De Quincey. LC 82-8517. (Banquo book). (Illus.). 5.95 (ISBN 0-912800-98-4). Woodbridge Press.

Klynts Law. Elliott Baker. LC 75-45144. 312p. 1976. 8.95 o.p. (ISBN 0-15-147283-1). HarBraceJ.

Klynt's Law: A Novel. Elliott Baker. LC 75-45144. 8.95. Harcourt, Brace, Jovanovich.

Klytaimnestra Who Stayed at Home. Nancy Bogen. LC 80-51052. 1980. 6.95 (ISBN 0-936726-00-8). Twickenham Press.

Klytia. A Story of Heidelberg Castle. Adolf Hausrath & Corkran, Sutton Fraser, Tr. (On cover: Seaside library. Pocket ed., no. 435). 1885. G. Munro.

Knave of Diamonds. Ethel May Dell. LC 21-16871. 1915. A. L. Burt Company.

Knave of Diamonds. Ethel May Dell. LC 12-268971. 1912. 1.35. G. P. Putnam's Sons.

Knave of Diamonds. Percy Marks. LC 43-10297. 1943. Reynal & Hitchcock.

Knave of Dreams. Alice Mary Norton. (Ace Book). 1977. 1.75. Ace Books.

Knave of Eagles. Bob Wade, pseud. LC 69-16472. 1969. 4.95. Random House.

Knave of Hearts. Philippa Carr, pseud. 288p. 1983. 13.95 (ISBN 0-399-12810-7, Putnam). Putnam Pub Group.

Knave of Hearts. Jean Plaidy. LC 82-21406. 13.95 (ISBN 0-399-12810-7). Putnam.

Knave of Hearts. Dell Shannon. 1962. 4.95 o.p. Morrow.

Knave of Hearts: A Fairy Story. Robert Grant. LC 6-44743. 1886. Ticknor and Company.

Knave of Hearts: By Dell Shannon Pseud. Elizabeth Linington. LC 62-14013. 1962. Morrow.

Kneel to the Prettiest. Berta Ruck. LC 25-25282. 1925. Dodd, Mead and Company.

Kneel to the Rising Sun. Erskine Caldwell. LC 75-315102. 1973. White Lion Publishers.

Kneel to the Rising Sun, and Other Stories. Erskine Caldwell. LC 51-10405. (uniform edition of the works of Erskine Caldwell). 1951. Duell, Sloan and Pearce.

Kneel to the Rising Sun and Other Stories. Erskine Caldwell. LC 35-8105. 1935. The Viking Press.

Knickerbocker Blood. Elisabeth Finley Thomas. LC 32-142102. Farrar & Rinehart, Incorporated.

Knickerbocker Gardens: A Pursuit of Happiness. Caleb Bruce. LC 41-212726. 1941. C. Scribner's Sons.

Knife. Peadar O'Donnell. LC 81-670153. (Illus.). 288p. 1981. 15.00 (ISBN 0-906462-02-9, Pub. by Irish Humanities Ireland); pap. 6.50 (ISBN 0-906462-03-7). Dufour.

Knife at My Back: By Adam Knight Pseud. Lawrence Lariar. LC 52-5668. 1952. Crown Publishers.

Knife Behind the Curtain: Tales of Crime and the Secret Service. Valentine Williams. LC 30-12135. 1930. Houghton Mifflin Company.

Knife Behind You. 1st Ed. James Walker Benet. LC 50-5149. 1950. Harper.

Knife Edge. William Ellis. LC 73-87453. (Illus.). 1973. 5.95 (ISBN 0-8027-5290-X). Walker.

Knife Edge. Donald MacKenzie. LC 61-5370. 1961. Houghton Mifflin.

Knife for the Juggler. Manning Coles, pseud. LC 64-24529. 1964. Published for the Crime Club by Doubleday.

Knife. Illustrated by Rus Anderson. Theon Wright. LC 55-987052. 1955. Gilbert Press; Distributed by Messner.

Knife in My Back. Sam Merwin. LC 45-2145. 1945. Mystery House.

Knife in My Hands. Keith Maillard. LC 81-38456. 13.95 (ISBN 0-8253-0082-7). Beaufort Books.

Knife in the Dark. George Douglas Howard Cole & Margaret Isabel Postgate Cole. LC 42-7953. 1942. The Macmillan Company.

Knife in the Night. William M James. (Apache series, #2). 1974. (pbk.) 0.95 (ISBN 0-523-00397-8). Pinnacle Books.

Knife Is Silent. Hoffman Birney. LC 47-761. 1947. Random House.

Knife of the Times, and Other Stories. William Carlos Williams. LC 73-12604. (Series: The Dragon Series.). 1973. (ISBN 0-8414-9402-9). Folcroft Library Editions.

Knife of the Times: And Other Stories. William Carlos Williams. LC 45-22515. (Half-title: The Dragon series, ed. by Angel Flores). 1932. The Dragon Press.

Knife on the Table. Jacques Godbout. LC 76-372786. (New Canadian library; no. 130). 2.50 (ISBN 0-7710-9230-X). McClelland and Stewart.

Knife Will Fall. Marten Cumberland. LC 44-6925. 1944. Pub. for the Crime Club by Doubleday, Doran & Co.

Knifeman. David Craig. LC 72-96295. 192p. 1973. 5.95 o.p. (ISBN 0-8128-1566-1). Stein & Day.

Knifeman. Allan James Tucker. LC 72-96295. 1973. 5.95 (ISBN 0-8128-1566-1). Stein and Day.

Knifeman: A Novel of Judas Iscariot. William Rayner. LC 77-79727. 1969. 5.50 o.p. Morrow.

Knight. George Shipway. LC 71-97689. 1970. 6.95. Doubleday.

Knight Among Ladies. Annie Edith Foster Jameson. LC 23-7007. 1.75. George H. Doran Company.

Knight at Arms. Henry Christopher Bailey. LC 25-13522. 1925. E. P. Dutton & Company.

Knight Comes Flying. Eustace L Adams. LC 31-367948. 1931. L. MacVeagh, The Dial Press.

Knight Conrad of Rheinstein: A Romance of the Days of Chivalry. Julius Ludovici. LC 99-5523. 1899. Rand, McNally & Company.

Knight-Errant. Ada Ellen Bayly. LC 6-10292. (On cover: Seaside library. Pocket ed., no. 1147.). G. Munroe.

Knight-Errant. Helen Mary Elizabeth Clamp. LC 43-4974. 1943. Hurst & Blackett Limited.

Knight-Errant. A Novel. Ada Ellen Bayly. (Harper's Franklin square library, no. 575.). 1887. Harper & Brothers.

Knight-Errant: A Novel. Ada Ellen Bayly. LC 6-10293. (On cover: Lovell's library, v. 20, no. 962.). J.W. Lovell Company.

Knight-Errant. A Novel. Ada Ellen Bayly. LC 42-471001. The F. M. Lupton Publishing Company.

Knight-Errant: A Novel of to-Day. Robert Alexander Wason. LC 11-23297. Small, Maynard & Company.

Knight for a Night. Carla Richter. 4.00 o.s.i. (ISBN 0-8181-0053-2). Pageant-Poseidon.

Knight in Denim. Ramsey I. E. Percival Ramsey Benson. LC 12-5549. 1912. 1.25. C. Scribner's Sons.

Knight in Grey: A Historical Novel. Marie E Richard. LC 13-227628. The Castle Press.

Knight in Homespun. John Charles Spoth. LC 9-7043. 1909. The C. M. Clark Publishing Company.

Knight Missing. Howard Barrington. LC 45-1558. 1945. The Macmillan Company.

Knight of Bloemendale, and Other Stories: Tales and Legends Reprinted from the "Ave Maria.". Ave. LC 7-22756. H. L. Kilner & Co.

Knight of Carolina. Annie Maria Barnes. LC 27-131222. 1927. The Penn Publishing Company.

Knight of Columbia: A Story of the War. Charles King. LC 4-7918. 1904. The Hobart Company.

Knight of Curtesy & the Fair Lady of Faguell. Elizabeth McCausland. 1922. ltd. ed. 10.00 (ISBN 0-8482-5159-8). Norwood Edns.

Knight of Delusion. Keith Laumer. 288p. 1983. pap. 2.75 (ISBN 0-523-48551-4). Pinnacle Bks.

Knight of Faith. Lydia Hoyt Farmer. LC 6-38669. (On cover: The fireside series, no. 96). 1889. J. S. Ogilvie.

Knight of Ghosts and Shadows. Poul Anderson. LC 75-318146. 1.25. Doubleday.

Knight of Ghosts and Shadows. Poul Anderson. (Signet book). 1975. (pbk.) 1.50. New American Library.

Knight of Ghosts and Shadows. Poul Anderson. LC 79-12860. (Gregg Press science fiction series). 1979. 12.50 (ISBN 0-8398-2523-4). Gregg Press.

Knight of Lonely Land. Evelyn Campbell. LC 21-471611. 1921. Little, Brown, and Company.

Knight of the Black Forest. Grace Denio Litchfield. 1885. G. P. Putnam's Sons.

Knight of the Cart. Constance B Hieatt. LC 70-78263. (Illus.). 1969. 3.95. Crowell.

Knight of the Cimarron. Charles Stanley Strong. LC 44-4102. 1944. Phoenix Press.

Knight of the Cumberland. John Fox. LC 6-37963. 1906. C. Scribner's Sons.

Knight of the Dixie Wilds. Walter E Taylor. LC 29-295240. Meador Publishing Company.

Knight of the Golden Chain. R. D Chetwode. LC 98-571. 1898. D. Appleton & Co.

Knight of the Golden Circle. Ulysses Samuel Leah. LC 11-18972. 1911. R. G. Badger.

Knight of the Golden Melice: A Historical Romance. John Turvill Adams. LC 5-42986. 1857. Derby & Yackson.

Knight of the Highway. Clinton Scollard. LC 3-29331. 1908. G. W. Browning.

Knight of the Key: Or, A Romance Amid Dots and Dashes. Edgar H Rancevau. LC 8-216. 1893. The Telegraphers' Pub. Co.

Knight of the Knot of Blue: The Legend of a Name. Mittie Owen McDavid. LC 30-33775. Done by the Bookfellows at the Torch Press.

Knight of the Mirrors. Thomas L. Taylor. 1970. 3.00 o.p. Carlton.

Knight of the Nets. Amelia Edith Huddleston Barr. LC 6-79881. 1896. Dodd, Mead and Company.

Knight of the Nineteenth Century. Edward Payson Roe. LC 7-40233. (On cover: Roe's works). Dodd, Mead, and Company.

Knight of the North. William Campbell. LC 44-1671. Bruce Publishing Company.

Knight of the Silver Star. Percy James Brebner. LC 7-34776. R. F. Fenno & Company.

Knight of the Third Estate. Hector Fezandie. LC 38-348037. 1938. T. F. Kyle.

Knight of the Thunderbolt. Robert LeGrand. 3.95 o.p. Vantage.

Knight of the Toilers. Arthur Newell. LC 5-41004. F. L. Marsh & Co.

Knight of the Virgin. Vicente Blasco Ibanez & Livingston, Arthur, 1883- Tr. LC 30-13354. E. P. Dutton & Co., Inc.

Knight of the Wilderness. Oliver Marble Gale & Wheeler, Harriet Martha. LC 10-146867. 1909. The Reilly & Britton Co.

Knight of Today. Elise Howard-Smith. LC 19-6481. 1919. The John C. Winston Company.

Knight on Wheels. John Hay Beith. LC 14-15566. 1914. Houghton Mifflin Company.

Knight on Wheels. John Hay Beith. LC 14-14540. 1914. Hodder and Stoughton.

Knight Returns, and Other Stories: A Collection of Thirteen Works. Victor Arico. LC 52-20980. 1952. William-Frederick Press.

Knight Sinister. Adam Hall. 1971. pap. 0.75 o.p. (T2463). Pyramid Pubns.

Knight with Armour. Alfred Leo Duggan. LC 51-11259. Coward-McCann.

Knightly Quest: A Novella and Four Short Stories. Tennessee Williams. LC 66-27615. (New Directions book). 1967. Published for J. Laughlin by New Directions Pub. Corp.

Knightly Quest & Other Stories. Tennessee Williams. LC 66-27615. 6.50 (ISBN 0-8112-0409-X). New Directions.

Knightly Years. W M Ardagh. LC 12-10622. 1912. John Lane.

Knight's Acre. Norah Robinson Lofts. LC 74-5918. 1975. 6.95 (ISBN 0-385-03551-9). Doubleday.

Knight's Acre. large print ed. Norah Robinson Lofts. LC 75-8662. 1975. 13.95 (ISBN 0-8161-6284-0). G. K. Hall.

Knight's Acre. Norah Robinson Lofts. (Fawcett Crest Book). 1976. (pbk.) 1.75. Fawcett.

Knights & Dragons. Elizabeth Spencer. 1965. 5.95 o.p. (ISBN 0-07-060145-3, GB). McGraw.

Knights & Dragons: A Novel. Elizabeth Spencer. LC 65-16154. bds., 3.95. McGraw.

Knight's Gambit. William Faulkner. LC 49-114728. 1949. Random House.

Knight's Gambit. William Faulkner. LC 78-4892. 1978. 1.95 (ISBN 0-394-72729-0). Vintage Books.

Knight's Gambit. Guy Noel Pocock. LC 29-294408. 1929. J. M. Dent & Sons Ltd.

Knight's Honor. Roberta Gellis. LC 64-11611. 1964. Doubleday.

Knight's Honor. Roberta Gellis. (Illus.). 1976. 1.75. Avon Books.

Knights in Fustian: A War Time Story of Indiana. Caroline Virginia Krout. LC 2062. 1900. Houghton, Mifflin and Company.

Knight's Landing. Francine Pinckert. LC 67-14676. 1967. McGraw-Hill.

Knight's Motto: A Novel. Sylvanus Cobb. (On cover: The popular series, no. 21). 1892. R. Bonner's Sons.

Knights of Arabia. San Antonio. Tr. by Cyril Buhler. (San Antonio Mystery Ser). 1970. pap. 0.60 o.p. (ISBN 0-446-63341-0, 63-341). Paperback Lib.

Knights of Athena. Robert Brahms. 4.95 o.p. Vantage.

Knights of Dark Renown. Graham Shelby. LC 76-90405. (Illus.). 1969. 6.95. Weybright and Talley.

Knights of the Cockpit: A Romantic Epic of the Flying Marines in Haiti. Irwin R Franklyn. LC 31-5709. 1931. L. MacVeagh, The Dial Press.

Knights of the Cross. Henryk Sienkiewicz. Tr. by Jeremiah Curtin. LC 696. 1900. Little, Brown, and Company.

Knights of the Cross (Krzyzacy) Historical Novel. Henryk Sienkiewicz & Soissons, S. C. De. Tr. R. F. Fenno & Company.

Knights of the Cross: Or, Krzyzacy; Historical Romance. Henryk Sienkiewicz. Tr. by Samuel Augustus Binion. LC 9-3869. R. F. Fenno & Company.

Knights of the Cross: Or, Krzyzacy; Historical Romance. Henryk Sienkiewicz. Tr. by Samuel Augustus Binion. LC 1-29119. 1899. R. F. Fenno & Company.

Knights of the Cross: The Crusaders) Henryk Sienkiewicz. LC 2143. Street & Smith.

Knights of the Desert. W. D Hoffman. 1927. A. C. McClurg & Co.

Knights of the Golden Horse-Shoe: A Traditionary Tale of the Cocked Hat Gentry in the Old Dominion. William Alexander Caruthers. LC 73-123107. (Southern literary classics series). 1970. 2.95 (ISBN 0-8078-4054-8). University of North Carolina Press.

Knights of the Green Cloth. Antonio Scalvini & Le Dyrol, Isabel, Tr. (On cover: Idle moments series, no. 10). 1891. The Price-McGill Company.

Knights of the Horseshoe: A Traditionary Tale of the Cocked Hat Gentryin the Old Dominion. William Alexander Caruthers. (Harper's Franklin square library. no. 269). 1882. Harper & Brothers.

Knights of the Horseshoe: A Traditionary Tale of the Cocked Hat Gentry in the Old Dominion. William Alexander Caruthers. LC 28-34158. (Burt's library of the world's best books). 1928. A. L. Burt Company.

Knights of the Horseshoe: A Traditional Tale of the Cocked Hat Gentry in the Old Dominion. William Alexander Caruthers. 1845. lib. bdg. 14.25 o.s.i. (ISBN 0-512-00088-3). Garrett Pr.

Knights of the Horseshoe: A Traditional Tale of the Cocked Hat Gentry in the Old Dominion. Ed. by Joseph V. Ridgely. LC 70-93601. (American Fiction Ser). (Illus.). 1970. lib. bdg. 12.50 o.s.i. (ISBN 0-512-00088-3). Garrett Pr.

Knights of the Range. Grey, Zane. LC 63-6982. (Great western edition, 16). 1963. Grosset & Dunlap.

Knights of the Range. Zane Grey. LC 73-1305. 1973. 10.95 (ISBN 0-8161-6088-0). G. K. Hall.

Knights of the Range. Zane Grey. LC 39-27063. 1939. Harper & Brothers.

Knights of the Seal: Or, The Mysteries of the Three Cities; a Romance of Men's Hearts and Habits... Augustine Joseph Hickey Duganne. LC 6-35667. 1845. Colon and Adriance.

Knights of to-Day: Or, Love and Science. Charles Barnard. LC 6-7207. 1881. C. Scribner's Sons.

Knights Who Fought the Dragon. Edwin Leslie. LC 6-44368. 1906. The Sunday School Times Co.

Knightsbridge Mystery, and The Picture: Also Tit for Tat. Charles Reade. (On cover: Lovell's library, v. 19, no. 917). 1887. J. W. Lovell Company.

Knitters in the Sun. Alice French. LC 69-11897. (American short story series, v. 55). 1969. Garrett Press.

Knitters in the Sun. Alice French. LC 4-151096. 1887. Houghton, Mifflin and Company.

Knitting of the Souls: A Tale of 17th Century Boston. Maude Clark Gay. LC 4-11532. 1904. Lee and Shepard.

Knives and Forks; or, Dwellers in Meridien. Mary Chappel Lee. LC 7-12595. Congregational Sunday-School and Publishing Society.

Knives Have Edges. Sara Woods, pseud. LC 76-103559. (Rinehart suspense novel). 1970. 4.50. Holt, Rinehart and Winston.

Knives Have Edges. Sara Woods. 1973. 0.75. Dell.

Knock and Wait a While. William Rawle Weeks. LC 57-5174. 1957. Houghton Mifflin.

Knock at Midnight. Charity L. Blackstock. 1968. 4.95 o.p. (73-740); pap. 0.60 o.p. (73-740). Lancer.

Knock at Midnight. James Reston. LC 75-305506. 1975. 6.95 (ISBN 0-393-08710-7). Norton.

Knock at Midnight: By Charity Blackstock. Ursula Torday. (73-740). 1968. Lancer.

Knock at Midnight: By Charity Blackstock. 1st Amer. Ed. Ursula Torday. LC 67-15279. 1967. 4.95. Coward.

Knock Four Times. Margaret Emma Faith Irwin. LC 27-18968. Harcourt, Brace & Company.

Knock, Knock, Knock, and Other Stories. Ivan Sergieevich Turgenev. Tr. by Constance Garnett. LC 21-20111. (novels of Ivan Turgenev. xvii). 1921. The Macmillan Company: Etc. Etc.

Knock, Knock, You're Dead: By V. J. Santiago. V. J Santiago. (Vigilante#4: Chicago). 1976. (pbk.) 1.25 (ISBN 0-523-00872-4). Pinnacle Books.

Knock on Any Door. Willard Motley. LC 47-3104. 1947. D. Appleton-Century Company, Inc.

Knock on Teak. Robin Maugham. LC 76-365260. 1976. 2.95 (ISBN 0-491-01676-X). Allen.

Knock on the Door: A Novel. Robert Smythe Hichens. LC 9-24956. 1909. J. B. Lippincott Company.

Knock on the Door: A Story of to-Day. Mary Caroline Holmes. LC 19-139. Fleming H. Revell Company.

Knock on the Nursery Door: Tales of the Dickens Children. Stuart Dickens McHugh. LC 72-197728. (Illus.). 1972. (ISBN 0-7181-1031-5). Joseph.

Knock Ten: A Novel of Mining Life. Kay Brown. LC 77-372243. 1976. 7.50 (ISBN 0-85587-091-5). Wentworth Books.

Knock Three - One - Two. Fredric Brown. 1961. 2.95 o.p. Dutton.

Knock Three-One-Two. 1st Ed. Fredric Brown. LC 59-10773. 1959. Dutton.

Knock Upon Silence. Carolyn Kizer. LC 65-19901. (O.s.i.). 2.95 o.s.i. (ISBN 0-385-04580-8). Doubleday.

Knockabout. Blaise Cendrars & Nina Rootes. LC 80-9057. 1982. 12.95 (ISBN 0-8128-2816-X). Stein and Day.

Knockdown. Dick Francis. LC 74-15870. 1975. 6.95 (ISBN 0-06-011339-1). Harper & Row.

Knocked for a Loop. Craig Rice. LC 57-13973. (Inner sanctum mystery). 1957. Simon and Schuster.

Knocker on Death's Door. Edith Pargeter. LC 74-142396. 1971. 5.50. Morrow.

Knocker on Death's Door. Ellis Peters. 1971. 5.50 (ISBN 0-688-01948-X). Morrow.

Knocking at God's Door. Oswald Chambers. 1957. pap. 1.50 (ISBN 0-87508-115-0). Chr Lit.

Knocking on the Door. Alan Paton. 308p. 1975. 30.00x (ISBN 0-901720-98-4, Pub. by Collins England). State Mutual Bk.

Knocknagow. Charles Joseph Kickham. LC 79-18425. (Ireland, from the Act of Union, 1800, to the death of Parnell, 1891). 1979. 42.00 (ISBN 0-8240-3517-8). Garland Pub.

Knocknagow; or, the Cabins of Tipperary. Charles Joseph Kickham. (Nineteenth Century Fiction Ser.: Ireland: No. 68). 1979. lib. bdg. 46.00 (ISBN 0-8240-3517-8). Garland Pub.

Knocknagow or the Homes of Tipperary. 2nd ed. Charles Joseph Kickham. (Sackville Library Edition Ser.). 1978. 32.50 o.p. (ISBN 0-7171-0941-0). Irish Bk Ctr.

Knockout. Charles Francis Coe. LC 36-103481. J. B. Lippincott Company.

Knockover. Newton Thornburg. 1975. (pbk.) 1.25 (ISBN 0-380-00303-1). Avon.

Knoll Island. George Agnew Chamberlain. LC 43-164364. 1943. The Bobbs-Merrill Company.

Knotted Cord: A Novel. Jerzy Pietrkiewicz. LC 53-9776. 1953. Roy Publishers.

Knout, a Tale of Poland. Tr. by Sadlier, Mary Ann (Madden) P. F. Cunningham.

Knout, a Tale of Poland. Tr. by Sadlier, Mary Ann (Madden) LC 7-141833. P. F. Cunningham.

Know Nothing? LC 7-14184. 1855. J. P. Jewett & Company; Etc., Etc.

Know Nothing. Mary Lee Settle. 1981. pap. 3.50 (ISBN 0-345-29313-4). Ballantine.

Know Nothing: A Novel. Mary Lee Settle. LC 60-13245. 1960. Viking Press.

Know Your Enemy. Delia Mares. 1962. pap. 0.95 o.p. (07392, Collier). Macmillan.

Known but to God. Quentin James Reynolds. LC 60-11300. 1960. John Day Co.

Known Homosexual. James Colton, pseud. (Orig.). 1968. pap. 1.25 o.p. (2074). Brandon.

Knuckle. David Hare. 1974. pap. 4.95 o.p. (ISBN 0-571-10467-3). Merrimack Bk Serv.

Knuckles. Clarence Budington Kelland. LC 28-9743. 1928. Harper & Brothers.

Knulp: Three Tales from the Life of Knulp. Hermann Hesse. LC 72-148710. 1971. 4.95 (ISBN 0-374-18216-7). Farrar, Straus and Giroux.

Knulp: Three Tales from the Life of Knulp. Hermann Hesse. Tr. by Ralph Manheim from Ger. 128p. 1971. pap. 4.95 (ISBN 0-374-50987-5, N423). FS&G.

Knute Hellson's Hard Luck: Complicated by His Wife Hulda in the Merry- Go-Round of Married Life. Fred G Shaffer. 1895. The Pioneer Publishing House.

Ko-Sang, a Korean Saga. Jim Sinnott. (Orig.). 1981. pap. cancelled (ISBN 0-671-41047-4). PB.

Koberg Link. Arthur Maling. LC 79-1802. 10.00 (ISBN 0-06-012709-0). Harper & Row.

Kobiety (Women) A Novel of Polish Life. Sofja Rygier-Nalkowska & Dziewicki, Michael Henry, Tr. LC 21-492. 1920. G. P. Putnam's Sons.

Kobra Manifesto. Adam Hall. 1977. lib. bdg. 13.50 o.p. (ISBN 0-8161-6454-1, Large Print Bks). G K Hall.

Kobra Manifesto. Adam Hall. LC 75-40703. 264p. 1976. 7.95 o.p. (ISBN 0-385-05108-5). Doubleday.

Kobra Manifesto. Elleston Trevor. LC 75-40703. 1976. 7.95 (ISBN 0-385-05108-5). Doubleday.

Kobra Manifesto. Elleston Trevor. LC 76-56251. 1977. 12.95 (ISBN 0-8161-6454-1). G. K. Hall.

Kocska Formula. Frank Riley. LC 78-151859. 1971. 5.95. Sherbourne Press.

Kodak Woman. Bertha N Clay. LC 6-21368. (On cover: The enterprise ser., no. 6). E. A. Weeks & Company.

Kohala of Hawaii. A Story of the Sandwich Islands Revolution. Alfred Rochefort Calhoun. (On cover: Once a week library, v. 1, no. 2). 1893. P. F. Collier.

Koheleth. A Novel. Lewis Austin Storrs. LC 8-16289. 1897. G. W. Dillingham Co.

Koiec Corollary. Homer N. Gholston. (Orig.). 1979. pap. 1.95 (ISBN 0-532-23253-4). Woodhill.

Kokin Waka-Shu: The 10th Century Anthology Edited by Imperial Edict. Tr. by H. H. Honda. 1970. 12.95 o.p. (ISBN 0-89346-072-9, Pub. by Hokuseido Pr). Heian Intl.

Kokle Tuksnesi. Reinhold Millers. 1978. 5.00x o.p. (ISBN 0-912852-22-4). Echo Pubs.

Kokoro. Natsume Soseki. Tr. by Edwin McClellan. 256p. 1957. pap. 4.95 (ISBN 0-89526-951-1). Regnery-Gateway.

Kokoro: A Novel; Translated from the Japanese, and with a Foreword by Edwin McClellan. Soseki Natsume. LC 57-10097. 1957. H. Regnery Co.

Kolchak's Gold. Barian Wynne Garfield. LC 73-84062. 1974. 7.95 (ISBN 0-679-50414-1). McKay.

Kolyma Tales. Varlamtikhonovich Shalamov. Tr. by John Glad from Rus. 224p. 1982. pap. 4.95 (ISBN 0-393-00077-X). Norton.

Kommersdorf Connection: A Suspense Thriller with Catastrophic Implications. Eric Ramsey, pseud. LC 77-15853. 1978. 1.95 (ISBN 0-87216-439-X). Playboy Press.

Kona: A Novel. Marjorie Jane Putnam Sinclair. LC 47-30161. 1947. The John Day Company.

Kona Caper. Nana Reeder Hall. LC 74-27605. Victoria Publishers.

Konarak: The Sun Temple of Love. Intro. by Rustam J. Mehta. (Illus.). 46p. 1981. text ed. 15.00x (ISBN 0-86590-065-5, Pub. by Taraporevala India). Apt Bks.

Kong. Harold Kingsley. LC 27-21347. 1927. Dodd, Mead & Company.

Kongo, the Gorilla-Man. Frank Orndorff. LC 47-8031. House of Field-Doubleday.

Konigsmark. Alfred Edward Woodley Mason. LC 39-2709. 1939. Doubleday, Doran & Company, Inc.

Koningsmarke: Or Old Times in, 2 Vols. James Kirke Paulding. Set. 16.00 o.s.i. (ISBN 0-403-00336-9). Scholarly.

Koningsmarke: Or, Old Times in the New World, Volumes I & II. James Kirke Paulding. LC 71-173932. 1971. 14.50 (ISBN 0-404-04919-2). AMS Press.

Koningsmarke, the Long Finne: A Story of the New World... James Kirke Paudling. LC 7-36487. 1823. C. Wiley.

Koningsmarke, the Long Finne: A Story of the New World. James Kirke Paulding. LC 78-93654. (American Fiction Ser). 1970. lib. bdg. 22.50 o.s.i. (ISBN 0-512-00539-7). Garrett Pr.

Konneautt Lake: A Story of Early Times in North-Western Pennsylvania. William McMichael. LC 7-20306. W. B. Smith & Co.

Konstantin Paustovskii: Selected Stories. Ed. by P. Henry. 1967. pap. 6.25 (ISBN 0-08-011859-3). Pergamon.

Kontinent. new ed. Solzhenitsyn et al. Ed. by Vladimir Maximov. LC 76-1328. (Eng.). 1976. 10.00 (ISBN 0-405-08104-9). Ayer Co.

Kontrol. Edmund Snell. LC 28-25626. 1928. J. B. Lippincott Company.

Konunga Sogur. Eirspennill. Ed. by C. R. Unger. LC 80-1975. Repr. of 1873 ed. 62.00 (ISBN 0-404-18636-X). AMS Pr.

Kopet, Alta. Edward Harper Thomas. LC 36-94633. 1936. The Caston Printers, Ltd.

Kophetua the Thirteenth. Julian Stafford Corbett. LC 7-4428. 1889. Macmillan & Co.

Koptic Court. Herbert D Kastle. LC 58-512411. 1958. Simon and Schuster.

Korean Conspiracy. Melford S. Weiss. 1978. pap. 1.95 (ISBN 0-532-19198-6). Woodhill.

Korean Tiger. Nick Carter. (Nick Carter Ser.). (O.s.i.). (Orig.). 1967. pap. 0.95 o.s.i. (AN1310, Award). Univ Pub & Dist.

Koren. Tim Lukeman. LC 79-7692. (Doubleday Science Fiction). 1981. 9.95 (ISBN 0-385-15239-6). Doubleday.

Korol, Dama, Valet. Vladimir Vladimirovich Nabokov. (Rus.). 1979. 15.00 (ISBN 0-88233-425-5); pap. 7.00 (ISBN 0-88233-426-3). Ardis Pubs.

Kosher Americans. Joseph D Rosenberg. LC 29-30553. 1929. Associated Publishers Company.

Koshopah. first ed. Phoebe Athey-Nater. 1972. 4.95. Vantage.

Kostia the Cossack: An Historical Novel. Petr Nikolaevich Krasnov. Tr. by Vitali, Olga. LC 30-27764. 1930. Duffield & Company.

Kosygin Is Coming. Tom Ardies. LC 73-82242. 1974. 6.95 (ISBN 0-385-08426-9). Doubleday.

Kotch. Katharine Topkins. LC 64-7872. bds., 4.50. McGraw.

Kothar & the Conjurer's Curse. Gardner F. Fox. (O.s.i.). (Orig.). 1970. pap. 0.75 o.s.i. (B75-2051). Belmont-Tower.

Kothar & the Demon Queen. Gardner F. Fox. 1974. pap. 0.75 o.p. (LB147SK). Leisure Bks.

Kothar & the Wizard Slayer. Gardner F. Fox. (Kothar Ser). (Orig.). 1970. pap. 0.75 o.p. (B75-2080). Belmont-Tower.

Kothar: Barbarian Swordsman. Gardner F. Fox. (Orig.). 1969. pap. 0.60 o.p. (B60-1003). Belmont-Tower.

Kothar-Barbarian Swordsman. Gardner F. Fox. 1974. pap. 0.75 o.p. (LB146SK). Leisure Bks.

Kothar of the Magic Sword. Gardner F. Fox. (Orig.). 1969. pap. 0.60 o.p. (B60-1043). Belmont-Tower.

Kotto. facs. ed. Lafcadio Hearn. LC 70-86144. (Short Story Index Reprint Ser.). 1902. 16.00 (ISBN 0-8369-3048-7). Ayer Co.

Kotto... Being Japanese Curios: With Sundry Cobwebs. Lafcadio Hearn. LC 2-25438. 1902. The Macmillan Company.

Kotto: Being Japanese Curios, with Sundry Cobwebs. Lafcadio Hearn. LC 78-172000. (Illus.). 1972. pap. 5.25 (ISBN 0-8048-1013-3). C E Tuttle.

Kowloon Contract. Philip Atlee. (Joe Gall). (Fawcett gold medal book: Vol. 19). 1974. (pbk.) 0.95. Fawcett.

Koyama's Diamond: A Novel of the Far Future. Adrian Berry. 1982. 11.95 (ISBN 0-533-04992-X). Vantage.

Kraal Baby: A Novel. Cynthia Stockley. LC 33-19399. 1933. Doubleday, Doran & Company, Inc.

Krakatit. Karel Capek. LC 74-16389. (Science Fiction). 1975. Arno Press.

Krakatit. Karel Capek & Hyde, Lawrence, 1800- Tr. 1925. The Macmillan Company.

Krakatoa, Hand of the Gods. H. E Raabe. LC 30-28401. 1930. Brewer and Warren Inc.

Kramer Girls. Ruth Suckow. LC 30-9308. 1930. A. A. Knopf.

Kramer Project. Robert A. Smith. LC 75-18858. 250p. 1976. 7.95 o.p. (ISBN 0-385-11451-6). Doubleday.

Kramer Versus Kramer: A Novel. Avery Corman. LC 77-5654. 7.95 (ISBN 0-394-41053-X). Randon House.

Kramer Versus Kramer: A Novel. Avery Corman. (Signet book). 1978. 2.50 (ISBN 0-451-08282-6). New American Library.

Kramer's War. Derek Robinson. LC 76-51776. 1977. 10.00 (ISBN 0-670-41516-2). Viking Press.

Krasnoe Derevo. Boris Pilnyak. 76p. (Orig., Rus.). 1980. pap. 3.00 (ISBN 0-88233-502-2). Ardis Pubs.

Krazy Kat. George Herriman. (Illus.). 165p. 1975. pap. 5.95 o.p. (ISBN 0-448-11951-X). G&D.

Krazy Kat & 76 More: Collected Stories, 1950-1976. Fielding Dawson. LC 82-14641. 1982. 14.00 (ISBN 0-87685-564-8) (ISBN 0-87685-565-6) (ISBN 0-87685-563-X). Black Sparrow Press.

Krazy Kat, The Unveiling & Other Stories. Fielding Dawson. LC 74-9270. 1969. Black Sparrow Press.

Kregel Reprint Library Series, 17 titles, 18 vols. Set. 243.00 o.p. (ISBN 0-8254-3035-6). Kregel.

Kremlin Conspiracy. Sean Flannery, pseud. 320p. 1982. pap. 2.75 (ISBN 0-441-45501-8, Pub. by Charter Bks). Ace Bks.

Kremlin Conspiracy. Sean Flannery, pseud. 288p. (Orig.). 1979. pap. 3.25 (ISBN 0-441-45502-6, Pub. by Charter Bks). Ace Bks.

Kremlin Letter. Noel Behn. LC 66-16149. 1966. Simon and Schuster.

Kremlin Watcher: A Novel of Suspense. Will Perry. LC 78-1428. 1978. 6.95 (ISBN 0-396-07529-0). Dodd, Mead.

Krestel. Lloyd Alexander. 256p. (gr. 5 up). 1982. 10.95 (ISBN 0-525-45110-2, 01063-320). Dutton.

Kreutzer Sonata. Lev Nikolaevich Tolstoi. LC 57-6499. (Modern library paperbacks, P29). 1957. Random House.

Kreutzer Sonata. Lev Nikolaevich Tolstoi. Tr. by Isai Kamen. pap. 1.65 o.p. (ISBN 0-394-70713-3, Vin, V713). Random.

Kreutzer Sonata. Lev Nikolaevich Tolstoi & Lyster, Frederic, Tr. LC 9-3450. (On cover: Pollard's popular publications. no. 1). 1890. The Pollard Publishing Company.

Kreutzer Sonata. Lev Nikolaevich Tolstoi & Tucker, Benjamin Ricketson, 1854- Tr. LC 12-37882. 1890. B. R. Tucker.

Kreutzer Sonata. Lev Nikolaevich Tolstoi & Tucker, Benjamin Ricketson, 1854- Tr. LC 4-356632. (On cover: The sunset series, no. 114). J. S. Ogilvie Publishing Company.

Kreutzer Sonata: And Other Stories. Lev Nikolaevich Tolstoi. LC 78-160951. (Short story index reprint series). 1971. (ISBN 0-8369-3930-1). Books for Libraries Press.

Kreutzer Sonata and Other Stories. Lev Nikolaevich Tolstoi & Maude, Aylmer, 1858-1938, Ed. (Half-title: The world's classics. CCLXVI). 1924. H. Milford, Oxford University Press.

Kreutzer Sonata, the Devil, & Other Tales. Lev Nikolaevich Tolstoi. (World's Classics Ser: No. 266). 5.95 o.p. (ISBN 0-19-250266-2). Oxford U Pr.

Kreutzman Formula. Virgil Scott & Dominic Koski. LC 74-119. 1974. 6.95 (ISBN 0-671-21737-2). Simon and Schuster.

Kriegie's Journey: A Novel of a Paratrooper in World War II. 1st Ed. Earl Hendricks. LC 54-90547. 1954. Exposition Press.

Kriegspiel: The War Game. Francis Hindes Groome. LC 9-8361. Ward, Lock & Bowden, Limited.

Krishna Fluting. John Berry. LC 59-137801. 1959. Macmillan.

Krishnakanta's Will. Translated from the Bengali by J. C. Ghosh. LC 62-12395. (Unesco collection of representative works: Indian series). 1962. New Directions.

Kristen's Passion. Sylvie F. Sommerfield. 1983. pap. 3.75 (ISBN 0-8217-1169-5). Zebra.

Kristiana Killers. Donald Quimby Burleigh. LC 37-16808. 1937. E. P. Dutton & Co., Inc.

Kristin Lavransdatter. Sigrid Undset. Tr. by Charles Archer. LC 47-38836. 1935. A. A. Knopf.

Kristin Lavransdatter I: The Bridal Wreath. Sigrid Undset. (gr. 10-12). 1978. pap. 2.25 (ISBN 0-553-14298-4). Bantam.

Kristin Lavransdatter II: The Mistress of Husaby. 1978. pap. 1.95 (ISBN 0-553-11030-6). Bantam.

Kristin Lavransdatter III: The Cross. (gr. 10-12). 1979. pap. 2.25 (ISBN 0-553-14299-2). Bantam.

Kristin Lavransdatter: The Bridal Wreath, The Mistress of Husaby, The Cross. Sigrid Undset. Tr. by Charles Archer. Scott, J. S., Tr. LC 29-13829. 1929. A. A. Knopf.

Kristin Lavransdatter: The Bridal Wreath. The Mistress of Husaby. The Cross. Sigrid Undset. Tr. by Charles Archer. Scott, J. S., Tr. LC 31-2977. 1930. A. A. Knopf.

Krokodil Tears. Nikolai Kavalerov. 1970. 3.75 o.p. Vantage.

Krom Zheltyi. Aldous Leonard Huxley. Tr. by G. Besserman from Eng. Orig. Title: Chrome Yellow. 190p. (Rus.). 1982. 14.50 (ISBN 0-88233-660-6); pap. 6.50 (ISBN 0-88233-661-4). Ardis Pubs.

Kronk: A Science Fiction Novel. Edmund Cooper. LC 78-147062. 1971. 4.95. Putnam.

Kronstadt: A Novel. Max Pemberton. LC 7-36378. 1898. D. Appleton and Company.

Krozair of Kregon. Alan Burt Akers. (Science Fiction Ser.). 1977. pap. 1.50 (ISBN 0-87997-288-2, UW1288). DAW Bks.

Kruitzner; or, The German's Tale. Harriet Lee. LC 16-19156. 1823. R. N. Henry.

Krull. Alan Dean Foster. 240p. 1983. pap. 2.95 (ISBN 0-446-30642-8). Warner Bks.
Krumnagel. Peter Ustinov. LC 77-160695. 1972. 1.25. New Amer. Lib.
Kryl'ia: Povest' V Trekh Chastiakh. Mikhail A. Kuzmin. (Rus.). 3.50 (ISBN 0-933884-05-2). Berkeley Slavic.
Kryptonite Kid: A Novel. Joseph Torchia. LC 79-1078. 7.95 (ISBN 0-03-046676-8). Holt, Rinehart and Winston.
Krystal Promise. Blaine M. Yorgason & Brenton G Yorgason. LC 81-69420. 4.95 (ISBN 0-88494-437-9). Bookcraft.
Ku Klux Ball: A Satire on the Younger Set. Glenn Gordon. LC 26-19262.
Ku-Klux Klan No. 40. A Novel. Thomas Jefferson Jerome. LC 7-9923. 1895. Edwards & Broughton, Printers.
Kubin's Dance of Death. Alfred Kubin. (Illus.). 7.50 (ISBN 0-8446-4766-7). Peter Smith.
Kubla Khan Caper: By Richard S. Prather. Richard S Prather. LC 66-26013. 1966. bds., 3.95. Trident.
Kubrik the Outlaw. Theodore Acland Harper & Harper, Winifred. LC 28-21742. 1928. Doubleday, Doran & Company, Inc.
Kubrik the Outlaw. Theodore Acland Harper & Harper, Winifred. LC 37-222202. (Young moderns bookshelf). 1937. The Sun Dial Press, Inc.
Kuchibue wo Fuku Toki see When I Whistle.
Kudjo Quatterman. Joseph Franklin Combs. LC 72-10368. (Illus.). 1972. (ISBN 0-8111-0471-0). Naylor Co.
Kukulcan. Terrazas Sanchez, Filiberto. LC 74-174411. 1974. 4.50 (ISBN 0-533-00495-0). Vantage Press.
Kulani & the Shama Thrush. Pierre Geauque. 1982. 5.00 (ISBN 0-87482-115-0). Wake-Brook.
Kuldesak. Richard Cowper, pseud. LC 72-76142. 216p. 1972. 5.95 o.p. (ISBN 0-385-00445-1). Doubleday.
Kullu and the Elephant. John Seymour Eyton. LC 29-168565. The Bobbs-Merrill Company.
Kullu of the Carts. John Seymour Eyton. LC 29-7395. The Bobbs-Merrill Company.
Kulubi. Edmund P Murray. LC 72-96658. 1973. 8.50 (ISBN 0-517-50423-5). Crown Publishers.
Kumanitu. 1974. pap. 2.50 (ISBN 0-916912-17-5, Bonewhistle Pr). Hellcoal Pr.
Kumari. William James De L'Aigle Buchan. LC 55-10061. 1955. Morrow.
Kummersdorf Connection. Eric Ramsey, pseud. LC 77-15853. 448p. 1978. pap. 3.50 (ISBN 0-86721-115-6). Playboy Pbks.
Kundu. Morris L West. LC 56-114977. (Dell first edition, A116). 1956. Dell Pub. Co.
Kundu. Morris L. West. LC 73-179647. 1973. 0.35 (ISBN 0-583-13028-3). Mayflower.
Kung of Nyae Nyae. Lorna Marshall. (Illus.). 416p. 1976. 22.50x (ISBN 0-674-50569-7). Harvard U Pr.
Kunnoo Sperits and Others. La Salle Corbell Pickett. LC 1-30923. (In de miz series, v. 1). 1900. The Neale Co.
Kurt Singer's Gothic Horror Book. Ed. by Kurt D. Singer. LC 74-196437. 1974. W. H. Allen.
Kutnar: Son of Pic. George Langford. LC 21-16539. (long ages ago series. v. 2). Boni and Liveright.
Kutzov Haul. Michael Kerr. LC 77-361326. 1976. 3.90 (ISBN 0-436-23312-6). Secker and Warburg.
Kuzneton, Babi Yar. A. Anatoli. 1977. pap. 3.95 (ISBN 0-671-81728-0). PB.
Kyle Contract. Donald MacKenzie. LC 75-120825. (Midnight novel of suspense). 1970. 4.95. Houghton Mifflin.
Kyoto in the Momoyama Period. Wendell Cole. (Centers of Civilization Ser.: No. 22). 1967. 3.95 o.p. (ISBN 0-8061-0748-0). U of Okla Pr.
Kyra Kyralina. Panait Istrati. LC 72-157777. (Short story index reprint series). 1971. (ISBN 0-8369-3889-5). Books for Libraries Press.
Kyra Kyralina. Panalt Istrati & Whitall, James Tr. LC 26-167085. 1926. A. A. Knopf.
Kyrik & the Lost Queen. Gardner F. Fox. 1976. pap. 1.25 o.p. (LB420ZK, Leisure Bks). Nordon Pubns.
Kyrik and the Lost Queen. Gardner F Fox. Leisure Books.
Kyrik & the Wizards Swords. Gardner F. Fox. (Orig.). 1976. pap. 1.25 o.p. (Leisure Bks). Nordon Pubns.
Kyrik Fights the Demon World. Gardner F. Fox. (Orig.). 1975. pap. 0.95 o.p. (LB284NK, Leisure Bks). Nordon Pubns.
Kyrik: Warlock Warrior. Gardner F. Fox. (Orig.). 1975. pap. 0.95 o.p. (LB252NK, Leisure Bks). Nordon Pubns.

L

L. A. & Others. Robert C. Frederiksen, Jr. 3.50 o.p. Vantage.
L. Baxter, Medicus. Knud Stouman. LC 42-7970. The Greystone Press, Inc.
L-One, L-Two, N, J, C. J J Sephoj. LC 76-154918. 1971. 6.95 (ISBN 0-394-47173-3). Knopf.
L. P. M.; the End of the Great War. John Stewart Barney. LC 15-15428. 1915. 1.35. G. P. Putnam's Sons.
La Aventura Equinocial De Lope De Aguirre, Antiepopeya. Ramon Jose Sender. LC 65-47741. 1965. 5.00. Las Americas.
La Bambolona. Alba De Cespedes. LC 76-101869. 1970. 6.50. Simon and Schuster.
La-Bas (Down There). Joris Karl Huysmans. LC 74-189352. 1972. (pbk) 2.50. Dover Publications.
La Belle Creole. M. P Green. (On cover: The Melbourne series, no. 14). 1893. E. A. Weeks & Company.
La Belle Edmee. Suzanne Prou. LC 77-3803. 8.95 (ISBN 0-06-013446-1). Harper & Row.
La Belle Lisa; or, The Paris Market Girls. Le Ventre De Paris. Emile Zola & Sherwood, Mrs. Mary (Neal) Tr. LC 9-1337. T. B. Peterson & Brothers.
La Belle-Nivernaise, and Other Stories. Alphonse Daudet. LC 77-130056. (Short story index reprint series). (Illus.). 1970. Books for Libraries Press.
La Belle-Nivernaise, and Other Stories. Alphonse Daudet. LC 6-33056. T. Y. Crowell & Co.
La Belle Sorel. Translated from the French by Richard and Clara Winston. Jacques Carton. LC 56-14201. 1956. I. Washburn.
La Belle Zoa: Or, the Insurrection of Hayti. Frances Hammond Pratt. LC 72-1820. (Black Heritage Library Collection). (Illus.). 1972. 8.50 (ISBN 0-8369-9049-8). Books for Libraries Press.
La Bete Humaine. Emile Zola. LC 77-379838. (Penguin classics). 1977. 3.95 (ISBN 0-14-044327-4). Penguin Books.
La Bete Humaine. The Human Animal. Emile Zola & Cox, Goerge D., Tr. LC 9-1336. T. B. Peterson & Brothers.
La Bodega (The Fruit of the Vine) A Novel. authorized american ed. Vicente Blasco Ibanez. Tr. by Isaac Goldberg. LC 19-10086. 1919. E. P. Dutton & Company.
La Boheme. Marie Coolidge-Rask & Puccini, Glacomo. LC 26-13346. Grosset & Dunlap.
La Casa Dorada. (Candlelight Regency special). 1978. 1.50 (ISBN 0-440-14617-8). Dell Pub. Co.
La Chamade. Francoise Sagan, pseud. 1974. (pbk.) 0.95. Popular Library.
La Chamade: By Francois Sagan. Tr. from French by Robert Westhoff. 1st Ed. Francoise Quoirez. LC 66-21294. 1966. bds., 3.95. Dutton.
La Chamade: By Francoise Sagan. Tr. from French by Robert Westhoff. Francoise Quoirez. (4610). 1967. Dell.
La Chance Mine Mystery. Susan Carleton Jones. LC 20-9277. 1920. Little, Brown, and Company.
La Chartreuse De Parme. Marie Henri Beyle. Tr. by Robins, E. P. LC 6-13109. 1895. G. H. Richmond & Co.
La Chingada. Jane Lewis Brandt. LC 79-4360. 12.95 (ISBN 0-07-007216-7). McGraw-Hill.
La Chingada. Jane Lewis Brandt. 1981. Pocket Books.
La Colmena. The Complete Novel Ed. with Notes and Vocabulary by Jose Ortega. Camilo Jose Cela. LC 66-31448. 1966. pap., 3.50. Las Americas.
La Comtesse. Joan Smith. (Fawcett Crest Book). 1978. 1.50 (ISBN 0-449-23490-8). Fawcett Books.
La Comtesse De Charny. Alexandre Dumas. LC 6-42836. 1890. Little, Brown and Company.
La Comtesse De Charny. Alexandre Dumas. LC 8-26655. 1894. Little, Brown and Company.
La Comtesse De Charny. Alexandre Dumas. LC 6-42832. (Half-title: The romances of Alexandre Dumas. Illustrated library ed. v. 34-37). 1894. Little, Brown and Company.
La Dame De Monsoreau. Alexandre Dumas & Maquet, Auguste. LC 6-42116. (Half-title: The Valois romances). 1889. Little, Brown and Company.
La Dame De Monsoreau. Alexandre Dumas & Maquet, Auguste. LC 4-17494. Little, Brown, & Company.
La Dame De Monsoreau. Alexandre Dumas & Maquet, Auguste. LC 6-42117. (Half-title: The romances of Alexandre Dumas. Illustrated library ed. v. 8-9). 1893. Little, Brown, and Company.
La Dame De Monsoreau. Alexandre Dumas & Maquet, Auguste. LC 8-26656. 1894. Little, Brown, and Company.
La Dame De Monsoreau. Alexandre Dumas & Maquet, Auguste. LC 5698. T. Y. Crowell & Co.
La Dame De Monsoreau. Alexandre Dumas & Auguste Maquet. LC 4563. T. Y. Crowell & Company.
La Dame De Monsoreau: Or, Chicot, the Jester. Being a Continuation of "Marguerite De Valois.". Alexandre Dumas & Maquet, Auguste. LC 6-42118. (On cover: Seaside library. Pocket ed. no. 2116). G. Munro's Sons.
La Dame De Sainte Hermine. Grace Elizabeth King. LC 24-7728. 1924. The Macmillan Company.
La Faustin. Edmond Louis Antoine Huot De Goncourt. LC 74-12379. (Series: The Lotus Library (London). 1974. 10.00. H. Fertig.
La Faustin. A Life Study. Edmond Louis Antoine Huot De Goncourt. Tr. by Sherwood, Mary (Neal) LC 6-43734. T. B. Peterson & Brothers.
La Femme 100 Tetes see Hundred Headless Woman.
La Fitte's Lieutenant. Prentiss Ingraham. The Arthur Westbrook Company.
La Gaviota: A Spanish Novel. Fernan Caballero. LC 6-2431. 1864. J. Bradburn.
La Golondrina (The Swallows) Interpreted and Written by Mabel J. Selby, from the Diary of Ralph Winston Written a Century Ago. Mabel Juanita Selby. LC 53-39591. 1952. Wetzel Pub. Co.
La Grande Florine. A Sequel to "The Stranglers.". Adolphe Belot. (Seaside library, v. 43, no. 876). G. Munro.
La Grande Florine: Sequel to "The Stranglers of Paris.". Adolphe Belot. Tr. by Cox, George D. LC 6-11683. T. B. Peterson & Brothers.
La Guerra: a Spanish Saga. Stephen Francis. LC 77-108661. 1970. 7.95. Delacorte Press.
La Hoya. Roberta Kalechofsky. LC 76-47292. (Illus.). 3.50 (ISBN 0-916288-03-X). Micah Publications.
La Maestra: A Novel. Mary Arkley Carter. LC 72-10289. 1973. 6.95 (ISBN 0-316-13044-3). Little, Brown.
La Maison De Rendez-Vous. Alain Robbe-Grillet. LC 66-19859. 1966. Grove Press.
La Mora: A Novel. Julia Markus. LC 75-33202. 4.95 (ISBN 0-916276-00-7). Decatur House Press.
La Nouvelle Femme. LC 7-203300. 1896. G. W. Dillingham.
La Parcelle 32. Ernest Perochon. Tr. by Fay, Frances C. LC 23-8241. George H. Doran Company.
La Petite Belle: Or The Life of an Adventurer. A Novel. LC 7-25486. 1877. Truair, Smith & Bruce, Printers.
La Quintrals. Magdelena Petit & Vargas Vila De Lee, Lulu, Tr. LC 42-24288. 1942. The Macmillan Company.
La Rhubarbe. Rene Victor Pilhes. LC 67-12887. 1969. 4.95. Doubleday.
La Rifa. Katia Saks. LC 68-28675. 1968. Morrow.
La Satyre. Virginie Des Rieux. LC 67-15222. 1967. World Pub. Co.
La Signora. Translated Form the Italian by Glauco Cambon. Elio Bartolini. LC 57-37111. (Lion book, LB163). 1957. Lion Books.
La Strega: And Other Stories. Louise De La Ramee. LC 72-101797. (Short story index reprint series). (Illus.). 1969. Books for Libraries Press.
La Terre. The Soil. Emile Zola & Cox, George D., Tr. LC 9-1303. T. B. Peterson & Brothers.
La Terre (The Soil) A Realistic Novel. Emile Zola & Chalmers, Edward Wharton, Ed. LC 9-1304. (pastime series v. 13). 1888. Laird & Lee.
La Tosca: A Novel. Arthur D Hall & Sardou, Victorien, 1831-1908. La Tosca. LC 7-326. 1888. Rand, McNally & Company.
La Tosca. Founded on the Famous Play of the Same Name. John Russell Coryell & Sardou, Victorien, 1831- (On cover: The sea and shore series, no. 10). 1889. Street & Smith.
La Vida es Sueno. Pedro Calderon De La Barca. Bd. with Alcalde de Zalamea; Magico Prodigioso. (Span.). pap. 1.95 o.s.i. French & Eur.
La Vie Passionnee of Rodney Buckthorne: A Tale of the Great American's Last Rally and Curious Death; a Novel, by R. V. Cassill. Robert Verlin Cassill. LC 68-16149. 1968. bds., 5.95. Geis.
La Vita Agra; It's a Hard Life: A Novel. Tr. from Italian by Eric Mosbacher. Luciano Bianciardi. LC 64-184824. bds., 3.95. Viking.
L.A. Woman. Eve Babitz. LC 81-20887. 12.95 (ISBN 0-671-42086-0). Linden Press/Simon & Schuster.
Laban's Will: A Novel. Albert Lebowitz. LC 66-10309. 1966. Random House.
L'abbe Constantin. Ludovic Halevy & Sullivan, Katherine, Tr. J. W. Lovell Company.
L'abbe Constantin. Ludovic Halevy & Sullivan, Katherine, Tr. LC 6-46213. (Lovell's library. v. 1, no. 15). 1882. J. W. Lovell Company.
Label My Love Lesbian. Marsha Alexander. (Orig.). 1969. pap. 1.75 o.p. (3051). Brandon.
LaBelle. Elizabeth Boatwright Coker. LC 59-7797. (O.s.i). 352p. 1976. pap. 1.95 o.s.i. (ISBN 0-89176-009-1, 6009). Mockingbird Bks.
Labels. Arthur Hamilton Gibbs. LC 26-15605. 1926. Little, Brown, and Company.
Labienus. F. K. Irvine. 1893. Olympic Publishing Company.
Labios Devoradores. new ed. Juan Castellanos. (Pimienta Collection Ser). (Illus.). 160p. (Span.). 1976. pap. 1.25 (ISBN 0-88473-246-0). Fiesta Pub.
Labor of Love. Barbara Roush. 1982. pap. 2.50 (ISBN 0-380-80879-X). Avon.
Labor: Or, The Money-God! Which! A Story of the Times. Charles Felton Pidgin. LC 8-14517. 1908. Mayhew Publishing Company.
Laborers Together. Bertha B. Moore McCurry. LC 52-4464. 1952. W. B. Eerdmans Pub. Co.
Labors of Hercules. Pietro Andrea De' Bassi. Tr. by William Kenneth Thompson. LC 76-142584. (Illus.). 1971. (ISBN 0-87636-020-7). Imprint Society.
Labors of Hercules. Agatha Miller Christie. 1975. (pbk.) 1.25. Dell.
Labors of Hercules: New Adventures in Crime. Agatha Miller Christie. LC 47-4481. 1947. Dodd, Mead.
Labors of Love. Robert Verlin Cassill. 288p. 1981. pap. 2.75 (ISBN 0-523-41552-4). Pinnacle Bks.
Labors of Love: A Novel. Robert Verlin Cassill. LC 79-56020. 10.95 (ISBN 0-87795-261-2). Arbor House.
Laboulaye's Fairy Book: Fairy Tales of All Nations. Edouard Rene Lefebvre De Laboulaye. Tr. by Mary Louise Booth. LC 44-11164. 1867. Harper & Brothers.
Labour Stands on Golden Foot. A Holiday Story, for Sensible Apprentices, Journeymen, and Masters. 4th ed., rev. ed. Heinrich Zschokke & Yeats, John, Tr. Cassell, Potter & Galpin.
Labours of Hercules. Agatha Miller Christie. (Greenway Edition). 1967. 8.95 (ISBN 0-396-05578-8). Dodd.
Labrador Days; Tales of the Sea Toilers. Wilfred Thomason Grenfell. LC 73-167451. (Short story index reprint series). (Illus.). 1971. (ISBN 0-8369-3977-8). Books for Libraries Press.
Labrador Days: Tales of the Sea Toilers. Wilfred Thomason Grenfell. LC 19-7919. 1919. Houghton Mifflin Company.
Labrador Nurse. William Edward Daniel Ross. LC 68-3406. 1968. Arcadia House.
LaBreeska. LaBreeska Hemphill. LC 75-42869. (Illus., Orig.). 1976. pap. 2.98 (ISBN 0-9600948-1-4). The Hemphills.
Labyrinth. Nicholas Brady. (Belmont Tower Books). 1.95. Tower Publications.
Labyrinth. Thomas William Duncan. LC 67-11176. 1967. Doubleday.
Labyrinth. Aaron Fletcher. 1977. pap. 1.95 o.s.i. (ISBN 0-505-51121-5, BT51121). Tower Bks.
Labyrinth. Stanton Forbes, pseud. Orig. Title: Go to Thy Deathbed. 1972. pap. 0.75 o.p. (T2610). Pyramid Pubns.
Labyrinth. Helen Rose Hull. LC 23-13891. 1923. The Macmillan Company.
Labyrinth. Bill Pronzini. LC 79-22856. 8.95 (ISBN 0-312-46352-9). St. Martin's Press.
Labyrinth. Eugene M. Propper & Taylor Branch. 656p. 1983. pap. 6.95 (ISBN 0-14-006683-7). Penguin.
Labyrinth. Cecil Roberts. LC 44-491854. 1944. Doubleday, Doran & Co., Inc.
Labyrinth. Ina Seidel Siedel & Williams Oakley, Tr. LC 32-29014. 1932. Farrar & Rinehart, Incorporated.
Labyrinth. Diane Stevens. LC 76-2821. 1976. 5.95 (ISBN 0-385-12201-2). Doubleday.
Labyrinth: A Novel. Gertrude Diamant. LC 29-771724. 1929. Coward-McCann, Inc.
Labyrinth: A Novel. Mackenzie-Lamb, Eric. LC 78-11875. 1979. 8.95 (ISBN 0-688-03422-5). Morrow.
Labyrinth Makers. Anthony Price. LC 74-150913. 1971. 4.95. Published for the Crime Club by Doubleday.
Labyrinth of Life. Edward Abram Uffington Valentine. LC 13-788648. 1912. E. P. Dutton & Company.
Labyrinth of Love. Louis Untermeyer. (O.S.I.). (Illus.). 1965. 2.50 o.s.i. (ISBN 0-671-40290-0). S&S.
Labyrinth of Silence. David S. Viscott. LC 71-116117. 1970. 5.95. Norton.
Labyrinthine Ways. Graham Greene. 1940. The Viking Press.
Labyrinths, Selected Stories & Other Writings. Jorge Luis Borges. Ed. by Donald A. Yates & James E. Irby. LC 64-25440. (Fr). 1969. pap. 4.95 (ISBN 0-8112-0012-4, NDP186). New Directions.
Lace: A Berlin Romance. Paul Lindau. LC 7-19019. (On cover: Appletons' town and country library. no. 30). 1889. D. Appleton and Company.

Lace, a Novel. Shirley Conran. LC 82-5741. 16.95 (ISBN 0-671-44662-2). Simon and Schuster.

Lace & a Bobbitt. Curt Johnson. Ed. by John Bennett. LC 76-51903. 1976. pap. 2.50 (ISBN 0-912824-15-8). Vagabond Pr.

Lace Curtain. Ellin Mackay Berlin. LC 48-7283. 1948. Doubleday.

Lace for Milady. Joan Smith. LC 80-51155. 1980. 11.95 (ISBN 0-8027-0659-2). Walker.

Lace for Milady. Joan Smith. LC 81-137. 1981. 12.95 (ISBN 0-8161-3182-1). G.K. Hall.

Lacemaker Lekholm Has an Idea. Gustaf Hellstrom & Lyon, F. H., Tr. LC 31-369351. 1931. L. MacVeagh, The Dial Press.

Lacey. Lorinda Hagen. (Belmont Tower Book). 1977. 1.95 (ISBN 0-505-51209-2). Tower Pubns.

Lacey. Claudette Williams. 1979. pap. 1.75 (ISBN 0-449-50007-1, Coventry). Fawcett.

Lachlan's Woman. Dwyer-Joyce, Alice. LC 78-19863. 1979. 7.95 (ISBN 0-312-46359-6). St. Martin's Press.

Lachmi Bai Rani of Jhansi, the Jeanne D'Arc of India. Michael White. 1901. J. F. Taylor & Company.

Lackawanna Elegy. Yvan Goll. Tr. by Galaway Kinnell. 1970. o. p. 7.50 (ISBN 0-912090-07-3); pap. 2.45 (ISBN 0-912090-06-5). Sumac Mich.

Laconia: Or, Legends of the White Mountains and Merry Meeting Bay. Isaac W Scribner. LC 14-22467. 1856. Borton, Kelley & Brother.

Lacquer Lady. Fryniwyd Tennyson Jesse. LC 30-26050. 1930. The Macmillan Company.

Lacquer Lady. Fryniwyd Tennyson Jesse. LC 80-28516. (Virago Modern Classic). 1981. 5.95 (ISBN 0-8037-4704-7). Dial Press.

Lacquer Screen. Robert V. Bulik. Ed. by J. Barzun & W. H. Taylor. LC 81-47391. (Crime Fiction 1950-1975 Ser.). 182p. 1981. lib. bdg. 14.95 (ISBN 0-8240-4951-9). Garland Pub.

Lacquer Screen. Robert Hans Van Gulik, pseud. LC 81-47391. (Fifty Classics of Crime Fiction, 1950-1975). 1982. 14.95 (ISBN 0-8240-4951-9). Garland Pub.

Lacquer Screen. Robert Van Gulik. 1982. 3.50 (ISBN 0-434-82560-3, Pub. by Heinemann). David & Charles.

Lacquer Screen. Robert Van Gulik. 1970. 3.95 o.p. (ISBN 0-684-10615-9). Scribner.

Lacquer Screen: A Chinese Dectective Story. Robert Hans Van Gulik, pseud. (Illus.). 1974. (pbk.) 0.95. Warner Paperback Library.

Lacquer Screen: A Chinese Detective Story. Robert Hans Van Gulik, pseud. LC 76-85257. (His New Judge Dee mysteries). (Illus.). 1970. 3.95. Scribner.

Lacquer Screen: A Judge Dee Mystery. Robert Van Gulik. 192p. 1982. pap. 2.95 (ISBN 0-684-17633-5, ScribT). Scribner.

Lacy Diamonds. A Novel. George James Atkinson Coulson. LC 11-7146. (The "Odd trump" series of novels). 1875. E. J. Hale & Son.

Lacy Wisps. Evelyn G. Penman. 1973. 2.95 o.p. (ISBN 0-8059-1922-8). Dorrance.

Lad and the Lion. Edgar Rice Burroughs. LC 64-15791. (Illus.). 1964. Canaveral Press.

Lad and the Lion. Edgar Rice Burroughs. LC 38-757910. E. R. Burroughs, Inc.

Lad and the Lion. Edgar Rice Burroughs. 1974. (pbk.) 0.95. Ace Books.

Lad of Kent. Herbert Harrison. LC 14-11801. 1914. The Macmillan Company.

Lad of the O'Friels. Seumas MacManus. LC 3-7164. 1903. McClure, Phillips & Co.

Ladder of Death: An Anthony Bathurst Story. Brian Flynn. LC 35-4873. 1935. Macrae-Smith Company.

Ladder of Folly. Muriel Hine Coxon. LC 29-7956. 1929. D. Appleton & Company.

Ladder of Fortune. Frances Courtenay Baylor Barnum. LC 99-1259. 1899. Houghton, Mifflin & Co.

Ladder of Love. Paul B. Newman. pap. 2.50 o.p. (ISBN 0-912292-15-6). Horizon.

Ladder of Love. Paul B. Newman. pap. 10.00 ltd. ed. o.p. The Smith.

Ladder of Promise. Susan M Griffith. LC 491. The Presbyterian Coummittee of Publication.

Ladder of Swords: A Tale of Love, Laughter and Tears. Gilbert Parker. LC 4-22674. 1904. Harper & Brothers.

Ladder: The Story of a Casual Man. Philip Everett Curtiss. LC 15-4666. 1915. 1.30. Harper & Brothers.

Ladder to the Stars. Jane Helen Findlater. 1906. D. Appleton and Company.

Ladders to Fire. Anais Nin. LC 66-6834. 3.50, 1.45 pap.,. Swallow.

Ladders to Fire. Anais Nin. LC 46-7091. 1946. E. P. Dutton & Company, Inc.

Laddie. Gene Stratton Porter. Repr. lib. bdg. 26.90x (ISBN 0-89190-933-8). Am Repr-Rivercity Pr.

Laddie. Evelyn Whitaker. LC 31-35228. 1894. T. Y. Crowell & Co.

Laddie. Evelyn Whitaker. (Altemus' good times series). Henry Altemus Company.

Laddie. Evelyn Whitaker. LC 43-434008. 1892. E. P. Dutton & Company.

Laddie: A True Blue Story. Gene Stratton Porter. LC 13-17971. 1913. Doubleday, Page & Company.

Laddie: A True Blue Story. Gene Stratton Porter. LC 20-15599. 1917. Grosset & Dunlap.

Laddie: A True Blue Story. Gene Stratton-Porter. 1974. Repr. of 1909 ed. lib. bdg. 25.00 (ISBN 0-8414-7979-8). Folcroft.

Ladies. Stanley Hopkins. LC 33-25691. 1933. Harper & Brothers.

Ladies!" A Shining Constellation of Wit and Beauty. Lily Moresby Adams Beck. LC 71-156612. (Essay index reprint series). (Illus.). 1971. (ISBN 0-8369-2268-9). Books for Libraries Press.

Ladies Advocate (Anonymous). LC 74-17032. (Flowering of the Novel). 1974. (ISBN 0-8240-1126-0). Garland Pub.

Ladies Advocate; or, Wit & Beauty a Match for Treachery & Inconstancy, 1749. Ed. by Michael F. Shugrue. (Novel in England 1700-1775 Ser.). 1974. lib. bdg. 50.00 (ISBN 0-8240-1126-0). Garland Pub.

Ladies and Gentlemen. Irvin Shrewsbury Cobb. LC 70-106266. (Short story index reprint series). 1970. Books for Libraries Press.

Ladies and Gentlemen. Irvin Shrewsbury Cobb. 1927. Cosmopolitan Book Company.

Ladies and Gentlemen: A Parcel of Reconsiderations. James Branch Cabell. LC 34-34569. 1934. R. M. McBride & Company.

Ladies & Gentlemen in Victorian Fiction. E. M. Delafield. (English Literature Ser., No. 33). 1974. lib. bdg. 27.95 o.p. (ISBN 0-8383-1842-8). Haskell.

Ladies and Gents. Vera Caspary. LC 29-17042. 2.00. The Century Co.

Ladies Bane. Patricia Wentworth. 1976. Repr. of 1952 ed. lib. bdg. 14.10x (ISBN 0-88411-737-5). Amereon Ltd.

Ladies Bane. 1st Ed. Patricia Wentworth. LC 52-7470. (Her A Miss Silver mystery). 1952. Lippincott.

Ladies C. O. D. Carrie Louis Shaw Seabury. LC 32-490718. W. Godwin, Inc.

Ladies' Choice. Ed. by Mavis Patterson. LC 82-5533. (Illus.). 96p. (Orig.). 1982. pap. 3.95 (ISBN 0-89621-066-9). Thorndike Pr.

Ladies' Close. Sarah Kilpatrick. LC 68-11794. 1968. Doubleday.

Ladies' Day. Elizabeth Frances Corbett. LC 68-28719. 1968. 4.95 o.p. (ISBN 0-696-67843-8). Hawthorn.

Ladies Day. Chard Powers Smith. 1941. C. Scribner's Sons.

Ladies' Day see This Crowded Earth.

Ladies' Day: A Novel. Elizabeth Frances Corbett. LC 68-28719. 1968. 4.95. Meredith Press.

Ladies' Delight. Emile Zola. LC 58-8013. 1958. Abelard-Schuman.

Ladies First!" A Novel. Dominique Francois Verdenal. (On cover: The welcome series, no. 6). 1896. The Home Publishing Company.

Ladies from Hell. Leslie T. White. 272p. 1974. pap. 1.50 (ISBN 0-532-15142-9). Woodhill.

Ladies' Gallery: A Novel. Justin McCarthy & Praed, Rosa Caroline (Murray-Prior) "Mrs. Campbell Praed," 1851- Joint Author. (On cover: Appletons' town and country library no. 26). 1895. D. Appleton and Company.

Ladies Go Masked. Margaret Widdemer. LC 39-8472. Farrar & Rinehart, Inc.

Ladies in Boxes. Gelett Burgess. 1942. Alliance Book Corporation.

Ladies in Hades: A Story of Hell's Smart Set. Frederic Arnold Kummer. LC 28-10096. J. H. Sears & Company, Inc.

Ladies in Love. Laszlo Bus Fekete & Katona, Victor, Tr. LC 37-846. E. P. Dutton & Co., Inc.

Ladies in the Parlor. Jim Tully. LC 35-985657. Greenberg.

Ladies in Waiting. Rian James. LC 34-3716. A. H. King.

Ladies in Waiting. Kate Douglas Smith Wiggin. LC 19-15559. 1919. Houghton Mifflin Company.

Ladies in Waiting: A Novel. Gwen Davis. LC 78-26192. 10.95 (ISBN 0-02-529850-X). Macmillan.

Ladies Juggernaut: A Novel. Archibald Clavering Gunter. LC 6-46699. 1895. The Home Publishing Co.

Ladies Lindores. Margaret Oliphant Wilson Oliphant. (Seaside library, v. 81, no. 1647). 1883. G. Munro.

Ladies Lindores. A Novel. Margaret Oliphant Wilson Oliphant. (Harper's Franklin square library, no. 313). 1883. Harper & Brothers.

Ladies Lindores. A Novel. Margaret Oliphant Wilson Oliphant. (On cover: Lovell's library, v. 3, no. 124). 1883. J. W. Lovell Company.

Ladies' Man. Hughes, Rupert. LC 30-12294. 1930. Harper & Brothers.

Ladies' Man. Richard Price. LC 78-17506. 1978. 8.95 (ISBN 0-395-27082-0). Houghton Mifflin.

Ladies Must Live. Alice Duer Miller. LC 17-244029. 1917. The Century Co.

Ladies of Chance. Davis Dresser. LC 36-35999. 1936. Godwin.

Ladies of Hanover Square. Rona Randall. LC 81-733. 12.95 (ISBN 0-698-11067-6). Coward, McCann & Geoghegan.

Ladies of Horror: Two Centuries of Supernatural Stories by the Gentle Sex. Ed. by Seon Manley. LC 77-148485. (Illus.). 1971. 5.95. Lothrop, Lee & Shepard Co.

Ladies of Levittown. Eugene Horowitz. 352p. 1981. pap. 2.95 (ISBN 0-449-24401-6, Crest). Fawcett.

Ladies of Levittown: A Novel. Eugene Horowitz. LC 79-24074. 11.95 (ISBN 0-399-90076-4). R. Marek.

Ladies of Locksley. Francis Vivian, pseud. LC 57-719038. 1957. Roy Publishers.

Ladies of Lyndon. Margaret Kennedy. LC 82-1443. (Virago Modern Classic). 1982. 7.95 (ISBN 0-385-27227-8). Dial Press.

Ladies of Pleasure. M. Von Luber. pap. 1.95 o.p. (6036). Brandon.

Ladies of St. Hedwig's. Martha Edith Almedingen. LC 67-26412. 1967. Vanguard Press.

Ladies of the Afternoon. Anita M. Fleagles. (Orig.). 1973. pap. 0.95 o.p. Curtis.

Ladies of the Evening. Milton Herbert Gropper. LC 31-20304. Greenberg.

Ladies of the Gothics: Tales of Romance and Terror by the Gentle Sex. Seon Manley & Gogo Lewis. LC 75-12879. 1975. 6.95 (ISBN 0-688-41715-9) (ISBN 0-688-51715-3). Lothrop, Lee & Shepard Co.

Ladies of the Rachmanioff Eyes. Henry Van Dyke. LC 65-10975. 1965. Farrar, Straus and Giroux.

Ladies of the Tang, Twenty-Two Classical Chinese Stories. E. Wang. (Illus.). 1966. pap. 2.50x o.p. Paragon.

Ladies of the T'ang: 22 Classical Chinese Stories. Elizabeth Te-Chen Wang. 350p. 1973. 10.00 (ISBN 0-89955-181-5, Pub. by Mei Ya China). Intl Schol Bk Serv.

Ladies of the Valley. Herbert D. Kastle. LC 78-73874. 1979. 10.95 (ISBN 0-87795-228-0). Arbor Hse.

Ladies of the Valley: A Novel. Herbert D Hastle. LC 78-73874. 10.95 (ISBN 0-87795-228-0). Arrbor House.

Ladies on the Loose. Peter Shelley, pseud. LC 35-940. W. Godwin, Inc.

Ladies' Paradise: Or, The Bonheur Des Dames. Emile Zola & Sherwood, Mrs. Mary (Neal) Tr. LC 12-40389. T. B. Peterson & Brothers.

Ladies Under Glass: A Novel. James Mandeville Neville. LC 38-3525. J. B. Lippincott Company.

Ladies Who Knit for a Living. Anthony E. Stockanes. LC 81-7421. (Illinois Short Fiction Ser.). 140p. 1981. 11.95 (ISBN 0-252-00904-5); pap. 4.95 (ISBN 0-252-00927-4). U of Ill Pr.

Ladies Who Knit for a Living: Stories. Anthony E. Stockanes. LC 81-7421. (Illinois Short Fiction). 11.95 (ISBN 0-252-00904-5) (ISBN 0-252-00927-4). University of Illinois Press.

Ladies Whose Bright Eyes. Ford Madox Ford. LC 35-6459. 1935. J. B. Lippincott Company.

Ladies with a Unicorn: A Novel. Monica Stirling. LC 53-10817. 1954. Simon and Schuster.

Ladies Won't Wait. Peter Cheyney. LC 51-11324. (Red badge detective). 1951. Dodd, Mead.

Ladle-Shaped Woman: A Story. Alice Rogoff & Nina Gaby Christina. LC 75-325679. (Illus.). 1975. Cassandra Publications.

Lad's Love. Arlo Bates. LC 6-9086. 1887. Roberts Brothers.

Lads' Love. Samuel Rutherford Crockett. LC 6-31595. 1897. D. Appleton and Company.

Lady. Anne Lambton. 352p. (Orig.). 1981. pap. 2.75 (ISBN 0-515-05532-8). Jove Pubns.

Lady. Thomas Tryon. LC 75-8663. 1975. 15.95 (ISBN 0-8161-6287-5). G. K. Hall.

Lady. Thomas Tryon. (Fawcett crest book). 1975. (pbk.) 1.95. Fawcett Publications.

Lady: A Novel. Thomas Tryon. LC 74-7748. 1974. 7.95 (ISBN 0-394-49093-2). Knopf; Distributed by Random House.

Lady Adelaide's Oath: Or, The Castle's Heir. Ellen Price Henry Wood Wood. (On cover: Seaside library. Pocket ed. no. 1001). 1887. G. Munro.

Lady Afraid. Lester Dent. LC 48-584142. 1948. Pub. for the Crime Club by Doubleday.

Lady Aft. Richard Matthews Hallet. LC 15-16895. Small, Maynard and Company.

Lady Agatha. Olive Katharine Parr. LC 22-2221. 1922. Longmans, Green and Co.

Lady Alice Lisle: The Last of the English Martyrs. Sarah Towne Martyn. LC 7-17815. American Tract Society.

Lady Alone. Peggy O'More, pseud. LC 53-7036. 1953. Arcadia House.

Lady and Her Doctor: By Evelyn Piper Pseud. 1st Ed. Merriam Modell. LC 56-6049. 1956. Harper.

Lady and Her Husband. Amber Reeves, pseud. LC 14-7728. 1914. G. P. Putnam's Sons.

Lady and Her Tree: A Story of Society. Charles Stokes Wayne. LC 8-367554. The Vortex Company.

Lady and Sada San: A Sequel to The Lady of the Decoration. Fannie Macaulay. LC 12-25461. 1912. The Century Co.

Lady and the Corsair. James Maurice Scott. LC 57-8988. 1958. Dutton.

Lady and the Deep Blue Sea. Garland Roark. LC 58-5659. 1958. Doubleday.

Lady and the Giant. Clarence Budington Kelland. LC 59-12154. 1959. Dodd, Mead.

Lady and the Ladder. Harrison Garfield Rhodes. LC 6-51365. 1906. Doubleday, Page & Company.

Lady and the Looking Glass. Frances Mallory Wykes. LC 55-136042. 1955. Macmillan.

Lady and the Mute. John St. Clair Muriel. LC 32-4340. W. Morrow & Co.

Lady and the Pirate: Being the Plain Tale of a Diligent Pirate and a Fair Captive. Emerson Hough. LC 13-167885. The Bobbs-Merrill Company.

Lady and the Sun. Elizabeth Dockman. LC 54-7542. 1954. Newman Press.

Lady and the Travelling Salesman: Stories. Leo Simpson. LC 76-383012. (Series: Canadian Short Stories Series.). (Canadian short story library). 1976. (ISBN 0-7766-4337-1). University of Ottawa Press.

Lady Ann. Donald Henderson Clarke. The Vanguard Press.

Lady Ann... Donald Henderson Clarke. LC 47-21835. (On cover: New Avon library. 105). 1946.

Lady Anna. Anthony Trollope. LC 37-27020. (Half-title: The world's classics, 443). 1936. H. Milford, Oxford University Press.

Lady Ashleigh: Or, The Rejected Inheritance. John Frederick Smith. LC 21-15373. (Seaside library, v. 81, no. 1631). 1883. G. Munro.

Lady Athlyne. Bram Stoker. LC 42-31840. 1906. P. R. Reynolds.

Lady Audley's Secret. M. E. Braddon. (Illus.). 320p. 1974. pap. 4.50 (ISBN 0-486-23011-2). Dover.

Lady Audley's Secret. Mary Elizabeth Braddon Maxwell. LC 73-90527. 1974. (pbk.) 3.00 (ISBN 0-486-23011-2). Dover Publications.

Lady Audley's Secret. 3d ed. Mary Elizabeth Braddon Maxwell. (Seaside library. v. 13, no. 251). 1878. G. Munro.

Lady Audley's Secret. Mary Elizabeth Braddon Maxwell. (On cover: Lovell's library. no. 104). 1883. J. W. Lovell Company.

Lady Audley's Secret. Mary Elizabeth Braddon Maxwell. (On cover: Seaside library. Pocket ed. no. 35). 1883. G. Munro.

Lady Audley's Secret. A Novel. Mary Elizabeth Braddon Maxwell. 1863. Dick & Fitzgerald.

Lady Avis Trewithen: A Romance of Dartmoor. Olive Katharine Parr. LC 22-24228. 1922. 2.00. Longmans, Green and Co.

Lady Baby: A Novel. Dorothea Gerard Longard De Longgarde. LC 7-15156. (On cover: Harper's Franklin square library. no. 668). 1890. Harper & Brothers.

Lady Bachelor. Harlan Page Halsey. (On cover: Parlor car series, no. 3). The Parlor Car Publishing Co.

Lady Baltimore. Owen Wister. LC 68-20024. (Americans in Fiction). (Illus.). 1968. Gregg Press.

Lady Baltimore. Owen Wister. LC 6-10312. 1906. The Macmillan Company.

Lady Baltimore. Owen Wister & Bailey, Vernon Howe, 1874- Illus. LC 21-8677. 1921. The Macmillan Company.

Lady Barbarina. Henry James. Bd. with Siege of London; International Episode; Pension Beaurepas; Bundle of Letters; Point of View. LC 73-158793. (Novels & Tales of Henry James: Vol. 14). xxi, 606p. Repr. of 1908 ed. 27.50x (ISBN 0-678-02814-1). Kelley.

Lady Barbarina & Other Stories. Henry James. 1908. 7.50 o.p. Scribner.

Lady Barbarina & Other Tales of Henry James. Henry James. 1961. pap. 2.25 o.p. (ISBN 0-448-00116-0, UL). G&D.

Lady Barberina & Other Tales. Henry James. Ed. by Herbert Ruhm. LC 62-51791. 8.95 o.s.i. (ISBN 0-8149-0126-3). Vanguard.

Lady Barberina, and Other Tales: Benvolic, Glasses, and Three Essays. With Variants, Notes, Introd., and Bibliography by Herbert Ruhm. 1st Ed. Henry James. LC 62-2072. (Universal library, UL116). 1961. Grosset & Dunlap.

Lady, Be Bad. Davis Dresser. (Mike Shayne mystery). 1974. (pbk.) 0.75. Dell.

Lady, Be Careful. Christopher Reeve. LC 50-5975. 1950. Mill.

Lady Be Good. Katharine Dunlap. LC 38-27620. 1938. W. Morrow and Company.

Lady Bell. A Story of Last Century. Henrietta Keddie. (Seaside library, v. 48, no. 977). G. Munro.

Lady Bell. A Story of the Last Century. Henrietta Keddie. LC 7-11417. 1884. H. A. Summer & Company.

Lady Betty Across the Water. Charles Norris Williamson & Williamson, Mrs. Alice Muriel (Livingston) 1869-1933, Joint Author. 1906. McClure, Phillips & Co.

Lady Betty Across the Water. Charles Norris Williamson & Alice Muriel Livingston Williamson. LC 13-235887. 1912. McClure, Phillips & Co.

Lady Betty's Governess: Or, The Corbet Chronicles. Lucy Ellen Guernsey. LC 7-148. 1872. T. Whittaker.

Lady Beware. Peter Arnold. LC 72-96271. 216p. 1974. 5.95 o.p. (ISBN 0-385-00951-8). Doubleday.

Lady, Beware. Peter Cheyney. LC 50-9275. (Red badge detective). 1950. Dodd, Mead.

Lady-Bird. A Tale. Georgiana Charlotte Leveson-Gower Fullerton. LC 42-26805. 1866. J. Murphy & Co.

Lady Blake's Love Letters. The Theme from Which Owen Meredith Took His Famous Poem of "Lucile"... George Sand & McCarty, Page, Tr. LC 6-34604. 1884. G. W. Carlton & Co.; Etc., Etc.

Lady Blanche Farm. Frances Parkinson Wheeler Keyes. 1969. pap. 0.75 o.p. (64-186). Paperback Lib.

Lady Blanche Farm. Frances Parkinson Wheeler Keyes. 272p. 1975. pap. 1.50 o.p. (532-15154-150). Manor Bks.

Lady Blanche Farm: A Romance of the Commonplace. Frances Parkinson Wheeler Keyes. LC 31-25221. H. Liveright, Inc.

Lady Blanche Farm, and Queen Anne's Lace: Two Full-Length Novels. One Volume Ed. Frances Parkinson Wheeler Keyes. LC 52-1038. 1952. Liveright.

Lady Blanche's Salon. A Story of Some Souls. Lloyd Stephens Bryce. F. T. Neely.

Lady Blanche's Salon: A Story of Some Souls. 2d ed. Lloyd Stephens Bryce. LC 3424. 1900. Harper & Brothers.

Lady Bliss. Maggie MacKeever. 1979. pap. 1.75 (ISBN 0-449-50010-1, Coventry). Fawcett.

Lady Blue. Florence Stevenson. LC 80-10755. 1980. 9.95 (ISBN 0-89340-253-2). J. Curley.

Lady Bluebeard: A Novel. Henry Curwen. LC 7-14177. (On cover: Harper's Franklin square library. no. 642). 1889. Harper & Brothers.

Lady Bobs, Her Brother, and I: A Romance of the Azores. Jean Chamblin. 1905. G. P. Putnam's Sons.

Lady Bonnie's Experiment. Tighe Hopkins. LC 7-52450. (Buckram series). 1895. H. Holt and Company.

Lady Bought with Rifles. Dorothy Jeanne Williams. LC 76-9842. 8.95 (ISBN 0-698-10745-4). Coward, McCann & Geoghegan.

Lady Bought with Rifles. Dorothy Jeanne Williams. (Kangaroo Book). 1977. 1.95 (ISBN 0-671-81235-1). Pocket Books.

Lady Bountiful. James Owen Hannay. LC 22-893878. George H. Doran Company.

Lady Branksmere. Margaret Wolfe Hungerford. (On cover: The seaside library. Pocket ed., no. 733). 1886. G. Munro.

Lady Buyer. Ruth Seinfel. LC 33-10595. 1933. Covici-Friede.

Lady by Change. Charles Green Shaw. LC 82-3295. The Macaulay Company.

Lady by Degrees. Edward L Delaney. LC 34-7419. The Reilly & Lee Co.

Lady by Marriage. Elizabeth Carfrae, pseud. LC 35-875114. G. P. Putnam's Sons.

Lady Byron Vindicated. Harriet Elizabeth Beecher Stowe. 1973. Repr. of 1870 ed. 13.50 o.p. R West.

Lady Can Do. Samuel Merwin. LC 29-22430. 1929. Houghton Mifflin Company.

Lady Car; the Sequel of a Life. Margaret Oliphant Wilson Oliphant. (On cover: Harper's Franklin square library, no. 657). 1889. Harper & Brothers.

Lady Carmichael's Will: And Other Christmas Stories. Mary Cecil Hay & Robinson, Frederick William, 1830-1901. LC 7-3759. (On cover: Harper's half-hour series. no. 89). 1879. Harper & Brothers.

Lady Caroline's Folly. Eva McDonald. Orig. Title: Lord Byron's Love. 1973. pap. 0.75 o.p. (07267). Curtis.

Lady Cassandra. Jessie Bell Vaizey. LC 14-13260. 1914. G. P. Putnam's Sons.

Lady Castlemaine's Divorce. By Bertha M. Clay Pseud.... Charlotte Mary Brame. (On cover: Lovell's library, v. 19, no. 923). J. W. Lovell Company.

Lady Castlemaine's Divorce; or, Put Asunder. Charlotte Mary Brame. LC 4666. (On cover: Bertha Clay library, no. 17). 1900. Street & Smith.

Lady Cavaliers. Andrea Lee. 1979. pap. 2.50 (ISBN 0-440-04807-9). Dell.

Lady Charlotte: A Novel. Adeline Sergeant. 1897. Rand, McNally & Company.

Lady Charlotte's Rune. Judith Harkness. 1982. pap. 2.25 (ISBN 0-451-11738-7, AE1738, Sig). NAL.

Lady Chatterley's Husbands: An Anonymous Sequel to the Celebrated Novel, Lady Chatterley's Lover. Samuel Roth. LC 31-317421. 1931. W. Faro, Inc.

Lady Chatterley's Lover. 2nd ed. / with an introduction by richard hoggart. ed. David Herbert Lawrence. LC 74-193801. 1973. 0.40 (ISBN 0-14-001484-5). Penguin.

Lady Chatterley's Lover. David Herbert Lawrence. LC 38-17283. Nesor Publishing Co.

Lady Chatterley's Lover. David Herbert Lawrence. LC 32-104527. (Modern amatory classics. no. 1). 1930. W. Faro, Inc.

Lady Chatterley's Second Husband. Jehanne D' Orliac. Tr. by Wells, Warre Bradley. LC 35-84689. R. M. McBride & Company.

Lady Chatterley's Second Lover: 2nd Other Erotica. rev. ed. Ted Mark, pseud. 1976. pap. 1.95 (ISBN 0-532-19115-3). Woodhill.

Lady Cicely. Sandra Wilson. LC 77-3660. 1977. 7.95 (ISBN 0-89340-068-8). John Curley.

Lady Cicely: The Story of Cicely Plantagenet. Sandra Wilson. LC 74-81467. 1974. 6.95. St. Martin's Press.

Lady Clara De Vere. A Story. Friedrich Spielhagen. LC 8-14064. (Appletons' new handy-volume series v. 67). 1881. D. Appleton and Company.

Lady Connie. Mary Augusta Arnold Humphry Ward Ward. LC 16-210515. 1916. Hearst's International Library Co.

Lady Corrigan's Love Match. Charles Stuart Welles. LC 17-235484. 1917. Fowler & Co.

Lady Damer's Secret. Charlotte Mary Brame. LC 4667. (Bertha Clay library, no. 15). 1900. Street & Smith.

Lady Damer's Secret: A Novel. Charlotte Mary Brame. (On cover: Lovell's library. v. 14, no. 701). J. W. Lovell Company.

Lady Damer's Secret. A Novel. Charlotte Mary Brame. LC 44-12247. 1881. G. W. Carleton & Co.

Lady Damer's Secret: A Novel. Charlotte Mary Brame. LC 44-116523. (On cover: Seaside library. Pocket ed. No. 469). G. Munro.

Lady Darlington. Fred M. Stewart. 1979. pap. 2.50 (ISBN 0-449-24182-3, Crest). Fawcett.

Lady Darlington: A Novel. Fred Mustard Stewart. LC 75-169924. 1971. 6.95 (ISBN 0-87795-023-7). Arbor House.

Lady Dean's Daughter: Or, The Confession of a Dying Woman. Judith Noot. LC 9-7828. 1909. Cochrane Publishing Company.

Lady Decides. 1st Ed. David Henry Keller. LC 50-7069. 1950. Prime Press.

Lady Detective. Harlan Page Halsey. (On cover: The calumet series, no. 19). G. Munro.

Lady Diana's Pride. Charlotte Mary Brame. LC 44-11268. (On cover: Lovell's library, v. 20, no. 985). John W. Lovell Company.

Lady Diana's Pride. Charlotte Mary Brame. LC 44-116555. (Seaside library. Pocket ed. No. 931). G. Munro.

Lady Dick. J. Joth. pap. 1.95 o.s.i. (OPS-38). Olympia.

Lady Doc. Caroline Lockhart. LC 12-23065. 1912. 1.25. J. B. Lippincott Company.

Lady Doctor. Peggy Gaddis, pseud. LC 56-124619. 1956. Arcadia House.

Lady, Don't Die on the Doorstep. Shallit, Joseph. LC 51-940. (Main line mysteries). 1951. Lippincott.

Lady, Drop Dead. Lawrence Treat. LC 60-7212. (Raven book). 1960. Abelard-Schuman.

Lady Edith: Or, Alton Towers. Thomas P May. LC 7-26239. T. B. Peterson & Brothers.

Lady Egeria: Or, Brought to Light. A Novel. John Berwick Harwood. LC 7-2632. (On cover: Lovell's international series, no. 67). 1890. J. W. Lovell Company.

Lady Eleanor: Lawbreaker. Robert Barr. LC 11-31965. 1.25. Rand, McNally & Company.

Lady Elect: A Chinese Romance. Norman Hinsdale Pitman. LC 13-22280. Fleming H. Revell Company.

Lady Ernestine: Or, The Absent Lord of Rocheforte. Catherine Ann Ware Warfield. LC 12-19555. T. B. Peterson & Brothers.

Lady Evelyn: A Story of to-Day. Max Pemberton. LC 6-23158. McLeod & Allen.

Lady Evelyn, or The Lord of Royal Rest. May Agnes Early Fleming. LC 860. (On cover: Eagle library, no. 141). Street & Smith.

Lady Ferry. With an Introd. by Annie E. Mower. Sarah Orne Jewett. LC 50-7813. 1950. Colby College Press.

Lady Finger. 1st Ed. George Malcolm-Smith. LC 62-12064. 1962. Published for the Crime Club by Doubleday.

Lady for Love. Alan Brener Schultz. LC 31-57006. H. Liveright.

Lady for Ransom. Alfred Leo Duggan. LC 53-8884. C.

Lady for Ransom. Alfred Leo Duggan. LC 68-12875. Weybright and Talley.

Lady Forgot. Margaret Sharp Marble. LC 47-661. 1947. Harper & Brothers.

Lady from Boston. Tom McHale. LC 76-42370. 1978. 8.95 (ISBN 0-385-01865-7). Doubleday.

Lady from Colorado: A Novel Based on the True Story of the Washerwoman Who Became the First Titled Lady of Colorado. 1st Ed. Homer Croy. LC 57-110506. 1957. Duell, Sloan and Pearce.

Lady from L. U. S. T. Rod Gray. (Lady from Lust Ser). (O.s.i.). 1976. pap. 1.25 o.s.i. (BT51102). Belmont-Tower.

Lady from Long Acre. Victor Bridges. LC 19-3594. 1919. G. P. Putnam's Sons.

Lady from L.U.S.T. see Lust,Be a Lady Tonight.

Lady from Stalingrad Mansions. Alan Coren. LC 77-76631. 1977. 7.95 o.p. (ISBN 0-312-46420-7). St Martin.

Lady from the Air. Alice Muriel Livingston Williamson & Williamson, Charles Norris, 1859-1920, Joint Author. LC 22-25010. 1922. Hodder and Stoughton Ltd.

Lady from the Air. Alice Muriel Livingston Williamson & Williamson, Charles Norris, 1859-1920, Joint Author. LC 23-14916. 1923. Doubleday, Page & Company.

Lady from Toledo. Illustrated by the Author. Angelico Chavez. LC 60-4487. 1960. Academy Guild Press.

Lady Gay's Pride: Or, The Miser's Treasure. Alexander McVeigh Miller. (On cover: Seaside library. Pocket ed., no. 268). 1884. G. Munro.

Lady Gay's Pride: Or, The Miser's Treasure. Alexander McVeigh Miller. (On cover: The library of American authors, no. 37). 1891. G. Munro.

Lady, Get Your Gun. Paul Ernst. LC 55-9713. (A Mill mystery). 1955. M. S. Mill Co., and W. Morrow.

Lady Godiva and Master Tom: A Novel. Raoul Cohen Faure. LC 48-5164. 1948.

Lady Gone Wild. Phyllis Gordon Demarest. LC 32-222419. The Macaulay Company.

Lady Good-for-Nothing: A Man's Portrait of a Woman. Arthur Thomas Quiller-Couch. LC 10-21639. 1910. 1.20. C. Scribner's Sons.

Lady Grace a Novel. Ellen Price Henry Wood Wood. (On cover: Lovell's library, no. 1093). 1887. J. W. Lovell Company.

Lady Grace a Novel. Ellen Price Henry Wood Wood. (On cover: Seaside library. Pocket ed. no. 1042). 1887. G. Munro.

Lady Hammond's Heredity. Mary F. S. Toy. LC 27-2157. 1927. The S. S. Scranton Company.

Lady Hancock" A Story of the American Revolution. Mary Elizabeth Springer. I. H. Blanchard Co.

Lady Hathaway's House Party. Jennie Gallant. 1980. pap. 1.75 (ISBN 0-449-50020-9, Coventry). Fawcett.

Lady Helena: Or, The Mysterious Lady. Gaston Leroux. LC 31-12123. 1931. E. P. Dutton & Co. Inc.

Lady Hobo. Beth Brown. LC 35-2537. Coward, McCann, Inc.

Lady Huckleberry Enlarges on Her Husband's Follies! A Continuation of the "Irene Macgillicuddy Papers." And A Romance of a Yachting Party, That Is More Than Romantic. James R. Sharpe & H. M. B., Joint Author. LC 8-4803. 1878. G. W. Carleton & Co.; Etc., Etc.

Lady in a Million. Harriette Ashbrook. LC 43-10686. 1943. Dodd, Mead & Company.

Lady in a Wedding Dress. Harriette Ashbrook. LC 43-979. 1943. Dodd, Mead & Company.

Lady in Armor. Octavus Roy Cohen. LC 41-15434. 1941. D. Appleton Century Company, Incorporated.

Lady in Berkshire. Mary Ann Gibbs. 1973. pap. 0.95 o.p. (95352-095). Beagle Bks.

Lady in Black. Anna Clarke. (General Ser.). 1979. lib. bdg. 11.50 (ISBN 0-8161-6712-5, Large Print Bks). G K Hall.

Lady in Black. Anna Clarke. (McKay-Washburn Novel of Suspense). 1978. 6.95 o.p. (ISBN 0-679-50832-5). McKay.

Lady in Black. Vida Hurst. LC 39-547168. M. S. Mill Co., Inc.

Lady in Black: A Novel of Suspense. Anna Clarke. LC 77-93503. (MW suspense). 1978. 6.95 (ISBN 0-679-50832-5). D. McKay Co.

Lady in Black: A Novel of Suspense. Anna Clarke. LC 79-11597. 1979. 11.50 (ISBN 0-8161-6712-5). G. K. Hall.

Lady in Blue: A Joseph Muller Story. Auguste Groner & Colborn, Grace Isabel. LC 22-966188. 1922. 1.75. Duffield and Company.

Lady in Blue: A Sitka Romance. John William Aretander. Lowman & Hanford Co.

Lady in Danger. Harriette Ashbrook. LC 42-4616. 1942. Dodd, Mead & Company.

Lady in Danger. Susannah Shane. LC 42-4616. 1942. Dodd, Mead & Company.

Lady in Darkness. easy eye ed. Evelyn Bond. pap. 0.75 o.p. Lancer.

Lady in Darkness. Evelyn Bond. (Berkley medallion book). 1974. (pbk.) 0.95 (ISBN 0-425-02701-5). Berkley Pub. Co.

Lady in Disguise. Jacqueline Diamond. LC 82-50335. 1983. 11.95 (ISBN 0-8027-0715-7). Walker.

Lady in Doubt. Annabel Wynne. LC 78-19395. 1979. 8.95 (ISBN 0-312-46424-X). St. Martin's Press.

Lady in Dread. Cover Painting by Barye Phillips. Walter Ryerson Johnson. LC 55-25857. (Gold medal books, 459). 1955. Fawcett Publications.

Lady in Gray: A Story of the Steps by Which We Climb. Clara Elizabeth Laughlin. LC 8-28311. 1908. F. H. Revell Company.

Lady in Heat. Rod Gray. (The Lady from L.U.S.T. Ser.). (O.s.i.). 1974. pap. 0.95 o.s.i. (BT50649). Belmont-Tower.

Lady in Heat see Dama en Calor.

Lady in Jade Green: By H. G. Freeman. H. G Freeman. 1974. 6.00 (ISBN 0-682-48061-4). Exposition Press.

Lady in Lilac. Harriette Ashbrook. LC 41-6232. 1941. Dodd, Mead & Company.

Lady in Lilac. Susannah Shane. LC 41-6232. 1941. Dodd, Mead & Company.

Lady in Love. Nellie Graf. LC 39-8726. Gramercy Publishing Co.

Lady in Marble. Robert E McClure. LC 28-12578. Doubleday, Doran & Company, Inc.

Lady in Mauve. Albert J Klinck. LC 11-16265. 1911. 1.00. Sherman, French & Company.

Lady in Shadows. easy eye ed. Antonia Lamb. 1968. pap. 0.60 o.p. (73-794). Lancer.

Lady in the Car with Glasses and a Gun. Sebastien Japrisot. LC 67-22938. (Inner sanctum mystery). 1967. Simon and Schuster.

Lady in the Car with Glasses and a Gun. Jean Baptiste Rossi. LC 67-2293. 1967. Simon and Schuster.

Lady in the Car with Glasses and a Gun. Jean Baptiste Rossi. LC 79-17097. (Penguin crime fiction). 1980. 2.50 (ISBN 0-14-005361-1). Penguin Books.

Lady in the Lake. Raymond Chandler. LC 75-44962. (Fifty Classics of Crime Fiction, 1900-1950; 9). 1976. 12.00 (ISBN 0-8240-2358-7). Garland Pub.

Lady in the Lake. Raymond Chandler. LC 76-10591. 1976. 1.95 (ISBN 0-394-72145-4). Vintage Books.

Lady in the Lake. Raymond Chandler. LC 43-157853. 1943. A. A. Knopf.

Lady in the Lightning. Katherine Tobias, pseud. pap. 0.60 o.p. Lancer.

Lady in the Mask. Anne Green. LC 42-5831. 1942. Harper & Brothers.

Lady in the Morgue. Jonathan Latimer. LC 53-7824. 1953. Published for the Crime Club by Doubleday.

Lady in the Morgue... Jonathan Latimer. LC 36-181573. 1936. Pub for the Crime Club, Inc., by Doubleday, Doran & Co., Inc.

Lady in the Morgue... Jonathan Latimer. LC 37-20211. 1937. The Sun Dial Press, Inc.

Lady in the Morgue. Jonathan Latimer. LC 46-21224. (Pocket books. 246). 1945.

Lady in the Straw. Maggie MacKeever. (Coventry Romance Ser.: No. 174). 224p. 1982. pap. 1.50 (ISBN 0-449-50275-9, Coventry). Fawcett.

Lady in the Tower. Katharine Newlin Burt. LC 46-2185. 1946. Macrae-Smith-Company.

Lady in the Tower. Katharine Newlin Burt. (Signet book). 1975. (pbk.) 0.95. New American Library.

Lady in the White Veil. Rose Cecil O'Neill. LC 9-12877. 1909. Harper & Brothers.

Lady in Waiting: A Novel. 1st American Ed. Rosemary Sutcliff. LC 57-6689. 1957. Coward-McCann.

Lady in Waiting: An Intimate Journal of A Labor of Love. Rory Gallagher. 3.50 o.p. (ISBN 0-8044-5400-0); pap. 1.50 o.p. (ISBN 0-8044-6171-6, Pub. by Stephen Daye Pr.). Ungar.

Lady in Waiting: Being Extracts from the Diary of Julie De Chesnil, Sometime Lady in Waiting to Her Majesty, Queen Marie Antoinette. Charles Woodcock- Savage. 1906. D. Appleton and Company.

Lady Ingram's Room. Jill Tattersall. LC 72-125606. 1971. 5.95. Morrow.

Lady Ingram's Room. Jill Tattersall. LC 78-11830. 1979. 10.95 (ISBN 0-89340-179-X). J. Curley.

Lady Interne. Charles Stanley Strong. LC 39-258724. Phoenix Press.

Lady into Fox. David Garnett. 1923. A. A. Knopf.

Lady into Fox. With an Author's Note to the Present Ed. Introd. by Vincent Starrett. Illus. with Wood Engravings by R. A. Garnett. David Garnett. LC 66-3435. (Seagull lib. of mystery and suspense). 1966. 3.95. Norton.

Lady Investigates. Patricia Craig & Mary Cadogan. 252p. 1982. 11.95 (ISBN 0-312-46426-6). St Martin.

Lady Is a Spy. Lionel Black. Orig. Title: Two Ladies in Verona. 1968. pap. 0.60 o.p. (53-664). Paperback Lib.

Lady Is Afraid. George Harmon Coxe. LC 40-269182. 1940. A. A. Knopf.

Lady Is Dead. Amelia Reynolds Long. LC 51-1593. 1951. Phoenix Press.

Lady Is Lethal. Paul Muller. LC 68-16328. 1968. Roy Publishers.
Lady Is Waiting. James Mitchell. LC 58-10311. 1958. Morrow.
Lady Jade. Leslie O'Grady. LC 80-29120. 1981. 12.95 (ISBN 0-312-46429-0). St. Martin's Press.
Lady Jane. Norma Lee Clark. LC 81-69710. 1982. 11.95 (ISBN 0-8027-0699-1). Walker.
Lady Jean. Frank Dilnot. LC 30-10258. H. Holt and Company.
Lady Jim of Curzon Street: A Novel. Fergus Hume. LC 6-7722. 1906. G. W. Dillingham Company.
Lady John. Madeleine Robins. (Coventry Romance Ser.: No. 175). 224p. 1982. pap. 1.50 (ISBN 0-449-50276-7, Coventry). Fawcett.
Lady Judith. A Tale of Two Continents. Justin McCarthy. LC 7-15282. Sheldon and Company.
Lady Kildare. A Novel. Harriet Lewis. (On cover: The popular series, no. 38). 1893. R. Bonner's Sons.
Lady Killer. Rod Gray. (Lady from L.U.S.T. Ser). (O.s.i.). (Orig.). 1975. pap. 1.25 o.s.i. (BT50838). Belmont-Tower.
Lady Killer. William M Hardy. LC 57-5868. (Red badge detective). 1957. Dodd, Mead.
Lady Killer. Rebecca Hicks. LC 7-47657. 1851. Lippincott, Grambo and Co.
Lady Killer. Elisabeth Sanxay Holding. LC 42-14364. 1942. Duell, Sloan and Pearce.
Lady Killer. Evan Hunter. (Signet book). 1974. (pbk.) 0.95. New American Library.
Lady Killer. Josiah Pitts Woolfolk. LC 35-19877. Godwin.
Lady Killer: By Ed McBain Pseud. Evan Hunter. LC 58-41172. (Permabook M3119. Mystery, 9). 1958. Permabooks.
Lady Killers. William T Brannon & Clarence Ivan Branton. LC 52-22906. (Handi-book mystery, 139). 1951. Quinn Pub. Co.
Lady Killers. Alan Riefe. (Cage#1). 1975. (pbk.) 0.95. Popular Library.
Lady Kills. Bruno Fischer. LC 51-22962. (Gold medal book, 148). 1951. Gold Medal Books.
Lady Kilpatrick. A Tale of to-Day. Robert Williams Buchanan. (On cover: Globe library, v. 1, no. 254). 1897. Rand, McNally & Company.
Lady L. Romain Gary, pseud. (Coll. Soleil). (Fr.). 1963. 11.50. French & Eur.
Lady, Lady, I Did It. Ed McBain. 1961. 3.50 o.p. (ISBN 0-671-40555-1). S&S.
Lady, Lady, I Did It! An 87th Precinct Inner Sanctum Mystery. Evan Hunter. 1961. Simon and Schuster.
Lady Larkspur. Meredith Nicholson. LC 19-4520. 1919. C. Scribner's Sons.
Lady Latimer's Escape: And Other Stories. Charlotte Mary Brame. (On cover: Seaside library. Pocket ed. no. 2086). G. Munro.
Lady Latimer's Escape, and Other Stories. Charlotte Mary Brame. LC 44-11266. (On cover: Seaside library. Pocket ed. No. 2088). G. Munro.
Lady Laughter. Ralph Henry Barbour. LC 13-25399. 1913. J. B. Lippincott Company.
Lady Lawyer. Teresa Holloway. 1964. Avalon Books.
Lady Lee's Widowhood. Edward Bruce Hamley. LC 7-93920. 1853. Harper & Brothers.
Lady Lee's Widowhood. A Novel. Edward Bruce Hamley. LC 7-937. (Franklin square library, no. 56). Harper & Brothers.
Lady Like the Moon. Genevieve Blanche Wimsatt. LC 45-959869. 1945. B. Ackerman Incorporated.
Lady Likes Blue White: And Other Stories. Irwin William Groh. LC 48-1785. 1948. Christopher Pub. House.
Lady Lilith. Stephen McKenna. LC 20-18657. George H. Doran Company.
Lady Lost Her Head. Manning Lee Stokes. LC 50-6868. 1950. Phoenix Press.
Lady Loved Too Well. Jackson Donahue. LC 77-17319. 9.95 (ISBN 0-07-017541-1). McGraw-Hill.
Lady Lovelace. A Novel. Catharine Louisa Pirkis. LC 7-39630. (Harper's Franklin square library. no. 483). 1885. Harper & Brothers.
Lady Loverly's Chatter. Connie Bertram. LC 45-8177. 1945. Arthur Yeoman Press.
Lady Luck. Hugh Wiley. LC 21-20187. 1921. A. A. Knopf.
Lady Luck: An Original Love Story. John Walsh Russell. LC 26-13383. American Press Publishing Co.
Lady Magic. Claudette Williams. 192p. (Orig.). 1983. pap. 2.25 (ISBN 0-449-20093-0, Crest). Fawcett.
Lady Marabout's Troubles: Or, The Worries of a Chaperone. Louise De La Ramee. (seaside library, v. 15, no. 281). 1878. G. Munro.
Lady Margery's Intrigue. Marion Chesney. 224p. 1980. pap. 1.75 (ISBN 0-449-50053-5, Coventry). Fawcett.
Lady Marion's Answer. Lydia L Rouse. LC 8-693250. American Tract Society.
Lady Mary. William Arthur Neubauer. LC 49-15686. 1946. Gramercy Publishing Company.
Lady Mary. William Arthur Neubauer. LC 46-15686. 1946. Grammercy Publishing Company.
Lady Mary. A Novel. Ann Sophia Winterbotham Stephens. (On cover: The idle hour series, no. 7). 1892. The F. M. Lupton Publishing Company.
Lady Mary: Or, Not of the World. 4th american ed. Charles Benjamin Tayler. (On cover: C. B. Tayler's works). 1850. Stanford and Swords.
"Lady Maud," Schooner Yacht. William Clark Russell. LC 8-1805. R. F. Fenno & Company.
"Lady Maud" Schooner Yacht. From the Account of a Guest on Board. William Clark Russell. (Harper's Franklin square library, no. 260). 1882. Harper & Brothers.
Lady Maude's Mania: A Tragedy in High Life. authorized ed. George Manville Fenn. LC 11-150907. (Lovell's international series, no. 136). United States Book Company, Successors to J. W. Lovell Company.
Lady Mechante: Or, Life As It Should Be: Being Divers Precious Episodes in the Life of a Naughty Nonpareille; a Farce in Filigree. Gelett Burgess. LC 9-28114. 1909. F. A. Stokes Company.
Lady Merton, Colonist. Mary Augusta Arnold Humphry Ward Ward. 1910. Doubleday, Page & Co.
Lady Mildred's Memoirs. 1972. pap. 1.75 o.s.i. (79-323). Lancer.
Lady Mislaid. Josiah Pitts Woolfolk. LC 37-2173. 1936. Godwin.
Lady Molly. Katherine Talbot. 160p. (Orig.). 1983. pap. 1.95 (ISBN 0-446-90762-6). Warner Bks.
Lady Molly of Scotland Yard. Emmuska Orczy. LC 75-32771. (Literature of Mystery and Detection). 1976. 17.00 (ISBN 0-405-07890-0). Arno Press.
Lady Molly of Scotland Yard. Emmuska Orczy. LC 81-83714. (IPL Library of Crime Classics). 5.00 (ISBN 0-930330-02-1). International Polygonics.
Lady Molly's. 1st American Ed. Anthony Dymoke Powell. LC 58-10681. (Music of time series). Little, Brown.
Lady Moreland's Mistake: Or, Blood Will Tell. Victorine Clarisse Jacquet Jones. LC 16-19220. 1916. 1.00. Jamaica Publishing Co.
Lady Muriel's Secret. Jean Middlemass. (On cover: Seaside library. Pocket ed., no. 155). 1884. G. Munro.
Lady Named Lou. Donald Henderson Clarke. LC 41-15913. The Vanguard Press.
Lady Noggs, Peeress. Edgar Jepson. LC 5-13027. 1905. McClure, Phillips & Co.
Lady of a Thousand Sorrows. Lee W Mason. LC 77-72967. 1977. 1.95. Playboy Press.
Lady of Arlac. Sandra Shulman. 1971. pap. 0.75 o.p. (ISBN 0-446-64744-6, 64-744-6). Paperback Lib.
Lady of Arlington: A Novel Based on the Life of Mrs. Robert E. Lee. 1st Ed. Harnett Thomas Kane. LC 53-913518. 1953. Doubleday.
Lady of Beauty: A Novel; Translated from the French by Katherine Woods. Foreword by Pearl S. Buck. Kiku Yamata. LC 54-10456. (Asia book). 1954. J. Day Co.
Lady of Big Shanty. Frank Berkeley Smith. LC 9-27447. 1909. Doubleday, Page & Company.
Lady of Castell March. Owen Vaughan. LC 98-640. 1898. Doubleday & McClure Company.
Lady of Castle Queer. David Skaats Foster. LC 19-15973. The Franklin Book Company.
Lady of Cawnpore: A Romance. Frank Vincent & Lancaster, Albert Edmund, Joint Author. LC 8-32703. 1891. Funk & Wagnalls.
Lady of Dreams. Una Lucy Silberrad. LC 6465. 1900. Doubleday, Page & Company.
Lady of Fan-Tan. Michael G Suba. LC 68-54482. 1969. 3.00. Dorrance.
Lady of Fire. Valerie Vayle, pseud. (Orig.). 1980. pap. 2.50 (ISBN 0-440-15444-8). Dell.
Lady of Fort St. John. Mary Hartwell Catherwood. LC 6-23113. 1891. Houghton, Mifflin and Company.
Lady of Fort St. John. Mary Hartwell Catherwood. 1892. Houghton, Mifflin and Company.
Lady of Fortune. Blanche Chenier. (Orig.). 1980. pap. 1.75 (ISBN 0-449-50028-4, Coventry). Fawcett.
Lady of France. Ella Madge Smith Conly. LC 8-373561. Homewood Publishing Company.
Lady of France. Grace Stair. LC 30-8607. 1930. Frederick A. Stokes Company.
Lady of Gestures. Charlton Andrews. LC 27-4645. The Macaulay Company.
Lady of Independence. Helen Argers. LC 81-43264. 1982. 11.95 (ISBN 0-385-17476-4). Doubleday.
Lady of King Arthur's Court: Being a Romance of the Holy Grail. Sara Hawks Sterling. 1907. G. W. Jacobs & Co.
Lady of Kingdoms. Inez Haynes Irwin. LC 17-25510. 1917. 1.50. George H. Doran Company.
Lady of Launay. Anthony Trollope. LC 8-28890. (On cover: Harper's half-hour series v. 74). 1878. Harper & Brothers.
Lady of Lawford: And Other Christmas Stories. Nathan Boughton Warren. LC 8-33686. H. B. Nims and Company.
Lady of Laws. Susanne G. Trautwein & Palmer, Herbert Edward, 1880- Tr. LC 29-18166. E. Holt.
Lady of Leisure. Ethel Sidgwick. LC 14-5040. Small, Maynard & Comapny.
Lady of Light & Darkness. Diane L. Parson. 256p. (Orig.). 1982. pap. 2.75 (ISBN 0-671-45597-4, Timescape). PB.
Lady of Loyalty House: A Novel. Justin Huntly McCarthy. LC 4-25387. 1904. Harper & Brothers.
Lady of Lynn. Walter Besant. LC 1-31696. 1901. Dodd Mead and Company.
Lady of Lyons. Taken from the Play. Edward George Earle Lytton Bulwer-Lytton Lytton. LC 7-8338. (On cover: Lovell's library, v. 3, no. 21). 1883. J. W. Lovell Company.
Lady of Mallow. Dorothy Eden. 1978. pap. 1.95 (ISBN 0-449-23167-4, Crest). Fawcett.
Lady of Monkswood Manor. Sarah Farrant. 1974. pap. 0.95 o.p. (26582-3-095). Beagle Bks.
Lady of Monkton. Elizabeth Byrd. LC 74-78519. 192p. 1975. pap. 2.50 (ISBN 0-8128-7053-0). Stein & Day.
Lady of Moray. Bonnie Copeland. LC 79-51400. 1979. 13.95 (ISBN 0-689-10996-2). Atheneum.
Lady of Mystery House. George Clifford Shedd. LC 17-8467. 1917. The Macaulay Company.
Lady of New Orleans. Edwina Levin MacDonald. LC 25-16899. 1925. The Macaulay Company.
Lady of New Orleans: A Novel of the Present. Marcellus Eugene Thornton. LC 2-8336. The Abbey Press.
Lady of Night. Barry, Jerome. LC 44-2707. 1944. Pub for the Crime Club by Doubleday, Doran and Co., Inc.
Lady of North Star. Ottwell Binns. LC 22-4239. 1922. A. A. Knopf.
Lady of Paris. William Vaughan Wilkins. LC 57-6932. 1957. St. Martin's Press.
Lady of Pentlands. Elizabeth Garver Jordan. LC 24-6456. 2.00. The Century Co.
Lady of Quality. Georgette Heyer. 1972. 6.95 o.p. (ISBN 0-525-14280-0). Dutton.
Lady of Quality. Claude P. Jolyot De Crebillon, Jr. 1964. pap. 0.95 o.p. (903). Brandon.
Lady of Quality: Being a Most Curious, Hitherto Unknown History, As Related to Mr. Isaac Bickerstaff but Not Presented to the World of Fashion Through the Pages of The Tatler, and Now for the First Time Written Down. Frances Hodgson Burnett. LC 1-2426. 1896. C. Scribner's Sons.
Lady of Quality: Being a Most Curious, Hitherto Unknown History, As Related by Mr. Issac Bickerstaff but Not Presented to the World of Fashion Through the Pages of the Tatler, and Now for the First Time Written Down. Frances Hodgson Burnett. LC 6-16424. 1897. C. Scribner's Sons.
Lady of Quality: Being a Most Curious, Hitherto Unknown History, As Related by Mr. Isaac Bickerstaff, but Not Presented to the World of Fashion Through the Pages of the Tatler, and Now for the First Time Written Down. Frances Hodgson Burnett. LC 16-6319. 1913. C. Scribner's Sons.
Lady of Repute. Janice James. LC 78-20079. 1980. 9.95 (ISBN 0-385-13507-6). Doubleday.
Lady of Resource. Arthur Somers Roche. LC 38-24146. 1938. Dodd, Mead & Company.
Lady of Rogan's Tower. Sarah Farrant. (Beagle books). 1975. (pbk.) 0.95 (ISBN 0-345-26667-6). Ballantine Books.
Lady of Rome. Francis Marion Crawford. LC 6-36630. 1906. The Macmillan Company.
Lady of Rome. Francis Marion Crawford. LC 41-123910. 1912. Hurst & Co.
Lady of St. Luke's. Mark Allerton. LC 18-17910. 1918. Dodd, Mead and Company.
Lady of Shenipsit: A Novel of New England. Frederic Pierpont Ladd. LC 10-18884. 1910. 1.25. Sturgis & Walton Company.
Lady of Stainless Raiment: By,Mathilde Eiker... Mathilde Eiker. LC 28-23112. 1928. Doubleday, Doran and Company, Inc.
Lady of Stantonwyck. Maye Barrett. 1981. pap. 2.50 (ISBN 0-89083-752-X). Zebra.
Lady of Taos. Richard L Luna. LC 74-170978. (Illus.). 1974. El Napeste Pub. Co.
Lady of the Abbey. James Owen Hannay. LC 26-4942. The Bobbs-Merrill Company.
Lady of the Aroostook. William Dean Howells. LC 75-145086. 1973. 19.50 (ISBN 0-403-01025-X). Scholarly Press.
Lady of the Aroostook. William Dean Howells. LC 70-98770. 1970. Greenwood Press.
Lady of the Aroostook. William Dean Howells. LC 4-15122. 1879. Houghton, Osgood and Company.
Lady of the Aroostook. Howells, William Dean. LC 6-456963. Houghton, Mifflin and Company.
Lady of the Aroostook. William Dean Howells. LC 24-279753. Houghton Mifflin Company.
Lady of the Barge. William Wymark Jacobs. LC 75-101815. (Short story index reprint series). (Illus.). 1969. Books for Libraries Press.
Lady of the Barge by W. W. Jacobs... William Wymark Jacobs. LC 2-23833. 1902. Dodd, Mead & Company.
Lady of the Bees. Thomas Burnett Swann. (Ace Science Fiction Special#7). 1976. (pbk.) 1.25. Ace Books.
Lady of the Blue Motor. George Sidney Paternoster. LC 7-16942. 1907. L. C. Page & Company.
Lady of the Camellias... Alexandre Dumas. Tr. by Walton, William. Janin, Jules Gabriel. LC 7-22752. (Added t.-p.: Roman contemporian. Realists. vol. vi). 1897. Printed Only for Subscribers by G. Barrie & Son.
Lady of the Crossing. Frederick John Niven. LC 19-84661. 1.50. George H. Doran Company.
Lady of the Crossing: A Novel of the New West. Frederick John Niven. LC 19-7720. 1919. Hodder and Stoughton.
Lady of the Decoration. Fannie Macaulay. 1906. The Century Co.
Lady of the Decoration. Fannie Macaulay. LC 8-11005. 1907. The Century Co.
Lady of the Decoration. Fannie Macaulay. 1908. The Century Co.
Lady of the Dynamos. Adele Marie Shaw & Beckwith, Carmelita, Joint Author. LC 9-8814. 1909. H. Holt and Company.
Lady of the Evening. Leslie Scott. LC 52-11257. 1952. Arco Pub. Co.
Lady of the Flag-Flowers. Florence Wilkinson Evans. LC 99-2368. 1899. H. S. Stone and Company.
Lady of the Green and Blue; or, The Magic Figure Head. Charles Carey. LC 6-22814. 1847. G. H. Williams.
Lady of the Haven. Graham Diamond. LC 78-55733. 384p. (Orig.). 1978. pap. 1.95 (ISBN 0-87216-477-2). Playboy Pbks.
Lady of the Heavens. Henry Rider Haggard. 1908. The Authors and Newspapers Association.
Lady of the Ice. James De Mille. (Toronto Reprint Library of Canadian Prose & Poetry). 1973. Repr. of 1870 ed. 15.00x (ISBN 0-8020-7517-7). U of Toronto Pr.
Lady of the Ice: A Novel. James De Mille. LC 74-168855. (Toronto reprint library of Canadian prose and poetry). (ISBN 0-8020-7517-7). University of Toronto Press.
Lady of the Ice. A Novel. James De Mille. LC 9-8347. 1870. D. Appleton and Company.
Lady of the Isle. A Romance from Real Life. Emma Dorothy Eliza Nevitte Southworth. LC 8-10822. 1859. T. B. Peterson and Brothers.
Lady of the Isle: Or, The Island Princess. Emma Dorothy Eliza Nevitte Southworth. T. B. Peterson & Brothers.
Lady of the Lens: A Novel. Frank Carleton Long. LC 7-15148. 1891. L. E. Crandall & Co.
Lady of the Lighthouse. Helen S Woodruff. LC 13-23879. George H. Doran Company.
Lady of the Lily Feet and Other Stories of China-Town. Helen F Clark. LC 1-29284. 1900. The Griffith & Rowland Press.
Lady of the Lotus. William Edmund Barrett. LC 73-15324. 1975. 7.95 (ISBN 0-385-02304-9). Doubleday.
Lady of the Lotus. William Edmund Barrett. 1976. (pbk.) 1.75 (ISBN 0-380-00594-8). Avon.
Lady of the Manor. Archibald Marshall. LC 32-22209. 1932. Dodd, Mead & Company.
Lady of the Mansion: A Novel: Originally Published As The Portent. George Macdonald. LC 82-48944. 1983. 5.95 (ISBN 0-06-250564-5). Harper & Row.
Lady of the Mohawks. 1st Ed. Margaret Widdemer. LC 51-13384. 1951. Doubleday.
Lady of the Moor. Pat Phillips. (YA) 1973. 4.95 o.p. (Avalon). Bouregy.
Lady of the Mount. Frederic Stewart Isham. 1908. The Bobbs-Merrill Company.
Lady of the Night. Sydney Horler. LC 30-19937. 1903. A. A. Knopf.
Lady of the Night Wind. Frederic Van Rensselaer Dey. LC 19-5849. 1919. 1.50. The Macaulay Company.
Lady of the Pool. Anthony Hope Hawkins. LC 7-3662. 1894. D. Appleton and Company.
Lady of the Robins: A Romance of Some of New York's 400. Adella Octavia Clouston & American Humane Education Society, Boston, Pub. LC 11-1433. 0.20. The American Humane Education Society.
Lady of the Shroud. Bram Stoker. Repr. lib. bdg. 12.70x (ISBN 0-88411-134-2). Amereon Ltd.
Lady of the Shroud. Bram Stoker. 1966. 4.95 (ISBN 0-09-080680-8, Pub. by Hutchinson). Merrimack Pub Cir.
Lady of the Snows: A Novel. (3d ed.) ed. Edith Ogden Harrison. LC 12-24488. 1912. 1.25. A. C. McClurg & Co.
Lady of the Spur. David Potter. LC 10-21299. 1910. 1.50. J. B. Lippincott Company.

Lady of the Tower: And Other Stories. George Barton. LC 9-12196. 1909. 1.25. Benziger Brothers.

Lady of the West: Or, The Gold Seekers... John Ballou. LC 6-60073. 1855. Author.

Lady of the Yellow River. Philip Hamilton Gibbs. LC 54-6745. Roy Publishers.

Lady of Wildersley. Josephine Edgar, pseud. (Kangaroo Book.). 1977. 1.50 (ISBN 0-671-81217-3). Pocket Books.

Lady Olivia. A Novel. William C Falkner. (On cover: The southern rose series). 1895. G. W. Dillingham.

Lady on a Train... Leslie Charteris. LC 45-10422. 1945.

Lady on Fire. James Michael Ullman. LC 68-16141. (Inner sanctum mystery). 1968. Simon and Schuster.

Lady on the Burning Deck. Catherine Heath. LC 78-27172. 1979. 8.95 (ISBN 0-8008-4528-5). Taplinger Pub. Co.

Lady on the Coin. Margaret Campbell Barnes & Elsna, Hebe, Joint Author. LC 63-20493. 1963. Macrae Smith.

Lady on the Drawing Room Floor. Mary Elizabeth Coleridge. LC 7-35195. 1906. Longmans, Green & Co.; Etc., Etc.

Lady on the Hunt. With Drawings by R. J. Davidson. 1st Ed. Clinch Calkins. LC 50-14404. 1950. Harper.

Lady on the Line. Teone Tone. 304p. (Orig.). 1983. pap. 2.75 (ISBN 0-449-12449-5, GM). Fawcett.

Lady on the Run. Lucille Schirman. 1982. pap. 2.95 (ISBN 0-451-11831-6, AE1831, Sig). NAL.

Lady, or the Tiger? And Other Stories. Frank Richard Stockton. LC 69-11918. (American short story series, v. 77). 1969. Garrett Press.

Lady, or the Tiger? and Other Stories. Frank Richard Stockton. LC 75-45015. 1976. (ISBN 0-403-03179-6). Scholarly Press.

Lady, or the Tiger? And Other Stories. Frank Richard Stockton. LC 4-15159. 1884. C. Scribner's Sons.

Lady or the Tiger: And Other Stories. Frank Richard Stockton. LC 8-2939. 1907. C. Scribner's Sons.

Lady, or the Tiger? And Other Stories, by Frank R. Stockton. Frank Richard Stockton. LC 41-81389. 1887. C. Scribner's Sons.

Lady or the Tiger: And Other Stories, by Frank Stockton. Introd. by Francis R. Gemme. Frank Richard Stockton. (Classics ser., CL163). 1968. Airmont.

Lady Oracle. Margaret Eleanor Atwood. LC 76-379253. 10.00 (ISBN 0-7710-0815-5). McClelland and Stewart.

Lady Oracle. Margaret Eleanor Atwood. 1978. 1.95 (ISBN 0-380-01799-7). Avon Books.

Lady Pamela. Clare Darcy. LC 75-12192. 1975. 8.95 (ISBN 0-8027-0504-9). Walker.

Lady Pamela. Clare Darcy. LC 75-42388. 1976. 10.95 (ISBN 0-8161-6340-5). G. K. Hall.

Lady Pamela. Clare Darcy. (Signet Book). 1977. 1.50 (ISBN 0-451-07282-0). New American Library.

Lady Paramount. Henry Harland. LC 2-11151. 1902. John Lane.

Lady Passenger. Arthur Williams Marchmont. LC 15-14921. 1915. Hodder and Stoughton.

Lady Proposes. Alma Sioux Scarberry. LC 41-4411. Gramercy Publishing Co.

Lady Regrets. James M. W. Knipscheer. LC 47-24203. 1947. Coward-McCann, Inc.

Lady Rich: A Novel of Penelope Devereus at the Court of Queen Elizabeth. Elizabeth Boatwright Coker. LC 63-7259. 1963. (Dutton.

Lady Rose's Daughter. Humphry Ward. 489p. 1977. Repr. of 1903 ed. lib. bdg. 20.10x (ISBN 0-89966-195-5). Buccaneer Bks.

Lady Rose's Daughter: A Novel. Mary Augusta Arnold Humphry Ward Ward. LC 41-41847. 1903. Grosset & Dunlap.

Lady Rose's Daughter: A Novel. Mary Augusta Arnold Humphry Ward Ward. LC 3-5780. 1903. Harper & Brothers.

Lady Royal. Molly Costain Haycraft. LC 64-23475. 1964. Lippincott.

Lady Royal. Molly Costain Haycraft. (Signet book). 1974. (pbk.) 1.25. New American Library.

Lady Rustler. Chad Calhoun, pseud. (Agent Brad Spear Ser.: No. 10). 304p. 1982. pap. 2.25 (ISBN 0-440-04628-9, Emerald). Dell.

Lady Ryhope's Lover. Emma Garrison Jones. (select series. no. 32). 1890. Street & Smith.

Lady Said No. Alan Allyson. LC 72-3664. 1972. 3.95 (ISBN 0-87749-313-8). Drake Publishers.

Lady Sativa. Frank Lauria. 1973. pap. 0.95 o.p. (09167). Curtis.

Lady Sativa. Frank Lauria. 1973. 0.95. Curtis Books.

Lady Saw Red. Amelia Reynolds Long. LC 52-6036. 1951. Phoenix Press.

Lady Scatterly's Lovers. Gene Fowler. LC 72-861705. 1973. 5.95. Lyle Stuart.

Lady Serena. Jeanne Duval. (Signet Book). 1978. 2.25 (ISBN 0-451-08163-3). New American Library.

Lady Silverdale's Sweetheart. And Other Tales. William Black. LC 6-12926. (Lovell's library, v. 5, no. 216). J. W. Lovell Company.

Lady Sinister. Paulette Warren. (Berkley Medallion) (ISBN 0-425-03258-2). Berkley.

Lady Slipper. Ella Wister Haines. LC 29-15928. A. L. Burt Company.

Lady Susan. Jane Austen. LC 26-3380. 1925. The Clarendon Press.

Lady Susan. Phyllis Ann Karr. 320p. (Based on the unfinished novel by Jane Austen). 1980. 11.95 o.p. (ISBN 0-89696-074-9, An Everest House Book). Dodd.

Lady Susan; The Watsons; Sanditon. Jane Austen & Margaret Drabble. LC 75-308566. (Penguin English library). 1974. 1.75 (ISBN 0-14-043102-0). Penguin.

Lady Susan: A Novel. Phyllis Ann Karr & Jane Austen. LC 80-80131. 11.95 (ISBN 0-89696-074-9). Everest House.

Lady, Susan, The Watsons. Jane Austen. Ed. by Auston-Leigh, James Edward. LC 7-34095. 1892. Roberts Brothers.

Lady Sweetbriar. Maggie MacKeever. (Coventry Romance Ser.: No. 169). 224p. 1982. pap. 1.50 (ISBN 0-449-50270-8, Coventry). Fawcett.

Lady Takes It All Off. Rod Gray. (Lady from L.U.S.T. Ser). (Orig., Osi). 1971. pap. 0.95 o.s.i. (B95-2114). Belmont-Tower.

Lady Takes It All off. Rod Gray. (The Lady from L.U.S.T. Ser.). (O.s.i.). 1974. pap. 0.95 o.s.i. (BT50636). Belmont-Tower.

Lady, That's My Skull. Wilburn O Hogue. LC 47-30780. 1947. Phoenix Press.

Lady to Kill. Lester Dent. LC 46-7666. 1946. Pub. for the Crime Club by Doubleday & Company, Inc.

Lady Trent's Daughter: A Novel. Isabel Constance Clarke. LC 20-4464. 1927. Benziger Brothers.

Lady Tumbles. Sally Chayes. LC 23-3185. Mason Publishing Co.

Lady Valiant. Freda Michel. 224p. 1981. pap. 1.95 (ISBN 0-449-50194-9, Coventry). Fawcett.

Lady Val's Elopement. Charles Henry Cook. LC 6-28087. (On cover: Lippincott's series of select novels). 1896. J.B. Lippincott Company.

Lady Valworth's Diamonds. Margaret Wolfe Hungerford. LC 7-9360. (On cover: Lovell's library. v. 17, no. 802). 1886. J. W. Lovell Company.

Lady Vanishes. Ethel L. White. Orig. Title: Wheel Spins. 1969. pap. 0.60 o.p. (ISBN 0-446-63188-4, 63-188). Paperback Lib.

Lady Verner's Flight. Margaret Wolfe Hamilton Hungerford. LC 7-9359. (On cover: Broadway series, no. 19). 1893. J. A. Taylor and Company.

Lady Viola's Secret. Dora Delmar. (On cover: Library of American authors. no. 74). G. Munro's Sons.

Lady Vixen. Shirlee Busbee. 544p. 1980. pap. 2.75 (ISBN 0-380-75382-0, 75382). Avon.

Lady Wedderburn's Wish: A Tale of the Crimean War. James Grant. LC 41-307379. G. Routledge and Sons.

Lady Wept Alone. Carolyn Byrd Dawson. LC 40-7932. 1940. Pub. for the Crime Club by Doubleday, Doran and Co., Inc.

Lady, What a Life? Mabel Margaret Clark. LC 28-1968. 1927. Harper & Brothers.

Lady Who Came to Stay. Robin Edgerton Spencer. LC 31-28167. 1931. A. A. Knopf.

Lady Who Lost. Alice Beal Parsons. LC 33-1449. Gotham House, Inc.

Lady Who Loved New York. Richard Laurence Gordon. LC 76-28359. 8.95 (ISBN 0-690-01213-6). Crowell.

Lady Who Smoked Cigars. Rupert Hughes. LC 13-2500. 0.50. D. FitzGerald, Inc.

Lady William. Margaret Oliphant Wilson Oliphant. LC 7-32610. 1893. Macmillan and Co.

Lady with a Flute to Be Tuned. Mark Harvey. 1971. pap. 0.75 (Pub. by Stone-Marrow Pr). SBD.

Lady with a Past. Harriet Henry, pseud. LC 31-150923. 1931. W. Morrow & Company.

Lady with Jade: A Novel. Margaret Mackprang Mackay. LC 39-25876. The John Day Company.

Lady with Lapdog: And Other Stories. Anton Pavlovich Chekhov. LC 64-55899. (Penguin classics). 1964. Penguin Books.

Lady with Lapdog & Other Stories. Anton Pavlovich Chekhov. Tr. by David Magarshack. (Classics Ser.). (Orig.). 1964. pap. 3.95 (ISBN 0-14-044143-3). Penguin.

Lady with Parasol. Elizabeth Frances Corbett. LC 46-8002. 1946. Doubleday & Company, Inc.

Lady with the Camellias. Alexandre Dumas. LC 6-42307. (On cover: Belford American novel series. vol. ii. no. 7). Belford Company.

Lady with the Camellias (Camille) connoisseur ed. Alexandre Dumas. LC 5-32479. (Added t.-p.: Comedie d'amour series). 1905. Societe Des Beaux-Arts.

Lady with the Dice: A New and Unusual Mystery Novel. Joel Townsley Rogers. LC 47-16999. (Handi-book mysteries. 56). 1946. Quinn Publishing Company, Inc.

Lady with the Dog. And Other Stories. Anton Pavlovich Chekhov. Tr. by Garnett, Constance (Black) LC 17-15285. (Half-title: The tales of Chekhov, vol. iii). 1917. 1.50. The Macmillan Company.

Lady with the Moving Parts: A Novel. Merrill Joan Gerber. LC 78-57322. 8.95 (ISBN 0-87795-193-4). Arbor House.

Lady with the Rubies. Eugenie John. Tr. by Wister, Annis Lee (Furness) LC 7-9906. 1885. J. B. Lippincott Company.

Lady with the Rubies. Eugenie John. Tr. by Miller, Hettie E. LC 7-990761. (On cover: The enterprise series, no. 29). E. A. Weeks & Company.

Lady with the X-Ray Eyes. Tr. by Krassimira Noneva. Svetoslav Minkov. LC 66-7634. 1965. bds., 3.60. Foreign Langs. Pr.

Lady with X-Ray Eyes. M. Svetoslav. 1965. 3.90x o.p. (B91). Vanous.

Lady Without Jewels. Arthur Frederick Goodrich. 1909. D. Appleton and Company.

Lady Without Mercy. Roman McDougald. LC 48-5729. (Inner sanctum mystery). 1948. Simon and Schuster.

Lady Wu: A Novel. Lin Yutang. LC 65-132935. bds., 4.95. Putnam.

Lady Zia. Patrick Wynnton. LC 28-19244. 1928. Doubleday, Doran and Company, Inc.

Lady. 1st Ed. Conrad Richter. LC 57-566041. 1957. Knopf.

Ladybird. Grace Livingston Hill. LC 75-35809. 1975. 9.95. American Reprint Co.

Ladybird. Grace Livingston Hill. LC 30-9486. 1930. J. B. Lippincott Company.

Ladybird Mystery. Eunice Pennington. 1974. 4.50; pap. 2.50. Pennington.

Ladybrook. Eleanor Farjeon. LC 31-6269. 1931. Frederick A. Stokes Company.

Ladycat: A Novel. Nancy Greenwald. LC 79-25665. 8.95 (ISBN 0-517-54102-5). Crown Publishers.

Ladye Nancye: Or, The Woman in Black. Eliza M. J. Humphreys. (On cover: Seaside library. Pocket ed., no. 1253). 1889. G. Munro.

Ladyfingers. Jackson Gregory. LC 20-8277. 1920. C. Scribner's Sons.

Ladyfingers. Suzanne White. LC 76-53028. 8.95 (ISBN 0-87223-473-8). Playboy Press.

Ladygrove. John Frederick Burke. LC 78-14539. 1978. 8.95 (ISBN 0-698-10933-3). Coward, McCann.

Lady's Drawing Room. LC 74-16069. (Flowering of the Novel). 1974. (ISBN 0-8240-1110-4). Garland Pub.

Lady's Drawing Room. Ed. by Michael F. Shugrue. (Novel in England 1700-1775). 1974. Repr. of 1744 ed. lib. bdg. 50.00 (ISBN 0-8240-1110-4). Garland Pub.

Lady's Fancy. Anne Tedlock Brooks. 1948. Gramercy Pub. Co.

Lady's Honor: A Chronical of Events in the Time of Marlborough. Bass Blake. LC 2-23413. (Appleton's town and country library. no. 316). 1902. D. Appleton and Company.

Lady's Lady. Ann Bell. LC 40-326101. House of Field, Inc.

Lady's Maid. Nella J. Benson. 1982. pap. 2.95 (ISBN 0-553-20479-3). Bantam.

Lady's Masquerade. Maggie Gladstone, pseud. LC 80-80988. 176p. (Orig.). 1980. pap. 1.75 (ISBN 0-87216-695-3). Playboy Pbks.

Lady's Mile. Mary Elizabeth Braddon Maxwell. (On cover: Seaside library. Pocked ed. no. 497). 1885. G. Munro.

Lady's Mile. Mary Elizabeth Braddon Maxwell. (On cover: Lovell's library. no. 880). 1887. J. W. Lovell Company.

Ladysmead. Jane Gillespie. LC 82-16773. 1983. 9.95 (ISBN 0-312-46433-9). St. Martin's Press.

Lafayette's Pigeons. Cole Atwood. LC 74-149417. 1971. 7.95. World Pub. Co.

Lafcadio's Adventures. Andre Paul Guillaume Gide. LC 79-24000. 1980. 10.00 (ISBN 0-8376-0452-4). R. Bentley.

Lafcadio's Adventures. Les Caves Du Vatican. Translated from the French by Dorothy Bussy. Andre Paul Guillaume Gide. LC 53-175857. (Doubleday anchor book, A 7). 1953. Doubleday.

L'affaire Jones: A Novel. Hillel Bernstein. LC 33-36720. 1934. Frederick A. Stokes Company.

Lafitte. Joseph Holt Ingraham. LC 70-104494. 1970. (ISBN 0-8398-0850-X). Literature House.

Lafitte of Louisiana. Mary Devereux. LC 2-15863. 1902. Little, Brown, and Company.

Lafitte: the Pirate of the Gulf. Joseph Holt Ingraham. LC 72-8170. 1972. (ISBN 0-8422-8078-2). MSS Information Corp.

Lafitte, the Pirate of the Gulf. Joseph Holt Ingraham. LC 79-93630. 1970. (ISBN 0-512-00360-2). Garrett Press.

Lafitte: The Pirate of the Gulf. Joseph Holt Ingraham. LC 20-23138. 1836. Harper & Brothers.

Lafitte, the Pirate of the Gulf. Prentiss Ingraham. (On cover: Pirate story series. no. 4). The Arthur Westbrook Company.

Laggard in Love. Mary Jean Hickling Gwynne Kernahan. LC 6-13113. (On cover: Lovell's Westminster series, no. 21). United States Book Company.

Lago. John Lee. LC 78-60293. (Illus.). 1980. 11.95 (ISBN 0-385-12993-9). Doubleday.

Lagoon of Desire. William Fisher Alder. LC 21-3289. 1921. Wayside Press.

Laguerre: A Gascon of the Black Border. Ambrose Elliott Gonzales. LC 71-37594. (Black Heritage Library Collection). 1972. (ISBN 0-8369-8970-8). Books for Libraries Press.

Laguerre: A Gascon of the Black Border. Ambrose Elliott Gonzales. LC 25-211. 1924. The State Company.

Laguna Contracts. Elizabeth C. Allen. (Orig.). 1973. pap. 1.25 o.p. (ISBN 0-515-03116-X, V3180). Pyramid Pubns.

Lahoma. John Breckenridge Ellis. LC 13-25401. 1.25. The Bobbs-Merrill Company.

Laicus: Or, The Experiences of a Layman in a Country Parish. Lyman Abbott. 1872. Dodd & Mead.

Laid Back in Washington. Art Buchwald. 1981. 12.95 (ISBN 0-399-12648-1). Putnam Pub Group.

Laid in the Future. Rod Gray. (The Lady from L.U.S.T. Ser.). (O.s.i). (Orig.). 1974. pap. 0.95 o.s.i. (BT50667). Belmont-Tower.

Laid Out. Joyce Eliason. LC 75-25081. 8.95 (ISBN 0-06-011119-4). Harper & Row.

Laid up in Lavender. Stanley John Weyman. LC 7-32320. 1907. Longmans, Green, and Co.

Laidlaw. William McIlvanney. LC 76-62708. 7.95 (ISBN 0-394-41253-2). Pantheon Books.

Laidlaw. William McIlvanney. 1979. 1.95 (ISBN 0-445-04334-2). Popular Library.

Lair. James Herbert. 1979. pap. 2.25 (ISBN 0-451-08650-3, E8650, Sig). NAL.

Lair of Ancient Dreams. Asa Drake. 240p. 1982. pap. 2.50 (ISBN 0-380-80325-9, 80325-9). Avon.

Lair of the White Worm. Bram Stoker. 1966. 4.95 (ISBN 0-09-080690-5, Pub. by Hutchinson). Merrimack Pub Cir.

Lair of the White Worm. Bram Stoker. (Orig.). 1979. pap. 1.95 (ISBN 0-89083-519-5). Zebra.

Laird and the Lady. Joan Marshall Grant. LC 78-20221. (Grant, Joan Marshall, 1907-. Works). (Works.). (Illus.). 1980. 23.00 (ISBN 0-405-12562-3). Arno Press.

Laird and the Lady and Royal Scot. Vivian Donald, pseud. (Signet Book). 1978. 1.75 (ISBN 0-451-08059-9). New American Library.

Laird O'Cockpen. authorized ed. Eliza Margaret J. Humphreys. LC 42-284328. (On cover: Lovell's international series, no. 151). 1891. United States Book Company.

Laird of Norlaw. A Scottish Story. Margaret Oliphant Wilson Oliphant. LC 41-31127. 1859. Harper & Brothers.

Laird's Choice: A Novel. Rosamond Van Der Zee Marshall. LC 51-1926. 1951. Prentice-Hall.

Laird's Luck: And Other Fireside Tales. Quiller-Couch, Arthur Thomas. LC 72-10767. (Short story index reprint series). 1973. (ISBN 0-8369-4223-X). Books for Libraries Press.

Laird's Luck: And Other Fireside Tales. Arthur Thomas Quiller-Couch. LC 1-25672. 1901. C. Scribner's Sons.

Lairds of Turriff Hall. Angela Jamison. (queen-size gothic). 1974. (pbk.) 0.95. Popular Library.

Laird's Son. Lydia L Rouse. LC 8-6940. 1888. Phillips & Hunt.

Lajla: A Tale of Finmark. Jens Andreas Friis. Tr. by Markhus, Ingerid (Egge) LC 6-44723. 1888. G. P. Putnam's Sons.

Lake. Hilde Abel. LC 47-2145. 1947. Dodd, Mead & Company.

Lake. Margaret Eliza Ashmun. LC 24-21920. 1924. The Macmillan Company.

Lake. Yasunari Kawabata. LC 73-89699. 1974. 6.95 (ISBN 0-87011-216-3). Kodansha International; Distributed by Harper & Row.

Lake. George Moore. LC 5-37156. 1906. D. Appleton and Company.

Lake Frome Mystery. Arthur William Upfield. (Napoleon Bonaperts Mysteries). Repr. lib. bdg. 11.75x (ISBN 0-89190-557-X). Am Repr-Rivercity Pr.

Lake Front. Ruth Russell. LC 74-22811. (Labor Movement in Fiction and Non-Fiction). (Illus.). 1977. 21.50 (ISBN 0-404-58467-5). AMS Press.

Lake Front. Ruth Russell. LC 31-20402. 1931. Thomas S. Rockwell Company.

Lake-House. Fanny Lewald-Stahr & Greene, Nathaniel, 1797-1877, Tr. LC 8-28110. 1861. Ticknor and Fields.

Lake Mystery. Marvin Dana. LC 23-13883. 1923. A. C. McClurg & Co.

Lake of Darkness. Frances Cowen. 1974. (pbk.) 0.95. Ace Books.

Lake of Darkness. Ruth Rendell. LC 79-6087. 1980. 10.00 (ISBN 0-385-17026-2). Published for the Crime Club by Doubleday.

Lake of Dreams. John Oxenham & Oxenham, Erica Isobel, Joint Author. LC 42-184351. 1940. Longmans, Green and Co.

Lake of Fire. Lionel Houser. LC 33-9092. C. Kendall.

Lake of Life. Edmond Hamilton. LC 79-113573. (Lost fantasies; # 8). (Illus.). 5.50. R. Weinberg.

Lake of Shadows. Georgia M. Shewmake. (YA) 1980. 6.95 (Avalon). Bouregy.

Lake of Wine: By Bernard Capes. Bernard Edward Joseph Capes. (Half-title: Appletons' town and country library no. 239). 1898. D. Appleton and Company.

Lakeland Vet. Joyce Stranger, pseud. LC 72-184787. 1972. 5.95 (ISBN 0-670-41642-8). Viking Press.

Lakes of Fire: A Novel. Joseph Letteriello. LC 74-83718. 1974. 8.95. Valor House.

Lakeside: A Memorial of the Planting of the Church in Northwestern Pennsylvania. Samuel John Mills Eaton. LC 6-36809. 1880. Presbyterian Board of Colportage.

Lakeside Cottage. George C Marsh. LC 7-24672. 1894. J. H. Earle.

Lakestown Rebellion. Kristin Hunter. LC 78-1085. 9.95 (ISBN 0-684-15572-9). Scribner.

Lakeville Lady. Jeanne Bowman, pseud. (Starlight Romance Ser.). 1971. pap. 0.60 o.p. (60-466). Manor Bks.

Lakeville Lady: By Jeanne Bowman Pseud. Peggy O'More, pseud. LC 55-118739. 1955. Arcadia House.

Lakeville: Or, Substance and Shadow. Marie Healy Bigot. LC 6-12734. 1873. D. Appleton and Company.

Lal. A Novel. William Alexander Hammond. LC 7-50061. 1884. D. Appleton and Company.

Lalage's Lovers. James Owen Hannay. LC 11-269542. Hodder & Stoughton, George H. Doran Company.

Laleen: And Other Stories. Myrtle Johnston. LC 78-157781. (Short story index reprint series). 1971. (ISBN 0-8369-3893-3). Books for Libraries Press.

Laleen, and Other Stories. Myrtle Johnston. LC 38-32025. 1937. D. Appleton-Century Company, Incorporated.

Lali Yuga. Robert Bohm. 1976. pap. 7.00 (ISBN 0-89924-003-8). Lynx Hse.

Lalla Rookh, an Oriental Romance. Thomas Moore. LC 74-141486. (Illus.). 179p. Repr. of 1930 ed. 14.50 o.p. (ISBN 0-8371-5871-0). Greenwood.

L'Allegro-Milton. (Classics Ser.). slip case 7.95 (ISBN 0-88088-937-3). Peter Pauper.

Lally of the Brigade: A Romance. L MacManus. LC 99-3595. 1899. L. C. Page and Company (Incorporated).

Lalor's Maples. Katherine Eleanor Conway. LC 1-27460. 1901. The Pilot Publishing Company.

Lamaar Ransom, Private Eye. David D Galloway. LC 79-63414. 1980. (u.s.) 11.95 (ISBN 0-7145-3686-5). J. Calder.

L'amante Anglaise. Marguerite Duras. LC 68-31618. 1968. 3.95. Grove Press.

L'amante Anglaise. Marguerite Duras. LC 79-21573. 1979. 11.00 (ISBN 0-8357-0472-6). Reprinted for Grove Press by University Microfilms International.

Lamarchos. Jo Clayton. (Science Fiction Ser.). 1981. pap. 2.25 (ISBN 0-87997-627-6, UE 1649). DAW Bks.

Lamarchos. Jo Clayton. (Science Fiction Ser). (Orig.). 1978. pap. 1.50 o.p. (ISBN 0-87997-354-4, UW1354). DAW Bks.

Lamarchos: A Novel of the Diadem. Jo Clayton. 1.50 (ISBN 0-87997-354-4). DAW Books.

Lamb. Bernard MacLaverty. LC 80-18167. 1980. 8.95 (ISBN 0-8076-0990-0). G. Braziller.

Lamb in His Bosom. Caroline Pafford Miller. LC 33-22931. 1933. Harper & Brothers.

Lamb in His Bosom: By Caroline Miller. Caroline Pafford Miller. LC 66-9740. 1966. 5.95, 4.98 lib. ed.,. N. S. Berg.

Lamb: L'agneau) Translated by Gerard Hopkins. Francois Mauriac. LC 56-5193. 1955. Farrar, Straus and Cudahy.

Lamb of Abyssalia. Joyce Carol Oates. LC 79-66104. (Illus.). 1980. softcover, handbound 15.00; softcover, handbound & signed 35.00. Pomegranate.

Lambda Five-Five-Five. William D. Miller. 1978. pap. 2.95 (ISBN 0-89185-176-3). Anthelion Pr.

Lambda I: And Other Stories; an Anthology. Ed. by John Carnell. LC 72-268401. (Penguin science fiction). 1965. Penguin Books.

Lambert Revels. Terence De Vere White. LC 75-91233. 1970. 5.95 o.p. (936006, Pub. by Atlantic Monthly Pr). Little.

Lambert Revels. Terence De Vere White. LC 75-91233. 1970. 5.95. Little, Brown.

Lambing Out, and Other Stories. Mary Clearman. LC 77-274. 1977. 8.00 (ISBN 0-8262-0227-6). University of Missouri Press.

Lambs in the Meadow. Lee Reay. LC 79-66222. (Illus.). 1979. 7.95 (ISBN 0-934826-00-5); pap. 5.95 (ISBN 0-934826-01-3). Meadow Lane.

Lambs of Fire. Pierre Gascar, pseud. Tr. by M. Lawrence. LC 65-12526. 1965. 5.00 (ISBN 0-8076-0285-X). Braziller.

Lambs to the Slaughter. Gladstone Abisdid. 3.50 o.p. Vantage.

Lamb's War. Jan De Hartog. 512p. 1983. pap. 3.95 (ISBN 0-449-20019-1, Crest). Fawcett.

Lamb's War: A Novel. Jan De Hartog. LC 78-20201. 8.95 (ISBN 0-06-010995-5). Harper & Row.

Lame Dog Murder. John Creasey. LC 70-185119. (Falcon's head mystery). 1972. 5.95 (ISBN 0-529-04481-1). World Pub.

Lame Dog's Diary: A Novel. Sarah Broom Macnaughtan. 1906. Dodd, Mead & Company.

Lame Duck. E. M. Beekman. LC 71-132795. 1971. 5.95. Houghton Mifflin.

Lame Englishman. Warwick Deeping. LC 11-8984. 1911. 1.20. Cassell and Company Ltd.

Lament: A Novel. David Sunset Carson. LC 73-7613. 1973. 5.95 (ISBN 0-8184-0175-3). Grove Press; Distributed by L. Stuart.

Lament for a City. 1st Ed. Henry Bettle Hough. LC 60-11033. 1960. Atheneum Publishers.

Lament for a Lady Laird. Margot Arnold, pseud. LC 81-86251. 224p. (Orig.). 1982. pap. 2.50 (ISBN 0-86721-132-6). Playboy Pbks.

Lament for a Lonesome Corpse. Ruth Elizabeth Traughber Reeves. LC 51-10925. 1951. Phoenix Press.

Lament for a Lost Lover. Philippa Carr, pseud. 1978. pap. 1.95 (ISBN 0-449-23657-9, Crest). Fawcett.

Lament for a Lost Lover. Philippa Carr, pseud. LC 77-9497. 1977. 8.95 (ISBN 0-399-12021-1). Putnam Pub Group.

Lament for a Lost Lover. Eleanor Hibbert. LC 77-9497. 8.95 (ISBN 0-399-12021-1). Putnam.

Lament for a Lousy Lover. Carter Brown, pseud. LC 61-7274. (Signet book, S5186). 1960. New American Library of World Literature.

Lament for a Lousy Lover. Alan Geoffrey Yates. LC 61-727. (Signet book, S1856). 1960. New American Library of World Literature.

Lament for a Maker. Michael Innes, pseud. pap. 0.95 o.p. (02143, Collier). Macmillan.

Lament for a Maker. John Innes MacKintosh Stewart. LC 74-159157. 1973. 0.35 (ISBN 0-14-003598-2). Penguin.

Lament for a Maker: A Detective Story. John Innes Mackintosh Stewart. LC 38-201184. 1938. Dodd, Mead & Company.

Lament for a Virgin. Lionel White. LC 60-23478. (Gold medal books, S949). 1960. Fawcett Publications.

Lament for Agnes. Jan Albert Goris. LC 74-34320. (Library of Netherlandic literature; v. 6). 1975. 6.95 (ISBN 0-8057-8150-1). Twayne Publishers.

Lament for Barney Stone. 1st Ed. Robert Glynn Kelly. LC 61-55004. 1961. Holt, Rinehart and Winston.

Lament for Four Brides. Evelyn Berckman. LC 59-8298. (Red badge detective). 1959. Dodd, Mead.

Lament for Four Brides. Evelyn Berckman. (Signet book). 1974. (pbk.) 1.25. New American Library.

Lament for Four Virgins. Lael Tucker Wertenbaker. LC 52-5169. 1952. Random House.

Lament for Four Virgins: A Novel. Lael Tucker, pseud. LC 52-5169. 1952. Random House.

Lament for Julie. Robert Colby. 1970. pap. 0.75 o.p. (75-317). Manor Bks.

Lament for Lost Lovers. Alanna Knight. (Belmont Tower Book). 1977. 1.25 (ISBN 0-505-51137-1). Tower Publications.

Lament for the Bride. Helen Kieran Reilly. LC 51-11443. 1951. Random House.

Lament for William. Charlotte Murray Russell, pseud. LC 47-4996. 1947. Pub. for the Crime Club by Doubleday.

Lament of Dives. Walter Besant. LC 6-12880. (On cover: Lovell's international series, no. 46). 1889. F. F. Lovell & Company.

Lament of Dives. Walter Besant. (On cover: Seaside library. Pocket ed., no. 1247). 1889. G. Munro.

Laments for the Living. Dorothy Rothschild Parker. LC 30-17714. 1930. The Viking Press.

Laments for the Living. Dorothy Rothschild Parker. LC 35-12202. 1935. The Viking Press.

Lamh Dearg Aboo, Battle Cry of the O'Neills, High Kings of Ancient Ireland: A Romantic Novel Based on Historical Legends of the Ancient Irish People. Carlton Greer George. LC 57-16786. C. G. George & Co.

Lamia. P. Thyraud De Vosjoli. LC 70-121424. 1970. 6.95 o.p. (ISBN 0-316-18160-9). Little.

Lamia: A Novel of Sexual Horror. Tristan Travis. LC 82-2415. 420p. 1982. 15.95 (ISBN 0-525-24113-2, 01549-460). Dutton.

Lamiel: By Stendhal Pseud. Translated and with an Introd. by T. W. Earp. Marie Henri Beyle. LC 52-10026. (Direction, 23). 1952. New Directions.

Lamiel: Or, The Ways of the Heart. Marie Henri Beyle. LC 77-11672. 1978. 15.50. H. Fertig.

Lamiel: Or, The Ways of the Heart, Translation and Preface. Marie Henri Beyle. Tr. by Le Clereq. Jacques Georges Clemenceau. LC 29-5225. 1929. Brentano's.

L'Amour Westerns, 4 bks. Louis L'Amour. Incl. To Tame a Land; Heller With a Gun; Tall Stranger; Last Stand at Papago Wells. (Western Fiction Ser.). 1981. Set. lib. bdg. 40.00 (ISBN 0-8398-2661-3, Gregg). G K Hall.

Lamp for Nightfall. Erskine Caldwell. 1965. pap. 0.50 o.p. (50-241). Manor Bks.

Lamp for Nightfall. Erskine Caldwell. 144p. 1972. pap. 0.75 o.p. (T2523, GM). Fawcett World.

Lamp for Nightfall. 1st Ed. Erskine Caldwell. LC 52-5516. 1952. Duell, Sloan and Pearce.

Lamp in Jerusalem: By Drayton Mayrant. Katherine Drayton Mayrant Simons. LC 57-10269. 1957. Appleton-Century-Crofts.

Lamp in the Desert. Ethel May Dell. LC 19-129831. 1919. G. P. Putnam's Sons.

Lamp in the Desert. Ethel May Dell. LC 22-4741. 1921. Grosset & Dunlap.

Lamp in the Valley: A Novel of Alaska. Arthur John Arbuthnott Stringer. LC 38-24562. The Bobbs-Merrill Company.

Lamp in the Window. Ethel Field Foster. LC 38-457252. De Vorss & Co.

Lamp in the Window. Edith Gividen. 1980. 5.75 (ISBN 0-8062-1537-2). Carlton.

Lamp in the Window. Wynder. 1970. pap. 1.25 o.p. Chr Lit.

Lamp of Destiny: A Novel. Isabel Constance Clarke. LC 27-25778. 1927. Benziger Brothers.

Lamp of Fate. Margaret Bass Pedler. LC 22-13398. George H. Doran Company.

Lamp of Fate. Margaret Bass Pedler. LC 28-179403. 1921. Grosset & Dunlap.

Lamp on the Plains. Paul Horgan. LC 37-3743. 1937. Harper & Brothers.

Lamp Post. Gregor-Dellin, Martin. LC 64-17702. 1964. Knopf.

Lamp Still Burns. 1st Ed. Edith Wherry. LC 54-13139. 1955. Vantage Press.

Lamp Unto My Feet. 1st Ed. Lyna Duncan Adams. LC 55-7179. 1955. Vantage Press.

Lamplighter. Maria Susanna Cummins. LC 70-93609. 1969. Garrett Press.

Lamplighter. Maria Susanna Cummins. LC 11-10566. 1882. Houghton, Mifflin and Compny.

Lamplighter. Maria Susanna Cummins. 1891. Houghton, Mifflin and Company.

Lamplighter. new and complete ed. Maria Susanna Cummins. LC 2-27515. 1902. Houghton, Mifflin and Company.

Lamplighter. Maria Susanna Cummins. LC 13-23591. (On cover: The Astor prose series). 1912. T. Y. Crowell Company.

Lamplighter. Ed. by Edward Foster. LC 70-93609. (American Fiction Ser). 1969. lib. bdg. 15.50 o.s.i. (ISBN 0-512-00119-7). Garrett Pr.

Lamplighter. 20th Thousand. Maria Susanna Cummins. LC 6-31737. 1854. J. P. Jewett & Company.

Lamplighter's Story: Hunted Down; The Detective Police: And Other Nouvellettes. Charles Dickens. LC 6-264451. T. B. Peterson and Brothers.

Lamprey's Legacy. Richard Shaw. LC 81-3858. 1981. 11.95 (ISBN 0-8253-0068-1). Beaufort Books.

Lamprey's Legacy: A Novel. Richard Shaw. LC 81-3858. 256p. 1981. 13.95 o.p. (ISBN 0-8253-0068-1). Beaufort Bks NY.

Lamps at High Noon: A Novel. Jack Balch. LC 41-9960. Modern Age.

Lamps of Fire and Flames: A Novel. Joe Van De Kattebeek. LC 51-13306. 1951. Exposition Press.

Lampton Dreamers. Leslie Purnell Davies. LC 67-14126. 1967. Published for the Crime Club by Doubleday.

Lamy Killer. George Harmon Coxe. LC 49-8191. 1949. A. A. Knopf.

Lanagan, Amateur Detective. Edward H Hurlburt. LC 13-156408. 1913. 1.25. Sturgis & Walton Company.

Lanark. Alasdair Gray. LC 80-7895. (Harper colophon book). 8.95. Harper & Row.

Lancaster Triple Thousand: A Novel of Suspense. 1st Ed. William B Woods. LC 56-7473. 1956. Exposition Press.

Lancasters: A Novel. Elizabeth Custer Nearing. LC 47-5149. 1947. Coward-McCann, Inc.

Lancaster's Choice. Alexander McVeigh Miller. (On cover: Seaside library. Pocket ed., no. 269). 1884. G. Munro.

Lancaster's Choice. Alexander McVeigh Miller. (On cover: The library of American authors, no. 42). 1892. G. Munro.

Lance, a Novel About Multicultural Men. Edward Froelich Haskell. LC 41-12247. The John Day Company.

Lance Falls in Love. Louise Platt Hauck. LC 41-514716. The Penn Publishing Company.

Lance of Longinus. Hubertus Prince Loewenstein. LC 46-234. 1946. The Macmillan Company.

Lanced in Light. Larry Rubin. LC 67-20329. 1967. 4.50 o.p. (ISBN 0-15-147675-6). HarBraceJ.

Lancelot. Walker Percy. LC 76-57197. 1977. 8.95 (ISBN 0-374-18313-9). Farrar, Straus and Giroux.

Lancelot. Walker Percy. 1978. 2.25 (ISBN 0-380-01861-6). Avon Books.

Lancelot Du Lac: The Non-Cyclic Old French Prose Romance, 2 vols. Ed. by Elspeth Kennedy. 1981. Set. 169.00x (ISBN 0-19-812064-8). Oxford U Pr.

Lancelot, or The Knight of the Cart. Chretien De Troyes. Ed. by William W. Kibler. (Garland Library of Medieval Literature). (O.s.i.). 1981. lib. bdg. 36.00 o.s.i. (ISBN 0-8240-9442-5). Garland Pub.

Lancelot: Scottish Metrical Romance of Lancelot Du Lak. Repr. of 1839 ed. 18.50 (ISBN 0-384-31180-6). Johnson Repr.

Lancelot Ward, M. P. A Love Story. Charles Joseph Galliari Rampini. LC 8-25967. (On cover: Seaside library. Pocket ed., no. 599). G. Munro.

Lances of Linwood: Chivalry in England a Story of Edward, the Black Prince. Charlotte Mary Yonge. 1881. D. Lothrop & Co.

Lances of Lynwood. Charlotte Mary Yonge. LC 8-30427. 1856. D. Appleton and Company.

Lances of Lynwood. Charlotte Mary Yonge. LC 4-17491. 1902. Macmillan and Co., Limited.

Lances of Lynwood. Charlotte Mary Yonge. (Half-title: Everyman's library, ed. by Ernest Rhys. For young people. no. 579). 1912. J. M. Dent & Sons. Ltd.

Lances of Lynwood. Charlotte Mary Yonge. LC 36-37497. (Half-title: Everyman's library, ed. by Ernest Rhys. For young people. no. 579). 1925. J. M. Dent & Sons, Ltd.

Lances of Lynwood. Charlotte Mary Yonge. LC 29-18264. (The Macmillan children's classics). 1929. The Macmillan Company.

Lancet: A Novel. Garet Rogers. LC 56-10243. 1956. Putnam.

Lanchester of Brazenose. Ronald MacDonald. LC 13-11513. 1913. John Lane Company.

Land. Mary Vigliante, pseud. (Orig.). 1979. pap. 1.95 (ISBN 0-532-19255-9). Woodhill.

Land: A Novel. Liam O'Flaherty. LC 46-38093. 1946. Random House.

Land and the Well. Hilda Wernher & Singh, Huthi. LC 46-6620. 1946. The John Day Company.

Land Baron. John Henry Reese. LC 76-181794. 1974. 4.95 (ISBN 0-385-03429-6). Doubleday.

Land Baron Mirage. Rosalind Earnest Dickenson. 1976. 4.00 o.p. (ISBN 0-682-48582-9). Exposition.

Land Behind God's Back: By A Den Doolaardpseud. Translated by N. C. Bruinwold Riedel. Cornelis Spoelstra. LC 58-11811. 1958. Simon and Schuster.

Land Beyond. William Corlett. LC 75-38207. 1976. 6.95 (ISBN 0-87888-091-7). Bradbury Press.

Land Beyond see Hungry Land.

Land Beyond: By Bill Gulick. Grover C Gulick. LC 57-9977. 1958. Houghton Mifflin.

Land Beyond the Mountains. Janice Holt Giles. LC 58-9062. 1974. 9.95 (ISBN 0-910220-62-X). Norman S. Berg.

Land Beyond the Mountains. janice holt giles. ed. Janice Holt Giles. 1.75 (ISBN 0-380-00593-X). Avon Books.

Land Beyond the River. Jesse Stuart. LC 72-7287. 1973. 7.95 (ISBN 0-07-062241-8). McGraw-Hill.

Land Beyond The Tempest: By Drayton Mayrant Pseud. Katherine Drayton Mayrant Simons. LC 59-11451. 1960. Coward-McCann.

Land Breakers. John Ehle. LC 63-10610. 1964. Harper & Row.

Land Claimers. John Fleming Wilson. LC 11-9155. 1911. Little, Brown, and Company.

Land Endures. Mary Emily Pearce. LC 80-28953. 1981. 10.95 (ISBN 0-312-46440-1). St. Martin's Press.

Land for My Sons: A Frontier Tale of the American Revolution. Maribelle Cormack & Alexander, William Prindle. LC 39-964789. 1939. D. Appleton-Century Company, Incorporated.

Land for Their Inheritance. Ethel Mary Granger Bennett. LC 55-13722. Bouregy & Curl.

Land-Girl's Love Story. Berta Ruck. LC 19-4789. 1919. 1.50. Dodd, Mead and Company.

Land God Gave to Cain: A Novel of Labrador. 1st American Ed. Hammond Innes. LC 58-12631. 1958. Knopf.

Land Grabbers. Peter Keyes. LC 75-13498. 0.95 (ISBN 0-89041-011-9). Major Books.

Land Grabbers. Lee D. Willoughby. 1981. pap. 2.75 (ISBN 0-440-04762-5). Dell.

Land Grabbers: By John S. Daniels Pseud. Wayne D Overholser. LC 54-94264. 1955. Lippincott.

Land Ho! Morgan Robertson. LC 76-101290. (Short story index reprint series). 1969. Books for Libraries Press.

Land Ho! Morgan Robertson. LC 5-35795. 1905. Harper & Brothers.

Land I Have Chosen. Ellin Mackay Berlin. LC 44-6036. 1944. Doubleday, Doran & Co., Inc.

Land I Have Chosen. Ellin Mackay Berlin. LC 45-9065. 1945. The Blakiston Company.

Land I Live: A Novel. Stephen Longstreet. LC 43-552722. 1943. Random House.

Land I Will Show Three: A Novel. Marian M Schoolland. LC 49-5158. 1949. W. B. Eerdmans Pub. Co.

Land in the Day. Julio Ortega. Tr. by Ewing Campbell from Span. LC 78-70338. 1978. cancelled (ISBN 0-918722-02-0); pap. text ed. 3.95 (ISBN 0-918722-03-9). Nefertiti.

Land Is Bright. Archie Binns. LC 39-27109. 1939. C. Scribner's Sons.

Land Is Bright. Noel Bertram Gerson. LC 61-12524. 1961. Doubleday.

Land Is Bright. James Arthur Kjelgaard. LC 58-8284. 1958. Dodd, Mead.

Land Killer. Lee Hoffman. LC 78-406. 1978. 7.95 (ISBN 0-385-13379-0). Doubleday.

Land Lay Waiting. 1st Ed. Ellanore J Parker. LC 55-10073. 1955. Pageant Press.

Land Leaguers: A Story of Irish Life in the Present Time. Anthony Trollope. (On cover: The seaside library. Pocket ed. no. 32). 1883. G. Munro.

Land Leviathan. Michael Moorcock. LC 74-1504. (Doubleday science fiction). 1974. 4.95 (ISBN 0-385-01473-2). Doubleday.

Land Lies Pretty. 'Op-Jah-Mo-Mak-Ya. A Story of the Great Sauk Trail in 1832 with an Introduction to the Northwest Territory. Chapter Head Drawings by Jane Penfold. Merritt Greene. LC 59-14503. 1959. Hillsdale School Supply.

Land O' the Leal a Novel. Helen Buckingham Mathers Reeves. LC 7-15436. 1896. Dodd, Mead and Company.

Land of a Million Elephants. Asa Baber. LC 71-103886. 1970. 4.95. Morrow.

Land of Big Rivers: A Story of the Northwest. Arthur Murray Chisholm. LC 24-28887. 20.00. Chelsea House.

Land of Cain. 1st Ed. Peter Lappin. LC 58-5946. 1958. Doubleday.

Land of Clouded Skies: V.2. by Ethan W. Bruce. Ethan W Bruce. (Reflection bk.). 1966. 8.50. Carlton.

Land of Cockayne: A Novel. Matilde Serao. LC 2-629851. 1901. Harper & Brothers.

Land of Content. Edith Barnard Delano. LC 13-376523. 1913. 1.30. D. Appleton and Company.

Land of Darkness, a Novel. 1st Ed. Roy J Hansen. LC 52-10989. 1952. Exposition Press.

Land of Darkness: Along with Some Further Chapters in the Experiences of the Little Pilgrim. Margaret Oliphant Wilson Oliphant. LC 1-164327. 1888. Macmillan and Co.

Land of Enchantment. Eleanor Craig. (Candlelight Romance). 1974. (pbk.) 0.75. Dell.

Land of Enough. Charles Edward Jefferson. LC 17-24813. 0.50. Thomas Y. Crowell Company.

Land of Fadeless Stars. rev. ed. Edwin Arnold. LC 48-11087. 1948. Christopher Pub. House.

Land of Fadeless Stars. Edwin Arnold. LC 45-22322. Alpha Law Brief Company.

Land of Forgotten Men. Edison Marshall. 1923. 1.75. Little, Brown, and Company.

Land of Frozen Suns; a Novel. Bertrand William Sinclair. LC 10-969558. G. W. Dillingham Company.

Land of Green Ginger. Winifred Holtby. LC 28-5558. 1928. R. M. McBride & Company.

Land of Green Ginger. Winifred Holtby. LC 77-12075. 1977. 7.50. (ISBN 0-915864-26-6) (ISBN 0-915864-25-8). Cassandra Editions.

Land of Green Ginger: A Romance. Winifred Holtby. LC 76-381293. 1976. 0.65 (ISBN 0-552-10119-2). Corgi.

Land of Hidden Men. Edgar Rice Burroughs. 1977. pap. 1.95 (ISBN 0-441-47016-5). Ace Bks.

Land of Joy: A Novel. Ralph Henry Barbour. LC 3-11818. 1903. Doubleday, Page & Company.

Land of Last Chance. George Washington Ogden. LC 19-15485. 1919. A. C. McClurg & Co.

Land of Laughs. Jonathan Carroll. LC 79-56269. 1980. 10.95 (ISBN 0-670-41755-6). Viking Press.

Land of Leys. Leslie Purnell Davies. LC 79-7121. 1979. 7.95 (ISBN 0-385-15358-9). Published for the Crime Club by Doubleday.

Land of Little Rain. Mary Hunter Austin. 1973. lib. bdg. 69.95 (ISBN 0-87968-182-9). Gordon Pr.

Land of Loneliness: And Other Stories. Seumas O'Kelly. LC 70-286427. 1969 (ISBN 0-7171-0270-X). Gill and Macmillan.

Land of Long Ago. Eliza Calvert Hall. LC 73-2938. (Short story index reprint series). 1973. (ISBN 0-8369-4252-3). Books for Libraries Press.

Land of Long Ago. Eliza Caroline Calvert Obenchain. LC 9-24960. 1909. Little, Brown & Company.

Land of Lost Content. Robert S Phillips. LC 70-134667. 1970. 5.95. Vanguard Press.

Land of Lure: A Story of the Columbia River Basin. Elliott Smith. LC 20-21001. 1920. Press of Smith-Kinney Company.

Land of Mist. Arthur Conan Doyle. LC 82-19642. 1927. A. L. Burt Company.

Land of Mist. Andrew Quiller. LC 80-71032. (Gladiators Ser.). 144p. 1981. pap. 2.95 (ISBN 0-87754-225-2). Chelsea Hse.

Land of Mystery. Cleveland Moffett. LC 13-23214. 1913. The Century Co.

Land of Nod: And Other Stories. Paul Green. LC 75-33880. 1976. 9.95 (ISBN 0-8078-1269-2). University of North Carolina Press.

Land of Oil. Robert V. Doak. 1978. pap. 3.95 (ISBN 0-89185-163-1). Anthelion Pr.

Land of Plenty. Robert Cantwell. LC 73-83664. (Crosscurrents/modern fiction). 1971. 10.00. Southern Illinois University Press.

Land of Plenty. Robert Cantwell. LC 34-103900.

Land of Pluck: Stories and Sketches for Young Folk. Mary Mapes Dodge. LC 4-16131. 1894. The Century Co.

Land of Promise. Paul Charles Joseph Bourget. LC 6-150041. F. T. Neely.

Land of Promise. Lazar Herrmann. Tr. by Henry, R. LC 35-2973. 1935. The Macmillan Company.

Land of Promise: A Novel. John Lawrence Barnard. LC 42-212363. 1942. Doubleday, Doran and Company, Inc.

Land of Promise: A Novelization of W. Somerset Maugham's Play. D Torbett & Maugham, William Somerset, 1874- LC 14-5819. E. J. Clode.

Land of Promises: By Joseph Wayne Pseud. 1st Ed. Wayne D Overholser. LC 62-8931. (Double D western). 1962. Doubleday.

Land of Purple Shadows. Idah Meacham Strobridge. LC 9-31479. 1909. The Artemisia Bindery.

Land of Rumblelow: A Fable in the Form of a Novel. Carlos Heard Baker. LC 63-13301. 1963. Scribner.

Land of Shadows. Frances C. Matranga. 1977. pap. 1.50 (ISBN 0-532-15292-1). Woodhill.

Land of Shvambrania: A Novel, with Maps, a Cost of Arms, and a Flag, from the Russian of Leo Kassil. Lev Abramovich Kassil' Tr. by Glass, Sylvia. LC 36-1009. 1935. The Viking Press.

Land of Spices: A Novel. Kate O'Brien. LC 41-10682. 1941. Doubleday, Doran & Company, Inc.

Land of Strangers. Lillian Budd. LC 53-8923. 1953. Lippincott.

Land of Strong Men. by frank tenney johnson. ed. Chisholm, Arthur Murray. LC 20-7301. The H. K. Fly Company.

Land of Sunny Days. Gerhard Lewis Wind. LC 26-14155. Concordia Publishing House.

Land of Tawny Beasts. Charles Causse & Vincent, Charles. Tr. by Cary, Elizabeth Luther. LC 9-34458. F. A. Stokes Company.

Land of Terror. Edgar Rice Burroughs. LC 63-21732. 1963. Canaveral Press.

Land of Terror. Edgar Rice Burroughs. LC 46-949. E. R. Burroughs, Inc.

Land of the Beautiful River. Helmer Linderholm. LC 62-11107. 1963. St Martin's Press.

Land of the Black Diamonds. Stanley Sluzalis. 2.75 o.p. Vantage.

Land of the Blue Flower. Frances Hodgson Burnett. LC 9-25815. 1909. Moffat, Yard and Company.

Land of the Blue Flower. Frances Hodgson Burnett. LC 16-22594. 1916. Moffat, Yard and Company.

Land of the Changing Sun. William Nathaniel Harben. LC 75-5648. (Gregg Press science fiction series). 1975. 11.50 (ISBN 0-8398-2305-3). Gregg Press.

Land of the Changing Sun. William Nathaniel Harben. LC 7-191813. The Merriam Company.

Land of the Children. Sergiel Ivanovich Gusev. Tr. by Selivanova, Nina Nikolaevna. LC 28-3370. 1928. Longmans, Green and Co.

Land of the Fathers. Sergey Ivanovich Gusev. Tr. by Selivanova, Nina Nikolaeyna. 1924. L. MacVeagh, The Dial Press.

Land of the Fathers. Sergei Ivanovich Gusev-Orenburgskii & Selivanova, Nina Nikolaevna, Tr. LC 24-23606. 1924. L. MacVeagh, The Dial Press.

Land of the Forgotten. Raymond J Lapanne. LC 64-57124. Author, Railroad St.

Land of the Forgotten. Raymond J Lapanne. LC 64-57124. 1964.

Land of the Fox. Jane Stuart. LC 74-14538. 1975. 6.95 (ISBN 0-07-062201-9). McGraw-Hill.

Land of the Free. Charles Alden Seltzer. LC 76-39977. 1976. 6.95 (ISBN 0-88411-112-1). Aeonian Press.

Land of the Free. Charles Alden Seltzer. LC 27-19221. 1927. Doubleday, Page & Company.

Land of the Giants, No. 2# The Hot Spot. Murray Leinster, pseud. (Orig.). 1969. pap. 0.60 o.p. (X1921). Pyramid Pubns.

Land of the Giants, No. 3# The Unknown Danger. Murray Leinster, pseud. (Orig.). 1969. pap. 0.60 o.p. (X2105). Pyramid Pubns.

Land of the Golden Mountain. Chin-Yang Li. LC 67-16511. 1967. Meredith Press.

Land of the Golden Scarabs. Diomedes De Pereyra. LC 28-236622. The Bobbs-Merrill Company.

Land of the Hidden Men. Edgar Rice Burroughs. 1982. pap. 2.25. Ace Bks.

Land of the Laurel: A Story of the Alleghanies. Oren Frederic Morton. LC 3-24206. (Arbor lodge series, III). 1903. The Acme Publishing Company.

Land of the Living: A Novel. Maude Lavinia Radford Warren. 1908. Harper & Brothers.

Land of the Living Dead. Neal Fyne. LC 77-84225. (Lost Race and Adult Fantasy Fiction). (Illus.). 1978. 17.00 (ISBN 0-405-10977-6). Arno Press.

Land of the Living Dead: A Narration of the Perilous Sojourn Therein of George Cowper, Mariner, in the Year 1835. Neal Fyne. Ed. by R. Reginald & Douglas Melville. LC 77-84224. (Lost Race & Adult Fantasy Ser.). (Illus.). 1978. Repr. of 1897 ed. lib. bdg. 17.00x (ISBN 0-405-10977-6). Ayer Co.

Land of the Living. 1st American Ed. 1962. Harper & Row.

Land of the Long Shadow. Oliver Lange. LC 80-54523. 10.95 (ISBN 0-87223-683-8). Seaview Books.

Land of the Pilgrims' Pride. Robert Paterson. LC 36-3534. 1936. Napier & Noyes.

Land of the Sky" Or, Adventures in Mountain Byways. Frances Christine Tiernan. LC 9-2483. 1876. D. Appleton and Company.

Land of the Snake Charmer. Ruth Seamonds. 1970. pap. 0.60 o.p. Moody.

Land of the Spirit. Thomas Nelson Page. LC 13-8250. 1913. C. Scribner's Sons.

Land of the Sun: Vistas Mexicanas a Novel. Frances Christine Tiernan. 1894. D. Appleton and Company.

Land of the Torreones. Clarence Budington Kelland. LC 46-313085. 1946. Harper & Brothers.

Land of Their Fathers. Marguerite Mooers Marshall. LC 38-8556. J. Messner, Inc.

Land of Tomorrow. Charlotte Margaret Kruger Bryant. LC 47-23208. 1947. Zondervan Publishing House.

Land of Tomorrow. Mons Daveson. (Harlequin Romances Ser.). 192p. 1982. pap. 1.50 (ISBN 0-373-02461-4). Harlequin Bks.

Land of Tomorrow. Charlotte Margaret Kruger. LC 47-23208. 1947. Zondervan Publishing House.

Land of Tomorrow: A Legend of Kentucky. Shirley Seifert. LC 37-375493. M. S. Mill Co., Inc.

Land of Tomorrow: A Novel of Kentucky in the Years Following the War Between the States. Louise Philipps. 336p. 1974. 8.50 o.p. (ISBN 0-682-47951-9). Exposition.

Land of Unreason. Lyon Sprague De Camp & Fletcher Pratt. 1979. pap. 1.75 (ISBN 0-440-14736-0). Dell.

Land of Unreason. Fletcher Pratt & De Camp, Lyon Sprague. LC 42-155478. 1942. H. Holt and Company.

Land of Waving Grass. J. H. Sellars, Jr. 1970. 3.50 o.p. Carlton.

Land of Youth. Richard Power. LC 63-19936. 1964. Dial Press.

Land Pirate: Or, The Wild Girl of the Beach. Benjamin Barker. LC 6-7210. 1847. F. Gleason.

Land Poor: A Chicago Parable. Robert C Givins. LC 6-43974. 1884. The Franklin Printing Company.

Land Poor: And Six Shorter Stories. Kate Mayhew Speake Penney. LC 28-11164. 1928. H. Vinal Limited.

Land Sharks. Robert Jesse Gresham. LC 34-22033. 1934. E. V. Brewster.

Land Spell. Gladys Hasty Carroll. LC 30-28895. 1930. The Macmillan Company.

Land That Drank the Rain: A Novel. William Hoffman. LC 81-18585. 1982. 14.95 (ISBN 0-8071-1004-3). Louisiana State University Press.

Land That Time Forgot. Edgar Rice Burroughs. LC 62-17747. 1962. Canaveral Press.

Land That Time Forgot. Edgar Rice Burroughs. LC 24-148829. 1924. A. C. McClurg & Co.

Land That Time Forgot. Edgar Rice Burroughs. LC 30-123348. 1925. Grosset & Dunlap.

Land That Time Forgot, and The Moon Maid: Two Science Fiction Novels. Edgar Rice Burroughs. LC 63-3183. 1963. Dover Publications.

Land That Touches Mine: A Novel. 1st Ed. John B Sanford. LC 53-5604. 1953. Doubleday.

Land They Loved. Geraldine D Cummins. LC 19-13643. 1919. The Macmillan Company.

Land They Possessed. Mary Worthy Breneman. LC 56-9617. 1956. Macmillan.

Land to Tame. Zola Helen Ross. LC 56-13046. 1956. Bobbs-Merrill.

Land Under England. Joseph O'Neill. LC 35-27365. 1935. Simon and Schuster.

Land Under England. Joseph O'Neill. LC 80-14273. 1980. 10.95 (ISBN 0-87951-117-6). Overlook Press.

Land Under Heaven. Pearl Ashby Tibbetts. LC 37-10494. 1937. Falmouth Book House.

Land Where Our Fathers Died. Helen S. Nuelle. 1978. pap. text ed. 1.50 (ISBN 0-532-15377-4). Woodhill.

Land Where the Sun Dies. Henry C. Carlisle. LC 74-16581. 1975. 8.95 (ISBN 0-399-11531-5). Putnam.

Land Without Moses: A Novel. Charles Curtis Munz. LC 38-7464. 1938. Harper & Brothers.

Land Without Shadow. Michael Mewshaw. LC 78-69661. 1979. 8.95 (ISBN 0-385-14504-7). Doubleday.

Land Without Thunder. Grae Ogot. 1968. 2.00 o.p. Northwestern U Pr.

Landed Gently. Alan Hunter. LC 60-110198. 1957. Roy Publishers.

Landed Gently. Alan Hunter. LC 76-17064. 1976. 6.95 (ISBN 0-02-557580-5). Macmillan.

Landfall. Julius Horwitz. LC 76-29904. 7.50. Holt, Rinehart and Winston.

Landfall. Helen Rose Hull. LC 52-13998. 1953. Coward-McCann.

Landfall. easy eye ed. Nevil Shute. pap. 0.75 o.p. (74-898). Lancer.

Landfall. Nevil Shute. 1959. Repr. of 1940 ed. 4.95 o.p. (ISBN 0-688-21867-9). Morrow.

Landfall: A Channel Story. Nevil Shute Norway. LC 40-27709. 1940. Morrow & Company.

Landfall Finesse. Daniel Da Cruz. 1975. (pbk.) 1.50 (ISBN 0-345-24362-5). Ballantine Books.

Landgrabbers. Dan J. Stevens. (Orig.). 1969. pap. 0.50 o.p. (B50-1013). Belmont-Tower.

Landings. Dennis Hamley. LC 78-74474. 1979. 6.95 (ISBN 0-233-97110-6). A Deutsch.

Landlady. William Arthur Neubauer. LC 45-863815. 1945. Phoenix Press.

Landlady. Constance Rauch. LC 74-30578. 1975. 6.95 (ISBN 0-399-11507-2). Putnam.

Landlady on Riverside Drive. Sally Chayes. LC 31-22235. The Vanguard Press.

Landler. Theodore Enslin. 1975. 16.00 o.p.; pap. 8.00 o.p. Elizabeth Pr.

Landlocked. Lessing, Doris May. LC 66-44902. (Her Children of violence, 4). 1965. MacGibbon & Kee.

Landlocked: A Complete Novel from Doris Lessing's Masterwork, Children of Violence. Doris May Lessing. 1970. pap. 3.95 (ISBN 0-452-25138-9, Z5138, Plume). NAL.

Landlocked Man. Alfred Coppel. LC 70-182326. 1972. 6.95 (ISBN 0-15-147680-2). Harcourt Brace Jovanovich.

Landlooker. William F Steuber. LC 57-9353. 1957. Bobbs-Merrill.

Landloper: The Romance of a Man on Foot. Holman Francis Day. LC 15-146703. 1915. 1.35. Harper & Brothers.

Landlord. Kristin Hunter. LC 66-15075. bds., 5.95. Scribners.

Landlord at Lion's Head. William Dean Howells. LC 82-17821. 1983. 8.95 (ISBN 0-486-24455-5). Dover.

Landlord at Lion's Head. William Dean Howells. Repr. of 1900 ed. lib. bdg. 30.00 (ISBN 0-8495-2248-X). Arden Lib.

Landlord at Lion's Head: A Novel. William Dean Howells. LC 75-41144. 1976. 27.50 (ISBN 0-404-14778-X). AMS Press.

Landlord at Lion's Head: A Novel. William Dean Howells. LC 7-5770. 1897. Harper & Brothers.

Landlord at Lion's Head: A Novel. William Dean Howells & Smedley, William Thomas, 1858-1920. Illus. LC 16-9379. 1908. Harper & Brothers.

Landlord's Daughter. Monica Dickens. LC 68-24830. 1968. 5.95. Doubleday.

Landlord's Daughter. Harrison Smith Morris. LC 23-9856. 1923. The Penn Publishing Company.

Landlubbers. Gertrude King. LC 9-8575. 1909. 1.50. Doubleday, Page & Company.

Landmark. James Lane Allen. LC 70-110177. (Short story index reprint series). 1970. Books for Libraries Press.

Landmark. James Lane Allen. LC 25-245879. 1925. The Macmillan Company.

Landmarks. Edward Verrall Lucas. LC 14-19689. 1914. The Macmillan Company.

Landmarks. Hilda Morris. LC 41-17326. G. P. Putnam's Sons.

Lando. Louis L'Amour. LC 62-20973. (Bantam western). 1962. Bantam Books.

Landolin. Berthold Auerbach. Tr. by Irish, Annie B. LC 6-4508. (Leisure hour series, v. 94). 1878. H. Holt and Company.

Landon Experiments. John Pendleton Kennedy. 1976. pap. 1.75 o.p. (ISBN 0-8439-0371-6, Leisure Bks). Nordon Pubns.

Landru. Tr. from French by Gillian Tindall. Rene Masson. LC 65-156623. 1965. 5.95. Doubleday.

Land's End. Kevin Starr. LC 78-26795. 1979. 14.95 (ISBN 0-07-060880-6). McGraw.

Land's End, and Other Stories. Wilbur Daniel Steele. LC 18-16554. 1918. Harper & Brothers.

Land's Lord. T. Obinkaram Echewa. LC 76-18327. 1976. 6.50. (ISBN 0-88208-069-5) (ISBN 0-88208-070-9). L. Hill.

Landscape in Concrete: A Novel. Tr. from German by Ralph Manheim. Jakov Lind. LC 66-141023. 4.50. Grove.

Landscape in Concrete. Tr. from the German by Ralph Manheim. Jakov Lind. (75236). 1968. Pocket Bks.

Landscape of Dreams. A Novel. Teo Savory. LC 60-5610. 1960. G. Braziller.

Landscape of the Heart. August William Derleth. 4.00 o.p. Arkham.

Landscape of the Heart. Elizabeth Renier. 1979. 1.75 (ISBN 0-449-23970-5). Fawcett Crest.

Landscape Painter. Henry James. LC 70-142265. (Short story index reprint series). 1970. (ISBN 0-8369-3749-X). Books for Libraries Press.

Landscape Painter. Henry James. LC 19-19849. 1919. Scott and Seltzer.

Landscape with Corpse: A Jane and Dagobert Brown Mystery. Delano L Ames. LC 56-23975. 1955. I. Washburn.

Landscape with Dead Dons. Robert Henry Robinson. LC 56-5724. 1956. Rinehart.

Landscape with Figures. Ronald Fraser, pseud. LC 26-8381. 1926. Boni & Liveright.

Landscape with Figures. Doreen Eileen Agnew Wallace, pseud. LC 77-352865. 1976. 3.50 (ISBN 0-00-222357-0). Collins.

Landscape with Traveler: The Pillow Book of Francis Reeves. Barry Gifford. LC 79-12823. 8.95 (ISBN 0-525-14344-0). Dutton.

Landscape with Violence. John William Wainwright. LC 75-10931. 1976. 7.95. St. Martin's Press.

Landscape with Violence. John William Wainwright. 1980. 1.95 (ISBN 0-425-04464-5). Berkley Publishing Corp.

Landscapes in Oils. J. M. Parramon. 1981. pap. 4.95 (ISBN 0-89586-093-7). H P Bks.

Landseekers. Allan Vaughan Elston. LC 63-20385. 1964. J. B. Lippincott.

Landsend Terror. Julia Trevelyan. (Signet book). 1979. 1.75 (ISBN 0-451-08526-4). New American Library.

Landslide. Desmond Bagley. (S1591). 1968. Berkley.

Landslide. 1st Ed. Desmond Bagley. LC 67-15369. 1967. 4.95. Doubleday.

Landsmen. Peter Martin. LC 77-5667. (Lost American fiction). 1977. 8.95 (ISBN 0-8093-0837-1). Southern Illinois University Press.

Landsmen. Peter Martin. LC 52-6799. 1952. Little, Brown.

Landtakers; the Story of an Epoch. Brian Con Penton. LC 35-8369. Farrar & Rinehart, Incorporated.

Lane. Helen Sherman Griffith. LC 25-6195. 1925. The Penn Publishing Company.

Lane That Had No Turning. Gilbert Parker. 1902. Doubleday, Page & Co.

Lane That Had No Turning: And Other Tales Concerning the People of Pontiac; Together with Certain "Parables of Provinces.". Gilbert Parker. LC 579925. 1900. Doubleday, Page & Company.

Lanes Lead to Cities. Georgina Garry. LC 29-18163. E. P. Dutton & Co., Inc.

Lanfer Case. A Tale of Hypnotic Passion. A Romance Founded on Life in New Orleans. Robert J. Ferrall. LC 6-38988. The Bow-Knot Publishing Co.

Lang Syne: Or, The Wards of Mount Vernon; a Tale of the Revolutionary Era. Mary Stuart Harrison Smith. LC 8-9618. 1889. J. B. Alden.

Langbarrow Hall. Theodora Wilson Wilson. LC 5-6942. 1905. D. Appleton and Company.

Langford of the Three Bars. Kate Boyles Bingham & Boyles, Virgil Dillin. LC 7-15542. 1907. A. C. McClurg & Co.

Langford's Luck. Donal Hamilton Haines. LC 39-438957. Farrar & Rinehart, Inc.

Langrische Go Down. Aidan Higgins. 1980. 10.95 (ISBN 0-7145-0328-2); pap. 6.95 (ISBN 0-7145-0329-0). Riverrun NY.

Langrishe, Go Down: A Novel. Aidan Higgins. LC 66-28731. 1966. Grove Press.

Language of Cats and Other Stories. Spencer Holst. LC 79-134479. 1971. 3.95. McCall Pub. Co.

Language of Goldfish. Zibby Oneal. 192p. 1981. pap. 1.95 (ISBN 0-449-70005-4, Juniper). Fawcett.

Language of Happiness. Ed. by Susan P. Schutz. LC 77-93903. (Illus., Orig.). 1978. pap. 4.95 (ISBN 0-88396-026-5). Blue Mtn Pr CO.

Language Tutor's Legacy's Legacy: A Novel of International Greed and Intrigue. John D. Healy. LC 80-12976. 1981. 10.95 (ISBN 0-87949-188-4). Ashley Books.

Languages of Pao. Jack Vance, pseud. (Science Fiction Ser.). pap. 1.75 o.p. (ISBN 0-87997-541-5, UE541). DAW Bks.

Languages of Pao. Jack Vance. 1974. (pbk.) 0.95. Ace Books.

Langworthy Family: A Novel of Mount Royal. Elizabeth Frances Corbett. 1937. D. Appleton-Century Company, Incorporated.

Lanier of the Cavalry: Or, A Week's Arrest. Charles King. LC 9-7831. 1901. J. B. Lippincott Company.

Lansing Legacy. Ann Hyman. LC 74-77332. 1974. 7.95 (ISBN 0-679-50465-6). D. McKay Co.

Lansing Legacy. Ann Hyman. 1977. 1.50 (ISBN 0-440-14706-9). Dell Pub. Co.

Lantern for Jeremy: A Novel. Victor Jeremy Jerome. LC 52-10137. 1952. Masses & Mainstream.

Lantern in Her Hand. Bess Streeter Aldrich. LC 28-209204. 1928. D. Appleton & Company.

Lantern in Her Hand. Bess Streeter Aldrich. LC 31-895741. 1931. D. Appleton & Company.

Lantern in Her Hand. Bess Streeter Aldrich. LC 32-632174. 1932. D. Appleton & Company.

Lantern in Her Hand. Bess Streeter Aldrich & Robinson, Nona, Ed. LC 44-1741. (Half-title: Appleton modern literature series). 1944. D. Appleton-Century Company, Incorporated.

Lantern in Her Hand: By Bess Streeter Aldrich... Bess Streeter Aldrich. LC 36-3546. 1935. D. Appleton-Century Company, Incorporated.

Lantern in the Night. Frances Barney. 1976. 4.95. Avalon Books.

Lantern Lane. Warwick Deeping. LC 21-10258. 1921. Cassell and Company, Ltd.

Lantern-Light. Anne Duffield. LC 43-15359. 1943. Arcadia House, Inc.

Lantern of Love: A Novel in Three Parts. Della Campbell MacLeod. LC 21-127051. 1921. 2.00. Houghton Mifflin Company.

Lantern of Luck. Della Campbell MacLeod. LC 9-28401. 1909. W. J. Watt & Company.

Lantern on the Plow. George Agnew Chamberlain. LC 24-19919. 1924. Harper & Brothers.

Lanty Hanlon. Patrick MacGill. LC 23-171203. 1923. Harper & Brothers.

Lanzas Coloradas. Arturo Uslar Pietri. Ed. by Donald D. Walsh. 1944. pap. 2.75 o.p. (ISBN 0-393-09455-3). Norton.

Laodicean. Thomas Hardy. (Seaside library, v. 56, no. 1147). 1881. G. Munro.

Laodicean. A Novel. Thomas Hardy. (Harper's Franklin square library, no. 215). 1881. Harper & Brothers.

Laodicean: A Story of to-Day. Thomas Hardy. LC 1-21952. 1896. Harper & Brothers.

Laodicean: A Story of to-Day. Thomas Hardy. LC 24-24967. Harper & Brothers.

Laodicean: Or, The Castle of the De Stancys. A Story of to-Day. Thomas Hardy. LC 44-15602. (Works v. 7). P. F. Collier.

Lap of Luxury. Berta Ruck. LC 31-32636. 1932. Dodd, Mead & Company.

Lapidaries and Aunt Deborah Hears "The Messiah,". Elizabeth Cheney. LC 1-29667. Eaton & Mains.

Lapidary. Jonathan Greene. pap. 6.00 o.p. (ISBN 0-87685-044-1). Black Sparrow.

Lapse of Enoch Wentworth. Isabel Gordon Curtis. LC 13-1379. 1913. F. G. Browne & Co.

Larabee of Big Spring. Charles Stanley Strong. LC 47-2846. 1947. Phoenix Press.

Laramee's Ranch. Max Brand. 1981. pap. 1.95 (ISBN 0-671-41558-1). PB.

Laramie Holds the Range. Frank Hamilton Spearman. 1921. C. Scribner's Sons.

Laramie" Or, The Queen of Bedlam. A Story of the Sioux War of 1876. Charles King. 1889. J. B. Lippincott Company.

Laramie" Or, The Queen of Bedlam. A Story of the Sioux War of 1876. Charles King. LC 16-131071. 1909. J. B. Lippincott Company.

Laramie Rides Alone. Harry Sinclair Drago. LC 34-135060. 1934. W. Morrow & Co.

Laramie Rides Alone. Will Ermine. pap. 0.60 o.p. Lancer.

Laramie River Crossing. Jack Ehrlich. 1973. (pbk.) 0.75 (ISBN 0-671-75780-6). Pocket Books.

Lararus. Olla Perkins Toph. 1895. Indianapolis Printing Co.

L'arbre Au Grand Coeur. Shel Silverstein. LC 73-4978. (Illus.). 1973. 3.79 (ISBN 0-06-025669-9) (ISBN 0-06-025670-2). Harper & Row.

Larcency on the Loose. Elaine Russell. 1970. 2.95 o.p. Vantage.

Lardners and the Laurelwoods: A Novel. Sheila Kaye-Smith. LC 47-31119. 1947. Harper.

Laredo Lawman. James R. Dowler. Ed. by Alice Sachs. 1970. 3.95 o.p. Lenox Hill.

Large Land. William Arthur Neubauer. LC 64-9279. 1964. Arcadia House.

Largemouth, Smallmouth & Close Kin. Dave Bowring. 176p. (Orig.). 1982. pap. 10.95 (ISBN 0-87691-363-X). Winchester Pr.

Larger Faith: A Novel. James W Coulter. C. H. Kerr & Company.

Larger Growth (Mothers and Fathers) Anne Constance Smedley Maxwell Armfield & Armfield. LC 11-17100. E. P. Dutton & Company.

Larger Leaves: Stories for the Young. Louise Snow. 1.25. Broadway Publishing Co.

Larger Than Life. Tr. by Henry Reed. Dino Buzzati. LC 67-23102. 1967. 3.95. Walker.

Larger Than the Cloud. Charlotte Margaret Kruger Bryant. LC 49-3338. 1949. Zondervan Pub. House.

Larger View. Veniamin Aleksandrovich Kaverin. Tr. by Swan, Edith Leda (Straznik) LC 38-107011. Stackpole Sons.

Largo: A Novel. Petr Nikolaevich Krasnov. Tr. by Vitali, Olga. LC 32-31308. Duffield & Green.

Lariat: A Novel. Jaime De Angulo. LC 73-78138. (His Library; v. 5). (Illus.). 1974. Turtle Island Foundation.

Lariat Law. Claude Rister. LC 39-335172. Phoenix Press.

Larissa. Lynn L. Hahn. 1979. pap. 2.50 (ISBN 0-553-12961-9). Bantam.

Lark. Dana Burnet. LC 21-17078. 1921. Little, Brown, and Company.

Lark. Helen Simmons. LC 42-253687. 1942. Smith & Durrell, Inc.

Lark Above, the Guns Below. Geoffrey Bocca. LC 79-50834. pap. 2.25 o.s.i. (ISBN 0-89516-076-5). Condor Pub Co.

Lark Against the Thunder. Bea Agard. LC 53-6966. 1953. Island Press.

Lark & Sky. Margaret S. Decker. 112p. 1972. pap. 3.00 (ISBN 0-913976-04-0). Discovery Bks.

Lark Ascending. Mazo De La Roche. LC 32-20616. 1932. Little, Brown, and Company.

Lark in an Alien Sky. Rebecca Stratton. (Harlequin Romance Ser.). 1979. pap. 1.25 (ISBN 0-373-02274-3, Pub. by Harlequin). PB.

Lark in the Clear Air. Dennis T. Patrick Sears. LC 77-362273. (Illus.). 1976. 3.95 (ISBN 0-7043-2100-9). Quartet Books.

Lark Legacy. Alice Caldwell Hegan Rice. LC 35-4296. 1935. D. Appleton-Century Company, Incorporated.

Lark, Radio Singer. Helen Diehl Olds & Wagstaff, Dorothy, Illus. LC 46-4019. 1946. J. Messner, Inc.

Lark Rise to Candleford: A Trilogy. Flora Thompson. (Illus.). 1979. Repr. of 1945 ed. text ed. 17.95x (ISBN 0-19-211759-9). Oxford U Pr.

Lark Shall Sing. Elizabeth Cadell. LC 55-9059. 1955. Morrow.

Larkins Wedding. Alice McAlilly. LC 5-32387. 1905. Moffat, Yard & Company.

Larks Creek. Andrew Francis Klarmann. LC 27-22061. Frederick Pustet Co., Inc.

Lark's Fate. John Owen. LC 29-20657. 1929. J. B. Lippincott Company.

Lark's on the Wing: A Novel. Mary Carlier. LC 55-115147. 1955. Bruce Pub. Co.

Larkspur Conspiracy. Judson Pentecost Philips. LC 73-7489. (Red Badge novel of suspense). 1973. 4.95 (ISBN 0-396-06837-5). Dodd, Mead.

Larkspur Conspiracy. Judson Pentecost Philips. (Peter Styles mystery series,#10). 1974. (pbk.) 0.95 (ISBN 0-523-00374-9). Pinnacle Books.

Larkspur Conspiracy: A Peter Styles Mystery Novel. new ed. Judson Pentecost Philips. LC 73-7489. 192p. 1973. 4.95 o.p. (ISBN 0-396-06837-5). Dodd.

Larky Furnace: And Other Adventures of Sue Betty. Hildegard Brooks. LC 6-5139. 1906. H. Holt and Company.

Larnin. Louise Rosalie Preysz. LC 39-458842. 1939. Meador Publishing Company.

Larramee's Ranch. Frederick Faust. LC 76-20825. 1976. 8.95 (ISBN 0-89340-033-5). J. Curley.

Larramee's Ranch. By Max Brand. Frederick Faust. LC 66-24268. (Dodd silver star westerns). 1966. 3.50. Dodd.

L'Arret De Mort see Death Sentence.

Larrikin. Louis Stone. LC 33-32288. 1933. R. Long & R. R. Smith, Inc.

Larrish Hundred. Arthur Raymond Beverley-Giddings. LC 42-5631. 1942. W. Morrow and Company.

Larruping Leather. Frank Chester Robertson. LC 33-239355. 1933. I. Washburn.

Larry of Lonesome Lake. Harold Bindloss. LC 29-18169. 1929. Frederick A. Stokes Company.

Larry Pennington. Basil Partridge. LC 54-5431. 1954. Westminster Press.

Lars. James Wyckoff. LC 65-17257. (Double D western). 1965. Doubleday.

Las Vegas. Arthur Moore & Clayton Matthews. 1974. (pbk.) 1.50 (ISBN 0-671-78737-3). Pocket Books.

Las Vegas Bad Boy. Jim Williams. pap. 1.95 o.p. (BH711). Holloway.

Las Vegas Connection. Neil Rounds. 6.95 o.p. Vantage.

Las Vegas Hillbilly & the Preacher. Douglas A. Harrell. LC 81-85804. 160p. 1983. 9.95 (ISBN 0-86666-050-X). GWP.

Las Vegas Madam. Matt Harding, pseud. 1971. pap. 0.75 o.p. (75-427). Manor Bks.

Las Vegas Strip. Morris Renek. LC 74-21302. 1975. 7.95 (ISBN 0-394-48355-3). Knopf: Distributed by Random House.

Las Vegas Strip. Morris Renek. 1976. 1.95. Avon.

Las Vegas Vengeance. Bruno Rossi, pseud. (Sharpshooter Ser: No. 14). (Orig.). 1975. pap. 1.25 o.p. (LB261ZK, Leisure Bks). Nordon Pubns.

Laser Shuttle. Philip Kirk. (Butler Ser.: No. 7). 240p. (Orig.). 1982. pap. 2.50 (ISBN 0-8439-1076-3, Leisure Bks). Dorchester Pub Co.

Laser War. Joseph Rosenberger. (Death Merchant,#9). 1974. (pbk.) 0.95 (ISBN 0-523-00399-4). Pinnacle Books.

Lash. Olin Linus Lyman. LC 9-29768. 1909. R. G. Badger.

Lash: A Thrilling Story of Law Enforcement. Harden Greaves. LC 29-136224. 1928. David C. Cook Publishing Company.

Lash of Vengeance. James Farnsworth, pseud. 1978. pap. 1.25 (ISBN 0-532-12563-0). Woodhill.

Lashed but Not Leashed. Mark McShane. LC 76-2801. 1976. 5.95 (ISBN 0-385-12154-7). Published for the Crime Club by Doubleday.

Lasko Tangent. Richard North Patterson. LC 78-27492. 9.95 (ISBN 0-393-01190-9). Norton.

Laslett Affair. Harold Begbie. LC 29-273827. The Macaulay Company.

Lass O' Laughter. Winifred Carter & Carter, Edith. 1923. C. Scribner's Sons.

Lass O' Lowrie's. Frances Hodgson Burnett. LC 6-17250. 1896. C. Scribner's Sons.

Lass O' Lowrie's. Frances Hodgson Burnett. LC 4-15420. 1902. C. Scribner's Sons.

Lass O' Mine. Hazel M Giertsen. LC 34-37086. Dorrance & Company, Inc.

Lass of the Sword. Charles Edward Lawrence. LC 24-30080. 1923. E. P. Dutton and Company.

Lass with the Delicate Air. Arthur Rhys Goring-Thomas. LC 11-4939. 1911. 1.50. John Lane.

Lasses of Leverhouse. A Story. Jessie Fothergill. (On cover: Seaside library. Pocket ed. no. 1099). 1888. G. Munro.

Lassie Come Home. Eric Knight. 1975. pap. 1.75 (ISBN 0-440-94651-4, LFL). Dell.

Lassiter. Jack Slade, pseud. (Lassiter Ser.: No. 1). 192p. 1982. pap. 2.25 o.p. (ISBN 0-505-51833-3). Tower Bks.

Lassiter: Funeral Bend. Jack Slade, pseud. 1973. pap. 0.75 o.p. (BT50622). Belmont-Tower.

Lassiter: Lust for Gold. Jack Slade, pseud. 1977. pap. 1.25 o.s.i. (ISBN 0-505-51127-4). Tower Bks.

Lassiter's Folly. Nathaniel Benchley. LC 78-124979. 1971. 6.95. Atheneum.

Lasso Round the Moon. Agnar Mykle. LC 59-12581. 1960. Dutton.

L'assommoir. Emile Zola. LC 62-51373. (Signet classic, OT128). 1962. New American Library.

L'Assommoir. Emile Zola. LC 70-18826. (Penguin classics). (Illus.). 1970 (ISBN 0-14-044231-6). Penguin.

L'assommoir. Emile Zola. LC 26-112568. 1924. A. A. Knopf.

L'assommoir. A Novel. Emile Zola & Sherwood, Mrs. Mary (Neal) Tr. LC 9-1338. T. B. Peterson & Brothers.

L'assommoir. Nana's Mother. Emile Zola & Sherwood, Mrs. Mary (Neal) Tr. LC 9-2233. T. B. Peterson & Brothers.

Last Act. Jane Aiken Hodge. LC 79-10663. 1979. 8.95 (ISBN 0-698-10988-0). Coward, McCann & Geoghegan.

Last Act. Joanne Marshall, pseud. LC 75-34385. 7.95 (ISBN 0-399-11719-9). Putnam.

Last Act in Bermuda: A Murder Mystery. David Burnham. LC 40-30522. 1940. C. Scribner's Sons.

Last Adam. James Gould Cozzens. LC 56-13731. (Harvest books, 12). 1956. Harcourt, Brace.

Last Adam. James Gould Cozzens. LC 33-135739. Harcourt, Brace and Company.

Last Ambassador. Bernard Kalb & Marvin Kalb. 267p. 1981. 12.95 (ISBN 0-316-48222-6). Little.

Last Ambassador: A Novel. Bernard Kalb & Marvin L Kalb. LC 81-8259. (Illus.). 13.50. Little, Brown.

Last American. John Ames Mitchell. LC 75-104529. (Illus.). 1970. Literature House.

Last American: A Fragment from the Journal of Khan-Li, Prince of Dimph-Yoo-Chur and Admiral in the Persian Navy. John Ames Mitchell. LC 42-29939. 1889. F. A. Stokes & Brother.

Last American: A Fragment from the Journal of Khan-Li, Prince of Dimph-Yoo-Chur and Admiral in the Persian Navy. 14th ed. John Ames Mitchell. LC 7-311013. 1893. F. A. Stokes Company.

Last American: A Fragment from the Journal of Khan-Li, Prince of Dimph-Yoo-Chur and Admiral in the Persian Navy. John Ames Mitchell. LC 2-24323. 1902. F. A. Stokes Company.

Last American: A Fragment from the Journal of Khan-Li, Prince of Dimph-Yoo-Chur and Admiral in the Persian Navy. John Ames Mitchell. LC 17-22991. 1916. Frederick A. Stokes Company.

Last Analysis, a Play. Saul Bellow. (O.s.i.). pap. 1.25 o.s.i. (ISBN 0-670-00192-9, Comp). Viking Pr.

Last and First Love. Abel Hermant. Tr. by Brown, Slater. LC 30-232022. 1930. The Macaulay Company.

Last & First Men. Olaf Stapledon. Bd. with Last Men in London. 1973. pap. 2.95 o.p. (ISBN 0-14-003506-0). Penguin.

Last & First Men. Olaf Stapledon. Bd. with Star Maker. 10.00 (ISBN 0-8446-2995-2). Peter Smith.

Last and First Men: A Story of the Near and Far Future. William Olaf Stapledon. LC 31-7638. 1931. J. Cape and H. Smith.

Last and First Men, and Last Men in London. William Olaf Stapledon. LC 73-159353. 1972. 2.45 (ISBN 0-14-003506-0). Penguin Books.

Last & First Men & Star Maker. William Olaf Stapeldon. pap. 5.00 (ISBN 0-486-21962-3). Dover.

Last and First Men, & Star Maker: Two Science-Fiction Novels. William Olaf Stapledon. LC 68-19448. (Illus.). 1968. 2.00. Dover Publications.

Last and the First. Compton-Burnett, Ivy. LC 75-154907. 1971. 5.95 (ISBN 0-394-47040-0). Knopf.

Last Angry Man. Gerald Green. 1976. Repr. of 1956 ed. lib. bdg. 22.80x (ISBN 0-89190-121-3). Am Repr-Rivercity Pr.

Last Angry Man. Gerald Green. 1980. pap. 3.50 (ISBN 0-425-04993-0). Berkley Pub.

Last Angry Man. Gerald Green. 1956. 6.95 o.p. Scribner.

Last Angry Man. Gerald Green. Repr. of 1956 ed. lib. bdg. 14.00 o.p. (1132). Am Repr-Rivercity Pr.

Last Angry Man: A Novel. Gerald Green. LC 56-12444. Scribner.

Last Apaches. William L Hopson. LC 51-14975. 1951. T. Bouregy.

Last Apaches. William L. Hopson. 1974. 4.50. Avalon.

Last Assembly Ball, and The Fate of a Voice. Mary Hallock Foote. LC 6-41410. 1889. Houghton, Mifflin and Company.

Last Assignment. Norman Fischer. 256p. 1973. 5.95 o.p. (ISBN 0-8027-5276-4). Walker & Co.

Last Assignment. Norman Fisher. LC 72-95794. 1973. 5.95 (ISBN 0-8027-5276-4). Walker.

Last Athenian. Viktor Rydberg & Thomas, William Widgery, 1839- Tr. LC 8-1359. T. B. Peterson & Brothers.

Last Athenian. Translated from the Swedish of Victor Rydberg. Viktor Rydberg & Thomas, William Widgery, Jr., 1839-1927, Tr. LC 8-1363. T. B. Peterson & Brothers.

Last Autumn. Herbert Gutterson. LC 58-8004. 1958. W. Morrow.

Last Ball. Charles Rigdon. LC 72-89202. 1972. 7.95 (ISBN 0-671-27091-5). Trident Press.

Last Battle. Cornelius Ryan. 576p. 1975. pap. 3.50 (ISBN 0-445-08381-6). Popular Lib.

Last Battle Ground. Margaret Stephenson Organ. LC 10-29411. 1.50. G. T. Long.

Last Believers. David Karp. LC 64-19940. 1964. Harcourt, Brace & World.

Last Best Friend. George Sims. LC 68-16042. 1968. Stein and Day.

Last Best Hope. Peter Tauber. LC 77-92705. 10.00 (ISBN 0-15-148377-9). Harcourt Brace Jovanovich.

Last Boat from Beyrouth. Royce Brier. LC 43-5578. 1943. D. Appleton-Century Company.

Last Boat Out of Cincinnati. Don Tracy. LC 79-105866. 1970. 6.50. Trident Press.

Last Book of Wonder. Edward John Moreton Drax Plunkett Dunsany. LC 76-101282. (Short story index reprint series). 1969. Books for Libraries Press.

Last Brand. Maxwell Smith. LC 33-4388. E. J. Clode, Inc.

Last Bridge: By Brian Garfield. Brian Wynne Garfield. 1966. bds., 4.95. McKay.

Last Brigade. Steven Ashley. 320p. 1982. pap. 2.95 (ISBN 0-515-05559-X). Jove Pubns.

Last Buccaneer: Or, The Trustees of Mrs. A. Leslie Cope Cornford. LC 2-26353. 1902. J. B. Lippincott Company.

Last Buffoon. Leonard Jordan. (Orig.). 1980. pap. text ed. 1.95 o.s.i. (ISBN 0-505-51537-7). Tower Bks.

Last Bullet. Morgan Hill. (Orig.). 1982. pap. 1.95 (ISBN 0-440-14664-X). Dell.

Last Bullet see Loco.

Last Bus to Woodstock. Colin Dexter. LC 74-24834. 1975. 7.95. St. Martin's Press.

Last Butterfly. Michael Jacot. 1974. 6.95. Bobbs-Merrill.

Last Butterfly. Michael Jacot. LC 73-16803. 1975. (pbk.) 1.50 (ISBN 0-345-24406-0). Ballantine Books.

Last Caesar. Edward McGhee. 320p. (Orig.). 1980. pap. 2.75 (ISBN 0-523-41425-0). Pinnacle Bks.

Last Call. Warren Murphy. (Destroyer: No. 35). 1978. pap. 1.95 (ISBN 0-523-41250-9). Pinnacle Bks.

Last Call for a Gunfighter. Harry Sinclair Drago. (Dell Book). 1978. 1.25 (ISBN 0-440-14656-9). Dell Pub. Co.

Last Call for Lissa. Dorothy Mayor. LC 48-2378. 1948. M. S. Mill Co.

Last Call for the Stars. new ed. Charles Nuetzel. Ed. by Alice Sachs. 1970. 3.95 o.p. Lenox Hill.

Last Call of Mourning. Charles L Grant. LC 78-20075. 1979. 7.95 (ISBN 0-385-14376-1). Doubleday.

Last Campaign. 1st Ed. Glen Ross. LC 62-9922. 1962. Harper.

Last Capitalist. Robert F Mirvish. LC 62-15767. 1963. W. Sloane Associates.

Last Card. Hans Hellmut Kirst. LC 67-3622. 1967. Pyramid Publications.

Last Caress. Dianna Booher. (Orig.). 1981. pap. 2.50 (ISBN 0-89083-722-8). Zebra.

Last Carnival. Alexandra Ellis. (Orig.). 1980. pap. 2.50 (ISBN 0-515-04816-X). Jove Pubns.

Last Carousel. Nelson Algren. LC 72-97289. 1973. 8.95 (ISBN 0-399-11131-X). Putnam.

Last Casquette Girl. Lorena Dureau. 288p. (Orig.). 1981. pap. 2.50 (ISBN 0-523-41266-5). Pinnacle Bks.

Last Catholic in America. John R. Powers. LC 79-24431. 1981. Repr. of 1973 ed. lib. bdg. 10.00x (ISBN 0-8376-0439-7). Bentley.

Last Catholic in America. John R. Powers. 224p. 1974. pap. 2.50 (ISBN 0-445-08528-2). Popular Lib.

Last Catholic in America. John R. Powers. 224p. 1982. pap. 2.75 (ISBN 0-446-31040-9). Warner Bks.

Last Catholic in America: A Fictionalized Memoir. John R. Powers. LC 72-88664. 1973. 6.95 (ISBN 0-8415-0218-8). Saturday Review Press.

Last Catholic in America: A Fictionalized Memoir. John R Powers. LC 79-24431. 1980. 10.00 (ISBN 0-8376-0439-7). R. Bentley.

Last Cattle Drive. Robert Day. LC 76-28173. 1977. 7.95 o.p. (ISBN 0-399-11883-7). Putnam Pub Group.

Last Cattle Drive: A Novel. Robert Day. LC 76-28173. 7.95 (ISBN 0-399-11883-7). Putnam.

Last Cattle Drive: A Novel. Robert Day. 1978. 1.95 (ISBN 0-380-01832-2). Avon.

Last Cavalier. Albert Morgan. 320p. 1980. 12.95 (ISBN 0-399-90079-9, Marek). Putnam Pub Group.

Last Cavalier: A Novel. Albert Morgan. LC 79-27530. 11.95. R. Marek.

Last Centennial. Patricia Kilina. 1971. 6.95 o.p. Dial.

Last Centennial. Patricia Nell Warren. LC 77-163583. 1971. 6.95. Dial Press.

Last Chance. Rona Jaffe. LC 76-7564. (ISBN 0-671-22274-0). Simon and Schuster.

Last Chance. Ed. by James Edwin Miller. LC 79-64656. 1980. 5.95 (ISBN 0-533-04318-2). Vantage.

Last Chance. Frank O'Rourke. LC 56-8360. (Dell first edition, 104). 1956. Dell Pub. Co.

Last Chance at Devil's Canyon. Barry Cord. (Leisure book). 1979. 1.25 (ISBN 0-8439-0613-8). Nordon Pubns.

Last Chance Valley. Heuman, William. LC 64-7332. 1962. Arcadia House.

Last Checkpoint. John Quigley. LC 77-146472. 1971. 5.95 (ISBN 0-8415-0108-4). McCall Pub. Co.

Last Christian. George Kibbe Turner. LC 14-17090. 1914. Heart's International Library Co.

Last Chronicle of Barset. Anthony Trollope. 1962. Harcourt, Brace & World.

Last Chronicle of Barset. edited with an introd. and notes by arthur mizener. ed. Anthony Trollope. LC 64-3431. (Riverside editions) "B74."). 1964. Houghton Mifflin Co.

Last Chronicle of Barset. Anthony Trollope. LC 4-16587. (On cover: The chronicles of Barsetshire). 1903. Dodd, Mead & Company.

Last Chronicle of Barset. Anthony Trollope. LC 32-266741. (Half-title: The world's classics. CCXXVIII, CCCXXXX). 1932. H. Milford, Oxford University Press.

Last Chronicle of Barset... Anthony Trollope. LC 38-17013. (Half-title: Everyman's library, ed. by Ernest Rhys. Fiction. no. 391-392). 1936. J. M. Dent & Sons, Ltd.

Last Chronicles of Ballyfungus. Mary Manning. LC 77-20176. 9.95 (ISBN 0-316-54523-6). Little, Brown.

Last Chukker. Illus. by Maurice Tulloch. John Keith Stanford. LC 54-10815. 1954. Devin-Adair.

Last Circle. Stephen Vincent Benet. LC 72-10776. (Short Story Index Reprint Ser.). 1973. Repr. of 1946 ed. 20.00 (ISBN 0-8369-4217-5). Ayer Co.

Last Circus. Ray Bradbury. 50p. 1980. 15.00 (ISBN 0-935716-03-3); deluxe signed ed. 50.00 (ISBN 0-935716-04-1). Lord John.

Last Civiliam. Ernst Glaeser. Tr. by David, Gwenda. LC 35-274386. R. M. McBride & Company.

Last Clash of Claymores: A Story of Scotland in the Time of Prince Charles. Maribelle Cormack & Alexander, William Prindle. LC 40-32076. 1940. D. Appleton-Century Company, Incorporated.

Last Clear Chance. 1st Ed. Burke Wilkinson. LC 54-5101. 1954. Little, Brown.

Last Collection. Seymour Blicker. LC 76-54309. 1977. 8.95 (ISBN 0-688-03156-0). Morrow.

Last Collection. Seymour Blicker. LC 76-366726. 10.00 (ISBN 0-7710-1568-2). McClelland and Stewart.

Last Comanchero. Ray Hogan. (Shaw Starbuck). (Signet brand western: Vol. 19). 1975. (pbk.) 0.95. New American Library.

Last Come the Children. David Hagberg. 352p. (Orig.). 1982. pap. 2.95 (ISBN 0-523-48036-9). Pinnacle Bks.

Last Coming. Gerald G. Griffin & Robin Moore. LC 78-78062. 1978. pap. 2.25 o.s.i. (ISBN 0-89516-062-5). Condor Pub Co.

Last Commandment. George Harmon Coxe. LC 60-12802. 1960. Knopf.

Last Communion. Nicholas Yermakov. 192p. 1981. pap. 2.25 (ISBN 0-451-09822-6, E9822, Sig). NAL.

Last Concubine. Frances Shelley Wees. LC 68-15220. (Raven book). 1970. 4.95 (ISBN 0-200-71550-X). Abelard-Schuman.

Last Confession: And The Blind Mother. Hall Caine. LC 6-21870. 1892. Tait, Sons & Company.

Last Convertible. Anton Myrer. 1979. pap. 3.75 (ISBN 0-425-05349-0). Berkley Pub.

Last Convertible. Anton Myrer. LC 77-15557. 1978. 10.95 (ISBN 0-399-12124-2). Putnam Pub Group.

Last Convertible: A Novel. Anton Myrer. (Berkley book). 1979. 2.50 (ISBN 0-425-04034-8). Berkley Pub. Co.

Last Cop Cut. Frank Morrison Spillane. LC 72-97714. 1973. 6.95 (ISBN 0-525-14353-X). Dutton.

Last Cop Out. Mickey Spillane, pseud. 192p. 1973. pap. 2.50 (ISBN 0-451-11905-3, AE1905, Sig). NAL.

Last Cop Out. Mickey Spillane, pseud. 1973. 6.95 o.p. (ISBN 0-525-14353-X). Dutton.

Last Courtesies and Other Stories. Ella Leffland. LC 79-3411. 15.00 (ISBN 0-06-012554-3). Harper & Row.

Last Cowboy. Jane Kramer. LC 77-6150. 1978. 9.95 o.p. (ISBN 0-06-012454-7, HarpT). Har-Row.

Last Crescendo: The Story of Paul Gray. Owen Francis Dudley. 1954. Longmans, Green.

Last Crusader. 1st Ed. Louis De Wohl. LC 56-108073. 1956. Lippincott.

Last Cry. Sallie Lee Bell. LC 67-11616. 1967. Zondervan Pub. House.

Last Day. Beatrice Kean Stapleton Seymour. LC 26-200559. 1926. A. & C. Boni.

Last Day & Other Stories. E. J. Fowler. 2.95 o.p. Carlton.

Last Day and Other Stories. Harold Everett Green. LC 39-215122. B. Humphries, Inc.

Last Day in Limbo. Peter O'Donnell. LC 77-364187. 1976. 3.25 (ISBN 0-285-62225-0). Souvenir Press.

Last Day of a Condemned. Victor Marie Hugo. Tr. by De B. Eugenia. LC 76-25870. 1977. Repr. of 1894 ed. 18.50x (ISBN 0-86527-269-7). Fertig.

Last Day of Ikhnaton: A Novel of Ancient Egypt. 1st Ed. Catherine Needham Severance. LC 52-12346. 1953. Exposition Press.

Last Day of Lincoln Charles. Gordon M Williams. LC 66-171536. 1966. bds., 4.95. Stein & Day.

Last Day the Dogbushes Bloomed. Lee Smith. LC 68-28226. 1968. 4.95. Harper & Row.

Last Day. 1st Ed. Raymond Lester Carter. LC 67-308865. 4.95. Threefools Pr.

Last Days. William Rayner. LC 69-11039. 1969. 5.95. Morrow.

Last Days at Apswich: A Novel ... LC 7-13848. (Harper's handy series. no. 47). 1886. Harper & Brothers.

Last Days of a King. An Historical Romance. Moritz Hartmann. Tr. by Niles, M. E. LC 7-3659. 1867. J. B. Lippincott & Co.

Last Days of America. large print ed. Paul Emil Erdman. LC 81-20091. 1982. 17.95 (ISBN 0-8161-3349-2). G.K. Hall.

Last Days of Atlantis. K. H Scheer. (Perry Rhodan, 62). 1975. (pbk.) 0.95. Ace Books.

Last Days of Dutch Schultz. William Burroughs. 1972. price not set o.p. Dutton.

Last Days of Louisiana Red. Ishmael Reed. LC 74-8699. 1974. 5.95 (ISBN 0-394-49188-2). Random House.

Last Days of Louisiana Red. ishmael reed. ed. Ishmael Reed. (Bard Book). 1.95 (ISBN 0-380-00736-3). Avon Books.

Last Days of Mr. Punch. D. H. Myers. LC 77-139540. 1971. 4.95 o.p. (ISBN 0-8415-0092-4). Sat Rev Pr.

Last Days of Oak Lane Plantation. Anne Labranche. LC 63-823. 1962.

Last Days of Pompeii. Edward George Bulwer-Lytton. 1976. 11.95x (ISBN 0-460-00080-2, Evman). Biblio Dist.

Last Days of Pompeii. Edward George Earle Lytton Bulwer-Lytton Lytton. LC 50-3267. (World's greatest literature). 1950. Fountain Press.

Last Days of Pompeii. library ed.... ed. Edward George Earle Lytton Bulwer-Lytton Lytton. LC 7-8336. (Half-title: Novels of Sir Edward Bulwer Lytton. Library ed. Historical romances, vol. XII-XIII). 1860. J. B. Lippincott & Co.

Last Days of Pompeii. Edward George Earle Lytton Bulwer-Lytton Lytton. LC 42-26813. 1867. J. B. Lippincott & Co.

Last Days of Pompeii. Edward George Earle Lytton Bulwer-Lytton Lytton & Johnson, Rossiter I.E. Edwin Rossiter, 1840- Ed. (Condensed classics. v. 4). 1876. H. Holt and Company.

Last Days of Pompeii. the lord lytton ed. Edward George Earle Lytton Bulwer-Lytton Lytton. LC 7-8335. 1877. J. B. Lippincott & Co.

Last Days of Pompeii. Edward George Earle Lytton Bulwer-Lytton Lytton. LC 8-26645. G. Routledge and Sons.

Last Days of Pompeii. Edward George Earle Lytton Bulwer-Lytton Lytton. LC 34-37784. 1881. A. Cogswell & Co.

Last Days of Pompeii. the lord lytton ed. Edward George Earle Lytton Bulwer-Lytton Lytton. LC 7-8334. 1882. J. B. Lippincott & Co.

Last Days of Pompeii. Edward George Earle Lytton Bulwer-Lytton Lytton. LC 7-8333. (Lovell's library, v. 2, no. 59). J. W. Lovell Company.

Last Days of Pompeii. Edward George Earle Lytton Bulwer-Lytton Lytton. (On cover: Seaside library. Pocket ed. no. 40). G. Munro.

Last Days of Pompeii. vignette ed. with one hundred new illustrations by joseph m. gleeson. ed. Edward George Earle Lytton Bulwer-Lytton Lytton. LC 7-8090. 1891. F. A. Stokes Company.

Last Days of Pompeii. Edward George Earle Lytton Bulwer-Lytton Lytton. (Half-title: Novels of Sir Edward Bulwer Lytton. Library ed. Historical romances, vol. III). 1893. Little, Brown, and Company.

Last Days of Pompeii. Edward George Earle Lytton Bulwer-Lytton Lytton. LC 99-4092. Rand, McNally & Company.

Last Days of Pompeii. Edward George Earle Lytton Bulwer-Lytton Lytton. LC 2-20633. 1902. C. Scribner's Sons.

Last Days of Pompeii. a complete ed., with notes. ed. Edward George Earle Lytton Bulwer-Lytton Lytton. LC 41-159193. Grosset & Dunlap.

Last Days of Pompeii. Edward George Earle Lytton Bulwer-Lytton Lytton. (Half-title: Everyman's library, ed. by Ernest Rhys. Fiction. no. 80). 1908. J. M. Dent & Co.

Last Days of Pompeii. Edward George Earle Lytton Bulwer-Lytton Lytton & Castleman, Josiah Hamilton, 1873- Ed. LC 8-16740. (Macmillan's pocket American and English classics). 1908. The Macmillan Company.

Last Days of Pompeii. Edward George Earle Lytton Bulwer-Lytton Lytton. LC 25-23751. 1922. Thomas Y. Crowell Company.

Last Days of Pompeii. Edward George Earle Lytton Bulwer-Lytton Lytton & Yohn, Frederick Coffay, 1875- Illus. LC 26-19155. 1926. C. Scribner's Sons.

Last Days of Pompeii. Edward George Earle Lytton Bulwer-Lytton Lytton. LC 79-425. 1979. 24.95 (ISBN 0-442-24744-3). Van Nostrand Reinhold.

Last Days of Pompeii. Adapted by Lou P. Bunce. Edward George Earle Lytton Bulwer-Lytton Lytton & Lou P Bunce. LC 60-206437. 1960. Globe Book Co.

Last Days of Pompeii. Harold: the Last of the Saxon Kings. The Caxtons: a Family Picture... Edward George Earle Lytton Bulwer-Lytton Lytton. LC 24-249963. (works of Edward Bulwer Lytton (Lord Lytton) vol. I). P. F. Collier.

Last Days of Pompeii. Introd. by Charles Dwoskin. Edward George Earle Lytton Bulwer-Lytton Lytton. LC 57-95168. Fine Editions Press.

Last Days of St. Pierre. Louis Smirnow. LC 11-1796. The C. M. Clark Publishing Company.

Last Days of September. Winifred Mary Scott. LC 31-213332. 1931. Doubleday, Doran & Company, Inc.

Last Days of Shylock. Ludwig Lewisohn. LC 31-98013. 1931. Harper & Brothers.

Last Days of Sodom and Gomorrah. Paul Ilton. LC 57-8655. (Signet book, 1399). 1957. New American Library.

TITLE INDEX LAST MAN.

Last Days of the American Empire. Bruce Powe. LC 73-91377. (Illus.). 1975. 8.95. St. Martin's Press.
Last Days of the Late, Great State of California. Curt Gentry. 1977. pap. 2.50 (ISBN 0-89174-021-X). Comstock Edns.
Last Days of the Late, Great State of California. Curt Gentry. 1974. pap. 1.25 o.p. (ISBN 0-345-22483-3, 22438-8-125). Comstock Edns.
Last Days of the Nineteenth Century: A Story of the Social Problem. Leon Greenbaum. (On cover: People's series, v. 6, no. 2). 1897. W. B. Conkey Company.
Last Days of the Republic. Pierton W Dooner. LC 15-21839. 1880. Alta California Publishing House.
Last Days of the Republic. Pierton W. Dooner. LC 78-54814. (Series: Asian Experience in North America: Chinese and Japanese.). 1978. 16.00 (ISBN 0-405-11270-X). Arno Press.
Last Days of the U.S.A. Felix Murat. LC 74-162833. (Illus.). 1971. Printed by Peninsula Print.
Last Days of Wolf Garnett. Clifton Adams. (Ace Western). 1973. (pbk.) 0.75. Ace.
Last Days of Wolf Garnett. Clifton Adams. LC 77-103728. (Doubleday western). 1970. 4.50. Doubleday.
Last Deal. Laurence Gonzales. LC 81-66017. 1981. 13.95 (ISBN 0-689-11199-1). Atheneum.
Last Decathalon. John Redgate. 1979. 8.95 o.s.i. (ISBN 0-440-04983-0). Delacorte.
Last Decathlon. Adam Kennedy. LC 79-15422. 8.95. Delacorte Press.
Last Defender of Camelot. Roger Zelazny. (Orig.). 1980. pap. 2.95 (ISBN 0-671-41773-8, Timescape). PB.
Last Delamar. Clementine B Allan. LC 6-475. (On cover: The crescent library. no. 6). The Price-McGill Company.
Last Detail. Darryl Ponicsan. LC 76-120469. 1970. 4.95. Dial Press.
Last Devil. Signe Toksvig. LC 27-23277. 1927. The John Day Company.
Last Diaries. abr ed. Lev Nikolaevich Tolstoi. Ed. by Leon Stilman. (Orig.). 1960. pap. 1.35 o.p. (21, Cap). Putnam.
Last Diary. W. N. Barbellion. Repr. of 1921 ed. lib. bdg. 20.00 (ISBN 0-8414-1674-5). Folcroft.
Last Directions. Alison Spitz. 1966. pap. 1.00x (ISBN 0-88020-079-0). Coach Hse.
Last Disaster. Hugh Walters, pseud. LC 78-308930. 1978. 8.95 (ISBN 0-571-11153-X). Faber.
Last Ditch. Will Levington Comfort. LC 16-22902. George H. Doran Company.
Last Ditch. Belle Willey Gue. LC 23-18068. 1923. The Stratford Company.
Last Ditch. Louis MacNiece. 52p. 1971. Repr. of 1940 ed. 11.00x (ISBN 0-7165-1389-7, Pub. by Cuala Press Ireland). Biblio Dist.
Last Ditch. Ngaio Marsh. LC 76-52287. 7.95 (ISBN 0-316-54674-7). Little, Brown.
Last Ditch. Ngaio Marsh. LC 77-15539. 1978. 12.95 (ISBN 0-8161-6537-8). G. K. Hall.
Last Ditch see Ngaio Marsh.
Last Dogfight. Martin Caidin. LC 74-6136. 1974. 7.95 (ISBN 0-395-19411-3). Houghton Mifflin.
Last Domino Contract. Philip Atlee. (Joe Gall). (Fawcett Gold Medal Book: Vol. 22). 1976. 1.50 (ISBN 0-449-13587-X). Fawcett.
Last Door to Aiya: A Selection of the Best New Science Fiction from the Soviet Union. Ed. by Mirra Ginsburg. LC 68-16347. 1968. S. G. Phillips.
Last Door to Aiya: A Selection of the Best New Science Fiction from the Soviet Union. Ed. by Mirra Ginsburg. 1968. S. G. Phillips.
Last Doorbell. Joseph Harrington. LC 69-16163. 1969. 4.50 o.p. (ISBN 0-397-00586-5). Lippincott.
Last Doorbell. Joseph Harrington. 1972. pap. 0.95 o.p. (95198). Beagle Bks.
Last Doorbell. John K Vedder, pseud. LC 41-20889. H. Holt and Company.
Last Doorbell: A Lieutenant Kerrigan Mystery. Joseph Harrington. LC 69-16163. 1969. 4.50. Lippincott.
Last Duchess of Belgarde. Molly Elliot Seawell. 1908. D. Appleton and Company.
Last Egyptian: A Romance of the Nile. LC 8-10435. 1908. E. Stern & Co., Inc.
Last Egyptian: A Romance of the Nile. Illus. by Francis P. Wightman. Lyman Frank Baum. LC 8-10435. 1908. E. Stern.
Last Enchantment. Mary Stewart. LC 79-12937. (Illus.). 1979. 11.95 (ISBN 0-688-03481-0). Morrow.
Last Enchantment. Mary Stewart. LC 82-11915. 1982. 19.95 (ISBN 0-8161-3340-9). G.K. Hall.
Last Enchantments. Robert Liddell. LC 49-107711. 1949. Appleton-Century-Crofts.
Last Encounter. Robin Maugham. LC 73-7534. 1973. 5.95 (ISBN 0-07-040967-6). McGraw-Hill.
Last Enemy. Keith Ayling. (Orig.). 1971. pap. 0.75 o.p. (T2567). Pyramid Pubns.
Last Enemy. Iris Barry. LC 29-200103. The Bobbs-Merrill Company.
Last Enemy. Hugh Mason. LC 77-352803. (ISBN 0-9598478-0-4). Inchcape Books.
Last Enemy. Alexander Judson Pettit. LC 19-577. 1918. Marshall Jones Company.
Last Enemy. Berton Roueche. LC 56-6757. (Dell first edition, D90). Dell Pub. Co.
Last Enemy. Berton Roueche. LC 56-120126. (Evergreen book, E-46). 1956. Grove Press.
Last Enemy. Berton Roueche. LC 75-6375. 1975. 6.95 (ISBN 0-06-013687-1). Harper & Row.
Last Enemy: A Study of Youth. Leonard Alfred George Strong. LC 36-235226. 1936. A. A. Knopf.
Last Englishman: The Story of Hereward the Wake. Hebe Weenolsen. LC 51-14059. 1951. Doubleday.
Last Escape. Edith Caroline Rivett. LC 59-8269. 1959. Published for the Crime Club by Doubleday.
Last Essays. facs. ed. Maurice Henry Hewlett. LC 68-54349. (Essay Index Reprint Ser). 1924. 16.00 (ISBN 0-8369-0539-3). Ayer Co.
Last Exam. Timothy David Takata. LC 76-52141. 6.95. Libra Publishers.
Last Exile. James Aldridge. LC 61-12489. 1961. Doubleday.
Last Exit to Brooklyn. Hubert Selby, Jr. 1964. pap. 2.95 (ISBN 0-394-17467-4, B313, BC). Grove.
Last Express... Baynard Hardwick Kendrick. LC 37-112445. 1937. Pub. for the Crime Club, Inc., by Doubleday, Doran & Co., Inc.
Last Express... Baynard Hardwick Kendrick. LC 37-11244. 1937. Pub. for the Crime Club, Inc., by Doubleday, Doran & Co., Inc.
Last Fair Deal Going Down. David Rhodes. LC 72-1125. (Illus.). 1972. 6.95 (ISBN 0-316-74233-3). Little, Brown.
Last Fathom. Martin Caidin. LC 67-18496. 1967. Meredith Press.
Last First. Paul Hutchens. LC 38-114748. Wm. B. Eerdmans Publ. Co.
Last Five Dollar Baby. Nancy C Wood. LC 71-156568. 1972. 6.95 (ISBN 0-06-014739-3). Harper & Row.
Last Flapper. George Zuckerman. LC 69-15070. 1969. Little, Brown.
Last Flight. Barbara Hall. LC 33-4312. 1936. Dodd, Mead & Company.
Last Flight: A Suspense Novel. Myrick Land. LC 74-32131. 1975. 6.95 (ISBN 0-393-08717-4). Norton.
Last Flower. Con Sellers. 1980. pap. 2.95 (ISBN 0-671-81749-3). PB.
Last Flower. James Thurber. (Illus.). 1971. pap. 3.50 o.p. (ISBN 0-06-090232-9, CN232, CN). Har-Row.
Last Flower. James Thurber. 1977. Repr. of 1939 ed. lib. bdg. 16.95x (ISBN 0-89244-057-0). Queens Hse.
Last Flowers. Michael Barrett. LC 56-581045. 1956. Longlans, Green.
Last Flowers. Michael Barrett. LC 57-5920. 1957. Farrar, Straus and Cudahy.
Last Flying Tiger: A Novel. David E. Fisher. LC 76-15610. 7.95 (ISBN 0-684-14751-3). Scribner.
Last Forest: Tales of the Allegheny Woods. Douglas McNeill. LC 40-197742. Fortuny's.
Last Freshet. Ben Field. LC 48-5766. 1948. N. Y., Doubleday.
Last Frontier. Courtney Ryley Cooper. LC 23-15622. 1923. Little, Brown and Company.
Last Frontier. Howard Melvin Fast. LC 41-13229. Duell, Sloan and Pearce.
Last Frontier: By Howard Fast, with a Foreword by Carl Van Doren. Howard Melvin Fast. LC 42-51125. 1942. The Press of the Readers Club.
Last Full Measure. Honore McCue Willsie Morrow. LC 30-19274. 1930. W. Morrow & Company.
Last Furlong, a Racing Novel. Mordaunt Milner. 4.95x o.s.i. (ISBN 0-8277-0457-7). British Bk Ctr.
Last Furlong, a Racing Novel. Mordaunt Milner. 4.95x o.s.i. (ISBN 0-8277-0457-7). British Bk Ctr.
Last Galley: Impressions and Tales. Arthur Conan Doyle. LC 11-15192. 1911. Doubleday, Page & Company.
Last Gamble. Harold Q. Masur. LC 58-521. (Inner sanctum mystery). 1958. Simon and Schuster.
Last Gamble: A Novel of Cornwall, 1792-1793. 1st Ed. Winston Graham. LC 55-5575. 1955. Doubleday.
Last Gamble: By Rae Foley Pseud. Elinore Denniston. (Red badge detective). 1956. Dodd, Mead.
Last Gas Station and Other Stories. Tom Clark. LC 80-36765. 1980. 14.00 (ISBN 0-87685-457-9) (ISBN 0-87685-458-7) (ISBN 0-87685-456-0). Black Sparrow Press.
Last Gene. Chris Longo. 1976. pap. 1.25 (ISBN 0-89041-117-4, 3117). Major Bks.
Last Gentleman. Shirley Barker. LC 60-6377. 1960. Random House.
Last Gentleman. Marguerite Krough. LC 42-25814. 1942. The Christopher Publishing House.
Last Gentleman. Walker Percy. LC 66-188614. bds., 5.95. Farrar.
Last Glencannon Omnibus: Including The Canny Mr. Glencannon and Mr. Glencannon Ignores the War. With an Introd. by Barnaby Conrad. Guy Gilpatric. LC 53-93677. 1953. Dodd, Mead.
Last Good Kiss. James Crumley. 1980. pap. 2.75 (ISBN 0-671-82813-4). PB.
Last Good Kiss. James Crumley. 1978. 8.95 o.p. (ISBN 0-394-41946-4). Random.
Last Good Kiss: A Novel. James Crumley. LC 77-90286. 8.95 (ISBN 0-394-41946-4). Random House.
Last Grain of Sand. Ivan E Green. LC 50-50352. 1949. Dorrance.
Last Great Death Stunt. Clark Howard. (Berkley Medallion Book). 1977. 1.50 (ISBN 0-425-03316-3). Berkley Pub. Corp.
Last Great Love. Marilyn Harris. LC 81-5199. 14.95 (ISBN 0-399-12649-X). Putnam.
Last Great Season. Donald Honig. LC 79-10403. 10.95 (ISBN 0-671-24197-4). Simon and Schuster.
Last Grey Wolf. Tom Townsend. 181p. 1982. 11.95 (ISBN 0-89896-009-6); pap. 6.95 (ISBN 0-89896-010-X). Larksdale.
Last Gun. Marion Christie. (Orig.). 1971. pap. 0.75 o.p. (B75-2131). Belmont-Tower.
Last Gun to Jericho. James Kane. Ed. by Alice Sachs. 1970. 3.95 o.p. Lenox Hill.
Last Gunsmoke. Stanton M. Lammers. 1979. 7.95 o.p. (ISBN 0-533-04252-6). Vantage.
Last Happy Hour. Charles J Hackett. LC 75-40728. 1976. 7.95 (ISBN 0-385-11471-0). Doubleday.
Last Hard Men. Brian Garfield. 1976. Fawcett Publications.
Last Heracles. Georgia Sallaska. LC 74-164724. 1971. 7.95. Doubleday.
Last Hero... Leslie Charteris. LC 30-31194. 1930. Pub. for the Crime Club, Inc., by Doubleday, Doran & Company, Inc.
Last Hero. Leslie Charteris. LC 36-17952. 1936. Doubleday, Doran & Company, Inc.
Last Hero see Saint Closes the Case.
Last Hero. 1st Ed. Peter W Denzer. LC 57-618656. 1957. Holt.
Last Heroes. John Gill. LC 73-5417. 1974. 6.95 (ISBN 0-394-48772-9). Random House.
Last Hill. Spencer Dunmore. LC 73-664. 1973. 5.95 (ISBN 0-688-00167-X). Morrow.
Last Hill. Spencer Dunmore. 1974. (pbk.) 0.95 (ISBN 0-523-00307-2). Pinnacle Books.
Last Hill to Climb & Other Tales. Clarence W. Granath. 3.75 o.p. Carlton.
Last Hope. Hugh Stowell Scott. LC 4-21990. 1904. C. Scribner's Sons.
Last Hope Ranch. Charles Alden Seltzer. LC 25-873727. The Century Co.
Last Hours of Sandra Lee. 1st American Ed. William Sansom. LC 62-8066. 1961. Little, Brown.
Last House. 1st Ed. Gina Dessart. LC 50-9033. 1950. Harper.
Last Houseparty. Peter Dickinson. LC 82-47892. 1982. 11.95 (ISBN 0-394-51795-4). Pantheon Books.
Last Hunt. Maurice Genevoix. Tr. by Wells, Warre Bradley. LC 40-6582. Random House.
Last Hunt. Milton Lott. LC 54-86953. 1954. Houghton Mifflin.
Last Hunt. Milton Lott. LC 79-14279. (Series: Gregg Press Western Fiction Series.). (Illus.). 1979. 12.95 (ISBN 0-8398-2581-1). Gregg Press.
Last Hunt. Luke Short. 128p. 1982. pap. 1.95 (ISBN 0-553-20677-X). Bantam.
Last Hurdle. Edward Bacon. LC 9-16922. 1909. 1.50. The Knickerbocker Press.
Last Hurrah. 1st. ed. Edwin O'Connor. Little, Brown.
Last Hurrah of the Golden Horde. Norman Spinrad. LC 72-18682. 1970. N. Doubleday.
Last Husband: And Other Stories. William Humphrey. LC 52-13826. 1953. Morrow.
Last Husband: And Other Stories. William Humphrey. LC 75-132118. (Short story index reprint series). 1970. (ISBN 0-8369-3675-2). Books for Libraries Press.
Last Husband, & Other Stories. facs. ed. William Humphrey. LC 75-132118. (Short Story Index Reprint Ser). 1953. 15.00 (ISBN 0-8369-3675-2). Ayer Co.
Last Immortal. J. O Jeppson. LC 79-23681. 1980. 9.95 (ISBN 0-395-28949-1). Houghton Mifflin.
Last in Convoy. James Pattinson. 1958. 8.95 (ISBN 0-8392-1060-4). Astor-Honor.
Last in Convoy: A Novel. James Pattinson. LC 58-869993. 1958. McDowell, Obolensky.
Last Incantation. Clark A. Smith. (Orig.). 1982. pap. 2.95 (ISBN 0-671-83543-2, Timescape). PB.
Last Inheritor. Geraldine Halls. LC 80-22071. 1980. 9.95 (ISBN 0-312-47087-8). St. Martin's Press.
Last Inmate. Thomas B Allen. LC 73-79957. 1973. 6.95. Charterhouse Books.
Last Innocence. Translated from the French by Marjorie Deans. Celia Bertin. LC 55-5683. 1955. McGraw-Hill.
Last Innocent Man. Phillip Margolin. LC 80-25786. 11.95 (ISBN 0-316-54617-8). Little, Brown.
Last Inspection. Alun Lewis. LC 43-9684. 1943. The Macmillan Company.
Last Inspection & Other Stories. Alun Lewis. 1942. text ed. 3.95x o.p. (ISBN 0-04-823032-4). Allen Unwin.
Last Invasion. Donal Hamilton Haines. LC 14-181164. 1914. Harper & Brothers.
Last Jew in America. Leslie A Fiedler. LC 66-17154. 1966. Stein and Day.
Last Kill. Charles Wells. LC 55-10448. (Signet book, 1225). 1955. New American Library.
Last King of Yewle: A Novelette in Nine Chapters. P. L. McDermott. LC 7-15420. (On cover: The "unknown" library no. 21). Cassell Publishing Company.
Last Knight of Europe: The Life of Don John of Austria. Gloria Goddard. 1932. Coventry House.
Last Known Address. Joseph Harrington. (Boxer Ser). 1971. pap. 0.95 o.p. (95126). Beagle Bks.
Last Known Address. Joseph Harrington. 1965. 3.50 o.p. (ISBN 0-397-00382-X). Lippincott.
Last Known Address: A Mystery Novel. Joseph Harrington. LC 65-14895. (Main Line mysteries). bds., 3.50. Lippincott.
Last Known Address: A Mystery Novel. Joseph Harrington. LC 65-14895. (Main Line mysteries). 1965. Lippincott.
Last Lady of Mulberry: A Story of Italian New York. Henry Wilton Thomas. LC 2575. 1900. D. Appleton & Company.
Last Lamp Burning. Gwyn Griffin. (YA) 1966. 6.95 o.p. (ISBN 0-399-10487-9). Putnam.
Last Lamp Burning: A Novel. Gwyn Griffin. LC 66-15106. 1966. Putnam.
Last Laugh: An Original Novel. Charles Einstein. LC 36-121666. (Dell first edition, A121). 1956. Dell Pub. Co.
Last Laugh for the Baron. John Creasey. LC 74-161111. 1971. 4.95 (ISBN 0-8027-5235-7). Walker.
Last Laugh, Mr Moto. John Phillips Marquand. LC 42-3381. 1942. Little, Brown and Company.
Last Leaf. Marjorie Bowen Munsterberg. LC 47-18970. 1947. Dial Press.
Last Legs: By Steve Marriner Pseud. Charles Francis Huston Miller. LC 52-68715. 1953. Marriner Publications.
Last Lemurian. G. Firth Scott. LC 77-84266. (Lost Race and Adult Fantasy Fiction). 1978. 20.00 (ISBN 0-405-11007-3). Arno Press.
Last Lemurian: A Westralian Romance. G. Firth Scott. Ed. by R. Reginald & Douglas Melville. LC 77-84266. (Lost Race & Adult Fantasy Ser.). (Illus.). 1978. Repr. of 1898 ed. lib. bdg. 20.00x (ISBN 0-405-11007-3). Ayer Co.
Last Letter Home. Vilhelm Moberg. Tr. by Gustaf Lannestock. 1978. 1.95 (ISBN 0-445-04320-2). Popular Library.
Last Letter Home. Vilhelm Mokerg. (Emigrants Saga Ser.: No. 4). 288p. 1982. pap. 2.95 (ISBN 0-445-04320-2). Popular Lib.
Last Liberator. John Clive. 1981. pap. 2.75 (ISBN 0-440-15071-X). Dell.
Last Liberator: A Novel. John Clive. LC 79-19161. 8.95. Delacorte Press.
Last Licks. Troy Conway, pseud. (Coxeman Ser). (Orig.). 1968. pap. 0.60 o.p. (53-759). Paperback Lib.
Last Light. August William Derleth. 5.00 o.p. Arkham.
Last Lion: And Other Tales. Vicente Blasco Ibanez. (Half-title: International pocket library, ed. by E. R. Brown). The Four Seas Company.
Last Lion & Other Tales. Vicente Blasco Ibanez. pap. 0.60 o.p. (6, IPL). Humphries.
Last, Long Journey. Roger Cleeve. LC 76-85265. 1969. 4.95. Scribner.
Last Love. Thomas B Costain. LC 63-15486. 1975. (pbk.) 1.75 (ISBN 0-380-00215-9). Avon.
Last Love. Thomas Bertram Costain. 6.95 o.p. (ISBN 0-385-00566-0). Doubleday.
Last Love. authorized ed. Georges Ohnet. LC 41-31381. 1890. J. B. Lippincott Company.
Last Love of Camille: A Novel. 1st Ed. Frances Winwar. LC 54-6038. 1954. Harper.
Last Lover. Kelsey Freeman. LC 32-21557. Greenberg.
Last Lover. Tish Martinson. 480p. (Orig.). 1981. pap. 2.95 (ISBN 0-446-93023-7). Warner Bks.
Last Lover. Helen Topping Miller. LC 44-699851. D. Appleton-Century Company, Incorporated.
Last Magic. N. Richard Nash. LC 78-55022. 1978. 10.95 (ISBN 0-689-10905-9). Atheneum.
Last Man. Mary Wollstonecraft Godwin Shelley. Ed. by Hugh J. Luke. LC 65-19465. 1965. University of Nebraska Press.
Last Man: A Novel. Nathan Monroe McLaughlin. LC 2724. 1900. The Neale Company.

Last Man Alive. Gordon D. Shirreffs. 1977. pap. 1.25 o.s.i. (ISBN 0-505-51167-3, BT51167). Tower Bks.

Last Man at Arlington. Joseph DiMona. LC 73-78966. 1973. 7.95 (ISBN 0-525-63006-6). A. Fields Books.

Last Man Is Out. Marvin Karlins. LC 69-13039. (Illus.). 1969. 5.95. Prentice-Hall.

Last Man on Earth. Ed. by Isaac Asimov & Martin Greenberg. (Orig.). 1982. pap. 2.95 (ISBN 0-449-24531-4, Crest). Fawcett.

Last Man: Or, Omegarus and Syderia. Jean Baptiste Francois Xavier Cousin De Grainville. LC 77-84246. (Lost Race and Adult Fantasy Fiction). 1978. 26.00 (ISBN 0-405-10992-X). Arno Press.

Last Man: Or, Omegarus & Syderia, a Romance in Futurity, 2 vols. in 1. Jean B. De Grainville. LC 77-84246. (Lost Race & Adult Fantasy Ser.). 1978. Repr. of 1806 ed. lib. bdg. 26.00x (ISBN 0-405-10992-X). Ayer Co.

Last Mandarin. Stephen D. Becker. LC 78-23844. 8.95 (ISBN 0-394-49927-1). Random House.

Last Mandarin. Stephen D. Becker. (Berkley book). 1980. 2.50 (ISBN 0-425-04543-9). Berkley Pub Corp.

Last Mansion. Hal Adams. LC 61-15461. 1961. Dorrance.

Last Massacre see Ute's Last Stand.

Last Mayday. Keith Wheeler. 1972. pap. 0.95 o.p. (N2630). Pyramid Pubns.

Last Mayday. 1st Ed. Keith Wheeler. LC 68-22627. 1968. 5.95. Doubleday.

Last Meeting: A Story. Brander Matthews. LC 7-24700. 1885. C. Scribner's Sons.

Last Member of the Family. Lois A. Sunagel. (Orig.). 1979. pap. 1.75 (ISBN 0-532-17245-0). Woodhill.

Last Men in London. William Olaf Stapledon. LC 76-9745. (Gregg Press science fiction series). 1976. 15.00 (ISBN 0-8398-2340-1). Gregg Press.

Last Men in London see Last & First Men.

Last Migration. Vincent Cronin. LC 57-11250. (Illus.). 1957. Dutton.

Last Migration. Frison-Roche, Roger. LC 67-28582. 1967. Harper & Row.

Last Mile. Frank A. McAlister. LC 22-20279. 1922. Doubleday, Page & Company.

Last Mile-Stone. Emma Rosalyn Sutemeier Saylor. LC 17-24270. 1917. P. Elder & Company.

Last Movement. Joan Aiken. LC 76-42055. 1977. 7.95 (ISBN 0-385-12620-4). Doubleday.

Last Movement. Joan Aiken. LC 78-7488. 1978. 12.95 (ISBN 0-8161-6586-6). G. K. Hall.

Last Movement. Joan Aiken. 1977. 1.95 (ISBN 0-446-89681-0). Warner Books.

Last Mughal. G. D. Khosla. 376p. 1969. pap. 2.40 o.p. (ISBN 0-88253-050-X). Ind-US Inc.

Last Mystery of Edgar Allan Poe: The Troy Dossier. Manny Meyers. LC 78-17283. 8.95 (ISBN 0-397-01315-9). Lippincott.

Last Nazi. Max Lamb & Harry Sanford. (Orig.). 1980. pap. 2.25 o.s.i. (ISBN 0-505-51486-9). Tower Bks.

Last Night at Black Hammer. Gene Olson. (Dodd Mead Silver star westerns). 1957. Dodd, Mead.

Last Night at Paradise. Anne Weale. (Harlequin Romances Ser.). 192p. 1981. pap. 1.25 (ISBN 0-373-02411-8, Pub. by Harlequin). PB.

Last Night at the Brain Thieves Ball. Scott Spencer. 1978. pap. 1.75 (ISBN 0-380-39883-4, 39883). Avon.

Last Night at the Brain Thieves Ball: A Novel. Scott Spencer. LC 73-4805. 1973. 5.95 (ISBN 0-395-17125-3). Houghton Mifflin.

Last Night at the Brain Thieves Ball: A Novel. Scott Spencer. 1978. 1.75 (ISBN 0-380-39883-4). Avon Books.

Last Night at the Ritz. Elizabeth Savage. 1973-1974. (pbk.) 1.25. Popular Library.

Last Night at the Ritz: A Novel. Elizabeth Savage. LC 73-4764. 1973. 6.95 (ISBN 0-316-77144-9). Little, Brown.

Last Night I Dreamed: Twenty One Short Plays. Richard Urdahl. LC 74-76919. (Open Book Ser). (Illus.). 80p. 1974. pap. 1.00x o.p. (ISBN 0-8006-0159-9). Fortress.

Last Night of Summer. Erskine Caldwell. LC 63-20017. 1963. Farrar, Straus.

Last Night's Farm: A Novel. Paul Kennebeck. LC 73-83529. 1973. 6.95 (ISBN 0-8402-1324-7). Nash Pub.

Last Nights of Paris. Philippe Soupault. Tr. by William Carlos Williams. LC 29-18330. (Transatlantic library). 1929. The Macaulay Company.

Last Nights of Paris. Philippe Soupault. Tr. by William Carlos Williams. LC 81-22137. (Illus.). 1982. 17.95 (ISBN 0-916190-18-8) (ISBN 0-916190-19-6). Full Court Press.

Last Night's Stranger: One Night Stands & Other Staples of Modern Life. Pat Rotter. LC 81-70460. 16.95 (ISBN 0-89479-104-4). A & W Publishers.

Last of All Possible Worlds: A Novel. Peter Ferdinand Drucker. LC 81-48034. 13.41 (ISBN 0-06-014974-4). Harper & Row.

Last of Britain: A Story. Meriol Trevor. LC 56-4988. 1956. Macmillan.

Last of Cheri. Sidonie Gabrielle Colette. LC 32-31618. G. P. Putnam's Sons.

Last of Days: A Novel. Moris Farhi. LC 82-19803. 16.95 (ISBN 0-517-54908-5). Crown.

Last of Ellman. James E Nash. LC 72-156579. 1971. 5.95 (ISBN 0-06-013158-6). Harper & Row.

Last of Her Line. A Novel. Eliza Tabor Stephenson. (Franklin square library, no. 42). 1879. Harper & Brothers.

Last of His Name. Elbert Perce. LC 7-36360. 1854. Biker, Thorne & &Co.

Last of Lazarus. Robert C Goldston. LC 66-12279. P. Cm.

Last of Mr. Norris. Christopher Isherwood. LC 35-6721. 1935. W. Morrow and Company.

Last of Mrs. Cheyney: Novelized. Guy Fowler & Lonsdale, Frederick. LC 29-138245. Grosset & Dunlap.

Last of Philip Banter. John Franklin Bardin. LC 47-176992. 1947. Dodd, Mead & Company.

Last of Sheila. Alexander Edwards. 1973. (pbk) 1.25. Warner.

Last of Summer: A Novel. Kate O'Brien. LC 43-51121. 1943. Doubleday, Doran and Company, Inc.

Last of the Arawaks: A Story of Adventures on the Island of San Domingo. Frederick Albion Ober. LC 1-23067. 1901. W. A. Wilde Company.

Last of the Arawaks: A Story of Adventure on the Island of San Domingo. Frederick Albion Ober. LC 1-23067. 1901. W. A. Wilde Company.

Last of the Aukas: A Romance. ed. and rev. by percy b. st. john. ed. Gustave Aimard & St. John, Percy Bolingbroke, 1821-1889, Ed. LC 5-42598. (On cover: Lovell's library, no 1081). 1887. J. W. Lovell Company.

Last of the Barons... Edward George Earle Lytton Bulwer-Lytton Lytton. LC 31-32286. (The novels and romances of Edward Bulwer Lytton. v. 6). Aldine Book Publishing Co.

Last of the Barons. Edward George Earle Lytton Bulwer-Lytton Lytton. LC 1-1530. (New world. Extra ser. no. 56, 57, 58. Feb., 1843). 1843. J. Winchester.

Last of the Barons. library ed.... ed. Edward George Earle Lytton Bulwer-Lytton Lytton. LC 7-8125. (Half-title: Novels of Sir Edward Bulwer Lytton. Library ed. Historical romances, vol. XVII-XVIII). 1861. J. B. Lippincott & Co.

Last of the Barons. Edward George Earle Lytton Bulwer-Lytton Lytton. LC 37-32814. 1867. J. B. Lippincott & Co.

Last of the Barons. Edward George Earle Lytton Bulwer-Lytton Lytton. G. Routledge and Sons.

Last of the Barons. the lord lytton ed.... ed. Edward George Earle Lytton Bulwer-Lytton Lytton. LC 7-8124. 1881. J. B. Lippincott & Co.

Last of the Barons. Edward George Earle Lytton Bulwer-Lytton Lytton. LC 21-15380. (Seaside library, v. 72, no. 1454). 1882. G. Munro.

Last of the Barons. Edward George Earle Lytton Bulwer-Lytton Lytton. LC 7-8122. (On cover: Lovell's library, v. 5, no. 255). 1883. J. W. Lovell Company.

Last of the Barons. Edward George Earle Lytton Bulwer-Lytton Lytton. (On cover: Seaside library. Pocket ed. no. 130). 1884. G. Munro.

Last of the Barons. Edward George Earle Lytton Bulwer-Lytton Lytton. (Half-title: Novels of Sir Edward Bulwer Lytton. Library ed. Historical romances. vol. VII-VIII). 1893. Little, Brown, and Company.

Last of the Barons. Edward George Earle Lytton Bulwer-Lytton Lytton. (Half-title: Novels of Sir Edward Bulwer Lytton. Library edition. Historical romances, vol. VII-VIII). 1900. Little, Brown, and Company.

Last of the Barons. Edward George Earle Lytton Bulwer-Lytton Lytton. LC 2-20034. 1902. C. Scribner's Sons.

Last of the Barons. Edward George Earle Lytton Bulwer-Lytton Lytton. LC 18-4344. (On cover: The home library). 1917. A. L. Burt Company.

Last of the Big Kite Flyers. Patrice Chaplin. LC 72-116195. 1971. 5.95. Doubleday.

Last of the Breed. easy eye ed. Don Rico. pap. 0.60 o.p. Lancer.

Last of the Breed. Les Savage. LC 54-8030. (Dell first edition, 37). 1954. Dell Pub. Co.

Last of the Conquerors. William Gardner Smith. 262p. 1973. Repr. of 1948 ed. 8.50x (ISBN 0-911860-40-1). Chatham Bkseller.

Last of the Conquerors. William Gardner Smith. pap. 0.50 o.p. (72-959). Lancer.

Last of the Country House Murders. Emma Tennant. LC 76-6976. 6.95 (ISBN 0-8407-6490-1). T. Nelson.

Last of the Cowboys: A Novel. Max Franklin, pseud. (Signet Book). (Illus.). 1977. 1.75 (ISBN 0-451-07734-2). New American Library.

Last of the Crazy People. Timothy Findley. 1967. 4.95 o.p. (ISBN 0-696-68031-9). Hawthorn.

Last of the Crazy People. 1st Ed. Timothy Findley. LC 67-14744. 1967. 4.95. Meredith.

Last of the Danvers: The Story Ofa Fatalist. Edward Lyman Bill. Keynote Publishing Company.

Last of the Dog Team. William W. Johnstone. 1981. pap. 2.75 (ISBN 0-89083-736-8). Zebra.

Last of the Fairies. George Payne Rainsford James. (Seaside library, v. 29, no. 607). 1879. G. Munro.

Last of the Foresters: Or, Humors on the Border; a Story of the Old Virginia Frontier. John Esten Cooke. 1856. Derby & Jackson.

Last of the Gnostic Masters: A Novel. Thomas Sawyer Spivey. LC 26-24559. T. S. Spivey.

Last of the Great Wampanoag Indian Sachems: A Factual Story of the Last Days of King Philip's War, 1676. Milton A Travers. LC 63-11507. 1963. Christopher Pub. Houst.

Last of the Greeks. Olivia Davis. LC 68-21740. 1968. 5.95 o.p. (ISBN 0-395-07596-3). HM.

Last of the Greeks: A Novel. Olivia Davis. LC 68-21740. 1968. 5.95. Houghton, Mifflin.

Last of the Greenwood. Sharon Whitby. 1976. pap. 1.50 o.p. (ISBN 0-515-03978-0). BJ Pub Group.

Last of the Greenwood. Sharon Whitby. 1976. (pbk.) 1.50 (ISBN 0-515-03978-0). Pyramid Books.

Last of the Grenvilles. Frederick Harcourt Kitchin. LC 20-1693. E. P. Dutton & Company.

Last of the Houghtons: A Novel. Richard Wallace Buckley. 1907. The Neale Publishing Company.

Last of the Japs and the Jews. Solomon Cruso. LC 33-30141. H. W. Lefkowitz, Inc.

Last of the Just. Schwarz-Bart, Andre. LC 79-24071. 1981. 12.50 (ISBN 0-8376-0456-7). R. Bentley.

Last of the Just. Translated from the French by Stephen Becker. 1st American Ed. Andre Schwarz-Bart. LC 60-119474. 1960. Atheneum Publishers.

Last of the Knickerbockers: A Comedy Romance. Herman Knickerbocker Viele. LC 1-256659. 1901. H. S. Stone & Company.

Last of the Lairds. John Galt. LC 72-172054. (His Works, v. 9). (Illus.). 1968. AMS Press.

Last of the Lairds: Or, The Life and Opinions of Malachi Mailings, Esq. of Auldbiggings. John Galt. LC 6-44477. 1827. Printed by J. & J. Harper.

Last of the Legions: And Other Tales of Long Ago. Arthur Conan Doyle. LC 26-8498. 1925. George H. Doran Company.

Last of the Levanos. Maurits Wertheim. LC 67-10593. 1967. T. Yoseloff.

Last of the Longhorns. Harry Sinclair Drago. LC 48-7572. 1948. Doubleday.

Last of the Macallisters: A Novel. Amelia Edith Huddleston Barr. LC 6-798719. (Harper's handy series. no. 58). 1886. Harper & Brothers.

Last of the Maidens: A Novel. Richard Dohrman. LC 75-80329. 1969. 6.95. Holt, Rinehart and Winston.

Last of the Mansions. Dorothy Daniels. Orig. Title: Bed of Ashes. pap. 0.60 o.p. (73-511). Lancer.

Last of the Middle West. John R. Humphreys. LC 66-17392. 1966. 4.95. Doubleday.

Last of the Mohicans. James Fenimore Cooper. LC 64-15708. (Classics to grow on). 1966. Parents' Magazine Press.

Last of the Mohicans. James Fenimore Cooper. LC 51-12403. (New American Edition of Everyman's Library, 79A). 1951. Dutton.

Last of the Mohicans. James Fenimore Cooper. (On cover: Lovell's library, no. 6). 1882. J. W. Lovell Company.

Last of the Mohicans. James Fenimore Cooper. LC 13-2074. (Standard literature ser. no. 29). University Publishing Company.

Last of the Mohicans. James Fenimore Cooper. Ed. by Wight, John Green. LC 99-4178. (Heath's English classic). 1899. D. C. Heath & Co.

Last of the Mohicans. James Fenimore Cooper. LC 99-3056. (Maynard's English classic series. Special no.)). Maynard, Merrill & Co.

Last of the Mohicans. Cooper, James Fenimore. Ed. by Morris, Mowbray Walter. LC 4-15430. (His Leather-stocking tales). 1900. Macmillan and Co., Limited.

Last of the Mohicans. James Fenimore Cooper. LC 28-485419. (reader's library). J. H. Sears & Company, Inc.

Last of the Mohicans. James Fenimore Cooper. LC 28-24569. (golden books). D. McKay.

Last of the Mohicans. James Fenimore Cooper & Haight, Margaret Nanette. LC 9-16921. (On cover: Eclectric readings). American Book Company.

Last of the Mohicans: A Narrative of 1757. Illustrated by James Daugherty. Introd. by May Lamberton Becker. James Fenimore Cooper. LC 57-7410. (Rainbow classics). 1957. World Pub. Co.

Last of the Mohicans: A Narrative of 1757. James Fenimore Cooper. LC 73-166424. (Scribner library, SL 451). (Illus.). 1973. (pbk.) 3.95 (ISBN 0-684-20778-8) (ISBN 0-684-20778-8). Scribner.

Last of the Mohicans: A Narrative of 1757. James Fenimore Cooper. LC 50-5569. (World's greatest literature). 1949. Fountain Press.

Last of the Mohicans: A Narrative of 1757. James Fenimore Cooper. LC 6-398347. (Leather-stocking tales). 1926. H. C. Carey & I. Lea.

Last of the Mohicans. A Narrative of 1757. new ed. James Fenimore Cooper. LC 11-10567. 1852. Stringer and Townsend.

Last of the Mohicans: A Narrative of 1757. James Fenimore Cooper. (Lether stocking tales). 1872. D. Appleton and Company.

Last of the Mohicans: A Narrative of 1757. James Fenimore Cooper. LC 31-35233. (Lettered on cover: Leather stocking tales. Household ed.). Houghton, Mifflin and Company.

Last of the Mohicans: A Narrative of 1757. James Fenimore Cooper. Ed. by Cooper, Susan Fenimore. LC 6-29882. (Leather-stocking tales). 1876. Hurd and Houghton.

Last of the Mohicans: A Narrative of 1757. Cooper, James Fenimore. LC 6-29880. 1896. T. Y. Crowell & Company.

Last of the Mohicans: A Narrative of 1757. ed. for school use by edwin herbert lewis ed. James Fenimore Cooper. Ed. by Lewis, Edwin Herbert. LC 99-2395. (Lake English classics). 1890. Scott, Foresman and Company.

Last of the Mohicans: A Narrative of 1757. James Fenimore Cooper. Ed. by Wickes, William Kerr. LC 90-5815. (Macmillan's pocket English classics). 1899. The Macmillan Company.

Last of the Mohicans: A Narrative of 1757. James Fenimore Cooper. Ed. by Strunk, William, Jr. LC 16-6993. (English classics--Star series). 1913. World Book Company.

Last of the Mohicans: A Narrative of 1757. James Fenimore Cooper. Ed. by Wickes, William Kerr. LC 41-34794. (Macmillan's pocket American and English classics). 1917. The Macmillan Company.

Last of the Mohicans: A Narrative of 1757. James Fenimore Cooper. Ed. by Lewis, Edwin Herbert. LC 19-5046. (Half-title: The Lake English classics. General editor: L. T. Damon). Foresman and Company.

Last of the Mohicans: A Narrative of 1757. James Fenimore Cooper. LC 20-264. 1919. C. Scribner's Sons.

Last of the Mohicans: A Narrative of 1757. James Fenimore Cooper. Ed. by Law, Frederick Houk. LC 25-25278. (Winston companion classics). The John C. Winston Company.

Last of the Mohicans: A Narrative of 1757. james fenimore cooper, edited by w. k. wickes, revised by h. y. moffett, illustrated by george m. richard. ed. James Fenimore Cooper. Ed. by Wickes, William Kerr. Moffett, Harold Young. LC 30-10973. (Half-title: New pocket classics). The Macmillan Company.

Last of the Mohicans: A Narrative of 1757. James Fenimore Cooper. Ed. by Pound, Louise. LC 31-175979. (western series of English and American classics). 1931. Harlow Publishing Co.

Last of the Mohicans: A Narrative of 1757. James Fenimore Cooper. 1937. Charles Scribner's Sons.

Last of the Mohicans: A Narrative of 1757. James Fenimore Cooper. (Half-title: Everyman's library, ed. by Ernest Rhys Fiction). J. M. Dent & Co.

Last of the Mohicans: A Narrative of 1757. James Fenimore Cooper & James A. Sappenfield. LC 82-21890. (writings of James Fenimore Cooper). ((Series: Cooper, James Fenimore, 1789-1851.). ((Series: 1981.). (Works.). 30.00 (ISBN 0-87395-362-2). State University of New York Press.

Last of the Mohicans: A Tale of 1757. James Fenimore Cooper. LC 6-39302. 1871. Hurd and Houghton.

Last of the Mohicans: Adapted by Verne B. Brown and Edited by Gertrude Moderow. Illustrated by Brinton Turkle. James Fenimore Cooper & Verne B Brown. LC 50-3337. 1950. Scott, Foresman.

Last of the Mohicans. Introd. by Charles Angoff. James Fenimore Cooper. LC 57-953. Fine Editions Press.

Last of the Mohicans: Or, A Narrative of 1757. James Fenimore Cooper. Ed. by Cooper, Susan Fenimore. (Half-title: The Leather stocking tales. Riverside ed.). 1899. Houghton, Mifflin and Company.

Last of the Mohicans: Or, A Narrative of 1757. James Fenimore Cooper. LC 10-240263. 1.35. H. Holt and Company.

Last of the Mohicans: Or, A Narrative of 1757. James Fenimore Cooper. Ed. by Cooper, Susan Fenimore. LC 6-29881. (Riverside literature series. no. 95-98). 1896. Houghton, Mifflin and Company.

Last of the Mohicans: Or, A Narrative of 1757. James Fenimore Cooper & Cooper, Susan Fenimore. Ed. by Blackmer, Alan Rogers. LC 30-102455. (Riverside literature series). Houghton Mifflin Company.

Last of the Mohicans: Or, A Narrative of 1757. James Fenimore Cooper & Pattee, Fred Lewis. LC 27-18325. (modern reader's series). 1927. The Macmillan Company.

Last of the Mohicans. With an Introd. and Captions by Basil Davenport. James Fenimore Cooper. LC 51-12403. (Great Illustrated Classics). 1951. Dodd, Mead.

Last of the Mohicawns. James Fenimore Cooper. Ed. by Noyes, Ernest Clapp. LC 27-84626. (Academy classics for junior high schools). Allyn and Bacon.

Last of the Mountain Men. Harold Peterson. (O.s.i.). 1975. pap. 1.25 o.s.i. (BT50792). Belmont-Tower.

Last of the Peterkins with Others of Their Kin & The Queen of the Red Chessman. Lucretia P. Hale. (Illus.). pap. 1.50 o.p. (ISBN 0-486-21468-0). Dover.

Last of the Peterkins with Others of Their Kin & The Queen of the Red Chessman. Lucretia P. Hale. (Illus.). pap. 1.50 o.p. (ISBN 0-486-21468-0). Dover.

Last of the Peterkins, with Others of Their Kin, and The Queen of the Red Chessmen. Lucretia Peabody Hale. LC 65-24024. 1965. Dover Publications.

Last of the Plainsmen. Grey, Zane. LC 66-1374. (Bantam pathfinder editions). 1964. Bantam Books.

Last of the Plainsmen. Zane Grey. LC 8-24293. 1908. The Outing Publishing Company.

Last of the Plainsmen. Zane Grey. LC 41-34802. (On cover: Every boy's library--Boy scout edtion). Grosset & Dunlap.

Last of the Plainsmen. Zane Grey. LC 21-16872. 1915. Grosset & Dunlap.

Last of the Plainsmen. Zane Grey. LC 29-30788. Grosset & Dunlap.

Last of the Plainsmen. Zane Grey. LC 81-5473. 1982. 11.95 (ISBN 0-89340-359-8). J. Curley.

Last of the Puritans: The Story of Benjamin Gilbert and His Friends. Frederic Pierpont Ladd. LC 12-9959. 1.00. F. M. Lupton, Publisher (Incorporated.

Last of the Quills: A Story of Welsh Life. David Pugh Griffiths. LC 2-11614. 1902. The Modern Press, Printers.

Last of the Redskins. Tr. from French by Grace T. Mayes. Drawings by Raymond Davidson. Jean Dutourd. LC 65-14000. 1965. 4.50. Doubleday.

Last of the Southern Girls. Willie Morris. LC 72-11040. 1973. 6.95 (ISBN 0-394-46101-0). Knopf.

Last of the Southern Girls. Willie Morris. 1974. (pbk.) 1.50. Avon.

Last of the Southern Winds. David Loovis. LC 61-7208. 1961. Scribner.

Last of the Untouchables. Paul Robsky. (O.s.i.). 1976. pap. 1.50 o.s.i. (AD1589, Award). Univ Pub & Dist.

Last of the Untouchables: By Oscar Fraley with Paul Robsky. Paul Robsky & Oscar Fraley. LC 62-1580. (Popular Library eagle books, G569). 1962. Popular Library.

Last of the Valois. Ross Williamson, Hugh. LC 72-93324. (Illus.). 1973. 6.50. St. Martin's Press.

Last of the Valois. Hugh R. Williamson. LC 72-93324. 260p. 1973. 6.50 o.p. (ISBN 0-312-47215-3). St Martin.

Last of the Van Slacks: A Story of to Day. Edward Sims Van Zile. (On cover: Cassell's sunshine series of choice fiction, no. 31). 1889. Cassell & Company, Limited.

Last of the Vikings. Johan Bojer & Muir, Jessie, Tr. LC 23-86053. 1923. The Century Co.

Last of the Vikings. Tr. from Norwegian by Jessie Muir. Afterword by Richard Vowles. Johan Bojer. (Signet classic, CP248) Bibl.). 1964. New Amer. Lib.

Last of the Whitcombes. Rosemary Schafer. (Orig.). 1978. pap. 1.95 (ISBN 0-89083-391-5). Zebra.

Last of the Whitfields. 1st Ed. Elise Ayers Sanguinetti. LC 61-183156. 1962. McGraw-Hill.

Last of the Wild Stallions. Barlow Meyers. LC 49-10458. 1949. Westminister Press.

Last of the Wine. Mary Renault, pseud. LC 75-4841. (Illus.). 1975. 2.95 (ISBN 0-394-71653-1). Vintage Books.

Last of the Wine. Mary Renault, pseud. LC 56-10409. (Illus.). 1956. Pantheon.

Last of the Zinja. Robert Shea. (Shike Ser.: Bk. 2). 460p. (Orig.). 1981. pap. 3.50 (ISBN 0-515-07145-5). Jove Pubns.

Last of the Zinja. Robert Shea. (Shike Ser.). 488p. 1982. 14.95 (ISBN 0-399-12729-1). Putnam Pub Group.

Last of Vicky. Allan Nixon. pap. 0.60 o.p. (53-929). Paperback Lib.

Last of Wisdom. Eleanor Chase. LC 32-22556. Sears Publishing Company, Inc.

Last One. Dion Henderson. 1974. pap. 0.95 o.p. (00113). Leisure Bks.

Last One, a Novel. 1st Ed. Dion Henderson. LC 56-10510. 1956. Holt.

Last One Home Sleeps in the Yellow Bed: Stories. Leon Rooke. LC 68-8940. 1968. 5.95. Louisiana State University Press.

Last One Kills. Whit Masterson, pseud. LC 72-84090. (Red badge mystery). 1969. 3.95. Dodd, Mead.

Last One Left. John Dann MacDonald. LC 67-10975. 1967. Doubleday.

Last One Left: By John D. MacDonald. John Dann MacDonald. (Crest bk., t1085). 1968. Fawcett.

Last Outlaw. Lawrence Cortesi, pseud. 1.75 (ISBN 0-505-51560-1). Tower Books.

Last Outlaw. Brian Wynne Garfield. 1970. pap. 0.60 o.p. (ISBN 0-447-73207-2). Lancer.

Last Passion. Helen Bartlett Bridgman. LC 26-6025. Cloister Publishing Company.

Last Picture Show. Larry McMurtry. (Laurel edition). 1974. (pbk.) 1.25. Dell.

Last Picture Show. Larry McMurtry. LC 66-22587. 1966. Dial Press.

Last Picture Show. Larry McMurtry. LC 79-10775. 1979. 1.95 (ISBN 0-14-005183-X). Penguin Books.

Last Picture Show. Larry McMurty. 1979. pap. 3.50 (ISBN 0-14-005183-X). Penguin.

Last Pioneers. Melvin P Levy. LC 34-9618. A. H. King.

Last Place God Made. Henry Higgins. (Crest Book, M1832). 1973. 0.95. Fawcett.

Last Place God Made. Henry Patterson. LC 78-182754. 1972. 5.95 (ISBN 0-03-091350-0). Holt, Rinehart and Winston.

Last Place in the World. Margarete Sparks. 1975. 4.95. Avalon Books.

Last Place Left. Marshall Pugh. LC 75-83635. 1969. 5.95. Harper & Row.

Last Plane from Uli. Charles Kearey. LC 72-78116. 1972. 5.95 (ISBN 0-03-001396-8). Holt, Rinehart and Winston.

Last Plane Out: A Novel. John Dudley Ball. LC 79-99906. 1970. 5.95. Little, Brown.

Last Plane to Shanghai. Richard William Tregaskis. LC 61-7903. 1961. Bobbs-Merrill.

Last Poor Man. Edward S Hyams. LC 66-16151. 1966. Simon and Schuster.

Last Port of Call: A Novel. Heinrich Hauser & Mussey, June Barrows, 1910- Tr. LC 38-296323. Stackpole Sons.

Last Post. Ford Madox Ford. LC 28-2237. 1928. A. & C. Boni.

Last Post... Ford Madox Ford. LC 42-28123. 1928. The Literary Guild of America.

Last Post for a Partisan. Clive Egleton. 1974. (pbk.) 1.25 (ISBN 0-523-00344-7). Pinnacle Books.

Last Post for a Partisan. Clive Egleton. LC 71-136447. 1971. 5.95. Coward, McCann & Geoghegan.

Last President. Michael Kurland & Barton Whaley. LC 79-29751. 1980. 11.95 (ISBN 0-688-03610-4). Morrow.

Last Princess: A Novel of the Incas. 1st Ed. Charles O Locke. LC 54-6716. Norton.

Last Professin. Jacques Laurent Bost. Tr. by L. Duym, Alfred Van Ameyden Van. LC 48-7570. 1948. Doubleday.

Last Puritan: A Memoir in the Form of a Novel. George Santayana. LC 35-31979. 1935. Constable & Co., Ltd.

Last Puritan: A Memoir in the Form of a Novel. George Santayana. LC 36-271194. 1936. C. Scribner's Sons.

Last Quadrant. Meira Chand. LC 81-14400. 1982. 10.95 (ISBN 0-89919-079-0). Ticknor & Fields.

Last Race. Jon Ewbank Manchip White. LC 53-9199. 1953. M. S. Mill Co., and W. Morrow.

Last Raider. Douglas Reeman. (Berkley Medallion Book). 1974. (pbk.) 1.25. Berkley Pub. Co.

Last Ranger. Zane Grey. LC 82-16224. 1983. 13.95 (ISBN 0-89340-544-2). J. Curley.

Last Ranger. Zane Grey. 272p. 1981. pap. 2.25 (ISBN 0-505-51748-5). Tower Bks.

Last Ranger. Zane Grey. (O.s.i.). 1976. pap. 1.25 o.s.i. (BT50945). Belmont-Tower.

Last Rebel. Joseph Alexander Altsheler. LC 99-5030. 1900. J. B. Lippincott Company.

Last Rebel. Joe Millard, pseud. (O.s.i.). (Orig.). 1971. pap. 0.75 o.s.i. (A776S, Award). Univ Pub & Dist.

Last Recollections of My Uncle Charles. Nigel Balchin. LC 57-5684. 1957. Rinehart.

Last Recruit of Clare's: Being Passages from Thememoirs of Anthony Dillon, Chevalier of St. Louis, and Late Colonel of Calre's Regiment in the Service of France. Samuel Robert Keightley. LC 7-11431. 1897. Harper & Brothers.

Last Refuge. Henry Blake Fuller. Ed. by Donald Pizer. LC 77-96558. (American Authors Ser). 1970. lib. bdg. 16.95 o.s.i. (ISBN 0-512-00217-7). Garrett Pr.

Last Refuge. Edward Ernest Smith. LC 73-163011. 1972. 1.65 (ISBN 0-7260-0032-9). Gold Star Publications.

Last Refuge see Collected Works.

Last Refuge: A Sicilian Romance. Henry Blake Fuller. LC 5708. 1900. Houghton, Mifflin and Company.

Last Refuge of a Scoundrel: And Other Stories. Wendell Howard. LC 52-5701. 1952. Exposition Press.

Last Resort. Henry Francis Prevost Battersby. LC 12-22817. 1912. John Lane.

Last Resort. Hilda Van Siller. LC 51-11210. (Main line mysteries). 1951. Lippincott.

Last Resort: A Novel. Pamela Hansford Johnson. LC 57-524. 1956. Macmillan.

Last Resort: A Novel. Scott Sommer. LC 81-48280. 12.50 (ISBN 0-394-52290-7). Random House.

Last Resorts. John Magurk. 1969. pap. 1.95 o.s.i. Tri-Ocean.

Last Respects. Catherine Aird, pseud. LC 82-45344. 1982. 11.95 (ISBN 0-385-18256-2). Published for the Crime Club by Doubleday.

Last Respects. Catherine Aird, pseud. LC 82-45344. (Crime Club Ser.). 192p. 1982. 11.95 (ISBN 0-385-18256-2). Doubleday.

Last Respects. Jerome Weidman. LC 77-156966. 1972. 6.95 (ISBN 0-394-46551-2). Random House.

Last Reveille. David Morrell. (Fawcett Crest book). 1977. 1.95 (ISBN 0-449-23527-0). Fawcett Books.

Last Reveille: A Novel. David Morrell. LC 76-56140. 8.95 (ISBN 0-87131-228-X). M. Evans.

Last Revolt: The Story of Rabbi Akiba. Joseph Opatoshu. LC 52-3275. 1952. Jewish Publication Society of America.

Last Ride. Robert E Howard. (Berkley Book). (Illus.). 1978. 1.95 (ISBN 0-425-03754-1). Berkley Pub. Corp.

Last Ride. Frank O'Rourke. LC 58-5678. 1958. Morrow.

Last Ride to Los Lobos. William Chamberlain. 1969. pap. 0.60 o.p. (R2111, GM). Fawcett World.

Last Rider from Lonesome Canyon. James Farnsworth, pseud. 1978. pap. 1.25 (ISBN 0-532-12587-8). Woodhill.

Last Rights. H. H. Dooley. 224p. 1981. pap. 2.50 (ISBN 0-449-24392-3, Crest). Fawcett.

Last Rights: A Novel. H. H Dooley. LC 79-6882. 1980. 10.00 (ISBN 0-385-15742-8). Doubleday.

Last Rights: Death & Dying in Texas Law & Experience. Robert J. Connelly. 196p. 1983. pap. 8.95 (ISBN 0-931722-21-7). Corona Pub.

Last Rites. Perry Michael Smith. LC 73-140774. 1971. 6.95 (ISBN 0-684-10554-3). Scribner.

Last Rites. Paul Spike. 1982. pap. 3.50 (ISBN 0-451-11612-7, AE1612, Sig). NAL.

Last Rites: A Novel. Paul Spike. LC 81-9440. 12.95 (ISBN 0-453-00410-5). New American Library.

Last Rodeo. Ernest Haycox. LC 57-1043. (Pockd) et book, 1148. Western,). 1957. Pocket Books.

Last Rodeo. 1st Ed. Ernest Haycox. LC 56-561537. Little, Brown.

Last Romans, "Ostatni Rzumianie" A Tale of the Time of Theodosius the Great. Teodor Jeske-Choinski. Tr. by O'Toole, George Barry. LC 36-15380. The Pittsburgher Printing & Publ. Co.

Last Romantic. Charles Bonner. LC 49-8522. 1949. Coward-McCann.

Last Romantic. Dorothea Buske. LC 78-3966. 8.95 (ISBN 0-312-47135-1). St. Martin's Press.

Last Romantics. Ruth Harris. LC 79-29753. 10.95 (ISBN 0-671-24595-3). Simon and Schuster.

Last Rose of Summer. Rupert Hughes. LC 14-18648. 1914. Harper & Brothers.

Last Round. Frank O'Rourke. LC 56-5298. 1956. Morrow.

Last Round. Frank O'Rourke. LC 57-104036. (Permabooks, M3069. Fiction,9). 1957. Permabooks.

Last Roundup. Harry V Johnston. LC 50-1925. H. V. Johnston Pub. Co.

Last Run South. Robin Hiscock. LC 58-5827. 1958. Knopf.

Last Running: A Story. John Graves & John Groth. LC 75-306312. (Illus.). 9.50. Encino Press.

Last Rush North. Bruce Dobler. 1976. 8.95 o.p. (ISBN 0-316-18916-2). Little.

Last Rush North: A Novel About the Trans Alaska Pipeline. Bruce Dobler. LC 76-13625. (ISBN 0-316-18916-2). Little, Brown.

Last Safari. Richard Rhodes. LC 79-7207. 1980. 10.95 (ISBN 0-385-14243-9). Doubleday.

Last Samuri. Nick Carter. (Nick Carter Ser.). (Illus.). 208p. 1982. pap. 2.50 (ISBN 0-441-47183-8, Pub. by Charter Bks). Ace Bks.

Last Scam: A Novel. David Harris. LC 81-5582. 13.95 (ISBN 0-440-04674-2). Delacorte Press/S. Lawrence.

Last Score. Ellery Queen, pseud. LC 65-6641. 1964. Pocket Books.

Last Score. Ellery Queen. (Signet book). 1974. (pbk.) 0.95. New American Library.

Last Score: Or, The Private Life of Sir Richard Ormston. 1st Ed. Margaret Storm Jameson. LC 61-759885. 1961. Harper.

Last Secret. Albert Leffingwell. LC 44-20107. 1943-1944. Dial Press.

Last Secret. Albert Leffingwell. LC 45-15784. (Handi-book mysteries). 1945.

Last Secret. Doris Manners-Sutton. LC 39-8723. 1939. Longmans, Green and Co.

Last Seen Alive. Jim McCormick. LC 79-7329. 1979. 8.95 (ISBN 0-385-15113-6). Doubleday.

Last Seen Hitchhiking. Brett Halliday. (Mike Shane mystery). 1974. (pbk.) 0.95. Dell.

Last Seen in Samarra. Janet Gregory Vermandel. LC 72-3926. (Red badge novel of suspense). 1972. 4.95 (ISBN 0-396-06655-0). Dodd, Mead.

Last Seen Wearing. Colin Dexter. LC 75-26179. 1976. 7.95. St. Martin's.

Last Seen Wearing... Hillary Waugh. LC 52-10043. 1952. Published for the Crime Club by Doubleday.

Last Sentence. Jonathan Goodman. LC 79-26870. 1980. 8.95 (ISBN 0-312-47151-3). St. Martin's Press.

Last Sentence. Mary Gleed Tuttiett. LC 8-32313. Sons & Company.

Last September. Elizabeth Bowen. LC 52-8509. 1952. Knopf.

Last September. Elizabeth Bowen. LC 29-3188. 1929. L. MacVeagh, The Dial Press.

Last September. Elizabeth Bowen. 1979. 2.25. Avon Books.

Last Shall Be First. S. W. Karl. 1978. pap. 1.50 (ISBN 0-532-15372-3). Woodhill.

Last Sherlock Holmes Story. Michael Dibdin. LC 77-88773. 1978. 7.95. Pantheon Books.

Last Shiksa. B. H Litwack. LC 77-23900. 10.00 (ISBN 0-399-12065-3). Putnam.

Last Shootout. William L. Hopson. 1970. pap. 0.60 o.p. (B60-2023). Belmont-Tower.

Last Shot. Frederick Palmer. LC 14-78762. 1914. 1.35. C. Scribner's Sons.

Last Shot. William MacLeod Raine. LC 26-22320. 1926. Garden City Publishing Co., Inc.

Last Shot. Lee Thayer, pseud. LC 31-522. Sears Publishing Company, Inc.

Last Showdown. Max Brand. 192p. 1975. 5.95 o.p. (ISBN 0-396-07082-5). Dodd.

Last Showdown. Max Brand. (Adult Ser.). 1976. Repr. lib. bdg. 11.95 o.p. (ISBN 0-8161-6338-3, Large Print Bks). G K Hall.

Last Showdown. Frederick Faust. LC 75-4512. (Silver star western). 1975. 5.95 (ISBN 0-396-07082-5). Dodd, Mead.

Last Showdown. Frederick Faust. LC 75-33134. 1976. 11.95 (ISBN 0-8161-6338-3). G. K. Hall.

Last Showdown. Frederick Faust. 1.25 (ISBN 0-671-80835-4). Pocket Books.

Last Signal. Dora Russell. LC 8-1337. (On cover: Broadway series, no. 16). 1892. J. A. Taylor and Company.

Last Slaver. George Suthie King. LC 33-29352. 1933. G. P. Putnam's Sons.

Last Space Ship. William Fitzgerald Jenkins. LC 49-6995. (Fell's science fiction library). 1949. F. Fell.

Last Spike, and Other Railroad Stories. Cy Warman. LC 6-4636. 1906. S. Scribner's Sons.

Last Squadron. Translated by Paul Findlay. Gerd Gaiser. LC 56-791143. 1956. Pantheon Books.

Last Stage from Opal. Kelly P. Gast. LC 77-26525. 1978. 7.95 o.p. (ISBN 0-385-13473-8). Doubleday.

Last Stage to Aspen. Allan Vaughan Elston. LC 56-11685. Lippincott.

Last Stage to Benbow. Greer Wagoner. 176p. (Orig.). 1978. pap. 1.50 (ISBN 0-89041-193-X, 3193). Major Bks.

Last Stage to Eternity. Morgan Hill. (Dan Colt Western Ser.: No. 7). 224p. (Orig.). 1983. pap. 2.50 (ISBN 0-440-14806-5). Dell.

Last Stage to Gomorrah. Barry Cord. 1979. pap. 1.25 o.s.i. (ISBN 0-505-51339-0). Tower Bks.

Last Stage West. Frank Bonham. 160p. 1981. pap. 1.95 (ISBN 0-425-04947-7). Berkley Pub.

Last Stand at Indigo Flats. Zane Grey. 1982. 18.00x (ISBN 0-86025-183-7, Pub. by Ian Henry Pubns England). State Mutual Bk.

Last Stand at Papago Wells. Louis L'Amour. LC 80-24980. (Series: Gregg Press Western Fiction Series,). 1981. 10.95 (ISBN 0-8398-2694-X). Gregg Press.

Last Stand at Papago Wells see Complete L'Amour.

Last Stand at Papago Wells see L'Amour Westerns.

Last Stand at Rio Blanco. Terrell L. Bowers. 1981. pap. 6.95 (Avalon). Bouregy.

Last Stand at Saber River. Elmore Leonard. 176p. 1980. pap. 1.75 (ISBN 0-553-13696-8). Bantam.

Last Stand Mesa. Leonard London Foreman. 1974. (pbk.) 0.95. Ace Books.

Last Stand of Father Felix. Leonard Patrick O'Connor Wibberley. LC 74-3441. 1974. 5.95 (ISBN 0-688-00285-4). Morrow.

Last Starship from Earth. John Boyd. 1978. pap. 1.95 o.p. (ISBN 0-14-004875-8). Penguin.

Last Starship from Earth. John Boyd. 1968. 4.95 o.p. Weybright.

Last Starship from Earth. Boyd Upchurch. LC 68-17752. 1968. Weybright and Talley.

Last Starship from Earth. Boyd Upchurch. LC 77-26235. 1978. 1.95 (ISBN 0-14-004875-8). Penguin Books.

Last Station: A Novel. Bobby Jack Nelson. LC 72-76316. 1972. 5.95 (ISBN 0-395-13948-1). Houghton-Mifflin.

Last Station: A Novel. Bobby Jack Nelson. (A Signet Book.). 1.50 (ISBN 0-451-07396-7). New American Library,

Last Stop. Ed. by Joseph Bruchac. perfect bdg. 2.25 (ISBN 0-912678-10-0). Greenfld Rev Pr.

Last Stop. Wilson Tucker. LC 63-13852. 1963. Published for the Crime Club by Doubleday.

Last Stop Camp 7. Hans Hellmut Kirst. LC 78-81001. 1969. 5.95. Coward-McCann.

Last Stop, Lunsbury: A Novel About the Depression. Stanley L Wojcik. LC 78-102916. 1970. 4.95. William-Frederick Press.

Last Stop Lunsbury: A Novel of the Depression. Stanley L. Wojcik. 1973. 4.95 (ISBN 0-87164-108-9). William-F.

Last Straw... Ione Sandberg Shriber. LC 46-639561. 1946. Rinehart & Company, Inc.

Last Straw. Harold Titus. LC 20-471142. Small, Maynard & Company.

Last Straw for Harriet. Elizabeth Cadell. LC 47-30145. 1947. W. Morrow & Company.

Last Straw. 1st Ed. Doris Miles Disney. LC 54-11153. (Crime Club selection). 1954. Published for the Crime Club by Doubleday.

Last Straws. Richard Aldington. LC 76-52454. 1976-1977. 15.00 (ISBN 0-8414-2973-1). Folcroft Library Editions.

Last Stroke. Emma Murdoch Van Deventer. (On cover: Pinkerton detective series, no. 29). Laird & Lee.

Last Struggle. Joseph Kromolicki. LC 39-2604. 1939. Meador Publishing Company.

Last Summer. Emma Tamzin Shaler Carr. LC 29-1064. The Grafton Press.

Last Summer. Evan Hunter. LC 68-14191. 1968. Doubleday.

Last Summer: A Novel. Elizabeth Gunn. LC 62-7490. 1962. Norton.

Last Summer at Bluefish Cove. Jane Chambers. LC 81-86655. (Illus.). 120p. (Orig.). 1982. 25.00 (ISBN 0-935672-04-4); pap. 6.95 (ISBN 0-935672-05-2). JH Pr.

Last Summer of Mata Hari. Edward Huebsch. LC 79-14576. 11.95 (ISBN 0-517-53306-5). Crown Publishers.

Last Summer of the Men Shortage. Geraldine Halls. LC 77-354719. 1976. 2.95 (ISBN 0-09-461030-4). Constable.

Last Supper. Chaim I Bermant. LC 73-78872. 1973. 7.95. St. Martin's Press.

Last Supper. Charles McCarry. 384p. 1983. 15.95 (ISBN 0-525-24173-6, 01549-460). Dutton.

Last Supper: A Novel. Charles McCarry. LC 82-18377. 15.95 (ISBN 0-525-24173-6). E.P. Dutton.

Last Supper: And Other Stories. Howard Melvin Fast. 1955. Blue Heron Press.

Last Surrender. new ed. Sallie Lee Bell. 192p. (Orig.). 1974. pap. 2.25 o.p. (ISBN 0-310-21002-X). Zondervan.

Last Surrender: A Romance of the War Between the States. Sallie Lee Bell. LC 59-4385. 1959. Zondervan Pub. House.

Last Survivor. Roger Myers & Albert Herbert. LC 76-377732. (Illus.). 1976. 1.75. Manor Books.

Last Survivor: By Estil Dale Pseud. 1st Ed. Albert Benjamin Cunningham. LC 52-10436. (Guilt edged mystery). 1952. Dutton.

Last Suspect. Street, Cecil John Charles. LC 51-9116. 1951. Dodd, Mead.

Last Tales. Karen Blixen. LC 75-9828. 1975. 2.95 (ISBN 0-394-71752-X). Vintage Books.

Last Tales. Karen Blixen. LC 77-356892. 1976. 5.40 (ISBN 0-226-15297-9). University of Chicago Press.

Last Tales. Karen Blixen. LC 57-10037. 1957. Random House.

Last Tales. Isak Dinesen, pseud. 1957. 8.95 (ISBN 0-394-43254-1). Random.

Last Tallyho: A Novel. Newhafer, Richard L. LC 64-18019. 1964. Putnam.

Last Temptation. Joseph Viertel. LC 54-9799. 1955. Simon and Schuster.

Last Temptation of Christ. Nikos Kazantzakis. LC 60-10985. 1960. Simon and Schuster.

Last Temptation of Christ. Nikos Kazantzakis. 1960. 14.95 o.p. (ISBN 0-671-40710-4). S&S.

Last Temptation of Christ. Tr. from Greek by P. A. Bien. Nikos Kazantzakis. (Essandess paperback). 1966. pap., 2.25. S. & S.

Last Tenant. Benjamin Leopold Farjeon. LC 6-38635. Cassell Publishing Company.

Last Thing We Talk About. rev. & enl. ed. Joseph Bayly. LC 70-87318. Orig. Title: View from a Hearse. 122p. 1973. pap. 2.50 (ISBN 0-912692-07-3). Cook.

Last Thing You'd Want to Know. Eric Koch. LC 75-44836. 1976. 8.95 (ISBN 0-912766-35-2). Tundra Books.

Last Things. Charles Percy Snow. LC 73-123332. (His Strangers and brothers 11). 1970. 7.95. Scribner.

Last Three Soldiers. William Henry Shelton. LC 8-5112. 1897. The Century Co.

Last Tiger Out. Jan Doward. LC 72-92689. 127p. 1973. 4.95 o.p. (12035-2). Pacific Pr Pub Assn.

Last Time I Saw Hell. Simon Quinn. (Inquisitor,#2). 1974. (pbk.) 0.95. Dell.

Last Titan. Charles A. Gauld. (Illus.). 1972. 5.50 o.s.i. (ISBN 0-911760-12-1). Glenwood.

Last to Die. William Herrick. LC 70-156152. 1971. 4.95 (ISBN 0-671-20985-X). Simon and Schuster.

Last To Know. John Craig Stewart. 1982. pap. 1.95 (ISBN 0-448-17003-5, Pub. by Tempo). Ace Bks.

Last to Rest. Ernest Raymond. LC 42-242619. 1942. H. C. Kinsey & Company, Inc.

Last Toke. Amos Brooke. (Orig.). 1977. pap. 1.75 (ISBN 0-87067-519-2, BH519). Holloway.

Last Tomb. John Lange. 1974. (pbk.) 1.25. Bantam Books.

Last Touchdown. J. Lance Gilmer. (Orig.). 1978. pap. 1.75 (ISBN 0-87067-517-6, BH040). Holloway.

Last Touches: And Other Stories. Lucy Lane Clifford. LC 76-150470. (Short story index reprint series). 1971. (ISBN 0-8369-3810-0). Books for Libraries Press.

Last Touches, and Other Stories. Lucy Lane Clifford. LC 6-20741. 1892. Macmillan and Co.

Last Town. Norman Marion. 1979. pap. 1.75 o.s.i. (ISBN 0-8439-0659-6, Leisure Bks). Nordon Pubns.

Last Trail. Zane Grey. 1976. Repr. of 1909 ed. lib. bdg. 14.40x (ISBN 0-89190-754-8). Am Repr-Rivercity Pr.

Last Trail. Zane Grey. 256p. 1981. pap. 2.25 (ISBN 0-505-51761-2). Tower Bks.

Last Trail. Zane Grey. 2.95 o.p. (ISBN 0-448-05117-6). G&D.

Last Trail. Zane Grey. 1976. 1.25. Belmont Tower Books.

Last Trail: A Story of Early Days in the Ohio Valley. Zane Grey. LC 9-11538. A. L. Burt Company.

Last Trail: A Story of Early Days in the Ohio Valley. Zane Grey. LC 22-474038. 1916. A. L. Burt Company.

Last Trail: An Abridged Edition of the Novel. Zane Grey. LC 40-113374. The Saalfield Publishing Company.

Last Trail: Edited for Young Readers. Illustrated by Earl Sherwan. Zane Grey. LC 50-12509. 1950. Whitman.

Last Trail: Retold for Young Readers; Illustrated by Earl Sherwan. Authorized Ed. Zane Grey. LC 54-4379. 1954. Whitman Pub. Co.

Last Train from Berlin. George Blagowidow. LC 76-23749. 1977. 7.95 (ISBN 0-385-12339-6). Doubleday.

Last Train from Canton. James Leonard Johnson. LC 81-11456. (Johnson, James Leonard, 1927- . Code Name Sebastian Adventure). 6.95 (ISBN 0-310-26631-9). Zondervan.

Last Train Out. Edward Phillips Oppenheim. LC 40-337883. 1940. Little, Brown, and Company.

Last Train to Limbo. Playboy Press Editors. LC 78-136576. pap. 0.75 o.p. (D16106). Playboy.

Last Trap: A Detective Story. Sinclair Gluck. LC 28-1280. 1928. Dodd, Mead and Company.

Last Tresilians: A Novel. John Innes Mackintosh Stewart. LC 64-10574. 1963. Norton.

Last Trophy. Brian Marsh. LC 81-16571. 10.95 (ISBN 0-312-47165-3). St. Martin's Press.

Last Trump. John E Gardner. LC 80-16560. 11.95 (ISBN 0-07-022852-3). McGraw-Hill.

Last Trump. Lee Thayer, pseud. LC 37-2384. 1937. Dodd, Mead & Company.

Last Trumpet: Murder in a Mexican Bull Ring. Todd Downing. LC 37-11245. 1937. Pub. for the Crime Club, Inc., by Coubleday, Doran & Co., Inc.

Last Trumpeters and Other Stories. Elmer Inglesby Ransom. LC 41-550010. 1941. University of Georgia Press.

Last Try. John Reed Scott. LC 12-995635. 1912. 1.25. J. B. Lippincott Company.

Last Twist of the Knife. Margerie Bonner. LC 46-5942. 1946. C. Scribner's Sons.

Last Two Weeks of Georges Rivac. Geoffrey Household. LC 79-18121. 1979. 1.95 (ISBN 0-14-005273-9). Penguin Books.

Last Two Weeks of Georges Rivac. Geoffrey Household. LC 79-16583. 1979. 12.95 (ISBN 0-8161-6744-3). G. K. Hall.

Last Tycoon. Francis Scott Key Fitzgerald. LC 75-304758. 1974. 0.40 (ISBN 0-14-001495-0). Penguin.

Last Tycoon: An Unfinished Novel. Francis Scott Key Fitzgerald. LC 41-21401. 1941. C. Scribner's Sons.

Last Tycoon: An Unfinished Novel, Together with The Great Gatsby. Francis Scott Key Fitzgerald. LC 51-5440. 1951. Scribner.

Last Unicorn. Peter S Beagle. LC 68-16075. 1968. Viking Press.

Last Valley. Alfred Bertram Guthrie. LC 75-17598. 1975. 8.95 (ISBN 0-395-21899-3). Houghton Mifflin.

Last Valley. Haas, Ben. LC 66-16150. 1966. Simon and Schuster.

Last Vendee: Or, The She-Wolves of Machecoul... Alexandre Dumas. Tr. by Wormeley, Katharine Prescott. LC 6-43603. 1894. Estes and Lauriat.

Last Victim. Ann Dramann. (Orig.). 1980. pap. text ed. 1.95 o.s.i. (ISBN 0-505-51595-4). Tower Bks.

Last View of Eden. Ralph Hayes. (Orig.). 1981. pap. 2.50 (ISBN 0-505-51705-1). Tower Bks.

Last Viking. Poul Anderson. 1980. pap. cancelled (ISBN 0-89083-573-X). Zebra.

Last Viking: Book One, The Golden Horn. Poul Anderson. 272p. (Orig.). 1980. pap. text ed. 2.50 (ISBN 0-89083-597-7). Zebra.

Last Von Reckenburg. first american from the third german edition. ed. Luise Von Francois. Tr. by Safford, Mary Joanna. LC 6-43261. 1887. Cupples and Hurd.

Last Voyage. Anna Clarke. LC 81-21419. 9.95 (ISBN 0-312-47187-4). St. Martin's Press.

Last Voyage: Book Three of the Torch-Bearers. facsimile ed. Alfred Noyes. LC 70-167477. (Granger Index Reprint Ser.). Repr. of 1930 ed. 14.00 (ISBN 0-8369-6282-6). Ayer Co.

Last Voyage: Captain Cook's Lost Diary. Hammond Innes. LC 78-20443. (Illus.). 1979. 9.95 (ISBN 0-394-50579-4). Knopf.

Last Voyage of the Donna Isabel: A Romance of the Sea. Randall Parrish. LC 8-26195. 1908. A. C. McClurg & Co.

Last Walk Is Alone. V. L Martinetz. LC 72-93583. 1973. 1.95 (ISBN 0-87707-125-X). Tarnhelm Press.

Last War Cry. Joseph Chadwick. (Orig.). 1971. pap. 0.60 o.p. (ISBN 0-446-63551-0, 63-551). Paperback Lib.

Last War of Mankind. Frank J. Parnes. 4.95 o.p. Vantage.

Last Warpath. Henry Allen. LC 66-11999. 1966. Random House.

Last Warpath. Will Henry, pseud. 1966. 6.95 o.p. (ISBN 0-394-43255-X). Random.

Last Warrior Queen. Mary Mackey. LC 82-19270. 15.95 (ISBN 0-399-31016-9). Seaview/Putnam.

Last Warrior: 1st Ed. in the U.S.A. Mary Elwyn Patchett. LC 66-15055. 1966. 4.50. Doubleday.

Last Weapon. Theodora Wilson Wilson. LC 17-13958. 1916.

Last Weapon: A Vision. Theodora Wilson Wilson. LC 18-8492. 1917. The John C. Winston Company.

Last Western. Thomas S Klise. LC 73-94482. 1974. 8.95 (ISBN 0-913592-31-5). Argus Communications.

Last Will and Testament. E. X Ferrars, pseud. LC 78-8209. 1978. 7.95 (ISBN 0-385-14455-5). Published for the Crime Club by Doubleday.

Last Will and Testament: Or, The Pendexter Saga, Second (and Last) Canto; Being a Further Episode in the Career of Dr. Benjamin Tancred, Related by His Friend, Paul Graham. George Douglas Howard Cole & Margaret Isabel Postgate Cole. LC 36-29837. 1936. Pub. for the Crime Club, Incorporated, by Doubleday, Doran & Company, Inc.

Last Wish. 1st Ed. Helene Greifinger. LC 56-5538. 1956. Vantage Press.

Last Woman. Ross Beeckman. 1909. W. J. Watt & Company.

Last Woman in His Life. Ellery Queen, pseud. LC 74-100109. (Illus.). 1970. 5.95. World Pub. Co.

Last Woman in His Life see Cop Out.

Last Word. Alice MacGowan. LC 2-23415. 1903. L. C. Page & Company.

Last Words. Alex Karmel. LC 68-15737. 1968. bds., 5.95. McGraw.

Last Words of Dutch Schultz. William S. Burroughs. LC 73-17676. (Richard Seaver Bk). (O.s.i.). (Illus.). 192p. 1975. 8.95 o.s.i. (ISBN 0-670-41950-8). Viking Pr.

Last Yankee. Arabella Wood. 3.75 o.s.i. (ISBN 0-8181-0292-6). Pageant-Poseidon.

Last Yankee. Woodman, Marguerite M. LC 64-5687. 1964. Pageant Press.

Last Year. William D'Harrel. LC 73-91536. 1974. 5.95 (ISBN 0-8059-1976-7). Dorrance.

Last Year of the War: A Novel. Shirley Nelson. LC 79-4183. 1979. pap. 4.95i (ISBN 0-06-066093-7, RD 303, HarpR). Har-Row.

Last Year's Blood. Henry C Branson. LC 47-12505. 1947. Simon and Schuster.

Last Year's Nest. Dorothy A Beckett Terrell. LC 25-16721. 1925. D. Appleton and Company.

Last Year's Snow. Don Tracy. LC 37-149298. M. S. Mill Co., Inc.

Last Yggdrasill. Robert F Young. LC 81-22840. 1982. 1.95 (ISBN 0-345-30420-9). Ballantine.

Last Yoncalla: The Legend of Sam Fearn. Dean Baker. LC 81-67395. (Illus.). 214p. (Orig.). (YA) 1981. pap. 6.50 (ISBN 0-940388-00-6). Blind John.

Lastborn of Elvinwood. Linda Haldeman. LC 77-27704. 1978. 7.95 (ISBN 0-385-14267-6). Doubleday.

Lastborn of Elvinwood. Linda Haldeman. 1980. 2.25 (ISBN 0-380-47985-0). Avon Books.

Lastchance Junction, Far, Far West: A Novel. Sarah Pratt McLean Greene. LC 6-45563. 1889. Cupples and Hurd.

Lasting Love. Antonia Blake. (Orig.). 1981. pap. 1.50 (ISBN 0-440-14968-1). Dell.

Lastingham Murder. Louis Tracy. LC 29-342974. E. J. Clode, Inc.

Latchstring Out. Skulda Vanadis Baner. LC 44-3390. 1944. Houghton Mifflin Company.

Late and Soon: A Novel. Edmee Elizabeth Monica De La Pasture. LC 43-9415. 1943. Harper & Brothers.

Late Bill Smith. Andrew Garve. LC 73-144197. (Novel of Suspense Ser). 1971. 5.95 o.p. (ISBN 0-06-011444-4, HarpT). Har-Row.

Late Bill Smith. Paul Winterton. LC 73-144197. 1971. 5.95 (ISBN 0-06-011444-4). Harper & Row.

Late Bloomer. David A Kaufelt. LC 79-4591. (ISBN 0-15-148792-8). Harcourt Brace Jovanovich.

Late-Blooming Flowers: And Other Stories. Anton Pavlovich Chekhov. LC 63-19775. 1964. McGraw-Hill.

Late Blossoming. Sylvia Parker. LC 38-633773. Gramercy Publishing Co.

Late Bourgeois World. Nadine Gordimer. LC 66-203381. bds., 3.50. Viking.

Late Bride: A Novel of Suspense. Theodora McCormick Du Bois. LC 64-23490. 1965. 3.95. Washburn Dist. McKay.

Late Call. Angus Wilson. LC 65-116311. 1965. 4.95. Viking.

Late Clara Beame. Taylor Caldwell. 1978. pap. 1.95 (ISBN 0-449-23725-7, Crest). Fawcett.

Late Climbs the Sun. Gladys Bagg Taber. LC 34-31985. 1934. Coward-McCann, Inc.

Late Colonel Judd. John De Meyer. LC 38-3952. J. B. Lippincott Company.

Late Day. Ole Sarvig. 52p. 1982. pap. 3.50 (ISBN 0-915306-05-0). Curbstone.

Late Flowering: A Love Story. Janet Curren Owen. LC 34-7412. 1934. Harper & Brothers.

Late George Apley. John Phillips Marquand. 1970. pap. 0.75 o.p. (ISBN 0-671-46921-5). WSP.

Late George Apley: A Novel in the Form of a Memoir. John Phillips Marquand. LC 37-646. 1937. Little, Brown, and Company.

Late George Apley: A Novel in the Form of a Memoir. John Phillips Marquand. LC 40-27102. (Half-title: The modern library of the world's best books). 1940. The Modern Library.

Late George Apley: A Novel in the Form of a Memoir... John Phillips Marquand. LC 45-15789. 1944.

Late Great Creature. Brock Brower. 1974. (pbk.) 1.25. Popular Library.

Late Great Creature. Brock Brower. LC 72-168255. 1972. 6.95. Atheneum.

Late Great Future. Gregory Fitz Gerald & John Dillon. LC 76-26804. (Fawcett Crest book). (Illus.). 1.75 (ISBN 0-449-23040-6). Fawcett Publications.

Late Great Me. Sandra Scoppettone. 256p. (Orig.). 1980. pap. 1.95 (ISBN 0-553-13359-4). Bantam.

Late Great Me. Sandra Scoppettone. LC 75-27416. 1976. 7.95 (ISBN 0-399-11620-6). Putnam Pub Group.

Late Great Pilgrim's Progress: John Bunyan's I.E. Bunyan's Immortal Classic. Edward P. Ware & John Bunyan. LC 73-82549. (Illus.). 1973. 1.50. Tee Jay Publications.

Late Harvest. Norman Douglas. LC 75-41082. Repr. of 1946 ed. 16.00 (ISBN 0-404-14717-8). AMS Pr.

Late Harvest. Olive Bernardine White. LC 40-12742. 1940. The Macmillan Company.

Late Harvest. Yvonne Whittal. (Harlequin Presents Ser.). 192p. 1983. pap. 1.75 (ISBN 0-373-10574-6). Harlequin Bks.

Late Harvey Grosbeck. Gilbert Millstein. LC 73-83658. 1974. 6.95 (ISBN 0-385-01133-4). Doubleday.

Late Have I Loved Thee. Ethel Edith Mannin. LC 48-8671. 1948. G. P. Putnam's Sons.

Late in the Season. Felice Picano. LC 80-39614. 10.95 (ISBN 0-440-04729-3). Delacorte Press.

Late Lamented Lady; an Eve MacWilliams Mystery. Marie Blizard. LC 46-5409. 1946. Mystery House.
Late Lamented. 1st Ed. Fredric Brown. LC 59-5808. (A Dutton mystery novel). 1959. Dutton.
Late Lark Singing. Gwinette Leigh. 3.50 o.p. Carlton.
Late Last Night. James Reach. LC 49-7206. 1949. W. Morrow.
Late, Late in the Evening. Gladys Mitchell. LC 76-375632. 1976. 3.25 (ISBN 0-7181-1420-5). Joseph.
Late Lily Shiel. Sheilah Graham. LC 77-87800. (Illus.). 1978. 10.00 (ISBN 0-448-12648-6). Grosset & Dunlap.
Late Lt. Dessin, and Other Stories. Richard H Blum. LC 67-29102. 1967. M. Jones Co.
Late Mattia Pascal (Il Fu Mattia Pascal) Luigi Pirandello & Livingston, Arthur, 1883- Tr. LC 23-11679. E. P. Dutton & Company.
Late Miss Guthrie. Ethel Edith Mannin. LC 76-373488. 1976. 3.95 (ISBN 0-09-125210-5). Hutchinson.
Late Miss Hollingford. Rosa Mulholland Gilbert. (On cover: Seaside library, Pocket ed., no. 921). 1887. G. Munro.
Late Miss Trimming. Edith Caroline Rivett. LC 57-6706. 1957. Published for the Crime Club by Doubleday.
Late Mrs. D. Hillary Waugh. LC 62-7695. 1962. Published for the Crime Club by Doubleday.
Late Mrs. Fonsell. Velda Johnston. 1973. (pbk.) 0.95. Dell.
Late Mrs. Fonsell: Novel of Suspense. Velda Johnston. LC 72-725. 1972. 4.95 (ISBN 0-396-06578-3). Dodd, Mead.
Late Mrs. Lane. Rona Randall. LC 46-441. 1946. Arcadia House, Inc.
Late Mrs. Null. Frank Richard Stockton. LC 8-15542. 1886. C. Scribner's Sons.
Late Mrs. Null. Frank Richard Stockton. LC 9-3861. 1891. C. Scribner's Sons.
Late Mrs. Null. Frank Richard Stockton. LC 8-2380. 1907. C. Scribner's Sons.
Late Phoenix. Catherine Aird, pseud. LC 78-131064. 1971. 4.50. Doubleday.
Late Rapture. Jane Arbor. (Harlequin Romances Ser). (O.s.i.). 1979. pap. 0.95 (ISBN 0-373-02251-4, Pub by Harlequin). PB.
Late Repentance: Or, The Little White Hand. Mary Andrews Denison. (Select series. no. 19). Street & Smith.
Late September. Gladys Etta Johnson. 1932. Macrae Smith Company.
Late Show. Ned Calmer. LC 73-9016. 1974. 6.95 (ISBN 0-385-08250-9). Doubleday.
Late Tenant. Louis Tracy. LC 6-34806. 1906. E. J. Clode.
Late Unlamented. Robert Alfred John Walling. LC 48-3713. (A Morrow mystery). 1948. W. Morrow.
Late Unlamented, by Harry Carmichael: Pseud. 1st Ed. Leopold Horace Ognall. LC 61-597658. 1961. Published for the Crime Club by Doubleday.
Late Winter Child. Vincent Buckley. (Orig.). 1980. pap. text ed. 6.50x (ISBN 0-85105-358-0, Dolmen Pr). Humanities.
Latecomer. Sarah Aldridge. (1974 ed. 4.50 o.p.). 1982. 5.00 (ISBN 0-930044-00-2). Naiad Pr.
Latecomer. Sarah Aldridge. 1974. NAIAD PRESS.
Latecomers. E. M. Nathanson. 1973. 1.25 (ISBN 0-671-78238-X). Pocket Books.
Latecomers. E. M. Nathanson. LC 71-123704. 1970. 6.95. Doubleday.
Later Adventures of Sherlock Holmes: A Definite Ive Text, Corrected and Edited by Edgar W. Smith. Illustrated with a Selctive Collation of the Original Illus. by Frederic Dorr Steele, Sidney Paget & Others. Arthur Conan Doyle. LC 52-13035. 1952. For the Members of the Limited Editions Club.
Later Adventures of Wee Macgreegor. John Joy Bell. 1904. Harper & Brothers.
Later Clara Beame. Taylor Caldwell. LC 63-12974. 1963. Published for the Crime Club by Doubleday.
Later Life. Lewis R. Aiken. LC 77-11326. (Illus.). 1978. pap. text ed. 8.95 o.p. (ISBN 0-7216-1070-6). Saunders.
Later Life. Louis Marie Anne Couperus. Tr. by Teixeira De Mattos, Alexander Louis. LC 15-24007. 1915. Dodd, Mead and Company.
Later Love Letters of a Musician. Myrtle Reed. LC 5124. 1900. G. P. Putnam's Sons.
Later Pratt Portraits: Sketched in a New England Suburb. Anna Fuller. LC 79-122709. (Short story index reprint series). (Illus.). 1970. Books for Libraries Press.
Later Pratt Portraits: Sketched in a New England Suburb. Anna Fuller. LC 11-7262. 1911. G. P. Putnam's Sons.
Later Son, a Different Daughter. Harry Atkins. LC 68-13621. 1968. McGraw-Hill.
Later Than You Think. Gawen Brownrigg. LC 38-15735. 1938. A. A. Knopf.
Later Than You Think. Mary Margaret Kaye. LC 58-4771. Rk.
Later Than You Think: By Mollie Hamilton. Mary Margaret Kaye. LC 58-121197. 1958. Coward-McCann.
Later Years. William Cowper Prime. LC 7-30097. 1854. Harper & Brothers.
Latest a Story. Harry Skinner & Skinner, Ed, Joint Author. 1900. Skinner Bros.?
Lathe of Heaven. Ursula K. Legium. 1971. 4.95 o.p. (ISBN 0-684-12529-3). Scribner.
Lathe of Heaven. Ursula K. Le Guin. LC 77-162760. 1971. (ISBN 0-684-12529-3). Scribner.
Lathe of Heaven. Ursula K. Le Guin. LC 81-18093. 1982. 12.50 (ISBN 0-8376-0464-8). R. Bentley.
Lathe of Heaven. Ursula K. Le Guin. 1973. pap. 2.95 (ISBN 0-380-01320-7, 60624). Avon.
Latigo. Frank O'Rourke. LC 53-6924. 1953. Random House.
Latigo: Dead Shot. Dean Owen. 224p. 1981. pap. 1.95 (ISBN 0-445-04690-2). Popular Lib.
Latigo: Double Eagle, No. 4. Dean Owen. 224p. 1982. pap. 2.25 (ISBN 0-445-04706-2). Popular Lib.
Latimer Big Three. Jonathan Latimer. LC 40-9139. 1940. The Sun Dial Press.
Latimer of the Flying B. Tony Adams. LC 42-1098. Phoenix Press.
Latimers: A Tale of the Western Insurrection of 1794. Henry Christopher McCook. LC 69-17935. (American classics in history & social science, 69). (Burt Franklin research & source works series, 335.). (Illus.). 1969. B. Franklin.
Latimers: A Tale of the Western Insurrection of 1794. Henry Christopher McCook. LC 7-15294. 1898. G. W. Jacobs & Co.
Latin Blood. LC 25-150521. 1925. Authors Publishing Corporation.
Latin Blood: The Best Crime and Detective Stories of South America. Ed. by Donald A. Yates. LC 76-181010. 1972. 6.95 (ISBN 0-665-00021-9). Herder and Herder.
Latin-Quarter Courtship, and Other Stories. Henry Harland. LC 70-178439. (Short story index reprint series). 1971. (ISBN 0-8369-4040-7). Books for Libraries Press.
Latin Quarter Courtship: And Other Stories. Henry Harland. LC 7-15260. Cassell & Company, Limited.
Latin-Quarter Courtship: And Other Stories. Henry Harland. LC 7-1527. (On cover: Cassell's sunshine series, no. 20). The Cassell Publishing Co.
Latin Quarter: Scenes De la Vie De Boheme, by Henri Murger; Translated by Elizabeth Ward Hugus, with an Introduction by D. B. Wyndham Lewis. Henri Murger. Tr. by Hugus, Elizabeth Ward. LC 31-979. 1930. E. V. Mitchell, Inc.
Latin Quarter: Scenes De la Vie De Boheme. Henri Murger & Elizabeth Ward Hugus. LC 76-48444. (Classics of European Literature). (Hyperion library of world literature). 1977. 12.95. (ISBN 0-88355-584-0) (ISBN 0-88355-585-9). Hyperion Press.
Latitude 19 Degree: A Romance of the West Indies in the Year of Our Lord Eighteen Hundred and Twenty; Being a Faithful Account and True, of the Painful Adventures of the Skipper, the Bo's'n, the Smith, the Mate, and Cynthia. Mary Bradford Crowninshield. LC 98-1489. 1898. D. Appleton and Company.
Latitudes of Love. Thomas E Doremus. LC 61-11764. C. N. Potter.
Latter-Day Dora. Jane Shaw. LC 77-359500. 1976. 3.50 (ISBN 0-432-05919-9). P. Davies.
Latter Day Saint. Alfred Almond McKay. LC 7-19988. F. H. Revell Company.
Latter-Day Sinners. Alice Kate Roland. 1906. The Neale Publishing Company.
Latter-Day Sweethearts. Constance Cary Harrison. LC 6-208561. 1906. The Authors and Newspapers Association.
Latter-Day Sweethearts. complimentary ed. Constance Cary Harrison. LC 7-7195. 1907. The Authors and Newspapers Association.
Latter End: A Miss Silver Mystery. Patricia Wentworth. LC 47-27083. 1947. J. B. Lippincott Company.
Latter Howe. Doreen Eileen Agnew Wallace, pseud. LC 35-8182. 1935. Macmillan Company.
Latterday Symphony. Florence Roma Muir Wilson O'Brien. LC 27-815233. 1927. A. A. Knopf.
Lattice Window. Frederic Rudolph Stearns. LC 48-11827. 1948. Dunne Press.
Lattimer Legend. Ann Hebson. LC 61-151821. 1961. Macmillan.
Lattimore Arch. Angela Gray, pseud. 1971. pap. 0.75 o.p. (ISBN 0-447-74744-4). Lancer.
Lauderdale Run. Jack Cummings. 1979. pap. 1.75 (ISBN 0-532-17208-6). Woodhill.
Laugh and Grow Rich. Jack Kahane. LC 23-129982. Brentano's.
Laugh and Lie Down. Robert Cantwell. LC 31-290133. Farrar & Rinehart Incorporated.
Laugh, Jew- Laugh; Short Humorous Stories. Jacob Adler & London, Abraham, Tr. LC 36-100524. 1936. Bloch Publishing Company.
Laugh, Jew, Laugh. facs. ed. Jacob Adler. Tr. by Abraham London. LC 77-116925. (Short Story Index Reprint Ser). 1936. 15.00 (ISBN 0-8369-3427-X). Ayer Co.
Laugh, Jew, Laugh: Short Humorous Stories. Jacob Adler. LC 77-116925. (Short story index reprint series). 1970. Books for Libraries Press.
Laugh People, Laugh! Short Humorous Stories. Jacob Adler & London, Abraham, Tr. LC 34-5693. N.J., A. London.
Laugh till You Cry, an Advertisement. Foreword by Malcolm Muggeridge; Illustrated by Heather Standring. 1st Ed. Wolf Mankowitz. LC 54-11700. 1955. Dutton.
Laugh with Me, Love with Me. Lee Damon. (Second Chance at Love Ser.: No. 120). 1983. pap. 1.75 (ISBN 0-515-07208-7). Jove Pubns.
Laughable Loves. Milan Kundera. LC 73-16156. 1974. 6.95 (ISBN 0-394-47412-0). Knopf; Distributed by Random House.
Laughable Loves. Milan Kundera. (Writers from the other Europe). 1975. (pbk.) 3.50 (ISBN 0-14-004044-7). Penguin Books.
Laughable Loves. Milan Kundera. LC 74-20836. 1975. (ISBN 0-394-71507-1). Vintage Books.
Laughing Bacchante. Cecil William Mercer. LC 50-2153. Putnam.
Laughing Bill Hyde: And Other Stories. Rex Ellingwood Beach. LC 17-301233. 1917. Harper & Brothers.
Laughing Boy. Oliver La Farge. LC 29-23247. 1929. Houghton Mifflin Company.
Laughing Buddha. Carl Glick. LC 37-4085. 1937. Lothrop, Lee & Shepard Company.
Laughing Buddha: A Tale of Love and Adventure in Western China. James Livingstone Stewart. LC 25-202551. Fleming H. Revell Company.
Laughing Cavalier. Shelton Lawrence. LC 30-11853. 1930. H. Vinal, Ltd.
Laughing Cavalier. Emmuska Orczy. LC 14-14913. 1.25. George H. Doran Company.
Laughing Death. Paul Edwards. 1973. (pbk) 0.95 (ISBN 0-515-03236-0). Pyramid.
Laughing Eyes. H. C. Hoffman. (On cover: Munro's library, popular novels, v. 1, no. 394). 1885. N. L. Munro.
Laughing Fox. Frank Gruber. LC 40-11297. Farrar & Rinehart, Inc.
Laughing Gas. Pelham Grenville Wodehouse. LC 37-27010. 1936. Doubleday, Doran & Company, Inc.
Laughing Gas. Pelham Grenville Wodehouse. LC 38-3734. 1937. The Sun Dial Press, Inc.
Laughing Ghost. Dorothy Eden. 1976. 1.75. Ace.
Laughing Girl. Peggy O'More, pseud. (Contemporary Teens Ser.). 224p. (Orig.). 1981. pap. 2.25 (ISBN 0-89531-143-7, 0146-96). Sharon Pubns.
Laughing Girl: A Mystery Novel. George Frank Worts. LC 41-728. 1941. H. C. Kinsey & Company, Inc.
Laughing Girl: A Novel. Robert William Chambers. LC 18-21372. 1918. 1.50. D. Appleton and Company.
Laughing Heart. Beatrice Sheepshanks. LC 26-6142. 1926. London, Harper & Brothers.
Laughing His Way to a Million: A True Story. Horace Alan Dunn. LC 48-8806. 1948. Continental Publishers.
Laughing House. Warwick Deeping. LC 47-31135. 1947. Dial Press.
Laughing House: A Novel. Meade Minnigerode. 1920. G. P. Putnam's Sons.
Laughing in the Hills. Bill Barich. 240p. 1981. pap. 3.95 (ISBN 0-14-005832-X). Penguin.
Laughing in the Hills. Bill Barich. 228p. 1980. 10.95 (ISBN 0-670-41997-4). Viking Pr.
Laughing into Glory. Hodge MacIlvain Eagleson. LC 47-3876. 1947. G. W. Stewart, Inc.
Laughing Journey. Thomas Lennon. LC 34-24857. The John Day Company.
Laughing Loon. Josiah E Greene. LC 39-20246. 1939. W. Morrow & Company.
Laughing Man of Woodmont Coves. Tom T Hall. LC 81-47865. 1982. 14.95 (ISBN 0-385-17369-5). Doubleday.
Laughing Matter: A Novel. William Saroyan. LC 52-13557. 1953. Doubleday.
Laughing Mountains. Kay Lynn. LC 36-12315. 1936. E. P. Dutton & Co., Inc.
Laughing Peril. Henry Leyford Gates. LC 33-2636. 1933. The Macaulay Company.
Laughing Pioneer. Paul Green. LC 32-28979. 1932. R. M. McBride & Company.
Laughing Policeman. Maj Sjowall & Per Wahloo. LC 76-43000. (Sjowall, Maj. 1935-. Martin Beck Police Mystery). 1977. 1.65 (ISBN 0-394-72341-4). Vintage Books.
Laughing Policeman. Maj Sjowall & Per Wahloo. LC 69-20182. 1970. 4.95. Pantheon Books.
Laughing Prince: A Book of Jugoslav Fairy Tales and Folk Tales. Parker Hoysted Fillmore. LC 21-18687. 1921. Harcourt, Brace and Company.
Laughing Prophet. Emile Cammaerts. 243p. 1980. Repr. of 1937 ed. lib. bdg. 30.00 (ISBN 0-8492-4047-6). R West.
Laughing Queen. Lily Moresby Adams Beck. LC 29-15483. 1929. Dodd, Mead & Company.
Laughing Rider. Laurie York Erskine. LC 24-6452. 1924. D. Appleton and Company.
Laughing Stranger. 1st Ed. Vina Delmar. LC 53-7842. 1953. Harcourt, Brace.
Laughing to Keep from Crying. 1st Ed. Langston Hughes. LC 52-7952. 1952. Holt.
Laughing Vaquero. William L Hopson. LC 43-5529. 1943. Phoenix Press.
Laughing Vaquero. William L Hopson. (Belmont Tower book). 1978. 1.25 (ISBN 0-505-51245-9). Tower Pubns.
Laughing War. Martyn Burke. LC 77-16901. 1980. 9.95 (ISBN 0-385-13332-4). Doubleday Canada Ltd.
Laughing Water. Bertha Sinclair. LC 31-28594. 1932. Little, Brown, and Company.
Laughing Whitefish: By Robert Traver. Pseud. 1st Ed. John Donaldson Voelker. LC 65-24264. bds., 5.50. McGraw.
Laughing Widow. George Warren. 1974. (pbk.) 1.95 (ISBN 0-87056-385-8). Brandon Books.
Laughing Willows. Teresa Gerbers. (Avalon Books). 1977. 4.95. Thomas Bouregy.
Laughing Woman. Carlos Keith. LC 33-17678. The Vanguard Press.
Laughingest Dog. Carolyn Jerauld. LC 72-93027. (Illus.). 1973. 1.95 o.p. (ISBN 0-8059-1786-1). Dorrance.
Laughingest Lady. Elinore Cowan Stone. LC 27-7927. 1927. D. Appleton and Company.
Laughter & Dispair: Readings in Ten Novels of the Victorial Era. Ulrich Camillus Knoepflmacher. LC 73-145789. (Campus 85). (Illus.). 1973. 2.95 (ISBN 0-520-02352-8). Univ. of California Pr.
Laughter at the Door. Geoffrey Trease. LC 74-79598. 1974. 8.95 o.p. (ISBN 0-312-47495-4). St Martin.
Laughter Ends. John Farrow. LC 33-14796. Harcourt, Brace and Company.
Laughter for Tomi. Peggy O'More, pseud. LC 38-22016. 1938. Hillman-Curl, Inc.
Laughter from Downstairs. Czenzi Ormonde. LC 48-8480. 1948. Farrar, Straus.
Laughter in Cheyne Walk: A Novel. Ursula Bloom. LC 37-17028. J. B. Lippincott Company.
Laughter in Darkness: A Novel. Robert O'Neil Bristow. LC 73-88215. 1974. 6.95 (ISBN 0-517-51477-X). Crown Publishers.
Laughter in Hell. Jim Tully. LC 32-31300. A. & C. Boni, Inc.
Laughter in the Alehouse. Henry Kane. LC 68-15267. (Cock Robin mystery). 1968. Macmillan.
Laughter in the Alehouse. Henry Kane. LC 78-2248. (Penguin crime fiction.). 1978. 1.95 (ISBN 0-14-004936-3). Penguin Books.
Laughter in the Dark. Vladimir Vladimirovich Nabokov. LC 73-165563. 1969. 0.20 (ISBN 0-14-001932-4). Penguin.
Laughter in the Dark. Vladimir Vladimirovich Nabokov. LC 38-116440. The Bobbs-Merrill Company.
Laughter in the Dark. New Ed. Vladimir Vladimirovich Nabokov. LC 60-16644. New Directions.
Laughter in the Sun. Pamela Frankau. LC 37-6310. 1937. W. Morrow and Company.
Laughter in the West. Leonard Alfred George Strong. LC 37-29932. 1937. A. A. Knopf.
Laughter Limited. Nina Wilcox Putnam. LC 22-19047. 1.75. George H. Doran Company.
Laughter of a Ghoul: What Every Young Ghoul Should Know. Robert Bloch. (F & FS Fragments Ser.: No. 2). 1977. pap. 1.00 o.p. Necronomicon.
Laughter of Aphrodite. Peter Green, pseud. LC 65-19903. 1966. 4.95. Doubleday.
Laughter of Fools. Idabel Williams. LC 38-12696. 1938. Godwin.
Laughter of Life. Effie Adelaide Maria Albanesi. The Cupples & Leon Co.
Laughter of My Father. Carlos Bulosan. LC 44-40087. 1944. Harcourt, Brace and Company.
Laughter of Niobe. Charlotte M Kelly. LC 49-496369. 1949. Ave. Maria Press.
Laughter of the Sphinx. Albert White - Vorse. LC 3589. 1900. D. Biddle.
Laughter on a Weekday. Obolensky. Louis Falstein. LC 65-179688. 3.95. World.
Laughter on the Hill. Margaret Parton. LC 45-4469. 1945. Whittlesey House, McGraw-Hill Book Company, Inc.
Laughter on the Stairs: With Drawings by William McLaren. 1st Ed. Beverley Nichols. LC 54-5048. 1954. Dutton.
Laughter Trap. Judson Pentecost Philips. LC 64-18740. (Red badge detective). 1964. Dodd, Mead.
Launcelot & the Ladies. Will Bradley. LC 27-7089. 1927. Harper & Brothers.
Launcelot: My Brother. Dorothy James Roberts. LC 54-101094. 1954. Appleton- Century-Crofts.

Launch! Edward Stewart. LC 76-3130. 1976. 8.95 (ISBN 0-385-11491-5). Doubleday.
Launch! Edward Stewart. 1977. 1.95 (ISBN 0-451-07743-1). New American Library.
Launching of Barbara Fabrikant. Louise Blecher Rose. LC 73-91119. 1974. 6.95 (ISBN 0-679-50453-2). McKay.
Launching of Barbara Fabrikant. Louise Blecher Rose. (Fawcett crest book). 1975. (pbk.) 1.75. Fawcett.
Launching of Linda Bell. William F. Hallstead. 160p. 1983. pap. 1.95 (ISBN 0-449-70053-4, Juniper). Fawcett.
Launching of Roger Brook. Dennis Yates Wheatley. (Roger Brook spy adventure). 1973. 1.50 (ISBN 0-345-03204-7). Ballantine.
Laura. Vera Caspary. LC 77-8859. 1977. 6.95 (ISBN 0-89244-066-X). Queens House.
Laura. Vera Caspary. LC 43-1294. 1943. Houghton Mifflin Company.
Laura. LC 11-17965. 1809. Bradford & Inskeep.
Laura; a Cautionary Story. Ethel Sidgwick. LC 24-29189. Small, Maynard & Company.
Laura: A Novel. G. M. T. Parsons. LC 77-99122. 1978. 7.95 (ISBN 0-312-47520-9). St. Martin's Press.
Laura: An American Girl. Elizabeth Edson Gibson Evans. LC 6-381391. 1884. J. B. Lippincott & Co.
Laura Arden. Francis Marion Cranford. LC 6-31615. 1892. Macmillan & Co.
Laura Brayton: Or, A Struggle to Rise. John Russell Coryell. LC 44-12291. (Select series...No. 65). 1890. Street & Smith.
Laura Brayton: Or, A Struggle to Rise. Julia Edwards, pseud. (select ser. no. 65). 1890. Street & Smith.
Laura Creichton. Elinor Mordaunt, pseud. LC 22-16600. Small, Maynard & Company.
Laura Everingham: Or, The Highlanders of Glen Ora. James Grant. LC 41-31317. G. Routledge and Son.
Laura Jean Libbey's... Latest and Greatest Romance, Wooden Wives. Is It a Story for Philandering Husbands? Laura Jean Libbey. LC 23-183894. Publishers Printing Co.
Laura Jordan. Dennis J. Higman. 448p. (Orig.). 1982. pap. 3.25 (ISBN 0-505-51769-8). Tower Bks.
Laura Middleton see Two Novels of the Victorian Underground.
Laura Possessed. Anthea Fraser. 1975. (pbk.) 1.50. Bantam Books.
Laura Possessed: A Novel of Suspense. Anthea Fraser. LC 74-3785. 1974. 5.95. Dodd, Mead.
Laura Reynolds, M. D. Virginia Evansen. 1973. pap. 0.75 o.s.i. (01-376). Lancer.
Laura, the Imperiled, No. 38. Katheryn Kimbrough, pseud. (Saga of the Phenwick Women). 224p. 1981. pap. 2.25 (ISBN 0-445-04676-7). Popular Lib.
Laura's Garden. Marie Aimery Comminges. Tr. by Miall, Bernard. LC 32-20052. 1932. The Macmillan Company.
Laura's Private Sex Survey. Laura Smith. pap. 1.95 o.p. (8033). Cameo.
Laurel: A Novel. Alice Fellows. LC 50-6385. 1950. Harcourt, Brace.
Laurel: A Novel. Elsie Grimm. LC 78-146570. 1971. 3.50. Zondervan Pub. House.
Laurel & Hardy Murders. Marvin Kaye. LC 78-12845. 1979. 10.95 (ISBN 0-89340-168-4). J. Curley.
Laurel and Hardy Murders: A Hilary Quayle Mystery Novel. Marvin Kaye. LC 77-6732. 7.95. Dutton.
Laurel and Straw. James Saxon Childers. LC 27-7180. 1927. D. Appleton & Company.
Laurel & the Poppy. Margaret Gillett & Monika Kehoe. LC 66-10681. 1967. 7.95 o.s.i. (ISBN 0-8149-0106-9). Vanguard.
Laurel Bush. An Old-Fashioned Love Story. Dinah Maria Mulock Craik. 1876. Harper & Brothers.
Laurel for the Undefeated. Murrell Edmunds. LC 64-13889. 1964. T. Yoseloff.
Laurel of Stonystream. Faith Baldwin Cuthrell. LC 23-13315. Small, Maynard & Company.
Laurel Vane: Or, The Girls' Conspiracy. Alexander McVeigh Miller. (On cover: Seaside library. Pocket ed., no. 267). 1884. G. Munro.
Laurels Are Cut Down. Archie Binns. LC 37-27262. Reynal & Hitchcock.
Laurels for the Dreamer. William Murdoch Duncan. 1975. 4.95 (ISBN 0-09-123540-5, Pub. by Hutchinson). Merrimack Pub Cir.
Laurels of Lake Constance. Marie Chaix. LC 76-47597. 1977. 8.95 (ISBN 0-670-41999-0). Viking Press.
Laurence. Didier Decoin. 1976. pap. 1.50 (ISBN 0-532-15218-2). Woodhill.
Laurence: A Love Story. Didier Decoin. 1973. (pbk.) 0.95. Manor Books.
Laurence: A Love Story. Didier Decoin. LC 78-146081. 1971. 5.95. Coward, McCann & Geoghegan.
Laurence, My Love. Denise Robins. 1972. pap. 0.75 o.p. (94192). Beagle Bks.
Laurian Kane. Kitt Brown. 320p. 1982. pap. 3.50 (ISBN 0-449-14466-6, GM). Fawcett.
Laurian Vale. Iris Bromige. (Beagle romance#33). 1975. (pbk.) 0.95. Ballantine Book.
Laurie. Rob Eden. LC 47-221740. 1947. Gramercy Publishing Co.
Lauriel, the Love Letters of an American Girl. Herbert Dickinson Ward. LC 1-27058. 1902. L. C. Page & Company.
Laurie's Legacy. Jacquelyn Aeby. (Candlelight mystery). 1974. (pbk.) 0.75. Dell.
Lava. Kevin O'Donnell, Jr. (Journeys of McGill Feighan: Bk. 3). (Orig.). 1982. pap. 2.25 (ISBN 0-425-05248-6). Berkley Pub.
Lava: A Saga of Hawaii. Armine Von Tempski. LC 30-295634. 1930. Frederick A. Stokes Company.
Lava Flow Murders. Max Long. LC 40-2395. J. B. Lippincott Company.
Lava: The Story of a Fighting Pastor. Frederic Zeigen. LC 29-8839. Chapple Publishing Company, Ltd.
Lavalite World. Philip Jose Farmer. (World of Tiers Ser.). 288p. 1982. pap. 2.25 (ISBN 0-441-47421-7). Ace Bks.
Lavalite World. Philip Jose Farmer. (World of Tiers Ser.: No. 5). 1983. 18.00 (ISBN 0-932096-21-2). Phantasia Pr.
Lavarons: A Novel. Clara Louise Root Burnham. LC 25-179331. 1925. Houghton Mifflin Company.
Lavelle from Locust Grove. C. M. Thacker. 5.00 o.p. Carlton.
Lavender. Dorothy Dixon. LC 75-11947. 1975. 5.95 (ISBN 0-8111-0584-9). Naylor Co.
Lavender & Old Lace. Robert T. Owens. 3.95 o.s.i. (ISBN 0-87667-071-0). Hallux.
Lavender and Old Lace. Myrtle Reed. LC 2-22858. 1902. G. P. Putnam's Sons.
Lavender and Old Lace. Myrtle Reed. LC 8-7667. 1907. G. P. Putnam's Sons.
Lavender and Old Lace: By Myrtle Reed... Myrtle Reed. LC 24-25000. 1908. Grosset & Dunlap.
Lavender Burning. Sasha Moorsom. LC 76-24901. 1976. 7.95 (ISBN 0-698-10761-6). Coward, McCann & Geoghegan.
Lavender Dragon. Eden Phillpotts. LC 24-3714. 1923. The Macmillan Company.
Lavender Lad. Dolf Wyllarde. LC 24-8793. 1923. The St. Botolph Society.
Lavender Trip. Sasha Moorsom. LC 76-380414. 1976. 3.50 (ISBN 0-370-10593-1). Bodley Head.
Lavengro. a new ed., containing the unaltered text fo the original issue; some suppressed episodes now printed for the first time; ma. variorum, vocabulary and notes, by the author of the life of george borrow. 2d impression. ed. George Henry Borrow. Ed. by William Ireland Knapp. 1903. G. P. Putnam's Sons; Etc., Etc.
Lavengro. George Henry Borrow. LC 36-293391. (Half-title: Everyman's library, ed. by Ernest Rhys. Fiction. no.119). 1933. J. M. Dent & Sons, Ltd.
Lavengro. George Henry Borrow & Parson, Paul S., Ed. LC 26-15717. (Riverside bookshelf). 1926. Houghton Mifflin Company.
Lavengro: The Scholar--the Gipsy--the Priest. George Henry Borrow. LC 7-3542. 1851. Harper & Brothers.
Lavengro: The Scholar--the Gipsy--the Priest. George Henry Borrow. (Half-title: Everyman's library, ed. by Ernest Rhys. Fiction, no. 110). 1969. J. M. Dent & Co.
Lavengro: The Scholar--the Gypsy--the Priest. 6th thousand. ed. George Henry Borrow. LC 6-15026. 1851. G. P. Putnam.
Lavengro: The Scholar, the Gipsy, the Priest. George Henry Borrow. LC 43-399579. (Half-title: The works of George Borrow--I). 1937. Oxford University Press, H. Milford.
Lavengro, the Scholar, the Gypsy, the Priest. George Henry Borrow & Whicher, George Friable, 1880- Ed. LC 27-19414. (Modern readers' series). 1927. The Macmillan Company.
L'aventure De Ted Bopp. Marc Ceppi. LC 39-18844. (Heath's modern language series). 1937. D. C. Heath and Company.
Lavinia. Rhoda Broughton. LC 18-7773. 1906. Macmillan and Co., Limited.
Lavinia. Toni Howard. LC 58-9715. 1958. Crowell.
Lavinia and the Devil. Camilla York. LC 26-15279. 1926. E. P. Dutton & Company.
L'avril: A Novel. Paul Marguerltte. Tr. by Dole, Helen James (Bennett) LC 7-20440. T. Y. Crowell & Company.
Law. Roger Vailland. LC 58-12630. 1958. Knopf.
Law and Jake Wade. Marvin H Albert. LC 56-1240. (Gold medal books, 553). 1956. Fawcett Publications.
Law and Order. Claude Ollier. LC 76-133248. 1971. 4.95 (ISBN 0-87376-015-8). Red Dust.
Law and Order: A Novel. Dorothy Uhnak. LC 72-14250. 1973. 8.95 (ISBN 0-671-21505-1). Simon and Schuster.
Law and Order on Halfaday Creek. Bar-H Books. James Beardsley Hendryx. LC 41-10969. Carlton House.
Law and Order, Unlimited: A Gregory Quist Story. 1st Ed. William Colt MacDonald. LC 53-5287. (Double D western). 1953. Doubleday.
Law and Outlaw. Cecily Ullmann Sidgwick. LC 22-1946. W. J. Watt & Company.
Law and Outlaw. William E Vance. LC 81-43374. (Double D western). 1982. 10.95 (ISBN 0-385-17460-8). Doubleday.
Law and the Lady. A Novel. Wilkie Collins. LC 3-27270. Harper & Brothers.
Law and the Letter: A Story of the Province of Louisiana. Mary Polk Winn & Hannis, Margaret, Joint Author. LC 7-8532. 1907. The Neale Publishing Company.
Law and the McLaughlins. Margaret Wilson. LC 36-28559. 1936. Doubleday, Doran & Company, Inc.
Law and the McLaughlins. Margaret Wilson. LC 37-39262. 1937. The Sun Dial Press, Inc.
Law at Randado. Elmore Leonard. LC 55-5214. 1955. Houghton Mifflin.
Law Badge. Peter Field. LC 40-7011. 1940. W. Morrow and Company.
Law-Breakers. Ridgwell Cullum. LC 14-22143. 1.35. G. W. Jacobs & Co.
Law-Breakers: And Other Stories. Robert Grant. LC 69-11900. (American short story series, v. 58). 1969. Garrett Press.
Law-Breakers, and Other Stories. Robert Grant. LC 72-8171. (American short story series, v. 58). 1972. (ISBN 0-8422-8060-X). MSS Information Corp.
Law-Breakers: And Other Stories. Robert Grant. LC 6-14226. 1906. C. Scribner's Sons.
Law Bringers. Harry Sinclair Drago. LC 37-2869. The Macaulay Company.
Law-Bringers. Edith J. Lyttleton. LC 13-12873. Hodder and Stoughton.
Law-Bringers. Edith J. Lyttleton. LC 13-156845. Hodder & Stoughton, George H. Doran Company.
Law Budge. Peter Field. LC 51-6516. (Triple-A western classic). 1951. Jefferson House.
Law Busters: By Bliss Lomax Pseud. Harry Sinclair Drago. LC 50-10166. (Silver star westerns). 1950. Dodd, Mead.
Law Comes to Cold Rain. Jake Logan. LC 82-60686. (Jake Logan Western Ser.). 1983. pap. 2.25 (ISBN 0-86721-243-8). Playboy Pbks.
Law Enforcement Inc. Sidney Becker. 208p. 1975. pap. 1.50 o.p. (ISBN 0-532-15141-0). Woodhill.
Law Enforcement Inc. Sidney Becker. 208p. 1975. pap. 1.50 o.p. (ISBN 0-532-15141-0). Manor Bks.
Law Enforcement Inc. An Autobiographical Novel. Sidney Becker. LC 73-83164. 1973. 7.95 (ISBN 0-89388-106-6). Third Press.
Law for the Lion. Louis Auchincloss. LC 53-5728. 1953. Houghton Mifflin Co.
Law for Tombstone. Charles Morris Martin. LC 37-5399. 1937. Greenberg.
Law for Tombstone. Charles Morris Martin. (Belmont Tower book). 1978. 1.25 (ISBN 0-505-51268-8). Tower Pubns.
Law in Cottonwood. Lewis B Patten. LC 78-7764. 1978. 7.95 (ISBN 0-385-14448-2). Doubleday.
Law in Cottonwood. Lewis B Patten. LC 82-9226. 1982. 11.95 (ISBN 0-8161-3365-4). G.K. Hall.
Law, Law, Law. 4th rev. ed. Paul Copeland et al. 109p. (Orig.). 1976. pap. 2.95 (ISBN 0-88784-611-4, Pub. by Hse Anansi Pr Canada). U of Toronto Pr.
Law Man. Lee Leighton, pseud. 1977. pap. 1.95 (ISBN 0-441-47492-6). Ace Bks.
Law Man. Wayne D. Overholser. 1977. 1.50 (ISBN 0-441-47491-8). Ace Books.
Law Man: By Lee Leighton Pseud. Wayne D Overholser. LC 53-12733. 1953. Ballantine Books.
Law Man of Lonesome River. Archie Joscelyn. LC 35-30050. Phoenix Press.
Law Man of Powder Valley. Peter Field. LC 42-22689. 1942. W. Morrow & Company.
Law O' the Lariat. Oliver Strange. LC 32-13791. 1932. L. MacVeagh, Dial Press, Inc.
Law of Destiny. Ralph William Wiles. LC 26-8192. Dorrance and Company.
Law of Destiny, a Novel of Two Brothers. Rev. Ed. Ralph William Wiles. LC 52-7538. 1952. William-Frederick Press.
Law of Hemlock Mountain. Hugh Lundsford. LC 20-186095. W. J. Watt & Company.
Law of Kyger Gorge. Llewellyn Perry Holmes. LC 36-8204. Greenberg.
Law of Larion. Peter Freuchen. LC 51-13606. 1952. McGraw-Hill.
Law of Life: A Novel. Carl Merner. LC 14-2298.
Law of Life: Novel. Anna McClure Sholl. LC 3-20585. 1903. D. Appleton and Company.
Law of Love. Charles St. Morris. LC 8-18367. 1908. The C. M. Clark Publishing Co.
Law of Return. Alice Bloch. 300p. (Orig.). 1983. pap. 7.95 (ISBN 0-930436-19-9). Persephone.
Law of the Forty-Fives. William Colt MacDonald. LC 33-224677. Covici, Friede.
Law of the Gun. Ridgwell Cullum. G. W. Jacobs & Company.
Law of the Gun. John Thomas Edson. (Orig.). 1982. pap. 1.95 (ISBN 0-425-05311-3). Berkley Pub.
Law of the Gun. Stoney Hardcastle. 176p. (Orig.). 1982. pap. 1.95 (ISBN 0-8439-1005-4, Leisure Bks). Nordon Pubns.
Law of the Gun. Paul Evan Lehman. 1971. pap. 0.50 o.p. (50-508). Manor Bks.
Law of the Gun: By Brett Rider Pseud. Arthur Henry Gooden. LC 50-7400. 1950. Macrae Smith.
Law of the Holster. Donald S Rowland. LC 67-1447. 1967. Arcadia House.
Law of the Jungle. Mary Wibberley. (Harlequin Presents Ser.). 192p. 1982. pap. 1.75 (ISBN 0-373-10526-6). Harlequin Bks.
Law of the Land. Marguerite Allis. LC 48-6158. 1948. G. P. Putnam's Sons.
Law of the Land: Of Miss Lady, Whom It Involved in Mystery, and of John Eddring, Gentleman of the South, Who Read Its Deeper Meaning; a Novel. Emerson Hough. LC 4-27358. 1904. The Bobbs-Merrill Company.
Law of the Lash. Norman Daniels. (Orig.). 1969. pap. 0.95 o.p. (75-063). Lancer.
Law of the Lawless. Wayne C Lee. 1977. 1.50. Ace Books.
Law of the Lean Lands: A Novel of the Fur Country. Chart Pitt. LC 25-16487. 1925. Frederick A. Stokes Company.
Law of the Prairie. Wayne C Lee. 1974. 4.95. Lenox Hill Press.
Law of the Primitive. Elmer LeRoy Baker. LC 38-211667. The Book Craft.
Law of the Range. Wayne Groves Barrows. LC 9-28692. 1909. The C. M. Clark Publishing Company.
Law of the River. Francis Gerard & Wallace, Edgar. LC 40-10295. 1940. E. P. Dutton & Co., Inc.
Law of the Six-Gun. Robert Sherman Lerch. LC 41-25664. Dodge Publishing Company.
Law of the Talon. Louis Tracy. LC 27-1242. E. J. Clode, Inc.
Law of the Three Just Men... Edgar Wallace. LC 31-192721. Pub. for the Crime Club, Inc., by Doubleday, Doran & Company, Inc.
Law of the Threshold. Flora Annie Webster Steel. LC 24-24952. 1924. The Macmillan Company.
Law of the Trail. Jesse Edward Grinstead. Dodge Publishing Company.
Law of the Trigger. Giles A Lutz. 1974. (pbk.) 0.95. Ace Books.
Law of the White Circle. Thornwell Jacobs. 1908. Taylor-Trotwood Publishing Co.
Law on Horseback and Other Stories. William Surrey Hart. LC 35-12781. The Times-Mirror Press.
Law Rides the Range. Walt Coburn. LC 35-6349. 1935. D. Appleton Century Company, Incorporated.
Law Takes the Count, & Other Short Stories. James H. Smith. 1970. 3.50 o.p. (ISBN 0-682-47152-6). Exposition.
Law Unto Themselves: A Tale of Old Austria. Lilian Faith Loveday Prior. LC 34-15305. 1934. Little, Brown, and Company.
Law Unwrit. Maud Gillette Phillips. F. H. Hitchcock.
Lawbringers. William Earl Porter. LC 54-9888. 1954. Appleton-Century-Crofts.
Lawd Sayin' the Same: Negro Folk Tales of the Creole Country. Hewitt Leonard Ballowe. LC 47-11368. 1947. Louisiana State Univ. Press.
Lawd Today. Richard Wright. LC 63-11769. 1963. Walker.
Lawdog of Skeleton Canyon. William Edmunds Claussen. LC 45-11431. 1945. Phoenix Press.
Lawford Hall and The Lady of Lawford: Or, The Boughtons of Warwickshire... Nathan Boughton Warren. LC 8-33685. 1873. M. H. Mallory, & Co.
Lawgiver: A Novel About Moses. 1st Ed. Julius Amos Leibert. LC 52-8633. 1953. Exposition Press.
Lawless. John W. Jakes. LC 77-91235. (Kent Family Chronicles; Vol. VII). (Jove / HBJ Book). 1978. 2.25 (ISBN 0-515-04125-4). Jove Pubns.
Lawless see Kent Family Chronicles.
Lawless: An Adventure of Sudden, the Outlaw. Strange, Oliver. LC 33-15945. L. MacVeagh, Dial Press, Inc.,
Lawless Breed. Lewis B Patten. (Signet Book). 1976. (pbk.) 1.25. New American Library.
Lawless Guns. Will Garth. LC 37-19451. Dodge Publishing Company.
Lawless Hand. William Le Queux. LC 28-10875. The Macaulay Company.
Lawless: Kent Family Chronicle. John Jakes. 1978. pap. 2.95 (ISBN 0-515-05892-0). Jove Pubns.
Lawless Legion. Harry Sinclair Drago. LC 38-12834. The Macaulay Company.
Lawless Ones. Chuck Adams, pseud. 1979. pap. 1.75 o.s.i. (ISBN 0-505-51399-4). Tower Bks.
Lawless Range. Charles N Heckelmann. LC 45-9830. 1945. Arcadia House, Inc.

TITLE INDEX LEAGUE OF GREY-EYED WOMEN.

Lawless Range. Stephen Payne. LC 34-332759. The Dial Press, Inc.
Lawless Trail. Tex Holt, pseud. LC 40-33292. 1940. Gateway Books.
Lawless Trail. Claude Rister. LC 40-33292. 1940. Gateway Books.
Lawley Road & Other Stories. R. K. Narayan. 159p. 1969. pap. 1.95 o.p. (ISBN 0-88253-062-3). Ind-US Inc.
Lawman. Grant Freeling. (O.si.). (Orig.). 1971. pap. 0.95 o.s.i. (AN1445, Award). Univ Pub & Dist.
Lawman for the Slaughter. Ray Hogan. Bd. with Passage to Dodge City. (Shawn Starbuck Ser.: No. 10). (Shawn Starbuck Ser.: No. 9). 1980. pap. 1.95 (ISBN 0-451-09173-6, Sig). NAL.
Lawman Without a Badge. Dorothy L Bonar. LC 55-35182. (Ace double novel books, D-106). 1955. Ace Books.
Lawman's Choice. Ray Hogan. LC 80-1122. 1980. 8.95 (ISBN 0-385-17263-X). Doubleday.
Lawman's Choice. Ray Hogan. LC 81-13215. 1981. 10.95 (ISBN 0-8161-3290-9). G.K. Hall.
Lawman's Pay. Frank Chester Robertson. LC 57-105148. (Ballantine books, 208). 1957. Ballantine Books.
Lawmen of Blue Rock. Dan Roberts. LC 67-3718. 1967. Arcadia House.
Lawndy & Edgie. Dollie C. Snyder. Ed. by P. W. Synder et al. (Illus.). 64p. (Orig.). 1982. pap. text ed. 3.95 (ISBN 0-941352-00-5). Pee Wee.
Lawrence Barrett. A Professional Sketch. Elwyn Alfred Barron & Barrett, Lawrence. LC 17-6630. 1889. Knight & Leonard Co., Printers.
Lawrence Clavering. Alfred Edward Woodley Mason. LC 7-25580. 1897. Dodd, Mead and Company.
Lawrence Vane: A Novel. Angela Du Maurier. LC 46-32908. 1946. Doubleday & Company, Inc.
Lawrences: a Twenty Years' History. Charlotte Turnbull. LC 8-32670. The American News Company.
Lawrenceville Stories. Owen McMahon Johnson. LC 67-25392. (Illus.). 1967. Simon and Schuster.
Lawrie Todd: Or, The Settlers in the Woods. John Galt. LC 6-44478. 1830. Printed by J. & J. Harper.
Law's Delay. Sara Woods, pseud. LC 76-28070. 1977. 7.95. St. Martin's.
Laws of Chance. Florence Ethel Mills Young. LC 18-213811. 1918. John Lane.
Laws of the Night. H. A Murena. LC 76-106550. 1970. 7.95. Scribner.
Law's Outlaw. Seth Ducane. LC 40-6440. Dodge Publishing Company.
Lawson's Best Stories see Australian Classics.
Lawton Girl. Harold Frederic. LC 6-43134. 1890. C. Scribner's Sons.
Lawton Girl see Collected Works.
Lawyer. Albert Benjamin Gerber. 1974. (pbk.) 1.50 (ISBN 0-380-00048-2). Avon.
Lawyer. Albert Benjamin Gerber. LC 70-183086. 1972. 8.95 (ISBN 0-529-04555-9). World Pub.
Lawyer and the Carpenter: A Novel of Murder. Estelle Thompson. LC 64-13966. 1964. I. Washburn.
Lawyer Man. Max Trell. LC 32-19040. The Macaulay Company.
Lawyers. Babette Rosmond. LC 62-12756. 1962. Walker.
Lawyer's Daughter. Joseph Alden. LC 44-27161. (On cover: Harper's fireside library). 1847. Harper & Brothers.
Lawyers Don't Hang. Glenn M Barns. LC 53-13061. 1953. Arcadia House.
Lawyers of Hell. Ron Gorton. LC 78-27011. 8.95 (ISBN 0-8119-0319-2). F. Fell Publishers.
Lawyer's Religion. Helen R Edson. LC 6-36599. American Tract Society.
Laxdale Hall: A Novel. Eric Robert Russell Linklater. LC 52-9852. 1952. Harcourt, Brace.
Laxdale Saga. Tr. by Muriel Press. 1965. Repr. of 1964 ed. 9.95x (ISBN 0-460-00597-9, Evman). Biblio Dist.
Lay Analyst. Anne Richter. LC 78-170136. 1971. 5.95 (ISBN 0-87777-032-8). R. W. Baron.
Lay Anthony: A Romance. Joseph Hergesheimer. LC 14-145374. 1914. 1.25. M. Kennerley.
Lay Anthony: A Romance. Joseph Hergesheimer. LC 19-15541. 1919. A. A. Knopf.
Lay Anthony: A Romance. Joseph Hergesheimer. LC 26-281813. 1919. A. A. Knopf.
Lay Confessor. Stephen Graham. LC 29-9095. 1929. A. A. Knopf.
Lay Down I Want to Talk to You. Donald Timoney. 1974. 4.00 o.p. (ISBN 0-682-47773-7). Exposition.
Lay Down My Sword and Shield. James Lee Burke. LC 79-170991. 1971. 5.95 (ISBN 0-690-48703-7). Crowell.
Lay Down Your Arms: The Autobiography of Martha Von Tilling. Bertha Felicie Sophie Kinsky Suttner. LC 79-147459. (Garland Library of War and Peace). 1972. (ISBN 0-8240-0318-7). Garland Pub.
Lay Down Your Arms: The Autobiography of Martha Von Tilling. 2d ed. new impression. ed. Bertha Felicie Sophie Kinsky Suttner & Holmes, T., Tr. LC 6-7350. 1906. Longmans, Green and Co.
Lay Me Down. Gordon Cervantes. (Orig.). 1972. pap. 1.95 o.s.i. (76-314). Lancer.
Lay Me Odds. Rod Gray. (Lady from L. U. S. T. Ser). 1970. pap. 0.95 o.p. (B95-2026). Belmont-Tower.
Lay Me Odds. Rod Gray. (The Lady from L.U.S.T. Ser.). (O.s.i.). 1973. pap. 0.95 o.s.i. (BT50542). Belmont-Tower.
Lay My Body on the Line. Floyd Salas. LC 78-53969. (O.s.i.). 1978. pap. 4.95 o.s.i. (ISBN 0-931676-02-9). Reed & Youngs Quilt.
Lay My Body on the Line: A Novel. Floyd Salas. LC 78-53969. 4.95 (ISBN 0-931676-02-9). Y'Bird.
Lay of the Land. F. W. Paul. pap. 0.75 o.p. Lancer.
Lay of the Land. Norman Singer. LC 74-7580. 1969. 2.25. Ophelia Press.
Lay of the Land: A Collection of Short Stories. Virginia Aylett Quintman McNealus. LC 16-213911. 1916. The Neale Publishing Company.
Lay on, Mac Duff! Charlotte Armstrong. LC 42-6829. 1942. Coward-McCann, Inc.
Lay That Pistol Down. Richard Pitts Powell. LC 45-5093. 1945. Simon and Schuster.
Lay Them Straight: 1st Amer. Ed. Mickey Phillips, pseud. LC 65-119928. 1965. 3.95. Harcourt.
Layers of Deceit. Bradshaw-Jones, Malcolm Henry. LC 70-123228. 1970. 4.95. Bobbs-Merrill Co.
Layers of Deceit. Bradshaw Jones. LC 70-123228. 1971. 4.95 o.p. Bobbs.
Laying on of Hands. Arthur Arent. LC 77-83736. 1969. 5.95. Little, Brown.
Layle Jonathan, of Mountain Springs. Ruby A. Newman. 140p. (Orig.). 1983. pap. 5.00 (ISBN 0-932964-07-9). MN Pubs.
Layoff: By Robert George Dean. Robert George Dean. LC 42-154921. 1942. C. Scribner's Sons.
Layout for a Corpse. Gene Goldsmith. LC 49-10113. 1949. M. S. Mill Co. Distributed by W. Morrow.
Lays of Ancient Rome: And Other Poems. Thomas Babington Macaulay Macaulay. (Seaside library. v. 45, no. 926). 1881. G. Munro.
Layton Court Mystery. Anthony Berkeley Cox. LC 29-6186. 1929. Pub. for The Crime Club, Inc., by Doubleday, Doran & Company, Inc.
Lazarre. Mary Hartwell Catherwood. LC 1-17003. The Bowen-Merrill Company.
Lazarre. Mary Hartwell Catherwood. LC 6-20175. The Bowen-Merrill Company.
Lazarus. Leonid Nikolaevich Andreev & Bunin, Ivan Aleksfeevich, 1870- LC 19-19360. (Stratford universal library. no. 7). 1918. The Stratford Company.
Lazarus. Jerome Hartenfels. 1966. 5.00 o.p. (ISBN 0-8090-6485-5). Hill & Wang.
Lazarus see Black Lazarus.
Lazarus: A Novel. Jerome Hartenfels. 1973. (pbk) 0.95. Popular Library.
Lazarus: A Novel. Jerome Hartenfels. LC 66-23864. 1966. Hill and Wang.
Lazarus: A Tale of the World's Great Miracle. Georgiana Kingscote. LC 6-154539. 1897. E. P. Dutton & Company.
Lazarus' Cue & Other Plays. Mariguita Platov. LC 80-65679. 1980. 12.95 (ISBN 0-89754-013-1); pap. 3.95 (ISBN 0-89754-012-3). Dan River Pr.
Lazarus Curse. Noel Vreeland Carter. (queen-size gothic). 1974. (pbk.) 1.25. Popular Library.
Lazarus in London. Frederick William Robinson. (On cover: The seaside library. Pocket ed. no. 455). 1885. G. Munro.
Lazarus in London. A Novel. Frederick William Robinson. LC 7-41965. (Harper's Franklin square library, no. 462). 1885. Harper & Brothers.
Lazarus in Vienna. Alfred Slote. LC 56-6970. 1956. McGraw-Hill.
Lazarus Man. John Lutz. LC 78-26967. 1979. 8.95 (ISBN 0-688-03468-3). Morrow.
Lazarus Number Seven. Richard Sale. LC 42-6837. 1942. Simon and Schuster.
Lazo De Purpura see Purple Sash.
Lazy Isle. George Frederick Hummel. LC 27-22480. 1927. Boni & Liveright.
Lazy L Brand. James Lyon Rubel. LC 38-6959. Phoenix Press.
Lazy Laughter. Peggy Smith Shane. LC 28-15583. 1923. C. Scribner's Sons.
Lazy Lawrence Murders. Todd Downing. LC 41-76473. 1941. Pub. for the Crime Club by Doubleday, Doran and Co., Inc.
Lazy Man's Work: A Novel. Frances Campbell Sparhawk. (Leisure hour series, no. 122). 1881. H. Holt and Company.
Lazy Ones: Translated by William Goyen. Albert Cossery. LC 52-13223. New Directions.
Lazy River. A Samad Said. Tr. by Harry Aveling. (Writing in Asia Ser.). x, 122p. (Orig.). 1981. pap. text ed. 4.50x (00265). Heinemann Ed.
Lazy Thoughts of a Lazy Girl. Sister of That "Idle Fellow.". Jenny Wren. (On cover: The world library, no. 13). 1891. The Waverly Company.
Lazy Tour of Two Idle Apprentices. Charles Dickens & Collins, Wilkie. LC 6-38444. (On cover: Lovell's library, v. 8, no. 437). 1884. J. W. Lovell Company.
Lazylegs: By Kim Savage Pseud. Kim Savage. LC 53-395885. 1953. Vixen Press.
LBJ Brigade. William Wilson. LC 65-28536. 4.00. Apocalypse Corp. Sunset Drive.
Le Beau Sabreur. authorized ed. Annie Hall Thomas Cudlip. LC 6-31174. (On cover: Lovell's Westminster ser. no. 16). United States Book Company, Successors to J. W. Lovell Company.
Le Bleuet. An Alsatian Romance. Wilhelmine Josephine Simonin Fould. Tr. by L., M. De. LC 6-43986. 1889. Brentano's.
Le Chevalier De Maison-Rouge. Alexandre Dumas & Maquet, Auguste. LC 3-26654. 1894. Little, Brown, and Company.
Le Chevalier De Maison-Rouge. Alexandre Dumas & Maquet, Auguste. LC 6-42104. 1896. Estes and Lauriat.
Le Chevalier De Maison Rouge. Alexandre Dumas & Maquet, Auguste. LC 36-37605. (Half-title: Everyman's library, ed. by Ernest Rhys. Fiction no. 614). 1928. J. M. Dent & Sons, Ltd.
Le Chevalier D'Harmental. Alexandre Dumas & Maquet, Auguste. LC 6-428459. (Half-title: The romances of Alexandre Dumas. Illustrated library, ed. v. 23). 1893. Little, Brown and Company.
Le Chevalier D'harmental. Alexandre Dumas & Maquet, Auguste. LC 8-7671. 1894. Little, Brown, and Company.
Le Cure Manque: Or, Social and Religious Customs in France. Eugene De Courcillon. LC 6-30205. 1855. Harper & Brothers.
Le Diable Boiteux: Or, The Devil Upon Two Sticks. Alain Rene Le Sage. LC 73-170518. (Foundations of the Novel). (Illus.). 1972. 22.00 (ISBN 0-8240-0525-2). Garland Pub.
Le Drole. Edited by Isabelle H. Clarke; Illustrated by Madeleine Charlety. drole ed. Francois Mauriac. LC 57-30343. 1957. Heath.
Le Mans: Twice Around the Clock. Michael Dara Gibson. LC 64-13044. 1964. Putnam.
Le Mans 24. Denne Bart Petitclerc. LC 72-142094. 1971. (ISBN 0-15-149820-2). Harcourt Brace Jovanovich.
Le Mans 24. Denne Bart Petitclerc. LC 78-187411. (Illus.). 1972. 0.95. Playboy Press.
Le Morte Darthur. Thomas Malory. Ed. by Heinrich Oskar Sommer. Andrew Lang. LC 78-172839. 1973. 85.00 (ISBN 0-404-04175-2). AMS Press.
Le Morte D'Arthur. Thomas Malory & P. J. C Field. LC 77-22498. 1977. 16.00 (ISBN 0-8419-0333-6). Holmes & Meier.
Le Morte Darthur. Thomas Malory & R. M Lumiansky. LC 82-10513. (Illus.). 50.00 (ISBN 0-684-17672-6). Scribner.
Le Morte D'Arthur: Printed by William Caxton, 1485. reproduced in facsimile from the copy in the pierpont morgan library, new york /with an introd. by paul needham. Ed. Thomas Malory. LC 77-366793. (Illus.). 1976. Scolar Press in Association with the Pierpont Morgan Library.
Le Morte Darthur: Sir Thomas Malory's Book of King Arthur and His Noble Knights of the Round Table. Thomas Malory. Ed. by Edward Strachey. LC 78-145139. 1972. 19.50 (ISBN 0-403-00808-5). Scholarly Press.
Le Petit Chien: Par Denise et Alain Trez. 1. ed. Denise Trez & Alain Trez. LC 61-12024. 1961. World Pub. Co.
Le Petit Poucet (Hop O' My Thumb) Translated from Jean Lee Latham's English Text by Michele Halverson and Illustrated by Arnalot. LC 61-14959. Bobbs-Merrill.
Le Petit Prince: With Illustrations Based Upon the Original Drawings of the Author. Educational Ed., with Introduction, Notes, Vocabulary, and Bibliography. Antoine De Saint Exupery & Miller, John Richardson, 1890- Ed. LC 47-151. 1946. Houghton Miffin Company.
Le Petit Tambour Rouge. Eunice Young Smith. LC 61-4948. 1961. A. Whitman.
Le Pont De La Riviere Kwai. Ed. by Georges J. Joyaux. Avant-Propos by Pierre Boulle. Illus. by Gil Walker. Pierre Boulle. LC 63-17235. pap., 2.95. Scribners.
Le Reve... Emile Zola & Cox, George D., Tr. LC 9-130823. T. B. Peterson & Brothers.
Le Tailleur De Gloucester: Par Beatrix Potter; Traduite De L'anglais Par Deborah Chattaway. Beatrix Potter. LC 68-10151. 1967. bds., 1.50. Warne.
Le Vilain Chat: Par Denise et Alain Trez. Denise Trez & Alain Illus Trez. LC 65-13075. 1.95, 2.17 lib. ed.,. World.
Leacock Medal Treasury: 3 Decades of the Best of Canadian Humour. Ralph L Curry. LC 77-355729. 11.95 (ISBN 0-919630-62-6). Lester and Orpen.
Lead Hungry Lobos. Burt Arthur, pseud. 1978. pap. 1.25 o.s.i. (ISBN 0-505-51255-6). Tower Bks.
Lead Law. Amos Moore. LC 34-581722. The Macaulay Company.
Lead Me into Temptation. Gunnar Serner & Lee, Robert Emmons, Tr. LC 27-2859. Thomas Y. Crowell Company.
Lead Mountain. Michele A. McQuaid. (Orig.). 1981. pap. 1.95 (ISBN 0-505-51687-X). Tower Bks.
Lead of Honour. Norval Richardson. LC 10-16006. 1910. L. C. Page & Company.
Lead Soldiers: A Novel. Uri Orlev. LC 79-26348. 1980. 9.95 (ISBN 0-8008-4576-5). Taplinger.
Lead Us into Temptation. Breandan O Heithir. 1978. 14.95 o.p. (ISBN 0-7100-0030-8). Routledge & Kegan.
Lead with Your Left. 1st Ed. Ed. by Ed Lacy. LC 56-12238. 1957. Harper.
Leadbetter's Luck. Holman Francis Day. LC 23-14920. 1923. Duffield and Company.
Leaden Bubble. Henry C Branson. LC 49-79813. (Inner sanctum mystery). 1949. Simon and Schuster.
Leaden Casket: A Novel. author's ed. Margaret Raine Hunt. LC 7-9042. (Leisure hour series--no. 121). 1881. H. Holt and Company.
Leader. Mary C Johnson Dillon. 1906. Doubleday, Page & Company.
Leader. Gillian Freeman. LC 66-11159. 1966. bds., 4.95. Lippincott.
Leader of the Resistance. Jules Verne. 1964. 3.95. Assoc Bk.
Leading Lady. Geraldine Bonner. The Bobbs-Merrill Company.
Leading Lady. Ruth Townsend Mills Teague. LC 37-1676. 1936. C. Kendall, Inc.
Leading Lady: A Novel with a Preface. William Morgan Hannon. LC 17-700. 1916. Latin Quarter Publishing Co.
Leading Man. Horace Annesley Vachell. LC 29-318231. 1929. G. P. Putnam's Sons.
Leadville. Edwin Booth. (Orig.). 1981. pap. 1.95 (ISBN 0-505-51643-8). Tower Bks.
Leadville Avengers. Thomas Albert Curry. 1973. pap. 0.75 o.p. (07289). Curtis.
Leaf Against the Sky. Paul Fassett Ader. LC 47-6679. 1947. Crown Publishers.
Leaf Gold. William Woodrow Chamberlain. LC 41-164851. The Bobbs-Merrill Company.
Leaf Gold. William Woodrow Chamberlain. LC 41-164859. The Bobbs-Merrill Company.
Leaf in the Storm. Clara E. Ballou. LC 6-6100. J. S. Ogilvie.
Leaf in the Storm. Clara E. Ballou. LC 99-165. (Criterion library, no. 38). 1898. Dike Book Company.
Leaf in the Storm: A Novel of War-Swept China. Lin Yutang. LC 41-23073. The John Day Company.
Leaf in the Storm: And Other Tales. Louise De La Ramee. (seaside library, v. 14, no. 279). 1878. G. Munro.
Leaf in the Wind. Marie Joseph. LC 82-5548. 12.95 (ISBN 0-312-47708-2). St. Martin's Press.
Leaf in the Wind. Marie Joseph. 304p. 1982. 12.95 (ISBN 0-312-47708-2). St Martin.
Leaf Is Green. John V Craven. LC 31-119171. 1931. A. A. Knopf.
Leaf Shall Be Green. Marion Chamberlain. 1948. Dodd, Mead.
Leaf Storm, and Other Stories. Garcia Marquez, Gabriel. LC 76-138784. 1972. 6.50 (ISBN 0-06-012779-1). Harper & Row.
Leaf Storm and Other Stories. Gabriel García Marquez. (Harper Colophon Books). 1979. 3.50 (ISBN 0-06-090699-5). Harper & Row.
Leaf Storm & Other Stories. Gabriel Garcia Marquez. Tr. by Gregory Rabassa from Span. LC 76-138784. (O.s.i.). 192p. 1972. 10.95i (ISBN 0-06-012779-1, HarpT). Har-Row.
Leafless Spring. Lula Kirschner. Tr. by Safford, Mary Joanna. LC 7-12822. 1893. J. B. Lippincott Company.
Leafy Rivers. Jessamyn West. LC 67-20325. 1967. Harcourt, Brace & World.
League of Dark Men. John Creasey. 1975. (pbk.) 0.95. Popular Library.
League of Discontent. Francis Beeding. LC 30-7301. 1930. Little, Brown, and Company.
League of Frightened Men. Rex Stout. LC 80-29498. 1981. 14.50 (ISBN 0-8161-3225-9) (ISBN 0-8161-3225-9). G. K. Hall.
League of Frightened Men: A Nero Wolfe Mystery. Rex Stout. LC 35-127757. Farrar & Rinehart, Inc.
League of Frightened Men: A Nero Wolfe Mystery. Rex Stout. LC 40-9141. 1940. Triangle Books.
League of Grey-Eyed Women. Julius Fast. LC 70-85112. 1970. 5.95. Lippincott.

League of Guilt: Or, A Great Detective's Greatest Case. Duke I. E. Alexander Duke Bailie. LC 6-5029. (On cover: The Pinkerton detective series, no. 4). 1892. Laird & Lee.
League of the Frightened Men. Rex Stout. LC 43-73612. (Avon pocket-size books). 1942. Avon Book Company.
League of the Leopard. Harold Bindloss. LC 14-112431. 1914. F. A. Stokes Company.
League of the Miami. new ed., enl. and rev. by the author. ed. Emerson Bennett. LC 7-344237. 1860. U. P. James.
League of the Scarlet Pimpernel. Emmuska Orczy. LC 19-25943. George H. Doran Company.
Leah: A Novel. Seymour Epstein. LC 64-15050. 1964. Little, Brown.
Leah: a Woman of Fashion. Annie Edwards. (Seaside library. v. 24, no. 471). 1879. G. Munro.
Leah: a Woman of Fashion. Annie Edwards. (On cover: Seaside library. Pocket ed. no. 839). 1886. G. Munro.
Leah of Jerusalem: A Story of the Time of Paul. Edward Payson Berry. A. D. F. Randolph & Company.
Leah's Journey. Gloria Goldreich. LC 77-92553. 10.00 (ISBN 0-15-149451-7). Harcourt Brace Jovanovich.
Leah's Journey. Gloria Goldreich. 1979. 2.50 (ISBN 0-425-04430-0). Berkley Publishing Corp.
Leah's Mistake; or, Marriage Without Love. H. C. Hoffman. (On cover: Clover ser. no. 130). Street & Smith.
Lean and Lank. Zelma H Tankersley. LC 29-250383. 1929. Foote and Davies Co.
Lean Lands. Agustin Yanez. Tr. by Ethel Brinton from Sp. (Texas Pan American Ser.). Orig. Title: Tierras Flacas. (Illus.). 338p. 1968. 14.50x (ISBN 0-292-78384-1). U of Tex Pr.
Lean Twilight. Edward Shenton. LC 28-242795. 1928. C. Scribner's Sons.
Lean with the Wind: A Novel of the South Seas. Earl Schenck. LC 45-8176. 1945. Whittlesey House, McGraw-Hill Book Company, Inc.
Lean Year Madness. Herman Irving Bloom. LC 37-17081. 1937. Hillman-Curl, Inc.
Lean Years. Richard Barnet. 1980. 12.95 (ISBN 0-671-22460-3, Fireside). S&S.
Leander: Or, Secrets of the Priesthood. Ernest Truman. LC 8-28480. 1869. Claxton, Remsen and Haffelfinger.
Leaning Man: A Ludovic Travers Mystery. Christopher Bush. LC 38-32414. H. Holt and Company.
Leaning Tower. Fred Rothermell. LC 34-5095. The John Day Company.
Leaning Tower: A Novel. Maria Talwick. LC 75-35960. 8.95. Putnam.
Leaning Tower, and Other Stories. Katherine Anne Porter. LC 44-7946. 1944. Harcourt, Brace and Company.
Leanna: A Novel in Six Movements. Doris Schwerin. LC 78-2283. 1978. 10.95 (ISBN 0-688-03309-1). Morrow.
Leap Before You Look. Mary Stolz. (Laurel-Leaf Library). 1973. (pbk.) 0.75. Dell.
Leap Before You Look. Alec Waugh. LC 33-29646. 1933. Farrar & Rinehart, Incorporated.
Leap for the Sun. Michael Hartmann. LC 77-76637. 7.95 (ISBN 0-312-47717-1). St. Martin's Press.
Leap in the Dark. Anthony McCandless. LC 79-27357. 1980. 10.95 (ISBN 0-312-47719-8). St. Martin's Press.
Leap in the Dark. Donald Gordon Payne. LC 76-142391. 1971. 5.95. Morrow.
Leap in the Dark. A Novel. Emma Dorothy Eliza Nevitte Southworth. LC 8-10823. 1890. R. Bonner's Sons.
Leap in the Dark. A Novel. Emma Dorothy Eliza Nevitte Southworth. LC 8-142502. (popular series, no. 39). 1893. R. Bonner's Sons.
Leap into the Future: Or, How Things Will Be; a Romance of the Year 2000. Donald McMartin. LC 7-204247. 1890. Weed, Parsons & Company.
Leap of Malta Dolphins. Francis Ebejer. (Illus.). 1982. 9.50 (ISBN 0-533-05053-7). Vantage.
Leap Year Bride. Laura Lou Brookman. LC 32-17145. Grosset & Dunlap.
Leap-Year Frolic. A Story of Facts and Fiction... Martha Klock & S. A. Timmerman. LC 7-14282. 1896. E. L. Adams.
Leap Year Girl. Berta Ruck. LC 24-26492. 1924. Dodd, Mead and Company.
Leap Year Romance. Berta Ruck. LC 57-113871. 1957. Dodd, Mead.
Leaping Flame, No. 70. Barbara Cartland. 256p. (Orig.). 1982. pap. 1.95 (ISBN 0-515-06386-X). Jove Pubns.
Leaping Flame, No. 70. Barbara Cartland. 1974. pap. 1.50 o.p. (ISBN 0-515-03450-9, V3450). BJ Pub Group.
Leaps the Live Thunder. Garald Lagard. 1955. Morrow.
Lear of the Steppes: And Other Stories. Ivan Sergeevich Turgenev. LC 76-10303. (His Novels, v. 12). 1970. AMS Press.
Learn to Be a Lady. Barbara Worsley-Gough. LC 38-239182. 1938. G. P. Putnam's Sons.
Learn to Say Goodbye. Jan Middleton. LC 65-20910. 3.75. Dodd.
Learn to Say Goodbye. Middleton, Jan. LC 65-20910. 1965. Dodd, Mead.
Learn to Wear Orchids. Kathleen Shepard & Monique, Jean, 1903- Joint Author. LC 35-16784. J. Messner, Inc.C.
Learner's Permit: A Novel. 1st Ed. Laurence Davis Lafore. LC 62-11462. 1962. Doubleday.
Learning About Health. Oliver Erasmus Byrd. LC 64-57356. (New road to health series). Laidlaw Bros.
Learning to Give. K. Russell & J. Tooke. (Cloth ed. 12.25 o.p.). 1968. pap. 6.50 o.p. (ISBN 0-08-012477-1). Pergamon.
Learning to Live. Fern Edwards. LC 22-25003. Washington Office Supply Co.
Learning to Live Again. Medard Laz. 1983. pap. 1.50 (ISBN 0-89243-176-8). Liguori Pubns.
Learning Tree. Gordon Parks. LC 63-16528. 1963. Harper & Row.
Least of All Evils. Helen Arvonen. 1975. (pbk.) 0.95. Ace Books.
Least of All Saints. Grace Irwin. 1957. pap. 2.65 o.p. (ISBN 0-8028-6015-X). Eerdmans.
Least of All Saints. Grace Lillian Irwin. (Spire Bk). 1976. pap. 1.75 o.p. (ISBN 0-8007-8240-2). Revell.
Least of All Saints: A Novel. Grace Lillian Iwin. LC 57-13041. 1957. Mich., Eerdmans.
Least of These. Celia Dale. LC 44-6130. 1943. Hurst & Blackett Ltd.
Least of These. Celia Dale. LC 44-7485. 1944. The Macmillan Company.
Least of These: A Novel. Translated by Bernt Jebsen and Douglas K. Stafford. Jens Bjorneboe. LC 59-102093. 1959. Bobbs-Merill.
Least One. Borden Deal. LC 67-19097. 1967. Doubleday.
Least Resistance. Kate L McLaurin. LC 16-9545. George H. Doran Company.
Leather & Lace, No. 1: The Lavender Blossom. Dorothy Dixon. (Orig.). 1982. pap. 2.50 (ISBN 0-8217-1029-X). Zebra.
Leather & Lace, No. 2: The Trembling Heart. Dorothy Dixon. (Orig.). 1982. pap. 2.50. Zebra.
Leather & Lace, No. 3: The Belle of the Rio Grande. Dorothy Dixon. (Orig.). 1982. pap. 2.50 (ISBN 0-8217-1059-1). Zebra.
Leather & Lace, No. 4: Flame of the West. Dorothy Dixon. 1982. pap. 2.50 (ISBN 0-8217-1091-5). Zebra.
Leather & Lace, No. 5: Cimarron Rose. Dorothy Dixon. 1982. pap. 2.50 (ISBN 0-8217-1106-7). Zebra.
Leather & Lace, No. 6: Honeysuckle Love. Carolyn T. Armstrong. 1983. pap. 2.50. Zebra.
Leather & Lace, No. 7: Diamond Queen. Dorothy Dixon. 1983. pap. 2.50 (ISBN 0-8217-1138-5). Zebra.
Leather & Lace, No. 8: Texas Wildflower. Tammie Lee. 1983. pap. 2.50 (ISBN 0-8217-1178-4). Zebra.
Leather Boots. Gershon Kranzler, pseud. saddle-stitched 3.00 (ISBN 0-87559-130-2). Shalom.
Leather Burners. A Double D Western. Harry Sinclair Drago. LC 40-5187. 1940. Doubleday, Doran & Company, Inc.
Leather Duke. Frank Gruber. LC 49-9040. (Murray Hill mystery). 1949. Rinehart.
Leather Man. Lawrence Treat. LC 44-512770. 1944. Duell, Sloan and Pearce.
Leather Pushers. Harry Charles Witwer. LC 21-18247. G. P. Putnam's Son.
Leather Slapper. Nelson Coral Nye. LC 37-186598. Greenberg.
Leather Stocking and Silk: Or, Hunter John Myers and His Times. A Story of the Valley of Virginia. John Esten Cooke. 1854. Harper & Brothers.
Leatherface: A Tale of Old Falders. Emmuska Orczy. LC 16-18331. 1.35. George H. Doran Company.
Leatherface: A Tale of Old Flanders. Emmuska Orczy. LC 16-16722. 1916. Hodder and Stoughton.
Leatherman's Handbook. Larry Townsend. 1972. pap. 2.95 o.s.i. (TC-3313, Travellers Comp). Olympia.
Leatherstocking. George Arthur Gray & Cooper, James Fenimore. LC 24-15965. Grosset & Dunlap.
Leatherstocking Saga. James Fenimore Cooper. Ed. by Allan Nevins. 840p. 1980. pap. 8.95 (ISBN 0-380-58453-0, 58453). Avon.
Leatherstocking Saga. James Fenimore Cooper. (Modern Library Giants). 4.95 o.p. (G94). Modern Lib.
Leatherstocking Saga: Being Those Parts of The Deerslayer, The Last of the Mohicans, The Pathfinder, The Pioneers, and The Prairie Which Specially Pertain to Natty Bumppo. Ed. by Allan Nevins. Illus. by Reginald Marsh. James Fenimore Cooper. Ed. by Allan Nevins. LC 66-1679. (Mod. lib. giants, G94). 1966. 3.95. Random.
Leatherstocking Saga: Being Those Parts of The Deerslayer, The Last of the Mohicans, The Pathfinder, The Pioneers, and The Prairie Which Specially Pertain to Natty Bumppo, Otherwise Known As Pathfinder, Deerslayer, or Hawkeye; the Whole Arranged in Chronological Order from Hawkeye's Youth on the New York Frontier in King George's War Until His Death on the Western Prairies in Jefferson's Administration. Edite by Allan Navins Illustrated by Reginald Marsh. James Fenimore Cooper. Ed. by Allan Nevins. LC 54-9502. 1954. Pantheon Books.
Leatherwood God. William Dean Howells. LC 76-120773. (Illus.). 1970. AMS Press.
Leatherwood God. William Dean Howells. LC 78-131754. (Illus.). 1970. (ISBN 4-03-006414-0). Scholarly Press.
Leatherwood God. William Dean Howells. LC 16-22401. 1916. The Century Co.
Leave Cancelled. Nicholas Monsarrat. LC 45-8114. 1945. A. A. Knopf.
Leave Her to Heaven. Ben Ames Williams. LC 44-401373. 1944. Houghton Mifflin Company.
Leave Her to Heaven. Ben Maes Williams. LC 47-2861. 1947. The Sun Dial Press.
Leave It to Amanda. Helen K Maxwell. 1974. (pbk.) 0.75. Bantam Books.
Leave It to Amanda. Helen K Maxwell. LC 72-1268. 1972. 6.95 (ISBN 0-316-55148-1). Little, Brown.
Leave It to Doris. Ethel Powelson Hueston. LC 19-14905. The Bobbs-Merrill Comapny.
Leave It to Love. Winifred Mary Scott. LC 37-4270. 1937. Doubleday, Doran & Company, Inc.
Leave It to Nurse Kathy. Arlene Hale. (Ace Nurse Romance Series). 1975. (pbk.) 0.95. Ace Books.
Leave It to Psmith. Pelham Grenville Wodehouse. LC 75-13377. 1975. 1.95 (ISBN 0-394-72026-1). Vintage Books.
Leave It to Psmith. Pelham Grenville Wodehouse. LC 24-8571. George H. Doran and Company.
Leave It to Psmith. Pelham Grenville Wodehouse. LC 35-28588. 1925. A. L Burt Company.
Leave It to the Hangman: 1st American Ed. Bill Knox. LC 60-168453. 1960. Published for the Crime Club by Doubleday.
Leave Me Alone. David Karp. LC 57-12070. 1957. Knopf.
Leave Me with a Smile. Elliott White Springs. LC 28-9051. 1928. Doubleday, Doran & Company, Inc.
Leave My Heart Alone. Kathleen Harris. LC 43-22861. 1943. Arcadia House.
Leave My Heart Alone. Kathleen Harris, pseud. LC 43-22861. 1943. Arcadia House, Inc.
Leave of Absence: A Novel. Theodore Morrison. 1981. 12.95 (ISBN 0-393-01439-8). Norton.
Leave-Taking: By George Milner. George Hardinge. LC 67-117301. 3.95. Dood.
Leave the Salt Earth. Richard Warren Hatch. LC 33-27329. Covici, Friede.
Leave to Psmith. P. G. Wodehouse. 1971. pap. 0.95 o.p. (95149). Beagle Bks.
Leaven of Love: A Novel. Clara Louise Root Burnham. LC 8-23559. 1908. Houghton Mifflin Company.
Leaven of Malice. William Robertson Davies. 1955. Scribner.
Leavenworth Case. Anna Katherine Green. 352p. 1982. pap. 5.00 (ISBN 0-486-23865-2). Dover.
Leavenworth Case. Anna Katherine Green. LC 79-104467. Repr. of 1878 ed. lib. bdg. 18.50 (ISBN 0-8398-0666-3). Irvington.
Leavenworth Case. Anna Katherine Green. 1976. lib. bdg. 12.95x (ISBN 0-89968-171-9). Lightyear.
Leavenworth Case. Anna Katherine Green. 1981. 18.95x (Pub. by Remploy England). State Mutual Bk.
Leavenworth Case. Anna Katherine Green. LC 79-104467. 1970. Repr. of 1878 ed. lib. bdg. 14.50x o.p. (ISBN 0-8398-0666-3). Gregg.
Leavenworth Case. Anna Katharine Green Rohlfs. LC 79-104467. (Illus.). 1970. (ISBN 0-8398-0666-3). Literature House.
Leavenworth Case: A Lawyer's Story. Anna Katharine Green. LC 81-65621. (Illus.). 1982. 5.00 (ISBN 0-486-23865-2). Dover Publications.
Leavenworth Case: A Lawyer's Story. 105th thousand. ed. Anna Katharine Green Rohlfs. LC 4-16105. 1901. G. P. Putnam's Sons.
Leavenworth Case: A Lawyer's Story. 105th thousand. ed. Anna Katharine Green Rohlfs. LC 6-34795. 1906. G. P. Putnam's Sons.
Leavenworth Case: A Lawyer's Story. Anna Katharine Green Rohlfs. LC 13-12940. 1913. G. P. Putnam's Sons.
Leavenworth Case: A Lawyer's Story. Anna Katharine Green Rohlfs. LC 34-230966. G. P. Putnam's Sons.
Leavenworth Irregulars. William D Blankenship. LC 73-16808. 1974. 6.95 (ISBN 0-672-51898-8). Bobbs-Merrill.
Leavenworth Irregulars. William D Blankenship. 1975. 1.50(pbk.). Bantam Books.
Leaves & Ashes. John Haines. 1974. pap. 2.00 o.p. (ISBN 0-87711-053-0). Kayak.
Leaves for the Burning: A Novel. Mervyn Wall. 1952. Devin-Adair Co.
Leaves from a Bachelor's Book of Life. Francis Copcutt. 1860. S. A. Rollo.
Leaves from a Bad Girl's Diary. Ella E Bower. 1884. Owens Publishing Company.
Leaves from a Drummer's Diary: Or, Twenty-Five Years on the Road. Charles S Plummer. LC 7-38192. (On cover: The household library. v. 4. no. 16)). 1888. Clarke & Company; Etc., Etc.
Leaves from a Family Journal. From the French of Emile Souvestre... Emile Souvestre. LC 8-14261. 1855. D. Appleton & Company.
Leaves from a Life-Book of to-Day. Jane Dearborn Mills. 1901. Swedenborg Publishing Association.
Leaves from a Note Book: A Collection of Miscellaneous Short Stories. special limited ed. Edmond Louis De Lestry. LC 9-2499. 1897.
Leaves from a Physician's Journal. Denis E Smith. LC 8-8632. 1867. New York Publishing Company.
Leaves from an Old Log. Pehe Nu-E, the Tiger Whale of the Pacific. Charles Martin Newell. LC 7-17278. 1877. D. Lothrop and Company.
Leaves from Arcady. Horace Annesley Vachell. LC 25-20834. 1924. Cassell and Company, Ltd.
Leaves from Margaret Smith's Journal. John Greenleaf Whittier. LC 75-104596. 1970. (ISBN 0-8398-2167-0). Literature House.
Leaves from the Diary of a Celebrated Burglar and Pick-Pocket. Being a Compilation of the Events and Occurrences of the Most Exciting, Interesting and Extraordinary Character in the Life of a Thief. 1865. G. W. Matsell & Co.
Leaves from the Life of a Good-for-Nothing: Translated from the German of Joseph, Freiherr Von Eichendorff. Joseph Karl Benedikt Freiherr Von Eichendorff & Wister, Mrs. Annis Lee (Furness) 1830-1908 Tr. LC 6-37547. 1889. J. B. Lippincott Company.
Leaves in the Sun. Yuki, pseud. (Illus.). 1968. 3.95 o.p. Walker & Co.
Leaves in the Wind. Gwyn Thomas. LC 68-838. 1968. MR Press.
Leaves in the Wind. Gwyn Thomas. LC 49-984448. 1949. Little, Brown.
Leaves of Fire, Flame of Love. Susan Chatfield. 1981. pap. 1.75 (ISBN 0-440-14937-1). Dell.
Leaves of Grass. Walt Whitman. 1971. pap. 2.95 (ISBN 0-451-51702-4, CE1702, Sig Classics). NAL.
Leaves of Grass. Walt Whitman. 1968. 3.95 (ISBN 0-88088-574-2). Peter Pauper.
Leaves of Hypnos. Rene Char. Tr. by Cid Corman. (Mushinsha Bks). 1973. pap. 5.95 o.p. (ISBN 0-670-42256-8, Grossman). Penguin.
Leaves of Time. Neal Barrett, Jr. 1971. pap. 0.75 o.p. (ISBN 0-447-74721-5). Lancer.
Leaves on Grey. Desmond Hogan. LC 80-25146. 8.95 (ISBN 0-89621-258-0). Thorndike Press.
Leaves on Grey: A Novel. Desmond Hogan. LC 79-23765. 1980. 8.95 (ISBN 0-8076-0948-X). G. Braziller.
Leaves Still Talk. David Kalugin. (Illus.). 1979. pap. 4.95 (ISBN 0-933586-04-3). Book Promo Unltd.
Leaves the People. Benjamin Saltman. 1974. pap. 2.50 (Pub. by Red Hill). SBD.
Leaves Unfold. Peter Marsh. LC 36-6960. Arcadia House.
Leavetaking. Anna Gilbert. LC 79-22648. 1980. 8.95 (ISBN 0-312-47730-9). St. Martin's Press.
Leavetaking. Anna Gilbert. LC 81-4773. 1981. 13.95 (ISBN 0-8161-3203-8). G.K. Hall.
Leavetaking. John McGahern. LC 74-18376. 1975. 6.95 (ISBN 0-316-55851-6). Little, Brown.
Leavetaking. Peter Weiss. LC 62-16739. 1962. Harcourt, Brace & World.
Leaving. Steven Hopkins. LC 78-70051. (Illus.). 1978. 12.00 (ISBN 0-930012-10-0) (ISBN 0-930012-09-7). Mudborn Press.
Leaving. Fran Pokras. LC 77-91237. (Jove / HBJ Book). 1978. 1.75 (ISBN 0-515-04526-8). Jove Pubns.
Leaving Cheyenne. Larry McMurtry. LC 79-16685. 1979. 1.95 (ISBN 0-14-005221-6). Penguin Books.
Leaving Cheyenne. Larry McMurtry. 1974. (pbk.) 1.25. Popular Library.
Leaving Home. Elizabeth Janeway. LC 53-9994. 1975. (pbk.) 1.50 (ISBN 0-345-24340-4). Ballantine Books.
Leaving Home: A Novel. Arthur Cavanaugh. LC 74-130468. 1971. 6.95. Simon and Schuster.
Leaving Home. 1st Ed. Elizabeth Janeway. LC 53-9994. 1953. Doubleday.

TITLE INDEX LEGEND OF SLEEPY HOLLOW.

Leaving Kansas. Frank Roderus. LC 82-48712. (Double D western). 1983. 11.95 (ISBN 0-385-18417-4). Doubleday.
Leaving Mount Venus. William Hanley. LC 76-26513. 1977. 1.75 (ISBN 0-345-25172-5). Ballantine Books.
Lebanon. Caroline Pafford Miller. LC 44-6204. 1944. Doubleday, Doran and Company, Inc.
Leben Des Galilei. 2nd ed. Bertolt Brecht. Ed. by H. F. Brookes & C. E. Fraenkel. (Orig., Ger.). 1981. pap. text ed. 7.00x (ISBN 0-435-38123-7). Heinemann Ed.
Lecciones Sexuales. Roberto Ramirez. (Pimienta Collection Ser.). 1977. pap. 1.00 (ISBN 0-88473-267-3). Fiesta Pub.
Lecherous Limericks. Isaac Asimov. LC 75-7922. (Illus.). 96p. 1975. 6.95 o.p. (ISBN 0-8027-0515-4); pap. 3.95 (ISBN 0-8027-7096-7). Walker & Co.
Lectures Before the Thompson Street Poker Club. Henry Guy Carleton. LC 6-19910. White and Allen.
Lecturess: Or, Woman's Sphere. 1839. Whipple and Damrell.
Led Astray: A Novel,. Octave Feuillet & Godfrey, Mrs. G. W. (On cover: Seaside library. Pocket ed., no. 386). 1885. G. Munro.
Led Astray: A Novel Also, The Sphinx: or, Julia De Trecaur, and Bellah. Octave Feuillet. Tr. by O. Vibeaur. LC 6-39521. 1881. G. W. Carlton & Co.
Led Astray; or, "La Petite Comtesse."-- The Sphinx; or,..Julia De Tressurs.""--"Belah.". Octave Feuillet. Tr. by O. Vibeaur. LC 6-39522. 1875. G. W. Carleton & Co.
Led Back. Mary Andrews Denison. 1891. American Baptist Publication Society.
Led-Horse Claim. Mary Hallock Foote. LC 68-20012. (Americans in Fiction Ser.). 1979. lib. bdg. 14.50 (ISBN 0-8398-0559-4); pap. text ed. 4.95x (ISBN 0-8290-0135-2). Irvington.
Led-Horse Claim: A Romance of a Mining Camp. Mary Hallock Foote. LC 68-20012. (Americans in Fiction). (Illus.). 1968. Gregg Press.
Led-Horse Claim: A Romance of a Mining Camp. Mary Hallock Foote. LC 4-16823. 1883. J. R. Osgood and Company.
Led into Sunlight. large print ed. Claire Evans. LC 82-14064. (Second Chance at Love). 1983. 11.95 (ISBN 0-89340-531-0). J. Curley.
Led to the Light. A Sequel to Opposite the Jail. Mary Andrews Denison. LC 21-153843. 1867. J. S. Claxton.
Leddy Marget. Lucy Bethia Colquhoun Walford. LC 8-32812. 1898. Longmans, Green, and Co.
Ledge. Gertrude Schweitzer. LC 77-178718. 1972. 6.95. Delacorte Press.
Ledger. Dorothy Uhnak. LC 81-3108. 1981. 12.95 (ISBN 0-89340-346-6). J. Curley & Associates.
Ledger: A Novel. Joan Hurling. LC 81-4763. 10.95 (ISBN 0-8149-0847-0). Vanguard Press.
Ledger of Lying Dog. William George Weekley. LC 47-304840. 1947. Doubleday.
Lee on the Levee. Ralph Cannon. LC 40-4883. The Saravan House.
Lee Shore. R Macaulay. LC 12-249203. Hodder & Stoughton, George H. Doran Company.
Leech Club: Or, The Mysteries of the Catskills. George Washington Owen. 1874. Lee & Shepard.
Leeden's League: Or, The Voyagers' Quest. James Albert Knowlton. LC 23-7730. 1923. J. O. Lee.
Leerie. Ruth Sawyer. LC 20-13146. Harper & Brothers.
Lees & Leaven: A New York Story of to-Day. Edward Waterman Townsend. LC 3-5533. 1903. McClure, Phillips & Co.
Leezie Lindsay. Marie Muir. LC 55-125765. 1955. Macmillan.
Leffert's Disease. Peter Lake. LC 76-11621. 1976. 8.95 o.p. (ISBN 0-672-52265-9). Bobbs.
Left Bank. Michel Georges-Michel. Tr. by Wallis, Keene. H. Liveright, Inc.
Left Bank & Other Stories. Jean Rhys. LC 79-134976. (Short story index reprint series). 1970. (ISBN 0-8369-3698-1). Books for Libraries Press.
Left Bank of Desire: By R. V. Cassill and Eric Protter. Ronald Verlin Cassill & Eric Protter. LC 55-33825. (Ace books, S-104). 1955. Ace Books.
Left Behind. Olive Ruth Brown Pattison. LC 78-9341. (Spire books). 1978. 1.95. Revell.
Left Hand Is the Dreamer. Nancy Wilson Ross. LC 47-30131. 1947. William Sloane Associates, Inc.
Left Hand Left: A Thornton Zane Story. Morrell Massey. LC 32-3413. The Penn Publishing Company.
Left Hand of Darkness. Ursula K. Le Guin. LC 72-86391. (Science Fiction Ser). 1969. 4.95 o.p. (11058). Walker & Co.
Left Hand of Darkness. Ursula K. Le Guin. LC 72-86391. 1969. 4.95. Walker.
Left Hand of Darkness. Ursula K. Le Guin. LC 79-2652. 1980. 10.95 (ISBN 0-06-012574-8). Harper & Row.
Left Hand of Darkness. Ursula K. Le Guin. 1974. (pbk.) 1.50. Ace Books.
Left Hand of God. William Edmund Barrett. LC 76-22719. 1976. 7.75 (ISBN 0-89244-017-1). Town House Press.
Left Hand of God. Jeremy Lane. LC 29-20645. 1929. I. Washburn.
Left Hand of God: By William E. Barrett. William Edmund Barrett. LC 51-905200. (Echo bk., E55). 1968. Doubleday.
Left Handed Hunter-Shadow at Jackson Hole. C. McCall Cole. 1980. pap. 2.25 o.s.i. (ISBN 0-8439-0715-0, Leisure Bks). Nordon Pubns.
Left Handed Law. Charles Morris Martin. LC 36-9934. 1936. Greenberg.
Left-Handed Passenger. Felix Riesenberg. LC 35-86703. 1935. Doubleday, Doran & Company, Inc.
Left-Handed Sleeper: A Novel. Ted Willis. LC 75-29021. 1976. 7.95 (ISBN 0-399-11621-4). Putnam.
Left-Handed Woman. Peter Handke. LC 78-5568. 1978. 6.95 (ISBN 0-374-18497-6). Farrar, Straus, and Giroux.
Left Hander: A Novel. Cornelius Francis Donovan. LC 25-17619. J. H. Meier.
Left in Charge. Clara Morris. LC 4-1818. G. W. Dillingham Company.
Left in Charge. Victor L Whitechurch. LC 12-225137. 1912. Doubleday, Page & Company.
Left in Trust. Juliet Wilbor Tompkins. LC 29-421556. The Bobbs-Merrill Company.
Left Lady. Margaret Turnbull. LC 26-18172. The Reilly & Lee Co.
Left Leg. Theodore Francis Powys. LC 72-140337. (Short story index reprint series). 1970. Books for Libraries Press.
Left Leg. Theodore Francis Powys. LC 23-12340. 1923. A. A. Knopf.
Left Leg. Alice Tilton. 1967. 4.50 o.p. (ISBN 0-393-08521-X). Norton.
Left Leg. A Leonidas Witherall Mystery by Alice Tilton Pseud. c.1940 ed. Phoebe Atwood Taylor. LC 40-30982. 4.50. Norton.
Left Seat. Robert J Serling. LC 66-122199. 4.95. Doubleday.
Left Seat. Robert J Serling. (75-1220). 1967. Popular Lib.
Left to Herself. Jennie Latham Stabler. LC 9-936. 1872. J. B. Lippincott & Co.
Left to Themselves: Being the Ordeal of Philip and Gerald. Edward Irenaeus Prime-Stevenson. LC 8-16093. 1891. Hunt & Eaton.
Leftover Girls. Keith Rockwell. 192p. (Orig.). 1973. pap. 1.95 o.p. (ISBN 0-87056-292-4, 6292). Brandon.
Lefty O' the Bush. Gilbert Patten. LC 14-2210. Barse & Hopkins.
Leg see Three Novels: Bibliotheca Neerlandica Ser.
Leg Artist. Gene Harvey. LC 42-1104. Phoenix Press.
Leg-Pullers: Or, Politics As She Is Applied. A Tale of the Puritan Commonwealth. Edward Belcher Callender. LC 6-21862. 1895. Pemberton Square Publishing Co.
Legacy. Sybille Bedford. LC 75-34600. 1976. 4.95 (ISBN 0-912946-26-1). Ecco Press.
Legacy. Charles Bonner. LC 40-6585. 1940. A. A. Knopf.
Legacy. John Coyne. 1979. pap. 2.95 (ISBN 0-425-05612-0). Berkley Pub.
Legacy. Jere Cunningham. (Fawcett Gold Medal Book). 1977. 1.75 (ISBN 0-449-13926-3). Fawcett Books.
Legacy. Howard Melvin Fast. LC 81-2906. 1981. 14.95 (ISBN 0-395-31260-4). Houghton Mifflin.
Legacy. Howard Melvin Fast. LC 81-13210. 16.95 (ISBN 0-8161-3292-5). G.K. Hall.
Legacy. Florence Hurd. LC 77-78141. 1977. 1.95 (ISBN 0-380-01677-X). Avon Books.
Legacy. Sonya Jones. 1977. pap. 3.95 o.s.i. Vanity.
Legacy. E. W Lovell. LC 34-272742. W. W. Norton & Company, Inc.
Legacy: A Novel. Sybille Bedford. LC 57-5671. 1957. Simon and Schuster.
Legacy: A Novel. Ronald Lawrence Bern. LC 75-23341. 1975. 8.95 (ISBN 0-88405-116-1). Mason/Charter.
Legacy: A Novel. John Coyne. 2.25 (ISBN 0-425-04183-2). Berkley Publishing Corp.
Legacy: A Novel. Nevil Shute Norway. LC 50-6909. 1950. Morrow.
Legacy: A Story of a Woman. Mary Stanbery Watts. LC 11-9942. 1911. The Macmillan Company.
Legacy and Other Stories. Rose Creighton. LC 39-13880. Dorrance and Company.
Legacy for a Doctor. Elizabeth Seifert. LC 63-9544. 1963. Dodd, Mead.
Legacy for Our Sons: A Novel. Albert Benjamin Cunningham. LC 52-5291. 1952. Dutton.
Legacy in Nylons. Jay G. Brenter. (Orig.). pap. 0.95 o.p. (1105). Brandon.
Legacy Lenders. Harold Q. Masur. (F3690). 1968. Bantam.
Legacy Lenders. Harold Q. Masur. LC 67-12764. 1967. Random House.
Legacy of a Gunfighter. William Frederick Bragg. 1980. pap. 1.75 (ISBN 0-8439-0790-8). Nordon Pubns.
Legacy of a Land Hog. John Henry Reese. LC 78-68347. 1979. 7.95 (ISBN 0-385-14727-9). Doubleday.
Legacy of a Spy. 1st Ed. Henry S Maxfield. LC 58-730260. 1958. Harper.
Legacy of Alicia Allen. Jean Woodward. (Avalon Books). 4.95. Thomas Bouregy.
Legacy of Beulah Land. William Laurence Coleman. LC 79-7516. 1979. 12.50 (ISBN 0-385-15459-3). Doubleday.
Legacy of Cain. Wilkie Collins. LC 6-26943. (On cover: Lovell's library. no. 1176). 1888. J. W. Lovell Company.
Legacy of Danger: A New Selena Mead Novel of Intrigue & Suspense. Patricia McGerr. 1970. Repr. 5.95 o.p. (ISBN 0-88331-035-X). Luce.
Legacy of Death. Robert Alfred John Walling. LC 34-33871. 1934. W. Morrow & Company.
Legacy of Dooley Jones. Steven C. Lawrence, pseud. 1974. pap. 0.75 o.p. (07342). Curtis.
Legacy of Evil. Lyda B. Long. (Orig.). 1973. pap. 0.75 o.p. (ISBN 0-345-20776-9). Beagle Bks.
Legacy of Evil. Ariadne Pritchett. 176p. (Orig.). 1973. pap. 0.75 o.p. (T2821, GM). Fawcett World.
Legacy of Evil. Ariadne Pritchett. (Gold medal, T2821). 1973. (pbk.) 0.75. Fawcett.
Legacy of Fear. Garnett Weston. LC 50-9431. 1950. M.S. Mill Co., and W. Morrow.
Legacy of Gabriel Martel. Marie L Nowinson. LC 50-9721. 1950. Appleton-Century-Crofts.
Legacy of Loneliness. Sharon B Wagner. (Avon gothic). 1974. (pbk.) 0.95. Avon.
Legacy of Love. Julia Davis. (Illus.). 1961. 4.95 o.p. (ISBN 0-15-149751-6). HarBraceJ.
Legacy of Love. Arlene Hale. LC 78-12834. 1979. 10.95 (ISBN 0-89340-165-X). J. Curley.
Legacy of Love. Arlene Hale. (Signet Book). 1977. 1.50 (ISBN 0-451-07411-4). New American Library.
Legacy of Love. Tate McKenna. (Candlelight Ecstasy Ser.: No. 126). (Orig.). 1983. pap. 1.95 (ISBN 0-440-15096-5). Dell.
Legacy of Love. Edyth E. Spriggs. (Illus.). 1972. 5.95 (ISBN 0-934988-04-8). Foun Bks.
Legacy of Love: By Frances Sarah Moore Pseud. Elsie Frances Wilson Mack. LC 57-8725. 1957. Avalon Books.
Legacy of Mendouba. large easy to read type. ed. Jennifer Reddoch. (Queen-Size Gothic). 1973. (pbk) 0.95. Popular Lib.
Legacy of Merton Manor. Dorothy Brenner Francis. 1976. 4.95. Avalon Books.
Legacy of Passion. Catherine Kay. 512p. 1982. pap. 3.50 (ISBN 0-373-97002-1). Harlequin Bks.
Legacy of Pride. Paula Allardyce, pseud. 1975. (pbk.) 1.75. Dell.
Legacy of Redfern. Jeanne Judson. 1972. pap. 0.75 o.s.i. (01-358). Lancer.
Legacy of Tears. Merrill A. Myers. 1978. pap. 1.95 (ISBN 0-532-19201-X). Woodhill.
Legacy of Terror. Kate Cameron, pseud. (Whispering hills gothic,#4). 1974. (pbk.) 0.95. Leisure Books.
Legacy of the Bloody Bride. Robert P. Richmond. (Orig.). 1979. pap. 1.95 (ISBN 0-532-23125-2). Woodhill.
Legacy of the Lake. Michael A. Smith. 1980. pap. 2.25 (ISBN 0-380-75879-2, 75879). Avon.
Legacy of the Lost. June Wetherell. 1970. pap. 0.75 o.p. (ISBN 0-447-74690-1). Lancer.
Legacy of the Past. Anne Mather. (Presents Ser.). 1974. pap. 1.25 (ISBN 0-373-70557-3, 70557). PB.
Legacy of the Stars. John Gregory. (Leisure Book). 1.50 (ISBN 0-8439-0634-0). Nordon Publications.
Legacy of the Wolf. Jean Raynes. LC 77-74307. 1977. 6.95 (ISBN 0-385-12624-7). Doubleday.
Legacy of Thorns. Robert Proctor Johnson. LC 65-22969. bds., 5.95. Morrow.
Legacy of Windhaven. Marie De Jourlet. (Windhaven Saga). 1978. pap. 3.50 (ISBN 0-523-41784-5). Pinnacle Bks.
Legacy of Winterwyck. Catherine Morland. 1976. (pbk.) 1.25 (ISBN 0-523-00851-1). Pinnacle Books.
Legal Relations. Laura Chapman. LC 76-14800. 8.95. Dutton.
Legal Wreck. William Hooker Gillette. LC 1-770. 1888. Rockwood Pub. Co.
Legal Wreck. William Hooker Gillette. LC 6221. (Eagle series. no. 182). 1900. Street & Smith.
Legality of Love. Jerry Sonenblick & Martha Sowerwine. 480p. (Orig.). 1981. pap. 3.95 (ISBN 0-515-05491-7). Jove Pubns.
Legatee. Alice Prescott Smith. LC 3-7658. 1903. Houghton, Mifflin and Company.
Legend. Evelyn Anthony. 1969. 5.95 o.p. (ISBN 0-698-10205-3). Coward.
Legend. Winifred Ashton. LC 20-817. 1920. The Macmillan Company.
Legend. Winifred Ashton. LC 35-27373. 1935. Doubleday, Doran & Company, Inc.
Legend. Winifred Ashton. LC 78-17053. 1978. 15.25 (ISBN 0-313-20572-8). Greenwood Press.
Legend. James T. McCafferty. LC 72-95295. 1973. 2.95 o.p. (ISBN 0-8059-1801-9). Dorrance.
Legend. Eve Stephens, pseud. LC 69-19028. 1969. 5.95. Coward-McCann.
Legend: A Novel. Frank Sette. (Signet book). 1979. 1.95 (ISBN 0-451-08605-8). New American Library.
Legend Called Meryom. Joseph Gaer. LC 28-1743. 1928. W. Morrow & Company.
Legend in Blue Steel. Spider Page. (Blue Steel: No. 1). 1978. pap. 1.50 (ISBN 0-89300-002-7). Python Pub.
Legend in Green Velvet. Elizabeth Peters, pseud. LC 76-3617. 7.95 (ISBN 0-396-07283-6). Dodd, Mead.
Legend in Green Velvet. Elizabeth Peters, pseud. (Fawcett Crest Book). 1977. 1.50 (ISBN 0-449-23109-7). Fawcett Publications.
Legend in Her Own Time. Chelsea Farraday. 1979. pap. 1.95 o.s.i. (ISBN 0-8439-0690-1, Leisure Bks). Nordon Pubns.
Legend in the Dust. Dwight Bennett. (1974 ed. o.p.). 208p. 1977. pap. 1.25 (ISBN 0-532-12494-4). Woodhill.
Legend in the Dust. Dwight Bennett. (Double D Western Ser). 1970. 4.95 o.p. Doubleday.
Legend in the Dust. Dwight Bennett. LC 78-111793. (Manor western). 1974. (pbk.) 0.95. Manor Books.
Legend in the Dust. Dwight Bennett Newton. LC 78-111179. (DD western). 1970. 4.95. Doubleday.
Legend in the Dust. Frank O'Rourke. LC 57-10516. (Ballantine books, 211). 1957. Ballantine Books.
Legend Makers. Harry Sinclair Drago. LC 74-10005. (Illus.). 264p. 1975. 8.50 o.p. (ISBN 0-396-07003-5). Dodd.
Legend of a Lady: The Story of Rita Martin. Robert Douglas Andrews, pseud. LC 49-899518. 1949. Coward-McCann.
Legend of a Mermaid. Jac Albert Leonard & Cashman, Francis Westinghouse. LC 48-4723.
Legend of Baverstock Manor. Nancy Buckingham. (Ace gothic). 1973. (pbk.) 0.95. Ace.
Legend of Big Plantation. Francis Norman Wagner. LC 76-100557. (Illus.). 1970. 6.95. Oliver Co.
Legend of Black-Jack Sam. Lee Hoffman. 1975. (pbk.) 0.95. Ace Books.
Legend of Crownpoint. Monica Heath. 1974. (pbk.) 0.95. New American Library.
Legend of Devil's Doom. Ruth McCarthy Sears. (Avalon Books). 4.95. Thomas Bouregy.
Legend of Duke Ernst. John Wesley Thomas & Carolyn Dussere. LC 79-19843. 11.50 (ISBN 0-8032-4406-1). University of Nebraska Press.
Legend of Helena Vaughan. Robert Speaight. LC 36-19252. 1936. G. P. Putnam's Sons.
Legend of Jerry Ladd. Roy Rolfe Gilson. 1913. 1.00. Doubleday, Page & Company.
Legend of Joseph Nokato. Lawrence Paul Bachmann. LC 70-143708. 1971. 5.95 o.p. (ISBN 0-316-07461-6). Little.
Legend of Joseph Nokato: A Novel. Lawrence Paul Bachmann. LC 70-143708. 1971. 5.95. Little, Brown.
Legend of Landsee. Harwell Goodwin Davis. LC 76-40829. 7.95 (ISBN 0-87397-106-X). Strode Publishers.
Legend of Loch. Alanna Knight. (O.s.i.). 1976. pap. 1.25 o.s.i. (BT51106). Belmont-Tower.
Legend of Lostwithiel. Elaine F. Wells. (Illus., Orig.). 1979. pap. 1.95 (ISBN 0-89083-446-6). Zebra.
Legend of McNutt: A Story of Early Home Life and Christianity in the Yazoo and Mississippi Delta. William Lee Anderson. LC 2-28515. 1902. Bigham & Smith.
Legend of Miaree. Zachary Hughes. (Science fiction original). 1974. (pbk.) 1.25 (ISBN 0-345-23888-5). Ballantine Books.
Legend of Montrose. Walter Scott. (On cover: Lovell's library, no. 493). 1885. J. W. Lovell Company.
Legend of Ogden Jenks. Robert Emmett. LC 80-52283. (Zia book). 1980. 5.95 (ISBN 0-8263-0559-8). University of New Mexico Press.
Legend of Olie Wildcatter & Other Stories. Max Picot. 1966. 2.50 o.p. (ISBN 0-8059-0230-9). Dorrance.
Legend of Piper's Hole. large easy-to-read & type. ed. Patricia Farmer. (Queen-Size Gothic). 1973. (pbk) 0.95. Popular Lib.
Legend of Shame. Ben Roche. (Dell Book). 1979. 2.25 (ISBN 0-440-14733-6). Dell Pub. Co.
Legend of She. Rider H. Haggard. 1982. pap. 3.95 (ISBN 0-14-005297-6). Penguin.
Legend of Sleepy Hollow. new ed. Washington Irving. Ed. by Joseph W. Nash. 1976. pap. 0.95 o.p. (ISBN 0-89319-010-1). Andor Pub.
Legend of Sleepy Hollow. Washington Irving. 1982. Repr. lib. bdg. 17.95x (ISBN 0-89966-410-5). Buccaneer Bks.

Legend of Sleepy Hollow & Other Selections from Washington Irving. Washington Irving. Ed. by Austin M. Fox. 288p. (YA) (gr. 9-12). pap. 2.50 (ISBN 0-671-43132-3). WSP.
Legend of Sleepy Hollow & Other Sketches. Washington Irving. (Legacy Library Ser). 1966. Repr. of 1880 ed. 4.95 o.p. (LL02007). Univ Microfilms.
Legend of Susan Dane. Ruth Comfort Mitchell. 1933. D. Appleton and Company.
Legend of the Bluegrass. Leigh Borden, pseud. LC 76-56266. 7.95 (ISBN 0-385-12308-6). Doubleday.
Legend of the Christmas Rose. Selma Ottiliana Lovisa Lagerlof. LC 42-25585. 1942. Doubleday, Doran and Co., Inc.
Legend of the Damned. Gordon D Shirreffs. (Fawcett Gold Medal Book). 1977. 1.50 (ISBN 0-449-13846-1). Fawcett Pubns.
Legend of the Deadly Doll. Elizabeth Hughes. (O.s.i.). 192p. (Orig.). 1973. pap. 0.95 o.s.i. (AN1124, Award). Univ Pub & Dist.
Legend of the Green Man. Sara Hely. (Fawcett crest book). 1974. (pbk.) 1.25. Fawcett.
Legend of the Loch. Alanna Knight. 1970. pap. 0.95 o.s.i. (75-297). Lancer.
Legend of the Lone Ranger: A Novelization. Gary McCarthy. 160p. (Orig.). 1981. pap. 2.25 (ISBN 0-345-29438-6). Ballantine.
Legend of the Rhine: Also, Rebecca and Rowena. William Makepeace Thackeray. LC 8-28199. (Lovell's library, v. 5, no. 285). 1883. J. W. Lovell Company.
Legend of the Seventh Son. Francois Plourde. 1970. 7.50 o.p. Vantage.
Legend of the Seventh Son. first ed. Francois Plourde. 1972. 7.50. Vantage.
Legend of the Seventh Virgin. Eleanor Hibbert. LC 65-10627. 1965. Doubleday.
Legend of the Seventh Virgin. Victoria Holt, pseud. LC 65-10627. 1965. 4.95. Doubleday.
Legend of the Seventh Virgin. Victoria Holt, pseud. (Crest bk., t902). 1966. Fawcett.
Legend of the Shaman. Paul J. Payack. 1974. pap. 1.00. Chthon Pr.
Legend of the Silver Bars. Neal Wakely. 112p. 1979. 5.95 (ISBN 0-8059-2592-9). Dorrance.
Legend of the Stonecutter. R. Kushnerovich. 15p. 1975. pap. 1.49 (ISBN 0-8285-1176-4, Pub. by Progress Pubs USSR). Imported Pubns.
Legend of the Thirteenth Pilgrim. Jessica North. LC 78-10281. 8.95 (ISBN 0-698-10944-9). Coward, McCann & Geoghegan.
Legend of the Thirteenth Pilgrim. Jessica North. ("a Signet Book"). 1980. 2.25 (ISBN 0-451-09068-3). New American Library.
Legend of the Waldenses: And Other Tales. 3d ed., enl. ed. Mary Jane Windle. LC 8-377774. 1852. J. W. Moore.
Legend of the Yellow River. Somerest Struben De Chair. LC 79-27311. 1980. 8.95 (ISBN 0-312-47885-2). St. Martin's Press.
Legend of Wolf Song. George Stone. LC 74-24673. (Illus.). 1975. 7.95 (ISBN 0-448-11879-3). Grosset & Dunlap.
Legend of Wolf Song. George Stone. (Illus.). 1976. 1.50. Dell.
Legend Was Born. Harmoni Warren. LC 77-77270. 7.95 (ISBN 0-87949-101-9). Ashley Books.
Legend Whispered. Dougall MacArthur. LC 43-17568. 1943. Binfords & Mort.
Legendary: Consisting of Original Pieces, Principally Illustrative of American History, Scenery, and Manners. Ed. by Nathaniel Parker Willis. LC 8-36900. 1828. S. G. Goodrich.
Legendary Fictions of the Irish Celts. Patrick Kennedy. LC 68-25518. 1968. Repr. of 1866 ed. 34.00x (ISBN 0-8103-3467-4). Gale.
Legendary History of Britain in Lope Garcia De Salazar's Libro De las Bienandanzas e Fortunas. Harvey L. Sharrer. LC 78-53334. (Haney Foundation Ser). 1979. 17.50x (ISBN 0-8122-7749-X). U of Pa Pr.
Legendary King of San Miguel. Elizabeth Lester. 1979. pap. 6.50 (ISBN 0-87461-027-3). McNally.
Legende Vom Heiligen Trinker in Paulsen, Wolfgang. 1910- Joseph Roth. LC 50-131142. 1950. Holt.
Legenden Von Gottfried Keller. Gottfried Keller. Ed. by Muller, Margarethe. Wenchkebach, Carla. LC 2-3939. 1902. H. Holt and Company.
Legends & Fishnets. Richard Carter Higgins. LC 76-151018. (Illus.). 1976. 15.00 (ISBN 0-914162-13-6) (ISBN 0-914162-12-8). Unpublished Editions.
Legends & Stories of Ireland. Samuel Lover. 280p. 1980. Repr. of 1902 ed. lib. bdg. 25.00 (ISBN 0-8482-1620-2). Norwood Edns.
Legends and Stories of Ireland: To Which Is Added Irish Sketches. Samuel Lover. LC 78-15789. 1978. 25.00 (ISBN 0-8414-5840-5). Folcroft Library Editions.
Legends and Tales of the Old West: By Members of the Western Writers of America. Western Writers of America. Ed. by Squire Omar Barker. LC 62-8084. 1962. Doubleday.
Legends from Invalid Street. Efraim Sevela. LC 73-81448. 1974. 6.95 (ISBN 0-385-01692-1). Doubleday.
Legends from the End of Time. Michael Moorcock. LC 75-6373. 7.95 (ISBN 0-06-013001-6). Harper & Row.
Legends from the End of Time. Michael Moorcock. (Illus.). 1977. 1.25 (ISBN 0-87997-281-5). DAWBooks.
Legends of a Log Cabin. Chandler Robbins Gilman. LC 75-104466. 1970. (ISBN 0-8398-0661-2). Literature House.
Legends of a Log Cabin. By a Western Man... Chandler Robbins Gilman. LC 6-44835. 1835. G. Dearborn.
Legends of Angria: Compiled from the Early Writings of Charlotte Bronte. Charlotte Bronte. Ed. by Fannie E. Ratchford & William C. DeVane. LC 72-85292. 384p. 1973. Repr. of 1933 ed. 14.50 o.p. (ISBN 0-8046-1727-9). Kennikat.
Legends of Fire Island Beach and the South Side. Edward Richard Shaw. LC 12-12216. Lovell, Coryell & Company.
Legends of Le Detroit. Marie C. Hamlin. Repr. of 1884 ed. price not set o.p. Gale.
Legends of Long Ago. facsimile ed. Gottfried Keller. Tr. by Charles H. Handschin from Ger. LC 71-167456. (Short Story Index Reprint Ser.). Repr. of 1911 ed. 10.00 (ISBN 0-8369-3982-4). Ayer Co.
Legends of Long Ago (Sieben Legenden). Gottfried Keller. LC 71-167456. (Short story index reprint series). 1971. (ISBN 0-8369-3982-4). Books for Libraries Press.
Legends of Mexico. George Lippard. 1847. T. B. Peterson.
Legends of Michigan & the Old North West. Flavius J. Littlejohn. 1969. Repr. of 1875 ed. 14.50 o.p. Singing Tree.
Legends of Ned Buntline. Jack Rosenberg. LC 76-13084. 1969.
Legends of Santo Nino De Cebu. Manuel Enriquez De La Calzada. 1965. wrps. 8.75 o.p. Cellar.
Legends of Smokeover. Lawrence Pearsall Jacks. LC 70-125222. (Short story index reprint series). 1970. Books for Libraries Press.
Legends of Texas, 2 vols. J. Frank Dobie. Incl. Vol. 1. Lost Mines & Buried Treasures. 132p (ISBN 0-88289-085-9); Vol. 2. Pirates Gold & Other Tales. 144p (ISBN 0-88289-086-7). 1975. pap. 3.95 ea. Pelican.
Legends of the California Bandidos. Angus MacLean. LC 77-73239. (Illus.). 1977. 12.50 (ISBN 0-914330-09-8); pap. 4.95. Pioneer Pub Co.
Legends of the California Bandidos. Angus MacLean. 235p. 1977. 4.95 (ISBN 0-914330-09-8). Western Tanager.
Legends of the Fall. James Harrison. LC 78-31475. 10.95 (ISBN 0-440-05461-3). Delacorte Press/S. Lawrence.
Legends of the Middle Ages. Helena A. Guerber. 1973. 14.95 o.p. R West.
Legends of the Middle Ages. Helene A. Guerber. (Illus.). 1896. 12.50 o.p. Singing Tree.
Legends of the Province House. Nathaniel Hawthorne. LC 37-5481. 1936. Printed for W. R. Scott by the Powgen Press.
Legends of the Province House: And Other Twice-Told Tales. Nathaniel Hawthorne. LC 3005. (On cover: Riverside Aldine classics). 1900. Houghton, Mifflin and Company.
Legends of the Rhine and of the Low Countries. Thomas Colley Grattan. LC 50-34927. E. L. Carey & A. Hart.
Legends of the South. Nathan Ryno Smith. LC 6-14301. 1869. Steam Press of W. K. Boyle.
Legends of the Wars in Ireland. Robert Dwyer Joyce. LC 7-11895. 1868. J. Campbell.
Legends of the West. James Hall. LC 7-317. 1832. H. Hall.
Legends of the West. James Hall. LC 7-316. 1854. T.L. Magagnos and Company.
Legends of Virginia. Helena Lefroy Caperton. LC 51-7. 1950. Garrett & Massie.
Legends of Virginia. Helena Lefroy Caperton. LC 31-24489. Garrett & Massie.
Legeng of Crown Point see Chateau of Shadows.
Legion. Charles L. Grant. 1979. pap. 1.75 (ISBN 0-425-04108-5). Berkley Pub.
Legion of Dishonor. Ivan Lebedeff. LC 40-32861. Liveright Publishing Corporation.
Legion of Noble Christians: Or, The Sweeney Survey. Gerald Green. (75243). 1967. Pocket Bks.
Legion of Noble Christians: Or, The Sweeney Survey. Gerald Green. LC 65-25700. 1965. Trident Press.
Legion of Space. Jack Williamson. LC 75-441. (Garland Library of Science Fiction). 1975. 11.00 (ISBN 0-8240-1443-X). Garland Pub.
Legion of Space. Jack Williamson. (Kangaroo Book). 1977. 1.50 (ISBN 0-671-81450-8). Pocket Books.
Legion of Space. Jack Williamson. LC 47-23202. 1947. Fantasy Press.
Legion of the Condemned. Eustace Hale Ball & Saunders, John Monk, 1897- LC 28-12548. Grosset & Dunlap.
Legion of the Damned. Sven Hassel. 1970. pap. 0.95 o.p. (ISBN 0-447-75120-4). Lancer.
Legion of the Damned. Sven Hazel. LC 57-8132. 1957. Farrar, Straus and Cudahy.
Legion of the Damned. Translated from the Danish by Maurice Michael. Sven Hassel. LC 57-8132. 1957. Farrar, Straus and Cudahy.
Legion of the Dead. Hugh Barnett Cave. 1979. pap. 1.95 (ISBN 0-380-44669-3, 44669). Avon.
Legion of the Lost. rev. ed. John Creasey. LC 74-80973. (Doctor Palfrey thriller). 1974. 5.95 (ISBN 0-8027-5311-6). Walker.
Legion of the Lost. John Creasey. LC 44-47953. 1944. S. Dayo.
Legion of the Lost: A Novel. Donald Barr Chidsey. LC 67-17703. 1967. Crown Publishers.
Legion of Time. Jack Williamson. LC 52-4799. 1952. Fantasy Press.
Legionaries. 4th ed.... ed. Millard F Cox. LC 3-712. The Bowen-Merrill Company.
Legionnaires. new ed. Per O. Enquist. 468p. 1973. 10.00 o.p. (ISBN 0-440-04725-0, Sey Lawr). Delacorte.
Legionnaires: A Documentary Novel. Per Olov Enquist. LC 73-10238. 1973. 10.00. Delacorte Press/S. Lawrence.
Legions of Antares. Dray Prescot. (Science Fiction Ser.). 192p. 1981. pap. 2.25 (ISBN 0-87997-648-9, UE1648). DAW Bks.
Legions of Insanities or Who Was Barabbas Jones. Daniel McLaughlin. 1979. pap. 3.50 (ISBN 0-9602124-2-6). Literary Herald.
Legions of the Mist: A Novel of Roman Britain. Amanda Cockrell. LC 79-51353. (Illus.). 1979. 12.95 (ISBN 0-689-10989-X). Atheneum.
Legislative Body. Joe L. Hensley. LC 76-186025. 1972. 4.95. Published for the Crime Club by Doubleday.
Legs,". James Francis Dwyer. LC 15-11997. 1915. Federal Printing Company.
Legs. William Kennedy. 1976. 1.75. Warner Books.
Legs. William Kennedy. LC 77-356881. 1976. 3.50 (ISBN 0-224-01270-3). Cape.
Legs: A Novel. William Kennedy. LC 74-30596. 1975. 8.95 (ISBN 0-698-10672-5). Coward, McCann & Geoghegan.
Legs: A Novel. William Kennedy. LC 82-13285. 1983. 5.95 (ISBN 0-14-006484-2). Penguin.
Legs" A Novel of Today. Lillian Alma Chamberlain. LC 39-28302. 1939. The Lund Press.
Legs of the Lame, and Other Stories. Hugh Garner. LC 77-352889. 1976. Borealis Press.
Legs Parsons: A Story of up-Country Africa. Ferdinand Berthoud. LC 24-9271. 1924. Minton, Batch & Company.
Leiden Eines Knaben. Meyer. 1969. pap. 2.95, s.p.2.36 o.p. (ISBN 0-07-035649-1). McGraw.
Leif Garrett. Connie Berman. (Tempo books). (Illus.). 1.50 (ISBN 0-448-16476-0). Grosset & Dunlap.
Leif the Lucky: A Romantic Saga of the Sons of Erik the Red, Here Set Down. Clara Sharpe Hough. LC 26-14909. The Century Co.
Leifar Fornra Kristinna Froetha Islenskra. Thorvaldur Bjarnarson. LC 80-1980. Repr. of 1878 ed. 33.00 (ISBN 0-404-18629-7). AMS Pr.
Leighton Court. A Country-House Story. Henry Kingsley. (On cover: Lovell's library, v. 14, no. 731). 1886. J. W. Lovell Company.
Leila. new ed. Judith Murray. (Illus.). 32p. (Orig.). 1976. pap. 1.85 (ISBN 0-915288-20-6). Shameless Hussy.
Leila Inherits Adventure. Rose Hooks & Hooks, Flora, Joint Author. LC 41-14664. Dorrance and Company.
Leila: Or, The Seige of Granada; Calderon the Courtier; and The Pilgrims of the Rhine. Edward George Earle Lytton Bulwer-Lytton Lytton. G. Routledge and Sons.
Leila: Or, The Siege of Granada. Edward George Earle Lytton Bulwer-Lytton Lytton. (On cover: Lovell's library, v. 1, no. 12). 1882. J. W. Lovell Company.
Leila: Or, The Siege of Granada. Calderon, the Courtier. And The Pilgrims of the Rhine. Edward George Earle Lytton Bulwer-Lytton Lytton. LC 34-377852. 1888. J. B. Lippincott Company.
Leila: Or, The Siege of Granada. To Which Are Added Calderon the Courtier and Pausanias the Spartan. Edward George Earle Lytton Bulwer-Lytton Lytton & Lytton, Edward Robert Bulwer-Lytton, 1st Earl of, 1831-1891, Ed. LC 7-8461. (Half-title: Novels of Sir Edward Bulwer Lytton. Library ed. Historical romances, vol. VI). 1893. Little, Brown, and Company.
Leisure Dying. Lillian O'Donnell. LC 75-43795. 6.95 (ISBN 0-399-11741-5). Putnam.
Leisure Hours. George W Wear. LC 33-11062. 1933. Meador Publishing Company.
Leisure Riots. Eric Koch. LC 73-76301. 192p. (Orig.). 1973. 9.95 (ISBN 0-912766-06-9). Tundra Bks.
Leland Legacy. Dorothy Daniels. 1974. pap. 0.95 o.p. (ISBN 0-515-03325-1, N3325). Pyramid Pubns.
Lelia. George Sand. LC 77-23639. (Illus.). 12.75 (ISBN 0-253-33318-0). Indiana University Press.
Lelia: The Compleat Ballerina. Harold G. Scott. LC 75-8768. (Illus.). 224p. 1975. 24.95 (ISBN 0-88289-075-1). Pelican.
Lem Allen. William Pinkney Lawson. LC 23-127445. Boni and Liveright.
Lemahra and Doreen: A Fairy Tale. Xenia L. McCouch. LC 49-262455.
Lemmings. Charity L. Blackstone. (Osi). 1970. pap. 0.75 o.s.i. (B75-2001). Belmont-Tower.
Lemmings. Ursula Torday. LC 69-19031. 1969. 5.95. Coward-McCann.
Lemon: A Novel. Mohammed Mrabet & Paul Frederic Bowles. LC 72-2906. 1972. 5.95 (ISBN 0-07-073743-6). McGraw-Hill Book Co.
Lemon Bite. Yolande Tomiuk. 1970. 3.00 o.p. (ISBN 0-8059-1448-X). Dorrance.
Lemon Eaters. Jerry Sohl. (4729). 1968. Dell.
Lemon Eaters: A Novel. Jerry Sohl. LC 67-14238. 1967. 5.95. S.&S.
Lemon Farm. Martin Boyd. LC 75-324446. 1973. 3.95 (ISBN 0-333-13945-3) (ISBN 0-7251-0154-7). Sun Books.
Lemon Farm. Martin Boyd. LC 37-814. 1936. W. W. Norton & Company, Inc.
Lemon in the Basket. Charlotte Armstrong. LC 67-24531. 1967. Coward-McCann.
Lemons Never Lie. Richard Stark. 5.95 o.p. (A3693). World Pub.
Lemons Never Lie. Donald E Westlake. LC 70-128487. (Falcon's head suspense novel). 1971. 5.95. World Pub. Co.
Len Gansett. Opie Percival Read. LC 12-38416. 1888. Ticknor and Company.
Lena. A. C McWhortle. LC 75-176123. (Venus library, V-1037-K). 1971. 1.75. Grove Press.
Lena. Roger Vercel & Wells, Warre Bradley, 1892- Tr. LC 37-16812. Random House.
Lena Hates Men. Margot Neville. LC 43-104175. 1943. Mystery House.
Lena; or, The Stark Family. A Sketch of Real Life. From the Swedish of H. ! Hofsten. Kristina Johanna Augusta Von Hofsten. LC 11-150635. 1876. Hitchcock and Walden.
Lena Rivers. Mary Jane Hawes Holmes. LC 74-129371. 1970. (ISBN 0-404-03315-6). AMS Press.
Lena Rivers. Mary Jane Hawes Holmes. LC 79-121318. 1970. Scholarly Press.
Lena Rivers. Mary Jane Hawes Holmes. LC 12-34389. 1856. Miller, Orton & Mulligan.
Lena Rivers. Mary Jane Hawes Holmes. LC 32-336204. (On cover:Select library no. 44). 1900. Street & Smith Corporation.
Lend a Hand. J. S Blazer. LC 73-22664. 1975. 6.95 (ISBN 0-672-51852-X). Bobbs-Merrill.
Lend a Hand. Charles Monroe Sheldon. LC 99-3304. (On cover: Revell's popular religious series, no. 209). 1899. Fleming H. Revell Company.
Lend Me Your Ears. LC 76-18368. (Crime Club Ser.). 1976. 5.95 o.p. (ISBN 0-385-12245-4). Doubleday.
Lend Me Your Ears. Aaron Marc Stein. LC 76-18368. 1976. 5.95 (ISBN 0-385-12245-4). Published for the Crime Club by Doubleday.
Lend Me Your Name! Francis Perry Elliott. LC 17-167282. 1.25. The Reilly & Britton Co.
Lendemain, C'est Vous. Georges Bernanos. 14.50. French & Eur.
Leng Tso. The Chinese Bible-Woman; a Sequel to "The Chinese Slave-Girl,". John A Davis. LC 6-32480. Presbyterian Board of Publication.
Length of Rope. Monroe Engel. LC 52-5164. 1952. Random House.
Lengthened Shadow. William John Locke. LC 23-12872. 1923. Dodd, Mead and Company.
Leni Leoti: Or Adventures in the Far West. A Sequel to "Prairie Flower.". new ed. rev. and cor. by the author ed. Emerson Bennett. 1850. J. A. & U. P. James.
Leni-Leoti: Or, Adventures in the Far West. Emerson Bennett. 1849. Stratton & Barnard.
Lenient Beast. Fredric Brown. LC 56-6754. (Guilt edged mystery). 1956. Dutton.
Lenient God. Naomi Ellington Jacob. 1938. The Macmillan Company.
Lenin in Zurich: Chapters. Aleksandr Isaevich Solzhenitsyn. LC 75-44086. 1976. 8.95. Farrar, Straus and Giroux.
Lenin in Zurich: Chapters. Aleksandr Isaevich Solzhenitsyn. 1976. 2.50 (ISBN 0-553-10079-3). Bantam Books.
Lenin in Zurich: Chapters. Aleksandr Isaevich Solzhenitsyn. LC 77-351548. 1976. 3.75 (ISBN 0-370-10607-5). Bodley Head.
Lenora. Ann Gimbel. LC 77-71894. (Destiny Ser.). 1977. pap. 4.95 o.p. (ISBN 0-8163-0303-7, 12121-0). Pacific Pr Pub Assn.
Lenore: A Novel. Lillian Lawrence Nelson. LC 51-13962. 1951. Humphries.

Lenore Annandale. Evelyn Everett Green. I. Bradley & Co.

Lenox Dare. Virginia Frances Townsend. LC 41-42356. 1881. Lee and Shepard.

Lenox Dare. Virginia Frances Townsend. LC 8-31467. Lothrop, Lee & Shepard Co.

Lens and Key. Illus. by the Author. Martin Bordock. LC 57-12166. (Pan Press fiction library book). Pan Press.

Lensman from Rigel. David A. Kyle. 224p. 1982. pap. 2.50 (ISBN 0-553-20499-8). Bantam.

Lentala of the South Seas: The Romantic Tale of a Lost Colony. W. C Morrow. LC 8-24468. 1908. F. A. Stokes Company.

L'Envers du Reve. Betty Roland. (Collection Colombine). 192p. 1983. pap. 1.95 (ISBN 0-373-48058-X). Harlequin Bks.

Lenz. Georg Buchner. Tr. by Michael Hamburger from Ger. 55p. 1970. pap. 1.00 o.p. Frontier Press Calif.

Leo & Theodore. Donald Newlove. LC 74-154265. 1973. 7.95 (ISBN 0-8415-0175-0). Saturday Review Press.

Leo Conversion. David Smith. LC 80-13316. (Illus.). 9.95 (ISBN 0-396-07854-0). Dodd, Mead.

Leo Conversion. David Smith. LC 81-4804. 11.95 (ISBN 0-89340-337-7). J. Curley.

Leo Man. Rebecca Stratton. (Harlequin Romances Ser.). 192p. 1981. pap. 1.25 (ISBN 0-373-02405-3, Pub. by Harlequin). PB.

Leo the Last. Leo Skir. (O.s.i.). (Orig.). 1970. pap. 0.75 o.s.i. (A611S, Award). Univ Pub & Dist.

Leo Wyoming Caper. Jamie Mandelkau. 1978. pap. 1.95 (ISBN 0-425-03590-5, Medallion). Berkley Pub.

Leofwine the Saxon: A Story of Hopes and Struggles. Emma Leslie. LC 7-14497. (Church history stories, v. 5). Nelson & Philips.

Leola. A Novel. John Carroll. LC 6-24223. 1888. J. B. Lippincott Company.

Leola: A Novel. John A Griffin. LC 6-45430. The Author.

Leon. Illus. by Victor G. Ambrus. 1st Ed. in the U. S. Helen Griffiths. LC 68-10602. 1968. 3.50. Doubleday.

Leon Pontifex. Sarah Pratt McLean Greene. LC 10-4190. De Wolfe, Fiske & Co.

Leon Roch: A Romance. authorized ed....rev. and corr. in the united states. ed. Galdos Benito Perez & Bell, Clara Courtenay (Poynter) 1834-1927, Tr. LC 7-36351. 1888. W. S. Gottsberger.

Leon Roch: A Romance. Perez Galdos, Benito. LC 73-21742. 1974. 22.00. H. Fertig.

Leon Roch: A Romance. authorized ed.... rev. and cor. in the united states. ed. Benito Perez Galdos. Tr. by Bell, Clara Courtenay (Poynter) LC 7-36351. 1888. W. S. Gottsberger.

Leona. Mary Louisa Stewart Molesworth. Cassell Publishing Company.

Leona Gregory R see Florida Nurse.

Leonard the Doolit. Doven Hayes. Ed. by Roberta Munro. (Tatterman Ser.). (Illus.). 1977. pap. 2.95 (ISBN 0-918774-02-0). Fig Leaf.

Leonardo. Ritchie-Calder. LC 70-130350. 1970. 12.95 o.p. (ISBN 0-671-20713-X). S&S.

Leonardo Touch. Jeannette Eyerly. 1980. pap. 1.75 (ISBN 0-425-04521-8). Berkley Pub.

Leonardo Touch: A Novel of Suspense. Jeanette Eyerly. (Berkley Medallion Book). 1977. 1.25 (ISBN 0-425-03594-8). Berkley Pub. Corp.

Leonardo Was Right. Roland Topor. Tr. by Barbara Wright. 1980. pap. 3.95 (ISBN 0-7145-3671-7). Riverrun NY.

Leone... Luigi Monti. LC 7-31805. (Round-Robin series, v. 12). 1882. J. R. Osgood and Company.

Leone Leoni. George Sand. LC 77-28240. 1978. 10.95 (ISBN 0-915864-62-2) (ISBN 0-915864-61-4). Cassandra Editions.

Leonella. Rosy Chabbert. LC 73-16870. 1974. 8.95 (ISBN 0-8371-7240-3). Delacorte Press.

Leonella. Rosy Chabbert. LC 73-20331. 1974. 8.95 (ISBN 0-440-04758-7). Delacorte Press.

Leonie Locke: Or, The Romance of a Beautiful New York Working-Girl. Laura Jean Libbey. (On cover: The library of American authors, no. 10). 1889. G. Munro.

Leonie of the Jungle. Joan Conquest. LC 21-15951. The Macaulay Company.

Leonie: Or, The Sweet Street Singer of New York. Thomas W. Hanshew. (On cover: Munro's library, popular novels, v. 1, no. 163). 1884. N.L. Munro.

Leonie: Or, The Sweet Street Singer of New York. Thomas W. Hanshew. (Lovell's library, no. 1346). 1889. J.W. Lovell Company.

Leonora. Arnold Bennett. LC 74-5379. (Collected Works of Arnold Bennett: Vol. 43). 1976. Repr. of 1903 ed. 18.75 (ISBN 0-518-19124-9). Ayer Co.

Leonora. Maria Edgeworth. LC 25-23770. (Half-title: The novels of Maria Edgeworth, vol. iii). 1893. J. M. Dent & Co.

Leonora. Catherine Fellows. (Fawcett regency romance). 1974. (pbk.) 0.95. Fawcett.

Leonora. Frances Rumsey. LC 10-21296. 1910. 1.50. D. Appleton and Company.

Leonora of the Yawmish: A Novel. Francis Dana. LC 6-33170. 1897. Harper & Brothers.

Leonore Stubbs. Lucy Bethia Colquhoun Walford. LC 9-35328. 1908. Longmans, Green, and Co.

Leopard. Giuseppe Di Lampedusa. (Modern Classics Ser.). 1982. pap. text ed. 5.95 (ISBN 0-394-74949-9). Pantheon.

Leopard. Giuseppe Di Lampedusa. Tr. by A. Colquhoun. LC 60-6794. 1960. 8.95 (ISBN 0-394-43291-6). Pantheon.

Leopard. Victor Stafford Reid. LC 58-7064. 1958. Viking Press.

Leopard. Victor Stafford Reid. LC 70-160085. (American Library). 1971. 1.50. Collier Books.

Leopard. Victor Stafford Reid. LC 74-180042. 1972. (ISBN 0-911860-08-8). Chatham Bookseller.

Leopard. Tomasi Di Lampedusa, Giuseppe. LC 60-6794. 1960. Pantheon.

Leopard. Tomasi Di Lampedusa, Giuseppe. LC 60-6794. 1975. (pbk.) 1.75 (ISBN 0-380-00377-5). Avon.

Leopard and the Cliff. Wallace Breem. LC 78-71884. 10.95 (ISBN 0-312-48008-3). St. Martin's Press.

Leopard and the Lily. Marjorie Bowen. LC 7-7520. 1907. McClure, Phillips & Co.

Leopard and the Lily. Marjorie Bowen. LC 9-24330. 1909. 1.20. Doubleday, Page & Company.

Leopard at Maytime. John Demory Martin. LC 66-14931. 4.50. Doubleday.

Leopard Cat's Cradle. Jerome Barry. LC 42-24666. 1942. Published for the Crime Club by Doubleday, Doran & Company, Inc.

Leopard in a Cage. Jacqueline Pierce. LC 76-980764. 1976. East African Pub. House.

Leopard in the Bush: A Sequel to "Dalla the Lion-Cub". Cynthia Stockley. LC 27-23451. 1927. G. P. Putnam's Sons.

Leopard in the Grass. Desmond Stirling Stewart. LC 52-5793. Farrar, Straus & Young.

Leopard in the Snow. Anne Mather. (Alpha Book Ser.). 96p. 1974. pap. 2.95 (ISBN 0-19-424166-1). Oxford U Pr.

Leopard Priestess. Robert Sutherland Rattray. LC 35-4800. 1935. D. Appleton-Century Company, Incorporated.

Leopard Prince: A Romance of Venice in the Fourteenth Century, at the Period of the Bosnian Conspiracy, by Nathan Gallizier... Pictures by the Kinneys; Decorations by P. Verburg. Nathan Gallizier. LC 20-194363. 1920. The Page Company.

Leopard Woman. Stewart Edward White. 1916. Doubleday, Page & Company.

Leopards and Lilies. Alfred Leo Duggan. LC 68-12874. Weybright and Talley.

Leopards and Lilies. Alfred Leo Duggan. LC 54-10142. 1954. Coward-McCann.

Leopard's Claw. George Washington Ellis. LC 70-99373. 1969. Repr. of 1917 ed. lib. bdg. 8.50 o.p. (ISBN 0-8411-0044-6). Metro Bks.

Leopard's Claw: A Thrilling Story of Love and Adventure from a European Castle Through the West African Jungle, Disclosing a Deep Insight into the Quality and Spiritual Influence of African Social Institutions and Condition and Revealing a Profound Psychic Interpretation of African Inner Life, All Clustered About the Mysterious Function and Significance of the Leopard's Claw. George Washington Ellis. LC 18-13112. International Authors' Association.

Leopards in the Garden. Nathaniel Burt. LC 68-17268. 1968. 5.95 o.p. (ISBN 0-316-11783-8). Little.

Leopards in the Garden: A Novel. Nathaniel Burt. LC 68-17268. 1968. Little, Brown.

Leopard's Sports: A Romance of the White Man's Burden--1865-1900. Thomas Dixon. LC 15-632440. 1906. Doubleday, Page & Co.

Leopard's Spots. Thomas Dixon, Jr. LC 67-29265. (Americans in Fiction Ser.). 1979. Repr. of 1902 ed. lib. bdg. 14.50 (ISBN 0-8398-0366-4). Irvington.

Leopard's Spots. A Romance of the White Man's Burden--1865-1900. Thomas Dixon. LC 2-7626. 1902. Doubleday, Page & Co.

Leopard's Spots: A Romance of the White Man's Burden--1865-1900. Thomas Dixon. LC 16-11045. Grosset & Dunlap.

Leopard's Spots: A Romance of the White Man's Burden--1865-1900. Thomas Dixon. 1903. Doubleday, Page & Co.

Leopard's Spots: A Romance of the White Man's Burden, 1865-1900. Illus. by C. D. Williams. Thomas Dixon. LC 67-29265. (Americans in Fic.). 1967. Gregg Pr.

Leopard's Tooth. William Kotzwinkle. 96p. 1983. pap. 2.95 (ISBN 0-380-62869-4, 62869-4, Bard). Avon.

Leopold Contract. George Wolk. LC 74-85637. 1969. 4.50. Random House.

Leota Foreman, R. N. Peggy Gaddis, pseud. 1970. pap. 0.50 o.p. (50-507). Manor Bks.

Leper & Other Stories. Milovan Djilas. Tr. by Lovett F. Edwards. LC 64-14641. 1964. 5.95 (ISBN 0-15-149859-8). HarBraceJ.

Leper, and Other Stories. Translated by Lovett F. Edwards. Milovan Dilas. LC 64-14641. 1964. Harcourt, Brace & World.

Leper King: A Novel. Zofia Kossak-Szczucka. Tr. by Floyd S. Placzek. LC 45-35120. 1945. Roy Publishers.

Leper of Saint Giles. Ellis Peters. 224p. 1982. 11.50 (ISBN 0-688-01097-0). Morrow.

Leper's Bell. Massicks Sparroy. LC 21-152519. 1921. G. P. Putnam's Sons.

Lepidus the Centurion. Edwin Lester Linden Arnold. LC 77-84195. (Lost Race and Adult Fantasy Fiction). 1978. 20.00 (ISBN 0-405-10954-7). Arno Press.

Lepidus the Centurion. Edwin Lester Linden Arnold. LC 77-84195. (Lost Race and Adult Fantasy Fiction). 1978. 68.00 (ISBN 0-405-10953-9). Arno Press.

Lepidus the Centurion: A Roman of to-Day. Edwin Lester Linden Arnold. LC 2-5581. 1901. T. Y. Crowell & Co.

Lepidus the Centurion: A Roman of Today. Edwin Lester Linden Arnold. Ed. by R. Reginald & Douglas Melville. LC 77-84196. (Lost Race & Adult Fantasy Ser.). 1978. Repr. of 1901 ed. lib. bdg. 20.00x (ISBN 0-405-10954-7). Ayer Co.

Lepke. Jack Pearl. 1975. (pbk.) 1.25 (ISBN 0-671-78916-3). Pocket Books.

L'Epouse De Juin. Janet Dailey. (Harlequin Romantique). 192p. 1983. pap. 1.95 (ISBN 0-373-41194-4). Harlequin Bks.

Leprechaun Murders. Amelia Reynolds Long. LC 50-10978. 1950. Phoenix Press.

Leprosy of Miriam. Ursula Newell Gestefeld. LC 6-44071. 1894. The Gestefeld Library & Publishing Co.

Lerios Mecca. Gene Lancour. LC 73-80731. (Doubleday science fiction). (Illus.). 1973. 4.95 (ISBN 0-385-06365-2). Doubleday.

Leroy, Headed for Stardom: With Danny Boy & Prince David. Mary S. Cox. LC 81-50943. (Illus.). 56p. (Orig.). 1981. pap. 2.99 (ISBN 0-939726-00-9). Sunflowers KS.

Les Adieux: A Novel. Translated from the French by Richard Howard. Francois Regis Bastide. LC 58-750811. 1958. Simon and Schuster.

Les Belles Images. Simone De Beauvoir. LC 68-12095. 1968. Putnam.

Les Choses: A Story of the Sixties. Georges Perec. LC 67-30110. 1968. Grove Press.

Les Cinq Freres Chinois. Illustre Par Kurt Weise. Claire Huchet Bishop & Wiese, Kurt, 1887- Illus. LC 61-13397. 1961. Coward-McCann.

Les Guerilleres. Monique Wittig. LC 70-158421. 1971. 4.95 (ISBN 0-670-42463-3). Viking Press.

Les Liaisons Dangereuses. Pierre Ambroise Francois Choderlos De Laclos. LC 61-66311. (Penguin classics, L116). 1972. 1.95 (ISBN 0-14-044116-6). Penguin.

Les Liaisons Dangereuses. Translated and with an Introd. by P. W. K. Stone. Pierre Ambrose Francois Choderlos de Laclos. LC 61-663118. (Penguin classics, L116). 1961. Penguin Books.

Les Mesaventures De Jean-Paul Chappart. Louis Claude Joseph Florence Desnoyers. Ed. by Fontaine, Camille. LC 9-13028. (Heath's modern language series). 1909. D. C. Heath & Co.

Les Miserable. illustrated ed.... ed. Victor Marie Hugo. Tr. by Isabel Florence Hapgood. LC 4-23587. T. Y. Crowell & Co.

Les Miserables. Victor Marie Hugo. Tr. by Frederick Charles Lascelles Wraxall. Hurst & Company.

Les Miserables. library ed.... ed. Victor Marie Hugo. Tr. by Frederick Charles Lascelles Wraxall. LC 7-5875. 1887. Little, Brown, and Company.

Les Miserables. Victor Marie Hugo. LC 7-58743. 1887. G. Routledge and Sons The De Vinne Press.

Les Miserables. Victor Marie Hugo. Tr. by Isabel Florence Hapgood. LC 4-17557. T. Y. Crowell & Co.

Les Miserables. Victor Marie Hugo. LC 8-22802. 1907. Little, Brown, and Company.

Les Miserables... Victor Marie Hugo. Tr. by Frederick Charles Lascelles Wraxall. LC 21-20599. (Half-title: Handy library ed.). Little, Brown and Company.

Les Miserables. Victor Marie Hugo. LC 46-44332. T. Nelson and Sons.

Les Miserables. Victor Marie Hugo. LC 43-40892. (On cover: Library of select romances). Worthington Company.

Les Miserables. Victor Marie Hugo & Benichou, Paul, Ed. LC 64-56554. 1964. Washington Square Press.

Les Miserables. Victor Marie Hugo & Crawford, Douglas Gordon, Ed. LC 15-15099. (Macmillan's pocket American and English classics). 1915. The Macmillan Company.

Les Miserables. Victor Marie Hugo & Crawford, Douglas Gordon, Ed. LC 32-225655. (Half-title: New Pocket classics). The Macmillan Company.

Les Miserables. Victor Marie Hugo & Norman George Denny. LC 77-484808. (Illus.). 1976. 22.50 (ISBN 0-85067-106-X). Folio Press.

Les Miserables. Victor Marie Hugo & Holmes, Mabel Dodge, 1883- LC 46-707055. (Cebco classics for enjoyment). 1946. College Entrance Book Company.

Les Miserables. Victor Marie Hugo & Jeanniot, Pierre Georges, 1848- Illus. LC 26-26997. (Rittenhouse classics). 1926. G. W. Jacobs & Company.

Les Miserables. Victor Marie Hugo & Schaeffer, Mead, 1898- Illus. 1925. Dodd, Mead and Company.

Les Miserables. Victor Marie Hugo & Wilbour, Charles Edwin, 1833-1896, Tr. LC 32-17680. (Half-title: The modern library of the world's best books). 1931. The Modern Library.

Les Miserables... A Novel. Victor Marie Hugo & Wilbour, Charles Edwin, 1833-1896, Tr. 1862. Carleton.

Les Miserables. A Novel. complete and unabridged ed. "carleton's royal copyright ed."... ed. Victor Marie Hugo & Wilbour, Charles Edwin, 1833-1896, Tr. LC 7-5873. 1880. G. W. Carleton & Co.; Etc., Etc.

Les Miserables: A Novel. Victor Marie Hugo & Wilbour, Charles Edwin, 1833-1896, Tr. (Half-title: Everyman's library, ed. by Ernest Rhys, Fiction). 1909. J. M. Dent & Co.

Les Miserables. A Novel. Victor Marie Hugo & Wilbour, Charles Edwin, 1833-1896, Tr. LC 21-16934. (Lettered on cover: The home library). A. L. Burt Company.

Les Miserables. A Novel. Victor Marie Hugo & Wraxall, Sir Frederick Charles Lascelles, Bart., 1828-1865, Tr. LC 42-34679. The F. M. Lupton Publishing Company.

Les Miserables: Adapted by Alice Cecilia Cooper and Agnes Augusta Frisius. Victor Marie Hugo & Cooper, Alice Cecilia, 1895- LC 47-29687. 1947. Globe Book Co.

Les Miserables. Designed to Be Read As a Modern Novel. Victor Marie Hugo & Wilbour, Charles Edwin, 1833-1896, Tr. LC 47-27906. 1947. Halcyon House.

Les Miserables: Illustrated by Lyle Justis. Hugo, Victor Marie. LC 54-5073. 1954. International Collectors Library, American Headquarters.

Les Miserables. (The Wretched.) A Novel. Victor Marie Hugo & F., A., Ed. LC 7-5861. 1863-64. West & Johnston.

Les Miserables. Tr. by Charles E. Wilbour. Abridged, Ed., Introd. by Paul Benichou. Victor Marie Hugo. (Collateral Classic, CC703). 1966. Washington Sq.

Les Miserables. Translated from the French by Charles E. Wilbour. Abridged with an Introd. by James K. Robinson. Victor Marie Hugo. LC 61-2908. (Premier world classic, d119). 1961. Fawcett Publications.

Les Onze Mille Verges: Or, The Amorous Adventures of Prince Mony Vibescu. Guillaume Apollinaire. LC 76-365812. (Illus.). 1976. 4.75 (ISBN 0-7206-0174-6). Owen.

Lesbian Blow-Up. Winston Smith. pap. 1.25 o.p. (2051). Brandon.

Lesbian Body. Monique Wittig. LC 75-7738. 1975. 5.95 (ISBN 0-688-02900-0). Morrow.

Lesbian Career Woman. Toby Thompson. (Orig.). 1968. pap. 1.75 o.p. (3037). Brandon.

Lesbian Casebook: Women & Young Girls. Patty Benson. pap. 2.45 o.p. (4024). Cameo.

Lesbian Fiction: An Anthology. Elly Bulkin. LC 81-12194. 1981. 10.95 (ISBN 0-930436-11-3). Persephone Press.

Lesbian for the Making. Tony Trelos, pseud. (Orig.). pap. 1.25 o.p. (2052). Brandon.

Lesbian Happening. Tony Trelos, pseud. pap. 1.25 o.p. (2502). Brandon.

Lesbian Peoples. Wittig & Sande Zeig. 1979. pap. 5.95 (ISBN 0-380-46441-1, 46441). Avon.

Lesbian Possessed. William C. Spatari. 192p. pap. 1.95 o.p. (6113). Brandon.

Lesbian Roulette. Tony Trelos, pseud. (Orig.). 1969. pap. 1.75 o.p. (3057). Brandon.

Lesbian Web of Evil. Harry Gregory, pseud. (Orig.). 1969. pap. 1.25 o.p. (2093). Brandon.

Lesbian Wives. Lisa Robbins. 192p. pap. 1.95 o.p. (7102). Barclay Hse.

Lesbians Home Journal: Stories from the Ladder. Barbara Grier & Coletta Reid. LC 76-53825. (Illus.). 5.00 (ISBN 0-88447-013-X). Diana Press.

Lesbos Is for Lonnie. Arthur Adlon. LC 63-21016. 1963. Beacon-Signal Books.

Lesby. Elizabeth Powers Willis. LC 31-29194. 1931. C. Scribner's Sons.

Leschi of the Nisquallies. Della Florence Gould Emmons. LC 65-20096. 4.75. Denison.

Lesley Chilton. Eliza Orne White. LC 3-23045. 1903. Houghton, Mifflin and Company.

Leslie. Dorothy Taylor. (Leisure Book). 1.95 (ISBN 0-8439-0566-2). Nordo N Pub.

Leslie. J. D. Weston. 1978. pap. 1.95 o.s.i. (ISBN 0-8439-0566-2, Leisure Bks). Nordon Pubns.

Leslie Charteris Count on the Saint: The Pastor's Problem & the Unsaintly Santa. Leslie Charteris. LC 80-939. (Crime Club Ser.). 192p. 1980. 10.95 (ISBN 0-385-17191-9). Doubleday.

Leslie Charteris' Send for the Saint: The Midas Double & the Pawn Gambit. Leslie Charteris. LC 77-92210. 1978. 7.95 o.p. (ISBN 0-385-14138-6). Doubleday.

Leslie Charteris' Send for the Saint: Two Original Stories. Peter Bloxsom & Leslie Charteris. LC 77-92210. 1978. 7.95 (ISBN 0-385-14138-6). Published for the Crime Club by Doubleday.

Leslie Charteris' The Saint Abroad. Fleming Lee & Leslie Charteris. LC 69-15193. 1969. 4.50. Published for the Crime Club by Doubleday.

Leslie Charteris' The Saint and the Hapsburg Necklace. Leslie Charteris & Christopher Short. LC 75-14811. (His The Saint series). 1976. 5.95 (ISBN 0-385-11226-2). Published for the Crime Club by Doubleday.

Leslie Charteris' The Saint in Trouble: Two Original Stories. Graham Weaver & Leslie Charteris. LC 78-18551. (Saint series). 1978. 7.95 (ISBN 0-385-14612-4). Published for the Crime Club by Doubleday.

Less Deceived. Philip Larkin. 1955. 3.95 o.p. St Martin.

Less Fortunate Than Fair. Sandra Wilson. LC 77-4128. 1977. 9.95 (ISBN 0-89340-066-1). J. Curley & Associates.

Less Fortunate Than Fair: The Story of Cicely Plantagenet. Sandra Wilson. LC 74-81466. 1974. 6.95. St. Martin's Press.

Less Than Angels. Barbara Pym. LC 57-7682. 1957. Vanguard Press.

Less Than Angels. Barbara Pym. LC 80-69788. 1980. 10.95 (ISBN 0-525-14440-4). Dutton.

Less Than Kin. Alice Duer Miller. LC 9-14451. 1909. H. Holt and Company.

Less Than Kin: A Novel. Charles Caldwell Dobie. LC 26-161959. 1926. The John Day Company.

Less Than Kin: A Novel. Charles Caldwell Dobie. LC 35-4298. 1935. D. Appleton-Century Company, Incorporated.

Less Than Kind. Samuel Rogers. LC 28-24277. 1928. Payson & Clarke Limited.

Less Than the Angels. Roger Burke Dooley. LC 46-7726. 1946. The Bruce Publishing Company.

Less Than the Dust. M. A Hamilton. LC 12-244912. 1912. 1.25. Houghton Mifflin Company.

Lesser Antilles Case. Rufus King. LC 34-8140. 1934. Pub. for the Crime Club, Inc., by Doubleday, Doran & Company, Inc.

Lesser Bourgeoisie. Honore De Balzac. Tr. by Katharine Prescott Wormeley. LC 3-23182. (Half-title: The comedy of human life... Scenes from Parisian life). 1896. Roberts Brothers.

Lesser Breed. Mary Wiltshire. 1926. Dodd, Mead & Company.

Lesser Destinies: A Novel. Samuel Gordon. 1899. H. S. Stone & Company; Etc., Etc.

Lesser Light a Story. Emily Davant Embree. LC 4-8583. 1904. Baylor College.

Lesser Lion. Lane Kauffmann. LC 58-5845. 1958. J. Lippincott Company.

Lesser Lives. Diane Johnson. (O.s.i.). (Illus.). 1972. 7.95 o.s.i. (ISBN 0-394-48034-1). Knopf.

Lesser's Daughter. Cecily Ullmann Sidgwick. LC 8-7313. (Half-title: The incognito library, III). 1894. G. P. Putnam's Sons.

Lessing, Doris May. LC 64-22409. Simon and Schuster.

Lesson for Today. J. Harris Pritchard. LC 66-29821. (Illus.). 1966. A.J.L. Pub. Co.

Lesson in Love. Marie-Terese Baird. LC 73-8726. 1973. 5.95 (ISBN 0-395-17706-5). Houghton Mifflin.

Lesson in Love. Marie-Terese Baird. LC 73-21920. 1974. (lib. bdg.). 8.95 (ISBN 0-8161-6179-8). G. K. Hall.

Lesson in Love. Sidonie Gabrielle Colette & Benet, Rosemary (Carr) LC 32-4902. Farrar & Rinehart, Incorporated.

Lesson in Love. Maggie Gladstone, pseud. LC 81-47254. 192p. (Orig.). 1981. pap. 1.95 (ISBN 0-87216-907-3). Playboy Pbks.

Lesson in Love. Claudia Jameson. (Harlequin Romances Ser.). 192p. 1983. pap. 1.50 (ISBN 0-373-02523-8). Harlequin Bks.

Lesson in Love... Ellen Warner Olney Kirk. LC 7-12357. (On cover: Round-robin series. no. 2). 1881. J. R. Osgood and Company.

Lesson in Love. Ellen Warner Olney Kirk. LC 9-10494. Houghton Mifflin Company.

Lesson in Love. Emile Zola. LC 61-66096. 1961. Pyramid Books.

Lesson in Love: A Novel. Margaret Creal. LC 57-12398. 1957. Simon and Schuster.

Lesson in Loving. Mollie Chappell. (Cameo Romance). (Fawcett gold medal book). 1975. (pbk.) 0.95. Fawcett.

Lesson in Music: Short Stories. Marianne Hauser. LC 64-10318. 1964. University of Texas Press.

Lesson in Passion. William Arthur Neubauer. LC 47-219478. 1947. Phoenix Press.

Lesson of the Master. Henry James. Bd. with Death of the Lion; Next Time; Figure in the Carpet; Coxon Fund. LC 77-158794. (Novels & Tales of Henry James: Vol. 15). xvii, 367p. Repr. of 1909 ed. 22.50x (ISBN 0-678-02813-3). Kelley.

Lesson of the Master see Seven Short Novel Masterpieces.

Lesson of the Master & Other Stories. Henry James. 1909. 7.50 o.p. Scribner.

Lesson of the Master, The Marriages, The Pupil, Brooksmith, The Solution, Sir Edmund Orme. Henry James. LC 7-7442. 1892. Macmillan and Co.

Lessons, a Novel. Lee Zacharias. LC 81-2902. 1981. 12.95 (ISBN 0-395-30546-2). Houghton Mifflin.

Lessons for the Teacher. Warren Bisig. pap. 1.95 o.p. (ISBN 0-87977-156-9, DBB156). Dansk Blue Bk.

Lessons in Life: For All Who Will Read Them. Timothy Shay Arthur. 1851. Lippincott, Grambo & Co.

Lessons in Life: For All Who Will Read Them. Timothy Shay Arthur. LC 6-3406. (On cover: Lovell's library, v. 11, no. 579). J. W. Lovell Company.

Lessons in Love. Barbara Cartland. 1974. (pbk.) 0.95. Bantam Books.

Lessons in Love. Vida Hurst. LC 38-197871. M. S. Mill Co., Inc.

Lessons in Love. Kate Nichols Trask. LC 73-94745. (Short story index reprint series). (Illus.). 1969. (ISBN 0-8369-3125-4). Books for Libraries Press.

Lessons in Love. Kate Nichols Trask. LC 1-29899. 1900. Harper & Brothers.

Lessons in Love see Rape of the Statue.

Lessons in Paradise. William Harrison. 1973. 0.95. Pocket Books.

Lessons in Paradise. William Harrison. LC 74-135649. 1971. 5.95. Morrow.

Lessons in Seduction. Michel Millot. Tr. by Rudolf Schleifer. (Orig.). pap. 1.75 o.p. (3012). Brandon.

Lest Darkness Fall. Lyon Sprague De Camp. 1949. Prime Press.

Lest Darkness Fall: With Decorations. Lyon Sprague De Camp. LC 41-2806. H. Holt and Company.

Lest We Forget;" A Romance of a Fateful Period. Joseph Hocking. LC 6648. 1900. Advance Publishing Company.

Lest Ye Die: A Story from the Past or of the Future. Cicely Mary Hamilton. LC 28-20419. 1928. C. Scribner's Sons.

Lester Affair. Andrew Garve. LC 73-14313. (Novel of Suspense Ser.). 158p. 1974. 7.95 o.p. (ISBN 0-06-011456-8, HarpT). Har-Row.

Lester Affair. Paul Winterton. LC 73-14313. 1974. 5.95 (ISBN 0-06-011456-8). Harper & Row.

Lester's Secret: A Novel. Mary Cecil Hay. (Harper's handy series, no. 49). 1886. Harper & Brothers.

Let a Lady Confess: By Ernest Frederick Chester. Ernest Frederick Chester. LC 32-12762. 1932. L. MacVeagh, Dial Press, Inc.

Let Courage Increase. Anne Stewart. LC 38-775. Gramercy Publishing Co.

Let Dead Enough Alone: A Captain Heimrich Mystery, by Richard and Frances Lockridge. 1st Ed. Richard Lockridge & Frances Louise Davis Lockridge. LC 55-12264. (Main line mysteries). 1956. Lippincott.

Let Down Your Hair. Ross Sloane. LC 34-28772. 1934. W. Godwin, Inc.

Let 'em Roll: Written and Illustrated by Charles Michael Daugherty. Charles Michael Daugherty. LC 50-7041. 1950. Viking Press.

Let Freedom Cringe: A Novel. Daniel Aloysius Lord. LC 37-24118. The Queen's Work.

Let Freedom Ring. Edna R. Webster. 1978. 8.95; pap. 5.00. Wilmar Pubs.

Let Freedom Ring! A Novel of These Turbulent Times. Harold Morrow Sherman. LC 32-32270. N. H. White, Jr., Inc.

Let George Do It! By John Foster Pseud. Foster Furcolo. LC 57-10068. 1957. Harcourt, Brace.

Let Go of Yesterday. Howard Breslin. LC 50-7178. 1950. Whittlesey House.

Let Him Die: A Novel. Eileen Helen Clements. LC 40-135504. 1940. E. P. Dutton & Co., Inc.

Let It All Bleed Out. Alfred Hitchcock. 1980. pap. 1.95 (ISBN 0-440-14755-7). Dell.

Let It All Bleed Out. Ed. by Alfred Joseph Hitchcock. (Dell book). 1973. (pbk) 0.75. Dell Publishing Co.

Let It All Hang Out! Curtis Dean. 160p. 1974. pap. 1.95 o.p. (ISBN 0-87682-404-1, 7404). Barclay Hse.

Let It Burn: A Novel. Enoch Anson More. (On cover: Idle moments series. no. 20). 1892. The Price-McGill Comapny.

Let It Come Down. Paul Frederic Bowles. LC 52-5141. 1952. Random House.

Let It Come Down. Paul Frederic Bowles. LC 80-24825. 1980. 14.00 (ISBN 0-87685-480-3) (ISBN 0-87685-481-1) (ISBN 0-87685-479-X). Black Sparrow Press.

Let It Lie. Sidney Floyd Gowing. LC 29-6790. 1929. G. P. Putnam's Sons.

Let Love Alone: By Kathleen Harris Pseud. Adelaide Humphries. LC 51-10906. 1951. Arcadia House.

Let Love Come Last. Taylor Caldwell. LC 75-707. 1975. (ISBN 0-88411-160-1). Onian Press.

Let Love Come Last. Taylor Caldwell. LC 49-9993. 1949. C. Scribner's Sons.

Let Me Alone. Anna Kavan. 320p. 1930. 14.95 (ISBN 0-7206-0243-2). Kesend Pub Ltd.

Let Me Assure You. Edward Vick. 178p. pap. 2.75 o.p. (12135-0). Pacific Pr Pub Assn.

Let Me Be Awake. Stuart Mitchner. LC 59-11383. 1959. Crowell.

Let Me Breathe Thunder. William Attaway. LC 70-96382. 1969. Chatham Bookseller.

Let Me Breathe Thunder. William Attaway. LC 39-17641. 1939. Doubleday, Doran & Company, Inc.

Let Me Count the Ways. Peter De Vries. LC 65-18130. bds., 5.00. Little.

Let Me Die Tuesday. Helen Topping Miller. LC 37-2948. 1937. D. Appleton-Century Company, Incorporated.

Let Me Do the Talking. Richard Mealand. LC 47-30482. 1947. Doubleday.

Let Me Go. Mabel Dana Lyon. LC 37-9931. 1937. Hillman Curl, Inc.

Let Me Go. Flora Sandstrom. LC 33-971. 1933. H. C. Kinsey & Company, Inc.

Let Me Have Wings. Margaret Widdemer. LC 41-13508. Farrar & Rinehart, Inc.

Let Me Kill You Sweetheart! Kirby Carr. (Hitman no. 2). 1974. (pbk.) 1.50. Canyon Books.

Let My Name Stand Fair. Shirley Seifert. 1976. Repr. of 1956 ed. lib. bdg. 8.95 (ISBN 0-89190-134-5). Am Repr-Rivercity Pr.

Let My Name Stand Fair. 1st Ed. Shirley Seifert. LC 56-8190. 1956. Lippincott.

Let No Man Write My Epitaph. Willard Motley. LC 58-7667. 1958. Random House.

Let Noon Be Fair. Willard Motley. (Laurel leaf lib., 4740). 1967. Dell.

Let Noon Be Fair: A Novel. Willard Motley. LC 65-20682. 5.95. Putnam.

Let Not Man Put Asunder: A Novel. Basil King. LC 1-24658. 1901. Harper & Brothers.

Let Not Man Put Asunder: A Novel. Basil King. LC 7-4739. 1902. Harper & Brothers.

Let Nothing You Dismay. Walter Besant. (On cover: Lowell's library, no. 103). 1883. J. W. Lowell Company.

Let Sleeping Dogs Die. Tim Heald. LC 77-357614. 1976. 3.50 (ISBN 0-09-126960-1). Hutchinson.

Let Sleeping Dogs Lie. Tim Heald. LC 76-6894. 1976. 6.95. Stein and Day.

Let Sleeping Girls Lie: By James Mayo Pseud. Stephen Coulter. LC 66-11235. 1966. bds., 3.95. Morrow.

Let the Band Play Dixie: And Other Stories. Roark Bradford. LC 70-128721. (Short story index reprint series). 1970. (ISBN 0-8369-3612-4). Books for Libraries Press.

Let the Band Play Dixie, & Other Stories. facs. ed. Roark Bradford. LC 70-128721. (Short Story Index Reprint Ser). 1934. 17.00 (ISBN 0-8369-3612-4). Ayer Co.

Let the Bank Play Dixie: And Other Stories. Roark Bradford. LC 34-31075. 1934. Harper & Brothers.

Let the Bastards Freeze in the Dark: A Novel. Diane Simmons. LC 80-15033. 11.95 (ISBN 0-671-61004-X). Wyndham Books.

Let the Chips Fall. Lew Lauria. LC 47-258. 1946. Radco Publishers.

Let the Day Perish. Saul K Padover. LC 32-8309. 1932. J. Cape & R. Ballou.

Let the Dead Past. John S. Strange. 1971. pap. 0.75 o.p. (07148). Curtis.

Let the Dead Past: By John Stephen Strange Pseud. 1st Ed. Dorothy Stockbridge Tillet. LC 53-5278. 1953. Published for the Crime Club by Doubleday.

Let the Earth Speak. Ann Schiear Steward. LC 40-335991. 1940. The Macmillan Company.

Let the Fire Fall. Kate Wilhelm. LC 69-12214. (Doubleday science fiction). 1969. 4.95. Doubleday.

Let the Guns Roar! Charles N Heckelmann. LC 50-9036. (Double D western). 1950. Doubleday.

Let the Hurricane Roar. Rose Wilder Lane. (Keith Jennison large type ed.). 1966. 6.95. Watts.

Let the Hurricane Roar. Rose Wilder Lane. LC 33-27029. 1933. Longmans, Green and Co.

Let the King Beware! Honore McCue Willsie Morrow. LC 36-27270. 1936. W. Morrow and Company.

Let the Lion Eat Straw. Ellease Southerland. LC 78-21021. 7.95 (ISBN 0-684-16070-6). Scribner.

Let the Lion Eat Straw. Ellease Southerland. LC 79-22100. 1979. 10.95. G. K. Hall.

Let the Music Play: A Novel. Ryan Abe. LC 75-9414. Farris Press.

Let the Night Cry. Charles Wells. LC 53-6815. 1953. Abelard Press.

Let the People Sing; a Novel. John Boynton Priestley. LC 40-27052. 1940. Harper & Brothers.

Let the Roof Fall in. Julia Davis Frankau. LC 10-23939. 1910. 1.50. D. Appleton and Company.

Let the Skeletons Rattle. Frederick Clyde Davis. LC 44-2191. 1944. Pub. for the Crime Club by Doubleday, Doran and Company, Inc.

Let the Spring Come. Henry Schindall. LC 53-5115. 1953. Appleton-Century-Crofts.

Let the Tide Run. Kathryn Ragan. LC 42-9795. 1942. Dorrance and Company.

Let the Tiger Die. 1st Ed. Manning Coles, pseud. LC 47-11520. 1947. Pub. for the Crime Club by Doubleday.

Let Them Prey. Henry Gibbs. LC 43-18434. 1942. Pub. for the Crime Book Society by Rich & Cowan.

Let There Be Reign. Johnny Hart & Brant Parker. (Wizard of Id Ser.). (Illus.). 1978. pap. 1.75 (ISBN 0-449-13892-5, GM). Fawcett.

Let Tomorrow Come. A. J. Barr. LC 29-8008. W. W. Norton & Company, Inc.

Let Us Be Faithful. Allene Soule Corliss. LC 34-824701. Farrar & Rinehart, Incorporated.

Let Us Consider One Another. Josephine Lawrence. LC 45-350837. 1945. D. Appleton-Century Company Incorporated.

Let Us Find Heroes. Gregory Solon. LC 58-5279. 1958. Random House.

Let Us Follow Him. Henryk Sienkiewicz. Tr. by Jeremiah Curtin. LC 8-6885. 1897. Little, Brown and Company.

Let Us Follow Him: And Other Stories. Henryk Sienkiewicz & Hlaska, Vatslaf A., Tr. LC 13-12910. R. F. Fenno & Company.

Let Us Follow Him, and Other Stories. Henryk Sienkiewicz & Slupski, Sigmund C., Tr. LC 98-1670. H. Altemus.

Let Us Go: The Narrative of Kamehameha II, King of the Hawaiian Islands, 1819-1824. Walter F Judd. LC 76-14386. (Illus.). 1976. 10.00 (ISBN 0-914916-16-5). Topgallant Pub. Co.

Let Us Not Forget. Ed. by Dana Corum & Jean Glover. Orig. Title: Unwanted. (Illus.). 126p. (Orig.). 1974. pap. 1.25 o.p. (ISBN 0-515-03262-X, V3262). BJ Pub Group.

Let Us Now Praise Famous Men. James Agee & Walker Evans. 1974. pap. 1.95 (ISBN 0-345-23765-X). Ballantine.

Let Us Prey: A Sister Mary Teresa Mystery. Ralph M McInerny. LC 81-23072. 9.95 (ISBN 0-8149-0861-6). Vanguard Press.

Let Us Prey: A Sister Mary Teresa Mystery. Monica Quill. LC 81-23072. 256p. 1982. 9.95 (ISBN 0-8149-0861-6). Vanguard.

Let Us Reason Together. Thomas A. Morrill. 2.00 o.p. Duquesne.

Let Winter Go. Isabel Wilder. LC 37-19462. 1937. Coward-McCann, Inc.

Let X Be Excitement. Christie Harris. LC 69-13522. (Illus.). 1969. 4.95. Atheneum.

Let X Equal Marjorie. Edward Hope Coffey. LC 38-8832. 1938. Macrae-Smith Company.

Let Your Heart Answer. William Edward Daniel Ross. 1969. pap. 0.60 o.p. (73-857). Lancer.

L'Ete Commence a Peine. Margaret Mayo. (Collection Harlequin Ser.). 192p. 1983. pap. 1.95 (ISBN 0-373-49333-9). Harlequin Bks.

Lethal Gas. Ron Kurz. LC 73-91885. 1974. 6.95 (ISBN 0-87131-147-X). M. Evans.

Lethal Lady. Rufus King. LC 47-11842. 1947. Pub. for the Crime Club by Doubleday.

Lethal Sex: The 1959 Anthology, Edited, with an Introd., by John D. MacDonald. Mystery Writers of America. Ed. by John Dann MacDonald. LC 60-2516. (Dell first edition, B141). 1959. Dell Pub. Co.

Lethe. A Novel. Jesse Charles Fremont Grumbine. LC 7-1564. 1883. Knight & Co. Steam Printing Works.

Letitia. Lorinda Hagen. (Belmont Tower Book). 1.95 (ISBN 0-505-51242-4). Tower Publications.

Letitia: A Thrilling Novel of Western Life. Charles Albert Macfarlane. LC 8-34222. 1908. The C. M. Clark Publishing Company.

Letitia Berkeley, A. M.; la Novel: By Josephine Bontecou Steffens. Josephine Bontecou Steffens. F. A. Stokes Company.

Letitia: Nursery Corps, U. S. A. George Madden Martin. LC 7-37709. 1907. The McClure Company.

Letitia: Unfulfilled Desire. Joseph Henry Amrein. LC 55-11772. 1955. Pageant Press.

L'etranger. Albert Camus. Ed. by G. Bree & C. Lynes. 1955. pap. 10.95 (ISBN 0-13-530790-2). P-H.

L'Etranger. Albert Camus. 1963. 5.95 o.p. Pantheon.

Let's All Make Mother. Clarke Hammond. pap. 1.95 o.p. (ISBN 0-87056-211-8, 6211). Brandon.

Let's Be Modern: Or, "What About the Social Experiment of Drinking"? Kathryn Richardson. LC 36-244035. 1936. The Torch Press.
Let's Burn Our Bridges. Mary Frances Doner. LC 35-258. 1935. A. H. King.
Let's Buy a Farm. Lewis Graham. LC 33-287286. The Macaulay Company.
Let's Call It Love. Sabra Lee Corbin, pseud. LC 38-6013. 1938. Hillman-Curl, Inc.
Let's Call It Love. Sabra Lee Corbin. LC 38-6013. 1938. Hillman-Curl, Inc.
Let's Call It Love. Vivien Grey. LC 48-100872. 1948. Arcadia House.
Let's Choose Executors. Sara Woods, pseud. LC 67-13706. 1967. Harper & Row.
Let's Eat. Gyo Fujikawa. 1975. 3.50 (ISBN 0-448-11922-6, 0-448-11922). Putnam Pub Group.
Let's Face It. Marshall B. Goding. 3.00 o.p. Carlton.
Let's Face It. Aaron E. Pierce. 3.95 o.p. Carlton.
Let's Face It! Wendell K. Wheelock. 5.95 o.p. Vantage.
Let's Fall in Love. Carol Hill. LC 73-17135. (Illus.). 1974. 5.95 (ISBN 0-394-48926-8). Random House.
Let's Go! Leander T De Celles. LC 28-27592. Stone & Burr Company.
Let's Go. E. J. Rath. LC 30-11282. 1930. G. H. Watt.
Let's Go for Broke. Mary Lasswell. LC 62-7254. (Illus.). 1962. Houghton Mifflin.
Let's Go Play at the Adams' Mendal W Johnson. LC 73-18000. 1974. 6.95 (ISBN 0-690-00193-2). Crowell.
Let's Go Play at the Adams' Mendal W Johnson. 1975. (pbk.) 1.50. Bantam Books.
Let's Go to a Football Game. Robert Hood. LC 74-21065. (Let's go series). (Illus.). 1975. 3.86. G. P. Putnam.
Let's Go, Yank! Robert McGregor. LC 32-22980. 1932. Meador Publishing Company.
Let's Have a Baby. Howard Buck. LC 34-37835. The Macaulay Company.
Let's Have Church, Children, No. 2. Ernest Quinley & Rachel Quinley. 1981. pap. 7.95 (ISBN 0-87148-513-3). Pathway Pr.
Let's Hear It for Prendergast: A Novel. Barry Oakley. LC 72-175574. 1970. 4.25 (ISBN 0-85561-026-3). Heinemann.
Let's Hear It for the Deaf Man. Ed McBain. LC 72-77000. 256p. 1973. 5.95 o.p. (ISBN 0-385-01600-X). Doubleday.
Let's Hear It for the Deaf Man: An 87th Precinct Mystery. Evan Hunter. LC 72-77000. (Illus.). 1973. 5.95 (ISBN 0-385-01600-X). Doubleday.
Let's Hear It for the Deaf Man: An 87th Precinct Mystery. Ed McBain. (Signet O 5794). 1974. (pbk.) 0.95. New American Library.
Let's Kill George. Lucy Michaella Cores. LC 46-4720. 1946. Duell, Sloan and Pearce.
Let's Kill Uncle. Rohan O'Grady, pseud. 1963. 3.95 o.p. Macmillan.
Let's Kill Uncle. by rohan o'grady (pseud. ed. June O'Grady Skinner. LC 63-17513. 1963. Macmillan.
Let's Kill Uncle Lionel. John Creasey. LC 75-37168. (Superintendent Folly mysteries). 1976. 6.95 (ISBN 0-679-50589-X). D. McKay Co.
Let's Laugh at Love. Davis Dresser. LC 37-235311. 1937. Hillman-Curl, Inc.
Let's Not Cry Until Tomorrow. Alice B. Whitman. 96p. 1972. 4.00 o.p. (ISBN 0-682-47487-8). Exposition.
Let's Play at Love. Robert N Webb. LC 35-5308. 1935. Arcadia House.
Let's Play Make Believe. Paul Ricchiuti. 1975. pap. 1.65 o.p. (ISBN 0-8163-0187-5, 12150-9). Pacific Pr Pub Assn.
Let's Pretend. Watkins Eppes Wright. LC 42-7975. 1942. Arcadia House, Inc.
Let's Read About Birds. Kay Ware & Sutherland, Lucille, Joint Author. (Webster classroom science library). Webster Pub. Co.
Let's Read About Flowers. Kay Ware & Sutherland, Lucille, Joint Author. (Webster classroom science library). Webster Pub. Co.
Let's Read About Insects. Kay Ware & Sutherland, Lucille, Joint Author. (Webster classroom science library). Webster Pub. Co.
Let's Read About Prehistoric Animals. Kay Ware & Sutherland, Lucille, Joint Author. (Webster classroom science library). Webster Pub. Co.
Let's Read About Reptiles and Amphibians. Kay Ware & Sutherland, Lucille, Joint Author. (Webster classroom science library). Webster Pub. Co.
Let's Read About Rocks and Minerals. Kay Ware & Sutherland, Lucille, Joint Author. (Webster classroom science library). Webster Pub. Co.
Let's Sit in the Sun: By Carol Holliston Pseud. James Noble Gifford. LC 55-102024. 1955. Arcadia House.
Let's Stay Married. Basil Boothroyd. LC 68-19937. (O.S.I.). (Illus.). 1968. 4.95 o.s.i. (ISBN 0-671-41515-8). S&S.
Letter. Isaak Emmanuilovich Babel. Ed. by Isaac Goldberg. Tr. by Babette Deutsch. (International Pocket Library). pap. 3.00. Branden.
Letter.". Mary Grace Halpine. LC 7-1204. (On cover: Munro's library. v. 1. no. 402). N. L. Munro.
Letter and the Spirit. Cora Maynard. LC 98-913. 1898. Stokes.
Letter D. Grace Denio Litchfield. LC 4-25682. 1904. Dodd, Mead and Company.
Letter for Tomorrow. Rosemary Ross Skinner. LC 63-15773. 1963. Dutton.
Letter from an Unknown Woman. Stefan Zweig & Paul, Eden, 1865- Tr. LC 32-17518. 1932. The Viking Press.
Letter from Annette: By Jeanne Bowman Pseud. Peggy O'More, pseud. LC 54-990117. 1954. Arcadia House.
Letter from Kiev. Hugh McDonald. 1977. pap. 1.75 o.p. (ISBN 0-515-03984-5). BJ Pub Group.
Letter from Peking. rev. ed. Pearl Sydenstricker Buck. (John Day Bk.). 1957. 7.95 o.p. (ISBN 0-381-98039-1, A42660, TYC-T). T Y Crowell.
Letter from Peking: A Novel. Pearl Sydenstricker Buck. LC 57-9389. 1957. J. Day Co.
Letter of Credit. Susan Warner. LC 8-33794. 1882. R. Carter and Brothers.
Letter of Intent. Ursula Reilly Curtiss. LC 70-145394. 1973. 0.95 (ISBN 0-671-77607-X). Pocket Books.
Letter of the Contract. Basil King. LC 14-142327. 1914. 1.00. Harper & Brothers.
Letter of the Law. Katherine A. Davis Roome. LC 79-4784. 8.95 (ISBN 0-394-50623-5). Random House.
Letter to a Child. Karen McKinley. LC 51-1858. 1951. Holt.
Letter to a Child Never Born. Oriana Fallaci. LC 76-45205. 6.95 (ISBN 0-671-22374-7). Simon and Schuster.
Letter to a Child Never Born. Oriana Fallaci. LC 77-472450. 1976. 2.25. Arlington Books.
Letter to a Stranger. Elswyth Thane. LC 74-4542. 1974. 6.95. Aeonian Press.
Letter to a Stranger. 1st Ed. Elswyth Thane. LC 54-11130. 1954. Duell, Sloan and Pearce.
Letter to a Younger Son. Christopher Leach. 1982. pap. 2.25 (ISBN 0-451-11920-7, AE1920, Sig). NAL.
Letter to an Unknown Woman. Sheila Ascher & Dennis Straus. (Story Ser.: No. 6). (Illus.). 48p. 1979. signed 8.00 (ISBN 0-914232-21-5); pap. 2.50 (ISBN 0-914232-20-7). McPherson & Co.
Letter to Elizabeth. 1st Ed. Bettina Linn. LC 57-6833. 1957. Lippincott.
Letter to Engelhardt see What Then Must We Do?.
Letter to Five Wives. John Klempner. LC 46-155476. 1946. C. Scribner's Sons.
Letter to Philemon: A Novel of a Man's Search for Faith, by Winthrop and Frances Neilson. Frances Fullerton Neilson. LC 62-10368. 1962. T. Nelson.
Letters: A Novel. John Barth. LC 79-13503. 8.95 (ISBN 0-399-12425-X). Putnam.
Letters from a Self-Made Merchant to His Son. George Horace Lorimer. LC 73-129971. (Illus.). 1970. 5.95. Outerbridge & Dienstfrey; Distributed by Dutton.
Letters from a Self-Made Merchant to His Son... George Horace Lorimer. LC 2-23991. 1902. Small, Maynard & Company.
Letters from a Self-Made Merchant to His Son... George Horace Lorimer. LC 38-177. 1903. Small, Maynard & Company.
Letters from a Self-Made Merchant to His Son see Letters from a Self-Made Pork Merchant to His Son.
Letters from a Self-Made Merchant to His Son see Letters from a Self-Made Pork Merchant.
Letters from a Self-Made Pork Merchant. George Horace Lorimer. Orig. Title: Letters from a Self-Made Merchant to His Son. 1970. Repr. of 1901 ed. 5.95 o.p. (ISBN 0-87690-022-8, Golden Pr). Western Pub.
Letters from a Self-Made Pork Merchant to His Son. George Horace Lorimer. Orig. Title: Letters from a Self-Made Merchant to His Son. 1970. Repr. 5.95 o.p. (ISBN 0-87690-022-8). Dial.
Letters from a Traveler. pap. 2.45 o.p. (TB 385, Torch). Har-Row.
Letters from Alf. Gladden Schrock. LC 73-6311. 1973. 6.95 (ISBN 0-06-127774-6). Harper's Magazine Press.
Letters from an Oregon Ranch. Louise G. Stephens. LC 5-16887. 1905. A. C. McClurg & Co.
Letters from G.G.... Grace Hall. LC 9-27269. 1909. H. Holt and Company.
Letters from Hell. Valdemar Adolph Thisted. 1885. Funk & Wagnalls.
Letters from Hell. Valdemar Adolph Thisted & Kollmyer, A. C., Tr. LC 8-27052. 1889. Hunter, Robinson & Co.
Letters from Hell. Valdemar Adolph Thisted & S., L. W. J., Tr. LC 28-165999. 1900. Funk & Wagnalls Company.
Letters from My Mill. Alphonse Daudet. LC 66-20235. (Illus.). 1967. Taplinger Pub. Co.
Letters from My Mill. tr. by frank hunter potter, with illustrations by madame madeleine lemaire, and decorative headpieces by george wharton edwards. ed. Alphonse Daudet. Tr. by Potter, Frank Hunter. 1893. Dodd, Mead and Company.
Letters from My Mill: & Letters to an Absent One. Alphonse Daudet. LC 72-37266. (Short story index reprint series). (Illus.). 1971. (ISBN 0-8369-4077-6). Books for Libraries Press.
Letters from My Mill & Letters to an Absent One. facsimile ed. Alphonse Daudet. LC 72-37266. (Short Story Index Reprint Ser.). Repr. of 1900 ed. 16.00 (ISBN 0-8369-4077-6). Ayer Co.
Letters from My Mill: To Which Are Added Letters to an Absent One Etc. Alphonse Daudet. Tr. by Wormeley, Katharine Prescott. LC 4-215493. 1900. Little, Brown, and Company.
Letters from My Windmill. Alphonse Daudet. LC 79-348878. (Penguin classics). (Illus.). 1978. 2.50 (ISBN 0-14-044334-7). Penguin.
Letters from the Early Church. Roger Bradshaigh Lloyd. LC 60-9266. 1960. Macmillan.
Letters from the Earth. Mark Twain. Ed. by Bernard DeVoto. 1973. pap. 0.95 o.p. (M1447, Crest). Fawcett World.
Letters from the Living to the Living, Vol. 7. LC 78-170511. (Novel in England, 1700-1775). lib. bdg. 50.00 (ISBN 0-8240-0519-8). Garland Pub.
Letters from the Living to the Living. Anonymous. Malcolm J. Bosse. LC 78-170511. (Foundations of the Novel.). 1973. 22.00 ea. (ISBN 0-8240-0519-8). Garland.
Letters Home. William Dean Howells. LC 3-22817. 1903. Harper & Brothers.
Letters of a Country Vicar: Tr. from the French of Yves Le Querdec Pseud. George Fonsegrive & Holmes, Mara Gorden, Tr. LC 1-13913. 1896. Dodd, Mead and Company.
Letters of a Dakota Divorcee. Jane Burr. LC 9-29507. The Roxburgh Publishing Co., Incorporated.
Letters of a Japanese Schoolboy. Wallace Irwin. LC 77-96889. (Illus.). 1969. Literature House.
Letters of an American Countess to Her Friend: By the Countess Herself... Helen Burrell D'Apery. LC 4-1648. J. S. Ogilvie Publishing Company.
Letters of an Expectant Grandmother. Boy of My Heart, Author of. LC 19-218667. Hodder and Stoughton.
Letters of an Unknown Lover. Ronald De Levington Kirkbride. LC 30-34412. R. G. Badger.
Letters of Her Mother to Elizabeth. William Rutherford Hayes Trowbridge. LC 1-8308. 1901. J. Lane.
Letters of Insurgents. Sophia Nachalo & Yarostan Vochek. LC 77-370303. 1976. Black & Red.
Letters of Jennie Allen to Her Friend Miss Musgrove. Grace Donworth. LC 8-30936. 1908. Small, Maynard and Company.
Letters of Lucius M. Piso Pseud. from Palmyra: To His Friend Marcus Curtius, at Rome. Now First Translated and Published... William Ware. LC 8-37769. 1837. C. S. Francis.
Letters of Madam De Remusat. 1804-1814. Edited, with Preface and Notes. Claire Elisabeth Jeanne Gravier De Vergennes Remusat & Remusat, Paul Louis Etienne De, 1831-1897, Ed. LC 27-13677. (Seaside library. v. 51, no. 1042). 1881. G. Munro.
Letters of Marque. Albert Payson Terhune. LC 34-7416. 1934. Harper & Brothers.
Letters of Mildred's Mother to Mildred. Satirical Sketches of Stage Life. Edward D Price. LC 1-27717. J. S. Ogilvie Publishing Company.
Letters of One; Study in Limitations. Charles Hare Plunkett. LC 7-12641. 1907. G. P. Putnam's Sons.
Letters of the Motor Girl. Ethellyn Gardner. The New England News Co.
Letters of Theodore. Adelaide Louise Rouse. LC 5-6484. 1905. The Macmillan Company.
Letters of Two; or, The True History of a Late Love Affair. James Hampton Lee. LC 1-24952. The Abbey Press.
Letters of William Green. James William Foley. LC 14-174848. 1914. 1.00. McBride, Nast & Co.
Letters of Women. authorized ed. Marcel Prevost. Tr. by Hornblow, Arthur. LC 7-30109. 1897. Meyer Brothers & Co.
Letters on an Elk Hunt by a Woman Homesteader. Elinore P. Stewart. LC 79-13840. (Illus.). xviii, 162p. 1979. 13.95x (ISBN 0-8032-4112-7); pap. 4.50 (ISBN 0-8032-9112-4, BB 703, Bison). U of Nebr Pr.
Letters to a Djinn. Grace Zaring Stone. LC 22-18088. 1922. The Century Co.
Letters to Marion. Elsie Wheeler Rupp. LC 39-5146. B. Humphries, Inc.
Letters to My Husband's Analyst. Barbara Kerr Davis. LC 78-65408. 10.95 (ISBN 0-8015-4518-8). Hawthorn Books.
Letters to My Son. Winifred Lewellin James. LC 10-14146. 1910. Houghton Mifflin Company.
Letters to Nanette. Bob Biderman. LC 82-5180. (Contemporary Literature Series). 11.95 (ISBN 0-915786-07-9) (ISBN 0-915786-08-7). Early Stages Press.
Letters to Pauline. Ippy Gizzi. (Illus.). 1975. pap. 3.00 (ISBN 0-930900-40-5). Burning Deck.
Letters to Sanchia Upon Things As They Are, Extracted from the Correspondence of Mr. John Maxwell Senhouse. Maurice Henry Hewlett. LC 10-11142. 1910. C. Scribner's Sons.
Letters Written by a Peruvian Princesse. Francoise D'Issembourg D'Happoncourt De Graffigny. LC 74-16070. (Flowering of the Novel). 1974. (ISBN 0-8240-1121-X). Garland Pub.
Lettie: Or, The Whirlwind's Reaper. Addie Lettie Peck Miller. LC 17-390. 1916. The Author.
Letting Go. Robin K Glazer. (Illus.). 320p. 1983. 17.95 (ISBN 0-8065-0833-7); pap. 9.95 (ISBN 0-8065-0844-2). Citadel Pr.
Letting Go. Philip Roth. LC 62-8472. 1962. Random House.
Letting Go. Philip Roth. LC 82-70091. 1982. 9.95 (ISBN 0-374-51701-0). Farrar, Straus, Giroux.
Letting Love in. James Scroggs. LC 77-27268. 1978. 11.95 o.p. (ISBN 0-13-531566-2, Spec); pap. 4.95 (ISBN 0-13-531558-1, Spec). P-H.
Lettres De Mon Moulin. Alphonse Daudet. Ed. by H. C. Bradby & E. V. Rieu. 1921. 1.75x o.p. (ISBN 0-19-832327-1). Oxford U Pr.
Lettres De Mon Moulin. Alphonse Daudet. Ed. by G. H. Clarke. (Fr). 1909. 1.95x o.p. St Martin.
Lettres Persanes. Charles-Louis De Montesquieu. Ed. by Verniere. 1956. pap. 6.95 o.p. French & Eur.
Letty. Clare Darcy. LC 79-92333. 1980. 12.95 (ISBN 0-8027-0656-8). Walker.
Letty. Norah Robinson Lofts. Orig. Title: Calf for Venus. 1968. pap. 0.95 o.p. (N2790). Pyramid Pubns.
Letty. Norah Robinson Lofts. Orig. Title: Calf for Venus. 1972. pap. 0.95 o.p. (ISBN 0-515-02790-1). Pyramid Pubns.
Letty. Norah Robinson Lofts. 1976. pap. 1.75 o.p. (ISBN 0-515-03923-3). BJ Pub Group.
Letty & the Law. Faith Baldwin. 1976. Repr. of 1940 ed. lib. bdg. 14.40x (ISBN 0-88411-610-7). Amereon Ltd.
Letty and the Law. Faith Cutherell Baldwin, pseud. 1974. (pbk.) 0.95. Warner Paperback Library.
Letty and the Law. Faith Baldwin Cuthrell. LC 74-82150. 1974. Aeonian Press.
Letty and the Law. Faith Baldwin Cuthrell. LC 40-12356. Farrar & Rinehart, Inc.
Letty Fox, Her Luck. Christina Stead. LC 46-7309. 1946. Harcourt, Brace and Company.
Letty Fox, Her Luck. Christina Stead. LC 78-23871. (Harvest/HBJ book). 1979. 5.95 (ISBN 0-15-650885-0). Harcourt, Brace, Jovanovich.
Letty Leigh. Charlotte Mary Brame. (On cover: Lovell's library. no. 1033). J. W. Lovell Company.
Letty Leigh. Bertha M. Clay. LC 45-47543. (On cover: Lovell's library, no. 1033). J. W. Lovell Company.
Letty Lynton. Marie Adelaide Belloc Lowndes. LC 31-1515. J. Cape & H. Smith.
Letzte Buddenbrook. Thomas Mann. Ed. by Thomas A. Riley. 1965. pap. text ed. 3.50x o.p. (ISBN 0-669-29587-6). Heath.
LEugenia. Clare Darcy. (Signet Book). 1978. 1.75 (ISBN 0-451-08081-5). New American Library.
Leukas Man. Hammond Innes. 1979. 1.95 (ISBN 0-345-27410-5). Ballantine Books.
Leuv-We of Kalmogoor (Light-of-the-Storm) A Romance of the North Australian Bush. Arthur Livingstone Brewer. LC 46-8186. 1946. A. L. Brewer.
L'evangeliste. A Parisian Novel. Alphonse Daudet. Tr. by Sherwood, Mary Neal. LC 6-33049. T. B. Peterson & Brothers.
Levant Trilogy. Olivia Manning. 576p. 1983. pap. 7.95 (ISBN 0-14-005962-8). Penguin.
Levanter. Eric Ambler. LC 72-10229. 1972. 9.95 (ISBN 0-8161-6058-9). G. K. Hall.
Levanter. Eric Ambler. 1973. 1.50. Bantam.
Levanter. Eric Ambler. LC 72-76902. 1972. 6.95. Atheneum.
Levean of Malice. William Robertson Davies. LC 54-44727. 1954. Clarke, Irwin.
Level Crossing. Phyllis Bottome. LC 36-29600. 1936. Frederick A. Stokes Company.
Level Five. Hart-Davis, Duff. LC 81-69145. 1982. 12.95 (ISBN 0-689-11257-2). Atheneum.
Level 7. 1st Ed. Mordechal Roschwald. LC 60-8115. McGraw-Hill.

Leveller. Alexander McArthur. LC 8-21918. C. H. Doscher & Co.
Levelling Wind. Margaret Benaya. LC 58-6096. 1958. Pantheon Books.
Levenworth. A Story of the Mississippi and the Prairies. James Duncan Nourse. 1848. G. W. Noble.
Lever: A Novel. William Dana Orcutt. LC 11-1007. 1911. 1.50. Harper & Brothers.
Levi Coffin and the Underground Railroad. Charles Ludwig. LC 75-12583. 1975. 4.95 (ISBN 0-8361-1770-0). Herald Press.
Leviathan. John Gordon Davis. LC 76-17618. (Illus.). 9.95 (ISBN 0-525-14460-9). Dutton.
Leviathan. John Gordon Davis. (Fawcett Crest Book). (Illus.). 1977. 1.95 (ISBN 0-449-23339-1). Fawcett Books.
Leviathan. Robert Shea & Robert Anton Wilson. (Illuminatus! Part III). 1975. (pbk.) 1.50. Dell.
Leviathan. Tute, Warren. LC 60-6538. 1960. Little, Brown.
Leviathan: An Indian Ocean Whale Herd Journal. Hugh Fox. LC 80-39823. 5.00 (ISBN 0-914140-10-8). Carpenter Press.
Leviathan: The Record of a Struggle and a Triumph. Jeannette Augustus Marks. Hodder & Stoughton, George H. Doran Company.
Leviathan's Deep. Jayge Carr. LC 78-62600. 1979. 7.95 (ISBN 0-385-13647-1). Doubleday.
Levine. James Hanley. LC 56-14272. 1956. Horizon Press.
Levine M Carl. A Novel of Love's Victory Over Religious Conflict by Vicier Haine Pseud. 1st Ed. LC 53-5633. 1953. Exposition Press.
Levitation, Five Fictions. Cynthia Ozick. LC 80-7997. 1981. 9.95 (ISBN 0-394-51413-0). Knopf: Distributed by Random House.
Levitation: Five Fictions. Cynthia Ozick. LC 81-48117. 176p. 1982. 11.50 (ISBN 0-394-51413-0). Knopf.
Levitation: Five Fictions. Cynthia Ozick. LC 80-7997. 256p. 1981. 4.99 (ISBN 0-394-94563-8). Knopf.
Levitation: Five Fictions. Cynthia Ozick. 176p. 1983. pap. 4.95 (ISBN 0-525-48027-7, 0481-140, Obelisk). Dutton.
Levkas Man. Hammond Innes. LC 78-136324. (Illus.). 1971. 6.95 (ISBN 0-394-44240-7). Knopf.
Lew Archer, Private Investigator. Ross Macdonald. LC 77-81870. 1977. 10.00 (ISBN 0-89296-033-7). Mysterious Pr.
Lew Ott. Martha Barr Totten. LC 9-11259.
Lew Tyler and the Ladies. Wallace Irwin. LC 28-21580. 1928. Doubleday, Doran and Company, Inc.
Lew Tyler's Wives: A Nobel. Wallace Irwin. LC 23-12454. 1923. G. P. Putnam's Sons.
Lewey and I: Or, Sailor Boys' Wandering; a Sequel to "On Land and Sea,". William Henry Thomes. (On cover: The library of choice fiction, no. 46). 1892. Laird & Lee.
Lewis a Zenith: A Three-Novel Omnibus: Main Street. Babbitt. Arrowsmith. Sinclair Harry Sinclair Lewis Lewis. LC 61-11907. 1961. 5.95. Harcourt, Brace & World.
Lewis & Clark Northwest Glory. James Raymond. (American Explorers Ser.: No. 2). 320p. (Orig.). 1981. pap. 2.75 (ISBN 0-440-04747-1, Banbury). Dell.
Lewis and Irene. Paul Morand. Tr. by V., H. B. & H. B. V. LC 25-17061. 1925. Boni & Liveright.
Lewis Arundel: Or, The Railroad of Life. Francis Edward Smedley. LC 41-32446. G. Routledge and Sons.
Lewis Arundel: Or, The Railroad of Life. Francis Edward Smedley. (Harper's Franklin square library, no. 485). 1885. Harper & Brothers.
Lewis Arundel: Or, The Railroad of Life. Francis Edward Smedley. (On cover: Seaside library. Pocket ed. no. 562). 1885. G. Munro.
Lewis Arundel: Or, The Railroad of Life. Francis Edward Smedley & Browne, Hablot Knight, 1815-1882, Illus. LC 17-208622. G. Routledge & Sons, Limited.
Lewis Carroll: Alice's Adventures in Wonderland & Through the Looking Glass. Lewis Carroll. Ed. by Roger L. Green. (Illus.). 260p. 1971. 11.25 o.p. Oxford U Pr.
Lewis Rand. Mary Johnston. LC 8-23560. 1908. Houghton Mifflin Company.
Lewis Seymour and Some Women. George Moore. LC 17-3153. 1917. Brentano's.
L'homme Facile see Man for the Asking.
Liability Limited. John A Saxon. LC 47-16338. 1947. M. S. Mill Co., Inc.
Liadain and Curithir: A Medieval Irish Love Story, and Four Tales from the Elf-Mounds. George Brandon Saul. LC 77-27955. Walton Press.
Liaison. Maria Matray & Answald Kruger. LC 75-27203. 1976. 8.95 (ISBN 0-688-02987-6). W. Morrow.
Liana. Martha Gellhorn. LC 44-743. 1944. C. Scribner's Sons.
Lianne's Island Love. Berta LaVan Barker. (YA) 1979. 6.95 (Avalon). Bouregy.
Liar. Martin Alfred Hansen. LC 73-99540. (Library of Scandinavian Literature, V. 5). (Illus.). 1969. 5.00. Twayne Publishers.
Liar see Aspern Papers.
Liar: A Novel. Thomas Savage. LC 69-15071. 1969. 5.95. Little, Brown.
Liar Dice. John S Mosher. LC 39-23528. 1939. Simon and Schuster.
Liars. Peter Hill. LC 77-16672. 1978. 6.95 (ISBN 0-395-26383-2). Houghton Mifflin.
Liars & Tyrants & People Who Turn Blue. Barbara Paul. LC 79-6664. (Crime Club Ser.). 1980. 10.95 (ISBN 0-385-15955-2). Doubleday.
Liars and Tyrants and People Who Turn Blue. Barbara Vstedal. LC 79-6664. 1980. 8.95 (ISBN 0-385-15955-2). Published for the Crime Club by Doubleday.
Liars in Love. Richard Yates. 256p. 1982. pap. 6.95 (ISBN 0-440-54697-4, Delta). Dell.
Liars in Love: Stories. Richard Yates. LC 81-7796. 1981. 13.95. Delacorte/S. Lawrence.
Lias's Wife: An Island Story. Martha Baker Dunn. LC 1-25695. (Page's commonwealth series, no. 4). 1901. L. C. Page & Company.
Libation. Edmund Keeley. LC 58-6219. 1958. Scribner.
Libby. Milt Machlin. (Orig.). 1980. pap. 2.75 (ISBN 0-505-51533-4). Tower Bks.
Libby Williams, Nurse-Practitioner. Virginia K. Smiley. 1975. 4.95. Avalon Books.
Libel. Edward Wooll. LC 36-491324. 1936. Macrae Smith Company.
Liber XXI, Khing Kang King - The Classic of Purity. Ko Yuen. LC 73-11427. (Illus.). 1976. 14.95x (ISBN 0-913576-16-6). Thelema Pubns.
Libera Me Domine. Robert Pinget. Tr. by Barbara Wright from Fr. LC 78-53831. (New French Writing Ser.). 1979. 10.50 (ISBN 0-87376-025-5). Red Dust.
Liberals: A Novel. John Hyde Preston. LC 74-22803. (Labor Movement in Fiction and Non-Fiction). 1976. 23.50 (ISBN 0-404-58460-8). AMS Press.
Liberals: A Novel. John Hyde Preston. LC 38-24914. The John Day Company.
Liberated. David R. Slavitt. LC 72-84947. 1973. 7.95 (ISBN 0-385-07888-9). Doubleday.
Liberated. Henry Sutton, pseud. LC 72-84947. 416p. 1973. 7.95 o.p. (ISBN 0-385-07888-9). Doubleday.
Liberated Future. Ed. by Robert Hoskins. LC 74-21730. 1974. (pbk.) 1.50. Fawcett.
Liberated Lady. Eleanor Hinman. LC 47-11137. 1947. Dorrance.
Liberation. Isabel Egenton Ostrander. LC 24-29531. 1924. R. M. McBride & Company.
Liberation of Lord Byron Jones. Jesse Hill Ford. LC 65-17854. 1965. Little, Brown.
Liberation of Manhattan. Edmund Demaitre & Appleman, Mark J. LC 49-11788. 1949. Doubleday.
Liberation of Paris: The Sergeant, No. 4. Gordon Davis, pseud. 192p. 1981. pap. 2.25 (ISBN 0-553-14708-0). Bantam.
Liberation of Samantha Carson: A Novel. Susan Seavy. LC 77-29233. 6.95 (ISBN 0-8407-6583-5). T. Nelson.
Liberator of Jedd. Jeffrey Lord. (Blade Ser., No. 5). 224p. 1973. pap. 1.50 (ISBN 0-523-40435-2). Pinnacle Bks.
Liberator of Jedd. Jeffrey Lord. (Orig.). 1971. pap. 0.75 o.p. (75-408). Manor Bks.
Liberators. Jon Cleary. LC 77-146945. 1971. 6.95. Morrow.
Liberators. Wesley Towner. LC 46-780677. 1946. A. A. Wyn, Inc.
Liberators: A Story of Future American Politics. illustrations by nella fountain binkley. ed. Isaac Newton Stevens. LC 8-6664. 1908. B. W. Dodge & Company.
Liberia: Or, Mr. Petyon's Experiments. Sarah Josepha Hale. LC 6-48306. 1853. Harper & Brothers.
Liberia: Or, Mr. Peyton's Experiments. Sarah Josepha Hale. LC 68-57528. (American novels of muckraking, propaganda, and social protest). 1968. Gregg Press.
Liberian Interlude. 1st Ed. Lawrence McCaughrey. LC 54-11811. 1954. Pageant Press.
Liberry". John Hay Beith. LC 24-19413. 1924. Houghton Mifflin Company.
Libertine. Charlotte Dacre. LC 73-22761. (Gothic Novels II). 1974. (ISBN 0-405-06012-2). Arno Press.
Libertine. Jacapo Massimo. (O.s.i.). (Orig.). 1969. pap. 0.75 o.s.i. (A494S, Award). Univ Pub & Dist.
Libertine Reader. Tr. by L. E. LaBan. Incl. Libertine's Manual. Therdigne De Mericourt; Gamiani, or Two Nights of Excess. Albert De Musset; Angelique. Pantonio Rocco; Amatory Adventures of a Surgeon. James C. Reddie. 240p. pap. 1.75 o.p. (2006). Brandon.
Libertines. Howard Clewes. LC 64-19280. 1964. Doubleday.
Libertine's Manual see Libertine Reader.
Liberty & Corporal Kincaid. 1st Ed. Ray Grant Toepfer. LC 68-10960. 4.50. Chilton.
Liberty Belle. Al Hine. 1975. (pbk.) 1.50 (ISBN 0-345-24353-6). Ballantine Books.
Liberty Boys & Belles. Richard Cloke. LC 80-84878. 1982. pap. text ed. 4.25 (ISBN 0-917458-07-9, Pub. by Cerulean Pr). Kent Pubns.
Liberty Lad. Maurice Leitch. LC 67-19172. 1967. Pantheon Books.
Liberty Maid: The Story of Abigail Adams. Helen L Morgan. LC 50-7109. 1950. Westminster Press.
Liberty or Death! Or, The Mother's Sacrifice. J. P Hardwick. LC 7-1907. 1862. Printed for the Authoress.
Liberty Square Station. Edward Hannibal. LC 77-21868. 8.95 (ISBN 0-399-12058-0). Putnam.
Liberty Street. William Andris. LC 80-51206. 460p. 1980. 14.95 (ISBN 0-9604278-0-5). St Basil Pr.
Liberty Street. Ira Victor Morris. LC 44-2022. 1944. Harper & Brothers.
Liberty Sword. Gardner F. Fox. 1976. pap. 1.25 o.p. (LB358ZK, Leisure Bks). Nordon Pubns.
Liberty Tavern. Thomas J. Fleming. (Illus.). 1977. 2.25. (ISBN 0-446-82367-8). Warner Books.
Liberty Tavern: A Novel. Thomas J Fleming. LC 74-18795. (Illus.). 1976. 10.00 (ISBN 0-385-04420-8). Doubleday.
Liberty Two. Robert Lipsyte. LC 73-20698. 1974. 7.95 (ISBN 0-671-21694-5). Simon and Schuster.
Libra: An Astrological Romance. Eleanor Maria Easterbrook Ames. 1896. E. Kirk.
Library Lady. Kate Kellogg. Ed. by Alice Sachs. 1970. 3.95 o.p. Lenox Hill.
Library of American Fiction ... 1904. The Success Company.
Library of Love. By Joan Garrison Pseud. William Arthur Neubauer. LC 56-12453. 1956. Arcadia House.
Library of the World's Best Mystery and Detective Stories. Ed. by Julian Hawthorne. LC 8-35888. 1908. The Review of Reviews Company.
Libro del Caualleró Zifar: El Libro Del Caualleró De Dios. Charles Philip Wagner. LC 80-14982. (Michigan. University. University of Michigan Publications. Language & Literature: Vol. 5). (Illus.). 1981. 48.00 (ISBN 0-527-17500-5). Kraus Reprints.
Libya Connection: The Executioner. Don Pendleton. 192p. 1982. pap. 1.95 (ISBN 0-373-61048-3). Harlequin Bks.
Libyan Contract. Don Smith. (Secret Mission Ser). (O.s.i.). 192p. (Orig.). 1974. pap. 1.25 o.s.i. (AQ1371, Award). Univ Pub & Dist.
Libyan Kill. Will O'Neil. LC 79-19492. 10.95 (ISBN 0-393-01319-7). Norton.
License Renewed. John Gardner. 1982. 2.95 (ISBN 0-425-05247-8). Berkley Pub. Co.
License Renewed. John E Gardner. LC 81-1284. 9.95 (ISBN 0-399-90118-3). R. Marek Publishers.
License Renewed. John E Gardner. LC 81-13303. 1981. 14.95 (ISBN 0-8161-3326-3). G.K. Hall.
License to Kill. Norman Daniels. (Orig.). 1972. pap. 0.75 o.p. (ISBN 0-515-02849-5, T2849). Pyramid Pubns.
License to Prowl. Peter Kanto. (Orig.). pap. 0.95 o.p. (1002). Brandon.
Licensed for Murder: By John Rhode. Cecil John Charles Street. LC 59-12087. (Red Badge detective). 1959. Dodd, Mead.
Lida Campbell: Or, Drama of a Life. A Novel. Jean Kate Ludlum. (choice series, no. 58). 1892. R. Bonner's Sons.
Lidenman's Daughters: By Synnove Christensen Pseud. Translated by Mervyn Savill, 1st Ed. Mai Lindegard. LC 58-8098. 1958. Doubleday.
Lidless Eye. Peter Romsey. LC 57-9669. Roy Publishers.
Lido Lady. Morris Gilbert. LC 31-2445. Sears Publishing Company, Inc.
Lie. Peggy Goodin. LC 53-6089. 1953. Dutton.
Lie. Helen Reimensnyder Martin. LC 28-4064. 1928. Dodd, Mead & Company.
Lie. Alberto Moravia. 1973. pap. 1.25 (ISBN 0-532-12163-5). Woodhill.
Lie. Alberto Pincherle. 1973. (pbk.) 1.25. Manor Books.
Lie: By Alberto Moravia Pseud. Tr. from Italian by Angus Davidson. Alberto Pincherle. LC 66-188621. 1966. 5.95. Farrar.
Lie Down, I Want to Talk to You. William P McGivern. LC 67-19226. 1967. Dodd, Mead.
Lie Down in Darkness. Hoffman Reynolds Hays. LC 44-6936. 1944. Reynal & Hitchcock.
Lie Down in Darkness. William Styron. LC 79-12859. 1979. 12.95 (ISBN 0-394-50659-6). Random House.
Lie Down in Darkness: A Novel. William Styron. LC 63-6921. (Compass books, C18). 1962. Viking Press.
Lie Down in Darkness: A Novel. William Styron. LC 51-12286. 1951. Bobbs-Merrill.
Lie Down in Me: A Novel. Andrew Jolly. LC 76-108058. 1970. 4.95. Crown Publishers.
Lie Like a Lady: By C. S. Cody Pseud. Leslie Waller. LC 55-37185. 1955. Ace Books.
Lie of the Age. William Schoeler. LC 23-12608. 1922. The Book Concern.
Lied for Life; or, The Honor of the House of Sourakoff. A Romance of Russian Life. Henry Gaines Turner. (On cover: The Gossip printing co's. dime library. no. 1). 1892. The Gossip Printing Company.
Liers in Wait: By Raymond Lawrence and Katharine Mount. Raymond Lawrence & Katharine Mount. LC 56-14237. 1956. Bruce Humphries.
Lies. Richard Neely. LC 77-25177. 8.95 (ISBN 0-399-12126-9). Putnam.
Lies. Richard Neely. 1979. 1.75 (ISBN 0-515-04879-8). Jove/HBJ Books.
Lies. Bernard Wolfe. LC 74-29808. 1975. 8.95 (ISBN 0-88381-011-5). Wollstonecraft: Distributed by Price/Stern/Sloan Publishers.
Lies & Stories. Glenda Adams. 1976. pap. 2.95 o.p. (ISBN 0-8180-0620-X). Horizon.
Lies & Stories. Glenda Adams. 1976. pap. 2.95 o.p. (ISBN 0-8180-0620-X). Horizon.
Lies. (Mesonges) A Novel. Paul Charles Joseph Bourget. LC 6-15003. (On cover: Primrose Series, no. 37). 1892. Street & Smith.
Lies My Father Told Me: A Novel. Norman Allan. (Signet book). (Illus.). 1975. (pbk.) 1.50. New American Library.
Lies of Passion. Alison Hart. (Girls in Trouble). (Signet book: Vol. 4). New American Library.
Lies to Live by. S. Gallick. (Orig.). 1983. pap. 2.95 (ISBN 0-440-04786-2). Dell.
Lieut. Gullivar Jones, His Vacation. Edwin Lester Linden Arnold. LC 74-15947. (Science Fiction). 1975. (ISBN 0-405-06273-7). Arno Press.
Lieut. Gulliver Jones: His Vacation. Edwin Lester Linden Arnold. LC 74-15947. (Science Fiction Ser). 304p. 1975. Repr. 17.00x (ISBN 0-405-06273-7). Ayer Co.
Lieutenant. Andre Dubus. LC 67-18092. 1967. Dial Press.
Lieutenant. Mary G Shannonhouse. LC 26-127193. 1926.
Lieutenant and Others. Herman Cyril McNeile. LC 16-3766. 1915. Hodder and Stoughton.
Lieutenant Barnabas. Frank Barrett. LC 6-8665. (On cover: Lovell's library. no. 1130). J. W. Lovell Company.
Lieutenant Bertram: A Novel of the Nazi Luftwaffe. Bodo Uhse. LC 44-5523. 1944. Simon and Schuster.
Lieutenant Carey's Luck: A Companion Story to "Cadet Carey.". Lionel Lounsberry. LC 99-1576. (On cover: Medal library. no. 4). 1899. Street & Smith.
Lieutenant-Governor: A Novel. Guy Wetmore Carryl. LC 3-6568. 1903. Houghton, Mifflin and Company.
Lieutenant Hornblower. Cecil Scott Forester. 1961. Grosset & Dunlap.
Lieutenant Hornblower. 1st Ed. Cecil Scott Forester. LC 52-5530. 1952. Little, Brown.
Lieutenant Lookest & Other Stories. Masuji Ibuse. Tr. by John Bester from Jap. LC 71-135143. 308p. 1971. 10.50x (ISBN 0-87011-147-7). Kodansha.
Lieutenant Must Be Mad: Translated from the German by Richard and Clara Winston. 1st American Ed. Hans Hellmut Kirst. LC 51-2356. 1951. Harcourt, Brace.
Lieutenant of the Line. Duncan MacNeil. LC 72-96134. 1973. 6.95. St. Martin's Press.
Lieutenant of the Line. Duncan MacNeil. (Illus.). 1974. (pbk.) 1.25 (ISBN 0-345-23710-2). Ballantine Books.
Lieutenant Pascal's Tastes in Homicides: By Hugh Pentecost Pseud. Judson Pentecost Philips. LC 54-5579. (Red badge detective). 1954. Dodd, Mead.
Lieutenant Sandy Ray. Charles King. LC 15-633119. R. F. Fenno & Company.
Lieutenant, the Girl and the Viceroy: The Story of the Adventurers of These Three with II Liberator in South America. Marshall Putnam Thompson. LC 7-11211. 1907. The C. M. Clark Publishing Co.
Lieutenant What's-His-Name: Elaborated from Jacques Futrelle's The Simple Case of Susan. May Peel Futrelle & Futrelle, Jacques. LC 15-538320. 1.25. The Bobbs-Merrill Company.
Lieutenant's Lady. Bess Streeter Aldrich. LC 75-29115. 1975. 6.95. Aeonian Press.
Lieutenant's Lady. Bess Streeter Aldrich. LC 42-20993. 1942. D. Appleton-Century Company, Incorporated.
Lieutenants's Lady. Bess Streeter Aldrich. 1961. Grosset & Dunlap.
Life. Maupassant, Guy De. Tr. by Marjorie Laurie. LC 76-48440. (Classics of European Literature). (Hyperion library of world literature). 1977. 11.95. (ISBN 0-88355-576-X) (ISBN 0-88355-577-8). Hyperion Press.
Life. Wright Morris. LC 73-4155. 1973. 5.95 (ISBN 0-06-013079-2). Harper & Row.
Life. Wright Morris. LC 79-18304. 1980. 11.95 (ISBN 0-8032-3061-3) (ISBN 0-8032-8106-4). University of Nebraska Press.
Life. Ettore Schmitz. LC 62-15565. 1963. Knopf.

TITLE INDEX LIFE AND DEATH OF

Life. William Budd Trites. LC 11-288183. 1911. The Green Lane Press.

Life: A Novel. William Wallace Wheeler. LC 8-37110. 1890. The Case, Lockwood & Brainard Co., Printers.

Life: A Novelization of Thompson Buchanan's Play. D. Torbett & Buchanan, Thompson. LC 15-4799. E. J. Clode.

Life-Adjustment of Harry Blake. Frances Shine. LC 68-9522. 1968. 4.95. Meredith Press.

Life, Adventures, & Amours of Sir Richard Perrot, 1770 see Life, Adventures, Intrigues & Amours of the Celebrated Jemmy Twitcher, 1770.

Life, Adventures, & Piracies of the Famous Captain Singleton. Daniel Defoe. LC 74-13433. (Illus.). 1974. (ISBN 0-404-07916-4). AMS Press.

Life Adventures & Piracies of the Famous Captain Singleton. Daniel Defoe. (Half-title: Everyman's library, edited by Ernest Rhys. Fiction. no. 74). 1906. J. M. Dent & Co.

Life, Adventures & Piracies of the Famous Captain Singleton. Daniel Defoe. LC 36-29325. (Half-title: The world's classics. 82). 1924. H. Milford, Oxford University Press.

Life, Adventures, and Pyracies of the Famous Captain Singleton. Daniel Defoe. LC 70-170544. (Foundations of the Novel). 1972. (ISBN 0-8240-0545-7). Garland Pub.

Life, Adventures, & Pyracies of the Famous Captain Singleton... Being Set on Shore in the Island of Madagascar. Daniel Defoe. LC 70-170544. (Foundations of the Novel Ser.: Vol. 33). lib. bdg. 50.00 (ISBN 0-8240-0545-7). Garland Pub.

Life, Adventures, and Pyracies, of the Famous Captain Singleton: Containing an Account of... His Many Adventures and Pyracies with the Fampus Captain Avery and Others. Daniel Defoe & Shiv Kumar Kumar. LC 72-452378. (Oxford English novels). (Oxford paperbacks, 304). 1973. (pbk) 3.25 (ISBN 0-19-281139-8). Oxford Univ. Pr.

Life, Adventures, Intrigues, and Amours of the Celebrated Jemmy Twitcher. LC 74-31492. (Flowering of the Novel). 1975. 25.00 (ISBN 0-8240-1191-0). Garland Pub.

Life, Adventures, Intrigues & Amours of the Celebrated Jemmy Twitcher, 1770. Ed. by Michael F. Shugrue. Bd. with Life, Adventures, & Amours of Sir Richard Perrot, 1770. LC 74-31492. (Novel in England, 1700-1775 Ser). 1974. lib. bdg. 50.00 (ISBN 0-8240-1191-0). Garland Pub.

Life-Adventures of Zamba, an African Negro King. facs. ed. Ed. by Peter Neilson. LC 70-133162. (Black Heritage Library Collection Ser). 1847. 13.50 (ISBN 0-8369-8717-9). Ayer Co.

Life Adventurous: And Other Stories. James Thomas Farrell. LC 47-11610. 1947. Vanguard Press.

Life After Life. Raymond A. Moody, Jr. 1976. pap. 2.95 (ISBN 0-553-20433-5). Bantam.

Life Along the Passaic River. William Carlos Williams. 1938. New Directions.

Life Amongst the Modocs: Unwritten History. Joaquin Miller. LC 81-7532. (Illus.). 1982. 7.95 (ISBN 0-913522-10-4). Urion Press.

Life and Achievements of Don Quixote De la Mancha. Miguel de Cervantes de Saavedra & Peter Anthony Motteux. LC 66-43289. 1902. Simpkin, Marshall, Hamilton, Kent; New York, Scribner's.

Life and Adventeures of Martin Chuzzlewit. Charles Dickens. LC 36-7374. 1935. Dodd, Mead & Company.

Life and Adventues of...Roger Sherman Potter: Together with an Accurate... Account of His Great Achievement in Politics, Diplomacy, and War... Francis Colburn Adams. LC 5-42622. 1858. Stanford & Delisser.

Life and Adventure of a Country Merchant. A Narrative of His Exploits at Home, During His Travels, and in the Cities... John Beauchamp Jones. LC 1-1334. 1854. Lippincott, Grambo & Co.

Life & Adventures of Aloysius O'Callaghan. Thomas Washington Metcalfe. LC 32-232855. (His Santa Anna trilogy, v. 2). 1932. W. Morrow & Co.

Life and Adventures of an Arkansaw Doctor. Marcus Lafayette Byrn. LC 6-16402. 1851. Lippincott, Grambo and Co.

Life and Adventures of an Arkansaw Doctor. Marcus Lafayette Byrn. LC 6-164036. M. L. Byrn.

Life and Adventures of Arthur Clenning... Timothy Flint. 1828. Towar & Hogan.

Life & Adventures of Arthur Clenning. Timothy Flint. Ed. by Douglas B. Hill, Jr. LC 70-93617. (American Fiction Ser). 1970. lib. bdg. 20.25 o.s.i. (ISBN 0-512-00180-4). Garrett Pr.

Life & Adventures of Captain John Avery, the Famous English Pirate... Now in Possession of Madagascar see Perfidious P.

Life and Adventures of Dr. Dodimus Duckworth, A.N.Q. To Which Is Added, The History of a Steam Doctor... Asa Green. LC 9-3037. 1833. P. Hill.

Life and Adventures of Jack of the Mill: Commonly Called Lord Othmill; Created, for His Eminent Services, Baron Waldeck, and Knight of Kitcottie. A Fireside Story. William Howitt. LC 43-260081. 1844. Harper & Brothers.

Life and Adventures of Joaquin Murieta, the Celebrated California Bandit. new ed. John Rollin Ridge. LC 55-6358. (Western frontier library, v. 4). (Illus.). 1955. University of Oklahoma Press.

Life & Adventures of Joe Thompson, 1750, 2 vols. in 1. Edward Kimber. LC 74-17302. (Novel in England, 1700-1775 Ser). 1974. lib. bdg. 50.00 (ISBN 0-8240-1130-9). Garland Pub.

Life and Adventures of Joseph T. Hare. The Bold Robber and Highwayman, with Sixteen... Engravings. H. R. Howard. LC 7-23659. 1847. H. ? Ong and Brother.

Life and Adventures of Martin Chuzzelwit. Charles Dickens. Ed. by Philip Nicholas Furbank. LC 73-364219. (Penguin English library.). (Illus.). 1975. (pbk.) 3.95. Penguin.

Life and Adventures of Martin Chuzzlewit. Charles Dickens. LC 52-655. (New Oxford illustrated Dickens). (Illus.). 1951. Oxford University Press.

Life and Adventures of Martin Chuzzlewit... Charles Dickens. J. Winchester.

Life and Adventures of Martin Chuzzlewit. diamond ed. Charles Dickens. 1867. Ticknor and Fields.

Life and Adventures of Martin Chuzzlewit. Charles Dickens. LC 6-26436. (On cover: Lovell's library, v. 5, no. 201). 1883. J. W. Lovell Company.

Life and Adventures of Martin Chuzzlewit. Charles Dickens. (Half-title: Everyman's library, ed. by Ernest Rhys. Fiction). 1907. J. M. Dent & Co.

Life and Adventures of Martin Chuzzlewit. Charles Dickens. (Half-title: The centenary edition of the works of Charles Dickens in 36 volumes). 1911. Chapman & Hall, Ltd.

Life and Adventures of Martin Chuzzlewit, His Relatives, Friends, and Enemies, Comprising All His Wills and Ways: The Whole Forming a Complete Key to the House of Chuzzlewit. Charles Dickens. LC 47-11752. 1947. A. A. Knopf.

Life and Adventures' of Michael Armstrong: The Factory Boy. Frances Milton Trollope. LC 42-26502. 1840. Harper & Brothers.

Life and Adventures of Mr. Francis Clive. Phoebe Gibbes. LC 75-1172. (Flowering of the Novel). 1975. 25.00 (ISBN 0-8240-1168-6). Garland Pub.

Life and Adventures of Nicholas Nickleby. illustrated household ed. Charles Dickens. LC 6-26428. 1870. Fields, Osgood & Co.

Life and Adventures of Nicholas Nickleby. Charles Dickens. LC 34-37767. 1873. J. R. Osgood and Company.

Life and Adventures of Nicholas Nickleby. household ed. Charles Dickens. LC 12-19562. (On cover: The works of Charles Dickens. Household ed.). 1873. Harper & Brothers.

Life and Adventures of Nicholas Nickleby. Charles Dickens. LC 9-825. Aldine Book Publishing Co.

Life and Adventures of Nicholas Nickleby. Charles Dickens. LC 6-26427. (On cover: Lovell's library, v. 5, no. 231). 1883. J. W. Lovell Company.

Life and Adventures of Nicholas Nickleby. Charles Dickens. Ed. by Whipple, Edwin Percy. LC 15-23132. (Half-title: Works of Charles Dickens. New illustrated library ed. vol. v-vi). Houghton Mifflin Company.

Life and Adventures of Nicholas Nickleby. Charles Dickens. Ed. by Dickens, Charles. LC 4-153012. 1898. Macmillan and Co., Limited.

Life and Adventures of Nicholas Nickleby. Charles Dickens. (Half-title: Everyman's library, ed. by Ernest Rhys. Fiction. no. 238). 1907. J. M. Dent & Co.

Life and Adventures of Nicholas Nickleby. Charles Dickens. (Half-title: The centenary edition of the works of Charles Dickens in 36 volumes). 1910. Chapman & Hall, Ltd.

Life and Adventures of Nicholas Nickleby. Charles Dickens. LC 36-37123. (Half-title: Everyman's library, ed. by Ernerst Rhys. Friction no. 238). 1930. J. M. Dent & Sons, Ltd.

Life and Adventures of Nicholas Nickleby. Charles Dickens. LC 41-609. The Heritage Press.

Life & Adventures of Nicholas Nickleby. With 39 Illus. by "Phiz" and an Introd. by Dame Sybil Thorndike. Charles Dickens. LC 50-893374. (New Oxford illustrated Dickens). 1950. Oxford University Press.

Life and Adventures of Percival Mayberry: An Autobiography... Joseph Holt Ingraham. LC 7-10354. 1854. T. B. Peterson.

Life & Adventures of Peter Porcupine. William Cobbett. 1972. Repr. of 1927 ed. lib. bdg. 7.50 o.p. Folcroft.

Life & Adventures of Peter Wilkins. Robert Paltock. LC 73-13261. 1973. 10.95 (ISBN 0-88355-115-2) (ISBN 0-88355-115-2). Hyperion Press.

Life and Adventures of Peter Wilkins. Robert Paltock. LC 74-163872. (Oxford English novels). (Illus.). 1973. 13.00 (ISBN 0-19-255329-1). Oxford University Press.

Life & Adventures of Peter Wilkins. Robert Paltock & Bawden, Edward, 1903- Illus. LC 44-111637. 1928. J. M. Dent & Sons Ltd.

Life & Adventures of Peter Wilkins, a Cornish Man, 1751, 2 vols. in 1. Robert Paltock. LC 74-16040. (Novel in England, 1700-1775 Ser). 1974. lib. bdg. 50.00 (ISBN 0-8240-1134-1). Garland Pub.

Life and Adventures of Robinson Crusoe. By Daniel Defoe. Daniel Defoe. (Seaside library, v. 18, no. 343). G. Munro.

Life and Adventures of Robinson Crusoe: From the Original Work. a new ed., carefully adapted to youth... ed. Daniel Defoe. LC 6-32871. 1835. Conrad and Parsons.

Life and Adventures of Robinson Crusoe. Daniel Defoe. Ed. by James Runcieman Sutherland. LC 68-7239. (Riverside editions, B104). 1968. 1.25. Houghton Mifflin.

Life and Adventures of Robinson Crusoe. Daniel Defoe. LC 4-31642. 1839. Robinson & Franklin.

Life and Adventures of Robinson Crusoe. the only complete american ed. Daniel Defoe. LC 6-32873. 1853. D. Appleton & Company.

Life and Adventures of Robinson Crusoe. Daniel Defoe. (On cover: Farm and fireside library, no. 1). 1881. Farm and Fireside Company.

Life and Adventures of Robinson Crusoe. Daniel Defoe. Ed. by Lambert, William H. LC 6-32885. 1883. Ginn, Heath, & Co.

Life and Adventures of Robinson Crusoe. Daniel Defoe. (On cover: Lovell's library, v. 8, no. 428). 1884. J. W. Lovell Company.

Life and Adventures of Robinson Crusoe. Daniel Defoe. Ed. by Goodrich, Samuel Griswold. LC 6-32884. E. Maynard & Co.

Life and Adventures of Robinson Crusoe. Daniel Defoe. Ed. by Stephens, Kate. LC 6-32880. (On cover: Eclectic school readings). American Book Company.

Life and Adventures of Robinson Crusoe. Daniel Defoe. Ed. by Johnson, Clifton. LC 4-32667. (On verso of half-title: Macmillan's pocket American and English classics). 1904. The Macmillan Company.

Life and Adventures of Robinson Crusoe. windermere ed. Daniel Defoe. LC 14-14804. 1.35. Rand McNally & Company.

Life and Adventures of Robinson Crusoe. Daniel Defoe. LC 25-2768. (On cover: Mayflower series). The Saalfield Publishing Company.

Life and Adventures of Robinson Crusoe. Daniel Defoe. LC 30-18309. (On cover: Companion series). 1930. The Saalfield Publishing Company.

Life and Adventures of Robinson Crusoe. Daniel Defoe. Mirsky, Dmitry Svyatopolk. LC 37-18300. (Library of English classics). 1935. Co-Operative Publishing Society of Foreign Workers in the U.S.S.R.

Life and Adventures of Robinson Crusoe. Daniel Defoe & Dobson, Austin. LC 6-32886. (On cover: The classic series). 1883. Roberts Brothers.

Life and Adventures of Robinson Crusoe. Daniel Defoe & Jean Ignace Isidore Gerard Grandville. LC 77-20995. (Paddington masterpieces of the illustrated book). (Illus.). 6.95 (ISBN 0-448-22193-4). Paddington Press: Distributed by Grosset & Dunlap.

Life and Adventures of Robinson Crusoe. Daniel Defoe & Mittell, Sherman Fabian, 1902- Ed. LC 43-26001. 1935. National Home Library Foundation.

Life and Adventures of Robinson Crusoe, Part I- Daniel Defoe. Ed. by Gaston, Charles Robert. (On verso of half-title: Macmillan's pocket American and English classics). 0.25. The Macmillan Company.

Life and Adventures of Robinson Crusoe, Pt. 1- Daniel Defoe. Ed. by Noyes, Ernest Clapp. LC 10-28636. (Merrill's English texts). Charles E. Merrill Company.

Life and Adventures of Robinson Crusoe, Part 1. Daniel Defoe. LC 37-27220. (Half-title: The world's classics. xvii). 1920. H. Milford, Oxford University Press.

Life and Adventures of Robinson Crusoe, of York, Mariner. Daniel Defoe. LC 99-3511. T. Y. Crowell & Company.

Life and Adventures of Robinson Crusoe, of York, Mariner. With an Account of His Travels Round Three Parts of the Globe. Daniel Defoe. LC 21-759726. Munroe & Francis.

Life and Adventures of Robinson Crusoe, of York, Mariner. With a Memoir of the Author... Daniel Defoe. LC 8-19725. (Half-title: Bohn's illustrated library). 1892. G. Bell & Sons.

Life and Adventures of Robinson Crusoe: With a Biographical Account of Defoe, Illustrated with Sixteen Characteristic Engravings. New Ed., Complete. Daniel Defoe. LC 31-2451. 1864. Lea and Shepard.

Life and Adventures of Robinson Crusoe: With a Life of the Author... Daniel Defoe & Robertson, William. LC 38-226943. 1836. J. Gladding & Co.

Life and Adventures of Roderick Douglas. D. B. Mackintosh. 1886. C. H. Whiting.

Life and Adventures of Rody the Rover: The Ribbonman of Ireland. complete and unabridged ed. William Carleton. LC 8-2122. T. B. Peterson & Brothers.

Life & Adventures of Santa Claus. Julie Lane. Repr. of 1932 ed. 9.00 o.s.i. Finch Pr.

Life and Adventures of Sir Bartholomew Sapskull. William Donaldson & Somebody. LC 74-26834. (Flowering of the Novel). (Illus.). 1975. (ISBN 0-8240-1183-X). Garland Pub.

Life and Adventures of Sir Launcelot Greaves. Tobias George Smollett. LC 74-162185. (Oxford English novels). (Illus.). 1973. 10.75 (ISBN 0-19-255364-X). Oxford University Press.

Life and Adventures of the Celebrated Oriental Traveler Hajji Baba in Persia, Turkey and Russia... With Numerous Episodes and Incidents Illustrating Life in Persia. James Justinian Morier. J. E. Potter and Company.

Life & Adventures of the Lady Lucy see Rash Resolve; or, the Untimely Discovery.

Life and Adventures of Valentine Vox: The Ventriloquist. Henry Cockton. LC 58-52807. (Warne's Crown' library, 1). 1889. F. Warne.

Life and Adventures of Valentine Vox, the Ventriloquist. Henry Cockton. LC 37-18313. G. Routledge & Sons.

Life and Adventures of Valentine Vox, the Ventriloquist. Henry Cockton. LC 42-26795. Ward, Lock, and Co.

Life and Adventures of Wm. Harvard Stinchfield: Or The Wanderings of a Traveling Merchant. "An Owre True Tale," of the Gaming Table and Bowl. John Hovey Robinson. LC 7-42159. 1851. For the Author, Printed by Thurston & Co.

Life and Alone. LC 7-19392. 1870. Lee and Shepard.

Life & Amours of Kate Percival. Intro. by A. Warner. pap. 1.75 o.p. (3013). Brandon.

Life and Andrew Otway. Stephen Sothwold. LC 32-1270. 1932. G. P. Putnam's Sons.

Life & Astonishing Adventures of John Daniel. Ralph Morris. LC 74-16398. (Science Fiction Ser). (Illus.). 276p. 1975. Repr. 18.00x (ISBN 0-405-06307-5). Ayer Co.

Life and Death: A Novel. by your humble servant. ed. Samuel Ward Francis. 1871. Carleton; Etc., Etc.

Life and Death: And Other Legends and Stories. Henryk Sienkiewicz. Tr. by Jeremiah Curtin. 1904. Little, Brown, and Company.

Life & Death of a Tough Guy. Benjamin Appel. 1973. (pbk) 0.95. Manor Books.

Life and Death of Cormac the Skald. W. G. Collingwood & Jon Stefansson. LC 76-43948. (Illus.). 1982. 16.00 (ISBN 0-404-60011-5). AMS Press.

Life and Death of Harriett Frean. May Sinclair. LC 22-2309. 1922. The Macmillan Company.

Life and Death of Little Jo. Robert Bright. LC 44-40035. 1944. Doubleday, Doran & Company, Inc.

Life and Death of Little Jo. Robert Bright. LC 78-64355. (Zia book). (Illus.). 1978. 3.95 (ISBN 0-8263-0492-3). University of New Mexico Press.

Life and Death of Mr. Badman. John Bunyan. LC 30-15579. (Half-title: The world's classics. 338). 1929. Oxford University Press, H. Milford.

Life and Death of Peter Wade. Dudley Barker. LC 73-88398. 1974. 5.95 (ISBN 0-8128-1649-8). Stein and Day.

Life & Death of Peter Wade. Lionel Black. 192p. 1974. 5.95 o.p. (ISBN 0-8128-1649-8). Stein & Day.

Life and Death of Richard Yea-and-Nay. Maurice Henry Hewlett. LC 6646. 1900. The Macmillan Company.

Life and Death of Sam, in Virginia. Gardner. LC 7-15187. A. Morris.

Life and Death of Sylvia: A Novel. 1st Americaned. Edgar Mittelholzer. LC 54-5014. (Illus.). J. Day.

Life and Death of the Mayor of Casterbridge: A Story of a Man of Character. Afterword by Walter Allen. Thomas Hardy. (Signet classic, CD110). 1962. New Amer. Lib.

Life and Death of the Mayor of Casterbridge: A Story of a Man of Character. Ed. by Andrew A. Orr, Vivian De Sola Pinto. Thomas Hardy. Ed. by Andrew A. Orr & Vivian De Sola Pinto. LC 67-8786. 1967. 1.80. St. Martin's.

Life and Death of the Mayor of Casterbridge: A Story of a Man of Character. standard ed. Thomas Hardy. LC 66-12789. (Perennial classic, P3065D). 1966. Harper & Row.

Life and Death of the Mayor of Casterbridge: A Story of a Man of Character. Thomas Hardy. 1977. 2.95 (ISBN 0-312-52326-2). St. Martin's Press.

Life and Death of the Wicked Lady Skelton. Magdalen King-Hall. LC 46-2310. 1946. Rinehart & Company, Inc.

Life & Death of the Wicked Lady Skelton: Official Movie Tie-in edition. Magdalen King-Hall. 1983. pap. 2.95 (ISBN 0-14-006779-5). Penguin.

Life and Erica. Gilbert Frankau. LC 24-28673. The Century Co.

Life and Exploits of the Noted Criminal: Bristol Bill. George Thompson. LC 44-39855. M. J. Ivers & Co.

Life and Exploits of the Scarlet Pimpernel: Sir Percy Blakeney, Bart. John Montagu Orcxy Barstow. LC 35-27214. 1935. I. Washburn.

Life and Extraordinary Adventures of Private Ivan Chonkin. Vladimir Voinovich. LC 76-47579. 1977. 8.95 (ISBN 0-374-18621-9). Farrar, Straus and Giroux.

Life and Its Aims: in Two Parts. Part First--Ideal Life. Part Second--Actual Life. Elise Osborne. LC 7-23693. 1854. Lippincott, Grambo & Co.

Life and Lingo. Marie MacKenzie & MacKenzie, Trix, 1906- Joint Author. LC 31-290134. The Stratford Company.

Life and Loves of Mr. Jiveass Nigger: A Novel. Cecil Brown. LC 76-102062. 1969. 5.50. Farrar, Straus & Giroux.

Life & Loves of Mister Jiveass Nigger. Cecil Brown. 1970. 5.50 o.p. (ISBN 0-374-18624-3). FS&G.

Life and Loves of Von Steuben. William Benson Richter. LC 52-1663. 1952. Christopher Pub. House.

Life and Mary Ann. Catherine Cookson. LC 76-51958. 1977. 7.95 (ISBN 0-688-03186-2). Morrow.

Life and Memoirs of Ephraim Tristram Bates. LC 74-17279. (Flowering of the Novel). 1974. (ISBN 0-8240-1146-5). Garland Pub.

Life and Miss Celeste. Florence Glass Palmer. LC 37-18101. The Bobbs-Merrill Company.

Life and Opinions of John Buncle, Esquire. Thomas Amory. (Library of early novelists, ed. by E. A. Baker, v. 1). 1904. G. Routledge and Sons, Limited.

Life & Public Services of an Army Straggler. Kittrell J. Warren. Ed. by Floyd C. Watkins. LC 61-17536. 1961. 5.00 o.p. (ISBN 0-8203-0117-5); pap. 3.50x o.p. (ISBN 0-8203-0118-3). U of Ga Pr.

Life and Reflections of Charles Observator: In Which Are Displayed, the Real Characters of Human Life. Elijah Robinson Sabin. LC 8-1364. 1816. Printed by Rowe & Hooper.

Life & Sayings of Mrs. Partington. Benjamin Penhallow Shillaber. LC 79-91092. (American Humorists Ser.). Repr. of 1854 ed. lib. bdg. 20.00 (ISBN 0-8398-1858-0). Irvington.

Life and Strange Adventures of Robinson Crusoe, of York, Mariner. Daniel Defoe. LC 6-32881. (On cover: Riverside literature series, no. 87). Houghton, Mifflin and Company.

Life and Strange Adventures of Robinson Crusoe of York, Mariner, by. Daniel Defoe. Ed. by Schubert, Arthur. LC 30-256217. (Riverside literature series). Houghton Mifflin Company.

Life and Strange Surprising Adventures of Robinson Crusoe. Daniel Defoe. LC 8-34600. Houghton Mifflin Company.

Life and Strange Surprising Adventures of Robinson Crusoe. Daniel Defoe. LC 9-28151. 1909. Houghton Mifflin Company.

Life and Strange Surprising Adventures of Robinson Crusoe. Daniel Defoe. Ed. by Hastings, William Thomson. LC 13-8907. (Lake English classics). 0.40. Scott, Foresman and Company.

Life and Strange Surprising Adventures of Robinson Crusoe. Daniel Defoe. Ed. by Trent, William Peterfield. LC 16-23210. 0.60. Ginn and Company.

Life and Strange Surprising Adventures of Robinson Crusoe. Daniel Defoe & Ward, Lynd Kendall, 1905- Illus. LC 46-22598. (Illustrated junior library). 1946. Grosset & Dunlap.

Life & Strange Surprising Adventures of Robinson Crusoe, of York, Mariner. Daniel Defoe. LC 74-13442. (Illus.). 1974. (ISBN 0-404-07911-3). AMS Press.

Life and Strange Surprising Adventures of Robinson Crusoe, of York, Mariner... Daniel Defoe. 1868. Hurd and Houghton.

Life and Strange Surprising Adventures of Robinson Crusoe, of York, Mariner. Daniel Defoe. LC 6378. 1900. R. H. Russell.

Life and Strange Surprising Adventures of Robinson Crusoe of New York, Mariner. Daniel Defoe. LC 23-265906. Harper & Brothers.

Life and Strange Surprising Adventures of Robinson Crusoe of York, Mariner: As Related by Himself. Daniel Defoe & Hale, Edward Everett. (On cover: Heath's home and school classics. The young reader's series.). 1902. D. C. Heath & Co.

Life and Strange Surprising Adventures of Robinson Crusoe of York, Mariner. As Related by Himself. Daniel Defoe & Howell, John. LC 6-32888. 1872. Hubbard Bros; Etc., Etc.

Life and Strange Surprizing Adventures of Robinson Crusoe of York, Mariner: Who Lived Eight and Twenty Years All Alone in an un-Inhabited Island on the Coast of America, Near the Mouth of the Great River of Oroonoque, Having Been Cast on Shore by Shipwreck Wherein All the Men Perished but Himself I.E. Daniel Defoe. Daniel Defoe. Ed. by Joseph Donald Crowley. LC 72-172417. (Oxford English novels). (Illus.). 1972. 8.50 (ISBN 0-19-255359-3). Oxford University Press.

Life and Surprising Adventures of Robinson Crusoe. Daniel Defoe. LC 24-26902. (The Macmillan classics.). 1926. The Macmillan Company.

Life and Surprising Adventures of Robinson Crusoe, of York, Mariner: With a Biographical Account of Defoe. Illustrated with Fifty Characteristic Cuts, from Drawings by William Harvey... and Engraved by Adams. Daniel Defoe. LC 16-1224. 1859. Derby & Jackson.

Life and Surprising Adventures of Robinson Crusoe of York, Mariner... Daniel Defoe. (Franklin square library, no. 180). 1881. Harper & Brothers.

Life and Surprising Adventures of Robinson Crusoe, of York, Mariner. From the Original, in Words of One Syllable. Daniel Defoe. Ed. by Schwacofer, Mary A. LC 6-32887. (Cassell's series of one syllable books). Cassell, Petter, Galpin & Co.

Life and Surprising Adventures of Robinson Crusoe of York, Mariner: From the Original in Words of One Syllable. Daniel Defoe. Ed. by Schwacofer, Mary A. (Cassell's series of one syllable books). Cassell & Company.

Life and Surprising Adventures of Robinson Crusoe of York, Mariner: From the Original in Words of One Syllable. Daniel Defoe. Ed. by Schwacofer, Mary A. (Cassell's series of one syllable books). 1891. Cassell Publishing Company.

Life and Times of Buckshot South and of His Friend and Colleague, Phineas J. Courtney: And Their Mutual Companion, Laura Morse, to Say Nothing of Their Intrepid Adversary, Mr. Aaron Cosgrove of the Starling Detective Agency. Frank Davis Adams. LC 59-7793. 1959. Dutton.

Life and Times of Gasparilla: The Pirate. All Illus. Are by the Author Except Photos. Jack Beater. LC 67-31063.

Life and Times of Horatio Hornblower. Cyril Northcote Parkinson. LC 73-149465. (Illus.). 1971. 6.95. Little, Brown.

Life and Travels of James Tudor Owen. LC 76-57157. (Garland Library of Narratives of North American Indiana Captivities ; V. 25). 1977. 25.00 (ISBN 0-8240-1649-1). Garland Pub.

Life and Words of Christ. John Cunningham Geikie. LC 32-35367. (Seaside library, vol. xxxv, no. 717). G. Munro.

Life Around Us: A Collection of Stories. Maurice Francis Egan. LC 6-37571. F. Pustet & Co.

Life As Carola. Joan Marshall Grant. LC 40-7416. 1940. Harper & Brothers.

Life As Carola. Joan Marshall Grant. LC 78-20222. (Grant, Joan Marshall, 1907-. Works). (Illus.). 1980. 26.00 (ISBN 0-405-11784-1). Arno Press.

Life As Hilda Found It. Emma C Oliver. LC 7-23195.

Life at an Early Age. Jack Welch. LC 81-82631. (pbk.) 4.95. Mountain State Press.

Life at Happy Knoll. Drawings by John Morris. 1st Ed. John Phillips Marquand. LC 57-7841. 1957. Little, Brown.

Life at High Tide... Ed. by William Dean Howells. Alden, Henry Mills, 1836-1919, Joint Ed. LC 9-1054. (Harper's novelettes). Harper & Brothers.

Life at Shut-in Valley: And Other Pacific Coast Tales. Clara Spalding Brown. LC 6-18946. The Editor Publishing Co.

Life at Stake. Marcel Berger. Tr. by Wray, W. Fitzwater. LC 19-8990. 1919. 1.50. G. P. Putnam's Sons.

Life at the Top. John Braine. LC 62-129711. 1962. Houghton Mifflin.

Life at the Top. John Braine. LC 79-24779. 9.95 (ISBN 0-416-00581-0) (ISBN 0-416-00591-8). Methuen.

Life at the White Sulphur Springs: Or, Pictures of a Pleasant Summer. Mary Jane Windle. LC 9-3429. 1857. J. B. Lippincott and Co.

Life Before Him. A Novel... Oliver Bell Bunce. LC 6-18676. 1860. W. A. Townsend & Company.

Life Before Man. Margaret Eleanor Atwood. LC 79-20281. 10.95 (ISBN 0-671-25115-5). Simon & Schuster.

Life Begins to-Morrow. Guido Da Verona & Grazebrook, Isabel, Tr. LC 25-16659. E.P. Dutton & Company.

Life Begins Tomorrow. Sydney Muller Parkman. LC 50-7881. 1950. Pellegrini & Cudahy.

Life-Builders: A Novel. Elizabeth Dejeans. LC 15-7817. 1915. 1.35. Harper & Brothers.

Life: By Johan Bojer... Johan Bojer & Muir, Jessie, Tr. LC 20-19764. 1920. Moffat, Yard and Company.

Life Can Never Be the Same. William Babington Maxwell. LC 19-14945. The Bobbs-Merrill Company.

Life Comes to Judith. Antoinette Spitzer. LC 31-4180. 1931. Brentano's.

Life Comes to Seathorpe. Neil Bell. 1977. 9.95 (ISBN 0-86025-051-2). State Mutual Bk.

Life Cry, Anonymous. Ingyard Marya Linden. LC 33-3297. The Macaulay Company.

Life Everlasting. Marie Corelli. LC 32-195413. 1931. A. L. Burt Company.

Life Everlasting: A Reality of Romance. Marie Corelli. LC 11-22545. Hodder & Stoughton. George H. Doran Company.

Life Everlasting: A Reality of Romance. Marie Corelli. LC 34-38281. 1920. Grosset & Dunlap.

Life Everlasting and Other Tales of Science, Fantasy, and Horror. David Henry Keller. LC 73-13256. (Classics of science fiction). (Illus.). 1974. 10.50 (ISBN 0-88355-111-X) (ISBN 0-88355-111-X). Hyperion Press.

Life Fashionable: A Modern Comedy. Guy Mainwaring Morton. LC 30-2766. 1929. Brentano.

Life for a Death. Gordon Ashe. LC 72-91584. 192p. 1973. 4.95 o.p. (ISBN 0-03-007556-4). HR&W.

Life for a Death. John Creasey. LC 72-91584. (Rinehart suspense novel). 1973. 4.95 (ISBN 0-03-007556-4). Holt, Rinehart and Winston.

Life for a Life. Anthony Bloomfield. LC 79-140770. 1971. 6.95 (ISBN 0-684-10026-6). Scribner.

Life for a Life. Dinah Maria Mulock Craik. LC 4-16511. 1903. Harper & Brothers.

Life for a Life. Robert Herrick. LC 72-84658. 1976. (ISBN 0-403-03197-4). Scholarly Press.

Life for a Life. Robert Herrick. LC 10-132164. 1910. The Macmillan Company.

Life for a Life see Collected Works.

Life for a Life. Translated from the German by Richard and Clara Winston. Horst Fanger. LC 54-130365. Ballantine Books.

Life for a Love. authorized ed. Elizabeth Thomasina Meade Smith. LC 8-8650. (Lovell's international series, no. 152). United States Book Company, Successors to J. W. Lovell Company.

Life for Africa: The Story of Bram Fischer. Naomi Haldane Mitchison. 1973. 8.95 (ISBN 0-85036-170-2). Dufour.

Life for Kregen. Dray Prescot. (Illus.). 1979. 1.75 (ISBN 0-87997-456-7). DAW Books.

Life for Sale. Sydney Horler. LC 28-16856. 1928. Doubleday, Doran & Company, Inc.

Life Full of Holes. Driss Ben Hamed Charhadi. Tr. by Paul Bowles. 1964. pap. 0.95 o.p. (ISBN 0-394-17435-6, B121, BC). Grove.

Life Full of Holes. Larbi Layachi. LC 81-47638. 128p. 1982. pap. 3.50 (ISBN 0-394-17946-3, B436, BC). Grove.

Life Full of Holes: A Novel Tape-Recorded in Moghrebi and Translated into English by Paul Bowles. Driss Ben Hamed Charhadi. LC 64-10599. 1964. Grove Press.

Life Full of Holes: A Novel Tape-Recorded in Moghrebi and Translated into English by Paul Bowles. Driss Ben Hamed Charhadi. LC 81-47638. 1982. 3.50 (ISBN 0-394-17946-3). Grove Press.

Life Goes on. William Gardland Rogers. LC 29-206842. 1929. H. Liveright.

Life Goes on: A Novel of Southern Alabama. 1st Ed. Edith Caraway Creel. LC 57-10659. 1957. Exposition Press.

Life, Here and There: Or, Sketches of Society and Adventure at Far-Apart Times and Places. Nathaniel Parker Willis. LC 8-36899. 1850. Baker & Scribner.

Life, Here and There: Or, Sketches of Society and Adventure at Far-Apart Times and Places. Nathaniel Parker Willis. LC 41-33256. 1856. Alden and Beardsley.

Life Hunt. Kurt Brand. (Perry Rhodan,#43). 1974. (pbk.) 0.75. Ace Books.

Life I Really Lived. Jessamyn West. LC 80-17516. (Series: Penguin Contemporary American Fiction Series.). 1981. 3.95 (ISBN 0-14-005702-1). Penguin Books.

Life I Really Lived: A Novel. Jessamyn West. LC 79-1853. 11.95 (ISBN 0-15-151562-X). Harcourt Brace Jovanovich.

Life Illumined. Lillian Stephenson De Waters. LC 13-19423. 1.25. Davis & Bond.

Life in a Garrison Town: The Military Novel Suppressed by the German Government. Oswald Fritz Bilse. 1904. J. Lane.

Life in a Garrison Town: The Military Novel Suppressed by the German Government. Oswald Fritz Bilse. LC 18-17295. 1909. John Lane.

Life in a Movie Club. Patrick H. Cappello. 1970. 3.75 o.p. Vantage.

Life in a Putty Knife Factory. Harry Allen Smith. 224p. Repr. lib. bdg. 13.25x (ISBN 0-89190-983-4). Am Repr-Rivercity Pr.

Life in a Thousand Worlds. W. S. Harris. LC 72-154444. (Utopian Literature Ser). 1971. Repr. of 1905 ed. 19.00 (ISBN 0-405-03527-6). Ayer Co.

Life in America. Ed. by Gladys Eliot Mansir. LC 41-15015. Harper & Brothers.

Life in America. William Gilmore Simms. 1974. Repr. of 1848 ed. lib. bdg. 35.00 (ISBN 0-8414-8064-8). Folcroft.

Life in Dalecarlia: The Parsonage of Mora. Fredrika Bremer. Tr. by Mary Botham Howitt. LC 7-16321. 1845. Harper & Brothers.

Life in Israel: Or, Portraitures of Hebrew Character. Maria Tolman Richards. LC 7-41214. 1857. Sheldon, Blakeman and Company.

Life in Judea: Or, Glimpses of the First Christian Age. Maria Tolman Richards. American Baptist Publication Society.

Life in London. John Meiklejohn. LC 7-25859. (On cover: Lovell's detective series. no. 7). 1890. J. W. Lovell Company.

Life in New York. Samuel Irenaeus Prime. LC 5-4154. 1847. R. Carter.

Life in Order. Arthur Twining Hadley. LC 71-146598. 1971. 7.95 (ISBN 0-670-42787-X). Viking Press.

Life in Rhyme. C. S. Quinn. 3.00 o.p. Carlton.

Life in Texas. Charles Sealsfield. Tr. by Mersch, Ch. Fr. LC 8-3385. 1845. Colon and Adriance; Etc., Etc.

Life in the Ark. Russell David Burge. LC 40-7802. Harrison-Hilton Books.

Life in the Closet, and Stories. Robert Rushmore. LC 72-89697. 1973. 6.95. Bobbs-Merrill.

Life in the Day of...& Other Short Stories. Ed. by Frank Robinson. 240p. (Orig.). 1981. pap. cancelled (ISBN 0-553-13455-8). Bantam.

Life in the East Indies. William Henry Thomes. LC 13-12914. (Added t.-p.: The ocean life series). 1873. Lee and Shepard.

Life in the East Indies. William Henry Thomes. (On cover: The library of choice fiction, no. 45). 1892. Laird & Lee.

Life in the East Indies. William Henry Thomes. LC 45-48714. (Ocean life series). 1874. Lee and Shepard.

Life in the East Indies. William Henry Thomes & Hayward, C. F. R. (On cover: The detective and adventure library, no. 13). 1890. A. T. Loyd & Company.

Life in the Far West. George Frederick Augustus Ruxton. LC 72-11539. (Rio Grande classic). (Illus.). 1972. (ISBN 0-87380-098-2). Rio Grande Press.

Life in the Far West: Or A Detective's Thrilling Adventures Among the Indians and Outlaws of Montana. Charles H Simpson. LC 8-9002. 1896. Rhodes & McClure Publishing Company.

Life in the Far West: Or, The Comical Quizzical, and Tragical Adventures of a Hoosier. Adolphus M Hart. LC 7-2866. H. B. Pearson.

Life in the Forest: Or, The Trials and Sufferings of a Pioneer. S. M Cooper. 1854. Perry and Erety.

Life in the Iron Mills: Or, The Korl Woman. Rebecca Harding Davis & Tillie Olsen. LC 72-8880. (Feminist Press reprint series, no. 1). 1972. 1.95 (ISBN 0-912670-05-3). Feminist Press.

Life in the Itinerancy: In Its Relations to the Circuit and Station, and to the Minister's Home and Family. Lucius Daniel Davis. LC 6-32475. 1856. Miller, Orton & Mulligan.

Life in the Laity: Or, The History of a Station. Lucius Daniel Davis. LC 6-32474. 1858. Published for the Author by Carlton & Porter.

Life in the Mines: Or, Crime Avenged. Including Thrilling Adventures Among Miners and Outlaws. Charles H Simpson. LC 99-420. 1898. Rhodes & McClure Publishing Company.

Life in the New World: Or, Sketches of American Society. Charles Sealsfield. Tr. by Hebbe, Gustaf Clemens. Mackay, James Aberigh. LC 9-3437. J. Winchester.

Life in the New World: Or, Sketches of American Society. Charles Sealsfield. Tr. by Hebbe, Gustaf Clemens. Mackay, James Aberigh. LC 8-3384. J. Winchester.

Life in the South: A Companion to Uncle Tom's Cabin. Calvin Henderson Wiley. LC 8-37021. 1852. T. B. Peterson.
Life in the United States: A Collection of Narratives of Contemporary American Life from First-Hand Experience or Observation. LC 33-246590. 1933. C. Scribner's Sons.
Life in the Wabash Valley: A Story of the Pioneers and Their Descendants, 1860-1907. George Francis Coburn.
Life in the West: Or, Stories of the Mississippi Valley. Nathan Cook Meeker. LC 7-18476. 1868. S. R. Wells.
Life in the Wilds. A Tale of the South African Settlement. Harriet Martineau. (On cover: Lovell's library, v. 7, no. 388). 1884. J. W. Lovell Company.
Life in Whitehall During the Ship Fever Times. David Wilson. LC 20-231622. 1900. Inglee & Tefft.
Life Interest. Annie French Hector. (On cover: Lovell's library, no. 1142). 1888. J. W. Lovell Company.
Life Interest. Annie French Hector. (On cover: Seaside library. Pocket ed., no. 1057). 1888. G. Munro.
Life Is a Dream. Richard Curle. LC 78-106284. (Short story index reprint series). 1970. Books for Libraries Press.
Life Is a Dream. Richard Curle. LC 14-191388. 1914. Doubleday, Page & Co.
Life Is a Four Letter Word. Rona January. 288p. 1976. 8.00 o.p. (ISBN 0-682-48491-1, Banner). Exposition.
Life Is a Fulfilling: The Story of a Mormon Pioneer Woman, Sarah Diantha Gardner Curtis and Her Part in the Colonization of the San Pedro Valley in Southern Arizona, the Homeland of the Powerful, Antagonistic Apache. Olive Kimball B Mitchell. LC 67-8846. (Illus.). 1967. Brigham Young University Press.
Life Is a Gift. Rusty Berkus. (Illus.). 32p. (Orig.). 1982. pap. 12.00 (ISBN 0-9609888-0-7). Red Rose Pr.
Life Is Elsewhere. Milan Kundera. LC 73-20778. 1974. 6.95 (ISBN 0-394-48010-4). Knopf; Distributed by Random House.
Life Is for Living: A Novel. Kay Lipke. LC 36-9080. 1936. Frederick A. Stokes Company.
Life Is for the Living. Katherine Ursula Parrott. LC 39-211804. 1939. Dodd, Mead & Company.
Life Is Life: And Other Tales and Episodes. Gwendoline Keats. LC 79-101816. (Short story index reprint series). 1969. Books for Libraries Press.
Life Is Life & Other Tales & Episodes. Gwendoline Keats. LC 79-101816. (Short Story Index Reprint Ser.). 1898. 17.00 (ISBN 0-8369-3204-8). Ayer Co.
Life Is Like That! Kaye Holden. LC 33-29348. Grosset & Dunlap.
Life Is Such a Rush. Christine Jope-Slade. LC 31-24775. The Bobbs-Merrill Company.
Life Is to Seek. Desemea Wilson. LC 40-35818. 1941-1940. E. P. Dutton & Company, Inc.
Life Is Worth Living, and Other Stories. Lev Nikolaevich Tolstoi & Norraikow, Adolphus, Tr. LC 8-26743. 1892. C. L. Webster & Co.
Life Isn't So Bad. Helen Marion Edginton. LC 30-129952. 1930. The Penn Publishing Company.
Life Line. Michael Breslow. LC 77-9055. 1977. 7.95 (ISBN 0-670-27972-2). Viking Press.
Life Line. Ella M Noller. LC 44-10706. 1944. Wm. B. Eerdmans Publishing Company.
Life-Line Lad. William Harley Fleming. LC 57-7015. 1957. Comet Press Books.
Life Lines: A Novel. Joseph Viertel. LC 82-673. 15.95 (ISBN 0-671-25426-X). Simon and Schuster.
Life, Love and Jeanette. Louise Platt Hauck. LC 33-304474. The Penn Publishing Company.
Life, Love, Nature & You. William C. Lennard. 1977. 4.50 o.p. (ISBN 0-533-02048-4). Vantage.
Life Makes Advances. Madeleine Elise Reynier Boyd. 1939. Little, Brown and Company.
Life Mask: A Novel. Alice Muriel Livingston Williamson. LC 13-3301. 1913. Frederick A. Stokes Company.
Life Mirror"... S. Jay Bowers. LC 6-189074. 1889.
Life of a Prig. Thomas Longueville. LC 75-459. (Victorian Fiction: Novels of Faith and Doubt; No. 14). 1975. 35.00 (ISBN 0-8240-1538-X). Garland Pub.
Life of a Refugee. Z. L. Perrault. 4.95 o.p. Carlton.
Life of a Sailor. Frederick Chamier. LC 6-20162. 1833. Key and Biddle.
Life of a Sailor. Frederick Chamier. LC 41-32195. G. Routledge and Sons.
Life of a Simple Man. Emile Guillaumin. LC 82-40339. 1982. 7.95 (ISBN 0-87451-246-8) (ISBN 0-87451-247-6). University Press of New England.
Life of a Tiger. Sainthill Eardley-Wilmot. 1911. Repr. 12.00 o.s.i. Finch Pr.
Life of a Tramp and a Trip Through Hell. L. A. Miller & Goolsby, C. V., Joint Author. 1894. C. S. Warnock & Co.
Life of a Useless Man. Maksim Gorkii. LC 71-144254. 1971. 6.95. Doubleday.
Life of a Useless Man. Maksim Gorkii. Tr. by Moura Budberg. LC 71-144254. 1971. 6.95 o.p. (ISBN 0-385-04339-2). Doubleday.
Life of an Alcoholic. 1st Ed. Vally Astoris. LC 59-13091. 1959. Pageant Press.
Life of an Amorous Man. Ihara Saikaku. Tr. by Kengi Hamada. LC 63-21505. (Illus.). 1963. pap. 5.50 (ISBN 0-8048-0381-1). C E Tuttle.
Life of an Amorous Woman, and Other Writings. Saikaku Ihara. (UNESCO collection of representative literary works). 1963. New Directions.
Life of Anson Bunker: "the Bloody Hand," the Perpetrator of No Less Than Fifteen Cold-Blooded Murders, Amongst Which Were the Great Nathan Murder of New York City, and Those of His Three Wives... His Horrible Confessions and Terrible Doom. Anson Bunker. LC 10-4186. Barclay & Co.
Life of Byron Jaynes: A Novel. James Howard Kunstler. 1983. 16.50 (ISBN 0-393-01721-4); pap. 7.95 (ISBN 0-393-30116-8). Norton.
Life of Christ. Frederic William Farrar. LC 32-33634. (Seaside library, vol. xxxv. no. 711). 1880. G. Munro.
Life of Elvina and Her Return After Death: A True and Marvelous Story of How I Met the Spirit Forces from an Unseen World. Viola Moore Hart. LC 32-253230. 1932.
Life of George Washington: With Curious Anecdotes, Equally Honourable to Himself, and Exemplary to His Young Countrymen. Mason Locke Weems. LC 15-106725. (Seaside library, vol. LXXIX, no.1596). G. Munroe.
Life of Gus Davis Trifler: A Story Founded on Facts. Solomon Woolworth. LC 5-40405. 1905.
Life of Her Own, and Other Stories. Maeve Kelly. LC 77-357522. 1.32 (ISBN 0-905169-04-2). Poolbeg Press.
Life of Humbug. Fredric Maffie. (Orig.). 1979. pap. 1.75 (ISBN 0-532-17217-5). Woodhill.
Life of Jefferson S. Batkins: Member from Canberry Centre. Joseph Stevens Jones. LC 7-11923. Loring.
Life of Jesus. Toby Olson. LC 76-8210. (New directions book; 417). 1976. 8.50 (ISBN 0-8112-0613-0) (ISBN 0-8112-0614-9). New Directions Pub. Corp.
Life of Jesus: An Apocryphal Novel. Toby Olson. LC 76-8210. 1976. 8.50 (ISBN 0-8112-0613-0); pap. 3.95 (ISBN 0-8112-0614-9, NDP417). New Directions.
Life of Jimmy Dolan. Bertram Millhauser & Dix, Beulah Marie, 1876- LC 33-8142. The Macualay Company.
Life of John Buncle, Esq. Thomas Amory. LC 74-31048. (Flowering of the Novel). 1975. 25.00 (ISBN 0-8240-1144-9). Garland Pub.
Life of John William Walshe, F. S. A.; Ed., with an Introduction. Montgomery Carmichael. LC 3-16353. 1902. E. P. Dutton & Co.
Life of Jonathan Wild. Henry Fielding. LC 32-26088. (Half-title: The world's classics. CCCLXXXII). 1932. H. Milford, Oxford University Press.
Life of Joshua Davidson: Or, The Modern Imitation of Christ. A Theoretical Novel. 2d ed.... ed. Elizabeth Lynn Linton. LC 7-19010. 1882. R. Worthington.
Life of Lazarillo De Tormes: His Fortunes & Adversities. Tr. by W. S. Merwin. 8.00 (ISBN 0-8446-0767-3). Peter Smith.
Life of Madam De Beaumount, a French Lady: And The Strange Adventures of the Count De Vinevil and His Family. Penelope Aubin. LC 75-170548. (Foundations of the novel). 1973. 22.00 ea. (ISBN 0-8240-0548-1). Garland Pub.
Life of Mansie Wauch: Tailor in Dalkeith. David Macbeth Moir. LC 5-410903. 1828. Printed by J. & J. Harper.
Life of Me. Ethel Shackelford. LC 10-16325. Dodge Publishing Company.
Life of Mr. Jonathan Wild. Henry Fielding. LC 74-17291. (Flowering of the Novel). 1974. (ISBN 0-8240-1108-2). Garland Pub.
Life of Monsieur De Moliere. Mikhail Bulgakov. Tr. by Mirra Ginsburg. LC 70-93921. 1970. 5.95 o.p. (711150). Funk & W.
Life of My Own. Charlotte Ruth Miller. (Dell book). 1974. (pbk.) 1.25. Dell.
Life of Nancy. Sarah Orne Jewett. LC 77-98579. (Short story index reprint series). 1969. Books for Libraries Press.
Life of Nancy. Sarah Orne Jewett. LC 7-9727. 1895. Houghton, Mifflin and Company.
Life of Nancy see Collected Works.
Life of Ones Own. Gerald Brenan. 1963. 4.95 o.p. (ISBN 0-374-18708-8). FS&G.
Life of Paddy O'Flarrity: Who, from a Shoe Black, Has by Perseverance and Good Conduct, Arrived to a Member of Congress... Paddy O'Flarrity. LC 7-36192. 1834.
Life of Riley. Anthony Cronin. LC 64-12313. 1964. Knopf.
Life of Riley. Harvey Fergusson. LC 27-14277. 1937. A. A. Knopf.
Life of Riley: Novelized from the Screenplay. Irving Brecher. LC 49-452414. (Movie readers library). 1949. Waverly House.
Life of Riot. Judith Johnson Sherwin. 1970. 5.95 o.p. (ISBN 0-689-10326-3). Atheneum.
Life of Riot: Stories. Judith Johnson Sherwin. LC 72-108826. 1970. 5.95. Atheneum.
Life of the Automobile. Ilia Grigorevich Ehrenburg. LC 76-22477. 1976. 8.95 (ISBN 0-916354-06-7) (ISBN 0-916354-07-5). Urizen Books.
Life of the Party. Irvin Shrewsbury Cobb. LC 19-10468. George H. Doran Company.
Life of the Party. Elizabeth Garver Jordan. LC 36-10608. 1936. D. Appleton-Century Company, Incorporated.
Life of Vicissitudes. A Story of Revolutionary Times. George Payne Rainsford James. LC 7-7993. 1852. Harper & Brothers.
Life of Wild Bill Hickok. James W. Buel. (Golden West Ser.). 1976. pap. 1.25 o.p. (LB422ZK, Leisure Bks). Nordon Pubns.
Life on a Backwoods Farm: Or, The Boyhood of Rueben Rodney Blannerhassett. William Riley Halstead. LC 7-967. 1894. Cranston & Curts.
Life on the Acre: As Told by Whitey the Owl. Pauline M. Logue. 1968. 2.50 o.p. Vantage.
Life on the Head End. 1st Ed. P M Adams. LC 56-5533. 1956. Vantage Press.
Life on the Mississippi. Mark Twain. (Illus., TV tie-in edition). 1980. pap. 1.75 (ISBN 0-451-51448-3, CE1448, Sig Classics). NAL.
Life on the Mississippi. Mark Twain. (Harper Modern Classics Ser). (gr. 9-12). text ed. 2.28, s.p. 1.71 o.p. (ISBN 0-06-534066-3). Har-Row.
Life on the Mississippi. Mark Twain. 1957. pap. 1.45 o.p. (ISBN 0-8090-0021-0, AmCen). Hill & Wang.
Life on the Mississippi. Mark Twain. Ed. by Harry Shefter. (YA) 1968. pap. 0.50 o.p. (CC519, CC). WSP.
Life on the Mountain and Prairie. Edward Sylvester Ellis. (Seaside library, v. 90. no 1820). 1884. G. Munro.
Life on the Road. Virginia Wales Johnson. LC 13-5593. 1913. 0.75. The A. S. Barnes Company.
Life or Death: A True Story. Otto Zurcher. LC 16-6057. 1916. The Knickerbocker Press.
Life: Or, Unto the Third and Fourth Generation. Charles Wathen Chase & Francis, Eugene. LC 6-10647. 1904. C. M. Benton.
Life, Real and Portrayed. Rebecca Foutz. LC 47-163467. 1946. Brethren Publishing House.
Life Real and Unreal. Frances Fay. LC 6-38775. American Sunday-School Union.
Life Returns to Die: A Novel. by edward a. herron. ed. Edward Albert Herron. LC 34-2143. 1934. Benziger Brothers.
Life Sentence. Olga Hesky. LC 72-79395. 1972. 4.95 (ISBN 0-385-00090-1). Published for the Crime Club by Doubleday.
Life Sentence. A Novel. Adeline Sergent. LC 8-6853. (On cover: Lovell's international series, no. 34). 1889. F. F. Lovell & Company.
Life Sentence: A Reggie Fortune Novel. Henry Christopher Bailey. LC 46-7186. 1946. Pub. for the Crime Club by Doubleday & Company, Inc.
Life Sentence. By Adeline Sergeant. Adeline Sergeant. (On cover: Seaside library. Pocket ed. no. 1231). 1889. G. Munro.
Life Sentence: Or, Duty in Dealing with Crime. William Watson Burgess. LC 6-747. 1905. R. G. Badger.
Life Sentences: A Novel. Elizabeth Forsythe Hailey. LC 82-7388. 15.95 (ISBN 0-440-04924-5). Delacorte Press.
Life She Wanted. Roger Conway. 1968. pap. 0.75 o.p. (74-968). Lancer.
Life Signs. Johanna Davis. LC 72-82689. 1973. 5.95 (ISBN 0-689-10532-0). Atheneum.
Life Signs. Johanna Davis. 1974. (pbk.) 1.50. Dell.
Life Sketches from Common Paths: A Series of American Tales. Julia Louisa Carey Dumont. LC 6-35874. 1856. D. Appleton & Company.
Life Steps in. Ruby Mildred Ayres. LC 29-11933. 1929. Doubleday, Doran & Company, Inc.
Life-Stories. Nonna Osipova. (O.s.i.). (Illus.). 60p. (Orig.). 1980. pap. 4.00 o.s.i. (ISBN 0-935500-02-2, TX198-101). Am Samizdat.
Life Story. Phyllis Eleanor Bentley. LC 48-8343. 1948. Macmillan Co.
Life Story of Aner: An Allegory. Frederic William Farrar. LC 6-38658. 1898. Longmans, Green and Co.
Life Swap. Curtis Richards. 1973. (pbk.) 1.25. Warner Paperback Library.
Life the Accuser: A Novel in Two Parts. Emma Frances Brooke. LC 6-19392. 1896. E. Arnold.
Life, the Loves, the Adventures of Omar Khayyam: By Manuel Komroff, and the Complete Text of the Rubaiyat of Omar Khayyam, Translated by Edward FitzGerald. Manuel Komroff. LC 57-80289. (Signet book, 1377). 1957. New American Library.
Life, the Universe & Everything: The Cosmic Conclusion to the Hitchhiker Trilogy. Douglas Adams. 1982. 9.95 (ISBN 0-517-54874-7, Harmony). Crown.
Life to Come, and Other Short Stories. Edward Morgan Forster. LC 72-13127. 1973. 7.95 (ISBN 0-393-08381-0). W. W. Norton.
Life to Come: And Other Short Stories. Edward Morgan Forster. (Bard Book). 2.50 (ISBN 0-380-00870-X). Avon.
Life to Come & Other Stories. E. M. Forster. 264p. 1973. 7.95 (ISBN 0-393-08381-0). Norton.
Life to Come & Other Stories. Edward Morgan Forster. 1976. pap. 2.95 (ISBN 0-380-00870-X, 48611, Bard). Avon.
Life to Live: A Novel. Yvonne Burgess. LC 80-17914. 1981. 8.95 (ISBN 0-8008-4816-0). Taplinger Pub. Co.
Life, Travels, and Adventures of Christopher Wagstaff (1762) John Dunton. LC 74-23184. (Sterneiana; 8). (Life & times of seven major British writers). 1974. 22.00 (ISBN 0-8240-1327-1). Garland Pub.
Life, Treason, and Death of James Blount of Breckenhow: Comp. from the Rowlestone Papers. Beulah Marie Dix. 1903. The Macmillan Company.
Life: Trial and Conviction of Zella De Chalue, Also, the Life, Confession and Startling Disclosures of the Notorious Clarence O. Alderman. The Interesting Trial. Many Secrets for the First Time Made Public. E. O Nye. 1873. Osborn & Acres.
Life We Live. Lawrence Richard Schmieder. LC 47-16619. 1946. R. H. Mitchell.
Life We Prize. Elton Trueblood. 241p. 1982. pap. 3.95 (ISBN 0-932970-25-7). Prinit Pr.
Life with a Small L. Sandra Berkley. 1971. 5.95 o.p. (ISBN 0-525-12634-1). Dutton.
Life with Father. Clarence Day. (YA) 1957. 8.95 (ISBN 0-394-43319-X). Knopf.
Life With Father. Clarence Day. 1981. Repr. lib. bdg. 15.95x (ISBN 0-89966-430-X). Buccaneer Bks.
Life with Father & Life with Mother. Clarence Day. 1970. pap. 0.95 o.p. (ISBN 0-671-47821-4). WSP.
Life with Its Sorrow, Life with Its Tear: A Novel. Lester Atwell. LC 75-139616. 1971. 7.95 (ISBN 0-671-20826-8). Simon and Schuster.
Life with Larry Thompson. Larry Thompson. (Illus.). 1975. 5.95 (ISBN 0-87482-047-2). Wake-Brook.
Life Within ... LC 3-3282. 1903. Lothrop Publishing Company.
Life Without Birth. Stanley Johnson. LC 74-117041. 1971. 7.95 o.p. (ISBN 0-316-46739-1). Little.
Life Without End. Graham Seton Hutchison. LC 34-34020. 1934. Farrar & Rinehart, Incorporated.
Life, Wonderful Life! Edita Morris. LC 73-156598. 1971. 5.95 (ISBN 0-8076-0614-6). G. Braziller.
Life Worth Living. Phyllis Karas. LC 80-29186. 12.95 (ISBN 0-312-48503-4). St. Martin's Press.
Lifeboat Number Two. Margaret Culkin Banning. LC 70-144188. (Cass Canfield book). 1971. 5.95 (ISBN 0-06-010204-7). Harper & Row.
Lifeguard. Thom Racina. 1976. (pbk.) 1.50. Warner Books.
Lifeline of Texas. Roe Richmond. (Lashtrow Ser.: No. 6). 1981. pap. 1.95 (ISBN 0-8439-0892-0, Leisure Bks). Nordon Pubns.
Lifelines. Caroline Leavitt. LC 81-84530. 13.50 (ISBN 0-87223-770-2). Seaview Books.
Lifelines. James Mossman. 1971. 6.95 o.p. (ISBN 0-316-58576-9). Little.
Lifelines. Joseph Viertel. 1982. 15.95 (ISBN 0-671-25426-X). S&S.
Lifelines: A Novel. James Mossman. LC 76-154950. 1971. 6.95. Little, Brown.
Life's Assize. A Novel. Charlotte Eliza Lawson Cowan Riddell. (Seaside library, v. 64, no. 1300). 1882. G. Munro.
Life's Atonement. A Novel. David Christie Murray. (Franklin square library, no. 210). 1881. Harper & Brothers.
Life's Atonement. A Novel. David Christie Murray. LC 7-324603. (On cover: Seaside library. Pocket ed., no. 698). 1886. G. Munro.
Life's Battle Won. Julia A W De Witt. LC 6-33394. 1893. Hunt & Eaton.
Life's Bittersweet. Josephine Halliburton. LC 38-19928. 1938. Artcraft Press.
Life's Detours. C. L. Paddock. (Uplook Ser.). 32p. 1952. pap. 0.75 (ISBN 0-8163-0074-7, 12225-9). Pacific Pr Pub Assn.
Life's Discipline: A Tale of the Annals of Hungary. Therese Albertine Louise Robinson. LC 7-42186. 1851. D. Appleton & Co.
Life's Fitful Hours"... Matthew Long. LC 31-343995. G. H. Zerbey Publishing Co.
Life's Full Summer. Andree Martinerie. LC 76-124835. 1970. Harcourt Brace Jovanovich.

Life's Handicap: Being Stories of Mine Own People. Rudyard Kipling. LC 3-19549. 1891. Macmillan and Co.
Life's Handicap: Being Stories of Mine Own People. copyright ed. Rudyard Kipling. LC 90-302958. 1899. Doubleday & McClure Co.
Life's Handicap: Being Stories of Mine Own People. Rudyard Kipling. LC 28-166418. 1921. Doubleday, Page & Company.
Life's Joys. La Joie De Vivfe. Emile Zola & Philip, Kenward, Tr. (On cover: Munro's library. v. 1, no. 155). 1834. N. L. Munro.
Life's Labyrinth. Mary Ellen Mannix. LC 1-27576. The Ave Maria.
Life's Lesson. A Tale. Martha McCannon Thomas. 1854. Harper & Brothers.
Life's Like That. Elizabeth Carfrae, pseud. LC 34-418714. 1934. G. P. Putnam's Sons.
Life's Little Day. Martha King Davis. LC 54-8356. 1954. Vantage Press.
Life's Little Ironies: A Set of Tales, with Some Colloquial Sketches, Entitled, A Few Crusted Characters. Thomas Hardy. 1894. Harper & Brothers.
Life's Little Ironies: A Set of Tales, with Some Colloquial Sketches, Entitled, A Few Crusted Characters. Thomas Hardy. LC 24-24096. Harper & Brothers.
Life's Little Ironies & a Few Crusted Characters. Thomas Hardy. 1894. 7.50 o.p. (ISBN 0-312-48580-8). St Martin.
Life's Lottery: Or, Life and Its Aims. 4th ed. Elise Osborne. LC 7-23694. 1869. Claxton, Remsen & Haffelfinger.
Life's Lure. John Gneisenau Neihardt. LC 14-17928. 1914. M. Kennerley.
Life's Mistake. Charles Garvice. (On cover: Laurel library, no. 19). G. Munro's Sons.
Life's Morning. George Robert Gissing. LC 76-75985. 1969. AMS Press.
Life's Other Side. Nick Drosopoulos. 1970. 2.75 o.p. Carlton.
Life's Parade. Louise Gerard. The Macaulay Company.
Life's Passionate Guest. Clark Jewett. LC 98-113116. (Dillingham's metropolitan library. no. 43). 1898. G. W. Dillingham Co.
Life's Progress Through the Passions. Eliza Fowler Haywood. LC 74-16053. (Flowering of the Novel). 1974. (ISBN 0-8240-1123-6). Garland Publishing.
Life's Promise to Pay. A Novel. Clara L Conway. LC 6-27202. 1876. J. B. Lippincott & Co.
Life's Puckering Strings. Grace Virginia Logan. LC 33-16999. 1931. Wetzel Publishing Co., Inc.
Life's Rainbow. 1st Ed. Gertrude M Wiebe. LC 56-12773. 1957. Vantage Press.
Life's Remorse. Margaret Wolfe Hamilton Hungerford. (On cover: Seaside library. Pocket ed., no. 1249). 1889. G. Munro.
Life's Secret. Ellen Price Henry Wood Wood. (On cover: Seaside library. Pocket ed. no. 1027). 1887. G. Munor.
Life's Secret. Ellen Price Henry Wood Wood. (On cover: Lovell's library, no. 1160). 1888. J. W. Lovell Company.
Life's Secret. By Mrs. Henry Wood... Ellen Price Henry Wood Wood. (Seaside library, v. 3, no. 45). 1877. G. Munro.
Life's Shop Window. Vivian Cory. LC 7-41585. M. Kennerley.
Life's Tragedy. Mable Naomi Harriet Thompson. LC 13-21055. 1913. Chapple Publishing Company, Ltd.
Life's Trivial Round. Rosa Nouchette Carey. LC 2793. 1909. J. B. Lippincott Company.
Life's Vagaries: Fourteen Short Stories. Stephen M Gill. LC 75-307649. 1974. 2.50 (ISBN 0-9690996-5-7). Vesta Publications.
Lifeship. Gordon R Dickson & Harry Harrison. LC 75-25079. 7.95 (ISBN 0-06-011764-8). Harper & Row.
Lifeship. Gordon R Dickson & Harry Harrison. (Kangaroo Book). 1977. 1.50. Pocket Books.
Lifetime. Mark McShane. 1978. pap. 1.95 (ISBN 0-532-19166-8). Woodhill.
Lifetime Burning. Ellen Douglas, pseud. LC 82-40141. 13.95 (ISBN 0-394-52719-4). Random House.
Lifetime High & Dead. Richard Wayne. 1970. 3.95 o.p. Vantage.
Lifetime of Service. David Reid. (Illus.). 1969. 5.50 o.p. (ISBN 0-682-40076-9). Exposition.
Lifetime on Clouds. Gerald Murnane. LC 77-360704. 1976. (ISBN 0-85561-040-9). William Heinemann Australia.
Lifetime to Love. Ann Dabney. (Candlelight Romance). 1.25 (ISBN 0-440-15018-3). Dell Pub. Co.
Liffey Lane. Maura Laverty. LC 47-30392. 1947. Longmans, Green.
Lift-off at Satan. Richard Butler. LC 78-19396. 8.95 (ISBN 0-312-48600-6). St. Martin's Press.
Lift These Shadows from Our Eyes. Rosemari Mealy. 1978. pap. 1.00 (ISBN 0-931122-13-9). West End.
Lift up the Glory. Richard Warren Hatch. LC 34-16181. Covici, Friede.
Lifted Curtain. Mirabeau. Tr. by Howard Nelson. pap. 1.75 o.p. (ISBN 0-87067-505-2). Holloway.
Lifted Latch. George Vane. LC 11-273065. 1912. John Lane.
Lifted Masks: Stories. Susan Glaspell. LC 12-225936. 1912. 1.00. Frederick A. Stokes Company.
Lifted Shadows. Charles Elmo Robinson. LC 38-37002. Zondervan Publishing House.
Lifted Veil. Basil King. LC 17-8203. 1917. 1.40. Harper & Brothers.
Lifting Mist. Austin Harrison. LC 25-8365. 1925. T. Seltzer.
Lifting the Veil... Mary Webster McLain. LC 7-16303. 1870. C. Scribner & Co.
Lige Golden: The Man Who Twinkled. William W Harvey. LC 24-15986. 1924. B. J. Brimmer Company.
Lige Mounts: Free Trapper. Frank Bird Linderman. LC 22-18893. 1922. C. Scribner's Sons.
Light. Henri Barbusse. Tr. by W. Fitzwater Wray. LC 19-15319. E. P. Dutton & Company.
Light. Nina Kennedy Gorst. LC 8-8305. 1907. B. W. Dodge and Company.
Light. Jeanne Bartholow Magoun. LC 11-317481. 1911. M. Kennerley.
Light a Fire. Frank John. (Heritage Ser). 1973. pap. 2.50x. Broadside.
Light a Penny Candle. Maeve Binchy. LC 82-19132. 1983. 17.95 (ISBN 0-670-42827-2). Viking Press.
Light Across the Praire: By Norman E. King Pseud. Kenneth Anderson. 1948. Zondervan Pub. House.
Light After Darkness. Floyd Warren Dodds. LC 54-2238. 1954. Christopher Pub. House.
Light Again: A Novel. Blair Niles. LC 33-36077. Liveright, Inc.
Light and Darkness. Soseki Natsume & V. H Viglielmo. LC 81-15426. 1982. 6.95 (ISBN 0-399-50610-1). Putnam.
Light and Darkness: An Unfinished Novel. Soseki Natsume. LC 73-122552. (UNESCO Collection of Representative Works: Japanese Series). 1971. (ISBN 0-87022-770-X). University of Hawaii Press.
Light and Darkness: Or, Fate's Shadow. Lizzie Pittit Cutler. LC 21-13962. (Seaside library, v. 80, no. 1621). 1883. G. Munro.
Light and Darkness: Or Mysteries of Life. a new ed. Catherine Stevens Crowe. LC 7-3071. 1856. G. Routledge & Co.
Light and Power: Stories. Ian T MacMillan. LC 79-3066. 1980. 9.95 (ISBN 0-8262-0289-6). University of Missouri Press.
Light and Shade. Carol Brooke. LC 48-4480. 1947. J. Long.
Light and Shade. A Novel. Charlotte Grace O'Brien. (Franklin square library, no. 29). 1878. Harper & Brothers.
Light and Shade 'round Gulf and Bayou. Corinne Hay. The Roxburgh Publishing Company, Inc.
Light and Shadow. Bergner, Herz. LC 63-18246. 1963. T. Yoseloff.
Light and the Dark. Charles Percy Snow. LC 61-953. (His Strangers and brothers 4). 1961. Scribner.
Light and the Dark: A Novel. Charles Percy Snow. LC 48-541733. 1948. Macmillan Co.
Light As the Morning. Bowen Ingram. LC 54-960453. 1954. Houghton Mifflin.
Light at the End of the Universe. Ed. by Terry Carr. (Orig.). 1976. pap. 1.25 o.p. (ISBN 0-515-03982-9). BJ Pub Group.
Light at the Top of the Stairs. Dorothy McKay Martin. 256p. 1974. pap. 3.95 (ISBN 0-8024-4748-1). Moody.
Light at the Tunnel End. Leonard Robinson. 1975. 8.00 (ISBN 0-87012-198-7). McClain.
Light-Bearer. Sam Nicholson. 1980. pap. 1.95 (ISBN 0-425-04587-0). Berkley Pub.
Light Behind. Josephine Mary Hope-Scott W. P. Ward Ward. LC 3-3563. 1903. J. Lane.
Light Beyond. Edmund H Brown. LC 41-1052. 1941. Meador Publishing Company.
Light Beyond. Edward Phillips Oppenheim. LC 28-672. 1928. Little, Brown, and Company.
Light Beyond. Edward Phillips Oppenheim. 1939. Triangle Books.
Light Beyond the Zodiac. Emilie Ida Friedli. LC 47-292366. 1947. Wetzel Pub. Co.
Light Brigade in Spain: Or, The Last Fight of Sir John Morre. Herbert Strang. 1904. G. P. Putnam's Sons.
Light Cavalry Action. John Harris. LC 67-15146. 1967. bds., 4.95. Morrow.
Light Down, Stranger. Anita Pettibone. LC 42-181594. 1942. Farrar & Rhinehart, Inc.
Light Dragoon: Or, The Rancheros of the Poisoned Lance. A Tale of the Battle Fields of Mexico. Justin Jones. LC 4-885. 1848. 'Star Spangled Banner' Office.
Light Fantastic. Alfred Bester. LC 76-7269. (great short fiction of Alfred Bester; v. 1). 7.95 (ISBN 0-399-11418-1). Berkley Pub. Corp.: Distributed by Putnam.
Light Fantastic. Harry Harrison. 1971. 5.95 o.p. (ISBN 0-684-10228-5). Scribner.
Light Fantastic. Peter Mason. 1983. pap. 5.95 (ISBN 0-14-022449-1). Penguin.
Light Fantastic see Never in This World.
Light Fantastic: Science Fiction Classics from the Mainstream. Ed. by Harry Harrison. LC 76-140772. 1971. 5.95 (ISBN 0-684-10228-5). Scribner.
Light-Fingered Gentry. David G. Philips. Ed. by Abe C. Ravitz. (American Authors Ser). 1907. 23.75 o.s.i. (ISBN 0-512-00555-9). Garrett Pr.
Light-Fingered Gentry. David Graham Phillips. LC 72-84631. (Illus.). 1974. (lib. ed.) 18.50 (ISBN 0-403-02996-1). Scholarly Press.
Light-Fingered Gentry. David Graham Phillips. LC 76-110385. (Series in American Studies). (Illus.). 1970. Johnson Reprint Corp.
Light-Fingered Gentry. David Graham Phillips. 1907. D. Appleton and Company.
Light-Fingered Gentry. David Graham Phillips. LC 16-9359. 1912. D. Appleton and Company.
Light Fingers. Frank Lord. LC 26-18507. The Bobbs-Merrill Company.
Light for Fools. Natalia Ginzburg. LC 56-5270. 1957. Dutton.
Light Freights. William Wymark Jacobs. LC 77-113678. (Short story index reprint series). (Illus.). 1970. Books for Libraries Press.
Light Freights. William Wymark Jacobs. LC 1-25445. 1901. Dodd, Mead & Company.
Light from Arcturus. Mildred Walker, pseud. LC 35-270976. Harcourt, Brace and Company.
Light from Heaven. Christmas Carol Miller Kauffman. LC 61-19090. 1961. Herald Press.
Light from Sealonia. Arthur W Barker. LC 28-11706. The Four Seas Company.
Light from the Dust: A Historical Novel. Winifred M Milner. LC 72-147023. 1971. 8.95 (ISBN 0-8309-0040-3). Herald Pub. House.
Light from the Hill. Sallie Lee Bell. LC 65-19511. 1965. Zondervan Pub House.
Light from the Second Story Window. David L. Allen. 91p. 1972. 4.00 o.p. (ISBN 0-682-47436-3). Exposition.
Light Growth. Peter Hjersman. LC 77-28554. (Illus.). 1978. pap. 4.00 (ISBN 0-916342-02-6, Pub. by Erewon Pr). Bookpeople.
Light Heart. Maurice Henry Hewlett. LC 20-8858. 1920. 1.75. H. Holt and Company.
Light Heart. Elswyth Thane. LC 74-4539. 1974. 6.95. Aeonian Press.
Light Heart. Elswyth Thane. LC 47-30164. 1947. Duell, Sloan and Pearce.
Light Heart. Elswyth Thane. LC 80-25599. 1981. 17.95 (ISBN 0-8161-3163-5). G. K. Hall.
Light Here Kindled. Gladys Hasty Carroll. LC 67-23831. 1967. Little, Brown.
Light Horse Harry's Legion. Everett Titsworth Tomlinson. LC 10-22061. 1910. Houghton, Mifflin Company.
Light in August. William Faulkner. (Mod. lib. coll. ed. T68). 1965. pap., 2.45. Random.
Light in August. William Faulkner. LC 50-14491. (Modern library of the world's best books 88). 1950. Modern Library.
Light in August. William Faulkner. LC 67-12716. 1967. Random House.
Light in August. William Faulkner. (Modern Readers Series). 1947. New Directions.
Light in August. William Faulkner. LC 32-255883. H. Smith & R. Haas.
Light in Eden. 2d ed. Edwin Ritchie. LC 77-149884. 1971. 4.95. Courthouse Square Enterprises.
Light in Holland. Anthony Bailey. LC 78-118705. 1970. 6.95 o.p. (ISBN 0-394-43321-1). Knopf.
Light in Silence. Claude F Koch. LC 58-8286. 1958. Dodd, Mead.
Light in the Clearing: A Tale of the North Country in the Time of Silas Wright. Irving Bacheller. LC 17-11215. The Bobbs-Merrill Company.
Light in the Darkness: A Story of the Franco-German War. Tr. by Burk, Alice F. LC 7-19390. (On cover: The Fatherland series). 1883. Lutheran Publication Society.
Light in the Forest. Conrad Richter. LC 67-146. 1966. Knopf.
Light in the Forest. Conrad Richter. LC 52-12207. 1953. Knopf.
Light in the Forest. Edited for School Use by Joseph Gallant. Conrad Richter. (Modern literature series). 1958. Oxford Book Co.
Light in the Jungle. Edison Marshall. LC 33-647619. 1933. H. C. Kinsey & Company, Inc.
Light in the Piazza. Elizabeth Spencer. LC 60-15005. 1960. McGraw-Hill.
Light in the Rigging. Helen Corse Barney. LC 55-7226. 1955. Crown Publishers.
Light in the Sky. Herbert Clock & Eric Boetzel. LC 29-13212. 1929. Coward-McCann, Inc.
Light in the Sky. Herbert Clock & Eric Boetzel. LC 77-84211. (Lost Race and Adult Fantasy Fiction). 1978. 20.00 (ISBN 0-405-10966-0). Arno Press.
Light in the Sky. Agnes Brooks Young. LC 48-768588. 1948. Random House.
Light in the Swamp. Velda Johnston. LC 74-121976. (Red badge novel of suspense). 1970. 4.50. Dodd, Mead.
Light in the Tower. Miriam Lynch. (Empress Gothic). 1973. 0.95. Curtis Books.
Light in the Valley: No. 1. Mary Mackie. (Starlight Romances Ser.). 144p. 1981. pap. cancelled (ISBN 0-553-14366-2). Bantam.
Light in the Window. Gladys Starkey Battye. LC 68-10582. 1968. Published for the Crime Club by Doubleday.
Light in the Window. John Porter Fort. LC 28-12810. 1928. Dodd, Mead and Company.
Light in the Window. Margaret Lynn. 1968. 3.95 o.p. Doubleday.
Light in the Window. Mary Roberts Rinehart. LC 47-305294. 1948. Rinehart.
Light in the Window: A Story of the Wanderings and Sufferings of a Wayward Boy. Jennie Freeman Bennett. LC 13-24830. 1913. 1.15. W. B. Conkey Company.
Light Infantry Ball. 1st Ed. Hamilton Basso. LC 59-9131. 1959. Doubleday.
Light Keepers: A Story of the United States Lighthouse Service. James Otis Kaler. LC 6-32105. 1906. E. P. Dutton and Company.
Light Lady. Elisabeth Finley Thomas. LC 30-305743. Farrar & Rinehart, Incorporated.
Light Light-House Lass: Or, The World Well Lost. Elizabeth Stiles. (On cover: Library of American authors, no. 35). 1891. G. Munro.
Light, More Light; or, Danger in the Dark... Isaac Kelso. LC 7-109785. 1855. E. Hampson.
Light My Fire. Jim Morrison. Ed. by Jim Mooney. 1978. pap. 7.95 (ISBN 0-915628-07-4). Zeppelin.
Light of Day. Eric Ambler. LC 63-7762. 1963. Knopf.
Light of Day. Eric Ambler. 1974. (pbk.) 1.25. Bantam.
Light of Eden: Or, A Historical Narrative of the Barbarian Age. A Scientific Discovery... Swan Burg. LC 6-18664. 1896. S. Burg.
Light of Egypt. Werner Jansen. Tr. by Drake, William A. LC 28-25027. 1928. Brentano's.
Light of Her Countenance. Hjalmar Hjorth Boyesen. LC 6-16079. (On cover: Appleton's town and country library, no. 34). 1889. D. Appleton and Company.
Light of His Countenance: A Tale of Rome in the Second Century After Christ. Jerome Harte. LC 10-9850. 1910. Benziger Brothers.
Light of One Day: Seen Through a Narrow Window. Isabella J Postgate. LC 26-22297. 1915. Society for Promoting Christian Knowledge.
Light of Other Days. Mrs. Bridges. LC 6-18268. (On cover: Lippincott's series of select novels). 1894. J. B. Lippincott Company.
Light of Other Days: A Novel of Mount Royal. Elizabeth Frances Corbett. LC 38-271786. 1928. D. Appleton-Century Company, Incorporated.
Light of Parnell. John Wilberforce Appel. LC 16-16255. 1916. The Heidelberg Press.
Light of Scarthey: A Romance. Egerton Castle. LC 245. 1899. Frederick A. Stokes Company.
Light of Scarthey: A Romance. Egerton Castle. LC 34-37762. 1901. International Association of Newspapers and Authors.
Light of Stars. Hattie Donovan Bohannon. LC 9-10789. R. F. Fenno & Company.
Light of Stars. Evelyn Voss Wise. LC 46-19687. 1946. The Bruce Publishing Company.
Light of the Gods. Barbara Cartland. (Camfield Ser.: No. 6). 192p. 1982. pap. 1.95 (ISBN 0-515-06297-9). Jove Pubns.
Light of the Star see Collected Works.
Light of the Star: A Novel. Hamlin Garland. LC 72-84708. (Illus.). 1974. (ISBN 0-403-02980-5). Scholarly Press.
Light of the Star: A Novel. Hamlin Garland. 1904. Harper & Brothers.
Light of the Vision. Frances Christine Tiernan. LC 12-152. The Ave Maria.
Light of the Western Stars. Zane Grey. 1982. 18.00x (ISBN 0-86025-184-5, Pub. by Ian Henry Pubns England). State Mutual Bk.
Light of Western Stars. Zane Grey. 1982. pap. 2.50 (ISBN 0-671-83498-3). PB.
Light of Western Stars: A Romance. Zane Grey. LC 17-18596. 1914. Grosset & Dunlap.
Light of Western Stars: A Romance. Zane Grey. LC 14-11112. 1914. 1.35. Harper & Brothers.
Light of Western Stars: A Romance. Zane Grey. LC 22-4739. 1916. Grosset & Dunlap.
Light on a Dark Path. Alida W Graves. LC 6-454381. 1893. The American Sunday-School Union.
Light on a Hill. Clark Duncan. LC 43-10301. 1943. Wm. B. Eerdmans Publishing Company.
Light on a Mountain. Gerald Warner Brace. LC 41-51620. G. P. Putnam's Sons.
Light on Lucrezia. Eleanor Hibbert. LC 75-45064. 1976. 8.95 (ISBN 0-399-11723-7). Putnam.
Light on Lucrezia. Jean Plaidy. LC 75-45064. 1976. 8.95 (ISBN 0-399-11723-7). Putnam Pub Group.

Light on the Deep. George Henry Grafton. LC 66353. 1900. The Neale Co.

Light on the Hill: A Romance of the Southern Mountains. Martha Sawyer Gielow. 1.00. Fleming H. Revell Company.

Light on the Lagoon: A Novel. Isabel Constance Clarke. LC 21-202664. 1921. Benziger Brothers.

Light on the Lookout: A Novel of Romance in the Ozarks. Edgar E Hulse. LC 72-90681. 5.75. S of O Press.

Light on the Moon. Barbara Cartland. LC 79-13487. 1980. 6.95 (ISBN 0-87272-078-0). Duron Books.

Light on the Sound. Somtow Sucharitkul. 224p. (Orig.). 1982. pap. 2.95 (ISBN 0-671-44028-4, Timescape). PB.

Light on the Three-Hill Road, a Novel. Nellie Beatrice Ritter. LC 58-8377. Bruce Humphries.

Light Out of Darkness. George P Goldie. LC 6-43740. 1895. Goldie Bros.

Light Out of Darkness: Or, The Blue and the Gray United. Ida Wood Stevens. LC 8-16095. 1887.

Light Out of the East. Samuel Rutherford Crockett. LC 20-22156. 1.90. George H. Doran Company.

Light Outside. Marc Savage. LC 75-33472. 8.95 (ISBN 0-06-013777-0). Harper & Row.

Light Over Ruby Street. Edward Harris Heth. LC 40-30102. 1940. Smith & Durrell, Inc.

Light Princess & Other Fantasy Stories. George MacDonald. Ed. by George G. Sadler. (Fantasy Stories of George MacDonald Ser.). 176p. 1980. pap. 2.95 (ISBN 0-8028-1861-7). Eerdmans.

Light Shines Through. Octavus Roy Cohen. LC 28-19132. 1928. Little, Brown and Company.

Light Shines Through. Octavus Roy Cohen. LC 43-20445. 1928. Grosset & Dunlap.

Light Sons and Dark. David Cornel De Jong. LC 40-32364. Harper & Brothers.

Light That Failed. authorized ed. Rudyard Kipling. (Lovell's Westminster series, no. 25). United States Book Company.

Light That Failed. Rudyard Kipling. LC 13-9375. 1898. Macmillan and Co.

Light That Failed. copyright ed. Rudyard Kipling. LC 99-3030. 1899. Doubleday & McClure Co.

Light That Failed. Rudyard Kipling. LC 4780. H. M. Caldwell Company.

Light That Failed. Rudyard Kipling. LC 19-722. A. L. Burt Company.

Light That Failed. Rudyard Kipling. W. B. Conkey Company.

Light That Failed. Rudyard Kipling. LC 15-20316. 1911. Doubleday, Page & Company.

Light That Failed. Rudyard Kipling. LC 22-14554. 1920. Doubleday, Page & Company.

Light That Failed. Rudyard Kipling. LC 28-166822. 1923. Doubleday, Page & Company.

Light That Failed: By Rudyard Kipling. Rudyard Kipling. LC 46-20641. 1946. Doubleday & Company, Inc.

Light That Failed. Captains Courageous, a Story of the Grand Banks. Rudyard Kipling. LC 52-48512. (Mandalay edition of the works of Rudyard Kipling). 1925. Doubleday, Page.

Light That Failed. The Works of Rudyard Kipling. Rudyard Kipling. 1909. The Nottingham Society.

Light That Lies. Cockburn Harvey. LC 7-2628. 1896. J. B. Lippincott Company.

Light That Lies. George Barr McCutcheon. LC 16-906570. 1916. Dodd, Mead and Company.

Light That Lures. Percy James Brebner. LC 11-23506. 1.50. The H. K. Fly Company.

Light That Never Was. Lloyd Biggle, Jr. 1973. 0.95. Daw Books.

Light That Never Was. Lloyd Biggle, Jr. LC 71-180060. (Doubleday science fiction). 1972. 4.95. Doubleday.

Light That Never Was. Katharine Fullerton Gerould. LC 31-26529. 1931. C. Scribner's Sons.

Light Thickens. Ngaio Marsh. LC 82-14029. 12.95 (ISBN 0-316-54675-5). Little, Brown.

Light Thickens. Ngaio Marsh. (General Ser.). 1983. lib. bdg. 16.95 (ISBN 0-8161-3509-6, Large Print Bks). G K Hall.

Light Through the Mist. Harry H. Fein. 2.50 o.p. (ISBN 0-8283-1570-1). Branden.

Light to the Heart. Barbara Cartland. 1973. pap. 1.25 o.p. (ISBN 0-515-03174-7, V3174). BJ Pub Group.

Light to the Heart, No. 56. Barbara Cartland. 256p. 1982. pap. 1.95 (ISBN 0-515-06387-8). Jove Pubns.

Light up the Cave. Denise Levertov. LC 81-11295. 224p. 1981. 15.95 (ISBN 0-8112-0813-3); pap. 6.95 (ISBN 0-8112-0814-1, NDP525). New Directions.

Light Within. Yvonne Whittal. (Harlequin Romances Ser.). 192p. 1981. pap. 1.50 (ISBN 0-373-02441-X). Harlequin Bks.

Light Woman. Zona Gale. LC 37-4086. 1937. D. Appleton-Century Company, Incorporated.

Light-Years. Serge Rezvani. LC 70-162816. 1971. (ISBN 0-15-151990-0). Harcourt Brace Jovanovich.

Light Years. James Salter. LC 74-29594. 1975. 7.95 (ISBN 0-394-49433-4). Random House.

Light Years. James Salter. 1977. 1.75. (ISBN 0-380-01644-3). Avon Books.

Lighted Candle. Joseph Overberg. 3.00 o.p. Vantage.

Lighted Cities. Ernest Frost. LC 52-7084. 1952. Harcourt, Brace.

Lighted Heart. Elizabeth Yates. (Illus.). 251p. 1972. pap. 3.50 o.s.i. (ISBN 0-87233-027-3). Bauhan.

Lighted Horizon. Edith Snyder Pedersen. LC 40-34072. 1940. Wm. B. Eerdmans Publishing Co.

Lighted Lamp. A Novel. Charles Hanford Henderson. LC 8-27806. 1908. Houghton Mifflin Company.

Lighted Lantern. Gilbert Munger Wright. LC 30-6726. 1930. D. Appleton and Company.

Lighted Match. Charles Neville Buck. LC 11-13729. 1.25. W. J. Watt & Company.

Lighted Way. Edward Phillips Oppenheim. LC 12-281779. 1912. Little, Brown, and Company.

Lighted Windows. Emilie Baker Loring. LC 30-22430. The Penn Publishing Company.

Lighter of Flames. William Surrey Hart. LC 23-13453. Thomas Y. Crowell Company.

Lighter Than a Feather; a Novel. David Westheimer. LC 74-154947. (Illus.). 1971. 7.95. Little, Brown.

Lighter Than Air. Dean Boyd. 1961. 3.95 o.p. (ISBN 0-15-151959-5). HarBraceJ.

Lighter Than Air. 1st Ed. Dean Boud. LC 61-12346. 1961. Harcourt, Brace & World.

Lighter Than Day. Desmond Hawkins. LC 40-35886. 1940. Longmans, Green and Co.

Lighter Than Day: By Desmond Hawkins. Desmond Hawkins. LC 41-2206. 1941. A. A. Knopf.

Lightfoot Island. Joseph Chamberlain Furnas. LC 68-27655. 1968. 5.95. Atheneum.

Lighthearted Quest: By Ann Bridge Pseud. Mary Dolling Sanders O'Malley. LC 56-134986. 1956. Macmillan.

Lighthorseman. Bill Burchardt, pseud. 192p. 1982. pap. 1.95 (ISBN 0-441-48316-X, Pub. by Charter Bks). Ace Bks.

Lighthouse. Eugenia Price. LC 72-1452. 1972. 12.95 (ISBN 0-8161-6035-X). G. K. Hall.

Lighthouse. Eugenia Price. LC 79-163223. (Illus.). 1971. 6.95. Lippincott.

Lighthouse. Millie Ragosta. pap. 0.75 o.s.i. (01-326). Lancer.

Lighthouse at the End of the World. Jules Verne & Metcalfe, Cranstoun, Tr. LC 24-193291. 1924. G. H. Watt.

Lighthouse in a Desert. D. Stemmler. 3.00 o.p. Carlton.

Lighting Seven Candles. Cynthia Lombardi. LC 26-18626. 1926. D. Appleton and Company.

Lighting the Night Sky. Kenneth O. Hanson. 1983. 14.95 (ISBN 0-932576-16-8); pap. 6.95 (ISBN 0-932576-15-X). Breitenbush Pubns.

Lightly. Chipman Hall. LC 77-377386. 9.95 (ISBN 0-7710-3770-8). McClelland and Stewart.

Lightly Lies the Earth: A Novel. 1st Ed. Orren Jack Turner. LC 55-11613. 1955. Vantage Press.

Lightnin' Frank Bacon & Smith, Winchell. LC 20-4438. Harper & Brothers.

Lightnin' Calvert. William Blair Morton Ferguson. LC 30-7571. 1930. R. M. McBride & Company.

Lightning. Abdallah Nacereddine. 1970. 2.95 o.p. Vantage.

Lightning Before Dawn. David McLaughlin. LC 38-25510. The Bobbs-Merrill Company.

Lightning Bug. Donald Harington. LC 70-108662. 1970. 5.95. Delacorte Press.

Lightning Bug. Donald Harington. 1975. pap. 1.50 o.p. (ISBN 0-515-03770-2). Pyramid Pubns.

Lightning Conductor Discovers America. Charles Norris Williamson & Alice Muriel Livingston Williamson. LC 16-13974. Doubleday, Page & Company.

Lightning Conductor: The Strange Adventures of a Motor-Car. 3d ed., rev. and enl. ed. Charles Norris Williamson & Alice Muriel Livingston Williamson. LC 3-7158. 1903. H. Holt and Company.

Lightning Conductor: The Strange Adventures of a Motor-Car. rev., enl. and illustrated. ed. Charles Norris Williamson & Alice Muriel Livingston Williamson. LC 5-6937. 1905. H. Holt and Company.

Lightning in the Fog: A Novel. Elaine Stienon. LC 76-54963. 9.50 (ISBN 0-8309-0171-X). Herald Pub. House.

Lightning in the Night. Fred Allhoff. LC 78-23538. (Illus.). 9.95 (ISBN 0-13-536557-0). Prentice-Hall.

Lightning Kid. Jesse Edward Grinstead. LC 41-9242. Dodge Publishing Company.

Lightning Ridge. Ion L. Idriess. 1968. pap. 1.80 o.s.i. Tri-Ocean.

Lightning Rod. Mullin Garr. (Orig.). 1968. pap. 1.95 o.s.i. (OPS-250, Ophelia). Olympia.

Lightning Strikes Twice. Jean Potts. LC 58-11649. 1958. Scribner.

Lightning Strikes Twice. Lee Thayer, pseud. LC 39-2714. 1939. Dodd, Mead & Company.

Lightning Swift. 1st Ed. William Colt MacDonald. LC 53-9985. (Double D western). 1953. Doubleday.

Lightning's Flash; an Unveiling of Mysteries. A Stenographic Episode. Edward E. Wright. A. R. Woodford, Printer.

Lightning's Flash; an Unveiling of Mysteries. A Stenographic Episode. 2d ed. Edward E. Wright. LC 8-37213. Nonpareil Printing and Publishing Co.

Lights Across the Delaware. David Taylor. LC 54-5600. (Illus.). 1954. Lippincott.

Lights! Action! Murder! Glen Chase, pseud. (Cherry Delight Ser.). (Orig.). 1975. pap. 1.25 o.p. (LB274ZK, Leisure Bks). Nordon Pubns.

Lights! Action! Murder! Glen Chase, pseud. (Cherry Delight#23). 1975. (pbk.) 1.25. Leisure Books.

Lights Along the Ledges. Elisabeth Stancy Payne. LC 24-7731. 1924. The Penn Publishing Company.

Lights and Shadows: A Novelette. Charles Grogan. LC 45-7608. 1945. B. Humphries, Inc.

Lights and Shadows of a Life: A Novel. Madeleine Vinton Dahlgren. LC 6-321813. 1887. Ticknor and Company.

Lights and Shadows of American Life. Ed. by Mary Russell Mitford. LC 72-8689. 1972. 16.65. MSS Information Corp.

Lights and Shadows of American Life. Ed. by Mary Russell Mitford. LC 71-93647. 1969. Garrett Press.

Lights and Shadows of Domestic Life: And Other Stories. LC 7-16040. 1850. Ticknor, Reed and Fields.

Lights and Shadows of German Life. M M Montgomery. LC 7-254610. 1833. Carey, Lea & Blanchard.

Lights and Shadows of Irish Life. Anna Maria Fielding Hall. LC 78-24226. (Ireland, from the Act of Union, 1800, to the Death of Parnell, 1891). 1979. 96.00 (ISBN 0-8240-3496-1). Garland Pub.

Lights and Shadows of Scottish Life. John Wilson. LC 46-370953. 1846. Saxton & Kelt.

Lights and Shadows of Scottish Life. John Wilson. LC 41-35151. (On cover: Fireside library. 1). 1868. R. Carter & Brothers.

Lights and Shadows of the Soul: Collected Sketches and Stories. Sylvan Drey. LC 6-34221. 1892. Cushing & Company.

Lights Are Bright. "Four Bells and the Lights Are Bright" Night Call of Lookout on the Ore-Boats of the Great Lakes. Louise Kennedy Mabie. LC 14-12484. 1914. Harper & Brothers.

Lights Are Low. Jack Charles Richard Aistrop. LC 47-4505. 1947. Farrar, Straus.

Lights Around the Shore. Jerome Weidman. LC 43-751302. 1943. Simon and Schuster.

Lights Burn Blue. Sally Pickrell Jones. LC 47-26678. 1947. Reynal & Hitchcock.

Lights, Camera... Murder. David Snell. LC 79-16542. 1979. 9.95 (ISBN 0-312-48605-7). St. Martin's Press.

Lights in the Sky Are Stars. Fredric Brown. LC 53-11520. 1953. Dutton.

Lights of Barbrin. Joseph Burgo. 1978. 1.75 (ISBN 0-671-82121-0). Pocket Books.

Lights of Brown Mountain. Philip B Mishoe. LC 73-185578. 1972. 5.95 (ISBN 0-8059-1665-2). Dorrance.

Lights of Fame. Thomas Walter Gilkyson. LC 30-10713. 1930. C. Scribner's Sons.

Lights of Love. Barbara Cartland. 1973. pap. 1.25 o.p. (V4274). BJ Pub Group.

Lights of Love. Barbara Cartland. 1973. 0.95 (ISBN 0-515-02965-3). Pyramid.

Lights of Skaro. David Dodge. LC 54-5733. 1954. Random House.

Lights of Zetar. (Balzan of the Cat People Ser.: No. 3). 1975. pap. 1.25 o.p. Pyramid Pubns.

Lights Out. Baynard Hardwick Kendrick. LC 45-95081. 1945. W. Morrow & Co.

Lights up. Grace Louise Smith Richmond. LC 27-19313. 1927. Doubleday, Page & Company.

Lightship. Archie Binns. LC 34-25912. Reynal and Hitchcock.

Lightship. Translated from the German by Michael Bullock. 1st American Ed. Siegfried Lenz. LC 62-108654. 1962. Hill and Wang.

Lightstruck. Wallace E. Knight. 1979. 8.95 o.p. (ISBN 0-316-49925-0). Little.

Lightstruck: A Novel. Wallace E Knight. LC 78-12049. 8.95 (ISBN 0-316-49925-0). Little, Brown.

Lightwood Tree. Berry Fleming. LC 47-4063. 1947. J. B. Lippincott Company.

Lightyears. Beth Brown. LC 81-82663. 70p. 1982. pap. 4.50 perfect bdg. (ISBN 0-916418-36-7). Lotus.

Ligny's Lake. Sidney Hobson Courtier. LC 76-139619. (Inner sanctum mystery). (Illus.). 1971. 4.95 (ISBN 0-671-20840-3). Simon and Schuster.

Like a Big Brave Man: A Novel. Celso Al Carunungan. LC 60-7629. 1960. Farrar, Straus and Cudahy.

Like a Falcon Flying. Helena Lefroy Caperton. LC 43-4737. 1943. Garrett and Massie.

Like a Gallant Lady. Kate M Cleary. LC 6-312604. 1897. Way & Williams.

Like a Gentleman. Mary Andrews Denison. LC 6-33987. 1882. Lee and Shepard.

Like a Guilty Thing. Belton Cobb. LC 38-106942. 1938. Longmans, Green and Co.

Like a Man. Jeremy Lane. LC 23-22955. 1928. I. Washburn.

Like a River Flowing. Ida L Moore. LC 41-2436. 1941. Doubleday, Doran and Company, Inc.

Like a River of Lions. Tana De Gamez, pseud. 1975. (pbk.) 1.50. Bantam Books.

Like a Wall. Carroll Arnett. 1969. 5.00 (Pub. by Elizabeth Pr). SBD.

Like an Ostrich. Joseph Pawlick. 3.50 o.p. Carlton.

Like and Unlike. authorized ed. Mary Elizabeth Braddon Maxwell. (On cover: Seaside library. Pocket ed. no. 1036). 1887. G. Munro.

Like Another Helen. Hilda Caroline Gregg. LC 3-3566. 1902. L. C. Page & Company.

Like Another Helen. George Horton. LC 2-12964. 1901. The Bowen-Merrill Company.

Like Any Other Fugitive. Joseph Arnold Hayes. LC 74-144382. 1971. 7.95. Dial Press.

Like Any Other Man. Patrick Boyle. LC 68-20636. 1968. Grove Press.

Like As We Are. Mattie M Boteler. 1903. The Standard Publishing Company.

Like Birds: Like Fishes, and Other Stories. Ruth Prawer Jhabvala. LC 64-10567. 1964. W. W. Norton.

Like Clean Winds. Louise Agnes Morin. LC 51-1697. 1951. Bookman Associates.

Like Dian's Kiss: A Novel. Eliza M. J. Humphreys. (On cover: Lovell's library, v. 11, no. 599). 1885. J. W. Lovell Company.

Like Father. David Black. LC 78-6841. 1978. 8.95 (ISBN 0-396-07587-8, Dist. by W.W. Norton). Dembner Bks.

Like Lesser Gods. Mari Tomasi. LC 49-11904. 1949. Bruce.

Like Love. Ed McBain. 1982. pap. 2.25 (ISBN 0-451-11628-3, AE1628, Sig). NAL.

Like Love: An 87th Precinct Inner Sanctum Myster. Evan Hunter. LC 62-19078. 1962. Simon and Schuster.

Like Love: An 87th Precinct Mystery. Evan Hunter. (Signet book). (Illus.). 1976. 1.25 (ISBN 0-451-07221-9). New American Library.

Like Lucifer. A Novel. Fanny Du Tertre. (On cover: Once a week library, v. 11, no. 5). 1893. P. F. Collier.

Like Men Betrayed. John Clifford Mortimer. LC 54-559813. 1954. Lippincott.

Like Men Betrayed. Frederic Raphael. LC 70-138489. 1971. 6.95 (ISBN 0-670-42907-4). Viking Press.

Like Mother, Like Me. Sheila Schwartz. (gr. 9-12). 1978. pap. 1.95 (ISBN 0-553-14464-2). Bantam.

Like No Other Love. Charlotte Mary Brame. (On cover: Lovell's library. v. 14, no. 739). J. W. Lovell Company.

Like Normal People. Robert Meyers. (Illus.). 1980. pap. 2.25 (ISBN 0-451-09112-4, E9112, Sig). NAL.

Like Now. David Chagall. Orig. Title: Century God Slept. 1967. pap. 0.60 o.p. (53-557). Paperback Lib.

Like Ships Upon the Sea. A Novel. Frances Eleanor Ternan Trollope. (Harper's Franklin square library, no. 310). 1883. Harper & Brothers.

Like the Lion's Tooth. Marjorie Kellogg. LC 72-81008. 1972. 5.95 (ISBN 0-374-18763-0). Farrar, Straus and Giroux.

Like the Lion's Tooth. Marjorie Kellogg. (Signet book, Y5655). 1973. (pbk.) 1.25. New American Library.

Like the Phoenix: A Novel. Anthony Bertram. LC 36-6472. 1936. W. Morrow & Co.

Like Unto a Merchant,". Mary Agatha Gray. LC 15-727922. 1915. 1.35. Benziger Brothers.

Like Unto Like: A Novel. Katherine Sherwood Bonner McDowell. LC 7-20101. (On cover: Harper's library of American fiction, no. 9). 1878. Harper & Brothers.

Like Water Flowing: A Novel. Margaret Mackprang Mackay. LC 33-11476. Reynal & Hitchcock.

Like Waves. Joseph A. Mills. 54p. (Orig.). 1980. pap. 3.75 (ISBN 0-943454-00-X). Jotarian.

Likely Stories: A Collection of Untraditional Fiction. Ascher, Straus & Bruce R McPherson. LC 81-12927. 1981. 14.50 (ISBN 0-914232-42-8) (ISBN 0-914232-41-X). Treacle Press.

Likely Stories: A Collection of Untraditional Fiction. Emilio De Grazia et al. Ed. by Bruce R. McPherson. LC 82-129270. 224p. 1981. 14.50 (ISBN 0-914232-42-8); pap. 7.95 (ISBN 0-914232-41-X). McPherson & Co.

Likely Story. William Frend De Morgan. LC 11-287396. 1911. H. Holt and Company.

Likes of Which. Eugene Walter. 1980. 15.00 (ISBN 0-916276-06-6). Decatur Hse.

Li'l Gal. Paul Laurence Dunbar. LC 73-164800. (Illus.). Repr. of 1904 ed. 12.50 (ISBN 0-404-00034-7). AMS Pr.

Lila Sari. William Lee Howard. LC 8-31162. 1908. R. G. Badger.

Lila the Werewolf. Peter S Beagle. LC 75-316521. (Yes! Capra chapbook series; no. 17). (Illus.). 1974. 2.50 (ISBN 0-912264-91-8) (ISBN 0-912264-90-X). Capra Press.

Lilac Awakening. Bonnie Drake. (Candlelight Ecstasy Ser.: No. 85). (Orig.). 1982. pap. 1.95 (ISBN 0-440-14588-0). Dell.

Lilac Caprice. Alberta Murphy. 1955. J. Messner.

Lilac Ghost. Irene Saylor. Ed. by Alice Sachs. 1970. 3.95 o.p. Lenox Hill.

Lilac Mansion. Eileen Hehl. (Orig.). 1981. pap. 1.95 (ISBN 0-89083-725-2). Zebra.

Lilac Night. Michael T. Hinkemeyer. 320p. (Orig.). 1982. pap. 3.25 (ISBN 0-441-48335-6). Ace Bks.

Lilac Night: A Novel. Michael T Hinkemeyer. LC 81-5502. 12.95 (ISBN 0-517-54183-1). Crown.

Lilac Sunbonnet see Raiders.

Lilac Sunbonnet: A Love Story. Samuel Rutherford Crockett. LC 4-15295. 1894. D. Appleton and Company.

Lilac Sunbonnet: A Love Story. Samuel Rutherford Crockett. LC 29-252930. 1895. D. Appleton and Company.

Lilac Time. Guy Fowler. LC 28-219805. Grosset & Dunlap.

Lilacs & the Bittersweet Vine. Adella E. Newcomb. 2.00 o.p. Carlton.

Lilacs Out of the Dead Land. Rachel Billington. LC 73-182470. 1972. 5.95 (ISBN 0-8415-0146-7). Saturday Review Press.

Lilacs Overgrow. Tai-Yi Lin. LC 60-11459. 1960. World Pub. Co.

Lilayandopal Tu. Jose Sanchez-Boudy. LC 77-78254. 1978. pap. 4.95 (ISBN 0-89729-168-9). Ediciones.

Li'l'gal. facs. ed. Paul Laurence Dunbar. LC 75-78992. (Black Heritage Library Collection Ser). (Illus.). 1904. 10.00 (ISBN 0-8369-8558-3). Ayer Co.

Lili Marlene: An Intimate Diary. Ruth Landshoff Yorck. LC 45-73492. 1945. The Readers Press, Inc.

Lilia Chenoworth. Lee Wilson Dodd. LC 22-792692. E. P. Dutton & Company.

Lilian. Arnold Bennett. LC 74-5330. (collected works of Arnold Benett). 1974. (ISBN 0-518-19126-5). Books for Libraries Press.

Lilian. Arnold Bennett. LC 22-23568. George H. Doran Company.

Lilian. A Novel. Sarah Dana Loring Greenough. LC 6-44862. 1863. Ticknor and Fields.

Lilian Dalzell. (On cover: Loring's select novels). 1874. Loring.

Lilian: Or, Did She Do Right! Martha Finley. W.B. Evans & Co.

Liliane. Annabel Erwin. 1.95 (ISBN 0-446-79941-6). Warner Books.

Lilias and Her Cousins: Or, A Tale of Planter Life in the Old Dominion. LC 7-16051. 1860. General Protestant Episcopal Sunday School Union, and Church Book Society.

Lilies for Madame. Hugh Austin. LC 38-201271. 1938. Pub. for the Crime Club, Inc. by Doubleday, Doran & Co., Inc.

Lilies in Her Garden Grew. 1st Ed. Frederick Clyde Davis. LC 51-9954. 1951. Published for the Crime Club by Doubleday.

Lilies of Florence: And Other Stories and Legends. George Sand & Vanderpoole, Lew, 1855- LC 6-34596. (On cover: Lovell's library. v. 20. no. 965). J. W. Lovell Company.

Lilies of the Alley. Octavus Roy Cohen. LC 31-6273. 1931. D. Appleton & Company.

Lilies of the Field. William Edmund Barrett. LC 62-8085. (Illus.). 1962. Doubleday.

Lilies, White and Red. Frances Wilson Huard. LC 19-686892. George H. Doran Company.

Lilith. George Macdonald. LC 76-6467. (Adult fantasy). 1969. 0.95. Ballantine Books.

Lilith. J. R. Salamanca. LC 61-701861. 1961. Simon and Schuster.

Lilith: A Romance. George Macdonald. LC 7-18783. 1895. Dodd, Mead and Company.

Lilith. A Sequel to "The Unloved Wife.". Emma Dorothy Eliza Nevitte Southworth. LC 8-14251. (Ledger library, no. 29). 1891. R. Bonner's Sons.

Lilith: A Snake in the Grass, Bk. 1. Jack L. Chalker. (Four Lords of the Diamond). 1981. pap. 2.50 (ISBN 0-345-29369-X, Del Rey). Ballantine.

Lilith: The Roundtree Women. Margaret Lewerth. (Orig.). 1981. pap. 3.25 (ISBN 0-440-14630-5). Dell.

Lilla: A Part of Her Life. Marie Adelaide Belloc Lowndes. 1.35. George H. Doran Company.

Lillelord: A Novel. Johan Borgen & Ronald E Peterson. LC 81-14216. 16.00 (ISBN 0-8112-0826-5) (ISBN 0-8112-0827-3). New Directions Pub. Corp.

Lillian. David Emery. 1973. pap. 0.95 o.p. (09168). Curtis.

Lillian and Lucile: A Novel. Maude Massey Ray. 1899. The Franklin Printing and Publishing Co.

Lillian Harley. Marian Cockrell. LC 43-13573. 1943. Harper & Brothers.

Lillian Morris, and Other Stories. Henryk Sienkiewicz. Tr. by Jeremiah Curtin. 1894. Little, Brown and Company.

Lillian; or, Woman's Endurance: A Narrative Connected with the Early History of Canada and the American Revolution. Charles Shrimpton. 1868. N. Tibbals & Co.

Lillian Simmons: Or, The Conflict of Sections: a Story. 2d ed. Otis M. Shackelford. LC 73-18607. (Illus.). 1975. 14.50 (ISBN 0-404-11417-2). AMS Press.

Lillian Simmons: Or, The Conflict of Sections. Otis M. Shackelford. LC 15-16441. Burton Publishing Company.

Lillian White Deer: A Novel. Carl Jonas. LC 63-15872. 1964. Norton.

Lillian's Lovers. The Speaker of the House) A Novel. Angeline Teal. LC 8-26030. (On cover: The Ivy series). Laird & Lee.

Lillian's Vow: Or, The Mystery of Raleigh House. Emma Augusta Sharkey. (On cover: The library of American authors, no. 38). G. Munro.

Lillibullero. Robert Neill. LC 75-40799. 7.95. St. Martin's Press.

Lillie. David Butler. (Orig.). 1979. pap. 2.75 (ISBN 0-446-95818-2). Warner Bks.

Lillie Ray: Or, Every Cloud Has Its Silver Lining. A Tale of Real Life. Also, Eva, the Prairie Flower. C. A Bartlett. 1874. Press of the Case, Lockwood & Brainard Co.

Lillie Seline's Confession. Larry G. Stenzel. 96p. (Orig.). 1982. pap. 5.75 (ISBN 0-910021-02-3). Samuel P Co.

Lilliesleaf: Being a Concluding Series of Passages in the Life of Mrs. Margaret Maitland, of Sunnyside. Margaret Oliphant Wilson Oliphant. LC 7-32607. 1862. T. O. H. P. Burnham.

Lilliesleaf: Or, Passages in the Life of Mrs. Margaret Maitland of Sunnyside. Margaret Oliphant Wilson Oliphant. (On cover: Seaside library Pocket ed., no. 402). 1885. G. Munro.

Lilly Crackell. Caroline Beach Slade. LC 43-8184. 1943. The Vanguard Press.

Lilly's Story. 1st American Ed. Ethel Davis Wilson. LC 53-5382. 1953. Harper.

Lilo's Diary: By Richard M. Elman. Richard M Elman. LC 68-277919. 1968. 4.95. Scribners.

Lilting House: A Novel. Ruth Doan MacDougall. LC 65-177004. bds., 3.95. Bobbs.

Lily. Sue Petigru Bowen. LC 6-16093. 1855. Harper & Brothers.

Lily. Sandrine Forge. 1969. 6.95 o.p. (GP522). Grove.

Lily. Vincent Sheean. LC 54-53693. 1954. Random House.

Lily. Hugh Wiley. LC 22-218012. 1922. A. A. Knopf.

Lily and the Bull: A Novel Set in Minoan Crete. Moyra Caldecott. LC 79-10805. 8.95 (ISBN 0-8090-6572-X). Hill and Wang.

Lily, and the Cross. A Tale of Acadia. James De Mille. LC 6-340055. 1875. Lee & Shepard.

Lily and the Leopards. Alice Harwood. LC 49-10017. 1949. Bobbs-Merrill Co.

Lily and the Sergeant. Martin Yoseloff. LC 57-10582. 1957. Funk & Wagnalls.

Lily and the Sword. Agnes Russell Weekes & Weekes, Rose Kirkpatrick, 1874- Joint Author. LC 29-22686. 1929. Dodd, Mead & Company.

Lily Christine: A Romance. Michael Arlen. LC 28-31018. 1928. Double Day, Doran & Company, Inc.

Lily Cigar. Tom Murphy. (Orig.). 1979. pap. 2.75 (ISBN 0-451-08810-7, E8810, Sig). NAL.

Lily Dale. Paul Tabori. 256p. 1982. pap. cancelled (ISBN 0-505-51853-8). Tower Bks.

Lily Dale. Paul Tabori. 256p. 1983. pap. 2.75 (ISBN 0-8439-2007-6, Leisure Bks). Dorchester Pub Co.

Lily Dale. Paul Tabori. 1975. (pbk.) 1.50. Belmont Tower Books.

Lily He Plucked. A Romance. Clara Bouvier. LC 6-14913. 1891. I. H. Brown & Company.

Lily in Her Coffin: A Wade Paris Mystery. Ben Benson. LC 52-9698. 1952. M. S. Mill Co. and W. Morrow.

Lily-Iron. Mary Biggs. LC 27-24345. 1927. R. M. McBride & Company.

Lily Lang. Robert Watson. LC 77-76656. 1977. 8.95 (ISBN 0-312-48625-1). St. Martin's Press.

Lily Lang. Robert Watson. 1979. 1.95 (ISBN 0-671-82207-1). Pocket Books.

Lily of Fort Garry. Jane Rolyat. LC 30-33621. 1930. J. M. Dent and Sons Ltd.

Lily of France. Caroline Atwater Mason. 1901. The Griffith & Rowland Press.

Lily of San Miniato. A Story of Florence. Cecilia Viets Dakin Jamison. 1878. G. W. Carleton & Co.

Lily of the Coal Fields. 2d ed. William Wilfrid Whalen. LC 11-1006. Mayhew Publishing Company.

Lily of the Field. Blanche Smith Ferguson. LC 37-224925. The Penn Publishing Company.

Lily of the Valley. Honore De Balzac. Tr. by Katharine Prescott Wormeley. LC 3-23198. (Half-title: The comedy of human life... Scenes from provincial life). 1891. Roberts Brothers.

Lily of the Valley: Le Lys Dans la Vallee) Tr. by James Waring, with a Preface by George Saintsbury. Honore De Balzac. Tr. by James Waring. LC 4-18468. (Half-title:... Comedie humaine...). 1897. J. M. Dent and Co.

Lily of the Valley. The Gallery of Antiquities... Honore De Balzac. Tr. by Katharine Prescott Wormeley. LC 26-26982. (The works of Balzac. Centenary ed. vol. ix). Little, Brown, and Company.

Lily Pearl and the Mistress of Rosedale. C. M. R Gorton. Ed. by Kirkland, Joseph. LC 6-27513. 1892. Dibble Publishing Co.

Lily Pond. Dorothy Daniels. 1969. pap. 0.60 o.p. (63-238). Paperback Lib.

Lily Pool. Louis Arthur Cunningham. LC 55-7934. 1955. Arcadia House.

Lily: The Diary of a French Girl in New York. Sandrine Forge. LC 68-58151. 1969. 6.95. Grove Press.

Lily's Lover: Or, A Trip Out of Season. Matilda Stewart. LC 8-15688. (On cover: Stachel series, no. 7). The Authors' Publishing Company.

Limanora: The Island of Progress. 2d ed. John Macmillan Brown. LC 31-28162. 1931. H. Milford, Oxford University Press.

Limanora: The Island of Progress. John Macmillan Brown. LC 3-17235. 1903. G. P. Putnam's Sons.

Limb to Limb. John Russo. (Orig.). 1981. pap. 2.75 (ISBN 0-671-41690-1). PB.

Limbo. Joel Hamill. 1982. pap. 2.75 (ISBN 0-671-42616-8). PB.

Limbo. Joan Silver & Linda Gottlieb. LC 74-178176. 1972. 6.95 (ISBN 0-670-42914-7). Viking Press.

Limbo. Bernard Wolfe. LC 52-5165. 1952. Random House.

Limbo: A Novel. Joel Hammil. LC 79-54011. 9.95 (ISBN 0-87795-254-X). Arbor House.

Limbo Affair. Anthony Firth. Orig. Title: Tall, Balding & Thirty-Five. 1968. pap. 0.60 o.p. (73-781). Lancer.

Limbo City: A Contemporary Novel. Edwin B Self. LC 47-1209. 1946. Herald Publishing Company.

Limbo Connection. Derry Quinn. LC 76-28054. 1977. 7.95 (ISBN 0-312-48650-2). St. Martin's Press.

Limbo Connection. Derry Quinn. LC 78-10938. 1979. 1.95 (ISBN 0-14-005118-X). Penguin Books.

Limbo Line. Victor Canning. LC 63-2875. (Award novel of intrigue). 1975. (pbk.) 1.50. Award Books.

Limbo Line. Victor Canning. LC 64-10511. 1964. W. Sloane Associates.

Limbo of the Lost Today. John W. Spencer. 1975. 6.95 o.s.i. Phillips Pub Co.

Limbo of the Lost Today. John W. Spencer. 1973. 5.95 o.p. Phillips Pub Co.

Limbo Tower. William Lindsay Gresham. LC 49-8811. 1949. Rinehart.

Lime-Kiln Man: Or, The Victim of Misfortune. Jason C Swayze. LC 38-11296. 1855. DeWitt & Davenport.

Lime Pit. Jonathan Valin. LC 79-28205. 8.95 (ISBN 0-396-07818-4). Dodd, Mead.

Lime Tree Prison. Ed. by Van K. Brock & Francis Poole. pap. 3.00 (ISBN 0-938078-00-3). Anhinga Pr.

Lime Twig. John Hawkes. LC 60-14719. 1961. New Directions.

Lime Works. Thomas Bernhard. LC 73-7286. 1973. 5.95 (ISBN 0-394-47926-2). Knopf; Distributed by Random House.

Limehouse Nights. Thomas Burke. LC 73-88661. 1974. 6.95 (ISBN 0-8180-0619-6). Horizon Press.

Limehouse Nights. Thomas Burke. LC 73-103498. (Short story index reprint series). 1969. Books for Libraries Press.

Limehouse Nights. Thomas Burke. LC 17-22292. 1917. R. M. McBride & Company.

Limehouse Nights. Thomas Burke. LC 26-19631. 1926. R. M. McBride & Company.

Limelight. Howard Rockey. LC 27-20429. Macrae Smith Company.

Limerick Veteran: Or, The Foster Sister. Agnes M Stewart. 1873. Kelley, Piet and Company.

Lime's Crisis. Ronald Bass. LC 81-22470. 352p. 1982. 15.50 (ISBN 0-688-01025-3). Morrow.

Limestone & Other Stories. Adalbert Stifter. Tr. by David Luke. LC 68-24398. (Helen & Kurt Wolff Book). 1968. 4.95 o.p. (ISBN 0-15-152167-0). HarBraceJ.

Limestone Tree. Joseph Hergesheimer. LC 46-42514. 1931. A. A. Knopf.

Limit. Ada Leverson. LC 51-7698. 1951. W. W. Norton.

Limit of Darkness: A Novel. Howard Hunt. LC 44-4917. 1944. Random House.

Limited Engagements. Karen Stabiner. LC 79-11562. 8.95 (ISBN 0-87223-529-7). Seaview Books: Trade Distribution by Simon and Schuster.

Limited Engagements. Karen Stabiner. 1980. 2.25 (ISBN 0-87216-670-8). Playboy Press.

Limited Murder. Robert Black. 208p. (Orig.). Date not set. pap. price not set o.p. (ISBN 0-505-51837-6). Tower Bks.

Limits and Renewals. Rudyard Kipling. LC 32-10835. 1932. Doubleday, Doran & Company, Inc.

Limits of Eden. Joyce Keener. 424p. (Orig.). 1981. pap. 2.95 (ISBN 0-441-48363-1). Ace Bks.

Limits of the Land. Curtis Harnack. LC 78-8191. 1978. 8.95 (ISBN 0-385-12502-X). Doubleday.

Limmerston Hall. Hester W. Chapman. LC 72-94947. 1973. 6.95 (ISBN 0-698-10514-1). Coward, McCann & Geoghegan.

Limmerston Hall. Hester W. Chapman. (Fawcett crest book). 1974. (pbk.) 1.25. Fawcett.

Limner. Paul Darcy Boles. LC 74-13959. 1975. 8.95 (ISBN 0-690-00559-8). Crowell.

Limo. Dan Jenkins & Edwin Shrake. LC 76-11576. 1976. 8.95 (ISBN 0-689-10734-X). Atheneum.

Limo. Dan Jenkins & Edwin Shrake. (Kangaroo Book). 1977. 1.95 (ISBN 0-671-81239-4). Pocket Books.

Limping Goose. Frank Gruber. LC 54-9855. (Murray Hill mystery). 1954. Rinehart.

Limping Man. Margaret Erskine, pseud. LC 39-4284. 1939. Pub. for the Crime Club, Inc., by Doubleday, Doran & Company, Inc.

Limping Man. Francis Durham Grierson. LC 26-182420. E. J. Clode, Inc.

Limping Man. Wetherby Williams. LC 39-4284. 1939. Pub. for the Crime Club, Inc., by Doubleday, Doran & Company, Inc.

Limping Sway. Joseph McCulloch. LC 37-381996. E. P. Dutton and Company, Inc.

Lin McLean. Owen Wister. LC 76-104600. (Illus.). 1970. Literature House.

Lin McLean. Owen Wister. LC 13-12911. 1898. Harper & Brothers.

Lin McLean. Owen Wister. LC 4-16484. 1903. Harper & Brothers.

Lin McLean. Owen Wister. 1907. Harper & Brothers.

Lin McLean. Owen Wister. A. L. Burt Company.

Lina Sarger. George William Marque Maier. LC 32-30128. 1932. The Christopher Publishing House.

Lincoln Diddle. Barbara Steward & Dwight Steward. LC 79-14601. 1979. 8.95 (ISBN 0-688-03498-5). Morrow.

Lincoln Hunters. Wilson Tucker. LC 58-5207. 1958. Rinehart.

Lincoln Lords. Cameron Hawley. 1960. 5.95 o.p. Little.

Lincoln Lords: A Novel. Cameron Hawley. LC 60-5858. 1960. Little, Brown.

Lincoln McKeever. Eleazar Lipsky. LC 53-9610. 1953. Appleton-Century-Crofts.

Lincoln's Mary and the Babies. Bernie Smade Babcock. LC 29-7204. 1929. J. B. Lippincott Company.

Lincoln's Mothers. Dorothy Clarke Wilson. LC 80-950. 1981. 13.95 (ISBN 0-385-15146-2). Doubleday.

Linda. Loise Marks Clancy. LC 49-2338. 1949. Gramercy Pub. Co.

Linda. Margaret Prescott Montague. LC 12-245616. 1912. Houghton Mifflin Company.

Linda. Virginia Swain. LC 28-235372. Grosset & Dunlap.

Linda Condon. Joseph Hergesheimer. LC 19-27595. 1919. A. A. Knopf.

Linda Lane's Problems. Josephine Lawrence. LC 28-140062. Barse & Co.

Linda Lee Incorporated: A Novel. Louis Joseph Vance. LC 22-8240. E. P. Dutton & Company.

Linda Loyd, a Tale of the Mountains. Marie E. Hoffman. LC 20-8234. 1920. Marshall Jones Company.

Linda More, and Poems. Daisy Zane Brennan. LC 65-19368. Greenwich Book Publishers.

Linda: Or, The Young Pilot of the Belle Creole. A Tale of Southern Life. by caroline lee hentz... ed. Caroline Lee Whiting Hentz. LC 7-4135. 1850. A. Hart.

Linda: Or, The Young Pilot of the Belle Creole. Caroline Lee Whiting Hentz. LC 7-4137. T. B. Peterson & Brothers.

Linda Shawn. Ethel Edith Mannin. LC 32-184323. 1932. A. A. Knopf.

Linda Tressel. Anthony Trollope. LC 80-1887. (Trollope, Anthony, 1815-1882. Selections. 1981). 1981. 45.00 (ISBN 0-405-14152-1). Arno Press.

Linda Vale: Fashion Designer by Frances Dean Hancock Pseud. Jeanne Judson. LC 56-13291. 1956. Avalon Books.

Linda's Homecoming. Phyllis A. Whitney. (Signet, T4793). 1973. (pbk.) 0.75. New American Lib.

Linda's Homecoming. Phyllis A. Whitney. LC 50-7645. 1950. McKay.

Linden Affair. Martha Albrand. LC 56-11271. 1956. Random House.

Linden Affair: By Martha Albrand Pseud. Heidi Huberta Freybe Loewengard. LC 56-11271. 1956. Random House.

Linden Hill: Or, The Vanquished Life-Dream. Louise S Harris. LC 7-2901. 1874. Southwestern Book and Publishing Company.

Linden Road. Miriam Bruce. LC 51-360. 1951. Harper.

Linden Walk Tradegy. Foxhall Daingerfield. LC 29-3973. 1929. D. Appleton & Company.

Lindisfarm Chase. A Novel. Thomas Adolphus Trollope. LC 20-12346. 1866. D. Appleton and Co.

Lindisfarn Chase. A Novel. Thomas Adolphus Trollope. LC 8-284983. 1864. Harper & Brothers.

Lindsay's Girl: A Novel. Herbert Martin. LC 7-25979. R. F. Fenno & Company.

Lindsay's Luck. Frances Hodgson Burnett. LC 6-16423. C. Scribner's Sons.

Lindsay's Luck. A Love Story. Frances Hodgson Burnett. LC 6-16422. T. B. Peterson & Brothers.

Lindsay's Luck. A Love Story. Frances Hodgson Burnett. LC 11-15058. T. B. Peterson & Brothers.

Lindseys. Pauline Marrington. (Signet Book.). 1976. 1.75. New American Library.

Line a Day. Juliet Wilbor Tompkins. LC 23-14915. The Bobbs-Merrill Company.

Line Between. Arthur Dorman Welton. LC 33-322276. Sears Publishing Company, Inc.

Line by Line. Amy Schor. LC 80-39822. 11.95 (ISBN 0-399-90083-7). R. Marek.

Line in the Water. Amrita Pritam. Tr. by Krishna Gorowara from Punjabi. (Mayfair Paperbacks). 141p. 1975. 5.95 (ISBN 0-89253-012-X); pap. 2.50 (ISBN 0-89253-023-5). Ind-US Inc.

Line Jungle. Ida Martucci. LC 56-5813. 1956. Vantage Press.

Line o' Cheer for Every Day o' the Year. John Kendrick Bangs. Repr. of 1915 ed. lib. bdg. 25.00 (ISBN 0-8414-1668-0). Folcroft.

Line of Chance: A Novel. Thomas Caplan. LC 78-10860. 1979. 9.95 (ISBN 0-688-03412-8). Morrow.

Line of David. Ken Hurwitz. LC 72-13672. 1973. 6.95 (ISBN 0-393-08380-2). Norton.

Line of Departure. Peter Viertel. LC 47-11503. 1947. Harcourt, Brace.

Line of Duty. Ernest Tidyman. 1976. (pbk.) 1.75. Bantam Books.

Line of Duty: A Novel. Ernest Tidyman. LC 74-8940. 1974. 6.95 (ISBN 0-316-84511-6). Little, Brown.

Line of Fire. Donald Hamilton. LC 55-751156. (Dell first edition 46). 1955. Dell Pub. Co.

Line of Love. James Branch Cabell. LC 5-32701. 1905. Harper & Brothers.

Line of Love, Dizain Des Mariages. facsimile ed. James B. Cabell. LC 79-996077. (Select Bibliographies Reprint Ser). 1921. 22.00 (ISBN 0-8369-5106-9). Ayer Co.

Line of Love: Dizain Des Mariages. James Branch Cabell. LC 70-114046. 1970. AMS Press.

Line of Love: Dizain Des Mariages. James Branch Cabell. LC 79-99677. (Select bibliographies reprint series). 1969. Books for Libraries Press.

Line of Love: Dizain Des Marriages. James Branch Cabell. LC 28-275943. 1926. R. M. McBride & Company.

Line of Love: Dizian Des Marriages. James Branch Cabell. LC 21-20264. 1921. R. M. McBride & Company.

Line of Succession. Brian Wynne Garfield. LC 78-38897. 1972. Delacorte Press.

Line on Ginger. William Somerset Maugham. LC 50-6431. 1950. Harcourt, Brace.

Line to Tomorrow and Other Stories of Fantasy and Science-Fiction: By Lewis Padgett Pseud. Henry Kuttner. LC 54-35673. (Bantam books, 1251). 1954. Bantam Books.

Line-up... Helen Kieran Reilly. 1934. Publ. for the Crime Club, Inc., by Doubleday, Doran & Company, Inc.

Line-up... Helen Kieran Reilly. LC 42-25554. 1942. The Sun Dial Press.

Line-up: A Collection of Crime Stories by Famous Mystery Writers. Cecil John Charles Street. LC 40-13737. 1940. Dodd, Mead & Company.

Line up for Murder. Marian Babson. LC 81-51979. 1981. 9.95 (ISBN 0-8027-5453-8). Walker.

Linebacker: A Novel of Professional Football, by Tex Maule. Hamilton Maule. LC 65-26319. 3.95. McKay.

Linen Suit: And Other Stories. Jerome Bahr. LC 57-355075. 1957. Trempealeau Press.

Liner. James Barlow. 1972. pap. 1.50 o.p. Lancer.

Liner: A Novel. James Barlow. LC 70-130464. 1970. 7.95. Simon and Schuster.

Liner: A Novel. Edouard Peisson. LC 55-14109. Norton.

Liner: A Novel About a Great Ship. Noel Bertram Gerson. LC 73-10537. 1977. 8.95 (ISBN 0-385-08281-9). Doubleday.

Lines & Mounds. Dave Oliphant. 1976. pap. 3.00x (ISBN 0-914476-54-8). Thorp Springs.

Line's Busy,". Albert Edward Ullman. LC 20-3576. Frederick A. Stokes Company.

Lines for Everyday Living. Chet Long. (O.s.i.). pap. 2.50 o.s.i. (ISBN 0-671-10508-6, Fireside). S&S.

Lines Long & Short see Collected Works.

Lines of Life: Destins) Translated by Gerard Hopkins. Francois Mauriac. LC 57-103155. 1957. Straus & Cudahy.

Lines of Time. Kenneth C. Kellar & Phyillis H. Kellar. LC 78-61180. (Illus.). 1978. pap. 4.95 (ISBN 0-87970-144-7). North Plains.

Lines on the Death of a Fisherman. J Inchardi. LC 77-29495. 1970. Sirius Books.

Lines to a Lady. Reita Lambert. LC 35-4299. 1935. Doubleday, Doran & Co., Inc.

Lingala Code. Warren Kiefer. LC 72-2003. 1972. 5.95 (ISBN 0-394-47956-4). Random House.

Lingard: A Novel. Colin Wilson. LC 77-108077. 1970. 5.95. Crown Publishers.

Lingering Faun: A Novel. Mabel Wood Martin. LC 27-50000. 1927. Frederick A. Stokes Company.

Lingering Laughter. Georgina Grey, pseud. (Coventry Romance Ser.: No. 172). 224p. 1982. pap. 1.50 (ISBN 0-449-50273-2, Coventry). Fawcett.

Lingering Light. Marjorie S. Scheuer. 4.00 o.p. (ISBN 0-8283-1283-4). Branden.

Lingering Moments. D. Z. Newton. 2.50 o.p. Vantage.

Lingering Shadows. Nancy MacDougall Kennedy. (Candlelight mystery). 1974. (pbk.) 0.75. Dell.

Lingering Shadows. Mohan Rakesh. Tr. by Jai Ratan. 214p. 1970. pap. 2.50 (ISBN 0-88253-075-5). Ind-US Inc.

Link. Marjorie A Clark. 1956. Augustana Press.

Link... Philip MacDonald. LC 30-24248. 1930. Pub. for the Crime Club, Inc., by Doubleday, Doran & Company, Inc.

Link. Robin Maugham. 1971. pap. 1.25 o.p. (V2422). Pyramid Pubns.

Link, a Victorian Mystery: A Novel. Robin Maugham. LC 75-85116. 1969. McGraw-Hill.

Link in the Chain. Dorothy Phoebe Ansle. LC 76-11876. 6.95 (ISBN 0-8415-0445-8). Dutton.

Link in the Chain. Laura Conway. LC 76-11876. 1976. 6.95 o.p. (ISBN 0-8415-0445-8). Dutton.

Linked Lives. Gertrude Douglas. LC 75-458. (Victorian Fiction: Novels of Faith and Doubt; No. 13). 1975. 35.00 (ISBN 0-8240-1537-1). Garland Pub. Co.

Linked with Fate. John Louis Berry. LC 6-10378. (On cover. The silver series, v. 2, no. 3). 1892. H. J. Smith & Co.

Links. Charles Panati. LC 77-26639. 1978. 8.95 (ISBN 0-395-26293-3). Houghton Mifflin Co.

Links: A Novel. Charles Panati. (Berkley book). 1979. 2.25 (ISBN 0-425-04048-8). Berkley Pub. Corp.

Links in a Chain. Margaret Sutton Briscoe Hopkins. LC 7-5249. 1893. Dodd, Mead and Company.

Links in the Chain. Cecil John Charles Street. LC 48-7775. (Red badge detective). 1948. Dodd, Mead.

Links in the Chain: Or, Who Killed Judge Noble. Frederick William Davis. LC 1-30043. (On cover: Magnet detective library, no. 167). 1901. Street & Smith.

Links of Gold. Jane Gater. LC 34-236533. 1934. Meador Publishing Company.

Links of the Chain. William Harnack. LC 80-54187. (Illus.). 116p. (Orig.). 1982. pap. 4.95 (ISBN 0-938838-04-0). Textile Bridge.

Linnet Estate. Dora Polk. LC 73-84070. 1973. 6.95 (ISBN 0-679-50425-7). D. McKay Co.

Linnets and Valerians. Elizabeth Goudge. 1978. 1.75 (ISBN 0-380-01934-5). Avon Books.

Linnet's Story. Betty Hale Hyatt. LC 80-82217. 208p. (Orig.). 1980. pap. 1.95 (ISBN 0-87216-758-5). Playboy Pbks.

Linton Family: Or, The Fashion of This World. Sarah Elizabeth Hopkins Bradford. LC 6-15208. 1860. Pudney & Russell.

Linton Memorial: A Novel. Lavender Lloyd. LC 57-38846. 1957. Longmans, Green.

Linwoods: Or, "Sixty Years Since" in America. by the author of "hope leslie", "redwood", &c.... ed. Catharine Maria Sedgewick. LC 8-6435. 1835. Harper & Brothers.

Lion. Joseph Kessel. LC 59-10061. 1959. Knopf.

Lion & Blue. Robert Vavra. LC 74-10319. 1974. 9.95 (ISBN 0-688-61164-8). Reynal.

Lion & Lambs. Rebecca West. 1928. 20.00 o.p. (ISBN 0-8274-3874-5). R West.

Lion and the Cross. Joan Lesley Hamilton. LC 78-69659. 1979. 10.00 (ISBN 0-385-14480-6). Doubleday.

Lion and the Honeycomb. Siegel Fleisher. LC 54-52556. 1954. Houghton Mifflin.

Lion and the Rose. 1st American Ed. Jane Oliver, pseud. LC 59-7848.

Lion & the Unicorn. Gary L. Blackwood. LC 82-90758. 291p. (Orig.). 1983. pap. 5.95 (ISBN 0-910971-00-5). Eagle Bks.

Lion and the Unicorn. Richard Harding Davis. LC 71-94715. (Short story index reprint series). (Illus.). 1969. Books for Libraries Press.

Lion at a Cocktail Party. Michael Hogan. 1978. pap. 4.00 (ISBN 0-916300-12-9). Gallimaufry.

Lion at Morning, a Novel: With Line Drawings by the Author. Stephen Longstreet. LC 54-9798. 1954. Simon and Schuster.

Lion at My Heart: A Novel. 1st Ed. Harry Mark Petrakis. LC 59-5286. 1959. Little, Brown.

Lion at Sea. Max Hennessy, pseud. LC 77-20779. 1978. 8.95 (ISBN 0-689-10845-1). Atheneum.

Lion by the Tail. 1st Ed. Claude O Clements. LC 55-10537. 1956. Blackmore Press.

Lion Country. Frederick Buechner. LC 70-135569. 1971. 5.95. Atheneum.

Lion Cub. Josef Skvorecky. Tr. by Peter Kussi from Chechoslovak. LC 73-7611. 6.95 o.p. (ISBN 0-8184-0179-6). Grove.

Lion De Venise. Margaret Rome. (Harlequin Romantique). 192p. 1983. pap. 1.95 (ISBN 0-373-41193-6). Harlequin Bks.

Lion Game. James H. Schmitz. 224p. 1982. pap. 2.25 (ISBN 0-441-48433-6). Ace Bks.

Lion Game. James H. Schmitz. (Orig.). 1973. pap. 0.95 o.p. (UQ1038). Daw Bks.

Lion Heart: A Tale of the War in Vietnam. Alan Clark. LC 69-11569. (Illus.). 1969. 5.95. Morrow.

Lion House. Marjorie Lee. LC 59-6570. 1959. Rinehart.

Lion. Illustrated by Harper Johnson. Joseph Kessel. LC 62-147743. 1962. Knopf.

Lion in a Den of Daniels. Caroline Wedgwood Benn. LC 62-164566. 1962. Macmillan.

Lion in the Box. Marguerite Lofft De Angeli. 1975. 4.95 (ISBN 0-385-03317-6). Doubleday.

Lion in the Evening. Alan Scholefield. LC 73-17591. 1974. 5.95 (ISBN 0-688-00242-0). Morrow.

Lion in the Garden. Gladys Bronwyn Stern. LC 40-11563. 1940. The Macmillan Company.

Lion in the Hills. John Brewster Prescott. LC 61-9125. 1961. Dodd, Mead.

Lion in the House. Lina E. Moore. 142p. 1981. pap. 4.25x (Pub. by New Day Publishers Philippines). Cellar.

Lion in the Lei Shop. Kaye Starbird. LC 71-117575. 1970. Harcourt, Brace, Jovanovich.

Lion in the Stone. Henrietta Buckmaster, pseud. 1968. 6.95 o.p. (ISBN 0-15-152515-3). HarBraceJ.

Lion in the Stone: A Novel. Henrietta Buckmaster, pseud. LC 68-23579. 1968. Harcourt, Brace & World.

Lion in the Way. Elizabeth Cadell. LC 81-16928. 1982. 13.00 (ISBN 0-688-01098-9). Morrow.

Lion in the Way. Elizabeth Cadell. LC 82-12152. 1982. 15.95 (ISBN 0-8161-3425-1). G.K. Hall.

Lion in Wait. Dorothy Gardiner. LC 63-11205. 1963. Published for the Crime Club by Doubleday.

Lion in Winter. James Goldman. 1966. 9.95 (ISBN 0-394-40615-X). Random.

Lion Is Come. 1st American Ed. Jane Oliver, pseud. LC 57-6734. Putnam.

Lion Is in the Streets. Adria Locke Langley. LC 45-4226. 1945. Whittlesey House, McGraw-Hill Book Company.

Lion Is in the Streets. Adria Locke Langley. LC 45-8762. 1945. The Blakiston Company.

Lion Is in the Streets. Adria Locke Langley. LC 46-456788. 1946. The Sun Dial Press.

Lion Jack: A Story of Perilous Adventures Among Wild Men and the Capturing of Wild Beasts; Showing How Menageries Are Made. Phineas Taylor Barnum. LC 4-33143. 1901. G. W. Dillingham Co.

Lion of Boaz-Jachin and Jachin-Boaz. Russell Hoban. LC 73-81396. 1973. 6.95 (ISBN 0-8128-1624-2). Stein and Day.

Lion of Boaz-Jachin and Jachin-Boaz. Russell Hoban. 1974. (pbk.) 1.25 (ISBN 0-671-78392-0). Pocket Books.

Lion of Christ. Margaret Butler. LC 76-58024. 320p. 1977. 9.95 o.p. (ISBN 0-698-10820-5, Coward). Putnam Pub Group.

Lion of Comarre. Arthur C. Clarke. Bd. with Against the Fall of Night. LC 68-28816. 214p. 1968. 5.75 (ISBN 0-15-152524-2). HarBraceJ.

Lion of Comarre & Against the Fall of Night. Arthur Charles Clarke. LC 68-28816. 1968. Harcourt, Brace & World.

Lion of Delos. Anne Worboys. LC 74-4196. 1974. 6.95 (ISBN 0-440-04814-1). Delacorte Press.

Lion of Delos. Anne Worboys. 1978. 1.95 (ISBN 0-441-48425-5). Ace Books.

Lion of England. Margaret Butler. LC 73-78741. (Illus.). 1973. 7.95 (ISBN 0-698-10555-9). Coward, McCann & Geoghegan.

Lion of Flanders. Translated from the Flemish. Introductory Essay on Flemish and Dutch Fiction by A Schade Van Westrum and a Biographical Sketch. Hendrik Conscience. LC 53-52547. (Foreign classical romances).

Lion of Ireland. Morgan Llywelyn. LC 80-84371. 560p. 1981. pap. 3.50 (ISBN 0-87216-825-5). Playboy Pbks.

Lion of Ireland: The Legend of Brian Boru. Morgan Llywelyn. LC 79-21768. (Illus.). 1980. 12.95 (ISBN 0-395-28588-7). Houghton Mifflin.

Lion of Islam. Howard Leoner Oleck. (Orig.). 1980. pap. 1.95 (ISBN 0-89083-615-9). Zebra.

Lion of Janina: Or, The Last Days of the Jamissaries, a Turkish Novel. Mor Jokai. Tr. by Bain, Robert Nisbet. LC 7-14308. 1898. Harper & Brothers.

Lion of Judah. John T Dorsey. LC 24-211511. Fouche Company, Inc.

Lion of Justice. Margaret Butler. LC 74-166471. (Illus.). 1975. 7.95. Coward, McCann & Geoghegan.

Lion of Justice. Margaret Butler. LC 75-326959. 1975. 3.50 (ISBN 0-333-14769-3). MacMillan London.

Lion of Justice. Eleanor Hibbert. LC 79-12572. (Illus.). 1979. 10.00 (ISBN 0-399-12355-5). Putnam.

Lion of Justice. Jean Plaidy. LC 79-12572. 1979. 10.00 o.p. (ISBN 0-399-12355-5). Putnam Pub Group.

Lion of la Roche. Yvonne Whittal. (Harlequin Presents Ser.). 192p. 1982. pap. 1.75 (ISBN 0-373-10498-7). Harlequin Bks.

Lion of Limerick. Dennis O'Sullivan. (On cover: Munro's library, popular novels, v. 1, no. 418). N. L. Munro.

Lion of Oakhurst. Walter Reed Johnson. (Orig.). 1979. pap. 2.95 (ISBN 0-451-11686-0, AE1686, Sig). NAL.

Lion Pit: A Novel. 1st Ed. Frank Harvey. 1961. Little, Brown.

Lion Story and Pictures. Du Bois, William Pene. (Viking Seafarer book). (Illus.). 1974. (pbk.) 1.50 (ISBN 0-670-05093-8). Viking.

Lion-Tamer. Edith Maude Hull. LC 28-178147. 1928. Dodd, Mead & Company.

Lion Tamer. Carroll E Robb. LC 25-5961. 1925. Harper & Brothers.

Lion-Tamer: And Other Stories. Bryan MacMahon. LC 49-7611. 1949. E. P. Dutton.

Lion Took Fright. Louis Umfreville Wilkinson. LC 31-8423. 1931. Doubleday, Doran & Company, Inc.

Lion Triumphant. Philippa Carr, pseud. 384p. 1977. pap. 2.50 (ISBN 0-449-23233-6, Crest). Fawcett.

Lion Triumphant. Philippa Carr, pseud. 384p. 1974. 7.95 (ISBN 0-399-11135-2). Putnam Pub Group.

Lion Triumphant. Eleanor Hibbert. LC 73-78602. 1973. 7.95 (ISBN 0-399-11135-2). Putnam.

Lion Unannounced: Twelve Stories and a Fable. Leonard Casper. LC 75-128125. (Illus.). 1971. 7.95. Southern Methodist University Press.

Lion Without Claws. Philippa Wiat. LC 77-73019. 1977. 7.95 (ISBN 0-312-48736-3). St. Martin's Press.

Lionel Ardon. Malcolm Dearborn. 1902. G. W. Dillingham Company.

Lionel Lincoln: Or, The Leaguer of Boston... James Fenimore Cooper. LC 6-32145. 1825. C. Wiley.

Lionel Lincoln: Or, The Leaguer of Boston... 5th ed. James Fenimore Cooper. LC 6-321463. 1832. Carey & Lea.

Lionel Lincoln: Or, The Leaguer of Boston... a new ed. James Fenimore Cooper. LC 14-22461. 1847. Lea & Blanchard.

Lionel Lincoln: Or, The Leaguer of Boston... James Fenimore Cooper. LC 6-32147. 1851. Stringer & Townsend.

Lionel Lincoln: Or, The Leaguer of Boston. new ed. James Fenimore Cooper. LC 6-32148. 1852. Stringer and Townsend.

Lionel Lincoln: Or, The Leaguer of Boston. James Fenimore Cooper. (On cover: Lovell's library, no. 527). 1885. J. W. Lovell Company.

Lionel Lincoln: Or, The Leaguer of Boston. James Fenimore Cooper. (On cover: Seaside library. Pocket ed. no. 397). 1885. G. Munro.

Lionel Lincoln: Or, The Leaguer of Boston. James Fenimore Cooper. LC 4-19568. 1897. D. Appleton and Company.

Lionel Lincoln: Or, The Leaguer of Boston... a new ed. James Fenimore Cooper. LC 42-470664. 1836. Carey, Lea, & Blanchard.

Lionello. A Sequel to the Jew of Verona. Antonio Bresciani. LC 6-17391. 1860. Kelly, Hedian & Piet.

Lioness. Michael Horbach. LC 77-29226. 8.95 (ISBN 0-397-01250-0). Lippincott.

Lioness: A Romance of the Riff Mountains. Ferdynand Antoni Ossendowski. LC 29-26339. E. P. Dutton & Company, Inc.

Lioness and the Lambs. 1st Ed. Anthony Spiezia. LC 56-9021. 1956. Pageant Press.
Lioness & the Lily, No. 135. Barbara Cartland. 144p. 1981. pap. 1.75 (ISBN 0-553-14503-7). Bantam.
Lionheads: A Novel. Josiah Bunting. LC 78-188356. 1972. 5.95 (ISBN 0-8076-0632-4). G. Braziller.
Lionheads: A Novel. Josiah Bunting. 1973. 1.25. Popular Lib.
Lionheart. Alexander Fullerton. LC 65-25934. 1966. 3.95. Norton.
Lionheart! Martha Rofheart. 1982. pap. 3.50 (ISBN 0-451-11617-8, AE1617, Sig). NAL.
Lionheart! A Novel of Richard I, King of England. Martha Rofheart. LC 81-9187. 15.95 (ISBN 0-671-43250-8). Simon and Schuster.
Lionhearted, a Story About the Jews in Medieval England. Charles Reznikoff. LC 44-7074. The Jewish Publication Society of America.
Lions & Shadows. Christopher Isherwood. LC 47-11810. 1977. pap. 3.75 o.p. (ISBN 0-8112-0649-1, NDP435). New Directions.
Lions and Shadows: An Education in the Twenties. Christopher Isherwood. LC 77-151325. 1977. 3.45 (ISBN 0-8112-0649-1). New Directions Pub. Corp.
Lions at Night. Richard Himmel. 1980. pap. 2.25 (ISBN 0-440-14980-0). Dell.
Lions at Night: A Novel. Richard Himmel. LC 79-592. (Illus.). 9.95 (ISBN 0-440-04980-6). Delacorte Press.
Lion's Brood. Duffield Osborne. LC 1-31484. 1901. Doubleday, Page & Co.
Lions' Den. Janet Ayer Fairbank. LC 30-33755. The Bobbs-Merrill Company.
Lions Fed the Tigers. With Decorations by Peter Spier. Douglas Angus. LC 58-9051. 1958. Houghton Mifflin.
Lions in the Way. Hughes Mearns. LC 27-6441. 1927. Simon and Schuster.
Lion's Mouse. Charles Norris Williamson & Alice Muriel Livingston Williamson. LC 19-14910. 1919. Doubleday, Page & Company.
Lions of Judah. Ted Willis. LC 79-22703. 1980. 10.95 (ISBN 0-03-039906-8). Holt, Rinehart and Winston.
Lions of the Lord: A Tale of the Old West. Harry Leon Wilson. LC 3-13822. 1903. Lothrop Publishing Company.
Lion's Paw. D. R Sherman. LC 74-25122. 1975. 6.95 (ISBN 0-385-07545-6). Doubleday.
Lion's Paw: A Story of Freemasonry. Carl Harry Claudy. LC 44-99186. 1944. The Temple Publishers.
Lion's Shadow. Elizabeth Hunter. 192p. (Orig.). 1980. pap. 1.50 (ISBN 0-671-57018-8). S&S.
Lion's Share. Arnold Bennett. LC 74-17027. (Collected works of Arnold Bennett). 1974. (ISBN 0-518-19127-3). Books for Libraries Press.
Lion's Share. Arnold Bennett. LC 16-228558. George H. Doran Company.
Lion's Share. Alice French. LC 7-31229. 1907. The Bobbs-Merrill Company.
Lion's Share. John Man. LC 81-21535. 1982. 12.95 (ISBN 0-312-48737-1). St. Martin's Press.
Lion's Share. Mark Steadman. LC 75-5468. 384p. 1976. 8.95 o.p. (ISBN 0-03-015086-8). HR&W.
Lion's Share. Malvina Sarah Black Clark Waring Waring. (On cover: The household library, v. 4, no. 25). 1888. Clark and Company: Etc., Etc.
Lion's Share: A Novel. Mark Steadman. LC 75-5468. 8.95 (ISBN 0-03-015086-8). Holt, Rinehart and Winston.
Lion's Share: A Novel. Mark Steadman. 1977. 1.75 (ISBN 0-380-00921-8). Avon Books.
Lion's Skin... Rafael Sabatini. LC 47-666. (On cover: A Bard house novel, 30). 1946.
Lion's Skin. Rafael Sabatini. LC 26-26231. Houghton Mifflin Company.
Lion's Skin. Darwin Le Ora Teilhet. LC 55-7107. (Illus.). 1955. W. Sloane Associates.
Lion's Skin: A Historical Novel and a Novel History. John Sergeant Wise. LC 72-2066. (Black Heritage Library Collection). 1972. 16.50 (ISBN 0-8369-9073-0). Books for Libraries Press.
Lion's Skin: A Historical Novel and a Novel History. John Sergeant Wise. LC 5-76230. 1905. Doubleday, Page & Company.
Lion's Skin: A Romance. Rafael Sabatini. LC 11-1965. 1911. D. Appleton and Company.
Lions Starve in Naples. Johan Wigmore Fabricius. Tr. by Blewitt, Phyllis. LC 35-1534. 1935. Little, Brown, and Company.
Lions, Three: Christians, Nothing. Ann Borowik. LC 64-18342. bds., 4.95. Pantheon.
Lions Three: Christians Nothing. Ann Borowik. 1967. Repr. pap. 0.60 o.p. (60-302). Manor Bks.
Lion's Way. Lewis Orde. 1982. pap. 3.75 (ISBN 0-89083-900-X). Zebra.
Lion's Way: A Novel. Lewis Orde. LC 80-66493. 13.95 (ISBN 0-87795-268-X). Arbor House.
Lion's Way: A Story of Men and Lions. Charles Thurley Stoneham. LC 32-333. 1932. Frederick A. Stokes Company.
Lion's Whelp: A Story of Cromwell's Time. Amelia Edith Huddleston Barr. LC 1-25683. 1901. Dodd, Mead & Company.
Lip Malvy's Wife: A Novel. George Agnew Chamberlain. LC 23-131009. 1923. Harper & Brothers.
Lip Service. Robert L. McRoberts. 1976. pap. 3.50 (ISBN 0-87886-078-9, Pub. by Ithaca Hse). SBD.
Lipstick: A Novel of Us and Our Young Sophisticates. Henry Leyford Gates. LC 29-132111. 1929. Barse & Co.
Lipstick Girl: A Romance of a Little Beauty. Edna Robb Webster. LC 32-9884. Grosset & Dunlap.
Liquid Fire. M Lucretia Hayden. LC 53-6463. 1953. Vantage Press.
Liquid from the Sun's Rays: A Story. Sue Greenleaf. LC 2-182. The Abbey Press.
Liquid Geometry. Cynthia Lasky. 1979. 8.95 (ISBN 0-915248-28-X); pap. 3.95 (ISBN 0-915248-26-3). Vermont Crossroads.
Liquid Man. C. B. Gilford. 1969. pap. 0.75 o.p. (74-560). Lancer.
Liquidated, and The Seer. By Rudolph Lindau... Rudolf Lindau. LC 7-19018. (Appletons' new handy-volume series v.15). 1878. D. Appleton and Company.
Liquidator. R. L. Brent. (Liquidator Ser.). (O.s.i.). 192p. 1975. pap. 1.25 o.s.i. (AQ1507, Award). Univ Pub & Dist.
Liquidator. Nick Carter. (Nick Carter Ser.). (O.s.i.). 192p. (Orig.). 1973. pap. 0.95 o.s.i. (AN1127, Award). Univ Pub & Dist.
Liquidator. John E Gardner. LC 64-23352. 1964. Viking Press.
Liquor, Loot and Ladies. Chester T Crowell. LC 30-140121. 1930. A. A. Knopf.
LIrsud. Jo Clayton. 1978. 1.75 (ISBN 0-87997-403-6). DAW Books.
Lisa. Joan Van Every Frost. (Leisure books). 1979. 1.95 (ISBN 0-8439-0616-2). Nordon Pubns.
Lisa. Matthew Lipman. 153p. (gr. 7-10). 1976. pap. 6.50 (ISBN 0-916834-03-4, TX482-514). Inst Adv Philo.
Lisa: A Novel of the Postwar Life of Adolf Hitler. Andre Richard. LC 56-7471. 1956. Exposition Press.
Lisa and David. Theodore Isaac Rubin. LC 61-8191. 1961. Macmillan.
Lisa Bastian. James Wood. LC 61-17540. 1961. Vanguard Press.
Lisa, Bright and Dark: A Novel. John Neufeld. (Signet novel, T4387). 1973. (pbk.) 0.75. New American Library.
Lisa, Bright and Dark: A Novel. John Neufeld. LC 75-85002. 1969. 4.50. S. G. Phillips.
Lisa: By Edith Young. Edith Young. LC 31-3505. 1931. W. Morrow & Co.
Lisa Lillywhite. Margery Sharp. LC 51-13571. 1951. Little, Brown.
Lisa Vale. Olive Higgins Prouty. LC 38-11079. 1938. Houghton Mifflin Company.
Lisa's Boy. Joseph Machlis. LC 82-6293. 13.95 (ISBN 0-393-01605-6). Norton.
Lisa's Boy: A Novel. Joseph Machlis. 416p. 1982. 13.95 (ISBN 0-393-01606-4). Norton.
Lisa's Sweet Body. Tony Trelos, pseud. (Orig.). 1968. pap. 1.75 o.p. (3039). Brandon.
Lisbeth. Grace L Keith Johnston. LC 7-10796. The Cassell Publishing Co.
Lisbeth; a Story of Two Worlds. Carolinn Edna Skinner Twing. 1900. Banner of Light Publishing Co.
Lisbeth, a Story of Two Worlds. 3d ed. Carolinn Edna Skinner Twing. LC 34-38303. 1901. Banner of Light Publishing Co.
Lisbeth of Jarnfjeld. Johan Falkberget. Tr. by Gjelsness, Rudolph. LC 30-6437. W. W. Norton & Co., Inc.
Lisbeth: The Story of a First Communion. Mary Teresa Waggaman. LC 14-20738. P. J. Kenedy & Sons.
Lisbeth Wilson: A Daughter of New Hampshire Hills. Eliza Nelson Blair. Lee and Shepard.
Lise Tavernier: Or, From Under the Veil. Alphonse Daudet. Tr. by Williams, Henry Llewellyn. LC 6-33048. (On cover: The cosmopolitan series, no. 51). Hurst & Co.
Lisheen: Or, The Test of the Spirits. Patrick Augustine Sheehan. LC 7-33595. 1907. Longmans, Green, and Co.
Lisping Man. Frank Rawlings. LC 42-23664. 1942. Gateway Books.
Lisping Man. Frank Rawlings. LC 44-6682. 1944. Hercules Publishing Corp.
List. Nick Carter. (Nick Carter Ser). (O.s.i.). 176p. 1976. pap. 1.25 o.s.i. (AQ1566, Award). Univ Pub & Dist.
List. Nick Carter. (Nick Carter Killmaster Series # AQ 1566). 1976. (pbk.) 1.25. Award Books.
List of Adrian Messenger. 1st Ed. Philip MacDonald. LC 59-13980. 1959. Published for the Crime Club by Doubleday.
List, Ye Landsmen! A Romance of Incident. William Clark Russell. LC 37-18322. Cassell Publishing Company.
Listen, Dr. Galahad. Dorothy Worley. LC 64-57252. (Avalon nurse stories). 1964. Avalon Books.
Listen for a Stranger. 1st Ed. Stewart Devine. LC 51-9422. 1951. Published for the Crime Club by Doubleday.
Listen for the Laughter. John Edward Thompson. LC 42-9797. 1942. Macrae-Smith-Company.
Listen for the Voices: A Novel of Concord. Anne Colver. LC 39-18505. Farrar & Rinehart, Inc.
Listen for the Whisperer. Phyllis A. Whitney. (Crest bk., P1774). 1973. 1.25. Fawcett.
Listen for the Whisperer. Phyllis A. Whitney. LC 76-168682. 1971-1972. 5.95. Doubleday.
Listen for the Whisperer. Phyllis A. Whitney. LC 75-39774. 1972. 11.95 (ISBN 0-8161-6024-4). G. K. Hall.
Listen, Lavinia! Watkins Eppes Wright. LC 41-15458. 1941. Arcadia House, Inc.
Listen, Listen. Kate Wilhelm. LC 81-4179. 1981. 13.95 (ISBN 0-395-31269-8). Houghton Mifflin.
Listen, Moon! Leonard Cline. LC 26-151861. 1926. The Viking Press.
Listen, Please Listen. Naomi A Hintze. LC 73-19677. 1974. 5.95 (ISBN 0-394-49072-X). Random House.
Listen, Please Listen. Naomi A Hintze. 1975. (pbk.) 1.50. Bantam.
Listen, Ruben Fontanez: A Novel. Jay Neugeboren. LC 68-14350. 1968. Houghton Mifflin.
Listen to Danger. Dorothy Eden. 1976. 1.75. Ace.
Listen to the Millrace. Barton Porter. LC 78-66449. (Illus.). 12.50 (ISBN 0-9601888-0-0). M. J. Stone Co.
Listen to the Mocking Bird. Sidney J. Perelman. 1970. pap. 2.45 (ISBN 0-671-20718-0, Fireside). S&S.
Listen to the Mocking Bird. Hester Pine. LC 40-3361. Farrar & Rinehart, Inc.
Listen to the Silence. David W. Elliott. (Signet, Q4513). 1973. (pbk.) 0.95. New American Lib.
Listen to the Skylark. Jane McCarthy. 192p. (YA) 1975. 6.95 (Avalon). Bouregy.
Listen to the Skylark. Jane McCarthy. 1975. 4.95. Avalon Books.
Listen to the Wind. E. H. Miller. 1970. 3.95 o.p. Vantage.
Listen to Your Heart. Dorothea J Snow. (Avalon Books). 4.95. Thomas Bouregy.
Listener. Taylor Caldwell. 288p. Repr. of 1960 ed. lib. bdg. 15.45x (ISBN 0-88411-166-0). Amereon Ltd.
Listener. Taylor Caldwell. 304p. 1980. pap. 2.95 (ISBN 0-553-14230-5). Bantam.
Listener. John Gill. LC 70-187520. 224p. 1972. 6.95 o.p. (ISBN 0-8128-1475-4). Stein & Day.
Listener. John Russell Gillies. LC 70-187520. 1972. 6.95 (ISBN 0-8128-1475-4). Stein and Day.
Listener. John Russell Gillies. 1.95 (ISBN 0-445-08555-X). Popular Library.
Listener. Anne Telscombe. LC 69-12557. 1969. 5.50. Weybright and Talley.
Listener, & Other Stories. facsimile ed. Algernon Blackwood. LC 70-150537. (Short Story Index Reprint Ser.). Repr. of 1907 ed. 17.00 (ISBN 0-8369-3834-8). Ayer Co.
Listener: And Other Stories. Helen Hudson. LC 68-25766. 1968. 4.95. Dutton.
Listener in Babel: Being a Series of Imaginary Conversations Held at the Close of the Last Century. Vida Dutton Scudder. LC 3-25551. 1903. Houghton, Mifflin and Company.
Listener. 1st Ed. Taylor Caldwell. LC 60-13727. 1960. Doubleday.
Listener. 1st Ed. Theodora McCormick Du Bois. LC 53-10655. 1953. Published for the Crime Club by Doubleday.
Listeners. James E. Gunn. LC 72-1219. (Illus.). 1972. 6.95 (ISBN 0-684-13013-0). Scribner.
Listeners. James E. Gunn. (Signet book). 1974. (pbk.) 1.25. New American Library.
Listeners. Herbert Whiting. LC 43-1686. 1943. D. Appleton-Century Company, Incorporated.
Listener's Lure: A Kensington Comedy. Edward Verrall Lucas. LC 6-32676. 1906. The Macmillan Company.
Listening Eye. Patricia Wentworth. 1976. Repr. of 1954 ed. lib. bdg. 15.45x (ISBN 0-88411-738-3). Amereon Ltd.
Listening Eye. Patricia Wentworth. 208p. 1980. pap. 1.95 (ISBN 0-553-13947-9). Bantam.
Listening Eye. 1st Ed. Patricia Wentworth. (Her A Miss Silver mystery). 1955. Lippincott.
Listening Heart. N. King. pap. 0.75 o.s.i. (01-324). Lancer.
Listening Heart. (Gifts of Gold Ser.). 1972. 3.95 (ISBN 0-88088-635-8). Peter Pauper.
Listening House. Mabel Seeley. LC 38-34139. 1938. Pub. for the Crime Club, Inc., by Doubleday, Doran & Company, Inc.
Listening Man. John Antonio Moroso. LC 24-9126. 1924. D. Appleton and Company.
Listening Post. Grace Louise Smith Richmond. LC 29-16662. 1929. Doubleday, Doran and Company, Inc.
Listening Silence. Marie Joseph. LC 83-2873. 10.95 (ISBN 0-312-48739-8). St. Martin's Press.
Listening Silence. Helen Lillie. 192p. 1972. 5.95 o.p. Hawthorn.
Listening Silence. Helen Lillie. 1975. (pbk.) 0.95. Dell.
Listening to Billie. Alice Boyd Adams. LC 77-2527. 1978. 7.95 (ISBN 0-394-41069-6). Knopf.
Listening to Billie. Alice Boyd Adams. 1979. 1.95 (ISBN 0-671-82316-7). Pocket Books.
Listening Valley. Dorothy Emily Stevenson. LC 44-7488. 1944. Farrar & Rinehart, Inc.
Listening Valley. 2d ed. Dorothy Emily Stevenson. LC 77-155953. 1978. 7.95 (ISBN 0-03-020446-1). Holt, Rinehart and Winston.
Listening Walls. Margaret Millar. LC 59-5728. 1959. Random House.
Listening Walls. Margaret Millar. 1975. (pbk.) 1.25 (ISBN 0-380-00414-3). Avon.
Listening Walls. Margaret Millar. LC 80-10662. 1980. 9.95 (ISBN 0-89340-285-0). J. Curley.
Listening Woman. Massicks Sparroy. LC 32-125229. 1932. Little, Brown and Company.
Listening Women. Tony Hillerman. LC 77-11788. (Harper Novel of Suspense Ser.). 1978. 10.53i (ISBN 0-06-011901-2, HarpT). Har-Row.
Listening World. Reginald Arthur Moore. LC 46-7931. 1946. Creative Age Press.
Lister Legacy. Jan Drabek. LC 81-148726. 1980. 13.95 (ISBN 0-8253-0015-0). Beaufort Books.
Lister's Great Adventure. Harold Bindloss. LC 21-1354. Frederick A. Stokes Company.
Lists of the Past: Stories. new ed. Julie Hayden. LC 76-3685. 144p. 1976. 7.95 o.p. (ISBN 0-670-43019-6). Viking Pr.
Litany of Evil. Alice Brennan. 1973. pap. 0.95 o.s.i. (75-480). Lancer.
Litany of Sh'reev. William Jon Watkins & Eugene V Snyder. LC 76-7698. 1976. 5.95 (ISBN 0-385-12328-0). Doubleday.
Literary Courtship Under the Auspicies of Pike's Peak. Anna Fuller. LC 4-16458. 1893. G. P. Putnam's Sons.
Literary Love-Letters: And Other Stories. Robert Herrick. LC 69-11902. (American short story series, v. 60). 1969. Garrett Press.
Literary Love-Letters: And Other Stories. Robert Herrick. LC 7-4307. (The Ivory series). 1897. C. Scribner's Sons.
Literary Love Letters & Other Stories see Collected Works.
Literary Review (Teaneck, N.J.) Modern Stories from Many Lands: The Literary Review Book Selected and Edited by Clarence R. Decker and Charles. Ed. by Decker, Clarence Raymond & Angoff, Charles. LC 62-21220.
Literary Review (Teaneck, N.J.) Modern Stories from Many Lands: The Literary Review Book Selected and Edited by Clarence R. Decker and Charles Angoff. Ed. by Clarence Raymond Decker & Angoff, Charles, 1902-LC 62-21220. 1963. Manyland Books.
Literary Tales. Dan Dramer. 240p. (Orig.). (gr. 9 up). 1980. pap. text ed. 6.00x (ISBN 0-89061-233-1, 761). Jamestown Pubs.
Literature in Bureaucracy: Readings in Administrative Fiction. Marc Holzer & Kenneth T Morris. LC 79-122695. 7.95. Avery Pub. Group.
Literature in Russia, Pt. 2. Paul Miliukov. pap. text ed. 3.95 o.p. (ISBN 0-498-04007-0, Prepta). A S Barnes.
Literature of Crime: Stories by World-Famous Authors. Ed. by Ellery Queen, pseud. LC 50-10909. 1950. Little, Brown.
Literature of Horror & the Supernatural. J. Olander & M. Greenberg. 1978. 8.95 (ISBN 0-13-537761-7); pap. 2.95 (ISBN 0-13-537753-6). P-H.
Literature of Mystery & Detection, 44 vols. 1976. 920.00 (ISBN 0-405-07860-9). Ayer Co.
Literature of the Fantastic. J. Olander & M. Greenberg. 1978. 8.95 (ISBN 0-13-537662-9); pap. 2.95 (ISBN 0-13-537654-8). P-H.
Lithium for Medea. Katherine Braverman. 288p. 1981. pap. 2.75 (ISBN 0-523-41185-5). Pinnacle Bks.
Lithium for Medea: A Novel. Katherine Braverman. LC 78-69617. 10.00 (ISBN 0-06-010441-4). Harper & Row.
Lithuanian Quartet. Ed. by Stepas Zobarskas. 4.95 o.p. (ISBN 0-87141-004-4). Manyland.
Lithuanian Quartet: By Aloyzas Baronas and Others. Ed. by Stepas Zobarskas. Baronas, Aloyzas. LC 62-15857. 1962. Maryland Books.
Lithuanian Short Story: Fifty Years. Stepas Zobarskas. LC 76-51607. (Illus.). 12.50 (ISBN 0-87141-050-8). Manyland Books.
Lithuanian Village. Leon Kobrin. Tr. by Goldberg, Isaac. LC 20-6127. Brentano's.
Litle Barefoot. A Tale. Berthold Auerbach. Tr. by Lee, Eliza Buckminster. LC 6-4497. 1867. H. B. Fuller and Company.

TITLE INDEX LITTLE DUKE, RICHARD THE

Litmore Snatch: By Henry Wade Pseud. Harry Lancelot Aubrey-Fletcher. LC 57-106784. (Cock Robin mystery). 1957. Macmillan.
Litoral: Short Stories of the Sea of P. R. Nestor A. Escudero. 3.75 o.p. Vantage.
Little. Louis Zukofsky. LC 74-121373. 1970. 10.95 (ISBN 0-670-43050-1, Grossman). Viking Pr.
Little Acorn: The Story Behind the Joy of Cooking. Marion R. Becker. LC 66-24072. 1966. pap. 2.95 o.p. (ISBN 0-672-50739-0). Bobbs.
Little Adventure. Barbara Cartland. (Bantam Barbara Cartland Library, 3). 1974. (pbk.) 0.95. Bantam Books.
Little Aliens. Myra Kelly. LC 74-27992. (Modern Jewish Experience). (Illus.). 1975. 18.00 (ISBN 0-405-06719-4). Arno Press.
Little Aliens. Myra Kelly. LC 10-9692. 1910. C. Scribner's Sons.
Little Aliens. Myra Kelly. LC 42-1552. 1927. C. Scribner's Sons.
Little America. Rob Swigart. 1977. 7.95 o.p. (ISBN 0-395-25172-9); pap. 3.95 o.p. (ISBN 0-395-25443-4). HM.
Little America: A Novel. Rob Swigart. LC 76-30289. 1977. 7.95 (ISBN 0-395-25172-9) (ISBN 0-395-25443-4) (ISBN 0-395-25443-4) (ISBN 0-395-25443-4). Houghton Mifflin.
Little America: A Novel. Rob Swigart. (Kangaroo Book). 1978 (ISBN 0-671-81920-8). Pocket Books.
Little Amy's Christmas. Wilson J Vance. 1880. The American News Company.
Little and Good. Ruby Mildred Ayres. LC 40-9516. 1940. Doubleday, Doran and Co.,Inc.
Little Angel, and Other Stories. Leonid Nikolaevich Andreev. LC 78-167439. (Short story index reprint series). 1971. (ISBN 0-8369-3965-4). Books for Libraries Press.
Little Angel: And Other Stories. Leonid Nikolaevich Andreev. LC 16-1084. 1916. A. A. Knopf.
Little Angel of Canyon Creek. Cyrus Townsend Brady. LC 14-15746. 1.25. Fleming H. Revell Company.
Little Angie. Emma Cave. LC 76-39924. 7.95 (ISBN 0-698-10806-X). Coward, McCann & Geoghegan.
Little Angie. Emma Cave. (Kangaroo Book). 1977. 1.95 (ISBN 0-671-81689-6). Pocket Books.
Little Apostle on Crutches. Henriette Eugenie Delamare. LC 12-1477. 1912. 0.45. Benziger Brothers.
Little Ark. Jan De Hartog. LC 53-11959. (Illus.). 1970. Repr. of 1953 ed. 5.95 o.p. (ISBN 0-689-10373-5). Atheneum.
Little Arlette: Or My Cousin Guy. Henri Ardel & Furey, Francis Thomas, 1852- Tr. LC 6-36. H.L. Kilner & Co.
Little Ask: Ars. Jan De Hartog. LC 53-11959. 1953. Harper.
Little Athletes. 1979. pap. 1.00 (ISBN 0-8351-0690-X). China Bks.
Little Augie's Lament. Mark McGarrity. LC 72-81082. 1973. 7.50 (ISBN 0-670-43056-0). Grossman Publishers.
Little Aversion. Louise Platt Hauck. LC 34-358804. The Penn Publishing Company.
Little Aversion. Clara I Martin. LC 15-8941. 1912. J. W. Arrowsmith Ltd.; Etc., Etc.
Little Benders. 1st Ed. Joe Knox. LC 52-9533. 1952. Lippincott.
Little Bessie. M. B. Smith. (On cover: Munro's library, no. 677). 1886. N. L. Munro.
Little Betty Blew: Her Strange Experiences and Aventures in Indian Land. Annie Maria Barnes. LC 3-13622. 1903. Lee and Shepard.
Little, Big. John Crowley. LC 81-2483. 8.95 (ISBN 0-553-01266-5). Bantam Books.
Little Big Man. Thomas Berger. LC 64-20284. 1964. Dial Press.
Little Big Man: A Novel. Thomas Berger. LC 78-11139. 1979. 10.95 (ISBN 0-440-05165-7). Delacorte Press /S. Lawrence.
Little Big Top. Doris Hiller, pseud. LC 78-72328. (Pacemaker bestsellers book). (Illus.). 3.32 (ISBN 0-8224-5366-5). Fearon Pitman Publishers.
Little Bird Lost in the Snow. Carolyn Cardinale. 3.00 o.s.i. (ISBN 0-8181-0102-4). Pageant-Poseidon.
Little Birds. Anais Nin. 1980. pap. 2.95 (ISBN 0-553-13465-5). Bantam.
Little Birds: Erotica. Anais Nin. LC 78-2226. 10.00. Harcourt, Brace, Jovanovich.
Little Bishop: Episodes in the Life of John Newmann. Paschal Turbet. LC 77-6232. (Illus.). 3.50. St. Paul Editions.
Little Bit of Eden. Mary Sanders Nelson. LC 66-23558. 1966. Dorrance.
Little Bit of Love: A Novel. Richard Underwood. LC 63-12610. 1963. Holt, Rinehart and Winston.
Little Bit of Luck. Anne Betteridge, pseud. 1973. pap. 0.75 o.p. (ISBN 0-345-20762-9). Beagle Bks.
Little Bit of Sand. John O'Rourke. 4.95 o.p. Vantage.
Little Black Dog see Collected Works.
Little Black Fish & Other Modern Persian Stories. Samad Behrangi. Tr. by Mary Hooglund & Eric Hooglund. LC 75-42512. 1982. 14.00 (ISBN 0-914478-21-4); pap. 7.00 (ISBN 0-914478-22-2). Three Continents.
Little Blind God on Rails. A Romaunt of the Gold Northwest. James Daly. LC 6-33173. 1888. Rand, McNally & Co.
Little Blue Heaven. Hertha Dial & Catherine Richter. 1972. 4.50 (ISBN 0-87516-111-1). De Vorss.
Little Bok, and Other Stories About Schools. Charles William Bardeen. LC 17-286041. C. W. Bardeen.
Little Book for Christmas: Containing a Greeting, a Word of Advice, Some Personal Adventures, a Carol, a Meditation, and Three Christmas Stories for All Ages. Cyrus Townsend Brady. LC 73-167443. (Short story index reprint series). (Illus.). 1971. (ISBN 0-8369-3969-7). Books for Libraries Press.
Little Book for Christmas: Containing a Greeting, a Word of Advice, Some Personal Adventures, a Carol, a Meditation, and Three Christmas Stories of All Ages. Cyrus Townsend Brady. LC 17-27749. 1917. G. P. Putnam's Sons.
Little Book of Christmas. Maturin Murray Ballou. LC 12-406045. 1942. Little, Brown, and Company.
Little Book of Christmas. John Kendrick Bangs. LC 77-116933. (Short story index reprint series). (Illus.). 1970. Books for Libraries Press.
Little Book of Profitable Tales. Eugene Field. LC 76-98568. (His The writings in prose and verse of Eugene Field, 2). (Illus.). 1969. Books for Libraries Press.
Little Book of Strange Tales. George Brandon Saul. LC 70-27956. Walton Press.
Little Book of Sylvanus. David Kossoff. 143p. 1975. 7.95 o.p. (ISBN 0-312-48825-4). St Martin.
Little Book of Sylvanus (Died 41 A.D.) David Kossoff. LC 76-2742. 1976. 9.95 (ISBN 0-8161-6363-4). G. K. Hall.
Little Book of Sylvanus (Died 41 A.D.) David Kossoff & Charles Keeping. LC 75-25548. 1975. 7.95. St. Martin's Press.
Little Book: The Tale & Revelation of the Seventh Angel. Warner Perry. (Illus.). 1979. 9.95 (ISBN 0-9603962-1-7); pap. 4.95 (ISBN 0-9603962-0-9). W Perry.
Little Bookshop. Florence Stonebraker. LC 52-8372. 1952. Arcadia House.
Little Boy Black, and Other Sketches. Betty Reynolds Cobb. LC 26-21901. 1926. The J. W. Burke Company.
Little Boy Blues. George William Willis. LC 47-579420. 1947. E. P. Dutton.
Little Boy Lost. Marghanita Laski. LC 49-503400. 1949. Houghton Mifflin.
Little Boy Lost. Jerry Ludwig. LC 77-24185. 7.95 (ISBN 0-440-04796-X). Delacorte Press.
Little Boy Lost. Terry Ludwig. (Dell Book). 1978. 1.95 (ISBN 0-440-14713-1). Dell Pub. Co.
Little Boy Lost. David Wolman. LC 81-84138. 288p. (Orig.). 1982. pap. 2.95 (ISBN 0-86721-060-5). Playboy Pbks.
Little Brick Church. William C. Falkner. LC 74-104447. 1970. (ISBN 0-8398-0550-0). Literature House.
Little Brick Church. A Novel. William C Falkner. LC 6-38423. 1882. J. B. Lippincott & Co.
Little Brother. Josiah Flynt Willard. LC 68-57562. (Muckrakers Ser.). Repr. of 1902 ed. lib. bdg. 16.50 (ISBN 0-8398-2170-0). Irvington.
Little Brother: A Story of Tramp Life. Josiah Flynt Willard. LC 68-57562. (American novels of muckraking, propaganda, and social protest). 1968. Gregg Press.
Little Brother: A Story of Tramp Life. Josiah Flynt Willard. LC 2-8863. 1902. The Century Co.
Little Brother: And Other Genre-Pictures. Fitz Hugh Ludlow. LC 7-14740. 1867. Lee and Shepard.
Little Brother Fate. Mary Carter Roberts. LC 57-7419. 1957. Farrar, Straus and Cudahy.
Little Brother Is Watching. Walter Dillon. LC 62-7846. (Illus.). 1962. Houghton Mifflin.
Little Brother O' Dreams. Elaine Goodale Eastman. LC 10-7831. 1910. 1.00. Houghton Mifflin Company.
Little Brother of the Rich. Joseph Medill Patterson. LC 68-57545. (Muckrakers Ser.). (Illus.). Repr. of 1908 ed. lib. bdg. 14.50 (ISBN 0-8398-1553-0). Irvington.
Little Brother of the Rich: A Novel. Joseph Medill Patterson. LC 68-57545. (American novels of muckraking, propaganda, and social protest). (Illus.). 1968. Gregg Press.
Little Brother of the Rich: A Novel. Joseph Medill Patterson. LC 8-23548. 1908. The Reilly & Britton Co.
Little Brothers. Dorothy Salisbury Davis. LC 72-11134. 1973. 5.95 (ISBN 0-684-13397-0). Scribner.
Little Brown Brother. Stanley Portal Hyatt. LC 8-24469. 1908. H. Holt and Company.
Little Brown Jug at Kildare. Meredith Nicholson. LC 8-25998. 1908. The Bobbs-Merrill Company.
Little Burr, the Warwick of America: A Tale of the Old Revolutionary Days. Charles Felton Pidgin. LC 5-4092. 1904. The Robinson Luce Company.
Little Caesar. William Riley Burnett. LC 29-12494. 1929. L. MacVeagh, The Dial Press; Etc., Etc.
Little Caesar. With a Foreword by Gilbert Seldes and a New Introd. by W. R. Burnett. William Riley Burnett. LC 58-1355. 1958. Dial Press.
Little Candle's Beam. Isa Glenn. LC 35-4528. 1935. Doubleday, Doran & Company, Inc.
Little Captive Lad. Beulah Marie Dix. LC 2-23906. 1902. The Macmillan Company.
Little Car. Leila Berg, pseud. 1974. pap. 0.95 o.p. (ISBN 0-14-030682-X, Puffin). Penguin.
Little Cardinal. Olive Katharine Parr. LC 12-23203. 1912. 1.25. Benziger Brothers.
Little Carp. 1978. 1.50 (ISBN 0-8351-0613-6). China Bks.
Little Chatelaine. William Ulick O'Connor Cuffe Desart. LC 6-33886. (On cover: Lovell's international ser. no. 69). F. F. Lovell & Company.
Little Chen & the Dragon Brothers. 1980. pap. 1.50 (ISBN 0-8351-0731-0). China Bks.
Little Chevalier. Mary Evelyn Moore Davis. LC 3-27968. 1903. Houghton, Mifflin and Company.
Little Chicken-Thieves. W. A Robinson. LC 7-42188. 1893. Cranston & Curts.
Little Child Shall Lead Them. Elizabeth C. Fife. 2.50 o.p. Vantage.
Little Child Shall Lead Them. 1st Ed. Leah Ramsdell Fuller. LC 51-2938. 1950. J. W. Luce Co.
Little Children. William Saroyan. LC 37-18112. Harcourt, Brace and Company.
Little Chronicle of Magdalena Bach. Esther Hallam Moorhouse Meynell. LC 78-129112. (Illus.). 1970. 5.95. F. Ungar Pub. Co.
Little Citizens: The Humors of School Life. Myra Kelly. LC 22-4746. 1912. Doubleday, Page & Company.
Little Citizens: The Humours of School Life. Myra Kelly. LC 70-163036. (Short story index reprint series). (Illus.). 1971. (ISBN 0-8369-3950-6). Books for Libraries Press.
Little Citizens; the Humours of School Life. Myra Kelly. LC 4-29195. 1904. McClure, Phillips & Co.
Little Citizens: The Humours of School Life. Myra Kelly. LC 26-187. 1925. Doubleday, Page & Company.
Little Citizens: The Humours of School Life. Myra Kelly. LC 32-26107. 1931. P. Smith.
Little Citizens: The Humours of School Life. Illus. by W. D. Stevens. Myra Kelly. 1966. 4.00. P. Smith.
Little City of Hope: A Christmas Story. Francis Marion Crawford. 1907. The Macmillan Company.
Little Clown Lost. Barry Benefield. LC 28-20760. 1928. 2.00. The Century Co.
Little Comedy and Other Stories. Arthur Schnitzler. LC 77-6952. 10.00. (ISBN 0-8044-2802-6) (ISBN 0-8044-6839-7). Ungar.
Little Comedy of Errors. S S Morton. LC 7-324791. (On cover: The golden library, no. 1). 1891. The Price-McGill Company.
Little Company. Eleanor O'Reilly Dark. LC 45-3923. 1945. The Macmillan Company.
Little Comrade: A Tale of the Great War. Burton Egbert Stevenson. LC 15-538246. 1915. 1.20. H. Holt and Company.
Little Conquerors. Ann Abelson. LC 60-121466. 1960. Random House.
Little Corky: A Novel. Edward Hungerford. LC 12-5556. 1912. 1.35. A. C. McClurg & Co.
Little Countess. A Novel. Emmy Dinklage-Campe. Ed. by Boggs, Sara Elisabeth (Siegrist) LC 6-36823. (On cover: Ledger library, no. 50). 1891. R. Bonner's Sons.
Little Countess. By Octave Feuillett...Tr. by Mary Neal Sherwood. Octave Feuillet & Sherwood, Mrs. Mary (Neal) Tr. LC 6-39520. T. B. Peterson & Brothers.
Little Country Schoolteacher. Janet G Slight. LC 40-33597. Fleming H. Revell Company.
Little Court of Yesterday. Minnie Reid French. The Abbey Press.
Little Daffydowndilly: And Other Stories. Nathaniel Hawthorne. LC 7-3875. (Riverside literature series, no. 28). 1887. Houghton, Mifflin and Company.
Little Dark Man... Upton Terrell. LC 34-302499. The Reilly & Lee Co.
Little Dark Man and Other Russian Sketches. Ernest Poole. LC 72-10768. (Short story index reprint series). 1973. (ISBN 0-8369-4222-1). Books for Libraries Press.
Little Dark Man and Other Russian Sketches. Ernest Poole. 1925. The Macmillan Company.
Little Darlings. Pilcer. pap. 2.25 (ISBN 0-345-28894-7). Ballantine.
Little Daughter of Jerusalem. Myriam Harry. Tr. by Allen, Phoebe. LC 19-730322. 1918. J. M. Dent & Sons, Ltd.
Little Daughter of Jerusalem. Myriam Harry. Tr. by Allen, Phoebe. LC 19-10087. E. P. Dutton & Company.
Little David. Robert Stuart Christie. LC 23-16662. 1923. T. Seltzer.
Little Days. Frances Gill. LC 19-2554. 1917. 1.50. Houghton Mifflin Company.
Little Demon. Fedor Kuznich Teternikov & Cournos, John, Tr. LC 16-21979. 1916. A. A. Knopf.
Little Destiny. Vera Cleaver & Bill Cleaver. (gr. 11 up). 1982. pap. 1.95 (ISBN 0-553-20047-X). Bantam.
Little Difference: By P. B. Abercrombie Pseud. Patricia Abercrombie Barnes. LC 59-923561. 1959. Doubleday.
Little Dinners with the Sphinx, and Other Prose Fancies. Richard Le Gallienne. LC 72-11932. (Short story index reprint series). 1973. (ISBN 0-8369-4239-6). Books for Libraries Press.
Little Dinners with the Sphinx, and Other Prose Fancies. Richard Le Gallienne. 1907. Moffat, Yard & Company.
Little Disturbances of Man. Grace Paley. LC 68-174214. 1968. 4.50. Viking.
Little Disturbances of Man. 1st Ed. Grace Paley. LC 59-7915. 1959. Doubleday.
Little Dixie Devil. Bernie Smade Babcock. LC 67-9929. 1937. Arcadia House.
Little Doctor. Louise Platt Hauck. LC 36-143258. The Penn Publishing Company.
Little Doctor. Frederick Herman Herman. LC 78-54149. 1979. 5.95 (ISBN 0-915010-21-6). Sutter House.
Little Doctor. 1981. 1.00 (ISBN 0-8351-0931-3). China Bks.
Little Doctor Victoria: A Southern Story for Boys and Girls. Louise Carnahan. 1899. Carnahan Publishing Co.
Little Dog Barked. Anne Van Melborn Rowe. LC 42-676273. 1942. W. Morrow and Company.
Little Dog Barked. Anne Von Melborn Rowe. LC 42-6762. 1942. W. Morrow and Company.
Little Dog Lost. Tiffany Thayer. LC 38-33562. 1938. J. Messner, Inc.
Little Dorrit. t. b. peterson's uniform ed.... ed. Charles Dickens. LC 6-26443. 1857. T. B. Peterson.
Little Dorrit. diamond ed. Charles Dickens. LC 6-26442. 1867. Ticknor and Fields.
Little Dorrit... Charles Dickens. LC 6-37040. 1867. Hurd and Houghton.
Little Dorrit... Charles Dickens. 1868. Hurd and Houghton.
Little Dorrit. Charles Dickens. LC 34-37768. 1873. J. R. Osgood and Company.
Little Dorrit. Charles Dickens. LC 9-826. Aldine Book Publishing Co.
Little Dorrit. Charles Dickens. LC 6-26440. (On cover: Lovell's library, v. 5, no. 223). 1883. J. W. Lovell Company.
Little Dorrit. Charles Dickens. (Half-title: The centenary edition of the works of Charles Dickens in 36 volumes). 1911. Chapman & Hall, Ltd.
Little Dorrit. Charles Dickens & Harvey Peter Sucksmith. LC 77-30368. (Clarendon Dickens). 1978. 59.50 (ISBN 0-19-812513-5). Clarendon Press.
Little Dorrit: Illustrated by Mimi Korach. Charles Dickens. LC 56-14118. 1956. Heritage Press.
Little Dorrit. With 16 Full-Page Illus. Including Reproductions of Drawings for Early Editions Together with an Introd. and Captions by John Cournos. Charles Dickens. LC 51-13036. (Great Illustrated Classics). 1951. Dodd, Mead.
Little Dorrit. With 40 Illus. by 'Phiz.' London. Charles Dickens. LC 53-419540. (New Oxford illustrated Dickens). 1953. Oxford University Press.
Little Dragon from Peking. James Eastwood. LC 67-21509. 1967. Coward-McCann.
Little Drops of Blood. 1st Ed. Bill Knox. LC 62-11448. 1962. Published for the Crime Club by Doubleday.
Little Drummer Girl. John Le Carre. LC 82-48733. 448p. 1983. 15.95 (ISBN 0-394-53015-2). Knopf.
Little Duke. Charlotte Mary Yonge. Ed. by Edward Lee Thorndike. (Thorndike library). D. Appleton-Century Company, Incorporated.
Little Duke: Richard the Fearless. Charlotte Mary Yonge. LC 9-2220. D. Lothrop & Company.
Little Duke, Richard the Fearless. Charlotte Mary Yonge. 1903. Macmillan and Co., Limited.
Little Duke, Richard the Fearless. Charlotte Mary Yonge. 1923. Duffield & Company.

Little Elephant's Christmas. Heluiz Chandler Washburne & McConnell, Jean, Illus. LC 38-32854. 1938. A. Whitman & Co.
Little Emperors. Alfred Leo Duggan. LC 52-11718. 1953. Coward-McCann.
Little Ethel: Or, A Sprig of Sumac. Philip Henry Smith. F. T. Neely.
Little Eve Edgarton. Eleanor Hallowell Abbott. LC 14-15565. 1914. 1.00. The Century Co.
Little Ferret. Raymond Foxall. LC 73-87404. 1974. 6.95. St. Martin's Press.
Little Fictions, Loving Lies. Hale Chatfield & Jeanne Meinke. LC 81-2813. 1981. 22.50 (ISBN 0-916906-34-5) (ISBN 0-916906-35-3). Konglomerati Press.
Little Fiddler of the Ozarks: A Novel. John Breckenridge Ellis. 1.25. Laird & Lee.
Little Fire: By Elisabeth Kyle Pseud. Agnes Mary Robertson Dunlop. LC 50-6939. 1950. Appleton-Century-Crofts.
Little Flat in the Temple. Winifred Mary Scott. LC 30-17707. 1930. Doubleday, Doran & Company, Inc.
Little Flower of the Street. Dion Clayton Calthrop. LC 23-13326. 1923. Hodder and Stoughton Ltd.
Little Flowers. Francis. 1967. 3.95 (ISBN 0-88088-483-5). Peter Pauper.
Little Flower's Desire. Karen A. Bale. (Sweet Medicine's Prophecy: No. 2). (Orig.). 1982. pap. 2.95 (ISBN 0-89083-910-7). Zebra.
Little Flowers of St. Francis. Tr. by Raphael Brown. 1971. pap. 4.95 (ISBN 0-385-07544-8, Im). Doubleday.
Little Flowers of St. Francis. 1976. pap. 1.95 (ISBN 0-8198-0434-7). Dghtrs St Paul.
Little Fool. Henrietta Eliza Vaughan Stannard. (On cover: Seaside library. Pocket ed. no. 1223). 1889. G. Munro.
Little Fortune. Frederic Arnold Kummer. LC 15-24885. 1915. 1.25. W. J. Watt & Company.
Little French Daughter of Joy. George C Foster. LC 30-10249. The Macaulay Company.
Little French Girl. Anne Douglas Sedgwick. LC 34-203837. 1924. Houghton Mifflin Company.
Little Friend. Ernst Lothar. Tr. by Muir, Willa. LC 33-20285. 1933. G. P. Putnam's Sons.
Little Friend. Bruce Marshall. LC 29-692. 1929. The Macaulay Company.
Little Game. Fielden Farrington. LC 68-16681. 1968. Walker.
Little Game with Destiny. Harriet Louise Lynch. LC 8-3401. 1892. Nocton & Co.
Little Garrison: A Realistic Novel of German Army Life of Today. Oswald Fritz Bilse. LC 4-2324. 1904. F. A. Stokes Company.
Little Gate. Annemarie Ewing. 1947. Rinehart & Company, Inc.
Little Gentleman Across the Road. Prentice Abbot. LC 14-19281. R.G. Badger; Etc., Etc.
Little Girl & Her Older Men. Darlene Goddard. 192p. pap. 1.95 o.p. (6162). Brandon.
Little Girl: And Other Stories. Katherine Mansfield. LC 24-269425. 1924. A. A. Knopf.
Little Girl Lost. Temple Bailey. LC 32-21639. The Penn Publishing Company.
Little Girl Lost. Carole Bolton. LC 79-25151. 7.95 (ISBN 0-525-66653-2). Elsevier/Nelson Books.
Little Girl Nobody Wanted. Dorothy T. Sorrells. 3.95 o.p. Vantage.
Little Girl Sex. Jack Benjamin. 192p. pap. 1.95 o.p. (7100). Barclay Hse.
Little Girl Under a Mosquito Net. Monique Lange. LC 73-6085. 1973. 4.95 (ISBN 0-670-43193-1). Viking Press.
Little Girl Who Couldn't Get-Over-It. Alfred Scott Barry. LC 18-13451. E. P. Dutton & Company.
Little Girl Who Lives Down the Lane. Laird Koenig. LC 73-87594. 1973. 6.95 (ISBN 0-698-10577-X). Coward, McCann & Geoghegan.
Little Girl with the Golden Heart. P. R. Castine. 3.00 o.p. Carlton.
Little Girls Breathe the Same Air As We Do. Paul Fournel. LC 78-24643. 1979. 7.95 (ISBN 0-8076-0916-1). G. Braziller.
Little Girls, Older Men & Sex. Brenda Hawthorne. pap. 2.45 o.p. (4030). Cameo.
Little God Ebisu. Beulah Marie Dix. 1914. 1.25. Duffield & Company.
Little Gods: A Masque of the Far East. Rowland Thomas. LC 9-6849. 1909. Little, Brown, and Company.
Little Gods Laugh. Louise Maunsell Field. LC 17-23975. 1917. 1.40. Little, Brown and Company.
Little Gold Miners of the Sierras. Joaquin Miller. LC 11-17967. 1886. D. Lothrop & Company.
Little Gold Ring: And Other Stories. Cosmo Hamilton. LC 70-121557. (Short story index reprint series). 1970. Books for Libraries Press.
Little Gold Ring: And Other Stories. Cosmo Hamilton. LC 29-22419. 1929. G. P. Putnam's Sons.
Little Gold Ring & Other Stories. Cosmo Hamilton. LC 70-121557. (Short Story Index Reprint Ser). 1929. 20.00 (ISBN 0-8369-3514-4). Ayer Co.
Little Golden Calf. Ilia Arnoldovich Ilf & Eugene Petrov. Tr. by Charles Malamuth. LC 61-17564. 1961. 11.50 (ISBN 0-8044-2412-8). Ungar.
Little Golden Calf: A Satiric Novel. Ilia Arnoldovich Ilf & Evgenii Petrovich Petrov. Tr. by Malamuth, Charles. LC 32-25317. Farrar & Rinehart, Incorporated.
Little Golden: Or, The Pride of the Family. Emma Garrison Jones. (On cover: Munro's library. v. 1, no. 86). 1883. N. L. Munro.
Little Golden's Daughter. Alexander McVeigh Miller & Ross, Percy. (Lovell's library, no. 1250). 1888. J. W. Lovell Company.
Little Golden's Daughter: Or, The Dream of Her Lifetime. Alexander McVeigh Miller. (On cover: Munro's library, v. 1, no. 6). N. L. Munro.
Little Goldie. A Story of Woman's Love. Sumner Hayden. (On cover: Seaside library. Pocket ed., no. 279). 1884. G. Munro.
Little Good-for-Nothing. Le Petit Chose), from the French of Alphonse Daudet. Alphonse Daudet. Tr. by Sherwood, Mrs. Mary Neal. LC 6-33047. (cobweb series of choice fiction). 1878. Estes and Lauriat.
Little Good-for-Nothing. Le Petit Chose) From the French of Alphonse Daudet... Alphonse Daudet. Tr. by Sherwood, Mrs. Mary Neal. (On cover: Lovell's library. v. 12, no. 615). J. W. Lovell Company.
Little Grand and the Marchioness: Or, Our Maltese Peerage and Other Stories. Louise De La Ramee. (seaside library. v. 12, no. 230). 1878. G. Munro.
Little Gray Home in the West. Margaretta D'Arcy & John Arden. 80p. 1982. pap. 4.95 (ISBN 0-86104-221-2). Pluto Pr.
Little Gray Lady: A Novel. Helen Burrell D'Apery & Pollock, Channing. LC 33-28369. (On cover: Play book series. no. 84). J. S. Ogilvie Publishing Company.
Little Gray Shoe: A Romance. Percy James Brebner. LC 13-629744. 1913. 1.25. Little Brown and Company.
Little Green Apples: Or, The Chronicle of a Fallen Man. Geoffrey McNeill-Moss. LC 31-14060. 1931. Brewer and Warren Inc.
Little Green Door: A Novel. Mary E. Stone Bassett. 1905. Lothrop Publishing Co.
Little Green Gate. Stella Callaghan. LC 11-260240. 1911. 1.35. G. P. Putnam's Sons.
Little Green God. Caroline Atwater Mason. 1902. F. H. Revell Company.
Little Green God. Caroline Atwater Mason. LC 33-31155. Fleming H. Revell Company.
Little Green House. Ellen K. Wood. 3.50 o.p. Vantage.
Little Greenhorn. John Madison. 1974. 3.95 o.s.i. (ISBN 0-8181-0326-4). Pageant-Poseidon.
Little Grey Girl. Mary Openshaw. LC 13-8763. 1.25. G. W. Dillingham Company.
Little Grey Lady. limited ed. Virginia Mackay-Smith. LC 15-6757. 1914. E. S. Gorham.
Little Guardian: A Novel of Life in a Scottish Fishing Village. 1st Ed. Dena Kerr. LC 60-40133. 1960. Exposition Press.
Little Guzzy and Other Stories. John Habberton. LC 6-46677. 1878. G. W. Carleton & Co.; Etc., Etc.
Little Heather-Blossom. Emilie Von Loga Von Ingersleben. Tr. by Safford, Mary Joanna. LC 7-8846. (Ledger library. no. 47). 1891. R. Bonner's Sons.
Little Heather-Blossom (Erica) Emilie Von Loga Von Ingersleben. Tr. by Safford, Mary Joanna, D. LC 7-8847. (choice series. no. 47). 1891. R. Bonner's Sons.
Little Hell, Big Heaven. Edith Kneipple Roberts. LC 42-210792. 1942. The Bobbs-Merrill Company.
Little Hercules. Frank Gruber. LC 65-19978. 1965. 3.95. Dutton.
Little Hercules. Francis Wallace. LC 39-32487. M. S. Mill Co., Inc.
Little Hero see Poor People.
Little Herr Friedemann, and Other Stories. Thomas Mann. LC 73-162146. (Penguin modern classics). 1972. 0.35 (ISBN 0-14-003398-X). Penguin.
Little Hills. Nancy Huston Banks. 1905. The Macmillan Company.
Little Horses of Tarquinia. Marguerite Duras. Tr. by Peter Den Beeg. 1980. pap. 4.95 (ISBN 0-7145-0348-7). Riverrun NY.
Little Hotel. Christina Stead. (Bard Book.). 1980. 2.50 (ISBN 0-380-48389-0). Avon Books.
Little Hotel: A Novel. Christina Stead. LC 74-6943. 1975. 6.95 (ISBN 0-03-013226-6). Holt, Rinehart and Winston.
Little House. Coningsby William Dawson. LC 20-161583. 1920. John Lane Company.
Little House. Helen S Woodruff. LC 14-16476. George H. Doran Company.
Little House & Other Stories. Dorothy B. Clary. 5.95 o.p. Vantage.
Little Houses: A Tale of Past Years. George Wilson Slaney. LC 19-14017. E. P. Dutton and Company.
Little Huguenot" A Romance of Fontainebleau. Max Pemberton. LC 3-21939. 1895. Dodd, Mead & Co.
Little Hunchback Zia. Frances Hodgson Burnett. LC 16-16689. Frederick A. Stokes Company.
Little Idyls of the Big World: By W. D. McCrackan... William Denison McCrackan. LC 7-15303. (On cover: Round table library). 1895. J. Knight Company.
Little Ike Templin, and Other Stories. Richard Malcolm Johnston. LC 72-3343. (Short story index reprint series). (Illus.). 1972. (ISBN 0-8369-4151-9). Books for Libraries Press.
Little Ike Templin: And Other Stories. Richard Malcolm Johnston. LC 7-10801. 1894. Lothrop Publishing Company.
Little Iliad. Maurice Henry Hewlett. LC 15-21414. 1915. J. B. Lippincott Company.
Little Injun. Lowell Otus Reese. LC 28-7633. 1927. Thomas Y. Crowell Company.
Little Ironies: Stories of Singapore. Catherine Lim. (Writing in Asia Ser.). 1978. pap. text ed. 3.95x (00244). Heinemann Ed.
Little Jade Lady. Doris Knight. LC 48-3515. 1948. Arcadia House.
Little Jewel: Or, Newport's Brightest Gem. Ella Randall. (Munro's twenty-five cent edition, no. 813). 1888. N. L. Munro.
Little Joanna. A Novel. Elizabeth Whitfield Croom Bellamy. LC 6-116987. (On cover: Appleton's library of American fiction). 1876. D. Appleton and Company.
Little Journey in the World. Charles Dudley Warner. LC 67-29283. (Americans in fic.). 1967. Gregg Pr.
Little Journey in the World. Charles Dudley Warner. LC 77-79664. (Series in American studies). 1969. Johnson Reprint Corp.
Little Journey in the World. biographical ed. Charles Dudley Warner. LC 99-5478. 1899. Harper & Brothers.
Little Journey in the World. A Novel. Charles Dudley Warner. LC 3-39715. 1889. Harper & Brothers.
Little Journey in the World. A Novel. Charles Dudley Warner. LC 13-12913. (Half-title: Harper's Franklin square library, no. 747). 1894. Harper & Brothers.
Little Karin. Marie Sofle Birath Schwartz. Tr. by Borg, Selma & Shipley, Marie Adelaide (Brown) LC 8-20654. 1873. R. W. Bliss & Company.
Little Karoo. Pauline Smith. LC 25-6390. George H. Doran Company.
Little Karoo: Stories. Pauline Smith. LC 59-9250. Vanguard Press.
Little King: A Story of the Childhood of Louis XIV, King of France. Charles Major. 1910. The Macmillan Company.
Little Kingdoms: A Novel. John H. Irsfeld. LC 75-42389. 7.95. Putnam.
Little Kit. A Novel. Effie Adelaide Maria Albanesi. (On cover: The choice series, no. 127). 1895. R. Bonner's Sons.
Little Knight of the X Bar B. Mary Katherine Finigan Maule. LC 10-4044. 1910. Lothrop, Lee & Shepard Co.
Little Knowledge. Michael Bishop. LC 76-50139. 8.95 (ISBN 0-399-11943-4). Berkley Pub. Corp.: Distributed by Putnam.
Little Knowledge. Michael Bishop. (Berkley Medallion Book). 1978. 1.50 (ISBN 0-425-03671-5). Berkley Pub. Corp.
Little Lady Bertha. Fanny Alricks Shugert. LC 11-29660. Every Where Publishing Company.
Little Lady Charles. Effie Adelaide Maria Albanesi. (On cover: Eagle library, no. 139). 1899. Street & Smith.
Little Lady Mildred's Inheritance. Constance Draper. 1890. New York, J. Pott & Co.
Little Lady of Lagunitas: A Franco-Californian Romance. Richard Henry Savage. LC 12-122131. 1892. The American News Company.
Little Lady of the Big House. Jack London. LC 16-7918. 1916. 1.50. The Macmillan Company.
Little Lady of the Big House. Jack London. LC 24-20471. 1919. The Macmillan Company.
Little Lady of the Hall. Nora Ryeman. LC 15-4860. 1915. Benziger Brothers.
Little Lass. Mary Moncure Paynter. LC 7-33762. 1886. H. M. Paynter, Jr.
Little Leafy, the Cloakmaker's Beautiful Daughter. A Romantic Story of a Lovely Working-Girl in the City of New York. Laura Jean Libbey. LC 7-14312. 1891. N. L. Munro.
Little Leaven. Katharine Grey. LC 22-6313. 1922. J. B. Lippincott Company.
Little Leaven: A Missionary Story. Elizabeth E Holding. LC 7-6123. 1890. Hunt & Eaton.
Little Legacy: & Other Stories. Lucy Bethia Colquhoun Walford. (Half-title: Blue cloth books). 1899. H. S. Stone and Company.
Little Less. Angela Du Maurier. LC 41-13932. 1941. Doubleday, Doran and Company, Inc.
Little Less. Aishie Pharall. LC 26-625613. 1926. D. Appleton and Company.
Little Less Than Gods. Ford Madox Ford. LC 26-23919. 1928. The Viking Press.
Little Less Than Kind. Charlotte Armstrong. LC 63-10153. 1963. Cpward-McCann.
Little Less Than Kind. Charlotte Armstrong. 1975. (pbk.) 1.25 (ISBN 0-425-03018-0). Berkley Pub. Co.
Little Lie. Jean Potts. LC 68-27784. 1968. 3.95. Scribner.
Little Life Stories. Harry Hamilton Johnston. LC 79-122725. (Short story index reprint series). 1970. Books for Libraries Press.
Little Life Stories. Harry Hamilton Johnston. LC 23-5358. 1923. The Macmillan Company.
Little Lightning, the Shadow Detective: Or, The Twenty-Third Street Mystery. William H. Van Orden. (secret service series, no. 8). 1888. Street & Smith.
Little Lion. Clifton Hicks. LC 46-495314. 1946. Island Press.
Little Lives. John Howland Spyker. LC 78-58067. 1978. 10.00 (ISBN 0-448-15164-2). Grosset & Dunlap.
Little Lives. John Howland Spyker. 1980. 2.25 (ISBN 0-380-48322-X). Avon Publishers.
Little Local Murder. Robert Barnard. LC 82-23027. 1983. 11.95 (ISBN 0-684-17882-6). Scribner.
Little Loo. William Clark Russell. (On cover: Seaside library. Pocket ed., no. 109). 1883. G. Munro.
Little Loo. A Novel. William Clark Russell. (Harper's Franklin square library, no. 360). 1884. Harper & Brothers.
Little Lord Fauntleroy. Frances Hodgson Burnett. LC 21-4150. 1887. C. Scribner's Sons.
Little Lords of Creation. Hersilia A Mitchell Copp Keays. 1900. H. S. Stone & Company.
Little Lost Sister. Virginia Brooks. LC 14-6230. 1914. Gazzolo and Ricksen.
Little Love. Herbert D Kastle. LC 73-167384. 1973. 2.50 (ISBN 0-491-00953-4). W. H. Allen.
Little Love, a Little Learning. Nina Bawden. LC 66-20611. 1966. Harper & Row.
Little Love and Laughter. Annie F S Cantwell. LC 6-21483. 1886. Shaw & Company.
Little Lower Than the Angels. Virginia Eggersten Sorensen. 1942. A. A. Knopf.
Little Maelstrom. Andrew Magnus Fleming. LC 31-338921. 1931. Meador Publishing Company.
Little Maid of Acadie. Marian Calhoun Legare Reeves. LC 7-30669. (On cover: The Gainsborough series). 1888. D. Appleton and Company.
Little Maid of Arcady. Frances Christine Tiernan. (On cover: Catholic library). H. L. Kilner & Co.
Little Maid of Boston Town. Harriet Mulford Stone Lothrop. LC 10-18954. 1910. 1.50. Lothrop, Lee & Shepard Co.
Little Maid of Israel. Emma Howard Wight. LC 4524. 1900. B. Herder.
Little Make-Believe. Benjamin Leopold Farjeon. (On cover: The seaside library. Pocket ed. no. 179). 1884. G. Munro.
Little Man, Little Man: A Story of Childhood. James Baldwin & Yoran Cazac. LC 76-10723. 7.95 (ISBN 0-8037-4859-0). Dial Press.
Little Man, Little Man: A Story of Childhood. James Baldwin & Yoran Cazac. LC 77-352241. (Illus.). 1976. 2.95 (ISBN 0-7181-1374-8). Joseph.
Little Man, What Now? Rudolf Ditzen, pseud. Tr. by Sutton, Eric. LC 33-14292. 1933. Simon and Schuster.
Little Man Who Wasn't There. Mildred Gordon. LC 46-3586. 1946. Pub. for the Crime Club by Doubleday & Company, Inc.
Little Man with Three Legs. Jim Stickter. LC 80-8771. (Illus.). 224p. (Orig.). 1980. 10.00 (ISBN 0-930770-17-X). Hemisphere Hse.
Little Maude and Her Mamma. Charles Battell Loomis. LC 9-28267. 1909. 0.50. Doubleday, Page & Company.
Little Me. Patrick Dennis, pseud. (Illus.). pap. 0.75 o.p. (T1005, Crest). Fawcett World.
Little Me: The Intimate Memoirs of That Great Star of Stage, Screen and Television. Belle Poitrine, As Told to Patrick Dennis. Photogs. by Cris Alexander. Edward Everett Tanner. (Crest bk., t1005). 1967. Fawcett.
Little Me: The Intimate Memoirs of That Great Star of Stage, Screen, and Television, Belle Poitrine, As Told to Patrick Dennis Pseud. With Photos. by Cris Alexander. 1st Ed. Edward Everett Tanner. LC 61-15133. 1961. Dutton.
Little Me: The Memoirs of Belle Poitrine. Patrick Dennis, pseud. (Illus.). 304p. 1982. pap. 8.95 (ISBN 0-525-48008-0, 0869-260). Dutton.
Little Meg's Children. Hesba Stretton. LC 77-127864. (Early Children's Books). (Illus.). 1970. Johnson Reprint Corp.
Little Meg's Children see Jessica's First Prayer.
Little Men, Big World. 1st Ed. William Riley Burnett. LC 51-3027. 1951. Knopf.
Little Messenger Birds: Or, The Chimes of the Silver Bells. Caroline H Butler. LC 6-15445. 1850. Phillips, Sampson, and Company.

Little Mininister. James Matthew Barrie. LC 98-1458. (Library of famous books by famous authors). H. M. Caldwell Company.
Little Minister. James Matthew Barrie. LC 56-58790. 1954. Scribner.
Little Minister. James Matthew Barrie. LC 59-16050. 1959. Grosset & Dunlap.
Little Minister. James Matthew Barrie. LC 6-8642. J. W. Lovell Company.
Little Minister. James Matthew Barrie. LC 6-8641. 1892. Lovell, Coryell and Company.
Little Minister. a new edition revised by the author. ed. James Matthew Barrie. LC 8-8640. (On cover: Fortnightly series, no. 1). American Publishers Corporation.
Little Minister. (maude adams ed.) ed. James Matthew Barrie. LC 99-156. 1898. R. H. Russell.
Little Minister. James Matthew Barrie. LC 20-56277. Thomas Y. Crowell Company.
Little Minister. James Matthew Barrie. 1921. Charles Scribner's Sons.
Little Minister. James Matthew Barrie. LC 9-2706. Lovell, Coryell & Company.
Little Minister. James Matthew Barrie. LC 43-26009. (Reader's library... Lucas Lexow, editor). J. H. Sears & Company, Inc.
Little Minx: A Sketch. Ada Cambridge Cross. LC 6-31958. (On cover: Appletons' town and country library, no. 114). 1893. D. Appleton and Company.
Little Miss By-the-Day. Lucille Baldwin Van Slyke. LC 19-15222. Frederick A. Stokes Company.
Little Miss Dee. Roswell Martin Field. LC 4-33219. 1904. F. H. Revell Company.
Little Miss Grouch: A Narrative Based Upon the Private Log of Alexander Forsyth Smith's Maiden Transatlantic Voyage, by Samuel Hopkins Adams. Samuel Hopkins Adams. LC 15-18692. 1915. Houghton Mifflin Company.
Little Miss Marker. Damon Runyon. Repr. lib. bdg. 11.50x (ISBN 0-89190-436-0). Am Repr-Rivercity Pr.
Little Miss Muffet: A Love Story for Grown-Ups. Elizabeth Kirby. LC 19-15682. 1919. Moffat, Yard and Company.
Little Miss Muffett. Rosa Nouchette Carey. LC 6-23105. 1893. J. B. Lippincott Company.
Little Miss Primrose. A Novel. Eliza Tabor Stephenson. (Seaside library, v. 32, no. 667). 1879. G. Munro.
Little Miss Primrose. A Novel. Eliza Tabor Stephenson. (Franklin square library, no. 94). 1879. Harper & Brothers.
Little Missioner. Nina Wilcox Putnam. LC 15-4804. 1915. 1.30. D. Appleton and Company.
Little Mr. Bouncer and His Friend Verdant Green: Also, Tales of College Life. Edward Bradley. LC 6-15199. 1893. Little, Brown and Company.
Little Moment of Happiness. Clarence Budington Kelland. LC 19-140043. Harper & Brothers.
Little Monsters: Children of Wonder & Dread. Ed. by Roger Elwood & Vic Ghidalia. 1971. pap. 0.75 o.p. (532-75282-075). Manor Bks.
Little Moorland Princess. Eugenie John. Tr. by Wister, Annis Lee (Furness) LC 1454. 1900. J. B. Lippincott Company.
Little More. William Babington Maxwell. LC 22-2604. 1922. Dodd, Mead and Company.
Little More Than Kin. Ernest Hebert. LC 81-24135. 1982. 13.95 (ISBN 0-670-43209-1). Viking Press.
Little More Than Kin: A Novel. Nelia Gardner White. LC 56-8565. 1956. Viking Press.
Little More Time: A Novel. David Chandler. LC 56-8347. 1956. J. Day Co.
Little Mother Who Sits at Home. Marguerite Florence Helene Evans. LC 15-5601. E. P. Dutton & Coompany.
Little Mrs. Manington. Cecil Roberts. LC 26-173075. George H. Doran Company.
Little Mule: A Novel. John Burress. LC 52-6779. 1952. Vanguard Press.
Little Natalie & Her Big Black Lover. Jerome Warr. pap. 1.95 o.p. (ISBN 0-87056-182-0, 6182). Brandon.
Little Nea's Engagement: A Sequel to "Nearest and Dearest,". Emma Dorothy Eliza Nevitte Southworth. LC 12-38904. (On cover: Southworth library. no. 134). Street & Smith.
Little Neighbor. Jim Kelly. (Small Star Stories). (Illus.). 1975. 5.95 o.p. (ISBN 0-02-645480-7, 64548); cassette 6.95 o.p. (ISBN 0-02-645490-4, 64549). Glencoe.
Little Night Music. Barbara Hunt. LC 47-3103. 1947. Rinehart & Company, Inc.
Little Nobody. Alexander McVeigh Miller. (On cover: The library of American authors, no. 51). 1893. G. Munro's Sons.
Little North of Everywhere. James Norman Schmidt. LC 51-13494. 1951. Pellegrini & Cudahy.
Little Novels. Wilkie Collins. LC 77-74566. 1977. 3.00 (ISBN 0-486-23506-8). Dover Publications.
Little Novels. Arthur Schnitzler. LC 77-175574. 1974. (ISBN 0-404-08277-7). AMS Press.
Little Novels of Italy. Maurice Henry Hewlett. LC 99-455010. 1899. The Macmillan Company.
Little Novels of Sicily. Giovanni Verga. Tr. by David Herbert Lawrence. LC 75-11483. 1975. 13.00 (ISBN 0-8371-8199-2). Greenwood Press.
Little Novels of Sicily. Giovanni Verga. Tr. by David Herbert Lawrence. LC 74-168626. (Penguin modern classics). 1973. 0.40 (ISBN 0-14-003250-9). Penguin.
Little Novels of Sicily. Giovanni Verga. Tr. by David Herbert Lawrence. LC 25-6701. 1925. T. Seltzer.
Little Novels of Sicily: Translated by D. H. Lawrence. Giovanni Verga. Tr. by David Herbert Lawrence. LC 53-119035. 1953. Grove Press.
Little Novels: Translated from the German by Eric Sutton. Arthur Schnitzler. Tr. by Sutton, Eric. LC 29-18001. 1929. Simon and Schuster.
Little Nugget. Pelham Grenville Wodehouse. LC 14-1107. W. J. Watt & Company.
Little Nugget. Pelham Grenville Wodehouse. LC 43-30670. The Curtiss Press.
Little of What You Fancy. Herbert Ernest Bates. LC 74-193864. 1973. 0.30 (ISBN 0-14-003702-0). Penguin.
Little Often Fanny. Norman Jackson. (Fanny Ser. Vol. 3). 1968. pap. 0.60 o.p. (73-798). Lancer.
Little Old Admiral. Louis Golding. 3.95 o.p. (ISBN 0-8149-0535-8). Vanguard.
Little Old Lady. Lynn Harold Hough. LC 17-233384. The Abingdon Press.
Little Old Man of Batignolles: And Other Stories. Emile Gaboriau. LC 6-44550. (On cover: Lovell's library. no. 1119). 1888. J. W. Lovell Company.
Little Old Man of the Batignolles. A Chapter from a Detective's Memoirs. Emile Gaboriau. LC 6-44549. (On cover: Seaside library. Pocket ed. no. 1083). 1888. G. Munro.
Little Old New York. Rida Johnson Young. LC 23-9687. Grosset & Dunalp.
Little Orvie. Booth Tarkington. LC 35-27014. 1934. Doubleday, Doran & Company, Inc.
Little Ottleys. Ada Leverson. LC 82-25246. 1983. 7.95 (ISBN 0-385-27918-3). Dial Press.
Little Ottleys: Love's Shadow. Tenterhooks. Love at Second Sight. With a Foreword by Colin MacInnes. Ada Leverson. LC 62-52081. 1962. Norton.
Little Pardner: And Other Stories. Eleanor Hodgman Porter. LC 26-16331. George H. Doran Company.
Little Pardner, & Other Stories. facs. ed. Eleanor Hodgman Porter. LC 70-142273. (Short Story Index Reprint Ser). 1926. 16.00 (ISBN 0-8369-3757-0). Ayer Co.
Little Pedlington and the Pedlingtonians. John Poole. (Half-title: Appletons' popular library of the best authors). 1852. D. Appleton & Company.
Little People. John Christopher. LC 66-21825. 1967. Simon and Schuster.
Little People. Albert Halper. LC 74-26110. (Labor Movement in Fiction and Non-Fiction). 1976. 24.50 (ISBN 0-404-58435-7). AMS Press.
Little People. Albert Halper. LC 42-22583. 1942. Harper & Brothers.
Little People of the Dust: A Novel. Joseph Burke Egan. LC 13-23413. The Pilgrim Press.
Little Peter in War & Peace. Gerhard Zwerenz. LC 78-111014. 1970. 6.95. Grove Press.
Little Peter's Task. Marie Healy Bigot. Tr. by Maguire, Hortense G. LC 31-18739. (Heath supplementary readers). D. C. Heath and Company.
Little Pierre and Big Peter. Frances Otis Ogden Ide. LC 15-16591. 1915. 1.35. Frederick A. Stokes Company.
Little Pierre, the Pedlar of Alsace: Or, The Reward of Filial Piety. Tr. by C., J. M. LC 7-16062. 1872. Catholic Publication Society.
Little Pilgrim. Margaret Oliphant Wilson Oliphant. (On cover: Lovell's library. v. 4. no. 179). 1883. J. W. Lovell Company.
Little Pilgrim. Margaret Oliphant Wilson Oliphant. (On cover: Seaside library. Pocket ed., no. 45). 1883. G. Munro.
Little Pilgrims: A Sequel to The Tailor's Apprentice. By the Author of "The Tailor's Apprentice.". Timothy Shay Arthur. LC 6-3407. 1843. Godey & McMichael.
Little Pitchers. Isa Glenn. LC 27-2002. 1927. A. A. Knopf.
Little Pitchers Have 'em: A Novel. Daisy Metcalfe Johnson. LC 51-15540. (Gusto issues). 1950. House-Warven.
Little Place Called King's Standing: A Novel. Illus. by Edward Norrington. Sheila Turner. LC 65-15060. 1965. 3.95. Holt.
Little Pretender. Barbara Cartland. 1975. pap. 1.25 o.p. (ISBN 0-515-03909-8, V3909). BJ Pub Group.
Little Pretender. Barbara Cartland. 1977. pap. 1.50 o.p. (ISBN 0-515-04381-8). BJ Pub Group.
Little Primrose. Florence Blackburn White Schoeffel. (On cover: American series no. 150). M. J. Ives & Co.
Little Prince. anniversary edition. ed. Antoine De Saint-Exupery. (Illus.). 1973. (boxed) 7.50 (ISBN 0-15-152820-9). Harcourt Brace.
Little Prince (Anniversary Edition) Antoine De Saint-Exupery. (Illus.). 1973. 7.50 o.p. (ISBN 0-15-152820-9). HarBraceJ.
Little Princess. Frances Hodgson Burnett. (Yearling book). 1975. (pbk.) 1.25. Dell.
Little Prodigals. Nannie Lee Frayser. LC 12-32361. 1910. 0.35. F. M. Barton Company.
Little Raw on Monday Mornings. Robert Cormier. 176p. 1980. pap. 1.95 (ISBN 0-380-51490-7, 51490). Avon.
Little Rebel. authorized ed. Margaret Wolfe Hungerford. LC 7-9358. (On cover: Lovell's Westminster series, no. 32). 1891. J. W. Lovell Company.
Little Rebel. Margaret Wolfe Hungerford. LC 7-17924. (On cover: Romantic series. no. 5). 1891. The Minerva Publishing Company.
Little Red Box. Ernest L. Norman. 1968. 4.95 (ISBN 0-932642-16-0); pap. 3.95 (ISBN 0-932642-47-0). Unarius.
Little Red Chimney: Being the Love Story of a Candy Man. Mary Finley Leonard. LC 14-148052. 1914. Duffield & Company.
Little Red Foot. Robert William Chambers. LC 21-95001. George H. Doran Company.
Little Red Foot. Robert William Chambers. LC 34-38279. 1923. A. L. Burt Company.
Little Red Hen. John McGrath. 64p. (Orig.). 1981. pap. 4.95 (ISBN 0-904383-31-8). Pluto Pr.
Little Red House in the Hollow. Amanda Benjamin Hall. LC 18-7405. G. W. Jacobs & Company.
Little Red Phone. Henry Kane. LC 81-71669. 12.95 (ISBN 0-87795-375-9). Arbor House.
Little Regiment, and Other Episodes of the American Civil War. Stephen Crane. LC 70-150471. (Short story index reprint series). 1971. (ISBN 0-8369-3811-9). Books for Libraries Press.
Little Regiment: And Other Episodes of the American Civil War. Stephen Crane. 1896. D. Appleton and Company.
Little Rogue, & Other Stories: Collected Novels & Stories, Vol. 10. facsimile ed. Guy De Maupassant. Ed. by Ernest Boyd. Tr. by Storm Jameson from Fr. LC 73-157788. (Short Story Index Reprint Ser.). Repr. of 1924 ed. 16.00 (ISBN 0-8369-3900-X). Ayer Co.
Little Rogue in Our Flesh. Yves Navarre. (Writers Fiction Ser.). 240p. 1982. 14.95 (ISBN 0-7145-3927-9); pap. 7.95 (ISBN 0-7145-3933-3). Riverrun NY.
Little Roque: And Other Stories. Guy De Maupassant. LC 73-157788. (Short story index reprint series). 1971. (ISBN 0-8369-3900-X). Books for Libraries Press.
Little Rosebud's Lovers: Or, A Cruel Revenge. Laura Jean Libbey. (On cover: The library of American authors, no. 16). 1890. G. Munro.
Little Russian Masterpieces. Zenaide Alexeievna Rogozin. LC 20-18302. 1920. G. P. Putnam's Sons.
Little Saint. Georges Simenon. LC 65-21035. 1965. Harcourt, Brace & World.
Little Saint of St. Domingue. Eleanor Louise Heckert. LC 73-79677. 1973. 7.95 (ISBN 0-385-02270-0). Doubleday.
Little Saint Sunshine. Charles Frederic Goss. LC 2-24243. 1902. The Bowen-Merrill Company.
Little Saints Annoy the Lord. Arthur Howard Hutchinson. LC 38-22955. 1938. The Greenwood Press.
Little Savage. Frederick Marryat. LC 7-24684. (On cover: Seaside library. Pocket ed. no. 272). G. Munro.
Little Schoolmaster Mark: A Spiritual Romance, 2 pts. in 1 vol. Joseph Henry Shorthouse. LC 79-8200. Repr. of 1884 ed. 44.50 (ISBN 0-404-62126-0). AMS Pr.
Little Schoolmistress. Cleburne Lee Hayes. The C. J. Bell Company.
Little Secretary. Louise Platt Hauck. LC 42-183631. 1942. Dodd, Mead & Company.
Little Shepherd. 16p. 1974. pap. 0.99 (ISBN 0-8285-1193-4, Pub. by Progress Pubs USSR). Imported Pubns.
Little Shepherd. Anna Potter Wright. LC 35-8293. The Bible Institute Colportage Ass'n.
Little Shepherd of Bargain Row. Howard McKent Barnes. The Reilly & Britton Co.
Little Shepherd of Kingdom Come. John Fox. LC 3-21292. 1903. C. Scribner's Sons.
Little Shepherd of Kingdom Come. John Fox. LC 12-31335. 1919. C. Scribner's Sons.
Little Shepherd of Kingdom Come. John Fox. LC 21-13712. 1920. Grosset & Dunlap.
Little Shepherd of Kingdom Come. John Fox & Wyeth, Newell Convers, 1882- Illus. LC 31-28117. 1931. C. Scribner's Sons.
Little Shepherd of Lava Lake. Albert Cooper Allen. LC 28-134531. 1928. G.H. Watt.
Little Ships. Kathleen Thompson Norris. 1971. pap. 0.95 o.p. (ISBN 0-446-65622-4, 65-622). Paperback Lib.
Little Ships: A Novel. Kathleen Thompson Norris. LC 25-185781. 1921. Doubleday, Page & Co.
Little Sin. William Arthur Neubauer. LC 46-870. 1946. Phoenix Press.
Little Sin. William M Yardy. LC 58-10767. (Red badge detective). 1958. Dodd, Mead.
Little Sinner. Ruby Mildred Ayres. LC 40-5842. 1940. Doubleday, Doran & Company, Inc.
Little Sins. Katharine Brush. LC 27-180059. 1927. Minton, Balch & Company.
Little Sir Galahad: A Novel. Phoebe Gray. LC 15-159108. Small, Maynard & Company.
Little Sister. Mary Burchell. LC 47-30657. 1947. Arcadia House.
Little Sister. Raymond Chandler. LC 49-10873. 1949. Houghton Mifflin Co.
Little Sister. Ida Cook. LC 47-30657. 1947. Arcadia House.
Little Sister. Reuven Kritz. 5.95 o.p. Vantage.
Little Sister. Jane Woolsey Yardley. LC 9-1471. (No name series. 3d series). 1882. Roberts Brothers.
Little Sister of Destiny. Gelett Burgess. LC 6-12133. 1906. Houghton, Mifflin & Company.
Little Sister Snow. Fannie Macaulay. 1909. The Century Co.
Little Sister to the Wilderness. Lilian Lida Bell. LC 6-9415.
Little Sisters Don't Count. Maysie Greig. LC 34-13900. 1934. Doubleday, Doran & Co., Inc.
Little Sleep: A Little Slumber. Norman Katkov. LC 49-101453. 1949. Doubleday.
Little Snoop. Betty I. Lovelace. LC 82-90020. 219p. 1982. 11.95 (ISBN 0-533-05213-0). Vantage.
Little Sorrowful. Glenn Allan. LC 46-118423. 1946. S. Curl, Inc.
Little Soul. Elinor Mordaunt, pseud. LC 21-17273. The James A. McCann Company.
Little Squire Jim. Robert K Marshall. LC 49-818351. 1949. Duell, Sloan and Pearce.
Little Star of Mexico. Hazel Hope. LC 44-990417. 1944. B. Humphries, Inc.
Little Steel. Upton Beall Sinclair. LC 74-26122. (Labor Movement in Fiction and Non-Fiction). 1976. 20.00 (ISBN 0-404-58470-5). AMS Press.
Little Steel. Upton Beall Sinclair. LC 38-27753. Farrar & Rinehart, Inc.
Little Stepson. Florence Marryat Church Lean. LC 7-13603. (On cover: Lovell's library. v. 19 no. 909). 1887. J. W. Lovell Company.
Little Stockade. 1st Ed. Natalie Anderson Scott. LC 53-10341. 1954. Dutton.
Little Stories. Silas Weir Mitchell. LC 76-85691. (Short story index reprint series). 1969. Books for Libraries Press.
Little Stories. Silas Weir Mitchell. LC 3-25877. 1903. The Century Co.
Little Stories from the Screen. William Addison Lathrop. LC 17-20180. Britton Publishing Company.
Little Stories of Courtship. Mary Stewart Doubleday Cutting. LC 79-98566. (Short story index reprint series). (Illus.). 1969. Books for Libraries Press.
Little Stories of Courtship. Mary Stewart Doubleday Cutting. LC 5-10922. 1905. McClure, Phillips & Co.
Little Stories of Married Life. Mary Stewart Doubleday Cutting. LC 70-152968. (Short story index reprint series). 1971. (ISBN 0-8369-3796-1). Books for Libraries Press.
Little Stories of Married Life. Mary Stewart Doubleday Cutting. LC 2-230892. 1902. McClure, Phillips & Co.
Little Stories of Married Life. Mary Stewart Doubleday Cutting. LC 13-9366. 1909. Doubleday, Page & Company.
Little Stories of Quebec. James Edward Le Rossignol. LC 8-37358. Jennings and Graham.
Little Striker. Russell G. Moore. LC 81-80507. (Illus.). 128p. (Orig.). 1981. pap. 5.00 (ISBN 0-936972-03-3). Lower Cape.
Little Sufferers: A Story of the Abuses of the Children's Societies. Gerhard Martin Jurgenson. LC 11-26806. 1.50. Broadway Publishing Co.
Little Sunshine. Adah M Howard. (Munro's library, v. 50. no. 821). N. L. Munro.
Little Sunshine: Or, The Secret of the Death Chamber. Adah M Howard. (On cover: Munro's library, v. 1., no. 655)). N. L. Munro.
Little Superman. Heinrich Mann. Tr. by Ernest Augustus Boyd. LC 45-8917. 1945. Creative Age Press, Inc.
Little Sweetheart: Or, Norman De Vere's Protegee. Alexander McVeigh Miller. (On cover: The library of American authors, no. 49). 1893. G. Munro.
Little Tales of Smethers & Other Stories. Dunsany. 1981. 18.95x (Pub. by Remploy England). State Mutual Bk.
Little Tea, a Little Chat. Christina Stead. 1948. Harcourt, Brace.

Little Thank You. Elizabeth Paschal O'Connor. LC 13-16387. 1913. 1.25. G. P. Putnam's Sons.
Little Things. 1970. 3.95 (ISBN 0-88088-399-5). Peter Pauper.
Little Things. George Spencer Merrill. LC 37-1272. Dorrance and Company.
Little Things. Garnett A. Schultz. 1964. 3.75 o.p. (ISBN 0-8059-0254-6). Dorrance.
Little Things: A Collection of Short Stories. 1st Ed. Joseph S Salzburg. LC 57-7925. 1957. Pageant Press.
Little Tiger. Anthony Hope Hawkins. LC 25-214178. George H. Doran Company.
Little Tigress: Tales Out of the Dust of Mexico. Wallace Smith. LC 74-144173. (Short story index reprint series). (Illus.). 1971. (ISBN 0-8369-3788-0). Books for Libraries Press.
Little Tigress: Tales Out of the Dust of Mexico. Wallace Smith. LC 23-141989. 1923. 2.50. G. P. Putnam's Sons.
Little Time for Laughter. Alfred Coppel. LC 76-78881. 1969. Harcourt, Brace & World.
Little to the East: A Novel. Robert Cenedella. LC 63-9655. 1963. Putnam.
Little Toot Through the Golden Gate. Hardy Gramatky. LC 75-10450. (Illus.). 1975. 6.95 (ISBN 0-399-20483-0). G. P. Putnam.
Little Touch of Drama. Valerian Petrovych Pidmohylnyi. LC 72-86407. (Ukrainian Classics in Translation, No. 1). 1972. (ISBN 0-87287-051-0). Ukrainian Academic Press.
Little Town. Heinrich Mann & Ray, Winifred, Tr. LC 31-5384. 1931. Houghton Mifflin Company.
Little Town. Beatrice Burton Morgan. LC 37-23787. Farrar & Rinehart, Inc.
Little Tragedy at Tien-Tsin. Frances Aymar Mathews. LC 4-9636. 1904. R. G. Cooke.
Little Traitor to the South: A War-Time Comedy, with a Tragic Interlude by Cyrus Townsend Brady. Cyrus Townsend Brady. LC 4-497493. 1904. The Macmillan Company.
Little Tu' Penny. A Tale. Sabine Baring-Gould. (On cover: The seaside library. Pocket ed. no. 878). G. Munro.
Little Tu'penny. Sabine Baring-Gould. LC 6-7597. (On cover: Lovell's library, v. 18, no. 875). 1887. J. W. Lovell Company.
Little Turning Aside. Lyda Farrington Krause. LC 98-1572. 1898. G. W. Jacobs & Co.
Little Tyke. Georges Westbeau. LC 56-13322. 115p. pap. 4.95 o.p. (ISBN 0-8163-0048-8, 12480-0). Pacific Pr Pub Assn.
Little Union Scout. Joel Chandler Harris. LC 72-2998. (Black Heritage Library Collection). (Illus.). 1972. (ISBN 0-8369-9075-7). Books for Libraries Press.
Little Union Scout. Joel Chandler Harris. LC 4-9630. 1904. McClure, Phillips & Co.
Little Upstart. A Novel. 2d ed. William Henry Rideing. LC 7-414381. 1885. Cupples, Upham, and Company.
Little Valley. Raymond Otis. LC 79-56813. (Zia book). (Illus.). 5.95 (ISBN 0-08-263053-4). University of New Mexico Press.
Little Valley of God. Translated by Campbell Nairne. Carlo Coccioli. LC 57-5672. 1957. Simon and Schuster.
Little Venice, and Other Stories. Grace Denio Litchfield. LC 72-98583. (Short story index reprint series). (Illus.). 1969. Books for Libraries Press.
Little Venice: And Other Stories. Grace Denio Litchfield. 1890. G. P. Putnam's Sons.
Little Virgin. Gladys Mary Attenborough. LC 33-110738. Frederick A. Stokes Company.
Little Voyage. Letitia Preston Osborne. LC 49-9379. 1949. J. B. Lippincott Co.
Little Walls. Winston Graham. LC 55-9230. 1955. Doubleday.
Little Warrior. Pelham Grenville Wodehouse. LC 20-18298. George H. Doran Company.
Little Warrior. Wodehouse, Pelham Grenville. LC 38-7787. 1923. A. L. Burt Company.
Little Wax Doll. Norah Robinson Lofts. LC 70-94117. 1970. 5.95. Doubleday.
Little Way Ahead. Alan Sullivan. LC 30-7683. E. P. Dutton & Co., Inc.
Little Welsh Girl. Howel Evans. LC 19-213. 1918. Hodder and Stoughton.
Little White Bird: Or, Adventures in Kensington Gardens. James Matthew Barrie. LC 73-4997. 1973. (lib. bdg.) 25.00 (ISBN 0-87821-122-5). Milford House.
Little White Bird: Or, Adventures in Kensington Gardens. James Matthew Barrie. LC 2-36769. 1909. C. Scribner's Sons.
Little White Bird: Or, Adventures in Kensington Gardens. James Matthew Barrie. LC 16-6895. 1915. C. Scribner's Sons.
Little White Bird: Or, Adventures in Kensington Gardens. James Matthew Barrie. LC 77-85624. (Illus.). 1977. 25.00 (ISBN 0-89341-451-4). Longwood Press.
Little White Bird or Adventures in Kensington Gardens. James Matthew Barrie. LC 77-85624. 1977. Repr. of 1902 ed. lib. bdg. 25.00 (ISBN 0-89341-451-4). Longwood Pr.
Little White Hag. Francis Beeding. LC 26-1451. 1926. Little, Brown, and Company.
Little White Horse. Elizabeth Goudge. LC 77-95091. (Illus.). 1978. 1.75 (ISBN 0-380-01875-6). Avon Books.
Little White Pagan, a Thrilling Missionary Story: Most Interesting to Adults, Intensely Fascinating to Young People. Anne Woodley. LC 42-32092. Light & Hope Publications.
Little White Shoes. Marie E. Moore. 80p. 1975. 4.00 o.p. (ISBN 0-682-48217-X). Exposition.
Little Widow: Or, The Fortune-Hunter's Doom. Julia Edwards, pseud. (select ser. no. 34). 1890. Street & Smith.
Little Window. Helen Merrill Hodsdon. LC 13-17973. 0.50. Thomas Y. Crowell Company.
Little Wizard. Stanley John Weyman. LC 12-100538. R. F. Fenno & Company.
Little Women: Good Wives. Louisa May Alcott. LC 36-37132. (Half-title: Everyman's library, ed. by Ernest Rhys. For young people. no. 248=5d). 1934. J. M. Dent & Sons, Ltd.
Little Women: Or, Meg, Jo, Beth and Amy. Louisa May Alcott. 1869. Roberts Brothers.
Little Women: Or, Meg, Jo, Beth and Amy. Louisa May Alcott. LC 2-23996. 1902. Little, Brown, and Company.
Little Women: Or, Meg, Jo, Beth, and Amy. Louisa May Alcott. LC 35-28559. 1932. A. L. Burt Company.
Little Wood Duck. Brian Wildsmith. LC 72-3828. (Illus.). 1973. 5.95 (ISBN 0-531-02593-4). F. Watts.
Little World. Rian James. LC 35-691871. A. H. King.
Little World: A Hospital Romance. Millicent Peppard De Mone. LC 20-19243. Burton Publishing Company.
Little World Apart. Squire Omar Barker. LC 66-14110. 4.50. Doubleday.
Little World Apart. George Stevenson. LC 17-7457. 1917. 1.25. John Lane.
Little World of Don Camillo. Giovanni Guareschi. (Washington Square Press Enriched Classics). (Illus.). 1973. (pbk.) 0.75. Pocket Books.
Little World of Don Camillo. Tr. from Italian by Una Vincenzo Tronbridge. Large Type Ed. Giovanni Guareschi. (Keith Jennison bk.). 1966. 6.95. Watts.
Little World of Don Camillo. Translated from the Italian by Una Vincenzo Troubridge. Giovanni Guareschi. LC 50-897531. 1950. Pellegrini & Cudahy.
Little World of the Past. Antonio Fogazzaro. Tr. by W. J. Strachan. 1962. 4.25 o.p. (ISBN 0-19-255107-8). Oxford U Pr.
Little World Waddies. Eugene Manlove Rhodes & Bugbee, Harold Dow, 1900- LC 47-11472. 1946.
Little Worldling: A Novel. Louise C. Ellsworth. LC 6-378391. 1890. The American News Co.
Little Wrinkled Old Man: A Christmas Extravaganza. And Other Trifles. Elizabeth A Thurston. LC 15-16816. 1866. W. V. Spencer.
Little Yellow House. Beatrice Burton Morgan. LC 28-21584. 1928. Doubleday, Doran and Company, Inc.
Littlehampton Bequest. Osbert Lancaster. LC 74-84419. (Illus.). 1974. 8.95 (ISBN 0-87645-087-7). Gambit.
Littlest Horse Thieves. Rosemary Anne Sisson. 1977. 1.50 (ISBN 0-671-80960-1). Pocket Books.
Littlest House. James Noble Gifford. LC 36-35991. 1936. Arcadia House.
Littlest House. Warren Howard. LC 36-35991. 1936. Arcadia House.
Littlest Neutral. David Lozell Martin. LC 66-26160. 1966. 4.95. Crown.
Littlest Orphan and Other Christmas Stories. Margaret Elizabeth Sangster. LC 35-274537. 1935. Round Table Press, Inc.
Littl'st Lover. Ruby Mildred Ayres. LC 25-24276. 1925. George H. Doran Company.
Liv. Kathleen Coyle. LC 29-854117. E. P. Dutton & Co., Inc.
Liv. James Pinckney Miller. LC 72-8977. 1973. 7.95. Dial Press.
Live and Kicking Ned. John Masefield. LC 39-27887. 1939. The Macmillan Company.
Live and Let Die. Ian Fleming. LC 55-1729. (Cock robin thriller). 1955. Macmillan.
Live and Let Die: Reissue. Ian Fleming. LC 66-54. 1966. bds., 3.95. Macmillan.
Live and Let Live: Or, Domestic Service Illustrated. Catharine Maria Sedgwick. LC 8-6436. 1837. Harper & Brothers.
Live and Let Love. Ruth Rosemary Corby. LC 42-795577. 1941. Arcadia House, Inc.
Live and Remember. Valentin Grigorevich Rasputin. LC 77-18884. 1978. 8.95 (ISBN 0-02-601130-1). Macmillan.
Live Bait. Bill Knox. LC 78-14684. 1979. 7.95 (ISBN 0-385-14872-0). Published for the Crime Club by Doubleday.
Live Bait. Thomas, Ronald Wills. LC 50-56415. (Questing owl detective story). 1950. Wingate.
Live Bait and Other Stories. Frank Tuohy. LC 78-4689. 1979. 7.95 (ISBN 0-03-043636-2). Holt, Rinehart, and Winston.
Live Bait for Murder. 1st Ed. William Herber. LC 55-6721. (Main line mysteries). 1955. Lippincott.
Live Bait: Shorter Romances. Ethel May Dell. LC 32-14439. 1932. G. P. Putnam's Sons.
Live for Today. Leigh R. Hardt. 288p. (Orig.). 1982. pap. 2.75 (ISBN 0-523-41172-3). Pinnacle Bks.
Live from the Devil. 1st Ed. Wyatt Blassingame. LC 59-8257. 1959. Doubleday.
Live Goat. Cecil Dawkins. LC 75-138781. 1971. 15.00 (ISBN 0-06-010998-X). Ultramarine Pub.
Live Goat. Cecil Dawkins. LC 75-138781. 1971. 6.95 o.p. (ISBN 0-06-010998-X, HarpT). Harper & Row.
Live Goat: A Novel. Cecil Dawkins. LC 75-138781. 1971. 6.95 (ISBN 0-06-010998-X). Harper & Row.
Live Love Laugh. Terri Conner & Joyce Sanderson. Ed. by Donna Dowdney & Conner Sanderson. (Illus.). 52p. (Orig.). 1981. pap. 6.95 (ISBN 0-9606904-0-9). Conner & Sanderson.
Live or Die. Thomas Ainsworth. 192p. 1983. 14.95 (ISBN 0-02-500640-1). Macmillan.
Live till Tomorrow. Victoria Catalani. LC 55-8324. 1955. Dutton.
Live with Lightning: A Novel. Mitchell A Wilson. LC 49-10443. 1949. Little, Brown.
Livelies, and Other Short Stories. Sarah Winter Kellogg. LC 7-10972. 1875. J. B. Lippincott & Co.
Liveliest Town in the West. Grover C Gulick. LC 68-22527. 1969. 4.95. Doubleday.
Lively Anatomy of God: Stories. Nancy Willard. LC 68-24021. 1968. 4.95. Eakins Press.
Lively Arts of Sister Gervaise. John Louis Bonn. LC 57-6668. 1957. P. J. Kenedy.
Lively Dead. Peter Dickinson. LC 74-25226. 1975. 5.95 (ISBN 0-394-49680-9). Pantheon Books.
Lively Dead. Peter Dickinson. 1977. 1.50 (ISBN 0-380-01706-7). Avon.
Lively Family: Major Lively, Will and Ben Lively, Esquimax Kooloose, Capt. Windward, Ship Raker and Crew. Their "Good Time" Adventures... Earnest Markman. (ten cent helper books,). 1875. Mercantile Publishing Company.
Lively Game of Death. Marvin Kaye. LC 72-79052. 1972. 5.95 (ISBN 0-8415-0185-8). Saturday Review Press.
Lively House. Blanche Faulkner. LC 75-32630. 4.95 (ISBN 0-89144-009-7). Crescent Publications.
Lively Lady. Kenneth Roberts. 15.95 (ISBN 0-385-04261-2). Doubleday.
Lively Lady. Kenneth Roberts. 1976. pap. 2.95 (ISBN 0-449-24482-2, Crest). Fawcett.
Lively Lady: A Chronicle of Arundel, of Privateering and of the Circular Prison on Dartmoor. Kenneth Lewis Roberts. LC 42-814377. 1938. Doubleday, Doran & Company, Inc.
Lively Lady: A Chronicle of Certain Men of Arundel in Maine, of Privateering During the War of Impressments, and of the Circular Prison on Dartmoor. Kenneth Lewis Roberts. LC 31-123691. 1931. Doubleday, Doran & Company, Inc.
Lively Lady: A Chronicle of Certain Men of Arundel in Maine of Privateering the War of Impressments and of the Circular Prison on Dartmoor. Kenneth Lewis Roberts. LC 34-382891. 1933. Doubleday, Doran & Company, Inc.
Lively Luke: Or, Keen As a Razor. A Story of a Boy's Brilliant Career. Harlan Page Halsey. (Old Sleuth's own; no. 102). 1897. The Parlor Car Publishing Co.
Lively Peggy. Stanley John Weyman. LC 28-20343. 1928. Longmans, Green, and Co.
Liverpool Jarge. William Herbert Nutter. LC 22-8044. 1922. Square Rigger Co.
Liverpool Jarge. William Herbert Nutter. LC 35-404331. Square Rigger Co.
Liverpool Jarge. William Herbert Nutter. LC 22-8044. 1922. Square Rigger Co.
Livery of Eve... Tr. from the Original Manuscript. Francis William Bain. LC 17-14951. 1917. 1.50. G. P. Putnam's Sons.
Livery of Heaven. R. H Sawyer. LC 10-5687. 1910. The C. M. Clark Publishing Company.
Lives and Adventures of the Desperadoes of the South West: Containing an Account of the Duelist and Dueling... Alfred W. Arrington. LC 6-2428. 1849. W. H. Graham.
Lives and Deaths of Roland Greer. Richard Lionel Pyke. LC 29-6180. 1929. A. and C. Boni.
Lives and Times of Bernardo Brown. Geoffrey Household. LC 73-13724. 1974. 7.95 (ISBN 0-316-37434-2). Little, Brown.
Lives and Times of Jerry Cornelius. Michael Moorcock. LC 76-376473. (Illus.). 1976. 3.50 (ISBN 0-85031-141-1). Allison and Busby.
Lives of a Woman: A Novel. Betsey Riddle Hutton Zum Stolzenberg. LC 35-6162. E. P. Dutton & Co., Inc.
Lives of Cleopatra and Octavia. Sarah Fielding. LC 74-17294. (Flowering of the Novel). 1974. (ISBN 0-8240-1147-3). Garland Pub.
Lives of Female Mormons: A Narrative of Facts Stranger Than Fiction. Metta Victoria Fuller Victor. LC 8-82797. 1860. G. G. Evans.
Lives of Girls & Women. Alice Munro. LC 73-12900. 1973. 10.95 (ISBN 0-8161-6142-9). G. K. Hall.
Lives of Girls and Women. Alice Munro. 1974. (pbk.) 1.25. New American Lib.
Lives of Girls and Women: A Novel. Alice Munro. LC 74-163605. 1971. (ISBN 0-07-092932-7). McGraw-Hill Ryerson.
Lives of Girls & Women: A Novel. Alice Munro. LC 72-1124. 1972. (ISBN 0-07-044043-3). McGraw-Hill.
Lives of Splendor. James C. Cox. 3.95 o.p. Carlton.
Lives of Wives. Laura Riding, pseud. LC 40-2378. 1939. Random House.
Lives That Die. Edward S Hanlon. LC 69-12216. (DD western). 1969. 3.95. Doubleday.
Lives to Give. Sanche De Gramont, pseud. (YA) 1971. 6.95 o.p. (ISBN 0-399-10499-2). Putnam.
Lives to Give. Sanche De Gramont. LC 72-136789. 1971. 6.95. Putnam.
Lives You Wished to Lead but Never Dared: A Series of Stories. La Fayette Ronald Hubbard & V. S Wilhite. LC 78-64364. 11.00 (ISBN 0-917972-00-7). Theta Books.
Livia. Emogak De Hazir. 176p. pap. 1.95 o.p. (6094). Brandon.
Livia. Lawrence Durrell. 1979. 12.95 (ISBN 0-670-43447-7). Viking Pr.
Livin' Is Easy. John Tranter. LC 65-3706. 1965. bds., 4.50. Oldbourne.
Living a Dream. Owen Elliotte Reiney. LC 39-20473. 1939. The Naylor Company.
Living: A Novel. Henry Green. LC 70-145058. 1971. (ISBN 0-403-01001-2). Scholarly Press.
Living Alone. John Givens. LC 80-69366. 1981. 9.95 (ISBN 0-689-11147-9). Atheneum.
Living Alone: Fictions. Robley Wilson. LC 78-50966. (Illus.). 5.00 (ISBN 0-931362-00-8). Fiction International.
Living & Learning in God's World. LaDonna Bogardus. 1961. pap. 2.00 o.p. (ISBN 0-687-22246-X). Abingdon.
Living and Loving. Virginia Frances Townsend. 1857. J. W. Bradley.
Living and Loving: Or, Ideal Letters About Life. Pauline Gregory. LC 6-44870. 1884. S. C. Toof & Co., Printers.
Living and the Dead. Konstantin Mikhailovich Simonov. LC 68-54438. 1968. Greenwood Press.
Living and the Dead. Patrick White. LC 41-1591. 1941. The Viking Press.
Living and the Dead. Patrick White. LC 76-13302. 1979. 28.50 (ISBN 0-404-15240-6). AMS Press.
Living and the Dead: By Pierre Boileau and Thomas Narcejac. Translated by Geoffrey Sainsbury. Pierre Boileau & Thomas Narcejac. LC 56-12826. (Chantecler novel of suspense). 1957. I. Washburn.
Living and the Dead. Translated from the Russian by R. Ainsztein. 1st Ed. Konstantin Mikhailovich Simonov. LC 62-15371. 1962. Doubleday.
Living and the Dying. Tom Stacey. LC 76-365289. 1976. 3.95 (ISBN 0-333-18769-5). Macmillan.
Living and the Lost. Translated from the French by J. M. Cohen. Michel Zeraffa. LC 53-9772. 1953. Roy.
Living Apart. Ruby Mildred Ayres. LC 37-22644. 1937. Doubleday, Doran & Company, Inc.
Living Arrows. Gillian Martin. LC 79-25534. 8.95 (ISBN 0-684-16450-7). Scribner.
Living Bomb. Michael Avallone. (Orig.). 1972. pap. 0.75 o.p. (07224). Curtis.
Living Buddha. Paul Morand. Tr. by Boyd, Madeleine Eilse (Reynier) LC 28-7496. H. Holt and Company.
Living China: Modern Chinese Short Stories. Ed. by Edgar Snow. LC 73-898. (Illus.). 1973. 16.50 (ISBN 0-88355-092-X). Hyperion Press.
Living China: Modern Chinese Short Stories. Ed. by Edgar Snow. Wales, Nym. LC 37-273195. 1937. Reynal & Hitchcock.
Living Dead Man. Leroy Scott. LC 29-9005. 1929. I. Washburn.
Living Death. Nick Carter. (Nick Carter Ser). (O.s.i.). 160p. 1976. pap. 1.25 o.s.i. (AQ1561, Award). Univ Pub & Dist.
Living Dog. Peter Somerville-Large. LC 81-43283. (Crime Club Ser.). 192p. 1982. 10.95 (ISBN 0-385-17861-1). Doubleday.
Living Earth. 1st Canadian Ed. Sheila MacKay Russell. 1954. Longmans, Green.
Living End. Frank Kane. LC 57-8532. (Dell first edition, A142). 1957. Dell Pub. Co.
Living Idol. Robert Switzer. LC 56-11325. (Signet book, 1335). 1956. New American Library.

Living Image. Gladys S Gallant. LC 77-15178. 1978. 7.95 (ISBN 0-385-13651-X). Doubleday.

Living in Ether: A Novel. Patricia Geary. LC 81-47685. 12.82 (ISBN 0-06-014931-0) (ISBN 0-06-090927-7). Harper & Row.

Living in the Clouds: By Charles Humana Pseud. Joseph Jacobs. LC 56-2934. 1955. Longmans, Green.

Living in the Maniototo. Janet Frame, pseud. LC 79-2358. 1979. 8.95 (ISBN 0-8076-0926-9). G. Braziller.

Living in the Maniototo. 2d ed. Janet Frame, pseud. LC 79-25418. 1980. 8.95 (ISBN 0-8076-0958-7). G. Braziller.

Living in the 25th Hour: A Novel. Richard Jones. LC 78-4692. 8.95 (ISBN 0-03-041921-2). Holt, Rinehart, and Winston.

Living Is Easy. Dorothy West. LC 71-94139. (American Negro, His History and Literature.). (Afro-American culture series.). 1969. Arno Press.

Living Is Easy. Dorothy West. LC 48-68718. 1948. Houghton, Mifflin Co.

Living Is Easy. Dorothy West. LC 81-22062. 6.95 (ISBN 0-912670-97-5). Feminist Press.

Living Legacy. Ruth Underwood. LC 12-28408. 1912. The John C. Winston Company.

Living Lie (Mesonges) Paul Charles Joseph Bourget. Tr. by John Abraham Jacob De Villier. LC 11-10513. R. F. Fenno & Company; Etc., Etc.

Living Link. A Novel. James De Mille. LC 13-12939. 1874. Harper & Brothers.

Living Lotus. Ethel Edith Mannin. LC 56-10238. 1956. Putnam.

Living Lotus. Ethel Edith Mannin. LC 73-119461. (Pergamon English Library). (Athena books.). 1970. Pergamon Press.

Living Miracles. Muriel Larson. 1973. (pbk) 0.95 (ISBN 0-87162-151-7). Warner Press.

Living Mummy. 2d ed. Ambrose Pratt. LC 22-10840. 1910. Frederick A. Stokes Company.

Living on: A Trilogy of Fate. F M Wilcox. LC 52-8950. 1952. William-Frederick Press.

Living on the Dead. Aharon Megged. LC 79-139538. (UNESCO Collection of Representative Works: Israel Series). 1971. 6.95 (ISBN 0-8415-0097-5). McCall Pub. Co.

Living or Dead. Frederick John Fargus. LC 6-384383. (On cover: Lovell's library. v. 14. no. 745). 1886. J. W. Lovell Company.

Living Pioneers: The Epic of the West by Those Who Lived It. Harold Preece. LC 52-5189. 1952. World Pub. Co.

Living Proof. Hank Williams, Jr. 1983. pap. 3.50 (ISBN 0-440-05213-0). Dell.

Living Quarters. Vincent Canby. LC 74-21287. 1975. 6.95 (ISBN 0-394-49513-6). Knopf.

Living Reed: A Novel. Pearl Sydenstricker Buck. LC 63-10220. 1963. John Day Co.

Living Room. Graham Greene. 1954. 2.50 o.p. Viking Pr.

Living Room. Sol Stein. 1975. (pbk.) 1.75. Bantam Books.

Living Room: A Novel. Sol Stein. LC 73-91499. 1974. 7.95 (ISBN 0-87795-077-6). Arbor House.

Living Shadow. Maxwell Grant, pseud. (Shadow Ser.: No. 1). 1974. pap. 0.95 o.p. (ISBN 0-515-03597-1, N3597). BJ Pub Group.

Living Shadow: From the Shadow's Private Annals. Maxwell Grant. LC 74-14285. 1974. (pbk.). 0.95 (ISBN 0-515-03597-1). Pyramid Books.

Living Shadows. Elizabeth Kutas. 1983. 9.50 (ISBN 0-8062-2160-7). Carlton.

Living Skeleton: A Novel. W. J Fraser. LC 99-4736. (On cover: Neely's imperial library, no. 43). 1899. F. T. Neely.

Living Sleep: A Novel. Kate Roberts. LC 77-361464. 1976. 3.95 (ISBN 0-902375-14-8). John Jones Cardiff Ltd.

Living Stone. Howell Roland, Jr. (Orig.). 1979. pap. 1.95 (ISBN 0-532-23138-4). Woodhill.

Living, the Dying & the Dead. George G. Gilman, pseud. (Edge Ser.: No. 29). 1979. pap. 1.95 (ISBN 0-523-41775-6). Pinnacle Bks.

Living Things. Paul L Bennett. LC 75-2958. 1975. 3.00. Orchard House.

Living Together. Carole Mortimer. (Harlequin Presents Ser.). 192p. 1981. pap. 1.50 (ISBN 0-373-10423-5, Pub. by Harlequin). PB.

Living up to Billy. Elizabeth Cooper. LC 15-18104. 1.00. Frederick A. Stokes Company.

Living Voice. Agnes Blundell. LC 31-31935. 1931. Benzinger Brothers.

Living Water. Linton Holland. LC 33-34615. The Stratford Company.

Living with Others. Carrie L. Goddard. pap. 1.25 leader's ed. o.p. (ISBN 0-687-22471-3); pap. 0.40 junior camper's ed. o.p. (ISBN 0-687-22472-1). Abingdon.

Living Wood: A Novel. Louis De Wohl. LC 47-5761. 1947. J. B. Lippincott Co.

Living Wood: A Novel. Ludwig Von Wohl. LC 47-5761. 1947. J. B. Lippincott Co.

Living Year: An Almanac for My Survivors. Mary Q. Steele. (Illus.). 109p. 1982. pap. 6.50 (ISBN 0-688-00992-1). Quill NY.

Livingston Heirs. Helen K Maxwell. LC 73-10189. 1973. 6.95 (ISBN 0-316-55150-3). Little, Brown.

Livingstones. Derrick Leon. LC 33-19965. The John Day Company.

Livingstone's Companions; Stories. Nadine Gordimer. LC 78-158415. 1971. 6.95 (ISBN 0-670-43570-8). Viking Press.

Livingstone's Still: A Story of Life on a Georgia Naval Stores Farm. Rosa Corley Hooks. LC 50-11171. 1950. Exposition Press.

Livre Blanc. Jean Cocteau. 12.95x (ISBN 0-8464-0576-8). Beekman Pubs.

Livre de Lancelot del Lac, 3 vols, Pts. IIII. Ed. by H. Oskar Sommer. LC 72-985. (The Vulgate Version of the Arthurian Romances Ser.: Nos. 3-5). Repr. of 1912 ed. Set. 172.50 (ISBN 0-404-10020-1); 57.50 ea. AMS Pr.

Livre De Mon Ami. Anatole France, pseud. 1926. 2.40 o.p. Oxford U Pr.

Liza. Elizabeth Hubbard. pap. 0.60 o.p. (ISBN 0-671-29338-9). Archway.

Liza. Ivan Sergieevich Turgenev. Tr. by William Ralston Shedden Ralston. (Half-title: Everyman's library, ed. by Ernest Rhys. no. 677). 1914. J. M. Dent & Sons, Ltd.

Liza Bowe. Shirley Barker. LC 56-8797. 1956. Random House.

Liza Hunt, Pediatric Nurse. Virginia K. Smiley. 1976. Avalon Books.

Liza of Lambeth. William Somerset Maugham. LC 67-112217. (B67-4164). 1967. Penquin in Association with Heinemann.

Liza of Lambeth. William Somerset Maugham. LC 75-25355. (Maugham, William Somserset, 1875-1965. Works. 1976). 1976. 15.00 (ISBN 0-405-07813-7). Arno Press.

Liza of Lambeth. William Somerset Maugham. LC 21-17985. 1921. George H. Doran Company.

Liza of Lambeth. William Somerset Maugham. LC 36-12117. 1936. Doubleday, Doran & Company Inc.

Liza of Lambeth. William Somerset Maugham. LC 38-31838. 1938. The Sun Dial Press, Inc.

Liza: Or, "A Nest of Nobles;" a Novel. Ivan Sergieevich Turgenev. Tr. by William Ralston Shedden Ralston. LC 8-32676. (On cover: Leisure hour series mo. 9). 1873. H. Holt and Company.

Liza: Or, "A Nest of Nobles," a Novel. Ivan Sergieevich Turgenev. Tr. by William Ralston Shedden Ralston. LC 8-32677. (On cover: Leisure hour series. no.9). 1873. Holt & Williams.

Lizard in the Cup. Peter Dickinson. LC 74-181669. 1972. 5.95 (ISBN 0-06-011041-4). Harper & Row.

Lizard Music. D. Manus Pinkwater. 1978. 1.25 (ISBN 0-440-95118-6). Dell.

Lizard of Oz. Richard W. Seltzer, Jr. LC 74-20172. (Illus.). 128p. (Orig.). (YA) 1974. pap. 2.95 (ISBN 0-915232-01-4). B & R Samizdat.

Lizards. Alessandra Lavagnino. LC 73-181658. 1972. 5.95 (ISBN 0-06-012537-3). Harper & Row.

Lizards of Trianada. Patricia N. Casciani. 1983. 10.00 (ISBN 0-533-05500-8). Vantage.

Lizard's Tail. Marc Brandel. LC 78-26816. 9.95 (ISBN 0-671-22475-1). Simon and Schuster.

Lizard's Tail. 1st Ed. William Fain. LC 54-5978. 1954. Knopf.

Lizbeth. Catherine Fitzpatrick. LC 6-4534. Broadway Publishing Co.

Lizbeth of the Dale. Mary Esther Macgregor. LC 10-28331. 1.20. Hodder & Stoughton, G. H. Doran Company.

Lizette: A Story of the Latin Quarter. Edward Marshall. LC 3-3873. 1902. Lewis, Scribner & Co.

Lizzie Adriance. Margaret Lee. (On cover: Library of American authors. no. 7). 1889. G. Munro.

Lizzie & Caroline. Ruth Moore. 1972. 6.95 (ISBN 0-688-00064-9). Morrow.

Lizzie and Caroline: A Novel. Ruth Moore. LC 72-186161. 1972. 6.95. Morrow.

Lizzie Borden: A Study in Conjecture. Marie Adelaide Belloc Lowndes. LC 39-9824. 1939. Longmaids, Green and Co.

Lizzie Leigh, and Other Tales. Elizabeth Cleghorn Stevenson Gaskell. LC 71-37543. (Short story index reprint series). (Illus.). 1972. (ISBN 0-8369-4102-0). Books for Libraries Press.

Lizzie Melton: A Self-Reliant Girl. Albert Chavannes. LC 2688. (On cover: New thought library, no. 12). 1900.

Lizzie Reynolds: Valiant New Englander, a Novel. 1st Ed. Mary C Kelly. LC 54-5751. 1954. Exposition Press.

Lizzy Glenn: Or, The Trials of a Seamstress. Timothy Shay Arthur. LC 6-3408. B. Peterson and Brothers.

Llana of Gathol. Edgar Rice Burroughs.

Llanfear Pattern. Francis Biddle. LC 27-22663. 1927. C. Scribner's Sons.

Llangobaith: A Story of North Wales. Erasmus W Jones. LC 7-119109. 1886. T. J. Griffiths.

Llegada. Jose L. Gonzalez. 144p. 1980. pap. 6.95 (ISBN 0-940238-56-X). Ediciones Huracan.

Llegaron los hippies. Manuel Abreu. 112p. 1978. pap. 3.00 (ISBN 0-940238-24-1). Ediciones Huracan.

LLLove Story. Kaye Lowman. LC 78-17336. (Illus.). 1978. pap. 5.95 (ISBN 0-912500-06-9). La Leche.

LO! Charles Fort. Ed. by Lester Del Rey. LC 75-407. (Library of Science Fiction). 1975. lib. bdg. 17.50 (ISBN 0-8240-1412-X). Garland Pub.

Lo, and Behold Ye! Seumas MacManus. LC 19-15487. Frederick A. Stokes Company.

Lo, Michael! Grace Livingston Hill. LC 75-37793. 1975. American Reprint Co.

Lo, Michael! Grace Livingston Hill. LC 13-12497. 1913. J. B. Lippincott Company.

Lo-to-Kah. Verner Zevola Reed. LC 11-16155. 1897. Continental Publishing Company.

Loaded Dice. Ellery Harding Clark. LC 9-9251. 1909. 1.50. The Bobbs-Merrill Company.

Loaded for Bare. Russell Smith. (Orig.). 1972. pap. price not set o.s.i. (TCP012, Travellers Comp). Olympia.

Loaded Gun. Francis Ryck. LC 76-160353. 1971. 4.95 (ISBN 0-8128-1401-0). Stein and Day.

Loaded Stick. Naomi Ellington Jacob. 1935. The Macmillan Company.

Loads of Love. Anne Parrish. LC 32-576. 1932. Harper & Brothers.

Loan Shark. J. W O'Dell. 1975. (pbk.) 1.50. Belmont Tower Books.

Loanshark. Peter McCurtin. (Belmont Tower Book). 1.75 (ISBN 0-505-51437-0). Tower Publications,C.

Loathsome Couple. Edward St. John Gorey. LC 76-13353. (Illus.). 4.95 (ISBN 0-396-07379-4). Dodd, Mead.

Loaves and Fishes. Elaine Myers. LC 34-30248. R. D. Henkle.

Loba. Diane Di Prima. (Capra Chapbook Ser.: No. 10). pap. 2.50 o.p. (ISBN 0-912264-69-1). Capra Pr.

Lobo. Frank Castle. (Orig.). 1969. pap. 0.60 o.p. (B60-1006). Belmont-Tower.

Lobo Brand. Oscar J Friend. (Avalon westerns). 1973. 4.50. Avalon Books.

Lobo Brand. Oscar Jerome Friend. LC 54-13441. 1954. Avalon Books.

Lobo Breed. Charles Morris Martin. LC 50-11860. 1950. Phoenix Press.

Lobo Breed. Charles Morris Martin. 1975. (pbk.) 0.95. Manor Books.

Lobo Gray. Leonard London Foreman. Date not set. pap. 1.75 (ISBN 0-451-09677-0, E9677, Sig). NAL.

Lobo Law. Harry Sinclair Drago. LC 35-8409. 1935. W. Morrow & Co.

Lobo Legacy: By Tom West Pseud. Fred East. LC 55-19319. (Ace double novel books, D-78). 1954. Ace Books.

Lobo Legion. Jackson Cole. 1974. (pbk.) 0.75. Popular Library.

Lobo of Lynx Valley. Tom West. 176p. 1981. pap. 1.95 (ISBN 0-441-48756-4, Pub. by Charter Bks). Ace Bks.

Lobo Trail. Larry Harris. 1970. pap. 0.60 o.p. (0502-06098). Curtis.

Lobo Valley. Lee Floren. 1970. pap. 0.50 o.p. (50-498). Manor Bks.

Lobo Valley: By Brett Austin Pseud. Lee Floren. LC 51-14493. 1951. Arcadia House.

Lobster and a Lady. Jeanne Whitmee. LC 79-4723. 1979. 8.95 (ISBN 0-312-49410-6). St. Martin's Press.

Lobster Catchers: A Story of the Coast of Maine. James Otis Kaler. LC 3031. 1900. E. P. Dutton & Company.

Lobster Pick Murder. Mary Violet Heberden. LC 41-3120. 1941. Pub. for the Crime Club by Doubleday, Doran and Co., Inc.

Lobster Post. Stafford Frank Hough. LC 44-36953. 1943. Hurst & Blackett, Ltd.

Lobster Pots & Sea Rocket Sandwiches. Derevitzky. (Illus.). 1979. pap. 4.50 (ISBN 0-89272-075-1). Down East.

Lobstick Trail. Douglas Leader Durkin. LC 22-7208. 1922. A. C. McClurg & Co.

Local Anaesthetic. Gunter Grass. LC 78-100501. 1970. 6.95. Harcourt, Brace & World.

Local Color. Irvin Shrewsbury Cobb. LC 16-22853. George H. Doran Company.

Local Color: Stories Foreword by Erakine Caldwell. John Andrew Rice. LC 55-120538. (Dell first edition, 71). 1955. Dell Pub. Co.

Local Colorist. Annie Trumbull Slosson. LC 70-144172. (Short story index reprint series). (Illus.). 1971. (ISBN 0-8369-3787-2). Books for Libraries Press.

Local Colorist. Annie Trumbull Slosson. LC 12-5152. 1912. C. Scribner's Sons.

Local Colorists: American Short Stores, 1867-1900. Ed. by Claude Mitchell Simpson. LC 59-13922. 12.00 o.p. Scholarly.

Local Colorists: American Short Stories, 1857-1900. Ed. by Claude Mitchell Simpson. LC 59-13922. 1960. Harper.

Local Doctor. Douglas Marshall, pseud. LC 42-15695. 1942. Gramercy Publishing Co.

Local Habitation. Walter Leon Sawyer. LC 99-4307. 1899. Small, Maynard & Company.

Local Hero: Official Movie Tie-in Edition. David Benedictus. 224p. 1983. pap. 3.50 (ISBN 0-14-006660-8). Penguin.

Local Lads. Jack S Scott, pseud. LC 82-12805. 12.95 (ISBN 0-525-24159-0). Dutton.

Local Lads: A Novel of Suspense. Jack S. Scott, pseud. 1983. 12.95 (ISBN 0-525-24159-0, 01258-370). Dutton.

Local Men. James Whitehead. LC 79-10660. 1979. 10.00 (ISBN 0-252-00763-8); pap. 3.95 o.p. (ISBN 0-252-00764-6). U of Ill Pr.

Local Talent. Marlene Fanta Shyer. LC 73-22655. 1974. 6.95 (ISBN 0-672-51980-1). Bobbs-Merrill Co.

Location. Russell O'Neil. 1974. (pbk.) 1.50. Warner Paperback Library.

Location Shots. J. F. Burke. LC 73-4144. 1974. 5.95 (ISBN 0-06-010582-8). Harper & Row.

Loch. Janet Caird. LC 70-78704. 1969. 4.50. Published for the Crime Club by Doubleday.

Loch. Janet Caird. (Signet book). 1974. (pbk.) 0.75. New American Library.

Loch Bras D'Or. Margaret MacPhail. LC 73-152126. 1970. 2.95. Lancelot Press.

Loch Ness Monster Watchers. new ed. Victor Perera. (Capra Chapbook Ser: No. 18). (Illus.). 1974. pap. 2.50 o.p. (ISBN 0-912264-92-6). Capra Pr.

Loch Sinister. Marilyn Ross. (queen-size gothic). 1974. (pbk.) 0.95. Popular Library.

Lochinvar: A Novel. Samuel Rutherford Crockett. LC 6-31593. 1898. Harper & Brothers.

Lochinvar. Illustrated by Vasiliu. Graham Porter. LC 59-11385. 1959. Crowell.

Lochinvar Luck. Albert Payson Terhune. (Illus.). 1961. Grosset & Dunlap.

Lochinvar: Or, Told by an Army Fireside. Alice King Hamilton. LC 7-1224. (On cover: United service library of original fiction. no. 1). 1889. The United Service Publishing Company.

Lock and Key. 2d ed. James M Galloway. (On cover: Dillingham's American authors library, no. 50). 1899. G. W. Dillingham Co.

Lock and Key. Aaron Marc Stein. LC 72-96259. 1973. 4.95 (ISBN 0-385-06732-1). Published for the Crime Club by Doubleday.

Lock and Key Library: Classic Mystery and Detective Stories. Ed. by Julian Hawthorne. LC 72-3560. (Short story index reprint series). (ISBN 0-8369-4149-7). Books for Libraries Press.

Lock and Key Library: Classic Mystery and Detective Stories. Ed. by Julian Hawthorne. LC 10-11468. 1909. The Review of Reviews Co.

Lock and the Key. Frank Gruber. LC 48-424744. (Murray Hill mystery). 1948. Rinehart.

Lock up My Heart. Rob Eden. LC 42-5123. Gramercy Publishing Co.

Locke Amsden: Or, The Schoolmaster, a Tale. Daniel Pierce Thompson. LC 49-320966. 1847. B. B. Mussey.

Locked Book. Frank Lucius Packard. LC 24-22005. George H. Doran Company.

Locked Corridor. Marilyn Ross. 1969. pap. 0.60 o.p. (63-169). Paperback Lib.

Locked Harbor. Gertie Evenhuis. (Illus.). 1967. Macmillan.

Locked in. Gerald Locklin. 1973. 3.00 (ISBN 0-917554-18-3). Maelstrom.

Locked Room. Maj Sjowall & Per Wahloo. LC 79-21993. 1980. pap. 1.95 (ISBN 0-394-74274-5, Vin). Random.

Locked Room Reader. Ed. by Hans S. Santesson. LC 68-28578. (O.s.i.). 1968. 8.95 o.s.i. (ISBN 0-394-43373-4). Random.

Locked Room Reader: Stories of Impossible Crimes and Escapes. Ed. by Hans Stefan Santesson. LC 68-28578. 1968. 6.95. Random House.

Locked Room: The Story of a Crime. Maj Sjowall & Per Wahloo. LC 73-7027. 1973. 5.95 (ISBN 0-394-48533-5). Pantheon Books.

Locked Room: The Story of a Crime. Maj Sjowall & Per Wahloo. LC 79-21993. (Sjowall, Maj. 1935-, Wahloo, per, 1926-1975. Martin Beck Police Mystery). 1980. 1.95 (ISBN 0-394-74274-5). Vintage Books.

Locked Rooms & Open Doors: Diaries & Letters of Anne Morrow Lindbergh, 1933-1935. Anne Morrow Lindbergh. (Adult Ser). 648p. 1974. Repr. lib. bdg. 13.95 o.p. (ISBN 0-8161-6231-X, Large Print Bks). G K Hall.

Locked Tower. Catherine Carfax, pseud. (Fawcett gold medal book). 1974. (pbk.) 0.95. Fawcett.

Locket & Other Stories. Ruth Tabor. 1980. 5.75 (ISBN 0-8062-1547-X). Carlton.

Lockhart Breed. Theodore V Olsen. LC 81-70967. 1982. 10.95. Walker.

Lockhart Breed. Theodore V. Olsen. 144p. 1982. Repr. 10.95 (ISBN 0-8027-4006-5). Walker & Co.

Lockhart's Trail. Albert Butler. 1981. 18.00x (ISBN 0-86025-197-7, Pub. by Ian Henry Pubns England). State Mutual Bk.

Lockhorns, No. 7: Let's Go for a Walk...And Bring your Wallet. Bill Hoest, pseud. 1982. pap. 1.75 (ISBN 0-451-11472-8, AE1472, Sig). NAL.

Lockhorns, No. 9: You Name It...I'm Guilty. Bill Hoest, pseud. 1982. pap. 1.95 (ISBN 0-451-11936-3, AJ1936, Sig). NAL.

Lockout. Kathryn Anger. LC 79-57121. (Feminist Novels Ser.). 100p. 1975. pap. 4.95 (ISBN 0-935772-02-2). Diotima Bks.

Locksmith of Lyons: Or, The Weavers' War. William Henry Peck. LC 7-36477. (On cover: Sea and shore series, no. 4). 1888. Street & Smith.

Lockwood. Joseph F Suessmuth. LC 77-353475. 1976. (ISBN 0-00-222085-7). Collins.

Lockwood Concern. John O'Hara. (Signet bk., Q2876). 1966. New Amer. Lib.

Lockwood Concern. John O'Hara. 1977. 1.95 (ISBN 0-445-08564-9). Popular Library.

Lockwood Concern: A Novel. John O'Hara. LC 65-21227. 5.95. Random.

Loco. Lee Hoffman. LC 73-91108. (Doubleday western). 1969. 4.50. Doubleday.

Loco. easy eye ed. Nelson Nye. Orig. Title: Last Bullet. 1969. pap. 0.60 o.p. (73-816). Lancer.

Loco and the Wolf. Willis Todhunter Ballard. LC 73-79642. (DD western). 1973. 4.95 (ISBN 0-385-05076-3). Doubleday.

Loco and the Wolf. Willis Todhunter Ballard. 1974. (pbk.) 0.95. Manor Books.

Locomotive Puffs from the Back Shop. Leon R Harris. LC 46-18741. 1946. B. Humphries, Inc.

Locura de Amor. new ed. Lino Martel. (Pimienta Collection Ser). 160p. (Span.). 1974. pap. 1.00 o.p. (ISBN 0-88473-197-9). Fiesta Pub.

Locus Solus. Raymond Roussel. LC 79-100023. 1970. 6.50 (ISBN 0-520-01645-9). University of California Press.

Locust Fire. Eugene Brown. LC 56-8092. 1957. Doubleday.

Locusts. Otto Schrag & Winston, Richard,Tr. LC 43-16041. 1943. Farrar & Rinehart, Inc.

Locusts and Wild Honey. Collin-Smith, Joyce. LC 54-6871. 1954. Little, Brown.

Locusts Have No King. Dawn Powell. LC 48-6638. 1948. C. Scribner's Sons.

Locusts' Years. Mary Helen Fee. LC 12-230631. 1912. 1.35. A. C. McClurg & Co.

Lodestar. Sidney Robinson Kennedy. LC 5-8071. 1905. The Macmillan Company.

Lodestar. Max Pemberton. LC 7-10291. 1907. The Authors and Newspapers Association.

Lodestar, Rocket Ship to Mars: The Record of the First Operation Sponsored by the Federal Commission for Interplanetary Exploration, June 1, 1971. Franklyn Mansfield Branley. LC 51-764. 1951. Crowell.

Lodge. Colleen Mahan. LC 79-8436. 1980. 10.95 (ISBN 0-385-15417-8). Doubleday.

Lodge for Lust. Norma Bradcock. pap. 1.95 o.p. (8050). Cameo.

Lodge in Friendship Village. P W George. LC 27-12298. 1927. The John Day Company.

Lodge in the Wilderness. John Buchan. LC 38-4654. 1933. T. Nelson and Sons, Ltd.

Lodge Sinister. Dana Fuller Ross. 1975. (pbk.) 0.95 (ISBN 0-671-68005-6). Pocket Books.

Lodger. Marie Adelaide Belloc Lowndes. LC 13-232163. 1913. 1.25. C. Scribner's Sons.

Lodger. Marie Adelaide Belloc Lowndes. LC 18-20842. 1914. C. Scribner's Sons.

Lodger. Marie Adelaide Belloc Lowndes. LC 31-180762. 1931. J. Cape & H. Smith.

Lodger Overhead: And Others. Charles Belmont Davis. LC 71-121533. (Short story index reprint series). (Illus.). 1970. Books for Libraries Press.

Lodger Overhead, and Others. Charles Belmont Davis. LC 9-10027. 1909. C. Scribner's Sons.

Lodgers in London. Adelaide Eden Phillpotts. LC 74-150483. (Short story index reprint series). 1971. (ISBN 0-8369-3824-0). Books for Libraries Press.

Lodgers in London. Adelaide Eden Phillpotts. LC 26-1538. 1926. Little, Brown, and Company.

Lodging at the Saint Cloud: A Tale of Occupied Nashville. Alfred Leland Crabb. LC 46-2717. 1946. The Bobbs-Merrill Company.

Lodging for the Night: A Tale. Robert Louis Stevenson. LC 3-17704. 1900. The Philosopher Press.

Lodore, 3 vols. in 1. Mary Wollstonecraft Godwin Shelley. LC 79-8197. Repr. of 1835 ed. 44.50 (ISBN 0-404-62118-X). AMS Pr.

Lodore. franklin library ed. Mary Wolstonecraft Shelley. LC 8-5104. 1835. Wallis & Newell.

Lofoten Run. Robert Middlemiss. 1.95. Fawcett Gold Medal Books.

Lofty and the Lowly: Or, Good in All and None All Good. Maria Jane McIntosh. LC 4-89486. 1853. D. Appleton & Company.

Lofty and the Lowly: Or, Good in All and None All Good. 11th ed. Maria Jane McIntosh. LC 17-7987. 1854. D. Appleton & Co.

Lofty Banners. Brenda Clarke. 2.25 (ISBN 0-445-04503-5). Popular Library.

Lofty Mountain Takes Tunisia. Eric Sundell. (Orig.). 1971. pap. 0.75 o.p. (B75-2108). Belmont-Tower.

Log Book. Frank Laskier. LC 43-13715. 1943. C. Scribner's Sons.

Log Cabin Noble. Francis Van Wyck Mason. LC 72-95716. (Illus.). 1973. 7.95 (ISBN 0-385-01279-9). Doubleday.

Log-Cabin Yarns of the Rocky Mountains. Edmund Deacon Peterson. LC 12-26898. 1912. 1.00. The Cosmopolitan Press.

Log College. Archibald Alexander. 4.00 o.p. Reiner.

Log Jam. 1st Ed. Leslie Turner White. LC 59-12661. 1959. Doubleday.

Log Meeting-House, and the McIlhanys. John Ellis Edwards. LC 6-36580. 1884. Southern Methodist Publishing House.

Log of a Cowboy. Andy Adams. LC 27-202512. 1927. Houghton Mifflin Company.

Log of a Cowboy: A Narrative of the Old Trail Days. Andy Adams. LC 3-12817. 1903. Houghton, Mifflin and Company.

Log of a Cowboy: A Narrative of the Old Trail Days. Andy Adams. LC 81-9065. (Classics of the Old West). 1981. 19.95. Time-Life Books.

Log of a Sea-Waif: Being Recollections of the First Four Years of My Sea Life. Frank Thomas Bullen. LC 99-5043. 1899. D. Appleton and Company.

Log of a Superfluous Son. Michael Henderson. LC 76-355494. 143p. 1975. 7.50x (ISBN 0-8002-1681-4). Intl Pubns Serv.

Log of a Superfluous Son: A Novel. Michael Henderson. LC 76-355494. 1975. J. McIndoe.

Log of the Maryland: Or, Adventures at Sea, by Douglas Frazar. Douglas Frazar. LC 6-43143. Lee and Shepard.

Log of the Mayflower. Philip Jerome Simon. 1956. Priam Press.

Log of the Skipper's Wife. Balano. LC 79-52446. (Illus.). 1979. pap. 6.95 (ISBN 0-89272-062-X). Down East.

Log of the S.S. The Mrs Unguentine. Stanley G. Crawford. LC 72-289. 1972. 3.50 (ISBN 0-394-48137-2). Knopf.

Log of Three Across the Sea. Helen Marie Smeeth. LC 10-24480. 1910. 1.00. The Henneberry Company.

Logan. Alan Joseph. 1970. pap. 0.60 o.p. (B60-1086). Belmont-Tower.

Logan, a Family History. John Neal. LC 7-23108. 1862. H. C. Carey & I. Lea.

Logan: A Family History, 2 Vols. John Neal. LC 73-93650. (American Fiction Ser). 1970. Set. lib. bdg. 22.50 o.s.i. (ISBN 0-512-00531-1). Garrett Pr.

Logan's Choice. Frank Bonham. 176p. 1981. pap. 1.95 (ISBN 0-425-05223-0). Berkley Pub.

Logan's Gone: A Novel. Bernard Wolfe. LC 73-92970. 1974. 7.95 (ISBN 0-8402-1341-7). Nash Pub.

Logan's Guns. Will Benton, pseud. LC 78-2413. (Western Novels Ser.). 1978. 7.95 o.p. (ISBN 0-312-49446-7); large type 9.95 o.p. St Martin.

Logan's Guns. Lauran Paine. LC 78-2413. 1978. 7.95 (ISBN 0-312-49446-7). St. Martin's Press.

Logan's Run. William F. Nolan & George C. Johnson. 1967. 3.95 o.p. Dial.

Logan's Run: A Novel by William F. Nolan, George Clayton Johnson. William F. Nolan & George Clayton Johnson. LC 66-27388. 1967. bds., 3.95. Dial.

Logan's Search. William F. Nolan. 160p. (Orig.). 1980. pap. 1.95 (ISBN 0-553-13805-7). Bantam.

Logging Chance. Mary Harmon Lasher. 1944. John C. Winston Company.

Logical Girl. Gerda Charles. LC 67-11123. 1967. Knopf.

Loins of Amon. rev. ed. Marcus Van Heller, pseud. pap. 1.25 o.p. (2031). Brandon.

Loins of Amon. Marcus Van Heller, pseud. pap. 1.95 o.s.i. (OPH-246, Ophelia). Olympia.

Lois. Laurence Walter Meynell. LC 27-12367. 1927. D. Appleton & Company.

Lois Carrol: Or, Her Two Selves. Susa S Vance. LC 8-302320. 1874. J. B. Lippincott & Co.

Lois Mallet's Dangerous Gift. Mary Catherine Jenkins Lee. LC 2-23305. 1902. Houghton, Mifflin and Company.

Lois Mills: By Maria Sias. Maria Sias. LC 28-22137. The Midwest Company.

Lois Morton's Investment. Eva Morley Murphy. LC 12-20630. 1912. 1.25. Crane & Company.

Lois Remembers. 8.00 o.p. Hazelden.

Loitering with Intent. Muriel Spark. LC 80-26049. 1981. 11.95 (ISBN 0-698-11047-1). Coward, McCann & Geoghegan.

Loitering with Intent. Muriel Spark. LC 82-5235. 1982. 5.95 (ISBN 0-399-50663-2). Perigee Books.

Lokotown & Other Stories. Cyprian Ekwensi. (African Writers Ser.). 1966. pap. text ed. 4.00x (ISBN 0-435-90019-6). Heinemann Ed.

Lokotown & Other Stories. Cyprian Ekwensi. (African Writers Ser: No. 19). 1966. pap. text ed. 1.75x o.p. (ISBN 0-435-90319-5). Humanities.

Lola. Owen Davis. LC 15-15951. 0.75. Grosset & Dunlap.

Lola. Heller Toren. 1978. pap. 1.95 (ISBN 0-425-03663-4, Medallion). Berkley Pub.

Lola: A Love Story. Philip Van Doren Stern. LC 49-8304. 1949. Rinehart.

Lola of London: A Tale of Summer Week-Ends in England. R. O Burt. 1945. B. Humphries, Inc.

Lolita. Vladimir Vladimirovich Nabokov. LC 58-10755. 1958. Putnam.

Lollard: a Story of the Wiclifites. Minnie K Davis. LC 6-324706. Lutheran Publication Society.

Lolly. Kelly L Segraves. LC 77-7399. 2.95 (ISBN 0-89293-024-1). Beta Books.

Lolly Willowes. Sylvia Townsend Warner. 1979. lib. bdg. 12.95 (ISBN 0-915864-92-4); pap. 5.00 (ISBN 0-915864-91-6). Academy Chi Ltd.

Lolly Willowes. Sylvia Townsend Warner. 3.95 (ISBN 0-7043-3824-6, Pub. by Quartet England). Charles River Bks.

Lolly Willowes, and Mr. Fortune's Maggot. Sylvia Townsend Warner. LC 66-31481. (Illus.). 1966. Viking Press.

Lolly Willowes: Or The Loving Huntsman. Sylvia Townsend Warner. (60-2994). 1968. Popular Lib.

Lolly Willowes: Or, The Loving Huntsman. Sylvia Townsend Warner. LC 26-262920. 1926. The Viking Press.

Lolly Willowes: Or, The Loving Huntsman. Sylvia Townsend Warner. LC 79-106790. 1978. 5.00. Academy Chicago.

Lombard Cavalcade: A Novel. Virginia Coffman. LC 81-67523. 15.50 (ISBN 0-87795-355-4). Arbor House.

Lombard Heiress. Virginia Coffman. LC 82-72071. 304p. 1982. 14.95 (ISBN 0-87795-434-8). Arbor Hse.

L'Ombra. Adele Lepic & Sherman, Mrs. Belle M., Tr. (On cover: Lovell's illustrated series. no. 12). 1892. Lovell, Coryell & Company.

L'Ombra. A Romance. From the French of A. Gennevraye Pseud. Adele Lepic & Ringwalk, Rosa B., Tr. (American series no. 258). 1891. M. J. Ivors & Co.

Lomokome Papers. Herman Wouk. (Illus.). 113p. 1976. Repr. of 1968 ed. lib. bdg. 14.95x o.p. (ISBN 0-89244-086-4). Queens Hse.

"Lomokome" Papers. Herman Wouk. (Illus.). 1974. (pbk.) 0.95 (ISBN 0-671-77749-1). Pocket Books.

Lona Hanson: A Novel. Thomas Savage. LC 48-4104. 1948. Simon and Schuster.

London. Gary Brandner. 1976. 1.95 (ISBN 0-671-80673-4). Pocket Books.

London Adventures of Mr. Collin. Gunnar Serner & De Chary, Pauline, Tr. LC 24-8654. Thomas Y. Crowell Company.

London Affair. Judi Lynn. (New Stewardesses Ser.). (O.s.i.). 1975. pap. 1.25 o.s.i. (AQ1443, Award). Univ Pub and Dist.

London Affair. Judi Lynn. (New Stewardess, #2). 1975. (pbk.) 1.25. Award Books.

London Affair. Anthony Stuart, pseud. LC 80-66500. 1981. 9.95 (ISBN 0-87795-275-2). Arbor Hse.

London After Midnight. Marie Coolidge-Rask. LC 28-5168. Grosset & Dunlap.

London Belle. Leona Collier. 240p. (Orig.). 1982. pap. cancelled (ISBN 0-505-51818-X). Tower Bks.

London, Bloody London. Michael Avallone. (Orig.). 1972. pap. 0.75 o.p. (07252). Curtis.

London Bridge Is Falling. Philip Lindsay. LC 34-19488. 1934. Little, Brown, and Company.

London Calling. Val Henry Gielgud & Maschwitz, Eric. LC 34-560527. 1934. Pub. for the Crime Club, Inc., by Doubleday, Doran & Company, Inc.

London Calling North Pole. H. J. Giskes. 208p. Date not set. 2.50 (ISBN 0-553-22703-3). Bantam.

London Crimes. Charles Dickens & Nadya Aisenberg. LC 81-84723. (Periwig mystery). (Illus.). 1982. 8.95 (ISBN 0-937672-05-X). Rowan Tree Press.

London Deal. N. J Crisp. LC 78-3987. 1978. 7.95 (ISBN 0-312-49483-1). St. Martin's Press.

London Embassy. Paul Theroux. LC 82-15663. 1983. 13.95 (ISBN 0-395-33107-2). Houghton Mifflin.

London from Laramie. Joseph Bushnell Ames. LC 25-2465. The Century Co.

London Ladies. Charlotte Grey. (Coventry Romance Ser: No. 192). 192p. 1982. pap. 1.50 (ISBN 0-449-50295-3, Coventry). Fawcett.

London Lavender: An Entertainment. Edward Verrall Lucas. LC 12-21324. 1912. The Macmillan Company.

London Life. Henry James. LC 57-6531. (Evergreen book, E-58). 1957. Grove Press.

London Life, The Patagonia, The Liar, Mrs. Temperly. Henry James. LC 73-312. (Short story index reprint series). 1973. (ISBN 0-8369-4247-7). Books for Libraries Press.

London Life, The Patagonia, The Liar, Mrs. Temperly. Henry James. LC 7-7441. 1889. Macmillan and Co.

London Lot. Albert Michael Neil Lyons & Unger, Gladys. LC 19-27581. 1919. John Lane.

London Magazine Stories. London Magazine Editors. 1967. pap. 3.50. Dufour.

London Nights' Entertainments: Forming a New Edition, with Additions, of Tales and Confessions. Leitch Ritchie. 1833. Carey, Lea & Blanchard.

London Nights of Belsize. Vernon Horace Rendall. LC 17-201817. 1917. John Lane.

London Novels: City of Spades. Absolute Beginners. Mr. Love and Justice. Colin MacInnes. LC 68-17293. 1969. 7.50. Farrar, Straus and Giroux.

London of Charles Dickens: Being an Account of the Haunts of His Characters and the Topographical Setting of His Novels. Edwin Beresford Chancellor. LC 78-14818. (Illus.). 1978. 35.00 (ISBN 0-8414-0053-9). Folcroft Library Editions.

London of Sherlock Holmes. Michael Harrison. LC 72-194877. (Illus.). 1972. 6.95 (ISBN 0-87749-223-9). Drake Publishers.

London Pride. Phyllis Bottome. LC 41-23964. 1941. Little, Brown and Company.

London Season. Sheila Bishop. 1978. 1.75 (ISBN 0-441-38900-7). Ace Books.

London Season. Joan Wolf. LC 81-17262. (Regency romances). 1982. 12.95 (ISBN 0-89340-325-3). J. Curley.

London Sparrow & Mignonette. C. M. Duncan-Jones. Repr. lib. bdg. 10.00 (ISBN 0-8414-3870-6). Folcroft.

London Story. George Buchanan. LC 35-8748. 1935. E. P. Dutton & Co., Inc.

London Switch. Robin Moore & Al Dempsey. (Pulsar international series,#1). 1974. (pbk.) 1.25 (ISBN 0-523-00351-X). Pinnacle Books.

London Venture. Michael Arlen. Dodd, Mead and Company.

Londoners. Robert Smythe Hichens. LC 7-4763. 1898. H. S. Stone & Company.

Londoners: An Absurdity. Robert Smythe Hichens. LC 76-24388. (Decadent Consciousness). 1977. 26.00 (ISBN 0-8240-2764-7). Garland Pub.

Lone Adventure. John T. Forsythe. 3.75 o.s.i. (ISBN 0-8181-0104-0). Pageant-Poseidon.

Lone Adventure. Halliwell Sutcliffe. LC 11-23495. Hodder & Stoughton, George H. Doran Company.

Lone Bull's Mistake: A Lodge Pole Chief Story. James Willard Schultz. LC 18-16488. 1918. Houghton Mifflin Company.

Lone Cowboy. Charlton Lawrence Edholm. LC 38-38713. Phoenix Press.

Lone Deputy. Wayne D Overholser. LC 57-112283. 1957. Macmillan.

Lone Dove: A Legend of Revolutionary Times. by a lady. ed. Diana Treat Killbourn. LC 7-15145. 1850. G. S. Appleton.

Lone Fighter. Mournful Martin Makes His Bow. Charles Wesley Sanders. LC 33-784633. A. H. King.

Lone Furrow. William Alexander Fraser. LC 7-6653. 1907. D. Appleton and Company.

Lone Grave of the Shenandoah: And Other Tales. Donn Piatt. LC 7-36047. 1888. Belford, Clarke & Co.

Lone Gun. easy eye ed. Eric Allen. 1968. pap. 0.60 o.p. (73-757). Lancer.

Lone Gun. Eric Allen. 1973. pap. 0.75 o.s.i. (74-796). Lancer.

Lone Gun. Clark Brooker, pseud. LC 55-12091. 1955. Ballantine Books.

Lone Gun. Tom West. 1974. pap. 0.75 o.p. (07341). Curtis.

Lone Gun. Cover Painting by Rob Schulz. Howard Rigsby. LC 56-22725. (Gold medal books, 542). 1955. Fawcett Publications.

Lone Gunhawk. Frank Gruber. 160p. 1983. pap. 2.25 (ISBN 0-451-12019-1, Sig). NAL.

Lone Hand. Joseph Bushnell Ames. LC 26-24510. The Century Co.

Lone Hand. Harold Bindloss. LC 28-7324. 1928. Frederick A. Stokes Company.

Lone Hand. Leonard London Foreman. LC 57-5950. (Dell first edition, A127). 1956. Dell Pub. Co.

Lone-Hand Tracker. William West Winter. LC 26-22305. (On cover: A pocket copyright. no. 66). 1926. Garden City Publishing Co., Inc.

Lone Hill Story: A Novel of the Pioneer West. 1st Ed. Edith Campbell Thomson. LC 55-868944. 1955. Exposition Press.

Lone House. Amelia Edith Huddleston Barr. LC 6-7986. Dodd, Mead & Company.

Lone Inn: A Mystery. Fergus Hume. LC 7-5842. (Half title: The "unknown" library. no. 35). The Cassell Publishing Co.

Lone Lodge Mystery. John Hawk. LC 26-8950. George H. Doran Company.

Lone Pilgrim. Laurie Colwin. LC 80-24572. 224p. 1981. 9.95 (ISBN 0-394-51453-X). Knopf.
Lone Pilgrim. Laurie Colwin. 1982. pap. 3.95 (ISBN 0-671-43489-6). WSP.
Lone Pine Ranch. Archie Joscelyn. LC 48-1237. 1947. Phoenix Press.
Lone Pine: The Story of a Lost Mine. Richard Baxter Townshend. LC 99-998. 1899. G. P. Putnam's Sons.
Lone Point. Grace Livingston Hill. Repr. lib. bdg. 16.60x (ISBN 0-89190-041-1). Am Repr-Rivercity Pr.
Lone Point: A Summer Outing. Grace Livingston Hill. LC 96-1544. A. J. Rowland.
Lone Ranger. Fran Striker. 1975. (pbk.) 0.95 (ISBN 0-523-00694-2). Pinnacle Books.
Lone Ranger and the Gold Robbery. Fran Striker. (Lone Ranger Series#3). 1976. (pbk.) 0.95 (ISBN 0-523-00801-5). Pinnacle Books.
Lone Ranger & the Mystery Ranch. Fran Striker. 1976. Repr. of 1938 ed. lib. bdg. 9.95 (ISBN 0-89190-501-4). Am Repr-Rivercity Pr.
Lone Ranger on Gunsight Mesa. Striker, Francis Hamilton. LC 52-8153. 1952. Grosset & Dunlap.
Lone Star. Eugene Percy Lyle. LC 7-25502. 1907. Doubleday, Page & Company.
Lone Star: A Novel of Presidential Assassination. J. David Andrews. 1978. cancelled o.p. (ISBN 0-682-49277-9). Exposition.
Lone Star & the Border Bandits, No. 3. Wesley Ellis. 192p. 1982. pap. 2.25 (ISBN 0-515-06228-6). Jove Pubns.
Lone Star & the Hardrock Payoff, No. 9. Wesley Ellis. 192p. 2.25 (ISBN 0-515-06234-0). Jove Pubns.
Lone Star & the Kansas Wolves, No. 4. Wesley Ellis. 192p. (Orig.). 1982. pap. 2.25 (ISBN 0-515-06229-4). Jove Pubns.
Lone Star & the Land Grabbers, No. 6. Wesley Ellis. 192p. 1982. pap. 2.25 (ISBN 0-515-06231-6). Jove Pubns.
Lone Star & the Opium Rustlers, No. 2. Wesley Ellis. 192p. 1982. pap. 2.25 (ISBN 0-515-06227-8). Jove Pubns.
Lone Star & the Renegade Comanches. Wesley Ellis. 192p. 1983. pap. 2.25 (ISBN 0-515-06235-9). Jove Pubns.
Lone Star & the Showdowners, No. 8. Wesley Ellis. 192p. 1983. pap. 2.25 (ISBN 0-515-06233-2). Jove Pubns.
Lone Star & the Timber Pirates, No. 5. Wesley Ellis. 192p. 1983. pap. 2.25 (ISBN 0-515-06232-4). Jove Pubns.
Lone Star & the Utah Kid, No. 5. Wesley Ellis. 192p. 1982. pap. 2.25 (ISBN 0-515-06230-8). Jove Pubns.
Lone Star Bo-Peep: And Other Tales of Texas Ranch Life. Howard Seely. LC 8-6442. 1885. W. L. Mershon & Co.
Lone Star Cowboy. Leslie Scott. LC 59-1575. 1959. Arcadia House.
Lone Star Law. Jackson Cole, pseud. LC 39-19153. M. S. Mill Co., Inc.
Lone Star Law. Oscar Schisgall. LC 39-19153. M. S. Mill Co., Inc.
Lone Star Legacy. Farris Fletcher. 288p. 1982. pap. 3.25 (ISBN 0-440-04679-3, Emerald). Dell.
Lone Star Legion. Jackson Cole, pseud. LC 40-32097. M. S. Mill Co., Inc.
Lone Star Legion. Oscar Schisgall. LC 40-32097. M. S. Mill Co., Inc.
Lone Star Massacre. J. D. Hardin. LC 82-80842. (J. D. Hardin Western Ser.). 224p. (Orig.). 1982. pap. 1.95 (ISBN 0-86721-178-4). Playboy Pbks.
Lone Star Omnibus: Containing Three Texas Novels. William MacLeod Raine. LC 37-11009. 1936. Grosset & Dunlap.
Lone Star on Outlaw Mountain, No. 11. Wesley Ellis. 192p. 1983. pap. 2.25 (ISBN 0-515-06236-7). Jove Pubns.
Lone Star on the Treachery Trail, No. 1. Wesley Ellis. 192p. 1982. pap. 2.25 (ISBN 0-515-06226-X). Jove Pubns.
Lone Star: Or, the Texas Bravo. A Tale of the Southwest. John Hovey Robinson & Baker, Joseph C. LC 7-42160. 1852. F. Gleason's Publishing Hall.
Lone Star Preacher: Being a Chronicle of the Acts of Praxiteles Swan, M. E. Church South, Sometime Captain, 5th Texas Regiment, Confederate States Provisional Army. John William Thomason. LC 41-51615. 1941. C. Scribner's Sons.
Lone Star Ranger. Zane Grey. 376p. Repr. of 1915 ed. lib. bdg. 18.55x (ISBN 0-89190-764-5). Am Repr-Rivercity Pr.
Lone Star Ranger. Zane Grey. 1973. (pbk.) 0.75. Pocket Books.
Lone Star Ranger: A Romance of the Border. Zane Grey. LC 15-1049. 1915. Harper & Brothers.
Lone Star Ranger: A Romance of the Border. Zane Grey. LC 21-136897. 1917. Grosset & Dunlap.
Lone Star Rider. George Parker Milne. LC 35-9702. E. J. Clode, Inc.
Lone Star Rises. Mabel Sturdivant Satterfield. LC 36-18134. The Story Book Press.
Lone Star Silver. Jackson Cole, pseud. LC 39-4164. M. S. Mill Co. Inc.
Lone Star Silver. Oscar Schisgall. LC 39-4164. M. S. Mill Co., Inc.
Lone Star Terror. Jackson Cole, pseud. LC 40-6707. M. S. Mill Co., Inc.
Lone Star Terror. Oscar Schisgall. LC 40-67075. M. S. Mill Co., Inc.
Lone Star Treasure. Oscar Schisgall. LC 44-5321. 1944. Arcadia House, Inc.
Lone Star Universe: Speculative Fiction and Fantasy from Texas. George W Proctor & Steven Utley. LC 76-7227. 1976-1977. 9.95 (ISBN 0-913206-08-3). Heidelberg Publishers.
Lone Star Universe: Speculative Fiction from Texas. Ed. by George W. Proctor & Steven Utley. 288p. 1976. 9.95 (ISBN 0-913206-08-3). Heidelberg Pub.
Lone Tree. Harry Leon Wilson. LC 29-18174. 1929. Cosmopolitan Book Corporation.
Lone Voyagers. Wanda Fraiken Neff. LC 29-15570. 1929. Houghton Mifflin Company.
Lone Wolf: A Melodrama. Louis Joseph Vance. LC 14-17926. 1914. Little, Brown, and Company.
Lone Wolf: A Melodrama. Louis Joseph Vance. LC 18-778577. 1915. A. L. Burt Company.
Lone Wolf: A Melodrama. Louis Joseph Vance. LC 33-175051. A. L. Burt Company.
Lone-Wolf Lawman. Galen C Colin. LC 42-7191. 1942. Phoenix Press.
Lone Wolf Returns. Louis Joseph Vance. LC 24-260281. 1923. E. P. Dutton & Company.
Lone Wolf's Last Prowl. Louis Joseph Vance. LC 34-35308. J. B. Lippincott Company.
Lone Wolf's Son. Louis Joseph Vance. LC 31-23673. 1931. J. B. Lippincott Company.
Loneliest Girl in the World, a Novel. 1st Ed. Kenneth Fearing. LC 51-11347. 1951. Harcourt, Brace.
Loneliness. Robert Hugh Benson. 1915. Dodd, Mead and Company.
Loneliness Is Rotting on a Bookrack. Johnny Hart. (B.C. Ser.). (Illus.). 1978. pap. 1.75 (ISBN 0-449-13942-5, GM). Fawcett.
Loneliness of the Long-Distance Runner. Alan Sillitoe. LC 60-8227. 1960. Knopf.
Lonely. Paul Gallico. LC 49-5592. 1949. A. A. Knopf.
Lonely. Besse Sprague. LC 37-35918. J. H. Hopkins & Son, Inc.
Lonely Boy Blues. Alan Kapelner. LC 44-8028. 1944. C. Scribner's Sons.
Lonely Breeze. Van Siller. 1970. pap. 0.60 o.p. (0502-06070). Curtis.
Lonely Breeze: By Van Siller. Hilda Van Siller. 3.50. Pub. for Crime Club by Doubleday.
Lonely Bride. Anne Duffield. LC 47-191871. 1947. Arcadia House.
Lonely Bride. Ruth Dewey Groves. LC 32-20048. A. L. Burt Company.
Lonely Carrot. Mannix Walker. LC 47-4998. 1947. Dodd, Mead.
Lonely Conqueror. Translated from the German by Sigrid Rock. Willi Heinrich. LC 62-13219. 1962. Dial Press.
Lonely Crusade. Chester B. Himes. LC 47-30774. 1947. A. A. Knopf.
Lonely Dark: By John B. Smithback. John B Smithback. LC 65-29269. 1965. Manzanita Press.
Lonely Earl. Vanessa Gray, pseud. (Signet Book). 1.75 (ISBN 0-451-07922-1). New American Library.
Lonely Earl. Vanessa Gray, pseud. LC 81-521. 1981. 12.95 (ISBN 0-89340-325-3). J. Curley.
Lonely for the Future. James Thomas Farrell. LC 66-11755. 1966. Doubleday.
Lonely for the Future. James Thomas Farrell. 1974. (pbk.) 1.50. Manor Books.
Lonely Furrow. Katherine Helen Maud Marshall Diver. LC 23-10552. 1923. Houghton Mifflin Company.
Lonely Furrow. Norah Robinson Lofts. LC 76-2793. 1977. 8.95 (ISBN 0-385-11649-7). Doubleday.
Lonely Furrow. Norah Robinson Lofts. (Fawcett Crest Book). 1978. 1.95 (ISBN 0-449-23572-6). Fawcett Pub.
Lonely Girl. Iris Evans. LC 77-84865. 1977. pap. 1.75 o.p. (ISBN 0-87216-428-4, K16428). Playboy.
Lonely Girl. Edna O'Brien. LC 62-8438. 1962. Random House.
Lonely Grass: A Novel of the American West. Nelson Coral Nye. LC 55-7823. 1955. Dodd, Mead.
Lonely Grave. Dave Waldo. 1971. pap. 0.60 o.p. (ISBN 0-447-73214-5). Lancer.
Lonely Graves. Christopher Monig, pseud. 1971. pap. 0.75 o.p. (ISBN 0-446-64654-7, 64-654-7). Paperback Lib.
Lonely Gun. Gordon D. Shirreffs. 1977. pap. 1.50 o.s.i. (ISBN 0-505-51175-4). Tower Bks.
Lonely Hearts Killers. Wenzell Brown. 1965. pap. 0.95 o.p. (01793, Collier). Macmillan.
Lonely Hill. Natalie Shipman. LC 46-3804. 1946. S. Curl, Inc.
Lonely House. Marie Adelaide Belloc Lowndes. LC 20-10307. 1.90. George H. Doran Company.
Lonely House: From the German of Adolf Streckfuss... Adolf Streckfuss & Wister, Mrs. Annie Lee (Furness) 1830-1908, Tr. LC 7-33203. 1907. J. B. Lippincott Company.
Lonely Hunter. Collin Wilcox. LC 70-85636. 1969. 4.50. Random House.
Lonely Key. Frank Roderus. LC 82-45303. 1982. 11.95 (ISBN 0-385-18029-2). Doubleday.
Lonely Lady. Harold Robbins. 1981. pap. 3.95 (ISBN 0-671-41713-4). PB.
Lonely Lady: A Novel. Harold Robbins. LC 76-1895. 9.95 (ISBN 0-671-22307-0). Simon and Schuster.
Lonely Lady of Dulwich. Maurice Baring. LC 34-31287. 1934. A. A. Knopf.
Lonely Lady of Grosvenor Square. Elizabeth Bonham De La Pasture. LC 6-41709. 1906. E. P. Dutton & Company.
Lonely Law. Llewellyn Perry Holmes. LC 57-7443. (Silver star westerns). 1957. Dodd, Mead.
Lonely Law. Matt Stuart. 1977. pap. 1.95 (ISBN 0-445-00434-7). Popular Lib.
Lonely Londoners. Samuel Selvon. St. Martin's Press.
Lonely Lovers: A Love-Story. Horace W. C Newte. M. Kennerley.
Lonely Maid. Margaret Wolfe Hamilton Hungerford. (On cover: Lippincott's select novels. no. 186). 1896. J. B. Lippincott Company.
Lonely Man. Faith Baldwin Cuthrell. LC 64-14368. 1964. Holt, Rinehart and Winston.
Lonely Man. Faith Baldwin Cuthrell. LC 64-14368. 1975. (pbk.) 0.95 (ISBN 0-446-75786-1). Warner Paperback Library.
Lonely Man. Gilbert Frankau. LC 33-6259. E. P. Dutton & Co., Inc.
Lonely Men. Louis L'Amour. 1976. pap. 2.25 (ISBN 0-553-20074-7). Bantam.
Lonely on the Mountain. large print ed. Louis L'Amour. LC 81-6213. 1981. 11.95 (ISBN 0-8161-3247-X). G.K. Hall.
Lonely Parade. Fannie Hurst. LC 42-1190. Harper & Brothers.
Lonely Passage. Loula Grace Erdman. LC 48-8701. 1948. Dodd, Mead.
Lonely Passion of Judith Hearne. Brian Moore. (Kangaroo Book). 1978. 1.95 (ISBN 0-671-81915-1). Pocket Books.
Lonely Passion of Judith Hearne. 1st American Ed. Brian Moore. LC 56-7053. 1956. Little, Brown.
Lonely Place. Dorothy Daniels. (Signet Book). 1978. 1.50 (ISBN 0-451-08031-9). New American Library.
Lonely Place. Ruth McCarthy Sears. (Orig.). 1976. pap. 1.25 o.p. (LB343ZK, Leisure Bks). Nordon Pubns.
Lonely Place to Die. Wessel Ebersohn. LC 79-2306. 1979. 7.95 (ISBN 0-394-50855-6). Pantheon Books.
Lonely Place to Die: A Novel of Suspense. Wessel Ebersohn. LC 80-12999. 1980. 2.50 (ISBN 0-394-74544-2). Vintage Books.
Lonely Rebels. Three Novelettes. Egon Hostovsky. LC 52-6070. (Golden griffin books, 6). Arts, Inc.
Lonely Ride. Giles A Lutz. 1973. (pbk) 0.75. Ace Books.
Lonely Ride. Giles A Lutz. LC 76-135715. 1971. 4.50. Doubleday.
Lonely Road. Elizabeth Carfrae, pseud. LC 41-208737. G. P. Putnam's Sons.
Lonely Road. Nevil Shute Norway. LC 32-6902. 1932. W. Morrow & Company.
Lonely Road: A Romance. Jeffery Farnol. LC 38-27923. 1938. Doubleday, Doran & Company, Inc.
Lonely Road Back. Leslie E Moser. LC 73-144371. 1971. 5.95. Word Books.
Lonely Room: A Novel. 1st Ed. Beatrice Levin. LC 50-7125. 1950. Bobbs- Merrill.
Lonely Rose. Penni Shubin. LC 78-10136. 1981. 12.95 (ISBN 0-87949-153-1). Ashley Bks.
Lonely Scoundrel: A Supplement to The Perishing Republic. Jerome Bahr. LC 73-80240. 1974. 4.95, 2.65 (pbk.). Trempealean Press.
Lonely Search. Miriam Schwarz. LC 78-124124. 1970. 6.95. Sabra Books.
Lonely Side of the River. Donald MacKenzie. LC 65-10534. 1965. 3.95. Houghton.
Lonely Sky. William Bridgeman & J. Hazard. (Illus.). 1955. 5.95 o.p. (ISBN 0-03-026750-1). HR&W.
Lonely Star. Donald S Rowland. LC 65-8249. 1964. Arcadia House.
Lonely Steeple. easy eye ed. Victor Wolfson. pap. 0.75 o.p. Lancer.
Lonely Steeple: A Novel. Victor Wolfson. LC 45-6107. 1945. Simon and Schuster.
Lonely Stranger. Paul E. Giguere. 108p. 1974. 4.95 o.p. (ISBN 0-8059-1936-8). Dorrance.
Lonely Strangers. Charity Blackstock. (Adult Ser.). 1973. Repr. lib. bdg. 10.95 o.p. (ISBN 0-8161-6093-7, Large Print Bks.). G K Hall.
Lonely Strangers. Charity Blackstock. (YA) 1972. 7.95 o.p. (ISBN 0-698-10478-1). Coward.
Lonely Strangers. Ursula Torday. LC 72-87575. 1972. 7.95 (ISBN 0-698-10478-1). Coward, McCann & Geoghegan.
Lonely Strangers. Ursula Torday. LC 73-3115. 1973. 10.95 (ISBN 0-8161-6093-7). G. K. Hall.
Lonely Stronghold. Gertrude M. Robins Reynolds. LC 18-760233. George H. Doran Company.
Lonely Target: By Hugh Pentecost Pseud. Judson Pentecost Philips. LC 59-147126. (Red badge detective). 1959. Dodd, Mead.
Lonely Terror. Serena Mayfield. (Ravenswood Gothic). 1973. (pbk.) 0.95 (ISBN 0-671-77693-2). Pocket Books.
Lonely the Autumn Bird: Two Novels. Richard McBride. LC 82-71231. 93p. (Orig.). 1963. pap. 3.75 (ISBN 0-8040-0189-8). Swallow.
Lonely Toys. Miriam Lynch. 1971. pap. 0.75 o.p. (ISBN 0-447-74746-0). Lancer.
Lonely Trail. Jackson Gregory. LC 43-3663. 1943. Dodd, Mead & Company.
Lonely Vigils. Manly Wade Wellman. (Illus.). 392p. 1981. 15.00 o.p. (ISBN 0-913796-03-4). Carcosa.
Lonely Walk. M. E. Chaber, pseud. (Milo March Series). pap. 0.60 o.p. (ISBN 0-446-63421-2, 63-241). Paperback Lib.
Lonely Walk: By M. E. Chaber Pseud. Kendell Foster Crossen. LC 56-72583. 1956. Rinehart.
Lonely Warrior. Claude Carlos Washburn. LC 22-231372. Harcourt, Brace and Company.
Lonely Way to Die. Hal Debrett. LC 50-8280. (Red badge detective). 1950. Dodd, Mead.
Lonely Women. Gerda Rhoads. LC 57-9038. 1957. Ballantine Books.
Lonely Women. Gerda Rhoads. LC 57-14439. (Ballantine books, 196). 1957. Ballantine Books.
Lonelyheart 4122. Colin Watson. (X1586). 1968. Berkley.
Loner. George G. Gilman, pseud. (Edge Ser.: No. 1). 144p. 1972. pap. 1.75 (ISBN 0-523-41279-7). Pinnacle Bks.
Loner. Frances Nichols Hanna. LC 56-135118. (Inner sanctum mystery). 1956. Simon and Schuster.
Loner. Fan Nichols. (O.s.i.). 1956. 2.75 o.s.i. (ISBN 0-671-42750-4). S&S.
Loner. James W. Smith. 1971. pap. 0.75 o.p. (T2598). Pyramid Pubns.
Loner: An Original Western, by Bliss Lomax Pseud. Harry Sinclair Drago. LC 56-675519. (Dell f2rst edition, 87). Dell.
Loners: Short Stories About the Young Alienated. Ed. by L. M. Schulman. LC 74-99125. 1970. Macmillan.
Lonesome Badger. Frank Gruber. LC 53-109229. (Murray Hill mystery). 1954. Rinehart.
Lonesome Cabin. Felicidad V Ocampo. LC 31-33893. 1931. Meador Publishing Company.
Lonesome Cowboy. John Reese. 1975. (pbk.) 0.95. Belmont Tower Books.
Lonesome Gods. Louis L'Amour. 464p. 1983. 14.95 (ISBN 0-553-05014-1). Bantam.
Lonesome Journey. Johnny Baranski. LC 73-85734. (Sunburst Originals Ser.: No. 2). 125p. (Orig.). 1973. pap. 2.00 (ISBN 0-934648-06-9). Sunburst Pr.
Lonesome Kid. Lewis C Merrill. LC 40-7107. Phoenix Press.
Lonesome Land. B. M. Bower. 1975. lib. bdg. 15.30x (ISBN 0-89966-022-3). Buccaneer Bks.
Lonesome Land. Bertha Muzzy Sinclair. LC 12-2461. 1912. 1.25. Little, Brown, and Company.
Lonesome Land. Bertha Muzzy Sinclair. LC 44-7831. 1943. Triangle Books.
Lonesome Longhorn. John H. Latham. LC 51-9834. (Illus.). 1951. Westminster Press.
Lonesome Places. August William Derleth. 1962. 3.50 o.p. Arkham.
Lonesome Quarter. Richard Edward Wormser. LC 51-10638. 1951. M. S. Mill Co. and W. Morrow.
Lonesome Ranch. Charles Alden Seltzer. LC 76-39974. 1976. 6.95. Aeonian Press.
Lonesome River. Frank Gruber. LC 57-6012. Rinehart.
Lonesome River Justice. Robert Maxwell Hankins. LC 43-2510. 1943. Macrae-Smith-Company.
Lonesome River Range. Robert Maxwell Hankins. LC 41-51768. 1941. Macrae-Smith Company.
Lonesome Road. Lucy Furman. LC 27-21143. 1927. Little, Brown, and Company.
Lonesome Road. Patricia Wentworth. LC 39-3408. J. B. Lippincott Company.
Lonesome Town. Ethel Arnold Smith Dorrance. LC 22-17064. The Macaulay Company.
Lonesome Trail. John Gneisenau Neihardt. 1907. John Lane Company.
Lonesome Trail. Bertha Muzzy Sinclair. LC 9-8812. G. W. Dillingham Company.
Lonesome Traveler. Weldon Hill, pseud. LC 75-114740. 1970. 6.95. D. McKay Co.
Lonesome Traveler. John Kerouac. 1970. pap. 3.95 (ISBN 0-394-17171-3, B253, BC). Grove.

Lonesome Traveler: And Other Stories. John William Corrington. LC 68-25430. 1968. 5.95. Putnam.
Lonesome Valley. Henry Hornsby. LC 49-8437. 1949. W. Sloane Associates.
Lonesome Valley Cowhand. Wayne North. LC 45-545412. 1945. Phoenix Press.
Long After Midnight. Ray Bradbury. LC 76-13689. 1976. 7.95 (ISBN 0-394-47942-4). Knopf.
Long After Summer. Robert Nathan. (Laurel leaf library). 1974. (pbk.). 0.95. Dell.
Long After Summer. Robert Nathan. LC 48-8246. 1948. A. A. Knopf.
Long Ago a Moonboat. Christopher Carroll. LC 74-24782. (Illus.). 1974. 4.95 (ISBN 0-915244-02-0). Silver Dog Press.
Long Ago, Far Away. Alice Lent Covert. LC 53-133901. 1953. Avalon Books.
Long Alert: A Novel. Philip Hamilton Gibbs. LC 42-957741. 1942. Doubleday, Doran & Company, Inc.
Long Anchorage: A New Bedford Story. Henry Beetle Hough. LC 47-30298. 1947. D. Appleton-Century Company, Inc.
Long and Happy Life. Reynolds Price. LC 61-12790. 1962. Atheneum.
Long & Living Shadow. Daoma Winston. (O.s.i.). 1971. pap. 0.75 o.s.i. (B75-2098). Belmont-Tower.
Long and Living Shadow. Daoma Winston. 1977. 1.95. Ace.
Long Arm. Henry Cecil. LC 57-117958. 1957. Harper.
Long Arm. Samuel Major Gardenhire. LC 6-2099. 1906. Harper & Brothers.
Long Arm and the Molly Maguires. Tabor Evans, pseud. 1979. 1.75 (ISBN 0-515-04753-8). Jove Publications.
Long Arm of Fantomas. Pierre Souvestre & Allain, Marcel, Joint Author. LC 24-5504. (A...Fantomas detective novel). The Macaulay Company.
Long Arm of Gil Hamilton. Larry Niven. LC 75-35969. 1.50 (ISBN 0-345-24868-6). Ballantine Books.
Long Arm of Mannister. Edward Phillips Oppenheim. 1908. Little, Brown and Company.
Long Arm of the Mounted. James French Dorrance. LC 26-6480. The Macaulay Company.
Long Arm of the Mounted. William Byron Mowery. LC 48-8869. 1948. Whittlesey House.
Long Black Coat. Jay Bennett. LC 73-7217. 1973. 5.95 o.p. (ISBN 0-440-04942-3). Delacorte.
Long Body. Helen McCloy. LC 55-815835. 1955. Random House.
Long Body of the Dream. Richard Grossinger. LC 74-177199. 1974. 5.00 (ISBN 0-913028-28-2). North Atlantic Books; Principal Distributor, Book People, Berkeley, Calif.
Long Bondage. Donald Joseph. LC 30-24844. 1930. Frederick A. Stokes Company.
Long Boots, Hard Boots. Carter Travis Young. LC 65-237934. (Double D. western). 3.50. Doubleday.
Long Bridge. Fannie Cook. LC 49-10801. 1949. Doubleday.
Long Chance. Max Brand. LC 41-10768. 1941. Dodd, Mead & Company.
Long Chance. Frederick Faust. LC 41-10768. 1944. Dodd, Mead & Company.
Long Chance. Peter Bernard Kyne. The H. K. Fly Company.
Long Chance. Peter Bernard Kyne. LC 21-19653. 1916. Grosset & Dunlap.
Long Chance: A Novel. David Mark. LC 55-9861. 1955. Messner.
Long Chase. Max Brand. 1975. (pbk.) 0.95. Warner Paperback Library.
Long Chase. John Morton Eshleman. LC 54-8734. 1954. I. Washburn.
Long Cold Wind. Giles A. Lutz. 1978. 1.50 (ISBN 0-671-82201-2). Pocket Books.
Long Cold Wind. 1st Ed. Giles A Lutz. LC 62-13348. (Double D western). 1962. Doubleday.
Long Cold Winter. Penny Jordan. (Harlequin Presents Ser.). 192p. 1982. pap. 1.75 (ISBN 0-373-10489-8). Harlequin Bks.
Long Communion. John Morressy. LC 73-90385. 1974. 7.95 (ISBN 0-8027-0448-4). Walker.
Long Corridor. Catherine Cookson. (Signet Book). 1976. (pbk.) 1.50. New American Library.
Long Corridor. Catherine Marchant, pseud. 1971. pap. 0.95 o.p. (95049). Beagle Bks.
Long Count. Ron Faust. 1.95 (ISBN 0-449-14270-1). Fawcett Gold Medal Books.
Long Crooked River. Albert Boardman Kerr. LC 29-29523. The Knickerbocker Press.
Long Cry. Mildred Offerle. LC 60-131146. 1960. Concordia Pub. House.
Long Dark Night. Joseph A. Hayes. (Dell Book). 1977. 1.95 (ISBN 0-440-14824-3). Dell Pub. Co.
Long Dark Night. Joseph Arnold Hayes. LC 73-93067. 1974. 8.95 (ISBN 0-399-11336-3). Putnam.
Long Dark Night of Baron Samedi. John Wyllie. LC 81-3229. (Crime Club Ser.). 192p. 1981. 10.95 (ISBN 0-385-17755-0). Doubleday.
Long Dark Night of the Soul. Susan Marvin. (Kangaroo Book). 1978. 1.50 (ISBN 0-671-82075-3). Pocket Books.
Long Day at Shiloh. Don Bannister. LC 80-24112. 1981. 11.95 (ISBN 0-394-50680-4). Knopf: Distributed by Random House.
Long Day Closes. Beatrice Tunstall. 1934. Doubleday, Doran & Company, Inc.
Long Day in a Short Life. Albert Maltz. LC 57-2903. 1957. International Publishers.
Long Day in Latigo. reissue ed. Wesley Ray, pseud. 1970. pap. 0.60 o.p. (63-295). Paperback Lib.
Long Day Wanes. Anthony Burgess. 1965. 6.95 o.p. (ISBN 0-393-08391-8). Norton.
Long Day Wanes: A Malayan Trilogy. Anthony Burgess. 1977. pap. 4.95 (ISBN 0-393-00864-9, Norton Lib). Norton.
Long Day Wanes: A Malayan Trilogy. John Anthony Burgess Wilson. LC 65-13324. 1965. 6.95. Norton.
Long Day Wanes: A Malayan Trilogy. John Anthony Burgess Wilson. LC 77-23535. (Norton library paperback series). 1977. 4.95 (ISBN 0-393-00864-9). Norton.
Long Day's Dying. Frederick Buechner. LC 60-6748. (Meridian fiction, MF7). 1960. Meridian Books.
Long Death: A Catalyst Club Murder Mystery. George Dyer. LC 37-3927. 1937. C. Scribner's Sons.
Long Defence. Friedrich Donaver. Tr. by Cooper, Frederic Taber. LC 31-10762. 1931. Longmans, Green and Co.
Long Desire. Evan S. Connell. LC 78-14175. 288p. 1980. pap. 4.95 (ISBN 0-03-057793-4). HR&W.
Long Dim Trail. Forrestine Cooper Hooker. LC 20-176516. (On verso of half-title: Borzol western stories). 1920. A. A. Knopf.
Long Discovery: A Novel. John Burgan. LC 50-6641. 1950. Farrar, Straus.
Long Distance. Penelope Mortimer. LC 74-2721. 1974. 6.95 (ISBN 0-385-02771-0). Doubleday.
Long Division. Anne Richardson Roiphe. LC 72-83905. 1972. 5.95 (ISBN 0-671-21363-6). Simon and Schuster.
Long Divorce. Edmund Crispin, pseud. (Penguin Crime Monthly Ser.). 256p. 1981. pap. 2.95 (ISBN 0-14-001304-0). Penguin.
Long Divorce. Robert Bruce Montgomery. LC 51-12094. (Red badge detective). 1951. Dodd, Mead.
Long Divorce. Robert Bruce Montgomery. LC 76-108397. 1970. (ISBN 0-8371-3820-5). Greenwood Press.
Long Divorce. Robert Bruce Montgomery. LC 80-24584. 1981. 2.95 (ISBN 0-14-001304-0). Penguin Books.
Long Draws: A Short Story of the Day. William Morton Preston. LC 44-398564. 1904. Hudson-Kimberly Publishing Company.
Long Dream. Sigrid Holmesland Boo & Nielsen, Edith M., Tr. LC 39-174114. 1939. E. P. Dutton & Co., Inc.
Long Dream. Richard Wright. 384p. 1969. Repr. of 1958 ed. 9.50x (ISBN 0-911860-02-9). Chatham Bkseller.
Long Dream: A Novel. Richard Wright. LC 58-12059. 1958. Doubleday.
Long Dream: A Novel. Richard Wright. LC 74-96383. 1969. Chatham Bookseller.
Long Drop. Alan White. LC 72-100505. 1970. Harcourt, Brace & World.
Long Dusk. Victor Serge & Manheim, Ralph, 1907- Tr. LC 47-2718. 1946. The Dial Press.
Long Echo: By Douglas Rutherford Pseud. James Douglas Rutherford McConnell. LC 57-12612. 1958. Abelard-Schuman.
Long Engagement. Ethel Stefana Stevens Drower. LC 12-206412. 1912. Hodder & Stoughton, George H. Doran Company.
Long Escape. David Dodge. LC 48-3591. 1948. Random House.
Long Escape. Irving Werstein. LC 64-21729. (Illus.). 1964. Scribner.
Long Ever Ago. Rupert Hughes. LC 18-5498. 1918. Harper & Brothers.
Long Exile. Eugene William Lohrke. 1936. D. Appleton-Century Company, Incorporated.
Long Exile. Georges Simenon. LC 81-48019. 15.95 (ISBN 0-15-152997-3). Harcourt Brace Jovanovich.
Long Farewell. Michael Innes, pseud. LC 81-47811. 224p. 1982. pap. 2.40 (ISBN 0-06-080575-7, P575, PL). Har-Row.
Long Farewell. John Innes Mackintosh Stewart. LC 58-5988. 1958. Dodd. Mead.
Long Fight. George Washington Ogden. LC 15-19188. 1915. Hearst's International Library Co.
Long Fight. Denys Arthur Rayner. LC 58-5663. 1958. Holt.
Long Fourth, and Other Stories. Peter Hillsman Taylor. LC 48-1781. 1948. Harcourt, Brace.
Long Furrows. Dora Aydelotte. LC 35-170124. 1935. D. Appleton-Century Company, Incorporated.
Long Fuse. Alan White. LC 74-3340. 1974. 5.95 (ISBN 0-15-153000-9). Harcourt Brace Jovanovich.
Long Gainer, a Novel. 1st Ed. William Raymond Manchester. LC 61-12817. 1961. Little, Brown.
Long Gallery. Eva Lathbury. LC 9-14515. 1909. H. Holt and Company.
Long Garden: By Emily Noble Pseud. James Noble Gifford. LC 52-13497. 1952. Arcadia House.
Long George Alley. Richard Hall. LC 73-178725. 1972. 6.95. Delacorte Press.
Long Gone. Paul Hemphill. 192p. pap. 2.25 (ISBN 0-445-04603-1). Popular Lib.
Long Gone: A Novel. Paul Hemphill. LC 79-10911. 1979. 8.95 (ISBN 0-670-44555-X). Viking Press.
Long Goodbye. Raymond Chandler. LC 54-52786. 1954. Houghton Mifflin.
Long Goodbye: A Trilogy. Yury V. Trifonov. Tr. by Helen Burlingame & Ellendea Proffer. 1978. 13.50 (ISBN 0-88233-281-3); pap. 4.95 (ISBN 0-88233-282-1). Ardis Pubs.
Long Goodbye: Three Novellas. Yury Valentinovich Trifonov. LC 78-104841. (ISBN 0-06-014371-1) (ISBN 0-88233-281-3). Harper & Row.
Long Goodnight. Carl D Burton. LC 61-8022. 1961. Morrow.
Long Green. Bart Spicer. LC 52-8101. 1952. Dodd, Mead.
Long Green Gaze: A Cross Word Puzzle Mystery. Vincent Fuller. LC 25-6517. 1925. B. W.S Huebsch, Inc.
Long Green Road. Sarah Pratt McLean Greene. LC 11-27648. 1911. 1.25. The Baker & Taylor Company.
Long Habit, a Novel. James Kern Feibleman. LC 48-9222. 1948. Duell, Sloan and Pearce.
Long-Haired Boy. Christopher Matthew. LC 79-55594. 1980. 8.95 (ISBN 0-689-11051-0). Atheneum.
Long Hard Ride. Robert E. Mills. (Kansan Ser.: No. 6). 208p. (Orig.). 1981. pap. 2.25 (ISBN 0-8439-0989-7, Leisure Bks). Nordon Pubns.
Long Haul. Albert Isaac Bezzerides. LC 38-8665. Carrick & Evans, Inc.
Long Haul. John Durham, pseud. (City Limits Ser., Bk. 2). (gr. 6). 1968. text ed. 2.20 o.p. (ISBN 0-07-018392-9, W). McGraw.
Long Haul. Oswaldo Franca. LC 79-18241. 10.95 (ISBN 0-525-14882-5). Dutton.
Long Haul. Rene Puget. LC 64-19932. 1964. Simon and Schuster.
Long Haul: A Novel. Mervyn Mills. LC 56-584642. 1956. Macmillan.
Long Haul: A Novel. Denys Arthur Rayner. LC 60-8038. 1960. McGraw-Hill.
Long Home. Neil S. Boardman. LC 48-6365. 1948. Harper.
Long Hot Days. Maynah Lewis. 1973. pap. 0.75 o.p. (26546-7-075). Beagle Bks.
Long Hunt. James Boyd. LC 30-10711. 1930. C. Scribner's Sons.
Long Hunter. Edd Winfield Parks & Shenton, Edward, 1895- Illus. LC 42-21759. 1942. Farrar & Rinehart Inc.
Long Is the Way: A Novel. Ruth Muirhead Berry. LC 58-5751. 1958. Muhlenberg Press.
Long Island Murders. Minna Wesselhoft Glidden. LC 38-5371. Phoenix Press.
Long Islanders. James P Hannibal. LC 77-99104. 3.95. Dunbar Publications.
Long John. Henry Newbold. 1979. 10.00 (ISBN 0-8184-0276-8). Lyle Stuart.
Long John: A Novel. Herbert Leon Newbold. LC 79-10122. 10.00 (ISBN 0-8184-0276-8). L. Stuart.
Long John Murray: A Novel of Northern Ireland. William Archer Sholto Douglas. LC 36-9227. Coward-McCann, Inc.
Long Journey. Johannes Vilhelm Jensen. Tr. by Chater, Arthur G. LC 33-27089. 1933. A. A. Knopf.
Long Journey. nobel prize ed. Johannes Vilhelm Jensen. Tr. by Arthur G. Chater. LC 45-35037. 1945. A. A. Knopf.
Long Journey. Elsie Singmaster. LC 17-63243. 1917. 1.00. Houghton Mifflin Company.
Long Journey Home. Mary Raymond. 1971. pap. 0.60 o.p. (ISBN 0-446-63574-X, 63-574). Paperback Lib.
Long Journey into Light. Marie St. John Sullivan. LC 70-100968. 1970. 5.95. Dorrance.
Long Knife... Edward Spence De Puy. LC 36-8613. 1936. Pub. for the Crime Club, Inc., by Doubleday, Doran and Company, Inc.
Long Knife. James Alexander Thom. 1979. pap. 2.75 (ISBN 0-380-44735-5, 44735). Avon.
Long Knife and Musket. Felix Lee Horton. 1973. (pbk) 0.95. Popular Lib.
Long Knives Walked. Mary Louise Mabie. LC 32-32021. The Bobbs-Merrill Company.
Long Lane. Philip Duffield Stong. LC 39-27055. Farrar & Rinehart, Incorporated.
Long Lane. Mary Virginia Terhune. LC 15-24855. 1915. 1.35. Hearst's International Library Co.
Long Lane: A Novel. Ethel Coxon. LC 6-28852. (Harper's handy series, no. 92). 1886. Harper & Brothers.
Long Lane's Turning. Hallie Erminie Rives. LC 17-22567. 1917. Dodd, Mead and Company.
Long Lash. Bertrand Leslie Shurtleff. LC 47-163529. 1947. The Bobbs-Merrill Company.
Long Lavender Look. John Dann MacDonald. LC 78-37010. (Travis McGee series). 1972. (ISBN 0-397-00739-6). Lippincott.
Long Light of Dawn. John Farris. 1962. 4.95 o.p. (ISBN 0-399-10503-4). Putnam.
Long Lightning. Norman A. Fox. (Silver star westerns). 1953. Dodo, Mead.
Long Lightning. Norman A. Fox. 1973. (pbk.) 0.75. Dell Pub. Co.
Long Live the King. Guy Newell Boothby. LC 5658. 1900. H. S. Stone and Company.
Long Live the King! Mary Roberts Rinehart. LC 17-24814. 1917. Houghton Mifflin Company.
Long Live the King. Lyn Tornabene. 1978. pap. 3.50 (ISBN 0-671-41324-4). PB.
Long Live the Republic: All About Me, and Julie, and the End of the Great War. Jan Prochazka. LC 72-76183. 1973. 4.50 (ISBN 0-385-04753-3) (ISBN 0-385-04753-3). Doubleday.
Long Loneliness. Dorothy Day. 1972. pap. 1.25 o.p. (01034). Curtis.
Long, Long Ago. Alexander Woollcott. Repr. lib. bdg. 15.15x (ISBN 0-89190-146-9). Am Repr-Rivercity Pr.
Long, Long Day for November. Moffitt Sinclair Henderson. LC 74-163727. (Illus.). 1972. 6.95 (ISBN 0-8059-1590-7). Dorrance.
Long Long Day in a Short Life. Albert Maltz. LC 57-2903. 1957. International Publishers.
Long, Long Love. Walter Sullivan. LC 59-7028. 1959. Holt.
Long, Long Summer. James Noble Gifford. LC 38-14889. 1938. Arcadia House.
Long, Long Summer. Warren Howard. LC 38-148891. 1938. Arcadia House.
Long, Long Trail. Max Brand. LC 74-6805. 212p. 1974. 5.95 o.p. (ISBN 0-396-06984-3). Dodd.
Long, Long Trail. Frederick Faust. LC 74-6805. (Silver star westerns). 1974. 5.95 (ISBN 0-396-06984-3). Dodd, Mead.
Long, Long Trail. Frederick Faust. LC 75-20447. 1975. 11.95 (ISBN 0-8161-6326-X). G. K. Hall.
Long, Long Trail. Frederick Faust. 1976. 1.25 (ISBN 0-671-80780-3). Pocket Books.
Long, Long Trail: A Western Story. George Owen Baxter. LC 23-12961. Chelsea House.
Long, Long Trail: A Western Story. Frederick Faust. LC 23-12961. 1923. Chelsea House.
Long Look Ahead: Or, The First Stroke and the Last. Azel Stevens Roe. LC 7-39822. 1855. J. C. Derby.
Long Loop. Bertha Muzzy Sinclair. LC 31-3634. 1931. Little, Brown, and Company.
Long Loop Raiders. Archie Joscelyn. LC 46-16628. 1946. Phoenix Press.
Long Lope to Lander. 1st Ed. Allan Vaughan Elston. LC 54-8747. 1954. Lippincott.
Long Lost Father: A Comedy. Gladys Bronwyn Stern. LC 33-10149. 1933. A. A. Knopf.
Long Lost Love. Julia Alcott. (Signet book). New American Library.
Long Loud Silence. Wilson Tucker. LC 52-8742. 1952. Rinehart.
Long Love. John Sedges, pseud. LC 49-10703. 1949. J. Day Co.
Long March. Jane Barry. LC 55-11160. 1955. Appleton-Century-Crofts.
Long March. William Styron. LC 68-21951. 3.95, 1.25 pap.,. Random.
Long March. William Styron. LC 56-104833. (Modern library paperbacks, P22). 1956. Random House.
Long March Nineteen Thirty-Five. Dick Wilson. 1982. pap. 5.95 (ISBN 0-14-006113-4). Penguin.
Long Masquerade. Madeleine Brent. LC 81-43048. 1982. 14.95 (ISBN 0-385-14597-7). Doubleday.
Long Masquerade. Madeleine Brent. LC 82-3086. 1982. 17.95 (ISBN 0-8161-3387-5). G.K. Hall.
Long Meadows. Minnie Hite Moody. LC 41-522277. 1941. The Macmillan Company.
Long Memory: A Novel. Howard Clewes. LC 52-5879. 1952. Doubleday.
Long Midnight. Alan White. LC 73-13952. 1974. 5.95. Harcourt Brace Jovanovich.
Long, Naked Descent into Boston. William Eastlake. LC 76-46932. 1977. 10.00 (ISBN 0-670-43852-9). Viking Press.
Long Night. Martin Caidin. LC 56-628795. Dodd, Mead.
Long Night. P. B. Gallagher. (Orig.). 1979. pap. 2.25. Zebra.
Long Night. Andrew Nelson Lytle. LC 36-27451. The Bobbs-Merrill Company.
Long Night. Julian Mayfield. LC 58-12188. 1958. Vanguard Press.
Long Night. Bellamy Partridge. LC 35-5782. Godwin.

Long Night. Stanley John Weyman. 1903. McClure, Phillips & Co.
Long Night of Waiting. Ed. by Roger Elwood. LC 72-85161. 1974. 6.95 (ISBN 0-87695-149-3). Aurora Publishers.
Long Night's Walk. Alan White. LC 68-24400. 1969. Harcourt, Brace & World.
Long Noose. Oscar Jerome Friend. LC 42-20338. 1942. Gateway Books.
Long Noose. Lee E Wells. LC 53-5354. 1953. Rinehart.
Long November. James Benson Nablo. LC 45-10475. 1946. E. P. Dutton & Co., Inc.
Long Odds. Harold Bindloss. LC 8-32330. 1908. Small, Maynard & Company.
Long Odds. Zeke Masters, pseud. (Faro Blake Ser.: No. 23). (Orig.). 1982. pap. 2.25 (ISBN 0-671-45182-0). PB.
Long Odds: A Novel. Hawley Smart. LC 8-9611. (Lovell's international series, no. 12). 1889. F. F. Lovell & Company.
Long Overcoat: By Pete Fry Pseud. Clifford King. LC 57-45359. (British bloodhound, no. 156). 1957. T. V. Boardman.
Long Patrol. Albert M Treynor. LC 26-151857. 1926. Dodd, Mead and Company.
Long Patrol: A Tale of the Mounted Police. Hiram Alfred Cody. 1.20. Hodder & Stoughton, George H. Doran Company.
Long Pennant: A Novel. Oliver La Farge. LC 33-29650. 1933. Houghton Mifflin Company.
Long Pig. Russell Foreman. LC 58-12999. 1958. McGraw-Hill.
Long Portage. Harold Bindloss. LC 12-7018. 1912. 1.25. Frederick A. Stokes Company.
Long Pursuit. Jon Cleary. 1967. 4.95 o.p. Morrow.
Long Pursuit. Joseph Freeman. LC 47-2726. 1947. Rinehart & Company, Inc.
Long Pursuit: A Novel. Jon Cleary. LC 67-20187. 1967. W. Morrow.
Long Quest. Christine Whiting Parmenter. LC 33-186593. Thomas Y. Crowell Company.
Long Reconnaissance. John Murphy. LC 70-94948. 1970. 5.95. Doubleday.
Long Remember. MacKinlay Kantor. LC 34-27082. Coward-McCann.
Long Result. John Brunner. 192p. (Orig.). 1981. pap. 2.25 (ISBN 0-345-29639-7, Del Rey). Ballantine.
Long Revenge. June Thomson. LC 74-18836. 1975. 5.95 (ISBN 0-385-09004-8). Published for the Crime Club by Doubleday.
Long Revenge. June Tompson. 160p. 1981. pap. 2.25 (ISBN 0-553-14723-4). Bantam.
Long Ride. Jonathan H. Glidden. LC 42-21088. 1942. Dodd, Mead & Company.
Long Ride. Lloyd Sumner. LC 77-28192. 1978. 8.95 o.p. (ISBN 0-8117-0952-3). Stackpole.
Long Ride Out. James Gribben. LC 58-5693. 1958. Putnam.
Long Ride. 1st Ed. Tom J Hopkins. LC 52-5757. (Double D western). 1952. Doubleday.
Long Riders. Dan Cushman. 1970. pap. 0.60 o.p. (R2300, GM). Fawcett World.
Long Riders. Clark Frost. LC 41-11983. Phoenix Press.
Long Rifle. Stewart Edward White. LC 57-141653. 1957. Doubleday.
Long Rifle. Stewart Edward White. LC 32-26260. 1932. Doubleday, Doran & Company, Inc.
Long Rifle. Stewart Edward White. LC 38-31835. 1938. The Sun Dial Press, Inc.
Long Rifle: The Saga of Andy Burnett. Stewart Edward White. 4.95 o.p. Doubleday.
Long Road. Laurie Nan Drake. LC 77-94360. 1970. 4.50. Dorrance.
Long Road. Frank Lateur. LC 75-44092. (Library of Netherlandic literature; v. 8). 7.95 (ISBN 0-8057-8155-2). Twayne Publishers.
Long Road. Natalie Shipman. LC 45-9783. 1945. Prentice-Hall, Inc.
Long Road. Alise Barton Whiticar. (Illus.). 1973. 7.95 o.p. (ISBN 0-87482-029-4). Wake-Brook.
Long Road: A Novel. John Oxenham, pseud. LC 7-10620. 1907. The Macmillan Company.
Long Road Home. J. R. Modansky. 7.50 o.p. Carlton.
Long Road Home. Ralph Delahaye Paine. LC 16-6290. 1916. C. Scribner's Sons.
Long Road to Eden. Arthur G. Garner. (Orig.). 1979. pap. 1.95 (ISBN 0-532-23248-8). Woodhill.
Long Roll. Mary Johnston. LC 11-13141. 1911. Houghton Mifflin Company.
Long Rope. Dane Coolidge. LC 35-2778. E. P. Dutton & Co., Inc.
Long Rope. Francis W Hilton. LC 35-2816. 1935. H. C. Kinsey & Company, Inc.
Long Rope. William Oliver Turner. LC 59-7005. (Double D western). Doubleday,
Long Roper. Jim Wilmeth. 208p. (Orig.). 1982. pap. 2.25 (ISBN 0-505-51775-2). Tower Bks.
Long Run. John Bigelow Clark. LC 52-8020. 1952. Coward-McCann.
Long Run. Rose Elizabeth Cleveland. LC 6-20752. 1886. F. B. Dickerson & Co.
Long Run. Nelson Coral Nye. LC 59-62921. 1959. Macmillan.
Long Run. large print ed. Nelson Coral Nye. LC 82-21374. 1983. 11.95 (ISBN 0-8161-3454-5). G.K. Hall.
Long Run South. 1st American Ed. Alan Williams. LC 62-17945. 1962. Little, Brown.
Long Run to Tobruk. Gordon Landsborough. 1978. pap. 1.50 (ISBN 0-532-15316-2). Woodhill.
Long S. Lee Floren. LC 45-957750. 1945. Phoenix Press.
Long Search. Sallie Lee Bell. LC 59-319071. Zondervan Pub. House.
Long Search. Mary Abigail Roe. LC 7-402569. Dodd, Mead & Company.
Long Search, a Novel. 1st Ed. William Bosworth. LC 56-12732. 1957. Advance Pub. Co.
Long Secret. Louise Fitzhugh. 1978. pap. 1.95 (ISBN 0-440-94977-7, LFL). Dell.
Long Shadow. Frank Bryan. LC 55-786. Comet Press Books.
Long Shadow. Jon Cleary. LC 77-357888. 1976. 3.15 (ISBN 0-7278-0134-1). Severn House: Distributed by Hutchinson.
Long Shadow. Celia Fremlin, pseud. LC 76-2771. 1976. 5.95 (ISBN 0-385-11590-3). Published for the Crime Club by Doubleday.
Long Shadow. Bertha Muzzy Sinclair. LC 9-26672. G. W. Dillingham Company.
Long Shadow. Bertha Muzzy Sinclair. LC 21-8692. Grosset & Dunlap.
Long Shadow: The Story of St. Jean De Brebeuf. Frances Taylor Patterson. LC 56-953382. 1956. Sheed and Ward.
Long Shadows. Adam P. Kephart. 3.50 o.s.i. (ISBN 0-8181-0044-3). Pageant-Poseidon.
Long Shadows. Laurence Snelling. LC 75-37526. 7.95 (ISBN 0-393-08738-7). Norton.
Long Shadows. Grace E. Thompson. LC 29-19456. International Fiction Library.
Long Ships: A Saga of the Viking Age. Frans Gunnar Bengtsson. LC 54-8763. (Illus.). 1954. Knopf.
Long Short Cut. Andrew Garve. 1968. 4.95 o.p. (ISBN 0-06-011451-7, HarpT). Har-Row.
Long Short Cut. Paul Winterton. LC 68-15982. 1968. Harper & Row.
Long Shot. Paul Monette. LC 80-69609. 5.95 (ISBN 0-380-76828-3). Avon Books.
Long Shot for Rosinante. Alexis A. Gilliland. 192p. 1981. pap. 2.25 (ISBN 0-345-29854-3, Del Rey). Ballantine.
Long Shots. Edwin Corley. LC 80-1089. 1981. 13.95 (ISBN 0-385-15922-6). Doubleday.
Long Shots. Leslie Winter. 300p. 1980. 9.95 o.p. (ISBN 0-440-05390-0). Delacorte.
Long Shots. Leslie Winter. (O.s.i.). 1980. 9.95 o.s.i. (ISBN 0-8037-5390-X). Dial.
Long Silence. Alan White. 1977. 7.95 o.p. (ISBN 0-442-80592-6). Van Nos Reinhold.
Long Silence: A Novel. Alan White. LC 77-22274. 1977. 7.95 (ISBN 0-88405-592-2). Mason/Charter.
Long Skeleton. Frances Louise Davis Lockridge & Richard Lockridge. 1975. Repr. of 1958 ed. lib. bdg. 12.05x (ISBN 0-89190-909-5). Am Repr-Rivercity Pr.
Long Skeleton: A Mr. & Mrs. North Mystery. Frances Louise Davis Lockridge & Richard Lockridge. LC 81-3105. 1981. 11.95 (ISBN 0-89340-344-X). J. Curley & Associates.
Long Skeleton: A Mr. and Mrs. North Mystery, by Frances and Richard Lockridge. 1st Ed. Frances Louise Davis Lockridge & Richard Lockridge. LC 58-690585. (Main line mysteries). 1958. Lippincott.
Long Spoon. Charles Bryce. LC 17-233415. 1917. 1.10. John Lane.
Long Storm. Ernest Haycox. LC 46-5157. 1946. Little, Brown and Company.
Long Storm. Ernest Haycox. (Signet, Y5525). 1973. (pbk.) 1.25. New American Lib.
Long Straight Road. George Horton. LC 2-21582. 1902. The Bowen-Merrill Company.
Long Summer. Alan White. LC 75-17601. 1975. 6.95 (ISBN 0-15-153079-3). Harcourt Brace Jovanovich.
Long Summer Day. Ronald Frederick Delderfield. LC 67-20800. 1974. (pbk.) 1.50 (ISBN 0-671-78672-5). Pocket Books.
Long Summer of George Adams. 1st Ed. Weldon Hill, pseud. LC 61-127518. 1961. D. McKay Co.
Long Sweetening: A Romance of the Red Woods. Grant Carpenter. LC 21-19768. 1921. R. M. McBride & Company.
Long Swim. Richard C Angell. LC 47-159594. 1947. G. P. Putnam's Sons.
Long Tails and Short. Gladys Bagg Taber & Dennis, Morgan, 1891- Illus. LC 33-35022. 1938. Macrae-Smith Company.
Long Talking Bad Conditions Blues. Ronald Sukenick. LC 79-52030. 9.95 (ISBN 0-914590-60-X) (ISBN 0-914590-61-8). Fiction Collective: Distributed by G. Braziller.
Long the Imperial Way. Hanama Tasaki. LC 72-104259. 1970. Greenwood Press.
Long, the Short & the All. Rajneesh. 1979. text ed. 11.50 (ISBN 0-89684-069-7, Pub. by Motilal Banarsidass Delhi); pap. text ed. 5.95 o.s.i. (ISBN 0-89684-064-6). Orient Bk Dist.
Long Thrill. Olga Rosmanith. LC 54-417125. (Lion book, 200). 1954. Lion Books by Arrangement with Prime Publications.
Long Time Ago. Margaret Kennedy. LC 32-310393. 1932. Doubleday, Doran & Company, Inc.
Long Time Ago: In Virginia and Maryland with a Glimpse of Old England. Alice Maude Ewell. LC 7-269575. 1907. The Neale Publishing Company.
Long Time Coming & a Long Time Gone. Richard Farina. LC 69-16409. (Illus.). 1969. 4.95 o.p. (ISBN 0-394-43396-3). Random.
Long Time No See. Ed McBain. 1977. 7.95 o.p. (ISBN 0-394-40293-6). Random.
Long Time No See: An 87th Precinct Mystery. Evan Hunter. LC 76-53534. 7.95 (ISBN 0-394-40293-6). Random House.
Long Time No See: 87th Precinct Mystery. Ed McBain. 1982. pap. 2.50 (ISBN 0-553-23130-8). Bantam.
Long Time Since Morning. Leon Odell Griffith. LC 54-7589. 1954. Random House.
Long Time Sleeping. Michael Sinclair. LC 76-10140. 1976. 6.95 (ISBN 0-393-08739-5). Norton.
Long Time to Hate. Willo Davis Roberts. 240p. (Orig.). 1982. pap. 2.50 (ISBN 0-380-79319-9, 79319). Avon.
Long Tomorrow. Leigh Brackett. LC 55-9983. 1974. (pbk.) 1.25 (ISBN 0-345-24289-0). Ballantine Books.
Long Tomorrow. Evelyn Voss Wise. LC 38-83429. 1938. D. Appleton-Century Company, Incorporated.
Long Tomorrow. 1st Ed. Leigh Brackett. LC 55-9983. (Doubleday science fiction). 1955. Doubleday.
Long Trail see Collected Works.
Long Trail Back. 1st Ed. Willis Todhunter Ballard. LC 60-867933. (Double D western). 1960. Doubleday.
Long Trail North. Kelly P Gast. LC 76-2993. 1976. 5.95 (ISBN 0-385-11501-6). Doubleday.
Long Trail to Devil's Pass. Lester Wayne Merha. (YA) 1978. 6.95 (Avalon). Bouregy.
Long Trail. 1st Ed. Arthur Henry Gooden. LC 52-7792. (Dutton Diamond D western). 1952. Dutton.
Long Traverse. Kathrene Sutherland Gedney Pinkerton & Pinkerton, Robert Eugene, 1882- Joint Author. LC 20-128113. 1920. Doubleday, Page & Company.
Long Trick. Lewis Anselin da Costa Ricci. LC 18-534. George H. Doran Company.
Long Trip Home & Other Short Stories. Charles F. Flowers. 1978. 4.95 o.p. Vantage.
Long Trip to Teatime. Anthony Burgess & Fulvio Testa. LC 76-56930. (Illus.). 8.95 (ISBN 0-88373-063-4). Stonehill Pub. Co.
Long Tunnel. Sidney Herbert Daukes. LC 36-1302. 1936. Doubleday, Doran & Co., Inc.
Long Twilight. Keith Laumer. LC 73-95237. 1969. 4.95. Putnam.
Long Vacation. Charlotte Mary Yonge. LC 9-1212. 1895. Macmillan and Co.
Long Valley. John Steinbeck. LC 38-27754. 1938. The Viking Press.
Long Valley... John Steinbeck. LC 46-3358. (New Avon library. 77). 1945.
Long View. Elizabeth Jane Howard. LC 56-7603. 1956. Reynal & Co.
Long View. Hilda Morris. LC 37-22639. 1937. G. P. Putnam's Sons.
Long View: The Final Volume in the Saga of Rissa. F. M Busby. LC 76-28472. 7.95 (ISBN 0-399-11875-6). Berkley Pub. Corp.: Distributed by Putnam.
Long Voyage Back. Luke Rhinehart. 416p. 1983. 15.95 (ISBN 0-440-04617-3). Delacorte.
Long Wait. Frank Morrison Spillane. LC 51-13576. (Guilt edged mystery). 1951. Dutton.
Long Walk. Richard Bachman. 1979. pap. 1.95 (ISBN 0-451-08754-2, J8754, Sig). NAL.
Long Walk. 1st. ed. Betsey Barton. LC 48-6225. 1948. Duel, Sloan and Pearce.
Long Walk Home from Town. David Duncan. LC 64-11281. 1964. Doubleday.
Long Walk of Samba Diouf. Jerome Thoraud & Tharaud, Jean, 1877- Joint Author. LC 24-6233. 1924. Duffield and Company.
Long Watch. Robert F Mirvish. LC 54-8069. 1954. W. Sloane Associates.
Long Watch. Alan White. LC 70-142100. 1971. (ISBN 0-15-152995-7). Harcourt Brace Jovanovich.
Long Watch: A Novel. Elizabeth Linington. LC 56-8563. 1956. Viking Press.
Long Way. Mary Imlay Taylor. LC 13-109892. 1913. Little, Brown and Company.
Long Way. Phyllis Yahnke. LC 54-131188. 1954. Arcadia House.
Long Way Back: 1st American Ed. Margot Bennett. LC 55-6515. 1955. Coward-McCann.
Long Way Down. Elizabeth Fenwick. LC 58-124769. 1959. Harper.
Long Way Down. Collin Wilcox. LC 73-20602. 1974. 4.95 (ISBN 0-394-48681-1). Random House.
Long Way Down. Collin Wilcox. 1979. 1.75 (ISBN 0-515-05195-0). Jove Publications.
Long Way Down: A Novel. Douglas Hall. LC 76-146575. 1971. 3.95. Zondervan Pub. House.
Long Way from Home. W. Cotter Murray. 1974. 5.95 o.p. (ISBN 0-395-18326-X). HM.
Long Way from Home. Desmond O'Grady. LC 66-18017. 1966. Cheshire.
Long Way from Home. Maureen C. Wartski. 1982. pap. 1.75 (ISBN 0-451-11434-5, AE1434, Vista). NAL.
Long Way from Home: A Novel. William Cotter Murray. LC 73-19890. 1974. 5.95 (ISBN 0-395-18326-X). Houghton Mifflin.
Long Way from Home: And Other Stories. Vern J Sneider. LC 56-6495. 1956. Putnam.
Long Way Home. Isabella Alden. LC 12-20629. 1912. Lothrop, Lee & Shepard Co.
Long Way Home. Poul Anderson. LC 78-561. (Gregg Press Science Fiction Series). (Worlds of Poul Anderson; 4). 1978. 8.50 (ISBN 0-8398-2431-9). Gregg Press.
Long Way Home. Sylvia Chatfield Bates. LC 37-30985. Harcourt, Barce and Company.
Long Way Home. Edith Snyder Pedersen. LC 42-12314. 1942. Wm. B. Eerdmans Publishing Company.
Long Way Home. Lisa St. Aubin de Teran. LC 82-48149. (Fiction Ser.). 192p. 1983. 12.45i (ISBN 0-06-015124-2, HarpT). Har-Row.
Long Way Home. St Aubin De Teran, Lisa. LC 82-48149. 1983. 12.95 (ISBN 0-06-015124-2). Harper & Row.
Long Way North. 1st Ed. Jim Bosworth. LC 59-13015. (Double D western). 1959. Doubleday.
Long Way Round. Leonard Levitt. LC 72-79055. 1972. 5.95 (ISBN 0-8415-0188-2). Saturday Review Press.
Long Way Round. Emerson Gifford Taylor. LC 21-471335. Small, Maynard & Company.
Long Way Through. James Ballard. LC 59-131072. 1959. Houghton Mifflin.
Long Way to Frisco: A Fold Adventure Novel of California and Oregon in 1852. Alfred Powers. LC 51-4263. 1951. Little, Brown.
Long Way to Go. Borden Deal. LC 65-19940. 4.50. Doubleday.
Long Way to Texas. Lee McElroy. LC 76-2786. 1976. 5.95 (ISBN 0-385-12128-8). Doubleday.
Long Way to Texas. Lee McElroy. 1979. 1.50 (ISBN 0-440-14639-9). Dell Publishing Co.
Long Week. Allan E Juenger. LC 66-135856. 3.00. Dorrance.
Long Week End. Harlow Estes. LC 41-197170. 1941. Dodd, Mead & Company.
Long West Trail. Herbert Arthur. LC 48-4964. 1948. Phoenix Press.
Long Whip. Eugene Campbell. LC 34-4195. 1934. C. Scribner's Sons.
Long Whip. John Hicks. LC 69-20207. 1969. 5.95. D. McKay Co.
Long White Cloud. Ray Mount Rogers. LC 60-6669. 1960. Dodd, Mead.
Long White Con. Robert Beck. (Orig.). 1977. pap. 2.25 (ISBN 0-87067-030-1, BH030). Holloway.
Long White Night. Katharine Scherman. LC 64-18783. 1964. Little, Brown.
Long Will: A Romance. Florence Converse. 1903. Houghton, Mifflin and Company.
Long Will: A Romance. Florence Converse. (Half-title: Everyman's library, ed. by Ernest Rhys. Fiction no. 328). 1908. J. M. Dent & Co.
Long Wind: By Joseph Wayne Pseud. 1st Ed.lNew York. 1953. ed. Wayne D Overholser. LC 52-129447. (Dutton Diamond D western).
Long Window. John Morton Eshleman. LC 53-1113. 1953. I. Washburn.
Long Wing: A Novel. Elizabeth Fenwick. LC 47-120518. 1947. Rinehart & Company, Inc.
Long Winter. John Christopher. LC 62-124112. 1962. Simon and Schuster.
Long Winter Ends. Newton George Thomas. LC 41-164944. 1941. The Macmillan Company.
Long Winters Night. Sondra Stanford. 192p. 1981. pap. 1.50 (ISBN 0-671-57058-7, Pub. by Silhouette Bks). S&S.
Long Wire. Barry Cord. 1978. pap. 1.25 o.s.i. (ISBN 0-505-51238-6). Tower Bks.
Long Year. Ann Chidester. LC 74-26097. (Labor Movement in Fiction and Non-Fiction). 1976. 21.50 (ISBN 0-404-58411-X). AMS Press.
Long Year. Ann Chidester. LC 46-3407. 1946. C. Scribner's Sons.
Long Yesterday. Nathan Starr. 64p. 1972. 3.00 o.s.i. (ISBN 0-87233-024-9). Bauhan.
Longarm. Tabor Evans. LC 78-60772. (Jove / HBJ book). 1978. 1.50 (ISBN 0-515-04750-3). Jove Pubns.
Longarm, 5 vols. Incl. No. 1. Longarm; No. 2. Longarm on the Border; No. 3. Longarm & the Avenging Angels; No. 4. Longarm & the Wendigo; No. 5. Longarm & the Indian Nation. Date not set. pap. 11.25 boxed set (ISBN 0-515-06815-2). Jove Pubns.
Longarm see Longarm.
Longarm & the Avenging Angels, No. 3. Tabor Evans, pseud. 1978. pap. 1.95 (ISBN 0-515-05899-8, 04791-0). Jove Pubns.

Longarm & the Avenging Angels see Longarm.
Longarm & the Blue Norther. Tabor Evans, pseud. 1981. pap. 1.95 (ISBN 0-515-05592-1). Jove Pubns.
Longarm & the Boot Hillers. Tabor Evans, pseud. (Longarm Ser.: No. 34). 208p. (Orig.). 1981. pap. 1.95 (ISBN 0-515-05590-5). Jove Pubns.
Longarm & the Buckskin Rogue, No. 53. Tabor Evans. 192p. pap. 2.25 (ISBN 0-515-06254-5). Jove Pubns.
Longarm & the Calico Kid. Tabor Evans, pseud. 192p. 1983. pap. 2.25 (ISBN 0-515-06255-3). Jove Pubns.
Longarm & the Comancheros. Tabor Evans, pseud. (Longarm Ser.: No. 17). 240p. (Orig.). 1981. pap. 1.95 (ISBN 0-515-05595-6). Jove Pubns.
Longarm & the Devil's Railroad. Tabor Evans, pseud. (Longarm Ser.: No. 39). (Orig.). 1981. pap. 1.95 (ISBN 0-515-05594-8). Jove Pubns.
Longarm & the Dragon Hunters. Tabor Evans, pseud. (Longarm Ser.: No. 26). 255p. (Orig.). 1980. pap. 1.95 (ISBN 0-515-06103-4). Jove Pubns.
Longarm & the Eastern Dudes, No. 49. Tabor Evans, pseud. 192p. 1982. pap. 2.25 (ISBN 0-515-06250-2). Jove Pubns.
Longarm & the French Actress, No. 55. Tabor Evans, pseud. 192p. 1983. pap. 2.25 (ISBN 0-515-06256-1). Jove Pubns.
Longarm & the Ghost Dancers. Tabor Evans, pseud. (Longarm Ser.: No. 22). 223p. (Orig.). 1980. pap. 1.75 (ISBN 0-515-05314-7). Jove Pubns.
Longarm & the Golden Lady. Tabor Evans, pseud. (Longarm Ser.: No. 32). (Orig.). 1981. pap. 1.95 (ISBN 0-515-05588-3). Jove Pubns.
Longarm & the Great Train Robbery. Tabor Evans, pseud. (Longarm Ser.). 192p. 1982. pap. 2.25 (ISBN 0-515-05602-2). Jove Pubns.
Longarm & the Hatchet Men, No. 9. Tabor Evans, pseud. 1979. pap. 1.95 (ISBN 0-515-05973-0). Jove Pubns.
Longarm and the Highgraders. Tabor Evans, pseud. LC 78-70788. 1979. 1.75 (ISBN 0-515-04752-X). Jove/HBJ.
Longarm & the Highgraders: No. 7. Tabor Evans, pseud. (Orig.). 1979. pap. 1.95 (ISBN 0-515-05901-3). Jove Pubns.
Longarm & the Indian Nation see Longarm.
Longarm & the Laredo Loop. Tabor Evans, pseud. (Longarm Ser.: No. 33). 224p. (Orig.). 1981. pap. 1.95 (ISBN 0-515-05589-1). Jove Pubns.
Longarm & the Loggers, No. 6. Tabor Evans, pseud. (Orig.). 1979. pap. 1.95 (ISBN 0-515-05900-5). Jove Pubns.
Longarm & the Lone Star Legend. Tabor Evans, pseud. 1982. pap. 2.75 (ISBN 0-515-06225-1). Jove Pubns.
Longarm & the Moonshiners. Tabor Evans, pseud. (Long Arm Ser.: No. 42). 192p. (Orig.). 1982. pap. 1.95 (ISBN 0-515-05598-0). Jove Pubns.
Longarm & the Mounties. Tabor Evans, pseud. (Longarm Ser.: No. 16). 252p. (Orig.). 1980. pap. 1.95 (ISBN 0-515-06104-2). Jove Pubns.
Longarm & the Nesters: No. 8. Tabor Evans, pseud. (Orig.). 1979. pap. 1.95 (ISBN 0-515-05985-4). Jove Pubns.
Longarm & the Railroaders. Tabor Evans, pseud. (Longarm Ser.: No. 24). 252p. (Orig.). 1980. pap. 1.75 (ISBN 0-515-05316-3). Jove Pubns.
Longarm & the Rurales. Tabor Evans, pseud. (Longarm Ser.: No. 27). (Orig.). pap. 1.75 (ISBN 0-515-05583-2). Jove Pubns.
Longarm & the Sheepherders. Tabor Evans, pseud. (Longarm Ser.: No. 21). 256p. (Orig.). 1980. pap. 1.95 (ISBN 0-515-05906-4). Jove Pubns.
Longarm & the Snake Dancers. Tabor Evans, pseud. (Longarm Ser.: No. 51). 192p. 1983. pap. 2.25 (ISBN 0-515-06252-9). Jove Pubns.
Longarm & the Stalking Corpse. Tabor Evans, pseud. (Longarm Ser.: No. 37). (Orig.). 1981. pap. 1.95 (ISBN 0-515-05593-X). Jove Pubns.
Longarm & the Texas Rangers. Tabor Evans, pseud. (Longarm Ser.: No. 11). (Orig.). 1979. pap. 1.95 (ISBN 0-515-05902-1). Jove Pubns.
Longarm & the Town Tamer. Tabor Evans, pseud. (Longarm Ser.: No. 23). 269p. (Orig.). 1980. pap. 1.95 (ISBN 0-515-05999-4). Jove Pubns.
Longarm & the Wendigo. Tabor Evans, pseud. (Longarm Ser.: No. 4). 256p. (Orig.). 1979. pap. 1.95 (ISBN 0-515-05972-2). Jove Pubns.
Longarm & the Wendigo see Longarm.
Longarm at Robber's Roost. Tabor Evans, pseud. (Longarm Ser.: No. 20). 256p. (Orig.). 1980. pap. 1.95 (ISBN 0-515-05931-5). Jove Pubns.
Longarm in Boulder Canyon. Tabor Evans, pseud. (Longarm Ser.: No. 44). (Orig.). 1982. pap. 2.25 (ISBN 0-515-05600-6). Jove Pubns.
Longarm in Deadwood. Tabor Evans, pseud. (Longarm Ser.: No. 43). (Orig.). 1982. pap. 2.25 (ISBN 0-515-05601-4). Jove Pubns.
Longarm in Leadville. Tabor Evans, pseud. (Longarm Ser.: No. 14). (Orig.). 1979. pap. 1.95 (ISBN 0-515-06070-4). Jove Pubns.
Longarm in Lincoln County. Tabor Evans, pseud. (Longarm Ser.: No. 12). 254p. (Orig.). 1979. pap. 1.95 (ISBN 0-515-05903-X). Jove Pubns.
Longarm in Northfield. Tabor Evans, pseud. (Longarm Ser.: No. 31). 208p. (Orig.). 1981. pap. 1.95 (ISBN 0-515-05586-7). Jove Pubns.
Longarm in Silver City. Tabor Evans, pseud. (Longarms Ser.: No. 40). 192p. (Orig.). 1982. pap. 2.25 (ISBN 0-515-05596-4). Jove Pubns.
Longarm in the Badlands, No. 47. Tabor Evans, pseud. 192p. 1982. pap. 2.25 (ISBN 0-515-05603-0). Jove Pubns.
Longarm in the Big Bend. Tabor Evans, pseud. (Longarm Ser.: No. 50). 192p. 1982. pap. 2.25 (ISBN 0-515-06251-0). Jove Pubns.
Longarm in the Big Thicket, No. 48. Tabor Evans, pseud. 192p. (Orig.). 1982. pap. 2.25 (ISBN 0-515-05604-9). Jove Pubns.
Longarm in the Four Corners. Tabor Evans, pseud. (Longarm Ser.: No. 19). 224p. (Orig.). 1980. pap. 1.95 (ISBN 0-515-05905-6). Jove Pubns.
Longarm in the Indian Nation. Tabor Evans, pseud. (Longarm Ser.: N0. 5). 272p. (Orig.). 1979. pap. 1.95 (ISBN 0-515-06063-1). Jove Pubns.
Longarm in the Sand Hills. Tabor Evans, pseud. (Longarm Ser.: No. 13). (Orig.). 1979. pap. 1.75 (ISBN 0-515-05305-8). Jove Pubns.
Longarm on the Barbary Coast. Tabor Evans, pseud. (Longarm Ser.: No. 41). 192p. (Orig.). 1982. pap. 1.95 (ISBN 0-515-05597-2). Jove Pubns.
Longarm on the Big Muddy. Tabor Evans, pseud. (Longarm Ser.: No. 29). 224p. (Orig.). 1981. pap. 1.95 (ISBN 0-515-05585-9). Jove Pubns.
Longarm on the Border see Longarm.
Longarm on the Border: No. 2. Tabor Evans, pseud. (Orig.). 1978. pap. 1.95 (ISBN 0-515-05378-3). Jove Pubns.
Longarm on the Devil's Trail. Tabor Evans, pseud. (Longarm Ser.: No. 15). 224p. (Orig.). 1979. pap. 1.95 (ISBN 0-515-05904-8). Jove Pubns.
Longarm on the Great Divide, No. 52. Tabor Evans, pseud. 192p. 1983. pap. 2.25 (ISBN 0-515-06253-7). Jove Pubns.
Longarm on the Humboldt. Tabor Evans, pseud. (Longarm Ser.: No. 28). 256p. (Orig.). 1981. pap. 1.95 (ISBN 0-515-05584-0). Jove Pubns.
Longarm on the Old Mission Trail. Tabor Evans, pseud. (Longarm Ser.: No. 25). 253p. (Orig.). 1980. pap. 1.95 (ISBN 0-515-05974-9). Jove Pubns.
Longarm on the Santa Fe. Tabor Evans, pseud. (Longarm Ser.: No.36). 256p. (Orig.). 1981. pap. 1.95 (ISBN 0-515-05591-3). Jove Pubns.
Longarm on the Yellowstone. Tabor Evans, pseud. (Longarm Ser.: No. 18). 256p. (Orig.). 1980. pap. 1.75 (ISBN 0-515-05310-4). Jove Pubns.
Longarm South of the Gila. Tabor Evans, pseud. (Longarm Ser.; Men's Western Ser.: No. 30). 256p. (Orig.). 1981. pap. 1.95 (ISBN 0-515-05587-5). Jove Pubns.
Longbow Murder. Victor Luhrs. LC 41-537496. W. W. Norton & Company, Inc.
Longcove Doings. Joseph Kennard Wilson. LC 18-27054. United Society of Christian Endeavor.
Longdens. David Rinaldo Compton. LC 24-74781. Dorrance & Company.
Longer. Otto Friedrich. LC 64-17845. 1964. Crown Publishers.
Longer Day. LC 30-31028. The Bobbs-Merrill Company.
Longer the Thread. Emma Lathan. 1980. pap. 2.75. PB.
Longer the Thread. Emma Lathen, pseud. LC 72-163102. (Inner sanctum mystery). 1971. 5.95 (ISBN 0-671-21113-7). Simon and Schuster.
Longer the Thread. Emma Lathen. (Inner Sanctum Mystery). 1973. (pbk.) 0.95. Pocket Books.
Longest Cocktail Party. Richard DiLello. LC 72-85965. 296p. 1974. pap. 2.95 (ISBN 0-87216-889-1). Playboy Pbks.
Longest Day. William Canfield Emerson. LC 65-19328. 1966. Dorrance.
Longest Day. Cornelius Ryan. 352p. 1975. pap. 2.95 (ISBN 0-445-08380-8). Popular Lib.
Longest Journey. Edward Morgan Forster. LC 22-133225. 1922. A. A. Knopf.
Longest Journey. Edward Morgan Forster. (New classics series). 1943. New Directions.
Longest Mile. Rena Gazaway. 1974. pap. 2.25 o.p. (ISBN 0-14-003814-0). Penguin.
Longest Night. Ada Cook Lewis. LC 58-724522. 1958. Rinehart.
Longest Night: A Novel. Kenneth O'Donnell Horan. LC 32-31722. 1932. D. C. Doran.
Longest Second. William Sanborn Ballinger. LC 57-11792. 1957. Harper.
Longest Shadow. Jeffery Eardley Marston. LC 27-3172. 1927. Little, Brown, and Company.
Longest Voyage. Robert Silverberg. LC 69-13089. (Illus.). 1972. 10.00 o.p. (ISBN 0-672-50741-2). Bobbs.
Longest Way Round. Marguerite Mooers Marshall. LC 51-9184. 1951. Macrae Smith.
Longhorn Brand. Wade Hamilton, pseud. 1978. pap. 1.25 o.s.i. (ISBN 0-505-51248-3). Tower Bks.
Longhorn Brand: By Wade Hamilton Pseud. Lee Floren. LC 52-8356. 1952. Arcadia House.
Longhorn Empire. Harry Sinclair Drago. LC 53-5050. (Double D western). 1953. Doubleday.
Longhorn Empire. Leslie Scott. LC 54-13357. 1954. Arcadia House.
Longhorn Feud. Max Brand. LC 33-16248. 1933. Dodd, Mead & Company.
Longhorn Feud. Frederick Faust. LC 33-16248. 1933. Dodd, Mead & Company.
Longhorn Feud. Frederick Faust. LC 41-4622. 1940. Triangle Books.
Longhorn Law. T. W. Ford. LC 48-2088. 1948. Phoenix Press.
Longhorn Stampede: A Western Novel. Philip Ketchum. LC 56-261741. (Popular Library eagle book, EB57). 1956.
Longhorn Trail. Hamilton Craigie. LC 32-2874. E. J. Clode, Inc.
Longhorn Trail. Donald B. Hobart. (Orig.). 1970. pap. 0.60 o.p. (06116). Curtis.
Longhorn Trail: By Richard Wormser and Dan Gordon. Richard Edward Wormser & Dnu Gordon. LC 55-26936. (Ace double novel books, D-92). 1955. Ace Books.
Longhorns of Hate. Frank Chester Robertson. LC 49-2095. (Dutton Diamond D western). 1949. E. P. Dutton.
Longing for Darkness: Kamante's Tales from Out of Africa. Ed. by Peter Beard. LC 74-19092. (Illus.). 242p. 1975. 19.95 o.p. (ISBN 0-15-153080-7). HarBraceJ.
Longings. Sylvia W. Greene. 352p. (Orig.). 1981. pap. 2.50 (ISBN 0-89083-706-6). Zebra.
Longleaf. Rose Brock, pseud. LC 72-9166. (Illus.). 1974. 6.95 (ISBN 0-06-010482-1). Harper & Row.
Long,Long Trail. Max Brand. (Adult Ser.). 1975. Repr. lib. bdg. 11.95 o.p. (ISBN 0-8161-6326-X, Large Print Bks). G K Hall.
Longrider. Johanas L. Bouma. (Leisure book). 1.50 (ISBN 0-8439-0597-2). Nordon Pubns.
Longs Peak: Its Story & a Climbing Guide. 8th ed. Paul W. Nesbit. (Illus.). 1972. 1.50 o.p. (ISBN 0-911746-02-1). Nesbit.
Longs Peak Tales. Randall. (Illus.). 93p. 1981. pap. 4.95 (ISBN 0-937050-20-2). Stonehenge.
Longshadow: And Nine Stories Tr. from Italian. Mauro Senesi. LC 65-269115. 4.50. Regnery.
Longstreet Legacy. Douglas Ashe. Orig. Title: Shroud for Grandmama. 1970. pap. 0.75 o.p. (ISBN 0-446-64322-X, 64-322). Paperback Lib.
Longsword. Victoria Thorne. LC 81-23220. 11.50 (ISBN 0-312-49679-6). St. Martin's Press.
Longsword, Earl of Salisbury. Thomas Leland & John Leland. LC 74-16058. (Flowering of the Novel). (Illus.). 1974. (ISBN 0-8240-1159-7). Garland Pub.
Longsword, Earl of Salisbury: An Historical Romance. Thomas Leland & John Leland. LC 75-1590. (Gothic Novels). (Illus.). 1974. (ISBN 0-405-06016-5). Arno Press.
Lonz Powers or, The Regulators. A Romance of Kentucky. Founded on Facts. James Weir. LC 9-2686. 1850. Lippincott, Grambo & Co.
Loo Sanction. Trevanian. LC 73-82951. 1973. 6.95 (ISBN 0-517-50610-6). Crown Publishers.
Loo Sanction. Trevanian. 1974. (pbk.) 1.75 (ISBN 0-380-00175-6). Avon.
Look Alive. Miles Burton. 1979. 11.00x (ISBN 0-86025-119-5, Pub. Ian Henry Pubns England). State Mutual Bk.
Look Alive. 1st American Ed. Miles Burton. LC 50-6595. 1950. Published for the Crime Club by Doubleday.
Look at All Those Roses. Elizabeth Bowen. LC 41-13225. A. A. Knopf,
Look at Home: Or, Life in the Poor-Houses of New England... new and rev. ed. Samuel Hayes Elliot. LC 6-37259. 1860. H. Dexter & Company.
Look at Me. Anita Brookner. LC 82-18968. 1983. 12.95 (ISBN 0-394-52944-8). Pantheon Books.
Look at the Harlequins! Vladimir Vladimirovich Nabokov. LC 74-10677. 1974. 7.95 (ISBN 0-07-045738-7). McGraw-Hill.
Look Away! George Nauman Shuster. LC 39-24723. 1939. The Macmillan Company.
Look Away, Beulah Land. Lonnie Coleman. (Dell book). 1979. 2.50 (ISBN 0-440-14642-9). Dell Pub. Co.
Look Away, Beulah Land: A Novel. William Laurence Coleman. LC 76-50759. 1977. 10.95 (ISBN 0-385-12826-6). Doubleday.
Look Away, Look Away. Ben Haas. (O.S.I.). 1964. 5.95 o.s.i. (42790). S&S.
Look Away, Look Away. Leslie Turner White. LC 44-702. 1943. Random House.
Look Away, Look Away: A Novel. Haas, Ben. LC 64-19934.
Look Back in Anger. John Jay Osborn. LC 57-9161. 1957. 7.95 o.s.i. (ISBN 0-87599-081-9). S G Phillips.
Look Back in Joy: A Celebration of Gay Lovers. Malcolm Boyd. (Illus.). 128p. (Orig.). 1981. 20.00 (ISBN 0-917342-85-2); pap. 6.95 (ISBN 0-917342-77-1). Gay Sunshine.
Look Back in Love. Edith F. Elliot. (Illus., Orig.). 1979. pap. 6.95 (ISBN 0-9602232-1-5). Gemaia Pr.
Look Back, Mrs. Lot. Ephraim Kishon. (YA) 1961. 4.50 o.p. Atheneum.
Look Back on Death. Lesley Egan, pseud. LC 77-27725. 1978. 7.95 o.p. (ISBN 0-385-14303-6). Doubleday.
Look Back on Death. new large print ed. Lesley Egan, pseud. LC 80-28019. 1981. Repr. of 1978 ed. 9.95x (ISBN 0-89621-267-X). Thorndike Pr.
Look Back on Death. Elizabeth Linington. LC 77-27725. 1978. 7.95 (ISBN 0-385-14303-6). Published for the Crime Club by Doubleday.
Look Back on Death. Elizabeth Linington. LC 80-28019. 9.95 (ISBN 0-89621-267-X). Thorndike Press.
Look Back on Happiness. Knut Hamsun & Wiking, Paula, Tr. LC 40-7240. Coward-McCann, Inc.
Look Back on Murder. doris miles disney. ed. Doris Miles Disney. 1.75. Ace Books.
Look Back on Murder. 1st Ed. Doris Miles Disney. LC 51-1624. 1951. Publishedfor the Crime Club by Doubleday.
Look Back to Earth. Don Pfeil. 1977. pap. 1.50 (ISBN 0-532-15299-9). Woodhill.
Look Back to Glory. Herbert Ravenel Sass. LC 33-31889. The Bobbs-Merrill Company.
Look Before You Leap. A Novel. Annie French Hector. (On cover: Seaside library. Pocket ed., no. 797). 1886. G. Munro.
Look Before You Love. Florence Stonebraker. LC 47-250332. 1947. Gramercy Pub. Co.
Look Behind You. Jay Barbette, pseud. LC 60-6171. (Red badge detective). 1960. Dodd, Mead.
Look Behind You, Lady. Wetherby Williams. LC 52-10999. 1952. Published for the Crime Club by Doubleday.
Look Behind You, Lady see Death of Our Dear One.
Look Cast Backward. Stephen D. Radford. 1970. 4.95 o.p. Vantage.
Look Down from Heaven: A Novel. Naomi Lane Babson. LC 42-20275. 1942. Reynal & Hitchcock.
Look Down in Mercy. Walter Baxter. LC 52-5265. 1952. Putnam.
Look Down, Look Down. Arthur Moore. 1977. pap. 1.50 (ISBN 0-532-15256-5). Woodhill.
Look for the Body. Matthew F Christopher. LC 52-7414. 1952. Phoenix Press.
Look Here: J. B.? Jean Cummings. LC 57-8471. 1957. Dorrance.
Look Homeward: A Novel. Rama Sarma, M. V. LC 77-902053. 1976. 5.00. Blackie & Son (India)
Look Homeward Angel. Thomas Wolfe. 359p. 1981. Repr. lib. bdg. 16.95 (ISBN 0-89966-293-5). Buccaneer Bks.
Look Homeward, Angel. Thomas Wolfe. 1979. 17.50 o.p. (ISBN 0-684-10678-7, ScribT). Scribner.
Look Homeward, Angel: A Story of the Buried Life. Thomas Wolfe. LC 52-10259. (Modern standard authors). (Illus.). 1952. Scribner.
Look Homeward, Angel: A Story of the Buried Life. Thomas Wolfe. LC 29-22336. 1929. C. Scribner's Sons.
Look Homeward, Angel: A Story of the Buried Life. Thomas Wolfe. LC 30-152164. 1930. C. Scribner's Sons.
Look Homeward, Angel: A Story of the Buried Life. Thomas Wolfe. LC 33-28342. 1931. C. Scribner's Sons.
Look Homeward, Angel: A Story of the Buried Life. Thomas Wolfe. LC 34-284367. (Half-title: The modern library of the world's best books). 1934. The Modern Library.
Look Homeward, Angel: II. The Adventures of Young Gant. Thomas Wolfe. LC 49-2901. (N. A. L. Signet books, 697). 1948. New American Library.
Look How the Fish Live. James Farl Powers. LC 75-8237. 1975. 6.95 (ISBN 0-394-49608-6). Knopf.
Look into Happiness. Roswell Gray Ham. LC 62-10968. 1962. Putnam.
Look into the Blue Tide, Pt. 2. Diter Rot. (Great Bear Pamphlets: No. 14). 1967. pap. 2.50 o.p. (ISBN 0-89366-079-5). Ultramarine Pub.
Look, Listen, and Love. Barbara Cartland. LC 77-670156. 1977. 6.95 (ISBN 0-87272-066-7). Duron Books.
Look Not Upon Me, a Novel. Denys Jones. LC 55-9241. Criterion Books.
Look of Eagles. John Taintor Foote. LC 16-17417. 1916. D. Appleton and Company.
Look of Innocence. Anna Gilbert. LC 76-29865. 8.95. St. Martin's Press.
Look of the Eagle. Robert Lee Scott. LC 55-11792. 1955. Dodd, Mead.

TITLE INDEX LORD GEOFFREY'S FANCY.

Look Out for Liza. Faith Baldwin. 1976. Repr. of 1950 ed. lib. bdg. 14.10x (ISBN 0-88411-620-4). Amereon Ltd.
Look Out for Liza. Faith Baldwin Cuthrell. LC 50-1108. 1950. Rinehart.
Look Out for Liza. Faith Baldwin Cuthrell. LC 76-41327. 1976. 6.95. Aeonian Press.
Look Out for Liza. Faith Baldwin Cuthrell. 1972. 0.95. Warner Paperback Lib.
Look-Out Girl. Alice Mary Ross Colver. LC 28-56403. The Penn Publishing Company.
Look Over Your Shoulder. Amanda McAllister. LC 76-43399. 1976. 1.50. Playboy Press.
Look Three Ways at Murder. John Creasey. LC 65-12689. 1965. bds., 3.50. Scribners.
Look to Beyond. Barbara Montagu Scott. LC 52-1721. 1951. Hutchinson.
Look to the Blue Horse. Marianne Ruuth. (Avalon romances). 1973. 4.50. Avalon Books.
Look to the Dawn. Julian R Drake. LC 52-6933. 1952. Vantage Press.
Look to the Lady see Margery Allingham Omnibus.
Look to the Lady! A Novel. Joseph L Bonney. LC 47-2489. 1947. J. B. Lippincott Company.
Look to the Mountain. Cannon. LC 43-17756. 1942. H. Holt and Company.
Look to the New Moon. Frances Fullerton Neilson. LC 53-1757. 1953. Abelard Press.
Look to the River. William A Owens. LC 63-7798. 1963. Ahteneum.
Look to the Rose. Shirley Seifert. 1976. Repr. of 1960 ed. lib. bdg. 7.95 (ISBN 0-89190-135-3). Am Repr-Rivercity Pr.
Look to the Rose: A Novel. 1st Ed. Shirley Seifert. LC 60-12220. 1960. Lippincott.
Look to the Sky. Wladyslaw Klekot. LC 46-225526. 1946. The Hobson Book Press.
Look to the Spring. Ruby Mildred Ayres. LC 33-9682.
Look to the Stars. Emilie Baker Loring. Repr. lib. bdg. 11.50x (ISBN 0-88411-371-X). Amereon Ltd.
Look to the Stars. Emilie Baker Loring. 1958. 2.95 o.p. (ISBN 0-448-06319-0). G&D.
Look to the Stars. 1st Ed. Emilie Baker Loring. LC 57-6441. 1957. Little, Brown.
Look to This Day: A Case History of Family Life. Phyllis B Heller. LC 55-12516. Pageant Press.
Look to Your Geese: A Novel of the Deflowering of New England. Jacquin Sanders. LC 60-5271. 1960. Putnam.
Look What Brains Can Do! Anne Benson Fisher. LC 32-11376. 1932. W. T. Lee Co., Inc.
Look What They Done to My Song: A Novel. John McCluskey. LC 74-8654. 1974. 5.95 (ISBN 0-394-48818-0). Random House.
Look Your Last. Dorothy Tillett. LC 43-16718. 1943. Pub. for the Crime Club by Doubleday, Doran & Co., Inc.
Looking After Joan. John Leslie Palmer, pseud. LC 24-130202. 1923. Harcourt, Brace and Company.
Looking Backward. Edward Bellamy. LC 81-21059. 1981. 3.95 (ISBN 0-394-32980-5). Modern Library.
Looking Backward & What I Saw. 2nd ed. W. W. Satterlee. LC 76-154461. (Utopian Literature Ser). 1971. Repr. of 1890 ed. 19.00 (ISBN 0-405-03543-8). Ayer Co.
Looking Backward; Miss Ludington's Sister; & Dr. Heidenhof's Process. Edward Bellamy. 1978. Repr. lib. bdg. 20.00 o.s.i. (ISBN 0-89760-034-7, Telegraph). Dynamic Learn Corp.
Looking Backward, 2000-1887. Edward Bellamy. LC 6-11710. 1888. Ticknor and Company.
Looking Backwards. Sidonie Gabrielle Colette. Tr. by David Le Vay. LC 74-29051. 216p. 1975. 8.95x (ISBN 0-253-14900-2). Ind U Pr.
Looking Beyond. Ludwig A Geissler. LC 6-442557. 1891. L. Graham & Son.
Looking Beyond. Lin Yutang. 387p. 1980. 5.95 (ISBN 0-89955-162-9, Pub. by Mei Ya China); pap. 4.95 (ISBN 0-89955-191-2). Intl Schol Bk Serv.
Looking Down Dark Holes & Climbing Mountains. Thomas Weinberg. (Illus.). 150p. (Orig.). 1979. pap. 6.95 (ISBN 0-9603484-0-9). Gordons & Weinberg.
Looking for a Star. Peggy O'More, pseud. LC 49-491198. 1949. Arcadia House.
Looking for a Wave. John Mill Couper. LC 75-11112. 1975. 6.95 (ISBN 0-87888-085-2). Bradbury Press.
Looking for Baby Paradise. John Speicher. LC 67-11976. 1967. Harcourt, Brace & World.
Looking for Fred Schmidt. Seymour Epstein. LC 72-92205. 1973. 6.95 (ISBN 0-385-05961-2). Doubleday.
Looking for Ginger North. John Dunning. 1.95 (ISBN 0-449-14317-1). Fawcett Gold Medal Books.
Looking for Grace. Horace Tremlett. LC 15-214414. 1915. John Lane.
Looking for Love: Seven Uncommon Love Stories. Peggy Woodford. LC 79-108218. 1979. 7.95 (ISBN 0-385-14784-8). Doubleday.
Looking for Miracles: A Memoir About Loving. A. E Hotchner. LC 73-4091. (Illus.). 1975. 7.95 (ISBN 0-06-011965-9). Harper & Row.
Looking for Miss Right. Allen Goodman. LC 81-85821. 224p. (Orig.). 1982. pap. 2.75 (ISBN 0-86721-109-1). Playboy Pbks.
Looking for Mr. Goodbar. Judith Rossner. LC 75-2317. 1975. 7.95 (ISBN 0-671-22025-X). Simon and Schuster.
Looking for Mr. Goodbar. Judith Rossner. 1976. (pbk.) 1.95 (ISBN 0-671-80409-X). Pocket Books.
Looking for Peace. R. L. Barth. 56p. (Orig.). 1982. pap. 3.25 o.p. (ISBN 0-941150-00-3). Barth.
Looking for Rachel Wallace. Robert B. Parker. 1983. pap. 2.95 (ISBN 0-440-15316-6). Dell.
Looking for Rachel Wallace. Robert S. Parker. (O.s.i.). 1980. 10.95 o.s.i. (ISBN 0-440-04764-1). Delacorte.
Looking for Rachel Wallace: A Spenser Novel. Robert B. Parker. LC 79-20776. 8.95 (ISBN 0-440-04764-1). Delacorte Press/S. Lawrence.
Looking for the General. Warren Miller. LC 63-21785. 1964. McGraw-Hill.
Looking for Tomorrow. JoAnn Pruitt. LC 79-66205. 4.95 (ISBN 0-8054-7311-4) (ISBN 0-8054-7311-4). Broadman Press.
Looking for Trouble: A School Story. William McAndrew. LC 8-1402. C. W. Bardeen.
Looking for Work. Susan Cheever. LC 79-18243. 8.95 (ISBN 0-671-25054-X). Simon and Schuster.
Looking for Work. Susan Cheever. 1981. 2.50 (ISBN 0-449-24389-3). Fawcett Crest Books.
Looking for Zoe. Daniel Boone Dodson. LC 80-16930. 12.95 (ISBN 0-396-07878-8). Dodd, Mead.
Looking Forward. Kenneth S Keyes & Jacque Fresco. LC 68-27189. (Illus.). 1969. 6.00. A. S. Barnes.
Looking Forward. Richard C Michaelis. (On cover: Globe library, v. 1, no. 129?). Rand, McNally & Company.
Looking Forward: An Anthology of Science Fiction. Ed. by Milton Lesser. LC 53-11680. 1953. Beechhurst Press.
Looking Forward: And Others. Booth Tarkington. LC 74-93381. (Essay index reprint series). 1969. Books for Libraries Press.
Looking Forward: Or, The Story of an American Farm. John Rankin Rogers. LC 99-2969. 1898. Spike Publishing Company.
Looking Forward: The Phenomenal Progress of Electricity in 1912. Harry W Hillman. LC 6-45176. 1906. Valley View Publishing Company.
Looking Forward to 1999. Louis Shores. LC 70-190736. 1972. South Pass Press.
Looking Further Backward. Arthur Dudley Vinton. LC 74-154466. (Utopian Literature Ser). 1971. Repr. of 1890 ed. 14.00 (ISBN 0-405-03548-9). Ayer Co.
Looking Further Forward. Richard C Michaelis. (On cover: Globe library, v. 1, no. 129?). 1890. Rand, McNally & Company.
Looking-Glass. William Edwards Campell. LC 43-158. 1943. Little, Brown and Company.
Looking-Glass. Virginia Coffman. (Dell Book.). 1978. Dell Publishing.
Looking-Glass. Minnie Teasdale. LC 13-15521.
Looking-Glass Conference: A Novel. Godfrey Blunden. LC 56-120296. 1956. Vanguard Press.
Looking Glass Heart. Myron Brinig. LC 58-6967. 1958. Sagamore Press.
Looking-Glass Murder. Anthony Gilbert, pseud. 1971. pap. 0.95 o.p. (95183). Beagle Bks.
Looking Glass Murder. Anthony Gilbert, pseud. 1967. 3.95 o.p. Random.
Looking Glass Murder. Lucy Beatrice Malleson. LC 67-12763. (Random House mystery). 1967. Random House.
Looking Glass Murders. Phillips Lore. LC 80-80997. (Phillips Lore Ser.: No. 3). 192p. (Orig.). 1980. pap. 1.95 (ISBN 0-87216-694-5). Playboy Pbks.
Looking Glass War. John Le Carre. LC 65-20401. 1965. Coward-McCann.
Looking Glass War: By John Le Carre Pseud. David John Moore Cornwell. (5024). 1966. Dell.
Looking Glass War: By John Le Carre. Pseud. 1st Amer. Ed. David John Moore Cornwell. LC 65-20401. 4.95. Coward.
Looking in. Ewald W. Schinitzer. LC 77-91620. (Illus.). 1977. pap. 4.95 (ISBN 0-913612-03-0). Strawberry Valley.
Looking on Darkness: A Novel. Andre Philippus Brink. LC 75-4515. 1975. 8.95. Morrow.
Looking Out for No. 1. Robert J. Ringer. 1978. pap. 2.95 (ISBN 0-449-23576-9, Crest). Fawcett.
Looking Out of Jimmie. Helen Hartness Flanders. LC 27-17778. E. P. Dutton & Co.
Looking Seaward. Jennie Maria Drinkwater Conklin. LC 6-30404. A. L. Bradley & Co.
Looking up. Elihu Blotnick. (Illus.). 72p. 1981. pap. 9.95 (ISBN 0-915090-01-5). Calif Street.
Looking up at Leaves. Barbara Howes. 1966. 4.50 o.p. Knopf.
Looking Wayward. Frank Dwyer. 1974. pap. 2.00 (ISBN 0-931848-04-0). Dryad Pr.
Lookout Cartridge. Joseph McElroy. LC 74-7744. 1974. (ISBN 0-394-49375-3). Knopf; Distributed by Random House.
Lookout Man. Bertha Muzzy Sinclair. LC 17-223059. 1917. 1.35. Little, Brown, and Company.
Looks Suspicious to Me. Playboy Press Editors. LC 76-184406. pap. 0.95 o.p. (ISBN 0-87216-160-9, A16160). Playboy.
Loom and the Web. Gibson-Jarvie, Clodagh. LC 79-5202. 1979. 8.95 (ISBN 0-312-49822-5). St. Martin's Press.
Loom O' Life. Josephine Cunnington Edwards. LC 39-30379. Pacific Press Publishing Association.
Loom of Destiny. Arthur John Arbuthnott Stringer. LC 74-103529. (Short story index reprint series). (Illus.). 1969. Books for Libraries Press.
Loom of Justice. Ernst Lothar. Tr. by Muir, Willis. LC 35-7669. 1935. G. P. Putnam's Sons.
Loom of Life. Charles Frederic Goss. 1902. The Bowen-Merrill Company.
Loom of Terror. easy eye ed. Paula Minton, pseud. (Orig.). 1968. pap. 0.75 o.p. (74-950). Lancer.
Loom of the Desert. Idah Meacham Strobridge. LC 8-26152. 1907. Artemisia Bindery.
Loom of the Fool. Austin MacLeod. LC 26-14516. George H. Doran Company.
Loom of the Land. Eleanor R Mayo. LC 46-25273. 1946. W. Morrow and Company.
Loom of Youth. Alec Waugh. LC 20-8276. 1920. George H. Doran Company.
Looming Shadow. Legson Kayira. LC 76-117962. (African/American library). 1970. 1.25. Collier Books.
Looming Shadow. 1st Ed. Legson Kayira. LC 67-15367. 1967. 3.95. Doubleday.
Loon Feather. Iola Fuller, pseud. LC 40-27210. Harcourt, Brace and Company.
Loon Lake. E. L. Doctorow. 304p. 1981. pap. 3.50 (ISBN 0-553-20027-5). Bantam.
Loon Lake. E. L. Doctorow. LC 79-5526. 1980. 11.95 o.p. (ISBN 0-394-50691-X); limited ed. 35.00 o.p. (ISBN 0-394-51176-X). Random.
Loona: A Strange Tail. Norman Walker. LC 31-244975. 1931. Longmans, Green and Co.
Loop. William Riley Burnett. LC 77-81175. 1977. cancelled o.s.i. (ISBN 0-88373-069-3). Stonehill Pub Co.
Looped Lariats. Claude Campbell. LC 57-59441. 1957. Arcadia House.
Loophole. Arthur Maling. LC 75-156577. 1971. 5.95 (ISBN 0-06-012774-0). Harper & Row.
Loophole: Or, How to Rob a Bank. Robert Pollock. (Fawcett crest book). 1975. (pbk.) 1.25. Fawcett.
Loophole: Or, How to Rob a Bank; a Novel. Robert Pollock. LC 72-94699. 1973. 5.95 (ISBN 0-525-14865-5). Dutton.
Loose Change. Sara Davidson. 1981. pap. 3.50 (ISBN 0-671-43119-6). PB.
Loose Ends. Peter Warner. LC 73-37573. 1972. (ISBN 0-07-068335-2). McGraw-Hill.
Loose Ladies. Vina Delmar. LC 29-11657. 1929. Harcourt, Brace and Company.
Loose Ladies... Vina Delmar. LC 46-21818. 1946.
Loose Ladies. Wright Williams. LC 39-127261. Phoenix Press.
Loose Ladies. Watkins Eppes Wright. LC 39-12726. 1939. Phoenix Press.
Loose Shoulder Straps. Alan Dubois. LC 32-759833. 1932. W. Faro, Inc.
Loose Shoulder Straps. Clement Wood. LC 32-7598. 1932. W. Faro, Inc.
Loosestrife City. Aleksandr Suslov. LC 80-14016. 1980. 10.00 (ISBN 0-88233-468-9) (ISBN 0-88233-586-3). Ardis.
Loot. Truman Hudson Alexander. LC 79-39077. (Black Heritage Library Collection). 1972. (ISBN 0-8369-9015-3). Books for Libraries Press.
Loot. Truman Hudson Alexander. LC 32-245451. Southwest Press.
Loot. Rob Eden. LC 32-3411. Grosset & Dunlap.
Loot. Arthur Somers Roche. LC 16-151327. The Bobbs-Merrill Company.
Loot! Albert Payson Terhune. LC 40-5401. 1940. Harper & Brothers.
Loot of Cities. Arnold Bennett. LC 74-17025. (Collected Works of Arnold Bennett: Vol. 49). 1976. Repr. of 1911 ed. 20.75 (ISBN 0-518-19130-3). Ayer Co.
Loot of Cities, Being the Adventures of a Millionaire in Search of Joy. A Fantasia. Arnold Bennett. LC 72-189747. 1972. 4.50. O. Train.
Looters. John Henry Reese. LC 68-14535. 1968. Random House.
Looters of Tharn. Jeffrey Lord. (Richard Blade Series#19). 1976. (pbk.) 1.25 (ISBN 0-523-00855-4). Pinnacle Books.
Lootvile: A Novel. Benedict Freedman & Nancy Mars Freedman. LC 57-6762. 1957. Holt.
Lope De Vega, Monster of Nature. Ed. by Angel Flores. LC 74-95098. (Illus.). 1969. Greenwood Press.
Lope De Vega: Monster of Nature. Ed. by Angel Flores. LC 79-93062. (Illus.). 1969. Kennikat Press.
Loquacious Mood. Nova T. Ashley. 1970. 3.00 o.p. (ISBN 0-8233-0143-5). Golden Quill.
Lora: The Major's Daughter. Bertha Behrens. LC 52-49170. 1889. Worthington Co.
Lord Alingham, Bankrupt. Marie Manning. LC 2-10719. 1902. Dodd, Mead and Company.
Lord Alistair's Rebellion. Allen Upward. LC 10-27673. 1910. M. Kennerley.
Lord and Mary Ann. Catherine Cookson. LC 74-24877. 1975. 5.95 (ISBN 0-688-02897-7). Morrow.
Lord and Mary Ann. Catherine Cookson. 1976. (pbk.) 1.50. Bantam Books.
Lord and the Gypsy. Patricia Veryan. LC 77-90135. 1978. 9.95 (ISBN 0-8027-0591-X). Walker.
Lord Apache. Robert J. Steelman. LC 76-53416. 1977. 6.95 (ISBN 0-385-12430-9). Doubleday.
Lord Arthur Savile's Crime and Other Stories. Oscar Wilde. LC 73-169381. (Penguin modern classics). 1973. (u.s.) 1.35 (ISBN 0-14-001021-1). Penguin Books.
Lord Bellinger: An Autobiography. Harry Graham. LC 11-5477. 1911. 1.20. Duffield & Company.
Lord Brackenbury. A Novel. Amelia Ann Blandford Edwards. (Franklin square library, no. 139). 1880. Harper & Brothers.
Lord Brandsley's Bride. Claire Lorel. 224p. 1981. pap. 1.95 (ISBN 0-449-50200-7, Crest). Fawcett.
Lord Byron of Broadway: A Novel. Nell Columbia Boyer Martin. LC 28-23875. 1928. Rae D. Henkle Co., Inc.
Lord Byron's Love see Lady Caroline's Folly.
Lord Cammarleigh's Secret: A Fairy Story of to-Day. Roy Horniman. LC 7-34173. 1907. Little, Brown, and Company.
Lord Carrisford's Mistress. Jasmine Cresswell. (Coventry Romance Ser.: No. 199). 192p. 1982. pap. 1.50 (ISBN 0-449-50303-8, Coventry). Fawcett.
Lord Clayborne's Fancy. Laura Matthews. 256p. (Orig.). 1980. pap. 1.75 (ISBN 0-446-94570-6). Warner Bks.
Lord Cobbleigh Disappears. John Collis Snaith. LC 36-759261. 1936. D. Appleton-Century Company, Incorporated.
Lord Courtney's Lady. Jane Morgan. (Berkley Medallion Book). 1.25 (ISBN 0-425-03349-X). Berkley Pub. Corp.
Lord Darcy Investigates. Randall Garrett. 192p. (Orig.). 1981. pap. 2.50 (ISBN 0-441-49141-3). Ace Bks.
Lord Dedringham's Divorce. Margaret SeBastian, pseud. 1978. 1.75 (ISBN 0-445-04248-6). Popular Library.
Lord Deverill's Heir. Catherine Coulter. 1980. pap. 2.25 (ISBN 0-451-11398-5, AE1398, Sig). NAL.
Lord Dismiss Us. Michael Campbell. LC 68-10826. 1968. Putnam.
Lord Dunmersey: His Recollections and Moral Reflections, by Himself. Leander P. Richardson. LC 7-412205. 1889. J. Delay.
Lord Edgware Dies. Agatha Miller Christie. (Greenway Edition). 1969. 8.95 (ISBN 0-396-06065-X). Dodd.
Lord Elesmere's Wife. Charlotte Mary Brame. LC 44-398372. (On cover: Seaside library. Pocket ed. No. 1134). G. Munro.
Lord Elgin's Lady: A Novel. Theodore Vrettos. LC 81-20059. 1982. 12.95 (ISBN 0-395-31333-3). Houghton Mifflin.
Lord Emsworth and Others. Pelham Grenville Wodehouse. LC 67-73672. (B 66-24483). 1966. Penguin.
Lord Fairchild's Daughter. Maggie MacKeever. (Fawcett Crest Book). 1976. (pbk.) 1.25. Fawcett.
Lord Fairfax: Or, The Master of Greenway Court. John Esten Cooke. 1892. G. W. Dillingham.
Lord Fairfax: Or, The Master of Greenway Court. John Esten Cooke. LC 16-9389. G. W. Dillingham Co.
Lord Fancy: 1st Ed. Leslie Turner White. LC 60-10686. 1960. Doubleday.
Lord Foul's Bane. Stephen R Donaldson. LC 77-3533. (Donaldson, Stephen R. The Chronicles of Thomas Covenant, the Unbeliever). (Del Rey book: Bk. 1). 1977. 1.95. Ballantine Books.
Lord Foul's Bane. Stephen R Donaldson. LC 77-73868. (Donaldson, Stephen R. The Chronicles of Thomas Covenant, the Unbeliever). (Illus.). 10.00. Holt, Rinehart and Winston.
Lord Foul's Bane: The Chronicles of Thomas Covenant, the Unbeliever, Vol. 1. Stephen R. Donaldson. (Del Rey Bk.). 1978. pap. 2.95 (ISBN 0-345-29657-5). Ballantine.
Lord Geoffrey's Fancy. Alfred Leo Duggan. LC 62-11086. 1962. Pantheon Books.

Lord Gilmore's Bride. Sheila Walsh. LC 80-29364. (Regency Romance). 1981. 11.50 (ISBN 0-89340-311-3). J. Curley & Associates.
Lord God of the Flesh: Translated from the French by John Rodker, with an Introd. by Lester G. Crocker. Jules Romains. LC 53-20514. (Pocket Book 919). 1953. Pocket Books.
Lord Grizzly. Frederick Feikema Manfred. LC 54-7365. 1954. McGraw-Hill.
Lord Grizzly. Frederick Feikema Manfred. LC 80-17752. (Series: Gregg Press Western Fiction Series.). 1980. 14.95 (ISBN 0-8398-2591-9). Gregg Press.
Lord Grizzly. Frederick Feikema Manfred. LC 82-24739. 1983. 7.95 (ISBN 0-8032-8118-8). University of Nebraska Press.
Lord Harry's Folly. Catherine Coulter. 1980. pap. 2.25 (ISBN 0-451-11534-1, AE1534, Sig). NAL.
Lord Have Mercy: By Shelley Smith Pseud. 1st Ed. Nancy Bodington. LC 56-11104. 1956. Harper.
Lord Heathbury's Revenge. Rachelle Edwards. 224p. 1980. pap. 1.75 (ISBN 0-449-50069-1, Coventry). Fawcett.
Lord Hermitage: A Novel. James Grant. LC 43-26605. 1878. G. Routledge and Sons Pref.
Lord Hope's Choice. Ann Sophia Winterbotham Stephens. LC 8-12413. T. B. Peterson & Brothers.
Lord Hornblower. Cecil Scott Forester. (Keith Jennison large type ed.). 1966. 6.95. Watts.
Lord Hornblower. Cecil Scott Forester. LC 46-251763. 1946. Little, Brown and Company.
Lord Hornblower see Indomitable Hornblower.
Lord How Different. Carolyn Pomonis. LC 80-299. 1980. 6.95 (ISBN 0-913270-85-7). Sundial Books: Distributed by Sunstone Press and Available from Carlo Co.
Lord, I've Been in Hell So Long. Sandee W. Tillee. 1978. pap. 2.50x o.p. (ISBN 0-8358-0375-9). Upper Room.
Lord Jacquelin Burkney: The Whitechapel Terror. Jacob Ringgold. LC 7-41652. 1889. The Anton Publishing Co.
Lord Jesus. Pierre Stephen Robert Payne. LC 64-20872. 1964. Abelard-Schuman.
Lord Jim. Joseph Conrad. (Reader's enrichment ser., RE 120). Washington Sq.
Lord Jim. Joseph Conrad. LC 75-184734. 1971. (ISBN 0-8376-0409-5). R. Bentley.
Lord Jim. Joseph Conrad. LC 18-4347. 1916. Doubleday, Page & Company.
Lord Jim. Joseph Conrad. LC 31-267558. (Half-title: The modern library of the world's best books). The Modern Library.
Lord Jim. educational ed. Joseph Conrad. LC 44-228437. Pub. by the Odyssey Press by Arrangement with Doubleday, Doran & Co., Inc.
Lord Jim: A Romance. Joseph Conrad. LC 22-10645. 1921. Doubleday, Page & Company.
Lord Jim: A Romance. Joseph Conrad & McFee, William, 1881. LC 22-247710. 1922. Doubleday, Page & Company.
Lord Jim: A Romance, by Joseph Conrad... Joseph Conrad. LC 6602. 1900. Doubleday & McClure Co.
Lord Jim: A Romance. Large Type Ed. Complete and Unabridged. Joseph Conrad. LC 66-4050. (Keith Jennison bk.). 1966. 6.95, 4.95 lib. ed.,. Watts.
Lord Jim: A Tale. Joseph Conrad. LC 28-10881. 1927. Doubleday, Page & Company.
Lord Jim. Afterword by Murray Krieger. Joseph Conrad. (Signet bk., D2641). 1965. New Amer. Lib.
Lord Jim: An Authoritative Text... Joseph Conrad. Ed. by Thomas C. Moser. LC 65-22077. (Norten critical editions). (Illus.). 1968. 4.97. Norton.
Lord Jim: An Authoritative Text. Ed. by Thomas Moser. 1st Ed. Joseph Conrad. Ed. by Thomas C Moser. LC 65-22077. (Norton critical eds.). 1968. pap., 1.95. Norton.
Lord Jim. Edited with Introd. and Notes by Robert B. Heilman. Joseph Conrad. LC 57-6455. (Rinehart editions, 85). 1957. Rinehart.
Lord Jim: Introd. by Francis R. Gemme. Joseph Conrad. (Classics ser., CL54). 1965. Airmont.
Lord Jim. Introd. by Thomas Moser. Joseph Conrad. (Scholastic lib. ed., T-580). 1965. Scholastic.
Lord Johnnie. Leslie Turner White. LC 49-3024. 1949. Crown Publishers.
Lord Kalvan of Otherwhen. H. Beam Piper. LC 75-421. (Garland Library of Science Fiction). 1975. 11.00 (ISBN 0-8240-1426-X). Garland Pub.
Lord Kalvan of Otherwhen. H. Beam Piper. 1977. 1.50 (ISBN 0-441-49051-4). Ace Books.
Lord Kilgobbin. Charles James Lever. (Seaside library, v. 25, no. 529). 1879. G. Munro.
Lord Kilgobbin. Charles James Lever & Wheeler, E. J., Illus. LC 16-7546. 1906. Little, Brown, and Company.
Lord Kilgobbin. A Novel. Charles James Lever. LC 7-14392. 1872. Harper & Brothers.
Lord Kilgobbin: A Tale of Ireland in Our Own Time, 3 vols. in 1. Charles James Lever. LC 79-8149. Repr. of 1872 ed. 44.50 (ISBN 0-404-61961-4). AMS Pr.
Lord Leonard the Luckless. William Edward Norris. LC 3-1582. 1903. H. Holt and Company.
Lord Libertine. Anthony Esler. (Fawcett Crest Book). 1977. 1.75 (ISBN 0-449-23170-4). Fawcett Pubns.
Lord Libertine: Or, The Memoirs of a Gentleman of Pleasure, Being a Rake's Progress from London to Paris in the Revolutionary Year 1792. Anthony Esler. LC 75-42231. 1976. 8.95 (ISBN 0-688-03047-5). Morrow.
Lord Linlithgow: A Novel. Morley Roberts. LC 6831. 1900. Harper & Brothers.
Lord Lisle's Daughter. Charlotte Mary Brame. LC 3627. (Bertha M. Clay library. no. 4). 1900. Street & Smith.
Lord London: A Tale of Achievement. John Keble Bell. LC 13-25717. 1913. McBride, Nast & Co.
Lord Love a Duck. 1st Ed. Al Hine. LC 61-6379. 1961. Atheneum.
Lord Love Us: A Novel. Arthur Mills P Stratton. LC 48-9114. 1948. C. Scribner's Sons.
Lord Loveland Discovers America. Charles Norris Williamson & Alice Muriel Livingston Williamson. LC 10-21482. 1910. Doubleday, Page & Co.
Lord Lynne's Choice. Charlotte Mary Brame. LC 6506. (Bertha Clay library. no. 32). 1900. Street & Smith.
Lord Lynne's Choice: Or, True Love Never Runs Smooth. Charlotte Mary Brame. (On cover: Lovell's library. v. 13. no. 692). J. W. Lovell Company.
Lord Malquist & Mr. Moon. Tom Stoppard. LC 75-13578. (Evergreen black cat book). 1975. 2.45 (ISBN 0-394-17886-6). Grove Press: Distributed by Random House.
Lord Malquist & Mr. Moon. Tom Stoppard. LC 68-12671. 1968. Knopf.
Lord Margrave's Deception. Diana Campbell. 1982. pap. 2.25 (ISBN 0-451-11460-4, AE1460, Sig). NAL.
Lord Mayor of Death. Marian Babson. LC 79-65165. 1979. 7.95 (ISBN 0-8027-5415-5). Walker.
Lord Mayor's Show. Vian Smith. LC 69-15178. 1969. 4.95. Doubleday.
Lord Montagu's Page: An Historical Romance of the Seventeenty Century. George Payne Rainsford James. 1858. Childs & Peterson.
Lord Mullion's Secret. Michael Innes, pseud. LC 81-5558. (Red badge novel of suspense). 8.95 (ISBN 0-396-08005-7). Dodd, Mead.
Lord Oakburn's Daughters. Ellen Price Henry Wood Wood. (Seaside library, v. 13, no.256). 1878. G. Munro.
Lord of Blood. Dave Van Arnam. 1970. pap. 0.75 o.p. (ISBN 0-447-74688-X). Lancer.
Lord of Creation. Rosalind Cowdray. (Harlequin Romances Ser.). 192p. (Orig.). 1981. pap. 1.25 (ISBN 0-373-02381-2, Pub. by Harlequin). PB.
Lord of Dark Places. Hal Z. Bennett. LC 70-112604. 1970. 5.95. Norton.
Lord of Darkness. Robert Silverberg. 575p. 1983. 15.95 (ISBN 0-87795-443-7). Arbor Hse.
Lord of Himself. Percy Marks. LC 27-199978. 2.00. The Century Co.
Lord of Himself. A Novel. Francis Henry Underwood. LC 8-32287. 1874. Lee and Shepard.
Lord of Lands. Ramsey I. E. Percival Ramsey Benson. 1908. H. Holt and Company.
Lord of Life. Stephen Southwold. LC 33-172772. 1933. Little, Brown and Company.
Lord of Light. Roger Zelazny. LC 67-19099. 1967. Doubleday.
Lord of Light. Roger Zelazny. LC 78-27140. (Gregg Press Science Fiction Series). (Illus.). 1979. 14.00 (ISBN 0-8398-2499-8). Gregg Press.
Lord of Light. 1st Ed. 1967. 4.95. Doubleday.
Lord of Lonely Valley. Peter Bernard Kyne. 1932. H. C. Kinsey & Company, Inc.
Lord of Lowedale: A Story of the Sixteenth Century. R. D Chetwode. LC 6-24207. Estes and Lauriat.
Lord of Misrule. Gareth Jones. LC 80-17069. 12.95 (ISBN 0-374-19120-4). Farrar, Straus, Giroux.
Lord of Ravensley. Constance Heaven. LC 77-11966. 1978. 9.95 (ISBN 0-698-10856-6). Coward, McCann & Geoghegan.
Lord of Shame Manor. Alexander Stewart. (Illus., Orig.). 1969. pap. 1.95 o.p. (6062). Brandon.
Lord of Terror. Marcel Allain. LC 25-19903. (Fantomas detective novel). David McKay Company.
Lord of the Apes. George Alec Effinger. (Planet of the Ape Ser.). (O.s.i.). 160p. (Orig.). 1975. pap. 0.95 o.s.i. (AN1488, Award). Univ Pub & Dist.
Lord of the Apes. George Alec Effinger. (Planet of the Apes#4). 1976. (pbk.) 0.95. Award Books.
Lord of the Dead. Robert E. Howard & G. Duncan Eagleson. LC 81-212468. (Illus.). 1981. 15.00 (ISBN 0-937986-35-6). D.M. Grant.
Lord of the Far Island. Eleanor Hibbert. LC 75-5262. 1975. 7.95. Doubleday.
Lord of the Far Island. Eleanor Hibbert. LC 75-45027. 1976. 13.95 (ISBN 0-8161-6350-2). G. K. Hall.
Lord of the Far Island. Victoria Holt, pseud. 320p. 1982. pap. 2.95 (ISBN 0-449-22874-6, Crest). Fawcett.
Lord of the Far Island. Victoria Holt, pseud. 1976. Repr. lib. bdg. 13.95 o.p. (ISBN 0-8161-6350-2, Large Print Bks). G K Hall.
Lord of the Flies: A Novel. William Gerald Golding. LC 55-10081. 1955. Coward-McCann.
Lord of the Flies: A Novel. William Gerald Golding. LC 59-11717. (Putnam Capricorn book, Cap 14). (Illus.). 1959. Capricorn Books.
Lord of the Golden Fan. Christopher Nicole. 1975. (pbk.) 1.50. Bantam Books.
Lord of the High Lonesome. Janet Dailey. (Harlequin Presents Ser.). (Orig.). 1980. pap. text ed. 1.50 (ISBN 0-373-10363-8, Pub. by Harlequin). PB.
Lord of the High Valley. Margaret Way. (Harlequin Romances Ser.). 192p. (Orig.). 1981. pap. 1.25 (ISBN 0-373-02387-1, Pub. by Harlequin). PB.
Lord of the Hollow Dark. Russell Kirk. LC 79-16428. 10.95 (ISBN 0-312-49844-6). St. Martin's Press.
Lord of the Island. Ruth Burnett. 1981. pap. 6.95 (Avalon). Bouregy.
Lord of the Isles. Donald Barr Chidsey. LC 54-6630. 1954. Crown Publishers.
Lord of the Isles. Henrietta Reid. (Harlequin Romances Ser.). 192p. 1981. pap. 1.50 (ISBN 0-373-02442-8). Harlequin Bks.
Lord of the Mountain: A Novel of Ireland. Walter Macken. LC 67-12224. 1967. Macmillan.
Lord of the Red Sun. William T Silent. LC 72-165935. 1972. 5.95 (ISBN 0-8027-5544-5). Walker.
Lord of the Rings. John Ronald Reuel Tolkien. LC 54-4943. Houghton Mifflin.
Lord of the Rings. 2d ed. collector's ed. John Ronald Reuel Tolkien. LC 75-308399. (Illus.). 1974. 35.00 (ISBN 0-395-19395-8). Houghton Mifflin.
Lord of the Rings. John Ronald Reuel Tolkien. LC 66-953. (Illus.). 1965. Ballantine Books.
Lord of the Rings. 2d ed. John Ronald Reuel Tolkien. LC 67-12274. (Illus.). 1967. Houghton Mifflin.
Lord of the Rings: Anniversary Edition, 3 vols. John Ronald Reuel Tolkien. 1981. Set. 50.00. HM.
Lord of the River. Bernard Clavel. LC 73-12800. 1974. 6.95 (ISBN 0-316-14706-0). Little, Brown.
Lord of the Sea. Matthew Phipps Shiel. LC 62-20047. (Xanadu library). 1963. Crown Publishers.
Lord of the Sea. Matthew Phipps Shiel. LC 74-16521. (Science Fiction). 1975. 28.00 (ISBN 0-405-06313-X). Arno Press.
Lord of the Sea. Matthew Phipps Shiel. LC 24-28226. 1924. A. A. Knopf.
Lord of the Silver Lode. Lee E. Wells. (Orig.). 1973. pap. 0.75 o.p. (07301). Curtis.
Lord of the Spiders. Michael Moorcock. (Science Fiction Ser). 1979. pap. 1.50 o.p. (ISBN 0-87997-443-5, UW1443). DAW Bks.
Lord of the Spiders. Michael Moorcock. 1971. pap. 0.75 o.p. (ISBN 0-447-74736-3). Lancer.
Lord of the Spiders. Michael Moorcock. 1973. pap. 0.75 o.s.i. (74-736). Lancer.
Lord of the Spiders or Blades of Mars. Michael Moorcock. 1979. 1.50 (ISBN 0-87997-443-5). DAW Books.
Lord of the Trees. Philip J. Farmer. Bd. with Mad Goblin. 1980. pap. 2.50 (ISBN 0-441-49252-5). Ace Bks.
Lord of the World. Robert Hugh Benson. LC 74-15951. (Science Fiction). 1975. 19.00 (ISBN 0-405-06277-X). Arno Press.
Lord of the World. Robert Hugh Benson. 1908. Dodd, Mead & Company.
Lord of Thunder. Alice Mary Norton. LC 62-14247. 1962. Harcourt, Brace & World.
Lord of Thundergate. Sidney Herschel Small. LC 23-536153. The Bobbs-Merrill Company.
Lord or the Doctor? A Story. William L Lockwood. LC 7-227400. 1892.
Lord Orlando's Protegee. Margaret SeBastian, pseud. (Berkley Medallion Book). 1977. 1.75 (ISBN 0-425-03408-9). Berkley Pub. Corp.
Lord Ormont and His Aminta. George Meredith. LC 1-19352. 1894. C. Scribner's Sons.
Lord Peter: A Collection of All the Lord Peter Wimsey Stories. Dorothy Leigh Sayers. (Flare Book). 1972. 3.95. Avon.
Lord Peter: A Collection of All the Lord Peter Wimsey Stories. Dorothy Leigh Sayers. LC 68-28234. 1971. 10.00 (ISBN 0-06-013787-8). Harper & Row.
Lord Protector: A Story. Sidney Kilner Levett-Yeats. LC 2-17484. 1902. Longmans, Green, and Co.
Lord Raingo. Arnold Bennett. LC 26-177651. George H. Doran Company.
Lord Ravenscar's Revenge. Barbara Cartland. LC 78-6464. 1978. 6.95 (ISBN 0-87272-040-3). Duron Books.
Lord Richard's Passion. Mervyn Jones. LC 73-20765. 1974. 7.95 (ISBN 0-394-49220-X). Knopf; Distributed by Random House.
Lord Rivington's Lady. Eileen Jackson. LC 75-40762. 1976. 7.95 (ISBN 0-8027-0533-2). Walker.
Lord Rivington's Lady. Eileen Jackson. 1977. 1.50 (ISBN 0-451-07612-5). New American Library.
Lord Rivington's Lady. Eileen Jackson. LC 78-15980. 1978. 10.95 (ISBN 0-8161-6596-3). G. K. Hall.
Lord Roldan. A Romance. Allan Cunningham. LC 6-31733. 1836. Harper & Brothers.
Lord Sin. Constance Gluyas. 1980. pap. 2.75 (ISBN 0-451-09521-9, E9521, Sig). NAL.
Lord Six-Gun. Norman A Fox. LC 43-12151. 1943. Phoenix Press.
Lord Stephen's Lady. Janette Radcliffe. 1976. 0.95. Dell Publishing Co.
Lord Strahan. A Novel. Marion White Wildrick. LC 8-37024. 1879. J. B. Lippincott & Co.
Lord Strathmore's Ruby. Ruth Harl. LC 15-8432. 1915. A. H. King.
Lord Tedric. E. E. Smith & Gordon Eklund. 1978. pap. 4.95 (ISBN 0-89437-021-9). Baronet.
Lord Tedric III: Black Knight of the Iron Sphere. Doc Smith & Gordon Eklund. (Lord Tedric Ser.). 224p. (Orig.). 1981. pap. 2.25 (ISBN 0-441-49256-8). Ace Bks.
Lord Tedric: Space Pirates, No. 2. Gordon Eklund. 1980. pap. 1.95 (ISBN 0-441-77760-0). Ace Bks.
Lord Tony's Wife: An Adventures of the Scarlet Pimpernel. Emmuska Orczy. LC 18-521. George H. Doran Company.
Lord Tyger. Philip Jose Farmer. LC 79-89108. (Doubleday science fiction). 1970. 5.95. Doubleday.
Lord Vanecourt's Daughter. A Novel. Mabel Collins Cook. LC 6-28080. (Harper's Franklin square library, no. 516). Harper & Brothers.
Lord Vanecourt's Daughter. A Novel. Mabel Collins Cook. LC 6-28081. G. Munro.
Lord Vanity. Samuel Shellabarger. LC 53-7330. 1953. Little, Brown.
Lord Was Their Sheperd, Stories. Mary Olive Wages. LC 52-5712. 1952. Exposition Press.
Lord Wicked Wolf. Margaret Summerville. (Candlelight Romance Ser.: No. 714). 256p. 1982. pap. 2.25 (ISBN 0-440-14996-7). Dell.
Lord Won't Mind. Gordon Merrick. 1971. pap. 2.95 (ISBN 0-380-01404-1, 58867). Avon.
Lord Won't Mind: A Novel. Gordon Merrick. LC 78-97590. 1970. 5.95. Bernard Geis Associates.
Lordless. Eleanor G Kneen. LC 36-19247. 1936. G. P. Putnam's Sons.
Lordly Ones. Benjamin Harrison Lehman. LC 27-21878. 1927. Harper & Brothers.
Lords and Ladies. Julia Cecilia Collinson Stretton. LC 23-24785. (On cover: Loring's railway novels). 1868. Loring.
Lords and Masters. Archibald Gordon Macdonnell. LC 37-647327. 1937. The Macmillan Company.
Lord's Anointed: A Novel of Hawaii. Ruth Eleanor McKee. LC 34-9626. 1934. Doubleday, Doran & Company, Inc.
Lord's Courtship: A Novel. Lee Meriwether. LC 2547. Laird & Lee.
Lords of Acadia. Harry James Chapman. LC 25-8317. Small, Maynard & Company.
Lords of Akchasaz: Murder in the Ironsmiths Market, Part 1. Yashar Kemal. Tr. by Thilda Kemal from Turkish. LC 79-25174. 1980. 15.00 (ISBN 0-688-03608-2). Morrow.
Lords of Castle Weirwyck. Elaine F. Wells. 256p. (Orig.). 1980. pap. 1.95 (ISBN 0-89083-668-X). Zebra.
Lords of Creation. Eando Binder. LC 49-6418. 1949. Prime Press.
Lords of Dair. Helen Wieselberg. LC 77-17313. 8.95. Putnam.
Lords of Dawn: A Novel. George Turner Marsh & Temple, Ronald. LC 16-15152. 1916. 1.50. J. J. Newbegin.
Lords of High Decision. Meredith Nicholson. LC 9-28248. 1909. Doubleday, Page & Company.
Lords of Lancaster. Pamela Bennetts. LC 72-96029. 1973. 5.95. St. Martin's Press.
Lords of Loone. John James. LC 72-84734. 1972. 7.50. St. Martin's Press.
Lords of Misrule: A Tale of Gods and of Men. William C Pomeroy. LC 7-381845. (On cover: Library of choice fiction. no. 73). 1894. Laird & Lee.
Lords of Power. Paul Weissman. 1973. (pbk.) 1.25. Bantam Books.
Lords of Power. Paul Weissman. LC 72-170235. 1972. 5.95. Morrow.

Lords of the Coast. Jackson Gregory. LC 35-16479. 1935. Dodd, Mead & Company.
Lords of the Crimson River. Jeffrey Lord. (Blade Ser.: No. 35). 192p. (Orig.). 1981. pap. 1.95 (ISBN 0-523-41209-6). Pinnacle Bks.
Lords of the Earth. Don Richardson. LC 77-74534. 368p. 1977. pap. 5.95 (ISBN 0-8307-0529-5, 54-057-18). Regal.
Lords of the Housetops: Thirteen Cat Tales. Ed. by Carl Van Vechten. LC 21-13067. 1921. A. A. Knopf.
Lords of the Land. Matthew Braun. (Dell Book). 1979. 2.25 (ISBN 0-440-14670-4). Dell Publishing Co.
Lords of the North. Agnes Christina Laut. LC 1-29339. 1900. J. F. Taylor & Company.
Lords of the North: A Romance of the Northwest. Agnes Christina Laut. (Added t.-p.: American classical romances. A-Fiction, v. 12). P. F. Collier & Son.
Lords of the Psychon. Daniel F Galouye. LC 63-9177. 1963. Bantam Books.
Lords of the Soil" A Romance of Indian Life Among the Early English Settlers. Lydia Annie Smith & Cuffee, Nathan Jeffrey, 1852- Joint Author. LC 5-32320. 1905. C. M. Clark Publishing Co., Inc.
Lords of the Starship. Mark S Geston. LC 78-21992. (Gregg Press science fiction series). 1978. 9.50 (ISBN 0-8398-2447-5). Gregg Press.
Lords of the Triple Moons. Ardath Mayhar. LC 82-16241. 156p. (gr. 6 up). 1983. 10.95 (ISBN 0-689-30978-3, Argo). Atheneum.
Lords of the World: A Story of the Fall of Carthage and Corinth. Alfred John Church. 1897. C. Scribner's Sons.
Lords of Underearth. 1980. pap. write for info. (ISBN 0-88074-018-3). Metagam.
Lord's Oysters. Gilbert Byron. LC 74-9246. 1967. 8.50. Tradition Press.
Lord's Oysters. rev. ed. Byron Gilbert. 330p. 1957. pap. 4.95. Md Hist.
Lord's Oysters. 1st Ed. Gilbert Byron. LC 57-644279. Little, Brown.
Lord's Pink Ocean. David Harry Walker. (Daw sf Books, no. 67). (Illus.). 1973. 0.95. Daw Books.
Lord's Pink Ocean. David Harry Walker. LC 72-189330. 1972. (ISBN 0-395-13940-6). Houghton Mifflin.
Lord's Pursebearers. Hesba Stretton. LC 8-16882. 1882. D. Lothrop and Company.
Lore of Proserpine. Maurice Henry Hewlett. LC 13-7848. 1913. 1.35. C. Scribner's Sons.
Lore of the Witch World. Andre Norton, pseud. (Science Fiction Ser.). 1980. pap. 2.50 (ISBN 0-87997-750-7, UE1750). Daw Bks.
Lorelei. Lynn Lowery. 432p. (Orig.). 1981. pap. 2.75 (ISBN 0-553-14150-3). Bantam.
Lorelei: And Other Stories. Mary Joanna Safford. LC 8-3397. (On cover: The golden library, no. 4). 1892. The Price-McGill Company.
Lorelei. 1st American Ed. Lawrence Paul Bachmann. LC 58-9382. 1958. Published for the Crime Club by Doubleday.
Lorena. Frank Gill Slaughter. LC 59-10882. 1959. Doubleday.
Lorenzino. Arvin Upton. LC 76-54262. 7.95 (ISBN 0-393-08762-X). Norton.
Lorenzo Benoni: Or, Passages in the Life of an Italian. Giovanni Domenico Ruffini. LC 41-38132. 1860. Redfield.
Lorenzo Bunch. Booth Tarkington. LC 36-27032. 1936. Doubleday, Doran & Company, Inc.
Lorenzo of Sarzana. Elizabeth Portia Goodson Lewis. LC 7-20618. 1907. R. G. Badger.
Lorenzo: Or The Empire of Religion. E. S. Deiende. LC 7-14783. 1844. J. Murphy.
Lorenzo the Magnificent: The Riders from Texas. Dane Coolidge. LC 25-10698. E. P. Dutton & Company.
Loretta, the Sunshine of the Convent: A Novel. Gilbert Guest. LC 21-142879. 1921. Burkley Printing Company.
Lorette. The History of Louise, Daughter of a Canadian Nun, Exhibiting the Interior of Female Convents. ...2d ed. George Bourne. LC 5-25860. 1834. C. Small.
Loretto; or, The Choice. a new rev. and enl. ed. George Henry Miles. LC 7-18429. 1870. Kelly Piet and Company.
Loretto; or, The Choice. A Story Written for the Old and for the Young. In Four Parts. 10th stereotype ed.--rev. and enl. by the author. ed. George Henry Miles. LC 7-18500. 1859. Kelly, Hedian & Piet.
Loretto: Sketches of a German War Volunteer. translated by charles ashleigh. ed. Max Heinz & Ashleigh, Charles, Tr. LC 30-53397. 1930. H. Liveright.
Lorgnette: Or, Studies of the Town. 2d ed., set off with mr. darley's designs. ed. Donald Grant Mitchell. LC 7-18722. Printed for Stringer and Townsend.
Lori. John Benton. LC 80-10139. (Spire books). 1.95 (ISBN 0-8007-8385-9). Revell.
Lori, Daughter of Kit. Harriet Theresa Smith Comstock. LC 38-8102. 1938. Doubleday, Doran & Company, Inc.
Lorielle. Marilyn Granbeck. (Historical Romance). 400p. (Orig.). 1980. pap. 2.75 (ISBN 0-515-04627-2). Jove Pubns.
Lorimer and Wife. A Novel. Margaret Lee. LC 7-12626. 1881. G. W. Harlan.
Lorimer and Wife. A Novel. Margaret Lee. (On cover: Lovell's library. no. 741). 1886. J. W. Lovell Company.
Lorimer Line. Anne Melville, pseud. LC 76-50783. 1977. 8.95 (ISBN 0-385-12132-6). Doubleday.
Lorimer of the Northwest. Harold Bindloss. LC 9-2261. 1909. F. A. Stokes Company.
Lorin Mooruck: And Other Indian Stories. Winifred Jennings Cowley. LC 6-28860. 1888. J. S. Smith & Co.
Lorinda. Marjorie Chalmers Carleton. LC 39-22446. 1939. Dodd, Mead & Company.
Loring Mystery. Jeffery Farnol. LC 24-22004. 1924. Little, Brown, and Company.
Loring Mystery. Jeffery Farnol. LC 25-23823. 1925. Little, Brown, and Company.
Lorita: An Alaskan Maiden. Susie Champney Clark. LC 6-214610. 1892. Lee and Shepard.
Lorley and Reinhard. Berthold Auerbach. Tr. by Brooks, Charles Timothy. LC 6-4509. (Leisure hour series, v. 76). 1877. H. Holt and Company.
Lormes of Castle Rising. Phyllis Cradock. LC 76-358. 1976. 8.95 (ISBN 0-8415-0437-7). Saturday Review Press.
Lormes of Castle Rising. 352p. 1976. 8.95 o.p. (ISBN 0-8415-0437-7). Dutton.
Lorna Carswell: A Story of the South. Comer Leonard Peek. 1903. Broadway Publishing Company.
Lorna Carswell: A Story of the South. 2d ed. Comer Leonard Peek. LC 6-23157. 1906. The Neale Publishing Company.
Lorna Doone. Richard Doddridge Blackmore. LC 66-1481. (Reader's enrichment series). 1964. Washington Square Press.
Lorna Doone. Richard Doddridge Blackmore. LC 14-22436. T. Y. Crowell & Co.
Lorna Doone. Richard Doddridge Blackmore. LC 36-37151. (Half-title: Everyman's library, ed. by Ernest Rhys. Fiction. no. 304). 1931. J. M. Dent & Sons, Ltd.
Lorna Doone. Richard Doddridge Blackmore. LC 43-16762. (On cover: Great illustrated classics). 1943. Dodd, Mead & Company.
Lorna Doone. Richard Doddridge Blackmore & Christ, Henry I. LC 46-6501. 1946. Globe Book Company.
Lorna Doone. Richard Doddridge Blackmore & Holmes, Mabel Dodge. Ed. by Randolph, Helen. LC 48-1189. (CEBCO classics for enjoyment). 1948. College Entrance Book Co.
Lorna Doone. Richard Doddridge Blackmore & Jordan, Rachel. LC 38-3047. Scott, Foreman and Company.
Lorna Doone. illustrated by mead schaefer. ed. Richard Doddridge Blackmore & Schaeffer, Mead, 1845- Illus. LC 30-298321. Dodd, Mead & Company.
Lorna Doone: A Romance of Exmoor. Richard Doddridge Blackmore. LC 42-26736. 1874. Harper & Brothers.
Lorna Doone: A Romance of Exmoor. Richard Doddridge Blackmore. LC 6-35025. (On cover:Franklin square library. Two column ed. no. 7). 1882. Harper & Brothers.
Lorna Doone: A Romance of Exmoor. Richard Doddridge Blackmore. LC 42-30838. 1891. Lovell Brothers & Company.
Lorna Doone: A Romance of Exmoor. with many drawings. ed. Richard Doddridge Blackmore. 1890. The Burrows Brothers Company.
Lorna Doone: A Romance of Exmoor. Richard Doddridge Blackmore. LC 6-13135. (On cover: Harper's Franklin square library. no. 666). 1890. Harper & Brothers.
Lorna Doone: A Romance of Exmoor. Richard Doddridge Blackmore. LC 6-13833. T. Y. Crowell & Co.
Lorna Doone: A Romance of Exmoor. Richard Doddridge Blackmore. LC 4825. W. B. Company.
Lorna Doone: A Romance of Exmoor. Richard Doddridge Blackmore. 1900. Harper & Bros.
Lorna Doone: A Romance of Exmoor. ed., with introduction and notes, by albert l. barbour... ed. Richard Doddridge Blackmore. LC 5-30661. (Macmillan's pocket American and English classics). 1905. The Macmillan Company.
Lorna Doone: A Romance of Exmoor. Richard Doddridge Blackmore. (Half-title: Everyman's library, ed. by Ernest Rhys. Fiction. (no. 304). 1909. J. M. Dent & Co.
Lorna Doone: A Romance of Exmoor. edited, with an introduction, notes, and study helps, by w. p. trent and w. t. brewster... ed. Richard Doddridge Blackmore. Ed. by William Peterfield Trent. Brewster, William Tenney, 1869- Joint Ed. LC 29-9993. (Standard English classics). Ginn and Company.
Lorna Doone, a Romance of Exmoor. Richard Doddridge Blackmore. LC 43-445516. (Half-title: Everyman's library, ed. by Ernest Rhys. Fiction. No. 304). J. M. Dent & Co.
Lorna Doone: A Romance of Exmoor. ed. by w. p. trent and w. t. brewster... ed. Richard Doddridge Blackmore. Ed. by William Peterfield Trent. Brewster, William Tenney, 1869- Joint Ed. LC 6-42375. (Standard English classics). Etc. Ginn & Company.
Lorna Doone, a Romance of Exmoor. Richard Doddridge Blackmore & Austen, John, Illus. LC 43-5435. 1943. The Heritage Press.
Lorna Doone: A Romance of Exmoor. ed. by carolyn sherwin bailey: illustrated by harold brett. ed. Richard Doddridge Blackmore & Bailey, Carolyn Sherwin, 1875- Ed. LC 21-12856. Milton Bradley Company.
Lorna Doone: A Romance of Exmoor. Richard Doddridge Blackmore & Grose, Helen Mason, Illus. LC 17-302777. (Rittenhouse classics). 1917. G. W. Jacobs & Company.
Lorna Doone: A Romance of Exmoor. abridged and edited by morton a. sturtevant... ed. Richard Doddridge Blackmore & Sturtevant, Morton Adams, Ed. LC 2-703517. (modern readers' series). 1928. The Macmillan Company.
Lorna Doone: A Romance of Exmoor. ed. by r. adelaide witham. ed. Richard Doddridge Blackmore & Witham, Rose Adelaide, 1873- Ed. LC 18-4152. (On cover: Academy classics). Allyn and Bacon.
Lorna Doone, a Romance of Exmoor: Doone-Land Ed. Richard Doddridge Blackmore. 1908. Harper & Brothers.
Lorna Doone: A Romance of Exmoor. Illus. by Broom Lynne. Richard Doddridge Blackmore. LC 66-5541. (Macdonald illus. classics, 12). 1966. 3.50. Macdonald.
Lorna Doone: A Romance of Exmoor. Introd. by Mary M. Threapleton. Richard Doddridge Blackmore. (Classics ser., CL149). 1967. Airmont.
Lorna Doone: A Romance of Exmore. abridged and ed. by harry c. davis... ed. Richard Doddridge Blackmore & Davis, Harry Carsell, 1856- Ed. LC 9-2767. 1908. Hinds, Noble & Eldredge.
Lorna Doone. With an Introd. by Maxwell H. Goldberg. Richard Doddridge Blackmore. LC 56-59152. (Pocket library, PL 508). 1956. Pocket Books.
Lorraine: A Novel. Dorothy Foster Gilman. LC 23-15031. 1923. The Macmillan Company.
Lorraine: A Romance. Robert William Chambers. Harper & Brothers.
Lorraine: A Romance. Robert William Chambers. LC 7-13294. 1898. Harper & Brothers.
Lorraine: A Romance. Robert William Chambers. LC 7-23537. 1906. Harper & Brothers.
Lorrie: A Novel. Jane Ludlow Drake Abbott. LC 41-9959. J. B. Lippincott Company.
Lorrimer Littlegood. Francis Edward Smedley. LC 16-1250. T. B. Peterson & Brothers.
Los Cerritos; a Romance of the Modern Time. Gertrude Franklin Horn Atherton. LC 68-23711. 1968. 10.00. Gregg Pr.
Los Cerritos. A Romance of the Modern Time. Gertrude Franklin Horn Atherton. LC 6-4517. J. W. Lovell Company.
Los Conquistadores: Novela. 1. Ed. Jose Nicaraguan Roman. LC 67-2752. 1966. pap., 2.00. Ediciones Centro.
Los Pazos De Ulloa: Novela. Emilia Pardo Bazan. (Her Obras completas, v.3). 1961. pap., 2.00. Las Americas Pub. Co.
Los Rios Profundos. Jose Maria Arguedas. Ed. by William Rowe. LC 73-4524. (Commonwealth and international library. Pergamon Oxford Latin-American series). 1973. (ISBN 0-08-017014-5) (ISBN 0-08-017015-3). Pergamon Press.
Loser. Peter De Polnay. LC 73-175855. 1973. 2.00 (ISBN 0-491-00964-X). W. H. Allen.
Loser. Gyorgy Konrad. LC 82-6205. 1982. 14.95 (ISBN 0-15-153442-X). Harcourt Brace Jovanovich.
Loser: A Novel. Borden Deal. LC 64-11397. Doubleday,
Loser, a Novel. Peter Ustinov. LC 60-8568. 1960. Little, Brown.
Loser Pays: A Story of the French Revolution. Mary Openshaw. LC 11-25679. 1.25. Small, Maynard & Company.
Loser Takes All. Graham Greene. LC 57-9494. 1957. Viking Press.
Loser Takes All. Graham Greene. LC 72-184803. 1971. 0.25 (ISBN 0-14-003277-0). Penguin.
Losers. George G. Gilman, pseud. (Steele Ser.: No. 10). 1978. pap. 1.50 (ISBN 0-523-40578-2). Pinnacle Bks.
Losers. Clifford Irving. LC 57-14523. 1957. Coward-McCann.
Loser's Choice. 1st Ed. Ruthven Todd. LC 53-9725. 1953. Hermitage House.
Losers Keepers. Alexander Mason. (Orig.). 1980. pap. 2.25 o.s.i. (ISBN 0-505-51505-9). Tower Bks.
Losers' Luck: Being the Questionable Enterprises of a Yatchtsman, a Princess, and Certain Filibusters in Central America. Charles Tenney Jackson. 1905. H. Holt and Company.
Losers, Weepers. Ellery Queen, pseud. LC 71-2003. 0.50. Dell Pub. Co.
Losers, Weepers. Edwin Silberstang. LC 74-9467. 1975. 6.95 (ISBN 0-385-00303-X). Doubleday.
Losing. Nancy Means Wright. 1973. (pbk.) 0.75. Ace Books.
Losing Battles. Eudora Welty. LC 74-102304. (Illus.). 1970. 7.95. Random House.
Losing Battles. Eudora Welty. LC 78-58857. 1978. 2.45 (ISBN 0-394-72668-5). Vintage Books.
Losing Gain. Blanche Upright. LC 23-7014. W. J. Watt & Company.
Losing Game. Freeman Wills Crofts. LC 41-218873. 1941. Dodd, Mead & Company.
Losing Game: A Novel. Will Payne. LC 10-702510. 1.50. G. W. Dillingham Company.
Losing People. Thomas P. Baird. LC 74-5757. 1974. 6.50 (ISBN 0-15-153468-3). Harcourt Brace Jovanovich.
Losing People. Thomas P. Baird. 1979. 1.75. Avon Books.
Losing to Win. A Novel. Theodore Davies. LC 6-32500. 1874. Sheldon & Company.
Loss and Gain: Callista. John Henry Newman. LC 75-450. (Victorian Fiction: Novels of Faith and Doubt). 1975. 35.00 (ISBN 0-8240-1530-4). Garland Pub.
Loss and Gain: The Story of a Convert. 15th impression. ed. John Henry Newman. (On cover: The works of Cardinal Newman). 1903. Longmans, Green, and Co.
Loss of El Dorado. Vidiadhar Surajprasad Naipaul. 1977. pap. 4.50 (ISBN 0-14-003641-5). Penguin.
Loss of El Dorado. Vidiadhar Surajprasad Naipaul. 1970. 7.50 o.p. (ISBN 0-394-43416-1). Knopf.
Loss of Heart. Robert McCrum. LC 81-69970. 1982. 13.95 (ISBN 0-670-44057-4). Viking Press.
Loss of Patients. Ralph M. McInerny. (Fathers Dowling Mystery Ser.). 256p. 1982. 10.95 (ISBN 0-8149-0864-0). Vanguard.
Loss of Patients: A Father Dowling Mystery. Ralph M McInerny. LC 82-8572. 11.95 (ISBN 0-8149-0826-8). Vanguard Press.
Loss of the Culion. Jeffrey Ashford, pseud. LC 81-51972. 1981. 9.95 (ISBN 0-8027-5445-7). Walker.
Loss of the Jane Vosper. Freeman Wills Crofts. LC 36-786. 1936. Dodd, Mead and Company.
Lost. Dale Collins. LC 33-4986. The Bobbs-Merrill Company.
Lost--a Pearle: A Novel. Sarah Elizabeth Forbush G. S. Downs Downs. LC 6-45948. (primrose series. no. 12). 1890. Street & Smith.
Lost Abroad... George Alfred Townsend. LC 8-29812. 1870. S. M. Betts and Company.
Lost Adventurer. Thomas Walter Gilkyson. LC 27-6202. 1927. C. Scribner's Sons.
Lost Ambassador: Or, The Search for the Missing Delora. Edward Phillips Oppenheim. LC 10-21747. 1910. 1.50. Little, Brown, and Company.
Lost Ambassador: Or, The Search for the Missing Delora. Edward Phillips Oppenheim. LC 21-137212. 1918. A. L. Burt Company.
Lost America. John Margolies. 6p. 1982. pap. 3.95 (ISBN 0-385-27800-4). Dial.
Lost American: A Tale of Cuba. Archibald Clavering Gunter. (On cover: The welcome series, no. 35). The Home Publishing Company.
Lost and Found. Julian Gloag. LC 81-934. 1981. 10.95 (ISBN 0-671-42828-4). Linden Press/Simon and Schuster.
Lost and Found. Sheldon Greene. LC 80-5274. 8.95 (ISBN 0-394-51250-2). Random House.
Lost and Found. large print ed. Sheldon Greene. LC 81-7432. 10.95 (ISBN 0-89621-289-0). Thorndike Press.
Lost and Found. Randall Reid. LC 75-4620. 1975. 7.95 (ISBN 0-671-22024-1). Simon and Schuster.
Lost & Found. Robert P. Smith. 164p. 1974. Repr. lib. bdg. 6.95 o.p. (ISBN 0-8161-6204-2, Large Print Bks). G K Hall.
Lost and Found. Besse Sprague. J. H. Hopkins & Son, Inc.
Lost and Found Man. Nicholas Guild. LC 75-9353. 1975. 6.95 (ISBN 0-06-122620-3). Harper's Magazine Press.
Lost and the Found. Ann Chidester. LC 63-11245. 1963. Doubleday.
Lost and the Lurking. Manly Wade Wellman. LC 81-65662. 1981. 10.95 (ISBN 0-385-17155-2). Doubleday.
Lost Angel. Elizabeth Goudge. 1972. Pyramid Bks.
Lost Angel. Elizabeth Goudge. LC 78-169137. (Illus.). 1971. 5.95. Coward, McCann & Geoghegan.
Lost Angel. Katharine Tynan Hinkson, pseud. 1908. J. B. Lippincott Company; Etc., Etc.

Lost April. Sydney Thompson. LC 38-295572. Thomas Y. Crowell Company.
Lost Areas. Helen Thorington. (Illus.). 1977. pap. 10.00. Oil Bks.
Lost Art. Burton Bernstein. LC 63-14786. 1963. Worlk Pub. Co.
Lost Atlantis. James Bramwell. 288p. 1974. pap. 4.95 (ISBN 0-87877-023-2, P-23). Newcastle Pub.
Lost Bank Note and Moat-Grange. Ellen Price Henry Wood Wood. (On cover: Seaside library. Pocket ed. no. 1235). 1889. G. Munro.
Lost Borders. Mary Hunter Austin. LC 9-28270. 1909. Harper & Brothers.
Lost Boy. Henry Van Dyke. LC 14-15403. 1914. Harper & Brothers.
Lost Boy. Thomas Wolfe & Edward Campbell Aswell. LC 65-19111. (Perennial library, P32). 1965. Harper & Row.
Lost Bride: Or, The Price of Silence. Clara Augusta Jones. LC 7-12139. (select series. no. 21). 1889. Street & Smith.
Lost Brother. Igor G. Walati. 1980. pap. 3.95 (ISBN 0-89185-202-6). Anthelion Pr.
Lost Buckaroo. Harry Sinclair Drago. LC 49-7635. (Silver star westerns).
Lost Cabin Mine. Frederick John Niven. LC 9-9250. 1909. J. Lane Company; Etc., Etc.
Lost Caesar. Ruth Fenisong. LC 45-76509. 1945. Pub. for the Crime Club by Doubleday, Doran & Company, Inc.
Lost Canyon. Clinton Dangerfield. 1932. G. H. Watt.
Lost Canyon. Germano, Peter. LC 64-7363. 1964. Arcadia House.
Lost Captain. Helen Ashton. LC 48-6151. 1948. Dodd, Mead.
Lost Caravan. Henry De Vere Stacpoole. LC 32-107777. Sears Publishing Company, Inc.
Lost Casket. Fortune Du Boisgobey. LC 6-34422. (On cover: Trans-Atlantic novels. 4). 1881. G. P. Putnam's Sons.
Lost Cavern: And Other Tales of the Fantastic. Gerald Heard. LC 48-5706. 1948. Vanguard Press.
Lost Chapel Picnic: And Other Stories. Margery Sharp. LC 73-6733. 1973. 6.95 (ISBN 0-316-78293-9). Little, Brown.
Lost Child. Rahel Sanzara & Katzin, Winifred, Tr. LC 29-22338. 1929. Longmans, Green and Co.
Lost Children. Tr. from Spanish by Joan Maclean. Ana Maria Matute. LC 65-11570. 6.95. Macmillan.
Lost Citadel. 1st Ed. Alexander Mathis. LC 54-10907. 1954. Pageant Press.
Lost Cities. Leonard Cottrell. (Illus.). 1963. pap. 2.95 o.p. (ISBN 0-448-00151-9, UL). G&D.
Lost Cities & Vanished Civilizations. Robert Silverberg. (Illus.). 1962. 4.50 o.p. (ISBN 0-8019-0837-X). Chilton.
Lost City. Carrie E. Myers Gruhn. Orig. Title: Trumpet in Zion. 1969. pap. 1.35 o.p. (38-22). Moody.
Lost City: A Novel. John Gunther. LC 63-20303. 1964. Harper & Row.
Lost Civilizations: Three Adventure Novels, Complete and Unabridged. Henry Rider Haggard. LC 53-99343. 1953. Dover Publications.
Lost Colony. Edison Marshall. (E130). 1965. pap., 5.95. Popular Lib.
Lost Colony. James F Raymond. LC 7-36637. T. B. Peterson & Brothers.
Lost Continent. Charles John Cutcliffe Wright Hyne. LC 74-176221. 1974. 6.50. O. Train.
Lost Continent. Charles John Cutcliffe Wright Hyne. LC 72-182492. 1972. 1.25. Ballantine Books.
Lost Continent. Charles John Cutcliffe Wright Hyne. LC 5071. 1900. Harper & Brothers.
Lost Countess Falka: A Story of the Orient. Richard Henry Savage. LC 8-2006. (On cover: Rialto series, no. 76). 1896. Rand, McNally & Company.
Lost Country: A Novel. J. R. Salamanca. LC 58-103541. 1958. Simon and Schuster.
Lost Creek: An Ozark Novel of the Civil War. 1st Ed. Minnie Jane Wyatt Forster. LC 52-8629. 1952. Exposition Press.
Lost Crucifix of Our Lady of Guadalupe. Fisher Alsup. LC 76-30774. (Illus.). 8.95 (ISBN 0-88319-028-1). Shoal Creek Publishers.
Lost Daughter. Louise Redfield Peattie. LC 38-29536. 1938. G. P. Putnam's Sons.
Lost Daughter: And Other Stories of the Heart. Caroline Lee Whiting Hentz. LC 4-22058. 1870. The Federal Book Company.
Lost Despatch. Friedrich Friedrich. Tr. by Williams, L. A. LC 6-44727. 1871. J. R. Osgood and Company.
Lost Diamond: The Blue Scarab) an...Interesting Story of Adventure. David Graham Adee. LC 99-34390. (On cover: Pinkerton detective series. no. 40). 1899. Laird & Lee.
Lost Diary: A Novel. 1st Ed. Joseph Sheban. LC 52-7660. 1953. Exposition Press.
Lost Discovery. Gertrude M. Robins Reynolds. LC 23-7003. George H. Doran Company.
Lost Dorsai. Gordon R Dickson. LC 80-134225. (Ace science fiction). (Illus.). 4.95 (ISBN 0-441-49299-1). Ace Books.
Lost Dutchman Mine: A Short Story of a Tall Tale. Harry G. Black. LC 75-2825. (Illus.). 110p. 1975. 7.95 o.p. (ISBN 0-8283-1613-9). Branden.
Lost Eagles. 1st Ed. Ralph A Graves. LC 55-9260. 1955. Knopf.
Lost Ecstasy. Mary Roberts Rinehart. (Dell Book). 1977. 1.75 (ISBN 0-440-15035-3). Dell Pub. Co.
Lost Ecstasy: A Novel. Mary Roberts Rinehart. LC 27-13977. George H. Doran Company.
Lost Eden. Paul McGinnis. LC 47-3263. 1947. R. M. McBride & Company.
Lost Eden: A Novel. Effie Breland Day. LC 49-2146. Chapman S Grimes.
Lost Eden: Noli Me Tangere. Jose Rizal Y Alonso. LC 60-53368. 1961. Indiana University Press.
Lost Eden: Noli Me Tangere) Jose Rizal Y Alonso. LC 68-9712. 1968. Greenwood Press.
Lost Eleven. Curtis Kent Bishop. LC 50-9512. 1950. Steck Co.
Lost Empires: Being Richard Herncastle's Account of His Life on the Variety Stage from November 1913 to August 1914 Together with a Prologue and Epilogue. John Boynton Priestley. (95-181). 1968. Popular Lib.
Lost Empires: Being Richard Herncastle's Account of His Life on the Variety Stage from November 1913 to August 1914, Together with a Prologue and Epilogue. John Boynton Priestley. LC 65-21351. 1965. Little, Brown.
Lost Empires: Being Richard Herncastle's Account of His Life on the Variety Stage from November 1913 to August 1914, Together with a Prologue and Epilogue. John Boynton Priestley. LC 66-50835. 1965. Heinemann.
Lost Enchantment. Barbara Cartland. 1976. pap. 1.25 o.p. (ISBN 0-515-04162-9). BJ Pub Group.
Lost Enchantment. Barbara Cartland. 1973. (pbk.) 0.95. Pyramid.
Lost Endeavor. Guy Newell Boothby. LC 6-15032. (Half-title" Iris series). 1895. Macmillan and Co.
Lost Endeavor. John Masefield. 1917. The Macmillan Company.
Lost Endeavour. John Masefield. LC 25-24277. 1925. The Macmillan Company.
Lost Face. Jack London. LC 10-6488. 1910. 1.50. The Macmillan Company.
Lost Face: Best Science Fiction from Czechoslovakia. Josef Nesvadba. LC 71-126982. 1971. 5.95 (ISBN 0-8008-5020-3). Taplinger Pub. Co.
Lost Farm Camp. Henry Herbert Knibbs. LC 12-6865. 1912. 1.25. Houghton Mifflin Company.
Lost Fields: A Novel. Michael McLaverty. LC 41-17325. 1941. Longmans, Green and Co.
Lost: Fifty Sun. Alfred Elton Van Vogt. (Daw Science Fiction Ser.). Orig. Title: Book of Van Vogt. 1979. pap. 1.75 o.p. (ISBN 0-87997-491-5, UE1491). Daw Bks.
Lost Fight. Hilda Frances Margaret Prescott. LC 28-22665. Dodd, Mead & Company.
Lost Footsteps. Silviu Craciunas. 318p. (Orig.). pap. 4.95 (ISBN 0-88264-176-X). Diane Bks.
Lost for a Woman. A Novel. May Agnes Early Fleming. LC 36-29334. 1880. G. W. Carleton & Co.
Lost for Love. Mary Elizabeth Braddon Maxwell. (Seaside library. v. 15, no. 295). 1878. G. Munro.
Lost Frangrance: A Novel. Alice Elinor Lambert. LC 33-208097. 1933. The Vanguard Press.
Lost Fraulein. Ben Haas. LC 74-102347. 1970. 4.95. Random House.
Lost Fraulein. Richard Meade, pseud. 1970. 4.95 o.p. (ISBN 0-394-43417-X). Random.
Lost Galleon. Bret Harte. 1976. Repr. of 1867 ed. lib. bdg. 8.95x (ISBN 0-88411-591-7). Amereon Ltd.
Lost Gallows. John Dickson Carr. LC 31-58823. 1931. Harper & Brothers.
Lost Garden. Jane Aiken Hodge. LC 82-73266. 1982. 13.95 (ISBN 0-698-11188-5). Coward, McCann & Geoghegan.
Lost Garden. Jane Aiken Hodge. 320p. 1982. 13.95 (ISBN 0-698-11188-5, Coward). Putnam Pub Group.
Lost General. Elswyth Thane. LC 74-4540. 1974. 6.95. Aeonian Press.
Lost General. 1st Ed. Elswyth Thane. LC 53-933011. 1953. Duell, Sloan and Pearce.
Lost Girl. D. H Lawrence & John Worthen. LC 82-70234. 1982. 22.95 (ISBN 0-670-44101-5). Viking Press.
Lost Girl. David Herbert Lawrence. LC 68-23405. (Viking compass book, C226). 1968. Viking Press.
Lost Girl. David Herbert Lawrence. LC 21-4161. 1921. T. Seltzer.
Lost Girl. David Herbert Lawrence & John Worthen. LC 80-40457. (Laurence, David Herbert, 1885-1930. Cambridge Edition of the Letters & Works of D.H. Laurence). 1981. 49.50 (ISBN 0-521-23303-8) (ISBN 0-521-29895-4). Cambridge University Press.
Lost Glove with Sequel: The Pale Young Maiden. Hendrik Conscience. LC 6-28062. 1887. J. Murphy & Co.
Lost Goddess. David Potter. LC 8-9523. 1908. H. Holt and Company.
Lost Gold. Mildred Fielder. LC 78-71706. (Illus.). 1978. pap. 7.95 (ISBN 0-87970-146-3). North Plains.
Lost Gospel. Arthur Cheney Train. LC 25-17275. 1925. C. Scribner's Sons.
Lost Guide. Joseph Elgon Norvell. LC 10-18379. 1.00. The Christian Witness Co.
Lost Half Hour. Laurence Walter Meynell. LC 77-361971. 1976. 3.25 (ISBN 0-333-19879-4). Macmillan.
Lost Half Hour. Laurence Walter Meynell. LC 77-15007. 1977. 7.95 (ISBN 0-8128-2420-2). Stein and Day.
Lost Haven. Kylie Tennant, pseud. LC 46-2674. 1946. The Macmillan Company.
Lost Heir of Linlithgow. Emma Dorothy Eliza Nevitte Southworth. LC 8-10825. T. B. Peterson & Brothers.
Lost Heiress. Emma Dorothy Eliza Nevitte Southworth. LC 12-38911. T. B. Peterson and Brothers.
Lost Heiress: A Tale of Love, Battle, and Adventure. Ernest Glanville. (On cover: Harper's Franklin square library. no. 692). 1891. Harper & Brothers.
Lost Heiress of Merriott Manor. Pamela Pacotti. (Orig.). 1982. pap. 2.25 (ISBN 0-89083-919-0). Zebra.
Lost Heritage. Bruno Frank. Tr. by Brooks, Cyrus Harry. LC 37-28690. 1937. The Viking Press.
Lost Heritage. Jan Herbrand. (Coronet Gothic Novles Ser). 192p. 1972. 5.95 o.p. (ISBN 0-448-02057-2). G&D.
Lost Hero. Elizabeth Stuart Phelps Ward & Herbert Dickinson Ward. LC 72-3106. (Black Heritage Library Collection). (Illus.). 1972. 12.50 (ISBN 0-8369-9090-0). Books for Libraries Press.
Lost Hero. Elizabeth Stuart Phelps H. D. Ward Ward & Ward, Herbert Dickinson, 1861- Joint Author. LC 8-33108. 1891. Roberts Brothers.
Lost Home. J. Avyzius. 544p. 1974. 7.45 (ISBN 0-8285-0945-X, Pub. by Progress Pubs USSR). Imported Pubns.
Lost Homecoming. Harry Harrison Kroll. LC 50-10398. 1950. Coward-McCann.
Lost Honor of Katharina Blum. Heinrich Boll. Tr. by Leila Vennewitz from Ger. LC 74-28138. (McGraw-Hill Paperbacks). 1976. pap. 4.95 (ISBN 0-07-006429-6, SP). McGraw.
Lost Honor of Katharina Blum: How Violence Develops and Where It Can Lead. Heinrich Boll. LC 74-28138. 1975. (ISBN 0-07-006425-3). McGraw-Hill.
Lost Horizon. Beorge Colby Borley. LC 21-17082. 1921. Dodd, Mead and Company.
Lost Horizon. James Hilton. LC 66-1483. (Reader's enrichment series). 1964. Washington Square Press.
Lost Horizon. James Hilton. 1973. 1.25 (ISBN 0-671-78307-6). Pocket Books.
Lost Horizon. James Hilton. LC 48-4398. (Living Library). 1948. World Pub. Co.
Lost Horizon. James Hilton. LC 33-25382. 1933. W. Morrow & Company.
Lost Horizon. James Hilton. LC 44-40365. 1944. Pocket Books Inc.
Lost Horizon. Introd. by Harold C. Martin. Suggestions for Reading and Discussion, by Frances Bantlett. School Ed. James Hilton. LC 62-52424. (Riverside literature series, R8). 1962. Published for Morrow by Houghton Mifflin.
Lost House. Frances Shelley Wees. LC 38-32620. 1938. Macrae Smith Company.
Lost Hunter. A Tale of Early Times... John Turvill Adams. 1856. Derby & Jackson.
Lost Hunters: A Story of Wild Man & Great Beasts. Joseph Alexander Altsheler. 311p. Repr. of 1918 ed. lib. bdg. 13.20x (ISBN 0-88411-949-1). Amereon Ltd.
Lost Ideal. Annie S Swan Smith. LC 8-8619. Ward, Lock & Bowden, Limited.
Lost Illusion. authorized ed. Grace L Keith Johnston. LC 7-10797. (On cover: Lovell's international series no. 146). 1891. United States Book Company.
Lost Illusions. Honore De Balzac. Tr. by Herbert J Hunt. (Penguin classics). 1976. 2.95 (ISBN 0-14-044251-0). Penguin Books.
Lost Illusions. Honore De Balzac. LC 67-11592. (Modern library giants G97). (Illus.). 1967. Modern Library.
Lost Illusions. Honore De Balzac. Tr. by Herbert James Hunt. LC 79-29738. (Penguin classics L251). 1971. 0.75 (ISBN 0-14-044251-0). Penguin.
Lost Illusions. Honore De Balzac. Tr. by Ellen Marriage. (Half-title: Everyman's library, ed. by Ernest Rhys. Fiction). 1913. J. M. Dent & Sons, Ltd.
Lost Illusions. Honore De Balzac. Tr. by Ellen Marriage. LC 37-5596. (Half-title: Everyman's library, ed. by Ernest Rhys. Fiction. no. 656). 1925. J. M. Dent & Sons, Ltd.
Lost Illusions. Honore De Balzac. Tr. by Herbert J. Hunt. (Classics Ser). 1971. pap. 3.45 o.p. (ISBN 0-14-044251-0, L251). Penguin.
Lost Illusions. Honore De Balzac. (Modern Library Giants). 4.95 o.p. (G97). Modern Lib.
Lost Illusions. Honore De Balzac. lib. bdg. 5.70x o.p. (ISBN 0-88307-069-3). Gannon.
Lost Illusions: The Two Poets; Eve and David. Honore De Balzac. Tr. by Katharine Prescott Wormeley. (Half-title: The comedy of human life... Scenes from provincial life). 1893. Roberts Brothers.
Lost in a Great City. Amanda Minnie Douglas. LC 6-33477. 1881. Lee and Shepard.
Lost in a Great City. Amanda Minnie Douglas. LC 8-31165. Lothrop, Lee & Shepard Co.
Lost in a Mist. Berta LaVan Barker. (YA) 1981. 6.95 (Avalon). Bouregy.
Lost in New York: Or, Meta's Misfortunes. Nathan D. Urner. (On cover: The select series, no. 84). 1891. Street & Smith.
Lost in Pompeii. Henry Howard Clark. LC 7-26234. (On cover: Peace Island series). 1883. D. Lothrop and Company.
Lost in the Canon. The Story of Sam Willett's Adventures on the Great Colorado of the West. Alfred Rochefort Calhoun. (On cover: Boy's home library, v u. no. 12). 1888. A. L. Burt.
Lost in the Funhouse. John Barth. 1969. pap. 2.95 (ISBN 0-553-14059-0). Bantam.
Lost in the Funhouse. John Barth. 1969. pap. 2.45 o.p. (ISBN 0-448-00239-6, UL). G&D.
Lost in the Funhouse: Fiction for Print, Tape, Live Voice. John Barth. LC 68-22615. 1968. 4.95. Doubleday.
Lost in the Great Atlantic Valley. Ed. by Everett Franklin Bleiler. (Frank Reade Library: Vol. 6). 1980. lib. bdg. 44.00 (ISBN 0-8240-3545-3). Garland Pub.
Lost in the Mammoth Cave. Daniel Riley Guernsey. LC 5-15690. Broadway Publishing Company.
Lost Inca. A Tale of Discovery in the Vale of the Inti-Mayu. Alfred F. Sears. LC 8-3378. Cassell & Company, Limited.
Lost Indian Magic: A Mystery Story of the Red Man As He Lived Before the White Man Came. G. Moon & C. Moon. 1977. lib. bdg. 39.95 (ISBN 0-8490-2185-5). Gordon Pr.
Lost Inheritance. Ann C. Addley. 1982. 8.95 (ISBN 0-533-05165-7). Vantage.
Lost Inheritance. Isabel Cabot. (Candlelight mystery). 1974. (pbk.) 0.75. Dell.
Lost Island. Mason Cabell. LC 41-38117.
Lost Island... James Norman Hall. LC 44-4714. 1944. Little, Brown and Company.
Lost Island. James Norman Hall. LC 45-9167. 1945. The Sun Dial Press.
Lost Island. Phyllis A. Whitney. LC 70-125545. 1970. 5.95. Doubleday.
Lost Jewels of Nabooti, No. 10. Raymond A. Montgomery. 128p. (Orig.). pap. 1.50 (ISBN 0-553-14358-1). Bantam.
Lost Kachina. Ruth Potts. (Orig.). 1979. pap. 1.75 (ISBN 0-532-17216-7). Woodhill.
Lost Key: Or, The Mysterious Box. Bessie C. Morris & Spear, Anne B., Joint Author. LC 7-32489. 1879. Grant, Faires & Rodgers, Printers.
Lost King. Raymond De Capite. LC 61-12752. 1961. D. McKay Co.
Lost King. Rafael Sabatini. LC 37-19156. 1937. Houghton Mifflin Company.
Lost King. Henry Shackelford. 1903. Brentano's.
Lost Lady. Willa Sibert Cather. LC 73-4265. 1973. 7.50 (ISBN 0-394-48558-0). Knopf Distributed by Random House.
Lost Lady. Willa Sibert Cather. LC 23-13012. 1923. A. A. Knopf.
Lost Lady. Willa Sibert Cather. LC 35-33395. 1932. A. A. Knopf.
Lost Lady. Octavus Roy Cohen. LC 51-35744. (Gold medal books, 172). 1951. Fawcett Publications.
Lost Lady. Eva McDonald. 1973. pap. 0.75 o.p. (07270). Curtis.
Lost Lady of Old Years: A Romance. John Buchan. LC 3-15222. 1899. J. Lane.
Lost Lamp. Sara Lucile Jenkins. LC 50-5992. 1950. Crowell.
Lost Land. Edison Marshall. Orig. Title: Dian of the Lost Land. 1972. pap. 0.75 o.p. (07227). Curtis.
Lost Land: A Novel. George H Freitag. LC 47-1228. 1947. Coward-McCann, Inc.
Lost Lands. Vansittart, Peter. LC 64-21104. bds. 4.95. Walker.
Lost Laughter. Barbara Cartland. LC 80-12897. 9.95 (ISBN 0-525-14891-4). Dutton.
Lost Laughter. Mateel Howe Farnham. LC 33-7689. 1933. Dodd, Mead & Company.

Lost Leader. Edward Phillips Oppenheim. LC 7-25082. 1907. Little, Brown & Company.
Lost Leader. Edward Phillips Oppenheim. LC 20-18817. 1919. Little, Brown & Company.
Lost Leader. Edward Phillips Oppenheim. LC 6-18998. 1906. Little, Brown & Company.
Lost Lectures or the Fruits of Experience. Maurice Baring. 1932. 25.00 (ISBN 0-8274-2995-9). R West.
Lost Legends of the Silver State. Jerry Higgs. 1976. 7.95 (ISBN 0-914740-20-2). Western Epics.
Lost Legion. Robert Valentine Mathews. LC 10-1777. 1909. 1.00. E. C. Hill.
Lost Legion. H. Warner Munn. LC 79-7051. 1980. 14.95 (ISBN 0-385-14828-3). Doubleday.
Lost Legions. Renzo Biasion et al. LC 67-11143. 1967. 7.95 o.p. Knopf.
Lost Legions: Three Italian War Novels, by. Biasion, Renzo. The Army of Love et al. Tr. by Archibald Colquhoun & Antonia Cowan. LC 67-11148. 1967. Knopf.
Lost Lenore. Thomas Mayne Reid. LC 44-22008. 1872. Carleton.
Lost Lenore: A Novel. Thomas Mayne Reid. LC 51-48706. (Capt. Mayne Reid's works). G. W. Dillingham.
Lost Life. A Novel. Emily H Moore. LC 7-26215. 1871. G. W. Carleton & Co.; Etc., Etc.
Lost Lineage: A Novel. Carrie Goldsmith Childs. LC 6-20976. 1897. Mayflower Publishing Co.
Lost Lode. by f. x. l. pseud. ed. Frances Christine Tiernan. (On cover: Catholic library). H. L. Kilner & Co.
Lost Love. Barbara Cartland. (Historical Romance Ser.). 1975. pap. 1.25 o.p. (ISBN 0-515-03588-2, V3588). BJ Pub Group.
Lost Love. new ed., rev. ed. Annie Ogle. LC 17-484. 1859. T. J. Crowen.
Lost Love, Last Love. Rosemary Rogers. 1981. pap. 2.95 (ISBN 0-380-75515-7, 75515). Avon.
Lost Madonna. Isabelle Holland. LC 80-5996. 1981. 11.95 (ISBN 0-89256-170-X). Rawson, Wade.
Lost Madonna. large print ed. Isabelle Holland. LC 82-4873. 1982. 11.95 (ISBN 0-89621-364-1). Thorndike Press.
Lost Mameluke: A Tale of Egypt. David M Beddoe. LC 13-19947. 1913. E.P. Dutton & Co.
Lost Man! Grant Watson, Elliot Lovegood. LC 34-12320. 1934. Harper & Brothers.
Lost Man's Lane: A Second Episode in the Life of Amelia Butterworth. Anna Katharine Green Rohlfs. LC 7-40744. 1898. G. P. Putnam's Sons.
Lost Manuscript: A Novel. authorized translation from the 16th german ed. Gustav Freytag. LC 51-46674. 1890. Open Court Pub. Co.
Lost Manuscript. A Novel. Gustav Freytag. LC 4-31650. 1892. The Open Court Publishing Company.
Lost Mark. Patrick Wynnton. LC 29-20104. 1929. J. B. Lippincott Company.
Lost Men. Benedict Thielen. LC 46-25116. 1946. D. Appleton-Century Co., Inc.
Lost Merry-Go-Round. Dorothy Pulis Lathrop. LC 34-35692. 1934. The Macmillan Company.
Lost Million. Winthrop Alden. LC 13-37549. 1913. Dodd, Mean and Company.
Lost Mine: A Story of the Western Plains and Mountain Lands. James H Connelly. LC 6-30687. (On cover: Once a week library, v. 9, no. 21-22). 1892. P.F. Collier.
Lost Mine Named Salvation. Nelson Nye. 1975. (pbk.) 0.95. Ace Books.
Lost Mine of the Mono: A Tale of the Sierra Nevada. Charles Herman Bruno Klette. LC 10-3287. 1909. Cochrane Publishing Company.
Lost Mr. Linthwaite. Joseph Smith Fletcher. LC 23-184015. 1921. Hodder and Stoughton.
Lost Mr. Linthwaite. Joseph Smith Fletcher. LC 23-20339. 1923. A. A. Knopf.
Lost Model. A Romance. Henry Hooper. LC 7-5264. 1874. J. B. Lippincott & Co.
Lost Moon Mystery. Leda A. Wadsworth. LC 45-9576. 1945. Farrar & Rinehart, Inc.
Lost Morning... Du Bose Heyward. LC 36-18258. Farrar & Rinehart, Incorporated.
Lost Musicians. William Heinesen. LC 70-163120. (Library of Scandinavian literature, v. 12). 1971. 6.95. Twayne.
Lost Name. Joseph Sheridan Le Fanu. LC 76-5272. (Le Fann, Joseph Sheridan, 1814-1873. Works. 1976). 1976. vols.) 59.00(3 (ISBN 0-405-09220-2). Arno Press.
Lost Name: A Novelette. Madeleine Vinton Dahlgren. LC 6-32180. 1886. Ticknor and Company.
Lost Nation. Noah Ephraim Aronstam. LC 37-176581. Duo-Art Press.
Lost Nation. Everett McNeil. LC 18-20478. E. P. Dutton & Co.
Lost Naval Papers. Frederick Harcourt Kitchin. LC 18-6310. 1918. E. P. Dutton & Company.
Lost on Grand River. G. O Bristow. LC 4410. 1900. Cherokee Air Publishing Company.
Lost on the Trail. Isabella Macdonald Alden. LC 11-4603. 1911. Lothrop, Lee & Shepard Co.
Lost on Venus. Edgar Rice Burroughs. LC 63-21731. (Illus.). 1963. Canaveral Press.
Lost on Venus. Edgar Rice Burroughs. LC 25-4994. Edgar Rice Burroughs, Inc.
Lost One. Mabel Dana Lyon. LC 58-6172. 1958. Harper.
Lost Ones. Samuel Beckett. LC 72-84341. (Evergreen original E-587). 1972. 1.65 (ISBN 0-394-17786-X). Grove Press.
Lost Ones. Ian Cameron, pseud. 1968. 5.95 o.p. Morrow.
Lost Ones. Donald Gordon Payne. LC 68-31912. (Illus.). 1968. W. Morrow.
Lost Packer Clan. 1st Ed. Francis Stone. LC 56-117815. 1956. Pageant Press.
Lost Paradise. Frederic Arnold Kummer. LC 14-756725. 1.25. W. J. Watt & Company.
Lost Paradise: A Boyhood on a Maine Coast Farm. Robert P. Coffin. LC 78-144951. 1971. Repr. of 1947 ed. 29.00 (ISBN 0-403-00904-9). Scholarly.
Lost Parchment: A Detective Story. Fergus Hume. LC 14-9409. G. W. Dillingham Company.
Lost Prince. Frances Hodgson Burnett. LC 15-214371. 1915. The Centry Co.
Lost Princess. William Frederick Dix. LC 7-26021. 1907. Moffat, Yard & Company.
Lost Profile. Francoise Quiorez. LC 75-37811. 6.95 (ISBN 0-440-05017-0). Delacorte Press.
Lost Profile. Francoise Quiorez. (Dell Book). 1977. 1.95 (ISBN 0-440-15072-8). Dell Pub. Co.
Lost Profile. Francoise Sagon, pseud. 192p. 1976. 6.95 o.p. (ISBN 0-440-05017-0). Delacorte.
Lost Profile: A Novel. Francoise Quiorez. LC 76-363912. 1976. 2.75 (ISBN 0-233-96706-0). Deutsch.
Lost Property. Ruby Mildred Ayres. LC 43-5037. 1943. Doubleday, Doran and Company, Inc.
Lost Provinces: A Novel. Stephen Glazier. LC 80-69635. 5.95 (ISBN 0-380-77255-8). Avon.
Lost Provinces: How Vansittart Came Back to France. Louis Tracy. LC 98-958. 1898. G. P. Putnam's Sons.
Lost Pueblo. Zane Grey. 1979. pap. 1.75 (ISBN 0-671-83106-2). PB.
Lost Pueblo. 1st Ed. Zane Grey. LC 54-8954. 1954. Harper.
Lost Queen. Norah Robinson Lofts. LC 69-13645. 1969. 5.95. Doubleday.
Lost Race & Adult Fantasy Fiction Series, 69 bks. Ed. by R. Reginald & Douglas Alver Menville. (Illus.). 1978. Set. lib. bdg. 1500.00 (ISBN 0-405-10950-4). Ayer Co.
Lost Range. Frank Chester Robertson. LC 46-3761. 1946. E. P. Dutton & Company, Inc.
Lost Rapture. Beulah Poynter. LC 34-17972. Greenberg.
Lost Rebellion: A Novel. James Wylie. LC 72-139748. 1971. 6.95 (ISBN 0-671-27077-X). Trident Press.
Lost River. Alice Walworth Graham. LC 38-8694. 1938. Dodd, Mead & Company.
Lost River. Alice Walworth, pseud. LC 38-8694. 1938. Dodd, Mead & Company.
Lost River Buckaroos. Charles Morris Martin. LC 37-16219. Greenberg.
Lost River Canyon. Archie Joscelyn. 1976. 4.95. Avalon Books.
Lost River Loot. Jackson Cole, pseud. 1974. (pbk.) 0.95. Popular Library.
Lost Road. Richard Harding Davis. LC 13-21706. 1913. C. Scribner's Sons.
Lost Road. Arthur Lee Leonard. LC 34-35315. The Macaulay Company.
Lost Road. Charles Elbert Scoggins. LC 41-2091. 1941. Doubleday, Doran & Co., Inc.
Lost Rosary: Or, Our Irish Girls: Their Trials, Temptations, and Triumphs. Con O'Leary. LC 7-32597. 1870. P. Donahoe.
Lost Salt Gift of Blood. Alistair MacLeod. LC 76-363775. 8.95 (ISBN 0-7710-5574-9). McClelland and Stewart Ltd.
Lost Sentinel. Translated from the French by Humphrey Hare. Rene Hardy. LC 60-124374. 3.95. Doubleday.
Lost Sheep. Vere Dawson Shortt. LC 15-5420. 1915. John Lane.
Lost Sheep. Translated by Frances Frenaye. Henry Bordeaux. LC 55-13587. 1955. Macmillan.
Lost Shepherd. 1st Ed. Agnes Mary White Sanford. LC 53-541995. 1953. Lippincott.
Lost Ship: Or, The Atlantic Steamer. William Johnson Neale. (On cover: Library of select novels. no. 18). 1843. Harper & Brothers.
Lost Silk Hat. Lord Dunsany. Ed. by Edmund R. Brown. (International Pocket Library). pap. 3.00. Branden.
Lost Silver of Briffault. Amelia Edith Huddleston Barr. LC 6-7985. 1885. Phillips & Hunt; Cincinnati, Cranston & Stowe.
Lost Sir Massingberd: A Romance of Real Life. James Payn. LC 75-32794. (Literature of Mystery and Detection). 1976. 19.00 (ISBN 0-405-07891-9). Arno Press.
Lost Skiff. Donald Wetzel. LC 69-14845. 1969. Harcourt, Brace & World.
Lost Son. Mary Linskill. (On cover: Seaside library. Pocket ed. no. 473). 1885. G. Munro.
Lost Song. Loren S Noblitt. LC 21-135034. 1921. Pillar of Fire.
Lost Sons. Translated from the German by Andrew Foster-Melliar. 1st Ed. Stefan Olivier. LC 60-13552. 1961. Doubleday.
Lost Souls. Gregory Bear. 320p. 1982. pap. 2.95 (ISBN 0-441-49492-7, Pub. by Charter Bks). Ace Bks.
Lost Speech of Abraham Lincoln: A Story. Honore McCue Willsie Morrow. 1925. Frederick A. Stokes Company.
Lost Springtime: The Chronicle of a Journey Far Away and Long Ago by Julian Dana. Julian Dana. LC 38-7059. 1938. The Macmillan Company.
Lost Squadron. Dick Grace. LC 32-8699. Grosset & Dunlap.
Lost Stage Valley. Frank Bonham. LC 48-4153. (Essandees western). 1948. Simon and Schuster.
Lost Star, and Other Stories. Maud Louise Hudnut Chapin. LC 49-14099. 1948. Falmouth Pub. House.
Lost Steps. 2d american ed. Alejo Carpentier. LC 67-24639. 1967. Knopf.
Lost Steps. Alejo Carpentier. (Illus.). 1979. 2.50 (ISBN 0-380-46177-3). Avon Books.
Lost Steps. Translated from the Spanish by Harriet De Onis. 1st Ed. Alejo Carpentier. LC 56-8906. 1956. Knopf.
Lost Stradivaruis. John Meade Falkner. (Detective Ser.). 93p. 1982. pap. 3.00 (ISBN 0-486-24334-6). Dover.
Lost Sunrise. Kathleen Thompson Norris. LC 39-30540. 1939. Doubleday, Doran & Company, Inc.
Lost Tales: Ales. Karen Blixen. LC 57-100373. 1957. Random House.
Lost Threshold: A Novel. Thomas Gerald Wheeler. (Illus.). 1968. S. G. Phillips.
Lost to the World. H. C. Hoffman. (On cover: Munro's library, popular novels. v. 1. no. 396). 1885. N. L. Munro.
Lost Trail. Edward Sylvester Ellis. LC 11-13615. 0.50. Hurst & Company.
Lost Trail of the Sahara, a Novel: Translated from the French by Paul Bowles. 1st American Ed. Frison-Roche, Roger. LC 52-9032. 1952. Prentice-Hall.
Lost Traveler. Sanora Babb. LC 58-7404. 1958. Reynal.
Lost Traveller. Ruthven Todd. LC 68-29041. (Illus.). 1968. 1.50. Dover Publications.
Lost Traveller. Antonia White. LC 80-20016. 1980. 5.95 (ISBN 0-8037-4935-X). Dial Press.
Lost Traveller. Steve Wilson. 1978. 2.95 (ISBN 0-441-49535-4). Ace Books.
Lost Traveller: A Motorcycle Grail Quest Epic and Science Fiction Western. Steve Wilson. LC 77-72008. (Illus.). 1977. 7.95 (ISBN 0-312-49890-X). St. Martin's Press.
Lost Traveller, a Novel. Antonia White. LC 50-6924. 1950. Viking Press.
Lost Treasure. Jacob Keel. LC 48-282574. 1948.
Lost Treasure Cave: Or, Adventures with the Cowboys of Colorado. Everett McNeil. LC 5-32834. 1905. E. P. Dutton and Company.
Lost Treasure Restored. William Chauncey Brookshire. LC 12-1798. Printed by Von Boeckmann-Jones Co.
Lost Tribes. James Owen Hannay. LC 14-44628. Hodder & Stoughton, George H. Doran Company.
Lost Tribes and the Land of Nod. An Original Natural Gas Story. Artemus P Kerr. 1897. Indiana Newspaper Union.
Lost Trumpet. James Leslie Mitchell. LC 32-29198. The Bobbs-Merrill Company.
Lost Valley: A Novel. Katharine Fullerton Gerould. LC 22-1722. 1922. Harper & Brothers.
Lost Valley, and Other Stories. Algernon Blackwood. LC 70-167442. (Short story index reprint series). (Illus.). 1971. (ISBN 0-8369-3968-9). Books for Libraries Press.
Lost Victim. T. A Waters. LC 73-5060. 1973. 5.95 (ISBN 0-394-48247-6). Random House.
Lost Viol. Matthew Phipps Shiel. LC 5-29531. 1905. E. J. Clode.
Lost Virgin. Peggy Gaddis, pseud. LC 45-6563. 1945. Phoenix Press.
Lost Virgin: A Novel. Charles Francis Bowen. LC 58-8443. 1959. B. Humphries.
Lost Wagon. James Arthur Kjelgaard. LC 55-7163. 1955. Dodd, Mead.
Lost Wagon Train. Grey, Zane. (Great western edition 21). 1962. Grosset & Dunlap.
Lost Wagon Train. Zane Grey. LC 36-20995. 1936. Harper & Brothers.
Lost Wagons. Dane Coolidge. LC 23-280332. E. P. Dutton & Company.
Lost Wedding-Ring. Jane Emmet Griswold. LC 7-165. 1887. G. P. Putnam's Sons.
Lost Weekend. Charles Jackson. 1973. (pbk.) 1.25. Manor Books.
Lost Weekend. Charles Reginald Jackson. LC 44-1290. 1944. Farrar & Rinehart, Inc.
Lost Weekend. Charles Reginald Jackson. (Modern Library of the World's best books 258). 1948. Modern Library.
Lost Weekend. Charles Reginald Jackson. LC 78-26163. 1979. 10.00 (ISBN 0-8376-0430-3). R. Bentley.
Lost Wife. Emily Sharp H. Cameron. LC 7-331257. (On cover: Seaside library. Pocket ed. no. 1205). G. Munro.
Lost Witness: Or, The Mystery of Leah Paget. Emma Murdoch Van Deventer. (library of choice fiction, v. 1). 1890. Laird & Lee.
Lost Wolf. Peter Henry Morland. LC 28-278072. 1928. Macy-Masius, The Vanguard Press.
Lost Wolf River. easy eye ed. Dwight Bennett. Orig. Title: When a Nurse a Doctor. 1968. pap. 0.60 o.p. (73-734). Lancer.
Lost Wolf River. Dwight Bennett Newton. LC 52-5226. (A Double D western). 1952. Doubleday.
Lost Word: A Christmas Legend of Long Ago. Henry Van Dyke. LC 98-127628. 1898. C. Scribner's Sons.
Lost World. Arthur Conan Doyle. LC 59-13339. (Looking glass library, 10). (Illus.). 1959. Looking Glass Library; Distributed by Random House.
Lost World. Arthur Conan Doyle. Hodder & Stoughton George H. Doran Company.
Lost World. Arthur Conan Doyle. LC 43-15357. 1943. Triangle Books.
Lost World. Intro. by Alistair MacLean. 240p. 1980. cancelled (ISBN 0-7195-3568-9). Transatlantic.
Lost World of the Colorado. Jack Heming. LC 46-409322. 1940. F. Warne & Co., Ltd.
Lost World of 2001. Arthur Charles Clarke. LC 79-16928. (Gregg Press science fiction series). (Illus.). 1979. 12.50 (ISBN 0-8398-2565-X). Gregg Press.
Lost Worlds. Lin Carter. (Science Fiction Ser.). 1980. pap. 1.95 o.p. (ISBN 0-87997-556-3, UJ1556). Daw Bks.
Lost Worlds. Leonard Cottrell. Orig. Title: Horizon Book of Lost Worlds. 1964. 20.00 o.p. Intl Pubns Serv.
Lost Worlds. Clark Ashton Smith. LC 44-9792. 1944. Arkham House.
Lost Worlds of 2001. Arthur C. Clarke. 1979. lib. bdg. 12.50 (ISBN 0-8398-2509-9, Gregg). G K Hall.
Lost Worlds, Unknown Horizons: Nine Stories of Science Fiction. Robert Silverberg. LC 78-18345. 6.95 (ISBN 0-8407-6601-7). T. Nelson.
Lost Year. 1st Ed. Robert Hazel. LC 52-132393. 1953. World Pub. Co.
Lost Years of Jesus. 1st Ed. John P Brown. LC 54-13214. Pageant Press.
Lot & Company. Will Levington Comfort. LC 15-24003. 1915. 1.25. George H. Doran Company.
Lot Leslie's Folks and Their Queer Adventures Among the French and Indians. A. D. 1755-1763. Eleanor Cecilia Donnelly. LC 124. H. L. Kilner & Co.
Lot of Her Neighbors. Bonner McMillion. LC 52-13730. 1953. Lippincott.
Lot 13. Dorothea Gerard Longard De Longgarde. LC 7-15157. (On cover: Appletons' town and country library. no. 135). 1894. D. Appleton and Company.
Lothair. Benjamin Disraeli Beaconsfield. LC 75-329012. (Oxford English novels). 1975. 16.00 (ISBN 0-19-255356-9). Oxford University Press.
Lothair. Benjamin Disraeli Beaconsfield. LC 75-98810. 1970. Greenwood Press.
Lothair. Benjamin Disraeli Beaconsfield. LC 75-478. (Victorian Fiction: Novels of Faith and Doubt). 1975. (ISBN 0-8240-1556-8). Garland Pub.
Lothair. Benjamin Disraeli Beaconsfield. LC 78-115230. 1970. (ISBN 0-403-00458-6). Scholarly Press.
Lothair. Benjamin Disraeli. LC 75-98810. Repr. of 1906 ed. lib. bdg. 17.25x (ISBN 0-8371-2846-3, BELO). Greenwood.
Lothair. Benjamin Disraeli. Ed. by Vernon Bogdanor. (Oxford English Novels Ser). 414p. 1975. 16.95x o.p. (ISBN 0-19-255356-9). Oxford U Pr.
Lothair. Benjamin Disraeli. LC 78-115230. 1971. Repr. 14.00 (ISBN 0-403-00458-6). Scholarly.
Lothair, Repr. Of 1870 Ed. Benjamin Disraeli. Ed. by Robert L. Wolff. Bd. with Lothaw; or, the Adventures of a Young Gentleman in Search of a Religion. Bret Harte. (Victorian Fiction Ser). 1975. lib. bdg. 66.00 (ISBN 0-8240-1556-8). Garland Pub.
Lothair. By the Right Honorable B. Disraeli... Benjamin Disraeli Beaconsfield. LC 31-19526. 1870. D. Appleton and Company.
Lothaw; or, the Adventures of a Young Gentleman in Search of a Religion see Lothair.
Lotta Embury's Career. Elia Wilkinson Peattie. LC 15-18966. 1915. 1.00. Houghton Mifflin Company.

Lotta Schmidt and Other Stories. Anthony Trollope. LC 80-1886. (Trollope, Anthony, 1815-1882. Selections. 1981). 1981. 45.00 (ISBN 0-405-14151-3). Arno Press.

Lotte in Weimar. Thomas Mann. Tr. by Helen Tracy Porter Lowe. LC 73-383793. (Penguin Modern classics, 2850). 1968. Penguin.

Lotteries. Daoma Winston. LC 79-19096. 1980. 10.95 (ISBN 0-688-03560-4). Morrow.

Lotteries. Daoma Winston. 320p. 1981. pap. 2.75 (ISBN 0-671-41277-9). PB.

Lottery. William E. Woodward. LC 24-24348. 1924. Harper & Brothers.

Lottery of Life. A Story of New York Twenty Years Ago. John Brougham. (On cover: Seaside library. Pocket ed., no. 354). 1885. G. Munro.

Lottery: Or, The Adventures of James Harris. Shirley Jackson. LC 79-24173. 1980. 12.50 (ISBN 0-8376-0455-9). R. Bentley.

Lottery: Or,The Adventures of James Harris. Shirley Jackson. LC 49-8263. 1949. Farrar, Straus.

Lottery Ticket. Fortune Du Boisgobey. LC 6-34421. (On cover: Seaside library. Pocket ed. no. 453). G. Munro.

Lottery Ticket: An American Tale. To Which Is Added, The Destructive Consequences of Dissipation and Luxury. LC 7-14772. 1827. D. F. Robinson & Co.

Lottery Ticket: Or, The Forlorn Hope. A Tale of the Present Times. Paul Richter. LC 7-41404. Barclay & Co.

Lottie and Victorine: Or, Working Their Own Way. Lucy Randall Comfort. LC 6-30661. (On cover: The library of American authors, no. 39). 1891. G. Munro.

Lottie Darling. A Novel. John Cordy Jeaffreson. LC 7-10813. (Seaside library, v. 79, no. 1609). 1883. G. Munro.

Lottie's Wooing. Francesca Maria Steele. LC 8-13428. Cassell Publishing Company.

Lotus and the Leopard: A Historical Novel. Argyle Kincaid. LC 51-11853. 1951. Exposition Press.

Lotus and the Wind: A Novel. John Masters. LC 52-12417. 1953. Viking Press.

Lotus Blossom. George Lancing. LC 39-19897. L. Furman, Inc.

Lotus Eaters. Gerald Green. LC 59-11321. 1959. Scribner.

Lotus Greek & Other Stories. Sun Li. 123p. (Orig.). 1982. pap. 2.95 (ISBN 0-8351-0972-0). China Bks.

Lotus Land. Monica Highland. LC 82-12606. 14.95 (ISBN 0-698-11202-4). Coward, McCann & Geoghegan.

Lotus Lantern. Mary Imlay Taylor & Sabine, Martin, Joint Author. LC 11-24400. 1911. Little, Brown & Company.

Lotus of the Dusk: A Romance of China. Dorothy Graham. LC 27-59443. 1927. Frederick A. Stokes Company.

Lotus Pond. Frank G. Flynn. 1970. 5.95 o.p. Carlton.

Lotus Position. Lotus Wienstock. 144p. 1982. pap. 2.95 (ISBN 0-553-14807-9). Bantam.

Lotus Salad. Mildred Cram. LC 20-10732. 1920. 1.75. Dodd, Mead and Company.

Lotus Seat. Victor Chapin. LC 55-9464. 1955. Rinehart.

Lotus Throne. Wendy Scarfe. LC 77-361824. 1976. (ISBN 0-909837-43-0). Spectrum.

Lotus Throne of Nirvana. Walter M Haushalter. LC 24-11555. Lucas Brothers.

Lotus Woman: A Romance of Byzantine Constantinople. Nathan Gallizier. LC 22-23260. 1922. The Page Company.

Lou. Alexander Roberts. Tr. by Haynes, Jessie. LC 7-41023. (On cover: Fortnightly series, no. 9). 1896. American Publishers Corporation.

Lou-Lan and Other Stories. Yasushi Inoue. LC 79-66239. 1979. 7.95 (ISBN 0-87011-389-5). Kodansha International.

Loud Halo. Lillian Beckwith. LC 64-19535. (Illus.). 1964-1965. Dutton.

Loud with Laughter: A Novel. Buena Vista Stine. LC 43-172377. 1943. Wetzel Publishing Co., Inc.

Louder & Funnier. P. G. Wodehouse. 1963. 11.95 o.s.i. (ISBN 0-8277-0219-1). British Bk Ctr.

Louder Than Guns; a Novel. 1st Ed. Paul Patterson. LC 56-10614. 1956. Pageant Press.

Louder Than Words: A Novel. Hugh MacMullan. LC 35-32769. Loring & Mussey.

Loudmouth. Rian James. A. H. King.

Loudwater Mystery. Edgar Jepson. LC 20-22232. 1920. A. A. Knopf.

Louie and Women. Todd Walton. LC 82-17771. 12.95 (ISBN 0-525-24167-1). Dutton.

Louie's Last Term at St. Mary's. Miriam Coles Harris. LC 11-16139. 1871. C. Scribner & Company.

Louis Beretti: A Novel. Donald Henderson Clarke. The Vanguard Press.

Louis Beretti: A Novel. Donald Henderson Clarke. LC 34-382800. Grosset & Dunlap.

Louis Bromfield Trilogy... Louis Bromfield. LC 36-28481. Blue Ribbon Books.

Louis Lambert: With an Introduction by George Frederic Parsons. Honore De Balzac. Tr. by Katharine Prescott Wormeley. LC 3-23167. (Half-title: The comedy of human life... Philosophical studies). 1889. Roberts Brothers.

Louis Norbert: A Two-Fold Romance. Violet Paget. LC 14-11362. 1914. John Lane Company; Etc., Etc.

Louis Wirth on Cities & Social Life. Louis Wirth. (O.s.i.). 1964. pap. 2.95 o.s.i. (ISBN 0-226-90241-2, P172, Phoen). U of Chicago Pr.

Louisa: A Novel. Susan Barrett. LC 79-78792. 1969. 4.95. Delacorte Press.

Louisa: A Novel. Katharine Sarah Gadsden Macquoid. (Harper's handy series, no. 4-5). 1885. Harper & Brothers.

Louisa. A Novel. Katharine Sarah Gadsden Macquoid. (On cover: Seaside library. Pocket ed., no. 479). 1885. G. Munro.

Louisa Avondale: Or, Two Southern Girls. Alice V Carey. LC 6-22816. The Irving Co.

Louisa Forrester. Mary Ann Fisher. 1905. Printed by J. J. Little & Co.

Louisa of Prussia and Her Times. Klara Muller Mundt. Tr. by Jordan, F. LC 16-1228. (historical romances of Louisa Muhlbach psued.). D. Appleton and Company.

Louisa of Prussia and Her Times. An Historical Novel. Klara Muller Mundt. Tr. by Jordan, F. LC 7-26108. 1867. D. Appleton and Company.

Louisa Van Benthusen. A Novel. Minnie L Harvey. 1882. W. H. Thompson.

Louisa Varena... Eliza Phillips Thruston Houk. LC 5-21562. Printed for the Author by the U.S. Publishing House.

Louisa Von Plettenhaus: The Journal of a Poor Young Lady. Tr. from the German... Marie Karoline Elisabeth Luise Scheele Von Nathusius. LC 7-23114. 1857. C. S. Francis & Co.

Louisa Williams: Or, The Orphan Bound-Girl. A Tale of the Queen City; Founded on Facts. P. W. Farmer. LC 6-38667. 1859. Printed for the Author at the Office of the "Cincinnatus.

Louisburg Square. Robert Cutler. LC 17-10857. 1917. 1.50. The Macmillan Company.

Louise. Joan Dering. LC 57-11040. (Chantecler novel of suspense). 1957. Washburn.

Louise. Sarah Shears. LC 76-383318. 1976. 7.95 (ISBN 0-236-40018-5). Elek.

Louise and Barnavaux. Pierre Mille & Drillien, Berengere, Tr. LC 16-135132. 1916. John Lane.

Louise and I: A Seaside Story. Charles Richards Dodge. LC 6-33861. 1879. G. W. Carleton & Co.

Louise De la Valliere. Alexandre Dumas. 3.00 o.p. (ISBN 0-00-422503-1); 1ea. 5.00 o.p. (ISBN 0-00-423503-7). Collins-World.

Louise De La Valliere: Being the Continuation of "The Three Guardsmen,""Twenty Years After," "The Vicomte De Bragelonne," and "Ten Years Later.". Alexandre Dumas & Maquet, Auguste. (On cover: Seaside library. Pocket ed. no. 2066). G. Munro.

Louise De La Valliere: Or. The Love of Bragellone ! A "Bragelonne, the Son of Athos". Alexandre Dumas & Maquet, Auguste. Tr. by Williams, Henry Llewellyn, Jr. (On cover: The elite series. no. 9). The F. M. Lupton Publishing Company.

Louise Elton: Or, Things Seen and Heard. A Novel. Mary ELiza Hicks Herndon. LC 7-4305. 1853. Lippincott, Grambo & Co.

Louise La Valliere: Or, the Second Series and Conclusion of The Iron Mask. Being the Final End of "The Three Guardsmen". "Twenty Years After". "Bragelonne". and "The Iron Mask". Alexandre Dumas & Auguste Maquet. Tr. by Williams, Thomas. LC 6-43627. T. B. Peterson.

Louise, the Restless. Katheryn Kimbrough, pseud. (Saga of the Phenwick Women: No. 24). pap. 1.75 (ISBN 0-445-04298-2). Popular Lib.

Louise's Daughters. Sarah Shears. LC 77-350209. 1976. 7.95 (ISBN 0-236-40034-7). Elek.

Louise's Inheritance. Sarah Shears. LC 77-370752. 1977. 7.95 (ISBN 0-236-40068-1). Elek.

Louisiana. Frances Hodgson Burnett. LC 4-15074. 1880. C. Scribner's Sons.

Louisiana. Frances Hodgson Burnett. LC 16-17423. 1915. C. Scribner's Sons.

Louisiana Cavalier. Everett Webber. LC 53-10850. 1955. Dutton.

Louisiana in the Short Story. Ed. by Lizzie Carter McVoy. LC 73-130264. 1971. (ISBN 0-8383-1171-7). Haskell House Publishers.

Louisiana in the Short Story. Ed. by Lizzie Carter McVoy. LC 40-28816. (Half-title: Louisiana state university studies. no. 41). 1940. Louisiana State University Press.

Louisiana Lady. Narena Easterling. LC 41-134974. Gramercy Publishing Co.

Louisiana Lady. Cynthia Van Hazinga. 320p. (Orig.). 1981. pap. 2.75 (ISBN 0-515-05152-7). Jove Pubns.

Louisiana Lil. Donald McGregor. (Orig.). 1980. pap. 1.75 o.s.i. (ISBN 0-8439-0737-1, Leisure Bks). Nordon Pubns.

Louisiana Lou; a Western Story. William West Winter. LC 22-21805. Chelsea House.

Louisville Saturday. Margaret Long. LC 50-9759. 1950. Random House.

Lourdes. Emile Zola & Vizetelly, Ernest Alfred, 1853-1922, Tr. LC 3-14796. (Neely's international library). 1894. F. T. Neely.

Lourdes see Trois Villes.

Lou'siana Man. D. Kershaw. 1971. pap. 2.95 o.p. (06105, Collier). Macmillan.

Lovable. Mary Raymond. LC 36-7039. J. H. Hopkins & Son, Inc.

Lovable Degenerate. William Bliss Stoddard. LC 8-34221. 1908. Cochrane Publishing Co.

Lovable Man. David Fletcher, pseud. LC 74-22659. 1975. 6.95 (ISBN 0-698-10645-8). Coward, McCann & Geoghegan.

Lovable Man. David Fletcher, pseud. 1976. 1.50 (ISBN 0-671-80692-0). Pocket Book.

Lovable Meddler. Leona Dalrymple. LC 15-152988. 1.35. The Reilly & Britton Co.

Lovable Stranger. Anne Duffield. LC 49-714702. 1949. Macrae-Smith-Co.

Love. Constance Leonie Caroline Borgstrom Aminoff. LC 22-20961. (Her Torchlight series of Napoleonic romances iii). E. P. Dutton & Company.

Love. Charlotte Campbell Bury. LC 6-16686. 1838. Carey, Lea and Blanchard.

Love. Leo F. Buscaglia. 208p. 1982. pap. 3.50 (ISBN 0-449-23452-5, Crest). Fawcett.

Love. Elizabeth. 1973. pap. 0.95 o.p. (09209). Curtis.

Love. Oakley, Hester Caldwell et al. LC 1-30777. 1901. McClure, Phillips & Co.

Love, Vol. V. Denise Robins. 736p. 1980. pap. 2.50 (ISBN 0-345-28519-0). Ballantine.

Love, Vol. VI. Denise Robins. 592p. 1980. pap. 2.75 (ISBN 0-345-28520-4). Ballantine.

Love, Vol. VII. Denise Robins. 720p. 1980. pap. 2.75 (ISBN 0-345-28521-2). Ballantine.

Love, Vol. VIII. Denise Robins. 624p. 1980. pap. cancelled (ISBN 0-345-28522-0). Ballantine.

Love. Mary Annette Beauchamp Russell Russell. LC 25-8738. 1925. Doubleday, Page & Company.

Love. William Saroyan. LC 56-268006. (Lion library editions, 56). 1955. Lion Library Editions.

Love. Susan Fromberg Schaeffer. LC 80-15438. 1980. 14.95 (ISBN 0-525-14902-3). Dutton.

Love. Stendhal. Tr. by Gilbert Sale & Suzanne Sale. (Classics Ser.). 336p. 1975. pap. 3.95 (ISBN 0-14-044307-X). Penguin.

Love, Vol. 4. Denise Robins. 608p. 1980. pap. 2.50 (ISBN 0-345-28518-2). Ballantine.

Love--and Diana. Concordia Merrel. LC 22-957249. 1922. T. Seltzer.

Love--and Helen. Selwyn Jepson. LC 28-27814. 1928. G. H. Watt.

Love,--and the Philosopher: A Study in Sentiment. Marie Corelli. LC 23-180712. George H. Doran Company.

Love--or a Name: A Story. Julian Hawthorne. LC 7-3890. 1885. Ticknor and Company.

Love, a Fearful Success. Elizabeth Baynes De Vegh. LC 82-20790. (Illus.). 3.95 (ISBN 0-9604152-7-0). Arrowhead Press.

Love Academy. Antonio Vignale. pap. 1.75 o.p. (3038). Brandon.

Love-Acre: An Idyl in Two Worlds. Edith M O Lees Ellis. LC 14-20740. 1914. 1.25. M. Kennerley.

Love-Act. Michael Austen. LC 82-976. 12.95 (ISBN 0-517-54674-4). Harmony Books.

Love Address. Eric Lee, pseud. pap. 0.95 o.p. (1154). Brandon.

Love Adventures of Al-Mansur. Archibald Clavering Gunter. LC 6-46704. (On cover: Rococo series. no. 1). The Home Publishing Company.

Love Affair. Ray Bradbury. 40p. DEC Limited signed ed. 35.00 (ISBN 0-935716-17-3). Lord John.

Love Affair. Dino Buzzati. Tr. by Joseph Green from It. 1963. 4.95 o.p. (ISBN 0-374-19268-5). FS&G.

Love Affair. Adrienne Clarkson. 1971. pap. 0.95 o.p. (N2501). Pyramid Pubns.

Love Affair. Seymour Epstein. LC 78-14700. 1979. 10.00 (ISBN 0-385-14831-3). Doubleday.

Love Affair. Eleanor Farjeon. LC 49-8293. 1949. Macmillan Co.

Love Affair. Emile Zola. 1957. 13.95 o.p. (ISBN 0-236-30905-6, Pub. by Paul Elek). Merrimack Pub Cir.

Love Affair of a Homely Girl. Jean Louise De Forest. LC 14-165762. 1914. Sully and Kleinteich.

Love Affair. Tr. from French by Jean Stewart. Emile Zola. 1963. 3.75. Elek Bks. Dist. Chester Springs, Pa., Dufour.

Love Affair. 1st Ed. Robert Carson. LC 58-11216. 1958. Holt.

Love Affairs in Our Village Twenty Years Ago. Anne Tuttle Jones Bullard. LC 4-8607. 1852. Printed and Pub. at Intelligencer Buildings.

Love Affairs of a Worldly Man. Maibelle Justice. LC 7-11661. 1894. F. T. Neely.

Love Affairs of an Old Maid. Lilian Lida Bell. LC 4-22064. 1893. Harper & Brothers.

Love Affairs of Captain John Smith: By John H. Gwathmey... John Hastings Gwathmey. LC 35-67173. 1935. Press of the Dietz Printing Co.

Love Affairs of Margaret Dale. Mary A Dixon. LC 99-2519. (On cover: Neely's imperial library. no. 31). F. T. Neely.

Love Afloat. A Story of the American Navy. Francis Henry Sheppard. LC 8-5119. Sheldon & Company.

Love After Hours. Barbara Brett. 2.50 (ISBN 0-380-76257-9). Avon Books.

Love Ain't Nothing but Sex Misspelled: Twenty-Two Stories. Harlan Ellison. LC 68-14286. 1968. 5.95. Trident Press.

Love: All. Molly Parkin. LC 74-28986. 1975. 6.95 (ISBN 0-8402-1365-4). Nash Pub.

Love Alone Is Lord. Frank Frankfort Moore. LC 5-19076. 1905. G. P. Putnam's Sons.

Love Among the Artists. George Bernard Shaw. LC 67065. 1900. H. S. Stone and Company.

Love Among the Artists. George Bernard Shaw. LC 45-28259. 1905. H. S. Stone and Company.

Love Among the Cannibals. Wright Morris. LC 76-16574. 1977. 10.95 (ISBN 0-8032-0880-4). University of Nebraska Press.

Love Among the Cannibals. 1st Ed. Wright Morris. LC 57-10060. 1957. Harcourt, Brace.

Love Among the Cape Enders. Harry Kemp. LC 31-23578. 1931. The Macaulay Company.

Love Among the Chickens. P. G. Wodehouse. 1963. 11.95 o.s.i. (ISBN 0-8277-0220-5). British Bk Ctr.

Love Among the Chickens: A Story of the Haps and Mishaps on an English Chicken Farm. Pelham Grenville Wodehouse. LC 9-18719. 1909. The Circle Publishing Company.

Love Among the Haystacks. D. H. Lawrence. (YA) Repr. lib. bdg. 12.35x (ISBN 0-88411-676-X). Amereon Ltd.

Love Among the Haystacks & Other Pieces. David Herbert Lawrence. LC 74-4124. 1974. 9.25 (ISBN 0-518-19074-9). Books for Libraries Press.

Love Among the Haystacks: & Other Pieces. David Herbert Lawrence & Garnett, David. LC 34-2499. 1933. The Viking Press.

Love Among the Mashed Potatoes. Gregory McDonald. LC 78-2861. 8.95. Dutton.

Love Among the Operators: A Novel. Rosemary Tonks. LC 76-98060. 1970. 4.95. Gambit.

Love Among the Ruins. Warwick Deeping. LC 4-8272. 1904. The Outlook Company.

Love Among the Ruins. Victor Kutchin. LC 25-3944. Printed by Worzalla Publishing Co.

Love Among the Ruins. Angela Mackail Thirkell. LC 48-8852. 1948. A. A. Knopf.

Love Among the Ruins. Angela Margaret Mackail Thirkell. 1972. 1.25 (ISBN 0-515-02871-1). Pyramid.

Love Among the Ruins: Little Novels of Hard Times. Elmer Holmes Davis. LC 35-487727. The Bobbs-Merrill Company.

Love and a Rich Girl. Berta Ruck. LC 60-16795. 1960. Dodd, Mead.

Love and Admiration. Louise Field Cooper. LC 44-51275. 1944. Duell, Sloan and Pearce.

Love and Be Silent. 1st Ed. Curtis Harnack. LC 62-805312. 1962. Harcourt, Brace World.

Love & Betrayal. Joanne Kaye. LC 81-47261. (Garment Center Ser.). 224p. (Orig.). 1981. pap. 2.25 (ISBN 0-87216-906-5). Playboy Pbks.

Love and Betty: A Love Story. Louisa Carter Lee. LC 31-8540. Chelsea House.

Love & Cherish. Dorothy Garlock. 1982. pap. 2.50 (ISBN 0-89083-897-6). Zebra.

Love and Consequences: By Peter V. K. Funk. 1st Ed. Peter V. K Funk. LC 66-27599. 1966. 4.95. Chilton.

Love & Death. Saneatsu Mushakoji. 3.00 o.p. Japan Pubns.

Love and Death: Ai to Shi. Saneatsu Mushakoji. LC 58-4889. 1958. Twayne Publishers.

Love & Discipline. Barbara Brenner. LC 82-90851. 224p. (Orig.). 1983. pap. 5.95 (ISBN 0-345-30520-5). Ballantine.

Love & Dreams. Nancy Bacon. 600p. 1980. pap. 2.75 (ISBN 0-345-28767-3). Ballantine.

Love and Forget. Peggy Gaddis, pseud. LC 41-19645. Phoenix Press.

Love and Forget. Gail Jordan. LC 41-196454. Phoenix Press.

Love & Friendship. Jane Austen. 2.95 (ISBN 0-7043-3823-8, Pub. by Quartet England). Charles River Bks.

Love and Friendship. Alison Lurie. LC 62-7996. 1962. Macmillan.

Love & Friendship & Other Early Works. Jane Austen. Pref. by G. K. Chesterton. LC 77-22471. Repr. of 1922 ed. lib. bdg. 12.50 (ISBN 0-8414-2936-7). Folcroft.

Love & Friendship & Other Early Works. Jane Austen & Harriet Bell. (Illus.). 128p. 1981. 8.95 (ISBN 0-517-54459-8, Harmony); pap. 3.95 (ISBN 0-517-54372-9). Crown.

Love & Glory. Patricia Hagan. 384p. (Orig.). 1982. pap. 3.50 (ISBN 0-380-79665-1, 79665). Avon.

Love & Glory. Robert L. Hecker. (Orig.). 1980. pap. text ed. 2.25 o.s.i. (ISBN 0-505-51592-X). Tower Bks.

Love and Hatred. Marie Adelaide Belloc Lowndes. LC 17-303513. 1.35. George H. Doran Company.

Love & Honor. Leslie Arlen. 384p. 1980. pap. 2.75 (ISBN 0-515-05480-1). Jove Pubns.

Love and Jealousy. Lucy Randall Comfort. LC 3-30212. (On cover: The library of American authors. no. 23). 1890. G. Munro.

Love and Joy in the Mabillon. Caroline Glyn. LC 66-13120. 1966. Coward-McCann.

Love & Kisses, Snoopy. Charles M. Schulz. 128p. pap. 1.75 (ISBN 0-449-24292-7, Crest). Fawcett.

Love & Lady Lovelace. Marion Chesney. 192p. (Orig.). 1982. pap. 1.50 (ISBN 0-449-50314-3, Coventry). Fawcett.

Love and Laughter. Claude M Griffith. LC 73-82419. 1973. 3.00 (ISBN 0-87012-148-0). McClain Print. Co.

Love and Learn: The Story of a Telephone Girl Who Loved Not Too Well but Wisely. Harry Charles Witwer. LC 24-29534. 1924. G. P. Putnam's Sons.

Love and Let Me Go. Maysie Greig. LC 35-3858. 1935. Doubleday, Doran and Co., Inc.

Love and Let Me Go. Maysie Greig. LC 37-32425. 1937. The Sun Dial Press, Inc.

Love and Liberty: A Romance of Anti-Slavery Days. William Capron Townsend. LC 1-19474. The Abbey Press.

Love and Liberty. A Thrilling Narrative of the French Revolution of 1792. Alexandre Dumas. LC 12-19575. T. B. Peterson & Brothers.

Love and Life. Louise Maunsell Field. LC 23-131017. E. P. Dutton & Company.

Love and Life. Charlotte Mary Yonge. (On cover: Lovell's library. v. 18, no. 899). 1887. J. W. Lovell Company.

Love and Life. An Old Story in Eighteenth Century Costume. Charlotte Mary Yonge. (On cover: Seaside library. Pocket ed. no. 742). 1886. G. Munro.

Love and Life. An Old Story in Eighteenth Century Costume by Charlotte M. Yonge... Charlotte Mary Yonge. (Franklin square library, no. 153). 1880. Harper & Brothers.

Love & Like. Herbert Gold. 1960. 4.95 o.p. Dial.

Love & Linda. Barbara Cartland. 1976. pap. 1.25 o.p. (ISBN 0-515-03989-6). BJ Pub Group.

Love and Luck; the Story of a Summer Loitering on the Great South Bay. Robert Barnwell Roosevelt. LC 7-40763. 1886. Harper & Brothers.

Love and Lucy. Maurice Henry Hewlett. LC 16-18028. 1916. 1.35. Dodd, Mead and Company.

Love & Lucy Granger, Moonlight & Magic: A Question of Marriage. Rachel Lindsay. (Harlequin Romances Ser.). 576p. 1981. pap. 3.50 (ISBN 0-373-20055-2). Harlequin Bks.

Love and Lure: Or, The Heart of a "Bad" Man; a Romance of Arizona. Cornelius Shea. LC 12-24917. 1912. Broadway Publishing Company.

Love & Lust. Ann Taylor. (Orig.). 1968. pap. 1.75 o.s.i. (116, Ophelia). Olympia.

Love and Marriage. Herbert M Katz. 1976. 1.75. Dell.

Love and Marriage: A Novel. Herbert M Katz. LC 75-11147. 7.95 (ISBN 0-87795-110-1). Arbor House.

Love and Mary Ann. Catherine Cookson. LC 76-11805. 1976. 6.95 (ISBN 0-688-03081-5). Morrow.

Love and Medicine. A Novel. Charles Frederic Gilliam. 1886. Gray & Clarkson.

Love and Mirage: Or, The Waiting on an Island. An Out-of-Door Romance. Matilda Barbara Edwards. (On cover: The seaside library. Pocket ed. no. 273). 1884. G. Munro.

Love & Mr. Lewisham. Herbert George Wells. 3.00 o.p. (688). Collins-World.

Love and Mr. Lewisham: The Story of a Very Young Couple. Herbert George Wells. LC 20-7426. George H. Doran Company.

Love and Mr. Lewisham: The Story of a Very Young Couple. Herbert George Wells. LC 24-277437. 1924. C. Scribner's Sons.

Love and Money. Erskine Caldwell. LC 54-8309. 1954. Duell, Sloan and Pearce.

Love and Money. Noel Clad. LC 59-6644. 1959. Random House.

Love and Money: Or, A Perilous Secret. Charles Reade. (On cover: Seaside library. Pocket ed., no. 232). 1884. G. Munro.

Love and Mr Lewisham: The Story of a Very Young Couple. Herbert George Wells. LC 1067. Frederick A. Stokes Company.

Love and Mrs. Candy. 1st Ed. Robert Tallant. LC 53-10647. 1953. Doubleday.

Love & Mrs. Sargent. Patrick Dennis, pseud. 1973. pap. 1.25 o.p. (ISBN 0-532-12155-4). Woodhill.

Love & Mrs. Sargent. Patrick Dennis, pseud. 1970. pap. 1.25 o.p. (12155). Manor Bks.

Love & Mrs. Sargent. Patrick Dennis, pseud. 1973. pap. 1.25 o.p. (ISBN 0-532-12155-4). Manor Bks.

Love & Naked Light see Goddess Game.

Love and Napalm: Export U.S.A. J. G. Ballard. LC 72-81790. 1972. 5.95 (ISBN 0-394-48277-8). Grove Press.

Love & Napalm: Export U.S.A. James G. Ballard. LC 72-81790. Orig. Title: Atrocity Exhibition. 156p. 1972. 5.95 o.p. (ISBN 0-394-48277-8, GP707). Grove.

Love & No Marriage. Rachel Lindsay. (Harlequin Presents Ser.). 192p. 1980. pap. 1.50 (ISBN 0-373-10381-6, Pub. by Harlequin). PB.

Love and Other Euphemisms. Norma Klein. LC 72-75956. 1972. 6.95 (ISBN 0-399-11009-7). Putnam.

Love: And Other Stories. Anton Pavlovich Chekhov. Tr. by Garnet, Constance (Black) LC 23-40071. (Half-title: The tales of Chekhov, vol. xiii). 1923. The Macmillan Company.

Love: And Other Stories, by Yuri Olyesha. Tr., Introd. by Robert Payne. IUrii Olesha & IUrii Karlovich Olesha. LC 67-17360. (Russian lib.). 1967. 4.95. Washington Sq.

Love and Patriotism! Or, The Extraordinary Adventures of M. Duportail, Late Major-General in the Armies of the United States. Interspersed with Many Surprising Incidents in the Life of the Late Count Pulaski. Jean Baptiste Louvet De Couvral. LC 7-14789. 1797. Printed by Carey & Markland.

Love and Patriotism! Or, The Extraordinary Adventures of Mons. Duportail, Late Major-General in the Army of the United States. Interspersed with Many Surprising Incidents in the Life of the Late Count Pulaski. Jean Baptiste Louvet De Couvral. LC 7-14781. 1825. Printed for the Purchasers.

Love and Politics: A Social Romance of a Prominent Orator and a Society Queen; Reproductions of Their Letters and Poems. Nellie Bingham Van Slingerland. LC 99-3735. Jersey City Printing Co.

Love and Pride. R Rosino Napoliello. The Abbey Press.

Love and Quiet Life" Somerset Idylls. Walter Raymond. LC 7-36631. 1894. Dodd, Mead and Company.

Love and Rebellion: A Story of the Civil War and Reconstruction. Martha Caroline Keller. LC 7-10969. (sunnyside series, no. 26). J. S. Ogilvie.

Love and Rocks. Laura Elizabeth Howe Richards. LC 7-41212. 1898. Estes and Lauriat.

Love & Safety. Empress of Asturia. pap. 1.45 o.p. (V1027Q, Venus). Grove.

Love & Sex Among the Very Rich. Aldo Lucchesi, pseud. LC 78-638. (Orig.). 1970. pap. 1.25 o.p. (ISBN 0-447-78640-7). Lancer.

Love and Shawl-Straps. Annette Lucile Noble & Coann, Pearl Clement. (On cover: The Hudson library, no. 1). 1894. G. P. Putnam's Sons.

Love & Sir John Falstaff. Louie B. McKay. 2.50 o.p. Carlton.

Love and Tears. Arsene Houssaye. (On cover: The silver series, no. 4-5). 1892. H. J. Smith & Co.

Love & Terror. William Herrick. LC 80-25140. 256p. 1981. 13.95 (ISBN 0-8112-0791-9); pap. 5.95 (ISBN 0-8112-0841-9, NDP538). New Directions.

Love and the Crescent: A Tale of the Near East. A Cunnick Inchbold. LC 20-112994. Frederick A. Stokes Company.

Love and the Ladies. Eleanor Hallowell Abbott. LC 28-6058. 1928. D. Appleton and Company.

Love and the Lieutenant. Robert William Chambers. LC 35-6348. 1935. D. Appleton-Century Company Incorporated.

Love and the Loathsome Leopard. Barbara Cartland. LC 77-16033. 1977. 6.95 (ISBN 0-87272-027-6). Duron Books.

Love & the Marquis. Barbara Cartland. (Camfield Romance Ser.: No. 4). 192p. 1982. pap. 1.95 (ISBN 0-515-06295-2). Jove Pubns.

Love and the Soul Hunters. Pearl Mary Teresa Richards Craigie. LC 2-21984. 1920. Funk & Wagnalls Company.

Love and the Twentieth Volunteers. 1st Ed. Charles P Breen. LC 61-88767. 1961. Doubleday.

Love & the Waiting Game: Eleven Stories. David Watmough. LC 75-331913. (ISBN 0-88750-170-2) (ISBN 0-88750-171-0). Oberon.

Love and the Wicked City. Thompson, John Burton. LC 51-14880. Arco Pub. Co.

Love and Theology: A Novel. Celia Parker Woolley. 1887. Ticknor and Company.

Love & Three Squares a Day in Montana. Alma P. Donald. 1964. 4.50 o.p. (ISBN 0-682-42107-3). Exposition.

Love and Treason. David Osborn. LC 82-12415. 13.95 (ISBN 0-453-00421-0). New American Library.

Love & War. Dan Allen. 1977. pap. 2.50 o.p. (ISBN 0-8059-2401-9). Dorrance.

Love & War. Dan Allen. 1977. pap. 2.50 o.p. (ISBN 0-8059-2401-9). Dorrance.

Love & War. Patricia Hagan. 1978. pap. 3.50 (ISBN 0-380-01947-7, 80044). Avon.

Love and War in Cuba. Including Many Thrilling Scenes of the Last Years of Spanish Rule. Peyton L Stanton. LC 1191. 1900. The Foote & Davis Company, Printers.

Love and Wisdom: A Novel About Solomon. by Richard G. Hubler. Richard Gibson Hubler. LC 68-27028. 1968. bds., 5.95. Crown.

Love and Work. Gwyneth Cravens. LC 81-13650. 1982. 13.50 (ISBN 0-394-52184-6). Knopf: Distributed by Random House.

Love and Work. Reynolds Price. LC 68-22422. 1968. Atheneum.

Love Arena. Tony Trelos, pseud. (Orig.). pap. 1.25 o.p. (2503). Brandon.

Love Artist. Florenz Branch. LC 39-258832. Phoenix Press.

Love Artist. Florenz Branch. LC 39-25883. 1939. Phoenix Press.

Love Astrologer. O. R. Bassett. 192p. (Orig.). 1973. pap. 1.95 o.p. (ISBN 0-87056-304-1, 6304). Brandon.

Love at a Festival. Berta Ruck. LC 52-20654. 1951. Hutchinson.

Love at a Festival. Berta Ruck. LC 52-6502. Dodd, Mead.

Love at a Price. Robert Norcross. LC 36-898168. Phoenix Press.

Love at All Ages. Angela Mackail Full Name Angela Margaret Mackail Thirkell Thirkell. LC 59-14052. 1959. Knopf.

Love at First Bite. Ed. by Staff of Fotonovel Publications. (Illus., Orig.). 1979. pap. 2.75. Fotonovel.

Love at Forty. Barbara Cartland. 1977. pap. 1.25 o.p. BJ Pub Group.

Love at Forty. Pierre Frondaie & Boyd, Madeleine Elise (Reynier) LC 30-24950. Sears Publishing Company, Inc.

Love at Large: Being the Amusing Chronicles of Julietta Carson. Sophie Kerr. LC 16-6607. 1916. Harper & Brothers.

Love at Last. Josiah Pitts Woolfolk. LC 37-706322. 1937. Godwin.

Love at Saratoga: Or, Married in Haste. Lucy Randall Comfort. (On cover: The library of American authors. no. 33). 1891. G. Munro.

Love at Sea. Patricia O'Hara. LC 39-15712. 1938. Hillman-Curl, Inc.

Love at Sea. Maxine Patrick. (Orig.). 1980. pap. 1.75 (ISBN 0-451-09261-9, E9261, Sig). NAL.

Love at Sea: The Chronicle of a Voyage by Mail Steamer. Herman Salomanson & Wyhe, Henrietta Van, Tr. LC 31-21906. E. P. Dutton & Co., Inc.

Love at Second Sight. Peggy Gaddis, pseud. LC 41-729772. 1941. Arcadia House, Inc.

Love at Second Sight. Ada Leverson. 1972. pap. 0.75 o.p. (07259). Curtis.

Love at Second Sight. Ada Leverson. 1973. 0.75. Curtis Books.

Love at Seventy. Linn Boyd Porter. (On cover: The albatross novels). 1894. G. W. Dillingham.

Love at Sunset. Jane Sheridan. LC 81-21537. 294p. 1982. 13.95 (ISBN 0-312-49941-8). St Martin.

Love at Sunset. Pauline Glen Winslow. LC 81-21537. 13.95 (ISBN 0-312-49941-8). St. Martin's Press.

Love at the Crossroads. Margaretta Brucker. LC 43-6904. 1943. Gramercy Publishing Co.

Love at the Helm. Barbara Cartland. 224p. 1981. 9.95 (ISBN 0-89696-126-5, An Everest House Book). Dodd.

Love at the Mission. R. Hernekin Baptist. LC 36-16389. 1938. Little, Brown and Company.

Love Baby! Oh Boy! Have You "It"?... Wilbert Le Roy Cosper. LC 42-28128. 1929. Cosmos Publishing House.

Love Bade Me Welcome: A Novel. John Lodwick. LC 53-9778. 1953. Roy Publishers.

Love Bargain. Vina Lawrence. LC 35-3117. G. H. Watt.

Love Barrier. Vera Craig. (Candlelight romance). 1974. (pbk.) 0.75. Dell.

Love Barrier. Florence Eberhard. LC 36-1546. G. H. Watt, Inc.

Love Beach. Leslie Thomas. LC 69-14422. 1969. 5.95. Delacorte Press.

Love Begins at Forty: A Romance. Winifred Mary Scott. LC 36-128143. 1936. Doubleday, Doran & Co., Inc.

Love Begins at Forty: A Romance. Winifred Mary Scott. LC 37-12767. 1937. The Sun Dial Press, Inc.

Love Besieged: A Romance of the Defense of Lucknow. Charles E Pearce. LC 11-35442. 1911. A. C. McClurg & Co.

Love Betrayed. Marcia Miller. Orig. Title: Tinsel Affair. 1971. 3.95 o.p. (Avalon). Bouregy.

Love Beyond Desire. Rachel Palmer. (Superromances Ser.). 384p. 1981. pap. 2.50 (ISBN 0-373-70004-0, Pub. by Worldwide). Harlequin Bks.

Love Beyond Life. Cozy Baker. 64p. 1982. 8.00 (ISBN 0-9608930-0-8). Beechcliff Bks.

Love Beyond Reason. Michael L. Delesio. 1982. 7.95 (ISBN 0-533-05392-7). Vantage.

Love Beyond Reason. Rachel Ryan. (Candlelight Ecstasy Ser.: No. 29). 192p. (Orig.). 1981. pap. 1.75 (ISBN 0-440-15062-0). Dell.

Love Beyond Reason. Karen Van Der Zee. (Harlequin Romances Ser.). 192p. 1981. pap. 1.25 (ISBN 0-373-02406-1, Pub. by Harlequin). PB.

Love Beyond Yesterday. Charlotte Tranbarger. 1982. 6.95 (Avalon). Bouregy.

Love-Birds in the Coco-Nuts. Peter Blundell. LC 15-13211. 1915. 1.25. John Lane.

Love-Birds in the Coco-Nuts. Frank Nestle Butterworth. LC 15-13211. 1915. John Lane Company.

Love Bite. David Sale. LC 73-156493. 1972. 2.00 (ISBN 0-491-00982-8). W. H. Allen.

Love, Black Love. George Davis. LC 74-33636. 1978. 7.95 o.p. (ISBN 0-385-09788-3). Doubleday.

Love Blind. Rob Eden. LC 30-29247. Gorsset & Dunlap.

Love Boat. Peter Kanto. (Orig.). pap. 0.95 o.p. (1115). Brandon.

Love Bomb. Henry Sackerman, pseud. LC 72-3190. 1972. 0.95. Bantam Books.

Love Bound. Beatrice Burton Morgan. LC 26-7844. Grosset & Dunlap.

Love: Brian Banaker's Autobiography up to the Age of Twenty-Four Years. William Budd Trites. LC 16-201075. 1917. A. A. Knopf.

Love Builds a Home: By Carol Holliston Pseud. James Noble Gifford. LC 56-134472. 1956. Arcadia House.

Love Business. William Arthur Neubauer. LC 46-24046. 1946. Phoenix Press.

Love by Accident: A Tragi-Farce. Lewis Umfreville Wilkinson. LC 30-10982. 1930. Doubleday, Doran and Company, Inc.

Love by Accident: By Emily Noble Pseud. James Noble Gifford. LC 56-702356. 1956. Arcadia House.

Love by Express: A Novel of California. Kate Douglas Smith Wiggin & Dorcas Society of Hollis and Buxton. LC 24-179703. 1924. Priv. Print. by the Dorcas Society of Hollis and Buxton, Maine.

Love by Fire. Violet Ashton. 256p. (Orig.). 1980. pap. 2.25 (ISBN 0-449-14360-0, GM). Fawcett.

Love Calls the Doctor. Elizabeth Seifert. LC 58-130927. 1958. Dodd, Mead.

Love Calls the Doctor. Elizabeth Seifert. LC 73-79175. 1974. 6.95. Aeonian Press.

Love Calls the Tune. Kathleen Thompson Norris. LC 44-7024. 1944. Sun Dial Press.

Love Calls the Tune. Kathleen Thompson Norris. LC 47-20015. 1947. Triangle Books, the Blakiston Company.

Love Came Along. William Arthur Neubauer. LC 66-475. 1966. Arcadia House.

Love Came Late. Rob Eden. LC 38-199352. M. S. Mill Co., Inc.

Love Came Laughing. Anne Tedlock Brooks. LC 47-120875. 1947. S. Curl.

Love Came Laughing by. Emilie Baker Loring. LC 49-117551. 1949. Little, Brown.

Love Can Be Dangerous: A Novel. Octavus Roy Cohen. LC 55-14045. (Cock Robin mystery). 1955. Macmillan.

Love Can Conquer Pride. Carrye Silvey Jacob. LC 7-94663. 1893. The University Press.

Love Can Wait. Peggy O'More, pseud. LC 37-9927. 1937. Hillman Curl, Inc.

Love Can Wait. Watkins Eppes Wright. LC 50-11453. 1950. Avalon Books.

Love Changes. Ruby Mildred Ayres. LC 29-13778. 1929. Doubleday, Doran & Company, Inc.

Love Changes. Barbara Bretton. (American Romance Ser.). 192p. 1983. pap. 2.25. Harlequin Bks.

Love Chase. Theresa Conway. (Tapestry Romance Ser.). 1983. pap. 2.50 (ISBN 0-671-46054-4). PB.

Love Chase. Felix Frendon. LC 22-107686. Small, Maynard & Company.

Love Chase: A Novel. James Barlow. LC 68-11010. 1968. Simon and Schuster.

Love, Cherish Me. Rebecca Brandewyne. 576p. 1983. pap. 3.95 (ISBN 0-446-30039-X). Warner Bks.

Love Child. Philippa Carr, pseud. 1979. pap. 2.75 (ISBN 0-449-24181-5, Crest). Fawcett.

Love Child. Philippa Carr, pseud. LC 78-16708. 1978. 9.95 (ISBN 0-399-12302-4). Putnam Pub Group.

Love Child. Maureen Duffy. LC 70-136322. 1971. 5.95 (ISBN 0-394-44236-9). Knopf.

Love Child. Eleanor Hibbert. LC 78-16708. 8.95. Putnam.

Love Child. Fiona Hill. LC 77-82863. 8.95 (ISBN 0-399-12061-0). Putnam.

Love Child. Fiona Hill. (Berkley book). 1979. 1.95 (ISBN 0-425-04102-6). Berkley Pub. Corp.

Love Child. Bertha Pearl Moore. LC 23-12715. 1923. T. Seltzer.

Love-Child. Edith Olivier. LC 27-18306. 1927. The Viking Press.

Love Child. Eve Shelnutt. LC 78-27484. 1979. 4.50. (ISBN 0-87685-384-X) (ISBN 0-87685-385-8). Black Sparrow Press.

Love Circle of the Suns. Paige McKenzie. (Orig.). 1980. pap. 1.95 (ISBN 0-505-51570-9). Tower Bks.

Love Climbs in. Barbara Cartland. LC 79-21292. 1979. 6.95 (ISBN 0-87272-082-9, Duron Bks). Brodart.

Love Clinic. Maurice Dekobra, pseud. Tr. by Atkinson, F. M. LC 29-6346. Payson & Clarke Ltd.

Love Clinic. Gil Hara. (O.s.i.). 160p. 1975. pap. 1.25 o.s.i. (AQ1516, Award). Univ Pub & Dist.

Love Clinic. Hugh Marner. (O.s.i.). 1968. pap. 0.75 o.s.i. (A390S, Award). Univ Pub & Dist.

Love Comes Again Later. Berta Ruck. LC 38-175616. 1938. Dodd, Mead & Company.

Love Comes Flying. Rob Eden. LC 40-132629. Gramercy Publishing Col.

Love Comes Home. Anna Robison. LC 38-22132. Gramercy Publishing Co.

Love Comes Last. Helen Topping Miller. LC 36-221779. The Penn Publishing Company.

Love Comes Softly. Janette Oke. LC 79-16421. 3.50 (ISBN 0-87123-342-8). Bethany Fellowship, Inc.

Love Comes to Sally. Achmed Abdullah. LC 33-120365. Chicago.

Love Comes to Susan. Winifred Mary Scott. LC 34-397432. 1934. Doubleday, Doran & Company, Inc.

Love Comes Unseen. Ruby Mildred Ayres. LC 43-1289. 1943. Doubleday, Doran & Company, Inc.

Love Complex. Thomas Dixon. LC 25-11486. 1925. Boni & Liveright.

Love Confessions of a Traveling Man. Harry Byron Magill. LC 7-441. 1906. The Chicago Press.

Love Connection. Brian Denny, pseud. (Orig.). 1972. pap. 1.95 o.s.i. (76-319). Lancer.

Love Courageous. Concordia Merrel. LC 23-176462. 1923. T. Seltzer.

Love Coward. Anne Gardner, pseud. LC 30-817369. E. J. Clode, Inc.

Love Crime. Paul Charles Joseph Bourget. (Added t.-p.: Comedie d'amour series)). 1905. Societe Des Beaux-Arts.

Love Crime. Paul Charles Joseph Bourget. LC 43-20448. (On cover: Wilson's Library of fiction... No. 4, June 10, 1891). G. E. Wilson.

Love, Dad. Evan Hunter. 1981. 12.95 o.p. (ISBN 0-517-54411-3). Crown.

Love, Dad. Evan Hunter. 1982. pap. 3.95 (ISBN 0-440-14998-3). Dell.

Love, Dad: A Novel. Evan Hunter. LC 80-27565. 12.95 (ISBN 0-517-54411-3). Crown Publishers.

Love Days: Susanna Moore's. Ettie Stettheimer. LC 23-142685. 1923. A. A. Knopf.

Love De Luxe: A Barometrical Novel. Reginald Wright Kauffman. LC 29-11644. 1929. The Macaulay Company.

Love, Death, and the Ladies' Drill Team. 1st Ed. Jessamyn West. LC 55-10809. 1955. Harcourt, Brace.

Love-Death Thing. Thomas Blanchard Dewey. LC 77-84122. (Inner sanctum mystery). 1969. 4.95. Simon and Schuster.

Love Debt: A Love Story. Claire Pomeroy. LC 32-11572. N. Y., Chelsea House.

Love Deferred. Anne Duffield. LC 51-10901. 1951. Macrae Smith.

Love Department. William Trevor. (U6130). 1968. Ballantine.

Love Department. William Trevor. LC 67-11262. 1967. Viking Press.

Love Deviates. Ursula Scheide. 192p. (Orig.). 1973. pap. 1.95 o.p. (ISBN 0-87682-333-9). Barclay Hse.

Love Doctor. Lilian Bennet- Thompson & Hubbard, George, 1884- Joint Author. LC 32-251724. The Macaulay Company.

Love Doctors. P. McCrady. 1972. 7.95 o.p. (ISBN 0-02-583370-7). Macmillan.

Love Dream. George Vane. LC 13-788733. 1913. John Lane.

Love Duel. Maggie Gladstone, pseud. LC 78-62019. (Lacebridge Ladies). 208p. 1979. pap. 1.75 (ISBN 0-87216-649-X). Playboy Pbks.

Love Eaters. Mary Lee Settle. LC 55-659689. Harper.

Love Eaters. Roy Bernard Sparkia. (Orig.). 1971. pap. 0.75 o.p. (75-409). Manor Bks.

Love Emerald of Colombia. Mary Elizabeth Conklin. LC 18-21375. 1918. Saulsbury Publishing Company.

Love Episode. Emile Zola. LC 48-3925. (New Avon library, 150). 1948. Avon Book Co.

Love, Etc. Bel Kaufman. 1981. 2.75 (ISBN 0-380-53629-3). Avon Books.

Love, Etc. A Novel. Bel Kaufman. LC 79-17269. 11.95 (ISBN 0-13-540906-3). Prentice-Hall.

Love Eternal. Henry Rider Haggard. LC 18-97773. 1918. Cassell and Company.

Love Eternal. Henry Rider Haggard. LC 18-10960. 1918. 1.50. Longmans, Green, and Co.

Love Explosion. Robert H. Rimmer. (SignetBook). 2.75 (ISBN 0-451-09519-7). New American Library.

Love Feast. Frederick Buechner. LC 74-77839. 1974. 7.95 (ISBN 0-689-10612-2). Atheneum.

Love Fetish. Evans Wall. LC 32-3297. The Macaulay Company.

Love Feud, Published Serially Under the Title Heart of Liane. Mabel McElliott. LC 31-31745. Grosset & Dunlap.

Love Finds Dr. Shelly. Isabel Cabot. (YA) 1978. 6.95 (Avalon). Bouregy.

Love Finds the Way. Paul Leicester Ford. LC 4-30954. 1904. Dodd, Mead & Company.

Love Finds the Way. Ruby Lorraine Radford. (Avalon careers). 1964. Avalon Books.

Love Finds the Way: And Other Stories. Walter Besant & Rice, James. (On cover: Seaside library. Pocket ed., no. 146). 1884. G. Munro.

Love Flies Out. Vida Hurst. LC 44-2362. 1944. Gramercy Publishing Co.

Love for a Convict. Veronica Henriques. LC 56-6298. 1956. Dutton.

Love for a Rogue. Glenna Finley. (Signet book). New American Library.

Love for a Rogue: Highwayman No. 16. Glenna Finley, pseud. pap. 1.95 (ISBN 0-451-11315-2, AJ1315, Sig). NAL.

Love for a Stranger. John Pleasant McCoy. LC 54-40284. (Avon, 601). 1954. Avon Publications.

Love for a Stranger. Daisy H. Thomson. 1974. pap. 0.95 o.p. (ISBN 0-515-03385-5, N3385). BJ Pub Group.

Love For All Time. Dorothy Garlock. (Loveswept Ser.: No. 6). 1983. pap. 1.95. Bantam.

Love for an Hour Is Love Forever. Amelia Edith Huddleston Barr. LC 6-7984. Dodd, Mead & Company.

Love for Each Other. Bernard Glemser. LC 47-222931. 1946. Creative Age Press.

Love for Lydia. Herbert Ernest Bates. LC 52-9066. 1953. Little, Brown.

Love for Sale. Barbara Cartland. LC 80-12898. 10.95 (ISBN 0-525-14906-6). Dutton.

Love for the Taking. Beth Christopher. (Finding Mr. Right Ser.). 1983. pap. 2.75. Avon.

Love for Today. James Noble Gifford. LC 56-12454. 1956. Arcadia House.

Love for Two. Mildred Evans Gilman. 1932. H. Smith.

Love Forbidden. Barbara Cartland. 1973. pap. 1.25 o.p. (ISBN 0-515-03196-8, V3196). BJ Pub Group.

Love Forbidden, No. 51. Barbara Cartland. (Orig.). 1982. pap. 1.95 (ISBN 0-515-06381-9). Jove Pubns.

Love Forever. Melanie James. 192p. (Orig.). 1983. pap. 2.50 (ISBN 0-449-12409-6, GM). Fawcett.

Love Forever Golden. Sara V. Myers. 164p. 1978. 6.95 (ISBN 0-8059-2564-3). Dorrance.

Love Forever More. Patricia Matthews. 1977. pap. 3.25 (ISBN 0-523-41857-4). Pinnacle Bks.

Love Formula. Peter Keyes. (Orig.). pap. 0.95 o.p. (1141). Brandon.

Love Forty. Robert Barker. LC 75-2241. 1975. 7.95 (ISBN 0-397-01069-9). Lippincott.

Love Freak. Chris Kazan. LC 71-178021. 1971. 5.95 (ISBN 0-8128-1442-8). Stein and Day.

Love from London. Gilbert Wolf Gabriel. LC 46-5530. 1946. The Macmillan Company.

Love from Sandy. 1st Ed. Elmer Berger. LC 53-10220. 1953. Lippincott.

Love Gamble. Harold Morrow. LC 32-16104. Grosset & Dunlap.

Love Game. Nancy Bacon. 320p. 1982. pap. 2.95 (ISBN 0-523-41400-5). Pinnacle Bks.

Love Garden. H. James Williams. 32p. 5.95 (ISBN 0-8059-2860-X). Dorrance.

Love Genie. Joanne Webster. 1980. 8.95. Elsevier/Nelson Books.

Love Girl. E. Marie Cooper. LC 48-6005. 1947. Exposition Press.

Love Girl. Helen Marion Edginton. LC 31-14420. The Macaulay Company.

Love Girl & the Innocent. Aleksandr Isaevich Solzhenitsyn. LC 72-97614. 131p. 1970. 5.95 (ISBN 0-374-19296-0); pap. 2.95 (ISBN 0-374-50840-2). FS&G.

Love Go with You. Dorothy Quentin. LC 44-7596. 1944. Arcadia House, Inc.

Love Goddess. David Hanna. (Belmont Tower Book.). 1977. 1.75. (ISBN 0-505-51130-4). Tower Publications.

Love Goes Past. Katherine Ursula Parrott. LC 31-20845. J. Cape & H. Smith.

Love Gone Astray. Linn Boyd Porter. LC 7-37767. (Dillingham's American authors library, no. 16). 1896. G. W. Dillingham.

Love Habit: The Sexual Confessions of an Older Women. Anne Cumming. 1980. pap. 2.95 o.p. (ISBN 0-14-005331-X). Penguin.

Love Happens Along. Marguerite Gahagan. LC 39-24973. 1939. Hillman-Curl, Inc.

Love Has His Way. Barbara Cartland. LC 80-108. 1980. 6.95 (ISBN 0-87272-085-3). Duron Books.

Love Has Many Faces. Angela Gordon. 1971. pap. 0.75 o.p. (94151). Beagle Bks.

Love Has No Mercy. Eleanor Woods. (Candlelight Ecstasy Ser.: No. 84). (Orig.). 1982. pap. 1.95 (ISBN 0-440-14611-9). Dell.

Love Has Silent Wings. Vera Holding & Joe Christy. (Contemporary Teens Ser.). 224p. (Orig.). 1981. pap. 2.25 (ISBN 0-89531-148-8, 0146-96). Sharon Pubns.

Love Has Wings. Janet Doran. LC 37-18437. Gramercy Publishing Co.

Love-Hater. Berta Ruck. 1930. Dodd, Mead & Company.

Love Head. Jackie Collins. 1975. (pbk.) 1.50. Warner Paperback Library.

Love Head see Love Killers.

Love, Here Is My Hat. William Saroyan. LC 38-669189. Modern Age Books, Inc.

Love Holds the Cards. Barbara Cartland. 1970. pap. 0.95 o.p. (N2249). Pyramid Pubns.

Love Holds the Cards. Barbara Cartland. 1974. pap. 1.25 o.p. (ISBN 0-515-03519-X, V3519). BJ Pub Group.

Love, Honor and Deceive! Howard Rockey. LC 34-56033. The Macaulay Company.

Love, Honor and Neglect. Vida Hurst. LC 37-202639. M. S. Mill Co., Inc.

Love, Honor & Submit. 192p. (Orig.). 1972. pap. 1.95 o.p. (ISBN 0-87977-169-0, DBB169). Dansk Blue Bk.

Love, Honour, and Obey. Maysie Greig. LC 33-354828. 1933. Doubleday, Doran & Company, Inc.

Love, Honour, and Obey. Maysie Greig. LC 43-13643. 1943. Triangle Books.

Love Hunter. Jon Hassler. LC 80-29693. 320p. 1981. 12.95 (ISBN 0-688-00483-0). Morrow.

Love Hunter. Jon Hassler. 1982. pap. 3.50 (ISBN 0-553-22945-1). Bantam.

Love Hunter: A Novel. Jon Hassler. LC 80-29693. 1981. 12.95 (ISBN 0-688-00483-0). Morrow.

Love I Dare Not. Allene Soule Corliss. LC 37-1525. Toronto, Farrar & Rinehart, Incorporated.

Love Idylls. Samuel Rutherford Crockett. LC 73-130055. (Short story index reprint series). 1970. Books for Libraries Press.

Love Idylls. Samuel Rutherford Crockett. LC 1-20946. 1901. Dodd, Mead and Company.

Love. Illus., Designed by Vanni. Story by Lowell A. Siff. Gian Berto Vanni. LC 64-24622. (Venture bk.). 1965. 5.00. Braziller.

Love Image. Valerie Taylor. LC 77-77987. (Illus.). 1977. 4.50 (ISBN 0-930044-08-8). Naiad Press.

Love in a Cold Climate: A Novel. Nancy Mitford. 1949. Random House.

Love in a Dark House. Merla Zellerbach. LC 61-12608. 1961. Doubleday.

Love in a Dry Season. Shelby Foote. LC 51-6514. 1951. Dial Press.

Love in a Dry Season. Shelby Foote. LC 79-12825. 1979. 10.00 (ISBN 0-394-40877-2). Random House.

Love in a Hot Climate. Edmund Schiddel. 224p. 1973. pap. 0.95 o.p. (ISBN 0-532-95234-0). Woodhill.

Love in a Hot Climate. Edmund Schiddel. 224p. 1973. pap. 0.95 o.p. (ISBN 0-532-95234-0). Manor Bks.

Love in a Hurry. Gelett Burgess. LC 13-19076. 1.25. The Bobbs-Merrill Company.

Love in a Little Town. J. E Buckrose. LC 11-24680. 1911. 1.35. G. P. Putman's Sons.

Love in a London Flat. Victor Jones. LC 63-14968. 1963. L. Stuart.

Love in a Major Key. Fiona Hill. (Berkley Medallion Book). 1976. (pbk.) 0.95 (ISBN 0-425-03019-9). Berkley Publishing Corp.

Love in a Mask: Or, Imprudence and Happiness; a Hitherto Unpublished Novel. Honore De Balzac. Tr. by Alice M. Ivimy. LC 11-279141. 1.25. Rand, McNally & Company.

Love in a Mist. Winifred Mary Scott. LC 32-107492. 1932. Doubleday, Doran & Company, Inc.

Love In a Mist, No. 38. Pamela Wynne. Ed. by Barbara Cartland. 160p. 1982. pap. 2.50 (ISBN 0-553-20500-5). Bantam.

Love in a Proper City. John Wahtera. LC 81-22365. 352p. 1982. 13.50 (ISBN 0-688-01104-7). Morrow.

Love in a Windy Space: A Novel. Wirt Williams. LC 57-5543. 1957. Reynal.

Love in All Its Disguises. Norman Rosten. LC 81-65135. 192p. 1981. 11.95 (ISBN 0-87795-324-4). Arbor Hse.

Love in Amber. Netta Muskett. LC 42-20090. 1942. Hutchinson & Co., Ltd.

Love in Amsterdam. Nicolas Freeling. LC 63-10616. (Harper novel of suspense). Harper & Row.

Love in Amsterdam. Nicolas Freeling. LC 76-360576. (Penguin crime fiction). 1975. 1.25 (ISBN 0-14-002281-3). Penguin.

Love in Atlantis: A Novel. B. L Barrett. LC 79-80417. 1969. 4.95. Houghton Mifflin.

Love in Black and White. 1st. ed. Irma Louise Banks. 1974. 5.95 (ISBN 0-533-00878-6). Vantage Press.

Love in Chartres. Nathan Asch. LC 27-24574. 1927. A. & C. Boni.

Love in Chicago. Albert Bein. LC 29-5599. Harcourt, Brace and Company.

Love in Chief: A Novel. Rose Kirkpatrick Weekes. 1904. Harper & Brothers.

Love in Danger. Glenna Finley, pseud. pap. 1.75 (ISBN 0-451-09190-6, E9190, Sig). NAL.

Love in Disguise. Rachel Lindsay. (Presents Ser.). 1975. pap. 1.25 (ISBN 0-373-70585-9, 705855, Pub by Harlequin). PB.

Love in Disguise. Nina Pykare. (Orig.). 1980. pap. 1.50 (ISBN 0-440-15229-1). Dell.

Love in Dishevelment. David Greenhood. LC 48-8174. 1948. Creative Age Press.

Love in Escrow. John O. Iversen & Mary Iversen. LC 78-61286. (Stories That Win Ser.). 1979. pap. 0.95 (ISBN 0-8163-0242-1). Pacific Pr Pub Assn.

Love in Exile. Blanche Chenier. (Orig.). 1980. pap. 1.75 (ISBN 0-449-50046-2, Coventry). Fawcett.

Love in Exile. Vivian Connolly. (Superromance Ser.). 295p. 1983. pap. 2.95 (ISBN 0-373-70063-6, Pub. by Worldwide). Harlequin Bks.

Love in Friendship: A Nameless Sentiment) Preface in Fragments from Stendhal... Hermine Lecomte du Nouy & Pene Du Bois, Henri, 1858-1906, Tr. LC 5-2556. Meyer Bros. & Co.

Love in Greenwich Village. Floyd Dell. LC 73-128730. (Short story index reprint series). 1970. Books for Libraries Press.

Love in Greenwich Village. Floyd Dell. LC 26-10802. George H. Doran Company.

Love in Her Heart. John Antonio Moroso. LC 34-6711. The Macaulay Company.

Love in Her Life. Angela Gordon. 1971. pap. 0.75 o.p. (94152). Beagle Bks.

Love in Hiding. Barbara Cartland. (Historical Romance Ser. No. 4). 1972. pap. 0.75 o.p. (ISBN 0-515-02751-0, N2750). Pyramid Pubns.

Love in Hiding. Barbara Cartland. 1976. pap. 1.25 o.p. (ISBN 0-515-04111-4). BJ Pub Group.

Love in Hiding. Barbara Cartland. 1977. pap. 1.50 o.p. (ISBN 0-515-04344-3). BJ Pub Group.

Love in Hot Climate. Edmund Schiddel. (O.s.i.). 1976. pap. 1.75 o.s.i. (AR1643, Award). Univ Pub & Dist.

Love in Idleness. A Bar Harbour Tale. Francis Marion Crawford. LC 6-31065. 1894. Macmillan and Company.

Love in Idleness.A Summer Story. By Ellen W. Olney. Ellen Warner Olney Kirk. 1877. J. B. Lippincott & Co.

Love in Its Empire: Illustrated in Seven Novels see Perfidious Brethren.

Love in Louisiana. Josiah Pitts Woolfolk. LC 51-12705. 1951. Arco Pub. Co.

Love in Old Cloathes & Other Stories. facsimile ed. Henry Cuyer Bunner. LC 78-94706. (Short Story Index Reprint Ser). 1896. 16.00 (ISBN 0-8369-3084-3). Ayer Co.

Love in Old Cloathes: And Other Stories. Henry Cuyler Bunner. LC 78-94706. (Short story index reprint series). (Illus.). 1969. Books for Libraries Press.

Love in Old Cloathes: And Other Stories. Henry Cuyler Bunner. 1896. C. Scribner's Sons.

Love in Old Cloathes & Other Stories. Henry Cuyler Bunner. Repr. of 1897 ed. lib. bdg. 12.50 (ISBN 0-8414-2523-X). Folcroft.

Love in Our Time. Norman Collins. LC 39-16405. 1939. Harper & Brothers.

Love in Paris. Murray Kalis. 224p. 1981. pap. 1.95 (ISBN 0-449-14382-1, GM). Fawcett.

Love in Pernicketty Town. Samuel Rutherford Crockett. LC 11-9235. Hodder and Stoughton.

Love in Pity. Barbara Cartland. 1976. pap. 1.25 o.p. (ISBN 0-515-03993-4). BJ Pub Group.

Love in Question. Rosalie Packard. LC 61-11955. 1961. Houghton, Mifflin.

Love in Style. Paula Little, pseud. (O.s.i.). 1976. pap. 0.95 o.s.i. (BT50900). Belmont-Tower.

Love in Style. Little, Paula. 1976. (pbk.) 0.95. Belmont Tower.

Love in the Afternoon. Ed Zimmerman. 1973. 0.95 (ISBN 0-671-77562-6). Pocket Books.

Love in the Afternoon. Ed. by Zimmermann. LC 70-142482. 1971. 5.95. Bobbs-Merrill.

Love in the Arctic. Orrie Hitt. LC 54-8761. Red Lantern Books.

Love in the Backwoods: Two Mormons from Muddlety, Alfred's Wife. Langdon Elwyn Mitchell. LC 7-31097. 1897. Harper & Brothers.

Love in the Clouds. Barbara Cartland. LC 78-26007. 8.95 (ISBN 0-525-14907-4). Dutton.

Love in the Dark. Barbara Cartland. LC 79-13855. 1980. 6.95 (ISBN 0-87272-081-0). Duron Books.

TITLE INDEX LOVE LIKE A SHADOW.

Love in the Environs of Voronezh & Other Poems. Alan Sillitoe. LC 68-9189. 1969. 3.95 o.p. Doubleday.
Love in the Family. Lydia Wilkinson. 192p. 1972. pap. 1.95 o.p. (ISBN 0-87056-223-1, 6223). Brandon.
Love in the Glade. rev. ed. Elizabeth Brennan. Ed. by Alice Sachs. (Orig.). 1970. Repr. of 1968 ed. 3.95 o.p. Lenox Hill.
Love in the Hot-Eye Country. Jane Lewis Brandt. 1975. (pbk.) 1.25. Bantam Books.
Love in the Latin Quarter: Amorous Episodes from Bohemians of the Latin Quarter. Henri Murger. LC 48-10603. (New Avon library, 163). 1948. Avon Book Co.
Love in the Mist. 1st American Ed. Rosalie Packard. LC 59-6927. 1959. Houghton Mifflin.
Love in the Mists. A Novel. Walter L Womble. LC 9-2508. 1892. Presses of Edwards & Broughton.
Love in the Moon, No. 138. Barbara Cartland. 160p. (Orig.). 1981. pap. 1.95 (ISBN 0-553-14585-1). Bantam.
Love in the Nineteenth Century. A Fragment. Harriet Waters Preston. LC 7-30940.
Love in the Ruins: The Adventure of a Bad Catholic at-a-Time Near the End of the World. Walker Percy. (Bard Book). 1981. 2.95 (ISBN 0-380-38984-3). Avon Books.
Love in the Ruins: The Adventures of a Bad Catholic at a Time Near the End of the World. Walker Percy. LC 71-143301. 1971. 7.95 (ISBN 0-374-19302-9). Farrar, Straus & Giroux.
Love in the Skies. Virginia Jordan. 80p. 1981. 5.50 o.p. (ISBN 0-682-49684-7). Exposition.
Love in the Springtime. Peggy Gaddis, pseud. LC 34-36402. W. Godwin, Inc.
Love in the Sun: A Novel. Leo Walmsley. LC 40-4225. 1940. Doubleday, Doran & Company, Inc.
Love in the Tropics: A Romance of the South Seas. Caroline Earle White. LC 8-36625. 1890. J. B. Lippincott Company.
Love in the Weaving. Edith Hall Orthwein. LC 10-17994. Broadway Publishing Co.
Love in the Winter. Daniel Curley. LC 76-7541. (Illinois Short Fiction Ser). 1976. 11.95 (ISBN 0-252-00551-1); pap. 4.95 (ISBN 0-252-00578-3). U of Ill Pr.
Love in These Days: A Modern Story. Alec Waugh. LC 27-3513. George H. Doran Company.
Love in Virginia. Josiah Pitts Woolfolk. LC 35-9331. Godwin.
Love in Waiting. Caroline Courtney. LC 82-15634. 1982. 8.95 (ISBN 0-8161-3463-4). G.K. Hall.
Love in White. James Noble Gifford. LC 40-30760. 1940. Gramercy Publishing Co.
Love in White. Gay Rutherford. LC 40-307601. Gramercy Publishing Co.
Love in Winter. Margaret Storm Jameson. LC 35-6533. 1935. A. A. Knopf.
Love in Winter. Storm Jameson. (Berkley Medallion). 1.95 (ISBN 0-425-03207-8). Berkley.
Love in Youth. Frank Harris. LC 16-9548. 1.25. George H. Doran Company.
Love Insurance. Earl Derr Biggers. LC 14-16206. The Bobbs-Merrill Company.
Love Is a Beggar. A. C. Phillips. 4.50 o.p. Vantage.
Love Is a Bridge. Bracelen Charles. (95-136). 1966. Popular Lib.
Love Is a Bridge. Charles Bracelen Flood. LC 52-8273. 1953. Houghton Mifflin.
Love Is a Bridge. Charles Bracelon Flood. 1974. (pbk.) 1.50 (ISBN 0-515-03535-1). Pyramid Books.
Love Is a Dangerous Game. Marjorie Lewty. (Harlequin Romances Ser.). 192p. 1981. pap. 1.25 (ISBN 0-373-02421-5). Harlequin Bks.
Love Is a Dirty Word. Yvonne MacManus. (O.s.i.). (Orig.). pap. 0.60 o.s.i. (A161X, Award). Univ Pub & Dist.
Love Is a Dream: By Carol Holliston Pseud. James Noble Gifford. LC 52-8359. 1952. Areadia House.
Love Is a Fever by Joan Sargent Pseud. Sara Lucile Jenkins. LC 53-13088. 1953. Avalon Books.
Love Is a Four Letter Word. Anita Rowe Block. LC 73-116940. (Short story index reprint series). 1970. Books for Libraries Press.
Love Is a Four Letter Word. 1st Ed. Anita Rowe Block. LC 58-5567. 1958. Doubleday.
Love Is a Frenzy. Charlotte Lamb, pseud. (Harlequin Presents Ser.). (Orig.). 1980. pap. 1.50 (ISBN 0-373-70834-3, Pub. by Harlequin). PB.
Love Is a Gamble: By Jennifer Ames Pseud. Maysie Greig. LC 54-7965. 1954. Avalon Books.
Love Is a Gambler. Maysie Greig. pap. 0.50 o.p. (50-285). Manor Bks.
Love Is a Lonely Thing: A Novel. Florence Jane Soman. LC 52-14158. 1953. Random House.
Love Is a Masquerade. Davis Dresser. LC 35-17236. Phoenix Press.
Love Is a Pie. Stories and Plays. Maude Phelps McVeigh Hutchins. LC 52-13036. 1952.
Love Is a Place. Margaret Thompson Bridgman. LC 53-10788. 1953. Funk & Wagnalls Co.
Love Is a Racket. Rian James. LC 31-29015. A. H. King.
Love Is a Riddle. Jane Rossiter, pseud. 1972. pap. 0.75 o.s.i. (01-356). Lancer.
Love Is a Sad Song. Ruskin Bond. 104p. 1976. pap. 1.80 (ISBN 0-89253-027-8). Ind-US Inc.
Love Is a Spirit: A Novel. Julian Hawthorne. LC 7-3891. 1896. Harper & Brothers.
Love Is a Tempest. Angela Gordon. 1972. pap. 0.75 o.p. (94306). Beagle Bks.
Love Is a Three Leter Word. William Johnston. LC 72-129735. (Tempo books, 5358). 1970. 0.75. Grosset & Dunlap.
Love Is a Wild Assault Elithe. Elithe Hamilton Kirkland. 1977. 2.25 (ISBN 0-380-01678-8). Avon Books.
Love Is a Wild Assault. 1st Ed. Elithe Hamilton Kirkland. LC 59-6362. 1959. Doubleday.
Love Is a Wound. Worth Tuttle Hedden. LC 52-5684. 1952. Crown Publishers.
Love Is All: Conversations of a Husband & Wife with God. Joseph W. Bird & Lois F. Bird. LC 67-22453. 1968. pap. 3.50 (ISBN 0-385-00779-5, Im). Doubleday.
Love Is Always New. Peggy Gaddis, pseud. LC 35-7018. Arcadia House.
Love Is an Eagle. Barbara Cartland. 1977. pap. 1.50 o.p. (ISBN 0-515-04380-X). BJ Pub Group.
Love Is an Eagle: No. 49. Barbara Cartland. 1975. pap. 1.25 o.p. (ISBN 0-515-03910-1, V3910). BJ Pub Group.
Love Is an Open Door. Bill Bair. 1975. pap. 1.45 o.p. (ISBN 0-88270-123-1). Logos.
Love Is Contraband. Barbara Cartland. (Historical Romance Ser: No. 13). 1974. pap. 1.25 o.p. (ISBN 0-515-03429-0, V3429). BJ Pub Group.
Love Is Dangerous. Barbara Cartland. (Romance Ser., No. 31). 1972. pap. 1.25 o.p. (V2611). Pyramid Pubns.
Love Is Dangerous. Barbara Cartland. 1976. pap. 1.25 o.p. (ISBN 0-515-04132-7). BJ Pub Group.
Love Is Enough. Denise Robins. 1975. (pbk.) 0.95 (ISBN 0-380-00305-8). Avon.
Love Is Enough. Francis Brett Young. LC 27-560585. 1927. A. A. Knopf.
Love Is Eternal: A Novel About Mary Todd Lincoln and Abraham Lincoln. Irving Stone. LC 54-9678. 1954. Doubleday.
Love Is Eternal. Edited for School Use by George W. Sullivan. Irving Stone. LC 57-140393. (Modern literature series). 1957. Oxford Book Co.
Love is Fire, Remedy for Love & The Legend of The Swans. Flora Kidd. (Harlequin Romances (3-in-1) Ser.). 576p. 1983. pap. 3.95 (ISBN 0-373-20071-4). Harlequin Bks.
Love Is for the Living. Agnes Mary Robertson Dunlop. LC 67-12646. 1967. Holt, Rinehart and Winston.
Love Is Forever. Margaret Elizabeth Bell. LC 54-7624. 1954. Morrow.
Love Is Forever. Norma Patterson. LC 41-232683. Farrar & Rinehart, Inc.
Love Is Forever. William Edward Daniel Ross. 1969. pap. 0.50 o.p. (62-090). Paperback Lib.
Love Is Forever. Jane Rossiter, pseud. LC 63-6872. 1963. Avalon Books.
Love Is Forever-We Are for Tonight. Robert M. Williams. 1970. pap. 0.60 o.p. (0502-06101). Curtis.
Love Is Free. Barbara Hedworth. LC 32-20227. E. P. Dutton Company, Inc.
Love Is Innocent. Barbara Cartland. (Barbara Cartland library, 26). 1975. (pbk.) 1.25. Bantam.
Love Is Just a Word. Johannes Mario Simmel. LC 69-12265. 1969. McGraw-Hill.
Love Is Just a Word. Johannes Mario Simmel. 1980. 2.95 (ISBN 0-445-04622-8). Fawcett Popular Library.
Love Is Just Around the Corner. Lester Atwell. LC 63-8154. 1963. Simon and Schuster.
Love Is Life. Lawrence Christopher Lee. LC 39-34158. Dorrance and Company.
Love Is Like an Acorn. Matsu Crawford. LC 73-179288. 1973. (pbk.) 1.25. Zondervan Pub. House.
Love Is Like an Acorn. Matsu Crawford. LC 69-11631. 1969. 2.95. Zondervan Pub. House.
Love Is Like Peanuts. Betty Bates. (gr. 7-9). 1981. pap. 1.75 (ISBN 0-671-56109-X). Archway.
Love Is Like That. Cecil Roberts. LC 58-6936. 1958. Coward-McCann.
Love Is Like This. James Noble Gifford. LC 46-6385. 1946. Gramercy Publishing Co.
Love Is Lord of All: Or, Neighboring Steppes. A Novel. Stephan Gatschenberger. Tr. by Safford, Mary Joanna. (choice series, no. 61). 1892. R. Bonner's Sons.
Love Is Master. Almey St. John Adcock. LC 29-6797. 1928. Little, Brown, and Company.
Love Is Mine. Barbara Cartland. LC 72-94183. 1972. 5.95 (ISBN 0-515-09377-7). Pyramid House.
Love Is My Business. Meredith Gorman. pap. 0.95 o.p. (1118). Brandon.
Love Is Never Late. Ruth Phillips. LC 33-220434. The Macaulay Company.
Love Is No Sin. Russell Higgins. LC 34-410599. W. Godwin, Inc.
Love Is No Sin. Albert Quandt. LC 34-41059. 1934. W. Godwin.
Love Is Not a Safe Country. Paige Mitchell, pseud. LC 66-21313. 1967. Dutton.
Love Is Not a Safe Country. Paige Mitchell. 1974. (pbk.) 1.25. Popular Library.
Love Is Not a Safe Country. By Inger and Lasse Sandberg. Tr. from Swedish by Nancy Swenson Leupold. 1st Amer. Ed. Paige Mitchell & Lasse Sandberg. 1968. 3.95. Delacorte.
Love Is Not Enough. Barbara Corcoran. 1981. pap. 1.95 (ISBN 0-345-29011-9). Ballantine.
Love Is Not Enough. Ruth Lyons. (Orig.). 1980. pap. 2.50 (ISBN 0-451-09196-5, E9196, Sig). NAL.
Love Is Not Enough: A Novel. Bob Shanks. LC 81-22582. 12.95 (ISBN 0-393-01586-6). W.W. Norton.
Love Is of the Valley. Jean Stubbs. LC 80-28198. 1981. 12.95 (ISBN 0-312-49942-6). St. Martin's Press.
Love Is One of the Choices. Norma Klein. 1982. pap. 1.95 (ISBN 0-449-24179-3, Crest). Fawcett.
Love Is One of the Choices: A Novel. Norma Klein. LC 78-51323. 7.95 (ISBN 0-8037-5019-6). Dial Press.
Love Is Out. Claudia De Lys. LC 32-15061. Mohawk Press, Inc.
Love Is So Blind. Ruby Mildred Ayres. LC 34-8354. 1934. Doubleday, Doran & Company, Inc.
Love Is the Anchor see Kiss for Elaine.
Love Is the Answer. Louise Bergstrom. (Candlelight Romance). 1.25 (ISBN 0-440-12058-6). Dell Pub. Co.
Love Is the Enemy. Barbara Cartland. (Romance Ser.: No. 9). 1972. pap. 1.25 o.p. (ISBN 0-515-02824-X, V2824). Pyramid Pubns.
Love Is the Enemy, No. 9. Barbara Cartland. 1977. pap. 1.25 o.p. (ISBN 0-515-04273-0). BJ Pub Group.
Love Is the Fulfilling. Drusilla Wildschut. LC 58-6722. 1958. Christopher Pub. House.
Love Is the Honey. Violet Winspear. (Harlequin Presents Ser.). (Orig.). 1980. pap. 1.50 (ISBN 0-373-10354-9, Pub. by Harlequin). PB.
Love Is the Message. Brent-Wood Scott. 1969. pap. 1.75 (ISBN 0-910140-20-0). Anthony.
Love Is the One with Wings: A Novel. Philip Van Doren Stern. LC 51-9568. 1951. Farrar, Straus, and Young.
Love Is the Sum of It All: A Plantation Romance. George Cary Eggleston. LC 7-23710. 1907. Lothrop, Lee & Shepard Co.
Love Is the Theme. Ed. by Douglas Angus. LC 78-115336. (Fawcett premier book). 1970. 0.95. Fawcett Publications.
Love Is the Winner. Gail Everett. (Candlelight romance, 211). 0.95. Dell.
Love Is Where You Find It. an original timely books ed. Paula Christian. LC 78-68727. 1979. 5.95 (ISBN 0-931328-05-5). Timely Books.
Love Is Where You Find It. Christine Conlin. 256p. (Orig.). 1982. pap. cancelled (ISBN 0-505-51816-3). Tower Bks.
Love Is Where You Find It. Cateau De Leeuw. LC 47-447888. 1947. Macrae-Smith Co.
Love Is Where You Find It. George W Seth. Burney Brothers Publishing Co.
Love Island. Barbara Max. LC 82-2850. (Nightingale Series). 1982. 6.95 (ISBN 0-8161-3379-4). G.K. Hall.
Love Island. Justine Valenti. (Orig.). 1981. pap. 1.50 (ISBN 0-440-14709-3). Dell.
Love Isn't Important: The Experiences of Gay Elwell. Louis Marks Clancy. LC 82-25174. Issued for the St. Botolph Society by L.C. Page & Company.
Love Kick. Fan Nichols. Orig. Title: Ask for Linda. 1970. pap. 0.75 o.p. (75-328). Manor Bks.
Love Killers. Jackie Collins. Orig. Title: Love Head. 192p. 1975. pap. 2.95 (ISBN 0-446-30816-1). Warner Bks.
Love Kills. Dan Greenburg. LC 77-92056. 7.95 (ISBN 0-15-154723-8). Harcourt Brace Jovanovich.
Love Kills. Dan Greenburg. 1979. 2.50 (ISBN 0-671-82756-1). Pocket Books.
Love Knows No Barriers (God Is for White Folks) Thomas, Will. LC 51-20335. (Signet book, 832). 1950. New American Library.
Love Knows No Law: A Love Story. Pearl Bank Steward. LC 34-14769. Chelsea House.
Love Knows No Law, by Leon De Tinseau. Leon De Tinseau & Curwen, Camden, Tr. (On cover: The fair library, no. 1). 1892. Worthington Company.
Love Laughs Gaily. James Noble Gifford. LC 33-193857. 1933. W. Godwin, Inc.
Love Laughs Last. Evelyn Beatrice Hall. LC 19-10145. George H. Doran Company.
Love Leaves at Midnight. Barbara Cartland. LC 78-3825. 1978. 1.50 (ISBN 0-553-11751-3). Duron Books.
Love Leaves No Choice. Sydney Thompson. LC 43-59487. 1943. Macrae-Smith-Company.
Love Legend. Peggy Smith Shane. LC 22-19298. 1922. C. Scribner's Sons.
Love (L'envers De L'histoire Contemporaine) 'a Novel, from the French. Honore De Balzac. Tr. by Myndart Vereist. (choice series, no. 94). 1893. R. Bonner's Sons.
Love Letter Hack. Michael Brondoli. LC 78-71990. (Gargoyle book). 3.00 (ISBN 0-9602424-0-6). Paycock Press.
Love Letter in the Dead-Letter Office: A Novel. Nora Johnson. LC 66-14889. bds., 4.95. Delacorte Dist. Dial.
Love Letters. large print ed. Eli Cantor. LC 82-16203. 1983. 13.95 (ISBN 0-89340-538-8). J. Curley & Associates.
Love Letters. Eli Cantor. 1982. pap. 3.50 (ISBN 0-8217-1068-0). Zebra.
Love Letters. Madeleine L'Engle. LC 66-201702. 1966. bds., 3.75. Farrar.
Love Letters. Madeleine L'Engle. (5059). 1967. Dell.
Love Letters. George Tsongas. 1975. pap. 2.50 (ISBN 0-915016-05-2). Second Coming.
Love Letters. Ann Warren. LC 80-50378. 5.95 (ISBN 0-8499-0263-0). Word Books.
Love Letters: A Novel. Eli Cantor. LC 78-27648. 8.95 (ISBN 0-517-53707-9). Crown Publishers.
Love Letters: A Novel. Chris Massie. LC 44-7922. 1944. Random House.
Love Letters: A Romance in Correspondence. Harold Richard Vynne. (Zimmerman's pocket library). 1898. Zimmerman's.
Love Letters: A Romance in Correspondence. Harold Richard Vynne. LC 27-15603. 1927. Rae D. Henkle Co., Inc.
Love Letters from the Nile. Mary Randolph. LC 10-28799. 1910. 1.50. The Knickerbocker Press.
Love Letters of a Divorced Couple. William Farquhar Payson. LC 15-6338. 1915. 1.00. Doubleday, Page & Company.
Love Letters of a Husband. James Milne. LC 28-14549. 1928. Doubleday, Doran & Company, Inc.
Love Letters of a Musician. Myrtle Reed. LC 99-53202. 1899. G. P. Putnam's Sons.
Love Letters of a Mystic. Alma Newton. LC 16-374. 1916. John Lane Company.
Love Letters of a Wordly Woman. Lucy Lane Clifford. LC 24-20476. H. M. Caldwell Co.
Love Letters of a Worldy Woman. Lucy Lane Clifford. (On cover: Neely's library of choice literature, no. 29). 1894. F.T. Neely.
Love, Letters of a Worldy Woman. Lucy Lane Clifford. (On cover: Seaside library. Pocket ed. no. 2104). 1895. G. Munro's Sons.
Love Letters of an Actress. Elsie Janis. LC 13-9794. 1913. 1.00. D. Appleton and Company.
Love-Letters of the King; or, The Life Romantic. Richard Le Gallienne. LC 1-31013. 1901. Little, Brown, and Company.
Love Letters on Blue Paper. Arnold Wesker. LC 74-20422. 1975. 7.95 (ISBN 0-06-014561-7). Harper & Row.
Love Letters That Caused a Divorce. A E Aldington. G. W. Dillingham Company.
Love Letters to a Dead Woman. Henry Devenish Harben. LC 24-4620. 1924. T. Seltzer.
Love Letters to Caitlin. August William Derleth. 10.00 o.p. Arkham.
Love-Lies-Bleeding. Jeff Bouck. 1976. 3.95 o.p. (ISBN 0-8059-2254-7). Dorrance.
Love Lies Bleeding. Edmund Crispin, pseud. LC 81-51170. 1981. 9.95 (ISBN 0-8027-5444-9). Walker.
Love Lies Bleeding. Edmund Crispin, pseud. LC 81-20999. 1982. 3.50 (ISBN 0-14-000974-4). Penguin Books.
Love Lies Bleeding: A Detective Story. Robert Bruce Montgomery. (Main line mysteries). 1948. J. B. Lippincott Co.
Love Lies Bleeding: A Novel. Peter Viertel. LC 64-19222. 1964. Doubleday.
Love Lies Dreaming. Cecil Scott Forester. LC 27-11961. The Bobbs-Merrill Company.
Love Life. Charlotte Vale Allen. (Dll Book). 1978. 1.95 (ISBN 0-440-14746-8). Dell Pub. Co.
Love Life: A Novel. Charlotte Vale Allen. LC 75-22166. 6.95 (ISBN 0-440-04292-5). Delacorte Press.
Love Life of a Cheltenham Lady. Dinah Brooke. LC 78-154771. 1971. 5.95. Coward, McCann & Geoghegan.
Love Life of Venus: La Vie Amoureuse De Venus. Francis De Miomandre & Girard, Daniel P., Tr. LC 30-7961. 1930. Brentano's.
Love Lightly. Margaret Elizabeth Sangster. LC 32-10934. 1932. Brewer, Warren & Putnam.
Love Like a Shadow. Lois Lodge. LC 35-3363. Phoenix Press.

Love Like an Arrow. Frances Y McHugh. 1972. 4.95. Lenox Hill Pr.

Love Like That. David Garth. LC 37-197552. 1937. H. C. Kinsey & Company, Inc.

Love Link. Pearl Doles Bell. LC 25-10146. W. J. Watt & Co.

Love Link. Pearl Doles Bell. LC 31-20658. 1926. A. L. Burt Company.

Love Listens. Don Hall. 288p. (Orig.). 1981. pap. 2.50 (ISBN 0-523-41034-4). Pinnacle Bks.

Love Locked in. Barbara Cartland. LC 76-57985. 6.95 (ISBN 0-525-14910-4). Dutton.

Love, Lords, and Lady-Birds. Barbara Cartland. LC 77-7027. 6.95 (ISBN 0-525-14920-1). Dutton.

Love Lottery. Bertil Fredrik Schutt. LC 73-166462. (Zebra books, Z-1089-T). 1971. 1.95. Grove Press.

Love, Love at the End. D. Berrigan. (O.s.i.). 1971. pap. 1.45 o.s.i. (ISBN 0-02-083750-X, Collier). Macmillan.

Love Machine. Jacqueline Susann. LC 70-75872. 1969. 6.95. Simon and Schuster.

Love Machinery. Karl Flinders. pap. 1.95 o.s.i. (OPS-24). Olympia.

Love Made Manifest. Guy Newell Boothby. 1899. H. S. Stone and Company.

Love Made the Choice. Mary Burchell. (Presents Ser.). 1975. pap. 1.25 (ISBN 0-373-70599-9, 70599, Pub by Harlequin). PB.

Love Madness: A Story of a Forbidden Love. Claire Pomeroy. LC 32-30525. Grosset & Dunlap.

Love Makers. Stark Cole. 176p. pap. 1.95 o.p. (6092). Brandon.

Love Makes the Difference. Ruth Watt. 1975. 4.95. Avalon Books.

Love-Making of Max-Robert (A Corner of the World) Robert Shaplen. LC 50-35207. (Signet book, 789). 1950. New American Library.

Love Making-Two. 192p. (Orig.). 1982. pap. 2.25 (ISBN 0-8439-1058-5, Leisure Bks). Nordon Pubns.

Love, Mary: A Novel of New York City at Its Most Hilarious. Mary Gwynn. LC 80-24996. 224p. 1981. 8.95 (ISBN 0-688-00429-6). Morrow.

Love Masque. Caroline Campbell. LC 81-70937. 1982. 11.95 (ISBN 0-8027-0703-3). Walker.

Love Match. Arnold Bennett. LC 74-16481. (Collected Works of Arnold Bennett: Vol. 50). 1976. Repr. of 1922 ed. 14.75 (ISBN 0-518-19131-1). Ayer Co.

Love Match. Hebe Elsna. 1971. pap. 0.95 o.p. (95074). Beagle Bks.

Love Match. Catherine Fellows. (Illus.). 1977. 1.25 (ISBN 0-440-13768-3). Dell Pub. Co.

Love Match. Ludovic Halevy & Cherbuliez, Victor, 1829-1899. LC 2-2470. (On cover: Gleanings from foreign authors. no. 1). 1889. J. Delay.

Love Match. Roberta Leigh. 352p. 1983. pap. 2.25 (ISBN 0-373-97003-X, Pub. by Worldwide). Harlequin Bks.

Love Match. Janet Quin-Harkin. 1982. pap. write for info. Bantam.

Love Match. A Novel. Sylvanus Cobb. (On cover: The choice series, no. 35). (On cover: Ledger library, no. 35). 1891. R. Bonner's Sons.

Love Me Again. Alexandra Scott. (Harlequin Romances Ser.). 192p. 1982. pap. 1.50 (ISBN 0-373-02506-8). Harlequin Bks.

Love Me & Die. Day Keene. 192p. 1973. pap. 0.95 o.p. (ISBN 0-532-95287-1). Woodhill.

Love Me & Die. Day Keene. 192p. 1973. pap. 0.95 o.p. (ISBN 0-532-95287-1). Manor Bks.

Love Me & Die. Day Keene. 1973. (pbk.) 0.95. Manor Books.

Love Me Anise. Arthur John Rees. LC 28-153788. Dodd, Mead & Company.

Love Me, Daddy. Christopher Robin. (Orig.). 1969. pap. 1.75 o.p. (3067). Brandon.

Love Me Forever. Barbara Cartland. 1974. pap. 1.25 o.p. (ISBN 0-515-03451-7, V3451). BJ Pub Group.

Love Me Forever. A Christmas Carol in Prose. Robert Williams Buchanan. (Seaside library, v. 74, no. 1506). 1883. G. Munro.

Love Me in Death: By D. B. Olsen. 1st Ed. Dolores Birk Hitchens. LC 51-1194. 1951. Published for the Crime Club by Doubleday.

Love Me Little. Amanda Vail. LC 57-943817. 1957. McGraw-Hill.

Love Me Little: By Amanda Vail Pseud. Warren Miller. LC 57-9438. 1957. Mc-Graw-Hill.

Love Me Little, Love Me Long.". Charles Reade. LC 7-39658. 1859. Harper & Brothers.

Love Me Little, Love Me Long.". household. ed. Charles Reade. 1869. Fields, Osgood & Co.

Love Me Little, Love Me Long. Charles Reade. LC 42-320870. (Works. Library edition). 1895. Metropolitan Publishing Company.

Love Me Little, Love Me Long. Charles Reade. LC 7-38600. (On back of cover: Large print library). 1907. Doubleday, Page & Company.

Love Me Little, Love Me Long." A Novel. Charles Reade. (On cover: Seaside library. Pocket ed., no. 2069). 1894. G. Munro.

Love Me, Love My Dog. Gus Stevens. (Orig.). 1969. pap. 1.95 o.s.i. (OPH-171, Ophelia). Olympia.

Love Me, Love My Doggerel. Louise F. Kerr. LC 70-107863. 1969. 3.00 (ISBN 0-937684-02-3). Tradd St Pr.

Love Me, Marietta. Jennifer Wilde. 560p. (Orig.). 1983. pap. 3.95 (ISBN 0-446-30723-8). Warner Bks.

Love Me No More. Denise Robins. LC 76-47858. 1.25 (ISBN 0-380-00825-4). Avon.

Love Me Now. Fan Nichols. pap. 0.60 o.p. (60-355). Manor Bks.

Love Me Sailor. Robert S Close. LC 50-10466. 1950. Fell.

Love Me to Death. Philip Kirk. (Butler: No. 5). 1980. pap. 1.75 o.s.i. (ISBN 0-8439-0712-6, Leisure Bks). Nordon Pubns.

Love Me Tomorrow. Robert Rimmer. (Orig.). 1978. pap. 2.50 (ISBN 0-451-08385-7, E8385, Sig). NAL.

Love Me Truly. S. C. Carew, pseud. (Orig.). 1969. pap. 1.75 o.p. (3060). Brandon.

Love Merchants. Stephen Lewis. 1974. (pbk.) 1.75. Ace Books.

Love Merger see Airport People.

Love-Minded. Denis Brian. LC 68-23896. 1968. Prentice-Hall.

Love Must Be Gay: A Novel, by Helen Ahern. Helen Ahern. LC 35-4297. The Macaulay Comapny.

Love Named Dan. William Arthur Neubauer. LC 66-4984. 1966. Arcadia House.

Love Needs a Nurse... Peggy O'More, pseud. LC 37-36099. Hillman, Curl, Inc.

Love Nest: And Other Stories. Ring Wilmer Lardner. LC 26-9020. 1926. C. Scribner's Sons.

Love Never Faileth: An Emotion Touched by Moralities. Carnegie Simpson. 1902. F. H. Revell Company.

Love Never Faileth: And Other Stories. Pearl L Simm. LC 55-12293. Comet Press Books.

Love Never Fails. Byrdie D. Meade. 2.50 o.p. Carlton.

Love Never Sleeps. Alan Williams. LC 35-15161. Godwin.

Love North & South. Susan N. Pulsifer. 174p. 1975. 7.50 o.p. (ISBN 0-682-48268-4). Exposition.

Love Not Afraid to Wait. J. C. Brown. 5.95 o.p. (ISBN 0-8062-1018-4). Carlton.

Love Not Human. Gordon R. Dickson. 256p. 1981. pap. 2.50 (ISBN 0-441-50414-0). Ace Bks.

Love Object. Edna O'Brien. 174p. (Orig.). 1970. pap. 3.50 (ISBN 0-14-003104-9, Pub. by Penguin England). Irish Bk Ctr.

Love Object. Edna O'Brien. 176p. 1975. pap. 1.95 o.p. (ISBN 0-14-003104-9). Penguin.

Love Object: Stories. Edna O'Brien. LC 69-10683. 1969. 4.95. Knopf.

Love Odds. Peter Keyes. (Orig.). pap. 0.95 o.p. (1136). Brandon.

Love of a Lady. Annie Hall Thomas Cudlip. LC 6-31167. (On cover: Lovell's international ser. no. 104). J. W. Lovell Company.

Love of a Lifetime. Caroline Gardiner Cary Curtis. LC 6-31716. 1884. Cupples, Upham and Company.

Love of Ali. Dorothea Chalmers. LC 41-122411. The Christopher Publishing House.

Love of an Unknown Soldier: Found in a Dug Out. LC 18-199251. 1918. John Lane Company.

Love of Azalea. Winnifred Eaton Babcock. LC 4-26878. 1904. Dodd, Mead & Company.

Love of Brothers. Katharine Tynan Hinkson, pseud. LC 20-3710. 1920. Benzinger Brothers.

Love of Comrades: A Romance. Frank James Mathew. 1900. J. Lane.

Love of Damocles. Angela Gordon. 1972. pap. 0.75 o.p. (94291). Beagle Bks.

Love of Elspeth Baker. Kaufmann, Myron S. LC 81-71681. 16.95 (ISBN 0-87795-390-2). Arbor House.

Love of Fingin O'Lea. Theodora McCormick Du Bois. LC 57-11763. 1957. Appleton-Century-Crofts.

Love of God. Oswald Chambers. 1965. pap. 2.50 (ISBN 0-87508-116-9). Chr Lit.

Love of Jeanne Ney. Ilya Grigorevich Ehrenburg & Matheson, Helen Chrouschoff, Tr. LC 30-4489. 1930. Doubleday, Doran and Company, Inc.

Love of Julie Borel. Kathleen Thompson Norris. LC 31-265579. Doubleday, Doran & Company, Inc.

Love of Landry. Paul Laurence Dunbar. LC 70-81113. 1969. Mnemosyne.

Love of Landry. Paul Laurence Dunbar. LC 72-88408. 1969. Negro Universities Press.

Love of Landry. Paul Laurence Dunbar. LC 76-104442. (Illus.). 1970. (ISBN 0-8398-0372-9). Literature House.

Love of Landry. Paul Laurence Dunbar. LC 6621. Dodd, Mead and Company.

Love of Life: And Other Stories. Jack London. LC 6-16513. 1906. The Macmillan Company.

Love of Life: And Other Stories. Jack London. LC 7-29686. 1907. The Macmillan Company.

Love of Long Ago: And Other Stories. Marie Corelli. LC 21-14134. 1921. Doubleday, Page & Company.

Love of Lucifer. Daoma Winston. 1970. pap. 0.95 o.s.i. (75-296). Lancer.

Love of Lucifer. Daoma Winston. 1976. (pbk.) 1.50. Ace Books.

Love of Mademoiselle. George Fort Gibbs. LC 26-7900. 1926. D. Appleton and Company.

Love of Mario Ferraro. Johan Wigmore Fabricius. Tr. by Katzin, Winifred. LC 31-240673. 1931. Simon and Schuster.

Love of Meltha Laone: Or, Beyond the Sun; a Novel. David Leroy Stump. LC 13-174088. The Roxburgh Publishing Company Inc.

Love of Monsieur. George Fort Gibbs. LC 3-12960. 1903. Harper & Brothers.

Love of Parson Lord, & Other Stories by Mary E. Wilkins. facs. ed. Mary Eleanor Wilkins Freeman. LC 76-75776. (Short Story Index Reprint Ser.). 1900. 15.00 (ISBN 0-8369-3001-0). Ayer Co.

Love of Parson Lord: And Other Stories. Mary Eleanor Wilkins Freeman. LC 76-75776. (Short story index reprint series). (Illus.). 1969. Books for Libraries Press.

Love of Parson Lord: And Other Stories. Mary Eleanor Wilkins Freeman. LC 4-15448. 1900. Harper & Brothers.

Love of Rich Women. William Hamilton. LC 81-6322. 1981. 11.95 (ISBN 0-395-31559-X). Houghton Mifflin.

Love of Seven Dolls. 1st Ed. Paul Gallico. LC 54-111573. 1954. Doubleday.

Love of Tanya. Claire Pomeroy. LC 33-136420. The Macaulay Company.

Love of the Foolish Angel. Helen Beauclerk. LC 29-18160. 1929. Cosmopolitan Book Corporation.

Love of the Wild. Archie P. McKishnie. LC 10-23741. Desmond Fitzgerald, Inc.

Love of Worker Bees. Aleksandra Mikhailovna Kollontai. Tr. by Cathy Porter from Russ. 1978. lib. bdg. 12.95 (ISBN 0-89733-002-1); pap. 5.00 (ISBN 0-89733-001-3). Academy Chi Ltd.

Love off Schedule. 1st Ed. Jack G Mauder. LC 56-9035. 1956. Vantage Press.

Love: Old and New. Ursula Bloom. LC 33-1359. E. P. Dutton & Co., Inc.

Love on a Dark Street. Irwin Shaw. 1966. pap. 2.95 (ISBN 0-440-15077-9). Dell.

Love on a Dark Street: And Other Stories. Irwin Shaw. LC 65-18626. 4.95. Delacorte Pr. Dist. Dial.

Love on a Holiday. I Torr. (Signet 451-P5620, a rainbow romance edition.). 1973. (pbk.) 0.60. New American Library.

Love on a Log and Other Stories. William Hosea Ballou. LC 6-6091. (On cover: Farm and fireside library, no. 113). 1895. Mast, Crowell & Kirkpatrick.

Love on a Trampoline. Sybah Darrich. LC 70-9872. (Traveller's companion series). 1968. 1.75. Traveller's Companion, Inc.

Love on a Tray. Minna Bardon. LC 49-496168. 1949. Arcadia House.

Love on Any Terms. Nell Kincaid. (Candlelight Ecstasy Ser.: No. 129). (Orig.). 1983. pap. 1.95 (ISBN 0-440-11927-8). Dell.

Love on Course. Kristin Michaels. (Adventures in Love Ser.: No. 26). 1982. pap. 1.75 (ISBN 0-451-11646-1, AE1646, Sig). NAL.

Love on Five Dollars a Day. (Stanyan Books Ser.). 1971. 3.00 o.p. (ISBN 0-394-47127-X). Random.

Love on Leave. James Noble Gifford. LC 43-202385. 1942. Phoenix Press.

Love on Second Thought. Berta Ruck. LC 37-4090. 1937. Dodd, Mead & Company.

Love on the Dole. A Tale of the Two Cities. Walter Greenwood. LC 34-28779. 1934. Doubleday, Doran & Company, Inc.

Love on the Ice. Deck Morgan. LC 37-17349. J. H. Hopkins & Son, Inc.

Love on the Landing. Samuel G. Werner. 3.95 o.p. Vantage.

Love on the Run. Barbara Cartland. 1973. pap. 1.25 o.p. (ISBN 0-515-03079-1, V3079). BJ Pub Group.

Love on the Run. Barbara Cartland. 1973. (pbk.) 0.95 (ISBN 0-515-03079-1). Pyramid.

Love on the Run. Peggy Gaddis, pseud. LC 44-2466. 1944. Phoenix Press.

Love on the Run. Gail Jordan. (Starlight Romance Ser). 160p. 1972. pap. 0.75 o.p. (532-00451-075). Manor Bks.

Love on Wings: By Jennifer Ames Pseud. Maysie Greig. 1958. Avalon Books.

Love Once Again. Jo Ann Simon. 400p. 1983. 3.50 (ISBN 0-380-83345-X). Avon.

Love Once in Passing. Jo Ann Simon. 320p. (Orig.). 1981. pap. 2.95 (ISBN 0-380-78154-9, 78154). Avon.

Love One & Love Two: Erotic Tales from Scandinavia. Ed. by Bengt Anderberg & Sven Holm. (Illus.). 1970. 10.00 o.p. (X1012). Grove.

Love One: Erotic Tales. Ed. by Bengt Anderberg. 1970. pap. 1.50 o.p. (Z1046D, Zebra). Grove.

Love or Diamonds; Was He to Blame? A Novel. Marshall Henry Underwood. (On cover: The enterprise series, no. 90). 1896. E. A. Weeks & Company.

Love or Duty, and Other Stories. Jesse C Rearick. LC 56-12114. (Pan Press fiction library book). 1956. Pan Press.

Love or Money. Rob Eden. LC 36-194411. J. H. Hopkins & Son, Inc.

Love or Whatever It Is: A Novel. 1st Ed. Warren Leslie. LC 60-80332. 1960. McGraw-Hill.

Love Out of Season. Ella Leffland. LC 74-77849. 1974. 8.95 (ISBN 0-689-10607-6). Atheneum.

Love Outrides the Storm: A Novel of the Civil War. George Brown Thomas. LC 64-5157. (Exposition-Lochinvar book). 1964. Exposition Press.

Love Pagoda. Intro. by Albert Ellis. 192p. 1972. pap. 1.95 o.p. (ISBN 0-87056-271-1, 6271). Brandon.

Love Parade. Russell Holman & Fourneau, Leon, 1867- The Prince Consort. LC 30-5173. Gorsset & Dunlap.

Love Party. Thomas J Jennings. LC 64-19282. 1964. Doubleday.

Love Passed This Way. Martha Ostenso. LC 42-6010. 1942. Dodd, Mead & Company.

Love Past Thirty. Besse Sprague. LC 32-9028. A. L. Burt Company.

Love Pavilion. Paul Scott. LC 60-117066. 1960. Morrow.

Love Pirate. Barbara Cartland. LC 77-156023. 1977. 6.95 (ISBN 0-87272-025-X). Duron Books.

Love Pirate. Heidi B. Jorgensen. 1981. 10.95 (ISBN 0-533-04835-4). Vantage.

Love Pirate. Paula Moore. (Orig.). 1980. pap. 2.50 (ISBN 0-440-14950-9). Dell.

Love Pirates. Paul Roan. 192p. (Orig.). 1973. pap. 1.95 o.p. (ISBN 0-87056-343-2, 6343). Brandon.

Love Play. Rosemary Rogers. LC 80-69930. 4.95 (ISBN 0-380-77917-X). Avon.

Love Play: A Novel Entertainment. Alexander Eliot. LC 66-19513. 5.95. New Amer. Lib.

Love Plays a Part. Nina Pykare. (Candlelight Regency Ser.: No. 675). (Orig.). 1981. pap. 1.75 (ISBN 0-440-14725-5). Dell.

Love Polynesian Flying: The Big Birds of Don Don Island - a Fantasy. J. H. Reinburg. 1979. 7.00 (ISBN 0-682-49454-2). Exposition.

Love Potion. Carlo Zezza. LC 75-15686. 416p. 1976. 8.95 (ISBN 0-87131-181-X). M Evans.

Love, Preferred: The Romance of a Business Girl. Edna Robb Webster. Grosset & Dunlap.

Love Proof. Robert Terry Shannon. LC 30-143897. E. J. Clode, Inc.

Love Quest. Jean Wick. LC 29-221507. A. L. Burt Company.

Love Rack: A Novel. Cecil Roberts. LC 25-19725. 1925. Frederick A. Stokes Company.

Love Regained. Jeanne Judson. 192p. (YA) 1974. 4.95 o.p. (Avalon). Bouregy.

Love Regained. Jeanne Judson. (Avalon romances). 1974. 4.50. Avalon Books.

Love Remembered. Elisabeth Beresford. LC 78-56096. 1978. pap. text ed. 1.50 o.s.i. (ISBN 0-89559-061-1). Dale Books Inc.

Love Respelt. Robert Graves. LC 66-15051. 1966. 3.95 o.p. (ISBN 0-385-06006-8). Doubleday.

Love Respelt. Robert Graves. 1965. 10.00 o.s.i. Ridgeway Bks.

Love Riddle: Novel. Translated by Eva Johnson from the Hungarian. 1st American Ed. Claire Kenneth. LC 62-12684. 1962. Appleton-Century-Crofts.

Love Rides the Rapids. Virginia Smiley. (YA) 1980. 6.95 (Avalon). Bouregy.

Love, Roger. Charles Richard Webb. LC 69-15031. 1969. 4.95. Houghton Mifflin.

Love Run: A Novel. Jay Parini. LC 79-27519. 10.95 (ISBN 0-316-69065-1). Little, Brown.

Love Runs Away. Peggy Gaddis, pseud. LC 37-19849. 1937. Hillman, Curl, Inc.

Love Sails at Dawn. Dorothy Quentin. LC 45-9820. 1945. Arcadia House, Inc.

Love Sandwich. Roger C. Kemp. 1970. 3.75 o.p. Vantage.

Love Scene. Jesse L. Lasky, Jr. & Pat Silver. 1981. pap. 2.75 (ISBN 0-425-05022-X). Berkley Pub.

Love Scent. Irving A. Greenfield. 1978. pap. 1.75 (ISBN 0-532-17174-8). Woodhill.

Love School. john hale. ed. John Hale. LC 75-9484. 1976. 8.95. St. Martin's.

Love Sect. Tr. by Andre Gilbert. pap. 1.95 o.p. (6017). Brandon.

Love-Seekers. Leonora Hornblow. LC 57-53935. 1957. Random House.

Love Sees Clearly. Diana Ridley. LC 47-1393. 1946. Arcadia House, Inc.

Love Shift. Florence Stonebraker. LC 43-2349. 1943. Phoenix Press.

Love Should Be Laughter. Elsie Frances Wilson Mack. LC 47-31026. 1947. S. Curl.

Love Should Be Laughter. Frances Sarah Moore. LC 47-310269. 1947. S. Curl.

Love Slave. Peggy Gaddis, pseud. LC 49-118337. 1949. Phoenix Press.
Love So Bold. Annelise Kamada. 1978. 2.50 (ISBN 0-446-81638-8). Warner Books.
Love So Fearful. Nina Coombs. (Rapture Romance Ser.: No. 1). 1983. pap. 1.95 (ISBN 0-451-12003-5, AJ2003, Sig). NAL.
Love So Fine. William H. Banks. (Orig.). 1974. pap. 1.25 o.p. (ISBN 0-515-03334-0, V3334). BJ Pub Group.
Love So Fine. William H Banks. LC 73-211187. 1974. (pbk.) 1.25. Pyramid Books.
Love So Proud. Rochel DeNore. 1977. 1.25 (ISBN 0-441-49723-3). Ace Books.
Love So Wild. Deborah Chester. LC 79-11874. 9.95 (ISBN 0-698-11007-2). Coward, McCann & Geoghegan.
Love Song. Philip Jose Farmer. 192p. pap. 1.95 o.p. (6134). Brandon.
Love Song. Rupert Hughes. LC 34-23274. 1934. Harper & Brothers.
Love Song. Adam Kennedy. LC 76-21052. 1976. 7.95 (ISBN 0-670-44298-4). Viking Press.
Love Song. Adam Kennedy. (Signet Book). 1977. 1.75 (ISBN 0-451-07535-8). New American Library.
Love Song. Prudence Martin. (Candlelight Ecstasy Ser.). (Orig.). 1983. pap. 1.95 (ISBN 0-440-14849-9). Dell.
Love Song. Anne Park. (Sweet Dreams Ser.: No. 19). 192p. 1982. 1.95 (ISBN 0-553-22542-1). Bantam.
Love Song. Karen Hansen Peyton. LC 64-20364. 1964. Chilton Books.
Love Song. Isabel Santana. (Illus.). 96p. 1981. pap. 1.95 (ISBN 0-380-76893-3, 76893). Avon.
Love Song. Leslie Tonner. LC 78-19397. 8.95 (ISBN 0-312-49948-5). St. Martin's Press.
Love Song for Two. Frances Nichols Hanna. LC 37-9479. 1937. Hillman Curl, Inc.
Love Song of Mara Lumera. Denti Di Pirajno Alberto. LC 64-13838. 1964. Doubleday.
Love Songs. Lawrence Sanders. 1973. (pbk.) 1.50. Dell.
Love Songs; a Novel. Lawrence Sanders. LC 76-187893. 1972. 6.95. Putnam.
Love, Spread Your Wings. Audrie Manley-Tucker. 1973. (pbk.) 0.75 (ISBN 0-671-75766-0). Pocket Books.
Love Standard. Peter Kanto. (Orig.). pap. 0.95 o.p. (1103). Brandon.
Love Star. Ruth Burnett. 1983. 6.95 (Avalon). Bouregy.
Love-Starved Divorcee. Wiley Dunbarton. 192p. 1972. pap. 1.95 o.p. (ISBN 0-87977-147-X, DBB147). Dansk Blue Bk.
Love Starved Wife. William Vaneer. 1969. pap. 0.60 o.p. (60-423). Manor Bks.
Love Stones. Howard Waldman. (V2206). 1968. Avon.
Love Stories. Martin Levin. LC 75-8293. 1975. 12.50 (ISBN 0-8129-0516-4). Quadrangle/The New York Times Book Co.
Love Stories. Mary Roberts Rinehart. LC 19-6869. 1.50. George H. Doran Company.
Love Stories by New Women. Charleen Swansea & Barbara Campbell. LC 78-111335. (Red Clay Reader; V. 13, No. 1). 5.50. Red Clay Books.
Love Stories-Love Poems. Ed. by Joe D. Bellamy & Roger Weingarten. 300p. (Orig.). 1982. pap. 12.95 (ISBN 0-931362-07-5). Fiction Intl.
Love Stories of India. Edison Marshall. LC 50-6507. 1950. Farrar, Straus.
Love Stories of Old California. facsimile ed. Cora Miranda Baggerly Older. LC 75-167465. (Short Story Index Reprint Ser.). Repr. of 1940 ed. 22.00 (ISBN 0-8369-3991-3). Ayer Co.
Love Stories of the Southwest. Ed. by Paul Leonard Heard. LC 34-18527. 1934. The Story Book Press.
Love Story. Judy Savoy. LC 80-21386. 3.95 (ISBN 0-8163-0396-7). Pacific Press Pub. Association.
Love Story. Erich W Segal. 1977. 1.75 (ISBN 0-380-01760-1). Avon Books.
Love Story. Erich W Segal. LC 71-96003. 1970. 4.95. Harper & Row.
Love Story. Thelma Woodhill. LC 29-178958. 1929. Simon and Schuster.
Love Story Black. William Demby. LC 77-93882. 1978. 4.95 (ISBN 0-918408-08-3). Reed, Cannon & Johnson Co.
Love Story Incidental. Sophie Kerr. LC 46-3291. 1946. Rinehart and Company, Inc.
Love Story of a Jewish Cat. Max Stein. (Illus.). 1979. pap. 3.95 o.p. (ISBN 0-8467-0582-6, Pub. by Two Continents). Hippocrene Bks.
Love Story of Abner Stone, Edwin Carlile Litsey. 1902. A. S. Barnes and Company.
Love-Story of Aliette Brunton. Gilbert Frankau. LC 22-11447. 1922. 2.00. The Century Co.
Love Story of Margaret Wynne. Adeline Sergeant. LC 8-6854. Rand, McNally & Company.
Love Talent. Ann Sumner. LC 29-124905. A. L. Burt Company.
Love Talker. Elizabeth Peters, pseud. LC 80-23786. 1980. 13.95 (ISBN 0-8161-3135-X). G. K. Hall.
Love Talker. Elizabeth Peters, pseud. LC 79-22104. 8.95 (ISBN 0-396-07780-3). Dodd, Mead.
Love-Tangle of Roots. Doug Flaherty. 45p. (Orig.). 1977. pap. 3.50 (ISBN 0-87886-080-0, Pub. by Ithaca Hse). SBD.
Love Tap. Leo Brady. 1979. 1.95 (ISBN 0-445-04339-3). Popular Library.
Love Tempter. Kevin James. pap. 1.95 o.p. (8051). Cameo.
Love Tested. Gunter Grass. 600.00. Johnson Repr.
Love Tested in the Fires of the Sixties. Robert I. E. Stephen Robert Ferguson. 1912. The Shakespeare Press.
Love That Lived. A Novel. Elizabeth C. J. Eiloart Eiloart. (Seaside library, v. 21, no. 411). 1878. G. Munro.
Love That Lives. Mabel Osgood Wright. LC 11-27104. 1911. The Macmillan Company.
Love That Loves Alway. A Novel. Elizabeth Casey. (Seaside library, v. 53, no. 1080). 1881. G. Munro.
Love That Never Was. Chigger. 3.00 o.p. Carlton.
Love That Prevailed. Frank Frankfort Moore. LC 8-5228. Empire Book Company.
Love That Spy. T. A. Waters. (Orig.). 1968. pap. 0.60 o.p. (73-713). Lancer.
Love the Criminal. John Burland Harris-Burland. LC 8-24301. The Cupples & Leon Co.
Love the Debt. Richard Ashe King. (Harper's Franklin square library. no. 234). 1882. G. Munro.
Love the Debt. Richard Ashe King. (Seaside library. v. 57, no. 1158). 1882. G. Munro.
Love, the Fiddler. Lloyd Osbourne. LC 73-103526. (Short story index reprint series). 1969. Books for Libraries Press.
Love, the Harvester: Being a Story of the Gleaners in the Winter of the Year, and of Those That Went a Hunting in the Days When George the Third Was King. Max Pemberton. LC 1-25670. 1901. Dodd, Mead and Co.
Love, the Judge. Wymond Carey. LC 10-7177. 1910. 1.50. Dodd, Mead and Company.
Love They Must. Jean Francis Webb. LC 33-6708. 1933. I. Washburn.
Love Thieves. 1st Ed. Peter Packer. LC 62-13612. 1962. Holt, Rinehart and Winston.
Love Thing. Hugh Barron. (Orig.). 1970. pap. 0.95 o.p. (N2244). Pyramid Pubns.
Love Thrives in War: A Romance of the Frontier in 1812. Mary Catherine Crowley. LC 3-13370. Little, Brown, and Company.
Love Throughout the Ages: Love Stories of All Nations, Edited. Ed. by Robert Lynd. LC 32-26289. Coward-McCann, Inc.
Love Thy Neighbor. Abraham Louis Scher & Redmond Flood, Thomas, 1876- Joint Author. LC 36-12120. DeVorss & Co.
Love Thy Neighbor - & His Wife. Lew Palmer. (Orig.). pap. 1.25 o.p. (2069). Brandon.
Love Tide. Parris Afton Bonds. 224p. (Orig.). 1982. pap. 2.50 (ISBN 0-445-04521-3). Popular Lib.
Love Time in Picardy. William Addison Lathrop. LC 19-6328. 1.50. Britton Publishing Company.
Love to be Loved. Pat Gaston. 464p. (Orig.). 1982. pap. 3.50 o.s.i. (ISBN 0-8439-1141-7, Leisure Bks). Dorchester Pub Co.
Love to Lean on. Blocklinger. pap. 0.75 o.s.i. (01-336). Lancer.
Love to Match These Mountains. Nancy Elaine Pindrus. 1979. 2.50 (ISBN 0-440-00163-3). Dell Pub. Co.
Love to Remember. large print ed. Ida Hills. LC 82-5478. 1982. 9.95. Thorndike Press.
Love to the Irish. Leatrice Fountain. LC 67-17544. 1967. Doubleday.
Love to the Rescue. Barbara Cartland. 1972. pap. 1.25 o.p. (ISBN 0-515-02864-9, V2864). BJ Pub Group.
Love to Vietnam: A Novel. Edita Morris. LC 68-22425. 1968. Monthly Review Press.
Love Toy: Anonymous. LC 25-11366. The Macaulay Company.
Love Trap. Barbara Andrews. (Candlelight Ecstasy Ser.: No. 86). (Orig.). 1982. pap. 1.95 (ISBN 0-440-14601-1). Dell.
Love Trap. Robert Terry Shannon. LC 32-287597. E. J. Clode, Inc.
Love Trap. Lionel White. LC 55-5472. (Signet book, 1204). 1955. New American Library.
Love Trap: Orginally Titled "Yellow Rose Farm.". Vina Delmar. LC 49-232166. (Avon, 187). 1949. Avon Pub. Co.
Love Trapeze. Lois Bull. LC 34-582118. The Macaulay Company.
Love Trial. Fawne Mallory. LC 81-20562. 2.95 (ISBN 0-345-29350-9). Ballantine Books.
Love Tribe. Peggy Swenson, pseud. 1968. pap. 1.25 o.p. (2068). Brandon.
Love Triumphant. Joan Conquest. LC 34-4858. The Macaulay Company.
Love Triumphant. Caroline Courtney. LC 81-5096. 1981. 11.95 (ISBN 0-8161-3243-7). G.K. Hall.
Love, True Love. 1974. 3.95 (ISBN 0-88088-423-1). Peter Pauper.
Love Two: Erotic Tales from Denmark. Ed. by Sven Holm. pap. 1.50 o.p. (Z1047D, Zebra). Grove.
Love Under Fire. Barbara Cartland. (Romance Ser, No. 39). 1972. pap. 1.25 o.p. (ISBN 0-515-02768-5, V2768). BJ Pub Group.
Love Under Fire. Randall Parrish. LC 11-5992. 1911. A. C. McClurg & Co.
Love Unmasked. Caroline Courtney. LC 80-16905. 1980. 11.95 (ISBN 0-8161-3096-5). G. K. Hall.
Love Unveiled. Ruth Watt. 1976. 4.95. Avalon Books.
Love Upon Tick: Implicit Gallantry see Highland Rogue: The Memorable Actions of the Celebrated Robert Mac-Gregor, Commonly Called Rob-Roy.
Love Ventures. A Novel with an Affidavit. Harry Julian. The Truth Seeker Company.
Love Victorian Style, 4 vols. 2400p. 1981. pap 15.35 boxed set (ISBN 0-394-17930-7, B465, BC). Grove.
Love Vs. Law: Les Dames Du Palais. Antoinette De Bergevin Huzard. Tr. by Gilman, Mary Rebecca (Foster) "Mrs. Bradley Gilman,". LC 11-273003. 1911. 1.35. G. P. Putnam's Sons.
Love Wager. Edna Robb Webster. LC 34-19182. A. L. Burt Company.
Love Waits at Penrhyn. Pat Phillips. 1975. 4.95. Avalon Books.
Love Watch. Michael Copeland. LC 36-35046. 1937. Frederick A. Stokes Company.
Love-Watch. William Allen Knight. LC 4-9129. 1904. The Pilgrim Press.
Love Watcher. Joe Caruso. pap. 0.95 o.p. (1156). Brandon.
Love While You May. Thomas Stone. LC 41-5678. Phoenix Press.
Love Wild & Fair. Bertrice Small. 1978. pap. 3.95 (ISBN 0-380-40030-8, 82867-7). Avon.
Love Wild & Free. Jocelyn Haley. (Superromances Ser.). 384p. 1982. pap. 2.50 (ISBN 0-373-70011-3, Pub. by Worldwide). Harlequin Bks.
Love Will Come Again. Lois Wyse. (Little Volumes of Love Ser). 1.95 o.p. (ISBN 0-529-01361-4, A4221). World Pub.
Love Will Come: Stories of Romance. Ed. by Aurelia Stowe. LC 59-6468. Random House,
Love Will Find a Way. Vivian Radcliffe. LC 39-5220. Gramercy Publishing Co.
Love Will Find Me. Ann Pinchot. 1976. pap. 1.25 o.p. (ISBN 0-515-04020-7). BJ Pub Group.
Love Will Never Die. Anne Maquire. 1974. 4.00 (ISBN 0-8233-0194-X). Golden Quill.
Love Will Remember. Bella Jarrett. (Orig.). 1981. pap. 2.50 (ISBN 0-8439-8029-X, Tiara Bks). Nordon Pubns.
Love Will Wait. Stella March. 1981. 18.95x (Pub. by Remploy England). State Mutual Bk.
Love Will Win. Jennifer Ames, pseud. 1972. pap. 0.75 o.p. (94232). Beagle Bks.
Love Wings. Rob Eden. LC 32-296851. Grosset & Dunlap.
Love with a Few Hairs. Mohammed Mrabet & Paul Frederic Bowles. LC 68-17389. 1968. G. Braziller.
Love with Honor. Emilie Baker Loring. LC 76-11822. 1976. 10.95 (ISBN 0-8161-6377-4). G. K. Hall.
Love with Honor. Emilie Baker Loring. LC 69-15073. 1969. 4.75. Little, Brown.
Love with Honour. Charles Marriott. LC 2-19017. 1903. J. Lane.
Love with Paprika: A Tale from Hungary. Maria Molnar. LC 58-7972. 1958. Harper.
Love with Tears. Hubert Lawrence. 1980. 6.95 (ISBN 0-8062-1492-9). Carlton.
Love Without Armor: By Bernice Ludwell Pseud. Manning Lee Stokes. LC 55-12495. 1955. Arcadia House.
Love Without Breakfast. Eunice Chapin. LC 34-36230. A. H. King.
Love Without Money. Floyd Dell. LC 31-29631. Farrar & Rinehart, Incorporated.
Love Without Music. Helen Welshimer. LC 40-298767. 1940. Arcadia House, Inc.
Love Without Wings. Ruby Mildred Ayres. LC 54-7496. 1954. Arcadia House.
Love Works Wonders. A Novel. Charlotte Mary Brame. J. W. Lovell Company.
Love Works Wonders. A Novel. Charlotte Mary Brame. LC 44-11140. 1878. G. W. Carleton & Co.
Love Ya Lots, by Mail. Connie M. Odenthal. 1974. 4.00 o.p. (ISBN 0-682-48042-8). Exposition.
Love, Yesterday & Forever. Elise Randolph. (Candlelight Ecstasy Ser.: No. 60). (Orig.). 1982. pap. 1.75 (ISBN 0-440-14715-8). Dell.
Love You Good, See You Later. Eugene Walter. LC 64-12839. 1964. Scribner.
Love You, Hate You, Just Don't Know. Ed. by Josie Karavasil. 112p. 1982. 32.00x (ISBN 0-237-45510-2, Pub. by Evans Bros). State Mutual Bk.
Love, 3000. Martin Harry Greenberg & Charles Waugh. LC 80-36790. 7.95 (ISBN 0-525-66691-5). Elsevier/Nelson Books.
Loved and Envied. Enid Bagnold. LC 75-110820. 1970. Greenwood Press.
Loved and Envied. 1st Ed. Enid Bagnold. LC 51-9211. 1951. Doubleday.
Loved and the Lost: A Novel. Morley Callaghan. LC 51-992120. 1951. Macmillan.
Loved and the Unloved. Francois Mauriac. LC 52-10290. 1952. Pellegrini & Cudahy.
Loved and the Unloved. Thomas Hal Phillips. LC 55-6590. 1955. Harper.
Loved and the Unloved: Tr. by Gerard Hopkins. Francois Mauriac. (Noonday Pr., 314). pap., 1.95. Farrar.
Loved One, an Anglo-American Tragedy. Evelyn Waugh. LC 58-3471. (Modern library paperbacks, P-41). 1958. Random House.
Lovefire. Julia Grice. 1977. pap. 2.75 (ISBN 0-380-01741-5, 79517). Avon.
Lovehead. Jackie Collins. LC 74-195587. 1974. W. H. Allen.
Lovejoy. Beatrice Burton Morgan. LC 30-19635. 1930. Doubleday, Doran & Company, Inc.
Lovel, the Widower. William Makepeace Thackeray. LC 8-28198. (On cover: Lovell's library, v. 4, no. 156). 1883. J. W. Lovell Company.
Lovel the Widower. A Novel. William Makepeace Thackeray. LC 8-27763. 1860. Harper & Brothers.
Loveland. Glendon Fred Swarthout. LC 68-22616. 1968. 4.95. Doubleday.
Loveletters. Susan Richards Shreve. 160p. 1981. pap. 1.75 (ISBN 0-553-13998-3). Bantam.
Loveliest of Friends! Gladys Sheila Donisthrope. LC 31-31341. C. Kendall.
Lovelife. Robert Muller. LC 76-170149. 1971. 5.95. New American Library.
Lovelife. Judith Searle. 1982. pap. 2.95 (ISBN 0-451-11822-7, AE1822, Sig). NAL.
Lovelife: A Novel. Judith Searle. LC 81-38422. 2.75 (ISBN 0-453-00409-1). NAL Books.
Lovell's Folly. A Novel. Caroline Lee Whiting Hentz. LC 7-3038. 1833. Hubbard and Edmonds.
Lovell's Whim. Ella J Curtis. (On cover: Lovell's household library. no. 69). 1887. F. F. Lovell & Company.
Lovelock Version. Maurice Shadbolt. LC 81-8720. 1981. 16.95 (ISBN 0-312-49953-1). St. Martin's Press.
Lovelorn. Vida Hurst. 1945. Gramercy Publishing Company.
Lovelorn Lady. Jeanne Bowman, pseud. pap. 0.75 o.s.i. (01-347). Lancer.
Lovelorn Parade. Bennie Caroline Hall. LC 36-29004. 1936. Godwin.
Lovelorn Parade. Bennie Caroline Hall. LC 36-29604. 1936. Godwin.
Lovelorners. William Hegner. 1976. 1.75 (ISBN 0-671-80578-9). Pocket Books.
Lovels of Arden. A Novel. Mary Elizabeth Braddon Maxwell. (Seaside library. v. 5, no. 89). 1877. G. Munro.
Lovely. David Meltzer. pap. 1.95 o.p. (0117). Essex Hse.
Lovely Ambition. Mary Ellen Chase. 1960. 5.95 (ISBN 0-393-08477-9). Norton.
Lovely Ambition: A Novel. 1st Ed. Mary Ellen Chase. LC 60-5843. 1960. W. W. Norton.
Lovely and the Wild. L. D. Lawrence. 1968. 6.95 o.p. (ISBN 0-07-036720-5). McGraw.
Lovely April: Novel. Margaret Howe Freydberg. LC 55-9023. 1955. Scribner.
Lovely Clay. Maysie Greig. LC 33-19975. 1933. Doubleday, Doran & Co., Inc.
Lovely Day. Henry Ceard. Tr. by Boyd, Ernest Augustus. LC 24-21397. 1924. A. A. Knopf.
Lovely Day. 1st Ed. Dorothy Evelyn Smith. LC 57-10539. 1957. Dutton.
Lovely Duckling. Lida Larrimore Turner Thomas. LC 51-10631. 1951. Macrae Smith.
Lovely Ducklings. Rupert Hughes. LC 28-13168. 1928. Harper & Brothers.
Lovely Fraud. Joe Weiss. LC 56-6548. 1956. Woodford Press.
Lovely Girl's Fetters. A Spicy Novel. Simon B. Paige. LC 7-35791. 1884. The American News Company.
Lovely Journey. Jessie Douglas Fox. LC 36-115472. Thomas Y. Crowell Company.
Lovely Ladies. Nicolas Freeling. 1973. (pbk) 1.25. Ballantine.
Lovely Ladies. Nicolas Freeling. LC 70-144196. 1971. 5.95 (ISBN 0-06-011349-9). Harper & Row.
Lovely Ladies. Nicolas Freeling. LC 80-6129. 1981. 2.50 (ISBN 0-394-74694-5). Vintage Books.
Lovely Lady. Mary Hunter Austin. LC 13-231981. 1913. 1.00. Doubleday, Page & Company.

Lovely Lady. David Herbert Lawrence. LC 77-38721. (Short story index reprint series). 1972. (ISBN 0-8369-4134-9). Books for Libraries Press.
Lovely Lady. David Herbert Lawrence. LC 33-3292. 1933. The Viking Press.
Lovely Lady Hamilton ("Emma Lyonna") Or, The Beauty and the Glory; an Historical Romance of Royalty and Revolution. Henry Llewellyn Williams & Dumas, Alexandre, 1803-1870. "Emma Lyonna.". LC 4-1887. 1903. Street & Smith.
Lovely Lady, Pity Me. Roy Huggins. LC 49-10740. 1949. Duell, Sloan and Pearce.
Lovely Lynchs. Magdalen King-Hall. LC 47-1208. 1947. Rinehart & Company, Inc.
Lovely Malincourt. Helen Buckingham Mathers Reeves. LC 29-19525. International Fiction Library.
Lovely Mask for Murder. Gerry Travis. LC 56-13318. Mystery House.
Lovely Monster. Rick De Marinis. (O.s.i.). 192p. 1976. 6.95 o.s.i. (ISBN 0-671-22175-2). S&S.
Lovely Monster: The Adventures of Claude Rains and Dr. Tellenbeck: a Novel. Rick De Marinis. LC 75-22199. 1975. 6.95 (ISBN 0-671-22175-2). Simon and Schuster.
Lovely Monster: The Adventures of Claude Rains and Dr. Tellenbeck. Rick De Marinis. (Dell Book). 1977. 1.75 (ISBN 0-440-14900-2). Dell Pub. Co.
Lovely Mrs. Pemberton. Florence Alice Price James. 1901. F. M. Buckles & Company.
Lovely People. Mary Manning. LC 53-9254. 1953. Houghton Mifflin.
Lovely Pretender. Besse Sprague. LC 38-5369. M. S. Mill Co., Inc.
Lovely Rebel. Muriel Marshall. LC 50-10199.
Lovely Season. Virginia Evans. LC 52-9805. 1952. Appleton-Century-Crofts.
Lovely She Goes: A Story of Arctic Trawling. William Mitford. LC 77-127987. (Illus.). 1970. 4.95 o.p. (ISBN 0-397-00653-5). Lippincott.
Lovely Ship. Margaret Storm Jameson. LC 27-10460. 1927. A. A. Knopf.
Lovely Ship. Storm Jameson. (Berkley medallion book). 1975. (pbk.) 1.50 (ISBN 0-425-02776-7). Berkley Pub. Co.
Lovely Time Was Had by All. Ruth Doan MacDougall. LC 82-71056. 1982. 13.95 (ISBN 0-689-11276-9). Atheneum.
Lovely to Look at. Anne Lee. LC 36-56402. Phoenix Press.
Lovemakers. Simon Cooper. (O.S.I.). 1971. pap. 0.95 o.s.i. (ISBN 0-446-65730-1, 65-730). Paperback Lib.
Lovemates. Justine Valenti. 320p. 1982. pap. 2.95 (ISBN 0-449-14453-4, GM). Fawcett.
Lovequest. Louise Vaughan. (Orig.). pap. 2.25 (ISBN 0-515-04696-5). Jove Pubns.
Lover. Carter Brown, pseud. Bd. with Bombshell. 1980. pap. 1.75 (ISBN 0-451-09121-3, E9121, Sig). NAL.
Lover. Bertha Harris. LC 76-7816. 4.50 (ISBN 0-913780-13-8). Daughters.
Lover. Abraham B. Yehoshua. LC 76-51996. 1978. 10.00 o.p. (ISBN 0-385-12134-2). Doubleday.
Lover and the Husband: The Woman of a Certain Age, &C. Charles De Bernard. Ed. by Gore, Catherine Grace (Moody) 1842. Lea and Blachard.
Lover at Forty. Charles Frederick Kenyon. LC 23-9462. 1923. 2.00. George H. Doran Company.
Lover Boy. Edward Reuben Huffman. LC 49-493. 1948. Edison Pub. Co.
Lover Come Back. Clair Blank. LC 40-4088. Gramercy Publishing Co.
Lover, Don't Come Back. Carter Brown, pseud. LC 62-521817. (Signet book, S2188). 1962. New American Library of World Literature.
Lover for Estelle. Daphne Rooke. LC 61-5374. 1961. Houghton Mifflin.
Lover from Across the Sea: And, In the Lands of the Enemy Also, The Fountain of Youth. Elisabeth Burstenbinder. Tr. by Safford, Mary Joanna. (choice series, no. 104). (ledger library, no. 104). 1894. R. Bonner's Sons.
Lover from the Sea. Bonnie Drake. (Candlelight Ecstasy Ser.: No. 114). (Orig.). 1983. pap. 1.95 (ISBN 0-440-14888-X). Dell.
Lover in Blue, No. 84. Aimee Duvall. 1982. pap. 1.75 (ISBN 0-515-06695-8). Jove Pubns.
Lover in Homespun: And Other Stories. F Clifford Smith. LC 8-8983. H. Altemus.
Lover Man. Alston Anderson. LC 59-10037. 1959. Doubleday.
Lover Next Door. Keith Alldritt. LC 77-5285. 1978. 8.95 (ISBN 0-312-49960-4). St. Martin's Press.
Lover Next Door. Keith Alldritt. LC 77-5285. 1978. 8.95 o.p. (ISBN 0-312-49960-4). St Martin.
Lover of Life. Zsolt Harsanyi. Tr. by Tabor, Paul. Muir, Edwin. LC 42-6284. 1942. G. P. Putnams's Sons.
Lover of Truth: A Health Novel. Marie Winchell Walker. LC 23-10103. S. Merritt.
Lover or Friend? Rosa Nouchette Carey. LC 6-231045. (Lovell's international series, no. 128). United States Book Company.
Lover Returns. Dominique Dunois. Tr. by Granberry, Edwin. The Macaulay Company.
Lover: The Confessions of a One-Night Stand. Lawrence Edwards. 304p. 1976. 8.95 o.p. (ISBN 0-374-19344-4). FS&G.
Lover Too Many. Roy Lewis. LC 71-148411. (Falcon's head mystery). 1971. 5.95. World Pub. Co.
Lover Under Another Name. Ethel Edith Man In. LC 54-166662. 1953. Jarrolds.
Lover Under Another Name. 1st American Ed. Ethel Edith Mannin. LC 53-8151. 1954. Putnam.
Lover Upon Trial. Also, The Will. Augusta Louisa Lyons. LC 7-16278. 1848. Stringer & Townsend.
Lover with a Killer's Instinct. Marcus A. Hart. 140p. 1975. 6.00 o.p. (ISBN 0-682-48257-9). Exposition.
Lover Would Be Nice. Frederick Hugh Herbert. LC 35-4117. The Macaulay Company.
Lovers. Ruby Mildred Ayres. LC 29-17925. Doubleday, Doran & Company, Inc.
Lovers. Philip Jose Farmer. LC 78-19723. 1979. 8.95 (ISBN 0-345-28032-6). Ballantine Books.
Lovers. Brian Friel. 1968. 4.50 o.p. (ISBN 0-374-19352-5). FS&G.
Lovers. Gina Kaus. Tr. by Head, June. LC 37-1707. 1937. The Macmillan Company.
Lovers. Richard Posner. 1978. 1.95 (ISBN 0-449-13989-1). Fawcett Gold Medal Books.
Lovers. Kathleen Winsor. LC 52-12010. 1952. Appleton-Century-Crofts.
Lovers: A Romance. Eden Phillpotts. LC 12-111614. 1.35. Rand, McNally & Company.
Lover's Alibi. Margaret Widdemer. LC 41-558250. Farrar & Rinehart, Inc.
Lovers All Untrue. Norah Robinson Lofts. LC 74-116229. 1970. 5.95. Doubleday.
Lovers & Agnostics. Kelly Cherry. (Red Clay Reader: Vol. 10, No. 2). 1975. pap. 2.95 (ISBN 0-911692-04-5). Red Clay.
Lovers and Exorcists. Wesley Simon York. 1974. (pbk.) 1.95 (ISBN 0-87056-370-X). Brandon Books.
Lovers and Fathers. Cressida Lindsay. LC 73-111341. 1970. C. N. Potter; Distributed by Crown Publishers.
Lovers and Friends. Edward Frederic Benson. LC 21-18165. 1.90. George H. Doran Company.
Lovers and Gamblers. Jackie Collins. LC 79-50647. 12.95 (ISBN 0-448-15179-0). Grosset & Dunlap.
Lovers and Heretics. John Hale. LC 77-356739. 1976. 4.20 (ISBN 0-575-02149-7). Gollancz.
Lovers and Heretics. John Hale. LC 77-27096. 1978. 6.95 (ISBN 0-8037-4771-3). Dial Press/James Wade.
Lovers & Liars. Doris Bingham. 1981. pap. 2.25 (ISBN 0-8439-0905-6, Leisure Bks). Nordon Pubns.
Lovers and Madmen. Barry Devlin. LC 53-20877. 1953. Vixen Press.
Lovers and Other Stories. Pearl Sydenstricker Buck. LC 76-56819. 7.95 (ISBN 0-381-97109-0). John Day Co.
Lovers and Other Stories. Pearl Sydenstricker Buck. LC 77-15573. 1977. 10.95 (ISBN 0-8161-6536-X). G. K. Hall.
Lovers and Strangers a Novel. 1st Ed. Joyce Marshall. LC 57-683455. 1957. Lippincott.
Lovers and Thinkers: A Novel. E. G. J. Clarke. 1865. Carleton.
Lovers and Tyrants. Francine Du Plessix Gray. LC 76-17614. 8.95 (ISBN 0-671-22338-0). Simon and Schuster.
Lovers and Tyrants. Francine Du Plessix Gray. (Kangaroo Book). 1977. 1.95 (ISBN 0-671-81473-7). Pocket Books.
Lovers and Warriors. Dial, Joan. 1978. 1.95 (ISBN 0-449-14072-5). Fawcett Pubns.
Lovers Are Losers: A Novel. Roland Pertwee. LC 41-440849. 1941. Doubleday, Doran and Company, Inc.
Lovers Are Never Losers. Jean Giono. Tr. by Le Clercq, Jacques Georges Clemenceau. LC 31-23462. 1931. Brentano's.
Lovers Are Not People. Timeri Murari. LC 77-21528. 1978. 7.95 (ISBN 0-688-03260-5). Morrow.
Lovers Are Not People. Timeri Murari. 1979. 2.25 (ISBN 0-515-04763-5). Jove Publicatons.
Lovers Aren't Company. Monica Stirling. LC 49-890185. 1949. Little, Brown.
Lover's Book: Thoughts, Dreams, & Fantasies. James Wagenvoord. 1981. pap. 7.95 (ISBN 0-89586-137-2). H P Bks.
Lover's Choice. Margaretta Brucker. LC 39-157064. Gramercy Publishing Co.
Lovers' Club. Philetus Brown. LC 7-164873. The Old Greek Press.
Lover's Creed. A Novel. Frances Sarah Johnston Cashel Hoey Hoey. (Harper's Franklin square library. no. 418). 1884. Harper & Brothers.
Lover's Creed. A Novel. Frances Sarah Johnston Cashel Hoey Hoey. (On cover: Seaside library. Pocket ed. no. 313). 1884. G. Munro.
Lovers' Crusade. Mary Sativa. pap. 1.95 o.s.i. (OPS-23). Olympia.
Lovers Cry for the Moon. Evans Wall. LC 35-4046. The Macaulay Company.
Lovers Four and Maidens Five: A Story of the Allegheny Mountains. 25th thousand ed. Julius Chambers. LC 6-23338. 1886. Porter & Coates.
Lovers in a Winter Circle. Jonathan Kirsch. (Signet Special). 1978. 1.75 (ISBN 0-451-08119-6). New American Library.
Lovers in Paradise. Barbara Cartland. LC 78-13317. 1978. 6.95 (ISBN 0-87272-045-4). Duron Books.
Lovers in the Sun. Arthur Moore. 192p. (Orig.). 1973. pap. 1.25 o.p. (ISBN 0-532-12198-8). Manor Bks.
Lover's Knot. Morris Hershman. LC 80-2083. 1981. 9.95 (ISBN 0-385-17209-5). Doubleday.
Lover's Knot. Janet Templeton. LC 80-2083. 192p. 1981. 10.95 (ISBN 0-385-17209-5). Doubleday.
Lover's Knot. Janet Templeton. 192p. 1982. pap. 1.50 (ISBN 0-449-50309-7, Coventry). Fawcett.
Lovers' Knots: The Whimsical Twists and Tangles of a Dozen Youthful Love Affairs. Elizabeth Garver Jordan. LC 16-21058. 1916. 1.25. Harper & Brothers.
Lover's Lair. Jeanette Ernest. (Rapture Romance Ser.: No. 3). 1983. pap. 1.95 (ISBN 0-451-12005-1, AJ2005). NAL.
Lover's Leap: A Story in Three Voices. Martin Donisthorpe Armstrong. LC 33-4991. Harcourt, Brace and Company.
Lovers Living, Lovers Dead. Richard Lortz. LC 77-13171. 1977. 7.95 (ISBN 0-399-12066-1). Putnan.
Lovers Living, Lovers Dead. Richard Lortz. 1979. 1.95 (ISBN 0-440-15149-X). Dell Publishing Co.
Lover's Loot. Eric Hatch. LC 31-21901. Farrar & Rinehart, Incorporated.
Lovers' Luck. Gertrude Knevels. LC 35-4526. The Penn Publishing Company.
Lovers Meeting. Mollie Hardwick. (General Ser.). 1980. lib. bdg. 15.95 (ISBN 0-8161-3064-7, Large Print Bks). G K Hall.
Lovers Meeting. Mollie Hardwick. LC 79-3993. 1979. 10.00 (ISBN 0-312-49970-1). St Martin.
Lovers' Meeting... Eleanor Furneaux Smith. LC 40-13631. 1940. Doubleday, Doran and Company, Inc.
Lovers Meeting: A Novel. Mollie Hardwick. LC 79-28851. 1980. 15.95 (ISBN 0-8161-3064-7). G. K. Hall.
Lovers Mist see Patterns of Love.
Lovers Must Learn. Irving Fineman. LC 32-26441. 1932. Longmans, Green and Co.
Lovers Must Live: A Romance. Pauline Stiles. LC 33-23177. 1933. Doubleday, Doran & Company, Inc.
Lovers Never Marry. Philo Jr Orton & Orton, Edith. LC 33-24192. 1933. W. Godwin, Inc.
Lovers No More. Peggy Gaddis, pseud. LC 34-28622. 1934. W. Godwin, Inc.
Lovers of Louisiana see Collected Works.
Lovers of Louisiana (to-Day) George Washington Cable. LC 18-17496. 1918. C. Scribner's Sons.
Lovers of Sanna: A Novel. Mary Stewart Doubleday Cutting. LC 12-11711. 1912. 1.00. McBride, Nast & Company.
Lovers of Skye. Frank Waller Allen. LC 13-4762. The Bobbs-Merrill Company.
Lovers of the Market-Place. Clotilde Inez Mary Graves. LC 28-28677. 1928. Little, Brown, and Company.
Lovers of the Woods. William Henry Boardman. LC 1-17006. 1901. McClure, Phillips & Co.
Lovers of Their Time and Other Stories. William Trevor. LC 78-23227. 1979. 10.95 (ISBN 0-670-44325-5). Viking Press.
Lover's Progress. Ernest Alfred Vizetelly. LC 2-55823. 1901. Brentano's.
Lover's Quest. Ernest Glanville. LC 98-71. (Globe library, no. 287). 1898. Rand, McNally & Co.
Lover's Replies to An Englishwoman's Love-Letters. 1901. Dodd, Mead and Company.
Lovers' Reunion. Arlene Hale. (Signet Book). 1977. 1.50 (ISBN 0-451-07771-7). New American Library.
Lover's Revolt. John William De Forest. LC 96-1201. 1898. Longmans, Green, and Co.
Lover's Reward. James Edwards. (On cover: Lucile ser. no. 1). E. A. Weeks & Company.
Lovers Should Marry. Nell Columbia Boyer Martin. LC 33-4542. The Macaulay Company.
Lovers' Tale. Maurice Henry Hewlett. 1915. C. Scribner's Sons.
Lover's Tale. Alfred Tennyson. (Illus.). 1977. 12.50. Porter.
Lover's Tale. Alfred Tennyson. (Illus.). 1970. 8.50 o.p. Porter.
Lover's Tales. Alfred Tennyson. 1975. 8.50 o.p. (0-911156-13-0). Porter.
Lover's Victory. Caroline Courtney. LC 82-9195. 1982. (ISBN 0-8161-3408-1). G.K. Hall.
Lovers' Vows. Joan Smith. LC 81-51970. 9.95 (ISBN 0-8027-0691-6). Walker.
Lovers Week see Love's Intrigues.
Lover's Week, and The Female Deserters. Mary Hearne. LC 70-170528. (Foundations of the Novel). 1973. 22.00 ea. (ISBN 0-8240-0531-7). Garland Pub.
Lovers. 1st Ed. Mitchell A Wilson. LC 54-7317. 1954. Doubleday.
Loversville: A Novel. Anees K Buckleh. LC 51-12075. 1951. Exposition Press.
Love's a Puzzle. Faith Baldwin Cuthrell. LC 33-23357. Farrar & Rinehart, Incorporated.
Love's a Puzzle. Faith Baldwin Cuthrell. 1973. (pbk.) 0.95. Warner Paperback Lib.
Love's Adventure. Besse Sprague. A. L. Burt Company.
Love's Agonies and Delights. Arthur Clark Ferguson. LC 90-3708. F.T. Neely.
Love's Agony. Violet Winspear. (Harlequin Presents Ser.). 192p. 1981. pap. 1.50 (ISBN 0-373-10450-2). Harlequin Bks.
Loves and Ambitions. Translated by Joseph Marek and H. C. Stevens. Herminia Fiszer Naglerowa. LC 54-52225. Roy Publishers.
Loves & Deaths: Novelists' Tales of the Nineteenth Century, from Scott to Hardy. Ed. by Peter Charles Bayley. LC 72-185801. 1972. 0.75 (ISBN 0-19-911021-2). Oxford University Press.
Love's Atonement: Or, Expiation. Tr. from the French. Marie Therese Blanc. LC 6-13844. (On cover: The bijou series, no. 6). 1892. The F. M. Lupton Publishing Company.
Love's Avenging Heart. Patricia Matthews. 1977. pap. text ed. 2.95 (ISBN 0-523-41513-3). Pinnacle Bks.
Love's Avenging Heart. Patricia Matthews. 1.95 (ISBN 0-523-00987-9). Pinnacle Books.
Love's Been Good to Me. Rod McKuen. Pocke Books.
Love's Blindness. Elinor Sutherland Glyn. LC 26-218251. The Authors' Press.
Love's Bold Embrace. Brynn Gilbert. 1979. pap. 2.25 o.s.i. (ISBN 0-505-51402-8). Tower Bks.
Love's Bold Journey. Patricia Matthews. 448p. (Orig.). 1980. pap. 2.95 (ISBN 0-523-40661-4). Pinnacle Bks.
Love's Broken Promises. Sharon Wagner. (Berkley Book). (Illus.). 1978. 1.95 (ISBN 0-425-03815-7). Berkley Pub. Corp.
Love's Burning Flame. Iris Bancroft. 1980. pap. cancelled. Bantam.
Love's Byways: A Love Story. Jane Davis. LC 30-32329. Chelsea House.
Love's Charade. Rachel C. Payes. LC 80-82661. (Seven Sisters Regency Romance Ser.: No. 1). 192p. (Orig.). 1981. pap. 1.95 (ISBN 0-87216-770-4). Playboy Pbks.
Love's Choice. Rosie Thomas. (Avon Romance Ser.). 352p. 1982. pap. 2.95 (ISBN 0-380-61713-7). Avon.
Love's Conflict... Florence Marryat Church Lean. LC 7-13604. (On cover: Lovell's library. v. 19. no. 952). 1887. J. W. Lovell Company.
Love's Conquest. Helen Rutherford Barton. LC 38-7800. The Dodge Publishing Company.
Love's Conquest. Anita Montaye. LC 33-693. A. L. Burt Company.
Love's Crooked Path: The Romances of Marriage to Reform, from Real Life in the Frozen North. Wilfrid Robert Smith. LC 22-106393. American Presses.
Love's Cross-Currents; a Year's Letters. Algernon Charles Swinburne. LC 64-4888. (Signet classic). 1964. New American Library.
Love's Cross-Currents: A Year's Letters. Algernon Charles Swinburne. LC 5-21570. 1905. Harper & Brothers.
Love's Crosses. A Novel. Frances Eliza Millett Notley. (Franklin square library, no. 28). 1878. Harper & Brothers.
Love's Crucible. Mary Shepardson Pomeroy. LC 11-303621. 1911. 1.35. Sherman, French & Company.
Love's Cruel Enigma. Cruelle Enigme. Paul Charles Joseph Bourget. Tr. by Julian Cray. LC 6-15002. The Waverly Company.
Love's Daring Dream. Patricia Matthews. 1978. 2.25 (ISBN 0-523-40346-1). Pinnacle Books.
Love's Dark Conquest. Ralph Hayes. (Belmont Tower Books). 1978. 1.95 (ISBN 0-505-51260-2). Tower Pubns.
Love's Dark Wilderness. Mary E. Webster. (YA) 1980. 6.95 (Avalon). Bouregy.
Love's Deadly Silhouette. Leslie Richards. (Vol. II). (Illus.). 1979. pap. 1.95 (ISBN 0-89083-438-5). Zebra.
Love's Defiant Prisoner. Patricia Phillips. LC 77-80697. (Jove/HBJ Book). 1978. 1.45 (ISBN 0-515-04375-3). Jove Publications.
Love's Delirium" Tr. from the German of Heinz Tovote. Heinz Tovote & Miller, Hettie E., Tr. LC 8-29834. (On cover: Idylwild series, no. 26). Morrill, Higgins & Co.
Love's Denial: Published Serially Under the Title The Shining Talent. Eleanor Early. LC 32-15432. Grosset & Dunlap.
Love's Destiny. Arlene Hale. LC 78-12837. 1979. 10.95 (ISBN 0-89340-164-1). J. Curley.
Love's Destiny. Arlene Hale. (Signet book). New American Library.

Love's Dilemmas. Robert Herrick. LC 73-113677. (Short story index reprint series). 1970. Books for Libraries Press.
Love's Dilemmas. Robert Herrick. LC 99-931. 1898. H. S. Stone & Company.
Love's Dilemmas see Collected Works.
Love's Dream: Or, Did He Mean to Wrong Her! Eben Freemont Champney. LC 1580. 1900. J. S. Ogilvie Publishing Company.
Love's Duel. Carole Mortimer. (Harlequin Presents Ser.). 192p. 1982. pap. 1.75 (ISBN 0-373-10510-X). Harlequin Bks.
Love's Duet. Patricia Veryan. LC 78-56289. 1979. 9.95 (ISBN 0-8027-0604-5). Walker.
Love's Echo. Kathryn White. LC 40-34601. The Penn Publishing Company.
Love's Ecstasy: A Novel. May Christie. LC 28-302640. Grosset & Dunlap.
Love's Emerald Flame. William Lambert. (Superromances). 384p. 1980. pap. 2.50 (ISBN 0-373-70002-4, Pub. by Worldwide). Harlequin Bks.
Love's Encore. Rachel Ryan. (Candlelight Ecstacy Ser.: No. 21). (Orig.). 1981. pap. 1.50 (ISBN 0-440-14932-0). Dell.
Love's Enduring Promise. Janette Oke. LC 80-22993. 3.50 (ISBN 0-87123-345-2). Bethany Fellowship, Inc.
Love's Escapade. Rachel C. Payes. LC 80-85108. (Seven Sisters Regency Romance Ser.: No. 5). 192p. (Orig.). 1981. pap. 1.95 (ISBN 0-87216-834-4). Playboy Pbks.
Love's Far Horizon. Lee Roddy. (Chime Ser.). (Illus.). 1981. pap. 2.50 (ISBN 0-89191-540-0, 55400). Cook.
Love's Far Horizon. Lee Roddy. (Chime Ser.). 1982. pap. 2.50 o.p. Caroline Hse.
Love's Fiery Dagger. Flora Hiller. 1978. 1.95 (ISBN 0-445-04211-7). Popular Library.
Love's Fiery Jewel. Elaine Barbieri. 1983. pap. 3.75 (ISBN 0-8217-1128-8). Zebra.
Love's Fine Edge. Jacqueline Cathcart. 1983. pap. 6.95 (Avalon). Bouregy.
Love's Folly. Anson Flower Robinson. 1898. O.E.Hungerford.
Love's Gentle Agony. Aaron Fletcher. (Dell/Lorelei Book). 1978. 2.25 (ISBN 0-440-04972-5). Lorelei Publishing Co., Inc.
Love's Gentle Fugitive. st edition. ed. Andrea Layton, pseud. LC 77-93130. 1.95 (ISBN 0-87216-455-1). Playboy Press Paperbacks.
Love's Gentle Smile. Anne Benson. LC 81-83256. 192p. (Orig.). 1982. pap. 1.95 (ISBN 0-86721-010-9). Playboy Pbks.
Love's Glittering Web. Kate Bowe. (Superromances Ser.). 384p. 1982. pap. 2.50 (ISBN 0-373-70028-8, Pub. by Worldwide). Harlequin Bks.
Love's Golden Circle. Margaret Maitland, pseud. 1978. pap. 1.95 o.s.i. (ISBN 0-8439-0557-3, Leisure Bks). Nordon Pubns.
Love's Golden Destiny. Patricia Matthews. 1979. pap. 2.95 (ISBN 0-523-41519-2). Pinnacle Bks.
Love's Golden Spell. Willa Lambert. (Superromances Ser.). 384p. 1983. pap. 2.95 (ISBN 0-373-70059-8, Pub. by Worldwide). Harlequin Bks.
Love's Greatest Mistake. Frederic Arnold Kummer. LC 27-13130. Grosset & Dunlap.
Love's Harvest. Benjamin Leopold Farjeon. LC 6-39539. (On cover: Lovell's library. v. 12. no. 654). 1885. J. W. Lovell Company.
Love's Harvest. E. S. Folmer. 4.50 o.p. Carlton.
Love's Hazard. Concordia Merrel. LC 35-5967. 1935. Doubleday, Doran & Company, Inc.
Love's Hidden Fire. Glenna Finley, pseud. pap. 1.95 (ISBN 0-451-11498-1, AJ1498, Sig). NAL.
Love's Hidden Glory. Lydia Lancaster. 576p. 1982. pap. 3.50 (ISBN 0-446-90580-1). Warner Bks.
Love's Hour. Elinor Sutherland Glyn. LC 32-162555. The Macaulay Company.
Love's Hour of Danger. Lisa Lenore. (Superromances Ser.). 384p. 1982. pap. 2.50 (ISBN 0-373-70039-3, Pub. by Worldwide). Harlequin Bks.
Love's Illusion. John Davys Beresford. LC 30-262689. 1930. The Viking Press.
Love's Impossible Dream. Ethel M. Comins. 1982. pap. 6.95 (Avalon). Bouregy.
Love's Inferno. Edward Stilgebauer & Thieme, Carol, Tr. LC 16-162608. 1916. Brentano's.
Love's Intrigues. Jane Barker. Bd. with Lovers Week. Mary Hearne; Female Deserters. Mary Hearne. LC 70-170528. (Foundations of the Novel 1700-1739). lib. bdg. 50.00 o.s.i. (ISBN 0-8240-0531-7). Garland Pub.
Love's Journey. Wendy Martin. 1976. 4.95. Avalon Books.
Love's Labor Won: A Novel. Emma Dorothy Eliza Nevitte Southworth. LC 33-7778. M. A. Donohue & Company.
Love's Labour's Won: A Novel About Shakespeare's Lost Years. Edward Fisher. LC 63-16294. 1963. Abelard-Schuman.
Love's Ladder: A Novel. W. DeWitt Wallace. LC 8-33279. 1886. Belford, Clarke & Company.
Love's Lady. Margaret Lyon Smith. LC 30-276872. E. J. Clode, Inc.
Love's Law. Dorothy Frooks. LC 28-8140. The Avondale Press, Incorporated.
Love's Little Hour. Sinclair Tousey. LC 35-38131. G. H. Watt.
Love's Logic: And Other Stories. Anthony Hope Hawkins. 1908. The McClure Company.
Love's Long Journey. Ana Leigh. 1981. pap. 2.250 (ISBN 0-8439-0884-X, Leisure Bks). Nordon Pubns.
Love's Long Journey. Janette Oke. LC 82-9469. 3.95 (ISBN 0-87123-315-0). Bethany House.
Love's Lotus Flower. Winifred Mary Scott. LC 40-2315. 1940. H. C. Kinsey & Company, Inc.
Love's Lovely Counterfeit. James Mallahan Cain. LC 57-3958. (Signet book, 1445). 1957. New American Library.
Love's Lovely Counterfeit. James Mallahan Cain. LC 48-12385. (Murder mystery monthly no. 44). 1947. Avon Book Co.
Love's Lovely Counterfeit. James Mallahan Cain. LC 48-105694. (New Avon library, 161). 1948. Avon Book Co.
Love's Lovely Counterfeit. James Mallahan Cain. LC 42-209914. 1942. A. A. Knopf.
Love's Lovely Counterfeit. James Mallahan Cain. LC 79-10778. 1979. 1.95 (ISBN 0-394-74213-3). Vintage Books.
Love's Magic. Louise Gerard. LC 28-11053. The Macaulay Company.
Love's Magic Moment. Patricia Matthews. 1979. pap. 3.25 (ISBN 0-523-41873-6). Pinnacle Bks.
Love's Magic Spell. Glenna Finley, pseud. 1974. pap. 1.95 (ISBN 0-451-11489-2, AJ1489, Sig). NAL.
Love's Majesty. Charles Beamer. LC 82-84071. 192p. 1983. pap. 4.95 (ISBN 0-89081-325-6). Harvest Hse.
Love's Martyr. Laurence Alma-Tadema. LC 6-58. (On cover: Seaside library. Pocket ed., no. 757). G. Munro.
Love's Masquerade. Caroline Courtney. LC 81-13156. 1981. 13.50 (ISBN 0-8161-3137-6). G.K. Hall.
Love's Masquerade. Lillian Marsh. (Second Chance at Love Ser.: No. 51). (Orig.). 1982. pap. 1.75 (ISBN 0-515-05851-3). Jove Pubns.
Love's Memory. Anne Duffield. LC 36-6961. Arcadia House.
Love's Miracle. May Christie. LC 30-13105. Grosset & Dunlap.
Love's Not Enough. Simonne Ratel. Tr. by Collins, Joseph. LC 30-24345. Farrar & Rinehart, Incorporated.
Loves of a Musical Student. 1969. pap. 1.75 o.p. (Z1039, Zebra). Grove.
Loves of Alice Brandt. John Hunter. 1970. pap. 0.75 o.p. (75-310). Manor Bks.
Loves of Ambrose. Margaret O'Bannon Womack Vandercook. LC 14-4494. 1914. Doubleday, Page & Company.
Loves of Cass Macguire. Brian Friel. 1967. 4.50 o.p. FS&G.
Loves of Edwy: Tale and Drawings. Rose Cecil O'Neill. LC 4-18892. 1904. Lothrop Publishing Company.
Loves of Lo-Foh. Frank Owen. LC 36-11548. C. Kendall, Inc.
Loves of Miss Anne. Samuel Rutherford Crockett. LC 4-23762. 1904. Dodd, Mead and Company.
Loves of Othniel & Achsah, Translated from the Chaldee, 1769, 2 vols. William Tooke. LC 74-14953. (Novel in England, 1700-1775 Ser). 1974. lib. bdg. 50.00 ea. (ISBN 0-8240-1188-0). Garland Pub.
Loves of Pelleas and Etarre. Zona Gale. LC 7-30832. 1907. The Macmillan Company.
Loves of the Lady Arabella. Molly Elliot Seawell. LC 41-42352. 1898. The Macmillan Company.
Loves of the Lady Arabella. Molly Elliot Seawell. LC 7-16410. 1898. The Macmillan Company.
Loves of the Lady Arabella. Molly Elliot Seawell. LC 6-36177. 1906. The Bobbs-Merrill Company.
Love's Only Deception. Carole Mortimer. (Harlequin Presents Ser.). 192p. 1983. pap. 1.95 (ISBN 0-373-10594-0). Harlequin Bks.
Love's Pagan Heart. Patricia Matthews. 1978. pap. 2.50 (ISBN 0-523-41834-5). Pinnacle Bks.
Love's Pilgrim. John Davys Beresford. LC 23-13487. The Bobbs-Merrill Company.
Love's Pilgrimage; a Novel. Upton Beall Sinclair. LC 11-11315. 1.35. M. Kennerley.
Love's Privilege. Stella M During. LC 9-12615. 1909. J. B. Lippincott Company.
Love's Progress. Floyd Lytle. 1969. 3.00 o.p. (ISBN 0-682-46916-5). Exposition.
Love's Progress. By the Author of "The Recollections of a New-England Housekeeper"... Etc.... Caroline Howard Gilman. 1840. Harper & Brothers.
Love's Promenade. Rachel C. Payes. LC 80-83568. (Seven Sisters Regency Romance Ser.: No. 3). 192p. (Orig.). 1981. pap. 1.95 (ISBN 0-87216-805-0). Playboy Pbks.
Love's Promise. Nina Pykare. (Candlelight Romance). 1.25 (ISBN 0-440-14641-0). Dell Publishing Co.
Love's Promised Land. Diana Hariland. 1978. pap. 2.95 (ISBN 0-449-14000-8, GM). Fawcett.
Love's Promised Land. Diana Haviland. 2.25. Fawcett Gold Medal Books.
Love's Proud Masquerade. Nomi Berger. 512p. (Orig.). 1982. pap. 3.50 (ISBN 0-8439-1055-0, Leisure Bks). Nordon Pubns.
Love's Proxy. Richard Bagot. 1904. Longman's, Green, and Co.
Love's Purple. S. Ella Wood Dean. LC 11-29662. 1911. 1.25. Forbes & Company.
Love's Raging Tide. Patricia Matthews. (Orig.). 1980. pap. 3.25 (ISBN 0-523-41969-4). Pinnacle Bks.
Love's Raging Torment. Alma Ashley. 1978. pap. 2.25 o.s.i. (ISBN 0-505-51250-5). Tower Bks.
Love's Rainbow Dream... William Lee Popham. LC 10-18879. 0.50. W. L. Popham.
Love's Random Shot: And Other Stories. Wilkie Collins. (On cover: The seaside library. Pocket ed., no. 175). 1884. G. Munro.
Love's Refrain. Jane Corby. (Starlight Romance Ser.). 144p. 1972. pap. 0.75 o.p. (532-75470-075). Manor Bks.
Love's Renegade. Rachel C. Payes. LC 80-83594. (Seven Sisters Regency Romance Ser.: No. 2). 192p. (Orig.). 1981. pap. 1.95 (ISBN 0-87216-809-3). Playboy Pbks.
Love's Secret Storm. Leonora Pruner. LC 81-2459. 3.95 (ISBN 0-87123-347-9). Bethany Fellowship.
Love's Serenade. Rachel C. Payes. LC 80-84374. (Seven Sisters Regency Romance Ser.). 192p. 1981. pap. 1.95 (ISBN 0-87216-817-4). Playboy Pbks.
Love's Shadow. Ada Leverson. 1972. pap. 0.75 o.p. (07235). Curtis.
Love's Shadow: A Novel. Ada Leverson. 1979. 1.75. Popular Library.
Love's Sound in Silence. Meg Hudson. (Superromances). 384p. 1982. pap. 2.50 (ISBN 0-373-70036-9, Pub. by Worldwide). Harlequin Bks.
Love's Strange Mysteries. Georgia M. Shewmake. 1982. pap. 6.95 (Avalon). Bouregy.
Love's Sweet Agony. Patricia Matthews. 448p. (Orig.). 1980. pap. 2.75 (ISBN 0-523-40660-6). Pinnacle Bks.
Love's Sweet Charity. Eva Zumwalt. LC 81-43537. 1982. 10.95 (ISBN 0-385-17866-2). Doubleday.
Love's Sweet Confusion. William Arthur Neubauer. LC 67-7881. 1967. Arcadia House.
Love's Tangled Web. Ethel M. Comins. (YA) 1978. 6.95 (Avalon). Bouregy.
Love's Tapestry. Kathleen Rollins. Arcadia House.
Love's Tempest. Elinor Larkin. (Orig.). 1981. pap. 1.50 (ISBN 0-440-14948-7). Dell.
Love's Temptation. Glenna Finley, pseud. 1979. pap. 1.95 (ISBN 0-451-11173-7, AJ1173, Sig). NAL.
Love's Tender Fury. Jennifer Wilde. 560p. (Orig.). 1983. pap. 3.95 (ISBN 0-446-30528-6). Warner Bks.
Love's Tender Fury. Jennifer Wilde. 1976. (pbk.) 1.95 (ISBN 0-446-79921-1). Warner Books.
Love's Tender Tears. Kate Ostrander. (Orig.). 1979. pap. 1.95 (ISBN 0-89083-504-7). Zebra.
Love's Toll: A Novel. Nell C Dillon. LC 18-12304. International Authors' Association.
Love's Torment. Helen Streny. (Orig.). 1979. pap. 1.95. Woodhill.
Love's Tormented Flame. Kate McBride. 352p. (Orig.). 1982. pap. 3.25 (ISBN 0-523-41465-X). Pinnacle Bks.
Love's Triumphant Heart. Violet Ashton. (Fawcett Gold Medal Book). 1977. 1.75 (ISBN 0-449-13771-6). Fawcett Publications.
Love's Turning Point. Kay Richardson. (Avalon Books). 4.95. Thomas Bouregy.
Love's Unveiling. Samantha Scott. (Candlelight Ecstasy Ser.: No. 147). (Orig.). 1983. pap. 1.95 (ISBN 0-440-15022-1). Dell.
Love's Vengeance. A Novel... Thomas Mayne Reid. LC 21-4157. 1880. G. W. Carleton & Co.
Love's Victory. Denise Robins. LC 34-42416. 1933. G. H. Watt.
Love's Warfare. Charlotte Mary Brame. G. Munro.
Love's Warfare. Charlotte Mary Brame. LC 1-29654. (Bertha Clay library, no. 88). 1900. Street & Smith.
Love's Warfare. Charlotte Mary Brame. (On cover: Lovell's library. v. 17, no. 803). J. W. Lovell Company.
Love's Warfare. A Novel... Frank Lee Benedict. LC 7-34452. 1884. G. W. Carleton & Co.; Etc., Etc.
Love's Warm Sun: The Story of a Bright Young Engineer. Wayne Kirk. 1982. 6.95 (ISBN 0-533-04988-1). Vantage.
Love's Way. Arthur Spalding. LC 76-19907. 1978. pap. 3.95 o.p. (ISBN 0-8163-0006-2, 12751-4). Pacific Pr Pub Assn.
Love's Way in Dixie: Some Short Stories from Cupid's Favorite Field. Katharine Hopkins Chapman. LC 5-24853. 1905. The Neale Publishing Company.
Love's Wicked Ways. Diana Summers. LC 78-61742. 448p. 1979. pap. 2.95 (ISBN 0-87216-502-7). Playboy Pbks.
Love's Wild Desire. Jennifer Blake. 384p. 1981. pap. 2.95 (ISBN 0-445-08616-5). Popular Lib.
Love's Wild Desire. Jennifer Blake. 1977. 1.95. (ISBN 0-445-08616-5). Popular Library.
Love's Wildest Fires. Christina Savage, pseud. 1977. 3.25 (ISBN 0-440-12895-1). Dell.
Love's Wildest Promise. Patricia Matthews. 1977. pap. 2.95 (ISBN 0-523-41514-1). Pinnacle Bks.
Love's Wine. Frances Flore. (Candlelight Ecstasy Ser.: No. 61). (Orig.). 1982. pap. 1.75 (ISBN 0-440-14785-9). Dell.
Love's Wondrous Ways. Dorothea J. Snow. 1981. pap. 6.95 (Avalon). Bouregy.
Love's Young Dream. Samuel Rutherford Crockett. LC 10-16391. 1910. 1.50. The Macmillan Company.
Lovesounds. Gail Sheehy. LC 74-102339. 1970. 5.95. Random House.
Lovestone. Deana James. (Orig.). 1982. pap. 3.50 (ISBN 0-8217-1202-0). Zebra.
Lovey Childs; a Philadelphian's Story: A Novel. John O'Hara. LC 73-85571. 1969. 5.95. Random House.
Lovey Mary. Alice Caldwell Hegan Rice. LC 3-57873. 1903. The Century Co.
Lovey Mary. Alice Caldwell Hegan Rice. LC 35-27378. 1935. D. Appleton-Century Company, Incorporated.
Lovice. Margaret Wolfe Hamilton Hungerford. LC 7-9356. 1897. J. B. Lippincott Company.
Loving. Henry Green. LC 49-10679. 1949. Viking Press.
Loving. J. M. Ryan. 1970. pap. 0.95 o.p. (N2188). Pyramid Pubns.
Loving. large print ed. Danielle Steel. LC 81-138. 1981. 13.95 (ISBN 0-8161-3237-2) (ISBN 0-8161-3279-8). G.K. Hall.
Loving; Living; Party Going. Henry Green. LC 78-11885. 1978. 4.95 (ISBN 0-14-004916-9). Penguin Books.
Loving Adversaries. Eileen Bryan. (Candlelight Ecstasy Ser.: No. 155). (Orig.). 1983. pap. 1.95 (ISBN 0-440-14885-5). Dell.
Loving and Giving. Denise Robins. (Beagle book). 1974. (pbk.) 0.95 (ISBN 0-345-26603-X). Ballantine Books.
Loving Are the Daring. Holman Francis Day. LC 23-13099. Harper & Brothers.
Loving Are the Daring. Marjorie Frickel. LC 47-3151. 1947. Prentice-Hall, Inc.
Loving Arrangement. Diana Blayne. (Candlelight Ecstacy Ser.: No. 113). (Orig.). 1983. pap. 1.95 (ISBN 0-440-15026-4). Dell.
Loving Couple: By Virginia Rowans Pseud. Edward Everett Tanner. LC 56-10793. 1956. Crowell.
Loving Cup. Allan Prior. LC 68-8125. (O.S.I.). 1969. 5.95 o.s.i. (ISBN 0-671-20112-3). S&S.
Loving Cup: A Novel. Allan Prior. LC 68-8125. 1969. 5.95. Simon and Schuster.
Loving Evie. Anthony Francis Caputi. LC 73-14308. 1974. 7.95 (ISBN 0-06-010611-5). Harper & Row.
Loving Exile. Eleanor Woods. (Candlelight Ecstasy Ser.: No. 141). (Orig.). 1983. pap. 1.95 (ISBN 0-440-14650-X). Dell.
Loving Eye: A Novel. William Sansom. LC 57-62072. Reynal.
Loving Friends: A Portrait of Bloomsbury. David Gadd. LC 74-26596. (Illus.). 210p. 1975. 6.95 o.p. (ISBN 0-15-154740-8). HarBraceJ.
Loving Hands at Home. Diane Johnson. LC 68-20068. 1968. 4.95. Harcourt, Brace & World.
Loving Heart. Elizabeth Inglis-Jones. LC 42-8277. 1942. J. Messner, Inc.
Loving Heart. William Arthur Neubauer. LC 63-6680. 1962. Arcadia House.
Loving Heart. Elsie Singmaster. LC 37-24115. 1937. Houghton Mifflin Company.
Loving Her. Ann Allen Shockley. LC 73-13227. 192p. 1974. 6.95 o.p. (ISBN 0-672-51835-X). Bobbs.
Loving Her: A Novel. Ann Allen Shockley. LC 73-13226. 1974. 6.95 (ISBN 0-672-51835-X). Bobbs-Merrill.
Loving Her: A Novel. Ann Allen Shockley. 1978. 1.75 (ISBN 0-380-38935-5). Avon Books.
Loving Highwayman. Helen Ashfield. 192p. 1983. 10.95 (ISBN 0-312-49973-6). St Martin.
Loving Highwayman. Pamela Bennetts. LC 83-2875. 1983. 10.95 (ISBN 0-312-49973-6). St. Martin's Press.
Loving Letty. Paul Darcy Boles. (Signet Book). 1976. (pbk.) 1.75. New American Library.
Loving Lips, Hot Flesh. John Logan. 192p. pap. 1.95 o.p. (2045). Intimate Lib.
Loving Little Stepdaughter. Nikki Marshall. pap. 1.95 o.s.i. (Venus). Grove.
Loving Meddler. 1st Ed. Rosamond Van Der Zee Marshall. LC 54-702269. 1954. Doubleday.
Loving Memory. James Hill, pseud. LC 37-33408. 1937. Little, Brown and Company.

Loving Mouthful. Joy Inman. 192p. (Orig.). 1971. pap. 1.95 o.s.i. (O*P*H257, Ophelia). Olympia.

Loving Partnership. Jean Marsh, pseud. Ed. by Gene DeRoin. (Aston Hall Presents Ser.). (Orig.). 1979. pap. 1.50 (ISBN 0-89936-015-7). Aston Hall.

Loving Sands, Deadly Sands: A Novel. Charlotte Keppel. LC 74-13801. 1975. 7.95 (ISBN 0-440-05085-5). Delacorte Press.

Loving Season. Rebecca Burton. 1979. pap. 2.25 o.s.i. (ISBN 0-505-51413-3). Tower Bks.

Loving Slave. Margaret Pargeter. (Harlequin Presents Ser.). 192p. 1982. pap. 1.75 (ISBN 0-373-10523-1). Harlequin Bks.

Loving Spirit. Daphne Du Maurier. LC 71-184733. 1971. 8.50 (ISBN 0-8376-0415-X). R. Bentley.

Loving Spirit. Daphne Du Maurier. LC 31-20151. 1931. Doubleday, Doran & Company, Inc.

Loving Spirit. Daphne Du Maurier. LC 39-15276. (A Mercury book, no. 18). The American Mercury, Inc.

Loving Strangers. Jack Mayfield. (Signet Book). 1978. 1.95 (ISBN 0-451-08216-8). New American Library.

Loving Strangers. Vri Owen. 1975. (pbk.) 1.50 (ISBN 0-380-00448-8). Avon.

Loving Trap. Daphne Clair. (Harlequin Presents Ser.). 192p. 1982. pap. 1.75 (ISBN 0-373-10506-1). Harlequin Bks.

Loving True, Living True. Marjorie Ford. 1975. (pbk.) 1.25 (ISBN 0-446-76438-8). Warner Paperback Library.

Loving Upward. mary richie. ed. Mary Richie. 1.75 (ISBN 0-380-00801-7). Avon Books.

Loving Upward: A Novel. Mary Richie. LC 74-3901. 1975. 7.95 (ISBN 0-06-127508-5). Harper's Magazine Press.

Loving Wife. Violet Weingarten. (Kangaroo Book). 1977. 1.75. Pocket Books.

Loving Wife. Violet Weingarten. LC 71-79329. 1969. 5.95. Knopf.

Loving with a Vengeance: Mass-Produced Fantasies for Women. Tania Modleski. LC 82-8687. 1982. 17.95 (ISBN 0-208-01945-6). Archon Books.

Loving You Always. Peggy Gaddis, pseud. 1946. Arcadia House, Inc.

Lovo-Maniacs: A Novel. Rona Barrett. LC 71-186904. 1972. 7.95 (ISBN 0-8402-1253-4). Nash Pub.

Low Breed. Joseph Johnson. LC 77-366583. 1976. (ISBN 0-17-005106-4). Nelson.

Low Bridge and Punk Pungs. Sam Hellman. LC 78-134965. (Short story index reprint series). (Illus.). 1970. Books for Libraries Press.

Low Bridge and Punk Pungs. Sam Hellman. LC 24-214058. 1924. 1.25. Little, Brown, and Company.

Low Ceilings: By W. Douglas Newton... Wilfrid Douglas Newton. LC 21-101762. 1921. D. Appleton and Company.

Low Company: A Novel. Daniel Fuchs. LC 37-2462. The Vanguard Press.

Low-Flying Aircraft, and Other Stories. J. G. Ballard. LC 77-357909. 1976. 3.50 (ISBN 0-224-01311-4). Cape.

Low Heaven. William J Walters. LC 39-5847. 1939. Dodd, Mead & Company.

Low Notes on a High Level. Story. John Boynton Priestley. LC 55-65912. Harper.

Low Road. Isabella Holt. LC 25-4858. 1925. The Macmillan Company.

Low Road: A Novel. Edward Havill. LC 44-2028. 1944. Harper & Brothers.

Low Run Tide and Lava Rock. Elliot Harold Paul. LC 29-20891. 1929. H. Liveright, Inc.

Low Society. Robert Halifax. LC 12-40506. 1912. E. P. Dutton & Company.

Low Tide. John Truesdell. LC 47-11208. 1947. Dodd, Mead.

Low Treason. Leonard D Tourney. LC 82-9414. 1982. 12.95 (ISBN 0-525-24153-1). E.P. Dutton.

Low Wit. Werner Low. LC 81-69718. 79p. (Orig.). 1982. pap. 3.95 (ISBN 0-917976-15-0). White Ewe.

Lowdown. Roy Chanslor. LC 31-19087. Farrar & Rinehart, Incorporated.

Lower and Husband. Bertha M. Clay. LC 1-29653. (Bertha Clay library, no. 45). 1900. Street & Smith.

Lower and Lower. John Speicher. LC 73-4160. 1973. 6.95 (ISBN 0-06-013964-1). Harper & Row.

Lower Bureau Drawer. Emma Upton Vaughn. LC 7-38025. The Editor Company.

Lower Lounge. Peter Kleman. 6.75 o.p. (ISBN 0-8062-0465-6). Carlton.

Lower Part of the Sky: A Novel of the Irony of Belief. Lenard Kaufman. LC 48-6004. 1948. Creative Age Press.

Lower Than Angels. Walter Karig. LC 45-122419. 1945. Farrar & Rinehart, Inc.

Lowest Trees Have Tops. Martha Gellhorn. LC 69-12470. 1969. 4.95. Dodd, Mead.

Lowland Beauty: George Washington's First Love; an Historical Novel. William Martin. LC 14-6006. The Raven Press.

Lowlife. Alexander Baron. 1979. 11.00x (ISBN 0-86025-076-8, Pub. by Ian Henry Pubns England). State Mutual Bk.

Lowlife. Alexander Baron. 1977. 7.25 o.p. State Mutual Bk.

Lowly Nazarene. A Story of Christ. J. Leroy Nixon. LC 7-23199. J. S. Ogilvie Publishing Company.

Loyal and Dedicated Servant. John Griffiths. LC 80-52411. 1981. 11.95 (ISBN 0-87223-659-5). Seaview Books.

Loyal Heart. William Arthur Neubauer. LC 55-124947. 1955. Arcadia House.

Loyal Hugenot Maid. Margaret Simpson Comrie. LC 2-21405. 1902. G. W. Jacobs & Co.

Loyal Lover. Emily Sharp H. Carmeron. (On cover: Broadway series, no. 8). J. A. Taylor and Company.

Loyal Lover. Margaret Widdemer. LC 30-14513. 1930. Farrar & Rinehart.

Loyal Ned: Or, The Last Cruise of the Alabama. A Rattling Romance of the Famous Rebel Privateer. A. F Grant. LC 6-27666. (War library Pocket ed. v. 1, no. 5). 1883. Novelist Publishing Co.

Loyal Traitors: A Story of Friendship for the Filipinos. Raymond Landon Bridgman. LC 3-2696. 1903. J. H. West Company.

Loyalist: A Story of the American Revolution. James Francis Barrett. LC 21-493. P. J. Kenedy & Sons.

Loyalists: An Historical Novel. Jane West. LC 8-34334. 1813. Published by Bradford and Read.

Loyalty. Phyllis Austin. LC 27-11032. 1927. Duffiled and Company.

Loyalty Is My Honour: A Novel. Ewan Butler. LC 64-18479. 1964. Viking Press.

Loyalty of Langstreth: A Novel. John R V Gilliat. LC 6-44044. Morrill, Higgins & Co.

Loys, Lord Beresford. Margaret Wolfe Hungerford. LC 7-9354. (Lovell's library. v. 3, no. 126). 1883. J. W. Lovell Company.

Loys, Lord Berresford. Margaret Wolfe Hungerford. (On cover: The Franklin library. no. 8). 1887. Franklin News Company.

Loys, Lord Beresford, and Other Tales. Margaret Wolfe Hamilton Hungerford. LC 7-9355. 1883. J. B. Lippincott & Co.

LSD Bullfight & Other Stories. Donald E. Brown. (Illus.). 28p. (Orig.). 1972. pap. 3.00 o.p. (ISBN 0-911156-27-5). Porter.

LSITT. Arthur Herzog. 1983. 14.95 (ISBN 0-87795-470-4). Arbor Hse.

Lsybeth: A Tale of the Dutch. Henry Rider Haggard. LC 1-27440. 1901. Longmans, Green, and Co.

Lu of the Ranges. Elinor Mordaunt, pseud. LC 13-15850. 1913. 1.35. Sturgis & Walton Company.

Lualda. Melville Shavelson. 1976. 1.75. Dell.

Lualda: A Novel. Melville Shavelson. LC 74-80709. 1975. 7.95 (ISBN 0-87795-088-1). Arbor House.

Lubbock Lights. David Wheeler. (O.si.). 1977. pap. 1.50 o.s.i. (AD1633, Award). Univ Pub & Dist.

Luca Sarto: A Novel, a History of His Perilous Journey into France in the Year Fourteen Hundred and Seventy-One. Charles Stephen Brooks. LC 20-38837. 1920. The Century Co.

Lucanus: A Friend of the Christ. James Frank Stout. 1904. Jennings and Graham.

Lucas' Annual. Ed. by Lucas, Edward Verrall. LC 14-15569. The Macmillan Company.

Lucas Garcia: And Other Stories. Original, Tr. and Selected. LC 7-14757. 1876. The Catholic Publication Society.

Lucas Tanner. Richard Posner. 1975. pap. 1.25 o.p. (ISBN 0-515-03928-4). Pyramid Pubns.

Lucasta. Sheila Bishop. (Fawcett Crest Book). 1.50 (ISBN 0-449-23458-4). Fawcett Books.

Lucasta. Richard Lovelace. 1975. Repr. of 1649 ed. text ed. 17.50x o.s.i. (ISBN 0-8277-3898-6). British Bk Ctr.

Luce the Foundling" An Anglo-American Tale... Frederic Bacon Cullens. LC 25-133034. 1925. Lewis Printing Co.

Luces De Bohemia: Bohemian Lights. Ramon del Valle-Inclan. Tr. by Anthony N. Zahareas & Gerald Gillespie. LC 75-36215. (Edinburgh Bilingual Library). (Cloth ed. 9.50 o.p.: No. 10). 278p. 1976. pap. 4.95x o.p. (ISBN 0-292-74610-5). U of Tex Pr.

Lucetta. Audrey Blanshard. 1979. 1.75 (ISBN 0-449-24189-0). Fawcett Crest.

Luchs Brothers' End-of-the-World Party Book. Kurt Luchs et al. LC 80-81216. (Illus., Orig.). 1980. pap. 6.95 (ISBN 0-936722-00-2). Prairie Sun.

Lucia Dare: A Novel. Sarah Anne Dorsey. LC 6-43127. 1867. M. Doolady.

Lucia: Her Problem. Amanda Minnie Douglas. 1872. Sheldon & Company.

Lucia, Hugh, & Another. A Novel. Mary Anna Lupton Needell. (Harper's Franklin square library, no. 386). 1884. Harper & Brothers.

Lucia Hugh and Another. A Novel. Mary Anna Lupton Needell. (On cover: The seaside library. Pocket ed. no. 582). 1885. G. Munro.

Lucia in London: A Novel. Edward Frederic Benson. LC 28-7950. 1928. Doubleday, Doran & Company, Inc.

Lucia Lascar. A Romance of Passion. Luman Allen. LC 6-47. (On cover: Dearborn series, no. 20). Donohue, Henneberry & Co.

Lucia, the Betrothed. From the Italian of Alessandro Manzoni... Alessandro Manzoni. LC 7-19680. 1834. G. Dearborn.

Luciano's Luck. Jack Higgins, pseud. LC 81-20129. 1982. 15.50 (ISBN 0-8161-3304-2). G.K. Hall.

Luciano's Luck. Jack Riggins. LC 81-40330. 1981. 12.95 (ISBN 0-8128-2827-5). Stein and Day.

Lucie Rodey. A Novel. Alice Marie Celeste Durand. Tr. by Sherwood, Mary (Neal) LC 6-356912. T. B. Peterson & Brothers.

Lucien. Vivian Parsons. LC 39-2711. 1939. Dodd, Mead & Company.

Lucien De Rubempre. Honore De Balzac. Tr. by Katharine Prescott Wormeley. LC 3-23186. (Half-title: The comedy of human life... Scenes from Parisian life). 1895. Roberts Brothers.

Lucien Leuwen. Marie Henri Beyle. LC 50-3663. 1950.

Lucien Leuwen, 2 vols. Stendhal. Tr. by H. L. Edwards. LC 82-73493. 645p. Repr. of 1951 ed. lib. bdg. 45.00x o.s.i. (ISBN 0-88116-011-3). Brenner Bks.

Lucienne. Jules Romains & Frank, Waldo David, 1880- Tr. LC 25-5458. 1925. Boni & Liveright.

Lucien's Tombs. Marion Rippon. LC 78-8217. 1979. 7.95 (ISBN 0-385-14429-6). Published for the Crime Club by Doubleday.

Lucifer & the Angel, No. 126. Barbara Cartland. 144p. (Orig.). 1980. pap. 1.75 (ISBN 0-553-13942-8). Bantam.

Lucifer & the Child. Ethel Edith Mannin. 1975. 4.95 (ISBN 0-09-122470-5, Pub. by Hutchinson). Merrimack Pub Cir.

Lucifer Cell. William Fennerton. LC 68-12537. 1968. Atheneum.

Lucifer Comet. Ian Wallace. 1980. 2.25 (ISBN 0-87997-581-4). DAW Books.

Lucifer Cove, No. 5: Chalet Diabolique. Virginia Coffman. 1973. pap. 1.25 o.s.i. (78-760). Lancer.

Lucifer Cove, No. 6: From Satan, with Love. Virginia Coffman. 1973. pap. 1.25 o.s.i. (78-761). Lancer.

Lucifer Cove Number Four: Masque of Satan. Virginia Coffman. 1971. pap. 1.25 o.s.i. (78-759). Lancer.

Lucifer Cove Number One: The Devil's Mistress. Virginia Coffman. (Orig.). 1970. pap. 1.25 o.s.i. (78-753). Lancer.

Lucifer Cove Number Three: The Devil's Virgin. Virginia Coffman. 1971. pap. 1.25 o.s.i. (78-755). Lancer.

Lucifer Cove Number Two: Priestess of the Damned. Virginia Coffman. 1970. pap. 1.25 o.s.i. (78-754). Lancer.

Lucifer Cult. Lynn Benedict. (Ravenswood gothic). 1974. (pbk.) 0.95 (ISBN 0-671-77785-8). Pocket Books.

Lucifer Falling. Terence De Vere White. LC 67-14831. 1967. bds., 4.95. World.

Lucifer in Pine Lake. Samuel Rogers. LC 37-2756. 1937. Little, Brown and Company.

Lucifer Key. Malcolm MacPherson. 1981. 13.50 o.p. (ISBN 0-525-14985-6, 01311-390). Dutton.

Lucifer Key: A Novel. Malcolm MacPherson. LC 80-27914. 13.50 (ISBN 0-525-14985-6). Dutton.

Lucifer Land. Mildred B Davis & Katherine Davis. LC 76-45859. 8.95 (ISBN 0-394-40932-9). Random House.

Lucifer Mask. Kathleen Rich. (Belmont Tower Book). 1977. 1.50 (ISBN 0-505-51186-X). Tower Pubns.

Lucifer Society. Ed. by Peter Haining. LC 73-150904. 1972. 2.50 (ISBN 0-491-00881-3). W. H. Allen.

Lucifer Society: Macabre Tales by Great Modern Writers. Ed. by Peter Haining. (Signet, Y5568). 1973. (pbk.) 1.25. New American Lib.

Lucifer Society: Macabre Tales by Great Modern Writers. Ed. by Peter Haining. LC 70-179949. 1972. 6.50 (ISBN 0-8008-5042-4). Taplinger Pub. Co.

Lucifer Wine. Ira Walker, pseud. LC 76-45575. 8.95 (ISBN 0-672-52313-2). Bobbs-Merrill.

Lucifer with a Book. John Horne Burns. 1977. pap. 2.25 (ISBN 0-380-01666-4, 33340, Bard). Avon.

Lucifer with a Book: A Novel. John Horne Burns. LC 49-8269. 1949. Harper.

Lucifer's Brand. Nicola West. (Harlequin Presents Ser.). 192p. 1983. pap. 1.95 (ISBN 0-373-10589-4). Harlequin Bks.

Lucifer's Dream: Translated from the French by Robin Chancellor. Jean Louis Curtis. LC 53-8149. 1953. Putnam.

Lucifer's Hammer. Larry Niven & J. E. Pournelle. LC 77-8074. 10.00 (ISBN 0-87223-487-8). Playboy Press.

Lucifer's Weekend. Warren Murphy. (Digger Ser.: No. 4). (Orig.). 1982. pap. 2.50 (ISBN 0-671-45095-6). PB.

Luciifer's Hammer. Larry Niven & Pournelle. J.E. 2.50 (ISBN 0-449-23599-8). Fawcett Crest.

Lucile Clery: A Woman of Intrigue. Joseph Shearing. LC 32-20231. 1932. Harper & Brothers.

Lucile Cranden: And the New Deal. Charles Francis Stocking. LC 34-18834. 1934. The Maestro Company.

Lucile of the Vineyard: A Temperance Romance. Nathan Hoyt Sheppard. LC 16-4426. 1915. N. H. Sheppard.

Lucinda. Anthony Hope Hawkins. LC 20-18612. 1920. D. Appleton and Company.

Lucinda Brayford. Martin Boyd. LC 48-556193. 1948. E. P. Dutton.

Lucinda Marries the Doctor. Elizabeth Seifert. LC 53-960135. 1953. Dodd, Mead.

Lucinda Marries the Doctor. Elizabeth Seifert. LC 73-79163. 1974. 6.95. Aeonian Press.

Lucinda: Or, The Mountain Mourner. Being Authentic Facts in a Series of Letters, from Mrs. Manvill, in the State of New York, to Her Sister in Pennsylvania. 3d ed. P. D Manvill. 1852. J. Munsell.

Lucinderella: A Novel. Berry Fleming. LC 67-108255. 4.50. John Day.

Lucinella: A Novel. Lore Groszmann Segal. LC 76-21877. 1976. 7.95 (ISBN 0-374-19425-4). Farrar, Straus, and Giroux.

Lucinie: A Novel. M L Pascal Dasque. LC 59-128976. 1959. Kenedy.

Lucius Flavus. An Historical Tale of the Time Immediately Preceeding the Destruction of Jerusalem. Joseph Spillmann. LC 2-473. 1901. B. Herder.

Lucius: The Centurion. Sara Elizabeth Gosselink. LC 44-40268. 1944. Wm. B. Eerdmans Publishing Company.

Luck. Mary Arden. LC 72-4425. (Short Story Index Reprint Ser). 1972. Repr. of 1927 ed. 17.00 (ISBN 0-8369-4167-5). Ayer Co.

Luck and Love and Tales of Marriage and Divorce. Thomas Edgar Willson. (On cover: Fireside series, no. 54). 1888. J. S. Ogilvie.

Luck, and Other Stories. Violet Middleton Murry. LC 72-4425. (Short story index reprint series). 1972. 11.00 (ISBN 0-8369-4167-5). Books for Libraries Press.

Luck and Pluck. Glendon Fred Swarthout. LC 72-90971. 1973. 5.95 (ISBN 0-385-03366-4). Doubleday.

Luck at Last, or the Happy Unfortunate see Four Before Richardson: Selected English Novels, 1720-1727.

Luck Be a Lady. Robert Terrall. LC 79-14128. 9.95 (ISBN 0-88326-161-8). Wyden Books: Trade Distribution by Simon and Schuster.

Luck in Disguise. Written in Good Faith. William J Yexter. (On cover: American novelists series, no. 16). 1889. J. W. Lovell Company.

Luck O' Lady Joan: A Fairy Tale for Women. Josephine Dodge Daskam Bacon. LC 13-205798. 1913. 0.25. F. G. Browne & Co.

Luck of a Lowland Laddie. Maria Henrietta De La Cherois Crommelin. LC 1-31714. F. M. Buckles & Company; Etc., Etc.

Luck of Barry Lyndon. a critical ed. edited, with an introd. and notes by martin f. anisman. ed. William Makepeace Thackeray. Ed. by Martin F. Anisman. LC 74-124517. 1970. New York University Press.

Luck of Brin's Five. Cherry Wilder, pseud. 1979. pap. 2.50 (ISBN 0-671-41637-5, Timescape). PB.

Luck of Ginger Coffey. Brian Moore. 1978. pap. 2.95 o.p. (ISBN 0-14-002115-9). Penguin.

Luck of Ginger Coffey: A Novel. 1st Ed. Brian Moore. LC 60-6533. 1960. Little, Brown.

Luck of Huemac: A Novel About the Aztec World. Daniel Peters. LC 81-40221. (Illus.). 688p. 1981. 16.95 (ISBN 0-394-51313-4). Random.

Luck of Laramie Ranch. John Harbottle. LC 13-21290. 1913. D. Appleton and Company.

Luck of Lost Canyon: Edited by Marya Tze Caraman. Clara M Blasingame. LC 55-16358. 1954. Bell Publications.

Luck of Rathcoole: Being the Romantic Adventures of Mistress Faith Wolcott (Sometime Known As "Miss Moppet") During Her Sojourn in New York an Early Period of the Republic. Jeanie Thomas Gould Lincoln. LC 12-3382. 1912. 1.20. Houghton Mifflin Company.

Luck of Roaring Camp. Bret Harte. Ed. by Walter Pauk & Raymond Harris. (Jamestown Classics Ser.). (Illus.). 35p. (gr. 6-12). 1976. pap. text ed. 2.00x (ISBN 0-89061-054-1, 529); tchrs. ed. 3.00 (ISBN 0-89061-055-X, 531). Jamestown Pubs.

Luck of Roaring Camp: And Other Sketches. Bret Harte. LC 50-5573. (World's greatest literature). 1949. Fountain Press.

Luck of Roaring Camp: And Other Sketches. Bret Harte. LC 21-4130. 1873. J. R. Osgood and Company.

TITLE INDEX LUDENDORFF PIRATES.

Luck of Roaring Camp: And Other Sketches. 33d ed. Bret Harte. LC 4-35668. Houghton, Mifflin and Company.
Luck of Roaring Camp: And Other Sketches. Bret Harte. LC 40-37527. 1899. Houghton Mifflin Company.
Luck of Roaring Camp: And Other Sketches. Bret Harte. (On cover: Souvenir edition). 1915. Houghton Mifflin Company.
Luck of Roaring Camp and Other Sketches. Bret Harte. LC 37-9721. (Classic romances of literature. vol. vi). The Spencer Press.
Luck of Roaring Camp: And Other Sketches. portland ed. Bret Harte. LC 43-39493. 1894. Houghton, Mifflin and Company.
Luck of Roaring Camp: And Other Sketches. Bret Harte. (Riverside Library). 1869. Houghton Mifflin Company.
Luck of Roaring Camp & Other Sketches, Including Outcasts of Poker Flat & Tennessee's Partner. Bret Harte. (Wild & Woolly West Ser: No. 29). (Illus.). 40p. 1974. 7.00 (ISBN 0-910584-48-6); pap. 1.50 (ISBN 0-910584-77-X). Filter.
Luck of Roaring Camp and Other Stories. Bret Harte & Angelo, Valenti, 1897- Illus. 1943. Peter Pauper Press.
Luck of Roaring Camp: And Other Stories; Including Earlier Papers, Spanish and American Legends, Tales of the Argonauts, Etc. Bret Harte. LC 597. (Half-title: The works of Bret Harte. Riverside ed.). 1899. Houghton, Mifflin and Company.
Luck of Roaring Camp: And Other Stories, Including Earlier Papers, Spanish and American Legends, Tales of the Argonauts, Etc. Bret Harte. LC 12-24359. (Half-title: The works of Bret Harte. Riverside edition... v. 2.). 1882. Houghton, Mifflin and Company; Etc., Etc.
Luck of Roaring Camp: And Other Stories, Including Earlier Papers, Spanish and American Legends, Tales of the Argonauts, Etc. Bret I. E. Francis Bret Harte. LC 12-24359. (Half-title: The works of Bret Harte. Riverside edition... v. 2). 1882. Houghton, Mifflin and Company; Etc., Etc.
Luck of Roaring Camp, and Other Tales. Bret Harte. LC 61-15035. (Great illustrated classics). (Illus.). 1961. Dodd, Mead.
Luck of Roaring Camp: And Other Tales, with Condensed Novels, Spanish and American Legends, and Earlier Papers. Bret Harte. LC 4-15451. (Half-title: Riverside ed. The writings of Bret Harte, vol. 1). 1902. Houghton, Mifflin and Company.
Luck of Roaring Camp: And Selected Stories and Poems. Bret Harte. Ed. by Stewart, George Rippey. LC 28-7034. (modern readers' series). 1928. The Macmillan Company.
Luck of Roaring Camp: & Three Other Stories. Bret Harte. LC 68-10285. (Illus.). 1968. F. Watts.
Luck of Roaring Camp & Three Other Stories. Bret Harte. (Illus.). 1968. F. Watts.
Luck of Roaring Comp. And Other Stories. 3d ed. Bret Harte. (Riverside Aldine series). 1886. Houghton, Mifflin and Company.
Luck of the Bodkins. Pelham Grenville Wodehouse. LC 36-488. 1936. Little, Brown, and Company.
Luck of the Darrells. James Payn. (On cover: Seaside library. Pocket ed. no. 589). 1885. G. Munro.
Luck of the Darrells: A Novel. James Payn. LC 7-33771. (Harper's handy series, no. 25). 1885. Harper & Brothers.
Luck of the Darrells: A Novel. James Payn. (On cover: Lovell's library, no. 659). 1885. J. W. Lovell Company.
Luck of the Draw. Zeke Masters, pseud. 1980. (ISBN 0-671-83378-2). Pocket Books.
Luck of the House. A Novel. Adeline Sergeant. LC 8-6855. (On cover: Lovell's international series, no. 26). 1889. F. F. Lovell & Company.
Luck of the House. By Adeline Sergeant. Adeline Sergeant. (On cover: Seaside library. Pocket ed. no. 1241). 1889. G. Munro.
Luck of the Irish: A Romance. Harold MacGrath. LC 17-250846. 1917. 1.40. Harper & Brothers.
Luck of the Kid. Ridgwell Cullum. LC 23-10226. 1923. 2.00. G. P. Putnam's Sons.
Luck of the Laird. Albert Payson Terhune. LC 27-19115. 1927. Harper & Brothers.
Luck of the Laird: A Highland Collie. Albert Payson Terhune. (Perennial library, P64A). 1965. Harper & Row.
Luck of the Linscotts: A Novel of Great New England Dynasty. Ann Pinchot. LC 81-71675. 1982. 14.95 (ISBN 0-87795-381-3). Arbor Hse.
Luck of the Lonely Sea. 1st Amer. Ed. Patrick O'Hara. LC 66-23424. 1966. bds., 4.95. McKay.
Luck of the Mounted; a Tale of the Royal Northwest Mounted Police. Ralph Selwood Kendall. LC 20-17967. 1920. John Lane Company.
Luck of the Road. Ruth Sawyer. LC 34-5602. 1934. D. Appleton-Century Company, Incorporated.
Luck of the Spindrift. Frederick Faust. LC 72-175310. 1972. 4.95 (ISBN 0-396-06470-1). Dodd, Mead.
Luck of the Spindrift: A Novel of Adventure. Frederick Faust. 1973. (pbk.) 0.95 (ISBN 0-671-77666-5). Pocket Books.
Luck of the Vails: A Novel. Edward Frederic Benson. LC 1-7284. 1901. D. Appleton and Company.
Luck of the Van Meers: A Tradition. Arona McHugh. LC 69-12217. 1969. 5.95. Doubleday.
Luck O'Lassendale. Walter Stafford Northcote Iddesleigh. LC 2-20470. 1902. J. Lane.
Luck Runs Out. Charlotte MacLeod. LC 79-7606. 1979. 7.95 (ISBN 0-385-15562-X). Published for the Crime Club by Doubleday.
Luck Runs Out. Charlotte MacLeod. LC 81-17293. 1982. 13.95 (ISBN 0-89340-381-4). J. Curley.
Luckiest Lady. Ruby Mildred Ayres. LC 27-21622. George H. Doran Company.
Lucky: A Tale of the Western Prairie. Eva Bell Botsford. LC 6-15018. 1895. The Peter Paul Book Company.
Lucky Bargee. Harry Lander. LC 7-14105. 1898. D. Appleton and Company.
Lucky Chance: The Story of a Mine. Matie Whitney Loraine. 1.00. Small, Maynard and Company.
Lucky Darryl. Bill Knott & James Tate. LC 76-45728. (Orig.). 1976. pap. 3.00 (ISBN 0-913722-10-3, Pub. by Release). SBD.
Lucky Devil. Arthur Maling. LC 77-11782. 8.95 (ISBN 0-06-012854-2). Harper & Row.
Lucky Devil. Arthur Maling. (Perennial Library). 1979. 1.95 (ISBN 0-06-080482-3). Harper & Row.
Lucky Disappointment. Florence Marryat Church Lean & De la Ramee, Louise. LC 7-13605. (On cover: Lovell's library. v. 19. no. 904). 1887. J. W. Lovell Company.
Lucky Fellow. Jeffrey Simmons. LC 79-22807. 1979. 10.95 (ISBN 0-312-50002-5). St. Martin's Press.
Lucky Girl. Besse Sprague. LC 39-314113. Gramercy Publishing Company.
Lucky in Love. Barbara Cartland. (Camfield Romance Ser.: No. 13). (Orig.). 1982. pap. 1.95 (ISBN 0-515-06292-8). Jove Pubns.
Lucky in Love" A Novel. Berta Ruck. LC 24-14172. 1924. Dodd, Mead and Company.
Lucky Jim. Kingsley Amis. 1976. pap. 3.95 (ISBN 0-14-001648-1). Penguin.
Lucky Jim. Kingsley Amis. 256p. 1976. Repr. of 1954 ed. lib. bdg. 15.95x (ISBN 0-89244-069-4). Queens Hse.
Lucky Jim: A Novel. Kingsley Amis. LC 54-5356. 1954. Doubleday.
Lucky Jim: A Novel. Kingsley Amis. LC 77-16238. 1977. 9.50 (ISBN 0-89244-069-4). Queens House.
Lucky Kristoffer. Martin Alfred Hansen. LC 73-9298. (Library of Scandinavian Literature, V. 25). 1974. 7.50 (ISBN 0-8057-3339-6). Twayne Publishers.
Lucky Lady. Rob Eden. LC 47-177. 1946. Gramercy Publishing Co.
Lucky Larribee. Max Brand. 1975. pap. 1.75 (ISBN 0-446-94456-4). Warner Bks.
Lucky Larribee: By Max Brand Pseud. Frederick Faust. LC 57-5869. (Dodd Mead silver star westerns). 1957. Dodd, Mead.
Lucky Lawrences. Kathleen Thompson Norris. LC 30-259061. 1930. Doubleday, Doran & Company, Inc.
Lucky Lover. John Habberton.
Lucky Mill. Ioan Slavici & Emperle, Alexandru Mircea, 1895- Tr. LC 19-7921. 1919. Duffield & Company.
Lucky Mishap: A Novel. Eva Katherine Clapp Gibson. LC 6-25373. 1883. Belford, Clarke & Co.
Lucky Miss Spaulding. Eleanor Arnett Nash. LC 52-8396. (Romance for young moderns). 1952. Messner.
Lucky Moores. Elsie Bass Guthrie. LC 73-10018. 1973. 6.95 (ISBN 0-8111-0501-6). Naylor Co.
Lucky Number. Ethel May Dell. LC 20-7648. 1920. 0.75. G. P. Putnam's Sons.
Lucky Number. Isaac Kahn Friedman. 1896. Way and Williams.
Lucky Number: Short Stories. John Hay Beith. LC 23-649989. 1923. Houghton Mifflin Company.
Lucky Number. With Drawings by Vasiliu. 1st Ed. Vera Henry. LC 57-6235. 1957. Lippincott.
Lucky Numbers. Montague Marsden Glass. LC 27-5008. 1927. Doubleday, Page & Company.
Lucky One. Anne Parrish. LC 58-8891. 1958. Harper.
Lucky Piece: A Tale of the North Woods. Albert Bigelow Paine. LC 6-10646. 1906. The Outing Publishing Company.
Lucky Prisoner. Joseph Arthur Gobineau. Tr. by Drake, William A. LC 30-9729. 1930. Brentano's.
Lucky Prisoner: Le Prisonnier Chanceux. Joseph Arthur Gobineau. Tr. by Atkinson, F. M. LC 26-15718. 1926. Doubleday, Page and Company.
Lucky Seven. John Taintor Foote. LC 18-3561. 1883. B. Bell and Sons.
Lucky Seventh: Tales of the Big League. Charles Emmett Van Loan. LC 78-130075. (Short story index reprint series). (Illus.). 1970. Books for Libraries Press.
Lucky-Seventh: Tales of the Big League. Charles Emmett Van Loan. LC 13-9243. Small, Maynard and Company.
Lucky Shuffles. Mark McGarrity. LC 73-5109. 1973. 7.95 (ISBN 0-670-44428-6). Grossman.
Lucky Star: Or, Three Episodes in the Life of Timothy Osborn, and Other Stories. Tristram Tupper. LC 29-20654. Grosset & Dunlap.
Lucky Starr and the Big Sun of Mercury: By Paul French Pseud. 1st Ed. Isaac Asimov. LC 56-5584. 1956. Doubleday.
Lucky Starr and the Big Sun of Mercury. Isaac Asimov. LC 78-14585. (The Lucky Starr Series). ((His). 1978. 7.95 (ISBN 0-8398-2489-0). Gregg Press.
Lucky Starr and the Moons of Jupiter. Isaac Asimov. LC 78-13136. (The Lucky Starr Series). ((His). 1978. 7.95 (ISBN 0-8398-2490-4). Gregg Press.
Lucky Starr and the Moons of Jupiter: By Paul French Pseud. 1st Ed. Isaac Asimov. LC 57-95044. 1957. Doubleday.
Lucky Starr and the Oceans of Venus. Isaac Asimov. LC 78-14506. 1978. 7.95 (ISBN 0-8398-2488-2). Gregg Press.
Lucky Starr and the Oceans of Venus: By Paul French Pseud. 1st Ed. Isaac Asimov. LC 54-983230. 1954. Doubleday.
Lucky Starr and the Pirates of the Asteroids: By Paul French Pseud. Illustrated by Richard Powers. 1st Ed. Isaac Asimov. 1953. Doubleday.
Lucky Starr and the Pirates of the Asteroids. Isaac Asimov. LC 78-13135. (The Lucky Starr Series). ((His). 1978. 7.95 (ISBN 0-8398-2487-4). Gregg Press.
Lucky Starr & the Rings of Saturn. Isaac Asimov. (Lucky Starr Ser.). 1978. pap. 2.25 (ISBN 0-449-23462-2, Crest). Fawcett.
Lucky Starr & the Rings of Saturn. Isaac Asimov. 9.95 (ISBN 0-8398-2491-2, Gregg). G K Hall.
Lucky Starr Series. Isaac Asimov. 50.00 (ISBN 0-444-47070-0, Gregg). G K Hall.
Lucky Stiff. Craig Rice. 1945. Simon and Schuster.
Lucky Ten Bar of Paradise Valley. His Humorous, Pathetic and Tragic Adventures. Charles McClellan Stevens. LC 1-30188. 1900. Rhodes & McClure Publishing Company.
Lucky the Bride: By Ann Carter Pseud. Anne Tedlock Brooks. LC 50-7910. 1950. Arcadia House.
Lucky Thirteen. Hank Bedard. 1980. pap. 1.50. Eldridge Pub.
Lucky Thirteen. Hank Bedard. 1980. pap. 1.50. Eldridge Pub.
Lucky to Be Alive? Alice Hamilton Cromie. LC 78-12483. 8.95 (ISBN 0-671-24081-1). Simon and Schuster.
Lucky Way: A Rmoantic Novel of Sporting Action for Young and Old Who Believe in Fair Play. Frank Orval Spohn. LC 51-14949. 1951. William-Frederick Press.
Luckybug Lode. Arthur Preston Hankins. LC 26-142227. The Macaulay Company.
Luckypenny: A Novel. Bruce Marshall. LC 38-16754. 1938. E. P. Dutton & Co., Inc.
Lucretia. Edward George Earle Lytton Bulwer-Lytton Lytton. (Lovell's library, v. 5, no. 253). 1883. J. W. Lovell Company.
Lucretia. Barbara Riefe. LC 81-85826. (Shackleford Legacy Ser.: Bk. 3). 352p. (Orig.). 1982. pap. 2.95 (ISBN 0-86721-076-1). Playboy Pbks.
Lucretia Borgia: A Dramatic Biography. Alfred Schirokauer & Griffin, Gerald, 1888- Tr. LC 37-22821. 1937. D. Appleton-Century Company, Incorporated.
Lucretia Lombard. Kathleen Thompson Norris. LC 22-7877. 1922. Doubleday, Page & Company.
Lucretia: Or, The Children of Night. Edward George Earle Lytton Bulwer-Lytton Lytton. LC 8-26647. G. Routledge and Sons.
Lucretia: Or, The Children of Night. the lord lytton ed. Edward George Earle Lytton Bulwer-Lytton Lytton. LC 7-8120. 1883. J. B. Lippincott & Co.
Lucretia: Or, The Children of Night. Edward George Earle Lytton Bulwer-Lytton Lytton. (Half-title: Novels of Sir Edward Bulwer Lytton. Library ed. Novels of life and manners, vol. XII). 1893. Little, Brown, and Company.
Lucy. Helen Ansell. LC 69-15270. 1969. 5.95. Harper & Row.
Lucy. Hester W. Chapman. LC 66-12613. 1966. bds., 5.75. Reynal Dist. Morrow.
Lucy. A Novel. Julie P. Smith. LC 8-8181. 1880. G. W. Carleton & Co.; Etc., Etc.
Lucy Amarillo Stories. Constance DeJong. 1978. pap. 5.00 (ISBN 0-918746-03-5). Standard Edns.
Lucy Amarillo Stories. Constance DeJong. 1978. pap. 3.50 (ISBN 0-918746-03-5). Urizen Bks.
Lucy and Their Majesties: A Comedy in Wax. Benjamin Leopold Farjeon. 1904. The Century Co.
Lucy and Three. Mary Granger. LC 30-6151. 1930. Brewer and Warren Inc., Psyson and Clarke Ltd.
Lucy Anderson: Portrait of a Wife. Helen Reimensnyder Martin. LC 32-3187. 1932. Dodd, Mead & Company.
Lucy Arden: Or, Hollywood Hall. James Grant. LC 41-30738. G. Routledge and Sons.
Lucy Arlyn. John Townsend Trowbridge. LC 12-39589. 1866. Ticknor and Fields.
Lucy Broad's Choice. Anna Maria Tolman Pickford. LC 7-35913. 1898. American Tract Society.
Lucy Carmichael. Margaret Kennedy. LC 51-5189. 1951. Rinehart.
Lucy Carmichael. Margaret Kennedy. LC 73-153890. 1972. 6.95 (ISBN 0-85617-521-8). White Lion Publishers.
Lucy Church, Amiably. Gertrude Stein. LC 78-82530. 1969. 6.95. Something Else Press.
Lucy Crofton. Margaret Oliphant Wilson Oliphant. (On cover: Seaside library. Pocket ed., no. 370). 1885. G. Munro.
Lucy Crofton. Margaret Oliphant Wilson Oliphant. (On cover: Lovell's library, v. 20, no. 994). 1887. J. W. Lovell Company.
Lucy Crofton: A Novel. Margaret Oliphant Wilson Oliphant. (Harper's handy series, no. 117). 1887. Harper & Brothers.
Lucy Crown. Irwin Shaw. LC 57-3959. (Signet book, D1438). 1957. New American Library.
Lucy Crown: A Novel. Irwin Shaw. LC 55-8168. 1956. Random House.
Lucy Emmett: Or, a Lady of Quality. Anita Bronson. LC 78-481. 10.95 (ISBN 0-698-10887-6). Coward, McCann & Geoghegan.
Lucy Gayheart. Willa Sibert Cather. LC 75-28046. 1976. 2.95 (ISBN 0-394-72051-2). Vintage Books.
Lucy Gayheart. Willa Sibert Cather. LC 35-114955. 1935. A. A. Knopf.
Lucy Gayheart. Willa Sibert Cather. LC 45-48721. 1935. A. A. Knopf.
Lucy Gelding: A Tale of Land and Sea; Showing the Evil Effects of Gambling, As It Is Practiced Upon the Atlantic Coast... Mary S. F. Slacom. LC 9-927. 1862. E. B. Myers.
Lucy Howard's Journal. Lydia Howard Huntley Sigourney. LC 8-14238. 1858. Harper & Brothers.
Lucy Maria. Abby Morton Diaz. LC 6-34203. 1874. J. R. Osgood and Company.
Lucy Novels: Early Sketches for a Room with a View. Edward Morgan Forster. Ed. by Oliver Stallybrass. (Abinger Edition of E. M. Forster Ser.). 1978. text ed. 26.00x o.p. (ISBN 0-8419-5805-X). Holmes & Meier.
Lucy of the Stars. Frederick Palmer. LC 6-139383. 1906. C. Scribner's Sons.
Lucy: Or, Married from Pique. A Story of Real Life From the German of E. Junker Pseud. Else Kobert Schmieden. Tr. by Sigmund, Joseph A. LC 8-2035. (On cover; Loring's tales of the day). Loring.
Lucy: Or, The Delaware Dialogues. Babette Rosmond. LC 52-6984. 1952. Simon and Schuster.
Lucy, Perhaps. Alfred Marshall Hitchcock. LC 35-16894. H. Holt and Company.
Lucy Temple: A Sequel to Charlotte Temple. Susanna Haswell Rowson. (On cover: Lovell's library, no. 1329). 1889. J. W. Lovell Company.
Lucy Winchester. Christmas Carol Miller Kauffman. LC 72-75018. 1969. 4.95. Herald Press.
Lucy Winchester. Christmas Carol Miller Kauffman. LC 46-744. 1945. Herald Press.
Lucy's Cottage. Pamela Bennetts. LC 80-28948. 1981. 8.95 (ISBN 0-312-50006-8). St. Martin's Press.
Lucy's Cottage. Margaret James. 184p. 1981. 9.95 (ISBN 0-312-50006-8). St Martin.
Lud Daingerfield: Life of a Young Man. Donald Joseph. LC 56-142207. 1956. Naylor Co.
Lud-in-the-Mist. Hope Mirrlees. LC 27-5683. 1927. A. A. Knopf.
Lud of Lunden, Vol. 1. Talbot Mundy. (Tros of Samothrace Ser.). 1978. pap. 2.25 (ISBN 0-89083-372-9). Zebra.
Luda, the Occult Girl: A Romance. Julia Webb Mays. LC 12-25205. Broadway Publishing Co.
Ludendorff Pirates: A Novel About the Hijacking of the Largest German Battleship of WW II. Al Ramrus & John Shaner. LC 77-76267. 1978. 8.95 (ISBN 0-385-11460-5). Doubleday.

Ludi Victor. James Leigh. LC 80-13626. 11.95 (ISBN 0-698-11038-2). Coward, McCann & Geoghegan.
Ludovic and Gertrude. Hendrik Conscience. 1875. J. Murphy & Co.
Ludwig Tieck, Der Heilige Von Dresden: Aus der Fruehzeit der Deutschen Novelle. Marianne Thalmann. (Quellen und Forschungen Zur Sprachgeschichte und Kulturgeschichte der Germanischen Voelker, No. 3). (Ger). 1960. 8.60 o.p. (ISBN 3-11-000194-2). De Gruyter.
Ludwig Von Wolfgang Vulture. Dolph Sharp. LC 73-76706. (Illus.). 1973. 1.50. Price/Stern/Sloan Publishers.
Luelle: A Southern Romance. Richard Penfield. LC 7-36363. 1884. E. Claxton & Company.
Luis & les Deux Coins. J. DuHadway Craig. 1976. 5.95 o.p. (ISBN 0-533-02406-4). Vantage.
Luis Armed Story. Tom Veitch, pseud. LC 78-9676. 9.95. (ISBN 0-916190-06-4) (ISBN 0-916190-07-2). Full Court Press.
Luise: A Gothic Tale of Old Alexandria. Dawn Stewart Field. LC 73-78609. 1974. 8.95 (ISBN 0-399-11169-7). Putnam.
Luise: A Gothic Tale of Old Alexandria. Dawn Stewart Field. (Berkley Book). 1978. 1.95 (ISBN 0-425-03767-3). Berkley Pub. Corp.
Luisita see Massage Parlor.
Lukan War. Michael Collins. (Orig.). 1969. pap. 0.60 o.p. (1023). Belmont-Tower.
Luke. Peter Winston. 1979. pap. 1.75 (ISBN 0-532-17126-8). Woodhill.
Luke Benedict. Michael Sidney Tyler-Whittle. LC 62-11168. 1962. Vanguard Press.
Luke Bennett's Hide Out: A Story of the War. C. B. Pseud. Ashley. LC 2928. (On cover: Medal library,no. 48). 1900. Street & Smith.
Luke Darby the "World" Detective: Or, Romance of the Dexter, Maine, Bank Robbery and Murder. Ernest A. Young. (On cover: The champion detective series, no. 19). 1887. J. S. Ogilvie & Company.
Luke Delmege. Patrick Augustine Sheehan. LC 55-9740. (Thomas More book to live). 1955. H. Regnery Co.
Luke Delmege. Patrick Augustine Sheehan. LC 1-27702. 1901. Longmans, Green, and Co.
Luke Hammond, the Miser: A Novel. William Henry Peck. LC 7-36476. (popular series. no. 7). 1891. R. Bonner's Sons.
Luke Hammond, the Miser: A Novel. William Henry Peck. LC 7-36475. (Ledger library. no. 131). 1896. R. Bonner's Sons.
Luke Sutton, Avenger. Leo P Kelley. LC 82-45560. (Double D western). 1983. 11.95 (ISBN 0-385-18396-8). Doubleday.
Luke Sutton, Gunfighter. Leo P Kelley. LC 81-43262. 1982. 9.95 (ISBN 0-385-17680-5). Doubleday.
Luke Sutton, Indian Fighter. Leo P Kelley. LC 81-43415. 1982. 10.95 (ISBN 0-385-17910-3). Doubleday.
Luke Sutton, Outlaw. Leo P Kelley. LC 80-2322. 1981. 9.95 (ISBN 0-385-17254-0). Doubleday.
Luke Sutton, Outlaw. large print ed. Leo P Kelley. LC 82-25169. 1983. 12.95 (ISBN 0-89340-563-9). J. Curley & Associates.
Luke Sutton: Outlaw. Leo P. Kelley. 1982. pap. 1.95 (ISBN 0-451-11522-8, AJ1522, Sig). NAL.
Lukong & the Leopard: The White Man of Cattle. Kenjo Jumban. (Secondary Readers Ser.). 1975. pap. text ed. 3.00x (ISBN 0-435-92425-7). Heinemann Ed.
Lull. Max Miller. LC 46-8289. 1946. Whittlesey House, McGraw-Hill Book Company, Inc.
Lullaby with Lugers. James Crockett. LC 46-8581. 1946. Crown Publishers.
Lulu. A Tale of the National Hotel Poisoning. Mansfield Tracy Walworth. LC 8-33123. 1863. Carleton.
Lumber. Louis Colman. LC 74-22773. (Labor Movement in Fiction and Non-Fiction). 1976. 17.50 (ISBN 0-404-58413-6). AMS Press.
Lumber. Louis Colman. LC 31-3407. 1931. Little, Brown, and Company.
Lumbering on the Cumberland: A Romance Taken from Life. A. A Brown. LC 18-208373. 1887. The Lumber Worker Company.
Luminous Face. Carolyn Wells. LC 21-154273. George H. Doran Company.
Luminous Isle. Eliot Bliss. LC 34-29540. Farrar & Rinhart, Incorporated.
Luminous Night: A Novel. George Lewis. LC 71-103433. 1970. 5.95. Dial Press.
Lumley: The Painter. Henrietta Eliza Vaughan Stannard. LC 8-13857. (On cover: Lovell's Westminster series. no. 40). 1891. J. W. Lovell Company.
Lummox. Fannie Hurst. LC 23-13730. 1923. Harper & Brothers.
Lump of Gold. Esther Baldwin Ferguson. LC 10-24712. Gilmartin Company.
Lump of Sugar & A Dash of Spice. Wauneta Hackleman. LC 80-80782. 1980. 9.95 (ISBN 0-89002-148-1); pap. 2.95 (ISBN 0-89002-147-3). Northwoods Pr.
Luna Benamor. Vicente Blasco Ibanez. Tr. by Isaac Goldberg. LC 19-12720. 1919. J. W. Luce & Company.
Lunar Attack. John Rankine, pseud. 1976. Repr. lib. bdg. 5.95 (ISBN 0-88411-675-1). Amereon Ltd.
Lunar Attack. John Rankine. (Space: 1999,#5). (Illus.). 1976. (pbk.) 1.50. Pocket Books.
Lunar Attractions. Clark Blaise. LC 77-16884. 1979. 8.95 (ISBN 0-385-13318-9). Doubleday.
Lunar Caustic. Malcolm Lowry. Ed. by Conrad Knickerbocker. LC 68-55826. (Cape Editions). 1968. 3.50 o.p. (ISBN 0-670-44439-1). Grossman.
Lunar Landscapes: Stories & Short Novels, 1949-1963. John Hawkes. LC 69-17827. (New Directions book). 1969. 5.95. New Directions.
Lunarian Professor and His Remarkable Revelations Concerning the Earth, the Moon and Mars: Together with an Account of the Cruise of the Sally Ann. James Bradun Alexander. LC 9-10024. 1909.
Lunatic at Large: A Novel. Joseph Storer Clouston. LC 5-11598. 1905. F. M. Buckles & Company.
Lunatic Fringe: A Novel Wherein Theodore Roosevelt Meets the Pink Angel. William L DeAndrea. LC 80-15065. 10.95 (ISBN 0-87131-325-1). M. Evans.
Lunatic in Charge. Joseph Storer Clouston. LC 26-14625. E. P. Dutton & Company.
Lunatic in Love. Joseph Storer Clouston. LC 27-21468. E. P. Dutton & Company.
Lunatic Still at Large. Joseph Storer Clouston. LC 24-14458. 1924. E. P. Dutton & Company.
Lunatic Time. John Roeburt. LC 56-4986. (Inner sanctum mystery). 1956. Simon and Schuster.
Lunatics & Other Lovers. Stan Hager. 1979. 10.00 o.p. (ISBN 0-912950-14-5); pap. 4.50 o.p. (ISBN 0-912950-13-7). Blue Oak.
Lupe. Gene Thompson. LC 77-6000. 8.95 (ISBN 0-394-41988-X). Random House.
Lupin Valley. (Harlequin Romances Ser.). 192p. 1983. pap. 1.75. Harlequin Bks.
Lupita: A Story of Mexico in Revolution. foreword by john a. mackay. ed. Alberto Rembao. LC 35-12190. Friendship Press.
Lurcher. Frank Walker. 1978. 8.95 o.p. (ISBN 0-440-05083-9). Delacorte.
Lure. Ethel Stefana Stevens Drower. LC 12-5840. 1912. John Lane Company.
Lure. Felice Picano. LC 79-12817. 9.95 (ISBN 0-440-05081-2). Delacorte Press.
Lure. George Scarborough. LC 14-9530. G. W. Dillingham Company.
Lure O' Gold. Bailey Millard. LC 4-15008. 1904. E. J. Clode.
Lure of a Dream. Neil Kiser Reid. LC 31-33896. 1931. Meador Publishing Company.
Lure of Crooning Water. Marion Hill. LC 13-199385. Small, Maynard and Company.
Lure of Distant Trails. John Clemons. LC 42-203244. 1942. Gateway Books.
Lure of Eagles. Anne Mather. (Harlequin Presents Ser.). (Orig.). 1979. pap. 1.50 (ISBN 0-373-70829-7). Harlequin Bks.
Lure of Fame. Clive Holland. LC 7-6132. 1896. New Amsterdam Book Company.
Lure of Hong Ke. James P Leynse. LC 51-15539. (Gusto classics). 1950. House-Warven.
Lure of Life. Agnes Sweetman Castle & Castle, Egerton. LC 12-24064. 1912. 1.35. N. Y., Doubleday, Page & Company.
Lure of the Bush. 1st Amer. Ed. Arthur William Upfield. LC 65-16180. 3.95. Pub. for the Crime Club by Doubleday.
Lure of the Cedars. Laurene E Henderson. LC 54-10242. 1954. Vantage Press.
Lure of the Dim Trails. Bertha Muzzy Sinclair. LC 7-328369. 1907. G. W. Dillingham Company.
Lure of the Dust: A Comedy of Rhodesia and the South Atlantic. Harding Forrester. LC 30-10716. The Century Co.
Lure of the Falcon. Juliette Benzoni. LC 78-13154. 1978. 8.95 (ISBN 0-399-12048-3). Putnam.
Lure of the Flame. Mark Danger. LC 13-22100. 1913. 1.25. The Macaulay Company.
Lure of the Hills: A Tale of Life in the Mountains of Kentucky. Mildred E Norbeck. LC 31-145496. Pub. for the Author by the Revivalist Press.
Lure of the Hills: A Tale of the Early Gold Days in the Black Hills. Will Henry Spindler. LC 37-19886. H. A. Burk & Co.
Lure of the Hills. 1st Ed. Frances Trippet Newell. LC 57-9292. 1957. Vantage Press.
Lure of the Indian Country. rev. ed. Aaron Abbott. LC 18-9865. A. Abbott.
Lure of the Indian Country: And a Romance of Its Great Resort. Aaron Abbott. LC 9-14823. A Abbot.
Lure of the Iron Trail. Ward William Adair. LC 13-381. 1912. Association Press.
Lure of the Land. Allena Joyce Webb. LC 34-34592. The Story Book Press.
Lure of the Little Drum. Margaret Peterson. LC 13-22820. 1913. 1.35. G. P. Putnam's Sons.
Lure of the Lorelei. Edward J Byrne. LC 40-11886. Dorrance and Company.
Lure of the Mask. Harold MacGrath. LC 8-177861. 1908. The Bobbs-Merrill Company.
Lure of the Mississippi. Dietrich Lange. LC 17-28332. 1917. 1.25. Lothrop, Lee & Shepard Co.
Lure of the North. Harold Bindloss. LC 18-74064. Frederick A. Stokes Company.
Lure of the North: A True Story of the Canadian Wilds. Albert Edward Jones. LC 47-16343. 1946.
Lure of the Outlaw Trail. Giles A Lutz. LC 78-19333. 1979. 7.95 (ISBN 0-385-14749-X). Doubleday.
Lure of the Purple Star. Maccowan Greenlee. LC 12-17800. 1.50. MacDaniel Publishing Company.
Lure of the West. Lillian Cawthra. LC 54-741287. 1954. Vantage Press.
Lure of the West. Mary Imeida Wallace. LC 24-28964. J. H. Meier.
Lure! Published Serially Under the Title Gems of Peril. Hazel Rose Hailey. LC 32-5747. Grosset & Dunlap.
Lured Away: Or, The Story of a Wedding-Ring. And The Heiress of Arne. Charlotte Mary Brame. (On cover: Seaside library. Pocket ed. no. 1155). 1889. G. Munro.
Lured from Home: Or, Alone in a Great City. Edna Winfield, pseud. LC 2367. (On cover: Holly library. no. 159)). 1900. The Mershon Co.
Lured into Dawn. Catherine Mills. (Second Chance at Love Ser.: No. 34). 192p. (Orig.). 1982. pap. 1.75 (ISBN 0-515-06162-X). Jove Pubns.
Lurker at the Threshold. Howard Phillips Lovecraft & August William Derleth. LC 46-439. (Arkham house novels of fantasy and terror). 1945. Arkham House.
Lurking Fear: And Other Stories. Howard Phillips Lovecraft. LC 48-20691. (New Avon library, 136). 1948. Avon Book Co.
Lurking Fear & Other Stories. Howard Phillips Lovecraft. 1982. pap. 2.25 (ISBN 0-345-30229-X, Del Rey). Ballantine.
Lurking Fear & Other Stories. Howard Phillips Lovecraft. 1971. pap. 0.95 o.p. (95042-095). Beagle Bks.
Luscious. James Noble Gifford. LC 39-33265. 1939. Phoenix Press.
Lush Valley. Patricia Campbell. LC 48-8170. 1948. Superior Pub. Co.
Lusiads. Camoens. Tr. by W. C. Atkinson. (Classics Ser.). (O.s.i.). 1973. pap. 2.25 o.p. (ISBN 0-14-044026-7, L26). Penguin.
Lusita. Sophie Treadwell. LC 31-25642. J. Cape & H. Smith.
Lusitania. David Butler. LC 82-40139. 1982. 17.95 (ISBN 0-394-52809-3). Random House.
Lust. Gerald Foster. LC 33-37453. 1934. W. Godwin, Inc.
Lust: A Novel. Gerald Foster. LC 49-51883. 1949. Balzac Press.
Lust & Liberty. Joseph Tusiani. 1963. 8.95 (ISBN 0-8392-1063-9). Astor-Honor.
Lust Club. Sylvia Sharon. pap. 0.95 o.p. Lancer.
Lust-Crazed Teen-Agers. Wilma Tarrant. 1974. (pbk.). 2.25 (ISBN 0-87682-415-7). Barclay House.
Lust for a Vampire. William Hughes. (Orig.). 1971. pap. 0.75 o.p. (94095). Beagle Bks.
Lust for Gold. Jack Slade. (Belmont Tower Books). 1.25. Tower Publications.
Lust for Life. Irving Stone. 1981. pap. 3.95 (ISBN 0-451-09898-6, E9898, Sig). NAL.
Lust for Life. Irving Stone. Ed. by Harry Shefter et al. (Illus.). pap. 0.75 o.p. (CC707, CC). WSP.
Lust for Life: A Novel of Vincent Van Gogh. Irving Stone. LC 54-12716. 1954. Doubleday.
Lust for Life: A Novel of Vincent Van Gogh. Irving Stone. LC 36-27320. The Heritage Press.
Lust for Life: The Novel of Vincent Van Gogh. Irving Stone. LC 39-27148. (Half-title: The modern library of the world's best books). 1939. The Modern Library.
Lust for Life: The Novel of Vincent Van Gogh. Irving Stone. LC 34-31642. 1934. Longmans, Green and Co.
Lust for Life: The Novel of Vincent Van Gogh. Irving Stone. LC 36-7194. 1935. Longmans, Green and Co.
Lust for Life: The Novel of Vincent Van Gogh... Irving Stone. LC 46-5745. (Pocketbooks. 344). 1945.
Lust for Murder. Henry Klinger. LC 66-24832. 1966. bds., 3.95. Trident.
Lust for Murder. Henry Klinger. (64006). 1968. Pocket Bks.
Lust Lovers. Geoffrey Kyle. 192p. pap. 1.95 o.p. (6117). Brandon.
Lust of Power. Henry Kane. LC 74-81283. 1975. 8.95 (ISBN 0-689-10642-4). Atheneum.
Lust of Power. Henry Kane. 1976. (pbk.) 1.75. Dell.
Lust Pit. Jason Dobbins. pap. 1.95 o.p. (8080). Cameo.
Lust Savages. Larry Booker. pap. 1.95 o.s.i. (Venus). Grove.
Lust Seekers. Peggy Gaddis, pseud. 1968. pap. 0.50 o.p. (B50-844). Belmont-Tower.
Lust Seekers. Robert E. Reynolds. Orig. Title: Backwoods Bride. 1970. pap. 0.75 o.p. (75-353). Manor Bks.
Lust Town. Marland M. Metcalf. pap. 1.95 o.p. (8046). Cameo.
Lust,Be a Lady Tonight. Rod Gray. (The Lady from L.U.S.T. Ser.). (O.s.i.). Orig. Title: Lady from L.U.S.T. 160p. 1973. pap. 0.95 o.s.i. (BT50516). Belmont-Tower.
Lustful Acts. Francoise Durer. 1972. pap. 1.95 o.s.i. (V1085T, Venus). Grove.
Lustful Female. Christopher Blue. 1972. pap. 1.75 o.s.i. (V10801T, Venus). Grove.
Lustful Maidens & Ascetic Kings: Buddhist & Hindu Stories of Life. Roy C. Amore & Larry D. Shinn. (Illus.). 176p. 1981. text ed. 16.95x (ISBN 0-19-502838-4); pap. 6.95 (ISBN 0-19-502839-2). Oxford U Pr.
Lustful Memoirs. pap. 1.75 o.p. (V1032K, Venus). Grove.
Lustful Memoirs of a Young and Passionate Girl & How We Lost Our Maidenheads & Realistic Pleasures. LC 70-180147. (Venus library). 1.75. Grove Press.
Lustmaster. A. Martinet. pap. 1.95 o.s.i. (Venus). Grove.
Lustre in the Sky: By R. G. Waldeck. Rosie Goldschmidt Waldeck. LC 46-3212. 1946. Doubleday & Company, Inc.
Lustres. Anne Parrish & Parrish, Dillwyn. LC 24-9272. George H. Doran Company.
Lustrous Heroine. Elizabeth Leavelle. LC 34-33669. Farrar & Rinehart, Incorporated.
Lusts of Don Dashell. 1st Ed. Edward Fisher Brown. LC 59-89976. 1959. Pageant Press.
Lusty. James Noble Gifford. 1949. Phoenix Press.
Lusty Wind for California. Inglis Clark Fletcher. 576p. 1980. pap. 2.95 (ISBN 0-553-13393-4). Bantam.
Lusty Wind for Carolina. Inglis Clark Fletcher. LC 52-974. 1951. Garden City Books.
Lusty Wind for Carolina. Inglis Clark Fletcher. LC 76-6506. 1976. 11.25 (ISBN 0-89244-003-1). Queens House.
Lusty Wind for Carolina. Inglis Clark Fletcher. LC 44-8968. 1944. The Bobbs-Merrill Company.
Lusty Winter. Max Braithwaite. LC 78-316891. 12.95 (ISBN 0-7710-1609-3). McClelland and Stewart.
Lutaniste of St. Jacobi's: A Tale. Catharine Drew. LC 6-34222. (Leisure hour series, no. 128). 1881. H. Holt and Company.
Lute Player. Norah Robinson Lofts. LC 51-13985. 1951. Doubleday.
Luther Nichols. Mary Stanbery Watts. LC 23-13574. 1923. The Macmillan Company.
Luther Strong: His Wooing and Madness. Thomas Jondrie Vivian. 1899. R. F. Fenno & Company.
Luttrell of Arran. Charles James Lever. LC 7-14479. (Seaside library, v. 43, no. 872). 1880. G. Munro.
Lux Crucis: A Tale of the Great Apostle. Samuel Major Gardenhire. LC 4-3586. 1904. Harper & Brothers.
Luxembourg Run. Stanley Ellin. LC 77-4751. 8.95 (ISBN 0-394-49646-9). Random House.
Luxury Cruise: A Novel. Joseph Deericks Bennett. LC 62-116679. 1962. G. Braziller.
Luxury Husband. Maysie Greig. LC 27-3100. Small, Maynard & Company.
Luxury Husband. Maysie Greig. LC 28-238286. 1928. L. MacVeagh, The Dial Press.
Luxury in a Tent. Carol M. Bohach & Susan Martin. LC 76-49395. 1977. pap. 1.75 o.p. (ISBN 0-87216-388-1, K16388). Playboy.
Luxury Liner. Gina Kaus. Tr. by Theis, Otto Frederick. LC 32-22981. 1932. R. Long & R. R. Smith, Inc.
Luxury Merchants. Richard Rosenthal. 1975. pap. 1.25 o.p. (ISBN 0-515-03683-8). Pyramid Pubns.
Luxury Nurse. Peggy Gaddis, pseud. 1970. pap. 0.50 o.p. (50-493). Manor Bks.
Luxury Nurse. Carol Morris. LC 46-36941. 1946. Arcadia House, Inc.
Luxury Sweetheart. Ann Sumner. LC 29-159322. A. L. Burt Company.
Lycanthia. Tanith Lee. (Science Fiction Ser). 1981. pap. 2.25 (ISBN 0-87997-610-1, UE1610). DAW Bks.
Lycanthrope: The Mystery of Sir William Wolf. Eden Phillpotts. 1938. The Macmillan Company.
Lyddy. Eugenia Jones Bacon. LC 77-37582. (Black Heritage Library Collection). 1972. (ISBN 0-8369-8958-9). Books for Libraries Press.
Lydeard Beauty. Audrey Blanshard. 1980. pap. 1.75 (ISBN 0-449-50016-0, Coventry). Fawcett.
Lydia. Clare Darcy. LC 77-14013. (Regency Romance). 1978. 9.95 (ISBN 0-89340-112-9). J. Curley.

Lydia. M. L. Lord. LC 6-20968. (Neely's popular library). 1895. F. T. Neely.
Lydia: A Novel. Lois T Henderson. LC 79-50946. 7.95 (ISBN 0-915684-32-2). Christian Herald Books.
Lydia: A Novel. Lois T Henderson. LC 82-48399. 1983. 6.89 (ISBN 0-06-063862-1). Harper & Row.
Lydia: A Tale of the Second Century. Hermann Geiger. LC 6-44256. 1867. E. Cummiskey.
Lydia: A Woman's Book. Camilla Dufour Toulmin Crosland. LC 6-31962. 1852. Ticknor, Reed, and Fields.
Lydia Bailey. Kenneth Lewis Roberts. LC 47-1541. 1947. Doubleday & Company, Inc.
Lydia Bailey. Kenneth Lewis Roberts. LC 46-11883. 1947. Doubleday & Company, Inc.
Lydia of Lebanon. E Palmer Smith. LC 19-18168. The Roxburgh Publishing Co., Inc.
Lydia of Old Cape Cod. Edith Bronson Tracy. LC 13-1902. 1912. The Matatuck Press Inc.
Lydia of the Pines. Honore McCue Willsie Morrow. LC 17-7817. Frederick A. Stokes Company.
Lydia of the Pines. Honore McCue Willsie Morrow. LC 21-12964. A. L. Burt Company.
Lydia; or, Filial Piety, Seventeen Fifty-Five, 4 vols. in 2. John Shebbeare. LC 74-17448. (Novel in England, 1700-1775 Ser). 1974. Set. lib. bdg. 90.00 (ISBN 0-8240-1143-0); lib. bdg. 50.00 ea. Garland Pub.
Lydia: Or, Love in Town. Clare Darcy. LC 72-95767. 1973. 6.95 (ISBN 0-8027-0408-5). Walker.
Lydia: Or Love in Town. Clare Darcy. (Signet book). 1974. (pbk.) 1.25. New American Library.
Lydia, or Love in Town. Clare Darcy. 256p. 1974. pap. 1.75 (ISBN 0-451-08272-9, E8272, Sig). NAL.
Lydia or Love in Town. Clare Darcy. (O.s.i.). 224p. 1973. 6.95 o.s.i. (ISBN 0-8027-0408-5). Walker & Co.
Lydia Trendennis. Frederick Smith. 1968. pap. 0.60 o.p. (53-715). Paperback Lib.
Lydian Inheritance. Iris Bromige. 1972. pap. 0.75 o.p. (94300). Beagle Bks.
Lydia's Little Plans. Elizabeth Hall Yates. LC 30-72009. The Penn Publishing Company.
Lying Days: A Novel. Nadine Gordimer. LC 53-108135. 1953. Simon and Schuster.
Lying Ladies. Robert Finnegan. LC 46-187977. 1946. Simon and Schuster.
Lying Low. Diane Johnson. LC 78-54910. 1978. 8.95 (ISBN 0-394-49890-9). Knopf.
Lying Prophets: A Novel. Eden Phillpotts. 1896. F. A. Stokes Company.
Lying Three. large print ed. Ralph M McInerny. LC 81-9001. 1981. 10.95 (ISBN 0-89621-304-8). Thorndike Press.
Lying Three: A Father Dowling Mystery. Ralph M McInerny. LC 78-68734. 8.95 (ISBN 0-8149-0819-5). Vanguard Press.
Lying Woman. Jean Giraudoux. Tr. by Richard Howard from Fr. Orig. Title: Menteuse. 1972. 6.95 o.s.i. (ISBN 0-87806-017-0). Winter Hse.
Lynch Lawyers. William Patterson White. LC 20-625. 1920. Little, Brown, and Company.
Lynch-Rope Law. Davis Dresser. LC 50-13683. (Triple-A western classic). 1950. Jefferson House.
Lynch-Rope Law. Davis Dresser. LC 41-14544. 1941. W. Morrow and Company.
Lynch Town. George G. Gilman, pseud. (Steele Ser.: No. 11). 1978. pap. 1.50 (ISBN 0-523-40370-4, Dist. by Independent News Co.). Pinnacle Bks.
Lynchers. John Edgar Wideman. LC 72-91841. 1973. 6.95 (ISBN 0-15-154800-5). Harcourt Brace Jovanovich.
Lynchers. John Edgar Wideman. 1974. (pbk.) 0.95. Dell.
Lynching at Broken Butte. Lewis B Patten. LC 73-22536. 1974. 4.95 (ISBN 0-385-01800-2). Doubleday.
Lynching at Broken Butte. Lewis B Patten. LC 83-203. 1983. 11.95 (ISBN 0-8161-3470-7). G.K. Hall.
Lynching of Orin Newfield. Gerald Jay Goldberg. LC 78-120464. 1970. 5.95. Dial Press.
Lynch's Daughter. Leonard Merrick. LC 8-29737. 1908. The McClure Company.
Lynchtree County. Robert H. Robinson. (Orig.). 1980. pap. 2.50 o.s.i. (ISBN 0-505-51553-9). Tower Bks.
Lyndall's Temptation: Or, Blinded by Love. A Story of Fashionable Life at Lenox. Laura Jean Libbey. LC 11-15076. 1892. N. L. Munro.
Lynde Weiss: An Autobiography... Thomas Bangs Thorpe. 1852. Lippincott, Grambo & Co.
Lyndell Sherburne: A Sequel to Sherburne House. Amanda Minnie Douglas. LC 6-33475. (The Sherburne series). Dodd, Mead & Company.
Lynette. Lorena Dureau. 352p. (Orig.). 1983. pap. 2.95 (ISBN 0-523-41638-5). Pinnacle Bks.
Lynette and the Innocent Bystanders. Elise Howard-Smith. LC 33-31882. 1933. The John C. Winston Company.
Lynmara Legacy. Catherine Gaskin. LC 75-14987. 1976. 8.95 (ISBN 0-385-11205-X). Doubleday.
Lynmara Legacy. Catherine Gaskin. 1977. 1.95 (ISBN 0-449-23060-0). Fawcett Crest.
Lynn Malone's Daughter: A Novel of Marriage. Kay Lipke. LC 35-6270. 1935. Frederick A. Stokes Company.
Lyonesse. Jack Vance, pseud. 448p. (Orig.). 1983. pap. 6.95 (ISBN 0-425-05873-5). Berkley Pub.
Lyonesse Abbey. Jill Tattersall. LC 68-28674. 1968. 5.50. W. Morrow.
Lyon's Pride. Mary S. Craig. 352p. 1983. pap. 3.50 (ISBN 0-515-05295-7). Jove Pubns.
Lyra, My Love. Jan Temest. 1969. 3.50 o.p. (50-4995). Moody.
Lyra, My Love. Jan Tempest. LC 79-80949. 1969. 3.50. Moody Press.
Lyre and Lancet: A Story in Scenes. Thomas Anstey Guthrie. LC 6-46690. 1895. Macmillan and Co.
Lyrics of Lowly Life. Paul Laurence Dunbar. LC 71-78573. lib. bdg. 16.00 (ISBN 0-8398-0373-7); pap. text ed. 5.25x (ISBN 0-89197-832-1). Irvington.
Lys dans la Vallee. Honore De Balzac. (Coll. Prestige). 27.95. French & Eur.
Lys Rouge see Romans et Contes.
Lysander. Francis Van Wyck Mason. LC 57-5161. (Pocket book, 1143 3). Pocket Books.
Lysbeth, a Tale of the Dutch. with twenty-six illustrations by g. p. jacomb hood... new impression. ed. Henry Rider Haggard. LC 20-18824. (Half-title: The silver library). 1918. Longmans, Green and Co.
Lysette. Ena Holliday. (Tapestry Romance Ser.). (Orig.). 1983. pap. 2.50 (ISBN 0-671-46165-6). PB.
Lyubka, the Cossack, and Other Stories. Isaak Emmanuilovich Babel. LC 63-25545. (Signet classic). 1963. New American Library.

M

M: A Detective Novel. Leonard Falkner. LC 31-5738. H. Holt and Company.
M. A. S. H. rev. ed. David S. Reiss. 176p. 1983. pap. 9.95 (ISBN 0-672-52762-6). Bobbs.
M. C. Higgins the Great. Virginia Hamilton. 1976. pap. 1.75 (ISBN 0-440-95598-X, LFL). Dell.
M. D. Neil Ravin. 1982. pap. 3.50 (ISBN 0-440-15307-7). Dell.
M. Fontaine's Establishment. LC 73-85145. (Venus library, V-1001). 1969. 1.75. Grove Press.
M. I. M. Morrow Wilson. 1974. 10.00. Liberation Bk.
M. or N. Whyte-Melville, George John. LC 75-32792. (Literature of Mystery and Detection). 1976. (2 vols. in one) 35.00 (ISBN 0-405-07908-7). Arno Press.
M. or N. "Similia Similibus Curantur.". new ed. George John Whyte-Melville. LC 44-33120. (On cover: Select library of fiction.). Ward, Lock and Co.
M. S. Bradford, Special: A Marvelous Story of the Day. Archibald Clavering Gunter. LC 99-2589. (On cover: The welcome series, no. 46). The Home Publishing Company.
M Thirty-Three in Andromeda. Alfred Elton Van Vogt. (Orig.). 1971. pap. 0.95 o.p. (ISBN 0-446-65584-8, 65-584). Paperback Lib.
Ma." A Companion to "Pa.". Jacob Ralph Abarbanell. LC 5-42189. (Munro's library. v. 50, no. 734). N.L. Munro.
Ma and Me. William Ornstein. LC 52-3991. 1952. Story Book Press.
Ma and Me. 2d Ed. William Ornstein. LC 54-209681. 1953. Story Book Press.
Ma Cinderella. Harold Bell Wright. LC 32-231341. 1932. Harper & Brothers.
Ma Dalton. Rene de Goscinny. (Lucky Luke Ser.). (French.). 1976. 5.95x (ISBN 2-205-00585-5). Intl Learn Syst.
Ma Jones and the Little White Cannibals. Kylie Tennant, pseud. LC 67-99394. (B 67-14850). 1967. Macmillan.
Ma Pettengill. Harry Leon Wilson. LC 19-584481. 1919. Doubleday, Page & Company.
Ma Pettengill. Harry Leon Wilson. LC 35-33421. 1924. Doubleday, Page & Company.
Mabel: A Story. Robert Creeley. 176p. 1979. 11.95 (ISBN 0-7145-2505-7, Pub. by M Boyars). Merrimack Pub Cir.
Mabel and May. A Novel. Dora Delmar. (On cover: Laurel library. no. 15). 1893. G. Munro's Sons.
Mabel Clement. John Milton Sallee. LC 3-18177. 1903. The National Baptist Publishing House.
Mabel Clifton. A Novel. Frank Brierwood. 1869. Claxton, Remsen & Haffelfinger.
Mabel Lee. A Novel. Frances Christine Tiernan. LC 3291. 1895. D. Appleton and Company.
Mabel Seymour: Or, A Strange Detective. Charles Matthew. (On cover: Secret service series, no. 41). 1891. Street & Smith.
Mabel Stanhope: A Story. Kathleen O'Meara. LC 7-24099. 1886. Roberts Brothers.
Mabel Tarner: An American Primitive. Harry Kemp. LC 36-30328. L. Furman, Inc.
Mabel Vaughan. new ed. Maria Susanna Cummins. LC 6-31735. 1885. Houghton, Mifflin and Company.
Mabinogi & Other Medieval Welsh Tales. Ed. by Patrick K. Ford. LC 76-3885. 1977. 20.00x (ISBN 0-520-03205-5); pap. 3.95 (ISBN 0-520-03414-7). U of Cal Pr.
Mabinogion. Tr. by Gwyn Jones & Thomas Jones. 1975. 9.95x (ISBN 0-460-00097-7, Evman); pap. 2.50x (ISBN 0-460-01097-2, Evman). Biblio Dist.
Mable's Fables. Mable Scott. 3.95 o.p. (ISBN 0-8111-0435-4). Naylor.
Mac: A Dog's True Story, with Portraits from Life. Mary Kellogg Johnson. LC 7-10545. 1895. H. H. Carter & Company.
Mac & the Princess. Bruce Calhoun. (O. s. i.). 1976. 9.95 o.p. (ISBN 0-933054-01-7); pap. 6.95 o.p. (ISBN 0-933054-02-5). Ricwalt Pub Co.
Mac & the Princess. Bruce Calhoun. (O. s. i.). 1976. 9.95 o.s.i. (ISBN 0-933054-01-7); pap. 6.95 o.s.i. (ISBN 0-933054-02-5). Ricwalt Pub Co.
Mc Lean Intervenes. George Goodchild. 256p. 1973. lib. bdg. 5.95 o.s.i. White Lion Pubs.
Mac of Placid. Thomas Morris Longstreth. LC 20-14293. 1920. The Century Co.
Mc Veys (an Episode) Joseph Kirkland. LC 7-12517. 1888. Houghton, Mifflin and Company.
Macabre Manor. Elizabeth Grayson. 1974. (pbk.) 0.95. Manor Books.
Macabre Mansion. Luanna Churchill. 1973. 4.95. Lenox Hill Pr.
McAfee County: A Chronicle. Mark Steadman. LC 77-155532. (Illus.). 1971. 6.95 (ISBN 0-03-080212-1). Holt, Rinehart and Winston.
McAllister. Matt Chisholm, pseud. 1971. pap. 0.75 o.p. (94072). Beagle Bks.
McAllister and His Double. Arthur Cheney Train. LC 76-110220. (Short story index reprint series). (Illus.). 1970. Books for Libraries Press.
McAllister and His Double. Arthur Cheney Train. LC 5-32328. 1905. C. Scribner's Sons.
McAllister Fights. Matt Chisholm, pseud. 1971. pap. 0.75 o.p. (94175). Beagle Bks.
McAllister Gambles. Matt Chisholm, pseud. 1971. pap. 0.75 o.p. (94947-075). Beagle Bks.
McAllister Justice. Matt Chisholm, pseud. (Western Ser). 1971. pap. 0.95 o.p. (94144). Beagle Bks.
McAllister Makes War. Matt Chisholm, pseud. 1971. pap. 0.75 o.p. (94084). Beagle Bks.
McAllister Rides. Matt Chisholm, pseud. (Boxer Ser). 1971. pap. 0.75 o.p. (94128). Beagle Bks.
McAllister Says No. Matt Chisholm, pseud. (Boxer Ser). 1971. pap. 0.75 o.p. (94112). Beagle Bks.
McAllister Strikes. Matt Chisholm, pseud. 1971. pap. 0.75 o.p. (94163). Beagle Bks.
McAllister's Grove. Marion Hill. LC 17-13950. 1917. D. Appleton and Company.
Macamba. Lilla Van Saher. LC 49-156719. 1949. E. P. Dutton.
McAndrew Chronicles. Charles Sheffield. (Tor Bks.). 288p. (Orig.). 1983. pap. 2.95 (ISBN 0-523-48566-2). Pinnacle Bks.
Macaria. Augusta Jane Evans Wilson. LC 4-868. 1868. Carleton.
Macaria: A Novel. Augusta Jane Evans Wilson. (On cover: Arrow library, no. 30). 1899. Street & Smith.
Macaria: Or, Altars of Sacrifice. 2d ed. Augusta Jane Evans Wilson. 1864. West & Johnston.
Macaria; or, Altars of Sacrifice. Augusta Jane Evans Wilson. LC 79-162234. (Confederate Imprints Collection Ser.). 183p. 1973. Repr. of 1864 ed. 8.00 o.p. (ISBN 0-405-04339-2). Arno.
McAuslan in the Rough, and Other Stories. George MacDonald Fraser. LC 74-7720. 1974. 6.95 (ISBN 0-394-49303-6). Knopf.
McAuslan in the Rough, and Other Stories. George MacDonald Fraser. LC 77-355611. 1976. 0.60 (ISBN 0-330-24633-X). Pan Books.
Macaw: The Story of a Parrot. Peggy Von Der Goltz. LC 37-18105. 1937. Farrar and Rinehart.
McBain's Brier Rose. Helen Campbell Dickson Reynolds. LC 57-126911. 1957. T. Bouregy.
McBee's Station. Elise Ayers Sanguinetti. LC 74-138868. 1971. 6.95 (ISBN 0-03-086013-X). Holt, Rinehart and Winston.
McBroom the Rainmaker. Albert Sidney Fleischman. LC 73-4458. (Thistle Book). (Illus.). 1973. 4.99 (ISBN 0-448-21479-2). Grosset & Dunlap.
McCabe: A Novel. Edmund Naughton. LC 59-9710. 1959. Macmillan.
McCaffery. Charles Gorham. 1970. pap. 0.75 o.p. (75-322). Manor Bks.
McCarthy's List. Mary Mackey. LC 78-73189. 1979. 10.00 (ISBN 0-385-14527-6). Doubleday.
McCarty Incog. Isabel Egenton Ostrander. 1922. R. M. McBride & Company.
McCloud. Collin Wilcox. (McCloud Ser.). (O.s.i.). 1973. pap. 0.95 o.s.i. (AN1203, Award). Univ Pub & Dist.
McCord. Gil Martin. (Berkley medallion book). 1974. (pbk) 0.75 (ISBN 0-425-02481-4). Berkley Pub. Co.
McCormack's Mountain. Amanda Hart Douglass. 1980. pap. 2.25 (ISBN 0-8439-0835-1). Nordon Pubns.
McDade. Wayne C. Ulsh. 1981. pap. 1.95 (ISBN 0-8439-0875-0, Leisure Bks). Nordon Pubns.
McDermot? A Story of Life in Ireland in the Eighteenth Century. Jonathan Periam. LC 7-36348. (On cover: Globe library. v. l, no. 169). 1892. Rand, McNally & Company.
Macdermots of Ballycloran. Anthony Trollope. LC 78-12604. (Ireland, from the Act of Union, 1800, to the Death of Parnell, 1891; 53). 1979. 96.00 (ISBN 0-8240-3502-X). Garland Pub.
Macdermots of Ballycloran. reprint ed. / introduction by n. john hall. ed. Anthony Trollope. LC 80-1874. (Trollope, Anthony, 1815-1882. Selections. 1981). 1981. (3 vol. set) 105.00 (ISBN 0-405-14118-1). Arno Press.
Macdermots of Ballycloran. Anthony Trollope & Thorold, Algar Labouchere, Ed. LC 12-39448. (Half-title: The new pocket library. xxxv). 1906. John Lane.
Macdermots of Ballyeloran. Anthony Trollope. (seaside library. v. 72, no. 1455). 1882. G. Munro.
McDermott's Sky. Robert J Serling. LC 77-14000. 1977. 8.95 (ISBN 0-930392-00-0). Laurel Group.
McDermott's Sky. Robert J Serling. 1980. 1.95 (ISBN 0-671-82869-X). Pocket Books.
McDonald of Oregon: A Tale of Two Shores. Eva Emery Dye. 1906. A. C. McClurg & Co.
McDonalds: Or, The Ashes of Southern Homes. A Tale of Sherman's March. William Henry Peck. LC 12-31368. 1867. Metropolitan Record Office.
McDonough: A Novel. 1st Ed. Francis T Field. LC 51-9611. 1951. Duell, Sloan and Pearce.
McDowell's Ghost. Jack Cady. LC 81-66974. 256p. 1981. 14.50 (ISBN 0-87795-343-0). Arbor Hse.
McDowell's Ghost: A Tale of the Border South. Jack Cady. LC 81-66974. 14.50 (ISBN 0-87795-343-0). Arbor House.
Mace & the Plume. Jeanne Lancour. (Age of Chivalry Ser.: Bk. 3). 320p. 1982. pap. 3.25 (ISBN 0-440-06457-0, Emerald). Dell.
McECKr'n. John F Hopkins. LC 79-22920. 10.00 (ISBN 0-312-52365-3). St. Martin's Press.
McElroy: A Novel. Marvin Richard O'Connell. LC 79-26067. 11.95 (ISBN 0-393-01358-8). Norton.
McFlannels United. Helen W Pryde. LC 50-1311. 1949. Nelson.
McGarr and the Politician's Wife. Bartholomew Gill. LC 81-15802. (Penguin crime fiction). 1982. 2.95 (ISBN 0-14-005984-9). Penguin.
McGarr and the Politician's Wife: A Mystery Novel. Mark McGarrity. LC 76-49831. 6.95 (ISBN 0-684-14851-X). Scribner.
McGarr & the Sienese Conspiracy. Bartholomew Gill. 1980. pap. 2.25 (ISBN 0-440-15784-6). Dell.
McGarr and the Sienese Conspiracy. Mark McGarrity. LC 77-24570. 1977. 7.95 (ISBN 0-684-15185-5). Scribner.
McGarr at the Dublin Horseshow. Mark McGarrity. LC 79-18232. 1979. 8.95 (ISBN 0-684-16388-8). Scribner.
McGarr on the Cliffs of Moher. Bartholomew Gill. LC 82-506. 1982. 2.95 (ISBN 0-14-006197-5). Penguin Books.
McGarr on the Cliffs of Moher. Mark McGarrity. LC 78-2645. 7.95 (ISBN 0-684-15570-2). Scribner.
McGarrity & the Pigeons. John Cecil Holm. LC 47-4755. 1947. Rinehart.
McGillicuddy McGotham. Illustrated by Aldren A. Watson. 1st Ed. Leonard Wibberley. LC 56-7964. Little, Brown.
McGillicuddy McGotham: ReissueIllus. by Aldren A. Watson. Leonard Patrick O'Connor Wibberley. LC 66-1809. 1966. 3.75. Morrow.
McGinnis Speaks. 1st Ed. Frank Rooney. LC 60-7429. 1960. Harcourt, Brace.
McGivern. Theodore V. Olsen. 160p. 1982. pap. 2.25 (ISBN 0-449-14465-8, GM). Fawcett.
McGlusky's Great Adventure. A. G. Hales. LC 17-16320. 1917. Hodder and Stoughton.
McGrandad an Elephant & Other Stories. Vokom M. Bashear. Tr. by R. E. Ascher from Malaym. 1981. 12.50x (ISBN 0-85224-386-3, Pub. by Edinburgh U Pr Scotland); pap. 6.50x (ISBN 0-85224-408-8, Pub. by Edinburgh U Pr Scotland). Columbia U Pr.
McGraw's Inheritance. John Thomas Edson. 176p. 1981. pap. 1.95 (ISBN 0-425-05073-4). Berkley Pub.
McGuires. Robert F. Wagner. 4.00 o.p. Carlton.
Mach One see Terror on Planet Ionus.

Mach 1: A Story of Planet Ionus. Allen A Adler. LC 57-121531. 1957. Farrar, Straus and Cudahy.

Macha Doon & Other Stories. T. Huntington. 4.95 o.p. (ISBN 0-8062-1132-6). Carlton.

M'hashish. Mohammed Mrabet. LC 70-88228. 1969. 1.50. City Lights Books.

Machiavellian Madam of Basin Street & Other Tales of New Orleans. Edward Larocque Tinker. 1969. 6.95 (ISBN 0-88426-019-4). Encino Pr.

Machiavellian Marquess. Freda Michel. (Fawcett Crest Book). 1977. 1.50 (ISBN 0-449-23348-0). Fawcett Books.

Machine-God Laughs. Pragnell. 3.50; pap. 1.50. Fantasy Pub Co.

Machine to Kill. Gaston Leroux. LC 36-4921. 1935. The Macaulay Company.

Machineries of Joy. Ray Bradbury. 1963. 6.95 o.p. (ISBN 0-671-43830-1). S&S.

Machineries of Joy: Short Stories. Ray Bradbury. (H2988). 1965. Bantam.

Machismo. Gramm Hall. 1971. pap. 0.95 o.p. (ISBN 0-447-75157-3). Lancer.

Macho! By Villasenor. Edmund Villasenor. LC 73-10044. 1973. (pbk) 0.95. Bantam Books.

Macho Callahan. Joe Millard, pseud. (O.s.i.). (Orig.). 1970. pap. 0.95 o.s.i. (AN1447, Award). Univ Pub & Dist.

Macho Camacho's Beat. Luis Rafael Sanchez. LC 80-7713. 10.00 (ISBN 0-394-50976-5). Pantheon Books.

McHugh. Jay Flynn. 1970. Repr. pap. 0.75 o.p. (75-342). Manor Bks.

McIvor Affair. Margaret Way. 192p. 1982. pap. 1.50 (ISBN 0-373-02454-1). Harlequin Bks.

MacIvor's Folly. Hugh MacNair Kahler & Herring, Donald Grant. LC 25-4987. 1925. D. Appleton and Company.

Mack. Carl Bruno Adams. LC 19-16360. Saulsbury Publishing Company.

McKay's Bees. Thomas McMahon. LC 78-20211. 8.95 (ISBN 0-06-012974-3). Harper & Row.

McKay's Bees. Thomas McMahon. (Bard Book). 1981. 2.75. Avon Books.

McKee of Centre Stree: A Detective Novel of the New York Police. Helen Kieran Reilly. LC 34-216. 1934. Pub. for the Crime Club, Inc., by Doubleday, Doran & Company, Inc.

McKee of Centre Street. Helen Kieran Reilly. 299p. 1980. Repr. of 1933 ed. lib. bdg. 14.25x (ISBN 0-89968-214-6). Lightyear.

McKee of Centre Street: A Detective Novel of the New York Police. Helen Kieran Reilly. LC 43-27168. 1943. The Sun Dial Press.

McKeever. Vina Delmar. LC 76-18210. 8.95 (ISBN 0-15-158320-X). Harcourt Brace Jovanovich.

MacKenna's Gold. Henry Allen. LC 63-8336. 1963. Random House.

Mackenzie Raid: By Red Reeder. Russell Potter Reeder & Ranald Slidell ---Fiction Mackenzie. LC 55-11309. 1955. Ballantine Books.

Mackerel Sky: A Conversation Piece. Helen Ashton. LC 31-3186. 1931. Doubleday, Doran and Company, Inc.

Mackin Cover. Diane K. Shah. 1977. 7.95 o.p. (ISBN 0-396-07511-8). Dodd.

Mackin Cover. Diane K. Shah. LC 79-88830. 240p. 1979. pap. 1.95 (ISBN 0-87216-518-3). Playboy Pbks.

Mackin Cover: A Novel of Suspense. Diane K Shah. LC 77-22710. 7.95. Dodd, Mead.

Mackinac and Lake Stories. Mary Hartwell Catherwood. LC 69-11881. (American short story series, v. 39). (Illus.). 1969. Garrett Press.

Mackinac and Lake Stories. Mary Hartwell Catherwood. LC 72-8309. (American short story series, v. 39). 1972. (ISBN 0-8422-8023-5). MSS Information Corp.

Mackinac and Lake Stories. Mary Hartwell Catherwood. LC 99-488785. 1899. Harper & Brother.

Macking Gangster. Charlie Avery Harris. 1976. (pbk.) 1.50 (ISBN 0-87067-491-9). Holloway House.

Maclarens. Clement Lister Skelton. LC 77-18715. (His The regiment quartet; v. 1). 9.95 (ISBN 0-8037-5131-1). Dial Press/J. Wade.

Maclarens. Clement Lister Skelton. 1979. 2.50 (ISBN 0-440-15703-X). Dell Pub. Co.

McLaren's Men. Robert W. Marsh. 1979. pap. 1.75 o.s.i. (ISBN 0-505-51435-4). Tower Bks.

McLean Deduces. George Goodchild. 256p. 1973. lib. bdg. 5.95 o.s.i. (ISBN 0-85617-063-1). White Lion Pubs.

McLean Investigates. George Goodchild. 280p. 1973. lib. bdg. 5.95 o.s.i. (ISBN 0-85617-681-8). White Lion Pubs.

McLean Scores Again. George Goodchild. 192p. 1973. lib. bdg. 5.95 o.s.i. (ISBN 0-85617-886-1). White Lion Pubs.

McLean Solves It. George Goodchild. 192p. 1973. lib. bdg. 5.95 o.s.i. (ISBN 0-85617-691-5). White Lion Pubs.

Macleod of Dare. William Black. LC 6-13856. (Lakeside library, v. 9, no. 242). Donnelley, Gassette & Loyd.

Macleod of Dare. William Black. (Franklin square library. no. 25). 1878. Harper & Brothers.

Macleod of Dare. William Black. (Seaside library, v. 21, no. 417). G. Munro.

Macleod of Dare. William Black. (Lovell's library, v. 3, no. 93). 1883. J. W. Lovell Company.

Macleod of Dare: A Novel. illustrated by j. pettie... t. graham, g. h. boughton and others... ed. William Black. LC 42-27475. 1879. Harper & Brothers.

Macleod of Dare: A Novel. illustrated by j. pettie... t. graham, g. h. boughton etc. ed. William Black. LC 4-16499. 1903. Harper & Brothers.

McLeod of the Camerons. M Hamilton. LC 7-945. (Half-title: Appletons' town and country library, no. 207). 1897. D. Appleton and Company.

M'lord, I Am Not Guilty. Frances Shelley Wees. LC 54-681728. 1954. Published for the Crime Club by Doubleday.

M'lord O' the White Road. Cedric Fraser. LC 22-15975. 1922. D. Appleton and Company.

McLoughlin and Old Oregon. Eva Emery Dye. LC 36-4102. 1936. Wilson-Erickson, Inc.

McLoughlin and Old Oregon: A Chronicle. Eva Emery Dye. LC 3335. 1900. A. C. McClurg & Co.

McLoughlin and Old Oregon: A Chronicle. Eva Emery Dye. 1921. Doubleday, Page & Company.

MacLyon: A Novel. Lolah Burford. LC 73-21292. 1974. 8.95 (ISBN 0-02-518190-4). Macmillan.

McMasters. Dean Owen. (O.s.i.). 1970. pap. 0.75 o.s.i. (A544S, Award). Univ Pub & Dist.

McMaster's Horses. Ken Redenius. 1980. pap. 1.75 (ISBN 0-8439-0848-3). Nordon Pubns.

MacNamara's Gold. Archie Joscelyn. (Avalon Books). 4.95. Thomas Bouregy.

McNeills Chase a Ghost. Theodora McCormick Du Bois. LC 41-19802. 1941. Houghton Mifflin Company.

MacOrvan Curse. Florence Bowes. LC 79-48086. 1980. 8.95 (ISBN 0-385-15844-0). Doubleday.

McQ: A Novel. Alexander Edwards. 1974. (pbk.) 1.25. Warner Paperback Lib.

MacQuaid. Shepard Rifkin. LC 73-87204. 1974. 5.95 (ISBN 0-399-11267-7). Putnam.

McQuaid in August. Shepard Rifkin. LC 78-69665. 1979. 7.95 (ISBN 0-385-14561-6). Published for the Crime Club by Doubleday.

Macrabre Manor. Elizabeth Grayson. 1978. pap. 1.25 o.p. (ISBN 0-532-12548-7). Woodhill.

Macrabre Manor. Elizabeth Grayson. 1978. pap. 1.25 o.p. (ISBN 0-532-12548-7). Manor Bks.

Macrolife. George Zebrowski. LC 76-26283. (Illus.). 12.50 (ISBN 0-06-014792-X). Harper & Row.

Macroscope. Piers Anthony, pseud. 1969. pap. 3.95 (ISBN 0-380-00209-4, 81992-9). Avon.

McSmash. Timothy Harris. LC 76-97666. 1970. 4.95. Doubleday.

McSorley's Wonderful Saloon. Joseph Mitchell. LC 43-11949. 1943. Duell, Sloan and Pearce.

McTaggart's Promise. Bernard Alvin Palmer. LC 77-78499. 2.95 (ISBN 0-89191-088-3). D. C. Cook Pub. Co.

MacTaggart's War. Ralph Dennis. 1980. 2.50 (ISBN 0-445-04546-9). Fawcett Popular Library.

McTeague. Frank Norris. LC 23-7733. (Half-title: The modern library of the world's best books). 1918. Boni and Liveright Inc.

McTeague: A Story of California. Frank Norris. LC 72-184736. 1971. lib. bdg. 12.50x (ISBN 0-8376-0406-0). Bentley.

McTeague: A Story of San Francisco. Frank Norris. LC 67-3229. (His Complete works, v. 8). 1967. Kennikat Press.

McTeague, a Story of San Francisco. Frank Norris. LC 50-12507. (Rinehart editions, 40). 1950. Rinehart.

McTeague: A Story of San Francisco. Frank Norris. LC 99-1053. 1899. Doubleday & McClure Co.

McTeague: A Story of San Francisco. Frank Norris. LC 20-19511. 1920. Doubleday, Page & Company.

McTeague: A Story of San Francisco. Frank Norris & Kevin Starr. LC 82-12307. (Penguin American library). 1982. 3.95 (ISBN 0-14-039017-0). Penguin Books.

McTeague: A Story of San Francisco: an Authoritative Text, Backgrounds and Sources, Criticism. Frank Norris & Donald Pizer. LC 77-479. (Norton critical edition). 12.95 (ISBN 0-393-04460-2). Norton.

McTodd. Charles John Cutcliffe Wright Hyne. LC 3-21015. 1903. The Macmillan Company.

Maculan's Daughter. Sarah Gainham. LC 73-87188. 1974. 8.95 (ISBN 0-399-11255-3). Putnam.

McVeys see Collected Works.

McVey's Valley. Ray Gaulden. LC 65-122399. (Double D western). 3.50. Doubleday.

Mad About a Boy. Jon Marsh. pap. 1.95 o.s.i. (TC-507, Travellers Comp). Olympia.

Mad, and Short Stories. Guy De Maupassant. LC 10-732090. 1910. The Pearson Publishing Co.

Mad Around the World. Frank Jacobs & Peter P. Porges. (Illus.). 192p. 1979. pap. 1.50 (ISBN 0-446-88390-5). Warner Bks.

Mad As the Mist and Snow: A Novel. Oliver Robinson. LC 54-668415. 1957. Bruce Humphries.

Mad Barbara. Warwick Deeping. LC 9-3879. 1909. 1.50. Harper & Brothers.

Mad Betrothal. A Novel. Laura Jean Libbey. (On cover: The popular series, no. 36). 1893. R. Bonner's Sons.

Mad Betrothal: Or, Nadine's Row. A Novel. Laura Jean Libbey. (On cover: The choice series, no. 1). 1890. R. Bonner's Sons.

Mad Book of Mysteries. Lou Silverstone & Jack Rickard. (Illus.). 192p. (Orig.). 1980. pap. 1.75 (ISBN 0-446-84843-3). Warner Bks.

Mad Book of Word Power. Max Brandel. (Illus.). 192p. 1973. pap. 1.50 (ISBN 0-446-88736-6). Warner Bks.

Mad Busman: And Other Stories. Ida Alexa Ross Wylie. LC 26-14518. George H. Doran Company.

Mad Camerons: A Novel of New Hampshire. 1st Ed. Agnes Finlay Sinniger. LC 55-7288. 1955. Exposition Press.

Mad Carews. Martha Ostenso. LC 27-21133. 1927. Dodd, Mead and Company.

Mad Dictator: A Novel of Adolph Hitler. Frances Bonker. LC 50-8049. 1950. Chapman & Grimes.

Mad Dog of Europe. Albert Nesor. LC 40-1220. 1939. Epic Publishers, Inc.

Mad Dog Press Archives. J. Spencer Grendahl. 1970. 5.95 o.p. (ISBN 0-399-10513-1). Putnam.

Mad Dog Press Archives: A Novel. J. Spencer Grendahl. LC 73-112933. 1970. 5.95. Putnam.

Mad Dumaresq. Florence Marryat Church Lean. LC 7-13607. (On cover: Lovell's library. v. 20. no. 991). 1887. J. W. Lovell Company.

Mad Empress of Callisto. Lin Carter. 1975. (pbk.) 0.95. Dell.

Mad Goblin see Lord of the Trees.

Mad God's Amulet. Michael Moorcock. (Science Fiction Ser.). 1977. pap. 1.95 (ISBN 0-87997-688-8, UJ1688). DAW Bks.

Mad Grandeur: A Novel. Oliver St. John Gogarty. LC 41-246256. J. B. Lippincott Company.

Mad-Gun Mesa. Francis W Hilton. 1937. H. C. Kinsey & Company, Inc.

Mad Hatter Mystery. John Dickson Carr. LC 33-30825. 1933. Harper & Brothers.

Mad Hatter's Holiday. Peter Lovesey. LC 73-6027. (Red badge novel of suspense). 1973. 4.95 (ISBN 0-396-06835-9). Dodd, Mead.

Mad Hatter's Holiday. Peter Lovesey. LC 77-3684. 1977. 7.95 (ISBN 0-89340-062-9). J. Curley.

Mad Hatter's Holiday. Peter Lovesey. LC 80-20878. 1981. 2.50 (ISBN 0-14-005804-4). Penguin Books.

Mad Hatter's Village. Mary Cavendish Gore. LC 34-2558. A. H. King.

Mad Heroes. facs. ed. Joseph Tenenbaum. LC 75-134983. (Short Story Index Reprint Ser.). 1931. 12.00 (ISBN 0-8369-3713-9). Ayer Co.

Mad Heroes: Skeletons and Sketches of the Eastern Front. Joseph Tenenbaum. LC 75-134983. (Short story index reprint series). 1970. Books for Libraries Press.

Mad Heroes: Skeletons and Sketches of the Eastern Front. Joseph Tenenbaum. LC 31-1719. 1931. A. A. Knopf.

Mad Honeymoon. Ella Wister Haines. LC 30-13234. A. L. Burt Company.

Mad Is the Heart. Denise Robins. 1972. pap. 0.75 o.p. (94305). Beagle Bks.

Mad King. Edgar Rice Burroughs. LC 26-16083. 1926. A. C. McClurg & Co.

Mad Lodge Mystery. G M Belloome. LC 64-8636. Greenwich Book Publishers.

Mad Look at the Future. Lou Silverstone & Jack Rickard. (Illus.). 192p. (Orig.). 1978. pap. 1.50 (ISBN 0-446-88174-0). Warner Bks.

Mad Love. Charlotte Mary Brame. LC 1-29655. (Bertha Clay library, no. 41). 1900. Street & Smith.

Mad Love. Courteney Grant. LC 6-44738. (On cover: Seaside library. Pocket ed no. 510). G. Munro.

Mad Love: Or, The Abbe and His Court. (La Conquete De Plassans. Emile Zola & Sherwood, Mrs. Mary (Neal) Tr. LC 9-1319. T. B. Peterson & Brothers.

Mad Love: The Strange Story of a Musician. Frank Harris. LC 20-7421. 1920. The Author.

Mad Lover. Richard Edward Connell. LC 27-6201. 1927. Minton, Balch & Company.

Mad Madonna, and Other Stories. Louise Clarkson Whitelock. LC 8-36554. 1895. J. Knight Company.

Mad Make-Out Book. Larry Siegel & Angelo Torres. (Illus.). 192p. (Orig.). 1979. pap. 1.75 (ISBN 0-446-94441-6). Warner Bks.

Mad Marriage. Laura Lou Brookman. LC 31-939014. Grosset & Dunlap.

Mad Marriage. George Fort Gibbs. LC 25-16817. 1925. D. Appleton and Company.

Mad Marriage. A Novel. May Agnes Early Fleming. LC 36-29333. 1875. G. W. Carleton & Co.

Mad Masquerade. Lorin Andrews Lathrop. LC 28-9052. 1928. Houghton Mifflin Company.

Mad Melody. William Charles Lengel. A.H. King, Inc.

Mad Monk. Reginald Thomas Maitland Scott. LC 31-29822. C. Kendall.

Mad Monkton & Other Stories. Wilkie Collins. Repr. lib. bdg. 11.15x (ISBN 0-89190-242-2). Am Repr-Rivercity Pr.

Mad Moon. Mary Ann Van Ness Austin. LC 42-1400. Press of Zion's Printing & Publishing Co.

Mad Murder. Richard Hill Wilkinson. LC 31-24650. 1931. Meador Publishing Company.

Mad O'Hara of Wild River. Jackson Gregory. LC 39-259570. 1939. Dodd, Mead & Company.

Mad Prank. Margaret Wolfe Hungerford. LC 7-9352. (On cover: Mayflower library, no. 12). 1893. J. A. Taylor & Company.

Mad Puppetstown. Mary Nesta Skrine Keane. LC 32-26950. Farrar & Rinehart, Incorporated.

Mad Puppetstown. Mary Lesta Skrine. LC 32-239591. 1932. Farrar & Rinehart, Incorporated.

Mad Rapture. Elizabeth Irons Folsom. LC 26-151898. The Macaulay Company.

Mad River. Donald Hamilton. LC 56-807713. (Dell first edition, 91). 1956. Dell Pub. Co.

Mad River Guns. Lee Floren. 176p. 1975. pap. 0.95 o.p. (ISBN 0-532-95384-3). Woodhill.

Mad River Guns. Lee Floren. 1965. pap. 0.50 o.p. (50-476). Manor Bks.

Mad River Guns. Lee Floren. 176p. 1975. pap. 0.95 o.p. (ISBN 0-532-95384-3). Manor Bks.

Mad Scientist: A Tale of the Future. Raymond McDonald. LC 8-20021. 1908. Cochrane Publishing Co.

Mad Shadows. Translated from the French by Merloyd Lawrence. Marie Claire Blais. LC 60-438286. 1960. McClelland & Stewart.

Mad Shepherdess. Hugh Brooke. LC 30-3767. 1930. Longmans, Green and Co.

Mad Shepherds, and Other Human Studies. Lawrence Pearsall Jacks. LC 73-125223. (Short story index reprint series). (Illus.). 1970. Books for Libraries Press.

Mad Shoemaker. John Batki. 1973. pap. 3.00 o.p. (ISBN 0-915124-01-7). Toothpaste.

Mad Sir Peter. Frank Dilnot. LC 32-20150. 1932. The Macmillan Company.

Mad Sir Uchtred of the Hills. Samuel Rutherford Crockett. LC 6-315921. 1894. Macmillan & Co.

Mad-Song. Mabel Wagnalls. LC 26-790550. 1926. Funk & Wagnalls Company.

Mad Stew. Nick Meglin. (Illus.). 192p. (Orig.). 1978. pap. 1.75 (ISBN 0-446-94437-8). Warner Bks.

Mad Stone. Lorna Doone Beers. LC 32-7123. 1932. E. P. Dutton & Co., Inc.

Mad Sucks. (Mad Ser.: No. 50). (Illus.). 192p. (Orig.). 1979. pap. 1.75 (ISBN 0-446-94377-0). Warner Bks.

Mad-Vertising. Dick DeBartolo & Bob Clarke. (Illus.). 192p. (Orig.). 1979. pap. 1.50 (ISBN 0-446-98100-1). Warner Bks.

Mad with Much Heart. Gerald Alfred Butler. LC 45-8633. 1945. Jarrolds Limited.

Mad with Much Heart. Gerald Alfred Butler. LC 46-18820. 1946. Rinehart & Company, Inc.

Madalena. Sheila Walsh. (Signet Book). 1977. 1.50 (ISBN 0-451-07457-2). New American Library.

Madam. Richmond Brooks Barrett. LC 32-17148. Liveright, Inc.

Madam. Margaret Oliphant Wilson Oliphant. (On cover: Seaside library. Pocket ed., no. 345). 1885. G. Munro.

Madam. Ethel Sidgwick. LC 21-4509. Small, Maynard & Company.

Madam. A Novel. Margaret Oliphant Wilson Oliphant. (Harper's Franklin square library, no. 435). 1884. Harper & Brothers.

Madam Ambassador. Ned Calmer. LC 74-24484. 1975. 7.95 (ISBN 0-385-05106-9). Doubleday.

Madam Big. Barry Devlin. LC 53-8842. 1953. Vixen Press.

Madam Cinderella. Maurice Carter. LC 31-25264. Arlington Publishing Co.

Madam Constantia: The Romance of a Prisoner of War in the Revolution (South Carolina. Jefferson Carter. LC 19-3702. 1919. 1.50. Longmans, Green and Co.

Madam Crowl's Ghost: And Other Tales of Mystery. Joseph Sheridan Le Fanu. LC 72-167459. (Short story index reprint series). 1971. (ISBN 0-8369-3985-9). Books for Libraries Press.

Madam Erika's Girls. Trisha Stevens. 1973. (pbk.) 1.25 (ISBN 0-671-78333-5). Pocket Books.

Madam, I'll Give You-- Kathleen Wallace. LC 35-14568. 1935. Doubleday, Doran and Company, Inc.

Madam Is Dead. Robert Terrall. LC 47-311363. (A bloodhound mystery). 1947. Duell, Sloan and Pearce.

Madam Jumel: By Ray Brown. Raymond Barrington Brown. LC 65-26227. 1966. pap., 1.95. Magna Carta.

Madam Kitty. Peter Norden. 1977. pap. 1.50 (ISBN 0-345-24228-9). Ballantine.

Madam Midas. A Realistic and Sensational Story of Australian Mining Life. Fergus Hume. (On cover: Seaside library. Pocket ed., no. 1127). 1888. G. Munro.

Madam of the Ivies. Elizabeth Phipps Train. LC 8-29729. 1898. J. B. Lippincott Company.

Madam President-Elect: A Novel. 1st Ed. Samuel Jonathan Warner. LC 56-8723. 1956. Exposition Press.

Madam Sapphira: A Fifth Avenue Story. Edgar Evertson Saltus. LC 77-113268. 1970. (ISBN 0-404-05533-8). AMS Press.

Madam Satan. Harry Sinclair Drago & MacPherson, Jeanie, Joint Author. LC 30-24057. A. L. Burt Company.

Madam Sex Thief. Robert Moore, pseud. pap. 1.95 o.s.i. (OPH-239, Ophelia). Olympia.

Madam Will Not Dine Tonight. Hillary Waugh. LC 47-11495. (gargoyle mystery). 1947. Coward-McCann.

Madam, Will You Talk? Mary Stewart. LC 56-5634. 1956. M. S. Mill Co. and W. Morrow.

Madame. John Selby. LC 61-13016. 1961. Dodd, Mead.

Madame. A Novel. Frank Lee Benedict. LC 7-34451. 1877. G. W. Carleton & Co.; Etc., Etc.

Madame Agnes. Charles Dubois. 1874. Catholic Publication Society.

Madame and Her Twelve Virgins. Edward Phillips Oppenheim. LC 27-1236. 1927. Little, Brown, and Company.

Madame Aubry and the Police: By Hugh Travers. 1st U. S. Ed. Hugh Travers Mills. LC 67-11338. bds., 4.50. Harper.

Madame Aubry Dines with Death. Hugh Travers Mills. LC 67-23282. 1967. Harper & Row.

Madame Baltimore. A Novel of Suspense. Helen Davis Herrick Knowland. LC 49-253587. (Red badge detective). 1949. Dodd, Mead.

Madame Blavatsky: Priestess of the Occult. Gertrude M. Williams. 1970. pap. 1.25 o.p. (ISBN 0-447-78651-2). Lancer.

Madame Bluebeard: A Case for Anatole Fox. Bruce Sanders. LC 57-6611. 1957. Roy Publishers.

Madame Bovary. Gustave Flaubert. LC 70-6894. (Riverside editions, C115). 1969. 1.50. Houghton Mifflin.

Madame Bovary. Gustave Flaubert. Tr. by Eleanor Marx Aveling. LC 71-2807. 1969. 4.95. F. Watts.

Madame Bovary. Gustave Flaubert. LC 57-5214. 1957. Random House.

Madame Bovary. Gustave Flaubert. Tr. by Eleanor Marx Aveling. LC 73-76838. (Great illustrated classics). (Illus.). 1969. Dodd, Mead.

Madame Bovary. Gustave Flaubert. Tr. by Aveling, Eleanor (Marx) LC 48-18939. (Living Library). 1948. World Pub. Co.

Madame Bovary. Gustave Flaubert. LC 48-8477. (Rinehart editions, 2). 1948. Rinehart.

Madame Bovary. Gustave Flaubert. Ed. by Maugham, William Somerset. LC 49-108020. (Ten Greatest Novels of the World). 1949. J. C. Winston Co.

Madame Bovary. Gustave Flaubert. Tr. by Eleanor Aveling. LC 19-65603. (Half-title: The modern library of the world's best books). 1918. Boni and Liveright, Inc.

Madame Bovary. Gustave Flaubert. Tr. by Eleanor Aveling. 1919. A. A. Knopf.

Madame Bovary. Gustave Flaubert. Tr. by Eleanor Aveling. Saintsbury, George Edward Bateman, 1845-1928. (Half-title: Everyman's library, ed. by Ernest Rhys. Fiction. no. 808). 1928. J. M. Dent & Sons, Ltd.

Madame Bovary. Gustave Flaubert. Tr. by Eleanor Aveling. (Universal library). 1931. Grosset & Dunlap.

Madame Bovary: A Story of Provincial Life. Gustave Flaubert. LC 76-6694. (Hart classics). (Illus.). 9.95 (ISBN 0-8055-1200-4). Hart Pub. Co.

Madame Bovary: A Study of Provincial Life. Gustave Flaubert & Ranous, Mrs. Dora Knowlton (Thompson) 1859-1916, Ed. LC 21-21696. (Lettered on cover: The iotus library). 1919. Brentano's.

Madame Bovary: A Tale of Provincial Life. Gustave Flaubert & Sherwood, Mrs. Mary (Neal) Tr. LC 6-39914. T. B. Peterson & Brothers.

Madame Bovary. Backgrounds and Sources; Essays in Criticism. Ed. with a Substantially New Tr. by Paul De Man. Gustave Flaubert. Ed. by Paul De Man. LC 65-22074. (Norton crit. eds.) Bibl.). pap., 1.95. Norton.

Madame Bovary: Life in a Country Town. Gustave Flaubert. Tr. by Hopkins, Gerard. LC 49-3232. (World's classics. Galaxy ed., 5). 1949. Oxford Univ. Press.

Madame Bovary: Or, Loved to the Last. Gustave Flaubert. Tr. by Eleanor Aveling. LC 6-39913. (library of choice fiction. no. 26). 1891. Laird & Lee.

Madame Bovary. Provincial Manners. Gustave Flaubert. Tr. by Aveling, Eleanor (Marx) LC 2-1093. (Seaside library. Pocket ed., mo. 2232). 1904. G. Munro's Sons.

Madame Bovary: Translated from the French by Marx Aveling; with an Introd. by Caroline Gordon. Gustave Flaubert. (Harper's modern classics). 1950. Harper.

Madame Bovery. Gustave Flaubert. Tr. by Eleanor Aveling. LC 44-15330. (Comedie d'armour series). 1915. Societe Des Beaux-Arts.

Madame Buccaneer. Gardner F Fox. LC 53-35244. (Gold medal books, 328). 1953. Fawcett Publications.

Madame Butterfly. japanese ed. John Luther Long. 1903. The Century Co.

Madame Butterfly; Purple Eyes; A Gentleman of Japan and a Lady; Kito; Glory. John Luther Long. LC 98-503. 1898. The Century Co.

Madame Butterfly: Purple Eyes, Etc. John Luther Long. LC 68-55684. (American short story series, v. 25). 1969. Garrett Press.

Madame Butterfly, Purple Eyes, Etc. John Luther Long. LC 72-8177. (American short story series, v. 25). 1972. (ISBN 0-8422-8092-8). MSS Information Corp.

Madame Casanova. Gaby Von Schonthan. LC 75-91016. 1969. 6.95. Meredith Press.

Madame Casanova. Gaby Von Schoenthan. 1969. 5.95 o.p. (ISBN 0-696-69658-4). Hawthorn.

Madame Castel's Lodger. Frances Parkinson Wheeler Keyes. LC 62-20209. 1962. Farrar, Straus and Cudahy.

Madame Chrysantheme. Pierre Loti. Tr. by Laura Ensor. LC 72-77522. (Illus.). 1973. pap. 2.50 o.p. (ISBN 0-8048-1025-7). C E Tuttle.

Madame Chrysantheme. Julien Viaud. LC 72-77522. (Tut books. L). (Illus.). 1973. 2.50 (ISBN 0-8048-1025-7). C. E. Tuttle Co.

Madame Chrysantheme. Julien Viaud. Tr. by Robins, E. P. LC 8-29994. (On cover: The optimus series, no. 18). 1892. Donohue, Henneberry & Co.

Madame Chrysantheme. Julien Viaud & Ensor, Laura, Tr. (Half-title: The modern library of the world's best books). The Modern Library.

Madame Claire. Susan Ertz. LC 23-752426. 1923. D. Appleton and Company.

Madame Claire. Susan Ertz. LC 24-371526. 1924. D. Appleton and Companu.

Madame Claire. Susan Ertz. LC 29-307813. 1926. A. L. Burt Company.

Madame Clapain. Edouard Estaunie. LC 33-25686. 1933. D. Appleton-Century Company, Incorporated.

Madame De. Louise De Vilmorin. LC 54-10596. 1954. J. Messner.

Madame De Beaupre. Henrietta Camilla Jackson Jenkin. LC 7-10197. 1869. Leypoldt & Holt.

Madame De Chamblay. Alexandre Dumas. LC 6-42330. (On cover: Turner's select series no. 1). Turner Brothers & Co.

Madame De Mailly: Or, The Love Affairs of King Louis Xv. Alexandre Dumas. LC 6-43608. (On cover: Seaside library. Pocket ed. no. 2096). G. Munro's Sons.

Madame De Maurescamp. A Story of Parisian Life. Octave Feuillet & Page, Beth, Tr. LC 6-39519. 1889. J. B. Lippincott Company.

Madame De Presnel. Eleanor Frances Poynter. (On cover: Seaside library Pocket ed. no. 526). 1885. G. Munro.

Madame De Stael. Bella Duffy. 1887. lib. bdg. 20.00 (ISBN 0-8414-9103-8). Folcroft.

Madame De Stael: An Historical Novel. Amely Bolte & Johnson, Theodore, Tr. LC 6-14183. 1869. G. P. Putnam & Son.

Madame De Treymes. Edith Newbold Jones Wharton. 1907. C. Scribner's Sons.

Madame de Treymes & Others. Edith Newbold Jones Wharton. LC 73-100130. 1973. pap. 5.95 (ISBN 0-684-13235-4, SL419, ScribT); lib. bdg. 20.00 (ISBN 0-684-17283-6). Scribner.

Madame De Treymes, and Others: Four Novelettes. Edith Newbold Jones Wharton. LC 73-100130. (Scribner lib. of contemporary classics). 1973. 2.95 (ISBN 0-684-13235-4). Scribner's.

Madame Delphine. George Washington Cable. LC 74-80649. 1969. AMS Press.

Madame Delphine. George Washington Cable. LC 71-121308. 1970. Scholarly Press.

Madame Delphine. George Washington Cable. LC 11-10533. 1881. C. Scribner's Sons.

Madame Delphine. George Washington Cable. (The ivory series). 1896. C. Scribner's Sons.

Madame Delphine. George Washington Cable. (The ivory series). 1909. C. Scribner's Sons.

Madame Delphine see Collected Works.

Madame D'Orgevaut's Husband. Henry Rabusson. Tr. by Potter, Frank Hunter. LC 7-42424. Dodd, Mead and Company.

Madame Dorthea. Sigrid Undset & Chater, Arthur G., Tr. LC 40-11818. 1940. A. A. Knopf.

Madame Flowery Sentiment. Albert Gervais. Tr. by Dixon, Campbell. LC 37-17027. Covic-Friede.

Madame Geneva. Elaine Dakers. LC 46-629991. 1946. Rinehart & Company, Inc.

Madame Gilbert's Cannibal. Frederick Harcourt Kitchin. LC 21-206777. E. P. Dutton & Company.

Madame Goldenflower. C. Y. Lee. LC 75-2697. 1975. 15.25 (ISBN 0-8371-8030-9). Greenwood Press.

Madame Izan: A Tourist Story. Rosa Caroline Murray-Prior Praed. LC 99-2149. (Half-title: Appleton's town and country library, no. 264). 1899. D. Appleton and Company.

Madame Jane Junk and Joe. A Novel. Mars Bornemann. LC 6-15028. 1876. A. L. Bancroft and Company.

Madame Judas. Margaret Turnbull. LC 26-12595. 1926. J. B. Lippincott Company.

Madame Jumel. Pauline Panzer. LC 61-18409. Rolton House Publishers.

Madame Lucas... Eleanor P. Bell Wells. LC 8-366464. (Round-robin series). 1882. J. R. Osgood and Company.

Madame Maigret's Own Case. Georges Simenon. LC 59-15002. 1959. Published for the Crime Club by Doubleday.

Madame Maillart. Claude Aveline. LC 33-3290. E. P. Dutton & Co., Inc.

Madame Margot: A Grotesque Legend of Old Charleston. John Bennett. LC 21-196523. (Lettered on cover: The bat series). 1931. 1.00. The Century Co.

Madame Margot: A Grotesque Legend of Old Charleston. John Bennett. LC 33-36229. (On cover: The bat series). 1933. The Century Co.,

Madame Margot: A Legend of Old Charleston. John Bennett. LC 51-13406. 1951. University of South Carolina Press.

Madame Paradox: A Novel. Maud W Ormerod. LC 99-3829. D. Biddle.

Madame Pompadour's Garter. A Thrilling and Historical Romance of the Reign of Louis Xv. Gabrielle De St. Andre. LC 6-39353. T. B. Peterson & Brothers.

Madame Prince. William Pett Ridge. LC 16-24204. George H. Doran Company.

Madame Rosa. Emile Ajar. (Berkley book). 1979. 1.95 (ISBN 0-425-04036-4). Berkley Pub. Corp.

Madame Rosely. Victorine Monniot. Tr. by Quintero, Elvira & Mack, Jean. LC 7-31118. 1893. Cassell Publishing Company.

Madame Sans-Gene: Founded on the Play. Edmond Adolphe de Bouhelier Lepelletier & Sardou, Victorien 1831-1908. LC 1-17012. (On cover: American series, no. 350). M. J. Ivers & Co.

Madame Sans-Gene: Historical Romance of the Revolution, the Consulate & the Empire by Victorien Sardou in Collaboration with Emile Moreau and Edmond Lepelletier. Edmond Adolphe De Bouhelier Lepelletier. LC 2-11479. 1895. Drallop Pub. Co.

Madame Sans-Gene: "Madame Don't-Care". Edmond Adolphe De Bouhelier Lepelletier & Sardou, Victorien, 1831- LC 1-17011. (On cover: Arcadian series, no. 33). 1895. Optimus Printing Company.

Madame Sans-Gene: "Madame Don't-Care". Edmond Adolphe de Bouhelier Lepelletier & Sardou, Victorien, 1831-1908. (On cover: Arrow library. no. 148). 1900. Street & Smith.

Madame Serpent. Eleanor Hibbert. LC 74-28549. 1975. 7.95 (ISBN 0-399-11506-4). Putnam.

Madame Serpent. Eleanor Hibbert. 1975. (pbk.) 1.50 (ISBN 0-425-03024-5). Berkley Pub. Co.

Madame Serpent. Jean Plaidy. LC 74-28549. 1975. 7.95 o.p. (ISBN 0-399-11506-4). Putnam Pub Group.

Madame Serpent: By Jean Plaidy Pseud. Eleanor Hibbert. LC 51-760. 1951. Appleton-Century-Crofts.

Madame Silva: Also The Ghost of Dred Power. Margaret Greenway McClelland. LC 7-15267. Cassell & Company, Limited.

Madame Solarie: A Novel. LC 56-8564. 1956. Viking Press.

Madame Solario. 1978. pap. 3.95 (ISBN 0-14-004199-0). Penguin.

Madame Solario: A Novel. Gladys Parish Huntington. LC 56-8564. 1956. Viking Press.

Madame Solario: A Novel. LC 56-856459. 1956. Viking Press.

Madame Storey. Hulbert Footner. LC 26-18504. George H. Dran Company.

Madame Tahiti: Decorations by Yvonne De Saint-Cyr. Andre De Wissant & Vernon, Grenville, 1883- Tr. LC 33-34991. W. F. Payson.

Madame Tellier's Establishment: And Short Stories. Guy De Maupassant. LC 10-7484. 1910. The Pearson Publishing Co.

Madame Tellier's Girls (La Maison Tellier) The Inheritance (L'heritage) Butter-Ball (Boule De Suif) Three Masterpieces. Guy De Maupassant. Tr. by Ellis, Edwin. (Dillingham's metropolitan library, no. 22). 1897. G. W. Dillingham Co.

Madame Therese. Emile Erckmann & Chatrian, Alexandre, 1826-1890, Joint Author. LC 6389. 1900. American Book Company.

Madame Therese. Emile Erckmann & Chatrian, Alexandre, 1826-1890, Joint Author. LC 10-7508. (Heath's modern language series). 1910. D. C. Heath & Co.

Madame Therese. Emile Erckmann & Chatrian, Alexandre, 1826-1890, Joint Author. Ed. by Florence B. Williams et al. LC 33-2209. (Chicago French Ser.). (Half-title: The Chicago French series). The University of Chicago Press.

Madame Therese. Emile Erckmann & Chatrian, Alexandre, 1826-1890, Joint Author. LC 33-25043. American Book Company.

Madame Therese. Emile Erckmann & Chatrian, Alexandre, 1826-1890, Joint Author. LC 27-5648. (International modern language series). Ginn and Company.

Madame Therese: Or, The Volunteers of '92. Emile Erckmann & Chatrian, Alexandre, I.E. Louis Gratien Charles Alexandre, 1826- 1890, Joint Author. LC 6-39364. 1869. C. Scribner and Company.

Madame Therese: Or, The Volunteers of '92. Emile Erckmann & Chatrian, Alexandre, 1826-1890, Joint Author. LC 6-39368. (Half-title: Erckmann-Chatrian national novels). 1889. C. Scribner's Sons.

Madame Therese: Or, The Volunteers of '92. Emile Erckmann & Chatrian, Alexandre, 1826-1890, Joint Author. LC 98-1211. 1898. C. Scribner's Sons.

Madame Therese: Ou Les Volontaires De '92. Emile Erckmann & Chatrian, Alexandre, 1826-1890, Joint Author. LC 12-26484. (Romans historiques, no. III.). 1866. H. Holt and Company Etc.

Madame Therese: Ou Les Volontaires De '92. Emile Erckmann & Chatrian, Alexandre, 1826-1890, Joint Author. LC 12-32147. 1897. H. Holt and Company.

Madame Treymes & Others: Four Novelettes. Edith Newbold Jones Wharton. 1970. 6.95 o.p. (ISBN 0-684-10642-6). Scribner.

Madame Valcour's Lodger. Florence Olmstead. LC 22-743973. 1922. C. Scribner's Sons.

Madame Valerie: A Novel. Francis Charles Philips. LC 7-36070. 1892. D. Appleton and Company.

Madame X: A Story of Mother-Love. J. W McConaughy & Bisson, Alexandre Charles Auguste, 1848-1912. LC 38-127561. 1911. Grosset & Dunlap.

Madame X: A Story of Motherlove. J. W McConaughy & Bisson, Alexandre Charles Auguste, 1848-1912. LC 11-6385. The H. K. Fly Company.

Madball. Fredric Brown. LC 53-10777. (Dell first edition, 2 E). 1953. Dell Pub. Co.

Madcap. George Fort Gibbs. LC 13-23734. 1913. 1.30. D. Appleton and Company.

Madcap. Peggy O'More, pseud. LC 40-6541. Gramercy Publishing Co.

Madcap Violet. William Black. LC 6-12325. (Lovell's library, v. 4, no. 178). J. W. Lovell Company.

Madcap Violet. William Black. LC 11-105383. (Seaside library. Pocket ed. no. 78). G. Munro.

Maddening Scar: A Mystery Novel. Dorothy Randle Clinton. LC 62-173171. 1962. Christopher Pub. House.

Madder Music. Mildred Cram. LC 30-3849. 1930. Little, Brown, and Company.

Madder Music. Peter De Vries. LC 77-9355. 1977. 8.95 (ISBN 0-316-18190-0). Little, Brown.

Madder Music. Peter De Vries. LC 81-19994. 1982. 3.95 (ISBN 0-14-006133-9). Penguin Books.

Madder Music. Peter DeVries. 1982. pap. 3.95 (ISBN 0-14-006133-9). Penguin.

Made for Love. James Noble Gifford. LC 32-193533. 1932. W. Godwin, Inc.

Made for Man. Alan Patrick Herbert. LC 58-12047. 1958. Doubleday.

Made for Murder. Fenn McGrew. LC 54-7075. (Murray Hill mystery). 1954. Rinehart.

Made for TV: A Novel. Richard Breen. LC 82-4325. 12.95 (ISBN 0-8253-0103-3). Beaufort Books.

Made in America. Peter Maas. LC 79-12789. 1979. 9.95 (ISBN 0-670-44555-X). Viking Press.

Made in America. George Madden Martin. LC 35-15039. 1935. D. Appleton-Century Company Incorporated.

Made in France. facs. ed. Henry Cuyer Bunner. LC 71-94707. (Short Story Index Reprint Ser.). 1893. 12.00 (ISBN 0-8369-3085-1). Ayer Co.

Made in France: French Tales Retold with a United States Twist. Henry Cuyler Bunner. LC 71-94707. (Short story index reprint series). (Illus.). 1969. Books for Libraries Press.
Made in France;" French Tales Retold with a United States Twist. Henry Cuyler Bunner & Taylor, Charles Jay, 1855-1929, Illus. LC 6-18672. (On Cover: Puck's Mulberry Series, No. 8). 1893. Keppler & Schwarzmann.
Made in Heaven. Rosie Blake. 1972. 5.95 o.p. (ISBN 0-316-09936-8). Little.
Made in Heaven: A Novel. Rosie Blake. LC 78-187785. 1972. 5.95. Little, Brown.
Made in Heaven: A Novel of a Famous Family Shattered by Tragedy. Tracy Hotchner. LC 81-4299. 1981. 11.95 (ISBN 0-688-00663-9). Morrow.
Made in His Image. Cyril Arthur Edward Ranger Gull. LC 6-34372. 1906. G. W. Jacobs & Co.
Made in Japan. Glen Chase, pseud. (Cherry Delight Ser.). 1976. pap. 1.25 o.p. (LB423ZK, Leisure Bks). Nordon Pubns.
Made in Japan. Glen Chase. 1976. 1.25 (ISBN 0-8439-0042-3). Leisure Books.
Made in USA: A Novel. Alfred Kern. LC 65-193175. 4.95. Houghton.
Made to Order: Short Stories from a College Course. Ed. by Gustavus Howard Maynadier. 1915. L. A. Noble.
Made up to Kill. Kelley Roos. LC 40-136291. 1940. Dodd, Mead & Company.
Madeira Party. Also, "A Little More Burgundy". Silas Weir Mitchell. LC 7-31094. 1895. The Century Co.
Madelaina. Michaela Morgan. 1977. 2.50. Pinnacle Books.
Madelaine Darth a Novel. E. L Ford. LC 6-41404. 1867. Western News Company.
Madeleine. Catherine Irvine Gavin. LC 57-11756. 1957. St. Martin's Press.
Madeleine. Celia Roberts. Ed. by John Milne. (Heinemann Guided Readers Ser.). 1978. pap. text ed. 1.75x (ISBN 0-435-27053-2). Heinemann Ed.
Madeleine. A Love Story. Jules Sandeau. LC 8-5795. T. B. Peterson & Brothers.
Madeleine: a Story of French Love. Crowned by the French Academy.) Translated from the French. Of Jules Sandeau. Jules Sandeau & Charlot, Francis, Tr. LC 8-4773. (On verso of half-title: Tales from foreign tongues. IV). 1879. Jansen, McClurg & Co.
Madeleine: A Tale of Auvergne, Founded on Fact. by julia kavanagh... ed. Julia Kavanagh. LC 7-11121. 1857. D. Appleton and Company.
Madeleine Austrian: A Novel. Robert R Kirsch. LC 60-10991. 1960. Simon and Schuster.
Madeleine Eparvier. Andre Theuriet. LC 8-27742. (On cover: Idylwild series, v. 1, no. 19). 1892. Morrill, Higgins & Co.
Madeleine Ferat. Emile Zola. 1957. 13.95 (ISBN 0-236-30907-2, Pub. by Paul Elek). Merrimack Pub Cir.
Madeleine Ferat. Tr. from French by Alec Brown. Emile Zola. LC 57-36257. 1965. bds., 3.95. Elek Bks.
Madeleine Heritage. Martin Boyd. LC 28-7754. The Bobbs-Merrill Company.
Madeline. Roswell Martin Field. LC 6-21389. 1906.
Madeline. A Novel. Mary Jane Hawes Holmes. LC 7-6023. G. W. Carleton & Co.
Madeline of the Desert. Arthur Edward Pearse Brome Weigall. LC 20-201892. 1920. Dodd, Mead and Company.
Madeline Payne, the Detective's Daughter. Emma Murdoch Van Deventer. (On cover: The detective and adventure library, no. 3). A. T. Loyd & Co.
Madeline, the Island Girl. Anna Johnson. LC 6-13937. Eaton & Mains.
Madelon. Florence Stonebraker. LC 44-80295. 1944. Phoenix Press.
Madelon: A Novel. Mary Eleanor Wilkins Freeman. LC 16-3400. Harper & Brothers.
Mademoiselle B. A Novel. Maurice Pons. LC 73-89042. 1974. 6.95. St. Martin's Press.
Mademoiselle Bismarck: From the French of Henri Rochefort, by Virginia Champlin Pseud. Victor Henri Rochefort-Lucay & Lord, Grace Virginia, D. 1885, Tr. LC 7-39794. (On cover: Trans-Atlantic novels. v. 5). 1881. G. P. Putmam's Sons.
Mademoiselle Blanche: A Novel. John Daniel Barry. LC 4-16262. (Half-title: Canvas-back library of popular fiction, vol. i). 1904. J. Lane.
Mademoiselle Celeste: A Romance of the French Revolution. Adele Ferguson Knight. LC 10-10698. 1910. 1.50. G. W. Jacobs & Company.
Mademoiselle Dahlia. Winifred Mary Scott. LC 28-21587. 1928. Doubleday, Doran & Company, Inc.
Mademoiselle De Berny: A Story of Valley Forge. Pauline Bradford Mackie Cavendish. LC 7-13309. 1897. Lamson, Wolffe and Company.
Mademoiselle De Berny: A Story of Valley Forge. Pauline Bradford Mackie Hopkins. LC 7-13309. 1897. Lamson, Wolffe and Company.
Mademoiselle De Maupin. Theophile Gautier. LC 49-9868. (Novel library). 1949. Pantheon Books.
Mademoiselle De Maupin. Theophile Gautier. (Half-title: The modern library of the world's best books). 1918. Boni and Liveright.
Mademoiselle De Maupin. Theophile Gautier. Tr. by Burton Rascoe. LC 20-21964. 1920. A. A. Knopf.
Mademoiselle De Maupin. Theophile Gautier. Tr. by Burton Rascoe. LC 26-3383. (Borosol classics). 1925. A. A. Knopf.
Mademoiselle De Maupin: A Romance of Love and Passion. Theophile Gautier. (On cover: The library of choice fiction, no. 2). 1890. Laird & Lee.
Mademoiselle De Maupin: Translation Revised and Amended. Theophile Gautier. Tr. by Alvah C. Bessie. Endore, S. Guy, 1901- LC 31-1197. 1930. C. Kendall.
Mademoiselle De Mersac. A Novel. William Edward Norris. (Franklin square library, no. 106). 1880. Harper & Brothers.
Mademoiselle De Mersac. A Novel. William Edward Norris. (Seaside library, v. 34, no. 698). 1880. G. Munro.
Mademoiselle Desroches, a Novel. Andre Theuriet & De Vere, Meta, Tr. (choice series. no. 44). 1891. R. Bonner's Sons.
Mademoiselle Fifi, and Other Stories. Guy De Maupassant. Ed. by Ernest Augustus Boyd. LC 77-157789. (Short story index reprint series). 1971. (ISBN 0-8369-3901-8). Books For Libraries Press.
Mademoiselle Fifi & Other Stories. Guy de Maupassant. Tr. by Ada Galsworthy. Incl. Old Mother Savage; Piece of String; Sale; Two Friends; Duel; Umbrella; At Sea. (Illus.). pap. 3.00 (ISBN 0-8283-1446-2, IPL). Branden.
Mademoiselle Fifi, & Other Stories: Collected Novels & Stories, Vol. 2. facsimile ed. Guy De Maupassant. Ed. by Ernest Boyd. LC 77-157789. (Short Story Index Reprint Ser.). Repr. of 1922 ed. 16.00 (ISBN 0-8369-3901-8). Ayer Co.
Mademoiselle Fifi, and Twelve Other Stories. Guy De Maupassant. LC 17-20962. (Half-title: The modern library of the world's best books). Boni and Liveright, Inc.
Mademoiselle Gizaud Gizaud. Adolphe Belot. Tr. by D., A. Zola, Emile. 1891. Laird & Lee.
Mademoiselle Ixe: By Lanoe Falconer Pseud. Mary Elizabeth Hawker. LC 7-2619. (Half title: The "unknown" library, v. 1). Cassell Publishing Company.
Mademoiselle Kid. Tod Williams. LC 35-19153. The Macaulay Company.
Mademoiselle Miss. Henry Harland. LC 4-16266. (Half-title: Canvas-back library of popular fiction, vol. vi). 1904. J. Lane.
Mademoiselle Miss, and Other Stories. Henry Harland. LC 76-24385. (Decadent Consciousness). 1977. 26.00 (ISBN 0-8240-2760-4). Garland Pub.
Mademoiselle Miss: To Which Is Added: The Funeral March of a Marionette.--The Prodigal Father.--A Sleeveless Errand.--A Light Soverign. Henry Harland. LC 12-24116. Lovell, Coryell & Company.
Mademoiselle Mori: A Tale of Modern Rome. Margaret Roberts. (Seaside library, v. 69, no. 1402). 1882. G. Munro.
Mademoiselle of Cambrai. David Skaats Foster. LC 20-16800. The Franklin Book Company.
Mademoiselle of Monte Carlo. William Le Queux. LC 21-15819. The Macaulay Company.
Mademoiselle of Monte Carlo: A Mystery of to-Day. William Le Queux. LC 21-836890. 1921. Cassell and Company, Ltd.
Mademoiselle Perle & Other Stories. Guy de Maupassant. (Fr. & Eng.). 2.50 o.p. French & Eur.
Mademoiselle Solange. Francois De Julliot. Tr. by Eaton, A. I. LC 1-18651. (On cover: Globe library, no. 96). 1889. Rand, McNally & Company.
Madge: A Girl in Earnest. S Jennie Smith. LC 2-18738. 1902. Lee and Shepard.
Madge, a Novel. Margaret Adams. LC 52-14823. 1952. Comet Press Books.
Madge Marland: An Every-Day Girl. Laura Francis. LC 6-43245. 1881. American Tract Society.
Madhouse. Angus Hall. (O.s.i.). 160p. 1974. pap. 0.95 o.s.i. (AN1280, Award). Univ Pub & Dist.
Madhouse in Washington Square. David Alexander. 1961. pap. 0.95 o.p. (01623, Collier). Macmillan.
Madhouse in Washington Square. 1st Ed. David Alexander. LC 58-131785. 1958. Lippincott.
Madigans. Miriam Michelson. LC 4-27356. 1904. The Century Co.
Madman at My Door. Hillary Waugh. 1979. pap. 2.25 (ISBN 0-380-47159-0, 47159). Avon.
Madman at My Door. Hillary Waugh. LC 78-3261. 1978. 7.95 o.p. (ISBN 0-385-12748-0). Doubleday.
Madman, the Kite, & the Island: A Novel. Felix Leclerc. LC 76-382643. (ISBN 0-88750-175-3). Oberon Press.
Madman Theory. Ellery Queen, pseud. LC 67-192. 1966. Pocket Books.
Madman Theory. Ellery Queen, pseud. (Signet book). 1975. (pbk.) 1.25. New American Library.
Madman's Buff. Rudolf Kagey. LC 41-17324. 1941. Little, Brown and Company.
Madman's Defense: Le Plaidoyer D'un Fou. August Strindberg. LC 67-10387. 1967. Anchor Books.
Madman's Defense. Le Plaidoyer D'un Fou. Tr. Based on Ellie Schleussner's Version. The Confession of a Fool Rev., Ed. by Evert Sprinchorn. August Strindberg. Tr. by Ellie Schleussner. Ed. by Evert Sprinchorn. (Anchor bk., A4926 rebound). 1968. 3.25. Peter Smith.
Madman's Memory. Roger Vercel & Wells, Warre Bradley, 1892- Tr. LC 47-30307. 1947. Random House.
Madmen Die Alone. Josiah E Greene. LC 38-18127. 1938. W. Morrow & Co.
Madmen Must. William Jovanovich. LC 77-11543. (Cass Canfield book). 9.95 (ISBN 0-06-012247-1). Harper & Row.
Madness at the Castle see Silent Voice.
Madness in the Heart. Edward Donahoe. LC 37-2565. 1937. Little, Brown, and Company.
Madness in the Spring. Elinore Denniston. LC 54-10577.
Madness of a Seduced Woman. Susan Fromberg Schaeffer. LC 82-17771. 16.95 (ISBN 0-525-24165-5). Dutton.
Madness of a Seduced Woman: A Novel. Susan Fromberg Schaeffer. LC 82-17771. 560p. 1983. 16.95 (ISBN 0-525-24165-5, 1646-490). Dutton.
Madness of May. Meredith Nicholson. LC 17-114684. 1917. C. Scribner's Sons.
Madness of Philip: And Other Tales of Childhood. Josephine Dodge Daskam Bacon. LC 75-98557. (Short story index reprint series). (Illus.). 1969. Books for Libraries Press.
Madness of Philip. And Other Tales of Childhood. Josephine Dodge Daskam Bacon. LC 2-7299. 1902. McClure, Phillips & Co.
Madness of Philip & Other Tales of Childhood. facsimile ed. Josephine Dodge Daskam Bacon. LC 75-98557. (Short Story Index Reprint Ser.). 1902. 15.00 (ISBN 0-8369-3131-9). Ayer Co.
Madness of the Heart. Richard Neely. LC 75-20338. 272p. 1976. 6.95 o.p. (ISBN 0-690-01016-8). T Y Crowell.
Madness of the Heart. Richard Neely. (Signet Book.). 1977. 1.50. New American Library.
Madness on Midsea Isle. John Albert Comstock. 3.75 o.p. Vantage.
Madolin Rivers: Or, The Little Beauty of Red Oak Seminary. A Love-Story. Laura Jean Libbey. (On cover: Seaside library. Pocket ed., no. 341). 1885. G. Munro.
Madolin Rivers: Or, The Little Beauty of Red Oak Seminary. A Love Story. Laura Jean Libbey. (On cover: The library of American authors, no. 8). 1889. G. Munro.
Madonna and the Student. Isabel Neilson. LC 25-10972. 1925. B. W. Huebsch, Inc.
Madonna Complex. Norman Bogner. (Berkley Medallion Book.). 1977. 1.95. (ISBN 0-425-03528-X). Berkley Pub. Corp.
Madonna Complex. Norman Bogner. LC 68-30948. 1968. 6.95. Coward-McCann.
Madonna Creek Witch. Jacqueline La Tourrette. 1973. (pbk.) 1.25. Dell.
Madonna Hall: The Story of Our Country's Peril. Emily Clemens Pearson. LC 7-33497. 1890. J. H. Earle.
Madonna Mary. Margaret Oliphant Wilson Oliphant. (Seaside library, v. 32, no. 651). 1879. G. Munro.
Madonna Mary: A Novel. Margaret Oliphant Wilson Oliphant. 1867. Littell, Son & Company.
Madonna of a Day. Lily Dougall. (Half-title: Appletons' town and country library, no. 194). 1895. D. Appleton and Company.
Madonna of Avenue A". A Heart Stirring Romance of Love and Pathos, Based on the Motion Picture Story. Mark Canfield. 1929. Jacobsen Publishing Company, Inc.
Madonna of Pass Christian: A Tale of the Resurrection. George F Ormsby. (On cover: The optimus series, no. 3). 1891. Donohue, Henneberry & Co.
Madonna of Sacrifice: A Story of Florence. William Dana Orcutt. LC 13-3813. 1913. 0.50. F. G. Browne & Co.
Madonna of Seven Moons. Margery H Lawrence. LC 33-10599. The Bobbs-Merrill Company.
Madonna of the Alps. Bernahardine Schulze-Smidt. Tr. by Dole, Nathan Haskell. LC 8-2052. 1895. Little, Brown, and Company.
Madonna of the Astrolabe: A Novel. John Innes Mackintosh Stewart. LC 77-24043. (His A staircase in Surrey; 4). 8.95 (ISBN 0-393-08801-4). Norton.
Madonna of the Curb. Anna Balmer Myers. LC 22-209939. G. W. Jacobs & Company.
Madonna of the Damned. Frank Owen. LC 35-11487. The Macaulay Company.
Madonna of the Future, and Other Early Stories. With a Foreword by Willard Thorp. Henry James. LC 62-2374. (Signet classic, CD105). 1962. New American Library.
Madonna of the Hills: A Story of a New York Cabaret Girl. Arthur Guy Empey. LC 21-1673. Harper & Brothers.
Madonna of the Peach-Tree: A Romance. Maurice Henry Hewlett. LC 90-556028. 1899. The Macmillan Co.
Madonna of the Seven Hills. Eleanor Hibbert. LC 74-13502. 1974. 6.95 (ISBN 0-399-11456-4). Putnam.
Madonna of the Seven Hills. jean plaidy. ed. Eleanor Hibbert. 1976. 1.75 (ISBN 0-449-23026-0). Fawcett Crest.
Madonna of the Seven Hills. Jean Plaidy. LC 74-13502. 304p. (YA) 1974. 6.95 o.p. (ISBN 0-399-11456-4). Putnam.
Madonna of the Slate and Other Short Stories. Laban Lacy Rice. LC 37-327931. 1923. The Baird-Ward Press.
Madonna of the Sleeping Cars. Maurice DeKobra, pseud. Tr. by Wainwright, Neal. LC 27-10320. Payson & Clarke. Ltd.
Madonna of the Snowflakes, and Other Convent Stories. Margaret Kenna. 1897. J. Murphy & Co.
Madonna of the Tubs. Elizabeth Stuart Phelps Ward. LC 74-85688. (American fiction reprint series). (Illus.). 1969. Books for Libraries Press.
Madonna of the Tubs: By Elizabeth Stuart Phelps. Elizabeth Stuart Phelps Ward. LC 8-2500. 1887. Hoghton, Mifflin and Company.
Madonna Red. James Carroll. LC 76-1999. 7.95 (ISBN 0-316-13007-9). Little, Brown.
Madonna Who Shifts For Herself. Lyn Lifshin. 64p. 1983. pap. 4.95 (ISBN 0-930090-18-7); 10.00 (ISBN 0-930090-19-5). Applezaba.
Madonna with the Cat. Paul Eldridge. LC 42-16842. 1942. Harbinger House.
Madonna Without Child. Myron Brinig. LC 29-5409. 1929. Doubleday, Doran & Company, Inc.
Madras-Type Jacket. 1st Ed. Evelyn Hawes. LC 67-19194. 1967. 4.50. Harcourt.
Madre. Maksim Gorkii. 423p. (Span.). 1979. 6.45 (ISBN 0-8285-1322-8, Pub. by Progress Pubs USSR). Imported Pubns.
Madrigal. John E Gardner. LC 68-16078. 1968. Viking Press.
Madrigal. Samuel Bertram Harrison. LC 73-95383. 1969. 6.95. Nash Pub. Corp.
Madrine Doucet: A Romance. Walter L. Jenkins.
Madrona Island. Elizabeth Graham, pseud. (Harlequin Presents Ser.). 192p. 1981. pap. 1.50 (ISBN 0-373-10446-4). Harlequin Bks.
Madrone Tree. David Duncan. LC 49-7289. 1949. Macmillan Co.
Madrugada see En la Ardiente Obscuridad.
Mad's Bizarre Bazaar. Don Edwing. (Illus.). 192p. (Orig.). 1980. pap. 1.75 (ISBN 0-446-94285-5). Warner Bks.
Mad's Don Martin Digs Deeper. Don Martin. (Illus.). 192p. (Orig.). 1979. pap. 1.95 (ISBN 0-446-30452-2). Warner Bks.
Mad's Sergio Aragones on Parade. Sergio Aragones. (Illus.). 160p. (Orig.). 1979. pap. 5.95 (ISBN 0-446-37369-9). Warner Bks.
Madselin. Norah Robinson Lofts. LC 81-43769. (Illus.). 216p. 1983. 13.95 (ISBN 0-385-18103-5). Doubleday.
Madsong. Serena Sue Hilsinger. LC 76-118210. 1970. 4.95. Gambit.
Madwand. Roger Zelazny. LC 81-210616. 1981. 35.00 (ISBN 0-932096-11-5). Phantasia Press.
Mae Madden: A Novel. Mary Murdoch Mason. LC 7-25571. 1876. Jansen, McClurg & Co.
Maelcho: A Sixteenth Century Narrative. Emily Lawless. LC 7-13623. 1894. D. Appleton and Company.
Maelstrom. Frank Froest. LC 16-8693. 1.25. E. J. Clode.
Maelstrom. Howard Hunt. LC 48-7665. 1948. Farrar, Straus.
Maelstrom: A Novel. George L Bauerfeind. LC 46-19196. 1946. Dorrance & Company.
Maestra. Mary Carter. 1973. 6.95 o.p. (ISBN 0-316-13044-3, Pub. by Atlantic Monthly Pr). Little.
Maestrica Pervertida. Danilo Cesto. (Pimienta Collection Ser.). 160p. (Span.). 1976. pap. 1.25 (ISBN 0-88473-245-2). Fiesta Pub.
Maestro. Felix Jackson. LC 57-9599. 1957. Dial Press.
Maestro Murders. Frances Shelley Wees. LC 31-216818. 1931. The Mystery League, Inc.
Maeve. Jo Clayton. 1979. 1.75 (ISBN 0-87997-469-9). DAW Books.

TITLE INDEX MAGIC MIRROR, AN ANTIQUE

Maeve: A Novel of the Diadem. Jo Clayton. (Science Fiction Ser.). 1979. pap. 2.25 (ISBN 0-87997-760-4, UE1760). DAW Bks.
Maeve, the Huntress. James Reynolds. LC 52-6981. 1952. Farrar, Staus and Young.
Mafia. Noel Clad. (O.s.i.). 1972. pap. 0.95 o.s.i. (BT50274). Belmont-Tower.
Mafia. Fred J. Cook. 1973. pap. 1.25 o.p. (P2695, GM). Fawcett World.
Mafia Death Watch. Bruno Rossi, pseud. (Sharpshooter Ser). (Orig.). 1975. pap. 1.25 o.p. (LB286ZK, Leisure Bks). Nordon Pubns.
Mafia Don. George W. Ziran. (Orig.). 1972. pap. 1.25 o.p. (ISBN 0-515-02756-1, V2756). BJ Pub Group.
Mafia Fix. Warren Murphy. (Destroyer Ser.: No. 4). 192p. (Orig.). 1980. pap. 2.25 (ISBN 0-523-41758-6). Pinnacle Bks.
Mafia Fix see Cargamento Mortifero.
Mafia Kiss. Philip Loraine. LC 69-16425. 1969. 4.95. Random House.
Mafia Man. Richard Posner. (Orig.). 1973. pap. 0.95 o.p. (M2671, GM). Fawcett World.
Mafia Massacre. Frank Scarpetta. (Marksman,#12). 1974. (pbk.) 0.95. Belmont Tower Books.
Mafia: Operation Cocaine. Don Romano, pseud. LC 73-21117. 1974. (pbk.) 1.25. Pyramid Books.
Mafia: Operation Cocaine. Don Romano, pseud. (Orig.). 1974. pap. 1.25 o.p. (0-515-03311-1). Pyramid Pubns.
Mafia: Operation Hijack. Don Romano, pseud. (Orig.). 1974. pap. 1.25 o.p. (ISBN 0-515-03339-1, V3339). BJ Pub Group.
Mafia: Operation Hit Man. Don Romano, pseud. (Orig.). 1974. pap. 1.25 o.p. (ISBN 0-515-03444-4, V3444). Pyramid Pubns.
Mafia: Operation Loan Shark. Don Romano, pseud. (Orig.). 1974. pap. 1.25 o.p. (ISBN 0-515-03510-6, V3510). BJ Pub Group.
Mafia: Operation Porno. Don Romano, pseud. (Orig.). 1973. pap. 1.25 o.p. (ISBN 0-515-03170-4, V3170). Pyramid Pubns.
Mafia Wife. Robin Moore & Barbara Fuca. LC 77-1840. 8.95 (ISBN 0-02-586180-8). Macmillan.
Mafia Women. Joseph Cenni. (O.s.i.). 192p. (Orig.). 1973. pap. 0.95 o.s.i. (AN1043, Award). Univ Pub & Dist.
Mafioso. Peter McCurtin. (Orig.). 1970. pap. 0.95 o.p. (B95-2029). Belmont-Tower.
Mafoota: A Romance of Jamaica. Dolf Wyllarde. LC 8-6988. 1907. J. Lane Company.
Mag: A Story of to-Day. LC 7-20271. (On cover: Harper's library of American fiction, no. 4). 1878. Harper & Brothers.
Mag Pye. Betsey Riddle Hutten Zum Stolzenberg. LC 17-4712. 1917. 1.50. D. Appleton and Company.
Maga Stories. Putnam's Magazine, 1853-1870. LC 7-16609. (Putnam's railway classics). 1867. G. P. Putnam & Sons.
Magazine. Diane Watson. (Orig.). 1981. pap. 2.50 (ISBN 0-505-51662-4). Tower Bks.
Magazine of Fantasy & Science Fiction: A Thirty Year Retrospective. Ed. by Edward L. Ferman. LC 79-8007. (Science Fiction Ser.). 320p. 1980. 10.95 (ISBN 0-385-15357-0). Doubleday.
Magazine of Fantasy and Science Fiction, April 1965. Edward L Ferman & Martin Greenberg. LC 81-187926. (Alternatives). 1981. (ISBN 0-8093-1007-4). Southern Illinois University.
Magazine of Fantasy and Science Fiction: A 30-Year Retrospective. Edward L Ferman. LC 79-8007. 10.00 (ISBN 0-385-15357-0). Doubleday.
Magazine of Fantasy and Science Fiction. The Best from: Fantasy and Science Fiction. 14th Ser. Ed. by Avram Davidson. LC 52-5510. 4.50. Doubleday.
Magazine of Fantasy and Science Fiction. The Best from Fantasy and Science Fiction. Ed. by William Anthony Parker White. LC 52-5510. 1952. Little, Brown.
Magda. Maurice Gerschon Hindus. LC 51-9429. 1951. Doubleday.
Magda. Lisa Wells. 224p. (Orig.). 1981. pap. 2.50 (ISBN 0-441-51526-6). Ace Bks.
Magdalen: Authorized Translation from the Bohemian of J. S. Machar, by Leo Wiener... Jan Svatopluk Machar & Wiener, Leo, 1862- Tr. LC 16-15316. (Half-title: The Slavic translations by L. Wiener). 1916. 1.25. M. Kennerley.
Magdalen Church-Yard, from the French of J. J. Regnault Warin... Tr. By Samuel Mackay... Jean Baptiste Joseph Innocent Philadelphe Regnault-Warin & Mackay, Samuel, Tr. LC 7-30660. 1809. Hastings, Etheridge and Bliss.
Magdalen Ferat. A Novel. Emile Zola & Sherwood, Mrs. Mary (Neal) Tr. LC 9-13182. T. B. Peterson & Brothers.
Magdalen Hepburn. A Story of Scottish Reformation. Margaret Oliphant Wilson Oliphant. LC 7-25766. Garrett & Co.
Magdalen Hepburn: A Story of the Scottish Reformation. Margaret Oliphant Wilson Oliphant. (On cover: Seaside library. Pocket ed., no. 377). 1885. G. Munro.
Magdalen: Or, The Penitent of Godstow. An Historical Novel... Elizabeth Helme. LC 7-411979. 1813. West and Blake.
Magdalen, the Enchantress. Founded on Fact. E. L. Laselle. LC 42-33511. 1858. J. B. Lippincott & Co.
Magdalena. LC 36-4084. 1936. The Macmillan Company.
Magdalena: From the Spanish of Perpetuo Ponslevi Pseud. Barbary Eduardo De Miery & Meghan, Joseph, Tr. LC 7-37413. (On cover: Globe library. v. 1, no. 186). 1894. Rand, McNally & Company.
Magdalene. Carolyn Slaughter. LC 78-27132. 204p. 1979. 8.95 (ISBN 0-87131-279-4). M Evans.
Magdalene: A Study in Methods. Ethel Stefana Stevens Drower. LC 19-16375. 1919. Cassell and Company, Ltd.
Magdalene Scrolls. Barbara Wood. LC 77-16854. 1978. 8.95 (ISBN 0-385-13550-5). Doubleday.
Magdalene Woman. Margaret Rogers. LC 79-28420. 10.95 (ISBN 0-312-50405-5). St. Martin's Press.
Magdalen's Vow. May Agnes Early Fleming. LC 6-39952. (On cover: The laurel library. no. 12). 1893. G. Munro's Sons.
Magdalen's Vow. May Agnes Early Fleming. LC 1431. (On cover: Eagle library, no. 146). 1900. Street & Smith.
Magellan. Colin Anderson. LC 79-103380. (Science Fiction Ser). 1970. 4.95 o.p. (ISBN 0-8027-5510-0). Walker & Co.
Magenta Stone. Terry G Haskin. (Berkley Medallion Book). 1975. (pbk.) 1.50 (ISBN 0-425-02938-7). Berkley Pub. Co.
Maggie. Stephen Crane. (Novel As American Social History Ser). 1970. text ed. 6.50 o.p. (ISBN 0-8131-1207-9). U Pr of Ky.
Maggie. Lena Kennedy. 1981. pap. 2.95 (ISBN 0-671-42378-9). PB.
Maggie. William Woolfolk. 1978. pap. 1.95 (ISBN 0-89041-178-6, 3178). Major Bks.
Maggie: A Girl of the Streets. Stephen Crane. LC 6-30866. 1896. D. Appleton and Company.
Maggie, a Girl of the Streets: A Story of New York. Stephen Crane. LC 66-20867. 1966. Scholars' Facsimiles & Reprints.
Maggie; a Girl of the Streets: A Story of New York). Stephen Crane. LC 68-10823. (Chandler facsimile editions in American literature). 1968. Chandler Pub. Co.; Science Research Associates, Distributors, Chicago.
Maggie, a Girl of the Streets: A Story of New York). Stephen Crane. LC 72-104764. 1970. 6.50. University Press of Kentucky.
Maggie, a Girl of the Streets: A Story of New York. Stephen Crane & Sigmund Abeles. LC 75-323842. (Illus.). 1974. Limited Editions Club.
Maggie, a Girl of the Streets: A Story of New York) Stephen Crane & Thomas A Gullason. LC 78-24596. (Norton critical edition). 20.95 (ISBN 0-393-01222-0). Norton.
Maggie. A Girl of the Streets: a Story of New York, by Stephen Crane (Johnston Smith Pseud.) Facsimile Reprod. of the 1st Ed. of 1893. Introd. by Joseph Katz. Stephen Crane. LC 66-20867. 1966. 6.00. Scholars' Facsimiles.
Maggie: A Girl of the Streets (Eighteen Ninety-Three) Stephen Crane. Ed. by Thomas A. Gullason. (Norton Critical Edition). 1980. 20.95x (ISBN 0-393-01222-0); pap. 5.95x (ISBN 0-393-95024-7). Norton.
Maggie: A Love Story. William Woolfolk. LC 72-139074. 1971. 5.95. Doubleday.
Maggie Adams, Dancer. Karen S. Dean. 176p. 1982. pap. 2.25 (ISBN 0-380-80200-7, 80200, Flare). Avon.
Maggie & David. Roger Erickson. 224p. 1981. pap. 2.50 (ISBN 0-449-14431-3). Fawcett.
Maggie: And Other Stories. Stephen Crane. (CL166). 1968. Airmont.
Maggie & Other Stories. Stephen Crane. Ed. by Austin M. Fox. (O.s.i.). (YA) (gr. 9-12). pap. 0.75 o.s.i. (ISBN 0-671-46574-0). WSP.
Maggie & Other Stories. Stephen Crane. Ed. by Austin M. Fox. (O.s.i.). (YA) (gr. 9-12). pap. 0.75 o.s.i. (ISBN 0-671-46574-0). WSP.
Maggie & Other Stories see Blue Hotel & Other Stories.
Maggie Cameron, Cruise Nurse. Addie Adam. (YA) 1978. 6.95 (Avalon). Bouregy.
Maggie Cassidy. John Kerouac. LC 77-25167. (McGraw-Hill paperbacks). 1978. 3.50 (ISBN 0-07-034203-2). McGraw-Hill.
Maggie Cassidy: Novel. John Kerouac. LC 59-3512. (Avon, G-1035). 1959. Avon Book Division, Hearst Corp.
Maggie Craig. Marie Joseph. LC 81-21458. 11.95 (ISBN 0-312-50407-1). St. Martin's Press.
Maggie D., a Sexual History: A Novel. Adam Kennedy. LC 72-93790. 1973. 8.95 (ISBN 0-671-27096-6). Trident Press.
Maggie D., a Sexual History: A Novel. Adam Kennedy. 1974. (pbk.) 1.50 (ISBN 0-671-78664-4). Pocket Books.
Maggie, Her Marriage. Taylor Caldwell. LC 53-27313. (Gold medal book, 288). 1953. Fawcett Publications.
Maggie: Her Marriage. Taylor Caldwell. 204p. Repr. of 1953 ed. lib. bdg. 12.70x (ISBN 0-88411-169-5). Amereon Ltd.
Maggie-Now. Betty Smith. LC 57-8214. 1958. Harper.
Maggie-Now. rev. ed. Betty Smith. LC 66-31228. (Perennial library, P98F). 1966. Harper & Row.
Maggie-Now. Betty Smith. LC 81-20329. 1982. 18.95 (ISBN 0-8161-3303-4). G.K. Hall.
Maggie of Virginsburg: A Story of the Pennsylvania Dutch. Helen Reimensnyder Martin. 1918. The Century Co.
Maggie: Or, The Loom Girl of Lowell. William Mason Turner. (On cover: Munro's library, popular novels, v. 1, no. 51). N. L. Munro.
Maggie Pepper. Charles Klein. LC 12-1164. 1.25. The H. K. Fly Company.
Maggie Pepper. Charles Klein. LC 38-350442. 1913. Grosset & Dunlap.
Maggie Rowan. Catherine Cookson. (Signet Book). 1975. (pbk.) 1.50. New American Library.
Maggie Rowan. Catherine Marchant, pseud. 1971. pap. 1.25 o.p. (96113). Beagle Bks.
Maggie Royal: A Novel. Jane McIlvaine McClary. LC 81-5339. 14.95 (ISBN 0-671-24968-1). Simon and Schuster.
Maggie Story. Edna M. LaVeigne. 3.00 o.p. Carlton.
Maggie: Text and Context. Stephen Crane. Ed. by Maurice Bassan. LC 66-20990. Wadsworth Pub. Co.
Maggie: Text and Context. Ed. by Maurice Bassan. Stephen Crane. LC 66-20990. 1966. Wadsworth.
Maggie, the Mouth Girl. John Racine. 192p. (Orig.). 1972. pap. 1.95 o.p. (ISBN 0-87682-284-7, 7284). Barclay Hse.
Maggie: Together with George's Mother and The Blue Hotel. Stephen Crane & Hazlitt, Henry. LC 31-281406. 1931. A. A. Knopf.
Maggie's Way. Martha Barron Barrett. (Signet Book)). 2.75 (ISBN 0-451-09601-0). New American Library, C.
Maggot. Robert Flanagan. 272p. 1971. pap. 3.50 (ISBN 0-446-30523-5). Warner Bks.
Maggot and Worm, and Eight Other Stories. Myron M Liberman. LC 78-12370. (Illus.). 1969. Cummington Press.
Magia De Amor. new ed. Evelio Rojas. (Pimienta Collection Ser). 160p. (Span.). 1974. pap. 1.00 (ISBN 0-88473-209-6). Fiesta Pub.
Magic. William Goldman. (Dell Book). 1977. 1.95 (ISBN 0-440-15141-4). Dell Pub. Co.
Magic. 1978. pap. 2.50 (ISBN 0-440-15141-4). Dell.
Magic: A Novel. William Goldman. LC 76-14871. 7.95 (ISBN 0-440-05159-2). Delacorte Press.
Magic and Mary Rose. Faith Baldwin Cuthrell. LC 24-249503. Small, Maynard & Company.
Magic at Sunset. Leslie Hatcher. 1.75 (ISBN 0-8439-8022-2). Nordon Publications.
Magic at Sunset. Leslie Hatcher. (Orig.). 1981. pap. 1.75 (ISBN 0-8439-8022-2, Tiara Bks). Nordon Pubns.
Magic Barrel. Bernard Malamud. LC 58-6841. 1958. Farrar, Straus & Cudahy.
Magic Barrel. Bernard Malamud. 1980. 2.50 (ISBN 0-380-49973-8). Avon Books.
Magic Bow: A Romance of Paganini. Manuel Komroff. LC 40-27734. Harper & Brothers.
Magic Bullet: A Novel of Presidential Assassination. J. David Andrews. 185p. (Orig.). 1980. pap. 7.50 (ISBN 0-938330-00-4). Planetary Pr.
Magic Casket. Richard Austin Freeman. LC 27-7183. 1927. Dodd, Mead & Company.
Magic Christian. Terry Southern. LC 60-7681. 1960. Random House.
Magic Circle. Gladys Eleanor Meyer. LC 44-2898. 1944. A. A. Knopf.
Magic City. James W. Buel. LC 74-15728. (Popular Culture in America Ser.). (Illus.). 294p. 1975. Repr. 60.00x (ISBN 0-405-06364-4). Ayer Co.
Magic City. Marsha Manning. (Fawcett Gold Medal Book). 1976. 1.25. (ISBN 0-449-13516-0). Fawcett.
Magic Cup: An Irish Legend. Andrew M. Greeley. LC 79-16720. 10.95 (ISBN 0-07-024250-X). McGraw-Hill.
Magic Dolls. Charline B. Kay & Kenneth Kay. LC 76-42916. (Illus.). 1976. 6.95 o.p. (ISBN 0-912760-27-3); pap. 4.95 o.p. Valkyrie Pr.
Magic Egg and Other Stories. Frank Richard Stockton. LC 75-132126. (Short story index reprint series). (Illus.). 1970. Books for Libraries Press.
Magic Egg: And Other Stories. Frank Richard Stockton. LC 8-2381. 1907. C. Scribner's Sons.
Magic Fallacy, a Novells. David Westheimer. LC 50-5178. 1950. Macmillan.
Magic Fern. Phillip Bonosky. LC 61-11065. 1961. International Publishers.
Magic Flute. W. H. Auden & Chester Kallman. (O.S.I.). 1956. 3.50 o.s.i. (ISBN 0-394-40384-3). Random.
Magic Flute. Sara Cone Bryant. LC 26-18624. 1926. Houghton Mifflin Company.
Magic for Marigold. Lucy Maud Montgomery. LC 29-20431. 1929. Frederick A. Stokes Company.
Magic Forest. Stewart E. White. 1976. lib. bdg. 9.95x (ISBN 0-89968-126-3). Lightyear.
Magic Forest: A Modern Fairy Story. Stewart Edward White. LC 3-25542. 1903. The Macmillan Company.
Magic Formula: And Other Stories. Lawrence Pearsall Jacks. LC 27-8776. Harper & Brothers.
Magic Fountain. Sadyebeth Lowitz & Anson Lowitz. 1979. pap. 0.95 (ISBN 0-440-45847-1, YB). Dell.
Magic Garden. Gene Stratton Porter. 1976. Repr. of 1927 ed. lib. bdg. 12.05x (ISBN 0-89190-942-7). Am Repr-Rivercity Pr.
Magic Garden of Stanley Sweetheart: A Novel. Robert Westbrook. LC 73-75088. 1969. 5.95. Crown Publishers.
Magic Goes Away. Ed. by Larry Niven. 1983. pap. 2.50 (ISBN 0-441-51547-9, Pub. by Ace Science Fiction). Ace Bks.
Magic Grandfather. Doris Miles Disney. (60-320). 1968. Macfadden.
Magic Grandfather. Doris Miles Disney. LC 66-24324. 1966. Published for the Crime Club by Doubleday.
Magic Ground. Joseph Csida. 3.50 (ISBN 0-671-83135-6). Pocket Books.
Magic Helmett. Angelo Belle-Cotic. 1970. 10.00 o.p. Vantage.
Magic House. Louise Harvey Butler. LC 29-9536. (A just right book). A. Whitman & Co.
Magic in May. Peggy Gaddis, pseud. LC 56-898093. 1956. Arcadia House.
Magic Ink, and Other Stories. William Black. LC 79-37537. (Short story index reprint series). (Illus.). 1972. (ISBN 0-8369-4096-2). Books for Libraries Press.
Magic Ink: And Other Stories. William Black. LC 11-10509. 1892. Harper & Brothers.
Magic Is Fragile. Elsie Frances Wilson Mack. LC 52-9204. 1952. Bouregy & Curl.
Magic Is Fragile. Elsie Frances Wilson Mack. (Avalon romances). 1972. 3.95. Avalon.
Magic Journey. John Treadwell Nichols. 1978. 11.95 (ISBN 0-03-015356-5); pap. 7.95 (ISBN 0-03-042866-1). HR&W.
Magic Journey: A Novel. John Treadwell Nichols. LC 77-13670. 11.95 (ISBN 0-03-015356-5). Holt, Rinehart, and Winston.
Magic Journey: A Novel. John Treadwell Nichols. 1979. 2.75 (ISBN 0-671-82311-6). Pocket Books.
Magic Journrey. John Treadwell Nichols. 640p. 1983. pap. 4.95. Ballantine.
Magic Labyrinth. Philip Jose Farmer. LC 80-144. (Riverworld series; v. 4). 1981. 10.95 (ISBN 0-399-12381-4). Berkley Pub. Corp.: Distributed by Putnam.
Magic Labyrinth see Philip Jose Farmer: The Complete Riverworld Novels.
Magic Lantern. Eleanor Furneaux Smith. LC 44-53422. 1944. Hutchinson & Co. Ltd.
Magic Lantern. Eleanor Furneaux Smith. LC 45-3732. 1945. Doubleday, Doran and Company, Inc.
Magic Lantern. 1st Ed. Robert Carson. LC 52-9047. 1952. Holt.
Magic Makers. David Carroll. LC 73-91503. 1974. 8.95 (ISBN 0-87795-080-6). Arbor Hse.
Magic Makes Murder. Harriette Russell Campbell. LC 43-5113. 1943. Harper & Brothers.
Magic Man. David Bannerman. 1983. pap. 3.50 (ISBN 0-8217-1158-X). Zebra.
Magic Man. Hallie Erminie Rives. LC 27-5421. 1927. Dodd, Mead and Company.
Magic Man, Magic Man. Fredrica Wagman. LC 74-5098. 1975. 6.95 (ISBN 0-03-012501-4). Holt, Rinehart and Winston.
Magic Margin. 1st Ed. Martin Yoseloff. LC 54-97852. 1954. Dutton.
Magic Mashie and Other Golfish Stories. Edwin Legrand Sabin. LC 2-21096. 1902. A. Wessels Company.
Magic May Return. Larry Niven. LC 81-202037. (Ace science fiction). (Illus.). 6.95 (ISBN 0-441-51548-7). Ace Books.
Magic Michael. Louis Slobodkin. (Collier juvenile paperbacks). (Illus.). 1973. (pbk.) 0.95. Collier Books.
Magic Mirror. by elsie singmaster. ed. Elsie Singmaster. LC 34-34974. 1934. Houghton Mifflin Company.
Magic Mirror. Elmer George Suhr. LC 65-280139. 1966. bds., 4.95. Helios Bks.
Magic Mirror, an Antique Optical Toy. McLoughlin Bros. pap. 2.50 (ISBN 0-486-23847-4). Dover.

Magic Mountain. Thomas Mann. Tr. by Helen Tracy Lowe. LC 32-26067. (Half-title: The modern library of the world's best books). 1932. The Modern Library.
Magic Mountain: Der Zauberberg... Translated from the German. Thomas Mann. Tr. by Helen Tracy Lowe. LC 39-1755. 1938. A. A. Knopf.
Magic Mountain. Der Zauberberg. Tr. from the German by H. T. Lowe-Porter. Thomas Mann. (Modern Lib. Coll. eds., T93). 1967. pap., 2.45. Random.
Magic Mountain: Der Zauberberg Translated from the German. Thomas Mann. Tr. by Helen Tracy Lowe. LC 27-10461. 1927. A. A. Knopf.
Magic Mountain: Der Zauberberg Translated from the German. Thomas Mann. Tr. by Helen Tracy Lowe. 1939. Alfred A. Knopf.
Magic Mountain. Translated from the German by H. T. Lowe-Porter, with an Introductory Essay by the Autohr. Illustrated with Wood Engravings by Felix Hoffmann. Thomas Mann. LC 62-5012. 1962. Heritage Press.
Magic, Mystery & Monsters. Jane V. Barker & Sybil Downing. (Colorado Heritage Ser.: Bk. 6). (Illus.). 45p. (gr. 3-4). 1979. pap. text ed. 3.50x (ISBN 0-87108-219-5). Pruett.
Magic Nest. Ralph Fletcher. 1980. 9.95 (ISBN 0-89002-136-8); pap. 2.95 (ISBN 0-89002-135-X). Northwoods Pr.
Magic Obsession. Sara Orwig. (Super Romances Ser.). 384p. 1983. pap. 2.95 (ISBN 0-373-70057-1, Pub. by Worldwide). Harlequin Bks.
Magic of a Voice: A Novel. Margaret Russell Macfarlane. LC 7-20096. Cassell & Company, Limited.
Magic of Atlantis. Lin Carter. 1970. pap. 0.75 o.p. (ISBN 0-447-74699-5). Lancer.
Magic of Dr. Farrar. Adeline McElfresh. (O.s.i.). 1976. pap. 0.95 o.s.i. (BT50993). Belmont-Tower.
Magic of Dr. Farrar. Adeline McElfresh. 1976. 0.95. Belmont Tower.
Magic of His Kiss. Jessica Steele. (Harlequin Romances). 192p. 1981. pap. 1.25 (ISBN 0-373-02394-4, Pub. by Harlequin). PB.
Magic of Honey. Barbara Cartland. 1977. pap. 1.25 o.p. (ISBN 0-515-04317-6). BJ Pub Group.
Magic of Limping John: A Story of the Mexican Border Country. Frank Goodwyn. LC 44-5717. 1944. Farrar & Rinehart, Inc.
Magic of Love. Vida Hurst. 1947. Gramercy Publishing Co.
Magic of Love. William Edward Daniel Ross. (YA) 1980. 6.95 (Avalon). Bouregy.
Magic of Oz. Lyman Frank Baum. 256p. 1981. pap. 2.25 (ISBN 0-345-28235-3, Del Rey). Ballantine.
Magic of Paris. Berta LaVan Barker. (YA) 1981. 6.95 (Avalon). Bouregy.
Magic of Shirley Jackson. Shirley Jackson. Ed. by Stanley E. Hyman. Incl. Bird's Nest; Life Among the Savages; Raising Demons. 753p. 1966. pap. 5.95 o.p. (ISBN 0-374-65100-0, S7, Sunburst). FS&G.
Magic of the Mistletoe. Peggy Gaddis, pseud. LC 36-29806. 1936. Arcadia House.
Magic of the Moon. Marsha Manning. pap. 0.45 o.p. (56-937). Paperback Lib.
Magic of the Sea: Or, Commodore John Barry in the Making. James Connolly. LC 11-16257. 1911. B. Herder.
Magic of Their Singing. Bernard Wolfe. LC 61-7211. 1961. Scribner.
Magic of Xanth, 3 vols. Piers Anthony, pseud. 1982. pap. 7.50 (ISBN 0-345-30073-4, Del Rey). Ballantine.
Magic or Mirage. Barbara Carltland. LC 78-7964. 1978. 6.95 (ISBN 0-87272-039-X, Duron Bks). Brodart.
Magic Penny. Babette Plechner Hughes. LC 48-606. 1948. Rinehart.
Magic Penny: By Babette Hughes. Babette Plechner Hall. LC 48-606. 1948. Rinehart.
Magic Ring. Dorothy Daniels. (Orig.). 1978. pap. 2.25 (ISBN 0-446-82789-4). Warner Bks.
Magic Ring. Pilar F. Legaspi. 3.00 o.p. Carlton.
Magic Ring. Ed. by Joseph McLaughlin. (Illus.). 1973. 5.50 o.p. (ISBN 0-89002-019-1); pap. 2.00 o.p. (ISBN 0-89002-010-8). Northwoods Pr.
Magic Shawl: And Other Stories. 1st Ed. Eleanor Holm. LC 55-9744. 1955. Pageant Press.
Magic Ship. Sandra Paretti. LC 78-19400. 11.95 (ISBN 0-312-50419-5). St. Martin's Press.
Magic Skin. Honore De Balzac. Tr. by Katharine Prescott Wormeley. LC 38-12759. (Half-title: The comedy of human life... Philosophical studies). 1891. Roberts Brothers.
Magic Skin. The Hidden Masterpiece. Illustrated by P. Avril. Honore De Balzac. Tr. by Katharine Prescott Wormeley. LC 26-26963. (Half-title: The works of Balzac. Centenary ed. vol. xxviii). Little, Brown, and Company.
Magic Skin. With an Introduction. Honore De Balzac. Wormeley, Katharine Prescott, 1830- Tr. LC 3-231649. (Half-title: The comedy of human life... Philosophical studies). 1888. Roberts Brothers.
Magic Skin. With an Introduction. Honore De Balzac. LC 3-23163. (Half-title: The comedy of human life... Philosophical studies). 1889. Roberts Brothers.
Magic Slippers. Weisner. 4.50 o.p. (21255). G&D.
Magic Sound of Om. Yogi Dhun. LC 74-25842. (Illus.). 1975. pap. 3.95 o.p. (ISBN 0-89087-015-2). Celestial Arts.
Magic Spring. Allen Eppes. LC 40-11403. Gramercy Publishing Co.
Magic Spring. Watkins Eppes Wright. LC 40-11493. 1940. Gramercy Pub. Co.
Magic Squares. Paul Calter. LC 77-1213. 6.95 (ISBN 0-8407-6546-0). T. Nelson.
Magic Story. Frederic Van Rensselaer Dey. LC 4-1647. 1903. The Success Company.
Magic Story. Frederic Van Rensselaer Dey. LC 32-33595. De Vorus & Co.
Magic Striptease. George Palmer Garrett. LC 73-79668. 1973. 7.95 (ISBN 0-385-05034-8). Doubleday.
Magic Summer. Ann Hamblen. 1973. pap. 0.75 o.s.i. (01-379). Lancer.
Magic Tale of Harvanger and Yolande. George Philip Baker. LC 14-12482. 1.35. George H. Doran Company.
Magic Time. Kit Reed, pseud. LC 79-14129. 9.95 (ISBN 0-399-12423-3). Berkley Pub. Corp.: Distributed by Putnam.
Magic Tortoise Ranch: A Novel. Annette King. LC 71-168315. 1971. 5.95. Crown Publishers.
Magic Toyshop. Angela Carter. LC 68-13031. 1968. Simon and Schuster.
Magic Valley. Margaret Bell Houston. LC 34-5590. 1934. D. Appleton-Century Company, Incorporated.
Magic Valley Travellers: Welsh Stories of Fantasy & Horror. Ed. by Peter Haining. LC 73-14368. 1974. 8.50 (ISBN 0-8008-5047-5). Taplinger.
Magic Water. Barbara Webster. LC 42-13729. 1942. C. Scribner's Sons.
Magic Wheel: A Novel. Henrietta Eliza Vaughan Stannard. LC 1-23087. 1901. J. B. Lippincott Company.
Magic Will. Herbert Gold. 1971. 7.95 o.p. (ISBN 0-394-46018-9). Random.
Magic Year: A Novel. Joachim Maass & Meyer, Erika M., Tr. LC 44-40220. 1944. L. B. Fischer.
Magical Carpenter of Japan. Masamochi Ishikawa. LC 65-22113. 1965. C. E. Tuttle Co.
Magical Carpenter of Japan: By Rokujiuyen Pseud. Tr. from the Japanese by Frederick Victor Dickins. With 70-Full-Page Woodcuts by Hokusai. Masamochi Ishikawa & Hokusai Katsushika. LC 65-22113. 5.95. Tuttle.
Magician. Raymond Feist. LC 80-2957. 1982. 19.95 (ISBN 0-385-17580-9). Doubleday.
Magician. William Somerset Maugham. LC 9-7829. 1909. Duffield & Company.
Magician; Together with A Fragment of Autobiography. William Somerset Maugham. LC 75-25356. (Maugham, William Somerset, 1814-1965. Works. 1976). 1977. 15.00 (ISBN 0-405-07814-5). Arno Press.
Magician: A Novel. Leitch Ritchie. LC 7-41673. 1836. Carey, Lea & Blanchard.
Magician: A Novel. Sol Stein. LC 70-163084. 1971. 6.95. Delacorte Press.
Magician: A Novel, Together with A Fragment of Autobiography. William Somerset Maugham. LC 73-414062. 1967. Penguin in Association with Heinemann.
Magician: And Other Stories. Bruno Frank. LC 47-419. 1946. The Viking Press.
Magician, and The Widow: Two Novels. 1st Ed. Georges Simenon. LC 55-5573. 1955. Doubleday.
Magician of Lublin. Isaac Bashevis Singer. 1979. pap. 2.50 (ISBN 0-449-24059-2, Crest). Fawcett.
Magician of Lublin. Isaac Bashevis Singer. Tr. by Elaine Gottlieb & Joseph Singer. 1960. 9.95 (ISBN 0-374-19633-8). FS&G.
Magician of Lublin. Isaac Bashevis Singer. Ed. by Joseph Singer. Tr. by Elaine Gottlieb. 1960. 5.95 o.p. (ISBN 0-374-19633-8). FS&G.
Magician of Lublin. Translated from the Yiddish by Elaine Gottlieb and Joseph Singer. Isaac Bashevis Singer. LC 60-10006. 1960. Noonday Press.
Magician of Naples: Or, Love and Necromancy. A Story of Italy and the East. Maturin Murray Ballou. LC 7-11439. (With Judson, Edward Z. C. The black avenger of the Spanish Main. New York, c1847). S. French.
Magician of Sunset Boulevard. Frederick Kohner. Ed. by C. N. Anderson. LC 78-175270. 10.00 (ISBN 0-89430-004-0). Morgan-Pacific.
Magician: Together with A Fragment of Autobiography. William Somerset Maugham. LC 57-5791. 1957. Doubleday.
Magicians. James E. Gunn. LC 76-17558. 6.95 (ISBN 0-684-14782-3). Scribner.
Magicians. John Boynton Priestley. LC 54-6024. 1954. Harper.
Magician's Bags. Carmino Aiello. 1980. 4.50 (ISBN 0-533-04172-4). Vantage.
Magician's Daughter. Lydia Charpentier. 1977. pap. 1.50 (ISBN 0-532-15258-1). Woodhill.
Magician's Feastletters. Diane Wakoski. 133p. 1982. 14.00 (ISBN 0-87685-532-X); pap. 6.00 (ISBN 0-87685-531-1); signed ed. 20.00 (ISBN 0-87685-533-8). Black Sparrow.
Magician's Garden and Other Stories. Geza Csath & Marianna D Birnbaum. LC 78-12345. (Illus.). 1980. 15.00 (ISBN 0-231-04732-0). Columbia University Press.
Magicians Sleeve. J. C Conaway. 1.75 (ISBN 0-449-14120-9). Fawcett Gold Medal.
Magician's Wife. James Mallahan Cain. LC 65-15329. bds., 3.95. Dial.
Magick of Camelot. Arthur H. Landis. (Science Fiction Ser.). 208p. 1981. pap. 2.25 (ISBN 0-87997-623-3, UE1623). DAW Bks.
Magico Prodigioso. Pedro Calderon De La Barca. Bd. with Casa con dos Puertas Mala Es de Guardar. (Span.). pap. 0.95 o.s.i. French & Eur.
Magico Prodigioso see La Vida es Sueno.
Magics: The Turn of the Screw, Covering End. Henry James. LC 25-237643. 1924. The Macmillan Company.
Magie D'Une Voix. Rebecca Stratton. (Collection Harlequin). 192p. 1983. pap. 1.95 (ISBN 0-373-49320-7). Harlequin Bks.
Magister Ludi: The Glass Bead Game. Hermann Hesse. 1970. pap. 3.50 (ISBN 0-553-20023-2). Bantam.
Magister Ludi: The Nobel Prize Novel Das Glasperlenspial. Hermann Hesse. LC 40-10878. 1949. H. Holt.
Magister Ludi. Translated from the German by Mervyn Savill. Hermann Hesse. LC 57-12322. 1957. F. Ungar Pub. Co.
Magistrate. Ernest Kellogg Gann. LC 81-66970. 304p. 1982. 14.50 (ISBN 0-87795-339-2). Arbor Hse.
Magistrate: A Novel. Ernest Kellogg Gann. LC 81-66970. 14.95 (ISBN 0-87795-339-2). Arbor House.
Magistrate's Own Case. Palle Adam Vilhelm Rosenkrantz. LC 8-2946. 1908. The McClure Company.
Magna. Zona Gale. LC 39-20167. 1939. D. Appleton-Century Company, Incorporated.
Magna Carta Two: Without Heroes or Villains. Sydney Rosenberg. 160p. 1976. 6.00 o.p. (ISBN 0-682-48510-1). Exposition.
Magnate. John Harriman. LC 46-6027. 1946. Random House.
Magnate. Jack Mayfield. 1980. pap. 1.95 (ISBN 0-451-09411-5, J9411, Sig). NAL.
Magnet. Maksim Gorkii & Bakshy, Aleksandr, Tr. LC 31-10369. J. Cape & H. Smith.
Magnet: A Romance of the Battles of Modern Giants. Alfred Owen Crozier. 1908. Funk & Wagnalls Company.
Magnet for Murder. Molly E Corne. LC 39-9940. M. S. Mill Co., Inc.
Magnet: Published Serially As "The Pilot-Fish") a Romance. Henry Cottrell Rowland. LC 11-1309. 1911. 1.25. Dodd, Mead and Company.
Magnetic Field(S) A Novel. Ron Loewinsohn. LC 82-48879. 1983. 12.95 (ISBN 0-394-53105-1). Knopf.
Magnetic Light. LC 79-54136. 1980. 5.00 (ISBN 0-935490-01-9). Euclid Pub.
Magnetic Man and Other Stories. Edward Sims Van Zile. (On cover: American authors' series, no. 6). F. F. Lovell & Company.
Magnetic North. Elizabeth Robins. LC 72-96893. (Illus.). 1969. Literature House.
Magnetic North. Elizabeth Robins. LC 4-6736. 1904. Frederick A. Stokes Company.
Magnhild. author's ed. Bjornstjerne Bjornson & Anderson, Rasmus Bjorn, 1846- Tr. LC 6-11717. 1883. Houghton, Mifflin and Company.
Magnhild: A Tale of Psychic Love. John Duncan Quackenbos. LC 19-2533. 1.50. R. G. Badger.
Magnifi-Cat. Carolyn Sheehan & Edmund Sheehan. LC 72-76204. 1972. 5.95 (ISBN 0-385-00296-3). Doubleday.
Magnifica Secretaria... En la Cama. new ed. Danilo Cesto. (Pimienta Collection Ser.). (Illus.). 160p. (Span.). 1976. pap. 1.25 (ISBN 0-88473-248-7). Fiesta Pub.
Magnificat. Rene Bazin. LC 32-24140. 1932. The Macmillan Company.
Magnificat: A Christian Phantasy. Gerald Michael Cushing Fitzgerald. Typography and Printing by C. A. Hack & Son, Inc.
Magnificence & Other Stories. Estrella D. Alfon. 1960. wrps. 5.00 o.p. Cellar.
Magnificent Adventure: This Being the Story of the World's Greatest Exploration, and the Romance of a Very Gallant Gentleman; a Novel. Emerson Hough. LC 16-167148. 1916. D. Appleton and Company.
Magnificent Ambersons. Booth Tarkington. LC 57-9754. (American century series, S-2). 1957. Sagamore Press.
Magnificent Ambersons. Booth Tarkington. (Bard Book). 1973. (pbk.) 1.50. Avon Books.
Magnificent Ambersons. Booth Tarkington. LC 67-2674. 1967. P. Smith.
Magnificent Ambersons. Booth Tarkington. LC 18-20166. 1918. Doubleday, Page & Company.
Magnificent Ambersons. Booth Tarkington. LC 22-16010. 1920. Doubleday, Page & Company.
Magnificent Ambersons. Booth Tarkington. LC 21-13724. 1920. Grosset & Dunlap.
Magnificent Ambersons. Booth Tarkington. LC 22-9197. 1922. Doubleday, Page & Company.
Magnificent Animals. Marina Mayson. pap. 1.95 o.s.i. (OPH-242, Ophelia). Olympia.
Magnificent Barb: A Novel. Dana Faralla. LC 47-30236. 1947. J. Messner, Inc.
Magnificent Bastards. Lucy Herndon Crockett. LC 54-5893. 1954. Farrar, Straus and Young.
Magnificent Century. Thomas Bertram Costain. (Plantagenets Ser.: No. 2). 1976. pap. 2.95 (ISBN 0-445-08512-6). Popular Lib.
Magnificent Challenge. Sue Alden. (Avalon Books). 4.95. Thomas Bouregy.
Magnificent Courtesan. Lozania Prole, pseud. LC 50-7113. 1950. McBride.
Magnificent Destiny: A Novel About the Great Secret Adventure of Andrew Jackson and Sam Houston. Paul Iselin Wellman. LC 63-14180. 1962. Doubleday.
Magnificent Dishonor: A Novel of Modern Life in the United States. Frank Newton & Ruby N. Wirth. LC 76-105955. 1970. HBM Book Publishers.
Magnificent Duchess. Sarah Stamford. LC 74-20707. 1975. 6.95 (ISBN 0-440-05252-1). Delacorte Press.
Magnificent Duchess. Sarah Stamford. (Dell Book). 1977. 1.75 (ISBN 0-440-15371-9). Dell Pub. Co.
Magnificent Enemies. Edgar Mass. LC 55-9024. 1955. Scribner.
Magnificent Failure. Giles A Lutz. LC 67-23569. 1967. Doubleday.
Magnificent Hoax. Edward Phillips Oppenheim. LC 36-156913. 1936. Little, Brown, and Company.
Magnificent Idiot. Peter De Polnay. LC 42-16840. 1942. Doubleday, Doran and Company, Inc.
Magnificent MacDarney. John Desmond Sheridan. LC 51-10312. 1951. Pellegrini & Cudahy.
Magnificent MacInnes. Shepherd Mead. LC 49-9709. 1949. Farrar, Straus.
Magnificent Maricon. William C. Spatari. (Orig.). 1969. pap. 1.75 o.p. (3052). Brandon.
Magnificent Marriage. Barbara Cartland. (Barbara Cartland library, 15). 1975. (pbk.) 1.25. Bantam Books.
Magnificent Moghuls. Tikam Ramnani. 1969. pap. 1.80 o.p. (ISBN 0-88253-177-8). InterCulture.
Magnificent Obcession. Lloyd Cassel Douglas. 1982. lib. bdg. 18.95x (ISBN 0-89966-387-7). Buccaneer Bks.
Magnificent Obsession. Lloyd Cassel Douglas. LC 62-53. 1961. Grosset & Dunlap.
Magnificent Obsession. Lloyd Cassel Douglas. LC 29-22201. 1920. Willett, Clark & Colby.
Magnificent Obsession. Lloyd Cassel Douglas. LC 32-19539. 1932. Willett, Clark & Company.
Magnificent Obsession. Lloyd Cassel Douglas. LC 33-17499. 1933. Willett, Clark & Company.
Magnificent Pimp. Francois Du Bourg. 3.95 o.p. Vantage.
Magnificent Plebian. Julia Magruder. LC 7-20131. 1888. Harper & Brothers.
Magnificent Strangers see Magnificos Visitantes, Los.
Magnificent Traitor: A Novel of Alcibiades and the Golden Age of Pericles, by Lynn and Gray Poole. Lynn Poole. LC 67-26149. 1968. 5.95. Dodd.
Magnificent Young Man. Henrietta Eliza Vaughan Stannard. LC 8-13856. (On cover: Lippincott's series of select novels). 1895. J. B. Lippincott Company.
Magnificient Hoax. Edward Phillips Oppenheim. Triangle Books.
Magnificient Sin. Andre Tellier. LC 30-14194. C. Kendall.
Magnifico. Joseph Stephens. LC 45-5194. 1945. Chapman & Grimes, Inc.
Magnificos Visitantes, Los. Ann Wedeworth. Ed. by Andy Carrodeguas & Esteban Marosi. Tr. by Antonio Valencia. Orig. Title: Magnificent Strangers. 135p. (Span.). 1981. pap. 2.00 (ISBN 0-8297-1079-5). Life Pubs Intl.
Magnolia Blossoms. Louretta Smith. 155p. 1973. 5.50 o.p. (ISBN 0-682-47759-1). Exposition.
Magnolia Blossoms: A Novel. Loretta Smith. 1973. 5.50 (ISBN 0-682-47759-1). Exposition Pr.
Magnolia Curse. Lidie Murfi. (Ravenswood gothic). 1973. (pbk) 0.95 (ISBN 0-671-77636-3). Pocket Books.
Magnolia Manor. J. S. Bradt. 3.50 o.p. Carlton.

TITLE INDEX MAIDEN VOYAGE.

Magnolia Plantation. Beverly Butler. (Orig.). 1982. pap. 3.50 (ISBN 0-89083-914-X). Zebra.
Magnolia Room. Annette Eyre. 1975. (pbk.) 1.25. New American Library.
Magnolia Siege. Pamela Pope. (Harlequin Presents Ser.). 192p. 1982. pap. 1.75 (ISBN 0-373-10525-8). Harlequin Bks.
Magnolia Square. Sara Christy. LC 36-12316. J. H. Hopkins & Sons, Inc.
Magnolia Street. Louis Golding. LC 73-152519. 1972. 7.95 (ISBN 0-85617-941-8). (Baker St., WM FA), White Lion Publishers Ltd.
Magnolia Street. Louis Golding. LC 32-6524. Farrar & Rinehart. Incorporated.
Magnolia Widow. Mannix Walker. LC 49-102786. 1949. Dodd, Mead.
Magnolias. Julie Ellis. LC 75-37830. (ISBN 0-671-22210-4). Simon and Schuster.
Magnolias Abloom. A Story of Butler's Reign in New Orleans and Other Stories. LC 8-2925. 1894. Press of Gazette Publishing Company.
Magnum Bonum. Charlotte Mary Yonge. LC 75-1526. (Victorian Fiction: Novels of Faith and Doubt). 1975. 35.00 (ISBN 0-8240-1598-3). Garland Pub.
Magnum Bonum: Or, Mother Carey's Brood a Novel. Charlotte Mary Yonge. (Seaside library, v. 38, no. 772). 1880. G. Munro.
Magnum Force. Mel Valley. 1974. (pbk.) 1.25. Warner Paperback Lib.
Magnus. George Mackay Brown. 206p. 1978. 8.95 o.p. (ISBN 0-7012-0382-X, Pub. by Chatto Bodley Jonathan). Merrimack Pub Cir.
Magnus Merriman. Eric Robert Russell Linklater. LC 34-5279. Farrar & Rinehart, Incorporated.
Magnus the Magnificent: A Novel. Leslie Turner White. LC 50-3034. 1950. Crown Publishers.
Magog: A Novel. Andrew Sinclair. LC 72-190255. 1972. (ISBN 0-297-99391-7). Weidenfeld and Nicolson.
Magog: A Novel. Andrew Sinclair. LC 72-181663. 1972. 6.95 (ISBN 0-06-013901-3). Harper & Row.
Magpie. Douglas Durkin. LC 73-91564. (Social history of Canada#23). 1974. 15.00 (ISBN 0-8020-2150-6). University of Toronto Press.
Magpie House. Andrew Soutar. LC 12-21824. 1913. Cassell and Company, Limited.
Magpie Murder. John Russell Warren. LC 42-4618. 1942. Sheridan House.
Magpie's Nest. Isabel Bowler Paterson. LC 17-981006. 1917. 1.40. John Lane Company.
Maguelone: Or, The Fair Maid of the Glen. A Tale of the Mountain Clan of Columbiana County, Ohio. George W Roof. 1880. E. J. Roberts.
Magus. John Fowles. (5162). 1967. Dell.
Magus. John Fowles. (Dell bk., 05162). 1973. 1.25. Dell.
Magus. John Fowles. LC 65-21357. 1966. Little, Brown.
Magus: A Revised Version. John Fowles. LC 77-17343. 1978. 12.95 (ISBN 0-316-29092-0). Little, Brown.
Magwitch. Michael Noonan. LC 82-16926. 1983. 11.95 (ISBN 0-312-50426-8). St. Martin's Press.
Magwitch. Michael Noonan. 224p. 1983. 11.95 (ISBN 0-312-50426-8). St Martin.
Mah Jongg Group. Susan Greene. LC 74-76435. 1975. 7.95 (ISBN 0-87949-033-0). Ashley Books.
Mahabharat. condensed ed. Ed. & tr. by Shanta Rameshwar Rao. 1975. lib. bdg. 4.50x o.p. South Asia Bks.
Mahabharata. William Buck. LC 70-153547. (Illus.). 1973. 10.00 (ISBN 0-520-02017-0). University of California Press.
Mahabharata, 12 vols. 3rd ed. Tr. by Kisari M. Ganguli from Sanskrit. 1975. Set. 220.00x (ISBN 0-8002-0332-1). Intl Pubns Serv.
Mahabharata. C. Rajagopalachari. 1979. pap. 3.95 (ISBN 0-89744-929-0). Auromere.
Mahabharata: A Shortened Modern Prose Version of the Indian Epic. R. K. Narayan. LC 77-21802. (Illus.). 1978. 10.00 (ISBN 0-670-45085-5). Viking Press.
Mahagony Trinrose: A Sime/Gen Novel. Jacqueline Lichtenberg. LC 79-8563. (Gen Series). 1981. 10.95 (ISBN 0-385-15476-3). Doubleday.
Mahalinda: Or, The Two Cousins... Nathaniel James Walter Le Cato. LC 6-26197. 1858. Printed for the Author by J. A. Gray.
Mahaly Sawyer: Or, "Putting Yourself in Her Place.". Sarah E. Douglas. LC 6-35882. 1888. Cupples and Hurd.
Mahanomah. Bertha Anna Kelsey Breckenridge. LC 11-179874. 1910. 1.25. Cochrane Publishing Company.
Mahanttan Primitive. Robert A. Carter. LC 75-122428. 1971. 6.95 o.p. (ISBN 0-8128-1381-2). Stein & Day.
Maharajah. Polan Banks. (Tourqull book). 1962. Distributed by Dodd, Mead.
Maharajah. Pierre Stephen Robert Payne. LC 51-13190. 1951. World Pub. Co.
Maharajah, and Other Stories. T. H White & Kurth Sprague. LC 81-5923. 1981. 12.95 (ISBN 0-399-12650-3). Putnam.
Mahars of Pellucidar. John Eric Holmes. 1976. (pbk.) 1.50. Ace Books.
Mahatma and the Hare. Henry Rider Haggard. LC 77-92411. (Lost Race and Adult Fantasy Fiction). (Illus.). 1978. 12.00 (ISBN 0-405-11021-9). Arno Press.
Mahatma and the Hare: A Dream Story. with 12 illustrations by messrs. w. t. horton and h. m. brock, r.i. ed. Henry Rider Haggard. LC 11-33256. 1911. 1.00. H. Holt and Company.
Mahattaners: A Story of the Hour. Edward Sims Van Zile. LC 8-30215. 1895. Lovell, Coryell & Company.
Mahattaners; A Story of the Hour: A Story of the Hour. Edward Sims Van Zile. (On cover: Eagle library, no. 167). Street & Smith.
Mahdi. A. J. Quinnell. 320p. 1983. pap. 3.50 (ISBN 0-449-20168-6, Crest). Fawcett.
Mahdi: A Novel. A J Quinnell. LC 81-14095. 1982. 12.95 (ISBN 0-688-00646-9). Morrow.
Mahdi: Or, Love and Race. Hall Caine. LC 6-19900. 1894. D. Appleton and Company.
Maheo's Children: The Legend of Little Dried River, by Will Henry. 1st Ed. Henry Allen. LC 68-17165. 1968. 4.50, 4.37 lib. ed.,. Chilton.
Mahetible Hopkins and Her Travels. D. H. Rlfrt. LC 6-37544. 1885. W. H. Lawrence & Company.
Mahetible Hopkins on Her Travels. D. H. Elder. (On cover: J. S. Ogilvie and company's Fireside series, no. 12). 1886. J. S. Ogilvie & Company.
Mahogany. Alfredo Segre. LC 44-2894. 1944. L. B. Fischer.
Mahogany. Burton Wohl. 1975. (pbk.) 1.50. Bantam Books.
Mahogany Battleship: By David D. Lewis. David D Lewis. LC 66-22788. 1966. 5.50. Luce.
Mahogany House. June Wetherell. 176p. 1976. pap. 1.25 (ISBN 0-532-12402-2). Woodhill.
Mahogany Table. A Novel. F Clifford Stevens. LC 5836. (peerless series. no. 118). J. S. Ogilvie Publishing Company.
Mahogany Trinrose. Jacqueline Lichtenberg. LC 79-8563. (Double D Science Fiction Ser.). 224p. 1981. 11.95 o.p. (ISBN 0-385-15476-3). Doubleday.
Mahogany Trinrose. Jacqueline Lichtenberg. LC 81-86258. 240p. (Orig.). 1982. pap. 2.50 (ISBN 0-86721-129-6). Playboy Pbks.
Mahomet, Mahmed, Mamish: A Novel. Chingiz Hasan Oghlu Huseinov. LC 78-12699. 8.95 (ISBN 0-02-546630-5). Macmillan.
Mahound. Lance Horner. 1978. pap. 2.95 (ISBN 0-449-13605-1, GM). Fawcett.
Mai-Dee of the Mountains: A Story of Present-Day China. Mary Brewster Hollister. LC 33-10980. Fleming H. Revell Company.
Maias. Eca De Queiroz, Jose Maria De. LC 65-24582. 1965. St. Martin's Press.
Maias: By Eca De Quieroz 1st. Amer. Ed. Tr. by Patricia McGowen Pinheiro, Ann Stevens. Jose Maria De Eca De Queiros. LC 65-24582. bds., 7.95. St. Martin's.
Maid. H. R. Kaye, pseud. 1968. 1.75 o.p.; pap. 1.95 o.p (3026). Brandon.
Maid Among Men. Alexander Wrexe. LC 27-19642. 1927. G. P. Putnam's Sons.
Maid and a Man. Ethel Arnold Smith Dorrance. LC 9-25187. 1909. Moffat, Yard & Company.
Maid and a Million Men: The Candid Confessions of Leona Canwick. James Gerald Dunton. LC 29-1201. J. H. Sears & Company, Inc.
Maid and a Million Men: The Candid Confession of Leona Camwick. James Gerald Dunton. LC 34-38282. 1930. Grosset & Dunlap.
Maid and Her Money. Joseph Smith Fletcher. LC 29-141111. 1929. Doubleday, Doran & Company, Inc.
Maid and the Miscreant. George Hembert Westley. LC 7-276093. 1906. Mayhew Publishing Co.
Maid and Wife. Carolyn Beecher. LC 19-3006. Britton Publishing Co.
Maid-at-Arms: A Novel. Robert William Chambers. LC 2-22844. 1902. Harper & Brothers.
Maid Ellice. A Novel. Theodora Havers Boulger. (Seaside library, v. 22, no. 425)). 1878. G. Munro.
Maid for Murder. Milton K Ozaki. LC 56-21102. (Ace double novel books, D-135). Ace Books.
Maid in Sweden. Maude Poiret. (O.s.i.). (Orig.). 1971. pap. 0.95 o.s.i. (A839N, Award). Univ Pub & Dist.
Maid in the Monte: A Novel. 1st Ed. Jorge Piedra. LC 60-16960. Greenwich Books.
Maid in Waiting. John Galsworthy. LC 31-28308. 1931. C. Scribner's Sons.
Maid Is Reckless. Rob Eden. LC 41-220442. Gramercy Publishing Col.
Maid Marian and Crotchet Castle. Thomas Love Peacock. Ed. by Saintsbury, George Edward Bateman. LC 7-33749. 1895. Macmillan and Co.
Maid Marian: And Other Stories. Molly Elliot Seawell. LC 5-2445. (On cover: Appletons' town and country library, no. 77). 1891. D. Appleton and Company.
Maid Melicent. Beulah Marie Dix. LC 14-16919. 1914. 1.25. Hearst's International Library Co.
Maid No More. Helen De Guerry Simpson. LC 40-11562. Reynal & Hitchcock.
Maid of Athens. Lafayette McLaws. LC 6-7398. 1906. Little, Brown, and Company.
Maid of Athens. A Novel. Justin McCarthy. (Harper's Franklin square library, no. 345). 1883. Harper & Brothers.
Maid of Athens: A Novel of Today. French Strother. LC 32-18433. 1932. Doubleday, Doran & Company, Inc.
Maid of Bar Harbor. Henrietta Gould Rowe. LC 2-16200. 1902. Little, Brown, and Company.
Maid of Bocasse. May Halsey Miller. LC 5102. G. W. Dillingham Company.
Maid of Canal Street: And The Bloxhams Also Barclay Compton. Eliza Leslie. 1851. A. Hart.
Maid of Delight. Florent D'Asherville. LC 77-237849. 1968. 1.75. Ophelia Press.
Maid of Gloucester. Henry Lane Eno. LC 23-7261. 1923. Duffield & Company.
Maid of Honor. Louise Platt Hauck. LC 36-20441. 1936. Macrae-Smith-Company.
Maid of Honor. Richard Sill Holmes. LC 7-38899. F. H. Revell Company.
Maid of Honor. Jean Randall. LC 36-20441. 1936. Macrae Smith Company.
Maid of Honour: A Novel Set in the Court of Mary Queen of Scots. Elizabeth Byrd. LC 78-19952. 1979. 8.95 (ISBN 0-312-50430-6). St. Martin's Press.
Maid of Israel. Tolbert R Ingram. LC 55-14327. 1955. Broadman Press.
Maid of Killeena, & Other Stories. facsimile ed. William Black. LC 71-152936. (Short Story Index Reprint Ser.). Repr. of 1874 ed. 16.00 (ISBN 0-8369-3794-5). Ayer Co.
Maid of Magdala. Lee Mays. LC 66-29253. 1967. Dorrance.
Maid of Maiden Lane: A Sequel to "The Bow of Orange Ribbon". A Love Story. Amelia Edith Huddleston Barr. LC 4965. 1900. Dodd, Mead and Company.
Maid of Many Moods. Virginia Stanton Sheard. LC 2-21978. 1902. J. Pott & Company.
Maid of Mettle. Louie Alien Baker. LC 2-29916. 1902.,G. W. Jacobs & Co.
Maid of Middies' Haven: A Story of Annapolis Life. Gabrielle Emilie Snow Jackson. LC 13-115. 1912. 1.20. McBride, Nast & Company.
Maid of Mirabelle: A Romance of Lorraine. Eliot Harlow Robinson. LC 20-12599. 1920. The Page Company.
Maid of Montauk a Story. Ferdinand Gerhard Wiechmann. LC 2-13113. 1902. W. R. Jenkins.
Maid of Moods: A Tale of the Maine Woods. Edith Woodell Shepherd. LC 10-23199. The C. M. Clark Publishing Company.
Maid of Nettuno. Ludwig Huna & Pemberton, Madge, Tr. LC 31-11915. 1931. Brewer and Warren Inc.
Maid of New Orleans. Minette Graham Smith. LC 54-10248. Vantage Press.
Maid of New Ulm. An Historical Tale of the Indian Uprising and Massacre in Minnesota in 1862. A Novel. James Milford Merrill. (On cover: The war series, v. 1, no. 3). 1895. Novelist Publishing Co.
Maid of Old New York: A Romance of Peter Stuyvesant's Time. Amelia Edith Huddleston Barr. LC 11-27299. 1911. 1.25. Dodd, Mead and Company.
Maid of Old Virginia: A Romance of Bacon's Rebellion. William Sage. LC 15-20587. Fleming H. Revell Company.
Maid of Orleans: Tr. from the German of Frederick Henning. Friedrich Henning & Upton, George Putnam, 1834-1919, Tr. LC 4-32320. (Life stories for young people). 1904. A. C. McClurg & Co.
Maid of Salem Towne. Lucy Foster Madison. LC 6-11309. 1906. The Penn Publishing Company.
Maid of Sark. Sibyl Collings Hathaway & Turner, Joseph Mallord William, 1775-1851, Illus. LC 39-27728. 1939. D. Appleton-Century Company, Incorporated.
Maid of Sher. Richard Doddridge Blackmore. LC 6-13831. (On cover: Lovell's library, v. 19, no. 936). J. W. Lovell Company.
Maid of Sker. A Novel. Richard Doddridge Blackmore. LC 7-23673. (On cover: Library of select novels. no. 381). 1872. Harper & Brothers.
Maid of Sonora. Charles Edmund Haas. LC 5-12159. 1905. Broadway Publishing Company.
Maid of Stralsund. A Story of the Thirty Years' War. Jacob B De Liefde. LC 7-15849. 1876. Lovell, Adam, Wesson & Co.
Maid of the Combahee: A Romance of the South. Israel Plummer Taft. LC 19-1491. Saulsbury Publishing Co.
Maid of the Foot-Hills: Or, Missing Links in the Story of Reconstruction. James Walter Daniel. LC 5-39864. 1905. The Neale Publishing Company.
Maid of the Forest: A Romance of St. Clair's Defeat. Randall Parrish. LC 13-20574. 1913. A. C. McClurg & Co.
Maid of the Kentucky Hills. Edwin Carlile Litsey. LC 13-247961. (Illus.). 1913. Browne & Howell Company.
Maid of the Mississippi: The Story of Susan John. 1st Ed. Josephine Grider Jacobs. LC 53-10543. 1953. Exposition Press.
Maid of the Mist. John Oxenham, pseud. LC 14-9884. Hodder and Stoughton.
Maid of the Mist. John Oxenham, pseud. LC 14-11091. 1914. John Lane Company.
Maid of the Mohawk. Frederick Augustus Ray. LC 6-39723. 1906. The C. M. Clark Publishing Co.
Maid of the Mountain. Jackson Gregory. 1976. Repr. of 1925 ed. lib. bdg. 17.15x (ISBN 0-88411-283-7). Amereon Ltd.
Maid of the Mountain: A Romance of the California Wilderness. Jackson Gregory. LC 25-15848. 1925. C. Scribner's Sons.
Maid of the North: Feminist Folk Tales from Around the World. Ethel Johnston Phelps. LC 80-21500. (Illus.). 10.95 (ISBN 0-03-056893-5). Holt, Rinehart, and Winston.
Maid of the Valley: Or, The Brothers's Revenge. A Tale of the Revolution. Andrew Jackson Herr. 1847. W. H. Graham.
Maid of the Whispering Hills. Vingie Eve Roe. LC 12-2459. 1912. Dodd, Mead and Company.
Maid of '76. Emilie Benson Knipe & Knipe, Alden Arthur. LC 15-19078. 1915. The Macmillan Company.
Maid or Mistress. James Noble Gifford. LC 43-164438. 1943. Phoenix Press.
Maid Silja. new ed. Frans Eemil Sillanpaa. Tr. by Alexander Matson from Finnish. LC 33-32586. 316p. 1974. 14.95 (ISBN 0-910220-66-2). Berg.
Maid Silja: The History of the Last Offshoot of an Old Family Tree. Frans Eemil Sillanpaa. LC 74-192547. 1974. 10.63 (ISBN 0-910220-66-2). N. S. Berg.
Maid Silja: The History of the Last Offshoot of an Old Family Tree. Frans Eemil Sillanpaa & Matson, Alexander, Tr. LC 33-32586. 1933. The Macmillan Company.
Maid to Marry see Killer & Other Plays.
Maid to Murder. Roy Vickers. LC 50-6629. 1950. Mill.
Maid Unafraid. Lovella Annette Pitts Woolfolk. LC 37-2834. 1937. Godwin.
Maid, Wife, or Widow! Annie French Hector. (On cover: Seaside library. Pocket ed., no. 229). 1884. G. Munro.
Maid, Wife, or Widow! Annie French Hector. (On cover: Lovell's library, v. 16, no. 799). 1886. J. W. Lovell Company.
Maidee, the Alchemist: Or, Turning All to Gold. Susan Cannon. LC 6-21474. 1871. M. Doolady.
Maiden. Cynthia Buchanan. LC 70-163446. 1972. (671-78255-x) 1.25. Popular Library.
Maiden All Forlorn: And Other Stories. Margaret Wolfe Hungerford. (On cover: Lovell's library, v. 12, no. 621). 1885. J. W. Lovell Company.
Maiden & Married Life of Mary Powell: Afterwards Mistress Milton. Anne Manning. LC 4-17545. Dodd & Mead.
Maiden Castle. John Cowper Powys. LC 66-3670. 1966. Colgate Univ. Pr.
Maiden Castle. John Cowper Powys. LC 36-32645. 1936. Simon and Schuster.
Maiden Effort. Samuel Hopkins Adams. LC 37-12437. Liveright Publishing Corp.
Maiden Fair. By Charles Gibbon. Charles Gibbon. (On cover: Seaside library. Pocket ed., no. 64). 1883. G. Munro.
Maiden Manifest. Della Campbell MacLeod. LC 13-3070. 1913. Little, Brown, and Company.
Maiden Mother: Or, Eugenia the Guiltless. A Thrilling History of Real Life, in Which Many Prominent Citizens of Louisiana Figure Conspicuously. Charles Zornow. Barclay & Co.
Maiden Murders. Mystery Writers of America. LC 52-7294. 1952. Harper.
Maiden of Glory Island. June Wetherell. (Berkley Medallion) (ISBN 0-425-03184-5). Berkley.
Maiden of Mars. F. M Clarke. LC 6-21377. (On cover: Sergel's international library, vol. i, no. 17)). 1892. C. H. Sergel & Company.
Maiden Rites: A Romance. Sonia Pilcer. LC 81-51888. 1982. 13.95 (ISBN 0-670-22460-X). Viking.
Maiden Voyage. Geoffrey Marcus. 1977. pap. 1.95 (ISBN 0-532-19143-9). Woodhill.
Maiden Voyage. Kathleen Thompson Norris. LC 75-33038. 1975. 9.95 (ISBN 0-89190-305-4). American Reprint Co.
Maiden Voyage. Kathleen Thompson Norris. LC 34-30874. 1934. Doubleday, Doran & Company, Inc.

Maiden Voyage. Felix Riesenberg & Binns, Archie. LC 31-5214. The John Day Company.
Maiden Voyage. Jeannie Sakol. 240p. (Orig.). 1981. pap. 2.25 (ISBN 0-8439-0943-9). Leisure Bks CT.
Maiden Voyage. Herbert Silvette. LC 50-8566. 1950. Dutton.
Maiden Voyage. Denton Welch. LC 80-16729. 1980. 9.95 (ISBN 0-8290-0358-4). Irvington Publishers.
Maiden Widow: A Novel. Emma Dorothy Eliza Nevitte Southworth. LC 8-10826. T. B. Peterson & Brothers.
Maiden Worlds Unconquered. Florizel Von Reuter. (Illus.). 1967. 9.50x (ISBN 0-910476-03-9). Cultural Pr.
Maiden Worlds Unconquered: Eleven Fiction Tales of Love Through the Ages. Florizel Von Reuter. LC 68-594. (Illus.). 1967. Cultural Press.
Maidenhead Stories. Intro. by J. S. Murphy. pap. 1.25 o.p. (2048). Brandon.
Maiden's Diary. Alexandra Guy. (O.s.i.). (Orig.). pap. 0.95 o.s.i. (A436, Award). Univ Pub & Dist.
Maiden's Heritage: A Story of Love and Idealism with an Understanding of Life's Universal Principle. Elizabeth Barbour Dickson. LC 29-6862. Dickson Publishing Company.
Maidens of Osiris & Other Stories. Brigitta Valentiner. 1970. 4.50 o.p. Vantage.
Maidens of the Rocks. Gabriele D' Annunzio & Antona, Annetta Halliday, Tr. LC 9-3441. (His The romances of the lily). 1898. G. H. Richmond & Son.
Maidens of the Rocks. Gabriele D' Annunzio & Antona, Annetta Halliday, Tr. LC 26-36535. (Half-title: The modern library of the world's best books.). 1926. The Modern Library.
Maiden's Progress: A Novel in Dialogue. Violet Hunt. LC 7-9382. 1894. Harper & Brothers.
Maids and Mistresses. Beatrice Kean Stapleton Seymour. LC 32-26502. 1932. A. A. Knopf.
Maids of Paradise: A Novel. Robert William Chambers. LC 2-24324. 1902. Harper & Brothers.
Maids of Paradise: A Novel. Robert William Chambers. LC 3-21291. 1903. Harper & Brothers.
Maids Will Be Wives. Hazel Bowker Cole. LC 29-13214. 1929. Little, Brown, and Company.
Maidstone: A Mystery. Norman Mailer. LC 79-30761. (Signet book). (Illus.). 1971. 1.50. New American Library.
Maigret Abroad. Georges Simenon & Sainsbury, Geoffrey, Tr. LC 40-31041. Harcourt, Brace and Company.
Maigret Abroad. Georges Simenon & Sainsbury, Geoffrey, Tr. LC 44-141801. (Murder mystery monthly. No. 8). 1943. The Avon Book Company.
Maigret Among the Rich. Georges Simenon. 1978. pap. 5.95 (ISBN 0-671-79051-X, Wallaby). PB.
Maigret and M. Labbe. Georges Simenon & Gilbert, Stuart, Tr. LC 42-20570. 1942. Harcourt, Brace and Company.
Maigret and the Apparition. Georges Simenon. LC 76-14382. 6.95. Harcourt Brace Jovanovich.
Maigret and the Apparition. Georges Simenon. LC 77-22449. 1977. 7.95 (ISBN 0-8161-6503-3). G. K. Hall.
Maigret and the Apparition. Georges Simenon. LC 80-14124. (Harvest/HBJ book). 1980. 2.95 (ISBN 0-15-655127-6). Harcourt Brace Jovanovich.
Maigret and the Black Sheep. Georges Simenon. LC 75-28384. Harcourt Brace Jovanovich.
Maigret and the Bum. Georges Simenon. LC 73-9850. 1973. 5.95 (ISBN 0-15-155141-3). Harcourt Brace Jovanovich.
Maigret & the Burglar's Wife. Georges Simenon. 1973. pap. 0.95 o.p. (09194). Curtis.
Maigret and the Calame Report. Georges Simenon. LC 70-78874. 1969. Harcourt, Brace & World.
Maigret & the Enigmatic Letter. Georges Simenon. 1964. pap. 2.95 (ISBN 0-14-002023-3). Penguin.
Maigret and the Ghost. Georges Simenon. LC 76-379527. 1976. 2.95 (ISBN 0-241-89455-7). Hamilton.
Maigret and the Headless Corpse. Georges Simenon. LC 68-12598. 1968. Harcourt, Brace & World.
Maigret and the Hotel Majestic. Georges Simenon. LC 77-84398. 1978. 7.95 (ISBN 0-15-155124-3). Harcourt, Brace, Jovanovich.
Maigret and the Hundred Gibbets. Georges Simenon. LC 63-25657. 1963. Penguin Books.
Maigret and the Informer. Georges Simenon. LC 72-91839. 1973. 5.95 (ISBN 0-15-155140-5). Harcourt Brace Jovanovich.
Maigret and the Killer. Georges Simenon. LC 73-153691. 1971. 5.50 (ISBN 0-15-155127-8). Harcourt Brace Jovanovich.
Maigret and the Killer. Georges Simenon. LC 79-10402. (Harvest/HBJ book). 1979. 2.95 (ISBN 0-15-655124-1). Harcourt Brace Jovanovich.
Maigret & the Killers. Georges Simenon. 1973. pap. 0.95 o.p. (09192). Curtis.
Maigret and the Loner. Georges Simenon. LC 74-23862. 1975. 5.95 (ISBN 0-15-155144-8). Harcourt Brace Jovanovich.
Maigret and the Madwoman. Georges Simenon. LC 72-75421. 1972. 5.95 (ISBN 0-15-155138-3). Harcourt Brace Jovanovich.
Maigret & the Madwomen. Georges Simenon. Tr. by Eileen Ellenbogen. LC 79-10401. (Helen & Kurt Wolff Bk.). 1979. pap. 2.95 (ISBN 0-15-655122-5, Harv). HarBraceJ.
Maigret and the Man on the Bench. Georges Simenon. LC 75-8566. 1975. (ISBN 0-15-155145-6). Harcourt Brace Jovanovich.
Maigret and the Man on the Bench. Georges Simenon. LC 78-13304. (Harvest/HBJ book). 1979. 2.50 (ISBN 0-15-655123-3). Harcourt Brace Jovanovich.
Maigret and the Millionaires. Georges Simenon. LC 74-7009. 1974. 5.95 (ISBN 0-15-155143-X). Harcourt Brace Jovanovich.
Maigret and the Nahour Case. Georges Simenon. LC 82-47661. 1982. 10.95 (ISBN 0-15-155559-1). Harcourt Brace Jovanovich.
Maigret and the Spinster. Georges Simenon. LC 76-27416. 6.95. Harcourt Brace Jovanovich.
Maigret & the Strangled Stripper. Georges Simenon. pap. 0.95 o.p. (09195). Curtis.
Maigret and the Toy Village. Georges Simenon. LC 79-1843. 1979. 7.95 (ISBN 0-15-155554-0). Harcourt Brace Jovanovich.
Maigret and the Wine Merchant. Georges Simenon. LC 73-142097. 1971. (ISBN 0-15-155136-7). Harcourt Brace Jovanovich.
Maigret and the Wine Merchant. Georges Simenon. LC 79-26173. (Harvest/HBJ book). 1980. 2.95. Harcourt Brace Jovanovich.
Maigret at the Coroner's. Georges Simenon. LC 80-81491. 8.95 (ISBN 0-15-155556-7). Harcourt Brace Jovanovich.
Maigret at the Crossroads. Georges Simenon. 1963. pap. 2.95 (ISBN 0-14-002028-4). Penguin.
Maigret Cinq: Maigret and the Young Girl, Maigret's Little Joke, Maigret and the Old Lady, Maigret's First Case, Maigret Takes a Room. Georges Simenon. LC 65-16954. (Helen & Kurt Wolff bk.). 1965. 5.95. Harcourt.
Maigret et L'affaire Nahour. Georges Simenon. pap. 3.95. French & Eur.
Maigret et le Fantome. Georges Simenon. pap. 3.95. French & Eur.
Maigret et le Fueur. Georges Simenon. pap. 3.95. French & Eur.
Maigret et le Marchand de Vin. Georges Simenon. pap. 3.95. French & Eur.
Maigret et l'homme tout seul. Georges Simenon. pap. 3.95. French & Eur.
Maigret Goes Home. Georges Simenon. LC 68-4999. 1967. Penguin Books.
Maigret Goes Home. Georges Simenon. LC 67-111056. 1967. Penguin.
Maigret Goes Home. Georges Simenon. LC 68-4999. 1967. Penguin Books.
Maigret Hesitates. Georges Simenon. LC 79-100504. 1970. Harcourt, Brace & World.
Maigret in Exile. Georges Simenon. LC 78-13771. 1979. 7.95. Harcourt Brace Jovanovich.
Maigret in New York's Underworld. Georges Simenon. 1973. pap. 0.95 o.p. (09197). Curtis.
Maigret in New York's Underworld. Maigret a New York) Translated from French by Adrienne Foulke. 1st Ed. Georges Simenon. LC 54-7325. 1955. Published for the Crime Club by Doubleday.
Maigret in Vichy. Georges Simenon. LC 69-12047. 1969. Harcourt, Brace & World.
Maigret Keeps a Rendezvous. Georges Simenon & Ludwig, Margaret, Tr. LC 41-13234. Harcourt, Brace and Company.
Maigret Loses His Temper. Georges Simenon. LC 68-94534. (B 67-25642). 1967. Penguin Books in Association with H. Hamilton.
Maigret Loses His Temper. Georges Simenon. LC 73-18301. 1974. 5.95 (ISBN 0-15-155142-1). Harcourt Brace Jovanovich.
Maigret Loses His Temper. Georges Simenon. LC 80-14212. (Harvest/HBJ book). 1980. 2.95 (ISBN 0-15-655128-4). Harcourt Brace Jovanovich.
Maigret Meets a Milord. Georges Simenon. 1963. pap. 2.95 (ISBN 0-14-002027-6). Penguin.
Maigret Mystified. Georges Simenon. Orig. Title: Shadow in the Courtyard. 1964. pap. 1.95 o.p. (ISBN 0-14-002024-1). Penguin.
Maigret on the Defensive. Georges Simenon. LC 71-402364. 1968. Penguin.
Maigret on the Defensive. Georges Simenon. LC 81-47576. 1981. 10.95 (ISBN 0-15-155557-5). Harcourt Brace Jovanovich.
Maigret Se Defend. Georges Simenon. pap. 3.95. French & Eur.
Maigret Sets a Trap. Simenon, Georges. 1973. 0.95. Curtis Books.
Maigret Sets a Trap. Georges Simenon. LC 70-182331. 1972. (ISBN 0-15-155137-5). Harcourt Brace Jovanovich.
Maigret Sets a Trap. Georges Simenon. LC 78-13655. (Harvest/HBJ book). 1979. 2.50 (ISBN 0-15-655126-8). Harcourt Brace Jovanovich.
Maigret Sits It Out: Translated from the French. Georges Simenon & Ludwig, Margaret, Tr. LC 41-24631. Harcourt, Brace and Company.
Maigret Stonewalled. Georges Simenon. LC 63-25659. 1963. Penguin Books.
Maigret to the Rescue. Georges Simenon & Sainsbury, Geoffrey, Tr. LC 41-613. Harcourt, Brace and Company.
Maigret Travels South. Georges Simenon & Sainsbury, Geoffrey, Tr. LC 40-9595. Harcourt, Brace and Company.
Maigret Trio. Georges Simenon. LC 72-88794. 1973. 6.95 o.p. (ISBN 0-15-155139-1). HarBraceJ.
Maigret Trio: Maigret's Failure, Maigret in Society, & Maigret & the Lazy Burglar. Georges Simenon. Tr. by Daphne Woodard & Robert Eglesfield. 288p. pap. 6.95 (ISBN 0-15-655137-3, Harv). HarBraceJ.
Maigret Trio: Maigret's Failure, Maigret in Society, Maigret and the Lazy Burglar. Georges Simenon. LC 72-88794. 1973. 6.95 (ISBN 0-15-155139-1). Harcourt Brace Jovanovich.
Maigret's Boyhood Friend. Georges Simenon. LC 79-124825. 1970. Harcourt Brace Jovanovich.
Maigret's Boyhood Friend. Georges Simenon. LC 80-25139. (Harvest/HBJ book). 1981. 2.95 (ISBN 0-15-655131-4). Harcourt Brace Jovanovich.
Maigret's Christmas. Georges Simenon. LC 77-367934. (His Complete Maigret short stories; v. 1). 1976. 4.95 (ISBN 0-241-89513-8). Hamilton.
Maigret's Christmas: Nine Stories. Georges Simenon. LC 77-1724. 1977. 8.95 (ISBN 0-15-155551-6). Harcourt Brace Jovanovich.
Maigret's Dead Man. Georges Simenon. LC 64-13104. 1964. Published for the Crime Club by Doubleday.
Maigret's Pickpocket. Georges Simenon. Tr. by Nigel Ryan. LC 68-20073. (Helen & Kurt Wolff Book). 1968. 3.95 o.p. (ISBN 0-15-155131-6). HarBraceJ.
Maigret's Pipe: Seventeen Stories. Georges Simenon. LC 78-4169. 1978. 8.95. Harcourt Brace Jovanovich.
Maigret's Rival. Georges Simenon. LC 79-3362. 1980. 7.95 (ISBN 0-15-155555-9). Harcourt Brace Jovanovich.
Mail Boat. 1st Ed. Alexander Randolph. LC 54-545974. 1954. Holt.
Mail Robber: Or, The Clever Capture of a Dishonest Postal Clerk. From the Diary of Chief Inspector James E. Stewart... James E. Stewart. LC 8-156907. (Pinkerton detective series, no. 34). 1889. Laird & Lee.
Maime O'th' Corner: A No el. Mary E. Sweetman Blundell. LC 6-14201. Printed by the Burr Printing House,
Main. Trevanian. LC 76-24896. 1976. 8.95 (ISBN 0-15-155549-4). Harcourt Brace Jovanovich.
Main Chance. Meredith Nicholson. 1903. The Bobbs-Merrill Company.
Main Chance. Edmund Ward. LC 76-30365. 1977. 7.95 (ISBN 0-698-10816-7). Coward, McCann & Geoghegan.
Main Chance. Jules Witcover. LC 78-26867. 1979. 10.00 (ISBN 0-670-45112-6). Viking Press.
Main Chance. Jules Witcover. 1981. 2.50 (ISBN 0-425-04646-X). Berkley Books.
Main Entrance, a Novel. Konrad Bercovici. Covici, Friede, Inc.
Main Experiment. Christopher Hodder-Williams. (U6049). 1966. Ballantine.
Main Experiment: 1st Amer. Ed. Christopher Hodder-Williams. LC 65-10854. 1965. 4.95. Putnam.
Main from the River, a Wilson Story. George Douglas Howard Cole & Margaret Isabel Postgate Cole. LC 28-21188. 1928. The Macmillan Company.
Main Line: A Philadelphia Novel. Livingston Biddle. LC 50-6927. 1950. Messner.
Main Line Girl. Robert Boyd. LC 57-11737. (Milestone book). 1957. Comet Press Books.
Main Line Kill. Roger Busby & Gerald Holtham. LC 68-30945. (Walker mystery.). 1968. 3.95. Walker.
Main Line West. Paul Horgan. LC 36-7370. 1936. Harper & Brothers.
Main Road: A Novel. Maude Lavinia Radford Warren. LC 13-210178. 1913. Harper & Brothers.
Main Stream. Hilda Morris. LC 39-27328. 1939. G. P. Putnam's Sons.
Main Street. Sinclair Lewis. LC 46-8601. (Half-title: The Living library). 1946. The World Publishing Company.
Main Street: The Story of Carol Kennicott. Sinclair Lewis. LC 20-189340. 1920. Harcourt, Brace and Howe.
Main Street: The Story of Carol Kennicott. Sinclair Lewis. LC 24-11843. 1921. Grosset & Dunlap.
Main Street: The Story of Carol Kennicott. Sinclair Lewis. LC 21-101791. 1921. Harcourt, Brace and Company.
Main Street: The Story of Carol Kennicott. Sinclair Lewis. LC 25-23747. 1923. Grosset & Dunlap.
Main-Traveled Roads. Hamlin Garland. (Harper Modern Classics Ser). (gr. 7 up). text ed. 2.00, s.p. 1.50 o.p. (ISBN 0-06-534024-8). Har-Row.
Main-Travelled Roads. sunset ed. Hamlin Garland. LC 72-84689. 1974. (lib. ed.) 10.50 (ISBN 0-403-02981-3). Scholarly Press.
Main-Travelled Roads. Hamlin Garland. LC 79-103888. (Charles E. Merrill standard editions). 1970. C. E. Merrill.
Main-Travelled Roads. new ed., with additional stories. ed. Hamlin Garland. LC 99-4062. 1899. The Macmillan Company.
Main-Travelled Roads. sunset ed. Hamlin Garland. LC 19-5047. Harper & Brothers.
Main-Travelled Roads. Hamlin Garland & Garland, Constance Hamlin, Illus. LC 30-28187. 1930. Harper & Brothers.
Main-Travelled Roads. Authorized Ed. Introd. by William Dean Howells. Afterword, Bibl. by B. R. McElderry, Jr. Hamlin Garland. LC 56-698016. (Perennial classic, HP6058V). 1966. 1.50. Harper.
Main-Travelled Roads: Being Six Stories of the Mississippi Valley. Hamlin Garland. LC 6-40719. 1893. Stone and Kimball.
Main-Travelled Roads: Six Mississippi Valley Stories. Ed., Intro. by Thomas A. Bledsoe. Hamlin Garland. (Rinehart eds., 66 rebound). 1965. 3.00. P. Smith.
Main-Travelled Roads: Six Mississippi Valley Stories. Edited with an Introd. by Thomas A. Bledsoe. Hamlin Garland. LC 54-5867. (Rinehart editions, 66). 1954. Rinehart.
Main-Travelled Roads. With a New Pref. by B. R. Mc-Elderry, Jr., and the 1893 Introd. by William Dean Howells. Hamlin Garland. LC 56-6980. (Harper's modern classics). 1956. Harper.
Mainboy. James Russell Johnson. 1978. 1.75 (ISBN 0-87067-540-0). Holloway House.
Maine Girl. A Realistic Romance of Down East. Erwin L Coolidge. LC 6-30195. 1892. G. W. Dillingham.
Maine Is in My Heart. William Murray Clark. LC 64-13108. 1964. D. McKay Co.
Maine Massacre. Janwillem Van De Wetering. LC 79-16939. 1979. 13.95 (ISBN 0-8161-6753-2). G. K. Hall.
Maine Massacre. Janwillem Van De Wetering. LC 78-10185. 1979. 8.95 (ISBN 0-395-27395-1). Houghton Mifflin.
Mainland. Grant Watson, Elliot Lovegood. LC 17-24853. 1917. A. A. Knopf.
Mainly Horses. Ed. by Ernest Rhys. Scott, Mrs. Catharine Amy (Dawson) Joint Ed. LC 29-148730. 1929. D. Appleton and Company.
Mainly on the Air. rev. ed. Max Beerbohm. 1958. 4.50 o.p. Knopf.
Mainprize: A Novel of Who We Are. Bruce Earlin McFarland. LC 72-181821. 1971. 9.50. Concord Press.
Mainsail Haul. John Masefield. LC 13-21106. 1913. The Macmillan Company.
Mainside. Paul Mandel. LC 62-8467. 1962. Random House.
Mainspring. Charles Agnew Maclean. LC 12-10813. 1912. Little, Brown, and Company.
Mainspring. Beatrice Burton Morgan. LC 36-74853. Farrar & Rinehart, Inc.
Mainsprings for Action. Ron Preece. 1979. pap. 1.50 (ISBN 0-85363-127-1). OMF Bks.
Mainstays of Maine. Coffin. 1978. pap. 3.75 (ISBN 0-89272-042-5). Down East.
Mainwaring. Maurice Henry Hewlett. LC 20-195060. 1920. Dodd, Mead and Company.
Maisie Derrick. Katharine Sarah Gadsden Macquoid. LC 7-20283. (On cover: Lovell's international series, no. 208). Lovell, Coryell & Company.
Maisie McFlannel's Romances. Helen W Pryde. LC 52-24664. 1951. T. Nelson.
Maison De Claudine. Sidonie Gabrielle Colette. 1977. pap. 3.95 (763). French & Eur.
Maison De Shine: More Stories of the Actors' Boarding House. Helen Green. LC 8-32338. 1908. B. W. Dodge & Company.
Maison du Chat qui Pelote - Le Bal de Sceaux - La Vendetta. Honore De Balzac. Ed. by Castex. (Coll. Prestige). 9.95 o.p. French & Eur.
Maitland Varne: Or, The Bells of De Thaumaturge. Du Bois H Loux. LC 11-636. 1911. 1.50. De Thaumaturge Company.
Maitland's Master Mystery. Melvin Linwood Severy. LC 13-1643. 1913. The Ball Publishing Company.
Maitre De Santiago. Henry De Montherlant. Ed. by Lucille Becker & Alba Della Fazia. 1965. pap. text ed. 2.50x o.p. (ISBN 0-669-28266-9). Heath.

Maiwa's Revenge. Henry Rider Haggard & Fargus, Frederick John, 1847-1885. LC 6-46145. (On cover: Lovell's library. no. 1200). 1888. J. W. Lovell Company.
Maiwa's Revenge: A Novel. Henry Rider Haggard. LC 6-46144. 1888. Harper & Brothers.
Maiwa's Revenge: Or, The War of the Little Hand, by H. Rider Haggard. Henry Rider Haggard. LC 23-6382. 1923. 1.25. Longmans, Green and Co.
Maiwa's Revenge: Or, The War of the Little Hand. Illus. by Hookway Cowles. Henry Rider Haggard. LC 66-5448. 1966. bds., 2.95. Macdonald.
Maj. G. T. Ellard. 5.95 o.p. Vantage.
Maj. G. T Ellard. 1973. 5.95 (ISBN 0-533-00748-8). Vantage.
Maje: A Love Story. Armistead Churchill Gordon. LC 14-39715. 1914. 0.75. C. Scribner's Sons.
Majella: Or, Nameless and Blind. A Story of the Susquehanna. Ella Maude Stewart. LC 8-15693. 1893. Printed by J. B. Lippincott Company.
Majestic. Ray Hubbard. 432p. (Orig.). 1981. pap. 2.75 (ISBN 0-553-13218-0). Bantam.
Majestic Mystery. Denis George Mackail. LC 24-21917. 1924. Houghton Mifflin Company.
Majesty: A Novel. Louis Marie Anne Couperus. Tr. by Teixeira De Mattos, Alexander Louis. LC 21-74061. 1921. Dodd, Mead and Company.
Majesty of the Law. Sinclair Gluck. LC 17-1009. 1916. Hodder and Stoughton.
Majesty's Rancho. Grey, Zane. LC 63-6978. (Great western edition, 22). 1963. Grosset & Dunlap.
Majesty's Rancho. Zane Grey. LC 42-208051. 1938. Harper & Brothers.
Majesty's Rancho. large print ed. Zane Grey. LC 82-709. 1982. 11.95 (ISBN 0-89621-347-1). Thorndike Press.
Majesty's Rancho. Zane Grey. 1980. pap. 1.95 (ISBN 0-671-83506-8). PB.
Majipoor Chronicles. Robert Silverberg. LC 81-67589. 304p. 1982. 12.95 (ISBN 0-87795-358-9); pap. 5.95 (ISBN 0-87795-359-7). Arbor Hse.
Majipoor Chronicles. Robert Silverberg. 1983. pap. 3.50. Bantam.
Major. Charles William Gordon. LC 17-301223. 1.40. George H. Doran Company.
Major--Diamond Buyer. L. Patrick Greene. LC 24-29997. 1924. Doubleday, Page & Company.
Major American Short Stories. A. Walton Litz. LC 74-83990. (Illus.). 1975. 6.95 (ISBN 0-19-501868-0). Oxford University Press.
Major American Short Stories. rev. ed. A. Walton Litz. LC 79-20446. 1980. 8.95 (ISBN 0-19-502701-9). Oxford University Press.
Major Crime. James H. Mantinband. LC 48-1824. 1948. Phoenix Press.
Major Dane's Garden. Margery Freda Perham. LC 76-131909. (Illus.). 1971. 12.50 (ISBN 0-8419-0056-6). Africana Pub. Corp.
Major Enquiry. Laurence Henderson. LC 76-1481. 1976. 7.95. St. Martin's Press.
Major Frank. A Novel. Basboom-Toussaint, Anna Louisa Geertruida & Akeroyd, James, Tr. LC 6-15023. (On cover: Seaside library. Pocket ed., no. 803). 1886. G. Munro.
Major Has Seven Guests: A Novel. Constance Wagner. LC 40-27419. 1940. Frederick A. Stokes Company.
Major Jones's Courtship. rev. and enl. to which are added thirteen humorous sketches. with illus. by cary. ed. William Tappan Thompson. LC 73-87312. (Illus.). 1973. 8.00 (ISBN 0-87797-025-4). Cherokee Pub. Co.
Major Jones's Courtship and Travels. Comprising All the Scenes, Incidents and Adventures of His Courtship, in a Series of Letters by Himself; As Well As the Humorous Narrative of His Travels from Georgia to Canada, and Back, Together with His Experience in Each Town He Passed Through. With Twenty-One Illustrations, from Original Designs. William Tappan Thompson. LC 43-43394. (On cover: Peterson's illustrated uniform edition of humorous American works). T. B. Peterson and Brothers.
Major Jones's Courtship. Detailed, with Humorous Scenes, Incidents and Adventures. rev. and enl. with twenty-one illustrations by darley and cary... ed. William Tappan Thompson. LC 8-19960. T. B. Peterson & Brothers.
Major Jones's Courtship: Detailed, with Other Scenes, Incidents, and Adventures, in a Series of Letters. 2d ed., greatly enl., with illustrations by darley... ed. William Tappan Thompson. LC 8-19961. 1844. Carey & Hart.
Major Jones's Georgia Scenes. Comprising His Celebrated Sketches of Scenes in Georgia. With Their Incidents and Characters. William Tappan Thompson. LC 8-19958. T. B. Peterson & Brothers.
Major Jones's Scenes in Georgia. William Tappan Thompson. LC 76-91094. (American humorists series). (Illus.). 1969. Literature House.
Major Ordeals of the Mind. Henri Michaux. LC 73-16237. (Helen & Kurt Wolff Bk.). 1974. 6.95 o.p. (ISBN 0-15-155720-9). HarBraceJ.
Major Matterson of Kentucky: A Novel. St. George Rathborne. (On cover: Idle moments series, no. 21). The Price-McGill Company.
Major Matterson of Kentucky. A Novel. St. George Rathborne. LC 8-5849. (On cover: Criterion series, no. 10). 1894. Street & Smith.
Major Operation. James White. 192p. 1981. pap. 2.25 (ISBN 0-345-29381-9). Ballantine.
Major Stepton's War. Matthew Vaughan. LC 77-11369. 1978. 7.95 (ISBN 0-385-13607-2). Doubleday.
Major Thompson Goes French: The New Notebooks of Major W. Marmaduke Thompson. Pierre Daninos. LC 71-863494. 1971. 1.50 (ISBN 0-491-00216-5). W. H. Allen.
Major Thorpe's Scenes in Arkansaw. Containing the Whole of the Quarter Race in Kentucky... and Other Sketches Illustrative of Scenes, Incidents, and Characters, Throughout "The Universal Yankee Nation." To Which Is Added, The Drama in Pokerville; A Night in a Swamp; and Other Stories. Ed. by William Trotter Porter. Field, Joseph M. LC 2-9866. T. B. Peterson & Brothers.
Major Tom. A Story of the Storming of Petersburg. A Novel. Edward S Brooks. LC 6-17385. (On cover: The war series, v. 1, no. 4). Novelist Publishing Company.
Major Vigoureaux. Arthur Thomas Quiller-Couch. LC 7-30166. 1907. C. Scribner's Sons.
Major: 1st Amer. Ed. David Hughes. LC 65-123088. 3.95. Coward.
Majorca. Sam Dodson. (Fawcett Gold Medal Book.). 1977. 1.75. (ISBN 0-449-13740-6). Fawcett Pub.
Majorca. Sam Dodson. (Fawcett Gold Medal Book.). 1977. 1.75. (ISBN 0-449-13740-6). Fawcett Pub.
Majorettes. John Russo. 1979. pap. 1.95 (ISBN 0-671-82315-9). PB.
Majorie Daw & Other Stories. Thomas Bailey Aldrich. 1972. Repr. of 1885 ed. lib. bdg. 15.00 (ISBN 0-8422-8001-4). Irvington.
Majors. W. E. Griffin. (Brotherhood of War Ser.: No. 3). 384p. 1983. pap. 3.50 (ISBN 0-515-05645-6). Jove Pubns.
Major's Candlesticks. James Owen Hannay. LC 29-161704. The Bobbs-Merrill Company.
Major's Christmas: And Other Stories. Patience Stapleton. LC 12-143542. 1886. News Printing Company.
Major's Favourite: A Novel. Henrietta Eliza Vaughan Stannard. LC 8-13855. 1895. J. S. Tait & Sons.
Major's Love: Or, The Sequel of a Crime. Ella Brown Price. LC 7-30104. 1888. T. B. Peterson & Brothers.
Major's Niece. Sara Van Buren & Brady, Adeline, Joint Author. LC 3-7165. 1903. The Abbey Press.
Makar's Dream, and Other Stories. Vladimir Galaktionovich Korolenko. LC 74-163037. (Short story index reprint series). (Illus.). 1971. (ISBN 0-8369-3951-4). Books for Libraries Press.
Makar's Dream, and Other Stories. Vladimir Galaktionovich Korolenko. Tr. by Fell, Marian. LC 16-6611. 1916. Duffield and Company.
Makassar Strait Contract. Philip Atlee. (Fawcett Gold Medal Book). 1976. (pbk.) 1.25. Fawcett.
Makbara. Juan. Goytisolo. LC 81-5808. 12.95 (ISBN 0-86579-014-0) (ISBN 0-394-51803-9). Seaver Books: Distributed by Grove Press.
Make a Killing. Harold Q Masur. LC 64-10294. (Random House mystery). 1964. Random House.
Make a Killing. Brad Williams. LC 61-14400. 1961. M. S. Mill Co., and W. Morrow.
Make a Run for Heaven. Walter Tipton. LC 53-33937. 1953. De Vorss.
Make a Wish. Don Robertson. LC 77-14531. 7.95 (ISBN 0-399-12043-2). Putnam.
Make-Believe. Faith Baldwin Cuthrell. LC 30-240433. 1930. Dodd, Mead & Company.
Make Believe. James Noble Gifford. LC 38-15230. 1938. Gramercy Pub. Co.
Make Believe. Carol Holliston. LC 38-152309. Gramercy Publishing Co.
Make-Believe Children. Arlene DeMarco. (Signet book). 1975. (pbk.) 1.75. New American Library.
Make-Believe Love. Kristin Michaels. (Signet Book). 1978. 1.50 (ISBN 0-451-08058-0). New American Library.
Make-Believe Man. Elizabeth Fenwick. LC 63-16530. 1963. Harper & Row.
Make-Believe Rainbow. Bennie Caroline Hall. LC 55-11879. 1955. Arcadia House.
Make-Believers. Berry Fleming. LC 72-91908. (Illus.). 1972. 7.95 (ISBN 0-911116-81-8). Pelican Pub. Co.
Make Death Love Me. Ruth Rendell. LC 78-22621. 1979. 8.95 (ISBN 0-385-15184-5). Doubleday.
Make Death Love Me. Ruth Rendell. LC 79-23061. 1979. 13.50 (ISBN 0-8161-3012-4). G. K. Hall.
Make Haste, My Beloved. Frances J. Roberts. 1978. 5.95 (ISBN 0-932814-25-5); pap. 3.95 (ISBN 0-932814-26-3). Kings Farspan.
Make Haste, My Beloved. Thelma Thompson. LC 52-6709. 1952. Austin-Phelps.
Make Haste: My Love. George Adolphus Edinger. LC 52-25671. 1951. Hutchinson.
Make Haste to Live: By the Gordons. 1st Ed. Mildred Gordon & Gordon Gordon. LC 50-6846. 1950. Published for the Crime Club by Doubleday.
Make Her Beg. Lee De Pepys. pap. 1.95 o.p. (ISBN 0-87977-161-5, DBB161). Dansk Blue Bk.
Make Love & War. Harold Ross. (Orig.). pap. 0.60 o.p. (B60-074). Belmont-Tower.
Make Love, Not Water. William Furber. LC 75-28504. (Traveller's companion series, TC 477). 1.95. Traveller's Companion.
Make Me a Falcon. Libby Marsh Campbell. LC 74-33070. 100p. 1974. 3.95 (ISBN 0-89227-011-X). Commonwealth Pr.
Make Me a Lady. E. Dammann. 3.75 o.p. Carlton.
Make Me a Lesbian. Polly Sherman. pap. 1.25 o.p. (2056). Brandon.
Make Me a Star. Chet Hagan. LC 81-202362. 5.95 (ISBN 0-441-51603-3). Ace Books.
Make Me an Offer: Illustrated by Leonard Rosoman. 1st American Ed. Wolf Mankowitz. LC 53-5209. 1953. Dutton.
Make Me Yours. Eleanore Browne. LC 34-445. 1934. The Macaulay Company.
Make Mine Maclain: The Silent Whistle, Melody in Death, The Murderer Who Wanted More. Baynard Hardwick Kendrick. LC 47-3321. 1947. W. Morrow & Company.
Make Mine Murder. Robert Sidney Bowen. LC 46-6949. 1946. Crown Publishers.
Make Mine Revenge. W. Crawford Thompson. 1973. pap. 0.95 o.p. (09216). Curtis.
Make Much of Time. Patrick Davidson. LC 66-18821. 1966. 5.95. Rigby.
Make My Bed: A Novel. 1st Ed. Nathaniel Burt. LC 57-11999. 1957. Little, Brown.
Make My Bed Soon. Dorothy Stockbridge Tillet. LC 47-12513. 1948. Pub. for the Crime Club by Doubleday.
Make My Bed Soon. Jack Webb. LC 63-18426. (Rinehart suspense novel). 1963. Holt, Rinehart and Winston.
Make My Coffin Strong. Cover Painting by Barye Phillips. William Robert Cox. LC 55-159892. (Gold medal book, 447). 1954. Fawcett Publications.
Make No Law. Donald Gilbert Taggart. LC 69-20099. 1969. 5.95. Doubleday.
Make One. Rod Witney. 1974. 6.95 (ISBN 0-533-01308-9). Vantage Press.
Make Out with Murder. Chip Harrison. LC 76-354081. (Fawcett gold medal book). 1974. 0.95. Fawcett Publications.
Make Room for the Jester. Stead Jones. LC 65-107986. 1965. 4.50. Doubleday.
Make Room! Make Room! Harry Harrison. (Medallion bk., X1416)., C.
Make Room! Make Room! Harry Harrison. LC 79-2562. (Series: Gregg Press Science Fiction Series.). (Illus.). 1979. 12.00 (ISBN 0-8398-2565-X). Gregg Press.
Make Room, Make Room. Jarr Harrison. LC 66-17406. 1966. Doubleday.
Make-Shift Marriage. Gertrude M. Robins Reynolds. LC 12-228152. Hodder and Stoughton.
Make-Shift Marriage. Gertrude M. Robins Reynolds. LC 12-24817. Hodder & Stoughton, George H. Doran Company.
Make the Corpse Walk. Rene Raymond. LC 46-21057. 1946. Pub. for the Crime Book Society by Jarrolds Limited.
Make the Love Tree Grow: A Novel. Martin O'Neill. LC 70-86649. 1969. 5.95. Crown Publishers.
Make the Man Notice You. Maysie Greig. LC 40-691075. 1940. Doubleday, Doran & Company, Inc.
Make the Man Pay. Bennie Caroline Hall. LC 45-7763. 1945. Phoenix Press.
Make-up: A Romance of the Footlights. Alma Sioux Scarberry. LC 31-41861. Grosset & Dunlap.
Make up and Kiss. Samuel Michael Fuller. LC 38-36742. 1938. Godwin.
Make-up for the Toff. John Creasey. LC 67-13220. 1967. bds., 3.95. Walker.
Make Us Happy. Arthur Herzog. LC 78-4770. 8.95 (ISBN 0-690-01460-0). Crowell.
Make Way, Darling. Belle Bruck. LC 47-177742. 1946. Arcadia House, Inc.
Make Way for Love. Ruth MacLeod. LC 73-3050. (Red rose romance 136). 1973. (pbk.) 0.75. Bantam Books.
Make Way for Lucia: The Complete Lucia, Including Queen Lucia, Lucia in London, Miss Mapp, The Male Impersonator, Mapp and Lucia, The Worshipful Lucia, and Trouble for Lucia. Edward Frederic Benson. LC 76-783. 1976. 10.00 (ISBN 0-690-01105-9). Crowell.
Make Way for Romance. Kathleen Harris. 1940. Arcadia House.
Make Way for Romance. Kathleen Harris, pseud. LC 43-27307. 1940. Arcadia House, Inc.
Make Way for Spring. Peggy O'More, pseud. LC 66-9244. 1966. Arcadia House.
Make Way for Tomorrow. Maynah Lewis. 1973. pap. 0.75 o.p. (345-26513-0-075). Beagle Bks.
Make with the Brains, Pierre... Dana Wilson. LC 46-7387. 1946. J. Messner, Inc.
Make Your Own World of Christmas. Claude Kailer & Rosemary Lowndes. LC 73-22563. (Illus.). 107p. 1974. pap. 5.95 o.p. (ISBN 0-672-51981-X). Bobbs.
Makebelieve Marriage. Flora Kidd. (Harlequin Presents Ser.). 192p. 1982. pap. 1.75 (ISBN 0-373-10520-7). Harlequin Bks.
Makepeace Experiment. Andrei Donat'Evich Siniavskii. LC 64-18351. 1965. Pantheon Books.
Makepeace Experiment. Tr. from Russian, Introd. by Manya Harari. Abram Terts, pseud. LC 64-18351. bds., 3.95. Pantheon.
Maker. Diana J. Austin. 4.95 (ISBN 0-8062-1995-5). Carlton.
Maker of Gods: Ten Lithuanian Stories. Stepas Zobarskas. LC 61-18249. 1961. Voyages Press.
Maker of Heavenly Trousers. Daniele Vare. LC 36-4989. 1936. Doubleday, Doran and Company, Inc.
Maker of History. Edward Phillips Oppenheim. LC 6-1024. 1906. Little, Brown, and Company.
Maker of Moons. Robert William Chambers. LC 75-98565. (Short story index reprint series). (Illus.). 1969. Books for Libraries Press.
Maker of Moons. Robert William Chambers. 1896. G. P. Putnam's Sons.
Maker of Nations. Guy Newell Boothby. LC 99-5177. 1899. D. Appleton and Company.
Maker of Opportunities. George Fort Gibbs. LC 12-9562. 1912. D. Appleton and Company.
Maker of Rainbows: And Other Fairy-Tales and Fables. Richard Le Gallienne. LC 77-167460. (Short story index reprint series). (Illus.). 1971. (ISBN 0-8369-3986-7). Books for Libraries Press.
Maker of Saints. Hamilton Drummond. LC 20-107311. E. P. Dutton & Company.
Maker of Shadows. Jack Mann. 1977. 5.00. Bookfinger.
Maker of Shadows. Charles E. Vivan. Ed. by R. Reginald & Douglas Menville. LC 75-46310. (Supernatural & Occult Fiction Ser.). 1976. Repr. of 1938 ed. lib. bdg. 16.00x (ISBN 0-405-08172-3). Ayer Co.
Maker of Shadows. Evelyn Charles H Vivian. LC 75-46310. (Supernatural and Occult Fiction). 1976. 16.00 (ISBN 0-405-08107-3). Arno Press.
Maker of Signs. facsimile ed. Whit Burnett. LC 79-106252. (Short Story Index Reprint Ser.). 1934. 16.00 (ISBN 0-8369-3289-7). Ayer Co.
Maker of Signs: A Variety. Whit Burnett. LC 79-106252. (Short story index reprint series). 1970. Books for Libraries Press.
Maker of Signs: A Variety. Whit Burnett. LC 34-32564. 1934. H. Smith and R. Haas.
Maker of Universes. Philip Jose Farmer. LC 75-403. (Garland Library of Science Fiction). 1975. 19.75 (ISBN 0-8240-1408-1). Garland Pub.
Maker's Name. Bruce Cutler. (W.N.J. Ser.: No. 14). 1980. 10.00; signed ed. 20.00; pap. 4.50. Juniper Pr WI.
Makes Me Think of Tall Green Grass. Daniel Casolaro. LC 70-146438. 1973. 3.00 (ISBN 0-8059-1541-9). Dorrance.
Makeshift Marriage. Marjorie Lewty. (Harlequin Romances Ser.). 192p. 1983. pap. 1.75 (ISBN 0-373-02546-7). Harlequin Bks.
Maki. R. James Minney. LC 22-137786. 1921. John Lane Company.
Makin' O' Joe. Louis Matthews Sweet. LC 19-15686. George H. Doran Company.
Making. Sherman Baker. LC 66-14045. 5.95. World.
Making an American Gentleman. Anne Travis Keating. LC 20-9716. The Roxburgh Publishing Co., Inc.
Making and Breaking of Almansur. cresswell. ed. Clarice M Cresswell. LC 16-263220. Dodd.
Making Do. Paul Goodman. LC 63-16105. Macmillan,
Making Ends Meet. Barbara Howar. LC 75-10276. 8.95 (ISBN 0-394-49617-5). Random House.

Making Good: A Story of Northwest Canada. by captain g. b. mckean... ed. George Burdon McKean. LC 20-18611. 1920. The Macmillan Company.
Making Good Again. Lionel Davidson. LC 68-26786. 1968. 5.95. Harper & Row.
Making Good with Margaret. E. Ward Strayer. LC 18-799316. 1918. G. Sully & Company.
Making Hate. Jacqueline Wilson. LC 77-16719. 1978. 7.95 (ISBN 0-312-50710-0). St. Martin's Press.
Making Her His Wife. Corra May White Harris. LC 18-6694. 1918. Doubleday, Page & Company.
Making His Mark. Horatio Alger, Jr. (Illus.). 307p. 1979. Repr. of 1901 ed. 30.00. G K Westgard.
Making Home Peaceful: Sequel to "Making Home Happy,". Lilla Dale Avery-Stuttle. 1899. Home Life Publishing Co.--Limited.
Making It Big. John Jakes. (Orig.). 1968. pap. 0.50 o.p. (B50-762). Belmont Prods.
Making Love. Norman Bogner. LC 76-136440. 1971. 6.95. Coward-McCann.
Making Love. Norman Bogner. LC 76-873894. 1971. 2.00 (ISBN 0-491-00387-0). W. H. Allen.
Making Love: A Novel. Leonore Fleischer. LC 81-19151. 1982. 2.50 (ISBN 0-345-30162-5). Ballantine Books.
Making Mary. Joan Markham. pap. 1.95 o.s.i. (OPH-252, Ophelia). Olympia.
Making Money. Owen McMahon Johnson. LC 15-19406. 1915. 1.35. Frederick A. Stokes Company.
Making of a Bigot. Rose Macaulay. LC 14-551392. Hodder and Stoughton.
Making of a Chief. R. Gordon Hepworth. (O.s.i.). 305p. 1974. 15.00 o.s.i. (ISBN 0-913600-33-4). Kanchenjunga Pr.
Making of a Country Home. Andrew Carpenter Wheeler. LC 1-27056. 1901. Doubleday, Page and Co.
Making of a Fortune: A Romance. Harriet Elizabeth Prescott Spofford. LC 11-5192. 1911. Harper & Brothers.
Making of a Frontier Missionary: The Early Years of Apostle William H. Kelley. Edmund G Kelley. LC 79-23719. (Illus.). 9.00 (ISBN 0-8309-0270-8). Herald Pub. House.
Making of a Gunman. Max Brand. LC 82-19940. 1983. 10.95 (ISBN 0-396-08128-2). Dodd.
Making of a Hero. Nikolai Alekseevich Ostrovskii. Tr. by Brown, Alec. LC 37-16535. 1937. E. P. Dutton & Co., Inc.
Making of a Lady. Sara Haardt. LC 31-4806. 1931. Doubleday, Doran & Company, Inc.
Making of a Lawman. John Thomas Edson. (Orig.). 1981. pap. 1.95 (ISBN 0-425-05089-0). Berkley Pub.
Making of a Man. By the Author of "His Majesty, Myself"... Etc.... William Mumford Baker. LC 6-68653. 1884. Roberts Brothers.
Making of a Marchioness. Frances Hodgson Burnett. LC 66-24805. (Doughty library, no. 4). 1967. Stein and Day.
Making of a Marchioness. Frances Hodgson Burnett. LC 1-20944. F. A. Stokes Company.
Making of a Millionaire. A B Montgomery. LC 13-129300. 1898. G. W. Dillingham Co.
Making of a Peasant Doctor. Hsiao Yang. LC 77-472305. (Illus.). 1976. Foreign Languages Press.
Making of a Saint. William Somerset Maugham. LC 7-25600. 1898. L. C. Page and Company (Incorporated.
Making of a Saint: A Romance of Mediaeval Italy. William Somerset Maugham. LC 75-30388. (Maugham, William Somerset, 1814-1965. Works. 1976). 1977. 10.00. Arno Press.
Making of a Saint. Foreword by John Farrar. William Somerset Maugham. (75-1272). 1968. Popular Lib.
Making of a Schoolgirl. Evelyn Sharp. LC 3-24508. (Bodley booklets, no. 2). 1897. J. Lane, The Bodley Head.
Making Of A Seaman. 3rd ed. Rowan O'Neill. (Illus.). 164p. 1982. pap. 2.95 (ISBN 0-933704-45-3). Dawn Pr.
Making of a Statesman, and Other Stories. Joel Chandler Harris. LC 79-113665. (Short story index reprint series). 1970. Books for Libraries Press.
Making of a Statesman: And Other Stories. Joel Chandler Harris. 1902. McClure, Phillips & Co.
Making of Americans: Being a History of a Family's Progress. Gertrude Stein. 1973. (ISBN 0-87110-028-2) (ISBN 0-87110-099-1). Something Else Pr.
Making of Americans: Being a History of a Family's Progress. complete version. ed. Gertrude Stein. LC 66-23136. 1966. Something Else Press.
Making of an American: An Adaptation of Memorable Tales by Charles Sealsfield. Ulrich Steindorff Carrington & Charles Sealsfield. LC 74-77736. (Bicentennial series in American studies, 2). 1974. 7.95 (ISBN 0-87074-143-8). SMU Press.
Making of an Englishman. Walter Lionel George. LC 14-4307. 1914. 1.35. Dodd, Mead and Company.
Making of Bobby Burnit. George Randolph Chester. LC 9-16442. 1909. The Bobbs-Merrill Company.
Making of Christopher Ferringham. Beulah Marie Dix. LC 1-309714. 1901. The Macmillan Company.
Making of England. John Richard Green. (Seaside library, v. 63, no. 1274). 1882. G. Munro.
Making of George Groton. Bruce Barton. LC 18-7991. 1918. Doubleday, Page & Company.
Making of Jane: A Novel. Sarah Barnwell Elliott. 1901. C. Scribner's Sons.
Making of Little Hippo. Grace Macouillard. LC 74-22657. 1975. 6.95 (ISBN 0-399-11406-8). Putnam.
Making of Major. Mary Chappel Lee. LC 13-24116. David C. Cook Publishing Co.
Making of Mary. Jean Newton McIlwraith. LC 7-19991. (On cover: The "unknown" library no. 39)). The Cassell Publishing Co.
Making of Peter Cray. William Heyliger. LC 27-181428. 1927. D. Appleton and Company.
Making of Star Trek. Stephen E. Whitfield & Gene Roddenberry. (Illus.). 416p. 1979. pap. 2.25 (ISBN 0-345-27638-8). Ballantine.
Making of the Exorcist Ii: The Heretic. Barbara Pallenberg. (Illus.). 1977. 1.95 (ISBN 0-446-89361-7). Warner Books.
Making of the Mayor. Ruth Harris. 1971. 5.95 o.p. (GP696). Grove.
Making of the Representative for Planet Eight: Canopus in Argos; Archives. Doris May Lessing. LC 82-40422. (Canopus Ser.). 160p. 1983. pap. 4.95 (ISBN 0-394-71377-X, Vin). Random.
Making of Thomas Barton. Anna Nicholas. LC 13-9289. The Bobbs-Merrill Company.
Making Out. Playboy Editors. LC 74-81745. 1974. pap. 1.25 o.p. (ISBN 0-87216-244-3, B16244). Playboy.
Making Over Martha. Julie Mathilde Lippmann. LC 13-22208. 1913. 1.20. H. Holt and Company.
Making People Happy. Thompson Buchanan. LC 11-25671. 1.25. W. J. Watt & Company.
Making Play. John Jacob. LC 75-41706. 1.00. (ISBN 0-915316-21-8) (ISBN 0-915316-22-6). Pentagram Press.
Making Progress: A Novel. Anthony Bailey. LC 59-7485. 1959. Dial Press.
Making the President. Carol Flinders. pap. 1.95 o.s.i. (OPS-32). Olympia.
Making Time. Eddie Constantine. (Orig.). 1980. pap. 2.25 (ISBN 0-440-16414-1). Dell.
Making Tracks. Rob Phillips. 1981. pap. 2.25 (ISBN 0-8439-0888-2, Leisure Bks). Nordon Pubns.
Making U-Hoo. Irving A Greenfield. 1973. (pbk) 1.25. Dell.
Makini's Coming of Age. Nwandu S. Matunde. (Illus.). 40p. (Orig.). (gr. 8-12). 1981. pap. text ed. 3.00 (ISBN 0-936868-01-5). Freeland Pubns.
Makin's of a Girl. Emma Elise Geiselman Meguire. LC 11-317. 1911. 1.50. R. G. Badger.
Makioka Sisters. Junichiro Tanigaki. LC 57-10311. (Berkley Windhover book). 1975. (pbk.) 2.95 (ISBN 0-425-02829-1). Berkley Pub. Co.
Makioka Sisters. Junichiro Tanizaki. LC 80-39721. 1981. 6.95 (ISBN 0-399-50520-2). Perigee Books.
Makioka Sisters. Tr. from Japanese by Edward G. Seidensticker. Jun'Ichiro Tanizaki. (Universal lib., UL190). 1966. pap., 2.45. Grosset.
Makioka Sisters. Translated from the Japanese by Edward G. Seidensticker. 1st American Ed. Jun'Ichiro Tanizaki. LC 57-10311. 1957. A. A. Knopf.
Maktoub: A Romance of French North Africa. Matthew Craig. LC 18-680142. 1918. 1.50. G. P. Putnam's Sons.
Mal Moulee. A Novel. Ella Wheeler Wilcox. LC 8-370292. 1886. G. W. Carleton & Co.; Etc., Etc.
Malabang Pearl. Richard O'Connor. LC 64-20986. 1964. Published for the Crime Club by Doubleday.
Malacca Cane. Mario Soldati. LC 73-78131. 1973. 8.95. St. Martin's Press.
Malachite Casket. Pavel Petrovich Bazhov. 219p. 1981. 9.00 (ISBN 0-8285-2042-9, Pub. by Progress Pubs USSR). Imported Pubns.
Malachite Casket: Tales from the Urals. 10th thousand. ed. Pavel Petrovich Bazhov & Williams, Alan Moray, Tr. LC 45-892020. 1944. Hutchinson & Co. Ltd.
Malachite Cross: A Romance of Two Countries. Frank Henry Norton. (Union square series no. 1). Cleveland Publishing Company.
Malacia Tapestry. Brian Wilson Aldiss. LC 76-377074. (Illus.). 1976. 3.95 (ISBN 0-224-01269-X). Jonathan Cape.
Malacia Tapestry. Brian Wilson Aldiss. (Illus.). 1978. 1.95 (ISBN 0-441-51647-5). Ace Books.
Malady at Madeira. Ann Bridge, pseud. 1969. 6.95 o.p. (ISBN 0-07-007740-1). McGraw.
Malady in Madeira. Mary Dolling Sanders O'Malley. LC 76-89788. 1969. McGraw-Hill.
Malady of the Century. Max Simon Nordau. LC 98-517. (Neely's continental library, no. 15). F. T. Neely.
Malaeska; the Indian Wife of the White Hunter. Ann Sophia Winterbotham Stephens. LC 75-175875. (Illus.). 1971. B. Blom.
Malaeska: The Indian Wife of the White Hunter. Ann Sophia Winterbotham Stephens & O'Brien, Frank P. LC 29-29969. The John Day Company.
Malafrena. Ursula K. Le Guin. LC 79-11042. 10.95 (ISBN 0-399-12410-1). Berkley Pub. Corp.: Distributed by Putnam.
Malafrena. Ursula K. Le Guin. 1980. pap. 2.50 (ISBN 0-425-04647-8). Berkley Pub.
Malago's Visit. Craig Salcido. (Orig.). 1980. pap. 1.75 o.s.i. (ISBN 0-505-51488-5). Tower Bks.
Malaisie. Henri Fauconnier. Tr. by Sutton, Eric. LC 31-31525. 1931. The Macmillan Company.
Malamud Reader. Bernard Malamud. LC 67-28799. 1967. Farrar, Straus and Giroux.
Malaret Mystery. Olga Hartley. LC 27-235142. 1926. Small, Maynard & Company.
Malayalam Short Stories: An Anthology. LC 76-901414. 1976. 8.50 (ISBN 0-88386-595-5). Kerala Sahitya Akademi.
Malayalam Short Stories: An Anthology. 1976. text ed. 8.50 o.p. (ISBN 0-88386-595-5). South Asia Bks.
Malayalam Short Stories: An Anthology. K. Ayyappa Panikkar. 157p. 1982. 37.00x (Pub. by Garlandfold England). State Mutual Bk.
Malayalam Short Stories: An Anthology. Ed. by K. Ayyappa Panikkar. 175p. 1982. text ed. 17.95x (ISBN 0-7069-1297-7, Pub. by Vikas India). Advent NY.
Malayan Monochromes. Hugh Charles Clifford. LC 13-21485. 1913. E. P. Dutton and Company.
Malaysian Short Stories. Ed. by Lloyd Fernanco. (Writing in Asia Ser.). xvii, 302p. (Orig.). 1981. pap. text ed. 7.50x (00264). Heinemann Ed.
Malbone: An Oldport Romance. Thomas Wentworth Higginson. LC 22-4760. 1869. Fields, Osgood, & Co.
Malbone: An Oldport Romance. Thomas Wentworth Higginson. LC 1-1118. 1871. J. R. Osgood and Company.
Malcolm. George Macdonald. LC 4-16557. G. Routledge & Sons, Limited.
Malcolm. George Macdonald. LC 12-18281. 1911. D. McKay.
Malcolm. James Purdy. LC 59-14689. 1959. Farrar, Straus & Cudahy.
Malcolm. James Purdy. LC 80-19147. 1980. 3.95 (ISBN 0-14-005595-9). Penguin Books.
Malcolm. A Romance. George Macdonald. LC 7-158563. 1877. J. B. Lippincott & Co.
Malcolm, a Romance. George Macdonald. (Seaside library. v. 43, no. 887). 1880. G. Munro.
Malcolm Sage, Detective. Herbert George Jenkins. LC 57-9667. (Herbert Jenkins' book). Roy Publishers.
Malcolm Sage: Detective. Herbert George Jenkins. LC 21-2758. George H. Doran Company.
Malcom Kirk: A Tale of Moral Heroism Overcoming the World. Charles Monroe Sheldon. LC 1655. 1900. Advance Publishing Co.
Malcontents. Steve Franklin, pseud. LC 79-111163. 1970. 4.50. Published for the Crime Club by Doubleday.
Malcontents. Brendan Gill. LC 74-157807. 1973. Harcourt, Brace, Jovanovich.
Malcontents. Charles Percy Snow. LC 70-37197. 1972. 6.95 (ISBN 0-684-12812-8). Scribner.
Male and Female. Josiah Pitts Woolfolk. LC 34-4344. 1934. W. Godwin, Inc.
Male Child. 1st American Ed. Paul Scott. LC 57-5330. 1957. Dutton.
Male Order. Clell Edgar Bowman. 149p. 1976. 6.50 o.p. (ISBN 0-682-48436-9). Exposition.
Male Virgin. Josiah Pitts Woolfolk & John Burton Thompson. LC 51-9398. 1950. Arco Pub. Co.
Malediction. Julian Claman. LC 68-12466. 1969. 5.95. Dutton.
Malediction De Chrichton. Jean S. MacLeod. (Harlequin Romantique Ser.). 192p. 1983. pap. 1.95 (ISBN 0-373-41190-1). Harlequin Bks.
Malediction. Translated from the French by Peter De Mendelssohn. Jean Giono. LC 55-7843. 1955. Criterion Books.
Malefactor. Edward Phillips Oppenheim. LC 7-984. 1907. Litle, Brown, and Company.
Malefactors. 1st Ed. Caroline Gordon. LC 56-66534. Harcourt, Brace C.
Malentendu see Caligula.
Malevil. Robert Merle. LC 73-11463. 1974. 10.00 (ISBN 0-671-21600-7). Simon and Schuster.
Malford Manor. Juliet Mann. Ed. by Alice Sachs. 1970. 3.95 o.p. Lenox Hill.
Malfreys. Catharine Whitcomb. LC 44-4958. 1944. Random House.
Malgudi Days. R. K. Narayan. LC 81-52204. 1982. 14.95 (ISBN 0-670-45178-9). Viking Press.
Malibar Farm. Louis Bromfield. 1976. Repr. of 1948 ed. lib. bdg. 19.95x (ISBN 0-88411-506-2). Amereon Ltd.
Malibu. William Murray. LC 79-14308. 9.95 (ISBN 0-698-10978-3). Coward, McCann & Geoghegan.
Malibu Cove. Peter O'Crotty. LC 48-6731. 1948. Murray & Gee.
Malibu Million Dollar Rock. Stefani B. Ninman. LC 79-53369. (Illus.). 36p. 1979. pap. 4.00 (ISBN 0-930422-21-X). Dennis-Landman.
Malice Aforethought. Francis Iles. LC 31-32419. 289p. 1980. pap. 2.95i (ISBN 0-06-080532-3, P 532, PL). Har-Row.
Malice Aforethought: The Story of a Commonplace Crime. Anthony Berkeley Cox. LC 31-32419. 1931. Harper & Brothers.
Malice Aforethought: The Story of a Commonplace Crime. Francis Iles. LC 31-37419. 1931. Harper & Brothers.
Malice Domestic. Evelyn Cameron. LC 40-33928. 1940. Pub. for the Crime Club by Doubleday, Doran and Company, Inc.
Malice Domestic. Elinore Denniston. LC 68-15413. (Red badge mystery). 1968. Dodd, Mead.
Malice in Wonderland. Day-Lewis, Cecil. LC 74-192877. 1973. 1.80 (ISBN 0-85617-314-2). White Lion Publishers.
Malice in Wonderland. Cecil Day-Lewis. LC 46-6542. (On cover: Penguin books. 592). 1946. Penguin Books, Inc.
Malice in Wonderland. 1st Ed. Rufus King. LC 58-8093. 1958. Published for the Crime Club by Doubleday.
Malice Matrimonial. Joan Margaret Fleming. 2.95 o.p. Washburn.
Malice with Murder. Nicholas Blake. 1971. pap. 0.75 o.p. (T2448). Pyramid Pubns.
Malicious Mischief. Lesley Egan, pseud. LC 74-156574. (Novel of Suspense). (L). 1971. 5.95 o.p. (ISBN 0-06-011156-9, HarpT). Har-Row.
Malicious Mischief. Elizabeth Linington. LC 74-156574. 1971. 5.95 (ISBN 0-06-011156-9). Harper & Row.
Malignant Heart. 1st Ed. Celestine Sibley. LC 58-8108. 1958. Published for The Crime Club by Doubleday.
Malignant Metaphysical Menace. Mallory T. Knight. (Man from T.O.M.C.A.T. Ser.). 160p. pap. 0.60 o.p. (A369X, Award). Univ Pub & Dist.
Malinche and Cortes. Margaret Cochran Shedd. LC 76-139059. 1971. 6.95. Doubleday.
Malinki of Malawi. Josephine Cunnington Edwards. LC 78-55903. (Destiny Ser.). 1978. pap. 4.95 o.p. (ISBN 0-8163-0089-5, 13054-2). Pacific Pr Pub Assn.
Malinsay Massacre: Dennis Wheatley Presents a Murder Mystery. J. G. Links. 101p. 1981. 17.95 (ISBN 0-8317-5798-1, Rutledge Pr). Smith Pubs.
Malko Versus the CIA. Gerard De Villiers. (Malko series,#4). 1974. (pbk.) 1.25 (ISBN 0-523-00316-1). Pinnacle Books.
Mallabec. David Harry Walker. LC 65-106849. 4.95. Houghton.
Mallen Girl. Catherine Cookson. LC 73-78097. 1973. 6.95 (ISBN 0-525-15072-2). Dutton.
Mallen Girl. Catherine Cookson. 1974. (pbk.) 1.50. Bantam Books.
Mallen Lot. Catherine Cookson. LC 73-16393. 1974. 7.95. Dutton.
Mallen Lot. Catherine Cookson. 1975. (pbk.) 1.50. Bantam Books.
Mallen Streak. Catherine Cookson. LC 72-82718. 1973. 6.95 (ISBN 0-525-15075-7). Dutton.
Mallen Streak. Catherine Cookson. 1974. (pbk.) 1.50. Bantam Books.
Mallet's Masterpiece. Edward Henry Peple. 1908. 0.75. Moffat, Yard and Company.
Malletts. Emily Hilda Young. LC 27-27783. 1927. Harcourt, Brace and Company.
Mallignant Stars. 1st Ed. Jerome Barry. LC 60-685755. 1960. Published for the Crime Club by Doubleday.
Mallodoce, the Briton. His Wanderings from Druidism to Christianity. Orlando B. Mayer & Chapman, John Abney, 1821- Joint Author. LC 7-262235. 1891. E. Waddey Co.
Malloonkai. Donald Stuart. LC 77-360697. 1976. (ISBN 0-85585-501-0). Georgian House.
Mallory. Norma Lee Clark. 1.75 (ISBN 0-449-23608-0). Fawcett Crest Books.
Mallory Grange. Christine Randell. (Orig.). 1971. pap. 0.75 o.p. (ISBN 0-446-64701-2, 64-701-2). Paperback Lib.
Mallory's Luck. Katherine Shoesmith. 1981. pap. 1.95 (ISBN 0-441-51634-3). Ace Bks.
Mallory's Luck. Kathleen A Shoesmith. (Ace Gothic). 1974. (pbk.) 0.95. Ace Books.
Mallot Diaries. Robert Nathan. LC 65-17384. bds., 3.95. Knopf.
Malloy of the Royal Mounted. Charles Stoddard. LC 44-3269. 1944. Arcadia House, Inc.

Malloy of the Royal Mounted. Charles Stanley Strong. LC 44-3269. 1944. Arcadia House.

Malloy's Subway. R. Wright Campbell. LC 81-66021. 1981. 12.95 (ISBN 0-689-11181-9). Atheneum.

Mallworld. Somtow Sucharitkul. LC 81-9827. 4.95 (ISBN 0-89865-161-1). Donning Co.

Mally. Sandra Heath. 224p. (Orig.). 1980. pap. 1.75 (ISBN 0-451-09342-9, E9342, Sig). NAL.

Mally Lee. Agnes Mary Robertson Dunlop. LC 47-5080. 1947. Pub. for the Crime Club by Doubleday.

Malmaison. Katherine N. Haffner. 1979. 8.95 (ISBN 0-533-03989-4). Vantage.

Malone Dies. Samuel Beckett. LC 57-733. 1956. Grove Press.

Malone Dies see Three Novels.

Malory to Mrs. Behn: Specimens of Early Prose Fiction. Ed. by Albert Morton Turner. Turner, Mrs. Percie (Hopkins) Joint Ed. LC 30-21940. (Half-title: Nelson's English series; general editor--E. Bernbaum). 1930. T. Nelson and Sons.

Malpais Rider. James Powell. LC 80-2978. (Double D western). 1981. 10.95 (ISBN 0-385-17588-4). Doubleday.

Malpas Legacy. Ariadne Pritchett. (Fawcett Gold Medal Book). 1976. 1.25. Fawcett.

Malpractice. John R. Feegel. 1982. pap. 3.50 (ISBN 0-451-11821-9, AE1821, Sig). NAL.

Malpractice. Eleazar Lipsky. (O.S.I.). 304p. 1973. pap. 1.25 o.s.i. (ISBN 0-446-76176-1). Paperback Lib.

Malpractice: A Novel. John R Feegel. LC 81-38420. 12.95 (ISBN 0-453-00406-7). New American Library.

Malpractice: A Novel. Eleazar Lipsky. 1973. (pbk) 1.50. Warner Paperback Lib.

Malpractice: A Novel. Eleazar Lipsky. LC 70-182456. 1972. 7.95. W. Morrow.

Malraux, Andre. Whale, Winifred Stephens, Tr. LC 29-219282. Harcourt, Brace and Company.

Malsy and I. Jeannette Ritchie Hadermann Walworth. LC 33-19486. 1883. Rogers & Co.

Maltaverne: Un Adolescent D'autrefois). Francois Mauriac. LC 70-113774. 1970. 5.95. Farrar, Straus and Giroux.

Maltese Boyhood: Stories. Philip Ward. 1976. pap. 6.50 (ISBN 0-902675-41-9). Oleander Pr.

Maltese Cross: Or, The Detective's Quest. Eugene T Sawyer. (On cover: The secret service library, no. 11). 1888. Street & Smith.

Maltese Falcon. Dashiell Hammett. LC 30-5989. 1930. A. A. Knopf.

Maltese Falcon. Dashiell Hammett. LC 34-8348. (Half-title: The modern library of the world's best books). 1934. The Modern Library.

Maltese Falcon... Dashiell Hammett. LC 45-13597. 1944.

Maltese Falcon. Dashiell Hammett. LC 81-17259. 1982. 12.95 (ISBN 0-89340-330-X). J. Curley.

Malverne Hall. Rachel Cosgrove Payes. 1976. 1.50. Ace.

Malverne Manor. Helen York. LC 73-14058. 1974. 5.95 (ISBN 0-385-09654-2). Published for the Crime Club by Doubleday.

Malvie Inheritance. Pamela Hill. (Fawcett crest book). 1975. (pbk.) 1.50. Fawcett.

Malvina of Brittany. Jerome Klapka Jerome. LC 16-22941. 1916. 2.60. Cassell and Company, Ltd.

Mam' Linda: A Novel. William Nathaniel Harben. LC 7-29431. 1907. Harper & Brothers.

Mama. Lee Bennett Hopkins. 1978. 1.25 (ISBN 0-440-96174-2). Dell Pub. Co.

Mama. Gregorio M. Sierra. (O.s.i.). 1937. pap. 2.95x o.s.i. (ISBN 0-393-09456-1, NortonC). Norton.

Mama and the Outlaw. Jean Littleton Gentry. LC 53-13172. 1953. R. R. Smith.

Mama Black Widow. Robert Beck. (Orig.). 1970. pap. 2.25 (ISBN 0-87067-708-X, BH708-X). Holloway.

Mama Doll. Martin Woodhouse. LC 75-185766. 1972. 6.95. Coward, McCann & Geoghegan.

Mama, I Love You. William Saroyan. LC 56-7051. 1956. Little, Brown.

Mama Liz Drinks Deep. Howard Rheingold. (The Acid Orgy Trilogy Ser). 192p. (Orig.). 1972. pap. 1.95 o.s.i. (O*P*S51). Olympia.

Mama Liz Tastes Flesh. Howard Rheingold. (Orig.). 1972. pap. 1.95 o.s.i. (Ophelia). Olympia.

Mama Maria's. Ann Chidester. LC 47-236143. 1947. C. Scribner's Sons.

Mama Tass Manifesto: A Novel. Roger Lichtenberg Simon. LC 76-108669. 1970. 4.95. Holt, Rinehart, and Winston.

Mama, the Preacher. Gladys Miller. LC 68-54699. 1968. 2.95. Dorrance.

Mama Was a Ballerina. Ilanon Moon & Shad E. Graham. LC 72-138838. (Illus.). 1971. F. Young Pub. Co.

Mama's Bank Account. Kathryn Anderson McLean. LC 43-4313. 1943. Harcourt, Brace and Company.

Mama's Bean Sweater & Other Stories. Roselyn Edwards. (YA) 1969. pap. 2.25 o.s.i. (130658). Review & Herald.

Mama's Choice. Elizabeth Mansfield, pseud. (Orig.). 1982. pap. 2.25. Berkley Pub.

Mama's Way. Thyra Ferre Bjorn. 1976. pap. 1.95 (ISBN 0-553-13791-3, Y13791-3). Bantam.

Mama's Way. Thyra Ferre Bjorn. 1959. 4.50 o.p. (ISBN 0-03-028600-X). HR&W.

Mamba. Stuart Cloete. LC 56-10190. 1956. Houghton Mifflin.

Mamba's Daughters. Du Bose Heyward. LC 29-349743. 1929. Doubleday, Doran & Company.

Mamba's Daughters: A Novel of Charleston. Du Bose Heyward. LC 74-173543. 1974. 9.95 (ISBN 0-910220-59-X). N. S. Berg.

Mambo. Robert Burdette Sweet. 1975. (pbk.) 1.95 (ISBN 0-912852-11-9). Echo Publishers West.

Mambo to Murder: By Dale Clark Pseud. Ronal Kayser. LC 55-371878. (Ace double novel books, D-109). 1955. Ace Books.

Mameluke: Or, The Sign of the Mystic Tie. A Tale of the Camp and Court of Bonaparte. Benjamin Perley Poore et al. LC 7-11434. (With Judson, Edward Z. C. The black avenger of the Spanish Main. New York, c1847). 1852. F. Gleason's Publishing Hall.

Mamigon. Jack Hashian. 320p. 1982. 16.95 (ISBN 0-698-11186-9, Coward). Putnam Pub Group.

Mamma: A Novel. Diana Tutton. LC 55-14276. 1955. Macmillan.

Mammon. Annie French Hector. J. W. Lovell Company.

Mammon: A Mystery Novel. Percival Christopher Wren. LC 30-7107. 1930. Frederick A. Stokes Company.

Mammon and Co. Edward Frederic Benson. LC 99-4156. 1899. D. Appleton and Company.

Mammon of Unrighteousness. Hjalmar Hjorth Boyesen. LC 78-104421. 1970. Literature House.

Mammon of Unrighteousness. Hjalmar Hjorth Boyesen. LC 6-15220. United States Book Company.

Mammoth Cave Romance. William Lee Popham. LC 11-32416. 1.00. The World Supply Company.

Mammoth Corridors. Earle Birney. 1980. pap. 5.00 (ISBN 0-936892-07-2). Stone Pr MI.

Mammoth Mystery Book: Three Complete Scotland Yard Novels. Edgar Wallace. LC 29-27528. 1929. Pub. for the Crime Club, Inc., by Doubleday, Doran & Company, Inc.

Mammuth see Gulliveriana, No. 4.

Mammy: A Memory, Being a True History Faithfully Set Down of One Life That Is a Type of the Many, That Existed in the Old South. Frances Hardin Hess. LC 14-107274. 1913. 0.50. Printed by California Press.

Mammy Dicey's Philosophy: A Story of Yesterday. Nancy Moore. LC 19-16365. The Roxburgh Publishing Company, Inc.

Mammy Jinny's Christmas Home-Coming. Frances Cannon Smith Porcher. LC 27-14964. The J. W. Burke Company.

Mammy Mystic. Margaret Greenway McClelland. The Merriam Company.

Mammy Rosie. Albert Morris Bagby. LC 71-38638. (Black Heritage Library Collection). 1972. (ISBN 0-8369-8996-1). Books for Libraries Press.

Mammy Rosie.". Albert Morris Bagby. LC 4-268622. 1904. The Author.

Mammy Tittleback & Her Family. Helen H. Jackson. 1976. lib. bdg. 8.50x (ISBN 0-89968-052-6). Lightyear.

Mamo Murders. Juanita Sheridan. LC 52-5545. 1952. Published for the Crime Club by Doubleday.

Mamselle. Nathan Butler. (Fawcett gold medal book). 1974. (pbk.) 1.25. Fawcett.

Mam'selle Jo. Harriet Theresa Smith Comstock. LC 18-188901. 1918. Doubleday, Page & Company.

Mamselle of the Wilderness: A Story of La Salle and His Pioneers. Augusta Huiell Seaman. LC 13-12283. 1913. Sturgis & Walton Company.

Mam'zelle Beauty. Marian Crawford. (On cover: Sergel's railway library, v. 1, no. 2). G. H. Sergel Company.

Mamzelle Fifine: A Romance of the Girlhood of the Empress Josephine on the Island of Martinique. Eleanor Stackhouse Atkinson. LC 3-26969. 1903. D. Appleton and Company.

Man. Oriana Fallaci. LC 80-17838. 14.95 (ISBN 0-671-25241-0). Simon and Schuster.

Man. Irving Wallace. 1974. (pbk) 1.75. Bantam Books.

Man: A Novel. Irving Wallace. LC 64-22411. 1964. Simon and Schuster.

Man. A Story of to-Day. With Facts, Fancies and Faults Peculiarly Its Own... Elbert Hubbard. LC 7-56625. (Sunnyside series, no. 47). 1891. J. S. Ogilvie.

Man About the House: A Novella. Ward Allison Dorrance. LC 72-79643. (Breakthrough book). 1972. 5.00 (ISBN 0-8262-0128-8) (ISBN 0-8262-0128-8). University of Missouri Press.

Man About the House: An Old Wives' Tale. Francis Brett Young. LC 42-184648. 1942. Reynal & Hitchcock.

Man About Town. Denison Halley Clift. LC 32-107555. 1932. The Macaulay Company.

Man About Woman. Leona Slottman. LC 46-12928. 1946. Phoenix Press.

Man About Women. Leona Slottman. LC 46-129289. 1946. Phoenix Press.

Man Abroad. with a new introd. / by lyman tower sargent. ed. LC 76-10996. (Gregg Press science fiction series). 1976. 11.00 (ISBN 0-8398-2349-5). Gregg Press.

Man Abroad: A Yarn of Some Other Century. LC 7-20463. 1887. G. W. Dillingham; Etc., Etc.

Man Abroad: A Yarn of Some Other Century. Ed. by Lyman T. Sargent. (Science Fiction Ser.). 80p. 1976. Repr. of 1887 ed. lib. bdg. cancelled o.s.i. (ISBN 0-8398-2349-5, Gregg). G K Hall.

Man Against Mustang. Robert Ames Bennet. LC 36-192651. I. Washburn.

Man Ain't Nothin' but a Man: The Adventures of John Henry. John Oliver Killens. LC 74-34414. 1975. 5.95 (ISBN 0-316-49278-7). Little, Brown.

Man Alone. George Agnew Chamberlain. LC 26-4706. 1926. G. P. Putnam's Sons.

Man Alone. Translated from the French by J. H. F. McEwen. Paul Pilotaz. LC 53-9775. Roy Publishers.

Man Among His Peers. pap. 1.00 (ISBN 0-89023-012-9). Forrest Printing.

Man and a Woman. Carl Henry Grabo. LC 31-5127. 2.00. The Century Co.

Man and a Woman. Stanley Waterloo. LC 8-367683. (On cover: The Aeriel library. no. 17). 1892. F. J. Schulte & Company.

Man and a Woman: A Human Story of Life. Dale Drummond. LC 18-18095. Britton Publishing Co.

Man and Beast. Phyllis Bottome. LC 79-122689. (Short story index reprint series). (Illus.). 1970. Books for Libraries Press.

Man and Beast, and Others Stories. Grace A. Baughman. LC 71-162878. 1971. Celestial Press.

Man and Beast. Illustrated by W. T. Mars. Phyllis Bottome. LC 54-9722. 1954. Harcourt, Brace.

Man and Boy. Morris, Wright. LC 51-2263. 1951. Knopf.

Man and Boy. Wright Morris. (Bison Book, BB575). 1974. (pbk.) 2.25 (ISBN 0-8032-5787-2). University of Nebraska Press.

Man and His Kingdom. Edward Phillips Oppenheim. LC 6-12559. 1906. Little, Brown, and Company.

Man and His Lesson. William Babington Maxwell. LC 19-15690. The Bobbs-Merrill Company.

Man & His Master. Francois Billetdoux. Tr. by Ralph Manheim. 1964. 3.50 o.p. (ISBN 0-8090-6700-5). Hill & Wang.

Man and His Money. Robert Boggs. LC 15-105091. 1913. Broadway Punlishing Co.

Man and His Money. Frederick Stewart Isham. LC 12-6862. The Bobbs-Merrill Company.

Man and Maid. Elinor Sutherland Glyn. LC 22-105452. 1922. J. B. Lippincott Company.

Man and Money. Emile Souvestre. LC 8-12378. 1892. Cassell Publishing Company.

Man and Monster. Karl-Herbert Scheer. (Perry Rhodan #36). 1973. (pbk) 0.75. Ace.

Man & Number. D. Smeltzer. 1962. pap. 0.95 o.p. (09412, Collier). Macmillan.

Man and the Dragon. Alexander Otis. LC 10-213002. 1910. 1.50. Little, Brown and Company.

Man and the Moment. Elinor Sutherland Glyn. LC 14-16200. 1914. 1.35. D. Appleton and Company.

Man and the Post. Anthony R Voigt. LC 33-14290. Printed by A. E. Kern & Co.

Man and the Woman. G A Perrigo. LC 7-36184. 1895. American Publishing & Engravings Co.

Man and Three Women. Vincent Samuel Stevens. LC 48-6834. Dorrance.

Man and Two Gods: A Novel. Jean Morris. LC 54-5704. 1954. Viking Press.

Man & Two Women. Doris May Lessing. 320p. 1975. pap. 2.75 (ISBN 0-445-03075-5). Popular Lib.

Man & Two Women. Doris May Lessing. 1963. write for info. o.p. (ISBN 0-671-44270-8). S&S.

Man and Two Women: Stories. Lessing, Doris May. LC 63-19277. 1963. Simon and Schuster.

Man and Two Women; Stories. Doris May Lessing. LC 63-19277. 1975. (pbk.) 1.50. Popular Library.

Man and Wife. Beth Brown. LC 33-8155. C. Kendall.

Man and Wife. Wilkie Collins. LC 82-17809. 1983. 5.00 (ISBN 0-486-24451-2). Dover.

Man and Wife. A Novel. Wilkie Collins. LC 3-27272. Harper & Brothers.

Man and Wife: A Novel. Wilkie Collins. LC 12-23251. 1911. Harper & Brothers.

Man and Wife: A Novel. Wilkie Collins. LC 16-7567. Harper & Brothers.

Man Apart. Jan Rabie. LC 69-17388. 1969. Macmillan.

Man As He Is. Robert Bage. LC 78-60848. 1979. 112.00 (ISBN 0-8240-3661-1). Garland Pub.

Man at Armageddon. James D. Johnson. 144p. 1976. 6.50 o.p. (ISBN 0-682-48551-9). Exposition.

Man-at-Arms: A Romance of the Days of Gian Galeazzo Visconti, the Great Viper. Clinton Scollard. LC 3-2526. 1898. Lamson, Wolffe and Company.

Man-at-Arms: Or, Henry De Cerons. A Romance. George Payne Rainsford James. (Seaside library, v. 30, no. 614). 1879. G. Munro.

Man at Lone Lake. Virginia Stanton Sheard. LC 16-21064. 1912. Cassell and Company, Ltd.

Man at the Carlton... Edgar Wallace. LC 32-2235. Pub. for the Crime Club, Inc., by Doubleday, Doran & Company, Inc.

Man at the Crossroads. Francis Nielson. 10.50 o.s.i. Roseman.

Man at the Door. Agnes Mary Biddle Dell. LC 44-168. 1943. The Wartburg Press.

Man at the Gate of the World: A Story of the Star. W E Cule. Hale, Cushman & Flint.

Man at the Wheel. Michael Kenyon. LC 82-45397. 1982. 11.95 (ISBN 0-385-18299-6). Published for the Crime Club by Doubleday.

Man at Willow Ranch. Harold Bindloss. Frederick A. Stokes Company,

Man Before the Morning. Cecil Maiden. LC 77-81625. 5.95 (ISBN 0-915684-20-9). Christian Herald Books.

Man Behind. John Hunter. LC 38-16226. 1938. E. P. Dutton & Co., Inc.

Man Behind: A Novel. 5th ed., ed. Thomas Stewart Denison. LC 99-5387. (On cover: Oriental library. v. 1. no. 17). 1899. Rand, McNally & Company.

Man Behind the Badge: The Fictionalized Experiences of a Small-Town Police Officer. 1st Ed. Myrtle Irene Snider. LC 59-44069. 1959. Exposition Press.

Man Behind the Mask: A Novel. Grace MacGowan Cooke. LC 27-7735. 1927. Frederick A. Stokes Company.

Man Between. Walter Archer Frost. LC 13-21297. 1913. 1.25. Doubleday, Page & Company.

Man Between: An International Romance. Amelia Edith Huddleston Barr. 1906. The Authors and Newspapers Association.

Man Born Again: Saint Thomas More. John Edward Beahn. LC 54-11424. 1954. Bruce Pub. Co.

Man Born of Woman. 1st. ed. James Ronald. LC 51-11184. 1951. Lippincott.

Man Branders. Frank Chester Robertson. LC 28-678. Barse & Co.

Man Called Alamo. Arthur Moore. 1975. (pbk.) 0.95 (ISBN 0-523-00776-0). Pinnacle Books.

Man Called Brazos. Theodore V. Olsen. 1978. pap. 1.50 (ISBN 0-449-14047-4, T2611, GM). Fawcett.

Man Called Brazos. Theodore V. Olsen. 1969. pap. 0.50 o.p. (D2110, GM). Fawcett World.

Man Called Cervantes. Bruno Frank. Tr. by Lowe, Helen Tracy (Porter) LC 35-3206. 1935. The Viking Press.

Man Called Coyote. Marc Savin. 320p. (Orig.). 1980. pap. 2.50 (ISBN 0-523-40500-6). Pinnacle Bks.

Man Called Eighty-Eight. Roy W Hinds. LC 30-7558. 1930. R. M. McBride & Company.

Man Called Harry Brent. Francis Durbridge. 1982. 18.00x (ISBN 0-86025-199-3, Pub. by Ian Henry Pubns England). State Mutual Bk.

Man Called Horse. Dorothy Johnson. LC 53-8871. 1973. pap. 1.75 (ISBN 0-345-29069-0). Ballantine.

Man Called Lenz. George Young. LC 55-28308. 1954. Hutchinson.

Man Called Lenz. 1st American Ed. George Young. LC 55-651496. 1955. Coward-McCann.

Man Called Noon. Louis L'Amour. 160p. 1973. pap. 2.25 (ISBN 0-553-14700-5). Bantam.

Man Called Paladin. Frank Chester Robertson. LC 63-15696. 1963. Macmillan.

Man Called Pedro. Barbara Westphal. LC 75-25227. (Destiny Ser.). 1975. pap. 4.95 o.p. (ISBN 0-8163-0214-6, 13075-7). Pacific Pr Pub Assn.

Man Called Sam. John Earl Lewis. LC 74-34399. 1975. 4.95 (ISBN 0-517-52161-X). Lenox Hill Press.

Man Called Spade. Dashiell Hammett. LC 46-20589. (Private detective mystery stories). Dell Publishing Company.

Man Can Build a House. Nathalie Sedgwick Colby. LC 28-249527. Harcourt, Brace and Company.

Man Cannot Tell. Philip Lightfoot Scruggs. LC 42-7204. 1942. The Bobbs-Merrill Company.

Man Chain. Robert Gillespie. LC 79-12276. 1979. 4.50 (ISBN 0-87886-102-5). Ithaca House.

Man Changes His Skin. Bruno Jasienski. Tr. by Scott, H. G. 1936. International Publishers.

Man-Chaser. Kirk Westley. Orig. Title: Pleasure Bound. 1969. pap. 0.60 o.p. (60-408). Manor Bks.
Man Chasers. Ann Pinchot. LC 79-115442. 1970. 6.95. McKay.
Man Cleansed by God: A Novel Based on St. Patrick's Confession. John Edward Beachn. LC 58-11461. 1959. Newman Press.
Man Condemned. Peter Alding. LC 80-54822. 1981. 9.95 (ISBN 0-8027-5443-0). Walker.
Man Condemned: Written and Illustrated by William Edw. Baubie. William Edward Baubie. LC 36-9968. The Stratford Company.
Man Could Get Killed That Way. Weldon Hill, pseud. LC 67-12498. 1967. D. McKay Co.
Man Could Stand up--a Novel. Ford Madox Ford. LC 26-181675. 1926. A. & C. Boni.
Man Dead. Selwyn Jepson. LC 51-12475. 1951. Published for the Crime Club by Doubleday.
Man Died Here. Gina Dessart. LC 47-30872. 1947. Harper.
Man Divided: By Dean Douglas Pseud. Douglas De Neen. LC 54-33171. (Gold medal books, 407). 1954. Fawcett Publications.
Man Dormant: A Novel. John Lodwick. LC 50-8034. 1950. Duell, Sloan and Pearce.
Man Downstairs. William F Hallstead. LC 79-4061. 7.95 (ISBN 0-525-66628-1). Elsevier/Nelson Books.
Man Drowning. 1st Ed. Henry Kuttner. LC 52-5458. 1952. Harper.
Man Eater. Vince Ducette. 1974. (pbk.) 1.95 (ISBN 0-87682-395-9). Barclay House.
Man Eater. Henry Milner Rideout. LC 24-28339. 1924. 1.50. Duffield and Company.
Man-Eater. Ted Willis. LC 77-359377. 1976. 3.25 (ISBN 0-333-19488-8). Macmillan.
Man-Eater. Ted Willis. LC 76-25009. 1977. 7.95 (ISBN 0-688-03124-2). Morrow.
Man-Eater of Malgudi. R. K. Narayan. LC 61-5919. 1961. Viking Press.
Man Eater of Manjari. Ruskin Bond. 112p. 1975. pap. 2.15 (ISBN 0-88253-734-2). Ind-US Inc.
Man-Eaters of Cascalon. Gene Lancour. LC 78-68352. (Doubleday science fiction). 1979. 7.95 (ISBN 0-385-13565-3). Doubleday.
Man-Eating Machine. John Sack. 1973. 6.95 o.p. (ISBN 0-374-20152-8). FS&G.
Man Everybody Was Afraid of. Joseph Hansen. LC 78-4190. (Rinehart suspense novel). 7.95 (ISBN 0-03-042376-7). Holt, Rinehart and Winston.
Man Everybody Was Afraid of. Joseph Hansen. LC 81-4836. 1981. 3.50 (ISBN 0-03-059894-X). Holt, Rinehart and Winston.
Man Fever. Florence Stonebraker. LC 44-9907. 1944. Phoenix Press.
Man for Marietta. Peggy O'More, pseud. LC 55-10190. 1955. Arcadia House.
Man for the Ages: A Story of the Builders of Democracy. Irving Bacheller. LC 19-18008. The Bobb-Merrill Company.
Man for the Asking. Catherine Breillat. Tr. by Harold J. Salemson. Orig. Title: L'homme Facile. 1969. 4.95 o.p. Morrow.
Man for the Asking: A Novel. Catherine Breillat. LC 74-81741. (Illus.). 1969. 4.95. Morrow.
Man Forbid. Else Reed. LC 35-201056. 1835. W. Morrow & Co.
Man Four-Square. William MacLeod Raine. LC 19-5199. 1919. Houghton Mifflin Company.
Man from America: A Sentimental Comedy. Elizabeth Bonham De La Pasture. LC 6-9622. 1906. E. P. Dutton & Company.
Man from Archangel: And Other Tales of Adventure. Arthur Conan Doyle. LC 73-101801. (Short story index reprint series). 1969. Books for Libraries Press.
Man from Archangel: And Other Tales of Adventure. Arthur Conan Doyle. LC 26-8499. 1925. George H. Doran Company.
Man from Archangel & Other Tales of Adventure. facsimile ed. Arthur Conan Doyle. LC 73-101801. (Short Story Index Reprint Ser.). 1925. 15.00 (ISBN 0-8369-3189-0). Ayer Co.
Man from Ashaluna. Henry Payson Dowst. LC 20-18763. Small, Maynard & Company.
Man from Atlantis. Kenneth Robeson. (Avenger,#25). 1974. (pbk.) 0.95. Warner Paperback Library.
Man from Atlantis. Richard Woodley. (Dell Book). 1977. 1.50 (ISBN 0-440-15368-9). Dell Pub. Co.
Man from Bar Twenty. Clarence Edward Mulford. (Hopalong Cassidy Ser). 1976. Repr. of 1922 ed. lib. bdg. 16.30x (ISBN 0-88411-229-2). Amereon Ltd.
Man from Bar 20: A Story of the Cow Country. Clarence Edward Mulford. LC 76-28254. 1976. 6.95 (ISBN 0-88411-229-2). Aeonian Press.
Man from Bar-20: A Story of the Cow-Country. Clarence Edward Mulford. LC 18-11941. 1918. 1.40. A. C. McClurg & Co.
Man from Bar 20: A Story of the Cow Country. Clarence Edward Mulford. LC 27-7326. 1918. A. L. Burt Company.
Man from Barranca Negra. Ray Hogan. 1976. (pbk.) 0.95. Ace Books.
Man from Blankley's, and Other Sketches: Reprinted from Punch. 2d ed. Thomas Anstey Guthrie. LC 3-26187. 1893. Longmans, Green, and Co.
Man from Bozeman. Don P Jenison. 1974. (pbk.) 0.95. Ace Books.
Man from Brazil. Edward Ballard Garside. LC 52-13760. 1953. Appleton-Century-Crofts.
Man from Brodney's. George Barr McCutcheon. LC 8-23920. 1908. Dodd, Mead & Company.
Man from Brodney's. George Barr McCutcheon. LC 15-174040. 1909. Dodd, Mead & Company.
Man from Butte City. Lauran Paine. LC 57-4458. 1957. Arcadia House.
Man from Cape Clear. Conchur O'Siochain. Tr. by Riobard P. Breatnach. 1975. pap. 6.25 o.p. Irish Bk Ctr.
Man from Cheyenne. Jack Slade, pseud. (Lassiter Ser.: No. 4). 192p. 1982. pap. write for info o.p. (ISBN 0-505-51860-0). Tower Bks.
Man from Cook's. Polan Banks. LC 33-19257. L. Furman, Inc.
Man from Corpus Christi: Or, The Adventures of Two Bird Hunters and Adog in Texan Bogs. Arthur C Peirce. LC 11-7171. 1894. Forest and Stream Publishing Company.
Man from Curdie's River: Or, Where Men Are Made. Donald Findlay MacLean. LC 74-79246. (Historical reprints series; no. 5). (Illus.). 1974-1975. 8.75 (ISBN 0-909706-29-8). Lowden Publishing.
Man from Cyrene: By Frans Venter. Francois Alwyn Venter. LC 62-15698. 1962. Muhlenberg Press.
Man from El Paso. W. D Hoffman. LC 26-18098. 1926. 2.00. A. C. McClurg & Co.
Man from Elbow River: By Chuck Stanley. Charles Stanley Strong. LC 56-11702. Arcadia House.
Man from Furnace Creek. Tom Ryan. (Brannigan Ser). (O.s.i.: No. 2). 1975. pap. 0.95 o.s.i. (LB227NK, Leisure Bks). Nordon Pubns.
Man from Glengarry: A Tale of the Ottawa. Charles William Gordon. 1901. F H. Revell Company.
Man from Glengarry: A Tale of the Ottawa. Charles William Gordon. LC 22-108380. Grosset & Dunlap.
Man from Greek and Roman: A Novel. James Goldman. LC 74-9066. 1974. 6.95 (ISBN 0-394-49391-5). Random House.
Man from Greek and Roman. A Novel by James Goldman. James Goldman. 1975. (pbk.) 1.75. Bantam Books.
Man from Home. Harry Leon Wilson. LC 15-8707. 1915. D. Appleton and Company.
Man from India. John Russell Coryell. LC 98-134. (On cover: Magnet detective library, no. 50). Street & Smith.
Man from Jericho. Edwin Carlile Litsey. LC 11-319649. 1911. 1.50. The Neale Publishing Company.
Man from Laramie. Thomas Theodore Flynn. LC 54-8046. (A Dell first edition, 14). 1954. Dell Pub. Co.
Man from Limbo. S. Guy Endore. LC 30-258223. Farrar & Rinehart, Incorporated.
Man from Lisbon: A Novel. Thomas Gifford. LC 77-24563. 10.00 (ISBN 0-07-023187-7). McGraw-Hill.
Man from Lisbon: A Novel. Thomas Gifford. 1978. 2.50 (ISBN 0-671-82070-2). Pocket Books.
Man from London Town. Sarah Stone Williams. LC 6-27352. 1906. The Neale Publishing Compnay.
Man from Lordsburg. Jack Slade, pseud. (Lassiter Ser.). 1978. pap. 1.25 o.s.i. (ISBN 0-505-51296-3). Tower Bks.
Man from Madura. Leslie Gillespie. LC 52-67081. 1952. T. V. Boardman.
Man from Maine: A Humorous Episode in the Life of Asa King. Frank Carlos Griffith. LC 5-37787. 1905. C. M. Clark Publishing Co., Inc.
Man from Manhattan: A Murder Mystery. Leonard Reginald Gribble. LC 35-3208. 1935. Pub. for the Crime Club, Inc., by Doubleday, Doran & Company, Inc.
Man from Mars: Or, Service, for Service's Sake. Henry Wallace Dowding. LC 10-268204. 1910. Cochrane Publishing Company.
Man from Mesabi. 1st Ed. Sarah McNeil Lockwood. LC 55-6481. 1955. Doubleday.
Man from Missouri. James D Salts. LC 16-13046. Authors Co-Operative Pub. Co.
Man from Morocco. Edgar Wallace. LC 75-12581. 1970. 4.50. London House & Maxwell.
Man from Moscow: A Commander Shaw Novel. 1st Amer. Ed. Philip McCutchan. LC 65-198506. 1965. 3.95. John Day.
Man from Mt. Vernon. 1st Ed. Burke Boyce. LC 61-568163. 1961. Harper.
Man from Mustang. large print ed. Max Brand. 1981. 18.00x o.p. (ISBN 0-89340-201-X, Pub. by Curley Assoc England). State Mutual Bk.
Man from Mustang. Frederick Faust. LC 79-1295. (Max Brand western). 1979. 10.95 (ISBN 0-89340-201-X). J. Curley.
Man from Mustang: A Silvertip Story. Max Brand. LC 42-161400. 1942. Dodd, Mead & Company.
Man from Mustang: A Silvertip Story. Frederick Faust. LC 42-16140. 1942. Dodd, Mead & Company.
Man from Next Door. Honor Lilibush Wingfield Tracy. 1977. 7.95 o.p. (ISBN 0-394-40279-0). Random.
Man from Next Door: A Novel. Honor Lilbush Wingfield Tracy. LC 76-53473. 7.95 (ISBN 0-394-40279-0). Random House.
Man from Nowhere. Oscar Chisgall. LC 35-21952. The Macaulay Company.
Man from Nowhere. Frank Hampson & Frank Bellamy. (Dan Dare Ser.: Vol. 1). 112p. 1981. pap. 9.95 (ISBN 0-8256-9555-4, Pub. by Dragon's Dream Holland). Music Sales.
Man from Nowhere. Elspeth Joscelin Grant Huxley. LC 65-20946. 1965. bds., 4.50. Morrow.
Man from Nowhere. Flora Haines Apponyi Loughead. LC 7-14774. (On cover: "The gold dust series." no. 1). 1891. C. A. Murdock & Co.
Man from Nowhere. Anna Theresa Sadlier. LC 18-6646. 1918. Benziger Brothers.
Man From Nowhere. Rebecca Stratton. (Harlequin Romances Ser.). 192p. 1983. pap. 1.75 (ISBN 0-373-02543-2). Harlequin Bks.
Man from O. R. G. Y. 3rd ed. Ted Mark, pseud. 1968. pap. 0.75 o.p. (75-210). Lancer.
Man from O.R.G.Y. Ted Mark. 1973. (pbk.) 1.25. Dell.
Man from O.R.G.Y. No. 2: The Tight End. Ted Mark, pseud. 1981. pap. 2.50 (ISBN 0-89083-823-2). Zebra.
Man from O.R.G.Y. Thy Neighbor's Orgy. Ted Mark, pseud. 272p. (Orig.). 1981. pap. 2.25 (ISBN 0-89083-701-5). Zebra.
Man from Oshkosh: A Story in Several Chapters and a Preface. John Hicks. LC 7-4764. (On cover: Sergel's international library, v. 1, no. 7. new series). 1894. C. H. Sergel Company; Etc., Etc.
Man from Outback. Lucy Walker, pseud. 1974. pap. 1.75 (ISBN 0-345-29500-5). Ballantine.
Man from Padera. Rory Calhoun. 1978. pap. 1.50 (ISBN 0-89041-199-9, 3199). Major Bks.
Man from Painted Rock. Jackson Gregory. LC 43-91928. 1943. Dodd, Mead & Company.
Man from Pansy. Don Rico. pap. 0.60 o.p. Lancer.
Man from Papago Wells. Jack Slade. Belmont Tower.
Man from Red Keg. Eugene Thwing. LC 5-33024. 1905. Dodd, Mead and Company.
Man from Riondo. Dudley Dean. 160p. 1981. pap. 1.75 (ISBN 0-449-14231-0, GM). Fawcett.
Man from Riondo. Dudley Dean. 1969. pap. 0.60 o.p. (R2184, GM). Fawcett World.
Man from Riondo: By Dudley Dean Pseud. Cover Painting by Frank McCarthy. Dudley Dean McGaughy. LC 55-15738. (Gold medal books, 486). 1954. Fawcett Publications.
Man from Robber's Roost: A Powder Valley Western. Peter Field. LC 57-8936. 1957. Jefferson House.
Man from S. T. U. D. in the Solid Gold Screw. F. W. Paul. (Man from S. T. U. D. Ser. No. 4). (Orig.). 1968. pap. 0.60 o.p. (73-782). Lancer.
Man from S. T. U. D. Sock It to Me, Zombie. F. W. Paul. (Orig.). 1968. pap. 0.60 o.p. (73-759). Lancer.
Man from S. T. U. D. The Orgy at Madame Dracula's. F. W. Paul. (Orig.). 1968. pap. 0.60 o.p. (73-754). Lancer.
Man from S. T. U. D. Three for an Orgy. F. W. Paul. (Orig.). 1968. pap. 0.60 o.p. (73-728). Lancer.
Man from St. Petersburg. Ken Follett. LC 81-22550. 1982. 14.50 (ISBN 0-688-01150-0). Morrow.
Man from St. Petersburg. large print ed. Ken Follett. LC 82-12143. 1982. 15.95 (ISBN 0-8161-3412-X). G.K. Hall.
Man from Salt Creek. Archie Joscelyn. LC 57-12670. 1957. Avalon Books.
Man from Savage Creek. Max Brand. 1977. 6.95 o.p. (ISBN 0-396-07422-7). Dodd.
Man from Savage Creek. Frederick Faust. LC 77-4384. (Silver star westerns). 1977. 6.95 (ISBN 0-396-07422-7). Dodd, Mead.
Man from Savage Creek. Frederick Faust. LC 77-14110. 1978. 9.95 (ISBN 0-89340-116-1). J. Curley & Associates.
Man from Scotland Yard. Zenith Jones Brown. LC 32-172560. Farrar & Rinehart, Incorporated.
Man from Sing Sing. Edward Phillips Oppenheim. LC 31-28604. 1932. Little, Brown, and Company.
Man from Skibbereen. Louis L'Amour. LC 73-14869. 1973. 8.95 (ISBN 0-8161-6161-5). G. K. Hall.
Man from Skibbereen. Louis L'Amour. LC 73-6941. 1973. 0.95. Bantam Books.
Man from Smiling Pass: Or: The Honorable Abe Blount. Eliot Harlow Robinson. LC 24-211509. 1924. L. C. Page & Company.
Man from Snowy River. Andrew B. Paterson. (Illus.). 1967. pap. 1.60 o.s.i. Tri-Ocean.
Man from Stony Lonesome. Jay Albert. LC 56-26717. (Ace double novel books, D-144). 1956. Ace Books.
Man from S.T.U.D. Vs. the Mafia. F. W. Paul. Bd. with The Lay of the Land; Sock It to Me, Zombie; The Orgy at Madam Dracula's. 1972. pap. 1.65 o.p. (70-403). Lancer.
Man from Tall Timber. Thomas K Holmes. LC 20-160. 1.75. G. Sully & Company.
Man From Tennessee. Jeanne Grant. (Second Chance at Love Ser.: No. 119). 1983. pap. 1.75 (ISBN 0-515-07207-9). Jove Pubns.
Man from Texas. Jackson Gregory. LC 42-238633. 1942. Dodd, Mead & Comapny.
Man from Texas. Edward Beverly Mann. LC 31-8636. 1931. W. Morrow & Co.
Man from Texas. Edward Beverly Mann. LC 43-2714. 1943. The Sun Dial Press.
Man from Texas. A Western Romance. Henry Oldham. LC 7-36488. T. B. Peterson & Brothers.
Man from the Bad Lands. George Washington Ogden. LC 33-6253. 1933. Dodd, Mead & Company.
Man from the Badlands. 1st Ed. Paul Evan Lehman. LC 51-3442. (Dutton Diamond D western). 1951. Dutton.
Man from the Bitter Roots. Caroline Lockhart. LC 37-328152. A. L. Burt Company.
Man from the Bitter Roots. Caroline Lockhart. LC 15-240045. 1915. 1.25. J. B. Lippincott Company.
Man from the Broken Hills. Louis L'Amour. 1975. (pbk.) 1.25. Bantam Books.
Man from the Broken Hills. Louis L'Amour. LC 76-9053. 1976. 10.95 (ISBN 0-8161-6375-8). G. K. Hall.
Man from the Clouds. Joseph Storer Clouston. LC 19-3700. George H. Doran Company.
Man from the Kimberleys. Margaret Pargeter. (Harlequin Presents Ser.). 192p. 1983. pap. 1.95 (ISBN 0-373-10595-9). Harlequin Bks.
Man from the Mist. Mary Elgin, pseud. LC 65-2213. (Illus.). 1965. M. S. Mill Co.; Distributed by W. Morrow.
Man from the Mountain: Stories. first ed. Robert K Swisher. 1973. 3.50 (ISBN 0-682-47779-6). Exposition Press.
Man from the Norlands. John Buchan. LC 39-24454. 1939. The Sun Dial Press, Inc.
Man from the Norlands. John Buchan. LC 36-17536. 1936. Houghton Mifflin Company.
Man from the North. Arnold Bennett. LC 74-17023. (Collected works of Arnold Bennett). 1974. Books for Libraries Press.
Man from the North. Arnold Bennett. LC 11-26258. 1911. George H. Doran Company.
Man from the Past. Andrew MacKenzie. LC 59-23065. (British bloodhound, no. 236). 1958. T. V. Boardman.
Man from the Sea. Michael Innes, pseud. LC 82-47566. 224p. 1982. pap. 2.84i (ISBN 0-06-080591-9, P-591, PL). Har-Row.
Man from the Sea: By Michael Innes Pseud. John Innes Mackintosh Stewart. LC 55-61986. (Red badge detective). 1955. Dodd, Mead.
Man from the Turkish Slave. Victor Canning. LC 54-5545. 1954. Sloane.
Man from the West. A Novel. Descriptive of Adventures from the Chaparral to Wall Street. David Law Proudfit. (On cover: Echo series, no. 86). 1889. Pollard & Moss.
Man from the West: Or, From the Chaparral to Wall Street. David Law Proudfit. LC 7-300863. (sunnyside series, no. 75). J. S. Ogilvie Publishing Company.
Man from the Wilderness. Max Brand. LC 82-9171. 1982. 13.95 (ISBN 0-8161-3351-4). G.K. Hall.
Man from the Wilderness. Frederick Faust. LC 80-14494. (Silver star western). 1980. 8.95 (ISBN 0-396-07863-X). Dodd, Mead.
Man from the Wilds. Harold Bindloss. LC 22-2316. Frederick A. Stokes Company.
Man from There. Ben-Ner, Isaac. LC 74-124123. 1970. 5.95. Sabra Books.
Man from Thief River. Peter Field. LC 49-6578. (Triple-A western classic). 1949. Jefferson House.
Man from Thief River. Peter Field. LC 40-33360. 1940. W. Morrow & Company.
Man from Tibet. Clyde B Clason. LC 38-146996. 1938. Pub. for the Crime Club, Inc., by Doubleday, Doran & Company, Inc.
Man from Tibet. Clyde B Clason. LC 39-24231. 1939. The Sun Dial Press, Inc.
Man from Tombstone. Jack Slade, pseud. (Lassiter Ser). (Orig.). 1971. pap. 0.75 o.p. (B75-2104). Belmont-Tower.
Man from Tombstone. Jack Slade. (Lassiter,#14). 1974. (pbk.) 0.95. Belmont Tower Books.
Man from Tombstone and Gunfight at Ringo Junction. Jack Slade, pseud. (Belmont Tower books). 1978. 2.25 (ISBN 0-505-51285-8). Tower Pubns.

TITLE INDEX MAN-KILLERS.

Man from Tripoli. Kay Thorpe. (Harlequin Presents Ser.). 1979. pap. 1.50 (ISBN 0-373-70811-4). Harlequin Bks.
Man from Tucson. Claude Cassady. LC 77-16733. 1978. 7.95 o.p. (ISBN 0-312-51019-5); large type 9.95 o.p. (ISBN 0-312-51020-9). St Martin.
Man from Tucson. Lauran Paine. LC 77-16733. 1978. 7.95. (ISBN 0-312-51019-5) (ISBN 0-312-51020-9). St. Martin's Press.
Man from Two Rivers. Luke Short. 1974. (pbk.) 0.95. Bantam Books.
Man from White Hat. Stuart Jason. (Butcher Ser.: No. 34). 208p. (Orig.). 1982. pap. 1.95 (ISBN 0-523-41665-2). Pinnacle Bks.
Man from Yesterday. Dorothy Daniels. (Orig.). 1970. pap. 0.60 o.p. (63-436). Paperback Lib.
Man from Yesterday. Will H Robinson. LC 15-20596. The Roxburgh Publishing Co., Inc.
Man from Yesterday: By John S. Daniels Pseud. Wayne D Overholser. LC 57-12137. (Signet books, 1435). 1957. New American Library.
Man from Yonder. Harold Titus. LC 34-10386. Macrae Smith Company.
Man from Yuma. Jack Slade, pseud. (Lassiter Ser.: No. 3). 192p. 1982. pap. 2.25 (ISBN 0-505-51851-1). Tower Bks.
Man from Yuma. Jack Slade, pseud. (Lassiter Ser.). 1973. pap. 0.75 o.p. (BT40152). Belmont-Tower.
Man Gets Around. John McNulty. LC 51-9719. 1951. Little, Brown.
Man Goes Alone. Neil Miller Gunn. LC 44-5773. 1944. G. W. Stewart, Inc.
Man Goeth Forth. Charles W Gillum. LC 33-225921. B. Humphries, Inc.
Man Had Tall Sons. Martha Ostenso. LC 58-10773. 1958. Dodd, Mead.
Man-Handled. Bennie Caroline Hall. LC 47-200067. 1947. Phoenix Press.
Man Hater. Joseph Calvitt Clarke. LC 34-41050. 1934. W. Godwin.
Man Higher up: A Story of the Fight, Which Is Life and the Force, Which Is Love. Henry Russell Miller. LC 10-113003. The Bobbs-Merrill Company.
Man Hunt. Giles A. Lutz. 1981. pap. 1.75 (ISBN 0-345-29218-9). Ballantine.
Man Hunt (Rogue Male) Geoffrey Household. LC 42-24283. 1942. Triangle Books.
Man Hunters. Mabel McElliott. LC 32-132442. Grosset & Dunlap.
Man I Love. Norma Patterson. LC 40-691441. Farrar & Rinehart.
Man I Want. Rob Eden. LC 42-196427. 1942. Gramercy Publishing Co.
Man in a Black Hat. Ernest Temple Thurston. LC 31-330188. 1931. Doubleday, Doran & Company, Inc.
Man in a Cage. Brian M Stableford. LC 74-22024. 1975. 13.95 (ISBN 0-381-98280-7). John Day Co.
Man in a Mirror. Richard Llewellyn. LC 61-9531. 1961. Doubleday.
Man in a Net. William Butler. 12.95x (ISBN 0-8464-0586-5). Beekman Pubs.
Man in Ambush. Maurice Procter. pap. 0.95 o.p. (02407, Collier). Macmillan.
Man in Ambush. 1st American Ed. Maurice Procter. LC 59-634154. 1959. Harper.
Man in Arms. Frank W Bail. LC 35-287336. J. Messner, Inc.
Man in Aspic. Constantine Fitz Gibbon. 1977. 8.95 o.p. (ISBN 0-393-08769-7). Norton.
Man in Black. Al Conroy. 1979. pap. 1.25 (ISBN 0-440-15875-3). Dell.
Man in Black. Stanley John Weyman. 1894. The Cassell Publishing Co.
Man in Black. Stanley John Weyman. LC 20-13981. 1901. Longmans, Green and Co.
Man in Black. An Historical Novel of the Days of Queen Anne. George Payne Rainsford James. LC 7-7992. (On cover: Library of sterling novels). T. B. Peterson and Brothers.
Man in Blue: Or, Which Did He Love? Mary Andrews Denison. (sea and shore series. no. 9). 1889. Street & Smith.
Man in Button Boots. Lucy Beatrice Malleson. LC 35-4334. H. Holt and Company.
Man in Charge: A Novel. Morris H. Philipson. LC 79-299. 9.95 (ISBN 0-671-24818-9). Simon and Schuster.
Man in Evening Clothes. John Reed Scott. LC 17-14179. 1917. G. P. Putnam's Sons.
Man in Gray: A Romance of North and South. Thomas Dixon & Lee, Robert Edward. 1807-1870--Fiction. LC 21-199245. 1921. D. Appleton and Comapny.
Man in Grey. Eleanor Furneaux Smith. LC 42-36090. 1942. Doubleday, Doran and Company, Inc.
Man in Grey: Being Episodes of the Chouan Conspiracies in Normandy During the First Empire. Emmuska Orczy. LC 18-13910. 1918. Cassell and Company, Ltd.
Man in Grey: Being Episodes of the Chouan Conspiracies in Normandy During the First Empire. Emmuska Orczy. 1.50. George H. Doran Company.
Man in Her Life. Ruby Mildred Ayres. LC 35-16320. 1935. Doubleday, Doran & Company, Inc.
Man in Her Life. Ruby Mildred Ayres. LC 37-2260. 1937. The Sun Dial Press, Inc.
Man in Her Life. Ruby Mildred Ayres. LC 43-3868. 1943. The Sun Dial Press.
Man in His Arms. Preston Harriman. 160p. 1974. pap. 1.95 o.p. (ISBN 0-87682-400-9, 7400). Barclay Hse.
Man in His Prime: A Novel. Gilbert Phelps. LC 55-17251. 1955. J. Day Co.
Man in His Prime: A Novel. Z Skujins. LC 82-103703. (Illus.). 6.00. Progress.
Man in Inner & Outer Space. S. T. Butler & H. Messel. 1969. pap. 4.40 o.p. (ISBN 0-08-013874-8). Pergamon.
Man in Lonely Land. Kate Lee Langley Bosher. LC 12-796596. 1912. Harper & Brothers.
Man in Lower Ten. Mary Roberts Rinehart. LC 9-7946. 1909. 1.50. The Bobbs-Merrill Company.
Man in Lower Ten. Mary Roberts Rinehart. LC 20-15609. Grosset & Dunlap.
Man in Lower Ten. Mary Roberts Rinehart. LC 40-9079. 1940. Triangle Books.
Man in Lower Ten. Mary Roberts Rinehart. LC 46-40168. (works of Mary Roberts Rinehart). The Review of Reviews Corp.
Man in Motion. Michael Mewshaw. LC 71-117654. 1970. 5.95. Random House.
Man in My Grave. Wilson Tucker. LC 55-11018. 1956. Rinehart.
Man in Our Lives. John Brodie. LC 47-24092. 1946. T. Nelson and Sons Ltd.
Man in Paradise: A Novel. Walker Winslow. LC 41-22361. Smith & Durrell.
Man in Possession. Eliza M. J. Humphreys. LC 7-5792. J. W. Lovell Company.
Man in Question: By John Godey Pseud. 1st Ed. Morton Freedgood. LC 51-13245. 1951. Published for the Crime Club by Doubleday.
Man in Revolt. Eva Taube. (gr. 9-12). 1971. text ed. price not set o.p. (5789); pap. price not set o.p. (ISBN 0-8104-5788-1). Hayden.
Man in Search of a Wife: Or, The Adventures of a Bachelor in New York... Walter Seaton. LC 8-3375. 1853. DeWitt & Davenport.
Man in the Basement. Palle Adam Wilhelm Rosenkrantz. LC 7-36227. Empire Book Company.
Man in the Bearskin. John H De Groot. LC 25-259871. Augustana Book Concern.
Man in the Blue Coat: From the German. Johannes, George, Tr. LC 11-6957. The Erie Printing Co.
Man in the Blue Mask. Anthony Morton, pseud. LC 37-812. J. B. Lippincott Company.
Man in the Blue Mask. Anthony Morton, pseud. LC 39-949. 1938. The Sun Dial Press, Inc.
Man in the Blue Vest and Other Stories. W. Gunther Plaut. LC 79-23762. 1980. 8.95 (ISBN 0-8008-5093-9). Taplinger Pub. Co.
Man in the Box. Peter Moss. 192p. (Orig.). 1973. pap. 1.95 o.p. (ISBN 0-87682-348-7, 7348). Barclay Hse.
Man in the Box: A Story from Vietnam. Mary Lois Dunn. (Laurel leaf library). (Illus.). 1975. (pbk.) 0.95. Dell.
Man in the Brown Derby. Wells Southworth Hastings. LC 11-25743. 1.25. The Bobbs-Merrill Company.
Man in the Brown Suit. Agatha Miller Christie. LC 24-25524. 1924. Dodd, Mead and Company.
Man in the Cage. John Holbrook Vance. LC 60-5545. (Random House mystery). 1960. Random House.
Man in the Cage see TaleSpinners I.
Man in the Camlet Cloak: Being an Old Writing Transcribed and Ed. Carlen Bateson. LC 3-18675. 1903. The Saalfield Publishing Company.
Man in the Cane. 1st Ed. Mentis Carrere. LC 56-5811. 1956. Vantage Press.
Man in the Case. Elizabeth Stuart Phelps H. D. Ward Ward. LC 6-32116. 1906. Houghton, Mifflin and Company.
Man in the Corner. Emmuska Orczy. LC 9-25630. 1909. Dodd, Mead & Company.
Man in the Corner: Introd. by Vincent Starrett. Illus. by H. M. Brock. Emmuska Orczy. LC 66-3388. (Seagull lib. of mystery and suspense). 3.95. Norton.
Man in the Dark. John Alexander Ferguson. LC 28-16165. 1928. Dodd, Mead and Company.
Man in the Dark. Douglas Orgill. LC 65-11489. bds., 3.95. Morrow.
Man in the Dark. Albert Payson Terhune. LC 21-262942. 1921. E. P. Dutton & Company.
Man in the Dark Suit: A Futuristic Mystery /by Dennis R. Caro. Dennis R Caro. 1.95 (ISBN 0-671-83153-4). Pocket Books.
Man in the Garden. Paule Mason. LC 70-91832. 1969. 3.95. McKay.
Man in the Glass Booth. Robert Shaw. LC 67-10770. 1967. Harcourt, Brace & World.
Man in the Glass Octopus. J. Michael Yates. 109p. 1974. pap. 4.95 o.p. (ISBN 0-913600-06-7). Kanchenjunga Pr.
Man in the Gray Flannel Suit. Sloan Wilson. LC 54-9811. 1955. Simon and Schuster.
Man in the Gray Flannel Suit. Sloan Wilson. LC 79-18970. 1979. 10.00 (ISBN 0-8376-0448-6). R. Bentley.
Man in the Gray Flannel Suit II. Sloan Wilson. 356p. 1983. 15.95 (ISBN 0-87795-474-7). Arbor Hse.
Man in the Green Hat. 1st Ed. Manning Coles, pseud. LC 55-558867. 1955. Published for the Crime Club by Doubleday.
Man in the High Castle. Philip K Dick. LC 78-32091. (Gregg Press science fiction series). 1979. 9.95 (ISBN 0-8398-2476-9). Gregg Press.
Man in the Holocene. Max Frisch. Tr. by Geoffrey Skelton. LC 79-3351. (Helen & Kurt Wolff Bk.). (Illus.). 1981. pap. 3.95 (ISBN 0-15-656952-3, Harv). HarBraceJ.
Man in the Holocene. Max Frisch. Tr. by Geoffrey Skelton. LC 79-3351. (Helen & Kurt Wolff Bk.). (Illus.). 120p. 1980. 7.95 (ISBN 0-15-156931-2). HarBraceJ.
Man in the House. Florence Stonebraker. 1947. Gramercy Publishing Co.
Man in the Iron Mask. Alexandre Dumas. LC 65-4063. 1965. Printed for the Members of the Limited Editions Club.
Man in the Iron Mask. Alexandre Dumas. LC 39-27638. 1939. Dodd, Mead and Company.
Man in the Iron Mask. Alexandre Dumas. LC 44-5938. (On cover: Great illustrated classics). 1944. Dodd, Mead & Company.
Man in the Iron Mask. Alexandre Dumas & Maquet, Auguste. LC 6-42302. (American series, no. 301). M. J. Ivers & Co.
Man in the Iron Mask. A Historical Romance. Alexandre Dumas & Maquet, Auguste. Tr. by Williams, Henry Llewellyn. LC 6-42300. The F. M. Lupton Publishing Company.
Man in the Iron Mask. Being the Completion of "The Three Guardsmen," "Twenty Years After," "The Vicomte De Bragelonne," "Ten Years Later" and "Louise De La Valliere,". Alexandre Dumas & Maquet, Auguste. LC 6-42301. (On cover: Seaside library. Pocket ed. no. 2067). G. Munro.
Man in the Jungle. David Rowbotham. LC 66-38595. 1964. Angus & Robertson.
Man in the Jury Box. Isabel Egenton Ostrander. LC 21-2069. 1921. R. M. McBride & Co.
Man in the Making. Harry Wagenseller Jones. LC 13-386. 1912. 1.35. Crane & Company.
Man in the Mews. Joy Packer. 1965. 4.50 o.p. Dutton.
Man in the Mews: A Novel. Joy Petersen Packer. LC 64-21861. 1965. bds., 4.50. Dutton.
Man in the Middle. Hugh Atkinson. LC 73-86474. 1973. 6.95 (ISBN 0-399-11247-2). Putnam.
Man in the Middle. M. E. Chaber, pseud. (Rinehart Suspense Novel). 1967. 3.95 o.p. (ISBN 0-03-063680-9). HR&W.
Man in the Middle. M. E. Chaber, pseud. (Milo March Mystery Ser). 1970. pap. 0.60 o.p. (ISBN 0-446-63203-1, 63-203). Paperback Lib.
Man in the Middle. Anthony Heal. LC 80-12653. 1980. 9.95 (ISBN 0-684-16642-9). Scribner.
Man in the Middle: A New Milo March Adventure. Kendell Foster Crossen. LC 67-12583. (Rinehart suspense novel). 1967. Holt, Rinehart and Winston.
Man in the Middle: By Ferguson Findley Pseud. 1st Ed. Charles Weiser Frey. LC 52-5863. 1952. Duell, Sloan and Pearce.
Man in the Middle. 1st Ed. David Wagoner. 1954. Harcourt, Brace.
Man in the Mirror. Robert Aitken. LC 10-225371. W. J. Watt & Company.
Man in the Mirror. Herman Tierlinck. 1963. 10.00x o.s.i. (ISBN 0-8277-0118-7). British Bk Ctr.
Man in the Mirror: A Biographical Reflection. William A Garrett. LC 31-18067. 1931. D. Appleton and Company.
Man in the Mirror: A Novel of Espionage. Frederick Ayer, Jr. LC 65-191631. 4.50. Regnery Co.
Man in the Mist. Audrey Walz. LC 51-13660. 1951. Duell, Sloan and Pearce.
Man in the Monkey Suit. Ann Hathaway. LC 33-3599. 1933. W. Godwin, Inc.
Man in the Moone: And Other Lunar Fantasies. Ed. by Faith K. Pizor. LC 73-136146. (Illus.). 1971. 8.95. Praeger.
Man in the Moone: Or a Discourse of a Voyage Thither. Francis Godwin. 1975. Repr. of 1638 ed. text ed. 6.95x o.s.i. (ISBN 0-8277-3842-0). British Bk Ctr.
Man in the Moonlight. Cecile Gilmore. LC 53-104915. 1953. Avalon Books.
Man in the Moonlight. Rupert Sargent Holland. LC 20-100515. G. W. Jacobs & Company.
Man in the Moonlight. Helen McCloy. LC 40-7803. 1940. W. Morrow & Company.
Man in the Net: A Novel of Suspense. Patrick Quentin. LC 56-142044. (Inner sanctum mystery). 1956. Simon and Schuster.
Man in the Open. Roger S Pocock. LC 12-17663. The Bobbs-Merrill Company.
Man in the Panther's Skin: A Romantic Epic. S. Rust'Haveli. Tr. by M. S. Wardrop. (Oriental Translation Fundseries, No. 21). 1966. Repr. 7.50 o.p. Verry.
Man in the Purple Gown. John Leslie Palmer, pseud. LC 39-14948. 1939. Dodd, Mead & Company.
Man in the Queue. Elizabeth Mackintosh. (Kangaroo Book). 1977. 1.75 (ISBN 0-671-80959-8). Pocket Books.
Man in the Queue. Elizabeth Mackintosh. LC 29-16556. E. P. Dutton & Co., Inc.
Man in the Queue. Elizabeth Mackintosh. LC 79-28589. 1980. 10.00 (ISBN 0-8376-0450-8). R. Bentley.
Man in the Queue. Josephine Tey. LC 79-28589. 1981. Repr. of 1929 ed. lib. bdg. 10.00x (ISBN 0-8376-0450-8). Bentley.
Man in the Queue. Josephine Tey. 1970. pap. 1.25 (ISBN 0-425-03220-5, Medallion). Berkley Pub.
Man in the Queue. Josephine Tey. 1982. pap. 2.95 (ISBN 0-671-43524-8). PB.
Man in the Red Hat. Clifford James Wheeler Hosken. LC 30-21869. 1930. Harper & Brothers.
Man in the Saddle. Ernest Haycox. LC 38-168703. 1938. Little, Brown and Company.
Man in the Saddle. Ernest Haycox. LC 82-9169. 1982. 10.95 (ISBN 0-8161-3358-1). G.K. Hall.
Man in the Saddle. Ernest Haycox. (Signet brand western, T5292). 1972. New American Lib.
Man in the Sandhills. Antony Marsden. LC 27-17358. 1927. A. & C. Boni.
Man in the Shadow. Richard Washburn Child. LC 11-25089. 1911. 1.25. The Macmillan Company.
Man in the Shadow: By Rae Foley Pseud. Elinore Denniston. (Red badge detective). 1953. Dodd, Mead.
Man in the Shadows. Rosemary Carter. (Harlequin Romances Ser.). 192p. (Orig.). 1981. pap. 1.25 (ISBN 0-373-02380-4). Harlequin Bks.
Man in the Shadows. Carroll John Daly. LC 28-219797. E. J. Clode, Inc.
Man in the Shadows. Elias Lieberman. 3.95 o.p. (ISBN 0-87140-892-9). Liveright.
Man in the Shower. Peter Arno. (Illus.). 128p. 1976. 13.50 (ISBN 0-7156-1149-6, Pub. by Duckworth England). Biblio Dist.
Man in the Sky. Richard Gibson Hubler. LC 56-9585. 1956. Duell, Sloan and Pearce.
Man in the Sopwith Camel: A Novel. Michael Butterworth. LC 74-12678. 1975. 4.95 (ISBN 0-385-02390-1). Published for the Crime Club by Doubleday.
Man in the Tower. Rupert Sargent Holland. LC 9-25178. 1909. J. B. Lippincott Company.
Man in the Tricorn Hat. Delano L. Ames. LC 66-17747. 1966. 3.95. Regnery.
Man in the Twilight. Ridgwell Cullum. LC 22-14575. 1922. 2.00. G. P. Putnam's Sons.
Man in the Wheatfield. Robert Laxalt. LC 64-18079. 1964. Harper & Row.
Man in the White Raincoat. Richard Lebherz. LC 63-21726. 1963. London House & Maxwell.
Man in the White Slicker. Leonard Hastings Nason. LC 29-10954. 1929. Doubleday, Doran & Company, Inc.
Man in the Yellow Raft. Cecil Scott Forester. LC 69-16972. 1969. 5.95. Little, Brown.
Man in the Yellow Raft: By C. S. Forester. Cecil Scott Forester. 1976. (pbk.) 1.25 (ISBN 0-523-00839-2). Pinnacle Books.
Man in the Zoo. David Garnett. LC 24-141711. 1924. A. A. Knopf.
Man in Yellow and The Empty House. Herman Cyril McNeile. LC 33-22226. 1933. Doubleday, Doran & Company, Inc.
Man Inside. M. E. Chaber, pseud. (Milo March Mystery). 1970. pap. 0.60 o.p. (ISBN 0-446-63213-9, 63-213). Paperback Lib.
Man Inside. Natalie Sumner Lincoln. LC 14-5196. 1914. 1.30. D. Appleton and Company.
Man Inside: A Novel of Suspense, by M. E. Chaber Pseud. 1st Ed. Kendell Foster Crossen. LC 54-5444. 1954. Holt.
Man Inside: Being the Record of the Strange Adventure of Allen Steele Among the Xulus. Victor Francis Calverton. LC 36-29612. 1936. C. Scribner's Sons.
Man Inside... Landry, Bob St. John. 1981. pap. 2.75 (ISBN 0-380-56481-5, 56481). Avon.
Man into Beast: Strange Tales of Transformation. Ed. by Auguste C. Spectorsky. LC 47-11097. 1947. Doubleday.
Man Is Always Right. Maysie Greig. LC 40-339311. 1940. Doubleday, Doran and Company Inc.
Man Is an Onion. D. J. Enright. LC 72-5280. 222p. 1973. 9.95 o.s.i. (ISBN 0-912050-31-4, Library Pr). Open Court.
Man Is Strong. Corrado Alvaro. LC 48-428797. 1948. A. A. Knopf.
Man-Killers. Dane Coolidge. LC 21-5477. E. P. Dutton & Company.

Man, Know Thy Future: Or, Tales from the Borderland. Sophia Beale McIntyre. LC 41-15447. Dorrance and Company.
Man Laughs Back. Tay Garnett. LC 35-2972. The Macaulay Company.
Man Lay Dead. Ngaio Marsh. LC 72-192854. 1972. 5.95. Little, Brown.
Man Lay Dead. Ngaio Marsh. LC 42-36026. 1942. Sheridan House.
Man Made Angry. Hugh Brooke. LC 32-23139. 1932. R. Long & R. R. Smith, Inc.
Man Made Angry: By Hugh Brooke... Hugh Brooke. 1932. Longmans, Green and Co.
Man Made for Trouble. James Powell. 1979. pap. 1.75 (ISBN 0-89041-249-9). Major Bks.
Man Made of Smoke. Stanley Middleton. 1973. 8.95 (ISBN 0-09-115060-4, Pub. by Hutchinson). Merrimack Pub Cir.
Man Made the Town. Ruby Mildred Ayres. LC 31-28919. 1931. Doubleday, Doran & Company, Inc.
Man Madness: A Novel. May Christie. LC 29-964326. Grosset & Dunlap.
Man Maid. Evis Joberg. LC 53-1770. (Arco sophisticate). 1952. Arco Pub. Co.
Man, Master or Slave. John Langley. 3.75 o.p. Vantage.
Man May Dream. Carl Avery Werner. LC 40-12363. Sheridan House.
Man Miss Susie Loved. Augusta Tucker. LC 42-36359. 1942. Harper & Brothers.
Man Missing. Mignon Good Eberhart. LC 54-5393. 1954. Random House.
Man Missing. Mignon Good Eberhart. LC 54-5393. 1974. (pbk.) 0.95. Popular Library.
Man Named Luke. Peggy Morrison. LC 33-10148. 1933. A. A. Knopf.
Man Named Murdo & Rough Road to Denver. Ray Gaulden. 1981. pap. 2.50 (ISBN 0-89083-771-6). Zebra.
Man Named Thin, and Other Stories. Collected and Edited with Introd. and Critical Notes by Ellery Queen. Dashiell Hammett. LC 62-11514. (Mercury mystery, no. 233). 1962. J. W. Ferman.
Man Named Yuma. Theodore V. Olsen. (Orig.). 1971. pap. 0.60 o.p. (R2414, GM). Fawcett World.
Man Next Door. Mignon Good Eberhart. LC 43-51152. 1943. Random House.
Man Next Door. Emerson Hough. LC 17-4711. 1917. D. Appleton and Company.
Man Next Door. Emanuel Litvinoff. LC 69-19787. 1969. 4.50. Norton.
Man Nobody Knew. Harold Everett Porter. LC 19-769. 1919. 1.50. Dodd, Mead and Company.
Man Nobody Saw. Peter Cheyney. LC 49-10587. (Red badge mystery). 1949. Dodd, Mead.
Man O' Men. Clyde C Cortright. LC 30-20457. Meador Publishing Company.
Man of a Hundred Faces. Gaston Leroux. LC 30-14090. The Macaulay Company.
Man of Affairs. John Dann MacDonald. 176p. 1978. pap. 2.25 (ISBN 0-449-14051-2, GM). Fawcett.
Man of Affairs: An Original Novel. John Dann MacDonald. LC 58-27454. (Dell first edition, B112). 1957. Dell Pub. Co.
Man of Athens. Julia D Dragoumis. LC 17-260778. 1916. Houghton Mifflin Company.
Man of Blood. Jose Luis De Vilallonga. LC 60-608835. 1960. Simon and Schuster.
Man of Brittany: A Novel. Selwyn James. LC 46-1080. 1946. Simon and Schuster.
Man of Bronze. A Superhero Adventure. Kenneth Robeson, pseud. (His the fantastic adventures of Doc Savage, 1). (Illus.). 1975. 1.75. (ISBN 0-307-02379-6). Golden Press.
Man of Clay: A Tale of Life. Hiram Wallace Hayes. LC 11-27456. Davis & Bond.
Man of Constantia: A Biographical Novel on the Life of Simon Van der Stel. Hymen Willem Johannes Picard. LC 73-76810. 1973. 11.29 (ISBN 0-360-00191-2). Purnell.
Man of Cyrene. Avin Harry Johnston. LC 60-155768. 1961. Concordia Pub. House.
Man of Dangerous Secrets... Maxwell March. LC 33-21129. 1933. Pub. for the Crime Club, Inc., by Doubleday, Doran & Company, Inc.
Man of Destiny. Thomas Gold Frost. LC 9-23729. 1909. The Gramercy Publishing Company.
Man of Destiny. Graham Masterton. 1981. 16.95 o.p. (ISBN 0-671-42054-2). S&S.
Man of Dollar, Which? A Novel. (On verso of t.-p.: Unity library, no. 55). 1896. C. H. Kerr & Company.
Man of Double Deed. Leonard Daventry. LC 65-23794. (Doubleday sci. fic.). 3.95. Doubleday.
Man of Earth. Algis Budrys, pseud. LC 58-8259. (Ballantine books, 243). 1958. Ballantine Books.
Man of Earth. Maggi Lidchi. LC 68-31909. 1968. W. Morrow.
Man of Feeling. Henry Mackenzie. LC 74-18367. (Flowering of the Novel). 1974. 25.00 (ISBN 0-8240-1196-1). Garland Pub.
Man of Feeling. Henry Mackenzie. LC 78-172709. (Mackenzie, Henry, 1745-1831. The Novels of Henry Mackenzie). 1976. 16.25 (ISBN 0-404-04093-4). AMS Press.
Man of Feeling see Novels of Henry Mackenzie.
Man of Feeling. Introd. by Kenneth C. Slagle. Henry Mackenzie. LC 59-259318. (Norton library, N14). 1958. Norton.
Man of Fire. Margaret Rome. (Harlequin Presents Ser.). 1974. pap. 1.25 (ISBN 0-373-70558-1, 70558). Harlequin Bks.
Man of Fortune. A Story of the Present Day. Albany De Grenier Fonblanque. LC 6-41418. 1865. Routledge, Warne and Routledge.
Man of Fortune: And Other Tales. Catherine Grace Frances Moody Gore. LC 6-27498. 1842. Lea & Blanchard.
Man of Forty. Gerald William Bullett. LC 40-62004. 1940. A. A. Knopf.
Man of Freedom. Ed. by Don R. Riso. 1975. 2.50 o.s.i. (ISBN 0-913390-12-7). Pathmark Bks.
Man of Genius: A Story of the Judgment of Paris. Mary Patricia Willcocks. LC 8-17245. 1908. J. Lane Company; Etc., Etc.
Man of Glass. Donald Zochert. LC 81-47466. (Nick Caine Adventure Ser.). 264p. 1982. 12.95 (ISBN 0-03-056222-8). HR&W.
Man of God. Eduard Heinrich Nikolaus Graf Von Keyserling. LC 30-15342. The Macaulay Company.
Man of Gold. Rufino Blanco Fombona. Tr. by Isaac Goldberg. 1977. lib. bdg. 59.95 (ISBN 0-8490-2200-2). Gordon Pr.
Man of Grace, Andy Capp. Smythe. 1979. pap. 1.50 (ISBN 0-449-14153-5, GM). Fawcett.
Man of Her Dreams. Renee Shann. Orig. Title: Meet Candy. pap. 0.45 o.p. (56-951). Paperback Lib.
Man of Her Dreams. Renee Shann. 1973. pap. 0.75 o.p. (94318). Beagle Bks.
Man of His Age. Hamilton Drummond. LC 7-28447. 1900. Harper & Brothers.
Man of His Own: And Other Dog Stories. Corey Ford & MacBain, Alastair. 1949. Whittlesey House.
Man of His Time: By Phhllis Bentley. Phyllis Eleanor Bentley. LC 66-25585. 1966. 4.95. Macmillan.
Man of His Word: And Other Stories. William Edward Norris. (Harper's Franklin square library, no. 454). 1885. Harper & Brothers.
Man of Honor. Laura Chambers. LC 51-487055. 1920. Knickerbocker Press.
Man of Honor. George Cary Eggleston. LC 76-137728. (American fiction reprint series). (Illus.). 1970. Books for Libraries Press.
Man of Honor. George Cary Eggleston. LC 12-19566. Orange Judd Company.
Man of Honor. Theodor Fontane. Tr. by E. M. Valk. LC 74-78439. 206p. 1975. 10.50 (ISBN 0-8044-2207-9); pap. 4.95 (ISBN 0-8044-6155-4). Ungar.
Man of Honor: A Novel. Ursula Tighe Hopkins. LC 55-10265. 1955. Morrow.
Man of Honor: A Novel. Henrietta Eliza Vaughan Stannard. LC 8-13854. (Harper's handy series, no. 50). 1886. Harper & Brothers.
Man of Honor: A Novel. Henrietta Eliza Vaughan Stannard. (On cover: The seaside library. Pocket ed. no. 688). 1886. G. Munro.
Man of Honor. "M. De Camors". Octave Feuillet. (On cover: The library of choice fiction, no. 27). 1891. Laird & Lee.
Man of Honor (Schach Von Wuthenow). Theodor Fontane. LC 74-78439. 1975. 7.50 (ISBN 0-8044-2207-9) (ISBN 0-8044-2207-9). Ungar.
Man of Ice. Rachel Lindsay. (Harlequin Presents Ser.). (Orig.). 1980. pap. 1.50 (ISBN 0-373-10359-X). Harlequin Bks.
Man of Iron. Clotilde Inez Mary Graves. LC 15-4807. 1915. Frederick A. Stokes Company.
Man of Last Resort. Melville Davisson Post. 284p. 1980. Repr. of 1897 ed. lib. bdg. 14.25x (ISBN 0-89968-198-0). Lightyear.
Man of Last Resort: Or, The Clients of Randolph Mason. Melville Davisson Post. LC 14-1828. G. P. Putnam's Sons.
Man of Law. John William Wainwright. LC 80-53086. 1980. 9.95 (ISBN 0-312-51088-8). St. Martin's Press.
Man of Little Evils. Stephen Dobyns. LC 73-78408. 1973. 6.95 (ISBN 0-689-10567-3). Atheneum.
Man of Little Faith. Reginald Wright Kauffman. LC 27-6815. 1927. The Penn Publishing Company.
Man of Malaysia. Kok Seng Tan. (Writing in Asia Ser.). 1974. pap. text ed. 4.00x (00221). Heinemann Ed.
Man of Malice Landing. Dorothy James Roberts. LC 43-11850. 1943. The Macmillan Company.
Man of Many Minds. Edward Everett Evans. 1976. Repr. of 1953 ed. lib. bdg. 4.95 (ISBN 0-88411-982-3). Amereon Ltd.
Man of Many Minds. With an Introd. by Edward E. Smith. 1st Ed. Edward Everett Evans. LC 53-12860. (FP science fiction). Fantasy Press.
Man of Many Parts. Raymond Steiber. 1974. (pbk.) 1.25. Dell.
Man of Mark. Anthony Hope Hawkins. (On cover: Seaside library. Pocket ed., no. 2147). 1895. G. Munro's Sons.
Man of Mark. Anthony Hope Hawkins. LC 872. (On cover: Arrow library, no. 98). Street & Smith.
Man of Mark. A Novel. Anthony Hope Hawkins. LC 12-254233. 1895. H. Holt and Company.
Man of Means. Kay Thorpe. (Harlequin Presents Ser.). 192p. 1983. pap. 1.75 (ISBN 0-373-10573-8). Harlequin Bks.
Man of Means. Tr. from Portuguese by Ann Stevens 1st Amer. Ed. Luis De Sttau Monteiro. LC 64-123017. 1965. bds., 3.95. Knopf.
Man of Metal. Pel Torro, pseud. Ed. by Alice Sachs. Orig. Title: Space No Barrier. 1970. 3.95 o.p. Lenox Hill.
Man of Middle Age. Patricia Zelver. LC 79-1929. 228p. 1980. 12.95 (ISBN 0-03-048986-5). HR&W.
Man of Middle Age & Twelve Stories. Patricia Zelver. LC 79-1929. 12.95 (ISBN 0-03-048986-5). Holt, Rinehart and Winston.
Man of Miracles. Maurice Leblanc. LC 31-18176. The Macaulay Company.
Man of Nazareth. Anthony Burgess. LC 78-27316. 10.95 (ISBN 0-07-008962-0). McGraw-Hill.
Man of Parts. Vivian Connell. LC 50-57970. (Gold medal book, 130). 1950. Fawcett Publications.
Man of Parts. Tr. from Italian by Julia Martines. 1st Amer. Ed. Piero Chiara. LC 68-14741. 1968. bds., 4.95. Little, Brown.
Man of Power. Mary Wibberley. (Harlequin Romances Ser.). 192p. (Orig.). 1981. pap. 1.25 (ISBN 0-373-02388-X, Pub. by Harlequin). PB.
Man of Promise. Willard Huntington Wright. LC 16-5193. 1916. John Lane Company.
Man of Promise. Willard Huntington Wright. LC 30-4239. 1930. C. Scribner's Sons.
Man of Property. John Galsworthy. LC 49-3881. (Modern standard authors). 1949. C. Scribner's Sons.
Man of Property. John Galsworthy. 1906. G. P. Putnam's Sons.
Man of Property. John Galsworthy & Limited Editions Club., Inc., New York. LC 64-5353. 1964. Printed by A. Colish for the Members of the Limited Editions Club.
Man of Property. Afterword by Louis Auchincloss. John Galsworthy. (Signet classic, CQ373). (His The Forsyte saga, 1). 1967. New Amer. Lib.
Man of Property, and Indian Summer of a Forsyte. Introd. and Study Guide by Marsden V. Dillenbeck, with Marian L. Warren Sch. Ed. John Galsworthy. (His Forsyte saga, v.1-2). 3.36. Scribners.
Man of Property. Introd. by Evelyn Waugh. Illus. by Charles Mozley. John Galsworthy & Charles Illus Mozley. LC 65-2033. 1965. 6.50. Heritage Dist. Dial.
Man of Purpose. Donald Randall Richberg. LC 22-13967. Thomas Y. Crowell Company.
Man of Purpose: A Novel. Donald Randall Richberg. LC 35-3544. 1934. Thomas Y. Crowell Company.
Man of Real Sensibility: Or, The History of Sir George Ellison. Founded on Fact... Sarah Robinson Scott. LC 19-2895. 1797. Printed by H. Kammer, Jr.
Man of Samples. Something About the Men He Met "on the Road.". William H Maher. 1887. Toledo Book Company.
Man of Sark. John Oxenham, pseud. LC 7-29685. 1907. The Baker and Taylor Company.
Man of Sensibility. Jean Dutourd. 1961. Simon and Schuster.
Man of Straw. Joy Cowley. LC 75-97655. 1970. 5.95. Doubleday.
Man of Strife. Grove Wilson. LC 25-21212. 1925. Frank-Maurice, Inc.
Man of Taste: And Other Stories. Philip Freund. LC 49-9705. Beechhurst Press.
Man of Teak. Sue Peters. (Harlequin Romances Ser.). 192p. 1982. pap. 1.50 (ISBN 0-373-02501-7). Harlequin Bks.
Man of the Desert. Grace Livingston Hill. LC 75-31643. 1975. 9.95. American Reprint Co.
Man of the Desert. Grace Livingston Hill. LC 22-4743. Grosset & Dunlap.
Man of the Desert. Grace Livingston Hill. LC 14-15742. Fleming H. Revell Company.
Man of the Desert. Grace Livingston Hill. LC 81-19270. 5.95 (ISBN 0-8007-1295-1). Revell.
Man of the Desert: A Western Story. Robert J Horton. LC 25-5542. Chelsea House.
Man of the Family. Ralph Moody. (Illus.). 1962. 8.95 o.s.i. (ISBN 0-393-07536-2, Norton Lib); pap. 3.95x (ISBN 0-393-00902-5). Norton.
Man of the Family; a Novel. Frances Christine Tiernan. LC 8-19808. 1897. G. P. Putnam's Sons.
Man of the Forest. Zane Grey. (Kangaroo Book). 1977. 1.50 (ISBN 0-671-81275-0). Pocket Books.
Man of the Forest: A Novel. Zane Grey. LC 20-2265. 1920. Harper & Brothers.
Man of the Forest: A Novel. Zane Grey. LC 22-247780. Grossett & Dunlap.
Man of the Hour. Alice French. LC 76-51666. (Recovered Fiction by American Women). 1977. 22.00 (ISBN 0-405-10045-0). Arno Press.
Man of the Hour. Alice French. The Bobbs-Merrill Company.
Man of the House. Muriel Hine Coxon. LC 40-7351. 1940. D. Appleton-Century Company, Incorporated.
Man of the Name of John. Florence M King. LC 7-12210. (On cover: Cassell's "rainbow" series. no. 30). 1889. Cassell & Company, Limited.
Man of the Name of John. Florence M King. LC 3219. (On cover: Eagle library. no. 162). 1900. Street & Smith.
Man of the North. James Beardsley Hendryx. LC 29-20793. 1929. Doubleday, Doran & Company, Inc.
Man of the Outback. Anne Hampson. 192p. (Orig.). 1980. pap. 1.50 (ISBN 0-671-57028-5, Pub. by Silhouette Bks). S&S.
Man of the People. Chinua Achebe. LC 66-22929. pap. 3.50 (ISBN 0-385-08616-4, A594, Anch). Doubleday.
Man of the People: A Novel. Chinua Achebe. LC 66-22929. 1966. John Day Co.
Man of the Storm: A Romance of Colter Who Discovered Yellowstone. Ethel Powelson Hueston. LC 36-7001. The Bobbs-Merrill Company.
Man of the West. Philip Yordan. LC 55-7131. 1955. Simon and Schuster.
Man of the World. Stanley Kauffmann. LC 56-572339. 1956. Rinehart.
Man of the World. Henry Mackenzie. LC 76-25569. (Mackenzie, Henry, 1745-1831. The Novels of Henry Mackenzie: Vols. 2-3). 16.95 (ISBN 0-404-04091-8). AMS Press.
Man of the World. Henry Mackenzie. LC 74-17142. (Flowering of the Novel). 1974. (ISBN 0-8240-1202-X). Garland Pub.
Man of the World see Novels of Henry Mackenzie.
Man of the World. A Novel. William North. LC 7-33282. (On cover: Peterson's dollar series). 1877. T. B. Peterson & Brothers.
Man of to-Day. A Novel. Helen Buckingham Mathers Reeves. LC 7-30679. (On cover: Lippincott's series of select novels). 1894. J. B. Lippincott Company.
Man of Two Coutries. Alice Harriman Browne. LC 10-26374. 1910. 1.50. The Alice Harriman Company.
Man of Two Lives. James Boaden. LC 6-14196. 1829. Wells and Lilly.
Man of Two Minds. Francis Tillou Buck. The Merriam Company.
Man of Two Tribes. 1st Ed. Arthur William Upfield. LC 56-6534. 1956. Published for the Crime Club by Doubleday.
Man of Two Worlds. Raymond F. Jones. 1971. pap. 0.75 o.p. (T2413). Pyramid Pubns.
Man of Two Worlds: The Novel of a Stranger. Ainsworth Morgan. LC 33-7085. The Bobbs-Merrill Company.
Man of Valor. Arthur W Spaulding. Review and Herald Publishing Assn.
Man of Vengeance. Lynsey Stevens. (Harlequin Presents Ser.). 192p. 1983. pap. 1.95 (ISBN 0-373-10606-8). Harlequin Bks.
Man of Yesterday: A Romance of a Vanishing Race. Mary Holland McNeish Kinkaid. LC 8-7595. 1908. F. A. Stokes Company.
Man off Beat. David Hughes. LC 58-540528. Reynal.
Man on a Donkey. Hilda Frances Margaret Prescott. 640p. 1981. pap. 9.95 (ISBN 0-02-023830-4, Collier). Macmillan.
Man on a Donkey. Hilda Frances Margaret Prescott. 1961. pap. 2.50 o.p. (02383, Collier). Macmillan.
Man on a Donkey: A Chronicle. Hilda Frances Margaret Prescott. LC 52-12372. 1952. Macmillan.
Man on a Leash. Charles Williams. LC 73-79601. (Red mask mystery). 1973. 4.95 (ISBN 0-399-11219-7). Putnam.
Man on a Mountain. Joe Barnes. LC 68-58686. (Illus.). 1969. Southern University Press.
Man on a Nylon String. Whit Masterson, pseud. 1975. (pbk.) 1.25 (ISBN 0-523-00681-0). Pinnacle Books.
Man on a Rope. 1st Ed. George Harmon Coxe. LC 56-89072. 1956. Knopf.
Man on a Short Leash. Oliver Jacks, pseud. LC 73-92189. 1974. 6.95 (ISBN 0-8128-1684-6). Stein and Day.
Man on a String. David J Aiello. LC 80-20345. 1982. 13.95 (ISBN 0-87949-193-0). Ashley Books.
Man on a String. Michael Wolfe, pseud. LC 73-4166. 1973. 5.95 (ISBN 0-06-014714-8). Harper & Row.
Man on a Trestle. Ken Kennedy. 285p. (Orig.). 1982. pap. 6.75 (ISBN 0-9608864-0-0). Saguaro.

TITLE INDEX MAN WHO CRIED.

Man on All Fours: A Judge Peck Mystery Story. August William Derleth. LC 34-35889. Loring & Mussey.
Man on Fire. A. J Quinnell. LC 80-16381. 1980. (ISBN 0-688-03743-7). Morrow.
Man on Fire. Bruce D. Reeves. 1971. pap. 0.95 o.p. (N2405). Pyramid Pubns.
Man on Fire: A Novel of the Life of St. Paul. Le Gette Blythe. LC 64-13738. 1964. Funk & Wagnalls.
Man on Her Hands. David Williams Luke. LC 41-6694. Gramercy Publishing Co.
Man on Horseback. Achmed Abdullah. LC 20-36336. 1919. The James A. McCann Company.
Man on Horseback. Pierre Drieu La Rochelle. Tr. by Thomas M. Hines. 14.00 (ISBN 0-917786-07-6). French Lit.
Man on Horseback. Bertha Muzzy Sinclair. LC 40-8824. 1940. Little, Brown and Company.
Man on Horseback: A Story of Life Among the West Virginia Hills. Floyd F Farnsworth. LC 21-19124. 1921. Tribune Printing Company.
Man on Horseback: Original Title, L'Homme a Cheval. Drieu La Rochelle, Pierre. LC 79-110370. 1978. 14.00 (ISBN 0-917786-07-6). French Literature Publications Co.
Man on Spikes. Eliot Asinof. LC 55-726619. 1955. McGraw-Hill.
Man on the Balcony. Maj Sjowall & Per Wahloo. 1976. pap. 2.95 (ISBN 0-394-71777-5, Vin). Random.
Man on the Balcony. Maj Sjowall & Per Wahloo. Tr. by Alan Blair. LC 68-20889. (Martin Beck Mysteries, Vol. 2). 1968. 4.50 o.p. (ISBN 0-394-41263-X). Pantheon.
Man on the Balcony: The Story of a Crime. Maj Sjowall & Per Wahloo. LC 75-34377. (Sjowall, Maj, 1935-, Wahloo, per, 1926-1975. Martin Beck Police Mystery). 1976. 1.65. Vintage Books.
Man on the Barge. Max Miller. LC 35-247533. 1935. E. P. Dutton & Co., Inc.
Man on the Bench in the Barn. Georges Simenon. LC 73-78875. 1969. Harcourt, Brace & World.
Man on the Blood Bay. Kyle Hollingshead. 1.50 (ISBN 0-441-51860-5). Ace Books.
Man on the Blue. Luke Short. 1975. (pbk.) 0.95. Dell.
Man on the Box. Harold MacGrath. LC 70-124776. (Illus.). 1970. AMS Press.
Man on the Box. Harold MacGrath. LC 78-145155. (Illus.). 1972. (ISBN 0-403-01083-7). Scholarly Press.
Man on the Box. Harold MacGrath. 1904. The Bobbs-Merrill Company.
Man on the Box. Harold MacGrath. LC 9-32296. Grosset & Dunlap.
Man on the Bridge. Ian Stuart Black. LC 76-5368. 7.95. St. Martin's Press.
Man on the Buckskin: By Peter Dawson Pseud. Jonathan H Glidden. LC 56-6871. 1957. Dodd, Mead.
Man on the Camel. Howard Morley Sachar. LC 79-91676. 10.95 (ISBN 0-8129-0909-7). Times Books.
Man on the Couch: George Pringle Who Lived Twice. Proctor, James D. LC 51-2812. 1951. Dial Press.
Man on the End of the Rope. Paul Townend. LC 60-152294. 1960. Dutton.
Man on the Mountain. Gladys Hasty Carroll. LC 79-92546. 1969. 5.95. Little, Brown.
Man on the Mountain. large print ed. Gladys Hasty Carroll. LC 81-12542. 1982. 11.95 (ISBN 0-89340-369-5). J. Curley.
Man on the Other Side. Ada Barnett. LC 22-7409. 1922. 1.75. Dodd, Mead and Company.
Man on the Raffles Verandah. Lydia Kirk. LC 69-15179. 1969. 4.95. Doubleday.
Man on the Rock: Novel. Francis Henry King. LC 57-13361. Pantheon Books.
Man on the Run. John Creasey. LC 72-80400. (Falcon's head mystery). 1972. 5.95 (ISBN 0-529-04484-6). World Pub.
Man on the Run. Giles A. Lutz. 128p. (Orig.). 1976. pap. 1.95 (ISBN 0-441-51883-4). Ace Bks.
Man on the Run. Giles A Lutz. 1.25. Ace Books.
Man on the Tightrope: A Short Novel. Neil Paterson. 1953. Random House.
Man on the Top. 1st Ed. Rose M Collins. LC 52-17546. 1951.
Man on the White Horse. Warwick Deeping. LC 34-34746. 1934. A. A. Knopf.
Man on the Wire. Edward Herbert Franklin. LC 77-20277. 6.95 (ISBN 0-517-53263-8). Crown Publishers.
Man Out of the Rain: And Other Stories. 1st Ed. Philip MacDonald. LC 55-11602. 1955. Published for the Crime Club by Doubleday.
Man Out There. Joy Petersen Packer. LC 67-20545. 1968. Dutton.
Man Out There: By Joy Packer. 1st Ed. Joy Petersen Packer. LC 67-20545. 1968. bds., 4.95. Dutton.
Man Outgunned. Lewis B Patten. (Signet Book). 1977. 1.25 (ISBN 0-451-07546-3). New American Library.
Man Outgunned. Lewis B Patten. LC 76-1643. 1976. 5.95 (ISBN 0-385-11641-1). Doubleday.
Man Outgunned. Lewis B Patten. LC 79-10523. 1979. 11.50 (ISBN 0-8161-6718-4). G. K. Hall.
Man Outside. Wyndham Martyn. LC 10-2606. 1910. Dodd, Mead and Company.
Man Over Forty: A Novel. Eric Robert Russell Linklater. LC 64-2570. 1963. Macmillan.
Man Overboard! Francis Marion Crawford. LC 3-64590. 1903. The Macmillan Company.
Man Overboard. Allan Mackinnon. LC 65-12822. 3.50. Pub. for the Crime Club by Doubleday.
Man Overboard. Norman Frederick Simpson. LC 76-40349. 1976. 5.95 o.p. (ISBN 0-688-03129-3). Morrow.
Man Overboard! A Naughty Novel. Hervey White. LC 33-20986. Maverick Press.
Man Overboard: An Inspector Freeman Detective Story. Freeman Wills Crofts. LC 36-216833. 1936. Dodd, Mead & Company.
Man Overbroad. Max De Grundy. 1973. pap. 1.95 o.s.i. (76-338). Lancer.
Man Plus. Frederik Pohl. LC 76-3484. 7.95 (ISBN 0-394-48676-5). Random House.
Man Proposes. Henry Benajah Russell. LC 40-628. Fleming H. Revell Company.
Man Proposes. A Novel. Francis Henry Underwood. LC 8-322880. 1880. Lee and Shepard.
Man Proposes: Or, The Romance of John Alden Shaw. Eliot Harlow Robinson. LC 16-17726. 1916. The Page Company.
Man Responsible. Stephen Robinett. 1978. 1.75. Ace Books.
Man Running: A Novel. Elliot West. LC 59-7635. 1959. Little, Brown.
Man Says Yes. Dan McCall. LC 69-15656. 1969. 5.95. Viking Press.
Man Scans His Past: Un Homme Se Penche Sur Son Passe. Maurice Constantin-Weyer & Brown, Slater, 1896- Tr. LC 29-13069. The Macaulay Company.
Man Scent. Samuel Alexander White. LC 36-17731. 1936. C. Scribner's Sons.
Man She Bought. Maysie Greig. LC 30-140943. 1930. L. MacVeah, The Dial Press.
Man She Cared for. Frederick William Robinson. (On cover: The seaside library. Pocket ed. no. 217). 1884. G. Munro.
Man She Cared for. A Novel. Frederick William Robinson. LC 7-41966. (Harper's Franklin square library, no. 375). 1884. Harper & Brothers.
Man She Loved. Effie Adelaide Maria Albanesi. (On cover: Eagle library, no. 149). 1900. Street & Smith.
Man She Married. Violet Winspear. (Harlequin Presents Ser.). 192p. 1983. pap. 1.75 (ISBN 0-373-10566-5). Harlequin Bks.
Man Should Rejoice. Virginia Gordon. LC 44-21226. The Westminster Press.
Man-Size. William MacLeod Raine. LC 22-10861. 1922. 1.75. Houghton Mifflin Company.
Man-Size. William MacLeod Raine. 1974. (pbk.) 0.95. Popular Library.
Man Sollte Dagegen Sein & Other Stories. Wolfdietrich Schnurre. Pref. by Roderick Watt & Ursula Smith. 176p. (Orig.). 1982. pap. text ed. 8.50x (ISBN 0-435-38750-2). Heinemann Ed.
Man Story. Edgar Watson Howe. LC 72-84674. 1974. 15.50 (ISBN 0-403-02961-9). Scholarly Press.
Man Story. Edgar Watson Howe. LC 7-71258. 1889. Ticknor and Company.
Man Story see Collected Works.
Man Story: The Best True Stories of the Year from True, the Man's Magazine. True. LC 50-2969. (Gold medal book, 102). 1950. Fawcett Publications.
Man Survives. Vladimir Emelianovich Maksimov, pseud. LC 75-15657. 1975. 8.75 (ISBN 0-8371-8217-4). Greenwood Press.
Man Ten Feet Tall. Helen Topping Miller. LC 57-9348. 1957. Bobbs--Merrill.
Man That Corrupted Hadleyburg. Samuel Langhorne Clemens. 1981. Repr. lib. bdg. 39.00 (ISBN 0-403-00103-X). Scholarly.
Man That Corrupted Hadleyburg: And Other Stories and Essays. Samuel Langhorne Clemens. LC 3182. 1900. Harper & Bros.
Man That Corrupted Hadleyburg: And Other Stories and Essays. Samuel Langhorne Clemens. LC 6-4916. 1901. Harper & Brothers.
Man That Corrupted Hadleyburg: And Other Stories and Essays. Samuel Langhorne Clemens. LC 28-16806. 1917. Harper & Brothers.
Man That I Marry. William Arthur Neubauer. LC 47-19787. 1947. Gramercy Publishing Co.
Man That Never Grew up: A Novel. Mabel C Lathrop & Lathrop, William Addison. LC 19-15966. Britton Publishing Company.
Man That She Married. Betty Wright. (Orig.). 1982. pap. 2.95 (ISBN 0-8217-1052-4). Zebra.
Man That Walks Like a Bear: A Novel. George P Bolotoff. LC 77-80277. 8.95 (ISBN 0-87949-082-9). Ashley Books.
Man the Devil Didn't Want. Percival Christopher Wren. LC 40-26997. 1940. Macrae-Smith-Company.
Man the Fugitive. George Alec Effinger. (Planet of the Apes Ser.). (O.s.i.). 160p. (Orig.). 1974. pap. 0.95 o.s.i. (AN1373, Award). Univ Pub & Dist.
Man the Maker: A First History of Tools and Machines. Anne Jolliffe. LC 67-18556. (Illus.). 1967. Hawthorn Books.
Man: The Sensual Male. Sigmund Lichter. (Orig.). 1970. pap. 1.50 (ISBN 0-87067-412-9, BH412). Holloway.
Man, the Tiger, and the Snake. Ferdinand Reyher. LC 21-15186. 1921. G. P. Putnam's Sons.
Man the World Needs Most. Arthur S. Maxwell. (Stories That Win Ser.). 96p. 1970. pap. 0.85 o.p. (13095-5). Pacific Pr Pub Assn.
Man There Was. Agnes Louise Provost. LC 37-4079. 1937. Macrae Smith Company.
Man They Called Mistai. DeWitt S Copp. LC 74-139010. 1971. 4.50. Doubleday.
Man They Called My Wife. Stark Cole. pap. 0.95 o.p. (1160). Brandon.
Man They Called the Messiah. Nicholas Damer. 1968. 6.00 o.p. (ISBN 0-682-46781-2). Exposition.
Man They Couldn't Arrest. Austin J Small. George H. Doran Company.
Man They Couldn't Hang. Herbert Oliver White. LC 33-362320. 1933. W. Morrow & Co.
Man They Hanged. Robert William Chambers. LC 26-14624. 1926. D. Appleton & Company.
Man They Hanged. Robert J Steelman. LC 80-1038. 1980. 8.95 (ISBN 0-385-15829-7). Doubleday.
Man Thou Gavest. Harriet Theresa Smith Comstock. LC 17-11705. 1917. Doubleday, Page & Company.
Man to Conjure with, a Novel. Jonathan Baumbach. LC 65-169695. bds., 4.95. Random.
Man to His Mate. Joseph Allan Elphinstone Dunn. LC 20-18765. The Bobbs-Merrill Company.
Man to Man. John Chesterm & Michael Marten. 1980. pap. text ed. 2.50 (ISBN 0-425-04278-2). Berkley Pub.
Man to Man. Jackson Gregory. LC 20-199191. 1920. C. Scribner's Sons.
Man to Man. Jacques Saison. 1968. pap. 1.75 o.p. (3040). Brandon.
Man to Man see Man's Man.
Man to Marry. William Arthur Neubauer. LC 54-990294. 1954. Arcadia House.
Man to Match the Hour. Seldon Truss, pseud. LC 59-7004. 1959. Published for the Crime Club by Doubleday.
Man to Protect You. Maysie Greig. LC 40-3850. 1939. Doubleday, Doran & Company, Inc.
Man to Ride with. Jack Farris. LC 57-13210. 1957. Lippincott.
Man to Send Rain Clouds: Contemporary Stories by American Indians. Ed. by Kenneth Rosen. LC 73-6086. (Illus.). 1974 (ISBN 0-670-45331-5). Viking Press.
Man to Send Rain Clouds: Contemporary Stories by American Indians. Ed. by Kenneth Rosen. LC 75-12582. (Illus.). 1975. 2.95. Vintage Books.
Man Tracks. Bennett Foster. LC 43-90963. 1943. Doubleday, Doran & Co., Inc.
Man-Trail. Henry Oyen. LC 15-19409. George H. Doran Company.
Man Trap. Joseph Allan Elphinstone Dunn. LC 21-4163. 1921. Doubleday, Page & Company.
Man Trap. Matt Harding, pseud. 1970. pap. 0.75 o.p. (75-361). Manor Bks.
Man-Trapper. A Story of Extraordinary Detective Devices. Harlan Page Halsey. LC 7-1186. (calument series, no. 21). G. Munro's Sons.
Man Under Authority. Ethel May Dell. 1925. Cassell and Company, Ltd.
Man Under Authority. Ethel May Dell. LC 26-1831. 1926. G. P. Putnam's Sons.
Man Unwept: Visions from the Inner Eye: An Anthology of Science and Fantasy Fiction. Ed. by Stephen V. Whaley. LC 73-14616. (Illus.). 1974. 4.95 (ISBN 0-07-069481-8). McGraw-Hill.
Man Unwept: Visions from the Inner Eye. Stephen Whaley & Stanley Cook. (Illus.). 384p. 1974. pap. text ed. 11.00 o.p. (ISBN 0-07-069481-8, C). McGraw.
Man Upstairs. Roscoe J Bailey. LC 72-97161. 1973. 5.95 (ISBN 0-87012-142-1). McClain Print. Co.
Man Walking on Eggshells. Herbert Alfred Simmons. LC 62-7389. 1962. Houghton Mifflin.
Man Went Over the Mountain. Thomas Benjamin Allen. LC 67-27875. 1967. Dorrance.
Man Who Asked Why. Jessica Ryan. LC 45-10157. 1945. Pub. for the Crime Club by Doubleday, Doran & Company, Inc.
Man Who Ate New York. Richard M. Elman. 1975. saddlestitched in wrappers 1.25 (Pub. by New Rivers Pr); signed ed. 5.00. SBD.
Man Who Ate the Money. Rosina Umelo. 1981. pap. 3.95x (ISBN 0-19-575458-1). Oxford U Pr.
Man Who Became a Savage: A Story of Our Own Times. William Temple Hornaday. 1896. The P. Paul Book Co.
Man Who Believed in the Code of the West. George L Voss. LC 74-21094. 1975. 6.95. St. Martin's Press.
Man Who Bit Snakes. J. D. Hardin. LC 79-92153. (J. D. Hardin Ser.: No. 6). 224p. (Orig.). 1980. pap. 1.95 (ISBN 0-87216-881-6). Playboy Pbks.
Man Who Broke Things. 1st Ed. John Nixon Brooks. LC 57-11794. 1958. Harper.
Man Who Brought the Dodgers Back to Brooklyn. David Ritz. LC 80-39796. 12.95 (ISBN 0-671-25356-5). Simon and Schuster.
Man Who Bucked up: A Fact Story. Arthur Platt Howard. LC 12-24067. 1912. Doubleday, Page & Company.
Man Who Called Himself Devlin. William M. Green. (Orig.). pap. 1.95 (ISBN 0-515-05245-0). Jove Pubns.
Man Who Called Himself Devlin: A Novel of Suspense. William M. Green. LC 78-55653. 1978. 8.95 (ISBN 0-672-52514-3). Bobbs-Merrill.
Man Who Came Back. John Rossiter. LC 78-23540. 1979. 8.95 (ISBN 0-395-27216-5). Houghton Mifflin.
Man Who Came Back. John Fleming Wilson. LC 12-246199. 1912. Sturgis & Walton Company.
Man Who Came Home. Louis Paul. LC 53-109462. 1953. Crown Publishers.
Man Who Cannot Die. Thames Ross Williamson. LC 26-20630. (His The American panorama). Small, Maynard & Company.
Man Who Captivated New York: The Further Adventures of Brother Angelo. 1st Ed. LC 60-15184. 1960. Doubleday.
Man Who Carved Women from Wood. Charles William White. LC 49-10529. 1949. Harper.
Man Who Caught the Weather, and Other Stories. Bess Streeter Aldrich. LC 75-29113. 1975. 6.95. Aeonian Press.
Man Who Caught the Weather: And Other Stories. Bess Streeter Aldrich. LC 36-19830. 1936. D. Appleton-Century Company, Incorporated.
Man Who Changed His Name. Edgar Wallace & Curtis, Robert G., Joint Author. LC 34-6041. 1934. Pub. for the Crime Club, Inc., by Doubleday, Doran & Company, Inc.
Man Who Changed Overnight. Fielding Dawson. 140p. (Orig.). 1978. pap. 4.00 o.p. (ISBN 0-87685-245-2). Black Sparrow.
Man Who Changed Overnight, and Other Stories & Dreams, 1970-1974. Fielding Dawson. LC 75-31976. (Illus.). 1976. 15.00. (ISBN 0-87685-246-0) (ISBN 0-87685-245-2). Black Sparrow Press.
Man Who Conquered Death. Franz V. Werfel. Tr. by Clifton P. Fadiman. Drake, William A., 1899- Joint Tr. LC 27-22491. 1927. Simon & Schuster.
Man Who Convicted Himself. Isabel Egenton Ostrander. LC 20-18253. 1920. R. M. McBride & Co.
Man Who Could Grow Hair: Or, Inside Andorra. Drawings by Roger Duvoisin. William Attwood. LC 51-27547. 1950. Wingate.
Man Who Could Grow Hair: Or, Inside Andorra. William Attwood. LC 49-9186. 1949. A. A. Knopf.
Man Who Could Make Things Vanish. Jack Cady. LC 82-72074. 1982. 14.95 (ISBN 0-87795-428-3). Arbor Hse.
Man Who Could Not Lose. Richard Harding Davis. 1911. 1.25. C. Scribner's Sons.
Man Who Could Not Shudder. John Dickson Carr. LC 40-9588. Harper & Brothers.
Man Who Could Not Sin. Newman Watts. LC 38-258764. Fleming H. Revell Company.
Man Who Could Read Cards. R. L. Broyles. (Orig.). 1980. pap. 1.95 (ISBN 0-532-23310-7). Woodhill.
Man Who Couldn't Sleep: Being a Relation of the Divers Strange Adventures Which Befell on Witter Kerfoot When, Sorely Troubled with Sleeplessness, He Ventured Forth at Midnight Along the Highways and Byways of Manhattan. Arthur John Arbuthnott Stringer. The Bobbs-Merrill Company.
Man Who Couldn't Sleep: By Charles Eric Maine Pseud. David McIlwain. LC 58-6908. 1958. Lippincott.
Man Who Covered Mirrors: A Saturnin Dax Mystery. Marten Cumberland. LC 49-11787. 1949. Published for the Crime Club by Doubleday.
Man Who Cried: A Novel. Catherine Cookson. LC 79-87976. 1979. 10.95 (ISBN 0-688-03520-5). W. Morrow.

Man Who Cried All the Way Home. Dolores Birk Hitchens. LC 66-202537. (Inner sanctum mystery). bds., 3.95. S. & S.

Man Who Cried I Am. John Alfred Williams. LC 67-18103. 1967. Little, Brown.

Man Who Cried I Am. John Alfred Williams. LC 67-18103. 1974. (pbk.) 0.95. New American Library.

Man Who Dared. John P Ritter. LC 99-3662. 1899. G. W. Dillingham Company.

Man Who Dealt in Blood. George Wolk. 1974. (pbk.) 1.75 (ISBN 0-446-59267-6). Warner Paperback Library.

Man Who Did the Right Thing: A Romance. Harry Hamilton Johnston. LC 21-5712. 1921. The Macmillan Company.

Man Who Didn't Answer. Inez Hildagard Oellrichs. LC 39-27461. 1939. Pub. for the Crime Club, Inc., by Doubleday, Doran & Company, Inc.

Man Who Didn't Count: A Novel by G. M. Glaskin. Gerald M. Glaskin. LC 67-17165. 1967. 4.95. Delacorte.

Man Who Didn't Exist. Daniel Mainwaring. LC 37-536728. 1937. W. Morrow & Company.

Man Who Didn't Fly. 1st Ed. Margot Bennett. LC 56-8774. Harper.

Man Who Didn't Mind Hanging... Nancy Barr Mavity. LC 32-169680. Pub. for the Crime Club, Inc., by Doubleday, Doran & Company, Inc.

Man Who Died. David Herbert Lawrence. LC 31-269903. 1931. A. A. Knopf.

Man Who Died see Saint Mawr.

Man Who Died on Friday. Michael Underwood. 1979. 15.00x (ISBN 0-86025-049-0, Pub. by Ian Henry Pubns England). State Mutual Bk.

Man Who Died Twice. Lois Paxton, pseud. LC 74-173662. 1968 (ISBN 0-09-089590-8). Hurst & Blackett.

Man Who Died Twice: A Novel About Hollywood's Most Baffling Murder. Samuel Anthony Peeples. LC 76-7085. 7.95. Putnam.

Man Who Died Twice. 1st Ed. George Harmon Coxe. LC 51-11095. 1951. Knopf.

Man Who Disappeared. Edgar Henry Bohle. (Random House mystery). 1958. Random House.

Man Who Discovered Himself. Willis George Emerson. LC 19-10975. 1919. Forbes & Company.

Man Who Ended War. Hollis Godfrey. LC 8-28057. 1908. Little, Brown, & Company.

Man Who Fell Through the Earth. Carolyn Wells. LC 19-15574. George H. Doran Company.

Man Who Fell to Earth. Walter S Tevis. LC 78-23821. (Gregg Press Science Fiction Series). 1978. 10.00 (ISBN 0-8398-2438-6). Gregg Press.

Man Who Folded Himself. David Gerrold. LC 72-8076. 1973. 4.95 (ISBN 0-394-47922-X). Random House.

Man Who Folded Himself. David Gerrold. 1974. (pbk.) 0.95. Popular Library.

Man Who Folded Himself. David Gerrold. LC 76-28305. 1976. 6.95 (ISBN 0-88411-191-1). Aeonian Press.

Man Who Forgot: A Novel. James Hay. LC 15-8153. 1915. Doubleday, Page & Company.

Man Who Forgot: A Novel. James Hay. LC 24-28527. Grosset & Dunlap.

Man Who Found Christmas. Walter Prichard Eaton. LC 13-25942. 1913. McBride Nast & Company.

Man Who Found Christmas. Walter Prichard Eaton. LC 28-8593. W. A. Wilde Company.

Man Who Found Christmas. Walter Prichard Eaton. LC 41-22956. W. A. Wilde Company.

Man Who Found Himself (Uncle Simon) Margaret Robson Stacpoole & Stacpoole, Henry De Vere, 1865- Joint Author. LC 20-19238. 1920. John Lane Company.

Man Who Found His Way. Frank O'Rourke. LC 57-7181. 1957. Morrow.

Man Who Gave Thunder to the Earth: A Taos Way of Seeing and Understanding. Nancy C Wood. LC 75-30462. 1976. 6.95 (ISBN 0-385-09682-8). Doubleday.

Man Who Got Away. Sumner Locke Elliott. LC 72-79706. 1972-1973. 6.95 (ISBN 0-06-011183-6). Harper & Row.

Man Who Got Away. Sumner Locke Elliott. 1973. pap. 1.50 o.p. (02021). Curtis.

Man Who Got Away with It. Bernice Carey. LC 50-96862. 1950. Published for the Crime Club by Doubleday.

Man Who Grew Younger, and Other Stories. Jerome Charyn. LC 67-11355. (Illus.). 1967. Harper & Row.

Man Who Had Everything. Louis Bromfield. LC 35-27189. 1935. Harper & Brothers.

Man Who Had Everything... Louis Bromfield. LC 44-51247. (New Avon library. 52). 1944.

Man Who Had Everything. Donald Morison Murray. LC 64-14578. 1964. New American Library.

Man Who Had His Hair Cut Short: A Novel by Johan Daisne. Johan Daisne. Tr. by S. J. N Sackett from Flemish. LC 75-5001. 224p. 1976. Repr. of 1965 ed. lib. bdg. 15.00x (ISBN 0-8371-7426-0, THMW). Greenwood.

Man Who Had His Hair Cut Short: A Novel, by Johan Daisne Pseud. Tr. by S. J. Sackett. Herman Thiery. LC 65-225600. 4.95. Horizon.

Man Who Had His Hair Cut Short: A Novel. Herman Thiery. LC 75-5001. 1975-1976. 12.50 (ISBN 0-8371-7426-0). Greenwood Press.

Man Who Had No Idea. Thomas M. Disch. 1982. pap. 2.95 (ISBN 0-553-22667-3). Bantam.

Man Who Had Power Over Women. Gordon M. Williams. (V2235). 1968. Avon.

Man Who Had Power Over Women: By Gordon M. Williams. Gordon M. Williams. LC 67-157621. 1967. 5.95. Stein & Day.

Man Who Had Too Much to Lose. Hampton Stone, pseud. (Hampton Stone Mystery Ser). 1972. pap. 0.75 o.p. (ISBN 0-446-64781-0, 64-781-0). Paperback Lib.

Man Who Had Too Much to Lose: By Hampton Stone Pseud. Aaron Marc Stein. LC 55-14314. (Inner sanctum mystery). 1955. Simon and Schuster.

Man Who Haunted Himself. Ralph Martin. (O.s.i.). (Illus., Orig.). 1971. pap. 0.75 o.s.i. (A816S, Award). Univ Pub & Dist.

Man Who Heard Too Much. Stockton Woods. 224p. (Orig.). 1983. pap. 2.50 (ISBN 0-449-12390-1, GM). Fawcett.

Man Who Held Five Aces. Jean Leslie. 1949. Pub. for the Crime Club by Doubleday.

Man Who Held the Queen to Ransom & Sent Parliament Packing. Peter V. Greenaway. 1969. 4.95 o.p. (ISBN 0-689-10101-5). Atheneum.

Man Who Held the Queen to Ransom & Sent Parliament Packing. Peter Van Greenaway. LC 69-18618. 1969. 4.95. Atheneum.

Man Who Insulted Somersville. Jennings Rice. LC 38-8224. 1938. Harper & Brothers.

Man Who Invented Sin & Other Stories. Sean O'Faolain. (Illus.). 1948. 4.50 o.p. Devin.

Man Who Japed. Philip K Dick. 1975. (pbk.) 0.95. Ace Books.

Man Who Keeps Going to Jail. Dell Erwin & John Erwin. (Illus.). 1980. pap. 2.50 (ISBN 0-89191-107-3). Cook.

Man Who Kept Cigars in His Cap. James Heynen. LC 77-95332. (Illus.). 9.00 (ISBN 0-915308-18-5). Graywolf Press.

Man Who Killed. Claude Farrere. Tr. by Schuyler, M. C. LC 17-29738. 1917. Brentano's.

Man Who Killed Fortescue. Dorothy Stockbridge Tillet. LC 28-21589. 1928. Pub. for the Crime Club, Inc., by Doubleday, Doran & Company, Inc.

Man Who Killed Fortescue. Dorothy Stockbridge Tillet. LC 80-8413. 320p. 1981. pap. 2.25i (ISBN 0-06-080536-6, P 536, PL). Har-Row.

Man Who Killed Himself. Julian Symons. LC 77-368792. (Penguin crime fiction). 1977. 1.95. Penguin Books.

Man Who Killed Himself. 1st Ed. Julian Symons. 1967. bds., 4.50. Harper.

Man Who Killed His Brother. Reed Stephens, pseud. 224p. (Orig.). 1980. pap. 1.95 (ISBN 0-345-28675-8). Ballantine.

Man Who Killed Mick Jagger: A Novel. David Littlejohn. LC 76-56752. 8.95 (ISBN 0-316-52782-3). Little, Brown.

Man Who Killed Mick Jagger: A Novel. David Littlejohn. (Kangaroo Book). 1978. (ISBN 0-671-81913-5). Pocket Books.

Man Who Killed the Deer. american library ed. Frank Waters. LC 51-9164. (American Fiction Library). University of Denver Press.

Man Who Killed the Deer. Frank Waters. LC 42-10943. 1942. Farrar & Rinehart, Inc.

Man Who Killed the King: 1st Amer. Ed. Dennis Yates Wheatley. LC 65-13300. 1965. 5.95. Putnam.

Man Who Knew. Patrick Leyton. LC 27-266120. 1926. Small, Maynard & Company.

Man Who Knew. Edgar Wallace. LC 18-18188. Small, Maynard & Company.

Man Who Knew Better: A Christmas Dream. Tom Gallon. LC 1-27057. 1901. D. Appleton and Company.

Man Who Knew Coolidge: Being the Soul of Lowell Schmaltz, Constructive and Nordic Citizen. Sinclair Lewis. LC 79-157784. (Short story index reprint series). 1971. (ISBN 0-8369-3896-8). Books for Libraries Press.

Man Who Knew Coolidge: Being the Soul of Lowell Schmaltz, Constructive and Nordic Citizen. Sinclair Lewis. LC 28-111618. Harcourt, Brace and Company.

Man Who Knew Kennedy. Vance Nye Bourjaily. (N3674). 1968. Bantam.

Man Who Knew Kennedy. Vance Nye Bourjaily. LC 67-12691. 1967. Dial Press.

Man Who Knew the Date. Sophie Kerr. LC 51-832. 1951. Rinehart.

Man Who Knew Too Much. Gilbert Keith Chesterton. LC 22-231714. 1922. Harper & Brothers.

Man Who Laughed. Gerard Fairlie. LC 28-21423. 1928. Little, Brown, and Company.

Man Who Laughs. Victor Marie Hugo. LC 67-30477. 1967. NBI Press.

Man Who Laughs. Victor Marie Hugo. Tr. by William Young. LC 7-5869. 1869. D. Appleton and Company.

Man Who Laughs. library ed. Victor Marie Hugo. LC 7-587051. 1888. Little, Brown, and Company.

Man Who Laughs. Victor Marie Hugo. LC 7-58718. 1889. G. Routledge and Sons.

Man Who Laughs (L'homme Qui Rit) By Order of the King. Victor Marie Hugo. Tr. by Isabel Florence Hapgood. LC 4-16881. T. Y. Crowell & Co.

Man Who Laughs. Pt. I Sea and Night. From the French. Victor Marie Hugo. Tr. by William Young. LC 20-23147. 1869. D. Appleton and Company.

Man Who Left Well Enough. Mark McShane. 1973. (pbk) 0.75. Curtis Books.

Man Who Left Well Enough. Mark McShane. LC 70-134482. 1971. 4.95. McCall Pub. Co.

Man Who Liked Cats, and Other Stories. Edwin Samuel. LC 79-157985. 1974. 5.95 (ISBN 0-200-71836-3). Abelard-Schuman.

Man Who Liked Slow Tomatoes. K. C Constantine. LC 82-16589. 1983. 2.95 (ISBN 0-14-006621-7). Penguin Books.

Man Who Liked to Look at Himself. K. C Constantine. LC 73-76493. 1973. 5.95 (ISBN 0-8415-0266-8). Saturday Review Press.

Man Who Liked to Look at Himself. K. C Constantine. LC 81-47346. (Fifty Classics of Crime Fiction, 1950-1975). 1982. 14.95 (ISBN 0-8240-4955-1). Garland.

Man Who Liked Women. Marcus Beresford. 1973. (pbk) 1.50 (ISBN 0-671-78626-1). Pocket Books.

Man Who Liked Women. Marc Brandel. LC 72-83912. 1972. 6.95 (ISBN 0-671-21364-4). Simon and Schuster.

Man Who Liked Women. Marc Brendel. (O.S.I.). 6.95 o.s.i. (ISBN 0-671-21364-4). S&S.

Man Who Limped, and Other Stories. Otis Adelbert Kline. (On cover: A Chartered collection. 22). 1946. Saint Enterprises Inc.

Man Who Lived at the Ritz: A Novel. A. E Hotchner. LC 81-10600. 13.95 (ISBN 0-399-12651-1). Putnam.

Man Who Lived Backward. Malcolm Harrison Ross. LC 50-8807. 1950. Farrar, Straus.

Man Who Lived in a Shoe. Henry James Forman. LC 22-18089. 1922. Little, Brown and Company.

Man Who Lived in Inner Space. Arnold Federbush. LC 72-9078. 1973. 5.95 (ISBN 0-395-14074-9). Hougton Mifflin.

Man Who Lived in Inner Space. Arnold Federbush. 1975. (pbk.) 1.25. Bantam Books.

Man Who Looked Back. 1st American Ed. Joan Fleming. LC 52-8049. 1952. Published for the Crime Club by Doubleday.

Man Who Looked Back. 1st American Ed. Joan Margaret Fleming. LC 52-8049. 1952. Published for the Crime Club by Doubleday.

Man Who Looked Death in the Eye. Aaron Marc Stein. LC 61-16556. (inner sanctum mystery). 1961. Simon and Schuster.

Man Who Looked Death in the Eye, No. 11. Hampton Stone, pseud. (Hampton Stone Mystery Ser). 1971. pap. 0.75 o.p. (ISBN 0-446-64652-0, 64-652-0). Paperback Lib.

Man Who Looked Like the Prince of Wales. Frederick Feikema Manfred. LC 65-21954. 3.95. Trident Dist. S. &S.

Man Who Lost Everything. Paul Kuttner. LC 76-17142. 8.95. (ISBN 0-8069-0152-7) (ISBN 0-8069-0153-5). Sterling Pub. Co.

Man Who Lost Himself. Osbert Sitwell. LC 71-131834. 1973. 14.50. Scholarly Press.

Man Who Lost Himself. Osbert Sitwell. LC 30-593732. 1930. Coward-McCann, Inc.

Man Who Lost Himself. Henry De Vere Stacpoole. LC 18-816377. 1918. John Lane Company; Etc., Etc.

Man Who Lost His Head. Claire Huohet Bishop. (Viking Seafarer Book). (Illus.). 1974. (pbk.) 1.25 (ISBN 0-670-05094-6). Viking.

Man Who Lost His Shadow. Fathy Chanem. Tr. by Desmond Stewart. (African Writers Ser.: No. 223). 352p. 1980. pap. text ed. 6.00x (ISBN 0-435-90223-7). Heinemann Ed.

Man Who Lost His Shadow. Bertie Denham. LC 79-11702. 7.95 (ISBN 0-684-16243-1). Scribner.

Man Who Lost His Shadow. Fathy Ghanem. Tr. by Desmond Stewart from Arabic. 352p. (Orig.). 1981. 14.00x (ISBN 0-89410-206-0); pap. 7.00x (ISBN 0-89410-207-9). Three Continents.

Man Who Lost His Shadow: By Fathy Ghanem. Tr. from Arabic by Desmond Stewart. 1st Amer. Ed. Fathy Ghanim. LC 66-11227. 4.95. Houghton.

Man Who Lost His Wife. Julian Symons. LC 77-368589. (Penguin crime fiction). 1977. 1.95 (ISBN 0-14-004348-9). Penguin Books.

Man Who Lost His Wife. Julian Symons. LC 76-125351. 1970. 5.95. Harper & Row.

Man Who Lost the War. W. T Tyler. LC 79-23675. 9.95 (ISBN 0-8037-5390-X). Dial Press.

Man Who Lost the War. W. T Tyler. 1981. 2.95 (ISBN 0-425-04852-7). Berkley Publishing Corp.

Man Who Loved Beauty. Leonard Wallace Robinson. LC 76-5527. 8.95 (ISBN 0-06-013584-0). Harper & Row.

Man Who Loved Beauty. Leonard Wallace Robinson. (Signet Book). 1977. 1.95 (ISBN 0-451-07788-1). New American Library.

Man Who Loved Cat Dancing. Marilyn Durham. 1973. (pbk.) 1.75. Dell.

Man Who Loved Cat Dancing. Marilyn Durham. LC 72-75415. 1972. (ISBN 0-15-156940-1). Harcourt Brace Jovanovich.

Man Who Loved Children. Christina Stead. LC 40-33108. 1940. Simon and Schuster.

Man Who Loved Children: Rev. Ed. Introd. by Randall Jarrell. Christina Stead. LC 65-101287. 1965. 5.95. Holt.

Man Who Loved His Wife. Vera Caspary. LC 66-104642. 4.95. Putnam.

Man Who Loved His Wife. Vera Caspary. (5292). 1967. Dell.

Man Who Loved His Wife. Vera Caspary. LC 73-163552. 1972. 1.80 (ISBN 0-85617-744-X). White Lion Publishers.

Man Who Loved Mars. Lin Carter. 1973. pap. 0.75 o.p. (T2690, GM). Fawcett World.

Man Who Loved the Midnight Lady. Barry N. Malzberg. LC 78-22618. (Science Fiction Ser.). 1980. 10.00 o.p. (ISBN 0-385-15020-2). Doubleday.

Man Who Loved the Midnight Lady: A Collection. Barry N Malzberg. LC 78-22626. 1980. 10.00 (ISBN 0-385-15020-2). Doubleday.

Man Who Loved Women: A Landscape with Nudes. Ernest Borneman. LC 68-17572. 1968. Coward-McCann.

Man Who Loved Zoos. Malcolm J. Bosse. LC 73-93723. (Red mask mystery). 1974. 5.95 (ISBN 0-399-11353-3). Putnam.

Man Who Made Friends with Himself: A Novel. Christopher Darlington Morley. LC 49-8864. 1949. Doubleday.

Man Who Made Gold. Hilaire Belloc. LC 31-2159. Harper & Brothers.

Man Who Made Wine. With Illus. by B. Biro. 1st American Ed. James Maurice Scott. LC 54-10315. 1954. Dutton.

Man Who Married His Cook, and Other Stories. Edgar Wallace. LC 77-350661. 1976. 3.10 (ISBN 0-7274-0138-6). White Lion Publishers.

Man Who Mastered Time. Ray Cummings. LC 74-15960. (Science Fiction). 1975. 20.00 (ISBN 0-405-06270-2). Arno Press.

Man Who Mastered Time. Ray Cummings. LC 29-22339. 1929. A. C. McClurg & Co.

Man Who Missed the War, a Novel. Dennis Yates Wheatley. LC 47-6751. 1946. Hutchinson.

Man Who Moved the World. Sheldon A. Jacobson. LC 80-83024. 10.95 (ISBN 0-9604800-0-5). Galley Press.

Man Who Murdered Goliath. Daniel Mainwaring. LC 38-669628. 1938. W. Morrow & Co.

Man Who Murdered Himself. Daniel Mainwaring. LC 36-271228. 1936. W. Morrow & Co.

Man Who Murdered Himself. Daniel Mainwaring. LC 43-7365. (Avon pocket-size books). Avon Book Company.

Man Who Must Not Die. Kenneth Kay & Marshall Goldberg. 336p. (Orig.). 1982. pap. 3.50 o.s.i. (ISBN 0-8439-1174-3, Leisure Bks). Nordon Pubns.

Man Who Needed Action. Michael Geller. 1979. pap. 1.75 o.s.i. (ISBN 0-505-51436-2). Tower Bks.

Man Who Never Blundered. Sinclair Gluck. LC 29-4206. 1929. Dodd, Mead & Company.

Man Who Never Changed. John Selby. LC 54-9348. 1954. Rinehart.

Man Who Never Laughed: A Novel. Arnold Hare. LC 62-7972. 1963. Norton.

Man Who Never Was. Sam Picard. (Notebooks Ser). (O.s.i.). (Orig.). 1971. pap. 0.75 o.s.i. (A820S, Award). Univ Pub & Dist.

Man Who Owned New York. John Jay Osborn, Jr. 1981. 10.95 (ISBN 0-395-30511-X). HM.

Man Who Owned New York. John Jay Osborn, Jr. 1982. pap. 3.25 (ISBN 0-445-04745-3). Popular Lib.

Man Who Owned New York: A Novel. John Jay Osborn. LC 80-28526. 1981. 10.95 (ISBN 0-395-30511-X). Houghton Mifflin.

Man Who Paid His Way. Walt Sheldon. LC 55-6297. 1955. Lippincott.

Man Who Played God. St. John, Robert. LC 62-15892. 1962-1963. Doubleday.

TITLE INDEX MAN WITH THE CHOCOLATE

Man Who Plundered the City. Sven Christofer Svendsen Elvestad & Martens, Frederick Herman, 1874- LC 24-29827. 1924. R. M. McBride & Company.
Man Who Pretended. William Babington Maxwell. LC 29-221321. 1929. Doubleday, Doran & Company, Inc.
Man Who Rang the Bell. Milward Rodon Kennedy Burge. LC 29-16991. 1929. Pub. for The Crime Club, Inc., Doubleday, Doran & Company, Inc.
Man Who Ranked Between Jesse and Frank. Jesse Emery Gossett. LC 66-28034. 1966. Christopher Pub. House.
Man Who Raped San Francisco. Norman Singer. (Orig.). 1969. pap. 1.95 o.s.i. (OPH169, Ophelia). Olympia.
Man Who Reaps: A Story. Katharine Jones. LC 12-3373. 1.20. D. FitzGerald, Inc.
Man Who Rocked the Earth. Arthur Cheney Train & Robert Williams Wood. LC 74-16523. (Science Fiction). (Illus.). 1975. (ISBN 0-405-06315-6). Arno Press.
Man Who Rocked the Earth. Arthur Cheney Train & Wood, Robert Williams, 1868- Joint Author. LC 15-10951. 1915. Doubleday, Page & Company.
Man Who Rode His 10-Speed Bicycle to the Moon. Bernard Fischman. LC 78-23730. (Illus.). 7.95 (ISBN 0-399-90038-1). R. Marek.
Man Who Said No. Walt Grove. LC 50-12090. (Gold medal book, 120). 1950. Fawcett Publications.
Man Who Saw Through Heaven and Other Stories. Wilbur Daniel Steele. LC 27-20813. 1927. Harper & Brothers.
Man Who Saw Wrong. Sabine W. Wood. LC 13-20751. The John C. Winston Company.
Man Who Searched for Love. Dino Segree & Wells, Warre Bradley, 1892- Tr. LC 31-31613. 1932. R. M. McBride & Company.
Man Who Shook Hands. Diane Wakoski. LC 77-80917. 1978. 6.95 o.p. (ISBN 0-385-13407-X); pap. 4.95 o.p. (ISBN 0-385-13408-8). Doubleday.
Man Who Shot Quantrill. 1st Ed. George Charles Appell. 1957. Doubleday.
Man Who Shot Rob Muldoon. Jason Calder. LC 77-358643. (Kea new fiction series; no. 4). 1976. (ISBN 0-908564-10-4). Dunmore Press.
Man Who Slept All Day. Craig Rice. LC 42-21897. 1942. Coward-McCann, Inc.
Man Who Sold Christmas. 1st Ed. Rosalie Lieberman. LC 51-13800. 1951. Longmans, Green.
Man Who Sold Death. Nick Carter. (Nick Carter Ser.). (O.s.i.). 208p. (Orig.). 1974. pap. 1.25 o.s.i. (AQ1297, Award). Univ Pub & Dist.
Man Who Sold Death. James Mitchell. LC 65-13321. 1965. Knopf.
Man Who Sold Death. James Munro. 1974. (pbk.) 0.95. Bantam Books.
Man Who Sold Death: 1st Amer. Ed. James Monro. LC 65-13321. 1965. bds., 4.95. Knopf.
Man Who Sold Leadville. Philip Ketchum. (Orig.). pap. 0.50 o.p. (72-176). Lancer.
Man Who Sold Out. E. H. Stracke. (Inflation Fighters Ser.). 176p. (Orig.). 1982. pap. cancelled o.s.i. (ISBN 0-8439-0964-1, Leisure Bks). Nordon Pubns.
Man Who Sold Prayers. Margaret Creal. LC 82-48142. 14.95 (ISBN 0-06-039017-4). Harper & Row.
Man Who Sold Prayers. Margaret Creal. (Bessie Bks.). 192p. 1983. 13.45i (ISBN 0-06-039017-4, HarpT). Har-Row.
Man Who Sold the Moon: Harriman and the Escape from Earth to the Moon! Introd. by John W. Campbell, Jr. 1st Ed. Robert Anson Heinlein. LC 50-6570. (His Future history series). 1950. Shasta Publishers.
Man Who Sold the Moon: Harriman and the Escape from Earth to the Moon! Introd. by John W. Campbell, Jr. 2d Ed. Robert Anson Heinlein. LC 51-8552. (His Future history series). 1951. Shasta Publishers.
Man Who Sold the Moon: Harriman and the Escape from the Earth to the Moon! Introd. by John W. Campbell, Jr. 3d Ed. Robert Anson Heinlein. LC 53-380439. (His Future history series). 1953. Shasta Publishers.
Man Who Started Clean. Thomas Owen Beachcroft. LC 37-22966. 1937. Harper & Brothers.
Man Who Stole a University. Phoebe Ballard & Willis Todhunter Ballard. LC 67-10979. 1967. Doubleday.
Man Who Stole Portugal. Thomas Gifford. LC 77-24563. 1977. 9.95 o.p. (ISBN 0-07-023187-7, GB). McGraw.
Man Who Survived. Marguerite Borel & Potter, Frank Hunter, 1851-Tr. LC 18-10005. 1918. Harper & Brothers.
Man Who Talked Babytalk. Brian Merriman. LC 77-352710. 1976. 4.00 (ISBN 0-85616-400-3). Brian & O'Keeffe.
Man Who Tamed Dodge. Philip Ketchum. pap. 0.60 o.p. Lancer.
Man Who Took the Next Train. Ed. by Jack L. Stoll. 365p. (Orig.). 1980. text ed. 14.95 (ISBN 0-918258-15-4); pap. text ed. 7.95. New Earth.
Man Who Took Trips. Roy Ald. 1971. 6.95 o.p. (5281-6). Delacorte.
Man Who Tramps. A Story of to-Day. Lee O Harris. LC 7-2898. 1878. Douglass & Carlon.
Man Who Travelled on Motorways. Trevor Hoyle. 280p. 1982. pap. 6.95 (ISBN 0-7145-3790-X). Riverrun NY.
Man Who Tried Out for Tarzan: Stories. Harry H. Taylor. LC 73-83911. 160p. 1973. 12.95x (ISBN 0-8071-0061-7). La State U Pr.
Man Who Tried to Be It. Cameron Mackenzie. LC 17-7928. 1.00. George H. Doran Company.
Man Who Turned into a Woman. Keith S. Gormezano. LC 81-69808. (New Authors Ser.: No. 3). 120p. 1981. pap. 6.95 (ISBN 0-935954-11-2). Beacon Presse IA.
Man Who Turned Mex: And Other Stories. Paul Bailey. LC 25-4210. Dorrance & Company.
Man Who Turned Outlaw. Philip Ketchum. (Cabot Western Ser). 1969. pap. 0.60 o.p. (73-859). Lancer.
Man Who Understood Women. Leonard Merrick. LC 11-29732. 1911. 1.20. M. Kennerley.
Man Who Vanished: A Novel. John Talbot Smith. LC 22-7101. 1922. B. Benziger & Co., Inc.
Man Who Vanished: A Psychological Phantasy. Fergus Hume. LC 7-5843. (On cover: Liberty library, no. 2). 1892. Liberty Book Company.
Man Who Vanished: Or, Bob Ferret's Complicated Case. John Russell Coryell. LC 842. (On cover: Magnet detective library, no. 114). 1900. Street & Smith.
Man Who Walked on Diamonds. James Quartermain, pseud. LC 78-131100. 1971. 5.95. Doubleday.
Man Who Walked with Death. Sydney Horler. LC 31-323417. 1931. A.A. Knopf.
Man Who Wanted a Bungalow: Being the Veracious Account of an Author Who Went Back to Nature to Get Inspiration and Reduce Expenses. Lionel Josaphare. LC 7-39996. Press of W. S. Van Cott.
Man Who Wanted Stars. Dean McLaughlin. (Orig.). 1968. pap. 0.75 o.p. (74-949). Lancer.
Man Who Wanted to Play Center Field for the New York Yankees: A Novel. Gary Morgenstein. LC 82-73020. 1983. 12.95. Atheneum.
Man Who Wanted Tomorrow: A Novel. Brian Freemantle. LC 75-15704. 1975. 7.95 (ISBN 0-8128-1870-9). Stein and Day.
Man Who Was Afraid: A Novel. Edward Semple Le Comte. LC 79-89873. 1969. 5.95. Crown Publishers.
Man Who Was Born Again. Paul Busson & Mirsky, Dmitry Svyatopolk, Prince Tr. LC 27-21616. 1927. The John Day Company.
Man Who Was Dead. Arthur Williams Marchmont. 1908. F. A. Stokes Company.
Man Who Was Dead. W. Stanley Sykes. LC 31-218943. 1931. Dodd, Mead and Company.
Man Who Was God. Glen Chase, pseud. (Cherry Delight Ser.). 1978. pap. 1.50 o.s.i. (ISBN 0-8439-0517-4, Leisure Bks). Nordon Pubns.
Man Who Was Good. Leonard Merrick. LC 33-17770. (Half-title: The works of Leonard Merrick). E. P. Dutton and Company.
Man Who Was Guilty. Flora Haines Apponyi Loughead. LC 7-14775. (The Riverside paper series, no. 18). 1886. Houghton, Mifflin and Company.
Man Who Was Loved. James Stern. LC 51-2839. 1951. Harcourt,Brace.
Man Who Was Magic: A Fable of Innocence. 1st Ed. Paul Gallico. LC 66-18064. 1966. 3.95. Doubleday.
Man Who Was Murdered Twice. Robert H Leitfred. LC 37-17234. Green Circle Books.
Man Who Was Not Himself. John Creasey. LC 76-6897. 1976. (ISBN 0-8128-1907-1). Stein and Day.
Man Who Was Not There. Ethel Lina White. LC 43-15365. 1943. Harper & Brothers.
Man Who Was Not with It. Herbert Gold. LC 65-15133. 1965. pap., 1.95. Random.
Man Who Was Not with It. 1st Ed. Herbert Gold. 1956. Little, Brown.
Man Who Was There. Donald Gabriel Barron. LC 73-79087. 1973. 4.95. Atheneum.
Man Who Was There. Neville Aldridge Holdaway. LC 30-16344. E. P. Dutton & Co., Inc.
Man Who Was There. Wright Morris. LC 75-37932. 1977. 10.95 (ISBN 0-8032-0878-2) (ISBN 0-8032-5813-5) (ISBN 0-8032-5813-5). University of Nebraska Press.
Man Who Was There. Wright Morris. LC 45-9990. 1945. C. Scribner's Sons.
Man Who Was Three Jumps Ahead. Aaron Marc Stein. LC 59-13149. (inner sanctum mystery). 1959. Simon and Schuster.
Man Who Was Three Jumps Ahead. Hampton Stone, pseud. 1972. pap. 0.75 o.p. (ISBN 0-446-64800-0). Paperback Lib.
Man Who Was Thursday. Gilbert Keith Chesterton. Repr. lib. bdg. 15.45x (ISBN 0-89190-577-4). Am Repr-Rivercity Pr.
Man Who Was Thursday. Gilbert Keith Chesterton. 1969. 3.95 o.p. (ISBN 0-396-00272-2). Dodd.
Man Who Was Thursday: A Nightmare. Gilbert Keith Chesterton. LC 60-9057. (Putnam Capricorn book, CAP27). 1960. Capricorn Books.
Man Who Was Thursday: A Nightmare. Gilbert Keith Chesterton. LC 74-10161. (Permanent Chesterton series). 7.95 (ISBN 0-8362-0594-4). Sheed and Ward.
Man Who Was Thursday: A Nightmare. Gilbert Keith Chesterton. LC 8-7896. 1908. Dodd, Mead and Company.
Man Who Wasn't There. Roderick MacLeish. LC 75-10333. 7.95 (ISBN 0-394-49361-3). Random House.
Man Who Wasn't There. Roderick MacLeish. (Fawcett Crest Book). 1977. 1.75 (ISBN 0-449-23168-2). Fawcett Pub.
Man Who Watched the Trains Go by. Georges Simenon & Gilbert, Stuart, Tr. LC 46-4175. 1946. Reynal & Hitchcock.
Man Who Went Away. Harold Bell Wright. LC 42-20651. 1942. Harper & Brothers.
Man Who Went Away: A Novel. 1st Ed. Themistocles Hoetis. LC 52-5375. 1952. Pellegrini & Cudahy.
Man Who Went Back. Warwick Deeping. LC 40-300993. 1940. A. A. Knopf.
Man Who Went up in Smoke. Maj Sjowall & Per Wahloo. LC 69-15536. 1969. 4.50. Pantheon Books.
Man Who Wins see Collected Works.
Man Who Wins: A Novel. Robert Herrick. LC 7-4308. (The Ivory series). 1897. C. Scribner's Sons.
Man Who Won. Cyrus Townsend Brady. LC 19-17479. A. C. McClurg & Co.
Man Who Won: Or, The Career and Adventures of the Younger Mr. Harrison. Leon David Hirsch. LC 18-19573. 1918. The Page Company.
Man Who Won the Medal of Honor. Len Giovannitti. LC 73-5003. 1973. 5.95 (ISBN 0-394-48776-1). Random House.
Man Who Won the Pools. John Innes Mackintosh Stewart. LC 61-5780. 1961. Norton.
Man Who Worked for Collister. Mary Tracy Earle. LC 71-101806. (Short story index reprint series). 1969. Books for Libraries Press.
Man Who Worked for Collister. Mary Tracy Earle & Tracy, Marguerite, 1875- Joint Author. LC 99-3922. 1898. Copeland and Day.
Man Who Would Be God. Haakon Maurice Chevalier. LC 59-12001. 1959. Putnam.
Man Who Would Be King. John Michael Drinkrow Hardwick. 1975. (pbk.) 1.50. Bantam Books.
Man Who Would Be King. Rudyard Kipling. LC 99-4250. 1899. Doubleday and McClure Company.
Man Who Would Be King: Without Benefit of Clergy. Rudyard Kipling. LC 19-18229. (Half-title: International pocket library, ed. by E. R. Brown). The Four Seas Company.
Man Who Would Do Anything. Ivan T Ross, pseud. LC 63-12385. (Crime Club selection). 1963. Published for the Crime Club by Doubleday.
Man Who Would Not Be King. Being the Adventures of One Fenimore Slavington, Who Was Neither Born Great nor Achieved Greatness, but Had Greatness Thrust Upon Him Much to His Own Discomfort and the Discomfort an the Discomfort of Many Others. Sidney Dark. LC 13-5694. 1913. John Lane.
Man Who Would Not Die. Thomas Page. LC 81-50332. 320p. 1981. 13.50 (ISBN 0-87223-716-8, Seaview Bks). Putnam Pub Group.
Man Who Would Not Die. Thomas Page. 1982. pap. 3.50 (ISBN 0-451-11763-8, AE1763, Sig). NAL.
Man Who Would Save the World. John Oxenham, pseud. LC 27-23456. 1927. Longmans, Green and Co., Ltd.
Man Who Wouldn't Say No. Albert Lebowitz. LC 69-16424. 1969. 4.95. Random House.
Man Who Wouldn't Talk. Quentin James Reynolds. LC 54-5403. 1953. Random House.
Man Who Wrote Detective Stories: And Other Stories. John Innes Mackintosh Stewart. LC 59-5623. 1959. W. W. Norton.
Man Who Wrote Dirty Books. Hal Dresner. LC 65-103884. 1965. bds., 3.95. S. & S.
Man Whose Dreams Came True. Julian Symons. LC 77-368994. (Penguin crime fiction). 1977. 1.95 (ISBN 0-14-004347-0). Penguin Books.
Man Whose Name Wouldn't Fit. Theodore Tyler. 1969. pap. 0.75 o.p. (0502-07020-075). Curtis.
Man Whose Name Wouldn't Fit: Or, The Case of Cartwright-Chickering. Theodore Tyler. LC 68-14195. (Doubleday science fiction.). 1968. Doubleday.
Man Will Be Kidnapped Tomorrow. Jeremy Ashford. LC 76-188472. (O.s.i.). 192p. 1972. 4.95 o.s.i. (ISBN 0-8027-5255-1). Walker & Co.
Man with a Background of Flames: By Richard Johns Pseud. Montagu Slater. LC 54-10465. Roy Publishers.
Man with a Calico Face: By Shelley Smith Pseud. 1st Ed. Nancy Bodington. LC 50-10581. 1950. Harper.
Man with a Knife. Stanley Winchester. LC 68-25469. 1968. Putnam.
Man with a Maid. 1974. pap. 1.95 (ISBN 0-345-23709-9). Ballantine.
Man with a Maid. 1968. 6.00 o.p. (GP514). Grove.
Man with a Maid, Bk. 2. LC 79-15758. 1979. pap. 2.95 (ISBN 0-394-17091-1, B434, BC). Grove.
Man with a Maid, Bk. 3. LC 8-27284. 1968. pap. 2.95 o.p. (ISBN 0-394-17479-8, B181, BC). Grove.
Man With a Maid, Bk. 3. LC 82-48004. (Grove Press Victorian Library). 240p. 1982. 3.95 (ISBN 0-394-17993-5, B476, BC). Grove.
Man with a Paper Skull... Dwight Marfield. LC 32-17258. E. P. Dutton & Co., Inc.
Man with a Star. Lawrence L. Goldman. LC 66-8153. 1966. Areadia House.
Man with a Thousand Names. A. B. Van Vogt. (Science Fiction Ser.). pap. 1.75 (ISBN 0-87997-502-4, UE1502). DAW Bks.
Man with a Thousand Names. Alfred Elton Van Vogt. 1974. (pbk.) 0.95. DAW Books.
Man with a Thousand Names. A. E. Van Vogt. (Science Fiction Ser.). 1975. pap. 1.25 o.p. (UY1202). DAW Bks.
Man with a Thumb. William Cadwalader Hudson. LC 754. (On cover: Magnet detective library. no. 113). Street & Smith.
Man with a Thumb. William Cadwalader Hudson. LC 11-15073. Cassell Publishing Company.
Man with a Weak Heart. Gordon Gardiner. LC 33-148091. 1932. Houghton Mifflin Company.
Man with an Honest Face: Being the Personal Experience of a Gentleman Who Signs the Name of Howard Dana, at a Critical Time in His Career. Paul Wells. LC 11-9157. 1911. D. Appleton and Company.
Man with Bated Breath. Joseph Baker Carr. LC 34-308790. 1934. The Viking Press.
Man with Bogart's Face. Andrew J. Fenady. 184p. 1978. pap. 1.95 (ISBN 0-380-01849-7, 49015). Avon.
Man with Bogart's Face. Andrew J. Fenady. LC 76-41917. 1977. 7.95 o.p. (ISBN 0-8092-7937-1). Contemp Bks.
Man with Bogart's Face: A Novel. Andrew J Fenady. LC 76-41917. 7.95 (ISBN 0-8092-7937-1). H. Regnery Co.
Man with Fifty Complaints. Mary McMullen. LC 80-11517. 12.95 (ISBN 0-8161-3084-1). G. K. Hall.
Man with Four Lives. William Joyce Cowen. LC 34-671583. Farrar & Rinehart, Inc.
Man with My Face. Samuel Woolley Taylor. LC 48-8442. 1948. A. A. Wyn.
Man with No Face. Margaret Neilson Armstrong. LC 41-975. Random House.
Man with No Name. Evelyn Davies & Peter Town. (Heinemann Guided Readers Ser.). 1977. pap. 2.00x (ISBN 0-435-27050-8). Heinemann Ed.
Man with No Shadow. Stephen Marlowe. LC 73-21668. 1974. 7.95 (ISBN 0-13-548321-2). Prentice-Hall.
Man with One Talent: A Novel. Josiah E Greene. LC 51-9678. 1951. McGraw-Hill.
Man with Seven Names: By Alves Redol. Translated from the Portuguese by Linton Lomas Barrett. Antonio Alves Redol. LC 64-12319. 1964. Knopf.
Man with the Black Cord. Auguste Groner. Tr. by Colbron, Grace Isabel. LC 11-5475. 1911. 1.20. Duffield & Company.
Man with the Black Feather. Gaston Leorux & Jepson, Edgar, 1864- Tr. LC 12-268626. Small, Maynard & Company.
Man with the Black Worrybeads. George N Rumanes. LC 72-94678. (Illus.). 1973. 8.95 (ISBN 0-525-63003-1). A. Fields Books.
Man with the Book: Or, The Bible Among the People. John Matthias Weylland & Shaftesbury, Anthony Ashley Cooper, 7th Earl of, 1801-1885. LC 8-34335. 1871. H. Hoyt.
Man with the Broken Ear. Edmond Francois Valentin About. LC 74-15941. (Science Fiction). 1975. (ISBN 0-405-06271-0). Arno Press.
Man with the Broken Ear. Edmond Francois Valentin About & Holt, Henry, 1840- Tr. LC 5-42612. 1867. Leypoldt & Holt.
Man with the Brooding Eyes. Sidney Floyd Gowing. LC 21-18246. 1921. G. P. Putnam's Sons.
Man with the Cane. Jean Potts. LC 57-12064. 1957. Scribner.
Man with the Chocolate Egg. John Noone. 1968. pap. 4.95 o.p. (GP401). Grove.

Man with the Chocolate Egg: A Novel. John Noone. LC 67-20343. 1967. Grove Press.
Man with the Clubfoot. Valentine Williams. LC 26-24713. 1919. Grosset & Dunlap.
Man With the Crimson Box. Harry Stephen Keeler. LC 40-11753. 1940. E. P. Dutton & Co., Inc.
Man with the Double Heart. Muriel Hine Coxon. LC 14-14912. 1914. 1.30. John Lane.
Man with the Face. Arthur Howard Gollmar. LC 24-2077. 1923. The Stratford Co.
Man with the Gash. Jack London. (Illus.). 299p. 1981. pap. 5.95 (ISBN 0-932458-04-1). Star Rover.
Man With the Getaway Face. Richard Stark. 1981. lib. bdg. 10.95 (ISBN 0-8398-2707-5, Gregg). G K Hall.
Man with the Gloved Hand. James McKimmey. LC 72-2505. 1972. 4.95 (ISBN 0-394-47417-1). Random House.
Man with the Golden Arm. Nelson Algren. LC 77-2265. 1977. 2.50 (ISBN 0-14-004523-6). Penguin Books.
Man with the Golden Arm: A Novel. 53ist ed. Nelson Algren. LC 49-10533. 1949. Doubleday.
Man with the Golden Arm: A Novel. Nelson Algren. LC 78-72524. 1978. 10.00 (ISBN 0-8376-0425-7). R. Bentley.
Man with the Golden Gun. Ian Fleming. LC 65-27967. bds., n3 4.50. New Amer. Lib.
Man with the Golden Touch. Mor Jokai. 5.00 o.p. (ISBN 0-8044-2428-4). Ungar.
Man with the Key. Virginia Eggertsen Sorensen. LC 73-22429. 1974. 7.95 (ISBN 0-15-156942-8). Harcourt Brace Jovanovich.
Man with the Lamp. Janet Laing. LC 19-12165. E. P. Dutton & Company.
Man with the Lantern. Henry Middleton Paxton. LC 33-28337. 1898. Banner of Light Publishing Co.
Man with the Lumpy Nose. Lawrence Lariar. LC 44-3411. 1944. Dodd, Mead & Company.
Man with the Magic Eardrums: A Mystery Novel. Harry Stephen Keeler. LC 39-31047. 1939. E. P. Dutton & Co., Inc.
Man with the Miracle Cure. Walter Ross. (O.s.i.) 1972. pap. 0.95 o.s.i. (532-95180-095). Manor Bks.
Man with the Miracle Cure, a Novel. Walter Ross. LC 64-13349. 1964. Simon and Schuster.
Man with the Miracle Cure: A Novel. Walter Sanford Ross. LC 64-13349. 1964. Simon and Schuster.
Man with the Monocle. Garnett Weston. LC 44-40005. 1943. Pub. for the Crime Club by Doubleday, Doran and Co., Inc.
Man with the Painted Head. Helen Kieran Reilly. LC 31-31931. Farrar & Rinehart, Incorporated.
Man with the Power. Leslie Thomas. LC 74-1895. 1974. (ISBN 0-06-014274-X). Harper & Row.
Man with the President's Mind. Ted Allbeury. LC 77-15494. 8.95 (ISBN 0-671-22908-7). Simon and Schuster.
Man with the Scar. Warren Fones & Fones, Alice, Joint Author. LC 11-470. 1911. R. G. Badger.
Man with the Scar. John E W Lomas. LC 26-15705. 1926. Houghton Mifflin Company.
Man with the Scarred Hand. Henry Kitchell Webster. The Bobbs-Merrill Company.
Man with the Squeaky Voice. Robert Alfred John Walling. LC 30-841301. 1930. W. Morrow & Company.
Man with the Talents. Stead Jones. 1970. pap. 0.75 o.p. (0502-07072). Curtis.
Man with the Talents. 1st Ed. in the U.S.A. Stead Jones. LC 67-15358. 1967. 4.95. Doubleday.
Man with the Tattooed Face. Miles Burton. LC 38-2822. 1937. Pub. for the Crime Club, Inc., by Doubleday, Doran & Co., Inc.
Man with the Tiny Head. Ivor Drummond. LC 77-95865. 1970. Harcourt, Brace & World.
Man with the Transplanted Brain. Victor Vicas & Alain Frank. (Raven Bk) 1971. price not set o.p. Abelard.
Man with the Wax Face. Richard Edward Wormser. LC 34-23280. 1934. H. Smith & R. Haas.
Man with the White Eyes. Leopold Tyrmand. LC 59-82343. 1959. Knopf.
Man with the Wooden Spectacles. Harry Stephen Keeler. LC 41-14052. 1941. E. P. Dutton & Company, Inc.
Man with Three Chins. Delano L. Ames. LC 68-18264. 1968. Regnery.
Man with Three Jaguars: By Delano Ames. Delano L. Ames. LC 67-14658. 1967. 3.95. Regnery.
Man with Three Names. Harold MacGrath. LC 20-261060. 1920. Doubleday, Page & Company.
Man with Two Clocks. Whit Masterson, pseud. LC 74-6808. (Red badge novel of suspense). 1974. 5.95 (ISBN 0-396-06988-6). Dodd, Mead.

Man with Two Faces. Kurt Brand. (Perry Rhodan, 104). (Illus.). Ace.
Man with Two Faces. Jane Corrie. (Harlequin Romances Ser.). 192p. 1983. pap. 1.75 (ISBN 0-373-02551-3). Harlequin Bks.
Man with Two Memories. John Burdon Sanderson Haldane. LC 77-366295. 1976. 2.80 (ISBN 0-85036-209-1). Merlin Press.
Man with Two Names. John Leslie Palmer, pseud. LC 40-200914. 1940. Dodd, Mead & Company.
Man with Two Shadows. Robin Maugham. LC 59-8249. 1959. Harper.
Man with Two Shadows: By Robin Maugham. Robin Maugham. LC 58-4594. 1958. Longmans, Green.
Man with Two Wives. Patrick Quentin. LC 55-3385. (Inner sanctum mystery). 1955. Simon and Schuster.
Man with Yellow Eyes. Bertram Atkey. LC 27-107273. 1927. L. MacVeagh, The Dial Press.
Man with Yellow Shoes. Anthony Heckstall-Smith. 1957. Roy Publishers.
Man with 2 Left Feet. Pelham Grenville Wodehouse. LC 33-9686. A. L. Burt Company.
Man Within. Graham Greene. LC 72-184804. 1971. 0.30 (ISBN 0-14-003283-5). Penguin.
Man Within. Graham Greene. LC 29-207922. 1929. Doubleday, Doran & Company, Inc.
Man Without a Church: The Story of James Millbrook. Henry Hughes. LC 16-98. 1915. Sherman, French & Company.
Man Without a Country. Edward Everett Hale. LC 59-11523. (Revell inspirational classic). 1959. Revell.
Man Without a Country. Edward Everett Hale. LC 74-19087. 1974. 7.50. Folcroft Library Editions.
Man Without a Country. Edward Everett Hale. LC 74-19087. (Illus.). 1974. (ISBN 0-8414-4889-2). Folcroft Library Editions.
Man Without a Country. Edward Everett Hale. LC 6-46183. 1889. Roberts Brothers.
Man Without a Country. new ed., with an introduction in the year of the war with spain. ed. Edward Everett Hale. LC 98-238. 1898. Little, Brown, and Company.
Man Without a Country. birthday ed. Edward Everett Hale. LC 2-10711. 1902. The Outlook Company.
Man Without a Country. Edward Everett Hale. LC 7-24034. H. M. Caldwell Co.
Man Without a Country. Edward Everett Hale. LC 7-24767. Hurst & Company.
Man Without a Country. Edward Everett Hale. LC 10-18958. The Platt & Peck Co.
Man Without a Country. Edward Everett Hale. LC 31-35215. (On cover: Home and school library). 1912. Ginn and Company.
Man Without a Country. Edward Everett Hale. LC 33-7797. 1917. The Platt & Nourse Co.
Man Without a Country. new ed., with an introduction in the year of the war with spain. ed. Edward Everett Hale. 1923. Little, Brown, and Company.
Man Without a Country. Edward Everett Hale. LC 27-19410. A. Whitman & Company.
Man Without a Country. Edward Everett Hale & Bradley, William Aspenwall, 1878, 1939, Ed. (Merrill's English texts). Charles E. Merrill Company.
Man Without a Country. Edward Everett Hale & Eberhardt, Walter F. LC 25-8273. Grosset & Dunlap.
Man Without a Country. Edward Everett Hale & Ellis, Richard, Ed. 1940. The Haddon Craftsmen.
Man Without a Country. Edward Everett Hale & Laughton, Norris Hastings, Ed. LC 8-19154. (On cover: Altemus' classics series). 1908. H. Altemus Company.
Man Without a Country. Edward Everett Hale & Revell, Ellen Isabel, 1867- Ed. LC 10-951913. 0.25. Educational Publishing Company.
Man Without a Country. Edward Everett Hale & Sharp, Russell Alger, Ed. LC 23-8361. (Riverside literature series. 141). Houghton Mifflin Company.
Man Without a Country. Edward Everett Hale & Shinn, Everett, 1876- Illus. LC 40-34745. Random House.
Man Without a Country. Edward Everett Hale & Skinner, Hubert Marshall, 1855- Ed. LC 5-38102. The O. Brewer Publishing Co.
Man Without a Country. Edward Everett Hale & Tapper, Thomas, 1864- Ed. LC 17-201791. (cozy corner series). 1917. The Page Company.
Man Without a Country. Hale, Edward Everett, 1822-1909. LC 37-15594. (Classic romances of literature. vol. IX). The Spencer Press.
Man Without a Country: And Its History. limited ed. Edward Everett Hale. LC 6-46184. J. S. Smith & Company.
Man Without a Country, and Other Stories... Edward Everett Hale. LC 47-16620. 1946.

Man Without a Country & Other Stories. Edward Everett Hale. 300p. 1977. Repr. of 1863 ed. lib. bdg. 15.25x (ISBN 0-89966-253-6). Buccaneer Bks.
Man Without a Country: And Other Stories. Edward Everett Hale & Tucker, Samuel Marion, Ed. LC 10-22723. (Macmillan's pocket American and English classics). 1910. The Macmillan Company.
Man Without a Country and Other Tales. Edward Everett Hale. LC 74-152942. (Short story index reprint series). 1971. (ISBN 0-8369-3801-1). Books for Libraries Press.
Man Without a Face. John Eugene Hasty. LC 58-13090. (Red badge detective). 1958. Dodd, Mead.
Man Without a Face, L'homme Sans Figure. Albert Boissiere & Crewe-Jones, Florence, Tr. LC 11-139803. G. W. Dillingham Company.
Man Without a Gun. Hal George Evarts. 1974. (pbk.) 0.75 (ISBN 0-671-75816-0). Pocket Boooks.
Man Without a Gun. Ray Hogan. LC 74-4. 1974. 4.95 (ISBN 0-385-06725-9). Doubleday.
Man Without a Gun. Ray Hogan. LC 81-23965. 1982. 10.95 (ISBN 0-8161-3363-8). G.K. Hall.
Man Without a Gun: Conger's Woman. Ray Hogan. 320p. 1983. pap. 2.95 (ISBN 0-451-12020-5, Sig). NAL.
Man Without a Head. Joseph Bowen. LC 37-217. Covici, Friede.
Man Without a Head. Tyler De Saix. LC 8-228006. 1908. Moffat, Yard and Company.
Man Without a Heart. Ruby Mildred Ayres. LC 24-9356. 1924. George H. Doran Company.
Man Without a Heart. Anne Hampson. 192p. 1981. pap. 1.50 (ISBN 0-671-57052-8, Pub. by Silhouette Bks). S&S.
Man Without a Home: A Novel. Rupert Hughes. LC 35-12777. 1935. Harper & Brothers.
Man Without a Memory, and Other Stories. William Henry Shelton. LC 8-5113. 1895. C. Scribner's Sons.
Man Without a Name. Martin James Russell. LC 77-4825. 7.95 (ISBN 0-698-10853-1). Coward, McCann & Geoghegan.
Man Without a Necktie: A Novel. Erminia Arbib Hauser & Jordan, Mrs. Charlotte Brewster, Tr. LC 30-553. 1929. Dickens Publishing Company, Inc.
Man Without a Planet. Lester Del Rey. pap. 0.75 o.p. Lancer.
Man Without a Shadow. Oliver Cabot. LC 9-11688. 1909. D. Appleton and Company.
Man Without a Star. Dee Linford. LC 52-9701. 1952. W. Morrow.
Man Without Armour. Barbara Hedworth. LC 33-12046. E. P. Dutton & Co., Inc.
Man Without Friends. Margaret Echard. LC 40-30606. 1940. Doubleday, Doran and Company, Inc.
Man Without Mercy. Margery Hilton. (Harlequin Presents Ser.). 1974. pap. 1.25 (ISBN 0-373-70552-2, 70552). Harlequin Bks.
Man Without Mercy. new ed. Margery Hilton. (World of Romance Ser.). 192p. 1972. 4.95 o.p. (ISBN 0-529-04891-4). World Pub.
Man Without Mercy. Concordia Merrel. LC 29-207940. 1929. Doubleday, Doran & Company, Inc.
Man Without Nerves. Edward Phillips Oppenheim. LC 34-12022. 1934. Little, Brown, and Company.
Man Without Principle? Lester Everret Broyles. 1.50. The Hoeking Publishing Co.
Man Without Principle? Lester Everret Broyles. LC 9-15996. The Hocking Publishing Co.
Man Without Qualities: Translated from the German and with a Foreword by Eithne Wilkins & Ernst Kaiser. 1st American Ed. Robert Musil. LC 53-5303. Coward-McCann.
Man Without Shoes. John Sanford. 454p. 1982. 25.00 (ISBN 0-87685-544-3). Black Sparrow.
Man Without Shoes: A Novel. John B Sanford. LC 51-5517. 1951. Plantin Press.
Man Without Uniform. Willy Corsari. Tr. by Salzedo, S. L. LC 41-16596. Greenberg.
Man-Wolf and Other Tales. Emile Erckmann & Alexandre Chatrian. LC 75-46268. (Supernatural and Occult Fiction). 1976. 14.00 (ISBN 0-405-08126-X). Arno Press.
Man, Woman, and Child. Erich W. Segal. LC 79-3414. 9.95 (ISBN 0-06-014031-3). Harper & Row.
Man, Woman, and Child. Erich W Segal. LC 80-19302. 1980. 10.95 (ISBN 0-8161-3124-4). G. K. Hall.
Manacle. Mario J Sagola. LC 77-26783. 7.95 (ISBN 0-02-606700-5). Macmillan.
Manacle. Mario J Sagola. 1979. 2.25 (ISBN 0-440-15460-X). Dell Pub. Co.
Manager of the B & A: A Novel. Vaughan Kester. LC 1-16997. 1901. Harper & Brothers.
Managing Somehow. John W McKinley. LC 42-8907. 1942. The Ingleside Press.
Manalive. Gilbert Keith Chesterton. LC 62-17710. (G. K. Chesterton reprint series, v. 3). 1962. Dufour Editions.
Manalive. Gilbert Keith Chesterton. LC 12-670689. 1912. T. Nelson and Sons.

Manalive. Gilbert Keith Chesterton. LC 12-6806. 1912. John Lane Company.
Manana Kid. Francis W Hilton. 1939. H. C. Kinsey & Company, Inc.
Manana Man. Irene Hattie McCain. LC 49-50214. 1949. Murray Gee.
Manasco Road. Victor Canning. LC 57-60893. 1957. W. Sloane Associates.
Manassas: A Novel of the War. Upton Beall Sinclair. LC 75-2449. 1968. Scholarly Press.
Manassas; a Novel of the War. Upton Beall Sinclair. LC 4-23761. 1904. The Macmillan Company.
Manassas: Theirs Be the Guilt. Upton Beall Sinclair. pap. 1.25 o.p. (ISBN 0-532-12145-7). Woodhill.
Manassas: Theirs Be the Guilt: A Novel of the War Between the States. Upton Beall Sinclair. 1973. (pbk.) 1.25. Manor Books.
Manasseh: A Romance of Transylvania, Retold from the Hungarian of. Mor Jokai. Tr. by Bicknell, Percy Favor. LC 1-7304. 1901. L. C. Page & Company.
Manatee. Nancy Bruff, pseud. 1945. E. P. Dutton & Co., Inc.
Manatee. Nancy Bruff Gardner. LC 45-8639. 1945. Dutton.
Manatitlans: Or, A Record of Recent Scientific Explorations in the Andean La Plata, S.A. Elton R. Smilie. LC 8-8186. 1877. Printed at the Riverside Press.
Manch. Mary Edwards Bryan. LC 12-12210. 1880. D. Appleton and Company.
Manch. Mary Edwards Bryan. (On cover: The library of American authors, no. 26). 1890. G. Munro.
Manchaug; a Historical Novel. Frederick Hubbard Sibley. LC 36-21646. The Christopher Publishing House.
Manchester Fourteen Miles. Margaret Penn. 244p. 1981. pap. 9.95 (ISBN 0-521-28065-6). Cambridge U Pr.
Manchilde: An Imaginary Tale. Almer John Davis. LC 80-81274. 1981. 10.95 (ISBN 0-936800-00-3). Ironwood Press.
Manchu. Robert S Elegant. LC 80-17452. 12.50 (ISBN 0-07-019163-8). McGraw-Hill.
Manchu Blood. Hugh Wiley. LC 75-160953. (Short story index reprint series). 1971. (ISBN 0-8369-3932-8). Books for Libraries Press.
Manchu Blood. Hugh Wiley. LC 27-17530. 1927. A. A. Knopf.
Manchu Cloud. James W Bennett. LC 27-1845. 1927. Duffield and Company.
Manchu Empress. Bluebell Matilda Hunter. LC 45-5842. 1945. Dial Press.
Manchurian Candidate. Richard Condon. 1974. (pbk.) 1.50. Dell Pub. Co.
Mandala. Pearl Sydenstricker Buck. LC 73-111648. 1970. 7.95. John Day Co.
Mandarin: And Other Stories. Tr. from Portuguese by Richard Franko Goldman. Jose Maria De Eca De Queiroz. LC 65-13907. 4.00. Ohio Univ. Pr.
Mandarin Cypher. Adam Hall. 1975. Repr. lib. bdg. 11.95 o.p. (ISBN 0-8161-6333-2, Large Print Bks). G K Hall.
Mandarin Cypher. Adam Hall. LC 74-25105. 240p. 1975. 7.95 o.p. (ISBN 0-385-05107-7). Doubleday.
Mandarin Cypher. Elleston Trevor. LC 74-25105. 1975. 7.95 (ISBN 0-385-05107-7). Doubleday.
Mandarin Cypher. Elleston Trevor. LC 75-31541. 1975. 11.95 (ISBN 0-8161-6333-2). G. K. Hall.
Mandarin Cypher. Elleston Trevor. 1.75. Dell.
Mandarin Ducks and Butterflies: Popular Fiction in Early Twentieth-Century Chinese Cities. Eugene Perry Link. LC 80-15149. 20.00 (ISBN 0-520-04111-9). University of California Press.
Mandarin from Salem. Richard O Patterson. LC 79-83608. (Illus.). 1979. 16.95 (ISBN 0-8022-2244-7). Philosophical Library.
Mandarin Gold: A Novel. James Leasor. LC 73-19502. 1974. 6.95 (ISBN 0-688-00246-3). Morrow.
Mandarin Gold: A Novel. James Leasor. 1975. (pbk.) 1.50. Dell.
Mandarin Orange Sunday. Angelique Durand. 384p. (Orig.) 1981. pap. 2.75 (ISBN 0-553-14709-9). Bantam.
Mandarin Summer: A Novel. Fiona Kidman. LC 82-139116. 1981. 16.95 (ISBN 0-86863-665-7). Heinemann.
Mandarins. Simone De Beauvoir. LC 79-65852. 610p. 1979. pap. 8.95 (ISBN 0-89526-898-1). Regnery-Gateway.
Mandarins. Simone De Beauvoir. pap. 3.95 o.p. (MF1, Mer). World Pub.
Mandarins: A Novel. Translated by Leonard M. Friedman. 1st Ed. Simone De Beauvoir. LC 56-531510. 1956. World Pub. Co.
Mandarins: A Novel. Translated from the French by Leonard M. Friedman. Simone De Beauvoir. LC 60-6741. (Meridian fiction, MF1). 1960. Meridian Fiction.
Mandarin's Bell. Edward Noble. LC 25-11395. 1925. Houghton Mifflin Company.

Mandarin's Fan. Fergus Hume. LC 4-34127. 1904. G. W. Dillingham Company.

Mandarin's Sapphire. Dwight Marfield. LC 38-8835. 1938. E. P. Dutton & Co., Inc.

Mandate for Murder. J. A. McCombie. 1978. pap. 1.50 (ISBN 0-532-15349-9). Woodhill.

Mandelbaum Gate. Muriel Spark. LC 64-190902. 5.95. Knopf.

Mandelbaum Gate. Muriel Spark. (Crest bk., t1014). 1967. Fawcett.

Manders: A Tale of Paris. Elwyn Alfred Barron. LC 16-250355. 1900. International Book and Publishing Co.

Mandevilla. Kate Thompson. LC 57-998473. 1957. Houghton Mifflin.

Mandeville. A Tale of the Seventeenth Century in England. William Godwin. LC 43-20229. 1848. Printed by M. Thomas, J. Maxwell, Printer.

Mandingo. Kyle Onstott. LC 57-23335. Denlinger.

Mandoa, Mandoa! A Comedy of Irrelevance: By Winifred Holtby. Winifred Holtby. LC 33-17936. 1933. The Macmillan Company.

Mandragon. R. M. Koster. LC 79-88122. 1979. 10.95 (ISBN 0-688-03513-2). W. Morrow.

Mandragon. R. M. Koster. LC 80-20503. 1981. 10.95 (ISBN 0-688-00348-6). Morrow Quill Paperbacks.

Mandrake Root. Joy Cowley. LC 74-2828. 1975. 7.95 (ISBN 0-385-04244-2). Doubleday.

Mandrake Root. Janet Oline Hart Diebold. LC 46-6541. 1946. H. Holt and Company.

Mandrake Root. Martha Ostenso. LC 38-318268. 1938. Dodd, Mead & Company.

Mandrake Root. Frederic Wakeman. LC 53-93230. 1953. Dial Press.

Mandrake Root: An Anthology of Fantastic Tales. Ed. by Jeremy Scott. LC 46-19939. 1946. Jarrolds Ltd.

Mandrake Scream. Melisand March. 1977. 1.75 (ISBN 0-380-00883-1). Avon.

Mandrake Scream: A Novel. Melisand March. LC 75-12610. 1975. 8.95 (ISBN 0-88405-112-9). Mason/Charter.

Mandrake the Magician in Hollywood. Lee Falk. Ed. by Leonard Brown. LC 76-159555. (Illus.). 1977. pap. 5.95 (ISBN 0-87897-009-6). Nostalgia Pr.

Mandrake's Book. Howard Pearlstein. LC 74-84450. 164p. (Orig.). 1974. pap. 3.00 (ISBN 0-912528-09-5). John Muir.

Mandy Wilkins' Vision. Grace Worrall Burleigh. LC 11-28816. Jennings and Graham.

Maneating Woman. Steve Alexander. (Illus.). pap. 4.75 o.p. (ISBN 0-87964-569-5). Academy-Parliament.

Manela, the Bull Elephant: A Story for the Young at Heart. Willem Andries Hickey. LC 76-367630. 1976. (ISBN 0-7986-0226-0). De Jager-Haum.

Manfred: Or, The Battle of Benevento. Francesco Domenico Guerrazzi. Tr. by Monti, Luigi. LC 12-24118. 1875. G. W. Carleton & Co. Etc.

Manfrone: Or the One-Handed Monk, 2 Vols. Mary-Anne Radcliffe. LC 79-131339. (Gothic Novels Ser). 1971. Repr. of 1828 ed. Set. 38.00 (ISBN 0-405-00818-X). Ayer Co.

Manfrone: Or, The One-Handed Monk; a Romance. Mary-Anne Radcliffe. LC 79-131339. (Gothic novels). 1972. (ISBN 0-405-00818-X). Arno Press.

Mangan Inheritance. Brian Moore. LC 79-13853. 10.95 (ISBN 0-374-20194-3). Farrar, Straus and Giroux.

Mangan Inheritance. Brian Moore. LC 80-16330. 1980. 3.50 (ISBN 0-14-005671-8). Penguin Books.

Mango on the Mango Tree. David Mathew. LC 51-11059. C.

Mango Season. Kathryn Grondahl. LC 54-7098. 1954. Morrow.

Manhandled. Arthur John Arbuthnott Stringer & Holman, Russell, Joint Author. LC 24-19020. Grosset & Dunlap.

Manhattan. Neal Travis. LC 78-25693. 10.00 (ISBN 0-517-53778-8). Crown Publishers.

Manhattan Acres: The Story of a New York Family. Virginia Cruse Watson. LC 34-365633. E. P. Dutton & Co., Inc.

Manhattan Cowboy. Alan Geoffrey Yates. (Signet, T5571). 1973. (pbk.) 0.75. New American Lib.

Manhattan East. Polan Banks. 1971. pap. 0.75 o.p. (532-75434-075). Manor Bks.

Manhattan Fever: A Girl's Story That's True. Sally Brookes. LC 30-7428. Sears Publishing Company, Inc.

Manhattan File. Ian Kennedy Martin, pseud. LC 75-21481. 1976. 6.95 (ISBN 0-03-089815-3). Holt, Rinehart and Winston.

Manhattan Furlough. Hiram Collins Haydn. LC 45-3731. 1945. The Bobbs-Merrill Company.

Manhattan Gambit. Benjamin Stein. LC 81-43637. 1983. 15.95 (ISBN 0-385-17225-7). Doubleday.

Manhattan Jungle: The Adventures of a Life Underwriter. Lowell King Randolph. LC 56-11596. 1956. Exposition Press.

Manhattan Jungle: The Adventures of a Life Underwriter. 1st Ed. Kip Ran. LC 56-11596. 1956. Exposition Press.

Manhattan Love. Ruth Phillips. LC 32-214314. The Macaulay Company.

Manhattan Love Song. Hopley-Woolrich, Cornell George. LC 80-19544. (Gregg Press Mystery Fiction Series). 1980. 10.95 (ISBN 0-8398-2720-2). Gregg Press.

Manhattan Love Song. Kathleen Thompson Norris. LC 34-559479. 1934. Doubleday, Doran & Company, Inc.

Manhattan Love Song. Cornell Woolrich, pseud. LC 32-219022. 1932. W. Godwin, Inc.

Manhattan Masquerade. Frederic Arnold Kummer. LC 34-802. Sears Publishing Company, Inc.

Manhattan Masquerade. large print ed. Joanna Scott. LC 82-9221. 1982. 6.95 (ISBN 0-8161-3411-1). G.K. Hall.

Manhattan Massacre. Peter McCurtin. (assassin,#7). 1973. (pbk.) 0.95. Dell Books.

Manhattan Murder. Arthur Cheney Train. LC 41-40525. (His Criminal court series, v. 3). C. Scribner's Sons.

Manhattan Murder. Arthur Cheney Train. LC 36-712041. 1936. C. Scribner's Sons.

Manhattan Night. William Almon Wolff. LC 30-15620. 1930. Minton, Balch & Company.

Manhattan Nights. Faith Baldwin Cuthrell. LC 37-39109. Farrar & Rinehart, Incorporated.

Manhattan North. Martha Albrand. LC 70-169659. 1971. 5.95. Coward, McCann & Geoghegan.

Manhattan Primitive: A Novel. Robert A Carter. LC 75-122428. 1971. 6.95 (ISBN 0-8128-1381-2). Stein and Day.

Manhattan Prodigal. George Tichenor. LC 34-12026. Farrar & Rinehart, Incorporated.

Manhattan Side Street. Jay Dratler. LC 36-7479. 1936. Longmans, Green and Co.

Manhattan Solo. Marjorie Muir Worthington. LC 37-30183. 1937. A. A. Knopf.

Manhattan: Stories from the Heart of a Great City. 1st Ed. Ed. by Seymour Krim. LC 54-20973. (Bantam giant, A1201). 1954. Bantam Books.

Manhattan Transfer. Dos Passos, John. LC 64-9120. 1963. Houghton Mifflin.

Manhattan Transfer. John Dos Passos. LC 25-23116. 1925. Harper & Brothers.

Manhattan Transfer. Dos Passos, John. LC 79-10459. 1979. 10.00 (ISBN 0-8376-0433-8). R. Bentley.

Manhattan Wipeout. Joseph Rosenberger. (Death merchant,#11). 1975. (pbk.) 1.25 (ISBN 0-523-00561-X). Pinnacle Books.

Manhatton Massacre. Peter McCurtin. (Assassin). (Dell/Lorelei Book: Vol. 1). 1973. (pbk) 0.95. Dell.

Manhold. Phyllis Eleanor Bentley. 1941. The Macmillan Company.

Manhood Ceremony. Ross Berliner. LC 77-12929. 8.95 (ISBN 0-671-22936-2). Simon and Schuster.

Manhood Ceremony. Ross Berliner. (Signet book). 1979. 2.25 (ISBN 0-451-08509-4). New American Library.

Manhounds of Antares. Alan Burt Akers. 1974. pap. 1.25 o.p. (UY1124). DAW Bks.

Manhunt. John Benteen. (Sundance Ser.: No. 17). 192p. 1982. pap. 2.25 (ISBN 0-8439-1133-6, Leisure Bks). Nordon Pubns.

Manhunt. John Benteen. (Sundance Ser.). (Orig.). 1976. pap. 1.25 o.p. (LB3322K, Leisure Bks). Nordon Pubns.

Manhunt. John Benteen. (Sundance series). 1976. (pbk.) 1.25. Leisure Books.

Manhunt. Donald MacKenzie. LC 56-118470. 1957. Houghton Mifflin.

Manhunt in Murder. Wyndham Martyn. LC 58-7547. Roy Publishers.

Manhunt Trail. Westmoreland Gray. LC 34-38716. J. B. Lippincott Company.

Manhunt Was a Biggie. Ava V. Anderson. (Illus.). 144p. 1983. 10.95 (ISBN 0-89962-327-1). Todd & Honeywell.

Manhunt West. Walker A Tompkins. LC 49-9460. 1949. Macrae-Smith-Co.

Manhunter. Matthew Gant. LC 57-11881. (Signet book, 1423). 1957. New American Library.

Manhunter. Gordon D. Shirreffs. (Orig.). 1970. pap. 0.60 o.p. (R2246, GM). Fawcett World.

Manhunter, No. 5. Matthew Braun. (Orig.). 1981. pap. 1.95 (ISBN 0-671-41992-7). PB.

Maniac Responsible. Gover, Robert. LC 63-12836. 1963. Grove Press.

Manifest Destiny. Barry B. Longyear. 1980. pap. 2.25 (ISBN 0-425-04530-7). Berkley Pub.

Manifest Destiny. Magruder, Julia. LC 1139. 1900. Harper & Brothers.

Manifest Destiny. Arthur Douglas Howden Smith. LC 26-15402. 1926. Brentano's.

Manifestos. John Giorno et al. (Great Bear Pamphlets: No. 18). 1967. pap. 3.50 (ISBN 0-89366-073-6). Ultramarine Pub.

Manila Galleon. Cameron Rogers. LC 36-17402. 1936. D. Appleton-Century Company, Incorporated.

Manila Galleon. Illustrated by John Alan Maxwell. 1st Ed. Francis Van Wyck Mason. 1961. Little, Brown.

Manila Hemp. Elinor Chamberlain. LC 47-49321. 1947. Dodd, Mead.

Manila Masquerade: And Other Stories. David Garth. LC 42-14360. 1942. H. C. Kinsey & Company, Inc.

Manila Romance: Or, Life in the East Indies. William Henry Thomes. (pastime series, no. 132). 1898. Laird & Lee.

Manila Rope. Veijo Meri. LC 67-11139. 1967. Knopf.

Manipulator. Diane Cilento. LC 67-24053. 1967. Scribner.

Manipulator. John Lennox Cook. LC 78-9353. 1978. 8.95 (ISBN 0-698-10927-9). Coward, McCann & Geoghegan.

Manipulator. Jeffrey M. Wallman. 368p. 1982. pap. 3.25 (ISBN 0-380-81166-9, 81166). Avon.

Manipulators. Gloria V. Basile. (Manipulators Bk.: No. I). 512p. (Orig.). 1982. pap. 3.50 (ISBN 0-523-41794-2). Pinnacle Bks.

Manipulators. William Garner. LC 73-108163. 1970. 5.95. Bobbs-Merrill.

Manipulators. John Rossiter. LC 73-8478. 1974. 6.95 (ISBN 0-671-21679-1). Simon and Schuster.

Manita of the Pictured Rocks: Or, The Copper Speculator. A Tale of Lake Superior. Osgood Bradbury. LC 9-1844. 1848. F. Gleason.

Manitou. Graham Masterton. 1977. pap. 2.95 (ISBN 0-523-48070-9). Pinnacle Bks.

Manitou Island: A Novel. Margaret Greenway McClelland. 1892. H. Holt and Company.

Manjiro, the Man Who Discovered America. Hisakazu Kaneko. LC 56-7239. 1956. Houghton Mifflin.

Manka, the Sky Gipsy: The Story of a Wild Goose. Denys James Watkins-Pitchford. LC 40-270176. 1939. C. Scribner's Sons.

Mankill Sport. Lionel Derrick. (Penetrator#14). 1976. (pbk.) 1.25. Pinnacle Books.

Mankiller. Collin Wilcox. LC 79-5548. 8.95 (ISBN 0-394-50550-6). Random House.

Manless World. Agnes Bond Yourell. LC 9-1190. 1891. G. W. Dillingham.

Manley: The Master of Millions. George L Crisp. LC 27-23635. The Business Collegian.

Manly-Hearted Woman. Frederick Feikema Manfred. LC 75-25887. 1975. 6.95 (ISBN 0-517-52374-4). Crown Publishers.

Manly-Hearted Woman. Frederick Feikema Manfred. (Signet Book). 1977. 1.75 (ISBN 0-451-07648-6). New American Library.

Manna Enzyme. Richard Hoyt. LC 81-16970. 1982. 11.50 (ISBN 0-688-00888-7). Morrow.

Mannequin. Fannie Hurst. LC 26-25426. A. A. Knopf.

Mannequin. Carolyn Kenmore. 5.95 o.p. Delacorte.

Mannequin. Julie Mathilde Lippmann. LC 17-123892. 1917. 1.30. Duffield and Company.

Mannequin d'Osier see Romans et Contes.

Manner Music. Charles Reznikoff. LC 77-14057. 1977. 14.00 (ISBN 0-87685-325-4) (ISBN 0-87685-326-2). Black Sparrow Press.

Mannerby's Lady. Sandra Heath. (Signet Book). 1977. 1.50 (ISBN 0-451-07492-0). New American Library.

Mannerings. Alice Brown. LC 3-7883. 1903. Houghton, Mifflin and Company.

Manning-Burke Murder. Louis Tracy. LC 30-4487. E. J. Clode, Inc.

Mannings. Fred M. Stewart. LC 72-82173. 1973. 8.95 (ISBN 0-87795-053-9). Arbor Hse.

Mannings: A Novel. Fred Mustard Stewart. LC 72-82173. 1973. 8.95 (ISBN 0-87795-053-9). Arbor House.

Mannings: A Novel. Fred Mustard Stewart. 1974. (pbk.) 1.95. Bantam Books.

Manny' Mongst the Wild Nations of Europe. Ruthella Mory Bibbins. 1904. Frederick A. Stokes Company.

Mano Cercenada. new ed. Errol Lecale, pseud. Tr. by John Reed from Eng. (Compadre Collection Ser., el Artifice: No. 3). Orig. Title: Severed Hand. (Illus.). 160p. (Span.). 1975. pap. 0.95 (ISBN 0-88473-623-7). Fiesta Pub.

Mano Majra. Khushwant Singh. LC 56-5725. (Evergreen books, E-28). 1956. Grove Press.

Manoeuvring, Madame De Fleury, & The Dun. Maria Edgeworth. LC 6-26302. 1856. G. Routledge & Co.

Manon Lescaut. Antoine Francois Prevost. Tr. by Helen Jane Waddell. LC 76-48453. (Classics of European Literature). (Hyperion library of world literature). 1977. 12.95. (ISBN 0-88355-600-6) (ISBN 0-88355-601-4). Hyperion Press.

Manon Lescaut. Antoine Francois Prevost. Tr. by Rascoe, Burton. LC 20-12453. 1919. A. A. Knopf.

Manon Lescaut. Antoine Francois Prevost. Tr. by Waddell, Helen Jane. Saintsbury, George Edward Bateman. LC 36-5109. 1935. E. P. Dutton and Co., Inc.

Manon Lescaut. A New Translation with an Introd. by Donald M. Frame. Antoine Francois Prevost. LC 62-802. (Signet classic, CP96). 1961. New American Library.

Manon's Daughter: The Love Story of an Outcast in Early St. Louis. Chaille Payne Robinson. LC 47-117612. 1947. Cloud.

Manor. Isaac Bashevis Singer. LC 67-25966. 1967. Farrar, Straus and Giroux.

Manor. Isaac Bashevis Singer. LC 79-114212. 15.00 (ISBN 0-374-20225-7). Farrar, Straus, and Giroux.

Manor & the Estate Complete. Isaac Bashevis Singer. 818p. 1979. 15.00 (ISBN 0-374-20225-7). FS&G.

Manor Farm: A Novel. Mary E. Sweetman Blundell. LC 2-16455. 1902. Longmans, Green, and Co.

Manor Farm: A Novel. Mary E. Sweetman Blundell. LC 2-20387. 1902. Longmans, Green, and Co.

Manor Farm: By Mary Douglas Warren Pseud. Maysie Greig. LC 51-4918. 1951. Arcadia House.

Manor House. Johannes Meintjes. LC 64-11902. 1964. Delacorte Press Book; Distributed by the Dial Press.

Manordale Mystery. A Strong Detective Story. Harlan Page Halsey. LC 12-32981. (Old Sleuth's own, no. 114). 1898. The Parlor Car Publishing Co.

Manowen. Esther Penny Boutcher. LC 51-10407. 1951. Duell, Sloan, and Pearce.

Manrissa Man. Peter Van Greenaway. 192p. 1982. 17.50 (ISBN 0-575-03100-X, Pub. by Gollancz England). David & Charles.

Man's a Man for A' That"... A Novel. LC 7-20452. (On cover: Knickerbocker novels). 1879. G. P. Putnam's Sons.

Man's Blessing. Leonardo Sciascia. LC 68-15978. 1968. Harper & Row.

Man's Choice. Frank R Wallace. LC 70-119325. 1970. 6.95. I & O Pub. Co.

Man's Code. William Blair Morton Ferguson. LC 15-11875. G. W. Dillingham Company.

Man's Conscience: A Novel. Avery MacAlpine. LC 7-15271. 1891. Harper & Brothers.

Man's Conscience: A Novel. Avery MacAlpine. LC 7-15270. (Half-title: Harper's Franklin square library, no. 724). 1892. Harper & Brothers.

Man's Country: The Story of a Great Love, of Which Business Was Jealous. Peter Clark Macfarlane. LC 23-887. 1923. Cosmopolitan Book Corporation.

Man's Courage. Joseph Vogel. LC 38-9836. 1938. A. A. Knopf.

Man's Enemies. Lee Thayer, pseud. LC 37-16069. 1937. Dodd, Mead & Company.

Man's Estate. Emyr Humphreys. LC 56-9629. 1956. McGraw-Hill.

Man's Estate. Mabel Emily Ince. LC 38-3951. Stackpole Sons.

Man's Fate. Andre Malraux. 1969. pap. 3.95 (ISBN 0-394-70479-7, Vin); pap. 3.95 (ISBN 0-394-30975-8). Random.

Man's Fate. Andre Malraux. Tr. by Haakon M. Chevalier. 1965. pap. 3.95 (Mod LibC). Modern Lib.

Man's Fate: La Condition Humaine. Andre Malraux. LC 68-7701. 1968. 4.95. Random House.

Man's Fate (La Condition Humaine) Andre Malraux. LC 72-7480. 1973. (ISBN 0-394-70479-7). Vintage Books.

Man's Fate (La Condition Humaine) Andre Malraux & Chevalier, Haakon M., Tr. LC 36-27493. (Half-title: The modern library of the world's best books). 1936. The Modern Library.

Man's Fate (La Condition Humaine) Andre Malraux & Chevalier Hankon M., Tr. LC 34-17970. 1934. H. Smith and R. Haas.

Man's Game. John Brent. LC 21-14796. 1921. 2.00. The Century Co.

Man's Heart Is Evil: A Novel. Morris Perman. LC 47-5593. 1947. House of Field-Doubleday.

Man's Hearth. Eleanor Marie Ingram. LC 15-23789. 1915. 1.25. J. B. Lippincott Company.

Man's Highest Duty: A Story and a Message. Irene Nylen. LC 20-12057. A. L. Schmoeger.

Man's Hope. Andre Malraux. LC 79-2333. 1979. 6.95 (ISBN 0-394-17093-8). Grove Press: Distributed by Random House.

Man's Hope. Andre Malraux & Gilbert, Stuart, Tr. LC 38-28904. Random House.

Man's Hope. Andre Malraux & Gilbert, Stuart, Tr. (Half-title: The Modern library of the world's best books). 1941. The Modern Library.

Man's Life: Amour Nuptial. Jacques De Lacretelle. Tr. by Granberry, Edwin. LC 31-8211. H. Holt and Company.

Man's Little Plot. Richard J. Aielli. 3.50 o.p. Carlton.

Man's Man. John Hay Beith. 1910. Houghton Mifflin Company.

Man's Man. Jacques Saison. Orig. Title: Man to Man. 192p. 1974. pap. 2.25 o.s.i. (ISBN 0-89053-105-6). Lambda Pr.

Man's Mortality. Michael Arlen. LC 33-70916. 1933. Doubleday, Doran & Company, Inc.

Man's Own Country. Katharine Newlin Burt. LC 31-255651. 1931. Houghton Mifflin Company.

Man's Perpetual Love Calendar. Peggy Burke & Evan Burke. 192p. (Orig.). 1974. pap. 1.95 o.p. (ISBN 0-87056-393-9, 6393). Brandon.
Man's Persuasion. Katherine Granger. LC 83-1974. 1983. 11.95 (ISBN 0-89340-603-1). J. Curley & Associates.
Man's Persuasion. Katherine Granger. (Second Chance at Love Ser.: No. 89). 1982. pap. 1.75 (ISBN 0-515-06851-9). Jove Pubns.
Man's Place. Ramon Jose Sender & La Farge, Oliver, 1901- Tr. LC 40-337067. Duell, Sloan and Pearce.
Man's Privilege. Dora Russell. (On cover: Globe library, v. 1, no. 257). 1897. Rand, Mc Nally & Company.
Man's Protection. Jayne Castle. (Candlelight Ecstasy Ser.: No. 36). (Orig.). 1982. pap. 1.75 (ISBN 0-440-15188-0). Dell.
Man's Reach. Sally Nelson Robins. LC 16-561709. 1916. 1.25. J. B. Lippincott Company.
Man's Reach. Thomas Alva Stubbins. LC 29-12489. Meador Publishing Company.
Man's Reach. Charles Morrow Wilson. LC 44-5429. 1944. H. Holt and Company.
Man's Reach. Muriel S Wright. LC 75-180124. 1972. 4.95 (ISBN 0-8059-1640-7). Dorrance.
Man's Undoing. Emily Sharp H. Cameron. LC 99-3478. 1899. F. M. Buckles & Co.
Man's Way. Muriel Hine Coxon. LC 34-2646. 1934. D. Appleton-Century Company, Incorporated.
Man's Will. A Novel. Edgar Fawcett. LC 6-38791. 1888. Funk & Wagnalls.
Man's Woman. Marianne Baer. LC 77-11679. 8.95. Putnam.
Man's Woman. Frank Norris. LC 71-108125. 1970. AMS Press.
Man's Woman. Frank Norris. LC 1157. 1900. Doubleday & McClure Co.
Man's Woman. Yvernelle; a Legend of Feudal France. Frank Norris. LC 67-3231. (His Complete works, v. 6). 1967. Kennikat Press.
Man's World. Arthur Bullard. LC 12-216121. 1912. 1.25. The Macmillan Company.
Man's World. Arthur Bullard. LC 15-239212. 1914. The Macmillan Company.
Man's World. Charlotte Haldane. LC 27-114851. George H. Doran Company.
Man's World. Charlotte Lamb, pseud. (Harlequin Presents Ser.). 192p. (Orig.). 1981. pap. 1.50 (ISBN 0-373-10412-X, Pub. by Harlequin). PB.
Man's World. Patricia Lee. LC 37-15785. 1937. Hillman-Curl, Inc.
Man's World: A Novel. Douglas Fairbairn. LC 56-7485. 1956. Simon and Schuster.
Mansart Builds a School see Black Flame; a Trilogy.
Manse at Barren Rocks. Albert Benjamin Cunningham. LC 18-18957. 1.40. George H. Doran Company.
Manse Dwellers. Luther Little. LC 27-14797. 1927. Presbyterian Standard Pub. Co.
Manseed. Jack Williamson. 192p. 1982. 10.95 (ISBN 0-345-30742-9, Del Rey). Ballantine.
Mansfield Park. Jane Austen. (Harcourt library of English and American classics). 1962. Harcourt, Brace & World.
Mansfield Park. Jane Austen. LC 75-540925. (Oxford English novels). 1970 (ISBN 0-19-255336-4). Oxford U.P.
Mansfield Park. Jane Austen. LC 49-9857. (Novel library). 1949. Pantheon Books.
Mansfield Park. Jane Austen. LC 6-3865. 1892. Roberts Brothers.
Mansfield Park. Jane Austen. LC 4-15274. 1897. Macmillan and Co., Limited.
Mansfield Park. Jane Austen. (Half-title: Everyman's library, ed. by Ernest Rhys. Fiction. no. 23). 1966. J. M. Dent & Co.
Mansfield Park. Jane Austen. LC 26-26508. (Rittenbouse classics). 1926. Macrae Smith Company.
Mansfield Park. Jane Austen. LC 36-37055. (Half-title: Everyman's library, ed. by Ernest Rhys. Fiction no. 23). 1931. J. M. Dent & Sons, Ltd.
Mansfield Park. Jane Austen & Bailey, John Cann. 1928. Dodd, Mead & Company.
Mansfield Park. Jane Austen & James Kinsley. LC 80-40259. (World's classics). 1980. 2.95 (ISBN 0-19-281526-1). Oxford University Press.
Mansfield Park see Oxford Illustrated Jane Austen.
Mansfield Park: Ed. by R. W. Chapman Introd. by Reuben A. Brower. Jane Austen. (Riverside eds., B90) Bibl.). pap., 1.35. Houghton.
Mansfield Park: Ed., Introd. by Tony Tanner. Jane Austen. (Penguin Eng. lib. EL16). 1966. pap., 1.45. Penguin.
Mansfield Park. Introd. by Q. D. Leavis. Illus. by by Philip Gough. Jane Austen. LC 57-585221. (Macdonald illus. classics, 34). 1966. 3.50. Macdonald.
Manshape. John Brunner. 160p. 1982. pap. 2.25 (ISBN 0-87997-764-7). DAW Bks.
Mansion. William Faulkner. LC 59-10811. 1959. Random House.
Mansion. Henry Van Dyke. LC 74-19077. 1974. 5.00. Folcroft Library Editions.
Mansion. Henry Van Dyke. LC 43-37801. 1911. Harper & Brothers.
Mansion see Snopes: A Trilogy.
Mansion for My Love. Robyn Donald. (Harlequin Presents Ser.). 192p. 1983. pap. 1.75 (ISBN 0-373-10567-3). Harlequin Bks.
Mansion House. Eleanor Mercein Kelly. LC 25-76683. 2.00. The Century Co.
Mansion Malevolent. Caroline Farr. (Signet book). 1974. (pbk.) 0.95. New American Library.
Mansion of Dark Mists. Eva Zumwalt. 1981. pap. 2.50 (ISBN 0-8439-0915-3, Leisure Bks). Nordon Pubns.
Mansion of Deadly Dreams. Grace Corren. (Queen-size gothic: large easy-to-read type). 1973. (pbk.) 0.95. Popular Lib.
Mansion of Evil. Joseph Millard. LC 51-15535. (Gold medal book, 129). Fawcett Publications.
Mansion of Golden Windows. easy eye ed. Elsie Lee. pap. 0.75 o.p. Lancer.
Mansion of Golden Windows. Elsie Lee. 1.25. Dell.
Mansion of Lost Memories see House of Stolen Memories.
Mansion of Menace. Caroline Farr. (Signet Book). 1976. 1.25. New American Library.
Mansion of Menace. Minerva Rossetti. 1974. 4.95 (ISBN 0-517-51560-1). Lenox Hill Press.
Mansion of Mystery: Being a Certain Case of Importance, Taken from the Note-Book of Adam Adams, Investigator and Detective. Chester K Steele. LC 11-7871. 0.90. Cupples & Leon Company.
Mansion of Peril. Caroline Farr. (Signet book.). 1975. (pbk.) 0.95. New American Library.
Mansion on the Moors. William Edward Daniel Ross. (Candlelight gothic). 1974. (pbk.) 0.75. Dell.
Mansion Tenebrosa. new ed. Thelma R. Bernard, pseud. Tr. by John A. Reed from Eng. (Compadre Collection Ser.). Orig. Title: Moonshadow Mansion. 160p. (Span.). 1974. pap. 0.75 (ISBN 0-88473-606-7). Fiesta Pub.
Mansion with One Door. Franklin Fillmore Farrington. LC 24-229433. Powell & White.
Mansions in the Cascades. Anne Shannon Monroe & Wood, Elizabeth (Lambert) LC 26-23006. 1936. The Macmillan Company.
Mansions of America. Rosemary Anne Sisson. 1981. pap. 3.50 (ISBN 0-440-15393-X). Dell.
Mansions of Unrest. Elizabeth Dejeans. LC 26-12289. 1926. Doubleday, Page & Company.
Manslaughter. Alice Duer Miller. LC 21-188018. 1921. Dodd, Mead and Company.
Manspell-Godspell. Sam Bradley. 1975. pap. 3.50 (Pub. by Anvil Pr). SBD.
Mansville Brand. W. G Schreiber. (Avalon Books). 4.95. Thomas Bouregy.
Mantee. Robert J. Hensler. (Orig.). 1969. pap. 0.95 o.p. (65-230). Paperback Lib.
Mantel-Piece Minstrels: And Other Stories. John Kendrick Bangs. LC 6-6125. 1896. R. H. Russell & Son.
Mantel-Piece Minstrels, & Other Stories. facs. ed. John Kendrick Bangs. LC 78-85689. (Short Story Index Reprint Ser.). 1896. 11.00 (ISBN 0-8369-3030-4). Ayer Co.
Manticore. William Robertson Davies. LC 72-81120. 1972. 7.95 (ISBN 0-670-45313-7). Viking Press.
Manticore. William Robertson Davies. LC 76-43018. 1976. 1.95 (ISBN 0-14-004388-8). Penguin Books.
Mantilla. Richard Aumerle Maher. LC 13-8909. 1913. B. Herder.
Mantis. Peter F Fox. LC 79-5335. 9.95 (ISBN 0-312-51295-3). St. Martin's Press.
Mantis: A Novel. Ethelreda Lewis. LC 29-5949. 1929. Simon and Schuster, Inc.
Mantis & the Moth see Crowded Loneliness.
Mantis and the Moth: A Novel. Max Weatherly. LC 64-17202. 1964. Houghton Mifflin.
Mantis Carol. Laurens Van Der Post. 166p. 1976. 6.95 o.p. (ISBN 0-688-03018-1). Morrow.
Mantissa. John Fowles. LC 82-7234. 13.95 (ISBN 0-316-28980-9). Little, Brown.
Mantle. Bill Stephens. LC 76-1325. 1976. 7.95 (ISBN 0-8423-4020-3). Tyndale House Publishers.
Mantle: And Other Stories. Nikolai Vasilevich Gogol. LC 77-152940. (Short story index reprint series). 1971. (ISBN 0-8369-3799-6). Books for Libraries Press.
Mantle: And Other Stories. Nikolai Vasilevich Gogol. Tr. by Field, Claud Herbert Alwyn. Merimee, Prosper. LC 16-10453. Frederick A. Stokes Co.
Mantle & Other Stories. facsimile ed. Nikolai Vasilevich Gogol. Tr. by Claud Field from Rus. LC 77-152940. (Short Story Index Reprint Ser.). Repr. of 1916 ed. 15.00 (ISBN 0-8369-3799-6). Ayer Co.
Mantle of Elijah: A Novel. Israel Zangwill. LC 1-29137. Harper & Brothers.
Mantle of Masquerade. Steuart M Emery. LC 26-12144. E. P. Dutton & Company.
Mantle of Silence. E. J. Rath. LC 20-14284. W. J. Watt & Company.
Mantrap. Sinclair Lewis. LC 26-12145. 1926. Harcourt, Brace and Company.
Mantrap. Sinclair Lewis. LC 38-32011. (A Mercury book, no. 11). The American Mercury, Inc.
Mantras: Sacred Words of Power. John Blofeld. 1977. pap. 4.50 o.p. (ISBN 0-525-47451-X). Dutton.
Manual for Manuel. Julio Cortazar. LC 77-88782. 10.95 (ISBN 0-394-49661-2). Pantheon Books.
Manual Labor: A Novel. Frederick Busch. LC 74-6286. (New Directions book). 1974. 8.50 (ISBN 0-8112-0535-5) (ISBN 0-8112-0535-5). New Directions.
Manuel De Jesus Galvan's Enriquillo: The Cross and the Sword; Translated by Robert Graves. Manuel De Jesus Galvan. LC 75-153323. (Series: UNESCO Collection of Representative Works: Latin American Series.). 1975. 17.00 (ISBN 0-404-02675-3). AMS Press.
Manuel De Jesus Galvan's Enriquillo: The Cross & the Sword. Manuel de Jesus Galvan. LC 75-153323. Repr. of 1954 ed. 28.00 (ISBN 0-404-02675-3). AMS Pr.
Manuel, the Mexican: A Novel. Translated from the French by Hans Koningsberger. Carlo Coccioli. LC 58-13172. 1958. Simon and Schuster.
Manuela: A Novel. William Howard Woods. LC 57-127578. 1957. Hill and Wang.
Manuela, la Caballeresa Del Sol: A Novel. Authorized Tr., Introd. by Willis Knapp Jones. Foreword by J. Cary Davis. Demetrio Aguilera Malta. (Contemp. Latin Amer. classics). 1967. 6.95. Univ. Pr.
Manuela, la Caballeresa Del Sol: A Novel. Aguilera Malta, Demetrio. LC 67-11700. (Contemporary Latin American classics). 1967. Southern Illinois University Press.
Manuela Paredes. William Mellen Chamberlain. LC 6-23342. (No name series, 2d series, v. S.). 1881. Roberts Brothers.
Manuelita: The Story of San Xavier Del Bac. Marian Calvert Wilson. LC 8-37092. United States Book Company.
Manulito; or, A Strange Friendship. William Bruce Leffingwell. LC 7-12605. 1892. J.B. Lippincott Company.
Manuscript for Murder. Richard Martin Stern. LC 76-106542. 1970. 4.95. Scribner.
Manuscript Murder. Lewis George Robinson. LC 34-1681. 1934. Published for the Crime Club, Inc., by Doubleday, Doran & Company, Inc.
Manuscript Murders. Roy Harley Lewis. LC 81-21467. 9.95 (ISBN 0-312-51391-7). St Martin's Press.
Manuscript of Youth: A Novel. Desemea Wilson. LC 23-9748. E. P. Dutton & Company.
Manuscripts of Pauline Archange: A Novel. Marie Claire Blais. LC 77-115751. 1970. 5.95. Farrar, Straus & Giroux.
Manville Murders. Cortland Fitzsimmons. LC 30-29643. 1930. R. M. McBride & Company.
Manx Cat. Fred Levon, pseud. LC 79-100110. 1970. 4.95. World Pub. Co.
Manxman. Hall Caine. LC 6-198993. 1894. D. Appleton and Company.
Manxman: A Novel. 13th ed. Hall Caine. LC 4-15289. 1896. D. Appleton and Company.
Manxmouse. Paul Gallico. LC 68-14308. (Illus.). 1968. Coward-McCann.
Many a Green Isle. Agnes Sligh Turnbull. LC 68-21739. 1968. 5.95. Houghton, Mifflin.
Many a Mile. Desmond Martin. LC 77-358447. (Illus.). 1976. (ISBN 0-17-005069-6). Thomas Nelson (Australia)
Many a Monster. Paul William Ryan. LC 48-5618. (Inner sanctum mystery). 1948. Simon and Schuster.
Many a Thorn: A Novel. Lois Young Nelson. LC 49-50189. 1949. W. B. Eerdmans Pub. Co.
Many a Voyage. Loula Grace Erdman. LC 67-25106. 1967. 3.95. Dodd.
Many Are Called: Forty-Two Short Stories. Edward Newhouse. LC 51-12159. 1951. Sloane.
Many Are the Hearts. Elisabeth Bertram Margetson. LC 46-3764. 1946. M. S. Mill Co., Inc.
Many Are the Hearts. Bruce Palmer. LC 61-15120. 1961. Simon and Schuster.
Many Are the Travelers. William Brown Meloney. LC 54-5705. 1954. Appleton-Century-Crofts.
Many Broken Hammers. Kelly Covin. LC 70-135381. 1971. 6.95. Delacorte Press.
Many Captives. John Owen. LC 30-307766. 1930. J. B. Lippincott Company.
Many Cargoes. William Wymark Jacobs. LC 71-103520. (Short story index reprint series). (Illus.). 1969. Books for Libraries Press.
Many Cargoes. William Wymark Jacobs. LC 7-7426. F. A. Stokes Company.
Many Cargoes. William Wymark Jacobs. LC 3-27962. 1903. F. A. Stokes Company.
Many Colored Coat. Morley Callaghan. LC 60-11285. 1960. Coward-McCann.
Many-Colored Fleece. Ed. by Mariella Gable. LC 50-10979. 1950. Sheed & Ward.
Many Deadly Returns. Patricia Moyes. LC 73-103550. (Rinehart suspense novel). 1970. 4.50. Holt, Rinehart and Winston.
Many Dimensions. Charles Williams. LC 49-10010. 1949. Pellegrini & Cudahy.
Many Dimensions. Charles Walter Stansby Williams. 1965. pap., 1.95. Eerdmans.
Many Dimensions see Novels.
Many Flies Have Feathers. Ivor Cutler. 1973. 7.00 (Pub. by Trigram Pr); signed ed. 15.00; pap. 4.00. SBD.
Many Happy Returns. Justin Scott. LC 72-92652. 1973. 5.95. McKay.
Many Happy Returns. Richard Strachey. LC 33-20279. Harcourt, Brace and Company.
Many Heavens: A New Mormon Novel. 1st Ed. Virginia Eggertsen Sorensen. LC 54-5258. 1954. Harcourt, Brace.
Many Inventions. Rudyard Kipling. LC 7-37393. 1893. Macmillan and Co.
Many Inventions. Rudyard Kipling. LC 4-15318. 1893. D. Appleton and Company.
Many Inventions. Rudyard Kipling. LC 16-936553. 1908. Doubleday, Page & Company.
Many Inventions. Rudyard Kipling. LC 24-22217. 1914. Doubleday, Page & Company for Review of Reviews Co.
Many Inventions. Rudyard Kipling. LC 16-16159. 1916. Doubleday, Page & Company.
Many Inventions. Rudyard Kipling. LC 28-166716. 1922. Doubleday, Page & Company.
Many Junes. Archibald Marshall. 1920. Dodd, Mead and Company.
Many Kingdoms. Elizabeth Garver Jordan. LC 8-30707. 1908. 1.50. Harper & Brothers.
Many Latitudes. Fryniwyd Tennyson Jesse. LC 76-116957. (Short story index reprint series). 1970. Books for Libraries Press.
Many Latitudes. Fryniwyd Tennyson Jesse. LC 28-15172. 1928. A. A. Knopf.
Many Long Years Ago. Ogden Nash. 1945. 4.95 o.p. (ISBN 0-316-59822-4). Little.
Many Loves of Dobie Gillis. Max Shulman. 220p. Repr. lib. bdg. 13.25x (ISBN 0-89190-982-6). Am Repr-Rivercity Pr.
Many Loves of Dobie Gillis: Eleven Campus Stories. Max Shulman. LC 51-12243. 1951. Doubleday.
Many Mansions. Gina Cerminara. 1972. pap. 2.50 (ISBN 0-451-09955-9, E9955, Sig). NAL.
Many Mansions. Donald L. Kimball. (Illus.). 300p. 1982. 14.95 (ISBN 0-942698-05-3); pap. 7.95 (ISBN 0-942698-06-1). Trends & Events.
Many Mansions. Sarah Warder MacConnell. LC 18-18405. 1918. Houghton Mifflin Company.
Many Mansions. Ed. by Robert M. Myers. (The Children of Pride Ser: Vol. 1). 1977. pap. 1.95 (ISBN 0-445-08592-4). Popular Lib.
Many Mansions. Henry Cottrell Rowland. LC 32-5300. 1932. R. Long & R. R. Smith, Inc.
Many Mansions of Sam Peeples. Howard McMillen. LC 74-172897. 1971. 7.95 (ISBN 0-670-45423-0). Viking Press.
Many Marriages. Sherwood Anderson. LC 23-731991. 1923. B. W. Huebsch, Inc.
Many Marriages. a critical ed. / edited by douglas g. rogers. ed. Sherwood Anderson & Douglas G. Rogers. LC 78-2353. 1978. 10.00 (ISBN 0-8108-1122-7). Scarecrow Press.
Many Marriages by Sherwood Anderson. Ed. by Douglas G. Rogers. LC 78-2353. 1978. 13.00 (ISBN 0-8108-1122-7). Scarecrow.
Many Missions. Mary Britton Miller. LC 52-12830. 1952. Scribner.
Many Mizners. Addison Mizner. LC 32-24133. Sears Publishing Company.
Many Moons. James Thurber. (Voyager book). (Illus.). 1972. 1.65 (ISBN 0-15-656980-9). Harcourt.
Many Murders. Inez Haynes Irwin. LC 41-7831. Random House.
Many People Prize It: A Novel. Joseph Chamberlain Furnas. LC 37-20058. 1937. W. Morrow and Company.
Many Rivers to Cross. Steve Frazee. 176p. 1981. pap. 1.95 (ISBN 0-449-14012-1, GM). Fawcett.
Many Rivers to Cross. Steve Frazee. 1970. pap. 0.60 o.p. (R2361, GM). Fawcett World.
Many Shall Come. Patrick Joseph Carroll. LC 37-22498. The Ave Maria Press.
Many Splendid Thing. Han Suyin, pseud. 336p. 1982. pap. 3.95 (ISBN 0-553-22736-X). Bantam.
Many-Splendored Thing. Suyin Han. (A love story). 1952. 6.95 o.p. (ISBN 0-316-34290-4, Pub. by Atlantic Monthly Pr). Little.
Many Thing You No Understand. Adaora L. Ulasi. 1970. pap. 1.25 o.p. (ISBN 0-531-06049-7, Fontana Pap). Watts.
Many Thousand Gone: An American Fable. Ronald L Fair. LC 65-11987. 3.50. Harcourt.
Many Thousands Gone. John Peale Bishop. LC 31-12018. 1931. C. Scribner's Sons.
Many Wars of Christopher Branch. Hank Stohl & Gary Hudson. 108p. (Orig.). 1976. 6.95 (ISBN 0-89185-031-7); pap. 2.25 (ISBN 0-89185-030-9). Anthelion Pr.

Many Waters. Elinor Chipp. LC 24-17832. 1924. D. Appleton and Company.
Many Waters. Marjorie Barkeley McClure. LC 28-21481. 1928. Minton, Balch & Company.
Many Waters. William Hardwick Ruth. LC 42-24775. 1942. The Christopher Publishing House.
Many Waters: A Story of New York. Robert Shackleton. LC 2-11731. 1902. D. Appleton and Company.
Many Windows: Seasons of the Heart. Faith Baldwin. 1958. 3.50 o.p. (ISBN 0-03-028460-0). HR&W.
Many Windows: 22 Stories from American Review. Ted Solotaroff. LC 81-47803. (Harper colophon books). 7.95 (ISBN 0-06-090923-4). Harper & Row.
Many Windows: 23 Stories from American Review. Ed. by Ted Solotaroff. 1982. pap. 7.64i (ISBN 0-06-090923-4, CN-923, HarpT). Har-Row.
Many Worlds of Andre Norton. Ed. by Roger Elwood. LC 74-10980. 232p. 1974. 7.95 o.p. (ISBN 0-8019-5927-6). Chilton.
Many Worlds of Andre Norton. Andre Norton, pseud. LC 74-10980. 1974. 6.95 (ISBN 0-8019-5927-6). Chilton Book Co.
Many Worlds of Magnus Ridolph. Jack Vance, pseud. (Science Fiction Ser.). 1980. pap. 1.75 (ISBN 0-7899-7531-9, UE1531). Daw Bks.
Many Worlds of Poul Anderson. Poul Anderson. Ed. by Roger Elwood. LC 74-3445. 1974. 6.95 (ISBN 0-8019-5950-0). Chilton Book Co.
Maori Girl. Noel Hilliard. LC 74-192750. 263p. 1971. pap. 4.50x (ISBN 0-8002-0072-1). Intl Pubns Serv.
Maori Murder Case. Andrew I Albert. LC 44-8826. 1944. Vulcan Publications, Inc.
Map of Days: A Novel, by Ethel Boileau... Ethel Mary Young Boileau. LC 35-64613. 1935. E. P. Dutton & Co., Inc.
Map of Mistrust. Allan MacKinnon. LC 48-7150. 1948. Pub. for the Crime Club by Doubleday.
Map on the Ceiling. John Leonard Pierce. LC 64-17605. Macmillan.
Maple Hall Mystery. A Romance. Enrique Parmer. LC 7-34729. (On cover: Satchel series, no. 25). The Authors' Publishing Company.
Maple Hill Folks. Wilber Haller. LC 29-6449. The Author.
Maple on the Hill. L. L. Ward. 5.95 o.p. Carlton.
Maple Princess. Susan E. Kirby. 1982. pap. 6.95 (Avalon). Bouregy.
Maple Range. Edna A Barnard. LC 6-7208. 1882. H.A. Sumner & Co.
Maplehurst: Or, Campbellism Not Christianity. Jenny Bland Beauchamp. LC 6-10357. 1867. P. M. Pinckard.
Mapleton: Or, More Work for the Maine Law... Pharcellus Church. LC 6-254000. 1853. Jenks, Hickling and Swan.
Mapmaker. Frank Gill Slaughter. (Kangaroo Book). 1978. 1.95 (ISBN 0-671-81192-4). Pocket Books.
Mapmaker: A Novel of the Days of Prince Henry, the Navigator. 1st Ed. Frank Gill Slaughter. LC 57-12475. 1957. Doubleday.
Mapondera, Soldier of Zimbabwe. Solomon M Mutswairo. LC 77-90992. (Illus.). 15.00 (ISBN 0-914478-19-2) (ISBN 0-914478-20-6). Three Continents Press.
Mapp and Lucia. Edward Frederic Benson. LC 31-28425. 1931. Doubleday, Doran & Company, Inc.
Maquisard: A Christmas Tale. Albert Joseph Guerard. LC 45-35196. 1945. A. A. Knopf.
Mara. Stoyan Christowe. LC 37-216890. Thomas Y. Crowell Company.
Mara. Kathleen Morris. (Dell/James A. Bryans Book). 1978. 2.25 (ISBN 0-440-04971-7). Dell Pub. Co.
Mara: A Novel. Tova Reich. LC 78-5837. 1978. 8.95 (ISBN 0-374-20286-9). Farrar, Straus, Giroux.
Mara & the Priest. Lorenzo D'Agostino. 272p. 1975. 7.95 o.p. (ISBN 0-682-48282-X, Banner). Exposition.
Mara, Mura. Benjamin Burack. LC 73-88097. 1974. 4.95 (ISBN 0-8059-1941-4). Dorrance.
Marabelle. T. E Huff. LC 79-22857. 11.95 (ISBN 0-312-51430-1). St. Martin's Press.
Marabi Dance. Modikwe Dikobe. (African Writers Ser.). 1973. pap. text ed. 4.50x (ISBN 0-435-90124-9). Heinemann Ed.
Marable Family. A Novel. Shaler Hillyer. LC 7-4680. 1879. J. B. Lippincott & Co.
Maracaibo. Stirling Silliphant. LC 55-721253. 1955. Farrar, Straus.
Maracaibo Affair. Rod Gray. (New Lady from L.U.S.T. Ser). (O.s.i.: No. 4). (Orig.). 1975. pap. 1.25 o.s.i. (BT50814). Belmont-Tower.
Maracaidb Mission. Francis Van Wyck Mason. LC 65-12370. 4.50. Doubleday.
Maracot Deep. Arthur Conan Doyle. LC 68-10892. (Seagull library of mystery and suspense). 1968. 4.95. Norton.
Maracot Deep. Arthur Conan Doyle. (Seagull Library of Mystery & Suspense). 1968. Repr. 4.95 o.p. Norton.
Maracot Deep: And Other Stories. Arthur Conan Doyle. 1929. Doubleday, Doran & Company, Inc.
Marah. Jean Merrill. LC 81-8776. 1981. 11.95 (ISBN 0-312-51435-2). St. Martin's Press.
Marah: A Story of Old Virginia. William Asbury Christian. LC 76-39079. (Black Heritage Library Collection). 1972. (ISBN 0-8369-9017-X). Books for Libraries Press.
Marah: A Story of Old Virginia. William Asbury Christian. LC 3-28129. 1903. L.H. Jenkins, Printer.
Marah: The Woman at the Well. Nina B. Mason. 1982. pap. 3.50 (ISBN 0-8423-4032-7). Tyndale.
Marahuna: A Romance. Henry Brereton Marriott Watson. LC 8-36760. 1888. Longmans, Green, and Co.
Marama: A Tale of the South Pacific. Ralph Stock. LC 13-22515. 1913. Little, Brown, and Company.
Maramar. Naguib Nahfouz. (Arabic.). 5.50x (ISBN 0-86685-159-3). Intl Bk Ctr.
Marannos: A Novel, Tr. from the German of Dr. Ludwig Philippson. Ludwig Philippson. Tr. by Koplowitz, Isidore. 1898. Press of the Levytype Company.
Maras Affair. Eliot Reed, pseud. LC 52-13572. 1953. Published for the Crime Club by Doubleday.
Marathon. David A. Smith. 256p. 1982. pap. 2.50 (ISBN 0-441-51943-1). Ace Bks.
Marathon Man. William Goldman. LC 74-10893. 1974. 7.95 (ISBN 0-440-05327-7). Delacorte Press.
Marathon Mystery: A Story of Manhattan. Burton Egbert Stevenson. LC 4-30588. 1904. H. Holt and Company.
Marathon Mystery: A Story of Manhattan. Burton Egbert Stevenson. LC 21-4119. 1920. H. Holt and Company.
Marauder. C. H. Haseloff. 176p. 1982. pap. 2.25 (ISBN 0-553-20400-9). Bantam.
Marauders. Lee Floren. (O.s.i.). Orig. Title: Burnt Wagon Ranch. 1975. pap. 0.95 o.s.i. Tower.
Marauders. Peter McCurtin. (Sundance Ser.: No. 31). 1980. pap. 1.75 o.s.i. (ISBN 0-8439-0740-1, Leisure Bks). Nordon Pubns.
Marauders. Gordon D Shirreffs. (Fawcett Gold Medal Book). 1.50 (ISBN 0-449-13723-6). Fawcett Publications.
Marauders at the Lazy Mare. Peter Field. LC 51-9253. 1951. Jefferson House.
Marauders of Gor. John Norman. (Science Fiction Ser). 1975. pap. 2.75 (ISBN 0-87997-676-4, UE1676). DAW Bks.
Marazan. Nevil Shute. 1982. 14.95 (ISBN 0-434-69901-2, Pub. by Heinemann). David & Charles.
Marbeau Cousins. Harry Stillwell Edwards. LC 21-8696. The J. W. Burke Company.
Marbeau Cousins. Harry Stillwell Edwards. Rand, McNally & Company.
Marbeck Inn. Harold Brighouse. LC 20-3713. 1920. Little, Brown, and Company.
Marble and Mud: A Novel. Jane Burr. LC 35-281740. 1935. The Parnasus Press.
Marble Angel. Dorothy Daniels. 1970. pap. 0.75 o.p. (ISBN 0-447-74678-2). Lancer.
Marble Angel. easy eye ed. Dorothy Daniels. Orig. Title: Marble Leaf. (Orig.). pap. 0.95 o.p. (73-482). Lancer.
Marble Faun. Nathaniel Hawthorne. pap. 2.95 (ISBN 0-451-51771-7, CE1771, Sig Classics). NAL.
Marble Faun. Nathaniel Hawthorne. Ed. by William Charvat et al. (Centenary Edition of the Works of Nathaniel Hawthorne: Vol. 4). (Illus.). 1968. 20.00 (ISBN 0-8142-0062-1). Ohio St U Pr.
Marble Faun, & a Green Bough. reissue ed. William Faulkner. 1965. 10.95 (ISBN 0-394-40385-1). Random.
Marble Faun: Or, The Romance of Monte Beni, a Romance. Nathaniel Hawthorne. Ed. by Richard H. Rupp. LC 73-134464. (Library of literature). (Illus.). 1971. 2.95. Bobbs-Merrill.
Marble Faun: Or The Romance of Monte Beni. Nathaniel Hawthorne. LC 66-1478. (Signet classic). 1961. New American Library.
Marble Faun: Or, The Romance of Monte Beni. Nathaniel Hawthorne. LC 7-3869. 1860. Ticknor and Fields.
Marble Faun: Or, The Romance of Monte Beni. Nathaniel Hawthorne. LC 4-16289. (Half-title: Riverside edition. The complete works of Nathaniel Hawthorne... v. 6). 1888. Houghton, Mifflin and Company.
Marble Faun: Or, The Romance of Monte Beni. Nathaniel Hawthorne. LC 7-3874. 1889. Houghton Mifflin and Company.
Marble Faun: Or, The Romance of Monte Beni. Nathaniel Hawthorne. LC 99-5077. 1899. Houghton, Mifflin & Co.
Marble Faun: Or, The Romance of Monte Beni. Nathaniel Hawthorne. LC 3-32797. (Half-title: The Unit books, no. 1). 1903. H. W. Bell.
Marble Faun: Or, The Romance of Monte Beni. Nathaniel Hawthorne & Katherine Lee Bates. LC 2-19991. 1902. T. Y. Crowell & Company.
Marble Faun: Or, The Romance of Monte Beni. Nathaniel Hawthorne & Marble, Mrs. Annie (Russell) 1864- Ed. LC 1-26276. (On cover: Riverside literature series, no. 148). 1901. Houghton, Mifflin and Company.
Marble Faun; or, The Romance of Monte Beni. Nathaniel Hawthorne & Ohio. State University, Columbus. Ohio State Center for Textual Studies. LC 68-6279. (His Centenary Ed. of the Works of Nathaniel Hawthorne, V. 4). 1968. 10.00. Ohio State Univ. Pr.
Marble Faun: Or, the Romance of Monte Beni. Ed. by Richard H. Rupp. LC 73-134464. 1971. pap. 7.60 o.p. (ISBN 0-672-61026-4). Bobbs.
Marble Faun: Or, The Romance of Monte Beni. With an Introd. by Maxwell Geismar. Nathaniel Hawthorne. LC 58-574. (Pocket library, PL59). 1958. Pocket Books.
Marble Forest. Eaton K Goldthwaite. LC 72-150898. 1971. 4.95. Published for the Crime Club by Doubleday.
Marble Forest. 1st Ed. Theo Durrant, pseud. LC 51-9345. 1951. Knopf.
Marble Leaf see Marble Angel.
Marble Orchard. Margaret Currier Boylen. LC 56-8792. 1956. Random House.
Marble Virgins. Stephanie King. (Beagle gothic). 1974. (pbk.) 0.95. Beagle Books.
Marbleface. Max Brand. LC 39-6487. 1939. Dodd, Mead & Company.
Marbleface. Frederick Faust. LC 39-6487. 1939. Dodd, Mead & Company.
Marblehead. Joan Thompson. LC 77-99127. (Illus.). 8.95 (ISBN 0-312-51438-7). St. Martin's Press.
Marc Dean, Mercenary, No. 5: School for Slaughter. Peter Buck. 1982. pap. 2.25 (ISBN 0-451-11457-4, AE1457, Sig). NAL.
Marc Dean, Mercenary, No. 6: Ready, Aim, Die. Peter Buck. Date not set. pap. 2.25 (ISBN 0-451-11619-4, Sig). NAL.
Marc Dean, Mercenary, No. 7: The Black Gold Briefing. Peter Buck. 224p. 1982. pap. 2.50 (ISBN 0-451-11824-3, Sig). NAL.
Marcaboth Women. 1st Ed. Vina Delmar. LC 51-13520. 1951. Harcourt, Brace.
Marcabrun: The Chronicle of a Foundling Who Spoke Evil of Women and of Love and Followed Unawed the Paths of Arrogance Until They Led to Madness: and of His Dealings with Women and of Ribald Words, the Which Brought Him Repute As a Great Rascal and As a Great Singer. Ramon Guthrie. LC 26-18502. George H. Doran Company.
Marcadia. Kay Ashby. 1974. (pbk.) 0.95. Dell.
Marceau Case. Harry Stephen Keeler. LC 36-7596. 1936. E. P. Dutton & Company, Inc.
Marcel Armand, a Romance of Old Louisiana: Being the Story of a Lieutenant of Jean Lafitte's Pirate Band and of Elbee Rochelle, a Lady of New Orleans, with Whom He Fell in Love and Thereby Acquired a Mortal Enemy. Sallie Lee Bell. LC 35-702775. L. C. Page & Company.
Marcel Levignet. Elwyn Alfred Barron. LC 6-36038. 1906. Duffield & Company.
Marcel Proust: An English Tribute. Scott-Moncrieff, Charles Kenneth. LC 73-1451. 1973. 15.00 (ISBN 0-8414-2318-0). Folcroft Library Editions.
Marcel Proust's Combray. Marcel Proust & Gabriel Seymour. LC 79-17314. 1979. 32.50 (ISBN 0-915998-04-1). Lime Rock Press.
Marcela: A Mexican Love Story. Mariano Azuela. LC 76-784. 1976. H. Fertig.
Marcela: A Mexican Love Story. Mariano Azuela. Tr. by Brenner, Anita. LC 32-24282. Farrar & Rinehart, Inc.
Marcella. Marilyn Coffey. LC 73-84082. 1973. 6.95 (ISBN 0-88327-028-5). Charterhouse.
Marcella. Mary Augusta Arnold Humphry Ward Ward. LC 3-21947. 1894. Macmillan and Co.
Marcella. Mary Augusta Arnold Humphry Ward Ward. LC 22-5162. (On cover: Macmillan's novalists' library, v. 1). 1895. Macmillan and Co.
Marcella Grace: An Irish Novel. Rosa Mulholland Gilbert. (Harper's handy series, no. 96). 1886. Harper & Brothers.
Marcelle the Mad. Seth Cook Comstock. LC 6-9276. 1906. D. Appleton and Company.
Marcello of the Quarter. Clive Holland. LC 2092. Frederick A. Stokes Company.
March. W. S. Kuniczak. LC 78-22598. 1979. 14.95 (ISBN 0-385-00204-1). Doubleday.
March Hare Murders. Morna Doris MacTaggart Brown. LC 49-11049. 1949. Published for the Crime Club by Doubleday.
March Hare Murders. E. X. Ferrars. 1971. pap. 0.75 o.p. (07176). Curtis.
March Hares. Harold Frederic. LC 72-84581. 1974. 11.50 (ISBN 0-403-02973-2). Scholarly Press.
March Hares. Harold Frederic. LC 3-2510. 1896. D. Appleton and Company.
March Hares see Collected Works.
March in the Ranks. Jessie Fothergill. LC 6-40015. (On cover: Lovell's international series, no. 56). 1889. F. F. Lovell & Company.
March-Man: A Novel. Keith Botsford. LC 64-13296. 1964. Viking Press.
March of the Hero. Richard Lee Marks. LC 52-12290. 1952. Appleton-Century-Crofts.
March of the Hundred. Manuel Komroff. LC 40-2196. 1939. Coward-McCann, Inc.
March of the White Guard. Gilbert Parker. LC 2-12963. 1901. R. F. Fenno & Co.
March of the White Guard. Gilbert Parker. LC 2-26751. 1902. R. F. Fenno & Company.
March of Truth: Twenty Historical Miniatures. Stephen Szabo. LC 44-8150. 1944. Wm. B. Eerdmans Publishing Co.
March on. George Madden Martin. LC 21-19576. 1921. D. Appleton and Company.
March the Ninth. Ray Coryton Hutchinson. LC 57-11474. 1957. Rinehart.
March to the Gallows. Mary Kelly. LC 65-22449. (Rinehart suspense novel). 1965. bds., 3.50. Holt.
March to the Monteria. B Traven. LC 74-163569. 1971. 5.95 (ISBN 0-8090-6748-X). Hill and Wang.
Marchand Woman. John Ives. 1981. pap. 2.75 (ISBN 0-425-04731-8). Berkley Pub.
Marchand Woman: A Novel. John Ives. LC 79-10399. 9.95 (ISBN 0-525-15285-7). Dutton.
Marchers of Valhalla. Robert E. Howard. LC 73-153531. (Illus.). 1972. 4.50. D. M. Grant.
Marchers of Valhalla. Robert E Howard. (Berkley Medallion Book). 1978. 1.95 (ISBN 0-425-03702-9). Berkley Pub. Corp.
Marchester Royal. Joseph Smith Fletcher. LC 27-10852. 1926. George H. Doran Company.
Marching Home. Donald Honig. LC 79-22771. 10.95 (ISBN 0-312-51443-3). St. Martin's Press.
Marching! Marching! Clara Weatherwax Strang. LC 74-22824. (Labor Movement in Fiction and Non-Fiction). 1976. 16.50 (ISBN 0-404-58483-7). AMS Press.
Marching! Marching! Clara Weatherwax Strang. LC 36-373. 1935. The John Day Company.
Marching! Marching! Clara Weatherwax. LC 36-373. The John Day Company.
Marching Men. Sherwood Anderson. LC 17-24200. 1917. John Lane Company.
Marching Men; a Critical Text. Sherwood Anderson. Ed. by Ray Lewis White. LC 73-149169. (His The major fiction of Sherwood Anderson). 1972. 9.95 (ISBN 0-8295-0216-5). Press of Case Western Reserve University.
Marching Morons: And Other Famous Science Fiction Stories. Cyril M Kornbluth. LC 59-100341. (Ballantine books, 303K). 1959. Ballantine Books.
Marching on. James Boyd. LC 27-11031. 1927. C. Scribner's Sons.
Marching on. Rachel Costelloe Strachey. LC 23-14911. Harcourt, Brace and Company.
Marching Orders. Olov Hartman. 1970. 4.50 o.p. (ISBN 0-8028-3385-3). Eerdmans.
Marching Orders. Ira Victor Morris. LC 38-295522. 1938. The Macmillan Company.
Marching Orders: A Novel. Olov Hartman. LC 73-103447. 1970. 4.50. Eerdmans.
Marching Sands. Harold Lamb. LC 73-13258. 1974. 9.50 (ISBN 0-88355-113-6) (ISBN 0-88355-113-6). Hyperion Press.
Marching Sands. Harold Lamb. LC 20-5227. 1920. D. Appleton and Company.
Marchington Inheritance. large print ed. Isabelle Holland. LC 81-5645. 439p. 1981. Repr. of 1979 ed. 12.95x (ISBN 0-89621-280-7). Thorndike Pr.
Marchington Inheritance: A Novel of Suspense. Isabelle Holland. LC 78-64802. 9.95 (ISBN 0-89256-084-3). Rawson, Wade Publishers.
Marchington Scandal. Jane Ashford. 1982. pap. 2.25 (ISBN 0-451-11623-2, AE1623, Sig). NAL.
Marchioness. James Broom Lynne. LC 69-15888. 1969. 4.95. Doubleday.
Marchioness: Or, A Marriage by Will. Octave Feuillet. (On cover: The echo series, no. 9). 1887. Pollard & Moss.
Marchwood. Iris Bromige. 1974. pap. 0.75 o.p. (26554-8-075). Beagle Bks.
Marcia: A Novel. Ellen Warner Olney Kirk. LC 7-9553. 1907. Houghton, Mifflin and Company.
Marcia: A Novel. William Edward Norris. LC 7-33291. (On cover: Harper's Franklin square library, no. 687). 1890. Harper & Brothers.
Marcia: A Novel. William Edward Norris. LC 7-33290. (Lovell's international series, no. 137). United States Book Company, Successors to J. W. Lovellcompany.
Marcia: Or, Cross Purposes. Mattie Dyer Britts. LC 13-17752. 1886. G.W. Ogilvie.
Marcia: Private Secretary. Zillah Katherine Macdonald. LC 49-1386. 1949. J. Messner.
Marcia Schuyler. Grace Livingston Hill. LC 8-5229. 1908. J. B. Lippincott Company.
Marcia, the Innocent. Katheryn Kimbrough, pseud. (The Saga of the Phenwick Women: No.12). 1977. pap. 1.75 (ISBN 0-445-00413-4). Popular Lib.

Marco: A Novel. Curtis Bill Pepper. LC 77-76997. 8.95 (ISBN 0-89256-027-4). Rawson Associates Publishers.
Marco Polo. Keith Miles & David Butler. 1982. pap. 3.50 (ISBN 0-440-15754-4). Dell.
Marco Polo, If You Can. William Frank Buckley. LC 81-43245. 1982. 13.95 (ISBN 0-385-15232-9). Doubleday.
Marco Polo, If You Can. large print ed. William Frank Buckley. LC 82-5470. 1982. 13.95 (ISBN 0-89621-361-7). Thorndike Press.
Marco the Magi's Production of Le Grand David & His Own Spectacular Magic Company: (A Stage Magic Extravaganza) Webster Bull et al. LC 81-51987. 112p. (Orig.). 1981. pap. write for info. (ISBN 0-940376-00-8). White Horse.
Marco Visconti. ed. de luxe ed. Tommaso Grossi. (Added t.-p.; The literature of Italy. 1265-1907. Ed. by Rossiter Johnson and Doran Knowiton Ranous). The National Alumni.
Marcore. Antonio Olavo Pereira. LC 75-111931. (Texas pan-American series). (Illus.). 1970. 6.50. University of Texas Press.
Marcus and Miriam: A Story of Jesus. Rebecca Ruter Springer. LC 8-346050. D. C. Cook Publishing Company.
Marcus Device. Ib Melchior. 288p. 1981. pap. 2.75 (ISBN 0-553-20030-5). Bantam.
Marcus Device: A Novel. Ib Melchior. LC 79-2654. 9.95 (ISBN 0-06-013038-5). Harper & Row.
Marcus Holbeach's Daughter. Alice Jones. LC 12-21279. 1912. 1.30. D. Appleton and Company.
Marcus Stratford's Charge: Or, Roy's Temptation. Evelyn Everett Green. LC 6-45549. Bradley & Woodruff.
Marcus Warland. Caroline Lee Whiting Hentz. Ed. by J. V. Ridgely. LC 76-93624. (American Fiction Ser). 1970. lib. bdg. 14.75 o.s.i. (ISBN 0-512-00303-3). Garrett Pr.
Marcus Warland: Or, The Long Moss Spring. by caroline lee hentz... ed. Caroline Lee Whiting Hentz. LC 7-4138. 1852. A. Hart.
Marcy Tarrant. Edith Engren, pseud. 1978. 1.95 (ISBN 0-449-13974-3). Fawcett Gold Medal Books.
Marden Fee. Gerald William Bullett. LC 31-13091. 1931. A. A. Knopf.
Mardi. Kathleen Hewitt. LC 32-25731. 1932. G. P. Putnam's Sons.
Mardi. Herman Melville. Ed. by Tyrus Hillway. (Masterworks of Literature Ser). 1973. 11.00x (ISBN 0-8084-0016-9); pap. 4.95x o.s.i. (ISBN 0-8084-0017-7, M37). Coll & U Pr.
Mardi. Herman Melville. Ed. by Nathalia Wright. (Complete Works of Herman Melville). 1983. 15.00 (ISBN 0-87532-015-5). Hendricks House.
Mardi and a Voyage Thither. Herman Melville. LC 67-21602. (Writings of Herman Melville, v. 3). (Illus.). 1970. (ISBN 0-8101-0015-0). Northwestern University Press.
Mardi, and a Voyage Thither. Herman Melville. LC 23-11040. The St. Botolph Society.
Mardi Gras: A Tale of Ante Bellum Times. James Curtis Waldo. LC 7-16047. 1871. P. F. Gogarty.
Mardi Gras Madness. Davis Dresser. LC 34-23279. W. Goodwin, Inc.
Mardi Gras Massacre. Lionel Derrick. (Penetrator,#5). 1974. (pbk.) 0.95 (ISBN 0-523-00378-1). Pinnacle Books.
Mardi Gras Murders. Gwen Bristow & Manning, Bruce, Pseud., Joint Author. LC 33-24123. 1932. The Mystery League.
Mardi Gras Mystery. Henry Bedford-Jones. LC 21-10334. 1921. Doubleday, Page & Company.
Mardios Beack: A Novel. Oakley M Hall. 1955. Viking Press.
Mare Nostrum (Our Sea) A Novel. Vicente Blasco Ibanez & Jordan, Mrs. Charlotte Brewster, Tr. LC 19-129822. 1919. E. P. Dutton & Company.
Mareca-Maria. Sophie Kerr. LC 29-26269. 1929. Doubleday, Doran & Company, Inc.
Mare's Nest. Paul Griffith. LC 50-9699. 1950. Macmillan.
Mare's Nest: A Mystery. Carlyn Coffin. LC 41-14660. Farrar & Rinehart, Inc.
Mare's Tales. Ruth B. Wells. 3.50 o.s.i. (ISBN 0-8181-0093-1). Pageant-Poseidon.
Marfe: A Story of the Opium Smugglers of the St. Clair River. Hulda Theodate St. Bernard Hollands. LC 7-6029. 1889.
Marga. Mark Dunster. (Rin Ser.: Pt. 4). 61p. (Orig.). 1982. pap. 4.00 (ISBN 0-89642-086-8). Linden Pubs.
Margaret. illus. by michael martchenko. ed. Dorothy Jane Goulding. LC 66-20907. 1966. McGraw-Hill.
Margaret. Henry Rider Haggard. LC 7-32845. 1907. Longmans, Green, and Co.
Margaret. Sylvester Judd. LC 68-57536. (Muckrakers Ser.). Repr. of 1845 ed. lib. bdg. 15.00 (ISBN 0-8398-0959-X). Irvington.
Margaret. Raymond Joseph Martinez. 76p. pap. 1.75 (ISBN 0-911116-88-5). Pelican.
Margaret. Caroline Beach Slade. LC 46-3697. 1946. The Vanguard Press.
Margaret: A Story of the Life in a Prairie Home. 5th thousand. ed. Reginald Hughes. LC 7-54243. 1868. C. Scribner & Co.
Margaret. A Tale of the Real and Ideal, Blight and Bloom; Including Sketches of a Place Not Before Described, Called Mons Christi... Sylvester Judd. LC 7-3525. 1845. Jordan and Wiley.
Margaret: A Tale of the Real and the Ideal, Blight and Bloom. Sylvester Judd. LC 68-57536. (American novels of muckraking, propaganda, and social protest). 1968. Gregg Press.
Margaret: A Tale of the Real and the Ideal, Blight and Bloom; Including Sketches of a Place Not Before Described, Called Mons Christi... Rev. Ed.... Sylvester Judd. LC 3-22366. 1851. Phillips, Sampson, and Company.
Margaret: A Tale of the Real and the Ideal, Blight and Bloom; Including Sketches of a Place Not Before Described, Called Mons Christi... Rev. Ed.... Sylvester Judd. LC 3-223676. 1857. Phillips, Sampson and Company.
Margaret and Her Bridesmaids. Julia Cecilia Stretton. (Lovell's library, v.2, no. 66). 1883. J. W. Lovell Company.
Margaret and I. Wilhelm, Kate. LC 70-154951. 1972. (345-02660-8) 1.25. Ballantine Books.
Margaret and I. Kate Wilhelm. 1978. 1.75 (ISBN 0-671-81449-4). Pocket Books.
Margaret Armstrong's Charity. LC 25-81359. Melrose Publishing Co.
Margaret Arnold's Christmas, and Other Stories. Mary Dow Northam Brine. LC 6-182533. 1894. E. P. Dutton & Company.
Margaret Ballentine: Or, The Fall of the Alamo; a Romance of the Texas Revolution. Frank Templeton. LC 7-9559. 1907. State Printing Company.
Margaret Bowlby: A Love Story. Edgar La Verne Vincent. LC 2-13396. 1902. Lothrop Publishing Company.
Margaret Brent, Adventurer: A Novel. Dorothy Fremont Grant. LC 44-8361. 1944. Longmans, Green and Co.
Margaret Byng. Francis Charles Philips. LC 7-36069. (On cover: Lovell's international series, no. 114). J. W. Lovell Company.
Margaret Hamilton. A Novel. Emma Barry Newby. LC 7-26117. (On cover: Turners' select novels, no. 7). Turner Brothers & Co.
Margaret Howth. Rebecca Harding Davis. LC 77-104437. Repr. of 1862 ed. lib. bdg. 14.50 (ISBN 0-8398-0353-2). Irvington.
Margaret Ives. Eli Barber. LC 15-255069. 1.35. The Gorham Press; Etc., Etc.
Margaret Maliphant: A Novel. Alice Vanbittart Strettel Carr. LC 6-24227. (On cover: Harper's Franklin square library, no. 655). 1889. Harper & Brothers.
Margaret Moncrieffe; the First Love of Aaron Burr. A Romance of the Revolution. With an Appendix Containing the Letters of Colonel Burr to "Kate" and "Eliza," and from "Leonora," Etc., Etc. Charles Burdett. 1860. Derby & Jackson.
Margaret Normanby. Josephine Edgar, pseud. LC 82-17052. 448p. 1983. 13.95 (ISBN 0-312-51444-1). St Martin.
Margaret Normanby. Mary Howard, pseud. LC 82-17052. 1983. 13.95 (ISBN 0-312-51444-1). St. Martin's Press.
Margaret: Or, The Pearl. 3d american ed. Charles Benjamin Tayler. LC 8-20126. (On cover: C. B. Taylers works). 1851. Stanford and Swords.
Margaret: Or, Was It Magnetism! Gilbert Guest. LC 20-227953. 1920. Burkley Printing Company.
Margaret Perceval; The Experience of Life. Elizabeth Missing Sewell. LC 75-472. (Victorian Fiction: Novels of Faith and Doubt). 1977. 40.00. Garland Pub.
Margaret Percival. By the Author of "Amy Herbert," Gertrude," "Laneton Parsonage," &C. Elizabeth Missing Sewell & Sewell, William, 1804-1874, Ed. LC 8-11250. 1847. D. Appleton & Company.
Margaret Percival, 1847. Elizabeth Missing Sewell. Bd. with Experience of Life; or, Aunt Sarah, 1852. (Victorian Fiction Ser). 1975. lib. bdg. 66.00 o.s.i. (ISBN 0-8240-1550-9). Garland Pub.
Margaret Steyne. A Romance of the New Virginia. 2d ed. Martha Frye Boggs. LC 99-5583. (Dillingham's metropolitan library, no. 56). 1899. G. W. Dillingham Co.
Margaret, the Faithful. Katheryn Kimbrough. (Saga of the Phenwick women,#3). 1975. (pbk.) 1.25. Popular Library.
Margaret, the Pearl of Navarre. A Narrative Compiled from Authentic Sources... Sarah Towne Martyn. LC 7-17814. American Tract Society.
Margaret Tudor: A Romance of Old St. Augustine. Annie T Colcock. LC 2-11613. Frederick A. Stokes Company.
Margaret Vincent: A Novel. Lucy Lane Clifford. LC 2-11890. 1902. Harper & Brothers.
Margaret Warrener. Alice Brown. LC 1-26207. 1901. Houghton, Mifflin and Company.
Margaret Yorke. Kathleen Thompson Norris. LC 30-17710. 1930. Doubleday, Doran & Company, Inc.
Margarethe: A Tale of the Sixteenth Century. Emma Leslie. LC 11-16141. 1879. Philips & Hunt.
Margarethe: Or, Life Problems; a Romance from the German of E. Juncker Pseud. Else Kobert Schmieden. Tr. by Wister, Annis Lee (Furness) LC 12-12215. 1878. J. B. Lippincott & Co.
Margarethe: Or, Life-Problems; a Romance from the German of E. Juncker Pseud. Else Kobert Schmieden. Tr. by Wister, Annis Lee (Furness) 1906. J. B. Lippincott Company.
Margaret's Bridal. Founded on Fact. 1st Thousand. Lucius Manlius Sargent. LC 8-1820. (On cover: Temperance tales, v. 7, no. 20). 1839. Whipple & Damrell.
Margaret's Influence: A Secret of the Confessional. Peter Geiermann. LC 10-107018. 1910. 1.00. B. Herder.
Margaret's Mead. Jane Harding. LC 21-19481. 1921. Doubleday, Page & Company.
Margaret's Plighted Troth. Linda Thayer Guilford. LC 1439. 1899. W. M. Bayne Printing Company.
Margaret's Story. Eugenia Price. LC 80-7870. 416p. 1980. 12.95i (ISBN 0-690-01939-4). Har-Row.
Margaret's Story. Eugenia Price. 432p. 1982. pap. 3.50 (ISBN 0-553-22583-9). Bantam.
Margaret's Story: A Novel. Eugenia Price. LC 80-7870. 12.95 (ISBN 0-690-01939-4). Lippincott & Crowell.
Margarita. Joan Wolf. 1982. pap. 2.25 (ISBN 0-451-11556-2, AE1556, Sig). NAL.
Margarita: A Legend of the Fight for the Great River. Elizabeth Williams Champney. LC 2-20466. (Her Dames and daughters of colonial days, v. 4). 1902. Dodd, Mead & Company.
Margarita's Soul: The Romantic Recollections of a Man of Fifty. Josephine Dodge Daskam Bacon. LC 9-36806. 1909. 1.50. J. Lane Company; Etc., Etc.
Margery Allingham Omnibus. Margery Allingham. Incl. Mystery Mile; Crime at Black Dudley; Look to the Lady. 592p. 1983. pap. 7.95 (ISBN 0-14-006058-8). Penguin.
Margery: By E. F. Benson. Edward Frederic Benson. LC 10-18882. 1910. 1.20. Doubleday, Page & Company.
Margery Daw. A Novel. Effie Adelaide Marie Albanesi. (On cover: The seaside library. Pocket ed. no. 755). 1886. G. Munro.
Margery (Gred) A Tale of Old Nuremberg. authorized ed., rev. and corr. in the united states. ed. Georg Moritz Ebers. Tr. by Clara Courtenay Bell. LC 43-260072. 1889. W. S. Gottsberger & Co.
Margery Morris in the Pine Woods. Violet Gordon Gray. LC 21-21142. 1921. The Penn Publishing Company.
Margery of Quether: And Other Stories. Sabine Baring-Gould. LC 6-7230. J. W. Lovell Company.
Margeurite Tanner. Beth Michel. 304p. (Orig.). 1982. pap. 2.95 (ISBN 0-8439-1037-2, Leisure Bks). Nordon Pubns.
Margey Wins the Game. John Van Alstyne Weaver. LC 22-10015. 1922. A. A. Knopf.
Margherita. Leon Kelley. LC 27-18259. 1927. G. P. Putnam's Sons.
Margie. E. V. Cunningham, pseud. 1966. 4.95 o.p. Morrow.
Margie: A Novel, by E. V. Cunningham. Howard Melvin Fast. LC 66-234619. 1966. bds., 4.95. Morrow.
Margie's Mistake, and Other Stories. Mary F. Strong. 1891. W. B. Conkey Company, Printers.
Margin. Pieyre De Mandiargues, Andre. LC 68-58146. 1969. 5.95. Grove Press.
Margin. John Dick Scott. LC 50-9177. 1950. Knopf.
Margin for Doubt. Miriam Borgenicht. LC 68-11762. 1968. Published for the Crime Club by Doubleday.
Margin of Error. Paul Henissart. LC 79-22864. 10.95 (ISBN 0-671-24029-3). Simon and Schuster.
Margin of Error. 1st Ed. Mary Borden. LC 54-10863. 1954. Longmans, Green.
Margin of Terror. William P McGivern. LC 53-124234. (Red badge detective). 1953. Dodd, Mead.
Marginal Land: A Novel. Horace Kramer. LC 39-5470. J. B. Lippincott Company.
Marginalia. Edgar Allan Poe. LC 80-22585. 235p. 1981. 11.95x (ISBN 0-8139-0812-4). U Pr of Va.
Margins. David Kranes. LC 72-2240. 1972. 6.95 (ISBN 0-394-47920-3). Knopf.
Margit Visconti: A Novel. Keith Clarke. LC 77-361175. 1976. 4.75 (ISBN 0-575-02150-0). Gollancz.
Margo Mystery. Jerry B Jenkins. LC 81-460. Moody Press.
Margoleen. Poca T. Smith. LC 8-9623. 1897. W. P. Titus, Printer.
Margot. Sidney Pickering. LC 7-35915. 1897. G. P. Putnam's Sons.
Margot la Ravaudeuse see Amorous Adventures of Margot.
Margot's Progress. Douglas Goldring. LC 20-9785. 1920. T. Seltzer.
Margret Howth: A Story of to-Day. Rebecca Harding Davis. LC 6-32467. 1862. Ticknor and Fields.
Marguerite: A Novel. Mathilde Georgina Elisabeth De Peyrebrune. LC 7-30575. Belford Company.
Marguerite De la Roque: A Story of Survival. Elizabeth Boyer. LC 75-20805. (Illus.). 9.95 (ISBN 0-915964-01-5). Veritie Press.
Marguerite De Valois. Alexandre Dumas & Maquet, Auguste. LC 1-515. 1889. Little, Brown and Company.
Marguerite De Valois. Alexandre Dumas & Maquet, Auguste. LC 1-516. (Half-title: The romances of Alexandre Dumas. Illustrated library edition. v. 6- 7). 1893. Little, Brown and Company.
Marguerite De Valois. Alexandre Dumas & Maquet, Auguste. LC 8-26658. 1894. Little, Brown, and Company.
Marguerite De Valois. Alexandre Dumas & Maquet, Auguste. LC 4-17496. 1899. Little, Brown, & Company.
Marguerite De Valois. Alexandre Dumas & Maquet, Auguste. T. Y. Crowell & Company.
Marguerite De Valois: An Historical Romance. new ed. Alexandre Dumas & Maquet, Auguste. LC 1-512. 1857. G. Routledge & Co.
Marguerite De Valois: An Historical Romance. Alexandre Dumas & Auguste Maquet. LC 3-27807. G. Routledge and Sons, Limited.
Marguerite De Valois: An Historical Romance. Alexandre Dumas & Maquet, Auguste. LC 1-514. (Seaside library, v. 79, no. 1592). G. Munro.
Marguerite; or, A Wild Flower. Rose Anna Leigh. LC 7-13150. The Showalter-Lincoln Co.
Marguerite Reilly. Inez Madge. LC 47-1819. 1947. Pilot Press.
Maria. Brian Cooper. LC 56-5031. Vanguard Press.
Maria. Betsey Riddle Hutton Zum Stolzenberg. LC 14-12073. 1914. 1.35. D. Appleton and Company.
Maria. Edward Kimber. LC 74-16057. (Flowering of the Novel). 1974. (ISBN 0-8240-1171-6). Garland Pub.
Maria. John C Neff. LC 51-13025. 1951. Washburn.
Maria. Eugenia Price. LC 77-1707. 10.00 (ISBN 0-397-01058-3). Lippincott.
Maria: A Romance of Santa Clara County, California, During the Days of Early Spanish Settlement. Josephine H Patton. Printed by Lederer, Street and Zeus Co., Inc.
Maria: A South American Romance. Jorge Isaacs. Tr. by Rollo Ogden. LC 75-44122. 1976. H. Fertig.
Maria: A South American Romance. Jorge Isaacs. Tr. by Rollo Ogden. 1890. Harper & Brothers.
Maria: A South American Romance. Jorge Isaacs. Tr. by Rollo Ogden. LC 25-2772. Harper & Brothers.
Maria: A South American Romance. Jorge Isaacs. Tr. by Rollo Ogden. LC 81-6951. (Latin American Literature Series). 1981. 79.95 (ISBN 0-8490-2208-8). Gordon Press.
Maria: A Tale of the Northeast Coast and of the North Atlantic. Curtis Bok. LC 62-15481. 1962. Knopf; Distributed by Random House.
Maria Again. Anna Eichberg Lane. LC 15-18429. 1915. 1.00. John Lane.
Maria and the Captain. Isabel Dunn. LC 51-3597. 1951. Bobbs-Merrill.
Maria Canossa. Sandra Paretti. LC 80-28926. 11.95 (ISBN 0-312-51449-2). St. Martin's Press.
Maria Capponi. Rene Schickele & Waller, Hannah, Tr. LC 28-6082. 1928. A. A. Knopf.
Maria Chapdelaine. Louis Hemon & Blake, W. H., Tr. LC 29-2132. (modern readers' series)). 1929. The Macmillan Company.
Maria Chapdelaine: A Tale of the Lake St. John Country. Louis Hemon & Blake, W. H., Tr. LC 24-282237. 1924. The Macmillan Company.
Maria Chapdelaine: A Tale of the Lake St. John Country. Louis Hemon & Blake, W. H., Tr. LC 34-40100. (Half title: The modern library of the world's best books). The Modern Library.
Maria Chapdelaine: A Tale of the Lake St. John Country. Translated by W. H. Blake. Louis Hemon. LC 56-461519. (Image books, D40). 1956. Image Books.
Maria De Guadalupe. 1st Ed. Kenneth R Campbell. LC 54-12877. 1954. Pageant Press.

Maria Fernanda. Perez De la Ossa, Huberto. Tr. by Peers, Edgar Allison. LC 31-25569. 1931. Little, Brown, and Company.
Maria: Or, The Wrongs of Woman. Mary Wollstonecraft. LC 74-30341. (Norton library, N761). 1975. 6.95 (ISBN 0-393-08713-1) (ISBN 0-393-00761-8). Norton.
Maria Paluna: A Novel. Blair Niles. LC 34-12173. 1934. Longmans, Green and Co.
Mariam: A Romance of Persia. Samuel Graham Wilson. LC 6-33572. American Tract Society.
Mariam: Or, Twenty-One Days. Horace Victor. 1891. Macmillan and Co.
Mariamne. Glen Petrie. LC 76-30604. 1977. 9.95 (ISBN 0-698-10769-1). Coward, McCann & Geoghegan.
Mariam'ne of the Cedars. Ida Helen McCarty. LC 11-31137. 1911. The Shakespeare Press.
Marian: A Story of the South. Mary A Palmer. LC 17-24706. 1917. The Neale Publishing Company.
Marian Elwood: Or, How Girls Live. Sarah M. Brownson. LC 6-17216. 1859. E. Dunigan & Brother.
Marian Elwood: Or, How Girls Live. A Tale. Sarah M Brownson. LC 6-17215. D. & J. Sadlier & Co.
Marian Grey. Mary Jane Hawes Holmes. LC 51-54798. J. H. Sears.
Marian Grey; or The Heiress of Redstone Hall. Mary Jane Hawes Holmes. LC 32-335924. 1863. Carleton.
Marian Grey; or, The Heiress of Redstone Hall. Mary Jane Hawes Holmes. LC 12-25952. G. W. Dillingham.
Marian Grey; or, The Heiress of Redstone Hall. Mary Jane Hawes Holmes. LC 99-279. 1899. G. W. Dillingham Co.
Marian Wallace; or, Life's Changes. A Tale of Truth. Rosa Scott. 1858. Derby and Jackson.
Mariana. Karen S. Dean. 176p. (YA) 1981. pap. 1.95 (ISBN 0-380-78345-2, 78345, Flare). Avon.
Mariana. Sally Salminen & Munsey, June Barrows, 1910- Tr. LC 40-27352. Toronto, Farrar & Rinehart, Inc.
Marianela. Benito Perez Galdos. Tr. by Bell, Clara. LC 7-36352. 1883. W. S. Gottsberger.
Marianela. Benito Perez Galdos. 1951. pap. 3.50 o.p. (ISBN 0-536-00418-8). Xerox College.
Marianela: A Story of Spanish Love. Helen W. Lester. Tr. by B. Perez Galdos. 1979. Repr. of 1892 ed. lib. bdg. 20.00 (ISBN 0-8495-2006-1). Arden Lib.
Marianela: A Story of Spanish Love. Galdos Benito Perez & Lester, Helen W., Tr. LC 23-17382. (Students' literal translations). 1923. The Translation Publishing Company, Inc.
Marianela: A Story of Spanish Love. Perez Galdos, Benito. LC 75-4621. 1975. H. Fertig.
Marianela: A Story of Spanish Love. Benito Perez Galdos. Tr. by Lester, Helen W. (On cover: Tales from foreign lands. v. 5). 1892. A. C. McClurg and Company.
Marianela: A Story of Spanish Love. Benito Perez Galdos. Tr. by Lester, Helen W. LC 23-173825. (students' literal translations). The Translation Publishing Company, Inc.
Marianela: A Story of Spanish Love. Benito Perez Galdos. Tr. by Helen W. Lester. 1960. pap. 1.50 o.p. (ISBN 0-389-02805-3, TPS16). B&N.
Marianna. Gleb Botkin. LC 31-24148. 1931. Longmans, Green and Co.
Marianne. Juliette Benzoni. LC 73-98945. 1970. 6.95. Putnam.
Marianne and the Crown of Fire. Juliette Benzoni. LC 76-10732. 1976. 7.95 (ISBN 0-399-11798-9). Putnam.
Marianne and the Lords of the East. Juliette Benzoni. LC 75-24594. 1975. 7.95 (ISBN 0-399-11578-1). Putnam.
Marianne and the Privateer. Juliette Benzoni. LC 72-84745. (Berkley medallion book). 1975. (pbk.) 1.50 (ISBN 0-425-02795-3). Berkley Pub. Co.
Marianne and the Rebels. Juliette Benzoni. LC 73-87176. 1974. 7.95 (ISBN 0-399-11194-8). Putnam.
Marianne in India: And Seven Other Tales. Lion Feuchtwanger & Creighton, Basil, Tr. LC 35-2974. 1935. The Viking Press.
Marianne. 1st American Ed. Rhys Davies. LC 52-5123. 1952. Doubleday.
Maridu. Sharon Wagner. 1970. pap. 0.75 o.p. (ISBN 0-447-74715-0). Lancer.
Maridu see Curse of Still Valley.
Marie. Henry Rider Haggard. LC 12-3795. 1912. Cassell and Company, Ltd.
Marie--of Circle-A: A Story of the Black Hills Country. Roy A Palmer. LC 28-250240. Meador Publishing Company.
Marie: A Book of Love. Peter Nansen. Tr. by Le Gallienne, Julia (Norregard) LC 25-8785. 1924. J. W. Luce and Company.
Marie; a Story of Russian Love. From the Russian of Alexander Pushkin. Aleksandr Sergeevich Pushkin. Tr. by Zielinska, Marie H. De. LC 8-580. 1877. Jansen, McClurg & Co.
Marie. A Story of the Morgue and Catacombs of Paris. By Lillian Herbert Andrews... Lillian Herbert Andrews. LC 6-2459. (On cover: Once a week library, v. 10, no. 24). 1893. P. F. Collier.
Marie: An Episode in the Life of the Late Allan Quatermain. Henry Rider Haggard. 1912. Longmans, Green, and Co.
Marie Antoinette, a Novel. Frank Wilson Kenyon. LC 56-5696. Crowell.
Marie Antoinette, a Novel. Frank Wilson Kenyon. LC 56-5696. Crowell.
Marie Antoinette and Her Son. Klara Muller Mundt. Tr. by Gage, William Leonard. LC 16-1241. (historical romances of Louisa Muhlbach pseud.). D. Appleton and Company.
Marie Antoinette and Her Son. An Historical Novel. Klara Muller Mundt. Tr. by Gage, William Leonard. LC 7-25469. 1867. D. Appleton and Company.
Marie Antoinette's Daughter. Alice Curtis Desmond. (Illus.). 1967. Dodd, Mead.
Marie Arnaud, Syp. Fielding Hope. LC 34-1826. The Macaulay Company.
Marie Beginning. Alfred Grossman. LC 65-14004. 1965. 4.50. Doubleday.
Marie Blithe. Howard Frank Mosher. LC 82-17428. 1983. 17.75 (ISBN 0-670-45705-1). Viking Press.
Marie Blythe. Howard Frank Mosher. 384p. 1983. 17.75 (ISBN 0-670-45705-1). Viking Pr.
Marie Bonifas. Jacques De Lacretelle. Tr. by Whale, Winifred (Stephens) LC 28-2244. 1927. G. P. Putnam's Sons, Ltd.
Marie-Claire. Marguerite Audoux. Tr. by Raphael, John N. LC 11-1929. Hodder & Stoughton Etc.
Marie Claire's Workshop. Marguerite Audoux. Tr. by Flint, F. S. LC 21-759. 1920. T. Seltzer.
Marie Fredericka. Marie Schmeiser. (Illus.). 1974. 3.50. Exposition Press.
Marie Grubbe. Jens Peter Jacobsen. Tr. by H. A. Larsen. 1917. 4.00 o.p. (ISBN 0-89067-001-3). Am-Scandinavian.
Marie Grubbe: A Lady of the Seventeenth Century. Jens Peter Jacobsen. LC 65-29428. (Scandinavian Classics, V. 7). 1962. American-Scandinavian Foundation.
Marie Grubbe, a Lady of the Seventeenth Century. 2d ed. Jens Peter Jacobsen. LC 75-330359. (Library of Scandinavian Literature; V. 30). 7.95 (ISBN 0-89067-053-6). Twayne Publishers.
Marie Grubbe: A Lady of the Seventeenth Century. Jens Peter Jacobsen. Tr. by Larsen, Hanna Astrup. LC 18-268. (Half-title: Scandinavian classics, vol. vii). 1917. The American-Scandinavian Foundation; Etc., Etc.
Marie Grubbe: A Lady of the Seventeenth Century. Jens Peter Jacobsen. Tr. by Larsen, Hanna Astrup. LC 25-279648. 1925. A. A. Knopf.
Marie Halkett. Robert William Chambers. LC 37-170867. 1937. D. Appleton-Century Company, Incorporated.
Marie, Island in Revolt. Robert Gaillard. 1974. (pbk.) 0.95. Avon.
Marie Laveau. Francine Prose. LC 76-28693. 8.95 (ISBN 0-399-11873-X). Berkley Pub. Corp.: Distributed by Putnam.
Marie of Arcady. F. Hewes Lancaster. 1909. 1.25. Small. Maynard & Company.
Marie of Circle-A: A Story of the Black Hills Country. 2d ed.... ed. Roy A Palmer. LC 30-18307. 1930. Meador Publishing Company.
Marie of the House D'Anters. Michael Earls. LC 16-8463. 1916. Benziger Brothers.
Marie of the Isles: Translated from the French by Merle Severy. Robert Gaillard. LC 53-5896. 1953. A. A. Wyn.
Marie: Or, Fort Beauharnois; and Historic Tale of Early Days in the Northwest, by E. G. L. E G Lindsey. A. C. Bausman.
Marie-Rose: Or, The Mystery. Fortune Du Boisgobey & Kendall, Laura E., Tr. (Seaside library, v. 79, no. 1602). G. Munro.
Marie Therese: Memoirs of a Prostitute. Marie Therese Cointre. LC 66-4359. 1966. Brussel & Brussel.
Mariella: Of Out-West. Ella Rhoads Higginson. LC 2-256049. 1902. The Macmillan Company.
Marielle. Ena Halliday. (Orig.). 1982. pap. 2.50 (ISBN 0-671-45962-7). PB.
Marienbad. Sholom Aleichem. Tr. by Aliza Shevin. 192p. 1982. 13.95 (ISBN 0-399-12732-1). Putnam Pub Group.
Marienbad. Sholem Aleichem. LC 82-5314. 14.95 (ISBN 0-399-12733-X). Putnam.
Marie's Mistake. A Woman's History. Agnese M. C Massena. LC 7-17811. 1868. Pratt Brothers.
Maries's Story. A Tale of the Days of Louis XIV. Mary Ellen Bamford. LC 6-62941. Congregational Sunday-School and Publishing Society.
Marietta. Anne Green. LC 32-26057. 1932. E. P. Dutton & Co., Inc.
Marietta: A Maid of Venice. Francis Marion Crawford. LC 1-25434. 1901. The Macmillan Company; London, Macmillan & Co., Ltd.
Marietta's Marriage. William Edward Norris. LC 7-33288. (Half-title: Appletons' town and country library, no. 218). 1897. D. Appleton and Company.
Mariflor. Espina De Serna, Concha & Douglas. Frances. 1870- Tr. LC 24-8371. 1924. The Macmillan Company.
Marigold. Jennie Maria Drinkwater Conklin. LC 6-30405. R. Carter & Brothers.
Marigold. Grace Livingston Hill. LC 61-66509. 1961. Grosset & Dunlap.
Marigold. Grace Livingston Hill. LC 38-5676. J. B. Lippincott Company.
Marigold Field. Diane Pearson. LC 78-77863. 1969. 6.50. Lippincott.
Marigold Mornings. Dorothy Evslin. LC 75-45856. 222p. 1976. 6.95 o.p. (ISBN 0-915684-02-0). Christian Herald.
Marihuana Myths & Realities. J. L. Simmons et al. (Orig.). pap. 1.75 o.p. (3076). Brandon.
Marijuana Double-Take. 2nd ed. Uri Dowbenko. 64p. (Orig.). 1982. pap. 3.95. Sirius Pubns.
Marijuana Mystery. Mary Sturdivant Stimson. LC 40-11564. Dorrance and Company.
Marika. Darwin Porter. LC 77-79538. 8.95 (ISBN 0-87795-175-6). Arbor House.
Marika. Darwin Porter. 1979. 2.50 (ISBN 0-425-04262-6). Berkley Publishing Corp.
Marilee. Con Sellers. (Kangaroo Book). 1978. 1.95 (ISBN 0-671-81211-4). Pocket Books.
Marilee: Three Stories. Elizabeth Spencer. LC 81-7444. 1981. 30.00 (ISBN 0-87805-140-6) (ISBN 0-87805-141-4). University Press of Mississippi.
Marilyn the Wild. Jerome Charyn. LC 75-31072. 1976. 8.95 (ISBN 0-87795-129-2). Arbor Hse.
Marilyn the Wild. Jerome Charyn. 208p. 1981. pap. 2.95 (ISBN 0-380-00964-1, 54536, Bard). Avon.
Marilyn the Wild: A Novel. Jerome Charyn. LC 76-31072. 8.95 (ISBN 0-87795-129-2). Arbor House.
Marilyn the Wild: A Novel. Jerome Charyn. 1977. 1.75 (ISBN 0-380-00964-1). Avon Books.
Marina. Robert Svensson. (Orig.). 1979. pap. 1.95 (ISBN 0-532-23162-7). Woodhill.
Marina Mystery. Constance Leonard. LC 80-2781. 7.95 (ISBN 0-396-07930-X). Dodd, Mead.
Marina Tower: A Novel. Charles Beardsley. 1978. 1.95 (ISBN 0-445-04198-6). Popular Library.
Marine. Winston Graham. 1979. 2.50 (ISBN 0-671-82190-3). Pocket Books.
Mariner's End. Elaine Booth Selig. (Kangaroo Book)). 1977. 1.50 (ISBN 0-671-81038-3). Pocket Books.
Mariners' Prison: A Novel. Michel Mohrt. LC 63-8857. 1963. Viking Press.
Marines! Robert Leckie. LC 60-128091. (Bantam book, A2171-1). 1960. Bantam Books.
Marines and Others. John William Thomason. LC 29-23888. 1929. C. Scribner's Sons.
Mario and the Magician: Translated from the German. Thomas Mann. Tr. by Helen Tracy Lowe. LC 31-1716. 1931. A. A. Knopf.
Marion: A Story. Florence Taylor Haselden. LC 8-37357. Broadway Publishing Company.
Marion Alive. Vicki Baum. LC 42-30020. 1942. Doubleday, Doran and Company, Inc.
Marion Berkley: A Story for Girls. Elizabeth Barker Comins. LC 6-30378. 1870. Loring.
Marion Darche. A Story Without Comment. Francis Marion Crawford. LC 6-30890. 1893. Macmillan and Co.
Marion Fay. reprint ed. / introduction by andrew wright. ed. Anthony Trollope. LC 80-1902. (Trollope, Anthony, 1815-1882. Selections. 1981). 1981. 90.00 (ISBN 0-405-14191-2). Arno Press.
Marion Fay: A Novel. Anthony Trollope & R. H Super. LC 82-7036. 25.00 (ISBN 0-472-10023-8). University of Michigan Press.
Marion Graham: Or, "Higher Than Happiness.". Margaret Oliver Woods Lawrence. 1861. Crosby, Nichols, Lee and Company.
Marion Graham: Or, "Higher Than Happiness,". Margaret Oliver Woods Lawrence. LC 7-13232. 1890. Lee and Shepard.
Marion Harvie: A Tale of Persecution in the Seventeenth Century. Martha Finley. LC 7-12337. Presbyterian Board of Publication.
Marion Howard: Or Trials and Triumphs. F S D Ames. LC 5-42975. 1872. P. F. Cunningham.
Marion Isle. Henry Rider Haggard. LC 29-11679. 1929. Doubleday, Doran & Company, Inc.
Marion Manning: A Novel. Edith Livingston Morton Eustis. LC 2-14430. 1902. Harper & Brothers.
Marion: Or, The Dawning Light. Mary S Rowley. LC 8-941292. 1888. Printed by J. B. Lippincott Company.
Marion: The Story of an Artist's Model. Winnifred Eaton Babcock & Bosse, Sara. 1.35. W. J. Watt & Company.
Marionette. Pamela Bennetts. LC 79-8445. 8.95 (ISBN 0-312-51524-3). St. Martin's Press.
Marionette. Pamela Bennetts. LC 80-17834. 1980. 11.95 (ISBN 0-8161-3113-9). G. K. Hall.
Marionette. Louis Arthur Cunningham. LC 41-341836. The Penn Publishing Company.
Marionette. Margaret James. (General Ser.). 1980. lib. bdg. 11.95 (ISBN 0-8161-3113-9, Large Print Bks). G K Hall.
Marionette. Margaret James. 1980. 8.95 (ISBN 0-312-51524-3). St Martin.
Marionettes. Julie Grinnell Storrow Cruger. LC 6-31584. Cassell Publishing Company.
Marion's Brigade: Or, The Light Dragoons. A Tale of the Revolution. John Hovey Robinson. LC 7-42161. 1852. F. Gleason's Publishing Hall.
Marion's Faith. Charles King. LC 12-23270. 1887. J. B. Lippincott Company.
Marion's Faith. Charles King. LC 3-22371. 1893. J. B. Lippincott Company.
Marion's Men: A Romance of the Revolution. LC 10-3731. 1843. A. J. Rockafellar.
Marion's Wall: A Novel. Jack Finney. LC 72-89251. 1973. 6.95 (ISBN 0-671-21467-5). Simon and Schuster.
Marion's Wall: A Novel. Jack Finney. LC 12-85291. 1974. (pbk.) 1.25. Warner Paperback Library.
Mariposa. Henry Philip Bernard Baerlein. LC 24-23482. Boni and Liveright.
Mariposa. Phyllis G. Leonard. 416p. (Orig.). 1983. pap. 3.95 (ISBN 0-440-16071-5). Dell.
Mariposa Gold. Albert Butler. (Avalon Books). 4.95. Thomas Bouregy.
Mariposilla: A Novel. Mary Stewart Daggett. LC 6-32225. 1895. Rand, McNally & Company.
Mariquita: A Novel. Francis Browning Drew Bickerstaffe-Drew. LC 22-14351. 1922. Benziger Brothers.
Maris. Grace Livingston Hill. LC 38-295376. J. B. Lippincott Company.
Maris: A Novel. Michael De Capite. LC 42-508524. The John Day Company.
Maris Stella. Marie Clothilde Balfour. LC 6-632324. (On cover: The keynotes series, no. 27). 1896. Roberts Bros.; Etc., Etc.
Marital Liability. Elizabeth Phipps Train. LC 8-29727. (Half-title: The lotus library). 1897. J. B. Lippincott Company.
Marital Messenger. Walter Ernest Gibson. LC 10-300361. 1910. 1.50. The Neale Publishing Company.
Marital Spanking. Will Henry, pseud. pap. 1.95 o.s.i. (Venus). Grove.
Maritta Wolff. Maritta Walff. pap. 0.60 o.p. (73-501). Lancer.
Mariu Saga, 2 vols. Ed. by C. R. Unger. LC 80-1957. 140.00 (ISBN 0-404-18707-2). AMS Pr.
Marius the Epicurean. Walter Horatio Pater. LC 75-481. (Victorian Fiction: Novels of Faith and Doubt). 1975. (ISBN 0-8240-1558-4). Garland Pub.
Marius the Epicurean: His Sensations and Ideas. Walter Horatio Pater. LC 72-10814. 1973. (ISBN 0-384-45082-2). Johnson Reprint Corp.
Marius the Epicurean: His Sensations and Ideas. Walter Horatio Pater. LC 72-97499. (Signet classic, CY476). 1970. 1.25. New American Library.
Marius the Epicurean: His Sensations and Ideas. Walter Horatio Pater & Reedy, William Marion. LC 2-24056. 1900. T. B. Mosher.
Marivosa. Emmuska Orczy. LC 31-8635. Doubleday, Doran and Company, Incorporated.
Marji and the Kidnap Plot. John Benton. LC 80-15571. (Spire book). 1980. 2.50 (ISBN 0-8007-8391-3). F. H. Revell Co.
Marjoire Daw. Thomas Bailey Aldrich. LC 8-29734. 1908. Houghton Mifflin Company.
Marjoribanks. Jessie Wright Whitcomb. LC 8-37210. Congregational Sunday-School and Publishing Society.
Marjorie. Charlotte Mary Brame. (On cover: Lovell's library. v. 18, no. 896). J. W. Lovell Company.
Marjorie. Charlotte Mary Brame. (On cover: Seaside library. Pocket ed. no. 922). G. Munro.
Marjorie. Charlotte Mary Brame. LC 44-392324. (On cover: Seaside library. Pocket ed. No. 922). G. Munro.
Marjorie. Bertha M. Clay. LC 44-39231. (On cover: Lovell's library, v. 18, no. 896). J. W. Lovell Company.
Marjorie. Justin Huntly McCarthy. LC 3-93381. 1903. R. H. Russell.
Marjorie Daw: And Other People. Thomas Bailey Aldrich. LC 76-103488. (Short story index reprint series). (Illus.). 1969. Books for Libraries Press.
Marjorie Daw: And Other People... Thomas Bailey Aldrich. LC 6-499. 1873. J. R. Osgood and Company.
Marjorie Daw and Other People. Thomas Bailey Aldrich. LC 1-208043. 1901. Houghton, Mifflin and Company.
Marjorie Daw, and Other Stories. Thomas Bailey Aldrich. LC 69-11878. (American short story series, v. 35). 1969. Garrett Press.

Marjorie Daw: And Other Stories. Thomas Bailey Aldrich. LC 70-103489. (Short story index reprint series). 1969. Books for Libraries Press.
Marjorie Daw: And Other Stories. Thomas Bailey Aldrich. LC 6-509. (Half-title: The Riverside Aldine series)). 1885. Houghton, Mifflin and Company.
Marjorie Daw: And Other Stories. Thomas Bailey Aldrich. LC 13-12933. 1894. Houghton, Mifflin and Company.
Marjorie Daw: And Other Stories. Thomas Bailey Aldrich. LC 2-20917. (Riverside Aldine series)). 1900. Houghton, Mifflin and Company.
Marjorie Deane. Charlotte Mary Brame. (Street & Smith's select series, no. 39). 1890. Street & Smith.
Marjorie Deane. Bertha M. Clay. LC 44-39233. (Select series... No. 39). 1890. Street & Smith.
Marjorie Huntingdon. A Novel. Harriett Pennawell Belt. LC 6-11347. 1884. J. B. Lippincott & Co.
Marjorie Morningstar. Herman Wouk. LC 55-6485. 1955. 15.95 (ISBN 0-385-04285-X). Doubleday.
Marjorie Morningstar. Herman Wouk. 1977. pap. 5.95 (ISBN 0-671-82629-8). PB.
Marjorie Morningstar: A Novel. Herman Wouk. LC 55-6485. 1973. (pbk.) 1.50. Pocket Books.
Marjorie Morningstar. 1st Ed. Herman Wouk. LC 55-6485. 1955. Doubleday.
Marjorie of Scotland. Pamela Hill. LC 56-13863. (Illus.). 1956. Putnam.
Marjorie: Or, Wild As a Hawk. A Novel. Katharine Sarah Gadsden Macquoid. (Harper's Franklin square library, no. 528). 1886. Harper & Brothers.
Marjorie's Child: Or, Shadowed for Years. John Russell Coryell. LC 6-39924. (On cover: Munro's library, v. 1, no. 124). 1884. N. L. Munro.
Marjorie's Child: Or, Shadowed for Years. John Russell Coryell. LC 6-39924. (On cover: Munro's library, v. 1, no. 124). 1884. N. L. Munro.
Marjorie's Fate. Bertha M. Clay. (On cover: Lovell's library. v. 20. no. 988). J. W. Lovell Company.
Marjorie's Fate. Bertha M. Clay. LC 1-29163. (Bertha Clay library. no. 39). 1900. Street & Smith.
Marjorie's Quest. Jeanie Thomas Gould Lincoln. LC 7-19023. 1872. J. R. Osgood and Company.
Marjorie's Quest. Jeanie Thomas Gould Lincoln. LC 3045. 1900. Houghton, Mifflin and Company.
Marjory: A Study of the Author of "James Gordon's Wife"... Frances Elizabeth Georgiana Brock. (Harper's Franklin square library, no. 258). 1882. Harper & Brothers.
Marjory Graham: A Novel... Isa E. Gray. LC 6-45538. 1882. G. P. Putnam's Sons.
Marjo's. H L Perry. LC 77-79428. 1.95. Playboy Press.
Mark. William Lodewick Doty. LC 53-1656. 1953. Bruce Pub. Co.
Mark. Aquila Kempster. LC 3-27964. 1903. Doubleday, Page and Co.
Mark. Frances Newbold Noyes. LC 13-38100. 1.25. E. J. Clode.
Mark: A Novel. Charles E Israel. LC 58-9047. 1958. Simon and Schuster.
Mark: A Novel. John Stone. 1973. 6.50 (ISBN 0-682-47622-6). Exposition Pr.
Mark Chester: or, A Mill and a Millon: A Tale of Southern California. Carlyle Petersilea. LC 37-32787. Banner of Light Publishing Co.
Mark Coffin, U. S. S. Allen Drury. 1980. pap. 2.75 (ISBN 0-441-51965-2). Ace Bks.
Mark Coffin, U.S.S. A Novel of Capitol Hill. Allen Drury. LC 78-69655. 1979. 10.00 (ISBN 0-385-14434-2). Doubleday.
Mark Dunning's Enemy. Mary Dwinell Chellis. LC 6-23409. (Added t.-p.: The standard series of temperance tales v. 3). 1870. H. A. Young & Co.
Mark Eminence. Edgar Harold Spedding Barnes Austin. LC 46-22693. 1946. J. Long Limited.
Mark Eminence. Edgar Harold Spedding Barnes Austin. LC 47-2061. 1947. R. M. McBride & Company.
Mark Enderby, Engineer. Robert Fulkerson Hoffman. LC 10-23943. 1910. 1.50. A. C. McClurg & Co.
Mark Everard: A Romance. Knox Magee. LC 1-24545. 1901. R. F. Fenno & Company.
Mark Gildersleeve. A Novel. John S. Sauzade. LC 8-1836. 1873. G. W. Carleton & Co.; Etc., Etc.
Mark Gray's Heritage. Eliot Harlow Robinson. LC 23-7831. 1923. The Page Company.
Mark Heffron. A Novel, by Alice Ward Bailey. Alice Ward Bailey. LC 6-5026. 1896. Harper & Brothers.
Mark It with a Stone. George Victor Martin. LC 47-11498. 1947. F. Fell.
Mark Logan, the Bourgeois. Juliette Augusta Kinzie. 1887. J. B. Lippincott Company.
Mark Manning's Mission; or, the Story of a Shoe Factory Boy. Horatio Alger. 268p. 1974. Repr. of 1905 ed. lib. bdg. 15.15x (ISBN 0-88411-804-5). Amereon Ltd.
Mark Maynard's Wife. Frankie Faling King. LC 7-12211. T. B. Peterson & Brothers.
Mark of Cain. Harriet Theresa Smith Comstock. LC 35-5197. 1935. Doubleday, Doran & Company, Inc.
Mark of Cain. Harriet Theresa Smith Comstock. LC 37-16231. 1937. The Sun Dial Press, Inc.
Mark of Cain. Sean A. Key. (Orig.). 1980. pap. 2.25 (ISBN 0-440-15192-9). Dell.
Mark of Cain. authorized ed. new york, scribner, 1886. ed. Andrew Lang. LC 68-54278. 1968. AMS Press.
Mark of Cain. Andrew Lang. LC 7-13865. (Lovell's library. no. 1395). 1889. J. W. Lovell Company.
Mark of Cain. Carolyn Wells. LC 17-7931. 1917. J. B. Lippincott Company.
Mark of Clover: By Judith B. Kelly, with Courtney Willard. Special Ed. Judith Barczy Kelly. LC 54-314035. 1953.
Mark of Cosa Nostra. Nick Carter. (Nick Carter Killmaster Ser.). (Orig.). 1971. pap. 0.75 o.p. (A847S, Award). Univ Pub & Dist.
Mark of Death Claw. Nyle Estes. 253p. 1983. 10.95x (ISBN 0-938936-15-8); pap. 3.95x (ISBN 0-938936-14-X). Daring Pr.
Mark of Demons. John Jakes. (Brak Ser.: No. 2). (Orig.). 1981. pap. 2.25 (ISBN 0-505-51651-9). Tower Bks.
Mark of Displeasure. Elizabeth Hely Younger. LC 60-14015. 1960. Scribner.
Mark of Merlin. McCaffrey, Anne. 1978. 1.95 (ISBN 0-441-51966-0). Ace Books.
Mark of Murder. Dell Shannon. (Lt. Luis Mendoza Mystery Ser). 1971. pap. 0.75 o.p. (T2541). Pyramid Pubns.
Mark of Murder: By Dell Shannon. Elizabeth Linington. LC 64-20295. 1964. Morrow.
Mark of Shadow. Maxwell Grant, pseud. (Orig.). pap. 0.50 o.p. (B50-683). Belmont-Tower.
Mark of Shame. Willi Henrich. 288p. 1981. pap. 2.75 (ISBN 0-553-20110-7). Bantam.
Mark of Shame: Translated from the German by Sigrid Rock. Willi Heinrich. LC 59-10018. 1959. Farrar, Straus and Cudahy.
Mark of the Beast. A. Degranamour. pap. 2.25 o.s.i. (Venus). Grove.
Mark of the Beast. Sydney Watson. LC 33-329183. Fleming H. Revell Company.
Mark of the Beast: A Novel. Reginald Wright Kauffman. LC 16-18293. 1916. 1.25. The Macaulay Company.
Mark of the Dead. The Aresbys. LC 30-843. 1929. I. Washburn.
Mark of the Hand. Armstrong, Charlotte. LC 63-50135. (Ace giant double novel book. G-526). 1963. Ace Books.
Mark of the Hand. Charlotte Armstrong. 1975. (pbk.) 1.25. Ace Books.
Mark of the Horse Lord. Rosemary Sutcliff. LC 65-23257. 4.50. Walck.
Mark of the Hunter. Gene Caesar. LC 53-8154. 1953. Sloane.
Mark of the Land. Ruth L. Anderson. 320p. (Orig.). 1983. pap. 5.95x (ISBN 0-933892-15-2). Child Focus Co.
Mark of the Rat. Frederic Arnold Kummer. LC 29-18934. J. H. Sears & Company, Inc.
Mark of the Rattler. Tom Ryan. (Brannigan Ser). (O.s.i.: No. 3). (Orig.). 1975. pap. 0.95 o.s.i. (LB257NK, Leisure Bks). Nordon Pubns.
Mark of the Rattler. Tom Ryan. (Brannigan # 3). 1975. (pbk.) 0.95. Leisure Books.
Mark of the Rebel. George L. Machoe. 3.50 o.p. Carlton.
Mark of the Sun. Elizabeth Catherine Webb. LC 59-11615. 1959. Doubleday.
Mark of the Taw. Jack Finegan. LC 72-1762. 1972. 5.95 (ISBN 0-8042-1951-6). John Knox Press.
Mark of the Warrior. Paul Scott. LC 58-5727. 1958. W. Morrow.
Mark of Zorro. Johnston McCulley. LC 76-6510. 1976. 7.95 (ISBN 0-89190-999-0). American Reprint Co.
Mark of Zorro. Johnston McCulley. LC 24-31099. Grosset & Dunlap.
Mark One: the Dummy. John Dudley Ball. LC 74-7365. 1974. 7.50 (ISBN 0-316-07950-2). Little, Brown.
Mark Only. Theodore Francis Powys. LC 73-131805. 1972. (ISBN 0-403-00692-9). Scholarly Press.
Mark Only. Theodore Francis Powys. LC 25-815. 1924. A. A. Knopf.
Mark Pfeiffer, M.D. John Weld. 1943. C. Scribner's Sons.
Mark Rowland. A Tale of the Sea. John Sherburne Sleeper. 1867. Loring.
Mark Rutherford's Deliverance: Being the Second Part of His Autobiography. William Hale White & Shapcott, Reuben, Ed. LC 36-30339. 1936. H. Milford, Oxford University Press.
Mark Seaworth. A Tale of the Indian Ocean. William Henry Giles Kingston. (Seaside library, v. 89, no. 1792). 1884. G. Munro.
Mark Seaworth's Voyage on the Indian Ocean. William Henry Giles Kingston. LC 6259. (On cover: Medal library, no. 71). 1900. Street & Smith.
Mark the Sparrow. Clark Howard. LC 75-2367. 1975. 8.95 (ISBN 0-8037-5431-0). Dial Press.
Mark Three for Murder. Robert P Hansen. LC 57-5848. 1957. M. S. Mill Co., and W. Morrow.
Mark Tidd, Editor. Clarence Budington Kelland. LC 17-30119. 1917. Harper & Brothers.
Mark Tidd in Business. Clarence Budington Kelland. LC 15-17978. 1915. Harper & Brothers.
Mark Twain. Mark Twain. Incl. Huckleberry Finn. 4.95 o.p. (G49). Modern Lib.
Mark Twain Every Child Should Know. Samuel Langhorne Clemens. LC 43-56. (What every child should know library. 4th ser.). 1942. Pub. by Doubleday, Doran & Co., Inc., for the Parents' Institute, Inc.
Mark Twain: God's Fool. Hamlin Hill. LC 72-9754. (Illus.). 336p. 1973. 10.95 o.p. (ISBN 0-06-011893-8, HarpT). Har-Row.
Mark Twain, Jackleg Novelist. Robert A Wiggins. LC 64-18428. 1964. University of Washington Press.
Mark Twain Proposition. Gina Cerminara. LC 77-13456. 4.95 (ISBN 0-915442-41-8). Unilaw Library.
Mark Twain's Adventures of Tom Sawyer: Retold in 96 Pages. Samuel Langhorne Clemens & Kline, Bennett. LC 40-32858. Whitman Publishing Company.
Mark Twain's Fables of Man. Mark Twain. Ed. & intro. by John S. Tuckey. LC 70-157823. (Mark Twain Papers). (£8.35). (Illus.). 600p. 1972. 24.50 (ISBN 0-520-02039-1). U of Cal Pr.
Mark Twain's First Story. Samuel Langhorne Clemens & Franklin Julius Meine. LC 73-18302. 1973. 4.00. Folcroft Library Editions.
Mark Twain's Hannibal, Huck & Tom. Mark Twain. Ed. by Walter Blair. LC 69-10575. (Mark Twain Papers). (-6.75). 1969. 37.50x (ISBN 0-520-01501-0). U of Cal Pr.
Mark Twain's Huckleberry Finn: Tom Sawyer's Comrade, Retold in 96 Pages. Samuel Langhorne Clemens & Kline, Bennett. LC 40-82611. Whitman Publishing Company.
Mark Twain's Mysterious Stranger Manuscripts. Samuel Langhorne Clemens. Ed. by William Merriam Gibson. LC 69-10576. (Mark Twain papers). (Illus.). 1969. 12.50. University of California Press.
Mark Twain's Sketches, New and Old. Now First Published in Complete Form... Samuel Langhorne Clemens. LC 3-14548. 1875. The American Pub. Company.
Mark Twain's The Adventures of Huckleberry Finn. Samuel Langhorne Clemens. LC 60-51651. 1960. Grosset & Dunlap.
Mark Twain's The Adventures of Huckleberry Finn: Simplified and Adapted by Robert J. Dixson in Collaboration with Lewis T. Davis. Drawings by Syd Browne. With Exercises for Study and Vocabulary Drill. Samuel Langhorne Clemens & Robert James Dixson. LC 54-5570. (American classics, book 9). 1954. Regents Pub. Co.
Mark Twain's The Prince and the Pauper: By Charles Leavitt. Charles L Leavitt. LC 66-27338. (Monarch notes & study gds., 878-9). pap., 1.00. Monarch Pr.
Mark Twain's Virginia City: Nevada Territory. Mark Twain. Ed. by William R. Jones. (Illus.). 64p. pap. 3.95 (ISBN 0-89646-074-6). Outbooks.
Mark Wilton. Charles Benjamin Tayler. LC 75-490. (Victorian Fiction: Novels of Faith and Doubt; 42). 1976. 40.00 (ISBN 0-8240-1566-5). Garland Pub.
Marked "Cancelled,". Natalie Sumner Lincoln. LC 30-10079. 1930. D. Appleton and Company.
Marked Destiny. Anita Brumback Rothgeb. LC 59-155468. Christopher Pub. Hourse.
Marked Down for Murder: By Spencer Dean Pseud. 1st Ed. Prentice Winchell. LC 56-115041. 1956. Published for the Crime Club by Doubelday.
Marked for a Victim." A Thrilling Story of Love and Mysticism. Stuart C Cumberland. (On Cover; Red Cover Ser. No. 41). 1889. J. S. Ogilvie.
Marked for Murder... Davis Dresser. LC 45-9823. 1945. Dodd, Mead & Company.
Marked for Murder. Wallace Reed. LC 41-13503. Phoenix Press.
Marked House. Jacob Twersky. LC 68-10316. 1968. 4.95. T. Yoseloff.
Marked "In Haste." A Story of to-Day... 3d ed. Blanche Roosevelt McChetta. LC 7-15177. 1883. Trow's Printing and Bookbinding Co.
Marked "In Haste." A Story of to-Day. Blanche Roosevelt Tucker Macchetta. (On cover: Lovell's library; v. 17, no. 837). 1886. J. W. Lovell Company.
Marked Man. Meriol Trevor. 1974. (pbk.) 0.95 (ISBN 0-671-77780-7). Pocket Books.
Marked Man. Harold Channing Wire. LC 34-21301. (Tired business man's library of adventure, detective, and mystery novels). 1934. D. Appleton-Century Company, Incorporated.
Marked Man: A Romance of the Great Lakes. Karl William Detzer. LC 27-16578. The Bobbs-Merrill Company.
Marked Man: By Harry Carmichael Pseud. 1st Ed. Leopold Horace Ognall. LC 59-12640. (Crime club selection). 1959. Published for the Crime Club by Doubleday.
Marked Man: Some Episodes in His Life. Ada Cambridge Cross. LC 6-31957. (On cover: Lovell's international series no. 113). 1890. J. W. Lovell Company.
Marked Men. Charles Neville Buck. LC 29-21206. 1929. Pub. for The Crime Club, Inc., by Doubleday, Doran & Company, Inc.
Marked Men. Aris Fakinos. LC 73-137868. 1971. 6.95 (ISBN 0-87140-516-4). Liveright.
Marked Men. 1st Ed. Allan Vaughan Elston. LC 56-6422. 1956. Lippincott.
Marked One: And Twelve Other Stories. Translated from the German, with an Introd. by Ludwig Lewisohn. Jacob Picard. LC 56-778491. 1956. Jewish Publication Society of America.
Marked "Personal,". Anna Katharine Green Rohlfs. LC 7-40745. 1893. G. P. Putnam's Sons.
Markenmore Mystery. Joseph Smith Fletcher. LC 23-133361. 1923. A. A. Knopf.
Market for Murder. 1st Ed. Charlotte Murray Russell, pseud. LC 53-65206. 1953. Published for the Crime Club by Doubleday.
Market Harborough: Or, How Mr. Sawyer Went to the Shires. Inside the Bar; or, Sketches at Soakington. George John Whyte-Melville. (On cover: The Seaside library. Pocket ed. no. 451). 1885. G. Munro.
Market Harborough: Or, How Mr. Sawyer Went to the Shires. Inside the Bar; or, Sketches at Soakington. new ed. George John Whyte-Melville. LC 42-27380. (On cover: Select library of fiction). Ward, Lock, and Co.
Market-Place. Harold Frederic. LC 72-84584. (Illus.). 1974. 16.50 (ISBN 0-403-02997-X). Scholarly Press.
Market-Place. Harold Frederic & Charlyne Dodge. LC 81-8853. (Harold Frederic edition; v. 2). ((Series: Frederic, Harold, 1856-1898.). (1977). (Works.). (V. 2.). 1981. 22.00 (ISBN 0-912646-60-8). Texas Christian University Press.
Market Place see Collected Works.
Market-Place: A Novel. Harold Frederic. LC 99-2405. Frederick A. Stokes Company.
Market Square. Miss Read. 1967. 4.00 o.p. (ISBN 0-395-08113-0). HM.
Market Square. Dora Jessie Saint. LC 67-10617. 1967. Houghton Mifflin.
Marketing Deb. Hughes Cornell. LC 26-14104. The Macaulay Company.
Markets of Paris. Le Ventre De Paris. Emile Zola & Sherwood, Mrs. Mary (Neal) Tr. LC 9-1317. T. B. Peterson & Brothers.
Markham Affair. Stanley Portal Hyatt. LC 25-18065. E. J. Clode, Inc.
Markof. The Russian Violinist. Alice Marie Celeste Durand. Tr. by Stanley, Helen. T. B. Peterson & Brothers.
Marks of Identity. Juan Goytisolo. LC 68-58153. 1969. Grove Press.
Marksman. A. J. Langguth. LC 73-14314. 1974. 6.95 (ISBN 0-06-012499-7). Harper & Row.
Marksmen of Monmouth: A Tale of the Revolution. Newton Mallory Curtis. 1843. L. Willard.
Marling Hall. Angela Mackail Thirkell. LC 42-222716. 1942. A. A. Knopf.
Marloe Mansions Murder. Adam Gordon MacLeod. LC 28-6395. 1928. L. MacVeagh, The Dial Press.
Marlou Chronicles. Lawrence Sanders. 1979. 2.25 (ISBN 0-425-04493-9). Berkley Publishing Corp.
Marlow Chronicles. Lawrence Sanders. LC 76-4889. 8.95. Putnam.
Marm Lisa. Kate Douglas Smith Wiggin. LC 8-37037. 1896. Houghton, Mifflin and Company.
Marmaduke of Tennessee. Edward Cummings. LC 14-14923. 1914. A. C. McClurg & Co.
Marmaduke Story As Featured in the Pages of Power. Steve Elonka. LC 55-474155. McGraw Hill.
Marmaduke Surfaceblow's Salty Technical Romanaces. Stephen Michael Elonka. LC 79-14107. (Illus.). 1979. 14.50 (ISBN 0-88275-967-1). R. E. Krieger Pub. Co.
Marmaduke Wyvil: Or, The Maid's Revenge. by henry william herbert... ed. Henry William Herbert. LC 7-4290. J. Winchester.

Marmalade Man. Charlotte Vale Allen. LC 80-29118. 14.08 (ISBN 0-525-15294-6). E. P. Dutton.

Marmali. Jeremiah McMahon. 1976. (pbk.) 1.25. Pyramid Books.

Marmalie. Jeremiah McMahon. (Orig.). 1976. pap. 1.25 o.p. (ISBN 0-515-03604-8). BJ Pub Group.

Marmorne. Philip Gilbert Hamerton. LC 7-956. (No name series). 1878. Roberts Brothers.

Marmot Drive. John Richard Hersey. LC 53-9476. 1953. Knopf.

Marne. Edith Newbold Jones Wharton. LC 18-228925. 1918. D. Appleton and Company.

Maron, the Christian Youth of the Lebanon. Adolf Von Berlichingen. LC 6-11332. 1895. St. Aemilianus' Orphan Asylum.

Maroon: A Legend of the Caribbees, and Other Tales. William Gilmore Simms. LC 8-8997. 1855. Lippincott, Grambo & Co.

Maroon Tales: University of Chicago Stories. William Jacob Cuppy. LC 10-738. 1910. Forbes & Company.

Marooned. William Clark Russell. (On cover: Seaside library. Pocket ed., no. 1210). 1889. G. Munro.

Marooned: A Novel. Martin Caidin. (S2965). 1965. Bantam.

Marooned: A Novel. William Clark Russell. (On cover: Harper's Franklin square library, no. 659). 1889. Harper & Brothers.

Marooned: A Sea Tale. William Clark Russell. LC 4-16313. Rand, McNally & Company.

Marooned in Crater Lake, Stories of the Skyline Trail: The Umpqua Trail, and the Old Oregon Trail. Alfred Powers. LC 30-15335. 1930. Metropolitan Press.

Marooned in Orbit. Arthur W Ballou. LC 68-13878. 1968. Little, Brown.

Marooned on Mars. Lester Del Rey. LC 52-5497. (Science fiction novel). 1952. Winston.

Marooned with Murder. Robert Alfred John Walling. LC 37-24567. 1937. W. Morrow and Company.

Marooner. Charles Frederick Holder. LC 8-32337. 1908. B. W. Dodge & Company.

Marotz. Francis Browning Drew Bickerstaffe-Drew. LC 9-18. 1908. G. P. Putnam's Sons.

Marplot. Sidney Royse Lysaght. LC 11-7172. 1893. Macmillan and Co.

Marquard Von Lindau: Die Zehe Gebot. Jacobus W. Van Maren. (Dutch.). 1980. pap. 52.50 (ISBN 90-6203-771-2). Humanities.

Marquee Ballyhoo: An American Novel. Maurice Lincoln Kusell & Merritt, Mal Sylvester. LC 32-30639. 1932. A. H. Chamberlain.

Marquis. Charles Garvice. (On cover: Laurel library, no. 21). 1895. G. Munro's Sons.

Marquis: A Novel. Joan Sanders. LC 63-8045. 1963. Houghton Mifflin.

Marquis and Miss Jones. Helen Ashfield. LC 82-5550. 9.95 (ISBN 0-312-51547-2). St. Martin's Press.

Marquis and Pamela. Edward Herbert Cooper. LC 8-8092. 1908. Duffield & Company.

Marquis De Bolibar. Leo Perutz. Tr. by Rawson, Graham Stanhope. LC 27-2966. 1927. The Viking Press.

Marquis of Carabas. Harriet Elizabeth Prescott Spofford. LC 8-14056. 1882. Roberts Brothers.

Marquis of Lossie. George Macdonald. LC 7-15857. A. L. Burt.

Marquis of Lossie. George Macdonald. G. Routledge & Sons, Limited.

Marquis of Lossie. George Macdonald. LC 12-18284. 1911. D. McKay.

Marquis of Lossie. A Romance. Sequel to "Malcolm". George Macdonald. (Seaside library, v. 46, no. 948). 1881. G. Munro.

Marquis of Loveland. Charles Norris Williamson & Alice Muriel Livingston Williamson. LC 14-10507. 1908. The McClure Company.

Marquis of Lumbria see Three Exemplary Novels.

Marquis of Penalta (Marta y Maria) A Realistic Social Novel. Palacio Valdes, Armando. Tr. by Nathan Haskell Dole. LC 8-319021. T. Y. Crowell & Co.

Marquis' Secret. George Macdonald & Michael Phillips. LC 82-12949. (Illus.). 5.95 (ISBN 0-87123-324-X). Bethany House.

Marquis' Secret: Sequel to The Fisherman's Lady. George MacDonald. Ed. by Mike Phillips. 228p. 1982. pap. 4.95 (ISBN 0-87123-324-X, 210324). Bethany Hse.

Marquis Who Hated Women. Barbara Cartland. LC 77-670155. 1977. 6.95 (ISBN 0-87272-065-9). Duron Books.

Marquise and the Novice. Victoria Ramstetter. LC 80-83118. (Illus.). 1981. 4.95 (ISBN 0-930044-16-9). Naiad Press.

Marquise De Brinvilliers. Emile Gaboriau. LC 6-44718. (On cover: Aldine series. no. 2). 1886. Aldine Book Publishing Company.

Marquise of O-, and Other Stories. Heinrich Von Kleist. LC 73-87441. 1973. 8.50 (ISBN 0-8044-2478-0) (ISBN 0-8044-2478-0). Ungar.

Marquise of O-, and Other Stories. Heinrich Von Kleist. LC 79-318619. (Penguin classics). 1978. 3.95 (ISBN 0-14-044359-2). Penguin.

Marquise of O: And Other Stories. Heinrich Von Kleist. LC 60-14139. 1960. Criterion Books.

Marquise Went Out at Five. Claude Mauriac. Tr. by Richard Howard. 1981. pap. 4.95 (ISBN 0-7145-0367-3). Riverrun NY.

Marquise's Millions: A Novel. Frances Aymar Mathews. LC 5-11071. 1905. Funk & Wagnalls Company.

Marrakesh. Graham Diamond. 288p. 1981. pap. 2.50 (ISBN 0-449-14443-7, GM). Fawcett.

Marrakesh One-Two. Richard Grenier. LC 82-15818. 1983. 14.95 (ISBN 0-395-33099-8). Houghton Mifflin.

Marranos. Liliane Webb. LC 80-10635. 13.95 (ISBN 0-8362-6112-7). Andrews and McMeel.

Marr'd in Making". Betsey Riddle Hutton Zum Stolzenberg. LC 6799. 1901. J. B. Lippincott Company.

Marrguerite Lacoste: Or, Fleur-De-Crime. Adolphe Belot. (Seaside library, v, 67, no. 1353). G. Munro.

Marriage. Gwen Davis. LC 81-66966. 288p. 1981. 12.95 (ISBN 0-87795-335-X). Arbor Hse.

Marriage. Gwen Davis. 1983. pap. 3.50 (ISBN 0-8217-1122-9). Zebra.

Marriage... Susan Edmonstone Ferrier. LC 6-39369. 1893. Roberts Brothers.

Marriage. Herbert George Wells. LC 12-21729. 1912. Duffield & Company.

Marriage see Passion of Amy Styron.

Marriage a la Mode. Mary Augusta Arnold Humphry Ward Ward. LC 9-13541. 1909. Doubleday, Page & Company.

Marriage a la Mode. Mary Augusta Arnold Humphry Ward Ward. LC 24-204939. 1911. A. L. Burt Company.

Marriage a la Mode: A Novel. Justin Smith. LC 47-11331. 1947. I. Washburn.

Marriage a la Mode: A Story of Romance, Love and Companionate Marriage. Vida Hurst. LC 29-220484. Grosset & Dunlap.

Marriage: a Novel. Susan Edmonstone Ferrier. LC 70-590491. (Oxford English novels). 1971. 3.50 (ISBN 0-19-255349-6). Oxford University Press.

Marriage. A Novel. Susan Edmonstone Ferrier. (Seaside library. v. 63, no. 1273). 1882. G. Munro.

Marriage, a Novel. Mona Goodwyn Williams. LC 58-612224. 1958. Putnam.

Marriage Above Zero. A Novel. Nevada McNeil. 1894. G. W. Dillingham.

Marriage Act. John Shebbeare. LC 74-17449. (Flowering of the Novel). 1974. 25.00 (ISBN 0-8240-1139-2). Garland Pub.

Marriage Agency. Russell Higgins. LC 35-233124. Godwin.

Marriage Agency. Albert Quandt. LC 35-23312. 1935. Godwin.

Marriage Agreement. Margaret MacWilliams. LC 81-14500. 1981. 9.95 (ISBN 0-89621-311-0). Thorndike Press.

Marriage Alliance. Mira Stubbles. (Fawcett Crest Book). 1977. 1.50 (ISBN 0-449-23142-9). Fawcett Publications.

Marriage and Mary Ann. Catherine Cookson. LC 77-10921. 1978. 7.95 (ISBN 0-688-03270-2). Morrow.

Marriage and the Family Through Science Fiction. Val Clear. LC 75-38023. 12.95. St. Martin's Press.

Marriage & the Sexual Kiss. Adrian Y. Meadows. pap. 1.95 o.p. (ISBN 0-87056-238-X, 6238). Brandon.

Marriage Arranged. Mira Stables. 224p. 1981. pap. 1.95 (ISBN 0-449-50192-2, Coventry). Fawcett.

Marriage at a Venture. From the French of Emile Gaboriau. Emile Gaboriau. Tr. by Calfa, Vincenzo. (On cover: Seaside library. Pocket ed. no. 1002). 1887. G. Munro.

Marriage at Sea. authorized ed. William Clark Russell. (On cover: Lovell's Westminster series, no. 17). 1890. United States Book Company.

Marriage Bargain. Rachelle Edwards. (Coventry Romance Ser.: No. 186). 224p. 1982. pap. 1.50 (ISBN 0-449-50288-0, Coventry). Fawcett.

Marriage Bargain. Joanna Scott. 192p. 1981. pap. 1.50 (ISBN 0-671-57068-4). S&S.

Marriage Bed. Beresford-Howe, Constance. LC 82-25267. 1983. 12.95 (ISBN 0-89340-571-X). J. Curley.

Marriage Bed. Jean Clark. LC 82-13134. 320p. 1983. 15.95 (ISBN 0-399-12746-1, Putnam). Putnam Pub Group.

Marriage Bed. (Illus.). 4.95 (ISBN 0-910550-43-3). Centurion Pr.

Marriage Bed. Ernest Pascal. LC 27-5133. Harcourt, Brace & Company.

Marriage Bed. Chayym Zeldis. LC 77-92376. 8.95. Putnam.

Marriage Below Zero. A Novel. Alfred J. Cohen. LC 6-26767. 1889. G. W. Dillingham.

Marriage Between Friends. Florence Eberhard. LC 35-3923. G. H. Watt.

Marriage Broker: Based on the Stories of Shulem the Shadchen, by Tashrak Pseud. Israel Joseph Zevin. LC 60-10304. 1960. Putnam.

Marriage by Bequest. Elizabeth Carey. (Coventry Romance Ser.: No. 165). 224p. 1982. pap. 1.50 (ISBN 0-449-50265-1, Coventry). Fawcett.

Marriage by Capture. Arthur John Arbuthnott Stringer. LC 33-10968. The Bobbs-Merrill Company.

Marriage by Capture: A Romance of to-Day. Robert Williams Buchanan. (On cover: The lotos library). 1896. J. B. Lippincott Company.

Marriage by Conquest. Warwick Deeping. LC 15-24891. 1915. McBride, Nast and Company.

Marriage by Conquest. Warwick Deeping. LC 36-8625. 1936. R. M. McBride & Company.

Marriage by Lot: A Novel Based on Moravian History. Elsa Koenig Nitzsche. LC 59-1940. (Pennsylvania German Folklore Society, v. 22). 1958.

Marriage Cage. William Johnston. LC 60-13211. 1960. L. Stuart.

Marriage Ceremony. Ada Cambridge Mrs. G. F. Cross Cross. LC 6-31956. (On cover: Appletons' town and country and library. no. 133). 1894. D. Appleton and Company.

Marriage Chest. Dorothy Eden. LC 66-20159. 1966. Coward-McCann.

Marriage Chest. 1st Amer. Ed. Mary Paradise. LC 66-20159. 1966. 4.50. Coward.

Marriage Clinic. Florence Btonebraker. LC 47-313872. 1947. Phoenix Press.

Marriage Contract. Honore De Balzac. Tr. by Katharine Prescott Wormeley. LC 3-23167. (Half-title: The comedy of human life... Scenes from private life). 1895. Roberts Brothers.

Marriage Contract. Virginia Nelson. (Orig.). 1980. pap. 1.95 (ISBN 0-449-14355-4, GM). Fawcett.

Marriage Exchange. Florence Stonebraker. LC 46-4963. 1946. Phoenix Press.

Marriage Feast. Par Fabian Lagerkvist. LC 73-75187. 1973. 5.95 (ISBN 0-8090-6786-2) (ISBN 0-8090-6786-2). Hill and Wang.

Marriage for Good. Leslie Lynd. LC 39-25559. Gramercy Publishing Co.

Marriage for Good. Albert Quandt. LC 39-25559. 1938. Gramercy Pub. C.

Marriage for Love. Ludovic Halevy & Hall, Arthur D. Tr. LC 6-46667. (On cover: Globe library. v. 1. no. 146). 1891. Rand, McNally & Company.

Marriage for Love. Ludovic Halevy & Potter, Frank Hunter, 1851- Tr. LC 6-46668. Dodd, Mead, and Company.

Marriage for Love: Tr. by Frank Hunter Potter, Illustrated by Wilson De Meza. Ludovic Halevy & Potter, Frank Hunter, 1851- Tr. LC 7-5401. 1890. Dodd, Mead & Company.

Marriage for One. Erno Szep & Lengyel, Emil, Tr. LC 29-124876. 1929. The Macaulay Company.

Marriage for Revenue. George Agnew Chamberlain. LC 34-55969. The Bobbs-Merrill Company.

Marriage for Rosamond. Louise Platt Hauck. LC 37-34665. 1937. The Penn Publishing Company.

Marriage for Three. Carlotta Baker. LC 38-6958. Phoenix Press.

Marriage for Three. Elizabeth Seifert. LC 54-105783. 1954. Dodd, Mead.

Marriage for Three. Elizabeth Seifert. LC 73-79165. 1974. 6.95. Aeonian Press.

Marriage for Two. Frederick Jackson. LC 33-13338. 1933. Macrae Smith Company.

Marriage for Two. Gladys Knight. LC 24-15423. Boni and Liveright.

Marriage Guest: A Novel. Konrad Bercovici. LC 25-20828. 1925. Boni & Liveright.

Marriage Hats. Mary Sue Hubbard. 1970. pap. 6.00 (ISBN 0-88404-068-2). Bridge Pubns Inc.

Marriage Huskers: A Novel. 1st Ed. W K Beach. LC 55-8615. 1955. Vantage Press.

Marriage in Blue. Edward Fisher. LC 31-21314. 1931. Cosmopolitan Book Corporation.

Marriage in Gotham. Ishbel Ross. LC 43-268942. 1933. A. L. Burt Company.

Marriage in Haste. Sue Peters. (Harlequin Romances Ser.). 192p. 1981. pap. 1.25 (ISBN 0-373-02410-X, Pub. by Harlequin). PB.

Marriage in Heaven. Ronald Fraser, pseud. LC 32-35790. 1933. C. Scribner's Sons.

Marriage in High Life. Octave Feuillet. Tr. by Celia Connelly. (Lovell's library, v. 2, no. 41). 1882. J. W. Lovell Company.

Marriage in High Life. From the French of Octave Feuillet... Octave Feuillet. Tr. by Celia Connelly. LC 6-39531. (On cover: International series of new approved novels). Porter and Coates.

Marriage in Philippsburg. Martin Walser. LC 61-10123. 1961. New Directions.

Marriage Is a Private Affair. Judith Kelly. LC 41-14433. Harper & Brothers.

Marriage Is for Two. Natalie Shipman. 1947. S. Curl.

Marriage Is Possible. Margaret Widdemer. LC 36-27124. Farrar & Rinehart, Incorporated.

Marriage Is Possible. Margaret Widdemer. LC 42-25483. 1942. The Sun Dial Press.

Marriage Is So Final. Winifred Halsted. LC 39-2512. 1938. H. C. Kinsey & Company, Inc.

Marriage Later. William Arthur Neubauer. LC 46-22351. 1946. Phoenix Press.

Marriage License. Hager-Smith, Joanna. LC 81-82198. 8.95 (ISBN 0-88270-522-9). Haven Books: Distributed by Logos International.

Marriage License. Strange, Cecil. LC 32-19498. Covici; Friede.

Marriage Machine. Gillian Freeman. LC 74-30237. 256p. 1975. pap. 1.95 (ISBN 0-8128-7017-4). Stein & Day.

Marriage Machine: A Novel. Gillian Freeman. LC 74-30237. 1975. 7.95 (ISBN 0-8128-1792-3). Stein and Day.

Marriage Made in Heaven. Barbara Cartland. (Romance Ser.: No. 165). 160p. 1982. pap. 2.25 (ISBN 0-553-22918-4). Bantam.

Marriage Mart. Elizabeth Carter. 256p. (Orig.). 1983. pap. 2.25 (ISBN 0-449-20082-5, Crest). Fawcett.

Marriage Masque. Catherine Fellows. (Regency romance). 1974. (pbk.) 0.95. Dell.

Marriage Merger. Glenna Finley, pseud. (Orig.). 1978. pap. 1.95 (ISBN 0-451-11718-2, AJ1718, Sig). NAL.

Marriage of a Young Stockbroker. Charles Richard Webb. LC 79-103601. 1970. 5.95. Lippincott.

Marriage of Anne. Concordia Merrel. LC 27-16477. George H. Doran Company.

Marriage of Barry Wicklow. Ruby Mildred Ayres. LC 22-2003. W. J. Watt & Company.

Marriage of Captain Kettle. Charles John Cutcliffe Wright Hyne. LC 12-10817. 1.25. The Bobbs-Merrill Company.

Marriage of Caroline Lindsay. Margaret Rome. (Presents Ser.). 1974. pap. 1.25 (ISBN 0-373-70562-X, 70562, Pub by Harlequin). PB.

Marriage of Cecilia. Maude Leeson. LC 14-473912. 1914. G. P. Putnam's Sons.

Marriage of Claudia. Rose Franken. LC 48-1420. 1948. Rinehart.

Marriage of Convenience. Anne Green. LC 33-284942. 1933. E. P. Dutton & Co., Inc.

Marriage of Convenience. Tim Jeal. LC 79-840. 10.95 (ISBN 0-671-22872-2). Simon and Schuster.

Marriage of Convenience. Elizabeth Rossiter. LC 75-189233. 1974. (pbk.) 1.50. Avon.

Marriage of Convenience. A Tale. Harriett Jay. LC 7-10181. (On cover: Seaside library. Pocket ed. no. 334). G. Munro.

Marriage of Don Quixote. Adeline Lobdell Pynchon. LC 31-5123. The Bobbs-Merrill Company.

Marriage of Elizabeth Whitacker. 1st Ed. Jacobine Hichens. LC 53-6450. 1953. Duell, Sloan and Pearce.

Marriage of Esther. Guy Newell Boothby. LC 6-15031. 1895. D. Appleton and Company.

Marriage of Gabrielle: Tr. from the French of Daniel Lesueur Pseud. Jeanne Loiseau Lapauze. Tr. by Kendall, Laura E. LC 7-14802. (On cover: Globe library. v. 1, no. 141). 1890. Rand, McNally & Company.

Marriage of Gerard. Andre Theuriet & Watkins, Mary Linsay, Tr. LC 8-27739. (library of choice fiction no. 28). 1891. Laird & Lee.

Marriage of Inconvenience. Diana Campbell. 1982. pap. 2.25 (ISBN 0-451-11867-7, AE1867, Sig). NAL.

Marriage of Josephine. Marjorie Coryn. LC 45-10147. 1945. D. Appleton-Century Company.

Marriage of Josephine. Marjorie Coryn. LC 47-20094. 1947. The Sun Dial Press.

Marriage of Katherine. Dorothy Emily Stevenson. LC 65-22468. 1965. Holt, Rinehart and Winston.

Marriage of Loti. Julien Viaud. LC 75-37685. (Illus.). 9.95 (ISBN 0-8248-0395-7). University Press of Hawaii.

Marriage of Mademoiselle Gimel: And Other Stories. Rene Bazin. LC 13-21298. 1913. C. Scribner's Sons.

Marriage of Mademoiselle Gimel, & Other Stories. facs. ed. Rene Bazin. Tr. by Edna K. Hoyt. LC 71-128719. (Short Story Index Reprint Ser). 1913. 15.00 (ISBN 0-8369-3610-8). Ayer Co.

Marriage of Meggotta. Edith Pargeter. 1979. Viking Press.

Marriage of Megotta. Edith Pargeter. 1980. 2.50 (ISBN 0-445-04549-3). Fawcett Popular Library.

Marriage of Mrs. Merlin. Charles Stokes Wayne. 1907. G. W. Dillingham Company.

Marriage of Patricia Pepperday. Grace Miller White. LC 22-443583. 1922. Little, Brown, and Company.

Marriage of Reason. Maurice Francis Egan. LC 6-37570. 1893. J. Murphy & Co.

Marriage of Susan. Helen Reimensnyder Martin. LC 21-15715. 1921. Doubleday, Page & Company.

Marriage of Theodora. Molly Elliot Seawell. LC 10-8535. 1910. 1.50. Dodd, Mead and Company.
Marriage of William Ashe. Mary Augusta Arnold Humphry Ward Ward. LC 34-37797. 1906. Harper & Brothers.
Marriage of William Ashe: A Novel. Mary Augusta Arnold Humphry Ward Ward. LC 5-7624. 1905. Harper & Brothers.
Marriage of Wisdom & Other Tales. Wilton Sankawulo. (Secondary Readers Ser.). 1974. pap. text ed. 3.00x (ISBN 0-435-92820-1). Heinemann Ed.
Marriage of Yussuf Khan. translated from the swedish by robert emmons lee. ed. Gunnar Serner & Lee, Robert Emmons, Tr. LC 23-15163. Thomas Y. Crowell Company.
Marriage on Approval. Besse Sprague. LC 30-23084. A. L. Burt Company.
Marriage; or, Nellie. Margaret Lee. (On cover: Library of American authors. no. 6). 1889. G. Munro.
Marriage Pact. Lillian Cheatham. LC 73-83620. 1974. 4.95 (ISBN 0-385-07199-X). Published for the Crime Club by Doubleday.
Marriage Portion: A Novel. Hersilia A. Mitchell Copp Keays. LC 11-27302. 1.35. Small, Maynard & Company.
Marriage Racket. Vina Delmar. LC 33-163511. Harcourt, Brace and Company.
Marriage Racket... Vina Delmar. LC 47-219508. (On cover: New Avon library. 107). 1946.
Marriage Rite. Evans Wall. LC 32-16973. A. H. King, Inc.
Marriage Season. Sally Dubois. (Candlelight Ecstasy Ser.: No. 13). (Orig.). 1981. pap. 1.75 (ISBN 0-440-16058-8). Dell.
Marriage: Short Stories of Married Life. LC 23-9170. 1923. Doubleday, Page & Company.
Marriage to a Stranger. Dorothy Phillips. (Candlelight Ecstasy Ser.: No. 71). (Orig.). 1982. pap. 1.95 (ISBN 0-440-15605-X). Dell.
Marriage Under the Terror. Patricia Wentworth. LC 10-101888. 1910. G. P. Putman's Sons.
Marriage Verdict: A Novel. Frank Hamilton Spearman. LC 23-655974. 1923. C. Scribner's Sons.
Marriage Voices: A Novel. Benjamin R. Barber. LC 80-18831. 10.95 (ISBN 0-671-44808-0). Summit Books.
Marriage Was Made. Elizabeth Gertrude Levin Stern. LC 28-5642. J. H. Sears & Company, Inc.
Marriage While You Wait. Annie Edith Foster Jameson. LC 19-16155. 1919. Hodder and Stoughton.
Marriage While You Wait. Annie Edith Foster Jameson. LC 19-10144. George H. Doran Company.
Marriage with Nina. Norman Charles Hunter. LC 34-176506. 1934. W. Morrow and Company.
Marriage Without Love. Penny Jordan. (Harlequin Presents Ser.). 192p. 1982. pap. 1.75 (ISBN 0-373-10484-7). Harlequin Bks.
Marriages. Peter Straub. LC 72-87595. 1973. 5.95 (ISBN 0-698-10486-2). Coward, McCann & Geoghegan.
Marriages. Peter Straub. (Kangaroo Book). 1977. 1.75 (ISBN 0-671-81276-9). Pocket Books.
Marriages and Infidelities: Short Stories. Joyce Carol Oates. LC 72-83348. (Fawcett Crest Book). 1973. (pbk) 1.25. Fawcett.
Marriages Between Zones Three, Four, and Five (As Narrated by the Chroniclers of Zone Three) Doris May Lessing. LC 79-16515. (Canopus in argos archives). 1980. 9.95 (ISBN 0-394-50914-5). Knopf: Distributed by Random House.
Marriages Between Zones Three, Four, & Five. Doris May Lessing. LC 81-40193. 256p. 1981. pap. 4.95 (ISBN 0-394-74978-2, Vin). Random.
Married? Marjorie Benton Cooke. LC 21-172692. 1921. Doubleday, Page & Comapany.
Married. August Strindberg. LC 17-20667. (Half-title: The modern library of the world's best books.). Boni and Liveright, Inc.
Married. A Domestic Novel. Emma Barry Newby. LC 7-26116. 1869. Turner Brothers & Co.
Married Above Her. A Society Romance. LC 7-24687. T. B. Peterson & Brothers.
Married Against Reason. Adelheid Mackenzie. LC 7-16310. Loring.
Married Alive. Ralph Straus. LC 25-8369. 1925. H. Holt and Company.
Married at Leisure. Virginia Lederer & Alajalov, Constantin, 1900- Illus. LC 44-8909. 1944. Doubleday, Doran & Co., Inc.
Married at Midnight. H. C. Hoffman. (On cover: Munro's library, popular novels. v. 1, no. 395). 1885. N. L. Munro.
Married at Sight. Charles Garvice. (On cover: Laurel library, no. 17). 1894. G. Munro's Sons.
Married Belle: Or, Our Red Cottage at Merry Bank. A Novel. Julie P. Smith. LC 26-235593. 1872. G. W. Carleton & Co.
Married Beneath Him. James Payn. (Seaside library. v. 31, no. 646). 1879. G. Munro.
Married by the Mayor; or, The Dark Page in His Life. H. C. Hoffman. (On cover: Munro's library, popular novels. v. 1. no. 392). 1885. N. L. Munro.
Married Flirts. Mabel McElliott. LC 34-469044. Grosset & Dunlap.
Married for Both Worlds. Lydia Ann Emerson Porter. LC 7-37755. 1871. Lee and Shepard.
Married for Fun. A Novel... Augustus Hoppin. LC 7-5238. (On cover: Riverside paper series, no. 8). 1885. Houghton, Mifflin and Company.
Married for Gold. Emma Augusta Sharkey. (select series, no. 31). 1889. Street & Smith.
Married for Money. Lucy Randall Comfort. LC 6-30214. (On cover: The library of American authors. no. 19). 1890. G. Munro.
Married for Money: And Other Stories. May Agnes Early Fleming. (Sunnyside series, no. 18). 1891. J. S. Ogilvie.
Married in Haste. Ann Sophia Winterbotham Stephens. LC 8-142681. T. B. Peterson & Brothers.
Married in Haste. A Novel. Mary Elizabeth Braddon Maxwell. (Seaside library. v. 81, no. 1638). 1883. G. Munro.
Married in Haste. A Novel. Mary Elizabeth Braddon Maxwell. (On cover: Seaside library. Pocket ed. no. 480). 1885. G. Munro.
Married in Mask. A Novel. Mansfield Tracy Walworth. (On cover: The Manhattan series, no. 2). A. L. Burt.
Married in Mask. A Novel. Mansfield Tracy Walworth. (select series, no. 50). 1890. Street & Smith.
Married Land. Charles G Bell. LC 62-141904. 1962. Houghton Mifflin.
Married Life. Edith Louise Coues O'Shaughnessy. LC 71-152952. (Short story index reprint series). 1971. (ISBN 0-8369-3867-4). Books for Libraries Press.
Married Life. Edith Louise Coues O'Shaughnessy. LC 25-182745. Harcourt, Brace and Company.
Married Life: Its Shadows and Sunshine. Timothy Shay Arthur. LC 6-3409. (On cover: Lovell's library, v. 10, no. 518). J. W. Lovell Company.
Married Life of Helen and Warren. Mabel Herbert Urner. LC 25-180592. Small, Maynard & Company.
Married Life of the Frederic Carrolls. Jesse Lynch Williams. LC 10-27859. 1910. C. Scribner's Sons.
Married Life: Or, The True Romance. Helen Marion Edginton. 1917. Cassell and Company, Ltd.
Married Life: Or, The True Romance. Helen Marion Edginton. LC 20-862618. 1.75. Small, Maynard & Company.
Married Look. Robert Nathan. LC 50-13123. 1950. Knopf.
Married Lovers. Julius Horwitz. LC 72-14245. 1973. 6.95. Dial Press.
Married Man. Piers Paul Read. LC 79-2590. 10.00 (ISBN 0-397-01379-5). Lippincott.
Married Man. Piers Paul Read. 1981. 2.95 (ISBN 0-380-55103-9). Avon Books.
Married Man: A Novel. Frances Aymar Mathews. LC 99-4096. Rand McNally & Company.
Married Man: The Reflections of a Married Man and The Opinions of a Philosopher. Robert Grant. LC 26-1825. 1925. C. Scribner's Sons.
Married Man. 1st Ed. Benjamin Demott. LC 68-243832. 1968. 3.95. Harcourt.
Married Men. Jane Burr. LC 26-7845. 1925. Frank-Maurice, Inc.
Married Men. Francis Gordon Hurrell. LC 35-2266. 1934. Coward-McCann, Inc.
Married Men: A Novel. Ira Wolfert. LC 53-10814. 1953. Simon and Schuster.
Married Miss Worth: A Novel. Louise Closser Hale. LC 11-1530. 1911. Harper & Brothers.
Married Money. Harford Willing Hare Powel. LC 29-21219. 1929. Little, Brown, and Company.
Married or Single? Bithia Mary Sheppard Croker. LC 6-32163. (On cover: The fortnightly library. v. 14, no. 14-15). P. F. Collier.
Married or Single? Catharine Maria Sedgwick. LC 8-11242. 1857. Harper & Brothers.
Married Past Redemption. Patricia Veryan. LC 82-17019. 1983. 13.95 (ISBN 0-312-51615-0). St. Martin's Press.
Married People. Mary Roberts Rinehart. (Dell Book). 1977. 1.50 (ISBN 0-440-15423-5). Dell Pub. Co.
Married People. Mary Roberts Rinehart. LC 37-2688. Farrar & Rinehart, Incorporated.
Married, Spoken for, & Involved. Ruby Dusina. 1976. pap. 3.00 o.p. (Freedom Pr). Valkyrie Pr.
Married Sweethearts: A Romance of the Rockies. Alfred Osmond. LC 29-925762. The Deseret News Press.
Married the Wrong Man. A True and Wonderful Story. Benoni Mendenhall. LC 7-258436. 1890.
Married to a Spy. Alec Waugh. LC 76-380943. 1976. 3.95 (ISBN 0-491-01837-1). Allen.
Marrige for Three. Leona Slottman. LC 38-6958. Phoenix Press.
Marriotts and the Powells. Isabella Holt. LC 21-176225. 1921. The Macmillan Company.
Marrow of Tradition. Charles Waddell Chesnutt. LC 69-18585. (American Negro, His History and Literature). (Afro-American culture series.). 1969. Arno Press.
Marrow of Tradition. Charles Waddell Chesnutt. LC 70-83927. 1969. Mnemosyne Pub. Co.
Marrow of Tradition. Charles Waddell Chesnutt. LC 73-3467. (Ann Arbor paperbacks, AA147). 1969. 1.95. University of Michigan Press.
Marrow of Tradition. Charles Waddell Chesnutt. LC 74-78571. 1968. Gregg Press.
Marrow of Tradition. Charles Waddell Chesnutt. LC 72-1564. 1972. (ISBN 0-404-00014-2). AMS Press.
Marrow of Tradition. Charles Waddell Chesnutt. 1901. Houghton, Mifflin and Company.
Marry at Leisure see Nice Girl Like Me.
Marry at Leisure. 1st Ed. Anne Piper. LC 59-11739. 1959. Norton.
Marry for Love. Allene Soule Corliss. LC 31-20745. Farrar & Rinehart Incorporated.
Marry for Money. Faith Baldwin. 1976. Repr. of 1948 ed. lib. bdg. 14.40x (ISBN 0-88411-621-2). Amereon Ltd.
Marry for Money. Faith Baldwin Cuthrell. LC 76-41699. 1976. 6.95 (ISBN 0-88411-621-2). Aeonian Press.
Marry for Money. Faith Baldwin Cuthrell. LC 48-5391.
Marry in Haste. Maysie Greig. LC 35-163215. 1935. Doubleday, Doran & Co., Inc.
Marry in Haste. Maysie Greig. LC 37-11010. The Sun Dial Press, Inc.
Marry in Haste. Jane Aiken Hodge. LC 72-89109. 1970. 4.95. Doubleday.
Marry Me! John Updike. 1977. pap. 2.95 (ISBN 0-449-23369-3, Crest). Fawcett.
Marry Me: A Romance. John Updike. LC 76-13722. 1976. 8.95 (ISBN 0-394-40856-X). Knopf.
Marry Me: A Romance. limited 1st ed. John Updike. LC 77-364853. (Illus.). 1976. Franklin Library.
Marry Me: A Romance. John Updike. (FawcettCrest Book). 1977. 1.95 (ISBN 0-449-23369-3). Fawcett Books.
Marry Me Before You Go. Katherine Ursula Parrott. LC 41-193124. 1941. Dodd, Mead & Company.
Marry Me, Carry Me. Ardyth Kennelly. LC 56-102908. 1956. Houghton Mifflin.
Marry Me!, Marry Me! Claude Berri. LC 73-90762. 1969. 4.50. W. Morrow.
Marry Me, Nurse. Virginia Nielsen, pseud. 1973. pap. 0.75 o.s.i. (01-393). Lancer.
Marry on Monday. Laura Saunders. LC 54-3652. 1954. Avalon Books.
Marryers: A History Gathered from a Brief of the Honorable Socrates Potter. Irving Bacheller. LC 14-7568. 1914. Harper & Brothers.
Marrying and Giving in Marriage. Mary Louisa Stewart Molesworth. (On cover: Lovell's library, no. 1008). J. W. Lovell Company.
Marrying and Giving in Marriage. A Novel. Mary Louisa Stewart Molesworth. LC 9-3891. (Harper's Franklin square library, no. 582). 1887. Harper & Brothers.
Marrying and Giving in Marriage. A Novel. Mary Louisa Stewart Molesworth. LC 7-25316. (On cover: Seaside library. Pocket ed. no. 992). G. Munro.
Marrying by Lot. A Tale of the Primitive Moravians. Charlotte B Mortimer. LC 7-26104. 1868. G. P. Putnam & Son.
Marrying Kind. Elizabeth Cadell. LC 79-20088. 1980. 9.95 (ISBN 0-688-03581-7). Morrow.
Marrying Kind. Elizabeth Cadell. LC 80-12153. 1980. 12.95 (ISBN 0-8161-3083-3). G. K. Hall.
Marrying Kind. Peggy Gaddis, pseud. LC 47-11513. 1947. Gramercy Pub. Co.
Marrying Kind. Helen Grose. LC 32-20525. 1932. L. MacVeagh, Dial Press, Inc.
Marrying Man. A Novel. Harriet Maria Gordon Smythies. LC 8-10198. 1841. R. Bentley.
Marrying Mark. Violette Kimball Dunn. LC 38-17006. 1938. E. P. Dutton & Co., Inc.
Mars: A Science Fiction Vision. Richard Grossinger. (Illus.). 230p. (Orig.). 1971. pap. 3.50 (ISBN 0-913028-00-2). North Atlantic.
Mars at Last! Mark Washburn. LC 77-8509. 1977. 8.95 o.p. (ISBN 0-399-11935-3). Putnam Pub Group.
Mars' Butterfly: A Tale of the Career of Major John Andre, Spy-Extraordinary of the British Army in the American Revolution. Henry Pleasants. LC 41-6231. The Christopher Publishing House.
Mars in the House of Death. Rex Ingram. LC 39-251461. 1939. A. A. Knopf.
Mars, We Love You. Jane Hipolito & Willis E. McNelly. (O.S.I.). 1973. pap. 1.25 o.s.i. (ISBN 0-515-03086-4). Pyramid Pubns.
Mars, We Love You. Herbert George Wells et al. Ed. by Willis E. McNelly & Jane Hipolito. (Science Fiction Ser). 1971. 6.95 o.p. Doubleday.
Mars, We Love You: Tales of Mars, Men, and Martians. Jane Hippolito. LC 77-166420. (Doubleday science fiction). 1971. 6.95. Doubleday.
Mars Wun. James Bob Miller. 1978. pap. 2.95 (ISBN 0-89185-175-5). Anthelion Pr.
Marsanne. Virginia Coffman. (Fawcett Crest Book). 1977. 1.75 (ISBN 0-449-23373-1). Fawcett Books.
Marsanne: A Novel. Virginia Coffman. LC 76-150633. 8.95 (ISBN 0-87795-138-1). Arbor House.
Marsanne: A Novel. Virginia Coffman. LC 80-36760. 1980. 14.95 (ISBN 0-8161-3049-3). G. K. Hall.
Marse Bob. 1st Ed. Leroy Barry Allen. LC 56-127685. 1957. Vantage Press.
Marse Chan: A Tale of Old Virginia. Thomas Nelson Page. LC 12-37646. 1892. C. Scribner's Sons.
Marseilles Enforcer. Don Smith. (Secret Mission Ser). (O.s.i.). 192p. (Orig.). 1974. pap. 0.95 o.s.i. (AN1041, Award). Univ Pub & Dist.
Marsena, and Other Stories of the Wartime. Harold Frederic. LC 72-110191. (Short story index reprint series). 1970. Books for Libraries Press.
Marsena: And Other Stories of the Wartime. Harold Frederic. LC 6-43132. 1894. C. Scribner's Sons.
Marsena & Other Stories of the Wartime see Collected Works.
Marsh. Ernest Raymond. LC 37-324212. 1937. Frederick A. Stokes Company.
Marsh. A Novel. Rosa Vertner Jeffrey. LC 7-10191. 1884. J. B. Lippincott & Co.
Marsh-Fire. Mateel Howe Farnham. LC 28-25955. 1928. Dodd, Mead & Company.
Marsh House. Mary Linn Roby. LC 73-10887. 1974. 6.95. Hawthorn Books.
Marsh House. Mary Linn Roby. 1975. (pbk.) 1.25 (ISBN 0-523-00576-8). Pinnacle Books.
Marsh Island see Collected Works.
Marsh Lights. Helen Manchester Gates Granville-Barker. LC 13-18597. 1913. 1.35. C. Scribner's Sons.
Marsh Lights. Rachel Swete Macnamara. LC 25-115912. Small, Maynard & Company.
Marsh Wife. James B Wharton. LC 30-7293. 1930. Coward-McCann, Inc.
Marsha. Margaret Maze Craig. LC 55-9209. 1955. Crowell.
Marsha & Her Uncle Jonathan. Lottie Henry. pap. 1.95 o.p. (8084). Cameo.
Marshal. Mary Raymond Shipman Andrews. LC 12-228723. The Bobbs-Merrill Company.
Marshal. Frank Gruber. LC 58-716653. 1958. Rinehart.
Marshal. Frank Gruber. (Signet brand western). 1974. (pbk.) 0.95. New American Library.
Marshal. Dennis St. Pierre. 272p. (Orig.). 1981. pap. 2.75 (ISBN 0-446-90832-0). Warner Bks.
Marshal Duke of Denver: Or, The Labor Revolution of 1920. A Novel. Ernest Hugh Fitzpatrick. LC 6-41120. Donohue & Henneberry Co.
Marshal of Bent Fork. Philip Morgan. LC 57-126874. 1957. Avalon Books.
Marshal of Deer Creek. Archie Joscelyn. LC 49-485023. (Silver star westerns). 1949. Dodd, Mead.
Marshal of Medicine Bend: By Brad Ward Pseud. 1st Ed. Samuel Anthony Peeples. LC 53-6076. (Dutton Diamond D western). 1953. Dutton.
Marshal of Packersville. Cy Martin. 1976. 4.95. Avalon Books.
Marshal of Sundown. Jackson Gregory. LC 38-177157. 1938. Dodd, Mead & Company.
Marshal of Wichita. Thomas Albert Curry. LC 46-3763. 1946. Arcadia House, Inc.
Marshal Sam Clay. Strong, Charles Stanley. LC 52-10212. 1952. Arcadia House.
Marshall from Texas. Owen G Irons. 1975. 4.95. Avalon Books.
Marshall of Babylon see Bullet for Mr Texas.
Marshall of Bitterroot. Michael Hammonds. (O.s.i.). Orig. Title: Among the Hunted. 1975. pap. 0.95 o.s.i. (BT50853). Belmont-Tower.
Marshall of Pioche. Nelson Nye. 1976. (pbk.) 0.95. Ace Books.
Marshal's Gun. Stack Sutton. 1978. pap. 1.75 (ISBN 0-89041-218-9, 3218). Major Bks.
Marshal's Lady. Sarah Stamford. LC 80-23290. 11.95 (ISBN 0-525-15320-9). Dutton.
Marshfield: The Observer & The Death-Dance; Studies of Character & Action. Egerton Castle. LC 2502. 1900. H. S. Stone & Company.
Marshland. Andre Paul Guillaume Gide. Bd. with Prometheus Misbound. 4.50 o.p. New Directions.
Marshland Brace: Two Louisiana Stories. Chris Segura. LC 82-15193. 1982. 15.95 (ISBN 0-8071-1040-X). Louisiana State University Press.

TITLE •NDEX MARY ANERLEY. A YORKSHIRE

Marshlands & Prometheus Misbound. Andre Paul Guillaume Gide. 1965. pap. 1.95 o.p. (ISBN 0-07-023194-X). McGraw.
Marshmallow Pie. Graham Lord. LC 78-113532. 1970. 4.95. Coward-McCann.
Marshwood. Monica Heath. (Signet Book). 1977. 1.50 (ISBN 0-451-07801-2). New American Library.
Marshwood. Dorothy James Roberts. LC 49-2705. 1949. Appleton-Century-Crofts.
Marston Hall. A Story Illustrative of Southern Life. Beryl Carr. LC 6-24225. 1880. G. W. Carleton & Co.; Etc., Etc.
Marston Murder Case. William Averill Stowell. LC 30-19506. 1930. D. Appleton and Company.
Marta. Rodolfo Celletti. LC 62-9936. (O.s.i.). 1962. 4.95 o.s.i. (ISBN 0-8076-0177-2). Braziller.
Marta. Peggy O'More, pseud. LC 56-10912. 1956. Arcadia House.
Marta in Love. Peggy O'More, pseud. (Starlight Romance Ser). 1971. pap. 0.60 o.p. (60-486). Manor Bks.
Martereau. Nathalie Sarraute. pap. 7.95. French & Eur.
Martereau: A Novel. Translated by Maria Jolas. Nathalie Sarraute. LC 59-12067. 1959. G. Braziller.
Martha. Ethel Edith Mannin. LC 23-14913. 1923. Duffield & Company.
Martha. Percy Marks. LC 25-5459. 2.00. The Century Co.
Martha. Nathan A Schiff. LC 74-163455. 1973. 5.95. Lyle Stuart.
Martha: A Novel. Maria Benedicto. LC 66-40067. 1964. J. M. Dent.
Martha and Cupid. Julie Mathilde Lippmann. LC 14-20503. 1914. 1.00. H. Holt and Company.
Martha and Mary. Johannes Anker-Larsen & Chater, Arthur G., Tr. LC 26-14672. 1926. A. A. Knopf.
Martha and Mary. Olive Mary Salter. LC 21-7407. 1921. G. P. Putnam's Sons.
Martha by-the-Day. Julie Mathilde Lippmann. LC 12-21275. 1912. H. Holt and Company.
Martha by-the-Day. Julie Mathilde Lippmann. LC 26-235672. 1914. Grosset & Dunlap.
Martha Corey: A Tale of the Salem Witchcraft. Constance Goddard Du Bois. LC 6-34912. 1890. A. C. McClurg and Company.
Martha Crane: A Novel. Charles O Gorham. 1953. Farrar, Straus and Young.
Martha, Eric, and George: A Novel. Margery Sharp. LC 64-12101. 1964. Little, Brown.
Martha, Martha: A Biblical Novel. Patricia McGerr. LC 60-7787. 1960. P. J. Kenedy.
Martha of India: A Missionary Story. Millie Bock Jacobson. LC 24-24696. Augustana Book Concern.
Martha of the Mennonite Country. Helen Reimensnyder Martin. LC 15-26131. 1915. 1.35. Doubleday, Page & Company.
Martha Quest. Doris May Lessing. LC 74-159969. (Her Children of violence, v. 1). 1973. 0.50 (ISBN 0-586-02115-9). Panther.
Martha Quest: A Complete Novel from Doris Lessing's Masterwork, Children of Violence. Doris May Lessing. 1970. pap. 4.95 (ISBN 0-452-25353-5, Z5353, Plume). NAL.
Martha the Parson's Daughter: And Under the Muses' Ban. Bertha Behrens. LC 6-9436. (primrose series, no. 22). 1891. Street & Smith.
Martha Wilton's Strong Tower. Mabel Hale. LC 25-22639. Gospel Trumpet Company.
Martha's Vineyard Affair. Stan Hart. (Orig.). 1980. pap. 2.25 (ISBN 0-440-15557-6). Dell.
Marthe and the Madman. Jean De Bosschere & Loving, Pierre, 1898- Tr. LC 28-29429. 1928. Covici, Friede.
Martial Spirit. Walter Millis. 6.50 o.p. HM.
Martian: A Novel. George Louis Palmella Busson Du Maurier. LC 77-144991. (Illus.). 1971. Scholarly Press.
Martian: A Novel. George Louis Palmella Busson Du Maurier. LC 6-35879. 1897. Harper & Brothers.
Martian, a Novel. George Louis Palmella Busson Du Maurier. 1979. Repr. of 1897 ed. lib. bdg. 20.00 (ISBN 0-8495-1045-7). Arden Lib.
Martian Chronicles. Ray Bradbury. LC 72-94171. (Illus.). 1973. 8.95 (ISBN 0-385-03862-3). Doubleday.
Martian Chronicles. Ray Bradbury. Ed. by Joseph A. Mugnaini. LC 75-321031. (Illus.). 1974. Cardavon Press.
Martian Chronicles. Ray Bradbury. LC 58-8207. 1958. Doubleday.
Martian Chronicles. 1st Ed. Ray Bradbury. LC 50-7660. 1950. Doubleday.
Martian Inca. Ian Watson. 1978. 1.95 (ISBN 0-441-52044-8). Ace Books.
Martian Odyssey. Ronald J. Ebner. 1981. 4.95 (ISBN 0-8062-1624-7). Carlton.
Martian Odyssey. Stanley Grauman Weinbaum. (Orig.). 1972. pap. 0.95 o.s.i. (75-399). Lancer.
Martian Odyssey and Other Science Fiction Tales. Stanley Grauman Weinbaum. LC 73-13269. (Classics of science fiction). 1974. (ISBN 0-88355-123-3) (ISBN 0-88355-152-7). Hyperion Press.
Martian Odyssey: And Others. Stanley Grauman Weinbaum. LC 49-8970. 1949. Fantasy Press.
Martian Tales, 4 vols. Edgar Rice Burroughs. 1982. pap. 7.80 (ISBN 0-345-26213-1, Del Rey). Ballantine.
Martian Time-Slip. 4th ed. Philip K. Dick. 224p. 1981. pap. 2.25 (ISBN 0-345-29560-9). Ballantine.
Martian Way: And Other Stories. Isaac Asimov. LC 55-5496. (Doubleday science fiction). 1955. Doubleday.
Martian Way and Other Stories. Isaac Asimov. LC 81-15009. 1982. 12.50 (ISBN 0-8376-0463-X). R. Bentley.
Martians, Go Home. Fredric Brown. LC 55-11672. 1955. Dutton.
Martie, the Unconquered. Kathleen Thompson Norris. LC 17-22088. 1917. Doubleday, Page & Company.
Martin. George A. Romero & Susan Sparrow. LC 77-94386. 7.95 o.p. (ISBN 0-8128-2478-4); pap. 1.95 (ISBN 0-8128-7020-4). Stein & Day.
Martin: A Novel. George A. Romero & Susan Sparrow. LC 77-78073. 1977. 7.95 (ISBN 0-8128-2478-4). Stein and Day.
Martin Birck's Youth. Hjalmar Emil Fredrik Soderberg. Tr. by Stork, Charles Wharton. LC 30-8264. 1930. Harper & Brothers.
Martin Brook. Morgan Bates. 1901. Harper & Brothers.
Martin Butterfield. John Burgan. LC 50-8985. 1950. Winston.
Martin Chuzzlewit... Charles Dickens. LC 6-26439. 1867. Hurd and Houghton.
Martin Chuzzlewit... Charles Dickens. LC 7-3633. 1873. Hurd and Houghton.
Martin Chuzzlewit. Charles Dickens. LC 9-824. Aldine Book Publishing Co.
Martin Chuzzlewit. Charles Dickens. LC 42-28981. (Complete works. The household edition). Estes and Lauriat.
Martin Chuzzlewit. Charles Dickens & Brock, Henry Matthew, 1875- Illus. LC 44-5770. (On cover: Great illustrated classics). 1944. Dodd, Mead & Company.
Martin Chuzzlewit. Ed., Introd. by Edgar Johnson. Charles Dickens. Ed. by Edgar Johnson. LC 65-1702. (Laurel Dickens, 5445). Dell.
Martin Chuzzlewitt. Charles Dickens. Ed. by P. N. Furbank. (English Library Ser.). 1975. pap. 5.95 (ISBN 0-14-043031-8). Penguin.
Martin Conisby's Vengeance. Jeffery Farnol. LC 21-17370. 1921. Little, Brown, and Company.
Martin, Conisby's Vengeance. Jeffery Farnol. LC 35-28558. 1923. A. L. Burt Company.
Martin Eden. Jack London. LC 9-22752. 1909. The Macmillan Company.
Martin Eden. Jack London. LC 16-6996. 1910. The Macmillan Company.
Martin Eden. Jack London. LC 46-8611. 1946. Penguin Books, Inc.
Martin Eden. Introd. and Notes by Sam S. Baskett. Jack London. LC 56-120474. (Rinehart editions, 80). 1956. Rinehart.
Martin Eden. Library Ed. Jack London. LC 57-734. 1957. Macmillan.
Martin Faber: The Story of a Criminal and Other Tales. William Gilmore Simms. LC 75-32784. (Literature of Mystery and Detection). 1976. (2 vols. 28.00 (ISBN 0-405-07899-4). Arno Press.
Martin Hanner: A Comedy. Kathleen Freeman. LC 27-8467. 1926. Harcourt, Brace and Company.
Martin Hewitt, Investigator. Arthur Morrison. LC 74-10488. (Illus.). 1975. 10.00 (ISBN 0-88355-203-5). Hyperion Press.
Martin Hewitt, Investigator. Arthur Morrison. LC 75-32769. (Literature of Mystery and Detection). (Illus.). 1976. 12.00 (ISBN 0-405-07888-9). Arno Press.
Martin Hewitt: Investigator. Arthur Morrison. LC 72-27079. 1971. 4.50. O. Train.
Martin Hewitt: Investigator. Arthur Morrison. LC 7-26100. (On cover: Harper's Franklin square library, no. 755). 1894. Harper & Brothers.
Martin Hyde: The Duke's Messenger. John Masefield. LC 10-22985. 1910. Little, Brown, and Company.
Martin Hyde: The Duke's Messenger. John Masefield. LC 24-2690. (Beacon Hill bookshelf). 1924. Little, Brown, and Company.
Martin Marauder & the Franklin Allens: A Wartime Love Story. Ed. by Donald J. Mrozek et al. 1980. 30.00x (ISBN 0-89745-007-8); pap. 18.00x. Sunflower U Pr.
Martin Pippin in the Apple Orchard. Eleanor Farjeon. LC 22-9875. Frederick A. Stokes Company.
Martin Rivas: Novela De Costumbres Chilenas. Gana Alerto Blest & Umphrey, George Wallace, 1878- Ed. LC 26-23393. (Heath's Modern Language Series). D.C. Heath and Company.
Martin Salander. Gottfried Keller. 1981. pap. 4.95 (ISBN 0-7145-0371-1). Riverrun NY.
Martin Schuler. Florence Roma Muir Wilson O'Brien. LC 19-26445. 1919. H. Holt and Company.
Martin Schuler: With an Introduction. Florence Roma Muir Wilson O'Brien. LC 28-5871. 1928. A. A. Knopf.
Martin the Founding: Or, The Adventures of a Valet De Chambre. Eugene Sue. (Seaside library, v. 75, no. 1540). 1883. G. Munro.
Martin Valliant. Warwick Deeping. LC 17-10202. 1917. R. M. McBride & Company.
Martin Wickramasinghe's Madol Doova. Martin Wickramasinghe. LC 76-904026. (Illus.). 1976. 8.00. Tisara Prakasakayo.
Martini-Henry Modification: A Novel. Barrie Hughes. LC 78-13148. 8.95 (ISBN 0-393-08840-5). Norton.
Martin's Land. Jess Shelton. 1970. pap. 0.75 o.p. (ISBN 0-446-64433-1, 64-433). Paperback Lib.
Martin's Land: A Novel. 1st Ed. Jess Shelton. LC 61-12692. 1961. Chilton Co., Book Division.
Martins of Cro' Martin. Charles James Lever. (Seaside library, v. 32, no. 65). 1879. G. Munro.
Martins of Cro' Martin: Paul Goslett's Confessions. Charles James Lever. 1906. Little, Brown, and Company.
Martin's Summer. Vicki Baum. Tr. by Creighton, Basil. LC 31-21180. 1931. Cosmopolitan Book Corporation.
Martir De Las Catacumbas: Martyr of the Catacombs. (Span). pap. 2.95 (ISBN 0-8024-1720-5). Moody.
Martlet's Tale. Nicholas Delbanco. LC 66-13361. 4.50. Lippincott.
Marty. P. Chayevsky. Ed. by Warren Halliburton. Bd. with Printer's Measure. (Reading Shelf 1 Ser.). 1968. pap. 2.12 o.p. (ISBN 0-07-025632-2). McGraw.
Martyr. pap. 0.75 o.p. (07150). Curtis.
Martyr. David Meltzer. pap. 1.95 o.p. (0116). Essex Hse.
Martyr. Liam O'Flaherty. LC 33-14406. 1933. The Macmillan Company.
Martyr. Brian R. Utley. 1970. pap. 0.75 o.p. (07150). Curtis.
Martyr of Destiny. Edgar Fawcett. LC 6-38790. (On cover: Once a week semi-monthly library. v. 11, no. 2). 1894. P. F. Collier.
Martyr of Golgotha: A Picture of Oriental Tradition. Enrique Perez Escruch. Tr. by Godoy, Adele Josephine. LC 7-36356. 1887. W. S. Gottsberger.
Martyr of the Catacombs. pap. 2.95 (ISBN 0-8024-0011-6). Moody.
Martyr to the Queen. Paul Feval & Lassez, M., Joint Author. LC 28-6309. (His The years between; adventures of D'Artagnan and Cyrano de Bergerac. II). 1928. Longmans, Green and Co.
Martyred: A Novel. Richard E Kim. LC 64-10785. 1964. G. Braziller.
Martyred Fool: A Novel. David Christie Murray. LC 7-31827. 1895. Harper & Brothers.
Martyred Souls. Wallace G Young. LC 36-8615. Chapman & Grimes.
Martyrs. Francois August Rene de Chateaubriand. LC 76-15294. 1976. 17.50. H. Fertig.
Martyrs: By M. De Chateaubriand. Francois Auguste Rene De Chateaubriand. Ed. by Wight, Orlando William. LC 6-23436. 1859. Derby & Jackson.
Martyrs Never Die. Precioso M Nicanor. LC 67-31119. 1968. Pre-Mer Pub. Co.
Martyrs of Empire: Or, Dinkinbar. Herbert C McIlwain. 1889. R. F. Fenno & Company; Etc., Etc.
Martyrs of Guanabara. John Gillies. LC 76-14954. 5.95 (ISBN 0-8024-5187-X). Moody Press.
Martyrs of Spain and the Liberators of Holland. Elizabeth Rundle Charles. LC 6-20158. 1865. R. Carter and Brothers.
Martyrs of the Oblong & Little Nine. Decost Smith. 6.00 o.p. Brown Bk.
Maru. Bessie Head. LC 73-154270. 1971. 4.50 (ISBN 0-8415-0117-3). McCall Pub. Co.
Maruja. Bret I. E. Francis Bret Harte. LC 13-7659. 1885. Houghton, Mifflin and Company.
Maruja: And Other Tales. Bret Harte. LC 71-113671. (His Stories of California and the frontier). (Short story index reprint series.). 1970. Books for Libraries Press.
Maruja: And Other Tales. Bret Harte. LC 12-24357. (Half-title: Standard library edition, The writings of Bret Harte... v. 5). Houghton, Mifflin and Company.
Maruja & Other Tales. facsimile ed. Bret Harte. LC 71-113671. (Short Story Index Reprint Ser.: Vol. 1). 1896. 25.00 (ISBN 0-8369-3400-8). Ayer Co.
Marune: Alastor Nine Hundred Thirty-Three. Jack Vance, pseud. 1981. pap. 2.25 (ISBN 0-87997-591-1, UE1591). Daw Bks.
Marune: Alastor 933. John Holbrook Vance. LC 75-19107. 1975. 1.50 (ISBN 0-345-24518-0). Ballantine Books.
Marusia. Grigoril Fedorovich Kvitka. Tr. by Livesay, Florence (Randal) LC 40-27274. 1940. E. P. Dutton & Co. Inc.
Marvel. Margaret Wolfe Hungerford. LC 7-8496. (On cover: Lovell's library, no. 1136). 1888. J. W. Lovell Company.
Marvella. Hazel Smith. LC 49-9432. 1949. Meador Pub. Co.
Marvellous Coincidence: Or, A Chain of Misadventures and Mysteries. Kinahan Cornwallis. LC 6-28729. 1891. G. W. Dillingham.
Marvellous in Our Eyes: A Story of Providence. Emma E Hornibrook. LC 7-5195. (On cover: Cassell's "rainbow" series of original novels. v. 1. no. 11). Cassell & Company, Limited.
Marvelous Evidence; or, A Witness from the Grave. A Psychological Study. A True Narrative of Thrilling Interest, Astounding Incident and Climax... Thomas Henry Bates. LC 6-9076. 1897. T. H. Bates.
Marvelous Mongolian. James Aldridge. LC 73-20234. (Illus.). 1974. 5.95 (ISBN 0-316-03120-8). Little, Brown.
Marvelous Mongolian. James Aldridge. (Illus.). 1976. (pbk.) 1.25. Bantam Books.
Marvelous Palace and Other Stories. Pierre Boulle. LC 78-103643. 8.95 (ISBN 0-8149-0788-1). Vanguard Press.
Marverick. A Double D. Western. Bennett Foster. LC 42-10303. 1942. Doubleday, Doran and Company, Inc.
Marvick Heart. Rebecca Marsh, pseud. (Alouette Romance Ser.). 224p. (Orig.). 1981. pap. 2.25 (ISBN 0-89531-134-8, 0198-96). Sharon Pubns.
Marvin and Tige. Frankcina Glass. LC 77-76634. 1977. 8.95 (ISBN 0-312-51783-1). St. Martin's Press.
Mary. Bjornstjerne Bjornson & Morison, Mary, Tr. (Half-title: The novels of Bjornstjerne Bjornson, ed. Edmund Gosse, vol. III). 1909. The Macmillan Company.
Mary. Winifred Graham Cory. LC 11-11316. 1910. M. Kennerley.
Mary. David W. Frasure. 128p. (Orig.). 1982. pap. 5.95 (ISBN 0-932298-26-5). Copple Hse.
Mary. David W. Frasure. 1982. pap. 5.95 o.p. Caroline Hse.
Mary. Vladimir Vladimirovich Nabokov. 1981. pap. 4.95 (ISBN 0-07-045698-4). McGraw.
Mary. Vladimir Vladimirovich Nabokov. 1971. pap. 0.95 o.p. (M1602, Crest). Fawcett World.
Mary. Vladimir Vladimirovich Nabokov. 1970. 6.95 o.p. (ISBN 0-07-045731-X). McGraw.
Mary. Wilis. pap. 3.95 o.p. (ISBN 0-910122-36-9). Amherst Pr.
Mary: A Fiction. Mary Wollstonecraft. LC 76-39618. 1977. 7.50. (ISBN 0-8052-3657-0). Schocken Books.
Mary: A Fiction. Mary Wollstonecraft. LC 73-22069. (Feminist Controversy in England, 1788-1810). 1974. (ISBN 0-8240-0888-X). Garland Pub.
Mary, a Fiction. Mary Wollstonecraft. LC 76-39618. 7.50x (ISBN 0-8052-3657-0); pap. 3.45 o.p. (ISBN 0-8052-0557-8). Schocken.
Mary, a Fiction and The Wrongs of Woman. Mary Wollstonecraft. LC 77-352233. 1976. 12.00 (ISBN 0-19-255367-4). Oxford University Press.
Mary: A Novel, Following Spira and Ray, Containing Suggestions for the Betterment of Aspiring Mankind. Monroe E Miller. LC 41-27722. Press of H. L. & J. B. McQueen, Inc.
Mary Adrianna. 1st. ed. Maren Sainte Marie. 1975. 5.00 (ISBN 0-682-47976-4). Exposition Press.
Mary Alice in the Palace. cancelled o.p. (ISBN 0-8092-8680-7). Regnery.
Mary and Bob's True Story Book. Bernarr Macfadden. LC 30-29255. 1930. Macfadden Book Company, Inc.
Mary & the Kansas Kid. Don A. Brosseau. 220p. 1978. 6.95 o.p. (ISBN 0-8059-2574-0). Dorrance.
Mary and the Seven Boys: A Story of the Heroic People of Holland Under the Nazi Occupation. Joan Speakman. LC 59-10377. 1959. Greenwich Book Publishers.
Mary and the Spinners. Elizabeth Hollister Frost. LC 46-11922. 1946. Coward-McCann, Inc.
Mary & the Wrongs of Woman. Mary Wollstonecraft. Ed. by Gary Kelly. (Oxford English Novels Ser.). 1976. 14.95x (ISBN 0-19-255367-4); pap. 3.95 (ISBN 0-19-281527-X). Oxford U Pr.
Mary Anerley. Richard Doddridge Blackmore. LC 6-13829. (On cover: Lovell's library, no. 1034). 1887. J. W. Lovell Company.
Mary Anerley. A Yorkshire Tale. Richard Doddridge Blackmore. LC 6-13858. (Harper's Franklin square library, no. 123). 1880. Harper and Brothers.

Mary Anerley. A Yorkshire Tale. Richard Doddridge Blackmore. LC 6-13830. (On cover: Seaside library. Pocket ed., no. 615). G. Munro.
Mary Ann. Alex Karmel. LC 58-54712. 1958. Viking Press.
Mary Ann and Bill. Catherine Cookson. LC 78-64881. 1979. 8.95 (ISBN 0-688-03393-8). Morrow.
Mary Anne. Daphne Du Maurier. LC 76-184729. 352p. 1971. Repr. of 1954 ed. lib. bdg. 12.50x (ISBN 0-8376-0411-7). Bentley.
Mary Anne, a Novel. Daphne Du Maurier. LC 54-6254. 1954. Doubleday.
Mary Anne: A Novel. Daphne Du Maurier. LC 76-184729. 1971-1972. 8.50 (ISBN 0-8376-0411-7). R. Bentley.
Mary Anne Carew: Wife, Mother, Spirit Angel. Carlyle Petersilea. 1893. Colby & Rich.
Mary Ann's Angels. Catherine Cookson. LC 78-53413. 1978. 7.95 (ISBN 0-688-03317-2). W. Morrow.
Mary Arden. Grace Livingston Hill. 1976. Repr. of 1948 ed. lib. bdg. 14.10x (ISBN 0-89190-021-7). Am Repr-Rivercity Pr.
Mary Arden. Grace Livingston Hill & Ruth R. Hill. 1948. 2.95 o.p. G&D.
Mary Arden: A Novel. Grace Livingston Hill. LC 48-7781. 1948. J. B. Lippincott Co.
Mary Arden: A Novel. Grace Livingston Hill & Ruth Livingston Hill Munce. LC 79-28143. 1980. 11.40 (ISBN 0-89190-021-7). Aeonian Press.
Mary Barton. Elizabeth Cleghorn Stevenson Gaskell. (Half-title: Everyman's library, ed. by Ernest Rhys. Fiction. no. 598). 1912. J. M. Dent & Sons, Ltd.
Mary Barton. Elizabeth Cleghorn Stevenson Gaskell. LC 33-344999. (Half-title: The novels and tales of Mrs. Gaskell--i). 1930. H. Milford, Oxford University Press.
Mary Barton. Elizabeth Cleghorn Stevenson Gaskell. Ed. by Adolphus William Ward. LC 6-31382. (Half-title: The works of Mrs. Gaskell... Knutsford ed. v. 1). 1906. G. P. Putnam Sons; Etc., Etc.
Mary Barton: a Tale of Manchester Life. Elizabeth Cleghorn Stevenson Gaskell. LC 76-18825. (Penguin English library). (Illus.). 1970. Penguin.
Mary Barton: A Tale of Manchester Life. Elizabeth Cleghorn Stevenson Gaskell. (Harper's Franklin square library, no. 308). 1883. Harper & Brothers.
Mary Barton. To Which Are Added: Libbie Marsh's Three Eras, Clopton House, The Sexton's Hero. knutsford ed. 1st ams ed. new york, putnam. ed. Elizabeth Cleghorn Stevenson Gaskell. LC 70-148782. (works of Mrs. Gaskell, v. 1). (Illus.). 1972. 24.00 (ISBN 0-404-07251-8). AMS Press.
Mary Bunyan, the Dreamer's Blind Daughter. A Tale of Religious Persecution. Sallie Rochester Ford. LC 6-41227. 1860. Sheldon & Co.
Mary: By Ruth Dewey Groves. Ruth Dewey Groves. LC 29-2967. A. L. Burt Company.
Mary Cameron: A Romance of Fisherman's Island. Edith Augusta Sawyer. LC 99-2973. 1899. B. H. Sanborn & Co.
Mary Cary "Frequently Martha,". Kate Lee Langley Bosher. LC 12-21682. 1910. Harper & Brothers.
Mary Celeste. J. G. Lockhart. (Mariners Library). 1952. text ed. 4.75x o.p. Humanities.
Mary Celeste: A Survivor's Tale. Stanley Miller. LC 80-51383. 9.95 (ISBN 0-312-51862-5). St. Martin's Press.
Mary Contrary. Peggy O'More, pseud. LC 64-9282. 1964. Arcadia House.
Mary Darlin' Evelyn Voss Wise. LC 43-12121. 1943. D. Appleton-Century Company, Incorporated.
Mary Derwent: A Novel. Ann Sophia Winterbotham Stephens. LC 8-12412. T. B. Peterson and Brothers.
Mary Donovan. Anne Miller Downes. LC 48-536619. 1948. J. B. Lippincott Co.
Mary Dove. Jane Gilmore Rushing. LC 73-9029. 216p. 1974. 9.95 (ISBN 0-385-08302-5). Doubleday.
Mary Dove: A Love Story. Jane Gilmore Rushing. LC 73-9029. 1974. 5.95 (ISBN 0-385-08302-5). Doubleday.
Mary Ellen's Diary. H. S. Lehman. LC 28-227788. Biola Book Room.
Mary Faith. Beatrice Burton Morgan. LC 31-14055. Farrar & Rinehart, Incorporated.
Mary Fenwick's Daughter: A Novel. Beatrice Whitby. LC 8-36038. (On cover: Appletons' town and country library, no. 143). 1894. D. Appleton and Company.
Mary Fran & Mo. Maureen Lynch. LC 79-16493. 1979. 8.95 (ISBN 0-312-51864-1). St Martin.
Mary Garvin: The Story of a New Hampshire Summer. Fred Lewis Pattee. LC 2-9793. 1902. T. Y. Crowell & Co.
Mary-Girl: A Posthumous Novel. Hope Butler-Wilkins Merrick. LC 20-8792. E. P. Dutton and Company.
Mary Glenn. Sarah Gertrude Liebson Millin. LC 26-183141. 1925. Boni and Liveright.
Mary Glenn. limited ed. Sarah Gertrude Liebson Millin. LC 79-18571. 1979. 11.95 (ISBN 0-89733-015-3) (ISBN 0-89733-014-5). Academy Chicago.
Mary Gray. Katharine Tynan Hinkson, pseud. LC 10-14253. 1909. Cassell and Company, Limited.
Mary Gresley and Other Stories. Anthony Trollope. LC 73-16190. 1973. (ISBN 0-8414-8562-3). Folcroft Library Editions.
Mary-'Gusta. Joseph Crosby Lincoln. LC 16-21935. 1916. D. Appleton and Company.
Mary-'Gusta. Joseph Crosby Lincoln. LC 21-13934. 1918. A. L. Burt Company.
Mary Hallam. Susan Ertz. LC 47-30176. 1947. Harper & Brothers.
Mary Jane's Pa. Norman Way & Ellis, Edith. 1909. The H. K. Fly Company.
Mary Lacey: A Novel. Maureen Connell. LC 80-7893. 10.95 (ISBN 0-690-01950-5). Harper & Row.
Mary Lavelle: A Novel. Kate O'Brien. LC 36-296093. 1936. Doubleday, Doran and Company, Inc.
Mary Lavin: Selected Stories. Mary Lavin. 288p. (Orig.). 1981. pap. 6.95 (ISBN 0-14-005602-5). Irish Bk Ctr.
Mary Lawson. Frank Swigart. LC 10-742. Roxburgh Publishing Company, Incorporated.
Mary Lee. Geoffrey Pomeroy Dennis. LC 22-17451. 1922. A. A. Knopf.
Mary Lee. Geoffrey Pomeroy Dennis. 1931. Simon and Schuster.
Mary Leith. Ernest Raymond. LC 32-6103. 1932. D. Appleton and Company.
Mary Magdalen, a Chronicle. Edgar Evertson Saltus. LC 78-116002. 1970. (ISBN 0-404-05517-6). AMS Press.
Mary Magdalen: A Chronicle. Edgar Evertson Saltus. LC 7-1648. (On cover: Windermere series. no. 21). 1896. United States Book Company.
Mary Magdalen Smith. Henry Rosendahl. LC 38-5870. The Macaulay Company.
Mary Magdalene. Edith Olivier. LC 35-3434. (Appleton biographies). 1935. D. Appleton-Century Company, Incorporated.
Mary Marie. Eleanor Hodgman Porter. LC 20-803506. 1920. Houghton Mifflin Company.
Mary Marston. A Novel. George Macdonald. (Seaside library. v. 45, no. 922). 1881. G. Munro.
Mary Marston. A Novel. George Macdonald. LC 12-18283. 1911. D. McKay.
Mary Marston. A Novel. George Macdonald. LC 43-40888. 1881. D. Appleton and Company.
Mary, Mary. James Stephens. LC 70-131839. 1970. Scholarly Press.
Mary, Mary. James Stephens. LC 12-10647. 1.25. Small, Maynard and Company.
Mary Mavourneen: Or, The Bright Child of Sorrow. Dennis O'Sullivan. (On cover: Munro's library, popular novels, v. 1, no. 417). N. L. Munro.
Mary Midthorne. George Barr McCutcheon. LC 11-23296. 1911. Dodd, Mead and Company.
Mary Midthorne. George Barr McCutcheon. LC 20-164713. 1913. Grosset & Dunlap.
Mary Milton: Or, The Conquests of Grace. A Brief Account of the Life, Experience and Labors of a Humble Servant of Christ. Mary N Lord. 1876. Printed by the Claremont Manufacturing Company.
Mary Minds Her Business. George Weston. LC 20-4960. 1920. Dodd, Mead and Company.
Mary Moreland: A Novel, by Marie Van Vorst... Marie Van Vorst. LC 15-11002. 1915. Little, Brown, and Company.
Mary Morton's Experiment. Janet G Sligh. LC 41-19816. Fleming H. Revell Company.
Mary North: A Novel. Lucy Jane Rider Meyer. LC 3-5782. F. H. Revell Company.
Mary of Carisbrook. Margaret Campbell Barnes. (Signet Book, Y5658). 1973. (pbk.) 1.25. New American Library.
Mary of Carisbrooke. Margaret Campbell Barnes. LC 55-10738. 1956. Macrae Smith.
Mary of Jerusalem. Jean Des Vallieres. Tr. by Hennessy, Katherine Alicia. LC 32-31605. 1932. Longmans, Green and Co.
Mary of Lorraine: An Historical Romance. James Grant. G. Routledge and Sons.
Mary of Magdala: A Tale of the First Century. Harriette Gunn Roberson. LC 9-11152. The Saalfield Publishing Company.
Mary of Magdala: Her Romantic Story. Archie Bell. LC 25-7276. Issued for the St. Botolph Society by L. C. Page & Company.
Mary of Nazareth. Esther Kellner. LC 58-8502. 1958. Appleton-Century-Crofts.
Mary of Scotland. Frank Wilson Kenyon. LC 57-5631. 1957. Crowell.
Mary of the Anthracite: A Story of the Pennsylvania Coal Region. Charles Edward Roudabush. LC 40-6442. Fortuny's.
Mary O'Gorman. Ruth Irma Low. LC 27-19213. H. L. Kilner & Co.
Mary O'Grady. Mary Lavin. LC 50-5260. 1950. Little, Brown.
Mary Oliver; a Life. May Sinclair. LC 19-11715. 1919. Cassell and Company, Ltd.
Mary Oliver: a Life. May Sinclair. LC 19-12252. 1919. The Macmillan Company.
Mary Oliver: A Life. May Sinclair. (Virago Modern Classic Ser.). 392p. 1982. pap. 8.95 (ISBN 0-385-27653-2). Dial.
Mary Olivier: a Life. May Sinclair. LC 74-169850. 1972. 14.50 (ISBN 0-8371-6244-0). Greenwood Press.
Mary Paget: A Romance of Old Bermuda. Minna Caroline Smith. LC 1187. 1900. The Macmillan Company.
Mary Patten's Daughters. Jane Ludlow Drake Abbott. LC 45-4142. 1945. J. B. Lippincott Company.
Mary Pechell. Marie Adelaide Belloc Lowndes. LC 12-191567. 1912. 1.30. C. Scribner's Sons.
Mary Peters. Mary Ellen Chase. LC 34-27262. 1934. The Macmillan Company.
Mary Plantagenet: An Improbable Story. John Collis Snaith. LC 18-16893. 1918. Cassell and Company, Ltd.
Mary Portrayed. Vincent Cronin. 12.50 (ISBN 0-87505-213-4). Borden.
Mary Powell, and Deborah's Diary. Anne Manning. (Half-title: Everyman's library, ed. by Ernest Rhys. Fiction. no. 324). 1908. J. M. Dent & Co.
Mary, Queen of Scots. Margarete Siebert Kurlbaum. Tr. by Hamilton, Mary Agnes (Adamson) LC 29-3262. Harcourt, Brace and Company.
Mary Raymond: And Other Tales. Catherine Grace Frances Moody Gore. LC 6-27497. 1838. Lea & Blanchard.
Mary Read, Buccaneer. Philip Rush. LC 45-10121. 1945. T.V. Boardman and Company Limited.
Mary Regan. Leroy Scott. LC 18-2905. 1918. 1.50. Houghton Mifflin Company.
Mary Roberts Rinehart Crime Book: The Door. Mary Roberts Rinehart. LC 57-109474. 1957. Rinehart.
Mary Roberts Rinehart's Crime Book: The After House; The Buckled Bag; Locked Doors; The Red Lamp; The Window at the White Cat. Mary Roberts Rinehart. LC 33-577906. 1933. Farrar & Rinehart, Incorporated.
Mary Roberts Rinehart's Mystery Book: The Circular Staircase; The Man in Lower Ten; The Case of Jennie Brice; The Confession. Mary Roberts Rinehart. LC 30-271170. 1930. Farrar & Rinehart, Inc.
Mary Roberts Rinehart's Mystery Book: The Circular Staircase, The Man in Lower Ten and The Case of Jennie Brice. Mary Roberts Rinehart. LC 47-31048. 1947. Rinehart.
Mary Roberts Rinehart's Romance Book: "K"; The Amazing Interlude; The Street of Seven Stars. Mary Roberts Rinehart. LC 31-26993. 1931. Farrar & Rinehart, Inc.
Mary Rose of Mifflin. Frances Roberta Sterrett. LC 16-6200. 1916. D. Appleton and Company.
Mary Schweidler: The Amber Witch. Wilhelm Meinhold. Tr. by Duff-Gordon, Lucie (Austin) LC 29-12769. (Half-title: The World's classics. ccxxv). 1928. H. Milford, Oxford University Press.
Mary Schweidler: The Amber Witch. The Most Interesting Trail for Witchcraft Ever Known, Printed from an Imperfect Manuscript by Her Father, Abraham Schweidler, the Pastor of Coserow, in the Island of Usedom. Wilhelm Meinhold. Tr. by Duff-Gordon, Lucie (Austin) LC 7-18475. (Half-title: Wiley and Putnam's library of choice reading). 1845. Wiley and Putnam.
Mary Shelley: Collected Tales & Stories with original engravings. Ed. by Charles E. Robinson. LC 75-36931. (Illus.). 424p. 1976. 25.00x (ISBN 0-8018-1706-4). Johns Hopkins.
Mary Smith. Pedro Juan Labarthe. LC 59-227. Whittier Books.
Mary Spencer: A Tale for the Times, 1844 see Sir Roland Ashton: A Tale of the Times, 1841.
Mary Starkweather. Corolin Crawford Williamson. LC 1-26949. The A-Bey Ress.
Mary Staunton: Or, The Pupils of Marvel Hall. Rhoda Elizabeth Waterman White. 1860. D. Appleton and Company.
Mary Stewart's Merlin Trilogy. Mary Stewart. LC 80-21019. 1980. 14.95 (ISBN 0-688-00347-8). Morrow.
Mary Sunshine. Bertha B. Moore McCurry. LC 39-6275. 1939. Wm. B. Eerdmans Publishing Company.
Mary Sunshine. Bertha B Moore. LC 39-627538. 1939. Wm. B. Eerdmans Publishing Company.
Mary, Sweet Mary. Claudette Williams. (Coventry Romance Ser.: No. 63). 224p. 1980. pap. 1.75 (ISBN 0-449-50094-2, Coventry). Fawcett.
Mary the Maniac: Or The Mother Her Own Victim! In Eight Letters, to a Young Lady of the South. M. Ro. Bar, -(Lev.), Pseud. 1843. Nafis & Cornish.
Mary, the Merry, and Other Tales. Leo Robbins. LC 52-52919. 1918. Stratford Co.
Mary: the Queen of the House of David and Mother of Jesus. The Story of Her Life... Alexander Stewart Walsh. LC 8-6771. 1886. H. S. Allen.
Mary: The Queen of the House of David, and Mother of Jesus. The Story of Her Life... Alexander Stewart Walsh. LC 203. 1899. H. S. Allen.
Mary. Translated by Leo Steinberg. Shalom Asch. LC 57-4106. (Cardinal edition, C255. Fiction, 5). 1957. Pocket Books.
Mary Vowell Adams: Reluctant Pioneer: One Woman-Without Rights-Caught in the Wave of an Historic Migration. Beatrice L Bliss. LC 70-188685. (Illus.). 1972. 7.50. Mail Printers.
Mary Wakefield. Mazo De La Roche. 1.50 (ISBN 0-449-23057-0). Fawcett Crest.
Mary Wakefield. 1st whiteoak ed. Mazo De La Roche. LC 48-28258. 1949. Little, Brown.
Mary Ware in Texas. Annie Fellows Johnston. LC 10-236747. (On verso of half-title: The Little Colonel series). 1910. 1.50. L. C. Page & Company.
Mary Was Love. Guy Fletcher. LC 27-605836. George H. Doran Company.
Mary Who? Daniel Winnifred Whipple. LC 43-17754. 1943. Meador Publishing Company.
Mary Wollaston. Henry Kitchell Webster. LC 20-18250. The Bobbs-Merrill Company.
Maryjane Tonight at Angels Twelve. Martin Caidin. 1973. (pbk) 1.50. Warner Paperback Library.
Maryjane Tonight at Angels Twelve. Martin Caidin. LC 78-186012. 1972. 6.95. Doubleday.
Maryland Manor: A Novel of Plantation Aristocracy and Its Fall. 3d ed. Frederic Emory. LC 1-31727. Frederick A. Stokes Company.
Mary's Children. Martha King Davis. LC 30-2685. 1930. Macrae Smith Company.
Mary's Garden: By Joan Garrison Pseud. William Arthur Neubauer. 1955. Arcadia House.
Mary's Little Donkey. Gunhild Sehlin. (Illus.). 1979. 10.95 (ISBN 0-903540-29-0, Pub. by Floris Books). St George Bk Serv.
Mary's Neck. Booth Tarkington. LC 31-28601. 1932. Doubleday, Doran and Company, Inc.
Mary's Secret: A Novel. Harriet Sibyl Collins. LC 26-15707. 1926. The Stratford Company.
Mary's Yankee Man. Henry Paul. LC 20-12449. The Philips Press.
Marzio's Crucifix. Francis Marion Crawford. LC 70-8004. Scholarly Press.
Marzio's Crucifix. Francis Marion Crawford. LC 79-80626. 1969. AMS Press.
Marzio's Crucifix. Francis Marion Crawford. LC 4-15090. 1887. Macmillan and Co.
Marzio's Crucifix. Francis Marion Crawford. LC 32-336104. 1892. Macmillan and Co.
Mas Vale Creerlo. Ed. by Esteban Marosi. Tr. by Shelly Kjellgreen. 159p. 1980. pap. 2.00 o.p. (ISBN 0-8297-0822-7). Life Pubs.
Masada. Ernest Kellogg Gann. Orig. Title: Antagonists. 320p. 1981. pap. 2.95 (ISBN 0-515-05443-7). Jove Pubns.
Masada Plan. Leonard Harris. 1981. pap. 2.75 (ISBN 0-445-04189-7). Popular Lib.
Masada Plan: A Novel. Leonard Harris. LC 76-22557. 8.95 (ISBN 0-517-52799-5). Crown Publishers.
Masada Plan: A Novel. Leonard Harris. 1978. 1.95 (ISBN 0-445-04189-7). Popular Library.
Masaniello: Or, The Fisherman of Naples: an Historical Romance. Alexandre Dumas. LC 6-42329. G. Munro.
Mascarada Pass: A Gregory Quist Story. 1st Ed. William Colt MacDonald. LC 54-6248. (Double D western). 1954. Doubleday.
Mascarose. Gordon Arthur Smith. LC 13-21703. 1913. C. Scribner's Sons.
Mascot of Sweet Briar Gulch. Henry Wallace Phillips. LC 8-30248. 1908. The Bobbs-Merrill Company.
Masculine Feminine. Jean-Luc Godard. (Illus.). 1969. pap. 2.45 o.p. (ISBN 0-394-17136-5, B188, BC). Grove.
MASH. Richard Hooker. LC 68-29610. 1968. 4.95. Morrow.
MASH Goes to Hollywood. Richard Hooker & William E. Butterworth. 1976. (pbk.) 1.50 (ISBN 0-671-80408-1). Pocket Books.
MASH Goes to Las Vegas. Richard Hooker & William E. Butterworth. 1976. (pbk.) 1.50 (ISBN 0-671-80265-8). Pocket Books.
MASH Goes to London. Richard Hooker & William E Butterworth. 1975. (pbk.) 1.50 (ISBN 0-671-78941-4). Pocket Books.
M.A.S.H. Goes to Maine. Richard Hooker. 1973. 1.25 (ISBN 0-671-78254-1). Pocket Books.
MASH Goes to Maine. Richard Hooker. LC 71-151912. 1972. 5.95. W. Morrow.

M.A.S.H. Goes to Miami. Richard Hooker & William E. Butterworth. (MASH series) (ISBN 0-671-80705-6). Pocket Books.
MASH Goes to Montreal. Richard Hooker & William E. Butterworth. (Kangaroo Book). 1977. 1.50 (ISBN 0-671-80910-5). Pocket Books.
MASH Goes to Morocco. Richard Hooker & William E Butterworth. 1976. (pbk.) 1.50. Pocket Books.
Mash Goes to Moscow. Richard Hooker & William E. Butterworth. (Kangaroo Book). 1977. 1.50 (ISBN 0-671-80911-3). Pocket Books.
MASH Goes to New Orleans. Richard Hooker & William E. Butterworth. 1975. (pbk.) 1.50 (ISBN 0-671-78490-0). Pocket Books.
MASH Goes to Paris. Richard Hooker & William E. Butterworth. 1974. (pbk.) 1.50 (ISBN 0-671-78491-9). Pocket Books.
MASH Goes to Texas. Richard Hooker & William E. Butterworth. (Mash). (Kangaroo Book). (Mash series). 1977. 1.50 (ISBN 0-671-80892-3). Pocket Books.
MASH Goes to Vienna. Richard Hooker & William E. Butterworth. 1976. (pbk.) 1.50 (ISBN 0-671-80458-8). Pocket Books.
MASH Mania. Richard Hooker. LC 77-22709. 1977. 7.95 (ISBN 0-396-07508-8). Dodd, Mead.
MASH Mania: Richard Hooker. Richard Hooker. 1979. 1.95 (ISBN 0-671-82178-4). Pocket Books.
Mashal U-Melisah. Meir L. Malbim. (Heb). 10.00 o.p. AMS Pr.
Masha's Awful Pillow. G. Lebedeva. 1980. pap. 1.49 (ISBN 0-8285-1780-0, Pub. by Progress Pubs USSR). Imported Pubns.
Mashenka. Vladimir Vladimirovich Nabokov. (Rus.). 1979. 15.00 (ISBN 0-88233-092-6); pap. 6.00 (ISBN 0-88233-093-4). Ardis Pubs.
Mashi: And Other Stories. Thakura Ravindranatha. LC 18-65192. 1918. The Macmillan Company.
Mashi, and Other Stories. Rabindranath Tagore. LC 70-37564. (Short story index reprint series). 1972. (ISBN 0-8369-4123-3). Books for Libraries Press.
Mask. Stuart Cloete. LC 57-9190. 1957. Houghton Mifflin.
Mask. John Cournos. LC 74-26098. (Labor Movement in Fiction and Non-Fiction). 1976. 20.00 (ISBN 0-404-58416-0). AMS Press.
Mask. John Cournos. LC 20-262. George H. Doran Company.
Mask. Will Scott. LC 29-20448. 1929. Macrae, Smith Company.
Mask. Clare Consuelo Frewen Sheridan. LC 42-23666. 1942. Hutchinson & Co., Ltd.
Mask. Owen West. (Orig.). 1981. pap. 2.95 (ISBN 0-515-05695-2). Jove Pubns.
Mask. William H. Woods. 1960. 3.50 o.p. (ISBN 0-8090-6795-1). Hill & Wang.
Mask: A Novel. Florence Irwin. LC 17-248167. 1917. 1.40. Little, Brown and Company.
Mask: A Novel. William Howard Woods. LC 60-7320. 1960. Hill and Wang.
Mask: A Novel. William Howard Woods. LC 51-7234. 1951. Longmans, Green.
Mask: A Story of Love and Adventure. Arthur Hornblow. LC 13-11306. G. W. Dillingham Company.
Mask for Murder. 1st Ed. Aaron Marc Stein. LC 52-6353. 1952. Published for the Crime Club by Doubleday.
Mask for the Toff. John Creasey. LC 66-12634. 1966. Walker.
Mask of a Lion. A. T. W. Simeons. LC 52-8513. 1952. Knopf.
Mask of Alexander. Martha Albrand. LC 55-5797.
Mask of Alexander: By Martha Albrand Pseud. Heidi Huberta Freybe Loewengard. LC 55-5797. Random House.
Mask of Apollo. Mary Renault, pseud. (95049). 1967. Pocket Bks.
Mask of Apollo. Mary Renault, pseud. 1974. (pbk.) 1.75. Bantam Books.
Mask of Apollo. Mary Renault, pseud. LC 66-24894. 1966. Pantheon Books.
Mask of Beauty. A Novel. Tr. from the German of Fanny Lewald. Fanny Lewald-Stahr & Pleasants, Mary M., Tr. (Ledger library, no. 113). 1894. R. Bonner's Sons.
Mask of Cthulhu. Howard Phillips Lovecraft & August William Derleth. (Boxer Ser). 1971. pap. 0.95 o.p. (95107). Beagle Bks.
Mask of Death. Anita Bachelin. LC 77-80985. (Illus.). 3.95 (ISBN 0-89343-030-7). Ermine Publishers.
Mask of Evil. Jo Anne Creighton. 1973. pap. 0.95 o.p. (09212). Curtis.
Mask of Fu Manchu. Sax Rohmer, pseud. 1976. Repr. of 1932 ed. lib. bdg. 17.15x (ISBN 0-89190-803-X). Am Repr-Rivercity Pr.
Mask of Fu Manchu. Sax Rohmer, pseud. 1970. pap. 0.60 o.p. (X2248). Pyramid Pubns.
Mask of Fu Manchu. Sax Rohmer, pseud. 1976. pap. 1.25 o.p. (ISBN 0-515-03942-X). BJ Pub Group.
Mask of Fu Manchu. Arthur Sarsfield Ward. LC 32-34790. 1932. Pub. for the Crime Club, Inc., Doubleday, Doran & Company, Inc.
Mask of Fu Manchu: By Sax Rohmer Pseud. Arthur Sarsfield Ward. LC 53-2404. (twenty-fifth anniversary Crime Club classic). 1953. Published for the Crime Club by Doubleday.
Mask of Glass. Holly Roth. LC 54-6988. 1954. Vanguard Press.
Mask of Glory. Dan Levin. LC 49-104087. 1949. Whittlesey House.
Mask of Gold. Rachel Lindsay. (Presents Ser.). 1974. pap. 1.25 (ISBN 0-373-70553-0, 70553, Pub by Harlequin). PB.
Mask of Innocence: Translated by Gerard Hopkins. Francois Mauriac. LC 53-108723. 1953. Straus & Young.
Mask of Jon Culon. Edward W. Ludwig. Ed. by Alice Sachs. 1970. 3.95 o.p. Lenox Hill.
Mask of Love. Barbara Cartland. (Barbara Cartland Library#29). 1975. (pbk.) 1.25. Bantam.
Mask of Love. Katherine Court. (Orig.). 1980. pap. 1.50 (ISBN 0-440-18559-9). Dell.
Mask of Medusa. Paula Minton, pseud. LC 75-17078. 160p. (Orig.). pap. 1.25 (ISBN 0-89041-026-7, 3026). Major Bks.
Mask of Memory. Victor Canning. LC 74-19774. 1975. 7.95 (ISBN 0-688-02889-6). Morrow.
Mask of Night. Michael Norday. LC 54-2424. 1954. Vixen Press.
Mask of Passion. Kay Hooper. (Candlelight Ecstasy Ser.: No. 77). (Orig.). 1982. pap. 1.95 (ISBN 0-440-15406-5). Dell.
Mask of Satan: A Novel of Spiritism, by Marsha Lavonda Pseud. 1st Ed. Martha Elizabeth Marshall Worester. LC 54-10338. 1954. Exposition Press.
Mask of Silence. easy eye ed. Sheila McErlean. 1968. pap. 0.60 o.p. (73-799). Lancer.
Mask of Silenus: A Novel About Socrates. Babette Deutach. LC 33-359857. 1933. Simon and Schuster.
Mask of the Enchantress. Eleanor Hibbert. LC 79-6088. 1980. 10.00 (ISBN 0-385-17024-6). Doubleday.
Mask of the Enchantress. Eleanor Hibbert. LC 80-22818. 1980. 16.95 (ISBN 0-8161-3142-2). G. K. Hall.
Mask of the Enchantress. Eleanor Hibbert. 1980. 3.25 (ISBN 0-449-24418-0). Fawcett Crest.
Mask of the Enchantress. Victoria Holt, pseud. LC 79-6088. 356p. 1980. 13.95 (ISBN 0-385-17024-6). Doubleday.
Mask of the Enchantress. Victoria Holt, pseud. 1981. pap. 3.25 (ISBN 0-449-24418-0, Crest). Fawcett.
Mask of the Enchantress. Victoria Holt, pseud. (General Ser.). 1980. lib. bdg. 16.95 (ISBN 0-8161-3142-2, Large Print Bks). G K Hall.
Mask of the Jaguar. Jessica North. LC 80-22668. 10.95 (ISBN 0-698-11050-1). Coward, McCann & Geoghegan.
Mask of the Sun. Fred Soberhagen. 240p. 1981. pap. 2.75 (ISBN 0-441-52078-2). Ace Bks.
Mask of Treason. Anne Stevenson, pseud. LC 79-14275. 10.00 (ISBN 0-399-12370-9). Putnam.
Mask of Violence. John Harris. LC 71-124831. 1970. (ISBN 0-15-193750-8). Harcourt, Brace, Jovanovich.
Mask of Violence. Mark Hebden, pseud. 1970. 5.75 o.p. (ISBN 0-15-193750-8). HarBraceJ.
Mask of Wisdom. Howard Clewes. LC 49-717428. 1949. E. P. Dutton.
Mask of Words. Jan Roffman. (Ace Gothic). 1973. (pbk.) 0.95. Ace Books.
Maske: Thaery. Jack Vance, pseud. LC 76-17610. (Berkley Medallion Book). 1977. 1.50 (ISBN 0-425-03503-4). Berkley Publishing Corp.
Maske: Thaery. John Holbrook Vance. LC 76-17610. (Illus.). 1.50 (ISBN 0-425-03503-4). Berkley Pub. Corp.: Distributed by Putnam.
Masked Detective. A Tale of Strange Mysteries. Harlan Page Halsey. LC 7-1185. (secret service series, no. 5). 1888. Street & Smith.
Masked Heiress. Vanessa Gray. (Signet Book). 1977. 1.50 (ISBN 0-451-07397-5). New American Library.
Masked Longing. Howard Rockey. LC 30-21172. The Macaulay Company.
Masked Man. Gaston Leroux & Bennett, Hannaford, Tr. LC 29-8548. 1929. The Macaulay Company.
Masked Prophet: A Psychological Romance. 2d ed. John Bowles. LC 37-327772. 1900. The Alliance Publishing Company.
Masked Prophet. One's Hidden Self. A Romance in Two Lives--Here and Hereafter. John Bowles. LC 6-16086. Caxton Company.
Masked Rider. Hoffman Birney. LC 26-23874. 1928. The Penn Publishing Company.
Masked Venus: A Story of Many Lands. Richard Henry Savage. LC 12-38410. 1893. The American News Company.
Masked Woman. Johnston McCulley. LC 20-7058. W. J. Watt & Company.
Masked Women. Rex Ellingwood Beach. LC 34-5067. Farrar & Rinehart, Incorporated.
Masks. Fumiko Enchi. Tr. by Juliet W. Carpenter from Japanese. LC 82-48726. 1983. 11.95 (ISBN 0-394-50945-5). Knopf.
Masks. Queen Maria. LC 37-1011. 1937. E. P. Dutton & Co., Inc.
Masks. Barry J Titus. LC 61-7119. 1961. Knopf.
Masks: A Novel. Gerald W Haslam. LC 76-12310. 4.95. Old Adobe Press.
Masks & Demons. K. Macgowan & H. Rosse. LC 29-28817. Repr. of 1923 ed. 18.00 (ISBN 0-527-59600-0). Kraus Repr.
Masks and Faces: A Book of Stories. Phyllis Bottome. LC 40-985965. 1940. Little, Brown and Company.
Masks of Love: A Novel. Margarita Spalding Gerry. LC 14-2480. 1914. 1.20. Harper & Brothers.
Masks of the Illuminati. Robert Anton Wilson. 336p. (Orig.). 1981. pap. 2.95 (ISBN 0-671-82585-2). PB.
Masks of Thespis. Mozelle Richardson. 1973. (pbk) 0.95. Warner.
Masks of Time. Robert Silverberg. 1978. pap. 1.95 (ISBN 0-425-03871-8, Dist. by Putnam). Berkley Pub.
Masks off at Midnight. Valentine Williams. LC 34-34577. 1934. Houghton Mifflin Company.
Mason County War. Wayne D. Overholser. 256p. 1981. pap. 1.95 (ISBN 0-441-52081-2). Ace Bks.
Mason County War. Wayne D Overholser. Ace.
Mason of Bar X. Harry Bennett. LC 20-23020. R. G. Badger.
Masonic City: A Novel. Joseph Thomas Francis. LC 22-3514. 1922. Morris County Press.
Masoud the Bedouin. Alfreda Post Carhart. LC 76-150541. (Short story index reprint series). (Illus.). 1971. (ISBN 0-8369-3838-0). Books for Libraries Press.
Masoud the Bedouin. Alfreda Post Carhart. LC 15-18426. 1915. 1.00. Missionary Education Movement of the United States and Canada.
Masque. Sheila Holland. (Orig.). 1979. pap. 1.95 (ISBN 0-89083-439-3). Zebra.
Masque of Chameleons. Joan V. Frost. 384p. 1981. pap. 2.95 (ISBN 0-449-24472-5, Crest). Fawcett.
Masque of Death: A Story of the Terror. John Ruse Larus. LC 17-25593. 1917. 1.50. The Neale Publishing Company.
Masque of Honor. Edward Linn & Jack Pearl. LC 78-77410. 1969. 5.95. W. W. Norton.
Masque of Honor. A Saratoga Romance. Caroline Washburn Rockwood. LC 7-39802. 1889. Funk & Wagnalls.
Masque of the Red Death. Edgar Allan Poe. Ed. by Raymond Harris. (Jamestown Classics Ser.). (Illus.). 48p. (Orig.). 1982. pap. text ed. 2.00x (ISBN 0-89061-271-4, 475); tchr's ed. 3.00x (ISBN 0-89061-272-2, 477). Jamestown Pubs.
Masque of Virtue. Louis A Brennan. LC 55-5791. 1955. Random House.
Masque World. Alexei Panshin. 1978. 1.75 (ISBN 0-441-52105-3). Ace Books.
Masquer. Denice Greenlea. 224p. (Orig.). 1980. pap. 1.75 (ISBN 0-449-50054-3, Coventry). Fawcett.
Masquerade. Vincenz Brun. LC 39-12438. Carrick & Evans, Inc.
Masquerade. Anne Gardner, pseud. LC 31-25220. Grosset & Dunlap.
Masquerade. Vida Hurst. LC 46-223567. 1946. Gramercy Publishing Co.
Masquerade. Murdock Stuart Jervis. LC 43-7234. 1943. Hurst & Blackett, Ltd.
Masquerade. Vera Murdock Juervis. LC 43-111424. 1943. Arcadia House, Inc.
Masquerade. Oscar Micheaux. LC 47-20647. 1947. Book Supply Company.
Masquerade. Cecilia Sternberg. LC 79-64209. 8.95 (ISBN 0-89256-111-4). Rawson, Wade.
Masquerade. Kit Williams. LC 80-14127. 1980. 9.95 (ISBN 0-8052-3747-X). Schocken Books.
Masquerade: An Historical Novel. Oscar Micheaux. LC 73-18595. 1975. 20.00 (ISBN 0-404-11406-7). AMS Press.
Masquerade at Monfalcone. Dorinne Moore. (Berkley medallion book). 1974. (pbk) 0.75 (ISBN 0-425-02507-1). Berkley Pub. Co.
Masquerade at Sea House. Elisabeth Ogilvie. Repr. lib. bdg. 11.50x (ISBN 0-88411-333-7). Amereon Ltd.
Masquerade for a Nurse see Secret of Greenwillows.
Masquerade in Venice. Velda Johnston. 1974. (pbk.) 1.25. Dell.
Masquerade in Venice: A Novel of Suspense. Velda Johnston. LC 72-11251. 1973. 4.95 (ISBN 0-396-06770-0). Dodd, Mead.
Masquerade into Madness. Russ Meservey. LC 53-31782. (Gold medal books, 302). 1953. Fawcett Publications.
Masquerade of Evil. Eva Zumwalt. (Ace Gothic#21). 1975. (pbk.) 0.95. Ace Books.
Masquerade of Love. Alice Morgan. (Candlelight Ecstasy Ser.: No. 48). (Orig.). 1982. pap. 1.75 (ISBN 0-440-15405-7). Dell.
Masquerade: Translated by Charlotte Bodde. Jo Van Ammers-Kuller. Tr. by Bodde, Charlotte. LC 32-165583. E. P. Dutton & Co., Inc.
Masquerade with Music. Mary Burchell. (Harlequin Romances Ser.). 192p. 1983. pap. 1.50 (ISBN 0-373-02528-9). Harlequin Bks.
Masquerader. Katherine Cecil Thurston. LC 24-279706. 1922. Grosset & Dunlap.
Masquerader: A Novel. Katherine Cecil Thurston. 1904. Harper & Brothers.
Masqueraders. Georgette Heyer. (Fawcett Crest Book). 1976. (pbk.) 1.50. Fawcett.
Masqueraders. Georgette Heyer. LC 67-20552. 1967. Dutton.
Masqueraders. Georgette Heyer. LC 29-119124. 1929. Longmans, Green and Co.
Masqueraders. Frances Y. McHugh. pap. 0.75 o.s.i. (01-343). Lancer.
Masquerading Heart. Caroline Courtney. (Regency Romance Ser.: No. 18). 208p. (Orig.). 1982. pap. 1.95 (ISBN 0-446-90612-3). Warner Bks.
Masquerading Mary. Emma Speed Sampson. LC 24-22008. Reilly & Lee Co.
Masquerading of Margaret. Cora Gottschalk Welty. LC 9-563. 1908. The C. M. Clark Publishing Co.
Masques. Bill Pronzini. 224p. 1983. pap. 2.95 (ISBN 0-425-05936-7). Berkley Pub.
Masques. Elizabeth Hall Yates. LC 23-9939. 1923. The Penn Publishing Company.
Mass for a Dead Witch. Alicia Grace. 1976. pap. 1.25 (ISBN 0-532-12413-8). Woodhill.
Mass for a Dead Witch. Alicia Grace. 1970. pap. 0.75 o.p. (ISBN 0-447-74682-0). Lancer.
Mass of Brother Michel. Michael Kent & Brown, Beatrice Bradshaw, Illus. LC 42-7961. (Illus.). 1942. The Bruce Publishing Company.
Massa John: Or, Life in the Old South. Charles Durfee. LC 57-9479. 1957. Meador Press.
Massacre. John J Vrooman. LC 55-15242. 1954. Baronet Litho Co.
Massacre at Fall Creek. Jessamyn West. LC 74-30377. 1975. 8.95 (ISBN 0-15-157820-6). Harcourt Brace Jovanovich.
Massacre at Fall Creek. Jessamyn West. LC 75-19106. 1975. 14.95 (ISBN 0-8161-6324-3). G. K. Hall.
Massacre at Fall Creek. Jessamyn West. (Fawcett Crest Book). 1976. (pbk.) 1.95. Fawcett.
Massacre at Fort Caid. W. G Schreiber. (Avalon Books). 4.95. Thomas Bouregy.
Massacre at Goliad. Elmer Kelton. 176p. 1981. pap. 1.95 (ISBN 0-553-20009-7). Bantam.
Massacre at Salt Creek. Blaine M. Yorgason. LC 78-22744. 1979. 7.95 (ISBN 0-385-15200-0). Doubleday.
Massacre at Tangini. Robert Lait. LC 62-8464. 1963. Random House.
Massacre at the Gorge. Mick Clumpner. 1982. pap. 2.25 (ISBN 0-451-11743-3, AE1743, Sig). NAL.
Massacre at Umtali. Peter McCurtin. (Soldier of Fortune Ser.: No. 1). 192p. 1981. pap. 1.95 (ISBN 0-505-51757-4). Tower Bks.
Massacre at Umtali. Peter McCurtin. (O.s.i.). 1976. pap. 1.25 o.s.i. (BT50915). Belmont-Tower.
Massacre at Umtali. Peter McCurtin. (Soldier of Fortune series). 1976. (pbk.) 1.25. Belmont Tower Books.
Massacre at Wounded Knee. Abby Mann. (Orig.). 1979. pap. 2.50 (ISBN 0-89083-542-X). Zebra.
Massacre in Milan. Nick Carter. (O.s.i.). 192p. 1975. pap. 1.25 o.s.i. (AQ1455, Award). Univ Pub & Dist.
Massacre Mission. George G. Gilman, pseud. (Edge Ser.: No. 38). 160p. 1982. pap. 1.95 (ISBN 0-523-41449-8). Pinnacle Bks.
Massacre of Glencoe. George William McArthur Reynolds. LC 7-30594. T. B. Peterson & Brothers.
Massacre of Innocents: A Novel. Christopher Brennan, pseud. LC 67-92823. (B 67-9229). 1967. Hart-Davis.
Massacre of the Innocents: And Other Tales. Maurice Maeterlinck et al. Tr. by Edith Wingate Rinder. LC 7-19656. (On cover: The green tree library). 1895. Stone & Kimball.
Massacre Ranch. Orlando Rigoni. LC 66-9242. 1966. Arcadia House.
Massacre River. John Benteen. 1970. pap. 0.60 o.p. (B60-1078). Belmont-Tower.
Massacre River. John Benteen. (Osi). 1971. pap. 0.75 o.s.i. (B75-2138). Belmont-Tower.
Massacre Trail. George Charles Appell. LC 55-8914. (Permabooks, M-313). 1955. Permabooks; Distributed by Pocket Books.
Massacre Trail: A Novel of the Pioneer Northwest. 1st Ed. Arnold H Schroeder. LC 54-11322. 1954. Exposition Press.
Massacre Valley. Dwight Bennett Newton. (Orig.). 1973. pap. 0.75 o.p. (07302). Curtis.
Massage Palace. J. J. Montague. 192p. (Orig.). 1973. pap. 1.95 o.p. (ISBN 0-87056-325-4, 6375). Brandon.
Massage Parlor. Rae Loomis, pseud. Orig. Title: Luisita. 1970. pap. 0.75 o.p. (75-327). Manor Bks.

Massage Specialist. Will Flint. 192p. (Orig.). 1973. pap. 1.95 o.p. (ISBN 0-87682-346-0, 7346). Barclay Hse.

Massarenes. Louise De La Ramee. LC 41-27496. R. F. Fenno & Company.

Massarenes. Ouida, pseud. LC 79-8186. Repr. of 1897 ed. 44.50 (ISBN 0-404-62087-6). AMS Pr.

Massasoit: A Romantic Story of the Indians of New England. Alma Holman Burton. LC 6-22257. 1896. The Morse Company.

Massasoit's Daughter. Augustine Joseph Hickey Duganne. LC 75-7102. (Garland Library of Narratives of North American Indian Captivities; V. 77). (Illus.). 1978. 29.50 (ISBN 0-8240-1701-3). Garland Pub.

Massasoit's Daughter; or, The French Captives. A Romance of Aboriginal New-England. Augustine Joseph Hickey Duganne. LC 43-47577. (Beadle's dime novels. No. 19). 1861. Beadle and Company.

Masseni: A Novel. Tidiane Dem. LC 82-36. 12.95 (ISBN 0-8071-1011-6). Louisiana State University Press.

Massey's Game. Jack Olsen, pseud. LC 75-17269. 8.95 (ISBN 0-87223-441-X). Playboy Press.

Massingham Butterfly, and Other Stories. Joseph Smith Fletcher. LC 76-122699. (Short story index reprint series). 1970. Books for Libraries Press.

Massingham Butterfly, and Other Stories. Joseph Smith Fletcher. LC 26-19344. Small, Maynard & Company.

Master. Malcolm Braly. 1973. (pbk.) 0.95 (ISBN 0-446-75117-0). Warner Paperback Library.

Master. Carter Brown, pseud. (Signet Mystery). 1973. 0.75. New American Lib.

Master. Tom Clark. 1979. 18.00 (ISBN 0-915316-65-X); pap. 5.00 (ISBN 0-915316-66-8). Pentagram.

Master. Mary Andrews Denison. LC 6-33986. 1862. Walker, Wise and Company.

Master: A Novel. Israel Zangwill. 1895. Harper & Brothers.

Master Adam the Calabrian. Alexandre Dumas. Tr. by Spurr, Harry A. LC 2-30267. 1902. R. F. Fenno & Company.

Master: An Adventure Story. Terence Hanbury White. 1957. Putnam.

Master and Commander. Patrick O'Brian. LC 77-85111. (Illus.). 1969. 6.95. Lippincott.

Master and Maid. Lizzie Allen Harker. LC 10-307355. 1911. 1.35. C. Scribner's Sons.

Master and Man. Lev Nikolaevich Tolstoi. LC 9-20916. (Neely's Booklet Library: No. 7). 1899. F. T. Neely.

Master and Man. Lev Nikolaevich Tolstoi & Beaman, Ardern George Hulme, 1857-1929, Tr. LC 8-25988. 1895. D. Appleton and Company.

Master and Man. Lev Nikolaevich Tolstoi & Ludwig, Yekaterina Alexandrovna, Tr. (Neomonic series, v. 2). 1895. The Neomon.

Master and Man. Lev Nikolaevich Tolstoi & Miller, Hettie E., Tr. (On cover: Melbourne series, no. 34). 1895. E. A. Weeks & Company.

Master & Man see Seven Short Novel Masterpieces.

Master and Man. A Tale of the Civil War. O O'B Strayer. (sunnyside series, no. 17). 1891. J.S. Ogilvie.

Master and Man", and Other Parables and Tales. Lev Nikolaevich Tolstoi. (Half-title: Everyman's library ed., by Ernest Rhys. Fiction.). 1910. J. M. Dent & Sons, Ltd.

Master & Man & Other Parables & Tales. Lev Nikolaevich Tolstoi. 1969. 9.95x (ISBN 0-460-00469-7, Evman); pap. 5.95x (ISBN 0-460-01469-2). Biblio Dist.

Master & Man & Other Stories. Lev Nikolaevich Tolstoi. Tr. by Paul Foote. (Classics Ser.). (Orig.). 1977. pap. 3.50 (ISBN 0-14-044331-2). Penguin.

Master and Man, and Other Stories. Lev Nikolaevich Tolstoi & Paul Foote. LC 78-305821. (Penguin classics). 1977. 2.50 (ISBN 0-14-044331-2). Penguin.

Master and Man: The Kreutzer Sonata; Miscellanies. Lev Nikolaevich Tolstoi. LC 26-26872. T. Y. Crowell Co.

Master and Margarita. Mikhail Afanasevich Bulgakov. LC 67-22898. 1967. Harper & Row.

Master, and Other Stories. Sue Kaufman. LC 75-44523. 1976. 7.95 (ISBN 0-385-12048-6). Doubleday.

Master and the Maiden. Alice Chetwynd Ley. LC 76-27369. 1977. 1.25 (ISBN 0-345-25560-7). Ballantine Books.

Master-at-Arms: A Romance. Rafael Sabatini. LC 40-114506. 1940. Houghton Mifflin Company.

Master Baiter. Troy Conway, pseud. (Coxeman Ser). (Orig.). 1970. pap. 0.75 o.p. (64-435). Paperback Lib.

Master-Beggars. Leslie Cope Cornford. LC 6-30207. 1897. J. B. Lippincott Company.

Master: Being in Part Copied from the Minutes of the School for Novelists, a Round Table of Good Fellows Who, Long Since, Dined Every Saturday at the Sign O' the Lanthorne, on Golden Hill in New York City. Irving Bacheller. LC 9-28042. 1909. Doubleday, Page & Company.

Master Bieland and His Workmen. Berthold Auerbach. Tr. by Hancock, E. LC 6-45106. (Leisure hour series, no. 153). 1883. H. Holt and Company.

Master Breed. Francis Dickie. LC 23-10098. George H. Doran Company.

Master Builders. James Edmund Dunning. 1909. D. Appleton and Company.

Master-Christian: A Question of the Time. Marie Corelli. LC 4684. 1900. Dodd, Mead and Company.

Master Christopher. Elizabeth Bonham De La Pasture. LC 11-15863. 1.35. E. P. Dutton & Company.

Master Craftsman. Walter Besant. (On cover: The fortnightly library, v. 14, no. 25). 1896. P. F. Collier.

Master Craftsman: A Novel. Walter Besant. LC 6-12407. F. A. Stokes Company.

Master Criminal. Joseph Jefferson Farjeon. LC 24-21153. 1924. L. MacVeagh, The Dial Press.

Master Criminal. George Sidney Paternoster. LC 7-42014. Empire Book Company.

Master Detective: Being Some Further Investigations of Christopher Quarles. Percy James Brebner. LC 16-822674. 1.35. E. P. Dutton & Company.

Master Detective Stories. Ed. by Arthur Neale. LC 29-148068. 1929. E. J. Clode, Inc.

Master Eustace. Henry James. LC 74-157780. (Short story index reprint series). 1971. (ISBN 0-8369-3892-5). Books for Libraries Press.

Master Eustace. Henry James. Ed. by Mordell, Albert. 1920. T. Seltzer.

Master from Afar. Florizel Von Reuter. 7.50 o.p. Carlton.

Master-Girl: A Romance. Ashton Hilliers. LC 10-9919. 1910. 1.25. G. P. Putnam's Sons.

Master Hand: The Story of a Crime. Nathan Winslow Williams. LC 3-22108. 1903. G. P. Putnam's Sons.

Master Humphrey's Clock. Charles Dickens. LC 22-145593. 1841. Lea and Blanchard.

Master Humphrey's Clock: New Christmas Stories, General Index of Characters and Their Appearances, Familiar Saying. Charles Dickens. LC 6-26435. 1869. Hurd and Houghton.

Master Influence: A Novel. Thomas McKean. LC 8-13277. 1908. J. B. Lippincott Company.

Master Key. John Fleming Wilson. LC 15-7816. Grosset & Dunlap.

Master Key: An Electrical Fairy Tale. Lyman Frank Baum. (Illus.). 1976. pap. 3.00 o.p. (ISBN 0-486-23382-0). Dover.

Master Key: An Electrical Fairy Tale. Lyman Frank Baum. LC 73-13247. (Classics of Science Fiction Ser.). (Illus.). 256p. 1973. 12.50 (ISBN 0-88355-103-9); pap. 3.75 (ISBN 0-88355-132-2). Hyperion Conn.

Master-Key for Life's Problems. Paul Albert Liebelt. LC 36-3603. The Christopher Publishing House.

Master-Knot and "Another Story,". Conover Duff. (On cover: Buckram series). 1895. H. Holt and Company.

Master-Knot of Human Fate. Ellis Meredith. LC 1-31338. 1901. Little, Brown, and Company.

Master-Man. Mary Howard Hoopes. LC 6-28224. 1906. John Lane Company.

Master Mariner: Darken Ship. Nicholas Monsarrat. LC 80-20222. (Illus.). 192p. 1981. 9.95 (ISBN 0-688-00017-7). Morrow.

Master Mariner: Running Proud. Nicholas Monsarrat. LC 78-71142. (Illus.). 1979. 12.95 (ISBN 0-688-03397-0). Morrow.

Master Mason's House. Frederick Philip Grove, pseud. LC 76-381310. (Illus.). (ISBN 0-88750-207-5). Oberon Press.

Master Mechanic. I. G Broat. LC 78-14518. 1979. 10.95 (ISBN 0-689-10935-0). Atheneum.

Master Mind. Marvin Dana & Carter, Daniel D. LC 14-11759. 1.25. The H. K. Fly Company.

Master Mind: A Detective Story. Cleveland Moffett. LC 27-20029. 1927. D. Appleton & Company.

Master Mind of Mars see Three Martian Novels.

Master Mind of Mars: Being a Tale of Weird and Wonderful Happenings on the Red Planet. Edgar Rice Burroughs. LC 28-8137. 1928. A. C. McClurg & Co.

Master Mind of Mars: Being a Tale of Weird and Wonderful Happenings on the Red Planet. Edgar Rice Burroughs. LC 40-375177. 1929. Grosset & Dunlap.

Master Mosaic-Workers. George Sand & Johnston, Charlotte C., Tr. LC 4-16889. 1895. Little, Brown, and Company.

Master Motive: A Tale of the Days of Champlain. F Angers & Gethin, Theresa A., Tr. LC 9-7392. 1909. B. Herder; Etc., Etc.

Master Mummer. Edward Phillips Oppenheim. LC 16-25042. 1912. Little, Brown & Company.

Master Mummer. Edward Phillips Oppenheim. LC 4-31604. 1904. Little, Brown, & Company.

Master Murderer. Carolyn Wells. LC 33-25198. J. B. Lippincott Company.

Master Mystery. Arthur Benjamin Reeve & Grey, John W., Joint Author. LC 19-730019. 1919. Grosset & Dunlap.

Master Mystery. Austin J Small. LC 28-231063. 1928. Pub. for the Crime Club, Inc., by Doubleday, Doran & Company, Inc.

Master Mystery Stories. Ed. by Leo Margulies. LC 45-7929. 1945. The Hampton Publishing Company.

Master of Appleby: A Novel Tale Concerning Itself in Part with the Great Struggle in the Two Carolinas; but Chiefly with the Adventure Therein of Two Gentlemen Who Loved One and the Same Lady. Francis Lynde. LC 2-24926. 1902. The Bowen-Merrill Company.

Master of Aysgarth. Margaret Mayhew. LC 75-40735. 1976. 5.95 (ISBN 0-385-11624-1). Doubleday.

Master of Badger's Hall. Henry Treece. LC 59-10817. 1959. Random House.

Master of Ballantrae. Robert Louis Stevenson. Ed. by White, H. Adelbert. LC 7-39196. (Macmillan's pocket American and English classics). 1907. The Macmillan Company.

Master of Ballantrae. Robert S. Stevenston. (Rinehart Editions). pap. text ed. 1.25 o.p. (ISBN 0-03-008420-2, HoltC). HR&W.

Master of Ballantrae: A Winter's Tale. Robert Louis Stevenson. (On cover: Seaside library. Pocket ed. no. 1228). 1889. G. Munro.

Master of Ballantrae: A Winter's Tale. Robert Louis Stevenson. LC 4-16581. 1904. C. Scribner's Sons.

Master of Ballantrae: A Winter's Tale. Robert Louis Stevenson. LC 5-16631. (Half-title: The biographical edition of the works of Robert Louis Stevenson). 1905. C. Scribner's Sons.

Master of Ballantrae: A Winter's Tale. Robert Louis Stevenson. LC 22-10237. (modern students library). C. Scribner's Sons.

Master of Ballantrae, a Winter's Tale. Introd. by Leslie A. Fiedler. Robert Louis Stevenson. LC 54-5868. (Rinehart editions, 67). 1954. Rinehart.

Master of Ballantrae. Introd. by G. B. Stern. Color 'ithographs by Lynd Ward. Robert Louis Stevenson & Lynd Kendall Ward. LC 66-6291. 1966. 6.95. Heritage Pr. Dist. Dial.

Master of Bengal. Norman Partington. LC 74-40498. 288p. 1975. 8.95 o.p. St Martin.

Master of Bengal: A Novel of Robert Clive of India. Norman Partington. LC 74-40498. (Illus.). 1975. 8.95. St. Martin's Press.

Master of Blackoaks. Ashley Carter, pseud. 1978. pap. 2.95 (ISBN 0-449-13585-3, GM). Fawcett.

Master of Blackoaks. Ashley Carter. (Fawcett Gold Medal Book). 1976. 1.95 (ISBN 0-449-13585-3). Fawcett.

Master of Blacktower. Barbara Michaels. 1975. (pbk.) 1.25. Bantam Books.

Master of Blacktower: By Barbara Michaels. Barbara Mertz. LC 66-19994. bds., 4.95. Appleton-Century Dist. Meredith.

Master of Bonne Terre. William Antony Kennedy. LC 17-14954. 1917. R. J. Shores.

Master of Boranga. Mike Sirota. (Ro-Lan Ser.: No. 1). 320p. (Orig.). 1980. pap. 1.95 (ISBN 0-89083-616-7). Zebra.

Master of Castile. S. Edwards. 1972. pap. 0.95 o.p. (09113). Curtis.

Master of Castile. Noel Bertram Gerson. LC 62-14367. 1962. Morrow.

Master of Caxton. Hildegard Brooks. LC 2-10342. 1902. C. Scribner's Sons.

Master of Chaos. Irving Addison Bacheller. LC 32-463719. The Bobbs-Merrill Company.

Master of Craft. William Wymark Jacobs. LC 3-2083. F. A. Stokes Company.

Master of Deeplawn. Hattie E Colter. LC 6-30673. (On cover: The crown series). American Baptist Publication Society.

Master of Destiny: Victor Tremaine. Ida F Powell. LC 39-31267. Chapman & Grimes.

Master of Ettersberg. Ei abeth Burstenbinder. (Primrose series, no. 24). 1891. Street & Smith.

Master of Evil. David C. Smith. 352p. (Orig.). 1983. pap. 2.95 (ISBN 0-523-41738-1). Pinnacle Bks.

Master of Evrington. Vanessa Blake. 1974. (pbk.) 0.95 (ISBN 0-671-77738-6). Pocket Books.

Master of Falconhurst. Kyle Onstott. 1977. pap. 2.95 (ISBN 0-449-23189-5, Crest). Fawcett.

Master of Falcon's Head. Anne Mather. (Presents Ser.). 1974. pap. 1.25 (70569, Pub by Harlequin). PB.

Master of Fortune. Julian Sturgis. LC 8-16858. ("The Newport series" of modern fiction). F. A. Stokes Company.

Master of Fortune: Being Further Adventures of Captain Kettle. Charles John Cutcliffe Wright Hyne. G. W. Dillingham Company.

Master of Foxhollow. Susan Claudia. (Orig.). 1973. pap. 0.95 o.p. (345-26524-6-095). Beagle Bks.

Master of Geneva: A Novel Based on the Life of John Calvin. 1st Ed. Gladys Hutchison Barr. LC 61-130774. 1961. Holt, Rinehart and Winston.

Master of Go. Yasunari Kawabata. (Berkley medallion book). 1974. (pbk.) 1.75 (ISBN 0-425-02645-0). Berkley Pub. Co.

Master of Go. Yasunari Kawabata. LC 72-2228. (Illus.). 1972. 5.95 (ISBN 0-394-47541-0). Knopf; Distributed by Random House.

Master of Go. Yasunari Kawabata. LC 80-39972. 1981. 4.95 (ISBN 0-399-50528-8). Perigee Books.

Master of Gray. Henry Christopher Bailey. LC 4-12219. 1903. Longmans, Green, and Co.

Master of Greylands. Ellen Price Henry Wood Wood. (Seaside library, v.6, no.106). 1877. G. Munro.

Master of Greylands: A Novel. Ellen Price Henry Wood Wood. T. B. Peterson & Brothers.

Master of Greystone. Glenda Carrington. (Berkley Medallion Book). 1977. 1.50 (ISBN 0-425-03443-7). Berkley Pub. Corp.

Master of Hawks. Linda Bushyager. 1979. pap. 1.95 (ISBN 0-440-15871-0). Dell.

Master of Hearts. Kendall Rivers. (Adventures in Love Ser.: No. 33). 1982. pap. 1.95 (ISBN 0-451-11840-5, AJ1840, Sig). NAL.

Master of Heronsbridge. Iris Bromige. 1971. pap. 0.75 o.p. (94091). Beagle Bks.

Master of Heronsbridge. Iris Bromige. 1974. pap. 0.75 o.p. (20491-3-075). Beagle Bks.

Master of Hestviken. Sigrid Undset & Chater, Arthur G., Tr. LC 32-26675. 1932. A. A. Knopf.

Master of Hestviken: The Axe, The Snake Pit, In the Wilderness, The Son Avenger. Sigrid Undset & Chater, Arthur G., Tr. 1934. Alfred A. Knopf.

Master of Hestviken. Translated from the Norwegian by Arthur G. Chaster. Sigrid Undset. LC 52-85123. 1952. Knopf.

Master of His Fate. Amelia Edith Huddleston Barr. LC 6-7983. Dodd, Mead & Company.

Master of His Fate. James Maclaren Coban. LC 6-26763. (On cover: Lovell's international series, no. 62). F. F. Lovell & Company.

Master of Jalna. Mazo De La Roche. LC 33-273931. 1933. Little, Brown, and Company.

Master of Jalna. Mazo De La Roche. (Jalna Ser.). 1979. pap. 1.95 (ISBN 0-449-23932-2, Crest). Fawcett.

Master of Jethart. Dwyer-Joyce, Alice. LC 76-2562. 7.95. St. Martin's Press.

Master of Jethart. Dwyer-Joyce, Alice. LC 77-4509. 1977. 9.95. G. K. Hall.

Master of Life. Zola M Boyle. 1900. G. W. Dillingham Co.

Master of Love. Glenna Finley, pseud. (Signet Book). 1978. 1.50 (ISBN 0-451-08016-5). New American Library.

Master of Mackenzie Station. Kathleen Yapp. (Orig.). pap. 2.50 (ISBN 0-89191-373-4, 53736). Cook.

Master of Mackenzie Station. Kathleen Yapp. (Chime Ser.). 1982. pap. 2.50 o.p. Caroline Hse.

Master of Mahia. Gloria Bevan. (Harlequin Romances Ser.). 192p. 1981. pap. 1.50 (ISBN 0-373-02426-6). Harlequin Bks.

Master of Man: The Story of a Sin. Hall Caine. LC 21-158263. 1921. J. B. Lippincott Company.

Master of Men. Harry Edward Anzer. LC 32-14335.

Master of Millions: A Novel. George Claude Lorimer. LC 3-14859. 1903. F. H. Revell Company.

Master of Millshaven. Clarence Hawkes. LC 36-326419. Chapman & Grimes.

Master of Misfit. John Cleve, pseud. LC 82-80258. (Spaceways Ser.: No. 5). 224p. (Orig.). 1982. pap. 2.50 (ISBN 0-86721-128-8). Playboy Pbks.

Master of Montrolfe Hall: By Rohan O'Grady Pseud. June O'Grady Skinner. 1975. (pbk.) 1.25. Ace Books.

Master of Morley. Kay Thorpe. (Harlequin Presents Ser.). 192p. 1983. pap. 1.95 (ISBN 0-373-10597-5). Harlequin Bks.

Master of Mysteries. Gelett Burgess. LC 75-32736. (Literature of Mystery and Detection). (Illus.). 1976. 27.00 (ISBN 0-405-07865-X). Arno Press.

Master of Mysteries: Being an Account of the Problems Solved by Astro, Seer of Secrets, and His Love Affair with Valeska Wynne, His Assistant. Gelett Burgess. LC 12-23756. 1.35. The Bobbs-Merrill Company.

Master of Mysteries: Problems Solved by Astro, Seer of Secrets & His Love Affair with Valeska Wynne, His Assistant. Gelett Burgess. LC 75-32736. (Literature of Mystery & Detection Ser.). (Illus.). 1976. Repr. of 1912 ed. 27.00x (ISBN 0-405-07865-X). Ayer Co.

Master of Oakwindsor. Douglas Kent Hall. 1976. 8.95 o.p. (ISBN 0-690-01171-7, TYC-T). T Y Crowell.

Master of Oakwindsor. Douglas Kent Hall. 1977. pap. 1.95 o.p. (ISBN 0-515-04411-3). BJ Pub Group.

Master of Occultism: Himalayi Mahatma Sakramagogo); Thesaurus of Occult Lore, from Personal Study and Experience in Phenomena of Higher Human Life. Dinshah Pestanji Framji Ghadiali. LC 36-481. 1935. Printed and Pub. by Spectro-Chrome Institute.

Master of Penrose. Jane Aiken Hodge. 1975. (pbk.) 0.95. Dell.

Master of Power. Brian Crozier. LC 77-79368. 1969. 8.95 o.p. (ISBN 0-316-16276-0). Little.

Master of Red Leaf: A Tale. Elizabeth Avery Meriwether. LC 7-25963. 1880. E. J. Hale & Son.

Master of Revels. Richard Howells Watkins. 1928. By Doubleday, Doran & Company, Inc.

Master of Roxton. Elisabeth Barr. (Candlelight Regency). 1976. (pbk.) 0.75. Dell.

Master of Silence. A Romance. Irving Bacheller. LC 6-5086. (Half-title: Fiction, fact, and fancy series). 1892. C. L. Webster & Co.

Master of Stair. Marjorie Bowen. LC 7-159246. 1907. McClure, Phillips & Co.

Master of the Dauntless. 1st Ed. Frank Robb. LC 53-11682. 1954. Longmans, Green.

Master of the Day of Judgement. Leo Perutz. Tr. by Singer, Hedwig. LC 30-9247. 1930. C. Boni.

Master of the Day of Judgment. Leo Perutz. LC 62-21799. (Collier mystery classics). Collier Books,, C.

Master of the Five Magics. Lyndon Hardy. 384p. 1980. pap. 2.25 (ISBN 0-345-27635-3). Ballantine.

Master of the Flesh. Lucy Hester Thurston Abbott. LC 35-672232. The Christopher Publishing House.

Master of the Forges. From the French of Georges Ohnet. Georges Ohnet. Tr. by P., J. Y. (On cover: Seaside library. Pocket ed., no. 219). 1884. G. Munro.

Master of the Hashomi. Jeffrey Lord. (Blade Ser.: No. 27). (Orig.). 1978. pap. 1.50 (ISBN 0-523-40205-8). Pinnacle Bks.

Master of the Hills: A Tale of the Georgia Mountain. Sarah Johnson Cocke. LC 17-17974. E. P. Dutton & Co.

Master of the House. Radclyffe Hall. LC 32-831426. 1932. J. Cape.

Master of the House. Radclyffe Hall. 1932. J. Cape and R. Ballon.

Master of the House: A Story of Modern American Life, Adapted from the Play of Edgar James. Edward Marshall & James, Edgar. LC 13-8392. 1.25. G. W. Dillingham Company.

Master of the Inn. Robert Herrick. LC 76-96886. 1969. Literature House.

Master of the Inn. Robert Herrick. LC 8-14332. 1908. C. Scribner's Sons.

Master of the Inn. Robert Herrick. LC 40-37529. 1911. C. Scribner's Sons.

Master of the Inner Court. Mary Polk Winn. LC 16-4387. Broadway Publishing Co.

Master of the Lash. Ford Bowne, pseud. 1974. 4.95. Lenox Hill Press.

Master of the Magicians. Elizabeth Stuart Phelps Ward & Ward, Herbert Dickinson, 1861- Joint Author. LC 8-331070. 1890. Houghton, Mifflin and Company.

Master of the Mesa. William Colt MacDonald. LC 47-3063. 1947. Doubleday & Co., Inc.

Master of the Microbe: A Fantastic Romance. Robert William Service. LC 26-14517. Barse & Hopkins.

Master of the Mine. Robert Williams Buchanan. (On cover: Seaside library. Pocket ed., no. 646). 1885. G. Munro.

Master of the Mine. Robert Williams Buchanan. (On cover: Lovell's library, v. 13, no. 696). 1886. J. W. Lovell Company.

Master of the Moor. Ruth Rendell. LC 82-18519. 1982. 13.95 (ISBN 0-8161-3437-5). G.K. Hall.

Master of "The Oaks" A Novel. Caroline Abbot Stanley. LC 13-314. Fleming H. Revell Company.

Master of the Red Buck and Bay Doe: A Story of Whig and Tory Warfare in North Carolina in 1781-83. William Lauriston Hill. LC 14-14808. 1913. Stone Publishing Co.

Master of the River. Felix-Antoine Savard. LC 77-551736. (French writers of Canada series). 9.95. (ISBN 0-88772-226-1) (ISBN 0-88772-170-2). Harvest House.

Master of the Sycamores. Lelia McAnally Batte. LC 47-1529. 1947. The Anson Jones Press.

Master of the Undead. Hugo Paul, pseud. (Orig.). 1968. pap. 0.60 o.p. (73-746). Lancer.

Master of the Undead. Hugo Paul, pseud. 1973. pap. 1.25 o.s.i. (78-726). Lancer.

Master of the Vineyard. Myrtle Reed. LC 10-22063. 1910. G. P. Putnam's Sons.

Master of the Vineyard. Myrtle Reed. LC 13-23586. 1911. G. P. Putnam's Sons.

Master of the World. Cothburn O'Neal. LC 52-10775. 1952. Crown Publishers.

Master of the World. Jules Verne. LC 66-557. (Airmont classic CL73). 1965. Airmont Pub. Co.

Master of This Vessel. Gwyn Griffin. LC 61-8426. 1961. Holt, Rinehart and Winston.

Master of Tinarua. Rosemary Carter. (Harlequin Presents Ser.). 192p. 1983. pap. 1.95 (ISBN 0-373-10575-4). Harlequin Bks.

Master of Urulu. Helen Bianchin. (Harlequin Romances Ser.). 192p. (Orig.). 1981. pap. 1.25 (ISBN 0-373-02378-2, Pub. by Harlequin). PB.

Master of Warlock: A Virginia War Story. George Cary Eggleston. LC 3-2227. 1903. Lothrop Publishing Company.

Master of Wyndward. Norman Daniels. (Orig.). 1969. pap. 0.95 o.p. (75071). Lancer.

Master Passion. Florence Marryat Church Lean. (On cover: Lovell's library. v. 19, no. 903). 1887. J. W. Lovell Company.

Master Passion. Florence Marryat Church Lean. LC 2843. (Arrow library. no. 116). 1900. Street & Smith.

Master Passion. Wilber Foster Yates. LC 46-3360. 1946. The William-Frederick Press.

Master Plan. Clifton Bullock. 1978. 6.00 (ISBN 0-682-48273-0). Exposition.

Master Planner. Nicholas Brady, pseud. (O.s.i.). 1976. pap. 1.50 o.s.i. (BT50990). Belmont-Tower.

Master Planner. Nicholas Brady. Belmont Tower.

Master Plot. Lou Smith. LC 77-22189. 1977. 7.95 (ISBN 0-312-52086-7). St. Martin's Press.

Master Plot. Lou Smith. 1981. 2.50 (ISBN 0-87216-771-2). Playboy Paperbacks.

Master Prim. James Whitfield Ellison. 1974. (pbk.) 0.95. Popular Library.

Master Prim: A Novel. James Whitfield Ellison. LC 68-11522. 1968. (pbk.) 0.95. Little, Brown.

Master Revenge. Hiram Alfred Cody. LC 24-24810. 2.00. George H. Doran Company.

Master Road. Carlin Eastwood. LC 10-24304. 1910. 1.35. The Alice Harriman Company.

Master-Rogue. David G. Philips. Ed. by Abe C. Ravitz. (American Authors Ser). 1903. 17.75 o.s.i. (ISBN 0-512-00547-8). Garrett Pr.

Master Rogue. David Graham Phillips. LC 68-23724. (Americans in Fiction Ser.). (Illus.). lib. bdg. 16.00 (ISBN 0-8398-1565-4); pap. text ed. 5.95x (ISBN 0-89197-841-0). Irvington.

Master-Rogue. David Graham Phillips. (American Author Ser.). 1981. Repr. lib. bdg. 19.00. Scholarly.

Master Rogue: The Autobiography of "Lord Jim" Manes "the Slickest Crook on Earth" As Told to Charles Somerville... Charles Somerville. J. B. Lippincott Company.

Master-Rogue: The Confessions of a Croesus. Illus. by Gordon H. Grant. David Graham Phillips. LC 68-23724. 1688. 10.00. Gregg Pr.

Master-Rogue: The Confessions of a Croesus. David Graham Phillips. LC 3-23893. 1903. McClure, Phillips & Co.

Master Sea Stories: Famous Stories by Russell, Jacobs, Bullen, Becke and Others. Russell, William Clarke, 1844-1911 & Jacobs, William Wymark, 1863- LC 29-163971. E. J. Clode, Inc.

Master Simon's Garden. Cornelia Lynde Meigs. LC 29-19518. 1929. The Macmillan Company.

Master Simon's Garden: A Story. Cornelia Lynde Meigs. LC 16-21398. 1916. The Macmillan Company.

Master Snickup's Cloak. Alexander Theroux. LC 79-1799. (Illus.). 1979. 7.95i (ISBN 0-06-014283-9, HarpT); lib. bdg. 7.89 (ISBN 0-06-014284-7). Har-Row.

Master Sniper. Stephen Hunter. LC 79-26065. 1980. 10.95 (ISBN 0-688-03591-4). Morrow.

Master Spirit. John Christopher Kleber. LC 10-4588. 1909. 1.50. Cochrane Publishing Company.

Master Spirit. William Magnay. LC 6-35732. 1906. Little, Brown, and Company.

Master Spirit. Harriet Elizabeth Prescott Spofford. LC 8-14055. (The ivory series). 1896. C. Scribner's Sons.

Master Spy. Arthur Gask. LC 37-36655. 1937. The Macaulay Company.

Master Tales of Mystery: By the World's Most Famous Authors of to-Day. Ed. by Francis Joseph Reynolds. LC 15-7733. P. F. Collier & Son.

Master. Translated from the German by Heinz Norden. Max Brod. LC 51-13644. 1951. Philosophical Library.

Master Tyll Owlglass: His Marvellous Adventures & Rare Conceits. Tr. by K. R. Mackenzie. 20.00 o.p. (ISBN 0-8274-4168-1). R West.

Master Weaver. Richard E. Early. LC 80-40475. 19.50 (ISBN 0-7100-0641-1). Routledge and Kegan Paul.

Master White Grass. Douglas Waugh. LC 76-355940. 1974. 5.95 (ISBN 0-17-005021-1). Thomas Nelson (Australia)

Master Wilberforce: The Study of a Boy. Eliza M. J. Humphreys. LC 7-5793. 1895. G. P. Putnam's Sons.

Master William Mitten: Or, A Youth of Brilliant Talents, Who Was Ruined by Bad Luck. Augustus Baldwin Longstreet. 1864. Burke, Boykin & Company.

Master William Mitten: Or, A Youth of Brilliant Talents, Who Was Ruined by Bad Luck. Augustus Baldwin Longstreet. 1889. J. W. Burke & Co.

Master William Mitten; or, A Youth of Brilliant Talents, Who Was Ruined by Bad Luck. Augustus Baldwin Longstreet. LC 75-162225. 239p. 1973. Repr. of 1864 ed. 10.00 o.p. (ISBN 0-405-04331-7). Arno.

Master Zacharius: A Winter Amid the Ice. Jules Verne. Repr. lib. bdg. 11.50x (ISBN 0-88411-916-5). Amereon Ltd.

Masterfolk: Wherein Is Attempted the Unravelling of the Strange Affair of My Lord Wyntwarde of Cavil and Miss Betty Modeyne. Haldane Macfall. LC 3-24294. 1903. Harper & Brothers.

Masterful: By Jack Woodford Pseud. & Todd Marshall Pseud. Josiah Pitts Woolfolk & John Burton Thompson. LC 54-22397. 1954. Signature Press.

Masterful Monk. Owen Francis Dudley. LC 29-21559. (His Problems of human happiness. iii). 1929. Longmans, Green and Co.

Mastering Marcus. Paul Hutchens. LC 38-133964. 1938. Wm. B. Eerdmans Publishing Company.

Masterless Man. Jules Verne. 3.95. Assoc Bk.

Masterless Man. Jules Verne. 11.95x (ISBN 0-8464-0616-0). Beekman Pubs.

Masterman and Son. William James Dawson. LC 9-27031. 1.20. F. H. Revell Company.

Masterman Ready. Frederick Marryat. (Half-title: Everyman's library, ed. by Ernest Rhys. For young people). 1907. J. M. Dent & Co.

Masterman Ready. Frederick Marryat. LC 23-26592. (Half-title: Children's classics. edited by Walter Jerrold). E. Nister.

Masterman Ready. Frederick Marryat. LC 28-29239. 1928. Harper and Brothers.

Masterman Ready: Or, The Wreck of the "Pacific.". Frederick Marryat. LC 7-17579. (On cover: Seaside library. Pocket ed. no. 1218). 1880. G. Munro.

Masterman Ready: Or, The Wreck of the "Pacific". Frederick Marryat. LC 7-24683. A. L. Burt.

Masterman Ready: Or, The Wreck of the "Pacific". Frederick Marryat. LC 22-5154. (On cover: The home library). A. L. Burt Company.

Masterpiece. Emile Zola. 1957. Macmillan.

Masterpiece. Emile Zola. LC 68-5529. (Ann Arbor paperbacks, AA145). 1968. 2.95. University of Michigan Press.

Masterpiece. Emile Zola & Woods, Katherine, 1886- Tr. LC 46-8467. 1946. Howell, Soskin.

Masterpiece Affair. Kenneth Royce. LC 73-6524. (Simon and Schuster novel of suspense). 1973. 6.95 (ISBN 0-671-21566-3). Simon and Schuster.

Masterpiece Library of Short Stories, 20 vols. Ed. by J. A. Hammerton. 1977. Repr. lib. bdg. 450.00 (ISBN 0-8414-4985-6). Folcroft.

Masterpiece of Adventure. Louis Morris. LC 66-15781. (Masterpiece Ser.). 256p. (Orig.). 1975. pap. 1.95 o.p. (ISBN 0-8055-0062-6). Hart.

Masterpiece of Imposture see Finished Rake: or Gallantry in Perfection.

Masterpiece of Mystery & Detection. Rosamund Morris. LC 66-1578. (Masterpiece Ser.). 256p. (Orig.). 1975. pap. 1.95 o.p. (ISBN 0-8055-0056-1). Hart.

Masterpiece of Nice Mr. Breen. new ed. Henry Hudvald. (Falcon's Head Mystery Ser.). 192p. 1972. 5.95 o.p. (ISBN 0-529-04821-3, A4106). World Pub.

Masterpiece of Nice Mr. Breen. Henry Hunvald. LC 72-86871. 1972. 5.95 (ISBN 0-529-04821-3). World Pub.

Masterpiece of Nice Mr. Breen. Henry Hunvald. (Harrow Books). 1973. (pbk) 0.95 (ISBN 0-06-087056-7). Harper & Row.

Masterpiece of Surprise. James L. Monahan. LC 66-23131. (Masterpiece Ser.). 256p. (Orig.). 1975. pap. 1.95 o.p. (ISBN 0-8055-0002-2). Hart.

Masterpiece of Suspense. Rosamund Morris. LC 66-15782. (Masterpiece Ser.). 256p. (Orig.). 1975. pap. 1.95 o.p. (ISBN 0-8055-0006-5). Hart.

Masterpiece. Tr. from French by Thomas Walton. Emile Zola. LC 64-740855. 1965. bds., 3.95. Elek Bks.

Masterpieces of Adventure... Ed. by Nella Braddy Henney. LC 37-25066. Garden City Publishing Co., Inc.

Masterpieces of Adventure. Ed. by Louis Morris. LC 66-15781. (Illus.). 1966. Hart Pub. Co.

Masterpieces of German Fiction. Rudolf Lindau et al. LC 7-19654. L. Schick.

Masterpieces of German Fiction. Golden-Rod Ed.. From the German of Rudolph Lindau, Fanny Lewald, Ernst Eckstein, Adolph Wilbrandt, Paul Heyse and Hans Hopfen. Lindau, Rudolf, 1829- et al. LC 7-19653. Laird & Lee C.

Masterpieces of Humor. Ed. by Rosamund Morris. LC 66-15780. (Illus.). 1966. Hart Pub. Co.

Masterpieces of Legal Fiction. Ed. by Maximilian Koessler. 1964. 12.50 o.p. Lawyers Coop.

Masterpieces of Murder. Agatha Miller Christie. LC 76-44421. 9.95 (ISBN 0-396-07412-X). Dodd, Mead.

Masterpieces of Mystery... Ed. by Joseph Lewis French. LC 21-381. 1920. Doubleday, Page & Company.

Masterpieces of Mystery... Ed. by Joseph Lewis French. LC 37-39538. 1937. Garden City Publishing Co., Inc.

Masterpieces of Mystery. Anna Katharine Green Rohlfs. LC 13-10502. 1913. Dodd, Mead and Company.

Masterpieces of Mystery & Detection. Ed. by Rosamund Morris. LC 66-15778. 1966. Hart.

Masterpieces of Mystery and Detection. Ed. by Rosamund Morris. 1975. (pbk.) 1.50. Hart Publishing.

Masterpieces of Science Fiction. Thomas Durwood & Armand Eisen. LC 78-58827. (Illus.). 1978. 7.95. Ariel Books.

Masterpieces of Science Fiction. hyperion reprint ed. Ed. by Samuel Moskowitz. LC 73-15070. 1973. 12.95 (ISBN 0-88355-127-6) (ISBN 0-88355-127-6). Hyperion Press.

Masterpieces of Science Fiction. Ed. by Samuel Moskowitz. LC 66-24995. 1967. World Pub. Co.

Masterpieces of Science Fiction. Ed. by Samuel Moskowitz. LC 73-15070. (Classics of science fiction). 1974. (ISBN 0-88355-127-6) (ISBN 0-88355-156-X). Hyperion Press.

Masterpieces of Surprise. Louis Morris. (Orig.). 1966. pap. 1.45 o.p. (ISBN 0-8055-0002-2). Hart.

Masterpieces of Suspense. Ed. by Rosamund Morris. LC 66-15782. 1966. Hart Pub. Co.

Masterpieces of Suspense. Ed. by Rosamund Morris. LC 66-15782. 1975. (pbk.) 1.50. Hart.

Masterpieces of the Spanish Golden Age. Ed. by Angel Flores. (Rinehart Editions). 1957. pap. text ed. 1.25 o.p. (ISBN 0-03-008425-3, HoltC). HR&W.

Masterplayers. Michael Sinclair. LC 78-9812. 8.95 (ISBN 0-393-08820-0). Norton.

Masters. Charles Percy Snow. (His Strangers and brothers, 4; SL104). 1965. pap., 1.65. Scribners.

Masters. Charles Percy Snow. LC 60-51308. (His Strangers and brothers, 4). Scribner.

Masters. Charles Percy Snow. LC 51-8194. (His Strangers and brothers, 5). 1951. Macmillan.

Masters. Charles Percy Snow. LC 60-51308. (His Strangers and brothers, 5). 1951. Scribner.

Masters Affair. Burt Hirschfeld. 1976. 1.95 (ISBN 0-671-80675-0). Pocket Book.

Masters Affair. Burt Hirschfeld. LC 70-139296. 1971. 6.50. Arbor House.

Masters & Martyrs. Robert Vaughan. 320p. 1983. pap. 3.50 (ISBN 0-440-06370-1, Emerald). Dell.

Masters & Masterpieces of the Short Story: 2nd Series. Ed. by Joshua McClennen. LC 57-5710. 1960. text ed. 5.25 o.p. (ISBN 0-03-010070-4, HoltC). HR&W.

Masters and Masterpieces of the Short Story. Ed. by Joshua McClennen. LC 57-5710. 1957. Holt.

Masters and Men: The Human Story in the Mahatma Letters (a Fictionalized Account) Virginia Hanson. LC 79-3665. (Quest book). 7.50 (ISBN 0-8356-0534-5). Theosophical Pub. House.

Masters and Peasants. Theodor Kallifatides. LC 75-40746. 1977. 6.95 (ISBN 0-385-09916-9). Doubleday.

Masters' Choice. Laurence M. Janifer. (O.s.i.). 1966. 5.95 o.s.i. (ISBN 0-671-45280-0). S&S.

Masters' Choice: The Best Science-Fiction Stories of All Time Chosen by the Masters of Science Fiction. Ed. by Laurence M. Janifer. LC 66-17602. bds., 5.95. S&S.

Master's Degree. Margaret Hill McCarter. LC 13-195042. 1913. A. C. McClurg & Co.

Master's Golden Years. John Oxenham, pseud. LC 32-869477. 1932. Longmans, Green and Co.

Master's House: A Tale of Southern Life. Thomas Bangs Thorpe. LC 7-15844. 1854. T. L. McElrath & Co.; Etc., Etc.

Master's Mission: Or, The Minister Who Dared. William Curtis Stiles. (Added t.-p.: Alliance library, no. 12). Street & Smith.

Masters of Bow Street. John Creasey. (O.s.i.). 1974. 9.95 o.s.i. (ISBN 0-671-21783-6). S&S.

Masters of Bow Street: A Novel. John Creasey. LC 74-944. 1974. 9.95 (ISBN 0-671-21783-6). Simon and Schuster.
Masters of Bow Street: A Novel. John Creasey. LC 74-944. 1975. (pbk.) 1.95 (ISBN 0-671-78935-X). Pocket Books.
Masters of Everon. Gordon R Dickson. LC 80-110067. (Ace Science Fiction). 2.25. Ace Books.
Masters of Mayhem: The 1965 Mystery Writers of America Anthology. Ed. by Edward D. Radin. LC 65-22976. 1965. Morrow.
Masters of Mayhem: The 1965 Mystery Writers of America Anthology. Ed. by Edward D. Radin. Mystery Writers of America. Ed. by Edward D. Radin. LC 65-22976. bds., 3.95. Morrow.
Masters of Men: A Romance of the New Navy. Morgan Robertson. 1901. Doubleday, Page & Co.
Masters of Men: A Romance of the New Navy. autograph ed. Morgan Robertson. LC 14-21585. McClure's Magazine and Metropolitan Magazine.
Masters of St. Benedict's. Frances Bridges Marshall. LC 7-24397. (On cover: Globe library, v. 1, no. 177). 1893. Rand, McNally & Company.
Masters of Shades and Shadows: An Anthology of Great Ghost Stories. Seon Manley & Gogo Lewis. LC 77-76255. 7.95. (ISBN 0-385-12743-X) (ISBN 0-385-12744-8). Doubleday.
Masters of Solitude. Marvin Kaye & Parke Godwin. LC 77-92217. (Illus.). 1978. 10.00 (ISBN 0-385-12480-5). Doubleday.
Masters of Space. Philip S. Hopkins. (Illus.). (YA) 1964. pap. 0.50 o.p. (ISBN 0-87474-013-4). Smithsonian.
Masters of the Dew. Jacques Roumain. LC 70-144148. (American Library). 1971. 1.50. Collier Books.
Masters of the Dew. Jacques Roumain. (O.s.i.). 1971. pap. 1.50 o.s.i. (ISBN 0-02-035550-5, Collier). Macmillan.
Masters of the Dew. Jacques Roumain & Hughes, Langston, 1902- Tr. LC 47-46970. 1947. Reynal & Hitchcock.
Masters of the Game. Sidney Sheldon. LC 82-60920. 448p. 1982. 15.95 (ISBN 0-688-01365-1). Morrow.
Masters of the Maze. Avram Davidson. 1976. pap. 1.25 (ISBN 0-532-12439-1). Woodhill.
Masters of the Modern Short Story. a new edition. ed. Ed. by Walter Havighurst. LC 55-409. 1955. Harcourt, Brace.
Masters of the Modern Short Story. Ed. by Walter Havighurst. LC 45-3743. 1945. Harcourt, Brace and Company.
Masters of the Peaks: A Story of the Great North Woods. Joseph Alexander Altsheler. 311p. Repr. of 1918 ed. lib. bdg. 13.20x (ISBN 0-88411-938-6). Amereon Ltd.
Masters of the Pit. Michael Moorcock. (Science Fiction Ser.). 1979. pap. 1.50 (ISBN 0-87997-450-8, UW1450). DAW Bks.
Masters of the Short Story. Ed. by Abraham Harold Lass. LC 74-156759. 1971. 1.95. New American Library.
Masters of the Vortex. Edward Elmer Smith. 1970. pap. 1.25 o.p. (V3000). BJ Pub Group.
Masters of the Wheat-Lands. Harold Bindloss. LC 10-17325. 1910. Frederick A. Stokes Company.
Masters of Time. Alfred Elton Van Vogt. LC 50-7467. 1950. Fantasy Press.
Master's Touch: By Helen Lloyd Dubuar Pseud. Helen Alkin Dubuar. LC 53-24371. 1952.
Master's Violin. Myrtle Reed. LC 4-229875. 1904. G. P. Putnam's Sons.
Master's Violin. Myrtle Reed. LC 24-25001. 1912. Grosset & Dunlap.
Masterson. Lee Wichelns. LC 43-5032. 1943. D. Appleton-Century, Incorporated.
Masterson: A Story of an English Gentleman. Gilbert Frankau. LC 26-7012. 1926. Harper & Brothers.
Masterstroke. Marilyn Sharp. LC 80-25318. 12.95. R. Marek.
Masterwork: A Novel. John Miglis. LC 80-7862. 11.95 (ISBN 0-690-01894-0). Lippincott & Crowell.
Masterworks of Crime & Mystery. Arthur Conan Doyle & Jack Tracy. LC 82-10312. 14.95 (ISBN 0-385-27688-5). Dial Press.
Mastery. Mark Lee Luther. LC 4-23763. 1904. The Macmillan Company.
Mastery of Love: A Narrative of Settlement Life. James Edward McCulloch. LC 11-550. Fleming H. Revell Company.
Mastery of Tess. Patrick Joseph Carroll. LC 35-15621. The Ave Maria Press.
Mastodonia. Clifford D. Simak. LC 77-26969. 1978. 7.95 (ISBN 0-345-27500-4). Ballantine Books.
Mastro-Don Gesualdo: A Novel. Giovanni Verga. LC 77-20331. 14.50 (ISBN 0-520-03598-4). University of California Press.
Mastro-Don Gesualdo. Giovanni Verga. LC 75-11486. 1976. 25.00 (ISBN 0-8371-8198-4). Greenwood Press.
Mastro-Don Gesualdo. Giovanni Verga. LC 73-874424. (Penguin modern classics). 1970 (ISBN 0-14-003168-5). Penguin.
Mastro-Don Gesualdo. Giovanni Verga & Lawrence, David Herbert, 1885-1930, Tr. LC 23-14912. 1923. T. Seltzer.
Mastro-Don Gesualdo. Translated by D. H. Lawrence. Giovanni Verga. LC 55-14808. 1955. Grove Press.
Masts to Spear the Stars. Stephen Longstreet. (95-188). 1968. Popular Lib.
Masts to Spear the Stars. 1st Ed. Stephen Longstreet. LC 67-15352. (Liberty tree ser.). 1967. 5.95. Doubleday.
Mata Hari. Kurt D. Singer. (O.s.i.). (Orig.). pap. 0.60 o.s.i. (A254, Award). Univ Pub & Dist.
Mata the Magician: A Romance of the New Era. Isabella Ingalese. LC 1-26950. The Abbey Press.
Matador. Barnaby Conrad. 1970. pap. 0.95 o.p. (ISBN 0-532-95136-0). Woodhill.
Matador. Barnaby Conrad. 1970. pap. 0.95 o.p. (ISBN 0-532-95136-0). Manor Bks.
Matador: A Novel. Marguerite Steen. LC 34-18189. 1934. Little, Brown, and Company.
Matador: Illustrated by the Author. Barnaby Conrad. LC 52-10142. 1952. Houghton Mifflin.
Matador of the Five Towns, and Other Stories. Arnold Bennett. LC 74-17024. (Collected works of Arnold Bennett). 1974. (ISBN 0-518-19134-6). Books for Libraries Press.
Matador of the Five Towns, and Other Stories. Arnold Bennett. LC 79-144875. 1970. (ISBN 0-403-00862-X). Scholarly Press.
Matador of the Five Towns. And Other Stories. Arnold Bennett. LC 12-9187. George H. Doran Company.
Matador. Tr. from French by Peter Wiles. Henry De Montherlant. LC 62-27943. 1965. bds., 3.50. Elek Bks.
Matadora, a Novel. Louise Tornquist. LC 58-145135. 1957. Exposition Press.
Matagorda. Louis L'Amour. 176p. (Orig.). 1981. pap. 2.25 (ISBN 0-553-14743-9). Bantam.
Matanza. Peter Gentry. 1979. pap. 2.25 (ISBN 0-449-14117-9, GM). Fawcett.
Matanza: A Novel. Peter Gentry. 1979. 2.25 (ISBN 0-449-14117-9). Fawcett Gold Medal Books.
Matanzas: Or, A Brother's Revenge. A Tale of Florida. Also Selling a Green 'un; or, A Sight at Louis Philippe. Edward Zane Carroll Judson. LC 7-12843. 1848. G. H. Williams.
Matapan Affair. Fortune Du Boisgobey. Tr. by Laura E. Kendall. (Seaside library. vol. lxi, no. 1241). 1882. G. Munro.
Matapan Affair. Fortune Du Boisgobey. Rand, McNally & Co.
Matarese Circle. Robert Ludlum. LC 78-31673. 12.50 (ISBN 0-399-90043-8). R. Marek Publishers.
Matata. Malcolm McConnell. LC 70-155660. 1971. 8.95 (ISBN 0-670-46219-5). Viking Press.
Match for a Murderer. Dorothy Dunnett. LC 74-144078. (Midnight novel of suspense). 1971. 5.95 (ISBN 0-395-12343-7). Houghton Mifflin.
Match for Elizabeth. Mira Stables. 1974. pap. 0.95 o.p. (26571-095). Beagle Bks.
Match King. Einar Thorvaldson. LC 32-15772. The Macaulay Company.
Match of the Season. Susan Gordon. LC 82-70761. 1982. 11.95 (ISBN 0-8027-0708-4). Walker.
Match Set. Orlando R Petrocelli. 1977. 1.95. Pinnacle Books.
Match Trick. Don Zacharia. LC 81-20808. 1982. 13.50 (ISBN 0-671-44017-9). Linden Press/Simon & Schuster.
Matched Pearls. Grace Livingston Hill. LC 33-15393. J. B. Lippincott Company.
Matches. Mary Evans Foster. 1937. The Naylor Company.
Matching Wits. Carla Neggers. (Loveswept Ser.: No. 5). 1983. pap. 1.95. Bantam.
Matchless Rogue; or, an Account of the Contrivances, Cheats, Stratagems & Amours of Tom Merryman, Commonly Called Newgate Tom see Highland Rogue: The Memorable Actions of the Celebrated Robert Mac-Gregor, Commonly Called Rob-Roy.
Matchmaker: A Novel. Lucy Bethia Colquhoun Walford. LC 8-328111. 1894. Longmans, Green, and Co.
Matchmakers. Rebecca Baldwin. 1980. pap. 1.75 (ISBN 0-449-50017-9, Coventry). Fawcett.
Matchmakers. Annie Edith Foster Jameson. LC 16-21706. 1.35. George H. Doran Company.
Matchmakers' Lament & Other Astonishments. ltd. ed. Leonard Nathan. (Gehenna Press Ser). (Illus.). 1967. 35.00 o.p. (ISBN 0-670-46227-6). Grossman.
Mate of the Daylight. Sarah O. Jewett. Ed. by Kenneth Lynn. Incl. Friends Ashore. LC 70-96654. (American Authors Ser, Collected). 1970. Repr. of 1689 ed. lib. bdg 11.95 o.s.i. (ISBN 0-512-00371-8). Garrett Pr.
Mate of the Daylight, and Friends Ashore. 3d ed. Sarah Orne Jewett. LC 43-394969. 1885. Houghton, Mifflin and Company.
Mate of the Daylight, and Friends Ashore. Sarah Orne Jewett. LC 7-9728. 1884. Houghton, Mifflin and Company.
Mate of the Daylight & Friends Ashore see Collected Works.
Mate of the "Easter Bell" And Other Stories. Amelia Edith Huddleston Barr. LC 6-7980. (choice series... no. 80). R. Bonner's Sonsc.
Mate of the Good Ship York: Or, The Ship's Adventure. William Clark Russell. LC 2-15204. 1902. L. C. Page & Company.
Mate of the Vancouver. Morley Roberts. (On cover: Cassell's sunshine series, no. 120, extra). 1892. Cassell Publishing Company.
Mate Takes Her Home. Oliver Ramsay Pilat. LC 39-30681. 1939. C. Scribner's Sons.
Mate to Mate. A Novel. Tallula K. Sharkey. LC 7-26237. 1879. G. P. Putnam's Sons.
Mated, by. Wallace Irwin. LC 26-4707. 1926. G. P. Putnam's Sons.
Materfamilias. Ada Cambridge Cross. LC 6-319552. (Half-title: Appletons' town and country library. no. 242). 1898. D. Appleton and Company.
Material Goods. Janet Burroway. LC 80-12381. 77p. 1980. 7.95 (ISBN 0-8130-0670-8). U Presses Fla.
Material Plane. Thomas Farber. LC 79-25419. 9.95 (ISBN 0-525-15424-8). Dutton.
Mathematics of Guilt. Isabel Egenton Ostrander. LC 26-19676. 1926. R. M. McBride & Company.
Mathematics of Murder. Kenneth Bedford. LC 73-78299. 1969. 3.95. Roy Publishers.
Matherson Marriage. Ruby Mildred Ayres. LC 23-94882. 1923. 1.75. George H. Doran Company.
Matheson Formula. Joseph Smith Fletcher. LC 29-129113. 1929. A. A. Knopf.
Mathew Swain: When Trouble Beckons. Mike McQuay. (Orig.). 1981. pap. 2.25 (ISBN 0-553-20041-0). Bantam.
Mathias Sandorf... Jules Verne. LC 2-8385. (Seaside library. v. 101, no. 2039). 1885. G. Munro.
Mathieu Ropars: Et Cetera Short Stories and Poems. William Young. LC 9-1195. 1868. G. P. Putnam & Son.
Mathilda. Mary Wollstonecraft Godwin Shelley. Ed. by Elizabeth Nitchie. 104p. 1982. Repr. of 1959 ed. lib. bdg. 40.00 (ISBN 0-8495-5053-X). Arden Lib.
Mathilda. Edited by Elizabeth Nitchie. Mary Wollstonecraft Godwin Shelley. LC 60-1154. University of North Carolina Press.
Mathilda of Canossa, and Yoland of Groningen. Antonio Bresciani & Sadlier, Anna Theresa, 1854- Tr. LC 6-17390. 1875. D. & J. Sadlier & Co.
Mathilde: A Novel. Leonhard Frank. Tr. by Trask, Willard Ropes. LC 48-5634. 1948. Simon and Schuster.
Matilda. Paul Gallico. LC 72-113528. 1970. 5.95. Coward-McCann.
Matilda. Paul Gallico. (Berkley Book). 1978. 1.95 (ISBN 0-425-03556-5). Berkley Pub. Corp.
Matilda Berkely, or, Family Anecdotes. Winifred Marshall Gales. LC 7-17594. 1804. Printed by J. Gales, Printer to the State.
Matilda: Governess of the English. Sophia Cleugh. LC 24-255252. 1924. The Macmillan Company.
Matilda Hunter Murder. Harry Stephen Keeler. LC 31-28148. E. P. Dutton & Co., Inc.
Matilda Montgomerie; or, The Prophecy Fulfilled. A Tale of the Late American War. Being the Sequel to "Wacousta.". John Richardson. LC 44-153594. 1851. Dewitt & Davenport.
Matilda: Princess of England. A Romance of the Crusades. Marie Risteau Cottin. LC 6-29011. 1885. W. S. Gottsberger.
Matin Des Magiciens. Louis Pauwels & Jacques Bergier. Ed. by Yvone Lenard. 1967. pap. text ed. 4.95x o.p. (ISBN 0-06-045064-9, HarpC). Har-Row.
Matinee. Donna Schuman & Judy Roche. 1980. pap. 2.75 (ISBN 0-440-15223-2). Dell.
Matinees see Coupled.
Mating Call. Rex Ellingwood Beach. LC 27-15708. 1927. Harper & Brothers.
Mating Cry. John Thurlow. LC 25-19726. 1925. T. Seltzer.
Mating Cry. By Frank Danjels Pseud. Cover Painting by Barye Philips. Dan Lindsay. LC 55-24552. (Gold medal book, 449). 1954. Fawcett Publications.
Mating Dance. Rona Randall. LC 78-31724. 9.95 (ISBN 0-698-10961-9). Coward, McCann & Geoghegan.
Mating in the Wilds. Ottwell Binns. LC 20-15961. (On verso of half-title: Borzoi western stories). 1920. A. A. Knopf.
Mating Merry-Go-Round. Garth Brandtson. 1974. (pbk.) 1.95 (ISBN 0-87056-400-5). Brandon Books.
Mating of Anthea. Arabella Kenealy. LC 11-271120. 1911. 1.25. John Lane Company.
Mating of Doris Dinsmore. Catherine Morris Plumer Bement. LC 27-24665. 1927. The Stratford Company.
Mating of Lydia. Mary Augusta Arnold Humphry Ward Ward. LC 13-625397. 1913. Doubleday, Page & Co.
Mating of the Blades. Achmed Abdullah. LC 20-212885. 1920. The James A. McCann Company.
Mating Place. Jamison Bruce. (Orig.). pap. 0.95 o.p. (1131). Brandon.
Mating Season. Janet Dailey. (Harlequin Presents Ser.). (Orig.). 1980. pap. 1.50 (ISBN 0-373-10356-5). Harlequin Bks.
Mating Season. Pelham Grenville Wodehouse. LC 49-50278. 1949. Didier.
Mating Woman. Lois Bull. LC 33-19964. The Macaulay Company.
Matira Manisha see House Undivided.
Matisse, Picasso, and Gertrude Stein, with Two Shorter Stories. Gertrude Stein. LC 72-78187. 1972. 10.00 (ISBN 0-87110-085-1) (ISBN 0-87110-085-1). Something Else Press.
Matka and Kotik: A Tale of the Mist-Islands. David Starr Jordan. LC 7-11691. 1897. The Whitaker & Ray Company (Incorporated.
Matlock Paper. Robert Ludlum. LC 72-13314. 1973. 7.95. Dial Press.
Matlock Paper. Robert Ludlum. 1974. (pbk.) 1.75. Dell.
Mato, Come Heal Me. Craig Volk. (Outlaws Ser.: Vol. 4). 1980. 4.95x (ISBN 0-917624-15-7). Lame Johnny.
Mato Grosso Horror. Joseph Rosenberger. (Death Merchant,#13). 1975. (pbk.) 1.25 (ISBN 0-523-00705-1). Pinnacle Books.
Matoaka: A Story of the Fight for Americanism. William Grant Burleigh. LC 24-295323. Dorrance & Company.
Matorni's Vineyard. Edward Phillips Oppenheim. LC 28-23100. 1928. Little, Brown, and Company.
Matriarch. Gladys Bronwyn Stern. (YA) (gr. 9-12). pap. 0.75 o.p. (T1501). Pyramid Pubns.
Matriarch: A Chronicle. Gladys Bronwyn Stern. LC 25-1015. 1925. A. A. Knopf.
Matriarch: A Novel. Charles Roy MacKinnon. LC 75-8881. 1975. 8.95 (ISBN 0-440-05459-1). Delacorte Press.
Matriarch Chronicles... Gladys Bronwyn Stern. LC 36-32113. 1936. A. A. Knopf.
Matrimonial Adventures of Deacon Stonewall Satan Bomb. John Salaman Cantelo. LC 38-13394. 1938. Meador Publishing Company.
Matrimonial Agent of Potsdam: A Humoro-Social Romance, from the German of A. Von Winterfeld. Adolf Wilhelm Ernst Von Winterfeld & Raphael, Henry, Tr. LC 8-37779. 1887. T. R. Knox & Co.
Matrimonial Infelicites, with an Occasional Felicity, by Way of Contrast. Robert Barry Coffin. LC 6-26745. 1865. Hurd and Houghton.
Matrimonial Infelicities, with an Occasional Felicity, by Way of Contrast. Robert Barry Coffin. LC 41-347896. 1869. Hurd and Houghton.
Matrimony. A Novel. William Edward Norris. (Harper's Franklin square library, no. 390). 1884. Harper & Brothers.
Matrimony Most Murderous: By Leslie Gargill Sic. Leslie Cargill. LC 58-778528. Roy Publishers.
Matrimony: Or, Love Affairs in Our Village Twenty Years Ago. 2d ed. Anne Tuttle Jones Bullard. LC 6-22269. 1853. M. W. Dodd.
Matrix. Maria Thompson Davies. LC 20-3881. 1920. The Century Co.
Matrix. Melvin P Levy. 1925. T. Seltzer.
Matrushka Doll: A Novel. Barbara Fischman Traub. LC 79-9807. 10.95 (ISBN 0-399-90044-6). R. Marek Publishers.
Matsu. John Paris, pseud. LC 32-182405. 1932. G. P. Putnam's Sons.
Matt: A Tale of a Caravan. Robert Williams Buchanan. (On cover: Seaside library. Pocket ed., no. 398). 1885. G. Munro.
Matt of the Water-Front. Florence Martin Eastland. LC 9-12879. Jennings and Graham.
Matt Quarterhill: Rifleman. William Chamberlain. LC 65-10744. 3.50. John Day.
Matt Reagan's Lady. Mary Brinker Post. 1981. pap. 2.75 (ISBN 0-441-52222-X). Ace Bks.
Matt Regan's Lady. 1st Ed. Mary Brinker Post. LC 55-5591. 1955. Doubleday.
Matter of Accent. Francis Steegmuller. LC 43-2712. 1943. Dodd, Mead & Company.
Matter of Blue Chips. William Wetmore. LC 65-10645. 1965. Doubleday.
Matter of Business: And Other Stories. Jeffery Farnol. LC 40-33108. 1940. Doubleday, Doran & Company, Inc.
Matter of Business: And Other Stories. William Curtis Stiles. 1899. Advance Publishing Co.
Matter of Choosing. Eda Lord. LC 63-9279. 1963. Simon and Schuster.

TITLE INDEX MAX BRAND'S BEST STORIES.

Matter of Confidence. Brad Williams & J. W. Ehrlich. (Sam Benedict Mystery). 1974. (pbk.) 0.95. Popular Library.
Matter of Confidence. Brad Williams & Jacob W. Ehrlich. LC 72-78138. (Rinehart suspense novel). 1973. 4.95 (ISBN 0-03-001446-8). Holt, Rinehart and Winston.
Matter of Conscience. Edwin Palmer Hoyt. LC 66-199959. bds., 5.95. Duell, Dist. Meredith.
Matter of Conscience: A Novel. Translated from the German Language Original, Der Grosstyrann und das Gericht, by Norman Cameron. Werner Bergengruen. LC 52-8997. 1952. Thames and Hudson.
Matter of Conviction. Evan Hunter. LC 59-9503. 1959. Simon and Schuster.
Matter of Conviction. Evan Hunter. 1.75 (ISBN 0-380-00695-2). Avon Books.
Matter of Diplomacy. Warren Tute. LC 78-96778. 1970. 4.95. Coward-McCann.
Matter of Duty: By Edward Cranston. Edward Cranston, pseud. 1943. Longmans, Green and Co.
Matter of Endurance: A Novel. James Hans Meisel. LC 75-105116. 1970. 5.95. Regnery.
Matter of Fact. Herbert Brean. LC 56-11039. 1956. Morrow.
Matter-of-Fact Girl: A Novel. Theodora Havers Boulger. (On cover: Leisure hour series no. 126)). 1881. H. Holt and Company.
Matter of Feeling. Janine Boissard. LC 79-21268. 7.95 (ISBN 0-316-10098-6). Little, Brown.
Matter of Honor. Rebecca Baldwin. 176p. (Orig.). 1983. pap. 2.25 (ISBN 0-449-20102-3, Crest). Fawcett.
Matter of Honor. Charles F. Powers. 176p. 1983. 12.99 (ISBN 0-910829-03-9); pap. 3.95 (ISBN 0-910829-04-7). First East.
Matter of Honor. Nina Pykare. (Candlelight Regency Ser.: No. 716). (Orig.). 1982. pap. 2.25 (ISBN 0-440-16128-2). Dell.
Matter of Intelligence. George Wittman. LC 75-11669. (O.s.i.). 252p. 1975. 7.95 o.s.i. (ISBN 0-02-630850-9). Macmillan.
Matter of Intelligence: A Novel. George Wittman. LC 75-11669. 1975. 8.95 (ISBN 0-02-630850-9). Macmillan.
Matter of Iodine. David Keith, pseud. LC 40-6203. 1940. Dodd, Mead & Company.
Matter of Life & Death. Jane Horatio. (General Hospital Ser). (Orig.). 1971. pap. 0.75 o.p. (A858S, Award). Univ Pub & Dist.
Matter of Life and Death. Johanna P. Vrugt. LC 73-3955. (Library of Netherlandic literature, v. 3). 1974. 6.95 (ISBN 0-8057-3441-4). Twayne Publishers.
Matter of Love and Death. Tobias Wells. LC 66-12222. 3.50. Pub. for the Crime Club by Doubleday.
Matter of Love, and Other Baroque Tales of the Provinces. MacKinley Helm. LC 46-7373. 1946. Harper & Brothers.
Matter of Mandrake. Barry Norman. LC 68-13250. 1968. Walker.
Matter of Marriage. Renee Shann. LC 82-19816. 1983. 11.95 (ISBN 0-89340-485-3). Chivers.
Matter of Millions. A Novel. Anna Katharine Green Rohlfs. LC 7-39818. (ledger library, no. 36). 1891. R. Bonner's Sons.
Matter of Miracles. Edward Fenton. (Illus.). 1967. Holt, Rinehart and Winston.
Matter of Morals. 1st Ed. Joseph Gies. LC 51-1375. 1951. Harper.
Matter of Opportunity. Catherine Arley. LC 68-25428. (Red mask mystery). 1968. 4.50. Putnam.
Matter of Paradise. Brown Meggs. 1976. 1.50 (ISBN 0-449-22942-4). Fawcett Crest.
Matter of Paradise: A Novel. Brown Meggs. LC 74-22343. 1975. 6.95. Random House.
Matter of Policy: An Amy Brewster Mystery. Sam Merwin. LC 47-17776. 1946. Mystery House.
Matter of Pride. Janet Mathewson. LC 57-12125. 1957. Dodd, Mead.
Matter of Priority. Harry Homewood. LC 75-34949. 192p. 1976. 6.95 o.p. (ISBN 0-87955-909-8). O'Hara.
Matter of Revenge. first ed. Christy Demaine. LC 77-73823. 1.50. Playboy Press.
Matter of Scents. Tom Fitzgerald. (Orig.). 1974. pap. 1.25 o.p. (ISBN 0-515-03488-6, V3488). BJ Pub Group.
Matter of Size. Harry Homewood. LC 74-25386. 6.95 (ISBN 0-87955-904-7). J. P. O'Hara.
Matter of Succession. Patrick Cruttwell. 1962. 3.95 o.p. (52902). Macmillan.
Matter of Taste. Richard Lockridge. LC 49-10005. 1949. J. B. Lippincott Co.
Matter of Taste: A Novel. George Henry Picard. LC 7-35925. 1884. White, Stokes, & Allen.
Matter of Temperament: Janus. Edward Irenaeus Prime- Stevenson. LC 8-16091. (Fortnightly series, no. 14). American Publishers Corporation.
Matter of Time. Maurice Druon. (Signet Book). (Illus.). 1976. 1.50. New American Library.
Matter of Time. 1st Ed. Jessamyn West. LC 66-22289. 1966. 5.75. Harcourt.
Matter of Trust. Rebecca Flanders. (American Romance Ser.). 192p. 1983. pap. 2.25 (ISBN 0-373-16006-2). Harlequin Bks.
Matters of Chance. Gail Albert. LC 82-5368. 14.95 (ISBN 0-399-12747-X). Putnam.
Matters of Concern. 1st Ed. Stanley Wade Baron. LC 58-100666. 1958. Little, Brown.
Matters of Life & Death: New American Stories. Ed. by Tobias Wolff. 256p. 1983. 12.95 (ISBN 0-931694-14-0). Wampeter Pr.
Matthew Brent. Hiram Wallace Hayes. LC 24-532. 1.75. The H. K. Fly Company.
Matthew Doyle. Will A. Garland. 1900. G. W. Dillingham Co.
Matthew Early. 1st Ed. Alexander Kinnan Laing. LC 57-11068. 1957. Duell, Sloan and Pearce.
Matthew Ferguson. Lida Clara Schem. G. W. Dillingham Company.
Matthew Hargraves. Evelyn Beatrice Hall. LC 14-9881. 1914. G.P. Putnam's Sons.
Matthew Porter: A Story of to-Day. Gamaliel Bradford. LC 8-10859. 1908. L. C. Page & Company.
Matthew Ratton. Anne Knowles. LC 81-8724. 1981. 9.95 (ISBN 0-312-52306-8). St. Martin's Press.
Matthew Swain: Hot Time in Old Town. Mike McQuay. 224p. 1981. pap. 2.25 (ISBN 0-553-14811-7). Bantam.
Matthew's Hand. Charles Larson. LC 74-5528. 1974. 4.95 (ISBN 0-385-05184-0). Doubleday.
Mattie the Mill Girl. A Tale of the Manchester Mills. Also, Fortune's Wheel, and The Rush Twins. Erwin L Coolidge. LC 6-33690. (Factory life library. Pocket ed. no. 3). Factory Publishing Co.
Mattock. James Stevens. LC 27-906710. 1927. A. A. Knopf.
Mattress Game. Matt Harding. 1970. pap. 0.75 o.p. (75-344). Manor Bks.
Matt's Follies: And Other Stories. Mary Newmarch Prescott. LC 12-377501. 1873. J. R. Osgood and Company.
Matty Doolin. Catherine Cookson. (Signet book). 1.25. New American Library.
Matty Doolin & Joe & the Gladiator. Catherine Cookson. 1979. pap. 1.75 (ISBN 0-451-08964-2, E8964, Sig). NAL.
Mau Mau Manhunt. Dennis Holman. pap. 0.75 o.p. (T1655). Pyramid Pubns.
Maud Harcourt: Or, How She Became an Artist. Charlotte Elizabeth Graves. LC 6-454400. 1897.
Maud Mansfield: A Novel. Frances Hamilton Hood. LC 7-5397. 1876. J. W. Burke & Company.
Maud Martha: A Novel. Gwendolyn Brooks. LC 73-18553. 1974. (ISBN 0-404-11368-0). AMS Press.
Maud Martha: A Novel 1st Ed. Gwendolyn Brooks. LC 53-772663. 1953. Harper.
Maud Morton. Alfred Rochefort Calhoun. (popular series, no. 33). 1893. R. Bonner's Sons.
Maud Muller's Ministry: Or, The Claims of Christian Socialism. James Lawrenson Smiley. LC 7-42012.
Maud of the Mississippi. A Companion to Pauline of the Potomac. Charles Wesley Alexander. LC 44-350218. 1864. C. W. Alexander & Co.
Maude and Miriam: Or, The Fair Crusader. Harriet Burn McKeever. LC 7-16315. 1871. Claxton, Remsen & Haffelfinger.
Maude Blackstone, the Millionaire's Daughter. Raymond R. Carew- Johnston. LC 1-12833. 1901. The Henneberry Company.
Maude Percy's Secret. A Novel. May Agnes Early Fleming. LC 6-39950. 1884. G. W. Carleton & Co.; Etc., Etc.
Maude: Prose and Verse. Christina Georgina Rossetti. LC 76-12597. (Illus.). 1976. 7.50 (ISBN 0-208-01591-4). Archon Books.
Maude: Prose and Verse. Christina Georgina Rossetti. LC 8-683. 1897. H. S. Stone & Company.
Maude Reed Tale. Norah Lofts. (Laurel Leaf Library). 1974. (pbk.) 0.95. Dell.
Maudite. Justine L. Mie d'Aghonne. 249p. (Fr.). 1982. Repr. of 1896 ed. lib. bdg. 100.00 (ISBN 0-8287-1792-3). Clearwater Pub.
Maulever Hall. Jane Aiken-Hodge. 356p. 1981. Repr. lib. bdg. 14.95 (ISBN 0-89968-235-9). Lightyear.
Maulever Hall. Jane Aiken Hodge. (O.S.I.). 1973. pap. 0.95 o.s.i. (ISBN 0-515-03131-3). Pyramid Pubns.
Mauleverer Murders. Arthur Charles Fox-Davies. LC 7-27614. J. Lane Company.
Mauleverer's Millions: A Yorkshire Romance. Wemyss Reid. LC 7-30655. (Harper's handy series, no. 56). 1886. Harper & Brothers.
Maum Guinea and Her Plantation "Children;" Or, Holiday-Week on a Louisiana Estate; a Slave Romance. Metta Victoria Fuller Victor. LC 72-3199. (Black Heritage Library Collection). (Illus.). 1972. 11.00 (ISBN 0-8369-9087-0). Books for Libraries Press.
Maunaloa Curse. Irma Walker. LC 78-55657. 1978. 8.95 o.p. (ISBN 0-672-52450-3). Bobbs.
Maundy. Julian Gloag. LC 69-12087. 1969. 5.95. Simon and Schuster.
Maupassant's Short Stories. Guy de Maupassant. 1971. pap. 1.35 o.p. (ISBN 0-460-01907-4, Evman). Dutton.
Maupassant's Short Stories. Guy de Maupassant. 1956. 3.50 o.p. (ISBN 0-460-00907-9, E907, Evman). Dutton.
Mauprat. George Sand. LC 4-17506. 1899. Little, Brown & Company.
Mauprat. George Sand. LC 77-23992. (Da Capo paperback). (Illus.). 1977. 4.95 (ISBN 0-306-80077-2). Da Capo Press.
Mauprat. George Sand. LC 77-21222. (Series: The French Classical Romances.). 1977. 7.50. (ISBN 0-915864-44-4) (ISBN 0-915864-43-6). Cassandra Editions.
Mauprat. George Sand & Miller, Henrietta E., Tr. (Library of choice fiction. no. 18). 1891. Laird & Lee.
Mauprat. A Novel. Tr. by Virginia Vaughan. Vaughan, Virgina, D. 1913, Tr. LC 6-35678. 1870. Roberts Brothers.
Maura's Dream. Joel Gross. LC 80-52416. 12.95 (ISBN 0-87223-654-4). Seaview Books.
Maureen. Patrick MacGill. LC 20-13698. 1920. R. M. McBride & Co.
Maureen Dhu, the Admiral's Daughter. A Tale of the Claddagh of Galway. Mary Anne Madden Sadlier. LC 8-1654. (On cover: Parlor & cottage library). 1870. D. & J. Sadlier & Co.
Maureen's Fairing. Jane Barlow. LC 6-7223. (Iris series). 1895. Macmillan and Co.
Maureen's Fairing, and Other Stories. Jane Barlow. LC 72-4418. (Short story index reprint series). (Illus.). 1972. (ISBN 0-8369-4169-1). Books for Libraries Press.
Mauriac Reader. Francois Mauriac. LC 68-24597. 1968. 7.95. Farrar, Straus, and Giroux.
Maurice. Edward Morgan Forster. (Signet bk., W5311). 1973. 1.50. New American Lib.
Maurice: A Novel. Edward Morgan Forster. LC 76-170181. 1971. 6.95 (ISBN 0-393-08657-7). Norton.
Maurice: A Novel. Edward Morgan Forster. LC 80-39612. 1981. 4.95 (ISBN 0-393-00026-5). Norton.
Maurice and Berghetta: Or, The Priest of Rahery. A Tale. William Parnell. LC 7-34728. 1820. Wells and Lilly.
Maurice Burton: Or, The Warp and Weft of Fate. John Benton Nathaniel Berry. LC 6-11313. 1882. Printed by J. Murphy & Co.
Maurice Dering: Or, The Quadrilateral. George Alfred Lawrence. LC 41-31114. G. Routledge and Sons.
Maurice Guest. Henrietta Richardson. LC 17-25590. 1908. P. R. Reynolds.
Maurice Guest. Henrietta Richardson. LC 9-7947. 1909. Duffield & Company.
Maurice Guest. Henrietta Richardson. LC 30-24056. W. W. Norton & Company, Inc.
Maurice Guest. Henrietta Richardson. LC 37-270149. (Half-title: The modern library of the world's best books. 65). 1936. The Modern Library.
Maurice Guest. Henry Handel Richardson. LC 17-25590. 1908. P. R. Reynolds.
Maurice Guest. Henry Handel Richardson. LC 9-7947. 1909. Duffield.
Maurice Guest. rev. ed. Henry Handel Richardson. LC 30-2406. 1930. W. W. Norton.
Maurice Guest. Henry Handel Richardson. LC 37-27014. (Modern library of the world's best books, 65). 1936. Modern Library.
Maurice Guest. Henry Handel Richardson. LC 82-12844. (Virago Modern Classic). 1983. 9.95 (ISBN 0-385-27787-3). Dial Press.
Maurice Mystery. John Esten Cooke. LC 6-27190. 1885. D. Appleton and Company.
Maurice Rossman's Leading. Mary Ruth Baldwin. LC 6-6331. 1889. J. B. Alden.
Maurice Tiernay, the Soldier of Fortune. Charles James Lever. (Seaside library, v. 26, no. 546). 1879. G. Munro.
Maurice Tiernay, the Soldier of Fortune. Charles James Lever. LC 4-16546. (On cover: Novels of adventure). 1901. Little, Brown, and Company.
Maurin the Illustrious. A Translation from the French of Jean Aicard, by Alfred Allinson... Jean Francois Victor Alcard & Allinson, Alfred, Tr. LC 10-22064. 1910. The John Lane Company.
Mauritius Command. Patrick O'Brian. LC 77-26234. (Illus.). 1978. 8.95 (ISBN 0-8128-2476-8). Stein and Day.
Maurizius Case. Jakob Wassermann. Tr. by Caroline Newton. LC 29-22204. 1929. H. Liveright.
Maurizius Forever. Henry Miller. LC 60-18162. 1959. Fridtjof-Karla Publications.
Mausoleum Key. Norman Daniels. LC 42-24972. 1942. Gateway Books.
Mauvais Reve. Georges Bernanos. 13.50. French & Eur.
Mavde Baxter. Chauncey Crafts Hotchkiss. LC 11-2966. W. J. Watt & Company.
Maverick. Verne Athanas. LC 56-107438. (Dell first edition, A115). 1956. Dell Pub. Co.
Maverick Canyon. Nelson Coral Nye. LC 44-4116. 1944. Phoenix Press.
Maverick Gold. Dean W. Ballenger. 1978. pap. 1.25 (ISBN 0-532-12532-0). Woodhill.
Maverick Guns. J. E. Grinstead. 1978. pap. 1.25 o.s.i. (ISBN 0-505-51269-6). Tower Bks.
Maverick Heritage. Roe Richmond. LC 51-9015. 1950. Phoenix Press.
Maverick Lawman. Margaret Ogan & George Ogan. 1979. pap. 1.75 (ISBN 0-89041-232-4, 3232). Major Bks.
Maverick Legion. Larry A Harris. LC 39-25561. Phoenix Press.
Maverick Makers. Dane Coolidge. LC 31-2259. 1931. E. P. Dutton & Co., Inc.
Maverick Marshal. James Wesley. (Avalon westerns). 1974. 4.50. Avalon Books.
Maverick Marshall. Nelson Nye. Bd. with Thirty Notches. Brad Ward. 1978. pap. 1.75 (ISBN 0-451-08356-3, E8356, Sig). NAL.
Maverick Medico. George Brydges Rodney. LC 41-5501. Phoenix Press.
Maverick Molloy. Archie Joscelyn. LC 38-220129. Phoenix Press.
Maverick Queen. Grey, Zane. LC 63-6979. (Great western edition, 24). 1963. Grosset & Dunlap.
Maverick Queen. Zane Grey. LC 50-8030. 1950. Harper.
Maverick Raid. Terrell L. Bowers. 1982. 6.95 (Avalon). Bouregy.
Maverick Renegade. Galen C. Colin. LC 44-6996. 1944. Phoenix Press.
Maverick Showdown. William Frederick Bragg. LC 54-9906. 1954. Arcadia House.
Maverick Showdown. Bradford Scott. 1973. pap. 0.75 o.p. (ISBN 0-515-03063-5, T3063). Pyramid Pubns.
Maverick Star. L. P Holmes. 1975. (pbk.) 0.95. Ace Books.
Maverick Tales: Stories of Early Texas. Jack Rittenhouse. 1971. 8.95 o.p. (ISBN 0-87691-052-5). Winchester Pr.
Maverick Trail. B. A. Collier. (YA) 1978. 6.95 (Avalon). Bouregy.
Maverick Trio. Strong, Charles Stanley. LC 52-3416. 1952. Arcadia House.
Mavericks. Walt Coburn. LC 29-18262. The Century Co.
Mavericks. William MacLeod Raine. LC 12-730233. 1.25. G. W. Dillingham Company.
Mavericks. William MacLeod Raine. LC 22-4737. 1917. Grosset & Dunlap.
Mavericks of the Plains. Harry Sinclair Drago. LC 38-7469. Greenberg.
Maverick's Return. Peter Field. LC 54-552298. (Triple-A western classic). 1954. Jefferson House.
Maverick's Return. Peter Field. LC 44-2815. 1944. Books Inc., Distributed by W. Morrow and Company.
Mavis. Justin Kent. LC 53-295863. 1953. Vixen Press.
Mavis of Green Hill. Faith Baldwin Cuthrell. LC 21-151013. Small, Maynard & Company.
Mavourneen. A Novelization. Arthur D Hall. LC 7-324. (On cover: Drama series, no. 24). Street & Smith.
Mavreen. Claire Lorrimer. 1977. pap. 2.95 (ISBN 0-553-14738-2). Bantam.
Mawrdew Czgowchwz. James McCourt. LC 73-81058. 1975. (ISBN 0-374-20461-6). Farrar, Straus and Giroux.
Maw's Vacation: The Story of a Human Being in the Yellowstone. Emerson Hough. LC 21-10019. 1921. J. E. Haynes.
Max. Howard Melvin Fast. 400p. 1982. 15.95 (ISBN 0-395-32506-4). HM.
Max. Howard Melvin Fast. (General Ser.). 1983. lib. bdg. 18.95 (ISBN 0-8161-3495-2, Large Print Bks). G K Hall.
Max. Charles Welsh Mason. LC 6-31964. 1897. J. Lane.
Max. A Cradle Mystery. Sarah Elizabeth Forbush G. S. Downs Downs. (On cover: The select series. no. 95). 1892. Street & Smith.
Max: A Novel. Howard Melvin Fast. LC 82-9308. 1982. 15.95 (ISBN 0-395-32506-4). Houghton Mifflin.
Max, a Novel. Katherine Cecil Thurston. LC 10-20853. 1910. Harper & Brothers.
Max & Moritz. Wilhelm Busch. Tr. by C. T. Brooks. 1977. lib. bdg. 59.95 (ISBN 0-8490-2215-0). Gordon Pr.
Max Brand, Five Complete Novels. Max Brand. LC 82-1698. 1982. 6.98 (ISBN 0-517-36243-0). Avenel Books: Distributed by Crown Publishers.
Guns of Dorking Holllow /Max Brand I.E. Frederick Faust. Frederick Faust. 1976. 1.25. Warner Books.
Max Brand: The Big Westerner. Robert Olney Easton. LC 69-16732. (Illus.). 1970. 7.95. University of Oklahoma Press.
Max Brand's Best Stories. Max Brand. Ed. by Robert Easton. (Illus.). 1967. 5.00 o.p. (ISBN 0-396-05553-2). Dodd.

Max Brand's Best Western Stories. Max Brand & William F. Nolan. LC 81-3204. 8.95 (ISBN 0-396-07984-9). Dodd, Mead.
Max Carrados. Ernest Bramah, pseud. LC 75-44959. (Crime Fiction Ser.). 1976. Repr. of 1914 ed. lib. bdg. 17.50 (ISBN 0-8240-2355-2). Garland Pub.
Max Carrados. Ernest Bramah, pseud. LC 74-10485. (Milestones of Mystery Ser.). v, 296p. 1975. Repr. of 1914 ed. 12.00 (ISBN 0-88355-200-0). Hyperion Conn.
Max Carrados. Ernest Bramah Smith. LC 74-10485. 1975. 10.50 (ISBN 0-88355-200-0). Hyperion Press.
Max Carrados Mysteries. Ernest Bramah, pseud. 1964. pap. 0.85 o.p. (ISBN 0-14-002158-2). Penguin.
Max Fargus. Owen McMahon Johnson. LC 6-32685. 1906. The Baker & Taylor Company.
Max Havelaar: Or, The Coffee Auctions of the Dutch Trading Company. Edward Douwes Dekker & David Herbert Lawrence. Ed. by Roy Edwards. LC 66-29435. (Bibliotheca Neeriandica). 1967. London House & Maxwell.
Max Havelaar: Or, The Coffee Sales of the Netherlands Trading Company, by Multatuli Pseud. (1860) Translated from the Dutch by W. Siebenhaar. Eduard Douwes Dekker. Tr. by Siebenhaar, W. LC 27-1232. (Half-title: Blue jade library). 1927. A. A. Knopf.
Max Holly. Robert Sims Reid. LC 81-52070. 12.02 (ISBN 0-87223-744-3). Seaview Books.
Max Jamison: A Novel. Wilfrid Sheed. LC 71-113777. 1970. 6.50. Farrar, Straus and Giroux.
Max of the North: A Novel. Magnus A Bruce. LC 15-27761. 1915. 1.25. Diederich-Schaefer Co.
Max Roper in Match Point for Murder. Kin Platt. LC 74-28113. 1975. 6.95 (ISBN 0-394-49011-8). Random House.
Max Smart and the Ghastly Ghost Affair. William Johnston. LC 78-86678. 1969. 0.60. Grosset & Dunlap.
Max Smart and the Perilous Pellets. William Johnston. (Tempo books, T-140). 1966. Grosset & Dunlap.
Max Smart, the Spy Who Went Out to the Cold. William Johnston. LC 68-15287. (Tempo books, T-174). 1968. Grosset & Dunlap.
Maxa: Episodes in a Woman's Life. Robert Elson. LC 22-16880. Small, Maynard & Company.
Maximilian's Gold. Jane Barry. LC 66-16931. (Illus.). 1966. Doubleday.
Maximilian's Phantom Crown. Nathan Hoffman. LC 40-5844. Wetzel Publishing Co. Inc.
Maximina. Palacio Valdes, Armando. Tr. by Nathan Haskell Dole. T. Y. Crowell Co.
Maximus Zone. Christopher Keane. (Orig.). 1975. pap. 1.75 o.p. (ISBN 0-515-03696-X). Pyramid Pubns.
Maxwell Drewitt. Charlotte Eliza Lawson Cowan Riddell. LC 79-16676. (Ireland, from the Act of Union, 1800, to the Death of Parnell, 1891). 1979. 42.00 (ISBN 0-8240-3511-9). Garland Pub.
Maxwell Mystery. Carolyn Wells. LC 13-6733. 1913. J. B. Lippincott Company.
Maxwells. Mannie I Berger. LC 73-183715. 1972. 5.00 (ISBN 0-8059-1657-1). Dorrance.
Maxwell's Demons. Benjamin Bova. LC 79-110954. 1978. 5.95 (ISBN 0-89437-043-X). Baronet Pub. Co.
May: A Novel. Margaret Oliphant Wilson Oliphant. (Seaside library, v. 45, no. 919). 1881. G. Munro.
May a Novel. Margaret Oliphant Wilson Oliphant. LC 7-32603. 1873. Scribner, Armstrong & Co.
May Blossom; or, Between Two Loves. Margaret Lee. (On cover: Library of American authors. no. 55). G. Munro's Sons.
May Blossom; or, Between Two Loves. Margaret Lee. (On cover: Seaside library. Pocket ed. no. 330). 1885. G. Munro.
May Bretton. Robert Raynolds. LC 44-3416. 1944. G. P. Putnam's Sons.
May Day Mystery. Octavus Roy Cohen. LC 29-14911. 1929. D. Appleton & Company.
May Dust. Louise Platt Hauck. LC 29-2608. The Penn Publishing Company.
May Eve: Or, The Tinker of Ballinatray. Ernest Temple Thurston. LC 23-160413. 1923. D. Appleton and Company.
May Fair: Being an Entertainment Purporting to Reveal to Gentlefolk the Real State of Affairs Existing in the Very Heart of London During the Fifteenth and Sixteenth Years of the Resign of His Majesty King George the Fifth. Michael Arlen. LC 25-10419. George H. Doran Company.
May Fault. Theodore Enslin. 24p. 1979. pap. 4.00. Great Raven Pr.
May Flavin. Myron Brinig. LC 33-27494. Farrar & Rinehart, Inc.
May Flower, and Miscellaneous Writings. Harriet Elizabeth Beecher Stowe. LC 72-4411. (Short story index reprint series). 1972. 15.00 (ISBN 0-8369-4189-6). Books for Libraries Press.
May Flower, and Miscellaneous Writings. Harriet Elizabeth Beecher Stowe. LC 8-16125. 1855. Phillips, Sampson, and Company.
May Flower: And Miscellaneous Writings, Vol. 1. Harriet B. Stowe. LC 72-4411. (Short Story Index Reprint Ser). Repr. of 1855 ed. 23.00 o.p. (ISBN 0-8369-4189-6). Ayer Co.
May Flower: And Miscellaneous Writings, Vol. 1. Harriet Elizabeth Beecher Stowe. LC 72-4411. (Short Story Index Reprint Ser). Repr. of 1855 ed. 23.00 o.p. (ISBN 0-8369-4189-6). Arno.
May in Manhattan. Translated by Thomas I. Nonn from the Hungarian. 1st Ed. Claire Kenneth. LC 63-10349. 1963. Appleton-Century.
May Iverson--Her Book. Elizabeth Garver Jordan. 1904. Harper & Brothers.
May Iverson-Ner Book. Elizabeth Garver Jordan. LC 75-103521. (Short story index reprint series). (Illus.). 1969. Books for Libraries Press.
May Iverson's Career. Elizabeth Garver Jordan. LC 14-18647. 1914. Harper & Brothers.
May Iveson Tackles Life. Elizabeth Garver Jordan. LC 12-18795. 1912. 1.25. Harper & Brothers.
May Johnson's Girls. Peter Kanto. (Orig.). pap. 0.95 o.p. (1108). Brandon.
May Margaret: Called "the Fair Maid of Galloway,". Samuel Rutherford Crockett. LC 5-17277. 1905. Dodd, Mead & Company.
May Martin: And Other Tales of the Green Mountains. new ed. rev. and cor. by the author. ed. Daniel Pierce Thompson. LC 8-19970.
May Martin: Or, The Money Diggers, a Green Mountain Tale. Daniel Pierce Thompson. LC 41-42359. 1849. H. Underhill.
May Queen see Ann Boleyn.
May We Borrow Your Husband? And Other Comedies of the Sexual Life. Graham Greene. LC 67-13500. 1967. bds., 4.50. Viking.
May Wine on Brooklyn Heights. Robert Leary. LC 64-14831. 1964. Random House.
May You Die in Ireland. Michael Kenyon. LC 65-20947. bds., 3.95. Morrow.
Maya: A Story of Yucatan. William Dudley Foulke. LC 1-29608. 1900. G. P. Putnam's Sons.
Mayab. M. S. Karl. 320p. (Orig.). 1981. pap. 3.25 (ISBN 0-8439-1021-6). Leisure Bks CT.
Mayan Enchantment. Lila Ford. (Second Chance at Love Ser.: No. 21). 192p. (Orig.). 1981. pap. 1.75 (ISBN 0-515-06059-3). Jove Pubns.
Mayan Enigma: The Search for a Lost Civilazation. Pierre Ivanoff. 1971. 5.95 o.p. (ISBN 0-440-05528-8). Delacorte.
Maybe-- Tomorrow: By Jay Little Pseud. 1st Ed. Clarence L Miller. LC 53-3735. 1952. Pageant Press.
Maybe: A Novel. Burt Blechman. LC 67-11248. 1967. Prentice-Hall.
Maybe: A Story. Lillian Hellman. 1980. 9.95 (ISBN 0-316-35512-7). Little.
Maybe: A Story. Lillian Hellman. 1982. pap. 4.95 (ISBN 0-316-35509-7). Little.
Maybe He's Dead. Simon Oakroyd. 1971. pap. 0.95 o.p. (B95-2191). Belmont-Tower.
Maybe I Sound Like a Nut, but That's the Way I See It. Ralph Michaels. LC 76-5256. (Illus.). 1.95 (ISBN 0-8361-1325-X). Herald Press.
Maybe I'm Dead. Joe Klaas. LC 55-14756. 1955. Macmillan.
Maybe It's Love. William Arthur Neubauer. LC 46-229141. 1946. Gramercy Publishing Co.
Maybe Next Year. Cicely Schiller. LC 47-2432. 1947. Prentice-Hall, Inc.
Maybe Tomorrow. Sharlie West. (Orig.). 1981. pap. 1.95 (ISBN 0-8439-8035-4, Tiara Bks). Nordon Pubns.
Maybe Tomorrow: A Nurse's Story. Irene Kroth. LC 40-3852. 1940. Meador Publishing Company.
Mayberly's Kill. William Oliver Turner. LC 69-14967. (DD western). 1969. 3.95. Doubleday.
Mayblossom: Romance of the Reconstruction Period in the South Following the Civil War. Lee B. J. Butler. LC 31-32339. Burton Publishing Compnay.
Mayday. Thomas H Block. LC 79-16933. 1979. 10.95 (ISBN 0-399-90057-8). R. Marek Publishers.
Mayday. Thomas H Block. 1981. 2.95 (ISBN 0-425-04729-6). Berkley Books.
Mayday. William Faulkner. LC 76-22410. (Illus.). 1980. text ed. 8.95x (ISBN 0-268-01339-X). U of Notre Dame Pr.
Mayday. Thomas Patrick McMahon & Brian Patrick McMahon. LC 73-6526. (Simon and Schuster novel of suspense). 1973. 6.95 (ISBN 0-671-21593-0). Simon and Schuster.
Mayday Over Manhattan. Stuart Jason. (Butcher Ser.: No. 19). 192p. 1976. pap. 1.25 (ISBN 0-523-22869-4). Pinnacle Bks.
Mayday Over Manhattan. Stuart Jason. (Butcher Series#19). 1976. (pbk.) 1.25 (ISBN 0-523-00869-4). Pinnacle Books.
Mayday Seven Forty Seven. Reynolds Locke. LC 73-91850. 1975. pap. 2.45 (ISBN 0-8128-1856-3). Stein & Day.
Mayenne. E. C. Tubb. (Science Fiction Ser.). (Orig.). 1973. pap. 0.95 o.p. (UQ1054). DAW Bks.
Mayfair. Nancy Fitzgerald. LC 77-81552. 1978. 8.95 (ISBN 0-385-12685-9). Doubleday.
Mayfair Mistress. Sheila Foster. pap. 1.95 o.s.i. (OPS-20). Olympia.
Mayfair Murder. Henry Holt. LC 29-3232. 1929. L. MacVeagh, The Dial Press.
Mayfair Squatters. Arista Mary Mostyn. LC 46-2915. 1946. Doubleday & Company, Inc.
Mayfair Wager. Victoria Heland. (Orig.). 1982. pap. 2.25 (ISBN 0-515-05706-1). Jove Pubns.
Mayflower (Flor De Mayo) A Tale of the Valencian Seashore. Vicente Blasco Ibanez & Livingston, Arthur, 1883- Tr. LC 21-571112. E. P. Dutton & Company.
Mayflower Maid. Emilie Benson Knipe & Knipe, Alden Arthur. LC 20-165015. 1920. The Century Co.
Mayflower: Or, Sketches of Scenes and Characters Among the Descendants of the Pilgrims. Harriet Elizabeth Beecher Stowe. 1853. J. P. Jewett & Company.
Mayhem in B-Flat. Elliot Harold Paul. pap. 0.95 o.p. (02335, Collier). Macmillan.
Mayhem in B-Flat: A Homer Evans Murder Mystery. Elliot Harold Paul. LC 40-30405. Random House.
Mayhem on Bear Creek. Robert E. Howard. 7.00 (ISBN 0-937986-19-4). D M Grant.
Mayhem on the Coney Beat. Michael Geller. (Belmont Tower book). 1.75 (ISBN 0-505-51353-6). Tower Pubns.
Maylou. Frances Raymond. LC 7-36638. 1898. G. W. Dillingham Co.; Etc., Etc.
Maynard Hayes Affair. Dorothea Bennett. LC 78-26801. 8.95 (ISBN 0-698-10971-6). Coward, McCann & Geoghegan.
Maynard, the Nehalem River White Duck: And Other Stories. Kitty Mitchell. (Illus.). 1974. 3.00 (ISBN 0-682-47771-0). Exposition Press.
Mayo Sergeant: A Novel. James B Hall. LC 67-24794. 1967. New American Library.
Mayor Harding of New York: A Novel. Stephen Endicott. LC 31-250419. 1931. The Mohawk Press.
Mayor Harding of New York: A Novel. Walter Adolphe Roberts. LC 73-18602. 1974. (ISBN 0-404-11412-1). AMS Press.
Mayor of Casterbridge. Thomas Hardy. LC 64-7105. (Harper's modern classics). 1964. Harper & Row.
Mayor of Casterbridge. Thomas Hardy. LC 64-2842.
Mayor of Casterbridge. Thomas Hardy. LC 11-33240. Hovendon Company.
Mayor of Casterbridge. Thomas Hardy. Ed. by Amy, Ernest Francis. LC 33-39324. (Half-title: Nelson's English series). 1933. T. Nelson and Sons.
Mayor of Casterbridge: A Novel. Thomas Hardy. (On cover: Lovell's library, v. 14, no. 749). 1886. J. W. Lovell Company.
Mayor of Casterbridge: A Story of a Man of Character. Thomas Hardy. LC 48-4688. (Rinehart editions, 9). 1948. Rinehart.
Mayor of Casterbridge: A Story of a Man of Character. Thomas Hardy. LC 16-130994. 1895. Harper & Brothers.
Mayor of Casterbridge: A Story of a Man of Character, by Thomas Hardy. Thomas Hardy. LC 22-10774. (Added t.-p.; Harper's modern classics, ed. for educational use by W. T. Brewster). Harper & Brothers.
Mayor of Casterbridge: A Story of a Man of Character. With an Introd. by Albert J. Guerard. Thomas Hardy. LC 56-56378. (Pocket library, 52). 1956. Pocket Books.
Mayor of Casterbridge: An Authoritative Text, Backgrounds Criticism. Thomas Hardy & James K Robinson. LC 76-57983. (Norton critical edition). (Illus.). 12.95 (ISBN 0-393-04459-9). Norton.
Mayor of Casterbridge: By Thomas Hardy; Introduction by Joyce Kilmer... Thomas Hardy. LC 33-830922. (Half-title: The modern library of the world's best books). 1917. The Modern Library.
Mayor of Casterbridge: By Thomas Hardy... Thomas Hardy. LC 1238. (On cover: Arrow library, no. 108). 1900. Street & Smith.
Mayor of Casterbridge. Ed., Introd., Notes by Frederick R. Karl. Standard Ed.: John Paterson, General Ed. Thomas Hardy. LC 64-7105. (Perennial classic). 1.95, .75 pap., Harper.
Mayor of Casterbridge. Edited with an Introd. by Robert B. Heilman. Thomas Hardy. LC 62-1552. (Riverside editions, B63). 1962. Houghton Mifflin.
Mayor of Casterbridge: The Life and Death of a Man of Character. Thomas Hardy. LC 50-12244. (Modern Library college editions, T20). (Illus.). 1950. Modern Library.
Mayor of Casterbridge: Thomas Hardy. George Glencairn Urwin. LC 64-54677. (Notes on Eng. lit.). Barnes & Noble.
Mayor of Filbert. Charles Francis Stocking. LC 17-45. 1916. The Maestro Co.
Mayor of Kanemeta. Jeanie Oliver Davidson Smith. LC 8-8169. 1891. The American News Company.
Mayor of New York. Laurence I Barrett. LC 65-14005. 1965. Doubleday.
Mayor of New York: A Romance of Days to Come. Louis Pope Gratacap. LC 10-27675. 1.50. G. W. Dillingham Company.
Mayor of Troy. Arthur Thomas Quiller-Couch. 1905. C. Scribner's Sons.
Mayor of Warwick. Herbert Muller Hopkins. LC 6-13936. 1906. Houghton, Mifflin and Company.
Mayor of Wind-Gap. John Banim & Michael Banim. LC 6111. 1835. Harper & Brothers.
Mayor of Wind-Gap & Canvassing, 3 vols. John Banim & Michael Banim. Ed. by Robert L. Wolff. (Ireland Nineteenth Century Fiction - Series2). 1066p. 1979. lib. bdg. 96.00 (ISBN 0-8240-3472-4). Garland Pub.
Mayor of Zalamea, or: THe Best Garotting Ever Done. Adrian Mitchell. 120p. 1982. 45.00x (ISBN 0-907540-12-0, Pub. by Salamander Pr Scotland). State Mutual bk.
Mayor on Horseback. Edward Phillips Oppenheim. LC 37-38862. 1937. Little, Brown and Company.
Mayor's Nest. Tony Morphett. 1965. bds., 3.15. Jacaranda Pr.
Mayor's Wife. Anna Katharine Green Rohlfs. LC 7-17385. 1907. The Bobbs-Merrill Company.
Maypoles and Morals. Frederic Arnold Kummer. LC 29-10302. J. H. Sears & Company, Inc.
Maza of the Moon. Otis Adelbert Kline. LC 30-6733. 1930. A. C. McClurg & Co.
Mazaroff Mystery. Joseph Smith Fletcher. LC 24-16562. 1924. A. A. Knopf.
Maze. A. H Garnet. LC 82-5878. 1982. 14.50 (ISBN 0-89919-091-X). Ticknor & Fields.
Maze. Ellen Orford. 1973. pap. 0.95 o.p. (09204). Curtis.
Maze. Maurice Yves Sandoz & Dali, Salvador, 1904- Illus. LC 45-35233. 1945. Doubleday, Doran and Co., Inc.
Maze. Eileen B Simpson. LC 74-23536. 1975. 7.95 (ISBN 0-671-21960-X). Simon and Schuster.
Maze Maker: A Novel. Michael Ayrton. LC 67-19050. 1967. Holt, Rinehart and Winston.
Maze of Dark Desires. Hannah Gibson. 256p. (Orig.). 1981. pap. 2.25 (ISBN 0-8439-0944-7). Leisure Bks CT.
Maze of Death. Philip K Dick. LC 70-111158. 1970. 4.95. Doubleday.
Mazes & Monsters. Rona Jaffe. (O.s.i.). 1981. 13.95 o.s.i. (ISBN 0-440-05536-9). Delacorte.
Mazes & Monsters. Rona Jaffe. 1982. pap. 3.50 (ISBN 0-440-15699-8). Dell.
Mazes & Monsters. Rona Jaffe. (General Ser.). 1981. lib. bdg. 16.95 (ISBN 0-8161-3324-7, Large Print Bks). G K Hall.
Mazes and Monsters: A Novel. Rona Jaffe. LC 81-2160. 13.95 (ISBN 0-440-05536-9). Delacorte Press.
Mazes of Order... Anson Doner Eby. LC 27-13382.
Mazes of Scorpio. Dray Prescot. 176p. 1982. pap. 2.25 (ISBN 0-87997-739-6). DAW Bks.
M.D. A Novel. Neil Ravin. LC 80-25779. 13.95 (ISBN 0-440-05468-0). Delacorte Press/S. Lawrence.
Me" ... LC 7-25869. (Electric Series No. 64). 1888. Butler Brothers (Incorporated).
Me. 288p. (Orig.). 1981. pap. 2.95 (ISBN 0-553-13646-1). Bantam.
Me. (ISBN 0-553-02727-1). Bantam.
Me--Gangster. Charles Francis Coe. LC 27-196366. 1927. G. P. Putnam's Sons.
Me--Smith". Caroline Lockhart. LC 11-2073. 1911. 1.20. J. B. Lippincott Company.
Me: A Book of Remembrance. Winnifred Eaton Babcock. LC 15-16589. 1915. 1.30. The Century Co.
Me Again: Uncollected Writings of Stevie Smith. Stevie Smith. LC 82-40430. (Illus.). 400p. 1983. pap. 6.95 (ISBN 0-394-71362-1, Vin). Random.
Me An' Methuselar, and Other Episodes. Harriet Ford. LC 3-2507. 1895. The Peter Paul Book Company.
Me An' Shorty. Clarence Edward Mulford. LC 73-89645. 1974. 6.95. Aeonian Press.
Me An' Shorty. Clarence Edward Mulford. LC 29-9882. 1929. Doubleday, Doran and Company, Inc.
Me An' You. Jay Thomas Caldwell. LC 54-42481. (Lion book, 220). 1954. Lion Books by Arrangement with Prime Publications.
Me and Chummy. Coyne Fletcher. 1890. Sterling Publishing Co.
Me and Gallagher: A Novel. Jack Farris. LC 82-5966. 14.50 (ISBN 0-671-45697-0). Simon & Schuster.
Me and Gus: By Frank S. Anthony and Francis Jackson, Illustrated by Nevile Lodge. Frank Sheldon Anthony. LC 52-19608. 1951. A. H. & A. W. Reed.

Me and Lawson: "Humpty" Hotfoot's Little Run in with Frenzied Copper, Amalgamated Gas and Scrambled Oil. Richard Webb. 1905. G. W. Dillingham Company.
Me & Me: A Love Story. Bill Dana. cancelled o.s.i. (ISBN 0-523-40621-5). Corwin.
Me & Mr. Stenner. Evan Hunter. 1978. pap. 1.75 (ISBN 0-440-95551-3, LFL). Dell.
Me and Old Kate, and Other Christmas Stories: 1st Ed. Samuel Thomas Peace. LC 57-9296. 1957. Vantage Press.
Me and the Arch Kook Petulia. John Haase. (S3634). 1968. Bantam.
Me and the Arch Kook Petulia. John Haase. LC 66-26532. 1966. Coward-McCann.
Me and the Liberal Arts. Drawings by the Author. 1st Ed. Dave Morrah. LC 62-7664. 1962. Doubleday.
Me and Thee. Robert W McCulloch. LC 37-4279. 1937. Lothrop, Lee and Shepard Company.
Me 'ayin U-Le'An: Whence or Whither. R A Braudes. (Literaria Judaica Section Ser.: No. 7). 21.50 (ISBN 0-404-13860-8). AMS Pr.
Me Bandy, You Cissie. Donald Lamont Jack. LC 78-18136. (His The journals of Bartholomew Bandy; 4). 1979. 8.95 (ISBN 0-385-14396-6). Doubleday Canada.
Me, Hood. Mickey Spillane, pseud. (Orig.). 1969. pap. 1.95 (ISBN 0-451-11679-8, AJ1679, Sig). NAL.
Me! July and August... Carrie M. Coe. LC 6-26750. 1877. G. W. Carleton & Co.
Me Nobody Knows: Children's Voices from the Ghetto. Ed. by Stephen M. Joseph. 1969. 4.95 o.p. (A3405, Mer); pap. 2.95 o.p. (M282). World Pub.
Me Tanner, You Jane. Lawrence Block. LC 79-93176. (Cock Robin mystery). 1970. Macmillan.
Me-Won-I-Toc. A Tale of Frontier Life and Indian Character; Exhibiting Traditions, Superstitions, and Character of a Race That Is Passing Away. A Romance of the Frontier. Solon Robinson. LC 7-42182. 1867. New York News Company.
Mea Culpa: A Woman's Last Word. Henry Harland. LC 7-1528. J. W. Lovell Company.
Mea Culpa: A Woman's Last Word. Henry Harland. Street & Smith.
Mea Culpa: A Woman's Last Word. Henry Harland. LC 76-24386. (Decadent Consciousness). 1978-1977. 26.00 (ISBN 0-8240-2761-2). Garland Pub.
Meadow-Brook. Mary Jane Hawes Holmes. LC 7-6024. 1857. Miller, Orton & Co.
Meadow Brook. Mary Jane Hawes Holmes. LC 43-20450. Grosset & Dunlap.
Meadow-Grass: Tales of New England Life. Alice Brown. LC 69-11879. (American short story series, v. 36). 1969. Garrett Press.
Meadow-Grass: Tales of New England Life. Alice Brown. LC 11-105363. 1895. Copeland and Day.
Meadow-Grass: Tales of New England Life. Alice Brown. LC 4-16285. 1899. Houghton, Mifflin and Company.
Meadow of Stars. Eiji Shono. 6.00 o.p. Japan Pubns.
Meadowlane. Laverne Adell. LC 67-13082. 1967. Dorrance.
Meadowlark Basin. Bertha Muzzy Sinclair. LC 25-16900. 1925. Little, Brown, and Company.
Meadowlark Calling. Patricia Martin. (Orig.). 1981. pap. 2.25 (ISBN 0-8439-8034-6, Tiara Bks). Nordon Pubns.
Meadows. Clarice L. Davis. 1974. 3.50 o.s.i. (ISBN 0-8181-0330-2). Pageant-Poseidon.
Meadows of Amethyst. Dorothy Pierson. 1970. 3.75 o.p. Vantage.
Meadows of Tallon. Estelle Thompson. (Ace gothic). 1974. (pbk.) 0.95. Ace Books.
Meadows of the Moon. James Hilton. LC 27-381756. Small, Maynard & Company.
Meadowsong. Phyllis Ann Karr. 224p. 1981. pap. 1.95 (ISBN 0-449-50209-0, Coventry). Fawcett.
Meadowsweet. Gwendoline Butler. LC 77-1726. 1977. 8.95 o.p. (ISBN 0-698-10824-8, Coward). Putnam Pub Group.
Meadowsweet. Emmuska Orczy. LC 12-20795. 1.25. Hodder & Stoughton, George H. Doran Company.
Meaghan. Jerry B Jenkins. LC 82-14328. 1983. 2.95 (ISBN 0-8024-4321-4). Moody Press.
Mean Sensual Man. Stephen McKenna. LC 43-15763. 1943. Hutchinson & Ltd.
Mean Streets. Thomas Blanchard Dewey. LC 54-12366. (Inner sanctum mystery). 1955. Simon and Schuster.
Mean Streets. Michael T. Kaufman. (O.s.i.). 1976. pap. 1.50 o.s.i. (AD1603, Award). Univ Pub & Dist.
Mean Time. Christopher T Leland. LC 82-5404. 12.95 (ISBN 0-394-52557-4). Random House.
Meandering Corpse. Richard S Prather. LC 65-28044. bds., 3.95. Trident.
Meanest Squirrel I Ever Met. Gene Zion, pseud. LC 62-19851. (Illus.). 1982. pap. 2.95 (ISBN 0-689-70756-8, A-132, Aladdin). Atheneum.
Meaning of Christmas: A Storybook in Sound. Joyce Dickin & Riki McLean. 1975. 8.95 o.p. (HarpR). Har-Row.
Meaningful Life. Lawrence J Davis. LC 74-157973. 1971. 6.50 (ISBN 0-670-46435-X). Viking Press.
Means Massacre: Molly Finney, the Canadian Captive. Charles P Illsley. LC 76-51258. (Garland Library of Narratives of North American Indian Captivities). (Series: Old Freeport series.: Vol. 109). (Illus.). 1977. (set) 25.00 (ISBN 0-8240-1733-1). Garland Pub.
Means of Escape. Spencer Dunmore. LC 78-26763. 1979. 8.95. Coward, McCann & Geoghegan.
Means of Evil. Ruth Rendell. LC 80-25315. 1981. 11.50 (ISBN 0-89340-315-6). J. Curley.
Means of Evil: Five Mystery Stories by an Edgar Award-Winning Writer. Ruth Rendell. LC 79-7567. 1980. 8.95 (ISBN 0-385-15529-8). Doubleday.
Means to an End. 1st Ed. John Rowan Wilson. LC 59-5778. 1959. Doubleday.
Meanwhile. Frank Cyril Davison. LC 27-22952. 1927. Duffield & Company.
Meanwhile Back at the Henhouse: A Novel. Thomas Bledsoe. LC 66-256702. 1966. 3.95. Swallow.
Meanwhile Back at the Sex Farm. Bill Starr. pap. 1.95 o.s.i. (OPS-31). Olympia.
Meanwhile (the Picture of a Lady) Herbert George Wells. LC 27-16234. 1927. George H. Doran Company.
Mearham. William Leonard Buxton. LC 27-3361. 1927. Longmans, Green and Co., Ltd.
Measure for Measure. A Novel. Mary Stanley. LC 8-13879. 1883. G. W. Carleton & Co.; Etc., Etc.
Measure for Murder. Clifford Witting. LC 75-46007. (Fifty Classics of Crime Fiction, 1900-1950; 50). 1976. 12.00. Garland Publishing.
Measure My Love. Helga Sandburg. LC 59-9883. 1959. McDowell, Obolensky.
Measure of a Man. Dora Aydelotte. LC 42-14362. 1942. D. Appleton-Century Company, Incorporated.
Measure of a Man. Amelia Edith Huddleston Barr. LC 15-18112. 1915. 1.35. D. Appleton and Company.
Measure of a Man: A Tale of the Big Woods. Norman Duncan. LC 11-266042. 1.25. Fleming H. Revell Company.
Measure of Days. Christa Wakefield. (Orig.). 1979. pap. 1.95. Woodhill.
Measure of Dust. Steve Turner. LC 70-107260. (O.s.i.). 1970. 5.50 o.s.i. (ISBN 0-671-20552-8). S&S.
Measure of Dust: A Novel. Steven Turner. LC 70-107260. 1970. 5.50. Simon and Schuster.
Measure of Fear: A Novel. Louis Demestichas. LC 55-7596. 1955. Dorrance.
Measure of Margaret: A Tale of India. Isabel Brown Rose. LC 27-19783. Fleming H. Revell Company.
Measure of Sliding Sand. Ira Glackens. LC 76-18450. 8.95 (ISBN 0-8397-5740-9). P. S. Eriksson.
Measure of the Rule. Robert Barr. LC 73-82584. (Literature of Canada; poetry and prose in reprint). 1973. 15.00 (ISBN 0-8020-2072-0) (ISBN 0-8020-2072-0). University of Toronto Press.
Measure of the Rule. Robert Barr. LC 9-8349. 1908. D. Appleton and Company.
Measure of the Years. Alice Mary Ross Colver. LC 54-11718. 1954. Dodd, Mead.
Measure of Time. Rosa Guy. LC 82-15461. 345p. 1983. 16.95 (ISBN 0-03-057653-9). HR&W.
Measured for Murder. Marion Lee & Saunders, Clare Castler, Joint Author. LC 44-2817. 1944. C. Scribner's Sons.
Measuring a Meridian. Jules Verne. 3.95. Assoc Bk.
Meat: A Novel. Wilbur Daniel Steele. LC 28-5529. 1928. Harper & Brothers.
Meat for Murder. Lange Lewis. LC 43-147714. 1943. The Bobbs-Merrill Company.
Meat Man: A Romance of Life, of Love, of Labor. Moses Jordan. LC 24-1180. Judy Publishing Company.
Mechanic: A Novel. Allan McIvor. W. Ritchie.
Mechanic a Story. Frances Harriet Whipple Greene McDougall. LC 7-16280. 1842. Burnett & King.
Mechanical Pianos: A Novel. Henri Francois Rey. LC 64-11932. 1965. Farrar, Straus and Giroux.
Mechasm. John Thomas Sladek. 1980. pap. 1.95 (ISBN 0-671-83130-5, Timescape). PB.
Med Series. Murray Leinster, pseud. 1983. pap. 2.95 (ISBN 0-441-52360-9, Pub. by Ace Science Fiction). Ace Bks.
Medal of Honor: A Story of Peace and War. King, Charles. 1905. The H. B. Claflin Company.
Medal of Honor: A Story of Peace and War. Charles King. LC 5-11902. 1905. The Hobart Company.
Medal Without Bar. Richard Blaker. LC 30-12989. 1930. Doubleday, Doran & Company, Inc.
Medals: And Other Stories. Luigi Pirandello. LC 39-11997. 1939. E. P. Dutton & Co., Inc.
Meda's Heritage. Maia Pettus. 1906. The Neale Publishing Company.
Medbury Fort Murder. Lewis George Robinson. LC 29-22050. 1929. Pub. for The Crime Club, Inc., by Doubleday, Doran & Company, Inc.
Meddler and Her Murder. Joyce Porter. LC 73-77295. (MW suspense). 1973. 4.95. D. McKay Co.
Meddlers. Jonathan Leonard. LC 29-17923. 1929. The Viking Press.
Meddling Maverick. Fred East. LC 44-771819. 1944. E. P. Dutton & Company, Inc.
Meddlings of Eve. William John Hopkins. LC 10-183807. 1910. 1.00. Houghton Mifflin Company.
Mediation of Ralph Hardelot. William Minto. LC 7-25448. (On cover: Harper's Franklin square library, no. 628). 1888. Harper & Brothers.
Mediator. Roy Norton. LC 13-17412. 1.25. W. J. Watt & Company.
Mediator: A Tale of the Old World and the New. Edward Alfred Steiner. LC 7-29568. F. H. Revell Company.
Mediaware: Selection, Operation & Maintenance. Raymond Wyman. 1969. pap. 4.95x o.p. (ISBN 0-697-06041-1). Wm C Brown.
Medical Center. Faith Baldwin Cuthrell. LC 40-333595. Farrar & Rinehart, Inc.
Medical Center. Faith Baldwin Cuthrell. 1975. (pbk.) 1.50 (ISBN 0-446-78826-0). Warner Paperback Library.
Medical Detectives. Berton Roueche. 400p. 1982. pap. 3.95 (ISBN 0-671-43243-5). WSP.
Medical Meeting. Mildred Walker, pseud. LC 49-111894. 1949. Harcourt, Brace.
Medical Sexual Mystique. J. P. Donaldson. 192p. (Orig.). 1972. pap. 1.95 o.p. (ISBN 0-87056-219-3, 6219). Brandon.
Medical Story. Abby Mann. (Signet Book). 1975. (pbk.) 1.50. New American Library.
Medical Union Number Six. William Harvey King. LC 4-7277. 1904. The Monograph Press.
Medical Witness. Gordon Ostlere. (Signet book, W5628). 1973. (pbk.) 1.50. New American Library.
Medicare Nurse. Peggy O'More, pseud. LC 68-181. 1967. Arcadia House.
Medici Emerald. Martin Woodhouse & Robert Ross. LC 76-11873. 8.95 (ISBN 0-525-15458-2). E.P. Dutton.
Medici Fountain. Joseph Kessel. pap. 0.75 o.p. (74-832). Lancer.
Medici Guns. Martin Woodhouse & Robert Ross. LC 74-22075. 1975. 7.95 (ISBN 0-525-15460-4). Dutton.
Medici Hawks. Martin Woodhouse & Robert Ross. LC 78-55051. 1978. 8.95 (ISBN 0-525-15463-9). Dutton.
Medici Ring. Norma Johnston. LC 74-26795. 1975. 6.95 (ISBN 0-394-49342-7). Random House.
Medici Ring. Norma Johnston. 1976. (pbk.) 1.95 (ISBN 0-671-80444-8). Pocket Books.
Medici Ring. Norma Johnston. LC 76-377979. 1976. 3.50 (ISBN 0-00-222384-8). Collins.
Medici Ring. Nicole St. John. 1975. 6.95 o.p. (ISBN 0-394-49342-7). Random.
Medici Ring. Nicole St. John. 1975. 6.95 o.p. (ISBN 0-394-49342-7). Random.
Medicine Calf: A Novel. Bill Hotchkiss. LC 80-15019. (Illus.). 11.95 (ISBN 0-393-01389-8). Norton.
Medicine Creek. William Oliver Turner. LC 74-6. 1974. 4.95 (ISBN 0-385-06718-6). Doubleday.
Medicine for Melancholy. Ray Bradbury. 1977. pap. 2.50 (ISBN 0-553-20426-2). Bantam.
Medicine for Melancholy. 1st Ed. Ray Bradbury. LC 59-6352. 1959. Doubleday.
Medicine Lady. Elizabeth Thomasina Meade Smith. LC 8-8651. Cassell Publishing Company.
Medicine Man. Bill Burchardt, pseud. LC 79-7192. 1980. 7.95 (ISBN 0-385-14903-4). Doubleday.
Medicine Man. Shirley Seifert. LC 71-151490. 1971. 6.95. Lippincott.
Medicine-Man: A Hashknife Story. Wilbur C Tuttle. LC 39-10245. 1939. Houghton Mifflin Company.
Medicine Man's Daughter. Ann Nolan Clark. LC 63-11182. (Illus.). 1973. (pbk) 0.75. Avon.
Medicine Men. James Balfour. LC 68-15245. 1968. John Day Co.
Medicine Wagon. John Legg. (Orig.). 1981. pap. 1.95 (ISBN 0-505-51730-2). Tower Bks.
Medicine Whip: By Margaret and John Harris. Margaret Plumlee Harris & John Harris. LC 52-13823. 1953. Morrow.
Medicine Wind. Stan Tysell. (Illus.). 120p. (Orig.). 1981. pap. text ed. 5.00x (ISBN 0-938642-00-6). Huh Pubns.
Medico of Painted Springs. James Lyon Rubel. LC 34-40095. Phoenix Press.
Medico of the Valley. Joan Hamilton-Stockford. LC 40-262. Dorrance and Company.
Medico on the Trail. James Lyon Rubel. LC 38-209860. Phoenix Press.
Medico Rides. James Lyon Rubel. LC 35-9294. Phoenix Press.
Medics. Robert Newton. 1978. pap. 1.50 (ISBN 0-532-15383-9). Woodhill.
Medicus in Love: A Novel of Student Life. Gustav Genrychowitch Taube. LC 9-1480. (On cover: The ideal series, no. 4). W. D. Rowland.
Medieval Regions & Their Cities. Josiah C. Russell. LC 70-172025. 240p. 1972. 10.00x o.p. (ISBN 0-253-33735-6). Ind U Pr.
Medieval Romances. Andrew Marvell. pap. 1.45 o.p. (ISBN 0-394-30100-5, T70). Modern Lib.
Medieval Russia's Epics, Chronicles & Tales. Ed. by Serge A. Zenkovsky. (Illus.). 1963. pap. 2.95 o.p. (ISBN 0-525-47117-0). Dutton.
Medieval Storybook. Ed. by Morris Bishop. LC 72-109334. (Illus.). 1970. 7.50. Cornell University Press.
Medieval Summer. Paul Robbins. 1980. pap. 5.00 (ISBN 0-89502-031-9). FEB.
Medieval Town. E. Ennen. (Europe in the Middle Ages Selected Studies Ser.: Vol. 8). 1978. 44.00 (ISBN 0-444-85133-X, North-Holland). Elsevier.
Medieval Town. John H. Mundy & Peter Riesenberg. LC 79-9718. (Anvil Ser.). 192p. 1979. pap. 5.95 (ISBN 0-88275-906-X). Krieger.
Medieval Town. John H. Mundy & Peter Riesenberg. (Orig.). 1958. pap. 3.95x o.p. (ISBN 0-442-00030-8, 30, Anv). Van Nos Reinhold.
Mediocrat. Nalbro Isadorah Bartley. 1928. Doubleday, Doran & Company, Inc.
Meditation: A Novel. Juan Benet. LC 82-297. 13.95 (ISBN 0-89255-062-7). Persea Books.
Meditation on the Sand. Alessandro Pronzato. LC 82-24513. 104p. (Orig., Ital.). 1983. pap. 5.95 (ISBN 0-8189-0457-7). Alba.
Meditative Maxims. Ed. by G. F. Edwards & Paul V. Breier. 1978. LEB1. pap. 1.00 (ISBN 0-932318-00-2, Little Economy Bks). G F Edwards.
Mediterranean Adventure. Pat Phillips. (YA) 1974. 4.95 o.p. (Avalon). Bouregy.
Mediterranean Adventure. Pat Phillips. (Avalon romances). 1974. 4.50. Avalon Books.
Mediterranean Blues. Yvonne Cloud, pseud. LC 34-203952. The Vanguard Press.
Mediterranean Caper. Johanas L. Bouma. (Leisure adventure.). (Illus.). 2.25. Nordon Publications.
Mediterranean Caper. Clive Cussler. 1977. pap. 2.75 (ISBN 0-553-13899-5). Bantam.
Mediterranean Caper. Clive Cussler. 1973. (pbk.) 1.25 (ISBN 0-515-03179-8). Pyramid Books.
Mediterranean Cruise. Rachel Ingalls. LC 73-81317. 1973. 6.95 (ISBN 0-87645-081-8). Gambit.
Mediterranean Mystery. Fred E Wynne. LC 23-11262. 1923. Duffield & Company.
Mediterranean Odyssey: An Amazing True Story of Adventure and Heroism. Amy Josephine Baker. LC 42-505866. 1942. Liveright Publishing Corporation.
Medium for Murder. Mignon Warner. LC 76-52562. (MW suspense). 1977. 6.95 (ISBN 0-679-50751-5). D. McKay Co.
Medley of Mystery. Lynn Williams. (Candlelight mystery). 1974. (pbk.) 0.75. Dell.
Medoc in the Moor. Georgia Willis Read. LC 14-16483. 1914. 1.25. Sherman, French & Company.
Medoline Selwyn's Work. Hattie E. Colter. LC 6-30672. I. Bradley & Co.
Medora. special autographed ed.... ed. Zena Irma Trinka. LC 41-4927. 1940. First Award Books.
Medusa: A Tiger by the Tail. Jack L. Chalker. (Four Lords of the Diamond Ser.: Bk. 4). 304p. (Orig.). 1983. pap. 2.95 (ISBN 0-345-29372-X, Del Rey). Ballantine.
Medusa Complex. Marvin H. Albert. LC 81-66972. 320p. 1981. 13.95 (ISBN 0-87795-341-4). Arbor Hse.
Medusa Conspiracy. Ethan I Shedley. LC 79-56261. 1980. 13.95 (ISBN 0-670-46571-2). Viking Press.
Medusa Emerald. George Fort Gibbs. LC 7-35622. 1907. D. Appleton and Company.
Medusa Kiss. Michael Woodman. (Boxer Ser). 1971. pap. 0.95 o.p. (95125). Beagle Bks.
Medusa Syndrome. Ron Cutler. 256p. 1983. pap. 2.95 (ISBN 0-451-12057-4, Sig). NAL.
Medusa Touch. Peter Van Greenaway. LC 73-79342. 1973. 6.95 (ISBN 0-8128-1632-3). Stein and Day.
Medusa's Children. Bob Shaw. LC 77-25608. 1979. 7.95 (ISBN 0-385-13537-8). Doubleday.
Medusa's Head. Josephine Dodge Daskam Bacon. LC 26-14123. 1926. D. Appleton and Company.
Meek Heritage. Frans Eemil Sillanpaa & Matson, Alexander, Tr. LC 38-25343. 1938. A. A. Knopf.
Meek Heritage: A Novel. american ed. Frans Eemil Sillanpaa. LC 72-87308. 1973. 5.95 (ISBN 0-8397-5782-4). P. S. Eriksson.

Meek Shall Inherit: A Novel. Zofia Kossak-Szczucka. Tr. by Maurice Michael. LC 48-10915. 1948. Roy Publishers.
Meekness of Isaac: A Novel. William O'Rourke. LC 74-8372. 1974. 5.95 (ISBN 0-690-00299-8). Crowell.
Meet--the Tiger! Leslie Charteris. LC 29-8649. 1929. Pub. for the Crime Club, Inc., by Doubleday, Doran & Company, Inc.
Meet--the Tiger! The Saint in Danger. Leslie Charteris. LC 41-6045. 1940. The Sun Dial Press.
Meet a Dark Stranger. Lee Belvedere. (Candlelight Mystery). 1973. (pbk.) 0.75. Dell.
Meet a Dark Stranger. T. E Huff. LC 73-14232. 1974. 6.95. Hawthorn Books.
Meet Andy Capp. Smythe. (Andy Capp Ser.). (Illus.). 128p. 1977. pap. 1.25 (ISBN 0-449-13716-3, GM). Fawcett.
Meet Burma. Milton Coniff. Ed. by Bill Chadbourne. LC 77-75669. (Milton Coniff's Terry & the Pirates Ser.: Vol. 3). (Illus.). 1977. pap. 6.95 (ISBN 0-87897-015-0). Nostalgia Pr.
Meet Candy see Man of Her Dreams.
Meet Corliss Archer. Frederick Hugh Herbert. LC 44-487627. 1944. Random House.
Meet 'em with Shorty McCabe. Sewell Ford. LC 21-662. E. J. Clode.
Meet in Darkness. Frederick Clyde Davis. LC 64-12762. (Red badge detective). 1964. Dodd, Mead.
Meet Me at the Melba. Bronte Woodard. LC 77-19316. 1978. 12.95 (ISBN 0-8161-6543-2). G. K. Hall.
Meet Me at the Melba: a Novel: Bronte Woodard. Bronte Woodard. 1978. 1.95. Dell Pub. Co.
Meet Me at the Melba: A Novel. Bronte Woodard. LC 76-45453. 8.95 (ISBN 0-440-05342-0). Delacorte Press.
Meet Me at the Morgue: By John Ross Macdonald Pseud. 1st Ed. Kenneth Millar. LC 52-122084. 1953. Knopf.
Meet Me in Monte Carlo. Denise Robins. LC 78-70869. 1979. 1.75 (ISBN 0-380-43620-5). Avon Books.
Meet Me in the Green Glen. Robert Penn Warren. 1971. 12.95 (ISBN 0-394-46141-X). Random.
Meet Me in Time. Charlotte Vale Allen. 1978. 2.25 (ISBN 0-446-82530-1). Warner Books.
Meet Me on the Barricades: A Novel. Charles Yale Harrison. LC 38-272732. 1938. C. Scribner's Sons.
Meet Me Tonight. Albrand, Martha. LC 60-12142. 1960. Random House.
Meet Me Tonight: By Martha Albrand Pseud. Heidi Huberta Freybe Loewengard. LC 60-121429. 1960. Random House.
Meet Mr. Fortune: A Reggie Fortune Omnibus. Henry Christopher Bailey. LC 42-15827. 1942. Published for the Crime Club by Doubleday, Doran & Company, Inc.
Meet Mr. Lochinvar. Marie Blizard. LC 37-109247. 1937. Arcadia House.
Meet Mister Mulliner. P. G. Wodehouse. 1956. 11.95 o.s.i. (ISBN 0-8277-0221-3). British Bk Ctr.
Meet Mr. Mulliner. Pelham Grenville Wodehouse. LC 28-9057. 1928. Doubleday, Doran & Company, Inc.
Meet Mr. Stegg. Kennett Harris. LC 21-495. 1920. 2.00. H. Holt and Company.
Meet My Maker the Mad Molecule. James Patrick Donleavy. (Seymour Lawrence bk.). 1967. 4.95. Delacorte.
Meet My Maker the Mad Molecule. James Patrick Donleavy. (5547). 1968. Dell.
Meet My Maker the Mad Molecule. James Patrick Donleavy. LC 64-17470. 1964. Little, Brown.
Meet My Maker the Mad Molecule and the Saddest Summer of Samuel S. James Patrick Donleavy. 1975. (pbk.) 1.75. Dell.
Meet Nookie. Ross Webb. 192p. 1975. pap. 1.50 (ISBN 0-532-15168-2). Woodhill.
Meet the Detective: Bull-Dog Drummond, Hanaud, Dr. Fu Manchu and Others ... LC 36-5333. The Telegraph Press.
Meet the Prince. Watkins Eppes Wright. LC 34-32942. 1934. W. Godwin.
Meet the Warrens. Lucy Agnes Hancock. LC 40-322963. 1940. Macrae-Smith Company.
Meeting at a Far Meridian. 1st Ed. Mitchell A Wilson. LC 61-7666. 1961. Doubleday.
Meeting at Midnight. Flora Kidd. (Harlequin Presents Ser.). 192p. 1982. pap. 1.75 (ISBN 0-373-10495-2). Harlequin Bks.
Meeting by Moonlight. Raymond Knotts. LC 46-8189. 1946. Pub. for the Crime Club by Doubleday & Company, Inc.
Meeting by the River. Christopher Isherwood. (74-943). 1968. Lancer.
Meeting by the River. Christopher Isherwood. LC 67-13030. 1967. Simon and Schuster.
Meeting Currents, Jupiter or Christ: A Tale of the Days of Julian the Apostate. Edmund Hamilton Sears. LC 30-18196. The Cornhill Publishing Company.
Meeting for Burial. Janet Hitchman. LC 68-27441. 1968. Atheneum.
Meeting Her Fate. Mary Elizabeth Braddon Maxwell. LC 7-25589. 1881. G. W. Carleton & Co.; Etc., Etc.
Meeting in Madrid. Dorothy Fletcher. 1970. pap. 0.75 o.p. (ISBN 0-447-74713-4). Lancer.
Meeting in Madrid. Jean S. MacLeod. (Harlequin Romances Ser.). 192p. 1982. pap. 1.50 (ISBN 0-373-02482-7). Harlequin Bks.
Meeting of Minds. Steve Allen. 1978. 10.00 o.p. (ISBN 0-517-53383-9). Crown.
Meeting Point. Austin Chesterfield Clarke. LC 70-183852. 1972. 6.95. Little, Brown.
Meeting the Bear: Journal of the Black Wars. Lloyd Zimpel. 1973. (pbk) 0.95 (ISBN 0-671-77564-2). Pocket Books.
Meeting the Bear: Journal of the Black Wars. Lloyd Zimpel. LC 71-134887. 1971. 5.95. Macmillan.
Meeting the Pieman. Victor Wartofsky. LC 77-125571. 1971. 7.50. John Day Co.
Meeting the Unforeseen. Edward Somerville Stevens. LC 40-6579. Essex Publishing Concern.
Meeting with a Great Beast. Leonard Wibberley. 1971. 4.50 o.p. (ISBN 0-688-02840-3). Morrow.
Meeting with a Great Beast: A Novel. Leonard Patrick O'Connor Wibberley. LC 71-142418. 1971. 4.50. Morrow.
Meeting with Murder. Miriam Lynch. LC 56-12931. 1956. Arcadia House.
Meeting with the Past. Caroline Halter. LC 82-2479. (Second Chance at Love). 1982. 11.95 (ISBN 0-89340-514-0). J. Curley & Associates.
Meg. Maurice Gee. LC 81-16749. 12.95 (ISBN 0-312-52861-2). St. Martin's Press.
Meg. Theodora Keogh. (O.s.i.). 144p. 1972. pap. 0.75 o.s.i. (532-75477-075). Manor Bks.
Meg: A Novel. Theodora Keogh. LC 50-5328. 1950. Creative Age Press.
Meg McIntyre's Raffle, and Other Stories. Alvan Francis Sanborn. 1896. Copeland and Day.
Meg Miller. Margaret Sebastian, pseud. 208p. 1981. pap. 1.95 (ISBN 0-515-05811-4). Jove Pubns.
Meg Miller. Margaret SeBastian. (Berkley Medallion). Berkley.
Meg Randall. Charles Ellsworth Grapewin. LC 42-50417. 1942. Liveright Publishing Corporation.
Meg Shannon. Louis Arthur Cunningham. LC 56-13442. 1956. Arcadia House.
Megacorp. Jonathan Black. (Orig.). 1981. pap. 3.50 (ISBN 0-451-09889-7, E9889, Sig). NAL.
Megadeath Option. Peter Buck. (Marc Dean, Mercenary Ser.: No. 8). 224p. 1983. pap. 2.50 (ISBN 0-451-12062-0, Sig). NAL.
Megalodon. Robin Brown. LC 80-26143. 1981. 13.95 (ISBN 0-698-11078-1). Coward, McCann & Geoghegan.
Megan. Norma Lee Clark. 1979. pap. 1.75 (ISBN 0-449-50005-5, Coventry). Fawcett.
Megawind Cancellation. Bernard Boucher. LC 78-72977. 1979. 8.95 (ISBN 0-689-10947-4). Atheneum.
Megda. Emma Dunham Kelley. LC 7-10970. 1891. J. H. Earle.
Megstone Plot: By Andrew Garve Pseud 1st Ed. Paul Winterton. LC 57-6148. Harper.
Mehalah. A Story of the Salt Marshes. Sabine Baring-Gould. (On cover: Lovell's international series, no. 22). F. F. Lovell & Company.
Mehalah, a Story of the Salt Marshes, 2 vols. in 1. Sabine Baring-Gould. LC 79-8231. Repr. of 1880 ed. 44.50 (ISBN 0-404-61769-7). AMS Pr.
Meher's Leela. Alan S. Levinson. 350p. 1982. pap. 5.95 (ISBN 0-940978-03-2). Sharral Pub.
Mehlah. A Story of the Salt Marshes. Sabine Baring-Gould. (On cover: Seaside library. Pocket ed., no. 1201). 1889. G. Munro.
Meir Ezofovitch: A Novel, from the Polish of Eliza Orzeszko. Eliza Orzeszkowa. Tr. by Young, Iza. W. L. Allison Co.
Meister Eckhart: A Modern Translation. Ed. by Raymond B. Blakney. pap. 3.95 o.p. (ISBN 0-06-130008-X, TB8, Torch). Har-Row.
Melamare Mystery. Maurice Leblanc. LC 30-50670. The Macaulay Company.
Melancholy Man: A Study of Dicken's Novels. 2d ed. John Lucas. LC 80-514024. (Illus.). 1980. 19.50 (ISBN 0-389-20033-6). Harvester Press.
Melancholy Surgeon. Gabor Kisfaludy. 150p. 1982. 8.95x (ISBN 0-941432-03-3); pap. 4.95x (ISBN 0-941432-04-1). Silvergirl Bks.
Melancholy Virgin. Annabel Laine. LC 81-16730. 9.95 (ISBN 0-312-52865-5). St. Martin's Press.
Melanie. Gina Kaus. Tr. by Head, June. LC 40-31878. 1940. Modern Age Books.
Melanie Quest. Rosemary Santini. 1973. pap. 1.50 o.s.i. (71-353). Lancer.
Melanie's Happy Secret. Joyce Kotch. 3.50 o.p. Vantage.
Melbury Square. Dorothy Eden. LC 74-125400. 1970. 6.95. Coward-McCann.
Melchisedec. Ramsey I. E. Percival Ramsey Benson. LC 9-21917. 1909. 1.50. H. Holt and Company.
Melchizedek Connection. Raymond E. Fowler. (Illus.). 313p. 1982. pap. 8.95 (ISBN 0-933656-15-7). Trinity Pub Hse.
Melchoir of Boston. Michael Earls. LC 10-263721. 1910. Benziger Brothers.
Melincourt: Or, Sir Oran Haut-Ton. Thomas Love Peacock. Ed. by Saintsbury, George Edward Bateman. LC 7-33747. 1896. Macmillan and Co.
Melinda. Caroline Arnett, pseud. LC 79-19618. 1980. 9.95 (ISBN 0-89340-241-9). J. Curley.
Melinda. Caroline Arnett, pseud. (Fawcett crest book). 1975. (pbk.) 1.25. Fawcett.
Melinda. Carla Lambert. (Orig.). 1979. pap. 1.95 (ISBN 0-532-23285-2). Woodhill.
Melinda. Gaia Servadio. LC 68-14913. 1968. Farrar, Straus and Giroux.
Melinite: The Lady's Maid. Adolphe Belot. Tr. by Le Rodeur, -- LC 6-45530. 1892. Melbourne Publishing Co.
Melissa. Taylor Caldwell. LC 75-706. 1975. (ISBN 0-88411-159-8). Onian Press.
Melissa. Joseph Calvitt Clarke. LC 34-385180. 1934. W. Godwin, Inc.
Melissa. Julie Davis. Belmont Tower.
Melissa Starke. Annulet Andrews. LC 35-559. 1935. E. P. Dutton & Co., Inc.
Melkii Bes. Fyodor Sologub. (Rus.). 1979. 13.00 o.p. (ISBN 0-88233-458-1); pap. 6.00 (ISBN 0-88233-459-X). Ardis Pubs.
Mellichampe. William Gilmore Simms. 1974. Repr. of 1882 ed. lib. bdg. 30.00 (ISBN 0-8414-8065-6). Folcroft.
Mellichampe: A Legend of the Santee. William Gilmore Simms. LC 76-8899. (Simms Revolutionary War novels; v. 3). 1976. 21.00 (ISBN 0-87152-237-3). The Reprint Company.
Mellichampe: A Legend of the Santee. new and rev. ed. William Gilmore Simms. LC 8-13057. 1854. Redfield.
Mellichampe, a Legend of the Santee. new and rev. ed. William Gilmore Simms. (With his The partisan. New York, 1882). 1882. A. C. Armstrong & Son.
Mellichampe, a Legend of the Santee. new and rev. ed. William Gilmore Simms. (On cover: Lovell's library, v. 12, no. 648). 1885. J. W. Lovell Company.
Mellona. Kathalyn Krause. (Belmont Tower Book). 2.25 (ISBN 0-505-51360-9). Tower Publications.
Mellowing Money. Francis Lynde. LC 25-15844. 1925. C. Scribner's Sons.
Melmoth the Wanderer: A Tale. Charles Robert Maturin. LC 70-362058. (Oxford English novels). 1968. Oxford U.P.
Melmoth the Wanderer: A Tale. Charles Robert Maturin. Ed. by Douglas Grant. 1972. pap. 4.95 o.p. (ISBN 0-19-281130-4, 291). Oxford U Pr.
Melmoth the Wanderer: A Tale. Introd. by William F. Axton. Charles Robert Maturin. LC 61-556140. (Bison book, BB114). 1961. University of Nebraska Press.
Melodie du Vent. Joyce Dingwell. (Harlequin Romantique). 192p. 1983. pap. 1.95 (ISBN 0-373-41180-4). Harlequin Bks.
Melodramatists. Howard Nemerov. LC 49-8180. 1949. Random House.
Melody. Emilia Luptak. LC 42-984712. 1942. The Tower Publishing Company.
Melody. Eula A. Morrison. 192p. (OSI). 1972. 4.95 o.s.i. Lenox Hill.
Melody. Elswyth Thane. 1974. Repr. of 1950 ed. lib. bdg. 12.05x (ISBN 0-88411-953-X). Amereon Ltd.
Melody, a Romance. Thane, Elswyth. LC 50-9225. 1950. Duell, Sloan and Pearce.
Melody: A Romance. Elswyth Thane. LC 74-4541. 1974. 6.95. Aeonian Press.
Melody from Mars. Lillian Leslie. LC 24-31098. Authors' International Publishing Co.
Melody in Darkness. Geneva Stephenson. LC 43-4315. 1943. The Macmillan Company.
Melody in Silver. Keene Abbott. LC 11-11217. 1911. Houghton Mifflin Company.
Melody in the Night. Mont Hurst. LC 52-9721. 1952. Beacon Hill Press.
Melody Jones. David D. Galloway. 1981. 9.95 (ISBN 0-7145-3807-8); pap. 4.95 (ISBN 0-7145-3733-0). Riverrun NY.
Melody Lingers on. Lowell Brentano. LC 34-251513. The Macaulay Company.
Melody Maker: The Life of Sir Arthur Sullivan, Composer of the Gilbert and Sullivan Operettas. 1st Ed. Alma Shelley Power-Waters. LC 58-9580. 1959. Dutton.
Melody Man: Tears, Laughter and Pathos Blended with Rare Artistry--a Drama That Plays Upon the Heart-Strings. A Conflict Between the Classics and Jazz, Based on the Motion Picture Story. Howard J Green. LC 30-14089. Jacobsen Publishing Company, Inc.
Melody of Earth. Gertrude M. Richards. 1918. Repr. 15.00 o.s.i. Finch Pr.
Melody of Malice. Susan Hufford. 1.75 (ISBN 0-445-04402-0). Popular Library.
Melody Unheard. Marian Niven & University Press, Sewanee, Tenn. LC 79-25434. 14.95. Published for the University Press, Sewanee, Tennessee by Seabury Press.
Melody Unheard. Frances Shelley Wees. LC 50-5063. 1950. Macrae Smith Co.
Melomaniacs. James Gibbons Huneker. LC 69-13941. 1969. Greenwood Press.
Melomaniacs. James Gibbons Huneker. LC 70-107768. 1969. (ISBN 0-404-03388-1). AMS Press.
Melomaniacs. James Gibbons Huneker. LC 2-607819. 1902. C. Scribner's Sons.
Melon for Ecstasy: A Novel. John Fortune & John Wells. LC 70-157062. 1971. 5.95. Putnam.
Melon for Ecstasy: An Ecological Love Story. John Wells & John Fortune. 1971. 5.95 o.p. (ISBN 0-399-10533-6). Putnam.
Meloon Farm: A Novel. Maria Louise Pool. 1900. Harper & Brothers.
Melpomene Surf: Or, The Little Middy. Septimus R Urban. LC 8-31931. F. A. Brady.
Melt a Frozen Heart. Lindsay Armstrong. (Harlequin Presents Ser.). 192p. 1983. pap. 1.75 (ISBN 0-373-10559-2). Harlequin Bks.
Meltdown. Ray Kytle. LC 76-10209. (Illus.). 7.95 (ISBN 0-679-50576-8). McKay.
Melted Like Snow. 1st Ed. Walter Myers. LC 56-13129. 1956. Pageant Press.
Melting Man. Victor Canning. LC 77-78754. 1969. 5.95. W. Morrow.
Melting of Molly. Maria Thompson Daviess. LC 12-12010. 1.00. The Bobbs-Merrill Company.
Melting Pot. Samuel Wheat. LC 79-93241. 194p. (Orig.). 1980. pap. 2.95 (ISBN 0-936114-00-2). Bk Pr Release.
Melusine: Or, Devil Take Her! Charlotte Franken Haldane. LC 77-84231. (Lost Race and Adult Fantasy Fiction). 1978. 20.00 (ISBN 0-405-10984-9). Arno Press.
Melusine or Devil Take Her! A Romantic Novel. Charlotte Haldane. Ed. by R. Reginald & Douglas Melville. LC 77-84231. (Lost Race & Adult Fantasy Ser.). 1978. Repr. of 1936 ed. lib. bdg. 20.00x (ISBN 0-405-10984-9). Ayer Co.
Melutovna: A Novel. Hannah Berman. LC 74-27963. (Modern Jewish Experience). 1975. 22.00 (ISBN 0-405-06694-5). Arno Press.
Melville Davisson Post: Man of Many Mysteries. Charles A. Norton. 270p. 1973. lib. bdg. 8.95 (ISBN 0-87972-056-5); pap. 3.95 (ISBN 0-87972-060-3). Bowling Green Univ.
Melville Goodwin, USA. John Phillips Marquand. LC 51-12737. 1951. Little, Brown.
Melville Sea Dictionary: A Glossed Concordance and Analysis of the Sea Language in Melville's Nautical Novels. Jill B Gidmark. LC 82-6122. 45.00 (ISBN 0-313-23330-6). Greenwood Press.
Melville's Moby Dick: Or, The White Whale, Abridged with Biographical Introduction and Notes. Herman Melville. Ed. by Hawley, Hattie Louise. LC 24-236021. (On cover: The Macmillan pocket classics). 1924. The Macmillan Company.
Melville's South Seas. Ed. by Arthur Grove Day. (Illus.). 1970. 10.00 o.p. Hawthorn.
Melvin Mace: A Story of a Zinc Mine. Harvey C Lowrance. LC 15-20144. 0.50. Press of Franklin Hudson Publishing Company.
Melwood Mystery. James Hay. LC 20-49581. 1920. Dodd, Mead and Company.
Melymbrosia: An Early Version of The Voyage Out. Virginia Woolf & Louise A. DeSalvo. LC 82-2315. 1982. 20.00 (ISBN 0-87104-277-0). New York Public Library: Distributed by the Pub. Center for Cultural Resources.
Melyonen. Anne Lowing. 1977. pap. 1.25 o.p. (ISBN 0-515-04250-1). BJ Pub Group.
Melzar: A Tale of the Jericho Road. Octavius Van Beverhoudt. LC 13-15852. 1913. Broadway Publishing Co.
Mem Kha's Love Story. Jane Kravig. (Daybreak Ser.). 122p. Date not set. pap. 3.95 (ISBN 0-8163-0480-7). Pacific Pr Pub Assn.
Member for Paris. Eustace Clare Grenville Murray. (Seaside library, v. 25 i. e. 26 no. 507). 1879. G. Munro.
Member for Paris: A Tale of the Second Empire. Eustace Clare Grenville Murray. LC 7-25472. 1871. J. R. Osgood and Company.
Member from Pasquobit. Walter O'Hearn. LC 65-83745. 1965. McClelland and Stewart.
Member of Congress. A Novel. Edwin Beckman. LC 6-10348. 1898. G. W. Dillingham Co.
Member of Tattersall's: A Novel. Hawley Smart. LC 8-9612. Lovell, Coryell & Company.
Member of the Club: A Novel. Peter Niesewand. LC 79-51652. 1979. 8.95 (ISBN 0-525-15495-7). Dutton.
Member of the Family. Mary Arkley Carter. LC 73-13085. 1974. 6.95 (ISBN 0-385-05086-0). Doubleday.

TITLE INDEX MEMOIRS OF MAISIE.

Member of the Third House. Hamlin Garland. LC 68-57526. (Muckrakers Ser.). Repr. of 1892 ed. lib. bdg. 18.50 (ISBN 0-8398-0656-6). Irvington.
Member of the Third House. Hamlin Garland. 1892. lib. bdg. 14.75 o.s.i. (ISBN 0-512-00230-4). Garrett Pr.
Member of the Third House: A Dramatic Story. Hamlin Garland. LC 68-57526. (Illus.). 1968. Gregg Press.
Member of the Third House: A Dramatic Story. Hamlin Garland. LC 3-14805. F. J. Schulte & Company.
Member of the Third House: A Story of Political Warfare. Hamlin Garland. 1897. D. Appleton and Company.
Member of the Tribe. Camille Baum. LC 70-84821. 1971. 5.95. L. Stuart.
Member of the Wedding. Carson Smith McCullers. LC 46-2022. 1946. Houghton Mifflin Company.
Member's Lobby. Kenneth Pugh Thompson. LC 67-7187. 1967. London House & Maxwell.
Members of the Family. Owen Wister. LC 11-10638. 1911. The Macmillan Company.
Members of the Tribe. Richard Kluger. LC 77-70982. 1977. 10.00 (ISBN 0-385-12989-0). Doubleday.
Members Only: A Novel. Patricia Welles. LC 80-66495. 12.50 (ISBN 0-87795-270-1). Arbor House.
Memed, My Hawk. Translated by Edouard Roditi. 1st American Ed. Yashar Kemal. LC 60-11761. 1961. Pantheon Books.
Memento. Michael Macdonald Mooney. LC 78-7762. 1979. 10.00 (ISBN 0-385-14474-1). Doubleday.
Memento: A Novel. Michael Macdonald Mooney. LC 77-13575. 8.95 (ISBN 0-690-01470-8). Crowell.
Memento Mori. Muriel Spark. LC 59-7778. 1959. Lippincott.
Memento Mori. Muriel Spark. LC 82-5234. 1982. 5.95 (ISBN 0-399-50665-9). Perigee Books.
Memento Mori, and The Ballad of Peckham Rye. Muriel Spark. LC 66-21507. (Modern library of the world's best books). 1966. Modern Library.
Memet. Murat Alpar. LC 80-16550. 1980. 3.50 (ISBN 0-915306-19-0). Curbstone Press.
Memlo the Persian Stable Boy. B. H. Pearson. pap. 1.25 o.p. (ISBN 0-89107-080-X). Good News.
Memmo. Joseph Spencer Kennard. LC 20-19583. 2.00. George H. Doran Company.
Memo for Murder. Dale Wilmer, pseud. LC 51-24855. (Graphic mystery, 29). 1951. Graphic Publications.
Memo to a Firing Squad. Frederick Hazlitt Brennan. 1943. A. A. Knopf.
Memo to Timothy Sheldon. Marian McCamy Sims. LC 38-33005. J. B. Lippincott Company.
Memoir of a Gambler. Jack Richardson. LC 79-9378. 9.95 (ISBN 0-671-22584-7). Simon and Schuster.
Memoir of an Aged Child: A Novel. Alfred Duhrssen. LC 67-19052. 1967. Holt, Rinehart and Winston.
Memoir of Nathaniel Hawthorne, with Stories Now First Published in This Country. Nathaniel Hawthorne & Alexander Hay Japp. LC 76-15613. 1976. 20.00 (ISBN 0-8414-6795-1). Folcroft Library Editions.
Memoirs and Resolutions of Adam Graeme of Mossgray. Including Some Chronicles of the Borough of Fendie. Margaret Oliphant Wilson Oliphant. (On cover: Seaside library. Pocket ed., no. 337). 1885. G. Munro.
Memoirs Concerning the Life and Manners of Captain Mackheath (Anonymous). A Trip to the Moon (Anonymous) The Adventures of Abdalla. LC 79-170573. (Foundations of the Novel). (Illus.). 1973. 22.00 ea. (ISBN 0-8240-0564-3). Garland Pub.
Memoirs Found in a Bathtub. Stanislaw Lem. LC 72-10586. (Continuum book). 1973. 6.95 (ISBN 0-8164-9128-3). Seabury Press.
Memoirs Found in a Bathtub. stanislaw lem; translated by michael kandel and christine rose. ed. Stanislaw Lem. 1.50 (ISBN 0-380-00456-9). Avon Books.
Memoirs from the House of the Dead. Fedor Mikhailovich Dostoevskii. Tr. by Jessie Senior Coulson. LC 65-4999. (World's classics, 597). 1965. Oxford University Press.
Memoirs from the House of the Dead. Fedor Mikhailovich Dostoevskii. Ed. by Ronald Hingley. Tr. by Jessie Coulson. (World's Classics Ser.). 384p. 1983. pap. 4.95 (ISBN 0-19-281613-6, GB). Oxford U Pr.
Memoirs from the House of the Dead. Fedor Mikhailovich Dostoevskii. Tr. by Jessie Coulson. (World's Classics Ser: No. 597). 1965. 4.50 o.p. (ISBN 0-19-250597-1). Oxford U Pr.
Memoirs from the House of the Ead. Translated by Coulson. Fedor Mikhailovich Dostoevskii. LC 56-584053. 1956. Oxford University Press.
Memoirs of a Baby. Josephine Dodge Daskam Bacon. LC 4-9116. 1904. Harper & Brothers.
Memoirs of a Banknote. Paco D'Arcos, Joaquim. LC 68-18273. 1968. H. Regnery.
Memoirs of a Beatnik. Diane Di Prima. LC 71-11307. (Traveller's companion series). 1969. 1.95. Traveller's Companion, Inc.
Memoirs of a Cavalier... Daniel Defoe. LC 73-152395. (Oxford English novels). 1972. 3.00. Oxford University Press.
Memoirs of a Cavalier. Daniel Defoe. LC 74-170545. (Foundations of the Novel). 1972. (ISBN 0-8240-0546-5). Garland Pub.
Memoirs of a Cavalier: Or, A Military Journal of the Wars in Germany and the Wars in England. Daniel Defoe. LC 74-13443. (Illus.). 1974. (ISBN 0-404-07915-6). AMS Press.
Memoirs of a Certain Island Adjacent to the Kingdom of Utopia. Eliza Fowler Haywood. LC 75-170564. (Foundations of the Novel). 1972. vol. 22.00 ea. (ISBN 0-8240-0557-0). Garland.
Memoirs of a Citizen Soldier. Gerald Kaminski. 56p. (Orig.). 1981. pap. 4.95 (ISBN 0-940584-01-8). Gull Bks.
Memoirs of a Coquet: Or, The History of Miss Harriot Airy. Emily Willis, Author of. LC 74-18368. (Flowering of the Novel). 1974. (ISBN 0-8240-1169-4). Garland Pub.
Memoirs of a Cow Pony: As Told by Himself... John Horne Burns. LC 6-27716. Eastern Publishing Co.
Memoirs of a Coxcomb. John Cleland. LC 74-14913. (Flowering of the Novel). 1974. (ISBN 0-8240-1132-5). Garland Pub.
Memoirs of a Cross-Eyed Man: A Novel. James Howard Wellard. LC 56-11878. 1956. Macmillan.
Memoirs of a Doctor's Wife. Betty Wright. 1982. pap. 2.95 (ISBN 0-8217-1005-2). Zebra.
Memoirs of a Failure: With an Account of the Man and His Manuscript. Daniel Wright Kittredge. LC 8-37064. 1908. U. P. James.
Memoirs of a Fox-Hunting Man. Siegfried Sassoon. LC 29-3979. 1929. Coward-McCann, Inc.
Memoirs of a Fox-Hunting Man. Siegfried Sassoon. LC 37-20324. The Sun Dial Press.
Memoirs of a Fox-Hunting Man. Siegfried Sassoon. LC 31-32417. Coward-McCann, Inc.
Memoirs of a Good-for-Nothing: By Joseph Von Eichendorff; Tr. by Ronald Taylor. Joseph Karl Benedikt Eichendorff. LC 67-984881. 1966. bds., 3.00. Calder & Boyar.
Memoirs of a Good-for-Nothing. From the German of Joseph Von Eichendorff. Joseph Karl Benedikt Freiherr Von Eichendorff & Leland, Charles Godfrey, 1824-1903, Tr. LC 6-37546. 1866. Leypoldt & Holt.
Memoirs of a Good-for-Nothing. Translated by Bayard Quincy Morgan. Joseph Karl Benedikt Elichendorff. LC 55-8746. (College Translations). 1955. Ungar.
Memoirs of a Gothic American. Anne Kavanagh-Priest. LC 29-120617. 1929. The Macmillan Company.
Memoirs of a Harem Girl. Ary C. Phillips. LC 75-1055. 1969. pap. 1.25 o.p. (B12-1055). Belmont-Tower.
Memoirs of a Little Girl. Winifred Wallace Tinker Johnes. 1896. Continental Publishing Co.
Memoirs of a Little Girl. Winifred Wallace Tinker Johnes. LC 7-9913. 1896. The Transatlantic Publishing Co.
Memoirs of a Magdalen, or, the History of Louisa Mildmay, 1767, 2 vols. in 1. Hugh Kelly. LC 74-16055. (Novel in England, 1700-1775 Ser). 1974. lib. bdg. 50.00 (ISBN 0-8240-1175-9). Garland Pub.
Memoirs of a Man of Honour. Antoine Francois Prevost. LC 74-23659. (Flowering of the Novel). 1975. (ISBN 0-8240-1119-8). Garland Pub.
Memoirs of a Man of Honour, 1747. Antoine Francois. (Novel in England, 1700-1775 Ser). 1974. lib. bdg. 45.00 (ISBN 0-8240-1119-8). Garland Pub.
Memoirs of a Man of Pleasure. James Graham, pseud. (O.s.i.). 1969. pap. 0.95 o.s.i. (A420N, Award). Univ Pub & Dist.
Memoirs of a Married Man. Richard K. Sharon. 1981. pap. 2.50 (ISBN 0-89083-902-6). Zebra.
Memoirs of a Married Man. Richard K. Sharon. (Orig.). 1978. pap. 2.25 (ISBN 0-89083-427-X). Zebra.
Memoirs of a Married Woman. Betty Wright. 1982. pap. 2.95 (ISBN 0-89083-983-2). Zebra.
Memoirs of a Midget. Walter John De La Mare. LC 22-8937. 1922. A. A. Knopf.
Memoirs of a Midget. Walter John De La Mare. LC 25-155094. 1924. A. A. Knopf.
Memoirs of a Midget. Walter John De La Mare. LC 42-2416. The Press of the Readers Club.
Memoirs of a Militia Sergeant. Manuel Antonio De Almeida. (Unesco Collection of Representative Works: Latin American Series). 1959. Pan American Union.
Memoirs of a Millionaire. Lucia True Ames Mead. LC 7-25866. 1889. Houghton, Mifflin and Company.
Memoirs of a Mother-in-Law. George Robert Sims. (On cover: The world library, no. 18). 1892. The Waverly Company.
Memoirs of a Natural-Born Expatriate: A Novel. Richard McBride. LC 66-25960. 1966. bds., 3.95. Swallow.
Memoirs of a Nullifier. Thomas Cooper. LC 6-308779. 1832. The Telescope Office.
Memoirs of a Nullifier. With a Historical Sketch of Nullification in 1832-33. With an Illustration. Thomas Cooper. LC 20-23151. 1860. J. O. Noyes.
Memoirs of a Nun. Denis Diderot. 1960. 3.95 o.p. Dufour.
Memoirs of a Peeress: Or, The Days of Fox. Catherine Grace Frances Moody Gore. Ed. by Bury, Lady Charlotte Susan Maria Campbell. LC 6-27499. 1837. E. L. Carey & A. Hart.
Memoirs of a Physician. Alexandre Dumas. (Half-title: Marie Antoinette romances). 1901. Little, Brown, and Company.
Memoirs of a Physician. Alexandre Dumas & Maquet, Auguste. LC 6-42328. T. B. Peterson.
Memoirs of a Physician... Alexandre Dumas & Maquet, Auguste. LC 4-17497. (Half-title: The romances of Alexandre Dumas. Handy library edition. The Marie Antoinette romances...). 1893. Little, Brown and Company.
Memoirs of a Physician. Alexandre Dumas & Maquet, Auguste. LC 6-42327. (Half-title: The romances of Alexandre Dumas. Illustrated library edition, vol. xxvii-xxix). 1893. Little, Brown and Company.
M,Emoirs of a Physician. Alexandre Dumas & Maquet, Auguste. LC 8-7673. 1894. Little, Brown, and Company.
Memoirs of a Physician. Alexandre Dumas & Auguste Maquet. LC 4-22489. (Half-title: The Marie Antoinette romances). 1901. Little, Brown, and Company.
Memoirs of a Physician: An Historical Romance. Alexandre Dumas & Maquet, Auguste. G. Routledge and Sons.
Memoirs of a Physician: An Historical Romance. Alexandre Dumas & Auguste Maquet. LC 3-27819. G. Routledge and Sons.
Memoirs of a Physician: Being a Continuation of Joseph Balsamo. Alexandre Dumas & Maquet, Auguste. LC 6-42326. (American series no. 312). M. J. Ivers & Co.
Memoirs of a Physician. Being a Continuation of "Joseph Balsamo.". Alexandre Dumas & Maquet, Auguste. LC 6-42325. (On cover: Seaside library. Pocket ed. No. 2119). G. Munro's Sons.
Memoirs of a Public Baby. Philip O'Connor. 1963. pap. 1.95 o.p. (ISBN 0-8277-0092-X). British Bk Ctr.
Memoirs of a Russian Ballet Girl. 1972. pap. 2.25 o.s.i. (V1069R, Venus). Grove.
Memoirs of a Russian Ballet Girl, Vol. 2. 1972. pap. 1.75 o.s.i. (V1082K, Venus). Grove.
Memoirs of a Russian Princess. Katoumbah Pasha. (Black Circle Ser). 1968. 4.50 o.p. (GP455). Grove.
Memoirs of a Russian Princess. Katoumbah Pasha. 1968. pap. 1.25 o.p. (Z1026, Zebra). Grove.
Memoirs of a Shy Pornographer... Kenneth Patchen. LC 45-8438. 1945. J. Laughlin.
Memoirs of a Shy Pornographer: An Amusement by Kenneth Patchen. New Directions. Kenneth Patchen. LC 45-8438. (New directions bk.). 1965. pap., 1.65. Lippincott.
Memoirs of a Shy Pornographer: An Amusement. Kenneth Patchen. LC 57-14790. (City Light books, CL100). 1958. City Light Books.
Memoirs of a Sportsman. Ivan Sergeevich Turgenev. LC 75-101823. (Short story index reprint series). 1969. Books for Libraries Press.
Memoirs of a Survivor. Doris May Lessing. LC 74-21294. 1975. 6.95 (ISBN 0-394-49633-7). Knopf: Distributed by Random House.
Memoirs of a Teenage Hobo in the Thirties. J. W. Hyde. 4.00 o.p. (ISBN 0-8062-0708-6). Carlton.
Memoirs of a Venus Lackey. Derek Marlowe. LC 68-16631. 1968. Viking Press.
Memoirs of a Victorian Gentleman, William Makepeace Thackeray. 1st. u.s. ed. Margaret Forster & William Makepeace Thackeray. LC 79-63011. (Illus.). 1979. 12.95 (ISBN 0-688-03440-3). Morrow.
Memoirs of a Voluptary: The Secret Life of an English Boarding School. 1971. pap. 1.95 o.p. (Z1066T, Zebra). Grove.
Memoirs of a Voluptuary: The Secret Life of an English Boarding-School. LC 75-149791. (Zebra books, Z-1066-T). 1971. 1.95. Grove Press.
Memoirs of a Woman of Pleasure. John Cleland. 1963. 6.00 o.p. (ISBN 0-399-10534-4). Putnam.
Memoirs of an American Citizen. Robert Herrick. LC 65-10864. (John Harvard Lib., JHL4) Bibl.). (D. by Daniel Aaron.). 1965. pap., 1.95. Belknap Pr. of Harvard.
Memoirs of an American Citizen. Robert Herrick. LC 72-84655. (Illus.). 1974. (ISBN 0-403-03091-9). Scholarly Press.
Memoirs of an American Citizen. Robert Herrick. 1905. The Macmillan Co., Ltd.
Memoirs of an American Citizen see Collected Works.
Memoirs of an Amsterdam Streetwalker. Albert Mol. (O.s.i.). 1967. pap. 0.95 o.s.i. (281N, Award). Univ Pub & Dist.
Memoirs of an English Officer & Other Stories. Daniel Defoe. 1981. 20.00x (ISBN 0-575-00421-5, Pub. by Gollancz England). State Mutual Bk.
Memoirs of an Erotic Bookseller. Armand Coppens. LC 72-77631. 6.50. Grove Press.
Memoirs of an Ex-Porno Queen. Sheila Brady. 1975. (pbk.) 1.50 (ISBN 0-671-78821-3). Pocket Books.
Memoirs of an Ex-Prom Queen: A Novel. Alix Kates Shulman. LC 74-171159. 1972. 6.95 (ISBN 0-394-47156-3). Knopf.
Memoirs of an Infantry Officer: By Siegfried Sassoon; with Illus. by Barnett Freedman. Siegfried Sassoon. LC 66-696639. 1966. 5.00. Faber.
Memoirs of an Oxford Scholar. LC 74-31077. (Flowering of the Novel). 1975. 25.00 (ISBN 0-8240-1145-7). Garland Pub.
Memoirs of an Oxford Scholar, Containing His Amour with the Beautiful Miss L., of Essex. LC 74-31077. (Novel in England, 1700-1775 Ser). 1974. Repr. of 1756 ed. lib. bdg. 50.00 (ISBN 0-8240-1145-7). Garland Pub.
Memoirs of an Unfortunate Young Nobleman. James Annesley. LC 75-16366. (Flowering of the Novel). 1975. 25.00 (ISBN 0-8240-1107-4). Garland Pub.
Memoirs of Arsene Lupin. Maurice Leblanc. LC 25-9294. The Macaulay Company.
Memoirs of Barry Lydnon, Esq. William Makepeace Thackeray. LC 76-351892. 1975. 2.50 (ISBN 0-14-004006-4). Penguin Books.
Memoirs of Barry Lyndon. William Makepeace Thackeray. LC 8-28250. (On cover: Lovell's library, v. (?), no. 164). 1883. John W. Lovell Company.
Memoirs of Barry Lyndon, Esq. Written by Himself; The Fitz-Boodle Papers; Catherine: a Story; Men's Wives; Etc. William Makepeace Thackeray. LC 4-16321. (Half-title: The biographical edition. The works of... Thackeray... vol. IV). 1898. Harper & Brothers.
Memoirs of Barry Lyndon, Esq. Written by Himself; with The History of Samuel Titmarsh and the Great Hoggarty Diamond. William Makepeace Thackeray. LC 8-2125. 1871. J. B. Lippincott and Co.
Memoirs of Barry Lyndon, Esq., Written by Himself. William Makepeace Thackeray. LC 62-8409. (Bison book, BB137). 1962. University of Nebraska Press.
Memoirs of Barry Lyndon: Great Hoggarty Diamond; Sketches and Travels in London; Character Sketches; Men's Wives. William Makepeace Thackeray. LC 31-265. Caxton Publishing Co.
Memoirs of Bryan Perdue. Thomas Holcroft. LC 78-60851. 1979. 84.00 (ISBN 0-8240-3664-6). Garland Pub.
Memoirs of Capt. John Creichton see Brothers; or, Treachery Punish'd.
Memoirs of Count Alexis. pap. 1.75 o.p. (V1030K, Venus). Grove.
Memoirs of Dunstan Barr. Jonathan Fields. LC 59-7124. 1959. Coward-McCann.
Memoirs of Emma Courtney. Mary Hays. LC 73-22193. (Feminist Controversy in England, 1788-1810). 1974. (ISBN 0-8240-0870-7). Garland Pub.
Memoirs of Fanny Hill. John Cleland. pap. 2.25 (ISBN 0-451-09634-7, E9634, Sig). NAL.
Memoirs of Hadrian. Marguerite Yourcenar. (Illus.). 347p. 1963. 17.95 (ISBN 0-374-20728-3); pap. 9.95 (ISBN 0-374-50348-6). FS&G.
Memoirs of Hadrian: And Reflection on the Composition of Memoirs of Hadrian. Marguerite Yourcenar. LC 62-18317. (Illus.). 1963. Farrar, Straus.
Memoirs of Hecate County. new ed. Edmund Wilson. LC 59-11989. 1959. L. C. Page.
Memoirs of Hecate County. Edmund Wilson. LC 46-211619. 1946. Doubleday & Company, Inc.
Memoirs of Hecate County. Edmund Wilson. LC 79-1789. 1979. 22.50 (ISBN 0-374-98656-8). Octagon Books.
Memoirs of Hecate County. Edmund Wilson. LC 79-90554. 1980. 7.95 (ISBN 0-87923-315-X). Nonpareil Books.
Memoirs of Hecate County: Rev. Ed. Edmund Wilson. (Noonday Pr., 270). 1965. pap., 2.25. Farrar.
Memoirs of Josephine Mutzenbacher, 2 vols. Felix Salten. pap. 1.95 ea. o.p. Vol. 1 (ISBN 0-87056-244-4, 6244). Vol. 2 (ISBN 0-87056-245-2, 6245). Brandon.
Memoirs of Maisie. Maude Phelps McVeigh Hutchins. LC 55-6664. 1955. Appleton-Century-Crofts.

Memoirs of Mr. C. J. Yellowplush: The Fitzboodle Papers: The Wolves and the Lamb: Stories and Sketches. William Makepeace Thackeray. LC 12-37892. (Half-title: Illustrated library edition. The complete works of... Thackeray... vol. V). 1889. Houghton, Mifflin and Company.

Memoirs of Mr. Charles J. Yellowplush: The History of Samuel Titmarsh and the Great Hoggarty Diamond; Cox's Diary, Etc. William Makepeace Thackeray & Cruikshank, George, 1792-1878, Illus. LC 12-31111. (Half-title: The biographical edition. The works of... Thackeray... vol. III). 1898. Harper & Brothers.

Memoirs of Mr. Chas. J. Yellowplush. William Makepeace Thackeray. LC 8-28197. (On cover: Lovell's library. v. 6. no. 307). 1883. J. W. Lovell Company.

Memoirs of Mitzy, 2 vols. M. Pelletils. Incl. Vol. 1. 272p (6085); Vol. 2. 256p (6103). pap. 1.95 ea o.p. Brandon.

Memoirs of Modern Philosophers: A Novel. Elizabeth Hamilton. LC 74-8071. (Feminist Controversy in England, 1788-1810). 1974. 22.00 (ISBN 0-8240-0866-9). Garland Pub.

Memoirs of Prince Metternich. 1773 -1829. Clemens Lothar Wenze Metternich-Winneburg. Ed. by Metternich-Winneburg. Richard Clemens Lothar. Klinkowstrom, Alfons, Frieherr. Tr. by Napier, Robina. Mrs. Alexander Napier,". LC 4-702. (Seaside library, vol. xlviii. no. 975). 1881. G. Munro.

Memoirs of Satan. William Alexander Gerhardie & Lunn, Brian. LC 33-4389. 1933. Doubleday, Doran & Company, Inc.

Memoirs of Schlock Holmes: A Bagel Street Dozen. Robert L. Fish. LC 73-22663. 192p. 1974. 6.50 o.p. (ISBN 0-672-51987-9). Bobbs.

Memoirs of Schlock Homes: A Bagel Street Dozen) Robert L Fish. LC 73-22663. 6.50 (ISBN 0-672-51987-9). Bobbs-Merrill.

Memoirs of Sherlock Holmes. Arthur Conan Doyle. LC 75-37007. (Illus.). 1976. 5.95 (ISBN 0-8052-3622-8). Schocken Books.

Memoirs of Sherlock Holmes. Arthur Conan Doyle. LC 75-18880. (Illus.). 3.95 (ISBN 0-89104-024-2). A & W Visual Library.

Memoirs of Sherlock Holmes. Arthur Conan Doyle. LC 75-23638. 1970. (u.s.) 1.25 (ISBN 0-14-000785-7). Penguin Books.

Memoirs of Sherlock Holmes. new and rev. ed. Arthur Conan Doyle. LC 12-18801. Harper & Brothers.

Memoirs of Sherlock Holmes. Arthur Conan Doyle. LC 9-3540. (Half-title: Author's edition. Works of Arthur Conan Doyle...). D. Appleton and Company.

Memoirs' of Sherlock Holmes. ... new and rev. ed. Arthur Conan Doyle. LC 4-18684. 1902. Harper & Brothers.

Memoirs of Sherlock Holmes. Arthur Conan Doyle. LC 20-186131. A. L. Burt Company.

Memoirs of Sherlock Holmes. ... new and rev. ed. Arthur Conan Doyle. LC 25-15488. Harper & Brothers.

Memoirs of Sherlock Holmes. Arthur Conan Doyle. 1962. pap. 0.95 o.p. (01975, Collier). Macmillan.

Memoirs of Sherlock Holmes. facsimile ed. Arthur Conan Doyle. LC 75-18880. (Illus.). 288p. 1975. pap. 3.95 o.p. (ISBN 0-89104-024-2). A & W Pubs.

Memoirs of Sherlock Holmes: Facsimile of the First Publication with All the Original Sidney Paget Illustrations. Arthur Conan Doyle. LC 75-37007. (Illus.). 176p. 1976. 5.95 o.p. (ISBN 0-8052-3622-8). Schocken.

Memoirs of Signior Gaudentio Di Lucca. Simon Berington. LC 74-170596. (Foundations of the Novel). 1973. 22.00 (ISBN 0-8240-0578-3). Garland Pub.

Memoirs of Solar Pons. August William Derleth. (Solar Pons series,#3). 1975. (pbk.) 1.25 (ISBN 0-523-00543-1). Pinnacle Books.

Memoirs of Student Life in Germany: And Vacation Trips in the Tyrol, Switzerland, and Austria. Walter R Gosewisch. LC 98-152. 1898. J. H. Train.

Memoirs of the Baron Du Tan. Madeleine Angelique Poisson De Gomez. LC 74-16060. (Flowering of the Novel). 1974. (ISBN 0-8240-1111-2). Garland Pub.

Memoirs of the First Baroness. Lucinda Baker. LC 78-1320. 8.95. Putnam.

Memoirs of the Life and Adventures of Tsonnonthouan. LC 74-17287. (Flowering of the Novel). 1974. (ISBN 0-8240-1164-3). Garland Pub.

Memoirs of the Life & Adventures of Tsonnonthouan, a King of the Indian Nation Called Roundheads, 1763, 2 vols. in 1. (Novel in England, 1700-1775 Ser). 1974. lib. bdg. 50.00 (ISBN 0-8240-1164-3). Garland Pub.

Memoirs of the Remarkable Life and Surprizing Adventures of Miss Jenny Cameron. Archibald Arbuthnot. LC 74-26901. (Flowering of the Novel). 1974. (ISBN 0-8240-1117-1). Garland Pub.

Memoirs of the Twentieth Century: Being Original Letters of State Under George the Sixth. Samuel Madden. LC 74-170588. (Foundations of the Novel). 1972. (ISBN 0-8240-0570-8). Garland Pub.

Memoirs of the Year Two Thousand Five Hundred. Louis Sebastien Mercier. LC 74-16201. (Flowering of the Novel). 1974. (ISBN 0-8240-1199-6). Garland Pub.

Memoirs of the Year Two Thousand Five Hundred... Louis Sebastien Mercier. Tr. by Hooper, William. LC 7-17936. 1795. Printed by T. Dobson.

Memoirs of the Year Two Thousand Five Hundred... Louis Sebastien Mercier. Tr. by Hooper, William. 1799. Published by N. Pritchard.

Memoirs of the Year 2500. Louis Sebastien Mercier. LC 68-56258. 1973. 15.00 (ISBN 0-678-00915-5). A. M. Kelley.

Memoirs of the Year 2500. Louis Sebastien Mercier. LC 77-6804. (Gregg Press Science fiction series). 1977. 22.00 (ISBN 0-8398-2380-0). Gregg Press.

Memoirs of Two Young Married Women. Honore De Balzac. Tr. by Katharine Prescott Wormeley. LC 3-23162. (Half-title: The comedy of human life... Scenes from private life). 1894. Roberts Brothers.

Memoirs of Zeus. Maurice Druon. LC 64-14661. 1964. Scribner.

Memorable Christmas Stories. Ed. by Leon R. Hartshorn. LC 74-15999. (Illus.). 1974. 5.95 (ISBN 0-87747-536-9). Deseret Book Co.

Memorable Voyages of Rebel and Victory. Albert Barnes King. LC 7-12225. 1895. J. H. Earle.

Memorandum of a Murder. Joseph Wright. 1977. pap. 1.50 (ISBN 0-532-15297-2). Woodhill.

Memorial. Christopher Isherwood. LC 72-106718. Repr. of 1946 ed. lib. bdg. 22.50x (ISBN 0-8371-3544-3). Irvington.

Memorial Day. Karen Osney Brownstein. LC 82-45594. 1983. 14.95 (ISBN 0-385-18427-1). Doubleday.

Memorial Day. John Ratti. LC 73-15065. 1974. pap. 2.95 o.p. (ISBN 0-670-00420-0). Penguin.

Memorial Hall Murder. Jane Langton. LC 77-15930. (Illus.). 8.95 (ISBN 0-06-012507-1). Harper & Row.

Memorial Hall Murder. Jane Langton. LC 80-20208. (Penguin crime fiction). (Illus.). 1981. 2.95 (ISBN 0-14-005704-8). Penguin Books.

Memorial: Portrait of a Family. Christopher Isherwood. LC 47-3152. 1946. New Directions.

Memorial Service. John Innes Mackintosh Stewart. LC 76-14966. 7.95 (ISBN 0-393-08751-4). Norton.

Memorial to the Duchess. Jocelyn Kettle. (Berkley medallion book). 1974. (pbk.) 1.25 (ISBN 0-425-02525-X). Berkley Pub. Co.

Memorias De Lazaro see Memories of Lazarus.

Memories. Desmond MacCarthy. 223p. 1980. Repr. of 1953 ed. lib. bdg. 25.00 (ISBN 0-8482-5150-4). Norwood Edns.

Memories. Alma Newton. LC 17-28072. 1917. Duffield and Company.

Memories: A Story of German Love. Friedrich Max Muller. Tr. by Upton, George Putnam. LC 13-33865. 1875. Jansen, McClurg & Co.

Memories: A Story of German Love. new illustrated ed., with pictures and decorations by margaret and helen maitland armstrong. ed. Friedrich Max Muller. Tr. by Upton, George Putnam. LC 6-39027. 1906. A. C. McClurg & Co.

Memories: A Story of German Love. Tr. from the German of Max Muller. Friedrich Max Muller. Tr. by Upton, George Putnam. LC 7-4448. (Tales from foreign tongues. i). 1879. Jansen, McClurg & Co.

Memories: From the German of Max Muller. Friedrich Max Muller. Tr. by Upton, George Putnam. LC 18-17648. (Tales from foreign lands. 1). 1914. A. C. McClurg & Co.

Memories of a Grandmother. A. M. Richards & K., G., Ed. LC 7-41210. 1854. Gould and Lincoln.

Memories of a Humble Man. James Drought. LC 64-22901. 1964. Skylight Press.

Memories of a Non-Jewish Childhood. Robert Byrne. LC 71-124109. 1970. 5.95. L. Stuart.

Memories of Another Day: A Novel. Harold Robbins. LC 79-20774. 9.95 (ISBN 0-671-22585-5). Simon and Schuster.

Memories of Another Day: A Novel. Harold Robbins. 1980. 3.50 (ISBN 0-671-82429-5). Pocket Books.

Memories of Dying. David Hughes. LC 76-382462. 1976. 2.75 (ISBN 0-09-460990-X). Constable.

Memories of Home. Caesar Johnson. LC 78-91818. (Illus.). 1971. boxed 3.50 o.p. (ISBN 0-8378-1782-X). Gibson.

Memories of Lazarus. Adonias Filho. Tr. by Fred P. Ellison. LC 77-75500. (Texas-Pan American Ser). Orig. Title: Memorias De Lazaro. 184p. 1969. 10.00x o.p. (ISBN 0-292-78401-5); pap. 3.45x o.p. (ISBN 0-292-75021-8). U of Tex Pr.

Memories of Lazarus. Adonias Aguiar. LC 77-75500. (Texas pan American series). (Illus.). 1969. 5.00. University of Texas Press.

Memories of Love. Alan Atwood. LC 62-28200.

Memories of the Alhambra. Nash Candelaria. LC 76-26410. 8.95 (ISBN 0-9601086-1-0). Cibola Press.

Memories of the Black Hills: The Story of Betty West. 1st Ed. Libbie Westover Williams. LC 56-80796. 1956. Vantage Press.

Memories of the Future. Paul Horgan. (72002). 1968. Ballantine.

Memories of the Future: Novel. Paul Horgan. LC 66-16295. 1966. Farrar, Straus and Giroux.

Memories of the Manse. Anna Mary MacLeon. LC 6-17933. 1885. H. B. Nims & Co.

Memories of the Manse: Glimpses of Scottish Life and Character. Anna Mary MacLeon. LC 6-17932. ("Cozy corner series"). 1895. J. Knight Company.

Memories of the Past Since Snooksie Died. Edwin Mumford. (Orig.). 1980. pap. 6.50 (ISBN 0-682-49539-5). Exposition.

Memories of Two Cities. David Masson. 1911. Repr. lib. bdg. 40.00 (ISBN 0-8414-6494-4). Folcroft.

Memoris of Arthur Hamilton, B. A. of Trinity College, Cambridge: Extracted from His Letters and Diaries. Arthur Christopher Benson. LC 7-26604. 1907. M. Kennerley.

Memorv of Autumn. Charles Angoff. LC 67-14280. 1968. 5.95. Yoseloff.

Memory & Desire. Bo Crane. 172p. 1981. pap. 4.95 (ISBN 0-89260-201-5). Hwong Pub.

Memory and Desire. Justine Harlowe. LC 82-4944. 15.50 (ISBN 0-446-51246-X). Warner Books.

Memory and Desire. Leonora Hornblow. LC 50-6376. 1950. Random House.

Memory and Desire. Mary Foster Main. LC 45-9733. 1945. Dial Press.

Memory and Other Stories. Mary Lavin. LC 73-5791. 1973. 5.95 (ISBN 0-395-17122-9). Houghton Mifflin.

Memory Boy. Victor Canning. LC 81-14093. 1981. 12.95 (ISBN 0-688-00774-0). Morrow.

Memory Boy: A Novel of International Espionage. Victor Canning. LC 81-14093. 1981. 10.95 (ISBN 0-688-00774-0). Morrow.

Memory Corner. Tom Gallon. LC 12-10268. 1.25. G. W. Dillingham Company.

Memory Man. John Griffiths. LC 81-50333. 12.95 (ISBN 0-87223-711-7). Playboy Press.

Memory of a Scream. David X Manners. LC 46-20738. 1946. Mystery House.

Memory of Darkness. 1st Ed. Margaret Summerton. LC 67-205471. 1967. 3.95. Dutton.

Memory of Eva Ryker. Donald A Stanwood. LC 77-23897. (Illus.). 8.95 (ISBN 0-698-10876-0). Coward, McCann & Geoghegan.

Memory of Eva Ryker. Donald A Stanwood. (Dell book). 1979. 2.50 (ISBN 0-440-15550-9). Dell Pub. Co.

Memory of Evil. Marilyn Ross. 1970. pap. 0.60 o.p. (63-334). Paperback Lib.

Memory of Lions. Parke Godwin. 288p. (Orig.). 1983. pap. 2.95 (ISBN 0-425-05824-7). Berkley Pub.

Memory of Love. Bessie Breuer. LC 36-755. 1934. Simon and Schuster.

Memory of Love. Bessie Breuer. 1935. Simon and Schuster.

Memory of Murder: Four Novelettes. Judson Pentecost Philips. LC 47-11528. (fingerprint mystery). 1947. Ziff-Davis Pub. Co.

Memory of Old Jack. Wendell Berry. LC 74-5013. 1974. (lib. bdg.) 9.95 (ISBN 0-8161-6210-7). G. K. Hall.

Memory of Old Jack. Wendell Berry. LC 75-6530. (Harbrace paperbound library; HPL 64). 1975. 6.95 (ISBN 0-15-658670-3). Harcourt Brace Jovanovich.

Memory of Summer. Audrie Manley-Tucker. pap. 0.50 o.p. (52-917). Paperback Lib.

Memory of the Moon. Peggy O'More, pseud. LC 39-20436. Gramercy Publishing Co.

Memory of Youth: A Novel. Vilhelm Moberg & Bjorkman, Edwin August, 1866- Tr. LC 38-197286. 1937. Simon and Schuster.

Memory Street: A Story of Life. Martha Baker Dunn. 1900. L. C. Page and Company.

Memory Without Pain. Scott Flohr. (Orig.). 1969. pap. 1.75 (ISBN 0-87067-177-4, BH177). Holloway.

Memphis. Shana Clermont. (Orig.). 1981. pap. 2.95 (ISBN 0-89083-807-0). Zebra.

Memphis Jackson's Son. Mary Beechwood. LC 56-10531. 1956. Houghton Mifflin.

Memsahib. Berkely Mather. LC 77-78115. 8.95 (ISBN 0-684-15186-3). Scribner.

Men. Angelika Schrobsdorff. LC 63-7755. 1964. Putnam.

Men Act That Way. Maysie Greig. LC 33-221810. 1933. Doubleday, Doran & Company, Inc.

Men Against the Sea. Charles Bernard Nordhoff & Hall, James Norman. 1934. Little, Brown, and Company.

Men Against the Stars. Ed. by Martin Greenberg. LC 50-6637. (Adventures in science fiction series). 1950. Gnome Press.

Men and Brethren. James Gould Cozzens. LC 70-16039. 1970. Harcourt Brace Jovanovich.

Men and Brethren... James Gould Cozzens. LC 36-755179. Harcourt, Brace and Company.

Men and Machines: Ten Stories of Science Fiction. Ed. by Robert Silverberg. LC 68-28721. 1968. 4.95. Hawthorn Books.

Men and Malice. Ed. by Dean W. Dickensheet. LC 72-89303. 1973. 5.95 (ISBN 0-385-02779-6). Published for the Crime Club by Doubleday.

Men & Rivers: A Novel. Humayun Kabir. 228p. 1981. pap. text ed. 4.25x (ISBN 0-86131-262-7, Pub. by Orient Longman Ltd India). Apt Bks.

Men and the Mirror. Ross Rocklynne. 1973. (pbk) 0.95. Ace Books.

Men and Wives. Ivy Compton-Burnett. LC 31-100800. Harcourt, Brace and Company.

Men & Women. Erskine Caldwell. 1965. pap. 0.60 o.p. (60-233). Manor Bks.

Men and Women. Paul Eldridge. LC 46-4293. 1946. B. Ackerman, Inc.

Men and Women. Ed. by William Kozlenko. LC 54-19833. (Lion book, 177). 1953. Lion Books by Arrangement with Atlas News Co.

Men & Women: An Anthology of Short Stories. Ed. by William Smart. 320p. 1975. pap. text ed. 6.95x o.p. St Martin.

Men and Women and Guns. Haerman Cyril McNeile. LC 16-20442. George H. Doran Company.

Men & Young Girls. Ward Fulton. 192p. pap. 1.95 o.p. (7163). Barclay Hse.

Men Are Like Street Cars. Graeme Lorimer & Sarah Lorimer. LC 78-122730. (Short story index reprint series). (Illus.). 1970. Books for Libraries Press.

Men Are Like Street Cars. Graeme Lorimer & Lorimer, Sarah. LC 32-34681. 1932. Little, Brown, and Company.

Men Are Not Stars... Clarence Arthur Millspaugh. LC 38-5894. 1938. Doubleday, Doran & Company, Inc.

Men Are Only Human. Denise Robins. LC 33-16730. The Macaulay Company.

Men Are So Ardent. Gerald Kersh. LC 36-11955. 1936. W. Morrow & Co.

Men Are So Selfish! Horace Annesley Vachell. LC 28-3169. 1928. G. P. Putnam's Sons.

Men Are Strange Lovers. Anne Van Melborn Rowe. LC 35-2540. A. H. King.

Men Are Such Fools. Faith Baldwin. 1976. Repr. of 1936 ed. lib. bdg. 15.15x (ISBN 0-88411-611-5). Amereon Ltd.

Men Are Such Fools! Faith Baldwin Cuthrell. LC 74-82151. 1975. 6.95 (ISBN 0-88411-611-5). Aeonian Press.

Men Are Such Fools! Faith Baldwin Cuthrell. LC 36-189683. Farrar & Rinehart, Incorporated.

Men Are Such Liars. Myron Keats. The Halsey Company.

Men Are Unwise... Ethel Edith Mannin. LC 34-671223. 1934. A. A. Knopf.

Men Are What Women Make Them: Or, The Drama of Rue De la Paix. Adolphe Belot. Tr. by Furbish, Julia Morton. LC 6-11681. 1872. H. N. McKinney & Co.

Men Around Hurley. Louise Blackwell. LC 57-12249. 1657. Vanguard Press.

Men As Her Stepping Stones. Maysie Greig. LC 39-258. 1938. Doubleday, Doran & Company, Inc.

Men at Arms. Evelyn Waugh. 1979. 10.95 (ISBN 0-316-92629-9); pap. 5.95 (ISBN 0-316-92628-0). Little.

Men at Arms: A Novel. Evelyn Waugh. LC 52-10941. 1952. Little, Brown.

Men at Arms and Officers and Gentlemen. Evelyn Waugh. (Laurel ed. LX136). 1961. Dell.

Men at Axlir. Dominic Cooper. LC 79-23062. 1980. 10.95 (ISBN 0-312-52873-6). St. Martin's Press.

Men at Her Feet. Rob Eden. LC 33-144720. Grosset & Dunlap.

Men at the Gate. Translated by I. M. Rawson. Ottiero Ottieri. LC 62-14186. 1962. Houghton Mifflin.

Men at War: The Best War Stories of All Time. bramhall 1979 ed. Ed. by Ernest Hemingway. LC 79-21785. 1979. 5.98 (ISBN 0-517-30779-0). Bramhall House.

Men at Work: A Novel. Honor Lilbush Wingfield Tracy. LC 66-21498. 1967. Random House.

Men Atwhiles Are Sober. Hilmar Stephen Raushenbush. LC 28-11392. 1928. A. & C. Boni.

Men Born Equal. Harry Perry Robinson. LC 74-22806. 1983. 37.50 (ISBN 0-404-58462-4). AMS Press.

Men Born Equal: A Novel. Harry Perry Robinson. LC 7-41990. 1895. Harper & Brothers.

Men Call It Love. Inez Sabastian. LC 26-13139. The Macaulay Company.

Men Call Me Fool. Dan Totheroh. LC 29-7208. 1929. Doubleday, Doran & Company, Inc.

Men Die. Harold Louis Humes. LC 59-13012. 1959. Random House.

Men Die at Cyprus Lodge... Cecil John Charles Street. LC 44-344780. 1944. Dodd, Mead & Company.

Men Dislike Women: A Romance. Michael Arlen. LC 31-26890. 1931. Doubleday, Doran & Company, Inc.

Men Do Not Weep. Beverley Nichols. LC 42-9584. 1942. Harcourt, Brace and Company.

Men Don't Know. Marjorie Deans. LC 47-18598. 1946. Arcadia House, Inc.

Men Forget:... by Helen St. Bernard. Helen St. Bernard. LC 32-29768.

Men from Ariel. Donald A Wollheim. LC 82-143624. (Illus.). 1982. 13.00 (ISBN 0-915368-19-6) (ISBN 0-915368-81-1). Nefsa Press.

Men from Nowhere. Jean Malaquais. LC 43-5521. 1943. L. B. Fischer.

Men from the Boys. 1st Ed. Ed Lacy. LC 55-10711. Harper.

Men from the Boys. 1st Ed. Ed Lacy. LC 55-10711. Harper.

Men from the Bush. 1st Ed. Ronald Hardy. LC 59-10670. 1959. Doubleday.

Men from the Sea. Kurt Martti Wallenius. LC 55-8124. (Illus.). 1955. Oxford University Press.

Men God Forgot. Albert Cossery. LC 63-22187. 1963. pap. 1.50 o.p. (ISBN 0-87286-009-4). City Lights.

Men In Arms. John Crosby. LC 82-40168. 256p. 1983. 14.95 (ISBN 0-8128-2885-2). Stein & Day.

Men in Black: A Novel About Lidice. Owen Elford. LC 43-2935. A Unger.

Men in Buckskin. Herbert E Stover. LC 50-9282. 1950. Dodd, Mead.

Men in Darkness: Five Stories. James Hanley. LC 78-121559. (Short story index reprint series). 1970. Books for Libraries Press.

Men in Darkness, Five Stories. James Hanley. LC 32-2463. 1932. A. A. Knopf.

Men in Her Death. Anne Morice. LC 80-27946. 1981. 9.95 (ISBN 0-312-52939-2). St. Martin's Press.

Men in Her Death; an Eve MacWilliams Mystery. Marie Blizard. LC 47-177730. 1947. Mystery House.

Men in Her Death: By Stephen Ransome Pseud. 1st Ed. Frederick Clyde Davis. LC 56-754129. 1956. Published for the Crime Club by Doubleday.

Men in Her Life. Warner Fabian. LC 30-28842. Sears Publishing Company, Inc.

Men in Her Life. Berta Ruck. LC 54-8499. 1954. Dodd, Mead.

Men in Shirt-Sleeves: "Some Scenes of Vanity". Benvenuto Sheard. LC 30-12527. 1930. The Viking Press.

Men in the Field: Eighteen Short Stories, with a Foreword by John T. Frederick. Leo Lewis Ward. LC 55-951554. 1955. University of Notre Dame Press.

Men in the Jungle. Norman Spinrad. LC 67-11179. (Doubleday science fiction). 1967. Doubleday.

Men in the Sun. Ghassan Kanafani. Tr. by Hilary Kilpatrik from Arabic. LC 78-72967. 1978. 10.00 (ISBN 0-89410-021-1); pap. 5.00 (ISBN 0-89410-022-X). Three Continents.

Men in War. Adolf Andreas Latzko. LC 71-116961. (Short story index reprint series). 1970. Books for Libraries Press.

Men in War. Adolf Andreas Latzko. Tr. by Seltzer, Adele Szold. LC 18-10538. 1918. Boni and Liveright.

Men Inside. Barry N. Malzberg. 1973. pap. 0.95 o.s.i. (75-486). Lancer.

Men Like Gods. Herbert George Wells. 1974. pap. 0.95 o.p. Leisure Bks.

Men Like Gods: A Novel. Herbert George Wells. LC 23-28063. 1923. The Macmillan Company.

Men Like Gods: A Novel of Men and Oil. Robert Sturgis. LC 44-6289. 1944. M. S. Mill Co., Inc.

Men Like Shadows. Dorothy Charques. LC 52-13994. 1953. Coward-McCann.

Men, Maids, and Mustard-Pot: A Collection of Tales. Gilbert Frankau. LC 70-163025. (Short story index reprint series). 1971. (ISBN 0-8369-3939-5). Books for Libraries Press.

Men, Maids and Mustard-Pot: A Collection of Tales. Gilbert Frankau. LC 24-21509. The Century Co.

Men Marooned. George Tracy Marsh. LC 25-204091. 1925. The Penn Publishing Company.

Men Must Pay. James Noble Gifford. LC 39-33005. 1939. Phoenix Press.

Men Must Pay. John Saxon. LC 39-33005. Phoenix Press.

Men Never Know. Vicki Baum. LC 35-8926. 1935. Doubleday, Doran & Company, Inc.

Men of Affairs. Roland Pertwee. LC 22-10767. 1922. A. A. Knopf.

Men of Albemarle. Inglis Clark Fletcher. LC 76-5503. 1976. 10.25 (ISBN 0-89244-004-X). Queens House.

Men of Albemarle. Inglis Clark Fletcher. LC 42-22996. 1942. The Bobbs-Merrill Company.

Men of Albemarle. Garden City Books Reprint Ed. Inglis Clark Fletcher. LC 52-20975. 1951. Garden City Books.

Men of Career. John Lorraine. LC 60-8630. 1960. Crown Publishers.

Men of Chesley. James Wolf. 1982. 9.95 (ISBN 0-8062-1920-3). Carlton.

Men of Dallas. Burt Hirchfield. (Dallas Ser.). 288p. (Orig.). 1981. pap. 2.75 (ISBN 0-553-20390-8). Bantam.

Men of Destiny. Emil Dionne. LC 45-10151. 1945. Priv. Print.

Men of Destiny. 1st Ed. Louis A Hill. LC 59-652086. 1959. Vantage Press.

Men of Earth. Bernice Brown. LC 70-122692. (Short story index reprint series). 1970. Books for Libraries Press.

Men of Earth. Bernice Brown. LC 24-9781. 1924. G. P. Putnam's Sons.

Men of Good Will. Jules Romains & Wells, Warre Bradley, 1892- Tr. LC 33-14289. A. A. Knopf.

Men of Iron. Howard Pyle. 1904. Harper & Brothers.

Men of Iron. Howard Pyle. Ed. by Tourison, Eleanor. LC 30-16249. (Harper's modern classics). Harper & Brothers.

Men of Kildonan: A Romance of the Selkirk Settlers. John Herries McCulloch. LC 26-23685. George H. Doran Company.

Men of Maize. Miguel Angel Asturias. LC 75-6629. 1975. 10.00 (ISBN 0-440-05583-0). Delacorte Press/S. Lawrence.

Men of Marlowe's. Alice Dudeney. LC 5028. 1900. Henry Holt and Company.

Men of Men. Wilbur A Smith. LC 82-45566. 1983. 17.95 (ISBN 0-385-17834-4). Doubleday.

Men of Moon Mountain. Katharine Newlin Burt. LC 38-29161. 1938. Macrae Smith Company.

Men of Mystery. Wilder Anthony. LC 26-6473. The Macaulay Company.

Men of Ness (The Saga of Thorlief Coalbiter's Sons) Eric Robert Russell Linklater. LC 33-6710. Farrar & Rinehart, Inc.

Men of No Property. Dorothy Salisbury Davis. LC 55-120476. 1956. Scribner.

Men of Principle: A Novel. Edward Loomis. LC 63-8854. 1963. Viking Press.

Men of Sapio Ranch. Horace Mellard Du Bose. 1909. Publishing House of the M. E. Church, South, Smith & Lamar, Agents.

Men of Silence. Louis Forgione & Littlefield, Walter, 1867- LC 28-292335. E. P. Dutton & Co., Inc.

Men of Stones: A Melodrama. Rex Warner. LC 50-5447. 1950. Lippincott.

Men of the Burma Road. I Chiang. LC 43-1019. 1942. Transatlantic Arts.

Men of the Enchantress. Frances W Campbell. LC 46-7705. 1946. The Bobbs-Merrill Company.

Men of the Frozen North. Peter Freuchen. LC 62-13946. (Illus.). 1962. World Pub. Co.

Men of the Harem. Ted Hudson. 160p. 1974. pap. 1.95 o.p. (ISBN 0-87682-410-6, 7410). Barclay Hse.

Men of the High Calling. Ed. by Charles Neider. LC 54-8241. 1954. Abingdon Press.

Men of the Mesquite. George Washington Ogden. LC 32-8082. 1932. Dodd, Mead & Company.

Men of the Moss-Hags: Being a History of Adventure Taken from the Papers of William Gordonm of Earlstown in Galloway and Told Over Again. Samuel Rutherford Crockett. LC 4-16298. 1895. Macmillan and Co.

Men of the Mountain. Samuel Rutherford Crockett. LC 9-22183. 1909. Harper & Brothers.

Men of the Mountains. Jesse Stuart. LC 41-4022. 1941. E. P. Dutton & Co.

Men of the Mountains. Jesse Stuart. LC 79-11419. 4.95 (ISBN 0-8131-0143-3). University Press of Kentucky.

Men of the Mounted. Ted McCall. LC 34-34427. (On cover: The big little book). Whitman Publishing Company.

Men of the Outer Islands. Rex Ellingwood Beach. LC 32-73492. Farrar & Rinehart, Incorporated.

Men of the West: A Romance of Ireland's Fight for Freedom. John Joseph Kennedy. LC 33-21524. The Review Printing & Publishing Co.

Men on Horseback. Blanche Weitbrec. LC 11-24824. D. FitzGerald, Inc.

Men on the Dead Man's Chest. Clifford Samuel Raymond. LC 30-42963. The Bobbs-Merrill Company.

Men Pass. Marcelle Capy. Tr. by Yakhontoff, Victor A. LC 32-10342. Liveright, Inc.

Men That God Forgot. Richard Butler. LC 76-29857. 8.95 (ISBN 0-312-52955-4). St. Martin's Press.

Men That God Made Mad: A Novel of Ireland's Easter Rising. William Howard Baker, pseud. LC 69-18163. 1969. 5.95. Putnam.

Men We Marry. Lewis Edward MacBrayne. LC 11-2687. The C. M. Clark Publishing Co.

Men Who Dared... Byron Elbert Veatch. LC 9-115. H. Harisun & Co.

Men Who Die Twice. Peter Heath. 1968. pap. 0.60 o.p. (73-783). Lancer.

Men Who Explained Miracles. John Dickson Carr. 1970. pap. 0.75 o.p. (T2224). Pyramid Pubns.

Men Who Explained Miracles: Six Short Stories and a Novelette. John Dickson Carr. LC 63-20313. 1963. Harper & Row.

Men Who Fought for Us" in the "Hungry Forties." A Tale of Pioneers and Beginnings. Allen Clarke. LC 14-14235. 1914. The Co-Operative Newspaper Society Ltd.

Men Who Wrought. Ridgwell Cullum. LC 16-13972. G. W. Jacobs & Company.

Men with Little Hammers: A Novel. Robert Canzoneri. LC 72-91113. 1969. 5.95. Dial Press.

Men with the Bark on. Frederic Remington. LC 2132. 1900. Harper & Brothers.

Men with Three Eyes. Louisa Revell. LC 55-978. (Cock Robin mystery). 1955. Macmillan.

Men Withering. Francis MacManus. LC 40-14081. 1940. Sheed & Ward.

Men Without Bones. Gerald Kersh. LC 62-41850. 1962. Paperback Library.

Men Without Country. Charles Bernard Nordhoff & Hall, James Norman. LC 42-15983. 1942. Little, Brown and Company.

Men Without Doubt. William Turton. LC 40-33711. 1940. Houghton Mifflin Company.

Men Without Mercy. Alfred Doblin. LC 75-31978. 1975. 16.00. H. Fertig.

Men Without Women. Ernest Hemingway. LC 27-220533. 1927. C. Scribner's Sons.

Men Without Women. Ernest Hemingway. LC 28-9165. 1928. C. Scribner's Sons.

Men Without Women. Ernest Hemingway. LC 34-1948. 1932. C. Scribner's Sons.

Men Without Women. Ernest Hemingway. LC 46-8602. (Half-title: The Living library). 1946. The World Publishing Company.

Men, Women and Boats. Stephen Crane. Ed. by Starrett. Vincent. LC 22-7211. (Half-title: The modern library of the world's best books.). Boni and Liveright.

Men, Women, and Children. Alan Sillitoe. LC 74-136. 1974. 6.95 (ISBN 0-684-13833-6). Scribner.

Men, Women, and Ghosts. Elizabeth Stuart Phelps Ward. LC 69-11925. (American short story series, v. 84). 1969. Garrett Press.

Men, Women, and Ghosts. Elizabeth Stuart Phelps Ward. LC 72-8146. (American short story series, v. 84). 1972. (ISBN 0-8422-8122-3). MSS Information Corp.

Men, Women, and Ghosts. Elizabeth Stuart Phelps H. D. Ward Ward. LC 8-33106. 1869. Fields, Osgood, & Co.

Men, Women, and Ghosts. 13th ed. Elizabeth Stuart Phelps H. D. Ward Ward. LC 8-33105. Houghton, Mifflin and Company.

Men, Women, and Rattlesnakes. Franklin P. Collier. LC 33-259761. 1933. W. Godwin, Inc.

Men Working. John Faulkner, pseud. LC 41-13934. Harcourt, Brace and Company.

Menace. Sydney Horler. LC 33-34786. 1933. Little, Brown, and Company.

Menace... Philip MacDonald. LC 33-284024. 1933. Pub. for the Crime Club, Inc., by Doubleday, Doran & Company, Inc.

Menace, Based on the Motion Picture Story. Rowland V Lee & Lee, Donald W., Joint Author. Jacobsen Publishing Company, Inc.

Menace from Earth. Robert Heinlein. 1976. Repr. of 1959 ed. lib. bdg. 14.40x (ISBN 0-88411-882-7). Amereon Ltd.

Menace from Earth. 1st Ed. Robert Anson Heinlein. LC 59-151871. Gnome Press.

Menace of Death. Edward Churchill. LC 88-2666. The Dodge Publishing Company.

Menace of Graystone House. Thomas J. Saunders. 4.50 o.p. Vantage.

Menace of Marble Hill. Mona Farnsworth. 1977. pap. 1.25 (ISBN 0-532-12507-X). Woodhill.

Menace of Marble Hill. Mona Farnsworth. 1974. (pbk.) 0.95. Manor Books.

Menace of the Saucers. Eando Binder, pseud. 1978. pap. 1.25 o.s.i. (ISBN 0-8439-0576-X, Leisure Bks). Nordon Pubns.

Menace of the Saucers. Eando Binder, pseud. LC 60-1050. (Orig.). 1969. pap. 0.60 o.p. (B60-1050). Belmont-Tower.

Menace Within: A Novel of Suspense. Ursula Reilly Curtiss. LC 78-13361. 6.95 (ISBN 0-396-07620-3). Dodd, Mead.

Menaced Assassin. Sheila Ascher & Dennis Straus. LC 82-2866. 160p. 1982. 8.95 (ISBN 0-914232-49-5); pap. 4.95 (ISBN 0-914232-48-7); ltd. signed 25.00x (ISBN 0-914232-50-9). McPherson & Co.

Menaces, Menaces. John Michael Evelyn. LC 75-22226. 1976. 7.95. St. Martin's Press.

Menaces, Menaces. Michael Underwood. LC 75-22226. 200p. 1976. 7.95 o.p. (ISBN 0-312-52885-X). St Martin.

Menaco to Mrs. Kershaw. Austen Allen. LC 31-5766. 1930. Harper & Brothers.

Menagerie. Catherine Cookson. 1975. (pbk.) 1.25. Bantam Books.

Mended Wings. John Reid Turnbull. LC 44-1742. 1943. Wm. B. Eerdmans Publishing Co.

Mendel. William Hoffman. LC 68-27246. 1969. 4.95. T. Yoseloff.

Mendel: A Story of Youth. Gilbert Cannan. LC 16-235864. 1916. George H. Doran Company.

Mendel Marantz. David Freedman. LC 26-3377. 1926. The Langdon Publishing Company, Inc.

Mendelman Fire: And Other Stories. Wolf Mankowitz. LC 57-6443. 1957. Little, Brown.

Mendelov Conspiracy. Martin Caidin. LC 77-85418. 1969. 5.95. Meredith Press.

Mender of Images. Norma Octavia Lorimer. LC 21-16928. Brentano's.

Menders. Benedict Joseph Murdoch. LC 54-37048. 1953. M. Jones Co.

Mendoza and a Little Lady. William Caine. LC 22-4756. 1921. G. P. Putnam's Sons, Limited.

Mendoza and a Little Lady. William Caine. LC 22-5895. 1922. 1.75. G. P. Putnam's Sons.

Mendoza's Treasure. Vince Danials. 1980. pap. 1.75 (ISBN 0-8439-0721-5, Leisure Bks). Nordon Pubns.

Menfreya in the Morning. Eleanor Hibbert. LC 66-12220. 1966. Doubleday.

Menfreya in the Morning. Victoria Holt, pseud. LC 66-12220. 1966. 5.95 (ISBN 0-385-06098-X). Doubleday.

Menfreya in the Morning. Victoria Holt, pseud. 256p. 1982. pap. 2.95 (ISBN 0-449-23757-5, Crest). Fawcett.

Meningitis. Yuriy Tarnawsky. LC 77-88231. 1978. 8.95 (ISBN 0-914590-48-0); pap. 3.95 (ISBN 0-914590-49-9). Fiction Coll.

Meningitis: A Work of Fiction. IUrii O Tarnavskyi. LC 77-88231. 8.95. (ISBN 0-914590-48-0) (ISBN 0-914590-49-9). Fiction Collective: Distributed by G. Braziller.

Mennonite Soldier. Kenneth Reed. LC 74-1355. 1974. 6.95 (ISBN 0-8361-1734-4). Herald Press.

Menorah Men. Lionel Davidson. (5565). 1967. Dell.

Menorah Men. Lionel Davidson. LC 66-21717. (Illus.). 1966. Harper & Row.

Menotomy; Romance of 1776. Margaret L Sears. LC 8-33154. 1908. R. G. Badger.

Men's Club. Leonard Michaels. LC 81-681. 1981. 10.95. Farrar Straus Giroux.

Men's Tragedies. Richard Voorhees Risley. LC 99-2029. 1899. The Macmillan Company.

Men's Wives. William Makepeace Thackeray. LC 22-4752. (Half-title: Appletons' popular library of the best authors). 1853. D. Appleton & Company.

Men's Wives. William Makepeace Thackeray. LC 8-28196. (On cover: Lovell's library, v. 5, no. 296). 1883. J. W. Lovell Company.

Mensch mit Namen Ziegler see Augustus.

Mensh! Teddy Bart. LC 75-14345. 1975. 6.95 (ISBN 0-8407-4045-X) (ISBN 0-8407-5593-7). T. Nelson.

Menshikoff: Or, The Peasant Prince. Adnre Henri Constant Van Hassett. 1890. H. L. Kilner & Co.

Mensonges. Francoise Mallet-Joris. 1968. pap. 1.10 o.s.i. Paris Pubns.

Mental Marvel. Frederick John MacIsaac. LC 30-890123. 1930. A. C. McClurg & Co.

Mental Struggle: A Novel. Margaret Wolfe Hamilton Hungerford. LC 7-9350. (On cover: Lovell's library, v. 14, no. 735). 1886. J. W. Lovell Company.

Menteuse see Lying Woman.

Mention My Name in Atlantis. John Jakes. (Science Fiction Ser). 1975. pap. 1.25 o.p. (UY1196). DAW Bks.

Mention My Name in Hawaii. Eddie Sherman & Bill Stuart. Ed. by J. Patrick O'Connell. 200p. (Orig.). 1972. 1.65 o.s.i. (ISBN 0-911776-14-1). Hogarth.

Mentons. Was It a Crime? C. F. R Hayward. LC 7-8467. 1887. R. R. Donnelley & Sons.

Menu Cypher. Richard M Elman. LC 82-15200. 14.95 (ISBN 0-02-544820-X). Macmillan.

Mephisto. Klaus Mann. LC 77-5964. 10.00 (ISBN 0-394-41654-6). Random House.

Mephisto. Klaus Mann. 1979. 2.25 (ISBN 0-345-25393-0). Ballantine Books.

Mephisto and the Eagle: A Novel, by George C. Ebbert. 1st Ed. George C Ebbert. LC 65-28689. 4.50. Harlo.

Mephisto: Movie Tie-In Edition. Klaus Mann. Tr. by Robin Smith from Ger. 1983. pap. 4.95 (ISBN 0-14-006578-4). Penguin.

Mephisto Waltz. Fred M. Steward. 1978. pap. 1.95 (ISBN 0-425-03886-5, Medallion). Berkley Pub.

Mephisto Waltz: A Novel. Fred Mustard Stewart. LC 69-17367. 1969. 4.95. Coward-McCann.

Mephisto Waltz: A Novel. Fred Mustard Stewart. (Berkley Book). 1978. (ISBN 0-425-03886-6). Berkley Publishing Corporation.

Mephistophiles ! in England: Or, The Confessions of a Prime Minister... Robert Folkestone Williams. 1835. Harper & Brothers.

Mephistophiles ! in England. Or, The Confessions of a Prime Minister... Robert Folkestone Williams. LC 1-585708. 1835. Carey, Lea & Blanchard.
Mer-Lion. Lee Arthur. 624p. (Orig.). 1982. pap. 3.50 (ISBN 0-446-90044-3). Warner Bks.
Mercado de Adulteras. new ed. Jairo Ibero. (Pimienta Collection Ser). 160p. (Span.). 1975. pap. 1.00 (ISBN 0-88473-221-5). Fiesta Pub.
Mercedes: A Story of Mexico. Sarah Josepha Hale. LC 6-46207. 1895. Baptist Book Concern.
Mercedes of Castile: Or, The Voyage to Cathay. James Fenimore Cooper. LC 6-29877. 1840. Lea and Blanchard.
Mercedes of Castile: Or, The Voyage to Cathay. new ed. James Fenimore Cooper. LC 6-29875. 1852. Stringer and Townsend.
Mercedes of Castile: Or, The Voyage to Cathay. James Fenimore Cooper. LC 42-26098. (On cover: Cooper's novels). 1861. W. A. Townsend and Company.
Mercedes of Castile: Or, The Voyage to Cathay. James Fenimore Cooper. LC 2-26837. (On cover: Lovell's library. v. 10, no. 548). 1885. J. W. Lovell Company.
Mercedes of Castile: Or, The Voyage to Cathay. James Fenimore Cooper. (On cover: Seaside library. Pocket ed. no. 424). 1885. G. Munro.
Mercedes of Castile: Or, The Voyage to Cathay. James Fenimore Cooper. LC 4-19574. 1888. D. Appleton and Company.
Mercenaries. John Harris. LC 78-446301. 1969. 4.00. Hutchinson of Australia.
Mercenaries. Giles Tippette. LC 76-10803. 8.95 (ISBN 0-440-05579-2). Delacorte Press/E. Friede.
Mercenaries. Giles Tippette. (Dell Book). 1977. 1.95 (ISBN 0-440-15174-0). Dell Pub. Co.
Mercenaries. Donald E Westlake. LC 60-12118. (Random House mystery). 1960. Random House.
Mercenaries. Donald E Westlake. LC 72-179578. 1970. 0.25 (ISBN 0-14-002453-0). Penguin.
Mercenaries. Jon M. White. 1979. pap. 1.95 (ISBN 0-89041-248-0, 3248). Major Bks.
Mercenary. Burt Hirschfeld. (Orig.). 1970. pap. 0.60 o.p. (ISBN 0-447-73884-4). Lancer.
Mercenary. Jerry Pournelle. 1980. pap. 2.50 (ISBN 0-671-83293-X). PB.
Mercenary. Jerry Pournelle. pap. 2.50 (ISBN 0-671-44245-7, Timescape). PB.
Mercenary. Jerry Pournelle. (Kangaroo Book). 1977. 1.75 (ISBN 0-671-80903-2). Pocket Books.
Mercenary: Genesis in the Desert. Harold Calin. (Leisure Books). 1977. 1.50 (ISBN 0-8439-0463-1). Nordon Pubns.
Mercenary-Green Hell. Leon DaSilva, pseud. 1976. pap. 1.50 o.p. (LB388, Leisure Bks). Nordon Pubns.
Mercenary Lover: or the Unfortunate Heiresses see Reform'd Coquet.
Mercenary: The Fortunes of Gianpaolo Baglioni of Perugia. Charles Durbin. LC 63-10656. 1963. Houghton Mifflin.
Merchant at Arms. Ronald Lewis Oakeshott. LC 20-186640. 1920. 2.00. Longmans, Green and Co.
Merchant of Antwerp. A Tale from the Flemish. Hendrik Conscience & Lyle, Revin, Tr. 1872. Kelly, Piet and Company.
Merchant of Berlin. Klara Muller Mundt. Tr. by Coffin, Amory. LC 16-1242. (historical romances of Louisa Muhlbach pseud.). D. Appleton and Company.
Merchant of Berlin. An Historical Novel. Also, Maria Theresa and Her Fireman. Klara Muller Mundt. Tr. by Coffin, Amery. 1868. D. Appleton and Company.
Merchant of Berlin. An Historical Novel. Klara Muller Mundt. Tr. by Coffin, Amory. LC 7-36662. 1867. D. Appleton and Company.
Merchant of Killogue. Edmund Downey. LC 6-34248. (On cover: Once-a-week library. v. 11, no. 25-26). 1894. P. F. Collier.
Merchant of Menace. John Stevenson. 1.75 (ISBN 0-505-51507-5). Tower Publications.
Merchant of Mount Vernon. John Leonard Smith. LC 7-362473. 1907. The Author.
Merchant of Murder: By Spencer Dean Pseud. 1st Ed. Prentice Winchell. LC 59-6263. 1959. Published for the Crime Club by Doubleday.
Merchant of the Ruby. Alice Harwood. LC 50-8853. 1950. Bobbs-Merrill.
Merchant of Valor. Clarence Budington Kelland. LC 48-7077. 1947. Harper.
Merchant Prince. Henry Christopher Bailey. LC 20-5456. E. P. Dutton & Co., Inc.
Merchant Princes. Leon Harris. 1980. pap. 3.25 (ISBN 0-425-04700-8). Berkley Pub.
Merchanter's Luck. C. J. Cherryh. 208p. 1982. pap. 2.95 (ISBN 0-87997-745-0). DAW Bks.
Merchants Clerk. Samuel Warren. (On cover: Seaside library. Pocket ed. no. 408). 1885. G. Munro.
Merchant's Daughter. Ellen Pickering. LC 7-35916. 1838. Carey, Lea & Blanchard.
Merchants of Menace. Hillary Waugh. 1969. 5.95 o.p. Doubleday.
Merchants of Menace: An Anthology of Mystery Stories. Ed. by Hillary Waugh. Mystery Writers of America. LC 73-84381. 1969. 5.95. Doubleday.
Merchants of Precious Goods: And Other Stories. Anton Gross. LC 21-14801. The Roxburgh Publishing Company Inc.
Merchant's Tale. Geoffrey Chaucer. Ed. by Robert J. Blanch. (Literary Casebook Ser). 1970. pap. 1.75x o.p. (ISBN 0-675-09346-5). Merrill.
Merchant's Tale. Geoffrey Chaucer. Ed. by A. Kent Hieatt. 1970. pap. text ed. price not set o.p. Odyssey Pr.
Merchant's Widow: And Other Tales. Caroline Mehetabel Fisher Sawyer. LC 42-27065. 1841. P. Price.
Mercier and Camier. Samuel Beckett. LC 74-21639. 1975. 6.95 (ISBN 0-8021-0078-3). Grove Press: Distributed by Random House.
Mercies of a Covenant God. John Warburton. pap. 5.95. Reiner.
Merciless Ladies. Winston Graham. LC 79-8008. 1980. 10.00 (ISBN 0-385-15743-6). Doubleday.
Merciless Ladies. Winston Graham. LC 80-17733. 1980. 14.95 (ISBN 0-8161-3119-8). G. K. Hall.
Mercury. Jonis Agee. LC 81-2998. 1981. 7.50 (ISBN 0-915124-50-5). Toothpaste Press.
Mercury. Jonis Agee. 1982. signed o. p. 30.00 (ISBN 0-915124-53-X); pap. 7.50 (ISBN 0-915124-50-5). Toothpaste.
Mercury Story Book. The London Mercury. LC 29-22435. 1929. 2.50. Longmans, Green and Co.
Mercy. Joyce Maciver. LC 76-49707 (ISBN 0-380-00843-2). Avon.
Mercy Deering: Or, Faith Against Infidelity. David Bartley. LC 6-9400. 1891. J. B. Alden.
Mercy Forever: A Novel. 1st Ed. Bertha B. Moore McCurry. LC 54-14939. 1954. W. B. Eerdmans Pub. Co.
Mercy Island. Theodore Pratt. LC 41-3686. 1941. A. A. Knopf.
Mercy Men. Alan Edward Nourse. 1968. D. McKay Co.
Mercy Nurse. Grace Lang, pseud. (Orig.). 1979. pap. 1.95. Woodhill.
Mercy of Allah. Hilaire Belloc. LC 22-11292. 1922. D. Appleton and Company.
Mercy of Fate. Thomas McKean. LC 10-21302. 1910. 1.20. Wessels & Bissell Co.
Mercy of God. Jean Cau. LC 63-7793. 1963. Atheneum.
Mercy of the Court: A Novel. 1st Ed. Monica E Porter. LC 55-14980. 1955. W. W. Norton.
Mercy Philbrick's Choice. Helen Maria Fiske Hunt Jackson. LC 70-128925. 1970. AMS Press.
Mercy Philbrick's Choice. Helen Maria Fiske Hunt Jackson. LC 7-9472. (No name series). 1876. Roberts Brothers.
Mercy Philbrick's Choice. Helen Maria Fiske Hunt Jackson. LC 4-19870. 1904. Little, Brown, and Company.
Mercy's Story. Dorothy Wakely. 224p. pap. cancelled (ISBN 0-441-52564-4). Ace Bks.
Mere Accident. George Moore. LC 21-41333. (Half-title: Vizetelly's one-volume novels. xxvi). 1887. Brentanos.
Mere Adventurer. A Novel. Eliza Frances Andrews. LC 6-512. 1879. J. B. Lippincott & Co.
Mere Caprice. Marie Healy Bigot. LC 11-10552. 1882. Jansen, McClurg & Company.
Mere Child. Lucy Bethia Colquhoun Walford. (On cover: Lovell's library. no. 1185). 1888. J. W. Lovell Company.
Mere Cypher: A Novel. Mary Angela Dickens. LC 6-36835. 1893. Macmillan and Co.
Mere Formality. Barbara Howell. LC 81-17460. 276p. 1982. 11.95 (ISBN 0-87131-367-7). M Evans.
Mere Living. Betty Bergson Spiro Miller. LC 33-23358. 1933. Frederick A. Stokes Company.
Mere Man. Edwin Bateman Morris. LC 14-13577. 1914. The Penn Publishing Company.
Mere Woman. Vera Nikto. LC 13-11034. 1913. 1.25. D. Appleton and Company.
Meredith Blake, M.D. By Peggy Gaddis... Peggy Gaddis, pseud. LC 43-22853. 1943. Arcadia House, Inc.
Meredith Legacy. Sharon Anne Salvato. LC 74-78525. 224p. 1975. 25.00x o.s.i. (ISBN 0-8128-1723-0). Stein & Day.
Meredith Marriage, a Novel. George C. Kelly. LC 8-30885. (Ledger library, no. 125). 1895. R. Bonner's Sons.
Meredith Mystery. Natalie Sumner Lincoln. LC 23-551510. 1923. D. Appleton and Company.
Meredith: Or, The Mystery of the Meschianza. A Tale of the American Revolution. James McHenry. LC 1-12781. 1831. Sold by the Principal Booksellers.
Mereford Tapestry. Charles Roy MacKinnon. LC 73-19618. (Illus.). 1974. 8.95 (ISBN 0-440-08496-2). Delacorte Press.
Mereford Tapestry. Charles Roy MacKinnon. 1976. (pbk.) 1.50. Dell.
Merely Mary Ann. Israel Zangwill. LC 4-4570. 1904. The Macmillan Company.
Merely Mary Ann." By I. Zangwill...Illustrated by Mark Zangwill. Israel Zangwill. R. Tuck & Sons Co., Ltd.
Merely Murder... Georgette Heyer. LC 35-16781. 1935. Pub. for the Crime Club, Inc., by Doubleday, Doran & Company, Inc.
Merely Players: Stories of Stage Life. Virginia Tracy. LC 74-130074. (Short story index reprint series). 1970. Books for Libraries Press.
Merely Players: Stories of Stage Life. Virginia Tracy. LC 9-8996. 1909. The Century Co.
Merged Blood and The Attic Chest: Two Errands, The Way Out, The Ivory Dart, Dubbing Season, The Placard, Testimony, At Ten O'clock, Doctor's Bills, Tonic, Cracked. Jay G Sigmund. LC 29-124835. 1929. The Maizeland Press.
Mergendeiler. Jules Feiffer. 1965. 2.95 o.p. Random.
Merger. 1st Ed. Sterling Quinlan. LC 58-132945. 1958. Doubleday.
Merideth House. Nina Stephens & Jo Stephens. LC 76-126541. 1970. 4.95 (ISBN 0-8059-1476-5). Dorrance.
Meridian. Alice Walker. LC 76-941. 7.95 (ISBN 0-15-159265-9). Harcourt Brace Jovanovich.
Meridian. Alice Walker. (Kangaroo Book). 1977. 1.50 (ISBN 0-671-80962-8). Pocket Books.
Meridian. Alice Walker. LC 80-24583. (Harvest/HBJ book). 1981. 7.95. Harcourt Brace Jovanovich.
Meridian. Aura Ginieres Watson. LC 51-10043. 1951. Houghton Mifflin.
Merit Versus Money. Garnett Marnell. LC 7-24688. (On cover: Munro's library. v. 1, no. 94). N. L. Munro.
Merivale Banks. Mary Jane Hawes Holmes. LC 3-23897. 1903. G. W. Dillingham Company.
Merivale: Or, Phases of Southern Life. James Robertshaw. 1898. G. W. Dillingham Co.
Merivales. George Barr McCutcheon. LC 29-18418. 1929. Dodd, Mead & Company.
Meriwether Mystery... Kay Cleaver Strahan. LC 33-968043. Pub. for the Crime Club Inc., by Doubleday, Doran & Company, Inc.
Merl of Medevon, and Other Prose Writings. John Preston Campbell. LC 6-21482. 1888. Rand, McNally & Co.
Merle Maxwell: A Novel. Lola Callie Talkington. LC 18-8984. 1918. O. M. Goddard.
Merle's Crusade. Rosa Nouchette Carey. (On cover: Seaside library, Pocket ed., no. 1208). G. Munro.
Merle's Crusade. Rosa Nouchette Carey. LC 16-13113. 1903. J. B. Lippincott Company.
Merlin. Robert Nye. LC 78-26799. 1979. 10.00 (ISBN 0-399-12331-8). Putnam.
Merlin, 3 vols. Intro. by C. E. Pickford. 1975. Repr. of 1498 ed. Set. text ed. 200.00x o.s.i. (ISBN 0-8277-3425-5). British Bk Ctr.
Merlin: Or, The Early History of King Arthur: a Prose Romance (About 1450-1460 A. D.). Edited from the Unique Ms. in the University Library, Cambridge. Ed. by Henry Benjamin Wheatley. William Edward Mead & David William Nash. LC 69-19527. (Early English Text Society. Publications. Original Ser.: No. 10). (Illus.). 1969. Greenwood Press.
Merlin: 1498. LC 74-32357. 1975. 160.00 (ISBN 0-8277-3425-5). Scholar Press.
Merlin's Godson. H. Warner Munn. LC 76-14960. 1.95 (ISBN 0-345-25298-5). Ballantine Books.
Merlin's Keep. Madeleine Brent. LC 76-56270. 1978. 8.95 (ISBN 0-385-11102-9). Doubleday.
Merlin's Keep: A Novel. Madeleine Brent. 1979. 2.25 (ISBN 0-449-23810-5). Fawcett Crest.
Merlin's Mirror. Andre Norton, pseud. (Science Fiction Ser). 1975. pap. 2.25 (ISBN 0-87997-641-1, UE1641). DAW Bks.
Merlin's Ring. H. Warner Munn. LC 74-8310. (Ballantine fantasy). (Illus.). 1974. 1.95 (ISBN 0-345-24010-3). Ballantine Books.
Mermaid. Margaret Millar. LC 81-9467. 1982. 10.95 (ISBN 0-688-00793-7). Morrow.
Mermaid. Margaret Millar. LC 82-16198. 11.95 (ISBN 0-89340-543-4). J. Curley.
Mermaid. Grant Martin Overton. LC 20-1891. 1920. Doubleday, Page & Company.
Mermaid: A Love Tale. Lily Dougall. LC 6-33694. (Appletons' town and country library, no. 163). 1895. D. Appleton and Company.
Mermaid and Centaur. Rupert Hughes. LC 29-12488. 1929. Harper & Brothers.
Mermaid Dance. Cyril Norman. LC 7-33310. Brown & Co.
Mermaid in Nikoli. William Woods. 1967. 4.95 o.p. (ISBN 0-8090-6895-8). Hill & Wang.
Mermaid in Nikoli: A Novel. William Howard Woods. LC 67-23514. 1967. Hill and Wang.
Mermaid in the Swimming Pool. Douglass Wallop. LC 68-10887. 1968. Norton.
Mermaid Madonna. Strates Myribeles. LC 59-7759. 1959. Crowell.
Mermaid of Druid Lake: And Other Stories. Charles Weathers Bump. LC 6-45357. 1906. Nunn & Company.
Mermaid Summer. Lucy Cores. LC 73-107403. 1970. 5.95 o.p. McKay.
Mermaid Tavern: Kit Marlowe's Story. by george w. cronyn. ed. George William Cronyn. LC 37-124340. 1937. Knight Publications.
Mermaids. Eva Boros. LC 56-12150. 1956. Farrar, Staus & Cudahy.
Merman's Children. Poul Anderson. LC 79-1187. 10.95 (ISBN 0-399-12375-X). Berkley Pub. Corp.: Distributed by Putnam.
Merope: Or, The Destruction of Atlantis. H H Buckman. LC 6-16113. 1898. Da Costa Printing and Publishing House.
Merrie. Grace South. LC 78-19338. 1979. 8.95 (ISBN 0-385-14537-3). Doubleday.
Merrie England. Paul Johnson. LC 64-16810. 1964. Macmillan.
Merrie Tales of Jacques Tournebroche: And Child Life in Town and Country. Anatole France, pseud. LC 77-121548. (Short story index reprint series). 1970. Books for Libraries Press.
Merrilie Dawes. Frank Hamilton Spearman. LC 13-189551. 1913. C. Scribner's Sons.
Merrill. Marjorie Talbot. LC 6-12854. 1906. Mayhew Publishing Co.
Merrill Clan: Diaguerreotypes and Vignettes. Sarah Estelle Hammond Greathead. LC 37-5994. The Christopher Publishing House.
Merrily I Go to Hell: Reminiscences of a Bishop's Daughter. Mary Lady Cameron. LC 31-235765. Brentano's.
Merrimack; or, Life at the Loom: A Tale. Day Kellogg Lee. 1854. Redfield.
Merrivale Mystery. James Corbett. LC 31-244963. 1931. The Mystery League, Inc.
Merrivale Will. L. M. N & N. L. M. LC 7-25800. American Baptist Publication Society.
Merrivale Will: By Author of "Old Bristol.". Maria Frances Hill Anderson. LC 7-25800. 1896. American Baptist Publ. Society.
Merrivales. Alice Mary Ross Colver. LC 43-9417. 1943. Macrae-Smith-Company.
Merrivales. Alice Mary Ross Colver. LC 45-13285. 1944. Triangle Books, the Blakiston Company.
Merriweather File. 1st Ed. Lionel White. LC 59-125809. 1959. Dutton.
Merry Andrew. Florence Roney Weir. LC 18-105364. Small, Maynard and Company.
Merry-Andrew: By Keble Howard Pseud. John Keble Bell. LC 15-10493. 1915. 1.35. John Lane Company.
Merry Anne. Samuel Merwin. LC 4-91203. 1904. The Macmillan Company; Etc., Etc.
Merry Chanter. Frank Richard Stockton. LC 8-155410. The Century Co.
Merry Christmas: Mr. Baxter. Drawings by Dorothea Warren Fox. 1st Ed. Edward Streeter. LC 56-8787. 1956. Harper.
Merry-Go-Round. D. H. Lawrence. 1973. Repr. of 1940 ed. 6.50 o.p. R West.
Merry-Go-Round. D. H. Lawrence. 1971. 7.50 o.p. Porter.
Merry-Go-Round. William Somerset Maugham. 1978. pap. 3.95 (ISBN 0-14-003373-4). Penguin.
Merry Go Round. Richard Martin Stern. LC 68-57075. 1969. 4.95. Scribner.
Merry-Go-Round. Joyce Thompson. LC 81-9903. 288p. 1982. 11.95 (ISBN 0-517-54341-9). Crown.
Merry-Go-Round: By John Guthrie Pseud. John Brodie. LC 51-12764. 1952. Pellegrini & Cudahy.
Merry-Go-Round in the Sea. Randolph Stow. LC 66-164064. 1966. bds., 4.50. Morrow.
Merry-Go-Round of Love. Luigi Pirandello. LC 64-1274. (Signet classic, CT210). 1964. New American Library.
Merry Heart. Helen Raymond Abbott Beals. LC 18-18531. 1918. The Century Co.
Merry Heart: A Gentle Melodrama. Frank Arthur Swinnerton. LC 29-26344. 1929. Doubleday, Doran & Company, Inc.
Merry Hearts and True. Stories from Life. Mary Catherine Crowley. LC 11-10506. 1889. D. & J. Sadlier & Co.
Merry Hearts: The Adventures of Two Bachelor Maids. Anne Story Allen. LC 3-197949. 1903. H. Holt and Company.
Merry Innocents. Nolan Miller. LC 47-31237. 1947. Harper.
Merry Maid of Arcady, His Lordship, and Other Stories. Constance Cary Harrison. LC 72-11938. (Short story index reprint series). 1973. (ISBN 0-8369-4234-5). Books for Libraries Press.
Merry Maid of Arcady: His Lordship, and Other Stories. Constance Cary Harrison. 1897. Lamson, Wolffe and Company.
Merry Maid of Arcady, His Lordship: And Other Stories. Constance Cary Harrison. LC 7-2886. 1897. Lamson, Wolffe and Company.
Merry Men: And Other Tales and Fables. Robert Louis Stevenson. (On cover: Lovell's library. v. 19, no. 921). 1887. J. W. Lovell Company.

Merry Men: And Other Tales and Fables. Robert Louis Stevenson. LC 20-15593. (On cover: Seaside library. Pocket ed. no. 940). 1887. G. Munroe.

Merry Men: And Other Tales and Fables. Robert Louis Stevenson. 1887. C. Scribner's Sons.

Merry Men: And Other Tales and Fables. Strange Case of Dr. Jekyll and Mr. Hyde. Robert Louis Stevenson. LC 4-16582. 1903. C. Scribner's Sons.

Merry Men: And Other Tales and Fables; Strange Case of Dr. Jekyll and Mr. Hyde. Robert Louis Stevenson. LC 5-27090. (Half-title: The biographical edition of the works of Robert Louis Stevenson). 1905. C. Scribner's Sons.

Merry, Merry Boys. Benjamin Leopold Farjeon. LC 6-38651. (On cover: Lovell's Westminster series. no. 24). 1890. United States Book Company.

Merry, Merry Maidens. Helen Grace Carlisle. LC 37-284614. Harcourt, Brace and Company.

Merry Midwife. Eugene C Teodorescu. LC 47-12723. 1947. Houghton Mifflin Company.

Merry Miracle. Mary Lawrence Shipman Mian. LC 49-11660. 1949. Houghton Mifflin Co.

Merry Month of May. James Jones. LC 71-135379. 1971. 7.95. Delacorte Press.

Merry Month of May: And Two Other Short Novels. Nelia Gardner White. LC 52-1740. 1952. Viking Press.

Merry Mount: A Romance of the Massachusetts Colony... John Lothrop Motley. LC 7-3011. 1849. J. Munroe and Company.

Merry O. Ethel Powelson Hueston. LC 23-7009. The Bobbs-Merrill Company.

Merry School. Harvey MacDonald Barr. LC 40-8414. 1940. Fortuny's.

Merry Suffolk, Master Archie & Other Tales. Lois A. Fison. (Folklore Ser). 12.50 (ISBN 0-8482-3992-X). Norwood Edns.

Merry Tales. Samuel Langhorne Clemens. LC 6-21355. (Half-title: Fiction, fact, and fancy ser.). 1892. C. L. Webster & Co.

Merry Tales. Mark Twain. 1892. lib. bdg. 15.00 (ISBN 0-8414-8411-2). Folcroft.

Merry Tales & Three Shrovetide Plays. Hans Sachs. Tr. by William Leighton from Ger. LC 76-48458. (Library of World Literature Ser.). 1978. Repr. of 1910 ed. 21.50 (ISBN 0-88355-610-3). Hyperion Conn.

Merry Tales of the Monks. Stephalius. LC 8-13423. 1892. Jordan Bros.

Merry Tales of the Three Wise Men of Gotham. James Kirke Paulding. LC 7-34067. 1839. Harper & Brothers.

Merry Widow: A Novel Founded on Franz Lehar's Viennese Opera, "Die Lustige Witwe," As Produced by Henry W. Savage; Illustrations from Scenes in the American Production. Ferenc Lehar. LC 9-11258. G. W. Dillingham Company.

Merry Wives of Massachusetts. James Reid Parker. LC 59-8665. 1959. Doubleday.

Merrylips. Beulah Marie Dix. LC 6-340819. 1906. The Macmillan Company.

Merrylips. Beulah Marie Dix. (Half-title: Every boy and girl series). 1924. The Macmillan Company.

Merrymen & Other Tales see Dr. Jekyl & Mr. Hyde.

Merry's Illustrated Book of Rhymes. Robert Merry & Hatchet, Hiram. 1859. Bartlett and Miles.

Merton of the Movies. Harry Leon Wilson. LC 22-10017. 1922. Doubleday, Page & Company.

Merveilleuse Odyssee. Jane Ayres. (Harlequin Seduction Ser.). 332p. 1983. pap. 3.25 (ISBN 0-373-45019-2). Harlequin Bks.

Meryl. William Tillinghast Eldridge. LC 8-9814. 1908. Dodd, Mead & Company.

Merze: The Story of an Actress. Marah Ellis Martin Ryan. LC 8-1356. 1889. Rand, McNally & Company.

Mesa. Charles Alden Seltzer. LC 76-39998. 1976. 6.95 (ISBN 0-88411-113-X). Aeonian Press.

Mesa. Charles Alden Seltzer. LC 28-25183. 1928. Doubleday, Doran & Company, Inc.

Mesa Gang. Edward Beverly Mann. LC 40-2392. 1940. W. Morrow & Company.

Mesa of Flowers. Harold Courlander. LC 76-54720. 8.95 (ISBN 0-517-52937-8). Crown Publishers.

Mesa of Flowers. Harold Courlander. 1979. 1.95 (ISBN 0-445-04349-0). Popular Library.

Mesa Springs Sentinel. Galen C Colin. LC 41-119808. Phoenix Press.

Mesa Trail. Henry Bedford-Jones. LC 20-16855. 1920. Doubleday, Page & Company.

Mesabi. Margaret Culkin Banning. LC 69-15271. 1969. 5.95. Harper & Row.

Mesalliance. Katharine Tynan Hinkson, pseud. LC 13-228719. 1913. 1.35. Duffield & Company.

Mesas to Mountains. Jane V. Barker & Sybil Downing. (Colorado Heritage Ser.: Bk. 4). (Illus.). 45p. (gr. 3-4). 1979. pap. text ed. 3.50x (ISBN 0-87108-215-2). Pruett.

Mesh. Lucien Marchal. LC 49-49329. 1949. Appleton-Century-Crofts.

Meskin Hound. John H Latham. LC 58-11292. 1958. Putnam.

Mesmerist. Felice Picano. LC 77-9529. 8.95 (ISBN 0-440-05542-3). Delacorte Press.

Mesmerist. Felice Picano. (Dell Book). 1978. 2.25 (ISBN 0-440-15213-5). Dell Pub. Co.

Mesopotamia. Stephen Tapscott. LC 75-11617. (Wesleyan Poetry Program: Vol. 78). 72p. (Orig.). 1975. pap. 4.95x (ISBN 0-8195-1078-5, Pub. by Wesleyan U Pr). Columbia U Pr.

Mesquite Cowboy. Dan T Keliher. LC 49-2097. 1949. Phoenix Press.

Mesquite Jenkins. Clarence Edward Mulford. LC 73-89655. 1973. 5.95. Aeonian Press.

Mesquite Jenkins. Clarence Edward Mulford. LC 28-215928. 1928. Doubleday, Doran and Company, Inc.

Mesquite Jenkins, Tumbleweed. Clarence Edward Mulford. LC 73-89646. 1974. Aeonian Press.

Mesquite Jenkins, Tumbleweed. Clarence Edward Mulford. LC 32-261531. 1932. Doubleday, Doran & Company, Incorporated.

Mesquite Johnny: By Barry Cord Pseud. Peter Germano. LC 52-2442. 1952. Arcadia House.

Mesquiteer Mavericks: A Three Mesquiteers Story. William Colt MacDonald. LC 50-10403. (Double D western). 1950. Doubleday.

Message. Alec John Dawson. LC 7-38262. 1907. D. Estes & Company; Etc., Etc.

Message. Louis Tracy. LC 9-4189. E. J. Clode.

Message Ends. David Craig. 1969. 4.95 o.p. (ISBN 0-8128-1216-6). Stein & Day.

Message Ends. Allan James Tucker. LC 69-17950. 1969. 4.95. Stein and Day.

Message from a Corpse: An Amy Brewster Mystery. Sam Merwin. LC 45-98332. 1945. Mystery House.

Message from a Ghost. Marilyn Ross. (Marilyn Ross Gothic Ser). (Orig.). 1971. pap. 0.95 o.p. (ISBN 0-446-65742-5, 65-742). Paperback Lib.

Message from a Lost Soul: Or, Letters from Hell; with an Introductory Chapter on Hell As God Has Revealed It in His Word. Valdemar Adolph Thisted & Torrey, Reuben Archer, 1856- LC 6-41712. P. W. Ziegler Co.

Message from a Stranger. Marya Mannes. LC 61-17496. (Collier books: fiction AS61). 1961. Collier Books.

Message from a Stranger: A Novel. Marya Mannes. LC 48-5308. 1948. Viking Press.

Message from Absalom. Anne Armstrong Thompson. LC 74-12825. 1975. 7.95 (ISBN 0-671-22067-5). Simon and Schuster.

Message from Absalom. Anne Armstrong Thompson. 1976. (pbk.) 1.75. Pocket Books.

Message from Earth. Kenneth W. Hassler. Ed. by Alice Sachs. 1970. 3.95 o.p. Lenox Hill.

Message from Hong Kong. Mignon Good Eberhart. LC 69-16421. 1969. 4.50. Random House.

Message from Julie. Sara North, pseud. LC 77-82169. 1978. pap. 1.50 o.p. (ISBN 0-87216-429-2, C16429). Playboy.

Message from Malaga. Helen MacInnes. LC 79-160406. 1971. (ISBN 0-15-159280-2). Harcourt Brace Jovanovich.

Message from Moscow. pap. 2.45 o.p. (ISBN 0-394-71689-2, V-689, Vin). Random.

Message from Nowhere. Christy Cunningham. LC 29-18331. The Stratford Company.

Message from Sirius. Cecil Jenkins. LC 61-13017. (Red badge detective). 1961. Dodd, Mead.

Message of April Fools'. Lee Foster. LC 76-129815. 1970. 2.95. Pacific Coast Publishers.

Message of the Mute Dog: A Jane Amanda Edwards Story. Charlotte Murray Russell, pseud. LC 42-7965. 1942. Published for the Crime Club by Doubleday, Doran & Co., Inc.

Messages from Mars: By the Aid of the Telescope Plant. Robert D Braine. LC 6-17939. (peeriess series, no. 62). 1892. J. S. Ogilvie.

Messages from Michael. Chelsea Quinn Yarbo. LC 80-82567. 288p. 1980. pap. 2.50 (ISBN 0-87216-766-6). Playboy Pbks.

Messages from the Asylum. Winston Weathers. 64p. 1970. pap. 2.00 o.p. (ISBN 0-912484-01-2). J Nichols.

Messages of Love. Samuel Youd. LC 61-7004. 1961. Simon and Schuster.

Messalina. Vivian Crockett. LC 24-30454. 1924. Boni and Liveright.

Messalina. Jack Oleck. LC 59-13599. 1959. L. Stuart.

Messalina of the Suburbs. Edmee Elizabeth Monica De La Pasture. LC 75-106286. (Short story index reprint series). 1970. (ISBN 0-8369-3323-0). Books for Libraries Press.

Messenger. Katharine Holland Brown. LC 10-7787. 1910. 0.50. C. Scribner's Sons.

Messenger. Elizabeth Robins. LC 19-14909. 1919. 1.75. The Century Co.

Messenger. Mona Goodwyn Williams. LC 76-53298. 8.95 (ISBN 0-89256-013-4). Rawson Associates Publishers.

Messenger. Mona Goodwyn Williams. (Signet Book). 1978. 1.95 (ISBN 0-451-08012-2). New American Library.

Messenger. Charles Wright. 1974. (pbk.) 1.25. Manor Books.

Messenger. Charles Stevenson Wright. LC 63-11709. 1963. Farrar, Straus.

Messenger: A Novel by Remy Pseud. Translated from the French by Viola Gerard Garvin. Gilbert Renault-Roulier. LC 54-13038. 1954. Newman Press.

Messenger from Munich. Noel Pierce. LC 72-94120. 1973. 6.95 (ISBN 0-698-10523-0). Coward McCann & Geoghegan.

Messenger of Darkness. Hugh Walker. (Science Fiction Ser.). pap. 1.50 (ISBN 0-87997-452-4, UW1452). DAW Bks.

Messenger of Love. Barbara Cartland. 1971. pap. 1.25 o.p. (V2997). BJ Pub Group.

Messenger of Napoleon: A Dramatic Historical Story. Robert Nethercoat Moffat. LC 19-10458. 1918. The Roxburgh Publishing Company (Inc.

Messenger of the Gods. Phyllis Bottome. LC 27-224832. George H. Doran Company.

Messenger to the Gods. Ivy Kellerman Reed. LC 54-131007. 1955. Vantage Press.

Messenger to the Pharaoh: A Story of Ancient Egypt. Thames Ross Williamson. LC 37-17024. 1937. Longmans, Green and Co.

Messengers of Evil: Being a Further Account of the Lures and Devices of Fantomas. Pierre Souvestre & Allain, Marcel, Joint Author. LC 17-15546. (Their The Fantomas detective novels) $1.35.). 1917. Brentano's.

Messengers of Peace. William S. Parker. (Illus.). 1967. 1.75 o.p. (ISBN 0-8283-1145-5). Branden.

Messengers Will Come No More. Leslie A Fiedler. LC 74-78540. 1974. 8.95 (ISBN 0-8128-1732-X). Stein and Day.

Messer fuer den Ehrlichen Finder. Jorg Steiner. (Suhrkamp Taschenbuecher: 583). 208p. (Ger.). 1980. pap. text ed. 3.90 (ISBN 3-518-37083-9, Pub. by Suhrkamp Verlag Germany). Suhrkamp.

Messer Marco Polo. Donn Byrne. LC 21-16009. 1921. The Century Co.

Messer Marco Polo. Donn Byrne. LC 42-36366. (Half-title: The Modern library of the world's best books. 43). 1942. Modern Library.

Messer Marco Polo. Donn Byrne. LC 47-23565. (On cover: Penguin books. 611). 1946. Penguin Books, Inc.

Messer Marco Polo. Donn Byrne & Charles Buckles Falls. LC 79-10460. 1979. 7.50 (ISBN 0-8376-0437-0). R. Bentley.

Messiah. Gore Vidal. LC 54-5053. 1954. Dutton.

Messiah at the End of Time:: or The Transformation of Miss Mavis Ming. Michael Moorcock. 1978. 1.50 (ISBN 0-87997-358-7). DAW Books.

Messiah of the Cylinder. Victor Rousseau Emanuel. LC 73-13264. (Classics of science fiction). (Illus.). 1974. (ISBN 0-88355-118-7) (ISBN 0-88355-147-0). Hyperion Press.

Messiah of the Cylinder. Victor Rousseau Emanuel. LC 17-295353. 1917. A.C. McClurg & Co.

Messiah of the Cylinder. Victor Rousseau. LC 73-13264. (Classics of Science Fiction Ser). 334p. 1973. 12.50 (ISBN 0-88355-118-7); pap. 3.85 (ISBN 0-88355-147-0). Hyperion Conn.

Messiah: Rev. Ed. Gore Vidal. LC 65-17660. bds., 5.00. Little.

Messiah's Chains. Arnold Posy. LC 63-11734. 1963. Bloch Pub. Co.

Messing up see Willis & His Friends Series.

Messrs. Simon and Schuster Invite the Attention of the Reader to This New Novel "Society". J. P McEvoy. LC 31-24779. 1931. Simon and Schuster, Inc.

Mestico: Or, The War-Path and Its Incidents. A Story of the Creek Indian Disturbances of 1836. M. C Hodges. LC 7-602123. 1850. W. H. Graham.

Mestizo. W C Parks. LC 55-14125. 1955. Macmillan.

Met by Moonlight. Leonora Dorothy Rivers Cook Mackesy. LC 51-10923. 1951. Arcadia House.

Meta Gray: Or, What Makes Home Happy. Maria Jane McIntosh. LC 7-16451. 1859. D. Appleton and Company.

Meta Holdenis: A Novel from the French of Victor Cherbuliez. Victor Cherbuliez. LC 6-27167. (Half-title: Collection of foreign authors, no. 5). 1877. D. Appleton and Company.

Metairie: And Other Old Aunt Tilda of New Orleans Sketches. M. Agnes Thompson. LC 8-19969.

Metal Mistress. Barbara Cameron. (Candlelight Ecstasy Ser.). (Orig.). 1982. pap. 1.75 (ISBN 0-440-15636-X). Dell.

Metal Monster. Abraham Merritt. LC 73-13259. (Classics of science fiction). 1974. (ISBN 0-88355-114-4) (ISBN 0-88355-143-8). Hyperion Press.

Metallic Muse. Lloyd Biggle. 1974. (pbk.) 1.25. DAW Books.

Metallic Muse. Lloyd Biggle, Jr. LC 79-186007. 192p. 1972. 5.95 o.p. (ISBN 0-385-03830-5). Doubleday.

Metallic Muse. Lloyd Biggle, Jr. (Science Fiction Ser). pap. 1.25 o.p. (UY1115). DAW Bks.

Metallic Muse: A Collection of Science Fiction Stories. Lloyd Biggle, Jr. LC 79-186007. (Doubleday science fiction). 1972. 5.95. Doubleday.

Metamorphoses of Ovid. Tr. by A. E. Watts from Latin. LC 80-36845. (Illus.). 432p. 1980. pap. 12.50 (ISBN 0-86547-019-7). N Point Pr.

Metamorphosis. Franz Kafka & Lloyd, Albert Lancaster, Tr. LC 46-8128. 1946. The Vanguard Press, Inc.

Metamorphosis see Seven Short Novel Masterpieces.

Metaphysical Tales: Stories. Eugene K Garber. LC 80-26057. 10.00 (ISBN 0-8262-0325-6). University of Missouri Press.

Metasex, Mirth & Madness. Marco Vassi. LC 75-165. 1975. 7.95 o.p. (ISBN 0-89110-002-4). Penthouse Pr.

Metasex, Mirth & Madness: Erotic Tales of the Absurdly Real. Marco Vassi. LC 75-163. 7.95 (ISBN 0-89110-002-4). Penthouse Press.

Metello: A Novel. Tr. from Italian by Raymond Rosenthal. 1st Amer. Ed. Vasco Pratolini. LC 67-144602. 1968. 5.95. Little, Brown.

Meterorite: Track Two Ninety-One. Gary Paulson. 1979. pap. 2.25 (ISBN 0-440-15583-5). Dell.

Methinks the Lady... S. Guy Endore. LC 45-9739. 1945. Duell, Sloan and Pearce.

Method in His Murder. Thurman Warriner. LC 50-9609. 1950. Macmillan.

Method in Madness. 1st Ed. Doris Miles Disney. LC 57-6306. (Crime Club selection). 1957. Published for the Crime Club by Doubleday.

Methodist Faun. Anne Parrish. LC 29-20108. 1929. Harper & Brothers.

Methodist: Or, Incidents and Characters from Life in the Baltimore Conference. A Novel. Miriam Fletcher. LC 6-41689. 1859. Derby & Jackson.

Methods of Dr. Scarlett. Alexander Kinnan Laing. LC 37-13972. Farrar & Rinehart.

Methods of Lady Walderhurst. Frances Hodgson Burnett. LC 1-27300. Frederick A. Stokes Company.

Methods of Lady Walderhurst. Frances Hodgson Burnett. LC 16-25017. 1916. Frederick A. Stokes Company.

Methods of Maigret. Translated by Nigel Ryan. Georges Simenon. LC 57-552555. 1957. Published for the Crime Club by Doubleday.

Methods of Mr. Ames. Frederic Carrel. LC 8-22560. M. Kennerley.

Methods of Uncle Abner. Melville Davisson Post. LC 75-313000. 1974. 6.95. Aspen Press.

Methusaleh Enzyme. Fred M. Stewart. LC 76-122333. 1970. 5.95 (ISBN 0-87795-002-4). Arbor Hse.

Methuselah Enzyme: A Novel. Fred Mustard Stewart. LC 76-122333. (Illus.). 1970. 5.95. Arbor House.

Methuselah; Fantasy on a Moral Theme. Kenneth Joseph Foreman. LC 68-30860. (Illus.). 1968. 1.95. John Knox Press.

Methuselah's Children. Robert Anson Heinlein. LC 58-6984. Gnome Press.

Methuselah's Children. Robert Anson Heinlein. (Signet science fiction, T4226). 1973. (pbk.) 0.75. New American Lib.

Metrical Visions. George Cavendish. Ed. by Anthony S. Edwards. (Renaissance English Text Society Ser.: Vol. 9). 1980. 19.50 (ISBN 0-911028-19-6). Newberry.

Metroland. Julian Barnes. LC 79-3797. 1980. 10.95 (ISBN 0-312-53169-9). St. Martin's Press.

Metronome, a Novel. 1st Ed. Frederick H Romig. LC 53-851691. 1953. Exposition Press.

Metropolis. Thea Von Harbou. LC 75-12608. (Gregg Press science fiction series). 1975. 12.50 (ISBN 0-8398-2317-7). Gregg Press.

Metropolis. Upton Beall Sinclair. LC 8-5582. 1908. Moffat, Yard & Company.

Metropolitan Love Story. 1st Ed. Sheila Greenwald, pseud. LC 62-7124. 1962. Doubleday.

Metropolitan Opera Murders. Helen Traubel. LC 51-13551. (Inner sanctum mystery). 1951. Simon and Schuster.

Metropolitans: By Jeanie Drake. Jeanie Drake. LC 11-15078. 1896. The Century Co.

Metropolitee. Alexandre Le Maitre. Repr. of 1682 ed. 23.00 o.p. Clearwater Pub.

Metropolites: Or, Know They Neighbor. A Novel. St. Clar, Robert. LC 8-5787. American News Company.

Metti Von der Insel: Eine Erzahlung. Dorothea Mass Hollatz. LC 54-39533. 1954. Franck.

Mettle of the Pasture. James Lane Allen. LC 74-94468. 1969. AMS Press.

Mettle of the Pasture. James Lane Allen. LC 3-15441. 1903. The Macmillan Company.

Mettle of the Pasture. James Lane Allen. LC 38-35068. (Half-title: Macmillan's standard library). 1912. Grosset & Dunlap.

Metzerott, Shoemaker... Katharine Pearson Woods. LC 8-37248. T. Y. Crowell & Co.

Mexican. Bill Burchardt, pseud. LC 76-45263. 1977. 5.95 o.p. (ISBN 0-385-12388-4). Doubleday.
Mexican Assassin. Richard H Blum. LC 78-3693. 8.95 (ISBN 0-684-15567-2). Scribner.
Mexican Assignment. James Kendall McClarren. LC 57-651013. 1957. Funk & Wagnalls.
Mexican Bill, the Cowboy Detective. E. O. Tillburn. (On cover: Pinkerton detective series, v. 26). 1889. Laird & Lee.
Mexican Connection. Alexander Mason. (Leisure Book). 1.50 (ISBN 0-8439-0486-0). Nordon Pubns.
Mexican Gallop. Gregory Mason & Carroll, Richard, Joint Author. LC 37-4014. Green Circle Books.
Mexican Girl. Frederick Thickstun Clark. LC 6-25345. (On cover: Ticknor's paper series of choice reading. no. 41). 1888. Ticknor & Company.
Mexican Gunhawk. Byron Highfill. 176p. (Orig.). 1980. pap. 1.95 (ISBN 0-89083-650-7). Zebra.
Mexican Hearth: A Story of Jean Hendricks Pseud. Dorothy Schultz. LC 52-11676. 1952. Exposition Press.
Mexican Masquerade. Charles Neville Brand. LC 38-137933. Dodge Publishing Company.
Mexican Ranch: Or, Beauty for Ashes. Janie Prichard Duggan. LC 6-34630. (On cover: The crown series). 1894. American Baptist Publication Society.
Mexican Romance. Edith Roelker Curtis. LC 68-55071. 1969. 4.50. Dorrance.
Mexican Short Stories. Arturo Torres-Rioseco & Sims, Elmer Richard, Joint Ed. 1932. Prentice-Hall, Inc.
Mexican Sin Trip. Curtiss Knox. 192p. pap. 1.95 o.p. (6128). Brandon.
Mexican Slay Ride. Sidney Weintraub. LC 62-21304. (Raven book). 1962. Abelard-Schuman.
Mexican Spy: Or, The Bride of Buena Vista. A Tale of the Mexican War. Harry Halyard. 1848. F. Gleason.
Mexican Standoff. Glen Chase, pseud. (Cherry Delight Ser: No. 21). (Orig.). 1975. pap. 1.25 o.p. (LB260ZK, Leisure Bks). Nordon Pubns.
Mexican Standoff. Glen Chase, pseud. (Cherry Delight, 21). 1975. (pbk.) 1.25. Leisure Books.
Mexican Standoff. Alex Hawk, pseud. (Orig.). 1970. pap. 0.60 o.p. (63-355). Paperback Lib.
Mexican Time. Zoe Lund Schiller. 1943. The Macmillan Company.
Mexican Trail. William Fitzgerald Jenkins. LC 33-783. A. H. King, Inc.
Mexican Village. Josephina Niggli. LC 45-35184. 1945. The University of North Carolina Press.
Mexican Village: By Josephina Niggli; Designs by Marion Fitz-Simons. Josephina Niggli. LC 45-35184. 1968. pap., 2.95. Univ. of N.C. Pr.
Mexico Bay. Paul Horgan. 240p. 1982. 12.95 (ISBN 0-374-20880-8). FS&G.
Mexico City Blues. John Kerouac. 1959. pap. 4.95 (ISBN 0-394-17287-6, E552, Ever). Grove.
Mexico Run. Lionel White. (Fawcett gold medal book). 1974. (&bk.) 0.95. Fawcett.
Mexico Versus Texas. Anthony Ganilh. LC 79-104459. 1970. (ISBN 0-8398-0652-3). Literature House.
Mexico Versus Texas, a Descriptive Novel, Most of the Characters of Which Consist of Living Persons. Anthony Ganilh & A Texian. LC 7-18725. 1838. N. Siegfried, Printer.
Mey Wing: A Romance of Cathay. Thomas Watson Houston. LC 12-4765. 1912. Crane & Company.
Meyer & Son: A Novel. Dwight Tilton & Addison, Thomas. LC 8-37191. 1908. The C. M. Clark Publishing Company.
Meyer, Meyer. Helen Hudson. LC 67-11361. 1967. Dutton.
Mezhdu Sobakoi I Volkom. Sasha Sokolov. 1980. 15.00 (ISBN 0-88233-339-9); pap. 5.00 (ISBN 0-88233-340-2). Ardis Pubs.
Mezzanine. Edward Frederic Benson. LC 16-20058. 1926. Cassell and Company, Ltd.
Mezzanine. Edward Frederic Benson. LC 26-177680. George H. Doran Company.
Mezzo Cammin. Winston Weathers. (Orig.). 1981. pap. 4.50 (ISBN 0-912484-20-9). Joseph Nichols.
Mezzogiorno. Francis Browning Drew Bickerstaffe-Drew. LC 11-945. 1911. B. Herder.
Mezzoni the Brigand: Or, The King of the Mountains. Maturin Murray Ballou. LC 6-6094. (On cover: The sea and shore series, no. 12). Street & Smith,
MF. Anthony Burgess. 1971. 5.95 o.p. (ISBN 0-394-43608-3). Knopf.
MF. John Anthony Burgess Wilson. LC 79-136319. 1971. 5.95 (ISBN 0-394-43608-3). Knopf.
Mhudi. new ed. Solomon Tshekisho Plaatje. 1978. pap. 5.00 (ISBN 0-89410-031-9, Co-Pub by Heinemann Educ. Bks). Three Continents.
Mhudi. new ed. Solomon Tshekisho Plaatje. Ed. by Tim Couzens. (Illus.). 165p. 1975. 22.00x (ISBN 0-909078-01-7, Pub. by Quagga Press). Three Continents.
Mhudi, an Epic of South African Native Life a Hundred Years Ago. Solomon Tshekisho Plaatje. LC 74-100298. 1970. Negro Universities Press.
Mhudi: An Epic of South African Native Life a Hundred Years Ago. Solomon Tshekisho Plaatje. LC 74-100298. Repr. of 1930 ed. 12.25x (ISBN 0-8371-2930-3, Pub. by Negro U Pr). Greenwood.
Mi Abuela Fumaba Puros. Sabine R. Ulibarri. (Illus.). 1977. pap. 6.00 (ISBN 0-88412-105-4). Tonatiuh-Quinto Sol Intl.
Mi Amigo: A Novel of the Southwest. 1st Ed. William Riley Burnett. LC 59-926125. 1959. A. A. Knopf.
Mi Amigo, Pablito. J. N. McCune. 4.00 o.p. Carlton.
Mi Amor Te Espera. new ed. Silvia Orejuela. (Pimienta Collection Ser). 160p. (Span.). 1974. pap. 1.00 (ISBN 0-88473-201-0). Fiesta Pub.
Mi Manera de Amar. new ed. Luisa Estrella. (Pimienta Collection Ser). 160p. (Span.). 1974. pap. 1.00 (ISBN 0-88473-196-0). Fiesta Pub.
Mi Querido Rafa. Rolando Hinojosa. LC 81-68066. 96p. (Orig.). 1981. pap. 7.50 (ISBN 0-934770-10-7). Arte Publico.
Mi Viene in Mente: A Story in Images. Gianfranco Baruchello. (Illus., Orig.). pap. 10.00x o.p. Wittenborn.
Mia. Robert Nathan. LC 70-98656. 1970. 4.95. Knopf.
Mia. 1st. Amer. Ed. Derek Monsey. LC 65-11107. 1966. bds., 4.95. Knopf.
Miami. Arthur Moore. (Heart of the City Series). 1975. 1.50 (ISBN 0-671-80175-9). Pocket Books.
Miami Beach. J. C. Conaway. (O.s.i.). 1976. pap. 1.50 o.s.i. (BT50987). Belmont-Tower.
Miami Beach. J. C Conaway. Belmont Tower.
Miami Golden Boy. Herbert D Kastle. LC 71-85237. 1969. 5.95. B. Geis Associates.
Miami Marauder. Mike Barry. (Lone Wolf). (Berkley medallion book: Vol. 9). 1974. (pbk.) 0.95 (ISBN 0-425-02715-5). Berkley Pub Co.
Miami Millions. John Maccabee. 416p. (Orig.). 1980. pap. 2.50 (ISBN 0-553-13313-6). Bantam.
Miami Murder-Go-Round. 1st Ed. Marston La France. LC 51-12886. 1951. World Pub. Co.
Miasma. Elisabeth Sanxay Holding. LC 29-6176. E. P. Dutton & Co., Inc.C.
Miau. Benito Perez Galdos. Tr. by J. M. Cohen. 1963. 5.95 o.p. Dufour.
Miau. Tr. from Spanish by J. M. Cohen. Benito Perez Galdos. LC 64-25516. 1965. bds., 5.95. Dufour.
Miau. Tr. from Spanish, Introd. by J. M. Cohen. Benito Perez Galdos. (L181). 1966. pap., 1.75. Penguin.
Micah Clarke. Arthur Conan Doyle. 5.25 o.p. Transatlantic.
Micah Clarke. edited by virginia kirkus, with illustrations by henry c. pitz. ed. Arthur Conan Doyle & Kirkus, Virginia, 1893- Ed. LC 29-26906. 1929. Harper & Brothers.
Micah Clarke: His Statement As Made to His Three Grandchildren, Joseph, Gervas, & Reuben, During the Hard Winter of 1734... Arthur Conan Doyle. (On cover: Harper's Franklin square library. no. 648). 1889. Harper & Brothers.
Micah Clarke: His Statement As Made to His Three Grandchildren, Joseph, Gervas, & Reuben, During the Hard Winter of 1734... Arthur Conan Doyle. LC 4-163033. 1894. Harper & Brothers.
Micah Clarke: His Statement, As Made to His Three Grandchildren, Joseph, Gervas, and Reuben, During the Hard Winter of 1734... Arthur Conan Doyle. (On cover: Seaside library. Pocket ed. no 2109). 1895. G. Munro's Sons.
Micah Clarke: His Statement As Made to His Three Grandchildren, Joseph, Gervas, & Reuben, During the Hard Winter of 1734... new impression. ed. Arthur Conan Doyle. LC 25-15496. 1919. Longmans, Greene and Co.
Mice Are Not Amused. Kathleen Douglas Hewitt. LC 43-7889. 1943. Mystery House.
Mice for Amusement: A Novel. Betsey Riddle Hutton Zum Stolzenberg. LC 35-67243. 1934. E. P. Dutton & Co., Inc.
Michael. Edward Frederic Benson. LC 16-19218. 1916. 1.35. George H. Doran Company.
Michael. Edward Frederic Benson. LC 24-285434. 1919. A. L. Burt Company.
Michael. Elizabeth Bonham De La Pasture. LC 13-9245. E. P. Dutton & Company.
Michael: A Tale of the Masterful Monk. Owen Francis Dudley. 1948. Longmans, Green.
Michael and the Magic Man. Kathleen M Sidney. LC 79-16946. 1.95 (ISBN 0-399-12473-X). Berkley Pub. Corp.: Distributed by Putnam.
Michael and Theodora: A Russian Story. Amelia Edith Huddleston Barr. LC 6-7982. Bradley & Woodruff.
Michael Anonymous. James Maurice Scott. LC 73-143689. (Illus.). 1971. (ISBN 0-8019-5619-6). Chilton Book Co.
Michael Beam. Richard Matthews Hallet. LC 39-300653. 1939. Houghton Mifflin Company.
Michael Bond's Book of Bears. Michael Bond. (Puffen book). (Illus.). 1974. (ISBN 0-14-030662-5). Penguin.
Michael Cassidy, Sergeant. Herman Cyril McNeile. LC 16-16301. George H. Doran Company.
Michael Dred, Detective: The Unravelling of a Mystery of Twenty Years. Marie Connor Leighton & Robert Leighton. LC 75-32761. (Literature of Mystery and Detection). (Illus.). 1976. 19.00 (ISBN 0-405-07882-X). Arno Press.
Michael Evil Deeds. Edward Phillips Oppenheim. 1979. Repr. of 1923 ed. lib. bdg. 15.00 (ISBN 0-8495-4212-X). Arden Lib.
Michael Forth. Mary Johnston. LC 19-25938. Harper & Brothers.
Michael Joe: A Novel of Irish Life. William Cotter Murray. LC 65-12606. bds., 5.95. Appleton Dist. Meredith.
Michael O'Halloran. Gene Stratton Porter. LC 15-16590. 1915. Doubleday, Page & Company.
Michael O'Halloran. Gene Stratton Porter. LC 16-21933. 1916. 0.50. C. Scribner's Sons.
Michael O'Halloran. Gene Stratton Porter. LC 21-168580. 1920. Grosset & Dunlap.
Michael Ross, Minister. Annie E Holdsworth. LC 2-833719. 1902. Dodd, Mead & Company.
Michael Ryan, Capitalist: A Story of Labor. Faxon Franklin Duane Albery. LC 74-22766. (Labor Movement in Fiction and Non-Fiction). 1976. 10.00 (ISBN 0-404-58402-0). AMS Press.
Michael Ryan, Capitalist: A Story of Labor. Faxon Franklin Duane Albery. LC 13-11539. 1913. Rowfant Press and Bindery.
Michael Scarlett: A History. James Gould Cozzens. LC 25-227543. 1925. A. & C. Boni.
Michael Shayne Takes Over. Davis Dresser. LC 42-20562. H. Holt and Company.
Michael Shayne's Long Chance. Davis Dresser. LC 44-1893. 1944. Dodd, Mead & Company.
Michael Shayne's Triple Mystery. Davis Dresser. LC 48-1650. (Fingerprint mystery). 1948. Ziff-Davis Pub. Co.
Michael Strogoff: A Courier of the Czar... Jules Verne & Wyeth, Newell Convers, 1882- LC 27-229491. C. Scribner's Sons.
Michael Strogoff: Courier of the Czar. Jules Verne. (Classic romances of literature. vol. 1). The Spencer Press.
Michael Strogoff: Or, The Courier of the Czar. Jules Verne. LC 52-46788. 1892. Phoenix Pub. Co.
Michael Strogoff: Or, The Courier of the Czar. Jules Verne. LC 1-9844. (Seaside library. Pocket ed. no. 1020). 1887. G. Munro.
Michael Strogoff: Or, The Courier of the Czar. Jules Verne. LC 4-17512. A. L. Burt.
Michael Strogoff, the Courier of the Czar. Jules Verne & Kingston, William Henry Giles, 1814-1880, Tr. LC 12-39780. 1877. Scribner, Armstrong & Company.
Michael Thwaites's Wife. Miriam Michelson. LC 9-15091. 1909. 1.50. Doubleday, Page & Company.
Michael Torey. 1st Ed. Janet Mathewson. LC 62-7661. 1962. Doubleday.
Michaeleen. Patrick Joseph Carroll. LC 44-21024. 1940. The Ave Maria Press.
Michaell Donavan. 1st Ed. Salvatore De Rose. LC 53-857436. 1952. Pageant Press.
Michaelmas. Algis Budrys, pseud. LC 76-56214. 7.95 (ISBN 0-399-11653-2). Berkley Pub. Corp.: Distributed by Putnam.
Michaelmas Tree. Helen Ashfield. LC 82-5659. 9.95 (ISBN 0-312-53225-3). St. Martin's Press.
Michaelmos. Algis Budrys. (Berkley Book). 1978. 1.95 (ISBN 0-425-03812-2). Berkley Pub. Corp.
Michael's Crag. Grant Allen. LC 6-480. 1893. Rand, McNally & Company.
Michael's Evil Deeds. Edward Phillips Oppenheim. LC 23-17473. 1923. 2.00. Little, Brown, and Company.
Michael's Girl. Sophie Kerr. LC 42-3952. 1942. Farrar & Rinehart.
Michael's Wife. Alice DeFord. LC 34-35481. 1934. Lothrop, Lee and Shepard Company.
Michael's Wife. Marlys Millhiser. LC 72-79526. (Fawcett world library). 1974. (pbk.) 0.95. Fawcett.
Michail Gourakin: The Heart of a Russian. Lappo-Danilevskaia, Nadezhda Aleksandrovna (Liutkevich) LC 18-3368. 1917. R. M. McBride & Company.
Michel Gulpe. Everit Bogert Terhune. 1902. G. W. Dillingham Company.
Michel, Michel: A Novel. Robert Lewis. LC 67-20799. 1967. Simon and Schuster.
Michelangelo, the Florentine. Sidney Alexander. LC 57-10045. 1957. Random House.
Michelangelo: The Florentine, a Novel. Sidney Alexander & Michel Angelo Buonarroti. LC 57-100459. 1957. Random House.
Michelangelo to Our Shores. Michael Pette. LC 46-37659. 1946. The Hobson Book Press.
Michele. Tr. by L. E. LaBan. pap. 1.95 o.p. (6034). Brandon.
Micheline. Hector Henri Malot & Miller, Hettie E., Tr. LC 7-24362. (On cover: The optimus series, no. 7). 1891. Donohue, Henneberry & Co.
Michelle! Barney Parris. 1973. (pbk.) 1.25. Dell.
Michelle Mustn't Know. Joy Chamberlain. 272p. 1983. pap. 2.95 (ISBN 0-515-05699-5). Jove Pubns.
Michigan Ghost Towns, Vol. 1. Roy L. Dodge. (Illus.). 191p. (Orig.). 5.00 (ISBN 0-934884-01-3). Glenson Pub.
Michigan Ghost Towns, Vol. 2. Roy L. Dodge. (Illus.). 120p. (Orig.). 5.50 (ISBN 0-934884-03-X). Glenson Pub.
Michigan Ghost Towns, Vol. 3. Roy L. Dodge. (Orig.). write for info. (ISBN 0-934884-02-1). Glenson Pub.
Michigan Murders. Edward Keyes. 1981. pap. 2.95 (ISBN 0-671-43787-9). PB.
Michigan on Mendammas. Millie Ellen Lyke. (Illus.). 1973. 20.00.
Michigan's Irish Hills. Lita Hindman. LC 36-202484. 1936. The Elite Publishing Company.
Mickelsson's Ghosts. John Gardner. LC 81-48114. (Illus.). 1982. 16.95 (ISBN 0-394-50468-2). Knopf.
Mickey Finn Idylls. Ernest Jarrold. LC 99-4933. 1899. Doubleday & McClure Co.
Mickey Peck: A Novel. Orville Elder. LC 19-2711. The Roxburgh Publishing Company, Inc.
Micky. Olin Linus Lyman. LC 5-39870. 1905. R. G. Badger.
Micky. Evelyn Sharp. LC 6-16642. 1905. Macmillan and Co., Limited.
Micky, Th' Tough Mugg O' the Slums. Olive Emma de Gonville Ure. LC 44-51206. 1944. The William-Frederick Press.
Micmac. Susan Carleton Jones. LC 4-10479. 1904. H. Holt and Company.
Micro-Techs. Clark Darlton. (Perry Rhodan#55). (Illus.). 1974. (pbk.) 0.95. Ace Books.
Microbe Murders. Frederick George Eberhard. LC 36-1426. The Macaulay Company.
Microcosm: A Novel. Maureen Duffy. LC 66-11064. 5.95. S. &S.
Microcosm: An Anthology of the Short Story. Ed. by Donna Lorine Gerstenberger. LC 69-13160. 1969. Chandler Pub. Co.; Distributors: Science Research Associates, Chicago.
Microcosmic God: And Other Stories from Modern Masterpieces of Science Fiction. Ed. by Samuel Moskowitz. (60-335). 1968. Macfadden.
Microcosmic God & Other Stories from Modern Masterpieces of Science Fiction. Ed. by Samuel Moskowitz. 1968. pap. 0.60 o.p. (60-335). Manor Bks.
Microcosmic Tales: One Hundred Wondrous Science Fiction Short-Short Stories. Ed. by Isaac Asimov et al. LC 79-66641. 1980. 12.95 (ISBN 0-8008-5238-9). Taplinger.
Microwave Factor. Nicholas Brady, pseud. (Belmont Tower Book). 1977. 1.75 (ISBN 0-505-51170-3). Tower Pubns.
Microwave Factor. Aaron Fletcher. 304p. 1982. pap. 3.25 cancelled (ISBN 0-505-51857-0). Tower Bks.
Microwave Factor. Aaron Fletcher. 304p. pap. 3.25 (ISBN 0-8439-2010-6, Kable Bks). Dorchester Pub Co.
Mid-Century. Charles Angoff. LC 72-9853. 1973. 6.95 (ISBN 0-498-01339-1). A. S. Barnes.
Mid-Century: An Anthology of Distinguished Contemporary American Short Stories. Ed. by Orville Prescott. LC 57-11177. (Pocket library, PL65). 1958. Pocket Books.
Mid-City Hospital, No. 4: Crisis. Virginia Barclay. 1982. pap. 2.25 (ISBN 0-451-11415-9, AE1415, Sig). NAL.
Mid-City Hospital, No. 5: Double Face. Virginia Barclay. 1982. pap. 2.25 (ISBN 0-451-11554-6, AE1554, Sig). NAL.
Mid-City Hospital, No. 6: Life Support. Virginia Barclay. 1982. pap. 2.50 (ISBN 0-451-11769-7, AE1769, Sig). NAL.
Mid Green Pastures. Erminda Esler. LC 6-38147. 1895. J. Pott & Company.
Mid-Ocean Tragedy. John Hawk. LC 27-16580. George H. Doran Company.
Mid Watch: A Novel. Edward Ellsberg. LC 54-5576. Dodd, Mead.
Midaq Alley. Najib Mahfuz. Tr. by Trevor Le Gassick from Arabic. LC 81-51658. ix, 246p. 1981. 12.00x o.s.i. (ISBN 0-89410-282-6); pap. 6.00x o.s.i. (ISBN 0-89410-281-8). Three Continents.
Midas. Piers Kelaart. 1982. pap. 2.50 (ISBN 0-451-11618-6, AE1618, Sig). NAL.
Midas and Son. Stephen McKenna. LC 19-542820. George H. Doran Company.
Midas Coffin. Simon Quinn. (Inquisitor#5). 1975. (pbk.) 0.95. Dell.
Midas Compulsion. Ivan Shaffer. LC 69-20445. 1969. 6.95. M. Evans; Distributed in Association with Dutton.
Midas Consequence: A Novel. Michael Ayrton. LC 75-14804. 1976. 6.95 (ISBN 0-385-08470-6). Doubleday.

Midas Touch. Walter Winward. LC 81-18533. 13.95 (ISBN 0-671-42569-2). Simon and Schuster.

Midas Touch: A Novel. Lucille Stern. LC 57-11768. 1957. Citadel Press.

Midas World. Frederik Pohl. LC 83-2896. 1983. 13.95 (ISBN 0-312-53182-6). St. Martin's.

Midcentury. Dos Passos, John. LC 61-5359. 1961. Houghton, Mifflin.

Midday Moon. Dorothy Daniels. pap. 0.60 o.p. Lancer.

Middle Age Madness. Marian Edna Dormitzer Shamock. LC 35-27042. 1935. D. Appleton-Century Company, Incorporated.

Middle Age of Mrs. Eliot. Angus Wilson. 350p. 1982. pap. 6.95 (ISBN 0-14-001502-7). Penguin.

Middle Age of Mrs. Eliot: A Novel. Angus Wilson. LC 59-6869. 1959. Viking Press.

Middle Aged Love Stories. Josephine Dodge Daskam Bacon. LC 74-169538. (Short story index reprint series). (Illus.). 1971. (ISBN 0-8369-3285-4). Books for Libraries Press.

Middle Aged Love Stories. Josephine Dodge Daskam Bacon. LC 3-10796. 1903. C. Scribner's Sons.

Middle-Aged Maidens. Gwen Kelly. LC 77-350016. 1976. (ISBN 0-17-005064-5). Thomas Nelson (Australia)

Middle-Aged Man on the Flying Trapeze. James Thurber. Repr. lib. bdg. 13.55x (ISBN 0-89190-268-6). Am Repr-Rivercity Pr.

Middle-Aged Man on the Flying Trapeze. James Thurber. 1977. Repr. of 1935 ed. lib. bdg. 17.95x (ISBN 0-89244-059-7). Queens Hse.

Middle Aged Princess & the Frog. Alison Zier. LC 78-51357. (Illus., Orig.). 1978. pap. text ed. 3.95 (ISBN 0-918606-01-2). Heidelberg Graph.

Middle Child. Eleanor Morse. LC 32-20524. 1932. H. C. Kinsey & Company, Inc.

Middle Class. Nanette Kutner. 1932. R. Long & R. R. Smith, Inc.

Middle Classes: Les Petits Bourgeois) Honore De Balzac. Tr. by Clara Courtenay Poynter Bell. LC 99-337. (Half-title: Comedie humaine, ed. by G. Saintsbury). 1898. J. M. Dent and Co.

Middle Course. Edith Evelyn Jaffray Bigelow. LC 3-20588. 1903. The Smart Set Publishing Co.

Middle Fork & the Sheepeater War. Cort Conley & John Carrey. LC 80-17367. 1977. pap. 9.95 (ISBN 0-9603566-1-4). Backeddy Bks.

Middle Generation. John Davys Beresford. LC 33-4732. E. P. Dutton & Co., Inc.

Middle Greyness. Alec John Dawson. LC 6-32252. J. Lane.

Middle Ground. Ursula Zilinsky. LC 68-24140. 1968. Lippincott.

Middle Heaven. 1st Ed. Mona Gardner. LC 50-13208. 1950. Doubleday.

Middle Mist. Mary Renault, pseud. LC 45-1022. 1945. W. Morrow and Company.

Middle Mist. Mary Renault, pseud. LC 78-3856. 1978. 9.95 (ISBN 0-89244-080-5). Queens House.

Middle Mist. Mary Renault. 1975. (pbk.) 1.50. Popular Library.

Middle of Midnight. William Gilmore Beymer. LC 47-757. 1947. Whittlesey House, McGraw-Hill Book Company, Inc.

Middle of the Fire: A Novel. Irwin R Blacker. LC 73-143934. 1971. 10.00 (ISBN 0-684-12340-1). Scribner.

Middle of the Journey. Lionel Trilling. LC 57-1039. (Doubleday anchor books. A 98). 1957. Doubleday.

Middle of the Journey. Lionel Trilling. LC 76-626. 1976. 8.95 (ISBN 0-684-14619-3). Scribner.

Middle of the Journey. Lionel Trilling. (Equinox Book). 1976. 3.95 (ISBN 0-380-00520-4). Avon Books.

Middle of the Journey. Lionel Trilling. LC 47-314726. 1947. Viking Press.

Middle of the Journey. uniform ed. Lionel Trilling. LC 79-3369. (works of Lionel Trilling). ((Series: Trilling, Lionel, 1905-1975.). (Works.). 1980. 14.95 (ISBN 0-15-159547-X). Harcourt Brace Jovanovich.

Middle of the Road. Philip Hamilton Gibbs. LC 29-8993. 1925. Grosset & Dunlap.

Middle of the Road: A Novel. by Philip Gibbs. Philip Hamilton Gibbs. LC 23-5517. George H. Doran Company.

Middle of Things. Joseph Smith Fletcher. LC 22-194835. 1922. A. A. Knopf.

Middle Parts of Fortune. Frederic Manning. 1979. pap. 4.95 (ISBN 0-452-25202-4, Z5202, Plume). NAL.

Middle Parts of Fortune. Frederic Manning. LC 77-72368. 1977. 8.95 (ISBN 0-312-53185-0). St Martin.

Middle Parts of Fortune: Somme & Ancre, 1916. Frederic Manning. LC 77-72368. 8.95 (ISBN 0-312-53185-0). St. Martin's Press.

Middle Passage. Roland Barker & Doerflinger, William, Joint Author. LC 39-5779. 1939. The Macmillan Company.

Middle Passage. Daniel Chase. LC 23-145609. 1923. The Macmillan Company.

Middle Passage. Paul Metcalf. LC 75-21931. 1976. 5.00 (ISBN 0-912330-33-3, Dist. by Inland Bk). Jargon Soc.

Middle Passage. Lewis Frank Tooker. LC 20-16345. 1920. The Century Co.

Middle Pasture. Mathilde Bilbro. LC 17-26262. 1.25. Small, Maynard and Company.

Middle Temple Murder. Joseph Smith Fletcher. LC 19-15735. 1919. A. A. Knopf.

Middle Temple Murder. Joseph Smith Fletcher. LC 79-54145. 1980. 3.00 (ISBN 0-486-23910-1). Dover Publications.

Middle Ten. Frances Murray. 1895. The World Publishing Company.

Middle Tree: A Novel. Joan O'Donovan. LC 61-2192. 1961. Morrow.

Middle Wall. Edward Marshall. LC 4-6739. 1904. G. W. Dillingham Company.

Middle Wall: By Betty Webster. Elisabeth Webster Peplow. LC 54-18555. 1953. Zondervan Pub. House.

Middle Watch: A Romance of the Navy. John Hay Beith & King-Hall, Stephen, 1893- Joint Author. LC 30-23086. 1930. Houghton Mifflin Company.

Middle Window. Elizabeth Goudge. LC 39-920509. Coward-McCann, Inc.

Middle Window. Elizabeth Goudge. 1973. (pbk) 1.50 (ISBN 0-515-03177-1). Pyramid Books.

Middle Years. Victor Rousseau Emanuel. LC 25-59607. 1925. Minton, Balch & Company.

Middle Years see Author of Beltraffio.

Middlearth: A Modern Pilgrimage by Foot and Greyhound to Middle-Earth, After J. R. R. Tolkien, with Nikon and Notepad. Ted Simmons. LC 74-24634. (Illus.). 4.95 (ISBN 0-912662-06-9). Fur Line Press,: Distributed by B & H Books.

Middlefolks: A Novel. Richard James Talbot. LC 28-22360. The John C. Winston Company.

Middleman. David Chandler. LC 80-66504. 1981. 12.95 (ISBN 0-87795-279-5). Arbor Hse.

Middleman. David Chandler. 368p. 1982. pap. 2.75 (ISBN 0-345-30024-6). Ballantine.

Middleman. Mark Smith. 1977. 1.95 (ISBN 0-380-01766-0). Avon Books.

Middleman. 1st Ed. Mark Smith. LC 67-112172. bds., 5.95. Little.

Middlemarch. George Eliot. (Harcourt library of English and American classics). 1962. Harcourt, Brace & World.

Middlemarch. George Eliot. 1963. Washington Square Press.

Middlemarch. George Eliot. LC 65-29849. (Penguin English library, EL2). 1965. Penguin Books.

Middlemarch. George Eliot. LC 56-13878. (Riverside editions, B6). 1956. Houghton Mifflin.

Middlemarch. George Eliot. (Seaside library, v. 4 no. 70). 1877. G. Munro.

Middlemarch. George Eliot. LC 7-3078. (On cover: Seaside library. Pocket ed. no. 31). 1883. G. Munro.

Middlemarch: A Story of Provincial Life. George Eliot. LC 1-31175. (personal edition of George Eliot's works). Doubleday, Page & Co.

Middlemarch: A Study of Provincial Life. harper's library ed. George Eliot. (Added t.-p.: Novels of George Eliot, v. 6-7). 1872-73. Harper & Brothers.

Middlemarch: A Study of Provincial Life. George Eliot. (On cover: Lovells library, v. 4, no. 174). 1883. J. W. Lovell Company.

Middlemarch: A Study of Provincial Life. George Eliot. LC 1-29910. (Half-title: The works of George Eliot. Foleshill edition. v.7-8). 1900. Little, Brown and Company.

Middlemarch: A Study of Provincial Life. George Eliot. LC 43-357763. 1873. Harper & Brothers.

Middlemarch: A Study of Provincial Life. harper's library ed. George Eliot. LC 6-40736. (Added t.-p.: Novels of George Eliot, v. 6-7). 1876. Harper & Brothers.

Middlemarch, a Study of Provincial Life. George Eliot. (Half-title: Everyman's library, ed. by Ernest Rhys. Fiction. no. 854 and 855). 1930. J. M. Dent & Sons, Ltd.

Middlemarch: A Study on Provincial Life. George Eliot. LC 99-2777. T. Y.Crowell & Co.

Middlemarch: A Studyof Provincial Life. George Eliot & Neff, Mrs. Wanda (Fraiken) 1880. LC 26-26547. (modern readers' series). 1926. The Macmillan Company.

Middlemarch: An Authoritative Text, Backgrounds, Reviews and Critism. George Eliot & Bert G. Hornback. LC 76-22805. (Norton critical edition). 15.95 (ISBN 0-393-04430-0). Norton.

Middlemen. Giuseppe Bianco. LC 26-7652. 1925. Cassell and Company, Ltd.

Middleway: Tales of a New England Village. Kate Whiting Patch. LC 7-34084. 1897. Copeland and Day.

Middy: Or, Scenes from the Life of Edward Lascelles... Edward Lascelles. LC 7-13844. 1838. E. L. Carey and A. Hart.

Midge. Henry Cuyler Bunner. LC 48-35762. 1886. C. Scribner's Sons.

Midge. Henry Cuyler Bunner. LC 4-15416. 1902. C. Scribner's Sons.

Midge & Decker. Robert Mayer. LC 81-62204. 10.95 (ISBN 0-89479-094-3). A&W Publishers.

Midhaven. William Edward Daniel Ross. 1975. 4.95. Avalon Books.

Midheaven. Ken Kuhlken. LC 79-23760. 1980. 10.95 (ISBN 0-670-41757-2). Viking Press.

Midland Saga: The Story of an Iowa Family. Miriam Monger. LC 31-9262. Dorrance & Company, Inc.

Midlander. Booth Tarkington. LC 24-535. 1923. Doubleday, Page & Company.

Midlander. Booth Tarkington. LC 24-5810. 1924. Doubleday, Page & Company.

Midlanders, by Charles Tenney Jackson... Charles Tenney Jackson. LC 12-23757. The Bobbs-Merrill Company.

Midnight. Octavus Roy Cohen. LC 22-2220. 1922. Dodd, Mead & Company.

Midnight. Mao Dun. 1980. 10.95 (ISBN 0-8351-0614-4). China Bks.

Midnight. John Russo. 1980. pap. 2.25 (ISBN 0-671-83432-0). PB.

Midnight. Yen-Ping Shen. LC 77-551858. (Illus.). 1976. (u.s.) 1.80. C & W Pub. Co.: Distributor, Era Book Co.

Midnight. Yen-Ping Shen. LC 72-5088. (Illus.). 1970. Center for Chinese Research Materials, Association of Research Libraries.

Midnight. Yen-Ping Shen. LC 75-36237. (Illus.). 1979. 45.00 (ISBN 0-404-14485-3). AMS Press.

Midnight and Percy Jones. Vincent Starrett. LC 38-17820. Covici, Friede.

Midnight at Mallyncourt. T. E Huff. LC 74-16607. 1975. 7.95 (ISBN 0-399-11445-9). Berkley Pub. Corp.: Distributed by Putnam.

Midnight at Mallyncourt. Edwina Marlow. (Berkley Medallion Book). 1976. (pbk.) 1.75 (ISBN 0-425-03114-4). Berkley Publishing Corp.

Midnight at Mears House: A Detective Story. Harrison Jewell Holt. LC 12-996084. 1912. 1.25. Dodd, Mead and Company.

Midnight at the Well of Souls. Jack L Chalker. LC 76-56148. 1977. 1.75 (ISBN 0-345-25768-5). Ballantine Books.

Midnight Auto. Educational Challenges, Inc. (Turning Point I Ser.). (gr. 7-12). pap. text ed. 3.40 (ISBN 0-8009-1891-6). McCormick-Mathers.

Midnight Bell. Patrick Hamilton. LC 29-29433. 1930. Little, Brown, and Company.

Midnight Bell: A German Story Founded on Incidents in Real Life. Francis Lathom. LC 68-98584. (Northanger Set of Jane Austen Horrid Novels). 1968. Folio Pr.

Midnight Birds: Stories by Contemporary Black Women Writers. Mary Helen Washington. LC 79-7627. 1980. 3.95 (ISBN 0-385-14878-X). Anchor Books.

Midnight Boy. George Agnew Chamberlain. LC 49-10044. 1949. Bobbs-Merrill Co.

Midnight Bridge. Mary N. Korte. 1970. pap. 2.50 (Pub. by Oyez). SBD.

Midnight Clear. William Wharton. LC 81-20897. 1982. 12.95 (ISBN 0-394-51967-1). Knopf: Distributed by Random House.

Midnight Colt. Glenn Balch. 4.00 o.p. (ISBN 0-8446-0020-2). Peter Smith.

Midnight Convoy & Other Stories. S. Yizhar. Tr. by Rueben Ben-Yosef et al from Heb. (Institute for Translation of Hebrew Literature Ser). 273p. 1971. 5.00 o.p. (Pub. by Keter Inc). Intl Schol Bk Serv.

Midnight Court & The Adventures of a Luckless Fellow. Brian Merriman. Tr. by Percy A. Ussher from Gaelic. LC 75-28825. (Illus.). 80p. Repr. of 1926 ed. 9.50 (ISBN 0-404-13817-9). AMS Pr.

Midnight Cowboy. James Leo Herlihy. 1976. (pbk.) 1.50 (ISBN 0-380-00576-X). Avon.

Midnight Cowboy: A Novel. James Leo Herlihy. LC 65-15022. 4.95. S. & S.

Midnight Creek: By A. M. Bell Pseud. Alladine Bell. LC 54-5608. 1954. Crowell.

Midnight Cry: A Novel. Permelia Jane Marsh Parker. Dodd, Mead & Company.

Midnight Dancers. Anne Maybury. LC 73-4623. 1973. 6.95 (ISBN 0-394-48407-X). Random House.

Midnight Dancers. Anne Maybury. 1974. (pbk.) 1.50. Bantam Books.

Midnight Diary. 1st Ed. Michael Burn. LC 53-8931. 1953. Lippincott.

Midnight Elopement: Or, Robert Wayne's Choice. An Emotional Novel. Emma Sanders. LC 8-47746. (peerless series, no. 71). 1893. J. S. Ogilvie.

Midnight Encounter. Glenna Finley, pseud. (Orig.). 1981. pap. 1.95 (ISBN 0-451-12095-7, AJ2095, Sig). NAL.

Midnight Express. Billy Hayes & William Hoffer. 1977. 7.95 o.p. (ISBN 0-525-15605-4). Dutton.

Midnight Ferry to Venice. Ben Healey. 189p. 1982. 10.95 (ISBN 0-8027-5461-9). Walker & Co.

Midnight Fires. Andrea Layton, pseud. LC 79-83964. 304p. 1979. pap. 2.95 (ISBN 0-86721-049-4). Playboy Pbks.

Midnight Flyer. Nanci H. Cochran. 224p. (Orig.). 1982. pap. 2.50 (ISBN 0-523-41329-7). Pinnacle Bks.

Midnight Folk. John Masefield. LC 32-26474. 1932. The Macmillan Company.

Midnight Fox. Betsy Cromer Byars. LC 68-27566. (Illus.). 1975. (pbk.) 1.25 (ISBN 0-380-00197-7). Avon.

Midnight Fury. Susan E. Gross. 320p. 1981. pap. 2.75 (ISBN 0-449-14392-9, GM). Fawcett.

Midnight Gardener. pseud. 1st ed. Charles William White. LC 48-7807. 1948. Harper.

Midnight Guest: A Detective Story. Fred Merrick White. LC 7-20516. 1907. T. J. McBride & Son.

Midnight Hag. Joan Margaret Fleming. LC 66-25143. 1966. I. Washburn.

Midnight Hangman. Morgan Hill. (Dan Colt Western Ser.: No. 6). (Orig.). 1982. pap. 2.25 (ISBN 0-440-16375-7). Dell.

Midnight Hearse and More Ghosts: A Second Collection of True Tales and Legends. Elliot O'Donnell. LC 72-85970. 1969. 4.95. Taplinger Pub. Co.

Midnight House and Other Tales. William Fryer Harvey. LC 75-46275. (Supernatural and Occult Fiction). 1976. 14.00 (ISBN 0-405-08133-2). Arno Press.

Midnight in Arcady. Peggy Gaddis, pseud. LC 40-31625. 1940. Arcadia House, Inc.

Midnight in Morocco. Charles Stanley Strong. LC 43-10303. 1943. Phoenix Press.

Midnight Intimacies. pap. 1.95 o.p. (V1041T, Venus). Grove.

Midnight Intimacies: Being the Secret Life of a Warm Blooded Woman in Search of Passionate Pleasures. LC 74-171037. (Venus library). 1.95. Grove Press.

Midnight King. Georges Delamare. Tr. by Bierman, I. Louis. LC 27-22995. 1927. Rae D. Henkle Co., Inc.

Midnight Lace: A Novel. MacKinlay Kantor. LC 48-5129. 1948. Random House.

Midnight Lady and the Mourning Man. David Anthony. 1973. (pbk.) 1.25. Warner Paperback Library.

Midnight Lady and the Mourning Man. David Anthony. LC 69-11501. 1969. 5.95. Bobbs-Merrill.

Midnight Line: A Novel. Thomas Savage. LC 75-28252. 7.95 (ISBN 0-316-77141-4). Little, Brown.

Midnight Lover. Charlotte Lamb, pseud. (Harlequin Presents Ser.). 192p. 1982. pap. 1.75 (ISBN 0-373-10528-2). Harlequin Bks.

Midnight Magic. Christine D. Cott. pap. price not set. Harlequin Bks.

Midnight Mail... Henry Holt. LC 31-14178. Pub. for the Crime Club, Inc., by Doubleday, Doran & Company, Inc.

Midnight Man. Loren D Estleman. LC 82-944. (Amos Walker Mystery). 1982. 12.95 (ISBN 0-395-32204-9). Houghton Mifflin.

Midnight Man. Henry Kane. (Raven House Mysteries Ser.). 224p. 1981. pap. 2.25 (ISBN 0-373-63009-3, Pub. by Worldwide). Harlequin Bks.

Midnight Man: 1st Amer. Ed. Henry Kane. LC 66-10696. (Cock robin mystery). 1966. bds., 3.95. Macmillan.

Midnight Marriage. A Novel. Amanda Minnie Douglas. (On cover: The Manhattan series, v. 1, no. 1). 1888. A. L. Burt.

Midnight Marriage. A Novel. Amanda Minnie Douglas. (On cover: The select series, no. 48). 1890. Street & Smith.

Midnight Marriage. A Novel. Michael Angelo Holmes. LC 7-5177. J. S. Oglivie & Company.

Midnight Mass. Paul Frederic Bowles. LC 81-4803. 1981. 14.00 (ISBN 0-87685-477-3) (ISBN 0-87685-478-1) (ISBN 0-87685-476-5). Black Sparrow Press.

Midnight Match. Florence Stevenson. LC 80-10664. 1980. 9.95 (ISBN 0-89340-254-0). J. Curley & Associates.

Midnight Movies. David A Kaufelt. LC 79-19664. 9.95 (ISBN 0-440-05244-0). Delacorte Press.

Midnight Murder. Paul Herring. LC 32-20615. (S. Low, Marston & co., ltd.) has title: The murder of Margot Midnight.). 1932. J. B. Lippincott Company.

Midnight Murder. Kenneth Robeson. (Avenger,#24). 1974. (pbk.) 0.95. Warner Paperback Library.

Midnight Mystery. Bertram Atkey. LC 28-676930. 1928. D. Appleton & Company.

Midnight Never Comes. Jack Higgins. (Fawcett gold medal book). 1975. (pbk.) 0.95. Fawcett.

Midnight of the Ranges. George Gilbert. 1920. 1.75. Little, Brown, and Company.

Midnight Oil. Victor Sawdon Pritchett. 1973. pap. 3.95 (ISBN 0-394-71952-2, Vin). Random.

Midnight Patient. Egon Hostovsky. LC 54-8694. 1954. Appleton-Century-Crofts.

Midnight Patriot. Emma Lillie Patterson. LC 49-9716. 1949. Longmans, Green.

Midnight People. John Knittel. LC 31-294899. 1931. Doubleday, Doran & Company, Inc.

Midnight People see Vampires at Midnight.

Midnight Plumber. 1st Ed. Maurice Procter. LC 57-118021. 1957. Harper.

Midnight Plus One. Gavin Lyall. LC 65-12299. 4.50. Scribners.

Midnight Queen. A Novel. May Agnes Early Fleming. LC 6-39949. 1888. G. W. Dillingham.

Midnight Queen: Or, Leaves from New-York Life. George Lippard. 1853. Garrett & Co.

Midnight Raymond Chandler. Raymond Chandler. LC 74-162005. 1971. 10.00 (ISBN 0-395-12712-2). Houghton Mifflin Co.

Midnight Reader: Great Stories of Haunting and Horror, Edited, and with an Introduction. Ed. by Philip Van Doren Stern. LC 42-10680. 1942. H. Holt and Company.

Midnight Riders. James D. Sayers. Orig. Title: Beyond Midnight Chasm. 1970. pap. 0.75 o.p. (ISBN 0-447-74624-3). Lancer.

Midnight, Rodeo Champion: Illustrated by C. W. Anderson. Robert Edward Gard. LC 51-9605. 1951. Duell, Sloan and Pearce.

Midnight Round-up: A Powder Valley Western. Peter Field. 1944. Jefferson House.

Midnight Sailing. Lawrence Goldtree Blochman. LC 38-18384. Harcourt, Brace and Company.

Midnight Sailing. Susan Hufford. (Queen-size gothic). 1975. (pbk.) 1.25. Popular Library.

Midnight Special. Richard M. Garvin & Edmond G. Addeo. LC 70-134214. 1971. 6.95 o.p. (ISBN 0-87035-020-X). Geis.

Midnight Specials: An Anthology for Train Buffs and Suspense Aficionados. Bill Pronzini. 1978. 1.75 (ISBN 0-380-01941-8). Avon Books.

Midnight Specials: An Anthology of Suspense Stories About Trains. Bill Pronzini. LC 76-46227. 1977. 10.95 (ISBN 0-672-52308-6). Bobbs-Merrill.

Midnight Sun: A Pilgrimage. Fredrika Bremer. Tr. by Mary Botham Howitt. LC 6-22827. (On cover: Seaside library. Pocket ed., no. 187). G. Munroe.

Midnight Sun: A Story of Russian Court Life, Based on the Motion-Picture Story Adapted. Holger Lundberg. LC 26-13382. (On cover: Popular plays and screen library). 1925. Jacobsen-Hodgkinson Corporation.

Midnight Sun's Magic. Betty Neels. (Harlequin Romances Ser.). (Orig.). 1980. pap. 1.25 (ISBN 0-373-02314-6, Pub. by Harlequin). PB.

Midnight Suppers. Susan Monsky. LC 82-12050. 1983. 13.95 (ISBN 0-395-32558-7). Houghton Mifflin.

Midnight Surrender. Margaret M. Cleaves. (Orig.). 1980. pap. 1.50 (ISBN 0-440-15023-X). Dell.

Midnight: Translated into English. Julien Green. Tr. by Holland, Vyvyan Beresford. LC 36-18876. 1936. Harper & Brothers.

Midnight Treasure. William Rollins. LC 29-6671. 1929. Coward-McCann, Inc.

Midnight Tree: A Fairy Tale of Terror. Charles Higham. 1.95 (ISBN 0-671-82183-0).

Midnight Water: A Novel. Geoffrey Norman. LC 82-25131. 13.50 (ISBN 0-525-15585-6). Dutton.

Midnight Whispers. Patricia Matthews & Clayton Matthews. 480p. (Orig.). 1981. pap. text ed. 3.50 (ISBN 0-553-13389-6). Bantam.

Midnighters: a Documentary Novel Based on the Memoirs of Martin Allen Ribakoff. Rowland Barber. LC 72-108065. 1970. 5.95. Crown Publishers.

Midnight's Children: A Novel. Salman Rushdie. LC 80-2712. 1981. 13.95 (ISBN 0-394-51470-X). Knopf.

Midnight's Children: A Novel. Salman Rushdie. LC 80-2712. 1982. 4.95 (ISBN 0-380-58099-3). Avon Books.

Midpoint. Isabella Holt. LC 55-10542. 1955. Bobbs-Merrill.

Midshipmaid: The Tale of a Naval Manoeuvre. John Hay Beith. LC 33-16240. 1933. Houghton Mifflin Company.

Midshipman. William Henry Giles Kingston. (Lovell's library, v. 7, no. 338). 1884. J. W. Lovell Company.

Midshipman Days. Virginia Cruse Watson. LC 13-19328. 1913. Houghton Mifflin Company.

Midshipman. Marmaduke Merry. William Henry Giles Kingston. (On cover: Seaside library. Pocket ed., no. 763). 1886. G. Munro.

Midshipman Plowright. James T Pole. LC 69-15552. (Illus.). 1969. 4.50. Dodd, Mead.

Midshipman Ralph Osborn at Sea: A Story of the U.S. Navy. Edward Latimer Beach. LC 10-28166. W. A. Wilde Company.

Midshipman Stanford: A Story of Midshipman Life at Annapolis. Henry Howard Clark. LC 16-140494. 1916. Lothrop, Lee & Shepard Co.

Midst of Life: A Romance. Mina K Curtiss. LC 33-10982. 1933. Houghton Mifflin Company.

Midst the Wild Carpathians: A Novel. Mor Jokai. Tr. by Bain, Robert Nisbet. LC 98-251. 1898. L. C. Page and Company (Incorporated.

Midstream View. 1974. (pbk.) 2.00. Published by University Palisades Community Adult School.

Midsummer Bride. Mary Christianna Milne Lewis. 192p. (Orig.). 1980. pap. 1.50 (ISBN 0-671-57007-2, Pub. by Silhouette Bks). S&S.

Midsummer Century. James Blish. 1974. (pbk.) 0.95. DAW Books.

Midsummer Century. James Blish. LC 75-180061. (Doubleday science fiction). 1972. 4.95. Doubleday.

Midsummer Day's Dream. Henry Brereton Marriott Watson. LC 6-31656. 1906. D. Appleton and Company.

Midsummer Eve. Louise Bergstrom. (Candlelight romance). 1974. (pbk.) 0.75. Dell.

Midsummer Fires: A Long Fiction. James Aswell. LC 48-3592. 1948. W. Morrow.

Midsummer Lokki. Eva-Lis Wuorio. LC 67-12578. (Rinehart suspense novel). 1967. Holt, Rinehart and Winston.

Midsummer Lokki see Explosion.

Midsummer Madness. Ellen Warner Olney Kirk. LC 7-12360. 1884. J. R. Osgood and Company.

Midsummer Madness. LC 50-6083. 1950. Published for the Crime Club by Doubleday.

Midsummer Madness. Sterling North. LC 33-647. Grosset & Dunlap.

Midsummer Madness. Victor Wolfson. pap. 0.50 o.p. Lancer.

Midsummer Madness: Tr. from the Spanish of Emilia Pardo Bazan. Pardo Bazan, Emilia. Tr. by Loring, Amparo. 1907. The C. M. Clark Publishing Co.

Midsummer Magic: By Walter Bamfylde Pseud.... Tom Bevan. LC 15-20590. 1915. G. P. Putnam's Sons.

Midsummer Masque. Jill Tattersall. LC 73-151926. 1972. 6.95. Morrow.

Midsummer Masque. Jill Tattersall. LC 80-12244. 1980. 11.95 (ISBN 0-89340-272-9). J. Curley & Associates.

Midsummer Music. Stephen Graham. LC 27-3369. George H. Doran Company.

Midsummer Mystery. Gordon Hall Gerould. LC 25-7072. 1925. D. Appleton and Company.

Midsummer Night Madness: And Other Stories. Sean O'Faolain & Garnett, Edward. LC 32-7616. 1932. The Viking Press.

Midsummer Nightmare. Frances Moyer Ross Stevens. LC 45-6793. 1945. Pub. for the Crime Club by Doubleday, Doran & Co., Inc.

Midsummer Night's Murder. Ware Torrey. LC 42-7634. 1942. E. P. Dutton and Co., Inc.

Midsummer Passion: And Other Stories from "Jackpot". Erskine Caldwell. LC 49-1754. (New Avon library 177). 1948. Avon Pub. Co.

Midsummer Tempest. Poul Anderson. LC 73-11696. (Doubleday science fiction). 1974. 5.95 (ISBN 0-385-05505-6). Doubleday.

Midsummer Wooing. Mary E. Stone Bassett. LC 13-8246. 1913. 1.25. Lothrop, Lee & Shepard Co.

Midsummernight. Carl Wilhelmson & Ward, Lynd Kendall, Illus. LC 30-30569. 1930. Farrar & Rinehart.

Midsummer's Nightmare. Elizabeth Shenkin. LC 60-5909. 1960. Rinehart.

Midtown North. Mike Curtis. 1976. (pbk.) 1.25. Leisure Books.

Midtown North. Myer Kutz. 1976. pap. 1.25 o.p. (LB351ZK, Leisure Bks). Nordon Pubns.

Midwatch. Keith Wilson. 1972. 7.50 (ISBN 0-912090-15-4); pap. 2.45 (ISBN 0-912090-14-6). Sumac Mich.

Midway. Donald S Sanford. (Illus.). 1976. (pbk.) 1.75 (ISBN 0-553-02824-3). Bantam Books.

Midway at Midnight. Ted Mark, pseud. 192p. (Orig.). 1975. pap. 1.50 o.p. (ISBN 0-532-15236-0). Woodhill.

Midway at Midnight. Ted Mark, pseud. 192p. (Orig.). 1975. pap. 1.50 o.p. (ISBN 0-532-15236-0). Manor Bks.

Midway Plaisance. The Experience of an Innocent Boy from Vermont in the Famous Midway. A. J Dockarty. LC 6-34208. 1894. Chicago World Book Co.

Midway to Murder. Margaret Tayler Yates. 1941. The Macmillan Company.

Midwest Story. Augusta Walker. LC 59-13821. 1959. Dial Press.

Midwestern Village. Richard A. Coffey. Ed. by Paul Deegan. LC 70-156065. (World's People Ser.). (Illus.). (gr. 5-9). 1971. text ed. 7.95 (ISBN 0-87191-077-2). Creative Ed.

Midwich Cuckoos. John Beynon Harris. LC 69-14658. 1969. 4.50. Walker.

Midwich Cuckoos. John Beynon Harris. LC 57-12242. 1958. Ballantine Books.

Midwich Cuckoos. John Wyndham, pseud. LC 69-14658. 1969. 4.50 o.p. (ISBN 0-8027-5511-9). Walker & Co.

Midwife. Gary Courtier. 1982. pap. 3.95 (ISBN 0-451-11503-1, AE1503, Sig). NAL.

Midwife: A Novel. Gay Courter. LC 80-26324. 1981. 13.95 (ISBN 0-395-29463-0). Houghton Mifflin.

Midwife of Pont Clery: A Novel. 1st American Ed. Flora Sandstrom. LC 57-5984. 1957. J. Day Co.

Midwinter. John Buchan. LC 73-144915. 1971. (ISBN 0-403-00878-6). Scholarly Press.

Midwinter. John Buchan. LC 23-12113. George H. Doran Company.

Midwinter Madness. Anthony Stuart, pseud. LC 79-52254. 1979. 8.95 (ISBN 0-87795-237-X). Arbor Hse.

Midwinter Madness. Anthony Stuart, pseud. 192p. 1981. pap. 2.25 (ISBN 0-445-04677-5). Popular Lib.

Midwinter Madness: A Novel. Julian Anthony Stuart Hale. LC 79-52254. 8.95 (ISBN 0-87795-237-X). Arbor House.

Midworld. Alan Dean Foster. LC 75-35865. 1976. 1.50 (ISBN 0-345-25364-7). Ballantine Books.

Miernik Dossier. Charles McCarry. LC 72-88662. 1973. 7.95 (ISBN 0-8415-0245-5). Saturday Review Press.

Mifanwy: A Welsh Singer. Beynon Puddicombe. LC 8-6604. (Half-title: Appleton's town and country library, no. 224). 1897. D. Appleton and Company.

Might As Well Be Dead. Rex Stout. 160p. 1980. pap. 1.95 (ISBN 0-553-14447-2). Bantam.

Might As Well Be Dead: A Nero Wolfe Novel. Rex Stout. LC 56-11950. 1956. Viking Press.

Might As Well Be Dead, a Nero Wolfe Novel. Rex Stout. 1974. (pbk.) 0.95. Bantam Books.

Mightiest Machine. John Wood Campbell. 1972. Ace.

Mightiest Machine: Illus. by Robert Pailthrope. John Wood Campbell. LC 47-11483. 1947. Hadley Pub. Co.

Mighty Afternoon. Charles Kris Mills. LC 80-1037. 1980. 8.95 (ISBN 0-385-17194-3). Doubleday.

Mighty Atom. Marie Corelli. LC 6-28743. 1896. J. B. Lippincott Company.

Mighty Barbarians: Great Sword & Sorcery Heroes. Ed. by Hans S. Santesson. 1969. pap. 0.75 o.p. (74-556). Lancer.

Mighty Blochead: A Johnny Fletcher Mystery. Frank Gruber. LC 42-6756. Farrar & Rinehart, Inc.

Mighty Distance. Georgia McKinley. LC 65-19298. 1965. 4.95. Houghton.

Mighty Fortress. Le Grand Cannon. LC 46-20988. 1946. H. Holt and Company.

Mighty Friend: A Modern Romance of Labor-War-Fare, Country-Life and Love... Edmond Loutil. Tr. by Hannon, John. LC 13-4146. 1913. 1.50. Benziger Brothers.

Mighty Hunters: Being an Account of Some of the Adventures of Richard and Helen Carson in the Forests and on the Plains of Chiapas in Mexico. Ashmore Russan. LC 9-28460. 1909. 1.35. Longmans, Green, and Co.

Mighty Land. Cliff Farrell. LC 74-12685. 216p. 1975. 6.95 o.p. (ISBN 0-385-09759-X). Doubleday.

Mighty Lobo. Frederick Faust. LC 62-14230. 1975. (pbk.) 1.25. Warner.

Mighty Man of Valor: Gideon, the Sword of the Lord. Weldon Phillip Keller. LC 78-26975. 5.95 (ISBN 0-8007-0997-7). F.H. Revell Co.

Mighty Manslayer. Harold Lamb. LC 69-12222. 1969. 5.95. Doubleday.

Mighty Marvel Treasury. Marvel Comics. 1976. pap. 5.95 (ISBN 0-671-22186-8, Fireside). S&S.

Mighty Milo: A Series of Incidents in His Now Famous Career by Fred Anspach, Also Known As Honeyboy Hackenschmidt, by Phillips Rogers Pseud. Albert Edward Idell. LC 54-6512. 1954. Hermitage House.

Mighty Mountain. Archie Binns. LC 40-33100. 1940. C. Scribner's Sons.

Mighty Oaks. Ann Stewart Griffey. LC 68-54480. 1969. 3.00. Dorrance.

Mighty Ones: Great Men and Women of Early Bible Days. Meindert De Jong. (Illus.). 1959. Harper.

Mighty Swordsmen. Ed. by Hans S. Santesson. 1970. pap. 0.75 o.p. (ISBN 0-447-74707-X). Lancer.

Mighty Thing. Denison Halley Clift. LC 33-782551. The Macaulay Company.

Mighty Thor. (Super Hero Collection). (Illus., Orig.). 1968. pap. 0.50 o.p. (72-125). Lancer.

Mighty Waters. 1st Ed. Harry W Dennis. LC 56-5513. Vantage Press.

Mignon. Mrs. Bridges. (On cover: Seaside library. Pocket ed., no. 729). 1886. G. Munro.

Mignon. Mrs. Bridges. 1887. J. W. Lovell Company.

Mignon. James Mallahan Cain. LC 62-12310. 1962. Dial Press.

Mignon. A Tale. Tr. from the French. Henrietta Eliza Vaughan Stannard. 1868. P. O'Shea.

Mignon G. Eberhart's Mystery Book. Mignon Good Eberhart. LC 45-6792. 1945. The World Publishing Company.

Mignon: Or, Bootles' Baby, a Novelette. Jules Romain Tradieu. LC 8-155251. (Harper's handy series, no. 3). 1885. Harper & Brothers.

Mignon: Or, Bootles' Baby. A Novelette. Jules Romain Tradieu. (On cover: The seaside library. Pocket ed. no. 492). 1885. G. Munro.

Mignonette. Joseph Shearing. pap. 0.95 o.p. (02511, Collier). Macmillan.

Mignonette: A Novel. Joseph Shearing. LC 48-753769. 1948. Harper.

Mignonnette. An Ideal Love Story. Linda Marguerite Sangree Allen. LC 6-44. 1885. G. W. Carleton & Co.; Etc., Etc.

Mignon's Husband. A Novelette. Henrietta Eliza Vaughan Stannard. (On cover: Seaside library. Pocket ed. no. 1032). 1887. G. Munro.

Mignon's Secret. Henrietta Eliza Vaughan Stannard. (On cover: The seaside library. Pocket ed. no. 876). 1886. G. Munro.

Mignon's Secret: And Wanted--a Wife. Henrietta Eliza Vaughan Stannard. LC 8-13851. (Harper's handy series, no. 118). 1887. Harper & Brothers.

Migrants of the Stars: Being an Account of the Discovery of the Marvelous Land of Niames, and the Secret of Its Inhabitants. A. H Barzevi & Keller, Marc F. LC 31-18180. The Classic Press.

Migration. David Grew. LC 28-5866. 1928. C. Scribner's Sons.

Migrations. Ken McCullough. 1972. pap. 1.00 (Pub. by Stone-Marrow Pr). SBD.

Migrations: An Arabesque in Histories. Evelyn Scott. LC 27-767127. 1927. A. & C. Boni.

Migrations of the Heart. Marita Golden. LC 82-45248. 264p. 1983. 15.95 (ISBN 0-385-17519-1, Anchor Pr). Doubleday.

Miguel De Cervantes-Saavedra: Two Cervantes Short Novels: El Curioso impertinente & El Celoso extremeno. Miguel de Cervantes de Saavedra. Ed. by F. F. Pierce. 1970. pap. 4.30 (ISBN 0-08-015781-5). Pergamon.

Miguel of the Bright Mountain. Raymond Otis. LC 76-57531. (Zia book). 1977. 3.95 (ISBN 0-8263-0447-8). University of New Mexico.

Miguel Street. Vidiadhar Surajprasad Naipaul. (Caribbean Writers Ser.). 1974. pap. 3.50x (ISBN 0-435-98645-7). Heinemann Ed.

Miguel Street. Vidiadhar Surajprasad Naipaul. 1977. pap. 3.95 (ISBN 0-14-003302-5). Penguin.

Miguel Street. Vidiadhar Surajprasad Naipaul. 1960. 3.95 o.p. (ISBN 0-8149-0167-0). Vanguard.

Mihu the Detective. 1982. pap. 2.50 (ISBN 0-87306-168-3). Feldheim.

Mike & Psmith. P. G. Wodehouse. 1967. 3.25 o.p. British Bk Ctr.

Mike & Psmith. Pelham Grenville Wodehouse. 1966. 2.75 o.p. Verry.

Mike Dime. Barry Fantoni. LC 80-24901. 1981. 9.95 (ISBN 0-531-09948-2). F. Watts.

Mike Fink. rev. ed. Emerson Bennett. LC 75-104415. 1970. (ISBN 0-8398-0162-9). Literature House.

Mike Fink: A Legand of the Ohio. rev. ed. Emerson Bennett. LC 7-34420. 1853. J. A. & U. P. James.

Mike Fink: A Legend of the Ohio. Emerson Bennett. LC 7-34421. 1848. Robinson & Jones.

Mike Flannery on Duty and off. Ellis Parker Butler. 1909. 0.50. Doubleday, Page & Company.

Mike Fletcher. George Moore. LC 76-20121. (Decadent Consciousness). 1977. 26.00 (ISBN 0-8240-2770-1). Garland Pub.

Mike Moriarty, Alderman. Hans Stevenson Beattie. 1894. Columbia Publishing Co.

Mike Shayne Mystery Magazine. V. 1- Sept. 1956- LC 59-31784. Renown Publications.

Mike Stevens, Teenage Sleuth. T. W. Lamb, Jr. 3.00 o.p. Carlton.

Mike Was Here. Connie M. Hunt. LC 81-68368. 1981. 4.95 (ISBN 0-8054-5648-1). Broadman.

Miklos Alexandrovitch Is Missing. Anne Edwards. LC 70-96781. 1970. 5.95. Coward-McCann.

Mila Eighteen. Leon M. Uris. 576p. 1981. pap. 3.50 (ISBN 0-553-14701-3). Bantam.

Mila Eighteen. Leon M. Uris. LC 61-9562. 14.95 (ISBN 0-385-02076-7). Doubleday.

Mila Nadaya. Michael Simko. LC 67-27357. 1968. Dorrance.

Miladi" Being Sundry Little Chapters Devoted to Your Day-Dreams, Dear Miladi, and Your Realizations,-Harking Back to Your Education, Your Experience in the Industrial World and Your Decision in Favor of the Claims of Home, and Coming Down to the Development of Your Love, the Building of Your House O'dreams, and Your Motherhood. Clara Elizabeth Laughlin. LC 3-28560. 1903. F. H. Revell Company.

Milagro Beanfield War. John Treadwell Nichols. LC 74-4409. (Illus.). 1974. 8.95 (ISBN 0-03-012251-1). Holt, Rinehart and Winston.

Milagro Beanfield War. John Treadwell Nichols. (Illus.). 1976. (pbk.) 1.95 (ISBN 0-345-24758-2). Ballantine.

Milan Grill Room. Edward Phillips Oppenheim. LC 41-1831. 1941. Little, Brown and Company.

Milbry: A Novel. Bowen Ingram. LC 78-185082. 1972. 5.95. Crown.
Mild Barbarian: A Novel. Edgar Fawcett. LC 6-38789. 1894. D. Appleton and Company.
Mild Oats. Florence Ryerson & Clements, Colin Campbell, 1894- Joint Author. LC 33-120441. 1933. D. Appleton and Company.
Mildew Manse. Belle Kanaris Maniates. LC 16-1107. 1916. Little, Brown, and Company.
Mildmay Park: Episodes of a Doughboy in a London Hospital. Granivlle Parks Sturgis. LC 20-15386. R. G. Badger.
Mildred. A Novel. Mary Jane Hawes Holmes. LC 13-12934. 1877. G. W. Carleton & Co.
Mildred Arkell. Ellen Price Henry Wood Wood. LC 9-500. T. B. Peterson & Brothers.
Mildred Brainridge: Or, Passing Through the "Vale of Tears.". A. A. Atlantis. LC 6-3841. J. E. Potter and Company.
Mildred Carver: U.S.A. Martha S. Bensley Bruere. LC 19-4967. 1919. The Macmillan Company.
Mildred Farroway's Fortune: Or, Money Not Chief in Christian Work. Maria Frances Hill Anderson. LC 7-25799. 1885. American Baptist Publ. Society.
Mildred Farroway's Fortune: Or, Money Not Chief in Christian Work. L. M. N & N. L. M. LC 7-25799. American Baptist Publication Society.
Mildred Marville: By George Fox Tucker... George Fox Tucker. 1898. G. B. Reed,
Mildred Pierce. James M. Cain. 1973. (pbk) 1.25. Bantam Books.
Mildred Pierce. James Mallahan Cain. LC 41-15433. 1941. A. A. Knopf.
Mildred Pierce. James Mallahan Cain. LC 47-6422. (Penguin books, 591). 1946.
Mildred Pierce. James Mallahan Cain. LC 77-92632. 1978. 1.65 (ISBN 0-394-72582-4). Vintage Books.
Mildred Pierce. Ed. by Albert J. LaValley. LC 80-5107. (Wisconsin - Warner Bros. Screenplay Ser.). (Illus.). 264p. 1980. 17.50 (ISBN 0-299-08370-5); pap. 6.95t (ISBN 0-299-08374-8). U of Wis Pr.
Mildred Trevanion. Margaret Wolfe Hungerford. (On cover: Seaside library. Pocket ed., no. 390). 1885. G. Munro.
Mildred Tucker. Emma Spencer Barber. LC 23-127436. 1923. Printed by the Baptist Banner Publishing Co.
Mildred's Cadet: Or, Hearts and Bell-Buttons. An Idyl of West Point. Alice King Hamilton. LC 7-1225. T. B. Peterson & Brothers.
Mildred's Married Life: And a Winter with Elsie Dinsmore. by martha finley... ed. Martha Finley. LC 12-87646. Dodd, Mead & Company.
Mile Above the Rim: A Novel. Charles Rosen. LC 76-8640. 8.95 (ISBN 0-87795-137-3). Arbor House.
Mile Beyond the Moon. Cyril M. Kornbluth. 176p. (Orig.). 1976. pap. 1.25 (ISBN 0-532-12395-6). Woodhill.
Mile Beyond the Moon. Cyril M. Kornbluth. 176p. 1972. pap. 0.75 o.p. (532-75483-075). Manor Bks.
Mile Beyond the Moon. 1st Ed. Cyril M Kornbluth. LC 58-11318. 1958. Doubleday.
Mile High. Richard Condon. LC 77-80497. (Illus.). 1969. 6.95. Dial Press.
Mile High. Richard Condon. LC 81-12648. 1982. 8.95 (ISBN 0-385-27641-9). Dial Press.
Mile High: A Novel. Henry Cottrell Rowland. LC 21-3504. Harper & Brothers.
Mile High, Mile Deep. Richard K O'Malley. LC 70-169029. 1971. 6.95. Mountain Press Pub. Co.
Mile-Long Spaceship. Kate Wilhelm. LC 79-9107. (Gregg Press science fiction series). (Illus.). 1980. 13.00 (ISBN 0-8398-2600-1). Gregg Press.
Miles to Go. Mark Kram. LC 81-11264. 1982. 10.95 (ISBN 0-688-00451-2). Morrow.
Miles Wallingford: Sequel to Afloat and Ashore. household ed. James Fenimore Cooper. Ed. by Cooper, Susan Fenimore. LC 11-10573. Houghton, Mifflin and Company.
Miles Wallingford. Sequel to "Afloat and Ashore.". James Fenimore Cooper. (On cover: Seaside library. Pocket ed. no. 414). 1885. G. Munro.
Miles Wallingford: Sequel to Afloat and Ashore. James Fenimore Cooper. LC 4-15431. (His Works. Mohawk ed.). 1896. G. P. Putman's Sons.
Miles Wallingford: Sequel to Afloat and Ashore. James Fenimore Cooper. LC 4-19555. 1897. D. Appleton and Company.
Miles Wallingford: Sequel to "Alfloat and Ashore,". James Fenimore Cooper. (On cover: Lovell's library. no. 539). 1885. J. W. Lovell Company.
Milesian Chief. Charles Robert Maturin. LC 79-12041. (Ireland, from the Act of Union, 1800, to the Death of Parnell, 1891). 1979. 128.00. Garland Pub.
Milesian Chief: A Romance, 4 vols. in 2. Charles Robert Maturin. LC 79-8172. Repr. of 1812 ed. Set. 84.50 (ISBN 0-404-62038-8). AMS Pr.
Milestones: A Novel of New Mexico. Maynor D. McGee. LC 26-124671. M. A. Donohue & Co.
Militants: Stories of Some Parsons, Soldiers, and Other Fighters in the World. Mary Raymond Shipman Andrews. LC 7-18098. 1907. C. Scribner's Sons.
Military Belle... Henry Clinton Parkhurst. (On cover: Neely's classic library. no. 1). 1898. F. T. Neely.
Military Foundling. Ben P. Mauborgne. LC 73-88866. 1974. 4.95 (ISBN 0-8059-1956-2). Dorrance.
Military Intelligence--8. Francis Van Wyck Mason. LC 41-6175. 1941. Frederick A. Stokes Company.
Military Life in Italy. Edmondo De Amicis. Tr. by Cady, Wilhelmina W. LC 5-12995. 1882. G. P. Putnam's Sons.
Military Philosophers. Anthony Dymoke Powell. LC 69-12629. (His The music of time). 1969. 4.95. Little, Brown.
Military Secret. Barry, Harry. LC 45-3525. 1944. The Hobson Book Press.
Milk 'n Honey. A. Mati Klarwein. 1973. pap. 5.00 o.p. (ISBN 0-517-50453-7, C N Potter Bks). Crown.
Milk of Wolves: A Novel. Frederick Feikema Manfred. LC 77-153820. (Illus.). 1976. 6.95. Avenue Victor Hugo.
Milk River Range. Lee Floren. LC 49-9521. 1949. Phoenix Press.
Milkbottle H. Gil Orlovitz. LC 67-20522. 1968. 7.50. Delacorte.
Milkbottle H. Gil Orlovitz. LC 67-20522. 1968. Dell Pub. Co.
Milkmaid's Millions. Hugh Austin Evans. LC 48-81073. (His A Sultan's harem mystery). 1948. C. Scribner's Sons.
Milkman of the Manor. Eduard Vilde. LC 77-357720. (Illus.). 1976. 0.91rub. Eesti Raamat.
Milkman's on His Way. David Rees. 128p. 1982. pap. 4.95 (ISBN 0-907040-12-8). Gay Mens Pr.
Milky Way. Fryniwyd Tennyson Jesse. LC 14-11141. 1.25. George H. Doran Company.
Mill. James F. Murphy, Jr. 320p. 1981. pap. 2.95 (ISBN 0-380-77198-5, 77198). Avon.
Mill. Bradley Robinson. LC 61-623566. 1961. Random House.
Mill. Norman Walker. LC 30-65526. 1930. Longmans, Green and Co.
Mill Creek Irregulars. August William Derleth. 3.50 o.p. Arkham.
Mill Girl of Tyrol. M. T. Caldor. (On cover: The idle hour series, no. 18). 1892. The F. M. Lupton Publishing Company.
Mill Girls. George Larkin. 304p. 1981. pap. 2.50 (ISBN 0-505-51618-7). Tower Bks.
Mill House Murder: Being the Last of the Adventures of Ronald Camberwell. Joseph Smith Fletcher & Mathers, Edward Powys, 1892- LC 37-4874. 1937. A. A. Knopf.
Mill in the Meadow, A Stranger Came, The Long Shadow. Jane Donnelly. (Harlequin Romances Ser.). 576p. 1982. pap. 3.50 (ISBN 0-373-20062-5). Harlequin Bks.
Mill Mystery. Anna Katharine Green Rohlfs. (On cover: Knickerbocker novels). 1886. G. P. Putnam's Sons.
Mill Mystery. 29th thousand. ed. Anna Katharine Green Rohlfs. LC 16-25040. 1911. G. P. Putnam's Sons.
Mill of Many Windows. Joseph Smith Fletcher. LC 25-8909. George H. Doran Company.
Mill of St. Herbot. A Breton Story. Katharine Sarah Gadsden Macquoid. LC 7-20280. (Added t.-p.: Harper's half-hour series, no. 21). 1877. Harper & Brothers.
Mill on Mad River. Howard Clark, pseud. LC 48-5966. 1948. Little, Brown.
Mill on the Creek: A Romance of the Hudson. Frederick John Thomas. LC 13-11299. 1913. Broadway Publishing Co.
Mill on the Floss. Eliot, George. LC 63-5994. 1963. Limited Editions Club.
Mill on the Floss. George Eliot. LC 65-2. 1964. Heritage Press.
Mill on the Floss. George Eliot. LC 65-9704. (Harper perennial classic). 1965. Harper & Row.
Mill on the Floss. George Eliot. LC 6-40735. 1860. Harper & Bros.
Mill on the Floss. George Eliot. LC 7-302. 1860. Harper & Brothers.
Mill on the Floss. George Eliot. (Seaside library, v. 1, no. 11). 1877. G. Munro.
Mill on the Floss. George Eliot. 1883. G. Munro.
Mill on the Floss. George Eliot. (Half-title Everyman's library, ed by Ernest Rhys. Fiction. no. 325). 1908. J. M. Dent & Co.
Mill on the Floss. George Eliot. LC 48-41610. (Nelson classics). T. Nelson.
Mill on the Floss. George Eliot. LC 1-29911. (In her works. Foleshill ed. v. 4). 1900. Little, Brown, and Company.
Mill on the Floss. George Eliot & Clark, Mary Elizabeth, 1901- LC 29-9644. (Lettered on cover: The Windsor English classics). F. M. Ambrose Company.
Mill on the Floss. George Eliot & Dorey, Joseph Milnor, 1876- Ed. LC 14-2901. (Standard English classics). Ginn and Company.
Mill on the Floss. George Eliot & Eaton, Harold Thomas, 1894- Ed. LC 28-22145. 1928. Little, Brown, and Company.
Mill on the Floss. George Eliot & Gordon Sherman Haight. LC 78-41113. (Series: Clarendon Edition of the Novels of George Eliot.). (Illus.). 1980. 55.00 (ISBN 0-19-812560-7). Clarendon Press.
Mill on the Floss. George Eliot & Holmes, Mabel Dodge, 1883- LC 46-20549. 1946. Globe Book Company.
Mill on the Floss. George Eliot & Kirkus, Virginia, 1893- Ed. LC 32-28172. 1932. Harper & Brothers.
Mill on the Floss. George Eliot & Ward, Charles Henshaw, Ed. LC 16-23624. (Lake English classics) $0.40). Scott, Foresman and Company.
Mill on the Floss. George Eliot & Ward, Charles Henshaw, 1872- Ed. LC 20-204284. (Half-title: The Lake English classics; general editor, L. T.Damon). Scott, Foresman and Company.
Mill on the Floss. Afterword by Morton Berman. George Eliot. (Signet bk., CT278) Bibl.). New Amer. Lib.
Mill on the Floss: Biographical Introduction. George Eliot. (personal edition of George Eliot's works). 1901. Doubleday, Page & Co.
Mill on the Floss: By George Eliot... George Eliot. LC 17-17434. (Harvard classics shelf of fiction selected byC. W. Eliot. 9). P. F. Collier & Son.
Mill on the Floss: By George Eliot; Ed. with Introduction and Notes. George Eliot & Ausherman, Ida, Ed. LC 13-24401. (Macmillan's pocket American and English classics $0.25). 1913. Macmillan Company.
Mill on the Floss. Introd. by David Daiches. Illus. with Paintings by Wray Manning. George Eliot. LC 65-2. 1964. 6.50. Heritage Dist. Dial.
Mill on the Floss. Introd. by Maxwell H. Goldberg. George Pseud. I. E. Marian Evans Afterwards Cross Eliot. LC 56-565163. (Pocket library, 509). 1956. Pocket Books.
Mill on the Po. Riccardo Bacchelli. LC 75-3800. 1975. 28.50 (ISBN 0-8371-7962-9). Greenwood Press.
Mill on the Po: Translated by Frances Frenaye. Riccardo Bacchelli. LC 50-9509. 1950. Pantheon.
Mill Reef Hall. Ariadne Pritchett. (Orig.). 1970. pap. 0.75 o.p. (T2291, GM). Fawcett World.
Mill Reef Hall. Ariadne Pritchett. 176p. 1973. pap. 0.75 o.p. (T2753, GM). Fawcett World.
Mill Stream. Hortense Lion. LC 41-4812. 1941. Houghton Mifflin Company.
Mill Village: A Novel. Alberic A Archambault. LC 43-16366. 1943. B. Humphries, Inc.
Millbank; or, Roger Irving's Ward: A Novel. Mary Jane Hawes Holmes. 1871. G. W. Carleton & Co.
Millbank; or, Roger Irving's Ward. A Novel. Mary Jane Hawes Holmes. LC 99-933. 1899. G. W. Dillingham Co.
Millbrook. Della Thompson Lutes. LC 38-289694. 1938. Little, Brown and Company.
Millbrook Romance: And Other Tales. A L Donaldson. LC 6-33849. 1893. T. Whittaker.
Millenium. Benjamin Bova. 304p. 1982. pap. 2.75 (ISBN 0-345-30248-6, Del Rey). Ballantine.
Millennial Women. Virginia Kidd. 1979. pap. 1.95 (ISBN 0-440-16301-3). Dell.
Millennium. Ernest Temple Thurston. LC 30-890041. 1930. Doubleday, Doran & Company, Inc.
Millennium: A Novel About People and Politics in the Year 1999. Benjamin Bova. LC 75-33785. 7.95 (ISBN 0-394-49421-0). Random House.
Millennium: A Novel About People and Politics in the Year 1999. Benjamin Bova. (Del Rey Book). 1977. 1.95 (ISBN 0-345-25556-9). Ballantine Books.
Miller and the Mayor's Wife. Pedro Antonio De Alarcon. LC 49-26763. 1949. Avon Pub. Co.
Miller and the Toad. Richard Clifton. LC 8-35965. 1909. Sherman, French & Company.
Miller of Angibault. George Sand. LC 99-2459. 1892. Roberts Brothers.
Miller of Angibault: A Novel. George Sand & Dewey, Mary Elizabeth, 1821-1910, Tr. LC 6-35676. 1871. Roberts Brothers.
Miller of Glanmire: An Irish Story. Con. T Murphy. LC 7-31833. 1895. G. W. Baker.
Miller of Old Church. Ellen Anderson Gholson Glasgow. LC 11-12503. 1911. Doubleday, Page & Company.
Miller of Silcott Mill. A Novel. Maria Darrington Deslonde. LC 6-33881. 1875. G. W. Carleton & Co.
Miller's Dance: A Novel of Cornwell 1812-1813. Winston Graham. LC 82-45596. (Poldark Ser.: No. 9). 384p. 1983. 15.95 (ISBN 0-385-18405-0). Doubleday.
Miller's Daughter. A Novel. Anne Beale. LC 6-10279. (Franklin square library, no. 184). 1881. Harper & Brothers.
Miller's Daughter. A Novel. Anne Beale. LC 28-4878. (Seaside library. v. 67, no. 1358). 1882. G. Munro.
Miller's Holiday: Short Stories from the Northwestern Miller. The Northwestern Miller. Ed. by Edgar, Randolph. LC 20-14297. 1920. The Miller Publishing Company.
Miller's Prologue & Tale. Geoffrey Chaucer. Ed. by J. Winny. LC 76-132283. (Selected Tales from Chaucer). 1970. text ed. 4.95x (ISBN 0-521-08033-9). Cambridge U Pr.
Miller's Tale. Geoffrey Chaucer. (Illus.). 1973. pap. 3.95 (ISBN 0-88388-022-9). Bellerophon Bks.
Millicent Blair. Sarah L Greene. LC 6-455611. 1887. Ingham County Democrat Job Print.
Millicent Halford. A Tale of the Dark Days of Kentucky in the Year 1861. Martha Remick. LC 7-39792. 1865. A Williams & Co.
Millie. Donald Henderson Clarke. LC 30-288882. The Vanguard Press.
Millie. E. V. Cunningham, pseud. 1973. 5.95 o.p. (ISBN 0-688-00150-5). Morrow.
Millie: A Novel. Howard Melvin Fast. LC 72-14363. 1973. 5.95 (ISBN 0-688-00150-5). Morrow.
Millie and Cleve. Jess Carr. 1979. 2.25 (ISBN 0-8439-0615-4). Nordon Pubns.
Millie Lee. Lydia Ann Emerson Porter. D. Lothrop & Co.
Millie Myerson and the Prince of Wales. Penina Spiegel. LC 81-21531. 12.95 (ISBN 0-312-53242-3). St. Martin's Press.
Millie's Boy. Robert Newton Peck. 1973. 5.95 (ISBN 0-394-82699-X). Knopf.
Millie's Daughter. Donald Henderson Clarke. LC 39-6241. The Vanguard Press.
Milliner and the Millionaire. Rebecca Hicks. LC 7-4766. 1852. Lippincott, Grambo & Co.
Million a Minute: A Romance of Modern New York and Paris. Robert Aitken. LC 8-30246. 1908. W. J. Watt & Company.
Million, an Entertainment. Robert Smythe Hichens. LC 41-312152. 1941. Doubleday, Doran and Company, Inc.
Million & One Nights. Terry Ramsaye. (Illus.). 1964. pap. 3.95 o.p. (ISBN 0-671-47337-9). S&S.
Million Dollar Bloodhunt. Joe Millard, pseud. (O.s.i.). 160p. 1975. pap. 1.25 o.s.i. (AQ1466, Award). Univ Pub & Dist.
Million Dollar Madness. Davis Dresser. LC 37-17019. 1937. Hillman-Curl, Inc.
Million Dollar Mare. Jack C Tarlton. LC 77-74588. 5.95 (ISBN 0-8283-1697-X). Branden Press.
Million Dollar Meal Ticket. Jane Littell. 1938. Hillman-Curl, Inc.
Million Dollar Murder. Edward Sidney Aarons. 1969. pap. 0.60 o.p. (R2162, GM). Fawcett World.
Million Dollar Murder: By Edward Ronns Pseud. Edward Sidney Aarons. LC 50-4678. (Gold medal book, 110). 1950. Fawcett Publications.
Million Dollar Mystery: Novelized from the Scenario of F. Lonergan. Harold MacGrath & Lonergan F. LC 15-5554. Grosset & Dunlap.
Million Dollar Nurse. William Arthur Neubauer. LC 66-6014. 1966. Arcadia House.
Million Dollar Snatch. Joseph Como. pap. 1.95 o.p. (8006). Cameo.
Million Dollar Story. Eunice Chapin. LC 38-17713. J. Messner, Inc.
Million-Dollar Suitcase. Alice MacGowan & Newberry, Perry, 1870- Joint Author. Frederick A. Stokes Company.
Million in Jewels. Harlan Page Halsey. LC 7-1184. (On cover: The calument series, no. 29). G. Munro's Sons.
Million Missing Maidens. Mallory T. Knight. (Man from Tomcat Ser). 1967. pap. 0.60 o.p. (A237X, Award). Univ Pub & Dist.
Million Pesos! 1st ed. Jose Romero. LC 64-11282. 1964. Doubleday.
Million Pound Deposit. Edward Phillips Oppenheim. LC 30-2052. 1930. Little, Brown, and Company.
Million Too Much: A Temperance Tale. Julia MacNair Wright. LC 26-23549. 1886. Porter & Coates.
Millionaire. Mikhail Petrovich Artsybashev. LC 78-103491. (Short story index reprint series). 1969. Books for Libraries Press.
Millionaire. Mikhail Petrovich Artsybashev & Pinkerton, Percy E., Tr. LC 15-13361. 1915. B. W. Huebsch.
Millionaire. Edwin Bateman Morris. LC 14-116. 1913. The Penn Publishing Company.
Millionaire. A Novel. Louis John Jennings. (Seaside library, v. 88, no. 1781). G. Munro.

Millionaire Baby. Anna Katharine Green Rohlfs. LC 5-1183. 1905. The Bobbs-Merrill Company.
Millionaire Mystery. Fergus Hume. LC 2-2761. 1901. F. M. Buckles & Company; Etc., Etc.
Millionaire of Rough-and-Ready and Devil's Ford. Bret Harte. LC 11-8216. 1887. Houghton, Mifflin and Company.
Millionaire of Yesterday. Edward Phillips Oppenheim. LC 6-12558. 1906. Little, Brown, and Company.
Millionaire Playboy: A Delirious and True Extravaganza of Inheriting a Fortune and Squandering It. Tom Boggs. LC 33-17935. 1933. The Vanguard Press.
Millionaire Shoemaker. Edward R Williams. LC 29-14374. Dorrance and Company.
Millionaire Tramp. Robert C Givins. LC 6-43972. 1886. Cook County Review.
Millionaire Tramp. Robert C Givins. 0.25. Around the World Publishing Co.
Millionaires. Herbert D Kastle. (Dell bk., 5630). 1973. 1.50. Dell.
Millionaires: A Novel. Herbert D Kastle. LC 76-172797. (Illus.). 1972. Delacorte Press.
Millionaires: A Novel. Frank Frankfort Moore. LC 7-25306. 1898. D. Appleton and Company.
Millionaire's Darling. Griffith James. LC 40-11550. Phoenix Press.
Millionaire's Daughter. Dorothy Eden. LC 74-18304. 1975. (ISBN 0-8161-6248-4). G. K. Hall.
Millionaire's Daughter. Dorothy Eden. LC 74-76234. (Fawcett crest book). 1975. (pbk.) 1.50. Fawcett.
Millionaire's Folly: Or, The Beautiful Unknown. A Sensational Tale of Criminal Life. James Mooney. LC 7-2622. (Mooney & Boland detective series, no. 2). 1888. J. S. Ogilvie.
Millionaire's Folly: Or, The Beautiful Unkown, a Sensational Tale of Criminal Life... L. E Smyles. LC 3108. (On cover: Magnet detective library. no. 139). 1900. Street & Smith.
Millionaire's Love Story. Guy Newell Boothby. LC 2-11738. 1901. F. M. Buckles & Company.
Millionaire's Revenge. Founded Upon Hal Reid's Great Play of New York Life. Helen Burrell D'Apery & Reid, James Halleck. LC 33-28366. (On cover: Play book series. no. 92). J. S. Ogilvie Publishing Company.
Millionaire's Son. Anna Robeson Brown Burr. LC 3-17237. D. Estes & Company.
Millionaire's Wife. A Story of New England Society Life. Prudence Lowell. LC 7-14747. T. B. Peterson & Brothers.
Millionairess. Julian Ralph. 1902. Lothrop Publishing Company.
Millions. Ernest Poole. LC 22-18298. 1922. The Macmillan Company.
Millions for Love. Colette Roberts. LC 32-164369. Covici, Friede.
Millions for Marty. Steuart Mackie Emery. LC 39-11753. 1939. Macrae-Smith Company.
Millions in Motors: A Big Business Story. William West Winter. LC 24-197021. Chelsea House.
Millon Dollar Doll... Alice Muriel Livingston Williamson. LC 24-8789. George H. Doran Company.
Millonarias Lascivas. Juan Casteleiro. (Pimienta Collection Ser). (Illus.). 1976. pap. 1.25 (ISBN 0-88473-250-9). Fiesta Pub.
Mills. Manning O'Brine. LC 79-86307. 1969. 4.95. Lippincott.
Mills Bomb. Clive Egleton. LC 78-55207. 1978. 8.95 (ISBN 0-689-10910-5). Atheneum.
Mills of Colne. Robert Neill. LC 59-10682. (Illus.). 1959. Doubleday.
Mills of God. Elinor Macartney Lane. LC 1-11751. 1901. D. Appleton and Company.
Mills of Mammon. James Hattan Brower. LC 9-27026. 1909. P. H. Murray & Company.
Mills of Man: A Novel. Philip Payne. LC 3-22510. 1903. Rand, McNally & Co.
Mills of the Gods. George P Dillenback. LC 12-14714. 1.50. Broadway Publishing Co.
Mills of the Gods. Louise Snow Dorr. 1900. A. S. Barnes & Co.
Mills of the Gods. Elizabeth Robins. LC 8-24458. 1908. Moffat, Yard & Company.
Mills of the Gods. Daoma Winston. LC 78-25837. 9.95 (ISBN 0-671-22913-3). Simon and Schuster.
Mills of the Gods. A Novel. Julia Helen Watts Twells. LC 8-32305. 1875. J. B. Lippincott & Co.
Mills of the Gods: A Tale of Tomorrow. Charles Franklin Wimberly. LC 30-2694. 1929. Pentecostal Publishing Co.
Millstone: A Novel. Harold Begbie. LC 15-14308. George H. Doran Company.
Millstone: A Novel. Margaret Drabble. LC 66-16401. 1966. 3.95. Morrow.
Millstones. Wilson Collison. LC 33-6790. 1933. R. M. McBride & Company.
Milly and Mei Kwei: Servants of the Master. Oma Karn. LC 13-752730. 1913. Brethren Publishing House.
Milly Aveling. Sara Trainer Smith. LC 1-30830. 1901. Benziger Brothers.
Milly's Hero. Frederick William Robinson. (seaside library. v. 87, no. 1762). 1883. G. Munro.
Milo March Mysteries, 8 Vols. M. E. Chaber, pseud. pap. 4.80, boxed set o.p. (MM-B). Paperback Lib.
Milo Talon. Louis L'Amour. LC 81-13217. 1981. 12.95 (ISBN 0-8161-3311-5). G.K. Hall.
Milord and I. Anthony Richardson. LC 31-2677. 1931. The Macmillan Company.
Milord's Liegewoman. Elizabeth Chater. (Coventry Romance Ser.: No. 176). 224p. 1982. pap. 1.50 (ISBN 0-449-50277-5, Coventry). Fawcett.
Milre: A Story of Shadow. Martha McCulloch Williams. (On cover: Once a week library, no. 17-18). P. F. Collier.
Milrose: Or, The Cotton-Planter's Daughter. A Tale of South Carolina. John Hovey Robinson. LC 7-42162. F. A. Brady.
Milton Blairlee and the Green Mountain Boys: A Story of the New Hampshire Grants. Willard Goss Davenport. LC 4-37046. 1904. The Grafton Press.
Milton: Paradise Lost. Ed. by Alan Rudrum. 1966. pap. 1.00 o.p. Fernhill.
Milton Tragedy. A Novel. Frank H Cassedy. LC 6-22793. 1891. G. W. Dillingham.
Mimi Bluette. Guido Da Verona & Grazebrook, Isabel, Tr. LC 29-104831. E. P. Dutton & Co., Inc.
Mimi Goes to New Orleans. Mary Locke. 1971. pap. 1.50 o.p. (ISBN 0-911116-94-X). Pelican.
Mimic Life: Or, Before and Behind the Curtain. A Series of Narratives. Anna Cora Ogden Mowatt Ritchie. 1856. Ticknor and Fields.
Mimic Men. Vidiadhar Surajprasad Naipaul. LC 67-22616. 1967. Macmillan.
Mimics of Dephene. Gregory Kern. (Cap Kennedy,#15). 1975. (pbk.) 1.25. DAW Books.
Miminetta. Lucie Lacoste. LC 17-290212. 1917. The Avondale Press.
Mimosa. Amy Carmichael. 1958. pap. 2.50 (ISBN 0-87508-074-X). Chr Lit.
Mimosa Smokers. Peter S Jennison. LC 59-5249. 1959. Crowell.
Min-Min. Mavis Thorpe Clark. LC 79-78086. 1969. Macmillan.
Mince Collop Close. George Blake. LC 24-545381. 1924. R.M. McBride & Company.
Mind Adrift. Daniel Wright Kittredge. LC 20-22446. 1920. S. F. Shorey.
Mind and Soul. Olga Erbsloh Muller. LC 72-85034. 1972. 4.75 (ISBN 0-8022-2100-9). Philosophical Library.
Mind Benders. Ed. by Rob Nelson & Robin Smith. (Illus., Orig.). (gr. 7-12). 1969. pap. text ed. 1.25 (ISBN 0-377-82941-2). Friend Pr.
Mind Benders: 1st American Ed. James Kennaway. LC 63-17847. 1963. Atheneum.
Mind Blower. Marco Vassi. 1979. pap. 2.25 (ISBN 0-532-22105-2). Woodhill.
Mind-Blower. Marco Vassi. 1976. pap. 2.25 o.p. Manor Bks.
Mind Cage. Alfred Elton Van Vogt. 1981. pap. 2.25 (ISBN 0-671-42424-6, Timescape). PB.
Mind Cage. Alfred Elton Van Vogt. 1970. pap. 0.75 o.p. (B75-1093). Belmont-Tower.
Mind Cage, a Science-Fiction Novel. Alfred Elton Van Vogt. LC 57-14594. 1957. Simon and Schuster.
Mind-Call. Neil Shapiro. 1978. pap. 1.75 (ISBN 0-89041-219-7, 3219). Major Bks.
Mind Flight. Stephen Goldin. (Fawcett Gold Medal Book). 1.75 (ISBN 0-449-13980-8). Fawcett Pub.
Mind Gods: A Novel of the Future. Marie Jakober. LC 76-372481. (ISBN 0-7705-1328-X). Macmillan of Canada.
Mind Healer. Ralph Anthony Durand. LC 21-184743. 1921. 1.75. G. P. Putnam's Sons.
Mind Killers. Nick Carter. (Nick Carter Ser.). (O.s.i.). (Orig.). 1970. pap. 0.95 o.s.i. (AN1093, Award). Univ Pub & Dist.
Mind Master. James E. Gunn. 1982. pap. 2.25 (ISBN 0-671-82923-8, Timescape). PB.
Mind Masters. John F Rossmann. 1974. (pbk.) 0.95. New American Library.
Mind-Murders. Van De Wetering, Janwillem. LC 80-26128. 1981. 9.95 (ISBN 0-395-30544-6). Houghton Mifflin.
Mind Net. Herbert W. Franke. 1974. (pbk.) 0.95. DAW Books.
Mind of a Minx: A Novel. Berta Ruck. LC 27-166744. 1927. Dodd, Mead and Company.
Mind of Jon Magnus. Mary S Jespersen. LC 75-16766. 7.95 (ISBN 0-8283-1632-5). Branden Press.
Mind of Max Duvine. Elleston Trevor. 1960. 2.95 o.p. Wehman.
Mind of Mr. J. G. Reeder. Edgar Wallace. Orig. Title: Murder Book of J. G. Reeder. 320p. 1973. Repr. of 1929 ed. 5.95 o.s.i. (ISBN 0-85617-930-2). White Lion Pubs.
Mind of Mister Soames. Charles Eric Maine. 1970. pap. 0.75 o.p. (T2161). Pyramid Pubns.
Mind of My Mind. Octavia E Butler. 1978. 1.75 (ISBN 0-380-40972-0). Avon Books.
Mind of the Maker. Dorothy Leigh Sayers. LC 78-19503. 1979. pap. 6.68i (ISBN 0-06-067071-1, RD 295, HarpR). Har-Row.
Mind Out of Time: A Novel. Angela Tonks. LC 59-5426. 1959. Knopf.
Mind Over Murder. William X Kienzle. LC 81-723. 9.95 (ISBN 0-8362-6114-3). Andrews and McMeel.
Mind Parasites. Colin Wilson. LC 67-6297. 1967. Arkham House.
Mind Poisoners. Nick Carter. (Nick Carter Ser.). (O.s.i.). (Orig.). pap. 0.60 o.s.i. (A314X, Award). Univ Pub & Dist.
Mind Reader. Lundern M Phillips. LC 98-1065. (On cover: Neely's universal library, no. 30). 1898. F. T. Neely.
Mind Reader. Alan Baer Rothenberg. LC 56-11386. 1956. Greenberg.
Mind Reader: A Mystery. Walter Adolphe Roberts. LC 73-18600. 1974. (ISBN 0-404-11410-5). AMS Press.
Mind Reader: A Mystery. Walter Adolphe Roberts. LC 29-7206. The Macaulay Company.
Mind Readers. Margery Allingham. LC 65-18520. bds., 4.50. Morrow.
Mind-Riders. Brian M Stableford. (Daw Science Fiction#194). 1976. (pbk.) 1.25. Daw Books.
Mind Spider and Other Stories. Fritz Leiber. 1976. 1.50. Ace.
"Mind the Paint" Girl: Being a Novelization of Sir Arthur Pinero's Comedy. Louis Tracy & Pinero, Sir Arthur Wing, 1855- LC 12-235132. E. J. Clode.
Mind Thing. Fredric Brown. LC 61-5105. (Bantam books, A2187). 1961. Bantam Books.
Mind to Mind: Nine Stories of Science Fiction. Ed. by Robert Silverberg. (Laurel leaf library). 1974. (pbk.) 0.95. Dell.
Mind to Murder. P. D James. 1976. 1.50. Popular Library.
Mind to Murder. P. D James. LC 67-12914. 1967. Scribner.
Mind to Murder. P. D James. LC 79-28629. 1980. 12.95 (ISBN 0-8161-3057-4). G. K. Hall.
Mind Traders. J. Hunter Holly. 1967. pap. 0.60 o.p. (60-291). Manor Bks.
Mind Traders. J. Hunter Holly. 1974. (pbk.) 0.95. Manor Books.
Mind War. Gene Snyder. LC 79-89314. 1980. pap. 2.50 (ISBN 0-87216-612-0). Playboy Pbks.
Mind Warp. Dave Sheridan & Fred Schrier. LC 74-34557. 1975. pap. 3.50 o.p. (ISBN 0-915904-08-X). And-or Pr.
Mind Wizards of Callisto. Lin Carter. 1975. (pbk.) 0.95. Dell.
Mind Wreckers, Limited. And Other Adventures of Barrow--Ace Insurance Detective. Frank J Price. LC 33-34618. The Spectator Co.
Mindbenders. Jake Quinn. (Shannon Ser: No. 3). 1975. pap. 1.25 o.p. (LB226ZK, Leisure Bks). Nordon Pubns.
Mindblock. Jerry Names. 224p. (Orig.). 1981. pap. 2.25 (ISBN 0-8439-0988-9, Leisure Bks). Nordon Pubns.
Mindblower. Charles McNaughton, Jr. pap. 1.95 o.p. (0120). Essex Hse.
Mindblower. Marco Vassi. 180p. 1972. pap. 1.95 o.s.i. (OPS6195). Olympia.
Mindbreaker. Arthur R Mather. LC 80-16242. 8.95 (ISBN 0-440-05294-7). Delacorte Press.
Mindbridge. Joe Haldeman. 1978. 1.95 (ISBN 0-380-01689-3). Avon.
Mindbridge. Joe W Haldeman. LC 75-26185. (Illus.). 7.95. St. Martin's Press.
Minder: The Story of the Courtship, Call & Conflicts of John Ledger, Minder & Minister, 1900. Frederick R. Smith. Ed. by Robert L. Wolff. Bd. with Coming of the Preachers: A Tale of the Rise of Methodism, 1901. (Victorian Fiction Ser). 1975. lib. bdg. 66.00 (ISBN 0-8240-1590-8). Garland Pub.
Mindfogger. Michael Rogers. LC 72-11026. 1973. 5.95 (ISBN 0-394-48401-0). Knopf; Distributed by Random House.
Mindkiller. Spider Robinson. LC 81-20132. 256p. 1982. 14.50 (ISBN 0-03-059018-3). HR&W.
Mindleberg Papers: A Novel. Jacob Hay. LC 64-11762. 1964. Macmillan.
Mindoro & Beyond: Twenty-One Stories. N. V. Gonzalez. 1979. 12.50x (ISBN 0-8248-0661-1); pap. 8.50x (ISBN 0-8248-0662-X). UH Pr.
Mindreader. C. Terry Cline. LC 80-2737. 1981. 13.95 (ISBN 0-385-17372-5). Doubleday.
Minds. David Black. LC 80-5190. 1982. 13.95 (ISBN 0-87223-609-9). Wyden Books.
Minds Meet. Walter Abish. (New Directions book). 1975. 9.50 (ISBN 0-8112-0557-6) (ISBN 0-8112-0558-4). New Directions Pub. Corp.
Minds of Billy Milligan. Daniel Keyes. 1982. pap. 3.95 (ISBN 0-553-22585-5). Bantam.
Mindship. Gerard F Conway. 1974. (pbk.) 0.95. Daw Books.
Mindsong. Joan Cox. LC 78-65317. 1979. 2.50 (ISBN 0-380-43638-8). Avon Books.
Mindsounds. E. J. Daniel. 1981. pap. 2.50 (ISBN 0-89083-731-7). Zebra.
Mindspell. Elizabeth Thomasina Meade Smith. 288p. 1983. 12.95 (ISBN 0-688-01928-5). Morrow.
Mindswap. Robert Sheckley. 1978. Ace Books.
Mindswap: A Novel. Robert Sheckley. LC 65-18627. 3.95. Delacorte Dist. Dial.
Mindwarpers. Eric Frank Russell. (Orig.). 1972. pap. 0.95 o.s.i. (75-414). Lancer.
Mindy. June Strong. LC 77-77429. 11.95 (ISBN 0-8127-0139-9). Southern Pub. Association.
Mindy Lindy May Surprise. Michael Erlanger. LC 69-16439. 1969. 4.95. Random House.
Mindy Lindy: May Surprise. Michael Erlanger. LC 69-16439. 1969. 4.95 o.p. (ISBN 0-394-43624-5). Random.
Mine. Ransom Jeffery & John Keeble. LC 73-7090. 1974. 7.95 (ISBN 0-670-47656-0). Grossman Publishers.
Mine at Lost Mountain. Al Cody, pseud. 1978. pap. 1.25 (ISBN 0-532-12567-3). Woodhill.
Mine Boy. Peter Abrahams. LC 75-126514. (African/American library). 1970. 1.50. Collier Books.
Mine Boy. 1st American Ed. Peter Abrahams. LC 55-8789. 1955. Knopf.
Mine Eyes Have Seen the Glory: A Novel. Tristram Coffin. LC 64-15464. 1964. Macmillan.
Mine for Keeps. Jean Little. (Illus.). (gr. 4-6). 1974. pap. 1.95 (ISBN 0-671-42455-6). Archway.
Mine Inheritance. Emily Davant Embree. The Cottage Home.
Mine Inheritance. Frederick John Niven. LC 40-33217. 1940. The Macmillan Company.
Mine Is the Judgement. Kathryn Breese. LC 25-21770. 1925. B. J. Brimmer Company.
Mine Is the Kingdom. Jane Oliver, pseud. LC 37-6377. J. B. Lippincott Company.
Mine Is Thine. A Novel. Laurence William Maxwell Lockart. (seaside library. v. 19, no. 376). 1878. G. Munro.
Mine of Faults... Tr. from the Original Manuscript. Francis William Bain. LC 10-25051. 1910. 1.25. G. P. Putnam's Sons.
Mine Own Executioner. Nigel Balchin. LC 46-11904. 1946. Houghton Mifflin Company.
Mine Own People. Rudyard Kipling. LC 4871. H. M. Caldwell Company.
Mine Own People. authorized ed. Rudyard Kipling & James, Henry, 1843-1916. (At head of title: Lovell's international series, no. 153). United States Book Company.
Mine Own People. Rudyard Kipling & James, Henry, 1843-1916. LC 9-302019. 1899. The Lovell Company.
Mine Own People. The Works of Rudyard Kipling. Rudyard Kipling & Henry James. LC 9-16372. 1909. The Nottingham Society.
Mine to Avenge: By Thomas Wills Pseud. Cover Painting by Jack Floherty. William Ard. LC 55-38184. (Gold medal books, 490). 1955. Fawcett Publications.
Mine to Follow. Beulah Powell Anderson. LC 55-13813. 1955. Broadman Press.
Mine to Love. Elsie Frances Wilson Mack. LC 50-7730. 1950. Avalon Books.
Mine with the Iron Door: A Romance. Harold Bell Wright. LC 23-10975. 1923. D. Appleton and Company.
Miner. Frederick C Boden. LC 32-11791. E. P. Dutton & Co., Inc.
Miners Day... Bert Lewis Coombes. LC 46-4125. 1945.
Miners Hill. 1st Ed. Michael O'Malley. LC 62-7908. 1962. Harper.
Miner's Pale Children. William S. Merwin. LC 76-124973. 1970. 6.50. Atheneum.
Miner's Right: A Tale of the Australian Goldfields. Thomas Alexander Browne. LC 42-26488. 1890. Macmillan and Co.
Miner's Tears: Or, The Red Cross Beauty of the Coal Region. Jay Brinley. LC 16-14836. The Laurel Press.
Minerva Stone. Anne Maybury. LC 68-24746. 1968. Holt, Rinehart & Winston.
Minerva's Turn. Helen Faye Rosenblum. LC 80-13073. 11.95 (ISBN 0-399-12532-9). Putnam.
Minette: A Story of the First Crusade. Cram, George Franklin. LC 1-26952. 1901. J. W. Iliff & Co.
Ming and Magnolia. Catherine Isabel Dodd. LC 31-30604. Sears Publishing Company.
Ming Yellow. John Phillips Marquand. LC 35-3360. 1935. Little, Brown, and Company.
Mingham Air. Elizabeth Fair. LC 60-5230. 1960. Rinehart.
Mingled Yarn. Willie Snow Ethridge. LC 38-27414. 1938. The Macmillan Company.
Mingled Yarn. William Mestrezat John. LC 33-22042. Sears Publishing Company.
Minglestreams. Jane Ludlow Drake Abbott. LC 23-7998. 1923. J. B. Lippincott Company.
Mingo. Joel Chandler Harris. LC 76-104477. 1970. Literature House.

Mingo, and Other Sketches in Black and White. 6th ed. boston, houghton mifflin, 1893. ed. Joel Chandler Harris. LC 70-83911. 1969. Mnemosyne Pub. Co.
Mingo, and Other Sketches in Black and White. Joel Chandler Harris. LC 72-113666. (Short story index reprint series). 1970. Books for Libraries Press.
Mingo: And Other Sketches in Black and White. Joel Chandler Harris. LC 12-83982. 1884. J. R. Osgood and Company.
Mingo Dabney. Street, James Howell. LC 49-50311. 1950. Dial Press.
Mini-Murders. Alan Geoffrey Yates. LC 68-7860. (Signet books). 1968. 0.50. New American Library.
Miniature. Eden Phillpotts. 1927. The Macmillan Company.
Miniature Mysteries: One Hundred Malicious Little Mystery Stories. Isaac Asimov et al. LC 80-28667. 256p. 1981. 14.95 (ISBN 0-8008-5251-6). Taplinger.
Miniature Romances from the German, with Other Prolusions of Light Literature... Thomas Tracy & La-Motte-Fongue, Friedrich Heinrich Karl, Freiherr De, 1777-1843. Selections. English. Tracy. LC 8-30863. 1841. C. C. Little & J. Brown.
Miniatures Frame. Kenneth Royce. LC 72-78543. (Inner sanctum mystery). 1972. 5.95 (ISBN 0-671-21350-4). Simon and Schuster.
Minikins of Yam. Thomas Burnett Swann. (Science Fiction Ser.). 1976. pap. 1.25 o.p. (UY1219). DAW Bks.
Minikins of Yam. Thomas Burnett Swann. (Daw Science Fiction no. 182). (Illus.). 1976. (pbk.) 1.25. Daw Books.
Mining Camps & Ghost Towns: Along the Lower Colorado in Arizona & California. Frank Love. LC 73-86960. (Great West & Indian Ser.: Vol. 42). (Illus.). 240p. 8.95 (ISBN 0-87026-031-6). Westernlore.
Mining Men. Otis E. Young. LC 75-320611. (Illus.). 9.95 (ISBN 0-913504-18-1). Lowell Press.
Minion of the Moon. Thomas Wilkinson Speight. LC 8-15509. New Amsterdam Book Co.
Minions of the Moon. Eden Phillpotts. LC 35-4416. 1935. The Macmillan Company.
Minions of the Moon: A Novel of the Future. 1st Ed. William Gray Beyer. LC 50-10453. 1950. Gnome Press.
Minisink: Kingdom Forbidding Loyality. Edgar Donald Lewis. LC 49-10165. 1949. Exposition Press.
Minister. Mae Eleanor Edick Frey. LC 39-29606. Gospel Publishing House.
Minister. Charles E Mercer. LC 69-18190. 1969. 6.95. Putnam.
Minister for Justice. Terence De Vere White. LC 72-160415. 1971. 5.95 o.p. (ISBN 0-87645-045-1). Gambit.
Minister for Justice: A Novel. Terence De Vere White. LC 72-160415. 1971. 5.95 (ISBN 0-87645-045-1). Gambit.
Minister of Carthage. Caroline Atwater Mason. LC 99-1325. (Ladies' home journal library of fiction). 1899. Curtis Publishing Company.
Minister of Grace. Margaret Widdemer. LC 77-131857. 1972. 15.00 (ISBN 0-403-00744-5). Scholarly Press.
Minister of Grace. Margaret Widdemer. LC 22-16974. Harcourt, Brace and Company.
Minister of Injustice. Maurice Culpan. LC 66-22497. bds., 3.50. Walker.
Minister of Police. Henry Mountjoy. LC 12-5155. 1.25. The Bobbs-Merrill Company.
Minister of State: A Novel. John Alexander Steuart. LC 98-801. 1898. Dodd, Mead & Company.
Minister of the World: A Novel. Caroline Atwater Mason. LC 7-25579. A. D. F. Randolph and Co.
Minister of the World: A Novel. Caroline Atwater Mason. LC 7-25578. (Ladies' home journal library of fiction. no. 2). Curtis Publishing Company.
Ministering to Alcoholics. rev. ed. John E. Keller. LC 66-22560. 1966. pap. 6.50 (ISBN 0-8066-0922-2, 10-4439). Augsburg.
Ministering to Single Adults. Gene Van Note. 109p. 1978. pap. 2.95 (ISBN 0-8341-0556-X). Beacon Hill.
Minister's Charge: Or, The Apprenticeship of Lemuel Barker. William Dean Howells. LC 73-8061. Scholarly Press.
Minister's Charge: Or, The Apprenticeship of Lemuel Barker. William Dean Howells. LC 4-15123. 1887. Ticknor and Company.
Minister's Charge: Or, The Apprenticeship of Lemuel Barker. William Dean Howells. LC 77-22213. (His A selected edition of W. D. Howells; v. 14). 1978. 20.00 (ISBN 0-253-33855-7). Indiana University Press.
Minister's Charge, or the Apprenticeship of Lemuel Barker. William Dean Howells. 1973. lib. bdg. 25.00 (ISBN 0-8414-5146-X). Folcroft.
Minister's Charge; or, the Apprenticeship of Lemuel Barker. William Dean Howells. LC 77-22213. (Selected Edition of W. D. Howells: Center for Editions of American Authors: Vol. 14). 400p. 1978. 20.00x (ISBN 0-253-33855-7). Ind U Pr.
Minister's Charge, or the Apprenticeship of Lemuel Barker. William Dean Howells. 1887. 18.00 (ISBN 0-403-00024-6). Scholarly.
Minister's Daughter. Hildur Dixelius. Tr. by Settergren, Anna Ch. LC 27-2549. E. P. Dutton & Company.
Minister's Daughter. Charles H. Knickerbocker. 170p. 1974. 6.95 o.p. (ISBN 0-8059-1969-4). Dorrance.
Minister's Daughter. William McMichael. LC 7-20305. W. B. Smith & Co.
Minister's Daughter. Mwangi Ruheni. (African Writers Ser.). 1975. pap. text ed. 4.00x (ISBN 0-435-90156-7). Heinemann Ed.
Minister's Daughter. Mwangi Ruheni. (African Writers Ser: No. 156). 186p. (Orig.). 1975. pap. 2.75x o.p. (ISBN 0-435-90156-7). Humanities.
Minister's Daughter: And Other Stories. Ida E Pengilly. LC 7-30569.
Minister's Daughter: By Ethel Hamill Pseud. Jean Francis Webb. LC 53-131099. 1953. Avalon Books.
Minister's Eldest Daughter. Pearl McAllaster. LC 35-7173.
Ministers of Grace: A Novellette. Eva Wilder McGlasson Brodhead. LC 6-17962. (On cover: Harper's little novels). 1894. Harper & Brothers.
Minister's Probation. Sarah Cannon Leamon. LC 99-714. 1899. Barbee & Smith.
Minister's Quest; a Novel. Isabel Smith. (Half-title: Appleton's town and country library, no. 286). 1900. D. Appleton and Company.
Minister's Secret. Kate Tannatt Woods. (On cover: Lovell's household library, no. 125). 1888. F. F. Lovell & Company.
Minister's Son: A Story of Our Own Time. Madison Stahr. LC 32-5742. Fleming H. Revell Company.
Minister's Son: And The Sign of Fidelity. Louis Warner Flanders. LC 27-25426. 1927. G. J. Foster & Co.
Minister's Wife. Marian Kenberg. (Orig.). 1981. pap. 2.25 (ISBN 0-8439-8021-4, Tiara Bks). Nordon Pubns.
Minister's Wife. Margaret Oliphant Wilson Oliphant. LC 20-23171. G. Munro.
Minister's Wife. A Story. Jean Kate Ludlum. 1889. Hunt & Eaton.
Minister's Wife: And Other Stories. Mary Anne Madden Sadlier. (Catholic library. v. 22). 1898. C. Wildermann.
Minister's Wooing. Harriet Elizabeth Beecher Stowe. LC 72-8180. Scholarly Press.
Minister's Wooing. Harriet Elizabeth Beecher Stowe. LC 8-16123. 1859. Derby and Jackson.
Minister's Wooing. Harriet Elizabeth Beecher Stowe. LC 7-29155. 1872. J. R. Osgood and Company.
Minister's Wooing. 24th ed. Harriet Elizabeth Beecher Stowe. LC 12-37862. 1887. Houghton, Mifflin and Company.
Minister's Wooing. Harriet Elizabeth Beecher Stowe. LC 77-13796. (Stowe, Harriet Elizabeth Beecher, 1811-1896. New England Novels). (Illus.). 1978. 6.95 (ISBN 0-917482-12-3). Stowe-Day Foundation.
Minister's Wooing see Three Novels.
Ministry of David Baldwin: A Novel. Henry Thomas Colestock. LC 7-10047. T. Y. Crowell & Co.
Ministry of Death. John Michael Ward Bingham Clanmorris. LC 77-80631. 1977. 6.95 (ISBN 0-8027-5377-9). Walker.
Ministry of Fear. Graham Greene. 272p. 1982. 17.95 (ISBN 0-670-47682-X). Viking Pr.
Ministry of Fear see Three by Graham Greene.
Ministry of Fear: An Entertainment. Graham Greene. LC 43-825046. 1943. The Viking Press.
Ministry of Life. Maria Louisa Charlesworth. LC 41-34787. 1864. D. Appleton and Company.
Ministry of Rolla Clark. John Arch Morrison. LC 25-22757. Gospel Trumpet Company.
Ministry with Single Adults. Robert A. Dow. LC 76-48518. 1977. pap. 5.95 (ISBN 0-8170-0693-1). Judson.
Mink Coat. Kathleen Thompson Norris. LC 46-4356. 1946. Doubleday & Company, Inc.
Mink Coat. Kathleen Thompson Norris. LC 47-6542. 1947. Sun Dial Press.
Mink on Weekdays, Ermine on Sunday. Felicia Lamport. LC 50-7487. 1950. Houghton, Mifflin.
Mink Poison: A Combined Trapping Story and Novelette of the Near South. David Pugh. LC 34-23809. 1934. Meador Publishing Company.
Minkie. Louis Tracy. LC 7-33596. 1907. E. J. Clode.
Minna Von Barnhelm. Gotthold E. Lessing. Ed. by Werner F. Leopold & C. R. Goedsche. 1961. pap. text ed. 4.95x o.p. (ISBN 0-669-29538-8). Heath.
Minna: Wife of the Young Rabbi, a Novel. Wilhelmina Wittigschlager. LC 6-10651. 1905. Consolidated Retail Booksellers.
Minnesota Gothic: A Novel. 1st Ed. Walter O'Meara. LC 56-10517. 1956. Holt.
Minnesota Stories: A Collection of Twenty Stories of College Life, Collected and Arranged by Charles F. McClumpha... and W. L. Thomas... Ed. by Charles Flint McClumpha. Thomas William Isaac, 1863- Joint Ed. LC 7-4811. 1903. The H. W. Wilson Company.
Minnesota Strip. Kent Cooper. 1978. pap. 1.95 (ISBN 0-532-19211-7). Woodhill.
Minnesota Strip. Peter McCurtin. (Belmont Tower book). 1979. 1.75 (ISBN 0-505-51333-1). Tower Pubns.
Minnie. Anne Medley, pseud. LC 68-25876. 1968. 4.95. Morrow.
Minnie Flynn. Frances Marion. LC 25-8731. 1925. Boni and Liveright.
Minnie Herman: Or, The Night and Its Morning... 5th thousand. ed. Thurlow Weed Brown. LC 6-17379. 1854. Miller, Orton & Mulligan.
Minnie Hermon: Or, The Curse of Rum. A Tale for the Times. Thurlow Weed Brown & Ferris, George T. LC 6-17380. 1878. H. S. Goodspeed & Company; Etc., Etc.
Minnie Pearl's Diary: By Minnie Pearl Pseud. Ophelia Colley Cannon. LC 53-12011. 1953. Greenberg.
Minnie Santangelo & the Evil Eye. Anthony Mancini. LC 77-4494. 7.95 (ISBN 0-698-10818-3). Coward, McCann & Geoghegan.
Minnie Santangelo's Mortal Sin. Anthony Mancini. LC 74-79693. 7.95 (ISBN 0-698-10618-0). Coward, McCann & Geoghegan.
Minnie Santangelo's Mortal Sin. anthony mancini. ed. Anthony Mancini. 1976. 1.50 (ISBN 0-449-23024-4). Fawcett Crest.
Minnie's Bishop. by george a. birmingham pseud. ed. James Owen Hannay. LC 15-135576. 1915. Hodder and Stoughton.
Minnie's Bishop: And Other Stories. James Owen Hannay. LC 15-152415. Hodder & Stoughton, George H. Doran Company.
Minniglen. Agnes Sweetman Castle & Castle, Egerton. LC 18-145353. 1918. D. Appleton and Company.
Minon: A Tale of Love and Intrigue. Frederick W Pearson. LC 7-33493. (elite library). The Welles Publishing Company.
Minor Chord: A Story of a Prima Donna. Joseph Mitchell Chapple. LC 6-24206. (On cover: Neely's library of choice literature, no. 41). 1895. F. T. Neely.
Minor Classics of Nineteenth-Century Fiction. Ed. by William Earl Buckler. LC 67-9320. (Riverside editions, B107-B108). 1967. Houghton Mifflin.
Minor Classics of Nineteenth-Century Fiction: Ed. by William E. Buckler. Ed. by William Earl Buckler. LC 67-932006. (Riverside eds., B107). 1967. pap., ea. 2.25. Houghton.
Minor Gods. Rod Townley. LC 76-13044. 8.95. St. Martin's Press.
Minor Knickerbockers. Kendall B. Taft. 1979. Repr. of 1947 ed. lib. bdg. 25.00 (ISBN 0-8492-2644-9). R West.
Minor Miracle. Albert Morgan. LC 61-12317. 1961. Dodd, Mead.
Minor Murders. Joe L. Hensley. LC 78-22735. 1979. 7.95 (ISBN 0-385-15136-5). Published for the Crime Club by Doubleday.
Minor Operation. Alfred Walter Stewart. LC 37-27432. 1937. Little, Brown and Company.
Minor Place. Anna Fredair. LC 6-431395. 1869. E. J. Hale & Sons.
Minotaur. Benjamin Tammuz. 1982. pap. 1.50 (ISBN 0-451-11582-1, AW1582, Sig). NAL.
Minotaur. Benjamin Tamuz. LC 80-29119. 11.95 (ISBN 0-453-00401-6). New American Library.
Minotaur Country: A Novel of Suspense. Helen McCloy. LC 74-28370. 1975. 5.95 (ISBN 0-396-07004-3). Dodd, Mead.
Minotaur Factor. Stuart Stern. LC 76-49403. 1977. 1.95. Playboy Press.
Minotaur Garden. Lewis Hosegood. LC 73-6603. 1973. 10.95 (ISBN 0-8161-6108-9). G. K. Hall.
Minotaur Garden. Lewis Hosegood. LC 72-5325. 1972. Delacorte Press.
Minotaur, Minotaur... William Mathes. LC 67-18373. 1967. Delacourte Press.
Minot's Folly. Rupert Sargent Holland. LC 25-20144. 1925. Macrae Smith Company.
Minstrel Boy. Vian Smith. LC 73-97692. 1970. 4.95. Doubleday.
Minstrel Man. Richard Shapiro & Esther Mayesh Shapiro. 1977. 1.50 (ISBN 0-445-03186-7). Popular Library.
Minstrel of the Mountains. William Grant Burleigh. LC 32-319. 1931. Kanawha Valley Publishing Co.
Minstrels in Satin. Elisabeth Cobb Chapman. LC 29-9879. 1929. Doubleday, Doran & Company, Inc.
Mint Julep. Martha Claire Doyle. LC 9-282661. 1909. W. D. Lane & Co.
Mint of Money. authorized ed. George Manville Fenn. LC 6-393801. (Lovell's international series, no. 145). United States Book Company.
Minuet. Louis Paul. Boon. LC 78-61063. 1980. 8.95 (ISBN 0-89255-039-2). Persea Books.
Minuet. Jennie Gallant. (Coventry Romance Ser.: No. 66). 224p. 1980. pap. 1.75 (ISBN 0-449-50097-7, Coventry). Fawcett.
Minus Man. Richard Maxwell. LC 74-16609. 1975. 6.95 (ISBN 0-399-11454-8). Putnam.
Minus One Corpse: By John Cleveland Pseud. Adeline McElfresh. LC 54-9898. 1954. Arcadia House.
Minus Pool. Walter Stovall. LC 79-27816. 12.95 (ISBN 0-671-61040-6). Wyndham Books.
Minute Boys of the Mohawk Valley. James Otis Kaler. LC 5-17287. (Illus.). 1905. D. Estes & Company.
Minute by Glass Minute. Anne Stevenson, pseud. 64p. 1983. pap. 12.95 (ISBN 0-19-211947-8). Oxford U Pr.
Minute for Murder. Nicholas Blake. lib. bdg. 13.95x (ISBN 0-89966-246-3). Buccaneer Bks.
Minute for Murder. Nicholas Blake. LC 75-44956. (Crime Fiction Ser). (O.s.i.). 1976. Repr. of 1947 ed. lib. bdg. 17.50 o.s.i. (ISBN 0-8240-2354-4). Garland Pub.
Minute for Murder. Nicholas Blake. 1977. Repr. pap. 1.95i o.p. (ISBN 0-06-080419-X, P418, PL). Har-Row.
Minute for Murder. Day-Lewis, Cecil. LC 75-44956. (Fifty Classics of Crime Fiction, 1900-1950; 5). 1976. 12.00 (ISBN 0-8240-2354-4). Garland Pub.
Minute for Murder. Cecil Day-Lewis. LC 48-7743. 1948. Harper.
Minute Mysteries. Austin Ripley. 1976. pap. 2.50i (ISBN 0-06-080387-8, P387, PL). Har-Row.
Minute to Pray, a Second to Die - Mondo. Anthony Destefano. (No. 3). 1977. pap. 1.50 (ISBN 0-532-15272-7). Woodhill.
Minuteman Murder. Jane Langton. 1.25. Dell.
Minutemen of the Sea: Illustrated by Tom O'Sullivan. Tom Cluff. LC 55-7498. 1955. Follett Pub. Co.
Minutes of a Murder: By Madeleine Polland. 1st Ed. Madeleine A Polland. LC 67-12580. (Rinehart suspense novel). 1967. bds., 3.95. Holt.
Minutes of the Night, a Novel. Mary Arkley Carter. LC 65-18131. bds., 5.95. Atlantic-Little.
Minx. Gardner F. Fox. (O.s.i.). (Orig.). 1969. pap. 0.75 o.s.i. (A555S, Award). Univ Pub & Dist.
Minx: A Novel. Kathleen Mannington Hunt Caffyn. LC 99-5600. F. A. Stokes Company.
Mipam. Lama Yongden. Tr. by Percy Lloyd & Bernard Miall. (Illus.). 384p. 1972. pap. 3.95 o.p. (ISBN 0-914726-07-2). Mudra.
Mira. Daoma Winston. LC 80-68544. 11.95 (ISBN 0-87795-300-7). Arbor House.
Mira Conquistador. Martin Ancel. 1974. 12.95x. Pleasure Trove.
Mira Conquistador: Or, Caribbean Pleasure Troves. Martin Ancel. LC 74-83390. (Illus.). 1974. 12.95. Pleasure Trove Books.
Mirabeau: Lover and Statesman. Pierre Nezelof & Wells, Warre Bradley, 1892- Tr. LC 37-10108. Liveright Publishing Corporation.
Mirabeau Plantation. Marcia Meredith. 352p. (Orig.). 1980. pap. 2.50 (ISBN 0-89083-596-9). Zebra.
Mirabelle of Pameluna. Antoinette De Bergevin Hazard Tr. by Smith, Lucy Humphrey. LC 19-13596. 1919. C. Scribner's Sons.
Mirabel's Island. Louis Tracy. LC 12-4769. E. J. Clode.
Mirabilis Diamond: By Jerome Odlum. Jerome Odlum. LC 45-922836. 1945. C. Scribners Sons.
Miracle. Clarence Budington Kelland. LC 25-3193. 1925. Harper & Brothers.
Miracle. Dotson Rader. 1978. 8.95 o.p. (ISBN 0-394-41270-2). Random.
Miracle. Ernest Temple Thurston. LC 22-20348. 1922. D. Appleton and Company.
Miracle: A Novel. Dotson Rader. 2.25 (ISBN 0-445-04333-4). Popular Library.
Miracle: A Romance. Vincent O'Sullivan. LC 77-463192. 1976. (ISBN 0-908565-14-3). J. McIndoe.
Miracle at Cardenrigg: A Novel. Tom Hanlin. LC 49-482782. 1949. Random House.
Miracle at City Hall. Al Palmquist & Kay Nelson. LC 74-11738. 160p. 1974. pap. 2.45 o.p. (ISBN 0-87123-364-9). Bethany Hse.
Miracle at Gopher Creek. Oscar Schisgall. LC 39-725. Green Circle Books.
Miracle at Markham: How Twelve Churches Became One. Charles Monroe Sheldon. LC 99-1482. (On cover: Forward series, no. 5). The Church Press.
Miracle at Markham: How Twelve Churches Became One. Charles Monroe Sheldon. 1900. Advance Publishing Co.
Miracle at St. Bruno's. Philippa Carr, pseud. 1973. (pbk) 1.50. Popular Library.
Miracle at St. Bruno's. Eleanor Hibbert. LC 78-187131. 1972. 6.95. Putnam.

Miracle at Seaside. Laura C. Raef. 192p. (YA) 1975. 4.95 o.p. (Avalon). Bouregy.
Miracle Boy. a. a. knopf. ed. Louis Golding. LC 27-210201. 1927. A. A. Knopf.
Miracle de la Rose see Oeuvres Completes.
Miracle Father. Francis Sylvin, pseud. LC 52-10493. 1952. Metcalf Associates.
Miracle for Caroline. Ruth Feiner. LC 51-1098. Coward-McCann.
Miracle for Nurse Louisa. Adelaide Humphries. (YA) 1978. 6.95 (Avalon). Bouregy.
Miracle in Alaska. Thelma Thompson Slayden. LC 63-21559. 1963. F. Fell.
Miracle in Brittany. 1st Ed. Mildred A Jordan. LC 50-12305. 1950. Knopf.
Miracle in the Drawing Room... Edwin Greenwood. LC 36-9379. 1936. Doubleday, Doran & Company, Inc.
Miracle in the Rain. Ben Hecht. LC 43-15180. 1943. A. A. Knopf.
Miracle in the Wilderness: A Christmas Story of Colonial America. Paul Gallico. LC 75-16277. 1975. 4.95 (ISBN 0-440-05714-0). Delacorte Press.
Miracle Merchant. Concordia Merrel. LC 28-290704. 1929. Doubleday, Doran & Company, Inc.
Miracle of a Four-Leaf Clover. Elsie Rose Feerschner. LC 53-11638. Vantage Press.
Miracle of Dommatina. Ira Avery. LC 77-28031. 7.95. Putnam.
Miracle of Love. Cosmo Hamilton. LC 15-11451. 1.25. George H. Doran Company.
Miracle of Love: A Novel. 1st Ed. Lillian E Monroe. LC 55-108451. 1955. Vantage Press.
Miracle of Marcelino. Jose Maria Sanchez-Silva. LC 63-20073. 1963. Scepter.
Miracle of Merriford: Illustrated by J. S. Goodall. Reginald Arkell. 1956. Reynal.
Miracle of Murlin Heights. Clifton E. Snodgrass & Wanda J. Herman. (Orig.). 1976. pap. 1.75 o.p. (ISBN 0-88368-073-4). Whitaker Hse.
Miracle of Peille. James Lawrence Campbell. LC 29-299828. E. P. Dutton & Co., Inc.
Miracle of Pelham Bay Park. Anthony Mancini. LC 81-12495. 13.50 (ISBN 0-525-03058-1). Dutton.
Miracle of Saint Jubanus. Rudyard Kipling. LC 30-31039. 1930. Doubleday, Doran & Company, Inc.
Miracle of the Bells. Russell Janney. LC 48-276497. 1946. Garden City Pub. Co.
Miracle of the Bells. Russell Janney. LC 46-27124. 1946. Prentice-Hall Inc.
Miracle of the Rose. Jean Genet. LC 66-14097. Grove Press.
Miracle of the Rose. Tr. from French by Bernard Frechtman. Jean Genet. LC 66-140970. (Evergreen black cat, B-145). 1968. pap., 1.25. Grove.
Miracle on Hermon: A Story of the Carpenter. John Marvin Dean. LC 21-21369. Chicago Etc. Fleming H. Revell Company.
Miracle on San Jaime: A Novel. 1st Ed. John Cantwell. LC 59-6286. 1959. Chilton Co., Book Division.
Miracle on Sinai, a Satirical Novel. Osbert Sitwell. LC 34-4674. H. Holt and Company.
Miracle on the Mountain. Ethel Lockwood. Ed. by Alice Sachs. 1971. 3.95 o.p. Lenox Hill.
Miracle on Thirty-Fourth Street. Valentine Davies. LC 47-4221. (YA) (gr. 7-12). 1967. pap. 2.50 (ISBN 0-15-660453-1, Harv). HarBraceJ.
Miracle on 34th Street. Valentine Davies. LC 47-422110. 1947. Harcourt, Brace.
Miracle Play. Susan Richards Shreve. LC 82-80845. 400p. 1982. pap. 3.50 (ISBN 0-86721-182-2). Playboy Pbks.
Miracle Play: A Novel. Susan Richards Shreve. LC 81-1481. 1981. 12.95 (ISBN 0-688-00482-2). W. Morrow.
Miracle Season. Linda Cline. LC 76-18070. 7.95 (ISBN 0-399-11654-0). Berkley Pub. Corp.: Distributed by Putnam.
Miracle Season. Linda Cline. (Berkley Medallion Book). 1977. 1.25 (ISBN 0-425-03447-X). Berkley Pub. Corp.
Miracle to Believe In. Barry N. Kaufman. 384p. 1982. pap. 2.95 (ISBN 0-449-24496-2, Crest). Fawcett.
Miracle Worker. Gerald Maxwell. LC 7-15322. 1907. J. W. Luce & Company.
Miraclejack. Michael Baldwin. LC 67-10943. 1967. 4.95. Holt.
Miracles. Martin Ebon. (Orig.). 1981. pap. 2.50 (ISBN 0-451-11222-9, AE1222, Sig). NAL.
Miracles: Genuine Cases Contact Box 340: A Novel. Philip Oakes. LC 75-140465. 1971. 5.95. John Day Co.
Miracles of Antichrist: A Novel. Selma Ottiliana Lovisa Lagerlof. Tr. by Flach, Pauline Bancroft. LC 99-1043. 1899. Little, Brown and Company.
Miracles of Clara Van Haag. Johannes Buchholtz. Tr. by Worster, William John Alexander. LC 22-268949. 1922. A. A. Knopf.
Miracles of the Red Altar Cloth. Herman L Hunter. LC 49-487693. 1949. Exposition Press.
Miracles Take Longer. Zelma Orr. (American Romance Ser.). 192p. 1983. pap. 2.25 (ISBN 0-373-16007-0). Harlequin Bks.
Miraculous Barber: Translated from the French by Eric Sutton. 1st American Ed. Marcel Ayme. LC 51-10186. 1951. Harper.
Miraculous Fish of Domingo Gonzales. Martin M Goldsmith. LC 50-7445. (Illus.). 1950. Norton.
Miraculous Stories from the Japanese Buddhist Tradition: The Nihon Ryoiki of the Monk Kyokai. Tr. by Kyoko M. Nakamura from Japanese. LC 72-87773. (Harvard-Yenching Institute Monograph Ser: No. 20). (Illus.). 337p. 1973. 16.50x (ISBN 0-674-57635-7). Harvard U Pr.
Mirage. Julia Constance Fletcher. LC 6-41687. (No Name Series). 1878. Roberts Brothers.
Mirage. William H Kofoed. LC 18-8165. R. J. Shores.
Mirage. Ruth McKenney. LC 56-11635. 1956. Farrar, Straus and Cudahy.
Mirage. Edgar Lee Masters. LC 24-7318. Boni and Liveright.
Mirage. Margie Michaels. 192p. 1982. pap. 1.75. Jove Pubns.
Mirage. Helen Topping Miller. LC 49-445166. 1949. Appleton-Century-Crofts.
Mirage. Andrea Newman. LC 66-12830. 1966. 3.95. Dial.
Mirage. Ida Jean Sherman. LC 40-111065. The Saravan House.
Mirage. Ernest Temple Thurston. LC 8-32388. 1908. Dodd, Mead & Company.
Mirage: A Novel of the First Florida Colonies. Margaret Evans Price. LC 55-8223. 1955. Library Publishers.
Mirage Ended in Poitiers. Antoine J Saba. LC 57-13955. 1957. Philosophical Library.
Mirage of Love. Ursula Bloom. 1978. pap. 1.95 (ISBN 0-89041-190-5, 3190). Major Bks.
Mirage of Marriage. Josiah Pitts Woolfolk. LC 35-821844. Godwin.
Mirage of Promise. Harriett Pennawell Belt. LC 6-11346. 1887. J. B. Lippincott Company.
Mirage of the Many. William Thomas Walsh. LC 10-18657. 1910. H. Holt and Company.
Mirage on the Horizon. Ursula Bloom. 1979. pap. 1.95 (ISBN 0-89041-267-7, 3267). Major Bks.
Miramar. Najib Mahfuz. Tr. by Fatma Moussa-Mahmoud from Arabic. LC 78-72968. (Orig.). 1978. pap. 5.00 (ISBN 0-89410-020-3). Three Continents.
Miramar Seduction. Keeling Jordan. LC 80-17981. 9.85 (ISBN 0-453-00385-0). New American Library.
Miramar Seduction. Keeling Jorden. 384p. 1981. pap. 3.25 (ISBN 0-441-53373-6). Ace Bks.
Miramichi. 2d ed. William T. Savage. LC 8-2012. 1865. Loring.
Miranda. Jane Blackmore. 1973. 0.75. Dell.
Miranda. Leonora Blythe. 1980. pap. 1.75 (ISBN 0-449-50048-9, Coventry). Fawcett.
Miranda. Grace Livingston Hill. LC 15-10723. 1915. J. B. Lippincott Company.
Miranda. Elinor Lockwood. (Leisure Book). 1977. 1.95 (ISBN 0-8439-0508-5). Nordon Pubns.
Miranda. Richard Peck. LC 79-23083. 1980. 13.95 (ISBN 0-670-11530-4). Viking Press.
Miranda: A Novel. Pamela Sanders. LC 78-18911. 10.00 (ISBN 0-316-77009-4). Little, Brown.
Miranda Elliot: Or, The Voice of the Spirit. M., S. H. LC 7-15290. 1855. Lippincott, Grambo & Co.
Miranda Masters. John Cournos. LC 26-7439. 1926. A. A. Knopf.
Miranda No. Sixty. Emilie Baker Loring. 208p. 1981. pap. cancelled (ISBN 0-553-14294-1). Bantam.
Miranda of the Balcony: A Story. Alfred Edward Woodley Mason. LC 99-4095. 1899. The Macmillan Company.
Miranda's Folly. Rachelle Edwards. (Georgian Romance). 1979. 1.75 (ISBN 0-449-23992-6). Fawcett Crest Books.
Mira's Passage. Marianne L. Zeitlin. 304p. (Orig.). 1981. pap. 2.75 (ISBN 0-440-15657-2). Dell.
Mirbah. Emma P. Dumas. (Novels by Franco-Americans in New England 1850-1940 Ser.). 246p. (Fr.). (gr. 10 up). 1979. pap. 4.50x (ISBN 0-911409-20-3). Natl Mat Dev.
Mired. Hugh Joseph Morley. LC 45-3539. 1945. The William-Frederick Press.
Mirella: A Novel. Isabel Constance Clarke. LC 33-38719. 1938. Longmans, Green & Co.
Mirgorad: Four Tales. Nikolai Vasilevich Gogol. Tr. by David Magarshack. (Funk & W Bk.). 1969. pap. 2.50 o.p. (ISBN 0-308-60067-3, M62, TYC-T). T Y Crowell.
Mirgorod. Nikolai Vasilevich Gogol. Tr. by David Magarshack. LC 62-19237. 1962. Farrar, Straus and Cudahy.
Mirgorod. Nikolai Vasilevich Gogol. Tr. by Garnett, Constance (Black) LC 29-13373. 1929. A. A. Knopf.
Mirgorod: Including The Old-World Landowners, Taras Bulba, Viy, Ivan Ivanovich and Ivan Nikiforovich. Nikolai Vasilevich Gogol. Tr. by David Magarshack. LC 76-6081. 1968. Minerva Press.
Miri: A Novel. Peter Sourian. LC 57-7317. 1957. Pantheon.
Miriam. Gustav Kobbe. LC 7-14193. T. Y. Crowell & Company.
Miriam: A Novel. Lois T Henderson. LC 82-48929. 10.95 (ISBN 0-06-063867-2). Harper & Row.
Miriam: A Novel. Lois T. Henderson. LC 82-48929. 256p. 1983. 10.53i (ISBN 0-06-063867-2, HarpR). Har-Row.
Miriam Alroy: A Romance of the Twelfth Century Also, The Rise of Iskander. Benjamin Disraeli Beaconsfield. (Seaside library, v. 49, no. 994). 1881. G. Munro.
Miriam at Thirty-Four. Alan Lelchuk. LC 74-13311. 1974. 7.95 (ISBN 0-374-20970-7). Farrar, Straus and Giroux.
Miriam Balestier: A Novel. Edgar Fawcett. LC 6-38787. (On cover: The household library. no. 10. v. 4)). 1888. Belford, Clarke & Company.
Miriam Coffin: Or the Whale-Fisherman, 2 vols in 1. Joseph C. Hart. 1972. Repr. of 1834 ed. lib. bdg. 18.00 (ISBN 0-8422-8071-5). Irvington.
Miriam Coffin, or the Whale-Fisherman. Joseph C. Hart. Ed. by Edward C. Foster. LC 79-93622. (American Fiction Ser). 1969. lib. bdg. 13.50 o.s.i. (ISBN 0-512-00298-3). Garrett Pr.
Miriam Coffin: Or, The Whale-Fishermen: a Tale. new ed.... ed. Joseph C Hart. LC 3-10904. 1872. Republished by H. R. Coleman.
Miriam Lucas. Patrick Augustine Sheehan. LC 12-24626. 1912. Longmans, Green, and Co.
Miriam Monfort: a Novel. Catherine Ann Ware Warfield. LC 8-34835. 1873. D. Appleton and Company.
Miriam of Magdala: A Study. Katherine Frances Mullany. LC 6-21391. Magdala Co.
Miriam of Queen's. Lilian Vaux MacKinnon. LC 21-17623. 1.90. George H. Doran Company.
Miriam Rivers, the Lady Soldier: Or, General Grant's Spy. P. M. C & M. C. P. LC 7-347054. 1865. Barclay & Co.
Miriam Vs. Milton: R, The Mystery of Everdale Lake. James Johnson Kane. LC 7-11665. 1894. The American News Company.
Miriam's Heritage: A Story of the Delaware River. Alma Calder Johnston. LC 7-10815. (On cover: Harper's library of American fiction, no. 3). 1878. Harper & Brothers.
Miriam's Memoirs. A Sequel to "Montfort Hall." Being a Romance of the House of Beauseincourt. Catherine Ann Ware Warfield. LC 8-34834. T. B. Peterson & Brothers.
Miriam's Schooling: And Other Papers. William Hale White & Shapcott, Reuben, Ed. LC 38-10855. 1936. Oxford University Press, H. Milford.
Miriam's Schooling, Eighteen Ninety see Revolution in Tanner's Lane, 1887.
Miriam's Tower. Harriet Loretta Knapp. LC 7-14278. (Dillingham's American authors library, no. 23). 1897. G. W. Dillingham Co.
Miriam's Tower. 2d ed. Harriet Loretta Knapp. LC 10-260414. 1909. 1.25. Wichita Publishing Co.
Mirkheim. Poul Anderson. LC 76-28807. 7.95 (ISBN 0-399-11868-3). Berkley Pub. Corp.: Distributed by Putnam.
Mirkheim. Poul Anderson. (Berkley Medallion Book). 1977. 1.50 (ISBN 0-425-03596-4). Berkley Pub. Corp.
Mirkheim. Poul Anderson. (Berkley Medallion Book). (Illus.). 1977. 1.50 (ISBN 0-425-03596-4). Berkley Pub. Corp.
Miro. Shaun Herron. LC 74-85629. 1969. 4.95. Random House.
Miromesnil Edition of Guy De Maupassant... Guy De Maupassant. Tr. by A. E. Henderson. Quesada, Mme., Tr. LC 10-6186. P. F. Collier & Son.
Mirrikh: Or, A Woman from Mars: a Tale of Occult Adventure. Francis Worcester Doughty. LC 75-46267. (Supernatural and Occult Fiction). 1976. 15.00 (ISBN 0-405-08125-1). Arno Press.
Mirrikh, or, a Woman from Mars: A Tale of Occult Adventure. Francis W. Doughty. LC 76-42808. Repr. of 1892 ed. 22.50 (ISBN 0-404-60062-X). AMS Pr.
Mirrikh: Or, A Woman From Mars; a Tale of Occult Adventure. Francis Worcester Doughty. LC 6-33492. 1892. The Burleigh & Johnston Company.
Mirror. Marlys Millhiser. LC 78-6141. 9.95. Putnam.
Mirror. Mary F. Nixon- Roulet. LC 15-5149. 1915. 0.60. B. Herder.
Mirror: A Novel. Leonard Gross. LC 80-8229. 10.00 (ISBN 0-06-011642-0). Harper & Row.
Mirror & the Garden. Evelyn J. Hinz. 123p. 1971. pap. 6.75 o.p. (ISBN 0-88215-021-9). Ohio St U Libs.
Mirror and the Lamp. William Babington Maxwell. LC 18-210840. The Bobbs-Merrill Company.
Mirror and the Lamp. William Babington Maxwell. LC 19-425. 1918. Cassell and Company, Ltd.
Mirror Crack'd. Agatha Miller Christie. LC 63-20005. 1963. Dodd, Mead.
Mirror Crack'd from Side to Side. Agatha Miller Christie. LC 76-353431. 1974. 0.35 (ISBN 0-14-003804-3). Penguin.
Mirror Crack'd from Side to Side. the greenway ed. Agatha Miller Christie. LC 81-67346. 1981. 8.95 (ISBN 0-396-08018-9). Dodd, Mead.
Mirror Dance. Agnes Mary Robertson Dunlop. LC 70-138867. 1971. 4.95 (ISBN 0-03-085661-2). Holt, Rinehart and Winston.
Mirror Dance. Elisabeth Kyle, pseud. 1971. 4.95 o.p. (ISBN 0-03-085966-2). HR&W.
Mirror for Observers. 1st Ed. Edgar Pangborn. LC 54-5352. 1954. Doubleday.
Mirror for Skylarks. Zoe Girling. LC 35-25381. 1935. Harper & Brothers.
Mirror for Toby. Cecily Rosemary Hallack. LC 33-6713. 1933. The Macmillan Company.
Mirror for Witches. Esther Forbes. (YA) (gr. 9-12). pap. 1.75 o.p. (ISBN 0-395-08378-8, 29, SenEd). HM.
Mirror for Witches in Which Is Reflected the Life, Machinations, and Death of Famous Doll Bilby, Who, with a More Than Feminine Perversity, Preferred a Demon to a Mortal Lover. Here Is Also Told How and Why a Righteous and Most Awfull Judgment Befell Her, Destroying Both Corporeal Body and Immortal Soul. Esther Forbes. LC 28-12074. 1928. Houghton Mifflin Company.
Mirror Friend, Mirror Foe. George Takei & Robert Asprin. LC 79-53085. (Orig.). 1979. pap. 1.95 (ISBN 0-87216-581-7). Playboy Pbks.
Mirror Image. Linda DuBreuil. 1979. pap. 1.75 o.s.i. (ISBN 0-505-51393-5). Tower Bks.
Mirror Image. Stephen Harper. LC 75-14824. 1976. 6.95 (ISBN 0-385-11072-3). Doubleday.
Mirror Image. Mark Sadler, pseud. 1974. (pbk.) 1.25. Manor Books.
Mirror Image. Mark Sadler, pseud. LC 70-37075. 1972. 4.95 (ISBN 0-394-47205-5). Random House.
Mirror Man: The Adventures of a Roving Sensualist. Paul Virdell. LC 78-57317. 9.95 (ISBN 0-87795-190-X). Arbor House.
Mirror, Mirror. Noel Bertram Gerson. LC 75-96300. 1970. Morrow.
Mirror, Mirror. Jill Moordian. 224p. (Orig.). 1981. pap. text ed. 2.25 (ISBN 0-553-20211-1). Bantam.
Mirror, Mirror. Elinor Rice. LC 46-8239. 1946. Duell, Sloan and Pearce.
Mirror Mirror. Harriet Waugh. LC 74-28139. 1975. 6.95 (ISBN 0-316-92604-3). Little, Brown.
Mirror, Mirror, Fatal Mirror. Ed. by Hans Stefan Santesson. Mystery Writers of America. LC 73-81986. 1973. 5.95 (ISBN 0-385-05073-9). Published for the Crime Club by Doubleday.
Mirror, Mirror, Fatal Mirror: An Anthology of Mystery Stories by the Mystery Writers of America. Ed. by Hans S. Santesson. LC 73-81986. (Crime Club Ser.). 264p. 1973. 5.95 o.p. (ISBN 0-385-05073-9). Doubleday.
Mirror, Mirror on the Wall. Stanley Ellin. LC 72-636. 1972. 5.95 (ISBN 0-394-47168-7). Random House.
Mirror, Mirror, on the Wall. Barbara Freeman. 1978. pap. 1.50 (ISBN 0-532-15367-7). Woodhill.
Mirror, Mirror on the Wall: A Novel. Mona Kent. LC 49-104201. 1949. Rinehart.
Mirror Murder. Leta Zoe Adams. LC 37-24836. Phoenix Press.
Mirror of a Dead Lady. LC 40-27642. 1940. Longmans, Green & Co.
Mirror of a Mage. Vicente Huidobro & Wells, Warre Bradley, 1892- Tr. LC 32-3751. 1931. Houghton Mifflin Company.
Mirror of Delusion. Mary Reisner. LC 46-3634. 1946. Dodd, Mead & Company.
Mirror of Dionysos see To Dream of Evil.
Mirror of Dreams: A Tale of Oriental Mystery. Martin Louis Alan Gompertz. LC 28-23110. 1928. Doubleday, Doran & Company, Inc.
Mirror of Fools: Translated from the German for the First Time. Alfred Neumann. Tr. by Blewitt, Trevor E. LC 33-1966. 1933. A. A. Knopf.
Mirror of Hell. Leonard Holton, pseud. LC 79-180929. (Red Badge Novel of Suspense Ser). 1972. 4.95 o.p. (ISBN 0-396-06486-8). Dodd.
Mirror of Hell. Leonard Patrick O'Connor Wibberley. LC 79-180929. (Red badge novel of suspense). 1972. 4.95 (ISBN 0-396-06486-8). Dodd, Mead.
Mirror of Infinity. Ed. by Robert Silverberg. 288p. 1973. pap. 1.95i o.p. (ISBN 0-06-080306-1, P306, PL). Har-Row.

Mirror of Infinity: A Critics' Anthology of Science Fiction. Ed. by Robert Silverberg. LC 75-96004. 1970. 6.95. Harper & Row.

Mirror of Kong Ho. Ernest Bramah, pseud. 321p. 1977. Repr. of 1903 ed. lib. bdg. 15.50x (ISBN 0-89966-270-6). Buccaneer Bks.

Mirror of Kong Ho. Ernest Bramah Smith. LC 30-25912. 1930. Doubleday, Doran & Company, Inc.

Mirror of Love: A Reinterpretation of the "Romance of the Rose". Alan M. Gunn. 1952. 24.00 (ISBN 0-89672-005-5). Tex Tech Pr.

Mirror of Mind. Russel W. McDougal. Frwd. by Arguelles, Jose. LC 76-17152. 1977. pap. 8.95 (ISBN 0-917694-01-5). Open Window.

Mirror of Passion. Marcia Alexander. 176p. pap. 1.95 o.p. (6101). Brandon.

Mirror of Shadows. Dorothy Daniels. 1977. 1.95 (ISBN 0-446-89327-7). Warner.

Mirror of Shalott: Being a Collection of Tales Told at an Unprofessional Symposium. Robert Hugh Benson. 1907. Benziger Brothers.

Mirror of the Giant: A Ghost Story. Penelope Shuttle. 160p. 1980. 12.00 (ISBN 0-7145-2679-7, Pub. by M. Boyars). Merrimack Pub Cir.

Mirror of the Invisible World: Tales from the Khamseh of Nizami. Peter J Chelkowski & Nizami Ganjavi. LC 75-28305. 1975. 17.50 (ISBN 0-87099-142-6). Metropolitan Museum of Art.

Mirror on Horseback. George Hitchcock. 1979. pap. 4.00. Kayak.

Mirror Room. Christopher Landon. LC 73-152516. 1972. 5.95 (ISBN 0-85617-740-7). (Baker St., WM FA), White Lion Publishers Ltd.

Mirrored Walls. Helene Mullins. 5.95 o.p. Twayne.

Mirrors. Kaye Wilson Klein. 1982. pap. 3.50 (ISBN 0-451-11862-6, AE1862, Sig). NAL.

Mirrors. Barbara Krasnoff. 464p. (Orig.). 1980. pap. 2.75 (ISBN 0-89083-690-6). Zebra.

Mirrors. James Lipton. LC 80-29076. 12.95 (ISBN 0-312-53438-8). St. Martin's Press.

Mirrors. Howard McCord. (Illus.). 1973. wrappers 1.50 (Pub. by Stone-Marrow Pr). SBD.

Mirrors: A Novel. Ken Edgar. LC 77-29230. 1978. 9.95 (ISBN 0-458-93390-2). Methuen.

Mirrors, a Novel. Najib Mahfuz. Tr. by Roger Allen. LC 76-47306. (Studies in Middle Eastern Literatures, 8). 1977. 18.00 (ISBN 0-88297-014-3); pap. 10.00 (ISBN 0-88297-016-X). Bibliotheca.

Mirrors of Chartres Street. William Faulkner. LC 77-18204. (Illus.). 1977. 17.50 (ISBN 0-8414-4352-1). Folcroft Library Editions.

Mirrors of Chartres Street. Introd. by William Van O'Connor. Illustrated by Mary Demopoulos. William Faulkner. LC 53-12315. 1953. Faulkner Studies.

Mirrors of the Apocalypse. Donald Lloyd Moore. 1978. pap. 4.95 o.s.i. (ISBN 0-8202-5011-2). Sherbourne.

Mirrors of the Heart. Elyse Dalton. (Adventures in Love Ser.: No. 35). 1982. pap. 1.95 (ISBN 0-451-11875-8, AJ1875, Sig). NAL.

Mirrors: Stories. Lucy Warner. LC 69-10697. 1969. 4.95. Knopf.

Mirrows of the Sea. Joseph Conrad. 1973. pap. 2.55 o.p. (ISBN 0-460-01189-8, EP1189, Evman). Dutton.

Mirthful Haven. Booth Tarkington. LC 30-25307. 1930. Doubleday, Doran & Company, Inc.

Mis' Bassett's Matrimony Bureau. Winifred I. E. Hannah Winifred Arnold. LC 12-26287. Fleming H. Revell Company.

Mis' Beauty. Helen S Woodruff. LC 11-311356. 1911. The Alice Harriman Company.

Mis Lecciones de Amor. new ed. Juanita Bastidas. (Pimienta Collection Ser). 160p. (Span.). 1974. pap. 1.00 (ISBN 0-88473-205-3). Fiesta Pub.

Mis' Melissa's Baby. Gladys Freeman. LC 15-17759. 1915. 0.50. Isaac H. Blanchard Company.

Misadventure. A Novel. William Edward Norris. (On cover: Lovell's international series, no. 58). 1890. F. F. Lovell & Company.

Misadventure of John Nicholson: A Christmas Story. Robert Louis Stevenson. (On cover: Lovell's library. no. 1102). 1887. J. W. Lovell Company.

Misadventures of Bethany Price. Marian Cockrell. LC 79-11869. 10.95 (ISBN 0-8129-0831-7). Times Books.

Misadventures of John Nicholson: A Christmas Story. Robert Louis Stevenson. LC 8-15701. (On cover: Seaside library. Pocket ed. no. 1051). 1887. G. Munro.

Misadventures of Joseph. John Joy Bell. LC 14-157454. 1.00. Fleming H. Revell Company.

Misadventures of Marjory. James Ball Naylor. LC 8-30536. 1908. The C. M. Clark Publishing Co.

Misadventures of Martin Guerre. Gaston Delayen. Tr. by Symons, Farrell. LC 29-29430. E. P. Dutton & Co., Inc.

Misadventures of Rufus Burdy. William Richard Bird. LC 75-318409. (ISBN 0-07-082240-9). McGraw-Hill Ryerson.

Misadventures of Sherlock Holmes. Ed. by Ellery Queen, pseud. LC 44-3391. 1944. Little, Brown and Company.

Misadventures of Tim McPick. Daniel Curzon. LC 75-32707. 3.50. John Parke Custis Press.

Misadventures of Tim McPick: A Gay Comedy. Daniel Curzon. LC 75-32707. 1980. pap. 4.00 (ISBN 0-930650-02-6). D Brown Bks.

Misalliance. Wilbur Finley Fauley. LC 34-10328. The Macaulay Company.

Miscalculated Risk. Virginia McDonnell. (Orig.). 1969. pap. 0.50 o.p. (Golden Pr). Western Pub.

Miscast for Murder. 1st Ed. Ruth Fenisong. LC 54-9484. 1954. Published for the Crime Club by Doubleday.

Miscast Gentleman. Edward Easton, pseud. 1978. pap. 2.25 (ISBN 0-532-22120-6). Woodhill.

Miscellaneous Essays: Impressions of Theophrastus Such; The Veil Lifted; Brother Jacob; Biographical Introduction. George Eliot. LC 1-31177. (Her Works Personal edition). Doubleday, Page & Co.

Miscellany of a Japanese Priest. Kenko Yoshida. Tr. by William H. Porter. Orig. Title: Tsurezure Gusa. (Illus.). 240p. 1973. pap. 5.50 (ISBN 0-8048-1119-9). C E Tuttle.

Mischa, the Immigrant. Edna Badanis. 145p. 1979. 4.50 (ISBN 0-8059-2683-6). Dorrance.

Mischianza. Henry Misrock. LC 67-21420. 1967. Macmillan.

Mischief. Charlotte Armstrong. LC 50-7473. 1950. Coward-McCann.

Mischief. Ben Travers. LC 25-171448. 1925. Doubleday, Page & Company.

Mischief. Ben Travers. LC 33-28734. 1933. Doubleday, Doran & Company, Inc.

Mischief. Ben Travers. LC 78-4746. 12.95 (ISBN 0-06-014347-9). Harper & Row.

Mischief. Ben Ames Williams. LC 33-32767. E. P. Dutton & Co., Inc.

Mischief in the Lane. August William Derleth. LC 44-6480. 1944. C. Scribner's Sons.

Mischief in the Wind. Isabel Constance Clarke. LC 39-4594.

Mischief-Maker. Edward Phillips Oppenheim. 1913. 1.25. Little, Brown, and Company.

Mischief-Maker. Edward Phillips Oppenheim. LC 12-224204. 1912. Little, Brown, and Company.

Mischief Makers. William Haggard. LC 81-71418. 1982. 10.95 (ISBN 0-8027-5471-6). Walker.

Mischief of Monica. Lucy Bethia Colguhoun Walford. LC 8-32810. (On cover: Lovell's international series. 180). 1891. J. W. Lovell Company.

Mischievous Genie. Charles L. McKinley. 3.50 o.p. Carlton.

Miscreant. Jean Cocteau. 12.95x (ISBN 0-8464-0634-9). Beekman Pubs.

Miscreant. Lawrence O'Sullivan. LC 69-10226. 1969. 6.95. Holt, Rinehart and Winston.

Miser. Lesley Egan, pseud. LC 80-2993. (Crime Club Ser.). 192p. 1981. 9.95 (ISBN 0-385-17626-0). Doubleday.

Miser. Elizabeth Linington. LC 80-2993. 1981. 9.95 (ISBN 0-385-17626-0). Published for the Crime Club by Doubleday.

Miser Farebrother. A Novel. Benjamin Leopold Farjeon. (Harper's Franklin square library. no. 614). 1887. Harper & Brothers.

Miser Hoadley's Secret: A Detective Story. Arthur Williams Marchmont. LC 2-16451. 1902. New Amsterdam Book Company.

Miser: Ricketicketack; and The Poor Gentleman. Three Tales. murphy & co.; ed. Hendrik Conscience & Mayer, Brantz, 1809-1879, Tr. LC 6-28060. 1856. J. B. Lippincott & Co.

Miserable Clerk. Steele Rudd. (O.s.i.). 1973. 2.25x o.s.i. (ISBN 0-7022-0822-1). U of Queensland Pr.

Miserable Sinner. Dolf Wyllarde. LC 32-10751. The Macaulay Company.

Miserable Woman. H. C. Hoffman. (On cover: Munro's library, popular novels. v. 1. no. 398). 1885. N. L. Munro.

Miserable Woman. H. C. Hoffman. (On cover: Clover ser. no. 123). Street & Smith.

Miserables: A Novel. Victor Marie Hugo. Tr. by Sir Frederick Charles Lascelles Wraxall & Charles Edwin Wilbour. A., H. L., Ed. LC 42-535. Donohue, Henneberry & Co.

Miserere: A Musical Story. Mabel Wagnalls. LC 8-32829. 1892. Funk & Wagnalls Company.

Miserere: A Musical Story. rev., 3d ed. Mabel Wagnalls. LC 6-34364. 1906. Funk & Wagnalls Company.

Misericordia. A Story. Elizabeth Lynn Linton. LC 7-19009. (Appletons' new handy-volume series v. 3). 1878. D. Appleton and Company.

Miseries of Fo Hi: A Celestial Functionary. Francisque Sarcey & H., H. R., Tr. LC 8-1813. 1883. Jansen, McClurg & Company.

Miseries of Marriage: Or, The Fair of May Fair. Catherine Grace Frances Moody Gore. LC 6-44741. 1834. E. L. Carey & A. Hart: Boston, Allen & Ticknoir.

Miseries of Paris. Eugene Sue. Tr. by Henry Llewellyn Williams. (Souvenir series no. 9). 1892. The F. M. Lupton Publishing Company.

Miser's Heir: Or, The Young Millionaire. Peter Hamilton Myers. LC 7-23121. T. B. Peterson.

Miser's Money. Eden Phillpotts. 1920. The Macmillan Company.

Misfire. Jonathan Evans. 512p. 1982. pap. 3.50 (ISBN 0-523-48032-6). Pinnacle Bks.

Misfit Christmas Puddings. Consolation Club. LC 6-45358. 1906. J. W. Luce & Company.

Misfits. Arthur Miller. LC 61-6089. 1961. Viking Press.

Misfits and Remnants. Luigi Donato Ventura & Shevitch, S., Joint Author. 1886. Ticknor and Company.

Misfortunes of a Chicano: A Search for Identity Amid Poverty and Discrimination. Rogelio Leonardo Carpintero. LC 76-47812. 1977. 6.50 (ISBN 0-87164-036-8). William-Frederick Press.

Misfortunes of Elphin and Crochet Castle. Thomas Love Peacock. LC 25-26585. (Half-title: The World's classics ccxliv). 1924. H. Milford.

Misfortunes of Elphin and Rhododaphne. Thomas Love Peacock. Ed. by Saintsbury, George Edward Bateman. LC 7-337462. 1897. Macmillan and Co.

Misfortunes of Mary. Kem, Arnold. LC 63-39715. 1959. Oceanic-Press.

Misfortunes of Mr. Teal. Leslie Charteris. (Saint Ser.). (Illus.). 336p. 1982. pap. 2.50 (ISBN 0-441-53476-7, Pub. by Charter Bks). Ace Bks.

Misfortunes of Mr. Teal: The New Saint Book. Leslie Charteris. LC 34-16902. 1934. Pub. for the Crime Club, Inc., by Doubleday, Doran & Company, Inc.

Mishaps of Mr. Ezekiel Pelter... Alvin S. Higgins. LC 7-4768. 1875. S. C. Griggs and Company.

Misjudged. Bertha Behrens. Tr. by Mary E. Almy. (On cover: Globe library, no. 164). 1891. Rand, McNally & Company.

Misjudged. Bertha Behrens & Davis, Mrs. J. W., Tr. LC 6-9437. (On cover: Worthington's international library, no. 20). 1891. Worthington Company.

Misjudged Hero. Lisabeth Dawson. The Neely Company.

Miskel: A Novel. Lundern M Phillips. LC 7-36058. 1895. The Editor Publishing Co.

Mislaid Charm. Alexander Moore Phillips. LC 47-23973. 1947. The Prime Press.

Misleading Lady. Charles William Goddard & Dickey, Paul, 1885-1933, Joint Author. LC 15-18574. 1915. Hearst's International Library Co.

Misleading Lady. S. Andrew Wood. LC 26-11319. 1926. Cassell and Company, Ltd.

Mismated Shoes: By Arthur J. Clark; Written and Edited by Vinton C. Arnold. Rev. Arthur J Clark. LC 54-44386.

Misplaced. Griffin, Elsie Hazeltine. LC 64-18619. 1964. Royal Pub. Co.

Misplaced Corpse. Sarah Rider. LC 40-33594. 1940. Houghton Mifflin Company.

Misplaced Love: Or, The Rector's Daughter. Charlotte M. Stanley McKenna. LC 8-28178. (On cover: The library of American authors. no. 32). 1891. G. Munro.

Misplaced Machine and Other Stories. Jose J Veiga. LC 75-111233. 1970. 4.95. Knopf.

Miss Abbie's Honor. Jan Isbell Fortune. LC 48-6919. 1948. Appleton-Century-Crofts.

Miss Adventure. Rob Eden. LC 48-182895. 1948. Gramercy Pub. Co.

Miss Agatha Doubles for Death: A Recommended Mystery. H. L. V Fletcher. LC 47-17969. 1947. J. Messner, Inc.

Miss Agatha Doubles for Death: A Recommended Mystery by H. L. V. Fletcher. Harry Lutf Verne Fletcher. LC 47-17969. 1947. J. Messner, Inc.

Miss Aladdin. Christine Whiting Paramenter. LC 32-318959. Thomas Y. Crowell Company.

Miss Allick. Rupert Croft-Cooke. LC 47-1964. 1947. H. Holt and Company.

Miss America. Daniel Stern. LC 59-5704. 1959. Random House.

Miss America. Daniel Stern. 1973. (pbk.) 1.50. Lancer.

Miss American Dollars: A Romance of Travel. Paul Myron Wentworth Linebarger. LC 16-15594. 1916. 1.25. Midnation Publishers.

Miss Amerikanka: A Story. Olive Gilbreath. LC 18-602365. 1913. 1.40. Harper & Brothers.

Miss Angel. A Novel. Anne Isabella Thackeray Ritchie. LC 7-41666. 1875. Harper & Brothers.

Miss Anna. Edith Patton Oliver. LC 67-30779. (Illus.). 1968. Broland Pub.

Miss Annie. Omar Fletcher. (Orig.). 1978. pap. 1.75 (ISBN 0-87067-528-1, BH528). Holloway.

Miss Archer Archer. A Novel. Clara Louise Root Burnham. LC 6-19676. 1897. Houghton, Mifflin and Company.

Miss Armstrong's and Other Circumstances. John Davidson. LC 6-32865. 1896. Stone & Kimball.

Miss Ayr of Virginia, & Other Stories: & Other Stories. Julia Magruder. LC 7-20130. 1896. H. S. Stone & Co.

Miss Ayr of Virginia, & Other Stories. Julia Magruder. LC 77-110207. (Short story index reprint series). 1970. Books for Libraries Press.

Miss Bagg's Secretary. A West Point Romance. Clara Louise Root Burnham. LC 6-19675. 1892. Houghton, Mifflin and Company.

Miss Bagshot Goes to Moscow. Anne Telscombe. 1960. 3.50 o.p. Washburn.

Miss Bagshot Goes to Moscow: A Novel. Anne Telscombe. LC 61-7983. 1961. Washburn.

Miss Bagshot Goes to Tibet: A Novel. Anne Telscombe. LC 62-14657. 1962. Washburn.

Miss Bannister's Girls. Louise Stickney Tanner. LC 63-9392. 1963. Farrar, Straus.

Miss Barrett's Elopement. Carola Mary Anima Levanton. H. Holt and Company.

Miss Bayle's Romance: A Story of to-Day. William Fraser Rae. LC 8-201. (Leisure moment series, no. 82). 1887. H. Holt and Company.

Miss Beck. A Novel. Tilbury Holt. LC 7-5186. G. W. Carleton & Co.

Miss Bede is Staying. Anna Gilbert. 320p. 1983. 12.95 (ISBN 0-312-53471-X). St Martin.

Miss Belinda's Friends. Mary Dwinell Chellis. LC 6-23408. (On cover: The Chellis library). 1885. National Temperance Society and Publication House.

Miss Belladonna: A Child of to-Day. Caroline Ticknor. LC 8-19938. 1897. Little, Brown, and Company.

Miss Belladonna: A Social Satire. New Ed., with Additional Chapters. Caroline Ticknor. LC 2-23302. 1902. Little, Brown, and Company.

Miss Bellard's Inspiration: A Novel. William Dean Howells. 1905. Harper & Brothers.

Miss Bertha & the Yankee & Other Stories. Wilkie Collins. Repr. lib. bdg. 10.30x (ISBN 0-89190-248-1). Am Repr-Rivercity Pr.

Miss Betty's Happy Songs for Little People. Betty G. Hiles. (Illus.). 1973. pap. 9.95 with record (ISBN 0-8497-6608-7, GE17, Pub. by GWM). Kjos.

Miss Bianca in the Antarctic. Margery Sharp. LC 75-158484. 1971. 8.95 (ISBN 0-316-78294-7). Little.

Miss Bianca in the Orient. Margery Sharp. LC 79-119110. (Illus.). 1970. 6.95 o.p. (ISBN 0-316-78319-6). Little.

Miss Billy. Eleanor Hodgman Porter. LC 11-112842. 1911. L. C. Page & Company.

Miss Billy. Eleanor Hodgman Porter. LC 20-12353. 1919. The Page Company.

Miss Billy--Married. Eleanor Hodgman Porter. LC 14-2274. 1914. 1.25. The Page Company.

Miss Billy--Married. Eleanor Hodgman Porter. LC 24-22208. 1920. The Page Company.

Miss Billy, a Neighborhood Story. Edith Keeley Stokely & Hurd, Marian Kent, Joint Author. LC 5-10918. 1905. Lothrop Publishing Company.

Miss Billy's Decision. Eleanor Hodgman Porter. LC 12-15632. 1912. L. C. Page & Company.

Miss Bishop. Bess Streeter Aldrich. LC 75-29116. 1975. 6.95. Aeonian Press.

Miss Bishop. Bess Streeter Aldrich. LC 33-220802. 1933. D. Appleton-Century Company, Incorporated.

Miss Blake's Husband: A Novel. Elizabeth Garver Jordan. 2.00. The Century Co.

Miss Blinker's Blinds: Containing an Interesting Account of Miss Blinker's Trials and Adventures in Endeavoring to Observe the Doings of Her Neighbors. Edward E. Ten Eyck. F. Tousey.

Miss Boo Is Sixteen. Margaret Lee Runbeck. LC 56-115787. 1957. Houghton Mifflin.

Miss Bracegirdle and Others. Stacy Aumonier. LC 23-160405. 1923. Doubleday, Page & Company.

Miss Breckenridge. A Daughter of Dixie. Itti Kinney Rcno. LC 7-306493. 1890. J. B. Lippincott Company.

Miss Bretherton. Ward, Mary Augusta (Arnold) "Humphry Ward & Gladstone, William Ewart, 1809-1898. (On cover: Lovell's library, no. 1308). 1888. J. W. Lovell Company.

Miss Bronska. Gene Henry. LC 42-1191. 1942. Dodd, Mead & Company.

Miss Bronska. Gene Henry. LC 42-119110. 1942. Dodd, Mead & Company.

Miss Brooks. A Story. Eliza Orne White. LC 8-36621. 1890. Roberts Brothers.

Miss Brown. Violet Paget. LC 76-20088. (Decadent Consciousness). 1979. 35.00 (ISBN 0-8240-2766-3). Garland.

Miss Brown. A Novel. Violet Paget. (Harper's Franklin square library, no. 453). 1885. Harper & Brothers.

Miss Brown. A Novel. Violet Paget. (On cover: Seaside library. Pocket ed. no 399). 1885. G. Munro.

Miss Brown of X. Y. O. Edward Phillips Oppenheim. LC 27-17229. 1927. Little, Brown, and Company.

Miss Buncle: Married. Dorothy Emily Stevenson. LC 37-284444. 1937. Farrar & Rinehart, Inc.

Miss Buncle, Married. Dorothy Emily Stevenson. LC 37-28444. 1937. Farrar & Rinehart, Inc.

Miss Buncle's Book. Dorothy Emily Stevenson. LC 37-274783. Farrar & Rinehart, Inc.

Miss Buncle's Book. Dorothy Emily Stevenson. LC 37-27478. Farrar & Rinehart, Inc.

Miss Bunting. Angela Mackail Thirkell. LC 46-808. 1946. A. A. Knopf.

Miss Busybody. Watkins Eppes Wright. LC 44-5021. 1944. Gramercy Pub. Co.

Miss Canary. Chara Broughton Conant. 1865. American Baptist Publication Society.

Miss Caprice. A Novel. St. George Rathborne. LC 8-585. (On cover: Primrose series, no. 38). 1893. Street & Smith.

Miss Carstairs Dress for Bloodings. Peter Redgrove. 112p. 1981. pap. 5.95 o.p. (ISBN 0-7145-2557-X, Pub. by M Boyars). Merrimack Pub Cir.

Miss Carter and the Ifrit. Elizabeth Burton. LC 77-84239. (Lost Race and Adult Fantasy Fiction). 1978. 12.00 (ISBN 0-405-10987-3). Arno Press.

Miss Carter Came with Us. Helen Bradley. 1974. 6.95 o.p. (ISBN 0-316-10540-6). Little.

Miss Catastrophe. Jane Corrie. (Collection Harlequin Ser.). 192p. 1983. pap. 1.95 (ISBN 0-373-49336-3). Harlequin Bks.

Miss Cayley's Adventures. Grant Allen. LC 79-8227. (Illus.). Repr. of 1899 ed. 44.50 (ISBN 0-404-61756-5). AMS Pr.

Miss Charlesworth. Mabel Louise Tyrrell. LC 33-27104. 1933. Frederick A. Stokes Company.

Miss Cherry-Blossom of Tokyo. John Luther Long. LC 7-15149. 1895. J. B. Lippincott Company.

Miss Cherry Blossom of Tokyo. John Luther Long. 1905. J. B. Lippincott Company.

Miss Cheyne of Essilmont. James Grant. LC 44-20555. G. Routledge and Sons.

Miss Chunk: A Tale of the Times. Walter Vrooman. LC 8-33100. (On cover: The volunteers quarterly, v 1. no. 3). 1897. W. Vrooman.

Miss Churchill; a Study. Frances Christine Tiernan. LC 8-19807. 1887. D. Appleton and Company.

Miss Clare Remembers. Miss Read. 1963. 3.75 o.p. (ISBN 0-395-08110-6). HM.

Miss Condon. Aline Frankau Bernstein. LC 47-1678. 1947. A. A. Knopf.

Miss Cordelia Harling. Darrell Husted. 1978. 1.75 (ISBN 0-445-04274-5). Popular Library.

Miss Cordelia Harling. Darrell Husted. LC 79-19641. (Series: Regency Romance.). 1980. 9.95 (ISBN 0-89340-239-7). J. Curley.

Miss Crespigny. Frances Hodgson Burnett. LC 6-17374. C. Scribner's Sons.

Miss Crespigny. A Love Story. Frances Hodgson Burnett. LC 6-17373. T. B. Peterson & Brothers.

Miss Curtis: A Sketch. Catherine Boott Gannett Wells. LC 8-36649. 1888. Ticknor and Company.

Miss Davis of Brooklyn: A Novel. Florence Blackburn White Schoeffel. LC 8-2040. 1888. N. L. Munro.

Miss Dean's Dilemma. Dorothy Emily Stevenson. LC 38-8221. Farrar & Rinehart, Inc.

Miss Dean's Dilemma. Dorothy Emily Stevenson. LC 38-8221. Farrar & Rinehart, Inc.

Miss Delicia Allen. Mary Johnston. LC 33-6786. 1933. Little, Brown, and Company.

Miss Derrick. A Boston Society Girl's Diary. Evelyn Chester. LC 6-24211. 1894. G. W. Dillingham.

Miss Desmond: An Impression. Marie Van Vorst. LC 5-34699. 1905. The Macmillan Company.

Miss Dilly Says No. Theodore Pratt. LC 45-2361. 1945. Duell Sloan & Pearce.

Miss Doctor. Elizabeth Seifert. LC 51-9877. 1951. Dodd, Mead.

Miss Doctor. Elizabeth Seifert. LC 73-79157. 1973. 6.95. Aeonian Press.

Miss Dulcie from Dixie. Lulah Ragsdale. LC 17-21975. 1917. 1.40. D. Appleton and Company.

Miss Eaton's Romance. A Story of the New Jersey Shore. Richard Allen. Dodd, Mead and Company.

Miss Elizabeth of Hell. Walter S Faulkner. LC 34-360344. Lebanon Banner Printing Co.

Miss Erin. A Novel. Mary E. Sweetman Blundell. LC 98-11873. 1898. Benziger Brothers.

Miss Esperance and Mr. Wycherly. Lizzie Allen Harker. 1908. C. Scribner's Sons.

Miss Eyon of Eyon Court. Katharine Sarah Gadsden Macquoid. LC 7-20282. F. F. Lovell & Company.

Miss Fairfax of Virginia: A Romance of Love and Adventure Under the Palmettos. St. George Rathborne. LC 99-4685. Street & Smith.

Miss Fallowfield's Fortune. Ellen Thorneycroft Fowler. LC 8-29869. 1908. Dodd, Mead & Company.

Miss Fingal. Lucy Lane Clifford. LC 19-910010. 1919. C. Scribner's Sons.

Miss Flavia Farmer. Cecile Elizabeth Little. LC 52-1599. 1952. Pageant Press.

Miss Forrester. A Novel. Annie Edwards. 1873. Sheldon & Co.

Miss Frances Baird, Detective: A Passage from Her Memoirs, As Narrated to and Now Set Down. Reginald Wright Kauffman. LC 6-22315. 1906. L. C., Page & Company.

Miss Frances Merley. A Novel. John Elliott Curran. LC 6-31724. (Half-title: Collection of American authors. American Tauchnitz ed. vol.1). 1888. Cupples and Hurd.

Miss Gascoigne. A Novel. Charlotte Eliza Lawson Cowan Riddell. (On cover; Seaside library. Pocket ed., no. 1007). 1887. G. Munro.

Miss Giardino. Dorothy Bryant. LC 78-54280. 1978. pap. 6.00 (ISBN 0-931688-01-9). Ata Bks.

Miss Gibbie Gault: A Story. Kate Lee Langley Bosher. LC 11-10051. 1911. Harper & Brothers.

Miss Gifford's: A Novel. Kathrine Jones. 1948. Exposition Press.

Miss Gilbert's Career: An American Story. Josiah Gilbert Holland. 1860. C. Scribner; Etc., Etc.

Miss Gilbert's Career: An American Story. Josiah Gilbert Holland. LC 4-15455. 1901. C. Scribner's Sons.

Miss Gilbert's Career: An American Story. Josiah Gilbert Holland. LC 21-4121. 1909. C. Scribner's Sons.

Miss Good-for-Nothing. Tr. from the German of W. Heimburg Pseud. Bertha Behrens & Miller, Hettie E., Tr. (On cover: The Marguerite series, no. 11). E. A. Weeks & Company.

Miss Gossip from Thrush Green. Read. 246p. 1981. 18.50x (ISBN 0-7181-2046-9). State Mutual Bk.

Miss Grace of All Souls' William Edward Tirebuck. LC 8-26764. 1895. Dodd, Mead and Company.

Miss Granby's Secret: Or, The Bastard of Pinsk. Eleanor Farjeon. LC 41-5874. 1941. Simon and Schuster.

Miss Gunton of Poughkeepsie see Author of Beltraffio.

Miss Gwynne, Bachelor. A Novel. Winifred Wallace Tinker Johnes. LC 7-9914. 1894. G. W. Dillingham.

Miss Hadley's Finishing School. Clara Irene Patten. LC 31-977. Meador Publishing Company.

Miss Hard-Boiled. Jane Dixon. LC 30-17938. Grosset & Dunlap.

Miss Hargreaves. Frank Baker. LC 41-51588. Coward-McCann Inc.

Miss Haroun Al-Raschid. Jessie Douglas Kerruish. LC 17-139546. George H. Doran Company.

Miss Haroun Al-Raschid. Jessie Douglas Kerruish. LC 17-12392. 1917. Hodder and Stoughton.

Miss Harriet Townsend. Large Print ed. Kathleen Thompson Norris. LC 81-21319. 527p. 1982. Repr. of 1955 ed. Write for Info. (ISBN 0-89621-333-1). Thorndike Pr.

Miss Harriet Townshend. Kathleen Thompson Norris. LC 81-21319. 1982. 12.95 (ISBN 0-89621-333-1). Thorndike Press.

Miss Harriet Townshend. 1st Ed. Kathleen Thompson Norris. LC 55-5268. 1955. Doubleday.

Miss Harriett, and Other Stories. Guy De Maupassant. LC 71-157790. (Short story index reprint series). 1971. (ISBN 0-8369-3902-6). Books for Libraries Press.

Miss Harriett, & Other Stories: Collected Novels & Stories, Vol. 6. facsimile ed. Guy De Maupassant. Ed. by Ernest Boyd. LC 71-157790. (Short Story Index Reprint Ser.). Repr. of 1923 ed. 16.00 (ISBN 0-8369-3902-6). Ayer Co.

Miss Harrington's Husband. Florence Marryat Church Lean. (On cover: The seaside library. Pocket ed. no. 866). 1886. G. Munro.

Miss Herbert (the Suburban Wife) Christina Stead. LC 75-40561. 8.95 (ISBN 0-394-40517-X). Random House.

Miss Herbert (the Suburban Wife) Christina Stead. LC 80-24614. (Harvest/HBJ book). 1981. 5.95 (ISBN 0-15-660762-X). Harcourt Brace Jovanovich.

Miss Herbert: The Suburban Wife. Christina Stead. 1976. 8.95 (ISBN 0-394-40517-X). Random.

Miss High and Mighty. Margaret Rome. (Harlequin Romances Ser.). 192p. 1981. pap. 1.50 (ISBN 0-373-02445-2). Harlequin Bks.

Miss High-Heels. 1969. 6.00 o.p. (GP573). Grove.

Miss High-Heels. 1969. pap. 1.75 o.p. (Z1041, Zebra). Grove.

Miss High-Heels: The Story of a Rich but Girlish Young Gentleman Under the Control of His Pretty Step-Sister and Her Aunt. LC 71-79869. 1969. 6.00. Grove Press.

Miss Hogg, the American Heiress: A Novel. Victorine Clarisse Jacquet Jones. LC 2102. 1900. G. W. Dillingham Co.

Miss Hurd: An Enigma. Anna Katharine Green Rohlfs. LC 7-40748. 1894. G. P. Putnam's Sons.

Miss Hutchinson Steps Out: Adventures of a Small Doll at Large. Alice Hutchins Drake. LC 48-20601. 1947. House of Field-Doubleday.

Miss Ingalis. Gertrude Hall Brownell. LC 18-17247. 1918. The Century Co.

Miss Innocence: Or, Ignorance Not Bliss. A Novel. Alfred J. Cohen. (On cover: Vanity fair series, no. 5). 1891. E. Brandus & Co.

Miss J. Looks on. Sophie Kerr. LC 35-7531. Farrar & Rinehart, Inc.

Miss Jeffdrey's Neighborhood. Lucy Lincoln Montgomery. LC 26-21114. W. A. Wilde Company.

Miss Jerry. Alexander Black. LC 6-12423. 1895. C. Scribner's Sons.

Miss Jill: A Novel. Emily Hahn. LC 47-120472. 1947. Doubleday.

Miss Jimmy. Laura Elizabeth Howe Richards. LC 13-1380. 1.00. D. Estes & Company.

Miss Jolley's Family. Jane Ludlow Drake Abbott. LC 33-154982. J. B. Lippincott Company.

Miss Jones' Quilting. Marietta Holley. LC 7-6081. (fireside series no. 20). 1887. J. S. Ogilvie and Company.

Miss Kate: Or, Confessions of a Caretaker. Eliza M. J. Humphreys. (On cover: Lovell's international series, no. 14). 1889. F. F. Lovell & Company.

Miss Kate: Or, Confessions of a Caretaker. Eliza M. J. Humphreys. (On cover: Seaside library. Pocket ed., no. 1192). 1889. G. Munro.

Miss Kate: Or, Confessions of a Caretaker. Eliza M. J. Humphreys. LC 3018. (Arrow library. no. 121). 1900. Street & Smith.

Miss Keating's Temptation, No. 153. Margaret Sebastian, pseud. 224p. 1981. pap. 1.50 (ISBN 0-449-50226-0, Coventry). Fawcett.

Miss Lavinia's Call. Grace Livingston Hill. 2.50 o.p. G&D.

Miss Lavinia's Call: And Other Stories. Grace Livingston Hill. LC 49-11983. Lippincott.

Miss Leighton's Perplexities: A Love Story. Alice C Hall. LC 7-548. 1882. Fords, Howard, & Hubert.

Miss Lenora When Last Seen & Fifteen Other Stories. Peter Taylor. 1963. 12.50 (ISBN 0-8392-1070-1). Astor-Honor.

Miss Lillian Russell: A Novel Memoir. James Brough. LC 78-6448. 11.95 (ISBN 0-07-008120-4). McGraw Hill.

Miss Linsey and Pa. Stella Gibbons. LC 36-18875. 1936. Longmans, Green and Co.

Miss Linsey and Pa. Stella Gibbons. LC 36-17130. 1936. Longmans, Green and Co.

Miss Livingston's Companion: A Love Story of Old New York. Mary C Johnson Dillon. LC 11-8981. 1911. 1.30. The Century Co.

Miss Livingston's Companion: A Love Story of Old New York. Mary C Johnson Dillon. LC 22-145601. 1917. The Century Co.

Miss Lonelyhearts. Nathanael West. LC 33-14139. 1933. Liveright, Inc.

Miss Lonelyhearts, & The Day of the Locust. Nathanael West. LC 62-16924. (New Directions paperbook, no. 125). 1962. J. Laughlin.

Miss Lou,". Edward Payson Roe. LC 7-40234. 1888. Dodd, Mead and Company.

Miss Lou.". Edward Payson Roe. (On cover: Dodd, Mead & company's library of fiction, no. 4). Dodd, Mead & Co.

Miss Lou. Edward Payson Roe. LC 16-25020. Dodd, Mead and Company.

Miss Ludington's Sister. Edward Bellamy. LC 71-104414. 1970. (ISBN 0-8398-0161-0). Literature House.

Miss Ludington's Sister: A Romance of Immortality. Edward Bellamy. LC 6-11696. 1884. J. R. Osgood and Company.

Miss Lulu Bett. Zona Gale. LC 76-26895. 1976. 17.00 (ISBN 0-8371-9021-5). Greenwood Press.

Miss Lulu Bett. Zona Gale. LC 20-4218. 1920. D. Appleton and Company.

Miss Lulu Bett. Zona Gale. Ed. by Kelsey, Lella B. (Half-title: Appleton modern literature series). D. Appleton and Company.

Miss McCrea (1784) A Novel of the American Revolution.A Facsimile Reproduction,Together with a Translation from the French by Eric La Guardia, and with an Introd.by Lewis Leary. Michel Rene Hilliard D Auberteuil. LC 56-9146. 1958. Scholars' Facsimiles & Reprints.

Miss MacIntosh. My Darling. Marguerite Young. (Signet bk., J3020). 1967. pap., 1.95. New Amer. Lib.

Miss MacIntosh, My Darling. Marguerite Young. LC 65-15542. 1965. Scribner.

Miss MacIntosh, My Darling. Marguerite Young. LC 79-12048. (Harvest/HBJ book). 1979. 12.95 (ISBN 0-15-177083-2). Harcourt Brace Jovanovich.

Miss Mackenzie. Anthony Trollope. LC 25-265889. (Half-title: The World's classics. cclxxviii). 1924. H. Milford.

Miss Mackenzie. reprint ed. / introduction by juliet mcmaster. ed. Anthony Trollope. LC 80-1882. (Trollope, Anthony, 1815-1882. Selections. 1981). 1981. 65.00 (ISBN 0-405-14143-2). Arno Press.

Miss Madelyn Mack: Detective. Hugh Weir. LC 14-10071. 1914. The Page Company.

Miss Maggie and the Doctor. Una Troy. LC 58-5244. 1958. Dutton.

Miss Maitland, Private Secretary. Geraldine Bonner. LC 19-527508. 1919. D. Appleton and Company.

Miss Mallett: A Novel. Burke Boyce. LC 48-5905. 1948. Harper.

Miss Mamma Aimee. Erskine - Caldwell. LC 67-16941. 1967. New American Library.

Miss Mapp. Edward Frederic Benson. George H. Doran Company.

Miss Margaret Ridpath and the Dismantling of the Universe. Don Robertson. LC 76-51423. 10.00 (ISBN 0-399-11925-6). Putnam.

Miss Margery's Roses. A Love Story. Robert Cornelius V Myers. LC 7-25872. T. B. Peterson & Brothers.

Miss Marjoribanks. Margaret Oliphant Wilson Oliphant. LC 75-1546. (Victorian Fiction: Novels of Faith and Doubt). 1976. 35.00 (ISBN 0-8240-1615-7). Garland Pub.

Miss Marjoribanks. A Novel... Margaret Oliphant Wilson Oliphant. (Seaside library, v. 47, no. 959). 1881. G. Munro.

Miss Marjorie of Silvermead. Evelyn Everett Green. LC 1-249172. 1901. G. W. Jacobs & Co.

Miss Marks & Miss Wooley. Anna Mary Wells. 1978. 10.95 o.p. (ISBN 0-395-25724-7). HM.

Miss Marshall's Boys. Edward Cary Bass. LC 10-1229. 1909. 1.00. R. G. Badger.

Miss Marston. Luther H Bickford. LC 6-12906. (On cover: American author's series, no. 9). J. W. Lovell Company.

Miss Martha Brownlow: Or, The Heroine of Tennessee. A Truthful and Graphic Account of the Many Perils and Privations Endured by Miss Martha Brownlow... Daughter of the Celebrated Parson Brownlow, During Her Residence with Her Father in Knoxville. William D Reynolds. LC 1-13905. Barclay & Co.

Miss Martha Mary Crawford. Catherine Cookson. LC 75-18753. 1976. 7.95 (ISBN 0-688-02915-9). Morrow.

Miss Martha Mary Crawford. Catherine Cookson. 1977. 1.95 (ISBN 0-440-15271-2). Dell Pub. Co.

Miss Martha Mary Crawford. Catherine Marchant, pseud. (Adult Ser.). 1977. lib. bdg. 14.95 o.p. (ISBN 0-8161-6493-2, Large Print Bks). G K Hall.

Miss Martha Mary Crawford. Catherine Marchant, pseud. LC 75-18753. 288p. 1976. 7.95 o.p. (ISBN 0-688-02915-9). Morrow.

Miss Marvel. Esther Forbes. LC 35-14885. 1935. Houghton Mifflin Company.

Miss Maxwell's Affections: A Novel. Richard Pryce. LC 7-30084. (On cover: Harper's Franklin square library, no. 709). 1891. Harper & Brothers.

Miss Mayhew and Ming Yun: A Story of East and West. Anne Duffield. LC 28-972. 1928. Frederick A. Stokes Company.

Miss Melinda's Opportunity: A Story. Helen Stuart Campbell. LC 6-21489. 1886. Roberts Brothers.

Miss Mephistopheles: A Novel. Fergus Hume. (On cover: Lovell's detective series. no. 1). 1890. J. W. Lovell Company.

Miss Middleton's Lover: Or Parted on Their Bridal Tour. Laura Jean Libbey. LC 11-15077. 1888. American News Company.

Miss Millie's Trying. Mary Ellen Bamford. LC 6-629345. 1893. Hunt & Eaton.

Miss Million's Maid: A Romance of Love and Fortune. Berta Ruck. LC 15-21422. 1915. 1.35. Dodd, Mead and Company.

Miss Milne and I. By the Author of "A Yellow Aster"... Kathleen Mannington Hunt Caffyn. (On cover: Seaside library. Pocket ed., no. 2090). 1895. G. Munro's Sons.

Miss Minerva and William Green Hill. a facsim. ed. / with and introd. by robert drake. ed. Frances Boyd Calhoun. LC 75-20498. (Tennesseana Editions). (Illus.). 6.50 (ISBN 0-87049-182-2). University of Tennessee Press.

Miss Minerva and William Green Hill. Frances Boyd Calhoun. 1909. The Reilly & Britton Co.

Miss Minerva and William Green Hill. Frances Boyd Calhoun. LC 16-9368. The Reilly & Britton Co.

Miss Minerva and William Green Hill. Frances Boyd Calhoun. LC 17-269935. 1916. The Reilly & Britton Co.
Miss Minerva and William Green Hill. Frances Boyd Calhoun. LC 38-31705. The Reilly & Lee Co.
Miss Minerva on the Old Plantation. Emma Speed Sampson. LC 23-782745. The Reilly & Lee Co.
Miss Mink's Soldier, and Other Stories. Alice Caldwell Hegan Rice. LC 18-17613. 1918. The Century Co.
Miss Misanthrope: A Novel. Justin McCarthy. LC 7-15283. 1877. Sheldon & Company.
Miss Mischief: A Novel. Bertha Behrens & Smith, Mrs. Mary Stuart (Harrison) 1834- Tr. LC 6-9434. (choice series. 82). 1893. R. Bonner's Sons.
Miss Mischief. A Novel. Bertha Behrens & Smith, Mrs. Mary Stuart (Harrison) 1834- Tr. LC 6-24379. (Ledger series. no. 82). 1893. R. Bonner's Sons.
Miss Mole. Emily Hilda Young. LC 30-305668. Harcourt, Brace and Company.
Miss Mole. Emily Hilda Young. LC 32-20232. 1931. Harcourt, Brance and Company.
Miss Molly. Beatrice May Butt. LC 6-16673. (On cover: Leisure sour series. no. 60). 1876. H. Holt and Company.
Miss Mordeck's Father. Fani Pusey Gooch. LC 6-43729. Dodd, Mead & Company.
Miss Morissa. Mari Sandoz. 1975. 7.50 (ISBN 0-8038-4628-2). Hastings.
Miss Morissa: Doctor of the Gold Trail. Mari Sandoz. LC 79-23761. vi, 249p. 1980. pap. 5.50 (ISBN 0-8032-9118-3, BB 739, Bison). U of Nebr Pr.
Miss Morissa: Doctor of the Gold Trail; a Novel. Mari Sandoz. LC 55-9551. 1955. McGraw-Hill.
Miss Mouse. Mira Stables. 224p. 1981. pap. 1.95 (ISBN 0-449-50178-7, Coventry). Fawcett.
Miss Munday: A Novel by Sophia Belzer Engstrand. Sophia Belzer Engstrand. LC 40-27385. 1940. The Dial Press.
Miss Muriel and Other Stories. Ann Lane Petry. LC 75-150139. 1971. 6.95 (ISBN 0-395-12671-1). Houghton Mifflin.
Miss Mystery. Sydney Horler. LC 36-14627. 1935. Little, Brown, and Company.
Miss Mystery: A Novel. Etta Anthony Baker. LC 13-6545. 1913. 1.25. Little, Brown, and Company.
Miss Nancy... Ida. Rahm. LC 8-204. 1884. D. McKay.
Miss Nancy's Christmas Carol. Jean Moore Smith. LC 46-7330. 1946. The Exposition Press.
Miss Nancy's Pilgrimage. A Story of Travel. Virginia Wales Johnson. LC 7-10557. (On cover: Library of select novels, no. 471). 1876. Harper & Brothers.
Miss New York. Edmund Blair Pancake. R. F. Fenno & Company.
Miss Nobody from Nowhere. Elizabeth Garver Jordan. LC 28-8518. 2.00. The Century Co.
Miss Nobody of Nowhere: A Novel. Archibald Clavering Gunter. LC 4-354519. 1892. The Home Publishing Company.
Miss Ogilvy Finds Herself. Radclyffe Hall. LC 34-529620. Harcourt, Brace and Company.
Miss One Thousand Spring Blossoms. John Dudley Ball. 1980. 1.95 (ISBN 0-380-42325-1). Avon Books.
Miss One Thousand Spring Blossoms: A Novel. John Dudley Ball. LC 77-22743. 1977. 6.95 (ISBN 0-912588-48-9). Brooke House Publishers.
Miss One Thousand Spring Blossoms: A Novel. John Dudley Ball. LC 68-24239. 1968. 5.95. Little, Brown.
Miss Oona McQuarrie: A Sequel to Alfred Hagart's Household. Alexander Smith. LC 8-8190. 1866. Ticknor and Fields.
Miss Owen-Owen. Margaret Forster. LC 74-81855. 1969. 5.95. Simon and Schuster.
Miss Owen-Owen Is at Home. Margaret Forster. (O.s.i.). 1969. 5.95 o.s.i. (ISBN 0-671-20198-0). S&S.
Miss Pandora. M E Norman. LC 17-8742. 1916. George H. Doran Company.
Miss Parkworth and Three Short Stories. Edward Charles Booth. LC 72-125204. (Short story index reprint series). 1970. Books for Libraries Press.
Miss Parkworth: And Three Short Stories. Edward Charles Booth. LC 24-18760. 1924. 2.00. Dodd, Mead and Company.
Miss Pat. Elenore Meherin. LC 30-10082. Grosset & Dunlap.
Miss Peach. Mell Lazarus. 128p. (Orig.). 1981. pap. 1.75 (ISBN 0-553-14789-7). Bantam.
Miss Petticoats. Dwight Tilton. LC 2-12960. 1902. C. M. Clark Publishing Company.
Miss Pettigrew Lives for a Day. Winifred Watson. LC 39-238712. 1939. D. Appleton-Century Company, Incorporated.
Miss Pettinger's Niece. Dorothy Erskine. LC 49-11072. 1949. Creative Age Press.
Miss Phena. Flora May Stafford Swetnam. LC 16-22597. American Tract Society.
Miss Philadelphia Smith. Paula Allardyce, pseud. 1977. 7.95 o.p. (ISBN 0-698-10811-6, Coward). Putnam Pub Group.
Miss Philadelphia Smith. Ursula Torday. LC 76-30632. 1977. 7.95 (ISBN 0-698-10811-6). Coward, McCann & Geohegan.
Miss Philura's Wedding Gown. Florence Morse Kingsley. LC 12-24627. 1912. Dodd, Mead and Company.
Miss Pickthorn & Mister Hare. May Sarton. (Illus.). 1966. 14.95 (ISBN 0-393-08541-4). Norton.
Miss Pickthorn and Mr. Hare: A Fable. 1st Ed. May Sarton. LC 66-251689. 1966. bds., 3.50. Norton.
Miss Pilgrim's Progress. Concordia Merrel. LC 24-25412. 1924. T. Seltzer.
Miss Pim's Camouflage. Dorothy Tennant Stanley. LC 18-7289. 1918. Houghton Mifflin Company.
Miss Pink at the Edge of the World. Gwen Moffat. 220p. 1975. 6.95 o.p. (ISBN 0-684-14336-4). Scribner.
Miss Pink at the Edge of the World: A Crime Novel. Gwen Moffat. LC 75-4437. 6.95 (ISBN 0-684-14336-4). Scribner.
Miss Pinkerton. Mary Roberts Rinehart. LC 32-26040. Farrar & Rinehart, Incorporated.
Miss Pinkerton: Adventures of a Nurse Detective. Mary Roberts Rinehart. LC 59-5460. 1959. Rinehart.
Miss Plum and Miss Penny. Dorothy Evelyn Smith. LC 59-5811. 1959. Dutton.
Miss Polly Fairfax. Joy Wheeler Dow. 1898. Printed at the Printing House of P. F. McBreen.
Miss Primrose: A Novel. Roy Rolfe Gilson. LC 6-7720. 1906. Harper & Brothers.
Miss Prissy: By Jeanne Bowman Pseud. Peggy O'More, pseud. LC 53-8562. 1953. Arcadia House.
Miss Prissy's Diamond Rings: And Other Tales. Eva Josephine Beede Odell. LC 14-21623. 1914. 0.50. Huntington Art Press.
Miss Providence: A Novel. Dorothea Gerard Longard De Longgarde. LC 7-15158. (Half-title: Appletons' town and country library, no. 229). 1897. D. Appleton and Company.
Miss Prudence. Jennie Maria Drinkwater Conklin. LC 6-30406. 1883. R. Carter & Brothers.
Miss Pym Disappears. Josephine Tey. 1982. pap. cancelled (ISBN 0-671-43523-X). PB.
Miss Pym Disposes. Elizabeth Mackintosh. LC 48-685234. 1948. Macmillan Co.
Miss Pym Disposes. Josephine Tey. LC 79-19665. 1981. Repr. of 1948 ed. lib. bdg. 10.00x (ISBN 0-8376-0447-8). Bentley.
Miss Pym Disposes. Josephine Tey. 1971. pap. 1.25 (ISBN 0-425-03222-1, Medallion). Berkley Pub.
Miss Pym Disposes. Josephine Tey. 224p. 1982. pap. 2.95 (ISBN 0-671-43523-X). WSP.
Miss Ranskill Comes Home: A Novel. Barbara Euphan Todd Bower, pseud. LC 46-6174. 1946. G. P. Putnam's Sons.
Miss Ravenel's Conversion. John William De Forest. Ed. by Arlin Turner. 1969. 6.95 o.p. (ISBN 0-675-09391-0); pap. 0.95 o.p. (ISBN 0-675-09390-2). Merrill.
Miss Ravenel's Conversion. John William De Forest. Ed. by Gordon S. Haight. (Rinehart Editions). 1955. pap. text ed. 3.95 o.p. (ISBN 0-03-008585-3, HoltC). HR&W.
Miss Ravenel's Conversion from Secession to Loyalty. John William De Forest. LC 72-84546. 1974. 19.50 (ISBN 0-403-03090-0). Scholarly Press.
Miss Ravenel's Conversion from Secession to Loyalty. John William De Forest. LC 75-100633. (Charles E. Merrill program in American literature). (Charles E. Merrill standard editions.). 1969. (ISBN 0-675-09390-2). C. E. Merrill Pub. Co.
Miss Ravenel's Conversion from Secession to Loyalty. John William De Forest. LC 42-43995. 1867. Harper & Brothers.
Miss Ravenel's Conversion from Secession to Loyalty. John William De Forest. LC 75-100633. (Merrill Standard Ser). 6.00 (ISBN 0-675-09391-0); pap. 4.00 (ISBN 0-675-09390-2). Brown Bk.
Miss Ravenel's Conversion from Secession to Loyalty: Edited with an Introd. by Gordon S. Haight. John William De Forest. LC 55-8419. (Rinehart editions, 74). 1955. Rinehart.
Miss Reckless. Rob Eden. LC 46-184189. 1946. Gramercy Publishing Co.
Miss Reporter. Florence Stonebraker. LC 64-7301. Arcadia House.
Miss Rhode Island. Norman Kotker. LC 78-7261. 1978. 8.95 (ISBN 0-374-21038-1). Farrar Straus Giroux.
Miss Robin Hood. Rob Eden. LC 43-10326. 1943. Gramercy Publishing Co.
Miss Rolling Stone. Peter Loring. LC 39-110822. 1939. Macrae-Smith Company.
Miss Rollins in Love. Garibaldi Marto Lapolla. The Vanguard Press.
Miss Ruby's Novel. Samuel Isaac Joseph Schereschewsky. LC 8-2029. 1889. T. Whittaker.
Miss Sally. Robert Joe Stout. LC 73-3910. 1973. 6.95. Bobbs-Merrill.
Miss Santa Claus of the Pullman. Annie Fellows Johnston. LC 13-22755. 1913. 1.00. The Century Co.
Miss Schuyler's Alias. George Horton. LC 13-16794. R. G. Badger.
Miss Seeton Draws the Line. Heron Carvic. LC 77-100620. 1970. 4.95. Harper & Row.
Miss Seeton Sings. Heron Carvic. LC 72-9094. 1973. 5.95 (ISBN 0-06-010653-0). Harper & Row.
Miss Seeton Sings. Heron Carvic. LC 73-8602. 1973. 9.95 (ISBN 0-8161-6120-8). G. K. Hall.
Miss Selina Lue and the Soap-Box Babies. Maria Thompson Daviess. LC 9-26670. 1909. 1.00. The Bobbs-Merrill Company.
Miss Shafto. William Edward Norris. (On cover: Seaside library. Pocket ed. no. 1203). 1889. G. Munro.
Miss Shumway Waves a Wand. Rene Raymond. LC 44-4436. 1944. Jarrolds Limited.
Miss Silver Comes to Stay: A Miss Silver Mystery. Patricia Wentworth. LC 48-9672. (Main line mysteries). 1949. J. B. Lippincott Co.
Miss Silver Deals with Death. Patricia Wentworth. LC 43-14763. 1943. J. B. Lippincott Company.
Miss Silver's Past. Josef Skvorecky. LC 73-21044. 1975. 8.95 (ISBN 0-394-49293-5). Grove Press: Distributed by Random House.
Miss Slimmens' Boarding House. Metta Victoria Victor. LC 8-32796. J. S. Ogilvie & Company.
Miss Slimmens' Window, and Other Papers. Metta Victoria Victor. LC 8-32795. 1859. Derby & Jackson.
Miss Spring. Cecily Crowe. LC 53-5029. 1953. Random House.
Miss Stanton of the Cryer. Kathryn White. LC 41-3690. The Penn Publishing Company.
Miss Stuart's Legacy. Flora Annie Webster Steel. LC 8-13435. 1893. Macmillan and Co.
Miss Sue & the Sheriff. Robert B. House. ix, 118p. 1941. 6.50 (ISBN 0-8078-0374-X). U of NC Pr.
Miss Susie Slagle's. Augusta Tucker. LC 39-27947. 1939. Harper & Brothers.
Miss Sylvester's Marriage. Cecil Charles. 1903. The Smart Set Publishing Co.
Miss Theodora: A West End Story. Helen Leah Reed. LC 7-30951. 1898. R. G. Badger & Co.
Miss Theodosia's Heartstrings. Annie Hamilton Donnell. LC 16-19416. 1916. 1.00. Little, Brown, and Company.
Miss Tiverton Goes Out. LC 26-264101. 1926. The Bobbs-Merrill Company.
Miss Tommy. A Mediaeval Romance. Dinah Maria Mulock Craik. (On cover: Lovell's library, v. 8, no. 435). J. W. Lovell Company.
Miss Tommy. A Mediaeval Romance. And, In a Houseboat. A Journal. Dinah Maria Mulock Craik. LC 6-31079. (On cover: Seaside library. Pocket ed. no. 245). G. Munro.
Miss Toosey's Mission. Evelyn Whitaker. LC 19-2893. 1891. E. P. Dutton & Company.
Miss Toosey's Mission. Evelyn Whitaker. (Altemus' good times series). 1903. H. Altemus Company.
Miss Traumerei." A Weimar Idyl. Albert Morris Bagby. LC 6-5021. 1895. Lamson, Wolffe, and Company.
Miss Traumerei." A Weimar Idyl. Albert Morris Bagby. LC 6-5020. 1895. The Author.
Miss Turquoise: A David Grant Story. George Brown Mair. LC 65-212472. (Random mystery). 1965. bds., 3.95. Random.
Miss Van Kortland. A Novel. Frank Lee Benedict. LC 7-34450. 1870. Harper & Brothers.
Miss Varian of New York. A Newport and New York Society Novel. Laura Daintrey. LC 6-331879. 1887. G. W. Dillingham.
Miss Varney's Experience: And Other Stories. Eleanor Cecilia Donnelly & Kilpatrick, Mary Genevieve. LC 1-27105. H. L. Kilner & Co.
Miss Warren's Son. Elizabeth Garver Jordan. LC 45-6049. 1945. D. Appleton-Century Company Incorporated.
Miss Washington, of Virginia. A Semi-Centennial Love-Story. Jeannie Wormley Blackburn Moran. LC 7-262112. 1889. The Author.
Miss Washington, of Virginia. A Semi-Centennial Love-Story. Jeannie Wormley Blackburn Moran. LC 42-27371. 1905. H. M. Suter Publishing Company.
Miss Watts: An Old-Fashioned Romance. Ernest James Oldmeadow. LC 23-15829. 1923. 2.00. Longmans, Green and Co.
Miss Wealthy: Deputy Sheriff. Elizabeth Hyer Neff. LC 12-40583. 1912. Frederick A. Stokes Company.
Miss Welby at Steen. Archibald Marshall. LC 30-68099. 1930. Dodd, Mead & Company.
Miss Wentworth's Idea. authorized ed. William Edward Norris. LC 7-33287. (On cover: Lovell's international series. no. 171). J. W. Lovell Company.
Miss Willie. 2d ed. Janice Holt Giles. LC 70-132792. 1971. 6.95. Houghton Mifflin.
Miss Willie. Janice Holt Giles. LC 51-9085. 1951. Westminster Press.
Miss Wilton. Cornelia Warren. LC 8-33689. 1892. Houghton, Mifflin & Company.
Miss Wings. Florence Stonebraker. LC 41-16891. Gramercy Publishing Company.
Miss Withers Regrets: By Stuart Palmer. Stuart Palmer. LC 47-366019. 1947. Pub. for the Crime Club by Doubleday & Company, Inc.
Miss Worden's Hero. A Novel. Henry Barnard Salisbury. LC 8-373952. 1890. G. W. Dillingham.
Miss 318: A Story in Season and Out of Season. Rupert Hughes. LC 11-249768. Fleming H. Revell Company.
Miss 318 and Mr. 37. Rupert Hughes. LC 12-406575. Fleming H. Revell Company.
Missa Solemnis. Adolphe Ribaux & Sheldon, Jean B., Tr. 1902. Small, Maynard & Company.
Missed Connections: A Novel. Elaine Ford. LC 82-13270. 1983. 13.95 (ISBN 0-394-52980-4). Random House.
Missed It by That Much! William Johnston. LC 67-18858. (Tempo books, T-154). 1967. Grosset & Dunlap.
Missed Trains: A Novel. Arthur Cavanaugh. LC 78-24535. 10.95 (ISBN 0-671-22479-4). Simon and Schuster.
Misses Elliot of Geneva. Warren Hunting Smith. LC 40-31635. Farrar & Rinehart, Inc.
Misses Millikin. Maggie MacKeever. 224p. (Orig.). 1980. pap. 1.75 (ISBN 0-449-50074-8, Coventry). Fawcett.
Missiles of Zajecar. William F Hallstead. LC 69-17436. 1969. Chilton Book Co.
Missing. Thomas Hauser. 272p. 1982. pap. 2.95 (58834). Avon.
Missing. Mary Cecil Hay. LC 7-3758. (On cover: Harper's half-hour series no. 145). 1880. Harper & Brothers.
Missing,' Mary Augusta Arnold Humphry Ward Ward. LC 17-28797. 1917. Dodd, Mead and Company.
Missing--a Young Girl. authorized ed. Florence Alice Price James. LC 7-7415. (On cover: Lovell's Westminister series, no. 15). 1890. United States Book Company.
Missing: A Novel, Translated from the Czech by Ewald Osers. Egon Hostovsky. LC 52-8817. 1952. Viking Press.
Missing, and Presumed Dead. Joseph Arnold Hayes. LC 76-355578. 1977. 1.95 (ISBN 0-451-07687-7). New American Library.
Missing & the Dead. Jack Lynch. (Bragg Ser.: No. 2). 192p. 1982. pap. 2.50 (ISBN 0-449-14462-3, GM). Fawcett.
Missing Aunt. George Douglas Howard Cole & Margaret Isabel Postgate Cole. LC 38-5367. 1938. The Macmillan Company.
Missing Chancellor. Joseph Smith Fletcher. LC 27-369434. 1927. A. A. Knopf.
Missing Chord. A Novel. Lucy Dillingham. LC 6-36821. 1894. G. W. Dillingham.
Missing Finger: A Story of Mystery. by albert boissiere; tr. by mary j. safford. ed. Albert Boissiere & Safford, Mary Joanna, Tr. LC 11-23298. 1911. Dodd, Mead and Company.
Missing from Her Home. Anthony Gilbert, pseud. 1971. pap. 0.95 o.p. (95137). Beagle Bks.
Missing from Her Home. Anthony Gilbert, pseud. 1969. 4.95 o.p. (ISBN 0-394-41259-1). Random.
Missing from Her Home. Lucy Beatrice Malleson. LC 69-16469. 1969. 4.50. Random House.
Missing from His Home. Clifford James Wheeler Hosken. LC 41-7651. (On cover: Penguin books. 218). 1939. Penguin Books Limited.
Missing German. David Rees. LC 77-352200. 1976. 2.50 (ISBN 0-234-77696-X). Dobson.
Missing Grandfather. Frances Y. McHugh. 1972. pap. 0.75 o.s.i. (01-363). Lancer.
Missing Heiress. Bernice Carey. LC 52-8056. 1952. Published for the Crime Club by Doubleday.
Missing Heiress. Bernice Carey Martin. LC 52-8056. 1952. Published for the Crime Club by Doubleday.
Missing Hero. Annie French Hector. LC 1-30677. R. F. Fenne & Company.
Missing in Action. Bill Linn. LC 80-68427. 2.25 (ISBN 0-380-77370-8). Avon Books.
Missing Initial. Natalie Sumner Lincoln. LC 25-951523. 1925. D. Appleton and Company.
Missing Island. Oswald Kendall. LC 26-18100. 1926. Houghton Mifflin Company.
Missing Link. Warren Murphy. (Destroyer Ser.: No. 39). (Orig.). 1980. pap. 1.95 (ISBN 0-523-41254-1). Pinnacle Bks.
Missing Link. Carolyn Wells. LC 38-352619. J. B. Lippincott Company.

Missing Link. Carolyn Wells. LC 39-320583. 1939. Triangle Books.

Missing Link; a Story of New England Life. Charles Prentiss Kittredge & Kittredge, Ellen Rebecca (Thomas) LC 13-15851. 1.00. Safeguard Publishing Company.

Missing Man. Mary R. Platt Hatch. (On cover: Good company series, no. 22). 1893. Lee and Shepard.

Missing Man. Katherine MacLean. LC 74-16610. 1975. 6.95 (ISBN 0-399-11474-2). Berkley Pub. Corp.: Distributed by Putnam.

Missing Man. Katherine MacLean. (Berkley Medallion Book)). 1976. (pbk.) 1.25 (ISBN 0-425-03040-7). Berkley Publishing Corp.

Missing Man. Hillary Waugh. LC 64-13105. 1964. Published for the Crime Club by Doubleday.

Missing Man. Hillary Waugh. LC 81-47392. (Fifty Classics of Crime Fiction, 1950-1975). 1982. 14.95 (ISBN 0-8240-4953-5). Garland Pub.

Missing Masterpiece: A Novel. Hilaire Belloc. LC 30-262. 1929. Harper & Brothers.

Missing Matisse. Barbara Levy. LC 68-24839. 1969. 4.95. Doubleday.

Missing Men of Saturn: By Philip Latham Pseud. Jacket and Endpaper Designs by Alex Schomburg. 1st Ed. Robert Shirley Richardson. LC 53-7336. (Science fiction novel). 1953. Winston.

Missing Men: The Return of Cheri-Bibi. Gaston Leroux. LC 23-118097. The Macaulay Company.

Missing Millions. Edgar Wallace. LC 25-5545. Small, Maynard & Company.

Missing Miniature: Or, The Adventures of a Sensitive Butcher. Erich Kastner. Tr. by Brooks, Cyrus Harry. LC 37-84333. 1937. A. A. Knopf.

Missing Miniature: Or, The Adventures of a Sensitive Butcher. Erich Kastner. LC 39-30331. (A Mercury book, no. 21). The American Mercury, Inc.

Missing Partners. Henry Lancelot Aubrey-Fletcher. LC 28-19959. Payson & Clarke, Ltd.

Missing Person. Doris Grumbach. LC 80-24797. 11.95 (ISBN 0-399-12587-6). Putnam.

Missing Person. Doris Grumbach. LC 82-561. 1982. 4.95 (ISBN 0-14-004461-2). Penguin Books.

Missing Person. Oscar E Millard. LC 72-80964. 1972. 4.95. McKay.

Missing Persons. Heinrich Boll. Tr. by Leila Vennewitz from German. LC 77-9351. 1977. 9.95 (ISBN 0-07-006424-5, GB). McGraw.

Missing Persons. C. Terry Cline. LC 80-70215. 12.95 (ISBN 0-87795-304-X). Arbor House.

Missing Persons. Jack Olsen, pseud. LC 80-69375. 1981. 12.95 (ISBN 0-689-11133-9). Atheneum.

Missing Persons. large print ed. Jack Olsen, pseud. LC 81-18406. 1982. 12.95 (ISBN 0-89621-340-4). Thorndike Press.

Missing, Presumed Dead. Carlton Keith, pseud. 1969. pap. 0.60 o.p. (0502-06021-060). Curtis.

Missing, Presumed Dead: By Carlton Keith Pseud. 1st Ed. Keith Robertson. LC 61-12613. 1961. Published for the Crime Club, by Doubleday.

Missing Ship: Or, Notes from the Log of the "Ouzel" Galley. 8th thousand. ed. William Henry Giles Kingston. LC 44-43130. (On cover: The Boy's own favourite series). 1883. Griffith, Farran, Okeden & Welsh.

Missing Sibyl: Or, Found. Julia Edith Woolsy. LC 35-7175. 1935. Meador Publishing Company.

Missing Two... Gertrude M. Robins Reynolds. LC 32-24139. Pub. for the Crime Club, Inc., by Doubleday, Doran & Company, Inc.

Missing Widow. Lucy Beatrice Malleson. LC 48-6358. 1948. A. S. Barnes.

Missing Widow see Die in the Dark.

Missing Woman. Michael Z. Lewin. LC 80-39925. 224p. 1981. 10.95 (ISBN 0-394-50007-5). Knopf.

Missing Woman. Michael Z. Lewin. 224p. 1982. pap. 2.25 (ISBN 0-425-05391-1). Berkley Pub.

Missing Years: A Novel. Walter Ze'Ev Laqueur. LC 80-80087. 10.95 (ISBN 0-316-51472-1). Little, Brown.

Missing Years: 1st Ed. Patricia McGerr. LC 53-6946. 1953. Doubleday.

Mission. Dean Brelis. LC 58-5276. 1958. Random House.

Mission. Frank Camper. (Orig.). 1979. pap. 1.75 (ISBN 0-532-17243-4). Woodhill.

Mission. Marcos Spinelli. 1965. 4.95 o.p. (ISBN 0-8149-0211-1). Vanguard.

Mission. Patrick Tilley. 1981. 14.95 (ISBN 0-316-84541-8); pap. 7.95 (ISBN 0-316-84542-6). Little.

Mission: A Novel. Marcos Spinelli. LC 65-261598. bds., 4.95. Vanguard.

Mission: A Novel by Hans Habe Pseud. Tr.from the German by Michael Bullock. 1st Amer. Ed. Jean Bekessy, pseud. LC 66-13123. 6.00. Coward.

Mission: A Novel by Hans Habe. Translated from the German by Michael Bullock. Hans Habe. LC 66-13123. 1966. Coward-McCann.

Mission Accomplished. Translated from the French by Peter Green. Mongo Beti. LC 58-124363. 1958. Macmillan.

Mission Code: Acropolis. Bryan Swift, pseud. (Mac Wingate Ser.: No. 7). 192p. (Orig.). 1982. pap. 2.25 (ISBN 0-515-06038-0). Jove Pubns.

Mission Code Granite Island. Brian Swift, pseud. (Mac Wingate Ser.: No. 4). (Orig.). 1981. pap. 2.25 (ISBN 0-515-05548-4). Jove Pubns.

Mission Code: King's Pawn. Bryan Swift, pseud. (Mac Wingate Ser.: No. 2). 192p. (Orig.). 1981. pap. 2.25 (ISBN 0-515-05546-8). Jove Pubns.

Mission Code: Minotaur. Bryan Swift, pseud. (Mac Wingate Ser.: No. 3). 192p. (Orig.). 1981. pap. 2.25 (ISBN 0-515-05547-6). Jove Pubns.

Mission Code: Scorpion. Bryan Swift, pseud. 192p. 1982. pap. 2.25 (ISBN 0-515-06036-4). Jove Pubns.

Mission Code: Snow Queen. Bryan Swift, pseud. (Mac Wingate Ser.: No. 6). 192p. (Orig.). 1982. pap. 2.25 (ISBN 0-515-06039-9). Jove Pubns.

Mission Code: Springboard. Bryan Swift, pseud. (Mac Wingate Ser.: No. 5). (Orig.). 1982. pap. 2.25 (ISBN 0-515-06037-2). Jove Pubns.

Mission Code: Survival. Bryan Swift, pseud. (Mac Wingate Ser.: No. 10). (Orig.). 1982. pap. 2.25 (ISBN 0-515-06317-7). Jove Pubns.

Mission Code: Symbol. Bryan Swift, pseud. (Mac Wingate Ser.: No. 1). 192p. (Orig.). 1981. pap. 2.25 (ISBN 0-515-05545-X). Jove Pubns.

Mission Code: Track & Destroy. Bryan Swift, pseud. (Mac Wingate Ser.: No. 9). (Orig.). 1982. pap. 2.25 (ISBN 0-515-06376-2). Jove Pubns.

Mission Code: Volcano. Bryanx Swift, pseud. (Mac Wingate Ser.: No. 8). 1982. pap. 2.25 (ISBN 0-515-06375-4). Jove Pubns.

Mission Dangereuse. Jean-Jacques Antier. 1967. pap. 2.85 o.s.i. Paris Pubns.

Mission Flower: An American Novel. George Henry Picard. LC 7-35926. 1885. White, Stokes, & Allen.

Mission for Vengeance. Peter Rabe. LC 58-347945. (Gold medal books, S773). 1958. Fawcett Publications.

Mission Hopeless. J. E. Macdonnell. 1979. pap. cancelled o.s.i. (ISBN 0-8439-0670-7, Leisure Bks). Nordon Pubns.

Mission in Black. Gordon Cotler. LC 67-12762. 1967. Random House.

Mission in Guemo. Stanley Bennett Hough. LC 64-18691. 1964. Walker.

Mission in Sparrow Bush Lane: A Novel of Suspense in Wartime London. Alfred Boller Stanford. LC 66-17184. 1966. Morrow.

Mission in Tunis. Jacques Pendower. pap. 0.60 o.p. (53-496). Paperback Lib.

Mission Incredible. Lawrence Cortesi, pseud. 1979. pap. 1.25 o.s.i. (ISBN 0-505-51346-3). Tower Bks.

Mission: Interplanetary. Alfred Elton Van Vogt. LC 52-30872. (Signet book, 914). 1952. New American Library.

Mission into Time. L. Ron Hubbard. 1973. 19.00 (ISBN 0-88404-023-2). Bridge Pubns Inc.

Mission M. I. A. J. C. Pollock. (Orig.). 1983. pap. 3.50 (ISBN 0-440-15819-2). Dell.

Mission: Manstop. Kris Neville. 1974. pap. 0.75 o.p. (LB22S). Leisure Bks.

Mission M.I.A. A Novel. J. C Pollock. LC 81-15275. 12.95 (ISBN 0-517-54579-9). Crown Publishers.

Mission of Death: A Tale of the New York Penal Laws. Mansfield Tracy Walworth. LC 8-33122. D. & S. Sadlier & Co.

Mission of Fear. George Harmon Coxe. 1962. 3.50 o.p. Knopf.

Mission of Gravity. Hal Clement. (Science Fiction Ser.). 1978. lib. bdg. 12.00 o.p. (ISBN 0-8398-2426-2, Gregg). G K Hall.

Mission of Gravity. Hal Clement. 1969. pap. 0.75 o.p. (T2063). Pyramid Pubns.

Mission of Gravity. Hal Clement. 1974. pap. 0.95 o.p. (ISBN 0-515-03479-7, N3479). BJ Pub Group.

Mission of Gravity. Harry C Stubbs. LC 78-804. (Gregg Press science fiction series). 1978. 12.00 (ISBN 0-8398-2426-2). Gregg Press.

Mission of Gravity. Harry C Stubbs. (Del Rey Book). 1978. 1.75 (ISBN 0-345-27092-4). Ballantine Books.

Mission of Gravity: By Hal Clement Pseud. 1st Ed. Harry C Stubbs. LC 54-5720. 1954. Doubleday.

Mission of Jeffery Tolamy. Darwin Le Ora Teilhet. LC 51-11312. 1951. Sloane.

Mission of Mercy. John Branfroot Simpson Pedler. LC 69-17947. 1969. 5.95. Stein and Day.

Mission of Mercy. Dominic Torr. LC 69-17947. 1969. 5.95 o.p. (ISBN 0-8128-1217-4). Stein & Day.

Mission of Mercy: An Adventure Story from the Mission Field. Bernard Alvin Palmer. LC 47-259. 1946. Van Kempen Press.

Mission of Ponbalov. Frederick Russell Burton. (On cover: Criterion series, no. 20). Street & Smith.

Mission of Victoria Wilhelmina. Jeanne Bartholow Magoun. LC 12-21914. 1912. B. W. Huebsch.

Mission: Or, Scenes in Africa. Frederick Marryat. LC 21-153696. (Seaside library, v. 44, no. 898). 1880. G. Munro.

Mission, or Scenes in Africa. Frederick Marryat. LC 72-131908. (Colonial Novel Ser). (Illus.). 1970. Repr. of 1845 ed. 25.00x (ISBN 0-8419-0057-4, Africana). Holmes & Meier.

Mission: Or, Scenes in Africa. Written for Young People. new ed. Frederick Marryat. LC 12-31397. G. Routledge & Sons.

Mission: Or, Scenes in Africa, Written for Young People. Frederick Marryat. LC 42-35606. 1887. G. Routledge and Sons.

Mission River Justice. Wilbur C. Tuttle. LC 55-14832. 1955. Avalon Books.

Mission: Sneaky Sam see Plague of Spies.

Mission Tales in the Days of the Dons. Harrie Rebecca Piper Smith Forbes. LC 71-128735. (Short story index reprint series). (Illus.). 1970. Books for Libraries Press.

Mission Tales in the Days of the Dons. Harrie Rebecca Piper Smith Forbes. LC 9-7438. 1909. A. C. McClurg & Co.

Mission to Allegewi. Wilfrid Laurier Burke. LC 72-83664. (Illus.). 1972. 5.95 (ISBN 0-8059-1729-2). Dorrance.

Mission to Circassia. Kathleen Odell. LC 77-3802. (Illus.). 10.00 (ISBN 0-06-013287-6). Harper & Row.

Mission to Claudius: A Novel of the Most Fascinating Years of the First Century, A.D. Leon Kolb. LC 63-12155. 1963. Genuart Publishers.

Mission to Hell. Edward Eells. LC 9-26957. 1909. Sherman, French & Company.

Mission to Kala. Mongo Beti. (African Writers Ser.). 1964. pap. text ed. 3.00x (ISBN 0-435-90013-7). Heinemann Ed.

Mission to Mackinac. Myron David Orp. LC 56-12213. 1956. Dodd, Mead.

Mission to Mackinac. Myron David Orr. LC 56-122138. 1956. Dodd, Mead.

Mission to Malaspiga. Eve Stephens, pseud. LC 74-79687. 1974. 7.95 (ISBN 0-698-10608-3). Coward, McCann & Geoghegan.

Mission to Monte Carlo, No. 161. Barbara Cartland. 160p. Date not set. 2.25. Bantam.

Mission to Moulokin. Alan Dean Foster. 1979. pap. 2.50 (ISBN 0-345-29661-3, Del Rey Bks.). Ballantine.

Mission to Murder. Cover Painting by Barye Phillips. Richard Glendinning. LC 55-20534. (Gold medal books, 444). 1954. Fawcett Publications.

Mission to the Stars. Alfred Elton Van Vogt. (Kangaroo Book). 1977. 1.50 (ISBN 0-671-81451-6). Pocket Books.

Mission to the West. Theodore V Olsen. LC 72-92235. (DD western). 1973. 4.95 (ISBN 0-385-06021-1). Doubleday.

Mission to the West. Theodore V Olsen. 1976. (pbk.) 1.25. Ace Books.

Mission to Universe. Gordon R Dickson. LC 76-56760. 1977. 1.50 (ISBN 0-345-25703-0). Ballantine Books.

Mission to Venice. Nick Carter. (Nick Carter Ser). (O.s.i.). 1966. pap. 0.60 o.s.i. (AX0632, Award). Univ Pub & Dist.

Missionaries. Geoffrey Moorhouse. (Illus.). 368p. 1973. 7.95 o.p. (ISBN 0-397-00801-5). Lippincott.

Missionary. Edison Marshall. LC 30-7103. 1930. Cosmopolitan Book Corporation.

Missionary. John Weld. 180p. (Orig.). 1980. 15.00 (ISBN 0-89002-176-7); pap. 5.00 (ISBN 0-89002-175-9). Am Hist Pr.

Missionary. Grace Yankey. LC 47-6623. 1947. J. Day Co.

Missionary, an Indian Tale. Sydney Owenson Morgan. LC 7-18749. 1811. Published by the Franklin Company, and by Butler and White, Corner of Wall and William Streets.

Missionary and the Witch-Doctor,". Henry Rider Haggard. LC 20-224479. 1920. Paget Literary Agency.

Missionary Sheriff. facs. ed. Alice French. LC 70-75777. (Short Story Index Reprint Ser.). 1897. 15.00 (ISBN 0-8369-3002-9). Ayer Co.

Missionary Sheriff: Being Incidents in the Life of a Plain Man Who Tried to Do His Duty. Alice French. LC 70-75777. (Short story index reprint series). (Illus.). 1969. Books for Libraries Press.

Missionary Sheriff: Being Incidents in the Life of a Plain Man Who Tried to Do His Duty. Alice French. LC 4-15110. 1897. Harper & Brothers.

Missionary: 1811. Sydney Owenson Morgan. LC 80-20308. (Illus.). 1981. 35.00 (ISBN 0-8201-1358-1). Scholar's Facsimiles & Reprints.

Missionary's Daughters. Benjamin McKnight. pap. 1.95 o.s.i. (Venus). Grove.

Missioner. Edward Phillips Oppenheim. LC 7-41581. 1907. Little, Brown, and Company.

Mississippi. Ben Lucien Burman. LC 29-181622. 1929. Cosmopolitan Book Corporation.

Mississippi Argonauts: A Tale of the South. John Henton Carter. LC 4-522. 1903. Dawn Publishing Company.

Mississippi Belle. Clements Ripley. LC 42-568836. 1942. D. Appleton-Century Company, Incorporated.

Mississippi Flame. Walter Ryerson Johnson. LC 53-25383. (Red seal book, 28). 1953. Fawcett Publications.

Mississippi Gambler: A Heart Stirring Romance of the South. Karl Brown & Fields, Leonard, Joint Author. LC 30-152117. Jacobsen Publishing Company, Inc.

Mississippi Hawk. Oscar J Friend. LC 29-25893. 1929. A. C. McClurg & Company.

Mississippi Jimmy. Clement Yore. LC 33-184761. The Macaulay Company.

Mississippi Mood. Francois De La Roche. LC 38-9625. 1937. H. A. Burk & Co.

Mississippi Odyssey. Chris Markham. 1980. 15.00; pap. 7.95. Northwoods Pr.

Mississippi Run. Paul Darcy Boles. LC 76-27875. 10.00 (ISBN 0-690-01158-X). Crowell.

Mississippi Schoolmaster. Henrietta Matson. LC 72-1511. (Black Heritage Library Collection). (Illus.). 1972. 12.50 (ISBN 0-8369-9035-8). Books for Libraries Press.

Mississippi Schoolmaster: A Story. Henrietta Matson. LC 7-25566. Congregational Sunday-School and Publishing Society.

Missma. Elliott Pendleton White. LC 54-13228. 1954. Derby City Pub. Co.

Missolonghi Manuscript. Frederic Prokosch. LC 68-10646. 1968. Farrar, Straus & Giroux.

Missouri". Cora McNeill. 1898. Mizzoura Publishing Company.

Missouri Blue: A Novel. Joseph E Finley. LC 75-28089. 7.95. Putnam.

Missouri Bound. Elva Dye McGee. LC 76-9307. 9.95 (ISBN 0-89161-018-9). Athena Pub. Co.

Missouri Breaks. Thomas McGuane. 1976. (pbk.) 1.75 (ISBN 0-345-25218-7). Ballantine Books.

Missouri Flame: Deborah Leigh. Jeanne Foster. (Frontier Woman Saga Ser.: No. 2). 1982. pap. 2.95 (GM). Fawcett.

Missouri Traveler. John Burress. LC 55-7886. 1955. Vanguard Press.

Missouri Yesterdays: Stories of the Romantic Days of Missouri. Louise Platt Hauck. LC 20-220863. Burton Publishing Company.

Missourian. Eugene Percy Lyle. LC 5-25619. 1905. Doubleday, Page.

Missourian. Samuel Anthony Peoples. LC 57-9898. 1957. Macmillan.

Missourian: By Brad Ward Pseud. Samuel Anthony Peeples. LC 57-98980. 1957. Macmillan.

Missourian's Honor: By Walter W. Arnold. Walter Watson Arnold. LC 5-2431. 1904. Broadway Publishing Company.

Missy. Dana Gatlin. LC 20-20320. 1920. Doubleday, Page & Company.

Missy. Dorothy James Roberts. LC 57-7796. 1957. Appleton-Century-Crofts.

Missy. A Novel. Miriam Coles Harris. 1880. G. W. Carleton & Co.; Etc., Etc.

Missy: A Novel. Miriam Coles Harris. LC 8-14661. Houghton, Mifflin and Company.

Mist: A Tragi-Comic Novel. Miguel De Unamuno. 1974. Repr. of 1928 ed. 13.50 o.p. Fertig.

Mist & Creature of Darkness. M. Vasudevan Nair. LC 75-901765. 1974. lib. bdg. 4.00x (ISBN 0-8364-0433-5); pap. text ed. 2.50 (ISBN 0-8364-0434-3). South Asia Bks.

Mist in the Tagus. Henry Thomas Hopkinson. LC 47-3206. 1947. Little, Brown and Company.

Mist Maiden. Nancy Gardner. 1975. (pbk.) 1.25. Dell.

Mist Niebla a Tragicomic Novel. Unamuno y Jugo, Miguel De. LC 73-8976. 1973. 10.50. H. Fertig.

Mist Niebla: A Tragicomic Novel. by migue de unamuno, translated from the spanish by warner fite. ed. Unamuno y Jugo Miguel & Fite, Warner, Tr. LC 28-23540. 1928. A. A. Knopf.

Mist of Evil. Patty Brisco, pseud. 1976. pap. 1.25 (ISBN 0-532-12417-0). Woodhill.

Mist of Memory. Ruth McCarthy Sears. 192p. (YA) 1974. 4.95 o.p. (Avalon). Bouregy.

Mist of Morning. Isabel Ecclestone Macpherson Mackay. LC 19-143456. George H. Doran Company.

Mist on the Hills. Mary Howard, pseud. LC 50-11187. 1950. Arcadia House.

Mist on the Moors: A Romance of North Cornwall. Joseph Hocking. LC 7-4954. R. F. Fenno & Company; Etc., Etc.

Mist on the Waters. Frederick Lawrence Green. LC 49-7756. 1949. Harcourt Brace.

Mist Over Pendle. Robert Neill. LC 51-6941. 1951. Hutchinson.

Mist Over Talla. 1st Ed. Audrey Erskine Lindop. LC 57-130207. 1957. Doubleday.

Mistake of a Life-Time: Or, The Robber of the Rhine Valley; a Story of the Mysteries of the Shore and the Vicissitudes of the Sea. Waldo Howard. LC 51-542239. 1850. F. Gleason.

Mistaken. Randy Mott. (Illus.). 1978. pap. 3.75 (ISBN 0-931910-00-5). Sea of Storms.

Mistaken Identity: A Romance of Love and War. Oscar F G Day. (On cover: Idle moments series, no. 7). 1891. The Price McGill Company.

Mistaken: Or, The Seeming and the Real. Lydia Fuller. LC 6-445729. 1870. J. B. Lippincott & Co.

Mistaken Paths. A Novel. Carrie A. Morgan. LC 7-262009. 1887. J. B. Lippincott Company.

Mistaken Virtues. Joanna Trollope. LC 80-80361. 1980. 9.95 (ISBN 0-525-17585-7). Dutton.

Misted Mirror: Translated from the French with a Preface. Henry Daniel-Rops. Tr. by Mottram, Ralph Hale. LC 31-11916. 1931. A. A. Knopf.

Mr. Absalom Billingslea, and Other Georgia Folk. Richard Malcolm Johnston. LC 72-110203. (Short story index reprint series). (Illus.). 1970. Books for Libraries Press.

Mr. Absalom Billingslea, and Other Georgia Folk. Richard Malcolm Johnston. LC 7-10802. 1888. Harper & Brothers.

Mr. Ace. Helen Christy & Finklehoffe, Fred Franklin. Mr. Ace. LC 47-17945. (On cover: A Bart house movie hit. 101). 1946. Bartholomew House, Inc.

Mr. Achilles. Jennette Barbour Perry Lee. LC 12-22136. 1912. Dodd, Mead and Company.

Mr. Adam. Pat Frank. LC 46-65430. 1946. J. B. Lippincott Company.

Mr. Adams: A Parable for Parents and Others. Carl Mays. LC 74-22936. (Illus.). 1975. 2.95 (ISBN 0-8054-5612-0). Broadman Press.

Mr. Allenby Loses the Way. Frank Baker. LC 45-58406. 1945. Coward-McCann, Inc.

Mr. Allenby Loses the Way: A Novel. Frank Baker. LC 45-5840. 1945. Coward-McCann, Inc.

Mr. and Mrs. Bewer: From the 8th German Ed. of Paul Lindau... Paul Lindau. Tr. by Lowres, D. M. Mrs. (On cover: Globe library. v. 1, no,. 172). 1892. Rand. McNally & Company.

Mr. and Mrs. Bo Jo Jones. Ann Head, pseud. LC 67-15109. 1967. Putnam.

Mr. and Mrs. Cugat: The Record of a Happy Marriage. Isabel Scott Rorick. LC 40-32137. 1940. Houghton Mifflin Company.

Mister & Mrs. Daventry. Frank Harris. 1956. 3.50 o.p. Dufour.

Mr. and Mrs. Haddock Aboard. Donald Ogden Stewart. LC 24-290730. George H. Doran Company.

Mr. & Mrs. Haddock Abroad: A Novel. Donald Ogden Stewart. LC 75-6555. (Lost American Fiction Ser.). 272p. 1975. Repr. of 1924 ed. 7.95 (ISBN 0-8093-0731-6). S Ill U Pr.

Mr. and Mrs. Haddock in Paris, France. Donald Ogden Stewart. LC 26-16045. 1926. Harper & Brothers.

Mr. and Mrs. Hannibal Hawkins. Belle C Greene. (On cover: Copyright series, no. 7). American Publishers Corporation.

Mr. and Mrs. Meigs. Elizabeth Frances Corbett. LC 40-27595. 1940. D. Appleton-Century Company, Incorporated.

Mr. and Mrs. Morton: A Novel. Harold Williams. LC 8-36916. 1883. Cupples, Upham & Co.

Mr. and Mrs. North: A Novel. Richard Lockridge. LC 36-27436. 1936. Frederick A. Stokes Company.

Mr. and Mrs. Pennington. Francis Brett Young. LC 31-333817. 1931. Harper & Brothers.

Mr. and Mrs. Pierce: A Story of Youth. Cameron Mackenzie. LC 16-9064. 1916. 1.35. Dodd, Mead and Company.

Mr. & Mrs. Sen. Louise Jordan Miln. LC 23-6288. 1923. Frederick A. Stokes Company.

Mr. & Mrs. Tomnoddy. Madeline Maud Bellamy Higham. LC 35-5385. 1934. Longmans, Green and Co.

Mr. and Mrs. Villiers. Hubert Wales. LC 8-13278. 1908. The Stuyvesant Press.

Mr. Angel... Aboard. Charles Gordon Booth. LC 44-5273. 1944. Pub. for the Crime Club by Doubleday Doran and Co., Inc.

Mr. Antiphilos: Satyr. Remy De Gourmont. Tr. by Howard, John & Lozowick, Louis. LC 22-8593. 1922. Lieber & Lewis.

Mr. Aristotle. Ignazio Silone & Putnam, Samuel, Tr. LC 35-28732. R. M. McBride & Company.

Mr. Arkadin: A Novel. Orson Welles. LC 57-665253. Crowell.

Mr. Arnold: A Romance of the Revolution. Francis Lynde. LC 23-13485. The Bobbs-Merrill Company.

Mr. Arrow. Austin Russell. LC 47-4817. 1947. Beechhurst Press.

Mr. Ass Comes to Town. Krishan Chander. Tr. by Helen H. Bouman. 167p. 1968. pap. 1.95 (ISBN 0-88253-026-7). Ind-US Inc.

Mr. Atom. Theodore Pratt. LC 69-20032. 1969. 5.95. Wake-Brook House.

Mr. Audubon's Lucy. Lucy Kennedy. LC 56-11374. 1957. Crown Publishers.

Mr. Bailey-Martin: A Novel. Percy White. LC 8-36615. Lovell, Coryell & Company.

Mister Ballerina. Ronn Marvin. 1968. pap. 0.60 o.p. (60-347). Manor Bks.

Mr. Barnes, American: A Sequel to "Mr. Barnes of New York,". Archibald Clavering Gunter. LC 7-98414. 1907. Dodd, Mead and Company.

Mr. Battle Pays the Bills. Mary Imlay Taylor. LC 28-19551. 1928. Thomas Y. Crowell Company.

Mr. Beamish. Hugh Richmond. LC 40-27235. Coward-McCann, Inc.

Mr. Beamish. Gordon Ray Young. LC 40-27235. 1940. Coward-McCann.

Mr. Beluncle: A Novel. Victor Sawdon Pritchett. LC 51-12719. 1951. Harcourt, Brace.

Mr. Big. Daniel Forbes. LC 74-30600. 288p. (YA) 1975. 7.95 o.p. (ISBN 0-698-10656-3). Coward.

Mr. Big. Michael Kenyon. LC 74-30600. 1975. 7.95 (ISBN 0-698-10656-3). Coward, McCann & Geoghegan.

Mister Bill, "a Man,". Albert Edwin Lyons. LC 6-16734. 1905. R. G. Badger.

Mr. Bill Show-Star of Satuday Night Live. Walter Williams, pseud. LC 79-5197. (Illus.). 1979. lib. bdg. 12.90 (ISBN 0-89471-088-5); pap. 4.95 (ISBN 0-89471-085-0). Running Pr.

Mr. Billingham, and Marquis and Madelon. Edward Phillips Oppenheim. LC 29-11012. 1929. Little, Brown, and Company.

Mr. Billy Buttons. A Novel. William A. McDermott. LC 7-15422. (American author series of Catholic novels). 1896. Benziger Brothers.

Mr. Billy Downs and His Likes. Richard Malcolm Johnston. LC 1-1327. (Half-title: Fiction, fact, and fancy series. no. 10). 1892. C. L. Webster & Co.

Mr. Bingle. George Barr McCutcheon. LC 15-188209. 1915. Dodd, Mead and Company.

Mr. Birdsall Breezes Through. Walter Hawley Mack. LC 37-2463. 1937. Hillman-Curl, Inc.

Mr. Bisbee's Princess: And Other Stories. Julian Leonard Street. LC 25-108833. 1925. Doubleday, Page & Company.

Mr. Blandings Builds His Dream House. Eric Hodgins. LC 47-30016. 1946. Simon and Schuster.

Mr. Blettsworthy on Rampole Island. Herbert George Wells. LC 28-28683. 1928. Doubleday, Doran & Company, Inc.

Mr. Bliss. John Ronald Reuel Tolkien. 1983. 11.95 (ISBN 0-395-32936-1). HM.

Mr. Blue. Myles Connolly. LC 28-19748. 1928. The Macmillan Company.

Mr. Boccaccio of Broadway. Kenneth MacAlpin. LC 30-204561. 1930. New Publishing Company.

Mr. Bonaparte of Corsica. John Kendrick Bangs. LC 70-166677. (Illus.). 1971. (ISBN 0-403-01416-6). Scholarly Press.

Mr. Bonaparte of Corsica. John Kendrick Bangs. 1895. Harper & Brothers.

Mr. Bone's Retreat. mister bones retreat ed. Margaret Forster. LC 74-133092. 1971. 6.95 (ISBN 0-671-20805-5). Simon and Schuster.

Mr. Bottleby Does Something. Ernest Temple Thurston. LC 26-720301. 1925. Cassell and Company, Ltd.

Mr. Bottleby Does Something. Ernest Temple Thurston. LC 26-10569. George H. Doran Company.

Mr. Bremble's Buttons. Dorothy Langley. LC 47-1627. 1947. Simon and Schuster.

Mr. Bremble's Buttons: A Novel by Dorothy Langley Pseud. Dorothy Hight Richardson Kissling. LC 47-1627. 1947. Simon and Schuster.

Mr. Bridge. Evan S. Connell. LC 69-11478. 1969. 5.95. Knopf.

Mister Bridge. Evan S. Connell, Jr. 1970. pap. 0.95 o.p. (M1451, Crest). Fawcett World.

Mister Bridge. Evan S. Connell, Jr. 1969. 6.95 o.p. (ISBN 0-394-43711-X). Knopf.

Mr. Bridge. Evans S. Connell. (Kangaroo Book). 1977. 1.95 (ISBN 0-671-81096-0). Pocket Books.

Mr. Britling Sees It Through. Herbert George Wells. LC 16-18291. 1916. The Macmillan Company.

Mr. Britling Sees It Through. Herbert George Wells. LC 17-22994. 1917. The Macmillan Company.

Mr. Bulkly on a Cargo Boat. Hugh Lound. LC 42-20655. 1942. Dorrance and Company.

Mr. Bump. Roger Hargreaves. LC 73-16665. (Illus.). 1974. 1.00 (ISBN 0-448-11687-1). Grosset & Dunlap.

Mr. Bunting in Peace and War. Robert Greenwood. LC 41-23062. The Bobbs-Merrill Company.

Mr. Butler's Ward, a Novel. Frances Mabel Robinson. LC 7-41979. (Harper's handy series, no. 8). 1885. Harper & Brothers.

Mr. Byculla. 1st American Ed. Eric Robert Russell Linklater. LC 51-9210. 1951. Harcourt, Brace.

Mr. Calder & Mr. Behrens. Michael Francis Gilbert. LC 81-47686. 12.95 (ISBN 0-06-014932-9). Harper & Row.

Mr. Calder and Mr. Behrens. large print ed. Michael Francis Gilbert. LC 82-18302. 1983. 12.95 (ISBN 0-89340-551-5). J. Curley.

Mr. Calder & Mr. Behrens. Michael Francis Gilbert. LC 82-22365. 1983. 2.95 (ISBN 0-14-006637-3). Penguin Books.

Mr. Campion and Others. Margery Allingham. 1973. (pbk.) 1.25 (ISBN 0-14-000762-8). Penguin Books.

Mr. Campion: Criminologist. Margery Allingham. LC 37-36923. 1937. Pub. for the Crime Club, Inc., by Doubleday, Doran & Company, Inc.

Mr. Campion: Criminologist. Margery Allingham. LC 39-7927. 1939. The Sun Dial Press, Inc.

Mister Campion: Criminologist. Margery Allingham. 1970. pap. 0.75 o.p. (75-373). Manor Bks.

Mister Campion's Farthing. Margery Allingham. (O.s.i.). 1970. pap. 0.75 o.s.i. (532-75341-075). Manor Bks.

Mr. Campion's Farthing. Youngman Carter. LC 78-78339. 1969. 4.95. Morrow.

Mister Campion's Farthing. Youngman Carter. LC 78-78339. 1969. 4.95 o.p. Morrow.

Mr. Campion's Quarry. Youngman Carter. LC 71-20836. 1971. 5.95. W. Morrow.

Mister Campion's Quarry. Youngman Carter. (Albert Campion Mystery Ser). 1971. 5.95 o.p. Morrow.

Mr. Cantonwine: A Moral Tale. 1st Ed. Lionel Barrymore. LC 53-64510. 1953. Little, Brown.

Mr. Capon. Jenni Hall. LC 65-19056. 3.95. Harcourt.

Mr. Carteret and Others. David Gray. LC 10-8930. 1910. 1.00. The Century Co.

Mister Cat. George Freedley. 1972. pap. 0.95 o.p. (09127). Curtis.

Mr. Chaine's Sons: A Novel. William Edward Norris. LC 7-33286. J. W. Lovell Company.

Mr. Chilvester's Daughters. Edith Olivier. LC 33-972. 1933. The Viking Press.

Mr. Christian! The Journal of Fletcher Christian, Former Lieutenant of His Majesty's Steam Vessel, Bounty. Stanley Miller. (Illus.). 1973. 7.95. John Day Co.

Mr. Cinderella. Rex Stout. LC 38-37923. Farrar & Rinehart, Incorporated.

Mr. Claghorn's Daughter. Hilary Trent. LC 3-10936. 1903. J. S. Ogilvie Publishing Company.

Mr. Clifton of Barrington: A Popular Novel. J. F. Reichhard. LC 7-30658. 1891. J. S. Ogilvie.

Mr. Clunk's Text. Henry Christopher Bailey. LC 39-29479. 1939. Pub. for the Crime Club, by Doubleday, Doran & Co., Inc.

Mr. Cohen Takes a Walk. Mary Roberts Rinehart. LC 34-35702. Farrar & Rinehart, Incorporated.

Mr. Collin Is Ruined: A Novel. Gunnar Serner & De Chary, Pauline, Tr. LC 25-4854. Thomas Y. Crowell Company.

Mr. Commissioner Sanders. Edgar Wallace. LC 30-33757. 1930. Doubleday, Doran & Company, Inc.

Mr. Crewe's Career. Winston Churchill. LC 68-59351. (American novels of muckraking, propaganda, and social protest). (Illus.). 1968. Gregg Press.

Mr. Crewe's Career. Winston Churchill. 1908. The Macmillan Company.

Mister Crewe's Career. Winston Churchill. LC 68-59351. (Muckrakers Ser.: Vol. 22). 1969. Repr. of 1908 ed. lib. bdg. 13.50x o.p. (ISBN 0-8398-0266-8). Gregg.

Mister Crook Lifts the Mask. Anthony Gilbert, pseud. 1971. pap. 0.95 o.p. (95172). Beagle Bks.

Mister Crook Lifts the Mask. Anthony Gilbert, pseud. 1970. 4.95 o.p. (ISBN 0-394-41268-0). Random.

Mr. Crook Lifts the Mask. Lucy Beatrice Malleson. LC 73-102344. 1970. 4.95. Random House.

Mr. Crusoe's Young Woman. Sheila Scobie Macdonald. LC 35-4910. Coward-McCann.

Mr. Cushing and Mlle. Du Chastel. Frances Rumsey. LC 17-11701. 1917. 1.40. John Lane Company.

Mr. Darlington's Dangerous Age. Isa Glenn. LC 33-29346. 1933. Doubleday, Doran & Company, Inc.

Mr. Dayton, Darling! Mary Lady Cameron. LC 33-239250. Coward-McCann, Inc.

Mr. De Lacy's Double. Francis Eugene Storke. 1898. Continental Publishing Co.

Mr. Death. Carlton Wallace. LC 34-214119. 1934. Pub. for the Crime Club, Inc., by Doubleday, Doran & Company, Inc.

Mr. Death: Four Stories. Anne Moody. LC 75-9391. 5.95 (ISBN 0-06-024311-2) (ISBN 0-06-024312-0). Harper & Row.

Mr. Denning Drives North. 1st American Ed. Alec Coppel. LC 51-10203. 1951. Dutton.

Mr. Desmond, U. S. A. John Coulter. LC 6-29001. 1886. A. C. McClurg and Company.

Mr. Despondency's Daughter. Anne Parrish. LC 38-276611. 1938. Harper & Brothers.

Mr. Dickens Goes to the Play. Alexander Woollcott. 1973. lib. bdg. 8.25 o.p. Folcroft.

Mr. Digby: Adventures of Mr. "Happy" Digby, Demon Photographer and Chronic Headache of the Central City Daily Informer, and of Other Genial Lunatics at Large. Douglass Welch. 1945. G. P. Putnam's Sons.

Mr. Dimock. Dennis O'Sullivan. LC 20-21190. 1920. John Lane Company.

Mister Dinghy. Arch Oboler. 1970. 5.95 o.p. Bartholomew.

Mister Doc. Bettye K Butler. LC 62-8335. 1962. Dodd, Mead.

Mister Doctor Blo. John Tyne. LC 72-4711. 1973. 5.95 (ISBN 0-395-15089-2). Houghton Mifflin.

Mr. Doctor-Man. Helen Smith Woodruff. LC 15-248868. George H. Doran Company.

Mr. Dooley in Peace & in War. Finley P. Dunne. 1898. lib. bdg. 12.00 (ISBN 0-8414-3872-2). Folcroft.

Mr. Dooley in the Hearts of His Countrymen. Finley P. Dunne. 69.95 (ISBN 0-87968-248-5). Gordon Pr.

Mister Dooley in the Hearts of His Countrymen. Finley P. Dunne. LC 69-13888. Repr. of 1899 ed. lib. bdg. 15.00x (ISBN 0-8371-0399-1, DUMD). Greenwood.

Mr. Dooley Says. Finley P. Dunne. 1910. lib. bdg. 12.50 o.p. Folcroft.

Mr. Dooley's Philosophy. Finley P. Dunne. (Illus.). 1900. lib. bdg. 20.00 (ISBN 0-8414-3873-0). Folcroft.

Mr. Durant of Salt Lake City: "That Mormon,". Benjamin E Rich. LC 46-33953. 1899. Press of Zion's Printing and Publishing Company.

Mr. Durant of Salt Lake City: "That Mormon". Benjamin E Rich & Young, Brigham, 1801-1877. LC 2-7564. 1893. G. Q. Cannon & Sons Co., Printers.

Mr. Emmanuel: A Novel. Louis Golding. LC 39-19544. 1939. The Viking Press.

Mr. Everyman: A Gay Adventure. Charles Hatton. LC 48-6750. 1948. Didier.

Mr. Facey Romford's Hounds. Robert Smith Surtees. LC 78-8459. (Illus.). 1952. Folio Society.

Mr. Fairlie's Final Journey. August William Derleth. LC 70-1263. 1968. 3.50. Mycroft & Moran.

Mister Fairlie's Final Journey. August William Derleth. 1968. 5.00 o.p. (ISBN 0-87054-004-1, Mycroft & Moran). Arkham.

Mr. Fairlie's Final Journey. August Williams Derleth. (Solar Pons#7). 1976. (pbk.) 1.50 (ISBN 0-523-00870-8). Pinnacle Books.

Mr. Faraday's Formula: A Dean Riam Suspense Story. David Oakes Woodbury. LC 65-18926. 3.95. Devin.

Mr. Faraday's Formula: A Dean Riam Suspense Story by David O. Woodbury. Woodbury, David Oakes. LC 65-18926. 1965. Devin-Adair Co.

Mr. Filfil's Love Story. George Eliot & Morgan, Lawrence N., Ed. LC 31-13741. (western series of English and American classics). 1831. Harlow Publishing Company.

Mr. Finchley Goes to Paris. Victor Canning. LC 38-32404. 1938. Carrick & Evans, Inc.

Mr. Finchley's Holiday. Victor Canning. LC 35-1836. 1935. Reynal & Hitchcock.

Mister Fish Kelly: A Novel. Robert McBlair. LC 24-9130. 1924. D. Appleton and Company.

Mister Fisherman. Jack Bennett. LC 65-108935. 1965. Little, Brown.

Mister Flint. Frank R. Wallace. 1971. 6.95 o.p. (ISBN 0-911752-13-7). I & O Pub.

Mr. Foley of Salmon: A Story of Life in California Village. John Joseph Curran. LC 7-25051. 1907. Printed by Melvin, Hillis & Black.

Mr. Fortescue: An Andean Romance. William Westall. (On cover: Lovell's library, no. 1269). 1888. J. W. Lovell Company.

Mr. Fortescue. An Andean Romance. William Westall. (On cover: Seaside library. Pocket ed. no. 1159). 1889. G. Munro.

Mr. Fortner's Marital Claims, and Other Stories. Richard Malcolm Johnston. LC 7-10803. 1892. D. Appleton and Company.

Mr. Fortune: Eight of His Adventures. Henry Christopher Bailey. (Fifty Classics of Crime Fiction, 1900-1950; No. 3). 1976. Garland Pub.

Mr. Fortune: Eight of His Adventures. Henry Christopher Bailey. LC 75-44958. (Fifty Classics of Crime Fiction, 1900-1950; No. 3). 1976. (ISBN 0-8240-2352-8). Garland Pub.

Mr. Fortune Explains. Henry Christopher Bailey. LC 31-5765. 1931. E. P. Dutton & Co., Inc.

Mr. Fortune Finds a Pig. Henry Christopher Bailey. LC 43-511514. 1943. Pub. for the Crime Club by Doubleday, Doran & Co., Inc.

Mr. Fortune Here. Henry Christopher Bailey. LC 40-12261. 1940. Pub. for the Crime Club by Doubleday, Doran and Company, Inc.

Mr. Fortune Objects. Henry Christopher Bailey. LC 35-5965. 1935. Pub. for the Crime Club, Inc., by Doubleday, Doran & Company, Inc.
Mr. Fortune, Please. Henry Christopher Bailey. LC 26-227735. E. P. Dutton & Company.
Mr. Fortune Speaking. Henry Christopher Bailey. LC 78-140325. (Short story index reprint series). 1970. Books for Libraries Press.
Mr. Fortune Speaking. Henry Christopher Bailey. LC 31-326403. E. P. Dutton & Co., Inc.
Mister Fortune Speaking. facs. ed. Henry Christopher Bailey. LC 78-140325. (Short Story Index Reprint Series). 1931. 13.25 (ISBN 0-8369-3717-1). Ayer Co.
Mr. Fortune Wonders. Henry Christopher Bailey. LC 33-37017. 1933. Pub. for the Crime Club, Inc., by Doubleday, Doran & Company, Inc.
Mr. Fortune's Maggot... Sylvia Townsend Warner. LC 27-26459. 1927. The Viking Press.
Mr. Fortune's Maggot. Sylvia Townsend Warner. LC 75-41290. 1980. 18.50 (ISBN 0-404-14627-9). AMS Press.
Mr. Fortune's Practice. Henry Christopher Bailey. LC 24-1974. E. P. Dutton & Company.
Mr. Fortune's Trials. Henry Christopher Bailey. LC 26-105919. E. P. Dutton & Company.
Mr. Fothergill's Plot: His Conspirators; Martin Armstrong--H. R. Barbor--Elizabeth Bowen and Others... Fothergill, John. LC 31-333828. Oxford University Press.
Mr. Frank Merriwell. Gilbert Patten. LC 41-80807. Alliance Book Corporation.
Mr. Frank, the Underground Mail-Agent. Vidi. LC 8-32708. 1853. Lippincott, Grambo & Co.
Mr. Fred. John Buxton Hilton. LC 83-2891. 1983. 10.95 (ISBN 0-312-55081-2). St. Martin's Press.
Mr. G. Strings Along. Robert Wilder. LC 44-3443. 1944. G. P. Putnam's Sons.
Mr. Gallion's School. Jesse Stuart. LC 63-12132. 1967. McGraw-Hill.
Mister Gallion's School. Jesse Stuart. 1967. 9.95 o.p. (ISBN 0-07-062262-0). McGraw.
Mr. Generous. Rob Eden. LC 50-10967. 1950. Gramercy Pub. Co.
Mr. George and Other Odd Persons. August William Derleth. LC 63-24546. 1963. Arkham House.
Mister George & Others. Stephen Grendon, pseud. 1963. 5.00 o.p. (ISBN 0-87054-042-4). Arkham.
Mr. Gilfil's Love Story. George Eliot. LC 6-407734. (On Cover: Harper's Half-Hour Series, V. 30). 1877. Harper & Brothers.
Mr. Gilhooley. Liam O'Flaherty. LC 27-265724. Harcourt, Brace and Company.
Mr. Glencannon. Guy Gilpatric. 1934. Dodd, & Mead & Company.
Mr. Glencannon Ignores the War. Guy Gilpatric. LC 44-666893. 1944. E. P. Dutton & Company, Inc.
Mister God, This Is Anna. Fynn. LC 75-541. 1975. (ISBN 0-03-014716-6). Holt, Rinehart and Winston.
Mister God, This Is Anna. Fynn. LC 76-2631. (Illus.). 1976. 10.95 (ISBN 0-8161-6362-6). G. K. Hall.
Mr. Godly Beside Himself. Gerald William Bullett. LC 25-214162. 1925. Boni and Liveright.
Mr. Goggles. Henry Collins Brown. LC 7-20867. 1907. B.W. Dodge & Company.
Mr. Gold and Her Neighborhood House. Lenora Mattingly Weber. LC 33-24723. 1933. Little, Brown, and Company.
Mr. Grantley's Idea. John Esten Cooke. LC 6-27189. (On cover: Harper's half-hour series, v. 108). 1879. Harper & Brothers.
Mr. Grantley's Idea. John Esten Cooke. LC 45-46880. 1879. Harper & Brothers.
Mr. Gresham and Olympus. Norman Lindsay. LC 32-5297. Farrar & Rinehart, Incorporated.
Mr. Grex of Monte Carlo. Edward Phillips Oppenheim. 1915. 1.35. Little, Brown, and Company.
Mr. Grex of Monte Carlo. Edward Phillips Oppenheim. LC 21-13705. 1920. A. L. Burt Company.
Mr. Grosvenor's Daughter. A Story of City Life. Julia MacNair Wright. LC 9-5383. American Tract Society.
Mr. Guelpa: The Famous French Detective, Visits America and Finds the Most Baffling Mystery of His Career Awaiting Him. Vance Thompson. LC 25-245823. The Bobbs-Merrill Company.
Mr. Hamish Gleave: A Novel. 1st Ed. Richard Llewellyn. LC 56-5588. 1956. Doubleday.
Mr. Has & Mr. Is. Anthony V. Mandekic. 5.00 o.p. Carlton.
Mr. Hawkins' Humorous Adventure. Edgar Franklin Stearns. Dodge Publishing Company.
Mr. Hercules: A Tale of Mystery and Millions. Gwyn Evans. LC 31-13475. 1931. L. MacVeagh, The Dial Press.
Mr. Hobbs' Vacation. Drawings by Dorothea Warren Fox, 1st Ed. Edward Streeter. LC 54-6030. 1954. Harper.
Mr. Hobby" A Cheerful Romance. Harold Kellock. LC 33-831737. 1913. 1.30. The Century Co.
Mr. Hodge & Mr. Hazard. Elinor Hoyt Wylie. LC 28-8711. 1928. A. A. Knopf.
Mr. Hodge & Mrs. Hazard. Elinor Hoyt Wylie. LC 78-52743. (BCL Ser.: Nos. I & II). Repr. of 1928 ed. 31.00 o.p. (ISBN 0-404-18078-7). AMS Pr.
Mr. Holmes & the Fair Armenian. Conrad V. Bark. 1982. 15.00x (ISBN 0-86025-107-1, Pub. by Ian Henry Pubns England). State Mutual Bk.
Mr. Holmes at Sea. Conrad Voss Bark. 1977. 15.00. State Mutual Bk.
Mr. Holroyd Takes a Holiday. William Stanley. LC 66-15594. (Raven bk.). bds., 3.50. Abelard.
Mr. Horn. D. R Benson. (Dell book). 1978. 2.25 (ISBN 0-440-15194-5). Dell Pub. Co.
Mr. Hudson's Diaries. John Michael Drinkrow Hardwick. 1975. (pbk.) 1.50 (ISBN 0-671-78790-X). Pocket Books.
Mr. Incoul's Misadventure. Edgar Evertson Saltus. LC 68-54292. (Works of Edgar Saltus). 1968. AMS Press.
Mr. Incoul's Misadventure... Edgar Evertson Saltus. LC 25-12736. 1925. Brentano's.
Mr. Incoul's Misadventure: A Novel. Edgar Evertson Saltus. LC 7-1649. 1888. W. E. Benjamin.
Mister Incoul's Misadventures. Edgar Evertson Saltus. LC 70-131823. 1970. Repr. of 1887 ed. 7.00 (ISBN 0-403-00710-0). Scholarly.
Mr. Incoul's Misadventures: A Novel. Edgar Evertson Saltus. LC 8-3743. 1887. Benjamin & Bell.
Mr. Ingle Comes Through. Robert Bruce Thurber. LC 31-23210. Southern Publishing Association.
Mr. Ingleside. Edward Verrall Lucas. LC 10-208982. 1910. The Macmillan Company.
Mr. Insoul's Misadventure. Edgar Everrson Saltus. LC 70-131823. (Works of Edgar Saltus). 1970. (ISBN 0-403-00710-0). Scholarly Press.
Mister Isaacs. Francis Marion Crawford. LC 71-92607. (BCL Ser. I). 1969. Repr. of 1882 ed. 12.50 (ISBN 0-404-01835-1). AMS Pr.
Mister Isaacs: A Tale of Modern India. Francis Marion Crawford. LC 72-7814. Scholarly Press.
Mr. Isaacs: A Tale of Modern India. Francis Marion Crawford. LC 4-15091. 1882. Macmillan and Co.
Mr. Isaacs: A Tale of Modern India. Francis Marion Crawford. 1883. Macmillan and Co.
Mr. Isaacs: A Tale of Modern India. Francis Marion Crawford. LC 33-77704. 1892. Macmillan and Co.
Mr. Isaacs: A Tale of Modern India. Francis Marion Crawford. LC 16-19151. (On cover: Works of F. Marion Crawford). 1910. The Macmillan Company.
Mr. Isolate of Lonelyville. Clarence Conyers Converse. LC 99-5814. 1899. R. H. Russell.
Mr. Jabi and Mr. Smythe: A Novel. Samuel Barclay Charters. LC 82-12818. 1982. 12.95 (ISBN 0-7145-2779-3). Marion Boyars.
Mister Jack & the Greenstalks. Gene Horowitz. LC 72-90979. 1970. 5.95 o.p. (ISBN 0-393-08593-7). Norton.
Mr. Jack & the Greenstalks see Velvet Jungle.
Mr. Jack and the Greenstalks: A Novel. Eugene Horowitz. LC 72-90979. 1970. 5.95. W. W. Norton.
Mr. Jack Hamlin's Mediation. Bret Harte. LC 72-10783. (Short Story Index Reprint Ser.). 1973. Repr. of 1899 ed. 20.00 (ISBN 0-8369-4218-3). Ayer Co.
Mr. Jack Hamlin's Mediation, and Other Stories. Bret Harte. LC 72-10783. (Short story index reprint series). 1973. (ISBN 0-8369-4218-3). Books for Libraries Press.
Mr. Jack Hamlin's Mediation: And Other Stories. Bret Harte. LC 99-5247. 1899. Houghton, Mifflin and Company.
Mr. Jack Hamlin's Mediation: And Other Stories. Bret Harte. LC 42-26884. Houghton Mifflin Company.
Mr. Jackson. Helen Green. LC 29-270282. 1909. 1.25. B. W. Dodge & Company.
Mr. Jacobson's War. large print ed. Richard Hammer. LC 81-16570. 11.95 (ISBN 0-89621-327-7). Thorndike Press.
Mr. Jacobson's War: A Novel. Richard Hammer. LC 80-8750. 9.95 (ISBN 0-15-162828-9). Harcourt Brace Jovanovich.
Mister Jelly's Business. Arthur William Upfield. 1964. 4.50 o.p. British Bk Ctr.
Mister Jelly's Business. Arthur William Upfield. pap. 1.60 o.s.i. Tri-Ocean.
Mr. Jelly's Business: "Murder Down Under". Arthur William Upfield. (Napoleon Bonaperte Mysteries). Repr. lib. bdg. 15.70x (ISBN 0-89190-558-8). Am Repr-Rivercity Pr.
Mr. Jervis: By B. M. Croker... Bithia Mary Sheppard Croker. (On cover: Lippincott's select novels. no. 163). 1895. J. B. Lippincott Company.
Mister Johnson. Joyce Cary. LC 80-39938. (Time reading program special edition). 1981. 12.95 (ISBN 0-8094-3610-8) (ISBN 0-8094-3611-6). Time-Life Books.
Mister Johnson: A Novel. Joyce Cary. LC 51-12810. Harper.
Mr. Jonnemacher's Machine. The Port to Which We Drifted. Walter Doty Reynolds. LC 98-936. Knickerbocker Book Company.
Mr. Jory. Wilbur Hall. LC 47-6357. 1947. Ziff-Davis Pub. Co.
Mr. Justice Rattles. Ernest William Hornung. LC 9-242583. 1909. C. Scribner's Sons.
Mr. Keegan's Elopement. Winston Churchill. LC 3-142683. (Half-title: Little novels by favourite authors). 1903. The Macmillan Company.
Mr. Kello. Ian Ferguson. LC 25-12251. 1925. D. Appleton and Company.
Mr. Klein's Kampf: Or, His Life As Hitler's Double. illustrated by harry o. diamond. ed. Harry Allen Smith. LC 59-20724. 1939. Stackpole Sons.
Mr. Ladybug: A Novel. Becky Crocker. LC 68-14282. 1968. Sherbourne Press.
Mr. Lake of Chicago. A Novel. 3d ed. Harry Dubois Milman. LC 7-31114. (On cover: The criterion series, no. 1). Street & Smith.
Mr. Langdon's Mistale: A Novel. Sarah Marshall Hayden. LC 1-31736. 1901. J. J. Hayden.
Mr. Lemon Hart's Tropical Treats. Virginia Heffington & Leonce Picot. (Orig.). 1973. pap. 0.95 o.p. (N3279). Pyramid Pubns.
Mr. Limpet. Theodore Pratt. LC 42-104. 1942. A. A. Knopf.
Mr. Lincoln's Wife. Anne Colver. LC 43-3200. 1943. Farrar & Rinehart, Inc.
Mister Lincoln's Wife. reissue ed. Anne Colver. 1965. 5.95 o.p. (ISBN 0-03-047245-8). HR&W.
Mr. Lincoln's Wife. Polly Anne Colver Graff, pseud. LC 64-21941. 1965. Holt, Rinehart and Winston.
Mr. Line. L. A Pavey. LC 31-16338. 1931. D. Appleton and Company.
Mr. Littlejohn. Martin Flavin. LC 40-32292. Harper & Brothers.
Mr. Littlejohn. Martin Flavin. LC 46-7372. 1946. Harper & Brothers.
Mr. Love and Justice. Colin MacInnes. LC 61-8187. 1961. Dutton.
Mr. Love & Justice. Colin MacInnes. 176p. 1980. 13.95 (ISBN 0-8052-8043-X, Pub. by Allison & Busby England); pap. 5.95 (ISBN 0-8052-8042-1). Schocken.
Mr. Madison's War. Henry Barnard Safford. LC 36-24951. J. Messner, Incorporated.
Mr. Majestyk. Elmore Leonard. 1974. (pbk.) 1.25. Dell.
Mr. Man. Victor Von Kubinyi. LC 20-4015. 1920. F. Weidner Printing and Publishing Co.
Mr. Manager. Hants A White. LC 73-87325. 1973. Merit Pub. Co.
Mr. Manley,". G. I Whitham. LC 18-817061. 1918. John Lane.
Mr. Marlow Chooses Wine. John Bentley. LC 41-1909. 1941. Houghton Mifflin Company.
Mr. Marlow Stops for Brandy. John Bentley. LC 40-11885. 1940. Houghton Mifflin Company.
Mr. Marlow Takes to Rye. John Bentley. LC 42-394218. 1942. Houghton Mifflin Company.
Mr. Marx's Secret. Edward Phillips Oppenheim. LC 16-13052. 1916. Little, Brown, and Company.
Mr. Meek Marches on. Homer Cry. LC 41-332692. Harper & Brothers.
Mr. Meeson's Will. Henry Rider Haggard. LC 75-32747. (Literature of Mystery and Detection). (Illus.). 1976. 16.00 (ISBN 0-405-07876-5). Arno Press.
Mr. Meeson's Will. with eighteen illustrations. new impression. ed. Henry Rider Haggard. LC 17-501. 1913. Longmans, Green, and Co.
Mr. Meeson's Will. A Story of Adventure. Henry Rider Haggard. LC 6-43152. (On cover: Fireside series, no. 53). 1888. J. S. Ogilvie.
Mr. Mercer of New York. A Novel. Annie Henri Wilson. LC 8-37107. (Dillingham's American authors library, no. 17). 1896. G. W. Dillingham Co.
Mr. Mergenthwirker's Lobblies, and Other Fantastic Tales. Nelson Slade Bond. LC 46-763927. 1946. Coward-McCann, Inc.
Mister Mergenthwirker's Lobblies, & Other Fantastic Tales. facs. ed. Nelson Slade Bond. LC 74-121523. (Short Story Index Reprint Ser). 1946. 16.00 (ISBN 0-8369-3479-2). Ayer Co.
Mister Midas. Max Catto. LC 76-379365. 1976. 4.50 (ISBN 0-7181-1524-4). Joseph.
Mr. Midshipman Easy. Frederick Marryat. LC 42-26888. G. Routledge and Sons.
Mr. Midshipman Easy. Frederick Marryat. LC 7-17578. 1880. D. Appleton and Company.
Mr. Midshipman Easy. Frederick Marryat. LC 7-24682. (On cover: Seaside library. Pocket ed. no. 991). G. Munro.
Mr. Midshipman Easy. malta ed. Frederick Marryat. LC 7-246819. G. P. Putnam's Sons.
Mr. Midshipman Easy. Frederick Marryat. LC 4-16841. (Famous novels of the sea). 1899. C. Scriber's Sons.
Mr. Midshipman Easy. Frederick Marryat. LC 4-21564. 1902. Macmillan and Co., Ltd.
Mr. Midshipman Easy. Frederick Marryat. LC 6-11677. (Half-title: The English Comedie humaine. 2d series). 1906. The Century Co.
Mr. Midshipman Easy. Frederick Marryat. (Half-title: Everyman's library. ed. by Ernest Rhys. Fiction). 1907. J. M. Dent & Co.
Mr. Midshipman Easy. Frederick Marryat. LC 18-4343. (On cover: The home library). 1917. A. L. Burt Company.
Mr. Midshipman Easy. by harry h. a. burne. ed. Frederick Marryat. (father and son library). J.H. Sears & Company Inc.
Mr. Midshipman Easy. Frederick Marryat. LC 36-37092. (Half-title: Everyman's library. ed. by Ernest Rhys. Fiction. no. 82). 1934. J. M. Dent & Sons, Ltd.
Mr. Midshipman Hornblower. Cecil Scott Forester. 1961. Grosset & Dunlap.
Mr. Midshipman Hornblower. 1st Ed. Cecil Scott Forester. LC 50-6407. 1950. Little, Brown.
Mr. Milo Bush and Other Worthies: Their Recollections. Hayden Carruth. LC 99-3251. 1899. Harper & Brothers.
Mr. Mirakel. Edward Phillips Oppenheim. LC 43-14882. 1943. Little, Brown and Company.
Mr. Moffatt. Chester Francis Cobb. LC 26-122886. George H. Doran Company.
Mr. Moon. Philip Knobel. (Jove Book). 1979. 1.75 (ISBN 0-515-04870-4). Jove Puublications.
Mr. Moonlight's Island. Robert Dean Frisbie. LC 39-209575. Farrar & Rinehart, Inc.
Mister Moses. Max Catto. LC 61-7791. 1961. Morrow.
Mr. Moto Is So Sorry. John Phillips Marquand. LC 38-19938. 1938. Little, Brown and Company.
Mister Mulliner Speaking. P. G. Wodehouse. 1961. 4.95 o.p. (ISBN 0-8277-0224-8). British Bk Ctr.
Mr. Mulliner Speaking. Pelham Grenville Wodehouse. LC 30-6539. 1930. Doubleday, Doran and Company, Incorporated.
Mister Munchausen. facs. ed. John Kendrick Bangs. LC 78-81261. (Short Story Index Reprint Ser.). 1901. 15.00 (ISBN 0-8369-3013-4). Ayer Co.
Mr. Munchausen. John Kendrick Bangs. Repr. of 1901 ed. lib. bdg. 12.50 (ISBN 0-8414-1669-9). Folcroft.
Mr. Munchausen: Being a True Account of Some of the Recent Adventures Beyond the Styx of the Late Hieronymus Carl Friedrich, Sometime Baron Munchausen of Bodenwerder... John Kendrick Bangs. LC 78-81261. (Short story index reprint series). (Illus.). 1969. Books for Libraries Press.
Mr. Munchausen: Being a True Account of Some of the Recent Adventures Beyond the Styx of the Late Hieronymus Carl Friedrich, Sometime Baron Munchausen of Bodenwerder, As Originally Reported for the Sunday Edition of the Gehenna Gazette by Its Special Interviewer the Late Mr. Ananias Formerly of Jerusalem, and Now First Transcribed from the Columns of That Journal. John Kendrick Bangs. LC 1-27701. 1901. Noyes, Platt & Company.
Mr. Nicholas. Thomas Willes Chitty. LC 52-37795. 1952. MacGibbon & Kee.
Mr. Nicholas. David Ely. LC 73-93726. 1974. 6.95. (ISBN 0-399-11335-5). Putnam.
Mr. Nicholas: By Thomas Hinde Pseud. Thomas Willes Chitty. LC 53-9205. 1953. Farrar, Straus and Young.
Mr. Noah & the Second Flood. Sheila Every Burnford. (O.s.i.). 1974. pap. 0.95 o.s.i. (ISBN 0-671-47916-4). WSP.
Mr. Nobody. A Novel. Lilian Headland Spender. (Harper's Franklin square library. no. 369). 1884. Harper & Brothers.
Mister Noodle: An Extravaganza by J. P. McEvoy... J. P McEvoy. LC 31-7412. 1931. Simon and Schuster.
Mr. October. Maury Allen. 1982. pap. 2.50 (ISBN 0-451-11420-5, AE1420, Sig). NAL.
Mr. O'Hara: Written and Illustrated by Jack Weaver. Jack Weaver. LC 53-1633. 1953. Viking Press.
Mr. Oldmixon. A Novel. William Alexander Hammond. LC 7-559. 1885. D. Appleton and Company.
Mr. On Loong. Digby George Gerahty. LC 47-1728. 1947. The Macmillan Company.
Mr. Opp. Alice Caldwell Hegan Rice. LC 9-8574. 1909. The Century Co.
Mr. Pan. Emily Hahn. LC 42-159822. 1942. Doubleday, Doran and Company, Inc.
Mr. Paname: A Paris Fantasia. Sisley Huddleston. LC 27-6443. George H. Doran Company.
Mr. Parker Pyne, Detective. Agatha Miller Christie. LC 34-211560. 1934. Dodd, Mead & Company.

Mr. Parker Pyne, Detective. Agatha Miller Christie. (Dell Book). 1.75 (ISBN 0-440-15888-5). Dell Pub. Co.

Mr. Peepers: A Sort of Novel, by Wally Cox with the Assistance of William Redfield. Wallace Cox. LC 54-9804. 1955. Simon and Schuster.

Mr. Penrose: The Journal of Penrose, Seaman. William Williams & David Howard Dickason. LC 69-16004. (Illus.). 1969. 10.00. Indiana University Press.

Mister Pepys' Navy. Leslie A. Wilcox. LC 68-14369. (Illus.). 1968. 7.50 o.p. (ISBN 0-498-06817-X). A S Barnes.

Mr. Pepys of Seething Lane. Cecil Abernethy. LC 75-300889. 1974. 2.95 (ISBN 0-85617-363-0). White Lion Publishers.

Mr. Pepys of Seething Lane: A Narrative. 1st Ed. Cecil Abernethy. LC 57-12889. 1957. McGraw-Hill.

Mr. Perkins' Daugter. Clara Hammond Lanza. LC 7-14083. (On cover: Knickerbocker novels). 1881. G. P. Putnam's Sons.

Mr. Perkins of New Jersey: Or, The Stolen Bonds. M. P Green. (On cover: The red cover series, no. 18). 1888. J. S. Ogilvie & Company.

Mr. Perkins of New Jersey: Or, The Stolen Bonds. M. P Green. LC 3869. (On cover: Princess series, no. 19). 1900. Street & Smith.

Mr. Perryman's Christmas Eve: The Story of a Life of Faithful Service. Frances Cannon Smith Porcher. LC 12-180634. 0.50. The Reilly & Britton Co.

Mr. Pete & Co. Alice Caldwell Hegan Rice. LC 33-22824. 1933. D. Appleton-Century Company, Incorporated.

Mr. Peter Crewitt. Mary Andrews Denison. LC 6-33985. 1878. Lee and Shepard.

Mr. Peters: A Novel. Riccardo Stephens. LC 8-12402. 1897. Harper & Brothers.

Mr. Petre: A Novel. Hilaire Belloc. LC 25-22114. 1925. R. M. McBride & Company.

Mr. Petunia. Oliver St. John Gogarty. LC 45-11436. 1945. Creative Age Press.

Mr. Philip St. Clare." A Novel of Fashionable Life. Roman Ivanovitch Zubof. LC 8-37860. 1893. G. W. Dillingham.

Mr. Pickett of Detroit. Theophil Stanger. LC 16-11735. Millard Press.

Mr. Pickwick: An Adaptation of Charles Dickens' Pickwick Papers, by Carolyn Pulcifer Timm. Charles Dickens & Carolyn Pulcifer Timm. LC 54-1277. 1954. Globe Book Co.

Mr. Pidgeon's Island: A Novel. Anthony Berkeley Cox. LC 34-23848. 1934. Pub. for the Crime Club, Inc. by Doubleday, Doran & Company, Inc.

Mr. Pim. Alan Alexander Milne. LC 22-7756. George H. Doran Company.

Mr. Pim. Alan Alexander Milne. LC 30-269935. E. P. Dutton & Co., Inc.

Mr. Pinkerton: A Scotland Yard Omnibus. Zenith Jones Brown. LC 35-15470. Farrar & Rinehart, Inc.

Mr. Pinkerton and Inspector Bull: A New Scotland Yard Omnibus. Zenith Jones Brown. LC 37-16229. Farrar & Rinehart, Inc.

Mr. Pinkerton at the Old Angel. Zenith Jones Brown. LC 39-27746. Farrar & Rinehart, Inc.

Mr. Pinkerton Finds a Body. Zenith Jones Brown. LC 34-40097. Farrar & Rinehart, Inc.

Mr. Pinkerton Goes to Scotland Yard. Zenith Jones Brown. LC 24-137624. Farrar & Rinehart, Inc.

Mr. Pinkerton Grows a Beard. Zenith Jones Brown. LC 35-8865. Farrar & Rinehart, Inc.

Mr. Pinkerton Has the Clue. Zenith Jones Brown. LC 36-30704. Farrar & Rinehart, Inc.

Mr. Pirate, a Romance. Abraham B. Shiffrin. 1937. M. Kennerley.

Mr. Pisistratus Brown, M.P. in the Highlands. William Black. (Lovell's library, v. 5, no. 218). J. W. Lovell Company.

Mr. Pisistratus Brown, M.P., in the Highlands. Reprinted from "The Daily News", with Additions. William Balck. LC 6-129228. 1871. Macmillan and Co.

Mister Pistol-John. Richard Cloke. LC 76-23360. 1976. pap. 4.75 (ISBN 0-917458-01-X). Kent Pubns.

Mr. Podd. Freeman Tilden. LC 23-9745. 1923. The Macmillan Company.

Mr. Polton Explains. Richard Austin Freeman. LC 40-620106. 1940. Dodd, Mead & Company.

Mr. Potter of Texas: A Novel. Archibald Clavering Gunter. LC 6-44740. The Home Publishing Company.

Mr. Pottermack's Oversight: A Detective Story. Richard Austin Freeman. LC 30-22755. 1930. Dodd, Mead & Company.

Mr. Pratt, a Novel. Joseph Crosby Lincoln. LC 6-16999. 1906. A. S. Barnes and Company.

Mr. Pratt: A Novel. by joseph c. lincoln... with frontispiece by horace taylor. ed. Joseph Crosby Lincoln. LC 21-13933. 1911. A. L. Burt Company.

Mr. Pratt's Patients. Joseph Crosby Lincoln. LC 13-10544. 1913. 1.30. D. Appleton and Company.

Mr. Pratt's Patients. Joseph Crosby Lincoln. LC 24-15932. 1915. A. L. Burt Company.

Mr. Preen's Salon. Robert Tallant. LC 49-997407. 1949. Doubleday.

Mr. Preston's Daughter. Thomas Cobb. LC 20-19510. 1920. John Lane.

Mr. Prohack. Arnold Bennett. LC 74-17127. (Collected works of Arnold Bennett). 1974. (ISBN 0-518-19138-9). Books for Libraries Press.

Mr. Prohack. Arnold Bennett. LC 22-6319. George H. Doran Company.

Mr. Punch's" Prize Novels, New Series. Rudolph Chambers Lehmann. National Book Company.

Mr. Quill's Crusade. George Abbe. LC 48-8574. 1948. Island Press.

Mr. Ramosi. Valentine Williams. LC 26-6141. 1926. Houghton Mifflin Company.

Mr. Reeder Returns... Edgar Wallace. LC 32-300188. Pub. for the Crime Club, Inc., by Doubleday, Doran & Company, Inc.

Mr. Right. Carolyn Banks. LC 78-13500. 1979. 9.95 (ISBN 0-670-49318-X). Viking Press.

Mr. Right Is Dead. Rona Jaffe. 1980. pap. 2.25 (ISBN 0-440-16420-6). Dell.

Mr. Right Is Dead: A Short Novel and Five Stories. Rona Jaffe. LC 65-15024. 4.50. S.&S.

Mr. Robbins Rides Again. Drawings by Marc Simont. Edward Streeter. LC 58-6176. 1958. Harper.

Mister Roberts. Thomas Heggen. LC 46-25229. 1946. Houghton Mifflin Company.

Mr. Robinson Crusoe". Elton Thomas. LC 32-234200. Printed by Strawberry-Hill Press, Inc.

Mr. Rowl". Dorothy Kathleen Broster. LC 24-943619. 1924. Doubleday, Page & Company.

Mister St. John. Loren D. Estleman. LC 82-45869. (D. D. Western Ser.). 192p. 1983. 11.95 (ISBN 0-385-18713-0). Doubleday.

Mister St. John: A Novel. Raoul Cohen Faure. 1947. Harper & Brothers.

Mr. Salt: A Novel. Will Payne. LC 3-26879. 1903. Houghton, Mifflin and Company.

Mr. Sammler's Planet. Saul Bellow. LC 74-87248. (Viking compass book). 1973. (pbk.) 2.95. Viking Press.

Mr. Sammler's Planet. Saul Bellow. LC 76-58850. 1977. 1.95 (ISBN 0-14-004419-1). Penguin Books.

Mr. Sampath-the Printer of Malgudi. R. K. Narayan. LC 80-27352. 1981. 15.00 (ISBN 0-226-56838-5) (ISBN 0-226-56839-3). University of Chicago Press.

Mr. Sandeman Loses His Life. Eugene P Healy. LC 40-8421. H. Holt and Company.

Mr. Scarborough's Family. Anthony Trollope. LC 73-176176. (World's classics, 503). 1973. 5.00 (ISBN 0-19-250503-3). Oxford University Press.

Mr. Scarborough's Family. A Novel. Anthony Trollope. (Harper's Franklin square library. no. 317). 1883. Harper & Brothers.

Mr. Scarborough's Family: A Novel. Anthony Trollope. LC 8-28887. (On cover: Lovell's library. v. 3, no. 133). 1883. J. W. Lovell Company.

Mr. Scraggs: Introduced by Red Saunders. Henry Wallace Phillips. LC 6-102144. 1906. The Grafton Press.

Mr. Seidman and the Geisha. Drawings by Fred Banbery. LC 62-14281. 1962. Simon and Schuster.

Mr. September: A Novel of South Africa. John Trengove. LC 81-109884. 1980. 8.95 (ISBN 0-8253-0018-5). Beaufort Books.

Mr. Sermon: A Novel. Ronald Frederick Delderfield. LC 73-84121. 1970. 5.95. Simon and Schuster.

Mr. Sermon: A Novel. Ronald Frederick Delderfield. LC 74-38810. 1972. (ISBN 0-8161-6012-0). G. K. Hall.

Mr. Silly. Roger Hargreaves. LC 73-16663. (Illus.). 1974. 1.00 (ISBN 0-448-11686-3). Grosset & Dunlap.

Mr. Skeffington. Elizabeth. 1973. pap. 0.95 o.p. (09176). Curtis.

Mr. Skeffington. Mary Annette Beauchamp Countess Russell. 1972. 0.95. Curtis Books.

Mr. Skeffington. Mary Annette Beauchamp Russell Russell. LC 40-4224. 1940. Douleday, Doran & Co., Inc.

Mr. Smith. Lucy Bethia Colguhoun Walford. (On cover: Lovell's library. no. 1055). 1887. J. W. Lovell Company.

Mr. Smith: A Part of His Life. new impression. ed. Lucy Bethia Colguhoun Walford. LC 4-16589. 1902. Longmans, Green and Co.

Mr. Smith, a Part of His Life. Lucy Bethia Colquhoun Walford. LC 4-22079. (Leisure hour series. v. 48). 1875. H. Holt and Company.

Mr. Smith: The Personnel Officer, a Novel. A. Thetford. LC 20-908233. 1920. Printed for the Author by Pepper Printing Company.

Mr. Smith. 1st Ed. Louis Bromfield. LC 51-12204. 1951. Harper.

Mr. Smith's Hat. Helen Kieran Reilly. 1978. pap. 1.50 (ISBN 0-532-15311-1). Woodhill.

Mister Smith's Hat. Helen Kieran Reilly. 1971. pap. 0.75 o.p. (75-403). Manor Bks.

Mr. Smith's Hat: A Case for Inspector McKee. Helen Kieran Reilly. LC 36-8132. 1936. Pub. for the Crime Club, Inc., by Doubleday, Doran & Company, Inc.

Mr. Smith's Hat: A Case for Inspector McKee. Helen Kieran Reilly. LC 36-334136. 1936. The Sun Dial Press.

Mr. South Burned His Mouth. Gentry Nyland. LC 40-353212. 1941-1940. W. Morrow & Company.

Mr. Splitfoot. Helen McCloy. LC 68-31335. (Red badge mystery). 1968. 3.95. Dodd, Mead.

Mr. Sponge's Sporting Tour. Robert Smith Surtees. LC 58-4070. (World's classics, 565). 1958. Oxford University Press.

Mr. Sponge's Sporting Tour. Robert Smith Surtees & Herbert, Henry William, 1807-1858, Ed. LC 27-6620. 1856. Stringer & Townsend.

Mr. Squem and Some Male Triangles. Arthur Russell Taylor. LC 18-185377. George H. Doran Company.

Mr. Standfast. John Buchan. LC 73-19503. 1973. (ISBN 0-403-00879-4). Scholarly Press.

Mr. Standfast. John Buchan. LC 19-9660. George H. Doran Company.

Mr. Standfast. John Buchan. LC 36-15168. 1928. Houghton Mifflin Company.

Mr. Stone & the Knights Companion. Vidiadhar Surajprasad Naipaul. 1977. pap. 2.95 (ISBN 0-14-003712-8). Penguin.

Mr. Strang. Carroll John Daly. LC 36-181437. 1936. Frederick A. Stokes Company.

Mr. Tangier's Vacations: A Novel. Edward Everett Hale. LC 6-46185. 1888. Roberts Brothers.

Mister Target. William Harrington. 1974. (pbk.) 1.50. Dell.

Mister Target: A Novel. William Harrington. LC 73-3477. 1973. 7.95. Delacorte Press.

Mr. Tasker's Gods. Theodore Francis Powys. LC 72-145246. 1972. (ISBN 0-403-01161-2). Scholarly Press.

Mr. Theobald's Devil. Anna Gordon Keown. LC 36-27118. 1936. W. Morrow & Company.

Mr. Theodore Mundstock. Ladislav Fuks. LC 68-11056. 1968. Orion Press.

Mister Theodore Mundstock. Ladislav Fuks. Tr. by Iris Urwin. 1968. 4.95 o.p. (ISBN 0-670-49364-3, Orion Pr). Grossman.

Mr. Theodore Mundstock. Tr. from Czech by Iris Urwin. Ladislav Fuks. LC 68-11056. 1968. 4.95. Orion.

Mr. Thompson in the Attic. Anna Gordon Keown. LC 34-26452. 1934. W. Morrow & Company.

Mr. Three: 1st Amer. Ed. William Butler. LC 66-15107. 1966. 4.50. Putnam.

Mr. Thurtle's Trolley: A Novel. Theodore Pratt. LC 47-30410. 1947. Duell, Sloan & Pearce.

Mr. Tibbs Passes Through. Robert Neumann. LC 43-1378. 1943. E. P. Dutton & Co., Inc.

Mr. Tickle. Roger Hargreaves. LC 73-16666. (Illus.). 1974. 1.00 (ISBN 0-448-11688-X). Grosset & Dunlap.

Mr. Tilley Takes a Walk. Bradford Ropes & Valentine Burton. LC 51-9564. 1951. Austin-Phelps.

Mr. Tommy Dove: And Other Stories. Margaret Wade Campbell Deland. LC 75-94716. (Short story index reprint series). 1969. Books for Libraries Press.

Mr. Tommy Dove: And Other Stories. Margaret Wade Campbell Deland. 1893. Houghton, Mifflin and Company.

Mr. Topsy-Turvy. Roger Hargreaves. LC 73-16667. (Illus.). 1974. 1.00 (ISBN 0-448-11689-8). Grosset & Dunlap.

Mr. Trouble. William Ard. LC 54-9557. (Murray Hill mystery). Rinehart.

Mr. Trumper Bromleigh Presents No Ugly Ducklings. George Agnew Chamberlain. LC 26-17806. G. P. Putnam's Sons.

Mr. Tutt at His Best: A Collection of His Most Famous Cases. Arthur Cheney Train. LC 61-6963. 1961. Scribner.

Mr. Tutt Comes Home. Arthur Cheney Train. LC 41-7662. 1941. C. Scribner's Sons.

Mr. Tutt Finds a Way. Arthur Cheney Train. LC 45-2565. 1945. C. Scribner's Sons.

Mr. Tutt Takes the Stand. Arthur Cheney Train. LC 36-19217. 1936. C. Scribner's Sons.

Mr. Tutt Takes the Stand. Arthur Cheney Train. LC 41-405261. (His Criminal court series, v. 4). C. Scribner's Sons.

Mr. Tutt's Case Book: Being a Collection of His Most Celebrated Trials. Arthur Cheney Train. LC 36-33402. 1936. C. Scribner's Sons.

Mr. Twining. 1st American Ed. Timothy Angus Jones. LC 53-6844. 1954. Knopf.

Mr. Underhill's Progress. Elizabeth Frances Corbett. LC 34-36042. 1934. Reynal & Hitchcock.

Mr. Vaughan's Heir. A Novel. Frank Lee Benedict. LC 7-34449. 1875. Harper & Brothers.

Mr. Waddington of Wyck. May Sinclair. LC 21-147012. 1921. The Macmillan Company.

Mr. Waddy's Return. Theodore Winthrop & Stevenson, Burton Egbert, 1872- Ed. LC 4-29364. 1904. H. Holt and Company.

Mr. Wayt's Wife's Sister. Mary Virginia Terhune. LC 8-260552. The Cassell Publishing Co.

Mr. Weld Retires. Arthur Dorman Welton. LC 33-135432. Sears Publishing Company, Inc.

Mr. Westerby Missing. Miles Burton. LC 40-11103. 1940. Pub. for the Crime Club, by Doubleday, Doran and Company, Inc.

Mr. Weston's Good Wine. Theodore Francis Powys. LC 28-8710. 1928. The Viking Press.

Mister Weston's Good Wine. Theodore Francis Powys. LC 70-145248. 317p. 1928. Repr. 39.00 (ISBN 0-403-01163-9). Scholarly.

Mr. Whatley Enjoys Himself. Russell Gordon Carter. LC 54-8654. 1954. Christopher Pub. House.

Mr. White: The Red Barn, Hell, and Bridewater. Booth Tarkington. LC 35-27454. 1935. Doubleday, Doran & Company, Inc.

Mr. Whitman: A Story of the Brigands. Elizabeth Jones Pullen. LC 2-13260. 1902. Lothrop Publishing Company.

Mr. Whittle and the Morning Star. Robert Nathan. LC 47-775. 1947. A. A. Knopf.

Mr. Wiggs of the Cabbage Patch. Alice Caldwell Hegan Rice. LC 34-40679. 1933. D. Appleton-Century Company, Incorporated.

Mr. Wildridge of the Bank. Leslie Alexander Montgomery. LC 16-16526. 1.30. Frederick A. Stokes Company.

Mr. Winkfield. A Novel. LC 7-25329. 1866. American News Company.

Mr. Winkle Goes to War. Theodore Pratt. LC 43-4268. 1943. Duell, Sloan and Pearce.

Mr. Witt Among the Rebels. Ramon Jose Sender & Mitchell, Sir Peter Chalmers, 1864- Tr. LC 38-27141. 1938. Houghton Mifflin Company.

Mr. Witt's Widow. A Frivolous Tale. Anthony Hope Hawkins. LC 13-129247. United States Book Company.

Mr. World and Miss Chruch-Member: A Twentieth Century Allegory. rev. ed. William Shuler Harris. LC 1-31188. 1901. Evangelical Press.

Mr. World and Miss Chruch-Member: A Twentieth Century Allegory. 3d ed. William Shuler Harris. LC 2-13254. 1902. G. Holzapfel.

Mr. World and Miss Church-Member. A Twentieth Century Allegory. William Shuler Harris. LC 2-20651. 1902. Gospel Worker Society.

Mr. World and Miss Church-Member: Or, The Secret Service of Satan. An Allegory. William Shuler Harris. LC 1-29720. 1900. G. Holzapfel.

Mr. Wrong: Short Stories. Elizabeth Jane Howard. LC 75-12886. 223p. 1976. 7.95 o.p. (ISBN 0-670-49439-9). Viking Pr.

Mr. Wu. Louise Jordan Miln. LC 20-752413. 1920. Frederick A. Stokes Company.

Mr. Wycherly's Wards. Lizzie Allen Harker. 1912. 1.25. C. Scribner's Sons.

Mister, You Got Yourself a Horse: Tales of Old-Time Horse Trading. Ed. by Roger L. Welsch. LC 81-436. xii, 207p. 1981. 14.95 (ISBN 0-8032-4711-7). U of Nebr Pr.

Mr. Zero. Patricia Wentworth. LC 38-16227. J. B. Lippincott Company.

Mister 44,". E. J. Rath. LC 16-13512. 1.25. W. J. Watt & Company.

Misterios y Pavor: Trece Cuentos. D. McKay. LC 73-17210. 1974. pap. text ed. 11.95 (ISBN 0-03-000996-0, HoltC). HR&W.

Mistletoe & Sword. Anya Seton. 1976. lib. bdg. 14.40x (ISBN 0-89190-442-5). Am Repr-Rivercity Pr.

Mistr Jory: A Novel. Milton R Bass. LC 75-34335. 7.95 (ISBN 0-399-11702-4). Putnam.

Mistral. Max Brand. LC 29-132133. 1929. Dodd, Mead & Company.

Mistral's Daughter. Judith Krantz. LC 82-17966. 1983. 15.95 (ISBN 0-517-54906-9). Crown Publishers.

Mistress. Gideon Clark. LC 32-20665. 1932. R.M. McBride & Company.

Mistress. Theodora Keogh. 1966. pap. 0.60 o.p. (60-261). Manor Bks.

Mistress. Theodora Keogh. 1972. pap. 0.75 o.p. (532-75465-075). Manor Bks.

Mistress and Maid. A Household Story. Dinah Maria Mulock Craik. (On cover: West & Johnston's standard novels). 1864. West & Johnston.

Mistress and Maid. A Household Story. Dinah Maria Mulock Craik. LC 6-31075. (On cover: Seadide library. Pocket ed. no. 1038). G. Munro.

Mistress and Maid. A Household Story. Dinah Maria Mulock Craik. LC 16-9371. (Lettered on cover: Miss Mulock's works). Harper & Brothers.

Mistress: And Other Stories. Gina Berriault. LC 65-19955. bds., 4.50. Dutton.

Mistress & the Slave. pap. 1.75 o.p. (V1056K, Venus). Grove.

Mistress Ann. Temple Bailey. LC 17-11213. 1917. The Penn Publishing Company.

Mistress Bayou Labelle. Lou Cameron. pap. 0.95 o.p. Lancer.

Mistress Beatrice Cope: Or, Passages in the Life of a Jacobite's Daughter. M. E Le Clerc. (On cover: Seaside library. Pocket ed. no. 1220). 1889. G. Munro.

Mistress Branican. Jules Verne. LC 79-28548. 1970. 1.25 (ISBN 0-7251-0098-2). Sun Books.

Mistress Branican. Jules Verne & Estoclet, A., Tr. 1891. Cassell Publishing Company.

Mistress Brent: A Story of Lord Baltimore's Colony in 1638. Lucy Meacham Kidd Thruston. LC 1-24438. 1901. Little, Brown, and Company.

Mistress Content Cradock. Annie Eliot Trumbull. 1899. A. S. Barnes and Company.

Mistress Devon. Virginia Coffman. (Crest Book, M1879). 1973. (pbk.) 0.95. Fawcett.

Mistress Devon: A Novel. Virginia Coffman. LC 72-82177. 1972. 6.95 (ISBN 0-87795-044-X). Arbor House.

Mistress Dorothy Marvin. John Collis Snaith. LC 2-8391. 1900. Ward, Lock & Co., Limited.

Mistress Dorothy Marvin: Being Excerpta from the Memoirs of Sir Edward Armstrong, Baronet, of Copeland Hall, in the County of Somerset. John Collis Snaith. LC 8-10201. (Half-title: Appletons' town and country library, no. 188). 1896. D. Appleton and Company.

Mistress Dorothy of Haddon Hall: Being the True Love Story of Dorothy Vernon of Haddon Hall. Henry Hastings. LC 2-16201. 1902. R. F. Fenno & Company.

Mistress from Martinique. Helene Thornton. 1979. 1.95 (ISBN 0-449-14195-0). Fawcett Gold Medal Books.

Mistress Glory. Audrey Emily Cross. LC 48-8579. 1948. Dial Press.

Mistress Joy: A Tale of Natchez in 1798. Grace MacGowan Cooke & McKinney, Annie Booth. LC 1-25036. 1901. The Century Co.

Mistress Judith: A Cambridgeshire Story. Christina Catherine Fraser-Tytler Liddell. (On cover: Leisure hour series no. 46). 1875. H. Holt and Company.

Mistress Masham's Repose. Terence Hanbury White. LC 46-25270. 1946. G. P. Putnam's Sons.

Mistress Masham's Repose. Terence Hanbury White & Fritz Eichenberg. LC 79-18994. (Gregg Press Children's Literature Series). 1979. 9.95 (ISBN 0-8398-2615-X). Gregg Press.

Mistress Nancy. Barbara Bently. 368p. 1982. pap. 3.50 (ISBN 0-380-56895-0, 56895). Avon.

Mistress Nancy Molesworth: A Tale of Adventure. Joseph Hocking. LC 98-882. 1898. Doubleday & McClure Co.

Mistress Nell: A Merry Tale of a Merry Time ('twixt Fact and Fancy. George Cochrane Hazelton. 1901. C. Scribner's Sons.

Mistress Nell Gwyn: A Novel. Marjorie Bowen. LC 27-7933. 1926. D. Appleton and Company.

Mistress Nell: Or, Restoration Divertimento; Being a Story Based on the Life and Adventures of One Eleanor Gwyn, Server of Strong Waters, Orange Girl, Actress, Lady of Pleasure and Royal Mistress. Frank Wilson Kenyon. LC 61-13879. 1961. Appleton Century-Crofts.

Mistress of Beech Knoll: A Novel. Clara Louise Root Burnham. LC 12-18726. Houghton, Mifflin and Company.

Mistress of Bonaventure. Harold Bindloss. LC 8-300220. 1907. F. A. Stokes Company.

Mistress of Brae Farm: A Novel. Rosa Nouchette Carey. LC 6-23102. 1897. J. B. Lippincott Company.

Mistress of Corey's Landing. Margaret Harmon. 256p. (Orig.). 1981. pap. 1.95 (ISBN 0-89083-711-2). Zebra.

Mistress of Court Regna. Charles Garvice. LC 11-15075. (On cover: The Laurel library, no. 29). G. Munro's Sons.

Mistress of Darkness. Christopher Nicole. LC 75-26188. (Illus.). 10.00. St. Martin's Press.

Mistress of Darkness. Christopher Nicole. LC 77-360365. (Illus.). 1976. 4.95 (ISBN 0-304-29725-9). Cassell.

Mistress of Darkness. Christopher Nicole. (Signet Book). 1977. 1.95 (ISBN 0-451-07782-2). New American Library.

Mistress of Death. Piers Anthony & Roberto Fuentes. (Jason Strikea). (Jason Striker,#2: Vol. 2). 1974. (pbk.) 0.95 (ISBN 0-425-02623-X). Berkley Pub. Co.

Mistress of Devil's Manor. Florence Stevenson. (Kitty Telefair Ser). (O.s.i.). 160p. (Orig.). 1973. pap. 0.95 o.s.i. (AN1130, Award). Univ Pub & Dist.

Mistress of Erebus. Margaret Ogan & George Ogan. 1979. pap. 1.75 (ISBN 0-89041-229-4, 3229). Major Bks.

Mistress of Falcon Hill. Dorothy Daniels. (O.s.i.). 1973. pap. 0.95 o.s.i. (ISBN 0-515-02773-1, N3273). Pyramid Pubns.

Mistress of Falconhurst. Lance Horner. (Falconhurst Plantation Ser.). 1978. pap. 2.95 (ISBN 0-449-13575-6, GM). Fawcett.

Mistress of Ghosthaven. easy eye ed. Jean Bellamy. (Orig.). 1969. pap. 0.75 o.p. (74-520). Lancer.

Mistress of Glory. Lorinda Hagen. 1978. pap. 1.95 o.s.i. (ISBN 0-505-51279-3). Tower Bks.

Mistress of Harrowgate. Jessica Laurie. 1981. pap. 2.25 (ISBN 0-89083-772-4). Zebra.

Mistress of Husaby: Translated from the Norwegian of Sigrid Undset. Sigrid Undset. Tr. by Charles Archer. LC 25-10145. 1925. A. A. Knopf.

Mistress of Ibichstein. Frederike Henkel & Safford, Mary Joanna, Tr. LC 7-4125. (On cover: Seaside library. Pocket ed. no. 1030). 1887. G. Munro.

Mistress of Ibichstein: A Novel. Friederike Henkel & Boggs, Mrs. Sara Elisabeth (Siegrist) 1843- Tr. (Leisure hour series.--no. 157). 1884. H. Holt and Company.

Mistress of Langford Court. Marnie Ellington. (Candlelight Regency Ser.: No. 700). (Orig.). pap. 1.75 (ISBN 0-440-15652-1). Dell.

Mistress of Leather. Robert B. Davenport. 1972. pap. 1.75 o.s.i. (V1073K, Venus). Grove.

Mistress of Lost River. Mary Craig. 192p. 1976. pap. 1.25 (ISBN 0-532-12396-4, 532-12396-125). Woodhill.

Mistress of Lydgate. Evelyn Everett Green. LC 42-28121. I. Bradley & Co.

Mistress of Many Moods. Andre Theuriet & Rogers, Charlotte Boardman, 1878- Tr. The Abbey Press.

Mistress of Mellyn. Eleanor Hibbert. LC 60-13739. 1960. Doubleday.

Mistress of Mellyn. Victoria Holt, pseud. 240p. 1978. pap. 2.75 (ISBN 0-449-23924-1, Crest). Fawcett.

Mistress of Mellyn. 1st Ed. Victoria Holt, pseud. LC 60-13739. 1960. Doubleday.

Mistress of Men: A Novel. Flora Annie Webster Steel. LC 18-26171. 1917. Frederick A. Stokes Company.

Mistress of Men: A Novel. 2d impression. ed. Flora Annie Webster Steel. LC 20-4017. 1918. Frederick A. Stokes Company.

Mistress of Mistresses. E. R. Eddison. (Del Rey Bk.). 1978. pap. 2.50 (ISBN 0-345-27220-X). Ballantine.

Mistress of Mistresses: A Vision of Zimiamvia. Eric Rucker Eddison. LC 35-10470. E. P. Dutton & Co., Inc.

Mistress of Monterey. Virginia Stivers Bartlett. LC 33-170088. The Bobbs-Merrill Company.

Mistress of Oakhurst. Walter Reed Johnson. (Signet Book). 1978. 1.95 (ISBN 0-451-08253-2). New American Library.

Mistress of Orion Hall. Claudette Nicole. (Orig.). 1970. pap. 0.75 o.p. (T2614, GM). Fawcett World.

Mistress of Priory Manor. Betty Hale Hyatt. (Candlelight regency romance). 1974. (pbk.) 0.75. Dell.

Mistress of Quest: A Novel. Adeline Sergeant. LC 8-6856.

Mistress of Ravenswood. William Edward Daniel Ross. LC 66-8151. 1966. Arcadia House.

Mistress of Shades. Nelle McFather. 1977. pap. 1.50 (ISBN 0-532-15268-9). Woodhill.

Mistress of Shenstone. Florence Louisa Charlesworth Barclay. LC 10-221372. 1910. G. P. Putnam's Sons.

Mistress of Shenstone. Florence Louisa Charlesworth Barclay & Townsend, Frederick Henry, 1868-1920, Illus. LC 20-15626. G. P. Putnam's Sons.

Mistress of Shenstone. Florence Louisa Charlesworth Barclay. LC 41-42388. Grosset & Dunlap.

Mistress of Shenstone. Florence Louisa Charlesworth Barclay. LC 22-3024. 1913. Grosset & Dunlap.

Mistress of Sherburne. Amanda Minnie Douglas. LC 6-33474. (The Sherburne series). 1896. Dodd, Mead and Company.

Mistress of Soundcliff Manor. Deborah Wood. 528p. (Orig.). 1980. pap. 2.95 (ISBN 0-89083-652-3). Zebra.

Mistress of Tara. Christina Laffeaty. Orig. Title: Reluctant Bride. 1967. pap. 0.50 o.p. (52-471). Paperback Lib.

Mistress of the Boards. Richard Sumner. LC 76-14183. 8.95 (ISBN 0-394-40857-8). Random House.

Mistress of the Forge. David Taylor. LC 64-10876. 1964. Lippincott.

Mistress of the Highlands. Chloe Gartner. LC 75-40136. 1976. 8.95 (ISBN 0-688-02998-1). Morrow.

Mistress of the King: A Novel. Richard Summer. LC 78-19527. 1979. 1.95 (ISBN 0-515-04836-4). Jove /HBJ.

Mistress of the Lash. Robert Vaughan. (Orig.). 1970. pap. 0.95 o.p. (ISBN 0-447-75135-2). Lancer.

Mistress of the Manor. Ethel Lockwood. 1977. pap. 1.25 (ISBN 0-532-12501-0). Woodhill.

Mistress of the Manor. Ethel Lockwood. 1973. 4.95. Lenox Hill Pr.

Mistress of the Moor. Abigail Clements. (Fawcett world library). 1974. (pbk.) 0.95. Fawcett.

Mistress of the Morning Star. Elizabeth Lane. 448p. 1980. 2.75 (ISBN 0-515-05467-4). Jove Pubns.

Mistress of the Ranch: A Novel. Frederick Thickstun Clark. 1897. Harper & Brothers.

Mistress of the Shadows. Ruth MacLeod. 1972. pap. 0.75 o.p. (BT40128). Belmont-Tower.

Mistress of the Sun King. Sandra DuBay. (Orig.). 1980. pap. 2.25 o.s.i. (ISBN 0-505-51495-8). Tower Bks.

Mistress of Thornhedge: A Novel. Caroline Harris Ward. LC 54-7157. 1955. Bruce Humphries.

Mistress of Willowvale. Patricia Veryan. LC 79-64816. 1980. 11.95 (ISBN 0-8027-0637-1). Walker.

Mistress of Wynds. Meg Haviland. (Orig.). 1981. pap. 2.95 (ISBN 0-440-15707-2). Dell.

Mistress Pat: A Novel of Silver Bush. Lucy Maud Montgomery. LC 35-13181. 1935. Frederick A. Stokes Company.

Mistress Penwick. Dutton Payne. LC 99-5712. R. F. Fenno & Company.

Mistress to the Regent. Helen Tucker. (Orig.). 1980. pap. 1.75 (ISBN 0-449-50027-6, Coventry). Fawcett.

Mistress Wilding: A Romance. Rafael Sabatini. LC 24-263203. 1924. Houghton Mifflin Company.

Mistress Wilding: A Romance. Rafael Sabatini. LC 26-6481. Houghton Mifflin Company.

Mistresses of Mystery: Two Centuries of Suspense Stories by the Gentle Sex. Ed. by Seon Manley. LC 73-17213. 1973. 8.95 (ISBN 0-8161-6167-4). G. K. Hall.

Mists of Avalon. Marion Zimmer Bradley. LC 82-47810. 1982. 17.50 (ISBN 0-394-52406-3). Knopf.

Mists of Avalon. Marion Zimmer Bradley. LC 82-47810. 1983. 17.50 (ISBN 0-394-52406-3). Knopf.

Mists of Dark Harbor. Clarissa Ross. (Illus.). 1975. (pbk.) 0.95 (ISBN 0-380-00335-X). Avon.

Mists of Dawn. Chad Oliver. 1979. lib. bdg. 9.50 (ISBN 0-8398-2520-X, Gregg). G K Hall.

Mists of Fear. John Creasey. LC 77-80203. 1977. 6.95 (ISBN 0-8027-5381-7). Walker.

Mists of Manitoo. Lois Swann. LC 76-2387. 8.95 (ISBN 0-684-14585-5). Scribner.

Mists of Manittoo. Lois Swann. 464p. 1977. pap. 2.95 (ISBN 0-380-01690-7, 57380). Avon.

Mists of Manittoo. Lois Swann. 448p. 1976. 8.95 o.p. (ISBN 0-684-14585-5). Scribner.

Mists of Memory. easy eye ed. Catherine Marchant, pseud. 1969. pap. 0.75 o.p. (74-992). Lancer.

Misty. James Mc Quade. 128p. 1972. 6.50 o.p. (ISBN 0-8202-0151-0). Sherbourne.

Misty Flats. Helen Woodbury. LC 25-17116. 1925. Little, Brown, and Company.

Misty Isles--Here, There, Nowhere Land. Elizabeth Allen. (Illus.). 1981. 4.50 o.p. (ISBN 0-682-48953-0). Exposition.

Misty Mountain. Barbara Webb. LC 35-8288. 1935. Doubleday, Doran & Company, Inc.

Misty Mountains. James Jean Steward. LC 52-33986. 1952. White Wing Pub. House & Press.

Misty Pathway. Florence Riddell. LC 34-194831. J. B. Lippincott Company.

Misty Valley. Joanna Cannan, pseud. LC 24-9670. 1924. George H. Doran Company.

Misty's Kaboodle. AHI. (AHI Ser.). (gr. 1 up). 1979. 4.25 (ISBN 0-931420-25-3); pap. 2.95 o.p. Pi Pr.

Misunderstanding see Three Great Classics.

Misused Love Letters. Gottfried Keller. LC 74-78442. 1974. 6.50. (ISBN 0-8044-2460-8) (ISBN 0-8044-6355-7). Ungar.

Mitch Miller. Edgar Lee Masters. LC 20-17009. 1920. The Macmillan Company.

Mitchelhurst Place. Margaret Veley. (On cover: Seaside library. Pocket ed. no. 298). 1884. G. Munro.

Mitchelhurst Place. A Novel. Margaret Veley. (Harper's Franklin square library, no. 411). 1884. Harper & Brothers.

Mito Yashiki, a Tale of Old Japan: Being a Feudal Romance Descriptive of the Decline of the Shogunate and of the Downfall of the Power of the Tokugawa Family. Arthur Collins Maclay. 1889. G. P. Putnam's Sons.

Mitre and Crook. Bryan Houghton. LC 78-23857. 9.95 (ISBN 0-87000-434-4). Arlington House.

Mitslav: Or, The Conversion or Pomerania. A True Story of the Shores of the Baltic in the Twelfth Century. Robert Milman. LC 7-311194. (home library)). 1882. Society for Promoting Christina Knowledge.

Mitsou & Music-Hall Sidelights. new ed. Sidonie Gabrielle Colette. Tr. by Raymond Postgate & Anne-Marie Callimachi. 242p. 1976. 10.00 (ISBN 0-374-21069-1); pap. 2.95 (ISBN 0-374-51377-5). FS&G.

Mitsou: Or, How Girls Grow Wise, by Colette. Sidonie Gabrielle Colette. Tr. by Terry, Jane. LC 31-5119. 1930. A. & C. Bonie.

Mittee. Daphne Rooke. LC 52-128. 1952. Houghton Mifflin.

Mittenwald Syndicate. Frederick W. Nolan. LC 75-43669. 1976. 8.95 (ISBN 0-688-03041-6). Morrow.

Mitya's Love. Ivan Alekseevich Bunin & Boyd, Mrs Madeleine Elise (Reynier) Tr. LC 26-18389. H. Holt and Company.

Mitzi & Fritzi. Louis Bouchon. 1972. pap. 1.95 o.s.i. (V1107T, Venus). Grove.

Mix Me a Person. Jack Trevor Story. LC 60-8940. (Cock Robin mystery). 1960. Macmillan.

Mixed Bag of Magic Tricks. (Elephant Bks.). (O.s.i.). 1.25 o.s.i. (ISBN 0-448-14008-X, G&D). Putnam Pub Group.

Mixed Bags. S. C Westerham. LC 29-10432. 1929. R. M. McBride & Company.

Mixed Blessing. Helen Van Slyke. LC 74-25129. 1975. 8.95 (ISBN 0-385-09739-5). Doubleday.

Mixed Blessing. Helen Van Slyke. 1976. 1.95. Popular Library.

Mixed Blessings: A Novel. Marian Cockrell. LC 77-87824. 8.95 (ISBN 0-8129-0740-X). Times Books.

Mixed Company. Eleanor Mercein Kelly. LC 36-10346. 1936. Harper & Brothers.

Mixed Company: Collected Short Stories. Irwin Shaw. LC 50-10065. 1950. Random House.

Mixed Dates. Robert Gunkle Barnhill. LC 15-2638. 0.50. Printed by the Neerman Press.

Mixed Doubles. Alona Friend. LC 40-33215. The Greystone Press.

Mixed Doubles, No. 72. Meredith Kingston. 1982. pap. 1.75 (ISBN 0-515-06683-4). Jove Pubns.

Mixed Emotions. Charlotte Vale Allen. 1977. 1.75 (ISBN 0-446-84364-4). Warner Books.

Mixed Faces. Roy Norton. LC 21-11494. W. J. Watt & Company.

Mixed Feelings. Kerry Allyne. (Harlequin Romances Ser.). 192p. 1982. pap. 1.50 (ISBN 0-373-02479-7). Harlequin Bks.

Mixed Feelings. George Alec Effinger. LC 74-4858. 256p. (YA) 1974. 7.95 o.p. (ISBN 0-06-011146-1, HarpT). Har-Row.

Mixed Feelings. William Hanley. LC 72-82607. 1972. 7.95 (ISBN 0-385-04280-9). Doubleday.

Mixed Harvest. W. E Blackhurst. LC 70-117599. 1970. 5.00 (ISBN 0-87012-082-4). McClain Print. Co.

Mixed Marriage. Janet Doran. LC 43-3885. 1943. Gramercy Publishing Co.

Mixed Marriage, Anonymous. Margaret Culkin Banning. LC 30-28186. 1930. Harper & Brothers.

Mixed Men. Alfred Elton Van Vogt. LC 52-10217. 1952. Gnome Press.

Mixed Motives. (On cover: Seaside library. Pocket ed. no. 584). 1885. G. Munro.

Mixed Singles. Douglass Wallop. LC 76-45789. 7.95 (ISBN 0-393-08755-7). Norton.

Mixing: What the Hillport Neighbors Did. Bouck White. LC 13-21293. 1913. Doubleday, Page & Company.

Mixture As Before. William Somerset Maugham. LC 75-26134. (Maugham, William Somerset, 1874-1965. Works. 1976). (works of W. Somerset Maugham). ((Series: Maugham, William Somerset, 1874-1965.). (Works. 1976.). 1977. 15.00 (ISBN 0-405-07855-2). Arno Press.

Mixture As Before. William Somerset Maugham. LC 40-12740. 1940. Doubleday, Doran & Co., Inc.

Mixture of Frailties. Robertson Davies. 1973. 0.95. Curtis Books.

Mixture of Frailties. William Robertson Davies. LC 78-74578. 1979. 12.50 (ISBN 0-89696-051-X, An Everest House Book). Dodd.

Mixture of Frailties. William Robertson Davies. 384p. 1980. pap. 3.95 (ISBN 0-14-005432-4). Penguin.

Mixture of Frailties. William Robertson Davies. 1972. pap. 0.95 o.p. (09155). Curtis.

Mizora: A Prophecy. Mary E. Bradley Lane. LC 75-5835. (Gregg Press science fiction series). 1975. 14.00 (ISBN 0-8398-2306-1). Gregg Press.

Mizora: A Prophecy. A Mss. ! Found Among the Private Papers of the Princess Vera Zarovitch. Being a True and Faithful Account of Her Journey to the Interior of the Earth, with a Careful Description of the Country and Its Inhabitants, Their Customs, Manners and Government. Written by Herself. Mary E. Bradley Lane. LC 6-15196. 1890. G. W. Dillingham.

Mizpah: Or, Drifting Away. M. McCullen Whiteside. 1885. A. R. Fleming & Co.

Mlle. Cecie. Sarah Carlisle. 224p. (Orig.). 1980. pap. 1.75 (ISBN 0-449-50038-1, Coventry). Fawcett.

Mlle. Fouchette: Or, The Monkey & the Tiger. Charles Theodore Murray. LC 2-2771. 1902. J. B. Lippincott Company.

Mlle. Savelli? Suzanne Prou. LC 75-144192. 1971. 5.95 (ISBN 0-06-013434-8). Harper & Row.

Mme. Maimee. Fern Tolley Brand. LC 22-106360. 1922. W. C. West.

Mneomi: Or, The Indian of the Connecticut. Austin Corbin. LC 9-1839. 1847. Gleason's Publishing Hall.

Mnimaia Zhizn' Inna Varlamova. (Rus.). 1979. 12.50 (ISBN 0-88233-481-6); pap. 4.00 (ISBN 0-88233-482-4). Ardis Pubs.

Moabite Boy. Audrey Adams. 1962. 2.00 (ISBN 0-88027-011-X). Firm Foun Pub.

Moan of the Tiber. Guy Fitch Phelps. LC 17-6328. 0.60. The Standard Publishing Company.

Moana: A Novel of Early New Zealand. Barry Mitcalfe. LC 76-365547. (Illus.). 1975. 8.95x (ISBN 0-85467-030-0). Intl Pubns Serv.

Mob in Show Business. Hank Messick, pseud. 1975. pap. 1.50 o.p. (ISBN 0-515-03697-8). Pyramid Pubns.

Mob, "La Horda". Vicente Blasco Ibanez & Lorente, Mariano Joaquin, 1883- Tr. LC 27-151951. E. P. Dutton & Company.

Mobilia, a Novel. George Ernest Miller. LC 7-25971.

Mobius Man. M. S. Karl. 224p. (Orig.). 1982. pap. 2.50 (ISBN 0-8439-1038-0, Leisure Bks). Nordon Pubns.

Mobius Trip. William Garner. LC 77-17939. 8.95. Putnam.

Mobsmen on the Spot. Maxwell Grant, pseud. (Shadow Ser.: No. 3). 1974. pap. 0.95 o.p. (ISBN 0-515-03554-8, N3554). BJ Pub Group.

Mobsmen on the Spot: From the Shadow's Private Annals As Told to Maxwell Grant. Maxwell Grant. LC 74-10043. (master of darkness, 3). 1974. (pbk.) 0.95 (ISBN 0-515-03554-8). Pyramid Books.

Mobster. Frank Arrigio. (O.s.i.). 1975. pap. 1.25 o.s.i. (BT50786). Belmont-Tower.

Mobtown Clipper. Samuel Supplee Rabl. LC 49-8485. 1949. Cornell Maritime Press.

Moby- Dick: Or, The White Whale. With a New Introd. by Quentin Anderson. Herman Melville. LC 62-12455. (Classic Collier books, AS247). 1962. Collier Books.

Moby Dick. Herman Melville. Ed. by Robert James Dixson. LC 53-11807. (American Classics Simplified and Adapted for Greater Reading Pleasure, Book 2). (Illus.). 1973. (pbk.) 1.25. Regents Pub. Co.

Moby Dick. Herman Melville. Ed. by Verne B. Browne. LC 48-28178. 1948. Scott, Foresman.

Moby Dick. Herman Melville. LC 26-14494. (Half-title: The modern library of the world's best books). 1926. The Modern Library.

Moby Dick. Herman Melville. Ed. by Bates, Sylvia Chatfield. Finley, John Huston. C. Scribner's Sons.

Moby Dick. Herman Melville. LC 29-1566. (father and son library). J. H. Sears & Company, Inc.

Moby Dick. Herman Melville. Ed. by Helen Maria Fiske Hunt Jackson. Crane, Stephen. LC 42-3996. (Prose and poetry individualized program. The novel). The L. W. Singer Company.

Moby-Dick: An Authoritative Text. Herman Melville. Ed. by Harrison Hayford & Hershel Parker. LC 66-11309. (Norton critical edition). (Illus.). 1967. W. W. Norton.

Moby Dick: As Adapted and Retold by Frank L. Beals from Herman Melville's Famous Story. Herman Melville. Retold by Frank Lee Beals. LC 64-662572. (Famous story ser.). 1965. 3.95. Naylor.

Moby Dick: By Herman Melville. Herman Melville. LC 29-15659. (modern reader's series). 1929. The Macmillan Company.

Moby Dick: Condensed & Adapted for Reading in Secondary Schools. Herman Melville. 1948.

Moby Dick. Illustrated by Robert Shore. Afterword by Clifton Fadiman. Herman Melville. LC 62-18393. (Macmillan classics, 30). 1962. Macmillan.

Moby-Dick: Or, The Whale. Herman Melville. LC 50-58247. (Everyman's library, 179A. Fiction). 1950. Dutton.

Moby-Dick: Or, The Whale. Herman Melville. LC 52-6994. (His Complete works). 1952. Hendricks House.

Moby-Dick: Or, The Whale. Herman Melville. Ed. by Harold Lowther Beaver. LC 73-156284. (Penguin English library). (Illus.). 1972. 3.50 (ISBN 0-14-043082-2). Penguin.

Moby-Dick: Or, The Whale. Herman Melville. Ed. by Howard Mumford Jones. Harrison Hayford & Hershel Parker. LC 75-20032. 1975. 15.00 (ISBN 0-393-04402-5). Norton.

Moby Dick or, the Whale. Herman Melville. LC 75-7639. (Illus.). 1975. 450.00. The Artist's Limited Edition.

Moby-Dick: Or, The Whale. Herman Melville. LC 55-10354. (Great books of the Western World, v. 48). 1955. Encyclopaedia Britannica.

Moby Dick: Or, The Whale. large type ed., complete and unabridged. ed. Herman Melville. LC 68-3371. F. Watts.

Moby Dick: Or, The Whale. Herman Melville. LC 50-11914. (Modern Library college editions, T26). 1950. Modern Library.

Moby Dick: Or, The Whale. Herman Melville. LC 56-14046. (Illus.). 1956. Heritage Press.

Moby-Dick: Or, The Whale. Herman Melville. LC 52-6994. (His Complete works). 1962. Hendricks House.

Moby Dick: Or, The Whale. Herman Melville. LC 48-4635. 1948. Rinehart.

Moby Dick: Or, The Whale. Herman Melville. Ed. by Max T. Hohn. Benscoter, Grace A. LC 51-599. (Classics for enjoyment). 1949. Laidlaw Bros.

Moby Dick: Or, The Whale. Herman Melville. LC 99-4953. (Famous novels of the sea). 1899. C. Scribner's Sons.

Moby-Dick: Or, The Whale. Herman Melville. LC 22-5610. (Half-title: The world's classics. ccxxv). 1921. H. Milford.

Moby-Dick: Or, The Whale. abridged and edited with an introduction, notes, and exercises by william s. ament... illustrated by sears gallagher. ed. Herman Melville. Ed. by Ament. William Sheffield. LC 28-297306. (Standard English classics). Ginn and Company.

Moby Dick: Or, The Whale. Herman Melville. LC 30-307729. 1930. Random House.

Moby Dick: Or, The Whale. Herman Melville. LC 31-15683. (Half-title: Every child's library). The Saalfield Publishing Company.

Moby-Dick: Or, The Whale. Herman Melville. LC 31-1822. 1931. A. and C. Boni.

Moby Dick: Or, The Whale. de luxe ed. Herman Melville. LC 38-3248. 1937. Garden City Publishing Co., Inc.

Moby Dick: Or, The Whale. Herman Melville. LC 44-400992. (Half-title: The Modern library of the world's best books). 1944. The Modern Library.

Moby-Dick: Or, The Whale. Herman Melville. Ed. by Willard Thorp. LC 47-6540. 1947. Oxford Univ. Press.

Moby-Dick: Or, The Whale. Herman Melville. Ed. by Raymond Melbourne Weaver. LC 26-16712. (Half-title: The Pequod edition of Herman Melville's Collected works). 1925. A. & C. Boni.

Moby Dick: Or, The Whale. Herman Melville. LC 30-30421. 1930. The Lakeside Press.

Moby Dick: Or, The Whale, Herman Melville. LC 30-30421. (Illus.). 1930. The Lakeside Press.

Moby-Dick, or, The Whale. Herman Melville. LC 81-40320. (Illus.). 1981. 24.95 (ISBN 0-520-04354-5). University of California Press.

Moby Dick: Or, The Whale. Afterword by Jerry Allen. Herman Melville. LC 66-2888. (Perennial classic). 1966. 1.95, .75 pap.,. Harper.

Moby Dick: Or, The Whale. Complete and Unabridged Ed. Herman Melville. LC 55-3885. (Signet book, D1229). 1955. New American Library.

Moby Dick: Or, The Whale, Ed. by M. W. and G. Thomas. Illus. by Exell. Herman Melville. Ed. by Maurice Walton Thomas & Gladys Thomas. (Shorter classics). 1962. 2.50. Ginn.

Moby-Dick: Or, The Whale. Edited with an Introd. by Alfred Kazin. Herman Melville. LC 56-140871. (Riverside editions, A9). 1956. Houghton Mifflin.

Moby Dick: Or, The White Whale. Herman Melville. LC 50-6155. (Harper's modern classics). 1950. Harper.

Moby Dick: Or the White Whale. Herman Melville. Ed. by Maxwell Geismar. (Washington Square Press Enriched Classic). (Illus.). 1975. (pbk.) 0.95 (ISBN 0-671-47915-6). Pocket Books.

Moby Dick: Or, The White Whale. Herman Melville. LC 49-273911. (Pocket book, 612). 1949. Pocket Books.

Moby Dick: Or, The White Whale. Herman Melville. LC 49-9575. (Ten greatest novels of the world). 1949. J. C. Winston Co.

Moby-Dick: Or, The White Whale. Herman Melville. 1892. Dana Estes & Co.

Moby-Dick: Or, The White Whale. Herman Melville. United States Book Company.

Moby Dick: Or, The White Whale. Herman Melville. (Half-title: Everyman's library, ed. by Ernest Rhys. Fiction). 1907. J. Dent & Co.

Moby Dick: Or, The White Whale. Herman Melville. LC 22-518017. (Half-title: Everyman's library, edited by Ernest Rhys. Fiction no. 179). 1921. J. M. Dent & Sons, Ltd.

Moby Dick: Or, The White Whale. Herman Melville. LC 22-22440. 1922. Dodd, Mead and Company.

Moby Dick: Or, The White Whale. Herman Melville. LC 25-27962. Grosset & Dunlap.

Moby Dick: Or, The White Whale. Herman Melville. Ed. by Benson, Earl Maltby. LC 28-128078. (Academy classics). Allyn and Bacon.

Moby Dick: Or, The White Whale. Herman Melville. Ed. by William McFee. LC 31-19680. The John C. Winston Company.

Moby Dick: Or, The White Whale. With an Afterword by Denham Sutcliffe. Herman Melville. LC 61-2190. (A' Signet classic, CT47). 1961. New American Library.

Moby Dick: Simplified and Adapted by Robert J. Dixson. Drawings by Syd Browne. Herman Melville. Ed. by Robert James Dixson. LC 53-11807. (American Classics, Book 2). Regents Pub. Co.

Moby Lane and Thereabouts. Albert Michael Neil Lyons. LC 16-5198. 1916. John Lane.

Moccasin Flower: An Historical Novel. John Bell. LC 35-24890. 1935. The Book Masters.

Moccasin Murders. Kenneth Perkins. LC 31-31847. A. H. King, Inc.

Moccasin Ranch see Collected Works.

Moccasin Ranch: A Story of Dakota. Hamlin Garland. LC 72-84715. (Illus.). 1974. (lib. ed.) 5.50 (ISBN 0-403-02282-7). Scholarly Press.

Moccasin Ranch: A Story of Dakota. Hamlin Garland. LC 9-24262. 1909. Harper & Brothers.

Moccasin Telegraph. Hal George Evarts. LC 27-19892. 1927. Little. Brown, and Company.

Moccasin Trail: The Story of a Boy Who Took the Trail with Kit Carson. Reed Fulton. LC 29-17825. 1929. Doubleday, Doran & Company, Inc.

Moccasin Trails. E. R. Nunemaker. 1974. 2.50 o.s.i. (ISBN 0-8181-0331-0). Pageant-Poseidon.

Moccasins of Gold. Norman Way. LC 12-23714. E. J. Clode.

Mocha Dick: Or, The White Whale of the Pacific. Jeremiah N. Reynolds. LC 32-24982. 1932. C. Scribner's Sons.

Mock-Honeymoon: A Novel. Berta Ruck. LC 46-768970. 1946. Triangle Books, the Blakiston Company.

Mock-Honeymoon: A Novel by. Berta Ruck. LC 39-155968. 1939. Dodd, Mead & Company.

Mock Orange. Raylyn Moore. LC 68-12489. 1968. Scribner.

Mock Turtle Soup. Peter Neill. LC 73-184475. 1972. 6.95 (ISBN 0-670-48243-9). Grossman Publishers.

Mockbeggar: A Novel. Laurence Walter Meynell. LC 25-3546. 1925. D. Appleton and Company.

Mockery Bird. Gerald Malcolm Durrell. LC 81-23268. 1982. 13.95 (ISBN 0-671-44131-0). Simon & Schuster.

Mockery Gap. Theodore Francis Powys. LC 26-72745. 1925. A. A. Knopf.

Mockery in Arms. James Aldridge. LC 74-19387. 1975. 7.95 o.p. (ISBN 0-316-03121-6). Little.

Mockery in Arms: A Novel. James Aldridge. LC 74-19387. 1975. 7.95 (ISBN 0-316-03121-6). Little, Brown.

Mocking Bird Is Singing. Emma Louise Mally. LC 44-305047. 1944. H. Holt and Company.

Mocking Bird's Breed. Jennie McMillan. LC 18-20097. R. J. Shores.

Mockingbird. Paul Hunter, pseud. 1981. pap. 4.00 (ISBN 0-918116-24-4). Jawbone Pr.

Mockingbird. Robert Waddy Ramsey. LC 51-5017. 1951. Dutton.

Mockingbird. Walter S Tevis. LC 78-22773. 1980. 10.00 (ISBN 0-385-14933-6). Doubleday.

Mockingbird Sang at Chickamauga: A Tale of Embattled Chattanooga. Alfred Leland Crabb. LC 49-10419. 1949. Bobbs-Merrill Co.

Mod Squad: Assignment: the Arranger. authorized ed. Richard Deming. LC 79-5484. 1969. 0.69. Whitman Pub. Division.

Mod Squad No. 1: The Greek God Affair. Richard Deming. 1970. pap. 0.60 o.p. (X2319). Pyramid Pubns.

Mod Squad No. 2: A Groovy Way to Die. Richard Deming. 1968. pap. 0.60 o.p. (X1908). Pyramid Pubns.

Mod Squad No. 3: The Sock-It-To-'em Murders. Richard Deming. 1968. pap. 0.60 o.p. (X1922). Pyramid Pubns.

Mod Squad No. 4: Spy-In. Richard Deming. (Orig.). 1969. pap. 0.60 o.p. (X1986). Pyramid Pubns.

Mod Squad No. 5: Hit. Richard Deming. (Orig.). 1970. pap. 0.60 o.p. (X2214). Pyramid Pubns.

Model Actress. Mary Ellis. Smith. Vollrath & Veronee.

Model Childhood. Christa Wolf. LC 80-13601. 12.95 (ISBN 0-374-21170-1). Farrar, Straus, and Giroux.

Model Corpse. Marian Buxton Clark. LC 42-10297. 1942. Cushman & Flint.

Model for Love: By Gerald Seton Pseud. Jerome Darwin Engel. LC 50-9005. 1950. Phoenix Press.

Model for Murder. Carter Brown, pseud. (Orig.). 1980. pap. 1.50 (ISBN 0-505-51527-X). Tower Bks.

Model for Murder: A Mystery Novel. Julius Fast. LC 56-725735. 1956. Rinehart.

Model Is Murdered. Marion Van Der Veer Lee. LC 42-20998. 1942. C. Scribner's Sons.

Model Wife. A Novel. William James Roe. 1885. J. B. Lippincott Company.

Models. Susanne Jaffe. 1973. (pbk) 1.25. Ace Books.

Moderate Murderer: And The Honest Quack. Gilbert Keith Chesterton. LC 29-17783. 1929. Dodd, Mead and Company.

Moderato Cantabile. Marguerite Duras. 3.75 o.p. Peter Smith.

Moderato Cantabile. Marguerite Duras. Ed. by Thomas Bishop. (Orig., Fr.). 1968. pap. 1.95x o.p. (ISBN 0-13-586123-3). P-H.

Moderato Cantabile see Four Novels.

Modern Accomplishments: Or, The March of Intellect. Catherine Sinclair. LC 42-27066. 1861. R. Carter & Brothers.

Modern Adam and Eve in a Garden. Amanda Minnie Douglas. LC 6-33473. 1889. Lee and Shepard.

Modern African Stories. Ezekiel Mphahlele. Ed. by Ellis A. Komey. 228p. (Orig.). 1966. pap. 5.95 (ISBN 0-571-11217-X). Faber & Faber.

Modern Agrippa. Patience Barker; a Tale of Old Nantucket. Caroline Earle White. LC 8-36624. 1893. J. B. Lippincott Company.

Modern Aladdin: Or, The Wonderful Adventures of Oliver Munier; an Extravaganza in Four Acts. Howard Pyle. LC 7-42405. 1892. Harper & Brothers.

Modern American and British Short Stories. Ed. by Leonard Brown. LC 29-22680. Harcourt, Brace and Company.

Modern American Classics: An Anthology of Short Fiction. Ed. by David Rhoads Weimer. LC 76-82701. 1969. Random House.

Modern American Short Stories. Ed. by Bennett Alfred Cerf. LC 45-35161. 1945. The World Publishing Company.

Modern American Short Stories. Ed. by Thomas R Cook. LC 29-10671. C. Scribner's Sons.

Modern American Short Stories. Ed. by Thomas R Cook. LC 39-15958. C. Scribner's Sons.

Modern American Short Stories. Ed. by Edward Joseph Harrington O'Brien. LC 32-198239. 1932. Dodd, Mead & Company.

Modern American Short Stories. A. Steele. Ed. by J. Hancock. Repr. of 1941 ed. 10.00 o.p. Folcroft.

Modern American Short Stories 1982. Ed. by Dorrance & Co. Editors. 1982. 9.95 (ISBN 0-8059-2850-2). Dorrance.

Modern Antaeus. Lawrence Housman. 1801. Doubleday, Page & Co.

Modern Arabic Short Stories. Ed. by Denys Johnson-Davies. Tr. by D. Johnson-Davies from Arabic. (Orig.). 1976. 9.00x (ISBN 0-89410-316-4, Co-Pub by Heinemann Educ. Bks); pap. 5.00x (ISBN 0-435-99403-4). Three Continents.

Modern Atlantic Stories. The Atlantic Monthly. Ed. by Thomas, Charles Swain. LC 32-9690. 1932. Little, Brown, and Company.

Modern Australian Short Stories: Ed. by John K. Ewers. Ed. by John Keith Ewers. LC 66-788252. 1965. 3.95. Georgian House.

Modern Babylon. A Tale of the Metropolis. Charles William Slater. LC 8-9021. 1897. Queen City Publishing Company.

Modern Banker: A Story of His Rapid Rise and Dangerous Designs. James B Goode. (Library of progress, no. 18). 1896. C. H. Kerr & Company.

Modern Becky Sharp. Ida May Linkins Broughton. LC 17-7813. R. G. Badger; Etc., Etc.

Modern Black Stories. Ed. by Martin Mirer. LC 70-162824. (Illus.). (gr. 9-12). 1971. pap. 3.95 (ISBN 0-8120-0425-6). Barron.

Modern Brazilian Short Stories. Ed. by William Leonard Grossman. 1974. (pbk.) 2.25 (ISBN 0-520-02766-3). University of California Press.

Modern Brazilian Short Stories: Tr., Introd. by William L. Grossman. William Leonard Grossman. LC 67-13379. 1967. bds., 4.95. Univ. of Calif. Pr.

Modern British Short Novels. Ed. by Robert Murray Davis. LC 75-157243. 1972. 5.95. Scott, Foresman.

Modern Buccaneer. Thomas Alexander Browne. LC 6-172288. 1894. Macmillan and Co.

Modern Chinese Stories. Ed. by William John Francis Jenner. LC 75-322793. (Galaxy book). 1974. (1.75, 2.95 u.s.). Oxford University Press.

Modern Chinese Stories and Novellas, 1919-1949. Joseph S. M. Lau & Chih-Tsing Hsia. LC 80-27572. (Modern Asian Literature Series). (Illus.). 1981. 35.00 (ISBN 0-231-04202-7) (ISBN 0-231-04203-5). Columbia University Press.

Modern Chivalry: Containing the Adventures of Captain John Farrago and Teague O'Regan, His Servant. Ed. for the Mod. Reader by Lewis Leary. Hugh Henry Brackenridge. Ed. by Lewis Gaston Leary. LC 65-282574. (Masterworks of lit. ser.). 1966. 6.00, 2.45 pap.,. Coll. & Univ. Pr.

Modern Chronicle. Winston Churchill. LC 10-8530. 1910. The Macmillan Company.

Modern Cinderella. Charlotte Mary Brame. (On cover: Seaside library. Pocket ed. no. 1091). G. Munro.

Modern Circe. Margaret Wolfe Hungerford. LC 7-8495. (On cover: Lovell's library, no. 1065). 1887. J. W. Lovell Company.
Modern Classics: Containing The Man Without a Country... and Other Stories from the "Atlantic Monthly.". The Atlantic Monthly. LC 44-34788. 1865. Porter & Coates.
Modern Classics of Suspense. LC 68-31574. (Illus.). 1968. Reader's Digest Association.
Modern Comedy. John Galsworthy. LC 75-332934. 1970. Scribner.
Modern Comedy. John Galsworthy. LC 29-26919. 1929. C. Scribner's Sons.
Modern Corsair: A Story of the Levant. Richard Henry Savage. (On cover: Rialto series, no. 77). 1897. Rand, McNally & Company.
Modern Cressida. Francis Asheton & Hallowell, Sarah C. LC 6-4527. 1875. J. B. Lippincott & Co.
Modern Daedalus. Tom Greer. LC 74-15977. (Science Fiction). 1975. 15.00 (ISBN 0-405-06294-X). Arno Press.
Modern Daedalus... Tom Greer. LC 7-2178. 1887. Griffith, Farran, Okeden & Welsh.
Modern Daughters: Conversations with Various American Girls and One Man. Alexander Black. LC 99-4875. 1899. C. Scribner's Sons.
Modern Despotism: A True Story of American Political Life in 1893. Marcus Petersen. LC 7-36170. 1894. C. W. Moulton.
Modern Dick Whittington. James Payn. (On cover: Broadway series, no. 12). J. A. Taylor and Company.
Modern English Short Stories. Ed. by Phyllis Maud Jones. LC 70-161949. (World's classics, 477). 1971. (ISBN 0-403-01323-2). Scholarly Press.
Modern English Short Stories. Ed. by Edward Joseph Harrington O'Brien. 1978. Repr. of 1930 ed. lib. bdg. 17.50 (ISBN 0-8482-2042-0). Norwood Edns.
Modern English Short Stories, 1930-1955. Ed. by Derek Hudson. LC 73-151263. (Oxford paperbacks, 273). 1972. 0.70 (ISBN 0-19-281121-5). Oxford University Press.
Modern Eve. Helen Marion Edginton. LC 13-16789. 1913. 1.25. Frederick A. Stokes Company.
Modern Evelin. 1970. pap. 1.75 o.p. (Z1058K, Zebra). Grove.
Modern Eveline. 1972. pap. 2.25 o.s.i. (V1099R, Venus). Grove.
Modern Evil. Minnie L Armstrong. (On cover: Idle moments series, no. 5). 1891. The Price-McGill Publishing Co.
Modern Evil. Evie Sartor Byrd. LC 7-15586. 1907. Broadway Publishing Co.
Modern Far Eastern Stories. Ed. by Chung Chong-wha. (Writing in Asia Ser.). 1978. pap. text ed. 6.95x (00205). Heinemann Ed.
Modern Fine Gentleman. LC 74-16157. (Flowering of the Novel). 1974. (ISBN 0-8240-1203-8). Garland Pub.
Modern Fishers of Men Among the Various Sexes, Sects, and Stes of Chartville Church and Community. George Lansing Raymond. LC 7-25319. 1879. D. Appleton and Company.
Modern Fishers of Men Among the Various Sets, Sects, and Sexes of Chartville Church and Community. 3d ed. George Lansing Raymond. LC 22-24756. 1911. G. P. Putnam's Sons, the Knickerbocker Press.
Modern French Short Stories. Ed. by Edouard Fanniere. LC 34-314288. 1933. The Clarendon Press.
Modern Galaxy. Dale Warren. LC 30-30229. 1930. Houghton Mifflin Company.
Modern German Short Stories. Ed. by Hans F Eggeling. LC 29-22276. 1929. The Clarendon Press.
Modern German Short Stories. Ed. by Hans F Eggeling. LC 33-27257. 1933. The Clarendon Press.
Modern German Short Stories. H. Steinhaver & H. Jessiman. Repr. of 1938 ed. 20.00 (ISBN 0-89987-172-0). Darby Bks.
Modern German Short Stories. H. Steinhaver & H. Jessiman. 1938. 15.00. Havertown Bks.
Modern German Short Stories: Translated. Tr. by Harry Steinhauer. LC 38-27292. (Half-title: The world's classics, cdlvi). 1938. Oxford University Press, H. Milford.
Modern German Stories. Ed. by Allen Wilson Porterfield. LC 28-11648. (Heath's modern language series). D. C. Heath and Company.
Modern Ghosts: Selected and Translated from the Works of Guy De Maupassant, Pedro Antonio De Alarcon, Alexander L. Kielland, Leopold Kompert, Gustavo Adolfo Becquer, and Giovanni Magherini-Graziani; the Introduction by George William Curtis. George William Curtis et al. LC 3-21949. 1890. Harper & Brothers.
Modern Girl. William Budd Trites. LC 29-872007. 1929. Frederick A. Stokes Company.
Modern Greek Stories. Demetra Vaka Brown & Phoutrides, Aristides Evangelus, 1887-1923, Joint Tr. LC 20-267561. (interpreter's series). 1920. Duffield and Company.
Modern Greek Stories. Tr. by Demetra Vaka Brown. LC 79-136414. 1971. (ISBN 0-404-01134-9). AMS Press.
Modern Gypsy: A Romance of Circus Life. Charles Theodore Murray. LC 7-31831. (On cover: American technical series, no. 4). 1897. American Technical Book Company.
Modern Hagar. A Drama. Charlotte Clark. LC 6-23855. (Kasterskill ser. no. 2 5d). 1882. G. W. Harlan & Co.
Modern Hamilton. Frank Gates Ellett. LC 12-15147. 1.00. Press of F.H. West.
Modern Hebrew Literature. Robert Alter. LC 75-9928. (Library of Jewish studies). 1975. 4.95 (ISBN 0-87441-235-8) (ISBN 0-87441-218-8). Behrman House.
Modern Heloise. Alfred Buchanan. 1.25. G. W. Dillingham Company.
Modern Hercules", the Tale of a Sculptress. Melvin G Winstock. LC 447. 1899. Herald Democrat Print.
Modern Hero. Louis Bromfield. LC 32-26501. 1932. Frederick A. Stokes Company.
Modern Hindi Short Stories. Ed. by Gordon C. Roadarmel. LC 75-24041. (UNESCO Collection of Representative Works: Indian Series). 1974. 2.85 (ISBN 0-520-02776-0). University of California Press.
Modern Image. Frederick Morgan. 1965. 4.50 o.p. (ISBN 0-393-04222-7). Norton.
Modern Image: Outstanding Stories from the Hudson Review. The Hudson Review. Ed. by Morgan, Frederick. LC 64-23873. (Norton library, N285). 1965. Norton.
Modern Indian Short Stories. Ed. by Saros Cowasjee & Shiv K. Kumar. 146p. 1982. pap. 4.95 (ISBN 0-19-561202-7). Oxford U Pr.
Modern Indian Short Stories. Ed. by Suresh Kohli. (Indian Short Stories Ser.). 164p. 1975. 5.00 (ISBN 0-88253-737-7). Ind-US Inc.
Modern Instance. William Dean Howells. Ed. by W. Gibson. LC 57-13839. (YA) (gr. 9 up). 1957. pap. 4.75 (ISBN 0-395-05119-3, 3-47655, RivEd, A21). HM.
Modern Instance. William Dean Howells. 1973. lib. bdg. 7.50 o.p. Folcroft.
Modern Instance, a Novel. William Dean Howells. LC 4-8624. 1882. J. R. Osgood and Company.
Modern Instance: A Novel. 26th ed. William Dean Howells. LC 4-15124. Houghton, Mifflin and Company.
Modern Instance. Edited with an Introd. and Notes by William M. Gibson. William Dean Howells. LC 57-13829. (Riverside editions, A21). 1957. Houghton Mifflin.
Modern Irish Short Stories. Ben Forkner. LC 80-16071. 1980. 14.95 (ISBN 0-670-48324-9). Viking Press.
Modern Irish Short Stories. Ben Forkner. LC 80-19292. 1980. 5.95 (ISBN 0-14-005669-6). Penguin Books.
Modern Italian Short Stories. Ed. by Mark L Vovich Slonim. LC 54-6670. 1954. Simon and Schuster.
Modern Italian Short Stories. Edited Withnotes, Exercises, and Vocabulary. Rev. and Enl. Ed. by Thomas Goddard Bergin. LC 59-6276. 1959. Heath.
Modern Italian Short Stories: Edited with Notes, Exercises, and Vocabulary. Ed. by Thomas Goddard Bergin. LC 39-2125. (Heath-Chicago language series). D. C. Heath and Company.
Modern Jacob. Helen Butler Smith. LC 8-8166. D. Lothrop Company.
Modern Japanese Fiction. Mitsuo Nakamura. (Japanese Life & Culture Ser). (Illus.). pap. 3.75 o.p. (ISBN 0-87040-082-7). Japan Pubns.
Modern Japanese Stories. Ed. by Ivan Morris. Tr. by Seidensticker et al. 1961. 6.00 o.p. Verry.
Modern Japanese Stories: An Anthology. Ed. by Ivan Morris. LC 61-11971. (Illus.). 1977. pap. 8.50 (ISBN 0-8048-1226-8). C E Tuttle.
Modern Japanese Stories: An Anthology. Tr. by Edward Seidensticker Others. Ed. by Ivan I. Morris. (UNESCO collection of representative works: Japanese ser.). 1965. 6.00. Eyre & Spottiswoode.
Modern Jewish Stories: 1st Amer. Ed. Ed. by Gerda Charles. LC 65-22196. 1965. bds., 4.95. Prentice.
Modern Jezebel. Irene Nemirovsky. Tr. by Dunbar, Barre. LC 37-3279. H. Holt and Company.
Modern Job. George Washington Pangle. 1899. Burkley Printing Company.
Modern Juliet. Charles Garvice. LC 3192. (On cover: The Laurel library, no. 39). 1898. G. Munro's Sons.
Modern Knight (a Trans-Atlantic Trifle) Daisy G. S. Holbrook. LC 12-623. 1911. The Case, Lockwood & Brainard Co.
Modern Korean Short Stories. Ed. by Chung Chong-Wha. (Writing in Asia Ser.). (Orig.). 1981. pap. text ed. 9.00x (00256). Heinemann Ed.
Modern Lady. Grace Perkins Oursler. LC 35-1943. Farrar & Rinehart Incorporated.
Modern Look at Monsters. Daniel Cohen. 1971. pap. 0.95 o.p. (T-095-134). Tower.
Modern Love. Constance DeJong. 1977. pap. 5.00 (ISBN 0-918746-01-9). Standard Edns.
Modern Love. Leslie Glass. LC 83-2936. 14.95 (ISBN 0-312-54090-6). St. Martin's Press.
Modern Love Story, Which Does Not End at the Altar. Harriet E Orcutt. LC 7-231903. 1894. C. H. Kerr & Company.
Modern Lover. David Herbert Lawrence. LC 70-38722. (Short story index reprint series). 1972. (ISBN 0-8369-4135-7). Books for Libraries Press.
Modern Lover. David Herbert Lawrence. LC 34-37429. 1934. The Viking Press.
Modern Lovers. Viola Meynell. LC 14-430115. 1.25. R. G. Badger.
Modern Madonna. Alice Mary Ross Colver. LC 32-18735. 1932. Dodd, Mead & Company.
Modern Madonna. Caroline Abbot Stanley. LC 6-30928. 1906. The Century Co.
Modern Magadalene. Virna Woods. LC 8-372398. 1894. Lee and Shepard.
Modern Magdalen. Sofia McQuaide De Bonis. LC 31-22577. Farrar & Rinehart, Incorporated.
Modern Magician. Joseph Fitzgerald Molloy. LC 7-25312. (On cover: Lovell's library, no. 1139). J. W. Lovell Company.
Modern Malaysian Chinese Stories. Ed. by Ly Singko & Leon Comber. 1967. pap. text ed. 4.00x (00230). Heinemann Ed.
Modern Man. Ella MacMahon. LC 7-20430. (Iris series). 1895. Macmillan and Co.
Modern Marriage. Rob Eden. LC 37-391193. M. S. Mill Co., Inc.
Modern Marriage. Emile Zola & Tucker, Benjamin Ricketson, 1854- Tr. LC 9-1316. 1893. B. R. Tucker.
Modern Marriage: A Novel. Clara Hammond Lanza. LC 7-13835. (On cover: American authors' series. no. 8). 1890. J. W. Lovell Company.
Modern Marriage: A Short Novel. Maurice B Vankin. LC 31-10516. Miller Brothers Co., Inc.
Modern Marriage Market. Corelli, Marie & Steel, Mrs., Flora Annie (Webster) 1847- LC 12-18730. (With Corelli, Marie. Jane. Philadelphia, 1900). 1900. J. B. Lippincott Company.
Modern Masterpieces of Science Fiction: Ed. by Sam Moskowitz. Ed. by Samuel Moskowitz. LC 65-18008. 6.00. World.
Modern Masterpieces of Science Fiction. Ed. by Samuel Moskowitz. LC 73-15071. (Classics of science fiction). 1974. 12.95 (ISBN 0-88355-126-8) (ISBN 0-88355-126-8). Hyperion Press.
Modern Masters of Horror. Frank Coffey. LC 80-17314. 1980. 11.95 (ISBN 0-698-11051-X). Coward, McCann & Geoghegan.
Modern Mephistopheles. Louisa May Alcott. LC 26-3673. (No Name Series). 1877. Roberts Brothers.
Modern Mephistopheles: And a Whisper in the Dark. Louisa May Alcott. LC 12-133201. 1889. Roberts Brothers.
Modern Mephistopheles: And A Whisper in the Dark. Louisa May Alcott. LC 5-8706. 1902. Little, Brown, and Company.
Modern Mercenary. Kate O'Brien Hesketh Prichard & Prichard, Hesketh Vernon Hesketh. LC 99-4297. 1899. Doubleday & McClure Co.
Modern Midas, a Romance. Mor Jokai. Tr. by Bullard, Laura Curtis. LC 7-11922. (On cover: Lovell's library. v. 15. no. 754). 1886. J. W. Lovell Company.
Modern Midas. A Romance. Mor Jokai. Tr. by Bullard, Laura Curtis. LC 4-16167. (peerless series, no. 117). J. S. Ogilvie Publishing Company.
Modern Miracle. James Franklin Fitts. (On cover: The select series, no. 72). 1890. Street & Smith.
Modern Miracle. A Dramatic Story. James Franklin Fitts. (On cover: The Manhattan series, no. 13). 1889. A. L. Burt.
Modern Mystery and Adventure Novels, Edited and Abridged by Jay E. Greene. Ed. by Jay Elihu Greene. LC 51-4139. 1951. Globe Book Co.
Modern Nigerian Novels. V. Klima. (Oriental Institute Czechoslovakia Dissertationes Orientales, Vol. 18). 1969. 6.00 o.p. Paragon.
Modern Novel Writing: Or, The Elegant Enthusiast. William Beckford. LC 74-7458. (Feminist Controversy in England, 1788-1810). 1974. (ISBN 0-8240-0851-0). Garland Pub.
Modern Novel Writing: 1796) and Azemia (1797) William Beckford. LC 74-81366. 1970. 15.00. Scholars' Facsimiles & Reprints.
Modern Novelette. Ed. by Ronald Paulson. LC 65-15150. (Prentice-Hall English literature series). 1965. Prentice-Hall.
Modern Novelists: Selected Readings. Ed. D. L. Hartley. (General Studies Library). 159p. 1972. pap. 3.75 o.p. Transatlantic.
Modern Obstacle. Alice Duer Miller. LC 3-11497. 1903. C. Scribner's Sons.
Modern Pagan: A Novel. Constance Goddard Du Bois. LC 6-34213. The Merriam Company.
Modern Pagans. Charles Monroe Sheldon. LC 17-23051. The Methodist Book Concern.
Modern Pariah, a Story of the South. Francis Fontaine. LC 6-41413. F. Fontaine.
Modern Persian Short Stories. Ed. by Minoo Southgate. LC 79-89930. 228p. (Orig.). 1980. 14.00x (ISBN 0-89410-032-7, 033-5); pap. 7.00x (ISBN 0-89410-033-5). Three Continents.
Modern Pharisee. A Novel. Edgar Clifton Bross. (Dillingham's metropolitan library, no. 3). 1895. G. W. Dillingham.
Modern Philippine Short Stories: By Francisco Arcellana and Others, 1st Ed. Ed. by Leonard Casper. LC 61-100481. 1962. University of New Mexico Press.
Modern Pilgrims: Showing the Improvements in Travel, and the Newest Methods of Reaching the Celestial City... George Wood. LC 8-37561. 1855. J. C. Derby.
Modern Polish Mind. Ed. by Maria Tristan Kuncewicz. 1963. pap. 2.95 o.p. (ISBN 0-448-00162-4, UL). G&D.
Modern Polish Mind: An Anthology. 1st Ed. Ed. by Maria Szczepanska Kuncewiczowa. LC 62-10531. 1962. Little, Brown.
Modern Prince from an Ancient House. Horace Wilson Bennett. LC 36-17116. The Christopher Publishing House.
Modern Prodigal. LC 25-19681. The Warner Press.
Modern Prodigal. Julia MacNair Wright. LC 9-537. 1892. The National Temperance Society and Publication House.
Modern Prometheus. Martha Gilbert Dickinson Bianchi. 1908. Duffield & Company.
Modern Prometheus. Edward Phillips Oppenheim. LC 7-23193. (Neely's prismatic library). F. T. Neely.
Modern Psychological Novel. Leon Edel. 1973. 4.75 (ISBN 0-8446-2020-3). Peter Smith.
Modern Rasselas. Keith Lindsay. LC 99-951. F. T. Neely.
Modern Revival: An Enigmatic Novel, with Fantastic Angles Which Make an Interesting and Entertaining Story. Clarence Melville Walker. LC 45-891612. House of Field-Doubleday, Inc.
Modern Revolt from Rome: A Novel. John Berkeley. LC 10-27582. 1.35. Jennings and Graham.
Modern Rosalind. A Story. F Xavier Calvert. LC 6-21860. (On cover: Rialto series, no. 34). 1891. Rand, McNally & Company.
Modern Russian Classics. Tr. by Isaac Goldberg. Incl. Silence. Leonid Andreyev; White Dog. Fyodor Sologub; Father. Anton Chekhov; Her Lover. Maxim Gorki; Letter. Isaac Babel. pap. 3.00 (ISBN 0-8283-1450-0, IPL). Branden.
Modern Russian Classics. Science: by L. N. Andreyev; The White Dog: by Feodor Sologub; The Doctor: by Michael Artzibashev; A Father: by Anton Tchekov; Her Lover: by Maxim Gorky. LC 19-182300. (Half-title: International pocket library, ed. by E. R. Brown). 1918. The Four Seas Company.
Modern Russian Short Stories. Ed. by George Gibian & M. Samilov. 1965. text ed. 8.95x o.p. (ISBN 0-06-042320-X, HarpC). Har-Row.
Modern Saint Christopher: Or, The Brothers. Rose Porter. LC 7-37746. A. D. F. Randolph & Company.
Modern Satiric Stories: The Impropriety Principle. Ed. by Gregory Fitz Gerald. LC 76-140504. (Illus.). 1971. Scott, Foresman.
Modern Science Fiction. Ed. by Norman Spinrad. LC 73-18782. 1974. (pbk.) 3.50 (ISBN 0-385-02263-8). Anchor Press.
Modern Science Fiction. Ed. by Norman Spinrad. LC 76-11823. (Gregg Press science fiction series). 1976. 25.00 (ISBN 0-8398-2339-8). Gregg Press.
Modern Scottish Short Stories. Fred Urquhart & Giles Gordon. LC 82-82755. 1982. 6.95 (ISBN 0-571-11953-0). Faber and Faber.
Modern Short Novel. Ed. by William Wasserstrom. LC 65-14862. pap., 4.50. Holt.
Modern Short Novel: With an Introd. and Notes. Ed. by William Wasserstrom. LC 65-14862. 1965. Holt, Rinehart and Winston.
Modern Short-Stories. Ed. by Margaret Eliza Ashmun. LC 14-2242. 1914. The Macmillan Company.
Modern Short Stories. enl. ed. Ed. by Leonard Brown. LC 37-9866. Harcourt, Brace and Company.
Modern Short Stories. Ed. by Alice Cecillia Cooper. LC 49-2202. 1949. Globe Book Co.

Modern Short Stories. John Hadfield. Repr. of 1939 ed. 15.00 (ISBN 0-89987-173-9). Darby Bks.

Modern Short Stories. Higgins, Frank Victor. LC 63-14398. 1963. Varsity Press.

Modern Short Stories. Ed. by Jim Hunter. LC 66-7643. (Faber educational bks.)). 1966. bds., 2.25. Faber & Faber.

Modern Short Stories. Ed. by Emma L Reppert. Stratton, Clarence, 1880- Joint Ed. LC 39-1385. McGraw-Hill Book Company, Inc.

Modern Short Stories: A Book for High Schools. Ed. by Frederick Houk Law. LC 18-100062. 1918. The Century Co.

Modern Short Stories; a Critical Anthology. Robert Bechtold Heilman. LC 73-106674. 1971. (ISBN 0-8371-3360-2). Greenwood Press.

Modern Short Stories: A Critical Anthology. Ed. by Robert Bechtold Heilman. LC 50-7609. 1950. Harcourt, Brace.

Modern Short Stories: By Marvin Felheim, Franklin B. Newman and William R. Steinhoff. Ed. by Marvin Felheim. LC 51-3598. 1951. Oxford University Press.

Modern Short Stories for Oral Interpretation: A Compilation of Stories Chosen for the Purpose of Adaptation for Oral Interpretation, Together with an Introduction on the Art of Reading Aloud, Adapting a Reading, and Arranging a Program. Ed. by Mabel Pearl Lloyd. LC 33-36719. Print. by G. Banta Publishing Company.

Modern Short Stories from Story Magazine. Story Magazine Editors. 1961. pap. 1.95 o.p. (ISBN 0-448-00108-X, UL). G&D.

Modern Short Stories from Story Magazine. Story (New York, 1931-) LC 62-2537. (Universal library). Grosset & Dunlap.

Modern Short Stories in English. rev. ed. Robert James Dixson. (Illus., Orig., Sequel to Easy Reading Selections in English). (gr. 9-11). 1971. pap. text ed. 3.25 (ISBN 0-88345-117-4, 17986); 35.00 o.p. tapes; cassettes 40.00. Regents Pub.

Modern Short Stories: The Fiction of Experience Ed. by M. X. Lesser, John N. Morris. Ed. by M. X. Lesser & John N. Morris. LC 62-17644. 4.95, 3.75 pap.,. McGraw.

Modern Short Stories: The Fiction of Experience Edited by M. X. Lesser and John N. Morris. Ed. by M. X. Lesser & John N. Morris. LC 62-17644. 1962. McGraw-Hill.

Modern Short Stories: The Fiction of Experience. Ed. by M. X. Lesser & John N. Morris. 1962. pap. 16.50 (ISBN 0-07-037336-1, C); teacher's manual 20.00 (ISBN 0-07-037334-5). McGraw.

Modern Short Stories: The Fiction of Experience. Ed. by M. X. Lesser & John N. Morris. (gr. 11-12). 1962. text ed. 4.95, s.p. 3.96 o.p.; teachers' manual. 1.00, s.p. 0.80 o.p. McGraw.

Modern Short Stories: The Uses of Imagination. Rev. Ed. Ed. by Arthur Mizener. LC 66-117906. 1967. 4.25. Norton.

Modern Short Stories: The Uses of Imagination. 1st Ed. Ed. by Arthur Mizener. LC 61-8919. 1962. Norton.

Modern Short Story. Ed. by Wilbur Huck. LC 68-1534. 1968. American Book Co.

Modern Short Story. Miceli. (gr. 10-12). 1970. pap. text ed. 1.72 o.p. (ISBN 0-03-083357-4, HoltC). HR&W.

Modern Society: Or, The March of Intellect, the Conclusion of Modern Accomplishments. 5th thousand. ed. Catherine Sinclair. LC 41-34812. 1838. W. Whyte and Co.

Modern Society: Or, The March of Intellect, the Conclusion of Modern Accomplishments. Catherine Sinclair. LC 42-270674. (With her Modern accomplishments: or The march of intellect. New York, 1861). 1861. R. Carter & Brothers.

Modern Stories from Holland and Flanders: An Anthology. Ed. by Egbert Krispyn. LC 72-3913. (Library of Netherlandic literature, v. 2). 1973. 7.50. Twayne Publishers.

Modern Stories from Holland & Flanders. Ed. by Egbert Krispyn. (International Studies & Translations Ser). lib. bdg. 9.95 o.p. (ISBN 0-8057-3449-X, Twayne). G K Hall.

Modern Stories from Many Lands. 2nd enl. ed. Ed. by Charles Angoff & Clarence R. Decker. 434p. 1972. 7.95 (ISBN 0-87141-040-0). Manyland.

Modern Stories from Many Lands. rev. ed. edited by charles angoff. 2d enl. ed. Ed. by Clarence Raymond Decker. LC 72-77856. 1972. 7.95 (ISBN 0-87141-040-0). Manyland Books.

Modern Stories in English. W. H. Mew & H. J. Rosengarten. 1975. pap. text ed. 5.95x o.p. (ISBN 0-690-00765-5); instructor's manual avail. o.p. (ISBN 0-690-00816-3). T Y Crowell.

Modern Stories in English. Ed. by William H. New. LC 74-28447. 1975. 3.95 (ISBN 0-690-00764-7). Crowell.

Modern Story-Teller: Embracing the Best Stories of the Best Authors. LC 7-4440. 1886. Porter & Coates.

Modern Story-Teller: Or, The Best Stories of the Best Authors, Now First Collected. LC 44-31058. (Putnam's story library). 1856. G. P. Putnam & Co.

Modern Swedish Masterpieces. Tr. by Charles Wharton Stork. LC 23-117041. E. P. Dutton & Company.

Modern Swedish Short Stories. Anglo-Swedish Literary Foundation, London. LC 74-3326. (Short story index reprint series). 1974. 22.75 (ISBN 0-8369-4261-2). Books for Libraries Press.

Modern Swedish Short Stories. 487p. 1981. Repr. of 1934 ed. lib. bdg. 30.00 (ISBN 0-89987-596-3). Darby Bks.

Modern Talent: An Anthology of Short Stories. Ed. by John Edward Hardy. LC 64-14690. pap., 3.75. Holt.

Modern Tales of the Greek Islands. Argyres Ephtaliotes & Rouse, William Henry Denhain, 1863- Tr. LC 43-7355. 1942. T. Nelson and Sons Ltd.

Modern Telemachus. Charlotte Mary Yonge. (On cover: Seaside library. Pocket ed. no. 887). 1886. G. Munro.

Modern Telemachus: A Novel. Charlotte Mary Yonge. LC 9-1211. (Harper's handy series, no. 106). 1886. Harper & Brothers.

Modern Telemachus: Also, Henrietta's Wish. Charlotte Mary Yonge. (On cover: Lovell's library. v. 18, no. 858). 1886. J. W. Lovell Company.

Modern Telugu Short Stories: An Anthology. Ed. by V. Patanjali & A. Muralidhar. Tr. by A. Muralidhar. 261p. 1968. pap. 2.45 (ISBN 0-88253-065-8). Ind-US Inc.

Modern Times: Bringing You All the Hits, August River, Moon Man, and Many More. Thomas Jackson. LC 74-78288. 1974. 2.95. Fleetwood.

Modern Tradition: An Anthology of Short Stories. 3d ed. Ed. by Daniel Francis Howard. LC 75-26033. 6.95 (ISBN 0-316-37459-8). Little, Brown.

Modern Tradition: An Anthology of Short Stories. Ed. by Daniel Francis Howard. LC 68-16311. 1968. Little, Brown.

Modern Tradition: An Anthology of Short Stories. 2d ed. Ed. by Daniel Francis Howard. LC 74-186062. (Illus.). 1972. Little, Brown.

Modern Tradition: An Anthology of Short Stories. 4th ed. Ed. by Daniel Francis Howard. LC 78-71866. (Illus.). 7.95. Little, Brown.

Modern Tragedy. Phyllis Eleanor Bentley. LC 33-274991. 1934. The Macmillan Company.

Modern Tragedy. Murray Montague. LC 7-31809. 1891. S. W. Barrows & Co.

Modern Tragedy: A Romance of Italy and America. John Merritte Driver. LC 6-6929. Laird & Lee.

Modern Trio in an Old Town. Katharine Haviland Taylor. Harcourt, Brace and Company.

Modern Ukrainian Short Stories. Ed. & tr. by George S. Luckyj. LC 72-95387. 228p. 1973. lib. bdg. 8.50 o.p. (ISBN 0-87287-061-8). Ukrainian Acad.

Modern Ukrainian Short Stories. Ed. & tr. by George S. Luckyj. LC 72-95387. 228p. 1973. lib. bdg. 8.50 o.p. (ISBN 0-87287-061-8). Ukrainian Acad.

Modern Ulysses: The Strange History of Horace Durand, His Loves and His Adventures. Joseph Hatton. LC 7-2200. United States Book Company.

Modern Urdu Stories. Tr. by A. I. Mirza from Urdu. (Writers Workshop Saffronbird Bk Ser.). 1977. flexible bdg. 4.80 (ISBN 0-89253-643-8); text ed. 10.00 (ISBN 0-89253-642-X). Ind-US Inc.

Modern Vikings: Stories of Life and Sport in the Norseland. Hjalmar Hjorth Boyesen. LC 74-3416. (Short story index reprint series). 1974. 15.00 (ISBN 0-8369-4266-3). Books for Libraries Press.

Modern Vikings: Stories of Life and Sport in the Norse, Land. Hjalmar Hjorth Boyesen. LC 4-16122. 1887. C. Scribner's Sons.

Modern Wizard. Rodrigues Ottolengui. LC 7-22776. 1894. G. P. Putnam's Sons.

Modern Women. Gustav Kobbe. LC 15-19264. 1915. 1.00. Moffat, Yard & Company.

Modern Women in Love. Ed. by Christina Stead. Blech, William James, 1894- Joint Ed. LC 47-2866. 1947. Garden City Publishing Co., Inc.

Modern Women in Love; Sixty Twentieth-Century Masterpieces of Fiction. Ed. by Christina Stead. Blech, William James, 1894- Joint Ed. LC 46-401. 1945. The Dryden Press.

Modernist. Francis Deming Hoyt. LC 15-178061. 1915. The Lakewood Press.

Moderns. Daoma Winston. (Orig.). pap. 0.60 o.p. (X1626). Pyramid Pubns.

Moderns & Contemporaries: Nine Masters of the Short Story. Jonathan Baumbach & A. Edelstein. 7.00 (ISBN 0-8446-1611-7). Peter Smith.

Moderns and Contemporaries: Nine Masters of the Short Story, Ed. by Jonathan Baumbach, Arthur Edelstein. Ed. by Jonathan Baumbach. 1968. 5.00. Peter Smith.

Moderns and Contemporaries: Nine Masters of the Short Story. Ed. by Jonathan Baumbach. LC 68-10669. 1968. Random House.

Moderns and Contemporaries: Twelve Masters of the Short Story. 2d ed. Ed. by Jonathan Baumbach. LC 76-56168. 1977. 5.95 (ISBN 0-394-31287-2). Random House.

Modes of Fiction. Ed. by Paul J. Dolan. LC 79-77318. (Illus.). 1970. Free Press.

Modest Little Sara. By Alan St. Aubyn Pseud.... Frances Bridges Marshall. LC 7-24396. (On cover: Globe library, v. 1, no. 176). 1892. Rand, McNally & Company.

Modest Proposal. Robert Sherrill. 5.00 o.p. Bobbs.

Modesta. Gladys Bronwyn Stern. LC 29-26898. 1929. A. A. Knopf.

Modeste Mignon. Honore De Balzac. Tr. by Katharine Prescott Wormeley. (Half-title: The comedy of human life... Scenes from private life). 1889. Roberts Brothers.

Modesty Blaise. Peter O'Donnell. LC 65-17258. 1965. Doubleday.

Modigliani: Prince of Montparnasee. Tadeusz Wittlin. LC 64-15661. 1964. Bobbs-Merrill.

Mods. Sandra Lawrence. (Illus.). pap. 0.50 o.p. (72-171). Lancer.

Mog & Glog. David Hubert Lloyd. LC 78-51718. (Illus.). 2.25 (ISBN 0-930090-01-2). Applezaba Press.

Mogens, and Other Stories. Jens Peter Jacobsen. LC 72-4452. (Series: The Sea Gull Library, V. 2.). (Short story index reprint series). 1972. 8.50 (ISBN 0-8369-4179-9). Books for Libraries Press.

Mogens: And Other Stories. Jens Peter Jacobsen. Tr. by Grabow, Anna. LC 21-1280. (On verso of half-title: The sea gull library, ed. by O. F. Theis vol. ii). 1921. N. L. Brown.

Moghul: A Novel of India. Thomas Hoover. LC 82-45146. 384p. 1983. 16.95 (ISBN 0-385-17576-0). Doubleday.

Mogollon Rim Vengeance. Charles E. Wheeler. (YA) 1979. 6.50 (Avalon). Bouregy.

Mogul Tales: or the Dreams of Man Awake, Pt. 2. Thomas S. Gueulette. LC 73-170593. (Novel in England, 1700-1775). lib. bdg. 50.00 (ISBN 0-8240-0576-7). Garland Pub.

Mohammed Ali and His House. Klara Muller Mundt. Tr. by Coleman, Chapman. LC 16-1239. (historical romances of Louisa Muhlbach pseud.). D. Appleton and Company.

Mohammed Ali and His House. An Historical Romance. Klara Muller Mundt. Tr. by Coleman, Chapman. LC 7-36660. 1872. D. Appleton and Company.

Mohawk Ladder. 1st Ed. Noel Bertram Gerson. LC 51-10433. 1951. Doubleday.

Mohawk Peter: Legends of the Adirondacks, and Civil War Memories. Henry Gustavus Dorr. LC 22-107029. The Cornhill Publishing Company.

Mohawks. Mary Elizabeth Braddon Maxwell. (On cover: Lovell's library, no. 814).

Mohawks. Mary Elizabeth Braddon Maxwell. (On cover: Seaside library. Pocket ed. no. 881). 1886. G. Munro.

Mohawks. A Novel. Mary Elizabeth Braddon Maxwell. (Harper's Franklin square library, no. 553). 1886. Harper & Brothers.

Mohicans of Paris. A Novel. Alexandre Dumas & Bocage. LC 6-42323. T. B. Peterson & Brothers.

Mohicans of Paris. By Alexandre Dumas... Alexandre Dumas & Bocage. LC 21-13964. (Seaside library, v. 77, no. 1565). 1883. G. Munro.

Mohole Menace. Hugh Walters, pseud. LC 68-15232. (Illus.). 1969. 3.95. Criterion Books.

Mohun. John Esten Cooke. LC 68-20008. (Americans in Fiction Ser.). (Illus.). lib. bdg. 16.00 (ISBN 0-8398-0271-4); pap. text ed. 4.95x (ISBN 0-89197-856-9). Irvington.

Mohun. John Esten Cooke. LC 68-20008. (Americans in Fiction Ser.). 1968. Repr. of 1869 ed. lib. bdg. 9.00x o.p. (ISBN 0-8398-0271-4). Gregg.

Mohun. A Novel. John Esten Cooke. LC 4-229473. 1893. G. W. Dillingham.

Mohun: Or, The Last Days of Lee and His Paladins. Final Memoirs of a Staff Officer Serving in Virginia. From the Mss. of Colonel Surry, of Eagle's Nest. John Esten Cooke. LC 68-20008. (Americans in Fic.). 1968. 10.00. Gregg Pr.

Mohun: Or. The Last Days of Lee and His Paladins. Final Memoirs of a Staff Officer Serving in Virginia. From the Mss. of Colonel Surry, of Eagle's Nest. John Esten Cooke. LC 36-25555. 1936. Historical Publishing Co., Inc.

Moi. Barry Sadler. LC 75-26255. 1977. 6.95 (ISBN 0-87695-183-3). Aurora Publishers.

Moina; or, Against the Mighty. Emma Murdoch Van Deventer. (On cover: The library of choice fiction, no. 20). 1891. Laird & Lee.

Moira. Julien Green. LC 51-13792. 1951. Macmillan.

Moira. Caroline Stafford, pseud. LC 76-25220. 7.95 (ISBN 0-671-22373-9). Simon and Schuster.

Moira. Caroline Stafford, pseud. 1978. 1.75 (ISBN 0-449-23530-0). Fawcett Crest Books.

Moiron, and Short Stories. Guy De Maupassant. LC 10-7485. 1910. The Pearson Publishing Co.

Moise and the World of Reason. Tennessee Williams. LC 74-31061. 1975. 6.95 (ISBN 0-671-21982-0) (ISBN 0-671-22066-7). Simon and Schuster.

Moise and the World of Reason. Tennessee Williams. LC 76-375915. 1976. 3.25 (ISBN 0-491-01935-1). W. H. Allen.

Mojave. Guy Russell. LC 77-27298. (Illus.). 36p. 1977. pap. 6.95 (ISBN 0-916348-17-2). Sigga Pr.

Mojave: A Book of Stories. Edwin Corle. LC 34-702435. Liveright Publishing Corporation.

Mojave Crossing. Louis L'Amour. LC 64-10937. 1964. Bantam Books.

Mojave Design. Oliver B. Patton. (Orig.). 1982. pap. 3.50 (ISBN 0-445-04741-0). Popular Lib.

Mojave Gold. Fred Berger. 160p. (Orig.). 1981. pap. 1.95 (ISBN 0-523-41663-6). Pinnacle Bks.

Mojave Guns. Roe Richmond. LC 52-10210. 1952. Arcadia House.

Mojo Hand. Jane Phillips. LC 66-24834. 1966. 4.95. Trident.

Moke River. Roy Loehr. LC 77-84559. 1970. 3.95. Dorrance.

Mokey. Jennie Harris Oliver. LC 36-177033. Burton Publishing Company.

Moksha. Aldous Leonard Huxley. 304p. 1982. pap. 7.95 (ISBN 0-87477-208-7). J P Tarcher.

Mole. William Hood. (Espionage-Intelligence Library). 320p. 1983. pap. 3.50 (ISBN 0-345-30491-8). Ballantine.

Mole. Dan Sherman. LC 76-50339. 7.95 (ISBN 0-87795-162-4). Arbor House.

Mole: A Novel. Dan Sherman. (Fawcett Crest Book). 1.75 (ISBN 0-449-23531-9). Fawcett Books.

Molecule Men. Fred Hoyle & Geoffrey Hoyle. LC 74-184380. 272p. 1972. 7.95 o.p. (ISBN 0-06-011974-8, HarpT). Har-Row.

Molecule Men. Fred Hoyle & Geoffrey Hoyle. 1971. 8.00 o.p. (ISBN 0-06-011974-8). Ultramarine Pub.

Molehill. Alice Ritchie. LC 29-14807. 1929. G. P. Putnam's Sons.

Molehill File. Michael Kenyon. LC 77-16707. 1978. 7.95 (ISBN 0-698-10862-0). Coward, McCann & Geoghegan.

Mole's Pity. Harold Jaffe. LC 78-68129. 8.95 (ISBN 0-914590-52-9). Fiction Collective: Distributed by G. Braziller.

Moleskin Joe. Patrick MacGill. LC 24-391817. 1924. Harper & Brothers.

Molino Viejo. Robert G. Cleland. 1971. limited ed. 4.95 o.p. (ISBN 0-378-02371-3); pap. 2.75 o.p. (ISBN 0-378-02372-1). Ritchie.

Molinoff: Or, The Count in the Kitchen, by Maurice Bedel, Translated from the French. Maurice Bedel & Morris, Lawrence Shackelford, 1894- Tr. LC 29-11675. 1929. The Viking Press.

Moll Flanders. Daniel Defoe. Ed. by J. Paul Hunter. LC 69-13257. (Crowell critical library). 1970. Crowell.

Moll Flanders. Daniel Defoe & Defoe Daniel. LC 26-26990. (Half-title: The Abbey classics. xxi). 1936. Small, Maynard and Co., Inc.

Moll Flanders and The Fortunate Mistress... Daniel Defoe. LC 41-35133. 1629. Minton, Balch & Company.

Moll Pitcher's Prophecies: Or, The American Sibyl. Ellen Mary Griffin Hoey. LC 7-6602. 1895. The Eastburn Press.

Mollie: A Novel. Eustace Hale Ball. LC 26-14102. Grosset & Dunlap.

Mollie and the Unwiseman. John Kendrick Bangs. LC 2-26754. (Lettered on cover: Children's library). 1902. H. T. Coates & Co.

Mollie Deverill. Susan Richmond Lee. LC 9-12082. J. Long.

Mollie's Prince: A Novel. Rosa Nouchette Carey. 1899. J. B. Lippincott Company.

Mollie's Prince: A Novel. Rosa Nouchette Carey. 1912. J. B. Lippincott Company.

Mollie's Substitute Husband. Charles Maxwell McConn. LC 20-14216. 1920. Dodd, Mead and Company.

Mollie's Year. Tana Reiff. LC 78-75220. (LifeTimes Ser.). 1979. pap. 3.32 (ISBN 0-8224-4316-3). Pitman Learning.

Molloy. Samuel Beckett. Tr. by Samuel Beckett & Patrick Bowles. 1955. 12.50 (ISBN 0-394-47515-1, GP641). Grove.

Molloy see Three Novels.

Molly. Teresa Crane. LC 82-10598. 1982. 13.95 (ISBN 0-698-11072-2). Coward, McCann & Geoghegan.

Molly. Jean Louise De Forest. LC 15-4212. 1915. 1.25. Sully and Kleinteich.
Molly and the Confidence Man. Stephen Overholser. LC 74-33737. 1975. 5.95 (ISBN 0-385-04706-1). Doubleday.
Molly & the Gold Baron. Stephen Overholser. 176p. (Orig.). 1981. pap. 1.95 (ISBN 0-553-20042-9). Bantam.
Molly Bawn. Margaret Wolfe Hungerford. LC 7-9348. (Lovell's library, v. 2, no. 76). 1883. J. W. Lovell Company.
Molly B'Dam: Or, The Cross of Gold. Charles A Menges. LC 32-3601. 1931. Wetzel Publishing Co., Inc.
Molly Beamish. Henry De Vere Stacpoole. LC 13-25439. 1913. 1.25. Duffield & Company.
Molly Bishop's Family. Helen Alice Matthews Nitsch. LC 7-33482. 1888. Houghton, Mifflin and Company.
Molly, Bless Her. Frances Marion. LC 37-27195. 1937. Harper & Brothers.
Molly Companion. Maura Stanton. 1979. 1.95 (ISBN 0-380-40436-2). Avon.
Molly Companion: A Novel. Maura Stanton. LC 77-5257. 1977. 8.95 (ISBN 0-672-52353-1). Bobbs-Merrill.
Molly Gallagher. Betty Layman Receveur. LC 81-20561. 1982. 3.50 (ISBN 0-345-29512-9). Ballantine Books.
Molly McDonald: A Tale of the Old Frontier. Randall Parrish. LC 12-9511. 1912. A. C. McClurg & Co.
Molly Maguires. Wayne G. Broehl, Jr. (Cherry Pie Ser.). (0.s.i.). 1970. pap. 2.45 o.s.i. (ISBN 0-394-70574-2). Chelsea Hse.
Molly Make-Believe. Eleanor Hallowell Abbott. 1910. The Century Co.
Molly Make-Believe. Eleanor Hallowell Abbott. LC 13-33872. 1912. The Century Co.
Molly Make-Believe. Eleanor Hallowell Abbott & Tittle, Walter, Illus. LC 28-1678. 1913. The Century Co.
Molly, Malone Dies and The Unnamable: Three Novels. Translated from the French. Samuel Beckett. LC 59-138866. 1960. 6.50. Grove Press.
Molly Moonshine. Gertrude Knevels. LC 30-123012. 1930. D. Appleton and Company.
Molly's Bible. Mary Dwinell Chellis. LC 6-23407. H. A. Young & Co.
Molokai. Oswald A Bushnell. LC 63-14792. 1963. World Pub. Co.
Molokai. Oswald A Bushnell. LC 74-31402. (Pacific Classics; No. 4). 1975. 5.95 (ISBN 0-8248-0287-X). University Press of Hawaii.
Molotov Cocktail. John O. Virtanen. (Orig.). 1980. pap. 2.25 o.s.i. (ISBN 0-505-51517-2). Tower Bks.
Molt Brother. Jacqueline Lichtenberg. LC 81-84145. 256p. (Orig.). 1982. pap. 2.50 (ISBN 0-86721-067-2). Playboy Pbks.
Molting Season. Chris Ferguson. LC 74-1885. 1974. 6.95 (ISBN 0-06-011236-0). Harper & Row.
Mom Counted Six. Mac Gardner. LC 44-4610. 1944. Harper & Brothers.
Mom Kills Kids & Self. Alan Saperstein. 256p. 1980. pap. 2.50 (ISBN 0-345-28886-6). Ballantine.
Mom Kills Kids and Self: A Novel. Alan Saperstein. LC 79-12039. 9.95 (ISBN 0-02-606880-X). Macmillan.
Mom, My Lover. Jerry Crowell. pap. 1.95 o.p. (ISBN 0-87682-212-X, 7212). Barclay Hse.
Mom, the Wolfman & Me. Norma Klein. 160p. 1982. pap. 1.95 (ISBN 0-380-00791-6, 59998-8, Flare). Avon.
Mom, You Gotta Be Kiddin. Mary D. Bowman. LC 68-28435. (Illus.). 1968. pap. 1.50 o.p. (ISBN 0-8007-0212-3). Revell.
Momchilovo Affair. Andrei Guliashki. LC 77-363619. 1976. 1v 3.10. Sofia-Press.
Moment After. Robert Williams Buchanan. (On cover: Lovell's Westminister series, no. 2). 1890. J. W. Lovell Company.
Moment After. Virginia Tracy. LC 30-8782. 1930. Pub. for The Crime Club, Inc., by Doubleday, Doran & Company, Inc.
Moment Before Summer. May Gray. 1970. 4.00 (ISBN 0-8233-0148-6). Golden Quill.
Moment Before the Rain. 1st Ed. Elizabeth Enright. LC 55-5244. 1955. Harcourt, Brace.
Moment for Murder. Alfred Eichler. LC 56-116959. 1956. Arcadia House.
Moment in Camelot. Maggie Rennert. LC 68-16151. 1968. 8.95. Bernard Geis Associates; Distributed by Grove Press.
Moment in Peking. Lin Yutang. 815p. 1980. 10.00 (ISBN 0-89955-166-1, Pub. by Mei Ya China); pap. 8.50 (ISBN 0-89955-195-5). Intl Schol Bk Serv.
Moment in Peking: A Novel of Contemporary Chinese Life. Lin Yutang. LC 44-4529. 1942. The Sun Dial Press.
Moment in Peking: A Novel of Contemporary Chinese Life. Lin Yutang. LC 39-279233. 1939. The John Day Company.
Moment in Time. Herbert Ernest Bates. LC 64-19516. 1964. Farrar, Straus.
Moment in Time. James Howard Wellard. LC 47-31051. 1947. Dodd, Mead.
Moment of Beauty. Samuel Merwin. LC 25-584941. 1925. Houghton Mifflin Company.
Moment of Eclipse. Brian Wilson Aldiss. LC 72-175353. 1972. 5.95 o.p. (ISBN 0-385-05254-5). Doubleday.
Moment of Freedom. Jens Bjorneboe. 217p. 1975. 9.95 o.p. (ISBN 0-393-08719-0). Norton.
Moment of Glory. Thomas Thompson. LC 61-6521. (Double D western). 1961. Doubleday.
Moment of Impact. 1st Ed. Joseph Baily. LC 58-106888. 1958. Little, Brown.
Moment of Love. Denise Robins. 1971. pap. 0.75 o.p. (T2576). Pyramid Pubns.
Moment of Love. Denise Robins. 1976. pap. 1.25 o.p. (ISBN 0-515-04295-1). BJ Pub Group.
Moment of Madness. Charles Joseph Bellamy. LC 6-11699. (On cover: the select series, no. 46). 1890. Street & Smith.
Moment of Madness. Patricia Lake. (Harlequin Presents Ser.). 192p. 1983. pap. 1.95 (ISBN 0-373-10593-2). Harlequin Bks.
Moment of Madness. A Novel. Charles Joseph Bellamy. LC 6-11700. (On Cover: The Manhattan Series, No. 8). 1888. A. L. Burt.
Moment of Madness. And Captain Norton's Diary. Florence Marryat Church Lean. (On cover: The seaside library. Pocket ed. no. 159). 1884. G. Munro.
Moment of Magic. Yvonne Gordon. 1979. 1.95 (ISBN 0-441-53510-0). ACE Books.
Moment of Need. Frederick Clyde Davis. LC 48-545764. (A Dutton guilt edged mystery). 1947. E. P. Dutton.
Moment of the Predator. George Bernard. 1980. pap. 2.50 (ISBN 0-8439-0807-6). Nordon Pubns.
Moment of the Rose. Maryhelen Clague. 448p. (Orig.). 1983. pap. 2.95 (ISBN 0-449-12444-4, GM). Fawcett.
Moment of the Rose. Lucy Kennedy. LC 54-662688. 1954. Crown Publishers.
Moment of Time. Sydney Robertson McLean. LC 45-2935. 1945. G. P. Putnam's Sons.
Moment of Triumph. Gyorgy Sebestyen. LC 58-8573. 1958. Harcourt, Brace.
Moment of True Felling. Peter Handke. LC 77-6616. 1977. 8.95 (ISBN 0-374-17291-9). Farrar, Straus and Giroux.
Moment of Truth. Dorothy Phoebe Ansle. LC 75-10081. 1975. 6.95. Saturday Review Press.
Moment of Truth. K. Arne Blom. LC 76-40941. 6.95 (ISBN 0-06-010409-0). Harper & Row.
Moment of Truth. Margaret Storm Jameson. LC 49-7551. 1949. Macmillan Co.
Moment of Truth. Arnold Rodin. 1969. pap. 0.60 o.p. (60-425). Manor Bks.
Moment of Warmth. Francis Irby Gwaltney. Rinehart.
Moment Passed. Eleanor Kehrer & Kathryn Klingman. (Illus.). pap. 1.00 o.p. (ISBN 0-912852-06-2). Echo Pubs.
Moments. Berthe Laurence. (Orig.). 1980. pap. 2.50. Zebra.
Moment's Error: Or, The Mystery of Mortimer Strange. Arthur Williams Marchmont. (Globe library. no. 293). 1898. Rand, McNally & Co.
Moments of Freedom: The Heiligenberg Manuscript. Jens Bjrneboe. LC 74-34032. 1975. 6.95 (ISBN 0-393-08719-0). Norton.
Moments of Light. Fred Chappell. LC 80-81219. 195p. 1980. 12.95 (ISBN 0-917990-05-6). New South Co.
Moments of Rising Mist. Ed. by Amintendranath Tagore. (OSI). 1973. pap. 5.95 o.s.i. (ISBN 0-670-48464-4). Grossman.
Moments of the Italian Summer. James Wright. LC 76-40994. 1976. 15.00 (ISBN 0-931848-06-7); pap. 5.75 (ISBN 0-931848-07-5). Dryad Pr.
Moments of Truth. Ed. by Dan Herr & Joel Wells. LC 66-24327. 1966. Doubleday.
Moment's Surrender. Donald Lindquist. LC 75-21627. 7.95 (ISBN 0-03-015341-7). Holt, Rinehart and Winston.
Moment's Surrender. Donald Lindquist. 1977. 1.50 (ISBN 0-380-00922-6). Avon Books.
Momma," and Other Unimportant People. Rupert Hughes. LC 20-20946. Harper & Brothers.
Mommy's Gone. Rachel Summers. 1976. pap. 1.25 o.p. (LB359ZK, Leisure Bks). Nordon Pubns.
Mommy's Way. Lester R. Caldwell. pap. 1.95 o.p. (8086). Cameo.
Momo. Emile Ajar. LC 77-76253. 1978. 6.95 (ISBN 0-385-12503-8). Doubleday.
Mon frere Yves. Julien Viaud. LC 75-41283. (Fr.). Repr. of 1893 ed. 18.00 (ISBN 0-404-14786-0). AMS Pr.
Mon Paul: The Private Life of a Privateer. Samuel Spewack. LC 28-13449. The Macaulay Company.
Mon: The Gate. Soseki Natsume. LC 81-15427. 1982. 4.95 (ISBN 0-399-50608-X). Putnam.
Mon: ("The Gate") Natsume Soseki. Tr. by Francis Mathy. 217p. 12.95 (ISBN 0-698-11145-1, Coward). Putnam Pub Group.
Mona. pap. 1.45 o.p. (V1026Q, Venus). Grove.
Mona Intercept. Donald Hamilton. 512p. 1980. pap. 2.75 (ISBN 0-449-14374-0, GM). Fawcett.
Mona Lisa. Tiffany Thayer. LC 56-8110. Dial Press.
Mona Lisa, the Woman in the Portrait: A Fictional Biography. Sara Mayfield. LC 72-90845. 1974. 10.00. Grosset & Dunlap.
Mona Maclean, Medical Student. Margaret Georgiana Todd. 1892. D. Appleton and Company.
Mona the Druidess: Or, The Astral Science of Old Britain. Alice Kimball Hopkins. 1904. Eastern Publishing Company.
Monaldi: A Tale... Washington Allston. LC 6-57. 1841. C. C. Little and J. Brown.
Monaldi: A Tale. Washington Allston. LC 6-59. 1856. Ticknor and Fields.
Monarch. Babette Rosmond. LC 77-27299. 9.95 (ISBN 0-399-90009-8). R. Marek Publishers.
Monarch. Babette Rosmond. (Berkley Book.). 1980. 2.25 (ISBN 0-425-04147-6). Berkley Publishing Corp.
Monarch. Vassilis Vassilikos. LC 75-29961. 7.95 (ISBN 0-672-52139-3). Bobbs-Merrill.
Monarch Billionaire. Morrison Isaac Swift. LC 3-20056. J. S. Ogilvie Publishing Company.
Monarch of Deadman Bay: The Life & Death of a Kodiak Bear. Roger A. Caras. (Illus.). 1977. pap. 2.50 (ISBN 0-14-004575-9). Penguin.
Monarch of Millions: Or, The Rise and Fall of the American Empire. John Grosvenor Wilson. LC 6344. (On cover: Neely's popular library. no. 1). The Neely Company.
Monarch of Mincing Lane. William Black. LC 6-129232. (Lovell's library, v. 5, no. 232). J. W. Lovell Company.
Monarch of Mincing Lane. William Black. LC 6-39304. Belford, Clarke & Co.
Monarch of Mincing Lane. A Novel. William Black. (Seaside library. Pocket ed. no. 125). G. Munro.
Monarch of the Glen. Compton MacKenzie. LC 51-2017. 1951. Mifflin.
Monarchist: An Historical Novel, Embracing Real Characters and Romantic Adventures. John Beauchamp Jones. LC 7-12849. 1853. A. Hart.
Monarchy of Passion. James Clark Bennett. LC 30-7300. The Macaulay Company.
Mona's Choice. Annie French Hector. (On cover: Lovell's library, no. 1105). 1887. J. W. Lovell Company.
Mona's Choice. A Novel. Annie French Hector. (On cover: Seaside library. Pocket ed., no. 1054). 1887. G. Munro.
Monastery. Walter Scott. LC 49-30240. (Waverley novels. Pocket ed., v. 10). 1873. Scribner, Welford & Armstrong.
Monastery. new ed., with the author's notes. ed. Walter Scott. LC 8-5776. 1875. G. Routledge & Sons.
Monastery. Walter Scott. (On cover: Lovell's library, no. 609). 1885. J. W. Lovell Company.
Monastery. Walter Scott. (On cover: Seaside library. Pocket ed. no. 201). 1884. G. Munro.
Monastery; a Romance. From the Last Rev. Ed., Containing the Author's Final Corrections, Notes, &S. parker's ed. Walter Scott. (Waverley novels: Library ed. v. 9). 1830. Bazin & Ellsworth.
Monastery; a Romance... Parker's Ed., Rev. and Cor., with a General Preface, an Introduction to Each Novel, and Notes Historical and Illustrative. Walter Scott. LC 8-5778. (Waverley novels, v. 17). 1836. Pub. by S. H. Parker for Desilver, Thomas, and Co., Philadelphia.
Monastery of St. Columb: Or, The Atonement. A Novel. Regina Maria Dalton Roche. LC 7-39649. 1813. Published by Inskeep & Bradford; and Bradford & Inskeep, Philadelphia.
Monastery: The Abbot. Walter Scott. (Waverley novels, v. 5). D. Appleton & Co.
Moncrieff. large type ed. Isabelle Holland. LC 82-10362. 431p. 1982. Repr. of 1975 ed. 10.95 (ISBN 0-89621-381-1). Thorndike Pr.
Moncrieff. Isabelle Holland. LC 75-19262. 1975. 8.95 o.p. (ISBN 0-679-40129-6, Weybright). McKay.
Moncrieff: A Novel. Isabelle Holland. LC 75-19262. 1975. 8.95 (ISBN 0-679-40129-6). Weybright and Talley.
Moncrieff: A Novel. Isabelle Holland. (Fawcett Crest Book). 1977. 1.50 (ISBN 0-449-23089-9). Fawcett Pubns.
Monday at McMurdo. David Burke. LC 68-721000. 1967. bds., 4.50. Auckland Etc.
Monday Begins on Saturday. Arkadii Natanovich Strugatskii & Boris Natanovich Strugatskii. (Science Fiction Ser). (Orig.). 1977. pap. 1.75 (ISBN 0-87997-336-6, UE1336). DAW Bks.
Monday Man. Ronnie Pearlman. 1981. pap. 2.50 (ISBN 0-8128-7054-9). Stein & Day.
Monday Man. Ronnie Pearlman. LC 71-122427. 1970. 5.95 o.p. (ISBN 0-8128-1313-8). Stein & Day.
Monday Morning. Patrick Hamilton. LC 26-260392. 1925. Houghton Mifflin Company.
Monday Morning Father. William Johnston. LC 74-114835. (Tempo books, 5342). 1970. 0.75. Grosset & Dunlap.
Monday Night. Kay Boyle. LC 77-70179. 1977. 10.00 (ISBN 0-911858-35-0). P. P. Appel.
Monday Night. Kay Boyle. LC 38-18278. Harcourt, Brace and Company.
Monday or Tuesday. Virginia Stephen Woolf. LC 21-22105. 1921. Harcourt, Brace and Company.
Monday Tales. Alphonse Daudet. LC 78-113654. (Short story index reprint series). (Illus.). 1970. Books for Libraries Press.
Monday Tales. Alphonse Daudet. LC 28-28066. 1927. Little, Brown, and Company.
Monday the Rabbi Took off. Harry Kemelman. (Crest bk., P1785). 1973. 1.25. Fawcett.
Monday the Rabbi Took off. Harry Kemelman. LC 75-175264. 1972. 5.95. Putnam.
Monday, Tuesday, Wednesday! Robert Houston. LC 77-95089. 1978. 1.50 (ISBN 0-380-01876-4). Avon Books.
Monday Voices. Joanne Greenberg. 1972. pap. 1.75 (ISBN 0-380-01417-3, 35212). Avon.
Monday Voices: A Novel. Joanne Greenberg. LC 65-15057. 4.95. Holt.
Monday's Child. Mollie Hardwick. LC 81-21501. 10.95 (ISBN 0-312-54408-1). St. Martin's Press.
Monday's Mob. Don Pendleton. (Executioner Ser.: No. 33). pap. 2.25 (ISBN 0-523-41815-9). Pinnacle Bks.
Mondo. Anthony Destefano. 192p. (Orig.). 1975. pap. 1.25 o.p. Woodhill.
Mondo. Anthony Destefano. 192p. (Orig.). 1975. pap. 1.25 o.p. Manor Bks.
Money. Emile Zola & Tucker, Benjamin Ricketson, 1854- Tr. LC 3-26199. 1891. B. R. Tucker.
Money: A Novel. Theodore Pratt. LC 65-24851. bds., 4.95. Duell Dist. Meredith.
Money and Other Stories. Karel Capek. LC 73-106256. (Short story index reprint series). 1970. Books for Libraries Press.
Money & Other Stories. Karel Capek. Tr. by Francis P. Marchant et al. LC 29-29102. 1930. Brentano's.
Money Captain. Will Payne. LC 98-775. 1898. H. S. Stone & Company.
Money Creek Mare. Patricia Calvert. 144p. 1983. pap. 2.25 (ISBN 0-451-12024-8, Sig Vista). NAL.
Money Doubler. Bai T. Moore. LC 77-368598. Unicom Books.
Money for Love. Josephine Herbst. LC 76-51670. (Recovered Fiction by American Women). 1977. 22.00. Arno Press.
Money for Love. Josephine Herbst. LC 29-19024. 1929. Coward-McCann, Inc.
Money for Nothing. Pelham Grenville Wodehouse. LC 28-25549. 1928. Doubleday, Doran & Company, Inc.
Money for One: A Love Story. Berta Ruck. LC 28-2233. 1928. Dodd, Mead and Company.
Money for the Taking. Doris Miles Disney. LC 68-11191. 1968. Published for the Crime Club by Doubleday.
Money from Holme. Michael Innes, pseud. (Crime Ser.). 1976. pap. 2.95 (ISBN 0-14-002484-0). Penguin.
Money from Holme. Michael Innes, pseud. 1969. pap. 0.95 o.p. (ISBN 0-14-002484-0, 2484). Penguin.
Money from Holme: By Michael Innes Pseud. John Innes Mackintosh Stewart. LC 65-111569. (Red badge detective). 1965. bds., 3.50. Dodd, Mead.
Money from Home. Damon Runyon. LC 35-19684. 1935. Frederick A. Stokes Company.
Money Galore. Solomon Alexander Amu Djoleto. LC 75-326936. (African writers series; 161). 1975. (ISBN 0-435-90161-3). Heinemann.
Money Gods. Ellery Harding Clark. LC 22-22775. 1922. The Cornhill Publishing Company.
Money Hanging. Dean W. Ballenger. 1978. pap. 1.25 (ISBN 0-532-12583-5). Woodhill.
Money Harvest. Ross Thomas. LC 74-31025. 1975. 8.95 (ISBN 0-688-02912-4). Morrow.
Money Hat & Other Hungarian Folk Tales. Peggy Hoffman & Gyuri Biro. (O.s.i.). 1969. 4.50 o.s.i. (ISBN 0-664-32458-4). Westminster.
Money, Honey. Linda Howard. LC 82-13693. 14.95 (ISBN 0-399-12694-5). Putnam.
Money Hunters: A Novel. Cothburn O'Neal. LC 66-15110. 4.50. Crown.
Money in the Bank. Pelham Grenville Wodehouse. LC 42-36025. 1942. Doubleday, Doran & Company.
Money Is Love. Richard Condon. LC 75-5556. 1975. 8.95 (ISBN 0-8037-5752-2). Dial Press.
Money Is Love. Brian Glanville. LC 72-83142. 1972. 6.95 (ISBN 0-385-06335-0). Doubleday.
Money Is Not Enough. Winston Howard. LC 80-53510. 1980. 8.95 (ISBN 0-914244-05-1). Epic Publications.
Money Isn't Everything. Berta Ruck. LC 40-10301. 1940. Dodd, Mead & Company.

Money (L'argent) A Realistic Novel. Emile Zola & Maury, Max, Pseud.? Tr. LC 3-26198. (On cover: The pastime series, no. 63). 1891. Laird & Lee.

Money-Lender, 3 vols. in 1. Catherine Grace Frances Moody Gore. LC 79-8275. Repr. of 1843 ed. 44.50 (ISBN 0-404-61883-9). AMS Pr.

Money-Lender's Destiny: A Novel. Babken D Sookias. LC 63-24756. (Geneva book). 1963. Carlton Press.

Money Love. Beatrice Burton Morgan. LC 28-11532. Grosset & Dunlap.

Money, Love and Kate: Together with the Story of a Nickel. Eleanor Hodgman Porter. LC 23-13324. George H. Doran Company.

Money Mad. Rex Ellingwood Beach. LC 31-15607. 1931. Cosmopolitan Book Corporation.

Money Mad: An American Novel by an American Citizen. Alois Ernest Ulrich. LC 24-14174. 1924. C. T. Dearing Printing Company, Incorporated.

Money Magic. sunset edition. new york, harper. ed. Hamlin Garland. LC 72-84712. 1974. (ISBN 0-403-02988-0). Scholarly Press.

Money Magic see Collected Works.

Money Magic: A Novel. Hamlin Garland. LC 7-32322. 1907. Harper & Brothers.

Money, Magic, & Marriage. Barbara Cartland. (Orig.). pap. 1.75 (ISBN 0-515-05565-4). Jove Pubns.

Money Maker. John J McNamara. 1973. (pbk.) 1.50. Popular Lib.

Money Maker. John J McNamara. LC 72-82859. 1972. 6.95 (ISBN 0-690-55377-3). Crowell.

Money-Maker, and Other Tales. Jane C Campbell. LC 6-21481. 1854. J. C. Derby.

Money Maker: Or, The Sins of the Fathers and Raggedy Maija. Kaarlo Korpela. LC 76-350147. Dahlbacka.

Money-Maker: Or, The Victory of the Basilisk. William Taylor Adams. LC 2-111411. (yacht club series, v. 3). 1901. Lee and Shepard.

Money-Maker: The Romance of a Ruthless Man. Irving Ross Allen. LC 18-17353. 1918. Dodd, Mead and Company.

Money-Makers: A Social Parable. Henry Francis Keenan. LC 68-57537. (Muckrakers). 1968. Gregg Press.

Money-Makers: A Social Parable. Henry Francis Keenan. LC 72-79660. (Series in American Studies). 1969. Johnson Reprint Corp.

Money Makers: A Social Parable. Henry Francis Keenan. LC 7-31120. 1885. D. Appleton and Company.

Money Makers: A Story of Today. Charles Klein & Hornblow, Arthur. LC 14-186493. 1.25. G. W. Dillingham Company.

Money Man: A Novel of a Bank Built on Quicksand. Herman Michelson. LC 31-19093. The Vanguard Press.

Money Market. Edward Frederic Benson. 1899. D. Biddle.

Money Marriage: A Novel. Elaine Suss. LC 79-23995. 1980. 8.95. Taplinger Pub. Co.

Money Master: Being the Curious Histoy of Jean Jacques Barbille, His Labours, His Loves, and His Ladies. Gilbert Parker. LC 15-17981. Harper & Brothers.

Money Men. William Haggard. LC 81-51974. 1981. 9.95 (ISBN 0-8027-5448-1). Walker.

Money Men. Gerald Petievich. 224p. 1983. pap. 2.50 (ISBN 0-523-41154-5). Pinnacle Bks.

Money Men; and, One-Shot Deal: Two Novels. Gerald. Petievich. LC 80-8756. 12.95 (ISBN 0-15-169892-9). Harcourt Brace Jovanovich.

Money! Money! Money! Helen Marion Edginton. LC 31-6488. The Macaulay Company.

Money, Money, Money: 1st Ed. David Wagoner. 1955. Harcourt, Brace.

Money Moon. Jeffrey Farnol. 1975. lib. bdg. 15.30x (ISBN 0-89966-090-8). Buccaneer Bks.

Money Moon: A Romance. Jeffery Farnol. LC 11-290822. 1911. Dodd, Mead and Company.

Money Moon: A Romance. Jeffery Farnol. LC 11-29081. 1911. Dodd, Mead & Company.

Money, Murder & the McNeills. Theodora McCormick Du Bois. LC 74-583. Orig. Title: It's Raining Violence. 1969. pap. 0.75 o.p. Lancer.

Money Murders. Eugene Franklin, pseud. LC 75-187882. (Stein and Day mystery). 1972. 5.95 (ISBN 0-8128-1485-1). Stein and Day.

Money Musk. Carolyn Wells. LC 36-599. J. B. Lippincott Company.

Money Musk. Ben Ames Williams. LC 32-30023. 1932. E. P. Dutton & Co., Inc.

Money of Her Own. Margaret Culkin Banning. LC 28-202256. 1928. Harper & Brothers.

Money on the Black. Allan MacKinnon. LC 46-1880. 1946. Pub. for the Crime Club by Doubleday & Company, Inc.

Money-Order; with, White Genesis. Sembene Ousmane. LC 72-197852. (African writers series, 92). 1972. (ISBN 0-435-90092-7). Heinemann.

Money People. MacMillan. Leo Katcher.

Money People. 1st Ed. Leo Katcher. LC 61-597031. 1961. Doubleday.

Money Plays. Morton Beckner. LC 80-17643. 10.95 (ISBN 0-671-25122-8). Simon and Schuster.

Money Song. Arnold Shaw. LC 52-126917. 1953. Random House.

Money-Spider. William Le Queux. LC 11-8983. R. G. Badger.

Money-Spider: A Mystery of the Arctic. William Le Queux. LC 11-4213. 1911. Cassell and Company, Limited.

Money-Spinner and Other Character Notes. Hugh Stowell Scott & Hall, E. V. LC 1-11798. 1901. A. Mackel & Company.

Money Stones. St. James, Ian. LC 80-65984. 1980. 9.95 (ISBN 0-689-11104-5). Atheneum.

Money. Taken from the Play. Edward George Earle Lytton Bulwer-Lytton Lytton. LC 7-8460. (On cover: Lovell's library, v. 3, no. 128). 1883. J. W. Lovell Company.

Money That Money Can't Buy. James Mitchell. LC 68-12668. 1968. Knopf.

Money That Money Can't Buy. James Munro. 288p. 1981. pap. 2.75 (ISBN 0-441-53698-0, Pub. by Charter Bks). Ace Bks.

Money That Money Can't Buy. James Munro. LC 68-12668. 1968. 4.95 o.p. Knopf.

Money to Burn. Elizabeth Cadell. LC 55-5600. 1955. Morrow.

Money to Burn. Peter Bernard Kyne. LC 28-22356. Grosset & Dunlap.

Money to Burn... Helen Rosen Woodward. LC 45-4379. 1945. David McKay Company.

Money to Burn: An Adventure Story. Reginald Wright Kauffman. LC 24-12520. 2.00. Chelsea House.

Money War. Terrence Lore Smith. LC 78-6787. (Illus.). 1978. 9.95 (ISBN 0-689-10900-8). Atheneum.

Money Wolves. Paul Erickson. 1979. 2.50. Berkley Publication Corp.

Money Wolves. Paul Erikson. LC 78-17730. 1978. 9.95 (ISBN 0-688-03378-4). Morrow.

Moneychangers. Arthur Hailey. LC 74-12689. 1975. 10.00 (ISBN 0-385-00896-1). Doubleday.

Moneychangers. Upton Beall Sinclair. LC 75-78574. 1968. Gregg Press.

Moneychangers. Upton Beall Sinclair. LC 8-248662. 1908. B. W. Dodge & Company.

Moneymakers: The Great Big New Rich in America. Kenneth Church Lamott. LC 69-16971. (Illus.). 1969. 6.75 o.p. (ISBN 0-316-51290-7). Little.

Moneyman. Thomas Bertram Costain. LC 47-4818. 1947. Doubleday.

Moneyman. Judith Liederman. LC 78-14511. 1978. 9.95 (ISBN 0-395-27099-5). Houghton Mifflin.

Moneymooners. Watkins Eppes Wright. LC 34-18191. 1934. W. Godwin, Inc.

Monfort Hall. A Novel. Catherine Ann Ware Warfield. LC 8-34833. T. B. Peterson & Brothers.

Mongol Mask. Howard Hunt. LC 68-17751. 1968. Weybright and Talley.

Mongol Mask. David St. John, pseud. LC 68-17751. 1968. 4.95. Weybright & Talley.

Mongolian Short Stories. Ed. by Henry G. Schwarz. LC 74-620031. (Washington (State). Western Washington State College, Bellingham. Program in East Asian Studies: Occasional Papers: No. 8). (Illus.). 1974. 4.00 (ISBN 0-914584-08-1). Western Washington State College, Program in East Asian Studies.

Mongo's Back in Town. E. Richard Johnson. LC 69-12272. 1969. 4.95. Harper & Row.

Mongrel Mettle: The Autobiography of a Dog. Jesse Stuart & Ishmael, Woodi, Illus. 1944. Books, Inc., Distributed by E. P. Dutton & Co., Inc.

Mongrels. Sigurd Jay Simonsen. LC 46-157684. 1946. Diana Press Publishing Co.

Mongst the Hills of Kentucky. Lizzie Arnett. 1909. Printed for the Author by R. H. Carothers & Son.

Moni der Geissbub. Johanna Heusser Spyri & Guerber, Helen Adeline. LC 12-38925. (Heath's modern language series). 1897. D. C. Heath & Co.

Monica. Margaret Wolfe Hungerford. LC 7-9347. (On cover: Lovell's library, v. 2, no. 86). 1883. J. W. Lovell Company.

Monica, and Other Stories. Paul Charles Joseph Bourget. LC 77-106249. (Short story index reprint series). 1970. Books for Libraries Press.

Monica: And Other Stories. Paul Charles Joseph Bourget. Tr. by William Marchant. LC 2-10107. 1902. C. Scribner's Sons.

Monikins. James Fenimore Cooper. LC 6-29874. 1835. Carey, Lea & Blanchard.

Monikins. new ed. James Fenimore Cooper. LC 6-298726. 1852. Stringer and Townsend.

Monikins. James Fenimore Cooper. LC 42-261627. (On cover: Cooper's novels). 1860. W. A. Townsend and Company.

Monikins. James Fenimore Cooper. (On cover: Lovell's library. no. 543). 1885. J. W. Lovell Company.

Monikins. James Fenimore Cooper. (On cover: Seaside library. Pocket ed. no. 431). 1885. G. Munro.

Monima: Or, The Beggar Girl. A Novel, Founded on Fact. LC 2-8392. 1803. Printed by Eaken & Mecum.

Monique. 1979. ed. Madelyn Cunningham. LC 78-70785. 2.50 (ISBN 0-515-05113-6).

Monique. Yvonne Dufour. LC 30-24843. E. P. Dutton & Co., Inc.

Monique. Maude Poiret. (O.s.i.). (Orig.). 1970. pap. 0.75 o.s.i. (A695S, Award). Univ Pub & Dist.

Moniter Found in Orbit. Michael G. Coney. (Science Fiction Ser). 176p. (Orig.). 1974. pap. 0.95 o.p. (UQ1132). DAW Bks.

Monitor Affair: A Novel of the Civil War. Clarence Budington Kelland. LC 60-11928. 1960. Dodd, Mead.

Monitor, the Miners & the Shree. Lee Killough. (Orig.). 1980. pap. 1.95 (ISBN 0-345-28456-9). Ballantine.

Monk. Matthew G Lewis. 1975. (pbk.) 1.95 (ISBN 0-380-00468-2). Avon.

Monk. Matthew Gregory Lewis. LC 7-13288. T. B. Peterson.

Monk. Matthew Gregory Lewis. LC 11-16143. T. B. Peterson & Brothers.

Monk: A Novel. William H Hallahan. LC 82-18782. 1983. 12.00 (ISBN 0-688-01112-8). Morrow.

Monk: A Romance. Matthew Gregory Lewis. Ed. by Howard Peter Anderson. LC 73-179618. (Oxford English novels). 1973. 4.00 (ISBN 0-19-255362-3). Oxford University Press.

Monk: A Romance by M. G. Lewis, Ed. by E. A. Baker... Matthew Gregory Lewis. LC 24-14930. (Library of early novelists, ed. by E. A. Baker, v. 9). 1907. G. Routledge & Sons, Limited.

Monk and Knight: An Historical Study in Fiction. Frank Wakeley Gunsaulus. LC 7-2850. 1891. A. C. McClurg and Company.

Monk and the Dancer. Arthur Cosslett Smith. LC 73-98594. (Short story index reprint series). 1969. Books for Libraries Press.

Monk and the Dancer. Arthur Cosslett Smith. LC 310656. 1900. C. Scribner's Sons.

Monk and the Hangman's Daughter. Ambrose Gwinnett Bierce. LC 76-6979. 1976. (ISBN 0-89190-183-3). American Reprint Co.

Monk and the Hangman's Daughter. Ambrose Gwinnett Bierce & De Castro, Adolphe Danziger. LC 6-12945. 1892. F. J. Schulte & Company.

Monk and the Hangman's Daughter. Ambrose Gwinnett Bierce & De Castro, Adolphe Danziger. LC 7-20620. 1907. The Neale Publishing Company.

Monk and the Hangman's Daughter. Ambrose Gwinnett Bierce et al. LC 67-6988. (Illus.). 1967. Printed for the Members of the Limited Editions Club.

Monk and the Hangman's Daughter: Fantastic Fables. Ambrose Bierce & De Castro, Adolphe Danziger. LC 29-9300. 1926. A. & C. Boni.

Monk and the Marines. Philip Kingry. 1974. (pbk.) 1.25. Bantam Books.

Monk Dawson. Piers Paul Read. (Bantam book, Q8207). 1974. (pbk.) 1.25. Bantam Books.

Monk Dawson. Piers Paul Read. LC 70-120332. 1970. 5.95. Lippincott.

Monk in Armour. Gladys Hutchison Barr. LC 50-10318. 1950. Abingdon-Cokesbury Press.

Monk of Cruta: A Novel. Edward Phillips Oppenheim. LC 7-231923. (Neely's international library). 1894. F. T. Neely.

Monk of Fife. Andrew Lang. LC 68-59287. Repr. of 1895 ed. 10.00 (ISBN 0-404-03847-6). AMS Pr.

Monk of Fife: A Romance of the Days of Jeanne D'Arc, Done into English from the Manuscript in the Scots College of Ratisbon by Andrew Lang. Andrew Lang. 1895. Longmans, Green, and Co.

Monk of Hambleton. Armstrong Livingston. LC 28-4239. 1928. R. D. Henkle Co., Inc.

Monk of the Aventine. Ernst Eckstein & Johnson, Helen Hunt, Tr. LC 7-2871. 1894. Roberts Brothers.

Monk of the Mountains: Or, A Description of the Joys of Paradise ... With the Destiny and Condition of the Nations of the Earth for One Hundred Years to Come. LC 7-25452. 1866. Downey & Brouse.

Monk of Udolpho: A Romance. T. J. Horsley Curties. LC 77-2037. (Gothic Novels; Ser. III). 1977. 70.00 (ISBN 0-405-10136-8). Arno Press.

Monkey. Joan Cooper. (Illus.). 1971. pap. 1.25 o.p. (ISBN 0-912472-10-3). Miller Bks.

Monkey. Cheng-En Wu. LC 58-10533. 1958. Grove Press.

Monkey: A Folk Novel of China. Wu Ch'Eng-En. Tr. by Arthur Waley. 7.50 o.p. (ISBN 0-8446-1847-0). Peter Smith.

Monkey: A Selection of Incidents from a 16th Century Chinese Novel. Cheng-En Wu & Eleanor Hazard. LC 80-116035. (Illus.). 14.95 (ISBN 0-914676-14-8). Green Tiger Press.

Monkey & the Tiger. Robert Van Gulik. 1966. 3.50 o.p. (ISBN 0-684-10617-5). Scribner.

Monkey and the Tiger: Two Chinese Detective Stories. With Eight Illus. Drawn by the Author in Chinese Style. Robert Hans Van Gulik, pseud. LC 66-16691. 1966. 3.50. Scribners.

Monkey: By Wu Ch'eng-En. Tr. from Chinese by Arthur Waley. Cheng-En Wu. Tr. by Arthur Waley. (Evergreen bk. rebound). 1967. 4.50. P. Smith.

Monkey Grip. Helen Garner. LC 78-303184. 1977. (ISBN 0-85914-007-5). McPhee Gribble Publishers.

Monkey Grip. american ed. Helen Garner. LC 80-54525. 1981. 10.95 (ISBN 0-87223-677-3). Seaview Books.

Monkey in Silk. Margaret Turnbull. LC 31-12129. 1931. J. B. Lippincott Company.

Monkey in Winter. Antoine Blondin. (Illus.). 1960. 3.50 o.p. Putnam.

Monkey in Winter: A Novel. Translated from the French by Robert Baldick. 1st American Ed. Antoine Blondin. LC 60-13668. 1960. Putnam.

Monkey King. Timothy Mo. LC 79-7875. 1980. 10.00 (ISBN 0-385-15621-9). Doubleday.

Monkey Mountain. Craig Hiler. 1979. pap. 2.25 o.s.i. (ISBN 0-505-51403-6). Tower Bks.

Monkey Murder: And Other ? Hildegarde Withers Stories. Stuart Palmer. LC 50-57060. (Bestseller mystery, no. B128). 1950. L. E. Spivak.

Monkey on a Chain. Charity Blackstock. LC 65-19849. 1974. (pbk.) 0.95 (ISBN 0-380-00066-0). Avon.

Monkey on a Chain. Edwin Moultrie Lanham. LC 63-17773. 1963. Harcourt, Brace & World.

Monkey on a Chain: By Charity Blackstock Pseud. 1st Amer. Ed. Ursula Torday. LC 65-19849. 4.95. Coward.

Monkey on a Stick: A Novel. Henry W Clune. LC 40-7009. 1940. W. Morrow and Company.

Monkey on a String. Joseph Viertel. LC 68-13436. 1968. Trident Press.

Monkey Planet. Pierre Boulle. LC 75-327325. 1975. 0.45 (ISBN 0-14-002401-8). Penguin.

Monkey Puzzle. John Davys Beresford. LC 25-14666. The Bobbs-Merrill Company.

Monkey Puzzle Tree. Florence Chanock Cohen. LC 79-14445. (Illinois Writers; No. 2). 10.50 (ISBN 0-931704-03-0) (ISBN 0-931704-02-2). Story Press.

Monkey-Puzzle Tree: A Novel. Nona Coxhead. LC 67-29690. 1968. B. Geis Associates; Distributed by Random House.

Monkey Watcher. Robert Towers. LC 64-18297. 1964. Harcourt, Brace & World.

Monkey Wrench. Jason Griffith. LC 33-30726. The Stratford Company.

Monkey Wrench Gang. Edward Abbey. LC 75-831. (Illus.). 1975. 8.95 (ISBN 0-397-01084-2). Lippincott.

Monkey Wrench Gang. edward abbey. ed. Edward Abbey. 1.95 (ISBN 0-380-00741-X). Avon Books.

Monkeys. Geoffrey Kedington Wilkinson. LC 62-16281. 1962. Farrar, Strauss & Cudahy.

Monkeys Have No Tails in Zamboanga. Sterner St. Paul Meek. LC 35-3925. 1935. W. Morrow & Company.

Monkey's Money. Mabel Louise Tyrrell. LC 35-10853. 1935. Minton, Balch & Company.

Monkey's Money. Mabel Louise Tyrrell. LC 35-10853. 1935. Minton, Balch & Company.

Monkey's Tail. Rebecca Scarlett. LC 34-220348. 1934. C. Scribner's Sons.

Monkeyshines for a Laughing Lunacy. Alfred D. Niess. 1978. pap. 4.95. S&S Co OR.

Monks' Court. Katherine Wigmore Eyre. LC 66-14957. bds., 4.95. Meredith.

Monks' Court: A Novel. Katherine Wigmore Eyre. LC 66-14957. 1966. Appleton-Century.

Monk's Hood. Ellis Peters. 224p. 1982. pap. 2.50 (ISBN 0-445-04713-5). Popular Lib.

Monk's Hood Murders. Arlo Channing Edington & Edington, Mrs. Carmen Ballen, 1894- Joint Author. LC 31-11909. 1931. Cosmopolitan Book Corporation.

Monk's-Hood: The Third Chronicle of Brother Cadfael. Edith Pargeter. LC 80-26326. 1981. 9.95 (ISBN 0-688-00452-0). Morrow.

Monk's Magic. Alexander De Comeau. LC 31-15546. E. P. Dutton & Co., Inc.

Monk's Magic. Alexander De Comeau. LC 77-84213. (Lost Race and Adult Fantasy Fiction). 1978. 16.00 (ISBN 0-405-10968-7). Arno Press.

Monk's Magic. Alexander De Comeau. Ed. by R. Reginald & Douglas Melville. LC 77-84213. (Lost Race & Adult Fantasy Ser.). 1978. Repr. of 1931 ed. lib. bdg. 16.00x (ISBN 0-405-10968-7). Ayer Co.

Monk's Marriage see Plautus in the Convent.

Monks of Monk Hall. George Lippard. LC 76-111078. (Popular American fiction). 1970. Odyssey Press.

Monks of War: The Military Religious Orders. Desmond Seward. 1972. 13.50 o.p. (ISBN 0-208-01266-4, Archon). Shoe String.

Monk's Pardon. A Historial Romance of the Time of Philip Iv. of Spain. by anna t. sadlier... ed. Marie De Saffron David. Tr. by Sadlier, Anna Theresa. LC 7-1239. 1883. Benziger Brothers.
Monk's Retreat. Susannah Curtis. LC 76-47860. 1.25 (ISBN 0-380-00857-2). Avon.
Monks' Treasure. George Horton. LC 5-6935. 1905. The Bobbs-Merrill Company.
Monk's Wedding. Conrad Ferdinand Meyer. Tr. by Adams, Sarah Holland. LC 7-258741. 1887. Cupples and Hurd.
Monksbridge. Francis Browning Drew Bickerstaffe-Drew. LC 14-5426. 1914. Longmans, Green, and Co.
Monkshood. Eden Phillpotts. LC 39-216607. 1939. The Macmillan Company.
Monmouth. Charles Bracelen Flood. 1977. pap. 1.95 o.p. (ISBN 0-515-04271-4). BJ Pub Group.
Monmouth: A Novel. Charles Bracelen Flood. LC 61-15065. 1961. Houghton Mifflin.
Monna Lisa: Or, The Quest of the Woman Soul. Guglielmo Scala. LC 11-185681. 1911. Thomas Y. Crowell Company.
Monochromes. Ella D'Arcy. (On cover: The keynotes series v. 12). 1895. Roberts Bros.; Etc., Etc.
Monochromes. Ella D'Arcy. LC 76-20056. (Decadent Consciousness). (Series: Keynotes series; 12.). 1977. 26.00 (ISBN 0-8240-2754-X). Garland Pub.
Monochromist: A Novel. Douglas Moon. LC 76-150894. (Illus.). 4.00 (ISBN 0-89171-000-0). Bay Books.
Monodromos. Marian Engel. LC 73-85572. (Anansi Fiction Ser.: No. 27). 250p. 1973. 12.95 (ISBN 0-88784-427-8, Pub. by Hse Anansi Pr Canada). U of Toronto Pr.
Monodyne Catastrophe. Joseph Renard. Intro. by Barry N. Malzberg. 1976. pap. 1.25 (ISBN 0-89041-122-0, 3122). Major Bks.
Monogamist. Thomas Michael Gallagher. LC 55-6654. 1955. Random House.
Monomaniac: Or, Shirley Hall Asylum. William Gilbert. LC 6-44060. 1864. J. S. Gregory.
Mononia. Justin McCarthy. LC 1-30338. 1900. Small, Maynard & Company.
Monopoly on Terror. Bruce Buck. 1978. pap. 1.95 (ISBN 0-89083-431-8). Zebra.
Monopoly Players. Alfred M. Groner. LC 81-22798. 1982. 14.95 (ISBN 0-87949-207-4). Ashley Books.
Monotonous Landscape: Seven Stories. Gunter Herburger. LC 68-12576. 1968. Harcourt, Brace & World.
Monpti. Gabor Vaszary & Instein, Harry, Tr. LC 38-352852. 1938. A. A. Knopf.
Monsieur. George Challis. LC 26-20415. The Bobbs-Merrill Company.
Monsieur. Lawrence Durrell. LC 74-4925. 1975. 7.95 (ISBN 0-670-48678-7). Viking Press.
Monsieur. Lawrence Durrell. 1976. (pbk.) 1.95 (ISBN 0-671-80304-2). Pocket Books.
Monsieur Beaucaire. Booth Tarkington. LC 62-1789. 1961. Limited Editions Club.
Monsieur Beaucaire. Booth Tarkington. LC 3289. 1900. McClure, Phillips & Co.
Monsieur Beaucaire. Booth Tarkington. LC 28-17920. 1900. Grosset & Dunlap.
Monsieur Beaucaire. Booth Tarkington. LC 8-25591. 1900. McClure, Philips & Co.
Monsieur Beaucaire. Booth Tarkington. LC 8-25592. 1900. McClure, Phillips & Co.
Monsieur Beaucaire. Booth Tarkington. LC 16-6988. 1915. Doubleday, Page & Co.
Monsieur Beaucaire. Booth Tarkington. LC 21-13949. 1920. Grosset & Dunlap.
Monsieur Beaucaire. The Beautiful Lady. His Own People. Booth Tarkington. LC 20-40185. 1915. C. Scribner's Sons.
Monsieur Beaucaire. The Beautiful Lady. His Own People. Booth Tarkington. LC 22-16009. 1920. Doubleday, Page & Company.
Monsieur Beaucaire: The Beautiful Lady, His Own People, and Other Stories... Booth Tarkington. LC 24-20469. (works of Booth Tarkington. vol. IX). 1918. Doubleday, Page and Company.
Monsieur Bergeret a Paris. Anatole France, pseud. 1966. pap. 3.95. French & Eur.
Monsieur Bergeret a Paris see Romans et Contes.
Monsieur Blakshirt. David Graeme, pseud. J. B. Lippincott Company.
Monsieur Bob: A Novel. St. George Rathborne. (On cover: Idle moments series, no. 11). 1891. The Price-McGill Company.
Monsieur Bob. A Novel. St. George Rathborne. LC 8-5879. (On cover: Criterion series, no. 8). 1894. Street & Smith.
Monsieur Bussy, the Celebrated Hamster. Claude-Lafontaine, Pascale. (Illus.). 1968. McGraw-Hill.
Monsieur De Camors: Monsieur De Camors. Octave Feuillet. LC 42-5684. 1910. Current Literat Are Publishing Company.
Monsieur De Chauvelin's Will. Alexandre Dumas. Tr. by Smith, Mary Stuart (Harrison) LC 4373. (On cover: Seaside library. Pocket ed. no. 1985). 1900. G. Munro's Sons.
Monsieur De Chauvelin's Will. To Which Is Added The Womas with the Velvet Necklace. Alexandre Dumas & Paul Lacroix. LC 6-43604. (Half-title: The romances of Alexandre Dumas. New series). 1897. Little, Brown and Company.
Monsieur de Phocas: Asarte. Jean Lorrain. 316p. (Fr.). 1982. Repr. of 1929 ed. lib. bdg. 125.00 (ISBN 0-8287-1784-2). Clearwater Pub.
Monsieur D'En Brochette: Being an Historical Account of Some of the Adventures of Huevos Pasada Par Aqua, Marquis of Pollio Grille, Count of Pate De Foie Gras, and Much Else Besides. Bert Leston Taylor & Folwell, Arthur Hamilton, Joint Author. LC 5-26924. 1905. Keppler & Schwarzmann.
Monsieur Dupin: The Detective Tales of Edgar Allan Poe. Edgar Allan Poe. LC 4-29187. 1904. McClure, Phillips & Co.
Monsieur Hulot's Holiday. With Illus. by Pierre Etaix. Translated from the French by A. E. Ellis. Jean Claude Carriere. LC 60-6243. 1959. Crowell.
Monsieur Jacques Bogue: The Man of a Club. S. P Hamilton. 1894. Franklin Printing and Publishing Co.
Monsieur Janvier. 1st Ed. Elizabeth Linnington. LC 57-12469. 1957. Doubleday.
Monsieur Jonquelle: Prefect of Police of Paris. Melville Davisson Post. LC 23-13658. 1923. D. Appleton and Company.
Monsieur Lecoq. Emile Gaboriau. LC 74-29016. (Illus.). 1975. 3.50 (ISBN 0-486-22570-4). Dover Publications.
Monsieur Lecoq: From the French of Emile Gaboriau; Tr. Emile Gaboriau. Tr. by Kendall, Laura E. LC 6-44554. (On cover: Once a week semi-monthly library. v. 11, no. 14-16). 1894. P. F. Collier.
Monsieur Lecoq. From the French of Emile Gaboriau... Emile Gaboriau. LC 6-44506. Estes and Lauriat.
Monsieur Lecoq: Tr. from the French of Emile Gaboriau. Emile Gaboriau. LC 28213. 1900. C. Scribner's Sons.
Monsieur Lecoq. Tr. from the French of Emile Gaboriau. Emile Gaboriau. LC 12-31314. 1910. C. Scribner's Sons.
Monsieur Lecoq: Translated from the French of Emile Gaboriau. Emile Gaboriau. LC 26-22290. 1904. C. Scribner's Sons.
Monsieur Levert: A Novel. Translated by Richard Howard. Robert Pinget. LC 61-5520. (Evergreen original, E-281). 1961. Grove Press.
Monsieur, Madame and the Baby. A Series of Confessions. Gustave Droz & Savage, Reavel, Tr. LC 6-34438. 1881. T. B. Peterson & Brothers.
Monsieur Martin: A Romance of the Great Swedish War. Wymond Carey. LC 2-8340. 1902. G. P. Putnam's Sons.
Monsieur Moliere: A Novel. Michael O'Shaughnessy. LC 58-14309. 1959. Crowell.
Monsieur Monde Vanishes. Georges Simenon. LC 76-39800. 1977. (ISBN 0-15-162098-9). Harcourt Brace Jovanovich.
Monsieur Motte. Grace Elizabeth King. LC 79-98582. (Short story index reprint series). 1969. Books for Libraries Press.
Monsieur Motte. Grace Elizabeth King. 1888. A. C. Armstrong and Son.
Monsieur Nasson and Others. Grace Howard Peirce. (On cover: The golden library of choice fiction, no. 7). 1893. The Price-McGill Company.
Monsieur of the Rainbows. Vingie Eve Roe. LC 27-3814. 1926. Doubleday, Page & Company.
Monsieur Parent, and Short Stories. Guy De Maupassant. LC 10-7483. 1910. The Pearson Publishing Co.
Monsieur Paul: Translated by Douglas McKee. 1st Ed. Henri Calet. LC 52-12968. 1953. Dutton.
Monsieur Ripois and Namesis. Louis Hemon. Tr. by William Aspenwall Bradley. LC 25-8732. 1925. The Macmillan Company.
Monsieur Sylvestre: A Novel. George Sand & Shaw, Francis George, 1809-1882, Tr. LC 6-35675. 1870. Roberts Brothers.
Monsieur Teste. P. Valery. 1964. pap. 1.65 o.p. (ISBN 0-07-066809-4). McGraw.
Monsieur Thogo-gnini. Bernard Binlin Dadie. pap. 5.95. French & Eur.
Monsieur Verite. Joan A. Flower. 292p. 1975. 7.50 o.p. (ISBN 0-682-48270-6). Exposition.
Monsieur X: A Novel of Mystery. Robert William Sneddon. LC 28-234626. 1928. L. MacVeagh, The Dial Press.
Monsieur Yankee. Leslie Turner White. LC 57-94525. 1957. Morrow.
Monsignor: A Novel. Doran Hurley. LC 36-6126. 1936. Longmans, Green and Co.
Monsignor Quixote. Graham Greene. 1982. 12.95 (ISBN 0-671-45818-3); deluxe ed. 75.00 o.p. (ISBN 0-671-45984-8). S&S.
Monsignor Villarosa. Pompeo Litta-Visconti-Arese. LC 14-11092. 1914. 1.35. G. P. Putnam's Sons.
Monsignore. Jack-Alain Leger. (Orig.). 1982. pap. 3.50 (ISBN 0-440-15752-8). Dell.
Monsigny a Novel. Justus Miles Forman. LC 3-20055. 1903. Doubleday, Page & Company.
Monsoon. Wilfrid David. LC 33-29358. 1933. Harper and Brothers.
Monsoon. George Henry Johnston. LC 50-8786. 1950. Dodd, Mead.
Monsoon Murder. Brian Cooper. LC 68-8081. 1968. 6.95 o.s.i. (ISBN 0-8149-0042-9). Vanguard.
Monsoon Quarter: A Novel. Marion S Lowndes. LC 52-11540. 1953. Westminster Press.
Monster. Horace William Bleackley. LC 21-12849. 1921. George H. Doran Company.
Monster. Robin Morgan. 1972. pap. 1.95 o.p. (ISBN 0-394-71851-8, Vin). Random.
Monster. Robin Morgan. 1972. pap. 1.95 o.p. (ISBN 0-394-71851-8, Vin). Random.
Monster. Eden Phillpotts. LC 25-7201. 1925. The Macmillan Company.
Monster. Edgar Evertson Saltus. LC 70-113266. 1970. (ISBN 0-404-05541-9). AMS Press.
Monster. Edgar Evertson Saltus. LC 22-14570. 1912. Pulitzer Publishing Company.
Monster. Edgar Evertson Saltus. LC 13-25372. 1913. Pulitzer Publishing Company.
Monster and Other Stories. Stephen Crane. 1899. Harper & Brothers.
Monster Festival. Illus. by Edward Gorey. Ed. by Eric Protter. Edward St. John Illus Gorey. LC 65-2136. (Edward Ernest bk.). 4.95. Vanguard.
Monster from Earth's End: An Original Gold Meda Novel, by Murray Leinster Pseud. William Fitzgerald Jenkins. LC 59-1295. (Gold medal books, S832). 1959. Fawcett Publications.
Monster in the Moat. Fran Priddy. (Orig.). 1979. pap. 1.95. Woodhill.
Monster in the Pool. Armstrong Livingston. LC 29-166693. The Bobbs-Merrill Company.
Monster Makers: Creators and Creations of Fantasy and Horror. Ed. by Peter Haining. LC 74-1961. (Illus.). 1974. 7.95 (ISBN 0-8008-5324-5). Taplinger Pub. Co.
Monster Men. Edgar Rice Burroughs. (Illus.). 1962. Canaveral Press.
Monster Men. Edgar Rice Burroughs. LC 29-6857. 1929. A. C. McClurg & Co.
Monster Midway: An Uninhibited Look at the Glittering World of the Carny. William Lindsay Gresham. LC 53-9239. 1953. Rinehart.
Monster Movie Game. Mal Whyte & John Stanley. (Illus.). 64p. 1974. pap. 2.00 o.p. (ISBN 0-912300-33-7, 33-7). Troubador Pr.
Monster of Grammont. George Goodchild. LC 30-31361. 1930. The Mystery League, Inc.
Monster of Lazy Hook. Thorne Lee. LC 49-4280. (Bloodhound mystery). 1949. Duell, Sloan and Pearce.
Monster of Metelaze. Kern Gregory. (Cap Kennedy Ser: No. 3). 1973. pap. 0.75 o.p. (UT1084). DAW Bks.
Monster of Metelaze. Gregory Kern. (Secret Agent of the Spaceways). (Daw sf Book, no. 75: Vol. 3). (Illus.). 1973. (pbk.) 0.75. Daw Books.
Monster of Snowdon Hall. Grove Wilson. LC 32-8803. 1932. I. Washburn.
Monster of the Maze. Jeffrey Lord. (Blade Ser., No. 6). 192p. 1973. pap. 1.50 (ISBN 0-523-40436-0). Pinnacle Bks.
Monster of the Maze. Jeffrey Lord. (Richard Blade Ser.). 192p. 1972. pap. 0.95 o.p. (95-168). Manor Bks.
Monster Tales. Ed. by Roger Elwood. (Illus.). 1973. pap. 2.50 o.p. (ISBN 0-528-87760-7). Rand.
Monsters. Alfred Elton Van Vogt. 1970. pap. 0.06 o.p. (ISBN 0-446-63406-9, 63-406). Paperback Lib.
Monsters and Medics. James White. LC 76-30333. 1977. 1.50 (ISBN 0-345-25623-9). Ballantine Books.
Monsters & Monsters. Rona Jaffe. 1981. cancelled o.p. (ISBN 0-440-05536-9). Delacorte.
Mont-Oriol: A Novel. Guy De Maupassant. LC 7-25597. 1891. Belford Company.
Montagu Wycherly: A Rev. Ed. of "His First Leavec. Lizzie Allen Harker. LC 21-7412. 1921. C. Scribner's Sons.
Montague Scandal. Judith Harkness. 1979. pap. 1.75 (ISBN 0-451-08922-7, E8922, Sig). NAL.
Montagues of Casa Grande. 1st Ed. P. M Salzer. LC 53-11957. 1953. Pageant Press.
Montana: A Romance of the Western Plains. Grace Evelyn Thorne & Carey, Harry D. Montana. The Harry D. Carey Amusement Co.
Montana Bad Man. Roe Richmond. LC 57-8441. (Permabooks, M-3086. Western, 6). 1957. Permabooks.
Montana Bound. Oscar Schisgall. LC 36-5641. Green Circle Books.
Montana Crossing. Giles A. Lutz. pap. 0.95 o.s.i. Lancer.
Montana Dead-Shot. Charles Morris Martin. pap. 0.60 o.p. (60-379). Manor Bks.
Montana Ermine. Oscar Jerome Friend. LC 55-14628. 1955. Avalon Books.
Montana Gothic. Dirck Van Sickle. LC 78-15283. 8.95. Harcourt Brace Jovanovich.
Montana Gothic. Dirck Van Sickle. 1980. 2.50 (ISBN 0-380-50211-9). Avon Books.
Montana, Here I Be! Dan Cushman. LC 50-8484. 1950. Macmillan.
Montana Maiden. Jon Sharpe. (Trailsman Ser.: No. 11). 1982. pap. 2.25 (ISBN 0-451-11632-1, Sig). NAL.
Montana Man. Paul Evan Lehman. LC 49-291. 1949. E. P. Dutton.
Montana Masquerade. Allan Vaughan Elston. LC 59-5402. 1959. Lippincott.
Montana Maverick: A Powder Valley Western. Peter Field. LC 52-138305. 1953. Jefferson House.
Montana Moon. Donald H Clewton. LC 30-183117. World Wide Publishing Co., Inc.
Montana Number Three. Al Cody, pseud. 92p. 1976. pap. text ed. 1.25 o.p. (ISBN 0-532-12388-3). Woodhill.
Montana Number Three. Al Cody, pseud. 92p. 1976. pap. text ed. 1.25 o.p. (ISBN 0-532-12388-3). Manor. Bks.
Montana Outlaw. Tom Roan. LC 34-16310. A. H. King.
Montana Passage. Allan Vaughan Elston. (Berkley Medallion Book). 1976. (pbk.) 0.95. Berkley Publishing Corp.
Montana Rides. Evan Evans, pseud. 300p. 1976. Repr. of 1933 ed. lib. bdg. 11.50x (ISBN 0-89190-203-1). Am Repr-Rivercity Pr.
Montana Rides! Frederick Faust. LC 75-33327. 1975. 9.95 (ISBN 0-89190-203-1). American Reprint Co.
Montana Rides Again. Max Brand. 1969. pap. 0.60 o.p. (63-276). Paperback Lib.
Montana Rides Again. Evan Evans, pseud. LC 34-30686. 1934. Harper & Brothers.
Montana Rides! By Evan Evans. Evan Evans, pseud. LC 33-14140. 1933. Harper & Brothers.
Montana Road. Harry Sinclair Drago. LC 35-841069. 1935. W. Morrow & Company.
Montana Showdown. Jake Logan. LC 77-79431. (John Slocum Ser.: No. 13). 176p. 1978. pap. 1.75. Playboy Pbks.
Montana Vigilantes. Thomas Albert Curry. 1973. pap. 0.60 o.p. (06187). Curtis.
Montana's Golden Gamble. Al Cody, pseud. 192p. 1976. pap. 1.25 o.p. (ISBN 0-532-12407-3). Woodhill.
Montana's Golden Gamble. Al Cody, pseud. Ed. by Alice Sachs. 1970. 3.95 o.p. Crown.
Montana's Golden Gamble. Al Cody, pseud. 192p. 1976. pap. 1.25 o.p. (ISBN 0-532-12407-3). Manor Bks.
Montanas: Or, Under the Stars. A Romance. Sallie J Hancock. LC 7-550. 1866. Carleton.
Montanas: Or, Under the Stars. A Romance. Sallie J Hancock. LC 41-32427. 1867. Carleton.
Montana's Territory. Cody. Ed. by Sachs. 1970. 3.95 o.p. B Franklin.
Montana's Territory. Al Cody, pseud. 1976. pap. 1.25 o.p. (ISBN 0-532-12381-6). Woodhill.
Montana's Territory. Al Cody, pseud. 3.95 o.p. Lenox Hill.
Montana's Territory. Al Cody, pseud. 1976. pap. 1.25 o.p. (ISBN 0-532-12381-6). Manor Bks.
Montanye: Or, The Slavers of Old New York; a Historical Romance. William Osborn Stoddard. LC 72-2928. (Black Heritage Library Collection). 1972. 15.00 (ISBN 0-8369-9081-1). Books for Libraries Press.
Montarges Legacy: A Tale. Mary Miller Meline. LC 7-18472. 1869. P. F. Cunningham.
Montauk Fault. Herbert Mitgang. LC 81-17501. 1982. 14.95 (ISBN 0-89340-535-3). J. Curley.
Montauk Fault, a Novel. Herbert Mitgang. LC 80-70744. 12.95 (ISBN 0-87795-320-1). Arbor House.
Monte Carlo. Dorothy Daniels. 1981. pap. 2.75 (ISBN 0-8439-0900-5, Leisure Bks). Nordon Pubns.
Monte Carlo: A Novel. Margaret Robson Stacpoole. LC 15-16345. 1914. Dodd, Mead and Company.
Monte Carlo: Its Sin and Splendor. Edgar De Valcourt-Vermont. (On cover: Lakeside series, v. 1, no. 2). 1893. N. C. Smith & Co.
Monte Carlo Rally. Michael Gibson. LC 59-11261. (Illus.). 1959. Watts.
Monte Cristo, No. 99. John Jakes. (Orig.). 1970. pap. 0.75 o.p. (0502-07100). Curtis.
Monte Cristo and His Wife: A Sequel to the Count of Monte Cristo. LC 7-34693. (On cover: Lovell's library. v. 18, no. 885). 1887. J. W. Lovell Company.
Monte-Cristo and the Countess. A Sequel to the Count of Monte- Cristo. authorized ed. tr. from the french by jacob abarbanell... ed. Jules Hippolyte Lermina & Abarbanell, Jacob Ralph, 1852- Tr. LC 7-34692. (On cover: Munro's library. v. 1. no. 217). 1884. N. L. Munro.

Monte Cristo Cover-up: The Fabulously Daring Adventures and Exquisite Cooking Recipes of the Involuntary Secret Agent Thomas Lieven. Johannes Mario Simmel. 1.95 (ISBN 0-445-08563-0). Popular Library.
Monte Felis. Mary Salkeld-Robinson Jayne. LC 23-13374. 1923. Little, Brown, and Company.
Monte Walsh. Jack Warner Schaefer. LC 63-13684. 1963. Houghton Mifflin.
Monte Walsh. bison book ed. Jack Warner Schaefer. LC 80-25036. 21.50 (ISBN 0-8032-4124-0) (ISBN 0-8032-9121-3). University of Nebraska Press.
Montego. Robert Dupont. 224p. (Orig.). 1975. pap. 1.50 o.p. Woodhill.
Montego. Robert Dupont. 224p. (Orig.). 1975. pap. 1.50 o.p. Manor Bks.
Monteiths. Jane M. Bosworth. LC 10-23125. 1910. 1.00. The Knickerbocker Press.
Montenegran Plot: A Pendragon Adventure. Robert Trevelyan. LC 78-4391. 1978. 8.95 o.p. (ISBN 0-312-54662-9). St Martin.
Montenegrin Gold. Brian N Ball. LC 77-99214. 1978. 7.95 (ISBN 0-8027-5384-1). Walker.
Montenegro. Milovan Dilas. LC 63-24141. 1963. Harcourt, Brace & World.
Montenegro. Milovan Djilas. Tr. by Kenneth Johnstone. LC 63-8090. 1963. 5.75 (ISBN 0-15-162102-0). HarBraceJ.
Monterant Affair. Richard Grayson. 182p. 1980. 9.95 o.p. (ISBN 0-312-54665-3). St Martin.
Montes the Matador. Frank Harris. LC 72-104476. 1970. (ISBN 0-8398-0761-9). Literature House.
Montes the Matador, and Other Stories. Frank Harris. LC 10-11138. 1910. 1.00. M. Kennerley.
Montezuma; the Last of the Aztecs. A Romance. Edward Maturin. LC 7-17933. 1845. Paine & Burgess.
Montezuma, the Serf, or: The Revolt of the Mexitili; a Tale of the Last Days of the Aztex Dynasty. Joseph Holt Ingraham. LC 7-10353. 1845. H. L. Williams.
Montezuma's Ball. Eugene Wildman. LC 74-112037. 1970. 6.00. Swallow Press.
Montezuma's Castle: And Other Weird Tales. author's ed. Charles Barney Cory. LC 99-3121. 1899. Press of Rockwell and Churchill.
Montezuma's Daughter. with 25 illustrations by maurice greiffenhagen. new impression. ed. Henry Rider Haggard. LC 20-16460. 1920. Longmans, Green and Co.
Montezuma's Daughter. Henry Rider Haggard. LC 12-24114. 1893. Longmans, Green and Co.
Montezuma's Daughter. Illus. by Hookway Cowles. Henry Rider Haggard. LC 66-5450. 1966. bds., 2.95. Macdonald.
Montezuma's Gold Mines. Frederick Albion Ober. LC 7-33190. D. Lothrop Company.
Montezuma's Revenge. Harry Harrison. LC 72-76166. 1975. (pbk.) 1.25. Manor Books.
Montgomery and I. Geoff Baker. LC 74-362154. 1968. 1.00. Georgian House.
Montgomery Street: A Novel. Mark Dintenfass. LC 77-11785. 8.95 (ISBN 0-06-011063-5). Harper & Row.
Month for Mankind. T. Owen Williams. 192p. 1971. 3.95 o.p. Lenox Hill.
Month in Gordon Square. 1st American Ed. Frank Arthur Swinnerton. LC 54-5370. 1954. Doubleday.
Month of May. Jane Dashwood. LC 82-1271. 2.00. The Century Company.
Month of September. Translated from the French by Irene Ash. 1st American Ed. Frederique Hebrard. LC 58-6034. 1958. Little, Brown.
Month of Sundays. Louis Kronenberger. LC 61-7272. 1961. Viking Press.
Month of Sundays. John Updike. LC 74-21327. 1975. 6.95 (ISBN 0-394-49551-9). Knopf: Distributed by Random House.
Month of the Brittle Star. Eileen L Soper. LC 73-150178. (Illus.). 1971. 3.30. McIndoe.
Month of the Pearl. Philip M. Jones. LC 65-12692. 1965. bds., 3.50. Holt.
Month Soon Goes. Margaret Storm Jameson. LC 62-20123. 1963. Harper & Row.
Monthly Nurse. Betty Singleton. 1979. 7.50 (ISBN 0-533-03839-1). Vantage.
Months: A Novel. Joseph Grafton. LC 65-14233. 4.50. Yoseloff.
Months of Rain. Alice Lent Covert. LC 41-2430. 1941. H. C. Kinsey & Company, Inc.
Monticello Fault. Archibald Rogers. LC 79-63913. 12.95 (ISBN 0-87716-098-8). Moore Pub. Co.
Montlivet. Alice Prescott Smith. LC 6-335733. 1906. Houghton, Mifflin and Company.
Montlivet. with frontispiece in color by jay hambridge. ed. Alice Prescott Smith. LC 7-294302. 1907. Houghton, Mifflin and Company.
Montmartre Murders: A Novel. Richard Grayson. LC 81-23216. 10.95 (ISBN 0-312-54502-9). St. Martin's Press.
Montresor: An English-American Love Story, 1854-1894. LC 7-14796. 1897. F. T. Neely.
Monument. Lloyd Biggle, Jr. LC 73-11627. (Doubleday science fiction). 1974. 4.95 (ISBN 0-385-03831-3). Doubleday.
Monument. Pamela Hansford Johnson. LC 38-23360. Carrick & Evans, Inc.
Monument. James Kubeck. LC 65-17663. 1965. McNally & Loftin.
Monument: A Satiric Novel. Nathaniel Benchley. LC 66-15174. bds., 4.95. McGraw.
Monument Maker. Ronald Joseph. LC 78-175384. 1972. 5.95. Doubleday.
Monument of Terror. Victor Jones. LC 69-12271. 1969. 4.95. L. Stuart.
Mood for Murder. Van Siller. 1969. pap. 0.60 o.p. (0502-06005-060). Curtis.
Mood for Murder: By Van Siller. Hilda Van Siller. LC 66-18617. 3.50. Pub. for the Crime Club by Doubleday.
Mood Indigo. Boris Vian. LC 68-29440. 1968. 4.95. Grove Press.
Moods. 2d ed. Louisa May Alcott. LC 12-90102. 1865. Loring.
Moods. A Novel. Louisa May Alcott. LC 12-23772. 1882. Roberts Brothers.
Moon. Henry D. Thoreau. LC 80-2521. Repr. of 1927 ed. 17.50 (ISBN 0-404-19069-3). AMS Pr.
Moon Also Rises. Elliott A. White. 3.95 o.s.i. (ISBN 0-8181-0128-8). Pageant-Poseidon.
Moon and Sixpence. William Somerset Maugham. LC 75-25357. (Maugham, William Somerset, 1874-1965. Works. 1976). 1976. 15.00 (ISBN 0-405-07816-1). Arno Press.
Moon and Sixpence. William Somerset Maugham. LC 19-9478. George H. Doran Company.
Moon and Sixpence. William Somerset Maugham. LC 35-13202. 1928. Grosset & Dunlap.
Moon and Sixpence. William Somerset Maugham. LC 36-18159. (Half-title: The modern library of the world's best books). 1935. The Modern Library.
Moon and the Bonfires. Cesare Pavese. LC 75-25262. 1975. 13.00 (ISBN 0-8371-8384-7). Greenwood Press.
Moon and the Bonfires: Translated from the Italian by Marianne Ceconi. With a Foreword by Paolo Milano. Cesare Pavese. LC 53-7083. 1953. Farrar, Straus and Young.
Moon and the Thorn. 1st Ed. Beatrice Joy Chute. LC 61-124775. 1961. Dutton.
Moon and the Wind. A. P Carroll. LC 38-697743. Green Circle Books.
Moon by Night: A Novel. Joy Petersen Packer. LC 57-108674. 1957. Lippincott.
Moon-Calf. Floyd Dell. LC 57-12438. (American century series, S-18). 1957. Sagamore Press.
Moon-Calf: A Novel. Floyd Dell. LC 20-19503. 1920. A. A. Knopf.
Moon-Calf: A Novel. Floyd Dell. LC 21-10610. 1921. A. A. Knopf.
Moon Cat. Esther Neely. 1977. pap. 1.25 o.p. (ISBN 0-515-04187-4). BJ Pub Group.
Moon Children. Jack Williamson. LC 73-186646. 1972. 5.95. G. P. Putnam's Sons.
Moon Country. Gladys Etta Johnson. LC 24-187635. 1924. The Penn Publishing Company.
Moon Dancers. Sara Nichols. (Orig.). 1973. pap. 0.95 o.p. (09184). Curtis.
Moon Dancers. Mary Wibberley. (Alpha Books). 1978. pap. text ed. 2.95x (ISBN 0-19-424162-9). Oxford U Pr.
Moon Endureth: Tales and Fancies. John Buchan. LC 12-151451. 1912. 1.25. Sturgis & Walton Company.
Moon Era. reprint ed. Murray Leinster et al. 1969. pap. 0.75 o.p. (0502-07014-075). Curtis.
Moon-Eyed Appaloosa. Bill Gulick, pseud. LC 62-15888. 1968. pap. 0.50 o.p. (52-673). Paperback Lib.
Moon-Face, and Other Stories. Jack London. LC 71-140334. (Short story index reprint series). 1970. Books for Libraries Press.
Moon-Face, and Other Stories. Jack London. LC 6-145512. 1906. The Macmillan Company.
Moon-Face: And Other Stories. Jack London. LC 6-323513. 1906. The Macmillan Company.
Moon for Sara. Haze Barleau. LC 38-330029. J. Messner, Inc.
Moon Gaffney. Harry Sylvester. LC 76-6367. (Irish-Americans). 1976. (ISBN 0-405-09359-4). Arno Press.
Moon Gaffney. Harry Sylvester. LC 47-3527. 1947. H. Holt and Company.
Moon Gap. Ann Chidester. LC 50-6058. 1950. Doubleday.
Moon Gate. 1st Ed. Carroll Cox Estes. LC 54-6781. 1954. Published for the Crime Club by Doubleday.
Moon Goddess. Ethel M. Comins. 192p. (YA) 1974. 4.95 o.p. (Avalon). Bouregy.
Moon Goddess. Ethel M Comins. (Avalon romances). 1974. 4.50. Avalon Books.
Moon Harvest. Giuseppe Cautela. LC 25-9511. 1925. L. MacVeagh, The Dial Press.
Moon Hill. Martin Woodhouse. LC 74-79679. 7.95 (ISBN 0-698-10601-6). Coward, McCann & Geoghegan.
Moon Hoax. Richard Adams Locke & Joseph Nicolas Nicollet. (Science Fiction Ser). 120p. 1975. Repr. of 1854 ed. lib. bdg. 9.95 o.p. (ISBN 0-8398-2308-8, Gregg). G K Hall.
Moon Hoax; or, A Discovery That the Moon Has a Vast Population of Human Beings. Richard Adams Locke & Joseph Nicolas Nicollet. LC 75-5836. (Gregg Press science fiction series). 1975. 7.50 (ISBN 0-8398-2308-8). Gregg Press.
Moon Hoax: Or, A Discovery That the Moon Has a Vast Population of Human Beings. Richard Adams Locke & Nicollet, Joseph Nicolas. LC 40-37532. 1859. W. Gowans.
Moon in Aries. Marie Blizard. LC 42-2902. 1941. Arcadia House, Inc.
Moon in Rahu: A Novel. Tara Ali Baig. 10.00x (ISBN 0-210-33812-1). Asia.
Moon in Rahu: An Account of the Bhowal Sannyasi Case. Tara Ali Baig. LC 76-906263. 1969. 25.00. Asia Pub. House.
Moon in Shadow. Aynn Westminster. (Dell book). 1974. (pbk.) 0.95. Dell.
Moon in the Cloud. Rosemary Harris. 1969. Macmillan.
Moon in the Pail: A Neopicaresque Tale. Mordecai Schreiber. LC 67-15773. 1967. 4.95. World.
Moon in the River. James Leo Phelan. LC 46-5256. 1946. A. A. Wyn, Inc.
Moon in the Water. Ruby Mildred Ayres. LC 39-112733. 1939. Doubleday, Doran & Company, Inc.
Moon in the Water. Ruby Mildred Ayres. LC 40-5531. 1940. The Sun Dial Press.
Moon in the West. Bertrand Collins. LC 33-3931. Liveright, Inc.
Moon into Blood. Catherine Gavin. 1970. pap. 1.25 o.p. (96010). Beagle Bks.
Moon Is a Harsh Mistress. Robert Anson Heinlein. (Medallion bk., N1601). 1968. Berkley.
Moon Is a Harsh Mistress. Robert Anson Heinlein. LC 66-15582. 1966. Putnam.
Moon Is Down. John Steinbeck. 1982. pap. 3.95 (ISBN 0-14-006222-X). Penguin.
Moon Is Down see Short Novels of John Steinbeck.
Moon Is Down: A Novel. John Steinbeck. LC 42-36103. 1942. The Viking Press.
Moon Is Down: A Novel. John Steinbeck. LC 81-23470. 1982. 3.95 (ISBN 0-14-006222-X). Penguin Books.
Moon Is Feminine: A Tale. Winifred Ashton. LC 38-27581. 1938. Doubleday, Doran & Company, Inc.
Moon Is Hell! 1st Ed. John Wood Campbell. LC 51-594. (FP science fiction). 1951. Fantasy Press.
Moon Is Making. Margaret Storm Jameson. LC 38-3238. 1938. The Macmillan Company.
Moon Is Mine. Arthemise Goertz. LC 48-8998. 1948. Whittlesey House.
Moon Is Mine & Other Tales. Jack Neilson. 1978. 8.00 (ISBN 0-682-49176-4). Exposition.
Moon Is Our Lantern: A Novel. Edward Tatum Wallace. LC 52-13381. 1953. Doubleday.
Moon Is Red. Sax Rohmer, pseud. 1976. 6.50. Bookfinger.
Moon Is Rising. Maddy Vegtel. LC 47-880. 1947. Whittlesey House, McGraw-Hill Book Company, Inc.
Moon-Kissed. Barbara Faith. 2.50 (ISBN 0-671-83331-6). Pocket Books.
Moon Lady. Helen Manchester Gates Granville-Barker. LC 11-27913. 1911. 1.25. C. Scribner's Sons.
Moon Lake. Stephan Gresham. 1982. pap. 2.95 (ISBN 0-8217-1004-4). Zebra.
Moon Lamp. Mark Smith. LC 75-37688. 1976. 7.95 (ISBN 0-394-49888-7). Knopf.
Moon Lies Fair. Gerrie Ollier Thielens. LC 42-123113. 1942. Harper & Brothers.
Moon-Madness, and Other Fantasies. Aimee Crocker Gouraud. LC 11-312. 1.00. Broadway Publishing Co.
Moon Maid. Edgar Rice Burroughs. LC 26-35707. 1926. A. C. McClurg & Co.
Moon Maid. Edgar Rice Burroughs. LC 27-27456. 1926. Grosset & Dunlap.
Moon Man. Edgar Rice Burroughs. 1982. pap. 2.25 (ISBN 0-441-53756-1). Ace Bks.
Moon Men. Edgar Rice Burroughs. 224p. 1977. pap. 2.25 (ISBN 0-441-53756-1). Ace Bks.
Moon Men. Edgar Rice Burroughs. LC 62-8706. (Illus.). 1975. Repr. 10.000 (ISBN 0-940724-07-3). Canaveral.
Moon Men. Illustrated by Mahlon Blaine. Edgar Rice Burroughs. 1962. Canaveral Press.
Moon Metal. Garrett Putman Serviss. LC 6464. 1900. Harper & Brothers.
Moon Odyssey. John Rankine, pseud. (Space - 1999). 156p. 1975. lib. bdg. 5.95 (ISBN 0-88411-672-7). Amereon Ltd.
Moon of Aphrodite. Sara Craven. (Harlequin Presents Ser.). 192p. (Orig.). 1981. pap. 1.50 (ISBN 0-373-10411-1, Pub. by Harlequin). PB.
Moon of Darkness. Miriam Lynch. 1971. pap. 0.75 o.p. (B75-2183). Belmont-Tower.
Moon of Delight. Margaret Bell Houston. LC 31-1819. 1931. Dodd, Mead & Company.
Moon of Enchantment. Peggy Gaddis, pseud. LC 53-13066. 1953. Arcadia House.
Moon of Hope: By Bernice Ludwell Pseud. Manning Lee Stokes. 1956. Arcadia House.
Moon of Isis: An Adventure Story. Jack Little, pseud. LC 76-8728. 1976. 1.50. Altair Press.
Moon of Israel: A Tale of the Exodus. Henry Rider Haggard. LC 18-21687. 1918. 1.50. Longmans, Green and Co.
Moon of Madness. Arthur Sarsfield Ward. LC 27-19129. 1927. Doubleday, Page & Company.
Moon of Madness. Arthur Sarsfield Ward. LC 31-19416. 1929. A. L. Burt Company.
Moon of Mutiny. Lester Del Rey. 192p. 1982. pap. 1.95 (ISBN 0-345-30606-6, Del Rey). Ballantine.
Moon of Mutiny. Lester Del Rey. 1979. lib. bdg. 9.50 (ISBN 0-8398-2518-8, Gregg). G K Hall.
Moon of Skulls. Robert E. Howard. (Time-Lost Ser). Orig. Title: Red Shadows. (Illus.). 1970. pap. 1.50 o.p. (ISBN 0-87818-001-X). Centaur.
Moon of the Lost Frenchman. Kitty Mendenhall. 1976. 4.95. Avalon Books.
Moon of the Tiger. Oswald Wynd. LC 58-5961. 1958. Doubleday.
Moon of the Witch: A Novel. Antony De Courcy. LC 57-9478. 1957. Meador Pub. Co.
Moon of the Wolf. Leslie H Whitten. LC 67-16798. 1967. Published for the Crime Club by Doubleday.
Moon of Three Rings. Alice Mary Norton. LC 66-69438. 1966. 3.75. Viking.
Moon on an Iron Meadow. Peter Tate. LC 73-10977. (Doubleday science fiction). 1974. 5.95 (ISBN 0-385-02422-3). Doubleday.
Moon Out of Reach. Margaret Bass Pedler. LC 23-195. George H. Doran Company.
Moon Out of the Sky. Netta Syrett. LC 32-8080. 1922. Dodd, Mead & Company.
Moon Over Acadie. Louis Arthur Cunningham. LC 37-77124. The Penn Publishing Company.
Moon Over Broadway. Mark Hellinger. LC 71-37271. (Short story index reprint series). 1971. (ISBN 0-8369-4082-2). Books for Libraries Press.
Moon Over Broadway. Mark Hellinger. LC 31-103602. 1931. W. Faro, Inc.
Moon Over Eden. Barbara Cartland. (Bantam Barbara Cartland Library#37). 1976. (pbk.) 1.25. Bantam Books.
Moon Over Miami. Jim Deane. (Decoy). (Signet Book: Vol. 2). 1975. (pbk.) 1.25. New American Library.
Moon Over Moncrieff. Iris Rowland. 1974. 4.95 (ISBN 0-517-51637-3). Lenox Hill.
Moon Over Stamboul. Anne Duffield. LC 37-25073. 1937. Arcadia House.
Moon Over the Rio Grande. Harriet C Evans. LC 57-167885. 1956. Zondervan Pub. House.
Moon Over the Water. Rob Eden. LC 51-3772. 1951. Gramercy Pub. Co.
Moon Over the Water: By Mary Douglas Warren Pseud. Maysie Greig. LC 56-11700. 1956. Arcadia House.
Moon Over Willow Run. Dan E. L Patch. LC 43-5570. 1943. Zondervan Publishing House.
Moon People. Stanton Arthur Coblentz. 1970. pap. 0.75 o.p. (B75-2024). Belmont-Tower.
Moon Pool. John Bishop Ballem. LC 78-314413. (Illus.). 12.95 (ISBN 0-7710-1004-4). McClelland and Stewart.
Moon Pool. Abraham Merritt. LC 19-15978. 1919. 1.60. G. P. Putnam's Sons.
Moon Pool. Abraham Merritt. LC 44-7842. (Murder mystery monthly. No. 18). Avon Book Company.
Moon Rock. Arthur John Rees. 1922. John Lane Ltd.
Moon Rock. Arthur John Rees. LC 22-753455. 1922. Dodd, Mead and Company.
Moon Rocket: By John E. Muller. John E Muller. 1967. Arcadia House.
Moon Sails: A Novel. Emmanuel P Varandyan. LC 78-156496. 1971. 6.00. Pinnacle.
Moon Saw Murder. Gail Oliver. LC 37-4387. 1937. The Macmillan Company.
Moon Shadow. John M. Kimbro. 1976. 1.50. (ISBN 0-425-03140-3). Berkley Publishing Corp.
Moon Shadows. Ann Boyle. 1978. pap. 1.50 (ISBN 0-532-15351-0). Woodhill.
Moon-Spinners. Mary Stewart. LC 63-7387. 1963. M. S. Mill Co. and Morrow.
Moon Stallion. Jim Berry. LC 81-19600. 288p. 1982. 11.95 (ISBN 0-87131-368-5). M Evans.
Moon Tenders. August William Derleth. 3.95 o.p. Arkham.
Moon Terror. by a. g. birch, and stories by anthony m. rud, vincent starrett and farnsworth wright. ed. A G Birch. LC 28-2374. Popular Fiction Publishing Co.
Moon Through Glass. Coningsby William Dawson. LC 34-690. 1934. A. A. Knopf.
Moon Tide. Willard Robertson. LC 40-12037. Carrick & Evans, Inc.
Moon Tide. Willard Robertson. LC 42-20657. 1942. Triangle Books.

Moon to Play with. Elizabeth Clarke Dunn. LC 39-25562. 1939. W. Morrow & Company.
Moon to Play with: A Novel. 1st American Ed. John Wiles. LC 55-5938. 1955. Day.
Moon Tree. Maud Lang, pseud. LC 77-10071. 8.95 (ISBN 0-698-10861-2). Coward, McCann & Geoghegan.
Moon Tree. Maud Lang, pseud. (Signet book). 1979. 2.25 (ISBN 0-451-08512-4). New American Library.
Moon Valley. John Francis Case. LC 32-11381. J. B. Lippincott Company.
Moon Vow. 1st Ed. Hazel Ai Chun Lin. LC 58-9612. 1958. Pageant Press.
Moon Was Low. Monica Dickens. LC 40-14186. Harper & Brothers.
Moon Was Red. Dana Sage. LC 44-38250. 1944. Simon and Schuster.
Moon Witch. new ed. Anne Mather. (World of Romance Ser.). 192p. 1972. 4.95 o.p. (ISBN 0-529-04893-0). World Pub.
Moonbathers. Richard Miles. 1974. (pbk.) 1.50 (ISBN 0-515-03263-8). Pyramid.
Moonbeams. R. Vernon Beste. pap. 0.60 o.p. (73-444). Lancer.
Moonbeams. 1st Ed. R. Vernon Beste. LC 61-14835. 1961. Harper.
Moonblight and Six Feet of Romance. Daniel Carter Beard. LC 74-22767. (Labor Movement in Fiction and Non-Fiction). (Illus.). 1976. 16.00 (ISBN 0-404-58405-5). AMS Press.
Moonblight and Six Feet of Romance. Daniel Carter Beard. 1892. C. I. Webster and Company.
Moonblight and Six Feet of Romance. Daniel Carter Beard. 1941. A. Brandt.
Moonblood. Parley J Cooper. 1975. (pbk.) 1.25 (ISBN 0-671-80059-0). Pocket Books.
Moonbog. Rick Hautala. 1982. pap. 2.95 (ISBN 0-8217-1087-7). Zebra.
Moonchild. Aleister Crowley, pseud. 1974. lib. bdg. 49.95 o.p. (ISBN 0-87968-112-8). Krishna Pr.
Moonchild. Kenneth McKenney. LC 77-13170. 8.95 (ISBN 0-671-22887-0). Simon and Schuster.
Moonchild; a Prologue. Aleister Crowley, pseud. LC 72-142496. 1970. 3.00 (ISBN 0-87728-036-3). S. Weiser.
Moonclock. Claudia Von Canon. LC 79-22292. 1979. (ISBN 0-8161-3008-6). G. K. Hall.
Mooncranker's Gift. Barry Unsworth. LC 73-15944. 1974. 5.95. Houghton Mifflin.
Moondancers. W. J. Weathby. (Orig.). 1983. pap. 3.50 (ISBN 0-440-06189-X). Dell.
Moondeath. Rick Hautala. 436p. (Orig.). 1981. pap. 2.75 (ISBN 0-89083-702-3). Zebra.
Moondreamer. Zoe Kamitses. LC 82-17178. 14.00 (ISBN 0-316-48260-9). Little, Brown.
Moondyne: A Story from the Under-World. John Boyle O'Reilly. LC 42-30189. 1879. The Pilot Publishing Company.
Moondyne: A Story from the Underworld. 4th ed. John Boyle O'Reilly. 1883. Roberts Brothers.
Mooney. William Brown Meloney. LC 50-10201. 1950. Appleton-Century-Crofts.
Mooney Moves Around. Kerry O'Neil. LC 39-24725. Reynal & Hitchcock.
Moonfire Melody. Lily Bradford. (Second Chance at Love Contemporary Ser.: No. 11). 192p. (Orig.). 1981. pap. 1.75 (ISBN 0-515-05638-3). Jove Pubns.
Moonfisher. Philip MacDonald. LC 32-21198. 1932. Doubleday, Doran & Company, Inc.
Moonfleet. John Meade Falkner. LC 51-4955. (Illus.). 1951. Little, Brown.
Moonfleet. J. Meade Faulkner. (Illus.). 256p. 1982. pap. 2.25 (ISBN 0-448-16966-5, Pub. by Tempo). Ace Bks.
Moonflower. Bessie Winifred Fairbanks. LC 33-8989. R. Wilder and Company.
Moonflower. Beverley Nichols. LC 74-171256. 1973. 2.25 (ISBN 0-491-01111-3). W. H. Allen.
Moonflower. Phyllis A Whitney. LC 58-12827. 1958. Appleton-Century-Crofts.
Moonflower Couple. John Fairchild. LC 67-15362. 1967. Doubleday.
Moonflower Murder. 1st Ed. Beverley Nichols. LC 55-834213. (Guilt edged mystery). 1955. Dutton.
Moonflower Vine. Jetta Carleton. LC 62-19080. 1962. Simon and Schuster.
Moonglade: A Novel. Marguerite De Godart Cunliffe-Owen. LC 15-3969. 1915. 1.35. Harper & Brothers.
Moonhill Mystery. Nancy Mann Waddel Wilson Woodrow Woodrow. LC 30-246251. The Macaulay Company.
Moonhorn: An Anthology of Poignant Short Stories. Dion O'Donnol. LC 42-25896. 1942. Calico Press.
Moonlady. Josef Washington Hall. LC 27-23450. 1927. G. P. Putnam's Sons.
Moonlake Manor. Luanna Churchill. 192p. (OSI). 1972. 3.95 o.s.i. Lenox Hill.
Moonless Night. Jennie Gallant. 224p. (Orig.). 1980. pap. 1.75 (ISBN 0-449-50040-3, Coventry). Fawcett.
Moonlight: A Novel. Joyce Cary. LC 47-4403. 1947. Harper.
Moonlight & Murder. Joyce E. Davis. (Orig.). 1981. pap. 1.95 (ISBN 0-8439-8036-2, Tiara Bks). Nordon Pubns.
Moonlight, and Other Stories. Clinton A Rowe. LC 19-13517. Saulsbury Publishing Company.
Moonlight at Greystone. Louisa Bronte. LC 76-11802. 1976. 1.50 (ISBN 0-345-25060-5). Ballantine Books.
Moonlight Boy. Edgar Watson Howe. (American Authors Ser). 1970. Repr. of 1886 ed. lib. bdg. 18.95 o.s.i. (ISBN 0-512-00344-0). Garrett Pr.
Moonlight Boy see Collected Works.
Moonlight Enough. Sandra Clark. (Harlequin Romances Ser.). 192p. 1983. pap. 1.75 (ISBN 0-373-02533-5). Harlequin Bks.
Moonlight in Greystone. Louisa Bronte. LC 76-20658. (Greystone Tavern series). 1976. 9.95 (ISBN 0-89340-004-1). J. Curley.
Moonlight Jewelers. Albert Vidalie. LC 58-8148. 1958. Farrar, Straus & Cudahy.
Moonlight Meeting. Peggy Gaddis & Rebecca Marsh. (Signet Double romance). 1976. (pbk.) 1.25. New American Library.
Moonlight on the Nile. Elizabeth Ashton. (Harlequin Romance Ser.). (Orig.). 1979. pap. 1.25 (ISBN 0-373-02300-6, Pub. by Harlequin). PB.
Moonlight Rapture. Prudence Martin. (Candlelight Ecstasy Ser.: No. 148). (Orig.). 1983. pap. 1.95 (ISBN 0-440-15825-7). Dell.
Moonlight Sonata: Quasi una Fantasia) a Novel. Johan Nordling. LC 12-20786. 1912. 1.25. Sturgis & Walton Company.
Moonlight Traveler: Great Tales of Fantasy and Imagination. Ed. by Philip Van Doren Stern. LC 43-51158. 1943. Doubleday, Doran and Co., Inc.
Moonlight Variations. Florence Stevenson. 224p. (Orig.). 1981. pap. 2.50 (ISBN 0-515-05655-3). Jove Pubns.
Moonlight War. Clifton Adams. 1969. pap. 0.50 o.p. (D2186, GM). Fawcett World.
Moonlighter. Henry Kane. LC 70-134211. 1971. 6.95. B. Geis Associates.
Moonlighters. LC 66-17399. 1966. 3.50. Pub. for the Crime Club by Doubleday.
Moonlighting Wives. Peter Kanto. pap. 0.95 o.p. (1159). Brandon.
Moonlit Door. Anne Maybury. (Orig.). 1968. pap. 0.75 o.p. Lancer.
Moonlit Door: A Novel. 1st Ed. Anne Maybury. LC 67-11805. 1967. 4.95. Holt.
Moonlit Trap. Ruth Willock. LC 72-7787. 1973. 5.95. Hawthorn Books.
Moonlit Way. Dwyer-Joyce, Alice. LC 74-80992. 1974. 6.95. St. Martin's Press.
Moonlit Way: A Novel. Robert William Chambers. LC 19-704055. 1919. D. Appleton and Company.
Moonlovers. Olaf Lornquest. 1975. (pbk.) 1.25 (ISBN 0-523-00518-0). Pinnacle Books.
Moonmilk and Murder. Aaron Marc Stein. LC 55-5499. 1955. Published for the Crime Club by Doubleday.
Moonpies & Martinis. Roland L. Greene, Jr. 3.50 o.p. Carlton.
Moonraker. Ian Fleming. LC 55-14955. 1955. Macmillan.
Moonraker Mutiny. Antony Trew. LC 79-185862. 1972. 6.95. St. Martin's Press.
Moonraker: Or, The Female Pirate and Her Friends. Fryniwyd Tennyson Jesse. LC 27-11484. 1927. A. A. Knopf.
Moonrakers & Mischief. G. J. Feakes. 1962. 3.50 o.p. Washburn.
Moonraker's Bride. Madeleine Brent. LC 73-79649. 360p. 1973. 8.95 o.p. (ISBN 0-385-06445-4). Doubleday.
Moonraker's Bride. Madeleine Brent. 1978. pap. 1.95 (ISBN 0-449-23594-7, Crest). Fawcett.
Moonraker's Bride. Madeleine Brent. 636p. 1974. Repr. lib. bdg. 12.95 o.p. (ISBN 0-8161-6190-9, Large Print Bks). G K Hall.
Moonraker's Bride. Madeleine Brent. (Fawcett crest book). 1974. (pbk.) 1.50. Fawcett.
Moonrise. Theodore Strauss. LC 46-7631. 1946. The Viking Press.
Moonrise on the Indus: A Novel. Dennis Kincaid. LC 34-29559. Harcourt, Brace and Company.
Moon's a Balloon. David Niven. 1983. pap. 3.50 (ISBN 0-440-15806-0). Dell.
Moon's Fire-Eating Daughter. John Myers Myers & Hank Stine. LC 80-23268. (Starblaze editions). (Illus.). 1981. 20.00 (ISBN 0-89865-080-1) (ISBN 0-89865-079-8). Donning Co.
Moons in Gold. Carleton Stevens Montanye. LC 36-18569. J. B. Lippincott Company.
Moon's Nodes. G. White. pap. 1.95 (ISBN 0-87728-277-3). Weiser.
Moons of Jupiter: Stories. Alice Munro. LC 82-48734. 1983. 12.95 (ISBN 0-394-52952-9). Knopf: Distributed by Random House.
Moons of Triopus. John Rankine, pseud. 1969. pap. 0.60 o.p. (ISBN 0-446-63228-7, 63-228). Paperback Lib.
Moon's Our Home. Faith Baldwin. 1976. Repr. of 1936 ed. lib. bdg. 16.60x (ISBN 0-88411-602-6). Amereon Ltd.
Moon's Our Home. Faith Baldwin Culthrell. 1974. (pbk.) 0.95. Warner Paperback Library.
Moon's Our Home. Faith Baldwin Cuthrell. LC 73-86736. 1973. 5.95. Aeonian Press.
Moon's Our Home. Faith Baldwin Cuthrell. LC 36-406. Farrar & Rinehart, Incorporated.
Moons Ride Over: A Novel. Karl Zuckmayer & Ross, William, 1894- Tr. LC 37-1867. 1937. The Viking Press.
Moonscape: And Other Stories. Mika Toimi Waltari. LC 54-10493. 1954. Putnam.
Moonset. Margaret Ellsworth Gruen. LC 43-9095. 1943. L. B. Fischer.
Moonshadow Mansion see Mansion Tenebrosa.
Moonshell. Louise Bergstrom. (Orig.). 1981. pap. 1.75 (ISBN 0-8439-8016-8, Tiara Bks). Nordon Pubns.
Moonshine. J. F Oertel. LC 26-14836. 1926. The J. W. Burke Company.
Moonshine: A Story of the Reconstruction Period. Frederic Allison Tupper. LC 72-2067. (Black Heritage Library Collection). 1972. 12.50 (ISBN 0-8369-9071-4). Books for Libraries Press.
Moonshine; a Story of the Reconstruction Period. Frederic Allison Tupper. (On cover: Lovell's library, v. 18, no. 895). 1887. J. W. Lovell Company.
Moonshine; a Story of the Reconstruction Period: By Frederic Allison Tupper... Frederic Allison Tupper. LC 8-34326. 1884. Cupples, Upham and Company.
Moonshine and Marguerites: And Other Tales. Margaret Wolfe Hungerford. (On cover: Lovell's library. v. 3, no. 132). 1883. J. W. Lovell Company.
Moonshine Light, Moonshine Bright: A Novel. 1st Ed. William Price Fox. LC 67-14364. 1967. bds., 5.95. Lippincott.
Moonshine Strategy: And Other Stories. Wells Hawks. LC 6-38554. 1906. I. & M. Ottenheimer.
Moonshine War. Elmore Leonard. LC 69-20081. 1969. 4.95. Doubleday.
Moonshiners. Jess Carr. LC 77-71601. 9.95 (ISBN 0-87695-202-3). Aurora Publishers.
Moonshiner's Folly: And Other Stories. Hannibal Albert Compton. LC 16-5194. 1.00. The Roxburgh Publishing Company, Inc.
Moonshiner's Son. William Allen Dromgoole. 1898. The Penn Publishing Company.
Moonsong Chronicles. Jessica Stuart. 384p. (Orig.). 1981. pap. 2.75 (ISBN 0-523-41167-7). Pinnacle Bks.
Moonsong Chronicles: Sins of Moonsong. Jessica Stuart. 384p. (Orig.). 1982. pap. 2.95 (ISBN 0-523-41169-3). Pinnacle Bks.
Moonstar Odyssey. David Gerrold. (Signet Book). 1977. 1.50 (ISBN 0-451-07372-X). New American Library.
Moonstone. Wilkie Collins. LC 65-6517. (Perennial classic). 1965. Harper & Row.
Moonstone. Wilkie Collins. LC 14-19355. (Half-title: The English comedie humaine). 1904. The Century Co.
Moonstone. Wilkie Collins. LC 6-39761. (Half-title: The English Comedie humaine). 1906. The Century Co.
Moonstone. Wilkie Collins. LC 31-27058. 1931. Harper & Brothers.
Moonstone. Wilkie Collins. LC 42-46329. (Sun dial library). Garden City Publishing Company, Inc.
Moonstone. Wilkie Collins. LC 43-2619. 1943. The Press of the Readers Club.
Moonstone. Wilkie Collins. LC 47-6420. (Everyman's library, no. 949). 1947. J. M. Dent.
Moonstone. A Novel. Wilkie Collins. LC 41-34793. 1868. Harper & Brothers.
Moonstone. A Novel. Wilkie Collins. LC 6-269413. 1869. Harper & Brothers.
Moonstone. A Novel. Wilkie Collins. LC 3-27275. Harper & Brothers.
Moonstone. A Novel. Wilkie Collins. LC 16-7538. 1874. Harper & Brothers.
Moonstone: A Novel. Wilkie Collins. LC 26-752911. Harper & Brothers.
Moonstone: A Romance. Wilkie Collins. LC 8-31168. 1908. C. Scribner's Sons.
Moonstone and The Woman in White. Wilkie Collins. LC 37-302623. (Half-title: The modern library of the world's best books). 1937. The Modern Library.
Moonstone. Ed. by J.I.M. Stewart. Wilkie Collins. LC 66-7651. (Penguin Eng. lib., EL14). 1966. pap., 1.25. Penguin.
Moonstone: Ed. by M. W. and G. Thomas, Illus. by John Sergeant. Wilkie Collins. Ed. by Gladys - Thomas. LC 66-74079. (Shorter classics). 1965. bds., 2.50. Ginn.
Moonstone. Modern Abridged Ed. Wilkie Collins. LC 50-4003. (Pyramid books, 19). Almat Pub. Corp.
Moonstone. With Illus. of the Author and the Setting of the Book Together with an Introd. and Descriptive Captions by Basil Davenport. Wilkie Collins. LC 55-4191. (Great illustrated classics). 1955. Dodd, Mead.
Moonstone: With Illustrations. Wilkie Collins & Sharp, William, 1900-Illus. LC 44-51205. 1944. Doubleday, Doran & Company, Inc.
Moonstone: With Illustrations by William Sharp. Wilkie Collins. LC 46-4902. 1946. Doubleday & Company, Inc.
Moonstruck Madness. Laurie McBain. LC 76-53310. 1977. 1.95 (ISBN 0-380-00871-8). Avon Books.
Moontrap. Don Berry. 1976. pap. 2.50 (ISBN 0-89174-000-7). Comstock Edns.
Moontrap: A Novel. Don Berry. LC 62-16783. 1962. Viking Press.
Moonwater. Claudia Nicole. (Orig.). 1970. pap. 0.60 o.p. (ISBN 0-446-63484-0, 63-484). Paperback Lib.
Moonwind. Sharon Wagner. (Orig.). 1972. pap. 0.95 o.s.i. (75-416). Lancer.
Moor Fires. Emily Hilda Young. LC 27-27784. 1927. Harcourt, Brace and Company.
Moor Fires Mystery. Harriette Russell Campbell. LC 39-3402. 1939. Harper & Brothers.
Moor of Granada. Henri Guenot. LC 7-150. (On cover: Premium library). H. L. Kilner & Co.
Moorland Cottages. Elizabeth Cleghorn Stevenson Gaskell. LC 9-3014. 1868. Harper & Brothers.
Moorland Grove. Herman August Schroeder. LC 38-16868. 1938. Wm. B. Eerdmans Publishing Co.
Moorland Monster. Glen Chase, pseud. (Cherry Delight Ser.). 1977. pap. 1.50 o.s.i. (ISBN 0-8439-0489-5, Leisure Bks). Nordon Pubns.
Moormist. Georgina Ferrand. LC 76-20669. (Zodiac gothic: Taurus). 1976. 8.95 (ISBN 0-89340-010-6). J. Curley.
Moormist: An Astrological Gothic Novel: Taurus. Georgina Ferrand. LC 75-46067. 1976. 1.25 (ISBN 0-345-25098-2). Ballantine Books.
Moors and Christians: And Other Tales. Pedro Antonio De Alarcon & Serrano, Mrs. Mary Jane (Christie) D. 1923, Tr. LC 5-42175. Cassell Publishing Company.
Moor's Gold. Ben Aronin. LC 36-559. 1935. Argus Books.
Moorsend Manor. Florence Hurd. pap. 0.95 o.p. (ISBN 0-532-95231-6). Woodhill.
Moorsend Manor. Florence Hurd. pap.' 0.95 o.p. (ISBN 0-532-95231-6). Manor Bks.
Moorsend Manor: A Gothic Novel. Florence Hurd. 1973. (pbk.) 0.95. Manor Books.
Moorwood Legacy. Iris Foster. pap. 0.95 o.s.i. (75-281). Lancer.
Moose: A Very Special Person. Chet Oden & W. Scott MacDonald. 1978. pap. 3.95 o.p. (ISBN 0-03-043936-1). Winston Pr.
Moose Call. Adolph Philip Lehner. LC 32-768. 1931. Meador Publishing Company.
Moose Meat and Wild Rice. Basil Johnston. LC 79-302600. 1978. 12.95 (ISBN 0-7710-4443-7). McClelland and Stewart.
Mooswa & Others of the Boundaries. William Alexander Fraser. LC 6628. 1900. C. Scribner's Sons.
Moot Point. Peter De Polnay. LC 48-5612. 1948. Creative Age Press.
Moral Blot. A Novel. Sigmund B Alexander. 1894. Arena Publishing Company.
Moral Busybody. An Episode of New York's to-Day. Alfred J. Cohen. (On cover: Mascot library, no. 7). 1894. The Mascot Publishing Co.
Moral Dilemma: A Novel. Annie Thompson. 1893. Longmans, Green, and Co.
Moral Fables of Robert Henryson. Robert Henryson. Ed. by Andrew Hart. LC 72-144423. (Maitland Club. Glasgow. Publications: No. 15). Repr. of 1832 ed. 12.50 (ISBN 0-404-52950-X). AMS Pr.
Moral Imbeciles. Sarah Pratt McLean Greene. LC 98-72. 1898. Harper & Brothers.
Moral Inheritance. Lydia Hoyt Farmer. (sunnyside series no. 16). 1891. J. S. Ogilvie.
Moral Sinner. Myrtilla N Daly. (On cover: Cassell's "rainbow" series. no. 14). Cassell & Company.
Moral Sinner. Myrtilla N Daly. LC 3443. 1900. Street & Smith.
Moral Tales. Lawrence Perry Spingarn. LC 83-3431. 4.75 (ISBN 0-912288-19-1). Perivale Press.
Moral Tales. Lawrence Perry Spingarn. LC 82-6216. (Illus.). 70p. 1983. pap. 4.75 (ISBN 0-912288-19-1). Perivale Pr.
Moral Tales for Young People. Maria Edgeworth. LC 73-22194. (Feminist Controversy in England, 1788-1810). 1974. (ISBN 0-8240-0856-1). Garland Pub.
Moral Tales: Or, A Selection on Interesting Stories. Samuel Griswold Goodrich. LC 42-435301. 1840. Nafis & Cornish.
Moralist. Walter Adolphe Roberts. LC 73-18601. 1974. (ISBN 0-404-11411-3). AMS Press.
Moralist. Walter Adolphe Roberts. LC 31-171282. 1931. The Mohawk Press.
Moralist. Allen Wheelis. LC 72-97403. (O.s.i.). 1973. 7.95x o.s.i. (ISBN 0-465-04717-3). Basic.
Morality Court. Bonnie Melbourne Busch. LC 21-16929. Burton Publishing Company.

Morals for Moderns. Elmer Holmes Davis. LC 30-28403. The Bobbs-Merrill Company.

Morals of Abou Ben Adhem. David Ross Locke. LC 76-91086. (American humorists series). 1969. Literature House.

Morals of Marcus Ordeyne: A Novel. William John Locke. 1905. J. Lane.

Morals of Marcus Ordeyne: A Novel. William John Locke. LC 20-15618. John Lane.

Morals of Marcus Ordeyne: A Novel. William John Locke. LC 7-32442. 1907. J. Lane Company; Etc., Etc.

Morals of Marcus Ordeyne: A Novel. William John Locke. LC 9-73392. 1909. J. Lane Company; Etc., Etc.

Morals of Marcus Ordeyne: A Novel. William John Locke. LC 43-37735. Grosset & Dunlap.

Moran Beats Back. William MacLeod Raine. LC 39-9397. 1939. Houghton Mifflin Company.

Moran of Saddle Butte. Lynn Gunnison. LC 24-29996. 1924. 2.00. A. C. McClurg & Co.

Moran of the Lady Letty. Frank Norris. LC 70-104533. 1970. (ISBN 0-8398-1351-1). Literature House.

Moran of the Lady Letty: A Story of Adventure off the California Coast. Frank Norris. LC 75-144665. 1971. (ISBN 0-404-04790-4). AMS Press.

Moran of the Lady Letty: A Story of Adventure off the California Coast. Frank Norris. LC 98-624792. 1898. Doubleday & McClure Co.

Morana. John T Yates. LC 35-928938. Christopher Publishing House.

Moravagine. Blaise Cendrars. 12.95x (ISBN 0-8464-0642-X). Beekman Pubs.

Moravagine. Blaise Cendrars. 1970. 5.95 o.p. Doubleday.

Moravagine: A Novel. Blaise Cendrars. LC 70-111150. (Illus.). 1970. 5.95. Doubleday Projections Books.

Morbid Taste for Bones. Ellis Peters. LC 78-15324. 1978. 8.95 (ISBN 0-688-03374-1). Morrow.

Morchester: A Story of American Society, Politics, and Affairs. Charles Datchet. LC 2-12107. 1902. G. P. Putnam's Sons.

Mordaunt: Sketches of Life, Characters, and Manners in Various Countries; Including The Memoirs of a French Lady of Quality. John Moore. LC 65-29775. (Oxford English novels). 1965. Oxford University Press.

Mordemly;" Or, By Order of the Magistrate. A Novel. William Pett Ridge. LC 7-41442. 1898. Harper & Brothers.

Mordred. John E. Holmes. 1980. pap. 1.95 (ISBN 0-441-54220-4). Ace Bks.

More Aces: A Collection of Short Stories. The Community Workers of the New York Guild for the Jewish Blind, Comp & Ade, George. LC 25-212098. 1925. G. P. Putnam's Sons.

More Adventures of an A. D. C. Shelland Bradley. LC 16-261271. 1915. John Lane.

More Adventures of Captain Kettle, Captain Kettle, K. C. B. Charles John Cutcliffe Wright Hyne. LC 3-12518. 1903. The Federal Book Company.

More Adventures of the Great Brain. John Dennis Fitzgerald. 1971. pap. 2.25 (ISBN 0-440-45822-6, YB). Dell.

More Beautiful Than Murder: A Novel. Octavus Roy Cohen. LC 48-9304. 1948. Macmillan Co.

More Bitter Than Death. Kate Wilhelm. (O.s.i.). 1962. 3.50 o.s.i. (ISBN 0-671-49040-0). S&S.

More Cargoes. William Wymark Jacobs. LC 71-75780. (Short story index reprint series). 1969. Books for Libraries Press.

More Cargoes. William Wymark Jacobs. LC 98-1228. Frederick A. Stokes Company.

More Cheerful Americans. Charles Battell Loomis. LC 72-101817. (Short story index reprint series). (Illus.). 1969. Books for Libraries Press.

More Cheerful Americans. Charles Battell Loomis. LC 4-25679. 1904. H. Holt and Company.

More Chucklebait: Funny Stories for Everyone. Margaret Clara Scoggin. LC 49-11090. (Borzol books for young people). 1949. Knopf.

More Combat Stories of World War II and Korea. William Chamberlain. LC 64-20728. 1964. John Day Co.

More Dangerous Than the Moon. Richard Butler. LC 68-16682. 1968. Walker.

More Deaths Than One. Stuart David Engstrand. LC 54-67646. 1955. J. Messner.

More Deaths Than One. Bruno Fischer. LC 47-24774. 1947. Ziff-Davis Pub. Co.

More Deserving Cases. Robert Graves. 1962. 10.00 o.s.i. Ridgeway Bks.

More E. K. Means. Eldred Kurtz Means. LC 72-4738. (Black Heritage Library Collection). (Illus.). 1972. 14.50 (ISBN 0-8369-9112-5). Books for Libraries Press.

More E. K. Means. Is This a Title? It Is Not. It Is the Name of a Writer of Negro Stories, Who Has Made Himself So Completely the Writer of Negro Stories That This Second Book, Like the First, Needs No Title. Illustrated by Kemble. Eldred Kurtz Means. LC 19-8992. 1919. G. P. Putnam's Sons.

More Ex-Tank Tales. Clarence Louis Cullen. LC 2-11149. J. S. Ogilvie Publishing Company.

More Excellent Way: Being the Determinative Episodes in the Life of Chrissey De Selden, Hedonist. Cyrus Townsend Brady. LC 16-20591. 1916. 1.35. G. P. Putnam's Sons.

More Fables. George Ade. LC 6497. 1900. H.S. Stone and Company.

More Five O'clock Stories in Prose and Verse. LC 6-27992. 1906. Benziger Brothers.

More from One Step Beyond: A Second Volume of Eerie Stories Chosen from the Television Program 'Alcoa Presents' and Retold Here by Lenore Bredeson. Alcoa Presents (Television Program) & Lenore Bredeson. LC 61-14678. 1961. Citadel Press.

More Fun for Young Fingers. Grace M. Gardner. pap. 2.75 (ISBN 0-87164-079-1). William-F.

More Ghost Stories of an Antiquary. Montague Rhodes James. LC 72-163031. (Short story index reprint series). 1971. (ISBN 0-8369-3945-X). Books for Libraries Press.

More Ghosts and Marvels: A Selection of Uncanny Tales from Sir Walter Scott to Michael Arlen. Ed. by Vere Henry Collins. LC 29-19788. (Half-title: The World's classics, cccxxiii). 1929. Oxford University Press, H. Milford.

More Ghosts in the Valley. Adi-Kent T. Jeffrey. LC 75-4659. 80p. 1973. pap. 1.50 (ISBN 0-915460-01-7). New Hope.

More Gilt-Edged Bonds. Ian Fleming. LC 65-27967.

More Goodly Country: A Personal History of America. John B. Sanford. LC 74-28317. 1975. 12.95 (ISBN 0-8180-0814-8). Horizon Press.

More Goon Show Scripts. Spike Milligan, pseud. LC 74-78491. 155p. 1974. 6.95 o.p. (ISBN 0-312-54810-9). St Martin.

More Guys and Dolls: Thirty-Four of the Best Short Stories. Damon Runyon. LC 51-14193. 1951. Garden City Books.

More Guys and Dolls: Thirty-Four of the Best Short Stories, With an Introd. by Clark Kinnaird. Damon Runyon. LC 59-78993. 1959. Lippincott.

More Happy Thoughts, &C. &C. Francis Cowley Burnand. (Half title: Handy volume series, no. 9). 1871. Roberts Brothers.

More Honorable Man. Arthur Somers Roche. LC 22-21106. 1922. The Macmillan Company.

More Hours in My Day. Emilie Barnes. (Orig.). 1982. pap. 4.95 (ISBN 0-89081-355-8). Harvest Hse.

More Innocent Time: A Novel. Eugenie Hill. LC 79-5128. 1979. 8.95 (ISBN 0-8008-5355-5). Taplinger Pub. Co.

More Jataka Tales. Ellen C. Babbitt. (Illus.). (gr. 7-12). 1922. text ed. 4.25 o.p. (ISBN 0-13-601047-4). P-H.

More Johanna Stories. Laura Clark Childs. LC 22-24581. 1.50. Free Press Printing Co.

More Joy in Heaven. Morley Callaghan. LC 37-369243. Random House.

More Jungle Tales: Adventures in India. Howard Anderson Musser. LC 23-13652. 1.50. George H. Doran Company.

More Knaves Than One. Frank Lucius Packard. LC 38-33736. 1938. Doubleday, Doran & Company, Inc.

More Letters to My Son. Winifred James. LC 11-26179. 1911. 1.00. Moffat, Yard and Company.

More Limehouse Nights. Thomas Burke. LC 22-656. George H. Doran Company.

More Little Monsters. Ed. by Roger Elwood & Vic Ghidalia. 192p. (Orig.). 1973. pap. 0.95 o.p. (ISBN 0-532-95235-9). Woodhill.

More Little Monsters. Ed. by Roger Elwood & Vic Ghidalia. 192p. (Orig.). 1973. pap. 0.95 o.p. (ISBN 0-532-95235-9). Manor Bks.

More Lives Than One. Charles Bracelen Flood. LC 67-11451. 1967. Houghton Mifflin.

More Lives Than One. Carolyn Wells. LC 23-144082. Boni and Liveright.

More Marginalia. Leigh Hunt. LC 74-11472. 1974. Repr. of 1931 ed. lib. bdg. 10.00 (ISBN 0-8414-4832-9). Folcroft.

More Money. Charles Grant. LC 34-2593. C. Kendall.

More Murder in a Nunnery. Eric Shepherd. LC 54-758421. 1954. Sheed and Ward.

More New Arabian Nights. The Dynamiter. Robert Louis Stevenson & Fanny Van De Grift Osbourne Stevenson. LC 6-18296. (Half-title: The biographical edition of the works of Robert Louis Stevenson). 1905. C. Scribner's Sons.

More New Arabian Nights. The Dynamiter. Robert Louis Stevenson & Fanny Van De Grift Osbourne Stevenson. 1887. C. Scribner's Sons.

More News from Middle East: Being Further Pages from the Records of Captain James Donald MacGregor. Robert Mason. LC 43-157685. 1943. Hurst & Blackett Ltd.

More of Little Top Sail. Claude V Holland. (wide world of seanuts, v. 2). (Illus.). 1973. (pbk) 1.25. Hol-Land Books and Posters.

More of Mark of the Beast. A. Degranamour. pap. 2.25 o.s.i. (Venus). Grove.

More of the Best: Stories for Girls. (Illus.). 1978. 0.95 (ISBN 0-307-21520-2). Golden Press.

More Pennsylvania Mountain Stories... Henry Wharton Shoemaker. LC 12-555812. 1912. The Bright Printing Company.

More Perfect Union. Robert Stapp. LC 73-106938. 1970. 7.50 o.p. (ISBN 0-06-127790-8, HarpT). Har-Row.

More Perfect Union: A Novel. Robert Stapp. LC 73-106938. 1970. 7.50. Harper's Magazine Press.

More Pricks Than Kicks. Samuel Beckett. LC 72-119923. (His Collected works). 1970. 5.00. Grove Press.

More Rawhides. Charles Marion Russell. LC 46-21782. 1946. Trail's End Publishing Co., Inc.

More Roman Tales. Alberto Moravia. Tr. by Angus Davidson. 1964. 4.75 o.p. FS&G.

More Seven Club Tales: Found in Mr. Jefferay's Papers Marked: "Some Strange Relatings, Sent by Divers of Mine Acquaintance, with a Desire That They Be Read Unto the Sevn Club"... limited ed. Ed. by John Osborne Austin. Jefferay, William. 1900. Press of Newport Daily News.

More Short Fictions. Richard Kostelanetz. LC 80-58969. (Illus.). 224p. (Orig.). 1981. 15.00; pap. 6.96. Assembling Pr.

More "Short Sixes.". Henry Cuyler Bunner. LC 68-55666. (American short story series, v. 6). (Illus.). 1968. Garrett Press.

More "Short Sixes.". Henry Cuyler Bunner. LC 72-8305. (American short story series, v. 6). 1972. (ISBN 0-8422-8015-4). MSS Information Corp.

More "Short Sixes". Henry Cuyler Bunner. LC 4-13815. 1894. Keppler & Schwarzmann.

More Snappy Answers to Stupid Questions. Al Jaffee. (Illus.). 1979. pap. 1.75 (ISBN 0-446-94410-6). Warner Bks.

More Songs to Be Sung. Ed. by J. Lorne Peachey. (A sequel to Songs to Be Sung). 1971. pap. 0.75x o.p. (ISBN 0-8361-1138-9). Herald Pr.

More Soviet Science Fiction. Ed. by Isaac Asimov. (YA) (gr. 7-12). 1962. pap. 1.95 o.s.i. (ISBN 0-02-016470-X, Collier). Macmillan.

More Stately Mansions. Bertha B. Moore McCurry. LC 42-24776. 1942. The Moody Press.

More Stately Mansions: A Novel. Pauline Benedict Fischer. LC 39-29446. The Penn Publishing Company.

More Stories. James Thomas Farrell. LC 46-22547. 1946. The Sun Dial Press.

More Stories. Frank O'Connor, pseud. 1954. 5.95 o.p. (ISBN 0-394-43687-3). Knopf.

More Stories: By Frank O'Connor Pseud. 1st Ed. Michael O'Donovan. LC 54-7199. 1954. Knopf.

More Stories from the Hugo Winners, Vol. 2. Ed. by Isaac Asimov. 1979. pap. 2.25 (ISBN 0-449-23883-0, Crest). Fawcett.

More Stories from the Twilight Zone. Rod Serling. LC 61-2474. (Bantam book, A2227). 1961. Bantam Books.

More Stories in the Modern Manner from Partisan Review. By James Agee and Others. Partisan Review. LC 54-2423. (Avon, T-77). 1954. Avon Publications.

More Stories of Married Life. Mary Stewart Doubleday Cutting. LC 75-37264. (Short story index reprint series). 1971. (ISBN 0-8369-4075-X). Books for Libraries Press.

More Stories of Married Life. Mary Stewart Doubleday Cutting. LC 6-12557. 1906. McClure, Phillips & Co.

More Stories of the New Land. Elma C. Ehrlich Levinger. LC 38-11330. 1938. Bloch Publishing Company.

More Stories to Remember: V.3 & 4, Selected by Thomas B. Costain. John Beecroft. Thomas Bertram Costain. Ed. by John Beecroft. (W1174, W1175). 1965. Popular Lib.

More Strange Unsolved Mysteries. Emile C. Schurmacher. (Orig.). 1969. pap. 0.60 o.p. (63-164). Paperback Lib.

More Swapping in Building A. Gene North. 192p. pap. 1.95 o.p. (6166). Brandon.

More Tales by Polish Authors. Tr. by Else Cecilia Mendelssohn Benecke. Szymanaki, Adam et al. 1916. Longmans, Green & Co.

More Tales from Grimm. Wanda Gag. 1981. pap. 5.95 (ISBN 0-698-20533-2, Coward). Putnam Pub Group.

More Tales from Slim Ellison. Glenn R. Ellison. 1981. 17.50 (ISBN 0-8165-0715-5); pap. 9.50 (ISBN 0-8165-0681-7). U of Ariz Pr.

More Tales from Tolstoi; Translated from the Russian with an Enlarged Biography of the Author. Lev Nikolaevich Tolstoi & Bain, Robert Nisbet, 1854-1909, Tr. LC 3-160703. 1903. Brentano's.

More Tales of Cedar River. William Clark. 1961. 3.95 o.p. McKay.

More Tales of Cedar River. 1st Ed. William Murray Clark. LC 61-12753. 1961. D. McKay Co.

More Tales of the Black Widowers. Isaac Asimov. LC 76-2750. 1976. 5.95 (ISBN 0-385-11176-2). Published for the Crime Club by Doubleday.

More Tales of the Uneasy. Violet Hunt. LC 77-2899. 1977. 25.00 (ISBN 0-8414-4751-9). Folcroft Library Editions.

More Tales to Tremble by: A Second Collection of Great Stories of Haunting and Suspense, Ed. by Stephen P. Sutton. Illus. by Gordon Laite. Ed. by Stephen P Sutton. (Whitman classics). 1968. Whitman Pub.

More Than Bread. Don L. Chaffee. 1968. 2.95 o.p. Vantage.

More Than Bread. Hulbert Footner. LC 38-25514. J. B. Lippincott Company.

More Than Conquerer. Grace Livingston Hill. 1944. 2.95 o.p. (ISBN 0-448-05244-X). G&D.

More Than Conqueror. Grace Livingston Hill. LC 44-2952. 1944. J. B. Lippincott Company.

More Than Dust. Clara Emelia Burr & Burr, Clarence Edward, Joint Author. LC 43-8271. 1943. Meador Publishing Company.

More Than Flesi. Louis A Brennan. LC 57-70022. (Dell first edition, B108). 1957. Dell Pub. Co.

More Than Friends. Ruth Turk. 256p. (Orig.). 1980. pap. 2.50 (ISBN 0-553-13661-5). Bantam.

More Than Harps of Gold. Penny Estes Wheeler. LC 80-28712. 1982 (ISBN 0-8163-0424-6). Pacific Press Pub. Association.

More Than Human. Theodore Sturgeon. 1981. pap. 3.95 (ISBN 0-345-29406-8, Del Rey). Ballantine.

More Than Human. Theodore Sturgeon. Ed. by Lester Del Ray. LC 75-435. (Library of Science Fiction). 1975. lib. bdg. 17.50 (ISBN 0-8240-1438-3). Garland Pub.

More Than Human. Edward Hamilton Waldo, pseud. LC 75-435. (Garland Library of Science Fiction). 1975. 11.00 (ISBN 0-8240-1438-3). Garland Pub.

More Than Human: By Theodore Sturgeon Pseud. Edward Hamilton Waldo, pseud. LC 53-11211. 1953. Farrar, Straus and Young.

More Than Kin. Patricia Wentworth. LC 11-7869. 1911. G. P. Putnam's Sons.

More Than Kin: A Book of Kindness... James Vila Blake. LC 6-13851. 1893. C. H. Kerr & Company.

More Than Land: Stories of New England Country Life & Surveying. Heman Chase. LC 74-78070. 1975. 5.95 o.p. H Chase.

More Than Melchisedech. R. A. Lafferty. Ed. by Hank Stine. LC 82-12870. (Illus.). 380p. (Orig.). 1983. pap. 5.95 (ISBN 0-89865-254-5). Donning Co.

More Than Music. Dorothy Lester Chadwick. LC 39-176547. 1939. Arcadia House.

More Than Once; a Novel. Clement Agunwa. LC 67-88831. 1967. pap., 1.50. Longmans.

More Than Once: A Novel. Clement Agunwa. (Orig.). 1967. pap. text ed. 2.00x o.p. Humanities.

More Than Satisfied. David Stone. pap. 1.95 o.s.i. (Venus). Grove.

More Than She Could Bear: A Story of the Gachupin War in Texas, A. D. 1812-13. George W Archer. LC 6-3838. 1872. Claxton, Remsen & Haffelfinger.

More Than Sun. Tim Davis. LC 72-96458. 1973. 2.50 o.p. (ISBN 0-8059-1816-7). Dorrance.

More Than Welcome. Dean Boyd. LC 63-8089. 1963. Harcourt, Brace & World.

More Than Wife. Margaret Widdemer. LC 27-20592. Harcourt, Brace and Company.

More Things. Ivan T. Sanderson. (Orig.). 1969. pap. 0.75 o.p. (T2005). Pyramid Pubns.

More Things in Heaven. John Brunner. 1973. (pbk) 0.95. Dell.

More Tish. Mary Roberts Rinehart. LC 21-20115. George H. Doran Company.

More Tish. Mary Roberts Rinehart. LC 42-25443. 1942. The Sun Dial Press.

More Wandering Stars. Jack Dann. LC 81-43007. 1981. 10.95 (ISBN 0-385-17072-6). Doubleday.

More Ways Than One. Alice Perry. LC 7-36179. D. Lothrop and Company.

More Ways Than One. Alice Perry. LC 7-36178. (On cover: The household library. no. 9). 1886. D. Lothrop and Company.

More Wise Men of Helm and Their Merry Tales. Ed. by Hannah Goodman. Illus. by Stephen Kraft. Solomon Simon. LC 65-14594. 1965. 3.50. Behrman.

More Women of Wonder: Science Fiction Novelettes by Women About Women. Pamela Sargent. LC 76-13239. 1976. 1.95 (ISBN 0-394-71876-3). Vintage Books.

More Women Than Men. Ivy Compton-Burnett. 1933. 14.95 (ISBN 0-575-01959-X, Pub. by Gollancz England). David & Charles.

More Women than Men. Ivy Compton-Burnett. 1981. 20.00x (ISBN 0-575-01959-X, Pub. by Gollancz England). State Mutual Bk.

More Work for the Undertake. Margery Allingham. LC 49-7505. 1949. Doubleday.

More Work for the Undertaker. Margery Allingham. (Orig.). 1952. pap. 1.95 o.p. (ISBN 0-14-000864-0). Penguin.

More Work for the Undertaker. Margery Allingham. 208p. 1974. pap. 1.50 (ISBN 0-532-12233-X). Woodhill.

More Work for the Undertaker. Margery Allingham. 1971. pap. 0.75 o.p. (75-453). Manor Bks.

More Work for the Undertaker. Margery Allingham. 1973. (ISBN 0-14-000864-0). Penguin Books in Association with William Heineman.

More World Stories Retold. William J. Sly. Repr. of 1936 ed. 10.00 (ISBN 0-8414-8052-4). Folcroft.

More Wow's (Words of Wisdom, Vol. II. Jim Lytle. (Orig.). 1979. pap. 3.75 (ISBN 0-935040-12-9). Tri-Science Pubs.

More...Family Sex Games. Charles Richards. 192p. pap. 1.95 o.p. (7145). Barclay Hse.

More...Hot Mouth People. Sue Varian. 192p. pap. 1.95 o.p. (7154). Barclay Hse.

Moreland Legacy. Diana Haviland. LC 77-76877. 1977. 10.00 (ISBN 0-672-52336-1). Bobbs-Merrill.

Moreland Legacy. Diana Haviland. 1979. 1.95 (ISBN 0-449-14159-4). Fawcett Gold Medal.

Moreland Vale: Or, The Fair Fugitive. 1805. Printed by J. Wallis.

More...Oral Wives. Musetta Cepri. 192p. pap. 1.95 o.p. (7166). Barclay Hse.

More...People Who Have Sex with Animals. Joseph Edenn. 192p. pap. 1.95 o.p. (7165). Barclay Hse.

Moreton Mystery. Elizabeth Dejeans. LC 20-13978. The Bobbs-Merrill Company.

Moreton Mystery. Elizabeth Dejeans. LC 24-20454. 1922. The Bobbs-Merrill Company.

Moreton's Kingdom. Jean S. MacLeod. (Harlequin Romances Ser.). 192p. 1982. pap. 1.50. Harlequin Bks.

Morgan. Matt Weston. (Orig.). 1970. pap. 0.60 o.p. (ISBN 0-446-63423-9, 63-423). Paperback Lib.

Morgan of the Mounted. Samuel Alexander White. LC 39-17104. Phoenix Press.

Morgan: Or, The Knight of the Black Flag. A Strange Story of by-Gone Times. Edward Zane Carroll Judson. LC 7-11448. F. A. Brady.

Morgan Rutledge. Shannon Graham. LC 77-90455. 1978. pap. 2.25 o.s.i. (ISBN 0-89516-020-X). Condor Pub Co.

Morgan Trail: A Story of Hashknife Hartley. Wilbur C. Tuttle. LC 28-6762. 1928. Houghton Mifflin Company.

Morgan Wade's Woman. Amii Lorin. (Orig.). 1981. pap. 1.75 (ISBN 0-440-15507-X). Dell.

Morgana: A Novel. Marie Buchanan. LC 76-56273. 1977. 8.95 (ISBN 0-385-12881-9). Doubleday.

Morgana's Fault. Susan Ries Lukas. LC 81-5037. 10.95 (ISBN 0-399-12584-1). Putnam.

Morgan's Assassin. John Whitlatch. 1973. (pbk) 0.95. Pocket Books.

Morgan's Castle. Hilda Kay Grant. LC 64-12735. 1964. Abelard-Schuman.

Morgan's Horror: A Romance of the "West Countree,". George Manville Fenn. LC 6-39382. (On cover: Cassell's "rainbow" series. Vol. I. no. 16). 1888. Cassell & Company, Limited.

Morgan's Men: Containing Adventures of Stuart Schuyler, Captain of Cavalry During the Revolution. John Preston True. LC 1-24497. 1901. Little, Brown and Company.

Morgan's Passing. Anne Tyler. LC 79-20272. 1980. 9.95 (ISBN 0-394-50958-7). Knopf.

Morgan's Revenge. Matt Weston. (Westerns Ser). (Orig.). 1971. pap. 0.60 o.p. (ISBN 0-446-63569-3, 63-569). Paperback Lib.

Morgan's Woman. Garland Roark. LC 71-116247. 1971. 5.95 o.p. Doubleday.

Morgan's Yard. Richard Pryce. LC 32-11114. 1932. Houghton Mifflin Company.

Morgan's Youngest Rifleman. original illustrations by h. s. de lay. ed. Frederick Hankerson Costello. LC 13-11300. 1.25. Laird & Lee.

Morgesons. Elizabeth Drew Barstow Mrs. R. H. Stoddard Stoddard. LC 8-16305. Cassell & Company, Limited.

Morgesons: A Novel. Elizabeth Drew Barstow Stoddard & Richard Jackson Foster. LC 76-153961. (Illus.). 1971. Johnson Reprint Corp.

Morgue for Venus: By Jonathan Craig Pseud. Frank E Smith. LC 56-4760. (Gold medal books, 582). 1956. Fawcett Publications.

Morgue Is Always Open. Jerome Odlum. LC 44-4442. 1944. C. Scribner's Sons.

Morgue of the Wage-Earners: Or, Jerry Sly's Republic. William H Stanton. LC 8-13451. 1890. The Author.

Morgue the Merrier. June Truesdell. LC 45-508519. 1945. Dodd, Mead & Company.

Moriah's Mourning. Ruth McEnery Stuart. LC 70-104573. (Illus.). 1970. Literature House.

Moriah's Mourning, and Other Half-Hour Sketches. Ruth McEnery Stuart. LC 71-98600. (Short story index reprint series). 1969. Books for Libraries Press.

Moriah's Mourning: And Other Half-Hour Sketches. Ruth McEnery Stuart. LC 4-15166. 1898. Harper & Brothers.

Morial the Mahatma: Or, The Black Master of Tibet. Mabel Collins Cook. (On cover: Canterbury series, no. 3). Lovell, Gestefeld & Company.

Morisco. Hilary Mason. LC 78-73071. 1979. 9.95 (ISBN 0-689-10960-1). Atheneum.

Morituri. Barry Sadler. 320p. (Orig.). 1982. pap. 2.95 (ISBN 0-523-48045-8). Pinnacle Bks.

Moritz! Bob Herron. 220p. 1983. pap. text ed. 6.95 (ISBN 0-930762-06-1). Calamus Bks.

Morley Mythology. Austin McGiffert Wright. LC 76-5553. (Illus.). 10.95. (ISBN 0-06-014751-2) (ISBN 0-06-014742-3). Harper & Row.

Morlock Night. J. W Jeter. 1979. 1.75 (ISBN 0-87997-468-0). DAW Books.

Mormon Girl. Pauline Browning Higgins Dykes. LC 13-1153. 1912. Herald Publishing House.

Mormon of the Little Manitou Island: An Historical Romance. Nehemiah Hawkins. LC 16-204445. 1916. 2.00. Uplift Company.

Mormon Prophet. Lily Dougall. LC 99-1109. 1899. D. Appleton and Company.

Mormon Trail. Thomas Albert Curry. LC 42-22447. 1942. Gateway Books.

Mormon Trail. George Brydges Rodney. LC 33-4385. E. J. Clode, Inc.

Mormon Wife. Grace Wilbur Trout. LC 8-28485. (On cover: The Enterprise series. no. 64). 1896. E. A. Weeks & Company.

Mormon Wife. 3d ed. illustrations by vida e. horton. ed. Grace Wilbur Trout. LC 12-263651. Van-American Press.

Mormon Wife. Grace Wilbur Trout. LC 8-28486. (On verso of t.-p.: Unity library, no. 47). 1895. C. H. Kerr & Company.

Mormon Wives. Ana Zavala. 352p. (Orig.). 1982. pap. 2.95 (ISBN 0-449-14489-5, GM). Fawcett.

Mormon Wives: A Narrative of Facts Stranger Than Fiction. Metta Victoria Fuller Victor. LC 8-22794. 1856. Derby & Jackson.

Morning. Julian Fane. LC 57-13960. 1957. Reynal.

Morning After. Eugene Thomas. LC 34-4562. Sears Publishing Company, Inc.

Morning After. Jack B. Weiner. LC 72-6662. 1973. 6.95. Delacorte Press.

Morning After. Jack B Weiner. 1974. (pbk.) 1.50. Dell.

Morning After Death. Nicholas Blake. (Perennial Library). 1980. 1.95 (ISBN 0-06-080520-X). Harper & Row.

Morning After Death: By Nicholas Blake. 1st Ed. Cecil Day-Lewis. LC 66-22042. 1966. bds., 4.95. Harper.

Morning Always Comes. Donna K. Vitek. (Candlelight Ecstasy Ser.: No. 87). (Orig.). 1982. pap. 1.95 (ISBN 0-440-16185-1). Dell.

Morning & Triumph. Rebecca Drury. (Women at War Ser.: No. 1). (Orig.). 1982. pap. 2.95 (ISBN 0-440-05478-8, Banbury). Dell.

Morning at Jalna. Mazo De La Roche. LC 60-13487. (Fawcett crest book). 1975. (pbk.) 1.25. Fawcett.

Morning at Jalna. Mazo De La Roche. (Jalna Ser.). 1978. pap. 1.75 (ISBN 0-449-23712-5, Crest). Fawcett.

Morning at the Office. Edgar Mittelholzer. (Caribbean Writers Ser.). 1974. pap. text ed. 4.50x (ISBN 0-435-98594-9). Heinemann Ed.

Morning Comes Early. Kathleen Coyle. LC 34-8056. 1934. E. P Dutton & Co. Inc.

Morning Cool. Mary Elizabeth Rhyne Witherspoon. LC 76-158164. 1972. 7.95. Macmillan.

Morning Face. Mulk Raj Anand. 571p. 1980. pap. 5.75 (ISBN 0-86578-062-5). Ind-US Inc.

Morning Face. Mulk Raj Anand. 571p. 1974. 11.50 o.p. (ISBN 0-88253-461-0). InterCulture.

Morning Flight. Paul Hutchens. LC 44-5095. 1944. Wm. B. Erdmans Publishing Company.

Morning for Mr. Prothero: A Novel. Jane Oliver, pseud. LC 51-10163. 1951. McKay.

Morning Glory. Natalie King. (YA) 1973. 4.50 o.p. (Avalon). Bouregy.

Morning Glory. Natalie King. (Avalon romances). 1973. 4.50. Avalon Books.

Morning Glory. Lucy Poate Stebbins. LC 36-9690. The Penn Publishing Company.

Morning Glory. Wildie Thayer. 1897. Press of the Morning Star.

Morning Glory Club. George Alexander Kyle. LC 7-12001. 1907. L. C. Page and Company.

Morning in America. Willard Wiener. LC 42-28671. 1942. Farrar & Rinehart, Inc.

Morning in Antibes: A Novel. John Knowles. LC 62-7519. 1962. Macmillan.

Morning in Gascony. Jay William Hudson. LC 35-4799. 1935. D. Appleton-Century Company, Incorporated.

Morning in Kansas. 1st Ed. Kenneth Sydney Davis. LC 52-10045. 1952. Doubleday.

Morning in Mazatlan. 1st Ed. Richard Willis. LC 55-12186. Pageant Pres.

Morning in Queensland. Margaret Lucas Trist. LC 58-11127. 1958. Lippincott.

Morning in Shanghai. Zhou Erfu. Tr. by A. C. Barnes from Chinese. 654p. 1981. text ed. 11.95 (ISBN 0-8351-0920-8). China Bks.

Morning in the Land. Jessica Nelson North MacDonald. LC 41-3334. The Greystone Press.

Morning in Trinidad. Edgar Mittelholzer. LC 50-7594. 1950. Doubleday.

Morning Is for Joy. Ruth L. Hill, pseud. 1976. Repr. of 1949 ed. lib. bdg. 14.65x (ISBN 0-89190-254-6). Am Repr-Rivercity Pr.

Morning Is for Joy. Ruth L. Hill, pseud. 2.95 o.p. (ISBN 0-448-05245-8). G&D.

Morning Is for Joy. Ruth Livingston Hill Munce. LC 61-65580. 1950. Grosset & Dunlap.

Morning Is for Joy. Ruth Livingston Hill Munce. LC 75-33331. 1975. 9.95 (ISBN 0-89190-254-6). American Reprint Co.

Morning Is for Joy. Ruth Livingston Hill Munce. LC 49-4977. 1949. J.B. Lippincott Co.

Morning Is Near Us: A Novel. Susan Glaspell. LC 40-270784. 1940. Frederick A. Stokes Company.

Morning Journey. James Hilton. LC 51-9261. 1951. Little, Brown.

Morning Light. Curtis L. Johnson. LC 76-50958. (Illus.). 5.00 (ISBN 0-914140-02-7). Carpenter Press.

Morning Light. Kathleen Thompson Norris. LC 52-10053. 1950. Doubleday.

Morning Light (Lige Mounts: Free Trapper) Frank Bird Linderman. LC 30-269463. The John Day Company.

Morning Light: The Islanders in the Days of Oak and Hemp. Henry Major Tomlinson. LC 47-4559. ("Copyright 1946."). 1947. Macmillan Co.

Morning Line. Don Meredith. 208p. 1980. pap. 2.25 (ISBN 0-380-75689-7, 75689). Avon.

Morning News. Cynthia Trembly. 1977. pap. 1.00 (ISBN 0-89924-005-4). Lynx Hse.

Morning, Noon and Night. Kenneth Phillips Britton. LC 27-8148. 1927. E.V. Mitchell.

Morning Noon & Night. James G. Cozzens. LC 68-20064. 1968. 5.95 o.p. (ISBN 0-15-162160-8). HarBraceJ.

Morning Noon & Night. James Gould Cozzens. LC 68-20064. 1968. 5.95 o.p. (ISBN 0-15-162160-8). HarBraceJ.

Morning, Noon, and Night: A Novel. Lars Lawrence. LC 54-10485. (His The seed, v. 1). 1954. Putnam.

Morning, Noon, and Night: A Novel. Philip Stevenson. LC 54-10485. 1954. Putnam.

Morning of a Hero: A Novel. Burke Boyce. LC 63-16523. 1963. Harper & Row.

Morning of Life. Kristmann Gudmundsson. Tr. by Sprigge, Elizabeth. LC 36-894253. 1936. Doubleday, Doran & Company, Inc.

Morning of the Magicians. Louis Pauwels & Jacques Bergier. 1964. 6.95 o.p. (ISBN 0-8128-1117-8). Stein & Day.

Morning of to-Day. Florence Bone. LC 7-33594. Eaton & Mains.

Morning Passage. Janine P. Vega. Ed. by Maureen Owen. LC 76-19056. (Illus., Orig.). 1977. pap. 1.50 o.p. (ISBN 0-916382-15-X); signed copy 10.00. Telephone Bks.

Morning Red: A Romance. Frederick Feikema Manfred. LC 56-14354. 1956. A. Swallow.

Morning Shows the Day. Evelyn Bolster. LC 40-273022. The Vanguard Press.

Morning Shows the Day. Helen Rose Hull. LC 34-28459. Coward-McCann, Inc.

Morning Song. Dorshka Raphaelson. LC 48-7052. 1948. Random House.

Morning Star. Catherina N. Bruno. 3.00 o.p. Carlton.

Morning Star. with three illustrations by a. c. michael. ed. Henry Rider Haggard. LC 10-13219. 1910. 1.50. Longmans, Green, and Co.

Morning Star. Ada Negri. Tr. by Day, Anne. LC 30-25162. 1930. The Macmillan Company.

Morning Star. Dorothy Quentin. 1945. Arcadia House, Inc.

Morning Star. Marian McCamy Sims. LC 34-33131. J. B. Lippincott Company.

Morning Star. Lorol E. Toy. 116p. 1959. 3.00 o.s.i. (ISBN 0-910348-05-7). Channel Pub.

Morning Star: A Novel. James Lansdale Hodson. LC 52-9995. 1952. Simon and Schuster.

Morning Star, Evening Star: Tales of Outback Australia. Donald Stuart. LC 74-169331. 1973. 4.25 (ISBN 0-85585-492-8). Georgian House.

Morning Star Is Mine. Sarah H. Pressly. 4.95 o.p. Vantage.

Morning Thunder. Nalbro Isadorah Bartley. LC 27-16472. George H. Doran Company.

Morning Tide. Neil Miller Gunn. LC 31-26577. Harcourt, Brace and Company.

Morning Time: A Novel. Charles Kendall O'Neill. LC 49-107721. 1949. Simon and Schuster.

Morning Twilight. Christine De Rivoyre. LC 75-80424. 1969. 4.95 o.p. (ISBN 0-395-07603-X). HM.

Morning Twilight. Christine De Rivoyre. LC 75-80424. 1969. 4.95. Houghton Mifflin.

Morning Watch. James Agee. LC 51-1831. 1951. Houghton Mifflin.

Morning Watch. James Agee. (Bard Book). 1976. (pbk.) 1.50 (ISBN 0-380-00569-7). Avon Books.

Morning, Winter, and Night. John Nairne Michaelson & Alfred Charles Michaud. LC 52-8650. 1952. Sloane.

Morning's at Seven. Mae Foster Jay. LC 31-28455. W. A. Wilde Company.

Morning's at Seven: A Novel. Eric Lawson Malpass. LC 66-11351. 1966. bds., 3.95. Viking.

Morning's Come Singing. James Facos. 1967. 3.00 o.p. (ISBN 0-8059-0091-8). Dorrance.

Morning's War: A Romance. Charles Edward Montague. LC 13-19933. 1913. 1.35. H. Holt and Company.

Morningside Heights. Mason Woolford. LC 36-14624. Thomas Y. Crowell Company.

Moroccan. C. A Haddad. LC 75-6367. 1975. 7.95 (ISBN 0-06-011712-5). Harper & Row.

Moroni's Message. Warren Barr Knox. LC 72-95570. 1973. 4.95 (ISBN 0-8059-1804-3). Dorrance.

Morphine. A Tale of the Present Day. Jean Louis Dubut De Laforest. LC 6-34628. (world library, no. 11). 1891. The Waverly Company.

Morphine Tablet. George Wesley Davis. LC 14-21198. 1.00. W. F. Brainard.

Morphodite. M. A. Foster. (Science Fiction Ser.). 1981. pap. 2.75 (ISBN 0-87997-669-1, U E 1669). DAW Bks.

Morrina: Homesickness. Pardo Bazan, Emilia. Tr. by Serrano, Mary Jane (Christie) LC 7-35610. Cassell Publishing Company.

Morris Julian's Wife: A Novel. Annie Elizabeth Loomis. (choice series. no. 64). (Ledger library. no. 64). 1892. R. Bonner's Sons.

Morry: A Portrait of a Lawyer. Robert Elson. LC 24-23491. Small, Maynard & Company.

Mort Artu: An Old French Prose Romance of the XIIIth Century, Being the Last Division of "Lancelot Du Lac". Ed. by James Douglas Bruce. Paris. Bibliotheque Nationale. LC 75-178546. 1974. 18.00 (ISBN 0-404-56649-9). AMS Press.

Mortal Affair. Stella Allan. LC 79-12826. 1979. 8.95 (ISBN 0-684-16230-X). Scribner.

Mortal Antipathy. Oliver Wendell Holmes. LC 70-96887. 1969. Literature House.

Mortal Antipathy, First Opening of the New Portfolio. 5th ed. Oliver Wendell Holmes. LC 34-37775. 1886. Houghton, Mifflin and Company.

Mortal, Be Proud; a Novel. Pendleton Hogan. LC 39-1639. I. Washburn, Inc.

Mortal Coil and Other Stories. David Herbert Lawrence. LC 72-188231. 1971. 0.30 (ISBN 0-14-003264-9). Penguin.

Mortal Coils. Aldous Leonard Huxley. LC 22-152153. George H. Doran Company.

Mortal Encounter. Patricia Sargent. LC 78-62040. 1979. 2.25 (ISBN 0-380-41509-7). Avon.

Mortal Engines. Stanislaw Lem. LC 76-54758. (Continuum book). 1977. 9.95 (ISBN 0-8164-9296-4). Seabury Press.

Mortal Flesh. Gilbert Phelps. LC 73-20596. 1974. 5.95 (ISBN 0-394-49147-5). Random House.

Mortal Friends. James Carroll. 1979. 2.75 (ISBN 0-440-15789-7). Dell Pub. Co.

Mortal Friends: A Novel. James Carroll. LC 78-1420. 9.95 (ISBN 0-316-13009-5). Little, Brown.

Mortal Gods. Maurice Dolbier. LC 79-144378. 1971. 5.95. Dial Press.

Mortal Gods: A Novel. Jonathan East. (Signet book). 1979. 1.75 (ISBN 0-451-08573-6). New American Library.

Mortal Gods: A Novel. Jonathan Fast. LC 77-15901. 8.95 (ISBN 0-06-011266-2). Harper & Row.

Mortal Hunger; a Novel Based on the Life of Lafcadio Hearn. Harry Ezekiel Wedeck. LC 47-30403. 1947. Sheridan House.

Mortal Immortals. Cristabel, pseud. LC 75-149306. 1971. 5.95 (ISBN 0-8027-5538-0). Walker.

Mortal Instruments. T. Ernesto Bethancourt, pseud. 160p. (gr. 8 up). 1979. pap. 1.75 (ISBN 0-553-11752-1). Bantam.

Mortal Leap. Macdonald Harris. LC 64-11141. 1964. Norton.

Mortal Lips. Willis Steell. LC 8-13425. (On cover: The Belford American novel series, no. 27). 1890. Belford Company.

Mortal Love: A Novel of Eleanor of Aquitaine. Linda Hutchins. LC 79-7866. 1980. 10.95 (ISBN 0-385-15076-8). Doubleday.

Mortal Men. Burnham Carter. LC 29-12493. 1929. A. & C. Boni.

Mortal Passion. George Mikes. LC 66-33114. 1966. bds., 4.00. A. Deutsch.

Mortal Passion: A Novel. George Mikes. 4.00x o.p. British Bk Ctr.

Mortal Spring. Francisco Umbral. LC 80-7946. 9.95 (ISBN 0-15-162338-4). Harcourt Brace Jovanovich.
Mortal Stakes. Robert B. Parker. LC 75-20273. (Midnight novel of suspense). 1975. 6.95 (ISBN 0-395-21969-8). Houghton Mifflin.
Mortal Stakes. Robert B. Parker. LC 75-42204. 1976. 9.95 (ISBN 0-8161-6339-1). G. K. Hall.
Mortal Stakes. Robert B Parker. (Berkley Medallion Book.). 1977. 1.50. (ISBN 0-425-03311-2). Berkley Pub. Corp.
Mortal Stakes. Robert B. Parker. LC 79-14985. 1979. 10.95 (ISBN 0-89340-219-2). J. Curley.
Mortal Storm. Phyllis Bottome. LC 38-27226. 1938. Little, Brown and Company.
Mortal Storm. Phyllis Bottome. LC 42-347359. 1938. Penguin Books Limited.
Mortal Wound. Raffaele LaCapria. LC 63-16470. 1964. Farrar, Straus.
Mortdecai's Endgame. Kyril Bonfiglioli. LC 72-93504. 1973. 6.95 (ISBN 0-671-21482-9). Simon and Schuster.
Morte Darthur. Thomas Malory & Charles Richard Sanders. LC 78-6453. 1978. 7.95 (ISBN 0-89197-308-7). Irvington Publishers.
Morte Darthur. Thomas Malory & Charles Richard Sanders. LC 78-6453. 1979. 8.95 (ISBN 0-89197-308-7). Irvington Publishers.
Morte D'Arthur: King Arthur & the Knights of the Round Table. Thomas Malory. Tr. by Keith Baines. (Orig.). 1962. pap. 3.95 (ISBN 0-451-62220-0, ME6220, Ment). NAL.
Morte Darthur, Parts Seven and Eight. Thomas Malory. Ed. by Derek Stanley Brewer. LC 68-22420. (York medieval texts). 1968. 5.00. Northwestern University Press.
Morte D'Urban. James Farl Powers. LC 62-15893. 1962. Doubleday.
Morte D'Urban. James Farl Powers. LC 79-7458. 1979. 2.95 (ISBN 0-394-74135-8). Vintage Books.
Mortgage on Life. Vicki Baum. LC 48-10571. 1948. Triangle Books.
Mortgage on Life. Vicki Baum. LC 46-7454. 1946. Doubleday & Company, Inc.
Mortgage on the Hip-Roof House. Albion Winegar Tourgee. LC 8-29846. 1896. Curts & Jennings.
Mortgage on the Moon. Peggy Gaddis, pseud. LC 40-296465. 1940. Arcadia House, Nc.
Mortgage Your Heart. Sophus Keith Winther. LC 37-1527. 1937. The Macmillan Company.
Mortgage Your Heart. Sophus Keith Winther. LC 78-15857. (Scandinavians in America). 1979. 23.00 (ISBN 0-405-11665-9). Arno Press.
Mortgaged Heart: The Previously Uncollected Writings of Carson McCullers. Carson Smith McCullers. Ed. by Margarita Smith. 1971. 7.95 o.p. (ISBN 0-395-10953-1). HM.
Mortgaged Venus. Aethur Ramsey. (Orig.). pap. 0.95 o.p. (1113). Brandon.
Mortimer Brice, a Bit of His Life. Robert Smythe Hichens. LC 32-257301. 1932. Doubleday, Doran & Company, Inc.
Mortissimo. P. E. H Durston. (Dell book). 1973. 1.25. Dell Publishing Co.
Mortissimo. P. E. H Durston. LC 67-22676. 1967. Random House.
Mortlake. Griffin Taylor. LC 60-8294. 1960. Houghton Mifflin.
Mortmain. H C Asterley. LC 32-6659. Sears Publishing Company, Inc.
Mortmain. Arthur Cheney Train. LC 7-33597. 1907. D. Appleton and Company.
Mortmain, a Romance. Mary Lucy Pendered. LC 28-28487. 1928. G. P. Putnam's Sons.
Morton Montagu: Or, A Young Christian's Choice. A Narrative Founded on Facts in the Early History of a Deceased Moravian Missionary Clergyman. Charlotte B Mortimer. LC 7-26099. 1850. D. Appleton & Company.
Morton's Hope: Or, The Memoirs of a Provincial... John Lothrop Mottey. LC 7-3033. 1839. Harper & Brothers.
Mortover Grange Affair. Joseph Smith Fletcher. LC 27-7728. 1927. A. A. Knopf.
Morwenna. Anne Goring. LC 75-9481. 8.95. St. Martin's Press.
Morwenna. Anne Goring. 1977. 1.95. (ISBN 0-445-08604-1). Popular Library.
Morwyn: Or, The Vengeance of God. John Cowper Powys. LC 75-46301. (Supernatural & Occult Fiction). 1976. 18.00 (ISBN 0-405-08161-8). Arno Press.
Mosaic. Gladys Skelton. LC 29-16665. 1929. D. Appleton and Company.
Mosaic. Gladys Bronwyn Stern. LC 30-26995. 1930. A. A. Knopf.
Mosaic Earring. Nell Columbia Boyer Martin. LC 43-27910. 1927. International Fiction Library.
Mosaic Workers; a Tale of Venice. Tr. from the French of George Sand. George Sand. 1845. E. Ferrett & Co.
Mosby's Last Ride. Ray Hogan. (Orig.). 1966. pap. 0.50 o.p. (50-296). Manor Bks.
Mosby's Memoirs and Other Stories. Saul Bellow. LC 77-1607. 1977. 1.95 (ISBN 0-14-004524-4). Penguin Books.
Moscow. Nick Carter. (Nick Carter Ser.). (O.s.i.). (Orig.). 1970. pap. 0.95 o.s.i. (AN1091, Award). Univ Pub & Dist.
Moscow: A Novel Translated from the German by Stuart Hood. Theodor Plivier. LC 54-16665. 1953. F. Muller.
Moscow: A Story of the French Invasion of 1812. Frederick J. Whishaw. LC 6-11311. 1905. Longmans, Green, and Co.
Moscow at Noon Is the Target. Paul Richards. (Hot Line Ser.). (O.s.i.). 192p. (Orig.). 1973. pap. 0.95 o.s.i. (AN1110, Award). Univ Pub & Dist.
Moscow by Nightmare. Joyce L Shub. LC 72-94116. 1973. 5.95 (ISBN 0-698-10527-3). Coward, McCann & Geoghegan.
Moscow by Nightmare. Joyce L Shub. 1975. (pbk.) 0.95. Dell.
Moscow Coach: A Commander Shaw Novel. 1st Amer. Ed. Philip McCutchan. LC 66-22928. 1966. 4.50. John Day.
Moscow Farewell. George Feifer. LC 75-28266. 1976. 10.00 (ISBN 0-670-48985-9). Viking Press.
Moscow Five Thousand. David Grant, pseud. LC 79-14183. 408p. 1979. 10.95 (ISBN 0-03-046680-6). HR&W.
Moscow in Flames. Grigovii Petrovich Danilevskii. Tr. by Rappoport, Angelo S. LC 17-31035. 1917. Brentano's.
Moscow Intercept. Harry Arvay. 1975. (pbk.) 1.25. Bantam.
Moscow Interlude: A Novel. Charles Wheeler Thayer. LC 62-7901. 1962. Harper.
Moscow Mists. Clarissa Ross, pseud. LC 76-52901. 1977. 1.95 (ISBN 0-380-00912-9). Avon Books.
Moscow Nights. Vlas Tenin. Tr. by Michel Le Masque from Rus. LC 70-186227. 288p. 1972. 6.95 o.s.i. Olympia.
Moscow Option: An Alternative Second World War. David Downing. LC 79-21723. (Illus.). 9.95 (ISBN 0-312-54891-5). St. Martin's Press.
Moscow Papers. John Manchip White. 1979. pap. 1.95 (ISBN 0-89041-235-9, 3235). Major Bks.
Moscow Quadrille. Ted Allbeury. LC 76-380950. 1976. 3.50 (ISBN 0-432-00425-4). P. Davies.
Moscow Requiem. John Simpson. LC 81-16716. 1982. 10.95 (ISBN 0-312-54902-4). St. Martin's Press.
Moscow Road. Henry Gibbs. 1973. 0.95. Manor Books.
Moscow Road. Henry Gibbs. LC 78-142843. 1971. 4.95 (ISBN 0-8027-5223-3). Walker.
Moscow Road. Simon Harvester. 208p. 1972. pap. 0.95 (ISBN 0-532-95217-0). Woodhill.
Moscow Road. Simon Harvester. 209p. 1983. pap. 2.95 (ISBN 0-8027-3012-4). Walker & Co.
Moscow Road. Simon Harvester. 1971. 4.95 o.p. (ISBN 0-8027-5223-3). Walker & Co.
Moscow Skies. Maurice Gerschon Hindus. LC 36-21006. Random House.
Moscow to the End of the Line. Venedikt Erofeev. LC 79-5169. 1980. 8.95 (ISBN 0-8008-5374-1). Taplinger Pub. Co.
Moscow: Translated from the German by Stuart Hood. 1st Ed. Theodor Plivier. LC 54-5712. 1954. Doubleday.
Moscow Yankee. Dorothy Myra Page. LC 35-4723. G. P. Putnam's Sons.
Moscow 1979. Erik Maria Von Kuhnelt-Leddihn & Kuhnelt-Leddihn, Christiane Von. LC 40-33587. 1940. Sheed & Ward.
Moscow, 1979. A New and Rev. Ed. Erik Maria Kuhnelt-Leddihn & Kuhnelt-Leddihn, Christiane Von, Joint Author. LC 46-860794. 1946. Sheed & Ward.
Moscow 5000. Craig Thomas. LC 78-14183. 9.95 (ISBN 0-03-046680-6). Holt, Rinehart, and Winston.
Mose Evans: A Simple Statement of the Singular Facts of His Case. William Mumford Baker. LC 6-6866. 1874. Hurd & Houghton.
Moses: A Novel. Louis Untermeyer. LC 28-21887. 1928. Harcourt, Brace and Company.
Moses and the Ten Commandments: By Paul Ilton and MacLennan Roberts. Paul Ilton & MacLennan Roberts. LC 56-12480. (Dell first edition, B105). 1956. Dell Pub. Co.
Moses: Man of the Mountain. Zora Neale Hurston. LC 39-30532. J. B. Lippincott Company.
Moses, Man of the Mountain. Zora Neale Hurston. 351p. 1975. Repr. of 1939 ed. 9.50x (ISBN 0-911860-45-2). Chatham Bkseller.
Moses the Lawgiver. Thomas Keneally. LC 75-9322. (Illus.). 12.00 (ISBN 0-06-064773-6). Harper & Row.
Moses the Man. Lawrence Alloway. LC 51-3717. 1951. Vantage Press.
Moses, the Near Eastener: A Novel. Leon Kolb. LC 56-41004. 1956. Genuart Co.
Moses: Translated by Maurice Samuel. Shalom Asch. LC 51-12035. 1951. Putnam.
Moses Wine in the Big Fix. Roger Lichtenberg Simon. (O.s.i.). pap. 3.00 o.s.i. (Straight Arrow). S&S.
Mosquito Coast. Paul Theroux. LC 82-138042. 1981. 3.95 (ISBN 0-241-10688-5). Hamish Hamilton.
Mosquito Coast. Paul Theroux. 416p. 1982. 13.95 (ISBN 0-395-31837-8); text ed. 50.00 ltd. Ed. (ISBN 0-395-32075-5). HM.
Mosquito Coast. Paul Theroux. 384p. 1983. pap. 3.95 (ISBN 0-380-61945-8, 61945-8). Avon.
Mosquito Coast: A Novel. Paul Theroux. LC 81-6787. 1982. 14.95 (ISBN 0-395-31837-8). Houghton Mifflin.
Mosquitoes. William Faulkner. LC 27-10732. 1927. Boni and Liveright.
Moss, Mallards, and Mules, and Other Hunting and Fishing Stories. Bob Brister. LC 73-78819. (Illus.). 1973. 8.95 (ISBN 0-87691-113-0). Winchester Press.
Moss Mystery. Carolyn Wells. LC 24-7321. (Famous authors series. no. 43). 1924. Garden City Publishing Co., Inc.
Moss on the North Side. Sylvia Wilkinson. LC 66-18621. 1966. Houghton Mifflin.
Moss Rose. Joseph Shearing. LC 35-1942. 1935. H. Smith and R. Haas.
Moss Rose. Day Taylor, pseud. 1980. pap. 2.75 (ISBN 0-440-15969-5). Dell.
Moss Troopers. Samuel Rutherford Crockett. LC 13-63072. 1912. Hodder and Stoughton.
Mosses from an Old Manse. Nathaniel Hawthorne. LC 79-122717. (Short story index reprint series). (Illus.). 1970. Books for Libraries Press.
Mosses from an Old Manse. new ed., carefully rev. by the author. ed. Nathaniel Hawthorne. LC 24-27966. 1857. Ticknor and Fields.
Mosses from an Old Manse. Nathaniel Hawthorne. LC 9-8359. (Half-title: Riverside ed. The complete works of Nathaniel Hawthorne... vol. ii). 1892. Houghton, Mifflin and Company.
Mosses from an Old Manse. Nathaniel Hawthorne. LC 4-15453. (Half-title: Riverside ed. The complete works of Nathaniel Hawthorne, with introductory notes, by G. P. Lathrop... vol. ii). Houghton, Mifflin and Company.
Mosses from an Old Manse. Nathaniel Hawthorne. LC 4581. W. B. Conkey Company.
Mosses from an Old Manse. Nathaniel Hawthorne & Katherine Lee Bates. LC 4715. T. Y. Crowell & Co.
Most Auspicious Star. Suzanne Evel. (Fawcett gold medal book). 1975. (pbk.) 0.95. Fawcett.
Most Beautiful Girls in the World. Russell O'Neil. LC 78-113820. 1970. 6.95. McKay.
Most Beautiful Lady: A Mystery. Dorothea Thompson Brande. LC 35-5369. Farrar & Rinehart, Incorporated.
Most Contagious Game. Catherine Aird, pseud. LC 67-23570. 1967. Published for the Crime Club by Doubleday.
Most Contagious Game. 1st Ed. Samuel Grafton. LC 55-647869. 1955. Doubleday.
Most Dangerous Game. Clifton Adams. (O.s.i.). (Orig.). pap. 0.60 o.s.i. (A378, Award). Univ Pub & Dist.
Most Dangerous Game. Gavin Lyall. LC 63-19874. 1963. Scribner.
Most Dangerous Profession. Clifton Adams. LC 67-19129. (Double D western). 1967. Doubleday.
Most Dangerous Profession. 1st Ed. Clifton Adams. LC 67-19129. (Double D western). 1967. 3.95. Doubleday.
Most Deadly Hate. Harry Carmichael. 1974. 5.95 o.p. (ISBN 0-8415-0291-9). Dutton.
Most Deadly Hate. Leopold Horace Ognall. LC 73-16793. 1974. 5.95 (ISBN 0-8415-0291-9). Saturday Review Press.
Most Difficult Area. Kenneth White. LC 68-27529. (Cape Goliard Poetry Ser). 1968. 4.00 o.p. (ISBN 0-670-48998-0, Grossma). Viking Pr.
Most Eloquent Music. Marion Naismith. (Signet book). 1975. (pbk.) 0.95. New American Library.
Most Famous Loba: A Romance. Nellie K Blissett. LC 1-24185. (Half-title: Appletons' town and country library, no. 305). 1901. D. Appleton and Company.
Most Grievous Murder. Sara Woods, pseud. LC 82-5779. 10.95 (ISBN 0-312-54908-3). St. Martin's Press.
Most Happy Con Man. John P Radford. (Illusionist,#1). 1974. (pbk.) 1.50 (ISBN 0-89014-102-9). Canyon Books.
Most Immoral Murder. Harriette Ashbrook. LC 35-156179. Coward-McCann.
Most Likely to Succeed. John Dos Passos. LC 54-8476. 1954. Prentice-Hall.
Most Likely to Succeed. Dos Passos, John. LC 66-17513. 1966. Houghton Mifflin.
Most Loving Mere Folly. Paul Bloomfield. LC 23-12752. 1923. Hodder and Stonghton, Ltd.
Most Men Don't Kill. David Alexander. LC 51-10103. 1951. Random House.
Most of A. J. Liebling. Abbott J. Liebling. (O.s.i.). pap. 2.45 o.s.i. (ISBN 0-671-20487-4, Touchstone Bks). S&S.
Most of P. G. Wodehouse. P. G. Wodehouse. 1960. 12.95 o.p. (ISBN 0-671-49325-6). S&S.
Most of P. G. Wodehouse. P. G. Wodehouse. 1969. pap. 3.95 (ISBN 0-671-20349-5, Fireside). S&S.
Most Precious Moments: All of Life Is One Long Chapter. Jezebelle. LC 73-81156. 1973. 4.50. Nuclassics and Science Pub. Co.
Most Private Intrigue. Leo Calvin Rosten. (Crest bk., t1116). 1968. Fawcett.
Most Private Intrigue. By Leo Rosten. 1st Ed. Leo Calvin Rosten. LC 67-14331. 1967. 5.95. Atheneum.
Most Probable World. Stuart Chase. pap. 1.45 o.p. (ISBN 0-14-021098-9, A1098, Pelican). Penguin.
Most Romantic City. Mary Ann Gibbs, pseud. LC 76-11819. 1976. 7.95 (ISBN 0-88405-376-8). Mason/Charter.
Most Romantic City. Mary Ann Gibbs, pseud. (Fawcett Crest Book). 1977. 1.50. Fawcett Pubns.
Most Romantic City. Mary Ann Gibbs, pseud. LC 78-6960. 1978. 9.95 (ISBN 0-8161-6583-1). G. K. Hall.
Most Sacred of All: A Novel. Jeffery Farnol. LC 48-8471. 1948. R.M. McBride.
Most Savage Animal. Hugh Atkinson. LC 71-139615. 1973. 8.95 (ISBN 0-671-20817-9). Simon and Schuster.
Most Secret. John Dickson Carr. LC 64-25125. 1964. Harper & Row.
Most Secret. Nevil Shute Norway. LC 45-8649. 1945. W. Morrow and Company.
Most Secret. Nevil Shute. 310p. 1976. Repr. of 1945 ed. lib. bdg. 16.50x (ISBN 0-89244-084-8). Queens Hse.
Most Secret, Most Immediate. Howard Swiggett. LC 44-3682. 1944. Houghton Mifflin Company.
Most Unholy Trade. Henry James. 1982. lib. bdg. 42.50. Porter.
Most Women. Waugh, Alec. LC 31-28043. Farrar & Rinehart, Incorporated.
Mostly by Moonlight. easy eye ed. Dorothy Daniels. 1968. pap. 0.60 o.p. (73-795). Lancer.
Mostly Canallers: Collected Stories. Walter Dumaux Edmonds. LC 34-2901. 1934. Little, Brown, and Company.
Mostly Fools: A Romance of Civilization Mostly Fools. Edmund Randolph. LC 75-461. (Victorian Fiction: Novels of Faith and Doubt). 1976. 40.00 (ISBN 0-8240-1539-8). Garland Pub.
Mostly Marjorie Day. Virginia Frances Townsend. LC 8-29819. 1892. Lee and Shepard.
Mostly Murder: Eighteen Stories. 1st Ed. Fredric Brown. LC 53-5207. (Guilt edged mystery). 1953. Dutton.
Mostly Sally. Pelham Grenville Wodehouse. LC 23-6753. George H. Doran Company.
Mostly Sally. Pelham Grenville Wodehouse. LC 35-285603. 1924. A. L. Burt Company.
Mostly Womenfolk and a Man or Two: A Collection. Mignon Holland Anderson. LC 77-353461. 2.95 (ISBN 0-88378-075-5). Third World Press.
Mote and the Beam. Percy Winner. LC 48-6124. 1948. Harcourt, Brace.
Mote and the Beam: A Romance of Two Egotists. Pauline Stiles. LC 30-17706. 1930. Doubleday, Doran & Company, Inc.
Mote House Mystery. Archibald Marshall & Vachell, Horace Annesley. LC 26-633672. 1926. Dodd, Mead and Company.
Mote in God's Eye. Larry Niven & Jerry Pournelle. 576p. 1982. pap. 3.50 (ISBN 0-671-45618-0). PB.
Mote in Time's Eye. Gerard Klein. 1975. (pbk.) 1.25. Daw Books.
Motel of the Mysteries. David Macauley. 1979. 8.95 (ISBN 0-395-28424-4); pap. 4.95 (ISBN 0-395-28425-2). HM.
Motel Tapes. Mike McGrady. 1977. 1.95 (ISBN 0-446-89332-3). Warner Books.
Motel Tramp. Mark S Wolin. 1974. (pbk.) 1.95 (ISBN 0-87682-388-6). Barclay House.
Moth. James Mallahan Cain. LC 48-2901. 1948. A. A. Knopf.
Moth. Joy Carroll. 1974. (pbk.) 1.25. Dell.
Moth: A Novel. William Dana Orcutt. LC 12-187931. 1912. 1.30. Harper & Brothers.
Moth and Rust. Stephen Paul Sheffield. LC 8-5090. 1869. The Sun Job Printing House.
Moth and Rust: And Other Stories. Mary Cholmondeley. LC 2-24924. 1902. Dodd, Mead & Company.
Moth & Rust & Other Stories. facsimile ed. Mary Cholmondeley. LC 71-101794. (Short Story Index Reprint Ser.). 1902. 16.00 (ISBN 0-8369-3182-3). Ayer Co.
Moth. Authorized Abridgment. James Mallahan Cain. LC 50-35210. (Signet book, 811). 1950. New American Library.
Moth Decides: A Novel. Edward Alden Jewell. LC 22-19484. 1922. A. A. Knopf.
"Moth" Murder. Lynton Blow. LC 32-13200. 1932. H. Holt and Company.

Moth of Time: A Novel. Nolan Miller. LC 46-46063. 1946. Harper & Brothers.
Mother. Shalom Asch. LC 73-114047. 1970. AMS Press.
Mother. Shalom Asch & Ausubel, Nathan, Tr. LC 30-25746. 1930. H. Liveright.
Mother. Shalom Asch & Krauch, Elsa, Tr. LC 37-287393. 1937. G. P. Putnam's Sons.
Mother. Pearl Sydenstricker Buck. LC 34-807. The John Day Company.
Mother. Grazia Deledda. LC 74-173633. 1974. 7.95 (ISBN 0-910220-57-3). N. S. Berg.
Mother. Grazia Deledda. Tr. by Steegmann, Mary G. LC 23-16660. 1923. The Macmillan Company.
Mother. Grazia Deledda. LC 82-13995. 1982. 16.00 (ISBN 0-89783-022-9). Larlin Corp.
Mother. Norman Duncan. LC 5-29106. F. H. Revell Company.
Mother. Jules Eckert Goodman. LC 11-2975. 1911. 1.20. Dodd, Mead and Company.
Mother. Maksim Gorkii. LC 21-19767. 1921. D. Appleton and Company.
Mother. Maksim Gorkii. Tr. by Isidore Schneider. 1972. pap. 4.95 (ISBN 0-8065-0275-4, C338). Citadel Pr.
Mother. Maksim Gorkii. Tr. by Margaret Wettlin. (Soviet Authors' Library Ser.). (Illus.). 1976. Repr. of 1949 ed. 4.40 (ISBN 0-8285-8080-4, Pub. by Progress Pubs USSR). Imported Pubns.
Mother. Maksim Gorkii & Schneider, Isidor, 1898- Tr. LC 47-11296. 1947. Citadel Press.
Mother. Bernice Kavinoky. LC 58-6254. 1958. Rinehart.
Mother. Hector Henri Malot & Schonberg, James, Tr. LC 7-24361. (On cover: The Belford American novel series. v. 2, no. 6). 1890. Belford Company.
Mother. Kathleen Thompson Norris. Repr. lib. bdg. 12.70x (ISBN 0-89190-308-9). Am Repr-Rivercity Pr.
Mother. Kathleen Thompson Norris. 1970. pap. 0.75 o.p. (ISBN 0-446-64383-1, 64-383). Paperback Lib.
Mother. Naomi Gwladys Royde-Smith. LC 32-955424. 1932. Doubleday, Doran & Company, Inc.
Mother. Yusuke Tsurumi & Beard, Charles Austin, 1874- LC 32-643243. R. D. Henkle.
Mother. Owen Wister. 1907. Dodd, Mead & Company.
Mother: A Novel of the Revolution. Pamela Millward. LC 76-78045. (Writing Ser.: No. 26). 64p. (Orig.). 1970. pap. 2.00 (ISBN 0-87704-015-X). Four Seasons Foun.
Mother, a Story. Kathleen Norris. LC 70-137319. Repr. of 1935 ed. 14.50 (ISBN 0-404-04792-0). AMS Pr.
Mother: A Story. Kathleen Thompson Norris. LC 11-26415. 1911. The Macmillan Company.
Mother: A Story. Kathleen Thompson Norris. LC 22-4732. 1916. Grosset & Dunlap.
Mother: A Story. Kathleen Thompson Norris. LC 33-36227. 1933. Doubleday, Doran & Company, Inc.
Mother and Daughter. Ann Lawrence. LC 34-462. 1934. W. Godwin, Inc.
Mother and Four. Isabel Wilder. LC 33-3280. Coward-McCann, Inc.
Mother and Her Children. A Story for Young Mothers. C. B. Sargetn. LC 8-1814. Presbyterian Board of Publication.
Mother & I. D. Carlisle. 1981. 4.50 (ISBN 0-8062-1028-1). Carlton.
Mother and Son. Ivy Compton-Burnett. LC 55-72621. 1955. J. Messner.
Mother and Son. Clarkson Crane. LC 46-1551. 1946. Harcourt, Brace and Company.
Mother and Son... Romain Rolland & Brooks, Van Wyck, 1886- Tr. LC 27-8281. (His The soul enchanted. III). H. Holt and Company.
Mother and Son: A Brazilian Tale. Gilberto Freyre. LC 67-11135. 1967. Knopf.
Mother and Son: A Novelette. Murray Brown. LC 58-8368. 1958. Chapman & Grimes.
Mother and the Flying Saucer & Other Fables. Mary McDermott Shideler & Charles Sippel. LC 75-30171. (Illus.). 1976. 2.95 (ISBN 0-916226-01-8) (ISBN 0-916226-00-X). Pegana Press.
Mother, Be Careful! Carman Dee Barnes. LC 32-25836. Liveright, Inc.
Mother Cheats Altars, a Novel. 1st Ed. Jose Caden. LC 59-11556. 1959. Greenwich Book Publishers.
Mother, Daughter, Sister, Lover: A Collection of Short Stories Dealing with Woman's Relations to Woman. Jan Clausen. LC 80-16386. (Crossing Press Feminist Ser.). (Orig.). 1980. 13.95 (ISBN 0-89594-034-5); pap. 4.95 (ISBN 0-89594-033-7). Crossing Pr.
Mother Delaney. Genoveva Ansom. LC 41-15431. 1938. Magnificat Press.
Mother Earth & Other Stories. Boris Pilnyak. (Orig.). (YA) (gr. 9-12). 1967. pap. 1.45 o.p. (ISBN 0-385-02815-6, A630, Anch). Doubleday.
Mother Earth & Other Stories. Boris Pilnyak. LC 68-26787. 1968. 6.95 o.p. Praeger.
Mother Earth: And Other Stories by Boris Pilnyak. Tr. from Russian, & Ed. by Vera T. Reck. Michael Green. Boris Andreevich Vogau. LC 68-26787. 1968. 6.95. Praeger.
Mother Finds a Body. Gypsy Rose Lee. LC 42-24237. 1942. Simon and Schuster.
Mother Goddam. Whitney Stine & Betty Davis. (Illus.). 432p. 1982. pap. 2.95 (ISBN 0-425-05394-6). Berkley Pub.
Mother Goose in Spanish. Poesias De la Madre Oca. Tr. by Alastair Reid & Anthony Kerrigan. LC 67-15401. (Illus.). 1968. T. Y. Crowell Co.
Mother Goose in Spanish. Poesias De la Madre Oca Trs. by Alastair Reid, Anthony Kerrigan. Pictures by Barbara Cooney. Mother Goose. Tr. by Alastair Reid & Anthony Kerrigan. LC 67-154018. 1968. 4.15. T. Y. Crowell.
Mother Hunt. Rex Stout. 144p. 1981. pap. 2.25 (ISBN 0-553-20115-8). Bantam.
Mother Hunt: A Nero Wolfe Novel. Rex Stout. LC 63-17070. 1963. Viking Press.
Mother in Exile. LC 14-115295. 1914. Little, Brown, and Company.
Mother in Modern Story. Ed. by Maud Van Buren. Bemis, Katharine Isabel, Joint Ed. LC 28-113206. The Century Co.
Mother Is a Country: A Popular Fantasy. Kathrin Perutz. LC 68-12594. 1967. Harcourt, Brace & World.
Mother Knows Best. Edna Ferber. LC 77-110187. (Short Story Index Reprint Ser.). 1927. 17.00 (ISBN 0-8369-3338-9). Ayer Co.
Mother Knows Best: A Fiction Book. Edna Ferber. LC 77-110187. (Short story index reprint series). (Illus.). 1970. Books for Libraries Press.
Mother Knows Best: A Fiction Book. Edna Ferber. LC 27-9453. 1927. Doubleday, Page & Co.
Mother-Light. David Graham Phillips. (American Author Ser.). 1981. Repr. lib. bdg. 19.00. Scholarly.
Mother-Light. David Graham Phillips. 1905. lib. bdg. 19.25 o.s.i. (ISBN 0-512-00262-2). Garrett Pr.
Mother Love. Richard B. Long. 192p. (Orig.). 1973. pap. 1.95 o.p. (ISBN 0-87682-340-1, 7340). Barclay Hse.
Mother Love. Alberto Moravia. LC 77-363094. 1976. 0.60 (ISBN 0-586-04188-5). Panther.
Mother Lovers. Hal Edwards. 192p. pap. 1.95 o.p. (ISBN 0-87056-156-1, 6156). Brandon.
Mother Loves Best. Keith Rockwell. 192p. (Orig.). 1972. pap. 1.95 o.p. (ISBN 0-87682-286-3, 7286). Barclay Hse.
Mother Luck. Paul Petersen. (Smugglers#4). 1974. (pbk.) 0.95. Pocket Books.
Mother Machree: A Novel. Martin Jerome Scott. LC 22-21772. 1922. The Macmillan Company.
Mother Market. Nancy Burns Brelis. (Harper Trophy book). (Illus.). 1975. (pbk.) 1.50. Harper & Row.
Mother Mary. Heinrich Mann & Chambers, Whittaker, Tr. LC 28-27591. 1928. Simon and Schuster.
Mother Mason. Bess Streeter Aldrich. LC 75-29207. 1975. 6.95. Aeonian Press.
Mother Mason. Bess Streeter Aldrich. 1944. Triangle Books.
Mother Night. Kurt Vonnegut. LC 66-13931. 1966. Harper & Row.
Mother Night. Kurt Vonnegut. 1974. (pbk.) 1.25. Dell.
Mother of a Marquise: And The Aunt's Stratagem. Edmond Francois Valentin About & Kingsbury, Mrs. Carlton A., Tr. LC 5-42613. (On cover: Cassell's sunshine series, no. 104 extra). Cassell Publishing Company.
Mother of All Living: A Novel of Africa. Robert Keable. LC 22-3495. E. P. Dutton & Company.
Mother of Fair Love. Translated from the Spanish by Veronica Kirtland. Agustina Schroeder. LC 57-8934. 1957. Burce Pub. Co.
Mother of Five. Gladys Henrietta Raphael Schutze. LC 34-251553. Minton, Balch & Company.
Mother of Gold. Emerson Hough. LC 24-3532. 1924. D. Appleton and Company.
Mother of Her Country: A Novel. Alan Baer Green. LC 73-5056. 1974. 5.95 (ISBN 0-394-48350-2). Random House.
Mother of Pauline. L. Parry Truscott. LC 4-17924. 1904. D. Appleton and Company.
Mother of Pearl. Anatole France, pseud. LC 70-142262. (Short story index reprint series). 1970. (ISBN 0-8369-3746-5). Books for Libraries Press.
Mother of Pearl. Anatole France, pseud. Tr. by Chapman, Frederic. LC 28-223183. 1925. Dodd, Mead and Company.
Mother of Royalty. 1982. pap. 6.95. Feldheim.
Mother of the Bride. Alice Grant Rosman. LC 36-27335. G. P. Putnam's Sons.
Mother of the Deb: By Petronella Portobello Pseud. With an Epilogue by Compton Mackenzie. Flavia Giffard Anderson. LC 57-115623. 1957. Houghton Mifflin.
Mother of the Groom. Harriet Fitts Ryan. LC 51-12265. (Illus.). 1951. Longmans, Green.
Mother of the Man. Eden Phillpotts. 1908. Dodd, Mead & Company.
Mother of the Smiths. Lorraine Carr. LC 40-272051. 1940. The Macmillan Company.
Mother of the Year. B. B. Johnson. (Superspade Series). pap. 0.75 o.p. (64-343). Paperback Lib.
Mother of Unborn Generations: A Novel. Stuart Kencarden. LC 12-15562. Broadway Publishing Company.
Mother Russia: A Novel. Robert Littell. LC 77-17014. 7.95. Harcourt Brace Jovanovich.
Mother Sea. Felix Riesenberg. LC 33-3926. C. Kendall.
Mother Takes a Sin Trip. Warren Bisig. pap. 1.95 o.p. (ISBN 0-87977-167-4, DBB167). Dansk Blue Bk.
Mother Tongue. Anthony Bailey. LC 61-13990. 1961. Macmillan.
M.O.T.H.E.R. Versus Mafia. Rosemary Santini. (Orig.). 1972. pap. 1.25 o.p. Lancer.
Mother Was a Lovely Beast: A Feral Man Anthology, Fiction and Fact About Humans Raised by Animals. Ed. by Philip Jose Farmer. LC 74-11117. 1974. 6.95 (ISBN 0-8019-5964-0). Chilton Book Co.
Mother Was Always in Love: A Novel. Philip Van Rensselaer. LC 60-9571. 1960. Duell, Sloan and Pearce.
Mother Was Always in Love: A Novel. Philip Van Rensselaer. LC 60-957166. 1960. 3.95. Duell, Sloan and Pearce.
Mother Went Mad on Monday. Ethel Powelson Hueston. LC 44-7515. 1944. The Bobbs-Merrill Company.
Mother West's Neighbors. Jane Dunbar Chaplin. LC 6-23124. 1876. American Tract Society Etc.
Mother, Will and I. Milton Coit. LC 6-25423. 1894. Arena Publishing Company.
Mother You Gave Me. Beatrice Phillips Cole & O-Pee-Chee, Wa-Be-No, Joint Author. LC 41-1972. Haynes Corporation, Printers, C.
Mothering on Perilous. Lucy Furman. LC 13-212651. 1913. The Macmillan Company.
Mothering Sunday. Streatfeild, Noel. LC 50-5890. 1950. Coward-McCann.
Motherland. Gwen Davis. LC 73-20547. 1974. 8.95 (ISBN 0-671-21738-0). Simon and Schuster.
Motherless. Bengt Magnus Kristoffer Berg. Tr. by Stork, Charles Wharton. LC 24-213571. 1924. Doubleday, Page & Company.
Motherlines. Suzy McKee Charnas. LC 77-18862. 8.95. Berkley Pub. Corp.: Distributed by Putnam.
Mothers. Elissa Dale. 1975. (pbk.) 1.50. Dell.
Mothers. Elissa Dale. LC 72-486. 1972. (ISBN 0-13-602870-5). Prentice-Hall.
Mothers. Vardis Fisher. 1976. Repr. of 1943 ed. lib. bdg. 17.15x (ISBN 0-89190-831-5). Am Repr-Rivercity Pr.
Mothers. Vardis Fisher. 1979. 9.95; pap. 4.95 (ISBN 0-918522-55-2). O L Holmes.
Mothers. Vardis Fisher. 1974. pap. cancelled o.p. (ISBN 0-515-03381-2). Pyramid Pubns.
Mothers: A Documentary Novel of the Donner Party. Vardis Fisher. LC 72-94404. 1973. pap. 2.95 o.p. (ISBN 0-8040-0218-5, SB). Swallow.
Mothers: A Novel. Edward Loomis. LC 62-8096. 1962. Viking Press.
Mothers, an American Saga of Courage. Vardis Fisher. LC 43-14815. 1943. The Vanguard Press.
Mothers and Daughters. Evan Hunter. LC 61-960003. 1961. Simon and Schuster.
Mothers and Fathers. Juliet Wilbor Tompkins. LC 10-232056. 1910. The Baker & Taylor Co.
Mothers Cry. Helen Grace Carlisle. LC 30-844. 1930. Harper & Brothers.
Mothers, Daughters. Carolyn See. LC 77-3305. 8.95 (ISBN 0-698-10837-X). Coward, McCann & Geoghegan.
Mothers, Daughters. Carolyn See. 1979. 2.29 (ISBN 0-671-82063-X). Pocket Books.
Mother's Day. Robert Miner. 1979. 1.95 (ISBN 0-671-82513-5). Pocket Books.
Mother's Day. J. M Ryan. LC 69-19109. 1969. 5.95. Prentice-Hall.
Mother's Day: A Novel. Robert Miner. LC 78-1831. 8.95 (ISBN 0-399-90012-8). R. Marek Publishers.
Mother's Helper. Maureen Freely. 1981. pap. 2.95 (ISBN 0-440-15696-3). Dell.
Mother's Helper: A Novel. Maureen Freely. LC 78-31482. 8.95 (ISBN 0-440-05928-3). Delacorte Press.
Mothers in Israel: A Study in Rustic Amenities. Joseph Smith Fletcher. LC 8-19023. 1908. Moffat, Yard & Co.
Mothers-in-Law. Betsey Riddle Hutton Zum Stolzenberg. LC 22-18895. 1922. Cassell and Company, Ltd.
Mothers-in-Laws. Betsey Riddle Hutton Zum Stolzenberg. LC 22-7882. 1.75. George H. Doran Company.
Mother's Kisses. Bruce Jay Friedman. (Cardinal ed., 75077). 1965. Pocket Bks.
Mother's Kisses see Stern.
Mother's Love. Ed. by Gibson Staff. (Illus.). 1970. 2.95 o.p. (ISBN 0-8378-1720-X). Gibson.
Mothers of Men. William Henry Warner & Kaplan, De Witte, Joint Author. LC 19-3997. 1919. T. Scott.
Mother's Recompense. Edith Newbold Jones Wharton. LC 25-8793. 1925. D. Appleton and Company.
Mother's Recompense: A Sequel to Home Influence. Grace Aguilar. LC 37-183053. 1851. D. Appleton & Company.
Mother's Recompense: A Sequel to Home Influence. Grace Aguilar. 1891. D. Appleton and Company.
Mother's Recompense: A Sequel to Home Influence. 39th thousand. ed. Grace Aquilar. 1864. D. Appleton & Company.
Mother's Rule: Or, The Right Way and the Wrong Way. Timothy Shay Arthur. LC 6-3411. T. Bliss & Co.
Mother's Son: A Novel. Beulah Marie Dix. LC 13-22210. 1913. 1.35. H. Holt and Company.
Mother's Special Kiss. William Seeds. 192p. (Orig.). 1973. pap. 1.95 o.p. (ISBN 0-87682-326-6, 7326). Barclay Hse.
Mother's Sweet Thighs. O. R. Bassett. pap. 1.95 o.p. (ISBN 0-87682-252-9, 7252). Barclay Hse.
Mother's Three Daughters. P. L. 1972. pap. 2.25 o.p. (Z1108R, Zebra). Grove.
Mothers to Men. Zona Gale. LC 11-25012. 1911. The Macmillan Company.
Mother's Wages. Elizabeth W. Strachen. (Quiet Time Bks). 1957. pap. 1.25 o.p. (ISBN 0-8024-5670-7). Moody.
Mother's Walter and Walter's Mother: A Story from Incidents of Real Life. Rose Carothers. LC 7-443. The Studio Press Company.
Mothersill and the Foxes. John Alfred Williams. LC 74-9469. 1975. 7.95 (ISBN 0-385-09454-X). Doubleday.
Mothman Prophecies. John Keel. 1975. 7.95 o.p. (ISBN 0-8415-0355-9). Dutton.
Moths. Rosalind Ashe. 1977. 1.95 (ISBN 0-446-89447-8). Warner Books.
Moths. Louise De La Ramee. LC 22-173426. Street & Smith.
Moths. A Novel. Louise De La Ramee. LC 4-31645. 1880. J. B. Lippincott & Co.
Moths in a Rag Shop. Robert Chambers. LC 68-27630. 1968. 4.95. Bobbs-Merrill Co.
Moths of the Limberlost. Gene Stratton Porter. 1980. Repr. lib. bdg. 18.95 (ISBN 0-89967-042-3). Harmony Raine.
Motion and the Act: A Novel. Jeanne Rejaunier. LC 72-81837. 1972. 7.95 (ISBN 0-8402-1262-3). Nash Pub.
Motionless Shadows... Kathleen Thompson Norris. LC 46-22484. (On cover: A Bart house novel. 20). 1945.
Motive. Harry Carmichael. 1977. 6.95 o.p. (ISBN 0-525-16030-2). Dutton.
Motive. Merriam Modell. LC 50-5452. (Inner sanctum mystery). 1950. Simon and Schuster.
Motive. Leopold Horace Ognall. LC 77-71330. 1976. 6.95 (ISBN 0-525-16030-2). Dutton.
Motive for Murder. Neill Graham. 1977. 4.95 (ISBN 0-09-128790-1, Pub. by Hutchinson). Merrimack Pub Cir.
Motive for Murder. Edson T. Hamill. (Ryker Ser). 1975. pap. 1.25 o.p. (LB315, Leisure Bks). Nordon Pubns.
Motive in Shadow. Lesley Egan, pseud. LC 79-7667. (Crime Club Ser.). 1980. 10.95 (ISBN 0-385-15605-7). Doubleday.
Motive in Shadow. Elizabeth Linington. LC 79-7667. 1980. 7.95 (ISBN 0-385-15605-7). Published for the Crime Club by Doubleday.
Motive Key: By Jack Woodford Pseud. Josiah Pitts Woolfolk. LC 56-39666. 1956. Dawn Press.
Motives of Nicholas Holtz: Being the Weird Tale of the Ironville Virus. Thomas Painter & Laing, Alexander Kinnan, 1903- Joint Author. LC 36-20870. Farrar & Rinehart, Incorporated.
Motley. John Galsworthy. LC 70-145031. 1970. (ISBN 0-403-00978-2). Scholarly Press.
Motley. John Galsworthy. LC 10-146497. 1910. C. Scribner's Sons.
Motley and Mr. Pinch. Pearson Choate. LC 33-5774. The Century Co.
Motley Book: A Series of Tales and Sketches. new ed. Cornelius Mathews. LC 7-17929. 1838. J. & H. G. Langley.
Motor Maid. Charles Norris Williamson. LC 42-43757. 1910. A. L. Burt Company.
Motor Maid. Charles Norris Williamson & Alice Muriel Livingston Williamson. LC 10-17598. 1910. Doubleday, Page & Company.
Motor Show. Steve Gooch & Paul Thompson. 88p. (Orig.). 1981. pap. 3.95 (ISBN 0-902818-64-3). Pluto Pr.
Motorcycle. Pieyre De Mandiargues, Andre. LC 76-40432. 1976. 13.25 (ISBN 0-8371-9061-4). Greenwood Press.
Motorcycle: Tr. from French by Richard Howard. Pieyre De Mandiargues, Andre. LC 65-141996. (Zebra bks., Z1001). 1966. Grove.

Motore Car Divorce. Louise Closser Hale. LC 6-10648. 1906. Dodd, Mead & Company.
Motorman. David Ohle. LC 77-171130. 1972. 3.50 (ISBN 0-394-47391-4). Knopf.
Motormaniacs. Lloyd Osbourne. LC 70-85692. (Short story index reprint series). (Illus.). 1969. Books for Libraries Press.
Motormaniacs. Lloyd Osbourne. LC 5-12706. (On cover: The pocket books). The Bobbs-Merrill Company.
Mott, the Hoople: A Novel. Willard Manus. LC 66-24580. 1966. McGraw-Hill.
Mottele: A Partisan Odyssey. Gertrude Samuels. LC 75-25101. 8.95 (ISBN 0-06-013759-2). Harper & Row.
Mottele: A Partisan Odyssey. Gertrude Samuels. (Signet Book). 1977. 1.50 (ISBN 0-451-07523-4). New American Library.
Mottke; the Thief. Shalom Asch. LC 73-98807. 1970. Greenwood Press.
Mottke: The Thief. Shalom Asch & Muir, Mrs. Willa, Tr. LC 35-19670. 1935. G. P. Putnam's Sons.
Mottke the Vagabond (Mottke Ganef) Shalom Asch & Goldberg, Isaac, 1887- Ed. and Tr. LC 17-30731. J. W. Luce and Company.
Mottled Lizard. Elspeth Joscelin Grant Huxley. 334p. 1982. pap. 3.95 (ISBN 0-14-005958-X). Penguin.
Motto Changed: A Novel. Jean Ingelow. LC 7-8851. 1894. Harper & Brothers.
Motto for Murder. Merlda Mace. LC 43-165473. 1943. J. Messner, Inc.
Mouche. Alain Demouzon. LC 78-54647. (Midnight library). 1979. 8.95 (ISBN 0-85690-076-1). Peebles Press International: Distributed in the U.S. by Farrar, Straus & Giroux.
Mouchette. Georges Bernanos. LC 66-24082. 1966. Holt, Rinehart and Winston.
Mouching Moose and Mumbling Men. Joe Back. LC 63-20617. Johnson Pub. Co.C.
Mould. Grace Kellogg Griffith. LC 23-176516. 1923. The Penn Publishing Company.
Moulded in Earth. Richard Vaughan. LC 50-11144. 1951. Dutton.
Moulding a Maiden. Linn Boyd Porter. LC 7-36656. 1891. G. W. Dillingham.
Moulding Forces. Samuel Shankman. LC 55-14017. 1954. Philosophical Library.
Moulin Rouge: A Novel Based on the Life of Henri De Toulouse-Lautrec. Pierre La Mure. LC 50-10457. 1950. Random House.
Mouls House Mystery. Charles Bryson. LC 27-3942. E. P. Dutton & Company.
Moultrie De Kalb. A Romance of a College Rebellion, and Army and Mercantile Life on the Indian Border. Thomas J Spencer. (Dillingham's American authors library. no. 34). 1898. G. W. Dillingham Co.
Mount Allegro. Jerre Mangione & Bacon, Peggy, 1895- Illus. LC 43-345. 1943. Houghton Mifflin Company.
Mount Allegro. Jerre Gerlando Mangione. LC 52-8507.
Mount Analogue. Rene Daumal. Tr. by Roger Shattuck. pap. 2.00 o.p. (ISBN 0-87286-011-6). City Lights.
Mount Analogue: A Novel of Symbolically Authentic Non-Euclidean Adventures in Mountain Climbing. Rene Daumal. (Penguin Meta physical Library). 1974. (pbk.) 2.50. Penguin.
Mount Analogue: An Authentic Narrative. Tr., Introd. by Roger Shattuck. Postface by Vera Daumal. Rene Daumal. 1968. pap., 2.00. City Lights.
Mount Eden. A Romance. Florence Marryat Church Lean. LC 7-13608. (On cover: Lovell's international series. no. 42). 1889. F. F. Lovell & Company.
Mount Henneth. Robert Bage. LC 78-60846. (Novel, 1720-1805). 1979. 56.00 (ISBN 0-8240-3657-3). Garland Pub.
Mount Hope: Or, Philip, King of the Wampanoga; an Historical Romance. Gideon Hiram Hollister. LC 6-45407. 1851. Harper & Brothers.
Mount Horeb. Russell Birdwell. LC 77-187991. (Illus.). 1972. 4.95 (ISBN 0-8315-0122-7). R. Speller.
Mount Music. Edith Anna CEnone Somerville & Violet Florence Martin. LC 20-1374. 1919. Longmans, Green and Co.
Mount Music. Edith Anna CEnone Somerville & Violet Florence Martin. LC 20-264413. 1920. Longmans, Green and Co.
Mount of the Lost Children. Roland Rene Martin. LC 54-12572. 1954. Christopher Pub. House.
Mount Royal. Mary Elizabeth Braddon Maxwell. (On cover: Seaside library. Pocket ed. no. 495). 1885. G. Munro.
Mount Royal. Mary Elizabeth Braddon Maxwell. (On cover: Lovell's library. no. 888). 1887. J. W. Lovell Company.
Mount Royal. A Novel. Mary Elizabeth Braddon Maxwell. (Harper's Franklin square library, no. 249). 1882. Harper & Brothers.
Mount Royal: Chronicles of an American Town. Elizabeth Frances Corbett. LC 36-4845. Reynal & Hitchcock.
Mount Venus. Mary Manning. LC 38-316203. 1938. Houghton Mifflin Company.
Mountain, a Novel. Clement Wood. LC 20-8518. E. P. Dutton & Company.
Mountain: A Novel; Translated from the French by Constantine Fitz Gibbon. Henri Troyat. 1953. Simon and Schuster.
Mountain: And Other Stories. Burnham Carter. LC 62-414320.
Mountain, and Other Stories. St. John Greer Ervine. LC 72-101809. (Short story index reprint series). 1969. Books for Libraries Press.
Mountain: And Other Stories. St. John Greer Ervine. 1928. The Macmillan Company.
Mountain and the Feather. John Ashmead. LC 61-10644. 1961. Houghton Mifflin.
Mountain and the Plain. Herbert Sherman Gorman. LC 36-179553. Farrar & Rinehart, Incorporated.
Mountain and the Tree. Helen Beauclerk. LC 37-12223. 1936. Coward-McCann, Inc.
Mountain and the Valley. Ernest Buckler. LC 52-10295. 1952. Holt.
Mountain Angels: Trials of the Mountaineers of the Blue Ridge and Shenandoah Valley. Richard Edward Beaty. LC 32-33616. 1928. R. E. Beaty.
Mountain Blood: A Novel. Joseph Hergesheimer. LC 15-11452. 1915. 1.25. M. Kennerley.
Mountain Blood: A Novel. Joseph Hergesheimer. LC 26-75303. 1919. A. A. Knopf.
Mountain Blood, a Novel. Joseph Hergesheimer. LC 26-7530. 368p. Repr. cancelled o.s.i. (ISBN 0-403-01768-8). Scholarly.
Mountain Born. Emmett Gowen. LC 32-28971. The Bobbs-Merrill Company.
Mountain Bred. John A Parris. LC 67-31154. 1967. Citizen-Times Pub. Co.
Mountain Bride: An Incredible Tale. Elizabeth Jane Coatsworth. LC 54-7068. (Illus.). 1954. Pantheon.
Mountain Cat: A Mystery Novel. Rex Stout. LC 39-27682. Farrar & Rinehart, Inc.
Mountain Cat Murders. Rex Stout. 176p. 1982. pap. 2.50 (ISBN 0-553-20826-8). Bantam.
Mountain Cat Murders. Rex Stout. 1971. pap. 0.75 o.p. (T2389). Pyramid Pubns.
Mountain Cat Murders. Rex Stout. 1973. pap. 0.95 o.p. (ISBN 0-515-03161-5, N3161). BJ Pub Group.
Mountain City. Upton Beall Sinclair. LC 30-121496. 1930. A. & C. Boni.
Mountain Cloud. Charles Marius Barbeau. LC 44-7132. 1944. The Caxton Printers, Ltd.
Mountain Code and Other Stories. Virginia T Mankin. LC 38-1819. Dorrance and Company.
Mountain Divide. Frank Hamilton Spearman. LC 12-21606. 1912. C. Scribner's Sons.
Mountain Doves. Ed. by Nola M. Zobarskas. 3.50 o.p. Twayne.
Mountain Farm. Ernest Raymond. LC 73-75344. 1973. 7.95 (ISBN 0-8415-0253-6). Saturday Review Press.
Mountain Farm. Ernest Raymond. 1975. (pbk.) 1.50. Bantam Books.
Mountain Girl. Payne Erskine. LC 12-5555. 1912. Little, Brown, and Company.
Mountain Gold. Basil Carey. LC 30-817225. E. J. Clode Inc.
Mountain Hearts. Mary Viola Lind. LC 33-8629. The Times-Mirror Press.
Mountain Inn Mystery: Or, Nat Ridley with the Forest Rangers. Nat Jr Ridley. LC 27-719. (His Nat Ridley series--14). 1927. Garden City Publishing Co., Inc.
Mountain Interlude. Peggy Gaddis, pseud. LC 48-9913. 1948. Arcadia House.
Mountain Is Young. Suyin Han. LC 58-11006. 1958. Putnam.
Mountain Journey. Dorothy James Roberts. LC 47-194281. 1947. D. Appleton-Century Company, Inc.
Mountain Justice: A Tale of the Cumberlands. Charles Neville Buck. LC 35-13674. 1935. Houghton Mifflin Company.
Mountain King: A Novel. George Ernsberger. LC 78-6674. 1978. 8.95 (ISBN 0-688-03346-6). Morrow.
Mountain Lake. Mildred Goebel. 2.95 o.p. Vantage.
Mountain Lion. Robert William Murphy. LC 69-13338. (Illus.). 1969. 3.95. Dutton.
Mountain Lion. Jean Stafford. LC 62-10337. 1962. Random House.
Mountain Lion. Jean Stafford. LC 76-21501. (Zia book). 1977. 3.45 (ISBN 0-8263-0432-X). University of New Mexico Press.
Mountain Lion. Jean Stafford. LC 74-183237. 1972. 6.95. Farrar, Straus and Giroux.
Mountain Lion. Jean Stafford. LC 47-196378. 1947. Harcourt, Brace and Company.
Mountain Lodge. Rob Eden. 1944. Gramercy Publishing Company.
Mountain Lovers. William Sharp. LC 8-47966. (On cover: Keynotes series, no. 17). 1895. Roberts Bros.; Etc., Etc.
Mountain Lovers. William Sharp. LC 79-8164. (Fiona Macleod, pseud.). Date not set. Repr. of 1895 ed. 44.50 (ISBN 0-404-62013-2). AMS Pr.
Mountain Madness. Anna Alice Chapin. LC 17-4471. 1.35. W. J. Watt & Company.
Mountain Man. Vardis Fisher. 1976. Repr. of 1967 ed. lib. bdg. 17.15x (ISBN 0-89190-832-3). Am Repr-Rivercity Pr.
Mountain Man. Vardis Fisher. 1977. 8.95 (ISBN 0-918522-52-8). O L Holmes.
Mountain Man. Vardis Fisher. 320p. (gr. 10 up). 1972. pap. 2.95 (ISBN 0-671-83696-X, 42288). PB.
Mountain Man. Harold Channing Wire. LC 29-16771. Thomas Y. Crowell Company.
Mountain Man: A Novel of Male and Female in the Early American West. Vardis Fisher. LC 65-22970. bds., 5.95. Morrow.
Mountain Man: A Novel of Male and Female in the Early American West. Vardis Fisher. LC 80-18279. 1980. 13.10 (ISBN 0-89190-832-3). Aeonian Press.
Mountain Man Kill. Jon Sharpe. (Trailsman Ser.: No. 3). (Orig.). 1980. pap. 2.50 (ISBN 0-451-12100-7, AE2100, Sig). NAL.
Mountain Mary: An Historical Tale of Early Pennsylvania. Ludwig August Wollenweber. LC 73-5412. (Illus.). 1974. 4.00 (ISBN 0-87387-058-1). Liberty Cap Books.
Mountain Mating. 1st Ed. Marian Parker. LC 54-123561. 1954. Pageant Press.
Mountain Maverick. William Frederick Bragg. LC 50-6857. 1950. Phoenix Press.
Mountain Meadow. John Buchan. LC 41-51560. 1941. Houghton Mifflin Company.
Mountain Meadow. John Buchan. 1972. 0.95. Popular Lib.
Mountain Men. Jackson Gregory. LC 36-419757. 1936. Dodd, Mead & Company.
Mountain Men. Strong, Charles Stanley. LC 51-10929. 1951. Phoenix Press.
Mountain Monster: A Doc Savage Adventure. Kenneth Robeson. 1.25 (ISBN 0-553-02239-3). Bantam.
Mountain Murder. Philip Mallory Conley. LC 40-2888. (On cover: Gold and blue series. no. 1). 1939. West Virginia Publishing Co.
Mountain Mystery. George Martin Nathaniel Parker. LC 31-6866. 1.30. Country Life.
Mountain Mystery: Or, The Outlaws of the Rockies. Emma Murdoch Van Deventer. (On cover: The detective and adventure library, no. 12). A. T. Loyd & Co.
Mountain Mystery: Or, The Outlaws of the Rockies. Emma Murdoch Van Deventer. (Library of choice fiction no. 50). 1892. Laird & Lee.
Mountain Nurse. Arlene Hale. 1975. (pbk.) 0.75. Ace Books.
Mountain of Fear. Rona Randall. (Ace gothic). 1974. (pbk.) 0.95. Ace Books.
Mountain of Fears. Henry Cottrell Rowland. LC 5-35299. 1905. A. S. Barnes & Co.
Mountain of God. Ethel Stefana Stevens Drower. LC 11-8242. 1911. Press of W. G. Hewitt, Brooklyn, N.Y.
Mountain of Gold. Max Evans. LC 83-6991. 1983. 4.95 (ISBN 0-8263-0696-9). University of New Mexico Press.
Mountain of Gold. Willis Steell. LC 13-17733. (On cover: Neely's popular library). F. T. Neely.
Mountain of Gold. Illus. by Hugh Cabot, III. Max Evans. LC 65-3985. 2.95. N. S. Berg, 'Sellenraa.
Mountain of Green Tea. Yahya Taher Abdullah. LC 82-74250. 130p. 1983. 15.00X (ISBN 0-89410-353-9); pap. 5.00X (ISBN 0-89410-352-0). Three Continents.
Mountain of Jade. Violet Mary Irwin & Stefansson, Vilhjalmur, 1879- Joint Author. LC 26-177722. 1926. The Macmillan Company.
Mountain of Light. Austin Coates. 1977. pap. text ed. 9.95x (00115). Heinemann Ed.
Mountain of Winter: A Novel. Shirley Schoonover. LC 64-17971. bds., 4.95. Coward.
Mountain of Winter: A Novel. Shirley Schoonover. 1980. 2.25 (ISBN 0-380-76513-6). Avon Books.
Mountain Path. Harriette Louisa Simpson Arnew. LC 64-1754. (Appalachian heritage book). 1963. Council of the Southern Mountains Publishers.
Mountain Path. Harriette Louisa Simpson Arnow. LC 36-27443. 1936. Covici-Friede.
Mountain Path. Harriette Simpson. LC 36-27443. Covici-Friede.
Mountain Pony: A Story of the Wyoming Rockies. Henry V Larom. LC 46-7448. 1946. Whittlesey House, McGraw-Hill Book Company, Inc.
Mountain Raiders. Bradford Scott. (Orig.). 1969. pap. 0.50 o.p. (R2068). Pyramid Pubns.
Mountain Rambles. J. W Kingsbury. (On cover: The satchel series. no. 33). W. B. Smith & Co.
Mountain Rampage. (Executioner Ser.). 192p. 1983. pap. 2.25 (ISBN 0-373-61054-8, Pub. by Worldwide). Harlequin Bks.
Mountain Riders. large print ed.. ed. Max Brand. LC 82-7357. 1982. 12.95 (ISBN 0-89340-504-3). J. Curley & Associates.
Mountain Riders... Frederick Faust. LC 46-5160. 1946. Dodd, Mead & Company.
Mountain Road. Theodore Harold White. LC 58-6394. 1958. W. Sloane Associates.
Mountain Sanctuary. May Chapman Starkey. LC 28-212764. 1928. The Canterbury Company.
Mountain School-Teacher. Melville Davisson Post. LC 22-16973. 1922. D. Appleton and Company.
Mountain Shadows. Magdelana Eggeston. LC 56-5075. Roy Publishers.
Mountain Standard Time. Paul Horgan. 595p. 1962. 7.95 (ISBN 0-374-21568-5). FS&G.
Mountain Standard Time: Main Line West, Far from Cibola and The Common Heart. Introd. by D. W. Brogan. Paul Horgan. LC 62-13072. 1962. Farrar, Straus and Cudahy.
Mountain Tavern. Andre Chamson. Tr. by Granberry, Edwin. LC 33-32588. H. Holt and Company.
Mountain Tavern and Other Stories. Liam O'Flaherty. LC 73-178453. (Short story index reprint series). 1971. (ISBN 0-8369-4054-7). Books for Libraries Press.
Mountain Tavern: And Other Stories. Liam O'Flaherty. LC 29-11444. Harcourt, Brace and Company.
Mountain That Moved. Gay Randall. LC 52-26367. 1952. Pageant Press.
Mountain That Went to the Sea. Lucy Walker. 1973. (pbk) 0.75. Beagle Books.
Mountain, the Stone. Kathleen Kranidas. 100p. 1975. pap. 3.50 (ISBN 0-913006-07-6). Puckerbrush.
Mountain Time. De Voto, Bernard Augustine. LC 47-300385. 1947. Little, Brown and Company.
Mountain Top. Claire Saint-Soline & Baur, Louise W. LC 39-30366. 1939. Dodd, Mead & Company.
Mountain Trails and Parks in Colorado. A Novel. Lewis B France. LC 6-43373. 1887. Chain, Hardy & Co.
Mountain Treasures. Jane V. Barker & Sybil Downing. (Colorado Heritage Ser.: Bk. 1). (Illus.). 45p. (gr. 3-4). 1978. pap. text ed. 3.50x (ISBN 0-87108-212-8); tchr's. ed. 3.00x (ISBN 0-87108-222-5). Pruett.
Mountain Troubadour: A Novel. 1st Ed. Charles Carson. LC 52-18386. 1951. Borden Pub. Co.
Mountain Valley War. Louis L'Amour. 208p. 1982. pap. 2.50 (ISBN 0-553-23219-3). Bantam.
Mountain Village: A Novel. Chun-Chan Yeh. LC 47-5595. 1947. G. P. Putnam's Sons.
Mountain-White Heroine. James Roberts Gilmore. (On cover: The Belford American novel series, no. 8). 1889. Belford, Clarke and Company.
Mountain Witch. Felicia Andrews. 352p. (Orig.). 1980. pap. 2.75 (ISBN 0-515-05846-7). Jove Pubns.
Mountain Without Stars. Translated by Salvator Attanasio. Maurice Zermatten. LC 60-15626. 1960. Helicon Press.
Mountain Woman. Elia Wilkinson Peattie. LC 79-98590. (Short story index reprint series). 1969. Books for Libraries Press.
Mountain Woman. Elia Wilkinson Peattie. 1896. Way & Williams.
Mountaineer Detective. A Thrilling Tale of the Moonshiners. J A Patten. (secret service series, no. 16). 1889. Street & Smith.
Mountainhead. Desmond Cory, pseud. (Johnny Fedora Ser., No. 4). (Orig.). 1968. pap. 0.60 o.p. (A373X, Award). Univ Pub & Dist.
Mountainhead. Desmond Cory, pseud. (O.s.i.). (Orig.). pap. 0.60 o.s.i. (A373, Award). Univ Pub & Dist.
Mountainhouse: A Novella. Patt C. McDermid. 137p. (Orig.). 8.25 o.s.i. (ISBN 0-912288-18-3); pap. 5.25. Perivale Pr.
Mountains Ahead: A Novel. Martha Ferguson McKeown. LC 61-5700. 1961. Putnam.
Mountains and the Stars. Valentin Tikhonov, pseud. LC 38-14448. 1938. Little, Brown and Company.
Mountains Are Mine. Helen Hinckley, pseud. LC 46-770357. 1946. The Vanguard Press, Inc.
Mountains Are My Kingdom. Oscar Schisgall. LC 37-630741. Green Circle Books.
Mountains at the Bottom of the World. Ian Cameron, pseud. 1972. 6.95 o.p. (ISBN 0-688-00002-9). Morrow.
Mountains at the Bottom of the World. Donald Gordon Payne. 1974. (pbk.) 1.25 (ISBN 0-380-00184-5). Avon.
Mountains at the Bottom of the World: A Novel of Adventure. Donald Gordon Payne. LC 70-170248. (Illus.). 1972. (ISBN 0-688-00002-9). Morrow.
Mountains Have a Secret. Arthur William Upfield. LC 48-4482. 1948. Pub. for the Crime Club by Doubleday.
Mountains Have No Shadow. Owen Cameron. LC 51-11891. 1952. Harper.
Mountains Moved. Adolph Henry Parr. LC 50-17826. Pre-Ferred Books Co.

Mountains of Allah. Paul Chavchavadze. LC 52-5114. 1952. Doubleday.

Mountains of Brega. Jeffrey Lord. (Blade Ser.: No. 17). 192p. (Orig.). 1976. pap. 1.75 (ISBN 0-523-40790-4). Pinnacle Bks.

Mountains of Mystery. Arthur Olney Friel. LC 25-7943. 1925. Harper & Brothers.

Mountains of the Morning. Guy Fitch Phelps. LC 16-23584. The Abingdon Press.

Mountains of the Sun. Christian Leourier. (Berkley medallion book). 1974. (pbk.) 0.95 (ISBN 0-425-02570-5). Berkley Pub. Co.

Mountains of Tomorrow. Rosalie Wells. 1978. pap. 1.95 (ISBN 0-532-19207-9). Woodhill.

Mountains West of Town. Warwick Downing. LC 75-6512. 1975. 6.95 (ISBN 0-8415-0378-8). Saturday Review Press.

Mountainside Acres. Elisabeth Welles. (Kangaroo Book). 1977. 1.50 (ISBN 0-671-81079-0). Pocket Books.

Mountainy Crack: Tales of Slieve Gullioners. Michael J Murphy. LC 77-358513. 2.65 (ISBN 0-85640-119-6). Blackstaff Press.

Mountainy Singer. Harry Harrison Kroll. LC 23-20223. 1928. W. Morrow & Company.

Mountebank. William John Locke. LC 21-29703. 1921. John Lane Company.

Mountebank. Duncan R Wallace. LC 76-177541. 1972. 6.95 (ISBN 0-395-13655-5). Houghton Mifflin.

Mountebank's Tale. Michael Redgrave. LC 60-9115. Harper.

Mounted Falcon. Fjeril Hess. LC 33-8987. 1933. The Macmillan Company.

Mountolive. Lawrence Durrell. 1961. pap. 4.95 (ISBN 0-525-47082-4, 0481-140). Dutton.

Mountolive: A Novel. Lawrence Durrell. LC 59-7792. 1959. Dutton.

Moura. Virginia Coffman. 1976. 1.75. Ace Books.

Moura. Virginia Coffman. LC 59-14021. 1959. Crown Publishers.

Mourned on Sunday. Helen Kieran Reilly. LC 41-5223. Random House.

Mourned One. Stanlake Samkange. (African writers series; 169). (Illus.). 1976. 2.75 (ISBN 0-435-90169-9). Heinemann.

Mourner. Richard Stark. 1981. lib. bdg. 10.95 (ISBN 0-8398-2708-3, Gregg). G K Hall.

Mourner. Donald E Westlake. LC 80-26882. (Gregg Press Mystery Fiction Series). 1981. 10.95 (ISBN 0-8398-2708-3). Gregg Press.

Mourners Below. James Purdy. LC 80-24995. 1981. 13.95 (ISBN 0-670-49142-X). Viking Press.

Mourners Below. James Purdy. LC 81-22640. 1982. 4.95 (ISBN 0-14-006193-2). Penguin Books.

Mourning After: A Singer Batts Mystery. Thomas Blanchard Dewey. LC 50-8971. 1950. Mill.

Mourning Crazy Horse: Stories. Harold Jaffe. LC 81-71645. 11.95 (ISBN 0-914590-72-3) (ISBN 0-914590-73-1). Fiction Collective: Order from Flatiron Book Distributors.

Mourning Raga. Edith Pargeter. LC 70-99735. 1970. 5.95. Morrow.

Mourning Raga. Ellis Peters. 1970. 5.95 o.p. (ISBN 0-688-02120-4). Morrow.

Mourning Road. Fred Mandell. LC 78-52586. 5.25 (ISBN 0-916288-04-8). Micah Publications.

Mourning the Death of Magic. Blanche M. Boyd. LC 77-2343. 7.95 (ISBN 0-02-514270-4). Macmillan.

Mourning Trees. Velda Johnston. 1973. 0.95. Dell Books.

Mourning Trees. Velda Johnston. LC 73-175313. (Red badge novel of suspense). 1972. 4.95 (ISBN 0-396-06477-9). Dodd, Mead.

Mouse. Georges Simenon. LC 66-77868. 1966. Penguin.

Mouse Hole & Other Stories. I. J. Allen. 3.75 o.p. (ISBN 0-8062-0246-7). Carlton.

Mouse in Eternity. Nedra Tyre. LC 51-11976. 1952. Knopf.

Mouse in the Mountain. Norbert Davis. LC 43-452. 1943. W. Morrow & Company.

Mouse Is Born. Anita Loos. LC 51-10650. 1951. Doubleday.

Mouse on the Moon. Leonard Patrick O'Connor Wibberley. LC 62-19411. 1962. Morrow.

Mouse on Wall Street. Leonard Patrick O'Connor Wibberley. LC 78-85130. 1969. 4.95. Morrow.

Mouse That Glowed. Wynelle B Gardner. LC 75-10243. (Illus.). 1975. 5.95. (ISBN 0-88270-128-2) (ISBN 0-88270-129-0). Logos International.

Mouse That Roared. Leonard Wibberley. LC 54-829454. Little, Brown.

Mouse That Roared. Leonard Patrick O'Connor Wibberley. LC 54-8294. Little, Brown.

Mouse That Saved the West. large print ed. Leonard Wibberley. LC 81-15219. 1982. 11.95 (ISBN 0-89340-374-1). J. Curley.

Mouse Trap. Mona Naomi Anne Hocking Messer. LC 31-20073. 1931. G. P. Putnam's Sons.

Mouse-Trap & Other Farces. William Dean Howells. 1978. Repr. of 1889 ed. lib. bdg. 25.00 (ISBN 0-8495-2250-1). Arden Lib.

Mouse Who Wouldn't Play Ball. Anthony Gilbert, pseud. 192p. 1972. Repr. of 1944 ed. 5.95 o.s.i. (ISBN 0-85617-751-2). White Lion Pubs.

Mouse with Red Eyes. Elizabeth Eastman. LC 48-71317. 1918. Farrar, Straus.

Mousechildren & the Famous Collector. Warren Fine. LC 79-96013. (Illus.). 1970. 7.50 o.p. (ISBN 0-06-011239-5, HarpT). Har-Row.

Mousetrap. Dame Agatha Miller Christie. 1974. (pbk.) 0.95. Dell.

Mouth As a Sensual Trap. Lydia Wilkinson. pap. 1.95 o.p. (ISBN 0-87056-249-5, 6249). Brandon.

Mouth Full of Earth. Branimir Scepanovic. LC 78-72283. 1980. 7.95 (ISBN 0-917712-07-2). Longship Press.

Mouth Full of Sugar. Chris Kazan. LC 69-10728. 1969. 5.95. Stein and Day.

Mouth Game. Geoffrey Kyle. 224p. pap. 1.95 o.p. (6147). Brandon.

Mouth Girl, Vol. 2. Peggy Swenson, pseud. pap. 1.95 o.p. (8049). Cameo.

Mouth Girls. Ed. by John W. Fitzgerald. pap. 2.95 o.p. (ISBN 0-87964-101-0). Academy-Parliament.

Mouth Girls: Oral Sex & the Young Female. Patty Benson. pap. 2.45 o.p. (4016). Cameo.

Mouth Lover. Peggy Swenson, pseud. 224p. pap. 1.95 o.p. (6136). Brandon.

Mouth Magic. Mark Bailey. 192p. (Orig.). 1972. pap. 1.95 o.p. (ISBN 0-87682-230-8, 7230). Barclay Hse.

Mouth Man. Nord Southgate. pap. 1.95 o.p. (8032). Cameo.

Mouth Master. Warren Bisig. 192p. (Orig.). 1972. pap. 1.95 o.p. (ISBN 0-87682-280-4, 7280). Barclay Hse.

Mouth Merchants. Gerald Summers. 192p. (Orig.). 1973. pap. 1.95 o.p. (ISBN 0-87682-345-2, 7345). Barclay Hse.

Mouth of the Kaw. 1st Ed. Matie Manard Hensley. LC 53-100776. 1953. Pageant Press.

Mouth of the Wolf: A Novel. William Murray. LC 76-48976. 8.95 (ISBN 0-316-59129-7). Little, Brown.

Mouth Seducers. Kyle. pap. 1.95 o.p. (ISBN 0-87056-173-1, 6173). Brandon.

Mouth Seducers. Geoffrey Kyle. 192p. pap. 1.95 o.p. (6173). Brandon.

Mouth Sinners. Franklin Folger. 192p. 1.95 o.p. (6144). Brandon.

Mouth Swingers. Dick Mountain. 192p. (Orig.). 1972. pap. 1.95 o.p. (ISBN 0-87682-218-9, 7218). Barclay Hse.

Mouth to Mouth. Deborah Metcalf. LC 80-14144. 10.95 (ISBN 0-399-90086-1). R. Marek.

Mouth Trick. Bill Charles. 192p. (Orig.). 1973. pap. 1.95 o.p. (ISBN 0-87682-338-X, 7338). Barclay Hse.

Mouthful of Life. Hastin Dobson. LC 64-20358. 1964. Dragon Press.

Mouthpiece. Edgar Wallace & Curtis, Robert G., Joint Author. LC 36-17323. Dodge Publishing Company.

Move! Joel Lieber. LC 68-19924. 1968. D. McKay Co.

Move. Georges Simenon. LC 68-20074. 1968. Harcourt, Brace & World.

Move in the Game. Kathleen Conlon. LC 78-66255. 1979. 9.95 (ISBN 0-8128-2603-5). Stein and Day.

Move Over: A Novel of Our "Better Classes". Ethel Pettit. LC 27-19325. 1927. J. H. Sears & Company.

Move Over, Mountain. John Ehle. LC 57-692450. 1957. W. Morrow.

Move Over Steve McQueen. Jeff Keith. Ed. by Sylvia Ashton. LC 76-41069. 1977. 10.95 (ISBN 0-87949-068-3). Ashley Bks.

Move Over, Steve McQueen: A Novel. Jeff Keith. LC 77-41069. 7.95 (ISBN 0-87949-068-3). Ashley Books.

Move up, Dress up, Drink up, Burn up. Bernard Wolfe. LC 68-14220. 1968. Doubleday.

Moveable Feast. Ernest Hemingway. LC 64-15441. (Illus.). 1964. 5.95 o.p. (ISBN 0-684-10234-X, ScribT); pap. 5.95 (ISBN 0-684-71804-9, SL260, ScribT). Scribner.

Moved by Love: A Novel of Remembrance. William Gellin. LC 80-52633. 10.00 (ISBN 0-88400-070-2). Shengold Publishers.

Moved Out on the Inside. Julia Vose. 1976. signed ed. 10.00 (Pub. by Figures); pap. 4.00. SBD.

Moved Outers. Florence Crannell Means. LC 45-2267. 1945. Houghton Mifflin Company.

Movement. Norman Garbo. LC 78-83692. 1969. 6.95. Morrow.

Movement, a Novel in Stories. Valerie Miner. LC 82-2543. (Crossing Press Feminist Series). 13.95 (ISBN 0-89594-079-5) (ISBN 0-89594-078-7). Crossing Press.

Movement Toward Eden. Clark Howard. LC 77-88523. 1969. 5.95. Moore Pub. Co.

Mover: A Modern Tragedy. James Drought. LC 65-871. 1963. Skylight Press.

Movie Boy's Outdoor Exhibition: Or, The Film That Solved a Mystery. Victor Appleton. LC 27-7341. (On cover: Movie boys series--14). 1926. Garden City Publishing Company, Inc.

Movie Fantastic: Beyond the Dream Machine. David Annan. (Illus.). 128p. 1974. pap. 2.95 o.p. (ISBN 0-517-51813-9). Crown.

Movie Lover. Richard Friedel. LC 80-28720. 12.95 (ISBN 0-698-11068-4). Coward, McCann & Geoghegan.

Movie Maker. Herbert D Kastle. LC 68-16153. 1968. 6.95. B. Geis Associates; Distributed by Grove Press.

Movie Starring the Late Cary Grant and an As-Yet Unsigned Actress. Tom Ahern, pseud. (Treacle Story Ser.: No. 1). (Illus.). 32p. 1976. signed ed. 8.00 (ISBN 0-914232-07-X); pap. 2.50 (ISBN 0-914232-06-1). McPherson & Co.

Movie Story Year Book. Hosking, Dorothy, Ed & Willey, Dorothy, Ed. LC 59-15161. Fawcett Publications.

Moviegoer. Walker Percy. LC 61-7754. 1961. Knopf.

Moviegoer. Walker Percy. 1980. 2.50 (ISBN 0-380-47076-4). Avon Books.

Movieland. Ramon Gomez De La Serna. Tr. by Flores, Angel. LC 30-6547. The Macaulay Company.

Moving Dream. Elizabeth Reinier. (Fawcett Crest Book). 1.50 (ISBN 0-449-23460-6). Fawcett Books.

Moving Finger. Agatha Miller Christie. LC 68-6253. (Greenway edition 8). 1968. 3.95. Dodd, Mead.

Moving Finger. Agatha Miller Christie. LC 48-10519. (New Avon library, 164). 1948. Avon Book Co.

Moving Finger... Agatha Miller Christie. LC 42-23228. 1942. Dodd, Mead & Company.

Moving Finger. Cortland Fitzsimmons. 1937. Frederick A. Stokes Company.

Moving Finger. Natalie Sumner Lincoln. LC 18-652282. 1918. D. Appleton and Company.

Moving Finger. Edward Phillips Oppenheim. LC 10-7953. 1910. 1.50. Little, Brown, and Company.

Moving Finger. Edward Phillips Oppenheim. LC 11-10641. 1911. Little, Brown, and Company.

Moving Finger Writes. Martia Leonard. LC 46-556919. 1946. The Christopher Publishing House.

Moving Finger Writes. Grace Denio Litchfield. LC 1-29076. 1900. G. P. Putnam's Sons.

Moving of the Waters: A Novel, by Jay Cady, with Illustrations. Jay Cady. LC 9-28039. 1909. 1.50. The J. McBride Company.

Moving on: A Novel. Larry McMurtry. LC 78-116498. 1970. 7.95. Simon and Schuster.

Moving Parts. Steve Katz. LC 76-47782. (Illus.). 8.95. (ISBN 0-914590-32-4) (ISBN 0-914590-33-2). Fiction Collective: Distributed by G. Braziller.

Moving Picture Boys. Max Wilk. LC 78-2484. 8.95 (ISBN 0-393-08814-6). Norton.

Moving Right Along. Kenward Elmslie. 1980. 10.00 (ISBN 0-915990-21-0); pap. 5.00 (ISBN 0-915990-20-2). Z Pr.

Moving Stairs: A Novel. Paul Murphy Pickrel. LC 48-517019. 1948. Harper.

Moving Target. Ross Macdonald. LC 78-12353. 1979. 9.95 (ISBN 0-89340-171-4). J. Curley.

Moving Target. Ross Macdonald. LC 79-10898. (Series: Gregg Press Mystery Fiction Series.). (Illus.). 1979. 9.95 (ISBN 0-8398-2538-2). Gregg Press.

Moving Target. Kenneth Millar. LC 49-3023. 1949. A. A. Knopf.

Moving Target. 1st Amer. Ed. Jack McClenaghan. LC 66-222812. 1966. 4.50. Harcourt.

Moving Through Here. Don McNeill. (YA) 1970. 5.95 o.p. (ISBN 0-394-43704-7). Knopf.

Moving Toyshop. Edmund Crispin, pseud. 1977. pap. 2.95 (ISBN 0-14-001315-6). Penguin.

Moving Toyshop: A Detective Story. Edmund Crispin, pseud. LC 80-54479. 1981. 9.95 (ISBN 0-8027-5434-1). Walker.

Moving Toyshop: A Detective Story. Robert Bruce Montgomery. LC 72-109535. 1970. 4.95 (ISBN 0-8277-0338-4). London House & Maxwell.

Moving Toyshop: A Detective Story. Robert Bruce Montgomery. LC 47-283. 1946. J. B. Lippincott Company.

Moving Up. Ron Montana. 224p. (Orig.). 1982. pap. 2.25 (ISBN 0-505-51783-3). Tower Bks.

Moving Waters: A Story of the Two Sea Services... Edward Noble. LC 28-30268. 1928. Houghton Mifflin Company.

Moviola. Garson Kanin. LC 79-17631. 9.95 (ISBN 0-671-24822-7). Simon and Schuster.

Moviola. Garson Kanin. 1980. 2.95 (ISBN 0-671-82794-4). Pocket Books.

Moviola Man. Bill Mahan & Colleen Mahan. LC 78-7761. 1979. 8.95 (ISBN 0-385-14453-9). Doubleday.

Movou Ov; or, Well-Nigh Reconstructed. Or, Well Nigh Reconstructed. A Political Novel. William Simpson Pearson. LC 7-33492. 1882. E. J. Hale & Son.

Mowgil Stories. Rudyard Kipling. LC 56-1339. 1956. The Junior Deluxe Editions.

Mox: From the Shadow's Private Annals As Told to Maxwell Grant. Maxwell Grant. (Shadow#8). 1975. (pbk.) 0.95 (ISBN 0-515-03876-8). Pyramid.

Mozart: A Biographical Romance. Herbert Rau. Tr. by Sill, Edward Rowland. LC 8-594. 1868. Leypoldt & Holt.

Mozart Leaves at Nine. Harris Greene. 1970. pap. 0.95 o.p. (0502-09034). Curtis.

'Mozart' Leaves at Nine. 1st Ed. Harris Greene. LC 60-137355. 1961. Doubleday.

Mozart on the Way to Prague. Eduard Friedrich Morike & Phillips, Walter Alison, 1864- Tr. LC 47-11374. 1947. Pantheon.

Mozart Score. Edwin Leather. LC 79-7603. (Crime club). 1979. 7.95 (ISBN 0-385-15564-6). Published for the Crime Club by Doubleday.

Mozart's Journey to Prague. Eduard Moerikke. Tr. by Loewenberg. 1981. pap. 3.95 (ISBN 0-7145-0389-4). Riverrun NY.

Mpdeste Mignon. Honore De Balzac. Tr. by Katharine Prescott Wormeley. LC 3-24486. (Half-title: The comedy of human life... Scenes from private life). 1888. Roberts Brothers.

Mr Amberthwaite. Louis Umfreville Wilkinson. LC 29-5598. 1929. A. A. Knopf.

Mr and Mrs Haddock Abroad. Donald Ogden Stewart. LC 75-6555. (Lost American fiction). (Illus.). 1975. 7.95 (ISBN 0-8093-0731-6). Southern Illinois University Press.

Mr Blessington's Imperialist Plot. John Sherwood. LC 51-9437. 1951. Published for the Crime Club ByDoubleday.

Mr Campion's Quarry. Margery Allingham & Youngman Carter. 1972. pap. 0.95 o.p. (532-95193-095). Manor Bks.

Mr Dunton's Invention: And Other Stories. Julian Hawthorne. LC 7-3882. (On cover: The Waldorf series, no. 25). 1896. The Merriam Company.

Mr Fothergill's Plot: His Conspirators: Martin Armstrong H. R. Barbor Elizabeth Bowen and Others. John Fothergill. LC 72-13245. (Short story index reprint series). 1973. (ISBN 0-8369-4243-4). Books for Libraries Press.

Mr Meeson's Will. Henry Rider Haggard. (On cover: Seaside library. Pocket ed. no. 1100). 1888. G. Munro.

Mr Meeson's Will: A Novel. Henry Rider Haggard. LC 6-46146. (On cover: Lovell's library. no. 1183). 1888. J. W. Lovell Company.

Mr., Miss, & Mrs. Charles Bloomingdale. LC 99-1080. 1899. J. B. Lippincott Company.

Mrs. Albert Grundy. Harold Frederic. 1896. lib. bdg. 25.00 o.p. Folcroft.

Mrs. Albert Grundy see Collected Works.

Mrs. Albert Grundy: Observations in Philistia. Harold Frederic. LC 6-43131. (Half-title: The Mayfair set, v. 6). 1896. J. Lane.

Mrs. Ames. Edward Frederic Benson. LC 13-217334. 1912. 1.35. Doubleday, Page & Company.

Mrs Ames. Edward Frederic Benson. LC 12-212833. Hodder and Stoughton.

Mrs. Annie Green: A Romance. Opie Percival Read. (On cover: Globe library, no. 111). 1890. Rand, McNally & Company.

Mrs. Apple Gate's Affair. Frederic Franklyn Van De Water. LC 44-40105. 1944. Duell, Sloan and Pearce.

Mrs. Appleyard's Year. Louise Andrews Kent. LC 41-231711. 1941. Houghton Mifflin Company.

Mrs. Armington's Ward: Or, The Inferior Sex. Daniel Thew Wright. LC 8-37216. 1874. Lee and Shepard.

Mrs. 'Arris Goes to Moscow. Paul Gallico. LC 74-19062. 1975. 6.95 (ISBN 0-440-05905-4). Delacorte Press.

Mrs. 'arris Goes to Paris. Paul Gallico. (Illus.). 1958. 3.50 o.p. (ISBN 0-385-05164-6). Doubleday.

Mrs. 'Arris Goes to Parliament. Drawings by Gioia Fiammenghi. 1st Ed. in the U. S. A. Paul Gallico. LC 65-14006. 2.95. Doubleday.

Mrs. Arthur. Margaret Oliphant Wilson Oliphant. (Union square library,, no. 10). 1878. N. L. Munro.

Mrs. Arthur. A Novel. Margaret Oliphant Wilson Oliphant. LC 24-25018. (Harper's library of select novels, no. 488). 1877. Harper & Brothers.

Mrs. Austin. Margaret Veley. (Half-title: Harper's half-hour series, no. 139). 1880. Harper & Brothers.

Mrs. Balfame. Gertrude Franklin Horn Atherton. LC 16-5195. 1916. Frederick A. Stokes Company.

Mrs. Barnes' Niece. Wilhelmina A. Saville. (On cover: The optimus series, no. 12). 1891. Donohue, Henneberry & Co.

TITLE INDEX MRS. MINIVER.

Mrs. Barnet--Robes. Dorothy C. Bayliff Peel. LC 15-11878. 1915. 1.25. John Lane.

Mrs. Barrenger's Dirty Book. Daoma Winston. (Orig.). 1970. pap. 0.75 o.p. (ISBN 0-447-74632-4). Lancer.

Mrs. Barr's Short Stories. Amelia Edith Huddleston Barr. LC 6-7979. (Ledger library, no. 53). R. Bonner's Sons.

Mrs. Barry. Frederick John Niven. LC 33-21521. 1933. E. P. Dutton & Co., Inc.

Mrs. Barthelme's Madness. Susan Claudia. LC 76-3522. (YA) 1976. 7.95 o.p. (ISBN 0-399-11761-X). Putnam.

Mrs. Barthelme's Madness. William Johnston. LC 76-3522. 7.95. Putnam.

Mrs. Barthelme's Madness. William Johnston. (Kangaroo Book). 1977. 1.95 (ISBN 0-671-81046-4). Pocket Books.

Mrs. Beauchamp Brown... Jane Goodwin Austin. LC 6-4495. (No name series. 2d series. v. 4.). 1880. Roberts Brothers.

Mrs. Ben Darby: Or, The Weal and Woe of Social Life. 2d ed. Anna Maria Collins. LC 6-25411. 1853. Moore, Anderson, Wilstach & Keys.

Mrs. Beneker: A Novel. Violet Weingarten. (Kangaroo Book). 1977. 1.50 (ISBN 0-671-81057-X). Pocket Books.

Mrs. Beneker: A Novel. Violet Weingarten. LC 68-11020. 1968. Simon and Schuster.

Mrs. Betsey; or, Widowed and Wed: By Francesca Marton Pseud. 1st American Ed. Mraaret Bellasis. LC 55-755. 1955. Coward-McCann.

Mrs. Blair, a Comedy of Indiscretions. Maud Keck. LC 38-720613. 1938. Harper & Brothers.

Mrs. Bligh: A Novel. Rhoda Broughton. LC 6-18953. (On cover: Appleton's town and country library, no. 105). 1892. D. Appleton and Company.

Mrs. Bligh: A Novel. Rhoda Broughton. LC 18-7772. (Macmillan's two shilling library. no. 22). 1899. Macmillan and Co., Limited.

Mrs. Blood. Audrey Callahan Thomas. LC 70-123236. 1970. 6.50. Bobbs-Merrill.

Mrs. Bob. Henrietta Eliza Vaughan Stannard. LC 8-138522. (On cover: Lovell's international series, no. 47). 1889. F. F. Lovell & Company.

Mrs. Bob. Henrietta Eliza Vaughan Stannard. (On cover: Seaside library. Pocket ed. no. 1246). 1889. G. Munro.

Mrs. Bob: A Novel. St. George Rathborne. LC 8-586. (On cover: Criterion series, no. 17). Street & Smith.

Mrs. Bobble's Trained Nurse. George Fox Tucker. 1916. R. J. Shores.

Mrs. Brand: A Novel. Hersilia A. Mitchell Copp Keays. LC 14-150229. 1.25. Small, Maynard & Company.

Mrs. Bratbe's August Picnic: A Novel. Jacqueline Wheldon. LC 65-19318. 1966. Houghton Mifflin.

Mrs. Bridge. Evan S Connell. (Kangaroo Book). 1977. 1.95 (ISBN 0-671-81093-6). Pocket Books.

Mrs. Bridge. Evan S. Connell. LC 59-5650. 1959. Viking Press.

Mrs. Budlong's Christmas Presents. Rupert Hughes. LC 12-24486. 1912. D. Appleton and Company.

Mrs. Caldwell Speaks to Her Son. Camilo Jose Cela. Tr. by J. S. Bernstein. LC 68-16379. 224p. 1968. 17.50x (ISBN 0-8014-0073-2). Cornell U Pr.

Mrs. Caldwell Speaks to Her Son. Mrs. Caldwell Habla Con Su Hijo. Camilo Jose Cela. LC 68-16379. 1968. Cornell University Press.

Mrs. Caliban. Rachel Ingalls. LC 81-84459. 1982. 7.95 (ISBN 0-87645-112-1). Gambit.

Mrs. Candy and Saturday Night. Robert Tallant. LC 47-5137. 1947. Doubleday.

Mrs. Candy Strikes It Rich. Robert Tallant. LC 54-7663. 1954. Doubleday.

Mrs. Captain Kidd. Dunbar Maury Hinrichs. LC 52-6935. 1952. Vantage Press.

Mrs. Carr's Companion. M. G Wightwick. (On cover: Seaside library. Pocket ed. no. 113). 1883. G. Munro.

Mrs. Cassatt's Children. Ruth Yeaton Power-O'Malley. LC 43-188467. 1943. Houghton Mifflin Company.

Mrs. Caudle's Curtain Lectures. Douglas William Gerrold. LC 52-50335. Optimus Print. Co.

Mrs. Caudle's Curtain Lectures. Douglas William Jerrold. LC 7-9927. (On cover: Fitch's popular library. no. 10). 1879. G. W. Fitch.

Mrs. Caudle's Curtain Lectures: And Other Stories and Essays. Douglas William Jerrold. (Half-title: The world's classics, cxxii). 1907. H. Frowde.

Mrs. Cherry's Sister: Or, Christian Science at Fairfax. Minnie Willis Baines Miller. LC 1-29350. Jennings & Pye.

Mrs. Christopher. Introd. by Gerald Vann. Elizabeth Myers. LC 58-14451. (Thomas More book to live). 1959. Sheed & Ward.

Mrs. Cliff's Yacht. Frank Richard Stockton. LC 4-15160. 1896. C. Scribner's Sons.

Mrs. Cliff's Yacht. Frank Richard Stockton. LC 8-2940. 1907. C. Scribner's Sons.

Mrs. Clift-Crosby's Niece. Ella Childs Hurlbut. LC 7-9035. (On cover: Sphinx series). 1893. Tait, Sons & Company.

Mrs. Clyde: The Story of a Social Career. Julie Grinnell Storrow Cruger. LC 1-29901. 1901. D. Appleton and Company.

Mrs. Condover. John Metcalfe. LC 28-16043. 1928. Boni & Liveright.

Mrs. Cooper's Boardinghouse. Joan Lindau. LC 79-25189. (Illus.). 9.95 (ISBN 0-07-037882-7). McGraw-Hill.

Mrs. Cooper's Boardinghouse. Joan Lindau. LC 80-22110. 1980. 13.95 (ISBN 0-8161-3150-3). G. K. Hall.

Mrs. Craddock. William Somerset Maugham. LC 75-25358. (works of W. Somerset Maugham). ((Series: Maugham, William Somerset, 1874-1965.). (Works. 1976.). 1976. 15.00 (ISBN 0-405-07817-X). Arno Press.

Mrs. Craddock. William Somerset Maugham. LC 20-26573. 1920. George H. Doran Company.

Mrs. Craddock. William Somerset Maugham. LC 28-7943. Doubleday, Doran & Company, Inc.

Mrs. Crichton's Creditor. Annie French Hector. LC 7-5169. (On cover: The lotos library). 1897. J. B. Lippincott Company.

Mrs. Curgenven of Curgenven. Sabine Baring-Gould. LC 6-7229. Lovell, Coryell & Company.

Mrs. Daffodil. 1st Ed. Gladys Bagg Taber. LC 57-9186. 1956. Lippincott.

Mrs. Dalloway. Virginia Stephen Woolf. LC 25-974922. Harcourt, Brace and Company.

Mrs. Dalloway. Virginia Stephen Woolf. LC 29-3975. (Half-title: The Modern library of the world's best books). The Modern Library.

Mrs. Dalloway's Party: A Short Story of Suspense. Virginia Stephen Woolf. LC 73-11234. 70p. 1975. pap. 2.95 (ISBN 0-15-662900-3, Harv). HarBraceJ.

Mrs Dalloway's Party: A Short Story Sequence. Virginia Stephen Woolf. LC 73-11234. (Original harvest book, HB279). 1975. (ISBN 0-15-662900-3). Harcourt Brace Jovanovich.

Mrs. Darrell. Molly Elliot Seawell. LC 5-14966. 1905. The Macmillan Company.

Mrs. Day's Daughters. Mary E. Rackham Mann. LC 13-26103. (Illus.). Hodder and Stoughton.

Mrs. Day's Daughters. Mary E. Rackham Mann. LC 14-151. Hodder & Stoughton, George H. Doran Company.

Mrs. Delire's Euchre Party: And Other Tales. Evelyn Snead Barnett. LC 6-7202. The Editor Publishing Co.

Mrs. Delmar at Palm Beach. Julia Anna Nenninger Balbach. LC 26-22414. The Christopher Publishing House.

Mrs. Dines's Jewels: A Mid-Atlantic Romance. William Clark Russell. (On cover: Harper's Franklin square library, no. 715). 1892. Harper & Brothers.

Mrs. Discombobulous. Margaret Mahy. LC 73-81339. (Illus.). 1969. 4.95. F. Watts.

Mrs. Donald Dyke Detective. Ernest A. Young. LC 1-29136. (On cover: Magnet detective library. no. 155). 1900. Street & Smith.

Mrs. Doratt: A Novel. John Erskine. LC 41-519712. Frederick A. Stokes Company.

Mrs. Drummond's Vocation. Mark Ryce. LC 11-189381. 1911. The Vail Company.

Mrs. Dufresne: A Romance. Barbara K. Hodges. LC 40-27083. G. P. Putnam's Sons.

Mrs. Dymond: A Novel. Anne Isabella Thackeray Ritchie. (Harper's handy series, no. 43). 1885. Harper & Brothers.

Mrs. Dymond. A Novel. Anne Isabella Thackeray Ritchie. (On cover: Seaside library. Pocket ed. no. 675). 1886. G. Munro.

Mrs. Eckdorf in O'Neill's Hotel. William Trevor. LC 78-94844. 1970. 5.95. Viking Press.

Mrs. Egg and Other Americans: Collected Stories. Thomas Beer. LC 47-31162. 1947. A. A. Knopf.

Mrs. Egg and Other Americans: Collected Stories of Thomas Beer. Thomas Beer. Ed. by Wilson Follett. LC 78-23682. (Illus.). 1979. 29.75 (ISBN 0-313-20648-1). Greenwood Press.

Mrs. Egg and Other Barbarians. Thomas Beer. LC 33-27249. 1933. A. A. Knopf.

Mrs. Eli and Policy Ann. Florence Olmstead. LC 12-17297. 1.00. The Reilly & Britton Co.

Mrs. Essington: The Romance of a House-Party. Esther Chamberlain & Chamberlain, Lucia. LC 5-19079. 1905. The Century Co.

Mrs. Falchion: A Novel. Gilbert Parker. LC 7-34995. 1893. The Home Publishing Company.

Mrs. Farrell: A Novel. William Dean Howells. LC 21-17086. Harper & Brothers.

Mrs. Fenton. William Edward Norris. (On cover: Seaside library. Pocket ed. no. 1258). 1889. G. Munro.

Mrs. Fischer's War. Gladys Henrietta Raphael Schutze. LC 31-3102. 1931. Houghton Mifflin Company.

Mrs. Fitz. John Collis Snaith. LC 10-23123. 1910. 1.35. Moffat, Yard and Company.

Mrs. Fizzlebury's New Girl: A Truly Domestic Story. Benjamin Franklin De Costa. LC 6-32892. 1878. G. W. Carleton & Co.

Mrs Flannagan's Trumpet. Catherine Cookson. LC 76-379473. (Illus.). 1976. 2.50 (ISBN 0-356-08442-6). Macdonald and Jane's.

Mrs. Fraser on the Fatal Shore. Michael Alexander. LC 78-139614. (O.s.i.). 1971. 6.95 o.s.i. (ISBN 0-671-20828-4). S&S.

Mrs. Frisby & the Rats of Nimh. Robert C. O'Brien, pseud. 1971. pap. 2.95 (ISBN 0-689-70413-5, A-44, Aladdin). Atheneum.

Mrs. Fuller. Marguerite Bryant. LC 25-9490. 1925. Duffield and Company.

Mrs. Gailey. 1st Ed. Kaye-Smith, Sheila. LC 51-9476. 1951. Harper.

Mrs. Gainsborough's Diamonds. A Story. Julian Hawthorne. LC 7-3881. (On cover: Appletons' new handy-volume series, 14). 1878. D. Appleton and Company.

Mrs. Gamp: A Facsimile of the Author's Prompt Copy. Foreword by Monica Dickens. Introd. and Notes by John D. Gordan. Charles Dickens. LC 57-1569. (Judge and Mrs. Samuel D. Levy Memorial Publication Fund. New York Publication No. 1). 1956. New York Public Library.

Mrs. Gaskell's Tales of Mystery & Horror. Ed. by Michael Ashley. 1979. 9.95 o.p. (ISBN 0-684-16105-2, ScribT). Scribner.

Mrs. Gaskell's Tales of Mystery and Horror. Elizabeth Cleghorn Stevenson Gaskell. Ed. by Michael Ashley. LC 78-11149. 9.95 (ISBN 0-684-16105-2). Scribner.

Mrs. Geoffrey. Margaret Wolfe Hungerford. (On cover: Lovell's library, v. 2, no. 90). 1883. J. W. Lovell Company.

Mrs. Geoffrey. A Novel. Margaret Wolfe Hungerford. LC 7-8330. 1882. J. B. Lippincott & Co.

Mrs. Gerald: A Novel. Maria Louise Pool. LC 7-38176. 1896. Harper & Brothers.

Mrs. Gerald's Niece. Georgiana Charlotte Leveson-Gower Fullerton. LC 75-455. (Victorian Fiction: Novels of Faith and Doubt). 1976. 35.00 (ISBN 0-8240-1534-7). Garland Pub.

Mrs. Gilbert Lancaster, 3rd. Jessie Emerson Moffat. LC 51-430. 1951. Austin-Phelps.

Mrs. Graddock. William Somerset Maugham. LC 72-413961. 1967. Penguin in Association with Heinemann.

Mrs. Green's Daughter-in-Law. Nelia Gardner White. LC 32-17790. 1932. Frederick A. Stokes Company.

Mrs. Hallam's Companion. And the Spring Farm, and Other Tales. Mary Jane Hawes Holmes. LC 7-60263. 1896. G. W. Dillingham.

Mrs. Halliburton's Troubles. Ellen Price Henry Wood Wood. (Seaside library, v.5, no. 92). 1877. G. Munro.

Mrs. Haney. Foxhall Daingerfield. LC 33-341447. W. F. Payson.

Mrs. Harold Stagg. A Novel. Robert Grant. LC 6-44753. (Choice series, no. 31). 1891. Robert Bonner's Sons.

Mrs. Harry St. John: A Realistic Novel of Boston Fashionable Life. 4th ed. Roman Ivanovitch Zubof. LC 8-37859. (On cover: Idylwild series. v. 1, no. 20). 1892. Morrill, Higgins & Co.

Mrs. Harter. Edmee Elizabeth Monica De La Pasture. LC 25-8265. Harper & Brothers.

Mrs. Heaton's Daughter. Dorsha Hayes. LC 43-172314. 1943. Ziff-Davis Publishing Company.

Mrs. Heriot's House. Barbara Webster. LC 45-16240. 1945. C. Scribner's Sons.

Mrs. Herndon's Income. A Novel. Helen Stuart Campbell. 1886. Roberts Brothers.

Mrs. Hollyer. A Novel. Georgiana Marion Craik May. (Harper's Franklin square library, no. 493). 1885. Harper & Brothers.

Mrs. Hollyer. A Novel. Georgiana Marion Craik May. (On cover: Seaside library. Pocket ed. no. 605). 1885. G. Muro.

Mrs. Hope's Husband. Gelett Burgess. LC 17-23049. 1917. The Century Co.

Mrs. Hulett. Bertram Bloch. LC 52-13564. 1953. Doubleday.

Mrs. Jack. A Tale. Frances Eleanor Ternan Trollope. LC 8-28515. (Appleton's new handy-volume series v. 19). 1878. D. Appleton and Company.

Mrs. Jim and Mrs. Jimmie: Certain Town Experiences of the Second Mrs. Jim As Related to Jimmie's Wife. Stephen Conrad Stuntz. LC 5-23035. L. C. Page & Company.

Mrs Job. Victoria Branden. LC 79-1697. 9.95 (ISBN 0-06-010521-6). Harper & Row.

Mrs. John Vernon. Julia De Wolf Gibbs Addison. LC 8-32645. 1909. R.G. Badger.

Mrs. Jones. Dorothy C. Bayliff Peel. LC 16-19070. 1916. John Lane.

Mrs. Keats Bradford: A Novel. Maria Louise Pool. LC 7-38175. 1892. Harper & Brothers.

Mrs. Keith's Crime. A Novel. Lucy Lane Clifford. (On cover: Seaside library. Pocket ed., no. 546). 1885. G. Munro.

Mrs. Keith's Crime: A Novel. Lucy Lane Clifford. LC 6-20740. (Harper's handy series, no. 17). 1885. Harper & Brothers.

Mrs. Keith's Crime: A Record. new 6th ed. Lucy Lane Clifford. LC 6-20738. 1897. Harper & Brothers.

Mrs. Killick's Luck. Christina Fitzgerald. LC 61-13118. (Illus.). 1961. F. Watts.

Mrs. Kimber. Osbert Sitwell. LC 77-5710. Repr. of 1937 ed. lib. bdg. 10.00 o.p. (ISBN 0-8414-7694-2). Folcroft.

Mrs. Knollys: And Other Stories. Frederic Jesup Stimson. 1897. C. Scribner's Sons.

Mrs. Knox's Profession. Jessica Mann. LC 72-87026. (MW suspense). 1972. 4.95. D. McKay Co.

Mrs. Lancelot: A Comedy of Assumptions. Maurice Henry Hewlett. LC 12-22520. 1912. The Century Co.

Mrs. Leslie and Mrs. Lennox: A Novel. John R V Gilliat. (On cover: Cassell's sunshine series, no. 101). 1892. Cassell Publishing Company.

Mrs. Limber's Raffle, or a Church Fair & Its Victims. facs. ed. William Allen Butler. LC 71-137724. (American Fiction Reprint Ser). 1876. 12.00 (ISBN 0-8369-7023-3). Ayer Co.

Mrs. Limber's Raffle: Or, A Church Fair and Its Victims; a Short Story. William Allen Butler. LC 71-137724. (American fiction reprint series). 1970. Books for Libraries Press.

Mrs. Limber's Raffle: Or, A Church Fair and Its Victims. A Short Story. William Allen Butler. LC 6-17377. 1876. D. Appleton and Company.

Mrs. Limber's Raffle: Or, A Church Fair and Its Victims: a Short Story. new ed. William Allen Butler. LC 6-17378. 1894. D. Appleton and Company.

Mrs. Lord's Moonstone: And Other Stories. Charles Stokes Wayne. 1888. Wynne & Wayne.

Mrs. Lorimer: A Sketch in Black and White. Mary St. Leger Kingsley Harrison. 1883. D. Appleton and Company.

Mrs. Lorimer: A Sketch in Black and White. Mary St. Leger Kingsley Harrison. (Seaside library. v. 76, no. 1531). 1883. G. Munro.

Mrs. Lorimer's Family. Molly Clavering. LC 53-11642. 1953. Longmans, Green.

Mrs. Loverly's Chatter. 1st. ed. Grace Wampler. 1974. 3.50 (ISBN 0-533-01002-0). Vantage.

Mrs. Lygon: A Domestic Detective Story. Shirley Brooks & Fiske, Stephen, 1840-1916, Ed. LC 6-19380. (On cover: Idle moments series, no. 13). 1892. The Price-McGill Company.

Mrs. McGinty's Dead. Agatha Miller Christie. LC 52-6875. (Red badge detective). 1952. Dodd, Mead.

Mrs. McGuinty's Dead. Agatha Miller Christie. 1980. pap. 2.50 (ISBN 0-671-43201-X). PB.

Mrs. M'Lerie. John Joy Bell. LC 4-2320. 1904. The Century Co.

Mrs. Mahoney of the Tenement. Louise Montgomery. LC 74-128741. (Short story index reprint series). (Illus.). 1970. Books for Libraries Press.

Mrs. Mahoney of the Tenement. Louise Montgomery. LC 12-223162. 1.00. The Pilgrim Press.

Mrs. Maitland's Affair. Gladys Starkey Battye. LC 63-8761. 1963. Published for the Crime Club by Doubleday.

Mrs. Manson's Daughters. Mathilde Eiker. LC 25-5965. 1925. The Macmillan Company.

Mrs. Marden. Robert Smythe Hichens. LC 19-15687. George H. Doran Company.

Mrs. Marden's Ordeal. James Hay. LC 18-9487. 1918. Little, Brown, and Company.

Mrs. Maxon Protests. Anthony Hope Hawkins. LC 11-113143. 1911. 1.35. Harper & Brothers.

Mrs. Mayburn's Twins. John Habberton. LC 18-10678. (With his Helen's babies. New York c1881). Hurst & Company.

Mrs. Mayburn's Twins: With Her Trials in the Morning, Noon, Afternoon, and Evening of Just One Day. John Habberton. LC 13-17723. 1882. T. B. Peterson & Brothers.

Mrs. Meeker's Money. Doris Miles Disney. LC 61-8882. 1961. Published for the Crime Club by Doubleday.

Mrs. Meigs and Mr. Cunningham. Elizabeth Frances Corbett. LC 36-19069. 1936. D. Appleton-Century Company, Incorporated.

Mrs. Merivale. Paul Kimball. LC 26-15713. E. J. Clode, Inc.

Mrs. Mike. Benedict Freedman & Nancy Mars Freedman. 1981. Repr. lib. bdg. 16.95x (ISBN 0-89966-396-6). Buccaneer Bks.

Mrs. Mike: The Story of Katherine Mary Flannigan. Benedict Freedman & Freedman, Nancy Mars. LC 48-10593. 1948. Sun Dial Press.

Mrs. Mike: The Story of Katherine Mary Flannigan. Benedict Freedman & Freedman, Nancy Mars, Joint Author. LC 47-301373. 1947. Coward-McCann, Inc.

Mrs. Miniver. Graham Joyce Maxtone. LC 40-27553. Harcourt, Brace and Company.

Mrs. Miniver. pseud. ed. Joyce Maxtone Graham. LC 42-21686. 1942. Harcourt, Brace and Company.
Mrs. Miniver. Jan Struther. LC 40-27553. 1966. pap. 0.50 (ISBN 0-15-663138-5, Harv). HarBraceJ.
Mrs. Morton of Mexico. Arthur Davison Ficke. LC 39-279024. Reynal & Hitchcock.
Mrs. Munck. Ella Leffland. LC 70-108304. 1970. 5.95. Houghton Mifflin.
Mrs. Murdock Takes a Case. George Harmon Coxe. LC 41-11682. 1941. A. A. Knopf.
Mrs. Murphy's Underpants. Fredric Brown. LC 63-15789. 1963. Dutton.
Mrs. Musgrave--and Her Husband. Richard Marsh. LC 7-24670. 1895. D. Appleton and Company.
Mrs. Newdigate's Window. C Lenanton. LC 27-10049. 1927. D. Appleton & Company.
Mrs. October Was Here. Coleman Dowell. LC 73-89479. 1974. 9.25 (ISBN 0-8112-0518-5) (ISBN 0-8112-0518-5). New Directions Pub. Corp.
Mrs. Palfrey at the Claremont. Elizabeth Taylor. LC 70-150119. 1971. 5.95 (ISBN 0-670-49497-6). Viking Press.
Mrs. Palmer's Honey. Fannie Cook. LC 46-25036. 1946. Doubleday & Company, Inc.
Mrs. Panopoulis. Jon Godden. 1959. 3.50 o.p. Knopf.
Mrs. Paramor. Louis Joseph Vance. LC 24-16808. 1924. E. P. Dutton & Company.
Mrs. Parkington. Louis Bromfield. LC 42-36416. 1943. Harper & Brothers.
Mrs. Parkington. Louis Bromfield. LC 80-14467. 1980. 13.75 (ISBN 0-88411-502-X). Aeonian Press.
Mrs. Partington's New Grip-Sack: Filled with Fresh Things. Benjamin Penhallow Shillaber. (Red cover series, no. 85). J. S. Ogilvie.
Mrs. Party's House. Caroline Beach Slade. LC 48-103557. 1948. Vanguard Press.
Mrs. Patty's Place. Edythe B. Mayes. LC 76-532. 1976. 8.95 (ISBN 0-89002-061-2); pap. 5.00 (ISBN 0-89002-060-4). Northwoods Pr.
Mrs. Peixada. Henry Harland. LC 37-18312. Cassell & Company, Limited.
Mrs. Peixada a Novel. Henry Harland. (On cover: Cassell's "rainbow" series, v.1. no. 22). 1888. Cassell & Comany.
Mrs. Pendleton's Four-in-Hand. Gertrude Franklin Horn Atherton. LC 3-15438. (Half-title: Little novels by favourite authors). 1903. The Macmillan Company.
Mrs. Pennington. Katharine Carson. LC 39-27428. G. P. Putnam's Sons.
Mrs. Phelps' Husband. Adriana Spadoni. LC 24-6687. The Bobbs-Merrill Company.
Mrs. Pollifax on Safari. Dorothy Gilman. LC 76-18346. 1977. 7.95 o.p. (ISBN 0-385-07506-5). Doubleday.
Mrs. Pollifax on Safari. Dorothy Gilman. 1978. pap. 1.95 (ISBN 0-449-23414-2, Crest). Fawcett.
Mrs. Pollifax on the China Station. Dorothy Gilman. (Illus.). 192p. 1983. 12.95 (ISBN 0-385-14525-X). Doubleday.
Mrs. Porter's Letter. Vicki P. McConnell. LC 81-22483. (Nyla Wade Ser.). 260p. (Orig.). 1982. pap. 6.95 (ISBN 0-930044-29-0). Naiad Pr.
Mrs. Pym, and Other Stories. Nigel Morland. LC 77-360368. 1976. 3.95 (ISBN 0-85628-031-3). A. Ellis.
Mrs. Raffles: Being the Adventures of an Amateur Crackswoman Narrated by Bunny. John Kendrick Bangs. LC 5-32856. 1905. Harper & Brothers.
Mrs. Rasher's Curtain Lectures... Metta Victoria Victor. LC 12-17870. J. E. Ogilvie & Company.
Mrs. Raven's Temptation. Isabella Fyvie Mayo. (seaside library, v. 74, no. 1497). 1883. G. Munro.
Mrs. Red Pepper. Grace Louise Smith Richmond. LC 13-10503. 1913. Doubleday, Page & Company.
Mrs. Reinhardt & Other Stories. Edna O'Brien. 224p. 1980. pap. 3.50 (ISBN 0-14-005128-7, Pub. by Penguin England). Irish Bk Ctr.
Mrs. Reynolds and Hamilton; a Romance. George Alfred Townsend. 1890. E. F. Bonaventure.
Mrs. Robert Elsmere. A Companion Story to Mrs. Humphrey Ward's Robert Elsmere... Florence Kennedy. LC 7-11107. 1889. N. L. Munro.
Mrs. Searwood's Secret Weapon. Illus. by Warren Chappell. 1st Ed. Leonard Wibberley. LC 54-5107. Little, Brown.
Mrs. Searwood's Secret Weapon. Illus. by Warren Chappell. 1st Ed. Leonard Patrick O'Connor Wibberley. LC 54-5107. Little, Brown.
Mrs. Sherman's Summer. Marjorie Fischer. LC 60-6463. 1960. Lippincott.
Mrs. Singleton. Cornelia S. Barclay. LC 6-721318. (On cover: Satchel series mo. 24). The Authors' Publishing Company.
Mrs. Skagg's Husband & Other Sketches. Bret Harte. 1873. 21.00 o.p. (ISBN 0-403-04185-6). Somerset Pub.
Mrs. Skagg's Husbands: And Other Sketches. Bret Harte. LC 6912. 1900. Houghton, Mifflin and Company.
Mrs. Skagg's Husbands & Other Sketches. Bret Harte. 1972. Repr. of 1873 ed. lib. bdg. 19.50 (ISBN 0-8422-8072-3). Irvington.
Mrs. Skaggs's Husbands: And Other Sketches. Bret Harte. LC 1-1006. 1873. J. R. Osgood and Company.
Mrs. Skaggs's Husbands & Other Sketches. Bret Harte. Ed. by Clarence Gohdes. LC 69-11901. (American Short Story Ser., Vol. 59). 1969. Repr. of 1873 ed. lib. bdg. 17.00 o.s.i. (ISBN 0-512-00299-1). Garrett Pr.
Mrs. Smith of Longmains. Rhoda Broughton & Oliphant, Mrs. Margaret Oliphant (Wilson) 1828-1897. (On cover: Seaside library. Pocket ed., no. 645). 1885. G. Munro.
Mrs. Socrates. Fritz Mauthner. Tr. by Jacob Wittmer Hartmann. LC 26-16271. 1926. International Publishers.
Mrs. Sparks of Paris. A Realistic Novel. A. Curtis Bond. LC 6-10374. (On cover: The echo series, no. 40). 1888. Pollard & Moss.
Mrs. Spring Fragrance. Edith Maud Eaton. LC 12-13484. 1912. 1.40. A. C. McClurg & Co.
Mrs. Starr Lives Alone. Jon Godden. LC 79-171152. 1972. 5.95 (ISBN 0-394-46595-4). Knopf.
Mrs. Stevens Hears the Mermaids Singing. May Sarton. 240p. 1974. 6.95 (ISBN 0-393-08695-X, Norton Lib); pap. 3.95 1975 (ISBN 0-393-00762-6). Norton.
Mrs. Stevens Hears the Mermaids Singing: A Novel. May Sarton. LC 65-18016. bds., 4.50. Norton.
Mrs. Stevens Hears the Mermaids Singing: A Novel. May Sarton. LC 74-1349. 1974. 6.95 (ISBN 0-393-08695-X). Norton.
Mrs. Sunday's Problem, and Other Stories. Harold L Fickett. LC 78-31469. 6.95 (ISBN 0-8007-0996-9). Revell.
Mrs. Taylor: A Novel. Marjorie Muir Worthington. LC 32-214277. 1932. A. A. Knopf.
Mrs. Thompson: A Novel. William Babington Maxwell. LC 11-9944. 1911. D. Appleton and Company.
Mrs. Tim Carries on. new ed. Dorothy Emily Stevenson. LC 72-91586. 1973. 6.95 (ISBN 0-03-007491-6). Holt, Rinehart and Winston.
Mrs. Tim Carries on. Dorothy Emily Stevenson. LC 79-17309. 1980. 14.95 (ISBN 0-8161-6784-2). G. K. Hall.
Mrs. Tim Carries on: Leaves from the Diary of an Officer's Wife in the Year 1940. Dorothy Emily Stevenson. LC 41-10684. Farrar & Rinehart, Inc.
Mrs. Tim Christie. Dorothy Emily Stevenson. LC 72-78141. 1973. 6.95 (ISBN 0-03-001436-0). Holt, Rinehart and Winston.
Mrs. Tim Christie. Dorothy Emily Stevenson. LC 79-17306. 1980. 14.95 (ISBN 0-8161-6786-9). G. K. Hall.
Mrs. Tim Flies Home. Dorothy Emily Stevenson. LC 74-4807. 1974. 7.95 (ISBN 0-03-013171-5). Holt, Rinehart and Winston.
Mrs. Tim Flies Home. Dorothy Emily Stevenson. LC 52-9598. 1952. Rinehart.
Mrs. Tim Flies Home. Dorothy Emily Stevenson. LC 79-17308. 1980. 14.95. G. K. Hall.
Mrs. Tim Gets a Job. new ed. Dorothy Emily Stevenson. LC 73-12860. 1974. 6.95 (ISBN 0-03-012256-2). Holt, Rinehart and Winston.
Mrs. Tim Gets a Job. Dorothy Emily Stevenson. LC 47-1582. 1947. Rinehart & Company, Inc.
Mrs. Tim Gets a Job. Dorothy Emily Stevenson. LC 79-17307. 1980. 13.95 (ISBN 0-8161-6787-7). G. K. Hall.
Mrs. Tim of the Regiment. Dorothy Emily Stevenson. 378p. 1976. lib. bdg. 17.95x (ISBN 0-89966-157-2). Buccaneer Bks.
Mrs. Tim of the Regiment: Leaves from the Diary of an Officer's Wife. Dorothy Emily Stevenson. LC 40-30383. Farrar & Rinehart, Inc.
Mrs. Tree. Laura Elizabeth Howe Richards. LC 2-17483. 1902. D. Estes & Company.
Mrs. Tree's Will. Laura Elizabeth Howe Richards. D. Estes & Company.
Mrs. Tregaskiss: A Novel of Angelo-Australian Life. Rosa Caroline Murray-Prior Praed. LC 7-30301. 1895. D. Appleton and Company.
Mrs. Van Kleek. Elinor Mordaunt, pseud. LC 33-2407. The John Day Company.
Mrs. Van Twiller's Salon. Lillie Hamilton French. LC 5-36290. 1905. J. Pott & Company.
Mrs. Vanderstein's Jewels. Charles Bryce. 1914. 1.25. John Lane.
Mrs. Wallop. Peter De Vries. LC 77-126169. 1974. (pbk.) 1.25. Popular Library.
Mrs. Warrender's Profession. George Douglas Howard Cole & Margaret Isabel Postgate Cole. LC 38-290666. 1939. The Macmillan Company.
Mrs. Warren's Daughter, a Story of the Woman's Movement. Harry Hamilton Johnston. LC 20-7923. 1920. The Macmillan Company.
Mrs. Westerby Changes Course. Elizabeth Cadell. LC 68-12146. 1968. W. Morrow.
Mrs. Whilling's Faith Cure. Elizabeth Annable Needham. LC 7-25792. Bradley & Woodruff.
Mrs. Wiggs of the Cabbage Patch. Alice Caldwell Hegan Rice. LC 50-6607. (Thrushwood book). 1950. Grosset & Dunlap.
Mrs. Wiggs of the Cabbage Patch. Alice Caldwell Hegan Rice. LC 1-24948. 1901. The Century Co.
Mrs. Wiggs of the Cabbage Patch. Alice Caldwell Hegan Rice. 1902. The Century Co.
Mrs. Wiggs of the Cabbage Patch. Alice Caldwell Hegan Rice. LC 7-25787. 1903. The Century Co.
Mrs. Wiggs of the Cabbage Patch. Alice Caldwell Hegan Rice. LC 28-192943. 1926. The Century Co.
Mrs. Wiggs of the Cabbage Patch. Alice Caldwell Hegan Rice. LC 79-9874. 5.50 (ISBN 0-8131-1391-1). University Press of Kentucky.
Mrs. Wiggs of the Cabbage Patch. Alice Caldwell Hegan Rice & Brindl, Helen M., Ed. LC 37-7078. (Half-title: Appleton modern literature series). D. Appleton-Century Company, Incorporated.
Mrs. William Horton Speaking. Fannie Kilbourne. LC 25-515419. 1925. Dodd, Mead and Company.
Mrs. W's Last Sandwich: A Romance. Edwin Denby. LC 72-86737. 1972. 6.95. Horizon Press.
Mrs.Vereker's Courier Maid. Annie French Hector. (On cover: Seaside library. Pocket ed., no. 339). 1885. G. Munro.
Mruder of a Redhaired Man. Mary Plum. LC 52-13534. 1952. Arcadia House.
Ms. Charlotte's Lovers. Paul Wainberg. LC 77-362059. 1976. 1.95 (ISBN 0-671-80371-9). Simon and Schuster of Canada.
Ms. in a Red Box. John Arthur Hamilton. LC 3-20893. 1903. J. Lane.
Ms. Murphy's Theater. Victor J. Emmett, Jr. 32p. 1975. pap. 1.25 (ISBN 0-914994-04-2, CB-005). Cider Pr.
Ms. Mysteries. Arthur Leibman. (Orig.). 1976. write for info o.p. WSP.
Ms. Mysteries: 19 Tales of Suspense Written by Women and Featuring Female Heroines. Arthur Liebman. LC 76-364378. 1976. 1.95 (ISBN 0-671-48770-1). Washington Square Press.
Ms. Mysteries: 19 Tales of Suspense Written by Women and Featuring Female Heroines. Ed. by Arthur Liebman. 1976. (pbk.) 1.95 (ISBN 0-671-48770-1). Pocket Books.
Ms. President. Elizabeth Hanley, pseud. (O.s.i.). 1977. pap. 1.50 o.s.i. (BT51109). Belmont-Tower.
Ms. President. Elizabeth Hanley. (Belmont Tower Book). 1.50. Tower Publications.
Mt. Blossom Girls: Or the New Paths from Blossom Shop. Isla May Hawley Mullins. LC 18-2909. 1918. The Page Company.
Mucca Scob; or, Threads of Prehistoric and Present History, Concatenated. Teague M Kelly. LC 7-10976. 1885. The Author.
Much Ado About John's Other Wife. Florence H. Morris. 1966. pap. 1.00x (ISBN 0-88020-077-4). Coach Hse.
Much Ado About Peter: By Jean Webster... Illustrated by Charlotte Harding and Harry Linnell. Jean Webster. LC 9-7143. 1909. Doubleday, Page & Company.
Much Honored Man. 1st Ed. Daniel Tamkus. LC 59-11610. 1959. Doubleday.
Much Less a Slave. Jean Ethel Turnley. LC 75-330372. 1974. 6.95 (ISBN 0-17-005006-8). Thomas Nelson (Australia)
Much Loved... Ruby Mildred Ayres. LC 34-30877. 1934. Doubleday, Doran & Co., Inc.
Much-Married Saints and Some Sinners: Sketches from Life Among Mormons and Gentiles in Utah. Grace Talbot. LC 2-30408. 1902. The Grafton Press.
Much of Magic & Miracles. Naomi Hardy. (Orig.). 1979. pap. 1.75 (ISBN 0-532-17202-7). Woodhill.
Muckaluck: A Curious Episode in the Cavalry's Winning of the West. Richard Andersen. LC 79-24437. 7.95 (ISBN 0-440-05577-6). Delacorte Press.
Mucker. Edgar Rice Burroughs. LC 63-10803. (Illus.). 1963. Canaveral Press.
Mucker. Edgar Rice Burroughs. LC 21-18945. 1921. A. C. McClurg & Co.
Mucker. Edgar Rice Burroughs. LC 40-37518. 1921. Grosset & Dunlap.
Mucker. Edgar Rice Burroughs. 1974. (pbk.) 0.95. Ace Books.
Muckraker. John Parsons Peditto. 1976. (pbk.) 1.50. Warner Books.
Muckrakers Series, 39 Novels, 40 Vols. Intro. by C. F. Gohdes. 1836-1917. Set. 485.00 o.p. (Lit Hse). Gregg.
Mud and Dust. Charles N. Aronson. LC 76-5966. (Illus.). 12.50. (ISBN 0-915736-09-8) (ISBN 0-915736-10-1). Aronson.
Mud and Glory: An Inside Story of Football. James Mandeville Neville. LC 29-18947. 1929. Duffield & Company.
Mud and Money. Mary Holbert Ellyson. 1973. 5.95 (ISBN 0-533-00446-2). Vantage Press.
Mud-Hut Dwellers. Mihail Sadoveanu. LC 64-25057. 1964. Twayne Publishers.
Mud Lark. Arthur John Arbuthnott Stringer. LC 32-3490. The Bobbs-Merrill Company.
Mud Larks. Crosbie Garstin. LC 19-146310. George H. Doran Company.
Mud on the Stars: A Novel. William Bradford Huie. LC 42-17149. 1942. L. B. Fischer.
Mud War. Lou Cameron. 1971. pap. 0.95 o.p. (ISBN 0-447-75174-3). Lancer.
Muddle. Constance Sybil Kent. LC 60-357. (Milestone book). Comet Press Books.
Muddy Wheels: By Wade Hamilton Pseud. Lee Floren. LC 53-621879. 1953. Arcadia House.
Muder Charge. Wade Miller, pseud. LC 50-10761. 1950. Farrar, Straus.
Mudfog Papers Etc. Charles Dickens. LC 6-26433. (Lovell's library, v. 5, no. 270). 1883. J. W. Lovell Company.
Mudland. Morley Adams. (Orig.). 1980. pap. 1.75 (ISBN 0-532-23146-5). Woodhill.
Mudlander. Claude W McKenzie. LC 66-20442. Greenwich Book Publishers.
Mudlark. Theodore Bonnet. LC 49-9639. Doubleday,
Mudlark. Theodore Bonnet. LC 78-3866. 1978. 9.95 (ISBN 0-89244-076-7). Queens House.
Muertalma; or, The Poisoned Pin. A Detective Story. Marmaduke Dey. (secret service series, no. 35). 1890. Street & Smith.
Muerte Anduvo Por el Guasio. rev. ed. Luis Hernandez Aquino. (UPREX, Ficcion: No. 1). pap. 1.85 (ISBN 0-8477-0001-1). U of PR Pr.
Muffin. Toni Stevens. Tr. by Rita Berman. 176p. (Orig.). 1975. pap. 1.25 o.p. (ISBN 0-532-12355-7). Woodhill.
Muffin. Toni Stevens. Tr. by Rita Berman. 176p. (Orig.). 1975. pap. 1.25 o.p. (ISBN 0-532-12355-7). Manor Bks.
Mufti. Herman Cyril McNeile. LC 16-16391. 1919. Hodder and Stoughton.
Mufti. Herman Cyril McNeile. LC 19-12876. Geoger H. Doran Company.
Mugger. Ed McBain. 1975. (pbk.) 1.25. Ballantine Books.
Mugger. F. C. A McBain. LC 56-97040. (Permabooks, M-3061. Mystery, 1). 1956. Permabooks.
Muggers Blood: Destroyer No. 30. Warren Murphy. LC 76-42891. (Destroyer Ser.). 1977. pap. 1.50 (ISBN 0-523-40110-8). Pinnacle Bks.
Mugger's Day. Aaron Marc Stein. LC 79-7326. 1979. 7.95 (ISBN 0-385-15421-6). Published for the Crime Club by Doubleday.
Muggers's Day. George Bagby, pseud. (Crime Club Ser.). 1979. 9.95 o.p. (ISBN 0-385-15421-6). Doubleday.
Muir's Blood. Charles Larson. LC 76-18357. 1976. 5.95 o.p. (ISBN 0-385-12033-8). Doubleday.
Mujeres y Agonias. Rima Vallbona. LC 81-68068. 120p. (Orig., Span.). 1981. pap. 5.00 (ISBN 0-934770-12-3). Arte Publico.
Mukara. Muriel Bruce. LC 77-84204. (Lost Race and Adult Fantasy Fiction). 1978. 18.00 (ISBN 0-405-10960-1). Arno Press.
Mukara: A Novel. Muriel Bruce. LC 30-122890. Rae D. Henkle Co., Inc.
Mulata. Miguel Angel Asturias. 352p. 1982. pap. 3.50 (ISBN 0-380-58552-9, 58552, Bard). Avon.
Mulata. Tr. from Spanish by Gregory Rabassa, 1st Amer. Ed. Miguel Angel Asturias. LC 67-17639. 1967. bds., 7.95. Delacorte.
Mulatto. Evans Wall. 192p. 1974. pap. 1.25 o.p. (ISBN 0-532-12227-5). Woodhill.
Mulatto. Evans Wall. 1974. (pbk.) 1.25. Manor Books.
Mulatto. Jeanne Wilson. LC 77-28946. 8.95 (ISBN 0-87131-250-6). M. Evans Co.
Mulberry Bush. facs. ed. Silvia Dryhurst Lynd. LC 78-142886. (Short Story Index Reprint Ser). 1925. 15.00 (ISBN 0-8369-3751-1). Ayer Co.
Mulberry Bush, and Other Stories. Sylvia Dryhurst Lynd. LC 78-142886. (Short story index reprint series). 1970. Books for Libraries Press.
Mulberry Square. Lida Larrimore Thomas. LC 30-10464. 1930. Macrae Smith Company.
Mulcarrey's Ridge. Richard Vaughan. 1980. 6.95 (ISBN 0-8062-1341-8). Carlton.
Muldoon: A Novel. Don Bredes. LC 81-20316. 15.50. Holt, Rinehart and Winston.
Muldoon Was Here. 1st Ed. Sterling Quinlan. LC 67-25652. 1967. bds., 4.95. Citadel.
Mule for the Marquesa. Frank O'Rourke. LC 64-21739. 1964. Morrow.
Mule on the Minaret. Alec Waugh. 506p. 1965. 6.95 o.p. (ISBN 0-374-21596-0). FS&G.

Mule on the Minaret: A Novel About the Middle East. 1st Amer. Ed. Alec Waugh. LC 65-23191. 6.95. Farrar.

Mules That Angels Ride. Page Edwards. LC 70-188737. 1972. 4.95 (ISBN 0-87955-900-4). J. P. O'Hara.

Muleskinner. Robert MacLeod, pseud. 1971. pap. 0.60 o.p. (R2253, GM). Fawcett World.

Mulford's Mammoth Hopalong Cassidy: Containing Hopalong Cassidy's Protege, Hopalong Cassidy Returns. Clarence Edward Mulford. 1937. A. L. Burt and Company.

Mullah from Kashmir. Duncan Macneil. LC 76-10558. 1976. 8.95 o.p. (ISBN 0-312-55230-0). St Martin.

Mullah from Kashmir: An "Ogilvie" Novel. Philip McCutchan. LC 76-10558. 8.95. St. Martin's Press.

Muller-Fokker Effect. John Thomas Sladek. 1973 (ISBN 0-671-77622-3). Pocket Bks.

Muller-Fokker Effect. John Thomas Sladek. LC 71-166345. 1971. 5.95. W. Morrow.

Muller Hill. Harriet McDoual Daniels. LC 43-513221. 1943. A. A. Knopf.

Mulligan Stew: A Novel. Gilbert Sorrentino. LC 78-67419. 1978. 12.50 (ISBN 0-8021-0173-9). Grove Press.

Mulligans. Edward Harrigan. LC 1-23685. 1901. G. W. Dillingham Company.

Mulligan's Pirates. Don Stanford, pseud. (O.s.i.). 1966. 4.50 o.s.i. (ISBN 0-671-49640-9). S&S.

Mulligan's Pirates: A Novel. Don Stanford, pseud. LC 65-262535. 4.50. S. & S.

Mulligan's Seed. Herbert Burkholz. LC 75-9550. 1975. 7.95 (ISBN 0-15-163250-2). Harcourt Brace Jovanovich.

Mulliner Nights. Pelham Grenville Wodehouse. LC 75-13378. 1975. 1.95 (ISBN 0-394-72027-X). Vintage Books.

Mulliner Nights. Pelham Grenville Wodehouse. LC 33-4496. 1933. Doubleday, Doran & Company, Inc.

Mulliner Nights: By P. G. Wodehouse. Pelham Grenville Wodehouse. LC 67-111030. (Autograph ed.). 1966. bds. 2.75. Jenkins.

Multi-Colored Walking Stick. Janet Riesen. 3.00 o.p. Carlton.

Multiface. Mark Adlard. 1978. 1.75 (ISBN 0-441-54500-9). Ace Books.

Multiple Choice. Laura Chapman. LC 77-17001. 1978. 7.95 (ISBN 0-385-14049-5). Doubleday.

Multiple Man. Benjamin Bova. (Del Rey Book). 1977. 1.75 (ISBN 0-345-25656-5). Ballantine Books.

Multiple Man. Benjamin Bova. LC 75-33505. 1976. (ISBN 0-672-52072-9). Bobbs-Merrill.

Multiple Man: A Novel of Suspense. Benjamin Bova. LC 75-33505. 224p. 1976. 6.95 o.p. (ISBN 0-672-52072-9). Bobbs.

Multiple Modern Gods and Other Stories. Pref. by Sir Herbert Read. Woodcuts by Herman Zaage. Stanley Berne. LC 64-21952. (Archives of modern literature series) "A Metier Editions book."). 1964. G. Wittenborn.

Multitude. William A Garrett. LC 27-98579. 1927. D. Appleton and Company.

Multitude and Solitude. John Masefield. LC 16-26782. 1916. The Macmillan Company.

Multitude of Men: A Novel. William Dale Smith. LC 59-9498. 1959. Simon and Schuster.

Multitude of Sins. John A. Cuddon. 4.50 o.p. (ISBN 0-8362-0051-9, Pub. by Sheed). Guild Bks.

Multitude of Sins. Robert Molloy. LC 53-6935. 1953. Doubleday.

Multitude of Sins. M. K Wren, pseud. LC 74-18839. 1975. 5.95 (ISBN 0-385-08398-X). Published for the Crime Club by Doubleday.

Mulvaney Stories. Rudyard Kipling. LC 70-178444. (Short story index reprint series). 1971. (ISBN 0-8369-4045-8). Books for Libraries Press.

Mumbo Jumbo. Ishmael Reed. LC 73-171314. (Illus.). 1972. 6.95. Doubleday.

Mumbo Jumbo. Ishmael Reed. (Bard Book). (Illus.). 1978. 2.25 (ISBN 0-380-01860-8). Avon.

Mummers in Mufti. Philip Everett Curtiss. LC 22-181010. 1922. 1.75. The Century.

Mummer's Wife. George Moore. LC 17-31023. 1917. Brentano's.

Mummer's Wife. Authorized Ed. George Moore. LC 66-128196. (Black & gold lib.). 4.95. Liveright.

Mummery, a Tale of Three Idealists. Gilbert Cannan. LC 19-9659. 1919. 1.50. George H. Doran Company.

Mummy! A Chrestomathy of Crypt-Ology. Bill Pronzini. LC 80-66496. 10.95 (ISBN 0-87795-271-X). Arbor House.

Mummy! A Chrestomathy of Cryptology. large print ed. Bill Pronzini. LC 81-12539. 11.95 (ISBN 0-89340-370-9). J. Curley.

Mummy and Miss Nitocris: A Phantasy of the Fourth Dimension. George Chetwynd Griffith. LC 75-46273. (Supernatural and Occult Fiction). 1976. 18.00 (ISBN 0-405-08131-6). Arno Press.

Mummy Case. Dermot Morrah. LC 75-44995. (Fifty Classics of Crime Fiction, 1900-1950; No. 38). 1976. 10.00 (ISBN 0-8240-2350-1). Garland Pub.

Mummy Case Mystery. Dermot Morrah. LC 33-16729. 1933. Harper & Brothers.

Mummy Market: By Nancy Brelis. Pictures by Ben Shecter. Nancy Burns Brelis & Ben Illus Schecter. LC 66-8277. 1966. 3.95, 3.79 lib. ed.,. Harper.

Mummy Moves. Mary Eliza Bakewell Gaunt. LC 25-1014. 1925. E.J. Clode,Inc.

Mummy of Birchen Bower & Other True Ghosts. Harry Ludlam. LC 67-19755. 1967. 3.95 o.p. (ISBN 0-8008-5426-8). Taplinger.

Mum's the Word for Murder. Asa Baker. LC 39-1392. 1938. Frederick A. Stokes Company.

Mumsy, Nanny, Sonny & Girly. Brian Comport. 1970. pap. 0.75 o.p. (ISBN 0-447-74635-9). Lancer.

Mumu. Ivan Sergeevich Turgenev. Tr. by J. Domb & Z. Shoenberg. (Harrap's Bilingual Ser.). 96p. 1946. 5.00 (ISBN 0-911268-54-5). Rogers Bk.

Mumu, and The Diary of a Superfluous Man. Ivan Sergieevich Tergenev & Gersonl, Henry, 1844-1807, Tr. (On cover: Standard library, no. 107). 1884. Funk & Wagnalls.

Munchmeyer & Prospero on the Island. Audrey Callahan Thomas. LC 75-161252. 1972. 5.95 o.p. (ISBN 0-672-51432-X). Bobbs.

Mundahoi. Don Roth. (Crown Ser.). 126p. 1975. pap. 4.50 o.p. (ISBN 0-8127-0098-8). Review & Herald.

Mundahoi. Don Roth. (Crown Ser.). 126p. 1975. pap. 4.50 o.p. (ISBN 0-8127-0098-8). Southern Pub.

Mundome. A. G. Mojtabai. LC 73-20699. 1974. 6.95 (ISBN 0-671-21731-3). Simon and Schuster.

Mundy's Child: A Romance of Everyday Life. Alice Lindley. LC 33-4985. 1933. Dodd, Mead & Company.

Muneca Menor. Rosario Ferre. (De Orilla a Orilla Ser.). (Illus.). 16p. 1979. pap. 3.00 (ISBN 0-940238-29-2). Ediciones Huracan.

Mungo Starke: A Novel. 1st Ed. Patrick Fitzgerald O'Connor. LC 55-14910. 1955. W. W. Norton.

Mungo's Dream. John Innes Mackintosh Stewart. LC 73-2933. 1973. 6.95 (ISBN 0-393-08669-0). Norton.

Munich: A Tale of Two Myths. Thomas B. Jones. 1977. 3.95 o.p. (ISBN 0-8059-2380-2). Dorrance.

Municipal Bonds: A Novel. Jerry Oster. LC 80-27578. 1981. 10.95 (ISBN 0-395-30538-1). Houghton Mifflin.

Munster Cottage Boy. A Tale... Regina Maria Dalton Roche. LC 7-39650. 1820. A. T. Goodrich & Co., W. B. Gilley (Etc.

Munster Song of Love & War. James Liddy. 1971. pap. 1.50. White Rabbit.

Mura, the Western Lady Detective. Harlan Page Halsey. LC 7-11836. (On cover: The calument series, no. 6). G. Munro.

Mural for a Later Day. Kathleen Pawle. LC 38-126952. 1938. Dodd, Mead & Company.

Muramasa Blade: A Story of Feudalism in Old Japan. Louise Wertheimber. LC 12-19556. 1887. Ticknor and Company.

Murder. Harold Adams. 256p. (Orig.). 1981. pap. 2.50 (ISBN 0-441-54706-0). Ace Bks.

Murder. Coover. 1971. price not set o.p.; pap. price not set o.p. Dutton.

Murder. David Solon Greenberg. LC 16-11740. 1916. The Hour Publisher.

Murder--As Usual. Oscar Jerome Friend. LC 42-20326. 1942. Gateway Books.

Murder--but Natch. 1st Ed. Miriam Ann Hagen. LC 51-9209. 1951. Published for the Crime Club by Doubleday.

Murder--First Edition. Truman Garrett. LC 56-12450. 1956. Arcadia House.

Murder--Made in Germany: A True Story of Present-Day Germany. Heinz Liepmann. Tr. by Burns, Emile. LC 34-3724. 1934. Harper & Brothers.

Murder- Murder--Murder-- A Mr. and Mrs. North Omnibus, Including The Norths Meet Murder, Murder Out of Turn and A Pinch of Poison, by Frances and Richard Lockridge. Frances Louise Davis Lockipridge & Richard Lockridge. LC 56-116868. 1956. Lippincott.

Murder a Day! Robert Avery. LC 41-665117. 1940. Mystery House.

Murder a la Mode. Patricia Moyes. LC 82-23260. (Inspector Henry Tibbett mystery). ((Series: Moyes, Patricia.). (Inspector Henry Tibbett mystery.). 1983. 3.95 (ISBN 0-03-063544-6). Holt, Rinehart, and Winston.

Murder A La Mode. Patricia Moyes. LC 63-12604. 224p. 1983. pap. 3.95 (ISBN 0-03-063544-6). HR&W.

Murder a la Mode. Eleanore Kelly Sellars. LC 41-18617. 1941. Dodd, Mead & Company.

Murder a la Richelieu: Introducing That Old Battle-Ax. Anita Blackmon Smith. LC 37-19345. 1937. Pub. for the Crime Club, Inc., by Doubleday, Doran & Co., Inc.

Murder a la Stroganoff. Doris Caroline Abrahams & Simon Jasha Skidelsky. LC 38-33565. 1938. Pub. for the Crime Club, Inc. by Doubleday, Doran & Co., Inc.

Murder: A Love Story. William S. Ruben. 1977. pap. 1.50 (ISBN 0-532-15238-7). Woodhill.

Murder a Mile High. Elizabeth Dean. LC 44-3966. 1944. Pub. for the Crime Club by Doubleday, Doran & Co., Inc.

Murder After a Fashion: By Spencer Dean Pseud. 1st Ed. Prentice Winchell. LC 60-10687. 1960. Published for the Crime Club by Doubleday.

Murder After Hours. Agatha Christie. 1.50. Dell.

Murder After Hours. Agatha Miller Christie. 1982. pap. 2.50 (ISBN 0-440-15922-9). Dell.

Murder After Hours. Agatha Miller Christie. 1973. (pbk.) 0.75. Dell.

Murder After Tea-Time. Leela Cutter. LC 81-8745. 1981. 9.95 (ISBN 0-312-55276-9). St. Martin's Press.

Murder Against the Grain. Emma Lathen, pseud. LC 67-20183. (Cock Robin mystery). 1967. Macmillan.

Murder Against the Grain. Emma Lathen, pseud. LC 67-20183. 1975. (pbk.) 1.25 (ISBN 0-671-78885-X). Pocket Books.

Murder Al Fresco. Jennifer Jones. LC 39-31530. 1939. Pub. for the Crime Club, Inc., by Doubleday, Doran & Co., Inc.

Murder Among Children. Tucker Coe. LC 67-22674. 1968. 4.95 o.p. (ISBN 0-394-41269-9). Random.

Murder Among Children: By Tucker Coe. Donald E. Westlake. LC 67-22674. 1968. 4.50. Random.

Murder Among Friends. Irving E Cox. LC 56-124325. 1957. Abelard-Schuman.

Murder Among Friends. Lange Lewis. LC 42-191344. 1942. The Bobbs-Merrill Company.

Murder Among Friends... Lange Lewis. LC 47-17007. (On cover: A Bart house mystery, 36). 1946.

Murder Among the Angells... Roger Scarlett. LC 32-32419. Pub. for the Crime Club, Inc., by Doubleday, Doran & Company, Inc.

Murder Among the Nudists. Peter Hunt, pseud. LC 34-14226. 1934. The Vanguard Press.

Murder Among Thieves. Peter Alding. LC 70-113179. 1970. 4.50. McCall Pub. Co.

Murder and Blueberry Pie: By Frances and Richard Lockridge. 1st Ed. Frances Louise Davis Lockridge & Richard Lockridge. LC 59-778414. (Main line mysteries). 1959. Lippincott.

Murder & Magic. Randall Garrett. 272p. 1981. pap. 2.50 (ISBN 0-441-54541-6). Ace Bks.

Murder and More Murder. William Roughead. LC 39-21178. Sheridan House.

Murder and the Married Virgin. Davis Dresser. LC 48-18941. (Red badge mystery). 1948. Triangle Books.

Murder and the Married Virgin... Davis Dresser. 1944. Dodd, Mead & Company.

Murder and the Red-Haired Girl. Hearnden Balfour. LC 33-7957. 1933. Houghton Mifflin Company.

Murder and the Shocking Miss Williams: 1st Ed. Harvey J Kennedy. LC 56-123031. 1957. Vantage Press.

Murder Anonymous. Anthony Gilbert, pseud. 1971. pap. 0.95 o.p. (95184). Beagle Bks.

Murder Anonymous. Anthony Gilbert, pseud. 1968. 4.50 o.p. Random.

Murder Anonymous. Lucy Beatrice Malleson. LC 68-28573. 1968. 4.50. Random House.

Murder Arranged. Judson Pentecost Philips. LC 78-18786. (Red badge novel of suspense). 6.95 (ISBN 0-396-07591-6). Dodd, Mead.

Murder As an Ornament. Marjorie Boniface. LC 40-8544. 1940. Pub. for the Crime Club by Doubleday, Doran and Company, Inc.

Murder As the Curtain Rises. Judson Pentecost Philips. (Peter Styles Mystery Novel-Red Badge Novel of Suspense Ser.). 1981. 8.95 o.p. (ISBN 0-396-07954-7). Dodd.

Murder As Usual. Oscar Jerome Friend. LC 45-135986. (Black cat detective series. 13). 1945.

Murder As Usual. Hugh Pentecost. LC 78-60739. 1978. pap. 1.95 o.s.i. (ISBN 0-89559-100-6). Dale Books Inc.

Murder As Usual. Hugh Pentecost. (Red Badge Novel of Suspense). 1977. 6.95 o.p. (ISBN 0-396-07408-1). Dodd.

Murder As Usual. Judson Pentecost Philips. LC 77-551. (badge novel of suspense). 6.95 (ISBN 0-396-07408-1). Dodd, Mead.

Murder at a Police Station. Joseph Jefferson Farjeon. LC 43-4728. 1943. The Bobbs-Merrill Company.

Murder at Arondale Farm. John Hawk. LC 32-422127. 1932. Farrar & Rinehart, Incorporated.

Murder at Arroways. Helen Kieran Reilly. LC 50-7152. 1950. Random House.

Murder at Avalon Arms. Oscar Jerome Friend. E. J. Clode, Inc.

Murder at Bayside. Raymond Robins. LC 33-18661. Thomas Y. Crowell Company.

Murder at Belle Camille. Monte Barrett. LC 43-11950. 1943. The Bobbs-Merrill Company.

Murder at Brambles. Gilbert Collins. LC 32-26641. 1932. H. Holt and Company.

Murder at Bratton Grange. Cecil John Charles Street. LC 29-16599. 1929. Dodd, Mead & Company.

Murder at Bridge: A Mystery Novel. Anne Austin. LC 31-4815. 1931. The Macmillan Company.

Murder at Buckingham Palace. Thomas Ernest Bennett Clarke. LC 81-16739. 9.95 (ISBN 0-312-55283-1). St. Martin's Press.

Murder at Calamity House. Jean Powley. LC 47-30649. 1947. Arcadia House.

Murder at Cambridge. Q. Patrick, pseud. LC 33-6475. Farrar & Rinehart. Incorporated.

Murder at Coney Island. James D O'Hanlon. LC 39-12732. Phoenix Press.

Murder at Crawford Notch. Mary Loveland Burns. LC 44-3316. 1944. B. Humphries, Inc.

Murder at Crome House. George Douglas Howard Cole & Margaret Isabel Postgate Cole. LC 75-44966. (Fifty Classics of Crime Fiction, 1900-1950: 12). 1976. 12.00 (ISBN 0-8240-2361-7). Garland Pub.

Murder at Crome House. George Douglas Howard Cole & Margaret Isabel Postgate Cole. 1927. The Macmillan Company.

Murder at Crome House. G. D. H & Margaret Cole. 1976. lib. bdg. 13.95x (ISBN 0-89968-167-0). Lightyear.

Murder at Cypress Hall. William Rollins. LC 33-779671. The Macaulay Company.

Murder at Deer Lick. Albert Benjamin Cunningham. LC 39-247288. 1939. E. P. Dutton & Co., Inc.

Murder at Derivale: By John Rhode. Cecil John Charles Street. LC 58-8292. (Red badge detective). 1958. Dodd, Mead.

Murder at Drake's Anchorage. Waddell, Eleanor Lee. LC 49-8691. (Guilt edged mystery). 1949. E. P. Dutton.

Murder at Elaine's: A Novel. Ron Rosenbaum. LC 78-64635. (Illus.). 7.95 (ISBN 0-88373-083-9). Stonehill.

Murder at Elstree: Or, Mr. Thurtell and His Gig. Thomas Burke. LC 37-4842. 1936. Longmans, Green and Co.

Murder at Endor. William Almon Wolff. LC 33-978. 1933. Minton, Balch & Company.

Murder at Exbridge. Victor Lorenzo Whitechurch. LC 32-187342. 1932. Dodd, Mead & Company.

Murder at Fleet. Eric Brett Young. LC 28-6759. 1928. J. B. Lippincott Company.

Murder at Glen Athol... Norman Lippincott. LC 35-3356. 1935. Pub. for the Crime Club, Inc., by Doubleday, Doran & Company, Inc.

Murder at Government House. Elspeth Joscelin Grant Huxley. LC 37-17084. 1937. Harper & Brothers.

Murder at Grand Bay. Willo Davis Roberts. 1955. Arcadia House.

Murder at Hazelmoor. Agatha Christie. 1.50. Dell.

Murder at Hazelmoor. Agatha Miller Christie. LC 31-21887. 1931. Dodd, Mead & Company.

Murder at Hazelmoor. Dame Agatha Miller Christie. 1973. (pbk) 0.75. Dell.

Murder at High Noon. Paul McGuire. LC 35-20298. 1935. Pub.for the Crime Club, Inc., by Doubleday, Doran & Company, Inc.

Murder at High Tide. Charles Gordon Booth. LC 30-4723. 1930. W. Morrow & Company.

Murder at Horsethief: A Jason and Pat Cordry Mystery. James D O'Hanlon. LC 41-26008. Phoenix Press.

Murder at Large. Lesley Frost. LC 32-12521. Coward-McCann, Inc.

Murder at Leisure. James William MacQueen. LC 37-138562. 1937. Pub. for the Crime Club, Inc., by Doubleday, Doran & Co., Inc.

Murder at Leisure. Hubert Monteilhet. LC 74-139648. (Inner sanctum mystery). 1971. 4.95 (ISBN 0-671-20848-9). Simon and Schuster.

Murder at Liberty Hall. Alan Francis Clutton-Brock. LC 41-12688. 1941. The Macmillan Company.

Murder at Lilac Cottage. Cecil John Charles Street. LC 40-10305. 1940. Dodd, Mead & Company.

Murder at Lovers Lake. Margaretta Brucker. LC 43-180072. 1943. Phoenix Press.

Murder at Magpie Flats. Kelly P Gast. LC 77-82450. 1978. 6.95 (ISBN 0-385-13157-7). Doubleday.

Murder at Malibu. James D O'Hanlon. LC 38-1085. Phoenix Press.

Murder at Maneuvers. Royce Howes. LC 38-20124. 1938. Pub. for the Crime Club, Inc., by Doubleday, Doran & Company.

Murder at Manson's. Rose Emmet Young. LC 27-246615. 1927. The John Day Company.

Murder at Marston Manor. Robin Forsythe. LC 35-53783. (Tired business man's library of adventure, detective, and mystery novels). 1935. D. Appleton-Century Company, Incorporated.

Murder at Midnight. John Blackburn. LC 65-11332. 1964. M. S. Mill; Distributed by W. Morrow.
Murder at Midnight. Robert Alfred John Walling. LC 32-179092. 1932. W. Morrow & Company.
Murder at Midyears. Marion Mainwaring. LC 53-12738. 1953. Macmillan.
Murder at Montank. Dorothy Wheelock. LC 40-104522. Phoenix Press.
Murder at Monte Carlo. Edward Phillips Oppenheim. LC 33-270400. 1933. Little, Brown, and Company.
Murder at Moose Jaw. Tim Heald. LC 81-43126. 1981. 10.95 (ISBN 0-385-17754-2). Published for the Crime Club by Doubleday.
Murder at Prospect, Kentucky. Augusta Wallace Lyons. LC 77-24462. 7.95 (ISBN 0-399-12067-X). Putnam.
Murder at Radio City: A Mrs. Pym Story. Nigel Morland. Farrar & Rinehart, Incorporated.
Murder at Red Pass. The Aresbys. LC 30-329013. 1930. I. Washburn.
Murder at St. Dennis. Margaret Ann Hubbard. LC 52-11477. 1952. Bruce Pub. Co.
Murder at Sea. Richard Edward Connell. LC 29-1189. 1929. Minton, Balch & Company.
Murder at Sinai. Seymour Peyton. 1970. 3.50 o.p. Vantage.
Murder at Stone House. Edith Howie. LC 42-7960. 1942. Farrar & Rinehart, Inc.
Murder at Sunset Gables. Dean Heffernan. LC 32-35024. 1932. Benziger Brothers.
Murder at Sunset Rock. Deta Petersen Neeley. LC 44-36923. 1944. Meador Publishing Company.
Murder at the ABA. Isaac Asimov. (Fawcett Crest Book). 1977. 1.75 (ISBN 0-449-23202-6). Fawcett Publications.
Murder at the ABA: A Puzzle in Four Days and Sixty Scenes. Isaac Asimov. LC 75-21206. 1976. 6.95 (ISBN 0-385-11305-6). Doubleday.
Murder at the Academy Awards. Joe Hyams. LC 83-2886. 1983. 11.95 (ISBN 0-312-55284-X). St. Martin's Press.
Murder at the "Angel". Hugh McCutcheon. LC 52-10601. (Guilt edged mystery). 1952. Dutton.
Murder at the Black Crook. Cecile Hulse Matschat. LC 43-6647. 1943. Farrar & Rinehart, Inc.
Murder at the Casino. Carolyn Wells. J. B. Lippincott Company.
Murder at the Dome. Gelett Burgess. LC 46-438843. (Contemporary California short stories, no.2). 1937. Pub. for Its Members by the Book Club of California.
Murder at the Flea Club. Matthew Head. LC 80-8716. 272p. 1981. pap. 2.50i (ISBN 0-06-080542-0, P542, PL). Har-Row.
Murder at the Frankfurt Book Fair: A Wicked, Witty Novel About the Publishing of an International Bestseller. Hubert Monteilhet. LC 73-22790. 1976. 6.95 (ISBN 0-385-03453-9). Doubleday.
Murder at the Hunting Club. Mary Plum. LC 32-14946. 1932. Harper & Brothers.
Murder at the Inn. Alister McAllister. LC 29-23790. 1929. Harper & Brothers.
Murder at the Kentucky Derby. Charles B Parmer. LC 42-21559. 1942. Published for the Crime Club by Doubleday, Doran & Company, Inc.
Murder at the Keyhole. Robert Alfred John Walling. LC 29-4415. W. Morrow & Co.
Murder at the Mardi Gras. Elisabet M Stone. LC 47-11323. 1947. Sheridan House.
Murder at the Met. Fred G Jarvis. LC 70-133920. 1971. 5.95. Coward-McCann.
Murder at the Mike. Charles Saxby. LC 38-38826. E. P. Dutton & Co., Inc.
Murder at the Moorings. Miles Burton. LC 34-921320. Sears Publishing Company.
Murder at the Motor Show. Cecil John Charles Street. LC 36-252810. 1936. Dodd, Mead & Company.
Murder at the Munition Works. George Douglas Howard Cole & Margaret Isabel Postgate Cole. LC 40-13520. 1940. The Macmillan Company.
Murder at the New York World's Fair. Freeman Dana. LC 39-611326. Random House.
Murder at the Nook. Archibald E. Fielding. LC 30-779085. 1930. A. A. Knopf.
Murder at the Old Stone House. Charlotte Murray Russell, pseud. LC 35-14569. 1935. Pub. for the Crime Club, Inc., by Doubleday, Doran and Company, Inc.
Murder at the Pageant. Victor Lorenzo Whitechurch. LC 31-265497. 1931. Duffield & Company.
Murder at the Piano. George A Bagby, pseud. LC 35-16780. Covici, Friede.
Murder at the Piano. Aaron Marc Stein. LC 35-16780. 1935. Covici, Friede.
Murder at the Red October. Anthony Olcott. LC 81-12694. 11.95 (ISBN 0-89733-048-X). Academy Chicago.
Murder at the Savoy. Maj Sjowall & Per Wahloo. LC 76-42999. 1977. 1.65 (ISBN 0-394-72342-2). Vintage Books.
Murder at the Savoy. Maj Sjowall & Per Wahloo. LC 77-162551. 1971. 4.95 (ISBN 0-394-47081-8). Pantheon Books.
Murder at the Schoolhouse: A Novel. Albert Benjamin Cunningham. LC 40-107672. 1940. E. P. Dutton & Co., Inc.
Murder at the UN: A Novel of Suspense. Will Perry. LC 76-23115. 1976. 6.95 (ISBN 0-396-07351-4). Dodd, Mead.
Murder at the 'varsity. Q. Patrick, pseud. LC 33-7192. 1933. Longmans, Green and Co.
Murder at the Vicarage. Agatha Miller Christie. LC 77-156184. (Greenway edition; 21). (Illus.). 1977. 6.95. Dodd, Mead.
Murder at the Vicarage. Dame Agatha Miller Christie. 1973. (pbk) 0.75. Dell.
Murder at the Vicarage: A Detective Story. Agatha Miller Christie. LC 30-29830. 1930. Dodd, Mead & Company.
Murder at the Villa Rose. Alfred Edward Woodley Mason. 1979. pap. 2.25 (ISBN 0-684-16403-5, SL 899, ScribT). Scribner.
Murder at the Women's City Club. Q. Patrick, pseud. LC 32-26662. 1932. Roland Swain Company.
Murder at the World's Fair. Mary Plum. LC 33-14021. 1933. Harper & Brothers.
Murder at Tomorrow. Penelope Karageorge. 200p. 1982. 11.95 (ISBN 0-8027-5477-5). Walker & Co.
Murder at Vista Point? Norman Fenton. 1977. 5.95 o.p. (ISBN 0-533-02700-4). Vantage.
Murder at Wrides Park, Being Entry Number One in the Case--Book of Ronald Camberwell. Joseph Smith Fletcher. LC 31-18273. 1931. A. A. Knopf.
Murder at 28: 10. Newton Gayle. LC 36-8544. 1936. C. Scribner's Sons.
Murder at 300 to 1. James D O'Hanlon. LC 38-209840. Phoenix Press.
Murder Backstairs. Anne Austin. LC 30-12377. 1930. The Macmillan Company.
Murder Beat. Raymond Drennen. LC 56-58702. 1956. Mystery House.
Murder Before Marriage. Margot Neville. LC 51-9268. 1951. Published for the Crime Club by Doubleday.
Murder Before Midnight. Albert Benjamin Cunningham. 1945. E. P. Dutton & Co., Inc.
Murder Begets Murder. Roderic Jeffries. LC 79-5108. 1979. 8.95 (ISBN 0-312-55288-2). St. Martin's Press.
Murder Begins at Home. Delano L Ames. LC 50-6077. (Murray Hill mystery). 1950. Rinehart.
Murder Behind Closed Doors. Phillips Lore. (Playboy Press Paperback.). 1.95 (ISBN 0-87216-652-X). Playboy Press.
Murder Behind the Mike. Raymond Leslie Goldman. LC 41-27719. Coward-McCann, Inc.
Murder Being Once Done. Ruth Rendell. LC 72-83149. 1972. 4.95 (ISBN 0-385-03913-1). Published for the Crime Club by Doubleday.
Murder Being Once Done. Ruth Rendell. 1975. (pbk.) 0.95. Bantam Books.
Murder Between Dark and Dark. Max Long. J. B. Lippincott Company.
Murder Between Drinks. Angelica Gibbs. LC 32-6662. 1932. W. Morrow & Company.
Murder Bicarb. Delia Van Deusen. LC 40-3966. The Bobbs-Merrill Company.
Murder Book of J. G. Reeder. Edgar Wallace. LC 29-12500. 1929. Pub. for The Crime Club, Inc., by Doubleday, Doran & Company, Inc.
Murder Book of J. G. Reeder see Mind of Mr. J. G. Reeder.
Murder Book of J.G. Reeder. Edgar Wallace. LC 82-9486. 1982. 3.50 (ISBN 0-486-24374-5). Dover.
Murder Bound. Poul Anderson. LC 62-7995. (Cock Robin mystery). 1962. Macmillan.
Murder Breaks Trail. Eunice Mays Boyd. LC 43-100669. 1943. Farrar & Rinehart, Inc.
Murder Business. Peter C. Herring. 176p. (Orig.). 1976. pap. 1.50 (ISBN 0-89041-076-3, 3076). Major Bks.
Murder Buttoned up. Paul A. Holmes. LC 48-11088. (Dutton guilt edged mystery). 1948. E. P. Dutton.
Murder by Accident. Joe E. Hensley. LC 79-83948. pap. 1.95 o.s.i. (ISBN 0-89516-063-3). Condor Pub Co.
Murder by an Aristocrat... Mignon Good Eberhart. LC 32-268715. Pub. for the Crime Club, Inc., by Doubleday, Doran & Company, Inc.
Murder by Appointment. Eleanore Browne. LC 34-182934. 1934. The Macaulay Company.
Murder by Burial. Stanley Casson. LC 38-22502. 1938. Harper & Brothers.
Murder by Death. Henry Keating. 1976. (pbk.) 1.50 (ISBN 0-446-88161-9). Warner Books.
Murder by Decree. Robert Weverka. LC 79-62921. (Illus.). 1979. 1.95 (ISBN 0-345-28062-8). Ballantine Books.
Murder by Experts. Lucy Beatrice Malleson. LC 37-27332. The Dial Press, Inc.
Murder by Experts. Mystery Writers of America & Queen, Ellery, Pseud., Ed. LC 47-4135. 1947. Ziff-Davis Pub. Co.
Murder by Formula. James Harold Wallis. LC 31-169075. E. P. Dutton & Co., Inc.
Murder by Gaslight: Victorian Tales. Ed. by Edward Charles Wagenknecht. Maxwell, Mary Elizabeth (Braddon) 1837-1915. Lady Audley's Secret. LC 49-68309. 1949. Prentice-Hall.
Murder by Inches. Stanley Hopkins. LC 43-51084. 1943. Harcourt, Brace and Company.
Murder by Jury. Ruth Burr Sanborn. LC 32-9442. 1932. Little, Brown, and Company.
Murder by Latitude... Rufus King. LC 30-32902. 1930. Pub. for the Crime Club, Inc., by Doubleday, Doran & Company, Inc.
Murder by Magic. Martin Joseph Freeman. LC 32-22540. 1932. E. P. Dutton & Co., Inc.
Murder by Magic. Amelia Reynolds Long. LC 47-157933. 1947. Phoenix Press.
Murder by Mail. Fenn McGrew. LC 51-9813. (Murray Hill mystery). 1951. Rinehart.
Murder by Marriage. Robert George Dean. LC 40-30528. 1940. C. Scribner's Sons.
Murder by Match Light. E. C. Lorac. 1979. 15.00x (ISBN 0-86025-097-0, Pub. by Ian Henry Pubns England). State Mutual Bk.
Murder by Matchlight. E. C. Lorac. 1977. 6.60 o.p. State Mutual Bk.
Murder by Matchlight: A Chief-Inspector MacDonald Mystery. Edith Caroline Rivett. 1946. Mystery House.
Murder by Microphone. John Reeves. LC 78-8216. (Illus.). 1978. 7.95 (ISBN 0-385-14217-X). Garden City, N.Y.: Doubleday.
Murder by Prescription. Jonathan Stagge, pseud. LC 33-3523. 1938. Pub. for the Crime Club, Inc., by Doubleday, Doran & Co., Inc.
Murder by Proxy. Bettina Boyers & Boyers, Audrey, Joint Author. LC 45-7216. 1945. Pub. for the Crime Club by Doubleday, Doran & Co., Inc.
Murder by Proxy. Anne Morice. LC 78-54106. 1978. 7.95 (ISBN 0-312-55292-0). St. Martin's.
Murder by Reflection. Gerald Heard. LC 42-228572. 1942. The Vanguard Press.
Murder by Request. 1st American Ed. Beverley Nichols. LC 60-12298. 1960. Dutton.
Murder by Schedule... Julian Hinckley. LC 47-21438. (On cover: A Golden willow mystery, no. 55). 1947.
Murder by Scripture. Amelia Reynolds Long. LC 42-117968. Phoenix Press.
Murder by the Arch: A Novel. Harold Wynyard Higginson. LC 31-976. Thomas Y. Crowell Company.
Murder by the Book. Rex Stout. 208p. 1981. pap. 1.95 (ISBN 0-553-14450-2). Bantam.
Murder by the Book see Royal Flush: A Nero Wolfe Omnibus.
Murder by the Book: A Mr. and Mrs. North Mystery, by Frances and Richard Lockridge. 1st Ed. Frances Louise Davis Lockridge & Lockridge, Richard. LC 63-8892. 1963. Lippincott.
Murder by the Book: A Nero Wolfe Novel. Rex Stout. LC 51-13498. 1951. Viking Press.
Murder by the Book: A Nero Wolfe Story. Rex Stout. LC 75-310632. (Penguin crime fiction). 1974. 0.30 (ISBN 0-14-003806-X). Penguin.
Murder by the Clock. Rufus King. LC 29-98764. 1929. Pub. for The Crime Club, Inc., by Doubleday, Doran & Company, Inc.
Murder by the Day. 1st Ed. Veronica Parker Johns. LC 53-553953. 1953. Published for the Crime Club by Doubleday.
Murder by the Dozen: The Cream of the "Mystery" Crop, Mystery Novels and Stories. Ed. by Durbin Lee Horner. LC 35-15310. 1935. Dingwall-Rock, Ltd.
Murder by the Yard. Margaret Tayler Yates. LC 42-50214. 1942. The Macmillan Company.
Murder by Treason. Amelia Reynolds Long. LC 44-5960. 1944. Phoenix Press.
Murder by 3's. Patricia Moyes. LC 65-22469. bds., 5.95. Holt.
Murder by 3's: Including Dead Men Don't Ski, Down Among the Dead Men, and Falling Star. Patricia Moyes. LC 65-22469. 1965. Holt, Rinehart and Winston.
Murder Calling. David Whitelaw. LC 34-374353. C. Kendall.
Murder Calling "50," An Inspector Schmidt Story. Aaron Marc Stein. LC 42-20321. 1942. Pub. for the Crime Club by Doubleday, Doran & Co., Inc.
Murder Calls Dr. Hailey. Robert McNair Wilson. LC 38-10323. J. B. Lippincott Company.
Murder Came Late. John Creasey. LC 75-75907. (Cock robin mystery). 1969. Macmillan.
Murder Came Late. Jeremy York. (Cock Robin Mystery Ser.). 1969. 8.95 o.p. (ISBN 0-02-633230-2). Macmillan.
Murder Can Be Fun. Fredric Brown. LC 48-102489. (A Dutton guilt edged mystery). 1948. E. P. Dutton.
Murder Cancels All Debts. Mary Violet Heberden. LC 46-2916. 1946. Pub. for the Crime Club by Doubleday & Company, Inc.
Murder Can't Stop. Willis Todhunter Ballard. LC 47-24312. 1946. David McKay Company.
Murder Can't Wait: A Captain Heimrich Mystery.1st Ed. Richard Lockridge. LC 64-22180. (Main line mysteries). 1964. Lippincott.
Murder Case Number 33: A Detective Novel from the Files of the Michael Joyce Agency. Louis Cornell. LC 32-71251. 1932. Brentano's.
Murder Cavalcade: An Anthology by Mystery Writers of America, Inc. Mystery Writers of America. LC 46-5905. 1946. Duell, Sloan and Pearce.
Murder Children: A Novel. John Dudley Ball. LC 79-15361. 8.95 (ISBN 0-396-07720-X). Dodd, Mead.
Murder, Chop Chop. James Norman Schmidt. LC 42-2017. 1942. W. Morrow and Company.
Murder City. Oakley M Hall. LC 49-7594. 1949. Farrar, Straus.
Murder Clear, Track Fast. Judson Pentecost Philips. LC 61-986854. (Red badge detective). 1961. Dodd, Mead.
Murder Club. Howel Evans. LC 26-501592. 1925. G. P. Putnam's Sons.
Murder Comes at Night: A Matt Winters Story. Inez Hildagard Oellrichs. LC 40-307584. 1940. Pub for the Crime Club by Doubleday, Doran and Company, Inc.
Murder Comes Back. Harriette Ashbrook. LC 40-32651. Coward-McCann, Inc.
Murder Comes First. Frances Louise Davis Lockridge & Richard Lockridge. 192p. 1975. Repr. of 1951 ed. lib. bdg. 12.05x (ISBN 0-89190-902-8). Am Repr-Rivercity Pr.
Murder Comes First. Richard Lockridge & Frances Louise Davis Lockridge. (Mr. & Mrs. North Mystery Ser.). 1982. pap. 2.95 (ISBN 0-671-44335-6). PB.
Murder Comes First: A Mr. and Mrs. North Mystery. Frances Louise Davis Lockridge & Richard Lockridge. LC 51-10617. (Main line mysteries). 1951. Lippincott.
Murder Comes First: A Mr. and Mrs. North Mystery. Frances Louise Davis Lockridge & Richard Lockridge. LC 76-75. 1976. 6.95 (ISBN 0-89190-902-8). Rivercity Press.
Murder Comes High. Hugh Lawrence Nelson. LC 50-9376. (Murray Hill mystery). 1950. Rinehart.
Murder Comes Home. Nellise Child. LC 33-116331. 1933. A. A. Knopf.
Murder Comes Home. Anthony Gilbert, pseud. 1970. pap. 0.75 o.p. (T2373). Pyramid Pubns.
Murder Comes Home: By Anthony Gilbert Pseud. Lucy Beatrice Malleson. LC 51-9479. Random House-
Murder Comes to Breakfast. Heather Murray & A. M. Niethammer-Scott. LC 80-42089. 32p. 1981. 14.00 (ISBN 0-08-027253-3). Pergamon.
Murder Comes to Eden: By Leslie Ford Pseud. Zenith Jones Brown. LC 55-104915. 1955. Scribner.
Murder Cum Laude. Joseph Francis Delany. LC 35-4804. 1935. H. Smith and R. Haas.
Murder Day by Day. Irvin Shrewsbury Cobb. LC 33-30449. The Bobbs-Merrill Company.
Murder Does Light Housekeeping. Minna Bardon. LC 41-79089. Phoenix Press.
Murder Down Under. Arthur William Upfield. LC 43-1375. 1943. Pub. for the Crime Club by Doubleday, Doran & Company, Inc.
Murder Draws a Line: A Christopher Storm Mystery. Willetta Ann Barber & Rudolph Frederick Schabelitz. LC 40-8151. 1940. Pub. for the Crime Club by Doubleday, Doran and Company, Inc.
Murder En Route. Brian Flynn. LC 33-11099. 1932. Macrae Smith Company.
Murder Ends the Song. Alfred Meyers. LC 41-2090. Reynal & Hitchcock.
Murder Enters the Picture: A Christopher Storm Mystery. Willetta Ann Barber & Rudolph Frederick Schabelitz. LC 42-50588. 1942. Pub. for the Crime Club by Doubleday, Doran & Company, Inc.
Murder Expert. Robert Portner Koehler. LC 45-101531. 1945. Phoenix Press.
Murder Fantastical. Patricia Moyes. LC 67-12584. (Rinehart suspense novel). 1967. Holt, Rinehart and Winston.
Murder First Class. Roger Simons. LC 77-133780. 1970. 3.95 o.p. Roy.
Murder Flies the Atlantic. Stanley Hart Page. LC 33-35484. A. H. King.
Murder Follows Desmond Shannon. Mary Violet Heberden. LC 42-10919. 1942. Published for the Crime Club by Doubleday. Doran & Co., Inc.
Murder for a Hollow Shell... Andrew I Albert. LC 45-34978. 1945.
Murder for a Wanton. Elwyn Whitman Chambers. LC 34-41047. 1934. Pub. for the Crime Club, Inc., by Doubleday, Doran & Company, Inc.

Murder for Art's Sake. 1st Ed. Richard Lockridge. LC 67-13301. 1967. 3.95. Lippincott.

Murder for Breakfast. Peter Hunt, pseud. LC 34-4680. 1934. The Vanguard Press.

Murder for Charity. Patricia Ponder. 1977. pap. 1.50 (ISBN 0-532-15281-6). Woodhill.

Murder for Christmas. Ed. by Thomas Godfrey. LC 82-60904. (Illus.). 480p. 1982. 19.95 (ISBN 0-89296-057-4); ltd. ed. 35.00 (ISBN 0-89296-058-2). Mysterious Pr.

Murder for Christmas. Edith Howie. LC 41-23669. Farr & Rinehart, Inc.

Murder for Christmas: A Poirot Story. Agatha Miller Christie. LC 39-271711. 1939. Dodd, Mead & Company.

Murder for Madame: By Adam Knight Pseud. Lawrence Lariar. LC 51-11792. 1951. Crown Publishers.

Murder for Profit. William Bolitho. 407p. 1982. 14.95 (ISBN 0-910395-02-0); pap. 7.95 (ISBN 0-910395-03-9). Marlboro Pr.

Murder for Sale. Michael Bardsley. LC 72-133779. 1970. 3.95. Roy Publishers.

Murder for the Asking. George Harmon Coxe. LC 39-209641. 1939. A. A. Knopf.

Murder for the Bride. John Dann MacDonald. LC 51-34000. (Gold medal books, 164). 1951. Fawcett Publications.

Murder for the Holidays. Howard Rigsby. LC 51-9075. 1951. Morrow.

Murder for the Millions: A Harvest of Horror and Homicide, Edited by Frank Owen. Ed. by Frank Owen. LC 46-252037. 1946. F. Fell.

Murder for Treasure. David Williams. LC 80-51899. 1981. 9.95 (ISBN 0-312-55296-3). St. Martin's Press.

Murder for Two. George Harmon Coxe. LC 43-738369. 1943. A. A. Knopf.

Murder for What? Rudolf Kagey. LC 36-332941. The Bobbs-Merrill Company.

Murder for What? Rudolf Kagey. LC 43-12458. (On cover: A Crime novel selection. No. 4). 1943. Select Publications, Inc.

Murder: Four Miles High. Reinhard A Braun. LC 54-7492. 1954. Arcadia House.

Murder from Beyond. Reginald Francis Foster. LC 31-6378. The Macaulay Company.

Murder from Heaven. Gloria Goddard. LC 40-6126. Phoenix Press.

Murder from the East: A Race Williams Story. Carroll John Daly. LC 35-840890. 1935. Frederick A. Stokes Company.

Murder from the East: A Race Williams Story. Carroll John Daly. LC 78-55862. (International Polygonics. The IPL Library of Crime Classics). 1978. 4.00 (ISBN 0-930330-01-3). International Polygonics.

Murder from the Grave. William Levine. LC 30-258253. 1930. R. M. McBride & Company.

Murder from the Mind. Amelia Reynolds Long. LC 46-156846. 1946. Phoenix Press.

Murder from Three Angles. John Russell Warren. LC 39-21775. L. Furman, Inc.

Murder Games. Lionel Davidson. LC 77-26790. 1978. 8.95 (ISBN 0-698-10908-2). Coward, McCann & Geoghegan.

Murder Gets Around. Robert Sidney Bowen. LC 47-6456. 1947. Crown Publishers.

Murder Gives a Lovely Light. Dorothy Stockbridge Tillet. LC 41-139464. 1941. Pub. for the Crime Club by Doubleday, Doran and Company, Inc.

Murder-Go-Round. Ed. by Alfred Hitchcock. (Dell Book). 1978. 1.50 (ISBN 0-440-15607-6). Dell Pub. Co.

Murder-Go-Round: Including, Thirteen at Dinner, The A.B.C. Murders, Funerals Are Fatal. Agatha Miller Christie. LC 71-39008. 1972. 7.95 (ISBN 0-396-06554-6). Dodd, Mead.

Murder Goes Astray. Mary Violet Heberden. LC 43-10422. 1943. Pub. for the Crime Club by Doubleday, Doran & Co., Inc.

Murder Goes Fishing: Anthony Adams's First Mystery. Theodore Pratt. LC 36-17527. 1937. E. P. Dutton & Co., Inc.

Murder Goes in a Trailer: Anthony Adams's Second Mystery. Theodore Pratt. LC 37-201976. 1937. E. P. Dutton & Co., Inc.

Murder Goes Mumming. Alisa Craig. LC 81-43369. (Crime Club Ser.). 192p. 1981. 10.95 (ISBN 0-385-17887-5). Doubleday.

Murder Goes Mumming. large print ed. Alisa Craig. LC 82-3276. 289p. 1982. Repr. of 1981 ed. 9.95x (ISBN 0-89621-354-4). Thorndike Pr.

Murder Goes Mumming. Alisa Craig. 192p. 1982. pap. 2.50 (ISBN 0-553-22702-5). Bantam.

Murder Goes Mumming. Charlotte MacLeod. LC 81-43369. 1981. 10.95 (ISBN 0-385-17887-5). Published for the Crime Club by Doubleday.

Murder Goes Rolling Along. Harry F. S Moore. LC 43-503143. 1942. Pub. for the Crime Club by Doubleday, Doran and Company, Inc.

Murder Goes South. Amelia Reynolds Long. LC 42-1108. Phoenix Press.

Murder Goes to Bank Night. Wesley Clarke Clark. LC 41-5873. 1940. Hale Cushman & Flint, Inc.

Murder Goes to College. Rudolf Kagey. LC 36-18559. The Bobbs-Merrill Company.

Murder Goes to College. Rudolf Kagey. LC 44-6010. 1944. Cornell Publishing Corp.

Murder Goes to Press. Cicely Cairns. LC 51-9883. 1951. Macmillan.

Murder Goes to Press. Noel M. Loomis. LC 37-28609. Phoenix Press.

Murder Goes to School. Helen Farrar. LC 48-681. (Fingerprint mystery). 1948. Ziff-Davis Pub. Co.

Murder Goes to the Dogs: Anthony Adams's Third Mystery. Theodore Pratt. LC 38-23205. E. P. Dutton & Co., Inc.

Murder Goes to the World's Fair: Anthony Adams's Fourth Mystery. Theodore Pratt. LC 39-168853. 1939. E. P. Dutton & Company, Inc.

Murder Gone Mad... Philip MacDonald. LC 31-213320. Pub. for the Crime Club, Inc., by Doubleday, Doran & Company, Inc.

Murder Gone Minoan. Clyde B Clason. LC 39-13362. 1939. Pub. for the Crime Club, Inc., by Doubleday, Doran & Co., Inc.

Murder Half Baked. George A Bagby, pseud. LC 37-771578. Covici-Friede.

Murder Half Baked. Aaron Marc Stein. LC 37-7715. 1937. Covici-Friede.

Murder Has an Echo: A Mystery Novel. John Franke Notley. LC 45-827043. 1945. Mystery House.

Murder Has Its Points; a Mr. and Mrs. North Mystery: By Frances and Richard Lockridge. 1st Ed. Frances Louise Davis Lockridge & Richard Lockridge. LC 61-12241. (Main line mysteries). 1961. Lippincott.

Murder Has No Friends: By Bradshaw Jones. Bradshaw-Jones, Malcolm Henry. LC 68-26793. 1968. 4.00. Bobbs.

Murder Helps. Inez Hildagard Oellrichs. LC 47-493094. 1947. D. McKay Co.

Murder Hunt. Pat Stadley. Orig. Title: Autumn of a Hunter. 1977. pap. 1.75 (ISBN 0-89041-172-7, 3172). Major Bks.

Murder in a Blue Moon. Margot Neville. 1949. N. Y., Pub. for the Crime Club by Doubleday.

Murder in a Dark Room. Neill Graham. 1973. 4.95 (ISBN 0-09-116720-5, Pub. by Hutchinson). Merrimack Pub Cir.

Murder in a Haystack. Dorothy Aldis. LC 31-3438. Farrar & Rinehart Incorporated.

Murder in a Hurry. Frances Louise Davis Lockridge & Richard Lockridge. LC 50-6996. (Their A Mr. and Mrs. North mystery). 1950. Lippincott.

Murder in a Library. Charles Judson Dutton. LC 31-841924. 1931. Dodd, Mead and Company.

Murder in a Shell. Maurice Beam & Britton, Sumner 1902- Joint Author. LC 39-7264. J. Messner, Inc.

Murder in a Walled Town: The Private Memoirs of Wayne Armitage. Katherine Woods. LC 34-34008. 1934. Houghton Mifflin Company.

Murder in Amber. Anne Colver. LC 38-4573. 1938. Hillman-Curl, Inc.

Murder in Amityville. Hans Holzer. (Illus.). 288p. 1982. pap. 3.25 (ISBN 0-8439-1165-4, Leisure Bks). Nordon Pubns.

Murder in Any Degree: One Hundred in the Dark: A Comedy for Wives: The Lie: Even Threes: A Man of No Imagination: Larry Moore: My Wife's Wedding Presents: The Surprises of the Lottery. Owen McMahon Johnson. LC 13-17653. 1913. 1.30. The Century Co.

Murder in Any Language. Kelley Roos. LC 48-8286. 1948. A. A. Wyn.

Murder in Beacon Street. Wyndham Martyn. LC 30-7562. 1930. R. M. McBride & Company.

Murder in Bermuda. Willoughby Sharp. LC 33-219311. C. Kendall.

Murder in Black. Francis Durham Grierson. LC 35-15038. (Tired business man's library of adventure, detective, and mystery novels). 1935. D. Appleton-Century Company Incorporated.

Murder in Black and White. David Alexander. LC 51-13436. 1951. Random House.

Murder in Black Letter. Poul Anderson. LC 59-569054. (Cock Robin mystery). 1960. Macmillan.

Murder in Blue. Paul Petersen. (Smugglers # 3). 1974. (pbk.) 0.95. Pocket Books.

Murder in Blue. Clifford Witting. LC 37-19457. 1937. C. Scribner's Sons.

Murder in Blue Street. Frances Kirkwood Crane. LC 51-13907. 1951. Random House.

Murder in Brief, by Merrill Trask: Pseud. Mel Colton. LC 56-451959. 1956. Mystery House.

Murder in Bright Red. Frances Kirkwood Crane. 1953. Random House.

Murder in Canton. Robert Van Gulik. 1967. 3.95 o.p. (ISBN 0-684-10616-7). Scribner.

Murder in Canton: A Chinese Detective Story, by Robert Van Gulik. With 12 Illus. Drawn by the Author in Chinese Style. Robert Hans Van Gulik, pseud. LC 67-240574. (New Judge Dee Mysteries). 1967. 3.95. Scribners.

Murder in Chelsea. Edith Caroline Rivett. LC 35-3120. The Macaulay Company.

Murder in Church. Babette Plechner Hughes. LC 34-21305. (Tired business man's library of adventure, detective, and mystery novels). 1934. D. Appleton-Century Company, Incorporated.

Murder in False Face. George Childerness. LC 43-6905. 1943. Phoenix Press.

Murder in False-Face. Richard Lockridge. LC 68-12485. (White Line mysteries). 1968. Lippincott.

Murder in Fancy Dress. Laurie Mantell. (O.s.i.). 1981. 9.95 o.s.i. (ISBN 0-8027-5446-5). Walker & Co.

Murder in Fiji: A Case in the Career of Bertram Lynch, P.C.B. John Womack Vandercook. LC 36-11549. 1936. Pub. for the Crime Club, Inc., by Doubleday, Doran & Co., Inc.

Murder in Fiji: A Case in the Career of Bertram Lynch, P.C.B. John Womack Vandercook. LC 37-5487. 1936. The Sun Dial Press, Inc.

Murder in Five Columns. Frank Diamond. LC 44-40377. 1944. Mystery House.

Murder in Focus. Dorothy Dunnett. LC 72-9021. (Midnight novel of suspense). 1973. 5.95 (ISBN 0-395-15594-0). Houghton Mifflin.

Murder in Focus. Robert Julian. (Raven House Mysteries Ser.). 224p. 1982. pap. 2.25 (ISBN 0-373-63039-5, Pub. by Worldwide). Harlequin Bks.

Murder in Four Degrees, Being Entry Number Two in the Case--Book of Ronald Camberwell. Joseph Smith Fletcher. LC 31-291981. 1931. A. A. Knopf.

Murder in Full Flight. Brian Hill. LC 33-1448. J. B. Lippincott Company.

Murder in G-Sharp. Rudolf Kagey. LC 37-12724. The Bobbs-Merrill Company.

Murder in Haiti. John Womack Vandercook. LC 56-13608. (Cock Robin mystery).

Murder in Haste. Davis Dresser. 1975. (pbk.) 0.95. Dell.

Murder in Haste. E. P Fenwick. LC 44-6753. 1944. Farrar & Rinehart, Inc.

Murder in Haste. Heather Gardiner. LC 54-10478. Roy Publishers.

Murder in Haste. Garnett Weston. LC 35-907337. 1935. Frederick A. Stokes Company.

Murder in Havana. George Harmon Coxe. LC 43-13008. 1943. A. A. Knopf.

Murder in High Place. R. B Dominic. LC 76-123688. 1970. 4.50. Published for the Crime Club by Doubleday.

Murder in High Places. Hugh Pentecost. LC 82-22134. (Red badge novel of suspense). 1983. 10.95 (ISBN 0-396-08146-0). Dodd, Mead.

Murder in Hollywood. Cromwell Gibbons. LC 36-10387. D. Kemp and Company.

Murder in Jackson Hole. Maude Parker. LC 55-5867. 1955. Rinehart.

Murder in Las Vegas: With a Special Foreword by Irving Shulman. Avon 1st Ed. Jack Waer. LC 55-41993. (Avon, 651). 1955. Avon Publications.

Murder in Luxury. Hugh Pentecost. LC 80-22250. (Pierre Chambrun Mystery Novel Ser.). 196p. 1981. 8.95 (ISBN 0-396-07921-0). Dodd.

Murder in Luxury. Judson Pentecost Philips. LC 80-22250. (Red badge novel of suspense). 8.95 (ISBN 0-396-07921-0). Dodd, Mead.

Murder in Make-up. Lorenz Heller. LC 37-21963. J. Messner, Inc.

Murder in Mallorca. William Angus. 1977. 7.50 o.p. (ISBN 0-533-02821-3). Vantage.

Murder in Manhattan. Arthur Wyman Procter. 1930. W. Morrow & Company.

Murder in Marble: A Detective Story. Judson Pentecost Philips. LC 40-5398. 1940. Dodd, Mead & Company.

Murder in Marble: A Mystery Novel. Judson Pentecost Philips. LC 44-4537. (Handi-book mysteries). 1944. Quinn Publishing Company, Inc.

Murder in Maryland. Zenith Jones Brown. LC 32-29192. Farrar & Rinehart, Incorporated.

Murder in Maryland. Zenith Jones Brown. LC 42-242841. 1942. Triangle Books.

Murder in Mayorca. Michael Bryan. LC 57-10798. (Dell first edition, A145). 1957. Dell Pub. Co.

Murder in Mesopotamia. Agatha Christie. 1.50. Dell.

Murder in Mesopotamia. Agatha Miller Christie. LC 36-19962. 1936. Dodd, Mead & Company.

Murder in Mesopotamia. Agatha Miller Christie. 1979. 1.95 (ISBN 0-440-15982-2). Dell Book.

Murder in Mesopotamia. Agatha Miller Christie. 1973. (pbk.) 0.75. Dell.

Murder in Millennium VI. 1st Ed. Curme Gray. LC 52-97463. Shasta Publishers.

Murder in Mimicry. Anne Morice. LC 76-28046. 1977. 7.95. St. Martin's.

Murder in Mind. Dulcie Gray. 190p. (O.S.I.). 1973. lib. bdg. 5.95 o.s.i. (ISBN 0-85617-951-5). White Lion Pubs.

Murder in Mind. Mystery Writers Of America. Ed. by Lawrence Treat. 3.95 o.p. Dutton.

Murder in Mind: An Anthology of Mystery Stories. Mystery Writers of America. Ed. by Lawrence Treat. LC 67-20544. 1967. Dutton.

Murder in Mind. 1st Ed. James A Howard. LC 60-5977. 1960. Dutton.

Murder in Miniatures. Sam Merwin. 1940. Pub. for the Crime Club by Doubleday, Doran & Co., Inc.

Murder in Mink. Robert George Dean. 1941. C. Scribner's Sons.

Murder in Mink: By Bert Iles Pseud. Zola Helen Ross. LC 56-8976. 1956. Arcadia House.

Murder in Montana. Muriel Bradley. LC 50-12234. 1950. Published for the Crime Club by Doubleday.

Murder in New Guinea: A Case in the Career of Bertram Lynch. John Womack Vandercook. LC 59-5632. (Cock Robin mystery). 1959. Macmillan.

Murder in Newport. Gerard Barnes Lambert. 1938. C. Scribner's Sons.

Murder in Okefenokee. Cecile Hulse Matschat. LC 41-23064. Farrar & Rinehart, Inc.

Murder in Our Midst. Agatha Miller Christie. LC 67-18228. 1967. Dodd, Mead.

Murder in Outline. Anne Morice. LC 79-63485. 1979. 8.95 o.p. (ISBN 0-312-55303-X). St Martin.

Murder in Paradise. Jocelyn Davey, pseud. LC 81-69899. 1982. 11.95 (ISBN 0-8027-5459-7). Walker.

Murder in Paris. Alice Ormond Campbell. LC 30-15103. Farrar & Rinehart, Incorporated.

Murder in Pastiche: Or, Nine Detectives All at Sea. Marion Mainwaring. LC 54-11836. (Cock Bobin mystery). 1954. Macmillan.

Murder in Peking. Vincent Starrett. LC 46-207644. 1946. Lantern Press, Inc.

Murder in Plain Sight. Gerald Brown. LC 45-4558. 1945. Phoenix Press.

Murder in Print. Ray Sonin. LC 56-9518. 1956. Roy Publishers.

Murder in Public. John Crozier. LC 35-4452. 1935. Houghton Mifflin Company.

Murder in Retrospect. Agatha Miller Christie. 1974. (pbk.) 0.95. Dell.

Murder in Retrospect... Agatha Miller Christie. LC 42-16139. 1942. Dodd, Mead & Company.

Murder in Room 700. murder in room seven hundred ed. Mary Hastings Bradley. LC 31-6272. 1931. D. Appleton and Company.

Murder in St. John's Wood. Edith Caroline Rivett. LC 34-20572. The Macaulay Company.

Murder in Shinbone Alley. Helen Kieran Reilly. LC 40-27170. 1940. Pub. for the Crime Club by Doubleday, Doran & Company, Inc.

Murder in Shinbone Alley... Helen Kieran Reilly. LC 41-154517. (Sun dial mysteries). 1941. The Sun Dial Press.

Murder in Silence. George Selmark, pseud. LC 40-5190. 1940. Pub. for the Crime Club by Doubleday Doran & Co., Inc.

Murder in Stained Glass. Margaret Neilson Armstrong. LC 39-274216. Random House.

Murder in Style. Emma Lou Fetta. LC 39-23301. 1939. Pub. for the Crime Club, Inc., by Doubleday, Doran & Company, Inc.

Murder in Suffolk. Archibald E. Fielding. 1938. H. C. Kinsey & Company, Inc.

Murder in Sydney. Leonard Mann. LC 38-1577. 1937. Doubleday, Doran & Company, Inc.

Murder in Texas, Ada E Lingo. LC 35-18849. (Illus.). 1935. Houghton Mifflin Company.

Murder in the Act. Elizabeth St. Clair. (Mystery Puzzlers Ser.: No. 8). (Illus., Orig.). 1978. pap. 1.95 (ISBN 0-89083-411-3). Zebra.

Murder in the Air. Darwin Le Ora Teilhet. LC 31-3502. 1931. W. Morrow and Company.

Murder in the Basement: A Case for Roger Sheringham... Anthony Berkeley Cox. LC 32-200403. Pub. for the Crime Club, Inc., by Doubleday, Doran & Company, Inc.

Murder in the Bath. Roger Francis Didelot. Tr. by Abbott, Elizabeth. LC 33-21277. J. B. Lippincott Company.

Murder in the Blackout. John Russell Warren. LC 40-33932. 1940. Sheridan House.

Murder in the Bookshop: A Fleming Stone Detective Novel. Carolyn Wells. LC 36-89403. J. B. Lippincott Company.

Murder in the Brownstone House: From the Records of a Young Lawyer. Wilson Collison. LC 29-20442. 1929. R. M. McBride & Company.

Murder in the Calais Coach. Agatha Miller Christie. LC 34-4677. 1934. Dodd, Mead & Company.

Murder in the Calais Coach. Agatha Miller Christie. LC 41-4915. 1940. Pocket Books, Inc.

Murder in the Calais Coach. Dame Agatha Miller Christie. 1974. (pbk.) 0.95 (ISBN 0-671-77448-4). Pocket Books.

Murder in the Cassava Patch. Bai T. Moore. (O.s.i.). 1976. pap. 3.00 o.p. (Pub by Ducor Publishing House). Three Continents.

Murder in the Cellar. Louise Eppley. LC 31-18591. 1931. W. Morrow & Company.

Murder in the Dentist Chair. Molly Thynne. LC 32-7608. Covici, Friede.

Murder in the Embassy. John Franklin Carter. LC 30-24621. J. Cape & H. Smith.

Murder in the English Department. Valerie Miner. LC 82-16904. 1983. 9.95 (ISBN 0-312-55310-2). St. Martin's Press.
Murder in the English Department. Valerie Miner. LC 82-16904. 176p. 1983. 9.95 (ISBN 0-312-55310-2). St Martin.
Murder in the Family. John Creasey. LC 76-1554. (Superintendent Folly mysteries). (MW suspense). 1976. 6.95 (ISBN 0-679-50609-8). D. McKay Co.
Murder in the Family. James Ronald. LC 40-33595. J. B. Lippincott Company.
Murder in the Family. 1st Ed. Mary Hastings Bradley. LC 51-12511. 1951. Longmans, Green.
Murder in the Fog. Henry Leyford Gates. LC 32-19273. 1932. The Macaulay Company.
Murder in the Fog. Paul Thorne. LC 29-8832. The Penn Publishing Company.
Murder in the French Room. Helen Joan Hultman. LC 31-31451. 1931. The Mystery League, Inc.
Murder in the Game Reserve. Philip Neville Walker-Taylor. LC 39-1041. 1938. M. S. Mill Co., Inc.
Murder in the Garden. Francis Durham Grierson. LC 27-3018. E. J. Clode, Inc.
Murder in the Gilded Cage. Samuel Spewack. LC 29-204409. 1929. Simon and Schuster.
Murder in the Green Sedan. Robert Portner Koehler. LC 42-7198. 1942. Phoenix Press.
Murder in the Hellfire Club. Donald Zochert. LC 78-4702. 7.95 (ISBN 0-03-022441-1). Holt, Rinehart, and Winston.
Murder in the Hellfire Club. Donald Zochert. LC 80-109. 1980. 1.95 (ISBN 0-14-005504-5). Penguin Books.
Murder in the House of Commons. Mary Agnes Adamson Hamilton. LC 32-2233. 1932. Houghton Mifflin Company.
Murder in the House with the Blue Eyes. Christine Noble Govan. LC 39-20166. The Bobbs-Merrill Company.
Murder in the House with the Blue Eyes. Christine Noble Govan. LC 44-6681. 1911. Margood Publishing Corp.
Murder in the Key Club. Carter Brown, pseud. LC 62-51374. (Signet book, S2140). 1962. New American Library of World Literature.
Murder in the Laboratory. Kate Brooks. (Orig.). 1979. pap. 1.75 (ISBN 0-532-17212-4). Woodhill.
Murder in the Laboratory. T L Davidson. LC 29-18544. E. P. Dutton & Co., Inc.
Murder in the Language Lab. M. L. Allen. (Readers Ser.: Stage 3). 1979. pap. text ed. 1.95 (ISBN 0-88377-130-6). Newbury Hse.
Murder in the Madhouse. Jonathan Latimer. LC 35-5964. 1935. Pub. for the Crime Club, Inc., by Doubleday, Doran & Company, Inc.
Murder in the Madhouse. Jonathan Latimer. LC 36-33143. The Sun Dial Press.
Murder in the Making. Herman Petersen. R. M. McBride & Company.
Murder in the Maze. Alfred Walter Stewart. LC 27-153908. 1927. Little, Brown, and Company.
Murder in the Mews... Helen Kieran Reilly. LC 31-190897. Pub. for the Crime Club, Inc., by Doubleday, Doran & Company, Inc.
Murder in the Mind. Kenneth Thomas Knoblock. LC 32-464015. 1932. Harper & Brothers.
Murder in the Mist. Zelda Popkin. LC 40-32090. J. B. Lippincott Company.
Murder in the Moor. Thomas Kindon. LC 75-44987. (Fifty Classics of Crime Fiction, 1900-1950; No. 30). (Illus.). 1976. 12.00 (ISBN 0-8240-2379-X). Garland Pub.
Murder in the Moor. Thomas Kindon. LC 29-256015. E. P. Dutton & Co., Inc.
Murder in the Morning. Gertrude Pahlow. LC 31-25919. E. J. Clode, Inc.
Murder in the Museum... Eric Heath. LC 39-10519. 1939. Hillman-Curl, Inc.
Murder in the Museum. Eric Heath. LC 41-6794. 1940. Mystery Book of the Month, Inc.
Murder in the Navy. Ed McBain. 1971. pap. 0.75 o.p. (T2466, GM). Fawcett World.
Murder in the Navy: By Richard Marsten Pseud. Cover Painting by Clark Hulings. Evan Hunter. LC 55-43680. (Gold medal books, 507). 1955. Fawcett Publications.
Murder in the News Room. Henry Charlton Beck. LC 31-8418. E. P. Dutton & Co., Inc.
Murder in the Newspaper Guild... Henry Charlton Beck. LC 37-336522. E. P. Dutton & Co., Inc.
Murder in the Night. Arthur Gask. LC 32-12990. 1932. The Macaulay Company.
Murder in the Opera House. Queena Mario. LC 34-358811. E. P. Dutton & Co., Inc.
Murder in the O.P.M. Zenith Jones Brown. LC 42-18461. 1942. C. Scribner's Sons.
Murder in the Outlands. James Beardsley Hendryx. LC 49-48611. (Double D western). 1949. Doubleday.
Murder in the Pallant. Joseph Smith Fletcher. 1928. A. A. Knopf.
Murder in the Park: An Inspector Higgins Story. Cecil Freeman Gregg. LC 35-11481. 1935. The Dial Press, Inc.
Murder in the Penthouse. Peter McCurtin. (Orig.). 1981. pap. 2.50 (ISBN 0-505-51645-4). Tower Bks.
Murder in the Radio Department. Alfred Eichler. LC 43-16216. 1943. Gold Label Books, Inc.
Murder in the Rain: The Chronicle of a Curious Crime. Wilson Collison. LC 30-5408. 1930. R. M. McBride & Company.
Murder in the Rough. Horace Brown. LC 46-22700. 1946. Five Star Mysteries, Inc.
Murder in the Round. Dorothy Dunnett. LC 75-100101. 1970. 4.95. Houghton Mifflin.
Murder in the Ruins. Neville Aldridge Holdaway. LC 36-34846. The Dial Press.
Murder in the Senate. Francis Van Wyck Mason. LC 36-354. Dodge Publishing Company.
Murder in the Smithsonian. Margaret Truman. 304p. 1983. 14.95 (ISBN 0-87795-475-5). Arbor Hse.
Murder in the Squire's Pew. Joseph Smith Fletcher. LC 32-5311. 1932. A.A. Knopf.
Murder in the Stacks. Marion M Boyd. LC 34-31987. 1934. Lothrop, Lee and Shepard Company.
Murder in the Stacks. Marion M. Boyd Havighurst. LC 34-81987. 1934. Lothrop, Lee and Shepard Company.
Murder in the Stars. John Creasey. 1982. 15.00x (ISBN 0-86025-175-6, Pub. by Ian Henry Pubns England). State Mutual Bk.
Murder in the Stars. new ed. John Creasey. 192p. 1972. 5.95 o.p. (ISBN 0-529-04483-8, A4309). World Pub.
Murder in the State Department. John Franklin Carter. LC 30-11382. 1930. J. Cape & H. Smith.
Murder in the Stratosphere. Gilbert Eldredge. LC 40-32290. 1940. Phoenix Press.
Murder in the Supreme Court. Margaret Truman. LC 81-71678. 1982. 12.95 (ISBN 0-87795-384-8). Arbor Hse.
Murder in the Supreme Court. Margaret Truman. (General Ser.). 1983. lib. bdg. 15.50 (ISBN 0-8161-3516-9, Large Print Bks). G K Hall.
Murder in the Supreme Court: A Novel. Margaret Truman. LC 81-71678. 13.50 (ISBN 0-87795-384-8). Arbor House.
Murder in the Surgery... James William MacQueen. LC 35-8861. 1935. Pub. for the Crime Club, Inc., by Doubleday, Doran & Company, Inc.
Murder in the Synagogue. Thomas V. Lo Cicero. Orig. Title: Murder of Rabbi Adler. 1970. 9.95 o.p. (ISBN 0-13-606590-2). P-H.
Murder in the Title: A Charles Paris Mystery. Simon Brett. 192p. 1983. 12.95 (ISBN 0-684-17898-2, ScribT). Scribner.
Murder in the Tomb. Lucian Austin Osgood. LC 37-23781. 1937. Unique Mystery Novels.
Murder in the Tower. Eleanor Hibbert. LC 74-78900. 1974. 6.95 (ISBN 0-399-11396-7). Putnam.
Murder in the Tower. Jean Plaidy. LC 74-78900. 288p. 1974. 6.95 o.p. (ISBN 0-399-11396-7). Putnam Pub Group.
Murder in the Town: Professor Dixon's First Case. Mary Richart. LC 49-4561. 1947. Farrar, Straus.
Murder in the Walls. Richard Martin Stern. LC 73-140285. 1971. 4.95 (ISBN 0-684-12346-0). Scribner.
Murder in the White House. Margaret Truman. LC 79-54004. 1980. 9.95 (ISBN 0-87795-245-0). Arbor Hse.
Murder in the White House. Margaret Truman. (General Ser.). 1980. lib. bdg. 13.95 (ISBN 0-8161-3171-6, Large Print Bks). G K Hall.
Murder in the White House. Margaret Truman. 256p. 1981. pap. 2.95 (ISBN 0-445-04661-9). Popular Lib.
Murder in the White House: A Novel. Margaret Truman. LC 79-54004. 9.95 (ISBN 0-87795-245-0). Arbor House.
Murder in the Willett Family... Rufus King. LC 31-190883. Pub. for the Crime Club, Inc., by Doubleday, Doran & Company, Inc.
Murder in the Wind. John Dann MacDonald. LC 56-10365. (Dell first edition, A113). Dell Pub. Co.,
Murder in the Wind. George Ogan. (Raven House Mysteries Ser.). 224p. 1981. pap. 2.25 (ISBN 0-373-63010-7, Pub. by Worldwide). Harlequin Bks.
Murder in the WPA. Alexander Hazard Williams. LC 37-813769. R. M. McBride & Company.
Murder in the Zoo. Babette Flechner Hughes. LC 32-1650. 1932. D. Appleton and Company.
Murder in the Zoo: By Babette Hughes. Babette Plechner Hall. LC 32-1650. 1932. D. Appleton.
Murder in Thin Air. Robert McNair Wilson. LC 37-35. J. B. Lippincott.
Murder in Three Acts. Agatha Miller Christie. LC 34-32216. Dodd, Mead & Company.
Murder in Three Acts: "a Hercule Poirot Mystery"... Agatha Miller Christie. LC 45-4560. (New Avon library. 61). 1944.
Murder in Time. Lillian Day. LC 36-3328. Green Circle Books.
Murder in Tow: A Lieut. Bill French Mystery. Frances Moyer Ross Stevens. LC 43-497693. 1943. Pub. for the Crime Club by Doubleday, Doran and Company, Inc.
Murder in Trinidad. John Womack Vandercook. LC 55-811. (Murder revisited series, no. 11). 1955. Macmillan.
Murder in Trinidad: A Case in the Career of Bertram Lynch, P.C.B.... John Womack Vandercook. LC 33-23674. 1933. Pub. for the Crime Club, Inc., by Doubleday, Doran & Company, Inc.
Murder in Triplicate. Hugh Austin. LC 35-356820. 1935. N. Y., Pub. for the Crime Club, Inc., by Doubleday, Doran & Company, Inc.
Murder in Triplicate. Hugh Austin. LC 36-323381. The Sun Dial Press.
Murder in Triplicate. P. D James. LC 80-18493. 1980. 15.00 (ISBN 0-684-16748-4). Scribner.
Murder in Twenty-Five Words or Less. Irma Walker. (Raven House Mysteries Ser.). 224p. 1982. pap. 2.25 (ISBN 0-373-63032-8, Pub. by Worldwide). Harlequin Bks.
Murder in Two Flats. Roy Vickers. LC 52-5056. 1952. M. S. Mill Co., and W. Morrow.
Murder in Venice. 1974. (pbk.) 1.25 (ISBN 0-523-00343-9). Pinnacle Books.
Murder in Waiting. Mignon Good Eberhart. LC 73-1697. 1974. (pbk.) 0.95. Popular Library.
Murder in Waiting. Mignon Good Eberhart. LC 77-13445. 1978. 9.95 (ISBN 0-89340-103-X). J. Curley.
Murder in Waiting: A Novel. Robert Murphy. LC 38-14449. 1938. C. Scribner's Sons.
Murder in Wardour Street: A Mrs. Pym Mystery. Nigel Morland. LC 40-10299. Farrar Rinehart Incorporated.
Murder in Wax. Leonard Worswick Clyde. LC 31-35311. 1931. The Macaulay Company.
Murder in White. Hugh Zachary. 1981. pap. 1.95 (ISBN 0-8439-0876-9, Leisure Bks). Nordon Pubns.
Murder, Inc. In a Keg. Harold J. Treherne. 6.95 o.p. Vantage.
Murder Incidental. Keith Trask. LC 31-268805. Farrar & Rinehart, Incorporated.
Murder Ink: The Mystery Reader's Companion. Dilys Winn. LC 77-5282. 12.50. (ISBN 0-89480-003-5) (ISBN 0-89480-004-3). Workman Pub. Co.
Murder Intended. Francis Beeding. LC 32-179105. 1932. Little, Brown & Company.
Murder International, Including So Many Steps to Death, Death Comes As the End, Evil Under the Sun. Agatha Miller Christie. LC 65-269741. 4.95. Dodd.
Murder Is a Collector's Item. Elizabeth Dean. LC 39-27264. 1939. Pub. for the Crime Club, Inc., by Doubleday, Doran & Company, Inc.
Murder Is a Gamble. Glenn M Barns. LC 52-6563. 1952. Phoenix Press.
Murder Is a Package Deal. Alan Geoffrey Yates. (Signet, T5532). 1973. (pbk.) 0.75. New American Lib.
Murder Is a Serious Business. Elizabeth Dean. LC 40-34423. 1940. Pub. for the Crime Club by Doubleday, Doran and Co.
Murder Is Absurd. Patricia McGerr. LC 66-22938. 1967. Published for the Crime Club by Doubleday.
Murder Is an Art. A. Boyd Correll. LC 50-7356. 1950. Phoenix Press.
Murder Is an Evil Business. Marion Bramhall. LC 48-7281. 1948. Pub. for the Crime Club by Doubleday.
Murder Is Announced. Agatha Miller Christie. LC 50-7830. (Red badge mystery). 1950. Dodd, Mead.
Murder Is Announced. Agatha Miller Christie. LC 52-25499. W. J. Black.
Murder Is Contagious. Marion Bramhall. 1949. Pub. for the Crime Club by Doubleday.
Murder Is Corny see Trio for Blunt Instruments: A Nero Woolfe Threesome.
Murder Is Dangerous. Saul Levinson. LC 49-1186. 1949. Phoenix Press.
Murder Is Easy. Agatha Miller Christie. LC 81-67344. (Greenway edition). 1981. 8.95 (ISBN 0-396-08016-2). Dodd, Mead.
Murder Is Easy! Armstrong Livingston. LC 37-1609. R. Speller.
Murder Is for Keeps: By Peter Chambers Pseud. Dennis John Andrew Phillips. LC 62-139208. (Raven book). 1962. Abelard -Schuman.
Murder Is Forgetful. William Bogart. LC 44-40378. 1944. Mystery House.
Murder Is Insane. 1st Ed. Glenn M Barnes. LC 56-108167. (Main line mysteries). 1956. Lippincott.
Murder Is Mutual: An Adventure in Murder Which Recounts the Further Exploits of Doc Connor and Katie Storm. Jack Dolph. LC 48-8320. 1948. W. Morrow.
Murder Is My Business. Davis Dresser. 1945. Dodd, Mead & Company.
Murder Is My Shadow. Chandler Nash. LC 59-5694. (Cock robin mystery). 1959. Macmillan.
Murder Is Not Enough. Susan Wells. LC 39-340536. 1939. Simon and Schuster.
Murder Is Not Mute. Audrey Newell. LC 40-34428. 1940. Macrae-Smith-Company.
Murder Is Out. Lee Thayer, pseud. LC 42-2428. 1942. Dodd, Mead & Company.
Murder Is Out... Lee Thayer, pseud. LC 46-21107. (On cover: Bart house mystery. 16). 1945.
Murder Is Served: A Mr. and Mrs. North Mystery. Frances Louise Davis Lockridge & Richard Lockridge. LC 48-8046. (Main line mysteries). 1948. J. B. Lippincott Co.
Murder Is Suggested: A Mr. and Mrs. North Mystery, by Frances and Richard Lockridge. 1st Ed. Frances Louise Davis Lockridge & Richard Lockridge. LC 59-139471. (Main line mysteries). 1959. Lippincott.
Murder Is Suspected. Peter Alding. LC 78-62995. 1978. 7.95 (ISBN 0-8027-5389-2). Walker.
Murder Is the Pay-off: By Leslie Ford Pseud. Zenith Jones Brown. LC 50-11033. 1951. Scribner.
Murder Is Where You Find It. Robert P Hansen. LC 56-6977. 1956. M. S. Mill Co. and W. Morrow.
Murder Island. Wyndham Martyn. LC 28-28362. 1928. R. M. McBride & Company.
Murder Isn't Easy. Richard Henry Sampson. LC 36-13460. G. P. Putnam's Sons.
Murder Isn't Enough. Don Flynn. 192p. 1983. 12.95 (ISBN 0-8027-5495-3). Walker & Co.
Murder Jigsaw; "Inspector Manson Again...". Edwin Radford & Radford, Mona A., Joint Author. LC 46-20553. 1944. Pub. for the Crime Book Society by A. Melrose, Limited.
Murder Las Vegas Style. Willis Todhunter Ballard. 1970. pap. 0.75 o.p. (B75-2049). Belmont-Tower.
Murder Laughs Last. Jeremy Ford. LC 56-337095. (Mystery house). 1956. Bouregy & Curl.
Murder Lays a Golden Egg. Eric Traviss Hull. LC 44-35307. 1944. Pub. for the Crime Club by Doubleday, Doran & Co., Inc.
Murder League. Robert L Fish. LC 68-14838. (Inner sanctum mystery). 1968. Simon and Schuster.
Murder Leaves a Ring. Fay Grissom Stanley. LC 50-12466. 1950. Rinehart.
Murder, London-Australia. John Creasey. LC 65-22812. 3.50. Scribners.
Murder, London-Miami. John Creasey. LC 69-17038. 1969. 3.95. Scribner.
Murder, London-South Africa. John Creasey. LC 66-22555. 1966. 3.95. Scribners.
Murder Loves Company. John Mersereau. LC 40-5224. J. B. Lippincott Company.
Murder Machine. Frank Scarpetta. (Marksman Ser.). (O.s.i.). 1975. pap. 1.25 o.s.i. Tower.
Murder Made Absolute. Michael Underwood. 1977. 5.40 o.p. State Mutual Bk.
Murder Made Absolute: By Michael Underwood Pseud. John Michael Evelyn. LC 57-8258. (Chantecler mystery novel). 1957. I. Washburn.
Murder Madness. William Fitzgerald Jenkins. LC 50-5636. 1949. Fantasy Pub. Co.
Murder Madness. William Fitzgerald Jenkins. LC 31-5698. 1931. Brewer and Warren Inc.
Murder Madness. Leinster, pseud. pap. 1.50 o.p. Borden.
Murder, Maestro, Please. Delano L Ames. LC 52-5559. (Murray Hill mystery). 1952. Rinehart.
Murder, Maestro Please. Jack Sharkey, pseud. LC 60-11688. (Raven book). 1960. Abelard-Schuman.
Murder Makers. John Rossiter. LC 76-57854. 1977. 6.95 (ISBN 0-8027-5371-X). Walker.
Murder Makes a Marriage. Schuyler Broocks. LC 47-300. 1946. Mystery House.
Murder Makes a Merry Widow. Robert George Dean. LC 38-201268. 1938. Pub. for the Crime Club, Inc., by Doubleday, Doran & Co., Inc.
Murder Makes a Racket. Mary Violet Heberden. LC 42-252364. 1942. Published for the Crime Club by Doubleday, Doran & Company, Inc.
Murder Makes a Villain. Denis Scott. LC 44-1300. 1944. The Bobbs-Merrill Company.
Murder Makes an Entrance. 1st Ed. Clarence Budington Kelland. LC 55-658412. 1955. Harper.
Murder Makes by-Lines. Kelliher Secrist. LC 41-769447. Mystery House.
Murder Makes Me Nervous. Margaret Scherf. LC 48-774749. 1948. Pub. for the Crime Club by Doubleday.
Murder Makes Murder. Harriette Ashbrook. LC 37-5566. Coward-McCann, Inc.
Murder Makes the Mare Go. 1st Ed. Jack Dolph. LC 50-8304. 1950. Published for the Crime Club by Doubleday.
Murder Makes the Wheels Go 'round. Emma Lathen, pseud. LC 66-13562. (Cock Robin mystery). 1966. Macmillan.
Murder Makes the Wheels Go 'round. Emma Lathen, pseud. LC 81-47337. (Fifty Classics of Crime Fiction, 1950-1975). 1982. 14.95 (ISBN 0-8240-4985-3). Garland Pub.

TITLE INDEX

MURDER ON SHARK ISLAND.

Murder Makes the Wheels Go Round. Emma Lathen. 1974. pap. cancelled o.p. (ISBN 0-515-03432-0). Pyramid Pubns.
Murder Makes the Wheels Go Round. Emma Lathen, pseud. 1976. 1.50 (ISBN 0-671-80545-2). Pocket Books.
Murder Makes Us Gay. Inez Hildagard Oellrichs. LC 41-201634. 1941. Pub. for the Crime Club by Doubleday, Doran & Company, Inc.
Murder Mansion. Herman Landon. LC 28-23461. 1928. H. Liveright.
Murder Mansion... James Harold Wallis. LC 34-194615. 1934. E. P. Dutton & Co., Inc.
Murder Mansion. Alexander Wilson. LC 29-19690. 1929. Longmans, Green and Co.
Murder Maritime. Claudia Cranston. LC 35-114855. J. B. Lippincott Company.
Murder Masks Miami. Rufus King. LC 39-891340. 1939. Pub. for the Crime Club, Inc., by Doubleday, Doran & Company, Inc.
Murder Masquerade. George Bellairs. (Orig.). 1981. pap. 1.95 (ISBN 0-505-51698-5). Tower Bks.
Murder Masquerade. Inez Haynes Irwin. LC 35-1829. 1935. H. Smith & R. Haas.
Murder May Follow. Susan Morrow. 1969. pap. 0.60 o.p. (0502-06044-060). Curtis.
Murder May Follow. 1st Ed. Susan Morrow. LC 59-7914. 1959. Published for the Crime Club by Doubleday.
Murder, M.D. Miles Burton. 1977. 5.55 o.p. State Mutual Bk.
Murder Me for Nickels. Peter Rabe. LC 60-374145. (Gold medal books, 996). 1960. Fawcett Publications.
Murder Meets Mephisto. Queena Mario. LC 42-1109. 1942. E. P. Dutton & Co., Inc.
Murder Meets Mephisto... Queena Mario. LC 45-15792. (Bart house books. 11). 1945.
Murder Melody. Kelliher Secrist. LC 39-15709. Phoenix Press.
Murder Memo to the Commissioner: The Carl Houston Case, Documents Included, Oct. 1949 -- Aug. 1950. William Charles Oursler. LC 50-14307. (Inner sanctum mystery). 1950. Simon and Schuster.
Murder Menagerie. Jeremy Lane. LC 46-594402. 1946. Phoenix Press.
Murder Mission! Al Conroy. (Lancer book). 1973. (pbk) 0.95. Lancer Books.
Murder Mixture: An Anthology of Crime Stories. Elizabeth Lee. 1963. 7.95 o.p. (ISBN 0-236-31122-0). Dufour.
Murder Money. Edward Sidney Aarons. LC 38-15229. Phoenix Press.
Murder Money. Edward Ronns, pseud. Phoenix Press.
Murder Moon. Paul H Dobbins. LC 49-105074. 1949. Murray & Gee.
Murder Most Foul. Kathleen Buddington Pseud Coxe. LC 47-15518. 1946. Phoenix Press.
Murder Most Foul: The 1971 Mystery Writers of America Anthology. Ed. by Harold Q. Masur. Mystery Writers of America. LC 72-161116. 1971. 5.95 (ISBN 0-8027-5238-1). Walker.
Murder Most Fouled up. Stanton Forbes, pseud. LC 68-18071. 1968. 3.95. Published for the Crime Club by Doubleday.
Murder Most Fouled up. 1st Ed. Tobias Wells. LC 68-18071. 1968. 3.95. Published for the Crime Club by Doubleday.
Murder Most Opportune. Robert George Dean. LC 39-19159. 1939. Pub. for the Crime Club, Inc., by Doubleday, Doran & Co., Inc.
Murder Most Royal. Eleanor Hibbert. LC 79-189782. 1972. 7.95. Putnam.
Murder Most Royal. Jean Plaidy. 230p. 1972. 7.95 (ISBN 0-399-10934-X). Putnam Pub Group.
Murder Most Strange. Elizabeth Linington. LC 80-24573. 1981. 9.95 (ISBN 0-688-00378-8). Morrow.
Murder Most Strange. Dell Shannon. LC 80-24573. 224p. 1981. 10.95 (ISBN 0-688-00378-8). Morrow.
Murder Most Strange. large type ed. Dell Shannon. LC 82-10340. 354p. 1982. 10.95 (ISBN 0-89621-377-3). Thorndike Pr.
Murder, Murder, Little Star. Marian Babson. LC 79-91254. 1980. 9.95 (ISBN 0-8027-5416-3). Walker.
Murder Must Advertise. Dorothy Leigh Sayers. LC 59-10622. 1959. Harper.
Murder Must Advertise. Dorothy Leigh Sayers. LC 80-21308. 1980. 15.95 (ISBN 0-8161-3045-0). G. K. Hall.
Murder Must Advertise see Wimsey Set II.
Murder Must Advertise: A Detective Story. Dorothy Leigh Sayers. LC 33-8543. Harcourt, Brace and Company.
Murder Must Advertise and Hangman's Holiday. Dorothy Leigh Sayers. Harcourt, Brace and Company.
Murder Must Wait. Arthur William Upfield. LC 53-5951. 1953. Published for the Crime Club by Doubleday.
Murder Mystery. Gene Thompson. LC 80-5295. 10.95 (ISBN 0-394-51264-2). Random House.
Murder Mystery. Gene Thompson. 1981 (ISBN 0-345-29892-6). Avon Books.
Murder Needs a Face: A Mystery Novel. Ruth Fenisong. LC 42-50422. 1942. Pub. for the Crime Club by Doubleday, Doran & Company, Inc.
Murder Needs a Name. Ruth Fenisong. LC 42-16056. 1942. Published for the Crime Club by Doubleday, Doran & Co., Inc.
Murder Now & Again. J. A. Knipe & Madeleine Haldimon. (Orig.). 1980. pap. text ed. 2.50 o.s.i. (ISBN 0-505-51548-2). Tower Bks.
Murder Now & Then. English Language Services. (Collier-Macmillan English Readers). pap. 1.60 (ISBN 0-02-971320-X). Macmillan.
Murder of a Bad Man. Hulbert Footner. LC 36-1427. 1936. Harper & Brothers.
Murder of a Banker. Joseph Smith Fletcher. LC 33-304482. A. A. Knopf.
Murder of a Cop. William Murdoch Duncan. 1976. 7.95 (ISBN 0-09-127190-8, Pub. by Hutchinson). Merrimack Pub Cir.
Murder of a Dead Man. Rudolf Kagey. LC 35-8102. The Bobbs-Merrill Company.
Murder of a Fifth Columnist. Zenith Jones Brown. LC 41-12686. 1941. C. Scribner's Sons.
Murder of a Little Girl. Samuel Roen. LC 73-82981. 343p. 1974. 8.95 (ISBN 0-88435-000-2). Chateau Pub.
Murder of a Matriarch... Hugh Austin. LC 36-130425. 1936. N. Y., Pub. for the Crime Club, Inc., by Doubleday, Doran & Company, Inc.
Murder of a Matriarch... Hugh Austin Evans. LC 36-13042. 1936. N.Y., Pub for the Crime Club, Inc., by Doubleday, Doran & Company, Inc.
Murder of a Midget. Martin Joseph Freeman. LC 31-14177. E. P. Dutton & Co., Inc.
Murder of a Missing Man. Arthur Minturn Chase. LC 34-1290. 1934. Dodd, Mead & Company.
Murder of a Mistress. Henry Kuttner. LC 57-8440. (Permabooks, M--4062. Mystery 2). 1957. Permabooks.
Murder of a Mystery Writer. John Hawk. LC 29-107399. 1929. Pub. for The Crime Club, Inc., by Doubleday, Doran & Company, Inc.
Murder of a Mystery Writer. Eric Heath. LC 55-7152. 1955. Arcadia House.
Murder of a Novelist. Sally Calkins Wood. LC 42-110532. 1941. Simon and Schuster.
Murder of a Professor. John Miller. LC 34-21539. 1937. G. P. Putnam's Sons.
Murder of a Quack. George Bellairs. LC 44-8552. 1944. The Macmillan Company.
Murder of a Stuffed Shirt. Mary Violet Herberden. LC 44-855535. 1944. Pub. for the Crime Club by Doubleday, Doran & Co., Inc.
Murder of a Suicide. Morna Doris MacTaggart Brown. LC 41-25822. 1941. Published for the Crime Club by Doubleday Doran.
Murder of a Suicide. E. X. Ferrars. LC 41-258221. 1941. Pub. for the Crime Club by Doubleday, Doran & Co., Inc.
Murder of a Suicide. E. X. Ferrars, pseud. 1972. pap. 0.75 o.p. (07211). Curtis.
Murder of a Wife. Henry Kuttner. LC 81-47403. (Fifty Classics of Crime Fiction, 1950-1975). 1982. 14.95 (ISBN 0-8240-4971-3). Garland Pub.
Murder of Ann Avery. Henry Kuttner. LC 56-10589. (Permabooks, 3038. Mystery 8). 1956. Permabooks.
Murder of Aziz Khan: A Novel. Zulfikar Ghose. LC 69-10806. 1969. 6.50. John Day Co.
Murder of Bishop Conrad. Louise Hebach. LC 41-2315. Fortuny's.
Murder of Caroline Bundy. Alice Ormond Campbell. LC 32-33837. Farrar & Rinehart, Incorporated.
Murder of Cecily Thane. Harriette Ashbrook. LC 30-19684. 1930. Coward-McCann, Inc.
Murder of Christine Wilmerding. William Blair Morton Ferguson. LC 31-28684. H. Liveright, Inc.
Murder of Convenience. Robert George Dean. LC 39-24. 1938. Pub. for the Crime Club, Inc., by Doubleday, Doran & Company, Inc.
Murder of Crows. Patrick Buchanan, pseud. LC 78-111345. 1970. 4.95 (ISBN 0-8128-1278-6). Stein and Day.
Murder of Delicia. Marie Corelli. LC 6-28742. 1896. J. B. Lippincott Company.
Murder of Eleanor Pope. Henry Kuttner. LC 56-6726. (Permabooks, M-3046. Mystery.6). 1956. Permabooks.
Murder of Estelle Cantor. Cecil Freeman Gregg. LC 36-7043. The Dial Press.
Murder of Lalla Lee. Helen Burnham. LC 31-10081. 1931. R. M. McBride & Company.
Murder of Lawrence of Arabia: A Novel. Matthew Eden. LC 78-69528. 9.95 (ISBN 0-690-01790-1). Crowell.
Murder of Love. Dulcie Gray. 1979. 15.00x (ISBN 0-86025-115-2, Pub. by Ian Henry Pubns England). State Mutual Bk.
Murder of Love. Dulcie Gray. 1977. 6.90 o.p. State Mutual Bk.
Murder of Mary Steers. Brian Cooper. LC 66-16980. 1966. 4.95. Vanguard.
Murder of Miranda. Margaret Millar. LC 78-21811. 8.95 (ISBN 0-394-50509-3). Random House.
Murder of Miranda. Margaret Millar. LC 80-10632. 1981. 11.50 (ISBN 0-89340-283-4). J. Curley.
Murder of Miss Betty Sloan. Sidney Clark Williams. (Tired business man's library of adventure, detective, and mystery novels). 1935. D. Appleton-Century Company, Incorporated.
Murder of Monsieur Fualdes. Armand Praviel. Tr. by Ashley, Doris. LC 24-62345. 1924. T. Seltzer.
Murder of Mrs. Davenport. Lucy Beatrice Malleson. LC 28-20344. 1928. L. MacVeagh, The Dial Press.
Murder of My Aunt. Richard Hull, pseud. LC 79-67276. (Library of Crime Classics). 1979. pap. 5.00 (ISBN 0-930330-02-1, IPL 10003). Intl Polygonics.
Murder of My Aunt. Richard Hull, pseud. (Seagull Library of Mystery & Suspense Ser). (O.s.i.). 1968. 4.95 o.p. (ISBN 0-393-08404-3). Norton.
Murder of My Aunt. Richard Henry Sampson. LC 34-35699. 1934. Minton, Balch & Company.
Murder of My Aunt. Richard Henry Sampson. LC 36-7195. Minton, Balch & Company.
Murder of Quality. John Le Carre. 1980. pap. 2.50 (ISBN 0-553-14855-9). Bantam.
Murder of Quality. John Le Carre. 1978. pap. 1.95 (ISBN 0-445-08374-3). Popular Lib.
Murder of Rabbi Adler see Murder in the Synagogue.
Murder of Roger Ackroyd. Agatha Miller Christie. LC 75-44964. (Fifty Classics of Crime Fiction, 1900-1950; 11). 1976. 12.00 (ISBN 0-8240-2360-9). Garland Pub.
Murder of Roger Ackroyd. Agatha Miller Christie. LC 26-21118. 1926. Dodd, Mead and Company.
Murder of Roger Ackroyd. Agatha Miller Christie. LC 29-8547. 1927. Grosset & Dunlap.
Murder of Roger Ackroyd. Agatha Miller Christie. LC 43-657422. 1943. Triangle Books.
Murder of Roger Ackroyd. Agatha Miller Christie. 1973. (pbk.) 0.95 (ISBN 0-671-77706-8). Pocket Books.
Murder of Sigurd Sharon. Harriette Ashbrook. LC 33-1360. 1933. Coward-McCann, Inc.
Murder of Sir Edmund Godfrey. John Dickson Carr. LC 74-10426. (Classics of Crime & Criminology Ser). (Illus.). 352p. 1975. Repr. of 1936 ed. 26.50 (ISBN 0-88355-193-4). Hyperion Conn.
Murder of Some Importance. Graham Montague Jeffries. LC 31-16004. 1931. J. B. Lippincott Company.
Murder of Steven Kester. Harriette Ashbrook. LC 31-20846. 1931. Coward-McCann, Inc.
Murder of Suzy Pommier. Emmanuel Bove. Tr. by Bradley Warre. LC 34-583. 1934. Little, Brown, and Company.
Murder of the Admiral. Stephen Gould Fisher. LC 36-10240. The Macaulay Company.
Murder of the Dainty-Footed Model: By Frank E. Hewens. Frank E Hewens. LC 68-106321. (Cock Robin mystery). bds., 4.50. Macmillan.
Murder of the Frogs and Other Stories. Don Carpenter. LC 76-78873. 1969. 5.95. Harcourt, Brace & World.
Murder of the Honest Broker. Willoughby Sharp. LC 34-234711. C. Kendall.
Murder of the Lawyer's Clerk. Joseph Smith Fletcher. LC 33-6401. 1933. A. A. Knopf.
Murder of the Maharajah. Henry Reymond Fitzwalter Keating. LC 81-141. 1981. 13.95 (ISBN 0-8161-3179-1). G.K. Hall.
Murder of the Ninth Baronet. Joseph Smith Fletcher. LC 32-18955. 1932. A. A. Knopf.
Murder of the Only Witness. Joseph Smith Fletcher. LC 33-18745. 1933. A. A. Knopf.
Murder of the Pigboat Skipper... Stephen Gould Fisher. Hillman Curl, Inc.
Murder of the Secret Agent. Joseph Smith Fletcher. LC 34-5823. 1934. A. A. Knopf.
Murder of the U.S.A. William Fitzgerald Jenkins. LC 46-20792. 1946. Crown Publishers.
Murder of the Well-Beloved. 1st Ed. Margot Neville. LC 53-10656. 1953. Published for the Crime Club by Doubleday.
Murder of Whistler's Brother. David Alexander. LC 56-880775. (His A Bart Hardin mystery novel). 1956. Random House.
Murder off Broadway. Leonard Falkner. LC 30-71623. H. Holt and Company.
Murder off Key... Kathleen Sproul. LC 34-10374. E. P. Dutton & Co., Inc.
Murder off Miami. Dennis Yates Wheatley. LC 78-20833. (Illus.). 14.95 (ISBN 0-8317-6264-0). Mayflower Books.
Murder off Stage. Monte Barrett. LC 31-143363. The Bobbs-Merrill Company.
Murder off the Record. John Michael Ward Bingham. LC 57-12130. (Red badge detective). 1957. Dodd, Mead.
Murder off the Record. John Michael Ward Bingham Clanmorris. LC 57-12130. (Red badge detective). 1957. Dodd, Mead.
Murder on a Bad Trip. June Drummond. LC 68-24756. (Rinehart suspense novel). 1968. 3.95. Holt, Rinehart, and Winston.
Murder on a Tangent. Doris Miles Disney. LC 45-4610. 1945. Pub. for the Crime Club by Doubleday, Doran and Co., Inc.
Murder on Alternate Tuesdays. Tech Davis. LC 38-8107. 1938. Pub. for the Crime Club, Inc., by Doubleday, Doran & Company, Inc.
Murder on Angler's Island. Helen Kieran Reilly. LC 45-3046. 1945. Random House.
Murder on "B" Deck. Vincent Starrett. LC 29-6793. 1929. Pub. for The Crime Club, Inc., by Doubleday, Doran & Company, Inc.
Murder on Beacon Hill. Gerald Brown. LC 41-20045. Phoenix Press.
Murder on Board: Including The Mystery of the Blue Train, What Mrs. McGillicudy Saw: Death in the Air. Agatha Miller Christie. LC 74-6554. 1974. 7.95 (ISBN 0-396-06992-4). Dodd, Mead.
Murder on Both Sides. Abner Sideman. LC 46-600. 1945. F. M. Charlton Co., Inc.
Murder on Cape Cod. Frank Shay. LC 31-20078. 1931. The Macaulay Company.
Murder on Capitol Hill. Margaret Truman. 1981. 3.50 (ISBN 0-445-04724-0). Popular Library.
Murder on Capitol Hill: A Novel. Margaret Truman. LC 81-13211. 1981. 19.95 (ISBN 0-8161-3323-9). G.K. Hall.
Murder on Capitol Hill: A Novel. Margaret Truman. LC 80-70223. 11.95 (ISBN 0-87795-312-0). Arbor House.
Murder on Cue. Jane Dentinger. LC 82-45595. 1983. 11.95 (ISBN 0-385-18411-5). Published for the Crime Club by Doubleday.
Murder on Delivery: By Spencer Dean Pseud. 1st Ed. Prentice Winchell. LC 57-7377. 1957. Published for the Crime Club by Doubleday.
Murder on Display. Frances Moyer Ross Stevens. LC 39-135414. 1939. Pub. for the Crime Club, Inc., by Doubleday, Doran and Company, Inc.
Murder on Every Floor. Florence Demarest Bond. LC 39-21670. 1939. Hillman-Curl, Inc.
Murder on Fifth Avenue. Claudia Cranston. LC 34-74142. 1934. J. B. Lippincott Company.
Murder on Ghost Tree Island. Katherine S Daiger. LC 34-51714. Macrae Smith Company.
Murder on Halfaday Creek. James Beardsley Hendryx. LC 51-12474. (Double D western). 1951. Doubleday.
Murder on High. Carter Brown, pseud. (Signet book T5429). 1973. 0.75. New American Library.
Murder on High Heels. Richard Burke. LC 40-32857. 1940. Gateway Books.
Murder on His Mind. Gene Goldsmith. LC 47-22177. 1947. M. S. Mill Co., Inc.
Murder-on-Hudson. Jennifer Jones. LC 37-13701. Thomas Y. Crowell Company.
Murder on Location. Lee Thayer, pseud. LC 42-195617. 1942. Dodd, Mead & Company.
Murder on Margin... Robert George Dean. LC 38-1960. 1937. Pub. for the Crime Club, Inc., by Doubleday, Doran & Co., Inc.
Murder on Martha's Vineyard. Kelley Roos. LC 80-54480. 1981. 9.95 (ISBN 0-8027-5436-8). Walker.
Murder on Martha's Vineyard. large print ed. Kelley Roos. LC 81-16617. 9.95 (ISBN 0-89621-320-X). Thorndike Press.
Murder on Monday...! Charles Bryson. LC 32-26573. E. P. Dutton & Co., Inc.
Murder on Monday: A Steve Considine Mystery. 1st Ed. Robert Patrick Wilmot. LC 53-5414. (Main line mysteries). 1953. Lippincott.
Murder on Mondays: By Christopher Bush. Christopher Bush. LC 36-7722. H. Holt and Company.
Murder on My Street. 1st Ed. Edwin Moultrie Lanham. LC 58-5472. Harcourt, Brace.
Murder on Pad 34. Erik Bergaust. (Illus.). (YA) 1968. 6.95 o.p. (ISBN 0-399-10563-8). Putnam.
Murder on Parade. Carolyn Wells. LC 40-2387. J. B. Lippincott Company.
Murder on Polopel. Mason Wright & Kane, William Reno, 1885- Joint Author. LC 29-28505. 1929. Pub. for The Crime Club, Inc., by Doubleday, Doran & Comapny, Inc.
Murder on Queer Street. Gene Evans. (Orig.). pap. 1.75 o.p. (3044). Brandon.
Murder on Route 40: A Mystery Novel. Helen Joan Hultman. LC 40-6539. Phoenix Press.
Murder on Russian Hill. Lenore Glen Offord. LC 38-5747. 1938. Macrae Smith Company.
Murder on Safari. Elspeth Joscelin Grant Huxley. LC 38-12954. 1938. Harper & Brothers.
Murder on Safari. Elspeth Joscelin Grant Huxley. (Prize mystery novels). 1944. Crestwood Publishing Co., Inc.
Murder on Shadow Island. Garnett Weston. LC 33-8541. Farrar & Rinehart, Incorporated.
Murder on Shark Island. Jack De Witt. LC 42-22416. Liveright Publishing Corporation.

Murder on Stilts. Jacob D. Posner. LC 39-105140. 1939. Hillman-Curl, Inc.

Murder on the Aphrodite. Ruth Burr Sanborn. LC 35-16057. 1935. The Macmillan Company.

Murder on the Blackboard. Stuart Palmer. LC 32-30127. 1932. Brentano's.

Murder on the Bluff. Esther Tyler. LC 36-20365. 1936. Simon and Schuster.

Murder on the Brain. Anthony Heckstall-Smith. LC 58-110697. 1958. Roy Publishers.

Murder on the Bridge: A Colonel Gore Case. Alister McAllister. LC 30-18559. Harper & Brothers.

Murder on the Burrows. Edith Caroline Rivett. LC 32-257364. 1932. The Macaulay Company.

Murder on the Bus. Cecil Freeman Gregg. LC 30-23902. 1930. L. MacVeagh, The Dial Press.

Murder on the Costa Brava. John Coulson & Felicity Winifred Carter. LC 68-13251. 1968. Walker.

Murder on the Dais. Robert Gale. LC 65-25326. 1965. RosebudPress.

Murder on the Day of Judgment. Virginia Rath. LC 36-7595. 1936. Pub. for the Crime Club, Inc., by Doubleday, Doran & Co., Inc.

Murder on the Downbeat. Robert Avery. LC 43-146491. 1943. Mystery House.

Murder on the Eighteenth Hole. Charles Miron. 1978. pap. 1.50 (ISBN 0-532-15373-1). Woodhill.

Murder on the "Enriqueta". Molly Thynne. LC 29-12131. T. Nelson & Sons, Ltd.

Murder on the Face of It. Emma Lou Fetta. LC 40-78583. 1940. Pub. for the Crime Club by Doubleday, Doran & Company, Inc.

Murder on the Frontier. 1st Ed. Ernest Haycox. LC 52-126227. Little, Brown.

Murder on the Glass Floor. Viola Brothers Shore. LC 32-29501. 1932. R. Long & R. R. Smith, Inc.

Murder on the House. Dorothy Cadwell. LC 77-350247. 1976. (ISBN 0-7737-0027-7) (ISBN 0-7737-7133-6). Musson.

Murder on the Left Bank: A Homer Evans Mystery. Elliot Harold Paul. LC 51-9188. 1951. Random House.

Murder on the Links. Agatha Miller Christie. LC 23-6380. 1923. Dodd, Mead and Company.

Murder on the Links. Agatha Miller Christie. 1974. (pbk.) 0.95. Dell.

Murder on the List. Neill Graham. 1975. 4.95 (ISBN 0-09-122320-2, Pub. by Hutchinson). Merrimack Pub Cir.

Murder on the Long Straight. Charlotte Yarborough. 1979. pap. 1.95 o.s.i. (ISBN 0-8439-0674-X, Leisure Bks). Nordon Pubns.

Murder on the Marsh. John Alexander Ferguson. LC 30-860516. 1930. Dodd, Mead & Company.

Murder on the Matterhorn: By Glyn Carr Pseud. 1st Ed. Showell Styles. LC 52-12264. (Guilt edge mystery). 1953. Dutton.

Murder on the Merry-Go-Round: By Josephine Bell. Doris Bell Collier Ball. LC 65-3435. (A Ballantine mystery original, U2159). 1965. Ballantine Book.

Murder on the Mistral. Vincent Gaspard Malo. LC 58-64283. 1958. Abelard-Schuman.

Murder on the Monte. Ross Richards. (Sexton Blake Ser). pap. 0.50 o.p. (50-443). Manor Bks.

Murder on the Moon. Charles M. Garrison. 1968. 3.95 o.p. Vantage.

Murder on the Mountain. Christine Noble Govan. LC 37-4017. 1937. Houghton Mifflin Company.

Murder on the Nose. George A Bagby, pseud. LC 38-6014. 1938. Pub. for the Crime Club, Inc., by Doubleday, Doran & Co., Inc.

Murder on the Nose. Aaron Marc Stein. LC 38-6014. 1938. Pub. for the Crime Club, Inc., by Doubleday, Doran & Co., Inc.

Murder on the Orient Express. Agatha Miller Christie. (Greenway Ed.). 1981. 8.95 (ISBN 0-396-05777-2). Dodd.

Murder on the Orient Express. Agatha Miller Christie. 1980. pap. 2.50 (ISBN 0-671-42212-X). PB.

Murder on the Orient Express. Agatha Miller Christie. (Greenway Ed). 3.95 o.p. (ISBN 0-396-05777-2). Dodd.

Murder on the Pacific. David Knox Patton. LC 40-12737. 1940. Dodd, Mead & Company.

Murder on the Palisades. William Levine. LC 30-5403. 1930. R. M. McBride & Company.

Murder on the Program. M. M. Mannon. LC 44-3665. 1944. The Bobbs-Merrill Company.

Murder on the Purple Water. Frances Kirkwood Crane. LC 47-40615. 1947. Random House.

Murder on the Rocks: By Robert Dietrich Pseud. Howard Hunt. LC 57-8468. (Dell first edition, A141). 1957. Dell Pub. Co.

Murder on the Salem Road. Katharine Metcalf Roof. LC 31-151294. 1931. Houghton Mifflin Company.

Murder on the Side. Cover Painting by Barye Phillips. Day Keene. LC 57-22162. (Gold medal books, 622). 1956. Fawcett Publications.

Murder on the Ten-Yard Line... Dorothy Stockbridge Tillet. LC 31-28913. Pub. for the Crime Club, Inc., by Doubleday, Doran & Company, Inc.

Murder on the Thirty-First Floor. Per Wahloo. LC 82-47886. 1982. 2.95 (ISBN 0-394-70840-7). Pantheon Books.

Murder on the Tropic. Todd Downing. LC 35-361752. 1935. Pub. for the Crime Club, Inc., by Doubleday Doran & Company, Inc.

Murder on the Tropic. Todd Downing. LC 36-83144. The Sun Dial Press.

Murder on the Way! Theodore Roscoe. LC 35-21951. Dodge Publishing Company.

Murder on the Wild Side. Jeff Jacks. (Orig.). 1971. pap. 0.75 o.p. (T2515, GM). Fawcett World.

Murder on the Yacht... Rufus King. LC 32-26358. Pub. for the Crime Club, Inc., by Doubleday, Doran & Company, Inc.

Murder on the Yellow Brick Road. Stuart M Kaminsky. LC 77-15825. 7.95 (ISBN 0-312-55318-8). St. Martin's Press.

Murder on the Yellow Brick Road. Stuart M Kaminsky. LC 79-1417. 1979. 1.95 (ISBN 0-14-046223-6). Penguin Books.

Murder on the Yellow Brick Road. Stuart M Kaminsky. LC 78-12847. 1979. 9.95 (ISBN 0-89340-167-6). J. Curley.

Murder on Their Minds. 1st Ed. George Harmon Coxe. LC 57-530401. 1957. Knopf.

Murder on Tour. Todd Downing. LC 33-22306. 1933. G. P. Putnam's Sons.

Murder on Trial. Michael Underwood. 1977. 6.20 o.p. State Mutual Bk.

Murder on Wheels. Stuart Palmer. LC 32-9441. 1932. Brentano's.

Murder on Wheels. Kenneth Robeson. (Avenger #13). 1973. (pbk) 0.75. Warner.

Murder on 47th Street... Beulah Poynter. LC 31-8213. Pub. for the Crime Club, Inc., by Doubleday, Doran & Company, Inc.

Murder One. M. E Cohane. 1975. (pbk.) 1.25 (ISBN 0-523-00775-2). Pinnacle Books.

Murder One. Eleazar Lipsky. LC 48-693249. 1948. Pub. for the Crime Club by Doubleday.

Murder or Manslaughter? A Novel. Helen Buckingham Mathers Reeves. (On cover: The seaside library. Pocket ed. no. 635). 1885. G. Munro.

Murder or Three. Laurie Mantell. LC 80-54278. 1981. 9.95 (ISBN 0-8027-5432-5). Walker.

Murder Out of Commission. R. B Dominic. LC 76-2768. 1976. 5.95 (ISBN 0-385-12058-3). Published for the Crime Club by Doubleday.

Murder Out of Commission. R. B Dominic. LC 77-356884. 1976. 3.25 (ISBN 0-333-19663-5). Macmillan.

Murder Out of School. Ivan T Ross, pseud. LC 60-6101. (Inner sanctum mystery). 1960. Simon and Schuster.

Murder Out of Tune. Brian Hill. LC 31-21905. 1931. J. B. Lippincott Company.

Murder Out of Turn: A Mr. and Mrs. North Mystery. Frances Louise Davis Lockridge & Lockridge, Richard. LC 41-528. 1941. Frederick A. Stokes Company.

Murder Over Broadway. Fred Malina. LC 48-3589. 1948. Phoenix Press.

Murder Party. Henry Bordeaux. LC 31-29191. 1931. L. MacVeagh, The Dial Press.

Murder Picks the Jury. Willis Todhunter Ballard. LC 47-11783. 1947. Published for Mystery House by S. Curl.

Murder, Plain and Fancy. Garland Lord, pseud. 1943. Pub. for the Crime Club by Doubleday, Doran and Company, Inc.

Murder Plan Six. John Michael Ward Bingham. LC 59-618657. (Red badge detective). 1959. Dodd, Mead.

Murder Plan Six. John Michael Ward Bingham Clanmorris. LC 59-6186. (Red badge detective). 1959. Dodd, Mead.

Murder Plays an Ugly Scene. Leonard Alfred George Strong. LC 45-7982. 1945. Pub. for the Crime Club by Doubleday, Doran & Co., Inc.

Murder, Please. Wayne David. 3.50 o.p. Carlton.

Murder Pluperfect. Kenneth Giles. LC 77-120402. 1970. 4.95 (ISBN 0-8027-5212-8). Walker.

Murder Plus. Carolyn Wells. LC 40-792346. J. B. Lippincott Company.

Murder Point: A Tale of Keewatin. Coningsby William Dawson. LC 10-7789. 1.50. Hodder & Stoughton, G. H. Doran Company.

Murder Points a Finger. David Alexander. LC 53-9709. 1953. Random House.

Murder Pool. Eric Heath. LC 54-11334. 1954. Arcadia House.

Murder Premeditated. Percival Henry Powell. LC 58-12560. Roy.

Murder R. F. D. Herman Petersen. LC 42-10426. 1942. Duell, Sloan and Pearce.

Murder Racquet. Ed. by Alfred Hitchcock. 1975. (pbk.) 0.95. Dell.

Murder Recalls Van Kill. Spencer Bayne. LC 39-149517. 1939. Harper and Brothers.

Murder Reflected. Janet Caird. LC 66-46800. 1965. G. Bles.

Murder Rehearsel. Roger d'Este Burford. LC 33-33952. 1933. A. A. Knopf.

Murder Remote. Janet Caird. LC 72-84896. 1973. 4.95 (ISBN 0-385-00475-3). Published for the Crime Club by Doubleday.

Murder Rents a Room. Sara Elizabeth Mason. LC 43-126523. 1943. Pub. for the Crime Club by Doubleday, Doran and Company, Inc.

Murder, Repeat Murder. Allan MacKinnon. LC 52-5851. 1952. Published for the Crime Club by Doubleday.

Murder R.F.D. Leslie Stephan. LC 77-27014. 8.95 (ISBN 0-684-15522-2). Scribner.

Murder R.F.D. Leslie Stephan. LC 78-11138. 1979. 10.95 (ISBN 0-89340-183-8). J. Curley.

Murder Rides a Rocket: A Ransome Dragoon-Vicky Gaines Mystery. Frank Diamond. LC 46-18488. 1946. Mystery House.

Murder Roundabout: A Captain Heimrich Mystery. Richard Lockridge. LC 66-18446. 3.95. Lippincott.

Murder Runs a Fever. Ruth Fenisong. LC 43-17348. 1943. Pub. for the Crime Club by Doubleday, Doran and Co., Inc.

Murder Runs in the Family. Hulbert Footner. 1934. Harper & Brothers.

Murder Scholastic. Janet Caird. LC 67-100800. 1967. Bles.

Murder Scholastic. Janet Caird. LC 68-11801. 1968. Published for the Crime Club by Doubleday.

Murder Seeks an Agent. Wenzell Brown. LC 46-629623. (On cover: Five star mystery, 6). 1945. Green Publishing Co.

Murder Seeks an Agent. Wenzell Brown. LC 47-19188. 1947. Arcadia House.

Murder Set to Music. Harriette Russell Campbell. LC 41-8355. Harper & Brothers.

Murder Sets the Pace. Elizabeth Woods Freeman. LC 53-883. 1952. Pageant Press.

Murder Shrieks Out. Lelia DiBenedetto & Harris, Jules E., Joint Author. LC 45-3452. House of Field-Doubleday, Inc.

Murder So Real. Al Bird. LC 78-1968. 8.95 (ISBN 0-698-10891-4). Coward, McCann & Geoghegan.

Murder Solves a Problem. Marion Bramhall. 1944. Pub. for the Crime Club by Doubleday, Doran & Co., Inc.

Murder Sonata. Francis Flercher. 1980. pap. 1.95 (ISBN 0-8439-0847-5). Nordon Pubns.

Murder Spoils Everything. Jeremy Lane. LC 49-9893. 1949. Phoenix Press.

Murder Squad. Everard Meade. 1979. pap. 1.75 (ISBN 0-89041-228-6, 3228). Major Bks.

Murder Stalks the Circle... Lee Thayer, pseud. LC 47-3706. 1947. Dodd, Mead & Company.

Murder Stalks the Mayor. Reginald Thomas Maitland Scott. LC 36-210. E. P. Dutton & Co., Inc.

Murder Stalks the Wakely Family: A Judge Peck Mystery Story. August William Derleth. LC 34-4196. Loring & Mussey.

Murder Steals the Show. Leon David Hirsch. LC 46-2505. 1946. F. Fell, Inc.

Murder Steps in. Charlotte Murray Russell, pseud. LC 42-25517. 1942. Published for the Crime Club by Doubleday, Doran & Company, Inc.

Murder Steps Out. Christopher Reeve. LC 51-9275. 1951. M. S. Mill Co. and W. Morrow.

Murder Story: A Tragedy of Our Time. Lester Velie. (Illus.). 352p. 1983. 15.95 (ISBN 0-02-621720-1). Macmillan.

Murder Strikes an Atomic Unit. Theodora McCormick Du Bois. LC 46-3138. 1946. Pub. for the Crime Club by Doubleday & Company, Inc.

Murder Strikes Three. David MacDuff. LC 37-28671. Modern Age Books, Inc.

Murder Stroke. Ann B. Ross. (Orig.). 1981. pap. 1.75 (ISBN 0-8439-8018-4, Tiara Bks). Nordon Pubns.

Murder, Sunny Side up. R. B Dominic. LC 68-18970. (Raven book.). 1968. 3.95. Abelard-Schuman.

Murder Takes a Honeymoon. Ethel Fleming. LC 40-315211. 1940. Gateway Books.

Murder Takes a Wife. James A. Howard. (Raven House Mysteries Ser.). 224p. 1982. pap. 2.25 (ISBN 0-373-63026-3, Pub. by Worldwide). Harlequin Bks.

Murder Takes a Wife. 1st Ed. James A Howard. LC 58-9592. 1958. Dutton.

Murder Takes No Holiday. Davis Dresser. (Mike Shayne mystery). 1973. (pbk.) 0.75. Dell.

Murder Takes the Baths. Lee Priestley. LC 52-148562. 1952. Arcadia House.

Murder Takes the Veil. Margaret Ann Hubbard. LC 50-9554. 1950. Bruce.

Murder That Had Everything. Hulbert Footner. LC 39-17236. 1939. Harper & Brothers.

Murder That Wouldn't Stay Solved. Aaron Marc Stein. LC 51-4593. (Inner sanctum mystery). 1951. Simon and Schuster.

Murder That Wouldn't Stay Solved. Hampton Stone, pseud. (Hampton Stone Mystery Ser.). 1971. pap. 0.75 o.p. (ISBN 0-446-64526-5, 64-526). Paperback Lib.

Murder: Thirty-Two Thrilling Crimes. Evelyn Davies Johnson & Palmer, Gretta. LC 28-25019. 1928. Covici, Friede.

Murder Through the Looking Glass. Robert George Dean. LC 40-5186. 1940. Pub. for the Crime Club by Doubleday, Doran & Company, Inc.

Murder Through the Looking Glass. Andrew Garve. 1978. pap. 1.95i (ISBN 0-06-080449-1, P 449, PL). Har-Row.

Murder Through the Looking Glass. Craig Rice. LC 43-2710. 1943. Coward-McCann, Inc.

Murder Through the Looking Glass. Paul Winterton. LC 52-5436. Harper.

Murder Through the Looking Glass. Paul Winterton. (Perennial library). 1978. 1.95 (ISBN 0-06-080449-1). Harper & Row.

Murder Through the Window. Francis William Stokes. LC 30-19275. (W. Collins sons & co., ltd.) has title: Murder at Plenders.). 1930. W. Morrow & Co.

Murder Times Five. Robert Colby. 176p. (Orig.). 1972. pap. 0.75 o.p. (T2622, GM). Fawcett World.

Murder Times Three. Amelia Reynolds Long. LC 40-2386. Phoenix Press.

Murder to Go. Emma Lathen, pseud. LC 79-84128. (Inner sanctum mystery). 1969. 4.95. Simon and Schuster.

Murder to Hounds. Edward Acheson. LC 39-3406. Harcourt, Brace and Company.

Murder to Make You Grow up Little Girl. Noelle Loriot. LC 78-184050. 1972. 5.95 (ISBN 0-529-04519-2). World Pub.

Murder to Make You Grow Up Little Girl. Laurence Oriol. 1972. 5.95 o.p. (ISBN 0-529-04519-2, A3126). World Pub.

Murder to Make You Grow Up Little Girl. Laurence Oriol. (Dell books). 1973. 0.95. Dell.

Murder to Music. Glen Burne. LC 34-3089. Dodd, Mead & Company.

Murder to Type. Amelia Reynolds Long. LC 43-456. 1943. Phoenix Press.

Murder Today, Money Tomorrow: A Novel. Jon Messman. (Jefferson Boone, handyman, 3). 1973. (pbk.) 0.95. Pyramid.

Murder Trap. Armstrong Livingston. The Bobbs-Merrill Co.

Murder Trapp. Eugene Franklin, pseud. 1974. (pbk.) 0.95. Dell.

Murder Trapp. Eugene Franklin, pseud. LC 73-150945. (A Stein and Day mystery). 1971. 4.95 (ISBN 0-8128-1378-2). Stein and Day.

Murder Tree. Leslie McFarlane. LC 31-205239. E. P. Dutton & Co., Inc.

Murder Trouble. Louis Trimble. LC 46-2008. (Black cat detective series. No. 18). 1945. Crestwood Publishing Co., Inc.

Murder Trouble. Louis Trimble. LC 45-3040. 1945. Phoenix Press.

Murder Twice Removed. Muriel Bradley. LC 51-14853. 1951. Published for the Crime Club by Doubleday.

Murder Twice Told. Donald Hamilton. LC 50-6941. 1950. Rinehart.

Murder Under Construction. Sue MacVeigh. LC 39-448425. 1939. Houghton Mifflin Company.

Murder Under Construction. Elizabeth Nearing. LC 39-4484. 1939. Houghton Mifflin Company.

Murder Under the Sun. Lillian O'Donnell. LC 64-12737. (Raven book). 1964. Abelard-Schuman.

Murder Unleashed. Dorothy Bennett. 1935. Pub. for the Crime Club, Inc., by Doubleday, Doran & Company, Inc.

Murder Unlimited! Nick Carter. LC 45-667338. 1945. Vital Publications, Inc.

Murder Unlimited. 1st Ed. Mary Violet Heberden. LC 53-5035. 1953. Published for the Crime Club by Doubleday.

Murder Unprompted: A Charles Paris Mystery. Simon Brett. 160p. 1982. 10.95 (ISBN 0-684-17659-9, ScribT). Scribner.

Murder up My Sleeve. Erle Stanley Gardner. LC 37-363912. 1937. W. Morrow & Company.

Murder up My Sleeve. Erle Stanley Gardner. LC 47-28822. (Pocket books, 368). 1946.

Murder Upstairs. Adam Bliss. LC 34-129718. 1934. Macrae Smith Company.

Murder Walks Alone. Clements Ripley. LC 35-66491. J. Messner, Inc.

Murder Walks the Corridors. James DeWolf Perry. LC 37-2570. 1937. The Macmillan Company.

Murder Walks the Stairs. Glenn M Barns. LC 54-11460. 1954. Arcadia House.

Murder Ward. Warren Murphy. (Destroyer Ser., No. 15). (Orig.). 1974. pap. 2.25 (ISBN 0-523-41768-3). Pinnacle Bks.

Murder Ward. Richard Sapir & Warren Murphy. (Destroyer,#15). 1974. (pbk.) 1.25 (ISBN 0-523-00331-5). Pinnacle Books.

Murder Wears a Mummer's Mask. Davis Dresser. LC 43-3662. 1943. Dodd, Mead & Company.

Murder Wears Mukluks. Eunice Mays Boyd. LC 45-3286. 1945. Farrar & Rinehart, Inc.

Murder Well Done. Ione Sandberg Shriber. LC 41-8359. Farrar and Rinehart, Inc.

TITLE INDEX MUSHROOM TOWN.

Murder Will in. Carolyn Wells. LC 42-14743. 1942. J. B. Lippincott Company.
Murder Will in. Carolyn Wells. LC 44-111586. 1944. Gem Publications, Inc.
Murder Will Speak... George Bellairs. LC 43-130461. 1943. The Macmillan Company.
Murder Will Speak. Alfred Walter Stewart. LC 38-324182. 1938. Little, Brown and Company.
Murder with a Difference: Three Unusual Crime Novels. Ed. by Christopher Darlington Morley. Sampson, Richard Henry, 1896- The Murder of My Aunt & Heard, Gerald, 1889- A Taste for Honey. LC 46-7565. 1946. Random House.
Murder with a Theme Song. Virginia Rath. LC 39-27330. 1939. Doubleday, Doran & Co., Inc.
Murder with Long Hair. H. Donald Spatz. LC 40-29469. Phoenix Press.
Murder with Love. Elizabeth Linington. LC 73-170881. (Her A Luis Mendoza mystery). 1972. 5.95. Morrow.
Murder with Love. Garland Lord, pseud. LC 43-15361. 1943. W. Morrow and Company.
Murder, with Love. Dell Shannon. 1972. 5.95 o.p. (ISBN 0-688-00120-3). Morrow.
Murder with Malice. Michael Underwood. LC 76-28064. 1977. 7.95. St. Martin's.
Murder with Mirrors. Agatha Miller Christie. LC 52-9955. (Red badge detective). 1952. Dodd, Mead.
Murder with Mushrooms. John Creasey. LC 73-3748. (Rinehart suspense novel). 1974. 4.95 (ISBN 0-03-011156-0). Holt, Rinehart and Winston.
Murder with Music. Gilbert Riddell. LC 35-15152. Alliance Press.
Murder with Orange Blossoms. Ruth Darby. LC 43-115469. 1943. Pub. for the Crime Club by Doubleday, Doran and Company, Inc.
Murder with Pictures. George Harmon Coxe. LC 35-31025. 1935. A. A. Knopf.
Murder with Pictures: By George Harmon Coxe. George Harmon Coxe. 1981. 2.25 (ISBN 0-06-080527-7). Harper & Row's.
Murder with Roses. Adeline McElfresh. LC 50-4414. 1950. Phoenix Press.
Murder with Southern Hospitality. Zenith Jones Brown. LC 42-36027. 1942. C. Scribner's Sons.
Murder with Your Malted. Jerome Barry. LC 41-25000. 1941. Pub. for the Crime Club, by Doubleday, Doran & Co., Inc.
Murder Within Murder. Frances Louise Davis Lockridge & Richard Lockridge. LC 46-40263. 1946. J. B. Lippincott Company.
Murder Without Clues. Joseph L Bonney. LC 40-53929. Carrick & Evans Inc.
Murder Without Icing. Emma Lathen, pseud. LC 72-83919. (Simon and Schuster novel of suspense). 1972. 5.95 (ISBN 0-671-21207-9). Simon and Schuster.
Murder Without Make-up. Edla Benjamin. LC 40-14183. Random House.
Murder Without Motive. Raymond Leslie Goldman. LC 38-5869. Coward-McCann Inc.
Murder Without Regret. E Louise Cushing. LC 54-13349. 1954. Arcadia House.
Murder Without Risk! Herbert Adams. LC 36-510733. J. B. Lippincott Company.
Murder Without Tears: An Anthology of Crime. Ed. by William Jacob Cuppy. LC 46-4901. 1946. Sheridan House.
Murder Without Weapon. Means Davis. LC 35-363. 1934. H. Smith and R. Haas.
Murder Without Weapons. Albert Benjamin Cunningham. LC 49-9562. (Guilt edged mystery). 1949. E. P. Dutton.
Murder Won't Wait. Carroll John Daly. LC 33-24092. 1933. I. Washburn.
Murder Won't Wait. Ramoncita Sayer O'Connor. LC 53-12920. 1953. Arcadia House.
Murder Yet to Come. Isabel Briggs Myers. LC 30-2773. 1930. Frederick A. Stokes Company.
Murder '97: A Simon Lash Mystery. Frank Gruber. LC 48-5132. (Murray Hill mystery). 1948. Rinehart.
Murdercon. Richard L. Purtill. LC 81-43386. 1982. 10.95 (ISBN 0-385-17334-2). Doubleday.
Murdered but Not Dead: A Mystery Novel. Anne Austin. LC 39-16110. 1939. The Macmillan Company.
Murdered: One by One. Francis Beeding. LC 37-845955. 1937. Harper & Brothers.
Murderer. Roy A. Heath. 190p. 1981. pap. 5.95 (ISBN 0-8052-8072-3, Pub. by Allison & Busby England); 9.95 (ISBN 0-8052-8002-2). Schocken.
Murderer. Anthony Shaffer. 96p. 1979. 9.95 (ISBN 0-7145-2544-8, Pub. by M Boyars); pap. 5.95 (ISBN 0-7145-2545-6). Merrimack Pub Cir.
Murderer Among Us. Alan Geoffrey Yates. LC 63-3887. (Signet book). 1962. New American Library of World Literature.
Murderer in the House. Katharine Clugston. LC 47-185459. 1947. A. A. Wyn, Inc.
Murderer Invisible. Philip Wylie. LC 75-10673. (Classics of science fiction). 1976. 12.50. (ISBN 0-88355-354-6) (ISBN 0-88355-467-4). Hyperion Press.
Murderer Invisible. Philip Wylie. LC 31-119531. Farrar & Rinehart Incorporated.
Murderer Is a Fox. Ellery Queen, pseud. LC 77-14125. (Ellery Queen mystery). 1977. 9.95 (ISBN 0-89340-105-6). J. Curley.
Murderer Is a Fox. Ellery Queen. 1975. (pbk.) 1.25 (ISBN 0-345-24364-1). Ballantine Books.
Murderer Is a Fox: A Novel. Ellery Queen, pseud. LC 45-4451. 1945. Little, Brown and Company.
Murderer Is a Fox: A Novel. Ellery Queen, pseud. LC 46-22508. 1946. The Sun Dial Press.
Murderer of Sleep. Milward Rodon Kennedy Burge. LC 33-47299. 1933. H. C. Kinsey & Company, Inc.
Murderer Returns. Edwin Dial Torgerson. LC 30-24241. 1930. R. R. Smith, Inc.
Murderer Vine. Shepard Rifkin. LC 74-127168. 1970. 5.95. Dodd, Mead.
Murderers. Fredric Brown. 1961. 2.95 o.p. Dutton.
Murderer's Choice. Anna Mary Wells. LC 43-10913. 1943. A. A. Knopf.
Murderer's Choice. Anna Mary Wells. LC 47-42360. (Dell book, no. 126).
Murderer's Choice. Anna Mary Wells. (Perennial Library). 2.50 (ISBN 0-06-080534-X)., C.
Murderer's Companion. William Roughead. (Seagull Library of Mystery & Suspense). 1968. Repr. 5.50 o.p. (ISBN 0-393-08566-X). Norton.
Murderer's Holiday... Donald Henderson Clarke. LC 40-330612. The Vanguard Press.
Murderer's Luck... Henry Holt. LC 32-28145. Pub. for the Crime Club, Inc., by Doubleday, Doran & Company, Inc.
Murderer's Mansion. Irene Shaw. LC 75-17074. 192p. 1976. 5.95 o.p. (ISBN 0-385-11384-6). Doubleday.
Murderer's Mansion: Original Title, Moonstone Manor. Irene Roberts. LC 75-17074. 1976. 5.95 (ISBN 0-385-11384-6). Doubleday.
Murderer's Mistake: A Chief Inspector Macdonald Mystery. Edith Caroline Rivett. LC 47-30646. 1947. Pub. for Mystery House by S. Curl.
Murderers of Monty. Richard Henry Sampson. LC 37-25067. 1937. G. P. Putnam's Sons.
Murderers' Row. Donald Hamilton. (Matt Helm Ser.). 1978. pap. 1.95 (ISBN 0-449-14088-1, GM). Fawcett.
Murderers' Row. Ed. by Alfred Joseph Hitchcock. 1975. (pbk.) 0.95. Dell.
Murderer's Vanity. Hulbert Footner. LC 40-32293. Harper & Brothers.
Murderous Journey. Kenneth Giles. LC 75-4403. 1975. 5.95. (ISBN 0-8027-5317-5). Walker.
Murderous Journey. Edmund McGirr. LC 75-4403. (Piron Private Eye Ser). 159p. 1975. 5.95 o.p. (ISBN 0-8027-5317-5). Walker & Co.
Murderous Move. Charles Plumb. (Orig.). 1981. pap. 2.25 (ISBN 0-505-51697-7). Tower Bks.
Murderous Welcome. Judy Irwin. LC 67-24918. 1967. Roy Publishers.
Murder's a Swine. Nap Lombard, pseud. LC 43-9800. 1943. Etc. Hutchinson & Co., Ltd.
Murder's a Waiting Game. Lucy Beatrice Malleson. LC 75-37039. 1972. 4.95 (ISBN 0-394-47933-5). Random House.
Murders Anonymous. E. X Ferrars, pseud. LC 77-89881. 1978. 6.95 (ISBN 0-385-13536-X). Published for the Crime Club by Doubleday.
Murders at Impasse Louvain. Richard Grayson. LC 79-5038. 1979. 8.95 o.p. (ISBN 0-312-55343-9). St Martin.
Murders at Impasse Louvain: A Novel. Richard Grindal. LC 79-5038. 1979. 8.95 (ISBN 0-312-55343-9). St. Martins Press.
Murders at Loon Lake. Kenneth Whipple. LC 33-318855. A. H. King.
Murders at Moon. Alfred Bertram Gutheir. LC 43-5434. E. P. Dutton & Co.
Murders at Scandal House. Peter Hunt, pseud. LC 33-21523. D. Appleton-Century Company, Incorporated.
Murder's Burning. Sidney Hobson Courtier. LC 68-14531. Random House.
Murder's Coming. Donald Clough Cameron. LC 39-211831. H. Holt and Company.
Murders in Lovers' Lane. James Gerald Dunton. LC 27-19980. Small, Maynard & Company.
Murders in Praed Street. Cecil John Charles Street. LC 28-5865. 1928. Dodd, Mead & Company.
Murders in Silk. Mike Teagle. LC 38-856256. 1938. Hillman-Curl, Inc.
Murders in Surrey Wood. John Arnold. LC 28-30706. 1928. E. P. Dutton & Co., Inc.
Murders in the Mortuary. Austin Stone. LC 36-30159. G. P. Putnam's Sons.
Murders in the Rue Morgue. Edgar Allan Poe. (Illus.). 111p. 1982. Repr. of 1841 ed. 39.85 (ISBN 0-89901-048-2). Found Class Reprints.
Murders in the Rue Morgue. Edgar Allan Poe. (Illus.). 1980. Repr. deluxe ed. 29.75 (ISBN 0-89901-011-3). Found Class Reprints.
Murders in the Rue Morgue. rev. ed. Edgar Allan Poe. Ed. by Robert J. Dixson. Bd. with Gold Bug. (American Classics Ser.: Bk. 3). (gr. 9 up). 1973. pap. text ed. 3.25 (ISBN 0-88345-199-9, 18122); cassettes 40.00; 40.00 o.p. tapes. Regents Pub.
Murders in the Rue Morgue: And A Tale of the Ragged Mountains. raven ed. Edgar Allan Poe. LC 951. R. F. Fenno & Company.
Murders in the Rue Morgue, and The Gold Bug. Edgar Allen Poe. Ed. by Robert James Dixson. LC 54-556485. (American Classics Simplified and Adapted for Greater Reading Pleasure, Book 3). (Illus.). 1973. (pbk.) 1.25. Regents Pub. Co.
Murders in Volume 2. Elizabeth Daly. LC 41-3115. Toronto, Farrar & Rinehart, Inc.
Murder's Little Helper. George Bagby, pseud. 1972. pap. 0.95 o.p. (ISBN 0-446-65838-3). Paperback Lib.
Murder's Little Helper. Garland Lord, pseud. LC 41-25666. N. Y.
Murder's Little Helper. Aaron Marc Stein. LC 63-11206. 1963. Published for the Crime Club by Doubleday.
Murder's Little Sister. Pamela Branch. 1963. pap. 0.85 o.p. (ISBN 0-14-001947-2). Penguin.
Murder's Money. Gilbert Ralston. (Dakota,#4). 1975. (pbk.) 1.25 (ISBN 0-523-00564-4). Pinnacle Books.
Murder's No Accident. Albert Sidney Fleischman. LC 49-9520. 1949. Phoenix Press.
Murder's No Accident. Fred Orpet. LC 54-11466. 1954. Arcadia House.
Murder's No Picnic. E Louise Cushing. LC 53-112983. 1953. Arcadia House.
Murder's Not an Odd Job. Ralph Dennis. (Hardman,#6). 1974. (pbk.) 0.95. Popular Library.
Murders of Richard III. Elizabeth Peters, pseud. LC 73-21160. 1974. 6.95 (ISBN 0-396-06936-3). Dodd, Mead.
Murders on the Square. Theodore George. LC 76-169734. (Red badge novel of suspense). 1971. 4.95 (ISBN 0-396-06406-X). Dodd, Mead.
Murder's So Permanent. Edith Howie. 1942. Farrar & Rinehart, Inc.
Murder's Waiting Game. Anthony Gilbert, pseud. 1972. 4.95 o.p. (ISBN 0-394-47933-5). Random.
Murder's Web. Dorothy Dunn. LC 50-7141. 1950. Harper.
Murdo. Konrad Bercovici. LC 23-6047. Boni and Liveright.
Murdo & Other Stories. Iain C. Smith. 141p. 1981. 11.95 (ISBN 0-575-02983-8, Pub. by Gollancz England). David & Charles.
Murdoch Legacy. Ira Walker, pseud. LC 75-6392. 1975. 7.95 (ISBN 0-672-52129-6). Bobbs-Merrill.
Murdock. Geoffrey S. Simmons. LC 82-72056. 224p. 1982. 14.25 (ISBN 0-87795-429-1). Arbor Hse.
Murdock's Law. Loren D Estleman. LC 81-43410. 1982. 10.95 (ISBN 0-385-17957-X). Doubleday.
Murfy's Men. Gerald Green. LC 80-52409. 12.95 (ISBN 0-87223-662-5). Seaview Books.
Murgatreud's Empire. Bamber Gascoigne. LC 72-75750. 1972. 5.95 (ISBN 0-670-49555-7). Viking Press.
Murgunstrumm & Others. Hugh Barnett Cave. (Illus.). 475p. 1977. 15.00 (ISBN 0-913796-02-6). Carcosa.
Muriel: A Novel. George P. Elliott. LC 74-158607. 1972. 5.95 (ISBN 0-525-16140-6). Dutton.
Muriel at Metropolitan. Miriam Tlali. 190p. (Orig.). 1979. 9.00 o.s.i. (ISBN 0-89410-101-3); pap. 5.00 o.s.i. (ISBN 0-89410-100-5). Three Continents.
Muriel Howe. Angeline Teal. LC 8-26031. 1892. Dodd, Mead & Company.
Muriel: Or, Because of His Love for Her. Christine Carlton. (On cover: Library of American authors, no. 20). G. Munro.
Muriel Sterling: A Tale of the African Veldt. A. Irene Jewell. LC 30260. 1900. International Book and Publishing Company.
Muriella: Or, Le Selve. Louise De La Ramee. LC 6-33316. 1897. L. C. Page and Company (Incorporated.
Murillo Mystery. Beulah Poynter. LC 27-15601. Henry Altemus Company.
Murky Business. Honore de Balzac. (Penguin Classics Ser.). 1978. pap. 3.95 (ISBN 0-14-044271-5). Penguin.
Murky Business. Honore De Balzac. Tr. by Herbert J. Hunt from Fr. (Classic Ser.). 1972. pap. 1.95 o.p. (ISBN 0-14-044271-5, L271). Penguin.
Murmur of Mutiny. Marshall Pugh. LC 70-138793. 1972. 5.95 (ISBN 0-06-013438-0). Harper & Row.
Murphy. Samuel Beckett. LC 57-6939. 1957. Grove Press.
Murphy. Kurt Unkelbach. LC 67-16394. 1967. Prentice-Hall.
Murphy Stories. Mark Costello. LC 72-86409. (Illini book, IB-89). 1973. 2.50 (ISBN 0-252-00303-9) (ISBN 0-252-00303-9). University of Illinois Press.
Murphy's Bend. Grace E. Wills. LC 47-48814. 1946. The Westminster Press.
Murphy's Game. Martin Tarmey. LC 74-160410. 1971. 5.50 (ISBN 0-15-163600-1). Harcourt Brace Jovanovich.
Murphy's Law: And Other Reasons Why Things Go Wrong. Arthur Bloch. (Orig.). 1977. pap. 2.95 (ISBN 0-8431-0428-7). Price Stern.
Murphy's Romance. Max Schott. LC 82-22137. 132p. 1983. pap. 5.95 (ISBN 0-88496-197-4). Capra Pr.
Murphy's Romance: A Novel. Max Schott. LC 79-2657. 8.95 (ISBN 0-06-013781-9). Harper & Row.
Murphy's Trail. Kelly P Gast. LC 75-14821. 1976. 5.95 (ISBN 0-385-01802-9). Doubleday.
Murphy's War. Max Catto. LC 69-14279. 1969. 5.95. Simon and Schuster.
Murray Hill. Charles E Mercer. LC 79-28648. 10.95 (ISBN 0-440-06223-3). Delacorte Press.
Murrey: A Novel. Nancy Nichols. LC 78-12400. 1979. 10.00 (ISBN 0-670-49559-X). Viking Press.
Murvale Eastman: Christian Socialist. Albion Winegar Tourgee. LC 8-29845. Fords, Howard, & Hulbert; Etc., Etc.
Musashi. Eiji Yoshikawa. Tr. by Charles S. Terry from Japanese. LC 80-8791. (Illus.). 1066p. 1981. 17.95i (ISBN 0-06-859851-3, HarpT). Har-Row.
Muscavado. Eleanor Louise Heckert. LC 68-11923. (Illus.). 1968. Doubleday.
Muscavado. Eleanor Louise Heckert. 1975. (pbk.) 1.50. Dell.
Muscle Beach. 1st Ed. Ira Jan Wallach. LC 59-7636. 1959. Little, Brown.
Muscoma; or, Faith Campbell. A Romance of the Revolution. Aria Ahsland. LC 9-1849. 1848. Hotchkiss & Co.
Muscovite. Alison Macleod. LC 73-124356. (Illus.). 1971. 5.95 (ISBN 0-395-12714-9). Houghton Mifflin.
Muscovites. Creighton Scott. LC 40-10449. 1940. C. Scribner's Sons.
Muse and Mint. Walter Seymour Percy. LC 14-21739. 1914. 1.25. Sherman, French & Company.
Muses Are Heard. Truman Capote. pap. 1.25 (ISBN 0-394-70148-8, V-148, Vin). Random.
Muses of Ruin. William Pearson. LC 65-24262. 1965. McGraw-Hill.
Muses Three. With Illus. by Alma K. Lee. Terence Kennedy. LC 54-10472. Roy Publishers.
Museum: A Novel. Bernard Harper Friedman. LC 74-77778. 1974. 7.95 (ISBN 0-914590-02-2) (ISBN 0-914590-02-2). Fiction Collective; Distributed by G. Braziller.
Museum Murder. John Thomas McIntyre. LC 29-22915. 1929. Pub. for the Crime Club, Inc., by Doubleday, Doran & Company, Inc.
Museum of Cheats. Sylvia Townsend Warner. LC 47-1782. 1947. The Viking Press.
Museum Piece. Eden Phillpotts. LC 43-12684. 1943. Hutchinson & Co., Ltd.
Museum Piece No. 13. Rufus King. LC 46-66034. 1946. Pub. for the Crime Club by Doubleday & Company, Inc.
Museum Pieces. William Charles Franklyn Plomer. LC 54-117251. Noonday Press.
Museums and Women, and Other Stories. John Updike. (Crest Book, P2007). (Illus.). 1973. (pbk.) 1.25. Fawcett Pubns.
Museums and Women, and Other Stories. John Updike. LC 72-2247. (Illus.). 1972. 6.95 (ISBN 0-394-48184-4). Knopf.
Museums and Women and Other Stories. John Updike. LC 81-40080. (Illus.). 1981. 4.95 (ISBN 0-394-74762-3). Vintage Books.
Musgrave Ritual. Arthur Conan Doyle. Ed. by Walter Pauk & Raymond Harris. (Jamestown Classics Ser.). (Illus.). 39p. (gr. 6-12). 1976. pap. text ed. 2.00x (ISBN 0-89061-056-8, 533); tchrs. ed. 3.00 (ISBN 0-89061-057-6, 535). Jamestown Pubs.
Musgraves. Dorothy Emily Stevenson. LC 60-12970. 1960. Holt, Rinehart and Winston.
Musgraves. Dorothy Emily Stevenson. 1978. 1.95. Ace Books.
Musgrove Ranch. A Tale of Southern California. Tryphena Matilda Archer Browne. LC 6-17222. 1888. T. Whitaker.
Mushroom Cave. Robert J Rosenblum. LC 72-84940. 1973. 4.95 (ISBN 0-385-08329-7). Published for the Crime Club by Doubleday.
Mushroom Cave. Robert J Rosenblum. LC 76-374689. (Penguin crime fiction). 1976. 1.95 (ISBN 0-14-004106-0). Penguin Books.
Mushroom Heaven. John Wilmot Wiley. LC 35-404847. 1935. D. Appleton-Century Company, Incorporated.
Mushroom Town. Oliver Onions. LC 14-20505. Hodder and Stoughton.

Mushroom Town. Oliver Onions. LC 14-22555. 1.25. George ! H. Doran Company, Publishers in America ForHodder & Stoughton.

Music & Silence. Anne Redmon. (Penguin Contemporary American Fiction Ser.). 1980. pap. 3.95 (ISBN 0-14-005642-4). Penguin.

Music and Silence: A Novel. Anne Redmon. LC 78-14172. 10.00 (ISBN 0-03-047176-1). Holt, Rinehart and Winston.

Music Box. Leonard McDonald. LC 37-106943. 1937. The Clough-Bush Press.

Music for Chameleons. Truman Capote. 1981. pap. 3.50 (ISBN 0-451-09934-6, E9934, Sig). NAL.

Music for Chameleons. Truman Capote. 1980. 11.95 (ISBN 0-394-50826-2). Random.

Music for Mohini. Bhabani Bhattacharya. LC 52-5686. 1952. Crown Publishers.

Music from a Broken Piano. James B. Hall. 1983. 11.95 (ISBN 0-914590-78-2); pap. 5.95 (ISBN 0-914590-79-0). Fiction Coll.

Music from Another Room. James Kelly. 1980. pap. 2.25 (ISBN 0-8439-0779-7). Nordon Pubns.

Music from Spain. Eudora Welty. LC 49-4125. 1948. Levee Press.

Music from the Past. Kate Cameron, pseud. (Holderly Hall Ser). (Orig.). 1975. pap. 1.25 o.p. (LB287ZK, Leisure Bks). Nordon Pubns.

Music from the Past. Kate Cameron, pseud. 1975. (pbk.) 0.95. Leisure Books.

Music Hath Charms. Flora Annie Webster Steel. LC 8-13436. 1895. Macmillan and Co.

Music in the Hills. Dorothy Emily Stevenson. LC 50-10195. 1950. Rinehart.

Music in the Hills. Dorothy Emily Stevenson. 1973. Popular Lib.

Music in the Hills. new ed. Dorothy Emily Stevenson. LC 76-160440. 1972. 5.95 (ISBN 0-03-080287-3). Holt, Rinehart and Winston.

Music in the Street. Vera Caspary. LC 30-1701. Sears Publishing Company, Inc.

Music Is Gone. Le Garde S Doughty. LC 45-445544. 1945. Duell, Sloan and Pearce.

Music-Makers: A Novel. Murrell Edmunds. LC 27-22948. 1927. H. Vinal, Ltd.

Music Man: A Novel. Meredith Willson. LC 62-6129. 1962. Pyramid Books.

Music Master. Charles Klein. LC 9-7830. 1909. Dodd, Mead & Company.

Music of Aquarius. Canella Lewis. (Berkely Medallion Book). 1.50 (ISBN 0-425-03292-2). Berkley Pub. Corp.,

Music of Love. Marcia Rose, pseud. LC 79-90272. 1980. 1.95 (ISBN 0-345-28682-0). Ballantine Books.

Music of Passion. Lynda Ward. 1981. pap. 2.50. Harlequin Bks.

Music of Passion. Lynda Ward. (Superromances Ser.). 384p. 1981. pap. 2.50 (ISBN 0-373-70003-2, Pub. by Worldwide). Harlequin Bks.

Music of Their Laughter. Rodrick Thorp & Robert Blake. pap. 3.95x o.p. (ISBN 0-06-388750-9). Canfield Pr.

Music Out of Dixie: A Novel. Harold Sinclair. LC 52-5574. 1952. Rinehart.

Music Room. William Edward Daniel Ross. 1978. pap. 1.50 o.s.i. (ISBN 0-505-51223-8). Tower Bks.

Music School. John Updike. 1966. 12.50 (ISBN 0-394-43727-6). Knopf.

Music School. John Updike. LC 80-10774. 260p. 1980. pap. 2.95 (ISBN 0-394-74510-8, Vin). Random.

Music School: Short Stories. John Updike. (Crest bk., R1071). 1967. Fawcett.

Music School: Short Stories. John Updike. LC 80-10774. 1980. 2.95 (ISBN 0-394-74510-8). Vintage Books.

Music Stops and the Waltz Continues: A Novel. David G. Smith. LC 80-18490. 1980. 9.95 (ISBN 0-8037-5719-0). Dial Press.

Music to Murder by. Vernon Hinkle. (Belmont Tower Books). 1.75 (ISBN 0-505-51262-9). Tower Pubns.

Music When Sweet Voices Die. Chelsea Quinn Yarbro. LC 78-13324. 9.95 (ISBN 0-399-12004-1). Putnam.

Music Within. Elizabeth B. De Trevino. LC 72-84905. 360p. 1973. 6.95 o.p. (ISBN 0-385-07050-0). Doubleday.

Music Within. Elizabeth Borton Trevino. LC 72-84905. 1973. 6.95 (ISBN 0-385-07050-0). Doubleday.

Musical Crotchets. Hubert J Schonacker. LC 8-2042. Cathcart, Cleland & Co.

Musical Crotchets. From Darkness to Light. Hubert J Schonacker. LC 8-2043. Printed by Carlon & Hollenbeck.

Musical Honors. Kitty Barne. LC 47-11174. 1947. Dodd, Mead.

Musical Romances. Aimee M Wood. LC 9-515. 1898. The Life Publishing Co.

Musicale. Francis Steegmuller. LC 30-23556. J. Cape & H. Smith.

Musicians Only. Fradel Stock. LC 27-184919. 1927. The Pelican Publishing Company.

Musing Wanderer. Anton Gross. LC 23-13726. The Roxburgh Publishing Company, Inc.

Musings. Bert W. Whitehurst. (Illus.). 1979. lib. bdg. 13.95 (ISBN 0-918602-24-6); pap. text ed. 8.95 (ISBN 0-918602-23-8). Galleon-Whitehurst.

Musk and Amber. Alfred Edward Woodley Mason. LC 42-19563. 1942. Doubleday, Doran and Company, Inc.

Musk-Ox & Other Tales. Nikolai Semenovich Leskov. Tr. by R. Norman from Rus. LC 76-23887. (Classics of Russian Literature). 1977. 11.50 (ISBN 0-88355-499-2); pap. 3.50 (ISBN 0-88355-500-X). Hyperion Conn.

Muskeg Marshal. Orlando Bigoni. 1973. 4.95. Lenox Hill Pr.

Musket and the Cross: The Struggle of France and England for North America, by Walter D. Edmonds. Maps and Devices by Samuel H. Bryant. 1st Ed. Walter Dumaux Edmonds. LC 68-11527. 1968. 10.00. Little, Brown.

Muskets on the Mississippi. Matthew Whitman Harding. 1974. (pbk.) 0.95. Popular Library.

Muskie Murder. x ed. Ted Vogel. 200p. 1982. pap. 5.95. Caroline Hse.

Muskrat Farm. Dan Cushman. LC 59-6988. 1977. 9.95 (ISBN 0-911436-05-7). Stay Away.

Muslim Cities in the Later Middle Ages. Ira M. Lapidus. (Middle Eastern Studies: No. 11). 1967. 10.00x o.p. (ISBN 0-674-59500-9). Harvard U Pr.

Muslim Sir Galahad: A Present Day Story of Islam in Turkey. Henry Otis Dwight. LC 13-12433. 1.00. Fleming H. Revell Company.

Muslin. George Moore. 1915. Brentano's.

Mussolini's Gold. John Kimmey. (Orig.). 1981. pap. 1.95 (ISBN 0-505-51608-X). Tower Bks.

Must Woman Ever and Man Never Forgive? Richard Lightfoot. LC 18-2411. Angelus Publishing Company.

Mustang. Cliff Hammond. LC 39-17415. Phoenix Press.

Mustang Country. Hettie Jones. 1976. (pbk.) 1.50 (ISBN 0-671-80429-4). Pocket Books.

Mustang Gray: A Romance. Jeremiah Clemens. LC 6-21357. 1858. J. B. Lippincott & Co.

Mustang: Life & Legends of Nevada's Wild Horses. Anthony A. Amaral. LC 76-53821. (Lancehead Ser.). (Illus.). xiv, 156p. 1977. 9.00 (ISBN 0-87417-046-X). U of Nev Pr.

Mustang Man. Louis L'Amour. 176p. 1976. pap. 2.25 (ISBN 0-553-20258-8). Bantam.

Mustang Marshall. Herbert Arthur, pseud. LC 43-8702. 1943. Phoenix Press.

Mustang Marshall. Herbert Shappiro. LC 43-8702. 1943. Phoenix Press.

Mustang Men. Thorne Douglas. (Fawcett Gold Medal Book). 1977. 1.25 (ISBN 0-449-13918-2). Fawcett Pubns.

Mustang Mesa. Peter Field. LC 52-5790. (Triple-A western classic). 1952. Jefferson House.

Mustang Mesa. Peter Field. LC 37-27086. 1937. W. Morrow & Co.

Mustang Trail. Leonard London Foreman. LC 65-19911. (Double D western). 3.50. Doubleday.

Mustang Trail. Leonard London Foreman. 1975. (pbk.) 0.95. Ace Books.

Mustang Trail. Thomas Ernest Mount. LC 59-7402. (Triple-A western classic). 1960. Jefferson House.

Mustang Trail. Thomas Ernest Mount. LC 33-37444. 1933. W. Morrow and Company.

Mustangers. Bennett Foster. LC 39-27165. 1939. W. Morrow and Co.

Mustangers. Owen G. Irons. (YA) 1978. 6.50 (Avalon). Bouregy.

Mustangs for Montana. B. A. Collier. (YA) 1980. 6.50 (Avalon). Bouregy.

Mustard Seed. Vicki Baum. LC 53-9317. 1953. Dial Press.

Mustard Seed. Charles C Mottley & Charles M. Mottley. 1977. 1.50 (ISBN 0-445-08608-4). Popular Library.

Mustee. Lance Horner. 1978. pap. 2.95 (ISBN 0-449-13808-9, GM). Fawcett.

Muster of the Vultures. Gerard Fairlie. LC 30-1566. 1930. Little, Brown, and Company.

Mustian: Two Novels & a Story. Reynolds Price. LC 82-73009. 320p. 1983. 14.95 (ISBN 0-689-11377-3). Atheneum.

Musty Corn. Denny Culbert. LC 25-23721. 1925. Dorrance and Company.

Mutable Many. A Novel. Robert Barr. F. A. Stokes Company.

Mutant. Henry Kuttner. LC 75-29286. (Garland Library of Science Fiction). 1975. (ISBN 0-8240-1420-0). Garland Pub.

Mutant. Henry Kuttner. LC 53-12601. 1953. Gnome Press.

Mutant 50: The Plastic-Eaters. by kit pedlar & gerry davis. ed. Kit Pedler & Gerry Davis. 1973. 1.50. Bantam.

Mutant 59: The Plastic-Eaters. Kit Pedler & Gerry Davis. LC 70-173353. 1972. 5.95 (ISBN 0-670-49662-6). Viking Press.

Mutants. Gordon R. Dickson. LC 70-92076. 256p. 1973. pap. 1.95 (ISBN 0-02-019540-0, Collier). Macmillan.

Mutants: A Science Fiction Adventure. Gordon R Dickson. LC 77-89028. 1973. (pbk.) 1.25. Collier Books.

Mutants: A Science Fiction Adventure. Gordon R Dickson. LC 70-92076. 1970. Macmillan.

Mute. Piers Anthony, pseud. 448p. 1981. pap. 3.50 (ISBN 0-380-82354-3, 77578). Avon.

Mute. Otto F Walter. LC 62-13056. 1962. Grove Press.

Mute & Mutilated. Heinz G. Stripp. 1970. 4.95 o.p. Vantage.

Mute Island: A Novel. Charles Fecker Conrad. LC 17-2343. 1917. The University Book Co.

Mute Singer. A Novel. Anna Cora Ogden Mowatt Ritchie. LC 7-416586. 1866. Carleton.

Mute Witness. Robert L Fish. LC 63-17273. 1963. Published for the Crime Club by Doubleday & Co.

Muted Murder. Sally Sinclair. LC 53-7044. 1953. Arcadia House.

Muted Voices. Eugen Relgis. 1972. Repr. of 1938 ed. lib. bdg. 69.95 (ISBN 0-87968-001-6). Gordon Pr.

Muted Voices (Glasuri in Surdina) Eugen Relgis. LC 79-190032. (Illus.). 1972. 14.95 (ISBN 0-87968-001-6). Gordon Press.

Muted Voices Glasuri in Surdina. Eugen Relgis & Freeman-Ishill, Rose, Tr. LC 39-1108. 1938. Pub. and Printed by the Oriole Press.

Mutes in the Sun. Lee Kok Liang. (Writing in Asia Ser.). 1974. pap. text ed. 3.50x (00232). Heinemann Ed.

Mutilators. Mervin Casey. 208p. (Orig.). 1976. pap. 1.50 (ISBN 0-89041-086-0, 3086). Major Bks.

Mutineer. Roselyn Edwards. (Crown Ser.). 1975. pap. 4.50 o.p. (ISBN 0-8127-0103-8). Review & Herald.

Mutineer. Roselyn Edwards. (Crown Ser.). 1975. pap. 4.50 o.p. (ISBN 0-8127-0103-8). Southern Pub.

Mutineers. Richard Armstrong. 1968. D. McKay Co.

Mutinous Wind. Elizabeth Reynard. LC 51-10994. (Illus.). 1951. Houghton Mifflin.

Mutiny. Frank Tilsley. LC 59-59962. 1958. Reynal.

Mutiny in Space. Avram Davidson. 1969. pap. 0.60 o.p. (X2079). Pyramid Pubns.

Mutiny in Space. Avram Davidson. 1974. pap. 0.95 o.p. (ISBN 0-515-03376-6, N3376). Pyramid Pubns.

Mutiny of Madame Yes. Dale Collins. LC 34-23849. The Bobbs-Merrill Company.

Mutiny of the Elsinore. Jack London. LC 14-151764. 1914. The Macmillan Company.

Mutiny of the Elsinore. Jack London. 1919. The Macmillan Company.

Mutiny on the Bounty. Charles Bernard Nordhoff & Hall, James Norman, 1887- Joint Author. LC 43-13631. 1943. Triangle Books.

Mutiny on the Bounty. Charles Bernard Nordhoff & Hall, James Norman. LC 32-255969. 1932. Little, Brown, and Company.

Mutiny on the Bounty. Charles Nordoff & James F. Hall. (Illus.). (YA) pap. 2.00 o.p. (2-48148, RivLit); pap. 2.40x duraflex ed. o.p. (2-48103, R3). HM.

Mutiny on the Bounty: By Charles Nordhoff and James Norman Hall. A School Ed. by Florence Doerr Jones. Charles Bernard Nordhoff & James Norman Hall. LC 52-14515. 1952. Globe Book Co.

Mutiny on the Bounty: By Charles Nordhoff and James Norman Hall. With an Introd. by Sterling North. Suggestions for Reading and Discussion by Stanley Kegler. School Ed. Charles Bernard Nordhoff & James Norman Hall. LC 62-52423. (Riverside literature series, R3). 1962. Published for Little, Brown, by Houghton Mifflin.

Mutiny on the Long Trail. Ella M Rea. LC 33-116322. 1933. Printed by the Metropolitan Press.

Mutterings. James A. Levee. 3.50 o.p. Vantage.

Mutual Arrangements. Nonie C Murphy, pseud. LC 76-13585. (ISBN 0-671-22305-4). Simon and Schuster.

Mutual Friend. Frederick Busch. LC 77-11793. 9.95 (ISBN 0-06-010527-5). Harper & Row.

Mutual Pair: An Omnibus Volume... Doris Caroline Abrahams & Simon Jasha Skidelsky. LC 77-359364. 1976. 5.50 (ISBN 0-7181-1538-4). Joseph.

Muzzle Blast. Bruno Rossi, pseud. (Sharpshooter Ser., No. 6). 1974. pap. 0.95 o.p. (LB170NK). Leisure Bks.

Muzzling the Tiger. John William Fay. LC 24-8255. Murray Hill Publishers, Inc.

My Actor-Husband. LC 12-8803. 1912. 1.30. John Lane Company.

My Adventure in the Flying Scotsman. Eden Phillpotts. Ed. by Tom Schantz. (Illus.). 40p. 1975. pap. 4.00 (ISBN 0-915230-09-7). Rue Morgue.

My Affinity: And Other Stories. Elizabeth Doten. LC 37-32781. 1870. W. White and Company.

My Aggravating Wife. A Novel ... LC 7-11826. (On cover: Parlor-car series, no. 1). G. Munro.

My Ain Laddie. David Plante McAstocker. LC 22-21946. 1922. The Stratford Publishing Co.

My Airman Over There. Aimee Bond. LC 18-9774. 1918. Moffat, Yard & Company.

My Allegiance. Cora Kelley Wheeler. LC 8-36054. 1896. The Editor Publishing Company.

My America! Eliot Wagner. LC 80-14122. 13.95 (ISBN 0-671-25332-8). Kenan Press.

My American. Stella Gibbons. LC 40-3477. 1939. Longmans, Green and Co.

My American. Stella Gibbons. LC 40-30529. 1940. C. Scribner's Sons.

My Antonia. Willa Sibert Cather. (Keith Jennison large type ed.). 1966. 6.95. Watts.

My Antonia. new ed. Willa Sibert Cather. LC 26-13915. 1926. Houghton Mifflin Company.

My Antonia. Willa Sibert Cather. LC 18-18398. 1918. Houghton Mifflin Company.

My Antonia. new ed. Willa Sibert Cather. LC 28-485828. Houghton Mifflin Company.

My Antonia. new ed. Willa Sibert Cather. LC 32-335998. Houghton Mifflin Company.

My Antonia. Willa Sibert Cather & Handlan, Bertha. LC 49-8708. 1949. Houghton Mifflin.

My Antonia. With Illus. by W. T. Benda. Willa Sibert Cather. LC 58-1819. Houghton Mifflin.

My Argument with the Gestapo: A Macaronic Journal. Thomas Merton. 1975. (pbk.) 3.95 (ISBN 0-8112-0586-X). New Directions.

My Argument with the Gestapo: A Macaronic Journal. Thomas Merton. LC 69-20082. 1969. 4.95. Doubleday.

My Aunt Angie. Roy Larcom McCardell. LC 30-5932. Farrar & Rinehart Incorporated.

My Aunt Jeanette. Sarah Milligan Kimball. LC 7-12237. 1884. Phillips & Hunt.

My Aunt Lucienne. Rose Caroline Feld. LC 55-9676. (Illus.). 1955. Scribner.

My Aunt's Match Making. LC 7-32290. (On cover: Cassell's "rainbow" series. v. 1. no. 26). 1888. Cassell & Company, Limited.

My Aunt's Rhinoceros. Peter Fleming. (O.S.I.). 1958. 3.50 o.s.i. (50260). S&S.

My Back Doesn't Hurt Anymore. Jack Tessman. (Illus.). 1980. pap. 6.95 (ISBN 0-8256-3175-0, Quick Fox). Putnam Pub Group.

My Beautiful White Roses. Michael Lechner. LC 75-169940. (Illus.). 1971. Smoketree Press.

My Bed Is My Castle. Henrik Tjele. pap. 1.75 o.p. (Z1054K, Zebra). Grove.

My Bed Is Not for Sleeping. Gerty Agoston. (O.s.i.). (Orig.). 1970. pap. 0.95 o.s.i. (A300N, Award). Univ Pub & Dist.

My Bed Is Not for Sleeping. Gerty Agoston. (O.s.i.). 256p. 1976. pap. 1.50 o.s.i. (AD1570, Award). Univ Pub & Dist.

My Beloved. Aline Blossom. LC 54-277956. 1953. N. H., M. Jones Co.

My Best Girl. Kathleen Thompson Norris. LC 27-216237. A. L. Burt Company.

My Best Murder Story: 14 Authors Choose Their Best. Ed. by David Coxe Cooke. LC 55-11544. 1955. Merlin Press.

My Best Science Fiction Story: As Selected by 25 Outstanding Authors. Ed. by Leo Margulies. Friend, Oscar Jerome, 1897- Joint Ed. LC 49-49362. 1949. Merlin Press.

My Best Story: An Anthology of Stories Chosen by Their Own Authors. LC 30-26887. 1930. The Bobbs-Merrill Company.

My Big Buck: Outdoor Stories of Maine. Gerald E Lewis. LC 78-26185. 9.50 (ISBN 0-89621-021-9) (ISBN 0-89621-020-0). Thorndike Press.

My Big Sister's Sin: Me. Peter Kevin. 192p. (Orig.). 1972. pap. 1.95 o.p. (ISBN 0-87682-278-2, 7278). Barclay Hse.

My Bird Sings. Oriel Malet. LC 46-7661. 1946. Doubleday & Company, Inc.

My Bird Sings. Auriel Rosemary Malet Vaughan. LC 46-7661. 1946. Doubleday & Company, Inc.

My Blond Princess of Space. John N. Will. 2.00 o.p. Carlton.

My Blood and My Treasure. Mary Schumann. LC 41-6659. 1941. The Dial Press.

My Body. E. Howard Hunt. 1973. (pbk.) 0.95. Lancer.

My Bonnie Lass. Cecilia Viets Dakin Jamison. LC 7-10326. Estes and Lauriat.

My Book of The Ugly Duckling. Pictures by Maraja. Hans Christian Andersen. LC 61-66505. (Giant Maxton book). Maxton Pub. Corp.

My Boy in Khaki: A Mother's Story. Della Thompson Lutes. LC 18-11145. 1918. Harper & Brothers.

My Boy John That Went to Sea. James Vance Marshall. (Illus.). 1967. Morrow.

My Boy John That Went to Sea. Donald Gordon Payne. LC 67-15153. (Illus.). 1967. Morrow.

My Boy, My Lover. Harry Paul. (Orig.). 1969. pap. 1.95 o.p. (6051). Brandon.

My Brave and Gallant Gentlemen: A Romance of British Columbia. Robert Watson. LC 18-19983. George H. Doran Company.

My Brillant Career. Pref. by Henry Lawson. Miles Franklin. LC 66-12761. 1966. 4.50. Angus & Robertson.

My Brilliant Career. Miles Franklin. LC 80-52658. 1980. 9.95 (ISBN 0-312-55599-7). St. Martin's Press.

My Broken Heart. 1st Ed. Sol Kantor. LC 55-11734. 1955. Comet Press Books.
My Brother: A Novel. Vincent Brown. Rand, McNally & Company.
My Brother Jack. George Henry Johnston. LC 65-15164. 1965. bds., 5.95. Morrow.
My Brother John. Herbert R Purdum. (G-685). 1968. Ace.
My Brother John. Herbert R Purdum. LC 66-11742. (Double D western). 1966. Doubleday.
My Brother Jonathan. Francis Brett Young. LC 28-23467. 1928. A. A. Knopf.
My Brother Michael. Mary Stewart. LC 60-7072. 1960. M. S. Mill Co., and W. Morrow.
My Brother, My Enemy. Mitchell A Wilson. LC 52-9073. 1952. Little, Brown.
My Brother, My Executioner. F. Sionil Jose. 1979. pap. 8.75x. Cellar.
My Brother Napoleon: The Confessions of Caroline Bonaparte. Frank Wilson Kenyon. LC 71-141027. 1971. 5.95 (ISBN 0-396-06309-8). Dodd, Mead.
My Brother, Oh, My Brother! 1st Ed. Agnes Cochran Bramblett. LC 53-12635. 1953. Pageant Press.
My Brother, the Druggist. Marvin Kaye. LC 78-7759. 1979. 7.95 (ISBN 0-385-14427-X). Published for the Crime Club by Doubleday.
My Brother the King: The Tale of James Darcy (King James I. of Yalmal) & His Sister, Wyemarke Darcy. Edward Herbert Cooper. LC 11-4104. 1911. 1.50. John Lane.
My Brother, the Wind. G. Clifton Wisler, pseud. LC 78-14690. 1979. 7.95 (ISBN 0-385-14822-4). Doubleday.
My Brother Tom: A Love Story. 1st Amer. Ed. James Aldridge. LC 67-14455. 1967. bds., 4.95. Little.
My Brother's Image. Mark Hamilton. 160p. 1983. pap. 2.50 (ISBN 0-380-82230-X, 82230-X). Avon.
My Brother's Keeper. Richard Thomas Devall Carpenter. LC 14-21587. 1914. 0.50. R. T. D. Carpenter.
My Brother's Keeper. Marcia Gluck Davenport. LC 54-6300. 1954. Scribner.
My Brother's Keeper. Marcia Gluck Davenport. LC 78-74646. 1979. 12.50 (ISBN 0-8376-0429-X). R. Bentley.
My Brother's Keeper. Charles Tenney Jackson. LC 10-22860. 1.50. The Bobbs-Merrill Company.
My Brother's Keeper. Stanislaus Joyce & Richard Ellman. 256p. 1982. pap. 7.95 (ISBN 0-571-11803-8). Faber & Faber.
My Brother's Keeper. Israel Katz. 1978. 5.95 (ISBN 0-533-03133-8). Vantage.
My Brother's Keeper. Giles A Lutz. 1975. (pbk.) 0.95. Ace Books.
My Brother's Killer. Dominic Devine. LC 81-47093. 256p. 1981. pap. 2.40i (ISBN 0-06-080558-7, P 558, PL). Har-Row.
My Brother's Killer. Jean Potts. LC 75-14358. 1975. 6.95 (ISBN 0-684-14349-6). Scribner.
My Brother's Wife. Amelia Ann Blanford Edwards. (Lovell's library, no. 1358). 1889. J. W. Lovell Company.
My Brother's Wife: By Harry Davis Pseud. Roberta Hill. LC 56-7977. 1956. Greenberg.
My Business Is Murder. Henry Kane. LC 54-40285. (Avon, 602). 1954. Avon Publications.
My Business: The Apple's Fall and Mary's Woe. Paul Kish. LC 26-19723. Roberts.
My Candle Burns... Frederick Stephani. LC 34-6040. The Macaulay Company.
My Captive: A Novel. Joseph Alexander Altsheler. LC 2-15214. 1902. D. Appleton and Company.
My Caravaggio Style. Doris Langley-Levy Moore. LC 59-777257. 1959. Lippincott.
My Carnal Confession. Gerty Agoston. (O.s.i.). 1969. pap. 0.95 o.s.i. (A483N, Award). Univ Pub & Dist.
My Carnal Confession. Gerty Agoston. (O.s.i.). 1976. pap. 1.50 o.s.i. (AD1584, Award). Univ Pub & Dist.
My Cat Sammy. Ethel Edith Mannin. 1972. pap. 0.95 o.p. (09144). Curtis.
My Child and I. A Woman's Story. Florence Alice Price James. LC 7-7414. (On cover: Lippincott's select novels, no. 152). 1894. J. B. Lippincott Company.
My Chum, Pres. William C Dear. LC 26-4418. Pittsburgh Printing Company.
My Connaught Cousins. A Novel. Harriett Jay. LC 7-10180. (Harper's Franklin square library, no. 292). Harper & Brothers.
My Country: A Story of Today. George Rothwell Brown. LC 17-23648. 1917. Small Maynard & Company.
My Cousin Death. Mary McMullen. LC 79-8048. 1980. 8.95 (ISBN 0-385-15748-7). Published for the Crime Club by Doubleday.
My Cousin Jaspar. Lillian R. Kraemer. 1968. 6.00 o.p. (ISBN 0-682-46811-8). Exposition.
My Cousin: Miss Cinderella (Ma Cousine Pot-Au-Feu); Tr. from the French of Leon De Tinseau. Leon De Tinseau & Naylor, Edward Woodall, 1867- Tr. (Gainsborough series). 1889. D. Appleton and Company.
My Cousin Nicholas. a new ed. Richard Harris Barham. LC 6-7196. 1856. G. Routledge & Co.
My Cousin Rachel. presentation ed. Daphne Du Maurier. LC 52-5231. 1952. Doubleday.
My Cousin Rachel. Daphne Du Maurier. LC 74-184731. 1971. (ISBN 0-8376-0413-3). R. Bentley.
My Crime. A Novel. Josephine Zeman. J. S. Ogilvie Publishing Company.
My Cris: A Novel. 1st Ed. James Gerald Craven. LC 53-6710. 1953. Exposition Press.
My Crowded Solitude. Jack McLaren. pap. 1.40 o.s.i. Tri-Ocean.
My Crown, My Love. Ruth Walgreen Stephan. LC 60-15436. 1960. Knopf.
My Daddy Is a Policeman. Elizabeth A. Doll. LC 73-7650. (Illus.). 32p. 1973. 3.95 o.p. (ISBN 0-13-608463-X). P-H.
My Danish Sweetheart: A Novel. William Clark Russell. (On cover: Harper's Franklin square library, no. 701). 1992. Harper & Brothers.
My Darling, Darling Doctors. Fay Baker. LC 74-25292. 6.95 (ISBN 0-8076-0774-6). G. Braziller.
My Darling Doll. Dorothy S. Coleman. 1972. 6.95 o.p. (ISBN 0-87069-148-1). Wallace-Homestead.
My Darling from the Lions. Alice Denham. LC 67-25173. 1968. 5.00 o.p. Bobbs.
My Darling from the Lions... Edita Morris. LC 43-8185. 1943. Little, Brown and Company.
My Darling from the Lions: A Novel. Alice Denham. LC 67-251733. 1967. 5.00. Bobbs.
My Darling, My Hamburger. Paul Zindel. (gr. 7-12). 1971. pap. 1.95 (ISBN 0-553-12741-1). Bantam.
My Darling Spitfire. Rosemary Carter. (Harlequin Presents Ser.). (Orig.). 1980. pap. 1.50 (ISBN 0-373-10337-9, Pub. by Harlequin). PB.
My Daughter. Kate Mayhew Speake Penney. LC 46-19671. 1946. Printed at Birmingham Publishing Company.
My Daughter Elinor. A Novel. Frank Lee Benedict. LC 7-34448. 1869. Harper & Brothers.
My Daughter Helen. Allan Noble Monkhouse. LC 24-20560. Harcourt, Brace and Company.
My Day. Jean Rhys. LC 75-26592. 1975. 7.50 (Pub. by F Hallman); pap. 3.00. SBD.
My Days of Anger. James Thomas Farrell. LC 43-16086. 1943. The Vanguard Press.
My Days of Anger: With a New Introd. Written by the Author for This Ed. World Reprint Ed. James Thomas Farrell. LC 47-5504. 1947. World Pub. Co.
My Dead Body. George Bagby, pseud. LC 76-2751. (Crime Club Ser.). 192p. 1976. 5.95 o.p. (ISBN 0-385-12057-5). Doubleday.
My Dead Body. Aaron Marc Stein. LC 76-2751. 1976. 5.95 (ISBN 0-385-12057-5). Published for the Crime Club by Doubleday.
My Dead Wife. William Worley. LC 48-4957. (Inner sanctum mystery). 1948. Simon and Schuster.
My Dear. Helen Marion Edginton. LC 29-5696. Penn Publishing Company.
My Dear Bella. Arthur Kober. LC 41-892224. Random House.
My Dear Cousin. Margaret Jones Hoffmann. LC 74-78878. 1970. Harcourt, Brace & World.
My Dear Elaine. Sturges Mason Schley. LC 40-35167. 1940. W. Funk, Inc.
My Dear Five Hundred Friends. George Price. 1963. 3.95 o.p. (ISBN 0-671-50390-1). S&S.
My Dear Innocent. Lindsay Armstrong. (Harlequin Romances Ser.). 192p. 1982. pap. 1.50 (ISBN 0-373-02497-5). Harlequin Bks.
My Dear Jenny. Madeleine Robins. 224p. 1980. pap. 1.75 (ISBN 0-449-50041-1, Coventry). Fawcett.
My Dear Lover England. Pamela Bennetts. LC 74-19858. 1975. 6.95. St. Martin's Press.
My Dear Miss Emma. Paula Allardyce, pseud. LC 80-80979. 224p. 1980. pap. 1.95 (ISBN 0-87216-686-4). Playboy Pbks.
My Dearest Love. Emilie Baker Loring. LC 76-41729. 1976. 6.95 (ISBN 0-88411-359-0). Aeonian Press.
My Dearest Love. Emilie Baker Loring. LC 82-9180. 1982. 12.95 (ISBN 0-8161-3403-0). G.K. Hall.
My Dearest Love. 1st Ed. Emilie Baker Loring. LC 54-582041. 1954. Little, Brown.
My Debut in Journalism and Other Odd Happenings. Walter Polk Phillips. LC 7-36056. The International Telegram Co.
My Desire. Susan Warner. 1879. R. Carter and Brothers.
My Diana. Mary Elisabeth McFarland. LC 51-3720. 1951. Vantage Press.
My Diary by Pat: Satire. Milt Rosen. 155p. pap. 0.95 o.p. (ISBN 0-87056-259-2, 6259). Bks for Bet Living.
My Disappearance in Providence, and Other Stories. Alfred Andersch. LC 73-9005. 1978. 7.95 (ISBN 0-385-01391-4). Doubleday.
My Dish Towel Flies at Half-Mast. Mary Kuczkir. LC 78-19624. (Illus.). 1979. 7.95 (ISBN 0-345-27857-7). Ballantine Books.
My Dog Lemon. Raymond Prunty Holland. LC 45-10491. 1945. A. S. Barnes and Company.
My Door Is Always Open: A Novel. 1st Ed. Marc Nail. LC 61-592588. 1961. Chilton Co., Book Division.
My Double & How He Undid Me. Edward Everett Hale. LC 6-46187. 1895. Lamson, Wolffe & Co.
My Ducats and My Daughter. A Novel... Peter Hay Hunter & Whyte, Walter, Joint Author. LC 7-9379. (Harper's Franklin square library, no. 383). 1884. Harper & Brothers.
My Early Adventures During the Peninsular Campaigns of Napoleon. Selina Bunbury. LC 45-46877. 1834. J. Loring.
My Enemy and I. Theresa Charles, pseud. LC 41-134969. 1941. Longmans, Green and Co.
My Enemy My Lord. first ed. Margaret Masland Lavin. 1972. 5.95 (ISBN 0-533-00189-7). Vantage.
My Enemy, My Love. Reginald Thomas Staples. LC 77-81789. 1979. 10.00 (ISBN 0-385-13606-4). Doubleday.
My Enemy, My Love. R. T. Stevens. LC 77-81789. 1979. 10.00 o.p. (ISBN 0-385-13606-4). Doubleday.
My Enemy, My Love. R. T. Stevens. 384p. 1982. pap. 2.95 (ISBN 0-446-80663-3). Warner Bks.
My Enemy, My Love: A Novel. Susan Evans McCloud. LC 80-53391. 5.95 (ISBN 0-88494-414-X). Bookcraft.
My Enemy, My Wife. Allen Haden & Paul Frischauer. LC 51-10023. 1951. Putnam.
My Enemy the Motor: A Tale in Eight Honks and One Crash. Julian Leonard Street. LC 8-7892. 1908. J. Lane Company.
My Enemy the Queen. Eleanor Hibbert. LC 77-11366. 1978. 8.95 (ISBN 0-385-14111-4). Doubleday.
My Enemy the Queen. Eleanor Hibbert. 1979. 2.25 (ISBN 0-449-23979-9). Fawcett Crest Books.
My Enemy the Queen. Eleanor Hibbert. LC 78-24148. 1980. (2 vol set.) 18.50 (ISBN 0-8161-6638-2). G. K. Hall.
My Enemy the Queen. Victoria Holt, pseud. 1979. pap. 2.25 (ISBN 0-449-23979-9, Crest). Fawcett.
My Enemy, the World: A Novel. Guido D'Agostino. LC 47-31403. 1947. Dial Press.
My Enemy's Enemy. Kingsley Amis. LC 63-11907. 1963. 4.50 (ISBN 0-15-163681-8). HarBraceJ.
My Enemy's Friend. Helena Osborne. 1973. (pbk.) 0.95. Dell.
My Enemy's Friend. Helena Osborne. LC 72-76665. 1972. 6.95 (ISBN 0-698-10448-X). Coward, McCann & Geoghegan.
My Escape from the CIA (and into CBS) Hughes Rudd. 1976. 3.95. E. P. Dutton.
My Escape from the CIA: And Other Improbable Events. Hughes Rudd. LC 66-128594. bds., 4.95. Dutton.
My Face for the World to See. 1st Ed. Alfred Hayes. LC 57-8208. Harper.
My Fair Lady. Louis Hemon. LC 72-10773. (Short story index reprint series). 1973. (ISBN 0-8369-4219-1). Books for Libraries Press.
My Fair Lady. Louis Hemon. Tr. by William Aspenwall Bradley. LC 23-17165. 1923. The Macmillan Company.
My Fair Lady. Alan J. Lerner. (YA) 1957. 4.95 o.p. (ISBN 0-698-10262-2). Coward.
My Fair Lady: By Georgius Pseud. Translated from the French by Philip John Stead. Georges Guibourg. LC 54-52311. 1954. Roy Publishers.
My Family Overthere, Pt. III. Mildred Walker, pseud. 323p. 1977. pap. 4.95 (ISBN 0-917200-17-9). ESPress.
My Family Sin Circle. Thomas Shire. 192p. (Orig.). 1973. pap. 1.95 o.p. (ISBN 0-87682-324-X, 7324). Barclay Hse.
My Fantoms. Theophile Gautier & Richard Holmes. LC 76-381548. (Illus.). 1976. 4.50 (ISBN 0-7043-2103-3). Quarter Books.
My Father & I. Carter Sprague. pap. 1.95 o.p. (ISBN 0-87682-262-6, 7262). Barclay Hse.
My Father and I. Also, Helva's Child. Katharine M March. LC 7-20448. (On cover: Spare-hour series). A. D. F. Randolph & Company.
My Father More or Less. Jonathan Baumbach. 256p. 1982. 11.95 (ISBN 0-914590-66-9); pap. 5.95 (ISBN 0-914590-67-7). Fiction Coll.
My Father Sits in the Dark: And Other Selected Stories. Jerome Weidman. LC 61-8955. 1961. Random House.
My Fathers and I. With Decorations by Hans Tisdall. 1st American Ed. Eric Robert Russell Linklater. LC 59-6430. 1959. Harcourt, Brace.
My Father's Diary: A Ghost Story. David O'Connor. 66p. (Orig.). 1978. pap. 2.50x (ISBN 0-931308-00-3). Molly Yes.
My Father's House. Meyer Levin. LC 47-30778. 1947. Viking Press.
My Father's House. Luis E. Yglesias. LC 67-17217. 1968. 3.25 o.s.i.; PLB 4.79 o.s.i.; pap. 2.25 o.s.i. Identity.
My Father's House: A Novel. Henri Troyat. LC 51-10417. (His While the earth endures1). 1951. Duell, Sloan and Pearce.
My Father's Keeper. Andre Couteaux. LC 68-23436. 1968. Houghton Mifflin.
My Favorite Christmas Stories. Doris Sheridan. LC 47-19151. 1946.
My Favorite Nurse. Arlene Hale. (Ace nurse novel). 1974. (pbk.) 0.75. Ace Books.
My Favorite Nurse. Arlene Hale. 1976. 1.25. Ace.
My Favorite Stories. Ed. by Maureen Daly. LC 48-9226. 1948. Dodd, Mead.
My Favorite Story. Ed. by Ray Long. LC 28-101013. 1928.
My Favorite Suspense Stories. Ed. by Maureen Daly McGivern. LC 68-9455. 1968. 4.00. Dodd, Mead.
My Favorite True Mystery: A Collection from the American Weekly by the World's Foremost Crime Writers. Edited and with an Introd. by Ernest V. Heyn. The American Weekly (New York) LC 53-8885. Coward-McCann.
My Favorites in Suspense. Ed. by Alfred Hitchcock. (YA) 1959. 10.00 o.p. (ISBN 0-394-41223-0, BYR). Random.
My Feet Upon a Rock. W. H. Canaway. 1978. 9.95 (ISBN 0-86025-058-X). State Mutual Bk.
My Felicia: A Novel. Paul Francis Driscoll. LC 45-8813. 1945. The Macmillan Company.
My Fellow Devils. Leslie Poles Hartley. 1959. British Book Centre.
My Fellow Laborer Also The Wreck of the "Copeland". Henry Rider Haggard. (On cover: Seaside library. Pocket ed. no. 1145). 1888. G. Munro.
My Fire Opal, and Other Tales. Sarah Warner Brooks. LC 6-19381. 1896. Estes and Lauriat.
My First Cousin or Myself. Annie E Barnare. LC 9-22751. 1909. Cochrane Publishing Company.
My First Husband. Marie Armstrong Essipor. LC 32-5296. Greenberg.
My First Love: And My Last Love a Sequel. authorized ed. Charlotte Eliza Lawson Cowan Riddell. LC 7-41423. (On cover: Lovell's internatonal series, no. 164). 1891. J. W. Lovell Company.
My First Love Wears Two Masks. Dora Barrett & Rose C. Miller. LC 80-54266. (Illus.). 408p. 1981. write for info. (ISBN 0-9606048-0-4). Seaview Pr.
My First Offer: And Other Stories. Mary Cecil Hay. (On cover: Lovell's library, v. 20, no. 674). 1887. J. W. Lovell Company.
My First Rehearsal & My Clerical Rival. George Robert Gissing. Ed. by Pierre Coustillas. 1970. 5.00 o.p. Enitharmon Pr.
My First Season. Beatrice Reynolds. LC 48-36945. 1856. W. P. Fetridge.
My First Two Thousand Years: The Autobiography of the Wandering Jew. George Sylvester Viereck & Paul Eldridge. LC 72-145345. 1972. (ISBN 0-403-01254-6). Scholarly Press.
My First Two Thousand Years: The Autobiography of the Wandering Jew. George Sylvester Viereck & Eldridge, Paul, 1888- Joint Author. LC 28-225773. 1928. The Macaulay Company.
My First Two Thousand Years: The Autobiography of the Wandering Jew. George Sylvester Viereck & Eldridge, Paul, 1888- Joint Author. LC 31-19522. 1929. The Macaulay Company.
My First Two Thousand Years: The Autobiography of the Wandering Jew. George Sylvester Viereck & Eldridge, Paul, 1888- Joint Author. LC 33-17498. 1932. Gold Label Books, Inc.
My First 14 Wives. William Turpin Comerford. LC 35-15463. Alliance Press.
My Five Tigers. Illustrated by Peggy Bacon. Lloyd Alexander. LC 56-5323. Crowell.
My Flesh Is Sweet. Day Keene. 1969. pap. 0.75 o.p. (532-75243-075). Manor Bks.
My Foe Outstretch'd Beneath the Tree. Clinton Baddeley. 1981. pap. 2.25 (ISBN 0-440-15685-8). Dell.
My Foe Outstretch'd Beneath the Tree. Clinton-Baddeley, Victor Clinton. LC 68-25875. 1968. 4.95. W. Morrow.
My Folks in Maine, Vol. 1. Charles Asbury Stephens. LC 72-3380. (Short Story Index Reprint Ser). Repr. of 1934 ed. 18.00 (ISBN 0-8369-4161-6). Ayer Co.
My Friend Annabel Lee. Mary MacLane. LC 3-20895. 1903. H. S. Stone and Company.
My Friend Annie. Jane Duncan, pseud. 1972. pap. 0.95 o.p. (95278). Beagle Bks.
My Friend Bill: Many Stories Told in the Telling of One. Anson Albert Gard. LC 4188. 1900. The Emerson Press.
My Friend Charles. Francis Durbridge. 1973. lib. bdg. 5.95 o.s.i. (ISBN 0-85617-430-0). White Lion Pubs.

My Friend, Cousin Emmie. Jane Duncan, pseud. LC 65-13193. 1965. bds., 4.95. St. Martin's.
My Friend Flora. Jane Duncan, pseud. 1963. 4.50 o.p. St Martin.
My Friend from Cairnton. Jane Duncan, pseud. 1966. 4.95 o.p. St Martin.
My Friend from Limousin. Jean Giraudoux. LC 76-27657. 1976. 13.50. H. Fertig.
My Friend from Limousin. Jean Giraudoux. Tr. by Wilcox, Louise (Collier) LC 23-9536. Harper & Brothers.
My Friend from Outer Space. Earl Forkel. 1970. 2.50 o.p. Carlton.
My Friend George & Tom. Jane Duncan, pseud. LC 76-5371. 1976. 8.95 o.p. (ISBN 0-312-55755-8). St Martin.
My Friend Jim. William Edward Norris. (On cover: Lovell's library, no. 779). 1886. J. W. Lovell Company.
My Friend Jim. William Edward Norris. (On cover: Seaside library. Pocket ed. no. 848). 1886. G. Munro.
My Friend Judas. Andrew Sinclair. 1961. 3.95 o.p. (ISBN 0-671-50510-6). S&S.
My Friend Madame Zora. Jane Duncan, pseud. 1972. pap. 0.95 o.p. (95202). Beagle Bks.
My Friend Martha's Aunt. Jane Duncan, pseud. 1962. 4.50 o.p. St Martin.
My Friend, Mr. Leakey. John Burdon Sanderson Haldane. LC 38-9884. 1938. Harper & Brothers.
My Friend Monica. Jane Duncan, pseud. 1972. pap. 0.95 o.p. (95239). Beagle Bks.
My Friend Murial. Jane Duncan, pseud. 1972. pap. 0.95 o.p. (95200). Beagle Bks.
My Friend Musa, and Other Stories. Edwin Samuel. LC 63-12463. 1963. Abelard-Schuman.
My Friend, My Father. Jane Duncan, pseud. LC 67-10204. 1967. St. Martin's Press.
My Friend Pasquale: And Other Stories. James Selwin Tait. LC 8-25579. Tait, Sons & Company.
My Friend Phil. Isabel Maud Peacocke. LC 15-23061. 1.25. Rand McNally & Company.
My Friend Prospero: A Novel. Henry Harland. LC 4-2143. 1904. McClure, Phillips & Co.
My Friend Rose. Jane Duncan, pseud. LC 64-7789.
My Friend Rose. LC 64-7789.
My Friend Sandy. Jane Duncan, pseud. 1962. 3.95 o.p. St Martin.
My Friend Sandy. Jane Duncan, pseud. 1972. pap. 0.95 o.p. (95258). Beagle Bks.
My Friend Sashie. Jane Duncan, pseud. LC 72-180623. 1972. 4.95. St. Martin's Press.
My Friend Says It's Bulletproof. Penelope Mortimer. LC 67-12723. 1968. Random House.
My Friend Says It's Bulletproof. 1st Amer. Ed. Penelope Mortimer. LC 67-12723. 1968. bds., 4.95. Random.
My Friend the Boss. A Story of to-Day. Edward Everett Hale. LC 6-46188. 1888. J. S. Smith & Company.
My Friend the Chauffeur. Charles Norris Williamson & Alice Muriel Livingston Williamson. LC 5-32338. 1905. McClure, Phillips & Co.
My Friend, the Enemy: A Novel. Frank Baker. LC 48-5836. 1948. Coward-McCann.
My Friend the Gullah. J. Gary Black. 5.95 o.p. Beaufort.
My Friend the Hungry Generation. Jane Duncan, pseud. 252p. 1968. 4.95 o.p. (ISBN 0-312-55650-0). St Martin.
My Friend the Murderer: And Other Mysteries and Adventures. Arthur Conan Doyle. LC 76-37267. (Short story index reprint series). 1971. (ISBN 0-8369-4078-4). Books for Libraries Press.
My Friend the Murderer: And Other Mysteries and Adventures. Arthur Conan Doyle. LC 7-1506. Lovell, Coryell & Company.
My Friend the Murderer: And Other Mysteries and Adventures. Arthur Conan Doyle. LC 16-3389. (flashlight detective series. no. 80). M. A. Donohue & Co.
My Friend the Murderer: & Other Mysteries & Adventures. facsimile ed. Arthur Conan Doyle. LC 76-37267. (Short Story Index Reprint Ser.). Repr. of 1893 ed. 16.00 (ISBN 0-8369-4078-4). Ayer Co.
My Friend the Swallow. Jane Duncan, pseud. LC 79-145438. 1972. 4.95 o.p. (M50700). St Martin.
My Friend Tony. William Matthews Johnson. (Orig.). 1969. pap. 0.60 o.p. (73-838). Lancer.
My Friend Will: Including "The Little Boy That Was,". Charles Fletcher Lummis. LC 11-6716. 1911. A. C. McClurg & Co.
My Friendly Contemporaries see Collected Works.
My Friends and I. Julian Sturgis. (On cover: Seaside library. Pocket ed., no. 405). 1885. G. Munro.
My Friend's Book. Anatole France, pseud. Tr. by May, James Lewis. LC 31-19513. (Half-title: The works of Anatole France in an English translation, edited by Frederic Chapman). 1926. John Lane.
My Friend's Book (Le Livre De Mon Ami) Translated by Rosalie Feltenstein. Anatole France, pseud. LC 51-38081. (Barron's translation series). 1950. Barron's Educational Series, Inc.
My Friends from Cairnton. Jane Duncan, pseud. LC 66-150574. 1966. bds., 4.95. St. Martin's.
My Friends George and Tom. Jane Duncan, pseud. LC 76-5371. 1976. 7.95. St. Martin's Press.
My Friends, George and Tom. Jane Duncan, pseud. LC 76-57982. 1977. 11.95 (ISBN 0-8161-6456-8). G. K. Hall.
My Friends the Hungry Generation. Jane Duncan, pseud. LC 68-28796. 1968. 4.95. St. Martin's Press.
My Friends the MacLeans. Jane Duncan, pseud. LC 67-25453. 1967. St. Martin's Press.
My Friends the Miss Boyds. Jane Duncan, pseud. 1972. pap. 0.95 o.p. (95267). Beagle Bks.
My Friends the Misses Kindness. Jane Duncan, pseud. LC 73-91601. 1974. 6.50. St. Martin's Press.
My Friends the Misses Kindness. Jane Duncan, pseud. LC 74-171231. 1974. (ISBN 0-333-15774-5). Macmillan.
My Friends, the Mrs. Millers. Jane Duncan, pseud. LC 65-250443. 1965. 4.95. St. Martin's.
My Garden Doctor. Frances Duncan. LC 14-547419. 1914. 1.00. Doubleday, Page & Company.
My Garden of Hearts. Margaret Elizabeth Munson Sangster. LC 13-23212. The Christian Herald.
My Generation. Sarah Anna Emery. LC 8-83071. 1893. M. H. Sargent.
My Gentle Macho. Betty I. Lovelace. 1983. 12.95 (ISBN 0-533-05671-3). Vantage.
My Girls. Lida Abbie Churchill. LC 6-253961. (On cover: V.I.F. series: (v. 4)54). D. Lothrop and Company.
My Girls. Lida Abbie Churchill. LC 6-253951. (On cover: The household library, no. 2). D. Lothrop and Company.
My Glimpse into Eternity. Betty Malz. 1980. pap. 1.95 (ISBN 0-425-04581-1). Berkley Pub.
My Glorious Brothers. Fast, Howard Melvin. LC 48-8762. 1948. Little, Brown.
My Glorious Brothers. Howard Melvin Fast. LC 77-11154. 1977. 4.95 (ISBN 0-88482-758-5). Bonim Books.
My God, My Country, & My Lions Club. Wallace Hoffman. 1977. 5.95 o.p. (ISBN 0-533-02439-0). Vantage.
My God! Whose Wife Am I? Or, The Lost Heir. Anna Eliza Clay Bailey. 1879.
My Golden Egg. 1st Ed. Mary Carmody. LC 56-5497. Vantage Press.
My Goodness!" Said the Princess, a Modern Fairy Tale for Grown-Ups. DeWitt Carson. LC 38-11069. 1938. H. C. Kinsey & Company, Inc.
My Grand Enemy. Jean Stubbs. LC 67-25617. 1967. bds., 5.95. Stein & Day.
My Grandpa Went West. Joseph O Ward. LC 56-5040. 1956. Caxton Printers.
My Gun Is My Law. Harry Sinclair Drago. LC 50-6361. (Triple-A western classic). 1950. Jefferson House.
My Gun Is My Law. Harry Sinclair Drago. LC 42-24044. 1942. W. Morrow & Company.
My Gun Is Quick. Frank Morrison Spillane. LC 50-5643. 1950. Dutton.
My Hapai Machine - the Flying Saucer. George Kaeck. 4.50 o.p. Vantage.
My Head! My Head! Robert Graves. LC 73-20386. 1974. (lib. bdg.). 10.95 (ISBN 0-8383-1757-X). Haskell House.
My Head's High from Proudness. Octavia Jordan Perry. LC 63-23248. 1963. J. F. Blair.
My Heart an Altar: A Novel. Alice Lent Covert. LC 55-2127. 1955. Avalon Books.
My Heart and My Flesh... A Novel. Elizabeth Madox Roberts. 1927. The Viking Press.
My Heart and Stephanie: A Novel. Reginald Wright Kauffman. LC 10-78269. 1910. 1.25. L. C. Page & Company.
My Heart for Hostage. Robert Silliman Hillyer. LC 42-36347. 1942. Random House.
My Heart Has Its Love. Louise Bergstrom. (Avalon Books). 4.95. Thomas Bouregy.
My Heart in Hiding. Lois Edwards. LC 51-10110. 1951. Morrow.
My Heart Is Broken: Eight Stories and a Short Novel. Mavis Gallant. LC 64-11985. 1964. Random House.
My Heart Is Fast see Dream Comes True.
My Heart Remembers. William Addleman Ganoe. LC 50-9697. 1950. Crowell.
My Heart Remembers How. Margaret Bradshaw. LC 1-3507. J. H. Earle.
My Heart Shall Not Fear. Josephine Lawrence. LC 49-837551. 1949. Whittlesey House.
My Heart Turns Back: By Oliver B. Patton. Oliver B Patton. (Illus.). 2.25 (ISBN 0-445-04241-9). Popular Library.
My Heart Went Dead. Adeline McElfresh. LC 49-49620. 1949. Phoenix Press.
My Heart's Darling. Bertha Behrens & Conder, E. V., Tr. LC 6-9433. (On cover: Seaside library. Pocket ed. no. 1188). 1889. G. Munro.
My Heart's Down Under: By Jennifer Ames Pseud. Maysie Greig. LC 51-14991. 1951. Bouregy & Curl.
My Heart's in the Highlands. Maria M Grant. LC 6-44849. (Franklin square library no. 5). Harper & Brothers.
My Heart's in the Highlands. Maria M Grant. LC 6-44848. (Seaside library, no. 617). G. Munro.
My Heart's in the Hills. Harry Harrison Kroll. LC 56-7224. 1956. Westminster Press.
My Heart's Right Here. Florence Louisa Charlesworth Barclay. LC 15-2945. 1915. G. P. Putnam's Sons.
My Heart's Right There. Florence Louisa Charlesworth Barclay. LC 15-129. 1914. G.P. Putnam's Sons.
My Hero. Mrs. Bridges. (On cover: Lovell's library, v. 17, no. 850). 1887. J. W. Lovell Company.
My Hero. Maude Phelps McVeigh Hutchins. LC 53-8203. 1953.
My Hero. A Love Story. Mrs. Bridges. (On cover: Seaside library. Pocket ed., no. 726). 1886. G. Munro.
My Hero: Or, Contrasted Lives. Lydia Ann Emerson Porter. LC 11-8215. 1872. D. Lothrop & Co.
My Hero. 1st Ed. Robert Carson. LC 60-53125. 1961. McGraw-Hill.
My High Love Calling. Emily Cary. (Avalon Books). 4.95. Thomas Bouregy.
My Home Is Far Away. Dawn Powell. LC 44-9629. 1944. C. Scribner's Sons.
My Honey. Evelyn Whitaker. LC 4-898. 1895. Roberts Brothers.
My Host the Enemy, & Other Tales. facs. ed. Franklin Welles Calkins. LC 72-81265. (Short Story Index Reprint Ser). 1901. 17.00 (ISBN 0-8369-3017-7). Ayer Co.
My Host the Enemy: And Other Tales; Sketches of Life and Adventure on the Border Line of the West. Franklin Welles Calkins. LC 72-81265. (Short story index reprint series). (Illus.). 1969. Books for Libraries Press.
My Host the Enemy and Other Tales: Sketches of Life and Adventure on the Border Line of the West. Franklin Welles Calkins. LC 1-22991. 1901. Fleming H. Revell Company.
My Hourse Gonzalez. Fernando Algria. LC 64-3345. 1964. Las Americas Pub. Co.
My Husband and I. Lev Nikolaevich Tolstoi. (On cover: Seaside library. Pocket ed. no. 1066). 1888. G. Munro.
My Husband and I: And Other Stories. Lev Nikolaevich Tolstoi. LC 43-42362. (Vizetelly's Russian novels). 1887. Vizetelly & Co.
My Husband and I, and The Death of Ivan Ilitch. Lev Nikolaevich Tolstoi. (On cover: Lovell's library, no. 1110). 1888. J. W. Lovell Company.
My Husband's Crime a Novel. M. R. Housekeeper. LC 7-7135. 1868. Harper & Brothers.
My Husband's Friends. Katherine Jones Bellamann. LC 31-3408. 1931. The Century Co.
My Illegal Wife. James Arthur Macknight. (On cover: Neely's continental library, no. 5). 1897. F. T. Neely.
My Imprisoned Heart. Ramona Wingate. (Dear Miss Lonelyhearts). 1974. (pbk.) 0.95 (ISBN 0-523-00376-5). Pinnacle Books.
My Indian Family. Hilda Wernher. LC 45-6398. 1945. The John Day Company.
My Indian Queen: Being a Record of the Adventures of Sir Charles Verrinder, Baronet, in the East Indies. Guy Newell Boothby. LC 1-29444. (Half-title: Appleton's town and country library, no. 294). 1901. D. Appleton and Company.
My Indian Son-in-Law. Hilda Wernher. LC 49-10813. 1949. Doubleday.
My Intimate Enemy. A Story. LC 7-32289. 1878. Claxton, Remsen & Haffelfinger.
My Intimate Friend. A Novel. Florence I Duncan. 1878. J. B. Lippincott & Co.
My Invincible Aunt. Dorothea Thompson Brande. LC 38-3730. Farrar & Rinehart, Inc.
My Invisible Partner. Thomas Stewart Denison. LC 98-856. Rand, McNally & Company.
My Irish Cinderella. Cecil Spooner & Charles Blaney. (Playbooks). 1.25 o.p. McKay.
My Island. Eilian Hughes. LC 7-738. 1902. J. M. Dent & Co.
My Japanese Prince: Being Some Startling Excerpts from the Diary of Hilda Patience Armstrong of Meriden, Connecticut, at Present Travelling in the Far East. Archibald Clavering Gunter. 1904. The Home Publishing Company.
My Japanese Wife: A Japanese Idyl. Clive Holland. LC 2-15350. 1902. Frederick A. Stokes Company.
My Jean. Patience Stapleton. (On cover: Idylwild series, v. 1, no. 32). 1893. Morrill, Higgins & Co.
My Jewish Brother Jesus. Rolf Gompertz. LC 76-55591. 1977. 6.95 (ISBN 0-918248-03-5); pap. 3.95 (ISBN 0-918248-02-7). WorDoctor.
My Jo, John: By Helen Mathers... Helen Buckingham Mathers Reeves. LC 7-30678. (On cover: Lovell's Westminster series. no. 36). 1891. J. W. Lovell Company.
My Journey Through Hell. Louise Van Der Velden-Mathia. 7.95 o.p. Vantage.
My Kentucky Cousins. Letitia Vertrees Sylvester. LC 33-285949. The Christopher Publishing House.
My Killer Doesn't Understand Me. Thomas P Mulkeen. LC 73-82113. 1973. 5.95 (ISBN 0-8128-1636-6). Stein and Day.
My Kind! My Country! Aldrich Blake. LC 50-8361. 1950. Dorrance.
My Kingdom for a Hearse. Craig Rice. LC 57-715. (Inner sanctum mystery). 1957. Simon and Schuster.
My Lady. Jennie Maria Drinkwater Conklin. 1892. Bradley & Woodruff.
My Lady: A Story of Long Ago. Marguerite Bouvet. LC 6-14914. 1894. A.C. McClurg and Company.
My Lady and Allan Darke. Charles Donnel Gibson. LC 99-1427. 1899. The Macmillan Company.
My Lady April. John Overton. LC 23-26138. 1922. Frederick A. Stokes Company.
My Lady Beatrice,". Frances Cooke. LC 8-4439. 1908. Benziger Brothers.
My Lady Benbrook. Constance Gluyas. LC 74-20997. 1975. 9.75 (ISBN 0-13-608992-5). Prentice-Hall.
My Lady Benbrook. Constance Gluyas. 1979. 2.50 (ISBN 0-446-91124-0). Warner Books Inc.
My Lady Caprice. Jeffery Farnol. LC 7-31282. 1907. Dodd, Mead & Company.
My Lady Cinderella. Alice Muriel Livingston Williamson. LC 6-16647. 1906. B. W. Dodge and Company.
My Lady Clancarty: Being the True Story of the Earl of Clancarty and Lady Elizabeth Spencer. Mary Imlay Taylor. LC 5-8069. 1905. Little, Brown and Company.
My Lady Coquette. Eliza M. J. Humphreys. (Seaside library, v. 41, no. 844). 1880. G. Munro.
My Lady Coquette. Eliza M. J. Humphreys. (On cover: Lovell's library, no. 1151). 1888. J. W. Lovell Company.
My Lady Evil: A Novel. Parley J Cooper. LC 73-14088. 1974. 6.95 (ISBN 0-671-27118-0). Simon and Schuster.
My Lady Frivol. Rosa Nouchette Carey. LC 99-4173. 1900. J. B. Lippincott Company.
My Lady Green Sleeves. Helen Buckingham Mathers Reeves. LC 7-30677. (On cover: Lovell's library, no. 1050). 1887. J. W. Lovell Company.
My Lady Greensleeves. Constance Beresford-Howe. LC 54-8216. 1955. Ballantine Books.
My Lady Hoyden. Jane Sheridan. 1982. pap. 2.95 (ISBN 0-451-11511-2, AE1511, Sig). NAL.
My Lady Hoyden: A Novel. Pauline Glen Winslow. LC 80-28182. 13.95 (ISBN 0-312-55776-0). St. Martin's Press.
My Lady Laughter, a Romance of Boston Town in the Days of the Great Siege. Dwight Tilton. 1904. C. M. Clark Publishing Co. (Inc.
My Lady Lee. Edith Ballinger Price. LC 25-18064. 1925. Greenberg, Inc.
My Lady Ludlow. Elizabeth Cleghorn Stevenson Gaskell. LC 6-39724. (Half-title: The works of Mrs. Gaskell. Knutsford ed. v. 5). 1906. G. P. Putnam's Sons; Etc., Etc.
My Lady Ludlow. To Which Are Added: An Accursed Race, The Doom of the Griffiths, Half a Lifetime Ago, The Poor Clare, The Half-Brothers, Mr. Harrison's Confessions, The Manchester Marriage. Elizabeth Cleghorn Stevenson Gaskell. LC 72-186540. (works of Mrs. Gaskell, v. 5). (Illus.). 1972. 24.00 (ISBN 0-404-07255-0). AMS Press.
My Lady Mischief. Janet Louise Roberts. 1978. pap. 1.50 (ISBN 0-440-16228-9). Dell.
My Lady Nicotine: A Study in Smoke. James Matthew Barrie. LC 23-168087. 1896. Joseph Knight Company.
My Lady Nobody: A Novel. Jozua Marius Willen Van Der Poorten Schwartz. LC 4-16872. 1895. Harper & Brothers.
My Lady of Cleeve. Percy J Hartley. LC 8-5574. 1908. Dodd, Mead & Company.
My Lady of Cleves. Margaret Campbell Barnes. 352p. 1972. 6.95 (ISBN 0-8255-1540-8). Macrae.
My Lady of Cleves: A Novel. Margaret Campbell Barnes. LC 46-25028. 1946. Macrae-Smith-Company.
My Lady of Doubt. Randall Parrish. LC 11-26254. 1911. 1.35. A. C. McClurg & Co.

My Lady of Doubt. Randall Parrish. LC 16-25024. 1911. A. L. Burt Company.
My Lady of Orange. Henry Christopher Bailey. LC 1-11773. 1901. Longmans, Green, and Co.
My Lady of the Fog. Ralph Henry Barbour. LC 8-25123. 1908. J. B. Lippincott Company.
My Lady of the Fuchsias. Essie Summers. (Harlequin Romance Ser.). 1979. pap. 1.25 (ISBN 0-373-02281-6, Pub. by Harlequin). PB.
My Lady of the Indian Purdah. Elizabeth Cooper. LC 27-18300. 1927. Frederick A. Stokes Company.
My Lady of the Island: A Tale of the South Seas. Beatrice Ethel Grimshaw. LC 16-6201. 1916. 1.25. A. C. McClurg & Co.
My Lady of the Moor. John Oxenham, pseud. LC 16-14871. 1916. Longmans, Green, and Co.
My Lady of the North. Randall Parrish. 1976. lib. bdg. 16.30x (ISBN 0-89968-086-0). Lightyear.
My Lady of the North: The Love Story of a Gray-Jacket. Randall Parrish. 1904. A. C. McClurg & Co.
My Lady of the North: The Love Story of a Gray Jacket. Randall Parrish. LC 28-4852. A. L. Burt Company.
My Lady of the Snows. Margaret A Brown. LC 74-168496. (Toronto reprint library of Canadian prose and poetry). 1973. (ISBN 0-8020-7504-5). University of Toronto Press.
My Lady of the South. Randall Parrish. 1976. lib. bdg. 16.30x (ISBN 0-89968-087-9). Lightyear.
My Lady of the South: A Story of the Civil War. Randall Parrish. LC 9-26140. 1909. A. C. McClurg & Co.
My Lady of the Yellow Domino. Arthur Williams Marchmont. LC 14-18883. Hodder and Stoughton.
My Lady Peggy Goes to Town. Frances Aymar Mathews. LC 1-23056. The Bowen-Merrill Company.
My Lady Peggy Leaves Town. Frances Aymar Mathews. LC 13-7517. 1913. 1.00. Moffat, Yard and Company.
My Lady Pokahontas. John Esten Cooke. LC 68-20009. (Americans in Fiction Ser.). lib. bdg. 15.00 (ISBN 0-8398-0272-2); pap. text ed. 4.95x (ISBN 0-89197-862-3). Irvington.
My Lady Pokahontas. John Esten Cooke. LC 68-20009. (Americans in Fiction Ser). 1968. Repr. of 1879 ed. lib. bdg. 7.50x o.p. (ISBN 0-8398-0272-2). Gregg.
My Lady Pokahontas. A True Relation of Virginia. John Esten Cooke. LC 6-27173. 1885. Houghton, Mifflin and Company.
My Lady Pokahontas: A True Relation of Virginia. John Esten Cooke. LC 41-32202. 1907. Houhgton, Mifflin and Company.
My Lady Pokahontas: A True Relation of Virginia,Written by Anas Todkill, Puritan and Pilgrim,with Notes by John Esten Cooke. John Esten Cooke. LC 68-200097. (Americans in Fic.). 1968. 10.00. Gregg Pr.
My Lady Queen. John Cleve. (Crusader). (Dell-Grove book: Vol. 4). 1975. (pbk.) 1.50. Dell.
My Lady Quixote. Phyllis Ann Karr. 224p. (Orig.). 1980. pap. 1.75 (ISBN 0-449-50037-3, Coventry). Fawcett.
My Lady Rotha: A Romance. Stanley John Weyman. LC 8-34337. 1894. Longmans, Green, and Co.
My Lady Rotha: A Romance. Stanley John Weyman. LC 4-16591. 1899. Longmans, Green, and Co.
My Lady Valentine. Octavia Roberts. LC 17-29519. 0.75. The A. M. Davis Co.
My Lady's Bargain. Elizabeth Hope. LC 23-2469. 1923. 1.75. The Century Co.
My Lady's Deception. Barbara Doyle. (Candlelight Regency Ser.: No. 705). (Orig.). 1982. pap. 1.75 (ISBN 0-440-15960-1). Dell.
My Lady's Fortune Hunt. Frederick Kinkade. LC 8-35962. 1908. The C. M. Clark Publishing Co.
My Lady's Garter. Jacques Futrelle. 1.35. Rand, McNally & Company.
My Lady's Heart. A Sketch. Ellis Markoe. LC 7-24691. 1896. Roberts Brothers.
My Lady's Kiss: A Romance. Norman Innes. LC 8-31823. Rand, McNally & Company.
My Lady's Master. A Novel. Maude Rutledge. T. B. Peterson & Brothers.
My Lady's Money. An Episode in the Life of a Young Girl. Wilkie Collins. LC 6-30391. (On cover: Harper's half-hour series v. 45). 1878. Harper & Brothers.
My Lamp Is Bright. Dorothy Evelyn Smith. LC 49-9905. 1949. E. P. Dutton.
My Land Has a Voice. 1st Ed. Jesse Stuart. LC 66-24583. 1966. bds., 5.50. McGraw.
My Land. My Country. My Home. Adam Albright. LC 15-5823. 1915. C. F. Williams & Son.
My Last Duchess. Browning. 1970. 2.95 o.p. (ISBN 0-442-82349-5). Peter Pauper.
My Last Two Thousand Years. Herbert Gold. LC 72-4087. 1972. 6.95 (ISBN 0-394-47098-2). Random House.
My Late Wives: Another Adventure of Sir Henry Merrivale. John Dickson Carr. LC 46-7348. 1946. W. Morrow & Company.
My Life. George Friedell. 1981. 6.95 (ISBN 0-8062-1735-9). Carlton.
My Life. Lyn Hejinian. (Burning Deck Fiction Ser.). 90p. (Orig.). 1980. 15.00 (ISBN 0-930900-79-0); pap. 4.00 (ISBN 0-930900-80-4). Burning Deck.
My Life. William Hamilton Maxwell. LC 7-19159. 1835. Harper & Brothers.
My Life & Loves. Linda Van Dalen. 1974. pap. 1.25 o.p. (LB192ZK, Leisure Bks). Nordon Pubns.
My Life, and Other Stories. Anton Pavlovich Chekhov. LC 77-169544. (Short story index reprint series). 1971. (ISBN 0-8369-4005-9). Books for Libraries Press.
My Life As a Man. Philip Roth. LC 73-20847. 1974. 8.95 (ISBN 0-03-012646-0). Holt, Rinehart and Winston.
My Life As a Man. Philip Roth. 1975. (pbk.) 1.95. Bantam Books.
My Life As an Indian. James Willard Schultz. 426p. 1973. Repr. of 1907 ed. 10.00 (ISBN 0-87928-047-6). Corner Hse.
My Life for My Sheep. Alfred Leo Duggan. (YA) 1968. 6.50 o.p. Weybright.
My Life in the Bush of Ghosts. Amos Tutuola. 1962. pap. 6.95 (ISBN 0-394-17324-4, E559, Ever). Grove.
My Life Is Done. Sara Woods, pseud. LC 76-13047. 7.95. St. Martin's Press.
My Life on the Plains. George Custer. (Men Who Made the West Ser.: No. 1). 288p. 1982. pap. 2.50 (ISBN 0-8439-1118-2, Leisure Bks). Nordon Pubns.
My Life with Sherlock Holmes: Conversations in Baker Street. John H. Watson & J. R. Hamilton. 1976. pap. 2.50 o.p. (ISBN 0-8015-5272-9). Hawthorn.
My Life with Sherlock Holmes: Conversations in Baker Street by John H. Watson, M.D. Arthur Conan Doyle & J. R Hamilton. LC 75-20911. (Illus.). 1976. 2.50 (ISBN 0-8015-5272-9). Hawthorn Books.
My Little Boy. Carl Ewald. Tr. by Teixeira De Mattos, Alexander Louis. LC 6-14548. 1906. C. Scribner's Sons.
My Little Boy. Carl Ewald. Tr. by Teixeira De Mattos, Alexander Louis. LC 14-10518. 1912. C. Scribner's Sons.
My Little Brother Gets Away with Murder. Alan Pesin & Harry Pesin. (Illus.). 2.50 o.s.i. (ISBN 0-911130-16-0). Perspective.
My Little Girl. library ed. Walter Besant & Rice, James. LC 3-27822. 1888. Dodd, Mead & Company.
My Little Lady. Eleanor Frances Poynter. (Seaside library. v. 52, no. 1052). 1881. G. Munro.
My Little Love. Mary Virginia Terhune. LC 8-26054. 1876. G. W. Carleton & Co.; Etc., Etc.
My Little Princess. Florence Blackburn White Schoeffel. (On cover: The laurel library no. 9). 1892. G. Munro.
My Little Sister. Elizabeth Robins. LC 13-951. 1913. Dodd, Mead and Company.
My Lives and How I Lost Them. Countee Cullen. LC 42-114471. Harper & Brothers.
My Lodger's Legacy: Or, The History of a Recluse. Robert W Hume. LC 7-5784. 1886. Funk & Wagnalls.
My Lord America. Alec Rackowe. LC 50-9273. 1950. Farrar, Straus.
My Lord and My Lady. Mrs. Bridges. (Seaside library, v. 57, no. 1163). 1881. G. Munro.
My Lord and My Lady. Mrs. Bridges. (On cover: Lovell's library, v. 17, no. 843). 1886. J. W. Lovell Company.
My Lord Barbarian. Andrew J Offutt. LC 76-56150. 1977. 1.50 (ISBN 0-345-25713-8). Ballantine Books.
My Lord Brother the Lion Heart. Molly Costain Haycraft. (Signet book.). 1974. (pbk.) 1.25. New American Library.
My Lord Brother the Lion Heart. Molly Costain Haycraft. LC 68-14130. 1968. Lippincott.
My Lord Conceit: A Novel. Eliza M. J. Humphreys. (On cover: Lovell's library, no. 1173). 1888. J. W. Lovell Company.
My Lord Duke: A Novel. Ernest William Hornung. LC 7-5193. 1897. C. Scribner's Sons.
My Lord Essex, a Novel. 1st Ed. Olive Eckerson. LC 55-6418. 1955. Holt.
My Lord Foxe. Constance Gluyas. LC 75-44063. 8.95 (ISBN 0-679-50568-7). D. McKay Co.
My Lord John. Georgette Heyer. LC 75-10074. 1975. 8.95 (ISBN 0-525-16242-9). Dutton.
My Lord Kasseem. Mons Daveson. (Harlequin Romances Ser.). 192p. 1983. pap. 1.75. Harlequin Bks.
My Lord Monleigh. 1st Ed. Jan Cox Speas. LC 56-9421. 1956. Bobbs-Merrill.
My Lord Murderer. Elizabeth Mansfield, pseud. (Berkley Book). 1.95 (ISBN 0-425-03806-8). Berkley Publishing Corp.
My Lord of Canterbury. Godfrey Edmund Turton. LC 67-10396. 1967. Doubleday.
My Lord Rakehell. Margaret Sebastian, pseud. 1977. 1.95 (ISBN 0-445-03211-1). Popular Library.
My Lords, Ladies & Marjorie. Marion Chesney. 224p. 1981. pap. 1.50 (ISBN 0-449-50216-3, Crest). Fawcett.
My Lost Duchess: An Idyl of the Town. Jesse Lynch Williams. LC 8-11087. 1908. The Century Co.
My Lost Self. Arthur Williams Marchmont. Cupples & Leon Company.
My Love. Elizabeth Lynn Linton. (Seaside library. v. 49, no. 991). 1881. G. Munro.
My Love. A Novel. Elizabeth Lynn Linton. (Franklin square library. no. 181). 1881. Harper & Brothers.
My Love and I. Alice Brown. LC 12-21281. 1912. The Macmillan Company.
My Love and I. Alice Brown. LC 24-20475. 1914. The Macmillan Company.
My Love Belongs to Me. Dorothy Black. LC 42-19447. 1942. Macrae-Smith-Company.
My Love Had a Black Speed Stripe. Henry Williams. LC 74-162651. 1973. 3.95 (ISBN 0-333-13944-5). Macmillan of Australia.
My Love Is Black. Miks Williams. LC 72-81604. 1972. 5.95 (ISBN 0-911024-10-7). New Voices Pub. Co.
My Love Is Violent: A Novel of Suspense. Thomas Blanchard Dewey. LC 56-26718. (Popular library, 780). 1956. Popular Library.
My Love Is Young. Peryl Wade Parsons. LC 45-269226. 1945. Macrae-Smith-Company.
My Love Must Wait. Ernestine Hemmings Hill. 1967. Repr. pap. 2.00 o.s.i. Tri-Ocean.
My Love Must Wait: The Story of Matthew Flinders. Ernestine Hemmings Hill. LC 44-1895. 1944. Doubleday, Doran & Company, Inc.
My Love, My Enemy. Jan Cox Speas. LC 61-8912. 1961. Morrow.
My Love Wears Black: A Novel. Octavus Roy Cohen. LC 48-602193. 1948. Macmillan.
My Lovely Carrie. D. H. Kling. 232p. 1975. 7.50 o.p. (ISBN 0-682-48328-1). Exposition.
My Lovely Executioner: An Original Gold Medal Novel. Peter Rabe. LC 60-29906. (Gold medal books, 967). 1960. Fawcett Publications.
My Lovely Mama. Mathilde Walewska. LC 56-11652. Bobbs-Merrill.
My Lustfull Adventures. Harry Temple. 1972. pap. 2.25 o.s.i. (V1108R, Venus). Grove.
My Main Mother. Barry Beckham. LC 71-86400. 1969. 5.95. Walker.
My Main Mother. Barry Beckham. LC 73-590441. 1970 (ISBN 0-85523-017-7). Allan Wingate.
My Main Squeeze. Maximilian Hornung. 224p. (Orig.). 1981. pap. 2.50 (ISBN 0-523-41522-2). Pinnacle Bks.
My Man Godfrey. Eric Hatch. LC 35-19418. 1935. Little, Brown, and Company.
My-Man: Letters from a Wife to a Husband "Somewhere in France,". L., C. E & C. E. L. LC 16-23088. 0.50. George H. Doran Company.
My Marriage. A Novel ... (seaside library. v. 61, no. 1238). 1882. G. Munro.
My Married Life at Hillside. Robert Barry Coffin. LC 17-13019. 1868. Hurd and Houghton.
My Married Life at Hillside. Robert Barry Coffin. LC 41-34791. 1871. Hurd and Houghton.
My Married Life at Hillside. Robert Barry Coffin. LC 6-26744. 1872. Hurd and Houghton.
My Married Life at Hillside. Robert Barry Coffin. LC 41-34790. 1865. Hurd and Houghton.
My Master, Columbus. Cedric Belfrage. LC 61-9479. 1961. Doubleday.
My Masterpiece. Max Wilk. LC 77-116121. 1970. Norton.
My Mate Dick. Ion L. Idriess. 1967. Repr. pap. 1.25 o.s.i. Tri-Ocean.
My Men. LC 31-3867. 1931. R. R. Smith, Inc.
My Mercedes Is Bigger Than Yours. Nkem Nwankwo. LC 75-6374. 6.95 (ISBN 0-06-013208-6). Harper & Row.
My Merry Rockhurst" Being Some Episodes in the Life of Viscount Rockhurst, a Friend of King Charles the Second, and at One Time Constable of His Majesty's Tower of London, Recounted. Agnes Sweetman Castle & Castle, Egerton. LC 7-34310. 1907. The Macmillan Company.
My Michael. tr. from hebrew by nicholas de lange with the author. ed. Amos Oz. 1976. (pbk.) 1.50. Bantam.
My Michael. Amos Oz. LC 70-171158. 1972. 6.95 (ISBN 0-394-47146-6). Knopf; Distributed by Random House.
My Miscellanies. Wilkie Collins. LC 3-27278. 1874. Harper & Brothers.
My Mistress, My Wife. Harrison Orkow. LC 34-12030. The Macaulay Company.
My Mistress, My Wife. Harold Ross. 1969. pap. 0.60 o.p. (B60-1002). Belmont-Tower.
My Monterey. Zena Holman. LC 73-181316. (Illus.). 1973.
My Mortal Enemy. Willa Sibert Cather. LC 61-65908. 1961. Vintage Books.
My Mortal Enemy. Willa Sibert Cather. LC 26-185082. 1926. A. A. Knopf.
My Mother and I. A Love Story. Dinah Maria Mulock Craik. LC 6-31076. 1874. Harper & Brothers.
My Mother and I. A Love Story. Dinah Maria Mulock Craik. LC 4-316408. 1874. Harper & Brothers.
My Mother and I. A Love Story. Dinah Maria Mulock Craik. LC 4-22917. (Miss Mulock's works). 1904. Harper & Brothers.
My Mother & Madame Edwards. Georges Bataille. Tr. by Austryn Wainhouse. 1970. price not set o.p. Grove.
My Mother Bids Me Bind My Hair. Elizabeth Sale. LC 44-9914. 1944. Dodd, Mead & Company.
My Mother-in-Law ... 1877. Lockwood, Brooks, and Company.
My Mother-in-Law ... LC 7-32287. (On cover: Columbian library, no. 7). 1890. Columbian Publishing Company.
My Mother, My Sister & I. Brighton. pap. 1.95 o.p. (ISBN 0-87056-174-X, 6174). Brandon.
My Mother Taught Me. Tor Kung. 1968. pap. 1.25 o.s.i. (214, Travellers Comp). Olympia.
My Mother's House & Sido. Sidonie Gabrielle Colette. 1975. pap. 3.95 o.p. (ISBN 0-374-51218-3). FS&G.
My Mother's House & Sido. Sidonie Gabrielle Colette. Tr. by Una V. Troubridge & Enid McLeod. Incl. Sido. 219p. 1975. 7.95 (ISBN 0-374-21735-1); pap. 5.25 (ISBN 0-374-51218-3). FS&G.
My Mother's House & Sido. Sidonie Gabrielle Colette. 1975. pap. 3.95 o.p. (ISBN 0-374-51218-3). FS&G.
My Mother's House, and The Vagabond. Sidonie Gabrielle Colette. LC 55-13559. (Doubleday anchor book, A62). 1955. Doubleday.
My Mother's People. Barry Gifford. LC 76-7885. 1976. 15.00 (ISBN 0-916870-02-2) (ISBN 0-916870-01-4). Creative Arts Book Co.
My Music Bent. Ed. by James L. Weil. 1973. 20.00 (Pub. by Elizabeth Pr); pap. 10.00. SBD.
My Name Aloud. Harold Uriel Ribalow. 4.98 o.p. (ISBN 0-498-06763-7, Encore). A S Barnes.
My Name If Morgan. Woolfolk, William. LC 63-7723. 1963. N.Y., Doubleday.
My Name Is Aram. Illus. by Don Freeman. Freeman, Don, Illus. Title. LC 40-34075. Harcourt, Brace and Company.
My Name Is Asher Lev. Chaim Potok. (Crest Book, Q1807). 1973. 1.50. Fawcett.
My Name Is Asher Lev. Chaim Potok. LC 70-171131. 1972. 7.95 (ISBN 0-394-46137-1). Knopf; Distributed by Random House.
My Name Is Celia: A Novel. Rayne Kruger. LC 55-50693. 1955. Macmillan.
My Name Is Clary Brown. Charlotte Keppel. LC 76-10195. 8.95 (ISBN 0-394-40677-X). Random House.
My Name Is Legion. Charles Morgan. LC 79-188308. 1971. (ISBN 0-403-01115-9). Scholarly Press.
My Name Is Legion. Charles Morgan. LC 25-7327. 1925. A. A. Knopf.
My Name Is Legion. Roger Zelany. 224p. (Orig.). 1981. pap. 2.25 (Del Rey). Ballantine.
My Name Is Legion. Roger Zelazny. LC 75-44242. 1976. 1.50 (ISBN 0-345-24867-8). Ballantine Books.
My Name Is Mary. Anita Katzman. LC 74-15874. 1975. 5.95 (ISBN 0-06-012258-7). Harper & Row.
My Name Is Michael Sibley. John Michael Ward Bingham. LC 52-8828. (Red badge detective). 1952. Dodd, Mead.
My Name Is Morgan. William Woolfolk. LC 63-7723. 1978. pap. text ed. 1.95 o.s.i. (ISBN 0-89559-014-X). Dale Books Inc.
My Name Is Norval: A Novel. Terence De Vere White. LC 79-1805. 1979. 8.95 (ISBN 0-06-014592-7). Harper & Row.
My Name Is Rose. Theodora Keogh. LC 56-11062. 1956. Farrar, Straus and Cudahy.
My Name Is Rose: A Novel. Theodora Keogh. 1973. (pbk.) 0.75. Manor Books.
My Name Is Sappho. Martha Rofheart. LC 74-79665. 1975. (pbk.) 1.50 (ISBN 0-425-02981-6). Berkley Pub. Co.
My Name Is Sappho: A Novel. Martha Rofheart. LC 74-79665. 1974. 8.95 (ISBN 0-399-11400-9). Putnam.
My Name on the Bullet. Brad Cordell. 1979. pap. 1.25 o.s.i. (ISBN 0-505-51411-7). Tower Bks.
My Neighbors: Stories of the Welsh People. Caradoc Evans. LC 73-121539. (Short story index reprint series). 1970. Books for Libraries Press.
My Neighbors: Stories of the Welsh People. Caradoc Evans. LC 20-3187. 1920. Harcourt, Brace and Howe.
My Neighbor's Wife. Doris Miles Disney. LC 57-12463. (Signet book). 1974. (pbk.) 0.95. New American Library.
My Neighbor's Wife. 1st Ed. Doris Miles Disney. LC 57-124633. 1957. Published for the Crime Club by Doubleday.

My Nephew Hamlet. Drawings by Jill McDonald. John Turing. LC 68-103197. 1967. 4.95. Dent.
My New Curate: A Story Gathered from the Stray Leaves of an Old Diary. Patrick Augustine Sheehan. LC 412. 1899. Marlier, Callanan, & Company.
My New Curate: A Story Gathered from the Stray Leaves of an Old Diary. 4th ed. Patrick Augustine Sheehan. 1902. Marlier & Company, Limited.
My New Found Land: A Novel. Dean Brelis. LC 63-10187. 1963. Houghton Mifflin.
My New Home in Northern Michigan: And Other Tales. Charles W Jay. LC 7-10176. 1874. Printed by W. S. & E. W.S Sharp.
My Novel" By Pisistratus Caxton Pseud.; or Varieties in English Life... Edward George Earle Lytton. LC 8-26648. G. Routledge and Sons.
My Novel," By Pisistratus Caxton Pseud. or, Varieties in English Life... Edward George Earle Lytton Bulwer-Lytton Lytton. LC 26-3639. 1857. G. Routledge & Co.
My Novel" By Pisistratus Caxton Pseud. Or, Varieties in English Life... Edward George Earle Lytton Bulwer-Lytton Lytton. LC 4-15322. (Half-title: Novels of Sir Edward Bulwer Lytton. Library ed. The Caxton novels, vol. III-VI). 1892. Little, Brown, and Company.
My Novel" Or, Varieties in English Life, by Pisistratus Caxton Pseud. library ed.... ed. Edward George Earle Lytton Bulwer-Lytton Lytton. (Half-title: Novels of Sir Edward Bulwer Lytton. Library ed. The Caxton novels, vols. III-VI). 1860-65. J. B. Lippincott & Co.
My Novel" Or, Varieties in English Life, by Pisistratus Caxton Pseud. the lord lytton ed. Edward George Earle Lytton Bulwer-Lytton Lytton. LC 7-8117. 1874. J. B. Lippincott & Co.
My Novel" Or, Varieties in English Life. By Pisistratus Caxton Pseud. the lord lytton ed. Edward George Earle Lytton Bulwer-Lytton Lytton. 1880. J. B. Lippincott & Co.
My Novel: Or, Varieties in English Life... Edward George Earle Lytton Bulwer-Lytton Lytton. LC 21-15379. (Seaside library, v. 56, 53, no. 1089). 1881. G. Munro.
My Odyssey in Mother's Womb: A Diary of an Embryo, the Memoirs of a Fetus, the Novel of a Baby. Ben-Porat, Josef. LC 79-65922. (Illus.). 1979. 6.95 (ISBN 0-9603256-0-3). Brighton House Publications.
My Oedipus Complex. Frank O'Connor, pseud. 239p. 1963. pap. 3.95 (ISBN 0-14-001956-1, Pub. by Penguin England). Irish Bk Ctr.
My Official Husband: Or, The Mystery of Hilliard Hall. J. F. Reichhard. LC 7-30657. (sunnyside series no. 71). 1893. J. S. Ogilvie.
My Official Wife: A Novel. Richard Henry Savage. LC 8-200819. 1891. The Home Publishing Company.
My Old Field. Garroway Renfrew. LC 25-10773. 1925. The Stratford Company.
My Old Maid's Corner. Lillie Hamilton French. LC 3-26364. 1903. The Century Co.
My Old Man. Richard B Erno. LC 55-10163. 1955. Crown Publishers.
My Old Man's Badge. Charles Weiser Frey. LC 50-5051. 1950. Duell, Sloan and Pearce.
My One & Only Love. Daisy H. Thomson. 1976. pap. 1.25 o.p. (ISBN 0-515-03926-8). BJ Pub Group.
My Only Love. Daisy H. Thomson. 1974. pap. 0.95 o.p. (N3267). BJ Pub Group.
My Opinions and Betsy Bobbet's. Designed As a Beacon Light, to Guide Women to Life, Liberty, and the Pursuit of Happiness, but Which May Be Read by Members of the Sterner Sect, Without Injury to Themselves or the Book. Marietta Holley. LC 7-6032. 1873. American Publishing Company; Etc., Etc.
My Orient Pearl: Being an Englishman's Story of Love and Adventure in Japan. Charles Colton. LC 21-689938. (Illus.). 1921. John Lane.
My Outrageous Cousin. Marian Richards Torrey. LC 29-24078. 1929. The Macmillan Company.
My Own Child,". Florence Marryat Church Lean. LC 7-13609. (On cover: Lovell's library. v. 19. no. 906). 1887. J. W. Lovell Company.
My Own Far Towers: By Mathilde Eiker. Mathilde Eiker. LC 30-268213. 1930. Doubleday, Doran & Company, Inc.
My Own Ground. Hugh Nissenson. LC 75-40496. 1976. 7.95 (ISBN 0-374-21747-5). Farrar, Straus and Giroux.
My Own Ground. Hugh Nissenson. 1977 (ISBN 0-380-00985-4). Avon Books.
My Own Home and Fireside: Being Illustrative of the Speculations of Martin Chuzzlewitt and Co., Among the "Wenom of the Valley of Eden.". Samuel A. Allen. LC 7-21683. 1846. J. W. Moore; Etc., Etc.
My Own Manhattan. Henrietta Fort Holland. LC 47-578. 1946. I. Washburn, Inc.
My Own Murderer. Richard Henry Sampson. LC 40-14499. J. Messner, Inc.
My Own, My Native Land. Thyra Samter Winslow. LC 35-13198. 1935. Doubleday, Doran & Company, Inc.
My Own New England: Tales of Vanishing Types. Burleigh Cushing Rodick. LC 29-10668. 1929. W. Neale.
My Own Sin: A Story of Life in New York. Mary Edwards Bryan. (On cover: The library of American authors, no. 1). 1889. G. Munro.
My Pal Al. Richard Cloke. LC 77-81442. 1978. 2.25 (ISBN 0-917458-05-2). Kent Publications.
My "Pardner" and I Gray Rocks) A Story of the Middle-West. Willis George Emerson. LC 99-3528. (On cover: The pastime series, no. 78). 1899. Laird & Lee.
My Particular Murder. David Sharp. LC 31-340073. 1931. Houghton Mifflin Company.
My Past & Thoughts, 4 Vols. Alexander Herzen. LC 68-12684. 1968. Boxed. 30.00 o.p. (ISBN 0-394-43754-3). Knopf.
My Past Was an Evil River. George Reid Millar. LC 47-755. 1947. Doubleday & Company, Inc.
My Pearl. Alida W Graves. LC 6-45439. 1886. R. Carter and Brothers.
My Petition for More Space. John Richard Hersey. LC 74-9929. 1974. 5.95 (ISBN 0-394-49466-0). Knopf; Distributed by Random House.
My Poor Dick. Henrietta Eliza Vaughan Stannard. (On cover: Seaside library. Pocket ed. no. 1158). 1889. G. Munro.
My Poor Relations: Stories of Dutch Peasant Life. Jozua Marius Willen Van Der Poorten Schwartz. LC 5-13961. 1905. D. Appleton and Company.
My Pride, My Folly. Suzanne Butler. LC 52-12631. 1953. Little, Brown.
My Private Hangman. Norman Herries. LC 56-26711. (Ace double novel books, D-147). 1956. Ace Books.
My Psychiatrist Says: Let Me Make This Perfectly Clear...: a New Book. Gertrude Cooper. LC 73-93229. (Illus.). 1975. 4.00. William-Frederick Press.
My Quaker Maid. Marah Ellis Martin Ryan. LC 6-5137. Rand, McNally & Company.
My Queen; A Romance of the Great Salt Lake. Marie A. Walsh. LC 12-17871. 1878. G. W. Carleton & Co.; Etc., Etc.
My Rabbi Doesn't Make House Calls. Albert Vorspan. LC 69-20083. 1969. 1.49 o.p. (ISBN 0-385-06573-6). Doubleday.
My Ragpicker. Mary Ella Waller. LC 11-27846. 1911. Little, Brown, and Company.
My Rappahannock Story Book. Mary E. Hite. LC 50-13328. (Illus.). 232p. 1950. Repr. of 1950 ed. 15.00. Va Bk.
My Republic" In Which Are Narrated the Adventures of a Bibliophile During the French Revolution and the Part Played Therein by a Rare Book. Paul Lacroix. Tr. by Koch, Theodore Wesley. LC 36-12663. 1936. The Caxton Club.
My Revolution: Promenades in Paris 1789-1794, the Diary of Restif De la Bretonne. Alex Karmel. 1970. 10.00 o.p. (ISBN 0-07-033336-X). McGraw.
My Ringside Seat in Moscow. Miklos Nyarady & Nelson Coral Nye. LC 51-12373. (Silver star westerns). 1952. Crowell.
My Roses: The Romance of a June Day. L Virginia Smith French. 1872. Claxton, Remsen & Haffelfinger.
My Roses: The Romance of a June Day. L Virginia Smith French. (On cover: Lovell's library. no. 485). 1885. J. W. Lovell Company.
My Royal Past: By Baroness Von Bulop Nee Princess Theodora Louise Alexina Ludmilla Sophie Von Eckermann-Waldstein, As Told to Cecil Beaton. Rev. Ed. Cecil Walter Hardy Beaton. LC 60-10947. 1960. John Day Co.
My Satchel and I: Or Literature on Foot. George Stanford Stebbins. LC 8-134415. D. E. Fisk and Company.
My Savage Muse: The Story of My Life: Edgar Allan Poe, an Imaginative Work. Bernhardt J Hurwood. LC 79-51196. 9.95 (ISBN 0-89696-058-7). Everest House.
My Scottish Sweetheart. Charles Reekle. LC 99-3841. (On cover: Neely's universal library, no. 78). F. T. Neely.
My Searching Heart. Crying Wind. LC 80-83846. 242p. 1981. pap. 5.95 (ISBN 0-89081-262-4). Harvest Hse.
My Secret Garden. Nancy Friday. 1981. pap. 3.75. PB.
My Secret Life. (Unexpurgated, Abridged ed.). 1967. pap. 4.95 (ISBN 0-394-17397-X, B334, BC). Grove.
My Secret Love. Cara Canady. (Dear Miss Lonely Hearts,#2). 1974. (pbk.) 0.95. Pinnacle Books.
My Seeds Lie Scattered. Salvatore Neri. 3.50 o.p. Carlton.
My Sensuous Diary. 1975. (pbk.) 1.25. Dell.
My Shadow As I Pass. Sybil Bolitho. LC 34-31297. 1934. The Viking Press.
My Shame, My Degradation. Marie Defouet. Bd. with Fire in the Flesh. Marcel Tourigot. 160p. pap. 1.95 o.p. (MP-107). Montmartre.
My Shipmate Louise: The Romance of a Wreck. William Clark Russell. (On cover: Harper's Franklin square library, no. 682). 1890. Harper & Brothers.
My Side. Walter H Wager. LC 76-49933. 1976. 4.95. Collier Books.
My Side. Walter H Wager. LC 76-49829. 7.95. Macmillan.
My Side, by King Kong. Walter H. Wager. LC 76-49829. (O.s.i.). 1976. 7.95 o.s.i. (ISBN 0-02-622420-8). Macmillan.
My Silent War. Kim Philby. (Espionage-Intelligence Library). 224p. 1983. pap. 2.75 (ISBN 0-345-30843-3). Ballantine.
My Sister & I. Carter Sprague. 192p. pap. 1.95 o.p. (6160). Brandon.
My Sister Angie. Legh-Jones, Allison. LC 78-21409. 7.95 (ISBN 0-312-55856-2). St. Martin's Press.
My Sister Eileen. Ruth McKenney. LC 38-17844. (YA) 1968. pap. 0.60 (ISBN 0-15-663890-8, Harv). HarBraceJ.
My Sister Erica. Jane Blackmore. 1975. (pbk.) 1.25. Ace Books.
My Sister Goldie. Sara Sandberg. 1970. pap. 0.60 o.p. (0502-06096). Curtis.
My Sister Gone. Kathryn Marshall. LC 74-15880. 1975. 7.95 (ISBN 0-06-012817-8). Harper & Row.
My Sister Kate. Charlotte Mary Brame & De la Ramee, Louise, 1839-1906. LC 44-11269. (On cover: Seaside library. Pocket ed. No. 433). G. Munro.
My Sister Kitty; a Story of Election Day. Fanny D. Bates. LC 13-177450. 1881. Lee and Shepard.
My Sister Marion. L. B Magie. LC 7-20269. Tibbals Book Company.
My Sister: My Beloved, by Edwina Mark Pseud. 1st Ed. Edwin Fadiman. LC 55-12165. 1955. Citadel Press.
My Sister, My Bride: A Novel. Cyril Hume. LC 32-30517. 1932. Doubleday, Doran & Company, Inc.
My Sister, My Bride: A Novel. Merriam Modell. LC 48-6914. 1948. Simon and Schuster.
My Sister, My Friend. Katherine Blake. LC 65-209577. bds., 3.50. Reynal.
My Sister, My Love. Lucille Iremonger. LC 80-21357. 1981. 9.95 (ISBN 0-688-00055-X). Morrow.
My Sister, My Mistress. Gene North. 192p. (Orig.). 1972. pap. 1.95 o.p. (ISBN 0-87682-268-5, 7268). Barclay Hse.
My Sister My Sin. Terence FitzBancroft. (Orig.). 1968. pap. 1.75 o.s.i. (114, Ophelia). Olympia.
My Sister Sophie. Josephine Edgar. 1974. (pbk.). 0.95 (ISBN 0-671-77757-2). Pocket Books.
My Sister the Actress. Florence Marryat Church Lean. LC 27-13680. (Seaside library. v. 53, no. 1086). 1881. G. Munro.
My Sister the Actress. Florence Marryat Church Lean. LC 7-13610. (On cover: Lovell's library. v. 19, no. 937). 1887. J. W. Lovell Company.
My Sister, the Panther. Djibi Thiam. LC 80-1016. 1980. 6.95 (ISBN 0-396-07890-7). Dodd, Mead.
My Sister, the Sex Pawn. Paul Roan. pap. 1.95 o.p. (ISBN 0-87977-165-8, DBB165). Dansk Blue Bk.
My Sister's Hand in Mine: An Expanded Edition of the Collected Works of Jane Bowles. Jane Auer Bowles. LC 77-71329. (Neglected Books of the Twentieth Century). 1978. pap. 9.95 (ISBN 0-912946-44-X). Ecco Pr.
My Sister's Husband. Patience Stapleton. (On cover: American authors' series, no. 4). 1889. J. W. Lovell Company.
My Sister's Keeper. Ted Allan. LC 76-45644. 1976. pap. 7.50 (ISBN 0-8020-2208-1). U of Toronto Pr.
My Sisters' Keeper. Leslie Poles Hartley. 5.95 o.p. (ISBN 0-241-01783-1). Dufour.
My Sister's Story. Mikhail Andreevich Il'In. LC 31-32342. 1931. L. MacVeagh, The Dial Press.
My Sky Is Blue. 1st Ed. Loula Grace Erdman. 1953. Longmans, Green.
My Smoking-Room Companions. William Harvey King. LC 99-4555. T. Whittaker.
My Soldier Lady. Ella Hamilton Durley. LC 8-34813. 1908. The C. M. Clark Publishing Company.
My Solomon: A Story of Modern New York. L Melyxia Brown. LC 6-10690. 1879. W.L. Hyde & Co.
My Son. Corra May White Harris. LC 21-680518. George H. Doran Company.
My Son Africa. Froma Sand. LC 65-166475. 5.95. Sherbourne Pr.
My Son and Foe. Josephine Pinckney. LC 52-6018. 1952. Viking Press.
My Son and Heir. Isabella Holt. LC 49-10521. 1949. Bobbs-Merrill Co.
My Son Charles. Elizabeth Mayhew. 1976. 1.95 (ISBN 0-671-80543-6). Pocket Books.
My Son Dan. Lettie W. Moore. LC 77-94241. (Destiny Ser.). 1978. pap. 4.95 o.p. (ISBN 0-8163-0007-0, 13875-0). Pacific Pr Pub Assn.
My Son Francis. Jessie Hopwood Hughes. LC 68-56956. 1969. 4.00. Dorrance.
My Son Is a Good Boy. Maurits Ignatius Boas. LC 65-238647. 5.95. Fell.
My Son Is a Splendid Driver. William Motter Inge. LC 79-147771. 1971. 5.95. Little, Brown.
My Son John. Elizabeth Bartol Dewing Kaup. LC 26-163301. 1926. Minton, Balch & Company.
My Son, My Brother, My Friend: A Novel in Letters. Dale C Willard. LC 77-27695. 3.95 (ISBN 0-87784-651-0). InterVarsity Press.
My Son, My Son. B. Palmer. pap. 1.50 o.p. Believers Bkshelf.
My Son, My Son. Bernard Alvin Palmer. 1970. 1.95 o.p. (ISBN 0-8024-5661-8). Moody.
My Son, My Son! Howard Spring. LC 38-27427. 1938. The Viking Press.
My Son, the Double Agent. Ted Mark, pseud. (Orig.). 1969. pap. 0.60 o.p. (73-485). Lancer.
My Son, the Double Agent. Ted Mark. (man from ORGY). 1973. (pbk.) 1.25. Dell.
My Son, the Druggist. Marvin Kaye. LC 76-56309. 1977. 6.95 (ISBN 0-385-11042-1). Published for the Crime Club by Doubleday.
My Son: The Lawyer. Henry Denker. LC 50-5416. 1950. Crowell.
My Son, the Murderer. Patrick Quentin. LC 54-292538. (Inner sanctum mystery). 1954. Simon and Schuster.
My Sons, My England. Dougal Duncan. LC 80-13555. 10.95 (ISBN 0-684-16603-8). Scribner.
My Sons, My England. Dougal Duncan. 320p. 1981. pap. 2.75 (ISBN 0-449-24441-5, Crest). Fawcett.
My Son's Wife. Rose Porter. LC 7-37745. A. D. F. Randolph & Co.
My Soul to Keep. Elizabeth Davis, pseud. (Orig.). 1970. pap. 0.60 o.p. (X2251). Pyramid Pubns.
My South Sea Sweetheart. Beatrice Ethel Grimshaw. LC 21-5076. 1921. The Macmillan Company.
My Southern Friends. James Roberts Gilmore. LC 72-101143. 1969. Haskell House.
My Southern Friends. James Roberts Gilmore. LC 78-83964. 1969. Mnemosyne Pub. Inc.
My Southern Friends... James Roberts Gilmore. LC 6-37820. 1863. Carleton.
My Southern Friends... James Roberts Gilmore. LC 8-2132. 1863. The Tribune Association.
My Spanish Sweetheart: An International Romance. Frederick Albion Ober. (On cover: Neely's popular library, no. 81). 1897. F. T. Neely.
My Stars! Michael Goodwin. (Illus., Orig.). 1977. pap. 2.50 o.s.i. (ISBN 0-930068-03-3). Heritage Pr.
My Stillness. Paul Griffith. LC 72-83347. 212p. 1972. 8.95 (ISBN 0-8149-0724-5). Vanguard.
My Story. T. H. Caine. 1973. Repr. of 1908 ed. 25.00 (ISBN 0-8274-1503-6). R West.
My Story. A Novel. Katharine Sarah Gadsden Macquoid. (On cover: Library of choice novels, no. 47). 1875. D. Appleton & Company.
My Story: Being the Memoirs of Benedict Arnold: Late Major-General in the Continental Army and Brigadier-General in That of His Britannic Majesty. Frederic Jesup Stimson. LC 17-28796. 1917. C. Scribner's Sons.
My Story That I Like Best. Edna Ferber et al. 1978. Repr. of 1925 ed. lib. bdg. 17.50 o.p. (ISBN 0-8482-1605-9). Norwood Edns.
My Strange Life: The Intimate Life Story of a Moving Pictures Actress; Illustrated with Photographs of America's Most Famous Motion Picture Actresses. LC 16-1272. 1.25. E. J. Clode.
My Struggle. Geoff Brown. LC 74-21086. 1975. 7.50. St. Martin's Press.
My Sweet Audrina. Virginia C. Andrews. LC 82-12213. 14.50 (ISBN 0-671-44327-5). Poseidon Press.
My Sweet Charlie. David Westheimer. LC 65-19912. 4.50. Doubleday.
My Sweet-Orange Tree. Jose Mauro De Vasconcelos. LC 70-106625. (Illus.). 1970. 4.95. Knopf.
My Sword for Lafayette: Being the Story of a Great Friendship: and of Certain Episodes in the Wars Waged for Liberty, Both in France and America, by One Who Took No Mean Part Therein. Max Pemberton. LC 6-10645. 1906. Dodd, Mead & Company.
My System for Ladies. E. P. Muller. bds. 1.50. Assoc Bk.
My Talks with Dean Spanley. Edward John Moreton Drax Plunkett Dunsany. LC 36-25286. 1936. G. P. Punam's Sons.
My Theodosia. Anya Seton. LC 41-368849. 1941. Houghton Mifflin Company.
My Theodosia. Anya Seton. 1976. 1.95 (ISBN 0-449-23034-1). Fawcett Crest.
My Third Book. A Collection of Tales. Louise Chandler Moulton. LC 7-26096. 1859. Harper & Brothers.

My Three Conversations with Miss Chester. Frederic Beecher Perkins. LC 7-36346. 1877. G. P. Putnam's Sons.

My Three Favorite Novels. John Boynton Priestley. LC 78-8786. 1978. 15.00 (ISBN 0-8128-2529-2). Stein and Day.

My Three Legged Story Teller. Adelaide Skeel. LC 8-9013. 1892. R. C. Hartranft.

My Three Years at Andover. Lee James Perrin. LC 8-23538. 1908. Mayhew Publishing Company.

My Time and What I've Done with It. Francis Cowley Burnand. LC 75-456. (Victorian Fiction: Novels of Faith and Doubt). 1976. 40.00 (ISBN 0-8240-1535-5). Garland Pub.

My Time & What I've Done with It: An Autobiography, Compiled from the Diary, Notes & Personal Recollections of Cecil Colvin, 1874. Francis C. Burnard. (Victorian Fiction Ser.). 1975. lib. bdg. 66.00 (ISBN 0-8240-1535-5). Garland Pub.

My Time in Hell. Patrick J. Lisi. LC 76-9013. 1977. 9.95 o.p. (ISBN 0-87949-070-5). Ashley Bks.

My Time, My Life. 1st Ed. George Camden. LC 50-6852. 1950. Doubleday.

My Time or Yours? William D. Blake. (Orig.). 1979. pap. 1.95 (ISBN 0-532-23286-0). Woodhill.

My Tower in Desmond. Sidney Royse Lysaght. LC 25-18054. 1925. The Macmillan Company.

My Transient Halo. William A. St. Louis. 3.00 o.p. Carlton.

My Treasure, My Love. Lynna Cooper, pseud. (Signet Book). 1978. 1.50 (ISBN 0-451-07936-1). New American Library.

My Treasure, My Love see Substitute Bride.

My Trivial Life and Misfortune. A Gossip with No Plot in Particular. LC 21-153678. (Seaside library v. 81, no. 1636). 1883. G. Munro.

My Troubles Began: A Novel. Tr. from Italian by Belen Sevareid. Paolo Volponi. LC 64-780565. 1964. 5.00. Grossman.

My True Faces: A Novel About India. Chaman Lal Nahal. 1978. 9.00x (ISBN 0-88253-254-5). South Asia Bks.

My True Love. Denise Robins. LC 77-72118. 1977. 1.25. (ISBN 0-380-01642-7). Avon Books.

My True Love. Darwin Le Ora Teilhet. LC 45-10158. 1945. D. Appleton-Century Company, Incorporated.

My True Love Lies. Lenore Glen Offord. LC 47-2539. 1947. Duell, Sloan and Pearce.

My Turn. Roz Avrett. 288p. 1983. 14.50 (ISBN 0-87795-476-3). Arbor Hse.

My Turn Next! Bil Keane. (Family Circus Ser.: No. 23). 128p. (Orig.). 1981. pap. 1.50 (ISBN 0-449-14412-7, GM). Fawcett.

My Tussle with the Devil & Other Stories, by O'Henry's Ghost. facsimile ed. LC 72-160947. (Short Story Index Reprint Ser.). Repr. of 1918 ed. 10.25 (ISBN 0-8369-3926-3). Ayer Co.

My Tussle with the Devil: And Other Stories. O'Henry'S & William Sydney Porter. LC 72-160947. (Short story index reprint series). 1971. (ISBN 0-8369-3926-3). Books for Libraries Press.

My Two Kings: A Novel of the Stuart Restoration. Evelyn Maud Reid Nepean. LC 18-3836. E. P. Dutton & Company.

My Two Wives: By One of Their Husbands; in Two Parts: Part 1, My First Wife, by Her Second Husband; Part 2, My Second Wife, by Her First Husband. LC 8-27768. (Half-title: The "unknown" library no. 30). The Cassell Publishing Co.

My Two Worlds. Alice Siwundhla. LC 79-155491. 198p. 1971. 4.50 o.p. (13920-4). Pacific Pr Pub Assn.

My Uncle and Miss Elizabeth. Robert Harkness Parrish. LC 48-5956. 1948. Beechhurst Press.

My Uncle and My Cure. Alice Cherbonnel & Clarkson, James W., Tr. LC 99-2942. T. Y. Crowell & Company.

My Uncle and My Cure. Alice Cherbonnel & Redwood, Ernest, Tr. LC 7-12826. 1892. Dodd, Mead and Company.

My Uncle and the Cure: By Jean De La Brete Pseud.Translated by N. St. Barbe Sladen. Alice Cherbonnel. LC 58-9244. Vanguard Press.

My Uncle Barbassou. Mario Uchard & Hall, Arthur D., Tr. LC 12-39790. 1889. Rand, McNally & Company.

My Uncle Benjamin. Claude Tillier & Lorenz, Marie, Tr. LC 41-8924. 1941. Coventry House.

My Uncle Benjamin. Claude Tillier & Seltzer, Mrs. Adele Szold, 1876- Tr. LC 18-4255. 1917. Boni and Liveright.

My Uncle Benjamin. Claude Tillier & Tucker, Benjamin Ricketson, 1854- Tr. (On cover: Idle moments series, no. 17). 1892. The Price-McGill Company.

My Uncle Benjamin: A Humorous, Satirical, and Philosophical Novel. Claude Tillier & Tucker, Benjamin Ricketson, 1854- Tr. LC 8-27026. 1890. B. R. Tucker.

My Uncle Dudley. Wright Morris. LC 75-5696. 1975. 2.95 (ISBN 0-8032-5804-6). University of Nebraska Press.

My Uncle Dudley. Wright Morris. LC 71-110050. 1970. Greenwood Press.

My Uncle Dudley. Wright Morris. LC 42-114509. 1942. Harcourt, Brace and Company.

My Uncle Hobson and I: Or, Slashes at Life with a Fre-Broad-Axe. Pascal Jones. 1845. D. Appleton & Co.

My Uncle Jacinto. Translated by Isabel Quigly. Illus. by Eduardo Vicente. 1st American Ed. Andras Laszlo. LC 58-10903. 1958. Harcourt, Brace.

My Uncle Jan: A Novel. Joseph Auslander & Wurdemann, Audrey. LC 48-5867. 1948. Longmans, Green.

My Uncle Louis. Robert Louis Fontaine. 1953. McGraw-Hill.

My Uncle Ned. Eric MacHaye. LC 32-32761. Sears Publishing Company, Inc.

My Uncle Newt. Frances Eisenberg. LC 42-24442. 1942. J. B. Lippincott Company.

My Uncle Oswald. Roald Dahl. LC 79-19811. 1980. 8.95 (ISBN 0-394-51011-9). Knopf: Distributed by Random House.

My Uncle Scipio. Andre I. E. Claude Adhemar Andre Theuriet & Robins, E. P., Tr. (On cover: Once a week semi-monthly library, v. 11. no. 3). 1893. P. F. Collier.

My Uncle the Curate. A Novel. Marmion W. Savage. LC 7-3066. (On cover: Library of select novels. no. 1281). 1849. Harper & Brothers.

My Uncle Thomas. A Romance... From the French of Pigault Lebrun... Charles Antoine Guillaume Pigault De L'Epinoy Pigault-Lebrun. 1810. Printed for J. Branuan.

My Unforgettable Parents. Kay Kuzma. LC 77-93134. (Redwood Ser.). 1978. pap. 3.50 o.p. (ISBN 0-8163-0008-9, 13925-3). Pacific Pr Pub Assn.

My Vacation: Or, The Millennium. A Novel. John L Fitzporter. LC 6-41121. 1891.

My Very Best Friend. Paul Ricchiuti. (Hello World Ser.). 1975. pap. 1.65 o.p. (ISBN 0-8163-0188-3, 13950-1). Pacific Pr Pub Assn.

My Village. Elmer Boyd Smith. LC 8-8634. 1896. C. Scribner's Sons.

My Vineyard. Dorothy Hoyer Scharlemann. LC 46-8610. 1946. Concordia Publishing House.

My Visit to Venus. T. Lobsang Rampa, pseud. pap. 4.95 o.p G Barker Bks.

My Watch Below: Or, Yarns Spun When off Duty. William Clark Russell. (Harper's Franklin square library, no. 264). 1882. Harper & Brothers.

My Watch Below: Or, Yarns Spun When off Duty. William Clark Russell. (Seaside library, v. 68, no. 1373). 1882. G. Munro.

My Wayward Pardner: Or, My Trials with Josiah, America, the Widow Bump, and Etcetery. Marietta Holley. LC 7-6083. 1880. American Publishing Company.

My Wickedness. A Psychological Study. Robert Harborough Sherard. 1893. The Cleveland Publishing Company.

My Wife. Edward Burke. LC 17-239809. 1917. E. P. Dutton & Co.

My Wife and I: Or, Harry Henderson's History. Harriet Elizabeth Beecher Stowe. LC 8-16121. 1871. J. B. Ford and Company.

My Wife and My Wife's Sister. Elizabeth Wormeley Latimer. LC 7-13860. (No name series. 2d series, v. 10). 1881. Roberts Brothers.

My Wife Ethel. Damon Runyon. LC 40-742687. David McKay Company.

My Wife Melissa. Francis Durbridge. LC 73-155115. 1972. 5.95 (ISBN 0-85617-972-8). (Baker St., WM FA): White Lion Publishers Ltd.

My Wife, the Condesa. Felix Abelard. 1978. 9.50 o.p. (ISBN 0-682-49054-7). Exposition.

My Wife's Hidden Life. LC 13-26685. 1.25. Rand, McNally & Company.

My Wife's Hidden Life. LC 13-266865. 0.60. Hodder and Stoughton.

My Wife's Husband: A Touch of Nature. Alice Wilkinson Sparks. LC 8-12385. (pastime series, no. 53). 1897. Laird & Lee.

My Wife's Niece. A Novel. Anne Elliot. LC 7-23126. (Harper's Franklin square library. no. 495). 1885. Harper /& Brothers.

My Wisdom: A Novel. Jean Thompson. LC 82-11107. 1982. 14.95 (ISBN 0-531-09870-2). F. Watts.

My Wives. LC 29-21689. Harper & Brothers.

My Wondrous Dream. Frank P Ball. LC 23-131109. F. P. Ball.

My Word! Stories. 1977. 7.95 o.s.i. (ISBN 0-8128-2280-3); pap. 3.95 o.s.i. (ISBN 0-8128-2281-1). Stein & Day.

My World Is an Island. Elisabeth Ogilvie. Repr. lib. bdg. 14.85x (ISBN 0-88411-334-5). Amereon Ltd.

My Young Alcides: A Faded Photograph. Charlotte Mary Yonge. LC 4-8614. 1876. Macmillan and Co.

My Young Alcides: A Faded Photograph. Charlotte Mary Yonge. LC 4-8613. (On cover: The seaside library. Pocket ed., no. 666). 1886. G. Munro.

My Young Master: A Novel. Opie Percival Read. (On cover: The pastime series, no. 45). 1896. Laird & Lee.

Myer for Hire. Lester S. Taube. LC 70-22925. 1970 (ISBN 0-491-00106-1). W. H. Allen.

Mykonos. Minnie Warburton. LC 79-67. 9.95 (ISBN 0-698-10922-8). Coward, McCann & Geoghegan.

Mynheer Joe. A Novel. St. George Rathborne. LC 8-588. (Ledger library, no. 88). 1893. R. Bonner's Sons.

Mynn's Mystery. George Manville Fenn. LC 41-30734. 1890. F. Warne and Co.

Mynns' Mystery. A Novel. George Manville Fenn. LC 6-39381. (On cover: Lovell's international series, no. 49). F. F. Lovell & Company.

Myra: A Novel. Mamie Lamkin Hatchett. LC 7-2839. 1884. J. W. Randolph & English.

Myra Breckinridge. Gore Vidal. LC 68-14745. 1968. Little, Brown.

Myra Mordaunt: A Story of Love and Constancy. William F McMillan. LC 7-20304. (On cover: Idlywild series. v. 1, no. 33). Morrill, Higgins & Co.

Myra: the Child of Adoption. A Romance of Real Life. Ann Sophia Winterbotham Stephens. LC 3-28190. (On cover: Beadle's dime novels, no. 3). 1860. I. P. Beadle and Company.

Myria, the Mad Actress: Or, The Mysterious Murder. A True Narrative of Love and Crime. William D Ritner. LC 7-41411. Barclay & Co.

Myriah. Claudette Williams. (Regency Romance). 1.50 (ISBN 0-449-23577-7). Fawcett Crest Books.

Myriam and the Mystic Brotherhood. Maude Lesseur Howard. LC 12-13904. J. W. Lovell.

Myriam and the Mystic Brotherhood. Maude Lesseur Howard. LC 15-285207. 1915. Occult Publishing Company.

Myrmidon Project. Chuck Scarborough & William Murray. LC 80-20639. 11.95 (ISBN 0-698-11054-4). Coward, McCann & Geoghegan.

Myrna. Jacob Jankelson. LC 43-126565. 1943. Wetzel Publishing Co., Inc.

Myron: A Novel. Gore Vidal. LC 74-9052. 1974. 6.95 (ISBN 0-394-49477-6). Random House.

Myrta. Walter Samuel Cramp. LC 15-16633. 1.35. R. G. Badger; Etc., Etc.

Myrtis, with Other Etchings and Sketchings. Lydia Howard Huntley Sigourney. LC 8-8988. Harper & Brothers.

Myrtle. Stephen Hudson. LC 25-26746. 1925. A. A. Knopf.

Myrtle Baldwin. Charles Clark Munn. 1908. Lothrop, Lee & Shepard Co.

Myrtle Greene Unfolds Her Life and Innermost Emotions to Thomas Light Reeve. Thomas Light Reeve. LC 42-120335. 1942. Light Publishing Company.

Myrtle Lawn. A Novel. Robert E Ballard. T. B. Peterson & Brother.

Myrtle Tree: A Novel. Robert Godfrey Goodyear. LC 37-2569. 1937. W. Morrow & Company.

Myself: A Romance of New England Life. Enoch Emery. LC 6-37830. 1872. J. B. Lippincott & Co.

Myself As Witness. James Goldman. LC 78-57121. 12.95 (ISBN 0-394-41923-5). Random House.

Myself, Christopher Wren. David Weiss. LC 73-78750. 1974. 15.00 (ISBN 0-698-10538-9). Coward, McCann & Geoghegan.

Mysteries. Knut Hamsun. LC 74-115733. (Bard book). 1975. (pbk.) 1.95 (ISBN 0-380-00504-2). Avon.

Mysteries. Knut Hamsun. LC 74-115753. 1971. 8.95 (ISBN 0-374-21764-5). Farrar, Straus and Giroux.

Mysteries. Knut Hamsun & Chater, Arthur G., Tr. LC 27-986152. 1927. A. A. Knopf.

Mysteries. Kunt Hamsun. Tr. by Gerry Bothmer from Nor. 340p. 1971. pap. 4.50 o.p. (ISBN 0-374-50888-7, N397, Noonday). FS&G.

Mysteries & Adventures Along the Atlantic Coast. facs. ed. Edward R. Snow. LC 72-80398. (Essay Index Reprint Ser). 1948. 21.25 o.p. (ISBN 0-8369-1066-4). Ayer Co.

Mysteries and Miseries of New Orleans. Edward Zane Carroll Judson. L. Ormsby.

Mysteries and Miseries of San Francisco. A Californian. LC 49-35554. 1853. Garrett.

Mysteries of Ann. Alice Brown. LC 25-8113. 1925. The Macmillan Company.

Mysteries of Blair House. Roy O. Eastman. LC 48-11834. 1948. Conjure House.

Mysteries of City Life: Or, Stray Leaves from the World's Book, Being a Series of Tales, Sketches, Incidents, and Scenes, Founded Upon the Notes of a Home Missionary. James Rees. 1849. J. W. Moore.

Mysteries of Destiny. Matao Kano. Ed. by Eiichi Yamamoto. (Matao Kano's Destiny Ser.). 206p. (Orig.). 1982. pap. 12.95 (ISBN 0-942512-00-6). Yama Trans.

Mysteries of Heron Dyke. A Novel of Incident. Thomas Wilkinson Speight. (Franklin square library. no. 212). 1881. Harper & Brothers.

Mysteries of Louis Napoleon's Court. Emile Zola & Philp, Kenward, Tr. 1884. N. L. Monro.

Mysteries of Marsailles. A Love Story. Emile Zola & Cox, George D., Tr. LC 12-37827. T. B. Peterson & Brothers.

Mysteries of Marseilles. Emile Zola & Cooney, Myron A., Tr. (Brookside library, no. 435). 1885. F. Tousey.

Mysteries of Marseilles: A Novel. Emile Zola & Edward Vizetelly. LC 76-24887. 1976. 16.00. H. Fertig.

Mysteries of Motion. Hortense Calisher. 1983. 22.50. Doubleday.

Mysteries of Paris. Eugene Sue. Tr. by Henry Llewellyn Williams. (Seaside library, v. 11, no. 205). 1878. G. Munro.

Mysteries of Paris. Eugene Sue. Tr. by Henry Llewellyn Williams. (On cover: The elite series, no. 29). 1892. The F. M. Lupton Publishing Company.

Mysteries of Paris. Eugene Sue. LC 8-21619. 1903. The Century Co.

Mysteries of Paris. A Romance of the Rich and Poor. Eugene Sue & Deming, Henry Champion, 1815-1872, Tr. LC 8-17676. (Lettered on cover: The new world. Extra series). 1844. J. Winchester.

Mysteries of the Backwoods. Thomas B. Thorpe. LC 71-104579. (Illus.). 1970. Repr. of 1846 ed. lib. bdg. 9.50x o.p. (ISBN 0-8398-1958-7). Gregg.

Mysteries of the Court of Louis Napoleon. Emile Zola & Sherwood, Mrs. Mary (Neal) Tr. LC 9-1315. T. B. Peterson & Brothers.

Mysteries of the Court of Napoleon III. Gilbert Augustin Thierry & R., E. I., Tr. LC 8-28121. (library of choice fiction no. 56). 1892. Laird & Lee.

Mysteries of the Deep. Ed. by Joseph J. Thorndike, Jr. LC 80-7804. (Illus.). 352p. 1980. 34.95 o.p. (ISBN 0-8281-0407-7, Dist. by Scribner); deluxe ed. 39.95 o.p. (ISBN 0-8281-0408-5, Dist. by Scribner). Am Heritage.

Mysteries of the People: Or, The Story of a Plebeian Family for 2,000 Years. Eugene Sue & Booth, Mary Louise, 1831-1889, Tr. LC 8-17675. 1867. Clark.

Mysteries of the Pulpit: Or, A Revelation of the Church and the Home. George Lippard. 1851. E. E. Barclay.

Mysteries of the Worm. Robert Bloch. 1981. pap. 2.95 (ISBN 0-89083-815-1). Zebra.

Mysteries of the Zimniy Dvoretz (Winter Palace) A Russian Historical Novel. Charles W Pafflow. LC 5-8340. 1905. The Neale Publishing Company.

Mysteries of Time & Space. Brad Steiger. pap. 2.50 (ISBN 0-440-05924-0). Dell.

Mysteries of Udolpho. Ann Ward Radcliffe & Bonamy Dobree. LC 79-42712. (World's classics). 1980. 5.95 (ISBN 0-19-281502-4). Oxford University Press.

Mysteries of Udolpho: A Romance. Ann Ward Radcliffe. Ed. by Bonamy Dobree. LC 72-570265. (Oxford paperbacks, 212). (Illus.). 1970 (ISBN 0-19-281079-0). Oxford U.P.

Mysteries of Udolpho: A Romance. Ann Ward Radcliffe. LC 35-334223. (Half-title: Everyman's library edited by E. Rhys. Fiction. no. 865-866). 1931. J. M. Dent & Sons Ltd.

Mysteries of Udolpho: A Romance Interspersed with Some Pieces of Poetry. Ann Ward Radcliffe. Ed. by Bonamy Dobree. LC 66-2628. (Oxford English Novels: B66-4248). 1966. Oxford U. P.

Mysterious Affair at Styles. Agatha Miller Christie. 192p. 1981. pap. text ed. 2.50 (ISBN 0-553-14981-4). Bantam.

Mysterious Affair at Styles. Agatha Miller Christie. 236p. 1975. 7.95 o.p. (ISBN 0-396-07224-0). Dodd.

Mysterious Affair at Styles. Agatha Miller Christie. 1980. pap. 8.95 o.p. (ISBN 0-8161-3105-8, Large Print Bks). G K Hall.

Mysterious Affair at Styles: A Detective Story. Agatha Miller Christie. LC 20-19240. 1920. John Lane Company.

Mysterious Affair at Styles: A Detective Story. Agatha Miller Christie. LC 29-243902. 1928. Grosset & Dunlap.

Mysterious Affair at Styles: A "Hercule Poirot Mystery"... Agatha Miller Christie. LC 45-4609. (Murder mystery monthly. No. 26). 1944.

Mysterious Affair at Styles: A "Hercule Poirot Mystery,". Agatha Miller Christie. LC 46-6182. (New Avon library. 75). 1945.

Mysterious Affair at Styles: Poirot's First Case. a commemorative ed. Agatha Miller Christie. LC 75-42272. 1976. 10.95 (ISBN 0-8161-6343-X). G. K. Hall.

Mysterious Aviator. Nevil Shute Norway. LC 28-229623. 1928. Houghton Mifflin Company.

Mysterious Beau Yeux. Hattie Buckley & Kenneth Kroger. 180p. 1982. 10.95 (ISBN 0-89962-266-6). Todd & Honeywell.
Mysterious Beggar: A Novel, Founded on Facts... Albert A. Day. LC 6-322463. J. S. Ogilvie.
Mysterious Card. Cleveland Moffett. LC 12-18791. Small, Maynard and Company.
Mysterious Case: Or, Tracing a Crime. K. F Hill. LC 7-4697. (secret service series--no. 23). 1889. Street & Smith.
Mysterious Castle. A Tale of the Middle Ages. Tr. from the French by. Kate Elizabeth Duval Hughes. LC 7-563957. 1878. Kelly, Piet & Company.
Mysterious Cavalier. Paul Feval & Lassez, M., Joint Author. LC 28-6308. (His The years between: adventures of D'Artagnan and cyrano de Bergerac. I). 1928. Longmans, Green and C.
Mysterious Chinese Mandrake: And Other Stories. 1st Ed. Ida Diana Ekbergh. LC 54-125926. 1954. Pageant Press.
Mysterious Commission. Michael Innes, pseud. 218p. 1975. 5.95 o.p. (ISBN 0-396-07134-1). Dodd.
Mysterious Commission. Michael Innes, pseud. (Crime Ser). (O.s.i). 1977. pap. 1.95 o.s.i. (ISBN 0-14-004437-X). Penguin.
Mysterious Commission. John Innes Mackintosh Stewart. LC 74-28007. (Red badge novel of suspense). 1975. 5.95 (ISBN 0-396-07134-1). Dodd, Mead.
Mysterious Commission. John Innes Mackintosh Stewart. LC 77-1215. (Penguin crime fiction). 1977. 1.95 (ISBN 0-14-004437-X). Penguin Books.
Mysterious Disappearance. Louis Tracy. LC 5-2437. 1905. E. J. Clode.
Mysterious Disappearance of Helen St. Vincent. A Story of the Vanished City. John Joseph Flinn. LC 6-41668. 1895. G.K. Hazlitt & Co.
Mysterious Disappearnace. Louis Tracy. LC 27-24489. E. J. Clode, Inc.
Mysterious Doctor. A Novel. Z. L Stanley. 1888. G. W. Dillingham; Etc., Etc.
Mysterious Dr. Oliver: A Mystery Story. John Breckenridge Ellis. LC 29-13070. 1929. The Macaulay Company.
Mysterious Document. Jules Verne. 3.95. Assoc Bk.
Mysterious Five. Marie E. Taylor. LC 30-126900. The Christopher Publishing House.
Mysterious Grotto. Louise Bergstrom. 1973. 4.50 o.p. (Avalon). Bouregy.
Mysterious Guest. Eliza Ann Dupuy. LC 6-24599. T. B. Peterson & Brothers.
Mysterious Hunter: Or, The Last of the Aztecs. Squire D Hopkins. The Jeune Hopkins Company.
Mysterious Island. Jules Verne. LC 56-585765. 1956. Grosset & Dunlap.
Mysterious Island. Jules Verne. LC 58-10786. (Great illustrated classics). 1958. Dodd, Mead.
Mysterious Island. Jules Verne. LC 59-3152. 1959. Printed for the Members of the Limited Editions Club at the Garamond Press.
Mysterious Island. Jules Verne. LC 59-162105. 1959. Heritage Press.
Mysterious Island... Jules Verne. LC 1-9823. (On cover: Seaside library. Pocket ed. no. 1238). 1889. G. Munro.
Mysterious Island. Jules Verne. LC 27-21619. (father and son library). J. H. Sears & Company, Inc.
Mysterious Island. Jules Verne. LC 35-16745. The Saalfield Publishing Company.
Mysterious Island. authorized ed. with forty-eight illustrations. ed. Jules Verne. LC 1-98246. 1875. Scribner, Armstrong & Co.
Mysterious Island. Jules Verne & Wyeth, Newell Convers. 1882- Illus. LC 18-20168. 1918. C. Scribner's Sons.
Mysterious Island. Illustrated by Henry C. Pitz; Introd. by May Lamberton Becker. Jules Verne. LC 57-7411. (Rainbow classics R-41). 1957. World Pub. Co.
Mysterious Island, the Modern Robinson Crusoe. Jules Verne. LC 12-23261. 1909. C. Scribner's Sons.
Mysterious Island: The Secret of the Island. Jules Verne & Kingston, William Henry Giles, 1814-1880, Tr. LC 42-26820. 1876. Scribner, Armstrong, & Co.
Mysterious Island; the Secret of the Island. Translated from the French by W. H. G. Kingston. Jules Verne. LC 42-26820. 1876. Scribner, Armstrong.
Mysterious Juror. tr. from the 3d ed. Fortune Du Boisgobey. LC 6-34419. (On cover: The midland series, v. 5. no. 41). Morrill, Higgins & Co.
Mysterious Kingdom. A. M. Winterhalt. 1974. 1.95 o.s.i. (ISBN 0-8181-0332-9). Pageant-Poseidon.
Mysterious Madame S... Simone D' Erigny & Abbott, Elisabeth, Tr. LC 34-1473. J. B. Lippincott Company.
Mysterious Marriage: A Sequel to A Leap in the Dark. Emma Dorothy Eliza Nevitte Southworth. LC 12-389031. (On cover: Southworth library. no. 168). Street & Smith.
Mysterious Martin: A Fiction Narrative Setting Forth the Development of Character Along Unusual Lines. Clarence Aaron Robbins. LC 12-7622. 1.00. J. S. Ogilvie Publishing Company.
Mysterious Mickey Finn. Elliot Harold Paul. LC 43-12820. (Murder of the month. No. 2). 1942. The Avon Book Company.
Mysterious Mickey Finn: Or, Murder at the Cafe Du Dome, an International Mystery. Elliot Harold Paul. LC 39-229292. Modern Age Books Inc.
Mysterious Miss Morrisot. Valentine Williams. 1930. Houghton Mifflin Company.
Mysterious Mr. Frame: A Novel. Mollie Merrick. LC 38-32628. I. Washburn, Inc.
Mysterious Mr. Howard. A Novel. John Roy Musick. LC 7-32293. (Ledger library, no. 129). 1896. R. Bonner's Sons.
Mysterious Mr. I: A Detective-Mystery Novel. Harry Stephen Keeler. LC 38-34807. 1938. E. P. Dutton & Co., Inc.
Mysterious Mr. Jarvis. Frederick R Giles. ((On cover: Leisure-time series, no. 16). 1892. W. D. Rowland.
Mysterious Mr. Quin. Agatha Miller Christie. LC 30-11715. 1930. Dodd, Mead & Company.
Mysterious Mr. Quinn. Agatha Miller Christie. (Dell book). 1979. 1.95 (ISBN 0-440-16246-7). Dell Pub. Co.
Mysterious Mr. Sabin. Edward Phillips Oppenheim. LC 1-5615. (Windsor magazine. v. ii, no. 1 Suppl.). 1899. Ward, Lock & Co., Limited.
Mysterious Mr. Sabin. Edward Phillips Oppenheim. LC 5-3789. 1905. Little Brown, and Company.
Mysterious Mr. Sabin. Edward Phillips Oppenheim. LC 21-14131. 1919. Little, Brown, and Company.
Mysterious Monogram... A Composite Story. The Lucky Friday Club, Quincy, Ill. LC 11-22328. Printed by Bradley & Anderson.
Mysterious Mrs. Wilkinson: And Other Stories. William Edward Norris. LC 7-33285. J. W. Lovell Company.
Mysterious Office. Jennette Barbour Perry Lee. LC 22-22702. 1922. C. Scribner's Sons.
Mysterious Orchid. Gertrude Mace. (YA) 1980. 6.50 (Avalon). Bouregy.
Mysterious Partner. Archibald E. Fielding. LC 29-172215. 1929. A. A. Knopf.
Mysterious Planet. Lester Del Rey. LC 52-14254. (Science fiction novel). 1953. Winston.
Mysterious Planet. Jacket and Endpaper Designs by Alex Schomburg. 1st Ed. Kenneth Wright, pseud. LC 52-14254. (Science fiction novel). 1953. Winston.
Mysterious Rancho. Jackson Gregory. LC 38-32613. 1938. Dodd, Mead & Company.
Mysterious Rider. Zane Grey. 1973. (pbk) 0.75. Pocket Books.
Mysterious Rider: A Novel. Zane Grey. 1921. Harper & Brothers.
Mysterious Rider: A Novel. Zane Grey. Grosset & Dunlap.
Mysterious Stranger. Samuel Langhorne Clemens. Ed. by William Merriam Gibson. LC 70-105218. (Mark Twain papers). (Illus.). 1970. 2.95. University of California Press.
Mysterious Stranger: A Romance. Samuel Langhorne Clemens. 1916. Harper & Brothers.
Mysterious Stranger: And Other Stories. Samuel Langhorne Clemens. LC 55-103934. 1922. Harper & Brothers.
Mysterious Stranger & Other Stories. Mark Twain. Repr. of 1916 ed. 10.00 o.p. (ISBN 0-06-014400-9, HarpT). Har-Row.
Mysterious Stranger: No. 44. Mark Twain. LC 81-40326. (Mark Twain Library). 200p. 1982. 12.95 (ISBN 0-520-04544-0, CAL 538); pap. 3.95 (ISBN 0-520-04545-9). U of Cal Pr.
Mysterious Suspect: By John Rhode Pseud. Cecil John Charles Street. LC 53-7533. (Red badge detective). 1953. Dodd, Mead.
Mysterious Sweetheart. Ella Wister Haines. LC 29-6175. A. L. Burt Company.
Mysterious Tales of Ivan Turgenev. Tr. by Robert Dessaix from Rus. LC 79-53661. (Orig.). (gr. 11-12). 1980. pap. text ed. 13.95 (ISBN 0-7081-1204-8, 0376, Pub. by ANUP Australia). Bks Australia.
Mysterious Tales of the New England Coast. Edward R. Snow. (Illus.). 1961. 5.00 o.p. (ISBN 0-396-04582-0). Dodd.
Mysterious Trail: A Story of Mystery and Romance in Which the East and West Meet. Elizabeth Jane Leonard. LC 25-24585. 1925. Published by Arrangement with the York Blank Book Company.
Mysterious Treasure of Cloud Rock. Jo Brewer. (Illus.). 1953. 2.95 o.p. Dutton.
Mysterious Vanishing. Joseph R. McCloskey. 56p. 1977. 3.95 o.p. (ISBN 0-8059-2480-9). Dorrance.
Mysterious Visions. Martin Harry Greenberg & Joseph D Olander. LC 78-3990. 1978. 8.95 (ISBN 0-312-55866-X). St. Martin's Press.
Mysterious Warning: A German Tale, by Eliza Parsons. Eliza Phelp Parsons. LC 68-98582. (Northanger Set of Jane Austen Horrid Novels). 1968. Folio Pr.
Mysterious Waye: The Story of "The Unsetting Sun". Percival Christopher Wren. LC 30-27769. 1930. Frederick A. Stokes Company.
Mysterious Wife: A Novel. Grove Wilson. LC 27-13121. Frank-Maurice, Inc.
Mysteriouser & Mysteriouser. George Bagby, pseud. 1969. pap. 0.60 o.p. (0502-06038-060). Curtis.
Mysteriouser and Mysteriouser: By George Bagby Pseud. Aaron Marc Stein. LC 65-128231. 3.50. Pub. for the Crime Club by Doubleday.
Mystery. LC 82-463265. (No-Frills Book). 1981. 1.50 (ISBN 0-515-06248-0). Jove Publications.
Mystery. Stewart Edward White & Samuel Hopkins Adams. LC 74-16525. (Science Fiction). (Illus.). 1975. 16.00 (ISBN 0-405-06317-2). Arno Press.
Mystery. Stewart Edward White & Adams, Samuel Hopkins, Joint Author. 1907. McClure, Phillips & Co.
Mystery. Stewart Edward White & Adams, Samuel Hopkins, 1871- Joint Author. LC 20-16803. 1920. Doubleday, Page & Company.
Mystery. Ellen Price Henry Wood Wood. (On cover: Seaside library. Pocket ed. no. 255). 1884. G. Munro.
Mystery. A Story of Domestic Life. Ellen Price Henry Wood Wood. LC 8-37883. T. B. Peterson & Brothers.
Mystery & Manners: Occasional Prose. Flannery O'Connor. Ed. by Robert Fitzgerald & Sally Fitzgerald. LC 69-15409. 1969. 10.95 (ISBN 0-374-21792-0); pap. 5.95 (ISBN 0-374-50804-6). FS&G.
Mystery and Minette. Herbert Adams. J. B. Lippincott Company.
Mystery and Suspense: Great Stories from The Saturday Evening Post. Ed. by Julie Eisenhower. LC 76-41561. 5.95 (ISBN 0-89387-005-6). Curtis Pub. Co.
Mystery and the Detective: A Collection of Stories. Ed. by Blanche Colton Williams. LC 38-5140. D. Appleton-Century Company, Incorporated.
Mystery at a Country Inn. Philip Owen. Ed. by Virginia Rowe. LC 79-52082. 1979. 7.95 o.p. (ISBN 0-912944-54-4); pap. 5.95 o.p. (ISBN 0-912944-60-9). Berkshire Traveller.
Mystery at a Country Inn. Judson Pentecost Philips. LC 79-52082. 7.95 (ISBN 0-912944-54-4). Berkshire Traveller Press.
Mystery at Chillery. Reginald Francis Foster. LC 32-12523. The Fiction League.
Mystery at Crane's Landing. Marcella Thum. (Willow Bks). 1971. pap. 0.75 o.p. (JT51). Pyramid Pubns.
Mystery at Cranes Landing. Marcella Thum. 1970. pap. 0.60 o.p. (JX38). Pyramid Pubns.
Mystery at Fay's Landing. Lyman Ellsworth Thompson. LC 29-13475. 1929. W. Neale.
Mystery at Friar's Pardon... Philip MacDonald. LC 32-261524. Pub. for the Crime Club, Inc., by Doubleday, Doran & Company, Inc.
Mystery at Geneva: An Improbable Tale of Singular Happenings. Rose Macaulay. LC 23-31370. Boni and Liveright.
Mystery at Hidden Harbor. Cortland Fitzsimmons. LC 38-25350. 1938. Frederick A. Stokes Company.
Mystery at Lonesome End. Myna Lockwood. LC 46-8238. 1946. Oxford University Press.
Mystery at Lovers' Cave. Anthony Berkeley Cox. LC 27-19311. 1927. Simon and Schuster.
Mystery at Lynden Sands. Alfred Walter Stewart. LC 28-19130. 1928. Little, Brown, and Company.
Mystery at Newton Ferry. Laurence Walter Meynell. LC 30-22429. 1930. J. B. Lippincott Company.
Mystery at Peak House. Arthur John Rees. LC 34-12703. 1933. Dodd, Mead & Company.
Mystery at Robbers' Rock: Illustrated by Sally Tate. 1st Ed. Samuel Duff McCoy. LC 50-14252. (His A. J. J. Jenks Jr. mystery). 1950. Lippincott.
Mystery at Shadow Mountain. Fred John Meldau. LC 49-9366. 1949. Zondervan.
Mystery at Spanish Hacienda. Jackson Gregory. LC 29-17087. 1929. Dodd, Mead & Company.
Mystery at Spindle Key. Ed. by Gene Sprouse. (YA) 1980. 6.50 (Avalon). Bouregy.
Mystery at the Black Cat. Leda A Wadsworth. LC 41-1590. Farrar & Rinehart, Inc.
Mystery at the Blue Villa. Melville Davisson Post. LC 20-1695. 1919. D. Appleton and Company.
Mystery at the Carrol Ranch: A Story of the Southwest. Carl Louis Kingsbury. LC 10-29131. David C. Cook Publishing Co.
Mystery at the Elms, and Condemned: By John and Irene Haig. John Haig & Irene Haig. LC 57-11968. (Milestone book). 1957. Comet Press Books.
Mystery at the JHC Ranch. Wilbur C Tuttle. LC 32-28184. 1932. Houghton Mifflin Company.
Mystery at the Rectory. Archibald E. Fielding. LC 37-2883. 1937. H. C. Kinsey & Company, Inc.
Mystery at the Summit of the Himalayas. Michel Garson. 1981. 8.95 (ISBN 0-8062-1625-5). Carlton.
Mystery at White Moccasins. Leda A. Wadsworth. LC 44-20854. 1944. Farrar & Rinehart, Inc.
Mystery Book: One Full-Length Novel and Four Novelettes. LC 40-2010. Farrar & Rinehart, Inc.
Mystery Cities of Central America. Thomas Gann. 1977. lib. bdg. 59.95 (ISBN 0-8490-2313-0). Gordon Pr.
Mystery Companion. 1st- Abraham Louis Furman. LC 44-165. Gold Label Books.
Mystery De Luxe. Rufus King. LC 27-3373. George H. Doran Company.
Mystery Evans. Beth Baker. LC 6-6885. 1890. De Wolfe, Fiske & Co.
Mystery Flowers. Grace Livingston Hill. LC 36-10527. 1936. J. B. Lippincott Company.
Mystery for Mary. Virginia Hanson. LC 42-132713. 1942. Published for the Crime Club by Doubleday, Doran and Company, Inc.
Mystery Girl. Carolyn Wells. LC 22-3498. 1922. J. B. Lippincott Company.
Mystery Gorge. Ellen J. Macleod. 1959. 1.50 o.p. (ISBN 0-87508-726-4). Chr Lit.
Mystery House. Kathleen Thompson Norris. Repr. lib. bdg. 16.30x (ISBN 0-89190-309-7). Am Repr-Rivercity Pr.
Mystery House. Special Ed. Kathleen Thompson Norris. 1939. Doubleday, Doran & Company, Inc.
Mystery in Green: By Aldin Vinton Pseud. Adelin Summer Briggs Linton. LC 38-1826. Phoenix Press.
Mystery in Hawaii. Marg Nelson. (gr. 7 up). 1969. 3.95 o.p. (ISBN 0-374-35115-5). FS&G.
Mystery in Hidden Hollow. Mary C. Jane. LC 72-101904. 1970. 7.95 o.p. (ISBN 0-397-31147-8, JBL-J). Har-Row.
Mystery in Palace Gardens. Charlotte Eliza Lawson Cowan Riddell. (Seaside library, v. 50, no. 1022). 1881. G. Munro.
Mystery in Red. Sidney Clark Williams. LC 25-6313. 1925. The Penn Publishing Company.
Mystery in the Channel. Freeman Wills Crofts. LC 65-4559. (Penguin crime). 1965. Penquin Books.
Mystery in the English Channel. Freeman Wills Crofts. LC 31-18073. 1931. Harper & Brothers.
Mystery in the Ritsmore. William Andrew Johnston. LC 20-10309. 1920. 1.75. Little, Brown, and Company.
Mystery in the Woodshed. Lucy Beatrice Malleson. LC 42-155482. 1942. Smith and Durrell.
Mystery in White. Joseph Jefferson Farjeon. LC 38-289777. 1938. The Bobbs-Merrill Company.
Mystery Island. Ethel M. Comins. 192p. (YA) 1973. 4.95 o.p. (Avalon). Bouregy.
Mystery Island. Edward Harry Hurst. LC 7-32318. 1907. L. C. Page and Company.
Mystery Keepers. Marion Fox. LC 19-10083. 1919. John Lane.
Mystery Lady. Robert William Chambers. LC 26-1827. Grosset & Dunlap.
Mystery Maker. Austin J Small. 1930. Pub. for the Crime Club, Inc., by Doubleday, Doran & Company, Inc.
Mystery Mile. Margery Allingham. LC 30-12293. 1930. Pub. for The Crime Club, Inc., by Doubleday, Doran & Company, Inc.
Mystery Mile. Margery Allingham. 1973. Penguin Books in Association with William Heinemann.
Mystery Mile see Margery Allingham Omnibus.
Mystery Mind. Arthur Benjamin Reeve & Grey, John W., Joint Author. LC 21-1894. Grosset & Dunlap.
Mystery Motive. John Creasey. LC 74-83456. (His Superintendent Folly mysteries). (MW suspense). 1974. 5.95 (ISBN 0-679-50486-9). McKay.
Mystery of a Butcher's Shop. Gladys Mitchell. LC 30-4241. 1930. L. MacVeagh, The Dial Press.
Mystery of a Hansom Cab. Fergus Hume. LC 75-32754. (Literature of Mystery and Detection). 1976. 18.00 (ISBN 0-405-07878-1). Arno Press.
Mystery of a Hansom Cab. Fergus Hume. LC 82-9461. 1982. 3.95 (ISBN 0-486-21956-9). Dover.
Mystery of a Hansom Cab. A Novel. Fergus Hume. (On cover: Seaside library. Pocket ed. no. 1075). G. Munro.

TITLE INDEX MYSTERY OF THE GOLDEN

Mystery of a Madstone: Or, The Commercial Traveler Detective. K. F Hill. (secret service series--no. 20). 1889. Street & Smith.
Mystery of a Pyramid. Frances A Hood. LC 15-21794. 1.00. The Author.
Mystery of a Turkish Bath. Eliza M. J. Humphreys. (On cover: Lovell's library, no. 1202). 1888. J. W. Lovell Company.
Mystery of a Turkish Bath. Eliza M. J. Humphreys. (On cover: Seaside library. Pocket ed., no. 1125). 1888. G. Munro.
Mystery of Allan Grale. Isabella Fyvie Mayo. (On cover: The seaside library. Pocket ed. no. 662). 1886. G. Munro.
Mystery of Allan Grale: A Novel. Isabella Fyvie Mayo. LC 7-18490. (Harper's Franklin square library. no. 518). 1886. Harper & Brothers.
Mystery of Allanwold. Elizabeth Van Loon. LC 8-30219. T. B. Peterson & Brothers.
Mystery of Aloha House. Lee Roddy. LC 80-66587. 1981. 2.50 (ISBN 0-89191-293-2). D.C. Cook Pub. Co.
Mystery of Angelina Frood. Richard Austin Freeman. LC 25-55405. 1925. 2.00. Dodd, Mead and Company.
Mystery of Arthur G. Pym. Edgar Allan Poe & Jules Verne. 3.95. Assoc Bk.
Mystery of Ashton Hall: By Benjamin Nitsua Pseud. Benjamin Fish Austin. LC 10-24178. 1.25. The Austin Publishing Co.
Mystery of Bonanza Trail. Francis Joseph Arkins. LC 11-549. The General Publishing Syndicate.
Mystery of Boshingham Castle. Edwin P. Gleason. 3.50 o.s.i. (ISBN 0-8181-0038-9). Pageant-Poseidon.
Mystery of Burnleigh Manor. Walter Livingston. LC 30-28178. 1930. The Mystery League, Inc.
Mystery of Castlegreen: A Louisiana Romance. Mary Kerr Duke. LC 13-414816. 1913. 1.50. Broadway Publishing Co.
Mystery of Cedar Bluff. Herbert Weeks. LC 28-28746. Colonial Publishing Co.
Mystery of Central Park. A Novel. Pink Elizabeth J. Cochrane. (On Cover: The "Nellie Bly" Series). 1889. G. W. Dillingham.
Mystery of Choice. Robert William Chambers. LC 73-94710. (Short story index reprint series). 1969. Books for Libraries Press.
Mystery of Choice. Robert William Chambers. LC 6-23334. 1897. D. Appleton and Company.
Mystery of Cloomber. Arthur Conan Doyle. LC 6-34239. R. F. Fenno & Company.
Mystery of Cloomber. Arthur Conan Doyle. (On cover: Seaside library. Pocket ed. no 2108). 1895. G. Munro's Sons.
Mystery of Cloomber. Arthur Conan Doyle. LC 20-15616. 1903. R. F. Fenno & Company.
Mystery of Cloomber. Arthur Conan Doyle. LC 80-65206. (Doyle, Arthur Conan, Sir, 1859-1930. Conan Doyle Centennial Ser.). (Illus.). 1980. 11.95 (ISBN 0-934468-41-9). Gaslight Publications.
Mystery of Cloomber. Arthur Conan Doyle. LC 80-65206. (Conan Doyle Centennial Ser.). (Illus.). 195p. 1980. 11.95 (ISBN 0-934468-41-9). Gaslight.
Mystery of Colde Fell: Or, Not Proven. Charlotte Mary Brame. (On cover: Lovell's library. no. 1013). J. W. Lovell Company.
Mystery of Colde Fell: Or, Not Proven. Charlotte Mary Brame. LC 44-11270. (On cover: Lovell's library, no. 1013). J. W. Lovell Company.
Mystery of Colde Fell: Or, Not Proven. Charlotte Mary Brame. LC 44-38171. (On cover: Seaside library. Pocket ed. No. 969). G. Munro.
Mystery of Colde Fell: Or, Not Proven. Charlotte Mary Brame. LC 3628. (Bertha M. Clay library, no. 5). 1900. Street & Smith.
Mystery of Collinwood. Marilyn Ross. (Orig.). 1968. pap. 0.50 o.p. (52-610). Paperback Lib.
Mystery of Daggett's Bank: A Detective Story. E. O. Tilburn. (On cover: Pinkerton detective series. Quarterly, no. 26). 1896. Laird & Lee.
Mystery of Dark Hollow. Emma Dorothy Eliza Nevitte Southworth. LC 12-38913. 1875. T. B. Peterson & Brothers.
Mystery of Dead Man's Heath. Joseph Jefferson Farjeon. LC 34-2565. 1934. Dodd, Mead & Company.
Mystery of Destiny. 1st Ed. Florence Axelrod. LC 52-6214. Pageant Press.
Mystery of East Mountain Temple. John Bechtel. LC 40-1228. Bica Press.
Mystery of Edwin Drood. Charles Dickens. Ed. by Margaret Cardwell. LC 72-192250. (His The Clarendon Dickens). (Illus.). 1972. 4.50 (ISBN 0-19-812439-2). Clarendon Press.
Mystery of Edwin Drood. Charles Dickens. LC 56-1865. (New Oxford illustrated Dickens). (Illus.). 1956. Oxford University Press.
Mystery of Edwin Drood. Charles Dickens. LC 6-35889. 1871. Hurd and Houghton.
Mystery of Edwin Drood. Charles Dickens. LC 6-35886. 1871. Hurd and Houghton.
Mystery of Edwin Drood. Charles Dickens. LC 6-26451. (On cover: Lovell's library, v. 5, no. 297). 1883. J. W. Lovell Company.
Mystery of Edwin Drood. Charles Dickens. LC 25-26576. (Half-title: The World's classics. cclxiii). 1924. H. Milford.
Mystery of Edwin Drood. Charles Dickens & Margaret Cardwell. LC 81-22344. (World's classics). (Illus.). 1982. 3.50 (ISBN 0-19-281593-8). Oxford University Press.
Mystery of Edwin Drood. Charles Dickens & Leon Garfield. LC 80-8850. (Illus.). 1980. 12.95 (ISBN 0-394-51918-3). Pantheon Books.
Mystery of Edwin Drood and Master Humphrey's Clock. people's duodecimo ed. Charles Dickens. LC 52-46783. (Peterson's uniform duodecimo edition of the complete works of Charles Dickens). T. B. Peterson.
Mystery of Edwin Drood: And Other Pieces. Charles Dickens. LC 34-37769. 1871. J. R. Osgood and Company.
Mystery of Edwin Drood: And, Some Uncollected Pieces. Charles Dickens. LC 12-19560. 1870. Fields, Osgood & Co.
Mystery of Edwin Drood. Complete. Charles Dickens & James, Thomas Power. LC 6-26417. 1873. T. P. James.
Mystery of Evangeline Fairfax. Earle Kunst. LC 10-792825. 1910. 1.00. The Metropolitan Press.
Mystery of Evelin Delorme: A Hypnotic Story. Albert Bigelow Paine. LC 75-46299. (Supernatural & Occult Fiction). (Series: Side pocket series.). 1976. 10.00 (ISBN 0-405-08159-6). Arno Press.
Mystery of Evelin Delorme: A Hypnotic Story. Albert Bigelow Paine. LC 7-357886. (On cover: Side pocket series). 1894. Arena Publishing Co.
Mystery of Fernridge Manor. Richard Bodwell, pseud. 5.95 o.p. Vantage.
Mystery of Fernridge Manor. Richard Bodwell, pseud. 1974. 5.95 (ISBN 0-533-00936-7). Vantage Press.
Mystery of Fifty-Two. Walter S Masterman. LC 31-22798. E. P. Dutton & Co., Inc.
Mystery of Five Finger Island. Jan Pierson. 1979. pap. 1.95 (ISBN 0-8423-4663-5). Tyndale.
Mystery of Flight 24. Gertrude Ethel Mallette. LC 47-311284. 1947. Doubleday.
Mystery of Fourways. Florence Alice Price James. LC 26-7521. 1900. R. F. Fenno and Company.
Mystery of Frances Farrington. Elizabeth L Banks. LC 9-7437. 1909.
Mystery of Fury Castle. Marilyn Ross. pap. 0.50 o.p. (52-452). Paperback Lib.
Mystery of Gabriel: By Michael Wood... Michael Wood. LC 17-29539. 1917. Longmans, Green and Co.
Mystery of God & Mankind. Cordelia S. Hutchinson. 1977. 6.95 o.p. (ISBN 0-8059-2399-3). Dorrance.
Mystery of Hartley House. Clifford Samuel Raymond. LC 18-18527. 1.50. George H. Doran Company.
Mystery of Hartley House. Clifford Samuel Raymond. LC 19-3596. George H. Doran Company.
Mystery of Hornby Hall. Anna Theresa Sadlier. 1906. Benziger Brothers.
Mystery of Hotel Brichet. A Novel. Eugene Vachette. (On cover: The choice series, no. 116). 1894. R. Bonner's Sons.
Mystery of Hunting's End... Mignon Good Eberhart. LC 30-27061. 1930. Pub. for the Crime Club, Inc., by Doubleday, Doran & Company, Inc.
Mystery of Jack London. Georgia Bamford. 1975. 12.50 o.p. (0-911156-14-6). Porter.
Mystery of Jessy Page, and Other Tales. Ellen Price Henry Wood Wood. (On cover: Seaside library. Pocket ed. no. 514). 1885. G. Munro.
Mystery of Khufu's Tomb. Talbot Mundy. LC 35-5368. (Tired business man's library of adventure, detective, and mystery novels). 1935. D. Appleton-Century Company, Incorporated.
Mystery of King Arthur. Elizabeth Jenkins. LC 74-29396. (Illus.). 240p. 1975. 20.00 o.p. (ISBN 0-698-10676-8, Coward). Putnam Pub Group.
Mystery of King Cobra. Dwight Marfield. LC 33-202833. E. P. Dutton & Co., Inc.
Mystery of Kun-Ja-Muck Cave. George Franklin Tibbitts. LC 24-4587. Brieger Press, Inc.
Mystery of Kun-Ja-Muck Cave: By George F. Tibbitts; a Strange Mystery Trailing Through the Beautiful Mountain and Lake Country of the Adirondacks, Frontispeice. George Franklin Tibbitts. LC 29-349079. The Cornwall Press, Inc.
Mystery of Lookout Mountain. Sumpter Lee Flowers. LC 35-3425. The Christopher Publishing House.
Mystery of Louise Pollard. Weldon Webster. LC 8-36741. 1893. Longwell & Cummings.
Mystery of Lucien Delorme. Edmond Gautier Teramond & Safford, Mary Joanna, Tr. LC 15-2849. 1915. D. Appleton and Company.
Mystery of Lynne Court. Joseph Smith Fletcher. LC 23-14272. 1923. The Norman, Remington Company.
Mystery of M. Felix. Benjamin Leopold Farjeon. LC 6-38630. (On cover: Lovell's international series. no. 96). 1890. J. W. Lovell Company.
Mystery of Maata. Patrick Anthony Lawlor. 40p. 1980. Repr. of 1946 ed. lib. bdg. 15.00 (ISBN 0-8492-1624-9). R West.
Mystery of Maata: A Katherine Mansfield Novel. Patrick Anthony Lawlor. LC 73-541. (Illus.). 1973. 10.00. Folcroft Library Editions.
Mystery of Madeline Le Blanc. Max Ehrmann. The Co-Operative Publishing Company.
Mystery of Mar Saba. James Hogg Hunter. LC 40-296499. 1940. Evangelical Publishers.
Mystery of Marie Roget. raven ed. Edgar Allan Poe. LC 3-385. R. F. Fenno & Company.
Mystery of Mary. Grace Livingston Hill. LC 12-5557. 1912. J. B. Lippincott Company.
Mystery of Metropolisville. Edward Eggleston. LC 72-84565. (Illus.). 1974. (lib. ed.) 12.95 (ISBN 0-403-02977-5). Scholarly Press.
Mystery of Metropolisville. Edward Eggleston. LC 70-104446. (Illus.). 1970. Literature House.
Mystery of Metropolisville. Edward Eggleston. LC 6-37563. O. Judd and Company.
Mystery of Mirbridge: A Novel. James Payn. (On cover: Harper's Franklin square library, no. 623). 1888. Harper & Brothers.
Mystery of Miriam. James Wesley Johnston. LC 4-10851. 1904. H. B. Turner & Co.
Mystery of Miss Motte. Caroline Atwater Mason. LC 9-11537. 1909. L. C. Page & Company.
Mystery of Mr. Cross. Clifton Robbins. LC 33-1843. 1933. D. Appleton & Company.
Mystery of Monastery Farm. Henry Rodley Naylor. LC 8-20347. Easton & Mains.
Mystery of Mortimer Strange: Or, A Moment's Error. Arthur Williams Marchmont. LC 8-974. Rand, McNally & Company.
Mystery of Mortimore Strange. Arthur Williams Marchmont. 1976. lib. bdg. 16.70x (ISBN 0-89968-068-2). Lightyear.
Mystery of Murray Davenport: A Story of New York at the Present Day. Robert Neilson Stephens. 1903. L. C. Page & Company.
Mystery of Mysteries; Why Did God Create? By Wheeler Boggess... Wheeler Boggess. LC 42-183576. 1942. Zondervan Publishing House.
Mystery of New Orleans. facsimile ed. William Henry Holcombe. LC 78-39090. (Black Heritage Library Collection). Repr. of 1890 ed. 18.25 (ISBN 0-8369-9028-5). Ayer Co.
Mystery of New Orleans a Novel. William Henry Holcombe. LC 7-6119. (On cover: American novels). 1892. J. B. Lippincott Company.
Mystery of New Orleans: Solved by New Methods. William Henry Holcombe. LC 78-39090. (Black Heritage Library Collection). 1972. (ISBN 0-8369-9028-5). Books for Libraries Press.
Mystery of New Orleans: Solved by New Methods a Novel. William Henry Holcombe. 1890. J. B. Lippincott Company.
Mystery of No. 13. Helen Buckingham Mathers Reeves. LC 7-30676. (On cover: Lovell's Westminster series. no. 26). 1890. United States Book Company.
Mystery of Norman's Court. Charles De Balzac Rideaux. LC 24-6731. Small, Maynard & Company.
Mystery of Number 47. Joseph Storer Clouston. LC 11-27106. 1911. 1.00. Moffat, Yard and Company.
Mystery of Number 47. Joseph Storer Clouston. LC 12-2927. 1912. 1.10. Moffat, Yard and Company.
Mystery of Orcival. Emile Gaboriau. (On cover: Lovell's library, v. 4, no. 155). 1883. J. W. Lovell Company.
Mystery of Orcival: Translated from the French of Emile Gaboriau. Emile Gaboriau. LC 2822. 1900. C. Scribner's Sons.
Mystery of Park View. Kenneth Anderson. LC 41-1122. Zondervan Publishing House.
Mystery of Paul Chadwick: A Bachelor's Story. John W Postgate. (On cover: Pinkerton detective series, no. 27). Laird & Lee.
Mystery of Rachel. Venus G Booth. LC 20-23023. The Stratford Company.
Mystery of Redmarsh Farm. Archibald Marshall. LC 25-26437. 1925. Dodd, Mead and Company.
Mystery of Rich Mountain. Ann Burkhart. 1977. 4.95 o.p. (ISBN 0-533-02719-5). Vantage.
Mystery of Rockdale: A Tale of the Eastern Shore, Maryland. Theodore W Currier. LC 30-24944. The Millersville Press.
Mystery of Silver Spring Ranch. Ada Carter Dart. LC 32-35783. 1932. The Caxton Printers Ltd.
Mystery of Swordfish Reef. Arthur William Upfield. LC 43-16089. 1943. Pub. for the Crime Club by Doubleday, Doran and Company, Inc.
Mystery of the Anti. K. H Scheer. (Perry Rhoden#88). 1976. (pbk.) 1.25. Ace Books.
Mystery of the Ashes. Robert McNair Wilson. LC 27-3418. 1927. J. B. Lippincott Company.
Mystery of the Baroque Pearl. Mary J. Goodwin. LC 78-61637. 1978. pap. 3.95 (ISBN 0-932632-00-9). MJG Co.
Mystery of the Barranca. Herman Whitaker. LC 13-23789. 1913. Harper & Brothers.
Mystery of the Barren Lands. Ridgwell Cullum. LC 28-20462. 1928. J. B. Lippincott Company.
Mystery of the Black Book. Ruth Russell. pap. 1.00 o.p. Gospel Pub.
Mystery of the Black Diamonds. Phyllis A Whitney. LC 53-8355. (young adult mystery). 1974. (pbk.) 0.95. New American Library.
Mystery of the Blue Inns: By Brigadier Edgar Anstey... Edgar Anstey. LC 37-79942. Longmans, Green and Co.
Mystery of the Blue Train. Agatha Miller Christie. LC 28-17812. 1928. Dodd, Mead and Company.
Mystery of the Boule Cabinet. Burton Egbert Stevenson. LC 75-32786. (Literature of Mystery and Detection). 1976. 21.00 (ISBN 0-405-07901-X). Arno Press.
Mystery of the Boule Cabinet: A Detective Story. Burton Egbert Stevenson. LC 12-686441. 1912. 1.30. Dodd, Mead & Company.
Mystery of the Boule Cabinet: A Detective Story. Burton Egbert Stevenson. LC 29-44192. 1929. Dodd, Mead & Company.
Mystery of the Buried Crosses. Hamlin Garland. Ed. by Donald Pizer. LC 77-96610. (American Authors Ser). 1970. lib. bdg. 18.95 o.s.i. (ISBN 0-512-00273-8). Garrett Pr.
Mystery of the Buried Crosses see Collected Works.
Mystery of the Campagna: And A Shadow on a Wave. Ann Crawford Von Rabe. LC 8-37852. ("unknown" library. v. 3). Cassell Publishing Company.
Mystery of the Cape Cod Players: An Asey Mayo Mystery. Phoebe Atwood Taylor. LC 33-19969. W. W. Norton & Company, Inc.
Mystery of the Cape Cod Players: An Asey Mayo Mystery. Phoebe Atwood Taylor. LC 80-10929. 1980. 9.95 (ISBN 0-89340-258-3). J. Curley.
Mystery of the Cape Cod Tavern. Phoebe Atwood Taylor. (Seagull Lib. of Mystery & Suspense Ser). (YA) 1968. 4.95 o.p. (ISBN 0-393-08556-2). Norton.
Mystery of the Cape Cod Tavern: An Asey Mayo Mystery by Phoebe Atwood Taylor. Phoebe Atwood Taylor. LC 34-4192. bds., 4.95. Norton.
Mystery of the Closed Car. Kathleen Sproul. LC 35-3119. 1935. E. P. Dutton & Co., Inc.
Mystery of the Colored Circles. Lloyd W. Badgett. 4.95 o.p. Vantage.
Mystery of the Creeping Man. Frances Shelley Wees. LC 31-29196. Macrae Smith Company.
Mystery of the Dead Police... Philip MacDonald. LC 33-196936. 1933. Pub. for the Crime Club, Inc., by Doubleday, Doran & Company, Inc.
Mystery of the Downs. John Reay Watson & Arthur John Rees. LC 18-2908. 1918. John Lane Company.
Mystery of the East Wind. Dwight Marfield. LC 30-7964. E. P. Dutton & Co., Inc.
Mystery of the Fast Mail. Byron D Adsit. LC 1-22402. (On cover: Lovell's detective series. no. 2). 1890. J.W. Lovell Co.
Mystery of the Fast Mail. Byron D Adsit. LC 5186. (On cover: Magnet detective library. no. 149). 1900. Street & Smith.
Mystery of the Fiddling Cracksman. Harry Stephen Keeler. LC 34-4068. E. P. Dutton & Co., Inc.
Mystery of the Flaming Hut. Herbert Best. LC 32-12015. 1932. Harper & Brothers.
Mystery of the Fog Man. Carol J. Farley, pseud. (Illus.). 132p. 1974. pap. 1.95 (ISBN 0-380-00102-0, 61663, Camelot). Avon.
Mystery of the Folded Paper. Hulbert Footner. LC 30-25155. Harper & Brothers.
Mystery of the Four Fingers. Fred Merrick White. LC 8-6665. 1908. W. J. Watt & Company.
Mystery of the French Milliner. Basil Home Thomson. LC 37-11247. 1937. Pub. for the Crime Club, Inc., by Doubleday, Doran & Co., Inc.
Mystery of the Frightened Lady... Edgar Wallace. LC 33-293919. 1933. Pub. for the Crime Club, Inc., by Doubleday, Doran & Company, Inc.
Mystery of the Girl in Blue. Frank Perry. LC 38-5363. Dodge Publishing Company.
Mystery of the Glass Bullet. Bertram Atkey. LC 31-231985. 1931. D. Appleton and Company.
Mystery of the Golconda. William Newell Vaile. LC 25-17618. 1925. Doubleday, Page & Company.
Mystery of the Gold Box, a Clubfoot Story. Valentine Williams. LC 32-30017. 1932. Houghton Mifflin Company.
Mystery of the Golden Horn. Phyllis A Whitney. LC 62-13874. (Young adult mystery). 1974. (pbk.) 0.95. New American Library.
Mystery of the Golden Key. Ed. by M. A. Jones. 1951. pap. 0.39 o.p. Moody.

Mystery of the Golden Wings. Rosa Lambert & Lambert, Dudley. LC 35-10748. 1935. T. Nelson and Sons, Ltd.
Mystery of the Golden Wings. Rosa Lambert & Lambert, Dudley. LC 36-19979. 1936. The Macaulay Company.
Mystery of the Green Heart. Max Pemberton. LC 10-20294. 1910. 1.50. Dodd, Mead and Company.
Mystery of the Green Quartette. Mabel Knowles Waldreaon & D'Ekna, Virginia De Strale, Joint Author. LC 42-188524. 1942. Printed by the Citizen-News Co.
Mystery of the Gulls. Phyllis A Whitney. (Young adult mystery). 1974. (pbk.) 0.95. New American Library.
Mystery of the Hasty Arrow. Anna Katharine Green Rohlfs. LC 17-29867. 1917. Dodd, Mead and Company.
Mystery of the Haunted Wing: And Other Stories. Maurice O'Regan Fitzgerald. LC 28-28678. 1928. The Stratford Company.
Mystery of the Hidden Hand. Phyllis A. Whitney. 1980. pap. 1.50 (ISBN 0-451-09028-4, W9028, Sig). NAL.
Mystery of the Hidden Room. Marion Harvey. LC 22-19472. E. J. Clode.
Mystery of the Holly-Tree. Charlotte Mary Brame. LC 44-11263. (On cover: Lovell's library, no. 1041). J. W. Lovell Company.
Mystery of the Holy Ghost. C. Johnson. 4.50 o.p. (ISBN 0-8062-0971-2). Carlton.
Mystery of the Hope Diamond: As Set Down. H. L Gates & Yohe, May, 1868- LC 21-6806. 1921. International Copyright Bureau.
Mystery of the Horse with the Wrong Harness. Orman L. Miller. 4.50 o.p. Vantage.
Mystery of the House of Commons. Fielding Hope. LC 30-12523. 1930. L. MacVeagh, The Dial Press.
Mystery of the Hushing Pool. Joseph Smith Fletcher. LC 40-1425. 1938. Hillman--Curl, Inc.
Mystery of the Inn by the Shore. A Novel. Florence Alice Price James. LC 7-7413. R. Bonner's Sons.
Mystery of the King Turtle. Alan Gregg. LC 43-15965. 1943. Doubleday, Doran and Co., Inc.
Mystery of the Kingdom. A. K. Mozumdar. 1.50 o.p. (ISBN 0-87516-065-4). De Vorss.
Mystery of the Kneeling Dolls. Lawrence J. Joos. 2.50 o.p. Carlton.
Mystery of The Locks. Edgar Watson Howe. LC 7-7124. 1885. J. R. Osgood and Company.
Mystery of the Locks see Collected Works.
Mystery of the Lodge. Mary Dwinell Chellis. LC 6-23406. 1873. D. Lothrop & Co.
Mystery of the Lost Dauphin: Louis Xvii. Pardo Bazan, Emilia. Tr. by Seeger, Annabel Hord. LC 6-18835. 1906. Funk & Wagnalls Company.
Mystery of the Mad Millionairess. Edward Fenton. (Partridge Family #13). 1972. 0.60. Curtis Books.
Mystery of the Marbletons: A Romance of Reality. Marie Mackin. LC 1-30120. The Abbey Press.
Mystery of the Marsh. Paul Hutchens. LC 52-1351. 1952. Van Kampen Press.
Mystery of the Mind. Bettie A. Fauth. 3.75 o.p. Vantage.
Mystery of the Miniature. Richard Kemble Edwards. LC 9-927. 1908. The C. M. Clark Publishing Company.
Mystery of the Monkey Gland Cocktail. Roger d'Este Burford. LC 32-16240. 1932. Putnam.
Mystery of the Montauk Mills. Erwin L Coolidge. LC 31-35336. (Hub ten cent library, v. 1, no. 3). Atlantic News Company.
Mystery of the Old Mill. Eliza Ann Webb. LC 24-31910. 1924. The Morgantown Printing and Binding Co.
Mystery of the "Opal". Rupert Sargent Holland. LC 24-239184. G. W. Jacobs & Company.
Mystery of the Open Window: A Detective Story. Lucy Beatrice Malleson. LC 30-1966. 1930. Dodd, Mead & Co.
Mystery of the Painted Nude. William Gore. LC 33-6974. 1938. Pub. for the Crime Club, Inc., by Doubleday, Doran & Co., Inc.
Mystery of the Patrician Club. Albert Dresden Vandam. LC 8-30230. 1894. J. B. Lippincott Company.
Mystery of the Phantom Billionaire: A Novel. Marjel Jean De Lauer. LC 72-83301. 1972. 6.95 (ISBN 0-87949-005-5). Ashley Books.
Mystery of the Promise. Ada Dawson. 3.95 o.p. Vantage.
Mystery of the Rabbit's Paw. Selwyn Jepson. LC 32-336902. 1932. Harper & Brothers.
Mystery of the Ravenspurs: A Romance and Detective Story of Thibet and England. Fred Merrick White. LC 11-24110. J. S. Ogilvie Publishing Company.
Mystery of the Red Flame. George Barton. LC 18-425828. 1918. The Page Company.
Mystery of the Red Suitcase: A Lula Day Series. Lula Madelaine Day. LC 46-724143. 1946. Pub. for Hip Books, Incorporated, Alexandria, Va., Under Arrangements with Owl Press, Inc.
Mystery of the Red Triangle. Wilbur C. Tuttle. LC 42-110452. 1942. Houghton Mifflin Company.
Mystery of the Red Triangle... Wilbur C Tuttle. LC 44-51242. (New Avon library. 53). 1944.
Mystery of the Sandal-Wood Box: Being an Adventure of Harlan Nims, the Amateur American Detective. Melville Clemens Barnard. LC 8-11708. 1907. Mayhew Publishing Co.
Mystery of the Sea; a Novel. Bram Stoker. LC 2-8118. 1902. Doubleday, Page & Co.
Mystery of the Second Shot. Rufus Hamilton Gillmore. 1912. 1.25. D. Appleton and Company.
Mystery of the Seven Murals. Enid Johnson & Johnson, Margaret. LC 40-33364. Random House.
Mystery of the Shadow. authorized ed., with sixteen illustrations by a. t. smith. ed. Fergus Hume. LC 6-31659. 1906. B. W. Dodge and Company.
Mystery of the Silver Buckle. Bob Wright. (Tom & Ricky Mystery Ser.: No. 2). (Illus.). 48p. 1983. pap. 2.00 (ISBN 0-87879-340-2). Acad Therapy.
Mystery of the Silver Cord. George Snelling. 80p. 1981. pap. 2.95 (ISBN 0-934142-00-9). Vancento Pub.
Mystery of the Silver Dagger. Randall Parrish. LC 20-9714. 1.75. George H. Doran Company.
Mystery of the Singing Walls. William Averill Stowell. LC 25-7944. 1925. D. Appleton and Company.
Mystery of the Six Clues. Vernon Linwood Howard. LC 52-11293. 1952. Van Kampen Press.
Mystery of the Smoking Gun. Carroll John Daly. LC 36-405. 1936. Frederick A. Stokes Company.
Mystery of the Stolen Hats: Another Story of Superintendent Stevens and Inspector Pierre Allain. Graham Montague Jeffries. LC 39-8021. J. B. Lippincott Company.
Mystery of the Strange Traveler. Phyllis A Whitney. LC 67-16532. (young adult mystery). 1974. (pbk) 0.95. New American Library.
Mystery of the Summer-House. Horace Hutchinson. LC 19-9474. 1.50. George H. Doran Company.
Mystery of the Sycamore. Carolyn Wells. LC 21-6265. 1921. J. B. Lippincott Company.
Mystery of the Tarn: A Fleming Stone Detective Novel. Carolyn Wells. LC 37-738. J. B. Lippincott Company.
Mystery of the Third Mine. Jacket Designed by Kenneth Fagg. Robert W Lowndes. LC 52-12901. (Science fiction novel). 1953. Winston.
Mystery of the Third Parrot... Marvin Dana. LC 24-16565. 1924. 1.90. A. C. McClurg & Co.
Mystery of the Thirteenth Floor. Lee Thayer, pseud. LC 19-3420. 1919. The Century Co.
Mystery of the Tolling Bell. Ellen J. Macleod. 1960. 1.50 o.p. (ISBN 0-87508-728-0). Chr Lit.
Mystery of the Twin Rubies. Armstrong Livingston. LC 23-297452. 1922. Moffat, Yard and Company.
Mystery of the Twisted Man. Lydia P De Bechevet. LC 27-27456. 1927. F. H. Hitchcock.
Mystery of the Vanished Victim. 2nd ed. Ellery Queen, Jr., pseud. (Griffon Ser). 1969. pap. 0.50 o.p. (5674, Golden Pr). Western Pub.
Mystery of the Wax Museum. Ed. & intro. by Richard Koszarski. LC 78-53296. (Wisconsin-Warner Bros. Screenplay Ser.). (Illus.). 164p. 1979. 17.50 (ISBN 0-299-07670-9); pap. 6.95t (ISBN 0-299-07674-1). U of Wis Pr.
Mystery of the Witch, Who Wouldn't. Kin Platt. LC 70-91658. 1969. Chilton Book Co.
Mystery of the Woman in Red: A Mystery Novel. Lucy Beatrice Malleson. LC 44-8912. (Handi-book mysteries). 1944. Quinn Publishing Co., Inc.
Mystery of the Woods: And The Man Who Missed It. William Henry Harrison Murray. LC 7-32491. De Wolfe, Fiske & Co.
Mystery of the Yellow Room. Gaston Leroux. LC 75-32762. (Literature of Mystery and Detection). 1976. 18.00 (ISBN 0-405-07883-8). Arno Press.
Mystery of the Yellow Room: Extraordinary Adventures of Joseph Rouletabille, Reporter. Leroux Gaston. LC 75-32762. (Literature of Mystery & Detection Ser.). 1976. Repr. of 1908 ed. 22.00x (ISBN 0-405-07883-8). Ayer Co.
Mystery of the Yellow Room: Extraordinary Adventures of Joseph Rouletabille, Reporter. Gaston Leroux. LC 76-46041. 1977. 3.00 (ISBN 0-486-23460-6). Dover Publications.
Mystery of the Yellow Room: Extraordinary Adventures of Joseph Rouletabille, Reporter. Gaston Leroux. LC 8-19097. 1908. Brentano's.
Mystery of the Yellow Room: Le Mystere De la Chambre Jaune) Extraordinary Adventures of Joseph Rouletabille, Reporter. Gaston Leroux. LC 28-24484. (S. S. Van Dine detective library). 1928. C. Scribner's Sons.
Mystery of the 7 Bad Men. Henry Leyford Gates. LC 33-10976. 1933. The Macaulay Company.
Mystery of Tinker's Well. Jean A. Davis. 1968. 1.00 o.p. (ISBN 0-87508-727-2). Chr Lit.
Mystery of Tumbling Reef. Beatrice Ethel Grimshaw. LC 32-19270. 1932. Houghton Mifflin Company.
Mystery of Tumult Rock. Louise Platt Hauck. LC 21-17274. Burton Publishing Company.
Mystery of Tunnel 51. Alexander Wilson. LC 28-7501. 1928. Longmans, Green, and Co., Ltd.
Mystery of Uncle Bollard. Henry De Vere Stacpoole. LC 28-14548. 1928. Pub. for The Crime Club, Inc., by Doubleday, Doran & Company, Inc.
Mystery of Vaucluse... James Harold Wallis. LC 33-2861. E. P. Dutton & Co., Inc.
Mystery of Villa Sineste. Walter Livingston. LC 31-227966. 1931. The Mystery League, Inc.
Mystery of Walderstein: A Story from the Life of Two Prussian Officers. Mary Elizabeth Jordan Lamb. LC 42-27296. Donohue, Henneberry & Co.
Mystery of Witch-Face Mountain: And Other Stories. Mary Noailles Murfree. LC 69-11913. (American short story series, v. 72). 1969. Garrett Press.
Mystery of Witch-Face Mountain: And Other Stories. Mary Noailles Murfree. LC 72-8197. (American short story series, v. 72). 1972. (ISBN 0-8422-8099-5). MSS Information Corp.
Mystery of Witch-Face Mountain: And Other Stories. Mary Noailles Murfree. LC 7-31836. 1895. Houghton, Mifflin and Company.
Mystery of Witch-Face Mountain & Other Stories. Mary Noailles Murfree. 1972. Repr. of 1895 ed. lib. bdg. 18.00 (ISBN 0-8422-8099-5). Irvington.
Mystery of Witch-Face Mountain & Other Stories. Mary Noailles Murfree. 1895. 19.00 o.p. (ISBN 0-403-04187-2). Somerset Pub.
Mystery of Witch-Face Mountain & Other Stories. Mary Noailles Murfree. Ed. by Clarence Gohdes. LC 69-11913. (American Short Story Ser., Vol. 72). (Illus.). 1969. Repr. of 1895 ed. lib. bdg. 14.50 o.s.i. (ISBN 0-512-00526-5). Garrett Pr.
Mystery of 31, New Inn. Richard Austin Freeman. LC 13-8075. 1913. 1.20. The John C. Winston Company.
Mystery of 31, New Inn. Richard Austin Freeman. LC 30-17097. 1930. Dodd, Mead & Co.
Mystery on the Isle of Skye. Phyllis A Whitney. LC 54-11627. (Young adult mystery). 1974. (pbk.) 0.95. New American Library.
Mystery on the Queen Mary. Graham Montague Jeffries. LC 38-2494. J. B. Lippincott Company.
Mystery: Or, Forty Years Ago. A Novel... Thomas Gaspey. 1820. E. Duyckinck Etc.
Mystery, or Platonic Love. George S Crosby. LC 6-31966. 1875. J. B. Lippincott & Co.
Mystery Queen. Fergus Hume. LC 12-5157. G. W. Dillingham Company.
Mystery Raider. Leslie Erenwein. 1975. pap. 0.95 o.p. (LB297NK, Leisure Bks). Nordon Pubns.
Mystery Raider. Lessie Charles Ernenwein. 1975. (pbk.) 0.95. Leisure Books.
Mystery Ranch. Max Brand. LC 30-193787. 1930. Dodd, Mead & Company.
Mystery Ranch. Arthur Chapman. LC 21-19577. 1921. Houghton Mifflin Company.
Mystery Ranch. Frederick Faust. LC 30-1937. 1930. Dodd, Mead & Company.
Mystery Ranch. Frederick Faust. 1976. (pbk.) 1.25. Warner Books.
Mystery Range. Charles Alden Seltzer. LC 76-39972. 1976. 6.95 (ISBN 0-88411-114-8). Aeonian Press.
Mystery Range. Charles Alden Seltzer. LC 28-148267. 1928. Doubleday, Doran & Company, Inc.
Mystery Reader: Stories of Detection, Adventure, and Horror. Nancy Ellen Talburt & Lyna Lee Montgomery. LC 74-14073. (Scribner student paperbacks; SSP 36). 1975. 4.75 (ISBN 0-684-14104-3). Scribner.
Mystery Reef. Harold Bindloss. LC 28-20415. 1928. Fredrick A. Stokes Company.
Mystery Road. Edward Phillips Oppenheim. LC 23-9855. 1923. Little, Brown, and Company.
Mystery Stories. Stanley Ellin. LC 56-6674. (Inner sanctum mystery). 1956. Simon and Schuster.
Mystery Stories. Ed. by Wells, Carolyn. LC 31-26749. The John Day Company.C.
Mystery Tour. James Douglas Rutherford McConnell. LC 76-24562. (Illus.). 1976. 6.95 (ISBN 0-8027-5356-6). Walker.
Mystery Walk. Robert R. McCammon. LC 82-15419. 396p. 1983. 13.45 (ISBN 0-03-061832-0). HR&W.
Mystery Week-End. Percival Wilde. LC 38-5284. Harcourt, Brace and Company.
Mystery Woman. John Ulrich Giesy & Smith, Junius B. LC 90-649. Whitman Publishing Co.C.
Mystery Woman. John Ulrich Giesy & Smith, Junius B. LC 30-849. Whitman Publishing Co.
Mystery Woman. Alice MacGowan & Newberry, Perry, 1870- Joint Author. LC 24-2896. 1924. Frederick A. Stokes Company.
Mystic Adventures of Roxie Stoner. Berry Morgan. LC 74-6213. 1974. 5.95 (ISBN 0-395-19424-5). Houghton Mifflin.
Mystic Adventures of Roxie Stoner. Berry Morgan. LC 74-18285. 1974. (ISBN 0-8161-6253-0). G. K. Hall.
Mystic Island. Renate Chapman. (YA) 1980. 6.50 (Avalon). Bouregy.
Mystic Masseur. Vidiadhar Surajprasad Naipaul. LC 59-92492. 1959. Vanguard Press.
Mystic Orange Blossom. Joseph S Schultz. LC 27-17418. 1927. Hipple Printing Co.
Mystic 'phone: Or, Winning a Millionaire. Louise Von Haffner. LC 7-2761. 1907.
Mystic Rose. Patricia Gallagher. 1977. pap. 3.50 (ISBN 0-380-82560-0, 79467). Avon.
Mystic Spell: A Metaphysical Romance. Ada White Taylor. LC 23-7393. The Austin Publishing Company.
Mystic Spring, and Other Tales of Western Life. new and rev. ed. David Williams Higgins. LC 8-37708. Broadway Publishing Co.
Mystical Union. Don Robertson. LC 78-2895. 8.95 (ISBN 0-399-12237-0). Putnam.
Mystics: A Novel. Katherine Cecil Thurston. LC 7-14253. 1907. Harper & Brothers.
Mystic's Romance. Marshall Loepke. 1970. 3.50 o.p. Carlton.
Mystified Magistrate & Other Stories. Donatien Alphonse Francois Sade. Tr. by Richard Seaver from Fr. 1971. pap. 1.25 o.p. (B279Z, BC). Grove.
Myth Conceptions. Robert L. Asprin & Polly Freas. LC 79-9216. (Starblaze editions). 1980. 4.95 (ISBN 0-915442-94-9). Donning.
Myth Directions. Robert Aspin. Ed. by Hank Stine. LC 82-12776. (Myth Trilogy Ser.: Vol. 3). (Illus.). 176p. (Orig.). 1982. pap. 5.95 (ISBN 0-89865-250-2, Starblaze). Donning Co.
Myth Maker: A Novel. Frank London Brown. LC 76-103165. 1969. 5.00. Path Press.
Myth of the Bagre. Jack Goody. (Oxford Library of African Literature). 410p. 1972. 34.50x o.p. (ISBN 0-19-815134-9). Oxford U Pr.
Myth or Legend. Glyn Edmund Daniel. (Illus.). 1968. pap. 1.85 o.p. (ISBN 0-399-50167-3, 148, Cap). Putnam.
Mythomania. Paul J. Payack. Ed. by Daniel M. Stokes. (Illus.). 1976. pap. 1.50. Chthon Pr.
Myths & Folk Tales of Ireland. Jeremiah Curtin. LC 69-18206. 256p. 1975. pap. 4.00 (ISBN 0-486-22430-9). Dover.
Myths & Legends of Australia. A. W. Reed. LC 72-779. (Illus.). 1973. 7.50 (ISBN 0-8008-5463-2). Taplinger.
Myths & Legends of Our New Possessions & Protectorate. Charles M. Skinner. LC 73-140399. 1971. Repr. of 1900 ed. 15.00 o.p. (ISBN 0-8103-3634-0). Gale.
Myths & Legends of the Swahili. Jan Knappert. (African Writers Ser). 1970. pap. text ed. 2.25x o.p. (ISBN 0-435-90375-6). Humanities.
Myths of the Red Children. Gilbert Livingstone Wilson. LC 7-37546. Ginn & Company.
Myths of the World. Padraic Colum. (Illus.). 1959. pap. 3.95 o.p. (ISBN 0-448-00050-4, UL). G&D.

N

N Is for Naked. (Illus.). 5.00 o.p. Elysium.
N or M? Agatha Miller Christie. (Dell Book). 1977. 1.50 (ISBN 0-440-16254-8). Dell Pub. Co.
N or M; see Death in the Clouds.
N or M? The New Mystery. Agatha Miller Christie. LC 41-10769. 1941. Dodd, Mead & Company.
N-Three Conspiracy. Nick Carter. (Nick Carter Ser.). (O.s.i.). 208p. (Orig.). 1974. pap. 1.25 o.s.i. (AQ1547, Award). Univ Pub & Dist.
N. Y. Is All Ours! And Other Stories. Charles Tekeyan. LC 56-4340. 1956. Beekman.
N. Y., N. Y. A Novel. Drawings by Georg T. Hartmann. William Charles Oursler. LC 54-6535. 1954. Coward-McCann.
Naaman the Leper: And Princess Sarah, the Captive Maid. M I Cash. LC 37. 1899. The Editor Publishing Co.
Naaman the Syrian. A. B Mackay. LC 7-16428. (On cover: The colportage library, v. 3, no. 58). The Bible Institute Colportage Association.
Nabab. Alphonse Daudet. 1966. 4.95 o.p. French & Eur.
Nabala: Na-Ba-la. Jacquelin Ambler Caskie. LC 22-20737. 1922. J. P. Bell Company, Inc.

Nabisco Warehouse. J. D. Whitney. (Pap ed. 5.00 o.p.). 1971. 10.00 (Pub. by Elizabeth Pr). SBD.

Nabob. Alphonse Daudet. Tr. by Ives, George Burnham. Matthews, Brander. LC 16-7536. (Half-title: The works of Alphonse Daudet. Limited ed. vol. i. ii). 1898. Little, Brown, and Company.

Nabob. Alphonse Daudet & W Blaydes. LC 76-25867. (Series: The French Classical Romances; V. 18.). 1976. 16.50. H. Fertig.

Nabob: A Story of Parisian Life and Manners. Alphonse Daudet. Tr. by Clevequin, E. (On cover: Seaside library. Pocket ed. no. 574). G. Munro.

Nabob. From the French of Alphonse Daudet... author's ed. Alphonse Daudet. Tr. by Hooper, Lucy Hamilton. (cobweb series of choice fiction). 1878. Estes and Lauriat.

Nabob: From the French of Alphonse Daudet... author's ed. Alphonse Daudet. Tr. by Hooper, Lucy Hamilton. LC 6-33045. (On cover: Lovell's library, v. 12, no. 645). J. W. Lovell Company.

Nabokov's Dozen. facs. ed. Vladimir Vladimirovich Nabokov. LC 75-91138. (Short Story Index Reprint Ser). 1958. 14.50 (ISBN 0-8369-3078-9). Ayer Co.

Nabokov's Dozen. Vladimir Vladimirovich Nabokov. 1973. pap. 2.95 (ISBN 0-380-01352-5, 58370, Bard). Avon.

Nabokov's Dozen: A Collection of Thirteen Stories. Vladimir Vladimirovich Nabokov. LC 75-91138. (Short story index reprint series). 1969. Books for Libraries Press.

Nabokov's Dozen: A Collection of Thirteen Stories. 1st Ed. Vladimir Vladimirovich Nabokov. LC 58-10032. 1958. Doubleday.

Nabokov's Novels in English. Lucy Maddox & Vladimir Vladimirovich Nabokov. LC 82-4893. 15.00 (ISBN 0-8203-0626-6). University of Georgia Press.

Nacha Regules. Manuel Galvez. LC 75-43912. 1976. H. Fertig.

Nacha Regules. Manuel Galvez. LC 75-43912. 1977. 37.00. H. Fertig.

Nacha Regules. Manuel Galvez & Ongley, Leo, Tr. LC 23-10466. E. P. Dutton & Company.

Nachette. Ned I. E. Edward Nye & Wason, Robert A., Joint Author. LC 9-24021. 1.50. J. H. Remick & Company.

Nachkriegserzahlungen: A Selection of Contemporary German Short Stories for College Students. Ed. by Melvin E Valk. LC 52-2571. 1952. R. F. Moore Co.

Nachlese. William Diamond & F. H. Reinsch. (Ger). 1927. 2.60 o.p. (ISBN 0-03-015255-0). HR&W.

Nachlese: Easy Short Stories from Contemporary German Literature, Edited with Introductions, Notes, Exercises and Vocabulary. Ed. by William Diamond & Reinsch, Frank Herman. LC 28-1538. H. Holt and Company.

Nachtwandler. Arthur Koestler. (Suhrkamp Taschenbuecher: 579). 576p. (Ger.). 1980. pap. text ed. 7.80 (ISBN 3-518-37079-0, Pub. by Suhrkamp Verlag Germany). Suhrkamp.

Nacio, His Affairs. Eleanor Mercein Kelly. 1931. Harper & Brothers.

Nackte Maedchen Auf der Strasse Erzaehlungen. Fritz Rudolf Fries. (Suhrkamp Taschenbuecher: St 577). 192p. (Ger.). 1980. pap. text ed. 3.90 (ISBN 3-518-37077-4, Pub. by Suhrkamp Verlag Germany). Suhrkamp.

Nacoochee. Thomas H. Chivers. LC 77-24233. 1977. Repr. of 1837 ed. 25.00x (ISBN 0-8201-1295-X). Schol Facsimilies.

Nada the Lily. Henry Rider Haggard. LC 7-2852. 1892. Longmans, Green, and Co.

Nada the Lily. Henry Rider Haggard. LC 17-6109. 1894. P. F. Collier.

Nada the Lily. Henry Rider Haggard. LC 7-2815. (On cover: Once a week semi-monthly library. v. 12, no. 1-2). 1894. P. F. Collier.

Nada the Lily. Henry Rider Haggard. LC 80-19282. 1980. 10.95. Borgo Press.

Nada, the Lily. Illus. by Hookway Cowles. Henry Rider Haggard. LC 66-5451. 1966. bds., 2.95. Macdonald.

Nadgrobie Antokolskogo. Felix Aranovich. (Illus.). 182p. (Rus.). 1982. pap. 9.00 (ISBN 0-938920-16-2). Hermitage MI.

Nadia. pap. 1.45 o.p. (V1053Q, Venus). Grove.

Nadia: A Russian Story of Love and Passion. LC 76-188326. (Venus library, V-1053-Q). 1972. 1.54. Venus Library.

Nadia Grey,M: A Novel. Hilda C Collins. LC 10-6490. 1909. 1.50.

Nadine: A Novel. Geoffrey Bocca. LC 74-79639. 1974. 7.95 (ISBN 0-399-11337-1). Putnam.

Nadine: A Romance of Two Live. Nina E Ellison. LC 6-37841. 1897. Gospel Advocate Publishing Co.

Nadine Narska. Mahrah Caracciolo De Meyer. LC 17-5402. 1916. 1.35. Wilmarth Publishing Company.

Nadja. Andre Breton. Tr. by Richard Howard. (Orig.). 1960. pap. 3.95 (ISBN 0-394-17393-7, E580, Ever). Grove.

Nadja: A Surrealist Romance. Andre Breton. Tr. by Richard Howard. (Illus.). 5.00 o.p. (ISBN 0-8446-1735-0). Peter Smith.

Nag: By Mendele Mocher Seforim Pseud. Translated from the Yuiddish by Moshe Spiegel. Illus. by Kurt Werth. Shalom Jacob Abramowitz. LC 54-10690. 1955. Beechhurst Press.

Nagasaki Vector. L. Neil Smith. 256p. (Orig.). 1983. pap. 2.75 (ISBN 0-345-30382-2, Del Rey). Ballantine.

Nag's Head, and Bertie: Two Novels. George Higby Throop. LC 59-3849. 1958. Heritage House.

Nah-Nee-Ta: A Tale of the Navajos. Henry R Brinkerhoff. LC 8-213371. 1886. J. H. Soule & Co.

Nahkom: the Woman of Waupaca. Malcolm Leviatt Rosholt. LC 74-79083. 1974. Rosholt House.

Naiad: A Ghost Story. From the French of George Sand. George Sand & Zerega, Mrs. Katherine Berry Di, Tr. LC 6-35673. W. R. Jenkins.

Nail Down the Stars. John Morressy. LC 72-95788. 1973. 6.95 (ISBN 0-8027-5559-3). Walker.

Nail Hotel. Deyan Sheldon. LC 74-11449. 1975. 7.95 (ISBN 0-690-00529-6). Crowell.

Nail Merchant at Nightfall, a Novel. Translated by Alan Beesley. Illustrated by Roland Pym. Mika Toimi Waltari. LC 55-1451. 1954. Putnam.

Nairobi. George Myers, Jr. LC 77-99271. 1978. pap. 3.00 (ISBN 0-917976-01-0). White Ewe.

Naissance de l'Odyssee see Oeuvres Romanesques.

Naissance du Jour. Sidonie Gabrielle Colette. pap. 3.95. French & Eur.

Naive and Sentimental Lover. David John Moore Cornwell. 1973. 1.50. Popular Lib.

Naive and Sentimental Lover. John Le Carre. LC 78-163133. 1972. 7.95 (ISBN 0-394-47336-1). Knopf.

Naive & Sentimental Lover. John Le Carre. 1979. pap. 3.50 (ISBN 0-553-13955-X). Bantam.

Naive Homosexual. (Orig.). 1969. pap. 1.75 o.p. (3065). Brandon.

Najib. Albert Payson Terhune. LC 25-8266. George H. Doran Company.

Naju of the Nile. H E Barns. LC 25-14721. 1924. Houghton Mifflin Company.

Nakagawa's Tenno Yugao. Yoiche Nakagawa. Tr. by Jeremy Ingalls. (International Studies & Translations Program). 1975. lib. bdg. 11.95 (ISBN 0-8057-5720-1, Twayne). G K Hall.

Nakagawa's Tenno Yugao: With a Commentary on the Relevance of Yoichi Nakagawa's Novel in Japanese Literature: Translation and Commentary. Yoichi Nakagawa & Jeremy Ingalls. LC 74-20573. (Illus.). 1975. 8.95 (ISBN 0-8057-5720-1). Twayne Publishers.

Naked. Mary David. 1968. 3.00 o.p. (ISBN 0-8059-0078-0). Dorrance.

Naked and. 1stamerican ed. Hammond Innes. LC 54-5269. 1954. Knopf.

Naked & Monique. Intro. by R. Conway. pap. 1.75 o.p. (3028). Brandon.

Naked and the Dead. Norman Mailer. LC 68-16611. (Rinehart editions). (Illus.). 1968. Holt, Rinehart and Winston.

Naked and the Dead. Norman Mailer. LC 48-6633. 1948. Rinehart.

Naked and the Dead. Norman Mailer. LC 80-25751. 1981. 7.95 (ISBN 0-03-059043-4) (ISBN 0-03-029590-4). Holt, Rinehart, and Winston.

Naked and the Lost. Franklin M Davis. LC 54-44834. (Lion book, 221). 1954. Lion Books by Arrangement with Canam Publishers Sales Corp.

Naked & the Nude. F. H. Turner. 176p. (Orig.). 1971. pap. 1.95 o.s.i. (O*P*H255, Ophelia). Olympia.

Naked & the Savage. William M. James, pseud. (Apache Ser.: No. 9). (Orig.). 1977. pap. 1.50 (ISBN 0-523-40558-8). Pinnacle Bks.

Naked & Together. Joe Webber & Diane Webber. 9.95 (ISBN 0-910550-06-9). Elysium.

Naked Angel. Jack Webb. LC 53-9241. (Murray Hill mystery). 1953. Rinehart.

Naked As the Wind from the Sea. Gustav Sandgren. (O.s.i.). Orig. Title: Som Havets Navka Vind. 1969. pap. 0.95 o.s.i. (A487N, Award). Univ Pub & Dist.

Naked at Night. Peter Shelley, pseud. LC 36-696456. Godwin.

Naked Author. Pietro Di Donato. LC 74-111407. 1970. 7.95. Phaedra.

Naked Battle. Barbara Cartland. 1977. 6.95 (ISBN 0-87272-028-4, Duron Bks.). Brodart.

Naked Before My Captors: A Novel. Bergen F Newell. LC 59-789084. 1959. F. Fell.

Naked Bishop. Mario J Sagola. LC 79-21270. 10.95 (ISBN 0-698-11017-X). Coward, McCann & Geoghegan.

Naked Blade. George Challis. LC 38-13405. The Greystone Press.

Naked Blade. easy eye ed. Frederick Faust. 1968. pap. 0.75 o.p. (74-910). Lancer.

Naked Branch. Elizabeth A Scholten. LC 40-104489. 1940. Arcadia House, Inc.

Naked Came I: A Novel of Rodin. David Weiss. LC 63-17687. 1963. Morrow.

Naked Came the Stranger. Penelope Ashe, pseud. LC 69-20279. 1969. 5.95. L. Stuart.

Naked Clowns. Dean Blehert. LC 81-80159. 64p. 1983. pap. 5.95 (ISBN 0-86666-017-8). GWP.

Naked Countess of Liechtenstein. John Colleton. 1976. 1.95 (ISBN 0-671-80532-0). Pocket Books.

Naked Crusader. Frank Archer, pseud. pap. 1.95 o.p. (ISBN 0-87056-251-7, 6251). Brandon.

Naked Days of the Lost Moon. Wilfried Laurier Burke. 1970. 5.95 o.p. Vantage.

Naked Ebony. Dan Cushman. LC 51-26908. (Gold medal books, 158). 1951. Fawcett Publications.

Naked Escape. Gerald Foster. LC 25-151541. Godwin.

Naked Eye. Henriette Martin & Gita Lewis. LC 50-6956. 1950. Greenberg.

Naked Face. Sidney Sheldon. 1975. (pbk.) 1.25. Dell.

Naked Face. Sidney Sheldon. LC 76-121691. 1970. 5.95. Morrow.

Naked Fear. Carl Ruthven Offord. LC 54-31852. (Ace books, S-54). 1954. Ace Books.

Naked Girl. Nikos Athanassiadis. LC 68-30772. 1968. 4.95. Orion Press.

Naked Girl. Nikos Athanassiadis. Tr. by Stephanos Zotos. LC 68-30772. 1968. 4.95 o.p. (ISBN 0-670-50386-X, Orion Pr). Grossman.

Naked Glory. Lawrence David. LC 32-11803. 1932. The Macaulay Company.

Naked Heart. John Lee Weldon. LC 53-7081. 1953. Farrar, Straus and Young.

Naked Hunter: A Novel. William Woolfolk. LC 55-20539. (Popular library, 627). 1954. Popular Library.

Naked I. Roy Chanslor. LC 53-9965. 1953. Crown Publishers.

Naked I: Fictions for the Seventies. Ed. by Frederick Robert Karl. LC 73-150369. (Fawcett premier book). 1971. 1.25. Fawcett Publications.

Naked I Leave: A Novel. Michael Novak. LC 77-93284. 1970. Macmillan.

Naked in a Cactus Garden. 1st Ed. Jesse Lenard Lasky. LC 61-7905. 1961. Bobbs-Merrill.

Naked in a Public Place. Elizabeth Gundy. LC 75-4295. 6.95. Harper & Row.

Naked in a Public Place. elizabeth gundy. ed. Elizabeth Gundy. 1.50 (ISBN 0-380-00800-9). Avon Books.

Naked in December. William Dale Smith. LC 68-11141. 1968. Bobbs-Merrill.

Naked in Garden Hills. Harry Crews. LC 69-11120. 1969. 5.95. Morrow.

Naked in Her Coffin. Tiny Alice. 160p. pap. 1.95 o.p. (6114). Brandon.

Naked in the Night: A Novel. Jon Cleary. LC 55-56518. (Popular library,634). 1955. Popular Library.

Naked in the Sun. Jan Cheux. pap. 1.95 o.p. (8061). Cameo.

Naked Is the Best Disguise. Samuel Rosenberg. LC 72-11802. 1974. 8.95 o.p. (ISBN 0-672-51914-3). Bobbs.

Naked Is the Best Disguise: The Death & Resurrection of Sherlock Holmes. Samuel Rosenberg. LC 73-11802. 1974. 8.95 (ISBN 0-672-51914-3). Bobbs-Merrill.

Naked Is the Best Disguise: The Death and Resurrection of Sherlock Holmes. Samuel Rosenberg. 1975. (pbk.) 2.25. Penguin.

Naked Island. Basil Heatter. LC 68-26710. 1968. 4.95. Trident Press.

Naked Island: A Romance of the West Indies. Georg Edward & Ashton, Arthur Jacob, 1855- Tr. The Macaulay Company.

Naked Joy. Peter Kanto. LC 76-28558. (Traveller's companion series, TC 472). 1.95. Ophelia Press.

Naked King. Albert Ades & Shipley, Joseph T., Tr. LC 25-1774. 1924. A. & C. Boni.

Naked Lady. Mullin Garr. (Orig.). pap. 1.75 o.s.i. (OPH-118, Ophelia). Olympia.

Naked Land: By Hammond Innes Pseud. 1st American Ed. Ralph Hammond-Innes. LC 54-5269. 1954. Knopf.

Naked Limbo. Stanley Dawson. (Orig.). pap. 0.95 o.p. (1102). Brandon.

Naked Lunch. William S. Burroughs. LC 60-11097. 1962. Grove Press.

Naked Lust. Shep Shepard. pap. 0.60 o.p. (60-371). Manor Bks.

Naked Maja. Noel Bertram Gerson. LC 59-7842. 1959. McGraw-Hill.

Naked Man. Vere Hutchinson. LC 25-17661. 2.00. The Century Co.

Naked Martini. Leonard, John. LC 64-11901. 1964. Delacorte Press Book; Distrib Uted by the Dial Press.

Naked Mistress. Walter Deptula. 1974. pap. 0.95 o.p. (09254). Curtis.

Naked Murder. Firth Erskine. LC 34-2225. The Macaulay Company.

Naked Murderer: By Evelyn Piper Pseud. 1st Ed. Merriam Modell. LC 62-17280. 1962. Atheneum.

Naked Neddle. Nuruddin Farah. LC 77-365324. (African writers series; 184). (HEB paperback). 1976. 1.60 (ISBN 0-435-90184-2). Heinemann Educational.

Naked Night. Dan Brennan. LC 54-377505. (Lion book, 197). 1954. Lion Books by Arrangement with Cornell Pub. Corp.

Naked on Roller Skates: A Novel. Maxwell Bodenheim. LC 31-1718. 1931. H. Liveright.

Naked Prisoner. Peggy Swenson, pseud. pap. 1.95 o.p. (ISBN 0-87977-162-3, DBB162). Dansk Blue Bk.

Naked Prodigal. William Dick. LC 79-487421. 1969. 3.90. Hutchinson of Australia.

Naked Range. Steven C. Lawrence, pseud. Orig. Title: Thruway West. 1976. pap. 0.95 o.p. (LB354NK, Leisure Bks). Nordon Pubns.

Naked Reason. George Buchanan. LC 71-117287. 1971. 4.95 (ISBN 0-03-085053-3). Holt, Rinehart and Winston.

Naked Risk. Phyllis Gordon Demarest. 1973. pap. 1.25 o.p. (01055). Curtis.

Naked Risk. 1st Ed. Phyllis Gordon Demarest. LC 54-5169. 1954. Doubleday.

Naked Runner. Francis Clifford. (YA) 1966. 4.95 o.p. Coward.

Naked Runner. Arthur Leonard Bell Thompson. LC 66-13115. 1966. Coward-McCann.

Naked Sinner. Bart Frame. 1968. pap. 0.50 o.p. (50-420). Manor Bks.

Naked Snow. John P. Salinger. Ed. by Sherwood E. Dickerman & Benjamin Barrett. 210p. 1983. 13.95 (ISBN 0-939502-01-1). St Luke Pub.

Naked Soul of Iceberg Slim. Robert Beck. (Orig.). 1971. pap. 1.95 (ISBN 0-87067-073-5, BH645). Holloway.

Naked Spotlight. Gloria Stokes. 4.50 o.p. Vantage.

Naked Spur: By Allan Ullman and Rolfe Bloom. Allan Ullman & Rolfe Bloom. LC 52-10930. Random House.

Naked Spurs by Larry Lawson. Clarence O Lawson. LC 57-8738. 1957. Avalon Books.

Naked Stewardess. Danny Land. 176p. pap. 1.95 o.p. (6090). Brandon.

Naked Streets. Vasco Pratolini. LC 52-11576. 1952. A. A. Wyn.

Naked Sun. Asimov, Isaac. LC 57-5534. 1972. Fawcett Publications.

Naked Sun. 1st Ed. Isaac Asimov. LC 57-5534. (Doubleday science fiction). 1957. Doubleday.

Naked Sword. Frank Wilson Kenyon. LC 68-30949. 1975. (pbk.) 1.50. Leisure Books.

Naked Sword: The Story of Lucrezia Borgia. Frank Wilson Kenyon. LC 68-30949. 1968. Dodd, Mead.

Naked Sword: The Story of Lucrezia Borgia. Frank Wilson Kenyon. LC 70-399726. 1968. 3.30. Hutchinson of Australia.

Naked Teacher. Ralph Kenyon. 1974. (pbk.) 1.95 (ISBN 0-87056-383-1). Brandon Books.

Naked Teacher. Ross Kenyon. 192p. 1974. pap. 1.95 o.p. (ISBN 0-87056-383-1, 6383). Brandon.

Naked to Her Enemies: The Girl from S. I. N. George H. Smith. (Orig.). pap. 0.95 o.p. (1137). Brandon.

Naked to Laughter. Dorothy McCleary. LC 37-532. 1937. Doubleday, Doran & Company, Inc.

Naked to the Grave. Harry Carmichael. 1973. 5.95 o.p. (ISBN 0-8415-0232-3). Sat Rev Pr.

Naked to the Grave. Leopold Horace Ognall. LC 72-95554. 1973. 5.95 (ISBN 0-8415-0232-3). Saturday Review Press.

Naked to the Stars. Gordon R. Dickson. (Science Fiction Ser.). 1977. pap. 1.50 (ISBN 0-87997-278-5, UW1278). DAW Bks.

Naked to the Stars. Gordon R. Dickson. 1970. Repr. pap. 0.75 o.p. (ISBN 0-447-74667-7). Lancer.

Naked to the Stars. Gordon R Dickson. 1.50 (ISBN 0-87997-278-5). Daw.

Naked Triangle: An Autobiographical Novel. Balwant Gargi. LC 79-907126. 3.95. Vikas.

Naked Truth. Linn Boyd Porter. LC 99-3082. (On cover: "Albatross" novels). 1899. G. W. Dillingham Co.

Naked Under Capricorn: A Novel. 1st Ed. Olaf Ruhen. LC 58-5847. 1958. Lippincott.

Naked Villany: An Entertainment, by Jocelyn Davey Pseud. 1st American Ed. Chaim Raphael. LC 58-9675. 1958. Knopf.

Naked Year. Boris Pilnyak. LC 70-174201. Repr. of 1928 ed. 12.50 (ISBN 0-404-06778-6). AMS Pr.

Naked Year. Boris Pilnyak. Tr. by Alexander Tulloch from Rus. 250p. 1975. 15.00 (ISBN 0-88233-077-2); pap. 4.50 (ISBN 0-88233-076-4). Ardis Pubs.

Naked Year. Boris Andreevich Vogan & Brown, Alec, Tr. LC 29-8007. (Half-title: The young Russians. 1). Payson & Clarke Ltd.

Naked Year. Boris Andreevich Vogau. LC 70-174201. 1971. (ISBN 0-404-06778-6). AMS Press.

Nakia. Lee Hays. 1975. (pbk.) 1.25. Popular Library.

Nakoa's Woman. Gayle Rogers. 1975. (pbk.) 1.50. Dell.

Nalice of Men. Warwick Deeping. LC 38-25512. 1938. A. A. Knopf.

Nam-Bok, the Liar. Jack London. Ed. by Walter Pauk & Raymond Harris. (Jamestown Classics Ser.). (Illus.). 43p. (gr. 6-12). 1976. pap. text ed. 2.00x (ISBN 0-89061-042-8, 505); tchrs. ed. 3.00 (ISBN 0-89061-043-6, 507). Jamestown Pubs.

Namaqua. Pierce Egan. LC 26-136. 1925. The Torch Press.

Nambe-Year One. Orlando Romero. LC 76-13385. (Illus.). 1976. 4.95 o.p. (ISBN 0-89229-004-8); pap. 6.50 (ISBN 0-89229-003-X). Tonatiuh-Quinto Sol Intl.

Name and Fame. authorized ed. Adeline Sergeant & Lester, Ewing I.E. A. S. Ewing, Joint Author. (On cover: Lovell's international series, no. 126). 1890. United States Book Company.

Name Encanyoned River. Clayton Eshleman. 1977. 8.00 o.p. (ISBN 0-916258-05-X); pap. 4.00 o.p. (ISBN 0-916258-06-8). Volaphon Bks.

Name for Evil: A Novel. Andrew Nelson Lytle. LC 47-30393. 1947. Bobbs-Merrill Co.

Name in Lights. Suzanne Ebel. (Fawcett Gold Medal Book). 1975. (pbk.) 0.95. Fawcett.

Name Is Archer. Kenneth Millar. LC 66-17144. 1966. Bantam Books.

Name Is Hart. Frank Roderus. (Orig.). 1979. pap. 1.95 (ISBN 0-441-56020-2). Ace Bks.

Name Is O'Brien. Ralph Hayes. 1972. 4.95. Lenox Hill Press.

Name Is Smith: By Eric North Pseud. Bernard Cronin. LC 57-113545. (Blue lamp mystery). 1957. Roy Publishers.

Name of a Shadow. Ann Maxwell. LC 79-57331. 1980. 2.25 (ISBN 0-380-75390-1). Avon Books.

Name of Action. Graham Greene. LC 31-57071. 1931. Doubleday, Doran & Company, Inc.

Name of Greene: A Novel. Jocelyn Brooke. LC 61-15475. 1961. Vanguard Press.

Name of Hero. Richard W. Seltzer. LC 81-50329. 290p. 1981. 12.95 (ISBN 0-87477-187-0). J P Tarcher.

Name of the Game. Eric Wilkins. LC 74-590. (Orig.). 1969. pap. 0.75 o.p. Lancer.

Name of the Game Is Murder. Eliot Asinof. (Inner Sanctum Mystery Ser). (O.S.I.). 1969. 4.50 o.s.i. (ISBN 0-671-20119-0). S&S.

Name to Conjure with: A Novel. Henrietta Eliza Vaughan Stannard. 1900. J. B. Lippincott Company.

Name Your Poison. Helen Kieran Reilly. LC 42-20994. 1942. Random House.

Nameless. A Novel. Frances Murdaugh Downing. LC 6-34245. 1865. W. B. Smith & Co.

Nameless Breed. C. S. Boyles. (Ace Book). 1977. 1.50 (ISBN 0-441-56025-3). Ace Books.

Nameless Castle. Mor Jokai. Tr. by Dassel, M. LC 7-12833. (On cover: Idle moments series. no. 12). 1891. The Price-McGill Company.

Nameless Castle: A Novel. Mor Jokai. Tr. by Boggs, Sara Elisabeth (Siegrist) Doubleday, Nellie Blanchan (De Graff) LC 98-1230. 1898. Doubleday and McClure Company.

Nameless City. A Rommany Romance. Stephen Grail. LC 6-27656. (Harper's Franklin square library, no. 737). 1893. Harper & Brothers.

Nameless Coffin. Gwendoline Butler. LC 67-13246. 1967. bds., 3.95. Walker.

Nameless Crime. Walter S Masterman. LC 32-327689. E. P. Dutton & Co., Inc.

Nameless Love: Or, The Roger Mansion Tragedy. Charles Lomon. Tr. by Loranger, Alexina. LC 7-15144. (On cover: Idylwild series. v. 1, no. 23). Morrill, Higgins & Cop.

Nameless Man. Natalie Sumner Lincoln. LC 17-241634. 1917. 1.40. D. Appleton and Company.

Nameless Nobleman... Jane Goodwin Austin. (Round-robin series). 1881. J. R. Osgood and Company.

Nameless Nobleman. Jane Goodwin Austin. LC 9-10086. Houghton Mifflin Company C.

Nameless Novel. Margaret Greenway McClelland. (On cover: The nameless series, no. 1). 1891. S. H. Moore & Company.

Nameless Novel. Mary Greenway McClelland. LC 44-240141. (On cover: The Nameless series. No. 1). 1891. S. H. Moore & Company.

Nameless Ones: A Secret Service Smith Novel. Reginald Thomas Maitland Scott. LC 47-3633. 1947. E. P. Dutton & Co., Inc.

Nameless Ones: By Lesley Egan. 1st Ed. Elizabeth Linington. LC 67-13700. 1967. 4.50. Harper.

Nameless Places. Ed. by Gerald W. Page. LC 75-2525. 1975. 7.50 (ISBN 0-87054-073-4). Arkham House.

Nameless River. Vingie Eve Roe. LC 23-12162. 1923. Duffield and Company.

Nameless Road. Henry Gibbs. LC 70-103378. 1970. 4.50. Walker.

Nameless Road. Simon Harvester. 1981. 18.95x (Pub. by Remploy England). State Mutual Bk.

Nameless Road. Simon Harvester. LC 70-103378. (Mystery Ser). 1970. 4.50 o.p. (ISBN 0-8027-5130-X). Walker & Co.

Nameless Sin. Charlotte Mary Brame. LC 44-11264. (On cover: Seaside library. Pocket ed. No. 1012). 1887. G. Munro.

Nameless Thing. Melville Davisson Post. 1912. 1.25. D. Appleton and Company.

Nameless Woman: A Story of My Life. Loulia Jackson. LC 10-9073. 2.50. Press of Burd & Fletcher.

Nameless Wrestler. Josephine White Bates. LC 11-10553. 1889. J. B. Lippincott Company.

Names. Michael Mooney. (Treacle Story Ser.: No. 10). 64p. 1979. signed ed. 8.00 (ISBN 0-914232-33-9); pap. 2.50 (ISBN 0-914232-32-0). McPherson & Co.

Names & Faces of Heroes. Reynolds Price. LC 63-12414. 1973. pap. 2.95 (ISBN 0-689-70364-3, 201). Atheneum.

Name's Buchanan. Jonas Ward. (Buchanan Ser.). 128p. 1978. pap. 1.75 (ISBN 0-449-14135-7, GM). Fawcett.

Name's Death, Remember Me? Stanton Forbes, pseud. LC 78-84377. 1969. 4.50. Published for the Crime Club by Doubleday.

Namesake. Valancy Hunter. 1974. (pbk.) 0.95. Dell.

Nami-Ko: A Realistic Novel. Kenjiro Tokutomi & Shioya, Sakae, Tr. 1904. H. B. Turner & Co.

Naming Things: Stories. Herbert Edward Francis. LC 80-19543. (Illinois short fiction.). 10.00 (ISBN 0-252-00830-8) (ISBN 0-252-00831-6). University of Illinois Press.

Nan Haggard, the Heiress of Dead Hopes Mine. Mary Edwards Bryan. (On cover: Library of American authors, no. 63). 1895. G. Munro's Sons.

Nan of Music Mountain. Frank Hamilton Spearman. 1916. C. Scribner's Sons.

Nan Thursday. Virginia Dale. LC 44-3053. 1944. Coward-McCann, Inc.

Nana. Emile Zola. LC 56-12648. (Harper's modern classics). Harper.

Nana. Emile Zola. LC 61-185785. (Classic Collier books, IIS27). 1962. Collier Books.

Nana. Emile Zola. LC 64-20905. 1964. Bantam Books.

Nana. Emile Zola. LC 72-169379. (Penguin classics). 1972. (u.s.) 2.95 (ISBN 0-14-044263-4). Penguin Books.

Nana. Emile Zola. LC 74-171906. (Illus.). 1973. (ISBN 0-460-04144-4). Folio Press Distributed by J. M. Dent.

Nana. Emile Zola. LC 72-169379. (Penguin classics). 1972. (u.s.) 2.95 (ISBN 0-14-044263-4). Penguin Books.

Nana. Emile Zola. LC 33-23513. Illustrated Editions Company.

Nana. Emile Zola. LC 46-8194. (Half-title: The Living library). 1946. The World Publishing Company.

Nana. Emile Zola & Boyd, Ernest Augustus, 1887- LC 28-10872. (Half-title: The modern library of the world's best books) "First Modern library edition."). The Modern Library.

Nana: A Realistic Novel. Emile Zola & Chalmers, Edward Wharton, Ed. LC 9-1312. (pastime series. v. 14). 1888. Laird & Lee.

Nana: Official Movie Tie-in edition. Emile Zola. 1983. pap. 4.95 (ISBN 0-14-006128-2). Penguin.

Nana. Sequel to "L'assommoir.". Emile Zola & Sherwood, Mrs. Mary (Neal) Tr. LC 9-1314. (Peterson's dollar series). T. B. Peterson & Brothers.

Nana. Sequel to "L'assommoir.". Emile Zola & Sherwood, Mrs. Mary (Neal) Tr. LC 9-1313. T. B. Peterson & Brothers.

Nana. Tr. from French by Victor Plarr. Introd. by Alec Brown. Emile Zola. LC 65-7765. 1965. bds., 3.95. Elek Bks.

Nana. With an Introd. by John C. Lapp. Emile Zola. LC 56-12648. (Harper's modern classics). Harper.

Nana's Daughter. A Continuation of and Sequel to Emile Zola's Novel of "Nana,". Alfred Sirven & Leverdier, Henri, 1840- Joint Author. LC 8-9009. T. B. Peterson & Brothers.

Nana's Mother (L'assommoir) Emile Zola. LC 51-27094. (Avon pocket-size books, 271). 1950. Avon Pub. Co.

Nanciebel: A Tale of Stratford-on-Avon. William Black. (Seaside library. Pocket ed. no. 1259). G. Munro.

Nancy. Rhoda Broughton. (On cover: Lovell's library, no. 1026). 1887. Lovell Company.

Nancy. Jack Pearl, pseud. (Orig.). 1970. pap. 0.75 o.p. (T2339). Pyramid Pubns.

Nancy: A Novel. Rhoda Broughton. LC 6-18952. 1874. D. Appleton & Company.

Nancy. A Novel. Rhoda Broughton. (Seaside library, v. 23, no. 458). G. Munro.

Nancy: A Novel. Rhoda Broughton. (On cover: Seaside library, Pocket ed., no. 227). 1884. G. Munro.

Nancy: A Novel. Rhoda Broughton. LC 18-7781. (Macmillan's two shilling library). 1900. Macmillan and Co., Limited.

Nancy Flyer: A Stagecoach Epic. Ernest Poole. LC 49-8012. 1949. T. Y. Crowell Co.

Nancy Goes to Town. Frances Roberta Sterrett. LC 20-18766. 1920. D. Appleton and Company.

Nancy Hart: An American Heroine. Freear, Robert Louis. LC 8-307067. 1908. The C. M. Clark Publishing Company.

Nancy: Her Life and Death. Louis Dodge. LC 21-16793. 1921. C. Scribner's Sons.

Nancy Kelsey. Decorations by Paul Lantz. Virginia Besaw Evansen. LC 65-141367. 3.95. McKay.

Nancy Naylor Flies South. Elisabeth Carleton Hubbard Lansing. LC 43-14970. 1943. Thomas Y. Crowell Company.

Nancy Noon. William Romaine Paterson. LC 7-34077. 1896. C. Scribner's Sons.

Nancy Owlett. Eden Phillpotts. LC 33-291974. 1933. The Macmillan Company.

Nancy Ross: Private Secretary. Jeanne Judson. LC 56-13303. 1956. Avalon Books.

Nancy Rutledge. Katharine Pyle. LC 6-340439. 1906. Little, Brown & Co.

Nancy Stair: A Novel. Elinor Macartney Lane. LC 5-599241. 1905. D. Appleton and Company.

Nancy Stair: A Novel. Elinor Macartney Lane. 1910. D. Appleton and Company.

Nancy, The Daring. Katheryn Kimbrough, pseud. (Saga of the Phenwick Women: Book 11). 256p. 1976. pap. 1.50 (ISBN 0-445-00399-5). Popular Lib.

Nancy the Joyous. Edith Stow. LC 14-11045. The Reilly & Britton Co.

Nancy Waterman: Or, Woman's Faith Triumphant. A Story of New York City. Charles F Barrington. S. French.

Nancy's Pilgrimage. Margaret Pollock Sherwood. LC 11-137329. 1911. The Westminster Press.

Nanette. Patricia Veryan. LC 80-51854. 1981. 11.95 (ISBN 0-8027-0664-9). Walker.

Nanna: A Story of Danish Love (Poul Og Virginie Under Nordlig Bredde. Holger Henrik Herholdt Drachmann & Browne, Francis Fisher, 1843-1913, Tr. LC 1-27051. (On vergo of half-title: Tales from foreign lands. ix). 1901. A. C. McClurg & Co.

Nanny. Merriam Modell. LC 64-14931.

Nanny Goat, Nanny Goat. Pauline Waugh. LC 65-124616. 4.95. Holt.

Nanon. George Sand & Latimer, Mrs. Elizabeth (Wormeley) 1822-1904, Tr. 1890. Roberts Brothers.

Nanook Who Loved a Woman. Marc Stactton. LC 79-281799. (Illus.). 1970. 2.00.

Nan's Valley. Frances E. Whitney. 3.75 o.p. Carlton.

Nantucket Rebel. Edouard A Stackpole. LC 63-16391. (Illus.). 1963. I. Washburn.

Nantucket Woman. Diana Gaines. LC 76-12601. 8.95. Dutton.

Naomi: A Friend of Jesus. Florence Delight McGrew. LC 656. Review & Herald Pub. Co.

Naomi, Daughter of Ruth. 1st Ed. Leon Bone. LC 53-385. 1952. Pageant Press.

Naomi Martin. Clarkson Crane. 1947. Harcourt, Brace and Company.

Naomi of the Island. Lucy Hester Thurston Abbott. LC 12-567172. 1912. L.C. Page & Company.

Naomi; or, Boston, Two Hundred Years Ago. Eliza Buckminster Lee. LC 7-126092. 1848. W. Crosby & H.P. Nichols.

Naomi; or, Boston Two Hundred Years Ago. 2d ed. Eliza Buckminster Lee. LC 7-12610. 1848. W. Crosby and H. P. Nichols.

Naomi Torrente: The History of a Woman. Gertrude Vingut. LC 8-32700. 1864. J. Bradburn.

Napolean Ring. Anne Lowing. 1977. pap. 1.25 o.p. (ISBN 0-515-04251-X). BJ Pub Group.

Napoleans of Eridanus. Pierre Barbet. (Science Fiction Ser.). 1976. pap. 1.25 o.p. (ISBN 0-87997-240-8, UY1240). DAW Bks.

Napoleon and Blucher. Klara Muller Mundt. Tr. by Jordan, F. LC 16-1238. (historical romances of Louisa Mublbach pseud.). D. Appleton and Company.

Napoleon and Blucher. An Historical Novel. Klara Muller Mundt. Tr. by Jordan, F. LC 7-26107. (Napoleon in Germany. pt. 3). 1867. D. Appleton and Company.

Napoleon and Blucher: An Historical Novel. Klara Muller Mundt. Tr. by Jordan, F. LC 7-17266. (Napoleon in Germany. pt. 3). 1893. D. Appleton and Company.

Napoleon and His Son. Pierre Nezelof & Wells, Warre Bradley, 1892- Tr. LC 37-30933. Liveright Publishing Corporation.

Napoleon and Love. Philip Mackie. 1976. (pbk.) 1.95 (ISBN 0-671-80306-9). Pocket Books.

Napoleon and the Cossacks. Petr Nikolaevich Krasnov. Tr. by Vitali, Olga. LC 31-31530. 1931. Duffield & Green.

Napoleon and the Queen of Prussia. An Historical Novel. Klara Muller Mundt. Tr. by Jordan, F. LC 7-26110. (Napoleon in Germany. part 2). 1867. D. Appleton and Company.

Napoleon and the Queen of Prussia. An Historical Novel. Klara Muller Mundt. Tr. by Jordan, F. (Napoleon in Germany. part 2). 1868. D. Appleton and Company.

Napoleon and the Queen of Prussia: An Historical Novel. Klara Muller Mundt. Tr. by Jordan, F. (Napoleon in Germany. pt. 2). 1893. D. Appleton and Company.

Napoleon and the Queen of Prussia: Tr. from the German by F. Jordan. Klara Muller Mundt. Tr. by Jordan, F. LC 16-1237. (historical romances of Louisa Muhlbach pseud.). D. Appleton and Company.

Napoleon Is Dead in Russia. Guido Artom. LC 72-108818. (Illus.). 1970. 5.95. Atheneum.

Napoleon Jackson, the Gentleman of the Plush Rocker. Ruth McEnery Stuart. LC 72-2069. (Black Heritage Library Collection). (Illus.). 1972. (ISBN 0-8369-9069-2). Books for Libraries Press.

Napoleon Jackson: The Gentleman of the Plush Rocker. Ruth McEnery Stuart. LC 2-22482. 1902. The Century Co.

Napoleon of Notting Hill. Gilbert Keith Chesterton. LC 4-11539. 1904. John Lane.

Napoleon of Notting Hill. Gilbert Keith Chesterton. LC 77-99307. (Illus.). 1978. 3.45 (ISBN 0-8091-2096-8). Paulist Press.

Napoleon of Notting Hill: By Gilbert K. Chesterton... with Seven Illustrations by William Graham Robertson, and a Map of the Seat of War. Gilbert Keith Chesterton. LC 41-54788. 1906. John Lane Company.

Napoleon Smith. William J. Arkell & Worden, A. T., Joint Author. LC 6-3837. 1888. The Judge Publishing Company.

Napoleon Symphony. Anthony Burgess. LC 77-350207. (Corgi book). 1976. 0.95 (ISBN 0-552-10111-7). Corgi.

Napoleon Symphony. Anthony Burgess. LC 79-23059. 1980. 4.95 (ISBN 0-393-00964-5). Norton.

Napoleon Symphony. John Anthony Burgess Wilson. LC 73-20750. 1974. 7.95 (ISBN 0-394-47614-X). Knopf; Distributed by Random House.

Napoleon Symphony. John Anthony Burgess Wilson. 1975. (pbk.) 1.95. Bantam Books.

Napoleonic Stories. Arthur Conan Doyle. 1959. 9.75 o.p. Transatlantic.

Napoleon's Marshals. Ronald Frederick Delderfield. LC 66-16287. (Illus.). 1980. pap. 7.95 (ISBN 0-8128-6055-1). Stein & Day.

Napoleon's Second Empress. Patrick Turnbull. 320p. 1977. pap. 1.95 (ISBN 0-532-19152-8). Woodhill.

Narc. Robert Hawkes. 1973. (pbk) 0.95. Lancer.

Narc No. One. Robert Hawkes. 1973. pap. 0.95 o.s.i. (75-499). Lancer.

Narcissa, and Other Fables. Louis Auchincloss. LC 82-12086. 1983. 13.45 (ISBN 0-395-33114-5). Houghton Mifflin.

Narcissa & Other Fables. Louis Auchincloss. 1984. 13.95 (ISBN 0-395-33114-5). HM.

Narcissus. John Hawley Roberts. LC 30-100866. Sears Publishing Company, Inc.

Narcissus. Evelyn Scott. LC 76-51676. (Recovered Fiction by American Women). 1977. 22.00 (ISBN 0-405-10054-X). Arno Press.

Narcissus. Evelyn Scott. LC 22-12397. Harcourt, Brace and Company.

Narcissus; a Belgian Legend of Van Dyck. Brand Whitlock. LC 31-22139. 1931. D. Appleton & Company.

Narcissus and Goldmund. Hermann Hesse. LC 68-17291. 1968. Farrar, Straus and Giroux.

Nareen. Charles Bruce Pitblado & Pitblado, Edwy Guthrie, Joint Author. LC 8-20717. The Hadley Press.

Nark! Joe Ezterhas. (O.s.i.). 1974. 7.95 o.s.i. (21885, Straight Arrow). S&S.

Narka, the Nihilist. Kathleen O'Meara. LC 44-25792. 1887. Harper & Brothers.

Narna Darrell. Beverley Randolph Tucker. LC 36-4028. The Stratford Company.

Narracong Riddle: A Judge Peck Mystery. August William Derleth. LC 40-6801. 1940. C. Scribner's Sons.

Narraganset Chief: Or, The Adventures of a Wanderer. Isaac Peirce. LC 7-36504. 1832. J. K. Porter.

Narrative Impulse: Short Stories for Analysis. Ed. by Mary Joe Purcell & Robert C. Wylder. LC 63-14021. 1963. Odyssey Press.

Narrative of A. Gordon Pym. Edgar Allan Poe. LC 7-38186. (On cover: Lovell's library. v. 8. no. 426). 1884. J. W. Lovell Company.

Narrative of a Young Woman Taken by the Indians in 1777. Abraham Panther. LC 75-7038. (Garland Library of Narratives of North American Indian Captivities; V. 17). 1978. 29.50 (ISBN 0-8240-1641-6). Garland Pub.

Narrative of Arthur Gordon Pym, of Nantucket... Introd. by Sidney Kaplan. Edgar Allan Poe. LC 60-10515. (American century series, AC29). 1960. Hill and Wang.

Narrative of Arthur Gordon Pym of Nantucket. Edgar Allan Poe. LC 76-359660. (Penguin English library). (Illus.). 1975. 0.65 (ISBN 0-14-043097-0). Penguin.

Narrative of the Life and Astonishing Adventures of John Daniel. Ralph Morris & John Daniel. LC 74-16398. (Science Fiction). 1975. 16.00. (ISBN 0-405-06307-5). Arno Press.

Narrative of the Shipwreck of the Sophia. C. Cochelet. 59.95 (ISBN 0-8490-0709-7). Gordon Pr.

Narrative of the Travels and Adventures of Paul Aermont Among the Planets. Paul Aermont. LC 6-18283. 1873. Press of Rand, Avery and Company.

Narrative Sensibility: An Introduction to Fiction. Reloy Garcia & Lloyd J Hubenka. LC 75-33664. 6.95 (ISBN 0-679-30295-6). McKay.

Narratives From America. Richard Ronan. LC 81-67639. 152p. 1982. 12.00x (ISBN 0-937872-04-0); pap. 6.00x (ISBN 0-937872-05-9). Dragon Gate.

Narrow Bridge. Pearl Frye. LC 47-5945. 1947. Little, Brown.

Narrow Cage: An American Family Saga. LC 80-687. 320p. 1980. 12.95 o.p. (ISBN 0-672-52655-7). Bobbs.

Narrow Cell. Ronal Kayser. LC 44-20105. 1944. J. B. Lippincott Company.

Narrow Corner. William Somerset Maugham. LC 75-25359. (Maugham, William Somerset, 1874-1965. Works. 1976). 1976. 15.00 (ISBN 0-405-07818-8). Arno Press.

Narrow Corner. William Somerset Maugham. LC 32-31610. 1932. Doubleday, Doran & Company, Inc.

Narrow Corner. William Somerset Maugham. LC 37-38312. 1937. The Sun Dial Press, Inc.

Narrow Corner. William Somerset Maugham. LC 42-20793. 1942. Triangle Books.

Narrow Corner. William Somerset Maugham. LC 44-7522. 1944. New Avon Library.

Narrow Covering. 1st Ed. Siebel, Julia. LC 56-8524. 1956. Harcourt, Brace.

Narrow Exit. Paul Henissart. LC 73-9351. 1973. 7.95 (ISBN 0-671-21579-5). Simon and Schuster.

Narrow Exit. Paul Henissart. (Kangaroo Book). 1978. 1.95 (ISBN 0-671-81721-3). Pocket Books.

Narrow Gate. Charles Monroe Sheldon. LC 4-2317. 1903. Advance Publishing Co.

Narrow Gauge to Murder: By Carolyn Thomas Pseud. 1st Ed. Actea Duncan. LC 52-10939. (Main line mysteries). 1953. Lippincott.

Narrow House. Evelyn Scott. LC 76-51677. (Recovered Fiction by American Women). 1977. 18.00 (ISBN 0-405-10055-8). Arno Press.

Narrow House. Evelyn Scott. LC 21-5273. Boni and Liveright.

Narrow Land. Jack Vance, pseud. 176p. 1982. pap. 2.25 (ISBN 0-87997-747-7). DAW Bks.

Narrow Ledge. Charles E Mercer. LC 51-1622. 1951. Morrow.

Narrow Lyre. Janice Warnke. LC 58-11395. 1958. Harper.

Narrow Path. Francis Selormey. (African Writers Ser: No.27). 185p. 1976. pap. text ed. 1.50x o.p. (ISBN 0-435-90027-7). Humanities.

Narrow Road. Robin Moore & F. L. Kafka. 1978. pap. 1.95 (ISBN 0-532-19176-5). Woodhill.

Narrow Rooms. James Purdy. LC 77-90667. 8.95 (ISBN 0-87795-183-7). Arbor House.

Narrow Search. Andrew Garve. pap. 0.95 o.p. (02055, Collier). Macmillan.

Narrow Search: By Andrew Garve Pseud. 1st American Ed. Paul Winterton. LC 57-8205. Harper.

Narrow Street. Edwin Bateman Morris. LC 24-7727. 1924. The Penn Publishing Company.

Narrow Streets. Jefferson Thurber Wing. LC 32-22548. R. G. Badger.

Narrow Time. Ralph M McInerny. LC 69-15889. 1969. 4.95. Doubleday.

Narrowest Circle: A Novel. Katherine Shattuck. LC 58-6505. 1958. McDowell, Obolensky.

Narrowing Circle. Julian Symons. LC 81-47352. (Fifty Classics of Crime Fiction, 1950-1975). 1982. 14.95 (ISBN 0-8240-4962-4). Garland.

Narrowing Circle. 1st American Ed. Julian Symons. LC 55-6597. Harper.

Narrowing Wind. Catherine Ann Lawrence. LC 44-9744. 1944. Dodd, Mead & Company.

Narrows. Kenneth H. Brown. 1970. 5.95 o.p. Dial.

Narrows. Ann Lane Petry. LC 53-5729. 1953. Houghton Mifflin.

Narrows: A Novel. Kenneth H Brown. LC 79-103435. (Illus.). 1970. 5.95. Dial Press.

Nasakenai: We Are Forsaken. James J Hannon. LC 77-78420. (Illus.). 8.95 (ISBN 0-913182-93-1). Grossmont Press.

Nash. John G Lees. 1972. 4.95. Lenox Hill Pr.

Nashoba. Edd Winfield Parks. LC 63-11186. 1963. Twayne Publishers.

Nashville Babylon. S. A. Martinez. (Orig.). 1977. pap. 1.95 (ISBN 0-89041-159-X, 3159). Major Bks.

Nashville Lady. B. C Hall. (Berkley Medallion Book). 1976. (pbk.) 1.25 (ISBN 0-425-03088-1). Berkley Publishing Corp.

Nashville with a Bullet. Barry Sadler & Billy Arr. 288p. 1981. pap. 2.95 (ISBN 0-441-56476-3, Pub. by Charter Bks). Ace Bks.

Nashville 98: A Novel. James Rice. LC 78-59113. 8.95 (ISBN 0-87716-089-9). Moore Pub. Co.

Nasty Name Murders. Royce Howes. LC 39-4163. 1939. Pub. for the Crime Club, Inc., by Doubleday, Doran & Co., Inc.

Nat Foster, The Boston Detective. A Thrilling Story of Detective Life. Ernest A. Young. J. S. Ogilvie & Company.

Nat Gregory: Or, The Old Maid's Secret. A Novel. William Seton. LC 8-6871. (On cover: Library of standard novels). 1867. Hilton & Company.

Nat" the Coal-Miner's Boy: Or, One Step at a Time. Thomas L Baily. LC 6-5009. 1890. The National Temperance Society and Publication House.

Natalia: A Novel of Old Alaska. Anne Miller Downes. LC 60-6394. 1960. Lippincott.

Natalie. Alexandra Orme. LC 57-7937. 1957. Simon and Schuster.

Natalie. Gerhard Lewis Wind. LC 26-958. 1925. Northwestern Publishing House Print.

Natalie Natalia. Nicholas Mosley. LC 72-154775. 1972. Popular Library.

Natalie: Or, A Gem Among the Sea--Weeds. E. V Hallett. 1858. Printed by W. F. Draper.

Natalie Page. Katharine Haviland Taylor. LC 21-6799. G. W. Jacobs & Company.

Natalya. Anabel Brooke. 352p. (Orig.). 1981. pap. 2.75 (ISBN 0-345-29254-5). Ballantine.

Natasqua. Rebecca Harding Davis. (On cover: Cassell's "rainbow" series, v. 1, no. 1). 1887. Cassell & Company, Limited.

Natchey Kingdom. Sebastian Watt. 2.25 (ISBN 0-440-16274-2). Dell Publishing Co.

Natchez. Shana Clermont. (Orig.). 1981. pap. 3.50 (ISBN 0-89083-891-7). Zebra.

Natchez. Louise MacKendrick. (Belmont Tower Book). 1977. 1.75 (ISBN 0-505-51138-X). Tower Pubns.

Natchez. Logan Winters. (Spectros Ser.: No. 3). (Orig.). 1981. pap. 1.75 (ISBN 0-505-51626-8). Tower Bks.

Natchez: An Indian Tale. Francois August Rene de Chateaubriand. LC 77-12527. 1978. (set) 55.00. H. Fertig.

Natchez Woman. Alice Walworth Graham. LC 50-5036. 1950. Doubleday.

Nate's Lady. Bernadette Parkin. 1981. pap. 2.75 (ISBN 0-380-78204-9, 78204). Avon.

Nathalie: A Tale. Julia Kavanagh. LC 41-206897. 1888. D. Appleton and Company.

Nathan Burke. Mary Stanbery Watts. LC 10-9261. 1910. The Macmillan Company.

Nathan Burke. Mary Stanbery Watts. LC 41-35150. (Half-title: Macmillan's standard library). 1912. Grosset & Dunlap.

Nathan Burke. Mary Stanbery Watts. LC 41-324489. 1919. The Macmillan Company.

Nathan Burke. Mary Stanbery Watts & Stratton, Clarence, 1880- Ed. LC 23-6421. (On cover: The modern readers' series). 1923. The Macmillan Company.

Nathan Coulter. Wendell Berry. LC 60-5146. 1960. Houghton Mifflin.

Nathan Todd: Or, The Fate of the Sioux' Captive. Edward Sylvester Ellis. LC 10-278551. Hurst & Company.

Nathan Todd: Or, The Fate of the Sioux Captive. Edward Sylvester Ellis. LC 79-11427. (Garland Library of Narratives of North American Indian Captivities; V. 90). (Illus.). 1979. 29.50 (ISBN 0-8240-1714-5). Garland Pub.

Nathaniel Hawthorne: Young Goodman Brown. Ed. by Thomas Edmund Connolly. LC 68-55804. (Merrill literary casebook series). 1968. C. E. Merrill.

Nathaniel Moleskin and the Chinese Princess and Other Stories. Marie Gallagher. LC 32-1647. Printed by the Alexander Press.

Nation Within. Francis Fytton. LC 68-20891. 1969. 4.95. Pantheon Books.

National Anthem. Richard Kluger. LC 69-15278. 1969. 6.95. Harper & Row.

National Anthem. Barbara Raskin. LC 76-18699. Dutton.

National Book Award Reader. Ed. by Robert John Clements. LC 66-2841. (Popular living classics library). 1966. Popular Library.

National Book Award Reader: Ed. Introd. by Robert J. Clements. Ed. by Robert John Clements. LC 66-2841. (Popular living classics lib.: 50-443). Popular Lib.

National Lampoon's Class Reunion. Sandra Choron & John Hughes. (Orig.). 1982. pap. 2.95 (ISBN 0-440-16717-5). Dell.

National Provincial. Lettice Ulpha Cooper. 1938. The Macmillan Company.

National Standard. Gerald Jay Goldberg. LC 68-12207. 1968. Holt, Rinehart and Winston.

National Velvet. Enid Bagnold. LC 66-6176. 1966. F. Watts.

National Velvet,". Enid Bagnold. LC 49-10997. 1949. W. Morrow.

National Velvet". Enid Bagnold. LC 35-37090. 1935. W. Morrow and Company.

National Velvet.' Front. by Walter Seaton. Illus. by Earle B. Winslow. Enid Bagnold. LC 58-274539. 1958. Junior Deluxe Editions.

Nation's Crime: A Novel. I Lowenberg. LC 10-30035. 1910. 1.50. The Neale Publishing Company.

Nation's Missing Guest. Hulbert Footner. LC 39-720. 1939. Harper & Brothers.

Native Argosy. Morley Callaghan. LC 70-106255. (Short story index reprint series). 1970. Books for Libraries Press.

Native Argosy. Morley Callaghan. LC 29-9880. 1929. C. Scribner's Sons.

Native Born: Or, the Rajah's People. Ida Alexa Ross Wylie. LC 10-16980. The Bobbs-Merrill Company.

Native Intelligence. Raymond A Sokolov. LC 74-15893. 1975. 7.95 (ISBN 0-06-013910-2). Harper & Row.

Native Intelligence: A Novel. Raymond A. Sokolov. 240p. 1983. pap. 5.95 (ISBN 0-525-48029-3, 0577-180, Obelisk). Dutton.

Native Moment. Anthony C. West. LC 59-13760. 1959. McDowell, Obolensky.

Native of Winby: And Other Tales. Sarah Orne Jewett. LC 70-113679. (Short story index reprint series). 1970. Books for Libraries Press.

Native of Winby, and Other Tales. Sarah Orne Jewett. LC 72-84610. 1976. (ISBN 0-403-03189-3). Scholarly Press.

Native of Winby: And Other Tales. Sarah Orne Jewett. LC 9-2481. 1893. Houghton, Mifflin and Company.

Native of Winby & Other Tales see Collected Works.

Native Soil: A Novel. Allan Eugene Updegraff. LC 30-7566. The John Day Company.

Native Son. Richard Wright. LC 66-1833. (Harper perennial classic). 1966. Harper & Row.

Native Son. Richard Wright. LC 79-86654. 1969. 7.50. Harper & Row.

Native Son. Richard Wright. LC 40-4862. 1940. Harper & Brothers.

Native Son. Richard Wright. LC 42-36140. (Half-title: The Modern library of the world's best books). 1942. The Modern Library.

Native Son of the Golden West: A Novel. James D Houston. LC 70-144381. 1971. 5.95. Dial Press.

Native Son Who Loses His Identity. Adelbert Selders. LC 24-254134. 1924. The Stanly Republican and Selders' Weekly.

Native Son: With an Introd, by William A. Owens. Richard Wright. LC 56-12647. (Harper's modern classics). 1957. Harper.

Native Stone. Edwin Gilbert. LC 56-5440. 1956. Doubleday.

Native to the Grain. George Troy. LC 61-6646. 1961. Harcourt, Brace.

Natives of Hemso; &, The Scapegoat. Tr. by Arvid Paulson. Introd. by Richard B. Vowles. August Strindberg. LC 67-28883. (Bantam classic, QC4043). 1967. pap., 1.25. Bantam.

Natives of My Person. George Lamming. LC 70-155522. 1971. 7.95 (ISBN 0-03-086647-2). Holt, Rinehart and Winston.

Natural. Bernard Malamud. LC 52-9853. 1952. Harcourt, Brace.

Natural Acts. James Fritzhand. (Signet Book). 2.50 (ISBN 0-451-08603-1). New American Library, C.

Natural Bone. David Warren. LC 78-31612. (Illus.). 1979. 5.50 (ISBN 0-87886-095-9). Ithaca House.

Natural Bridge Romance. William Lee Popham. LC 11-324213. 1.00. The World Supply Company.

Natural Causes. Henry Cecil. 1974. Repr. of 1953 ed. 5.95 o.s.i. (ISBN 0-8277-3349-6). British Bk Ctr.

Natural Causes. Nicholas Roland, pseud. LC 74-125581. 1971. 4.95 (ISBN 0-87695-029-2). Aurora Publishers.

Natural Child. Calder Willingham. LC 52-10094. 1952. Dial Press.

Natural Collection. Steven C. Wilson. LC 81-65683. (Illus.). 220p. (Orig.). 1981. 19.95 (ISBN 0-939750-00-7); pap. 14.95 (ISBN 0-939750-01-5). Entheos.

Natural Death: A Novel. Nancy Price. LC 73-7896. 1973. 8.95 (ISBN 0-316-71852-1). Little, Brown.

Natural Enemies. Julius Horwitz. LC 74-15476. 1975. 6.95 (ISBN 0-03-013826-4). Holt, Rinehart and Winston.

Natural Enemy. Jane Langton. LC 81-16618. (Illus.). 1982. 11.95 (ISBN 0-89919-081-2). Ticknor & Fields.

Natural History. Constance Urdang. LC 69-15285. 1969. 4.95. Harper & Row.

Natural Law. Charles William Collins & Hall, Howard Girard. LC 16-18919. 1916. 1.25. The Macaulay Company.

Natural Man. Ed McClanahan. LC 82-21056. 11.50 (ISBN 0-374-21969-9). Farrar, Straus, and Giroux.

Natural Man. Patrick Miller. LC 24-25638. Brentano's.

Natural Mother. Dominique Dunois. Tr. by Rappoport, Angelo S. LC 29-23494. 1929. The Macaulay Company.

Natural Shocks. Richard Stern. 1981. 2.95 (ISBN 0-671-82269-1). Pocket Books.

Natural Shocks. Richard G. Stern. LC 77-22952. 8.95 (ISBN 0-698-10865-5). Coward, McCann & Geoghegan.

Natural Victims. Isabel Eberstadt. LC 82-48730. 1983. 15.95 (ISBN 0-394-52951-0). Knopf.

Natural Weapon. Garry Mitchelmore. (Orig.). 1981. pap. 1.95 (ISBN 0-505-51623-3). Tower Bks.

Naturally. David Kalugin. (Illus.). 1979. pap. 4.95 (ISBN 0-933586-02-7). Book Promo Unltd.

Nature and Art... Elizabeth Simpson Inchbald. LC 20-18840. 1796. Printed for H. & P. Rice.

Nature and Human Nature. Thomas Chandler Haliburton. LC 23-16031. 1855. Stringer and Townsend.

Nature Fantasies: A Coloring Book. William Rowe. (Illus.). pap. 2.00 (ISBN 0-486-23446-0). Dover.

Nature Girl. Bennie Caroline Hall. LC 49-11950. 1949. Phoenix Press.

Nature Mystic's Clue. Dwight Goddard. LC 25-5156. 1925.

Nature of a Crime. Joseph Conrad & Ford Madox Ford. LC 24-23735. 1924. Doubleday, Page & Company.

Nature of Love. 1st American Ed. Herbert Ernest Bates. LC 54-6866. 1954. Little, Brown.

Nature of Passion: A Novel. Ruth Prawer Jhabvala. LC 57-5504. 1957. W. W. Norton.

Nature of the Beast. Len Giovannitti. LC 76-53480. 8.95 (ISBN 0-394-40220-0). Random House.

Nature of the Beast. Rosemary Sibell Guest Boyd Kilmarnock. LC 53-8150. 1953. Putnam.

Nature of the Beast. Peter Menegas. 1975. (pbk.) 1.75. Bantam Books.

Nature of Witches. easy eye ed. Joan Sanders. 1969. pap. 0.75 o.p. Lancer.

Nature of Witches: A Novel. Joan Sanders. LC 64-10162. 1964. Houghton Mifflin.

Nature on the Road. Einar Rognebakke. LC 53-12152. 1954. Vantage Press.

Nature's Comedian. William Edward Norris. LC 4-66. 1904. D. Appleton and Company.

Nature's Revenge: Eerie Stories of Revolt Against the Human Race. Seon Manley & Gogo Lewis. LC 77-18892. 6.95 (ISBN 0-688-41843-0) (ISBN 0-688-51843-5). Lothrop, Lee & Shepard Co.

Nature's Serial Story. Edward Payson Roe. LC 7-40235. 1885. Harper & Brothers.

Nature's Serial Story. Edward Payson Roe. LC 7-40236. (On cover: Dodd, Mead & company's library of fiction, no. 12). Dodd, Mead, and Company.

Nature's Way. Herman Wouk. LC 58-8463. 3.50. Doubleday.

Naughty but Nice. Gerry Blumenfeld & Harold Blumenfeld. 1976. pap. 1.25 o.p. (LB374ZK, Leisure Bks). Nordon Pubns.

Naughty Girls. Arthur Wise. LC 73-158887. 1972. 1.85 (ISBN 0-491-00552-0). W. H. Allen.

Naughty Lady Ness. Claudette Williams. 224p. (Orig.). 1980. pap. 1.75 (ISBN 0-449-50045-4, Coventry). Fawcett.

Naughty Mary. William Arthur Neubauer. LC 50-5962. 1950. Phoenix Press.

Naughty Nan. John Luther Long. LC 2-6207. 1902. The Century Co.

Naughty Victorians. LC 75-33714. (Illus.). 1975. pap. 1.95 o.p. (ISBN 0-8021-4000-9, GP4000, Dist. by Whirlwind Bk. Co.). Grove.

Naulahka: A Story of West and East. Rudyard Kipling & Balestier, Wolcott. LC 7-12344. 1892. Macmillan and Co.

Naulahka: A Story of West and East. authorized ed. Rudyard Kipling & Wolcott Balestier. LC 99-3580. (works of Rudyard Kipling). 1899. Doubleday & McClure Company.

Naulahka: A Story of West and East. Rudyard Kipling & Wolcott Balestier. LC 28-1672. 1922. Doubleday, Page & Company.

Nausea. Jean Paul Sartre. LC 66-70332. (Penguin modern clasics) 4/-). 1965. Penguin.

Nausea. Jean Paul Sartre. LC 49-8942. 1949. New Directions.

Nausea. Jean-Paul Sartre & Lloyd Alexander. LC 79-17598. 1979. 10.00 (ISBN 0-8376-0443-5). R. Bentley.

Nausea, No. 1. Ed. by Reuben Brewster. 1968. pap. 3.95 o.p. Blue Oak.

Nausea, No. 2. Ed. by Reuben Brewster. 1969. pap. 3.95 o.p. Blue Oak.

Nauthty New York; or, The Apronstrings Relaxed. A Novel of the Period. Being a Truthful Narrative of a Weeks Jollification of Three Young Benedicts ... 1882. The American News Company.

Nautilus: Or Cruising Under Canvas. John Newland Maffitt. 1871. United States Publishing Company.
Nautilus: Or, The American Privateer. A Tale of Land and Sea During the Last War. Frank Clewline. LC 6-20749. 1847. F. Gleason.
Nautz Family. Southworth Shelley. (On cover: Lovell's library, no. 191). 1883. J. W. Lovell Company.
Navajo Canyon. Thomas Wakefield Blackburn. LC 52-6306. (Double D western). 1952. Doubleday.
Navajo Escapade. Lynn Temple. 4.95 o.p. Vantage.
Navajo Slave. Lynne Gessner. (signet book). 1978. 1.50 (ISBN 0-451-08128-5). New American Library.
Navajo Symbols of Healing. Donald Sandner. 1979. pap. 8.95 (ISBN 0-15-665445-8, Harv). HarBraceJ.
Naval Annual: Or, Stories of the Sea for M.Dccc.Xxxvi. Containing The Pirate, and The Three Cutters. Frederick Marryat. LC 7-17577. 1836. Longmans, Rees, Orme, Brown, Green, and Longman.
Naval Cadet Carlyle's Glove. Iona Oakley Gorham. LC 6-27512. (On cover: Tait's Kenilworth series, no. 10). J. S. Tait and Sons.
Naval Detective's Chast: Or, Nick, the Steeple-Climber. A Thrilling Tale of Real Life. Edward Zane Carroll Judson. LC 7-11451. (secret service series--no. 25). 1889. Street & Smith.
Naval Engagement: A Marine Narrative of Love and War. Elbridge Gerry Roberts. LC 18-7927. 1918.
Naval Lads and Lassies in War with Dixie. William Henry Winslow. LC 12-7300. The C. M. Clark Publishing Co.
Naval Mutiny. Rudyard Kipling. LC 31-33556. 1931. Doubleday, Doran & Company, Inc.
Naval Occasions and Some Traits of the Sailor-Man. Lewis Anselm Da Costa Ritchie. LC 70-130070. (Short story index reprint series). 1970. Books for Libraries Press.
Naval Officer: Or, The Pirate's Cave. A Thrilling Story of the Last War. Maturin Murray Ballou & Ames, Nathan, D. 1865. LC 7-129421. (With Judson, Edward E. C. The black avenger of the Spanish Main. New York. c1847). S. French.
Navarro. Carse Boyd, pseud. LC 62-11433. (Double D western). 1962. Doubleday.
Navigator. Morris L. West. LC 76-5504. 1976. 8.95 (ISBN 0-688-03061-0). Morrow.
Navigator. Morris L. West. LC 77-5651. 1977. 17.95 (ISBN 0-8161-6481-9). G. K. Hall.
Navigator. Morris L. West. (Kangaroo Book). 1977. 2.50 (ISBN 0-671-80986-5). Pocket Books.
Navigator. Morris L. West. LC 77-351887. (Illus.). 1976. 3.95 (ISBN 0-00-222267-1). Collins.
Navigator of Rhada. Alfred Coppel. LC 69-13774. 1968. Harcourt, Brace & World.
Navigator: The Story of Nathaniel Bowditch. Alfred Boller Stanford. LC 27-202557. 1927. W. Morrow & Company.
Navigator. Translated from the French by Mervyn Savill. 1st American Ed. Jules Roy. LC 55-9268. 1955. Knopf.
Navigators. Anthony Burton. LC 76-376181. (Troubadour). 1976. 3.95 (ISBN 0-356-08351-9). Macdonald and Jane's.
Navigator's Syndrome. Jayge Carr. LC 81-43446. (Science Fiction Ser.). 192p. 1983. 11.95 (ISBN 0-385-17221-4). Doubleday.
Navona One Thousand: A Novel. Mel Arrighi. LC 75-31607. 192p. 1976. 7.95 o.p. (ISBN 0-672-52211-X). Bobbs.
Navona 1000: A Novel. Mel Arrighi. LC 75-31607. 7.95 (ISBN 0-672-52211-X). Bobbs-Merrill.
Navvies Are Coming. Frank Walker. LC 77-360134. 1976. 4.25 (ISBN 0-7181-1500-7). Joseph.
Navy Blue: A Story of Cadet Life in the United Stated Naval Academy at Annapolis. Willis Boyd Allen. LC 10-7792. 1898. E. P. Dutton & Company.
Navy Blue and Gold: A Story of the Naval Academy. George Bruce. LC 37-3447. The William Caslon Company, Inc.
Navy Blue Lady. Kathleen Harris. LC 45-3454. 1945. Arcadia House.
Navy Blue Lady. Kathleen Harris, pseud. LC 45-345443. 1945. Arcadia House, Inc.
Navy Colt: A Johnny Fletcher Mystery. Frank Gruber. LC 41-194152. 1941. Farrar & Rinehart, Inc.
Navy Eternal. facsimile ed. Lewis Ainselm da Costa Ritchie. LC 72-134977. (Short Story Index Reprint Ser). 1918. 15.00 (ISBN 0-8369-3706-6). Ayer Co.
Navy Eternal. Which Is the Navy-That-Floats, the Navy-That-Flies and the Navy-Under-the-Sea. Lewis Anselm da Costa Ricci. LC 19-7044. 1918. Hodder and Stoughton.
Navy Eternal: Which Is the Navy-That-Floats, the Navy-That-Flies and the Navy-Under-the-Sea. Lewis Anselm da Costa Ricci. LC 19-7701. George H. Doran Company.
Navy Eternal: Which Is the Navy-That-Floats, the Navy-That-Flies, and the Navy-Under-the-Sea. Lewis Anselm Da Costa Ritchie. LC 72-134977. (Short story index reprint series). (Illus.). 1970. Books for Libraries Press.
Navy Eternal: Which Is the Navy-That-Floats, the Navy-That-Flies and the Navy-Under-the-Sea. Lewis Anselm da Costa Ritchie. LC 19-7044. 1918. Hodder and Stoughton.
Navy Eternal: Which Is the Navy-That-Floats, the Navy-That-Flies and the Navy-Under-the-Sea. Lewis Anselm da Costa Ritchie. LC 19-770. George H. Doran Company.
Navy Landing. L. J Stanton. LC 35-70329. J. Messner, Inc.
Navy Murders. Elwyn Whitman Chambers. LC 32-5310. Dodd, Mead & Company.
Navy Nurse. Adelaide Humphries. LC 54-9312. 1954. Avalon Books.
Navy Nurse. Virginia McCall. LC 68-14940. 1969. pap. 0.60 o.p. (63-080). Paperback Lib.
Navy Nurse. Katherine Ursula Parrott. LC 43-9189. 1943. Dodd, Mead & Company.
Navy Spy Murders. George Fielding Eliot. LC 87-19454. Dodge Publishing Company.
Navy Tramp. Elwyn Whitman Chambers. LC 36-25550. Godwin.
Navy Wives. Elwyn Whitman Chambers. LC 30-7797. Rae D. Henkle Co.
Naw Su: A Story of Burma. Harry Ignatius Marshall. LC 48-5310. 1947. Falmouth Pub. House.
Naya: A Story of the Bighorn Country. Elizabeth Trowbridge Egleston Hinman. LC 10-27713. 1910. Rand, McNally & Company.
Nayar. Miguel Angel Menendez. Tr. by Flores, Angel. LC 41-26005. Farrar & Rinehart, Inc.
Nazarene. Shalom Asch & Samuel, Maurice, 1895- Tr. LC 39-27842. G. P. Putnam's Sons.
Nazarene: Or, The Last of the Washingtons, a Revelation of Philadelphia, New York, and Washington, in the Year 1844. George Lippard. LC 7-16042. 1846. G. Lippard and Co.
Nazarene: Or, The Last of the Washingtons. A Revelation of Philadelphia, New York, and Washington, in the Year 1844. George Lippard. 1854. T. B. Peterson.
Nazarini: A Missionary Story. Ella M Noller. LC 42-20802. 1942. Wm. B. Eerdmans Publishing Company.
Nazi and the Barber. Edgar Hilsenrath. 1973. (pbk) 1.50. Manor Books.
Nazi and the Barber. Edgar Hilsenrath. LC 78-111187. 1971. 6.95. Doubleday.
Nazi Connection. F. W. Winterbotham. 1979. pap. 2.50 (ISBN 0-440-16197-5). Dell.
Nazi Hunter. Bynum Shaw. LC 68-20823. 1968. W. W. Norton.
Nazi Hunter, No .1. Mark Mandell. 213p. 1981. pap. 2.50 (ISBN 0-523-41049-2). Pinnacle Bks.
Nazi Hunter: Killer Instinct, No. 3. Mark Mandell. 192p. (Orig.). 1982. pap. 2.25 (ISBN 0-523-41446-3). Pinnacle Bks.
Nazi Interrogator. Raymond F. Tolliver. 464p. 1980. pap. 2.95 (ISBN 0-89083-649-3). Zebra.
Nazi Who Lived As a Jew. Edgar Hilsenrath. 1977. pap. 1.95 (ISBN 0-532-19145-5). Woodhill.
Nd Signposts in the Sea: A Novel. 1st Ed. Victoria Mary Sackville-West. LC 61-8903. 1961. Doubleday.
Ndidi, the African Businessman. John A. Iechukwu. 1978. 7.95 o.p. (ISBN 0-533-03245-8). Vantage.
Ne-Bo-Shone: At the Bend of the River. Hal L Cutler. LC 17-297326. 1.35. The Reilly & Britton Co.
Nea-Th Texas Stars: A Novel. 1st Ed. Yetive H Dean. LC 55-955. 1955. W. B. Eerdmans Pub. Co.
Neanderthal Planet. Brian Wilson Aldiss. 192p. 1981. pap. 2.25 (ISBN 0-380-54197-1, 54197). Avon.
Neapolitan Ice. Renee Haynes. LC 29-138314. 1929. L. MacVeagh, The Dial Press.
Neapolitan Lovers. Alexandre Dumas. Ed. by Garnett, Robert Singleton. LC 17-307229. 1917. Brentano's.
Neapolitan Streak. Timothy Holme. LC 80-14145. 1980. 10.95 (ISBN 0-698-11052-8). Coward, McCann & Geoghegan.
Near a Whole City Full. Edward Waterman Townsend. LC 76-166909. (Illus.). 1971. (ISBN 0-403-01434-4). Scholarly Press.
Near a Whole City Full. Edward Waterman Townsend. LC 8-29828. 1897. G. W. Dillingham & Co.
Near and the Far. Leopold Hamilton Myers. LC 30-4238. Harcourt, Brace and Company.
Near-Fatal Attraction: A Novel. Hursty Richey. LC 76-26783. 8.95 (ISBN 0-87949-076-4). Ashley Books.
Near Relation. Christabel Rose Coleridge. (On cover: Lovell's library, no. 1028). 1887. J. W. Lovell Company.
Near Relation. A Novel. Christabel Rose Coleridge. (Harper's Franklin square library, no. 563). 1887. Harper & Brothers.
Near the Fire. Philip K. Jason. Date not set. 10.00 (ISBN 0-931848-56-3); pap. 4.95 (ISBN 0-931848-55-5). Dryad Pr.
Near the Throne. W. J Thorold. Meyer Bros. & Company.
Near to Happiness (A Cote Du Bonheur) Tr. by Potter, Frank Hunter. LC 7-34695. (On cover: Appleton's town and country library. no. 28). 1889. D. Appleton and Company.
Near to Nature's Heart. Edward Payson Roe. LC 7-40237. Dodd, Mead & Company.
Near to Nature's Heart. Edward Payson Roe. LC 7-40238. (On cover: Dodd, Mead, & company's library of fiction, no. 18). Dodd, Mead & Company.
Near to Nature's Heart. new ed., with illustrations by frederick dielman. ed. Edward Payson Roe. LC 13-9377. 1891. Dodd, Mead & Company.
Near to Nature's Heart. Edward Payson Roe. LC 4-26115. 1904. Dodd, Mead and Company.
Nearby: A Novel. Elizabeth Yates. LC 47-662. 1947. Coward-McCann, Inc.
Nearer and Dearer: A Novelette... Edward Bradley. LC 6-15198. 1864. Carleton; Etc., Etc.
Nearer the Earth. Beatrice Borst. LC 42-209955. 1942. Random House.
Nearer to Heaven. Frank Baker. LC 55-9712. 1955. Westminster Press.
Nearest and Dearest. A Novel. Emma Dorothy Eliza Nevitte Southworth. R. Bonner's Sons.
Nearest and Dearest: A Novel. Emma Dorothy Eliza Nevitte Southworth. LC 43-319601. (On cover: Southworth library, no. 133). Street & Smith.
Nearest Fire. Cherry Wilder, pseud. 1982. pap. 2.75 (ISBN 0-671-44703-3). PB.
Nearing's Grace. Scott Sommer. 192p. 1981. pap. 2.25 (ISBN 0-449-24438-5, Crest). Fawcett.
Nearing's Grace. Scott Sommer. LC 79-5131. 1979. 8.95 (ISBN 0-8008-5476-4). Taplinger.
Nearing's Grace: A Novel. Scott Sommer. LC 79-5131. 1979. 8.95 (ISBN 0-8008-5476-4). Taplinger.
Nearly Heaven. John Palnud. LC 30-15703. Hecla Press.
Nearly Home: Or, The Shelving Rock. A Story in Real Life. John H Farris. LC 6-38966. 1892. Casebeer & Copeland, Printers.
Nearly Lost. A Novel. Annie M Hucker. LC 7-5653. 1890. G. W. Dillingham.
Nearness of Evil. Carley Mills. 1961. bds. 3.95 o.p. Coward.
Nearness of Evil: A Novel. Carley Mills. LC 61-54253. 1961. Coward McCann.
Neat Little Corpse. Max Murray. LC 50-7148. 1950. Farrar, Straus.
Neath Silver Mask: Or, The Cloudland of Life. William O'Brien. 1872. P. Donahoe.
Neath Sunny Southern Skies. Clara Marion Young Williamson. 1908. Press of Palfrey-Rodd-Pursell Co., Ltd.
Nebe. Ignatz Sahula-Dycke. 1978. 4.50 o.p. (ISBN 0-682-49069-5). Exposition.
Nebraska Coast. Clyde Brion Davis. LC 39-27580. Farrar & Rinehart.
Nebula Award Stories, No. 6. Ed. by Clifford D. Simak. 1971. 5.95 o.p. (ISBN 0-385-05753-9). Doubleday.
Nebula Award Stories, No. 7. Ed. by Lloyd Biggle, Jr. LC 66-20974. 288p. (YA) 1973. 6.95 o.p. (ISBN 0-06-010328-0, HarpT). Har-Row.
Nebula Award Stories, No. 7. Ed. by Lloyd Biggle, Jr. 320p. 1974. pap. 1.25 o.p. (ISBN 0-06-080438-6, P438, PL). Har-Row.
Nebula Award Stories Eleven. Ed. by Ursula K. LeGuin. LC 66-20974. (YA) 1977. 8.95 o.p. (ISBN 0-06-012564-0, HarpT). Har-Row.
Nebula Award Stories Five. Ed. by James Blish. LC 66-20974. 1970. 4.95 o.p. (ISBN 0-385-03851-8). Doubleday.
Nebula Award Stories Four. Ed. by Paul Anderson. 1969. 5.95 o.p. Doubleday.
Nebula Award Stories No. 10, Anniversary Issue. Ed. by James Gunn. LC 66-20974. 268p. (YA) 1975. 10.95 o.p. (ISBN 0-06-011628-5, HarpT). Har-Row.
Nebula Award Stories, No. 8. Ed. by Isaac Asimov. LC 66-20974. 268p. (YA) 1973. 9.95 o.p. (ISBN 0-06-010151-2, HarpT). Har-Row.
Nebula Award Stories, No. 9. Ed. by Kate Wilhelm. LC 66-20974. 268p. (YA) 1975. 9.95 o.p. (ISBN 0-06-014652-4, HarpT). Har-Row.
Nebula Award Stories: Number Two. Ed. by Brian W. Aldiss, Harry Harrison. Ed. by Damon Francis Knight & Brian Wilson Aldiss. Science Fiction Writers of America. (75114). 1968. Pocket Bks.
Nebula Award Stories Sixteen. Ed. by Jerry Pournelle & John F. Carr. LC 66-20974. 259p. 1982. 14.95 (ISBN 0-03-059787-0). HR&W.
Nebula Award Stories Three. Ed. by Roger Zelazny. LC 68-27141. 1968. 4.95 o.p. Doubleday.
Nebula Award Stories: Two. 1967. Ed. by Damon Francis Knight & Brian Wilson Aldiss. Science Fiction Writers of America. LC 66-20974. 1967. 4.95. Doubleday.
Nebula Award Stories. 1965- Ed. by Damon Francis Knight. Science Fiction Writers of America. LC 66-20974. 1966. 4.95. Doubleday.
Nebula Maker". William Olaf Stapledon. LC 77-363096. 1976. 3.50 (ISBN 0-905220-06-4). Bran's Head Books.
Nebula Maker & Four Encounters. William Olaf Stapledon. LC 82-17684. (Illus.). 288p. 1983. 14.95 (ISBN 0-396-08105-3); pap. 7.95 (ISBN 0-396-08167-3). Dodd.
Nebula Winners Fifteen. Ed. by Frank Herbert. LC 78-645226. 256p. 1981. 13.41i (ISBN 0-06-014830-6, HarpT). Har-Row.
Nebula Winners Fourteen. Frederik Pohl. LC 66-20974. (Harper Science Fiction Ser.). 240p. 1980. 13.41i (ISBN 0-06-013382-1, HarpT). Har-Row.
Nebula Winners Fourteen. Ed. by Frederik Pohl. 240p. 1982. pap. 2.25 (ISBN 0-553-20931-0). Bantam.
Nebula Winners Thirteen. Samuel R. Delany. 224p. 1981. pap. 2.50 (ISBN 0-553-14726-9). Bantam.
Nebula Winners Twelve. Ed. by Gordon R. Dickson. LC 66-20974. 1978. 12.45i (ISBN 0-06-011078-3, HarpT). Har-Row.
Necessary Action. Per Wahloo. LC 69-14187. 1969. 4.95. Pantheon.
Necessary Corpse. Ralph Carter Woodthorpe. LC 39-15795. 1939. Pub. for the Crime Club, Inc., by Doubleday, Doran & Company Inc.
Necessary Doubt. Colin Wilson. LC 64-16579. 1964. Trident Press.
Necessary End. 1st Ed. Anita Rowe Block. LC 60-5915. 1960. Doubleday.
Necessary Evil. Kelley Pseud Roos. LC 65-14521. (Red badge detective). bds., 3.50. Dodd.
Necessary Evil. Kelley Pseud Roos. LC 65-14521. (Red badge detective). 1965. Dodd, Mead.
Necessary Man. Agnes Louise Logan Adams. LC 29-17924. 1929. The Bobbs-Merrill Company.
Necessary Objects. Lois Gould. 1973. (pbk.) 1.75. Dell.
Necessary Objects. Lois Gould. LC 72-2696. 1972. 6.95 (ISBN 0-394-46847-3). Random House.
Necessary Objects. Lois Gould. LC 72-4471. 1972. Random House.
Necessary Woman. Helen Van Slyke. LC 78-62606. 1979. 10.95 (ISBN 0-385-12777-4). Doubleday.
Necessary Woman. Helen Van Slyke. LC 81-14479. 1981. 13.95 (ISBN 0-89621-322-6). Thorndike Press.
Neck & Neck. Leo Bruce, pseud. 224p. 1980. Repr. of 1951 ed. 14.95 (ISBN 0-89733-041-2). Academy Chi Ltd.
Neck & Neck. Leo Bruce, pseud. 224p. 1976. Repr. of 1951 ed. 7.95 o.p. (ISBN 0-86025-025-3, Pub. by Ian Henry Pubns England). Academy Chi Ltd.
Neck & Neck. Leo Bruce, pseud. 1979. 11.00x o.p. (ISBN 0-86025-025-3, Pub. by Ian Henry Pubns England). State Mutual Bk.
Neck & Neck. Leo Bruce, pseud. 1977. 6.50 o.p. State Mutual Bk.
Neck in a Noose. Morna Doris MacTaggart Brown. LC 43-4269. 1943. Published for the Crime Club by Doubleday, Doran.
Neck in a Noose. Elizabeth Ferrars, pseud. LC 43-4269. 1943. Pub. for the Crime Club by Doubleday, Doran & Co., Inc.
Necklace. Florence Stonebraker. LC 50-11859. 1950. Arcadia House.
Necklace & Calabash. Robert Van Gulik. (Judge Dee Mystery Ser.). (Orig.). 1979. pap. 2.25 (ISBN 0-684-16329-2, SL 888, ScribT). Scribner.
Necklace and Calabash: A Chinese Detective Story. Robert Hans Van Gulik, pseud. LC 78-140392. (His New Judge Dee mysteries). (Illus.). 1971. 4.95 (ISBN 0-684-10620-5). Scribner.
Necklace of Death... Henry Holt. LC 31-318492. Pub. for the Crime Club, Inc., by Doubleday, Doran & Company, Inc.
Necklace of Kali. Robert Towers. LC 60-10932. 1960. Harcourt, Brace.
Necklace of Pandura. Reginald Gourlay. LC 7-25162. Broadway Publishing Co.
Necklace of Princess Florimonde. Mary De Morgan. 1963. 12.50 (ISBN 0-575-01100-9, Pub. by Gollancz England). David & Charles.
Necklace of Skulls. Ivor Drummond. LC 76-62763. 1977. 7.95 (ISBN 0-312-56262-4). St. Martin's Press.
Necktie in Greenwich Village. Myron Levoy. LC 68-14334. 1968. Vanguard Press.
Necktie Party. Jake Logan. LC 81-86259. (Jake Logan Western Ser.). 224p. (Orig.). 1982. pap. 1.95 (ISBN 0-86721-134-2). Playboy Pbks.
Necromancer. Gordon R. Dickson. 189p. 1981. pap. 2.25 (ISBN 0-441-56851-3). Ace Bks.

Necromancer. Gordon R. Dickson. (Science Fiction Ser). 1978. pap. 1.75 o.p. (ISBN 0-87997-353-6, UE1353). DAW Bks.

Necromancer. Robert Holdstock. 1979. pap. 2.50 (ISBN 0-380-48082-4, 48082). Avon.

Necromancer see No Room for Man.

Necromancer: A Romance. George William McArthur Reynolds. LC 75-46304. (Supernatural and Occult Fiction). 1976. 15.00 (ISBN 0-405-08164-2). Arno Press.

Necromancer: Or The Tale of the Black Forest, Founded on Facts, Tr. from the German of Lawrence Flammenberg, by Peter Teuthold. Karl Friedrich Kahlert. LC 68-98585. (Northanger Set of Jane Austen Horrid Novels). 1968. Folio Pr.

Necromancer: Or, Voo-Doo Doctor: a Story Based on Facts. Handy Nereus Brown. LC 77-39544. (Illus.). 1976. 11.50 (ISBN 0-404-00008-8). AMS Press.

Necromancer: Or, Voo-Doo Doctor; a Story Based on Facts. Handy Nereus Brown. LC 6-5143.

Necromancers. Robert Hugh Benson. LC 75-36826. (Series: The Occult (New York, 1976-). 1976. 18.00 (ISBN 0-405-07939-7). Arno Press.

Necromancers. Robert Hugh Benson. LC 9-25620. 1909. B. Herder.

Necrophiles. David Gurney. LC 75-96280. 1970. 5.95 o.p. Geis.

Necrophiles. David Gurney. 1971. pap. 0.95 o.p. (N2384). Pyramid Pubns.

Necropolis. Basil Copper. LC 79-20723. (Illus.). 10.95 (ISBN 0-87054-088-2). Arkham House Publishers.

Nectar & the Night. Joe Thorn. 1976. 9.70 (ISBN 0-87012-232-0). McClain.

Nectar in a Sieve. Kamala Markandaya, pseud. pap. 2.50 (ISBN 0-451-12291-7, AE2291, Sig). NAL.

Nectar in a Sieve. Kamala Purnaiya Taylor. LC 55-5937. 1955. J. Day Co.

Nectar in a Sieve: A Novel by Kamala Markandaya Pseud. Kamala Purnaiya Taylor. LC 56-58088. (Signet books, S1336). 1956. New American Library.

Nectar of Heaven. E. C Tubb. 1981. 1.95 (ISBN 0-87997-613-6). DAW Books.

Ned Bachman, the New Orleans Detective. Alfred J. Cohen. (On cover: The champion detective series no. 10). 1887. J. S. Ogilvie and Company.

Ned Brewster's Bear Hunt. Chauncey Jeddie Hawkins. LC 13-20208. 1913. 1.20. Little, Brown, and Company.

Ned Brewster's Caribou Hunt. Chauncey Jeddie Hawkins. LC 14-17923. 1914. 1.20. Little, Brown, and Company.

Ned Brewster's Year in the Big Woods. Chauncey Jeddie Hawkins. LC 12-24683. 1912. 1.20. Little, Brown, and Company.

Ned Hampden: Or, The Ravages of Intemperance. With a Plea for Prohibition of the Liquor Traffic. I. A Sites. LC 8-9011. 1893. D. Miller.

Ned Kelly's Last Stand. Frank Clune, pseud. 1967. Repr. pap. 1.60 o.s.i. Tri-Ocean.

Ned Myers: Or, A Life Before the Mast. James Fenimore Cooper. 1843. Lea and Blanchard.

Ned Myers: Or A Life Before the Mast. new ed. James Fenimore Cooper. LC 6-29870. 1857. Stringer and Townsend.

Ned, Nigger An' Gent'man: A Story of War and Reconstruction Days. Norman Goree Kittrell. LC 7-25078. 1907. The Neale Publishing Company.

Nedra. Grace Lang, pseud. 1978. pap. 1.50 (ISBN 0-532-15380-4). Woodhill.

Nedra. George Barr McCutcheon. 1905. Dodd, Mead & Company.

Need. Russell O'Neil. 1974. (pbk.) 1.75. Dell.

Need. Tom Powers. LC 34-6836. 1932. Pegasus Publishing Company.

Need for Love: A Novel. B Trainor. LC 60-53491. 1961. Greenwich Book Publishers.

Need for the Magisterium of the Church. K. D. Whitehead. (Synthesis Ser.). 1979. 0.75 (ISBN 0-8199-0747-2). Franciscan Herald.

Need of Change. Julian Leonard Street. LC 9-21866. 1909. J. Lane Company.

Need of Change. 5th anniversary ed. Julian Leonard Street. LC 14-19164. 1914. John Lane Company; Etc., Etc.

Need of Change. twenty-fifth anniversary edition, 1909-1934. ed. Julian Leonard Street & Darrow, Whitney, 1909- Illus. LC 34-33479. 1934. Dodd, Mead & Company.

Need to Love. Amrtha Buren. 1964. Dod, Mead.

Need We Have. Arthur Hamilton Gibbs. LC 36-17723. 1936. Little, Brown, and Company.

Needle. Hal Clement. 1979. pap. 1.95 (ISBN 0-380-00635-9, 44263). Avon.

Needle. Hal Clement. 1972. pap. 0.95 o.p. (75-385). Lancer.

Needle. Francis Henry King. LC 76-11821. 1976. (ISBN 0-88405-358-X). Mason/Charter.

Needle That Wouldn't Hold Still. Aaron Marc Stein. LC 50-9181. (Inner sanctum mystery). 1950. Simon and Schuster.

Needle That Wouldn't Hold Still. Hampton Stone, pseud. (Hampton Stone Mystery Ser). 1971. pap. 0.75 o.p. (ISBN 0-446-64735-7, 64-735-7). Paperback Lib.

Needle-Watcher. Richard Blaker. LC 32-21194. 1932. Doubleday, Doran & Company, Inc.

Needle-Watcher: The Will Adams Story, British Samurai. Richard Blaker. LC 72-89743. (Tut books. L). 1973. 3.50 (ISBN 0-8048-1094-X). C. E. Tuttle Co.

Needles. William Deverell. LC 79-89716. 9.95. Little, Brown.

Needles and Pins: A Novel. Justin Huntly McCarthy. LC 7-18594. 1907. Harper & Brothers.

Needle's Eye. Margaret Drabble. 1973. (pbk.) 1.25. Popular Lib.

Needle's Eye. Edward Lee Fouts. LC 44-9630. 1944. Pub. for the Crime Club by Doubleday, Doran and Co., Inc.

Needle's Eye. Florence Morse Kingsley. LC 2-22850. 1902. Funk & Wagnalls Company.

Needle's Eye. 1977. 1.95. (ISBN 0-445-08590-8). Popular Library.

Needle's Eye. Arthur Cheney Train. LC 24-23091. 1924. C. Scribner's Sons.

Needle's Eye, a Novel. Margaret Drabble. LC 79-178957. 1972. 6.95 (ISBN 0-394-47966-1). Knopf.

Needle's Eye: A Novel. Timothy Pember. LC 47-31281. 1947. Reynal & Hitchcock.

Needle's Kiss. Austin J Small. LC 29-88313. 1929. Pub.for the Crime Club, Inc., by Doubleday, Doran & Company, Inc.

Neely. Walter Karig. LC 52-9604. 1953. Rinehart.

Neena: A Novel of the Navajos of New Mexico. 1st Ed. Ruth Hookham. LC 56-11592. 1956. Exposition Press.

Ne'er-Do-Much. Eleanor Hallowell Abbott. LC 18-692213. 1918. Dodd, Mead and Company.

Ne'er-Do-Well. Rex Ellingwood Beach. LC 20-8633. 1911. A. L. Burt Company.

Nefasti Noche (Unlucky Night) Emhill Burke. LC 39-36. 1938. L. & G. Gouget.

Negative in Blue. Carter Brown, pseud. (Signet book). 1974. (pbk.) 0.95. New American Library.

Negatives. Peter Everett. (Crest bk., R1139). 1968. Fawcett.

Negatives. Peter Everett. LC 65-11162. 1965. Simon and Schuster.

Neggar Journeys into Nightmares. Saggittarus. LC 72-96167. 144p. 4.50 (ISBN 0-912444-18-5). Gaus.

Neglected Clue. Isabel Egenton Ostrander. LC 25-8786. 1925. R. M. McBride & Company.

Neglected Lives. Stephen Alter. LC 78-5838. 1978. 8.95 (ISBN 0-374-22024-7). Farrar Straus Giroux.

Neglected Visions. Barry N Malzberg & Martin Harry Greenberg. LC 78-22797. 1980. 8.95 (ISBN 0-385-14613-2). Doubleday.

Negligent Daughter: A Novel. Edith De Born. LC 79-305998. 1978. 13.50 (ISBN 0-04-823146-0). Allen & Unwin.

Negotiable. Edwin M Thomas. LC 9-320605. 1908.

Negotiated Surrender. Jayne Castle. (Candlelight Ecstasy Ser.: No. 68). (Orig.). 1982. pap. 1.95 (ISBN 0-440-16498-2). Dell.

Negotiator. Clayton Matthews. (Orig.). 1975. pap. 1.50 o.p. (ISBN 0-515-03612-9). Pyramid Pubns.

Negotiator. Ray Mount Rogers. LC 75-1360. 1975. (ISBN 0-679-50537-7). D. McKay Co.

Negotiators. Francis Walder. LC 59-13758. 1959. McDowell, Obolensky.

Negro As He Is: A Realistic Story of Negro Life. Robert Cunningham. LC 6-31725. 1893. Independence Sentinel Print.

Negro Caravan. Sterling A. Brown et al. pap. 4.95 o.p. (ISBN 0-394-71094-0, V94, Vin). Random.

Negro Mystic Lore. Mamie Hunt Sims. LC 8-3517. 1907. To-Morrow Press.

Negro Question see Collected Works.

Negro Tales. Joseph Seamon Cotter. LC 75-83923. (Illus.). 1969. Mnemosyne Pub. Co.

Negro Tales. Joseph Seamon Cotter. LC 13-384. 1912. 1.00. The Cosmopolitan Press.

Nehalem Tillamook Tales. Elizabeth D. Jacobs & Melville Jacobs. LC 60-62647. (O.s.i.). 1959. pap. 3.00 o.s.i. (ISBN 0-87114-006-3). U of Oreg Bks.

Nehe; a Tale of the Times of Artaxerxes. Anna Pierpont Siviter. LC 1-23081. 1901. W. A. Wilde Company.

Neighbor. Edmund Brown. LC 76-9469. 1969. 4.95. Pageant Press.

Neighbor. Laird Koenig. LC 78-60674. 1978. 1.75 (ISBN 0-380-41285-3). Avon.

Neighbor Jackwood. rev. ed., with a chapter of autobiography. ed. John Townsend Trowbridge. LC 68-57556. (Illus.). 1968. Gregg Press.

Neighbor Jackwood. rev. ed., with a chapter of autobiography. ed. John Townsend Trowbridge. 1899. Lee and Shepard.

Neighbor to the Sky. Gladys Hasty Carroll. LC 37-27296. 1937. The Macmillan Company.

Neighborhood Nurse. Peggy O'More, pseud. LC 68-1544. 1968. Arcadia House.

Neighborhood of Girls. Lellie C Southwick. LC 8-10808. 1896. Jewell Publishing Company.

Neighborhood Stories. Zona Gale. LC 14-179882. 1914. The Macmillan Company.

Neighborhood Story (Hekayat Haretna) Najib Mahfuz. (Arabic.). 5.50x (ISBN 0-86685-156-9). Intl Bk Ctr.

Neighborhood. 1st Ed. David Mark. LC 59-7911. 1959. Doubleday.

Neighborly Lover. Peter Kanto. (Orig.). pap. 0.95 o.p. (1139). Brandon.

Neighborly Relations: And Other Stories of Bygone Times on a Saltwater Farm. Edwin D. Merry. LC 80-19823. (Illus.). 96p. (Orig.). 1980. pap. 3.95 (ISBN 0-89621-060-X). Thorndike Pr.

Neighbors. Michael Allwright. LC 68-15905. 1968. Walker.

Neighbors. Thomas Berger. (O.s.i.). 1980. 9.95 o.s.i. (ISBN 0-440-06556-9, Sey Lawr). Delacorte.

Neighbors. Thomas Berger. 1981. pap. 5.95 (ISBN 0-440-55975-8). Dell.

Neighbors. Thomas Berger. 1981. pap. 2.95 (ISBN 0-440-16306-4). Dell.

Neighbors. Edmund Brown. 4.00 o.p. (ISBN 0-8181-0030-3). Pageant-Poseidon.

Neighbors. Jim Kelly. (Small Star Stories). (Illus.). 5.95 o.p. (ISBN 0-02-645450-5, 64545); cassette 6.95 o.p. (ISBN 0-02-645460-2, 64546). Glencoe.

Neighbors. Florence Morse Kingsley. LC 17-24704. 1917. Dodd, Mead and Company.

Neighbors. Claude Houghton Oldfield. LC 27-17359. H. Holt and Company.

Neighbors: A Novel. Thomas Berger. LC 79-20307. 9.95 (ISBN 0-440-06556-9). Delacorte Press/Seymour Lawrence.

Neighbors: A Novel. Russell O'Neil. LC 72-76805. 1972. 1.25. Paperback Library.

Neighbors: A Novel. Virginia Eggersten Sorensen. LC 47-31092. 1947. Reynal & Hitchcock.

Neighbors and Other People: More of the Best of Douglass Welch. Douglass Welch & Ruth Welch. LC 77-20285. 1977. 4.95 (ISBN 0-914842-24-2). Madrona Publishers.

Neighbors Needn't Know. Sylvia Golden. LC 53-9495. 1953. Macmillan.

Neighbors of Ours: Slum Stories of London. Henry Woodd Nevinson. LC 7-17289. (On cover: Buckram series). 1895. H. Holt and Company.

Neighbors Unknown. Charles George Douglas Roberts. LC 11-846. 1911. 1.00. The Macmillan Company.

Neighbors' Wives. John Townsend Trowbridge. LC 12-39591. 1895. Lee and Shepard.

Neighbours: a Story of Every-Day Life. 4th ed., carefully rev. and corr. by the latest swedish ed. Fredrika Bremer. LC 74-150538. (Short story index reprint series). (Illus.). 1971. (ISBN 0-8369-3835-6). Books for Libraries Press.

Neighbours: A Story of Every-Day Life. 4th ed., carefully rev. and cor. by the latest swedish ed. Fredrika Bremer. Tr. by Mary Botham Howitt. LC 4-16867. (On cover: Bohn's standard library). 1892. G. Bell & Sons.

Neighbours in Barton Square. Alice Eddy Curtiss. LC 6-317060. Congregational Sunday-School and Publishing Society.

Neighbours on the Green. Margaret Oliphant Wilson Oliphant. LC 41-311291. 1889. Macmillan and Co.

Neil Nelson, the Veteran Detective: Or, Tracking Mail Robbers. Ernest A. Young. G. W. Ogilvie.

Neila Sen and My Casual Death. James H Connelly. LC 6-30686. (Lovell's occult series, no. 8). United States Book Company.

Neils Klim: Being an Incomplete Translation by Thomas De Quincey. Ludwig Holberg. Ed. by S. Musgrave. Tr. by Thomas De Quincey. 1977. Repr. of 1953 ed. lib. bdg. 10.00 (ISBN 0-8482-1127-8). Norwood Edns.

Neither a Candle nor a Pitchfork. Joyce Porter. LC 70-96304. 1970. 4.95. McCall Pub. Co.

Neither Bond nor Free. George Langhorne Pryor. LC 79-144674. Repr. of 1902 ed. 18.50 (ISBN 0-404-00208-0). AMS Pr.

Neither Bond nor Free. A Plea.)... George Langhorne Pryor, pseud. 1902. J. S. Ogilvie Publishing Company.

Neither Do I. Elizabeth Adamson Redford. LC 10-14647. 1910. 1.50. Broadway Publishing Company.

Neither Do They Reap. Frank B Howery. LC 68-57106. (Illus.). Vienna Typesetting Co.

Neither Five nor Three. Helen MacInnes. 1978. pap. 2.75 (ISBN 0-449-23566-1, Crest). Fawcett.

Neither Five nor Three. 1st Ed. Helen MacInnes Highet. LC 51-1551. 1951. Harcourt, Brace.

Neither Man nor Angel. Susan Seavy. LC 51-12268. 1951. Bobbs-Merrill.

Neither Rome nor Judah. Fanny Hooker. LC 7-5266. Presbyterian Board of Publications.

Neither Sun nor Storm. Michael Scott Stone. LC 40-98657. L. Raley, Incorporated.

Neither the Sea nor the Sand. Gordon Honeycombe. 1970. 6.95 o.p. Weybright.

Nelegko byt' ruskim shpionom. Aleksei Korotyukov. 132p. (Rus.). 1982. pap. 8.00 (ISBN 0-938920-18-9). Hermitage MI.

Nell Beverly, Farmer: A Story of Farm Life. Elizabeth Deborah Jewett Brown & Howe, Mrs. Susan Howard (Jewett) 1872- Joint Author. LC 9-1525. The Rural Publishing Co.

Nell Gwyn--Comedian: A Novel. Frank Frankfort Moore. LC 1-31557. 1901. Brentano's.

Nell Gwyn. "Sweet Nell of Old Drury." A Romantic Story Founded on the Life of Nell Gwyn. George Morehead. (peerless series, no. 120). 1901. J. S. Ogilvie Publishing Company.

Nell Gwynn: Or, The Court of the Stuarts. William Harrison Ainsworth. LC 9-2692. Street & Smith.

Nell Haffenden. Tighe Hopkins. (On cover: Seaside library. Pocket ed. no. 509). G. Munro.

Nell Haffenden: A Strictly Conventional Story. Tighe Hopkins. LC 7-5243. 1896. Dodd, Mead and Company.

Nell of Narragansett Bay. Augustus Mansfield Spies. LC 25-14512. 1925. The Stratford Co.

Nell of Shorne Mills. Charles Garvice. LC 6217. (laurel library, no. 40). 1900. G. Munro's Sons.

Nella. John Godey. LC 80-26386. 12.95 (ISBN 0-440-06509-7). Delacorte Press.

Nella: The Heart of the Army. a novel. ed. Philip Verrill Mighels. LC 5780. R. F. Fenno.

Nella Waits. Marlys Millhiser. LC 74-796627. (Fawcett Crest Book). 1975. 1.50. Fawcett.

Nella Waits: A Novel of the Supernatural. Marlys Millhiser. LC 74-79662. 256p. 1974. 6.95 o.p. (ISBN 0-399-11319-3). Putnam.

Nellie. Katheryn Kimbrough, pseud. (Saga of the Phenwick Women No. 21). 1978. pap. 1.75 (ISBN 0-445-04202-8). Popular Lib.

Nellie Bloom and Other Stories. Margery Latimer. LC 29-831683. J. H. Sears & Company, Inc.

Nellie Harland. A Romance of Rail and Wire. Elmer Ellsworth Vance. LC 8-30234. 1888. G. W. Dillingham, Successor to G. W. Carleton & Co.

Nellie Kelly: Or, The Little Mother of Five. Henriette Eugenie Delamare. LC 12-27600. 1.00. H. L. Kilner & Co.

Nellie Of Truro. Hornblower. LC 7-5196. 1856. R. Carter & Brothers.

Nellie Without Hugo. Janet Hobhouse. LC 81-69997. 1982. 12.95 (ISBN 0-670-50591-9). Viking Press.

Nellie's Memories. A Novel. Rosa Nouchette Carey. (Seaside library. v. 34, no. 708). G. Munro.

Nellie's Memories: A Novel. Rosa Nouchette Carey. LC 4-15424. (On cover: The home library). A. L. Burt.

Nell's Hospital. Louisa May Alcott. 1976. Repr. of 1865 ed. 25.00 o.p. (ISBN 0-403-05871-6, Regency). Scholarly.

Nell's Story. Henrietta Eliza Vaughan Stannard. (seaside library. v. 57. no. 1151). 1881. G. Munro.

Nelly Bracken: A Tale of Forty Years Ago. Annie Chambers Ketchum. LC 6-15205. 1855. Lippincott, Grambo & Co.

Nelly Kinnard's Kingdom. Amanda Minnie Douglas. LC 6-33472. 1876. Lee and Shepard.

Nelly Kinnard's Kingdom. Amanda Minnie Douglas. LC 4-29193. (On cover: American girl's series. v. 14). 1904. Lee and Shepard.

Nelly's Silver Mine: A Story of Colorado Life. Helen Maria Fiske Hunt Jackson. LC 10-24180. 2.00. Little, Brown, and Company.

Nels Oskar. Jolie Paylin. LC 78-14579. 1979. 6.95 (ISBN 0-8138-0980-0). Iowa State University Press.

Nelson Algren's Own Book of Lonesome Monsters. Nelson Algren. pap. 1.25 o.s.i. (33-016). Lancer.

Nelson Touch. Noel Bertram Gerson. LC 60-14113. 1960. Holt, Rinehart and Winston.

Nelson Touch. 1st Ed. Paul Lewis, pseud. 1960. Holt, Rinehart and Winston.

Nemesis. Agatha Miller Christie. 1973. Pocket Bks.

Nemesis. Agatha Miller Christie. LC 72-173454. 1971. 6.95 (ISBN 0-396-06423-X). Dodd, Mead.

Nemesis Club. Jenny Savage. LC 78-3991. 1978. 7.95 (ISBN 0-312-56379-5). St. Martin's Press.

Nemesis Conjecture. William Cooke. 1980. pap. 2.25 (ISBN 0-8439-0802-5). Nordon Pubns.

Nemesis from Terra. Leigh Brackett. 1976. 1.50. Ace.

Nemesis of Circle A. Giles A. Lutz. 1981. pap. 1.95 (ISBN 0-441-56921-8). Ace Bks.

Nemesis of Evil. Lin Carter. LC 74-25097. 192p. 1975. 5.95 o.p. (ISBN 0-385-00583-0). Doubleday.

Nemesis of Faith; Shadows of the Clouds. James Anthony Froude. LC 75-1519. (Victorian Fiction: Novels of Faith and Doubt; V. 68). 1975. (ISBN 0-8240-1592-4). Garland Pub.
Nemesis of Faith, 1849. James Anthony Froude. Ed. by Robert L. Wolff. Bd. with Shadows of the Clouds, 1847. LC 75-1519. (Victorian Fiction Ser.). 1975. lib. bdg. 66.00 o.s.i. (ISBN 0-8240-1592-4). Garland Pub.
Nemesis: Or, Tinted Vapors. James MacLaren Cobban. The F. M. Lupton Publishing Company.
Nemesis Wife. Cicely Louise Evans. LC 68-11802. 1970. 5.95. Doubleday.
Nemo. Ron Goulart. (Berkley Medallion Book). 1977. 1.25 (ISBN 0-425-03395-3). Berkley Pub. Corp.
Nemo, the Shadow Detective. F. Lusk Broughton. (On cover: The champion detectie series). J. S. Ogilvie & Company.
Nemorama the Nautchnee: A Story of India. Edwin MacMinn. LC 7-20302. 1890. Hunt & Eaton.
Nene. Ernest Perochon. LC 22-26242. George H. Doran Company.
Neon. Joe Goldberg. (Dell Book). 1977. 1.75 (ISBN 0-440-11836-0). Dell Pub. Co.
Neon Graveyard. George Baxt. LC 79-16429. 8.95 (ISBN 0-312-56412-0). St. Martin's Press.
Neon Haystack. James Michael Ullman. LC 63-17726. (Inner sanctum mystery). 1963. Simon and Schuster.
Neon Jungle. John Dann MacDonald. LC 53-33928. (Gold medal books, 323). 1953. Fawcett Publications.
Neon Preacher. Robert Chambers. LC 76-44335. 1977. 7.95 (ISBN 0-88405-373-3). Mason/Charter Publishers.
Neon Rainbow. 1st American Ed. Charles Terrot. LC 56-5006. 1956. Dutton.
Neon Wilderness. Nelson Algren. LC 68-3014. 1968. P. Smith.
Neon Wilderness. Nelson Algren. LC 60-10513. (American Century series). 1960. Hill and Wang.
Neon Wilderness. Nelson Algren. LC 47-772. 1947. Doubleday & Co., Inc.
Nepalese Short Stories. Ed. by Karuna Kar Vaidya. LC 75-12436. 7.95 (ISBN 0-913622-03-6). Gallery Press.
Nephele: A Novel. Francis William Bourdillon & Gerald, Endymion Pseud. LC 3-22388. 1896. New Amsterdam Book Company.
Nephew. James Purdy. LC 60-15672. 1960. Farrar, Straus & Cudahy.
Neptune. Noel Bertram Gerson. LC 76-6876. 7.95 (ISBN 0-396-07325-5). Dodd, Mead.
Neptune Vase. A Novel. Virginia Wales Johnson. (Franklin square library, no. 198). 1881. Harper & Brothers.
Neptune's Cauldron. Michael G. Coney. 240p. (Orig.). 1981. pap. 2.25 (ISBN 0-505-51755-8). Tower Bks.
Neptune's Children. Sherman M. Woodward. (Illus.). 5.00 o.p. (ISBN 0-87482-071-5). Wake-Brook.
Nequa: Or, The Problem of the Ages. Alcanoan O Grigsby. LC 6226. (Equity library series. v. 1). 1900. Equity Publishing Company.
Nereid. Mary Faith Floyd. LC 6-41427. 1871. J.W. Burke & Company.
Nero. Mary Teresa Ronalds. LC 72-76835. 1969. 5.95. Doubleday.
Nero: A Romance. authorized ed. Ernst Eckstein & Bell, Clara Courtenay (Poynter) 1834-1927, Tr. LC 6-26319. W. S. Gottsberger & Co.
Nero Wolfe Mystery Magazine. V. 1, No. 1-3; Jan.-June 1954. Rex Stout. LC 58-33034. Hillman Periodicals.
Nero Wolfe of West Thirty-Fifth Street. William S. Baring-Gould. (Crime Ser.). 1982. pap. 4.95 (ISBN 0-14-006194-0). Penguin.
Nero Wolfe of West 35th Street. William S. Baring-Gould, pseud. 1969. 5.50 o.p. (ISBN 0-670-50602-8). Viking Pr.
Nerve. Dick Francis. 1975. pap. 2.95 (ISBN 0-671-80142-2). PB.
Nerve. Dick Francis. 1975. (pbk.) 1.50 (ISBN 0-671-80142-2). Pocket Books.
Nerve of Foley: And Other Railroad Stories. Frank Hamilton Spearman. LC 1353. 1900. Harper & Brothers.
Nerves. Lester Del Rey. 1976. (pbk.) 1.50 (ISBN 0-345-24995-X). Ballantine Books.
Nerves: A Novel. Blanche M. Boyd. LC 73-86273. 1973. 3.00 (ISBN 0-913780-04-9). Daughters, Inc.
Nerves: Novel. Lester Del Rey. LC 56-9579. (Ballantine books, H-151). 1956. Ballantine Books.
Nervous People, and Other Satires. Mikhail Mikhailovich Zoshchenko. LC 75-8834. 1975. 21.50 (ISBN 0-8371-8106-2). Greenwood Press.
Nervous People, and Other Satires. Mikhail Mikhailovich Zoshchenko. LC 75-9131. 1975. 4.95 (ISBN 0-253-20192-6). Indiana University Press.
Nervous People, and Other Satires. Ed. Introd., by Hugh McLean. Tr. from Russian by Maria Gordon, Hugh McLean. Mikhail Mikhailovich Zoshchenko. (Vintage bks., V-751). 1965. pap., 1.95. Random.
Nervous Wreck. E. J. Rath. LC 29-116584. 1923. Grosset & Dunlap.
Nervous Wreck. E. J. Rath. LC 23-16819. 1923. G. H. Watt.
NESFA Index: Science Fiction Magazines & Original Anthologies 1977. NESFA. Date not set. cancelled o.s.i. NESFA Pr.
Nest Among the Stars. Louise Harrison McCraw. LC 42-184340. 1942. Zondervan Publishing House.
Nest and Other Stories. Anne Douglas Sedgwick. LC 26-27500. 1926. Houghton Mifflin Company.
Nest Builder. Beatrice Forbes-Robertson Hale. LC 43-36614. A. L. Burt Company.
Nest-Builder: A Novel. Beatrice Forbes-Robertson Hale. LC 16-267714. 1.35. Frederick A. Stokes Company.
Nest in a Falling Tree. Joy Cowley. 1969. pap. 0.75 o.p. (0502-07016-075). Curtis.
Nest in a Falling Tree. 1st Ed. Joy Cowley. LC 67-141212. 1967. 4.95. Doubleday.
Nest of Dragons. Maxine Hart. LC 78-59350. 1978. 15.00 (ISBN 0-89002-106-6); pap. 5.00 (ISBN 0-89002-105-8). Northwoods Pr.
Nest of Eagles: A Special Plural Presidency. rev. ed. Sally Short & Ralph Short. LC 74-76491. 1974. 10.00. Short Methods & Systems.
Nest of Gentlefolk & Other Stories. Ivan Sergeevich Turgenev. (W.C.570). 3.50 o.p. Oxford U Pr.
Nest of Hawks. Juanita Tyree Osborne. (YA) 1981. 6.50 (Avalon). Bouregy.
Nest of Hooks. Lon Otto. LC 78-16507. (Iowa School of Letters Award for Short Fiction). 8.95. (ISBN 0-87745-089-7) (ISBN 0-87745-090-0). University of Iowa Press.
Nest of Linnets: A Novel. Frank Frankfort Moore. LC 1-25451. 1901. D. Appleton and Company.
Nest of Ninnies. John Ashbery & James Schuyler. LC 75-28625. 1975. (pbk.) 3.50 (ISBN 0-915990-02-4). Z Press.
Nest of Ninnies. John Ashbery & James Schuyler. LC 69-17307. 1969. 4.95. Dutton.
Nest of Rats. John William Wainwright. LC 76-57892. 1977. 7.95 (ISBN 0-312-56438-4). St. Martin's.
Nest of Rattlers. Martin Ryerson. (Orig.). 1981. pap. 1.95 (ISBN 0-8439-0924-2, Leisure Bks). Nordon Pubns.
Nest of Simple Folk. Sean O'Faolain. LC 33-27269. 1934. The Viking Press.
Nest of Spies. Pierre Souvestre & Allain, Marcel, Joint Author. LC 17-27903. (Their The Fantomas detective novels). 1917. Brentano's.
Nest of the Kildeer. Ethel Van Pelt. 1976. 4.95. Avalon Books.
Nest of the Sparrowhawk: A Romance of the Xviith Century. Emmuska Orczy. LC 9-28213. 1909. 1.50. F. A. Stokes Company.
Nest of Traitors. Gordon Ashe. 1971. 4.95 o.p. (ISBN 0-03-085982-4). HR&W.
Nest of Traitors. John Creasey. LC 74-151062. (Rinehart suspense novel). 1971. 4.95 (ISBN 0-03-085982-4). Holt, Rinehart and Winston.
Nest of Vipers. Morgan D Jones. LC 11-947. 1.50. Broadway Publishing Co.
Nester: By John S. Daniels Pseud. 1st Ed. Wayne D Overholser. LC 53-8925. 1953. Lippincott.
Nester's Revenge. B. J. Whapeles. (Orig.). 1981. pap. 1.95 (ISBN 0-505-51702-7). Tower Bks.
Nesting Place. Sarah Aldridge. 320p. (Orig.). 1982. pap. 6.95 (ISBN 0-930044-26-6). Naiad Pr.
Nesting Place: A Novel. Sarah Aldridge. LC 81-22475. 1982. 6.95 (ISBN 0-930044-26-6). Naiad Press.
Nestlenook: A Tale. Leonard Kip. LC 7-12543. (On cover: Knickerbocker novels). 1880. G. P. Putnam's Sons.
Nestling. Charles Grant. 432p. (Orig.). 1982. pap. 3.50 (ISBN 0-671-41989-7). PB.
Nestors: A Story of Homesteading in the Southwest. William Carl Case. LC 20-192444. Burton Publishing Company.
Net. Edward Sidney Aarons. (O.s.i.). 1972. pap. 0.75 o.s.i. (532-75461-075). Manor Bks.
Net. Rex Ellingwood Beach. 1975. lib. bdg. 15.30x (ISBN 0-89966-014-2). Buccaneer Bks.
Net. Jean Renvoize. LC 72-96547. 1973. 6.95 (ISBN 0-8128-1536-X). Stein and Day.
Net: A Novel. Rex Ellingwood Beach. LC 12-23509. 1912. 1.30. Harper & Brothers.
Net Net. Isadore Barmash. LC 77-180292. 1972. 6.95. Macmillan.
Net of Cobwebs. Elisabeth Sanxay Holding. LC 45-16973. 1945. Simon and Schuster.
Net of Sex. Danny Namssorg. pap. 1.95 o.s.i. (Venus). Grove.
Net to Catch the Stars. Julian M. Hoadley. 1968. 3.00 o.p. (ISBN 0-8059-0133-7). Dorrance.
Neta. William E Hurd. LC 26-184. The Christopher Publishing House.
Nether Applewhite: A Story of Strange Lives in an English Village. Horace Annesley Vachell. LC 34-6834. 1934. Houghton Mifflin Company.
Nether Millstone. Fred Merrick White. LC 7-36980. 1907. Little, Brown, and Company.
Nether World. George Robert Gissing. 1975. pap. 8.95x (ISBN 0-460-00362-3, Evman). Biblio Dist.
Nether World. George Robert Gissing. Ed. by John Goode. 469p. 24.50 (ISBN 0-8386-1543-0). Fairleigh Dickinson.
Nether World, 3 Vols. George Robert Gissing. Set. cancelled o.s.i. (ISBN 0-403-00405-5). Scholarly.
Nether World. George Robert Gissing. 412p. 1982. pap. text ed. 6.95x (ISBN 0-460-01362-9, Pub. by Evman England). Biblio Dist.
Nether World. George Robert Gissing. 1978. text ed. 19.80x o.s.i. (ISBN 0-8277-5587-2). British Bk Ctr.
Nether World: A Novel. George Robert Gissing. LC 74-499. 1974. 18.00 (ISBN 0-8386-1543-0). Fairleigh Dickinson University Press.
Nether World: A Novel. George Robert Gissing. LC 6-43979. (On cover: Harper's Franklin square library, no. 646). 1889. Harper & Brothers.
Nether World: A Novel. George Robert Gissing. 1929. E. P. Dutton & Company.
Nethergate. Norah Robinson Lofts. LC 72-89950. 1973. 6.95 (ISBN 0-385-00891-0). Doubleday.
Nethergate. Norah Robinson Lofts. LC 73-7748. 1973. 11.95 (ISBN 0-8161-6115-1). G. K. Hall.
Netherleigh. W Riley. LC 16-4584. 1916. G. P. Putnam's Sons.
Netley Abbey: A Gothic Story. Richard Warner. LC 73-22771. (Gothic Novels). 1974. (ISBN 0-405-06021-1). Arno Press.
Nets to Catch the Wind. 1st Ed. Dolores Birk Hitchens. LC 52-8747. 1952. Published for the Crime Club by Doubleday.
Netsuke. Frieder Aichele & Gert Nagel. (Collectors Library). 1977. pap. 2.50 (ISBN 0-445-04096-3). Popular Lib.
Nettle Harvest. Sylvia Denys Hooke. LC 28-10294. 1928. Doubleday, Doran & Company, Inc.
Network. Sam Hedrin (ISBN 0-671-80767-6). Pocket Books.
Network. Jim Lowe & Curtis Brown Taylor. LC 75-44360. 1976. 1.25. Ballantine Books.
Network Jungle. David Levy. 224p. 1976. pap. 1.95 (ISBN 0-89041-067-4, 3067). Major Bks.
Network Nurse. Rose Dana, pseud. 1970. pap. 0.50 o.p. (ISBN 0-447-72179-8). Lancer.
Neue Marchen und Erzahlungen. Ed. by Hildegard Rose & Rose, Ernst Andreas. LC 34-31115. 1934. Prentice-Hall, Inc.
Neuen Liedew Des Jungen W. Ulrich Plenzdorf. 1978. pap. text ed. 13.50x (ISBN 0-471-02855-X). Wiley.
Neurotic Takes a Wife: A Novel. Susan Bond. LC 51-5515. 1951. Exposition Press.
Neustrian Cycle. Leslie Barringer. LC 76-6463. (Newcastle Forgotten Fantasy library; v. 7-). (Illus.). 3.95 (ISBN 0-87877-106-9). Newcastle Pub. Co.
Neutral French: Or, The Exiles of Nova Scotia. 2d ed. Catherine Read Arnold Williams. LC 8-36917. 1841. The Author.
Neutral Ground. Belle Willey Gue. LC 22-25803. 1922. The Stratford Company.
Neutral Ground. Frank Olney Hough. LC 41-6174. J. B. Lippincott Company.
Neutral Stars. Dan Morgan & Kippax, John. (Ballantine Books: science fiction). 1973. (pbk.) 1.25 (ISBN 0-345-03086-9). Ballantine.
Neutron Beam Murder. Terry Johnson King. LC 65-15797. (Raven book). 1965. Abelard-Schuman.
Neutron Two Is Critical. Lawrence Dunning. 1977. pap. 1.75 (ISBN 0-380-01775-X, 35089). Avon.
Neutron Two Is Critical: A Novel. Lawrence Dunning. LC 77-84309. 1977. 1.75 (ISBN 0-380-01775-X). Avon.
Nevada. Herbert Arthur, pseud. LC 49-10130. (Double D western). 1949. Doubleduy.
Nevada.". Grey, Zane. 1962. Grosset & Dunlap.
Nevada. Lorinda Hagen. (Orig.). 1981. pap. 2.50 (ISBN 0-505-51691-8). Tower Bks.
Nevada! Dana Fuller Ross. LC 82-9198. (Ross, Dana Fuller. Wagons West: Vol. 8). 1982. 15.95 (ISBN 0-8161-3396-4). G.K. Hall.
Nevada, No. 8. (Wagons West). 1982. pap. write for info. Bantam.
Nevada" A Romance of the West. Zane Grey. LC 28-9467. 1928. Harper & Brothers.
Nevada Jones. Hamilton Craigie. LC 35-336216. Phoenix Press.
Nevada Queen High. Roe Richmond. (Lashtrow Ser.: No. 5). 1980. pap. 1.95 (ISBN 0-8439-0831-9). Nordon Pubns.
Nevada Rampage. Llewellyn Perry Holmes. 1972. pap. 0.75 o.s.i. (74-790). Lancer.
Never a Bride. Charles Stanley Strong. LC 42-21308. 1942. Phoenix Press.
Never a Dull Moment. Curt Gerling. 210p. 1974. 6.95. Plaza Pubs.
Never Again. William Starbuck Mayo. LC 44-43265. 1873. G. P. Putnam & Sons.
Never Again. Renee Shann. 1971. pap. 0.75 o.p. (94132). Beagle Bks.
Never Again: And Other Stories. St. John, Adela Rogers. 1949. Doubleday.
Never Another Love. Cecile Gilmore. LC 50-8324. 1950. Bouregy & Curl.
Never Another Love. Tempest, Jan. LC 50-7419. 1950. Arcadia House.
Never Another Moon. Helen Topping Miller. LC 38-21320. 1938. D. Appleton-Century Company, Incorporated.
Never Any More. Nancy Hale. LC 34-30051. 1934. C. Scribner's Sons.
Never As Strangers. Suzanne Simmons. (Candlelight Ecstasy Ser.: No. 44). (Orig.). 1982. pap. 1.75 (ISBN 0-440-16278-5). Dell.
Never Ask a Policeman. D. J Olivy. LC 70-111406. 1970. 4.95. Coward-McCann.
Never Ask the End. Isabel Bowler Paterson. LC 33-774. 1933. W. Morrow & Co.
Never Been Kissed. Allan Prior. LC 78-2065. 1979. 12.95i (ISBN 0-06-013385-6, HarpT). Har-Row.
Never Been Kissed. Allan Prior. 448p. pap. 2.75 (ISBN 0-445-04598-1). Popular Lib.
Never Bet Your Life. 1st Ed. George Harmon Coxe. LC 52-10615. 1952. Knopf.
Never by Chance. Sylvia Tate. LC 47-5150. 1947. Harper.
Never Call It Loving. Dorothy Eden. 1978. pap. 2.25 (ISBN 0-449-23143-7, Crest). Fawcett.
Never Call It Loving: A Biographical Novel of Katharine O'Shea and Charles Stewart Parnell. Dorothy Eden. LC 66-13117., Coward-McCann.
Never Call Retreat. Joseph Freeman. LC 43-2472. 1943. Farrar & Rinehart, Inc.
Never Call Retreat. Anne Sayre. LC 57-11900. 1957. Crowell.
Never Close the Door. Ada Miller. LC 72-75153. 1972. 5.95 (ISBN 0-911024-00-X). New Voices Pub. Co.
Never Come Back. John Mair. LC 41-191934. 1941. Little, Brown and Company.
Never Come Back. Frank O'Rourke. LC 52-7515. (Barnes sports novel series). 1952. A. S. Barnes.
Never Come Morning. Nelson Algren. LC 49-1766. (New York library 185). 1948. Avon Pub. Co.
Never Contract. David J Gerrity. (Signet book). 1975. (pbk.) 1.25. New American Library.
Never Count Tomorrow. Daphne Clair. (Harlequin Romances Ser.). 192p. 1981. pap. 1.25 (ISBN 0-373-02420-7). Harlequin Bks.
Never Despair: A Tale of the Emigrants. Founded on Fact. 1837. Scofield & Voorhies.
Never Die Alone. Donald Goines. (Orig.). 1974. pap. 1.95 (ISBN 0-87067-623-7, BH018). Holloway.
Never Die in Honolulu. Ian Hamilton. LC 72-75172. 1969. 4.50. Lippincott.
Never Dies the Dream. Margaret Dorothea Mortenson Landon. LC 49-48290. 1949. Doubleday.
Never Distrust an Asparagus. Elihu Blotnick. (Complete Blot Ser.). (Illus.). 1979. pap. 3.45 (ISBN 0-915090-10-4). Calif Street.
Never Ending Wrong. Katherine Anne Porter. (Illus.). 1977. 5.95 o.p. (ISBN 0-316-71391-0, Atlantic-Little, Brown). Little.
Never Enough: A Novel. Leane Zugsmith. LC 32-31301. Liveright, Inc.
Never Fight a Lady. Seldon Truss, pseud. LC 50-10878. 1950. Published for the Crime Club by Doubleday.
Never Fire First: A Canadian Northwest Mounted Story. James French Dorrance. LC 24-615451. The Macaulay Company.
Never Forget Love: By Carol Holliston Pseud. James Noble Gifford. LC 52-12726. 1952. Arcadia House.
Never Forgotten. Bertha B. Moore McCurry. LC 40-34747. 1940. Wm. B. Eerdmans Publishing Co.
Never Forgotten. Bertha B. Moore. LC 40-34747. 1940. Wm. B. Eerdmans Publishing Co.
Never Give a Millionaire an Even Break see Don't Just Die There.
Never Give All. Denise Robins. LC 34-137607. The Macaulay Company.
Never Give All. Maude Lavinia Radford Warren. LC 27-432153. The Bobbs-Merrill Company.
Never Give the Heart. Ann Willets. LC 51-9197. 1951. Random House.
Never Give the Heart. Ann Willets. 1973. (pbk) 0.95. Popular Library.
Never Go Back: A Novel Without a Plot. George Boas. LC 28-21971. 1928. Harper & Brothers.
Never in This World. Ed. by Idella P. Stone. Orig. Title: Light Fantastic. (Orig.). 1971. pap. 0.75 o.p. (T2406, GM). Fawcett World.
Never in Vain. Jocelyn Lee Hardy. LC 36-7481. 1936. Doubleday, Doran & Company, Inc.

Never in Vain. Jocelyn Lee Hardy. LC 40-8746. (A Mercury book, no. 28). The American Mercury, Inc.
Never Kill Santa Claus. L. W. Douglas. 3.00 o.p. Carlton.
Never Leave Me. Harold Robbins. 1978. pap. 2.95 (ISBN 0-380-00179-9, 58875). Avon.
Never Leave Me: By Harold Robbins Pseud. Complete and Unabridged. Harold Rubin. LC 54-288078. (Avon red-and-gold library, T-74). 1954. Avon Publications.
Never Leave Shadow Wood. Sally Tyree Smith. (Avalon Books). 1977. 4.95. Thomas Bouregy.
Never Let Her Go. John Crosby. LC 70-104940. 1970. 5.95. McCall Pub. Co.
Never Let Me Go. Gale Wilhelm. LC 45-9837. 1945. W. Morrow and Company.
Never Let the Sun Set on a Quarrel. (Stanyan Books Ser). 1971. 3.00 o.p. (ISBN 0-394-47377-9). Random.
Never Look Back. Jacquelyn Aeby. (Candlelight Historical Romance, 205). Dell.
Never Look Back. Mignon Good Eberhart. LC 51-9711. 1951. Random House.
Never Look Back. Mignon Good Eberhart. LC 77-13550. 1978. 9.95 (ISBN 0-89340-102-1). J. Curley.
Never Look Back. Mignon Good Eberhart. 1973. (pbk) 0.75. Popular Library.
Never Look Back. Jack D Sanford. LC 72-94398. 1973. (pbk.) 0.75 (ISBN 0-8054-7307-6). Broadman Press.
Never Love a Stranger. Harold Robbins. 1977. pap. 3.95 (ISBN 0-671-41714-2). PB.
Never Love a Stranger: A Novel. Harold Rubins. LC 48-349. 1948. A. A. Knopf.
Never Meet a Stranger. Molly Castle. LC 64-55609. 1964. Hurst & Blackett.
Never Mind the Lady. David Garth. LC 35-10043. 1935. Dodd. Mead & Company.
Never Miss a Trick. Maggie DiMarco. 1977. pap. 1.50 o.s.i. (ISBN 0-8439-0446-1, Leisure Bks). Nordon Pubns.
Never Need an Enemy. Aaron Marc Stein. LC 59-10691. 1959. Published for the Crime Club by Doubleday.
Never No More. Shirley Seifert. 1976. Repr. of 1964 ed. lib. bdg. 6.95 (ISBN 0-89190-137-X). Am Repr-Rivercity Pr.
Never No More: A Novel. Maura Laverty. LC 62-2716. 1962. Templegate.
Never No More: A Novel. Maura Laverty. LC 42-827820. 1942. Longmans, Green and Co.
Never No More: A Novel. Shirley Seifert. LC 64-14469. 1964. Lippincott.
Never Past the Gate: A Novel. Emma Lou Thayne. LC 75-33580. 7.95 (ISBN 0-87905-047-0). Peregrine Smith.
Never Pick up Hitch-Hikers! Edith Pargeter. LC 76-6045. 1976. 7.95 (ISBN 0-688-03049-1). Morrow.
Never Put off till Tomorrow What You Can Kill Today. Morton Freedgood. LC 77-102345. 1970. 4.95. Random House.
Never Put off till Tomorrow What You Can Kill Today. John Godey. 1970. 4.95 o.p. (ISBN 0-394-43794-2). Random.
Never Say Die. Julia Davis. LC 79-91915. 1980. 15.00 (ISBN 0-89002-130-9); pap. 4.95 (ISBN 0-89002-129-5). Northwoods Pr.
Never Say Die. Foote-Smith, Elizabeth. LC 76-43257. (Red mask mystery). 6.95. Putnam.
Never Say Die. McKnight Malmar. LC 43-8248. 1943. Coward-McCann, Inc.
Never Say Die: An Autonecrographical Novel. Robert Grossbach. LC 78-69502. 8.95 (ISBN 0-06-011629-3). Harper & Row.
Never Say Good-by. Hetherington, George. LC 34-36040. 1934. Play-Novel Publishers.
Never Say Good-Bye: A Novel. Julia Truitt Yenni. LC 37-9723. Reynal & Hitchcock.
Never Say No to the Navy. Bennie Caroline Hall. LC 44-375. 1944. Phoenix Press.
Never Shake a Skeleton. Alfred Flett. LC 78-58410. 1978. 7.95 (ISBN 0-8027-5392-2). Walker.
Never So Few. Tom T Chamles. LC 57-60623. 1957. Scribner.
Never So Proud: Crete: May, 1941, the Battle and Evacuation. 1st U.E. Ed. John Wingate. LC 67-16512. 1966. 4.95. Meredith.
Never So Young Again. Dan Brennan. LC 46-1518. 1946. Rinehart & Company, Inc.
Never Speak of Love. Adrienne Martine-Barnes. 256p. 1982. pap. 2.50 (ISBN 0-380-78956-6, 78956). Avon.
Never Step on a Rainbow. Winifred Wolfe. LC 65-21383. 1975. (pbk.) 1.25 (ISBN 0-446-76843-X). Warner Paperback Library.
Never Summer Mystery. Tyline Perry. LC 32-2227. A. H. King.
Never Take a Short Price. Andrew Dowdy. LC 72-3924. 1972. 5.95 (ISBN 0-396-06648-8). Dodd, Mead.
Never the Twain: A Novel. G. D. Khosla. 177p. 1981. text ed. 15.00x (ISBN 0-7069-1270-5, Pub by Vikas India). Advent NY.
Never the Twain: A Novel. G. D. Khosla. 208p. 1982. 32.00x (ISBN 0-7069-1270-5, Pub. by Garlandfold England). State Mutual Bk.
Never the Twain: Novel. Max Wylie. LC 61-11210. 1961. Morrow.
Never the Twain Shall Meet. Peter Bernard Kyne. LC 23-15036. 1923. Cosmopolitan Book Corporation.
Never the Twain Shall Meet. Peter Bernard Kyne. LC 37-22398. Grosset & Dunlap.
Never the White Rose. Carroll Voss. LC 57-5755. 1957. Muhlenberg Press.
Never Throw Anything Over Your Shoulder. William K. Hathaway. 1967. 5.50 o.p. (ISBN 0-682-45721-3). Exposition.
Never to Be Alone. Laura Saunders. LC 51-3861. 1951. Bouregy & Curl.
Never to Be Alone. Laura Saunders. (Candlelight romance, 120). 1973. (pbk.) 0.75. Dell.
Never Too Late. 1st American Ed. Angela Mackail Thirkell. LC 56-891450. 1956. Knopf.
Never Trust a Handsome Man. Marlene Fanta Shyer. LC 78-11220. 8.95 (ISBN 0-698-10963-5). Coward, McCann & Geoghegan.
Never Trust Love. Peggy Gaddis, pseud. LC 42-814246. 1942. Arcadia House, Inc.
Never Turn Your Back. 1st Ed. Margaret Scherf. LC 59-637153. 1959. Published for the Crime Club by Doubleday.
Never Victorious, Never Defeated. Taylor Caldwell. LC 54-673174. 1954. McGraw-Hill.
Never Wake a Dead Man. Brandon Bird. LC 50-9576. (Red badge detective). 1950. Dodd, Mead.
Never Wed an Old Man. Helen Rayburn Caswell. LC 74-9479. 1975. 5.95 (ISBN 0-385-01124-5). Published for the Crime Club by Doubleday.
Never Wed an Old Man. LC 74-9479. (Crime Club Ser). 192p. 1975. 5.95 o.p. (ISBN 0-385-01124-5). Doubleday.
Never Without You. Achmed Abdullah. LC 34-236591. 1934. Farrar & Rinehart, Incorporated.
Neverlight. Donald Pfarrer. LC 81-84777. 12.95 (ISBN 0-87223-773-7). Seaview Books.
Nevermore. Thomas Alexander Browne. LC 22-145562. 1892. Macmillan and Co.
Nevermore Affair. Kate Wilhelm. 1969. pap. 0.75 o.p. (0502-07011-075). Curtis.
Nevermore Affair. 1st Ed. Kate Wilhelm. LC 66-22939. 1966. 4.50. Doubleday.
Nevertheless the Duke. Elisabeth Finley Thomas. LC 30-14006. The White House.
Neveryona: The Tale of Signs & Cities. Samuel R. Delany. LC 82-90321. 400p. 1982. pap. 6.95 (ISBN 0-553-01434-X). Bantam.
Nevidimaia Kniga. Sergei Dovlatov. (Rus.). 1979. 12.00 o.p. (ISBN 0-88233-381-X); pap. 3.50 o.p. (ISBN 0-88233-382-8). Ardis Pubs.
Nevilles of Garretstown. A Tale of 1760. Mortimer O'Sullivan & Marsh-Caldwell, Anne (Caldwell) LC 18-11272. 1844. Harper & Brothers.
Nevlo. Kenneth Robeson. (Avenger #17). 1973. (pbk.) 0.75. Warner Paperback Lib.
Nevoc: A Tale of Love & Survival. Elma E. Karki. 44p. 1979. 4.50 (ISBN 0-8059-2700-X). Dorrance.
Nevsky's Demon. Dimitri V. Gat. 304p. 1983. pap. 2.95 (ISBN 0-380-82248-2). Avon.
Nevsky's Return. Dimitri V Gat. 240p. 1982. pap. 2.50 (ISBN 0-380-79863-8, 79863). Avon.
New Abelard. Robert Williams Buchanan. LC 75-1531. (Victorian Fiction: Novels of Faith and Doubt). 1976. 35.00. Garland Pub.
New Abelard. A Romance. Robert Williams Buchanan. (On cover: Lovell's library, v. 6, no. 318). 1883. J. W. Lovell Comany.
New Abelard. A Romance. Robert Williams Buchanan. LC 43-39047. (On cover: Munro's library). N. L. Munro.
New Adam. Stanley Grauman Weinbaum. LC 39-31793. 1939. Ziff-Davis Publishing Company.
New Adam and Eva. A Love Story. Mary Van Lennup Ives Todd. LC 8-26754. 1890. G. W. Dillingham.
New Adventures of Bantan. Maurice B Gardner. LC 77-72501. (Illus.). 1977. 5.00. T. Gaus.
New Adventures of D'Artagan. Lucien Pemjean. Tr. by Boyd, Madeleine Elise (Reynier) LC 33-314228. 1933. The Junior Literary Guild and Doubleday, Doran & Co., Inc.
New Adventures of Ellery Queen. Ellery Queen. LC 68-108327. (Signet mystery, Q5320). 1973. New American Lib.
New Adventures of Ellery Queen: Including an Amazing Short Novel "The Lamp of God". Ellery Queen, pseud. LC 40-27050. 1940. Frederick A. Stokes Company.
New Adventures of the Actresses. Susan Parrish. 1974. (pbk.) 1.25. Ace Books.
New Adventures of the Models. Susanne Jaffe. (Modern career girl series). 1974. (pbk.) 1.25. Ace Books.
New Adventures of the Nurses. Nancy Wood. 1973. (pbk.) 1.25. Ace.
New Adventures of the Secretaries. Natalie West. (Modern Career Girl Series). 1974. (pbk.) 1.25. Ace Books.
New Adventures of the Teachers. Susan Parrish. 1974. (pbk.) 1.25. Ace Books.
New Age of Gold: Or, The Life and Adventures of Robert Dexter Romaine Pseud. George Payson. LC 7-33760. 1856. Phillips, Sampson and Company.
New Alaskans. Anthony Hawkes. LC 77-15848. 1978. pap. 1.95 o.p. (ISBN 0-87216-440-3, E16440). Playboy.
New America. Poul Anderson. 288p. 1983. pap. 2.95 (ISBN 0-523-48553-0). Pinnacle Bks.
New American Short Stories. Ed. by Tobias Wolff. 176p. 1982. pap. 7.95 (ISBN 0-931694-17-5). Wampeter Pr.
New American Story. Ed. by Donald M. Allen & Robert Creeley. (Orig.). (YA) (gr. 9 up). 1965. pap. 1.95 o.p. (ISBN 0-394-17298-1, B77). Grove.
New American Story. Ed. by Donald M. Allen, Robert Creeley. With an Introd. by Warren Tallman. Ed. by Donald M. Allen & Robert Creeley. (Evergreen black cat bk., BC-77). 1966. pap., 1.45. Grove.
New Americans. Alfred Hodder. LC 1-241820. 1901. The Macmillan Company.
New and Amusing History of Sandford and Merton... Francis Cowley Burnand. LC 5204. (On cover: Medal library. no. 70). Street & Smith.
New Antigone. William Francis Barry. LC 75-462. (Victorian Fiction: Novels of Faith and Doubt). 1976. 40.00 (ISBN 0-8240-1540-1). Garland Pub.
New Antigone. A Romance... William Francis Barry. LC 6-97400. 1887-88. Macmillan and Co.
New Arabian Nights. Robert Louis Stevenson. LC 8-15700. (Leisure moment series). 1882. H. Holt and Company.
New Arabian Nights. Robert Louis Stevenson. LC 4-23588. (Leisure hour series, no. 141). 1882. H. Holt and Company.
New Arabian Nights. Robert Louis Stevenson. (On cover: Lovell's library no. 793). 1886. J. W. Lovell Company.
New Arabian Nights. Robert Louis Stevenson. (On cover: Seaside library. Pocket ed. no. 856). 1886. G. Munro.
New Arabian Nights. author's ed. Robert Louis Stevenson. LC 4-17818. 1903. C. Scribner's Sons.
New Arabian Nights. Robert Louis Stevenson. LC 5-13037. (Half-title: The biographical edited of the works of Robert Louis Stevenson). 1905. C. Scribner's Sons.
New Arabian Nights. Robert Louis Stevenson. (On cover: The sunset series. no. 210). J. S. Ogilvie Publishing Company.
New Aristocracy. Alice Elinor Bowen Bartlett. LC 6-9405. 1891. Bartlett Publishing Company.
New Aristocracy. Alice Elinor Bowen Bartlett. LC 11-10556. (On cover: Neely's library of choice literature. no. 69). 1897. F. T. Neely.
New Arrivals, Old Encounters. Brian Wilson Aldiss. 208p. 1981. pap. 2.25 (ISBN 0-380-56101-8, 56101). Avon.
New Arrivals, Old Encounters. Brian Wilson Aldiss. LC 79-2642. 1980. 11.49i (ISBN 0-06-010055-9, HarpT). Har-Row.
New Arrivals, Old Encounters: Twelve Stories. Brian Wilson Aldiss. LC 79-2642. 224p. 1979. 15.00. Ultramarine Pub.
New at It. Blake Tremaine. pap. 2.25 o.s.i. (Venus). Grove.
New Atlantis & Other Novellas of Science Fiction. Ed. by Robert Silverberg. 224p. 1975. 7.95 o.p. (ISBN 0-8015-5359-8). Hawthorn.
New Atlantis and Other Novellas of Science Fiction. Gene Wolfe & Ursula K. Le Guin. LC 74-15636. 1975. 7.95 (ISBN 0-8015-5359-8). Hawthorn Books.
New Atlantis and Other Novellas of Science Fiction. Gene Wolfe & Ursula K. Le Guin. 1976. (pbk.) 1.50. Warner Books.
New Australian Short Stories. Craig Munro. LC 81-1147. 1981. 14.95 (ISBN 0-7022-1597-X) (ISBN 0-7022-1595-3). University of Queensland Press.
New Axis. Newman, Charles Hamilton. LC 66-14760. 1966. Houghton Mifflin.
New Bed. Edith Brill. LC 34-5091. Greenberg.
New Bess Streeter Aldrich Reader. Bess Streeter Aldrich. 320p. Repr. of 1979 ed. lib. bdg. 16.60x (ISBN 0-88411-263-2). Amereon Ltd.
New Bethlehem. Iser Tolush. LC 35-14389. B. G. Guerney.
New Birth of Freedom: Abraham Lincoln in the White House. Virginia Louise Snider Eifert. LC 59-5666. (Illus.). 1959. Dodd, Mead.
New Blend. John C. Campbell. 3.50 o.p. Carlton.
New Blood. Richard Salem. 1982. pap. 2.50 (ISBN 0-451-11615-1, AE1615, Sig). NAL.
New Blood: A Story of the Folks That Make America. Louise Guest Rice. LC 23-606169. Fleming H. Revell Company.
New Bodies for Old. Maurice Renard. LC 23-16462. The Macaulay Company.
New Body. James Fritzhand. 1976. (pbk.) 1.95 (ISBN 0-380-00547-6). Avon Books.
New Boss at Birchfields. Henrietta Reid. (Harlequin Romances Ser.). 192p. 1983. pap. 1.50 (ISBN 0-373-02524-6). Harlequin Bks.
New Breed. Douglass Elliot. 1981. pap. 6.95 (ISBN 0-345-29846-2); pap. 2.95 (ISBN 0-345-29822-5). Ballantine.
New Breed. Stan Fischler. LC 82-60969. (Illus.). 160p. (Orig.). 1982. pap. text ed. 8.95 (ISBN 0-688-01696-0). Quill NY.
New Bridge: A Novel. Meyer Levin. LC 33-8418. 1933. Covici, Friede.
New Canaan: In Which Onon Bjornson Tells the Saga of the Early Norse Migration to America and the Story of a Great Love. Martin Wendell Odland. LC 83-22828. 1933. Augsburg Publishing House.
New Candide. John Cournos. LC 24-106418. 1924. Boni and Liveright.
New Canterbury Tales. Maurice Henry Hewlett. LC 72-98575. (Short story index reprint series). 1969. Books for Libraries Press.
New Canterbury Tales. Maurice Henry Hewlett. LC 1-23700. 1901. The Macmillan Company.
New Carthage: La Nouvelle Carthage. Georges Eekhoud & Morris, Lloyd R., 1903- Tr. LC 17-17971. 1917. Duffield and Company.
New Catalan Short Story: An Anthology. Albert Porqueras-Mayo et al. LC 82-21927. 278p. (Orig.). 1983. lib. bdg. 22.50 (ISBN 0-8191-2899-6); pap. text ed. 11.75 (ISBN 0-8191-2900-3). U Pr of Amer.
New Centurions. Joseph Wambaugh. LC 77-131254. 1970. 6.95. Little, Brown.
New Chronicles of Rebecca. Kate Douglas Smith Wiggin. LC 7-11587. 1907. Houghton, Mifflin and Company.
New Clarion: A Novel. William Nathaniel Harben. LC 14-15182. 1914. Harper & Brothers.
New Commandment a Novel. Anthony Verrall. LC 9-22753. E. J. Clode.
New Confederate Short Stories. Ed. by Katharine M Jones. LC 54-10674. 1954. University of South Carolina Press.
New Constellations: An Anthology of Tomorrow's Mythologies. Thomas M Disch & Charles Naylor. LC 76-9205. 8.95 (ISBN 0-06-011036-8). Harper & Row.
New Continent. Worthey. LC 7-1634. 1890. Macmillan and Co.
New Country: A Selection of Western Australian Short Stories. Bruce Bennett. LC 77-370769. (Illus.). 1976. (ISBN 0-909144-01-X). Fremantle Arts Centre Press.
New Cowhand. William L. Hopson. LC 49-989027. 1947. Phoenix Press.
New Creation. Andrew Magnus Fleming. LC 32-227133. 1932. Meador Publishing Company.
New Creature. Prudence Andrew. LC 68-8846. 1968. 5.95. Putnam.
New Crime Club Golden Book of Best Detective Stories. LC 36-13700. 1934. Pub. for the Crime Club, Inc., by Doubleday, Doran & Company, Inc.
New Crusade. Anthony Gibbs. LC 32-3606. 1932. Doubleday, Doran & Company, Inc.
New Dawn. Agnes Christina Laut. LC 14-118. 1913. 1.35. Moffat, Yard and Company.
New Dawn: A Philosophical Story of the Unfolding of Man Through the Power of Evolution. Annie Lewis-Johnson. LC 11-671403. 1911. 1.00. Roger Brothers; Etc., Etc.
New Day. Emma Rebecca Jacobs Beall. LC 41-5977. Federal Printing Co.
New Day. Victor Stafford Reid. LC 78-182683. 1972. (ISBN 0-911860-09-6). Chatham Bookseller.
New Day. Victor Stafford Reid. LC 49-1576. 1949. A. A. Knopf.
New Day's Dawning: A Novel of the West That Still Dares to Cross New Frontiers. Peter Maentz. LC 34-18188. Williams Publishing Company.
New Days, New Ways. Jeannette Covert Nolan. LC 36-20840. Green Circle Books.
New Decameron. LC 20-8740. 1919. R. M. McBride & Co.
New Decameron: Further Tales from the Saragossa Manuscript. Jan Potocki. LC 66-26538. 1967. Orion Press.
New Departure. Kevin Connor. LC 62-19410. 1962. Jefferson House.
New Dimensions. Ed. by Robert Silverberg. (Avon science fiction). Avon.
New Dimensions. Ed. by Robert Silverberg. LC 73-157623. (Doubleday science fiction). (v. 1) varies 5.95. Doubleday.
New Dimensions III. Ed. by Robert Silverberg. (Signet, O 5805). 1974. (pbk.) 0.95. New American Library.
New Dimensions, No. 5: Science Fiction. Ed. by Robert Silverberg. 240p. 1976. pap. 1.95 o.p. (ISBN 0-06-080354-1, P354, PL). Har-Row.
New Dimensions One: Fourteen Original Science Fiction Stories. Ed. by Robert Silverberg. LC 73-157623. 1971. 5.95 o.p. (ISBN 0-385-07016-0). Doubleday.
New Dimensions: Science Fiction. Harper & Row.

New Dimensions: Science Fiction. Ed. by Robert Silverberg. LC 75-25103. 8.95 (ISBN 0-06-013864-5). Harper & Row.

New Dimensions Two. Ed. by Robert Silverberg. LC 72-79423. 263p. 1972. 5.95 o.p. (ISBN 0-385-09141-9). Doubleday.

New Doctor. James Noble Gifford. LC 41-20051. 1941. Gramercy Publishing Co.

New Doctor. Gay Rutherford. LC 41-200511. Gramercy Publishing Co.

New Doctor. Elizabeth Seifert. LC 58-828858. 1958. Dodd, Mead.

New Doctor. Elizabeth Seifert. LC 73-79173. 1974. 6.95. Aeonian Press.

New Doctor: Or, Health and Happiness; a Story. Sara Melissa Biddle. 1900. Published for the Author by F. E. Ormsby & Co.

New Doctrine: Or, Teachings and Tendencies. Elhanan Winchester Reynolds. LC 7-30600. 1848. Printed at the Censor Office.

New Don Quixote. A Continuatoin of Cervantes' Faithful Relation to the Most Marvelous Adventures of the Gallant Knight and His Faithful Squire. Harry B Smith. LC 8-8165. The Matthews-Northrup Co.

New Dream for Kendra. Sharon Wagner. (Adventures in Love Ser.: No. 24). 1982. pap. 1.75 (ISBN 0-451-11705-0, AE1705, Sig). NAL.

New Dreams for Old. Mary Badger Wilson. LC 31-4959. The Penn Publishing Company.

New "East Lynne". Clara Morris. LC 8-19021. C. H. Doschler & Co.

New England Born. Sara Ware Bassett. LC 36-27769. 1938. Doubleday. Doran & Co., Inc.

New England Boyhood. Edward Everett Hale. 267p. 1977. Repr. of 1893 ed. lib. bdg. 14.75x (ISBN 0-89966-255-2). Buccaneer Bks.

New England Boyhood. Edward Everett Hale. LC 76-104469. Repr. of 1900 ed. lib. bdg. 13.50 (ISBN 0-8398-0750-3). Irvington.

New England Boys. by a. l. stimson. with original designs by mclenan, engraved by n. orr. ed. Alexander Lovett Stimson. LC 8-15682. 1856. J. C. Derby.

New England Cactus: And Other Tales. Frank Pope Humphrey. LC 7-57855. (On cover: The Unknown library no. 16). Cassell Publishing Company.

New England Conscience. Belle C Greene. 1885. G. P. Putnam's Sons.

New England Folks: A Love Story... Eugene Wiley Presbrey. 1901. G. W. Dillingham Co.

New England Gothic, a Novel. 1st Ed. Addison J Allen. LC 60-14003. 1960. Chilton Co., Book Division.

New England Holiday: A Novel. Charles Allen Smart. LC 31-218883. W. W. Norton & Co., Inc.

New England Idyl. Belle C Greene. 1886. D. Lothrop and Company.

New England Nun: And Other Stories. Mary Eleanor Wilkins Freeman. LC 4-15108. 1891. Harper & Brothers.

New England Nun: And Other Stories. Mary Eleanor Wilkins Freeman. LC 20-18608. (Harper's modern classics). Harper & Brothers.

New England Nurse. Adelaide Humphries. LC 56-13296. 1956. Avalon Books.

New England Primrose. Adele Sarpy Morrison. LC 18-19576. The Branch Publishing Co.

New England Short Stories... Ed. by Conway, Paul Gerard & Thomas, Roger. LC 34-176532. J. B. Pomfret.

New England Story: A Novel. Henry Beetle Hough. LC 57-100461. 1958. Random House.

New England Tale. Catherine Maria Sedgwick. LC 78-64096. Repr. of 1822 ed. 37.50 (ISBN 0-404-17169-9). AMS Pr.

New England Tale, and Miscellanies. Catharine Maria Sedgwick. 1854. J. C. Derby.

New-England Tale: Or, Sketches of New-England Character and Manners. Catharine Maria Sedgwick. LC 8-64376. 1822. E. Bliss & E. White.

New England Woman: Or, The Confessions of a Modern Jean-Jacques Rousseau. Richard A. Soalfield. LC 8-1362. (On cover: The Socrates series, v. 1). 1894. The Socrates Publishing Company.

New England's Chattels: Or, Life in the Northern Poor-House... Samuel Hayes Elliott. LC 9-21407. 1858. H. Dayton.

New Epicurean: & The Adventures of a School-Boy; Two Tales from the Victorian Underground. Edward Sellon. LC 78-93847. 1969. 5.95. Grove Press.

New Epicureans. Bd. with Adventures of a School Boy. 5.95 o.p. (GP527); pap. 1.75 o.p. (Z1044, Zebra). Grove.

New Evadne. Frank Howard Howe. LC 7-6625. (On cover: American novelists' series, no. 40). J. W. Lovell Company.

New Exodus see Collected Works.

New Faces. Myra Kelly. LC 10-173272. 1.50. G. W. Dillingham Company.

New Female. (Illus.). softcover 5.00 (ISBN 0-910550-48-4). Centurion Pr.

New Flag see Collected Works.

New Fraternity: A Novel of University Life. George Frederick Gundelfinger. LC 16-235893. 1916. 1.35. The New Fraternity.

New Friend. Rob Eden. LC 50-562828. 1949. Gramercy Pub. Co.

New Friends in Old Chester. Margaret Wade Campbell Deland. LC 24-111403. Harper & Brothers.

New Gethsemane. Edward Lyell Fox. LC 17-25121. 1917. R. M. McBride & Co.

New Girl in Town. Faith Baldwin. (General Ser.). 1975. Repr. lib. bdg. 10.95 (ISBN 0-8161-6305-7, Large Print Bks). G K Hall.

New Girl in Town. Faith Baldwin Cuthrell. LC 74-15464. 1975. 6.95 (ISBN 0-03-013461-7). Holt, Rinehart and Winston.

New Girl in Town. Faith Baldwin Cuthrell. LC 75-19485. 1975. 6.95 (ISBN 0-8161-6305-7). G. K. Hall.

New Girl in Town. Faith Baldwin Cuthrell. (Kangaroo Book). 1977. 1.50 (ISBN 0-671-81052-9). Pocket Books.

New Girls. Beth Richardson Gutcheon. LC 79-12245. 9.95 (ISBN 0-399-12362-8). Putnam.

New God: A Tale of the Early Christmas. Richard Voss & Robinson, Mary A., Tr. LC 98-2033. (On verso of t.p.: The odd number series). 1899. Harper & Brothers.

New Godiva. Sidney Hodges. LC 7-4958. 1876. J. B. Lippincott & Co.

New Ground. Katharine Haviland Taylor. J. B. Lippincott Company.

New Grub Street. George Robert Gissing. LC 63-173. (Riverside editions, B73). Houghton Mifflin.

New Grub Street. George Robert Gissing. LC 27-877. (Half-title: The Modern library of the world's best books). 1926. The Modern Library.

New Grub Street: A Novel. George Robert Gissing. 1905. R. F. Fenno & Company.

New Gulliver. Esme Doderidge. LC 79-65728. 220p. 1980. pap. 3.95 (ISBN 0-8008-5507-8). Taplinger.

New Gulliver. Wendell Phillips Garrison. LC 99-37. 1898. The Marion Press.

New Gulliver: Or, The Adventure of Lemuel Gulliver, Jr. in Capovolta: a Novel. Esme Dodderidge. LC 79-65728. 9.95 (ISBN 0-8008-5506-X). Taplinger Pub. Co.

New Gun Runners. Archibald Gordon Macdonnell. LC 28-21977. Harcourt, Brace and Company.

New Hampshire Folk Tales. Eva A. Speare. LC 74-27628. 279p. 1975. Repr. of 1932 ed. 6.95 o.p. (ISBN 0-914016-12-1). Phoenix Pub.

New Harry and Lucy: A Story of Boston in the Summer of 1891. Edward Everett Hale & Hale, Lucretia Peabody, 1820-1900, Joint Author. LC 6-46189. 1892. Roberts Brothers.

New Head Nurse. Janet Lane Walters. 1974. 4.95 (ISBN 0-517-51561-X). Lenox Hill Press.

New Heaven & a New Earth. Robert Tripician. 200p. 1975. 5.95 o.p. (ISBN 0-8059-2189-3). Dorrance.

New Heaven, New Earth... Phoebe Fenwick Gaye. LC 32-18241. 1932. C. Scribner's Sons.

New Heaven, New Earth. Arthemise Goertz. LC 52-13464. 1953. McGraw-Hill.

New Heaven, New Earth. Joyce Carol Oates. 1978. pap. 2.50 (ISBN 0-449-23662-5, Crest). Fawcett.

New Holland Heritage (an Early West Australian Romance) Rix Weaver. LC 43-14885. 1941. W. A., Patersons Printing Press Ltd.

New Home. Caroline Kirkland. LC 70-93633. (American Fiction Ser). 1969. lib. bdg. 16.50 o.s.i. (ISBN 0-512-00444-7). Garrett Pr.

New Home--Who'll Follow? Glimpses of Western Life. By Caroline Matilda Kirkland (Mrs. Mary Clavers, Pseud.) Ed. for the Modern Reader by William S. Osborne. Caroline Matilda Stansbury Kirkland. LC 65-256292. (Masterworks of lit. ser., M-11). pap., 1.95. Coll. & Univ. Pr.

New Home--Who'll Follow? Or, Glimpses of Western Life. Caroline Matilda Stansbury Kirkland. LC 13-9373. 1839. C. S. Francis.

New Home--Who'll Follow? Or, Glimpses of Western Life. 2d ed. Caroline Matilda Stansbury Kirkland. LC 22-24753. 1840. C. S. Francis.

New Home--Who'll Follow? Or, Glimpses of Western Life. 5th ed. rev. by the author, and illustrated by engravings from designs by f. o. c. darley. ed. Caroline Matilda Stansbury Kirkland. LC 7-13207. 1855. C. S. Francis & Co.

New Home for Snow Ball. Joan Bowden. (Eger Reader). (Golden book). (Illus.). 1974. 0.39. Golden Press.

New Home: Or, Life in the Clearings. Edited and with an Introd. by John Nerber. Caroline Matilda Stansbury Kirkland. 1953. Putnam.

New Home-Who'll Follow? Or, Glimpses of Western Life. Caroline Matilda Stansbury Kirkland. LC 70-93633. 1969. Garrett Press.

New Home-Who'll Follow? Or, Glimpses of Western Life. Caroline Matilda Stansbury Kirkland. LC 72-8161. 1972. (ISBN 0-8422-8087-1). MSS Information Corp.

New Hope. Lawrence Josephson. 384p. 1973. 7.95 o.p. Putnam.

New Hope. Joseph Crosby Lincoln & Lincoln, Freeman. LC 41-21282. Coward-McCann, Inc.

New Hope. Ruth Suckow. LC 42-3175. Farrar & Rinehart, Inc.

New Hope: Or, The Rescue. John Lewis. LC 9-1192. 1855. Bunce.

New Hope; or, The Rescue. A Tale of the Great Kanawha ... LC 9-1192. 1855. Bunce & Brother.

New House. Lettice Ulpha Cooper. LC 36-22182. 1936. The Macmillan Company.

New House. Marc Kaminsky. 64p. 1975. pap. 1.95 o.p. (ISBN 0-8180-1574-8). Horizon.

New House. Nancy Noon Kendall. LC 34-12977. 1934. The Caxton Printers, Ltd.

New Improved Sun: An Anthology of Utopian S-F. Thomas M Disch. LC 74-15866. 1975. 8.95. Harper & Row.

New Improved Sun: An Anthology of Utopian Science Fiction. Thomas M Disch. LC 77-355922. 1976. 3.95 (ISBN 0-09-124200-2). Hutchinson.

New Incest. H. Hadley Williams. pap. 1.95 o.p. (ISBN 0-87682-120-4, 7120). Barclay Hse.

New Interns: A Novel. William Johnston & Wilton Schiller. LC 64-19575. 1964. Bantam Books.

New Ireland. Ella Burns. LC 13-41. 1.00. Angel Guardian Press.

New Israeli Writers: Short Stories of the First Generation. Ed. by Dalia Rabikovitz. LC 69-13467. (Sabra books). 1969. 5.95. Funk and Wagnalls.

New Jersey Showdown. Roosevelt Mallory. (Radcliff#4). 1976. (pbk.) 1.50 (ISBN 0-87067-472-2). Holloway House Publishing Co.

New Jerusalem. Gilbert Keith Chesterton. 1976. lib. bdg. 59.95 (ISBN 0-8490-2339-4). Gordon Pr.

New Job. Leopold Sacher-Masoch & Cohen, Harriet Lieber, Tr. Cassell Publishing Company.

New Juice. M. T. Brown. (Illus.). 1980. pap. 9.95 o.p. (ISBN 0-930490-32-0). Future Shop.

New June. Henry John Newbolt. LC 10-15196. 1909. E. P. Dutton and Company.

New Kind of Killer. Jennie Melville, pseud. LC 70-150947. 1971. 4.95. McKay.

New Kind of Life. Kenneth J. Holland. LC 73-87033. 64p. 1973. pap. 0.95 o.p. (ISBN 0-8163-0058-5, 14410-5). Pacific Pr Pub Assn.

New Kind of Light. Hal Adams. LC 65-27972. 4.00. Dorrance.

New Kind of Love. Patricia Aks. 160p. 1982. pap. 1.95 (ISBN 0-449-70019-4, Juniper). Fawcett.

New Kingmakers. David Chagall. LC 80-7932. 1981. 14.95 (ISBN 0-15-165203-1). HarBraceJ.

New Klondike: A Story of a Southern Baseball Training Camp, Based on the Motion Picture Story. Peggy Griffith. LC 26-131413. (On cover: Popular plays and screen library). Jacobsen-Hodgkin-Son-Corporation.

New Kona Tales, Vol. 1. Robyn Saintclaire. (Illus.). 1969. pap. 1.75 o.p. (ISBN 0-912180-09-9). Petroglyph.

New Kona Tales, Vol. 2. Robyn Saint Claire. (Illus.). 1970. pap. 1.75 o.p. (ISBN 0-912180-10-2). Petroglyph.

New Ladies' Tickler. 1970. pap. 1.45 o.p. (V1013Q, Venus). Grove.

New Lamps. Alberta Stedman Eagan. LC 30-335134. The Macaulay Company.

New Land Needs Singing: A Story of Grand Coulee. Sarah Kiner Hardy. LC 54-9132. 1954. Vantage Press.

New Land, Stories of Jews Who Had a Part in the Making of Our Country. Elma C. Ehrlich Levinger. LC 20-10306. 1920. Bloch Publishing Company.

New Lands. Charles Fort. Ed. by Lester Del Rey. LC 75-409. (Library of Science Fiction). 1975. lib. bdg. 17.50 (ISBN 0-8240-1413-8). Garland Pub.

New Leaf Mills. William Dean Howells. LC 13-35064. 1913. Harper & Brothers.

New Lease of Death. Ruth Rendell. LC 76-20815. 1976. 8.95 (ISBN 0-89340-020-3). J. Curley.

New Lease of Death. 1st Ed. in the U.S.A. Ruth Rendell. LC 67-14127. 1967. 3.95. Pub. for the Crime Club by Doubleday.

New Lease of Life, and Saving a Daughter's Dowry. Edmond Francois Valetin About. LC 5-42611. (On cover: Lovell's library, v. 3, no. 118). J. W. Lovell Company.

New Lease on Life. Georges Simenon. LC 63-12977. 1963. Doubleday.

New Life. Bernard Malamud. 1973. (pbk.) 1.25 (ISBN 0-671-78311-4). Pocket Books.

New Life. Bernard Malamud. LC 61-11416. 1961. Farrar, Straus and Cudahy.

New Life. Bernard Malamud. 1980. 2.75. (ISBN 0-380-52530-5). Avon Books.

New Life - a Day on a Collective Farm. Fedor Aleksandrovich Abramov. Tr. by George Reavey from Russian. (YA) (gr. 9 up). 1963. pap. 0.75 o.p. (ISBN 0-394-17423-2, B58). Grove.

New Life & Vindication of Robert Burns. James MacKenzie. 1973. Repr. of 1924 ed. 35.00 o.p. (ISBN 0-8274-0110-8). R West.

New Life for Joanna. Iris Bromige. 1973. pap. 0.75 o.p. (345-26507-6-075). Beagle Bks.

New Life for Nurse Paula. Jeanette Laura. 1975. 4.95. Avalon Books.

New Life of Mr. Martin. Robert Briffault. 1947. C. Scribner's Sons.

New Life Testament see Testamento "Nueva Vida".

New Lights: Or, Life in Galway. A Tale. Mary Anne Madden Sadlier. LC 8-1655. 1867. D. & J. Sadlier & Co.

New Lights: Or, Life in Galway. A Tale. Mary Anne Madden Sadlier. LC 8-1656. (On cover: Cottage and parlor library). D. & J. Sadlier & Co.

New Line. Translated by Archibald Colquhoun. Mario Pomilio. LC 61-6463. 1961. Harper.

New Lives, New Landscapes: Planning for the Twenty-First Century. Nan Fairbrother. (Illus.). 1970. 12.50 o.p. (ISBN 0-394-43810-8). Knopf.

New Love for Old. Ruth McCarthy Sears. 1975. 4.95. Avalon Books.

New Love or the Old? Dora Delmar. (On cover: Library of American authors. no. 73). G. Munro's Sons.

New Machiavelli. Herbert George Wells. LC 11-553. Duffield & Company.

New Machiavelli. Herbert George Wells. LC 20-16468. 1919. Duffield & Company.

New Magdalen. Wilkie Collins. LC 6-26939. (Lovell's library v. 1, no. 24). 1882. J. W. Lovell Company.

New Magdalen. Wilkie Collins. LC 8-31169. 1908. C. Scribner's Sons.

New Magdalen. A Novel. Wilkie Collins. 1873. Harper & Brothers.

New Magdalen. A Novel. Wilkie Collins. LC 3-27279. Harper & Brothers.

New Man. James Noble Gifford. LC 13-19077. 1913. Thomas Y. Crowell Company.

New Man. James Noble Gifford. LC 46-15683. 1946. Gramercy Publishing Co.

New Man: A Chronicle of the Modern Time. Ellis Paxson Oberholtzer. LC 7-33188. 1897. The Levytype Company.

New Man at Rossmere. Jeannette Ritchie Hadermann Walworth. LC 8-33134. Cassell & Company, Limited.

New Matron of Noah's Ark: A Story from the Northwest. Oluf Tandberg. LC 32-19501. 1932. Meador Publishing Company.

New Mayor. Albert Payson Terhune & Broadhurst, George H., 1866- LC 8-8309. J. S. Ogilvie Publishing Company.

New Meat. Mike Carter. 176p. pap. 1.95 o.p. (6089). Brandon.

New Men. Charles Percy Snow. LC 54-12906. 1955. Scribner.

New Men for Old. Howard Vincent O'Brien. LC 14-9766. 1914. 1.25. M. Kennerley.

New Mend, Vol. 2. Ed. by Roger Elwood. LC 73-6060. (Frontiers). 192p. 1973. 5.95 o.s.i. (ISBN 0-02-535410-8); pap. 1.50 o.s.i. (ISBN 0-02-019810-8). Macmillan.

New Mexico Connection. Collin Wilcox. (McCloud Ser). (O.s.i.). 160p. (Orig.). 1974. pap. 0.95 o.s.i. (AN1259, Award). Univ Pub & Dist.

New Mexico David: And Other Stories and Sketches of the Southwest. Charles Fletcher Lummis. LC 76-90586. (Short story index reprint series). (Illus.). 1969. Books for Libraries Press.

New Mexico David: And Other Stories and Sketches of the Southwest. Charles Fletcher Lummis. 1891. C. Scribner's Sons.

New Mexico Triptych: Being Three Panels and Three Accounts. Angelico Chavez. LC 75-31416. (Illus.). 1976. 8.50 (ISBN 0-88307-520-2) (ISBN 0-88307-521-0). W. Gannon.

New Mind. R. Elwood. 1973. pap. 1.50 o.p. (01980, Collier). Macmillan.

New Mind: Original Science Fiction. Ed. by Roger Elwood. LC 73-179317. (Frontiers, 2). 1973. (pbk.) 1.50. Collier Books.

New Minister. Louis L Miller. LC 53-583714. 1952. Pageant Press.

New Missioner. Nancy Mann Waddel Wilson Woodrow Woodrow. LC 7-33209. 1907. The McClure Company.

New Mr. Howerson. Opie Percival Read. LC 14-12629. 1.35. The Reilly & Britton Co.

New Moon. Elizabeth Robins. LC 7-41971. 1895. D. Appleton and Company.

New Moon: A Romance of Reconstruction. Oliver Onions. LC 18-17356. 1918. Hodder and Stoughton.

New Moon Rising. Eugenia Price. LC 72-11643. 1973. 11.95 (ISBN 0-8161-6063-5). G. K. Hall.

TITLE INDEX NEW WRITING & WRITERS

New Moon Rising. Eugenia Price. LC 69-14496. 1969. 5.95. Lippincott.
New Moon Through a Window. Maysie Greig. LC 37-29382. 1937. Doubleday, Doran & Co., Inc.
New Moon Through a Window. Maysie Greig. LC 39-7930. 1939. The Sun Dial Press, Inc.
New Moon Through a Window. Julia Grice. 1971. pap. 0.75 o.p. (94169). Beagle Bks.
New Moon with the Old: A Novel. Dorothy Gladys Smith. LC 63-18506. 1963. Little Brown.
New Mrs. Aldrich. Vivian Stuart. 1976. pap. 1.50 o.p. (ISBN 0-515-04049-5). BJ Pub Group.
New Name. Grace Livingston Hill. LC 26-12138. 1926. J. B. Lippincott Company.
New Name. Grace Livingston Hill. 1975. (pbk.) 1.25. Bantam Books.
New Narratives. enl. ed. Blanche Colton Williams. LC 44-8407. 1944. D. Appleton-Century Company Incorporated.
New Narratives. Ed. by Blanche Colton Williams. LC 30-15226. D. Appleton Company.
New Neighbors. Edmund Plante. (Orig.). 1979. pap. 1.95. Woodhill.
New Nero: A Realistic Romance. Edgar Fawcett. LC 6-38788. (On cover: Once a week semi-monthly library. v. 10, no. 22). 1893. P. F. Collier.
New Nobility. A Story of Europe and America. John Wien Forney. LC 6-40379. 1881. D. Appleton and Company.
New Northland. Louis Pope Gratacap. LC 15-10285. 1915. T. Benton.
New Note. Ella MacMahon. LC 7-20429. R. F. Fenno & Company; Etc., Etc.
New Novalis? Short Brilliant Thought-Flashes & Great Unity. J. E. Von Emmichoven. Tr. by Elizabeth Spaey. 1976. pap. 2.00 o.p. (ISBN 0-916786-17-X, Pub by Elizabeth Spaey). St George Bk Serv.
New Nurse. Florence Stonebraker. LC 47-202243. 1947. Gramercy Publishing Co.
New Nurse at Crest View. Arlene Hale. (Ace Nurse Romance Series). 1975. (pbk.) 0.95. Ace Books.
New Nurse at Noonday. Ray Dorian. pap. 0.50 o.p. Lancer.
New Nurse in Town. Janet Lane Walters. 1973. 4.95. Lenox Hill Pr.
New Olympia Reader. Maurice Girodias. 896p. 1970. 15.00 o.p. (ISBN 0-8202-0035-2). Sherbourne.
New Olympia Reader: Selections from the Traveller's Companion Series. Ed. by Maurice Girodias. LC 73-87042. (Illus.). 1975. 17.50 (ISBN 0-88486-001-9). Black Watch.
New Olympia Reader: Selections from the Traveller's Companion Series, Ophelia Press, Inc., and the Olympia Press, Inc. Ed. by Maurice Girodias. LC 71-114092. (Illus.). 1970. 15.00. Olympia Press Distributed by Sherbourne Press, Los Angeles.
New Orleans. Miriam Pace. (Orig.). 1981. pap. 3.50 (ISBN 0-89083-826-7). Zebra.
New Orleans Adventure: A Story of the Last Romantic Flicker of Piracy-Privateering in the Gulf and New Orleans of the 1830's. Charles Tenney Jackson. LC 55-100663. 1955. Dorrance.
New Orleans Holocaust. Peter McCurtin. (Assassin). (Dell/Lorelei Book: Vol. 2). 1973. (pbk) 0.95. Dell.
New Orleans Nurse. Diana Douglas. (Signet book). 1974. (pbk.) 0.95. New American Library.
New Orleans of Possibilities. David Madden. 144p. 1982. 14.95x (ISBN 0-8071-1008-6); pap. 7.95 (ISBN 0-8071-1015-9). La State U Pr.
New Orleans Sketch Book. George M. Wharton. LC 8-36216. 1853. A. Hart.
New Orleans Sketches. Ed. by Carvel Collins. William. Faulkner. LC 68-144956. 1968. 4.95. Random.
New Orleans Woman. Harnett Thomas Kane. 1972. pap. 0.95 o.p. (09141). Curtis.
New Orleans Woman: A Biographical Novel of Myra Clark Gaines. Harnett Thomas Kane. LC 46-7630. 1946. Doubleday & Company, Inc.
New Owner. Kay Thorpe. (Harlequin Presents Ser.). 192p. 1982. pap. 1.75 (ISBN 0-373-10534-7). Harlequin Bks.
New Paolo and Francesca: A Novel. Annie E. E. J. Lee Hamilton Holdsworth. LC 4-31322. 1904. J. Lane.
New Paul and Virginia: Or, Positivism on an Island. 4th ed. William Hurrell Mallock. 1878. Scribner and Welford.
New Paul and Virginia: Or, Positivism on an Island. William Hurrell Mallock & John D. Margolis. LC 74-88087. 1970. 4.50. University of Nebraska Press.
New Penguin Book of Scottish Short Stories. Ian Murray. 336p. 1983. pap. 4.95 (ISBN 0-14-006411-7). Penguin.
New People at the Hollies: By Josephine Bell Pseud. Doris Bell Collier Ball. LC 61-143429. (Cock Robin mystery). 1961. Macmillan.
New Pilgrim's Progress: Or, The Pious Indian Convert. James Walcot. LC 74-16309. (Flowering of the Novel). 1974. (ISBN 0-8240-1122-8). Garland Pub.
New Pocket Dictionary of the Latin and English Languages: Latin-English and English-Latin. With the Addition of a Copious Selection of Latin Phrases, with Their Translations and Equivalents in English. J Macfarlane. LC 34-4919. (E. F. G. pocket series). 1933. D. Appleton and Company.
New Poor. Clarissa Fairchild Cushman. LC 27-4639. 1927. Harper & Brothers.
New Priest in Conception Bay. Robert Traill Spence Lowell. LC 72-104520. 1970. (ISBN 0-8398-1173-X). Literature House.
New Priest in Conception Bay. Robert Traill Spence Lowell. LC 21-12971. 1889. Roberts Brothers.
New Priests: A Novel Tr. from French. Michel De Saint-Pierre. LC 66-18522. pap., 1.95. B. Herder.
New Prison Nurse. Warren Bisig. 192p. (Orig.). 1973. pap. 1.95 o.p. (ISBN 0-87977-182-8, DBB182). Dansk Blue Bk.
New Prodigal. A Novel. Stephen Paul Sheffield. (On cover: The Rialto series, no. 20). 1890. Rand, McNally & Company.
New Prometheans: Readings for the Future. Ed. by John S. Lambert. 1973. pap. text ed. 7.95x o.p. (ISBN 0-06-043831-2, HarpC). Har-Row.
New Prometheans: Readings for the Future. Ed. by John S. Lambert. 1973. pap. text ed. 7.95x o.p. (ISBN 0-06-043831-2, HarpC). Har-Row.
New Queens for Old. Gabriel Fielding, pseud. 1972. 6.95 o.p. (ISBN 0-688-00054-1). Morrow.
New Queens for Old: A Novella and Nine Stories. Alan Gabriel Barnsley. LC 73-182951. 1972. 6.95. Morrow.
New Race: A Romance from the German of Golo Raimund Pseud. Bertha Heyn Frederich. Tr. by Wister, Annis Lee (Furness) 1880. Lippincott & Co.
New Race: A Romance from the German of Golo Raimund Psued. Bertha Heyn Frederich. Tr. by Wister, Annis Lee (Furness) 1908. J. B. Lippincott Company.
New Religion: A Modern Novel. Jozua Marius Willen Van Der Poorten Schwartz. LC 7-29090. 1907. D. Appleton and Company.
New Republic: Culture, Faith, and Philosophy in an English Country House. 4th ed. reprinted; with an introduction by john lucas. ed. William Hurrell Mallock & John Lucas. LC 76-360556. (Victorian library). (Illus.). 1975. 13.00 (ISBN 0-7185-5030-7). Leicester University Press.
New Republic: Or, Culture, Faith and Philosophy in an English Country House. William Hurrell Mallock. Ed. by J. Max Patrick. LC 50-9045. 1950. University of Florida Press.
New Republic: Or, Culture, Faith, and Philosophy in an English Country House. new ed. William Hurrell Mallock. LC 7-16806. 1878. Scribner and Welford.
New Republic: Or Culture, Faith and Philosophy in an English Country House. William Hurrell Mallock. (On cover: Fitch's popular library, no. 6). 1879. G. W. Fitch.
New Reveries of a Bachelor: Or, Bob, Belle, and That Mule. A Meadowgrass Idyl. Mary Wonderly Parks. Printed by J. B. Piet.
New Rivers Calling. James Beardsley Hendryx. LC 43-10062. 1943. Doubelday, Doran & Co., Inc.
New Road. Merle Estes Colby. LC 33-8145. 1933. The Viking Press.
New Road. Judy Cooke. LC 75-9473. 191p. 1976. 7.95 o.p. (ISBN 0-312-56945-9). St Martin.
New Rose Garden Mystery & The Book of Slaves. M. Iqbal. 1969. pap. 6.25x (ISBN 0-87902-166-7). Orientalia.
New Russian Stories. Ed. by Bernard Guilbert Guerney. LC 53-10128. 1953. New Directions.
New Saint's Tragedy: A Novel. Thomas A Pinkerton. (On cover: Harper's Franklin square library. no. 718). 1892. Harper & Brothers.
New Samaria: And The Summer of St. Martin. Silas Weir Mitchell. LC 4-23717. 1904. J. B. Lippincott Company.
New Samaritan. The Story of an Heiress. Julia MacNair Wright. LC 9-535. 1895. American Tract Society.
New School for Sex. Michael Karnow. pap. 1.95 o.s.i. (OPH-226, Ophelia). Olympia.
New Schoolgirl. David G. Winlett. 192p. (Orig.). 1973. pap. 1.95 o.p. (ISBN 0-87977-189-5, DBB-189). Dansk Blue Bk.
New Schoolma'am: A Summer in North Sparta. Horatio Alger, Jr. 140p. 1976. Repr. of 1877 ed. 18.75. G K Westgard.
New Shoe. Arthur William Upfield. LC 76-40681. (Mystery Library; 1). (Illus.). 1976. (ISBN 0-89163-021-X). University Extension, University of California, San Diego.
New Shoe. Arthur William Upfield. LC 51-11592. 1951. Published for the Crime Club by Doubleday.
New Short Novels. V. 1- LC 54-6477. Ballantine Books.
New Sir Galahad. James Lawrenson Smiley. LC 31-117309. The Christopher Publishing House.
New Soldier: Or, Nature and Life. Henryk Sienkiewicz & Ray, Jens Christian, 1871- Tr. LC 38-12758. 1901. Hurst & Company.
New Solution of The Mystery of Edwin Drood. Mary Kavanagh & Charles Dickens. LC 73-1693. 1973. 4.00 (ISBN 0-8414-2200-1). Folcroft Library Editions.
New Song. Boone. LC 75-131441. 1970. 4.95 o.p. (ISBN 0-88419-075-7); pap. 1.95 o.p. (ISBN 0-88419-045-5). Creation Hse.
New Song. Bertha B. Moore McCurry. LC 47-359574. 1946. Wm. I. Eerdmans Publishing Company.
New South Creed: A Study in Southern Mythmaking. Paul M. Gaston. 1970. 7.95 o.p. (ISBN 0-394-43813-2). Knopf.
New Southern Harvest: An Anthology, Edited by Robert Penn Warren and Albert Erskine. Ed. by Robert Penn Warren & Albert Erskine. LC 57-5193. (Bantam book, F1556). 1957. Bantam Books.
New Soviet Science Fiction. Macmillan. Tr. by Alexander Nakhimovsky & Alice S. Nakhimovsky. (Best of Soviet Science Fiction Ser.). 1979. 12.95 o.s.i. (ISBN 0-02-578220-7). Macmillan.
New Soviet Science Fiction. Macmillan. Tr. by Helen S. Jacobson & Alexander Nakhimovsky. LC 80-10790. (Best of Soviet Science Fiction Ser.). 312p. 1980. pap. 4.95 o.s.i. (ISBN 0-02-022650-0, Collier). Macmillan.
New Star Over Hollywood. Nancy Anderson. 192p. 1975. 4.95 (ISBN 0-86694-037-5). Omega Pubns OR.
New Star Rising: The Story of Jesus of Nazareth. Rowena Rand. LC 51-11862. 1951. Exposition Press.
New Stewardesses. Judi Lynn. (New Stewardesses Ser.). (O.s.i.). 224p. (Orig.). 1974. pap. 1.25 o.s.i. (AQ1348, Award). Univ Pub & Dist.
New Stories by Guy De Maupassant. Guy De Maupassant. (On cover: Minerva series, no. 18). 1890. The Minerva Publishing Company.
New Stories for Men. Ed. by Charles Grayson. LC 41-208813. Doubleday, Doran & Company, Inc.
New Sufferings of Young W. Ulrich Plenzdorf. Tr. by Kenneth P. Wilcox from Ger. LC 78-20928. 1979. 8.95 (ISBN 0-8044-2735-6); pap. 3.95 (ISBN 0-8044-6656-4). Ungar.
New Swiss Family Robinson: Or, Our Unknown Inheritance. Helen Pomeroy. The Abbey Press.
New Tales of Space and Time: Introd. by Anthony Boucher. 1st Ed. Ed. by Raymond J. Healy. LC 51-14220. 1951. Holt.
New Tales of the Cthulhu Mythos. J. Ramsey Campbell. LC 80-14265. 1980. 11.95 (ISBN 0-87054-085-8). Arkham House.
New Tales of the Cthulhu Mythos. Howard Phillips Lovecraft et al. (Illus.). 300p. 1980. 11.95 (ISBN 0-87054-085-8). Arkham.
New Tavern Tales. Robert David Abrahams. LC 30-29013. 1930. W. Neale.
New Temple. Johan Bojer & Archer, Charles, 1863- Tr. LC 28-22464. The Century Co.
New Tenant see Three Plays.
New Tenant: A Daughter of Astrea. Edward Phillips Oppenheim. LC 15-4862. 1912. P. F. Collier & Son.
New Terror. Gaston Leroux. LC 26-9747. The Macaulay Company.
New Terrors, Vol. I. Ramsey Campbell. 1982. pap. 2.95 (ISBN 0-671-45116-2). PB.
New Terrors, Vol. 1. Ed. by R. Campbell. 1982. pap. 10.00x (ISBN 0-330-26126-6, Pub. by Pan Bks). State Mutual Bk.
New Terrors, Vol. 2. Ed. by R. Campbell. 1982. pap. 10.00x (ISBN 0-330-26127-4, Pub. by Pan Bks). State Mutual Bk.
New Thing Breathing. Gavin Bantock. 4.00 (Pub. by Anvil Pr); signed ed. 50 copies 15.00; pap. 2.00. SBD.
New Time--New People. Julia Schumann-Bender. LC 41-6371. Fortuny's.
New Timothy. A Novel. William Mumford Baker. LC 6-6867. 1870. Harper & Brothers.
New Timothy. A Novel. William Mumford Baker. LC 6-6868. (Harper's Franklin square library, no. 333). 1883. Harper & Brothers.
New Trade Winds for the Seven Seas. Alaric J Roberts. LC 42-14738. 1942. J. F. Rowny Press.
New Travels to the Westward. Alonso Decalves. LC 77-18883. (Garland Library of Narratives of North American Indian Captivities; V. 18). 1979. 29.50 (ISBN 0-8240-1642-4). Garland.
New Triangle: Modern Way of Bisexual Love. Toni Vaughan & Jon Mark. 224p. (Orig.). 1975. pap. 1.50 (ISBN 0-532-15145-3). Woodhill.
New Vigilantes. James David Horan. LC 75-1416. 1975. 7.95 (ISBN 0-517-51871-6). Crown Publishers.
New Vigilantes. james d. horan. ed. James David Horan. 1.95 (ISBN 0-380-00685-5). Avon Books.
New Virtue. Oscar Berringer. LC 62-11317. (Pioneer series). 1896. E. Arnold.
New Voices III. George R. R. Martin. (Orig.). 1980. pap. 2.25 (ISBN 0-425-05033-5). Berkley Pub.
New Voices in Science Fiction: Stories by Campbell Award Nominees. George R. R Martin. LC 76-16028. 8.95 (ISBN 0-02-580870-2). Macmillan.
New Voices, '64. Hayes B Jacobs. LC 64-16029. 1964. Macmillan.
New Voyage Round the World: By a Course Never Sailed Before. Daniel Defoe. LC 74-13444. 1974. 11.00 (ISBN 0-404-07924-5). AMS Press.
New Voyage to the Country of the Houyhnhnms: Being the Fifth Part of the Travels into Several Remote Parts of the World by Lemuel Gulliver, Wherein the Author Returns and Finds a New State of Liberal Horses and Revolting Yahoos. Matthew John Caldwell Hodgart & Jonathan Swift. LC 79-114228. (Illus.). 1970. 2.95. Putnam.
New Waggings of Old Tales. John Kendrick Bangs & Sherman, Frank Dempster, 1860- Joint Author. LC 6-6123. 1888. Ticknor and Company.
New War. Don Pendleton. (Executioner Ser.). 192p. 1982. pap. 1.95 (ISBN 0-373-61039-4, Pub. by Worldwide). Harlequin Bks.
New Way of Life: A Novel in Three Phases. Robert Smythe Hichens. LC 42-7339. 1942. Doubleday, Doran and Co., Inc.
New Way to Win a Fortune. Eliza Ann Dupuy. LC 6-35705. T. B. Peterson & Brothers.
New Winds Are Blowing. Molly Castle. LC 46-6622. 1946. Thomas Y. Crowell Company.
New Wine. Agnes Sweetman Castle & Castle, Egerton. LC 19-18222. 1919. 1.75. D. Appleton and Company.
New Wine at Cock-Crow. Geoffrey Uther Ellis. LC 37-652718. 1937. W. Morrow & Co.
New Woman. John Hund. LC 98-885. W. B. Conkey Company.
New Woman. A Novel. Jessie De Foliart Hamblin. C. H. Kerr & Company.
New Woman: In Haste and at Leisure. Elizabeth Lynn Linton. LC 7-19008. The Merriam Company.
New Womans Broken Heart: Short Stories. Andrea Dworkin. LC 79-55919. 1980. 3.00 (ISBN 0-9603628-0-0). Frog in the Well.
New Women of Wonder: Recent Science Fiction Stories by Woman About Women. Pamela Sargent. LC 77-76577. 1978. 2.95 (ISBN 0-394-72438-0). Vintage Books.
New World. G Murray Atkin. LC 21-15336. Thomas Y. Crowell Company.
New World for Simon Ashkenazy. David Peretsovich Markish. LC 76-3332. 1976. 8.95 (ISBN 0-525-16640-8). Dutton.
New World of Reform. Temkin. 6.95 (ISBN 0-87677-044-8). Hartmore.
New World or Old? A Tale of the French Refugees of 1793 and Their Azilum on the Susquehanna. Elsie Murray & Tioga Point Museum, Athens, Pa. LC 45-8186. 1945. Tioga Point Museum.
New World: Or, The Way to Win. Elizabeth Irving. 1905.
New World: Tale. Russell Banks. LC 78-10646. (Illinois short fiction). 3.95. (ISBN 0-252-00722-0) (ISBN 0-252-00721-2). University of Illinois Press.
New Worlds from the Lowlands: Fantasy & Science Fiction of Dutch & Flemish Writers. Compiled by Manuel Van Loggem. 256p. 1982. pap. 20.00 (ISBN 0-89304-053-3). Cross Cult.
New Wounds for Old Prairies: The Garrison Diversion Unit. Glen Sherwood. 64p. 1972. pap. 2.65. Country Print.
New Writers, No. 2. Incl. My Brown Friend. Simon Vestdijk; Return. Keith Johnstone; Lovers. Miodrag Bulatovic; The Old Tune. Robert Pinget. 4.50 o.p.; pap. 2.45 o.p. Transatlantic.
New Writers, No. 3. Incl. Four Stories. Alexander Trocchi; Texts. Nick Rawson; Four Poems. Sinclair Belles; Long Crawl Through Time. David Mercer. 4.50 o.p.; pap. 2.45 o.p. Transatlantic.
New Writers, No. 5. Incl. Unlikely Meeting. Daniel Castelain; Which Land Is Mine. Nazli Nour; Before the Undertaker Comes. Alex Naish. 4.50 o.p. (ISBN 0-7145-0404-1); pap. 2.45 o.p. (ISBN 0-7145-0405-X). Transatlantic.
New Writers, No. 6. Incl. Infatuation. Carol Burns; Road. J. A. Dooley; Excusable Vengence. Penelope Shuttle. 4.50 o.p. (ISBN 0-7145-0406-8); pap. 2.45 o.p. (ISBN 0-7145-0407-6). Transatlantic.
New Writing & Writers Nineteen: Contains Complete Novel Beyond All Love by Martin Walser & Work by 5 Others. Martin Walser. 350p. 1982. 11.95 (ISBN 0-7145-3811-6); pap. 5.95 (ISBN 0-7145-3815-9). Riverrun NY.

New Year: A Novel. Pearl Sydenstricker Buck. LC 68-11296. 1968. John Day Co.
New Year's Day see Old New York.
New Year's Day: The 'seventies. Edith Newbold Jones Wharton. LC 24-11470. (Her Old New York. v. 4). 1924. D. Appleton and Company.
New Year's Eve: A Novel. Jeannie Sakol. LC 74-10892. 1974. 8.95 (ISBN 0-397-01027-3). Lippincott.
New Year's Eve: A Novel. Jeannie Sakol. (Fawcett crest book). 1975. (pbk.) 1.75. Fawcett Publications.
New Year's Eve, Nineteen Twenty Nine. James Thomas Farrell. 4.50 o.p. (ISBN 0-8180-0603-X). Horizon.
New Year's Eve, 1929. James Thomas Farrell. LC 67-30058. 1967. The Smith, by Arrangement with Horizon Press.
New York. A Novel. Edgar Fawcett. LC 98-4768. (On cover: Nealy's continental library. no. 17 5d). 1898. F. T. Neely.
New York: A Novel. Nat Joseph Ferber. LC 29-19524. 1929. Covici, Friede.
New York Bible-Woman. Julia MacNair Wright. LC 9-534. Presbyterian Publication Committee.
New York Call Girl. 1st Ed. Robert James Collas Lowrey. LC 58-10029. 1958. Doubleday.
New York Detective: Or, Startling Phases of City Life. Harlan Page Halsey. LC 7-1181. (On cover: The calumet series, no. 7). 1892. G. Munro.
New York, Etc. New American Library Etc. EQMM Annual. Ed. by Ellery Queen. Ellery Queen's Mystery Magazine. LC 68-21367.
New York Family: A Novel. Edgar Fawcett. LC 6-38786. Cassell Publishing Company.
New York Girl in Virginia. David Joshua Wilson. LC 22-552557. Hartford Printing and Publishing Company.
New York Hooroarer: A Story of Newspaper Enterprise. Containing a Visit to the Infernal Regions and Return. 2d ed. by charles edwards... ed. Charles Edwards. LC 6-36572. 1894. The Humboldt Publishing Co.
New York: Its Upper Ten and Lower Million. George Lippard. LC 70-104514. (Illus.). 1970. (ISBN 0-8398-1161-6). Literature House.
New York: Its Upper Ten and Lower Million. George Lippard. LC 36-29315. 1854. H. M. Rulison.
New York Madness. Maxwell Bodenheim. LC 33-211331. The Macaulay Company.
New York Murders: An Ellery Queen Omnibus. Ellery Queen, pseud. LC 58-10692. 1958. Little, Brown.
New York Needle-Woman: Or Elsie's Stars. Julia MacNair Wright. LC 9-533. Presbyterian Publication Committee.
New York, New York. Earl Mac Rauch. LC 76-55701. 7.95 (ISBN 0-671-22633-9). Simon and Schuster.
New York Nights. Evert Alexander Louhi. LC 41-27721. 1941. The Humanity Press.
New York, N.Y. 10022. Steve Kahn, pseud. 2.50 (ISBN 0-671-82938-6). Pocket Books.
New York One. Lawrence Levine. (Orig.). 1979. pap. 2.50 (ISBN 0-89083-556-X). Zebra.
New York Ride. Anne Bernays. LC 65-16317. bds., 4.95. Trident.
New York Tempest. Manuel Komroff. LC 32-214283. Coward McCann, Inc.
New York Twenty Two. Ilka Chase. LC 73-112322. 308p. Repr. of 1951 ed. lib. bdg. 16.25x (ISBN 0-8371-4710-7, CHNY). Greenwood.
New York Without Gentiles: A Symbolic Phantasy by James A. Bell Pseud. Peter Caruso. LC 56-33960. 1956. Columbia's Pub. Co.
New York 22: That District of the City Which Lies Between Fiftieth and Sixtieth Streets, Fifth Avenue, and the East River. Ilka Chase. LC 51-1835. 1951. Doubleday.
New York 22: That District of the City Which Lies Between Fiftieth and Sixtieth Streets, Fith Avenue, and the East River. Ilka Chase. LC 73-112322. 1971. (ISBN 0-8371-4710-7). Greenwood Press.
New Yorkers. Hortense Calisher. LC 69-15066. 1969. 7.95. Little, Brown.
New Yorkers and Other People. Frances Aymar Mathews. LC 1625. 1900. G. A. S. Wieners.
New Zealand Short Stories: Second Series. Ed. by Christian Karlson Stead. LC 66-68237. (World's Classics, 613: B66-21366). 1966. Oxford U.P.
New Zealanders: A Sequence of Stories. Maurice Shadbolt. 1974. (ISBN 0-7233-0389-4). Whitcombe and Tombs.
Newcomer. Helen I. Troyanovich. 160p. 1979. 6.95 o.p. (ISBN 0-8059-2658-5). Dorrance.
Newcomer. 1st Ed. Clyde Brion Davis. LC 54-6100. 1954. Lippincott.
Newcomers. Elia Wilkinson Peattie. LC 17-24275. 1917. 1.25. Houghton Mifflin Company.
Newcomes. William Makepeace Thackeray. (Half-title: Everyman's library, ed. by Ernest Rhys. Fiction. no. 465-466). 1910. J. M. Dent & Sons, Ltd.
Newcomes: Memoirs of a Most Respectable Family. centenary ed. William Makepeace Thackeray. LC 57-1659. Printed for the Heritage Press at the University Press.
Newcomes. Memoirs of a Most Respectable Family. William Makepeace Thackeray. LC 26-364682. 1867. M. Doolady.
Newcomes: Memoirs of a Most Respectable Family. by william makepeace thackeray; with illustrations by richard doyle. ed. William Makepeace Thackeray & Doyle, Richard, 1824-1883, Illus. LC 31-261. Caxton Publishing Co.
Newcomes: Memoirs of a Most Respectable Family. William Makepeace Thackeray & Doyle, Richard, 1824-1883, Illus. LC 4-16322. (Half-title: The biographical edition. The works of... Thackeray... vol. VIII). 1899. Harper & Brothers.
Newcomes: Memoirs of a Most Respectable Family. William Makepeace Thackery. LC 8-33278. 1855. Harper & Brothers.
Newel Post. Cicely Louise Evans. LC 66-15442. 1967. Doubleday.
Newel Post. Rachel Ann Fish. LC 50-8128. 1950. Coward-McCann.
Newness of the Unchanging: A Spontaneous Unfoldment. Kenneth G. Mills. 1978. pap. 14.95 incl. cassette (ISBN 0-919842-02-X). Sun-Scape Pubns.
Newport. George Parsons Lathrop. LC 7-13852. 1884. C. Scribner's Sons.
Newport; a Novel. Edwin Gilbert. LC 70-154946. 1971. 7.95. Little, Brown.
Newport Squarelle. Maud Elliott. LC 6-37781. 1883. Roberts Brothers.
Newport Woman. Delphine Washburn. LC 67-23781. 1967. Newport Press.
News. Nicholas Delbanco. LC 72-107364. 1970. 5.95. Morrow.
News at Six & Other Stories & Essays. Bill Ensor. 1982. 6.95 (ISBN 0-533-05377-3). Vantage.
News Centurions. Joseph Wambaugh. (Dell Book). 1979. 2.50 (ISBN 0-440-16417-6). Dell Pub. Co.
News from Jerusalem: Stories. David Shahar. LC 73-22227. 1974. 6.95 (ISBN 0-395-18480-0). Houghton Mifflin.
News from Karachi: A Novel. William Wood. LC 62-12421. 1962. Macmillan.
News from Karachi: A Novel. Wood, William Parker. LC 62-12421. 1962. Macmillan.
News from Notown. Eleanor Ellis Perkins. LC 19-15593. 1919. 1.75. Houghton Mifflin Company.
News from Nowhere. William Morris. Ed. by James Redmond. (Routledge English Texts). (Cloth ed. 8.75 o.p.). 1970. pap. 6.95x (ISBN 0-7100-6799-2). Routledge & Kegan.
News from Thrush Green. Miss Read. (O.s.i.). 1971. 5.00 o.s.i. (ISBN 0-395-12102-7). HM.
News from Thrush Green. Dora Jessie Saint. LC 70-143325. (Illus.). 1971. 5.00. Houghton Mifflin.
News Reel. Robert Joseph Casey. LC 32-10933. The Bobbs-Merrill Company.
News Reel Murder. Prosper Buranelli. LC 40-32856. 1940. W. Funk, Inc.
Newsboy. 7th thousand ed. Elizabeth Oakes Prince Smith. LC 8-8639. 1854. J. C. Derby.
Newscasters. Rohn Powers. pap. 2.50 (ISBN 0-8439-0806-8). Nordon Pubns.
Newsdeath. Ray Connolly. LC 77-15840. 1978. 8.95 (ISBN 0-689-10872-9). Atheneum Publishers.
Newsman. Charles Parker. (Orig.). 1981. pap. 2.25 (ISBN 0-505-51611-X). Tower Bks.
Newspaper Editor & Other Stories. Rebecca Chua. (Writing in Asia Ser.). vi, 180p. (Orig.). 1982. pap. text ed. 5.50x (ISBN 9-971-64031-7, 00266). Heinemann Ed.
Newsreel. Irvin Faust. LC 79-3349. 10.95 (ISBN 0-15-165421-2). Harcourt Brace Jovanovich.
Newton and the Quasi-Apple. Stanley Schmidt. LC 74-9464. (Doubleday science fiction). 1975. 4.95 (ISBN 0-385-05598-6). Doubleday.
Newton Forster: Or, The Merchant Service. Frederick Marryat. LC 7-17575. 1873. D. Appleton and Company.
Next Best Thing. Charles Henry Mergendahl. LC 60-8478. 1960. Putnam.
Next-Besters. Lulah Ragsdale. LC 20-11498. 1920. C. Scribner's Sons.
Next Bullet. Karl H. Meyer. 1979. pap. 1.25 (ISBN 0-532-12592-4). Woodhill.
Next Chapter: The War Against the Moon. Andre Maurois. LC 28-108826. (Today and tomorrow). 1927. K. Paul, Trench, Trubner & Co., Ltd.
Next Christmas. Byron Elbert Veatch. LC 13-211085. 1913. Browne & Howell Co.
Next Corner. Kate Jordan. LC 21-664. 1921. 2.00. Little, Brown, and Company.
Next Door. Clara Louise Root Burnham. LC 4-154228. Houghton, Mifflin and Company.
Next Door. Johanna Moosdorf. LC 64-12308. 1964. Knopf.
Next Door, Down the Road, Around the Corner. Richard Balzer. (Illus.). 294p. 1973. 12.95 o.p. (ISBN 0-385-05345-2); pap. 5.95 o.p. (ISBN 0-385-05407-6). Doubleday.
Next Encounter. Donald Thompson. 224p. 1982. pap. 2.50 (ISBN 0-449-14458-5, GM). Fawcett.
Next Fine Day: A Novel. With Line Drawings by Nora S. Unwin. Elizabeth Yates. LC 61-15662. 1962. John Day Co.
Next Man. Michael Z Lewin (ISBN 0-446-88269-0). Warner Books.
Next of Kin. Gladys Hasty Carroll. LC 74-12269. 1974. 7.95 (ISBN 0-316-13005-2). Little, Brown.
Next of Kin. Gladys Hasty Carroll. LC 81-12509. 1982. 12.95 (ISBN 0-89340-366-0). J. Curley.
Next of Kin. Al Dewlen. LC 76-48603. 1977. 7.95 (ISBN 0-385-00251-3). Doubleday.
Next of Kin. Mignon Good Eberhart. LC 81-28299. 10.00 (ISBN 0-394-52433-0). Random House.
Next of Kin. Oliver Lange. LC 79-66080. 9.95 (ISBN 0-87223-560-2). Seaview Books.
Next of Kin. Colin Mackenzie. LC 78-68865. 1979. 7.95 o.p. (ISBN 0-533-04201-1). Vantage.
Next of Kin. Warren Murphy. (Destroyer Ser.: No. 46). 192p. (Orig.). 1981. pap. 1.95 (ISBN 0-523-40720-3). Pinnacle Bks.
Next of Kin--Wanted. by miss m. betham-edwards... ed. Matilda Barbara Betham-Edwards, pseud. (Harper's Franklin square library, no. 581). 1887. Harper & Brothers.
Next of Kin--Wanted. Matilda Barbara Betham-Edwards, pseud. (On cover: Lovell's library. no. 1005). 1887. J. W. Lovell Company.
Next of Kin--Wanted. A Novel. Matilda Barbara Betham- Edwards, pseud. (On cover: Seaside library. Pocket ed. no. 1023). 1887. G. Munro.
Next of Kin: A Suspense Novel. Mignon Good Eberhart. 1982. 10.50 (ISBN 0-394-52433-0). Random.
Next Season: A Novel. Michael Blakemore. LC 68-14833. 1968. Simon and Schuster.
Next Stop--Paradise. Translated from the Polish by Norbert Guterman. 1st Ed. Marek Hlasko. LC 60-5982. 1960. Dutton.
Next Stop the Stars. Robert Silverberg. 1977. 1.50. Ace Books.
Next Ten Thousand Years: A Vision of Man's Future in the Universe. Adrian Berry. 1974. 8.95 o.p. (ISBN 0-8415-0302-8). Dutton.
Next Time see Lesson of the Master.
Next Time I'll Pay My Own Fare. R. Vernon Beste. LC 77-107246. 1969. 5.95. Simon and Schuster.
Next Time We Live. Katherine Ursula Parrott. LC 35-7017. 1935. Longmans, Green and Co.
Next-to-Last Train Ride. Charles Dennis. LC 74-79596. 1974. 6.95. St. Martin's Press.
Next to My Heart. Helen Topping Miller. LC 39-249463. 1939. D. Appleton-Century Company.
Next-to-Nothing House. Alice V. Carrick. 1922. Repr. 13.00 o.s.i. Finch Pr.
Next to These Ladies. Margaret Hassett. LC 40-11548. 1940. Longmans, Green and Co.
Next to Valour: A Novel. John Edward Jennings. LC 39-27453. 1939. The Macmillan Company.
Next Witness see Royal Flush: A Nero Wolfe Omnibus.
Next Year Will Be Different. Maude Williamson. LC 39-27922. Farrar & Rinehart, Incorporated.
Next Year's Rose. Desemea Wilson. LC 34-22755. E. P. Dutton & Co., Inc.
Nexus. Henry Miller. (Orig.). 1965. pap. 3.95 (ISBN 0-394-17429-1, B326, BC). Grove.
Nez-Bits. Paul W. Nesbit. (Illus.). 1946. pap. 0.75x (ISBN 0-911746-04-8). Nesbit.
Nez Perce Buffalo Horse. William Elwood Sanderson. LC 77-137771. (Illus.). 1972. 4.95 (ISBN 0-87004-212-2). Caxton Printers.
Nez Perce Legend. Mick Clumpner. (Orig.). 1983. pap. 2.95 (ISBN 0-440-06330-2, Banbury). Dell.
Ngaio Marsh, 5 vols. Incl. Vol. 1. Black As He's Painted; Vol. 2. Enter a Murder; Vol. 3. Killer Dolphin; Vol. 4. Last Ditch; Vol. 5. Overture to Death. Date not set. pap. 12.50 boxed set (ISBN 0-515-06816-0). Jove Pubns.
Niagara. Robert Lewis Taylor. LC 79-21620. 12.95 (ISBN 0-399-12432-2). Putnam.
Niagara: A Stereophonic Novel. Michel Butor. Tr. by Elinor S. Miller. LC 69-15704. 1969. 7.95 o.p. (ISBN 0-8092-9692-6). Regnery.
Niagara Falls Romance. William Lee Popham. LC 11-32422. 1.00. The World Supply Company.
Nibelungenlied. A. T. Hatto. (Classics Ser.). 1965. pap. 3.95 (ISBN 0-14-044137-9). Penguin.
Nibsy's Christmas. Jacob August Riis. LC 71-90590. (Short story index reprint series). 1969. Books for Libraries Press.
Nibsy's Christmas. Jacob August Riis. LC 7-41645. 1893. C. Scribner's Sons.
Nicanor of Athens: The Autobiography of an Unknown Citizen. Owen Francis Grazebrook. LC 47-15853. 1946. University Press.
Nicanor of Athens: The Autobiography of an Unknown Citizen. Owen Francis Grazebrook. LC 47-469696. 1947. University Press.
Nicanor, Teller of Tales: A Story of Roman Britain. C. Bryson Taylor. LC 6-15107. 1906. A. C. McClvrg & Co.
Nicchia. Geoffrey Atheling Wagner. 352p. (Orig.). 1982. pap. 2.75 (ISBN 0-505-51782-5). Tower Bks.
Nicchia: A Novel. Geoffrey Atheling Wagner. LC 59-11455. 1959. J. Day Co.
Nice American. Gerald Sykes. LC 51-1591. 1951. Creative Age Press.
Nice American. Gerald Sykes. (M2029). 1963. Popular Lib.
Nice and Nasty: Tales. John A Why. LC 77-374919. Why.
Nice and Naughty. William Arthur Neubauer. LC 45-261. 1944. Phoenix Press.
Nice and the Good. Iris Murdoch. LC 68-11412. 1968. Viking Press.
Nice and the Good. Iris Murdoch. 1978. 2.95 (ISBN 0-14-003034-4). Penguin Books.
Nice Day for Screaming: And Other Tales of the Hub. James H Schmitz. LC 65-22543. 1965. Chilton Books.
Nice Deity. Martha Baird. LC 55-11012. 1955. 2.75 (ISBN 0-910492-04-2). Definition.
Nice Enough to Murder. Enid S Russell. LC 77-144293. 1971. 4.95. Published for the Crime Club by Doubleday.
Nice Fillies Finish Last. Davis Dresser. (Mike Shayne Mystery). 1973. (pbk.) 0.75. Dell.
Nice Fillies Finish Last. Brett Halliday. 1.25. Dell.
Nice Girl Comes to Town. Maysie Greig. LC 30-302438. 1930. L. MacVeagh, The Dial Press.
Nice Girl Like Me. Anne Piper. Orig. Title: Marry at Leisure. 1969. pap. 0.75 o.p. (T2044). Pyramid Pubns.
Nice Girls Do. Irene Kassorla. LC 80-53202. 1980. 9.95 (ISBN 0-936906-01-4). Stratford Pr.
Nice Guys Finish Last. Robert Kyle, pseud. LC 54-8051. (Dell first edition 51). 1955. Dell Pub. Co.
Nice Italian Girl. Elizabeth Christman. LC 75-38357. 4.95 (ISBN 0-396-07295-X). Dodd, Mead.
Nice Lady. Katharine Carson. LC 40-8313. G. P. Putnam's Sons.
Nice Little Killing. Anthony Gilbert, pseud. LC 73-15566. 1974. 4.95 (ISBN 0-394-48991-8). Random House.
Nice Long Evening. Elizabeth Frances Corbett. 1933. D. Appleton-Century Company, Incorporated.
Nice Long Vacation. William Arthur Neubauer. LC 49-48968. 1949. Arcadia House.
Nice Murderers. David Delman. LC 77-2911. 1977. 7.95 (ISBN 0-688-03211-7). Morrow.
Nice Neighborhood. Edith-Jane Bahr. 1975. (pbk.) 0.95. Dell.
Nice People Don't Kill. Francis Woolsey Bronson. LC 40-31516. Farrar & Rinehart, Inc.
Nice People Murder. 1st Ed. Mary Hastings Bradley. LC 52-5647. 1952. Longmans, Green.
Nice People Poison. 1st Ed. Mary Hastings Bradley. LC 52-11033. 1952. Longmans, Green.
Nice Place to Live. Robert C. Sloan. 1982. pap. 2.95 (ISBN 0-553-22507-3). Bantam.
Nice Sound Alibi. Philip Lauben. LC 81-8758. 1981. 9.95 (ISBN 0-312-57253-0). St. Martin's Press.
Nice to See You, Andy Capp! Smythe. 1977. pap. 1.50 (ISBN 0-449-13848-8, GM). Fawcett.
Nice Try. Thomas P Baird. LC 65-14710. 1965. Harcourt, Brace & World.
Nice Way to Die. Mignon Warner. LC 77-357659. 1976. 2.95 (ISBN 0-7091-5553-0). Hale.
Nicholas Blood, Candidate. Arthur Henry. LC 71-38654. (Black Heritage Library Collection). 1972. (ISBN 0-8369-9012-9). Books for Libraries Press.
Nicholas Comenius: Or Ye Pennsylvania Schoolmaster of Ye Olden Time. William Riddle. LC 7-41437. 1897. Wickersham Printing Company.
Nicholas Comenius: Or, Ye Pennsylvania Schoolmaster of Ye Olden Time. 2d ed. William Riddle. LC 98-99. 1898. T. B. & H. B. Cochran, Printers.
Nicholas Crabbe: Or, The One and the Many: a Romance. Frederick William Rolfe. LC 77-11680. 1977. 17.50 (ISBN 0-8371-9816-X). Greenwood Press.
Nicholas Crabbe: Or, The One and the Many, a Romance, by Fr. Rolfe (Baron Corvo) With an Introd. by Cecil Woolf. Frederick William Rolfe. 1958. New Directions.
Nicholas Goade: Detective. Edward Phillips Oppenheim. LC 29-23791. 1929. Little, Brown, and Company.
Nicholas Minturn. A Study in a Story. Josiah Gilbert Holland. LC 7-61395. 1877. Scribner, Armstrong & Co.

Nicholas Minturn: A Study in a Story. Josiah Gilbert Holland. LC 7-614018. 1882. C. Scribner's Sons.

Nicholas Minturn, a Study in a Story. Josiah Gilbert Holland. LC 4-18897. 1904. C. Scribner's Sons.

Nicholas Nickelby. Charles Dickens. 1977. 10.95x (ISBN 0-460-00238-4, Evman); pap. 3.95x (ISBN 0-460-01238-X, Evman). Biblio Dist.

Nicholas Nickelby. Charles Dickens. 1982. pap. 10.00x (ISBN 0-330-26424-9, Pub. by Pan Bks). State Mutual Bk.

Nicholas Nickleby. people american ed.... ed. Charles Dickens. LC 25-23746. (Letter on cover: Peterson's uniform duodecimo edition of the complete works of Charles Dickens.). T. B. Peterson.

Nicholas Nickleby... Charles Dickens. LC 6-26431. 1861. W. A. Townsend and Company.

Nicholas Nickleby... Charles Dickens. LC 6-37039. 1867. Hurd and Houghton.

Nicholas Nickleby... Charles Dickens. LC 6-26429. 1867. Hurd and Houghton.

Nicholas Nickleby. Charles Dickens. LC 26-27673. (Rittenhouse classics). 1926. Macrae Smith Company.

Nicholas Nickleby. Charles Dickens & Michael Slater. LC 78-314378. (Penguin English library). (Illus.). 1978. 3.95 (ISBN 0-14-043113-6). Penguin.

Nicholas Simon: A Romance of Revolution. D. P MacDonald. LC 15-21144. 1915. Hodder & Stoughton.

Nicholl's Forest of Dean. H. G. Nicholls. Repr. 3.95 (ISBN 0-7153-4047-6). David & Charles.

Nicholson at Large: A Novel. Ward S Just. LC 75-12639. 1975. 8.95 (ISBN 0-316-47722-2). Little, Brown.

Nichovev Plot. Nick Carter. (Nick Carter Ser.). (O.s.i.). (Orig.). 1976. pap. 1.50 o.s.i. (AD1623, Award). Univ Pub & Dist.

Nick Adams Stories. Ernest Hemingway. LC 77-159759. 1972. 7.95 (ISBN 0-684-12485-8). Scribner.

Nick Baba's Last Drink, and Other Sketches. George Paul Goff. LC 17-13018. 1879. Inquirer Printing and Publishing Company.

Nick Carter, Detective: Fiction's Most Celebrated Detective; Six Astonishing Adventures. Nick Carter. LC 63-16099. 1963. Macmillan.

Nick Carter Down East: Or, Lively Times in the Rural Districts. John Russell Coryell. LC 4268. (On cover: Magnet detective library. no. 141). 1900. Street & Smith.

Nick Carter's Clever Protege: Or, The Making of a Detective. John Russell Coryell. LC 259. (On cover: Magnet detective library. no. 108). 1899. Street & Smith.

Nick Carter's Clever Ruse: Or, Setting a Thief to Catch a Thief. Frederick William Davis. LC 6517. (On cover: Magnet detective library. no. 153). 1900. Street & Smith.

Nick Carter's Girl Detective: Or, Roxy's Great Triumph. John Russell Coryell. LC 3184. (On cover: Magnet detective library, no. 132). 1900. Street & Smith.

Nick Carter's Retainer: Or, The Clever Plan of an up-to-Date Crook. John Russell Coryell. LC 5215. (On cover: Magnet detective library, no. 147). 1900. Street & Smith.

Nick Carter's Star Pupil: Or, "Roxy" and Bob Ferrett After Big Game. John Russell Coryell. LC 1-29677. (On cover: Magnet detective library, no. 162). 1900. Street & Smith.

Nick of the Woods. Robert Montgomery Bird. Ed. by Curtis Dahl. (Masterworks of Literature Ser.). 1967. 7.50x (ISBN 0-8084-0234-X); pap. 4.45x (ISBN 0-8084-0235-8, M20). Coll & U Pr.

Nick of the Woods. George Edwards Lewis. LC 17-5980. 1916. Jensen Publishing Company Press.

Nick of the Woods: Or, The Jibbenainosay; a Tale of Kentucky. Robert Montgomery Bird. Ed. by Curtis Dahl. LC 66-24152. (Masterworks of literature series). 1967. College & University Press.

Nick of the Woods: Or the Jibbenainosay. A Tale of Kentucky. Robert Montgomery Bird. 1837. Carey Lea & Blanchard.

Nick of the Woods: Or, The Jibbenainosay; a Tale of Kentucky. a new ed., rev. by the author. ed. Robert Montgomery Bird. LC 8-34324. 1853. Redfield.

Nick of the Woods: Or, The Jibbenainosay; a Tale of Kentucky. Robert Montgomery Bird. LC 28-22868. (American bookshelf). 1928. Macy-Masiua.

Nick of the Woods: Or, The Jibbenainosay; a Tale of Kentucky. Robert Montgomery Bird. Ed. by Williams, Cecil Brown. LC 39-15206. (Half-title: American fiction series: general editor, H. H. Clark). American Book Company.

Nick of the Woods: Or, The Jibbenainosay; a Tale of Kentucky. Robert Montgomery Bird. Ed. by McClintock, Marshall. LC 41-22772. The Vanguard Press.

Nick of the Woods: Or, The Jibbenainosay; a Tale of Kentucky. a new ed., rev. by the author. ed. Robert Montgomery Bird. LC 42-4468. 1881. A. C. Armstrong & Son.

Nick Putzel; or, Arthur Curney's Ruin. A Narrative Showing the Ins and Outs, the Tricks and Devices, the Frauds and Falsehoods, Practiced by Adepts in the Art of Political Wire Pulling, and Especially Exposing the the Resistless Power of the Bar-Room and the Beer-Saloon... George Koehler. Hubbard Bros.; Etc., Etc.

Nick, the Click. Geoffrey Kedington Wilkinson. LC 69-11470. (Red mask mystery). 1968. 4.50. Putnam.

Nick the Greek. Harry Mark Petrakis. LC 77-80909. 1979. 10.00 (ISBN 0-385-04909-9). Doubleday.

Nickel Jackpot. J. J Lamb. LC 75-38861. 1976. 1.50 (ISBN 0-345-24921-6). Ballantine Books.

Nickel Miseries, a Collection. Ivan Gold. LC 63-11860. 1963. Viking Press.

Nickel Mountain. John Gardner. 304p. 1982. pap. 3.50 (ISBN 0-345-29294-4). Ballantine.

Nickel Mountain: A Pastoral Novel. John Champlin Gardner. LC 73-7293. (Illus.). 1973. 6.95 (ISBN 0-394-48883-0). Knopf; Distributed by Random House.

Nickel Ride. Michael Kaufman. (O.s.i.). (Orig.). 1974. pap. 1.25 o.s.i. (AQ1351, Award). Univ Pub & Dist.

Nickel Under Your Foot. Charles Robbins. LC 41-66582. J. B. Lippincott Company.

Nickel's Worth of Ice. Samuel H. Patterson. 1972. pap. 0.95 o.p. (09145). Curtis.

Nickel's Worth of Ice: By Sam Patterson. 1st Ed. Samuel H Patterson. LC 66-193946. 1966. 4.95. Knopf.

Nicky-Nan, Reservist. Arthur Thomas Quiller-Couch. LC 15-18110. 1915. 1.35. D. Appleton and Company.

Nicky, Son of Egg. Gerald William Bullett. LC 29-185432. 1929. A. A. Knopf.

Nicky: The Story of a Long Christmas. Winfred Van Atta. LC 65-25084. bds., 3.95. Eriksson Dist. Hill & Wang.

Nicodemus. W. Sybel Lester. 2.50 o.p. Carlton.

Nicodemus. Dorothy Walworth. LC 46-1793. 1946. Houghton Mifflin Company.

Nicola. 1st Ed. Audrey Erskine Lindop. LC 59-11603. 1959. Doubleday.

Nicolai Fechin. Mary Balcomb. LC 75-11161. (Illus.). 176p. 1975. 40.00 o.p. (ISBN 0-87358-140-7). Northland.

Nicole. Morgan St. Michel. (Orig.). 1982. pap. 2.95 (ISBN 0-515-06345-2). Jove Pubns.

Nicole, No. 5. Morgan St. Michel. 256p. 1983. pap. 2.95 (ISBN 0-515-06647-8). Jove Pubns.

Nicole Around the World. Morgan St. Michel. 256p. 2.95 (ISBN 0-515-06824-1). Jove Pubns.

Nicole Down Under. Morgan St. Michel. 240p. 1983. pap. 2.95 (ISBN 0-515-06886-1). Jove Pubns.

Nicole in Captivity. Morgan St. Michel. 240p. 1982. pap. 2.95 (ISBN 0-515-06347-9). Jove Pubns.

Nicole in Flight. Morgan St. Michel. 240p. (Orig.). 1982. pap. 2.95 (ISBN 0-515-06346-0). Jove Pubns.

Nicole Nobody. Duchess Of Bedford. LC 74-14378. (Illus.). 408p. 1975. 10.95 o.p. (ISBN 0-385-09773-5). Doubleday.

Nicole's Love Cruise, No. 6. Morgan St. Michel. 256p. 1983. pap. 2.95 (ISBN 0-515-06800-4). Jove Pubns.

Nicole's Pleasure Hunt. Morgan St. Michel. 256p. 1982. pap. 2.25 (ISBN 0-515-06348-7). Jove Pubns.

Nicole's Summer Pleasures. Morgan St. Michel. 256p. 1983. pap. 2.95 (ISBN 0-515-06891-8). Jove Pubns.

Nicolette. Herbert M Katz. (Berkley Medallion Book). 1977. 1.50 (ISBN 0-425-03588-3). Berkley Pub. Corp.

Nicolette: A Novel. Herbert M Katz. LC 76-8636. 7.95 (ISBN 0-87795-144-6). Arbor House.

Nicolette: A Tale of Old Provence. Emmuska Orczy. LC 22-26886. George H. Doran Company.

Niece of Abraham Pein. James Harold Wallis. LC 42-51778. 1943. E. P. Dutton & Co., Inc.

Nieces & Uncles. Preston Harriman. pap. 1.95 o.p. (ISBN 0-87682-194-8, 7194). Barclay Hse.

Niels Lyhne. Jens Peter Jacobsen. LC 66-28157. (Library of Scandinavian literature v. 2). 1967. Twayne Publishers.

Niels Lyhne. Jens Peter Jacobsen. Tr. by Larsen, Hanna Astrup. LC 20-1700. (Half-title: Scandinavian classics, vol. xiii). 1919. The American-Scandivavian Foundation; Etc., Etc.

Nielsen's Children. James Brady. LC 78-7058. 9.95 (ISBN 0-399-12165-X). Putnam.

Nifft the Lean. Michael Shea. 304p. 1982. pap. 2.95. DAW Bks.

Nigger: A Novel. Clement Wood. LC 22-20876. E. P. Dutton & Company.

Nigger Factory: A Novel. Scott-Heron, Gil. LC 78-37439. 1972. 5.95. Dial Press.

Nigger Heaven. Carl Van Vechten. LC 73-3471. 1973. (lib. ed.) 11.00 (ISBN 0-374-98069-1). Octagon Books.

Nigger Heaven. Carl Van Vechten. LC 26-15403. 1926. A. A. Knopf.

Nigger of the Narcissus. Joseph Conrad. 1936. Doubleday, Doran & Company, Inc.

Nigger of the Narcissus. Joseph Conrad. LC 38-32642. 1938. The Sun Dial-Press, Inc.

Nigger of the Narcissus see Youth.

Nigger of the Narcissus: A Tale of the Forecastle. Joseph Conrad. LC 14-97657. 1914. Doubleday, Page & Company.

Nigger of the Narcissus: A Tale of the Forecastle. Joseph Conrad. LC 22-10646. 1921. Doubleday, Page & Company.

Nigger of the Narcissus: A Tale of the Sea. Joseph Conrad. LC 42-28436. 1926. Doubleday, Page & Company.

Nigger of the "Narcissus," A Tale of the Sea; with an Introd. by Morton Dauwen Zabel. Joseph Conrad. LC 51-6230. (Harper's modern classics). 1951. Harper.

Nigger of the Narcissus. Narcissus. Introd. by Howard Mumford Jones, Illus. by Millard Sheets. Joseph Conrad. LC 66-973. bds., 6.95. Heritage Dist. Dial.

Nigger of the Narcissus, Typhoon & Other Stories. Joseph Conrad. 1963. pap. 2.75 (ISBN 0-14-002061-6). Penguin.

Nigger to Nigger. Edward Clarkson Leverett Adams. LC 28-24280. 1928. C. Scribner's Sons.

Nigh. Cid Corman, pseud. 1970. pap. 4.00 (Pub. by Elizabeth Pr). SBD.

Night. Edgar Hilsenrath. LC 66-20975. 1974. (pbk.) 1.75. Manor Books.

Night. Edna O'Brien. LC 72-2257. 1973. 5.95 (ISBN 0-394-48230-1). Knopf.

Night. Edna O'Brien. 1976. (pbk.) 1.75. Bantam.

Night. Elie Wiesel. Tr. by Stella Rodway. 1960. 3.00 o.p. (ISBN 0-8090-7350-1). Hill & Wang.

Night-Action. Sydney Muller Parkman. LC 36-174751. 1936. Harper & Brother.

Night Action. Bruce Douglas Reeves. LC 66-26043. 1966. 5.95. New Amer. Lib.

Night After the Wedding. Mildred Gordon & Gordon Gordon. LC 78-20073. 1979. 8.95 (ISBN 0-385-14012-6). Doubleday.

Night Air. Harrison Dowd. LC 50-9207. 1950. Dial Press.

Night Among the Horses. Djuna Barnes. LC 29-18120. 1929. H. Liveright.

Night and Day. Virginia Stephen Woolf. LC 73-5730. (Harvest book, HB 263). 1973. 3.95. Harcourt Brace Jovanovich.

Night and Day. Virginia Stephen Woolf. LC 20-19042. George H. Doran Company.

Night & Day & Night. Warja Honegger-Lavater. (Folded Story Ser: No. 9). (Illus., Eng., Fr. & Ger.). 1964. bds. 4.50 o.p. Wittenborn.

Night and Hope. Arnost Lustig. LC 76-39999. (His Children of the Holocaust). 1976. 8.95 (ISBN 0-87953-400-1). Inscape.

Night and Hope. Arnost Lustig. 1978. 1.75 (ISBN 0-380-01954-X). Avon Books.

Night and Hope. Translated from the Czech by George Theiner. Arnost Lustig. LC 62-4574. 1962. Dutton.

Night and Morning. Edward George Earle Lytton Bulwer-Lytton Lytton. LC 8-26649. G. Routledge and Sons.

Night and Morning... Edward George Earle Lytton Bulwer-Lytton Lytton. LC 7-8113. (Lovell's library, v. 2, no. 84). 1883. J. W. Lovell Company.

Night and Morning. Edward George Earle Lytton Bulwer-Lytton Lytton. LC 7-8112. (Half-title: Novels of Sir Edward Bulwer Lytton. Library ed. Novels of life and manners, vol. X-XI). 1893. Little, Brown, and Company.

Night and Morning: A Novel. lord lytton ed. Edward George Earle Lytton Bulwer-Lytton Lytton. LC 49-320944. 1879. J.B. Lippincott.

Night and Morning, a Novel. library ed.... ed. Edward George Earle Lytton Bulwer-Lytton Lytton. (Half-title: Novels of Sir Edward Bulwer Lytton. Library ed. Novels of life and manners, vol. XXXVII-XXXVIII). 1862. J. B. Lippincott & Co.

Night and Morning, Leila: Or, The Siege of Granada, Pausanias the Spartan. Edward George Earle Lytton Bulwer-Lytton Lytton & Lytton, Edward Robert Bulwer-Lytton, 1st Earl of, 1831-1891, Ed. LC 31-32288. (The novels and romances of Edward Bulwer Lytton. v. 9). Aldine Book Publishing Co.

Night and No Moon: A Novel. Jerome Odlum. LC 42-15978. 1942. Howell, Soskin.

Night and Silence: Who Is Here? an American Comedy. Pamela Hansford Johnson. LC 63-14895. 1963. Scribner.

Night and the City. Gerald Kersh. LC 46-2642. 1946. Simon and Schuster.

Night Angel Street. Bernard Dekle. LC 64-16742. 1965. 3.50. Tuttle.

Night at Hogwallow. Theodore Strauss. LC 37-23536. 1937. Little, Brown and Company.

Night at Lost End. George Agnew Chamberlain. LC 31-31125. 1931. Brewer, Warren & Putnam, Inc.

Night at Sea. Margaret Lane. (Signet bk., T3103). 1967. New Amer. Lib.

Night at Sea Abbey. Virginia Coffman. (Signet Book). 1978. 1.50 (ISBN 0-451-08093-9). New American Library.

Night at Sea Abbey see Black Heather.

Night at the Airport: Stories. Mark Aleksandrovich Aldanov. LC 49-10437. 1949. C. Scribner's Sons.

Night at the Mocking Widow: By Carter Dickson Pseud. John Dickson Carr. LC 50-7949. 1950. Morrow.

Night at the Vulcan. Ngaio Marsh. LC 51-11439. (London Ed. (Collins) Has Title: Opening Night.). 1951. Little, Brown.

Night Attack, a Novel by Lee Crosby Pseud. Ware Torrey. LC 43-121232. 1943. E. P. Dutton & Co., Inc.

Night Beat. William Camp. LC 68-14333. 1968. Vanguard Press.

Night Before Chancellorsville: And Other Civil War Stories. Ed. by Shelby Foote. LC 57-10074. (Signet books, S1415). 1957. New American Library.

Night Before Murder. Stephen Gould Fisher. LC 39-2154. 1939. Hillman Curl, Inc.

Night Before Thanksgiving: A White Heron and Selected Stories. Sarah Orne Jewett & Shute, Katherine H. LC 11-2074. (Riverside Literature Series. No. 202). 0.15. Houghton Mifflin Company.

Night Before the Wedding. Mildred Gordon & Gordon Gordon. LC 68-22621. 1969. 4.95. Doubleday.

Night Before the Wedding. Mildred Gordon & Gordon Gordon. LC 68-22621. 1969. 5.50 o.p. (ISBN 0-385-04130-6). Doubleday.

Night Bell. Kenneth O'Donnell Horan. LC 40-27329. 1940. C. Scribner's Sons.

Night Between the Rivers. Robert Luther Duffus. LC 37-132678. 1937. The Macmillan Company.

Night Boat. Robert A. McCammon. 1980. 2.50 (ISBN 0-380-75598-X, 75598). Avon.

Night Boat. Timothy Trent, pseud. LC 34-14227. 1934. W. Godwin, Inc.

Night Boat from Puerto Bedra. Donald MacKenzie. LC 69-15021. 1970. 4.95. Houghton Mifflin Co.

Night Boat to Paris. Richard Jessup. LC 56-7802. (Dell first edition, 92). Dell Pub. Co.,

Night-Born: And Also The Madness of John Harned, When the World Was Young, The Benefit of the Doubt, Winged Blackmail, Bunches of Knuckles, War, Under the Deck Awnings, To Kill a Man, The Mexican. Jack London. LC 13-3759. 1913. The Century Co.

Night Branders. Walt Coburn. 1979. pap. 1.50 o.s.i. (ISBN 0-505-51348-X). Tower Bks.

Night Branders. Walt Coburn. 176p. 1974. pap. 0.95 o.p. (ISBN 0-532-95354-1). Woodhill.

Night Branders. Walt Coburn. 176p. 1974. pap. 0.95 o.p. (ISBN 0-532-95354-1). Manor Bks.

Night Branders. Walt Coburn. 1974. (pbk.) 0.95. Manor Books.

Night Call from a Distant Time Zone. Herbert H. Lieberman. 320p. 1983. pap. 3.50 (ISBN 0-451-22994-0, Sig). NAL.

Night Call from a Distant Time Zone: A Novel. Herbert H. Lieberman. LC 81-9863. 12.95 (ISBN 0-517-54571-3). Crown Publishers.

Night Caller. Brennan Patrick. (Orig.). 1981. pap. 2.25 (ISBN 0-440-16674-8). Dell.

Night Cats. Anthony Taber. (Illus.). 64p. Date not set. 9.95 (ISBN 0-312-92571-9). Congdon & Weed.

Night Chant. Clee Woods. 1980. pap. 1.95 (ISBN 0-8439-0812-2). Nordon Pubns.

Night Child. Celeste De Blasis. LC 74-16643. 1975. 7.95 (ISBN 0-698-10632-6). Coward, McCann & Geoghegan.

Night Child. Celeste DeBlasis. LC 74-16643. 1976. 1.50 (ISBN 0-449-22941-6). Fawcett Crest.

Night Chills. Dean Koontz. LC 75-33122. 1976. 8.95 (ISBN 0-689-10660-2). Atheneum.

Night Chills. Dean R Koontz. (Fawcett Crest Book). 1977. 1.75 (ISBN 0-449-23087-2). Fawcett Publications.

Night Clerk. Gerald Foster. LC 35-3816. W. Godwin, Inc.

Night Climb. Frank Harper. LC 46-8275. 1946. Longmans, Green & Co.

Night Club. Katharine Brush. LC 29-17994. 1929. Minton, Balch & Company.

Night Club. Katharine Brush. LC 33-283472. 1932. A. L. Burt Company.

Night Club Daughter. Katharine Haviland Taylor. LC 33-4541. J. B. Lippincott Company.

Night Club Lady. William Arthur Neubauer. LC 47-17760. 1947. Phoenix Press.

Night Club Mystery: The Experiences of a Highly Unconventional Young Man Unexpectedly Brought into Contact with Sinister Forces. Elizabeth Garver Jordan. LC 30-7680. The Century Co.

Night Cometh. Paul Charles Joseph Bourget. Tr. by George Frederic William Lees. LC 16-112290. 1916. 1.35. G. P. Putnam's Sons.
Night Cometh. Laurence James McCauley. LC 59-13739. 1959. Duell, Sloan and Pearce.
Night Cover. Michael Z Lewin. LC 75-36784. 1976. 7.95 (ISBN 0-394-49644-2). Knopf.
Night Cover. Michael Z Lewin. 1.95 (ISBN 0-425-04030-5).
Night Crayons Talked. Vick Knight. LC 74-78585. (Illus.). 1974. 4.95 (ISBN 0-378-62726-0). Ward Ritchie Press.
Night Creature. Ball, Brian. (Fawcett gold medal book). 1974. (pbk.) 0.95. Fawcett.
Night Crew. J. R Goddard. LC 75-117028. (Illus.). 1970. 5.95. Little, Brown.
Night Crossing. Ken Kolb. 1975. (pbk.) 1.50. Playboy Press.
Night Crossing. Jurgen Petschull. 224p. 1982. pap. 2.50 (ISBN 0-523-41865-5). Pinnacle Bks.
Night Crossing: A Novel. Ken Kolb. LC 74-82486. 1974. 8.95 (ISBN 0-87223-420-7). Playboy Press.
Night Cry: A Novel. William L Stuart. LC 48-515552. 1948. Dial Press.
Night Cry: A Novel. William L Stuart. LC 49-1759. (New Avon library 186). 1949. Avon Pub. Co.
Night, Dawn, the Accident. Elie Wiesel. 1972. 7.95 o.p. (ISBN 0-8090-7352-8). Hill & Wang.
Night, Dawn, The Accident: Three Tales. Eliezer Wiesel. LC 72-81290. 1972. 7.95 (ISBN 0-8090-7352-8). Hill and Wang.
Night Desk: A Novel. George Ryga. LC 76-383785. 1976. 2.95 (ISBN 0-88922-089-1). Talonbooks.
Night Drop. 1st Ed. Frederick Clyde Davis. LC 55-93831. 1955. Published for the Crime Club by Doubleday.
Night Drums. Achmed Abdullah. LC 21-176245. The James A. McCann Company.
Night Duty. John Stuart Arey. LC 43-5110. 1943. Doubleday, Doran & Co., Inc.
Night Duty. David Michael De Reuda Winser. LC 43-5110. 1943. Doubleday, Doran.
Night-Express. James Dabney McCabe. LC 7-15274. 1879. J. M. Stoddart & Co.
Night Extra. William P. McGivern. 1975. pap. 1.25 o.p. (ISBN 0-515-03795-8). BJ Pub Group.
Night Extra. LC 57-7442. (Red badge detective). 1957. Dodd, Mead.
Night Face and Other Stories. Poul Anderson. LC 77-28644. (Gregg Press Science Fiction Series). (worlds of Poul Anderson; 1). 1978. 9.95 (ISBN 0-8398-2412-2). Gregg Press.
Night Fails on Siva's Hill. Edward John Thompson. LC 30-37681. 1929. L. MacVeagh, The Dial Press.
Night Falls at Bitterhill. Paulette Warren. 1976. pap. 1.25 (ISBN 0-532-12412-X). Woodhill.
Night Falls at Bitterhill. easy eye ed. Paulette Warren. (Orig.). 1969. pap. 0.75 o.p. (74-530). Lancer.
Night Falls on the City. Sarah Gainham. LC 67-11287. 1967. Holt, Rinehart and Winston.
Night Falls on the City. Sarah Gainham. LC 67-11287. 1975. (pbk.) 1.95 (ISBN 0-380-00442-9). Avon.
Night Falls Too Soon. Francesca Chimenti. (Orig.). 1972. pap. 0.75 o.p. (T2634). Pyramid Pubns.
Night Fear. Frank Belnap Long. Ed. by Roy Torgeson. 1979. pap. 2.25 (ISBN 0-89083-489-X). Zebra.
Night Fighter. C. F. Rawnsley & Robert Wright. (War Library). 320p. 1983. pap. 2.95 (ISBN 0-345-31025-X). Ballantine.
Night Fire. Edward Kimbrough. LC 46-20739. 1946. Rinehart & Company, Inc.
Night Fire. Abridged Ed. Edward Kimbrough. LC 54-34203. (Ace double novel books, D-65). 1954. Ace Books.
Night Flight. Saint Exupery, Antoine De. LC 73-16016. (Harbrace paperbound library, HPL63). 1974. (pbk.) 1.25 (ISBN 0-15-665605-1). Harcourt Brace Jovanovich.
Night Flight. Antoine De Saint Exupery & Gilbert, Stuart, Tr. LC 32-20300. The Century Co.
Night Flight for Ransom. Leroy H. Gray. Ed. by Gayle Ellis. LC 76-50909. (Illus.). 160p. 1980. pap. 5.95 (ISBN 0-9603976-0-4). L Gray Pub.
Night Flight for Ransom: The Legend of D. B. Cooper. Leroy H Gray & Gale Ellis. LC 76-505909. (Illus.). 5.95. Lee Gray Pub.: Christ Life Fellowship.
Night Flights: Stories New and Selected. Matthew Cohen. LC 77-89879. 1978. 7.95. (ISBN 0-385-13333-2) (ISBN 0-385-13334-0). Doubleday Canada.
Night Flower. Walter C Butler. LC 36-16935. The Macaulay Company.
Night for a Lady. Charles Beahan. LC 32-11456. 1932. H. Smith.
Night for Treason. John W Jakes. LC 56-133002. (Mystery house). 1956. Bouregy & Curl.
Night Freight Murders. Robert Fleming. LC 42-12028. 1942. Smith & Durrell.
Night Gallery 2. Rod Serling. LC 72-8885. (Bantam pathfinder editions). 1972. 0.75. Bantam Books.
Night Games. Ralph Markfield. 192p. 1972. pap. 1.95 o.p. (ISBN 0-87056-220-7, 6220). Brandon.
Night Games. Charles Rigdon. (O.s.i.). Orig. Title: Castrators. 1969. pap. 0.75 o.s.i. (A510S, Award). Univ Pub & Dist.
Night Games. Mai Zetterling. LC 67-10570. 1966. Coward-McCann.
Night Glow. Mary Lupton. 1982. pap. 6.95 (Avalon). Bouregy.
Night Has a Thousand Eyes. Cornell George Hopley-Woolrich. LC 45-10479. 1945. Farrar & Rinehart, Inc.
Night Has a Thousand Eyes. Cornell Woolrich, pseud. 304p. 1983. pap. 2.50 (ISBN 0-345-30667-8). Ballantine.
Night Hawk. Desmond Cory, pseud. 188p. 1983. pap. 2.95 (ISBN 0-8027-3024-8). Walker & Co.
Night Hawk. Desmond Cory. LC 69-15717. 1969. 4.50 o.p. (ISBN 0-8027-5132-6). Walker & Co.
Night Hawk. Shaun McCarthy. LC 69-15717. (Illus.). 1969. 4.50. Walker.
Night Hawk: A Novel. Arthur John Arouthnott Stringer. LC 26-5628. A. L. Burt Company.
Night Hell's Corners Died. Clay Ringold, pseud. 1978. Repr. of 1972 ed. 1.25 o.s.i. (ISBN 0-505-51328-5). Tower Bks.
Night Horseman. Max Brand. LC 20-20942. 1920. G. P. Putnam's Sons.
Night Horseman. Frederick Faust. LC 20-20942. 1920. G. P. Putnam's Sons.
Night Horseman: By Max Brand Pseud. Frederick Faust. LC 52-11154. (Silver star westerns). 1952. Dodd, Mead.
Night Hunt. Mara Rostov. LC 78-24034. 8.95 (ISBN 0-399-12311-3). Putnam.
Night Hunters. Jack M Bickham. LC 72-89689. (Black bat mystery). 1973. 5.95 (ISBN 0-672-51810-4). Bobbs-Merrill.
Night Hunters. Jack M Bickham. LC 73-13679. 1973. 7.95 (ISBN 0-8161-6153-4). G. K. Hall.
Night Hunters. Jack M Bickham. LC 81-47342. (Fifty Classics of Crime Fiction, 1950-1975). 1982. 14.95 (ISBN 0-8240-4995-0). Garland Pub.
Night Hunters. John Miles, pseud. Ed. by J. Barzun & W. h. Taylor. LC 81-47342. (Crime Fiction 1950-1975 Ser.). 200p. 1982. lib. bdg. 14.95 (ISBN 0-8240-4995-0). Garland Pub.
Night Hunters. John Miles, pseud. 5.95 o.p. (ISBN 0-672-51795-7). Bobbs.
Night Hunters. John Miles, pseud. (Adult Ser.). 1973. Repr. lib. bdg. 7.95 o.p. (ISBN 0-8161-6153-4, Large Print Bks). G K Hall.
Night Hunters: Winter Keeper. Jeanne Crecy, pseud. 1982. pap. 2.50 (ISBN 0-451-11581-3, AE1581, Sig). NAL.
Night Hurdling. James Dickey. 1982. ltd. ed. 14.95 (ISBN 0-89723-040-X). Bruccoli.
Night I Caught the Santa Fe Chief. Edward Thorpe. LC 73-81033. 1973. 6.50. St. Martin's Press.
Night in a Moorish Harem. George Herbert. (Illus.). pap. 1.25 o.p. (2021). Brandon.
Night in Acadie. Kate O'Flaherty Chopin. LC 68-55668. (American short story series, v. 8). (Illus.). 1968. Garrett Press.
Night in Acadie. 2d ed. Kate O'Flaherty Chopin. LC 74-23034. 1975. (ISBN 0-403-03156-7). Scholarly Press.
Night in Acadie. Kate O'Flaherty Chopin. LC 72-8201. (American short story series, v. 8). 1972. (ISBN 0-8422-8025-1). MSS Information Corp.
Night in Acadie: By Kate Chopin... Kate O'Flaherty Chopin. LC 6-20909. 1897. Way & Williams.
Night in Babylon: A Novel. James Howard Wellard. LC 53-1568. 1953. Macmillan Label.
Night in Bombay. Louis Bromfield. LC 40-8657. 1940. Harper & Brothers.
Night in Cold Harbor. Margaret Kennedy. LC 60-12176. 1960. Macmillan.
Night in Cold Harbour. Margaret Kennedy. LC 60-50894. 1960. Macmillan.
Night in Distant Motion. Irina Korschunow. LC 81-47325. 159p. 1983. 10.00 (ISBN 0-87923-399-0). Godine.
Night in Dixie: Or, Kilpatrick's Ride to Richmond. A Startling Tale of a Famous Raid. James Milford Merrill. (On cover: The war library. Pocket ed., v. 1, no. 8). 1883. Novelist Publishing Co.
Night in Funland, and Other Stories. William Harwood Peden. LC 68-13453. 1968. Louisiana State University Press.
Night in Glengyle. John Alexander Ferguson. LC 33-253700. 1933. Dodd, Mead & Company.
Night in Kurdistan. Jean Richard Bloch & Guest, Stephen Haden, Tr. LC 31-8212. 1931. Simon and Schuster.
Night in Lisbon. Erich Maria Remarque. Tr. by Ralph Manheim. LC 64-11538. 1964. 4.95 o.p. (ISBN 0-15-165595-2). HarBraceJ.
Night in Lisbon. Erich Maria Remarque. 1968. pap. 0.75 o.p. (T1216, Crest). Fawcett World.
Night in Manhattan. Alan Williams. LC 39-2153. 1939. Godwin.
Night in the Hotel. Eliot Crawshay-Williams. LC 31-156861. 1931. H. Liverright, Inc.
Night in Tunisia, and Other Stories. Neil Jordan. LC 77-357098. 1976. 1.00. Co-Op Books.
Night in Tunisia, and Other Stories. Neil Jordan. LC 79-25664. 8.95 (ISBN 0-8076-0955-2). G. Braziller.
Night Is a Child. Richard Llewellyn. LC 76-142036. 1972. 5.95. Doubleday.
Night Is a Time for Listening: A Novel. Elliot West. LC 66-12023. 1966. Random House.
Night Is Coming: A Novel. Marthedith Furans. LC 39-6473. 1939. Harper & Brothers.
Night Is Ending: A Novel. James Ronald. LC 44-3690. 1944. J. B. Lippincott Company.
Night Is for Music. George Selcamm. LC 64-13994. 1964. W. W. Norton.
Night Is Long. William R Lipman. LC 31-9261. 1931. I. Washburn.
Night Jasmine. Mary Lou Widmer. 1980. pap. 2.75 (ISBN 0-440-16558-X). Dell.
Night Journey. Winston Graham. LC 68-10677. 1968. Doubleday.
Night Journey. Albert Joseph Guerard. LC 50-7013. 1950. Knopf.
Night Journey From Rome. Clark Butterfield. 208p. (Orig.). 1982. pap. 4.95 (ISBN 0-937958-11-5). Chick Pubns.
Night Judgement at Sinos. Jack Higgins, pseud. LC 78-131080. 1971. 4.50 o.p. (ISBN 0-385-01036-2). Doubleday.
Night Judgement at Sinos. Henry Patterson. LC 78-131080. 1971. 4.50. Doubleday.
Night Land. William Hope Hodgson. LC 72-190576. 1972. per vol. 1.25. Ballantine Books.
Night Land: A Love Tale. William Hope Hodgson. LC 75-28858. (Classics of science fiction). 1976. 16.50. (ISBN 0-88355-372-4) (ISBN 0-88355-457-7). Hyperion Press.
Night Letter. Paul Spike. LC 78-18379. 9.95. Putnam.
Night Life of the Gods. Thorne Smith. LC 31-8536. 1931. Doubleday, Doran & Company, Incorporated.
Night Life of the Gods. Thorne Smith. LC 35-7680. 1934. Doubleday, Doran & Company, Incorporated.
Night Life of the Gods. Thorne Smith. LC 38-35054. 1935. Doubleday, Doran & Company, Incorporated.
Night Light. Marie Bardos. LC 64-21727. 1964. Doubleday.
Night Light. 1st Ed. Douglass Wallop. LC 53-6594. 1953. Norton.
Night Lights. Mindy Aloff. Ed. by Vi Gale. LC 79-84510. (Prescott First Book). (Illus.). 1979. ltd. ed. 20.00 (ISBN 0-915986-13-2); pap. 5.00 (ISBN 0-915986-14-0). Prescott St Pr.
Night Lords. Nicolas Freeling. LC 78-55242. 7.95 (ISBN 0-394-50281-7). Pantheon Books.
Night Lords. Nicolas Freeling. LC 79-22921. 1.95 (ISBN 0-394-74552-3). Vintage Books.
Night Lust. Philip Straker. 1982. pap. 2.95 (ISBN 0-8217-1090-7). Zebra.
Night Mail: Or, The Passenger from Scotland Yard. H. Freeman Wood. (On cover: The Calumet series, no. 17). 1894. G. Munro's Sons.
Night Manhattan Burned. Basil Jackson. LC 79-14756. 9.95 (ISBN 0-393-01248-4). Norton.
Night March. 1st Ed. Bruce Lancaster. LC 58-7866. 1958. Little, Brown.
Night Marchers: A Tale of the Huaka'i Po. Helen P. Hoyt. LC 76-4303. (Illus.). 1977. 6.95 o.p. (ISBN 0-89610-028-6). Island Her.
Night Mare. Piers Anthony, pseud. 320p. 1983. pap. 2.95 (ISBN 0-345-30456-X, Del Rey). Ballantine.
Night Marshal. Llewellyn Perry Holmes. LC 61-7170. (Dodd, Mead silver star westerns). 1961. Dodd, Mead.
Night Moves: A Novel. Alan Sharp. 1975. (pbk.) 1.25 (ISBN 0-446-76626-7). Warner Paperback Library.
Night Music. Charlotte Lamb, pseud. (Harlequin Presents Ser.). 192p. (Orig.). 1981. pap. 1.50 (ISBN 0-373-10404-9, Pub. by Harlequin). PB.
Night Music, a Fiction. Sven Stolpe. LC 60-7316. 1960. Sheed and Ward.
Night Music: A Novel. Lilli Palmer. LC 82-48148. 14.95 (ISBN 0-06-015105-6). Harper & Row.
Night Must End. Margaret Evans Price. LC 38-19924. 1938. Little, Brown and Company.
Night Must End. Alan Williams. LC 35-526215. Godwin.
Night My Enemy. Anne Maybury. 1976. (pbk.) 1.25. Ace Books.
Night Never Ends: By Frederick Lorenz Pseud. Lorenz Heller. LC 54-37055. (Lion book, 193). 1954. Lion Books.
Night Nurse. Grace Perkins Oursler. LC 30-14512. 1930. Brentano's.
Night of a Thousand Stars. Mona Newman. Ed. by Gene DeRoin. (Aston Hall Presents Ser.). 1979. pap. 1.50 (ISBN 0-89936-000-9). Aston Hall.
Night of a Thousand Suicides: The Japanese Outbreak at Cowra. Teruhiko Asada. LC 72-171851. (Illus.). 1972. 4.95. St. Martin's Press.
Night of Bright Stars. Richard Llewellyn. LC 78-60295. 1979. 8.95 (ISBN 0-385-13504-1). Doubleday.
Night of Camp David. Fletcher Knebel. LC 65-16259. 4.95. Harper.
Night of Camp David. Fletcher Knebel. (N3152). 1967. Bantam.
Night of Clear Choice. Doris Miles Disney. LC 67-15363. 1967. Published for the Crime Club by Doubleday.
Night of Dark Fires. Lionel Webb. 1977. pap. 1.75 (ISBN 0-425-03417-8, Medallion). Berkley Pub.
Night of Darkness & Other Stories. Paul Zeleza. (Malawian Writers Ser.: No. 2). (Illus.). 217p. (Orig.). (gr. 9-12). 1976. pap. 7.00x. Three Continents.
Night of Death. Marie Bregendahl. Tr. by Blanchard, Margery. LC 31-199121. 1931. A. A. Knopf.
Night of Decision: A Novel of Colonial New York,by Dorothy Fremont Grant. Dorothy Fremont Grant. LC 46-7816. 1946. Longmans, Green and Co.
Night of Delusions. Keith Laumer. LC 72-79515. 1972. 5.95 (ISBN 0-399-11011-9). Putnam.
Night of Errors. John Innes Mackintosh Stewart. LC 47-313365. 1947. Dodd, Mead.
Night of Fear. Moray Dalton. LC 31-842023. 1931. Harper & Brothers.
Night of Fire and Blood. Leo P Kelley. LC 78-72325. (Pacemaker bestellers book). (Illus.). 3.32 (ISBN 0-8224-5367-3). Fearon Pitman Publishers.
Night of Fire and Snow. Alfred Coppel. LC 57-56734. 1957. Simon and Schuster.
Night of Flame. Herbert Dyson Carter. LC 42-13380. 1942. Reynal & Hitchcock.
Night of Flames. Arthur K. Houston-Brown. 1978. 8.50 (ISBN 0-533-03436-1). Vantage.
Night of Four Hundred Rabbits. Elizabeth Peters, pseud. LC 77-145396. 1971. 5.95 (ISBN 0-396-06323-3). Dodd, Mead.
Night of Gaiety, No. 142. Barbara Cartland. (Orig.). 1981. pap. 1.95 (ISBN 0-553-14791-9). Bantam.
Night of Gold. Jill Moore. (Circle of Love Ser.: No. 25). 192p. Date not set. 1.75 (ISBN 0-553-21539-6). Bantam.
Night of Joseph's Lamentation & Joy. Harriet Lewis. 1974. 2.50 o.s.i. (ISBN 0-8181-0336-1). Pageant-Poseidon.
Night of Light. Philip Jose Farmer. LC 75-404. (Garland Library of Science Fiction). 1975. 11.00 (ISBN 0-8240-1409-X). Garland Pub.
Night of Love. John M. Haffert. 176p. 1966. pap. 3.95 (ISBN 0-911988-34-3). AMI Pr.
Night of Love. Roberta Leigh. 1978. 1.75 (ISBN 0-449-14071-7). Fawcett Gold Medal.
Night of Masks. Alice Mary Norton. LC 64-16266. 1964. Harcourt, Brace & World.
Night of Masks. Alice Mary Norton. 1973. (pbk.) 0.95. Ace.
Night of May Third. 1st Ed. Anna Mary Wells. LC 56-6533. 1956. Published for the Crime Club by Doubleday.
Night of Reckoning. Peter Ordway. LC 65-150346. (Inner sanctum mystery). bds., 3.50. S. & S.
Night of Reckoning: By John Stephen Strange Pseud. Dorothy Stockbridge Tillet. LC 58-8111. 1958. Published for the Crime Club by Doubleday.
Night of Secrets. June Pat Wetherell. (Dell Book). 1977. 1.25 (ISBN 0-440-12468-9). Dell Pub Co.
Night of Serious Drinking. Rene Daumal. 1979. 10.95. (ISBN 0-394-50766-5) (ISBN 0-394-73731-8). Shambhala.
Night of Shadows: By Frances and Richard Lockridge. 1st Ed. Frances Louise Davis Lockridge & Lockridge, Richard. LC 62-15208. 1962. Lippincott.
Night of Stones. George MacBeth. LC 69-15506. 1968. pap. 2.45 o.p. (ISBN 0-689-10173-2). Atheneum.
Night of Tears. John M. Kimbro. LC 75-34221. 1.50 (ISBN 0-345-24814-7). Ballantine Books.
Night of Temptation. Vivian Cory. LC 14-3969. 1914. 1.25. The Macaulay Company.
Night of the Apache. Warren T. Longtree. (Ruff Justice: No. 2). (Orig.). 1981. pap. 2.50 (ISBN 0-451-11029-3, AE1029, Sig). NAL.
Night of the Assassin. Don Smith. (Secret Mission Ser). (O.s.i.). 192p. (Orig.). 1973. pap. 0.95 o.s.i. (AN1148, Award). Univ Pub & Dist.
Night of the Assassins. Bruno Rossi. (Sharpshooter,#5). 1974. (pbk.) 0.95. Leisure Books.
Night of the Aurochs. Dalton Trumbo. LC 79-12786. 1979. 9.95 (ISBN 0-670-51412-8). Viking Press.

Night of the Aurocks. Dalton Trumbo. (Windstone Ser.). 224p. Date not set. pap. 3.95 (ISBN 0-553-13919-3). Bantam.

Night of the Avenger. Nick Carter. (Nick Carter Ser.). (O.s.i.). 192p. 1973. pap. 1.50 o.s.i. (ISBN 0-441-57496-3, Award). Univ Pub & Dist.

Night of the Avenger. Nick Carter. (Nick Carter/Killmaster Series). 1973. (pbk) 0.95. Award Books.

Night of the Axe. William Mulvihill, pseud. LC 72-172623. 1972. 5.95 (ISBN 0-395-13650-4). Houghton Mifflin.

Night of the Big Heat. John Lymington, pseud. pap. 0.60 o.p. (60-384). Manor Bks.

Night of the Big Snow. Charles Brooks. LC 62-106357. 1962. Macmillan.

Night of the Black Tower. Olga Sinclair. 1970. pap. 0.75 o.p. (ISBN 0-447-74679-0). Lancer.

Night of the Bonfire. Jane Blackmore. (Ace gothic). 1974. (pbk.) 0.95. Ace Books.

Night of the Bowstring. 1st Ed. D B Olsen. LC 62-11450. (Double D western). 1962. Doubleday.

Night of the Bulls. Anne Mather. (Presents Ser.). 1974. pap. 1.25 (ISBN 0-373-70554-9, 70554, Pub by Harlequin). PB.

Night of the Candles. Patricia Maxwell. 1978. 1.95 (ISBN 0-449-14093-8). Fawcett Gold Medal Books.

Night of the Cattlemen. Giles A Lutz. LC 76-22897. 1976. 5.95 (ISBN 0-385-12440-6). Doubleday.

Night of the Cattlemen. Giles A Lutz. 1979. 1.50 (ISBN 0-671-82199-7). Pocket Books.

Night of the Comet. Daniel Telfer. LC 69-10981. 1969. 5.95. Doubleday.

Night of the Coyotes. Philip Ketchum. LC 56-11222. 1956. Ballantine Books.

Night of the Darkest Moon. Jane Peart. (Orig.). 1972. pap. 0.95 o.s.i. (75-428). Lancer.

Night of the Dead. large easy-to-read type. ed. Dana Fuller Ross. (Queen-size gothic). 1973. pap. 0.95. Popular Library.

Night of the Falcon. James Oxford. LC 81-8859. 1981. 10.95 (ISBN 0-312-57302-2). St. Martin's.

Night of the Fires. Louise Bergstrom. 1973. 4.95 o.p. (Avalon). Bouregy.

Night of the Flaming Guns. P. A Bechko. LC 73-13084. 1974. 4.95 (ISBN 0-385-09570-8). Doubleday.

Night of the Flood. George Woodman. LC 57-8519. 1957. Dutton.

Night of the Flood. George Woodman. LC 57-8519. 1957. Dutton.

Night of the Fog. Lucy Beatrice Malleson. LC 30-29629. 1930. Dodd, Mead & Company.

Night of the Funny Hats. Elspeth Davie. 192p. 1980. 18.50 o.p. (ISBN 0-241-10377-0, Pub. by Hamish Hamilton England). David & Charles.

Night of the Garter Murder. Royce Howes. LC 37-2174. 1937. Pub. for the Crime Club, Inc., by Doubleday, Doran & Co., Inc.

Night of the Generals. Hans Hellmut Kirst. 1964. 9.95 o.p. (ISBN 0-06-012400-8, HarpT). Har-Row.

Night of the Ghulstak Races. Albert J. Manachino. 1979. pap. 1.00 (ISBN 0-932318-03-7, LEB4, Little Economy Bk). G F Edwards.

Night of the Giraffe & Other Stories. Translated from the German by Christa Armstrong. Alfred Andersch. LC 64-18340. 1964. Pantheon Books.

Night of the Good Children. Marjorie Chalmers Carleton. LC 57-11889. (Morrow mystery). 1957. W. Morrow.

Night of the Great Butcher. John Bennett. LC 75-19571. (Illus.). 4.00 (ISBN 0-913204-05-6). December Press.

Night of the Grizzlies. Jack Olsen, pseud. 1971. pap. 2.95 (ISBN 0-451-12304-2, AE2304, Sig). NAL.

Night of the Half-Moon. J. H. Rhodes. (YA) 1980. 6.50 (Avalon). Bouregy.

Night of the Hawk. Richard Raine. 1968. 4.75 o.p. (ISBN 0-15-165629-0). HarBraceJ.

Night of the Hawk. 1st Amer. Ed. Richard Raine. LC 68-12595. 1968. 4.75. Harcourt.

Night of the Hellebore. Jennifer Reddoch. 1974. (pbk.) 0.95. Popular Library.

Night of the Hunter. Davis Grubb. LC 77-1711. 1.95 (ISBN 0-14-004426-4). Penguin Books.

Night of the Hunter. 1st Ed. Davis Grubb. LC 53-11836. 1953. Harper.

Night of the Jabberwock. 1st Ed. Fredric Brown. LC 50-10851. (Guilt edged mystery). 1950. Dutton.

Night of the Juggler. William P McGivern. (Berkley Medallion Book). (Illus.). 1976. (pbk.) 1.95. Berkley Publishing Corp.

Night of the Juggler: A Novel. William P McGivern. LC 74-30565. (Illus.). 1975. 7.95 (ISBN 0-399-11498-X). Putnam.

Night of the Kill. Breni James. LC 61-9602. (Inner sanctum mystery). 1961. Simon and Schuster.

Night of the Letter. Dorothy Enid Eden. 1976. 1.75. Ace Books.

Night of the Living Dead. John Russo. 1981. 2.25 (ISBN 0-671-83573-4). Pocket Books.

Night of the Living Dead. John Russo. (Illus.). 1974. (pbk.) 1.25. Warner Paperback Library.

Night of the Long Knives. Hans Hellmut Kirst. LC 76-25006. 1976. 8.95 o.p. (ISBN 0-698-10760-8). Coward.

Night of the Mutilates: Space Probe 6. Charles Huntington, III. 160p. (Orig.). 1972. pap. 0.75 o.p. (A963S, Award). Univ Pub & Dist.

Night of the Party. Dorothy Phoebe Ansle. LC 70-146470. 1971. 5.95 (ISBN 0-8415-0107-6). McCall Pub. Co.

Night of the Party. Laura Conway. 1971. 5.95 o.p. (ISBN 0-8415-0107-6). Sat Rev Pr.

Night of the Peacock. Joseph Rosenberger. (Death Merchant Ser.: No. 49). 208p. (Orig.). 1982. pap. 1.95 (ISBN 0-523-41645-8). Pinnacle Bks.

Night of the Phoenix. Nelson De Mille. (Keller Ser: No. 3). 224p. (Orig.). 1975. pap. 1.25 o.p. (ISBN 0-532-12301-8). Woodhill.

Night of the Phoenix. Nelson De Mille. (Keller Ser: No. 3). 224p. (Orig.). 1975. pap. 1.25 o.p. (ISBN 0-532-12301-8). Manor Bks.

Night of the Pig-Killing. Tr. from Hungarian by Kathleen Szasz. 1st Amer. Ed. Magda Szabo. LC 65-111149. 1966. 4.95. Knopf.

Night of the Poor. Frederic Prokosch. LC 71-178789. 1972. 14.25 (ISBN 0-8371-6288-2). Greenwood Press.

Night of the Poor. Frederic Prokosch. LC 39-24223. 1939. Harper & Brothers.

Night of the Prom. Debra Spector. (Sweet Dreams: No. 12). 1982. pap. write for info. Bantam.

Night of the Rape. Lionel White. LC 67-11384. 1967. Dutton.

Night of the Running Man. Lee Well. LC 81-8886. 1981. 13.95 (ISBN 0-312-57310-3). St. Martin's Press.

Night of the Running Man. Lee Wells. LC 81-8886. 378p. 1981. 14.95 (ISBN 0-312-57310-3). St Martin.

Night of the Satyr. H. L. Owens. (Orig.). 1969. pap. 1.95 o.p. (6029). Brandon.

Night of the Saucers. Eando Binder, pseud. (Orig.). 1971. pap. 0.75 o.p. (B75-2116). Belmont-Tower.

Night of the Saucers. Eano Binder. 1975. (pbk.) 0.95. Belmont Tower Books.

Night of the Scorpion. Saliee O'Brien. (Berkley Medallion) (ISBN 0-425-03238-8). Berkley.

Night of the Seven Dawns-a Novel. Anita Kumar. 1980. text ed. 8.95x (ISBN 0-7069-0817-1, Pub. by Vikas India). Advent NY.

Night of the Shadow. Maxwell Grant, pseud. (Orig.). pap. 0.50 o.p. (B50-725). Belmont-Tower.

Night of the Shooting Star: A Novel of Suspense. Don Vipond. LC 74-17667. 6.95 (ISBN 0-672-52084-2). Bobbs-Merrill.

Night of the Silent Drums. John Lonzo Anderson. LC 75-4137. (Illus.). 1975. 9.95 (ISBN 0-684-14324-0). Scribner.

Night of the Silent Drums: A Narrative of Slave Rebellion in the Virgin Islands. John L. Anderson. (Illus.). 400p. 1975. 9.95 o.p. (ISBN 0-684-14324-0). Scribner.

Night of the Stanger. Jane Blackmore. (Ace Gothic). 1974. (pbk.) 0.95. Ace Books.

Night of the Summer Solstice: & Other Stories of the Russian War. Mark Van Doren. LC 43-13578. 1943. H. Holt and Company.

Night of the Tiger. Al Dewlen. LC 56-10308. 1956. McGraw-Hill.

Night of the Tiger. Mary Kistler. (Orig.). 1972. pap. 0.95 o.s.i. (75-380). Lancer.

Night of the Toads. Michael Collins, pseud. LC 80-82655. (Dan Fortune Detective Mystery Ser.). 192p. 1981. pap. 2.25 (ISBN 0-87216-773-9). Playboy Pbks.

Night of the Toads. Michael Collins, pseud. 1970. 4.50 o.p. Dodd.

Night of the Toads. Dennis Lynds. LC 70-114239. (Red badge novel of suspense). 1970. 4.50. Dodd, Mead.

Night of the Toy Dragons. Barney Cohen. (Berkley Medallion Book). 1977. 1.50 (ISBN 0-425-03452-6). Berkley Pub. Corp.

Night of the Toy Dragons. 1977. pap. 1.50 (ISBN 0-425-03452-6, Medallion). Berkley Pub.

Night of the Twelfth. Michael Francis Gilbert. LC 75-30351. 8.95 (ISBN 0-06-011534-3). Harper & Row.

Night of the Twelfth. Michael Francis Gilbert. 1978. 1.95 (ISBN 0-14-004615-1). Penguin Books.

Night of the Warlock. Raymond Giles. (Orig.). 1968. pap. 0.60 o.p. (53-677). Paperback Lib.

Night of the Wedding. Alice Muriel Livingston Williamson & Williamson, Charles Norris, 1859-1920. LC 23-109053. George H. Doran Company.

Night of the White Bear. Alexander Knox. LC 71-158416. 1971. 5.95 (ISBN 0-670-51139-0). Viking Press.

Night of the Willow. Maureen Peters. LC 81-16727. 1982. 10.95 (ISBN 0-312-57318-9). St. Martin's Press.

Night of the Wolf. easy eye ed. W. Howard Baker. 1967. pap. 0.60 o.p. (73-659). Lancer.

Night of the Wolf. James Conway. 1979. pap. 1.75 o.s.i. (ISBN 0-8439-0700-2, Leisure Bks). Nordon Pubns.

Night of the Wolf. Constance Fecher, pseud. LC 74-1310. 1974. 6.95 (ISBN 0-440-06176-8). Delacorte Press.

Night of the Wolf. Salambo Forest. (Orig.). 1969. pap. 1.95 o.s.i. (OPH162, Ophelia). Olympia.

Night of the Wolf: A Novel. Christopher Bryan. LC 82-48920. 10.53 (ISBN 0-06-250106-2). Harper & Row.

Night of the 12th-13th. Stanislas Andre Steeman. Tr. by Abbott, Elisabeth. J. B. Lippincott Company.

Night of the 3d Ult. H. Freeman Wood. (On cover: Lovell's international series, 118). 1890. J. W. Lovell Company.

Night of Their Own: 1st Amer. Ed. Peter Abrahams. LC 65-12051. bds., 4.95. Knopf.

Night of Time. Translated from the German by Richard and Clara Winston. 1st Ed. Rene Fulop-Miller. LC 55-753348. 1955. Bobbs-Merrill.

Night of Trees. Thomas Williams. LC 61-11952. 1961. Macmillan.

Night of Trees. Thomas Williams. LC 78-23832. 1978. 8.95 (ISBN 0-399-90026-8). R. Marek Publishers.

Night of Violence. Louis H Charbonneau. (Torquil book). 1959. Distributed by Dodd, Mead.

Night of Watching. Elliott Arnold. LC 67-21334. 1967. 5.95. Scribners.

Night of Watching. Elliott Arnold. (Crest bk., M1159). 1968. Fawcett.

Night of Wenceslas. Lionel Davidson. 1977. pap. 1.95 o.p. (ISBN 0-14-001758-5). Penguin.

Night of Wenceslas. Lionel Davidson. LC 82-47557. 224p. 1982. pap. 2.84i (ISBN 0-06-080595-1, P595, PL). Har-Row.

Night on the Pathway: A Jane Amanda Edwards Story. Charlotte Murray Russell, pseud. LC 36-21698. 1938. Pub. for the Crime Club, Inc., by Doubleday, Doran & Company, Inc.

Night Operator. Frank Lucius Packard. LC 22-5148. A. L. Burt Company.

Night Operator. Frank Lucius Packard. LC 19-12164. George H. Doran Company.

Night Out. Rupert Croft-Cooke. LC 32-17511. 1932. L. MacVeagh, Dial Press, Inc.

Night Outlasts the Whippoorwill. Sterling North. LC 36-246773. 1936. The Macmillan Company.

Night Over Fitch's Pond. Cora Hardy Jarrett. LC 33-24083. 1933. Houghton Mifflin Company.

Night Over Java. Johan Wigmore Fabricius. LC 46-1868. 1946. Greenberg.

Night Over Maple City. Marguerita Smart. LC 51-34. 1950. Vantage Press.

Night Over Mexico. Todd Downing. LC 37-83115. 1937. Pub. for the Crime Club, Inc., by Doubleday, Doran & Company, Inc.

Night Over the East. Von Kuhnelt-Leddihn Erik Maria. Tr. by Muir, Edwin. LC 36-17406. 1936. Sheed and Ward Inc.

Night Over the Wood. Hugh Addis. LC 43-36591. 1943. Dodd, Mead & Company.

Night Passage. Norman A Fox. LC 56-574115. (Silver star western). 1956. Dodd, Mead.

Night People. Jack Finney. LC 77-74269. 1977. 7.95 (ISBN 0-385-13029-5). Doubleday.

Night People. Jack Finney. 1978. Pocket Books.

Night-Pieces: Eighteen Tales. Thomas Burke. LC 78-150539. (Short story index reprint series). 1971. (ISBN 0-8369-3836-4). Books for Libraries Press.

Night Pieces: Eighteen Tales. Thomas Burke. 1936. D. Appleton Century Company, Incorporated.

Night Pillow: A Novel, by Hugh C. Rae. Hugh C Rae. LC 67-13496. 1967. bds., 5.50. Viking.

Night Probe! Clive Cussler. LC 81-43094. 13.95 (ISBN 0-553-05004-4). Bantam Books.

Night Probe! Clive Cussler. LC 82-881. 1982. 17.95 (ISBN 0-8161-3346-8). G.K. Hall.

Night Prowlers. Amita Malin. LC 81-21242. (Adult Readers Library). 1.98 (ISBN 0-673-24141-6). Scott, Foresman.

Night Raid. Frank Bonham. LC 54-6547. 1954. Ballantine Books.

Night Raid. Eugene William Lohrke. LC 41-5879. H. Holt and Company.

Night Raid. 1981. pap. 1.95 (ISBN 0-425-04814-4). Berkley Pub.

Night Ride: And Other Journeys. Charles Beaumont. LC 60-6434. (Bantam book A2087-7). 1960. Bantam Books.

Night Rider. Robert Penn Warren. LC 48-7805. (Signet book, 804). 1950. New American Library.

Night Rider. Robert Penn Warren. LC 39-58488. 1939. Houghton Mifflin Company.

Night Rider. Robert Penn Warren. LC 78-23586. 1979. 4.95 (ISBN 0-394-72817-3). Vintage Books.

Night Rider: A Novel. Tom Ingram, pseud. LC 74-29010. 1975. 6.95 (ISBN 0-87888-082-8). Bradbury Press.

Night Riders. Willis Todhunter Ballard. LC 61-7637. (Double D western). 1961. Doubleday.

Night Riders. Thorne Douglas. (Fawcett gold medal book.). 1975. (pbk.) 0.95. Fawcett.

Night Riders. Lee Floren. 1976. (pbk.) 0.95. Leisure Books.

Night Riders. Keith Jarrod. LC 78-14682. 1979. 7.95 (ISBN 0-385-14750-3). Doubleday.

Night Riders. Peter McCurtin. (Leisure books). (Sundance; #26). 1979. 1.75 (ISBN 0-8439-0653-7). Nordon Pubns.

Night Riders. Abel Short. LC 47-24303. 1947. Arcadia House.

Night-Riders: A Romance of Early Montana. Ridgwell Cullum. LC 13-73388. 1913. G. W. Jacobs & Company.

Night Riders: A Thrilling Story of Love, Hate and Adventure, Graphically Depicting the Tobacco Uprising in Kentucky. Henry Cleveland Wood. LC 8-19573. Laird & Lee.

Night Riders Moon. Robert J Hogan. LC 54-6127. (Silver star westerns). 1954. Dodd, Mead.

Night Riders of Cave Knob. Quincy Scott. LC 11-248212. 1911. 1.25. A. C. McClurg & Co.

Night Riders of Reelfoot Lake. Paul J. Vanderwood. LC 79-91959. (Illus.). 172p. 1969. 8.95 o.p. (ISBN 0-87870-002-1). Memphis St Univ.

Night Riders of Tonopah. Bill Martin. LC 51-38088. (Five point Western novel). 1951. T. V. Boardman.

Night Rituals: A Novel. Mike Jahn. LC 82-8277. 12.95 (ISBN 0-393-01630-7). Norton.

Night Rounds. Patrick Modiano. LC 79-136343. 1971. 4.95 (ISBN 0-394-44326-8). Knopf.

Night Sailing. S. F. Whitaker. LC 75-34598. pap. 5.95 (ISBN 0-87799-056-5). Aztex.

Night Sale. Richard Broderick. LC 82-61652. (Minnesota Voices Project Ser.: No. 8). (Illus.). 135p. 1982. pap. 5.00 (ISBN 0-89823-040-3). New Rivers Pr.

Night Sanctuary. Monique Van Vooren. 502p. 1981. 15.50 (ISBN 0-671-40093-2). Summit Bks.

Night Sanctuary. Monique Van Vooren. 560p. 1983. pap. 3.95 (ISBN 0-451-12055-8, Sig). NAL.

Night Screams. Bill Pronzini & Barry N. Malzberg. LC 78-27166. 5.95 (ISBN 0-87223-525-4). Playboy Press; Trade Distribution by Simon and Schuster.

Night Screams. Bill Pronzini & Barry N. Malzberg. 2.75 (ISBN 0-87216-788-7).

Night Search. Jerre Gerlando Mangione. LC 65-24317. 4.95. Crown.

Night Season. Robert O'Neil Bristow. LC 71-118268. 1970. 5.95. Morrow.

Night Season. Ed. by Robert Manson Myers. (Children of Pride: Vol. 6). 1978. pap. 2.25 (ISBN 0-445-04175-7). Popular Lib.

Night Shade. Dorothy Daniels. 1976. (pbk.) 1.25 (ISBN 0-671-80283-6). Pocket Books.

Night Shadows. Mary Sellers. (Berkley Medallion Book). 1977. 1.75 (ISBN 0-425-03459-3). Berkley Pub. Corp.

Night She Died. Dorothy Simpson. LC 81-877. 8.95 (ISBN 0-684-16869-3). Scribner.

Night She Died. large print ed. Dorothy Simpson. LC 82-9165. 1982. 8.95 (ISBN 0-8161-3329-8). G.K. Hall.

Night Shift. Richard Blaker. LC 34-19486. 1934. D. Appleton-Century Company, Incorporated.

Night Shift. Stephen King. LC 77-75146. 1978. 8.95 (ISBN 0-385-12991-2). Doubleday.

Night Shift. Maritta Martin Wolff. LC 43-15472. 1942. Random House.

Night Shift. Maritta Martin Wolff. LC 42-504343. 1942. Random House.

Night Shineth. Rudolph O Covey. LC 52-33983. 1952. White Wing Pub. House and Press.

Night-Side. Joyce Carol Oates. 1980. pap. 2.50 (ISBN 0-449-24206-4, Crest). Fawcett.

Night-Side: Eighteen Tales. Joyce Carol Oates. LC 77-77416. 10.00 (ISBN 0-8149-0793-8). Vanguard Press.

Night Side: Masterpieces of the Strange & Terrible. Ed. by August William Derleth. LC 47-1903. 1947. Rinehart & Company, Inc.

Night Song. John A. Williams. 219p. 1975. Repr. of 1961 ed. 7.95x (ISBN 0-911860-51-7). Chatham Bkseller.

Night Spiders. John Lymington, pseud. LC 67-10400. 1967. Doubleday.

Night Stage. William Heuman. LC 55-10188. 1955. Arcadia House.

Night Stalker. Jeff Rice. 1973. (pbk.) 1.25 (ISBN 0-671-78343-2). Pocket Books.

Night Stalks the Mansion. Harold Cameron & Constance Westbie. LC 77-27630. (O.s.i). 1978. 8.95 o.s.i. (ISBN 0-8117-1043-2). Stackpole.

Night Stalks the Mansion. Harold Cameron & Constance Westbie. LC 77-27630. (O.s.i). 1978. 8.95 o.s.i. (ISBN 0-8117-1043-2). Stackpole.

Night Stand: A Book of Stories. James McConkey. LC 64-253901. bds., 3.95. Cornell.

Night Stands at the Door: A Novel. Katherine Blake. LC 73-90706. 1974. 7.95 (ISBN 0-8128-1665-X). Stein and Day.

Night Stick. Derick Jansen. 192p. (Orig.). 1972. pap. 1.95 o.s.i. (OPH 4128). Olympia.

Night Still in Your Kiss. Norman N. McWhinney. 1975. pap. 2.50 o.p. (ISBN 0-916684-04-0). Rook Pr.

Night Stop. Elleston Trevor. LC 74-12859. 1975. 6.95. (ISBN 0-385-07472-7). Doubleday.

Night Strangler. Jeff Rice. 1974. (pbk.) 1.25. Pocket Books.

Night Studies: A Novel. 1 st ed. Cyrus Colter. LC 79-91893. 15.00 (ISBN 0-8040-0827-2). Swallow Press.

Night Swimmers. Nancy Hallinan. LC 75-25084. 8.95 (ISBN 0-06-011711-7). Harper & Row.

Night Tennis. Davis-Goff, Annabel. LC 78-7334. 8.95 (ISBN 0-698-10924-4). Coward, McCann & Geoghegan.

Night Tennis. Annabel D. Goff. pap. cancelled o.s.i. (ISBN 0-515-05123-3, Jove). BJ Pub Group.

Night the Fog Came Down. John Bude. LC 58-12246. (Chantecier mystery novel). 1958. I. Washburn.

Night, the Woman. Frederick Clyde Davis. LC 63-10241. (Red badge detective). 1963. Dodd, Mead.

Night They Raided Minsky's. Rowland Barber. (O.s.i.). 1968. pap. 0.75 o.s.i. (A377S, Award). Univ Pub & Dist.

Night They Stole Manhattan. Lewis Orde & Bill Michaels. LC 79-25392. 10.95 (ISBN 0-399-12489-6). Putnam.

Night Things. Thomas F. Monteleone. 320p. 1980. pap. 2.25 (ISBN 0-445-04624-4). Popular Lib.

Night Thorn: A Novel. Ian Gordon, pseud. LC 52-5947. 1952. Dial Press.

Night Thoughts. Edmund Wilson. 1961. pap. 1.65 o.p. (ISBN 0-374-50388-5, N253, Noonday). FS&G.

Night Tide: A Story of Old Chinatown. Grant Carpenter. LC 30-12378. 1920. The H. K. Fly Company.

Night Train to Paris. 1st Ed. Manning Coles, pseud. LC 52-5534. 1952. Published for the Crime Club by Doubleday.

Night Trains. Peter Heath Fine. LC 79-10166. 9.95 (ISBN 0-397-01363-9). Lippincott.

Night Trains. Barbara Wood & Gareth Wootton. LC 79-14286. 1979. 9.95 (ISBN 0-688-03470-5). Morrow.

Night. Translated by L. L. Barrett. Erico Verissimo. LC 56-13605. 1956. Macmillan.

Night Unto Night. Philip Wylie. LC 44-8153. 1944. Farrar & Rinehart, Inc.

Night Vision. Frank King. LC 78-24599. 9.95 (ISBN 0-399-90039-X). R. Marek.

Night Visions. Joseph F. Murphy. (O.s.i.). 5.00 o.s.i. (ISBN 0-8159-6304-1). Devin.

Night Visitor. B. Traven. Repr. lib. bdg. 14.95x (ISBN 0-89190-160-4). Am Repr-Rivercity Pr.

Night Visitor, and Other Stories. Arnold Bennett. LC 74-17062. (Collected works of Arnold Bennett). 1974. (ISBN 0-518-19140-0). Books for Libraries Press.

Night Visitor: And Other Stories. Arnold Bennett. LC 31-312271. 1931. Doubleday, Doran & Company, Inc.

Night Visitor, and Other Stories. B Traven. LC 66-15892. 1966. Hill and Wang.

Night Visitor: And Other Stories. Introd. by Charles H. Miller. B Traven. (75235). 1968. Pocket Bks.

Night Visitors. Julia Briggs. LC 77-370852. 1977. 15.95 (ISBN 0-571-11113-0). Faber.

Night Voyagers. Sybil Leek. (Adult Ser.). 1976. Repr. lib. bdg. 9.95 o.p. (ISBN 0-8161-6346-4, Large Print Bks). G K Hall.

Night Waking. Kathleen Snow. LC 78-17509. 9.95 (ISBN 0-671-23055-7). Simon and Schuster.

Night Walk. Elizabeth Daly. LC 47-30853. 1947. Rinehart.

Night Walker. Donald Hamilton. LC 54-804813. (Dell first edition, 27). 1954. Dell Pub. Co.

Night Walking. Kathleen Snow. 1979. 2.25 (ISBN 0-445-04464-0). Popular Library.

Night Walks. Joyce Carol Oates. 304p. 1982. 14.95 (ISBN 0-86538-022-8). Ontario Rev NJ.

Night Warrior and Other Stories from Papua New Guinea. LC 74-189307. (Pacific writers series). 1972. 1.50 (ISBN 0-7016-8180-2). Jacaranda.

Night Watch. Stephen Koch. LC 69-15279. 1969. 5.95. Harper & Row.

Night Watch. Jack Olsen, pseud. 1980. pap. 2.75 (ISBN 0-445-04609-0). Popular Lib.

Night Watch. Thomas Walsh. LC 52-5016. 1952. Little, Brown.

Night Watch: A Novel. Jack Olsen, pseud. LC 79-12011. 10.95 (ISBN 0-8129-0829-5). Times Books.

Night Watch: A Timeless Christmas Story. Paul Darcy Boles. LC 80-8778. (Illus.). 5.95 (ISBN 0-931948-15-0). Peachtree Publishers.

Night Watcher. James F. Murray, Jr. (Orig.). 1982. pap. 2.50 (ISBN 0-440-16527-X). Dell.

Night Watches. William Wymark Jacobs. LC 14-17981. 1914. C. Scribner's Sons.

Night Watchman. Simonne Jacquemard. LC 64-14360. 1964. Holt, Rinehart and Winston.

Night Way. Janet Dailey. (Orig.). 1981. pap. 2.95 (ISBN 0-671-83605-6). Pb.

Night Wheeler. Carter Brown, pseud. (Signet book). 1974. (pbk.) 0.95. New American Library.

Night Wheeler see Aseptic Murders.

Night Whispers. Charles Veley. LC 79-8946. 1980. 10.00 (ISBN 0-385-15124-1). Doubleday.

Night Will End. Henri Frenay. LC 75-11807. 512p. 1976. 12.95 o.p. (ISBN 0-07-022135-9). McGraw.

Night Wind. Roberta J. Moutjoy. 512p. 1983. pap. 3.50 (ISBN 0-515-06802-0). Jove Pubns.

Night Wind: A Novel. Roberta Jean Mountjoy. LC 81-4407. 14.95 (ISBN 0-698-11102-8). Coward, McCann & Geoghegan.

Night Wind at North Riding. Florence Hurd. (Signet Book). 1977. 1.50 (ISBN 0-451-07626-5). New American Library.

Night Winds. Brian Talbot Cleeve. LC 54-5698. 1954. Houghton Mifflin.

Night Winds. Karl Edward Wagner. (Orig.). 1983. pap. 2.95 (ISBN 0-446-30812-9). Warner Bks.

Night Wind's Promise. Frederic Van Rensselaer Dey. LC 14-18650. 1.25. G. W. Dillingham Company.

Night Wings. John Jessop Teague. LC 18-194049. 1915. Hodder and Stoughton.

Night with Alessandro: An Episode in Florence Under Her Last Medici. Treadwell Cleveland. 1904. H. Holt and Company.

Night with Jupiter: And Other Fantastic Stories. Ed. by Charles Henri Ford. 1945. View Editions, Distributed by the Vanguard Press.

Night Without Darkness. Kenneth Orvis. (YA) 1966. 4.50 o.p. (ISBN 0-698-10274-6). Coward.

Night Without Darkness: By Kenneth Orvis Pseud. 1st Amer. Ed. Kenneth Lemieux. LC 66-131261. 1966. 4.50. Coward.

Night Without End. Alistair MacLean. 1978. pap. 2.50 (ISBN 0-449-14129-2, GM). Fawcett.

Night Without End. Alistar MacLean. Repr. lib. bdg. 13.55x (ISBN 0-89190-174-4). Am Repr-Rivercity Pr.

Night Without End. 1st Ed. Alistair MacLean. LC 60-689315. 1960. Doubleday.

Night Without Sleep. Elick Moll. LC 50-9319. 1950. Little, Brown.

Night Without Stars. Luanna Churchill. 1975. (pbk.) 1.25. Belmont Tower Books.

Night Without Stars. Winston Graham. LC 50-9369. 1950. Doubleday.

Night Work. Irwin Shaw. LC 75-16205. 1975. 8.95 (ISBN 0-440-05757-4). Delacorte Press.

Night-World. Robert Bloch. LC 70-189750. (Inner sanctum mystery). 1972. 4.95 (ISBN 0-671-21282-6). Simon and Schuster.

Nightbait. Philip Straker. 1982. pap. 2.95 (ISBN 0-8217-1008-7). Zebra.

Nightbook. William Kotzwinkle. (Equinox book.). 1974. (pbk.) 2.45. Avon.

Nightchild. Scott Baker. LC 79-4358. 9.95 (ISBN 0-399-12377-6). Berkley Pub. Corp.: Distributed by Putnam.

Nightchild. John Meyer. 1978. 1.75 (ISBN 0-671-81379-X). Pocket Books.

Nightclerk. Stephen Schneck. 1965. 4.95 o.p. (GP344). Grove.

Nightclimber. Jon Ewbank Manchip White. LC 68-30866. 1968. 5.95. W. Morrow.

Nightclub. Georges Simenon. LC 79-1845. 7.95 (ISBN 0-15-165589-8). Harcourt Brace Jovanovich.

Nightcomers: A Speculation. Michael Hastings. LC 73-38893. 1972. 5.95. Delacorte Press.

Nightdive. Colin D Peel. LC 77-9120. 1978. 7.95 (ISBN 0-312-57278-6). St. Martin's Press.

Nightdreamers: A Novel. Paul Sedlock. LC 75-12585. 1975. 3.00 (ISBN 0-914476-39-4). Thorp Springs Press.

Nightface. Poul Anderson. 160p. 1981. pap. 1.95 (ISBN 0-441-57451-3). Ace Bks.

Nightfall. John Crosby. LC 76-12602. 1976. 8.95 o.s.i. Stein & Day.

Nightfall. Dorothy Daniels (ISBN 0-671-80831-1). Pocket Books.

Nightfall. David Goodis. LC 47-11897. 1947. J. Messner.

Nightfall. LC 21-19128. 1921. Dodd, Mead and Company.

Nightfall: A Novel. John Crosby. LC 76-12602. 1976. 8.95. Stein and Day.

Nightfall: A Novel. John Crosby. 1977. 1.95 (ISBN 0-446-89354-4). Warner Books.

Nightfall & Other Stories. Isaac Asimov. LC 77-78711. 1969. 7.95 (ISBN 0-385-08104-9). Doubleday.

Nightfall & Other Stories. Isaac Asimov. 1978. pap. 2.25 (ISBN 0-449-23672-2, Crest). Fawcett.

Nightfall at Noon. Marcel Hamon. LC 49-104565. 1949. Ziff-Davis Pub. Co.

Nightfall in Vienna. Carolyn Darling. LC 41-4623. 1941. D. Appleton-Century Company, Incorporated.

Nightfire. Mark Aultman. LC 77-362785. (Illus.). 8.95 (ISBN 0-8091-0213-7) (ISBN 0-8091-1973-0). Paulist Press.

Nightflyer. Christopher Fahy. 288p. 1982. pap. 2.95 (ISBN 0-515-06217-0). Jove Pubns.

Nightfrights; Occult Stories for All Ages. Ed. by Peter Haining. LC 72-7793. (Illus.). 1973. 6.50 (ISBN 0-8008-5556-6). Taplinger Pub. Co.

Nightgame Ranch. Don P Jenison. 1974. (pbk.) 0.75. Ace Books.

Nightgleams. Julia Thatcher, pseud. LC 76-44856. (Zodiac gothic: Sagittarius). 1977. 8.95 (ISBN 0-89340-017-3). J. Curley & Associates.

Nightgleams: An Astrological Gothic Novel, Sagittarius. Julia Thatcher, pseud. LC 76-21282. 1976. 1.25 (ISBN 0-345-25310-8). Ballantine Books.

Nighthawk. F. M Parker. LC 82-45603. (Double D Western). 1983. 11.95 (ISBN 0-385-18412-3). Doubleday.

Nighthawk Blues. Peter Guralnick. LC 80-50513. 10.95 (ISBN 0-87223-634-X). Seaview Books.

Nighthawk of the Northwest. Samuel Alexander White. LC 39-155951. Phoenix Press.

Nighthawks! John Gordon Brandon. LC 30-3074. 1930. Brentano's.

Nighthawk's Gold. Kim Knight. LC 39-21860. Dodge Publishing Company.

Nightime Guy. Tony Kenrick. LC 78-12899. 1979. 8.95 (ISBN 0-688-03414-4). Morrow.

Nightime Guy. Tony Kenrick. ("A Signet Book"). 1980. 2.75 (ISBN 0-451-09111-6). New American Library.

Nightingale. Eric Pace. LC 78-11269. 8.95 (ISBN 0-394-48420-7). Random House.

Nightingale. Agnes Sligh Turnbull. 1974. (pbk.) 1.25 (ISBN 0-380-00181-0). Avon.

Nightingale: A Lark. Ella Stoothoff Hulst Greenslet. LC 14-18498. 1914. 1.25. Houghton Mifflin Company.

Nightingale, a Romance. Agnes Sligh Turnbull. LC 60-13000. 1960. Houghton Mifflin.

Nightingale & the Rose. Ralph Moreno. (Illus.). 1958. pap. 1.50x o.p. Hartmus Pr.

Nightingale of Broadway. Stanley Tocci. LC 44-8370. 1944. E. Hopkins.

Nightingale Park. Moira Lord. (Signet Book.). 1977. 1.75 (ISBN 0-451-07617-6). New American Library.

Nightingale Sang. Barbara Cartland. LC 79-21752. 1979. 6.95 (ISBN 0-87272-083-7, Duron Bks). Brodart.

Nightingale Trivet. Russell Mead. (Raven House Mysteries Ser.). 224p. 1982. pap. 2.25 (ISBN 0-373-63034-4, Pub. by Worldwide). Harlequin Bks.

Nightingale Wood. Stella Gibbons. LC 38-154837. 1938. Longmans, Green and Co.

Nightingales. Mary Burchell. (Harlequin Romances Ser.). 192p. 1980. pap. 1.25 (ISBN 0-373-02359-6, Pub. by Harlequin). PB.

Nightingales. M. Dudin. 263p. 1981. 5.00 (ISBN 0-8285-2045-3, Pub. by Progress Pubs USSR). Imported Pubns.

Nightingales Are Singing. 1st American Ed. Monica Dickens. LC 53-10232. 1953. Little, Brown.

Nightingale's Song. Dorothy Alofsin. LC 45-90961. The Jewish Publication Society of America.

Nightingale's Song. Denise Robbins. 1971. pap. 0.75 o.p. (N2506). Pyramid Pubns.

Nightingale's Song. Denise Robins. 1974. pap. 0.95 o.p. (ISBN 0-515-03345-6, N3345). BJ Pub Group.

Nightland Spell. Benjamin Grimm. (Orig.). 1969. pap. 1.75 o.s.i. (TC446, Travellers Comp). Olympia.

Nightless City. Intro. by G. Lowndes. pap. 1.75 o.p. (3019). Brandon.

Nightlines: Stories. John McGahern. LC 71-135431. 1971. 4.95. Little, Brown.

Nightly She Sings. Edwin Olmstead. LC 37-17245. 1937. A. A. Knopf.

Nightmare. Edward Sidney Aarons. LC 48-15592. (Armchair mystery). 1948. D. McKay Co.

Nightmare. Edward S. Arrons. 160p. 1974. pap. 0.95 (ISBN 0-532-95363-0). Woodhill.

Nightmare. Mihaly Babits. Tr. by Eva Racz. 6.50x (ISBN 0-89918-348-4, H348). Vanous.

Nightmare. Anne Blaisdell, pseud. 1967. pap. 0.60 o.p. Lancer.

Nightmare. Leslie Dunkling. (Readers Ser.: Stage 1). 1979. pap. text ed. 1.80 o.p. (ISBN 0-88377-135-7). Newbury Hse.

Nightmare. Russell H Greenan. LC 71-117709. 1970. 5.95. Random House.

Nightmare. Gerld Mygatt. LC 29-2612. The Penn Publishing Company.

Nightmare. Richard Owen. LC 79-16339. 9.95 (ISBN 0-312-57328-6). St. Martin's Press.

Nightmare. rev. ed. Marcus Van Heller, pseud. pap. 1.75 o.p. (2042). Brandon.

Nightmare. Marcus Van Heller, pseud. pap. 1.95 o.s.i. (OPH-234, Ophelia). Olympia.

Nightmare Abbey & Crochet Castle. Thomas Love Peacock. Ed. by Raymond Wright. 1969. pap. 1.45 o.p. (ISBN 0-14-043045-8). Penguin.

Nightmare Abbey and Crotchet Castle. Thomas Love Peacock. LC 75-454914. (Penguin English library EL 45). 1969. Penguin.

Nightmare Abbey. The Misfortunes of Elphin. Crotchet Castle. Thomas Love Peacock. Ed. by Charles Brooks Dodson. LC 74-169972. (Rinehart editions, 148). (Illus.). 1971. (ISBN 0-03-083025-7). Holt, Rinehart, and Winston.

Nightmare Alley. William Lindsay Gresham. LC 48-1132. 1948. Sun Dial Press.

Nightmare Alley. William Lindsay Gresham. LC 46-5411. 1946. Rinehart and Company, Inc.

Nightmare and Dawn. Mark Aleksandrovich Aldanov. LC 73-21489. 1974. 14.75 (ISBN 0-8371-6406-0). Greenwood Press.

Nightmare and Dawn. Translated by Joel Carmichael. 1st Ed. Mark Aleksandrovich Aldanov. LC 57-756552. 1957. Duell, Sloan and Pearce.

Nightmare at Danger Island. Eric Mann. (Perspectives II Ser.). (Illus.). 48p. (Orig.). (gr. 7-12). 1982. pap. 2.50 (ISBN 0-87879-312-7); Set. 22.50 (ISBN 0-87879-311-9). Acad Therapy.

Nightmare at Dawn: A Peter Styles Mystery Novel. Judson Pentecost Philips. LC 78-102731. (Red badge novel of suspense). 1970. 4.50. Dodd, Mead.

Nightmare at Mountain Aerie. Florence Hurd. 192p. (Orig.). 1974. pap. 1.25 o.p. (ISBN 0-532-12513-4). Woodhill.

Nightmare at Mountain Aerie. Florence Hurd. 1974. (pbk.) 0.95. Manor Books.

Nightmare at Noon: A Marshal Pedley Story. pseud. 1st ed. Prentice Winchell. LC 51-11050. 1951. Dutton.

Nightmare at Riverview. Angela Gray, pseud. 1973. pap. 0.95 o.s.i. (75-469). Lancer.

Nightmare Baby. Linda DuBreuil. 1970. pap. 0.75 o.p. (B75-2058). Belmont-Tower.

Nightmare Baby. Linda DuBreuil. 1974. pap. 0.75 o.p. (LB107SK). Leisure Bks.

Nightmare: By Anne Blaisdell Pseud. 1st Ed. Elizabeth Linington. LC 61-9705. 1961. Harper.

Nightmare by Cornell Woolrich Pseud. Cornell George Hopley-Woolrich. LC 56-10055. (Red badge detective). 1956. Dodd, Mead.

Nightmare Chase. Evelyn Berckman. LC 74-33082. 1975. 7.95 (ISBN 0-385-03751-1). Doubleday.

Nightmare Chase. Evelyn Berckman. 1978. 1.75 (ISBN 0-380-40501-6). Avon Books.

Nightmare Chrysalis: A Novel of Suspense. Rosemary Gatenby. LC 77-21531. 6.95 (ISBN 0-396-07490-1). Dodd, Mead.

Nightmare Country. Marlys Millhiser. LC 81-1932. 12.95 (ISBN 0-399-12595-7). Putnam.

Nightmare County: A Novel. Harvey, Frank. LC 64-19576. 1964. Bantam Books.

Nightmare Factor. Thomas N. Scortia & Frank M. Robinson. LC 77-11760. 1978. 10.00 (ISBN 0-385-11462-1). Doubleday.

Nightmare Farm. Jack Mann. 1975. 5.00. Bookfinger.

Nightmare for a Virgin. Carr. pap. 1.95 o.p. (ISBN 0-87977-128-3, DBB128). Dansk Blue Bk.

Nightmare Garden. Ed. by Vic Ghidalia. 1976. pap. 1.25 (ISBN 0-532-12411-1). Woodhill.

Nightmare Hall. Annie Laurie McMurdie. (Lancer occult-gothic easy-eye). 1973. (pbk.) 1.25. Lancer Books.

Nightmare Has Triplets: Smirt, Smith & Smire. James B. Cabell. LC 70-156179. 311p. 1972. Repr. of 1971 ed. lib. bdg. 40.00x (ISBN 0-8371-6122-3, CANT). Greenwood.

Nightmare Has Triplets: Smirt, Smith, and Smire. James Branch Cabell. LC 70-156179. 1972. (ISBN 0-8371-6122-3). Greenwood Press.

Nightmare House. Elinore Denniston. LC 68-8277. (Red badge mystery). 1968. 3.95. Dodd, Mead.

Nightmare House. Rae Foley. (Red Badge Mystery Ser). 1968. 3.95 o.p. Dodd.

Nightmare in Algeria. Joseph Rosenberger. (Death Merchant series, 18) (ISBN 0-523-00911-9). Pinnacle Books.

Nightmare in Brown. Marcia Miller. (YA) 1978. 6.50 (Avalon). Bouregy.

Nightmare in Copenhagen. Martha Albrand. LC 53-9716. 1954. Random House.

Nightmare in Copenhagen: By Martha Albrand Pseud. Heidi Huberta Freybe Loewengard. LC 53-9716. 1954. Random House.

Nightmare in Dublin. Philip Loraine. 1977. 6.60 o.p. (ISBN 0-86025-087-3). State Mutual Bk.

Nightmare in Dublin: A Novel. Philip Loraine. LC 52-9693. 1952. M. S. Mill Co., and W. Morrow.

Nightmare in Eden. Miriam Asher. (Ravenswood gothic). 1974. (pbk.) 0.95 (ISBN 0-671-77751-3). Pocket Books.

Nightmare in Manhattan. Thomas Walsh. LC 50-6755. 1950. Little, Brown.

Nightmare in Pewter. Gene DeWeese. LC 78-3257. 1978. 7.95. Doubleday.
Nightmare in Pink. John Dann MacDonald. LC 76-10151. 1976. 9.95 (ISBN 0-8161-6382-0). G. K. Hall.
Nightmare in Pink. John Dann MacDonald. LC 75-31753. (His The Travis McGee series). 1976. (ISBN 0-397-01116-4). Lippincott.
Nightmare in Red. Jacqueline Marten. LC 81-47265. 368p. (Orig.). 1981. pap. 2.95 (ISBN 0-87216-894-8). Playboy Pbks.
Nightmare Island. Ralph Hayes. 176p. 1975. pap. 0.95 o.p. (ISBN 0-532-95402-5). Woodhill.
Nightmare Island. Ralph Hayes. 176p. 1975. pap. 0.95 o.p. (ISBN 0-532-95402-5). Manor Bks.
Nightmare Journey. Dean Koontz. LC 74-79653. 1975. 6.95 (ISBN 0-399-11388-6). Berkley Pub. Corp.: Distributed by Putnam.
Nightmare Journey. Dean R Koontz. LC 74-79653. 1975. (pbk.) 0.95 (ISBN 0-425-02923-9). Berkley.
Nightmare Machine. John Nicholas Datesh. (Belmont Tower books). 1.75 (ISBN 0-505-51372-2). Tower Pubns.
Nightmare Notebook. Henry Miller. LC 75-4746. (Illus.). 220p. 1975. limited ed. 150.00 (ISBN 0-8112-0576-2). New Directions.
Nightmare of the Dark. Edwin Silberstang. LC 67-11126. 1967. Knopf.
Nightmare of the Eyes. Don Rico. pap. 0.60 o.p. Lancer.
Nightmare on Vega Three. Charles Huntington, III. (Space Probe Six). (O.s.i.). 160p. (Orig.). 1972. pap. 0.75 o.s.i. (AS1045, Award). Univ Pub & Dist.
Nightmare Reader. Ed. by Peter Haining. LC 72-92215. 1973. 5.95 (ISBN 0-385-02215-8). Doubleday.
Nightmare Riders. Archie Joscelyn. LC 40-132631. Phoenix Press.
Nightmare Season. Arnold J. Mandell. 1976. 7.95 o.p. (ISBN 0-394-40252-9). Random.
Nightmare Seasons. Charles L Grant. LC 80-2051. 1982. 10.95 (ISBN 0-385-15956-0). Doubleday.
Nightmare Street. Margaret Tabor. 1982. pap. 2.75 (ISBN 0-671-41103-9). PB.
Nightmare Tales. Helene Petrovna Hahn-Hahn Blavatsky. 1892. Theosophical Publishing Society.
Nightmare. 1st Ed. Cecil Scott Forester. LC 54-8285. 1954. Little, Brown.
Nightmares. Charles L. Grant. LC 79-83966. (Orig.). 1979. pap. 2.25 (ISBN 0-87216-868-9). Playboy Pbks.
Nightmares and Daydreams. Nelson Slade Bond. LC 68-5214. 1968. Arkham House.
Nightmare's Nest: A Novel. Joen Arliss. 1.75 (ISBN 0-445-04454-3) (ISBN 0-445-04454-3). Popular Library.
Nightmares of Eminent Persons: And Other Stories. Illustrated by Charles W. Stewart. Bertrand Russell Russell. LC 54-12360. 1955. Simon and Schuster.
Nightmovers. Jack Dunphy. LC 68-12147. 1967-1968. W. Morrow.
Nightriders. Lee D. Willoughby. (Making of America Ser.: No. 26). 368p. (Orig.). 1982. pap. 3.25 (ISBN 0-440-06255-1, Bryans). Dell.
Nightriders' Feud. Walter Caruth McConnell. LC 12-7187. 1912. The Cosmopolitan Press.
Nightrunners. Michael Collins, pseud. (Dan Fortune Mystery Novel - Red Badge Mystery Ser.). 1978. 6.95 o.p. (ISBN 0-396-07569-X). Dodd.
Nightrunners. Michael Collins, pseud. LC 80-84369. 224p. 1981. pap. 2.25 (ISBN 0-87216-822-0). Playboy Pbks.
Nightrunners. Dennis Lynds. LC 82-1583. 1982. 12.95 (ISBN 0-89340-397-0). J. Curley.
Nightrunners: A Novel of Suspense. Dennis Lynds. LC 78-5782. 1978. 6.95 (ISBN 0-396-07569-X). Dodd, Mead.
Nightrunners of Bengal: A Novel. John Masters. LC 50-11094. 1951. Viking Press.
Nights and Daze in Hollywood. Richard Henry Lee. LC 34-22367. The Macaulay Company.
Night's Black Agent. John Michael Ward Bingham. LC 61-528421. (Red badge detective). 1961. Dodd, Mead.
Night's Black Agent. John Michael Ward Bingham Clanmorris. LC 61-5284. (Red badge detective). 1961. Dodd, Mead.
Night's Black Agent. Fritz Leiber, Jr. 1976. Repr. of 1947 ed. lib. bdg. 13.85x (ISBN 0-88411-932-7). Amereon Ltd.
Night's Black Agents. Fritz Leiber. 1947. Arkham House.
Night's Black Agents. Fritz Leiber. LC 80-17010. (Series: Gregg Press Science Fiction Series.). 1980. 15.00 (ISBN 0-8398-2640-0). Gregg Press.
Night's Cloak. Ernest Robertson Punshon. 1944. The Macmillan Company.
Night's Dark Secrets: The Story of a Lady Novelist. Margaret Campbell. (Signet Book). 1975. (pbk.) 1.50. New American Library.
Night's Evil. Mark McShane. LC 66-11743. 3.50. Pub. for the Crime Club by Doubleday.
Nights in the Garden of Love. Peggy Aldrich. (Orig.). 1975. pap. 1.50 o.p. (LB256NK, Leisure Bks). Nordon Pubns.
Nights in the Gardens of Brooklyn. Harvey Swados. LC 61-5316. 1961. Little, Brown.
Nights in the Gardens of Brooklyn. Harvey Swados. LC 71-128751. (Short story index reprint series). 1970. Books for Libraries Press.
Night's Master. Tanith Lee. (Science Fiction Ser.). (Orig.). 1978. pap. 2.25 (ISBN 0-87997-657-8, UE1657). DAW Bks.
Nights of an Old Child: A Novel. Heinz Liepmann. Tr. by Hudson, Lynton Alfred. LC 37-503193. J. B. Lippincott Company.
Nights of Crass. Martin Havela. LC 69-16275. 1969. 4.95. Christopher Pub. House.
Nights of Love and Laughter. With an Introd. by Kenneth Rexroth. Henry Miller. LC 55-116411. (Signet book, 1246). 1955. New American Library.
Nights of Malta. Gina Zammit. LC 70-79890. 1969. 0.95. Holloway House Pub. Co.
Nights of the Long Knives. Hans Hellmut Kirst. LC 76-25006. 1976. 8.95 (ISBN 0-698-10760-8). Coward, McCann & Geoghegan.
Nights of the Long Knives. Hans Hellmut Kirst. LC 77-350107. 1976. 3.95 (ISBN 0-00-222409-7). Collins.
Nights with Uncle Remus. Joel Chandler Harris. LC 17-25512. 1917. Houghton Millfin Company.
Nights with Uncle Remus: Myths and Legends of the Old Plantation. Joel Chandler Harris. LC 8-23921. 1883. J. R. Osgood and Company.
Nights with Uncle Remus: Myths and Legends of the Old Plantation. 22d ed. Joel Chandler Harris. LC 42-26420. Houghton, Mifflin and Company.
Night's Yawning Peal. Ed. by August William Derleth. (Signet book.). 1974. (pbk.) 1.25. New American Library.
Night's Yawning Peal: A Ghostly Company. Ed. by August William Derleth. LC 52-5051. 1952. Arkham House.
Nightscape. Thomas Chastain. LC 81-14900. 1982. 11.95 (ISBN 0-689-11236-X). Atheneum.
Nightschool for Saints. Ursule Molinaro. 128p. 1981. 10.95 (ISBN 0-89097-021-1); pap. 6.95 (ISBN 0-89097-022-X). Archer Edns.
Nightseed and Other Tales. Harold Alfred Manhood. LC 28-22352. 1928. The Viking Press.
Nightshade. Iris Foster, pseud. (Orig.). 1973. pap. 0.95 o.s.i. (75-425). Lancer.
Nightshade. Jay McCormick. LC 48-5919. 1948. Doubleday.
Nightshade. Derek Marlowe. LC 76-2396. 1976. 8.95 (ISBN 0-670-51418-7). Viking Press.
Nightshade. Derek Marlowe. (Signet Book). 1977. 1.50 (ISBN 0-451-07613-3). New American Library.
Nightshade: A Story of an Orphan Boy and His Sweetheart, Who Were Not Afraid, on the Platte, the Southwest Country, and Mexico. Sara L Baisinger. LC 14-2209. 1914. W. B. Conkey Publishing Co.
Nightshade: Or, The Masked Robber of Hounslow Heath. A Romance of the Road. John Hovey Robinson. LC 7-42164. F. A. Brady.
Nightshade Ring. Lindsay Hardy. LC 54-6256. 1954. Appleton-Century-Crofts.
Nightshade: The Confessions of a Reasoning Animal. LC 24-7532. E. P. Dutton & Company.
Nightshade. 1st Ed. Helen Topping Miller. LC 60-7157. 1960. Bobbs-Merrill.
Nightshool for Saints, 11short stories. Ursule Molinaro. 181p. 1981. pap. 6.95 o.p. (ISBN 0-89097-022-X). Berkshire Traveller.
Nightside. Thomas Collins. (Orig.). 1979. pap. 2.25 (ISBN 0-532-23143-0). Woodhill.
Nightspawn. John Banville. LC 70-152653. 1971. 5.95 (ISBN 0-393-08646-1). Norton.
Nightstar. Mari Evans. LC 79-54308. (California. University. University at Los Angeles. Center for Afro-American Studies. CAAS Special Publication). 4.50 (ISBN 0-934934-07-X). Center for Afro-American Studies, University of California, Los Angeles.
Nightstar. Fern Michaels. LC 82-15637. 1982. 6.95 (ISBN 0-8161-3462-6). G.K. Hall.
Nightwalk. Bob Shaw. 1979. pap. 1.75 (ISBN 0-440-15996-2). Dell.
Nightwalker. Louis Aragon. Tr. by Frederick Brown from Fr. LC 70-108323. (Illus.). 1970. 7.95 o.p. (ISBN 0-13-622480-6). P-H.
Nightwalker. Thomas Tessier. LC 79-23983. 1980. 9.95 (ISBN 0-689-11058-8). Atheneum.
Nightwalker: Le Paysan De Paris). Louis Aragon. LC 70-108323. (New library of French classics). 1970. 7.95. Prentice-Hall.
Nightwalkers. James Norman Schmidt. LC 47-12027. 1947. Ziff-Davis Pub. Co.
Nightwalkers. 1st American Ed. Beberley Cross. LC 57-5509. 1957. Little,Brown.
Nightwatch. Barbara Shoup. LC 82-47543. 12.95 (ISBN 0-06-039012-3). Harper & Row.
Nightwatchmen. Barry Hannah. LC 73-2038. 1973. 6.95 (ISBN 0-670-51223-0). Viking Press.
Nightwebs. Hopley-Woolrich, Cornell George. Ed. by Francis M. Nevins. LC 70-144199. 1971. 8.95 (ISBN 0-06-013173-X). Harper & Row.
Nightwebs: A Collection of Stories by Cornell Woolrich. Ed. by Francis M. Nevins, Jr. LC 70-144199. 1971. 8.95 o.p. (HarpT). Har-Row.
Nightwind. Sarah Allis. LC 74-17670. 1975. 7.95 (ISBN 0-672-52044-3). Bobbs-Merrill.
Nightwind. Mark Washburn. (Orig.). 1982. pap. 2.95 (ISBN 0-440-15757-9). Dell.
Nightwing. Ed. by Fotonovel Publications Staff. (Illus., Orig.). 1979. pap. 2.75. Fotonovel.
Nightwing. Martin Cruz Smith. LC 77-5035. 8.95 (ISBN 0-393-08783-2). Norton.
Nightwing. Martin Cruz Smith. (Jove1HBJ Book.). 1978. 2.25 (ISBN 0-515-04543-8). Jove Pubns.
Nightwing: A Novel. Martin Cruz Smith. 1977. 10.95 o.p. (ISBN 0-393-08783-2). Norton.
Nightwings. Robert Silverberg. LC 70-109186. 1970. 4.95. Walker.
Nightwings. Robert Silverberg. 1979. 1.50 (ISBN 0-380-41467-8). Avon.
Nightwitch Devil. Kenneth Robeson. 1974. (pbk.) 0.95. Warner Paperback Library.
Nightwood. Djuna Barnes. LC 49-1384. (New Classics Series 11). 1946. New Directions.
Nightwood. Djuna Barnes. LC 37-3021. 1937. Harcourt, Brace and Company.
Nightwork. Irwin Shaw. LC 75-43954. 1976. 14.95 (ISBN 0-8161-6347-2). G. K. Hall.
Niheem Glover's Short Stories - 3. Niheem Glover. (Illus.). 1973. 1.50 o.p. (ISBN 0-87976-208-X). Amuru Pr.
Nihilist Princess. Tr. from the French of M. L. Gagneur. Louise Mignerot Gagneur. LC 6-44493. 1881. Jansen, McClurg & Company.
Nijushi no Hitomi see Twenty-Four Eyes.
Nikanor. Alice Marie Celeste Durand. Tr. by Chase, Eliza E. LC 6-35689. (On cover: The Rialto series, no. 8). 1889. Rand, McNally & Company.
Nikki. Allan Nixon. LC 76-49394. 1977. pap. 1.95 o.p. (ISBN 0-87216-383-0, E 16383). Playboy.
Nikki: By Jack Woodford Pseud. & Conrad Carter. Josiah Pitts Woolfolk & Conrad Carter. LC 53-2478. 1953. Signature Press.
Nikki. 1st Ed. Kevin MacRae. LC 55-570754. 1955. Vantage Press.
Nikola Tesla: Man or Spaceman? Michael X. 1970. pap. 3.00 o.p. Saucerian.
Nikolai Negorev: Or, The Successful Russian. Ivan Afanasevich Kushschevskii. LC 73-189439. 1972. 6.95. St. Martin's Press.
Nile. Laurie Devine. LC 82-16960. 17.50 (ISBN 0-671-45170-7). Simon and Schuster.
Nile Days; or Egyptian Bonds. A Novel. E. Katharine Bates. LC 6-9082. 1879. J. B. Lippincott & Co.
Nile Fever: A Tale of Adventure and Intrigue in North Africa. Elmer J Carpenter. LC 59-15634. 1959. Pan Press.
Nile Gold: A Legend of Modern Egypt. John Knittel. LC 29-18943. 1929. Doubleday, Doran and Company, Inc.
Nile Green. David Jordan. LC 73-16176. 1974. 6.95 (ISBN 0-381-98259-9). John Day Co.
Niles. Michael Rogers. 1973. 5.95 o.p. Knopf.
Nimble Dollar: With Other Stories. Charles Miner Thompson. LC 8-19972. 1895. Houghton, Mifflin and Company.
Nimblefoot the Ant. Vytas Tamulaitis. 1965. 3.95 o.p. (ISBN 0-87141-015-X). Manyland.
Nimbus: The Creation Story According to Mr. G. LC 78-58330. (Illus.). 1978. pap. 4.95 o.p. (ISBN 0-89556-008-9). IDHHB.
Nimport. Edwin Lassetter Bynner. (Half-title: Wayside series). 1877. Lockwood, Brooks and Company.
Nimport. Edwin Lassetter Bynner. LC 6-16409. (On cover: Lovell's library, v. 3, no. 100). 1883. J. W. Lovell Company.
Nimrod & Co. Georges Ohnet. Tr. by Serrano, Mary Jane (Christie) (On cover: Cassell's sunshine series, no. 131). 1892. Cassell Publishing Company.
Nina. Alfred Bourne. LC 35-939. The Vanguard Press.
Nina. Donald Henderson Clarke. LC 35-939. 1935. Vanguard Press.
Nina. Donald Henderson Clarke. LC 48-411839. (Triangle books, 406). 1948. Triangle Books.
Nina. Susan Ertz. LC 24-215825. 1924. D. Appleton and Company.
Nina Balatka: The Story of a Maiden of Prague, 2 vols. Anthony Trollope. Ed. by N. John Hall. LC 80-1885. (Selected Works of Anthony Trollope Ser.). 1981. Repr. of 1867 ed. 50.00 (ISBN 0-405-14148-3). Ayer Co.
Nina: By Warren Howard Pseud. James Noble Gifford. LC 54-9903. 1954. Arcadia House.
Nina Gordon: A Tale of the Great Dismal Swamp. Harriet Elizabeth Beecher Stowe. 1866. Ticknor and Fields.
Nina Grant, Pediatric Nurse. Pattie Wright Stone. 1973. pap. 0.75 o.s.i. (01-380). Lancer.
Nina Huanca. Gonzalez Aller, Faustino. LC 76-46525. 10.00 (ISBN 0-670-51338-5). Viking Press.
Nina: Or Life's Caprices. A Story Founded on Fact. Frances Irene Burge Smith Griswold. LC 7-167. 1861. D. Dana.
Nina. Translated by Richard and Clara Winston. Luise Rinser. LC 56-113823. 1956. H. Regnery Co.
Nina Upstairs. Beverley Gasner. LC 64-12298. 1964. Knopf.
Nina's Book. Eugene Burdick. LC 64-25231. 1965. Houghton Mifflin.
Nina's Peril: A Novel. Alexander McVeigh Miller. (On cover: American author's series, no. 37). 1891. United States Book Company.
Nine--and Death Makes Ten. John Dickson Carr. 1940. W. Morrow & Company.
Nine Against New York. Albert Leffingwell. LC 41-92433. H. Holt and Company.
Nine Billion Names of God. Arthur C. Clarke. LC 67-16086. 1967. 7.95 o.p. (ISBN 0-15-165890-0). HarBraceJ.
Nine Billion Names of God. Arthur C. Clarke. 1974. pap. 2.50 (ISBN 0-451-11715-8, AE1715, Sig). NAL.
Nine Billion Names of God. Arthur C. Clarke. 1971. pap. 1.45 o.p. (ISBN 0-15-665895-X, HPL50, HPL). HarBraceJ.
Nine Billion Names of God: The Best Short Stories of Arthur C. Clarke. Arthur Charles Clarke. LC 67-16086. 1967. Harcourt, Brace & World.
Nine Billion Names of God: The Best Short Stories of Arthur C. Clarke. Arthur Charles Clarke. LC 67-16086. 1974. (pbk.) 1.25. New American Library.
Nine Blessings. Mary Harriott Norris. LC 7-33301. 1895. Hunt & Eaton.
Nine Brides and Granny Hite. Neill Compton Wilson. LC 52-5896. 1952. Morrow.
Nine Buck's Row. T. E Huff. LC 73-342. 1973. 5.95. Hawthorn Books.
Nine by Laumer. Keith Laumer. LC 67-10401. (Doubleday science fiction). 1967. Doubleday.
Nine Chains to the Moon. R. Buckminster Fuller. 1971. pap. 2.95 o.p. (ISBN 0-385-01149-0, Anch). Doubleday.
Nine Coaches Waiting. Mary Stewart. LC 59-5139. 1959. M. S. Mill and W. Morrow.
Nine Days of Father Serra. Isabelle Gibson Ziegler. LC 51-2723. 1951. Longmans, Green.
Nine Days' Panic. Reginald Davis. LC 38-9731. 1938. Pub. for the Crime Club, Inc., by Doubleday, Doran & Co., Inc.
Nine Days to Mukalla: A Novel. Frederic Prokosch. LC 52-14033. 1953. Viking Press.
Nine Doctors and a Madman. Elizabeth Curtiss. LC 37-294548. 1937. Simon and Schuster.
Nine Dragon Man. David DeReszke. 1975. pap. 1.25 o.p. (ISBN 0-515-03838-5). Pyramid Pubns.
Nine Good Men. O'Rourke, Frank. LC 52-8303. (Barnes sports novel series). 1952. A. S. Barnes.
Nine Guardians, a Novel. Translated by Irene Nicholson. Rosario Castellanos. LC 60-9716. 1960. Vanguard Press.
Nine Holes of Jade. Su Ling. (Orig.). pap. 1.75 (ISBN 0-87067-510-9, BH510). Holloway.
Nine Horrors. Joseph Payne Brennan. 3.00 o.p. Arkham.
Nine Horrors and a Dream. Joseph Payne Brennan. LC 58-49078. 1958. Arkham House.
Nine Hours to Rama. Stanley A Wolpert. LC 62-8436. 1962. Randon House.
Nine Humorous Tales. 2d ed., rev. ed. Anton Pavlovich Chekhov. Tr. by Isaac Goldberg & Henry Thomas Schnittkind. LC 76-106262. (Short story index reprint series). 1970. Books for Libraries Press.
Nine Humorous Tales. Anton Pavlovich Chekhov. Tr. by Goldberg, Isaac. LC 18-69249. (Stratford universal library). 1918. The Stratford Company.
Nine-Hundred Block. Katharine Haviland Taylor. LC 32-8426. 1932. J. B. Lippincott Company.
Nine Hundred Eleven: A Novel. Thomas Chastain. LC 75-41319. 1976. 7.95 (ISBN 0-88405-135-8). Mason/Charter.
Nine Hundred Fifty-Two King: A Christmas Eve Story. Karl H Krause. LC 75-307174. (Illus.). 1974. Rook Press.
Nine Hundred Grandmothers. R. A. Lafferty. 320p. 1982. pap. 2.50 (ISBN 0-441-58051-3). Ace Bks.
Nine Hundred Ninety-Eight: A Novel. Edward S Hyams. LC 52-7935. 1952. Pantheon Books.
Nine Lives. Ursula Bloom. LC 82-19815. 1983. 11.95 (ISBN 0-89340-486-1). J. Curley.
Nine Lives. Mark Channing. LC 37-226423. J. B. Lippincott Company.
Nine Lives. E. F. Miller, pseud. 1978. pap. 1.50 (ISBN 0-532-15334-0). Woodhill.
Nine Lives Are Not Enough. Jerome Odlum. LC 40-358164. Sheridan House.

Nine Lives of Alphonse. James Leonard Johnson. pap. 1.75 o.p. (ISBN 0-310-37422-7). Zondervan.

Nine Lives of Alphonse. James Leonard Johnson. (Code Name Sebastian Ser). (Illus.). 1968. 4.95 o.p. (ISBN 0-397-10063-9). Lippincott.

Nine Lives of Alphonse. James Leonard Johnson. 1969. pap. 1.95 o.p. (ISBN 0-8423-4700-3). Tyndale.

Nine Lives of Alphonse: A Code Name Sebastian Adventure. James Leonard Johnson. LC 68-19835. (Illus.). 1968. Lippincott.

Nine Lives of Deaf Smith. Illustrated by James T. Jones. Faye Campbell Griffis. LC 58-4890. 1958. Banks Upshaw.

Nine Lives to Pompeii: A Novel of Suspense. William Melton. LC 73-87842. (Illus.). 1974. 6.95 (ISBN 0-679-50438-9). D. McKay Co.

Nine Mile Circle. Patricia Hill. LC 57-6773. 1957. Houghton Mifflin.

Nine-Mile Swamp: A Story of the Loomis Gang. Harriet McDoual Daniels. LC 41-518442. The Penn Publishing Company.

Nine Mile Walk: The Nicky Welt Stories of Harry Kemelman. Harry Kemelman. LC 67-23130. (Red mask mystery). 1967. Putnam.

Nine Minus Nine Equals Nine. first ed. Michael Tanzillo. 1972. 4.95 (ISBN 0-533-00421-7). Vantage.

Nine Miracles. Carmine C. Argilo. 1979. 8.00 (ISBN 0-933744-00-5). Literati Pr.

Nine Modern Classics: An Anthology of Short Novels. Ed. by Sylvan Barnet. LC 72-14218. (Illus.). 1973. Little, Brown.

Nine Month Caper. 3rd ed. Ted Mark, pseud. (Orig.). 1968. pap. 0.75 o.p. (73-488). Lancer.

Nine-Month Caper. Ted Mark. 1973. (pbk.) 1.25. Dell.

Nine Months. Hilde Maria Kraus. Tr. by Gullick, Norman. LC 32-253247. Liveright, Inc.

Nine Months in the Life of an Old Maid. Judith Rossner. LC 70-80498. 1969. 4.95. Dial Press.

Nine Moons Wasted. Marianne Lamont, pseud. LC 76-43147. 1976. 8.95 o.p. (ISBN 0-399-11848-9). Putnam Pub Group.

Nine Moons Wasted. Anne Rundle. LC 76-43147. 1977. 8.95 (ISBN 0-399-11848-9). Putnam.

Nine More Lives. Michael Morgan. LC 47-3525. 1947. Random House.

Nine O'clock Parade. Peggy Gaddis, pseud. LC 38-777. 1937. Hillman-Curl, Inc.

Nine O'clock Tide. Mignon Good Eberhart. LC 77-12341. 6.95 (ISBN 0-394-42016-0). Random House.

Nine O'clock Tide. Mignon Good Eberhart. LC 79-13136. 1979. 10.95 (ISBN 0-89340-217-6). J. Curley.

Nine of Hearts: A Novel. Benjamin Leopold Farjeon. LC 6-38649. (Harper's handy series. no. 107). 1886. Harper & Brothers.

Nine of Hearts: And The Brighter Star of Life. Benjamin Leopold Farjeon. LC 6-38648. (On cover: Lovell's library. v. 18. no. 874). 1887. J. W. Lovell Company.

Nine Poems. James Den Boer. 1972. pap. 3.00 o.p. (ISBN 0-87922-008-2, Pub. by Christopher's Bks). SBD.

Nine Princes in Amber. Roger Zelazny. LC 77-103787. 1970. 4.50. Doubleday.

Nine Princes in Amber. Roger Zelazny. LC 78-23739. (Gregg Press Science Fiction Series). (Illus.). 1979. 15.00 (ISBN 0-8398-2427-0). Gregg Press.

Nine Saturdays Make a Year. 1st Ed. David M Camerer. LC 62-11307. 1962. Doubleday.

Nine Seven Juliet: A Mystery Novel. Laurence Davis Lafore. LC 69-20084. 1969. 5.95. Doubleday.

Nine Ships: A Book of Tales. Tony Cohan. (Illus.). 1975. 12.00 o.s.i. (ISBN 0-918226-02-3); pap. 5.95 o.s.i. (ISBN 0-918226-00-7). Acrobat.

Nine Short Novels. 2nd ed. Richard M. Ludwig & Marvin B. Perry, Jr. 1964. pap. text ed. 11.95x o.p. (ISBN 0-669-21238-5). Heath.

Nine Short Novels. 2d ed. Ed. by Richard M Ludwig & Perry, Marvin B. LC 61-15583. Heath.

Nine Short Novels: Edited by Richard M. Ludwig and Marvin B. Perry, Jr. Ed. by Richard M Ludwig. LC 52-12828. 1952. Heath.

Nine Stories. J. D. Salinger. LC 52-12626. 1953. Little, Brown.

Nine Stories. 1st Ed. J. D. Salinger. LC 59-10908. (Modern library of the world's best books 301). 1959. Modern Library.

Nine Stories, 1855-1863. Lev Nikolaevich Tolstoi. (W.C.420). 1.75 o.p. (ISBN 0-19-250420-7). Oxford U Pr.

Nine Stories, 1855-63. Lev Nikolaevich Tolstoi & Maude, Mrs. Louise (Shanks) 1855- Tr. LC 34-27224. (Half-title: The world's classics. 420). 1934. Oxford University Press, H. Milford.

Nine Strings to Your Bow. Maurice Walsh. LC 45-8769. 1945. J. B. Lippincott Company.

Nine Swords of Morales: The Story of an Old-Time California Feud. George Homer Meyer. LC 6-6486. 1905. H. Altemus Company.

Nine Tailors: Changes Rung on an Old Theme in Two Short Touches and Two Full Peals. Dorothy Leigh Sayers. LC 34-6048. Harcourt, Brace and Company.

Nine Tailors: Changes Rung on an Old Theme in Two Short Touches and Two Full Peals. Dorothy Leigh Sayers. LC 81-6925. 1981. 15.95 (ISBN 0-8161-3036-1). G.K. Hall.

Nine Tales. Hugh De Selincourt. LC 79-103506. (Short story index reprint series). 1969. Books for Libraries Press.

Nine Tales of Space & Time. Ed. by Raymond J. Healy. LC 54-7026. 1954. Holt.

Nine-Tenths. James Oppenheim. LC 68-57543. (Muckrakers Ser.). 1979. Repr. of 1911 ed. lib. bdg. 16.00 (ISBN 0-8398-1453-4). Irvington.

Nine-Tenths: A Novel. James Oppenheim. LC 68-57543. (American novels of muckraking, propaganda, and social protest). 1968. Gregg Press.

Nine Thirty Fifty-Five: A Novel. John Minahan. LC 77-83668. 1977. 1.75 (ISBN 0-380-00970-6). Avon Books.

Nine-Thousand & Nine. James Marie Hopper & Frederick Ritchie Bechdolt. LC 68-57532. (Muckrakers Ser). Repr. of 1908 ed. lib. bdg. 16.50 (ISBN 0-8398-0790-2). Irvington.

Nine Thousand-Nine. James Marie Hopper & Frederick Ritchie Bechdolt. LC 68-57532. (American novels of muckraking, propaganda, and social protest). 1968. Gregg Press.

Nine Thousand-Nine. James Marie Hopper & Frederick Ritchie Bechdolt. LC 8-27364. 1908. The McClure Company.

Nine-Tiger Man: A Tale of Low Behavior in High Places. Lesley Blanch. LC 65-15906. bds., 4.50. Atheneum.

Nine Times Nine. William Anthony Parker White. LC 40-32373. Duell, Sloan and Pearce.

Nine to Five. William Harrison Prosser. LC 52-12629. 1953. Little, Brown.

Nine to Five. Thom Racina. 160p. (Orig.). 1980. pap. 2.25 (ISBN 0-553-14496-0). Bantam.

Nine to Five. Harvey Hassall Smith. LC 44-3243. 1944. C. Scribner's Sons.

Nine Tomorrows. Isaac Asimov. 1978. pap. 2.25 (ISBN 0-449-24084-3, Crest). Fawcett.

Nine Tomorrows: Tales of the Near Future. 1st Ed. Isaac Asimov. LC 59-6347. (Doubleday science fiction). 1959. Doubleday.

Nine Unknown. Talbot Mundy. LC 24-6686. The Bobbs-Merrill Company.

Nine Waxed Faces. Francis Beeding. LC 36-20994. 1936. Harper & Brothers.

Nine White Roses. Morris J. Frank. 10.00 o.p. Carlton.

Ninepenny Flute: Twenty-One Tales. Alfred Edgar Coppard. LC 71-106277. (Short story index reprint series). 1970. Books for Libraries Press.

Nineteen. Aleksandr Aleksandrovich Fadeev. LC 72-90293. 1973. 13.50 (ISBN 0-88355-003-2). Hyperion Press.

Nineteen. Aleksandr Aleksandrovich Fadeev & Charques, Richard Denis, 1899- Tr. LC 30-31805. 1929. International Publishers.

Nineteen. Alexandrovich Fadeev. Tr. by Charques, R. D. LC 30-31805. 1929. International Publishers.

Nineteen. Roger Hall. 1973. 0.95. Warner Paperback Lib.

Nineteen. Roger Hall. LC 79-86591. 1970. 5.95. Norton.

Nineteen Eighties Countdown to Armageddon. Hal Lindsey. 1982. pap. 2.95 (ISBN 0-553-20102-6). Bantam.

Nineteen Eighty-Five. Anthony Burgess. LC 78-9583. 8.95 (ISBN 0-316-11651-3). Little, Brown.

Nineteen Eighty-Four. George Orwell. 1982. Repr. lib. bdg. 11.95x (ISBN 0-89966-368-0). Buccaneer Bks.

Nineteen Eighty-One Annual World's Best Science Fiction. Ed. by Donald A. Wollheim. (Science Fiction Ser.). 1981. pap. 2.25 o.p. DAW Bks.

Nineteen Eighty-One Annual World's Best SF. Ed. by Donald A. Wollheim. (Science Fiction Ser.). 1981. pap. 2.50 (ISBN 0-87997-617-9, UE1617). DAW Bks.

Nineteen Fifteen: A Novel. Roger McDonald. LC 79-26253. 1980. 10.95 (ISBN 0-8076-0949-8). G. Braziller.

Nineteen Hundred Years: Or, The Power of Christ. Winfield W Thiesing. LC 8-27055. W. W. Thiesing.

Nineteen Impressions. John Davys Beresford. LC 71-103492. (Short story index reprint series). 1969. Books for Libraries Press.

Nineteen Nineteen. John Dos Passos. LC 32-26235. Harcourt, Brace and Company.

Nineteen Nineteen. John Dos Passos. pap. 3.50 (ISBN 0-451-51508-0, CE1508, Sig Classics). NAL.

Nineteen Purchase Street. Gerald A. Browne. LC 82-72051. 1982. 14.95 (ISBN 0-87795-413-5). Arbor Hse.

Nineteen Purchase Street. Gerald A. Browne. 1983. pap. 3.50 (ISBN 0-425-06154-X). Berkley Pub.

Nineteen Seventy-Six. E. Gordon Dickie. 1971. 10.00 o.p. (ISBN 0-682-47231-X). Exposition.

Nineteen Sixty? Otis Carney. 1964. pap. 1.25 o.p. (A96). Apollo Eds.

Nineteen Sixty-Eight: A Short Novel, an Urban Idyll, Five Stories, & Two Trade Notes. Richard Stern. LC 70-105432. 1970. 5.95 o.p. (ISBN 0-03-084529-7). HR&W.

Nineteen Sixty-Eight: Short Novel, an Urban Idyll, Five Stories, & Two Trade Notes. Richard G. Stern. LC 70-105432. 1970. 5.95 (ISBN 0-03-084529-7). Holt, Rinehart, and Winston.

Nineteen Stories. Graham Greene. LC 49-594. 1949. Viking Press.

Nineteen Tales of Terror: Edited by Whit and Hallie Burnett. Ed. by Whit Burnett & Hallie Southgate Burnett. LC 57-5191. (Bantam giant, A1550). 1957. Bantam Books.

Nineteen Thirty-Nine: A Novel. Kay Boyle. LC 48-55873. Simon and Schuster.

Nineteen Twenty Nine Parents Tomorrow. Winnifred S. Lloyd. 64p. 1973. 3.00 o.p. (ISBN 0-682-47705-2). Exposition.

Nineteenth-Century American Short Fiction. Ed. by William James Holmes. LC 69-11520. 1970. Scott, Foresman.

Nineteenth Century Canadian Stories. David Arnason. LC 76-365288. (ISBN 0-7705-1345-X) (ISBN 0-7705-1346-8). Macmillan.

Nineteenth Century French Tales. Ed. by Angel Flores. LC 67-31051. 1967. 5.75, 2.45 pap.,. Ungar.

Nineteenth Century German Tales. Ed. by Angel Flores. LC 66-251106. 1966. 5.50. Ungar.

Nineteenth Hole: Being Tales of the Fair Green. William Gilbert Van Tassel Sutphen. LC 1-16989. (On cover: Harper's portrait collection of short stories, v.3). 1901. Harper & Brothers.

Ninette, an Idyll of Provence. Charlotte Louisa Hawkins Dempster. LC 44-22012. 1888. D. Appleton and Company.

Ninety and Nine. William Brinkley. LC 66-13194. 5.95. Doubleday.

Ninety and Nine. William Brinkley. (N162). 1967. Avon.

Ninety Degrees in the Shade. Clarence Cason. (Illus.). 240p. 1983. pap. text ed. 11.75 (ISBN 0-8173-0170-4). U of Ala Pr.

Ninety-Eight Point Six: A Novel. Ronald Sukenick. LC 74-24913. 1975. 7.95. (ISBN 0-914590-08-1) (ISBN 0-914590-09-X). Fiction Collective: Distributed by G. Braziller.

Ninety-Eight Point Six Degrees. Leon Z Surmelian. LC 50-8769. 1950. Dutton.

Ninety-Five File. James E. Martin. 1975. pap. 1.50 o.p. (ISBN 0-515-03583-1, A3583). Pyramid Pubns.

Ninety-Nine & Forty-Four One-Hundreds Percent Dead. Max Franklin, pseud. (O.s.i.). 160p. (Orig.). 1974. pap. 0.95 o.s.i. (AN1301, Award). Univ Pub & Dist.

Ninety-Nine Dark Street: A Novel. Frederick William Robinson. (On cover: Seaside library. Pocket ed. no. 1005). 1887. G. Munro.

Ninety-Nine Days. Clara Roxana Bush. LC 6-16682. (On cover: Satchel series no. 19). Authors' Publishing Company.

Ninety-Second Tiger. Michael Francis Gilbert. LC 73-4148. 1973. 6.95 (ISBN 0-06-011533-5). Harper & Row.

Ninety Six. Elliott Crayton McCants. LC 30-569421. Thomas Y. Crowell Company.

Ninety-Six: A Romance of Utopia. Frank Rosewater. LC 72-154460. (Utopian Literature Ser). 1971. Repr. of 1894 ed. 16.00 (ISBN 0-405-03542-X). Ayer Co.

Ninety-Six Hours' Leave. Stephen McKenna. LC 17-296222. George H. Doran Company.

Ninety-Three. Victor Marie Hugo. LC 26-27624. 1888. Little, Brown, and Company.

Ninety-Three. Victor Marie Hugo. Tr. by Frank Lee Benedict. 1889. G. Routledge and Sons.

Ninety-Three. Victor Marie Hugo. LC 26-26899. (Half-title: The romances of Victor Hugo. Handy library edition). Little, Brown and Company.

Ninety-Three. Victor Marie Hugo & Dole, Mrs. Helen James (Bennett) Tr. LC 16-19145. T. Y. Crowell & Co.

Ninety-Three. Victor Marie Hugo & Dole, Mrs. Helen James (Bennett) Tr. LC 4-16882. 1888. T. Y. Crowell & Co.

Ninety-Three. Victor Marie Hugo & Picot, E. B. D'Espinville, Tr. LC 7-585630. 1874. "The Evening Telegraph,

Ninety-Three: A Novel. Victor Marie Hugo. Tr. by Frank Lee Benedict. LC 7-5876. 1874. Harper & Brothers.

Ninety-Three: A Novel. Victor Marie Hugo. Tr. by Frank Lee Benedict. LC 7-5877. 1874. Harper & Brothers.

Ninety-Three: A Novel. Victor Marie Hugo. Tr. by Frank Lee Benedict. (On cover: Seaside library. Pocket ed., no. 2148). 1895. G. Munro's Sons.

Ninety-Three: A Story of the French Revolution. Victor Marie Hugo & Magee, Mrs. Katherine E. LC 7-5858. (On cover: Standard literature series, no. 18). 1896. University Publishing Company.

Ninety-Three. Translated by Lowell Bair. With an Introd. by Ayn Rand. Victor Marie Hugo. LC 62-19344. (Bantam books, S2453). 1962. Bantam Books.

Ninety-Two in the Shade. Thomas McGuane. LC 79-21606. 1980. 2.50 (ISBN 0-14-005319-0). Penguin Books.

Ninety-Two in the Shade. first ed. Thomas McGuane. LC 73-76222. 1973. 6.95 (ISBN 0-374-22259-2). Farrar, Straus and Giroux.

Ninety-Two in the Shade. Thomas McGuane. 1974. (pbk.) 1.50. Bantam Books.

Nineveh House. Desemea Wilson. LC 35-635016. E. P. Dutton & Co., Inc.

Ninfa Enloquecedora. Jaime Maldonado. (Pimienta Collection Ser). (Span.). 1977. pap. 1.00 (ISBN 0-88473-257-6). Fiesta Pub.

Ninfa Para Uso y Abuso. Silvia Orejuela. (Pimienta Collection Ser). (Sp.). 1977. pap. 1.00 (ISBN 0-88473-254-1). Fiesta Pub.

Ninja. Andrew Adams. (Illus.). 1970. 6.95x. Wehman.

Ninja. John Jacob. 1979. pap. 2.50 (ISBN 0-931498-11-2). DuBois Zone Pr.

Ninja. Eric Van Lustbader. 1981. 3.50 (ISBN 0-449-24367-2). Fawcett Crest Books.

Ninja. Eric Van Lustbader. 512p. 1981. pap. 3.50 (ISBN 0-449-24367-2, Crest). Fawcett.

Ninja. Eric Van Lustbader. 448p. 1980. 12.95 (ISBN 0-87131-314-6). M Evans.

Ninja: A Novel. Eric Van Lustbader. LC 79-25674. 12.95 (ISBN 0-87131-314-6). M. Evans.

Ninja Master, No. 3: Borderland of Hell. Wade Barker. (Men of Acton Ser.). 176p. (Orig.). 1982. pap. 1.95 (ISBN 0-446-30127-2). Warner Bks.

Ninja Master, No. 4: Million-Dollar Massacre. Wade Barker. (Men of Action Ser.). 176p. (Orig.). 1982. pap. 1.95 (ISBN 0-446-30177-9). Warner Bks.

Ninja Master No. 5: Black Magician. Wade Barker. (Men of Action Ser.). 160p. (Orig.). 1982. pap. 1.95 (ISBN 0-446-30178-7). Warner Bks.

Ninja Master, No. 7: The Skin Swindle. Wade Barker. (Men of Action Ser.). 176p. (Orig.). 1983. pap. 1.95 (ISBN 0-446-30227-9). Warner Bks.

Ninja Master, No. 8: Only the Good Die. Wade Barker. 176p. (Orig.). 1983. pap. 2.25 (ISBN 0-446-30239-2). Warner Bks.

Ninja's Revenge. Piers Anthony & Roberto Fuentes. (Berkley medallion book). 1975. (pbk.) 0.95 (ISBN 0-425-02821-6). Berkley Pub. Co.

Nino; the Legend of 'Apache Kid,' By Clay Fisher Pseud. Henry Allen. LC 61-8913. 1961. Morrow.

Nino y Grande. Gabriel Miro Ferrer. pap. 1.95 o.s.i. French & Eur.

Ninth Avenue. Maxwell Bodenheim. LC 26-21294. 1926. Boni & Liveright.

Ninth Car. Anne Reed Rooth & James P. White. LC 78-9515. 8.95. Putnam.

Ninth Circle. Harwood Elmes Robert Steele. LC 28-6524. 1928. Doubleday, Doran & Company, Inc.

Ninth Configuration. William Peter Blatty. LC 78-4741. 7.95 (ISBN 0-06-010359-0). Harper and Row.

Ninth Directive. Adam Hall. 1970. pap. 0.95 o.p. (N2212). Pyramid Pubns.

Ninth Directive. Adam Hall, pseud. 1977. pap. 1.50 o.p. BJ Pub Group.

Ninth Directive. Adam Hall, pseud. (O.S.I.). 1967. 4.95 o.s.i. (52818). S&S.

Ninth Floor: Middle City Tower; a Jerry Mooney Story. Kerry O'Neil. LC 43-10684. 1943. Farrar & Rinehart, Inc.

Ninth Hour. Ben Benson. LC 56-8434. 1956. M. S. Mill Co., and W. Morrow.

Ninth Life. Frances J. Eden. Ed. by Alice Sachs. 1969. lib. bdg. 3.50 o.p. Arcadia.

Ninth Life. Frances J. Eden. 1972. pap. 0.75 o.s.i. (01-357). Lancer.

Ninth Life. Jack Mann. 1970. 5.00. Bookfinger.

Ninth Man. John Lee. LC 75-14989. 1976. 8.95 (ISBN 0-385-11261-0). Doubleday.

Ninth Man. John Lee. 1.95. Dell.

Ninth Man: A Story. Mary Marvin Heaton Vorse. LC 20-15068. 1920. Harper & Brothers.

Ninth Marquess. Jon Cleary. LC 74-170222. 1972. 6.95. Morrow.

Ninth Netsuke. James Melville. LC 82-16782. 9.95 (ISBN 0-312-57476-2). St. Martin's Press.

Ninth of November. Bernhard Kellermann. Tr. by Kerr, Caroline V. LC 25-1017. 1925. R. M. McBride & Company.

Ninth Tentacle. Marion Rippon. LC 74-5536. 1974. 4.95 (ISBN 0-385-07995-8). Published for the Crime Club by Doubleday.

TITLE INDEX NO FRIENDLY DROP

Ninth Thermidor. Mark Aleksandrovich Aldanov. Tr. by Chamot, Alfred Edward. LC 26-12238. 1926. A. A. Knopf.
Ninth Thermidor: Translated from the Russian. Mark Aleksandrovich Landau. Tr. by Chamot, Alfred Edward. LC 26-12238. 1926. A. A. Knopf.
Ninth Vibration and Other Stories. Lily Moresby Adams Beck. LC 75-46251. (Supernatural and Occult Fiction). 1976. 18.00 (ISBN 0-405-08111-1). Arno Press.
Ninth Vibration: And Other Stories. Lily Moresby Adams Beck. LC 22-10392. 1922. Dodd, Mead and Company.
Ninth Wave. Eugene Burdick. LC 56-5055. 1956. Houghton Mifflin.
Ninth Wave. new ed. Eugene Burdick. 1975. (pbk.) 1.75. Dell.
Ninth Wave. Agnes Sweetman Castle & Castle, Egerton. LC 11-112143. 1911. 0.25. R. H. Paget.
Ninth Wave. Ilia Grigorevich Ehrenburg. LC 74-10358. (Series: Library of Contemporary Soviet Novels.). 1974. (ISBN 0-8371-7672-7). Greenwood Press.
Ninth Wave. Carl Clinton Van Doren. LC 26-16536. Harcourt, Brace and Company.
Ninth Wave for Nurse Kendall. Ruth McCarthy Sears. pap. 0.75 o.s.i. (01-345). Lancer.
Ninth Week. Irene Alexander. The Penn Publishing Company.
Niphrata Has Spoken! J. R. B Messenger. LC 38-38824. 1938. The Tipharet Publishing Co., Inc.
Nipped in the Bud: A Miss Withers Mystery. Stuart Palmer. LC 51-13986. 1951. M. S. Mill Co. and W. Morrow.
Nipper & Nipper's Secret Power. Morrie Turner. 1974. (pbk.) 0.75. New American Library.
Nipples: A Story of Fiction Describing a Political Mammal and Dramatizing a Contest Between Taxpayers and Politicians. Thomas Highley Morris. LC 46-3480. 1946. Hobson Book Press.
Nipples: A Story of Fiction Describing a Political Mammal and Dramatizing a Contest Between Taxpayers and Politicians. Tom Morris. LC 46-3480. 1946. The Hobson Book Press.
Nipsya. Georges Bugnet. Tr. by Woodrow, Constance Davies. LC 30-7100. L. Carrier & Co.
Niquin el Cesante. Jose Sanchez-Boudy. LC 78-74694. (Coleccion Caniqui). (Illus.). 157p. (Orig., Span.). 1980. pap. 5.95 (ISBN 0-89729-217-0). Ediciones.
Niram: A Dusky Idyl. Laisdell Mitchell. LC 72-1513. (Black Heritage Library Collection). (Illus.). 1972. 9.50 (ISBN 0-8369-9038-2). Books for Libraries Press.
Niram. A Dusky Idyl. Laisdell Mitchell. LC 7-31099. 1895. C. H. Banes.
Nirvana Blues. John Treadwell Nichols. LC 80-22376. 540p. 1981. 16.95 (ISBN 0-03-059256-9). HR&W.
Nirvana Blues. John Treadwell Nichols. 608p. 1983. pap. 4.95 (ISBN 0-345-30465-9). Ballantine.
Nirvana Contracts: A Novel of Suspense. James P Wohl. LC 78-17893. 8.95 (ISBN 0-672-52340-X). Bobbs-Merrill.
Nisi Prius. John Caldwell Browder. LC 12-275933. 1912. The Neale Publishing Company.
Nitchey Tilley: A Novel. Roy Addison Helton. 1934. Harper & Brothers.
Nitrogen Fix. Hal Clement. LC 81-112570. (Ace science fiction). (Illus.). 6.95 (ISBN 0-441-58116-1). Ace Books.
Nixe. Herbert Kuhner. LC 68-22269 1968. 4.95. Funk & Wagnalls.
Nixey's Harlequin. Alfred Edgar Coppard. LC 31-28597. 1932. A. A. Knopf.
Nixola of Wall Street. Felix Grendon. LC 19-656973. 1919. 1.50. The Century Co.
Nixon Recession Caper. Ralph Maloney. LC 70-173630. 1972. 5.95 (ISBN 0-393-08666-6). Norton.
Nix's Mate: An Historical Romance of America. Rufus Dawes. LC 29-25303. 1839 S. Colman.
Nizra, the Flower of the Parsa, the Visit of the Wisemen. Andrew Francis Klarmann. LC 8-30017. 1908. B. Herder.
Njal's Saga. Carl Frank Bayerschmidt & Lee Milton Hollander. LC 79-10657. 1979. 29.25. Greenwood Press.
No. Rose Terry Cooke. LC 11-10505. 1886. Phillips & Hunt.
No Acting Please. Eric Morris & Joan Hotchkis. 1979. pap. 6.95 (ISBN 0-8256-3150-5, Quick Fox). Putnam Pub Group.
No Adam in Eden. Grace Metalious. LC 63-18547. 1963. Trident Press.
No Americans Wanted. Sam Mims. 1969. 3.00. Claitors.
No Angels for Me: A Novel of Suspense. William Ard. LC 54-3333. (Popular library. 591). 1954. Popular Library.
No Angels in Heaven. Jesse Lenard Lasky. LC 38-3527. The Macaulay Company.
No Appointment in Heaven. Nicholas Arevalos. LC 57-10641. (Milestone book). 1957. Comet Press Books.
No Armour Against Fate... Margaret Bass Pedler. LC 38-37581. 1938. Doubleday, Doran & Company, Inc.
No Arms, No Armour. Robert David Quixano Henriques. LC 39-29453. Farrar & Rinehart, Inc.
No Bail for Dalton. Miriam Borgenicht. LC 73-10705. (Black bat mystery). 1974. 5.95 (ISBN 0-672-51881-3). Bobbs-Merrill.
No Bail for the Judge. Henry Cecil. LC 53-5374. 1953. Harper.
No Beast So Fierce. Edward Bunker. 192p. 1975. pap. 1.50 (ISBN 0-532-15146-1). Woodhill.
No Beast So Fierce: A Novel. Edward Bunker. LC 72-3281. 1972. (ISBN 0-393-08454-X). Norton.
No Beast So Fierce: A Novel About the Underground. Edward Bunker. LC 72-3281. 283p. 1973. 6.95 o.p. (ISBN 0-393-08454-X). Norton.
No Beast So Fierce: By Charles Rushton Pseud. Shortt, Charles Rushton. LC 58-7549. 1958. Roy Publishers.
No Beautiful Nights. Vasillii Semenovich Grossman & Donnelly, Elizabeth, Tr. LC 44-5521. 1944. J. Messner, Inc.
No Bed in Deseret. Juanita B. Anderson & Nickolae Gerstner. 352p. (Orig.). 1981. pap. 2.75 (ISBN 0-441-58863-8). Ace Bks.
No Bed of Her Own. Val Lewton. LC 48-10780. 1948. Triangle Books.
No Bed of Her Own. Val Lewton. LC 32-3289. 1932. The Vanguard Press.
No Bed of Her Own. Rex Weldon, pseud. (Orig.). pap. 0.95 o.p. (1110). Brandon.
No Bed of Roses. Faith Baldwin. 224p. 1980. pap. 2.50 (ISBN 0-671-83096-1). PB.
No Bed of Roses. Faith Baldwin. LC 72-91591. 224p. 1973. 6.95 o.p. (ISBN 0-03-007681-1). HR&W.
No Bed of Roses. Faith Baldwin Cuthrell. LC 72-91591. 1973. 6.95 (ISBN 0-03-007681-1). Holt, Rinehart and Winston.
No Bed of Roses: The Diary of a Lost Soul. Marjorie Erskine Smith. LC 30-198335. The Macaulay Company.
No Benefit of Law: A Western Novel. Arthur Henry Gooden. LC 49-9457. 1949. Macrae-Smith-Co.
No Better Fiend. Kenneth Giles. LC 71-142844. 1971. 4.95 (ISBN 0-8027-5224-1). Walker.
No Better Fiend. Edmund McGirr. 1971. 4.95 o.p. (ISBN 0-8027-5224-1). Walker & Co.
No Better Land. Laban C. Smith. LC 46-4286. 1946. The Macmillan Company.
No Better World. Irving A. Greenfield. LC 82-82117. 304p. 1982. pap. 2.95 (ISBN 0-86721-219-5). Playboy Pbks.
No Birds Sang. John Buxton Hilton. LC 75-18720. 1976. 7.95. St. Martin's Press.
No Blade of Grass: A Novel. John Christopher. LC 57-5674. 1957. Simon and Schuster.
No Blade of Grass: John Christopher. John Christopher. 1980. 1.95 (ISBN 0-380-48009-3). Avon Books.
No Blond Is an Island. Alan Geoffrey Yates. LC 65-2792. (Signet book). 1965. New American Library of World Literature.
No Bones About It. Joan Margaret Fleming. LC 67-22396. 1967. I. Washburn.
No Bones About It... Ruth Otis Sawtell Wallis. LC 44-6436. 1944. Dodd, Mead & Company.
No Bones About It. Ruth Otis Sawtell Wallis. LC 47-6112. (Bantam books, 72). 1946.
No Borderland: A Novel. Martha Marlow Morris & Speer, Mrs. Laura Belle (Napier) 1883- Joint Author. LC 39-152801. Mathis, Van Nort & Co.
No Boundaries: By Henry Kuttner and C. L. Moore. Henry Kuttner & Catherine L. Moore. LC 55-12406. 1955. Ballantine Books.
No Boundary Line. Esther Birdsall Darling. LC 42-137340. 1942. Wm. Penn Publishing Corp.
No Bride Price. David Rubadiri. 1967. pap. 2.00 o.p. (Pub. by East African Publ Hse). Northwestern U Pr.
No Brighter Dawn. Vera Murdock Stuart Jervis. LC 43-558272. 1943. Arcadia House, Inc.
No Brighter Glory: By Armstrong Sperry. Armstrong Sperry. LC 42-21515. 1942. The Macmillan Company.
No Brother, No Friend. Richard C Meredith. LC 75-38167. (Doubleday science fiction). 1976. 5.95 (ISBN 0-385-11109-6). Doubleday.
No Brother, No Friend. Richard Meridith. LC 75-38167. 192p. 1976. 6.95 o.p. (ISBN 0-385-11109-6). Doubleday.
No Bugle Call. Charles A McCarthy. LC 45-22126. 1945. The Hobson Book Press.
No Bugles, No Drums. Charles Durden. LC 76-91. 1976. 8.95 (ISBN 0-670-51419-5). Viking Press.
No Bugles, No Drums. Charles Durden. 1978. 1.95 (ISBN 0-441-58320-2). Charter Books.
No Bugles Tonight. Bruce Lancaster. LC 48-362335. 1948. Little, Brown.
No Business Being a Cop. Lillian O'Donnell. LC 78-18341. 8.95. Putnam.
No Business for a Lady. James Lyon Rubel. LC 50-13514. 1950. Fawcett Publications.
No, but I Saw the Movie. 1st Ed. Peter De Vries. LC 52-9777. Little, Brown.
No Case for the Police. Clinton-Baddeley, Victor Clinton. LC 77-120611. 1970. 4.95. W. Morrow.
No Case for the Police. Victor Clinton Clinton-Baddeley. (Murder Ink Mystery Ser.: No. 35). 1982. pap. 2.25 (ISBN 0-440-16424-9). Dell.
No Castanets: By Caryl Brahms Pseud. Doris Caroline Abrahams. LC 63-9335. 1963. Macmillan.
No Castle of Dreams. Marjorie McEvoy. 1977. pap. 1.25 (ISBN 0-532-12500-2). Woodhill.
No Castles in Spain. William McFee. LC 33-273333. 1933. Doubleday, Doran & Company, Inc.
No Certain Answer. Aubrey Toulmin Carney. LC 47-30900. 1947. Harper.
No Church. Frederick William Robinson. LC 75-499. (Victorian Fiction: Novels of Faith and Doubt; V. 50). 1975. 35.00 (ISBN 0-8240-1574-6). Garland Pub.
No Clouds of Glory. Marian Engel. LC 68-12572. 1968. Harcourt, Brace & World.
No Clue!" A Mystery Story. James Hay. LC 20-157031. 1920. Dodd, Mead and Company.
No Coffin for the Corpse. Clayton Rawson. LC 42-17219. 1942. Little, Brown and Company.
No Coffin for the Corpse. Clayton Rawson. LC 79-11594. (Gregg Press Mystery Fiction Series). 1979. 9.95 (ISBN 0-8398-2545-5). Gregg Press.
No Comebacks. large print ed. Frederick Forsyth. LC 82-13988. 1983. 13.95 (ISBN 0-89340-535-3). J. Curley.
No Comebacks: Collected Short Stories. Frederick Forsyth. LC 81-71238. 1982. 12.95 (ISBN 0-670-51420-9). Viking Press.
No Comment. Vahan Shirvanian. 288p. (Orig.). 1982. pap. 2.50 (ISBN 0-523-49005-4). Pinnacle Bks.
No Comment: A Novel. 1st Ed. John Rogers Shuman. LC 56-12504. 1956. Pageant Press.
No Common Glory. David Pilgrim, pseud. LC 42-912461. Harper & Brothers.
No Costumes or Masks. Grace Freeman. (Red Clay Reader: Vol. 10, No. 1). 1975. pap. 2.95 o.p. Red Clay.
No Country for Old Men. Warren Eyster. LC 54-5965. 1955. Random House.
No Country for Old Men. Alan Schwartz. LC 80-15496. 9.95 (ISBN 0-453-00390-7). New American Library.
No Country Without Grandfathers. Roch Carrier. Tr. by Sheila Fischman from Fr. (Anansi Fiction Ser.: No. 45). Orig. Title: Il NY a Pas De Pays Sans Grand-Pere. 156p. (Orig.). 1981. pap. 8.95 (ISBN 0-88784-090-6, Pub. by Hse Anansi Pr Canada). U of Toronto Pr.
No Crime for a Lady. Zelda Popkin. LC 42-193521. 1942. J. B. Lippincott Company.
No Crime Like the Present. Audrey Gaines. LC 52-11388. 1952. Arcadia House.
No Cure for Death. Max Collins. 192p. 1983. 12.95 (ISBN 0-8027-5488-0). Walker & Co.
No Darkness for Love. Barbara Cartland. LC 74-9965. 1974. (lib. bdg.) 10.95 (ISBN 0-8161-6229-8). G. K. Hall.
No Darkness for Love. Barbara Cartland. (Bantam Barbara Cartland Library, 2). 1974. (pbk.) 0.95. Bantam Books.
No Deadly Drug. James Kerr. LC 73-146088. 1972. 6.95. Coward, McCann & Geoghegan.
No Dearth of Horses. Carl L. Wagner. 1971. 6.95 o.p. (ISBN 0-87799-013-1). Haessner Lit Serv.
No Defence. Gilbert Parker. LC 20-17085. J. B. Lippincott Company.
No Deposit, No Return. Mary Patterson. (Orig.). 1973. pap. 1.25 o.p. Curtis.
No Desire Too Strange. H. R. Kaye, pseud. 1968. pap. 1.95 o.p. (6013). Brandon.
No Diamonds for a Doll. Peter Cagney. LC 61-129279. 1961. Roy Publishers.
No-Din: Romance, History and Science of the Preshistoric Races of America and Other Lands... Erastus S Curry. LC 582. 1899. The Author.
No Direction Home: An Anthology of Science-Fiction Stories. Norman Spinard. 1975. (pbk.) 1.25. Pocket Books.
No Direction Home: An Anthology of Science Fiction Stories. Norman Spinrad. LC 77-355891. 1976. 3.50 (ISBN 0-86000-054-0). Millington.
No Doubt Mad Idea. Stephen Minkin. LC 78-23602. 4.95 (ISBN 0-931272-00-9). Ross/Back Roads Books.
No Down Payment. John McPartland. LC 57-12411. 1957. Simon and Schuster.
No Dowry for Jennifer. Maysie Greig. LC 57-12681. 1957. Avalon Books.
No Dust in the Attic. Anthony Gilbert, pseud. 192p. 1973. Repr. of 1963 ed. 5.95 o.s.i. (ISBN 0-85617-540-4). White Lion Pubs.
No Dust in the Attic. Lucy Beatrice Malleson. LC 73-153554. 1971. 5.95 (ISBN 0-85617-540-4). White Lion.
No Earth for Foxes. Manning O'Brine. 1976. 1.75. Dell.
No Earth for Foxes: A Novel. Manning O'Brine. LC 74-17138. 1975. 6.95 (ISBN 0-440-06208-X). Delacorte Press.
No Earthly Shore. Francine Mezo. LC 80-68425. 2.50 (ISBN 0-380-77347-3). Avon Books.
No Easter for East Germany? Alvin C Currier. LC 68-13424. 1968. Augsburg Pub. House.
No Easy Answers. Carolyn G Hart. LC 74-122819. (Illus.). 1970. 4.95. M. Evans; Distributed in Association with Lippincott, Philadelphia.
No Easy Way Out. Elaine R. Chase. (Candlelight Ecstasy Ser.: No. 100). (Orig.). 1982. pap. 1.95 (ISBN 0-440-16119-3). Dell.
No End of Blame. Howard Barker. 1981. pap. 7.95 (ISBN 0-7145-3912-0). Riverrun NY.
No End of Nonsense. W. Blecher. (O.s.i.). 1968. 3.95g o.s.i. (ISBN 0-02-710900-3). Macmillan.
No End to the Way. Neville Jackson, pseud. (O.s.i.). 1969. pap. 0.75 o.s.i. (532-75259-075). Manor Bks.
No End to Yesterday. Shelagh Macdonald. LC 77-368272. 1979. 6.50 (ISBN 0-233-96865-2). Deutsch.
No Enemy (but Himself) Elbert Hubbard. LC 7-5663. 1894. G. P. Putnam's Sons.
No Enemy but Time. Evelyn Wilde Mayerson. LC 82-45260. 1983. 15.95 (ISBN 0-385-17966-9). Doubleday.
No Enemy but Time: A Novel. Michael Bishop. LC 81-18534. 16.95 (ISBN 0-671-83576-9). Timescape: Distributed by Simon and Schuster.
No Enemy but Winter. Sarah Prinsep. LC 63-24171. 1963. R. Hale.
No Enemy but Winter: A Novel. Richard Allen. LC 72-84315. 1972. 6.95 (ISBN 0-517-50057-4). Crown.
No Errant Winds. Eliza Willets. LC 31-324129. Sears Publishing Company, Inc.
No Escape: A Novel. Joseph Arnold Hayes. LC 81-12470. 14.95 (ISBN 0-440-06438-4). Delacorte Press.
No Escape: By Josephine Bell. Pseud. 1st Amer. Ed. Doris Bell Collier Ball. LC 66-123461. (Cock Robin mystery). 1966. bds., 3.95. Macmillan.
No Escape from Brooklyn. Hanan J. Ayalti. 1966. 3.95 o.p. Twayne.
No Escape from Brooklyn: A Novel. Tr. from Yiddish by Jacob Sloan, Jackson Mac Low. Hanan J. Ayalti. LC 66-16110. 3.95. Twayne.
No Escape from Love. Barbara Cartland. LC 77-21225. 1977. 6.95 (ISBN 0-87272-029-2, Duron Bks.). Brodart.
No Evil Angel. Elizabeth Linington. LC 64-25133. 1964. Harper & Row.
No Evil Angel. Elisabeth Ogilvie. LC 56-110536. 1956. McGraw-Hill.
No Face in the Mirror. Hugh McLeave. LC 80-7566. 1980. 9.95 (ISBN 0-8027-5421-X). Walker.
No Face to Murder. Edith Howie. LC 46-872. 1946. M. S. Mill Co.
No Farewell: A Novel. Gerda Lerner. LC 55-937414. 1955. Associated Authors.
No Fatherland. Hans Hellmut Kirst. LC 76-113529. 1970. 5.95. Coward-McCann.
No Fiction: Or, The Test of Friendship: a Narrative Founded on Recent and Interesting Facts. 2d genuine ed., from the 5th london ed., with additions. ed. Andrew B. A. Reed. LC 49-39801. 1821. W. Turner.
No Fiction: Or, The Test of Friendship: a Narrative Founded on Recent and Interesting Facts... Andrew B. A. Reed. LC 7-4672. 1821. W. Turner.
No Fire Can Warm Me. Margaret P. Gaddis. 1970. pap. 0.75 o.p. (ISBN 0-447-74704-5). Lancer.
No Flowers for a Clown. Stanley Noyes. LC 61-810956. 1961. Macmillan.
No Fond Return of Love. Barbara Pym. 250p. 1983. 12.95 (ISBN 0-525-24145-0, 01258-370). Dutton.
No Footprints in the Bush. Arthur William Upfield. LC 44-9573. 1944. Pub. for the Crime Club by Doubleday, Doran and Company, Inc.
No Fraternization: A Novel. Linda Marie Hubner. LC 51-4870. 1951. Exposition Press.
No Fresh Air. Peter Shelley, pseud. LC 37-328369. 1937. Godwin.
No Friend Like a Sister. Rosa Nouchette Carey. LC 6-32855. 1906. J. B. Lippincott Company.
No Friendly Drop. Henry Lancelot Aubrey-Fletcher. LC 32-7342. 1932. Brewer, Warren & Putnam.
No Friendly Drop: By Henry Wade Pseud. Henry Lancelot Aubrey-Fletcher. LC 57-6358. (Murder revisited mystery novel, no. 17). 1957. Macmillan.
No Friendly Drop by Henry Wade Pseud. Henry Lancelot Aubrey-Fletcher. LC 57-6358. (Murder revisited mystery novel, no. 17). 1957. Macmillan.

No Future for Luana: A Judge Peck Mystery. August William Derleth. LC 45-3111. 1945. C. Scribner's Sons.

No Future in It. John Brunner. 1969. pap. 0.75 o.p. (0502-07008-075). Curtis.

No Future, No Memory. Richard O'Brien. (Jazz Age Ser.: No. 1). 1982. pap. 2.95 (ISBN 0-440-06564-X). Dell.

No Gentle Love. Rebecca Brandewyne. 592p. (Orig.). 1983. pap. 3.95 (ISBN 0-446-30619-3). Warner Bks.

No Gentle Streets. Charles W. Sasser. LC 78-31638. 1983. 16.95 (ISBN 0-87949-166-3). Ashley Bks.

No Gentlemen,". Clara Louise Root Burnham. LC 16-6998. Houghton Mifflin Company.

No Gifts from Chance. Margaret Bass Pedler. LC 44-9913.

No Girls Allowed & Other Stories. Reinold Shubert. 2.50 o.p. Vantage.

No Gloves for the Groom. Flora F. T Bryant. LC 68-22633. 1969. 5.95. Doubleday.

No Gloves for the Groom. Peregrine Pace. LC 68-22633. 1968. 5.95 o.p. Doubleday.

No God in Saguaro. Lewis B Patten. LC 66-12226. (Double D western). 3.50. Doubleday.

No Good-Byes. Adela R. St. Johns. 1982. pap. 3.50 (ISBN 0-451-11740-9, AE1740, Sig). NAL.

No Good from a Corpse... Leigh Brackett. LC 45-3496. (Handi-book mysteries. 32).

No Goodness in the Worm. Gay Taylor. LC 30-32845. Harcourt, Brace and Company.

No Goose So Gray: A Short Story. Geddes Magrane. LC 50-6129. 1950. Writers' Fund.

No Grave for March. M. E. Chaber, pseud. (Milo March). 1970. pap. 0.60 o.p. (63-440). Paperback Lib.

No Grave for March: A Novel of Suspense, by M. E. Chaber Pseud. 1st Ed. Kendell Foster Crossen. LC 52-11041. 1953. Holt.

No Graven Image: A Novel. Elisabeth Elliot. (S321). 1968. Avon.

No Graven Image: A Novel. Elisabeth Elliot. LC 66-11487. 1966. Harper & Row.

No Greater Challenge. 1st Ed. Rose Talbot. LC 55-10850. 1955. Vantage Press.

No Greater Fury. Lila Thomson. 1978. pap. 2.25 (ISBN 0-532-22133-8). Woodhill.

No Greater Love. Patricia Gallagher. 1979. pap. 2.50 (ISBN 0-380-44743-6, 44743). Avon.

No Greater Love. Mary Arleville Lobdell Palmer. LC 61-13248. 1961. Dorrance.

No Greater Love: A Romance. Lola Verrill Cintron. LC 77-2260. 11.95 (ISBN 0-679-50637-3). McKay.

No Ground see No hay Lugar.

No-Gun Fighter. Nelson Coral Nye. LC 81-17517. 11.95 (ISBN 0-89340-379-2). J. Curley & Associates.

No-Gun Nelson. Tony Adams. LC 39-25884. Phoenix Press.

No Haloes for Hoods. Craig Cooper. LC 73-78300. 1969. 3.95. Roy Publishers.

No Handicap: A Novel. Marion Ames Taggart. LC 22-21321. 1922. Benziger Brothers.

No Hands on the Clock. Daniel Mainwaring. LC 39-152654. 1939. W. Morrow & Co.

No Harm in One. Lawrence Nelson. LC 37-542. 1937. Godwin.

No hay Lugar. Evelyn Carter. Ed. by Andy Carrodeguas & Esteban Marosi. Tr. by Virginia A. De Lobo. Orig. Title: No Ground. 182p. (Span.). 1981. pap. 2.25 (ISBN 0-8297-1142-2). Life Pubs Intl.

No Head for Her Pillow. Taylor, Sam S. LC 52-5286. (Guilt edged mystery). 1952. Dutton.

No Heart Is Free. Barbara Cartland. (Romance Ser.: No. 42). 1975. pap. 1.25 o.p. (ISBN 0-515-03830-X, V3830). BJ Pub Group.

No Hearts to Break. Susan Ertz. LC 37-286611. 1937. D. Appleton-Century Company, Incorporated.

No Heaven for Gunga Din: Consisting of the British and American Officers' Book. Ali Mirdrekvandi. LC 65-23748. 1965. Dutton.

No Hero. Ernest William Hornung. LC 3-9337. 1903. C. Scribner's Sons.

No Hero. John Phillips Marquand. LC 35-11490. 1935. Little, Brown, and Company.

No Hero--This. Warwick Deeping. LC 36-27489. 1936. A. A. Knopf.

No Hiding Place. Elinore Denniston. LC 69-17602. (Red badge mystery). 1969. 3.95. Dodd, Mead.

No Hiding Place. Rae Foley. (Red Badge Mystery Ser). 1969. 3.95 o.p. (ISBN 0-396-05877-9). Dodd.

No Hiding Place. Terry Morris. LC 45-53501. 1945. A. A. Knopf.

No Hiding Place. 1st Ed. Edwin Moultrie Lanham. LC 62-14465. Harcourt, Brace & World.

No Highway. Nevil Shute Norway. LC 48-3534. 1948. W. Morrow.

No Highway. Nevil Shute. (O.s.i.). 1977. pap. 1.95 o.s.i. (AY1653, Award). Univ Pub & Dist.

No Holds Barred. Barry Devlin. LC 54-407648. 1954. Vixen Press.

No Holiday for Crime. Elizabeth Linington. LC 72-13048. 1973. 5.95 (ISBN 0-688-00145-9). Morrow.

No Holiday for Crime. Dell Shannon. 1973. 5.95 o.p. (ISBN 0-688-00145-9). Morrow.

No Holiday for Death. Lee Thayer, pseud. LC 54-566457. (Red badge detective). 1954. Dodd, Mead.

No Holly for Miss Quinn. LC 76-17327. (Illus.). 1976. 6.95 (ISBN 0-395-24768-3). Houghton Mifflin.

No Holly for Miss Quinn. Read. 1976. 6.95 (ISBN 0-395-24768-3). HM.

No Homeward Course. Walter Havighurst. LC 41-390514. 1941. Doubleday, Doran & Co., Inc.

No Honour Amongst Spies. H. T Rothwell. LC 69-15421. 1969. 3.95. Roy Publishers.

No Hour of History: A Novel. Elizabeth Ford. LC 40-31874. I. Washburn.

No House of Peace. Elizabeth Connor. LC 37-27457. 1937. D. Appleton Century Company, Incorporated.

No, I'm Not Tired. Playboy Press Editors. LC 72-90423. pap. 1.25 o.p. (ISBN 0-87216-200-1, B16200). Playboy.

No! in Thunder. Lester A. Fiedler. LC 72-82146. 1972. pap. 4.95 (ISBN 0-8128-1480-0). Stein & Day.

No Intentions,". Florence Marryat Church Lean. (On cover: Lovell's library. v. 19. no. 907). 1887. J. W. Lovell Company.

No, John, No. 1st Amer. Ed. Cressida Lindsay. LC 67-16519. 1967. 4.50. Potter.

No King but Caesar. Anne Powers. 1974. (pbk.) 1.25 (ISBN 0-523-00337-4). Pinnacle Books.

No King but Caesar. 1st Ed. Anne Powers, pseud. LC 60-16847. 1960. Doubleday.

No Known Grave. Evelyn Berckman. LC 58-10768. (Red badge detective). 1958. Dodd, Mead.

No Lady, This see Duke's Mistress.

No Laggards We. Ross Raymond. LC 7-36636. 1881. G. W. Harlan.

No Land Is Free. Joseph Chadwick. LC 61-5961. (Double D western). 1961. Doubleday.

No Land Is Free. William Thomas Person. LC 47-490. 1946. The Westminster Press.

No Laughing Matter. Angus Wilson. LC 67-26185. 1967. Viking Press.

No Leave for the Captain. Translated from the Danish by Mervyn Savill. Gerhard Rasmussen. 1958. Crowell.

No Less. Cid Corman, pseud. 1968. pap. 4.00 (Pub. by Elizabeth Pr). SBD.

No Letters for the Dead. Gale Wilhelm. LC 36-17705. Random House.

No Life So Happy. Edwin Lewis Peterson. LC 40-5566. 1940. Dodd, Mead & Company.

No Light Came on. Alice Ormond Campbell. LC 45-3351. 1945. C. Scirbner's Sons.

No Little Enemy. Oliver Weld Bayer, pseud. LC 44-3885. 1944. Pub. for the Crime Club by Doubleday, Doran & Co., Inc.

No Longer at Ease. Chinua Achebe. LC 61-7356. 1961. I. Obolensky.

No Longer Fugitive. Ann Chidester. LC 43-13078. 1943. C. Scribner's Sons.

No Longer Human. Osamu Dazai. LC 56-13350. (New Direction paperbook, NDP357). 1973. (pbk.) 2.25 (ISBN 0-8112-0481-2). New Directions.

No Love. David Garnett. LC 29-12060. 1929. A. A. Knopf.

No Love Denied. John Meehan. pap. 0.95 o.p. (1158). Brandon.

No Love for Johnnie. Wilfred Fienburgh. LC 59-10613. 1959. Harper.

No Love Lost. Margery Allingham. 176p. 1975. pap. 1.50 (ISBN 0-532-15309-X). Woodhill.

No Love Lost. Margery Allingham. 1971. pap. 0.75 o.p. (75-428). Manor Bks.

No Love Lost. 4th ed. Margery Allingham. 176p. 1974. pap. 0.95 o.p. (532-95314-095). Manor Bks.

No Love Lost. Robert Reeves. LC 41-115023. H. Holt and Company.

No Love Lost. Helen Van Slyke. LC 79-26056. 10.95 (ISBN 0-690-01897-5). Lippincott & Crowell.

No Love Lost: Two Stories of Suspense The Patient at Peacocks Hall and Safer Than Love. 1st Ed. Margery Allingham. LC 54-7842. 1954. Published for the Crime Club by Doubleday.

No Love Without Sorrow. Translated by Charlotte Lord. 1st Ed. Amabile Ranucci. LC 54-13216. 1954. Pageant Press.

No Lovelier Spring. Lida Larrimore Thomas. LC 35-135454. 1935. Macrae Smith Company.

No Mama No. Verity Bargate. LC 78-2174. 7.95 (ISBN 0-06-010229-2). Harper & Row.

No Man Alone. Edwin L Mayer. LC 48-11713. 1948. Boni and Gaer.

No Man Her Age. Vida Hurst. LC 34-25938. Grosset & Dunlap.

No Man in Eden. Harold Lawrence Myra. LC 68-56989. 1969. 4.95. Word Books.

No Man Is an Island. Johannes Mario Simmel. 512p. 1982. pap. 3.25 (ISBN 0-445-04699-6). Popular Lib.

No Man Is Single. Stuart Hawkins. LC 34-29901. 1934. Houghton Mifflin Company.

No Man of Her Own. Violet Winspear. (Harlequin Presents Ser.). 192p. 1982. pap. 1.75 (ISBN 0-373-10492-8). PB.

No Man Sings: A Novel by Alexander Krislov Pseud. Leigh Howard, pseud. LC 56-36366. 1956. Longmans, Green.

No Man Tells Everything: Edited by Pat Duggan. 1st Ed. Libbie Block. LC 59-9778. 1959. Doubleday.

No Man's Child. Elizabeth Nicol Hutton. LC 31-9389. Wetzel Publishing Co., Inc.

No Man's Friend. A Novel. Frederick William Robinson. (seaside library, v. 65, no. 1325). 1882. G. Munro.

No Man's Land. Herman Cyril McNeile. LC 17-22291. 1917. Hodder and Stoughton.

No Man's Land. Herman Cyril McNeile. LC 17-23333. George H. Doran Company.

No Man's Land: A Romance. Louis Joseph Vance. LC 10-23316. 1910. Dodd, Mead and Company.

No Man's Son. Doris Sutcliffe Adams. LC 70-87070. 1969. 4.95. Walker.

No Man's Street. 1st American Ed. Beverley Nichols. LC 54-109142. (Guilt edged mystery). 1954. Dutton.

No Man's Time: A Novel, by V. S. Yanovsky. Tr. from Russian by Isabella Levitin,Roger Nyle Parris. With a Foreword by W. H. Auden. Basile S. Yanovsky. LC 67-20366. 1967. 5.00. Weybright &Talley.

No Man's Woman. Aubrey Boyd. LC 31-22589. E. P. Dutton & Company, Inc.

No Man's World: A Novel. Martin Caidin. LC 67-10065. 1967. Dutton.

No Marks for Trying. Stella Allan. 208p. (Orig.). 1982. pap. 2.25 (ISBN 0-380-57836-0, 57836). Avon.

No Marriage in Paradise. Myron Brinig. LC 48-973623. 1949. Rinehart.

No Match for Murder. Jean Francis Webb. LC 42-2429. 1942. The Macmillan Company.

No Matter Where. Arthur Cheney Train. LC 33-211282. 1933. C. Scribner's Sons.

No Matter Where You Travel, You Still Be Black. Houston A. Baker, Jr. LC 78-61608. 58p. 1979. pap. 3.00 perfect bdg. (ISBN 0-916418-18-9). Lotus.

No Mean City: A Story of the Glasgow Slums. Alexander McArthur & Long, H. Kingsley, Joint Author. LC 37-884. 1936. Longmans, Green and Co.

No Measure Danced. Harry Lee. LC 41-11194. 1941. The Macmillan Company.

No Medium: A Novel. Annie Hall Thomas Cudlip. (Harper's handy ser. no. 20). 1885. Harper & Brothers.

No Medium. A Novel. Annie Hall Thomas Cudlip. (On cover: Seaside library. Pocket ed. no. 565). 1885. G. Munro.

No Mind of Man. Carr et al. 1976. pap. 1.50 (ISBN 0-532-15220-4). Woodhill.

No Mind of Man. Ed. by Robert Silverberg. 224p. 1973. 5.95 o.p. Hawthorn.

No Mind of Man: Three Original Novellas of Science Fiction. Terry Carr & Richard A. Lupoff. LC 73-334. 1973. 5.95. Hawthorn Books.

No Minor Vices. Edmund S Whitman. A. & C. Boni, Inc.

No. Mr. Brown. Gertrude Knevels. LC 38-601830. The Penn Publishing Company.

No Money: An Odd Fellows' Story. James H Kinkead. 1876. J. H. Kinkead & Co.

No Moon but This. Helen Partridge. LC 35-82169. Arcadia House.

No Moon Last Summer, Bk. 1. Joyce McKennon. (Orig.). 1979. pap. 1.75 (ISBN 0-532-23234-8). Woodhill.

No Moon Last Summer, Bk. 2. Joyce McKennon. (Orig.). 1979. pap. 1.95. Woodhill.

No More. Cid Corman, pseud. 1969. pap. 4.00 (Pub. by Elizabeth Pr). SBD.

No More a Corpse: An Astounding Story. George Frank Worts. LC 32-16107. A. H. King, Inc.

No More a-Roving. Simon Troy. 1977. 6.20 o.p. State Mutual Bk.

No More Bugles in the Sky. Richard L Newhafer. LC 66-22216. 5.95. New Amer. Lib.

No More Candy: A Novel. Patricia Aks. 1.50 (ISBN 0-448-16491-4). Tempo Books.

No More Dreams. William Jeremiah Coughlin. LC 81-70461. 13.95 (ISBN 0-89479-105-2). A & W Publishers.

No More Dying Then. Ruth Rendell. LC 72-175396. 1972. 4.95 (ISBN 0-385-00575-X). Published for the Crime Club by Doubleday.

No More Dying Then. Ruth Rendell. 1974. (pbk.) 0.95. Bantam Books.

No More Gas. Charles Bernard Nordhoff & Hall, James Norman. LC 40-270518. 1940. Little, Brown and Company.

No More into the Garden: The Chronicles of Davey Bryant. David Watmough. LC 78-320711. 1978. 7.95 (ISBN 0-385-13452-5). Doubleday Canada.

No More Monday Mornings. C. P Crow. LC 79-23243. 1980. 10.95 (ISBN 0-670-51438-1). Viking Press.

No More, No Less. Harriet Henry, pseud. 1938. E. P. Dutton and Company, Inc.

No More Orchids. Grace Perkins Oursler. LC 32-19496. Covici, Friede.

No More Parades: A Novel. Ford Madox Ford. 1979. Repr. of 1925 ed. lib. bdg. 25.00 (ISBN 0-8495-1646-3). Arden Lib.

No More Parades!: A Novel. Ford Madox Ford. LC 25-233722. A. & C. Boni.

No More Remains. Leonard Oswald Mosley. LC 37-15350. 1937. Doubleday, Doran & Company, Inc.

No More Reunions. John Bowers. LC 72-94688. 1973. 6.50 (ISBN 0-525-16805-2). Dutton.

No More Sea. Wilson Follett. LC 33-805684. H. Holt and Company.

No More Septembers. Maurade Glennon. LC 68-14199. 1968. 4.95. Doubleday.

No More Than a Mustard Seed. Carol Greene. 1980. pap. 0.89 (ISBN 0-570-06134-2, 59-1252, Arch Bk). Concordia.

No More Than Human: A Novel. Maura Laverty. LC 44-40208. 1944. Longmans, Green and Co.

No More Tomorrow: A Novel. John Sonntag. LC 52-6100. 1952. Exposition Press.

No More Trains to Tottenville. Hope Campbell. LC 70-154245. 1971. 5.95 o.p. (ISBN 0-8415-0115-7). Sat Rev Pr.

No More Trains to Tottenville: A Novel. Geraldine Wallis. LC 70-154245. 1971. 5.95 (ISBN 0-8415-0115-7). McCall Pub. Co.

No More Trumpets, and Other Stories. George Milburn. LC 79-134968. (Short stories index reprint series). 1970. Books for Libraries Press.

No More Trumpets: And Other Stories. George Milburn. LC 33-24350. Harcourt, Brace and Company.

No More with Me. Russell Morsby La Due. LC 47-2414. 1947. Doubleday & Company, Inc.

No Mortal Fire. Elsa Valentine. LC 44-4959. 1944. Simon and Schuster.

No Mother to Guide Her. 1st Ed. Anita Loos. LC 61-10468. 1961. McGraw-Hill.

No Motive for Murder. William Earl Johns. LC 58-138415. (Chantecler mystery novel). 1959. Washburn.

No Mourning for the Matador. Delano L Ames. LC 53-11355. 1953. I. Washburn.

No Murder of Mine. Alice Ormond Campbell. LC 41-361051. 1941. C. Scribner's Sons.

No Music for Generals. Frederick James Howard. LC 51-6443. 1951. Wingate.

No Music for Generals: A Novel. Frederick James Howard. LC 51-10406. 1951. Duell, Sloan and Pearce.

No, My Darling Daughter. Sally Newman. LC 74-15883. 1975. 6.95 (ISBN 0-06-013179-9). Harper & Row.

No Name. Wilkie Collins. LC 66-24803. (Doughty library no. 2). 1967. Stein and Day.

No Name. A Novel. Wilkie Collins. LC 3-27276. Harper & Brothers.

No Name. A Novel. Wilkie Collins. LC 16-7540. (On verso of t.-p.: Harper's illustrated library edition). 1874.

No Name: A Novel. Wilkie Collins. LC 12-232528. 1911. Harper & Brothers.

No Name in the Street. James B. Baldwin. (O.s.i.). 216p. 1972. 6.95 o.s.i. (ISBN 0-8037-6451-0). Dial.

No Name in the Street. Kay Cicellis. Grove Press.

No-Nation Girl. Evans Wall. LC 29-21542. The Century Co.

No Need for Fear. Amanda McAllister. LC 76-14024. 1.50. Playboy Press.

No Need of Glory: A Novel. Helen Tucker. LC 72-80346. 1972. 6.95 (ISBN 0-8128-1510-6). Stein and Day.

No Need of Sun. Ruth Strahm Hoien. LC 51-34002. 1951. West Pub. Co.

No New Thing. William Edward Norris. (On cover: Lovell's library, no. 108). 1883. J. W. Lovell Company.

No New Thing. A Novel. William Edward Norris. (Harper's Franklin square library, no. 309). 1883. Harper & Brothers.

No New Thing: A Novel. William Edward Norris. (Leisure hour series, no. 148). 1883. H. Holt and Company.

No News from Helen. Louis Golding. LC 44-4919. 1943. Hutchinson & Co., Ltd.

No News from Helen. Louis Golding. LC 43-513408. 1943. Dial Press.

No News on Monday. Richard Clapperton. Orig. Title: Your're a Long Time Dead. 1970. pap. 0.95 o.p. (95011). Beagle Bks.

No Nice Girl. Peggy Gaddis, pseud. LC 46-6981. 1946. Phoenix Press.

No Night Without Stars. Andre Norton, pseud. 1978. pap. 1.75 (ISBN 0-449-23264-6, Crest). Fawcett.

No-No Boy. John Okada. LC 79-55834. 176p. 1980. pap. 6.95 (ISBN 0-295-95525-2). U of Wash Pr.
No-No Boy: A Novel. 1st Ed. John Okada. LC 57-8791. 1957. C. E. Tuttle Co.
No! No! The Woman! Norman Klein. Farrar & Rinehart, Incorporated.
No Nudes Is Good Nudes. Pelham Grenville Wodehouse. LC 73-101887. 1970. 4.95. Simon and Schuster.
No Number Is Greater Than One. David Weiss. LC 70-188729. 1972. 6.95. Coward, McCann & Geoghegan.
No Odds, No Victory. Aubrey Toulmin Carney. LC 51-1292. 1951. Scribner.
No One Bears but Him. Taylor Caldwell. LC 66-122272. 4.95. Doubleday.
No One Goes There Now. William Walling. LC 71-150923. (Doubleday science fiction). 1971. 5.95. Doubleday.
No One Has to Die. Roy Masters. LC 76-20023. 1977. pap. 6.50 (ISBN 0-933900-03-1). Foun Human Under.
No One Hears but Him. Taylor Caldwell. (Crest bk., 11054). 1967. Fawcett.
No One Hears but Him. Taylor Caldwell. LC 66-12227. 1966. Doubleday.
No One Knows My Name. Joyce Harrington. LC 80-14644. 10.95 (ISBN 0-312-57568-8). St. Martin's Press.
No One Man. Rupert Hughes. LC 31-9707. 1931. Harper & Brothers.
No One Now Will Know. Edmee Elizabeth Monica De La Pasture. LC 41-8169. Harper & Brothers.
No One of That Name: A Novel. William Merrick. LC 64-15306. 1964. Holt, Rinehart and Winston.
No One Was Killed: Convention Week, Chicago, August, 1968. John Schultz. (Big Table Book Ser). (Illus.). 1969. 4.95 o.p. (ISBN 0-695-80102-3); pap. 2.95 o.p. (ISBN 0-695-80101-5). Follett.
No One Writes to the Colonel, and Other Stories. Garcia Marquez, Gabriel. LC 68-15977. 1968. 5.95. Harper & Row.
No One Writes to the Colonel and Other Stories. Garcia Marquez, Gabriel. (Harper Colophon Books). 1979. 2.95. Harper & Row.
No One Writes to the Colonel & Other Stories. Gabriel Garcia Marquez. Tr. by J. S. Bernstein from Span. LC 68-15977. 1979. pap. 4.95i (ISBN 0-06-090700-2, CN 700, CN). Har-Row.
No One Writes to the Colonel & Other Stories. Gabriel Garcia Marquez. LC 68-15977. 1968. 9.95i (ISBN 0-06-011417-7, HarpT). Har-Row.
No One's Kindness. George Loveridge. LC 45-5352. 1945. D. Appleton-Century Company Incorporated.
No Orchids for Miss Blandish. James Hadley Chase. LC 42-2946. 1942. Howell, Soskin.
No Orchids for Miss Blandish. James Hadley Chase. LC 42-3946. 1942. Howell, Soskin.
No Ordinary Sun. Hone Tuwhare. 42p. 1964. 5.00x (ISBN 0-582-71687-X). Intl Pubns Serv.
No Other Gods: A Novel of Saskatchewan. Albert H Munday. LC 34-22369. 1934. Meador Publishing Company.
No Other Gods. 1st Ed. Wilder Penfield. LC 54-5114. 1954. Little, Brown.
No Other Harvest. 1st Ed. Richard L Hardman. LC 62-764356. 1962. Doubleday.
No Other Hunger. Frederic Mullally. LC 66-25148. 1966. D. McKay Co.
No Other Love: By Kathleen Harris Pseud. Adelaide Humphries. LC 52-7404. 1952. Arcadia House.
No Other Man. Alfred Noyes. LC 40-12660. 1940. Frederick A. Stokes Company.
No Other Man. Alfred Noyes & Savage, Steele, Illus. LC 40-12660. 1940. Frederick A. Stokes Company.
No Other Star: A Novel. Jane Williams. LC 48-28256. 1948. Conjure House.
No Other Tiger. Alfred Edward Woodley Mason. LC 27-25429. 1927. George H. Doran Company.
No Other Tiger. Alfred Edward Woodley Mason. 1931. Grosset & Dunlap.
No Other Way. Walter Besant. LC 2-22176. 1902. Dodd, Mead and Company.
No Other Way. Louis Tracy. LC 12-20198. E. J. Clode.
No Other Way. Dolf Wyllarde. LC 35-8750. 1935. The Macaulay Company.
No Other Wisdom. Violette Kimball Dunn. LC 40-30303. 1940. E. P. Dutton & Company, Inc.
No Outlet: A Detective Story. Arthur Minturn Chase. LC 40-5398. 1940. Dodd, Mead & Company.
No Parade for Mrs. Greenia. Anne Miller Downes. LC 62-11336. 1962. Lippincott.
No Parking This Side of Heaven: Fourteen Tales. Karin Dovring. 180p. 1982. 10.00 (ISBN 0-8059-2838-3). Dorrance.
No Pasaran! They Shall Not Pass) A Story of the Battle of Madrid. Upton Beall Sinclair. LC 37-5413. The Author.
No Passenger on the River. LC 65-1241. 1965. Vantage Press.
No Past Is Dead. Alfred Walter Stewart. LC 42-15979. 1942. Little, Brown and Company.
No Past, No Present, No Future. Yulisa Amadu Maddy. LC 73-21793. 1974. 9.50 (ISBN 0-87953-016-2). Black Orpheus Press.
No Patent on Murder. Akimitsu Takagi. 1977. 1.50. Playboy Press.
No Pattern for Love. Beryl Williams Epstein. LC 51-2677. (Romance for young moderns). 1951. Messner.
No Pattern for Love. Beryl Williams, pseud. pap. 0.50 o.p. (52-887). Paperback Lib.
No Peace for the Wicked. Peter Chambers, pseud. 1968. 3.75 o.p. Roy.
No Peace for the Wicked. Dennis John Andrew Phillips. LC 68-22660. 1968. Roy Publishers.
No Peace for the Wicked: A Novel. Ursula Torday. LC 37-5984. 1937. T. Nelson & Sons, Limited.
No Peace for the Wicked: By Elizabeth Ferrars. Morna Doris MacTaggart Brown. LC 66-11476. 1966. Harper & Row.
No Phantoms Here. James L. Hodson. 1932. 25.00 (ISBN 0-932062-84-9). Sharon Hill.
No Place for a Duke. Paul Moss. LC 49-109783. 1949. Mathis, Van Nort.
No Place for a Lady. A. Degranamour. pap. 1.95 o.s.i. (Venus). Grove.
No Place for a Woman. Laura Saunders. LC 53-13395. 1953. Avalon Books.
No Place for an Angel: A Novel. Elizabeth Spencer. LC 67-22970. 1967. McGraw-Hill.
No Place for Love. Maynah Lewis. 1974. pap. 0.75 o.p. (26570-075). Beagle Bks.
No Place for Murder. George Harmon Coxe. LC 75-8239. 1975. 6.95 (ISBN 0-394-49768-6). Knopf: Distributed by Random House.
No Place for Murder. George Harmon Coxe. LC 76-10152. 1976. 10.95 (ISBN 0-8161-6380-4). G. K. Hall.
No Place for Women: A Tom Gill Tropical Romance. Tom Gill. LC 46-3065. 1946. G. P. Putnam's Sons.
No Place Like Home. J. Bradford Olesker. LC 75-42355. (Red mask mystery). 6.95 (ISBN 0-399-11628-1). Putnam.
No Place Like Home. J. Bradford Olesker. (Kangaroo Book). 1978. 1.75 (ISBN 0-671-81349-8). Pocket Books.
No Place on Earth. Louis H Charbonneau. LC 66-1618. (Doubleday science fiction). 1966. Doubleday.
No Place on Earth. Christa Wolf. LC 82-7300. 11.95 (ISBN 0-374-22298-3). Farrar, Straus, Giroux.
No Place on Earth. 1st Ed. Louis H Charbonneau. LC 58-11306. 1958. Doubleday.
No Place to Die. Joseph Nazel. (Orig.). 1979. pap. 1.95 (ISBN 0-87067-634-2, BH634). Holloway.
No Place to Hide. Dorothy McKay Martin. 1975. pap. 3.95 (ISBN 0-8024-5939-0). Moody.
No Place to Live. Edward Sidney Aarons. LC 47-12151. (armchair mystery). 1947. D. McKay Co.
No Place to Live. Edward Sidney Aarons. 1971. pap. 0.75 o.p. (75-396). Manor Bks.
No Place to Run,a Novel. Philip Alston Stone. LC 59-8350. 1959. Viking Press.
No Playboy at Heart. 1st Ed. Mark Anthony Belian. LC 55-9807. 1955. CometPress Books.
No Pockets in a Shroud. Horace McCoy. LC 49-217262. (N.A.L. Signet books.). 1948. New American Library.
No Pockets in Shrouds. Louisa Revell. LC 48-6536. 1948. Macmillan Co.
No Private Heaven. Faith Baldwin. 1976. Repr. of 1946 ed. lib. bdg. 13.25x (ISBN 0-88411-622-0). Amereon Ltd.
No Private Heaven. Faith Baldwin Cuthrell. LC 76-41330. 1976. 6.95. Aeonian Press.
No Private Heaven. Faith Baldwin Cuthrell. LC 48-611. 1947. Sun Dial Press.
No Private Heaven. Faith Baldwin Cuthrell. LC 46-445. 1946. Farrar & Rinehart, Inc.
No Proof. Emma Murdoch Van Deventer. (On cover: Globe library, v. 1, no. 221). Rand, McNally & Company.
No Proof. A Novel. Alice O'Hanlon. (Harper's Franklin square library, no. 284). 1882. Harper & Brothers.
No Quarter. Nels Jorgensen. LC 54-8724. 1954. Avalon Books.
No Quarter. Nels Jorgensen. 1974. 4.50. Avalon.
No Quarter Given. Paul Horgan. 1935. Harper & Brothers.
No Question of Murder: By Peter Curtis Pseud. 1st Ed. Norah Robinson Lofts. LC 59-6266. 1959. Published for the Crime Club by Doubleday.
No Questions Asked. Oliver Bleeck. LC 75-38871. 1976. 6.95 o.p. (ISBN 0-688-03011-4). Morrow.
No Questions Asked. Forbes Rydell, pseud. LC 63-9438. 1963. Published for the Crime Club by Doubleday.
No Questions Asked. Edna Sherry. (Red badge mystery). 1949. Dodd, Mead.
No Questions Asked. Ross Thomas. LC 75-38871. 1976. 6.95 (ISBN 0-688-03011-4). Morrow.
No Range Is Free. Eugene E. Halleran. LC 44-95900. 1944. Macrae-Smith-Company.
No Red Ribbons. John E Quirk. LC 62-20033. 1962. Devin-Adair Co.
No Reference Intended. Barry Crump. (Illus.). 1971. 4.50 o.p. (ISBN 0-589-00645-2). Reed.
No Regrets. Vida Hurst. LC 36-312414. J. H. Hopkins & Son, Inc.
No Regrets. Kathleen Shepard. LC 33-31883. 1933. A. H. King.
No Relations. From the French of Hector Malot. Hector Henri Malot & Hartley, Mrs. May (Laffan) Tr. (seaside library, v. 37. no. 763). 1880. G. Munro.
No Relief. Stephen Dixon. LC 76-16004. 1976. 3.95 (ISBN 0-914908-28-6). Street Fiction Press.
No Remedy. rev. ed. Bubba Free John. LC 75-21551. 1976. pap. 3.95 o.p. (ISBN 0-913922-20-X). Dawn Horse Pr.
No Requiem. Tadashi Moriya. 10.50 o.p. Japan Pubns.
No Rest for Heroes. Harold Calin. pap. 0.50 o.p. Lancer.
No Rest for the Dying. James Kelly. 256p. 1981. pap. 2.25 (ISBN 0-8439-0998-6, Leisure Bks). Nordon Pubns.
No Resting Place. John McNellie. LC 48-8259. 1948. Knopf.
No Resting Place. Eugene Mirabelli. LC 75-181976. 1972. 6.95 (ISBN 0-670-51455-1). Viking Press.
No Retreat from Love. Maysie Greig. LC 42-19564. 1942. Doubleday, Doran & Company, Inc.
No Retreat from Love. Maysie Greig. LC 44-7714. 1944. Triangle Books.
No Ring on Her Finger. Mildred Woodford. LC 70-104821. 1970. 3.95. Moody Press.
No River So Wide. Pierre Danton. (Dell Book). 1978. 1.95 (ISBN 0-440-10215-4). Dell Pub. Co.
No Room for Man. 2nd ed. Gordon R. Dickson. (Necromancer). 1974. pap. 0.75 (ISBN 0-532-95367-3). Woodhill.
No Room for Man. Gordon R. Dickson. Orig. Title: Necromancer. 160p. 1972. pap. 0.75 o.p. (532-00482-075). Manor Bks.
No Room for Man: Population and the Future Through Science Fiction. Ralph S Clem & Martin Harry Greenberg. LC 79-14112. 1979. 11.50 (ISBN 0-8476-6181-4). Rowman and Littlefield.
No Room for Man: Population and the Future Through Science Fiction. Ralph S Clem & Martin Harry Greenberg. LC 79-14191. (Littlefield Adams quality paperbacks; no. 346). 4.50 (ISBN 0-8226-0346-2). Littlefield, Adams.
No Room in the Inn. William Allen Knight. LC 10-19622. 1910. 0.50. The Pilgrim Press.
No Room in the Kitchen. Lewis A. Blustin. 1979. pap. 2.95. Anthelion Pr.
No Ruined Castles: A Novel. James McGovern. LC 57-6732. 1957. Putnam.
No Sacrifice. Denise Robins. LC 34-154936. 1934. G. H. Watt.
No Sad Song, My Love. Ruth McCarthy Sears. (YA) 1973. 4.50 o.p. (Avalon). Bouregy.
No Sad Songs for Me. Ruth Southard. LC 44-40004. 1944. Doubleday, Doran and Company, Inc.
No Saint." A Novel. Anne Bozeman Lyon. J. P. Morton and Company.
No Saint. A Study. Adeline Sergeant. (On cover: Seaside library, Pocket ed. no. 812). G. Munro.
No Sauce for the Gander. first ed. Merle Thomas. 1974. 6.95 (ISBN 0-533-00820-4). Vantage Press.
No Scarlet Ribbons. Susan Terris. 160p. 1983. pap. 2.25 (ISBN 0-380-62844-9, Flare). Avon.
No Score. Chip Harrison. 1970. pap. 0.75 o.p. (T2285, GM). Fawcett World.
No Sea, No Music. M. J. Lowny. 1970. 4.95 o.p. Vantage.
No Second Spring. Susanna Valentine Mitchell. LC 42-9122. 1942. Harper & Brothers.
No Second Spring: A Novel. Janet Beith. LC 33-27308. 1938. Frederick A. Stokes Company.
No Second Wind. Alfred Bertram Guthrie. LC 79-23119. 1980. 9.95 (ISBN 0-395-29069-4). Houghton Mifflin.
No Secret Can Be Told. Natalie Shipman. LC 46-4508. 1946. Prentice-Hall, Inc.
No Secret So Close. Renee Farrington. (Candlelight Romance). 1973. (pbk) 0.75. Dell.
No Shelter for the Heart. Dana Lyon. M. S. Mill Co., Inc.
No Shelter for the Heart. Mabel Dana Lyon. LC 40-32084. 1940. M. S. Mill Co., Inc.
No Ship May Sail. Charles Fry Haywood. LC 42-132753. 1942. Nichols-Ellis Press.
No Shortage of Men. Ethel Powelson Hueston. LC 45-775975. 1945. The Bobbs-Merrill Company.
No Sign of Life. Jay Williams. LC 78-8200. 1979. 7.95 (ISBN 0-385-14599-3). Published for the Crime Club by Doubleday.
No Sign of Murder. Wallace Reed. LC 40-132683. Phoenix Press.
No Silver Bells. Phyllis Rambledon. LC 40-12032. 1940. E. P. Dutton & Co., Inc.
No Slacker, 1917-18: A Chronicle of the War at Home. Philip W Tiemann. LC 64-3778. 1964. Vantage Press.
No Sleep at All. James Warren. LC 41-22520. Alliance Book Corporation.
No Slightest Whisper: A Mystery. Dean Evans. LC 55-11293. 1955. Abelard- Schuman.
No Small Tempest: A Modern Sea Tale in a Great Tradition. 1st Ed. Alan F Carter. LC 51-13412. 1951. Abelard Press.
No Smoke, No Flame: A Tale of Detection, by Quentin Downes Pseud. Michael Harrison. Roy Publishers.
No Smoke Without Fire: The Tragedy of Mary Stuart's Brother James. Alice Harwood. LC 64-25304. 1964. Bobbs-Merrill.
No Son of Mine. Gladys Bronwyn Stern. LC 48-6860. 1948. Macmillan Co.
No Song to Sing. Donald Honig. LC 62-7328. 1962. W. Sloane Associates.
No Soul of My Own a Novel About the South. 1st Ed. J I Moir. LC 59-6524. Greenwich Book Publishers.
No Star Is Lost. James Thomas Farrell. LC 38-17566. The Vanguard Press.
No Star Is Lost. James Thomas Farrell. LC 47-5594. 1947. World Pub. Co.
No Stars So Bright. Mary Faid. Ed. by Gene DeRoin. (Aston Hall Presents Ser.). (Orig.). 1979. pap. 1.50 (ISBN 0-89936-007-6). Aston Hall.
No Steadyjob for Papa. Marion Benasutti. LC 66-28726. 1966. 4.95. Vanguard.
No Steeper Wall: A Novel. Percy Marks. LC 40-305787. 1940. Frederick A. Stokes Company.
No Stepping Backward. Vera Wheatley. LC 37-27367. 1937. E. P. Dutton & Company.
No Stone Unturned. Josephine Lawrence. LC 41-612. 1941. Little, Brown and Company.
No Stone Unturned: A Comedy. Patrick Carleton. LC 39-27307. 1939. E. P. Dutton and Company, Inc.
No Stork at Nine. John Klempner. LC 38-103365. 1938. C. Scribner's Sons.
No Stranger to My Heart. Louise Hathaway. LC 42-8906. 1942. Liveright Publishing Corporation.
No Stranger to My Heart. Lois Seyster Montross. LC 37-3025. 1937. D. Appleton-Century Company, Incorporated.
No Stranger to My Heart. Lois Seyster Montross. LC 42-17836. 1942. Triangle Books.
No Stranger to My Neighbor. Lewis B France. LC 6-44360. Outdoor Life Publishing Company.
No Strangers in Exile. Hans Harder. (Illus.). 1979. pap. 7.95 (ISBN 0-8361-1898-7). Herald Pr.
No Such Girl. Vida Hurst. LC 32-171414. Grosset & Dunlap.
No Surrender. Jo Van Ammers-Kuller. Tr. by Robson-Scott, William Douglas. LC 31-10861. E. P. Dutton & Co., Inc.
No Surrender. Elisabeth Burstenbinder. Tr. by Tyrrell, Christna. (Seaside library, v. 75, no. 1525). 1883. G. Munro.
No Surrender. Heidi Huberta Loewengard. LC 42-22267. 1942. Little, Brown and Company.
No Surrender. Constance Elizabeth Maud. LC 12-12379. 1912. The John Lane Company.
No Surrender. Emma Gelders Sterne. LC 32-253217. Duffield and Green.
No Surrender: A Novel. Katharine Newlin Burt. LC 40-33101. 1940. Macrae-Smith Compnay.
No Survivors. Edwyn Gray. 1975. (pbk.) 1.25 (ISBN 0-523-00568-7). Pinnacle Books.
No Survivors: A Novel by Will Henry Pseud. Henry Allen. LC 50-10477. 1950. Random House.
No Sweeter Song. Rachel Palmer. (Superromances Ser.). 384p. 1983. pap. 2.95 (ISBN 0-373-70058-X, Pub. by Worldwide). Harlequin Bks.
No Sweetness Here. Ama Ata Aidoo. LC 74-144244. 1971. 5.95. Doubleday.
No Sympathy for the Devil. Frederick Snow. 224p. 1982. pap. 2.75 (ISBN 0-449-14461-5, GM). Fawcett.
No Tears at the Funeral, by Helen Arre Pseud. Zola Helen Ross. LC 54-9904. 1954. Arcadia House.
No Tears for Christmas. Helen Topping Miller. LC 54-11441. 1954. Longmans, Green.
No Tears for Hilda. Andrew Garve. LC 75-44975. (Crime Fiction Ser). 1976. Repr. of 1950 ed. lib. bdg. 17.50 (ISBN 0-8240-2369-2). Garland Pub.
No Tears for Hilda. Andrew Garve. 1978. pap. 1.95i (ISBN 0-06-080441-6, P 441, PL). Har-Row.
No Tears for Hilda. Paul Winterton. LC 51-429. Harper.

No Tears for Hilda. Paul Winterton. LC 75-44975. (Fifty Classics of Crime Fiction, 1900-1950; No. 20). 1976. 12.00. Garland Pub.
No Tears for Shirley Minton: By Kenneth Lowe Pseud. 1st Ed. Elma K Lobaugh. LC 55-10513. 1955. Published for the Crime Club by Doubleday.
No Tears for the Dead. Elinore Denniston. LC 48-1019. (Red badge detective). 1948. Dodd, Mead.
No Tears for Yesterday: A Novel. 1st Ed. Abby Taylor Townsend. LC 56-9570. 1956. Exposition Press.
No Tears Shed. Alfred Betts Caldwell. LC 37-299347. 1937. Pub. for the Crime Club Inc., by Doubleday, Doran & Co., Inc.
No Thanks to the Duke. Alastair MacTavish Dunnett. LC 80-1984. 1981. 9.95 (ISBN 0-385-17389-X). Published for the Crime Club by Doubleday.
No Thoroughfare. Charles Dickens & Collins, Wilkie. LC 6-26426. (On cover: Lovell's library, v. 6. no. 302). 1883. J. W. Lovell Company.
No Thoroughfare. Denise Egerton. LC 55-6137. 1955. Coward-McCann.
No Through Road. Clifford John Druce. LC 35-5466. H. Holt and Company.
No Through Road. Martin James Russell. LC 66-20160. 1966. Coward-McCann.
No Time at All. Charles Einstein. LC 57-10974. 1957. Simon and Schuster.
No Time for Crime. Charlotte Murray Russell, pseud. LC 45-4607. 1945. Pub. for the Crime Club by Doubleday, Doran and Company, Inc.
No Time for Fear. Davenport Steward. LC 50-14310. 1950. Hale Pub. Co.
No Time for Glory: Stories of World War II. Ed. by Phyllis Reid Fenner. LC 62-11900. 1962. Morrow.
No Time for Love. Barbara Cartland. (Bantam Barbara Cartland Library #40). 1976. (pbk.) 1.25 (ISBN 0-553-02807-3). Bantam Books.
No Time for Love. Kay Clifford. (Harlequin Romances Ser.). 192p. 1982. pap. 1.50 (ISBN 0-373-02468-1). PB.
No Time for Love. Lori Herter. LC 81-14624. 1981. 9.95 (ISBN 0-89621-316-1). Thorndike Press.
No Time for Love. Emilie Baker Loring. LC 72-99907. 1970. 4.95. Little, Brown.
No Time for Passion. John Saxon. LC 41-13504. Phoenix Press.
No Time for Sergeants. Mac Hyman. LC 54-9435. 1954. Random House.
No Time for Tears. Cynthia Freeman. LC 80-70542. 448p. 1981. 14.95 (ISBN 0-87795-317-1). Arbor Hse.
No Time for Tears. Cynthia Freeman. 448p. 1982. pap. 3.95 (ISBN 0-553-22656-8). Bantam.
No Time for Tears. Peter Neagoe. LC 58-7701. 1958. Kamin Publishers.
No Time for Tears: A Novel. Cynthia Freeman. LC 82-6060. 1982. 17.95 (ISBN 0-8161-3386-7). G.K. Hall.
No Time Like the Future. Nelson Slade Bond. LC 54-32734. (Avon, T-80). 1954. Avon Publications.
No Time to Die. Ronald Kemp. LC 54-443594. 1954. Staples Press.
No Time to Kill. John Bonett & Emery Bonett. LC 70-186191. (O.s.i.). 192p. 1972. 4.95 o.s.i. (ISBN 0-8027-5251-9). Walker & Co.
No Time to Kill. John Coulson & Felicity Winifred Carter. LC 70-186191. 1972. 4.95 (ISBN 0-8027-5251-9). Walker.
No Time to Kill. George Harmon Coxe. LC 41-398242. 1941. A. A. Knopf.
No Time to Look Back. Leslie Greener. LC 50-7821. 1950. Viking Press.
No Tomorrow. Brigit Patmore. LC 29-18259. 2.00. The Century Co.
No Trains on Sunday: A Boyhood Reminiscence. Willie Kohlmann & Edwin A Schurmann. LC 68-28659. (Illus.). 1968. 3.95. Taplinger Pub. Co.
No Transfer. Stephen Walton. LC 66-28880. 1967. Vanguard Press.
No Traveler Returns: A Novel. 1st American Ed. James Lord. LC 56-59806. 1956. J. Day Co.
No Traveller Returns. Amber Dean. LC 49-7003. 1948. Pub. for the Crime Club by Doubleday.
No Trespassing. Sondra Stanford. 192p. (Orig.). 1980. pap. 1.50 (ISBN 0-671-57046-3, Pub. by Silhouette Bks). S&S.
No Trip Like This, and Other Stories. Clifford Comer Cawley. LC 51-24856. 1951. House of Edinboro.
No Truce with Time: By Alec Waugh. Alec Waugh. LC 40-35425. Farrar & Rinehart, Inc.
No Trumpet Before Him. Nelia Gardner White. LC 50-3335. Peoples Book Club.
No Trumpet Before Him. Nelia Gardner White. LC 50-3335. 1949. Sun Dial Press.
No Turning Back. Ceil Goldstein. LC 70-106350. 1970. 4.95. Dorrance.
No Two Sexes Are Alike. Johnny Hart. 128p. 1981. pap. 1.75 (ISBN 0-449-14428-3, Crest). Fawcett.

No Uncertain Sound. Illus. by Delor Erickson. Lillian Cummins Proctor. LC 66-22565. 1966. 4.95. Augsburg.
No Use Cryin' Henry L Anderson. LC 67-18905. 1967. International Scope.
No Use Cryin' A Novel. Henry L Anderson. LC 61-16229. 1961. Western Publisher.
No Vacancy. Mary Jane Rolfs. LC 51-6721. 1951. Houghton Mifflin.
No Vacation from Murder. Elizabeth Lemarchand. LC 73-90727. 1974. 5.95 (ISBN 0-8027-5287-X). Walker.
No Victory for the Soldier. James Hill, pseud. LC 39-448808. 1939. Doubleday, Doran & Co., Inc.
No Villian Need Be. Vardis Fisher. LC 36-17485. 1936. Doubleday, Doran & Company, Inc., and Caldwell, Id., The Caxton Printers. Ltd.
No Villian Need Be. Elizabeth Linington. LC 78-8197. 1979. 7.95 (ISBN 0-385-14600-0). Published for the Crime Club by Doubleday.
No Wall So High. Anne Powers, pseud. LC 49-8899. 1949. Bobbs-Merrill Co.
No Wall So High: A Novel. Frances Illotson. LC 56-11689. 1957. Lippincott.
No Wall So High: A Novel. Frances Tillotson. LC 56-11689. 1957. Lippincott.
No Walls of Jasper. Joanna Cannan, pseud. LC 31-8331. 1931. Doubleday, Doran & Company, Inc.
No Way. Natalia Ginzburg. LC 74-7069. 1974. 5.95 (ISBN 0-15-167674-7). Harcourt Brace Jovanovich.
No Way. natalia ginzburg; translated by sheila cudahy. ed. Natalia Ginzburg. (Bard Book). 1.75 (ISBN 0-380-00838-6). Avon Books.
No Way Back: A Novella. Teresa Ellis. 1973. 3.00 (ISBN 0-682-47716-8). Exposition Pr.
No Way Out. Jane Donnelly. (Harlequin Romances Ser.). 192p. 1980. pap. 1.25 (ISBN 0-373-02373-1, Pub. by Harlequin). PB.
No Way Out. Wilfred McNeilly. pap. 0.50 o.p. (50-320). Manor Bks.
No Way to Treat a Lady. William Goldman. LC 68-1279. 4.50. Harcourt, Brace & World.
No Weeds for the Widow. Milton Michael Raison. LC 47-359. 1946. Murray & Gee, Inc.
No Where Else in the World. Jay William Hudson. LC 23-14481. 1923. D. Appleton and Company.
No Wider Than the Heart: A Novel by N. B. Lamont Pseud. 1st Ed. Nedda Lemmon Barnitt. LC 61-7656. 1961. Doubleday.
No Will to Die. William Ellis. LC 74-82399. 1975. 5.95 o.p. (ISBN 0-8027-5307-8). Walker & Co.
No Wind of Blame. Georgette Heyer. LC 78-122781. 1970. 4.95. Dutton.
No Wind of Blame... Georgette Heyer. LC 39-33013. 1939. Pub. for the Crime Club by Doubleday, Doran & Co., Inc.
No Wind of Blame... Georgette Heyer. LC 41-4551. 1940. The Sun Dial Press.
No Wind of Healing. Dorothy Palmer Hines. LC 46-3946. 1946. Doubleday & Company, Inc.
No Wings on a Cop. Cleve Franklin Adams. LC 50-32364. (Handi-book mystery, 112). 1950. Quinn Pub. Co.
No Winners: The Blue Mumbling of Ray Lee Stankey: Fiction. Roger Larson. LC 78-78143. 3.95. Ipse Dixit Press.
No Witness! Cortland Fitzsimmons. LC 32-307832. 1932. Frederick A. Stokes Company.
No Witnesses. Paul Monette. 1981. pap. 5.95 (ISBN 0-380-76802-X, 76802). Avon.
No Woman Has Gone. Gretchen J. Corbitt. 56p. 1976. 4.00 o.p. (ISBN 0-682-48508-X). Exposition.
No Women Wanted. Gerald Foster. LC 36-86886. Godwin.
No World of Their Own. Poul Anderson. LC 55-37190. (Ace double novel books. D-110). 1955. Ace Books.
No. Xiii: Or, The Story of the Lost Vestal. Emma Martin Marshall. LC 7-24666. (On cover: Cassell's "rainbow" series, no. 19). Cassell & Company, Limited.
No. 101,". Wymond Carey. LC 5-37155. 1905. G. P. Putnam's Sons.
No. 13, Rue Du Bon Diable. Arthur Sherburne Hardy. LC 17-28186. 1917. Houghton Mifflin Company.
No 13 Rue Marlot. Leon Rene Delmas. Tr. by Lord, Grace Virginia. LC 7-37419. 1880. Lee and Shepard.
No. 13 Toroni: A Mystery. Julius Regis. LC 22-20734.
No. 13 Washington Square. Leroy Scott. LC 14-113562. 1914. 1.35. Houghton Mifflin Company.
No. 21 Castle Street. no. twenty-one castle street ed. H W Katz. Tr. by Guterman, Norbert. LC 40-337062. 1940. The Viking Press.
No. 26 Jayne Street. Mary Hunter Austin. LC 20-9713. 1920. Houghton Mifflin Company.
No. 40.". number fortty. ed. LC 8-28268. 1884. C. McCarthy & Co.
No. 40." A Romance of Fortress Monroe and the Hygeis. 2d ed. LC 43-40132. 1884. J. W. Randolph & English.

No. 40." A Romance of Fortress Monroe and the Hygeia. 3d ed. Nannie Whitmell Tunstall. 1890. J. W. Randolph & English.
No. 44, the Mysterious Stranger: Being an Ancient Tale Found in a Jug and Freely Translated from the Jug: a Selection from Mark Twain's Mysterious Stranger Manuscripts. Mark Twain. LC 81-40326. (Twain, Mark, 1835-1910. Mark Twain Library). 1981. 13.50 (ISBN 0-520-04544-0) (ISBN 0-520-04545-9). University of California Press.
No. 5 John Street. 30th thousand. ed. Richard Whiteing. LC 12-241102. 1899. The Century Co.
No. 9 Belmont Square. Wetherby Williams. LC 63-11218. 1963. Published for the Crime Club by Doubleday.
No. 99. Arthur George Frederick Griffiths. (On cover: Seaside library. Pocket ed. no. 614). 1885. G. Munro.
No. 99. Arthur George Frederick Griffiths. (On cover: Lovell's library. no. 706). 1866. J. W. Lovell Company.
Noa Noa. Paul Gauguin. Tr. by O. F. Theis. 1978. Repr. of 1920 ed. 25.00 (ISBN 0-8492-4913-9). R West.
Noachidae: or, Noah, and His Descendants. Jerome Bonaparte Holgate. LC 7-6129. 1860. Breed, Butler & Co.
Noah. J. F. Burke. 288p. 1968. 4.95 o.p. (ISBN 0-8202-0036-0). Sherbourne.
Noah: A Novel. J. F. Burke. LC 68-18746. 1968. Sherbourne Press.
Noah & the Waters. Lewis Day. 1.00 o.p. Transatlantic.
Noah Pandre: A Novel. Zalman Shneur & Leftwich, Joseph, Tr. LC 36-12811. L. Furman, Inc.
Noah's Ark. Darryl Francis Zanuck & De Haas, Arline. LC 28-25460. Grosset & Dunlap.
Noah's Ark: Or, The Love Story of a Respectable Young Couple. Amabel Williams-Ellis. LC 26-5829. George H. Doran Company.
Noahs Ark: The Deluge of Atlantis. Lillian Elizabeth Becker Roy. LC 28-21056. 1928. Macoy Publishing & Masonic Supply Co.
Noah's Ark, Tourist Class. Ephraim Kishon. (YA) 1962. 4.50 o.p. Atheneum.
Noah's Confession. George Byrne Smith. LC 99-4465. 1898. The Cicerone Publishing Company.
Noah's Grandchildren. Julier C Chevalier. LC 29-17891. 1929. Doubleday, Doran & Company, Inc.
Noah's Stowaway. Being the Journal of One Zadek, Who by His Own Testimony, Was Noah's Stowaway in the Ark. Laster Martin. LC 54-44722. 1954.
Nobel Price Reader. rev. ed. Ed. by Leo Hamalian. Volpe, Edmond Loris, Joint Ed. LC 65-5472. (Eagle books, Z28). 1965. Popular Library.
Nobel Prize. IUrii Krotkov. LC 80-10374. 10.95 (ISBN 0-671-24255-5). Simon and Schuster.
Nobel Prize Reader. Ed. by Leo Hamalian, Edmond L. Volpe. Introd. by Robert J. Clements Rev. Ed. Ed. by Leo Hamalian & Edmond Loris Volpe. LC 65-5472. (Eagle bks., Z28). pap., 1.25. Popular Lib.
Nobility in the Rough: An Historical Novel. David Bering. LC 41-11007. D. Ryerson, Inc.
Nobility Lost. James Leonard Johnson. LC 70-144275. 1971. 5.95 o.p. Doubleday.
Noble Art. Reita Lambert. LC 35-139015. 1935. Doubleday, Doran & Co., Inc.
Noble Blood. Julian Hawthorne. LC 7-3883. 1885. D. Appleton and Company.
Noble Blood: A Prussian Cadet Story, Translated from the German of Ernst Von Wildenbruch...by Charles King...and Anne Williston Ward; and A West Point Parallel; an American Cadet Story, by Captain Charles King; Ernst Wildenbruch & King, Charles, 1844-1933. LC 12-19559. 1896. F. T. Neely.
Noble Courtesan. Gerve Baronti. LC 30-11720. The Macaulay Company.
Noble Criminal: A Strange Tale Taken from the Notes and Memoirs of Hadlock Jones by His Friend, Dr. Lawrence L. Langdon. Albert Holland Rhodes. LC 12-111552. 1912. Holland Publishing Company.
Noble Descents. Gerald Hanley. 352p. 1983. 12.95 (ISBN 0-312-57618-8). St Martin.
Noble Earl of Fleetwood: Or, Kathryn's Promise. Sarah Frances Foster Annis. LC 13-15165. Broadway Publishing Company.
Noble Enemy: A Novel. Charles Fox. LC 78-22770. 1980. 12.50 (ISBN 0-385-14526-8). Doubleday.
Noble Fool. Florence Everard. LC 6-15732. 1906. Stitt Publishing Company.
Noble Girl: A Book Devoted to the Uplifting of Character and Modern Society. Ada Cornelius Brannon. LC 6-22861. Collie Printing Company.
Noble House. James Clavell. 1981. 22.95 (ISBN 0-440-06456-2). Delacorte.

Noble House. James Clavell. 1982. pap. 5.95 (ISBN 0-440-16483-4). Dell.
Noble House: A Novel of Contemporary Hong Kong. James Clavell. LC 80-26889. 17.95 (ISBN 0-440-06456-2). Delacorte Press.
Noble in Reason. Phyllis Eleanor Bentley. LC 55-14489. 1955. Macmillan.
Noble Life. Dinah Maria Mulock Craik. LC 4-15294. 1866. Harper & Brothers.
Noble Life. Dinah Maria Mulock Craik. LC 16-9373. (Lettered on cover: Miss Mulock's works). Harper & Brothers.
Noble Lord. The Sequel to "The Lost Heir of Linlithgow.". Emma Dorothy Eliza Nevitte Southworth. LC 8-10828. T. B. Peterson & Brothers.
Noble Outlaw. Matthew Braun. (Orig.) 1979. pap. 2.25 (ISBN 0-671-44014-4). PB.
Noble Outlaw. Matthew Braun. 1975. (pbk.) 1.25. Popular Library.
Noble Pirate. Raymond Foxall. (Signet Book.). 1978. 1.95 (ISBN 0-451-08291-5). New American Library.
Noble Profession. Translated from the French by Xan Fielding. Pierre Boulle. LC 60-15063. 1960. Vanguard Press.
Noble Rogue: A Cavelier's Romance. Emmuska Orczy. LC 12-5843. 1.35. Hodder & Stoughton, George H. Doran Company.
Noble Slaves. Being an Entertaining History of the Surprising Adventures, and Remarkable Deliverances, from Algerine Slavery, of Several Spanish Noblemen and Ladies of Quality. Penelope Aubin. LC 19-11340. 1806. Printed for Everet Duyckinck.
Noble Stallion. Translated from the German by James and Marika Cleugh. Illustrated by B. Biro. Arthur Heinz Lehmann. LC 55-641985. 1955. Holt.
Noble Wife. A Novel. John Saunders. (Harper's Franklin square library, no. 343). 1883. Harper & Brothers.
Noble Wife. A Novel. John Saunders. (On cover: Seaside library. Pocket ed., no. 105). 1883. G. Munro.
Noble Woman. Ann Sophia Winterbotham Stephens. T. B. Peterson & Brothers.
Nobleman of '89: An Episode of the French Revolution. Abel Quinton & Legarde, Ernst, Tr. LC 8-231. 1874. Kelly, Piet & Company.
Nobler Sex. Florence Marryat Church Lean. LC 7-13612. United States Book Company.
Noblesse Oblige. Margaret Roberts. LC 7-41041. (On cover: Leisure hour series. no. 71). 1876. H. Holt and Company.
Noblesse Oblige. Margaret Roberts. (Seaside library, v. 60, no. 1223). 1882. G. Munro.
Noblest Form. Victor B. A. Burner. LC 81-80167. (Illus.). 64p. 1983. pap. 5.95 (ISBN 0-86666-020-8). GWP.
Noblest Roman. David Halberstam. 1961. 3.95 o.p. (ISBN 0-395-07767-2). HM.
Noblest Roman: A Story of Political Debauchery and Prostituted Allegiance. Sinclair Moreland. LC 10-19616. 1910. Noblest Roman Pub. Co.
Noblest Roman: A Story of Political Debauchery and Prostituted Allegiance. 2d ed. illustrated by betty baugh. ed. Sinclair Moreland. LC 11-22757. The Noblest Roman Publishing Co.
Nobody. Louis Joseph Vance. LC 15-20561. George H. Doran Company.
Nobody. Susan Warner. LC 8-33702. 1883. R. Carter & Brothers.
Nobody Answered the Bell. Rhys Davies. LC 74-158816. 1971. 5.95 (ISBN 0-396-06373-X). Dodd, Mead.
Nobody Called Me Mine: Black Memories. Frederick Ward. LC 75-44838. 1977. 8.95 (ISBN 0-912766-37-9). Tundra Books.
Nobody Calls Me Doctor. William C. Davis. 1972. pap. 5.95 o.p. (ISBN 0-87108-065-6). Pruett.
Nobody Calls Me Doctor. William C. Davis. 1972. pap. 5.95 o.p. (ISBN 0-87108-065-6). Pruett.
Nobody Does You Any Favors. James Yaffe. LC 66-203019. bds., 5.95. Putnam.
Nobody Gathers Seashells & Gunshells Anymore: Sketches of an Island Town. E. Vallado Daroy. 203p. 1981. pap. 6.25x (Pub. by New Day Philippines). Cellar.
Nobody Gets to the Pre Catalan. Barbara Probst Solomon. Date not set. 8.95 o.p. (ISBN 0-06-013898-X, HarpT). Har-Row.
Nobody Heard the Shot: An Aleck West Detective Story. Donald Barr Chidsey. LC 41-110094. (On cover: Bantam books. 25). Bantam Publications, Inc.
Nobody Home. Jennifer Lloyd Paul. 1977. 7.95 (ISBN 0-393-08766-2). Norton.
Nobody Home: A Novel. Jennifer Lloyd Paul. LC 76-55729. 7.95. Norton.
Nobody Home: A Novel. Jennifer Lloyd Paul. 1978. 1.95 (ISBN 0-446-89591-1). Warner Books.
Nobody Is Safe: A Saturnin Dax Mystery. 1st Ed. Marten Cumberland. LC 53-5538. 1953. Published for the Crime Club by Doubleday.
Nobody Knew They Were There! Evan Hunter. LC 71-131081. 1971. 5.95. Doubleday.

Nobody Knows. Douglas Goldring. LC 23-8188. Small, Maynard and Company.
Nobody Likes Trina. Phyllis A. Whitney. 292p. (YA) 1973. lib. bdg. 7.95 o.p. (ISBN 0-8161-6074-0, Large Print Bks). G K Hall.
Nobody Lives Forever. William Riley Burnett. LC 43-18855. 1943. A. A. Knopf.
Nobody Loves a Dead Man. Milton Michael Raison. LC 46-3760. 1945. Murray & Gee, Inc.
Nobody Loves a Drunken Indian. Clair Huffaker. LC 67-24555. 1967. McKay.
Nobody Loves a Drunken Indian see Flap.
Nobody Loves a Loser see Who Dies There.
Nobody Loves Forever. Margaretta Brucker. LC 46-602699. 1946. Arcadia House, Inc.
Nobody Makes Me Cry. Shelley Steinmann List. LC 75-6514. 1975. (ISBN 0-8415-0381-8). Saturday Review Press.
Nobody on the Road. Geoffrey Rose. LC 75-26193. 1976. 7.95. St. Martin's Press.
Nobody on the Road: A Mission of Death into an Unknown Country. Geoffrey Rose. LC 75-26193. 190p. 1976. 7.95 o.p. (ISBN 0-312-57645-5). St Martin.
Nobody Say a Word: And Other Stories. Mark Van Doren. LC 53-8985. 1953. Holt.
Nobody Starves: A Novel by Catharine Brody... Catharine Brody. LC 32-270598. 1932. Longmans, Green and Co.
Nobody Wants My Resume. Robert Jagoda. LC 79-14986. 9.95 (ISBN 0-07-039870-4). McGraw-Hill.
Nobody Wins. C. P. Kennealy. 1978. pap. 1.75 (ISBN 0-532-17171-3). Woodhill.
Nobody's: A Novel. Virginia Demarest. LC 11-18062. 1911. 1.20. Harper & Brothers.
Nobody's Angel. Thomas McGuane. LC 81-13885. 14.50 (ISBN 0-394-52264-8) (ISBN 0-394-70565-3). Random House.
Nobody's Baby. Wright Williams. LC 43-11751. Phoenix Press.
Nobody's Baby. Watkins Eppes Wright. LC 43-11751. 1943. Phoenix Press.
Nobody's Boy (Sans Famille) Hector Henri Malot & Crewe-Jones, Florence, Tr. LC 16-176571. 1916. Cupples & Leon Company.
Nobody's Business. Jeannette Ritchie Hadermann Walworth. LC 8-33133. (On cover: Satchel series, no. 9). The Authors' Publishing Company.
Nobody's Business; Stories. Penelope Gilliatt. LC 77-186943. 1972. 6.95 (ISBN 0-670-51497-7). Viking Press.
Nobody's Child. Elizabeth Dejeans. LC 18-521313. 1.50. The Bobbs-Merrill Company.
Nobody's Child. Phyllis Hambledon. LC 51-11434. 1951. Rinehart.
Nobody's Children. Rose Kuszmaul. LC 42-24438. 1942. Houghton Mifflin Company.
Nobody's Children. Intro. by D. Norsky. pap. 1.95 o.p. (6028). Brandon.
Nobody's Cousin. A Van Ogle. LC 10-11475. 1910. Cochrane Publishing Company.
Nobody's Daughter: Or, The Hidden Crime at Fernwood. Clara Augusta Jones. LC 7-12140. (select series. no. 82). 1891. Street & Smith.
Nobody's Fault. Netta Syrett. LC 8-25585. 1896. Roberts Bros.; Etc., Etc.
Nobody's Fault: A Novel. Mervyn Jones. LC 76-57770. 1977. 7.95 (ISBN 0-88405-492-6). Mason/Charter.
Nobody's Fool: A Novel. Harrison, Charles Yale. LC 48-821850. 1948. H. Holt.
Nobody's Girl. Fannie Heaslip Lea. LC 40-315283. 1940. Dodd, Mead & Company.
Nobody's Husband. Samuel Woodworth Cozzens. LC 6-288503. 1878. Lee and Shepard.
Nobody's in Town: Two Short Novels... Edna Ferber. LC 44-51246. (New Avon library. 51). 1944.
Nobody's Island. Beatrice Ethel Grimshaw. LC 23-9944. 1923. Doubleday, Page & Company.
Nobody's Man. Edward Phillips Oppenheim. LC 21-19848. 1921. Little, Brown, and Company.
Nobody's Perfect. Douglas Clark. LC 79-84826. (A Stein and Day mystery). 1969. 4.95. Stein and Day.
Nobody's Perfect. Curtis L. Johnson. LC 73-87508. (Illus.). 1974. (pbk.) 6.00 (ISBN 0-914140-01-9). Carpenter Press.
Nobody's Perfect. Donald E Westlake. LC 77-24180. 7.95 (ISBN 0-87131-249-2). M. Evans.
Nobody's Son: Or, The Life and Adventures of Percival Mayberry. Joseph Holt Ingraham. LC 7-10352. 1851. A. Hart, Late Carey & Hart.
Nobody's Sorry He Got Killed. Arthur D Goldstein. LC 75-33162. 6.95 (ISBN 0-394-40028-3). Random House.
Nobody's Vineyard: A Joshua Clunk Story. Henry Christopher Bailey. LC 42-222681. 1942. Doubleday, Doran and Co., Inc.
Noches De Vudu. new ed. Danilo Cesto. (Pimienta Collection). (Illus.). 160p. (Span.). pap. 1.25 (ISBN 0-88473-239-8). Fiesta Pub.
Noches Violentes. new ed. W. B. Murphy. Tr. by Javier Lopez from Eng. (Compadre Collection Ser., Rivera y Razoni: No. 3). Orig. Title: One Night Stand. 160p. (Span.). 1975. pap. 0.85 (ISBN 0-88473-610-5). Fiesta Pub.
Nocola. Dorothy Dabiels. 1980. pap. 2.50 (ISBN 0-8439-0783-5). Nordon Pubns.
Nocturnal Minstrel: Or, The Spirit of the Wood. Eleanor Sleath. LC 70-131342. (Gothic novels). 1972. (ISBN 0-405-00821-X). Arno Press.
Nocturnal Vaudeville. Stephen Schneck. LC 74-133581. 1971. 6.95 (ISBN 0-525-16822-2). E. P. Dutton.
Nocturnal Visit: A Tale. Regina Maria Dalton Roche. LC 77-2045. (Gothic Novels III). 1977. 75.00 (ISBN 0-405-10143-0). Arno Press.
Nocturne. Frank Arthur Swinnerton. LC 17-23047. George H. Doran Company.
Nocturne. Frank Arthur Swinnerton. LC 33-31066. 1938. The Sun Dial Press, Inc.
Nocturne: From the Notes of Lt. Amiran Amilakhvari, Retired. Bulat Shalvovich Okudzhava. LC 77-11544. 10.95 (ISBN 0-06-013289-2). Harper & Row.
Nocturne Militaire. Elliott White Springs. LC 27-11719. George H. Doran Company.
Nocturne of a Night Rider. Neil Shea. 32p. 1973. 3.95 o.p. (ISBN 0-8059-1889-2). Dorrance.
Nocturnes. Thomas Mann. LC 79-140336. (Short story index reprint series). (Illus.). 1970. Books for Libraries Press.
Nocturnes for the King of Naples. Edmund White. LC 78-4384. 1978. 7.95 (ISBN 0-312-57653-6). St. Martin's Press.
Nocturnes for the King of Naples. Edmund White. LC 79-22059. 1980. 2.95 (ISBN 0-14-005330-1). Penguin Books.
Nod. Freeman Lincoln. Coward-McCann, Inc.
Noelle. LC 76-40674. 1976. pap. 2.95 o.p. (F00041). Playboy.
Noemi. Sabine Baring-Gould. LC 6-7228. 1894. D. Appleton and Company.
Nog: A Novel. Rudolph Wurlitzer. LC 68-28552. 1969. 4.95. Random House.
Noise in the Night. Selwyn Jepson. LC 57-13212. 1957. Lippincott.
Noise of the World. Adriana Spadoni. LC 21-6798. Boni and Liveright.
Noise of Their Wings. MacKinlay Kantor. LC 38-27867. 1938. Coward-McCann, Inc.
Nolan, No. 6: Scratch Fever. Max Collins. 192p. (Orig.). 1982. pap. 1.95 (ISBN 0-523-41164-2). Pinnacle Bks.
Nolan Number Three: Fly Paper. Max Collins. 192p. (Orig.). 1981. pap. 1.95 (ISBN 0-523-41161-8). Pinnacle Bks.
Nolan, Number Two: Blood Money. rev. ed. Max Collins. 192p. 1981. pap. 1.95 (ISBN 0-523-41160-X). Pinnacle Bks.
Nomad. Paul Jordan Smith, pseud. LC 25-8911. 1925. Minton, Balch & Company.
Nomad Harp. Elizabeth N. Walker. 224p. (Orig.). 1980. pap. 1.75 (ISBN 0-449-50070-5, Coventry). Fawcett.
Nomads of the Night: The Latest Adventures of Cheri-Bibi. Gaston Leroux. LC 25-128514. 1925. The Macaulay Company.
Nomads of the North. James O. Curwood. 1919. 15.00 (ISBN 0-403-00802-6). Scholarly.
Nomads of the North: A Story of Romance and Adventure Under the Open Stars. James Oliver Curwood. LC 75-144961. (Illus.). 1972. 19.50 (ISBN 0-403-00802-6). Scholarly Press.
Nomads of the North: A Story of Romance and Adventure Under the Open Stars. James Oliver Curwood. LC 78-127911. (Illus.). 1973. 12.00 (ISBN 0-404-01896-3). AMS Press.
Nomads of the North: A Story of Romance and Adventure Under the Open Stars. James Oliver Curwood. LC 19-5694. 1919. Doubleday, Page & Company.
Nombres. Jaime Carrero. (UPREX, Ficcion: No. 13). pap. 1.85 (ISBN 0-8477-0013-5). U of PR Pr.
Nommo: African Fiction in French South of the Sahara. John D Erickson. LC 78-73310. (Illus.). 1979. 17.00 (ISBN 0-917786-08-4). French Literature Publications Co.
Non-Believer's Journey. S. Nyamfukudza. LC 81-112481. (African Writers Series; 233). 1980. 6.50 (ISBN 0-435-90233-4). Heinemann.
Non-Conformist. George Abbe. 5.95 o.p. (ISBN 0-8283-1159-5). Branden.
Non-Scheduled Flight: A Novel. Robert Luther Duffus. LC 49-49686. 1950. Macmillan.
Non-Stop Connolly Show, Nos. 1 & 2. Margaretta D'Arcy & John Arden. (The Non-Stop Connolly Show Ser.). 64p. (Orig.). 1981. pap. 4.95 (ISBN 0-904383-80-6). Pluto Pr.
Non-Stop Connolly Show, No. 3. Margaretta D'Arcy & John Arden. (Non-Stop Connolly Show Ser.). 77p. (Orig.). 1981. pap. 4.95 (ISBN 0-904383-81-4). Pluto Pr.
Non-Stop Connolly Show, No. 4. Margaretta D'Arcy & John Arden. (Non-Stop Connolly Show Ser.). 87p. (Orig.). 1981. pap. 4.95 (ISBN 0-904383-82-2). Pluto Pr.
Non-Stop Connolly Show, No. 5. Margaretta D'Arcy & John Arden. (Non-Stop Connolly Show Ser.). 112p. (Orig.). 1981. pap. 4.95 (ISBN 0-904383-83-0). Pluto Pr.
Non-Stop Connolly Show, No. 6. Margaretta D'Arcy & John Arden. (Non-Stop Connolly Show Ser.). 128p. (Orig.). 1981. pap. 4.95 (ISBN 0-904383-84-9). Pluto Pr.
Nonborn King. Julian May. LC 82-11950. (saga of Pliocene exile; v. 3). ((Series: May, Julian.). (Saga of Pliocene exile; v. 3.). (Illus.). 1983. 16.95 (ISBN 0-395-32211-1). Houghton Mifflin.
Nonce. Cid Corman, pseud. 1965. pap. 6.00 o.p. (Pub. by Elizabeth Pr). SBD.
Nonce: A Novel. Michael Brandon. LC 44-2358. 1944. Coward-McCann, Inc.
Nonchalante: Casual Data Touching the Career of Dixie Bilton, Operettensangerin at Beilmar. Stanley Olmsted. LC 6-7773. 1906. H. Holt and Company.
Nonconformist and Other Stories. Clara Schechad. LC 73-78116. (Illus.). 1973. 3.95. Shengold Publishers.
None but Man. Gordon R Dickson. LC 69-12224. (Doubleday science fiction). 1969. 4.95. Doubleday.
None but Man. Gordon R Dickson. 1977. 1.75 (ISBN 0-87997-337-4). DAW Books.
None but My Foe. David Duncan. LC 50-10571. 1950. Macmillan.
None but the Brave". Arthur Schnitzler. Tr. by Simon, Richard L. LC 26-16706. 1926. Simon and Schuster.
None but the Brave. Joseph Hamblen Sears. LC 2-10716. 1902. Dodd, Mead & Co.
None but the Brave: A Novel of Recovery. Marguerite Mooers Marshall. LC 34-251537. 1934. Doubleday, Doran & Company, Inc.
None but the Lonely Heart. Eleanore D. Greene. LC 40-6537. House of Field, Inc.
None but the Lonely Heart. Richard Llewellyn. LC 69-18812. 1969. Macmillan.
None but the Lonely Heart. Richard Llewellyn. LC 43-14647. 1943. The Macmillan Company.
None Dare Call It Treason. Catherine Irvine Gavin. LC 77-99124. 1978. 8.95 (ISBN 0-312-57706-0). St. Martin's Press.
None of Maigret's Business. Georges Simenon. LC 58-7367. 1958. Published for the Crime Club by Doubleday.
None of the Above. Rosemary Wells. 1975. (pbk.) 1.25 (ISBN 0-380-00554-9). Avon.
None of Us Cared for Kate. John Haythorne. LC 68-12463. 1968. 3.95. Dutton.
None of Us Will Return. Charlotte Delbo. Tr. by John Githens. LC 68-20635. 1968. 3.95 o.p. (GP454). Grove.
None Other Gods. Robert Hugh Benson. LC 11-773562. 1911. B. Herder.
None Shall Know. Martha Albrand. (O.s.i.). 1967. pap. 0.60 o.s.i. (A257X, Award). Univ Pub & Dist.
None Shall Know. Peter De Polnay. LC 76-25526. 7.95. St. Martin's Press.
None Shall Know. Peter De Polnay. LC 76-367712. 1976. 3.50 (ISBN 0-491-01566-6). W. H. Allen.
None Shall Look Back. Caroline Gordon. LC 72-164528. 1971. (ISBN 0-8154-0397-6). Cooper Square Publishers.
None Shall Look Back... Caroline Gordon. LC 37-27189. 1937. C. Scribner's Sons.
None Shall Sleep Tonight. 1st Ed. Hugh McCutcheon. LC 53-6075. (Guilt edged mystery). 1953. Dutton.
None So Blind. Lee Bergman. LC 58-5362. 1957. Crowell.
None So Blind,". Ethel Deane. LC 10-107767. 1910. Reid Publishing Company.
None So Blind. Albert Parker Fitch. LC 24-4008. 1924. The Macmillan Company.
None So Blind. J. Aaron Norwood. 3.75 o.p. Vantage.
None So Blind. Fritz Thomas. LC 81-80156. 416p. 1983. 10.95 (ISBN 0-86666-007-0). GWP.
None So Blind: A Novel. Mitchell A Wilson. LC 45-9239. 1945. Simon and Schuster.
None So Pretty. Margaret Emma Faith Irwin. LC 30-8260. Harcourt, Brace and Company.
None Such? There Will Yet Be Thousands. Emory James Haynes. LC 7-3748. 1893. The North Publishing Co.
None to Comfort Me. Anne Mallard Davis. LC 78-21963. 8.95 (ISBN 0-89587-005-3). J. F. Blair.
Nonesuch. Georgette Heyer. 1976. 1.50 (ISBN 0-449-22940-8). Fawcett Crest.
Nonexistent Knight & The Cloven Viscount. Italo Calvino. LC 76-39699. (Harbrace paperbound library; 73). 1977. 2.95 (ISBN 0-15-665975-1). Harcourt Brace Jovanovich.
Nonexistent Knight and The Cloven Viscount: Two Short Novels. Italo Calvino & Italo Calvino. LC 62-8445. 1962. Random House.
Nonie. Leoti Leigh. 1899. The Editor Publishing Company.
Nono, Love and the Soil (Nono) Gaston Roupnel. Tr. by Beyer, Barnet Julius. LC 19-2015. (Half-title: The library of French fiction, ed. by B. J. Beyer). E. P. Dutton & Company.
Nonrequiem. Mel Konner. 1976. pap. 2.50 o.p. (ISBN 0-8180-1531-4). Horizon.
Nonsense ABC's, Verses. Illus. by Helen Endres and Robert Bonfils. Edward Lear. LC 56-11562. (Rand McNally elf book, 550). Rand McNally.
Nonsense Novels. Stephen Leacock. 4.75 o.p. (ISBN 0-8446-0176-4). Peter Smith.
Nonsuch Lure. Mary M Luke. LC 76-12605. 8.95 (ISBN 0-698-10750-0). Coward, McCann & Geoghegan.
Nonsuch Lure. Mary M. Luke. 1977. 1.95 (ISBN 0-425-03552-2). Berkley Pub. Corp.
Noon & Night. Hadrian Keene. (O.s.i.). (Orig.). 1969. pap. 0.60 o.s.i. (A554X, Award). Univ Pub & Dist.
Noon at a Country Inn. Antanas Vaiciulaitis. 1965. 3.95 (ISBN 0-87141-013-3). Manyland.
Noon at a Country Inn: Short Stories Tr. from Lithuanian ByAlbinas Baranauskas Others Foreword by Clark Mills. Antanas Vaiciulaitis. LC 66-552. 1966. 3.95. Manyland.
Noon Balloon to Rangoon. John Haase. (O.S.I.). 1967. 3.95 o.s.i. (ISBN 0-671-52937-4). S&S.
Noon Balloon to Rangoon: A Novel. John Haase. LC 67-25375. 1967. Simon and Schuster.
Noon-Mark. Mary Stanbery Watts. LC 20-18922. 1920. The Macmillan Company.
Noon on the Third Day. James Hulbert. LC 62-16931. 1962. Holt, Rinehart and Winston.
Noon Shouts. Margielea S. See. 1969. 4.00 (ISBN 0-87012-030-1). McClain.
Noon: Twenty-Second Century. Arkadii Natanovich Strugatskii & Boris Natanovich Strugatskii. 1979. pap. 3.95 o.s.i. (ISBN 0-02-025600-0, Collier). Macmillan.
Noon Wine see Six Great Modern Short Novels.
Noon, 22nd Century. Arkadii Natanovich Strugatskii & Boris Natanovich Strugatskii. LC 78-17444. (Macmillan's Best of Soviet Science Fiction). 10.95 (ISBN 0-02-615150-2). Macmillan.
Noon: 22nd Century. Arkadii Natanovich Strugatskii & Boris Natanovich Strugatskii. 1978. 12.95 o.s.i. (ISBN 0-02-615150-2). Macmillan.
Noonblaze. Milan Chiba. 288p. (Orig.). 1981. pap. 2.95 (ISBN 0-8439-1013-5, Leisure Bks). Nordon Pubns.
Noonday Height. Bruce Byers. LC 65-16569. 1965. 3.95. Morrow.
Noonday Night: A Romance of the Weak and the Strong. Albert Weber Sheffield. LC 7-440. 1906. The Southland Company.
Nooriabad File. Geoffrey Watson. LC 79-19637. 1979. 8.95 (ISBN 0-684-16292-X). Scribner.
Noose: A Detective Story. Philip MacDonald. LC 30-8265. 1930. L. MacVeagh, The Dial Press.
Noose at Big Iron. Terrell L. Bowers. (YA) 1980. 6.50 (Avalon). Bouregy.
Noose for Slattery: Walk a Narrow Trail. Steven G Lawrence. (Slattery#3). 1975. (pbk.) 0.95. Leisure Books.
Noose for the Desperado. Clifton Adams. LC 51-31789. (Gold medal books, 168). 1951. Fawcett Publications.
Noose for the Marshal. A. A. Baker. 1977. pap. 1.50 (ISBN 0-89041-140-9, 3140). Major Bks.
Noose Hangs High. Frank Chester Robertson. LC 45-2057. 1945. E. P. Dutton & Company, Inc.
Noose Is Drawn: A Christopher Storm Mystery. Willetta Ann Barber & Rudolph Frederick Schabelitz. LC 45-9159. 1945. C. Scribner's Sons.
Noose of Emeralds. Bevis Winter. LC 56-4040. 1956. Mystery House.
Noose of Red Beads. Terry J. King. LC 68-15221. (Raven Book Mystery). 1969. 4.25 o.p. (B61740). Abelard.
Noose Report. Alfred Hitchcock. 1.50. Dell.
Nopalgarth. Jack Vance, pseud. (Science Fiction Ser.). 1980. pap. 2.25 (ISBN 0-87997-563-6, UE1563). Daw Bks.
Nor All Thy Tears". Constance Antonina Boyle. LC 24-31914. 1924. T. Seltzer.
Nor All Thy Tears. Frank Arthur Swinnerton. LC 72-76210. 1972. 6.95. Doubleday.
Nor All Your Tears. Louis H Charbonneau. LC 59-14323. (Torquil book). 1959. Distributed by Dodd, Mead.
Nor All Your Tears. Maud H Yardley. LC 8-16716. R. F. Fenno & Company.
Nor Any Dawn. Netta Muskett. 1975. pap. 1.25 o.p. (ISBN 0-515-03760-5). BJ Pub Group.
Nor Crystal Tears. Alan Dean Foster. LC 82-8836. 1982. 2.75 (ISBN 0-345-29141-7). Ballantine.
Nor Iron Bars. Sylvia G. L. Dannett & Bennett, Edwin. LC 40-3028. Fortuny's.
Nor Spell nor Charm. Alicen White. 1971. pap. 0.75 o.p. (ISBN 0-447-74753-3). Lancer.
Nor Time nor Space. S. M Berthold. LC 47-572944. 1947. Meador Pub. Co.
Nor Time, nor Space. Dallas Reed. LC 31-14623. Dorrance & Company, Inc.
Nor Time nor Tide. Edward Carroll Sibley. LC 42-4716. 1937. Robert Speller Publishing Corporation.
Nor Wife, nor Maid. Margaret Wolfe Hamilton Hungerford. LC 7-9345. 1892. J. W. Lovell Company.

Nor Wife nor Maid. Margaret Wolfe Hamilton Hungerford. LC 7-90628. (On cover: Fortnightly series, no. 19). 1896. American Publishers Corporation.

Nora Brady's Vow: And Mona, the Vestal. Anna Hanson McKenney Dorsey. LC 6-33711. 1869. J. B. Lippincott & Co.

Nora. By Carl Detlef Pseud. Klara Bauer & Ford, Marian,Tr. LC 6-10340. (On cover: Seaside library. Pocket ed., no. 1086). 1888. G. Munro.

Nora Creina. Margaret Wolfe Hamilton Hungerford. LC 7-90613. (On cover: Fortnightly series, no. 20). 1897. American Publishers Corporation.

Nora Drake Story. Cornelia Blair. LC 50-10604. 1950. Duell, Sloan and Pearce.

Nora Lee. Elenore Meherin. LC 27-14708. Grosset & Dunlap.

Nora: Or, The Missing Heir of Callonby. Sarah Elizabeth Forbush G. S. Downs Downs. LC 2-85316. (On cover: Eagle series, no. 233). Street & Smith.

Nora Pays. Lucille Baldwin Van Slyke. LC 25-2348. 1925. Frederick A. Stokes Company.

Nora Was a Nurse. Peggy Gaddis, pseud. 1970. pap. 0.50 o.p. (50-495). Manor Bks.

Nora Was a Nurse: By Peggy Dern Pseud. Peggy Gaddis, pseud. 1953. Arcadia House.

Norab Conough. Walter George Henderson. LC 9-15204. 1909. The Outing Publishing Company.

Norah. Pamela Hill. LC 76-28038. 8.95. St. Martin's Press.

Norah. Pamela Hill. (Fawcett Crest Book). 1978. 1.95 (ISBN 0-449-23482-7). Fawcett Pub.

Norah of Waterford. Rosa Mulholland Gilbert. LC 15-19265. 1915. P. J. Kenedy & Sons.

Nora's Innocents. Barbara Szold. 448p. 1982. pap. 3.50 (ISBN 0-523-48008-3). Pinnacle Bks.

Nora's Love Test. Mary Cecil Hay. (Seaside library, v. 22, no. 421). 1878. G. Munro.

Nora's Return: A Sequel to "The Doll's House" of Henry Ibsen. Ednah Dow Littlehale Cheney. LC 6-233498. 1890. Lee and Shepard.

Nordic Twilight. Edward Morgan Forster. LC 77-28146. Repr. of 1940 ed. lib. bdg. 10.00 (ISBN 0-8414-4358-0). Folcroft.

Nordic Twilight. Edward Morgan Forster. 1940. 4.50 o.s.i. Ridgeway Bks.

Norgil, More Tales of Prestidigitection. Walter Brown Gibson. LC 78-53497. 1979. 10.00. (ISBN 0-89296-041-8) (ISBN 0-89296-042-6). Mysterious Press.

Norgil: More Tales of Prestidigitection. Maxwell Grant, pseud. LC 78-53497. (Illus.). 1979. 10.00 (ISBN 0-89296-041-8); limited ed. o.p. 25.00 (ISBN 0-89296-042-6). Mysterious Pr.

Norgil the Magician. Walter Brown Gibson. LC 76-16891. 1977. 10.00. (ISBN 0-89296-031-0) (ISBN 0-89296-032-9). Mysterious Press.

Norgil the Magician. Maxwell Grant, pseud. LC 76-16891. 1977. 10.00 (ISBN 0-89296-006-X). Mysterious Pr.

Norine's Revenge, and Sir Noel's Heir. May Agnes Early Fleming. LC 6-39948. 1888. G. W. Dillingham; Etc., Etc.

Norma Ashe: A Novel. Susan Glaspell. LC 42-22856. 1942. J. B. Lippincott Company.

Norma Jean, the Termite Queen. Sheila Ballantyne. LC 74-27448. 1975. 7.95 (ISBN 0-385-03264-1). Doubleday.

Norma Jean, the Termite Queen. Sheila Ballantyne. 1976. (pbk.) 1.75. Bantam Books.

Norma Jean, the Termite Queen. Sheila Ballantyne. LC 82-22254. (Penguin Contemporary American Fiction Series). 1983. 5.95 (ISBN 0-14-006551-2). Penguin Books.

Norma Lane: The Daughter of an Elk. Samuel Newton Cook. LC 9-24018. 1909. Wayne-Cook Publishing Co.

Norma Trist: Or, Pure Carbon: a Story of the Inversion of the Sexes. John Wesley Carhart. 1895. E. Von Boeckmann.

Normal Heart. Madelon S. Gohlke. LC 81-8379. (Minnesota Voices Project Ser.: No. 4). (Illus.). 78p. 1981. pap. 3.00 (ISBN 0-89823-027-6). New Rivers Pr.

Norman Bugles Blow No More. Clifford Dowdey. 1967. 7.50, 6.48 lib. ed.,. S. Berg.

Norman Conquests: Table Manners, Living Together, Round & Round the Garden. Alan Ayckbourn. LC 78-73051. 1979. pap. 3.95 (ISBN 0-394-17082-2, B422, BC). Grove.

Norman Holt: A Story of the Army of the Cumberland. Charles King. LC 1-31747. G. W. Dillingham Company.

Norman Leslie: A New York Story. Theodore Sedgwick Fay. LC 6-387719. 1869. G. P. Putnam and Son.

Norman Leslie: A Tale of Present Times. Theodore Sedgwick Fay. LC 79-93614. 1969. Garrett Press.

Norman Leslie: A Tale of Present Times. Theodore Sedgwick Fay. LC 72-8159. 1972. (ISBN 0-8422-8044-8). MSS Information Corp.

Norman Leslie. A Tale of the Present Times... Theodore Sedgwick Fay. 1835. Harper & Brothers.

Norman Macdonald. Jessie Hunter Brown. LC 6-18939. 1887. Standard Publishing Co.

Norman Macdonald. Jessie Hunter Brown Pounds. LC 6-18939. 1887. Standard Publishing Co.

Norman Pretender. Valerie Anand. LC 79-26365. 12.50 (ISBN 0-684-16099-4). Scribner.

Norman Reid, M.A. Jessie Patrick Findlay. 1891. Cranston and Stowe.

Normandie Affair. Milton Caniff. Ed. by Bill Chadbourne. LC 77-75668. (Milton Caniff's Terry & the Pirates Ser.: Vol. 2). (Illus.). 1977. pap. 6.95. Nostalgia Pr.

Normandie Triangle. Justin Scott. LC 81-67220. 480p. 1981. 13.95 (ISBN 0-87795-346-5). Arbor Hse.

Normandie Triangle. Justin Scott. 576p. 1982. pap. 3.95 (ISBN 0-345-30640-6). Ballantine.

Norman's Bridge: Or, The Modern Midas. Anne Caldwell Marsh-Caldwell. LC 52-56002. 1867. Harper.

Norman's Letter. Gavin Lambert. LC 66-20155. 1966. Coward-McCann.

Norman's Letter: Postscript by Lady D. Gavin Lambert. (74-985). 1967. Lancer.

Norman's Letter: Postscript by Lady D. 1st Amer. Ed. Gavin Lambert. LC 66-20155. bds., 5.50. Coward.

Normanton. A. J. Barrowcliffe. LC 79-8235. Repr. of 1862 ed. 44.50 (ISBN 0-404-61779-4). AMS Pr.

Norma's House. Paula MacFie. LC 75-2145. 1975. 4.95 (ISBN 0-517-521€8-7). Lenox Hill Press.

Normo-Saxon: Or, A Romance of English History. Alexander D Penfold. 1899. The Knickerbocker Press.

Norns Are Spinning. Andreas Haukland & Ten Eyck, Barent, Tr. LC 28-11815. 1928. Macy-Masius.

Norodom, King of Cambodia. A Romance of the East. Frank McGloin. 1882. D. Appleton and Company.

Norroy, Diplomatic Agent. George Fitzalan Bronson Howard. LC 7-5683. The Saalfield Publishing Co.

Norseman's Pilgrimage. Hjalmar Hjorth Boyesen. LC 6-15219. 1875. Sheldon & Company.

Norsk Gopher: A Story of the Northwest. Charles Nelson Sinnett. LC 8-9008. Hunt & Eaton.

Norston's Rest. Ann Sophia Winterbotham Stephens. LC 8-12410. T. B. Peterson & Brothers.

Norstrilia. Cordwainer Smith, pseud. 1978. pap. 1.95 (ISBN 0-345-27800-3, Del Rey Bks.). Ballantine.

Norstrilia. Cordwainer Smith. 1975. (pbk.) 1.50 (ISBN 0-345-24366-8). Ballantine Books.

North. Louis-Ferdinand Celine, pseud. 1972. 10.00 o.p. (ISBN 0-440-06420-1, Sey Lawr). Delacorte.

North. Louis-Ferdinand Celine, pseud. Tr. by Ralph Manheim. 1976. pap. 2.95 (ISBN 0-14-004342-X). Penguin.

North. Louis Ferdinand Destouches. LC 76-46530. 1976. 2.95 (ISBN 0-14-004342-X). Penguin Books.

North. Louis Ferdinand Destouches. LC 75-164849. 1972. 10.00. Delacorte Press.

North. James Beardsley Hendryx. LC 23-2804. 1923. G. P. Putnam's Sons.

North Against the Sioux. Kenneth Ulyatt. (60-2317). 1968. Popular Lib.

North Against the Sioux. Kenneth Ulyatt. LC 67-16393. (Illus.). 1967. Prentice-Hall.

North and South. Elizabeth Cleghorn Stevenson Gaskell. LC 73-169373. (Oxford English novels). 1973. 13.00 (ISBN 0-19-255340-2). Oxford University Press.

North & South. Elizabeth Cleghorn Stevenson Gaskell. LC 70-145039. (Everyman's library. Fiction no. 680). 1971. (ISBN 0-403-00985-5). Scholarly Press.

North and South. Elizabeth Cleghorn Stevenson Gaskell. LC 72-186541. (works of Mrs. Gaskell, v. 4). (Illus.). 1972. 24.00 (ISBN 0-404-07254-2). AMS Press.

North and South. Elizabeth Cleghorn Stevenson Gaskell. LC 74-19240. (Penguin English library). (Illus.). 1970. Penguin.

North and South. Elizabeth Cleghorn Stevenson Gaskell. Ed. by Adolphus William Ward. LC 7-5065. (Half-title: The works of Mrs. Gaskell. Knutsford ed. v. 4). 1906. G. P. Putnam's Sons; Etc., Etc.

North and South. Elizabeth Cleghorn Stevenson Gaskell. Ed. by Clement King Shorter. (Half-title: The world's classics. cliv). 1909. H. Frowde.

North and South: Or, Scenes and Adventures in Mexico. Charles Sealsfield. Tr. by Headley, Joel Tyler. LC 8-3383. 1844. J. Winchester.

North and South: Or, Slavery and Its Contrasts; a Tale of Real Life. Caroline E Rush. LC 68-58067. (Illus.). 1968. Negro Universities Press.

North and South: Or, Slavery and Its Contrasts. A Tale of Real Life. Caroline E Rush. LC 8-9695. 1852. Crissy & Markley.

North and South: Or, Slavery and Its Contrasts. Caroline E Rush. LC 70-149877. (Black Heritage Library Collection). (Illus.). 1971. (ISBN 0-8369-8757-8). Books for Libraries Press.

North Atlantic Tribune. Edward Dorn. 1967. 7.50 (ISBN 0-89760-135-1). Telegraph Bks.

North Beach Girl see Strange Lovers.

North by West. R. D. Symons. LC 73-79717. (Illus.). 192p. 1973. 5.95 o.p. (ISBN 0-385-07475-1). Doubleday.

North Cape. Joe Poyer, pseud. LC 69-20085. (Doubleday science fiction). 1969. 4.95. Doubleday.

North Carolina in the Short Story... Ed. by Richard Gaither Walser. LC 48-5605. 1948. Univ. of North Carolina Press.

North Carolina Sketches: Phrases of Life Where the Galax Grows. Mary Nelson Carter. 1900. A. C. McClurg & Co.

North Country Comedy. Matilda Barbara Betham- Edwards, pseud. LC 6-36590. (On cover: Lippincott's copyright foreign novels). 1892. J. B. Lippincott Company.

North Country Maid. A Novel. Emily Sharp H. Cameron. LC 6-21851. (Harper's Franklin square library, no. 409). Harper & Brothers.

North Country Maid. A Novel. Emily Sharp H. Cameron. LC 6-21852. (On cover: Seaside library. Pocket ed., no. 595). G. Munro.

North Dallas Forty. Peter Gent. LC 73-5815. 1973. 7.95 (ISBN 0-688-00183-1). Morrow.

North Dallas Forty. Peter Gent. (Signet book). 1974. (pbk.) 1.95. New American Library.

North Door, a Romance. Greville Macdonald. LC 20-269871. 1920. Houghton Mifflin Company.

North Face. Mary Renault, pseud. 1974. (pbk.) 1.25. Popular Library.

North Face. Mary Renault, pseud. LC 78-3849. 1978. 9.95 (ISBN 0-89244-081-3). Queens House.

North Face: A Novel. Mary Renault, pseud. LC 48-4120. 1948. W. Morrow.

North from Montana. Archie Joscelyn. LC 48-15319. 1948. Phoenix Press.

North from Rome. Helen MacInnes. 288p. 1982. pap. 2.95 (ISBN 0-449-24009-6, Crest). Fawcett.

North from Rome. 1st Ed. Helen MacInnes. LC 58-5922. 1958. Harcourt, Brace.

North from Thursday. John Cleary. 1981. 18.95x (Pub. by Remploy England). State Mutual Bk.

North Land. William J McNulty. LC 26-186. The Christopher Publishing House.

North of Copper Creek. Craig Massey. (YA) (gr. 9-12). 1963. pap. 0.95 o.p. (37-35, MG). Moody.

North of Fifty-Three. Bertrand William Sinclair. LC 14-623817. 1914. Little, Brown, and Company.

North of Fifty-Three. Bertrand William Sinclair. 1916. Little, Brown, and Company.

North of Grand Central: Three Novels of New England: The Late George Apley, Wickford Point, H. M. Pulham, Esquire. With New Prefaces by the Author, and with an Introd. by Kenneth Roberts. 1st Ed. John Phillips Marquand. LC 56-907628. 1956. Little, Brown.

North of Heaven. Biloine Grace Whiting & Skelton, Josephine Adelle. LC 48-216153. 1948. Herald House.

North of Market. 1st Ed. Arthur Foff. LC 57-10057. 1957. Harcourt, Brace.

North of Saginaw Bay: By E. J. (Pete) Petersen. Ernest J Petersen. LC 53-20028. 1952. Tall Tibber Press.

North of Santa Fe. Charles Stanley Strong. LC 49-6364. 1949. Phoenix Press.

North of the Border. Samuel Alexander White. LC 40-323725. Phoenix Press.

North of the Law. Samuel Alexander White. LC 20-7294. 1920. Doubleday, Page & Company.

North of the Platte. Robert F. Barger. 1970. 2.95 o.p. Vantage.

North of the Rio Grande: A Romance of Texas Pioneer Days. Roy Lander Lightfoot. LC 49-9986. 1949. Naylor Co.

North of the Stars. Charles Stoddard. LC 36-2637. The Dodge Publishing Company.

North of the Stars. Charles Stanley Strong. LC 38-2667. 1937. Dodge Pub. Co.

North of the Yukon. Arthur Robert Willis. LC 55-13908. 1955. Avalon Books.

North of Welfare, a Novel. 1st Ed. William Krasner. LC 54-8964. 1954. Harper.

North of 36. Emerson Hough. LC 24-10971. 1923. D. Appleton and Company.

North of 36. Emerson Hough & Hart, Olive Ely, Ed. (Half-title: Appleton modern literature series). D. Appleton and Company.

North of 62: A Story of Adventure. George Witeman Tweedd Le. LC 46-7786. 1946. Foster & Stewart Publishing Corp.

North Sea Mistress. Katrinka Blickle. 1978. 1.75 (ISBN 0-523-40326-7). Pinnacle Books.

North Sea Mistress: Romance and Revolution in Modern-Day Scotland. Katrinka Blickle. LC 76-45262. (Illus.). 1977. 7.95 (ISBN 0-385-12749-9). Doubleday.

North Shore. Wallace Irwin. LC 32-21897. 1932. Houghton Mifflin Company.

North Side Nurse. Lucy Agnes Hancock. LC 40-4500. 1940. Macrae-Smith-Company.

North Star. Henry Wilson Allen. LC 56-5222. 1956. Random House.

North Star. Will Henry, pseud. LC 56-5222. 1956. Random House.

North Star. Hammond Innes. LC 74-21292. (Illus.). 1975. 7.95 (ISBN 0-394-49578-0). Knopf.

North Star: A Dog Story of the Canadian Northwest. Rufus King. LC 25-11152. 1925. G. H. Watt.

North Star: A Tale of Norway in the Tenth Century. Margaret Ellen Henry Ruffin. LC 4-9212. 1904. Little, Brown, and Company.

North Star: By Will Henry Pseud. Henry Allen. LC 56-5222. 1956. Random House.

North Star Crusade. William Katz. LC 76-355809. 7.95 (ISBN 0-399-11646-X). Putnam.

North Star Sage: The Story OfIgnatius Donnelly. Oscar Matthias Sullivan. LC 53-11554. 1953. Vantage Press.

North to Cheyenne. Lou Cameron. 1975. (pbk.) 0.95. Dell.

North to Dakota. Jake Logan. LC 76-9581. (Jake Logan Ser.: No. 8). 176p. 1976. pap. 1.95 (ISBN 0-86721-051-6). Playboy Pbks.

North to Danger. Tom Gill. LC 42-182903. 1942. G. P. Putnam's Sons.

North to Freedom. Anne Sophie Holm. LC 65-12612. 1965. Harcourt, Brace & World.

North to Hanoi. Richard Parque. 150p. (Orig.). (YA) 1982. pap. 3.95 (ISBN 0-939066-04-1). Rapier Pr.

North to Montana. Steven C. Lawrence, pseud. 160p. 1981. pap. 1.95 (ISBN 0-8439-0985-4, Leisure Bks). Nordon Pubns.

North to Rabaul. Christopher Wood. LC 79-52253. 1979. 9.95 (ISBN 0-87795-233-7). Arbor Hse.

North to Rabaul: A Novel. Christopher Wood. LC 79-52253. 9.95 (ISBN 0-87795-233-7). Arbor House.

North to Texas. Noel M Loomis. LC 56-6651. Ballantine Books.

North to the Promised Land. Harold Channing Wire. LC 48-1415. 1948. Westminster Press.

North to the Rails. Louis L'Amour. 208p. 1975. pap. 2.25 (ISBN 0-553-14829-X). Bantam.

North to Toronto. Martin Maltese. 1978. pap. 1.75 (ISBN 0-532-17180-2). Woodhill.

North to Yesterday. Robert Flynn. LC 67-11121. 1967. Knopf.

North Town. Lorenz B Graham. LC 65-12503. 3.95. Crowell.

North Town. Lorenz B Graham. 1977. 1.25 (ISBN 0-451-07624-9). New American Library.

North Trail. Lester L. Whitmore. 1966. 4.00 o.p. (ISBN 0-682-44101-5). Exposition.

North Wall. Roger Hubank. LC 77-28426. (Illus.). 1978. 8.95 (ISBN 0-670-51551-5). Viking Press.

North Wilderness & Other Stories. Margaret Kolste. (Illus.). 1976. 3.95 o.p. (ISBN 0-8059-2301-2). Dorrance.

North Wind Do Blow. Bertha Muzzy Sinclair. LC 37-350. 1937. Little, Brown, and Company.

North Wind of Love. Compton Mackenzie. LC 45-8308. 1945. Dodd, Mead & Company.

North Woods Rendezvous. Eugene Edward Wilson, pseud. LC 53-39529. 1953.

Northanger Abbey. Jane Austen. LC 50-1514. 1950. Doric Books.

Northanger Abbey. Jane Austen. (Harcourt library of English and American classics). 1962. Harcourt, Brace & World.

Northanger Abbey. Jane Austen. Ed. by Anne Henry Ehrenpreis. LC 73-161820. (Penguin English library). (Illus.). 1972. 0.30 (ISBN 0-14-043074-1). Penguin.

Northanger Abbey. Jane Austen. LC 7078. 1833. Carey & Lea.

Northanger Abbey. Jane Austen. LC 7080. (Seaside library, vol. ii no. 1050). 1881. G. Munro.

Northanger Abbey. Jane Austen. LC 7081. 1892. Roberts Brothers.

Northanger Abbey. Jane Austen. Ed. by Sadleir, Michael. LC 31-26967. (Half-title: The World's classics. occlv). 1930. H. Milford, Oxford University Press.

Northanger Abbey. Jane Austen & Limited Editions Club, Inc., New York. LC 71-29866. (Illus.). 1971. Printed for the Members of the Limited Editions Club by the Garamond Press.

Northanger Abbey; Lady Susan; The Watsons and Sanditon. Jane Austen & James Kinsley. LC 80-40257. (World's classics). 1980. 4.50 (ISBN 0-19-281525-3). Oxford University Press.

Northanger Abbey and Persuasion. Jane Austen. LC 7-1509. 1897. Macmillan and Co., Limited.

Northanger Abbey & Persuasion. Jane Austen. (Half-title: Everyman's library, ed. by Ernest Rhys. Fiction). 1906. J. M. Dent & Co.

TITLE INDEX NOT IN THE PROSPECTUS.

Northanger Abbey & Persuasion. Jane Austen. LC 36-37057. (Half-title: Everyman's library, ed. by Ernest Rhys. Fiction. no. 25). 1932. J. M. Dent & Sons, Ltd.
Northanger Abbey & Persuasion see Oxford Illustrated Jane Austen.
Northanger Abbey & Persuasion: And, Persuasion. Jane Austen. LC 70-870112. (Oxford English novels). 1971. 2.50 (ISBN 0-19-255343-7). Oxford University Press.
Northanger Abbey. Introd. by Malcolm Elwin. Illus. by Philip Gough. Jane Austen. LC 66-5486. (Macdonald illus. classics, 40). 1966. 3.50. Macdonald.
Northanger Abbey, Persuasion, Lady Susan, The Watsons. Jane Austen & Bailey, John Cann. LC 29-25048. 1928. Dodd, Mead & Company.
Northanger Set of the Jane Austen Horrid Novels. Ed. by Devendra P. Varma. 1968. slipcase 75.00 o.p. Dufour.
Northbridge Rectory. Angela Mackail Thirkell. LC 42-214. 1942. A. A. Knopf.
Norther. Emilio Carballido. Tr. by Margaret S. Peden from Sp. (Texas Pan American Ser.). Orig. Title: El norte. (Illus.). 101p. 1968. 7.95x (ISBN 0-292-78389-2). U of Tex Pr.
Norther: El Norte). Emilio Carballido. LC 68-54901. (Texas pan-American series). (Illus.). 1968. 3.50. University of Texas Press.
Northern Affair. David K Findlay. LC 63-20044. (Illus.). 1963. Morrow.
Northern Exposure. Michael Kilian. LC 82-17045. 1983. 14.95 (ISBN 0-312-57896-2). St. Martin's Press.
Northern Georgia Sketches. William Nathaniel Harben. LC 73-110194. (Short story index reprint series). 1970. Books for Libraries Press.
Northern Georgia Sketches. William Nathaniel Harben. 1900. A.C. McClurg & Co.
Northern Georgia Sketches. William Nathaniel Harben. LC 5722. 1900. A. C. McClurg & Co.
Northern Girl. Elizabeth A Lynn. LC 79-25887. 10.95 (ISBN 0-399-12409-8). Berkley Pub. Corp.: Distributed by Putman.
Northern Light. Elisabeth Burstenbinder. Tr. by Lowrey, D. M. (choice series, no 33). 1891. R. Bonner's Sons.
Northern Light. Archibald Joseph Cronin. 1974. pap. 1.50 o.p. (ISBN 0-515-03324-3, A3395). BJ Pub Group.
Northern Lights. Tim O'Brien. LC 75-6881. 1975. 8.95 (ISBN 0-440-06664-6). Delacorte Press/S. Lawrence.
Northern Lights. Robert Olmsted. 1969. pap. 2.50 o.p. Northwoods Pr.
Northern Lights. Gilbert Parker. LC 9-24321. 1909. Harper & Brothers.
Northern Lights. Roger Vercel & Woods, Katherine, 1886- Tr. LC 48-3219. 1948. Random House.
Northern Lights: A New Collection of Distinguished Writing by Canadian Authors. With an Introd. by Mazo De La Roche. 1st Ed. Ed. by George Edmondson Nelson. LC 60-9741. 1960. Doubleday.
Northern Lights: A Tale of Spitzbergen. Jayne, Edith M. G., Tr & Jayne, Edith M. G. Tr. LC 31-208474. 1931. Longmans, Green and Co.
Northern Lights. From the Romantic American Drama. Arthur D Hall & Harkins, James W., Jr. Northern Lights. LC 7-531. (On cover; Drama series, no. 28). Street & Smith.
Northern Lights. Stories from Swedish and Finnish Authors. Tr. by Borg, Selma. LC 7-34713. 1873. Porter & Coates.
Northern Lights to Fields of Gold. Stanley Scearce. LC 40-255. 1939. The Caxton Printers, Ltd.
Northern Magic. Janet Dailey. 192p. 1982. pap. 1.75 (ISBN 0-373-10475-8). PB.
Northern Nurse. Elliott Merrick. 1982. pap. 8.95 (ISBN 0-9603324-2-1). Sherry Urie.
Northern Palmyra Affair. Harrison Evans Salisbury. LC 62-9923. 1962. Harper.
Northern Saga. Steven C Lawrence, pseud. LC 76-24251. 1.75. Playboy Press.
Northern Sunrise: A Novel. Haakon Bugge Mahrt & Mussey, June Barrows, 1910- Tr. LC 39-271444. Reynal & Hitchcock.
Northern Sunset. Penny Jordan. (Harlequin Presents Ser.). 192p. 1982. pap. 1.75 (ISBN 0-373-10508-8). PB.
Northerner. Norah Davis. LC 5-326833. 1905. The Century Co.
Northerner: A Novel. Joan Colebrook. LC 48-109476. 1948. C. Scribner's Sons.
Northing Tramp. Edgar Wallace. LC 29-18420. 1929. Pub. for The Crime Club, Inc., by Doubleday, Doran & Company, Inc.
Northington Dollar. Elizabeth Levin. LC 30-125718. The Guthrie Publishing House.
Northland Stories: Tales of Trapping Life in the Canadian Wilderness. William MacMillan. LC 23-9414. The Peltries Publishing Company, Inc.
Northlight. Erik Riis-Carstensen. LC 61-17970. 1962. Philosophical Library.
Northlight, Lovelight. Folch-Ribas, Jacques E. LC 76-20521. 1976. 6.95 (ISBN 0-88349-106-0). Reader's Digest Press: Distributed by Crowell.
Northlight, Lovelight. Jacques E. Folch-Ribas. LC 77-365029. 1976. 8.95 (ISBN 0-88902-400-6). Fitzhenry & Whiteside.
Norths Meet Murder. Frances Louise Lockridge & Lockridge, Richard. LC 40-27108. 1940. Frederick A. Stokes Company.
Northward the Coast by Edward Lindall. Edward Ernest Smith. LC 65-25809. 1966. W. Morrow.
Northwater. Cecily Crowe. LC 68-12205. 1968. Holt, Rinehart and Winston.
Northwest! Harold Bindloss. LC 22-16874. Frederick A. Stokes Company.
Northwest Contract. Lionel Derrick. (Penetrator,#8). 1975. (pbk.) 1.25 (ISBN 0-523-00540-7). Pinnacle Books.
Northwest Crossing. Samuel Alexander White. LC 44-64992. 1944. Phoenix Press.
Northwest Disaster: Fire & Avalanche. Ruby E. Hult. (Cloth ed. 6.50 o.p.). (Illus.). 244p. 1975. pap. 5.95 (ISBN 0-8323-0224-4). Binford.
Northwest Law. Samuel Alexander White. LC 42-1117. Phoenix Press.
Northwest of Earth. 1st Ed. Catherine L Moore. LC 54-12145. Gnome Press.
Northwest Passage. Kenneth Lewis Robert. LC 37-20753. 1937. Doubleday, Doran & Company, Inc.
Northwest Passage. Kenneth Lewis Roberts. LC 38-13109. 1937. Doubleday, Doran & Company, Inc.
Northwest Patrol. Samuel Alexander White. LC 43-16525. 1943. Phoenix Press.
Northwest Raiders. Samuel Alexander White. LC 45-221293. 1945. Phoenix Press.
Northwest Smith: The Legendary Hero of the Spaceway. Catherine L. Moore. 1982. pap. 2.75 (ISBN 0-441-58613-9, Pub. by Ace Science Fiction). Ace Bks.
Northwest the Coast: By Edward Lindall Pseud. Edward Ernest Smith. LC 65-258097. bds., 3.95. Morrow.
Northwest Trouble. Charles Stanley Strong. LC 48-981767. 1948. Phoenix Press.
Northwest Wagons. Samuel Alexander White. LC 41-5581. Phoenix Press.
Northwestern Arizona Ghost Towns. Stanley W. Paher. LC 75-138320. (Illus.). 1970. 3.95 o.p. (ISBN 0-913814-00-8); pap. 2.95 o.p. Nevada Pubns.
Northwood. facsimile ed. Sarah Josepha Hale. LC 74-38652. (Black Heritage Library Collection). Repr. of 1852 ed. 21.00 (ISBN 0-8369-9010-2). Ayer Co.
Northwood: A Tale of New England. Sarah Josepha Hale. LC 24-27963. 1827. Bowles & Dearborn.
Northwood: Or, Life North and South. Sarah Josepha Buell Hale. LC 70-105092. (Series in American studies). (Illus.). 1970. Johnson Reprint Corp.
Northwood; or, Life North and South: Showing the True Character of Both. Sarah Josepha Hale. LC 6-46209. H. Long & Brother.
Northwoods Reader. Cully Gage. LC 77-73934. (Illus.). 1977. Avery Color Studios.
Northwoods Romance. Craig Massey. LC 56-42783. 1956. Zondervan Pub. House.
Norton Anthology of Short Fiction. Robert Verlin Cassill. LC 77-11970. 5.95 (ISBN 0-393-09072-8). Norton.
Norton Anthology of Short Fiction. shorter ed. Robert Verlin Cassill. LC 77-17235. 4.95 (ISBN 0-393-09075-2). Norton.
Norton Anthology of Short Fiction. 2nd ed., shorter. ed. Robert Verlin Cassill. LC 81-18792. 10.95 (ISBN 0-393-95182-0). Norton.
Norton Hardin: Or, The Knight of the Xx. Century, by Mrs. Minnye Creighton Cottrell. Minnye Creighton Cottrell. LC 7-6404. 1907. Mayhew Publishing Co.
Norva: A Tale of the Roman Empire, and Other Stories. Emile Souvestre. LC 8-12379. 1857. Crosby, Nichols & Co.
Norvel Hastings: Or, The Frigate in the Offing. A Nautical Tale of the War of 1812. LC 7-33167. 1850. A. Hart, Late Carey and Hart.
Norwayman. Joseph O'Connor. LC 49-7828. 1949. Macmillan Co.
Norway's Best Stories: An Introduction to Modern Norwegian Fiction. Ed. by Hanna Astrup Larsen. Tr. by Orbeck, Anders. (Half-title: Scandinavian classics, vol. xxix). 1927. The American-Scandinavian Foundation; W. W. Norton & Company, Inc.
Norwegian Lady & the Wreck of the Dictator. William O. Foss. LC 77-4941. (Illus.). 1977. pap. 4.95 o.p. (ISBN 0-915442-29-9). Donning Co.
Norwegian Typhoon. Nick Carter. (Nick Carter Ser.). (Illus.). 224p. 1982. pap. 2.50 (ISBN 0-441-58866-2, Pub. by Charter Bks). Ace Bks.
Norwich Cadets: A Tale of the Rebellion. Homer White. LC 9-3421. 1873. A. Clarke.
Norwich Victims. Francis Beeding. LC 35-172336. 1935. Harper & Brothers.
Norwood. Charles Portis. LC 66-21822. 1966. Simon and Schuster.
Norwood: Or, Life on the Prairie. Edward Z C Judson. LC 7-11452. 1850. W. F. Burgess.
Norwood: Or, Village Life in New England. Henry Ward Beecher. LC 6-9763. 1868. C. Scribner & Company.
Norwood: Or, Village Life in New England. Henry Ward Beecher. LC 6-97653. 1874. J.B. Ford and Company.
Nos Veremos en la Cumbre. Zig Ziglar. LC 82-9093. 382p. (Span.). 1982. pap. 9.95 (ISBN 0-88289-323-8). Pelican.
Nose for Trouble. Jim Kjelgaard, pseud. (Skylark Ser.). 208p. 1982. pap. 1.95 (ISBN 0-553-15124-X, Skylark). Bantam.
Nose Jobs for Peace. Selma Diamond. LC 71-115834. 1970. 5.95 o.p. P-H.
Nose Knows. E. W. Hildick. 1979. pap. 1.25 (ISBN 0-448-17053-1, Pub. by Tempo). Ace Bks.
Nosotros Tres. new ed. Demetrio Veliz. (Pimienta Collection Ser.). 160p. (Span.). 1975. pap. 1.00 (ISBN 0-88473-227-4). Fiesta Pub.
Nostalgia. Genevieve Gennari. LC 64-22870. 1964. McKay.
Nostalgia. Heller McAlpin. LC 82-10494. 12.95 (ISBN 0-684-17768-4). Scribner.
Nostradamus: The Man Who Saw Through Time. Lee McCann. 1982. 23.50 (ISBN 0-374-22317-3); pap. 7.95 (ISBN 0-374-51754-1). FS&G.
Nostradamus Traitor. John E Gardner. LC 78-60291. 1979. 10.00 (ISBN 0-385-13601-3). Doubleday.
Nostromo. Joseph Conrad. LC 51-13938. (Modern library of the world's best books 275). 1951. Modern Library.
Nostromo: A Tale of the Seaboard. Joseph Conrad. LC 4-33122. 1904. Harper & Brothers.
Nostromo: A Tale of the Seaboard. Joseph Conrad. 1921. Doubleday, Page & Company.
Not a Blessed Thing! Monica Quill. (Sister Mary Teresa Mystery). 1981. 9.95 (ISBN 0-8149-0849-7). Vanguard.
Not a Cloud in the Sky. Josephine Lawrence. LC 64-18287. 1964. Harcourt, Brace & World.
Not a Clue. Arto DeMirjian. 1974. (pbk.) 0.95. Popular Library.
Not a Hero. A Novel. Eliza Lofton Phillips Pugh. LC 7-42392. 1867. Blelock & Co.
Not a Joy Forever: A Novel. Buena Vista Stine. LC 45-10544. 1945. Wetzel Publihsing Co., Inc.
Not a Leg to Stand on. Miles Burton. LC 45-5455. 1945. Pub. for the Crime Club by Doubleday, Doran and Co., Inc.
Not a Penny More, Not a Penny Less. Jeffrey Archer. LC 75-21203. 1976. 6.95 (ISBN 0-385-11222-X). Doubleday.
Not a Station but a Place. Judith Clancy & M. F. Fisher. LC 79-20885. (Illus.). 72p. 1979. bds. 9.95 (ISBN 0-912184-03-5); pap. 5.95. Synergistic Pr.
Not a Word About Nightingales. Maureen Howard. LC 62-7540. 1962. Atheneum.
Not-Afraid. Dane Coolidge. LC 26-16266. E. P. Dutton & Company.
Not All Angels: Or, The Influence of the Dead Upon the Living. Sophia Beale McIntyre. LC 42-20806. 1942. Dorrance and Company.
Not All Ashes. William J Tucker. Southwest Press.
Not All in Vain. Ada Cambridge Cross. LC 6-31954. 1892. D. Appleton and Company.
Not All of Your Laughter: Not All of Your Tears. Steve Allen. LC 62-16686. 1962. B. Geis Associates, Distributed by Random House.
Not All Our Pride. Vokes Richardson. LC 65-14600. 4.50. Braziller.
Not All Rivers. Adriana Spadoni. LC 74-22816. (Labor Movement in Fiction and Non-Fiction). 1976. 21.00 (ISBN 0-404-58475-6). AMS Press.
Not All Rivers. Adriana Spadoni. LC 37-1665. 1937. Doubleday, Doran & Company, Inc.
Not All Saints. Elizabeth Rayner. LC 33-289309. 1933. Longmans, Green and Co.
Not All That Glitters. Louise Harrison McCraw. LC 45-2940. 1945. Fleming H. Revell Company.
Not All the King's Horses: A Novel. George Agnew Chamberlain. LC 19-15557. 1.75. The Bobbs-Merrill Company.
Not All the King's Horses: A Novel of Washington Society. Katherine Elwes Thomas. LC 8-27046. ("unknown" library). The Cassell Publishing Co.
Not All Your Laughter. Sally Gibbs. LC 39-15794. 1939. D. Appleton-Century Company, Incorporated.
Not Angels Quite. Nathan Haskell Dole. LC 6-33850. 1893. Lee and Shepard.
Not As a Stranger. Morton Thompson. LC 53-13297. 1954. Scribner.
Not Ashamed: A Romance of the Tropics. John Preston Buschlen. LC 34-4564. Sears Publishing Company, Inc.
Not at Home. Parr Cooper. 1940. W. Morrow & Company.
Not at Night! Ed. by Herbert Asbury. 1928. Macy-Masius.
Not at These Hands. Manly Wade Wellman. LC 62-7356. 1962. Putnam.
Not Bad. Peggy Gaddis, pseud. LC 44-9094. 1944. Phoenix Press.
Not Built with Hands. Helen Constance White. LC 35-7568. 1935. The Macmillan Company.
Not by Any Single Man. 1st Ed. Brigid Knight. LC 50-7843. 1950. Doubleday.
Not by Bread Alone. Mary Frances Doner. LC 41-11805. 1941. Doubleday, Doran and Company, Inc.
Not by Bread Alone by Vladimir Dudintsev. Vladimir Dmitrievich Dudintsev. LC 57-11252. 1957. Dutton.
Not by Strange Gods. Elizabeth Madox Roberts. LC 76-12119. Repr. of 1941 ed. 20.50 (ISBN 0-404-15237-6). AMS Pr.
Not by Strange Gods: Stories. Elizabeth Madox Roberts. LC 41-5114. 1941. The Viking Press.
Not by Strange Gods: Stories. Elizabeth Madox Roberts. LC 76-12119. 1979. 20.50 (ISBN 0-404-15237-6). AMS Press.
Not by the Door. James B Hall. LC 54-5954. 1954. Random House.
Not Comin' Home to You. Paul Kavanagh. LC 73-93348. (Illus.). 1974. 6.95 (ISBN 0-399-11357-6). Putnam.
Not Counting the Cost. Jessie Catherine Huybers Couvreur. LC 3-26197. (Half-titled town and country library, no. 175). 1895. D. Appleton and Company.
Not Dead Yet. Daniel Banko. (Orig.). 1972. pap. 0.75 o.p. (T2581, GM). Fawcett World.
Not Ever to Regret. Mons Daveson. LC 73-167374. 3.99 (ISBN 0-9598924-0-0). Henson's Publishing Company.
Not Far Enough. Margaret Pargeter. (Harlequin Presents Ser.). 192p. 1982. pap. 1.75 (ISBN 0-373-10540-1). Harlequin Bks.
Not for Heaven. Dorothy McCleary. LC 35-63513. 1935. Doubleday, Doran & Co., Inc.
Not for Just an Hour. Fannie Heaslip Lea. LC 39-8346. 1939. Dodd, Mead & Company.
Not for Love. Alice Duer Miller. LC 37-30399. 1937. Dodd, Mead & Company.
Not for Love. Spencer Whedon. LC 54-12071. 1954. Crown.
Not for Publication. Clara Sharpe Hough. LC 27-196356. The Century Co.
Not for Publication: And Other Stories. Nadine Gordimer. LC 65-128292. bds., 4.95. Viking.
Not for the Meek. Elizabeth Bartol Dewing Kaup. LC 41-1829. 1941. The Macmillan Company.
Not Grass Alone. Nelson Nye. 224p. (Orig.). 1981. pap. 2.25 (ISBN 0-441-58876-X). Ace Bks.
Not Grass Alone, a Novel. Nelson Coral Nye. LC 61-151851. 1961. Macmillan.
Not Guilty. Charles Meyer. 3.50 o.p. Carlton.
Not Guilty!". Etta W Pierce. (American series no. 265). 1891. M. J. Ivers & Co.
Not Heaven: A Novel in the Form of Prelude, Variations, and Theme. 1st Ed. Waldo David Frank. 1953. Hermitage House.
Not Heaven Itself. Margaret Bass Pedler. LC 41-530. 1941. Doubleday, Doran and Company, Inc.
Not Hers Alone. Sally Elliott Allen. LC 42-25505. 1942. Liveright Publishing Corporation.
Not His Daughter. An American Novel. Will Herbert. LC 7-4298. T. B. Peterson & Brothers.
Not Honour More: A Novel. 1st Ed. Joyce Cary. LC 55-6570. 1955. Harper.
Not I, Said the Sparrow: An Inspector Heimrich Mystery. Richard Lockridge. LC 73-1818. 1973. 5.95 (ISBN 0-397-00962-3). Lippincott.
Not Impossible She: A Novel. Arthur Edward Pearse Brome Weigall. LC 26-238911. 1926. Frank-Maurice, Inc.
Not in a Day. George Sumner Albee. LC 35-2818. 1935. A. A. Knopf.
Not in His Steps: A Story of the Ministerial Dead-Line of Fifty Years. Francis Trout Hoover. LC 11-8477. 1911. 1.00. Holzapfel Publishing Company.
Not in It. Anna Olcott Commelin. LC 6-30380. Fowler & Wells Co.; Etc., Etc.
Not in Our Stars. Josiah E. Greene. LC 45-7612. 1945. The Macmillan Company.
Not in Our Stars. Edward S Hyams. LC 50-801815. 1949. Longmans, Green.
Not in Our Stars. Marguerite Mooers Marshall. LC 37-8761. J. Messner, Inc.
Not in Our Stars: A Novel. Jill Stern. LC 57-135502. 1957. D. McKay Co.
Not in Solitude. Kenneth Franklin Gantz. LC 59-6355. (Doubleday science fiction). 1959. Doubleday.
Not in the Calendar. Margaret Kennedy. LC 64-14526. 1964. Macmillan.
Not in the Prospectus. Hannah Lincoln Talbot. LC 8-25577. (On cover: The Riverside paper series, no. 23). 1886. Houghton, Mifflin and Company.

Not in the Script. John Bonett & Emery Bonett. LC 81-47396. 1982. 14.95 (ISBN 0-8240-4963-2). Garland.

Not in the Script: By John Bonett, Pseud. and Emery Bonett Pseud. 1st Ed. John Coulson. LC 52-301. 1951. Published for the Crime Club by Doubleday.

Not in Their Class. Arthur Irdell Ross. LC 31-3183. R. G. Badger.

Not in Their Set: Or, In Different Circles of Society. Maria Sebregondi Lenzen & M. S., Tr. LC 7-13161. 1874. Lee & Shepard.

Not in Utter Nakedness. Delano L. Ames. LC 32-12766. 1932. L. MacVeagh, Dial Press, Inc.

Not in Utter Nakedness: A Novel Depicting a Spiritual Pilgrimage. Thomas Alva Stubbins. LC 36-359962. 1936. Meador Publishing Company.

Not Included in a Sheepskin: Stanford Stories. Davida French & Stevens, Esther. The Stanford Book Store.

Not into Clean Hands. Translated by Bernard Miall. 1st American Ed. Louis Pauwels. LC 59-125935. 1959. Academy Library Guild.

Not Just to Remember. Alice Mary Ross Colver. LC 41-21399. 1941. Macrae-Smith-Company.

Not Knowing Whither He Went. Thornwell Jacobs. LC 33-25972. 1933. Oglethorpe University Press.

Not Less Than All, The Lonely Road, Cherish the Wayward Heart. Margaret Malcolm, pseud. (Harlequin Romance Ser.). 192p. 1983. pap. 1.75 (ISBN 0-373-20072-2). Harlequin Bks.

Not Like Other Girls: A Novel. Rosa Nouchette Carey. (Seaside library v. 90 no. 1815). G. Munro.

Not Like Other Girls. A Novel. Rosa Nouchette Carey. LC 9-8207. 1907. J. B. Lippincott Company.

Not Like Other Men. Rhoby S. Williams. J. S. Ogilvie Publishing Company.

Not Long for This World. Cynthia Mary Evelyn Charteris Asquith. LC 36-758419. The Telegraph Press.

Not Long for This World. Stories. August William Derleth. LC 49-733684. 1948. Arkham House.

Not Looked Upon with Favor. Velma B Clark. LC 51-9827. 1951. A. Swallpw.

Not Made in Heaven. Rian James. LC 36-341643. J. Messner, Inc.

Not Made of Iron. Christine Staggs Douglas. LC 54-15414. 1953. White Wing Pub. House.

Not Magnolia. Edith Everett Taylor. LC 28-4882. E. P. Dutton & Company.

Not Me, Inspector. Helen Kieran Reilly. LC 59-10802. (Random House Mystery). 1959. Random House.

Not My Own. Ethel Matson. LC 49-8773. 1949. F. H. Revell Co.

Not My Way;" Or, Good Out of Evil; a Tale. Tryphena Matilda Archer Brown. LC 6-17221. 1884. T. Whittaker.

Not My Will. Francena Harriet Arnold. LC 47-145793. 1946. Moody Press.

Not Native. W. R. Moses. (Juniper Bks: No. 27). 1979. pap. 3.00. Juniper Pr WI.

Not Now but Now. Mary Frances Kennedy Fisher. LC 47-30568. 1947. Viking Press.

Not Now but Now. Mary Frances Parrish, pseud. LC 47-30568. 1947. Viking Press.

Not Now, Not Ever. James Vizas. LC 75-75016. 1969. 3.50. Walden Press.

Not of Her Father's Race. William T Meredith. LC 7-26226. Cassell Publishing Company.

Not of Her Race. Nancy Kier Foster. LC 10-24023. 1911. 1.50. R. G. Badger.

Not of This Time, Not of This Place. Tr. from Hebrew by Shlomo Katz. 1st Ed. Yehuda Amichai. LC 67-28816. 1968. 6.95. Harper.

Not on the Chart: A Novel. Algernon Sydney Logan. LC 34-24491.

Not on the Chart: A Novel of to-Day, by. Algernon Sydney Logan. LC 99-717. 1899. G. W. Dillingham Co.

Not on the Chart: A Romance of the Pacific. Charles Leonard Marsh. LC 2-15203. 1902. F. A. Stokes Company.

Not on the Records: Or, Nick Carter's Gumshoe Case. Nick Carter & Dey, Frederic Van Rensselaer. LC 34-38273. (On cover: New magnet library. no. 849). Street & Smith.

Not on the Screen. Henry Blake Fuller. 1930. A. A. Knopf.

Not on the Screen see Collected Works.

Not Once but Twice. Betty Neels. (Harlequin Romances Ser.). 192p. 1981. pap. 1.50 (ISBN 0-373-02440-1). PB.

Not One of Us. Maysie Greig. LC 39-32602. 1939. Doubleday, Doran and Company, Inc.

Not One of Us. Maysie Greig. LC 42-17386. 1941. The Sun Dial Press.

Not One of Us. Margaret Roberts. LC 7-41042. 1892. National Society's Depository.

Not One of Us. June Thomson. LC 77-160660. 1971. 5.95 (ISBN 0-06-014266-9). Harper & Row.

Not Only That. Carroll Arnett. 1967. 3.00 (Pub. by Elizabeth Pr). SBD.

Not Only War: A Story of Two Great Conflicts. Victor Daly. LC 72-126689. 1970. AMS Press.

Not Only War: A Story of Two Great Conflicts. Victor Daly. LC 75-76099. 1969. McGrath Pub. Co.

Not Only War: A Story of Two Great Conflicts. Victor Daly. LC 32-1646. The Christopher Publishing House.

Not Peace but a Sword. Vance Havner. LC 76-160274. 1971. 4.95 (ISBN 0-8007-0470-3). Revell.

Not Quite a Dream. Kathleen Thelma Hughes. LC 48-5269. 1948. Doubleday.

Not Quite a Hero: A Novel. Milton R Bass. LC 77-4749. 8.95 (ISBN 0-399-12007-6). Putnam.

Not Quite Dead Enough. Rex Stout. 160p. 1982. pap. 2.50 (ISBN 0-553-22589-8). Bantam.

Not Quite Dead Enough. Rex Stout. 1973. pap. 0.95 o.p. (ISBN 0-515-03195-X, N3195). Pyramid Pubns.

Not Quite Dead Enough. Rex Stout. 1976. pap. 1.25 o.p. (ISBN 0-515-04158-0). BJ Pub Group.

Not Quite Dead Enough: A Nero Wolfe Double Mystery. Rex Stout. LC 44-7191. 1944. Farrar & Rinehart, Inc.

Not Regina. Christmas Carol Miller Kauffman. LC 54-10828. 1954. Herald Press.

Not Respectable. Wright Williams. LC 39-332683. Phoenix Press.

Not Respectable. Watkins Eppes Wright. LC 39-33268. 1939. Phoenix Press.

Not Seldom Talismans: A Collection of Short Stories by Students in English 372, Wells College. Ed. by Jeanne Munning. Verwiebe, Jennifer, Joint Ed & Wells College, Aurora, N.Y. LC 50-4668. 1948. Talisman Press.

Not Sleeping, Just Dead. Charles E Alverson. LC 77-8958. 1977. 7.95 (ISBN 0-395-25728-X). Houghton Mifflin.

Not Sleeping, Just Dead. Charles E Alverson. 1980. Playboy Paperbacks.

Not So Much Love of Flowers. Allan Appel. LC 75-23389. 1975. pap. 4.00 o.p. (ISBN 0-915124-07-6). Toothpaste.

Not Soldiers All. Robert T Crowley. LC 66-20982. 1967. Doubleday.

Not the Critic: A Novel of Psychiatry and the Law. H B Dearman. LC 65-18344. 1965. House of Wingate.

Not the Glory. Pierre Boulle. 1974. (pbk.) 1.25. Manor Books.

Not the Glory. Pierre Boulle. LC 55-10687. 1955. Vanguard Press.

Not the Marrying Kind. Netta Muskett. 1974. pap. 0.75 o.p. (26581-5-075). Beagle Bks.

Not This August. Cyril M. Kornbluth. 256p. 1982. pap. 2.75 (ISBN 0-523-48518-2). Pinnacle Bks.

Not This August. 1st Ed. Cyril M Kornbluth. LC 55-8406. (Doubleday science fiction). 1955. Doubleday.

Not to Be Opened. Lloyd Osbourne. LC 28-8592. 1928. Cosmopolitan Book Corporation.

Not to Be Trusted. Jessica Ayre. (Harlequin Romances Ser.). 192p. 1982. pap. 1.50 (ISBN 0-373-02504-1). Harlequin Bks.

Not to Be Won. Lenox Bell. LC 6-9417. (On cover: Munro's library, popular novels, v. 1 no. 93). N. L. Munro.

Not to Disturb. Muriel Spark. LC 73-178820. 1972. 5.00 (ISBN 0-670-51667-8). Viking Press.

Not to Eat, Not for Love: By George Anthony Weller. George Anthony Weller. LC 33-110781. 1933. H. Smith and R. Hass.

Not to Have and to Hold. Priscilla Norton Thomson. LC 9-30634. 1909. Broadway Publishing Co.

Not to Mention Camels: A Science Fiction Fantasy. R. A Lafferty. LC 75-30817. 1976. 6.95 (ISBN 0-672-52178-4). Bobbs-Merrill.

Not to the Strong. Jeanie Paine Thorndike. LC 41-637233. 1941. Thomas Y. Crowell Company.

Not to the Swift, a Novel. 1st Ed. Tristram Coffin. LC 61-929655. Norton.

Not to the Swift: A Tale of Two Continents. Lewis H Watson. 1891. Welch, Fracker Company.

Not Tonight. Parkhurst Whitney. LC 37-12430. Farrar & Rinehart, Incorporated.

Not Too Narrow, Not Too Deep. Richard Sale. LC 36-6127. 1936. Simon and Schuster.

Not Too Soon for Love. Angela Gordon. 1972. pap. 0.75 o.p. (94307). Beagle Bks.

Not Under Forty. Willa Sibert Cather. (O.s.i.). (YA) 1936. 7.95 o.s.i. (ISBN 0-394-43871-X). Knopf.

Not Under the Law. Grace Livingston Hill. LC 76-41278. 1976. 8.95 (ISBN 0-89190-022-5). American Reprint Co.

Not Under the Law. Grace Livingston Hill. LC 25-9636. 1925. J. B. Lippincott Company.

Not Unto Ourselves Alone. Irva Farnham Copp. LC 50-5039. 1949. Dorrance.

Not Wanted. Jesse Lynch Williams. LC 23-17923. 1923. C. Scribner's Sons.

Not Wisely, but Too Well. A Novel... Rhoda Broughton. LC 25-23759. 1868. D. Appleton and Company.

Not Wisely, but Too Well. A Novel. Rhoda Broughton. (Seaside library, v. 21 no. 402). 1878. G. Munro.

Not Wisely, but Too Well. A Novel. Rhoda Broughton. (On cover: Seaside library. Pocket ed., no. 765). 1886. G. Munro.

Not Wisely but Too Well: A Novel. Rhoda Broughton. LC 18-11269. (Macmillan's two shilling library, no. 6). 1899. Macmillan and Co., Limited.

Not Wisely, but Too Well. A Novel. Rhoda Broughton. LC 42-448074. 1870. D. Appleton and Company.

Not Wisely,but Too Well. Rhoda Broughton. (On cover: Lovell's library, no. 1026). 1887. J. W. Lovell Company.

Not with a Bang. Chapman Pincher. LC 65-14331. (NAL-World book). 1965. New American Library.

Not with Dreams: A Historical Novel. Edward Roe Eastman. LC 55-21. 1954. Greenberg.

Not with My Heart. Sarah Elizabeth Rodger. LC 41-118032. 1941. Doubleday, Doran and Co., Inc.

Not with My Neck... Tom Van Dycke & Kerner, Ben, Joint Author. LC 47-18672. 1947. J. Messner, Inc.

Not Without Dust: A Novel. 1st Ed. Seginald Chantrelle. LC 54-12467. 1954. Exposition Press.

Not Without Honor. Vivian Parsons. LC 41-16064. 1941. Dodd, Mead & Company.

Not Without Honor: A Historical Romance in the Time of Columbus. 1st Ed. Ida Mills Wilhelm. LC 54-13179. 1955. Exposition Press.

Not Without Laughter. Langston Hughes. LC 30-19627. 1930. A. A. Knopf.

Not Without Love. Angela Gordon. 1971. pap. 0.75 o.p. (94170). Beagle Bks.

Not Without Peril: A Novel. Marguerite Allis. LC 41-514369. 1941. G. P. Putnam's Sons.

Not Without Tears. 1st Ed. Estelle Miller Holmes. LC 57-9014. 1957. Citadel Press.

Not Without the Wedding: A Novel. Theodore Pratt. LC 35-1205. (Selwyn and Blount, ltd.) has title: Without the wedding.). 1935. E. P. Dutton & Co., Inc.

Not Working. George H. Szanto. LC 82-5810. 1982. 12.95 (ISBN 0-312-57962-4). St Martin's.

Not-World. Thomas Burnett Swann. (Science Fiction Ser). 1975. pap. 1.25 o.p. (UY1158). DAW Bks.

Not Yet... Tereska Torres. LC 57-8776. 1957. Crown Publishers.

Not Yet: A Theosophical Romance. Mary Weller Robbins. (On cover: Library of choice fiction, no. 3). 1895. Laird & Lee.

Not Yet the Moon. Eve Langley. LC 46-2023. 1946. E. P. Dutton and Company, Inc.

Notable Short Stories of Today. Ed. by Edwin Van Berghen Knickerbocker. LC 29-9874. 1929. Harper & Brothers.

Notary's Nose. Edmond Francois Valentin About & Holt, Henry, 1840- Tr. (Leisure hour series. (no. 42). 1874. H. Holt and Company.

Notch on the Knife. Richard Clayton. LC 73-83192. 1973. 4.95 (ISBN 0-8027-5285-3). Walker.

Notch on the Knife. William Haggard. 288p. 1973. 4.95 o.p. (ISBN 0-8027-5285-3). Walker & Co.

Notched Guns. William L. Hopson. (O.s.i.). 1977. pap. 1.25 o.s.i. (AQ1659, Award). Univ Pub & Dist.

Notched Hairpin: A Mycroft Mystery by H. F. Heard. Gerald Heard. LC 49-11290. 1949. Vanguard Press.

Note Book of a Country Clergyman... Samuel Wilberforce. LC 8-37031. 1833. Harper & Brothers.

Note of Grace. Betty Singleton. LC 58-5774. 1958. World Pub. Co.

Notebook of Malte Laurids Brigge. Rainer Maria Rilke. 1959. Repr. of 1930 ed. text ed. 6.75x o.p. Humanities.

Notebooks. Sam Picard. (Notebooks Ser). (O.s.i.). (Orig.). 1971. pap. 0.75 o.s.i. (A767S, Award). Univ Pub & Dist.

Notebooks of Captain Georges: A Novel. Jean Renoir. LC 66-21984. 1966. Little, Brown.

Notebooks of Captain Georges. Tr. by Norman Denny. Jean Renoir. (75-023). 1967. Lancer.

Notebooks of Henry James. Henry James & Matthiessen, Francis Otto, 1902- Ed. LC 47-11461. 1947. Oxford Univ. Press.

Notebooks of Major Thompson: An Englishman Discovers France & the French. Translated by Robin Farn. Illustrated by Walter Goetz. 1st American Ed. Pierre Daninos. 1955. Knopf.

Notebooks of Malte Laurids Brigge. Rainer Maria Rilke. LC 49-50028. 1949. W. W. Norton.

Notebooks of Malte Laurids Brigge. Translated by M. D. Herter Norton. Rainer Maria Rilke. LC 58-597575. (Putnam Capricorn book, CAP2). 1958. Capricorn Books.

Notes for the Two-Dollar Window: Portraits from an American Neighborhood. Leonard Kriegel. LC 75-29141. 8.95. Saturday Review Press.

Notes for the Two Dollar Window: Portraits of an American Neighborhood. Leonard Kregel. LC 75-2914. 224p. 1976. 8.95 o.p. (ISBN 0-8415-0406-7). Dutton.

Notes from a Dark Street. Edward Adler. LC 61-14572. 1962. Knopf.

Notes from Africa. H. S Aynor. LC 72-83783. 1969. 5.95. Praeger.

Notes from the Diaspora. With Pen and Ink Drawings by Nancy Marmer. Gerald Jay Goldberg. LC 62-46332. 1962. Atelier.

Notes from the Underground. Fedor Dostoyevsky et al. Ed. by Robert G. Durgy. Tr. by Serge Shishkoff. 1969. pap. 4.50x o.p. (ISBN 0-690-58821-6, HarpC). Har-Row.

Notes from the Underground see Three Short Novels of Dostoyevsky.

Notes from Underground. Fedor Mikhailovich Dostoevskii. 1974. (pbk.) 1.25. Bantam Books.

Notes from Underground. Fedor Mikhailovich Dostoevskii. Tr. by Mirra Ginsburg from Russian. (Bantam Classics Ser.). 192p. (gr. 9-12). 1981. pap. 1.95 (ISBN 0-553-21043-2). Bantam.

Notes from Underground & Selected Stories: White Nights, Dream of a Ridiculous Man, House of the Dead. Fedor Mikhailovich Dostoevskii. Tr. by Andrew R. MacAndrew. pap. 2.50 (ISBN 0-451-51442-4, CE1442, Sig Classics). NAL.

Notes from Underground: And The Grand Inquisitor. Fedor Mikhailovich Dostoevskii. LC 60-9687. 1960. Dutton.

Notes from Underground. The Double. Fedor Mikhailovich Dostoevskii. LC 72-192863. (Penguin classics). 1972. (u.s.) 1.65 (ISBN 0-14-044252-9). Penguin Books.

Notes of a Dirty Old Man. Charles Bukowski. LC 73-84226. 1973. (pbk.) 3.00 (ISBN 0-87286-074-4). City Lights Books.

Notes of a Guilty Bystander. Robert Sylvester. LC 75-110670. (Illus.). 1970. 7.95 o.p. (ISBN 0-13-624932-9). P-H.

Notes of a Native Son. James B. Baldwin. (Modern Classic Ser). 1971. pap. 1.95 (ISBN 0-553-13058-7). Bantam.

Notes of a Volunteer. An Autobiography. Charles Manby Smith. LC 8-8626. 1856. A. Burke.

Notes of Guilt: An Astrological Gothic Novel, Scorpio. Gene DeWeese. LC 76-11818. 1.25. Ballantine Books.

Notes of the Siege Year. George Hitchcock. 1974. pap. 2.00 o.p. (ISBN 0-87711-053-0). Kayak.

Notes on an Endangered Species and Others. Mordecai Richler. LC 73-20735. 1974. 6.95 (ISBN 0-394-48969-1). Knopf; Distributed by Random House.

Notes to a Bald Buffalo. John R Milton. LC 76-45681. 1976. 5.95 (ISBN 0-914982-03-6). Spirit Mound Press.

Notes to Help Me Hang in There. Jim Worthame. LC 79-91345. 1980. 12.50 (ISBN 0-89002-128-7); pap. 5.00 (ISBN 0-89002-127-9). Northwoods Pr.

Noteven, the Mouse: A Christmas Story. Thomas J. Riley. LC 82-61683. (Illus.). 32p. 1982. pap. 3.00 (ISBN 0-933050-13-5). New Eng Pr VT.

Nothin' but the 'Boo. Donald Ransom. (Illus.). 20p. (Orig.). 1981. pap. text ed. 2.50. Skydog OR.

Nothing. Henry Green. LC 50-6495. 1950. Viking Press.

Nothing. Henry Green. LC 72-122052. (Viking reprint editions). 1970. A. M. Kelley.

Nothing a Year: A Novel. Charles Belmont Davis. LC 16-4747. 1916. 1.30. Harper & Brothers.

Nothing As Before. Dorothy Elizabeth Sparks. LC 44-4325. 1944. Harper & Brothers.

Nothing Black but a Cadillac: A Novel. Raymond Spence. LC 69-14388. 1969. 5.00. Putnam.

Nothing Book. 272p. 1977. pap. 2.95 (ISBN 0-446-30251-1). Warner Bks.

Nothing but a Buggy. Philip Poole. 1970. 4.50 o.p. Vantage.

Nothing but a Drifter. Lee Hoffman. LC 76-22896. 1976. 5.95 (ISBN 0-385-12177-6). Doubleday.

Nothing but Foxes. Roy Lewis. LC 78-19406. 1979. 7.95 (ISBN 0-312-57964-0). St. Martin's Press.

Nothing but the Best. Diane Balson. LC 77-92528. 7.95 (ISBN 0-15-167327-6). Harcourt Brace Jovanovich.

Nothing but the Night. James Yaffe. LC 57-5518. (Atlantic Monthly Press book). 1957. Little Brown.

Nothing but the Truth. Frederic Stewart Isham. LC 14-17166. The Bobbs-Merrill Company.

Nothing but the Truth. Poul Rum. LC 76-9604. 7.95 (ISBN 0-394-49779-1). Pantheon Books.

Nothing but Wodehouse. Pelham Grenville Wodehouse & Nash, Ogden, 1902- Ed. LC 32-189578. 1932. Doubleday, Doran & Company, Inc.

Nothing but Wodehouse. Pelham Grenville Wodehouse & Nash, Ogden, 1902- Ed. LC 36-18571. Garden City Publishing Company, Inc.

Nothing but Wodehouse. Pelham Grenville Wodehouse & Nash, Ogden, 1902- Ed. LC 47-2843. 1946. Doubleday & Company, Inc.

Nothing Can Rescue Me. Elizabeth Daly. LC 43-451774. 1943. Farrar & Rinehart, Inc.

Nothing Can Rescue Me. Elizabeth Daly. LC 47-27907. (Bantam books 53). 1946.

Nothing Certain. S A Aldon. LC 48-9747. Beechhurst Press.

Nothing Doing. Michael Campbell. LC 74-132612. 1971. 5.95. Putnam.

Nothing Else Matters: A Novel. William Samuel Johnson. LC 14-11090. 1914. 1.35. M. Kennerley.

Nothing Ever Breaks Except the Heart. Kay Boyle. LC 66-15667. 1966. Doubleday.

Nothing Ever Ends. Katherine Ursula Parrott. LC 42-16184. 1942. Dodd, Mead & Company.

Nothing Ever Happens Sunday Morning. Blanche Cannon. LC 48-154249. 1948. G. P. Putnam's Sons.

Nothing from Nothing. George P. Elliott. 5.95 o.p. (ISBN 0-525-16930-X). Dutton.

Nothing Goes to Waste. 1st Ed. Jack Posner. LC 56-11782. 1956. Pageant Press.

Nothing Happens in Small Towns. William Gordon Ross. LC 72-96981. 1973. 4.95. Christopher Pub. House.

Nothing Happens to Children in Beverly Hills. Vi Wolfson. LC 74-30590. (Red mask mystery). 1975. 6.95 (ISBN 0-399-11516-1). Putnam.

Nothing Hid. Archibald Marshall. LC 35-25307. 1935. Houghton Mifflin Company.

Nothing in Her Way. Charles Williams. LC 54-19840. (Gold medal books, 340). 1953. Fawcett Publications.

Nothing in Life Is Free: Through Naches Pass to Puget Sound, a Historical Novel of the Pioneer West. Selected As the Official Book Commemorating the Washington Territorial Centennial. Della Florence Gould Emmons. LC 53-7881. 1953. Northwestern Press.

Nothing Is Impossible: The Story of Beatrix Potter. Dorothy Keeley Aldis. LC 69-13528. (Illus.). 1969. 4.50. Atheneum.

Nothing Is Lost. Beatrice Hawley. 1979. 8.95 (ISBN 0-918222-05-2); pap. 3.95 (ISBN 0-918222-06-0). Apple Wood.

Nothing Is Sacred. Josephine Herbst. LC 28-227762. 1928. Coward-McCann, Inc.

Nothing Is Sacred. Josephine Herbst. LC 76-51671. (Rediscovered Fiction by American Women). 1977. 20.00 (ISBN 0-405-10050-7). Arno Press.

Nothing Is Safe. Edmee Elizabeth Monica De La Pasture. LC 37-16656. 1937. Harper & Brothers.

Nothing Is the Number When You Die. Joan Margaret Fleming. LC 65-23222. 1965. I. Washburn.

Nothing Lasts Forever. Roderick Thorp. LC 79-15366. 9.95 (ISBN 0-393-01249-2). Norton.

Nothing Less Than a Man see Three Exemplary Novels.

Nothing Like It: Or, Steps to the Kingdom. Lois Waisbrooker. LC 8-32826. 1875. Colby & Rich.

Nothing Like Leather. Victor Sawdon Pritchett. LC 35-6532. 1935. The Macmillan Company.

Nothing Like the Sun. Anthony Burgess. 240p. 1975. pap. 5.95 (ISBN 0-393-00795-2, N795, Norton Lib). Norton.

Nothing Like the Sun: A Story of Shakespeare's Love-Life by Anthony Burgess. John Anthony Burgess Wilson. LC 64-20416. 1964. W. W. Norton.

Nothing Like the Sun: A Story of Shakespeare's Love-Style. John Anthony Burgess Wilson. LC 75-17759. (Norton library). 1975. 2.95 (ISBN 0-393-00795-2). Norton.

Nothing Man. James Myerd Thompson. LC 54-80383. (Dell first edition, 22). 1954. Dell Pub. Co.

Nothing Matters, and Other Stories. Herbert Beerbohm Tree. LC 70-132130. (Short story index reprint series). 1970. Books for Libraries Press.

Nothing Matters, and Other Stories. Herbert Beerbohm Tree. LC 17-13222. 1917. Houghton Mifflin Company.

Nothing More Than Murder. James Myers Thompson. LC 49-8009. 1949. Harper.

Nothing New Under the Sun. Riccardo Bacchelli. LC 55-5547. 1955. Pantheon.

Nothing on Earth. Idolene Hooper Hale. LC 55-56599. Abelard-Schuman.

Nothing Personal: A Novel. Seymour Wishman. LC 78-17045. 8.95. Delacorte Press.

Nothing Serious. Pelham Grenville Wodehouse. LC 51-10948. 1951. Doubleday.

Nothing So Monstrous. John Steinbeck. LC 77-16195. 1977. Repr. of 1936 ed. lib. bdg. 10.00 (ISBN 0-8414-7866-X). Folcroft.

Nothing So Monstrous. John Steinbeck. 1979. 28.50. Porter.

Nothing So Monstrous. John Steinbeck. 1936. 4.00 o.p. Folcroft.

Nothing So Monstrous: A Story. John Steinbeck. LC 77-16195. (Illus.). 1977. 8.50 (ISBN 0-8414-7866-X). Folcroft Library Editions.

Nothing So Strange. James Hilton. LC 47-31200. 1947. Little, Brown.

Nothing to Chance: Translated from the French. Charles Plisnier & Morris, Pamela, Tr. LC 38-36255. Reynal & Hitchcock.

Nothing to Do with Love. Joyce Reiser Kornblatt. LC 80-52006. 1981. 11.95 (ISBN 0-670-48020-7). Viking Press.

Nothing to Do with the Case. Elizabeth Lemarchand. LC 81-51975. (Illus.). 1981. 9.95 (ISBN 0-8027-5450-3). Walker.

Nothing to Drink. A Temperance Sea Story. Julia MacNair Wright. LC 9-11894. 1873. National Temperance Society and Publication House.

Nothing to Fear. Genevieve Gilfry. 1977. 5.95 o.p. (ISBN 0-533-02953-8). Vantage.

Nothing to Lose. Consuelo Baehr. LC 82-7519. 14.95 (ISBN 0-399-12744-5). Putnam.

Nothing to Pay. Caradoc Evans. LC 30-258161. W. W. Norton & Comapny.

Nothing to Report. Robert McLaughlin & Phil Foran. LC 74-30400. 1975. 7.95 (ISBN 0-316-56094-4). Little, Brown.

Nothing Venture. Patricia Wentworth. LC 32-4636. 1932. J. B. Lippincott Company.

Nothing's Certain but Death. M. K Wren, pseud. LC 77-76962. 1978. 6.95 (ISBN 0-385-13283-2). Published for the Crime Club by Doubleday.

Notion of Sin. Robert McLaughlin. LC 59-6016. 1959. Simon and Schuster.

Notions: Unlimited. Robert Sheckley. LC 60-50940. (Bantam book, A2003). 1960. Bantam Books.

Notorious. Day Keene. 1972. pap. 0.75 o.p. (532-75466-075). Manor Bks.

Notorious Angel. Patricia Maxwell. (Fawcett Gold Medal Book). 1.95 (ISBN 0-449-13825-9). Fawcett Pubns.

Notorious Eliza: A Novel About the Woman Who Married Aaron Burr. Basil Beyea. LC 78-2629. 10.00 (ISBN 0-671-24143-5). Simon and Schuster.

Notorious Lady. Maggie MacKeever. (Fawcett Crest Book). 1978. 1.50 (ISBN 0-449-23491-6). Fawcett Books.

Notorious Lady: The Life and Times of the Countess of Blessington. Doris Oppenheim Leslie. LC 77-355704. 1976. 3.90 (ISBN 0-434-41827-7). Heinemann.

Notorious Miss Lisle. Gertrude M. Robins Reynolds. LC 11-23505. Hodder and Stoughton.

Notre Coeur (The Human Heart) tr. by alexina loranger donovan. ed. Guy De Maupassant. Tr. by Donovan, Alexina (Loranger) (library of choice fiction. no. 5). 1890. Laird & Lee.

Notre Dame. Victor Marie Hugo. LC 7-5859. 1888. G. Routledge and Sons.

Notre Dame De Paris. library ed.... ed. Victor Marie Hugo. LC 7-5860. 1888. Little, Brown, and Company.

Notre Dame De Paris. Victor Marie Hugo. LC 4-16883. T. Y. Crowell & Co.

Notre Dame De Paris. Victor Marie Hugo. Tr. by Isabel Florence Hapgood. LC 18-17313. T. Y. Crowell & Co.

Notre Dame De Paris. Victor Marie Hugo. LC 3-12520. 1902. A. Wessels Company.

Notre Dame De Paris. Victor Marie Hugo. (Half title: Everyman's library, ed. by Ernest Rhys. Fiction). 1910. J. M. Dent & Sons, Ltd.

Notre Dame De Paris. Victor Marie Hugo. LC 17-17431. (Harvard classics shelf of fiction, selected by C. W. Eliot. 12). P. F. Collier & Son.

Notre Dame De Paris: The Hunchback of Notre Dame. Victor Marie Hugo. 1979. Repr. of 1910 ed. 14.95x (ISBN 0-460-00422-0, Evman). Biblio Dist.

Notre-Dame des Fleurs see Oeuvres Completes.

Notre-Dame of Paris. Victor Marie Hugo & John Sturrock. LC 79-300035. (Penguin classics). 1978. 3.95 (ISBN 0-14-044353-3). Penguin.

Notting Hill Mystery. Charles Felix. LC 75-32744. (Literature of Mystery and Detection). 1976. 8.00 (ISBN 0-405-07870-6). Arno Press.

Noughts & Crosses. Arthur Thomas Quiller-Couch. LC 77-103527. (Short Story Index Reprint Ser.). 1888. 15.00 (ISBN 0-8369-3269-2). Ayer Co.

Noughts and Crosses: A Child's Game for Two Players. Helen Muir. LC 76-382461. 1976. 3.45 (ISBN 0-7156-0963-7). Duckworth.

Noughts and Crosses: Stories, Studies, and Sketches. Quiller-Couch, Arthur Thomas. LC 77-103527. (Short story index reprint series). 1969. Books for Libraries Press.

Nouveau Roman Reader. Intro. by John Calder. 1983. 11.95 (ISBN 0-7145-3719-5); pap. 5.95 (ISBN 0-7145-3720-9). Riverrun NY.

Nouveaux Discours du Docteur O'Grady. Andre Maurois. pap. 7.95. French & Eur.

Nouvelle Anthologie Francaise. rev. ed. Ed. by Albert Schinz et al. 1943. text ed. 10.95 o.p. (ISBN 0-15-566643-6, HC). HarBraceJ.

Nouvelle Histoire De Mouchette. Georges Bernanos. 1960. 13.50. French & Eur.

Nouvelles, Contes et Recits Contemporains. Michael Pargment. 1956. 5.00 o.p. (ISBN 0-03-016060-X). HR&W.

Nouvelles et Recits Du XXIeme Siecle. Ed. by G. Mernier & M. Spingler. 1971. pap. 7.95 o.p. (ISBN 0-13-625335-0). P-H.

Nouvelles Francaises. Ed. by Marie-Louise M. Hall. 1959. 5.25 o.p. (ISBN 0-672-63186-5). Odyssey Pr.

Nouvelles: Textes Pour Rien. Samuel Beckett. 1955. pap. 2.40 o.s.i. Paris Pubns.

Nova. Samuel R Delany. LC 68-18083. (Doubleday science fiction). 1968. Doubleday.

Nova. Samuel R Delany. LC 77-17215. (Gregg Press science fiction series). (Illus.). 1977. 12.00 (ISBN 0-8398-2397-5). Gregg Press.

Nova Express. William S. Burroughs. 1964. pap. 2.45 (ISBN 0-394-17103-9, B102, BC). Grove.

Nova Four. Ed. by Harry Harrison. 224p. 1977. pap. 1.25 (ISBN 0-532-12351-4, 12351). Woodhill.

Nova Four. Ed. by Harry Harrison. LC 74-79212. (O.s.i.). 256p. 1975. 7.95 o.s.i. (ISBN 0-8027-5563-1). Walker & Co.

Nova One: An Anthology of Original SF Stories. Ed. by Harry Harrison. 1970. 4.95 o.p. (6499-6). Delacorte.

Nova Three. Ed. by Harry Harrison. LC 72-95775. (O.s.i.). 288p. 1973. 6.95 o.s.i. (ISBN 0-8027-5558-5). Walker & Co.

Nova 1: A an Anthology of Original Science Fiction Stories. Ed. by Harry Harrison. LC 79-103443. 1970. 4.95. Delacorte Press.

Nova 2. Ed. by Harry Harrison. 1974. (pbk.) 0.95. Dell.

Nova 2. Ed. by Harry Harrison. LC 79-188470. 1972. (ISBN 0-8027-5550-X). Walker.

Nova 3. Ed. by Harry Harrison. LC 72-95775. 1973. 6.95 (ISBN 0-8027-5558-5). Walker.

Nova 4. Harry Harrison. LC 74-79212. 1974. 7.95 (ISBN 0-8027-5563-1). Walker.

Novalis "Two Tales" & "Sacred Songs". Maria Selinger. 1978. pap. 6.95 o.p. (ISBN 0-916786-21-8). St George Bk Serv.

Novel, a Novella, and Four Stories. Andrew Nelson Lytle. LC 58-12577. 1958. McDowell, Obolensky.

Novel About a White Man and a Black Man: In the Deep South. James Saxon Childers. LC 36-8137. Farrar & Rinehart, Incorporated.

Novel and Story, a Book of Modern Readings. Ellery Sedgwick et al. Ed. by Harry A. Domincovich. LC 39-13542. 1939. Little, Brown, and Company.

Novel Called Heritage. Margaret Mitchell Dukore. LC 81-21336. 12.95 (ISBN 0-684-17428-6). Scribner.

Novel in Letters: Epistolary Fiction in the Early English Novel, 1678-1740. Ed. by Natascha Wurzbach. LC 70-81618. 1969. 8.50 (ISBN 0-87024-116-8). University of Miami Press.

Novel Notes. Jerome Klapka Jerome. LC 7-9920. 1893. H. Holt and Company.

Novel of the Century. Captain Trueman's Last Prisoner, a Tale of the Sixties. M. E Porter. LC 9-24699. 1909. J. N. Reynolds.

Novel on Yellow Paper. Stevie Smith. 288p. 1982. pap. 3.50 (ISBN 0-523-41683-0). Pinnacle Bks.

Novel on Yellow Paper: Or, Work It Out for Yourself. Florence Margaret Smith. LC 37-1013. 1937. W. Morrow & Company.

Novel To-Day. Anthony Burgess. 1963. 4.00 o.p. Folcroft.

Novel Writers. Emily Sisley. LC 80-81487. 78p. (Orig.). 1980. pap. 2.95 o.p. (ISBN 0-934696-01-2). Mosaic Pr.

Novelas. Angel M. De Lera. 7.95 o.s.i. French & Eur.

Novelas Completas. Ciro Alegria. 8.95 o.s.i. French & Eur.

Novelas de Ciro Alegria see Novelistica de Ciro Alegria.

Novelas y Cuentos. Voltaire. (Biblioteca De Cultura Basica Ser.). pap. 3.75 (ISBN 0-8477-0720-2). U of PR Pr.

Novelette Before Nineteen Hundred. Ed. by Ronald Paulson. 1965. text ed. 9.95 o.p. (ISBN 0-13-625327-X). P-H.

Novelette Before 1900. Ed. by Ronald Paulson. LC 65-13174. (Prentice-Hall English literature series). Prentice-Hall.

Novelette: The Black Hand. Sarah Jane Harper. LC 12-84105. 1911. 1.25. C. F. Williams & Son.

Novelette Trilogy. A Bachelor's Box: How He Got in and How He Was Gotten Out. A Jelous God: the Story of Hereditaments. The Chrustus Sonata: a Romance of the Rhine and the Hudson. Thomas Cooper De Leon. LC 6-34185. F. T. Neely.

Novelette: With Other Stories. A. L. Barker. LC 51-7091. 1951. Scribner.

Novelist in the Making: A Collection of Student Themes and the Novels Blix and Vandover and the Brute. Frank Norris. LC 72-129124. (John Harvard Library). (Illus.). 1970. 12.50 (ISBN 0-674-62820-9). Belknap Press of Harvard University Press.

Novelistica de Ciro Alegria. 2nd enlarged ed. Matilde Vilarino De Olivieri. LC 79-22294. (Coleccion Mente y Palabra). Orig. Title: Novelas de Ciro Alegria. 283p. (Sp.). 1980. 6.25 (ISBN 0-8477-0566-8); pap. 5.00 (ISBN 0-8477-0567-6). U of PR Pr.

Novella see Sorrows of Young Werther.

Novella Box. Smith Experimental Fiction Project. Incl. Invisibles. Hugh Fox. pap. 3.00; Same Thing Happened Over & Over. Leonard Chabrowe. pap. 3.00; Teak. Robert Reinhold. pap. 2.00. 1976. Boxed Set. pap. 5.00 (ISBN 0-912292-40-7). The Smith.

Novelle Italiane Moderne: Civinini, Serao, Pirandello, Zuccoli, Panzini. Ed. by John Revell Reinhard. De Filippis, Michele, 1896- Joint Ed. LC 27-15910. (Century modern language series, K. McKenzie, editor). The Century Co.

Novelle Italiane Moderne: Civinini, Serao, Pirandello, Zuccoli, Panzini. rev. ed. Ed. by John Revell Reinhard. De Filippis, Michael, Joint Ed. LC 33-5939. (Century modern language series, K. McKenzie editor). The Century Co.

Novellen, Tales & Entertainments. Johann Wolfgang Von Goethe. Tr. by Susanne Flatauer. 224p. 1982. 50.00x (ISBN 0-284-98634-8, Pub. by C Skilton Scotland). State Mutual Bk.

Novellettes of a Traveller: Or, Odds and Ends from the Knapsack of Thomas Singularity, Journeyman Printer. Henry Junius Nott. 1834. Harper & Brothers.

Novels. Charles Brockden Brown. LC 70-125016. (American classics in history & social science, 137). (Burt Franklin research & source work series, 523.). 1970. B. Franklin.

Novels. Dashiell Hammett. LC 65-20520. 6.95. Knopf.

Novels. Nathaniel Hawthorne. Ed. by Millicent Bell. LC 82-18031. 1272p. 1983. 25.00 (ISBN 0-940450-08-9). Literary Classics.

Novels. Wilhelm Karl Raabe & Volkmar Sander. LC 82-22097. (German Library; V. 45). 1983. 17.50 (ISBN 0-8264-0280-1) (ISBN 0-8264-0281-X). Continuum.

Novels. Ann Ward Radcliffe. 1971. Repr. of 1824 ed. 30.80 o.p. Adler.

Novels, 15 Vols. Ivan Sergeevich Turgenev. Tr. & illus. by Constance Garnett. LC 1-26225. Set. 375.00 o.p. (ISBN 0-403-00267-2). Scholarly.

Novels. Charles Williams. Incl. War in Heaven. pap. 3.95 (ISBN 0-8028-1219-8); Many Dimensions. pap. 4.95 (ISBN 0-8028-1221-X); Place of the Lion. pap. 3.95 (ISBN 0-8028-1222-8); Shadows of Ecstacy. pap. 3.95 (ISBN 0-8028-1223-6); Descent into Hell. pap. 3.95 (ISBN 0-8028-1220-1). 1965. pap. 32.95 boxed set (ISBN 0-8028-1215-5). Eerdmans.

Novels and Romances of Edward Bulwer Lytton (Lord Lytton)... the sidney library ed. Edward George Earle Lytton Bulwer-Lytton Lytton. LC 7-8327. 1896. G. D. Sproul.

Novels & Short Stories of Anatole France, 19 vols. Ed. by Frederic Chapman. 1980. Set. lib. bdg. 425.00 (ISBN 0-8495-0790-1). Arden Lib.

Novels & Stories. Jack London. Ed. by Donald Pizer. LC 82-249. 1026p. 1982. 25.00 (ISBN 0-940450-05-4). Literary Classics.

Novels & Stories of Frank Richard Stockton, 23 Vols. Frank Richard Stockton. LC 70-153598. Repr. of 1904 ed. Set. 345.00 o.p. (ISBN 0-404-09700-6); 15.00 ea. o.p. AMS Pr.

Novels and Stories of Ivan Turgenieff... Isabel Florence Hapgood & Isabel Florence Hapgood. LC 3-24207. 1903-04. C. Scribner's Sons.

Novels and Stories of Ivan Turgenieff... V. 1-16 Tr. from the Russian by Isabel F. Hapgood. Ivan Sergeievich Turgenev & Hapgood, Isabel Florence, 1850-1928 Tr. LC 3-24207. 1903-04. C. Scribner's Sons.

Novels and Stories of Richard Harding Davis... Richard Harding Davis. LC 16-22595. 1916. C. Scribner's Sons.

Novels & Tales. Johann Wolfgang Von Goethe. Ed. & tr. by R. D. Boylar. 1890. 45.00 (ISBN 0-8274-3052-3). R West.

Novels & Tales of Goethe. Johann Wolfgang Von Goethe. 1976. lib. bdg. 69.95 (ISBN 0-8490-2360-2). Gordon Pr.

Novels and Tales of Henry James. Henry James. LC 70-158792. (Scribner reprint editions). A. M. Kelley.

Novels by Eminent Hands: Also The Diary of C. Jeames De la Pluche, Esq., with His Letters. William Makepeace Thackeray. LC 8-28195. (On cover: Lovell's library, v. 6, no. 300). 1883. J. W. Lovell Company.

Novels by Hugo Wast, 4 vols. Hugo Wast. Incl. Black Valley: A Romance of the Argentine; Stone Desert; Peach Blossom; Strength of Lovers. 1977. lib. bdg. 200.00 set (ISBN 0-8490-2361-0). Gordon Pr.

Nevels Eighteen Seventy-Five to Eighteen Eighty-Six. William Dean Howells. Ed. by Edwin H. Cady. LC 82-112. 1218p. 1982. 25.00 (ISBN 0-940450-04-6). Literary Classics.

Novels: Love's Cross-Currents. Lesbia Brandon. With an Introd. by Edmund Wilson. Algernon Charles Swinburne. LC 62-213381. 1962. Farrar, Straus and Cudahy.

Novels of A. C. Swinburne. Algernon Charles Swinburne. LC 77-20107. 1978. 21.75 (ISBN 0-313-20010-6). Greenwood Press.

Novels of A.C. Swinburne: Love's Cross-Currents, Lesbia Brandon. Algernon Charles Swinburne. LC 77-20107. 1978. Repr. of 1962 ed. lib. bdg. 28.50x (ISBN 0-313-20010-6, SWNO). Greenwood.

Novels of Anthony Trollope. James R Kincaid. LC 77-368275. 1977. 21.50 (ISBN 0-19-812077-X). Clarendon Press.

Novels of Bjornstjerne Bjornson... Bjornstjerne Bjornson. Ed. by Edmund William Gosse. Tr. by Julie Sutter et al. LC 3-27260. 1895. Macmillan and Co.

Novels of Captain Marryat, 24 vols. Frederick Marryat. Ed. by Johnson R. Brimley. 1978. Repr. of 1895 ed. lib. bdg. 600.00 ltd. ed. (ISBN 0-8495-3720-7). Arden Lib.

Novels of Charles Dickens, 16 Vols. Charles Dickens. Set. 48.00 o.p. (ISBN 0-00-422003-X); 1ea. 80.00 o.p. (ISBN 0-00-423003-5). Collins-World.

Novels of Charles Williams, 7 vols. 1981. Set. pap. 32.95 (1215-5). Eerdmans.

Novels of Dashiell Hammett. rev. ed. Dashiell Hammett. (YA) 1965. 17.95 (ISBN 0-394-43860-4). Knopf.

Novels of George Eliot... George Eliot. LC 41-35135. Harper & Brothers.

Novels of George Eliot... George Eliot. LC 8-304115. Harper & Brothers.

Novels of George Meredith. Elmer J. Bailey. LC 75-163892. (Studies in George Meredith, No. 21). 1971. Repr. of 1908 ed. lib. bdg. 33.95x (ISBN 0-8383-1312-4). Haskell.

Novels of Gomberville. Philip A. Wadsworth. LC 72-1669. (Yale Romanic Studies: No. 21). Repr. of 1942 ed. 11.00 (ISBN 0-404-53221-7). AMS Pr.

Novels of Henry Mackenzie, 4 vols. Henry Mackenzie. Incl. Vol. 1. Man of Feeling. LC 78-172709. Repr. of 1771 ed (ISBN 0-404-04091-8); Vols. 2-3. Man of the World. LC 76-25569. Repr. of 1773 ed. Vol. 2 (ISBN 0-404-04092-6). Vol. 3 (ISBN 0-404-04093-4); Vol. 4. Julia de Roubigne. LC 76-25570. Repr. of 1815 ed (ISBN 0-404-04094-2). 1976. 16.25 ea.; 65.00 set (ISBN 0-404-04090-X). AMS Pr.

Novels of Ivan Turgenev. Ivan Sergeevich Turgenev. LC 70-104348. (Illus.). 1970. AMS Press.

Novels of Jane Austen, 5 Vols. Jane Austen. Set. leatheroid canterbury 15.00 o.p.; 1ea. 25.00 o.p. (ISBN 0-00-423001-9) (ISBN 0-00-422001-3). Collins-World.

Novels of Julio Cortazar. Steven Boldy. LC 79-41579. (Cambridge Iberian and Latin American Studies). 1980. 13.50 (ISBN 0-7100-0522-9) (ISBN 0-7100-0523-7). Cambridge University Press.

Novels of Mark Aleksandrovic Aldanov. C. Nicholas Lee. (Slavistic Printings & Reprintings Ser: No. 76). 1969. text ed. 24.75x o.p. Mouton.

Novels of Mary Delariviere Manley. Mary De La Riviere Manley. LC 75-161934. (Illus.). 1971. (ISBN 0-8201-1094-9). Scholars' Facsimiles & Reprints.

Novels of Mrs. Aphra Behn. Aphra Amis Behn. LC 72-98812. 1969. Greenwood Press.

Novels of Mystery: The Lodger; The Story of Ivy; What Really Happened. Marie Adelaide Belloc Lowndes. LC 33-270981. 1933. Longmans, Green and Co.

Novels of Pierre Loti. Clive Wake. LC 73-80224. (De Proprietatibus Litterarum. Series Practica, 82). 1974. Mouton.

Novels of Robert Surtees, 10 Vols. Robert Smith Surtees. LC 73-148311. Repr. of 1930 ed. Set. 240.00 (ISBN 0-404-08900-3); 24.00 ea. AMS Pr.

Novels of Samuel Richardson, 19 Vols. Samuel Richardson. LC 75-114357. 1970. Repr. of 1902 ed. Set. 665.00 (ISBN 0-404-05310-6); 35.00 ea. AMS Pr.

Novels of Victor Hugo: Fully Translated. national ed. Victor Marie Hugo. Tr. by James Carroll Beckwith et al. LC 7-6604. G. Barrie.

Novels of Virginia Woolf: Fact & Vision. Alice V. Kelley. LC 73-77134. 1973. 17.50x (ISBN 0-226-42985-7). U of Chicago Pr.

Novels of Wright Morris: A Critical Interpretation. Gail Bruce Crump. LC 77-15796. 12.95 (ISBN 0-8032-0962-2). University of Nebraska Press.

Novels. The Text Based on Collation of the Early Editions, by R. W. Chapman. With Notes, Indexes, and Illus. from Contemporary Sources. 3d Ed. Jane Austen. LC 54-12216. 1952. Oxford University Press.

Novels, Wilhelm Raabe. Ed. by Volkmar Sander. LC 82-22097. (German Library). 320p. 1983. 17.50 (ISBN 0-8264-0280-1); pap. 8.95 (ISBN 0-8264-0281-X). Continuum.

Novels, 1705-1714, 7 Vols. in Two. Mary De La Riviere Manley. LC 75-161934. 1971. 150.00x set (ISBN 0-8201-1094-9). Schol Facsimiles.

Novelty and Romancement: A Story. Charles Lutwidge Dodgson. LC 75-44107. 1975. 12.50 (ISBN 0-88305-848-0). Norwood Editions.

Novelty and Romancement: A Story. Charles Lutwidge Dodgson. LC 73-4442. 1973. (ISBN 0-8414-1825-X). Folcroft Library Editions.

November. Gustave Flaubert & Jellinek, Frank, Tr. LC 32-42188. Roman Press.

November. Georges Simenon. LC 72-124826. 1970. Harcourt Brace Jovanovich.

November. Georges Simenon. LC 78-6067. (Harvest/HBJ book). 1978. 2.50 (ISBN 0-15-667582-X). Harcourt Brace Jovanovich.

November. A New Ed. of an Early Novel by the Author. Gustave Flaubert. Ed. by Francis Steegmuller. Tr. by Frank Jellinek. LC 66-16502. 1967. Serendipity Press; Distributed by Crown Publishers.

November: A Novel. Rolf Schneider. LC 80-22770. 1981. 10.95 (ISBN 0-394-51440-8). Knopf: Distributed by Random House.

November Joe, Detective of the Woods. Hesketh Vernon Hesketh Prichard. LC 13-193325. 1913. 1.25. Houghton Mifflin Company.

November Man. Brian Freemantle. LC 76-363806. 1976. 2.95 (ISBN 0-224-01233-9). J. Cape.

November Man. Bill Granger. 1979. pap. 1.95 (ISBN 0-449-14245-0, GM). Fawcett.

November Night. Miss Tiverton Goes Out, Author of. LC 28-3429. The Bobbs-Merrill Company.

November Night Tales: A Book of Short Stories. Henry Chapman Mercer. LC 29-1663. W. Neale.

November Storm. Jay McCormick. LC 43-38765. 1943. Doubleday, Doran and Company Inc.

November Twenty-Second. Bryan Woolley. LC 80-54524. 13.45 (ISBN 0-87223-690-0). Seaview Books.

November Twenty-Second. Bryan Woolley. 304p. 1983. pap. 2.95 (ISBN 0-425-05748-8). Berkley Pub.

November Violets. Otto L. Chase. 1973. 4.00 (ISBN 0-8233-0190-7). Golden Quill.

November Wind. Paul Geddes. LC 77-136443. 1971. 4.95. Coward-McCann.

Novice. Oreon Mann Smith. LC 8-96223. 1894. Cox & Ward.

Novice Sex Queen. Jeremy August. (Orig.). 1968. pap. 0.95 o.p. (1147). Brandon.

Novice. Translated Form the Italian by Peter Green. Giovanni Arpino. LC 62-9935. 1962. G. Braziller.

Now. Bryan Hinshaw. LC 43-7353. 1943. The Parthenon Press.

Now"! Charles Marriott. LC 11-9149. 1910. 1.50. The John Lane Co.

Now-a-Days. Laura J. Bullard. 309p. 1980. pap. 4.95 (ISBN 0-89101-042-4). U Maine Orono.

Now: A Narrative Document. Norman Solomon. LC 76-16326. 1.00 (ISBN 0-912874-11-2). Out of the Ashes Press.

Now a Stranger. Humbert Wolfe. 1933. Repr. 12.50 (ISBN 0-8274-3053-1). R West.

Now and Always. Tempest, Jan. LC 51-9303. 1950. Arcadia House.

Now and Another Time. Shelby Hearon. LC 75-36594. 1976. 7.95 (ISBN 0-385-11200-9). Doubleday.

Now and Another Time. Shelby Hearon. 1977. 1.75 (ISBN 0-671-81049-9). Pocket Books.

Now & at the Hour. Robert Cormier. 144p. 1980. pap. 1.95 (ISBN 0-380-50195-3, 50195). Avon.

Now & at the Hour. Robert Cormier. 1960. 3.00 o.p. Coward.

Now, and at the Hour. T. A. James. 3.50 o.p. Carlton.

Now and Forever. Vera Craig. (Candlelight Romance). 1973. (pbk) 0.75. Dell.

Now and Forever. Mary V Jordan. LC 45-99320. 1945. The Bruce Publishing Company.

Now & Forever. Sharon McCaeeree. (American Romance Ser.). 192p. 1983. pap. 2.25 (ISBN 0-373-16004-6). Harlequin Bks.

Now and Forever. Danielle Steel. LC 82-15750. 1982. 16.95 (ISBN 0-8161-3330-1). G.K. Hall.

Now & Forever. Danielle Steel. 432p. 1982. pap. 3.95 (ISBN 0-440-11743-7). Dell.

Now and on Earth. James Myers Thompson. LC 42-12603. 1942. Modernage Books.

Now Barabbas Was a Robber: An Historical Romance of the First Century, A.D. William Franklin Schoch. LC 45-7644. 1945. Burton Publishing Company.

Now, Be a Little Lady. LaReine W. Clayton. (Illus.). 1967. 6.00 o.p. (ISBN 0-682-45734-5). Exposition.

Now Begins Tomorrow. Ed. by Damon Francis Knight. Orig. Title: First Flight. 1969. pap. 0.75 o.p. (74-585). Lancer.

Now Bless Thyself: 1st Ed. Elizabeth Missing Sewell. LC 62-11451. 1962. Doubleday.

Now Come the Spring. Andrea Edwards. 240p. 1983. pap. 2.95 (ISBN 0-380-83329-8). Avon.

Now Comes Theodora. Daniel Ford. (V2155). 1966. Avon.

Now Comes Theodora: A Novel. Daniel Ford. LC 65-14007. 4.95. Doubleday.

Now Comes Tomorrow. Robert M. Williams. (Orig.). 1971. pap. 0.75 o.p. (07115). Curtis.

Now East, Now West. Susan Ertz. LC 27-17656. 1927. D. Appleton and Company.

Now for the Turbulence. Alma Stone. LC 82-45642. (Illus.). 216p. 1983. 13.95 (ISBN 0-385-18203-1). Doubleday.

Now, God Be Thanked: A Novel. John Masters. LC 78-27829. (Masters, John, 1914-. Loss of Eden). (Illus.). 12.95 (ISBN 0-07-040781-9). McGraw-Hill.

Now He Is Legend. Gordon D. Shirreffs. 1979. pap. 1.50 (ISBN 0-449-14233-7, GM). Fawcett.

Now He Is Legend. Gordon D. Shirreffs. 1971. pap. 0.60 o.p. (R2445, GM). Fawcett World.

Now Hear This. Daniel V. Gallery. pap. 0.75 o.p. (ISBN 0-446-64412-9, 64-412). Paperback Lib.

Now Here's My Plan. Shel Silverstein. 1976. pap. 2.95 (Fireside). S&S.

Now I Lav Me Down to Die. Elizabeth Tebbetts-Taylor. LC 55-10193. 1955. Arcadia House.

Now I Lay Me Down: A Novel. Frank Brookhouser. LC 55-13850. 1955. A. Swallow.

Now I Lay Me Down to Sleep. Ludwig Bemelmans. LC 43-15465. 1943. The Viking Press.

Now I See. Charley Boswell & Curt Anders. 1969. 5.95 o.p. (ISBN 0-8015-5460-8). Hawthorn.

Now in November. Josephine Winslow Johnson. LC 77-364852. (Illus.). 1976. Franklin Library.

Now in November. Josephine Winslow Johnson. LC 77-9993. 1970. 5.95. Simon and Schuster.

Now in November. Josephine Winslow Johnson. LC 34-27271. 1934. Simon and Schuster.

Now in November. Josephine Winslow Johnson. LC 35-11506. 1935. Simon and Schuster.

Now Is the Time. Leo Katcher. LC 64-11765. 1964. Macmillan.

Now Let's Talk About Music. Gordon Merrick. 432p. 1981. pap. 3.50 (ISBN 0-380-77867-X, 82651-8). Avon.

Now Listen, Warden. Raymond Prunty Holland & Dennis, Wesley, Illus. LC 46-51581. 1946. A. S. Barnes & Company.

Now Listen, Warden. Raymond Prunty Holland & Dennis, Wesley, Illus. LC 46-180120. 1946. The Countryman Press.

Now Molly Knows. Merrill Joan Gerber. 1975. (pbk.) 1.50. Dell.

Now Molly Knows: A Novel. Merrill Joan Gerber. LC 73-89567. 1974. 7.50 (ISBN 0-87795-074-1). Arbor House.

Now Newman Was Old. Chaim I Bermant. LC 78-3993. 1978. 8.95 (ISBN 0-312-57971-3). St. Martin's Press.

Now or Never. 1st Ed. Manning Coles, pseud. LC 51-3931. 1951. Published for the Crime Club by Doubleday.

Now Playing at Canterbury. Vance Nye Bourjaily. LC 76-24902. 1976. 10.00 (ISBN 0-8037-6450-2). Dial Press.

Now That April's Here: And Other Stories. Morley Callaghan. LC 36-19250. 1936. Random House.

Now That April's There. Daisy Neumann. LC 45-12257. 1945. J. B. Lippincott Company.

Now That April's There: A Novel by Daisy Neumann. Daisy Newman. LC 45-1225. 1945. J. B.Lippincott Company.

Now That Summer's Come. Harry Philip Kemberton. LC 50-9014. 1950. Macmillan.

Now, the Gods. Robert French. 1979. pap. 1.50 (ISBN 0-532-15388-X). Woodhill.

Now, Voyager. Olive Higgins Prouty. LC 41-19417. 1941. Houghton Mifflin Company.

Now Wait for Last Year. Philip K Dick. LC 66-17393. (Doubleday sci. fic.). 3.95. Doubleday.

Now We Are Free. Marguerite Allis. LC 52-5264. 1952. Putnam.

Now We Set Out. Susan Ertz. LC 35-5036. 1935. D. Appleton-Century Company, Incorporated.

Now, Will You Try for Murder? Harry Olesker. LC 58-14684. (inner sanctum mystery). 1958. Simon and Schuster.

Now with the Morning Star. Thomas Dickenson Kernan. LC 44-401861. 1944. C. Scribner's Sons.

Now Yours, Now Mine. Elisabeth Bertram Margetson. LC 45-906. 1944. Arcadia House Inc.

Nowadays: And Other Stories. George Abiah Hibbard. LC 74-142885. (Short story index reprint series). (Illus.). 1970. Books for Libraries Press.

Nowadays, and Other Stories. George Abiah Hibbard. LC 7-4756. 1893. Harper & Brothers.

Nowhere? Aaron Marc Stein. LC 77-76268. 1978. 6.95 (ISBN 0-385-13065-1). Published for the Crime Club by Doubleday.

Nowhere City: 1st Amer. Ed. Alison Lurie. LC 66-10424. 1966. 4.50. Coward.

Nowhere Fast. Margoe Jane. Ed. by Craig H. Hastings. LC 80-85061. (Illus.). 64p. (Orig.). 1980. pap. 4.00x (ISBN 0-9602330-1-6). Margoe Jane.

Nowhere for Vallejo. Nathaniel Tarn. 1971. pap. 2.95 o.p. (ISBN 0-394-70954-3). Random.

Nowhere Hunt. Jo Clayton. 1981. pap. 2.25 (ISBN 0-87997-665-9, UE1665). DAW Bks.

Nowhere Left to Run. Willis Todhunter Ballard. LC 72-14104. 1973. 7.95 (ISBN 0-8161-6084-8). G. K. Hall.

Nowhere Left to Run. Willis Todhunter Ballard. LC 70-186002. (Doubleday western). 1972. 4.95. Doubleday.

Nowhere Man. Thomas Curley. LC 67-19637. 1967. Holt, Rinehart and Winston.

Nowhere Man. Kamala Markandaya, pseud. LC 72-2404. 320p. 1972. 8.95 o.p. (ISBN 0-381-98154-1, A56300). John Day.

Nowhere Man: A Novel. Kamala Markandaya, pseud. LC 72-2404. 1972. 8.95. John Day Co.

Nowhere Place. John Lymington, pseud. LC 74-150905. (Doubleday science fiction). 1971. 4.95. Doubleday.

Nowhere Street. Julian Mayfield. LC 61-5233. Orig. Title: Grand Parade. 1968. pap. 0.75 o.p. (54-589). Paperback Lib.

Nowhere to Go. Geraldine Kaye. Ed. by John Tedman & Alison Tedman. (Illus.). 48p. 1971. pap. 0.75 o.p. (ISBN 0-19-422382-5, OxC). Oxford U Pr.

Nowhere to Go but Home. Carmen Cortazzo. 176p. (Orig.). 1982. pap. cancelled (ISBN 0-523-41626-1). Pinnacle Bks.

Nowhere to Run. Ron Faust. 192p. 1981. pap. 2.25 (ISBN 0-449-14439-9, GM). Fawcett.

Nowhere Weapon. Nick Carter. (Nick Carter Ser.). 256p. (Orig.). 1979. pap. 1.95 o.p. (ISBN 0-441-58895-6). Charter Bks.

Nowhere with Music. Jack Iams. LC 38-32847. 1938. Longmans, Green and Co.

NP Puncher. William L Hopson. LC 48-5849. 1948. Phoenix Press.

N'th Foot in War. Merch Bradt Stewart. LC 1-90189. The Abbey Press.

Nuances. Anais Nin. LC 72-176709. 1970. Sans Souci Press.

Nuclear Catastrophe. Bett Pohnka & Barbara C. Griffin. LC 76-12249. 7.95 (ISBN 0-87949-056-X). Ashley Books.

Nuclear Letters. Graham Lancaster. LC 78-10658. 1979. 8.95 (ISBN 0-689-10940-7). Atheneum.

Nuclear Love. Eugene Wildman. LC 70-189193. (Illus.). 1972. 5.00 (ISBN 0-8040-0568-0) (ISBN 0-8040-0569-9). Swallow Press.

Nuclear Terror Novel see Ultimatum: PU 94.

Nude Assassins. Wayne Lawrence. (Orig.). pap. 0.95 o.p. (1107). Brandon.

Nude Croquet. Lester A. Fiedler. LC 71-87956. 288p. 1974. pap. 1.95 (ISBN 0-8128-1747-8). Stein & Day.

Nude Croquet: The Collected Stories of Leslie A. Fiedler. LC 71-87956. 1969. 5.95 o.p. (ISBN 0-8128-1244-1). Stein & Day.

Nude Croquet: The Stories of Leslie A. Fiedler. Ed. by Leslie A. Fiedler. 1974. (pbk.) 1.95. Stein and Day.

Nude Diana. hunter rowe. ed. Hunter Rowe. 1.75 (ISBN 0-380-00677-4). Avon Books.

Nude in Mink. Arthur Sarsfield Ward. LC 50-4297. (Gold medal book, 105). 1950. Fawcett Publications.

Nude in Nevada. Thomas Blanchard Dewey. LC 66-4979. (Dell mystery). 1965. Dell Pub. Co.

Nude in the Mirror. Ted Hudson. 192p. (Orig.). 1973. pap. 1.95 o.p. (ISBN 0-87682-357-6, 7357). Barclay Hse.

Nude in the Mirror. George Sylvester Viereck. LC 54-40767. Woodford Press.

Nude Look. (Illus.). softcover 4.95 (ISBN 0-910550-07-7). Elysium.

Nude Model. Orrie Hitt. (Orig.). 1970. pap. 0.75 o.p. (75-375). Manor Bks.

Nude Photography Annual. (Illus.). 6.95 (ISBN 0-910550-08-5). Elysium.

Nude Running. Clayton Matthews. 1970. pap. 0.75 o.p. (75-300). Manor Bks.

Nude Who Never. Ted Mark, pseud. 192p. 1976. pap. 1.50 o.p. (ISBN 0-532-15178-X). Woodhill.

Nude Who Never. 3rd ed. Ted Mark, pseud. (Orig.). 1968. pap. 0.60 o.p. (73-489). Lancer.

Nude Who Never. Ted Mark, pseud. 192p. 1976. pap. 1.50 o.p. (ISBN 0-532-15178-X). Manor Bks.

Nude Wore Black. Ted Mark, pseud. 1976. pap. 1.50 o.p. (ISBN 0-532-15170-4). Woodhill.

Nude Wore Black. Ted Mark, pseud. (Orig.). pap. 0.60 o.p. (73-546). Lancer.

Nude Wore Black. Ted Mark, pseud. 1976. pap. 1.50 o.p. (ISBN 0-532-15170-4). Manor Bks.

Nuder Gender. Joseph Hilton Smyth. LC 34-6037. 1934. R. M. McBride & Company.

Nudism, Obscenity & the Law. Eduard Frankhauser. Tr. by Alozis Knapp. (Illus.). 1.95 (ISBN 0-910550-09-3). Elysium.

Nudist Nudes. Ed Lange. 4.95 (ISBN 0-910550-12-3). Elysium.

Nuevo Amor. Salvador Novo. Tr. by E. W. Underwood. 1977. lib. bdg. 59.95 (ISBN 0-8490-2364-5). Gordon Pr.

Nugents of Carriconna: An Irish Story. Tighe Hopkins. LC 41-31328. (On cover: Appletons' town and country library). 1891. D. Appleton and Company.

Nugget. Ruth Potts. (Orig.). 1979. pap. 1.95 (ISBN 0-532-23256-9). Woodhill.

Nuggets of Gold. Mike C Wheat. LC 38-251610. 1938. The Naylor Company.

N.U.K.E.E. A Novel. Don Widener. LC 73-10643. 1974. 6.95. Hawthorn Books.

Null Set. George Chambers. LC 76-47788. 1977. 8.95 (ISBN 0-914590-34-0, Dist. by Braziller); pap. 3.95 (ISBN 0-914590-35-9). Fiction Coll.

Nulma: An Anglo-Australian Romance. Rosa Caroline Murray-Prior Praed. LC 7-30299. (Half-title: Appletons' town and country library, no. 220). 1897. D. Appleton and Company.

Numa Roumestan. Alphonse Daudet. Tr. by Lord, Grace Virginia. LC 11-10527. (On cover: The Rialto series. v. 1, no. 24 cm.). 1890. Rand, McNally & Company.

Numa Roumestan. Alphonse Daudet. Tr. by De Kay, Charles. LC 4271. 1900. Little, Brown and Company.

Numa Roumestan. Alphonse Daudet & Lord, Grace Virginia, D. 1885, Tr. LC 6-33044. 1882. Lee and Shepard.

Numa's Vision: An Allegory... Nicholas Michels. N. Michels.

Number B, Sixty-Seven Million. Frank Dunlap Frisbie. 1900. The Circuit Press.

Number Eighty-Seven. Eden Phillpotts. LC 22-3697. 1922. The Macmillan Company.

Number Naught: A Detective Story. Seldon Truss, pseud. LC 30-18862. 1930. Dodd, Mead & Company.

Number Nine; or, The Mind Sweepers. 1st American Ed. Alan Patrick Herbert. LC 52-5126. 1952. Doubleday.

Number of the Beast. Robert Anson Heinlein. LC 80-16844. 6.95 (ISBN 0-449-90019-3). Fawcett Columbine.

Number of Things: A Novel. Honor Lilbush Wingfield Tracy. LC 60-12126. 1960. Random House.

Number One. John Dos Passos. LC 43-3612. 1943. Houghton Mifflin Company.

Number One. John Dos Passos. LC 45-908129. 1944. The Sun Dial Press.

Number One. David Moessinger. pap. 0.75 o.p. Lancer.

Number One. Leslie Waller. LC 72-5232. 1972. 1.50. Bantam Books.

Number One Boy. John Taintor Foote. LC 26-6734. 1926. D. Appleton and Company.

Number One or Number Two. Mary Ellen Bamford. LC 6-6292. 1891. Hunt & Eaton.

Number One Son. Monfoon Leong. LC 74-84460. (Illus.). 1975. East/West Pub. Co.

Number One Sunset Blvd. Mickie Silverstein & Teddi Sanford. (Orig.). 1982. pap. 3.50 (ISBN 0-89083-929-8). Zebra.

Number One with a Bullet: A Novel. Elaine Jesmer. LC 73-90518. 1974. 8.95 (ISBN 0-374-22347-5). Farrar, Straus and Giroux.

Number One with a Bullet: A Novel. Elaine Jesmer. 1975. (pbk.) 1.75. Bantam Books.

Number Seven, Queer Street. Margery H Lawrence. LC 73-6083. 1969. 4.00. Mycroft & Moran.

Number Seventeen. Louis Tracy. LC 19-20184. E. J. Clode.

Number Stories of Long Ago. David E. Smith. Repr. of 1919 ed. 12.50 o.p. Folcroft.

Number Ten. William Clark. 1967. 4.50 o.p. HM.

Number Thirty: Being Some Relation of What Happened to Chivvy. Edward Asher Jonas. LC 20-22793. Stewart & Kidd Company.

Number Thiry-Six: A Novel. Gerald White Johnson. LC 33-89881. 1933. Minton, Balch & Company.

Number to Call Is... Raymond Thompson & Daley, Treve. 1981. Avon Books.

Number to Call Is... Raymond Thompson & Treve Daly. LC 79-5034. 10.00 (ISBN 0-312-57984-5). St. Martin's Press.

Number Two Man. Jack H Bailey. LC 68-57443. 1968. 5.95. D. McKay Co.

Number Two Wife. Georgia Craig. LC 40-8932. 1940. Gateway Books.

Number Two Wife. Peggy Gaddis, pseud. LC 40-8932. 1940. Gateway Books.

Number 10: A Novel. William Clark. LC 67-969. 1967. Houghton Mifflin.

Number 44, & Other Football Stories, Vol. 1. Harold Morrow Sherman. LC 72-4408. (Short Story Index Reprint Ser). Repr. of 1930 ed. 17.00 (ISBN 0-8369-4188-8). Ayer Co.

Number 49 Tinkham Street. Clara Emma Griswold Cheney. 1895. A. C. McClurg and Company.

Number 91: The Adventures of A New York Telegraph Boy. Horatio Alger, Jr. (Illus.). 205p. 1977. Repr. of 1889 ed. 19.50. G K Westgard.

Numbered Years: Five Decades at James City. Margaret Collins Denny Dixon. LC 57-10483. 1957. Garrett & Massie.

Numbers. large type ed. 1970. pap. 1.00 o.p. (ISBN 0-8055-0044-8). Hart.

Numbers. John Rechy. LC 67-28972. 1967. Grove Press.

Numbers for Lovers. Arlene J. Fitzgerald. 192p. (Orig.). 1974. pap. 1.25 o.p. (ISBN 0-532-12220-8). Woodhill.

Numbers for Lovers. Arlene J. Fitzgerald. 192p. (Orig.). 1974. pap. 1.25 o.p. (ISBN 0-532-12220-8). Manor Bks.

Numbers Man. David J Gerrity. (Signet Book.). 1977. 1.50. (ISBN 0-451-07456-4). New American Library.

Numbers of Our Days: A Novel. Francis Irby Gwaltney. LC 58-9887. 1959. Random House.

Numerous Treasure: A Romantic Novel. Robert Keable. LC 25-6519. 1925. G. P. Putnam's Sons.

Numin's Curse. Roger Lewis. (Berkley Medallion) (ISBN 0-425-03189-6). Berkley.

Nun. Denis Diderot. LC 74-172728. (Penguin classics). 1974. (0.35, 1.25 u.s.) (ISBN 0-14-044300-2). Penguin Books.

Nun and the Bandit. Elliot Lovegood Grant Watson. LC 41-25255. Smith & Durrell.

Nun in the Closet. Dorothy Gilman Butters. LC 74-6992. 1975. 5.95 (ISBN 0-385-05635-4). Doubleday.

Nun in the Closet. Dorothy Gilman. 1979. pap. 1.95 (ISBN 0-449-23632-3, Crest). Fawcett.

Nun in the Closet. Dorothy Gilman. 1975. lib. bdg. 10.95 o.p. (ISBN 0-8161-6296-4, Large Print Bks). G K Hall.

Nun (La Religieuse) Denis Diderot. LC 68-23187. 1968. Holloway House Pub. Co.

Nun (L'isolee) From the French of Rene Bazin... Rene Bazin. LC 8-15729. 1908. C. Scribner's Sons.

Nun of St. Ursula: Or, The Burning of the Convent. A Romance of Mount Benedict. Justin Jones. LC 11-7164. 1845. F. Gleason.

Nun: Saint Margaret Mary and the Sacred Heart, a Novel. Foreword by Columba Cary-Elwes. Margaret Lahey Trouncer. LC 55-108737. 1955. Sheed and Ward.

Nun, Witch, Playmate. Herbert W. Richardson. pap. 2.50 o.p. (RD67, HarpR). Har-Row.

Nuna, the Bramin Girl. Henry Willard French. LC 6-40366. 1882. Lee and Shepard.

Nuncle, and Other Stories. John Barrington Wain. LC 61-19889. 1961. St. Martin's Press.

Nuni. John Howard Griffin. LC 53-9256. 1956. Houghton Mifflin.

Nunnery. Dorothy Charques. LC 59-7123. 1960. Coward-McCann.

Nunquam: A Novel. Lawrence Durrell. LC 70-87181. 1970. 7.95. E. P. Dutton.

Nunquam: A Novel. Lawrence Durrell. LC 79-15616. 1979. 3.95 (ISBN 0-14-005189-9). Penguin Books.

Nuns. Eduardo Manet. Tr. by Robert Baldick from Sp. 91p. 1981. pap. 4.95 (ISBN 0-7145-0722-9). Riverrun NY.

Nun's Castle. Jennie Melville, pseud. LC 73-84060. 1973. 5.95 (ISBN 0-679-50411-7). McKay.

Nun's Curse. Charlotte Eliza Lawson Cowan Riddell. (On cover: Seaside library. Pocket ed., no. 1077). 1888. G. Munro.

Nun's Curse. Charlotte Eliza Lawson Cowan Riddell. (On cover: Lovell's library, no. 1134). 1888. J. W. Lovell Company.

Nun's Curse. Charlotte Eliza Lawson Cowan Riddell. LC 78-24149. (Ireland, from the Act of Union, 1800, to the Death of Parnell, 1891). 1979. 42.00 (ISBN 0-8240-3512-7). Garland Pub.

Nuns in Jeopardy. Martin Boyd. LC 74-17476. 1975. (ISBN 0-15-167740-9). Harcourt Brace Jovanovich.

Nun's Story. Kathryn Cavarly Hulme. LC 56-6768. 1956. Little, Brown.

Nun's Story. Large Type Ed. Kathryn Cavarly Hulme. (Keith Jennison bk.). 1966. 6.95. Watts.

Nunsuch: Stories About Sisters. Candida Lund. LC 82-139374. 12.95 (ISBN 0-88347-139-6). T. More Press.

Nunzio: A Novel. John Minahan. 1978. 1.95 (ISBN 0-345-27526-8). Ballantine Books.

Nuova; or, The New Bee: A Story for Children of Five to Fifty. Vernon Lyman Kellogg & Kellogg, Charlotte (Hoffman) LC 20-176038. Houghton Mifflin Company.

Nuplex Red. Simon Quinn. (Inquisitor,#5). 1974. (pbk.) 0.95. Dell.

Nuptial Flight. Edgar Lee Masters. LC 23-127450. Boni and Liveright.

Nuptial Night. Dolf Wyllarde. LC 31-11726. The Macaulay Company.

Nuptials. John Haase. 1970. pap. 0.75 o.p. (T2276). Pyramid Pubns.

Nuptials. John Haase. (O.S.I.). 1969. 4.95 o.s.i. (ISBN 0-671-20202-2). S&S.

Nuptials: A Novel. John Haase. LC 76-75863. 1969. 4.95. Simon and Schuster.

Nuptials of Corbal. Rafael Sabatini. LC 27-21135. 1927. Houghton Mifflin Company.

Nur Mahal. Harold Lamb. LC 32-24543. 1932. Doubleday, Doran & Company, Inc.

Nureyev Valantino. Alexander Bland, pseud. 1977. pap. 6.95 (ISBN 0-440-56478-6). Dell.

Nurse. Peggy Anderson. 1980. pap. 2.95 (ISBN 0-425-05351-2). Berkley Pub.

Nurse. Louise Logan. LC 40-31632. 1940. Arcadia House, Inc.

Nurse Abroad. Marion Marsh Brown. 1963. Avalon Books.

Nurse Adriane: A Novel. Norah C James. 1933. Covici, Friede.

Nurse & the Crystal Ball. Florence Stuart. 1972. pap. 0.75 o.s.i. (01-350). Lancer.

Nurse & the Talisman. Ruth Burnett. 192p. (YA) 1974. 4.95 o.p. (Avalon). Bouregy.

Nurse and the Talisman. Ruth Burnett. (Avalon nurse stories). 1974. 4.50. Avalon Books.

Nurse Andrea Takes a Flier. Annie L. Gelsthorpe. (YA) 1973. 4.50 o.p. (Avalon). Bouregy.

Nurse Anne's Emergency. William Arthur Neubauer. LC 54-7984. 1965. Arcadia House.

Nurse Ann's Secret. William Edward Daniel Ross. (YA) 1981. 6.50 (Avalon). Bouregy.

Nurse April's Dilemma. Jane McCarthy. 1974. 4.50. Avalon.

Nurse at Breakwater Hotel. Ann Gilmer, pseud. 1982. pap. 6.95 (Avalon). Bouregy.

Nurse at Burford's Landing. Peggy Dern, pseud. 1971. pap. 0.60 o.p. (60-475). Manor Bks.

Nurse at Burford's Landing. Peggy Gaddis, pseud. LC 66-474. 1966. Arcadia House.

Nurse at Burford's Landing. LC 66-474. 1966. Arcadia House.

Nurse at Danger Mansion. Dorothy Daniels. 1971. pap. 0.75 o.p. (ISBN 0-447-74938-2). Lancer.

Nurse at Danger Mansion. easy eye ed. Dorothy Daniels. (Orig.). 1968. pap. 0.75 o.p. (74-938). Lancer.

Nurse at Deer Hollow. Christine Bush. (Avalon Books). 4.95. Thomas Bouregy.

Nurse at Lookout Rock. Colleen Lewis. 1982. pap. 6.95 (Avalon). Bouregy.

Nurse at Mystery Villa. Willo Davis Roberts. (Ace nurse series). 1973. (pbk.) 0.75. Ace.

Nurse at Orchard Hill. Callie Buckingham. (YA) 1978. 6.50 (Avalon). Bouregy.

Nurse at Playland Park. Dorothy Brenner Francis. 1976. 4.95. Avalon Books.

Nurse at Sea Lair. Isabel Cabot. 192p. (YA) 1975. 4.95 o.p. (Avalon). Bouregy.

Nurse at Sea Lair. Isabel Cabot. 1975. 4.95. Avalon Books.

Nurse at Seaview. Polly Mark, pseud. (Avalon Books). 1977. 4.95. Thomas Bouregy.

Nurse at Shadow Manor. Sharon Heath. (Ace Nurse Romance Series). 1973. (pbk.) 0.75. Ace Books.

Nurse at Sundown. Peggy Gaddis, pseud. 1971. pap. 0.60 o.p. (60-470). Manor Bks.

Nurse at the Fair. Dorothy Cole. Ed. by Alice Sachs. 1971. 3.95 o.p. Lenox Hill.

Nurse at the Fair. Dorothy Cole. (Signet Nurse Book). 1973. 0.75. New American Library.

Nurse at Towpath Lodge. Anne Maguire, pseud. 1976. 4.95. Avalon Books.

Nurse at Whittle's. Lucy Agnes Hancock. LC 45-5086. 1945. Macrae-Smith-Company.

Nurse at Whittle's. Lucy Agnes Hancock. LC 47-2709. 1946. Triangle Books, the Blakiston Company.

Nurse Autumn's Secret Love. Colleen L. Reece. (YA) 1979. 6.95 (Avalon). Bouregy.

Nurse Barclay's Dilemma. Adelaide Humphries. LC 54-12956. 1954. Avalon Books.

Nurse Barlow. Lucy Agnes Hancock. LC 46-6023. 1946. Macrae-Smith-Company.

Nurse Beckie's New World. Mary C. Bowers. 1982. 6.95 (Avalon). Bouregy.

Nurse Benson. Justin Huntly McCarthy & Critchett, R. C., 1853- Nurse Benson. LC 19-4690. 1919. John Lane Company.

Nurse Blake at the Front. William Starret. LC 44-41183. 1944. Gramercy Publishing Company.

Nurse Blake Overseas. William Starret. LC 43-117504. 1943. Gramercy Publishing Co.

Nurse Blake, U.S.A. William Starret. LC 42-249635. 1942. Gramercy Publishing Co.

Nurse Camilla's Love. Colleen L. Reece. (YA) 6.95 (Avalon). Bouregy.

Nurse Carol. Maud McCurdy Welch. LC 55-999. 1955. Avalon Books.

Nurse Charly's New Love. Mary C. Bowers. 1982. pap. 6.95 (Avalon). Bouregy.

Nurse Christine. Peggy Gaddis, pseud. 1971. pap. 0.60 o.p. (60-487). Manor Bks.

Nurse Comes Home. Peggy Gaddis, pseud. LC 63-6968. 1963. Arcadia House.

Nurse Comes Home: By Ethel Hamill Pseud. Jean Francis Webb. 1954. Avalon Books.

Nurse Delia's Choice. Virginia K. Smiley. (Avalon Books). 4.95. Thomas Bouregy.

Nurse Elisia. George Manville Fenn. LC 6-393836. Cassell Publishing Company.

Nurse Ellen. Peggy Dern, pseud. 1970. pap. 0.50 o.p. (50-499). Manor Bks.

Nurse Ellen: By Peggy Dern. Peggy Gaddis, pseud. LC 56-8985. 1956. Arcadia House.

Nurse Errant. Lucilla Andrews. LC 74-34047. 1975. 4.95 (ISBN 0-517-52162-8). Lenox Hill Press.

Nurse Felicity. Peggy Dern, pseud. 1971. pap. 0.60 o.p. (60-474). Manor Bks.

Nurse Felicity. Peggy Gaddis, pseud. LC 66-7179. 1966. Arcadia House.

Nurse for Apple Valley. Peggy Gaddis, pseud. pap. 0.50 o.p. (50-458). Manor Bks.

Nurse for Galleon Key: By Ethel Hamill Pseud. Jean Francis Webb. LC 57-126739. 1957. Avalon Books.

Nurse for Mercy's Mission. Adeline McElfresh. 1976. 0.95. Belmont Tower Books.

Nurse for Rebels' Run: By Jane Scott Pseud. Adeline McElfresh. LC 60-3780. 1960. Avalon Books.

Nurse for the Civic Center. Virginia K. Smiley. 1974. 4.50. Avalon.

Nurse for the Fishermen. Teresa Holloway. (YA) 1974. 4.95 o.p. (Avalon). Bouregy.

Nurse for the Fishermen. Teresa Holloway. (Avalon nurse stories). 1974. 4.50. Avalon Books.

Nurse Freda. Rose Dana, pseud. 1969. pap. 0.50 o.p. (50-483). Manor Bks.

Nurse from Alaska. Florence Stonebraker. LC 64-25968. 1964. Arcadia House.

Nurse from Alaska. Florence Stuart. 1971. pap. 0.60 o.p. (60.491). Manor Bks.

Nurse from Hawaii. Webb, Jean Francis. (Avalon nurse stories). 1964. Avalon Books.

Nurse Grace's Dilemma. William Edward Daniel Ross. 1982. pap. 6.95 (Avalon). Bouregy.

Nurse Greer: By Joan Garrison Pseud. William Arthur Neubauer. LC 54-113398. 1954. Arcadia House.

Nurse Had Red Hair. Adelaide Humphries. LC 57-12684. 1957. Avalon Books.

Nurse Hilary. Peggy Gaddis & Florence Stuart. (Manor Books doible volume). 1973. (pbk.) 0.95. Manor Books.

Nurse Hilary - Research Nurse. Peggy Gaddis & Florence Stuart. 1972. pap. 0.95 o.p. (532-00499-060). Manor Bks.

Nurse Howard's Assignment: By Virginia Roberts Pseud. Nell Marr Dean. LC 57-8735. 1957. Avalon Books.

Nurse in a Nightmare. Adelaide Humphries. 1972. pap. 0.75 o.s.i. (01-364). Lancer.

Nurse in Australia. Mary C. Bowers. 1981. pap. 6.95 (Avalon). Bouregy.

Nurse in Blue. Gladys Bagg Taber. LC 43-160024. 1943. Macrae-Smith-Company.

Nurse in Blue. Gladys Bagg Taber. 1944. Triangle Books, the Blackiston Company.

Nurse in Danger. Fern Shepard. 1969. Repr. pap. 0.50 o.p. (50-475). Manor Bks.

Nurse in Fashion. Laura C. Raef. (YA) 1972. 4.50 o.p. (Avalon). Bouregy.

Nurse in Flight. Peggy Gaddis, pseud. 1969. Repr. pap. 0.50 o.p. (50-491). Manor Bks.

Nurse in Flight. Adelaide Humphries. pap. 0.75 o.s.i. (01-339). Lancer.

Nurse in Istanbul. R. E. Hayes. 1972. text ed. 0.75 o.s.i. (01-355). Lancer.

Nurse in Jeopardy. William Edward Daniel Ross. LC 68-611. 1967. Arcadia House.

Nurse in las Palmas. Anne Maguire, pseud. (YA) 1980. 6.95 (Avalon). Bouregy.

Nurse in Las Vegas. Jane Converse. (Signet Q 6272). 1975. (pbk.) 0.95. New American Library.

Nurse in Nassau. William Edward Daniel Ross. LC 67-2437. 1967. Arcadia House.

Nurse in Nassau. easy eye ed. Rose Williams, pseud. pap. 0.60 o.p. Lancer.

Nurse in Paris. easy eye ed. Renee Shann. (Orig.). 1968. pap. 0.60 o.p. (73-775). Lancer.

Nurse in Peril. Marcia Miller. 1975. 4.95. Avalon Books.

Nurse in Peru. Mary C. Bowers. 1981. pap. 6.95 (Avalon). Bouregy.

Nurse in Research. Helene Chambers Schellenberg. 192p. (YA) 1974. 4.95 o.p. (Avalon). Bouregy.

Nurse in Research. Helene Chambers Schellenberg. (Avalon nurse stories). 1974. 4.50. Avalon Books.

Nurse in Residence. Arlene Hale. (Candlelight Romance). 1977. 0.95 (ISBN 0-440-16620-9). Dell Pub Co.

Nurse in Spain. Diana Douglas. (Signet book). 1975. (pbk.) 0.95. New American Library.

Nurse in the Caribbean. Dorothy Brenner Francis. 192p. (YA) 1974. 4.95 o.p. (Avalon). Bouregy.
Nurse in the Caribbean. Dorothy Brenner Francis. (Avalon nurse stories). 1974. 4.50. Avalon Books.
Nurse in the Shadows. Peggy Gaddis, pseud. 1970. Repr. pap. 0.50 o.p. (50-489). Manor Bks.
Nurse in the Tropics. Peggy Dern, pseud. 1971. pap. 0.60 o.p. (60-479). Manor Bks.
Nurse in the Tropics. easy eye ed. Ann Gilmer, pseud. pap. 0.60 o.p. Lancer.
Nurse in the Tropics: By Peggy Dern Pseud. Peggy Gaddis, pseud. LC 57-114666. 1957. Arcadia House.
Nurse in Turmoil. Jane Converse. 1974. (pbk.) 0.75. New American Library.
Nurse in Waiting. William Edward Daniel Ross. LC 67-9488. 1967. Arcadia House.
Nurse in White. Lucy Agnes Hancock. LC 39-4490. 1939. The Penn Publishing Company.
Nurse in Yosemite. Beatrice Warren. 1982. pap. 6.95 (Avalon). Bouregy.
Nurse into Woman. Marguerite Mooers Marshall. LC 41-765535. 1941. Macrae-Smith-Company.
Nurse Jan & the Legacy. Laura C. Raef. 192p. (YA) 1974. 4.95 o.p. (Avalon). Bouregy.
Nurse Jan and the Legacy. Laura C Raef. (Avalon nurse stories.). 1974. 4.50. Avalon Books.
Nurse Jean's Strange Case. Arlene Hale. 1974. (pbk.) 0.75. Ace Books.
Nurse Jean's Strange Case: A Novel of Romantic Suspense. Arlene Hale. LC 80-26058. 1980. 8.95 (ISBN 0-89621-259-9). Thorndike Press.
Nurse Jessica's Cruise. Elnora Donarico. (YA) 1980. 6.95 (Avalon). Bouregy.
Nurse Julia's Tangled Loves. Arlene Hale. 1976. (pbk.) 0.95. Ace Books.
Nurse Julie's Sacrifice. Colleen L. Reece. (YA) 1980. 6.95 (Avalon). Bouregy.
Nurse Karen's Masquerade. Mary C. Bowers. 1982. pap. 6.95 (Avalon). Bouregy.
Nurse Kathryn. Peggy O'More, pseud. LC 65-7329. 1965. Arcadia House.
Nurse Kathryn and Disaster Nurse. Peggy O'More. (MB double volume). 1972. 0.95. Manor Books.
Nurse Kathy. Adeline McElfresh. LC 56-13302. 1956. Avalon Books.
Nurse Kathy Decides. Lucy Agnes Hancock. LC 51-1552. 1951. Macrae Smith.
Nurse Kilmer's Vow. Virginia C Holmgren. 1963. Avalon Books.
Nurse Knows Best. Adelaide Humphries. LC 53-12784. 1953. Avalon Books.
Nurse Kris's Trust. Marcia Miller. (Avalon nurse stories). 1973. 4.50. Avalon Books.
Nurse Lady. Adelaide Humphries. LC 53-8447. 1953. Bouregy & Curl.
Nurse Landon's Challenge. Adelaide Humphries. LC 52-12537. 1952. Bouregy & Curl.
Nurse Laurie's Cruise. Adelaide Humphries. LC 56-13314. 1956. Avalon Books.
Nurse Lora's Love. Arlene Hale. Ace.
Nurse Loreen's Nightmare. Merle C. Overholtzer. 1981. pap. 6.95 (Avalon). Bouregy.
Nurse Lucie. Georgia Craig. 0.50 o.p. (50-454). Manor Bks.
Nurse March. William Arthur Neubauer. LC 57-7717. 1957. Arcadia House.
Nurse Merton: Army Spy. Louise Logan. LC 42-14630. 1942. Arcadia House, Inc.
Nurse Merton Comes Home. Louise Logan. LC 46-819. 1946. Arcadia House, Inc.
Nurse Merton: Desert Captive. Louise Logan. LC 43-9101. 1943. Arcadia House, Inc.
Nurse Merton in the Caribbean. Louise Logan. LC 43-2626. 1943. Arcadia House, Inc.
Nurse Merton in the Pacific. Louise Logan. LC 44-751626. 1944. Arcadia House, Inc.
Nurse Merton on the Russian Front. Louise Logan. LC 45-12236. 1945. Arcadia House Inc.
Nurse Nicole's Decision. Arlene Hale. LC 81-14454. 1981. 9.95 (ISBN 0-89621-313-7). Thorndike Press.
Nurse Nolan's Private Duty. Adeline McElfresh. 1976. 0.95. Belmont Tower.
Nurse Nora's Folly. Ruth McCarthy Sears. (YA) 1979. 6.95 (Avalon). Bouregy.
Nurse of Brooding Mansion. Paulette Warren. (Orig.). 1970. pap. 0.60 o.p. (ISBN 0-447-73877-1). Lancer.
Nurse of Glen Lock. Ruth McCarthy Sears. 1973. 4.95. Lenox Hill Pr.
Nurse of Mount Juliet. Ruth Burnett. 192p. (YA) 1975. 4.95 o.p. (Avalon). Bouregy.
Nurse of Mount Juliet. Ruth Burnett. 1975. 4.95. Avalon Books.
Nurse of Polka Dot Island. Jeanne Bowman, pseud. 1968. pap. 0.50 o.p. (50-422). Manor Bks.
Nurse of St. John. Sue Alden. (Avalon Books). 4.95. Thomas Bouregy.
Nurse of Spirit Lake. Dorothy Brenner Francis. 1975. 4.95. Avalon Books.
Nurse of the Crossroads. Colleen L Reece. (Avalon Books). 4.95. Thomas Bouregy.
Nurse of the Crystalline Valley. Mary Collins Dunne. (Avalon Books). 4.95. Thomas Bouregy.
Nurse of the Grand Canyon. Virginia K. Smiley. 192p. (YA) 1973. 4.95 o.p. (Avalon). Bouregy.
Nurse of the Grand Canyon. Virginia K. Smiley. (Fawcett Gold Medal Book). 1975. (pbk.) 0.95. Fawcett.
Nurse of the High Sierras. Marcia Miller. (Avalon nurse stories). 1973. 4.50. Avalon Books.
Nurse of the Keys. Dorothy Brenner Francis. (Illus.). 1974. 4.50. Avalon Books.
Nurse of the Midnight Sun. Mary Collins Dunne. (YA) 1973. 4.95 o.p. (Avalon). Bouregy.
Nurse of the Ozarks. Patricia Logsdon. 192p. (YA) 1974. 4.95 o.p. (Avalon). Bouregy.
Nurse of the Ozarks. Patricia Logsdon. (Avalon nurse stories). 1974. 4.50. Avalon Books.
Nurse of the Vineyards. Mary Collins Dunne. 1975. 4.95. Avalon Books.
Nurse of Thorne Grotto. Jane McCarthy. (Avalon Books). 1977. 4.95. Avalon Books.
Nurse of Ward B. William Arthur Neubauer. LC 63-22876. Arcadia House.
Nurse on Assignment. Dorothy Brenner Francis. (YA) 1973. 4.95 o.p. (Avalon). Bouregy.
Nurse on Call. Ann Gilmer, pseud. LC 73-860. (Valentine Ser). 1969. pap. 0.60 o.p. Lancer.
Nurse on Call. Fay Stone. 1970. 3.95 o.p. Lenox Hill.
Nurse on Dark Island. Teresa Holloway. (Ace nurse romance series). 1972. 0.60. Ace.
Nurse on Holiday. Adelaide Humphries. LC 64-9017. (Avalon nurse stories). 1964. Avalon Books.
Nurse on Horseback. Jean Francis Webb. LC 52-13532. 1952. Bouregy & Curl.
Nurse on Leave. Arlene Hale. LC 80-28022. 1981. 8.95 (ISBN 0-89621-270-X). Thorndike Press.
Nurse on Paradise Isle. Nell Marr Dean. LC 64-25979. 1964. Avalon Books.
Nurse on Trial. Katherina McComb. (Avalon nurse stories). 1973. 4.50. Avalon Books.
Nurse on Trial. Katherine McComb. (YA) 1973. 4.95 o.p. (Avalon). Bouregy.
Nurse Paige's Triumph. Teresa Holloway. 1973. pap. 0.75 o.s.i. (01-384). Lancer.
Nurse Patsy's Last Chance. Luella Irving. (YA) 1980. 6.95 (Avalon). Bouregy.
Nurse Paula'a New Look. Beatrice Warren. 1982. 6.95 (Avalon). Bouregy.
Nurse Pro Tem. Glenna Finley, pseud. LC 67-1371. 1967. Arcadia House.
Nurse Revel's Mistake. Florence Alice Price James. (On cover: Seaside library. Pocket ed., no. 1272). 1890. G. Munro.
Nurse Robin. Willo Davis Roberts. 1973. 4.95 (ISBN 0-517-51504-0). Lenox Hill Press.
Nurse Said Yes. Carol Morris. LC 47-30647. 1947. Arcadia House.
Nurse Sally Dean. Dorothy Quentin. LC 43-143165. 1943. Arcadia House, Inc.
Nurse Sue's Romance. Arlene Hale. 1975. (pbk.) 0.75. Ace Books.
Nurse Suzanne's Bold Journey. Ethel E. Bangert. 192p. (YA) 1975. 4.95 o.p. (Avalon). Bouregy.
Nurse Suzanne's Bold Journey. Ethel E. Bangert. 1975. 4.95. Avalon Books.
Nurse Takes a Chance. Ruth Dorset, pseud. 1973. pap. 0.75 o.s.i. (01-396). Lancer.
Nurse to Marry. William Arthur Neubauer. LC 67-9638. 1967. Arcadia House.
Nurse to Remember. Teresa Holloway. 1976. 1.25. Ace Books.
Nurse Under Fire. Dorothy Brenner Francis. (YA) 1973. 4.95 o.p. (Avalon). Bouregy.
Nurse Under Fire. Florence Stonebraker. LC 64-9301. 1964. Arcadia House.
Nurse Under Suspicion. Ethel E. Bangert. (YA) 1973. 4.95 o.p. (Avalon). Bouregy.
Nurse Vicky's Love. Elnora Donarico. (YA) 1979. 6.95 (Avalon). Bouregy.
Nurse Was Juliet. Peggy Gaddis, pseud. 1970. pap. 0.50 o.p. (50-503). Manor Bks.
Nurse Was Kidnapped. Adelaide Humphries. 192p. (YA) 1976. 4.95 o.p. (Avalon). Bouregy.
Nurse Whitney's Paradise. Betty R. Gunn. (YA) 1981. 6.95 (Avalon). Bouregy.
Nurse with Wings. Adelaide Humphries. LC 55-135676. 1955. Avalon Books.
Nurse with Wings. Marguerite Mooers Marshall. LC 52-10366. 1952. Macrae Smith.
Nursery Rhyme Murders: An Anthology. Agatha Christie. Incl. Crooked House; Hickory Dickory Dock; Pocket Full of Rye. LC 77-111910. 1970. 6.95 o.p. (ISBN 0-396-06181-8). Dodd.
Nursery Rhyme Murders: Including: A Pocket Full of Rye, Hickory Dickory Death. The Crooked House. Agatha Miller Christie. LC 72-117622. 1970. Dodd, Mead.
Nursery Tale. T. M. Wright. LC 81-86261. 288p. (Orig.). 1982. pap. 2.95 (ISBN 0-86721-077-X). Playboy Pbks.
Nursery Tea and Poison. Anne Morice. LC 74-33908. 1975. 6.95. St. Martin's.
Nurses. William Johnston. LC 63-8349. (Bantam books). 1963. Bantam Books.
Nurse's Aide. Lucy Agnes Hancock. LC 43-14579. 1943. Macrae-Smith-Company.
Nurse's Aide. Lucy Anges Hancock. LC 44-8144. 1944. Triangle Books.
Nurses Are People. Lucy Agnes Hancock. LC 41-3330. 1941. Macrae-Smith-Company.
Nurses Are People. Lucy Agnes Hancock. LC 42-241007. 1942. Triangle Books.
Nurses Are People. Adelaide Humphries. LC 51-4034. 1951. Bouregy & Curl.
Nurse's Choice. Peggy Gaddis, pseud. 1971. pap. 0.60 o.p. (60-490). Manor Bks.
Nurse's Choice. Dan Ross, pseud. (YA) 1972. 4.50 o.p. (Avalon). Bouregy.
Nurse's Dilemma. Peggy Dern, pseud. 1971. pap. 0.60 o.p. (60-472). Manor Bks.
Nurse's Dilemma. Peggy Gaddis, pseud. LC 66-1866. 1966. Arcadia House.
Nurse's Heritage. easy eye ed. Jeanne Bowman, pseud. Orig. Title: When a Nurse Needs a Doctor. 1968. pap. 0.60 o.p. (73-731). Lancer.
Nurse's Holiday. Jennifer Ames, pseud. 1972. pap. 0.75 o.p. Beagle Bks.
Nurses' Home. Charles Stanley Strong. LC 39-12728. Phoenix Press.
Nurse's Journey. Helene Chambers Schellenberg. LC 67-1446. 1967. Arcadia House.
Nurses Marry Doctors. Maud McCurdy Welch. LC 56-345622. 1956. Avalon Books.
Nurses, Nurses, Nurses. Ed. by Helen Hoke. LC 60-11446. (Terrific triple title series). 1961. F. Watts.
Nurse's Secret. easy eye ed. Peggy Gaddis, pseud. 1968. pap. 0.60 o.p. (73-745). Lancer.
Nurse's Story. Carol Gino. 352p. 1982. 14.95 (ISBN 0-671-45390-4, Linden Pr). S&S.
Nurse's Story: In Which Reality Meets Romance. Adele Bleneau. LC 15-15950. 1.25. The Bobbs-Merrill Company.
Nurse's Training. Portia Maxwell. LC 41-1978. Gramercy Publishing Company.
Nursing-Home Murder. Ngaio Marsh & Jellett, Henry, 1872- Joint Author. 1941. Sheridan House.
Nurture & Evangelism of Children. Gideon Yoder. LC 59-7877. (Conrad Grebel Lecture Ser.). 1959. 4.00 o.p. (ISBN 0-8361-1409-4). Herald Pr.
Nut-Brown Maid and Nut-Brown Mare. A. G. Hales. 1919. Hodder and Stoughton.
Nut Cracker. Frederic Stewart Isham. LC 20-75133. The Bobbs-Merrill Company.
Nutcracker Sweet. Dale Greggsen. (Orig.). 1972. pap. 1.95 o.s.i. (76-321). Lancer.
Nuthin.". Harry Edward Webb. LC 52-28538. 1952.
Nutley Syndrome. Alexander Rose. 1971. 5.95 o.p. Impress Hse.
Nutley Syndrome: A Novel. Alexander Rose. LC 77-116846. 1970. 5.95. Impress House.
Nutmeg Tree. Margery Sharp. 1937. Little, Brown and Company.
Nutmeg Tree. Margery Sharp. LC 38-773379. 1938. Little, Brown and Company.
Nutro 29, a Romance. Frank Callan Norris. LC 50-7231. 1950. Rinehart.
Nuttie's Father. Charlotte Mary Yonge. (On cover: Seaside library. Pocket ed. no. 640). 1885. G. Munro.
Nutzenbolts and More Troubles with Machines. Ron Goulart. LC 74-18308. 1975. 5.95. Macmillan Pub. Co.
Nya. Stephen Haggard. LC 38-31047. 1938. Little, Brown and Company.
Nyangeta: The Name from the Calabash. Abel K Mwanga. LC 77-980019. (Illus.). 1976. East African Literature Bureau.
Nylon Net. Matt Harding, pseud. 1970. pap. 0.75 o.p. (75-319). Manor Bks.
Nylon Pirates. Nicholas Monsarrat. LC 60-14542. 1960. W. Sloane Associates.
Nylon Trap. Stan O'Dair. 192p. (Orig.). 1973. pap. 1.95 o.p. (ISBN 0-87682-350-9, 7350). Barclay Hse.
Nymph and Shepherds. 1st Ed. Richard Cavendish. LC 59-7902. 1959. Doubleday.
Nymph and the Lamp: A Novel. Thomas Head Raddall. LC 50-10175. 1950. Little, Brown.
Nymph de Sioux Lake. Jocelyn Haley. (Harlequin Seduction Ser.). 332p. 1983. pap. 3.25 (ISBN 0-373-45016-8). Harlequin Bks.
Nymph Errant. James Laver. LC 32-22560. 1932. A. A. Knopf.
Nymph Island Affair. Sean O'Shea, pseud. (Orig.). 1967. pap. 0.50 o.p. (B50-782). Belmont-Tower.
Nymph of the West: A Novel. Howard Seely. LC 8-6443. 1888. D. Appleton and Company.
Nymph Syndrome. Jean Francis. (Orig.). 1969. pap. 0.95 o.p. (75-082). Lancer.
Nymph Was Mortal. Ysabel De Teresa. LC 64-19481. 1964. Dodd, Mead.
Nymphet Confesses. William Danch. pap. 1.95 o.p. (8036). Cameo.
Nymphets & Their Lovers. Ralph Stoker. 192p. (Orig.). 1973. pap. 1.95 o.p. (ISBN 0-87682-293-6, 7293). Barclay Hse.
Nymphos. Ed. by John W. Fitzgerald. pap. 2.95 o.p. (ISBN 0-87964-105-3). Academy-Parliament.
Nymph's Conquest: By Jack Woodford Pseud. & Graham Roberts. Josiah Pitts Woolfolk & Graham Roberts. LC 53-1772. 1953. Signature Press.
Nymphs, Horses, & Athletes. Franklin. pap. 1.95 o.s.i. (OPH-209, Ophelia). Olympia.
Nymphs of the Valley. Kahlil Gibran & Nahmad, H. M., Tr. LC 48-5471. 1948. A. A. Knopf.

O

O American Embassy: A Novel of Suspense. David Coxe Cooke. LC 67-19231. 1967. Dodd, Mead.
O As in Omen: By Lawrence Treat. Lawrence Treat. LC 43-14282. 1943. Duell, Sloan and Pearce.
O Beulah Land. Mary Lee Settle. 304p. 1981. pap. 3.50 (ISBN 0-345-29311-8). Ballantine.
O Big Earth! Leon Harold Tebbetts. LC 39-112. 1938. Falmouth Book House.
O Buelah Land: A Novel. Mary Lee Settle. LC 56-8562. 1956. Viking Press.
O Canaan! A Novel. Waters Edward Turpin. LC 73-18610. 1975. 15.50 (ISBN 0-404-11420-2). AMS Press.
O Canaan! A Novel. Waters Edward Turpin. LC 72-6485. (Black Heritage Library Collection). 1972. (ISBN 0-8369-9179-6). Books for Libraries Press.
O Canaan! A Novel. Waters Edward Turpin. LC 39-27696. 1939. Doubleday, Doran & Company, Inc.
O Careless Love! Rex Stout. LC 35-22836. Farrar & Rinehart, Inc.
O Charitable Death. Rachel Cosgrove Payes. LC 68-14200. 1968. Published for the Crime Club by Doubleday.
O, Chautauqua: A Novel. Thomas William Duncan. LC 35-27092. 1935. Coward, McCann, Inc.
O Congress. Don Riegle & Trevor Armbrister. 1976. pap. 1.75 (ISBN 0-445-03141-7). Popular Lib.
O. D. at Sweet Claude's. Matt Gattzden. (Orig.). 1970. pap. 0.95 o.p. (B95-2064). Belmont-Tower.
O Distant Star! Mary Frances Doner. LC 44-2190. 1944. Doubleday, Doran and Co., Inc.
O for a Master of Magic. Josh Greenfeld. LC 68-28115. 1968. 4.95. World Pub. Co.
O Genesee. 1st Ed. Janet O'Daniel. LC 57-11949. 1958. Lippincott.
O Genteel Lady! Esther Forbes. LC 26-9023. 1926. Houghton Mifflin Company.
O. Henry Memorial Award Prize Stories... Ed. by Williams, Blanche Colton & Hansen, Harry. Society of Arts and Sciences, New York. LC 21-9372. Doubleday, Doran & Company, Inc.
O. Henry Stories. William Sydney Porter. LC 62-12640. (Platt & Munk great writers collection). 1962. Platt & Munk.
O. Henry's Best Stories: Edited by Lou P. Bunce. School Ed. William Sydney Porter. LC 53-4250. 1953. Globe Book Co.
O. Henry's New York. Selected, with an Introd., by J. Donald Adams. William Sydney Porter. LC 62-2155. (Premier book, d151). 1962. Fawcett Publications.
O, Huge Angel. Howard Baer. LC 49-4282. 1949. Roy Publishers.
O KAPLAN! My KAPLAN! Leo Calvin Rosten. LC 74-15891. (Cass Canfield book). 10.95 (ISBN 0-06-013676-6). Harper & Row.
O King, Live Forever: A Novel. Henry Myers. LC 53-5675. 1953. Crown Publishers.
O Master Caliban! A Novel. Phyllis Bloom Gotlieb. LC 76-5540. 8.95 (ISBN 0-06-011621-8). Harper & Row.
O My America! A Novel. Joanna Kaplan. LC 79-2649. 10.00 (ISBN 0-06-012289-7). Harper & Row.
O. P. Man. 3rd ed. Jim Stickter. LC 78-59344. (Illus.). 1978. pap. 15.00 (ISBN 0-930770-10-2). Hemisphere Hse.
O Pioneers. Willa Sibert Cather. LC 33-27137. 1933. Houghton Mifflin Company.
O Pioneers! Willa Sibert Cather. LC 13-15167. 1913. Houghton Mifflin Company.
O River, Remember! Martha Ostenso. LC 43-143682. 1943. Dodd, Mead & Company.
O, Rosie. Lusk Daniel. LC 78-23579. (Illus., Orig.). 1979. pap. 5.95x (ISBN 0-914140-04-3). Carpenter Pr.
O Rosie. Daniel Lusk. LC 78-23579. (Illus.). 5.00 (ISBN 0-914140-04-3). Carpenter Press.
O Shana, Shana. Eunice Loncoske McCloskey. LC 72-95807. 1973. 4.95 (ISBN 0-8059-1807-8). Dorrance.
O Shepard Speak. Upton Beall Sinclair. 1973. pap. 1.50 o.p. (02020). Curtis.
O Shepherd, Speak. Upton Beall Sinclair. LC 49-9981. 1949. Viking Press.

O Sinteze v Iskusste. Ernst Neizestny. Tr. by Alice Nichols. (Illus.). 102p. (Eng. & Rus.). 1982. pap. 12.00 (ISBN 0-938920-22-7). Hermitage MI.

O-So-Ge-To, the Hopi Maiden, and Other Stories. Ella Blake Stone. LC 7-33598. 1907. W. B. Conkey Company.

O Splendid Sorcery. James Francis Dwyer. LC 30-14661. The Vanguard Press.

O. T. A Danish Romance. author's ed. Hans Christian Andersen. LC 45-42396. 1878. Houghton, Osgood and Company.

O, the Brave Music. Dorothy Evelyn Smith. LC 51-11794. 1951. Dutton.

O Western Wind. John Anthony Devon, pseud. (New Plymouth)--Fiction.). 1957. Putnam.

Oak and Iron, of These by the Breed of the North. James Beardsley Hendryx. LC 25-827279.

Oak and the Room. Michael Moorcock. (Chronicles of Cirum). (Berkley medallion book: Vol. 5). 1974. (pbk.) 0.75 (ISBN 0-425-02534-9). Berkley Pub. Co.

Oak-Openings: Or, The Bee-Hunter. new ed. James Fenimore Cooper. 1852. Stringer and Townsend.

Oak-Openings: Or, The Bee-Hunter. James Fenimore Cooper. (On cover: Lovell's library. no. 562). 1885. J. W. Lovell Company.

Oak-Openings: Or, The Bee-Hunter. James Fenimore Cooper. (On cover: Seaside library. Pocket ed. no. 425). 1885. G. Munro.

Oak Shade: Or, Records of a Village Literary Association. Maurice Eugene. LC 6-38142. 1855. W. P. Hazzard.

Oakdale Affair. Edgar Rice Burroughs. 244p. 1979. pap. 1.95 (ISBN 0-441-60565-6, Pub. by Charter Bks). Ace Bks.

Oakdale Affair. Edgar Rice Burroughs. 1976. Repr. of 1937 ed. lib. bdg. 14.95 (ISBN 0-89966-041-X). Buccaneer Bks.

Oakdale Affair. Edgar Rice Burroughs. 1974. (pbk.) 1.25. Ace Books.

Oakdale Affair: The Rider. Edgar Rice Burroughs. Edgar Rice Burroughs, Inc.

Oakfield; or, Fellowship in the East, 1854. 2nd ed. William Delafield Arnold. Ed. by Robert L. Wolff. LC 75-1522. (Victorian Fiction Ser.). 1975. lib. bdg. 66.00 (ISBN 0-8240-1594-0). Garland Pub.

Oakhurst. Walter Reed Johnson. (Signet Book). 1978. 1.95 (ISBN 0-451-07874-8). New American Library.

Oakland County Child Killer. Michael L. Parrott. LC 80-80655. (Illus.). 176p. 1980. pap. 5.00 (ISBN 0-8187-0036-X). Harlo Pr.

Oaklawn Manor. Lucile B. Holmes. (Illus.). 84p. 1983. pap. 5.00 (ISBN 0-88289-418-8). Pelican.

Oakleyites. Edward Frederic Benson. LC 15-19079. Hodder and Stoughton.

Oakleyites. Edward Frederic Benson. LC 15-214165. 1.35. George H. Doran Company.

Oakridge: an Old-Time Story. Joseph Emerson Smith. LC 8-8175. 1875. J. R. Osgood and Company (Late Ticknor & Fields, and Fields, Osgood & Co.

Oaks of Bashan. Ruth Power Pond. LC 68-56170. 1969. 3.95. Dorrance.

Oaks of Eden: A Novel. Allen Pelzer Turner. LC 51-11875. 1951. Exposition Press.

Oakwood. A Story of True Love and Mystery. Agnes Louise Pratt. LC 99-1187. (Neely's popular library. no. 134). 1899. F. T. Neely.

Oases for Troubled Times. Robert O. Laaser. 1970. pap. 1.50 o.s.i. Eden.

Oasis. John Creasey. 1972. pap. 0.95 o.p. (75-384). Lancer.

Oasis. Mary Therese McCarthy. LC 49-10152. 1949. Random House.

Oasis. Willard Robertson. LC 44-7509. 1944. J. B. Lippincott Company.

Oasis: A Story of Dr. Palfrey. John Creasey. LC 70-103383. 1970. 4.50. Walker.

Oasis Nine: Four Short Novels. Victor Canning. LC 59-53463. 1959. W. Sloane Associates.

Oasis of Fear. Kenneth Evans. LC 68-15899. 1968. Roy Publishers.

Oasis Project. David Stuart Arthur. LC 80-54845. 12.95 (ISBN 0-939086-00-X). Sword & Stone Press.

Oath. Eliezer Wiesel. LC 73-5042. 1973. 7.95 (ISBN 0-394-48779-6). Random House.

Oath and the Sword: The Villains of the Piece. Graham Shelby. LC 72-87709. (Illus.). 1972. 6.95. Weybright and Talley.

Oath-Keeper of Forano. A Tale of Italy and Her Evangel. Julia MacNair Wright. LC 9-5327. The American Sunday-School Union.

Oath of Allegiance, and Other Stories. Elizabeth Stuart Phelps Ward. LC 9-35852. 1909. Houghton Mifflin Company.

Oath of Dishonor: A Novel. LC 64-20282. 4.95. Dial.

Oath of Dishonor: A Novel. Garet Rogers. LC 64-20282. 1965. Dial Press.

Oath of Fealty. Larry Niven & Jerry Pournelle. LC 81-9222. 2.95 (ISBN 0-671-45699-7). Timescape Books: Distributed by Simon and Schuster.

Oath of Fealty. Jerry Pournelle & Larry Niven. 1981. 2.95 (ISBN 0-671-22695-9, Timescape). PB.

Oath of Seven. George Maywin. pap. 0.60 o.p. (60-382). Manor Bks.

Obbligato. Elsie Frances Wilson Mack. LC 52-14737. 1952. Bouregy & Curl.

Obeah Murders. Hulbert Footner. LC 37-197577. 1937. Harper & Brothers.

Obeah, the God of Voodoo. Ted G Cooper. LC 76-49287. 8.95. Nuclassics and Science Pub. Co.

Obedience: A Tale. Michael Sadleir. LC 25-7198. 1925. Houghton Mifflin Company.

Obedience to the Moon. 1st Ed. Arthur Hamilton Gibbs. LC 56-5614. Little, Brown.

Obelisk. William Rollins. LC 30-12141. 1930. Brewer & Warren Ltd.

Obelisk Conspiracy. George Martin & Michael Burren. 224p. 1976. 7.95 (ISBN 0-8065-0513-3). Citadel Pr.

Obelisk Conspiracy: A Novel. George Marton & Michael Burren. LC 75-44075. 1976. 7.95 (ISBN 0-8065-0513-3). Citadel Press.

Obelists at Sea. Charles Daly King. LC 33-137588. 1933. A. A. Knopf.

Oberland. Dorothy Miller Richardson. LC 28-14833. (Her Pilgrimage. pt. IX). 1928. A. A. Knopf.

Oberlin's Three Stages. Jakob Wassermann & Porterfield, Allen Wilson, 1877- Tr. LC 26-9748. Harcourt, Brace and Company.

Obermann: Selections from Letters to a Friend. Etienne Pivert De Senancour. LC 76-48460. (Classics of European Literature). (Hyperion library of world literature). 1977. 13.95. (ISBN 0-88355-614-6) (ISBN 0-88355-615-4). Hyperion Press.

Obession of Emmet Booth. Martha Albrand & Martha Albrand. LC 57-5381. 1957. Random House.

Obey They Heart. Marie Blizard. LC 45-2142. 1945. Arcadia House, Inc.

Obi. John Munonye. (African Writers Ser.). 1969. pap. text ed. 3.00x (ISBN 0-435-90045-5). Heinemann Ed.

Obit Delayed. Helen Nielsen. LC 52-10659. 1952. I. Washburn.

Obituaries: Fiction. Bernard Kaplan. LC 75-28077. 1976. 8.95 (ISBN 0-670-52007-1). Grossman Publishers.

Obituary Club: By Hugh Pentecost Pseud. Judson Pentecost Philips. LC 58-130846. (Red badge detective). 1958. Dodd, Mead.

Object: Matrimony. Montague Marsden Glass. LC 12-22310. 1912. 0.50. Doubleday, Page & Company.

Objector. E. R. Stuart. 1970. pap. 0.95 o.p. (ISBN 0-447-75107-7). Lancer.

Objects. Jeff Nuttall. 1976. 6.00 (Pub. by Trigram Pr); pap. 3.50. SBD.

Oblate. Joris Karl Huysmans. Tr. by Perceval, Edward. LC 24-229488. 1924. K. Paul, Trench, Trubner & Co., Ltd.

Oblate. Joris Karl Huysmans. LC 77-11670. 1978. 15.75. H. Fertig.

Obligation. Jerome L Tiras. LC 76-2296. 7.95 (ISBN 0-87949-057-8). Ashley Books.

Obligations. Elizabeth York Miller. LC 24-20555. The Century Co.

Obliging Housemaid. David Emerson. 1981. 18.95x (Pub. by Remploy England). State Mutual Bk.

Oblivion. Mary Greenway McClelland. LC 7-15429. (Leisure hour series. No. 175). 1885. H. Holt and Company.

Oblivion: An Episode. Margaret Greenway McClelland. LC 7-15429. (On cover: Leisure hour series. no. 175). 1885. H. Holt and Company.

Oblivion Tapes. Timeri Murari. (Berkley Medallion Book). 1978. 1.75 (ISBN 0-425-03457-7). Berkley Pub. Corp.

Oblivious Host. Barrie Myers. 1973. (pbk.) 0.95. Popular Library.

Oblomov. Ivan Aleksandrovich Goncharov. LC 64-377. (Signet classic). (Illus.). 1963. New American Library.

Oblomov. Ivan Aleksandrovich Goncharov. Tr. by Duddington, Nathalie Alexandrovna (Ertel) LC 30-12158. 1929. The Macmillan Company.

Oblomov. Ivan Aleksandrovich Goncharov. Tr. by Duddington, Nathalie Alexandrovna (Ertel) (Half-title: Everyman's library, ed. by Ernest Rhys. Fiction. no. 878). 1932. J. M. Dent & Sons, Ltd.

Oblomov. Ivan Aleksandrovich Goncharov. LC 79-19061. 1979. 12.50 (ISBN 0-8376-0451-6). R. Bentley.

Oblomov. Ivan Aleksandrovich Goncharov & Magarshack, David, Ed. LC 67-7206. (Penguin classics, L40). 1967. Penguin Books.

Oboler Omnibus. Arch Oboler. 1974. pap. 0.75 o.p. (LB00121). Leisure Bks.

O'Briens and the O'Flahertys. Sydney Owenson Morgan. LC 78-14013. (Ireland, from the Act of Union, 1800, to the Death of Parnell, 1891). 1979. 128.00 (ISBN 0-8240-3458-9). Garland Pub.

O'Briens & the O'Flahertys. Morgan S. Owenson. Ed. by Robert L. Wolff. (Ireland-Nineteenth Century Fiction, Ser. Two: Vol. 9). 1979. lib. bdg. 184.00 (ISBN 0-8240-3458-9); lib. bdg. 46.00 ea. Garland Pub.

O'Briens & the O'Flahertys: A Naional Tale, 4 vols. in 2. Sydney Owenson Morgan. LC 79-8175. Repr. of 1827 ed. Set. 84.50 o.p. (ISBN 0-404-62055-8); Vol. 1. (ISBN 0-404-62056-6); Vol. 2. (ISBN 0-404-62057-4). AMS Pr.

O'Briens and the O'Flahertys: A National Tale. Sydney Owenson Morgan. LC 7-18746. 1828. Carey, Lea & Carey.

O'Briens and the O'Flahertys: A National Tale. Sydney Owenson Morgan & Mackenzie, Robert Shelton, 1809-1880, Ed. LC 7-18744. (Half-title: Lady Morgan's national stories, vol. I-II). 1856. Redfield.

OB's. Virginia Fletcher Mercer. LC 64-10799. Chilton Books.

Obscene Bird of Night. Jose Donoso. LC 70-171112. 1973. 7.95 (ISBN 0-394-46916-X). Knopf; Distributed by Random House.

Obscene Bird of Night. Jose Donoso. LC 79-88419. 1979. 7.50 (ISBN 0-87923-191-2). Nonpareil Books.

Obscene Freddie. William Horton. pap. 1.95 o.p. (8073). Cameo.

Obscenity. Donald Wetzel. LC 68-12605. 1968. Harcourt, Brace & World.

Obscure Destinies. Willa Sibert Cather. LC 74-5324. 1974. (pbk.) 1.95 (ISBN 0-394-71179-3). Vintage Books.

Obscure Destinies. Willa Sibert Cather. LC 32-26864. 1932. A. A. Knopf.

Obscure Enemy. Robert Raynolds. LC 45-4448. 1945. Margent Press.

Obsequies at Oxford. Robert Bruce Montgomery. LC 45-220381. 1945. J. B. Lippincott Company.

Observations by Mr. Dooley. Finley P. Dunne. 1906. lib. bdg. 20.00 (ISBN 0-8414-3874-9). Folcroft.

Observations by Mr. Dooley. Finley P. Dunne. LC 69-13889. Repr. of 1902 ed. lib. bdg. 15.00x (ISBN 0-8371-1636-8, DUOB). Greenwood.

Observations of Henry. Jerome Klapka Jerome. LC 72-94734. (Short story index reprint series). (Illus.). 1969. Books for Libraries Press.

Observations of Henry. Jerome Klapka Jerome. LC 1-31324. 1901. Dodd, Mead and Company.

Observatory: A Novel. 1st Ed. Carl Jonas. LC 66-18079. 1966. 4.95. Norton.

Observer. John Jenkins Espey. LC 65-21028. 1965. Harcourt, Brace & World.

Obsessed. Gertrude Schweitzer. LC 50-39499. (Gold medal book, 125). 1950. Fawcett Publications.

Obsession. Katherine Hale. 352p. (Orig.). 1980. pap. 2.25 (ISBN 0-345-28451-8). Ballantine.

Obsession. George Hayim. LC 76-124397. 1971. 5.95. Grove Press.

Obsession: An American Love Story. Yves Berger. LC 77-21666. 1978. 8.95 (ISBN 0-399-12049-1). Putnam.

Obsession of Emmet Booth. Martha Albrand. 1974. (pbk.) 0.95. Avon.

Obsession of Emmet Booth: By Martha Albrand Pseud. Heidi Huberta Freybe Loewengard. LC 57-5381. Random House.

Obsession of Sally Wing. Russell W. Martin. 288p. (Orig.). 1983. pap. 2.95 (ISBN 0-523-48054-7). Tor Bks.

Obsession of Victoria Gracen. Grace Livingston Hill. LC 63-2149. Grosset & Dunlap.

Obsession of Victoria Gracen: By Grace Livingston Hill Lutz... with Illustrations by Edwin F. Bayha. Grace Livingston Hill. LC 15-21433. 1915. J. B. Lippincott Company.

Obsession. 1st Ed. Lionel White. LC 62-7818. 1962. Dutton.

Obsessions. Cesar J Rotondi. LC 79-22863. 8.95 (ISBN 0-312-58052-5). St. Martin's Press.

Obsessions. St. Clair, Leonard. LC 79-24079. 10.95 (ISBN 0-671-24732-8). Simon and Schuster.

Obsidian Ape. Robert Neal Leath & Edward John Moreton Drax Plunkett Dunsany. (Fantasy Classics, 3). (Illus.). 1973. (pbk.) 1.95. Fantasy House.

Obsidian Mirror. James Norman. LC 77-72806. (Illus.). 5.00 (ISBN 0-914140-03-5). Carpenter Press.

Obstacle Race. Ethel May Dell. 1921. Cassell and Company, Ltd.

Obstacle Race. Ethel May Dell. 1921. 2.00. G. P. Putnam's Sons.

Obstacles. Reinhard Lettau. LC 65-11627. 1965. Pantheon Books.

Obstacles. Tr. from German by Ursule Molinaro. Reinhard Lettau. LC 65-116276. bds., 3.95. Pantheon.

Obstinate Captain Samson. Gavin Douglas. LC 37-2684. G. P. Putnam's Sons.

Obstinate Lady. William Edward Norris. LC 20-3064. 1919. Brentano's.

Obstinate Murderer. Elisabeth Sanxay Holding. LC 38-9835. 1938. Dodd, Mead & Company.

O'Byrne: Or, The Expatriated. Mary Anne Madden Sadlier. (Catholic library. v. 12). 1898. C. Wildermann.

Occam's Razor. David Duncan. LC 57-13096. (Ballantine books, 230). 1957. Ballantine Books.

Occasion for Loving: A Novel. Gordimer, Nadine. LC 63-8852. 1963. Viking Press.

Occasion of Sin. Rachel Billington. LC 82-19624. 14.95 (ISBN 0-671-45938-4). Summit Books.

Occasional Man. James Barr. pap. 0.75 o.p. (54-918). Paperback Lib.

Occasional Wife; Married--Yet Living Apart. Edna Robb Webster. LC 32-296823. Grosset & Dunlap.

Occidental Sketches. Benjamin Cummings Truman. LC 19-18909. 1881. San Francisco News Company.

Occupation. David Caute. 304p. 1972. 6.95 o.p. (ISBN 0-07-010290-2). McGraw.

Occupation. Robert Graves. 1977. Repr. of 1950 ed. lib. bdg. 22.50x (ISBN 0-374-93237-9). Octagon.

Occupation: A Novel. David Caute. LC 72-1056. 1972. (ISBN 0-07-010290-2). McGraw-Hill.

Occupation: Housewife: A Novel. Dorothy Les Tina. LC 47-31367. 1947. W. Morrow.

Occupational Hazards. Henry H. Roberts. 1981. pap. 2.50 (ISBN 0-8439-0904-8, Leisure Bks). Nordon Pubns.

Occupational Health Nurse. Beatrice Warren. 1981. pap. 6.95 (Avalon). Bouregy.

Occupations of a Retired Life. Isabella Fyvie Mayo. LC 24-24998. 1868. G. Routledge and Sons.

Occupied Spaces. Brad Johannsen. (Illus.). 1977. pap. 5.95 o.p. (ISBN 0-517-53083-X). Harmony.

Occupied Territory. Alice Ritchie. LC 30-23555. Harcourt, Brace and Company.

Occupiers. Julia Edwards, pseud. LC 67-15017. 1967. 5.95 o.p. (ISBN 0-8303-0018-X). Fleet.

Occupiers; a Novel. Julia Edwards, pseud. LC 67-150175. 1967. 5.95. Fleet.

Occupying Power. Gwyn Griffin. LC 68-26797. 1968. 6.95. Putnam.

Occurrence at Norman's Burger Castle: From the Adventures of Charlie Bates. James D Houston. LC 75-316519. (Yes! Capra chapbook series; no. 2). 1972. (ISBN 0-912264-42-X) (ISBN 0-912264-41-1). Capra Press.

Ocean. Pavel Georgievick Tupikov. LC 36-27208. 1936. Harper & Brothers.

Ocean: By James Hanley. James Hanley. LC 41-11979. 1941. W. Morrow & Company.

Ocean Free Lance. From a Privateersman's Log, 1812. A Novel. William Clark Russell. (Franklin square library, no. 194). 1881. Harper & Brothers.

Ocean Free Lance. From a Privateersman's Log, 1812. A Novel. William Clark Russell. (Seaside library, v. 51, no. 1034). 1881. G. Munro.

Ocean Front. Douglass Wallop. LC 62-19016. 1963. Norton.

Ocean Heritage. Sara Ware Bassett. LC 40-9439. 1940. Doubleday, Doran & Co., Inc.

Ocean Knight: Or, The Corsairs and Their Conquerors. Fortune Du Boisgobey. LC 7-3316. 1891. F. Warne and Co.

Ocean Monarch: Or, The Ranger of the Gulf. A Mexican Romance. Harry Halyard. 1848. F. Gleason.

Ocean Mystery. Caroline Earle White. LC 3-26871. 1903. J. B. Lippincott Company.

Ocean of Fear. Anne J Griffin. (Avon gothic). 1974. (pbk.) 0.95. Avon.

Ocean of Regrets. Noelle B. McCue. (Orig.). 1981. pap. 1.75 (ISBN 0-440-16592-X). Dell.

Ocean on Top. Hal Clement. (Orig.). 1973. pap. 0.95 o.p. (UQ1057). Daw Bks.

Ocean on Top. Hal Clement. 1973. (pbk.) 0.95. DAW Books.

Ocean Road. 1st Ed. Jack Bennett. LC 66-21987. 1966. bds., 4.95. Little.

Ocean Rovers. William Henry Thomes. (On cover: Pastime series, no. 29 171). 1896. Laird & Lee.

Ocean Sketches. Frederick W Wendt. LC 8-36237. The Colonial Book Co.

Ocean Tragedy. William Clark Russell. (On cover: Seaside library. Pocket edition, no. 1260). 1889. G. Munro.

Ocean Tragedy: A Novel. William Clark Russell. LC 3-68256. (On cover: Harper's Franklin square library, no. 662). 1889. Harper & Brothers.

Ocean Tramp. Philip D Heywood. LC 7-4751. D. Lothrop Company.

Oceana's Girlhood. Elizabeth Thomasina Meade Smith. LC 9-18156. Hurst & Company.

Oceanides: A Psychical Novel. Carlyle Petersilea. LC 7-36164. 1890. E. Von Himmel Publishing Co.

Oceanides: A Psychical Novel. Carlyle Petersilea. LC 7-36165. Colby & Rich.

Oceola Kid. Clay Randall, pseud. 144p. 1981. pap. 1.75 (ISBN 0-8439-0984-6, Leisure Bks). Nordon Pubns.
Ochikubo Monogatari, or the Tale of the Lady Ochikubo: A Tenth Century Japanese Novel. 7.00 o.p. Japan Pubns.
Ochiltree Walls. W. Irvine Cummings. LC 26-12142. 1926. R. M. McBride & Company.
Ocho Casos Extranos y Dos Casos Mas: Cuentos, 1930-1970. Gustavo Agrait. (UPREX, Ficcion: No. 4). pap. 1.85 (ISBN 0-8477-0004-6). U of PR Pr.
O'Conners. Mary Astor. LC 64-14281. 1964. Doubleday.
O'Conner's Career. Robert Cosmo Harding. LC 19-11714. Saulsbury Publishing Company.
O'Connors. Mary Astor. 1969. pap. 0.75 o.p. (0502-07031-075). Curtis.
O'Connors of Ballinchinch. Margaret Wolfe Hamilton Hungerford. LC 7-9060. J. W. Lovell Company.
Ocotpus of Paris. Gaston Leroux. LC 27-649. The Macaulay Company.
Octagon Club: A Character Study. Ellen Marvin Heaton. LC 7-5037. 1880. G. P. Putnam's Sons.
Octagon House. Gertrude Knevels. LC 25-159830. 1925. D. Appleton and Company.
Octagon House. Phoebe Atwood Taylor. (Foul Play Press Bks.). 1979. pap. 4.50 (ISBN 0-914378-47-3). Countryman.
Octagon House. Phoebe Atwood Taylor. 1970. pap. 0.60 o.p. (X2205). Pyramid Pubns.
Octagon House: An Asey Mayo Mystery of Cape Cod. Phoebe Atwood Taylor. LC 37-191546. W. W. Norton & Company, Inc.
Octagonal Heart. Drawings by Artur Marokvia. Ariadne Thompson. LC 56-9379. 1956. Bobbs-Merrill.
Octangle. Emanie Louise Nahm Sachs. LC 30-31037. J. Cape & H. Smith.
Octava. Jeffery Eardley Marston. LC 25-15847. 1925. Little, Brown and Company.
Octave, a Book of Stories. Helen Rose Hull. LC 47-312893. 1947. Coward-McCann.
Octavia. Jilly Cooper. 224p. 1982. pap. 2.25 (ISBN 0-449-24545-4, Crest). Fawcett.
Octavia. Oxford and Asquith, Margot Asquith. LC 28-10302. 1928. Frederick A. Stokes Company.
Octavia: A Tale of Ancient Rome. Seymour Van Santvoord. LC 23-10467. E. P. Dutton & Company.
Octavia, the Octoroon. J F Lee. LC 1-29934. The Abbey Press.
Octavia's Hill: A Novel. Margaret Dickson. LC 82-15830. 1983. 14.95 (ISBN 0-395-33159-5). Houghton Mifflin.
Octavia's Pride: Or, The Missing Witness. Charles T Manners. LC 7-20454. (Street & Smith's select series. no. 10). 1888. Street & Smith.
October Cabaret. Erica Quest. LC 79-7507. 1979. 7.95. Published for the Crime Club by Doubleday.
October Circle. Robert Littell. LC 75-26955. (Illus.). 1976. 7.95 (ISBN 0-395-21502-1). Houghton Mifflin.
October Circle. Robert Littell. 1977. 1.75 (ISBN 0-380-00872-6). Avon.
October Country. Ray Bradbury. (YA) 1970. 12.50 (ISBN 0-394-43892-2). Knopf.
October Country. Illustrated by Joe Mugnaini. Ray Bradbury. LC 55-12167. 1955. Ballantine Books.
October Country: Stories. Ray Bradbury. LC 73-106623. (Illus.). 1970. 6.95. Knopf.
October Ferry to Gabriola. Malcolm Lowry. LC 70-128492. 1970. 6.95. World Pub. Co.
October Fire. Eleanor R. Mayo. LC 51-761. 1951. Crowell.
October Fires. Margaret Flint. LC 41-19642. 1941. Dodd, Mead & Company.
October Fox. Clark McMeekin. LC 55-10095. Putnam.
October Heat. Gordon DeMarco. LC 80-125469. 1979. 8.95 (ISBN 0-918064-04-X) (ISBN 0-918064-05-8). Germinal Perss.
October Horse. Pauline Marrington. LC 74-14152. 1975. 6.95. St. Martin's Press.
October House. Kay Cleaver Strahan. LC 31-33327. 1931. By Doubleday, Doran & Company, Inc.
October Island: By William March Pseud. 1st American Ed. William Edward March Campbell. LC 52-9778. 1952. Little, Brown.
October Journey. Margaret Walker. LC 73-82444. 1973. (pbk.) 1.50 (ISBN 0-910296-95-2) (ISBN 0-910296-95-2). Broadside Press.
October Light. John Champlin Gardner. LC 76-13718. 1977. 10.00 (ISBN 0-394-49912-3). Knopf: Distributed by Random House.
October Men. Anthony Price. LC 73-20526. 1974. 4.95 (ISBN 0-385-00764-7). Published for the Crime Club by Doubleday.
October the First Is Too Late. Fred Hoyle. LC 66-20764. 1966. Harper & Row.
October Witch. Alanna Knight. 1971. pap. 0.75 o.p. (ISBN 0-447-74733-9). Lancer.
October's Baby. Glen Cook. (Orig.). 1980. pap. 1.95 (ISBN 0-425-04532-3). Berkley Pub.
October's Child. Donald Joseph. LC 29-182697. 1929. Frederick A. Stokes Company.
Octopus. Rupert Croft-Cooke. LC 47-16956. 1946. Jarrolds, Ltd.
Octopus. Frank Norris. 1976. lib. bdg. 19.50x (ISBN 0-89968-070-4). Lightyear.
Octopus. Frank Norris. pap. 3.50 (ISBN 0-451-51711-3, CE1711, Sig Classics). NAL.
Octopus. Frank Norris. Ed. by K. S. Lynn. pap. 1.50x o.p. (A33, RivEd, 3-47667). HM.
Octopus. Frank Norris. LC 50-2095. 1947. 7.95 o.p. (ISBN 0-385-04333-3). Doubleday.
Octopus: A Story of California. Frank Norris. LC 76-184737. (Illus.). 1971. (ISBN 0-8376-0405-2). R. Bentley.
Octopus: A Story of California. Frank Norris. LC 8-82500. (His The epic of the wheat. 1). 1903. Doubleday, Page & Co.
Octopus: A Story of California. Frank Norris. LC 16-25025. (His The epic of the wheat). 1914. Doubleday, Page & Company.
Octopus: A Story of California. Frank Norris. LC 30-26622. 1930. Doubleday, Doran & Company, Inc.
Octopus: A Story of California. Frank Norris. LC 38-62425. 1938. The Sun Dial Press, Inc.
Octopus: A Story of California. Edited with an Introd. by Kenneth S. Lynn. Frank Norris. LC 58-2300. (Riverside editions, A33). 1958. Houghton Mifflin.
Octopus: A Story of California. Foreword by Irvin S. Cobb. Frank Norris. LC 67-16621. (His complete works, v. 1-2). 1967. in complete set, 125.00. Kennikat.
Octopus. Introd. by Robert D. Lundy. Frank Norris. LC 57-12440. (American century series, S-20). 1957. Sagamore Press.
Octopus Papers: Selected, Adapted, Comp., Annotated by Burt Blechman. Burt Blechman. LC 65-22557. bds., 3.95. Horizon.
Octopus: The Story of California. Frank Norris. LC 1-31432. (His The epic of the wheat. 1). 1901. Doubleday, Page & Co.
Octopussy. Fleming, Ian. LC 66-17259. 1966. New American Library.
Octopussy: The Last Great Adventures of James Bond 007. Ian Fleming. (Signet bk., P3200). 1967. New Amer. Lib.
Octoroon. Dion Boucicault. LC 74-104420. 1977. lib. bdg. 15.00 (ISBN 0-8398-0168-8); pap. text ed. 4.75x (ISBN 0-89197-870-4). Irvington.
Octoroon. Mary Elizabeth Braddon Maxwell. (On cover: Seaside library. Pocket ed. no. 211). 1884. G. Munro.
Octoroon. Mary Elizabeth Braddon Maxwell. (On cover: Lovell's library, v. 16, no. 783). 1886. J. W. Lovell Company.
Ocular Delusion. Frank Howard Howe. LC 7-6624. (On cover: American novelists' series, no. 38). J. W. Lovell Company.
Odalisque. L M Hussey. LC 27-950. 1927. A. A. Knopf.
Odd--but Even So: Stories Stranger Than Fiction. Percival Christopher Wren. LC 42-12035. 1942. Macrae Smith Company.
Odd Craft. William Wymark Jacobs. LC 3-25881. 1903. C. Scribner's Sons.
Odd Fish: Being a Casual Selection of London Residents Described & Drawn. Stacy Aumonier. LC 71-116929. (Short story index reprint series). (Illus.). 1970. Books for Libraries Press.
Odd Folks. Opie Percival Read. (On cover: Neely's popular library, no. 93). 1897. F. T. Neely.
Odd Girl Out. Ann Bannon. LC 75-13735. (Homosexuality). (Reprint of the ed. published by Fawcett, Greenwich, Conn., in series: Gold medal books.). 1975. 9.00 (ISBN 0-405-07405-0). Arno Press.
Odd Girl Out. facsimile ed. Ann Dannox. Ed. by Jonathan Katz. LC 75-13735. (Homosexuality Ser.). 1975. Repr. of 1957 ed. 12.00x (ISBN 0-405-07405-0). Ayer Co.
Odd Girl Out. Elizabeth Jane Howard. 1974. (pbk.) 1.50. Dell.
Odd Girl Out. Elizabeth Jane Howard. LC 72-171894. 1972. 6.95 (ISBN 0-670-52028-4). Viking Press.
Odd Jewel: A Postnuptial Tale of a World-Wide Passion. Warren M Macleod. LC 1-29531. The Abbey Press.
Odd Job. Pat Flower. LC 77-18046. (Jubilee mystery). 1978. 7.95 (ISBN 0-8128-2413-X). Stein and Day.
Odd Job Man. N. J Crisp. LC 78-21410. 8.95 (ISBN 0-312-58114-9). St. Martin's Press.
Odd Job Number One Hundred-One. Ron Goulart. LC 74-10853. 1974. (ISBN 0-684-13996-0). Scribner.
Odd Job Number One Hundred-One: And Other Future Crimes & Intrigues. Ron Goulart. 186p. 1975. 6.95 o.p. (ISBN 0-684-13996-0). Scribner.
Odd John. William Olaf Stapledon. Ed. by Lester Del Rey. LC 75-434. (Library of Science Fiction). 1975. lib. bdg. 17.50 (ISBN 0-8240-1437-5). Garland Pub.
Odd John: A Story Between Jest and Earnest. William Olaf Stapledon. LC 75-434. (Garland Library of Science Fiction). 1975. 11.00 (ISBN 0-8240-1437-5). Garland Pub. Co.
Odd John: A Story Between Jest and Earnest. William Olaf Stapledon. LC 36-15690. E. P. Dutton & Co., Inc.
Odd John & Sirius: Two Science-Fiction Novels. William Olaf Stapledon. LC 72-77999. 1972. 2.50 (ISBN 0-486-21133-9). Dover Publications.
Odd Leaves from the Life of a Louisiana Swamp Doctor. Henry Clay Lewis. LC 79-91084. (American humorists series). 1969. Literature House.
Odd Leaves from the Life of a Louisiana "Swamp Doctor"... Henry Clay Lewis. LC 8-30880. (On cover: Library of humorous American works). 1850. A. Hart.
Odd Leaves from the Life of a Louisiana "Swamp Doctor"... Henry Clay Lewis. LC 29-25275. (On cover: Library of humorous American works). 1852. A. Hart.
Odd Leaves from the Life of a Louisiana "Swamp Doctor". Henry Clay Lewis. LC 29-25277. (Added t.-p.: The swamp doctor's adventures in the Southwest). 1858. T. B. Peterson.
Odd Man Out. Frederick Lawrence Green. LC 47-133685. 1947. Reynal & Hitchcock.
Odd Man Pays. Darwin Le Ora Teilhet. LC 44-5032. 1944. Little, Brown and Company.
Odd Number: Thirteen Tales. Guy De Maupassant. Tr. by Jonathan Sturges. James, Henry, 1843-1916. LC 4-16886. 1889. Harper & Brothers.
Odd Number; Thirteen Tales: By Guy De Maupassant; the Translation by Jonathan Sturges; an Introduction by Henry James. Guy De Maupassant. Tr. by Jonathan Sturges. Harper & Brothers.
Odd Numbers: Being Further Chronicles of Shorty McCabe. Sewell Ford. E. J. Clode.
Odd One. Fannie E Newberry. LC 7-17284. 1893. A. I. Bradley & Company.
Odd or Even? Adeline Dutton Train Whitney. 1880. Houghton, Osgood, and Company.
Odd, or Even? Adeline Dutton Train Whitney. LC 8-14663. Houghton, Mifflin and Company.
Odd Pairs: A Book of Tales. Laurence Housman. LC 78-169555. (Short story index reprint series). 1971. (ISBN 0-8369-4017-2). Books for Libraries Press.
Odd Situation. Stanley Waterloo. (On cover: Idylwild series. v. 1, no. 37). 1893. Morrill, Higgins & Co.
Odd Spot of Bother. Illus. by John Crawley. Barry Crump. LC 68-79688. 1967. bds., 3.50. Auckland, Reed.
Odd Tales: 13 Short Stories by Walter Beverley Crane. Walter Beverley Crane. LC 5013. 1900. M. Witmark & Sons.
Odd Trump. A Novel. George James Atkinson Coulson. LC 6-29000. (The "Odd trump" series of novels). 1875. E. J. Hale & Son.
Odd Types: A Character Comedy. Burnjam Kalisch. LC 6-14755. Broadway Publishing Company.
Odd Woman. Gail Godwin. LC 74-8552. 1974. 8.95 (ISBN 0-394-48928-4). Knopf; Distributed by Random House.
Odd Woman. Gail Godwin. (Berkley Medallion Book). 1976. 1.95. Berkley Publishng Corp.
Odd Woman Out. Joseph Linklater. LC 56-13312. Mystery House.
Odd Women. George Robert Gissing. LC 68-22595. (Doughty library, 10). 1968. 5.95. Stein and Day.
Odd Women. George Robert Gissing. LC 70-29689. 1971. 1.95 (ISBN 0-393-00610-7). Norton.
Odd Women. George Robert Gissing. LC 70-75986. 1969. AMS Press.
Odd Women. George Robert Gissing. LC 6-43978. 1893. Macmillan and Co.
Odd Women. George Robert Gissing. LC 77-10956. 3.25 (ISBN 0-393-00610-7). Norton.
Oddballs. Ed. by Vic Ghidalia. 1973. pap. 0.95 o.p. (ISBN 0-532-95266-9). Woodhill.
Oddballs. Ed. by Vic Ghidalia. 1973. pap. 0.95 o.p. (ISBN 0-532-95266-9). Manor Bks.
Oddballs. Ed. by Vic Ghidalia. 1973. (pbk) 0.95. Manor Books.
Oddest of Courtships: Or, The Bloody Chasm. A Novel. John William De Forest. LC 6-33391. (On cover: Appletons' popular series). 1882. D. Appleton and Company.
Oddities in Southern Life and Character. Henry Watterson. 1900. Houghton, Mifflin and Company; Etc., Etc.
Oddities in Southern Life and Character. Ed. by Henry Watterson. LC 7-174329. 1883. Houghton, Mifflin and Company.
Oddities of Short-Hand: Or, The Coroner and His Friends. John B Carey. LC 6-22813. 1891. Excelsior Publishing House.
Odditorium. Hob Broun. LC 82-48101. 13.41 (ISBN 0-06-015027-0). Harper & Row.
Odds Against. Dick Francis. LC 66-13935. 1966. bds., 4.95. Harper.
Odds Against. Dick Francis. 1975. (pbk.) 1.50 (ISBN 0-671-78967-8). Pocket Books.
Odds Against Her. Margaret Russell Macfarlane. LC 7-20095. Cassell & Company, Limited.
Odds Against Tomorrow. William P McGivern. LC 57-11395. 1957. Dodd, Mead.
Odds & Ends: A Collection of Essays, Short Stories, & Observations. Walter E. Klippert. 1976. 4.50 o.p. (ISBN 0-682-48645-0, Banner). Exposition.
Odds, and Other Stories. Ethel May Dell. LC 22-12633. Cassell and Company, Limited.
Odds, and Other Stories. Ethel May Dell. LC 22-10240. 1922. 2.00. G. P. Putnam's Sons.
Odds Are Murder. Mike McQuay. (Mathew Swain Ser.: No. 4). 213p. 1983. pap. 2.50. Bantam.
Odd's End. Wynne-Jones, Tim. LC 80-82040. (Illus.). 11.95 (ISBN 0-316-96308-9). Little, Brown.
Odds on Bluefeather: Being the Further Adventures of Mr. George Berkley. Laurence Walter Meynell. LC 35-754. J. B. Lippincott Company.
Odds on Death. Charles Drummond. LC 78-103006. (Mystery Ser). 1970. 4.50 o.p. (ISBN 0-8027-5135-0). Walker & Co.
Odds on Death. Kenneth Giles. LC 78-103006. 1970. 4.50. Walker.
Odds on Love. Maysie Greig. LC 36-2981. 1936. Doubleday, Doran and Co., Inc.
Odds on Love. Maysie Greig. LC 38-3735. 1937. The Sun Dial Press, Inc.
Odds on Miss Seeton. Heron Carvic. LC 75-9348. 1975. 5.95 (ISBN 0-06-010874-6). Harper and Row.
Odds on Miss Seeton. Heron Carvic. LC 76-7971. 1976. 6.95 (ISBN 0-8161-6374-X). G. K. Hall.
Odds on Miss Seton. Heron Carvic. 279p. 1981. Repr. lib. bdg. 14.95x (ISBN 0-89966-307-9). Buccaneer Bks.
Odds-on Murder. Jack Dolph. LC 48-1829. 1948. W. Morrow.
Odds on Murder. Marion Levien. LC 73-90641. 1974. 7.95 (ISBN 0-8059-1971-6). Dorrance.
Odds on the Hot Seat. Judson Pentecost Philips. LC 41-3335. 1941. Dodd, Mead & Company.
Odds Run Out. Hillary Waugh. LC 49-8946. (Gargoyle mystery). 1949. Coward-McCann.
Oddsfish! Edited, and with a Foreword, by Anne Fremantle. Robert Hugh Benson. LC 57-100923. 1957. Kenedy.
Oddways. Adams, Herbert. LC 29-20796. 1929. J. B. Lippincott Company.
O'dean Graves: Or, Womanhood's Supreme Test. B. H Hancock. LC 26-23131. The Christopher Publishing House.
Odessa File. Frederick Forsyth. LC 72-12596. 1973. 11.95 (ISBN 0-8161-6069-4). G. K. Hall.
Odessa File. Frederick Forsyth. 1974. (pbk.) 1.75. Bantam Books.
Odessa File. Frederick Forsyth. LC 72-81252. 1972. 7.95 (ISBN 0-670-52042-X). Viking Press.
Odette. Reuben Bercovitch. 1976. 1.50 (ISBN 0-87949-007-1). Popular Library.
Odette. Reuben Bercovitch. LC 73-78706. 1973. 7.95 (ISBN 0-87949-007-1). Ashley Books.
Odette's Marriage. Albert Delpit. Tr. by Prescott, Emily. LC 6-34172. 1880. H. A. Sumner and Company.
Odile. Robert F Joseph. LC 77-6939. 1977. 1.95. Ballantine Books.
Odious Duke. Barbara Cartland. 1975. pap. 1.25 o.p. (ISBN 0-515-03911-X, V3911). BJ Pub Group.
Odious Duke. Barbara Cartland. 1977. pap. 1.50 o.p. (ISBN 0-515-04350-8). BJ Pub Group.
Odious Ones. Jerry Sohl. LC 59-13404. 1959. Rinehart.
Odissea Finita. Gerald Fabian. 1969. signed ed. 5.00; pap. 2.00. Man-Root.
O'Donnel. Sydney Owenson Morgan. LC 78-26759. (Ireland, from the Act of Union, 1800, to the Death of Parnell, 1891; No. 7). 1979. 96.00 (ISBN 0-8240-3456-2). Garland Pub.
O'Donnel: A National Tale, 3 vols. in 2. Sydney Owenson Morgan. LC 79-8176. Repr. of 1814 ed. Set. 84.50 o.p. (ISBN 0-404-62060-4); Vol. 1. (ISBN 0-404-62061-2); Vol. 2. (ISBN 0-404-62062-0). AMS Pr.
O'Donnel: A National Tale. Morgan S. Owenson. Ed. by Robert L. Wolff. (Ireland-Nineteenth Century Fiction, Ser. Two: Vol. 7). 1979. lib. bdg. 126.00 (ISBN 0-8240-3456-2); lib. bdg. 42.00 ea. Garland Pub.
O'Donnells of Glen Cottage. A Tale of the Famine Years in Ireland. David Power Conyngham. LC 6-28089. 1874. D. & J. Sadlier & Co.
O'Donoghue: A Tale of Ireland Fifty Years Ago. Charles James Lever. LC 12-24354. (On cover: Lever's works). 1872. G. Routledge and Sons.

O'Donoghue: St. Patrick's Eve. Charles James Lever. LC 24-11864. (Lettered on cover: Novels of Irish life). 1907. Little, Brown, and Company.

Odor of Bitter Almonds. James William MacQueen. LC 38-12838. 1938. Pub. for the Crime Club, Inc., by Doubleday, Doran & Co., Inc.

Odor of Sanctity: A Novel of Medieval Moorish Spain. Frank Yerby. LC 65-23964. 1965. Dial Press.

Odor of Violets. Baynard Hardwick Kendrick. LC 40-31631. 1941-1940. Little, Brown and Company.

O'Driscoll of Darra. A Novel. Dennis O'Sullivan. (On cover: Munro's library, popular novels, v. 1, no. 414). N. L. Munro.

Odtaa. John Masefield. LC 26-7270. 1926. The Macmillan Company.

Odysseus: The Complete Adventures. Dennis J. Hartzell. (Illus.). 92p. (Orig.). (gr. 7-9). 1978. pap. text ed. 3.00x (ISBN 0-88334-110-7). Ind Sch Pr.

Odyssey. Homer. Tr. by S. O. Andrew. 1953. 5.00x o.p. (ISBN 0-460-00454-9, Evman). Biblio Dist.

Odyssey. Homer. LC 61-8886. 1961. 12.50 o.p. (ISBN 0-385-09553-8). Doubleday.

Odyssey, 2 Vols. Homer. (Loeb Classical Library: No. 104-105). 12.00x ea. Vol. 1, Bks. 1-12 (ISBN 0-674-99116-8). Vol. 2, Bks. 13-24 (ISBN 0-674-99117-6). Harvard U Pr.

Odyssey. Homer. Ed. by S. H. Butcher & A. Lang. 1947. 9.95 o.s.i. (ISBN 0-02-553600-1). Macmillan.

Odyssey. LC 42-7371. (Prose and poetry individualized program. Myths and legends). 1942. The L. W. Singer Company.

Odyssey, Bks. 6 & 7. Homer. Ed. by Gerald M. Edwards. (Gr.). 1915. text ed. 6.50x (ISBN 0-521-05322-6). Cambridge U Pr.

Odyssey: A Modern Sequel. Nikos Kazantzakis. 1961. pap. 9.95 (ISBN 0-671-20247-2, Touchstone Bks). S&S.

Odyssey of a Hero. Vardis Fisher. LC 40-9073. 1937. Ritten House.

Odyssey of a Nice Girl. Ruth Suckow. LC 25-21589. 1925. A. A. Knopf.

Odyssey of a Torpedoed Transport. Maurice Larrouy. Tr. by Norton, Grace Fallow. LC 18-11814. 1918. Houghton Mifflin Company.

Odyssey of a Torpedoed Transport. Maurice Larrouy. Tr. by Norton, Grace Fallow. LC 23-11049. 1923. Houghton Mifflin Company.

Odyssey of Katinou Kalokovich. Natalie L. M. Petesch. 199p. 1979. pap. 5.00 (ISBN 0-934238-01-4). Motheroot.

Odyssey of Katinou Kalokovich: A Novel. Natalie L. M. Petesch. LC 74-168290. (Illus.). 1974. 3.95. United Sisters.

Odyssey of Kostas Volakis. Harry Mark Petrakis. LC 63-14947. 1963. D. McKay Co.

Odyssey of Love. Janet Ayres. (Superromances Ser.). 384p. 1982. pap. 2.50 (ISBN 0-373-70026-1, Pub. by Worldwide). Harlequin Bks.

Odyssey of Thaddeus Baxter: A Novel. Robert Lund. LC 57-5982. 1957. J. Day Co.

Odyssey to Earth Death. Leo P. Kelley. (Orig.). 1968. pap. 0.60 o.p. (B60-085). Belmont-Tower.

Odyssey. Tr. by Samuel Butler. (Reader's enrichment ser., RE327). Washington Sq.

Oedipus. Marwan B. Ramadan. LC 82-70566. 86p. 1982. text ed. 10.95 (ISBN 0-931494-16-8); pap. 4.95 (ISBN 0-931494-15-X). Brunswick Pub.

Oedipus & Ahknaton. Immanuel Velikovsky. 1980. pap. 2.95 (ISBN 0-671-83193-3). PB.

Oedipus Burning: A Novel. David Lang. LC 80-5408. 1981. 11.95 (ISBN 0-8128-2722-8). Stein and Day.

Oedipus in Disneyland: Queen Victoria's Reincarnation As Superman. Hercules Molloy. LC 72-188907. (Illus.). 1972. 4.95. Paranoid Press.

Oedipus in Nottingham: D. H. Lawrence. Daniel A Weiss. LC 62-17149. (Illus.). 1962. University of Washington.

O'er Moor and Fen. A Novel. Charlotte Walsingham. LC 8-33256. 1876. Claxton, Remsen & Haffelfinger.

Oeuvres. Jean-Francois de Pons. 354p. (Fr.). 1982. Repr. of 1738 ed. lib. bdg. 135.00 (ISBN 0-8287-1805-9). Clearwater Pub.

Oeuvres Completes, 12 tomes. Alfred De Vigny. Ed. by Baldensperger. Incl. Poemes; Servitude et Grandeur Militaires; Cinq-Mars; Theatre, 2 tomes; Stella, Daphne; Journal d'une Poete, 3 tomes; Correspondance, 3 tomes. 1914. Set. 67.50 o.p. French & Eur.

Oeuvres Completes, Tome II. Jean Genet. Incl. Notre-Dame des Fleurs; Condamne a Mort; Miracle de la Rose; Chant d'Amour. 1951-53. 16.50. French & Eur.

Oeuvres Romanesques, Tome I. Jean Giono. Incl. Naissance de l'Odyssee; Colline; Un de Beaumugnes; Regain; Solitude de la Pitie; Grand Troupeau. (Bibliotheque de la Pleiade). 41.50. French & Eur.

Oeuvres Romanesques, Tome II. Jean Giono. Incl. Jean le Bleu; Chant de la Montagne; Que Ma Joie Demeure; Batailles dans la Montagne. (Bibliotheque de la Pleiade). 41.50. French & Eur.

Of. Carl Fredricks. 1976. pap. 4.95t o.s.i. (ISBN 0-917686-00-4). C Fredericks.

Of a World That Is No More. Israel Joshua Singer. LC 73-134665. 1970. 10.00 o.s.i. (ISBN 0-8149-0683-4). Vanguard.

Of Age & Innocence. George Lamming. 414p. 1981. 13.95 (ISBN 0-8052-8095-2, Pub. by Allison & Busby England); pap. 7.95 (ISBN 0-8052-8094-4). Schocken.

Of All Our Yesterdays. Elsie Frances Wilson Mack. LC 45-9505. 1945. Arcadia House, Inc.

Of All Our Yesterdays. Frances Sarah Moore. LC 45-9505. 1945. Arcadia House, Inc.

Of All Possible Worlds: Stories by William Tenn Pseud. Philip Klass. 1955. Ballantine Books.

Of Angels & Dreamers. Carson E. Bench. Ed. by Kathy Galchutt. (Illus.). 36p. (Orig.). 1982. pap. 3.95 (ISBN 0-9608146-4-7). Western Sun Pubns.

Of Angels and Men. 1st Ed. William P Farrell. LC 52-675300. 1952. Pageant Press.

Of Bank Burning: A Documentary Novel from Isla Vista. Edward Loomis. LC 75-312983. 1970. Capricorn Press.

Of Blood and Oil: With the Israeli Underground, a Novel. Erwin Arnovitz. LC 51-4869. 1951. Exposition Press.

Of Bombs & Mice: A Story of the Warsaw Ghetto. Mina Tomkiewicz. LC 70-107106. 1970. 6.95 o.p. (ISBN 0-498-07357-2, Yoseloff). A S Barnes.

Of Brightness Gone. Holly Watterson. LC 42-24967. 1942. Arcadia House, Inc.

Of Cheat and Charmer: A Novel. Elliott Nugent. LC 62-118780. 1962. Simon and Schuster.

Of Clear Intent: A Novel. Henry Cottrell Rowland. LC 23-126729. Harper & Brothers.

Of David and Eva: A Love Story. Gertrude Samuels. (Signet Book). 1978. 1.75 (ISBN 0-451-08262-1). New American Library.

Of Desert Bondage. Bedros Margosian. LC 40-8936. 1940. The Van Press.

Of Dope and Dervishes: A Novel. Louis Gainsborough. LC 79-56209. 8.95 (ISBN 0-9603670-0-4). Rapollo Books.

Of Dreams & Danger. Lucile V. Stevens. 1981. pap. 6.95 (Avalon). Bouregy.

Of Fighting Blood. E J Hoskins. LC 58-57622. 1958. B. Humphries.

Of Former Love. Emma Laird. LC 51-6722. 1951. Houghton Mifflin.

Of Good and Evil: A Novel. Ernest Kellogg Gann. LC 63-19276. 1963. Simon and Schuster.

Of Great Riches. Rose Franken. LC 37-273492. 1937. Longmans, Green and Co.

Of Heaven's Benediction. Margaret Gorman Nichols. LC 40-31187. 1940. Arcadia House, Inc.

Of Hell a Heaven: The Story of a Wilderness Preacher and His Traveling Church. Charles Thomas Morgan. LC 52-6095. 1952. Exposition Press.

Of High Degree. A Story. Charles Gibbon. (Harper's Franklin square library, no. 280). 1882. Harper & Brothers.

Of Horses and Men: An Anthology of Horse-Racing Stories. 1st Ed. Ed. by W Georg Issak. LC 61-14160. (Dolphin original, C347). 1961. Dulphin Books.

Of Human Bondage. text ed. William Somerset Maugham. LC 56-6696. (Modern library paperbacks, P16). (Illus.). 1956. Random House.

Of Human Bondage. William Somerset Maugham. LC 15-16343. George H. Doran Company.

Of Human Bondage. William Somerset Maugham. LC 27-24582. (On cover: Murray Hill library). 1927. George H. Doran Company.

Of Human Bondage. William Somerset Maugham. LC 30-534544. 1929. Doubleday, Doran & Company, Inc.

Of Human Bondage. William Somerset Maugham. LC 31-261224. (Half-title: The modern library of the world's best books). 1930. The Modern Library.

Of Human Bondage. William Somerset Maugham. LC 33-16067. 1933. Garden City Publishing Company, Inc.

Of Human Kindness. Ruth Comfort Mitchell. LC 74-22798. (Labor Movement in Fiction and Non-Fiction). 1976. 21.50 (ISBN 0-404-58454-3). AMS Press.

Of Human Kindness. Ruth Comfort Mitchell. LC 40-735439. 1940. D. Appleton-Century Company Incorporated.

Of Human Miseries. Osceola Aleese Dawson. LC 41-212769. Fortuny's.

Of Lena Geyer. Marcia Gluck Davenport. LC 36-23529. 1936. C. Scribner's Sons.

Of Lena Geyer. Marcia Gluck Davenport. LC 44-35027. Grosset & Dunlap.

Of Life & Love & Things. Alma C. Blake. 1971. 4.95 (ISBN 0-87012-075-1). McClain.

Of Life's Essence. 1st Ed. Willard C Anderson. LC 53-374. 1952. Pageant Press.

Of Light & Sounding Brass. Basile S. Yanovsky. Tr. by Isabella Levitin from Rus. LC 72-83353. 296p. 1972. 8.95 (ISBN 0-8149-0719-9). Vanguard.

Of Loin & Cloth. Tr. by Henrik Van Breda from Fr. 206p. 1972. pap. 1.95 o.p. (ISBN 0-87056-275-4, 6274). Brandon.

Of Love & Battle. Hugh Zachary & Elizabeth Zachary. 480p. (Orig.). 1981. pap. 2.75 (ISBN 0-345-28610-3). Ballantine.

Of Love and Dust. Ernest J. Gaines. LC 67-25308. 1967. Dial Press.

Of Love and Dust. Ernest J. Gaines. LC 78-26032. 1979. 2.95 (ISBN 0-393-00914-9). Norton.

Of Love & Intrigue. Virginia Coffman. Bd. with Chinese Door. 1980. pap. 1.95 (ISBN 0-451-09313-5, J9313, Sig). NAL.

Of Love & Longing. Lauren Skye. (Orig.). 1978. pap. 2.25 (ISBN 0-89083-360-5). Zebra.

Of Love and Lovers. E Deborah Atkin. LC 52-9676. 1952. Vantage Press.

Of Love and the Kennebec. Clifford S Reynolds. LC 53-16403. 1952. Falmouth Pub. House.

Of Love Beware. Gertrude Knevels. LC 36-9859. The Penn Publishing Company.

Of Love Remembered. Ethel Delston. 1973. (pbk) 1.25. Dell.

Of Love Remembered. Ethel Delston. LC 70-164636. 1972. 5.95. Delacorte Press.

Of Many Men. James Aldridge. LC 46-1869. 1946. Little, Brown and Company.

Of Men and a Might Mountain. W. E Blackhurst. LC 65-2352. 1965. McClain Print. Co.

Of Men and Angels. Joy Cowley. LC 70-180068. 1972. 6.95 (ISBN 0-385-04243-4). Doubleday.

Of Men and Crabs. Josue De Castro. LC 75-139683. 1970. 5.95 (ISBN 0-8149-0667-2). Vanguard Press.

Of Men and Medicine. George Alexis Bankoff. LC 76-373492. 1976. 3.10 (ISBN 0-7091-5229-9). Hale.

Of Men and Monsters. Philip Klass. LC 73-86394. 1969. 4.95. Walker.

Of Men & Monsters. William Tenn. 256p. (Orig.). 1981. pap. 2.50 (ISBN 0-345-29523-4, Del Rey). Ballantine.

Of Men & Monsters. William Tenn. LC 73-86394. 1969. Repr. 4.95 o.p. (11065). Walker & Co.

Of Men and of Angels: A Novel. Lon Riley Woodrum. LC 52-8015. 1952. Zondervan Pub. House.

Of Mice and Men. John Steinbeck. LC 66-1309. 1963. Bantam Books.

Of Mice and Men. John Steinbeck. LC 37-2568. Covici-Friede.

Of Mice and Men. John Steinbeck. LC 38-6623. (Half-title: The modern library of the world's best books). 1938. The Modern Library.

Of Mice and Men. John Steinbeck. LC 38-6024. 1938. Triangle Books.

Of Mice and Men. John Steinbeck. LC 40-701893. 1939. The Sun Dial Press, Inc.

Of Mice & Men see Short Novels of John Steinbeck.

Of Mice and Men; Cannery Row. John Steinbeck. LC 78-1412. 1978. 1.95 (ISBN 0-14-004891-X). Penguin Books.

Of Midnight Honor. Janet Gregory Vermandel. LC 71-183003. (Red badge novel of suspense). 1972. 4.95 (ISBN 0-396-06494-9). Dodd, Mead.

Of Midnight Honor. Janet Gregory Vermandel. 1973. 0.95. Dell.

Of Mikes and Men: Illustrated by Paul Galdone. LC 51-10637. 1951. McGraw-Hill.

Of Missing Persons. David Goodis. LC 50-7483. (A Morrow mystery). 1950. Morrow.

Of Mortal Love. definitive rev. ed. / pref. by michael holroyd. ed. William Alexander Gerhardie. LC 73-92456. 1974. 7.95. St. Martin's Press.

Of One Blood. Charles Monroe Sheldon. Small, Maynard & Company.

Of Outlaws, Whores, Politicians, Con Men & Other Artists. Larry L. King. 288p. 1981. pap. 4.50 (ISBN 0-14-005755-2). Penguin.

Of Power and Faith, and Other Stories. Joseph S. Salzburg. LC 66-28843. 1967. Exposition Press.

Of Roots & Petals. Jessie S. Grigg. LC 79-57290. 1980. 10.95 (ISBN 0-89754-009-3); pap. 3.50 (ISBN 0-89754-008-5). Dan River Pr.

Of Sheep and Girls. Robert M Duffy. LC 70-7607. (Traveller's companion series, TC-2222). 1968. 1.25. Traveller's Companion, Inc.

Of Smiling Peace. Stefan Heym. LC 44-6712. 1944. Little, Brown and Company.

Of Streets and Stars. Alan Marcus. LC 63-7542. 1963. Houghton Mifflin.

Of Such Is the Kingdom: A Novel. Leslie Chauncey Sheppard. LC 64-11486. 1964. Greenwich Book Publishers.

Of the Farm. John Updike. LC 65-18763. 1965. Knopf.

Of the Lineage of David: A Sequel to The Unused Cradle. Esther T Barker. LC 77-354127. (Illus.). 1.25. Adams Press.

Of the World, Worldly. Mrs. Bridges. LC 6-18267. Lovell, Coryell & Company.

Of This Day's Journey. Constance Beresford-Howe. LC 47-2973. 1947. Dodd, Mead & Company.

Of This Time, of That Place, and Other Stories. uniform ed, 1st ed. Lionel Trilling & Diana Trilling. LC 78-65748. (Works of Lionel Trilling). ((Series: Trilling, Lionel, 1905-1975.). (Works.). 7.95 (ISBN 0-15-168054-X). Harcourt Brace Jovanovich.

Of This Time, of That Place, and Other Stories. Lionel Trilling & Diana Trilling. LC 80-14022. (Works of Lionel Trilling). (Harvest/HBJ book). ((Series: Trilling, Lionel, 1905-1975.). (Works.). 1980. 59.95 (ISBN 0-15-168054-X). Harcourt Brace Jovanovich.

Of Time & Space & Other Things. Isaac Asimov. (YA) 1968. pap. 0.75 o.p. (33-023). Lancer.

Of Time & the River. Thomas Wolfe. 1935. lib.rep.ed. 17.50x o.p. (ISBN 0-684-14739-4, ScribT). Scribner.

Of Time & the River. Thomas Wolfe. 1979. 17.50 o.p. (ISBN 0-684-10680-9, ScribT). Scribner.

Of Time and the River: A Legend of Man's Hunger in His Youth. Thomas Wolfe. LC 35-27095. 1935. C. Scribner's Sons.

Of Time and the River: Young Faustus. Telemachus. Thomas Wolfe. LC 65-537. (Scribner library books, SL106). 1953. Scribner.

Of Time and the River: Young Faustus. Telemachus. Introd. by C. Hugh Holman. Thomas Wolfe. LC 65-537. (Scribner lib. bks., SL106). pap., 1.65. Scribners.

Of Time & Tide. Georgia H. Hart. LC 66-30574. (Illus.). 1966. 4.00 o.p. State Ptg.

Of Unsound Mind: By Harry Carmichael Pseud. 1st Ed. Leopold Horace Ognall. LC 62-16740. 1962. Published for the Crime Club by Doubleday.

Of Vice & Virtue. Intro. by G. Lowndes. pap. 1.95 o.p. (6012). Brandon.

Of Water and the Spirit. Margaret Prescott Montague. LC 16-250999. 0.50. E. P. Dutton & Company.

Of What Was, Nothing Is Left. Fred Starr. LC 72-78902. (Illus.). 1972. 4.95. Christopher Pub. House.

Of Wind and Fire. Jane Blackmore. 1979. 2.25 (ISBN 0-440-15963-6). Dell Publishing Co.

Of Wind and Song: A Novel. Evelyn Voss Wise. LC 56-8197. 1956. Bruce Pub. Co.

Of Women and Their Elegance. Norman Mailer & Milton H Greene. LC 80-15138. (Illus.). 29.95 (ISBN 0-671-24020-X). Simon and Schuster.

Of Worlds Beyond. Ed. by Lloyd Eshbach. LC 64-57013. 1964. 7.50 (ISBN 0-911682-05-8); pap. 4.00 (ISBN 0-911682-14-7). Advent.

Of Wrath and Praise. Tom Taylor. LC 80-29453. 2.95 (ISBN 0-8024-9249-5). Moody Press.

Ofay. Earl Shorris. LC 66-12530. bds., 4.50. Delacorte Dist. Dial.

Ofay. Earl Shorris. (6533). 1967. Dell.

Off Center. Damon Francis Knight. LC 78-66665. pap. 1.95 o.s.i. (ISBN 0-89516-046-3). Condor Pub Co.

Off Center. Damon Francis Knight. (O.s.i.). 160p. 1973. pap. 0.75 o.s.i. (AS1071, Award). Univ Pub & Dist.

Off Duty. Andrew Coburn. LC 79-24670. 10.95 (ISBN 0-393-01369-3). Norton.

Off Duty: A Dozen Yarns for Soldiers and Sailors. Ed. by Wilhelmina Harper. LC 19-121669. 1919. The Century Co.

Off-Hand Sketches. Timothy Shay Arthur. LC 6-3412. (On cover: Lovell's library, v. 11, no. 582). J. W. Lovell Company.

Off-Islander: A Story of Wesquo by the Sea. Florence Mary Bennett Anderson. LC 21-15628. 1921. The Stratford Company.

Off-Islanders. 1st Ed. Nathaniel Benchley. LC 61-11646. 1961. McGraw-Hill.

Off Key. Betty J. Hudson. (Orig.). 1979. pap. 1.75 (ISBN 0-532-23150-3). Woodhill.

Off Limits: A Novel. Hans Habe. LC 56-11971. 1957. F. Fell.

Off Limits: A Novel, by Hans Habe Pseud. Translated from the German by Ewald Osers. Jean Bekessy, pseud. LC 56-11971. 1957. F. Fell.

Off Lynnport Light: A Novel. Augusta Campbell Watson. LC 8-36761. 1895. E. P. Dutton & Company.

Off on a Comet see To the Sun?.

Off on a Comet: A Journey Through Planetary Space. Jules Verne. 520p. Repr. of 1878 ed. lib. bdg. 24.45x (ISBN 0-88411-902-5). Amereon Ltd.

Off on a Comet! A Journey Through Planetary Space. (A Sequel to "To the Sun?". Jules Verne & Roth, Edward, 1826-1911, Tr. LC 1-9821. 1878. Claxton, Remsen & Haffelfinger.

Off Sandy Hook: And Other Stories. Clotilde Inez Mary Graves. LC 15-19407. 1915. 1.25. Frederick A. Stokes Company.

Off Season. Jack Ketchum. 1981. pap. 2.50 (ISBN 0-345-29427-0). Ballantine.
Off the Arm. Don Marquis. LC 30-153383. 1930. Doubleday, Doran & Company, Inc.
Off the Beaten Path. 4.45 (ISBN 0-448-06976-8, G&D). Putnam Pub Group.
Off the Beaten Trek. Ed. by John Du Maurier. (Anthology of Science Fidtion Stories Ser: Vol. 3). (Illus.). 1977. pap. 5.00 (ISBN 0-89502-010-6). FEB.
Off the Beaten Trek. Ed. by Trinette Kern. (Anthology of Science Fiction Stories Ser: Vol. 1). 3.00x o.p. (ISBN 0-89502-006-8). FEB.
Off the Beaten Trek. Ed. by Trinette Kern. (Anthology of Science Fiction Ser: Vol. 2). pap. 4.50 o.p. (ISBN 0-89502-009-2). FEB.
Off the Beaten Trek. Ed. by Trinette Kern. (Anthology of Science Fiction Stories Ser: Vol. 1). 3.00x o.p. (ISBN 0-89502-006-8). FEB.
Off the High Road: Stories of English Village Life. Annette Reid & Brock, Charles Edmund, 1870- LC 24-7109. 1924. D. Appleton and Company.
Off the Highway. Alice Prescott Smith. LC 4-29185. 1904. Houghton, Mifflin and Company.
Off the Highway. Bessie A Van Dyke. LC 39-33516. The Christopher Publishing House.
Off the Record. Robert H. Ferrell. 1982. pap. 6.95 (ISBN 0-14-006080-4). Penguin.
Off the Rocks: A Novel. Emily Fox. LC 6-43281. ("Hammock series" no. 3). 1882. H. A. Sumner & Company.
Off the Rocks: Stories of the Deep-Sea Fisherfolk of Labrador. Wilfred Thomason Grenfell. LC 70-134963. (Short story index reprint series). (Illus.). 1970. Books for Libraries Press.
Off the Rocks: Stories of the Deep-Sea Fisherfolk of Labbrador. Wilfred Thomason Grenfell. LC 6-18836. 1906. The Sunday School Times Company.
Off the Skelligs, 4 vols. in 2. Jean Ingelow. LC 79-8138. Repr. of 1872 ed. Set. 84.50 (ISBN 0-404-61931-2). AMS Pr.
Off the Skelligs. A Novel. author's ed. Jean Ingelow. LC 4-153152. 1872. Roberts Brothers.
Off the Skelligs. A Novel. Jean Ingelow. LC 22-514131. 1873. Roberts Brothers.
Off the Skelligs. A Novel. Jean Ingelow. LC 16-9356. 1910. Little, Brown, and Co.
Off the Streets. 1st Ed. Joseph Hendryx. LC 55-9806. 1955. Comet Press Books.
Off to California: A Tale of the Gold Country. Hendrik Conscience & Cobb, James Francis, 1829- Tr. LC 26-22325. E. and J. B. Young and Co.
Off to Laramie. Charles Stanley Strong. LC 49-119398. 1949. Phoenix Press.
Off to See the Wizard: A Novel. Daniel Ort. LC 75-2084. 1975. 6.95 (ISBN 0-88405-104-8). Mason/Charter.
Off with Her Head. George Douglas Howard Cole & Margaret Isabel Postgate Cole. LC 39-11271. 1939. The Macmillan Company.
Off with the Old Love: A War Story. Guy Fleming, pseud. LC 17-219726. 1917. Longmans, Green and Co.
Offenders. Sandy Lafoca. 2.50 o.p. Carlton.
Offenders. Giles A Lutz. LC 73-10971. 1974. 4.95 (ISBN 0-385-05251-0). Doubleday.
Offending Brother. Sayd Anderson. LC 1-29884. 1900. F. Tennyson Neely Company.
Offense Against the Persons. Harriett Gilbert. LC 74-20419. 1975. 6.95 (ISBN 0-06-011536-X). Harper & Row.
Offer. Jesse L. Lasky & Pat Silver. LC 80-1813. 1981. 15.95 (ISBN 0-385-15767-3). Doubleday.
Offer of Marriage. Lynna Cooper. (Signet book). New American Library.
Offer of Marriage see Her Hearts Desire.
Offer of Marriage, by Berta Ruck. Berta Ruck. LC 31-3874. 1931. Dodd, Mead & Company.
Offering. James W Reid. LC 77-11632. 8.95 (ISBN 0-399-12074-2). Putnam.
Office. Nathan Asch. LC 25-19171. Harcourt, Brace and Company.
Office. Gathorne-Hardy, Jonathan. LC 70-149448. 1971. 4.95. Dial Press.
Office Affair. Charles Beardsley. 1975. (pbk.) 1.50. New American Library.
Office Game. Matt Harding, pseud. 1971. pap. 0.75 o.p. (75-404). Manor Bks.
Office Hours. Jacob Manuel Mayer. LC 40-3033. 1939. The Boro Publishing Company.
Office Nurse. Adelaide Humphries. LC 47-229384. 1947. Arcadia House.
Office Party. Michael A Gilbert. LC 81-8394. 1981. 11.95 (ISBN 0-671-43636-8). Linden Press/Simon & Schuster.
Office Party. Jonathan Quist. pap. 2.25 o.s.i. (Venus). Grove.
Office Politics. Wilfrid Shead. (95073). 1967. Pocket Bks.
Office Politics. Wilfrid Sheed. 339p. 1966. 5.95 (ISBN 0-374-22464-1). FS&G.
Office Politics: A Novel. Wilfrid Sheed. LC 66-20168. 1966. Farrar, Straus and Giroux.
Office Wife. Faith Baldwin. 1976. Repr. of 1930 ed. lib. bdg. 15.70x (ISBN 0-88411-603-4). Amereon Ltd.
Office Wife. Faith Baldwin Cuthrell. LC 73-86738. 1973. 5.95. Aeonian Press.
Office Wife. Faith Baldwin Cuthrell. LC 30-6729. 1930. Dodd, Mead, & Company.
Office Wife. Jerry Weil. LC 57-6279. (Signet book, 1350). 1957. New American Library.
Office. 1st Ed. Fredric Brown. LC 58-523054. 1958. Dutton.
Officer! Hulbert Footner. LC 24-20609. George H. Doran Company.
Officer and a Gentleman. Steven Phillip Smith. LC 82-90499. 1982. 2.75 (ISBN 0-380-80853-6). Avon Books.
Officer and a Lady. Peggy O'More, pseud. LC 42-21234. 1942. Grammercy Publishing Co.
Officer and Gentleman. Delves-Broughton, Josephine. LC 51-9470. 1951. McGraw Hill Book Co.
Officer Factory. Hans Hellmut Kirst. (Illus.). 1968. pap. 0.75 o.p. (T1807). Pyramid Pubns.
Officer from Special Branch. Tom Lilley. 1973. 1.25. Manor Bks.
Officer from Special Branch. Tom Lilley. LC 79-131091. 1971. 5.95. Doubleday.
Officer 666. Barton Wood Currie & McHugh, Augustia. LC 12-278521. The H. K. Fly Company.
Officers & Gentlemen. Evelyn Waugh. 1979. 10.95 (ISBN 0-316-92631-0); pap. 5.95 (ISBN 0-316-92630-2). Little.
Officers and Gentlemen. 1st Ed. Evelyn Waugh. LC 55-9832. 1955. Little, Brown.
Officers and Ladies. Richard O'Connor. LC 58-13289. 1958. Doubleday.
Officers' Wives. Thomas J Fleming. LC 80-1063. 1981. 15.95 (ISBN 0-385-14805-4). Doubleday.
Official Chaperon. Natalie Sumner Lincoln. LC 20-12359. The Macaulay Company.
Official Detective Omnibus. Official Detective Stories & Keller, Harry, Ed. LC 48-11525. 1948. Duell, Sloan and Pearce.
Official Secret. Allan Duncan. LC 37-33670. Thomas Y. Crowell Company.
Official Sgt. Pepper's Lonely Hearts Club Band Scrapbook. Robert Stigwood & Dee Anthony. 1978. pap. 5.95 (ISBN 0-671-79038-2, Wallaby). PB.
Offshore. Stephen Coulter. LC 66-19922. 1966. bds., 4.95. Morrow.
Offshore Light: By Eliot Naylor Pseud. 1st American Ed. Pamela Frankau. LC 53-10228. 1953. Duell, Sloan and Pearce.
Offspring. Clare Consuelo Frewen Sheridan. LC 36-7187. G. P. Putnam's Sons.
Offtrack. Steven G Crist. LC 79-6662. 1980. 9.95 (ISBN 0-385-15215-9). Doubleday.
Oficina de Placeres. new ed. Reynaldo Rengifo. (Pimienta Collection Ser). (Illus.). 160p. (Span.). 1975. pap. 1.25 (ISBN 0-88473-229-0). Fiesta Pub.
O'Flaherty the Great: A Tragi-Comedy. John Cournos. LC 27-12825. 1927. A. A. Knopf.
O'Flynn: A Novel. Justin Huntly McCarthy. LC 10-11471. 1910. Harper & Brothers.
Ogden Enigma. Gene Snyder. LC 80-81007. 320p. (Orig.). 1980. pap. 2.95 (ISBN 0-86721-118-0). Playboy Pbks.
Ogden's Strange Story. Edison Marshall. LC 34-2643. 1934. H. C. Kinsey & Company, Inc.
Ogeechee Cross-Firings: A Novel. Richard Malcolm Johnston. LC 7-10804. (On cover: Harper's Franklin square library, no. 656). 1889. Harper & Brothers.
OGF: Being the Private Papers of George Cockburn, Bus Conductor, a Resident of Hurstfield, a Suburb of Sydney, Australia. Illus. by Wep. Sydney, U. Smith. Keith Smith. LC 65-29108. 1966. bds., 4.50. Tri-Ocean.
Ogilvie, Tallant & Moon. Chelsea Quinn Yarbro. LC 75-30658. (Red mask mystery). 6.95 (ISBN 0-399-11630-3). Putnam.
Ogilvies. A Novel. Dinah Maria Mulock Craik. LC 4-16512. 1902. Harper & Brothers.
Ogre. Michel Tournier. LC 75-186310. 1972. 7.95. Doubleday.
Ogre. Michel Tournier. (Laurel Editions). 1973. (pbk.) 1.50. Dell.
Oh, Be Careful. Lee Colgate. LC 64-18073. 1965. Harper & Row.
Oh Boy! Here Comes Walt". Vahan Gregory. LC 74-76813. 1974. 6.95 (ISBN 0-87949-034-9). Ashley Books.
Oh, Bury Me Not. M. K Wren, pseud. LC 76-18376. 1976. 5.95 (ISBN 0-385-12078-8). Published for the Crime Club by Doubleday.
Oh Careless Love. Maurice Zolotow. LC 59-10244. 1959. Harcourt, Brace.
Oh Christina. John Joy Bell. F. H. Revell Company.
Oh Cynthia! Norma Knight. LC 32-225591. The Bobbs--Merrill Company.
Oh Definitely. Maurice Lincoln. LC 34-344289. 1934. R. M. McBride & Company.
Oh, Doctor! A Novel. Harry Leon Wilson. LC 23-13196. 1923. Cosmopolitan Book Corporation.
Oh, Eden! David Rogers. 1974. (pbk.) 1.50. Warner Paperback Lib.
Oh Glittering Promise: A Novel of the California Gold Rush. Anne Benson Fisher. LC 49-8019. 1949. Bobbs-Merrill Co.
Oh Glory! Harford Willing Hare Powel. LC 31-16672. The Bobbs-Merrill Company.
Oh, God! A Novel. Avery Corman. LC 79-159127. 1971. 5.95 (ISBN 0-671-21029-7). Simon and Schuster.
Oh Happy Youth. Kay Cleaver Strahan. LC 31-28063. 1931. Doubleday, Doran & Company Inc.
Oh! Hugh Pecker. Mark Clinton. 1973. pap. 1.95 o.s.i. (76-329). Lancer.
Oh! James! Helen Marion Edginton. LC 14-153711. 1914. 1.30. Little, Brown, and Company.
Oh, King, Live Forever. Polly A. Hutchison. LC 77-1988. 2.95 (ISBN 0-89293-025-X). Beta Books.
Oh Man! Clare A. Briggs. Repr. of 1919 ed. 10.00 o.s.i. Finch Pr.
Oh, Mary, Be Careful! George Weston. LC 17-26265. 1917. J. B. Lippincott Company.
Oh, Mr. Bidgood! A Nautical Comedy. Peter Blundell. LC 14-7693. 1914. net 1.25. John Lane.
Oh, Money! Money! Eleanor Hodgman Porter. LC 18-6306. 1918. Houghton Mifflin Company.
Oh, Murderer Mine: A New Mystery. Norbert Davis. LC 47-776. (Handi-book mysteries). 1946. Quinn Publishing Co., Inc.
Oh, My Darling. 1st Ed. Frank Rochna. LC 55-9257. 1955. Pageant Press.
Oh, Pal: A New Novel. Agnes Rachel Rider. LC 52-6310. 1952. William-Frederick Press.
Oh! PASCAL! Doug Cooper & Michael Clancy. 1982. pap. 17.95x (ISBN 0-393-95205-3). Norton.
Oh, Promised Land. James Howell Street. LC 40-27414. 1940. The Dial Press.
Oh Say, Can You See? Richard J. Aielli. 3.75 o.p. Carlton.
Oh, Say, Can You See (!) A Novel. Lewis Browne. LC 37-27455. 1937. The Macmillan Company.
Oh, Son!" A Tale of Two Worlds. Elsie Goerner Friedlander. LC 26-12464. 1926. C. H. Cochrane.
Oh, Susanna! A Romance of the Old American Merchant Marine. Meade Minnigerode. LC 22-349627. 1922. G. P. Putnam's Sons.
Oh, Susannah! large print ed. Kate Wilhelm. LC 82-25168. 1983. 12.95 (ISBN 0-89340-573-6). John Curley & Associates.
Oh, Susannah! A Novel. Kate Wilhelm. LC 81-23959. 1982. 12.95 (ISBN 0-395-32054-2). Houghton Mifflin.
Oh, the Brave Music! Richard Blaker. LC 25-191051. George H. Doran Company.
Oh, the Family! Clare Simon. LC 56-5985. 1956. Coward-McCann.
Oh to Be in England. Herbert Ernest Bates. 167p. 1963. 4.50 o.p. (ISBN 0-374-22492-7). FS&G.
Oh, Valley Green! John H Culp. LC 77-155508. 1972. (ISBN 0-03-086645-6). Holt, Rinehart and Winston.
Oh, Watchman! A Novel. Agnes Mary White Sanford. LC 51-9040. 1951. Lippincott.
Oh, What a Paradise It Seems. John Cheever. LC 81-48109. 1982. 10.00 (ISBN 0-394-51334-7). Knopf: Distributed by Random House.
Oh, What a Paradise It Seems. John Cheever. LC 82-12146. 1982. 11.95 (ISBN 0-8161-3423-5). G.K. Hall.
Oh, What a Wonderful Wedding: By Virginia Rowans Pseud. Illustrated by N. M. Bodecker. Edward Everett Tanner. LC 52-13116. 1953. Crowell.
Oh Where Are Bloody Mary's Earrings? Robert Player. LC 72-9100. 224p. (YA) 1973. 6.95 o.p. (ISBN 0-06-013353-8, HarpT). Har-Row.
Oh! Where Are Bloody Mary's Earrings? Robert Player. LC 72-9100. 1972. 6.95. Harper & Row.
Oh Wicked Country! Tr. by Celeste Piano from Fr. LC 82-84059. (Grove Press Victorian Library). 144p. (Orig.). 1983. pap. 3.25 (ISBN 0-394-62447-5, B485, BC). Grove.
Oh, You English. Emma Shelton Robbins. LC 16-5190. 1915. 1.25. The Neale Publishing Company.
Oh, You Tex! William MacLeod Raine. LC 20-6711. 1920. Houghton Mifflin Company.
Oh, You Tex. William MacLeod Raine. 1973. (pbk) 0.75. Popular Library.
Oh, You Wretch! Harry Miles. John M Schwarz. LC 67-27893. 1967. Grove Press.
Oh Youth of Mine. Ralph F. Rhoads. LC 81-86211. 64p. pap. 2.95. GWP.
O'Hara Generation. John O'Hara. LC 70-76277. 1969. 6.95. Random House.
O'Hara: Or, 1798. William Hamilton Maxwell. LC 78-12124. (Ireland, from the Act of Union, 1800, to the Death of Parnell, 1891). 1979. 64.00 (ISBN 0-8240-3499-6). Garland Pub.
O'Hara's Mission: Or, Hope on--Hope Ever. William O'Brien. (Munro's twenty-five cent edition. v. 50, no. 806). N. L. Munro.
O'Higgins. (Young Americans Ser). (Illus.). 1972. pap. 1.00 (ISBN 0-8270-4875-0). OAS.
O'Higgins and Don Bernardo. Edna Deu Pree Nelson. LC 54-10925. 1954. Dutton.
Ohio. Helen L. Poole. (Whitewater Dynasty Ser.). (Orig.). 1981. pap. 2.75 (ISBN 0-89083-733-3). Zebra.
Ohio's Ghostly Greats: An Anthology of Ohio Ghost Stories. David J. Gerrick. 1973. pap. 4.95 (ISBN 0-916750-40-X). Dayton Labs.
O'Houlihan's Jest: A Lament for the Irish, by Rohan O'Grady Pseud. June O'Grady Skinner. LC 61-5950. 1961. Macmillan.
Oh's Profit. John Goulet. LC 75-8571. 1975. 6.95 (ISBN 0-688-02935-3). Morrow.
Oic-? Science Fiction. Joe Thorn. LC 74-152279. 1971. (ISBN 0-87012-097-2). McClain Printing Co.
Oil. Jonathan Black. LC 74-10503. 600p. 1974. 8.95 o.p. (ISBN 0-688-00293-5). Morrow.
Oil. Jonathan Black. 1975. (pbk.) 1.75. Bantam.
Oil. Thomas Walter Gilkyson. LC 74-26108. (Labor Movement in Fiction and Non-Fiction). 1976. 17.50 (ISBN 0-404-58432-2). AMS Press.
Oil. Thomas Walter Gilkyson. LC 24-20559. 1924. C. Scribner's Sons.
Oil! Upton Sinclair. LC 79-24682. 1981. Repr. of 1927 ed. lib. bdg. 15.00x (ISBN 0-8376-0444-3). Bentley.
Oil. B. W Von Block. LC 74-10503. 1974. Morrow.
Oil! A Novel. Upton Beall Sinclair. LC 27-7669. 1927. A. & C. Boni.
Oil! A Novel. Upton Beall Sinclair. LC 32-19522. The Author.
Oil! A Novel. Upton Beall Sinclair. LC 79-24682. 1981. 15.00 (ISBN 0-8376-0444-3). R. Bentley.
Oil Creek Tales. E George Lindstrom. LC 38-38720. High Twelve Publishing Company.
Oil for the Lamps of China. Alice Tisdale Nourse Hobart. LC 33-27330. The Bobbs-Merrill Company.
Oil for the Light of the World. 1st Ed. Frank William Hart. LC 56-5504. 1956. Vantage Press.
Oil Man of Obange. John Munonye. (African Writers Ser.). 1971. pap. text ed. 4.50x (ISBN 0-435-90094-3); pap. text ed. 4.50x. Heinemann Ed.
Oil Slick. Richard Sapir & Warren Murphy. (Destroyer,#16). 1974. (pbk.) 1.25 (ISBN 0-523-00418-4). Pinnacle Books.
Oil Strike. John Wingate. LC 76-5382. (Illus.). 1976. 7.95. St. Martin's Press.
Oil Tide: A Tale of Ranger. Esther McCord Terrell. LC 45-5364. 1945. Dorrance & Company.
Oil Wells in the Woods. John Christopher O'Day. 1905. The Oquaga Press.
Oilers and Sweepers and Other Stories. George Dennison. LC 78-23732. 7.95 (ISBN 0-394-48416-9). Random House.
Oilfield Stories. Joseph Costa. 1983. 8.95 (ISBN 0-533-05513-X). Vantage.
Oilskin Packet: A Tale of the Southern Seas. Reginald Cheyne Berkeley & Dixon, James. LC 19-12171. 1918. 1.50. Frederick A. Stokes Co.
Ojibway: A Novel of Indian Life of the Period of the Early Advance of Civilization in the Great Northwest. Joseph Alexander Gilfillan. LC 4-29781. 1904. The Neale Publishing Company.
Okapi Fever, a Novel. Tr. from French by Peter Green. Philippe Diole. LC 65-239525. bds., 4.95. Viking.
Okara Mask. Rex Wiseman. 1979. pap. 1.95 o.s.i. (ISBN 0-505-51434-6). Tower Bks.
O'Kelly. Arthur Weiss. LC 68-13136. Orig. Title: O'Kelly's Eclipse. 1969. pap. 0.95 o.p. (ISBN 0-446-65056-0, 65-056). Paperback Lib.
O'Kelly's Eclipse. Arthur Weiss. LC 68-13136. 1968. Doubleday.
O'Kelly's Eclipse see O'Kelly.
Okewood of the Secret Service. Valentine Williams. LC 19-5815. 1919. R. M. McBride & Company.
Okies: Selected Short Stories. Gerald W. Haslam. LC 75-26947. (Illus.). 130p. 1975. pap. 4.95 (ISBN 0-87905-042-X). Peregrine Smith.
Okies: Selected Stories. Gerald W Haslam. LC 73-86006. 1973. (pbk.) 2.95. New West Publications.
Okiki. Ed. by Chinua Achebe. 4.00 o.p. Panther Hse.
Okla Hannali. R. A Lafferty. 1973. (pbk) 1.25 (ISBN 0-671-78301-7). Pocket Books.
Okla Hannali. R. A Lafferty. LC 73-186035. 1972. 5.95. Doubleday.
Oklahoma: A Novel. Courtney Ryley Cooper. LC 26-14910. 1926. Little, Brown, and Company.

TITLE INDEX OLD DORSET.

Oklahoma Crude. Marc Norman. LC 72-94683. 1973. 6.95 (ISBN 0-525-16995-4). E. P. Dutton.
Oklahoma Crude. Marc Norman. 1973. (pbk) 1.25. Popular Library.
Oklahoma Crude. Marc Norman. LC 73-9987. 1973. 8.95 (ISBN 0-8161-6139-9). G. K. Hall.
Oklahoma Fiddlefoot. Lauran Paine. LC 66-9239. 1966. Arcadia House.
Oklahoma Firefight. Lionel Derrick, pseud. (Penetrator Ser.: No. 31). 1979. pap. 1.50 (ISBN 0-523-40363-1). Pinnacle Bks.
Oklahoma Law. Tex Holt, pseud. LC 44-2702. 1944. Arcadia House.
Oklahoma Laws. Claude Rister. LC 44-2702. 1944. Arcadia House, Inc.
Oklahoma Punk. Loren D. Estleman. LC 75-40780. 192p. (Orig.). 1976. pap. 1.50 (ISBN 0-89041-052-6, 3052). Major Bks.
Oklahoma Romance. Helen Churchill Hungerford Candee. LC 1-25673. 1901. The Century Co.
Oklahoma Run. Alberta Wilson Constant. LC 55-5395. Crowell.
Oklahoma Town. George Milburn. LC 72-134969. (Short story index reprint series). 1970. Books for Libraries Press.
Oklahoma Town. George Milburn. LC 31-265389. Harcourt, Brace and Company.
Oklahoma Wildcat. Augusta Belle Weaver. LC 38-8902. The Macaulay Company.
Oklahomans. Whitney Stine. 448p. 1980. pap. 2.95 (ISBN 0-523-41886-8). Pinnacle Bks.
Oklahomans: The Second Generation. Whitney Stine. (The Oklahomans Ser.: No. 2). 464p. (Orig.). 1981. pap. 2.95 (ISBN 0-523-41488-9). Pinnacle Bks.
Oklahomans: The Third Generation. Whitney Stine. 512p. (Orig.). 1982. pap. 3.50 (ISBN 0-523-41662-8). Pinnacle Bks.
Okra. Sam Harrison. pap. 3.00. Anhinga Pr.
Oktoberfest. Frank De Felitta. LC 73-80012. 1973. 5.95 (ISBN 0-385-07060-8). Doubleday.
Oktoberfest. Frank De Felitta. 1974. (pbk.) 1.50. Warner Paperback Library.
Oktoberfest. Frank DeFilitta. LC 73-82243. 240p. 1973. 5.95 o.p. (ISBN 0-385-07060-8). Doubleday.
Ol' Bill, and Other Stories. John Alden Knight & Weller, Milton C., Illus. LC 42-51183. 1942. C. Scribner's Sons.
Ol' Man Adam An' His Chillun. Roark Bradford. (Illus.). 1928. 7.95 o.p. (ISBN 0-06-010445-7, HarpT). Har-Row.
Ol' Prophet Nat. Daniel Panger. LC 67-30725. 1967. J. F. Blair.
Ola & the Sea Wolf, No. 127. Barbara Cartland. 144p. (Orig.). 1980. pap. 1.75 (ISBN 0-553-14084-1). Bantam.
Olaf Sagas: Vol. I - Heimskringla. Snorri Sturluson. 1974. Repr. of 1964 ed. 9.95x (ISBN 0-460-00717-3, Evman). Biblio Dist.
Olaf Sagas: Vol. II - Heimskringla. Snorri Sturluson. 1974. Repr. of 1964 ed. 9.95x (ISBN 0-460-00722-X, Evman). Biblio Dist.
Old Abe Dead & Other Stories. Eston Meade. 1981. 6.95 (ISBN 0-533-04800-1). Vantage.
Old Abe's Jokes, Fresh from Abraham's Bosom. LC 79-91089. (American Humorists Ser.). 1979. Repr. of 1864 ed. lib. bdg. 17.00 (ISBN 0-8398-1450-X). Irvington.
Old Acquaintance. Nicholas Guild. LC 78-10383. 9.95 (ISBN 0-87223-517-3). Seaview Books.
Old Acquaintance. David Stacton. LC 64-13018. 1964. Putnam.
Old Adam. Arnold Bennett. LC 74-17296. (Collected Works of Arnold Bennett: Vol. 60). 1976. Repr. of 1913 ed. 27.00 (ISBN 0-518-19141-9). Ayer Co.
Old Adam: A Story of Adventure. Arnold Bennett. LC 13-13538. George H. Doran Company.
Old Adam: A Story of Adventure. Arnold Bennett. LC 13-135280. George H. Doran Company.
Old Adam and the New Eve. Rudolf Golm & Fowler, Edith, Tr. LC 98-1816. 1898. G. H. Richmond & Son.
Old Adam's Likeness. Lucy Poate Stebbins. LC 28-172012. 1928. Houghton Mifflin Company.
Old Age of Monsieur Lecoq. Fortune Du Boisgobey & Garnett, F. E., Tr. LC 6-34418. (On cover: Seaside library. Pocket ed. no. 1088). G. Munro.
Old Allegiance. Hubert Wales. M. Kennerley.
Old and New: Or, Taste Versus Fashion. Mary Anne Madden Sadlier. LC 8-1657. (On cover: Parlor & cottage library). 1862. D. & J. Sadlier & Co.
Old and New: Or, Taste Versus Fashion. Mary Anne Madden Sadlier. LC 8-16583. (On cover: Parlor & cottage library). 1863. D. & J. Sadlier & Co.
Old and the Young: I Vecchi E I Giovani. Luigi Pirandello & Scott-Moncrieff, Charles Kenneth, 1889-1930, Tr. LC 28-14115. E. P. Dutton & Company.
Old Anthony's Secret: A Kentucky Love Tale, Based on Our System of Judicial Robbery and a Crime Unparalleled. W. J Shaw. 1888. The Author.
Old As Cain. M. E. Chaber, pseud. (Milo March Mystery, No. 19 Ser). 1971. pap. 0.60 o.p. (ISBN 0-446-63527-8, 63-527). Paperback Lib.
Old Ashburn Place. Margaret Flint. LC 36-22342. 1936. Dodd, Mead & Company.
Old Ballads in Prose. Eva March Tappan. LC 1-22018. 1901. Houghton, Mifflin and Co.
Old Bank House. Angela Mackail Thirkell. LC 49-102268. 1949. A. A. Knopf.
Old Bank House: By Angela Thirkell. Angela Mackail Thirkell. 1973. 1.25 (ISBN 0-515-02922-X). Pyramid.
Old Battle-Ax. Elisabeth Sanxay Holding. LC 43-172337. 1943. Simon and Schuster.
Old Baxter Place. Adeline McElfresh. LC 54-10727. 1954. Arcadic House.
Old Bayberry Road. Lucy Lincoln Montgomery. LC 28-851926. W. A. Wilde Company.
Old Beau, and Other Stories. John Seymour Wood. LC 8-37551. Cassell Publishing Company.
Old Beauty, and Others. Willa Sibert Cather. LC 76-7362. 1976. 2.45 (ISBN 0-394-72122-5). Vintage Books.
Old Beauty: And Others. Willa Sibert Cather. LC 48-8145. 1948. A. A. Knopf.
Old Benches with New Props. Mary Dwinell Chellis. LC 6-23405. 1891. The National Temperance Society and Publication House.
Old Blackfriars: A Story of the Days of Sir Anthony Van Dyck. Beatrice Marshall. LC 2-15741. 1902. E. P. Dutton and Co.
Old Blaine Farm. Ethelyn B. Thornton. LC 47-2264. 1947. Meador Publishing Company.
Old Blood. Frederick Palmer. LC 16-22259. 1916. 1.40. Dodd, Mead and Company.
Old Blood. 1st Ed. Edgar Mittelholzer. LC 58-8104. 1958. Doubleday.
Old Bones. Herman Petersen. LC 43-512993. 1943. Duell, Sloan and Pearce.
Old Boniface: A Novel. George Henry Picard. LC 7-35927. 1886. White, Stokes, & Allen.
Old Bowen's Legacy: A Novel. Edwin Asa Dix. LC 1-31284. 1901. The Century Co.
Old Boys. William Trevor. 1981. pap. 4.95 (ISBN 0-14-002428-X). Irish Bk Ctr.
Old Brick House: And Other Stories. Charlotte Beath Brown. LC 36-15569. 1936. Boothbay Register Press.
Old Bristol: A Story of the Early English Baptists. Maria Frances Hill Anderson. LC 7-25798. 1880. American Baptist Publ. Society.
Old Bristol: a Story of the Early English Baptists. N., L. M & N., L. M. LC 7-25798. American Baptist Publication Society.
Old Bunch. Meyer Levin. LC 58-1388. 1958. Simon and Schuster.
Old Bunch. Meyer Levin. LC 37-3820. 1937. The Viking Press.
Old Bureau, and Other Tales. Daniel Clement Colesworthy. LC 6-25412. 1861. Antique Book Store.
Old Burma Road. Frank Anthony Long & Long, Gertrude Joyce. LC 41-14080. 1942. Burton Publishing Company.
Old Callahan Place: A Novel. Elizabeth Frances Corbett. LC 66-25967. 1966. Appleton-Century.
Old Captivity. Nevil Shute Norway. LC 10-27173. 1940. W. Morrow and Co.
Old Captivity. Nevil Shute. 1982. 13.95 (ISBN 0-434-69906-3, Pub. by Heinemann). David & Charles.
Old Captivity. Nevil Shute. 1970. pap. 0.95 o.p. (ISBN 0-447-75126-3). Lancer.
Old Card. Roland Pertwee. LC 19-14914. 1919. Boni and Liveright.
Old Charlmont's Seed-Bed. Sara Trainer Smith. LC 1-29392. 1900. Benziger Bros.
Old Chateau. Harriet Burn McKeever. LC 7-16314. 1870. Presbyterian Publication Committee.
Old Chest: Or, The Journal of a Family of the French People, from the Merovingian Times to Our Own Days. Tr. by Sadlier, Anna Theresa. 1875. D. & J. Sadlier & Co.
Old Chester Days. Margaret Wade Campbell Deland. LC 79-113657. (Short story index reprint series). 1970. Books for Libraries Press.
Old Chester Days. Margaret Wade Campbell Deland. LC 37-182524. 1937. Harper & Brothers.
Old Chester Secret. Margaret Wade Campbell Deland. LC 20-18606. Harper & Brothers.
Old Chester Tales. Margaret Wade Campbell Deland. LC 69-11887. (American short story series, v. 45). (Illus.). 1969. Garrett Press.
Old Chester Tales. Margaret Wade Campbell Deland. LC 69-13879. (Illus.). 1969. Greenwood Press.
Old Chester Tales. Margaret Wade Campbell Deland. LC 70-97884. (Illus.). 1969. AMS Press.
Old Chester Tales. Margaret Wade Campbell Deland. LC 72-8310. (American short story series, v. 45). 1972. (ISBN 0-8422-8037-5). MSS Information Corp.
Old Chester Tales. Margaret Wade Campbell Deland. LC 9-32362. Harper & Brothers.
Old Chester Tales. Margaret Wade Campbell Deland. LC 98-1805. 1899. Harper & Brothers.
Old Chester Tales. Margaret Wade Campbell Deland. LC 19-147978. (Harper's modern classics). Harper & Brothers.
Old Chicago... Mary Hastings Bradley. LC 33-10147. 1933. D. Appleton and Company.
Old Christmas-Bracebridge Hall. Washington Irving. (Illus.). 528p. 1980. boxed set 22.00 (ISBN 0-912882-43-3). Sleepy Hollow.
Old Cimarron. Harry H. Halsell. LC 44-33935. 1944.
Old Clinkers: A Story of the New York Fire Department. Harvey Jerrold O'Higgins. LC 9-27992. 1.50. Small, Maynard & Company.
Old Cobblestone House: A Ghost Story. Charlotte Curtis Smith. LC 17-27900. 1917. The Craftsman Press.
Old Continental: Or, The Price of Liberty. James Kirke Paulding. LC 6-28747. 1846. Paine and Burgess.
Old Continental: Or, The Price of Liberty. 2d ed. James Kirke Paulding. LC 6-28748. 1851. Cady and Burgess.
Old Contrairy: And Other Stories. Florence Marryat Church Lean. (On cover: The seaside library. Pocket ed. no. 183). 1884. G. Munro.
Old Copper Collar. Dan Cushman. LC 57-10515. 1957. Ballantine Books.
Old Corner Cupboard: Or, The Every-Day Life of Every People... Susan W Jewett. LC 7-9731. Truman and Spofford.
Old Countess. Anne Douglas Sedgwick. LC 27-7000. 1927. Houghton Mifflin Company.
Old Countess: Or, The Two Proposals. Ann Sophia Winterbotham Stephens. LC 8-12409. T. B. Peterson & Brothers.
Old Country. 1956. 2.98 o.p. (ISBN 0-517-03052-7); deluxe ed. 5.00 o.p. (ISBN 0-517-50705-6). Crown.
Old Country. de luxe illustrated ed. Shalom Rabinowitz. LC 65-7746. (Collected stories of Sholom Aleichem). 1965. Crown Publishers.
Old Country: A Romance. Henry John Newbolt. LC 8-4466. 1907. E. P. Dutton and Company.
Old Country & Seven More Years. Siegfried Sassoon. LC 76-6598. (BCL Ser.: No. I & II). Repr. of 1939 ed. 34.50 (ISBN 0-404-15295-3). AMS Pr.
Old Country House. Richard Le Gallienne. LC 2-27735. 1902. Harper & Brothers.
Old Country Idylls. John Stafford. LC 8-13886. 1896. Dodd, Mead and Company.
Old Country Tales. Sholom Aleichem. LC 79-13846. 1979. pap. 4.95 (ISBN 0-399-50394-3, Perige). Putnam Pub Group.
Old Country Tales. Sholom Aleichem. Tr. by Curt Leviant. 1969. pap. 0.95 o.p. (ISBN 0-446-65160-5, 65-160). Paperback Lib.
Old Country Tales. Sholom Aleichem. Tr. by Curt Leviant. (YA) 1966. 5.95 o.p. Putnam.
Old Country Tales. Shalom Rabinowitz. Ed. by Curt Leviant. LC 66-20261.
Old Country Tales: By Sholom Aleichem. Selected, Tr., Introd., by Curt Leviant. Shalom Rabinowitz. Ed. by Curt Leviant. LC 66-202696. 1966. 5.95. Putnam.
Old Courtyard. Katharine Sarah Gadsden Macquoid. (On cover: Lovell's Westminister series, no. 7). J. W. Lovell Company.
Old Creole Days. George Washington Cable. LC 72-84524. (Illus.). 1974. 9.50 (ISBN 0-403-03056-0). Scholarly Press.
Old Creole Days. George Washington Cable. LC 73-96486. (works of George W. Cable). (Illus.). 1970. Garrett Press.
Old Creole Days. George Washington Cable. LC 79-83932. 1969. Mnemosyne Pub. Co.
Old Creole Days. George Washington Cable. 1879. C. Scribner's Sons.
Old Creole Days... George Washington Cable. LC 12-15058. 1883. C. Scribner's Sons.
Old Creole Days. George Washington Cable. 1883. C. Scribner's Sons.
Old Creole Days. George Washington Cable. 1890. C. Scribner's Sons.
Old Creole Days. George Washington Cable. LC 6-21886. 1897. C. Scribner's Sons.
Old Creole Days. George Washington Cable & Bikle, Lucy Leffingwell (Cable) LC 37-10490. 1937. C. Scribner's Sons.
Old Creole Days see Collected Works.
Old Creole Days: A Story of Creole Life. George Washington Cable. LC 7-48146. 1907. C. Scribner's Sons.
Old Cronnak. Joseph Haldane. The Decker Publishing Company.
Old Crow. Alice Brown. LC 22-19052. 1922. The Macmillan Company.
Old Crow. Shena Mackay. LC 68-11932. 1968. McGraw-Hill.
Old Crowd. William F Fitzgerald. LC 31-27195. 1931. Longmans, Green and Co.
Old Curiosity Shop. Charles Dickens. LC 72-192922. (Penguin English library EL75). (Illus.). 1972. (0.60, 3.75 u.s.) (ISBN 0-14-043075-X). Penguin.
Old Curiosity Shop. Charles Dickens. LC 6-26422. (On cover: Lovell's library, v. 4, no. 144). 1883. J. W. Lovell Company.
Old Curiosity Shop. Charles Dickens. Ed. by Whipple, Edwin Percy. LC 15-23133. (Half-title: Works of Charles Dickens. New illustrated library ed. vol. vii). Houghton Mifflin Company.
Old-Curiosity Shop. Charles Dickens. (Half-title: Everyman's library, ed. by Ernest Rhys. Fiction. no. 173). 1908. J. M. Dent & Co.
Old Curiosity Shop. Charles Dickens. (Centenary Edition of the Works of Charles Dickens in Thirty-Six Volumes). (Half-title: The centenary edition of the works of Charles Dickens in 36 volumes). 1910. Chapman & Hall, Ltd.
Old Curiosity Shop. Charles Dickens. LC 25-27464. (Rittenhouse classics). 1925. Macrae, Smith Company.
Old Curiosity Shop. Charles Dickens. LC 36-37035. (Half-title: Everyman's library, ed. by Ernest Rhys. Fiction. no. 173). 1933. J. M. Dent & Sons, Ltd.
Old Curiosity Shop. Charles Dickens. LC 41-5029. The Heritage Press.
Old Curiosity Shop. Charles Dickens & Becker, May (Lamberton) 1873- LC 43-18838. (On cover: Great illustrated classics). 1943. Dodd, Mead & Company.
Old Curiosity Shop: And Master Humphrey's Clock. Charles Dickens. Ed. by Dickens, Charles. LC 4-15303. 1892. Macmillan and Co.
Old Curiosity Shop: And Reprinted Pieces. diamond ed. Charles Dickens. LC 6-26424. 1867. Ticknor and Fields.
Old Curiosity Shop: And Reprinted Pieces. illustrated household ed. Charles Dickens. LC 6-26423. 1870. Fields, Osgood & Co.
Old Curiosity Shop: And Reprinted Pieces. Charles Dickens & Whipple, Edwin Percy. LC 6-37243. (Half-title: Works... New illustrated library ed. vol. vi-vii). 1876. Hurd and Houghton.
Old Curiosity Shop. Hard Times. Charles Dickens. LC 9-820. Aldine Book Publishing Co.
Old Curiosity Shop. Sketches. Charles Dickens. LC 15-203051. (Works of Charles Dickens. Globe ed.). 1870. Hurd and Hougton.
Old Curiosity Shop: Sketches.--Pt. I... Charles Dickens. LC 8-30893. 1867. Hurd and Houghton.
Old Curiosity Shop. With the Orig Illus by Phiz. Charles Dickens & Hablot Knight Browne. LC 66-5543. (Macdonald illus. classics, 13). 1966. 3.50. Macdonald.
Old Curiousity Shop: T. V. Tie-in. Charles Dickens. Ed. by Angus Easson. 1979. pap. 3.95 (ISBN 0-14-005436-7). Penguin.
Old Dacres' Darling: A Novel. Annie Hall Thomas Cudlip. LC 6-31165. (On cover: Lippincott's series of select novels. no. 133). 1892. J. B. Lippincott Company.
Old Dance Master. William Romaine Paterson. LC 11-11322. 1911. 1.25. Little, Brown, and Company.
Old Dark House. John Boynton Priestley. LC 28-3978. 1928. Harper & Brothers.
Old Dark House. John Boynton Priestley. LC 41-38131. Harper & Brothers.
Old Darman: A Story of New England. Charles LeRoy Goodell. LC 6-46349. 1906. Funk & Wagnalls Company.
Old Delabole. Eden Phillpotts. LC 15-20559. 1915. 1.50. The Macmillan Company.
Old Detective's Pupil: Or, The Mysterious Crime of Madison Square. John Russell Coryell. (On cover: The secret service series, no. 17). 1889. Street & Smith.
Old Devotions. Ursula Perrin. LC 82-9663. 15.95 (ISBN 0-385-27656-7). Dial Press.
Old Dick. L. A. Morse. 240p. 1981. pap. 2.25 (ISBN 0-380-78329-0, 78329). Avon.
Old Die Rich: And Other Science Fiction Stories, with Working Notes and an Analysis of Each Story. H. L Gold. LC 55-7217. 1955. Crown Publishers.
Old Die Young. Richard Lockridge. LC 80-7775. 9.95 (ISBN 0-690-01948-3). Lippincott & Crowell.
Old Doc. Oliver Hazard Perry Pepper. LC 57-11950. 1957. Lippincott.
Old Doc. Elizabeth Seifert. LC 73-79147. 1973. 5.95. Aeonian Press.
Old Doc. Elizabeth Seifert. LC 46-3699. 1946. Dodd, Mead & Company.
Old Doctor. Gaddis, Peggy, pseud. 1943. Arcadia House, Inc.
Old Doctor. A Romance of Queer Village. John Vance Cheney. LC 6-27171. 1885. D. Appleton and Company.
Old Doctor's Son. Mary Dwinell Chellis. LC 6-23404. (Added t.-p.: The standard series of temperance tales v. 2). H. A. Young & Co.
Old Dorset. facs. ed. Robert Cameron Rogers. LC 76-140338. (Short Story Index Reprint Ser). 1896. 12.00 (ISBN 0-8369-3730-9). Ayer Co.

Old Dorset: Chronicles of a New York Country-Side. Robert Cameron Rogers. LC 76-140338. (Short story index reprint series). 1970. Books for Libraries Press.
Old Dorset: Chronicles of a New York Countryside. Robert Cameron Rogers. LC 7-40735. 1897. G. P. Putnam's Sons.
Old Ebenezer. Opie Percival Read. LC 7-36500. Laird & Lee.
Old Electricity, the Lighting Detective: Or, Through by Night. Harlan Page Halsey. LC 7-1180. (On cover: The calumet series, no. 12). G. Munro.
Old Enchantment. Larry Barretto. LC 28-905068. 1928. The John Day Company.
Old English Baron. Clara Reeve & Morley, Henry, 1822-1894, Ed. LC 25-7160. (Cassell's national library, vol. III, no. 129). 1888. Cassell & Company, Limited.
Old English Baron: A Gothic Story. Clara Reeve. Ed. by James Trainer. LC 77-30182. (Oxford paperbacks). 1977. 4.75 (ISBN 0-19-281226-2). Oxford University Press.
Old English Baron: A Gothic Story; Ed., Introd. by James Trainer. Clara Reeve. Ed. by James Trainer. LC 67-109149. (Oxford English novels). 1967. 3.40. Oxford Univ. Pr.
Old English Peep Show. Peter Dickinson. LC 69-12273. 1969. 4.95. Harper & Row.
Old Faces & New Wine. Alejandro Morales. Ed. by Alurista & Jose Monleon. Tr. by Max Martinez from Sp. LC 81-89601. (Illus.). 132p. (Orig.). 1981. pap. 5.00 (ISBN 0-939558-00-9). Maize Pr.
Old Factory: A Lancashire Story. William Westall. LC 44-35369. 1885. Cassell & Company, Limited.
Old Family Doctor. Henry Clark Brainerd. LC 5-2439. 1905. The A. H. Clark Company.
Old Farm: A Novel. Ettie Stephens Prichard. LC 34-223708. 1934. D. Appleton-Century Company, Incorporated.
Old Farm House. Caroline H Butler Laing. LC 7-14109. 1855. C. H. Davis.
Old-Fashioned Darling. Charles Simmons. (Signet bk., Q5355). 1973. 0.95. New American Lib.
Old-Fashioned Darling. Charles Simmons. LC 77-169658. 1971. 5.95. Coward, McCann & Geoghegan.
Old-Fashioned Heart. Ruby Mildred Ayres. LC 53-7223. 1953. Arcadia House.
Old-Fashioned Love Story. Mildred E. Reeves. 224p. 1974. 7.50 o.p. (ISBN 0-682-47928-4). Exposition.
Old-Fashioned Romance. Alma Newton. LC 24-113336. 1924. Minton, Balch & Company.
Old-Fashioned Tales. Zona Gale. LC 33-28505. 1933. D. Appleton-Century Company, Incorporated.
Old-Fashioned Woman. Amasa Pierce Thornton. LC 13-23024. 1913. Printed for the Author by Burr Printing House.
Old Father Antic. Philip Stevenson. LC 61-17418. International Publishers.
Old Father Frost. V. Odoyevsky. 22p. 1981. pap. 2.00 (ISBN 0-8285-2216-2, Pub. by Progress Pubs USSR). Imported Pubns.
Old Father of Waters. Alan Le May. LC 28-7951. 1928. Doubleday, Doran & Company, Inc.
Old Father Waters. Andrew Magnus Fleming. LC 36-736631. 1936. Meador Publishing Company.
Old Fears. John Wooley & Ron Wolfe. LC 81-21801. 1982. 13.95 (ISBN 0-531-04387-8). Watts.
Old-Field School-Girl. Mary Virginia Terhune. 1897. C. Scribner's Sons.
Old Fighting Days. Ernest Robertson Punshon. LC 21-268958. 1921. A. A. Knopf.
Old Fires and Profitable Ghosts: A Book of Stories. Quiller-Couch, Arthur Thomas. LC 72-10813. (Short story index reprint series). 1973. (ISBN 0-8369-4224-8). Books for Libraries Press.
Old Fires and Profitable Ghosts: A Book of Stories. Arthur Thomas Quiller-Couch. LC 1-30039. 1900. C. Scribner's Sons.
Old Firm. Francis Morton Howard. LC 24-172516. 1924. E. P. Dutton & Company.
Old First. Lawrence Perry. LC 31-6595. Farrar & Rinehart Incorporated.
Old First: The Biography of a Protestant Church. Edwin C. Coon. 1973. 4.00 (ISBN 0-87164-071-6). William-F.
Old Fish Hawk. Mitchell F Jayne. LC 71-85115. 1970. 5.95. Lippincott.
Old Flame. Alan Patrick Herbert. LC 25-8054. 1925. Doubleday, Page & Company.
Old Flute-Player: A Romance of to-Day. Edward Marshall & Dazey, Charles Turner. LC 10-22795. 1.50. G. W. Dillingham Company.
Old Fogy. Jeannette Ritchie Hadermann Walworth. LC 8-33132. The Merriam Company.
Old Folks' Wooing. Alice Marie Celeste Durand. Tr. by Robins, E. P. (On cover: Once a week library, v. 11, no. 19). P. F. Collier.
Old For-Ever" An Epic of Beyond the Indus. Alfred Ollivant. LC 23-9241. 1923. Doubleday, Page & Company.
Old Fort Duquesne: A Tale of the Early Toils, Struggles and Adventures of the First Settlers at the Forks of Ohio, 1754 ... 1844. Cook's Literary Depot.
Old Fort Duquesne: Or, Captain Jack, the Scout. An Historical Novel with Copious Notes. Charles McKnight. LC 7-20107. 1873. Peoples Monthly Publishing Co.
Old Frame School-House: Or, Surmounting the Barrier. An Illustrated Story... Allen H Olin. LC 99-4000. 1899. The Daily Herald.
Old Friend. Van Siller. LC 73-79723. 192p. 1973. 4.95 o.p. (ISBN 0-385-04681-2). Doubleday.
Old Friend. Hilda Van Siller. LC 73-79723. 1973. 4.95 (ISBN 0-385-04681-2). Published for the Crime Club by Doubleday.
Old Friend of the Family. Fred Saberhagen. 256p. 1981. pap. 2.50 (ISBN 0-441-62161-9). Ace Bks.
Old Friends. Andrew Lang. LC 70-101914. Repr. of 1890 ed. 10.00 (ISBN 0-404-03838-7). AMS Pr.
Old Friends. A Remembrancer of Beloved Companions: and Years Bygone ... LC 7-32598. 1835. Bliss, Wadsworth and Co.
Old Friends and New. Sarah Orne Jewett. LC 79-90584. (Short story index reprint series). 1969. Books for Libraries Press.
Old Friends and New. Sarah Orne Jewett. LC 4-15130. 1879. Houghton, Osgood and Company.
Old Friends and New. Sarah Orne Jewett. LC 79-10816. 1979. 25.00. Scholarly Press.
Old Friends & New see Collected Works.
Old Fritz and the New Era. Klara Muller Mundt. Tr. by Langley, Peter. LC 7-24121. (Germany in storm and stress). 1868. D. Appleton & Company.
Old Fritz and the New Era. Klara Muller Mundt. Tr. by Langley, Peter. LC 16-1236. (historical romances of Louisa Muhlbach pseud.). D. Appleton and Company.
Old Fulkerson's Clerk. Jeannette Ritchie Hadermann Walworth. (On cover: Cassell's "rainbow" series, no. 12). 1888. Cassell & Company, Limited.
Old Fusee: Or, The Cannoneer's Last Shot. A Tale of Bloody Antietam. Anthony P Morris. (War library Pocket ed. v. 1, no. 4). 1883. Novelist Publishing Co.
Old Garth: A Story of Sicily. James De Mille. (Seaside library. v. 75, no. 1512). 1883. G. Munro.
Old Gentleman of the Black Stock. Thomas Nelson Page. LC 4-15146. (The ivory series). 1897. C. Scribner's Sons.
Old Gentleman of the Black Stock. Thomas Nelson Page. LC 6041. 1900. C. Scribner's Sons.
Old Gentleman of the Black Stock. Thomas Nelson Page & Christy, Howard Chandler, 1873- Illus. LC 27-136551. 1901. C. Scribner's Sons.
Old Girl. Joshua Gidding. LC 81-1479. 1981. 12.95 (ISBN 0-89340-339-3). J. Curley & Associates.
Old Girl: A Novel. Joshua Gidding. LC 79-26850. 12.95 (ISBN 0-03-052196-3) (ISBN 0-03-057998-8). Holt, Rinehart and Winston.
Old Glory. Mary Raymond Shipman Andrews. LC 16-15660. 1916. C. Scribner's Sons.
Old Glory. Anne Duffield. LC 43-418571. 1943. Arcadia House, Inc.
Old Glory and the Real-Time Freaks. Ralph Blum. (Dell book. 6652). 1973. 1.25. Dell.
Old Glory and the Real-Time Freaks: A Children's Story and Patriotic Good Time Book, with Maps. Ralph Blum. LC 79-178721. 1972. Delacorte Press.
Old Goat: A Simple Picture of Home Life in America. Tiffany Thayer. LC 37-6378. 1937. J. Messner, Inc.
Old Gods Laugh. Frank Yerby. 1973. (pbk) 1.50. Dell Pub. Co.
Old Gods Laugh, a Modern Romance. Frank Yerby. LC 64-15225. 1964. Dial Press.
Old Gods Waken. Manly Wade Wellman. LC 78-22804. 1979. 7.95 (ISBN 0-385-14807-0). Doubleday.
Old Gorgon Graham: More Letters from a Self-Made Merchant to His Son. George Horace Lorimer. LC 4-228609. 1904. Doubleday, Page & Company.
Old Goriot. Honore De Balzac. Tr. by Ellen Marriage. Saintsbury, George Eduard Bateman, 1845-1933. Translation of Le Pere Goriot. (Half-title: Everyman's library, ed. by Ernest Rhys. Fiction. no. 170). 1908. J. M. Dent & Co.
Old Goriot. Honore De Balzac. 1972. pap. 1.35 o.p. (ISBN 0-460-01170-7, EP1170, Evman). Dutton.
Old Goriot (Le Pere Goriot) Tr. by Ellen Marriage, with a Preface by George Saintsbury. Honore De Balzac. Tr. by Ellen Marriage. LC 4-18469. (Half-title:... Comedie humaine...). 1901. J. M. Dent and Co.
Old Graham Place. Etta M Gardner. LC 1-30287. The Abbey Press.
Old Gray Homestead. Frances Parkinson Wheeler Keyes. LC 19-5197. 1919. Houghton Mifflin Company.
Old Gray Homestead, and The Career of David Noble: Two Full-Length Novels. One Volume Ed. Frances Parkinson Wheeler Keyes. LC 52-1039. Liveright.
Old Greasybeard: Tales from the Cumberland Gap. Leonard Roberts. LC 69-20398. (Illus.). 1980. pap. text ed. 7.95 (ISBN 0-933302-04-5). Pikeville Coll.
Old Greenbottom Inn and Other Stories. George Marion McClellan. LC 74-144654. (Illus.). 1975. 8.00 (ISBN 0-404-00199-8). AMS Press.
Old Grey Gods. Alfred Greenwood Hales. 1922. Hodder and Stoughton, Ltd.
Old Grey Homestead. Frances Parkinson Wheeler Keyes. 304p. 1974. pap. 1.50 o.p. (532-15135-150). Manor Bks.
Old Gumber's Mill: A Mystery Story. Ella Jane Kyle. LC 29-13371. 1928. The Ben Hur Press.
Old Harbor. William John Hopkins. LC 9-28708. 1909. Houghton Mifflin Company.
Old Harbor Town. A Novel. Augusta Campbell Watson. LC 8-34345. 1892. G. W. Dillingham.
Old Harbor Town: A Novel. Augusta Campbell Watson. LC 42-28434. 1907. H. D. Utley.
Old Haven. David Cornel De Jong. LC 38-27774. 1938. Houghton Mifflin Company.
Old Heart Goes a-Journeying. Rudolf Ditzen, pseud. LC 36-30627. 1936. Simon and Schuster.
Old Heidelberg. Wilhelm Meyer-Forster. Tr. by Chapelle, Max. LC 3-32588. 1903. Dodge & Metcalf.
Old Heidelberg. Wilhelm Meyer-Forster & Chapelle, Max, Tr. LC 4-35076. 1904. A. Wessels Company.
Old Hell. Emmett Gowen. LC 37-23966. (Modern age books. Blue seal books, no. 4). Modern Age Books.
Old Helmet. Susan Warner. LC 8-33701. 1864. R. Carter & Brothers.
Old Hepsy. Mary Andrews Denison. LC 6-407895. 1858. A. B. Burdick.
Old Herbaceous. 1st American Ed. Reginald Arkell. LC 51-9199. 1951. Harcourt, Brace.
Old Hickory. Noel Bertram Gerson. LC 64-11540. 1964. Doubleday.
Old Hicks the Guide. Charles Wilkins Webber. LC 77-104591. 1970. (ISBN 0-8398-2158-1). Literature House.
Old Hicks, the Guide: Or, Adventures in the Camanche Country in Search of a Gold Mine. Charles Wilkins Webber. LC 8-36747. 1848. Harper & Brothers.
Old Home. Rebecca Wells. LC 13-21266. Roxburgh Publishing Company, Inc.
"Old Home House". Joseph Crosby Lincoln. 1907. A. S. Barnes & Company.
Old Home Town. Rose Wilder Lane. LC 35-18417. 1935. Longmans, Green and Co.
Old Home Town. Agnes Sligh Turnbull. LC 33-31311. Fleming H. Revell Company.
Old Home Town: A Novel. Rupert Hughes. LC 26-10693. 1926. Harper & Brothers.
Old Home Week. Minnie Hite Moody. LC 38-27553. J. Messner, Inc.
Old Homestead: Novelized from Denman Thompson's Great Play: with Illustrations from Scenes in the Play. authorized ed. John Russell Coryell & Thompson, Denman. LC 8-5227. G. W. Dillingham Company.
Old Homstead. Ann Sophia Winterbotham Stephens. LC 8-14267. 1855. Bunce & Brother.
Old House: A Novel. Cecile Tormay & Torday, E., Tr. LC 22-20687. 1922. R. M. McBride & Company.
Old House, and Other Tales. Fedor Kuzmich Teternikov. LC 74-11995. (Series: New Adelphi Library, V. 44.). 1974. (ISBN 0-8371-7715-4). Greenwood Press.
Old House at "Four Corners,". Margaret K Parker. A. D. F. Randolph & Co.
Old House at Glenaran. Anna Hanson McKenney Dorsey. LC 43-21297. John Murphy Company.
Old House by the Boyne: Or, Recollections of an Irish Borough. Mary Anne Madden Sadlier. LC 42-26369. 1865. D. & J. Sadlier & Co.
Old House by the River. William Cowper Prime. 1853. Harper & Brothers.
Old House of Fear. Russell Kirk. 1961. 4.95 o.p. (ISBN 0-8303-0015-5). Fleet.
Old House of Fear: 2nd Ed. Russell Kirk. 1965. 4.95. Fleet.
Old House on Briar Hill. Isabella Grant Meredith. LC 11-15071. Dodd & Mead.
Old Hurricane: A Novel. Julia A Flisch. LC 25-5389. Thomas Y. Crowell Company.
Old Indianola: Life in a Frontier Seaport. Native Texan Ed. Lois Lucille Gray. LC 50-4318. 1950. Naylor.
Old Infant, and Similar Stories. Will Carleton. LC 6-19909. 1896. Harper & Brothers.
Old Inn: Or, The Travellers' Entertainment. Josiah Barnes. LC 6-7204. 1855. J. C. Derby.
Old Ironsides. rev. ed. Thomas P. Horgan. Ed. by Paul Quinn. LC 72-89565. (Illus.). 128p. (Orig.). 1980. pap. 9.95 (ISBN 0-911658-10-6). Yankee Bks.
Old Ironsides". Anna Maria Rose Wright & Carr, Harry, 1877-1936. LC 26-9565. Grosset & Dunalp.
Old Italian Version of the Navigatio Sancti Brendani. LC 31-35525. (Publications of the Philological society. X). 1931. Oxford University Press, H. Milford.
Old Jest. Jennifer Johnston. LC 79-7518. 1980. 8.95 (ISBN 0-385-15447-X). Doubleday.
Old Jest. Jennifer Johnston. LC 80-12178. 1980. 10.95 (ISBN 0-8161-3091-4). G. K. Hall.
Old Jim Case of South Hollow. Edward Irving Rice. 1909. Doubleday, Page & Company.
Old Joe: And Other Vesper Stories. Shepherd Knapp. The Abingdon Press.
Old Jolliffe: Not a Goblin Story. By the Spirit of a Little Bell, Awakened by "the Chimes". By the Author of "A Trap to Catch a Sunbeam," "Only"... Matilda Anne MacKarness. 1850. J. Munroe and Company.
Old Judge: Or, Life in a Colony. Thomas Chandler Haliburton. LC 7-3087. 1849. Stringer & Townsend.
Old Judge Priest. Irvin Shrewsbury Cobb. LC 75-120561. 1970. AMS Press.
Old Judge Priest. Irvin Shrewsbury Cobb. LC 16-9778. George H. Doran Company.
Old Judge Priest. Irvin Shrewsbury Cobb. LC 32-10941. 1932. Doubleday, Doran & Company, Inc.
Old Judge Priest. Irvin Shrewsbury Cobb. LC 37-225093. 1935. Doubleday, Doran & Company, Inc.
Old Jules. Mari Sandoz. 1975. Repr. 10.95 (ISBN 0-8038-5344-0). Hastings.
Old Jules Country. Mari Sandoz. 1965. 7.95 (ISBN 0-8038-5345-9). Hastings.
Old June Weather. Ernest Raymond. LC 74-5418. 1974. 6.95. Saturday Review Press.
Old Kaskaskia: A Novel. Mary Hartwell Catherwood. 1893. Houghton, Mifflin and Company.
Old 'Kaskia Days. Elizabeth Holbrook. LC 7-6118. 1893. The Schulte Publishing Company.
Old Kensington. A Novel. Anne Isabella Thackeray Ritchie. LC 7-41668. 1873. Harper & Brothers.
Old Knowledge. Stephen Lucius Gwynn. LC 1-25417. 1901. The Macmillan Company.
Old Kyle's Boy. Frank Roderus. LC 80-1661. 1981. 9.95 (ISBN 0-385-15937-4). Doubleday.
Old Kyle's Boy. Frank Roderus. LC 82-4628. 1982. 12.95 (ISBN 0-89340-509-4). J. Curley.
Old Ladies. Hugh Walpole. LC 24-23734. George H. Doran Company.
Old Lady see Old New York.
Old Lady: A Novel. Anne Green. LC 47-30285. 1947. Harper & Brothers.
Old Lady Esteroy. Edith Everett Taylor. LC 34-691. E. P. Dutton & Co., Inc.
Old Lady Mary. A Story of the Seen and the Unseen. Margaret Oliphant Wilson Oliphant. 1884. Roberts Brothers.
Old Lady Mary. A Story of the Seen and the Unseen. Margaret Oliphant Wilson Oliphant. (On cover: Lovell's library, v. 7, no. 368). 1884. J. W. Lovell Company.
Old Lady Mary. A Story of the Seen and Unseen. Margaret Oliphant Wilson Oliphant. (On cover: Seaside library. Pocket ed., no. 410). 1885. G. Munro.
Old Lady Number 31. old lady number thirty-one ed. Mary Louise Foster. LC 9-7140. 1909. The Century Co.
Old Lady's Shoes. Samuel Tupper. 1934. R. M. McBride & Company.
Old Lattimer's Legacy. Joseph Smith Fletcher. LC 29-18008. E. J. Clode,Inc.
Old Leaves: Gathered from Household Words. William Henry Wills. LC 8-36889. 1860. Harper & Brothers.
Old Liberty. Marshall Terry. LC 61-7276. 1961. Viking Press.
Old Liberty see Don't Blow Your Cool.
Old Lim Jucklin: The Opinions of an Open-Air Philosopher. Opie Percival Read. LC 5-34696. 1905. Doubleday, Page & Company.
Old Log School House. Furnitured with Incidents of School Life, Notes of Travel, Poetry, Hints to Teachers and Pupils, and Miscellaneous Sketches... Alexander Clark. LC 6-25365. 1861. Leary, Getz & Co.
Old London... Edward Frederic Benson. LC 37-21955. D. Appleton-Century Company, Incorporated.
Old Love. Isaac Bashevis Singer. LC 79-18765. 10.95 (ISBN 0-374-22581-8). Farrar, Straus & Giroux.
Old Love. Isaac Bashevis Singer. LC 80-15144. 1980. 10.95 (ISBN 0-89340-266-4). J. Curley.
Old Love & Other Stories. Isaac Bashevis Singer. 273p. 1979. 10.95 (ISBN 0-374-22581-8). FS&G.
Old Love for New. James Noble Gifford. LC 39-15274. 1938. Gramercy Publishing Co.

Old Love for New. Gay Rutherford. LC 39-152743. Gramercy Publishing Co.

Old Love or the New? Henrietta Eliza Vaughan Stannard. (seaside library. v. 36. no. 732). 1880. G. Munro.

Old Love Stories with New Variations: Or, The Reward of a Useful, Unselfish Life. Laura Isabel Ireland. LC 19-10686. Austin Publishing Company.

Old Lover's Ghost. Zenith Jones Brown. LC 40-118169. 1940. C. Scribner's Sons.

Old Loves. Weymer Jay Mills. LC 12-24061. 1912. Dodd, Mead and Company.

Old M'sieur's Secret. Henriette Etiennette Fanny Reybaud & Armand, Louise, Tr. LC 16-7551. 1882. G. W. Carleton & Co.; Etc., Etc.

Old Madame: & Other Tragedies. Harriet Elizabeth Prescott Spofford. LC 2343. 1900. R. G. Badger & Co.

Old Madhouse. William Frend De Morgan & De Morgan, Evelyn (Pickering) LC 19-12984. 1919. H. Holt and Company.

Old Maid Kindled. Alfred J. Cohen. LC 6-26736. 1890. G. W. Dillingham.

Old Maid Street. Elizabeth C. Morton. 4.50 o.p. Vantage.

Old Maid: The 'fifties. Edith Newbold Jones Wharton. LC 24-114691. (Her Old New York. v. 2). 1924. D. Appleton and Company.

Old Maids, and Burglars in Paradise. Elizabeth Stuart Phelps H. D. Ward Ward. LC 8-36036. 1887. Houghton, Mifflin and Company.

Old Maids' Club. Israel Zangwill. LC 8-37869. Tait, Sons & Company.

Old Maid's Love: A Dutch Tale Told in English. Jozua Marius Willen Van Der Poorten Schwartz. LC 8-2901. (On cover: Harper's Franklin square library, no. 709). 1891. Harper & Brothers.

Old Maid's Love: A Dutch Tale Told in English. authorized ed. Jozua Marius Willen Van Der Poorten Schwartz. LC 8-29001. (Lovell's international series, no. 153). J. W. Lovell Company.

Old Maid's Love: A Dutch Tale Told in English. Jozua Marius Willen Van Der Poorten Schwartz. LC 3-5761. 1891. United States Book Company.

Old Maid's Paradise. Elizabeth Stuart Phelps Ward. (On cover: Riverside paper series, no. 9). 1885. Houghton, Mifflin and Company.

Old Maid's Vengeance. Frances Powell Case. LC 11-5408. 1911. 1.25. C. Scribner's Sons.

Old Main, The Cabinet of Antiquities. Honore De Balzac. Tr. by William Walton. LC 42-281313. The Neale Company.

Old Mali and the Boy. D. R. Sherman. LC 64-21457. 1964. Little, Brown.

Old Mammy Tales from Dixieland. S. J. Cocke. Repr. of 1926 ed. 18.00 (ISBN 0-527-18400-4). Kraus Repr.

Old Mam'selle's Secret. Malitt E. & H., E., Tr. LC 43-40886. (On cover: The Bijou series). 1892. The F. M. Lupton Publishing Company.

Old Mamselle's Secret. Eugenie John. Tr. by Smith, Mary Stuart (Harrison) LC 27-13693. (Seaside library. v. 59, no. 1210). 1882. G. Munro.

Old Ma'm'selle's Secret. Eugenie John. Tr. by Smith, Mary Stuart (Harrison) LC 7-9908. (On cover: Seaside library. Pocket ed. no. 858). G. Munro.

Old Mam'selle's Secret. After the German of E. Marlitt Pseud. Eugenie John. Tr. by Wister, Annis Lee (Furness) 1869. J. B. Lippincott & Co.

Old Mam'selle's Secret. After the German of E. Marlitt Pseud.... Eugenie John. Tr. by Wister, Annis Lee (Furness) LC 4-16863. 1896. J. B. Lippincott Company.

Old Mam'selle's Secret: After the German of E. Marlitt Pseud.... Eugenie John. Tr. by Wister, Annis Lee (Furness) LC 12-16082. 1911. J. B. Lippincott Company.

Old Man. Eugene MacLean. LC 29-11443. 1929. Coward-McCann, Inc.

Old Man & His Sons. Heoin Bru. Tr. by John F. West from Faroese. (Illus.). 1970. 5.95 (ISBN 0-8397-8412-0). Eriksson.

Old Man and Me. Elaine Dundy. LC 64-13763. 1964. Dutton.

Old Man & the Boy. Robert Chester Ruark. LC 57-10425. 1957. 8.95 (ISBN 0-03-027910-0). HR&W.

Old Man and the Bureaucrats. Mircea Eliade. LC 79-18963. 8.95 (ISBN 0-268-01497-3). University of Notre Dame Press.

Old Man and the Girl. Ernest Gebler. LC 68-14201. 1968. Doubleday.

Old Man and the Medal. Ferdinand Oyono. LC 73-146613. (American Library). 1971. 1.50. Collier Books.

Old Man & the Monkey King. Robert Durand. (Illus.). 96p. (Orig.). 1972. pap. 3.50 o.p. (ISBN 0-912264-32-2). Capra Pr.

Old Man and the Monkey-King: Legend. Robert Durand. LC 75-314241. (Illus.). 1972. (ISBN 0-912264-31-4) (ISBN 0-912264-32-2). Capricorn Press.

Old Man and the Sea. Ernest Hemingway. LC 52-11935. 1952. Scribner.

Old Man and the Sea. illustrated ed. Ernest Hemingway. LC 60-16337. 1960. Scribner.

Old Man and the Sea. school ed. Ernest Hemingway. LC 61-65751. 1961. Scribner.

Old Man and the Sky. Robert Portune. LC 58-5466. 1958. Putnam.

Old Man at the Railroad Crossing, and Other Tales. 1st Ed. William Maxwell. LC 66-107561. 1966. 3.95. Knopf.

Old Man at the Zoo. Angus Wilson. 1961. 4.50 o.p. (ISBN 0-670-52302-X). Viking Pr.

Old Man Curry. Charles Emmett Van Loan. LC 17-255137. George H. Doran Company.

Old Man Dies. Elizabeth Sprigge. LC 33-20286. 1933. The Macmillan Company.

Old Man Dies. Tr. from French by Bernard Frechtman. 1st Ed. Georges Simenon. LC 67-160851. 1967. 4.50. Harcourt.

Old Man Gilbert. Elizabeth Whitfield Croom Bellamy. LC 6-11692. Belford, Clarke & Company.

Old Man Goriot. Honore De Balzac. Ed. by Maugham, William Somerset. Tr. by Underwood, Charlotte. (Ten Greatest Novels of the World). 1949. J. C. Winston Co.

Old Man Greenhut and His Friends. David A Curtis. LC 11-23054. 1911. 1.20. Duffield and Company.

Old Man Greenlaw. Kenneth Payson Kempton. LC 36-4067. Farrar and Rinehart, Incorporated.

Old Man in the Corner. Emmuska Orczy. 340p. 1980. Repr. of 1908 ed. lib. bdg. 15.95x (ISBN 0-89968-196-4). Lightyear.

Old Man in the Corner: Twelve Mysteries by the Baroness Orczy. Emmuska Orczy. Ed. by E. G. Bleiler. (Orig.). 1980. pap. 3.50 (ISBN 0-486-23972-1). Dover.

Old Man in the Corner Unravels the Mystery of Brundenell Court and the Tytherton Case. Emmuska Orczy. LC 24-14170. George H. Doran Company.

Old Man in the Corner Unravels the Mystery of the Fulton Gardens Mystery, and the Moorland Tragedy. Emmuska Orczy. LC 25-14663. George H. Doran Company.

Old Man in the Corner Unravels the Mystery of the Pearl Necklace and the Tragedy in Bishop's Road. Emmuska Orczy. George H. Doran Company.

Old Man in the Corner Unravels the Mystery of the Russian Prince: And of Dog's Tooth Cliff. Emmuska Orczy. LC 24-710731. George H. Doran Company.

Old Man in the Corner Unravels the Mystery of the White Carnation and the Montmartre Hat. Emmuska Orczy. LC 25-812071. George H. Doran Company.

Old Man Jim's Book of Knowledge. Dick Dabney. (Berkley Medallion Book). 1977. 1.25 (ISBN 0-425-03320-1). Berkley Pub. Corp.

Old Man Jim's Book of Knowledge: A Novel. Dick Dabney. LC 72-13084. 1973. (ISBN 0-394-48418-5). Random House.

Old Man of the Mountain, and Seventeen Other Stories. Allan Seager. LC 50-7000. 1950. Simon and Schuster.

Old Man Savarin: And Other Stories. Edward William Thomson. LC 8-19957. (Half-title: Off-hand stories no. 1). T. Y. Crowell & Company.

Old Man Savarin Stories: Tales of Canada and Canadians. Edward William Thomson. LC 73-91557. (Literature of Canada: poetry and prose in reprint, 10). 1974. 15.00 (ISBN 0-8020-2077-1) (ISBN 0-8020-2077-1). University of Toronto Press.

Old Man Savarin Stories: Tales of Canada and Canadians. Edward William Thomson. LC 70-37567. (Short story index reprint series). (Illus.). 1972. (ISBN 0-8369-4126-8). Books for Libraries Press.

Old Man Savarin Stories: Tales of Canada and Canadians. Edward William Thomson. LC 17-24211. George H. Doran Company.

Old Man Tutt. Arthur Cheney Train. LC 41-40527. (His Criminal court series, v. 5). C. Scribner's Sons.

Old Man Whickutt's Donkey. Mary Calhoun. (Illus.). 1975. Parents' Magazine Press.

Old Manoa: A Novel. Glenn Allan. LC 32-19274. 1932. D. Appleton and Company.

Old Manor: A Tale of Inspector Higgins. Cecil Freeman Gregg. LC 46-7242. 1946. W. L. McNaughton.

Old Manor House. Charlotte Turner Smith. Ed. by Anne Henry Ehrenpreis. LC 79-378200. (Oxford English novels). (Illus.). 1969. Oxford U.P.

Old Manor House: A Novel. Charlotte Turner Smith. LC 74-8008. (Feminist Controversy in England, 1788-1810). 1974. (ISBN 0-8240-0880-4). Garland Pub.

Old Man's Birthday. Richmal Crompton Lamburn. LC 35-1533. 1935. Little, Brown and Company.

Old Man's Bride. Timothy Shay Arthur. LC 6-34132. 1853. C. Scribner.

Old Man's Coming by Gosta Gustaf-Janson: Translated from the Swedish for the First Time by Claude Napier. Gosta Gustaf-Janson. Tr. by Napier, Claude. LC 36-13877. 1936. A. A. Knopf.

Old Man's Darling. Alexander McVeigh Miller. (On cover: Munro's library, v. 1, no. 3). N. L. Munro.

Old Man's Darling. Alexander McVeigh Miller. (On cover: Lovell's library, no. 1247). 1888. J. W. Lovell Company.

Old Man's Darling. Alexander McVeigh Miller. LC 1-30131. (On cover: Eagle series, no. 192). 1900. Street & Smith.

Old Man's Darling. Allan Turpin. LC 76-41336. 1977. 7.95 (ISBN 0-698-10804-3). Coward, McCann & Geoghegan.

Old Man's Darling: And Jaquelina. Alexander McVeigh Miller. (On cover: Clover series, no. 119). 1896. Street & Smith.

Old Man's Diary Forty Years Ago, 1823-33, 4 Vols. in 1. J. Payne Collier. Repr. of 1872 ed. 29.00 (ISBN 0-404-07289-5). AMS Pr.

Old Man's Folly: A Novel. Floyd Dell. LC 26-17767. George H. Doran Company.

Old Man's Gold, and Other Stories. Ovid Williams Pierce. LC 75-19101. 6.95 (ISBN 0-8078-1257-9). University of North Carolina Press.

Old Man's Love. reprint ed. / introduction by a.l. rowse. ed. Anthony Trollope. LC 80-1905. (Selected Works of Anthony Trollope). ((Series: Trollope, Anthony, 1815-1882. Selections. 1981.). 1981. 50.00 (ISBN 0-405-14202-1). Arno Press.

Old Man's Love: A Novel. Anthony Trollope. LC 8-28885. (On cover: Lovell's library, v. 7, no. 367). 1884. J. W. Lovell Company.

Old Man's Love: By Anthony Trollope. Anthony Trollope. LC 37-27124. (Half-title: The world's classics, ccxliv). 1936. H. Milford, Oxford University Press.

Old Man's Place. John B Sanford. LC 36-1044. A. and C. Boni, Inc.

Old Man's Romances: A Tale. William Morse Cole. 1895. Copeland and Day.

Old Man's Youth and the Young Man's Old Age. William Frend De Morgan & De Morgan, Evelyn (Pickering) LC 21-4504. 1920. 2.00. H. Holt and Company.

Old Manse. G. L Johns. LC 75-22946. Johns.

Old Manse and a Few Mosses. Nathaniel Hawthorne. LC 7-3873. (On cover: Riverside literature series, no. 69). Houghton, Mifflin and Company.

Old Mark Langston: A Tale of Duke's Creek. Richard Malcolm Johnston. LC 7-10805. 1884. Harper & Brothers.

Old Martin Boscawen's Jest. Marian Calhoun Legare Reeves & Read, Emily, Joint Author. (On cover: Library of choice novels. no. 59). 1878. D. Appleton and Company.

Old Masters. Thomas P Baird. LC 63-13502. 1963. Harcourt, Brace & World.

Old Masters: A Novel. Thomas P Baird. 1979. 2.25 (ISBN 0-380-45088-7). Avon Books.

Old May Coyote. Clara Kern Bayliss. LC 8-21867. 1908. T.Y. Crowell & Co.

Old Men at the Zoo. Angus Wilson. LC 61-13729. 1961. Viking Press.

Old Men of the Sea: A Romance of Adventure in the South Pacific. Compton Mackenzie. LC 24-23173. 1924. Frederick A. Stokes Company.

Old Mill. Allen Eppes. LC 45-270. 1944. Gramercy Publishing Company.

Old Mill... Philip Whitwell Wilson. LC 46-8523. 1946. Rinehart & Company, Inc.

Old Mill. Watkins Eppes Wright. LC 45-270. 1944. Gramercy Pub. Co.

Old Mill Mystery. Arthur Williams Marchmont. LC 7-20447. (On cover: Mayflower library, no. 7). 1892. J. A. Taylor and Company.

Old Mill on the Withrose. Henry Stanislaus Spalding. LC 10-25678. 1910. Benziger Brothers.

Old Misery. Hugh Pendexter. The Bobbs-Merrill Company.

Old Miss, a Novel. Thomas Bowyer Campbell. LC 29-185453. 1929. Houghton Mifflin Company.

Old Missionary. A Narrative in Four Chapters. William Wilson Hunter. LC 3-12425. A. D. F. Randolph & Company.

Old Mr. Davenant's Money. Frances Powell Case. 1908. C. Scribner's Sons.

Old Mr. Flood. Joseph Mitchell. LC 48-10354. 1948. Duell, Sloan and Pearce.

Old Mistresses' Apologue. Benjamin Franklin. Ed. by Whitfield Bell. 1956. pap. 3.50 (ISBN 0-939084-05-8). Rosenbach Mus and Lib.

Old Mitt Laughs Last. Clara Childs Puckette. 1944. The Bobbs-Merrill Company.

Old Mole: Being the Surprising Adventures in England of Herbert Jocelyn Beenham, M.A., Sometime Sixthform Master at Thrigsby Grammar School in the County of Lancaster. Gilbert Cannan. LC 14-1419. 1914. 1.35. D. Appleton and Company.

Old Moneypenny's. David Murphy. LC 3063. 1900. Cleveland Plain Dealer Print.

Old Monk's House Mystery. 1st. ed. Myrtle Adams. (Illus.). 1974. 4.50 (ISBN 0-533-01444-1). Vantage Press.

Old Morals, Small Continents, Darker Times. Philip F O'Connor. LC 70-158043. 1971. 5.95 (ISBN 0-87745-023-4). University of Iowa Press.

Old Mortality. Walter Scott. Ed. by Alexander. Welsh. LC 66-9577. (Riverside editions, B 98). 1966. Houghton Mifflin.

Old Mortality. Walter Scott. (On cover: Lovell's library, no. 641). 1885. J. W. Lovell Company.

Old Mortality. Walter Scott. Ed. by Montgomery, David Henry. LC 3-3027. (On cover: Classics for children). 1891. Ginn & Company.

Old Mortality... Walter Scott. LC 8-3026. 1893. Estes and Lauriat.

Old Mortality. Walter Scott. LC 2-242524.

Old Mortality. Walter Scott. (Half-title: Everyman's library, ed. by Ernest Rhys. Fiction no. 137). 1908. J. M. Dent & Co.

Old Mortality. Walter Scott. LC 36-37008. (Half-title: Everyman's library, ed. by Ernest Rhys. Fiction. no. 137). 1932. J. M. Dent & Sons, Ltd.

Old Mortality. Walter Scott & Angus Calder. LC 75-322754. (Penguin English library; EL 98). 1975. 3.95 (ISBN 0-14-043098-9). Penguin Books.

Old Mortality: King of Detectives; or, Piping the New York Mystery. (On cover: The secret service series, no. 9). 1888. Street & Smith.

Old Motley. Audrey Lucas. LC 38-27550. 1938. The Macmillan Company.

Old Mountain Hermit. James F Raymond. LC 5-6285. Broadway Publishing Company.

Old Mrs. Camelot. Felicity Winifred Carter. LC 44-8233. 1944. The Blakiston Company.

Old Mrs. Chundle and Other Stories with The Famous Tragedy of the Queen of Cornwall. Thomas Hardy & F. B Pinion. LC 78-322986. (New Wessex edition; v. 3). (Illus.). 1977. 5.50 (ISBN 0-333-19983-9). Macmillan.

Old Mrs. Ommanney Is Dead: By Margaret Erskine Pseud. 1st Ed. Wetherby Williams. LC 55-5269. 1955. Published for the Crime Club by by Doubleday.

Old Must Die. Audrey Gaines. LC 39-22342. 1939. Thomas Y. Crowell Company.

Old Myddelton's Money. Mary Cecil Hay. (Seaside library, v. 22, no. 427). G. Munro.

Old Myddelton's Money: A Novel. Mary Cecil Hay. (On cover: Lovell's library, v. 11, no. 590). 1885. J. W. Lovell Company.

Old Neighborhood. Avery Corman. 224p. 1981. pap. 2.95 (ISBN 0-553-14891-5). Bantam.

Old Neighborhood. Avery Corman. (General Ser.). 1980. lib. bdg. 12.95 (ISBN 0-8161-3146-5, Large Print Bks). G K Hall.

Old Neighborhood. Avery Corman. 1980. 10.95 o.p. (ISBN 0-671-41475-5, 41475, Linden Pr). S&S.

Old Neighborhood: A Novel. Avery Corman. LC 80-16946. 1980. 10.95 (ISBN 0-671-41475-5). Linden Press/Simon & Schuster.

Old Neighborhood: By Carol Holliston Pseud. James Noble Gifford. LC 51-13762. 1951. Arcadia House.

Old Neighbourhoods and New Settlements: Or, Christmas Evening Legends. Emma Dorothy Eliza Nevitte Southworth. LC 8-14253. 1853. A. Hart.

Old Nest. Rupert Hughes. LC 12-6558. 1912. The Century Co.

Old New-England Days. A Story of True Life. Sophie M Damon. LC 6-33172. 1887. Cupples and Hurd.

Old-New Land ("Alneuland") Theodor Herzl. Tr. by Levensohn, Lotta. LC 41-892144. 1941. Bloch Publishing Co.

Old New Orleans... Frances Tinker & Tinker, Edward Larocque, 1861- Joint Author. LC 31-2674. 1931. D. Appleton and Company.

Old New York, 4 bks in 1. Edith Wharton. Incl. False Dawn; Old Lady; Spark; New Year's Day. 1964. 4.95 o.p. (ISBN 0-684-10640-X, 140). Scribner.

Old Nick. Francis Woolsey Bronson. LC 28-6521. Doubleday, Doran & Company, Inc.

Old Nick: The Secret from an Old Wooden Box. Tim Burr. (Illus.). 16p. 1981. pap. 6.95. Dill Ent.

Old Nick's Camp-Meetin'. A Narration of Occurrences Thereat, in Which M. Satan Did Not Take a Hand, but Other People Did--Several in Fact. Thomas Pilgrim. (On cover: Satchel series no. 23). The Authors' Publishing Company.

Old Ninety-Nine's Cave. Elizabeth H Gray. LC 9-11153. 1909. The C. M. Clark Publishing Co.

Old Noll: Or, The Days of the Ironsides. A Tale of Oliver Cromwell's Times. Frederick William Robinson. (seaside library, v. 79, no. 1599). 1883. G. Munro.

Old Number Four. George Israel Putman. LC 65-22707. 1965. 4.50. Equity Pub. Corp.

Old Oak Chest. George Payne Richard Rainsford James. (Seaside library, v. 40, no. 814). 1880. G. Munro.
Old, Old Story: A Novel. Rosa Nouchette Carey. 1894. J. B. Lippincott Company.
Old One. David Middlebrook. LC 73-80996. 1973. 5.95 (ISBN 0-913522-01-5) (ISBN 0-913522-02-3). Urion Press.
Old One Looks on. Charles Pelton Jacobs. LC 27-2988. E. J. Clode, Inc.
Old Order and the New: A Novel of Africa. Wilfred Fowler. LC 65-11573. 1965. Macmillan.
Old Order Changes. William Hurrell Mallock. LC 75-1533. (Victorian Fiction: Novels of Faith and Doubt; 81). 1976. 40.00 (ISBN 0-8240-1605-X). Garland Pub.
Old Order Changes. William Hurrell Mallock. LC 354. Street & Smith.
Old Order Changeth: A Novel. Archibald Marshall. LC 15-162313. 1915. Dodd, Mead and Company.
Old Order: Stories of the South, from Flowering Judas, Pale Horse, Pale Rider, and The Leaning Tower. Katherine Anne Porter. LC 56-3944. (Harvest book, HB6). 1955. Harcourt, Brace.
Old Parish. Doran Hurley. LC 75-122724. (Short story index reprint series). 1970. Books for Libraries Press.
Old Parish. Doran Hurley. LC 38-27866. 1938. Longmans, Green and Co.
Old Peabody Pew: A Christmas Romance of a Country Church. Kate Douglas Smith Wiggin. LC 7-32837. 1907. Houghton, Mifflin and Company.
Old People. John Davys Beresford. LC 32-9673. E. P. Dutton & Co., Inc.
Old People and the Things That Pass. Louis Marie Anne Couperus. Tr. by Teixeira De Mattos, Alexander Louis. LC 18-66447. 1918. Dodd, Mead and Company.
Old Philadelphia... George Fort Gibbs. LC 31-22241. 1931. D. Appleton and Company.
Old Pines: And Other Stories. James Boyd. LC 52-12702. 1952. University of North Carolina Press.
Old Plantation: And What I Gathered There in an Autumn Month. James Hungerford. LC 7-9368. 1859. Harper & Brothers.
Old Plantation Days. Martha Sawyer Gielow. LC 2-28286. 1902. R. H. Russell.
Old Post-Road. Margaret Greenway McClelland. LC 7-15430. The Merriam Company.
Old Post-Road. Mary Greenway McClelland. LC 7-15430. 1894. The Merriam Company.
Old Powder Man. Joan Williams. LC 66-12377. 5.95. Harcourt.
Old Priory. Norah Robinson Lofts. LC 81-43066. 1982. 13.95 (ISBN 0-385-17581-7). Doubleday.
Old Priory. Norah Robinson Lofts. LC 82-15473. 1982. 14.95 (ISBN 0-8161-3422-7). G.K. Hall.
Old Pybus. Warwick Deeping. LC 28-23544. 1928. A. A. Knopf.
Old Quartz: The Nevada Detective. Eugene T Sawyer. LC 1341. (On cover: Magnet detective library. no. 118). 1900. Street & Smith.
Old Raclot's Million (Le Million Du Pere Raclot) From the French of Emile Richebourg. Emile I. E. Jules Emile Richebourg & Lewis, Mrs. Benjamin, Tr. LC 11-16147. Cassell Publishing Company.
Old Ramon. Jack Warner Schaefer. (Sandpiper Books). (Illus.). 1973. 0.95 (ISBN 0-395-15056-6). Houghton.
Old Ramon. Illustrated by Harold West. Jack Warner Schaefer. LC 60-5211. 1960. Houghton Mifflin.
Old Red, and Other Stories. Caroline Gordon. LC 79-164527. 1971. (ISBN 0-8154-0396-8). Cooper Square Publishers.
Old Red, and Other Stories. Edited by Lord Elton. Caroline Gordon & Charles George Gordon. 1963. Scribner.
Old Red Tavern... Mary A Ellison. 1849. Sabbath School Society.
Old Regime in France: The Court, Salons, and Theaters. Catherine Hannah Charlotte Elliott Jackson. (Seaside library, v. 62, no. 1270). 1882. G. Munro.
Old Reliable. Harris Dickson. LC 11-11320. 1.25. The Bobbs-Merrill Company.
Old Reliable. Pelham Grenville Wodehouse. LC 51-12860. 1951. Doubleday.
Old Reliable in Africa. Harris Dickson. LC 20-17655. 1.90. Frederick A. Stokes Company.
Old Road from Spain. Constance Holme. LC 48-17038. 1943. Penguin Books.
Old Room. Carl Ewald. Tr. by Teixeria De Mattos, Alexander Louis. LC 8-102753. 1908. C., Scribner's Sons.
Old Rose and Silver. Myrtle Reed. 1909. G. P. Putnam's Sons.
Old Rose and Silver. Myrtle Reed. LC 24-5832. 1914. Grosset & Dunlap.
Old Sailor's Yarns. Tale of Many Seas. Roland Folger Coffin. (On cover: Standard library, no. 125). 1884. Funk & Wagnalls.
Old Saint Mary's New Assistant. Joseph A Young. LC 30-6430. 1930. Benziger Brothers.
Old Saint Paul's: A Tale of the Plague & Fire. William Harrison Ainsworth. LC 36-37331. (Half-title: Everyman's library, ed. by Ernest Rhys. Fiction. no. 522). 1932. J. M. Dent & Sons, Ltd.
Old San Francisco... Ruth Comfort Mitchell. LC 33-291951. 1933. D. Appleton-Century Company, Incorporated.
Old San Francisco: Based on the Motion Picture Story, Adapted. Allie Lowe Miles. LC 27-19322. Grosset & Dunlap.
Old Settler and His Tales of Sugar Swamp. Edward Harold Mott. (On cover: Household library. v. 4, no. 45). 1889. Belford, Clarke & Co.; Etc., Etc.
Old Settler: The Squire and Little Peleg. Edward Harold Mott. LC 7-32311. (On cover: Belgravia series, no. 8). United States Book Company.
Old Sheepskin Coat. 1st Ed. Mary L Hotchkiss. LC 57-9688. 1957. Vantage Press.
Old Ship: A Novel. Lennox Kerr. LC 31-4810. 1931. The Macmillan Company.
Old Ship Warehouse: A Novel. Mary Andrews Denison. (On cover: Harper's library of American fiction. no. 8). 1878. Harper & Brothers.
Old Sleuth the Detective: Or, The Bay Ridge Mystery. Harlan Page Halsey. (On cover: Calumet series, no. 2). G. Munro.
Old Sleuth's Triumph: Or, "Piping" the Bronx Mystery. Harlan Page Halsey. LC 7-117866. (On cover: Calumet series, no. 9). 1892. G. Munro.
Old Soldiers Never Die: A Novel. James Ronald. LC 42-14629. 1942. J. B. Lippincott Company.
Old Soldiers Never Die. 1st American Ed. Wolf Mankowitz. LC 56-10636. (Atlantic Monthly Press Book). 1956. Little, Brown.
Old South: "A Summer Tragedy" and Other Stories of the Thirties. Arna Wendell Bontemps. LC 73-2136. 1973. 6.95 (ISBN 0-396-06788-3). Dodd, Mead.
Old Specie, the Treasury Detective: Or, The Harbor Lights of New York. A Startling Story of Night Life in the Great Metropolis. Alexander Robertson. LC 7-41678. (secret service series, no. 33). 1890. Street & Smith.
Old Squire: The Romance of a Black Virginian. Blackwood Ketcham Benson. LC 3-10720. 1903. The Macmillan Company.
Old Stag. Henry Williamson. LC 27-7188. E. P. Dutton & Company.
Old Stag, Stories. Henry Williamson. LC 27-15609. 1926. G. P. Putnam's Sons, Ltd.
Old Stone House. Nellie J Meeker. LC 7-25863. 1883. The St. Louis News Company.
Old Stone House, & Other Stories. facs. ed. Anna K. Green. LC 71-132117. (Short Story Index Reprint Ser). 1891. 11.00 (ISBN 0-8369-3674-4). Ayer Co.
Old Stone House and Other Stories. Anna Katharine Green Rohlfs. LC 71-132117. (Short story index reprint series). 1970. Books for Libraries Press.
Old Stone House and Other Stories. Anna Katharine Green Rohlfs. LC 7-40749. 1891. G. P. Putnam's Sons.
Old Stone Mansion. Charles Jacobs Peterson. LC 7-36158. T. B. Peterson and Brothers.
Old Stonewall, the Colorado Detective. Harlan Page Halsey. (secret service series, no. 6). 1888. Street & Smith.
Old Story in Tsin: Or, A Portrayal of China's Struggle for Freedom and Reform. Jesse Coleman Owen. LC 38-77280. The Christopher Publishing House.
Old Suit Case. Della Clarke. LC 30-292431. 1930. Della Clarke.
Old Sweet Song. William Arthur Neubauer. LC 47-307734. 1947. Gramercy Pub. Co.
Old Swords. Val Henry Gielgud. LC 28-7325. 1928. Houghton Mifflin Company.
Old Tavern: And Other Stories. Mary Dwinell Chellis. LC 6-23360. 1886. The National Temperance Society and Publication House.
Old Tayles Newlye Relayted. Joseph Crawhall. 1883. Repr. 15.00 o.s.i. Finch Pr.
Old Time Bottles Found in the Ghost Towns. rev. ed. Lynn Blumenstein. (Current Values Ser). (Illus., Orig.). 1974. pap. 2.95 (ISBN 0-911068-01-5, A666974). Old Time.
Old-Time Cowhand. Ramon F. Adams. 1971. pap. 2.45 o.s.i. (ISBN 0-02-097100-1, Collier). Macmillan.
Old-Time Mill. Martin Tresher. LC 46-6142. 1946. The Hobson Book Press.
Old Timer Talks Back. Allen R. Foley. LC 75-16578. (Illus.). 80p. 1975. pap. 3.95 (ISBN 0-8289-0258-5). Greene.
Old Times in Georgia. Good Times and Bad Times. A M Weir. 1889. Constitution Publishing Company.
Old Times in Middle Georgia. Richard Malcolm Johnston. LC 4-15131. 1897. The Macmillan Company.
Old Toney & His Master; or, the Abolitionist & the Land Pirate. Desmos. LC 74-162214. (Confederate Imprints Collection Ser.). 405p. 1973. Repr. of 1861 ed. 17.00 o.p. (ISBN 0-405-04320-1). Arno.
Old Trade of Killing. John Harris. LC 66-16314. bds., 4.95. Sloane, Dist. Morrow.
Old Trail: A Story of Rebekah. James Walter Morris. LC 14-2299. R. G. Badger.
Old Trails on Fire. Paul Wilkes. LC 29-3484. Odin Publishing Co.
Old Ugly-Face. Talbot Mundy. LC 40-4503. 1940. D. Appleton-Century Company, Incorporated.
Old Valentines: A Love Story. Munson Havens. LC 14-310398. 1914. Houghton Mifflin Company.
Old Washington. Harriet Elizabeth Prescott Spofford. 1906. Little, Brown, and Company.
Old Ways and New: Stories. Viola Roseboro' LC 7-41006. 1892. The Century Co.
Old West--and New: A Novel. Caroline Lockhart. LC 33-9681. 1933. Doubleday, Doran and Company, Inc.
Old West in Fiction. Ed. by Irwin R Blacker. 1961. I. Obolensky.
Old Wine. Phyllis Bottome. George H. Doran Company.
Old Wine. Phyllis Bottome. LC 37-27410. 1937. Frederick A. Stokes Company.
Old Wine and New. Warwick Deeping. LC 32-26489. 1932. A. A. Knopf.
Old Wine in New Bottles. Samuel Tilden Larkin. LC 15-163425. 1915. 1.00. Monfort & Company Press.
Old Wive Tale. Arnold Bennett. LC 31-26754. (Half-title: The modern library of the world's best books). 1931. The Modern Library.
Old Wives for New: A Novel. David Graham Phillips. LC 8-8091. 1908. D. Appleton and Company.
Old Wives for New. A Novel. David Graham Phillips. LC 11-17961. 1910. D. Appleton and Company.
Old Wives for New: A Novel. David Graham Phillips. LC 16-9353. 1912. D. Appleton and Company.
Old Wives' Tale. Arnold Bennett. LC 74-17060. (Collected works of Arnold Bennett). 1974. (ISBN 0-518-19142-7). Books for Libraries Press.
Old Wives' Tale. Arnold Bennett. LC 11-36289. Hodder & Toughton, G. H. Doran Company.
Old Wives' Tale. Arnold Bennett. LC 24-11870. George H. Doran Company.
Old Wives' Tale. Arnold Bennett. LC 28-166118. 1927. George H. Doran Company.
Old Wives' Tale. a new ed., with preface. by arnold bennett. ed. Arnold Bennett. LC 47-36815. Doubleday & Company, Inc.
Old Wives' Tale. a new ed., with preface. by arnold bennett. ed. Arnold Bennett. LC 43-30372. George H. Doran Company.
Old Wives' Tale. Arnold Bennett. LC 36-17486. (Half-title: The modern library of the world's best books). The Modern Library.
Old Wives' Tale. Arnold Bennett. LC 79-20285. (Pandora books). 1980. 15.95 (ISBN 0-915864-78-9) (ISBN 0-915864-77-0). Academy Chicago.
Old Wives Tale. George Peele. 1976. text ed. 7.50x o.s.i. (ISBN 0-8277-3937-0); pap. text ed. 4.95x o.s.i. (ISBN 0-8277-2291-5). British Bk Ctr.
Old Wives' Tale: With an Introd. by J. B. Priestley. Arnold Bennett. LC 50-6257. (Harper's modern classics). 1950. Harper.
Old Wives Tales. Arnold Bennett. LC 28-17938. 1928. Doubleday, Doran & Company, Inc.
Old Wolfville. Chapters from the Fiction of Alfred Henry Lewis, Selected, Ed., Introd., Commentary by Louis Filler. Illus. by Frederic Remington. Alfred Henry Lewis. Ed. by Louis Filler. LC 68-13363. 1968. 6.00, 2.50 pap.,. Antioch.
Old Woman of the Movies: And Other Stories. Vicente Blasco Ibanez. LC 25-9692. E. P. Dutton & Company.
Old Woman Out. Wendy Simons. LC 81-8887. 1981. 9.95 (ISBN 0-312-58120-3). St. Martin's Press.
Old Woman Talks. Francis Oscar Mann. LC 32-2877. Harcourt, Brace and Company.
Old Woman, the Wife, and the Archer: Three Modern Japanese Short Novels. Ed. by Donald Keene. LC 61-16603. 1961. Viking Press.
Old World, New World. Mark Dintenfass. LC 81-14044. 480p. 1982. 14.50 (ISBN 0-688-00811-9). Morrow.
Old World Wonder Stories. Ed. by Michael Vincent O'Shea. LC 2-188. (On cover: Heath's home and school classics). 1902. D. C. Heath & Co.
Old Yeller. Frederick Benjamin Gipson. LC 56-8780. (Illus.). 1956. Harper.
Old Yeller. large type ed. Frederick Benjamin Gipson. LC 68-1507. (Illus.). 1966. Harper & Row.
Old Yeller by Fred Gipson. Drawings by Carl Burger. Frederick Benjamin Gipson. LC 68-1507. 1966. Harper & Row.
Old Yet Ever New Robinson Crusoe. Daniel Defoe & Stayton, Belle Manley. LC 3-11599. 1902.
Old-Young Sex. Carl Stanton. 160p. pap. 1.95 o.p. (ISBN 0-87682-412-2, 7412). Barclay Hse.
Old Youth: A Novel. Coningsby William Dawson. LC 25-171193. 1925. Cosmopolitan Book Corporation.
Oldbury. Annie Keary. LC 7-11130. (Seaside library, v. 35, no. 715). G. Munro.
Olde Tayles Newlye Related: Enryched with All Ye Ancyente Embellythmentes. John Ashton. (Illus.). 12.50 o.p. Blom.
Older Lovers Only for Doris. Samantha Lasch. pap. 1.95 o.p. (ISBN 0-87682-234-0, 7234). Barclay Hse.
Older Man's Girl. Jerri Dugan. pap. 1.95 o.p. (8092). Cameo.
Older Men & Younger Girls. Christopher J. Markham. pap. 4.75 o.p. (ISBN 0-87964-531-8). Academy-Parliament.
Older Sister. William Arthur Neubauer. LC 47-12332. 1947. Gramercy Pub. Co.
Older Soldier. Jack M. Lambert. 1959. 3.50 o.p. (ISBN 0-671-53230-8). S&S.
Older Soldier: A Novel. Jack M Lambert. LC 59-9502. 1959. Simon and Schuster.
Older Women & Younger Boys. Christopher J. Markham. pap. 4.75 o.p. (ISBN 0-87964-532-6). Academy-Parliament.
Older Women's Young Studs. Sybil Sainte-Claire. Orig. Title: Young Boys & Their Older Women. 192p. 1974. pap. 2.25 o.p. (ISBN 0-87056-420-X, 6420). Brandon.
Oldest April. Sarah Litsey. 1956. 2.50 (ISBN 0-8233-0060-9). Golden Quill.
Oldest God: A Novel. Stephen McKenna. LC 26-1286. 1926. Little, Brown and Company.
Oldest Inhabitant: A Comedy. Eden Phillpotts. LC 34-20802. 1934. The Macmillan Company.
Oldest Maiden Lady in New Mexico, and Other Stories. Henry Allen. LC 62-19423. 1962. Macmillan.
Oldest Profession. Richard Condon. 1974. (pbk.) 1.50. Dell.
Oldfield: A Kentucky Tale of the Last Century. Nancy Huston Banks. LC 2-152076. 1902. The Macmillan Company.
Oldham. Catherine M Verschoyle. LC 27-173638. 1927. Longmans, Green and Co., Ltd.
Oldham: Or, Beside All Waters. Lucy Ellen Guernsey. LC 7-146. 1886. T. Whittaker.
Oldtown Folks. Harriet Elizabeth Beecher Stowe. LC 77-2783. 1968. Scholarly Press.
Oldtown Folks. Harriet Elizabeth Beecher Stowe. LC 70-127455. 1971. (ISBN 0-404-06293-8). AMS Press.
Oldtown Folks. Harriet Elizabeth Beecher Stowe. LC 8-16119. 1869. Fields, Osgood & Co.
Oldtown Folks. 25th ed. Harriet Elizabeth Beecher Stowe. LC 42-271038. 1883. Houghton, Mifflin and Company.
Oldtown Folks. Harriet Elizabeth Beecher Stowe. LC 3-4420. Houghton, Mifflin and Company.
Oldtown Folks. Harriet Elizabeth Beecher Stowe & May, Henry Farnham, 1915- Ed. LC 66-18257. (John Harvard Library). 1966. Belknap Press of Harvard University Press.
Oldtown Folks see Three Novels.
Ole Ann, and Others Stories. Jeanette Grace Watkins Watson. LC 5-29104. The Saalfield Publishing Company.
Ole Doc Methuselah. La Fayette Ronald Hubbard. LC 70-19578. 1970. 4.95. Theta Press.
Ole Man Mose: A Novel of the Tennessee Valley. 1st Ed. W Reginald Montague. LC 57-10665. 1957. Exposition Press.
Ole Mars An' Ole Miss. Edmund K. Goldsborough. LC 74-37592. (Black Heritage Library Collection). (Illus.). 1972. (ISBN 0-8369-8968-6). Books for Libraries Press.
Ole Mars An'ole Miss. Edmund K Goldsborough. LC 42-27363. 1900. National Publishing Co.
Olea: A Story of the Norsemen in Pennsylvania. Samuel Haven Glassmire. LC 13-18069. 1913. 1.00. The Knickerbocker Press.
Oleander Cove: By Peggy Dern Pseud. Peggy Gaddis, pseud. 1954. Arcadia House.
Oleander River. Gladys Bronwyn Stern. LC 37-28529. 1937. The Macmillan Company.
O'Leary's Panacea. John W. Patterson. LC 75-30163. 112p. (Orig.). 1976. 6.95 (ISBN 0-89185-009-0); pap. 2.25 (ISBN 0-89185-008-2). Anthelion Pr.
Olga. Marquise De St. Innocent. (O.s.i.). 1974. 9.95 o.s.i. (ISBN 0-8027-0414-X). Walker & Co.
Olga. Marquise De St. Innocent. (O.s.i.). 1974. 9.95 o.s.i. (ISBN 0-8027-0414-X). Walker & Co.
Olga Bardel. Stacy Aumonier. LC 16-18906. 1916. 1.35. The Century Co.

TITLE INDEX

OMNIBUS.

Olga Romanoff: Or, The Syren of the Skies. A Sequel to The Angel of the Revolution. George Chetwynd Griffith. LC 73-13255. (Classics of science fiction). (Illus.). 1974. (ISBN 0-88355-110-1) (ISBN 0-88355-139-X). Hyperion Press.

Olga's Crime. Frank Barrett. LC 6-866476. (Lovell's international series, no. 174). J. W. Lovell Company.

Olinda's Adventures: Or, The Amours of a Young Lady (1718. Catharine Trotter Cockburn. LC 71-7558. (Augustan Reprint Society. Publication: No. 138). (Illus.). 1969. William Andrews Clark Memorial Library, University of California.

Olinger Stories. John Updike. (Orig.). pap. 1.65 o.p. (ISBN 0-394-70257-3, V257, Vin). Random.

Olinger Stories: A Selection. John Updike. LC 64-18935. (Vintage Bks., V-257). 1964. pap., 1.65. Random.

Olive. Dinah Maria Mulock Craik. Ed. by Robert L. Wolff. LC 75-1521. (Victorian Fiction Ser.). 1975. Repr. of 1850 ed. lib. bdg. 66.00 (ISBN 0-8240-1593-2). Garland Pub.

Olive: A Novel. Dinah Maria Mulock Craik. LC 75-1521. (Victorian Fiction: Novels of Faith and Doubt; V. 69). 1975. 35.00 (ISBN 0-8240-1593-2). Garland Pub.

Olive Blake's Good Work. A Novel. John Cordy Jeaffreson. LC 7-10182. (On cover: Library of select novels). 1862. Harper & Brothers.

Olive Branch. abr. ed. Irene Shaw. Ed. by Alice Sachs. (Orig.). 1970. Repr. 3.95 o.p. Lenox Hill.

Olive-Branch: Or, White Oak Farm ... LC 7-24116. 1857. J. B. Lippincott & Co.

Olive Field. Ralph Bates. bds., 6.95. Washington Sq.

Olive Field. Ralph Bates. LC 66-4546. 1966. Washington Square Press.

Olive Field. Ralph Bates. LC 36-27372. E. P. Dutton & Co., Inc.

Olive Grove. Maria Szczepanska Kuncewiczowa. LC 63-11770. 1963. Walker and Co.

Olive Lacey; a Tale of the Irish Rebellion of 1798. Anna Argyle. LC 6-4525. 1874. J. B. Lippincott & Co.

Olive Latham. Ethel Lillian Boole Voynich. 1904. J. B. Lippincott Company.

Olive Logan's Christmas Story: Somebody's Stocking... Olive Logan Sikes Logan. LC 8-28116. The American News Company.

Olive Logan's New Christmas Story. John Morris's Money... Olive Logan Sikes Logan. LC 8-28117. 1867. The American News Company.

Olive of Minerva: Or, The Comedy of a Cuckold. Edward Dahlberg. LC 75-20358. 6.95 (ISBN 0-690-00697-7) (ISBN 0-690-01082-6). Crowell.

Olive Orchard: And Other Stories. Guy De Maupassant. LC 75-157791. (Short story index reprint series). 1971. (ISBN 0-8369-3903-4). Books for Libraries Press.

Olive Orchard, & Other Stories: Collected Novels & Stories, Vol. 14. facsimile ed. Guy De Maupassant. Ed. by Ernest Boyd. Tr. by Storm Jameson from Fr. LC 75-157791. (Short Story Index Reprint Ser.). Repr. of 1925 ed. 16.00 (ISBN 0-8369-3903-4). Ayer Co.

Olive Tracy. Amy Le Feuvre. LC 6421. 1901. Dodd, Mead & Company.

Olive Tree. Robin Estridge. LC 53-5334. 1953. Morrow.

Olive Winked Back. Cecil Barker. LC 64-3346. 1964. Exposition Press.

Oliver and the Jew Fagin from the Oliver Twist of Charles Dickens. Charles Dickens. LC 46-31655. (Half-title: Dickens' little folks). 1878. J. R. Anderson.

Oliver and the Seven Sinners. William Hubbart Bradley. LC 49-15635. Vickers Pub. Co.

Oliver Cromwell: Or, England's Great Protector. Henry William Herbert. LC 7-4286. 1856. Miller, Orton & Mulligan.

Oliver Ellis: Or, The Fusiliers. James Grant. LC 44-20554. 1861. G. Routledge and Sons.

Oliver Goldsmith's The Vicar of Wakefield. Oliver Goldsmith. Ed. by Jordan, Mary Augusta. LC 1-8258. (Longmans' English classics. v. 15). Longmans, Green and Co.

Oliver Iverson: His Adventures During Four Days and Nights in the City of New York in April of the Year 1890. Ann Devoore. LC 99-1819. (On cover: Blue cloth books). 1899. H. S. Stone and Company.

Oliver October. George Barr McCutcheon. LC 23-12065. 1923. Dodd, Mead and Company.

Oliver Perry Wiggins. Lorene B. Englert & Kenneth Englert. (Wild & Woolly West Ser., No. 6). (Illus., Orig.). 1968. 4.00 o.p.; pap. 2.00 o.p. (ISBN 0-910584-06-0). Filter.

Oliver Poges Lives! Max Handley. LC 79-127843. 1970. 5.95. Stein and Day.

Oliver, the Wayward Owl. August William Derleth. 3.95 o.p. (ISBN 0-87054-114-5). Arkham.

Oliver: The Wayward Owl. August William Derleth. 3.95 o.p. (ISBN 0-88361-059-0). Stanton & Lee.

Oliver Twist. Charles Dickens. LC 65-6515. (Perennial classic). 1965. Harper & Row.

Oliver Twist. Charles Dickens. Ed. by Peter Fairclough. LC 66-78223. (Penguin English library, EL 17) 6/-). 1966. Penguin.

Oliver Twist... Charles Dickens. LC 6-26420. 1867. Hurd and Houghton.

Oliver Twist. Charles Dickens. LC 7-38602. (Half-title: The "prairie" classics). 1907. A. C. McClurg & Co.

Oliver Twist. Charles Dickens. LC 26-18509. Minton, Balch & Company.

Oliver Twist. Charles Dickens. LC 41-16058. (On cover: Great illustrated classics). 1941. Dodd, Mead & Company.

Oliver Twist. Charles Dickens. LC 51-50182. 1839. Lea & Blanchard.

Oliver Twist. Charles Dickens. (Rittenhouse classics). 1922. G. W. Jacobs & Company.

Oliver Twist. Charles Dickens & Holmes, Mabel Dodge, 1883- LC 47-2434. (Cebco classics for enjoyment). 1947. College Entrance Book Company.

Oliver Twist. an abridged edition, ed. by fred reinfeld. ed. Charles Dickens & Reinfeld, Fred, 1910- LC 48-20296. (Pocket book 519). 1948. Pocket Books.

Oliver Twist. Charles Dickens & Teague, Donald, 1897- Illus. LC 42-517791. 1942. Garden City Publishing Co., Inc.

Oliver Twist. Charles Dickens & Kathleen Mary Tillotson. LC 81-16958. (World's classics). (Illus.). 1982. 4.95 (ISBN 0-19-281591-1). Oxford University Press.

Oliver Twist. Abridged and Edited for Use in Schools by David Holbrook. Charles Dickens. Ed. by David Holbrook. LC 65-4610. (Broadstream books, no. 1). 1965. University Press.

Oliver Twist: Ed. by Kathleen Tillotson. Charles Dickens. Ed. by Kathleen Mary Tillotson. LC 66-76648. (Clarendon Dickens). 1966. 12.00. Clarendon Pr.

Oliver Twist: Ed. by M. W. and G. Thomas. Illus. by John Sergeant. Charles Dickens. Ed. by Maurice Walton Thomas & Gladys Thomas. LC 66-6588. (Shorter classics). 1963. bds., 2.50. Ginn.

Oliver Twist: Or, The Parish Boy's Progress. Charles Dickens & Bentley's Miscellany. LC 6-37239. 1837. Carey, Lea and Blanchard.

Oliver Twist: 2v. Abridged, Ed. for Use in Schools by David Holbrook. Charles Dickens & David Holbrook. LC 65-461065. (Broadstream bks., no.1). 1.95 ea.,. Cambridge.

Oliver Wiswell. Kenneth Lewis Roberts. LC 40-340739. 1940. Doubleday, Doran & Company, Inc.

Oliver's Bride: A New Novel. Margaret Oliphant Wilson Oliphant. (On cover: Lovell's library, v. 12, no. 602). 1885. J. W. Lovell Company.

Oliver's Story. Erich W Segal. LC 75-6359. 7.95 (ISBN 0-06-013852-1). Harper & Row.

Oliver's Story. Erich W Segal. LC 77-22620. 1977. 10.95 (ISBN 0-8161-6500-9). G. K. Hall.

Olivers: The Story of an Artist and His Family. Robert Bright. LC 47-3262. 1947. Doubleday & Company, Inc.

Olives on the Apple Tree. Guido D'Agostino. LC 74-17924. (Italian American Experience). 1975. 17.00 (ISBN 0-405-06397-0). Arno Press.

Olives on the Apple Tree: A Novel. Guido D'Agostino. LC 40-33214. 1940. Doubleday, Doran & Company, Inc.

Olivia. Dorothy Strachey Bussy. LC 75-12342. (Homosexuality). 1975. 9.00 (ISBN 0-405-07382-8). Arno Press.

Olivia. Dorothy Strachey Bussy. LC 66-77859. (Penguin modern classics). 1966. Penguin.

Olivia. Dorothy Strachey Bussy. LC 49-2752. 1949. Sloane.

Olivia. Gwendoline Butler. LC 74-14388. 1974. 5.95 (ISBN 0-698-10638-5). Coward, McCann & Geoghegan.

Olivia. Gwendoline Butler. 1975. (pbk.) 1.50. Ballantine Books.

Olivia. Barbara Riefe. LC 81-47267. (Shackleford Legacy: No.1). 352p. (Orig.). 1981. pap. 2.95 (ISBN 0-87216-865-4). Playboy Pbks.

Olivia Delaplaine: A Novel. Edgar Fawcett. LC 6-38785. 1888. Ticknor and Company.

Olivia's Story. Abigail Winter. Dell.

Ollie Miss. George Wylie Henderson. 276p. 1973. Repr. of 1935 ed. 7.95x (ISBN 0-911860-41-X). Chatham Bkseller.

Ollie Miss: A Novel. George Wylie Henderson. LC 35-2970. 1935. Frederck A. Stokes Company.

Ollivant Orphans. Inez Haynes Irwin. LC 15-23791. 1915. 1.35. H. Holt and Company.

Olmec Head. David Westheimer. LC 73-12282. 1974. 6.95 (ISBN 0-316-93153-5). Little, Brown.

O'Loghlin of Clare. Rosa Mulholland Gilbert. LC 17-20673. 1916. P. J. Kenedy & Sons.

Olowalu Massacre & Other Hawaiian Tales. Aubrey P. Janion. LC 76-1508. (Illus.). 1977. 9.00 (ISBN 0-89610-029-4). Island Her.

Olt. Kenneth Gangemi. LC 78-94091. 1969. 3.95. Orion Press.

Olura. Geoffrey Household. 1965. 5.95 o.p. (Pub. by Atlantic Monthly Pr). Little.

Olura: A Novel. 1st Amer. Ed. IBoston. c.1965 ed. Geoffrey Household. LC 65-18134. 5.95.

Olvidados. Peter McCurtin. (Sundance Ser.: No. 30). 1980. pap. 1.75 (ISBN 0-8439-0724-X). Nordon Pubns.

Olympe De Cleves. Alexandre Dumas & Lacroix, Paul. LC 6-43964. (Half-title: The romances of Alexandre Dumas. Illustrated library ed. vol. xxv-xxvi). 1893. Little, Brown, and Company.

Olympe De Cleves. Alexandre Dumas & Lacroix, Paul. (On cover: Seaside library. Pocket ed., no. 2112). G. Munro's Sons.

Olympe De Cleves: A Romance of the Court of Louis, the Fifteenth. ed. de medicis. ed. Alexandre Dumas & Lacroix, Paul. LC 4-12776. 1904. D. Estes & Company.

Olympia. Elgin Earl Groseclose. LC 80-121371. 1980. 8.95. D. C. Cook Pub. Co.

Olympia: A Novel of the Reformation. Florence Whitfield Barton. LC 65-20340. 4.95. Fortress.

Olympia Reader: Selections from the Traveller's Companion Series. Ed. by Maurice Girodias. LC 73-87041. (Illus.). 15.00 (ISBN 0-88486-000-0). Black Watch.

Olympia Reader: Selections from the Traveller's Companion Series. Ed. by Maurice Girodias. LC 79-19841. (Illus.). 1979. 32.75 (ISBN 0-8357-0466-1). Reprinted for Grove Press by University Microfilms International.

Olympia Reader: Selections from the Traveller's Companion Series. Ed. by Maurice Girodias. LC 65-14205. 1980. 3.50 (ISBN 0-394-17648-0). Grove Press.

Olympia Reader: Selections from the Traveller's Companion Series. Ed. by Maurice Girodias. Illus. by Norman Rubington. Ed. by Maurice Girodias. The Traveller's Companion Series. (U8601). 1967. pap., 1.65. Ballantine.

Olympiad of Knowledge, 1984: A Novel. O. A. Battista. LC 75-8352. 1981. 9.95 (ISBN 0-915074-09-5). Research Servs Corp.

Olympian. Brian Glanville. LC 69-17785. 1969. 5.95. Coward-McCann.

Olympian. Brian Glanville. LC 79-26550. 1980. 5.95 (ISBN 0-395-29086-4). Houghton Mifflin.

Olympian: A Story of the City. James Oppenheim. 1912. 1.35. Harper & Brothers.

Olympian Nights. John Kendrick Bangs. LC 2-169265. 1902. Harper & Brothers.

Olympians. 1st Ed. Guy Reginald Bolton. LC 61-5810. 1961. World Pub. Co.

Olympia's Inheritance. Orlando R Petrocelli. LC 74-6802. 1974. 6.95 (ISBN 0-396-06989-4). Dodd, Mead.

Olympic Hope: A Story from the Olympic Games, 1996. Translated from the Danish by Eiler Hansen and William Luscombe. Kund Lundberg. LC 59-4041. Stamped: Distributed by Sportshelf. New Rochelle, N. Y.

Olympic Sleeper. Barling, Tom. 1980. 2.25 (ISBN 0-449-14330-9). Fawcett Gold Medal.

Olympic Torch. Dorothy Frooks. LC 47-17698. 1946. House of Ideas Publishing Company.

Olympic Victor: A Story of the Modern Games, by James Brendan Connolly; with Illustrations by A. Castaigne. James Brendan Connolly. 1908. C. Scribner's Sons.

Olympica. 1980. pap. write for info. (ISBN 0-88074-007-8). Metagam.

Olympio. Andre Maurois. 1968. pap. 1.25 o.p. (V1764). Pyramid Pubns.

Om Olav Den Helliges Saga. Sigurthur Nordal. LC 80-1953. Repr. of 1914 ed. 31.00 (ISBN 0-404-18712-9). AMS Pr.

Om: The Secret of Ahbor Vallet. Talbot Mundy. Repr. lib. bdg. 19.40x (ISBN 0-89190-490-5). Am Repr-Rivercity Pr.

Om: The Secret of Ahbor Valley. Talbot Mundy. LC 24-27998. The Bobbs-Merrill Company.

Om, the Secret of Ahbor Valley. Talbot Mundy. (Xanadu Library). pap. 1.65 o.p. Crown.

Omaha Crossing. Ray Hogan. 1977. pap. 1.95 (ISBN 0-441-62341-7). Ace Bks.

Omaha Crossing. Ray Hogan. 160p. 1981. pap. 1.95 (ISBN 0-441-62342-5, Pub. by Charter Bks). Ace Bks.

Omaha Indian Myths & Trickster Tales. Roger Welsch. 1975. 10.00 o.p. (ISBN 0-8040-0700-4). Swallow.

O'Mahony, Chief of the Comeraghs: A Tale of the Rebellion of .98. David Power Conyngham. 1879. D. & J. Sadlier & Co.

O'Malley of Shanganagh. Donn Byrne. LC 25-661900. 1.25. The Century Co.

Omar: A Fantasy for Animal Lovers. Wilfrid Blunt. LC 68-22524. (Illus.). 1968. 3.95. Doubleday.

Omar Khayyam: A Life. Harold Lamb. LC 34-32405. 1934. Doubleday, Doran & Company, Inc.

Omar Khayyam: A Life by. Harold Lamb. LC 36-33414. 1936. Doubleday, Doran & Company, Inc.

Omar Khayyam Revisted. Hakim Yama Khayyam. (Illus.). 122p. 1974. 8.95 (ISBN 0-8184-0167-2). Lyle Stuart.

Omar, the Tentmaker: A Romance of Old Persia. Nathan Haskell Dole. LC 98-1807. 1899. L. C. Page and Company.

O'Mara: A Novel. Laurence Greene. LC 38-6766. The Bobbs-Merrill Company.

Ombak Bukan Biru. Fatimah Busu. (Karyawan Malaysia Ser.). (Malay.). 1979. pap. text ed. 5.50x o.p. (00350). Heinemann Ed.

Ombra. Margaret Oliphant Wilson Oliphant. (On cover: Seaside library. Pocket ed., no. 605). 1885. G. Munro.

Ombre de mon Amour. Guillaume Apollinaire. (Coll. Le Bonguet). 12.15 o.p. French & Eur.

Ombu & Other South American Stories. William Henry Hudson. Repr. of 1923 ed. 21.50 (ISBN 0-404-03400-4). AMS Pr.

Ombu & Other South American Stories. William Henry Hudson. 1973. lib. bdg. 20.00 (ISBN 0-8414-5195-8). Folcroft.

Omega. Ed. by Roger Elwood. LC 73-83311. 1973. 6.95 (ISBN 0-8027-5561-5). Walker.

Omega. Stewart Farrar. 1980. 10.95 o.p. Times Bks.

Omega: A Collection of Original Science Fiction Stories. Roger Elwood. 1973. 6.95 o.p. (ISBN 0-8027-5561-5). Walker & Co.

Omega: A Novel. Stewart Farrar. LC 79-64453. 11.95 (ISBN 0-8129-0861-9). Times Books.

Omega: A Tale of Love, Death, and the Millennium. E. D. Elmer. LC 98-862. 1898. F. T. Neely.

Omega Document. J. Alexander McKenzie. LC 79-53442. (J. Alexander. Canaan Trilogy: 1st). 2.50 (ISBN 0-87123-416-5). Bethany Fellowship.

Omega-Minus. Ted Allbeury. LC 74-30387. 1975. 6.95 (ISBN 0-670-52408-5). Viking Press.

Omega Operation. Norman Conway. (Hunter#1). 1974. (pbk.) 1.50. Canyon Books.

Omega Street. Bernard Ash. LC 54-31250. 1954. Staples Press.

Omega Terror. Nick Carter. (Nick Carter Ser). (O.s.i.). 1976. pap. 1.50 o.s.i. (AD1648, Award). Univ Pub & Dist.

Omega Terror. Nick Carter. (Killmaster Series). 1972. 0.95. Award Books.

Omega: the Last Days of the World. Camille Flammarion. LC 74-15971. (Science Fiction). (Illus.). 1975. 16.00 (ISBN 0-405-06291-5). Arno Press.

Omega: The Last Days of the World. Camille Flammarion. LC 6-41143. The Cosmopolitan Publishing Company.

Omen. Mary N Dolim. LC 67-12203. 1967. Morrow.

Omen. Marie Eyre. (queen-size gothic). 1974. (pbk.) 0.95. Popular Library.

Omen. David Seltzer. (signet Book). (Illus.). 1976. 1.50. New American Library.

Omen Four: Armageddon Two Thousand. Gordon McGill. 1982. pap. 3.50 (ISBN 0-451-11818-9, AE1818, Sig). NAL.

Omensetter's Luck. William H. Gass. pap. 5.95 (ISBN 0-452-25349-7, Z5349, Plume). NAL.

Omensetter's Luck. William H. Gass. 1969. pap. 3.95 o.p. (MF23, Mer). World Pub.

Omensetter's Luck. William H. Gass. 1966. 6.95 o.p. (HO59, NAL). Norton.

Omensetter's Luck: A Novel. William H. Gass. LC 66-13373. 5.95. New Amer. Lib.

Omha Abides. C. C. MacApp. (Orig.). 1968. pap. 0.50 o.p. (52-649). Paperback Lib.

Ominous Orgy. Mallory T. Knight. (Man from T.O.M.C.A.T. Ser.). (O.s.i.: No. 7). (Orig.). 1969. pap. 0.60 o.s.i. (A432X, Award). Univ Pub & Dist.

Ominous Star. Elinore Denniston. LC 72-156859. (Red badge novel of suspense). 1971. 4.95 (ISBN 0-396-06361-6). Dodd, Mead.

Ominous Star. Rae Foley. (Red Badge Suspense Novel Ser). 1971. 4.95 o.p. Dodd.

Ominous Years. James Boswell. Ed. by C. A. Ryskamp & Frederick A. Pottle. 1963. 4.75 o.p. (ISBN 0-07-054367-4, P&RB). McGraw.

Omit Flowers... Stuart Palmer. LC 37-533. 1937. Pub. for the Crime Club, Inc., by Doubleday, Doran & Co., Inc.

Omit Flowers... Stuart Palmer. LC 38-6244. 1938. The Sun Dial Press, Inc.

Omit Flowers, Please... Audrey Gaines. LC 46-21109. 1946. J. Messner, Inc.

Ommirandy: Plantation Life at Kingsmill. Armistead Churchill Gordon. LC 17-25975. 1917. C. Scribner's Sons.

Omneros. Mohammad Dib. Tr. by Carol Lettieri & Paul Vangelisti. 1978. pap. 3.00 sewn in wrappers (Pub. by Red Hill). SBD.

Omni Strain. Cliff Patton. (Illus.). 432p. (Orig.). 1981. pap. 2.75 (ISBN 0-89083-689-2). Zebra.

Omnia Vanitas: A Tale of Society. Mrs. Bridges. (On cover: Seaside library. Pocket ed., no. 280). 1884. G. Munro.

Omnia Vanitas. A Tale of Society. Mrs. Bridges. (On cover: Lovell's library, v. 18, no. 860). 1887. J. W. Lovell Company.

Omnibus. Verne, Jules. LC 36-12318. 1933. Blue Ribbon Books, Inc.

Omnibus: Containing Whose Body? The Unpleasantness at the Bellona Club, Suspicious Characters. Dorothy Leigh Sayers. 1937. Harcourt, Brace and Company.

Omnibus Fleming Stone... Carolyn Wells. LC 32-26676. 1932. J. B. Lippincott Company.

Omnibus Jules Verne. Jules Verne. LC 31-220661. 1931. J. B. Lippincott Company.

Omnibus of Adventure. Ed. by John R. Colter. LC 31-26106. 1930. Dodd, Mead & Company.

Omnibus of Crime. Ed. by Dorothy Leigh Sayers. LC 31-28476. Garden City Publishing Company.

Omnibus of Romance: Complete Novelettes and Stories by Heyse, Cable, Stevenson, Gobineau, Doyle, Hergersheimer, Tarkington, Le Gallienne, L'Isle-Adam, Anthony, Hope, Halevy, Pushkin, Chateaubrid, Harts, F. Hopkinson Smith and Others. Ed. by John R. Colter. LC 31-16452. 1931. Dodd, Mead & Company.

Omnibus of Science Fiction. Ed. by Groff Conklin. LC 52-10778. 1952. Crown Publishers.

Omnibus of Science Fiction. Ed. by Groff Conklin. LC 80-15314. 1980. 6.98 (ISBN 0-517-32097-5). Bonanza Books.

Omnibus of Short Stories. James T. Arrell. 1956. 7.50 o.p. (ISBN 0-8149-0497-1). Vanguard.

Omnibus of Short Stories. James Thomas Farrell. LC 56-12033. 1956. Vanguard Press.

Omnibus of Sport. Ed. by Grantland Rice. Powel, Harford Willing Hare, 1887- Joint Ed. LC 32-18956. 1932. Harper & Brothers.

Omnibus of Terror. Dorothy Belle Flanagan Hughes. LC 43-11139. 1942. Duell, Sloan and Pearce.

Omnibus of Time. Farley. 1972. 8.00 o.p. Fantasy Pub Co.

Omnibus of Time: By Ralph Milne Farley Pseud. Roger Sherman Hoar. LC 50-7228. 1950. Fantasy Pub. Co.

Omnivore. Piers Anthony, pseud. 1978. pap. 2.95 (ISBN 0-380-00262-0, 82362-4). Avon.

Omoo. Herman Melville. LC 25-5777. 1924. Dodd, Mead and Company.

Omoo: A Narrative of Adventures in the South Seas. Herman Melville. LC 58-5530. (Evergreen books, E-94). Grove Press.

Omoo; a Narrative of Adventures in the South Seas. Herman Melville. LC 67-11991. (writings of Herman Melville. Northwestern-Newberry ed. v. 2). (Illus.). 1968. Northwestern University Press.

Omoo: A Narrative of Adventures in the South Seas. 5th ed. pt. 1 ed. Herman Melville. 1847. Harper & Brothers; Etc., Etc.

Omoo: A Narrative of Adventures in the South Seas. 6th ed. Herman Melville. LC 6-15438. 1855. Harper & Brothers.

Omoo: A Narrative of Adventures in the South Seas. 6th ed. Herman Melville. LC 18-20856. 1863. Harper & Brothers.

Omoo: A Narrative of Adventures in the South Seas. Herman Melville. LC 13-7658. United States Book Company.

Omoo: A Narrative of Adventures in the South Seas. Herman Melville. (Half-title: Everyman's library, ed. by Ernest Rhys. Fiction. no. 297). 1907. J. M. Dent & Co.

Omoo: A Narrative of Adventures in the South Seas. Herman Melville. LC 22-5179. (Half-title: Everyman's library, edited by Ernest Rhys. Fiction. no. 297). 1921. J. M. Dent & Sons, Ltd.

Omoo: A Narrative of Adventures in the South Seas. Herman Melville. LC 25-26582. (Half-title: The World's classics, cclxxv). 1924. H. Milford.

Omoo: A Narrative of Adventures in the South Seas. Herman Melville. LC 36-37148. (Half-title: Everyman's library, ed. by Ernest Rhys. Fiction. no. 297). 1925. J. M. Dent & Sons, Ltd.

Omoo: A Narrative of Adventures in the South Seas. Herman Melville. LC 42-33235. Harper & Brothers.

On a Balcony. David Staton. LC 59-16424. 1959. London House & Maxwell.

On a Dark Night: Three Canticles. Richard Bankowsky. LC 64-10355. 1964. Random House.

On a Darkling Plain... Wallace Earle Stegner. LC 40-27119. Harcourt, Brace and Company.

On a Darkling Plain: A Novel. Daniel Boone Dodson. LC 76-4829. 1976. 8.95 (ISBN 0-88405-140-4). Mason/Charter.

On a Darkling Plain: A Novel. Clifford Irving. LC 56-6490. 1956. Putnam.

On a False Charge: A Novel. Seward W Hopkins. (choice series, no. 121). 1895. R. Bonner's Sons.

On a Fated Night. Dorothea Malm. LC 64-22322. 5.95. Doubleday.

On a Field Azure. Aleksei Mikhailovich Remizov. LC 75-25267. (Series: Russian Literature Library; 6.). 1975. 9.75 (ISBN 0-8371-8387-1). Greenwood Press.

On a Field Azure. Aleksei Mikhailovich Remizov. LC 76-23896. (Series: Russian Literature Library; 6.). (Classsics of Russian literature). (Hyperion library of world literature). (Illus.). 1977. 2.95 (ISBN 0-88355-513-1). Hyperion Press.

On a Field of Black. Gerald Tomlinson. LC 79-16761. 1979. 8.00 (ISBN 0-8424-0151-2). Nellen Pub. Co.

On a Higher Plane. Moritz Loth. The Monitor Company.

On a Lark to the Planets: A Sequel to "The Wonderful Electric Elephant". Frances Trego Montgomery. LC 4-26872. 1904. The Saalfield Publishing Co.

On a Lonesome Porch. 1st Ed. Ovid Williams Pierce. LC 60-8681. 1960. Doubleday.

On a Margin... Julius Chambers. 1884. Fords, Howard & Hulbert.

On a Margin: A Novel. Julius Chambers. LC 8-12967. M. Kennerley.

On a Mountain Trail. Ray A. Neptune. 4.95 o.p. Vantage.

On a Passing Frontier: Sketches from the Northwest. Frank Bird Linderman. LC 20-10052. 1920. C. Scribner's Sons.

On a Planet Alien. Barry N Malzberg. 1974. (pbk.) 0.95 (ISBN 0-671-77766-1). Pocket Books.

On a Scottish Island. Mabel Grey MacGlashan Gehring. LC 49-9135. 1949. World Pub. Co.

On a Snow-Bound Train. A Winter's Tale. Julia MacNair Wright. LC 9-531. American Tract Society.

On a Western Campus. Stories and Sketches of Undergraduate Life. Grinnell College, Grinnell, Ia. Class of 1898. LC 7-34700. 1897. C. W. Moulton.

On Alien Wings. Ron Goulart. (Vampirella#2). 1975. (pbk.) 1.25. Warner Books.

On All Fronts. Jay Robert Nash. LC 74-81911. (Illus.). 5.00 (ISBN 0-913204-03-X). December Press.

On All Fronts. Ralph B. Perry. (O.s.i.). 1.75 o.s.i. (ISBN 0-8149-0592-7). Vanguard.

On an Island That Cost Twenty-Four Dollars. Irvin Shrewsbury Cobb. LC 26-1780. George H. Doran Company.

On and off the Bread Wagon: Being the Hard Luck Tales, Doings and Adventures of an Amateur Hobo. Charles Dryden. LC 5-37786. Star Publishing Company.

On Any Given Sunday. Ben Elisco. 384p. 1982. pap. 3.25 (ISBN 0-441-62674-2, Pub. by Charter Bks). Ace Bks.

On Behalf of Children. Linda Isham. LC 74-17842. 48p. (Orig.). 1975. pap. 1.95 (ISBN 0-8170-0666-4). Judson.

On Being Told That Her Second Husband Has Taken His First Lover, and Other Stories. Tess Slesinger. 1974. (pbk.) 3.95 (ISBN 0-8129-6242-7). Quadrangle, The New York Times Book Co.

On Board a Whaler: An Adventurous Cruise Through Southern Seas. Thomas West Hammond. 1901. G. P. Putnam's Sons.

On Board the Beatic. Anna Chapin Ray. LC 13-2842. 1913. Little, Brown, and Company.

On Board the Mary Sands. Laura Elizabeth Howe Richards. LC 11-26251. 1.25. D. Estes & Company.

On Board the Morning Star. Pierre MacOrlan & Cowley, Malcolm, 1898- LC 25-3199. 1924. A. & C. Boni.

On Borrowed Time. Lawrence Edward Watkin. A. A. Knopf.

On Both Sides. A Novel. 8th ed. Frances Courtenay Baylor Barnum. LC 3-281915. 1887. J. B. Lippincott Company.

On Both Sides of the Sea: A Story of the Commonwealth and the Restoration. A Sequel to "The Draytons and the Davenants.". Elizabeth Rundle Charles. 1867. Dodd & Mead.

On Both Sides of the Sea: A Story of the Commonwealth and the Restoration by the Author of "Chronicles of the Schonberg-Cotta Family." &C., &C. Elizabeth Rundle Charles. LC 41-381186. 1887. T. Nelson and Sons.

On Christmas Day in the Evening. Grace Louise Smith Richmond. LC 10-24713. 1910. Doubleday, Page and Company.

On Christmas Day in the Morning. Grace Louise Smith Richmond. 1908. Doubleday, Page & Company.

On Circumstantial Evidence. Florence Marryat Church Lean. LC 7-13613. F. F. Lovell & Company.

On Cloud Mountain: A Novel. Frederick Thickstun Clark. LC 6-25383. 1894. Harper & Brothers.

On Common Ground. Sydney Herman Preston. LC 6-14747. 1906. H. Holt and Company.

On Contract. Millie Bruhl Fredrick. LC 31-4184. The Stratford Company.

On Dangerous Ground: Or, Agatha's Friendship. A Romance of American Society. Clara Sophia Jessup Bloomfield-Moore. LC 7-26216. (On Cover: International Series of New Approved Novels. No. 165d). Porter and Coates.

On Dearborn Street. Miles Franklin. LC 81-11570. 14.95 (ISBN 0-7022-1636-4). University of Queensland Press.

On Drink. Kingsley Amis. LC 73-4276. 1973. 4.95 o.p. (ISBN 0-15-168995-4). HarBraceJ.

On Earth Peace: A Christmas Fairy Story. Rockwell Kent. LC 43-6173. (American artists group gift books, no. 12). American Artists Group.

On Easy Terms. Kay Martin. 1968. pap. 0.60 o.p. (60-333). Manor Bks.

On Emu Creek. Steele Rudd. (O.s.i.). (Illus.). 180p. 1972. pap. 2.50x o.s.i. (ISBN 0-7022-0746-2). U of Queensland Pr.

On Emu Creek & We Kaytons. Steele Rudd. (Illus.). 368p. 1972. 10.25x (ISBN 0-7022-0748-9). U of Queensland Pr.

On Etna. Norma Octavia Lorimer. LC 4-28200. 1904. H. Holt and Company.

On Flows the River. William Aden French. Vantage Press.

On Forsyte Change. John Galsworthy. LC 30-27763. 1930. C. Scribner's Sons.

On Fortune's Road: Stories of Business. Will Payne. 1902. A. C. McClurg & Co.

On Furlough. Florence Olmstead. LC 18-16896. 1918. 1.50. C. Scribner's Sons.

On Golden Hinges. Metta Folger Townsend. LC 18-4257. 1917. Broadway Publishing Co.

On Golden Pond. Movie tie-in ed. Ernest Thompson. 1981. pap. 2.50 (ISBN 0-451-11223-7, AE 1223, Sig). NAL.

On Her Majesty's Orders. Alex Stuart, pseud. 1977. pap. 1.95 (ISBN 0-89041-155-7, 3155). Major Bks.

On Her Majesty's Secret Service. Ian Fleming. pap. 4.50 fr. ed. French & Eur.

On Her Majesty's Secret Service. Ian Fleming. pap. 2.50 (ISBN 0-451-12107-4, AE2107, Sig). NAL.

On Her Wedding Morn. Charlotte Mary Brame. LC 1-5236. (On cover: Lovell's library, no. 1030). 1887. John W. Lovell Company.

On Her Wedding Morn. Charlotte Mary Brame. LC 1-29015. (Bertha Clay library, no. 36). 1900. Street & Smith.

On Her Wedding Morn: And, The Mystery of the Holly-Tree, a Christmas Story. Charlotte Mary Brame. LC 1-5235. (On cover: Seaside library. Pocket ed. no. 985). G. Munro.

On Her Wedding Morn: And The Mystery of the Holly-Tree. Charlotte Mary Brame. LC 1-5235. (On cover: Seaside library. Pocket ed. No. 985). G. Munro.

On Heroes and Tombs. Ernesto R. Sabato. LC 80-83957. 1981. 17.95 (ISBN 0-87923-381-8). Godine.

On Human Finery. 2nd rev. & en. ed. Quentin Bell. LC 76-9129. (Illus.). 1978. 14.95x o.p. (ISBN 0-8052-3629-5); pap. 6.95 (ISBN 0-8052-0606-X). Schocken.

On Ice. Robert George Dean. LC 42-17990. 1942. C. Scribner's Sons.

On Ice. Jack Gelber. LC 64-16045. 1964. Macmillan.

On Instructions of My Government. Pierre Salinger. LC 78-97688. 1971. 6.95. Doubleday.

On Jeweled Wings. Barbara Hedworth. LC 39-32054. 1938. Arcadia House.

On Jordon's Stormy Banks: A Novel of Sam Davis, the Confederate Scout. Adelaide Corinne Rowell. LC 48-6913. 1948. Bobbs-Merrill Co.

On Keeping Women. Hortense Calisher. LC 77-79531. 9.95 (ISBN 0-87795-169-1). Arbor House.

On Keeping Women. Hortense Calisher. (Berkley Book). 1979. 2.75 (ISBN 0-425-03936-6). Berkley Pub. Corp.

On Land and Sea. William Henry Thomes. LC 74-104577. (Illus.). 1970. (ISBN 0-8398-1954-4). Literature House.

On Land and Sea: Danger Ashore and Danger at Sea ByVictor Kosta Pseud. 1st Ed. Georges Simenon. LC 54-8392. 1954. Hanover House.

On Land and Sea: Or, California in the Years 1943, '44, and '45. William Henry Thomes. LC 8-20094. 1884. De Wolfe, Fiske & Company.

On Land and Sea: Or, California in the Years 1943, '44 and '45. William Henry Thomes. (On cover: The library of choice fiction, no. 44). 1892. Laird & Lee.

On Leave from Heaven. Abel Moreau. 2.50 o.p. (L38575). Franciscan Herald.

On Leaving Paradise. Frank Hercules. LC 79-3354. 324p. 1980. 10.95 (ISBN 0-15-169921-6). HarBraceJ.

On Loneman's Island. Mary Hubbard Howell. LC 7-661720. The American Sunday-School Union.

On Love's Altar: Or, A Fatal Fancy. Charles Garvice. (On cover: Laurel library, no. 6). 1892. G. Munro.

On Maiden Lane. Bruce Nicolaysen. 560p. 1981. pap. 2.95 (ISBN 0-380-77800-9, 77800). Avon.

On Mother's Lap. Ann Herbert Scott. LC 76-39726. (Illus.). 1972. 4.95 (ISBN 0-07-055896-5) (ISBN 0-07-055897-3). McGraw-Hill.

On Murder's Skirts. Terry Adler. LC 48-1241. 1947. Phoenix Press.

On Newfound River. Thomas Nelson Page. LC 78-110427. 1970. AMS Press.

On Newfound River. Thomas Nelson Page. LC 7-35796. 1891. C. Scribner's Sons.

On Newfound River. new ed. Thomas Nelson Page. 1906. C. Scribner's Sons.

On Newfound River. New York, Scribner, 1893. Thomas Nelson Page. LC 70-131795. 1970. Scholarly Press.

On Not Knowing How to Live. Allen Wheelis. LC 75-4294. 1975. 5.95 (ISBN 0-06-014562-5). Harper & Row.

On Not Knowing How to Live. Allen Wheelis. 1976. (ISBN 0-06-090535-2). Harper & Row.

On or About the First Day in June. John Colleton. (Signet Book). 1978. 1.95 (ISBN 0-451-08046-7). New American Library.

On Out. Lew Welch. pap. 1.00 o.p. Oyez.

On Overgrown Paths. Knut Hamsun. Tr. by Carl Anderson. 1967. 5.00 o.p. (ISBN 0-8397-6459-6). Eriksson.

On Pa's Farm. Mary Willis. (Destiny Ser.). 1980. pap. 4.95 (ISBN 0-8163-0393-2). Pacific Pr Pub Assn.

On Pegasus He Rode. Richard Blaker. LC 38-29159. Carrick & Evans, Inc.

On Peter's Island. Arthur Reed Ropes & Ropes, Mary Emily. LC 1-316708. 1901. C. Scribner's Sons.

On Picket & Other Tales. Louisa May Alcott. 1972. Repr. of 1864 ed. lib. bdg. 18.00 (ISBN 0-8422-8000-6). Irvington.

On Picket Duty: And Other Tales. Louisa May Alcott. LC 69-11876. (American short story series, v. 33). 1969. Garrett Press.

On Picket Duty, and Other Tales. Louisa May Alcott. LC 21-16866. 1864. J. Redpath.

On Rainbow Wings. Etta Pegues. (Orig.). 1981. pap. 1.75 (ISBN 0-8439-8031-1, Tiara Bks). Nordon Pubns.

On Sarpy Creek. Ira Stephens Nelson. LC 38-27304. 1938. Little, Brown and Company.

On Secret Air Service. Laurence La Tourette Driggs. LC 30-29340. 1930. Little, Brown, and Company.

On Skidd's Branch, a Tale of the Kentucky Mountains. Marion Stuart Cann. LC 6-21477. 1884. Printed at the Republican Job Rooms.

On Socialist Realism see Trial Begins.

On Some Fair Morning. Catherine Hutter. LC 46-7189. 1946. Dodd, Mead & Company.

On Spider Creek. Robert Roper. (O.s.i.). 1978. 9.95 o.s.i. (ISBN 0-671-22909-5). S&S.

On Spider Creek: a Novel. Robert Roper. LC 77-20183. 10.95 (ISBN 0-671-22909-5). Simon and Schuster.

On Spider Creek: A Novel. Robert Roper. 1979. 2.25 (ISBN 0-449-23903-9). Fawcett Crest Books.

On Such As We. Perry Adams. LC 44-334209. 1944. The Bobbs-Merrill Company.

On Sundays We Visit the In-Laws. Steven Schrader. LC 79-63182. (Orig.). 1979. pap. 3.00 (ISBN 0-913722-16-2, Pub. by Release). SBD.

On Sweetwater Trail. Sabra Conner. LC 28-209302. The Reilly & Lee Co.

On Swift's Remarks on the Barrier Treaty, & His Conduct of the Allies see Swiftiana.

On That Night. Elizabeth Yates. LC 70-81984. (Illus.). 1969. 3.95. Dutton.

On the Air. Paul Deresco Augsburg. LC 27-17228. 1927. D. Appleton and Company.

On the Altar of Mammon. Marie Petravsky. LC 7-36156. (On cover: Ideal series, no. 3). W. D. Rowland.

On the Anvil. Leslie Ingram Crawford. LC 29-181482. 1929. W. Morrow & Company.

On the Banks of the Big Fork. Dorothy Manske. (Illus.). 1976. 10.95 o.p. (ISBN 0-89002-077-9); pap. 3.95 o.p. (ISBN 0-89002-076-0). Northwoods Pr.

On the Battery: Or, Mildred's Dishes. A Story of New York City and Other Places... A. E. Corey Baldwin. 1879. The Author.

On the Beach. Norway, Nevil Shute. 1974. (pbk.) 1.25 (ISBN 0-345-23732-3). Ballantine Books.

On the Beach. Nevil Shute. 1978. pap. 2.50 (ISBN 0-345-29732-6). Ballantine.

On the Beach. Nevil Shute. 1957. 12.95 (ISBN 0-688-02223-5). Morrow.

On the Beach. Nevil Shute. 1964. pap. 2.50 o.p. (A97). Apollo Eds.

On the Beach: By Nevil Shute Pseud. Nevil Shute Norway. LC 57-9158. 1957. W. Morrow.

On the Big Wind. David Madden. LC 80-13629. 9.95 (ISBN 0-03-053276-0). Holt, Rinehart, and Winston.

On the Black Hill. Bruce Chatwin. LC 82-10923. 1983. 14.75 (ISBN 0-670-52492-1). Viking Press.

On the Border. James Roberts Gilmore. LC 6-44714. 1867. Lee and Shepard.

On the Borderland. Frederick Britten Austin. LC 23-17475. 1923. Doubleday, Page & Company.

On the Borderland: A Novel. Harriette A Keyser. LC 7-10828. 1882. G. P. Putnam's Sons.

On the Bottom. Edward Ellsberg. (Illus.). 1937. 4.50 o.p. (ISBN 0-396-00469-5). Dodd.
On the Boundaries of Darkness. Niel Hancock. (Wilderness of Four Ser.: No. 3). 288p. 1982. pap. 2.95 (ISBN 0-445-04722-4). Popular Lib.
On the Branch: From the French of Pierre De Coulevain Pseud. Helene Favre de Couvelain & Ward, Alice Hall, Tr. 1910. E. P. Dutton & Company.
On the Bright Shore. To Which Is Added, That Third Woman. Henryk Sienkiewicz. Tr. by Jeremiah Curtin. LC 9-3451. (On cover: The beacon series). 1898. Little, Brown, and Company.
On the Brink. Mercedes Endfield. (Ms squad no. 2). 1975. (pbk.) 0.95. Bantam Books.
On the Brink: A Novel. Benjamin Stein & Herbert Stein. LC 76-30823. 8.95 (ISBN 0-671-22609-6). Simon and Schuster.
On the Brink of the Precipice: A Story for Young People Author Unknown. Tr. by E. C. Eld. LC 32-23419. Augustana Book Concern.
On the Cards: An Entertaining Volume of Original Literature ... LC 37-18302. G. Routledge and Sons.
On the Company's Service. Ellis K Meacham. LC 75-143712. (Illus.). 1971. 6.95. Little, Brown.
On the Contrary. Mary Therese McCarthy. 321p. 1976. Repr. of 1961 ed. lib. bdg. 15.00x (ISBN 0-374-95440-2). Octagon.
On the Cross: A Romance of the Passion Play at Oberammergau. Wilhelmine Birch Von Hillern & Safford, Mary Joanna, Tr. LC 7-46756. 1893. G. G. Peck.
On the Damascus Road. Avin Harry Johnson. LC 64-8839. bds., 2.95. Zondervan.
On the Danger Line. Georges Simenon & Gilbert, Stuart, Tr. LC 44-7492. 1944. Harcourt, Brace and Company.
On the Darkening Green. Jerome Charyn. LC 64-66262. 1965. McGraw-Hill.
On the Dodge. William MacLeod Raine. LC 38-9425. 1938. Houghton Mifflin Company.
On the Dodge. William MacLeod Raine. 1974. (pbk.) 0.95. Popular Library.
On the Dover Road: A Narration of the Adventures of Master Jack Merrywaithe... Powell Thruston Manning. Stonebraker Brothers.
On the Drapier's Letters see Swiftiana.
On the Edge. Walter John De La Mare. LC 31-3683. 1931. A. A. Knopf.
On the Edge: A Novel. Roy Doliner. LC 77-22230. 8.95 (ISBN 0-670-52494-8). Viking Press.
On the Edge of a Moor. Amy Le Feuvre. LC 7-12604. F. H. Revell Company.
On the Edge of Love. Sheila Strutt. (Harlequin Romances Ser.). 192p. 1981. pap. 1.50 (ISBN 0-373-02447-9). PB.
On the Edge of Reason: A Novel. Miroslav Krleza. LC 74-81810. 1977. 8.95 (ISBN 0-8149-0747-4). Vanguard Press.
On the Edge of the Cliff & Other Stories. Victor Sawdon Pritchett. LC 79-4805. 1979. 11.95 (ISBN 0-394-50485-2). Random.
On the Edge of the Cliff: Short Stories. Victor Sawdon Pritchett. LC 80-11970. 1981. 3.95 (ISBN 0-394-74047-5). Vintage Books.
On the Edge of the Desert: Stories. Gladys Swan. LC 79-15858. (Illinois short fiction). 10.00 (ISBN 0-252-00780-8) (ISBN 0-252-00781-6). University of Illinois Press.
On the Edge of the Empire. Edgar Jepson & Beames, David. LC 99-1857. 1899. C. Scribner's Sons.
On the Edge of the Storm. Margaret Roberts. 1869. F. Warne and Co.
On the Edge of the Storm. Margaret Roberts. LC 7-41044. 1869. G. P. Putnam and Son.
On the Eighth Day. Lawrence E. Okun. LC 81-80093. 224p. 1981. pap. 2.25 (ISBN 0-87216-852-2). Playboy Pbks.
On the Establishment of the Chun-Chi Chu. L. Fang. 1963. pap. 0.75 o.p. (Pub. by Austral Natl U Pr). Intl Schol Bk Serv.
On the Eve. Ivan Sergeevich Turgenev. Tr. by Gilbert Gardiner. (Classics Ser.). 1950. pap. 2.95 (ISBN 0-14-044009-7). Penguin.
On the Eve: A Novel. Ivan Sergeevich Turgenev. LC 71-10318. (His Novels, v. 3). 1970. AMS Press.
On the Eve: A Tale. american ed. with amendments. ed. Ivan Sergeevich Turgenev. Tr. by Charles Edward Turner. LC 8-32675. (On cover: Leisure hour series no. 12). 1878. Holt & Williams.
On the Eve: A Tale. american ed. with amendments. ed. Ivan Sergieevich Turgenev. Tr. by Charles Edward Turner. LC 41-27435. (Leisure hour series). 1875. H. Holt and Company.
On the Eve: A Tale, by Ivan S. Turgenieff. american ed. with amendments. ed. Ivan Sergeevich Turgenev. Tr. by Charles Edward Turner. LC 41-27435. (Leisure hour series). 1875. H. Holt and Company.
On the Face of the Waters. Flora Annie Webster Steel. LC 8-13437. 1896. The Mershon Company.
On the Face of the Waters: A Tale of the Mutiny. Flora Annie Webster Steel. 1897. The Macmillan Company.
On the Farm. Edward William Dolch & Marguerite Perice Dolch. (First reading book). Garrard Press.
On the Field of Glory: An Historical Novel of the Time of King John Sobieski. Henryk Sienkiewicz. Tr. by Jeremiah Curtin. LC 6-2341. 1906. Little, Brown, and Company.
On the Fighting Line. Anne Constance Smedley Maxwell Armfield Armfield. LC 15-4798. 1915. G. P. Putnam's Sons.
On the Firing Line: A Romance of South Africa. Anna Chapin Ray & Fuller, Hamilton Brock. LC 5-9277. 1905. Little, Brown, and Company.
On the Fo'k'sle Head. William Clark Russell. (On cover: Lovell's library. v. 17, no. 836). 1886. J. W. Lovell Company.
On the Frontier. Bret Harte. LC 72-3290. (Short story index reprint series). 1972. 11.25 (ISBN 0-8369-4147-0). Books for Libraries Press.
On the Frontier. Bret Harte. LC 7-3645. 1884. Houghton, Mifflin and Company.
On the Fur Trail. Dietrich Lange. LC 31-20920. 1931. Newson & Company.
On the Gravy Train. Anne Ingalls. 2.95 o.p. Vantage.
On the Great-Circle Route: A Novel. Lucienne S Bloch. LC 79-13874. 9.95 (ISBN 0-671-24817-0). Simon and Schuster.
On the Heights. Berthold Auerbach & Bunnett, Fanny Elizabeth, 1832 or 3-1875, Tr. LC 43-37802. (Manhattan library... Vol. I, no. 2). 1891. A. L. Burt.
On the Heights. A Novel... rev. ed. Berthold Auerbach. Tr. by Bunnett, Fanny Elizabeth. LC 6-4512. 1869. Roberts Brothers.
On the Heights. A Novel... Berthold Auerbach. Tr. by Bunnett, Fanny Elizabeth. LC 34-37758. 1871. Roberts Brothers.
On the Heights: A Novel. Berthold Auerbach. Tr. by Stern, Simon Adler. LC 12-13515. 1875. H. Holt and Company.
On the Heights: A Novel. Berthold Auerbach. Tr. by Stern, Simon Adler. LC 4-21548. (On cover: Leisure hour series). 1899. H. Holt and Company.
On the Heights: A Novel. Berthold Auerbach. Tr. by Stern, Simon Adler. LC 16-6827. 1912. H. Holt and Company.
On the Heights of Himalay. Albert Van Der Naillen. LC 8-30228. (On cover: American novelists' series no. 35). United States Book Company, Successors to J. W. Lovell Company.
On the Heights of Himalay. Albert Van Der Naillen. LC 3-30227. (On cover: New occult series, no. 2). American Publishers Corporation.
On the Highest Hill. Roderick Langmere Haig Haig-Brown. LC 49-2628. 1949. W. Morrow.
On the Highest Hill. H. M Stephenson. LC 29-17894. International Fiction Library.
On the Hill. Joseph Walter Cove. LC 33-6707. 1933. D. Appleton and Company.
On the Hurricane Deck: A Novel. W. H. Wright. (On cover: Thistledown series, no. 1). 1894. The Mascot Publishing Co.
On the Indian Trail. Anna Lyle Van Dyne. LC 21-7723. Printed for the Author by the Abingdon Press.
On the Inside. Florence Finch Kelly. LC 7-10974. 1890. Sanford & Company.
On the Iron at Big Cloud. Frank Lucius Packard. LC 11-20544. 1911. Thomas Y. Crowell Company.
On the Job: Fiction About Work by Contemporary American Writers. William O'Rourke. LC 76-56433. 1977. 3.95 (ISBN 0-394-72083-0). Vintage Books.
On the King's Couch. Octave Aubry. Tr. by Johnson, Evelyn. LC 27-23448. Boni & Liveright.
On the Knees of the Gods. Anna Bowman Blake Dodd. LC 8-3428. 1908. Dodd, Mead & Company.
On the Lackawanna: A Tale of Northern Pennsylvania. Caleb Earl Wright. LC 8-37218. 1886. McGinty, Printer.
On the Lake of Lucerne and Other Stories. Beatrice Whitby. LC 8-36039. 1891. D. Appleton and Company.
On the Lightship. Herman Knickerbocker Viele. LC 9-24696. 1909. Duffield & Company.
On the Line: New Gay Fiction. LC 81-640. 11.95 (ISBN 0-89594-048-5) (ISBN 0-89594-049-3). Crossing Press.
On the Line. 1st Ed. Harvey Swados. LC 57-111525. 1957. Little, Brown.
On the Long Tide. Laura Smith Krey. LC 40-335862. 1940. Houghton Mifflin Company.
On the Loose. Happy Deams. pap. 1.95 o.p. (6031). Brandon.
On the Lot and off. George Randolph Chester & Chester, Mrs. Lilian Eleanor (Hauser) 1889- Joint Author. LC 24-8558. Harper & Brothers.
On the Makaloa Mat. Jack London. LC 19-15569. 1919. The Macmillan Company.
On the Make. Ann Lawrence. LC 35-353764. Godwin.
On the Make. John Riordan. LC 29-20970. Farrar & Rinehart Incorporated.
On the Marble Cliffs. Ernst Juenger. 1970. pap. 1.25 o.p. (ISBN 0-14-002985-0, 2985). Penguin.
On the Marble Cliffs. Ernst Junger. LC 75-22480. (Penguin modern classics,2985). 1970 (ISBN 0-14-002985-0). Penguin.
On the Marble Cliffs: A Novel. Ernst Junger & Hood, Stuart O., Tr. LC 48-2722. 1947. New Directions.
On the Margins of Old Books. Jules Lemaitre. LC 70-163041. (Short story index reprint series). 1971. (ISBN 0-8369-3955-7). Books for Libraries Press.
On the Midnight Tide. Don Tracy. LC 57-12643. 1957. Dial Press.
On the Monitor. Meredith Brucker. 1978. pap. 1.95 (ISBN 0-532-19189-7). Woodhill.
On the Mountain. Dion Henderson. LC 68-31282. 1969. 3.95. McKay.
On the Move. Harriet M. Savitz. (YA) 1979. pap. 1.75 (ISBN 0-380-46169-2, 46169). Avon.
On the Nail. Joseph Pyle. LC 50-1786. 1949. Humphries.
On the Night of the Fire. Frederick Lawrence Green. LC 39-14805. 1939. The Macmillan Company.
On the Night of the Seventh Moon. Eleanor Hibbert. LC 72-76170. 1972. 6.95 (ISBN 0-385-08579-6). Doubleday.
On the Night of the Seventh Moon. Eleanor Hibbert. LC 72-10471. 1972. 11.95 (ISBN 0-8161-6060-0). G. K. Hall.
On the Night of the Seventh Moon. Victoria Holt, pseud. LC 72-76170. 360p. 1972. 13.95 (ISBN 0-385-08579-6). Doubleday.
On the Night of the Seventh Moon. Victoria Holt, pseud. 384p. 1981. pap. 2.95 (ISBN 0-449-23568-8, Crest). Fawcett.
On the Night of the Seventh Moon. Victoria Holt, pseud. (Adult Ser.). 1972. Repr. lib. bdg. 11.95 o.p. (ISBN 0-8161-6060-0, Large Print Bks). G K Hall.
On the Night of the 18th..." A Novel. Laurence Walter Meynell. LC 36-372991. Harper & Brothers.
On the Offensive: An Army Story. George Israel Putnam. LC 12-38412. 1894. C. Scribner's Sons.
On the Old Frontier: Or, The Last Raid of the Iroquois. William Osborn Stoddard. LC 4-16469. 1893. D. Appleton and Company.
On the Other Side of the Bridge. Gertrude Capen Whitney. LC 22-213241. 1922. The Four Seas Company.
On the Overland Stage: Or, Terry As a King Whip Cub. Edwin Legrand Sabin. LC 18-181001. Thomas Y. Crowell Company.
On the Periphery. Veronica Forrest-Thompson. (Illus.). 1976. pap. 4.00 (Pub. by St Edns). SBD.
On the Plains with Custer: The Western Life and Deeds of the Chief with the Yellow Hair, Under Whom Served Boy Bugler Ned Fletcher, When in the Troublous Years 1866-1876 the Fighting Seventh Cavalry Helped to Win Pioneer Kansas, Nebraska, and Dakota for White Civilization and Today's Peace. Edwin Legrand Sabin. LC 13-210633. 1913. J. B. Lippincott Company.
On the Plains with Custer: The Western Life and Deeds of the Chief with the Yellow Hair, Under Whom Served Boy Bugler Ned Fletcher, When in the Troublous Years 1866-1876 the Fighting Seventh Cavalry Helped to Win Pioneer-Kansas, Nebraska, and Dakota for White Civilization and Today's Peace. Edwin Legrand Sabin. LC 25-23740. (Lettered on cover: Trail blazers series). 1923. J. B. Lippincott Company.
On the Plantation: A Story of a Georgia Boy's Adventures During the War. Joel Chandler Harris. 1892. D. Appleton and Company.
On the Plantation: A Story of a Georgia Boy's Adventures During the War. Joel Chandler Harris. LC 79-5189. (Illus.). 1980. 15.00 (ISBN 0-8203-0494-8) (ISBN 0-8203-0495-6). University of Georgia Press.
On the Point: A Summer Idyl. Nathan Haskell Dole. LC 7-1241. 1895. J. Knight Company.
On the Prime Minister's Account. Olle E. Hogstrand. 1975. (pbk.) 1.25. Dell.
On the Prime Minister's Account. Olle E. Hogstrand. LC 72-38681. 1972. 4.95 (ISBN 0-394-47904-1). Pantheon Books.
On the Prod. Richard Edward Wormser. (Orig.). 1970. pap. 0.60 o.p. (R2341, GM). Fawcett World.
On the Qucksands. M. B. Smith. (On cover: Clover series, no. 128). Street & Smith.
On the Rack: A Novel. William Cadwalader Hudson. LC 7-564695. (On cover: Cassell's sunshine series. no. 106). 1892. Cassell Publishing Company.
On the Rack: A Novel. William Cadwalader Hudson. LC 99-3366. (On cover: Magnet detective library, no. 90). 1899. Street & Smith.
On the Red Staircase. Mary Imlay Taylor. LC 8-25663. 1896. A. C. McClurg and Company.
On the Red World. Leo P. Kelley. LC 78-68227. (Galaxy 5 Ser.: Bk. 2). 1979. pap. 4.24 (ISBN 0-8224-3202-1). Pitman Learning.
On the Rim of the Arctic. James Beardsley Hendryx. LC 48-8577. 1948. Doubleday.
On the River Amour. Joseph Delteil. Tr. by Putnam, Samuel. LC 29-17280. 1929. Covici, Friede.
On the Road. John Kerouac. LC 57-9425. 1957. Viking Press.
On the Road. John Kerouac & Scott Donaldson. LC 78-12205. (Viking critical library). 1979. 5.95 (ISBN 0-14-015511-2). Penguin Books.
On the Road: Tales Told by a Commercial Traveller. Bracebridge Hemying. LC 7-4121. 1868. G. Routldege and Sons.
On the Road to Anahuac: An Incident in the Conquest of Mexico. 1st Ed. Rozelle S Parra. LC 56-7520. 1956. Vantage Press.
On the Road to Arcady. Mabel Nelson Thurston. LC 3-25722. 1903. F. H. Revell Company.
On the Road to Arden. Margaret Fessenden Morse. LC 9-7948. 1909. Houghton Mifflin Company.
On the Road to the Lake. Sam Flint. 1895. C.H. Kerr & Company.
On the Ropes. William Monson & Murray McLean. (Orig.). 1970. pap. 0.95 o.p. (B95-2063). Belmont-Tower.
On the Run. John Dann MacDonald. 1978. pap. 2.25 (ISBN 0-449-13983-2, GM). Fawcett.
On the Run. John Dann MacDonald. 1970. pap. 0.60 o.p. (R2241, GM). Fawcett World.
On the Rustler Trail. Robert Ames Bennet. LC 27-5006. 1927. A. C. McClurg & Co.
On the Seaboard: A Novel of the Baltic Islands. August Strindberg. Tr. by Elizabeth E. Westergren from Swedish. LC 74-13073. 304p. 1975. Repr. of 1913 ed. 19.50 o.p. (ISBN 0-86527-286-7). Fertig.
On the Seaboard: A Novel of the Baltic Islands, from the Swedish of August Strindberg. August Strindberg. Tr. by Elizabeth Clarke Westergren. LC 74-13073. 1974. H. Fertig.
On the Secret Service of His Majesty, the Queen: A Thrilling Adventure of Hebrew Secret Agent Oy-Oy-7, Israel Bond. Sol Weinstein. LC 66-9315. (PB special). 1966. Pocket Books.
On the Shady Side. Frank Arthur Swinnerton. 1973. 1.25. Lancer Books.
On the Shady Side. Frank Arthur Swinnerton. LC 73-132514. 1971. 5.95. Doubleday.
On the Shady Side. Frank Arthur Swinnerton. LC 81-47388. (Fifty Classics of Crime Fiction, 1950-1975). 1982. 14.95 (ISBN 0-8240-4999-3). Garland Pub.
On the Shore: Young Writer Remembering Chicago. Albert Halper. LC 34-3287. 1934. The Viking Press.
On the Shores of Night. Adrienne Mans. LC 67-23104. 1967. Walker.
On the Side of Romance. Eleanor Browne. LC 38-22015. 1938. Arcadia House.
On the Sixth Day. Giuseppe Bianco. LC 28-17818. The Bobbs-Merrill Company.
On the Slain Collegians. Herman Melville. Ed. by Antonio Frasconi. (Illus.). 48p. 1971. 5.95 o.p. (ISBN 0-374-22637-7); pap. 1.95 o.p. (ISBN 0-374-50954-9). FS&G.
On the Spanish Main. Herbert Strang. LC 7-33201. 1907. The Bobbs-Merrill Company.
On the Spot. Edgar Wallace. LC 49-1760. (New Avon library 173). 1948. Avon Pub. Co.
On the Spot... Edgar Wallace. LC 31-33329. Pub. for the Crime Club, Inc., by Doubleday, Doran & Company, Inc.
On the Staircase. Frank Arthur Swinnerton. LC 14-8475. George W. Doran Company.
On the Stairs. Henry Blake Fuller. LC 18-6019. 1918. Houghton Mifflin Company.
On the Stairs see Collected Works.
On the State House Steps. Mary Redfield Potter. LC 7-303145. 1896. Student Publishing Co.
On the Sunny Shore. Henryk Sienkiewicz & Soissons, Guy Jean Raoul Eugene Charles Emmanuel De Savoie- Carignan, Comte De, 1860- Tr. LC 8-6884. 1897. R. F. Fenno & Company.
On the Susquehanna: A Novel. William Alexander Hammond. LC 7-558. 1887. D. Appleton and Company.
On the Suwanee River: A Romance. golden rod ed. Opie Percival Read. Laird & Lee.
On the Take. William Riordan. (Orig.). 1976. pap. 1.25 o.p. (LB342ZK, Leisure Bks). Nordon Pubns.
On the Take. William Riordan. 1976. (pbk.) 1.25 (ISBN 0-8439-0034-2). Leisure Books.
On the Tale of a Tub see Swiftiana.

On the Threshold. Cigliana-Von Piazza, Doria. LC 65-18321. Walker.

On the Threshold. Albert F. Olivier. 5.95 o.p. Vantage.

On the Track of Death: By Douglas Rutherford Pseud. James Douglas Rutherford McConnell. LC 59-5361. 1959. Abelard-Schuman.

On the Trail of Four. Max Brand. 1982. pap. 1.95 (ISBN 0-671-44709-2). PB.

On the Trail of Four: By Max Brand. Frederick Faust. LC 67-22721. 1967. bds., 3.75. Dodd.

On the Trail of the Space Pirates. Willy Ley, Technical Adviser. Carey Rockwell. LC 53-2256. (His A Tom Corbett space cadet adventure.3). 1953. Grosset & Dunlap.

On the Trail of the Tumbling T. Clarence Edward Mulford. LC 73-89656. 1973. 6.95. Aeonian Press.

On the Trail of the Tumbling T. Clarence Edward Mulford. 1935. Doubleday, Doran & Company, Inc.

On the Trail of 1960: A Utopian Novel. Ray H Wiley. LC 50-11330. 1950. Exposition Press.

On the Trail to Sunset. Thomas William Wilby & Wilby, Mrs. Agnes Andrews, Joint Author. LC 12-9186. 1912. Moffat, Yard and Company.

On the Verge. Dikkon Eberhart. LC 79-9810. 1979. 9.95 (ISBN 0-916144-40-2). Stemmer House Publishers.

On the Verge: A Romance of the Centennial. A. L. Townsend. LC 8-298115. 1879. A. L. Bancroft & Company.

On the Volga and Other Stories. Panteleimon Sergeevich Romanov. Tr. by Ann Gretton. LC 34-36043. 1934. C. Scribner's Sons.

On the Volga and Other Stories. Panteleimon Sergeevich Romanov. LC 75-39013. (Early Soviet Literature in English Translation). 1978. 19.50 (ISBN 0-88355-415-1). Hyperion Press.

On the Warpath. James Willard Schultz. LC 14-20776. 1914. 1.25. Houghton Mifflin Company.

On the Way: Ten Stories by Members of English 7, Amherst College. Ed. by David Morton. LC 42-34884. 1934. Pub. by English.

On the Way to Perignan. Jennings Cropper Wise. LC 37-39112. 1937. The Paisley Press, Inc.

On the Way to the Sky. Douglas Kent Hall. LC 73-160059. 1972. 5.95 (ISBN 0-8415-0125-4). McCall Books.

On the Way to the Zoo. Linda Pastan. LC 74-34123. (Illus.). 1975. pap. 4.00 o.p. Dryad Pr.

On the We-a Trail: A Story of the Great Wilderness. Caroline Virginia Krout. LC 3-26967. 1903. The Macmillan Company.

On the Wing of Occasions. Joel Chandler Harris. LC 75-96883. (Illus.). 1969. (ISBN 0-8398-0765-1). Literature House.

On the Wing of Occasions: Being the Authorized Version of Certain Curious Episodes of the Late Civil War, Including the Hitherto Suppressed Narrative of the Kidnapping of President Lincoln. Joel Chandler Harris. LC 71-90582. (Short story index reprint series). (Illus.). 1969. (ISBN 0-8369-3065-7). Books for Libraries Press.

On the Wing of Occasions: Being the Authorized Version of Certain Cruious Episodes of the Late Civil War, Including the Hitherto Suppressed Narrative of the Kidnapping of President Lincoln. Joel Chandler Harris. LC 5726. 1900. Doubleday, Page & Co.

On the Wings of Eternity. 2nd ed. LC 74-162833. 550p. 15.00 (ISBN 0-9600356-3-X). F Murat.

On the Wings of Magic. Kay Hooper. (Candlelight Ecstasy Ser.: No. 153). (Orig.). 1983. pap. 1.95 (ISBN 0-440-16720-5). Dell.

On the Wings of the Morning. Louise Harrison McCraw. LC 43-18556. 1943. Fleming H. Revell Company.

On the Wings of the Storm. Richard L. Newhafer. 1970. pap. 0.95 o.p. (N2258). Pyramid Pubns.

On the Wings of the Storm: A Novel. Richard L Newhafer. LC 69-14480. 1969. 6.95. W. Morrow.

On the Wings of the Wind. Mary Virginia Stern. LC 51-2276. Chapman & Grimes.

On the Wings of Truth. J. B. Boydstun. 1978. 6.50 o.p. (ISBN 0-533-03261-X). Vantage.

On the Winning Side: A Southern Story of Ante-Bellum Times. Jeannette Ritchie Hadermann Walworth. LC 72-2927. (Black heritage library collection). (Illus.). 1972. 12.50 (ISBN 0-8369-9088-9). Books for Libraries Press.

On the Winning Side. A Southern Story of Ante-Bellum Times. Jeannette Ritchie Hadermann Walworth. (Once a week library. no. 20). 1893. P. F. Collier.

On the Yard. Malcolm Braly. (Crest bk., T1163). 1968. Fawcett.

On the Yard. Malcolm Braly. LC 77-2391. 1977. 1.95 (ISBN 0-14-004455-8). Penguin Books.

On the Yard: A Novel. 1st Ed. Malcolm Braly. LC 67-21099. 1967. bds., 5.95. Little, Brown.

On the 8th Day. Lawrence E. Okun. LC 78-74206. 9.95 (ISBN 0-89087-278-3). Celestial Arts.

On These I Stand. Countee Cullen. LC 47-30109. 1947. 10.95i (ISBN 0-06-010925-4, HarpT). Har-Row.

On Thin Ice. Fred Deem. LC 30-13807. The Warner Press.

On This Side Nothing. Alexander Comfort. LC 48-282169. 1949. Viking Press.

On This Star. Virginia Eggersten Sorensen. LC 46-25172. 1946. Reynal & Hitchcock.

On Tiptoe: A Romance of the Redwoods. Stewart Edward White. LC 22-19158. George H. Doran Company.

On to Berlin. James M. Gavin. 1979. pap. 2.95 (ISBN 0-553-13137-0). Bantam.

On to Oregon! The Story of a Pioneer Boy. Honore McCue Willsie Morrow. LC 26-160492. 1926. W. Morrow and Company, Inc.

On to the White House. Ben J Abson. LC 32-1936. 1931. The True Truth Publishing Company.

On to Widecombe Fair. Patricia Lee Gauch & Trina Schart Hyman. LC 76-48151. (Illus.). 7.95 (ISBN 0-399-20563-2). Putnam.

On Toplecote Bayou. Catherine Postell. LC 72-1518. (Black Heritage Library Collection). 1972. 8.00 (ISBN 0-8369-9048-X). Books for Libraries Press.

On Tour. Mel Arrighi. LC 79-7315. 1979. (ISBN 0-689-10984-9). Atheneum.

On Tour: An Autobiographical Novel of the 20's. Noel Streatfeild. LC 65-24181. 1965. F. Watts.

On Trial. Gwendoline Keats. LC 99-4816. 1899. C. Scribner's Sons.

On Trial for His Life. A Starring Novel of Military Life in the West Adapted from A H. Wood's Thrilling Play of the Same Name. Helen Burrell D'Apery & Davis, Owen. LC 33-28363. (On cover: Play book series. no. 125). 1908. J. S. Ogilvie Publishing Company.

On Trial: The Story of a Woman at Bay. D. Torbett & Reizenstein, Elmer L. LC 15-188182. 1915. Dodd, Mead & Company.

On Troublesome Creek. James Still. LC 41-19418. 1941. The Viking Press.

On Two Frontiers. George Tower Buffum. 1918. Lothrop, Lee & Shepard Co.

On Tybee Knoll: A Story of the Georgia Coast. James Brendan Connolly. 1905. A.S. Barnes & Company.

On Us. Douglas Woolf. LC 76-52385. 1977. 15.00. (ISBN 0-87685-285-1) (ISBN 0-87685-284-3). Black Sparrow Press.

On Virgin Soil: A Novel of Exotic Africa. Balder Olden. Tr. by Dietz, Loran. LC 30-5066. The Macaulay Company.

On We Go... A Novel. 1st Ed. Ashley N. Fordwick. LC 56-11393. 1956. Pageant Press.

On What Strange Stuff. Elisa Bialk. LC 35-10319. 1935. Doubleday, Doran & Company, Inc.

On Wheels. John Jakes. 1973. (pbk) 0.95. Warner Paperback Library.

On Wings of Faith; Stories of Kansas Pioneers and Other Tales. 1st Ed. E Lois English. LC 56-115897. 1956. Exposition Press.

On Wings of Fire. Evan Rhodes. (Orig.). 1981. pap. 3.50 (ISBN 0-440-16671-3). Dell.

On Wings of Magic. Susanna Collins. 192p. 1982. pap. 1.75 (ISBN 0-515-06650-8). Jove Pubns.

On Wings of Song. Thomas M Disch. LC 78-21411. 10.00 (ISBN 0-312-58466-0). St. Martin's Press.

On Wings of the Lion. Malcolm Kent. (O.s.i.). 289p. 1974. 7.95 o.s.i. (ISBN 0-913806-54-4). Laddin Pr.

On Winter's Traces: Decorations by Elmore Brown. Mathi Kohler Boynton-Hamilton. LC 45-9070. 1945. D. Appleton-Century Company, Incorporated.

On with the Dance. John Michael Drinkrow Hardwick. LC 79-23068. 1980. 10.95. G. K. Hall.

On with the Dance! Michael Norday. LC 54-31851. 1954. Vixen Press.

On with the Dance: Endings & Beginnings. Michael Hardwick. 1980. pap. 2.25 (ISBN 0-440-16599-7). Dell.

On with the Shoe. Jeff MacNelly. (Illus.). 1982. pap. 5.95 (ISBN 0-03-061656-5, Owl Bks). HR&W.

On with Torchy. Sewell Ford. LC 75-125210. (Short story index reprint series). (Illus.). 1970. Books for Libraries Press.

On with Torchy. Sewell Ford. LC 14-505. 1.25. E. J. Clode.

On You It Looks Good: A Novel. Marjorie Lee. LC 63-17684. 1963. W. Morrow.

Onar... Edwin Faxon Osborn. 1.50. Sylvan Press.

Onawago: Or, The Betrayer of Pontiac. Will Cumback Ludlow. LC 12-1212. 1911. Antiquarian Publishing Company.

Once. John Matter. LC 10-21298. 1910. H. Holt and Company.

Once a Fighter... Les Savage. LC 56-5863. (Pocket book 1104. Western 4). 1956. Pocket Books.

Once a Fool. Patricia Frane. LC 37-35647. 1937. Hillman-Curl, Inc.

Once a Greek. Friedrich Duerrenmatt. Tr. by R. Winston. 1965. 4.95 o.p. Knopf.

Once a Greek:...Tr. from German by Richard and Clara Winston. Friedrich Durrenmatt, pseud. LC 65-11110. 3.95bds.,. Knopf.

Once a Jolly Black Man. John McGarrity. LC 74-195835. 1973. (ISBN 0-85885-081-8). Wren.

Once a Junkie. Sonny Arguinzoni. LC 79-126917. Orig. Title: God's Junkie & the Addict Church. 212p. 1971. pap. 1.25 o.p. (ISBN 0-912106-46-8). Logos.

Once: a Novel. Samuel Miller Hageman. LC 6-45972. W. B. Smith & Co.

Once a Pony Time. Rodger E. Drake. 208p. 1975. 5.95 o.p. (ISBN 0-8059-2148-6). Dorrance.

Once a Pony Time. Rodger E. Drake. 208p. 1975. 5.95 o.p. (ISBN 0-8059-2148-6). Dorrance.

Once a Ranger... William Crawford. 1973. 4.95. Lenox Hill Pr.

Once a Ranger. James Wynbourne Routh. 1958. Avalon Books.

Once a Runner. John L. Parker, Jr. 1978. pap. 4.95. Cedarwinds.

Once a Sheriff. Al Cody, pseud. 1977. pap. 1.25 (ISBN 0-532-12497-9). Woodhill.

Once a Sheriff. Al Cody, pseud. 192p. 1973. pap. 0.95 o.p. (532-95337-095). Manor Bks.

Once a Sinner... Peggy Gaddis, pseud. LC 47-158541. 1947. Phoenix Press.

Once a Smuggler. Jewel Hatcher Henrickson. LC 65-28848. (Destiny book, D-106). Pacific Press Pub. Association.

Once a Spy. Robert Footman. LC 80-15748. 8.95 (ISBN 0-396-07864-8). Dodd, Mead.

Once a Thief. new ed. John Trinian. 160p. 1973. pap. 0.95 o.p. (ISBN 0-532-95272-3). Woodhill.

Once a Thief. John Trinian. 1973. (pbk.) 0.95. Manor Books.

Once a Week. Alan Alexander Milne. LC 26-12468. 1925. E. P. Dutton and Company.

Once a Week. Alan Alexander Milne. LC 77-91380. (Short Story Index in Reprint). 1978. 18.75 (ISBN 0-8486-5002-6). Core Collection Books.

Once a Widow: By Lee Roberts Pseud. Robert Lee Martin. LC 57-121299. (Red badge detective). 1957. Dodd, Mead.

Once a Wilderness: A Novel. Arthur Pound. 1934. Reynal & Hitchcock.

Once Aboard the Lugger -- The History of George and His Mary. Arthur Stuart-Menteth Hutchinson. LC 9-9506. M. Kennerley.

Once Aboard the Lugger-- The History of George and His Mary. Arthur Stuart-Menteth Hutchinson. LC 22-42141. 1922. Little, Brown, and Company.

Once Aboard the Lugger-- The History of George and Mary. Arthur Stuart-Menteth Hutchinson. LC 22-658. 1921. Little, Brown, and Company.

Once Acquitted... Amelia Reynolds Long. LC 45-114233. 1945. Phoenix Press.

Once Again. E. J. Rath. LC 29-169188. 1929. G. H. Watt.

Once Again. By Mrs. Forrester Pseud. Mrs. Bridges. (On cover: Seaside library. Pocket ed., no. 883). 1886. G. Munro.

Once Again. By Mrs. Forrester Pseud.... Mrs. Bridges. (On cover: Lovell's library, v. 17, no. 818). 1886. J. W. Lovell Company.

Once Again in Chicago. Minnie Hite Moody. LC 33-16584. A. H. King.

Once Against the Law. Ed. by Philip Klass. LC 67-26253. 1968. Macmillan.

Once Against the Law. William Tenn & D. Westlake. (O.s.i.). 1968. 6.95 o.s.i. (ISBN 0-02-616900-2). Macmillan.

Once an Eagle. Anton Myrer. (Berkley Medallion). 2.75 (ISBN 0-425-03330-9). Berkley.

Once & for All. Cid Corman, pseud. 1975. 16.00 o.p. (Pub. by Elizabeth Pr). SBD.

Once and Forever. Ethel E Bangert. LC 50-5935. 1950. Arcadia House.

Once and Forever: Or, Bright Morning. A Novel. Maria M Grant. 1878. G. W. Carleton & Co.; Etc., Etc.

Once and Future King. Terence Hanbury White. LC 58-10760. 1958. Putnam.

Once and Future Tales: From the Magazine of Fantasy and Science Fiction. Ed. by Edward L. Ferman. LC 67-30931. 1968. 5.95. Delphi Press.

Once Around Lightly. Robert St. John. LC 69-20086. (Illus.). 1.49 o.p. (ISBN 0-385-03397-4). Doubleday.

Once Around the Block. John Klempner. LC 39-7581. C. Scribner's Sons.

Once Around the Clock. Chikuyo Alimayo. (Illus.). 1974. 5.95. EKO Publications.

Once Around the Park: By Frank Shannonpseud. Illustrated by Leo Hershfield. Dennis Francis Joseph Shine. LC 52-13824. 1953. Morrow.

Once Beyond the Reef. Edith Austin Holton. LC 38-3537. The Penn Publishing Company.

Once Bitten. Anne J. Townsend. (Orig.). 1971. pap. 1.45 o.p. (ISBN 0-8307-0109-5, 5003407). Regal.

Once Burned. Rick West. pap. 1.95 o.p. (8060). Cameo.

Once Departed. Mack Reynolds. (Orig.). 1970. pap. 0.60 o.p. (0502-06122). Curtis.

Once I Had a Baby Debbie. 1982. 1.75. Cherubim.

Once in a Blue Moon. Frank Condon. LC 29-8314. J. H. Sears & Company, Inc.

Once in a Blue Moon. Mary Wentworth King. LC 39-299636. M. S. Mill Co., Inc.

Once in a Life. Charles Garvice. (On cover: Laurel library, no. 18). 1894. G. Munro's Sons.

Once in a Lifetime. Danielle Steel. LC 81-19579. 6.95 (ISBN 0-440-56682-7). Dell Pub. Co.

Once in a Lifetime. Danielle Steel. LC 82-21362. 1983. 14.95 (ISBN 0-8161-3407-3). G.K. Hall.

Once in a Lifetime see Sergeant Death.

Once in a Red Moon. Joel Townsley Rogers. LC 23-13650. Brentano's.

Once in Aleppo. Donald Richmond Barton. LC 54-6297. 1955. Scribner.

Once in Every Lifetime. Tom Hanlin. LC 45-9736. 1945. The Viking Press.

Once in Love Is Forever. Florence Glass Kaufman. LC 79-186598. 1972. 4.00. Dorrance.

Once in My Saddle. David Albert Lamson. LC 40-32083. 1940. C. Scribner's Sons.

Once in Six Thousand Years. Eloise R. Rees. (Orig.). 1980. pap. 1.95 (ISBN 0-532-23185-6). Woodhill.

Once in the Saddle. Nelson Nye. 176p. 1975. pap. 0.95 o.p. (ISBN 0-532-95408-4). Woodhill.

Once in the Saddle. Nelson Nye. 176p. 1975. pap. 0.95 o.p. (ISBN 0-532-95408-4). Manor Bks.

Once in the Saddle. Nelson Coral Nye. LC 46-191035. 1946. Arcadia House, Inc.

Once in the Saddle: And Paso Por Aqui. Eugene Manlove Rhodes. LC 27-9855. 1927. Houghton Mifflin Company.

Once in Vienna... Vicki Baum & Harvey, Felice, Tr. LC 45-2842. 1945. Didier.

Once Is Enough. Jeanne Cambrai. 224p. (Orig.). 1974. pap. 1.50 o.p. (ISBN 0-532-15126-7). Woodhill.

Once Is Enough. Jeanne Cambrai. 224p. (Orig.). 1974. pap. 1.50 o.p. (ISBN 0-532-15126-7). Manor Bks.

Once Is Not Enough. Jacqueline Susann. LC 72-14251. 1973. 7.95 (ISBN 0-688-00156-4). Morrow.

Once Is Not Enough. Jacqueline Susann. 1974. (pbk.) 1.95. Bantam Books.

Once More, Miranda. Jennifer Wilde. 576p. (Orig.). 1983. pap. 3.95 (ISBN 0-345-30694-5). Ballantine.

Once More the Hero. William Overgard. (Orig.). 1974. pap. 1.25 o.p. (ISBN 0-515-03348-0, V3348). Pyramid Pubns.

Once More the Sun. Vivian Lord. 352p. 1982. pap. 3.50 (ISBN 0-449-14460-7, GM). Fawcett.

Once More: Ye Laurels. David Cort. LC 28-23458. 1928. The John Day Company.

Once off Guard. James Harold Wallis. LC 42-395758. 1942. E. P. Dutton & Co., Inc.

Once on a Time. Alan Alexander Milne. LC 70-366594. (Puffin books, PS 377). (Illus.). 1968. Penguin.

Once on a Time. Alan Alexander Milne. LC 22-18784. 1922. G. P. Putnam's Sons.

Once on a Time. Illus. by Susan Perl. Alan Alexander Milne. LC 62-101169. 1962. New York Graphic Society.

Once on an Island: By Sara Sloane Pseud. Ursula Bloom. LC 50-13850. 1950. Arcadia House.

Once on the Summer Range. Francis Hill. LC 18-19295. 1918. The Macmillan Company.

Once Over Deadly. Ed McNamara. LC 58-6792. 1958. Abelard-Schuman.

Once Over Lightly. David Niven. LC 51-7575. 1951. Prentice-Hall.

Once There Was a Fat Girl. Cynthia Blair. 1981. pap. 1.95 (ISBN 0-449-14394-5, GM). Fawcett.

Once There Was a Giant. Keith Laumer. LC 76-139040. (Doubleday science fiction). 1971. 5.95. Doubleday.

Once There Was a Village. Katharine Dunlap. LC 40-35460. 1941. W. Morrow and Company.

Once There Was a Waltz. Paul Cooper Murray. LC 47-11453. 1947. M.S. Mill Co.

Once They Were Rich. David Leslie Murray. LC 33-17939. E. P. Dutton & Co., Inc.

Once to Every Man. Larry Evans. LC 15-152962. The H. K. Fly Company.

Once to Every Man. Paul Good. LC 77-127718. 1970. 6.95. Putnam.

Once to Every Man. Fannie Heaslip Lea. 1938. Dodd, Mead & Company.

Once to Every Woman. Davis Dresser. LC 38-30792. 1938. Godwin.

Once to Shout. Agnes Sligh Turnbull. LC 43-16233. 1943. The Macmillan Company.

Once to Tiger Bay. William Townend. LC 29-21205. 1929. I. Washburn.

Once Too Often. Elwyn Whitman Chambers. LC 38-24907. 1938. Doubleday, Doran & Company, Inc.
Once Upon a Christmas. Pearl Sydenstricker Buck. LC 72-2410. (Illus.). 1972. 8.95. John Day Co.
Once Upon a Crime. Christopher Monig, pseud. 1971. pap. 0.75 o.p. (ISBN 0-446-64631-8, 64-631-8). Paperback Lib.
Once Upon a Crime. Robert Selman. LC 47-31073. 1947. W. Morrow.
Once Upon a Dream. Patricia Bird. (Avalon Books). 4.95. Thomas Bouregy.
Once Upon a Lake. Thelma Jones. 7.95 o.p. (ISBN 0-87018-034-7). Ross.
Once upon a Medieval Time. John Myers. Ed. by Hank Stine. (Illus.). 176p. (Orig.). 1983. pap. 5.95 (ISBN 0-89865-291-X). Donning Co.
Once Upon a Star. Gerald Leroy Geering. (Illus.). 1973. 3.50 (ISBN 0-533-00474-8). Vantage.
Once Upon a Star: A Novel of the Future. 1st Ed. Kendell Foster Crossen. LC 53-549888. 1953. Holt.
Once Upon a Summer. Janette Oke. LC 81-10183. 3.50 (ISBN 0-87123-413-0). Bethany House.
Once Upon a Summer. Natalie Shipman. LC 50-5843. 1950. Avalon Books.
Once Upon a Time. Richard Harding Davis. LC 10-18653. 1910. C. Scribner's Sons.
Once Upon a Time. Gyula Illyes. 1975. 7.50 o.p. (ISBN 0-8283-1635-X). Branden.
Once Upon a Time. S. L. Miller. 3.00 o.p. Carlton.
Once Upon a Time, an Adventure. William Vaughan Wilkins. LC 49-11019. 1949. Macmillan Co.
Once Upon a Time in Lebanon. Roseanne Khalaf. LC 82-1193. (Illus.). 10.00 (ISBN 0-88206-051-1). Caravan Books.
Once Upon a Time Is Enough. Will Stanton. LC 76-124547. (Illus.). 1970. Lippincott.
Once Upon a Time, They Lived Happily Ever After. Ernest Rook & David Cavagnaro. LC 73-80426. 1973. pap. 3.95 o.p. (ISBN 0-912310-31-6). Celestial Arts.
Once Upon a Tombstone. (read easy large-type ed.) ed. Elizabeth Salter. (Ace gothic, 6278). 1972. Ace.
Once upon a Train & Other Stories. Stuart Palmer & Craig Rice. Ed. by Harold Straubing. 256p. 1981. pap. 5.95 (ISBN 0-87786-008-4). Gold Penny.
Once We Had a Child. Rudolf Ditzen, pseud. Tr. by Sutton, Eric. LC 36-6999. 1936. Simon and Schuster.
Once You Cared. Barbara Hedworth. LC 43-165. 1942. Arcadia House, Inc.
Once You Shave a Cactus: A Novel by E. E. Spitzer. Erwin Edwin Spitzer. LC 66-261742. 1966. 4.95. Crown.
Once You Stop, You're Dead. Eaton K Goldthwaite. LC 68-55997. 1968. 4.95. Morrow.
Ondine. Charles Kozloff. LC 79-23065. 11.95 (ISBN 0-312-58502-0). St. Martin's Press.
One. David Karp. 1962. pap. 1.95 o.p. (ISBN 0-448-00126-8, UL). G&D.
One. Sarah Warder MacConnell. LC 22-145219. 1922. The Macmillan Company.
One: A Novel. David Karp. LC 53-10801. 1953. Vanguard Press.
One Across, Two Down. Ruth Rendell. 1974. (pbk.) 0.95. Bantam Books.
One Across, Two Down. Ruth Rendell. LC 78-150914. 1971. 4.95. Published for the Crime Club by Doubleday.
One After Another. Stacy Aumonier. LC 20-15345. 1920. The Macmillan Company.
One Afternoon: And Other Stories. Marion Ames Taggart. LC 5-39867. 1905. Benziger Brothers.
One Afternoon with Mark Twain. George Ade. LC 74-3426. 1939. lib. bdg. 8.50 (ISBN 0-8414-2958-8). Folcroft.
One Against a Wilderness. Chester, William L. 1977. 1.50 (ISBN 0-87997-280-7). DAW Books.
One Against Many; or, Lady Diana's Pride. Bertha M. Clay. LC 4366. (Bertha M. Clay library, no. 10). 1900. Street & Smith.
One Against the Earth. Daniel Mainwaring. LC 33-2411. 1933. R. Long & R. R. Smith, Inc.
One Against the Odds. Cover Painting by Ray Johnson. Norbert Fagan. LC 54-255787. (Gold medal books, 382). 1954. Fawcett Publications.
One Against Time. Astron Del Martia. 1970. pap. 0.60 o.p. (ISBN 0-446-63270-8, 63-270). Paperback Lib.
One Alone. Hilda Van Siller. LC 46-6907. 1946. Pub. for the Crime Club by Doubleday & Company, Inc.
One Alone. Hilda Van Siller. LC 46-69072. 1946. Pub. for the Crime Club by Doubleday & Company Inc.
One American Girl. Hattie H. Rhodes. LC 1-39930. (On cover: Dillingham's American authors library, no. 70). 1901. G. W. Dillingham Company.
One Among None. Roy Olin Stratton. LC 65-20960. (Mass. State Police Mystery, 2). bds., 3.50. Mill, Dist. Morrow.
One and All. Retta Augusta Garland. LC 22-25001. 1922. The Schauer Printing Studio.
One, and I. Elizabeth Rockford Covey. LC 8-23925. 1908. G. W. Jacobs & Co.
One and Only. Ron De Christoforo. 1978. 1.75 (ISBN 0-671-81917-8). Pocket Books.
One and Only. Elizabeth Sherwood. LC 38-11886. Gramercy Publishing Co.
One and the Other. Richard Curle. LC 28-231139. 1928. Doubleday, Doran & Company, Inc.
One and the Other. F. Hewes Lancaster. LC 12-4766. 1.00. Small, Maynard and Company.
One-and-Twenty. A Novel. Frederick William Robinson. (seaside library. v. 45. no. 912). 1881. G. Munro.
One Angel Less. Henry Wisdom Roden. LC 45-3350. 1945. W. Morrow & Company.
One Angry Man. Norman Daniels. (Orig.). 1971. pap. 0.95 o.p. (N2486). Pyramid Pubns.
One Arm and Other Stories. Tennessee Williams. LC 57-31974. 1954. New Directions.
One Basket. Edna Ferber. LC 57-5531. 1957. 3.95. Doubleday.
One Basket. Edna Ferber. 1972. 1.25. Manor Books.
One Basket, Vol. 1. Edna Ferber. 288p. 1972. pap. 1.25 o.p. (ISBN 0-532-12143-0). Woodhill.
One Basket, Vol. 2. Edna Ferber. 336p. 1972. pap. 1.25 o.p. (ISBN 0-532-12144-9). Woodhill.
One Basket: Short Stories, 1913-40. Edna Ferber. LC 57-5531. 3.95 o.s.i. Doubleday.
One Basket: Thirty-One Short Stories. Edna Ferber. LC 57-5581. 1957. Doubleday.
One Basket: Thirty-One Short Stories. Edna Ferber. LC 47-30149. 1947. Simon and Schuster.
One Before. Barry Eric Odell Pain. LC 2-18035. 1902. C. Scribner's Sons.
One Before Bedtime: A Novel. Richard Linkroum. LC 68-10219. 1968. 4.50. Lippincott.
One Being Living. Ross Edwin. LC 35-6654. The Macaulay Company.
One Bell Calls the Watch. William Winter. 1940. The Caxton Printers, Ltd.
One Big Family: By Garth Hale Pseud. 1st Ed. Albert Benjamin Cunningham. LC 50-8564. 1950. Dutton.
One Big Happy Family. Irene Tiersten. LC 81-16712. 13.95 (ISBN 0-312-58515-2). St. Martin's Press.
One Black Summer. Barbara Jefferis. LC 67-12985. 1967. Morrow.
One Braver Thing. Clotilde Inez Mary Graves. LC 10-135837. 1910. Duffield & Company.
One Braver Thing. Cyril Harris. LC 42-21301. 1942. C. Scribner's Sons.
One Breath, a Novel. Patrick Carleton. E. P. Dutton & Co., Inc.
One Brief Sweet Hour. Jane Arbor. (Harlequin Romances Ser.). 192p. 1981. pap. 1.25 (ISBN 0-373-02419-3). PB.
One Bright Summer Morning. Rene Raymond. 1974. (pbk.) 0.95 (ISBN 0-671-77923-0). Pocket Books.
One Bullet for the General. Patrick Turnbull. LC 67-13485. 1968. Holt, Rinehart and Winston.
One by One. Penelope Gilliatt. LC 65-15924. 1965. Atheneum.
One by One. Linda Lee. LC 77-21427. 9.95 (ISBN 0-671-22822-6). Simon and Schuster.
One by One. Linda Lee. (Illus.). 1979. 2.50. Pocket Books.
One by One. Bill Webster. LC 71-186048. 1972. 5.95 (ISBN 0-385-08006-9). Doubleday.
One by One: A New Novel, by Fan Nichols. Frances Nichols Hanna. LC 51-4410. 1951. Arco Pub. Co.
One by One They Disappeared. Moray Dalton. LC 29-5956. 1929. Harper & Brothers.
One Came Out. Margaret Wilson. LC 32-2237. 1932. Harper & Brothers.
One Chance in a Hundred: A Novel. Elizabeth Winthrop Johnson. LC 11-283611. 1.25. R. G. Badger.
One Clear Call. Frances Nimmo Greene. LC 14-17925. 1914. C. Scribner's Sons.
One Clear Call. Frances Nimmo Greene. LC 22-160421. 1915. C. Scribner's Sons.
One Clear Call. Edwin Ryan. LC 62-106463. 1962. Macmillan.
One Clear Call. Upton Beall Sinclair. LC 48-8056. 1948. Viking Press.
One Coffee With. Margaret B. Maron. (Raven House Mysteries Ser.). 224p. 1983. pap. cancelled (ISBN 0-373-63052-2, Pub. by Worldwide). Harlequin Bks.
One Corpse Missing: A Beau and Pogy Murder Mystey. Zola Helen Ross. LC 48-5340. 1948. Bobbs-Merrill Co.
One Corpse Too Many. Ellis Peters. LC 80-176. 192p. 1980. 8.95 (ISBN 0-688-03630-9). Morrow.
One Corpse Too Many. Ellis Peters. 192p. 1981. pap. 2.25 (ISBN 0-445-04653-8). Popular Lib.
One Corpse Too Many. Ellis Peters. 1982. 15.00x (ISBN 0-333-27003-7, Pub. by Macmillan England). State Mutual Bk.
One Corpse Too Many: A Medieval Novel of Suspense. Edith Pargeter. LC 80-176. (Illus.). 1980. 8.95 (ISBN 0-688-03630-9). Morrow.
One Crazy Cowboy. Charles Horace Snow. LC 33-18224. 1933. W. Morrow and Company.
One Cried Murder. Sidney Hobson Courtier. LC 53-9432. (Murray Hill mystery). 1954. Rinehart.
One Cried Murder. Jean Leslie. LC 45-5015. 1945. Pub. for the Crime Club, by Doubleday, Doran & Company, Inc.
One Crow, Two Crow. Virginia Chase. LC 78-8164. 1978. lib. bdg. 9.50 o.p. (ISBN 0-89621-009-X); pap. 4.95 (ISBN 0-89621-008-1). Thorndike Pr.
One Crow, Two Crow. Virginia Chase Perkins. LC 70-155663. 1971. 5.95 (ISBN 0-8149-0691-5). Vanguard Press.
One Crowded Hour. Augusta Dillman Thomas. LC 42-43759. 1940. Schlechter's.
One Crystal and a Mother. Ellen Du Poise Taylor. LC 27-3695. 1927. Harper & Brothers.
One Dark Night. Wallace White. (Hi Lo Ser.). 96p. 1981. pap. 1.50 (ISBN 0-553-14822-2). Bantam.
One Day. Wright Morris. LC 65-12403. 5.95. Atheneum.
One Day. Wright Morris. LC 76-3766. 1976. 13.95 (ISBN 0-8032-0879-0) (ISBN 0-8032-5841-0). University of Nebraska Press.
One Day: A Sequel to "Three Weeks.". LC 9-19172. 1909. The Macaulay Company.
One Day a Stranger. Betty Swinford. LC 71-123160. 1970. 3.95. Moody Press.
One Day: A Tale of the Prairies. Elbert Hubbard. LC 7-5660. (On cover: Side pocket series). 1893. Arena Publishing Co.
One Day: A Tale of the Prairies. Elbert Hubbard. LC 18-2604. 1917. The Roycrofters.
One Day at Teton Marsh. Sally Carrighar. LC 78-26679. (Illus.). 1979. pap. 4.25 (ISBN 0-8032-6302-3, BB 692, Bison). U of Nebr Pr.
One Day in October. Sigurd Hoel & Bateson, Solvi, Tr. LC 32-30933. 1932. Coward-McCann, Inc.
One Day in the Afternoon of the World. William Saroyan. LC 64-20194. 1964. Harcourt, Brace & World.
One Day in the Life of Ivan Denisovich. Aleksandr Isaevich Solzhenitsyn. LC 63-12769. (Books that matter). 1963. Praeger.
One Day in the Life of Ivan Denisovich. Aleksandr Isaevich Solzhenitsyn. (Signet modern classic, CQ470). 1973. New American Lib.
One Day in the Life of Ivan Denisovich. Aleksandr Isaevich Solzhenitsyn. LC 63-12266. 1963. Dutton.
One Day in the Life of Ivan Denisovitch. Aleksandr Isaevich Solzhenitsyn. 1973. pap. 1.25 o.s.i. (33-037). Lancer.
One Day in the "New Life." Translated by David Floyd. Fedor Aleksandrovich Abramov. LC 63-18177. 1963. Praeger.
One Day More. John Womack Vandercook. LC 50-10149. 1950. Houghton Mifflin.
One Day, My Love. Iris Bromige. LC 80-146429. 1980. 26.50 (ISBN 0-340-25182-4). Hodder and Stoughton.
One Day of the Week. Translated from the Spanish by J. M. Cohen. Rafael Sanchez Feriosio. LC 62-11782. 1962. Abelard-Schuman.
One Day on Beetle Rock. Sally Carrighar. LC 78-18854. viii, 196p. 1978. pap. 3.25 (ISBN 0-8032-6301-5, BB 691, Bison). U of Nebr Pr.
One Day's Courtship: And The Heralds of Fame. Robert Barr. LC 12-306902. ("The Newport series" of modern fiction). F. A. Stokes Companyy.
One Dead Debutante. Heywood Gould. LC 75-9483. 1975. 7.95. St. Martin's Press.
One Deadly Summer. Sebastien Japrisot. Tr. by Alan Sheridan. LC 79-3356. (Helen & Kurt Wolff Bk.). 288p. 1980. 9.95 (ISBN 0-15-169381-1). HarBraceJ.
One Deadly Summer. Sebastien Japrisot. 320p. 1981. pap. 2.95 (ISBN 0-14-005846-X). Penguin.
One Deadly Summer. Jean Baptiste Rossi. LC 79-3356. 9.95 (ISBN 0-15-169381-1). Harcourt Brace Jovanovich.
One Deadly Summer. Jean Baptiste Rossi. LC 80-25170. 1981. 2.95 (ISBN 0-14-005846-X). Penguin Books.
One Destiny. Philip Duffield Stong. LC 42-24773. 1942. Reynal & Hitchcock, Inc.
One Dip Dead. Aaron Marc Stein. LC 78-22760. (Crime Club Ser.). 1979. 9.95 o.p. (ISBN 0-385-15226-4). Doubleday.
One Dollar Death. Richard Barth. LC 82-2555. 13.95 (ISBN 0-385-27633-8). Dial Press.
One Dollar's Worth... Fred H Brown.
One Down. Anders Bodelsen. LC 71-105367. 1970. 5.95. Harper & Row.
One Dozen & One Short Stories. Gladys Bagg Taber. 1966. 5.95 o.p. (ISBN 0-397-00437-0). Lippincott.
One Dozen and One: Short Stories, by Gladys Taber. Ed. Gladys Bagg Taber. LC 66-23249. 4.95. Lippincott.
One Dragon Too Many. Louise Field Cooper. 1973. (pbk.) 1.25. Warner Paperback Library.
One Dragon Too Many. Louise Field Cooper. LC 79-123426. 1971. 5.95. Knopf.
One Dragon Too Many. Louise Field Cooper. LC 77-13674. 1978. 9.95 (ISBN 0-89340-123-4). J. Curley & Associates.
One Drop of Blood: A Mystery Novel. Anne Austin. LC 32-8899. 1932. The Macmillan Company.
One Easy Piece. Don Merritt. LC 81-5493. 1981. 12.95 (ISBN 0-698-11112-5). Coward, McCann & Geoghegan.
One Enduring Purpose. Henry Lieferant & Sylvia Saltzberg Lieferant. LC 41-183049. 1941. E. P. Dutton & Co., Inc.
One-Eye. Stuart Gordon. (Science Fiction Ser.). pap. 0.95 o.p. (UQ1077). DAW Bks.
One-Eye. Stuart Gordon. 1973. (pbk) 0.95. DAW Books.
One-Eyed King. Edwin Fadiman, Jr. 1971. 6.95 o.p. (ISBN 0-87035-023-4). Geis.
One-Eyed King: A Novel. Edwin Fadiman. LC 73-134212. 1971. 6.95. B. Geis Associates.
One-Eyed Man. Larry L King. LC 66-188133. (Signet bk., Q3240). 1967. New Amer. Lib.
One-Eyed Moon. Marguerite Steen. LC 35-537581. 1935. Little, Brown, and Company.
One-Eyed Sky. Max Evans. LC 74-82064. (Illus.). 1974. 5.95 (ISBN 0-8402-1361-1). Nash Pub.
One Fair Daughter: A Story. Frederic Pierpont Ladd. LC 9-4955. M. Kennerley.
One Fair Daughter: Her Story. Frank Frankfort Moore. LC 7-25305. E. A. Weeks & Company.
One Fair Daughter: Translated from the German Manuscript. Bruno Frank & Trask, Claire, Tr. LC 43-14766. 1943. The Viking Press.
One False, Both Fair: Or, A Hard Knot. John Berwick Harwood. (On cover: Lovell's library, v. 5, no. 269). 1883. J. W. Lovell Company.
One False, Both Fair: Or, A Hard Knot. John Berwick Harwood. (On cover: Seaside library. Pocket ed., no. 143). 1884. G. Munro.
One False, Both Fair: Or, A Hard Knot. A Novel. John Berwick Harwood. (Harper's Franklin square library, no. 358). 1884. Harper & Brothers.
One False Move. Kelley Pseud Roos. LC 66-217334. (Red badge mystery). 1966. bds., 3.50. Dodd.
One Fat Englishman. Kingsley Amis. LC 64-11532. 1964. Harcourt, Brace & World.
One Fat Summer. Robert Lipsyte. (gr. 5-12). 1978. pap. 1.95 (ISBN 0-553-14306-9). Bantam.
One Fearful Yellow Eye. John Dann MacDonald. LC 77-24165. (Travis McGee series). 1977. 8.95 (ISBN 0-397-01191-1). Lippincott.
One Fearful Yellow Eye. John Dann MacDonald. LC 83-202. 1983. 14.95 (ISBN 0-8161-3380-8). G.K. Hall.
One Fell Soup: or I'm Just a Bug on the Windshield of Life. Roy J. Blount. 255p. 1982. 12.95 (ISBN 0-316-10005-6, Pub. by Atlantic Monthly Pr). Little.
One Fight More. Susan Ertz. LC 39-25441. 1939. D. Appleton-Century Company, Incorporated.
One Fine Spring. James Harold Turner. LC 52-7266. 1951. Pelican Pub. Co.
One Five Three Oakland Street. Dora Highland. (Queen-size gothic: large, easy-to-read type). 1973. (pbk.) 0.95. Popular Lib.
One Flesh. Rosita Torr Forbes. LC 31-383628. 1930. G. P. Putnam's Sons.
One Flew Over the Cuckoo's Nest. Ken Kesey. Ed. by John Clark Pratt. LC 72-78993. (Viking critical library). 1973. 7.95 (ISBN 0-670-52605-3) (ISBN 0-670-52605-3). Viking Press.
One Flew Over the Cuckoo's Nest. Ken Kesey. 1975. (pbk.) 1.50. New American Library.
One Flew Over the Cuckoo's Nest. Ken Kesey & John Clark Pratt. LC 77-22235. (Viking critical library). 1977. 3.95 (ISBN 0-14-015509-0). Penguin Books.
One Flew Over the Cuckoo's Nest: A Novel. Ken Kesey. LC 76-28166. 1976. 7.95 (ISBN 0-670-52604-5) (ISBN 0-670-00161-9). Penguin Books.
One Flew Over the Cuckoo's Nest: A Novel. Ken Kesey. LC 62-8602. 1962. Viking Press.
One Foot in America. Yuri Suhl. LC 50-9837. 1950. Macmillan.
One Foot in Eden. Albert Kovetz. 1981. pap. 2.75 (ISBN 0-89083-792-9). Zebra.
One Foot in the Grave. Peter Dickinson. LC 79-5354. 8.95. Pantheon Books.
One Foot in the Grave. Peter Dickinson. LC 80-21889. 1981. 2.95 (ISBN 0-14-005779-X). Penguin Books.
One Foot in the Grave: A Saturnin Dax Detective Novel. Marten Cumberland. LC 52-28540. 1952. Hurst & Blackett.

One for Many. Confessions of a Young Girl. Henny Bernstein. Tr. by Britoff, Henry. LC 12-39769. J. S. Ogilvie Publishing Company.

One for My Baby: A Novel. Alvah Cecil Bessie. LC 79-3441. 10.95 (ISBN 0-03-053851-3). Holt, Rinehart, and Winston.

One for My Dame. 1st Ed. Jack Webb. LC 61-5206. (Rinehart suspense novel). 1961. Holt, Rinehart and Winston.

One for New York. John A. Williams. 184p. 1975. Repr. of 1960 ed. 7.95x (ISBN 0-911860-52-5). Chatham Bkseller.

One for the Devil. Etienne Leroux. Tr. by Charles Eglington. LC 68-15024. 1970. 2.95 o.p. (Mer); pap. 2.95 o.p. (M295). World Pub.

One for the Devil. Translated from Afrikaans by Charles Eglington. Etienne Leroux. LC 68-15024. 1968. Houghton Mifflin.

One for the Gods. Gordon Merrick. 1972. pap. 2.95 (ISBN 0-380-01366-5, 55749). Avon.

One for the Gods: A Novel. Gordon Merrick. LC 79-148673. 1971. 6.95. B. Geis Associates.

One for the Money. Hazel Iris Addis. LC 41-6364. 1941. Arcadia House, Inc.

One for the Road. Clara Lee Brown. LC 72-112338. 1970. Christopher Pub. House.

One for the Road. 1st Ed. Fredric Brown. LC 58-9586. 1958. Dutton.

One Forty-Two: The Reformed Messenger Boy. Henry Morrow Hyde. LC 1-27068. 1901. H. S. Stone and Company.

One Game. Joan C Oviatt. LC 82-19817. 6.95 (ISBN 0-87747-949-6). Deseret Book Co.

One Generation. Roy A. Heathe. 176p. 1981. 13.95 (ISBN 0-8052-8074-X, Pub. by Allison & Busby England); pap. 5.95 (ISBN 0-8052-8073-1). Schocken.

One Generation After. Elie Wiesel. LC 82-3226. 198p. 1982. pap. 6.95 (ISBN 0-8052-0713-9). Schocken.

One Generation Away. Leslie Gordon Barnard. LC 32-346844. 1932. Holborn House.

One Girl Found: A Sequel to "Three Girls Lost". Robert Douglas Andrews, pseud. LC 30-29551. Grosset & Dunlap.

One Girl in the World. Charles Garvice. LC 16-23147. Hodder and Stoughton.

One Girl's Morals: The Romance of a Dime-a-Dance Girl. Joan Clayton. LC 32-9887. Grosset & Dunlap.

One Golden Earring. Ann Boyle. (YA) 1974. 4.95 o.p. (Avalon). Bouregy.

One Golden Earring. Ann Boyle. (Avalon romances). 1974. 4.50. Avalon Books.

One Good Death Deserves Another. Ritchie Perry. LC 76-54326. 1977. 6.95 (ISBN 0-395-25295-4). Houghton Mifflin.

One Good Death Deserves Another. Ritchie Perry. LC 77-354870. 1976. 2.95 (ISBN 0-00-231608-0). Collins for the Crime Club.

One Good Guest. Lucy Bethia Colquhoun Walford. LC 8-328092. 1892. Longmans, Green, and Co.

One Grave Too Many. Ron Goulart. (John Easy Mystery). 1974. (pbk.) 0.95. Ace Books.

One Green Bottle. 1st American Ed. Elizabeth Coxhead. LC 51-11188. 1951. Lippincott.

One Half of Robertson Davies. William Robertson Davies. 1978. pap. 4.95 (ISBN 0-14-004967-3). Penguin.

One Half of the World. 1st Ed. James Barlow. LC 56-11097. 1957. Harper.

One Half So Precious. Kate Farness. LC 55-9724. 1955. Dodd, Mead.

One Hand Clapping. Anthony Burgess. 1972. 5.95 o.p. (ISBN 0-394-47280-2). Knopf.

One Hand Clapping. John Anthony Burgess Wilson. 1973. 1.25 (ISBN 0-345-03151-2). Ballantine.

One Hand Clapping. John Anthony Burgess Wilson. LC 73-125826. 1972. 5.95 (ISBN 0-394-47280-2). Knopf.

One Happy Family. Gertrude Jobes. LC 55-12023. 1955. Pageant Press.

One Happy Jew. Nat Joseph Ferber. LC 34-13901. Farrar & Rinehart, Incorporated.

One Heart, One Vote. Ted Torkelson. LC 75-25224. (Stories That Win Ser.). 1975. pap. 0.95 o.p. (ISBN 0-8163-0182-4, 15199-3). Pacific Pr Pub Assn.

One Heart That Never Ached. J B Parrack. LC 11-18940. 1.25. The Roxburgh Publishing Company (Incorporated.

One Heavenly Night. Lynn Farnol & Bromfield, Louis. LC 31-3095. Grosset & Dunlap.

One Hell of an Actor: A Novel. Garson Kanin. LC 76-47252. 8.95 (ISBN 0-06-012249-8). Harper & Row.

One Hot Summer in Kyoto. John Haylock. 183p. 1980. 17.50x (ISBN 0-904388-31-X). Intl Pubns Serv.

One Hour. Lillian Eugenia Smith. LC 57-5299. 1959. Harcourt, Brace.

One Hour and Forever: The Story of a Woman and a Love Supreme. T Everett Harre. LC 25-6943. The Macaulay Company.

One Hour to Kill. George Harmon Coxe. 1963. 3.95 o.p. Knopf.

One House Contains Us. Oscar Leonard & Theodorescu, Dimitri. Robul. LC 40-99003. Liveright Publishing Corporation.

One Hundred and Twelve Elm Street. Henrietta Sperry Ripperger. LC 43-6808. 1943. G. P. Putnam's Sons.

One Hundred Bear Stories. Historical, Romantic, Biblical, Classical... Related, Selected. Murat Halstead. (sunnyside series, no. 87). J. S. Ogilvie Publishing Company.

One Hundred Best Novels Condensed. Ed. by Edwin Atkins Grozier & Wingate, Charles Edgar Lewis. LC 20-6498. 1920. Harper & Brothers.

One Hundred Best Novels Condensed. Ed. by Edwin Atkins Grozier & Wingate, Charles Edgar Lewis. LC 31-21758. W. J. Black Inc.

One Hundred Best Novels Condensed. Ed. by Edwin Atkins Grozier & Wingate, Charles Edgar Lewis. LC 31-140563. Harper & Brothers.

One Hundred Dollar Misunderstanding: A Novel. Robert Gover. LC 80-19795. 1980. 2.95 (ISBN 0-394-17764-9). Grove Press: Distributed by Random House.

One Hundred Fifty Eight Pound Marriage. John Irving. 1978. pap. 2.95 (ISBN 0-671-44000-4). PB.

One Hundred Forty-Four Piccadilly. Samuel Michael Fuller. LC 71-170137. 1971. 5.95 (ISBN 0-87777-033-6). R. W. Baron.

One Hundred French Romances. LC 31-93055. Preferred Publications, Inc.

One Hundred Great Science Fiction Short Short Stories. Ed. by Isaac Asimov et al. 1980. pap. 2.95 (ISBN 0-380-58735-1, 60483-3). Avon.

One Hundred Great Science Fiction Short Short Stories. Ed. by Isaac Asimov et al. LC 77-76221. 1978. 8.95 (ISBN 0-385-13044-9). Doubleday.

One Hundred Megaton Kill. Ralph Hayes. (Check Force Ser.: No. 1). 192p. 1975. pap. 1.25 o.p. (ISBN 0-532-12269-0). Woodhill.

One Hundred Megaton Kill. Ralph Hayes. (Check Force Ser.: No. 1). 192p. 1975. pap. 1.25 o.p. (ISBN 0-532-12269-0). Manor Bks.

One Hundred Nineteen Great Porter Square. Benjamin Leopold Farjeon. (seaside library. v. 49. no. 992). 1881. G. Munro.

One Hundred One Ghost Town Relics. Ed. by Wes Bressie & Ruby Bressie. (Current Values Ser.). (Illus.). 1976. pap. 2.95 (ISBN 0-911068-04-X, A962063). Old Time.

One Hundred One Years' Entertainment: The Great Detective Stories, 1841-1941. (G69). 4.95 o.p. (G69); PLB 3.89 o.p. Modern Lib.

One Hundred One Years' Entertainment: The Great Detective Stories. Ellery Queen, pseud. (Modern library of the world's best books). 1946. Modern Library.

One Hundred One Years' Entertainment: The Great Detective Stories, 1841-1941. Ed. by Ellery Queen, pseud. LC 41-24967.

One Hundred One Years' Entertainment: The Great Detective Stories, 1841-1941. Ed. by Ellery Queen, pseud. LC 45-35104. 1945. Garden City Publishing Co., Inc.

One Hundred Percent. Upton Beall Sinclair. LC 21-1179. The Author.

One Hundred Scenes from Married Life: A Selection. Giles Gordon. LC 76-383284. 1976. 3.95 (ISBN 0-09-127010-3). Hutchinson.

One Hundred Stories in Black: A Collection of Bright, Breezy, Humorous Stories of the Colored Race As Seen in the Sunny South. Bridges Smith. LC 72-4598. (Black Heritage Library Collection). (Illus.). 1972. (ISBN 0-8369-9126-5). Books for Libraries Press.

One Hundred Stories in Black: A Collection of Bright, Breezy, Humorous Stories of the Colored Race As Seen in the Sunny South. Bridges Smith. LC 48-30433. J. S. Ogilvie Pub. Co.

One Hundred Thousand Welcomes. Michael Kenyon. (YA) 1970. 4.95 o.p. (ISBN 0-698-10283-5). Coward.

One Hundred Times to China. Lloyd Kropp. LC 78-19711. 1979. 10.00 (ISBN 0-385-05708-3). Doubleday.

One Hundred True Crime Stories. Sam D. Cohen. Repr. of 1946 ed. 20.00 (ISBN 0-89987-179-8). Darby Bks.

One Hundred Twenty Days of Sodom & Other Writings. Donatien Alphonse Francois Sade. Ed. by Austryn Wainhouse & Richard Seaver. (Illus.). 1966. pap. 12.50 (ISBN 0-394-17119-5, B138, BC). Grove.

One-Hundred-Twenty Million. facsimile ed. Michael Gold. LC 77-178438. (Short Story Index Reprint Ser.). Repr. of 1929 ed. 12.50 (ISBN 0-8369-4039-3). Ayer Co.

One Hundred Twenty Six Days of Continuous Sunshine. Gerald Jay Goldberg. LC 72-37459. 1972. 6.95. Dial Press.

One Hundred World's Best Novels Condensed. Ed. by Edwin Atkins Grozier & Wingate, Charles Edgar Lewis. LC 33-5089. Blue Ribbon Books, Inc.

One Hundred Years of Science Fiction. Ed. by Damon Francis Knight. LC 68-28913. 1968. 6.50. Simon and Schuster.

One Hundred Years of Science Fiction Illustration. Anthony Freus'N. 1975. pap. 4.95 o.p. (ISBN 0-515-03863-6, Harv). HarBraceJ.

One Hundred Years of Solitude. Garcia Marquez, Gabriel. LC 74-83632. 1970. 7.95. Harper & Row.

One Hundred Years of Solitude. Gabriel Garcia Marquez. Tr. by Gregory Rabassa. LC 74-83632. 1970. 17.95i (ISBN 0-06-011418-5, HarpT). Har-Row.

One I Knew the Best of All: A Memory of the Mind of a Child. Frances Hodgson Burnett. 1893. C. Scribner's Sons.

One Immortality. Harold Fielding-Hall. LC 9-4434. 1909. The Macmillan Company.

One in a Minyan, and Other Stories. Max J. Routtenberg. LC 77-25319. 1977. 7.95 (ISBN 0-87068-342-X). Ktav Pub. House.

One in a Thousand: Or, The Days of Henri Quatre. George Payne Rainsford James. LC 7-7987. 1936. Harper & Brothers.

One in a Thousand; or, The Days of Henri Quatre. George Payne Ramsford James. LC 7-7987. 1836. Harper & Brothers.

One in Four. Leonard Patrick O'Connor Wibberley. LC 76-221. 1976. 7.95 (ISBN 0-688-03048-3). Morrow.

One in Four: A Prophecy in the Form of a Novel. Leonard Wibberly, pseud. 288p. 1976. 7.95 o.p. (ISBN 0-688-03048-3). Morrow.

One in Ten Thousand. Gerhard Lewis Wind. LC 38-39433. Zondervan Publishing House.

One in the Back Is Medea. Millicent Dillon. LC 72-81497. 1973. 6.95 (ISBN 0-670-52616-9). Viking Press.

One in Thine Hand. Gerald N Lund. LC 81-19418. 7.95 (ISBN 0-87747-894-5). Deseret Book Co.

One in Three Hundred: By J. T. McIntosh Pseud. James Murdoch Macgregor. LC 55-42202. (Ace double novel books, D-113). 1955. Ace Books.

One in Three Hundred: By J. T. McIntosh Pseud. 1st Ed. James Murdoch Macgregor. LC 54-9186. (Doubleday science fiction). 1954. Doubleday.

One Increasing Purpose. Arthur Stuart-Menteth Hutchinson. LC 25-18579. 1925. Little, Brown, and Company.

One Is a Lonely Number. Bruce Elliott. 1968. pap. 0.60 o.p. (60-316). Manor Bks.

One Is a Lonesome Number. William Manners. LC 50-5765. 1950. Dutton.

One Is Beloved. Louise Platt Hauck. LC 37-15469. The Penn Publishing Company.

One Is One. Barbara Leonie Picard. LC 66-8340. 1966. Holt, Rinehart and Winston.

One Just Man. James Mills. LC 74-18364. (O.s.i.). 1975. 7.95 o.s.i. (ISBN 0-671-21837-9). S&S.

One Just Man. James Mills. LC 74-18364. 1976. (pbk.) 1.95 (ISBN 0-671-80247-X). Pocket Books.

One Kiss for France. Marilyn F Tate. LC 61-12589. 1963. Doubleday.

One Last Glimpse. James Aldridge. LC 77-71629. 7.95. Little, Brown.

One Last Glimpse. James Aldridge. LC 78-316188. 1978. 2.50 (ISBN 0-14-004727-1). Penguin Books.

One Last Kiss. Carol Dean. 1982. pap. 2.95 (ISBN 0-8217-1112-1). Zebra.

One Life, One Kopeck: A Novel. Walter Duranty. LC 37-27458. 1937. Simon and Schuster.

One Light Burning: A Romantic Story. Ray Coryton Hutchinson. Farrar & Rinehart, Incorporated.

One Link in the Chain of Opostolic Succession: Or, The Crimes of Alexander Borgia. a Story, 1854. E. W. Hinks & Co.

One Link Was Golden: A Novel. 1st Ed. Ruth McAuliff Livingston. LC 55-7185. 1956. Vantage Press.

One Little Boy. Hugh De Selincourt. LC 24-1966. 1924. A. & C. Boni.

One Little Indian. Roy Maitland. LC 7-20121. (On cover: Satchel series, no. 22). 1879. The Authors' Publishing Company.

One Little Man. Christopher Ward. LC 26-9265. 1926. Harper & Brothers.

One Lonely Night. Frank Morrison Spillane. LC 51-1378. 1951. Dutton.

One Louisburg Square. William Edward Daniel Ross. (Inflation Fighter Ser.). 192p. 1982. pap. 1.50 o.s.i. (ISBN 0-8439-1148-4, Leisure Bks). Nordon Pubns.

One Louisburg Square. William Edward Daniel Ross. (O.s.i.). 1975. pap. 1.25 o.s.i. (BT50850). Belmont-Tower.

One Louisburg Square. William Edward Daniel Ross. 1974. 4.95. Lenox Hill Press.

One Love Have I. Beatrix. LC 74-82688. 128p. 1974. 5.95 o.p. (ISBN 0-914184-13-X). Crescent Pubns.

One Love Is Too Many for an Agent. Javad Mirkarimi. 1978. 5.95 o.p. (ISBN 0-533-03690-9). Vantage.

One Love Lost. Helen Holt, pseud. Ed. by Gene DeRoin. (Aston Hall Presents Ser.). (Orig.). 1979. pap. 1.50 (ISBN 0-89936-013-0). Aston Hall.

One Love Too Many. Max Fischer. Ed. by Sylvia Ashton. LC 77-78383. 1979. 12.95 (ISBN 0-87949-100-0). Ashley Bks.

One Lovely Moron. Lucian Cary. LC 30-354288. 1930. Doubleday, Doran and Company, Inc.

One Maid's Mischief. George Manville Fenn. (On cover: Lovell's library, no. 1132). 1888. J. W. Lovell Company.

One Maid's Mischief: A Novel. George Manville Fenn. LC 42-265759. 1888. D. Appleton and Company.

One Man. Flora L. S Aldrich. LC 10-227961. The Roxburgh Publishing Company (Incorporated.

One Man: A Novel. Robert Steele. LC 15-8821. 1915. 1.50. M. Kennerley.

One Man Dog. William F. Schilling. LC 37-1010. The Christopher Publishing House.

One-Man Girl. Maysie Greig. LC 31-22905. 1931. L. MacVeagh, The Dial Press.

One Man in His Time. Ellen Anderson Gholson Glasgow. LC 22-11443. 1922. Doubleday, Page & Company.

One Man in the World. James Barlow. (N3660). 1968. Bantam.

One Man in the World. James Barlow. LC 67-10521. Simon and Schuster.

One-Man Jury. Frederick Clyde Davis. LC 64-19482. (Red badge detective). 1964. Dodd, Mead.

One Man Loved. Marguerite Mooers Marshall. LC 52-6262. 1952. Macrae Smith.

One Man Must Die. Albert Benjamin Cunningham. LC 46-706910. 1946. E. P. Dutton & Company, Inc.

One Man Must Die. Jean Montaurier. 1966. 5.95 o.p. (ISBN 0-03-057600-8). HR&W.

One Man Must Die: By Jean Montaurier Pseud. Tr. from French by Irene Uribe. Edmond Fleury. LC 66-15262. bds., 5.95. Holt.

One Man, One Matchet. T. MofOlorynso Aluko. LC 65-80832. 1965. bds., 3.50. Heinemann.

One Man, One Matchete. T. MofOlorynso Aluko. (African Writers Ser.). 1965. pap. text ed. 2.50x (ISBN 0-435-90011-0). Heinemann Ed.

One Man, One Wife. T. MofOlorynso Aluko. (African Writers Ser.). 1967. pap. text ed. 3.00x (ISBN 0-435-90030-7). Heinemann Ed.

One Man, One Wife: By T. M. Aluko. 2nd Ed.. T. MofOlorynso Aluko. LC 67-112237. (African writers ser., 30). 1967. pap., 1.25. Heinemann.

One Man Power, Plus. George Olcott Phelps. LC 9-28953. 1.00. The Roxburgh Publishing Company (Incorporated.

One Man Show. Paul Eldridge. LC 33-6788. Liveright, Inc.

One-Man Show. John Innes Mackintosh Stewart. LC 52-7215. (Red badge detective). 1952. Dodd, Mead.

One-Man Show. Tiffany Thayer. 1937. J. Messner, Inc.

One-Man Show see Appleby Intervenes.

One Man Too Many. Virginia Coffman. (Orig.). pap. 0.75 o.p. (74-909). Lancer.

One Man Who Was Content. Mariana Griswold Van Rensselaer. LC 77-94746. (Short Story Reprint Ser). 1897. 11.00 (ISBN 0-8369-3126-2). Ayer Co.

One Man Who Was Content, Mary, The Lustigs, Corinna's Fiammetta. Mariana Griswold Van Rensselaer. LC 77-94746. (Short story index reprint series). 1969. Books for Libraries Press.

One Man Who Was Content: "Mary;" The Lustigs; Corinna's Fiammetta. Van Rensselaer, May (King) 1897. The Century Co.

One Man Woman. Vida Hurst. Grosset & Dunlap.

One Man's Destiny. Clarence E Hatfield. LC 37-12229. Burney Brothers Publishing Co.

One Man's Enemies. Seldon Truss, pseud. LC 60-5947. 1960. Published for the Crime Club by Doubleday.

One Man's Folly: A Novel. Peter B Maxwell. (On cover: Dearborn series, no. 54). 1891. Donohue, Henneberry & Co.

One Man's Inheritance. John Attenborough. 1979. 11.95 o.p. (ISBN 0-312-58536-5). St Martin.

One Man's Initiation: 1917: A Novel. authorized ed., complete and unexpurgated. ed. John Dos Passos. LC 69-15945. (Illus.). 1969. 5.95. Cornell University Press.

One Man's Life. 1st Ed. Eunice Finstrom Stoik. LC 56-12322. 1957. Vantage Press.

One Man's Muddle. Eleanor Baker Quinn. LC 37-814418. 1937. The Macmillan Company.

One Man's Murder. David Delman. LC 74-20322. (MW suspense). 1975. 5.95. (ISBN 0-679-50533-4). D. McKay Co.

One Man's Poison. Cortland Fitzsimmons. LC 40-7352. 1940. Frederick A. Stokes Company.

One Man's Struggle. George Washington Gallagher. LC 6-44490. 1890. Funk & Wagnalls.

One Master. Bertha B. Moore McCurry. LC 45-2697. 1944. Pinebrook Book Club.

One Master. Bertha B. Moore McCurry. LC 45-370. 1944. Wm. B. Eerdmans Publishing Company.

One May Day. A Sketch in Summer-Time. A Novel. Maria M Grant. (Harper's Franklin square library. no. 229). Harper & Brothers.

One May Day. A Sketch in Summer-Time. A Novel. Maria M Grant. LC 27-136915. (Seaside library. v. 59, no. 1206). 1882. G. Munro.

One Mexican Sunday. Mike Oehler. LC 80-82949. (Illus.). 8.50 (ISBN 0-9604464-1-9). Mole Pub. Co.

One Million. Hendrik Hertzberg. LC 77-125772. (Gemini Smith Bk). 1970. 4.95 o.p. (20754). S&S.

One Million Centuries. Richard A. Lupoff. 288p. 1981. pap. 2.75 (ISBN 0-671-83226-3, Timescape). PB.

One Million Centuries. Richard A. Lupoff. (Orig.). 1968. pap. 0.75 o.p. (74-892). Lancer.

One Million Dead. Jose Maria Gironella. LC 63-18207. 1963. Doubleday.

One Million Francs. Frederic Arnold Kummer. LC 12-10133. 1.25. W. J. Watt & Company.

One Million Pound Bank-Note & Other New Stories. Samuel Langhorne Clemens. LC 76-121529. (Short Story Index Reprint Ser). 1893. 16.00 (ISBN 0-8369-3485-7). Ayer Co.

One Minus One. Ruth Doan MacDougall. LC 73-157063. 1971. 5.95. Putnam.

One Minus Two: A Novel. Henri Troyat & Whitall, James, 1888- Tr. LC 38-5362. I. Washburn, Inc.

One-Minute Murder. John Gordon Brandon. 1935. The Dial Press.

One Minute Past Eight. 1st Ed. George Harmon Coxe. LC 57-868540. 1957. Knopf.

One Minute to Eternity. Robert Weverka. LC 69-19470. 1969. 5.50. W. Morrow.

One Moment, Please. Mort Crim. (Family Lib Ser). 1972. pap. 0.95 o.p. (FN2722). Pyramid Pubns.

One Monday We Killed Them All. John Dann MacDonald. 1978. pap. 2.25 (ISBN 0-449-13620-5, GM). Fawcett.

One More Bridge to Cross. Arlene Hale. LC 75-2368. 1975. 6.95 (ISBN 0-316-33856-7). Little, Brown.

One More Bridge to Cross. Arlene Hale. LC 76-15587. 1976. 12.95. G. K. Hall.

One More Camellia. Anne Tedlock Brooks. Ed. by Alice Sachs. 1971. 3.95 o.p. Lenox Hill.

One More Camellia. 1972. pap. 0.75 o.s.i. (01-362). Lancer.

One More Lover. Florence Stonebraker. LC 48-152121. 1947. Phoenix Press.

One More River. John Galsworthy. LC 74-113925. (His The Forsyte chronicles, v. 9). (Scribner library. Contemporary classics.). 1970. 2.45. Scribner.

One More River. John Galsworthy. LC 33-28406. 1933. C. Scribner's Sons.

One More River: Stories. Lester Goldberg. LC 77-9058. (Illinois short fiction). 7.50. (ISBN 0-252-00674-7) (ISBN 0-252-00673-9). University of Illinois Press.

One More River to Cross. Henry Wilson Allen. LC 79-13787. (Series: Gregg Press Western Fiction Series.). 1979. 9.95 (ISBN 0-8398-2585-4). Gregg Press.

One More River to Cross. Will Henry, pseud. 1979. lib. bdg. 9.95 (ISBN 0-8398-2585-4, Gregg). G K Hall.

One More River to Cross. Will Henry, pseud. 1967. 5.95 o.p. (ISBN 0-394-43926-0). Random.

One More River to Cross: The Life and Legend of Isom Dart. Henry Allen. LC 67-12755. 1967. Random House.

One More Spring. Robert Nathan. LC 33-3086. 1933. A. A. Knopf.

One More Such Victory. Katherine Ursula Parrott. LC 42-155491. 1942. Smith & Durrell.

One More Summer. Susan Lennox. LC 58-12510. 1958. Avalon Books.

One More Summer. Edward Carl Stephens. LC 60-7885. 1960. Doubleday.

One More Time. Faith Baldwin. LC 78-182770. 1972. 6.95 o.p. (ISBN 0-03-091385-3). HR&W.

One More Time. Faith Baldwin Cuthrell. LC 78-182770. 1975. (pbk.) 0.95 (ISBN 0-446-75859-0). Warner Paperback Library.

One More Time. Faith Baldwin Cuthrell. LC 78-182770. 1972. 6.95 (ISBN 0-03-091385-3). Holt, Rinehart and Winston.

One More Unfortunate. Edgar Marcus Lustgarten. LC 47-11093. 1947. C. Scribner's Sons.

One More Unfortunate. Edgar Marcus Lustgarten. LC 80-17167. (Gregg Press Mystery Fiction Series). (Illus.). 1980. 11.95 (ISBN 0-8398-2651-6). Gregg Press.

One More Woman. Peggy Gaddis, pseud. LC 35-353770. Godwin.

One More Year. Bertha B. Moore McCurry. LC 40-4665. 1940. Wm. B. Eerdmans Publishing Company.

One More Year. Bertha B Moore. LC 40-466575. 1940. Wm. B. Eerdmans Publishing Company.

One Morning, for Pleasure. John N Deck. LC 68-20065. 1968. Harcourt, Brace & World.

One Murder Too Many. 1st Ed. Edwin Moultrie Lanham. LC 52-11343. 1952. Harcourt, Brace.

One Murdered: Two Dead. Milton Morris Propper. LC 36-25285. 1936. Harper & Brothers.

One Must Love. Charles Pelton Jacobs. LC 31-213301. The John Day Company.

One Never Knows. Francis Charles Philips. LC 7-36068. 1893. Cleveland Publishing Company.

One Night Girl. Jacques Vieux. 65p. (Orig.). 1980. pap. 2.95 o.p. (ISBN 0-89260-184-1). Hwong Pub.

One Night in Bethlehem: A Christmas Story. William James Dawson. LC 10-26375. 0.75. Hodder and Stoughton, George H. Doran Company.

One Night in Newport. Elizabeth Villars, pseud. LC 80-718. 1981. 12.95 (ISBN 0-385-15328-7). Doubleday.

One Night in Newport. Elizabeth Villars, pseud. LC 81-6871. 1981. 15.95 (ISBN 0-8161-3271-2). G.K. Hall.

One Night in Santa Anna. Thomas Washington Metcalfe. LC 31-32953. (His Santa Anna trilogy, v. 1). 1931. The Macmillan Company.

One Night of Murder. Hamish Boyd. LC 58-9121. 1958. Mystery House.

One Night Stand see Noches Violentes.

One Night Stood. Richard Kostelanetz. LC 77-81597. 1977. 12.00; signed & lettered, a-z 50.00; pap. 2.50 (ISBN 0-918406-04-8). Future Pr.

One Night Stood: Newsprint Edition. Richard Kostelanetz. LC 77-87142. 1977. signed & lettered, a-z 25.00 (ISBN 0-918406-06-4); pap. 1.00. Future Pr.

One Night with Nancy. Wilson Collison. LC 33-109792. The Macaulay Company.

One Night with Nora. By Brett Halliday Pseud. Davis Dresser. LC 53-9303. 1953. Distributed by Dodd, Mead.

One Night's Play of Fox & Hare: A Novel. Chester Anderson & Charles Stevenson. LC 80-15642. 20.00 (ISBN 0-9601428-0-0) (ISBN 0-9601428-9-4). Entwhistle Books.

One, None and a Hundred-Thousand: A Novel. Luigi Pirandello & Putnam, Samuel, Tr. LC 33-8146. E. P. Dutton & Co., Inc.

One O'clock at the Gotham. Elinore Denniston. LC 73-17863. (Red badge novel of suspense). 1974. 4.95 (ISBN 0-396-06908-8). Dodd, Mead.

One O'Clock at the Gotham. Rae Foley. LC 73-17863. 194p. 1974. 4.95 o.p. (ISBN 0-396-06908-8). Dodd.

One of a City. Emma Marr Petersen. LC 72-88513. (Illus.). 1972. 2.95. Bookcraft.

One of a Kind. Jo Calloway. (Candlelight Ecstasy Ser.: No. 150). (Orig.). 1983. pap. 1.95 (ISBN 0-440-16689-6). Dell.

One of a Kind: The Many Faces & Voices of America. Harry Barba. LC 76-375102. 1976. 6.95 (ISBN 0-911906-11-8) (ISBN 0-911906-12-6). Harian Press.

One of "Berrian's" Novels. C. H. Stone. 1890. Welch, Fracker Company.

One of Cleopatra's Nights, and Other Fantastic Romances. Theophile Gautier & Hearn, Lafcadio, 1850-1904, Tr. 1882. R. Worthington.

One of Cleopatra's Nights, and Other Fantastic Romances. Theophile Gautier & Hearn, Lafcadio, 1850-1904, Tr. LC 99-3537. 1900. Brentano's.

One of Cleopatra's Nights, and Other Fantastic Romances. Theophile Gautier & Hearn, Lafcadio, 1850-1904, Tr. LC 17-496. 1915. Brentano's.

One of Cleopatra's Nights, and Other Fantastic Romances, Translated from the French. Theophile Gautier & Hearn, Lafcadio, 1850-1904, Tr. LC 28-3428. Brentano's.

One of Four. James Leslie Roberts.

One of God's Dilemmas. Allen Upward. LC 8-32282. (Pioneer series). 1896. E. Arnold.

One of My Sons. Anna Katharine Green Rohlfs. LC 1-27059. 1901. G. P. Putnam's Sons.

One of Our Bombers Is Missing. Dan Brennan. 1977. pap. 1.50 o.s.i. (ISBN 0-505-51140-1). Tower Bks.

One of Our Brains Is Draining. Max Wilk. LC 68-10889. 1968. W. W. Norton.

One of Our Conquerors. George Meredith. Ed. by Margaret Harris. LC 76-383418. (Victorian texts; 3). 1975. 12.90 (ISBN 0-7022-0966-X). University of Queensland Press.

One of Our Conquerors. author's ed. George Meredith. LC 1-19354. 1891. Roberts Brothers.

One of Our Conquerors. rev. ed. George Meredith. LC 1-19355. 1897. C. Scribner's Sons.

One of Our Dinosaurs Is Missing. David Forrest. 1975. (pbk.) 1.25 (ISBN 0-380-00363-5). Avon.

One of Our H Bombs Is Missing. Cover Painting by Stan Meltzoff. Frederick Hazlitt Brennan. LC 55-42719. (Gold medal books, 498). 1955. Fawcett Publications.

One of Our Millionaires Is Missing. Tr. from Danish by Carl Malmberg. Leif Panduro. LC 67-2637. (Evergreen Black Cat Bk. B-183). 1968. Grove.

One of Our Own. Maud Willis. (Doctors' hospital no. 1). 1975. (pbk.) 1.50 (ISBN 0-671-80231-3). Pocket Books.

One of Our Priests Is Missing: A Novel. William J Weatherby. LC 68-11804. 1968. Doubleday.

One of Our Spacecraft Is Missing. Paul Richards. (Hotline Ser). (O.s.i.). 160p. 1973. pap. 0.95 o.s.i. (AN1197, Award). Univ Pub & Dist.

One of Ours. Willa Sibert Cather. LC 71-31688. 1971. 1.95 (ISBN 0-394-71252-8). Vintage Books.

One of Ours. Willa Sibert Cather. LC 22-26887. A. A. Knopf,.

One of Ours. Willa Sibert Cather. LC 31-19527. 1926. A. A. Knopf.

One of Ours. Willa Sibert Cather. LC 22-26887. 1922. A. A. Knopf.

One of Ours. Willa Sibert Cather & Williams, Stanley Thomas. LC 31-195272. 1926. A. A. Knopf.

One of the Blue Hen's Chickens. Virginia Durant Young. LC 1-30558. 1901. C. W. Close.

One of the Boys. Janet Dailey. LC 82-19814. 1983. 11.95 (ISBN 0-89340-484-5). J. Curley.

One of the Boys. Janet Dailey. (Harlequin Presents Ser.). 192p. 1980. pap. 1.50 (ISBN 0-373-10399-9, Pub. by Harlequin). PB.

One of the Casualties. Weldon Hill, pseud. LC 64-11615. 1964. Doubleday.

One of the Children Is Crying. Coleman Dowell. LC 67-22675. 1968. Random House.

One of the Crowd: A Novel. Paul Gillette. LC 77-90669. 12.95 (ISBN 0-87795-184-5). Arbor House.

One of the Cunning Men of San Francisco: Or, Woman's Wrongs. Amelia Z. Caton. 1977. Repr. 15.00 o.p. (ISBN 0-403-07274-3). Scholarly.

One of the Dark Places. Paxton Davis. pap. 0.75 o.p. (54-398). Paperback Lib.

One of the Dark Places: A Novel. Paxton Davis. LC 65-22185. 1965. Morrow.

One of the Dunanes. A Novel. Alice King Hamilton. LC 7-1223. 1885. J. B. Lippincott Company.

One of the "Forty." L'immortel. Alphonse Daudet. LC 6-33043. (On cover: The continental series. no. 1). 1888. Continental Publishing Corporation.

One of the Founders: A Novel, by P. H. Newby. Percy Howard Newby. LC 65-23207. bds., 4.95. Lippincott.

One of the Grayjackets, and Other Stories. Elliott Crayton McCants. LC 9-18437. 1908. The State Company.

One of the Guilty. Walter Lionel George. Harper & Brothers.

One of the Multitude. George Acorn. LC 13-368. 1912. Dodd, Mead and Company.

One of the Raymonds. Jean Rikhoff. LC 73-19617. 1974. 8.95 (ISBN 0-8037-6674-2). Dial Press.

One of the Viconti: A Novelette. Eva Wilder McGlasson Brodhead. (The ivory series). 1896. C. Scribner's Sons.

One of Them. Charles James Lever. LC 24-11863. (Lettered on cover: Novels of foreign life). 1904. Little, Brown and Company.

One of Them: A Novel. Charles James Lever. LC 7-14394. 1861. Harpers & Brothers.

One of These Days. Michael Trappes-Lomax. LC 27-23877. 1927. George H. Doran Company.

One of These Seven: A Justus Drum Mystery. Carolynne Chitwood Logan & Malcolm Roderick Logan. LC 46-610039. 1946. Mystery House.

One of These Seven. Abridged Ed.... Carolynne Chitwood Logan & Logan, Malcolm Roderick, 1901- Joint Author. LC 47-23057. (On cover: Handi-book mysteries. No. 59). 1947.

One of Those Coincidences and Ten Other Stories. Julian Hawthorne. LC 71-116953. (Short story index reprint series). (Illus.). 1970. Books for Libraries Press.

One of Those Coincidences: And Ten Other Stories. Julian Hawthorne. LC 99-5250. 1899. Funk & Wagnalls Company.

One of Those Things. Peter Cheyney. LC 50-5399. (Red badge mystery). 1950. Dodd, Mead.

One of Those Ways. Marie Adelaide Belloc Lowndes. LC 29-10670. 1929. A. A. Knopf.

One of Three. Clifford Samuel Raymond. LC 19-27597. 1.75. George H. Doran Company.

One of Three," and Made or Marred. Jessie Fothergill. LC 6-40016. (Leisure hour series. no. 129). 1881. H. Holt and Company.

One of Us. Ezra Selig Brudno. LC 12-9963. 1912. 1.25. J. B. Lippincott Company.

One of Us. Lula Kirschner. Tr. by Waugh, Ellen. LC 7-12824. (On cover: Once a week library, v. 11, no. 2). 1893. P. F. Collier.

One of Us. Ernest Poole. LC 34-25934. 1934. The Macmillan Company.

One of Us Is a Murderer... Alan Le May. LC 30-16606. 1930. Pub. for The Crime Club, Inc., by Doubleday, Doran & Company, Inc.

One of Us Must Die. Anna Clarke. LC 80-1669. 1980. 8.95 (ISBN 0-385-17295-8). Published for the Crime Club by Doubleday.

One of Us Works for Them. Jack D Hunter. (S3633). 1968. Bantam.

One of Us Works for Them. Jack D Hunter. LC 67-11367. 1967. Dutton.

One Old Reb. Malvina Sarah Black Clark Waring Waring. LC 29-29424. 1929. The State Company.

One on Me. Tim Huntley. 1980. 2.25 (ISBN 0-87997-508-3). DAW Books.

One on One. Pat Nobel. (Orig.). 1980. pap. 2.25 (ISBN 0-532-23186-4). Woodhill.

One on One. Jerry Segal. 1977. 1.75 (ISBN 0-446-84450-0). Warner Books.

One on One: A Novel. Lawrence Shainberg. LC 70-117276. 1970. 5.95. Hold, Rinehart and Winston.

One on the House. Mary Lasswell. LC 49-11894. 1949. Houghton Mifflin.

One or Another. Rosalyn Drexler. LC 75-108891. 1970. 4.95. E. P. Dutton.

One Over One. William Harrington. LC 75-134802. 1970. McKay.

One Page Missing. Hans Jaray & Hapgood, Elizabeth Reynolds, Tr. LC 48-5719. 1948. H. Holt.

One Pearl of Great Price. William Fay Luder. LC 58-10545. 1958. Farnsworth Books.

One Place After Another: A Little Volume of Travel and Romance Meant to Entertain the Old As Well As the Young. Maybeth Darling. Enterprise Press.

One Poor Girl: The Story of Thousands. Wirt i. e. William Wirt Sikes. LC 8-28087. 1869. J. B. Lippincott & Co.

One Poor Scruple: A Seven Weeks' Story. Josephine Mary Hope-Scott W. P. Ward Ward. 1899. Longmans, Green and Co.

One Purple Week; and Then--- Harry Brazee Wandell. LC 99-861. 1898. Pub. by the Author.

One Queen Triumphant. Frank James Mathew. LC 61. 1899. John Lane.

One Reader-Check: Validity Card Update -Cards Punched Out 13 22cm. Margaret Storm Jameson. LC 58-113925.

One Reason Why. Beatrice Whitby. LC 8-36040. (On cover: Appletons' town and country library, no. 81). 1891. D. Appleton and Company.

One Reckless Night. Peter Shelley, pseud. LC 38-21853. 1938. Godwin.

One Red Rose for Christmas. 1st Ed. Paul Horgan. LC 52-9667. 1952. Longmans, Green.

One Red Rose Forever. Mildred A. Jordan. LC 41-11497. 1941. A. A. Knopf.

One Rich Man's Son. Emma Lefferts Super. LC 8-176583. 1895. Cranston & Curts.

One Romantic Summer. Archie Joscelyn. LC 37-678. Phoenix Press.

One Sane Man. Francis Beeding. LC 34-2592. 1934. Little, Brown, and Company.

One Schoolma'am Less. Ella L. McDougall. 1895. R. R. Donnelley & Sons Co., Printers.

One Shot. Richard Greenfield. 1977. pap. 1.75 (ISBN 0-532-17156-X). Woodhill.

One-Shot Deal. Gerald Petievich. 224p. 1983. pap. 2.50 (ISBN 0-523-41155-3). Pinnacle Bks.

One-Shot Kid. Nelson Nye. 1976. 1.25. Ace.

One-Shot War. Brian O'Connor. 1982. pap. 2.50 (ISBN 0-345-29885-3). Ballantine.

One-Shot War: A Novel. Brian O'Connor. LC 80-5147. 9.95 (ISBN 0-8129-0939-9). Times Books.

One Sided Shoot-Out. Don L. Lee. pap. 0.50 o.p. Broadside.

One Small Candle. Mary Linehan MacKinnon. LC 56-113631. 1956. Crown Publishers.

One Small Candle. Cecil Roberts. 1942. The Macmillan Company.

One Smart Indian. Robert J Seidman. LC 77-1174. 9.95 (ISBN 0-399-11929-9). Putnam.

One Smart Indian. Robert J Seidman. LC 79-14987. 1979. 4.95 (ISBN 0-87951-099-4). Overlook Press.

One Smart Kid: A Novel. Edwin Moses. LC 81-15623. 1981. 11.95 (ISBN 0-02-587570-1). Macmillan.

One-Smoke Stories. Mary Hunter Austin. LC 34-270711. 1934. Houghton Mifflin Company.

One Son-Indivisible. Helen V Simpson. LC 48-11063. 1948. Christopher Pub. House.

One Squeaking Straw. Richard Lyons. LC 58-13589. 24p. 1958. pap. 1.00 (ISBN 0-911042-04-0). N Dak Inst.

One Star General: A Novel. Albert Morgan. LC 59-9998. 1959. Rinehart.

One Star Jew: Short Stories by David Evanier. LC 82-73714. 256p. (Orig.). 1983. pap. 15.00 (ISBN 0-86547-098-7). N Point Pr.

One Stayed at Welcome. Maud Hart Lovelace & Lovelace, Delos W. LC 34-30688. The John Day Company.

One Step Apart. Joan L. Oppenheimer. 1978. pap. 1.50 (ISBN 0-448-14664-9, Pub. by Tempo). Ace Bks.

One Step Better. Allan G. Darnel. 7.95 o.p. Carlton.

One Step Beyond: Great Stories of the Psychic World Selected from the Television Series 'Alcoa Presents' and Retold Here for Reading Pleasure by Lenore Bredeson. Alcoa Presents (Television Program) & Lenore Bredeson. LC 60-9380. 1960. Citadel Press.

One Step Forward: A Novel. 1st Ed. Paul Erickson. LC 57-9619. 1957. Pageant Press.

One Step from Earth. Harry Harrison. LC 71-107049. 1970. Macmillan.

One Step, Two Step: A Novel. Earl W Hubbard. LC 51-12520. 1951. Exposition Prese.

One Summer. Ruby Mildred Ayres. LC 30-7795. 1930. Doubleday, Doran & Company, Inc.

One Summer. Kate Weldon Brown. LC 13-13539. 1913. 1.00. Broadway Publishing Co.

One Summer. Albert Drake. LC 79-63672. (Illus.). 1979. 4.00 (ISBN 0-917976-06-1). White Ewe Press.

One Summer... Blanche Willis Teuffel. LC 33-7790. 1875. J. R. Osgood and Company.

One Summer... Blanche Willis Teuffel. LC 8-26068. 1878. J. R. Osgood and Company.

One Summer. Blanche Willis Howard Von Teuffel. LC 2-94509. 1900. Houghton, Mifflin and Co.

One Summer. Blanche Willis Howard Von Teuffel. LC 12-213534. 1912. Houghton Mifflin Company.

One Summer Love. N. Richard Nash. 1976. (pbk.) 1.50 (ISBN 0-553-02813-8). Bantam Books.

One Summer. With Illustrations. Blanche Willis Howard Von Teuffel. LC 13-12920. 1878. J. R. Osgood and Company.

One Sunny Day. Joan Alexander, pseud. LC 73-87593. 1974. 6.95 (ISBN 0-698-10569-9). Coward, McCann & Geoghegan.

One Sunny Day. Joan Alexander, pseud. (Berkley Medallion Book). 1978. 1.95 (ISBN 0-425-03619-7). Berkley Pub. Corp.

One Tear for My Grave: By Mike Roscoe Pseud. John Roscoe. LC 55-104181. 1955. Crown Publishers.

One That Got Away. Helen McCloy. LC 45-9162. 1945. W. Morrow & Company.

One That Wins. The Story of a Holiday in Italy. Mona Alison Caird. (Harper's Franklin square library. no. 606). 1887. Harper & Brothers.

One Thing I Know. Patricia Hill. LC 62-14195. 1962. Houghton Mifflin.

One Thing in Common: A Collection of Three Novels. Mary Annette Beauchamp Russell Russell. LC 41-4410. 1941. Doubleday, Doran and Company, Inc.

One Thing Is Certain: A Novel. Sophie Kerr. LC 22-19172. George H. Doran Company.

One Thing Needful. Mary Elizabeth Braddon Maxwell. (On cover: Lovell's library, no. 868). 1887. J. W. Lovell Company.

One Thing Needful. A Novel. Mary Elizabeth Braddon Maxwell. (Harper's Franklin square library, no. 538). 1886. Harper & Brothers.

One Thing Needful: Or, The Penalty of Fate. Mary Elizabeth Braddon Maxwell. (On cover: Seaside library. Pocket ed. no. 840). 1886. G. Munro.

One Thing Worth Having. Lona B. Kennedy & Allen Bennington. LC 81-83207. 236p. 1982. 12.50 (ISBN 0-937884-02-2); pap. 8.50 (ISBN 0-937884-03-0). Hyst'ry Myst'ry.

One Third off. Irvin Shrewsbury Cobb. LC 21-14550. George H. Doran Company.

One Thousand: A Novel on the Millennium Years. Salem Kirban. LC 72-97136. (Illus.). 1973. (ISBN 0-912582-09-X).

One Thousand American Fungi. Charles McIlvaine & Robert MacAdam. (Illus.). 729p. 1973. pap. 9.95 (ISBN 0-486-22782-0). Dover.

One Thousand Dollars a Day. Studies in Practical Economics. Adeline Knapp. LC 7-14283. 1894. The Arena Publishing Company.

One Thousand Dollars a Week, & Other Stories. James Thomas Farrell. 1942. The Vanguard Press.

One Thousand Dollars a Week, & Other Stories. James Thomas Farrell. 1943. The Sun Dial Press.

One Thousand Men for a Christmas Present. Mary B Sheldon. LC 8-5098. 1898. Estes and Lauriat.

One Thousand Souls. Aleksei Feofilaktovich Pisemskii. LC 76-23892. (Classics of Russian literature). (Hyperion library of world literature). 1977. 5.95 (ISBN 0-88355-508-5). Hyperion Press.

One Thousand Souls. Aleksei Feofilaktovich Pisemskii. LC 69-14035. 1969. Greenwood Press.

One Thousand Souls. Translated from the Russian by Ivy Litvinov. 1st American Ed. Aleksei Feofilaktovich Pisemskii. LC 59-12217. 1959. Grove Press.

One Thousand Three Hundred Thirty-Nine...or So: Being an Apology for a Pedlar. Rod Whitaker. LC 75-11732. (Illus.). 1975. 7.95 (ISBN 0-15-189935-5). Harcourt Brace Jovanovich.

One Time, I Saw Morning Come Home: A Remembrance. Clair Huffaker. LC 74-8342. 1974. (ISBN 0-671-21827-1). Simon and Schuster.

One to Count Cadence. James Crumley. LC 68-14518. 1969. 6.95. Random House.

One to Fifty Book. Ed. by Anne Wyse & Alex Wyse. LC 73-85360. 1973. pap. 3.00 o.p. (ISBN 0-8020-6222-9). U of Toronto Pr.

One to Go. Harley Hess. (Orig.). 1979. pap. 1.75. Woodhill.

One to Grow on. 1st Ed. Nathaniel Benchley. LC 58-119751. 1958. McGraw-Hill.

One to Live with. Ruby Mildred Ayres. LC 38-13183. 1938. Doubleday, Doran and Company, Inc.

One to Ride the River with. Michael Hammonds. LC 74-2717. 1974. 4.95 (ISBN 0-385-09631-3). Doubleday.

One Too Many. Elizabeth Lynn Linton. LC 7-19007. 1894. F. T. Neely.

One Too Many Mornings. Robert G. Armstong. 1982. 8.95 (ISBN 0-533-05021-9). Vantage.

One Touch of Ecstasy: A Novel. Gwynne Wimberly. LC 59-65090. 1959. F. Fell.

One Touch of Murder. Hermia Harris Fraser. LC 53-8557. 1953. Arcadia House.

One Touch of Nature: And Other Stories. Beatrice Joy Chute. LC 65-14816. 1965. Dutton.

One Touch of Nature, by Margaret Lee... Margaret Lee. LC 7-12777. (On cover: Mayflower library. no. 3). J. A. Taylor and Company.

One Tree. A. M Allen. LC 26-62613. 1926. Little, Brown, and Company.

One Tree. Stephen R Donaldson. LC 81-17596. (Donaldson, Stephen R. The Second Chronicles of Thomas Covenant: Bk. 2). 1982. 14.50 (ISBN 0-345-29898-5). Ballantine Books.

One True Love. Paula Little, pseud. (O.s.i.). (Orig.). 1976. pap. 0.95 o.s.i. Belmont-Tower.

One True Love. Paula Little. 1976. (pbk.) 0.95. Belmont Tower Books.

One-Two-Three. Ulf Lofgren. Tr. by Alison Winn. Ray Broekel. LC 73-8442. (Illus.). Addison-Wesley.

One, Two, Three. Paul Selver. LC 27-1993. George H. Doran Company.

One-Two-Three-Four: A Nocturne. James Lafayette Hutchison. LC 35-12183. 1935. Lothrop, Lee and Shepard Company.

One, Two, Three, Four, Six, Seven, Eight, Nine, Zero. Arthur Okamura & Robert Creeley. (Illus.). signed 12.50 o.p. (ISBN 0-914726-03-X). Mudra.

One Unknown. Reinhold Conrad Muschler. Tr. by Barker, Muriel Alice (Barclay) LC 36-877567. G. P. Putnam's Sons.

One Very Hot Day. David Halberstam. LC 67-27510. 1967. 4.95 o.p. (ISBN 0-395-07768-0). HM.

One Very Hot Day: A Novel. David Halberstam. LC 67-27510. 1968. 4.95. Houghton.

One Vision Only. Carolyn Canfield. 1959. pap. 3.50 o.p. (ISBN 0-340-24607-3). OMF Bks.

One Voyage and Its Consequences. Julius Auboineau Palmer. LC 7-35774. D. Lothrop Company.

One Walked Out of Two & Forgot It. Toby MacLennan. LC 75-189887. 1972. 5.00 (ISBN 0-87110-083-5) (ISBN 0-87110-084-3). Something Else Press.

One Walked Out of Two & Forgot It. Toby MacLennan. LC 75-189887. 1972. 10.00 (ISBN 0-87110-083-5). Ultramarine Pub.

One Was a Marine. 1st Ed. Doyle A New. LC 56-8476. 1956. Greenwich Book Publishers.

One Was Glamorous. Bennie Caroline Hall. LC 55-140295. 1955. Arcadia House.

One Was Valiant. Doris Kent LeBlanc. LC 40-5950. 1939. Arcadia House.

One Way. Dick Anthony. 1972. pap. 2.95 o.p. (ISBN 0-8024-9221-5); record 5.98 o.p. (ISBN 0-8024-9223-1). Moody.

One Way or Another. Leonardo Sciascia. LC 76-26274. (Illus.). 7.95 (ISBN 0-06-013804-1). Harper & Row.

One Way Out. George Harmon Coxe. pap. 0.50 o.p. (R1662). Pyramid Pubns.

One Way Out. Betsey Riddle Hutton Zum Stolzenberg. LC 6-38553. 1906. Dodd, Mead and Company.

One Way Street. Beale Davis. LC 24-21807. Brentano's.

One-Way Street. Alexander T. Holmsen. 1967. 5.95 o.p. Hawthorn.

One Way Street. Joseph McCord. LC 36-4041. 1936. Macrae Smith Company.

One Way Street. Nick Marino. LC 52-6634.

One-Way Street: By Alexander T. Holmsen. 1st Ed. Alexander T Holmsen. LC 67-214126. 1967. bds., 5.95. Meredith.

One Way Ticket. Eugene O'Brien. LC 40-5631. 1940. Doubleday, Doran & Co., Inc.

One Way Ticket. Alec Thackery. (Orig.). 1976. pap. 1.75 o.p. (ISBN 0-515-03902-0). Pyramid Pubns.

One-Way Ticket. Ethel Turner. LC 34-5179. 1934. H. Smith and R. Haas.

One-Way Ticket: By Bert and Dolores Hitchens. 1st Ed. Hubert Hitchens & Dolores Birk Hitchens. LC 56-133693. 1956. Published for the Crime Club by Doubleday.

One Way to Eldorado. 1st Ed. Hollister Noble. LC 54-51785. 1954. Doubleday.

One Way to Heaven. Countee Cullen. LC 73-18572. 1975. 15.00 (ISBN 0-404-11383-4). AMS Press.

One Way to Heaven. Countee Cullen. LC 32-4559. 1932. Harper & Brothers.

One Way to Love, No. 30. Glenna Finley, pseud. 1982. pap. 1.95 (ISBN 0-451-11426-4, AJ1426, Sig). NAL.

One-Way to New York: A Novel. Claude Roy. LC 66-27889. 1966. Bobbs-Merrill Co.

One Way to Spell Man. Wallace Earle Stegner. LC 81-43428. 192p. 1982. 14.95 (ISBN 0-385-17720-8). Doubleday.

One Way to Venice. Jane Aiken Hodge. LC 74-79683. 1975. 7.95 (ISBN 0-698-10615-6). Coward, McCann & Geoghegan.

One-Way Trail: A Story of the Cattle Country. Ridgwell Cullum. LC 11-158619. 1.25. G. W. Jacobs & Company.

One Way Weekend. Edith B Wile. LC 80-22892. 1981. 12.95 (ISBN 0-87949-196-5). Ashley Books.

One Wet Season. Ion L. Idriess. pap. 1.60 o.s.i. Tri-Ocean.

One White Star. Gladys Hasty Carroll. LC 54-13018. 1954. Macmillan.

One Who Kills: A Novel. Ridgwell Cullum. LC 38-133991. J. B. Lippincott Company.

One Who Looked on. Frances Frederica Montresor. LC 7-31125. 1895. D. Appleton and Company.

One Who Returned. 1st Ed. Josephine Blackstock. LC 53-123163. 1953. Pageant Press.

One Who Saw. Francis Edward Grainger. LC 5-40807. 1905. The Victoria Press.

One Who Stays Virgin: A Story of Desire for the Love of Pete! Delbert Essex Davenport. LC 40-37520. 1939. Recorder Printing and Publishing Co.

One Wide River to Cross. Christine Whiting Paramenter. LC 28-23278. 1928. Thomas Y. Crowell Company.

One Wild Oat. Mackinlay Kantor. LC 50-39497. (Gold medal book, 122). 1950. Fawcett Publication.

One Winter in Boston: A Novel. Robert Miller Smith. LC 50-6423. 1950. Simon and Schuster.

One Woman. Tiffany Thayer. LC 33-241901. 1933. W. Morrow and Company.

One Woman. Tiffany Thayer. 1947. The Sun Dial Press.

One Woman: A Story of Modern Utopa. Thomas Dixon. LC 11-14327. 1907. Doubleday, Page & Company.

One Woman: A Story of Modern Utopia. Thomas Dixon. LC 3-17535. 1903. Doubleday, Page & Company.

One Woman: Being the Second Part of a Romance of Sussex. Alfred Ollivant. LC 22-4209. 1922. Doubleday, Page & Company.

One Woman: Story of Modern Utopia. Thomas Dixon. LC 9-32306. 1906. A. Wessels Comdpany.

One Woman's Fate: And Other Stories. Marion Weir. LC 99-3873. F. T. Neely.

One Woman's Freedom. Helen Zenna Smith. LC 32-3419. 1932. Longmans, Green and Co.

One Woman's Land. Gertrude E Bridgeman Finney. LC 65-20936. 1965. D. McKay.

One Woman's Life. Robert Herrick. LC 70-145082. 1974. (lib. ed.) 16.50 (ISBN 0-403-02995-3). Scholarly Press.

One Woman's Life. Robert Herrick. LC 13-3067. 1913. The Macmillan Company.

One Woman's Life see Collected Works.

One Woman's Story: A Novel. Carolyn Beecher. LC 19-14627. Britton Publishing Company.

One Woman's Story: Or, The Chronicles of a Quiet Life, As Told in Dorothea's Diary. Ellen A Lutz. LC 7-14514. 1895. Cranston & Curte.

One Woman's Two Lovers: Or, Jacqueline Thayne's Choice. Virginia Frances Townsend. LC 8-29814. 1875. J. B. Lippincott & Co.

One Woman's Way: A Novel. Edmund Pendleton. (On cover: Appletons' town and country library. no. 78). 1891. D. Appleton and Company.

One Wonderful Night: A Romance of New York. Louis Tracy. LC 12-16965. E. J. Clode.

One Wonderful Rose. Bertha J. Weeks Griffiths & Griffiths, Arthur Llewellyn. LC 20-220843. R. G. Badger.

One Wonderful Week. Cecil Scott Forester. LC 27-22954. The Bobbs-Merrill Company.

One World at a Time. Margaret Witter Fuller. LC 22-18679. 1922. The Century Co.

One Wreath with Love. Jan Roffman. LC 77-92230. 1978. 7.95 o.p. (ISBN 0-385-14103-3). Doubleday.

One Wreath with Love. Margaret Summerton. LC 77-92230. 1978. 6.95 (ISBN 0-385-14103-3). Published for the Crime Club by Doubleday.

One Year. Dorothea Gerard Longard De Longgarde. LC 5-7621. 1900. Dodd, Mead & Company.

One Year Affair. Byron Preiss & Ralph Reese. LC 76-25798. (Illus., Orig.). 1976. pap. 2.50 o.p. (ISBN 0-911104-86-0). Workman Pub.

One Year in Autumn. Kathleen Kranidas. LC 64-23476. 1965. Lippincott.

One Year of Love. Alice Mary Ross Colver. LC 37-30403. 1937. Dodd, Mead & Company.

One Year of Pierrot. Frederick Orin Bartlett. LC 14-6286. 1914. 1.35. G. P. Putnam's Sons.

One Year of Pierrot: With Illustrations. Frederick Orin Bartlett. LC 17-13449. 1917. Houghton Mifflin Company.

One Year with Grace. Martin Mooney. LC 42-16624. 1942. J. Swift.

Onedin Line: The Iron Ships. Cyril Abraham. (Signet book). 1975. (pbk.) 1.25. New American Library.

Onedin Line: The Shipmaster. Cyril Abraham. (Signet book). 1975. (pbk.) 1.25. New American Library.

O'Neil McDarragh, the Detective: Or, The Strategy of a Brave Man. Harlan Page Halsey. The American News Company.

Oneness Equals Alone. David O. Judd. 3.95 o.p. Vantage.

Oneness Trial: A Novel of the Washoe Indians. 1st Ed. Walter C Wilson. LC 56-9573. (Expositlion--Lochinvar book). 1956. Exposition Press.

Onesimus: Christ's Freedman: A Tale of the Pauline Epistle. Charles Edward Corwin. LC 5688. Fleming H. Revell Company.

Onesimus: Memoirs of a Disciple of St. Paul. Edwin Abbott Abbott. LC 42-267885. ("Ecce homo" series). 1882. Roberts Brothers.

Onesimus: The Runaway Slave. Henry Boyer Brumbaugh. LC 10-14148. 1909. 0.75. Brethren Publishing House.

Onesimus the Slave: A Romance of the Days of Nero. Laurel M Hoyt. LC 15-26977. 1915. 1.35. Sherman, French & Company.

Ongon: A Tale of Early Chicago. DuBois Henry Loux. LC 2-19384. 1902. C. Francis Press.

Oni: Or, Averted Vengeance. Florence Blackburn White Schoeffel. (On cover: Munro's library v. 50 no. 741). 1887. N. L. Munro.

Onion Eaters. James Patrick Donleavy. (O.s.i.). 1971. 7.95 o.s.i. (ISBN 0-440-06669-7, Sey Lawr). Delacorte.

Onion Eaters. James Patrick Donleavy. pap. 2.75 (ISBN 0-440-36643-7). Dell.

Onion Eaters, a Novel. James Patrick Donleavy. LC 73-152241. 1971. 7.95. Delacorte Press.

Onion Field. Joseph Wambaugh. 1979. 2.50 (ISBN 0-440-17350-7). Dell Pub. Co.

Onion Peel. K. M. Trishanku. (Indian Novels Ser, Vol. 2). 175p. 1974. 4.95 (ISBN 0-88253-465-3). Ind-US Inc.

Onionhead. Weldon Hill, pseud. LC 57-13552. 1957. D. McKay Co.

Onions & Tulips. Margaret M. Scariano. 1980. pap. 3.95 (ISBN 0-89293-071-3). Beta Bk.

Onliness: A Novel. Dave Smith. LC 81-255. 1981. 12.95 (ISBN 0-8071-0871-5). Louisiana State University Press.

Onliness: A Novel by Dave Smith. Dave Smith. LC 80-255. 1981. 12.95 (ISBN 0-8071-0871-5). La State U Pr.

Only a Boy. Eugene Field. (Illus.). 1968. Repr. of 1967 ed. pap. 0.95 o.p. (Z1014, Zebra). Grove.

Only a Brewer's Daughter. Jane Gater. LC 34-23632. 1934. Meador Publishing Company.

Only a Clod. Mary Elizabeth Braddon Maxwell. (Seaside library. v. 31, no. 641). 1879. G. Munro.

Only a Clod. Mary Elizabeth Braddon Maxwell. (On cover: Seaside library. Pocket ed. no. 498). 1885. G. Munro.

Only a Clod. Mary Elizabeth Braddon Maxwell. (On cover: Lovell's library, no. 878). 1887. H. W. Lovell Company.

Only a Commoner. Nathaniel Gould. LC 6-27645. (On cover: The Lafayette library, no. 1). G. Routledge & Sons, Limited.

Only a Coral Girl. A Novel. Gertrude Forde. (On cover: Harper's Franklin square library. 617). 1888. Harper & Brothers.

Only a Coral Girl. A Novel. Gertrude Forde. LC 6-403819. (On cover: Lovell's library, no. 1162). 1888. J. W. Lovell Company.

Only a Coral Girl. A Novel. Gertrude Forde. (On cover: Seaside library. Pocket ed. no. 1072). 1888. G. Munro.

Only a Fiddler: A Danish Romance. author's ed. Hans Christian Andersen. LC 9-3337. Houghton Mifflin Company.

Only a Fiddler. A Danish Romance. author's ed. Hans Christian Andersen. LC 44-516015. 1876. Hurd and Houghton.

Only a Game. Robert Daley. LC 67-29730. 1967. New American Library.

Only a Girl: Or, A Physician for the Soul. Wilhelmine Birch Von Hillern & Wister, Mrs. Annie Lee (Furness) 1830-1908, Tr. 1872. J. B. Lippincott & Co.

Only a Girl's Heart: A Novel. Emma Dorothy Eliza Nevitte Southworth. LC 8-14254. (Ledger library, no. 99). 1893. R. Bonner's Sons.

Only a Girl's Love. John Russell Coryell. LC 6-39923. (On cover: Lovell's library, no. 1261). 1888. J. W. Lovell's Company.

Only a Girl's Love. Geraldine Fleming. LC 6-39923. (On cover: Lovell's library, no. 1261). 1888. J. W. Lovell Company.

Only a Girl's Love. Geraldine Fleming. LC 6-39922. (On cover: Clover series. no. 124). 1896. Street & Smith.

Only a Girl's Love. Geraldine Fleming. LC 6-39922. (On cover: Clover series, no. 124). 1897. Street & Smith.

Only a Horse: Or, Tom's Reform. Lottie McCord. 1905. McCord & McCord.

Only a Love-Story. Iza Duffus Hardy. (Seaside library, v. 37, no. 753). 1880. G. Munro.

Only a Matter of Time. Clinton-Baddeley, Victor Clinton. LC 70-102406. 1970. 4.95. Morrow.

Only a Mechanic's Daughter. A Charming Story of Love and Passion. Laura Jean Libbey. LC 7-14313. 1892. N. L. Munro.

Only a Pin! An Instructive Moral Story. Tr. from the French of J. T. De Saint-Germaine Pseud. Jules Romain Tarieu & Stump, Pauline. LC 8-200997. 1873. The Catholic Publication Society.

Only a Substitute Wife. Adah Viola Rohrer Bienz. LC 39-9401. The Ruter Press.

Only a Tramp. Edgar William Robinson. LC 7-41975. (On cover: Satchel series no. 13). The Author's Publishing Company.

Only a Waif. Rose Anne Braendle. LC 6-17945. 1880. D. & J. Sadlier & Co.

Only a Waif: The Romance of an Earthquake. Eliza Jaquith Page. LC 7-22772. L. E. Kline.

Only a Woman. Mary Elizabeth Braddon Maxwell. (On cover: Seaside library. Pocket ed. no. 496). 1885. G. Munro.

Only a Woman: Translated from the French by Ralph Manheim. Francis Carco. LC 55-58952. (Berkley books, 337). 1955. Berkley Pub. Corp.

Only a Woman's Heart a Novel. Jane McElhinney. LC 7-16462. 1866. M. Doolady.

Only a Word. Georg Moritz Ebers. Tr. by Clara Courtenay Bell. (On cover: Seaside library. Pocket ed., in. 1112). 1888. G. Munro.

Only Akiko. Thorp, Duncan. LC 58-7855. 1958. Little, Brown.

Only an Inch from Glory. Albert Halper. LC 43-14786. 1943. Harper & Brothers.

Only an Incident. Grace Denio Litchfield. LC 7-189971. 1883. G. P. Putnam's Sons.

Only an Irish Girl. Margaret Wolfe Hungerford & Poe, Edgar Allan, 1809-1849. LC 20-23154. (On cover: Wakefield series. no. 64). The Prudential Book Co.

Only Anne: A Novel. Isabel Constance Clarke. LC 16-8806. 1946. Benziger Brothers.

Only As Far As Brooklyn. Maurice Kenney. 1977. pap. 4.00 (ISBN 0-915480-13-1). Good Gay.

Only." By the Author of A Trap to Catch a Sunbeam. author's ed. Matilda Anne MacKarness. LC 7-16437. 1850. J. Munroe and Company.

Only Child. Marguerite Stockman Dickson. LC 52-6901. (Illus.). 1952. Longmans, Green.

Only Children. Alison Lurie. LC 78-21994. 1979. 8.95 (ISBN 0-394-50471-2). Random House.

Only Children. Alison Lurie. LC 79-24984. 1980. 13.95 (ISBN 0-8161-3021-3). G. K. Hall.

Only Chilren. Allison Lewis. 1980. 2.50 (ISBN 0-445-04557-4). Popular Library.

Only Couples Need Apply. Doris Miles Disney. LC 72-92401. 1973. 4.95 (ISBN 0-385-02027-9). Published for the Crime Club by Doubleday.

Only Daughter. M. B. Smith. (On cover: Munro's library, no. 669). 1886. N. L. Munro.

Only Fade Away. Bruce Marshall. LC 54-10760. 1954. Houghton Mifflin.

Only Game in Town. Charles Einstein. LC 54-8053. (Dell first edition 47). 1955. Dell Pub. Co.

Only Gentlemen Can Play. Hugh McLeave. LC 73-21928. 1974. 5.95 (ISBN 0-15-169940-2). Harcourt Brace Jovanovich.

Only Gift. Jane Eklund Ball. LC 49-11577. 1949. Houghton Mifflin.

Only Gift. Jane Mary Eklund. LC 49-11577. 1949. Houghton Mifflin Co.

Only Girl. Jeanne Judson. (Cameo Romance). (Fawcett gold medal book). 1975. (pbk.) 0.95. Fawcett.

Only Girl in the Game. John Dann MacDonald. 224p. 1982. pap. 2.50 (ISBN 0-449-12358-8, GM). Fawcett.

Only Good Body's a Dead One. Tony Kenrick. LC 79-155424. (Inner sanctum suspense novel). 1971. 5.95 (ISBN 0-671-21008-4). Simon and Schuster.

Only Good German. Ted Allbeury. LC 76-361581. 1976. 3.50 (ISBN 0-432-00424-6). P. Davies.

Only Good Secretary. Jean Potts. LC 65-193614. 3.50. Scribners.

Only Gun in Town. Kenneth L Olsen. 1973. 4.95. Lenox Hill Pr.

Only Her Hairdresser Knew--- Carleton Carpenter. 1973. (pbk) 0.75. Curtis Books.

Only Human. Carroll Graham & Graham, Garrett. LC 32-5748. 1932. The Vanguard Press.

Only Human: Or, Justice. A Novel. Henrietta Eliza Vaughan Stannard. LC 8-13850. (On cover: Lippincott's series of select novels. no. 130). 1892. J. B. Lippincott Company.

Only Human: Or, Justice. A Novel. Henrietta Eliza Vaughan Stannard. LC 29-30761. 1903. J. B. Lippincott Company.

Only in New England: The Story of a Gaslight Crime. Theodore Roscoe. LC 59-113235. 1959. Scribner.

Only in Time. Helen Bratton. LC 67-21186. (Illus.). 1967. D. McKay Co.

Only Judith. Lydia L Rouse. 1893. Hunt & Eaton.

Only Just Above the Ground: Special Issues 28. Stuart Z. Perkoff. pap. 1.00 o.p. The Smith.

Only Let Me Live. Alice Mary Ross Colver. 1937. Dodd, Mead & Company.

Only Love. James Noble Gifford. LC 42-25361. 1942. Gramercy Pub. Co.

Only Love. Carol Holliston. LC 42-25361. 1942. Gramercy Publishing Co.

Only Love Counts. Vivian Radcliffe. LC 51-9306. 1950. Gramercy Pub. Co.

Only Love Lasts: A Novel. Rosamond Neal Du Jardin. LC 37-1116. J. B. Lippincott Company.

Only Lovers Left Alive. Dave Wallis. 1982. 15.00x (ISBN 0-86025-137-3, Pub. by Ian Henry Pubns England). State Mutual Bk.

Only Lovers Left Alive: A Novel. Dave Wallis. LC 64-21309. 1964. Dutton.

Only Make-Believe. Clarissa Ross, pseud. 1980. pap. 2.50 (ISBN 0-8439-0813-0, LB813). Leisure Bks CT.

Only Make-Believe. William Edward Daniel Ross. 1980. pap. 2.50 (ISBN 0-8439-0813-0). Nordon Pubns.

Only Man in Hollywood: Mark Roberts. Mark Roberts. 2.75 (ISBN 0-671-82048-6). Pocket Books.

Only Me. Thomas L Baily. LC 6-5010. D. Lothrop Company.

Only My Dreams. Denise Robins. 1976. (pbk.) 1.25 (ISBN 0-380-00597-2). Avon.

Only Nancy: A Tale of the Kentucky Mountains. Francis George. LC 17-31424. Fleming H. Revell Company.

Only Nellie Fayle: A Novel. 1st Ed. Bertram Bloch. LC 60-10664. 1960. Doubleday.

Only on Friday. Lee Torrance. LC 80-51312. 1981. 9.95 (ISBN 0-312-58580-2). St. Martin's Press.

Only on Sunday. Linda DuBreuil. 1977. pap. 1.50 o.s.i. (ISBN 0-8439-0459-3, Leisure Bks). Nordon Pubns.

Only One. Henry Willard French. LC 11-161621. 1884. Lee and Shepard.

Only One. Milton Paul Magly. LC 73-75156. 1973. 5.95 (ISBN 0-8059-1836-1). Dorrance.

Only One Heart. James Noble Gifford. LC 43-18009. 1943. Gramercy Publishing Co.

Only One Storm. Granville Hicks. LC 42-6009. 1942. The Macmillan Company.

Only Our Love. Iris Bromige. 1971. pap. 0.75 o.p. (94090). Beagle Bks.

Only Perfect. Rochelle Larkin. (Orig.). 1981. pap. 2.50 (ISBN 0-505-51704-3). Tower Bks.

Only Place to Be: A Novel. Joan Juliet Buck. LC 81-48291. 14.95 (ISBN 0-394-52300-8). Random House.

Only Place We Live. August William Derleth. 4.95 o.s.i. (ISBN 0-88451-013-1). Edco-Vis Assoc.

Only Reason. Tereska Torres. LC 61-12843. 1961. Simon and Schuster.

Only Relatives Invited: A Social and a Socialistic Satire. Charles Sherman. LC 16-67583. 1916. The Bobbs-Merrill Company.

Only Seven Were Hanged. Stuart Martin. LC 29-10298. 1929. Harper & Brothers.

Only Shorter. Ross Feld. LC 81-83971. 288p. 1982. 15.00 (ISBN 0-86547-061-8). N Point Pr.

Only Sin: A Novel. Anne Powers, pseud. LC 53-9864. 1953. Bobbs-Merrill.

Only Skin Deep. George Kimball. (Orig.). 1968. pap. 1.75 o.s.i. (115, Ophelia). Olympia.

Only Son. John Munonye. (African Writers Ser.). 1966. pap. text ed. 2.50x (ISBN 0-435-90021-8). Heinemann Ed.

Only Temper. A Novel. Emma Barry Newby. (On cover: Turners' select novels, no. 8). Turner Brothers & Co.

Only the Brave. Paul Evan Lehman. LC 47-22940. 1947. S. Curl, Inc.

Only the Brave: An Historical Novel. Allan R Bosworth. LC 55-439860. (Popular library, 684). 1955. Popular Library.

Only the Brave Are Great. Mabelle Stephenson Quine. LC 39-174288. Fleming H. Revell Company.

Only the Earth and the Mountains: A Novel of the Cheyenne Nation. George Heinzman. LC 64-17009. 1964. Macmillan.

Only the Good. Mary Garden Collins. LC 42-200922. 1942. C. Scribner's Sons.

Only the Governess. Rosa Nouchette Carey. (On cover: Lovell's library. no. 1140). 1888. J. W. Lovell Company.

Only the Governess. Rosa Nouchette Carey. LC 16-13111. 1915. J. B. Lippincott Company.

Only the Guilty. Aaron Marc Stein. LC 42-7370. 1942. Published for the Crime Club by Doubleday, Doran and Company, Inc.

Only the Gulls Cry. Anne Tedlock Brooks. LC 47-31028. 1947. Arcadia House.

Only the Hyenas Laugh. Robin Moore, pseud. 1978. pap. 2.25 (ISBN 0-532-22115-X). Woodhill.

Only the Land Endures. Brain MacKrell. 178p. 1975. 8.50x (ISBN 0-8002-0476-X). Intl Pubns Serv.

Only the Loving. Evelyn Perkins Ames. LC 52-10913. 1952. Dodd, Mead.

Only the Present. Noelle McGue. 1981. pap. 1.50 (ISBN 0-440-16597-0). Dell.

Only the Rich. Brux Fletcher. LC 32-14948. 1932. A. H. King.

Only the Strong. Mike Minehan. (Orig.). 1981. pap. 2.25 (ISBN 0-505-51683-7). Tower Bks.

Only the Unafraid. 1st Ed. Ronald De Levington Kirkbride. LC 52-12619. Duell, Sloane and Pearce.

Only the Valiant. Charles Marquis Warren. LC 43-2466. 1943. The Macmillan Company.

Only the Young. Elliott Arnold. LC 39-24730. H. Holt and Company.

Only Thing I've Done Wrong. John Jay Osborn. 1978. 1.75 (ISBN 0-380-01870-5). Avon.

Only Thing I've Done Wrong: A Novel. John Jay Osborn. LC 76-56406. 1977. 7.95 (ISBN 0-395-25174-5). Houghton Mifflin.

Only Thing That Matters. John Symonds. LC 61-66285. 1961. Horizon Press.

Only War We've Got. Derek Maitland. LC 70-128764. 1970. 5.95. Morrow.

Only Way Out. Leander Sylvester Keyser. LC 7-10946. A. D. F. Randolph & Company.

Only Way Out. 2d ed. Leander Sylvester Keyser. LC 6-29782. 1906. O. L. Youngen & Company.

Only with a Bargepole: A Novel. Joyce Porter. LC 73-91724. (MW suspense). 1974. 4.95 (ISBN 0-679-50439-7). McKay.

Only Woman in the Town: And Other Tales of the American Revolution. Sarah Johnson Prichard. LC 98-1638. 1898. Melicent Porter Chapter, Daughters of the American Revolution.

Only Yankee. Richard B. Wathen. LC 73-124731. 1970. 5.95. Regnery.

Only Youth Knows. Richard Whittington. LC 38-35048. The Fiction Guild.

Onoqua. Frances Campbell Sparhawk. LC 8-12383. (On cover: Good company series, no. 18). 1892. Lee and Shepard.

Onslaught. Joan Sutherland. LC 28-3980. 1928. Harper & Brothers.

Onstage for Love. William Edward Daniel Ross. (YA) 1981. 6.95 (Avalon). Bouregy.

Onward Christian Soldiers. Donald Day, pseud. 210p. (Orig.). 1982. pap. 7.00 (ISBN 0-939482-03-7). Noontide.

Onward, Mr. Casey: The Misadventures of a Gentle Man. Brassil Fitzgerald. LC 52-10385. 1952. Newman Press.

Onward Virgin Soldiers. Leslie Thomas. LC 71-176295. 1972. 5.95. New American Library; Distributed by Norton.

Onwards! A Novel. Nat Hentoff. LC 68-19942. 1968. Simon and Schuster.

Onyx. Jacqueline Briskin. LC 81-19583. 15.95 (ISBN 0-440-06738-3). Delacorte Press.

Onyx Ring. John Sterling & Hale, Charles. LC 7-3054. 1856. Whittemore, Niles, and Hall.

Onze Contes. Olin H. Moore & Walter Meiden. LC 57-674. (Fr). 1957. pap. text ed. 10.50 (ISBN 0-395-04941-5). HM.

Oo-Yoo-an Al-Sam-Ma Stories: As Told to Retsehc Ruhtra Seyek. Chester Arthur Keyes. LC 57-10653. 1957. Comet Press Books.

Oocytes. Alan Glasser. (Orig.). pap. cancelled (3175). Major Bks.

Ood-le-Uk the Wanderer. Alice Alison Lide & Margaret Alison Johansen. LC 30-21773. 1930. Little, Brown, and Company.

Oodles of Droodles. Roger Price. 1975. pap. 1.25 o.p. (ISBN 0-8431-0251-9). Price Stern.

Oona O' Thomas Michael Gallagher. LC 75-33938. (Harbrace paperbound library; HPL 67). 1976. 2.95 (ISBN 0-15-671371-3). Harcourt Brace Jovanovich.

Oona O. Thomas Michael Gallagher. LC 63-17852. 1964. Atheneum.

Oonomoo, the Huron. Edward Sylvester Ellis. LC 11-13359. 0.50. Hurst & Company.

Oooh. What You Said! Illustrated by Frederick E. Ban Bery. Arthur Kober. LC 58-9042. 1958. Simon and Schuster.

Oowikapun: Or, How the Gospel Reached the Nelson River Indians. Egerton Ryerson Young. LC 9-1202. 1894. Hunt & Eaton.

O.P. Man. 2nd ed. Jim Stickter. (Illus.). 1976. pap. 7.50 o.p. (ISBN 0-930770-07-2). Hemisphere Hse.

O.P. Man. Jim Stickter. (Illus., Orig.). 1976. pap. 7.50 o.p. (ISBN 0-930770-00-5). Hemisphere Hse.

Opal. Bessie Ray Hoover. LC 10-276767. 1910. 1.20. Harper & Brothers.

Opal. Ed. by Mallon. 4.50 o.p. Carlton.

Opal Canyon. William L Hawkins. LC 35-7178. Phoenix Press.

Opal-Eyed Fan. Andre Norton, pseud. LC 77-3679. 1977. 7.95 (ISBN 0-525-17180-0). Dutton.

Opal Legacy. Fortune Kent. LC 75-22383. (Birthstone gothic; no. 10). 1975. 1.25. Ballantine Books.

Opal Matrix. Wallace Jerome Chambers. LC 37-10491. 1937. The Salisbury Hill Press.

Opal Pendant. Elisabeth Barr. (Candlelight regency romance). 1974. (pbk.) 0.75. Dell.

Opal Pin. Rufus Hamilton Gillmore. LC 14-5429. 1914. 1.35. D. Appleton and Company.

Opal Queen. Eliza B Swan. LC 8-25645. 1892. R. Clarke & Co.

Opal Serpent. Fergus Hume. LC 5-22614. G. W. Dillingham Company.

Opal Street. June Wetherell. 1976. pap. 1.50 (ISBN 0-532-15216-6). Woodhill.

Opals from a Mexican Mine. George F. Duysters. LC 6-36397. 1896. New Amsterdam Book Company.

Opaque Shadows & Other Stories from Contemporary Africa. Charles R Larson. LC 76-7071. 256p. 1977. 12.50 o.s.i. (ISBN 0-87953-403-6, BO). Inscape Corp.

Open All Night. Paul Morand. Tr. by Holland, Vivian B. LC 23-149182. 1923. T. Seltzer.

Open and Shut. Edward Sefton Porter. LC 33-7853. The Christopher Publishing House.

Open at Random. Bruce Beaver. 1968. 7.95 o.s.i. Tri-Ocean.

Open at Your Own Risk. Joan Kahn. LC 75-15908. 1975. 12.95 (ISBN 0-395-20718-5). Houghton Mifflin.

Open Boat: And Other Tales of Adventure. Stephen Crane. LC 79-7805. 1969. Scholarly Press.

Open Boat: And Other Tales of Adventure. Stephen Crane. 1898. Doubleday & McClure Co.

Open Boat, & Other Tales of Adventure. Stephen Crane. LC 6-30865. 1898. 39.00 (ISBN 0-403-00012-2). Scholarly.

Open Boat, and Three Other Stories. Stephen Crane. LC 68-10280. (Illus.). 1968. F. Watts.

Open Boat: And Three Other Stories. Stephen Crane. (Illus.). 1968. F. Watts.

Open Cage: An Anzia Yezierska Collection. Anzia Yezierska & Alice Kessler Harris. LC 78-61060. 12.95 (ISBN 0-89255-035-X) (ISBN 0-89255-036-8). Persea Books.

Open City. Shelley Smith Mydans. LC 45-35017. 1945. Doubleday, Doran and Company, Inc.

Open Contract. Frank Scarpetta. (Marksman,#10). 1974. (pbk.) 0.95. Belmont Tower Books.

Open Country: A Comedy with a Sting. Maurice Henry Hewlett. LC 9-35789. 1909. C. Scribner's Sons.

Open Door. Edwin Bateman Morris. LC 32-3414. The Penn Publishing Company.

Open Door. W. A Sturdy. LC 5-37788. 1905. The Author, J. D. Bonnell & Son, Printers.

Open Door. Blanche Willis Howard Von Teuffel. 1889. Houghton, Mifflin and Company.

Open Door. Blanche Willis Howard Von Teuffel. LC 12-213520. 1912. Houghton Mifflin Company.

Open Door. Floyd Van Keuren. LC 42-25807. 1942. Harper & Brothers.

Open Door. Richardson Little Wright. LC 14-18117. 1914. McBride, Nast & Company.

Open Door: A Romance of Mystery, Time, 1905. Earle Ashley Walcott. LC 10-206083. 1910. Dodd, Mead and Company.

Open Door, and The Portrait. Two Stories of the Seen and the Unseen. Margaret Oliphant Wilson Oliphant. (On cover: Seaside library. Pocket ed., no. 635). 1886. G. Munro.
Open Door: Or, Light and Liberty. John Hyatt Smith. LC 8-8172. 1870. T. E. Perkins.
Open Doors: A Novel. Tereska Torres. LC 68-55953. 1968. 4.95. Simon and Schuster.
Open Eye, Open Heart. Lawrence Ferlinghetti. LC 73-78783. (Cloth ed. 6.95 o.p.). 160p. 1973. pap. 2.95 o.p. (ISBN 0-8112-0489-8, NDP361). New Directions.
Open-Eyed Conspiracy: An Idyl of Saratoga. William Dean Howells. LC 7-5769. 1897. Harper & Brothers.
Open Fire!... Wilfred Jay Holmes. LC 42-15691. 1942. The Macmillan Company.
Open Grave. Alan Hull Walton. LC 76-143494. 1971. 5.95 (ISBN 0-8008-5835-2). Taplinger.
Open Heart. Nikolai Mikhailovich Amosov. (O.s.i.). 1967. 4.95 o.s.i. (ISBN 0-671-54178-1). S&S.
Open Heart. Mary Bringle. LC 82-12416. 13.95 (ISBN 0-453-00423-7). New American Library.
Open Heart. Frederick Buechner. LC 76-190401. 1972. 5.95. Atheneum.
Open Heart: By N. Amosoff. Tr. from Russian by George St. George. Nikolai Mikhailovich Amosov. LC 67-108980. 1967. 4.95. S.&S.
Open Heart: By N. Amosoff. Tr. from Russian by George St. George. Nikolai Mikhailovich Amosov. (U6123). 1968. Ballantine.
Open House. Michael Innes, pseud. LC 82-5431. 1982. 2.95. Penguin Books.
Open House. Joan Kahn. LC 46-4002. 1946. J. B. Lippincott Company.
Open House. James Reid Parker. LC 51-11358. 1951. Doubleday.
Open House. Rebecca Newman Porter. LC 55-43391. 1955. Christopher Pub. House.
Open House. John Innes Mackintosh Stewart. LC 74-39128. (Red badge novel of suspense). 1972. 4.95 (ISBN 0-396-06524-4). Dodd, Mead.
Open House. Juliet Wilbor Tompkins. LC 9-2262. 1909. The Baker & Taylor Company.
Open Land. Bertha Muzzy Sinclair. LC 33-147923. 1933. Little, Brown, and Company.
Open Man. Dave Debusschere. pap. 1.50 o.p. (Zebra). Grove.
Open Mandala Journey. Mary L. Campbell. LC 79-63633. (Illus.). 1980. 50.00 (ISBN 0-8048-1314-0). C E Tuttle.
Open Market. Josephine Dodge Daskam Bacon. LC 15-119966. 1915. 1.35. D. Appleton and Company.
Open My Eyes. Dorothy C. Haskin. spiral bdg. 2.00 o.p. Warner Pr.
Open Question. A Novel. James De Mille. LC 9-8345. 1873. D. Appleton and Company.
Open Question: A Tale of Two Temperaments. Elizabeth Robins. LC 98-1653. 1899. Harper & Brothers.
Open Question: A Tale of Two Temperaments. Elizabeth Robins. LC 7-41972. 1899. Harper & Brothers.
Open Range. Hildegarde Hawthorne. LC 22-23562. 1932. Longmans, Green and Co.
Open Range. George Metcalf. LC 35-157341. E. J. Clode, Inc.
Open Season. David Osborn. 1974. (pbk.) 1.50. Dell.
Open Season: A Novel. David Osborn. LC 73-20235. 1974. 6.95 (ISBN 0-8037-6181-3). Dial Press.
Open Secret. Oliver Onions. LC 30-30573. 1930. Houghton Mifflin Company.
Open Secret. Wei Wei-Wu. 206p. 1965. pap. 6.75 o.p. (ISBN 0-19-643122-0). Oxford U Pr.
Open Sesame. Florence Marryat Church Lean. LC 7-13614. (On cover: Lovell's library. v. 20. no. 990). 1887. J. W. Lovell Company.
Open, Sesame!". Gertrude M. Robins Reynolds. LC 20-589935. George H. Doran Company.
Open Shadow. Brad Solomon. LC 78-13486. 10.00 (ISBN 0-671-40057-6). Summit Books.
Open Sky. Leonard Alfred George Strong. LC 39-15797. 1939. The Macmillan Company.
Open Swimmer. Tim Winton. LC 82-196991. 1982. 14.95 (ISBN 0-86861-220-0). Allen & Unwin.
Open the Door. Dolson, Hildegarde. LC 66-19986. 1966. Lippincott.
Open the Door: A Novel. Catherine MacFarlane Carswell. LC 20-10736. 1920. Harcourt, Brace and Howe.
Open the Door! A Volume of Stories. Osbert Sitwell. LC 75-142277. (Short story index reprint series). 1970. (ISBN 0-8369-3761-9). Books for Libraries Press.
Open the Door! A Volume of Stories. Osbert Sitwell. LC 42-107. 1941. Smith & Durrell.
Open the Gates! Ehud Avriel. 1975. 10.00 o.p. (ISBN 0-689-10590-8). Atheneum.
Open Then the Door. Dorothee Carousso. LC 42-110290. 1942. W. Morrow & Company.
Open Trail. George Brydges Rodney. LC 32-334166. E. J. Clode, Inc.
Open Verdict. Mary Elizabeth Braddon Maxwell. (Seaside library. v. 12, no. 235). 1878. G. Munro.
Open Verdict: By John Rhode Pseud. Cecil John Charles Street. LC 57-5874. (Red badge detective). 1957. Dodd, Mead.
Open Vistas. Nell K Walker. LC 51-21212. 1951. Vantage Press.
Open Water. James Brendan Connolly. LC 10-23747. 1910. C. Scribner's Sons.
Open Way. Jane Ludlow Drake Abbott. LC 55-6295. 1955. Lippincott.
Open Ways. Thomas L Baily. LC 6-209594. American Baptist Publication Society.
Open Window. Ernest Temple Thurston. LC 13-13537. 1918. D. Appleton and Company.
Open Window: Tales of the Months. Mabel Wright. 1908. The Macmillan Company.
Open Windows. Clara Bernhardt. LC 49-248039. 1947. W. B. Eerdmans Pub. Co.
Open Wings. Barbara Cartland. 1976. pap. 1.25 o.p. (ISBN 0-515-04029-0). BJ Pub Group.
Open Wings. Barbara Cartland. 1977. pap. 1.50 o.p. (ISBN 0-515-04343-5). BJ Pub Group.
Open Wings. Barbara Cartland. (Historical Romance Ser. No. 37). (O.s.i.). 1972. pap. 0.95 o.s.i. (N2734). Pyramid Pubns.
Open Wings, No. 37. Barbara Cartland. 256p. 1982. pap. 1.95 (ISBN 0-515-06388-6). Jove Pubns.
Open Wings, a Twenty-Third Novel. Barbara Cartland. LC 42-161440. 1942. Etc. Hutchinson & Co. Ltd.
Opened Shutters: A Novel. Clara Louise Root Burnham. LC 6-36632. 1906. Houghton, Mifflin and Company.
Opener of the Way. Robert Bloch. LC 77-354808. 1976. 0.60 (ISBN 0-586-04221-0). Panther.
Opener of the Way. Robert Bloch. LC 45-206911. 1945. Arkham House.
Openers of the Gate: Stories of the Occult. Lily Moresby Adams Beck. LC 30-23901. 1930. Cosmopolitan Book Corporation.
Opening a Chestnut Burr. Edward Payson Roe. 1874. Dodd & Mead.
Opening a Chestnut Burr. new and rev. ed.... ed. Edward Payson Roe. LC 13-9376. 1885. Dodd, Mead & Company.
Opening a Chestnut Burr. Edward Payson Roe. LC 2-19291. 1902. Dodd, Mead and Company.
Opening a Chestnut Burr. Edward Payson Roe. LC 42-435333. Dodd, Mead and Company.
Opening Door. Helen Kieran Reilly. LC 44-2895. 1944. Random House.
Opening Door: A Story of the Woman's Movement. Justus Miles Forman. LC 13-8077. 1913. Harper & Brothers.
Opening Gambit. Norman D. Kent. LC 78-76736. 1969. 4.95. Dorrance.
Opening Gate. Alice Maud Ellen Sampson. LC 33-4502. 1933. A. A. Knopf.
Opening of a Door. George Davis. LC 31-22398. 1931. Harper & Brothers.
Opening of the Cube. Rutherford Willems. pap. 3.00. Tree Bks.
Opening of the Light. Schwaller De Lubicz, Isha. LC 82-11894. 1982. 8.95 (ISBN 0-89281-038-6). Inner Traditions International.
Opening of the Light: The Three Principles of Man's Awakening. Isha Schwaller de Lubicz. Tr. by Susan Resnick from Fr. 350p. (Orig.). 1984. pap. price not set (ISBN 0-89281-038-6). Inner Tradit.
Opening the Oyster: A Story of Adventure. Charles Leonard Marsh. LC 7-24673. 1889. A. C. McClurg and Company.
Openings & Closings. Richard Kostelanetz. 1978. pap. 5.95 (ISBN 0-932360-18-1); pap. 50.00 signed & lettered, a-z; audiocassette 10.00. RK Edns.
Openings in the Old Trail. Bret Harte. LC 75-113672. (Short story index reprint series). 1970. Books for Libraries Press.
Openings in the Old Trail. Bret Harte. LC 2-12106. 1902. Houghton, Mifflin and Company.
Opera Dancer. Sandra Heath. (Orig.). 1981. pap. 2.25 (ISBN 0-451-11112-5, AE1112, Sig). NAL.
Opera House Murders. David Hanna. 256p. (Orig.). Date not set. pap. cancelled o.s.i. (ISBN 0-8439-1027-5, Leisure Bks). Nordon Pubns.
Opera Lover. David Kirby. pap. 3.00 o.s.i. Anhinga Pr.
Opera Murders. Kirby Williams. LC 33-5771. 1933. C. Scribner's Sons.
Opera Tomus III: Libelli 44-68. Lucian. (Oxford Classical Texts Ser.). 1980. text ed. 24.00x (ISBN 0-19-814592-6). Oxford U Pr.
Operacion Castro. Joseph Rosenberger. (Compadre Collection, El Mercader de la Muerte Ser: No. 7). 1976. pap. 0.95 (ISBN 0-88473-507-9). Fiesta Pub.
Operataion Hong Kong. Peter McCurtin. (Belmont Tower Book). 1977. 1.50 (ISBN 0-505-51161-4). Tower Pubns.
Operating Room - Four. Roy Bernard Sparkia. (Orig.). 1973. pap. 1.25 o.p. (ISBN 0-515-03078-3, V3078). Pyramid Pubns.
Operating Theater: A Novel. Vincent Brome. LC 68-12164. 1968. 5.95. S.&S.
Operation. Russell Boltar. LC 61-6824. 1961. Dodd, Mead.
Operation. Albert Kovetz. (Orig.). 1982. pap. 2.95 (ISBN 0-89083-938-7). Zebra.
Operation. A. Q Mowbray. (Signet Book, W5696). 1973. (pbk.) 1.50. New American Library.
Operation. A. Q Mowbray. LC 72-1561. 1972. 6.95. John Day Co.
Operation Africa. Charles Whiting. 1975. (pbk.) 1.25 (ISBN 0-523-00757-4). Pinnacle Books.
Operation Alcestis. Maggie Rennert. LC 75-2006. 1975. 7.95 (ISBN 0-13-637926-5). Prentice-Hall.
Operation: Alpha Death. Norman Conway. (Hunter#2). 1975. (pbk.) 1.50 (ISBN 0-89014-118-5). Canyon Books.
Operation Apricot. C. A Haddad. LC 77-3792. 7.95 (ISBN 0-06-011707-9). Harper & Row.
Operation Artemis. Douglas Scott. LC 79-2077. 10.95 (ISBN 0-672-52610-7). Bobbs-Merrill.
Operation Axe-Handle. Jacob McCroskey. pap. 0.60 o.p. Lancer.
Operation Bodenplatte. Lawrence Cortesi, pseud. 288p. (Orig.). 1981. pap. 2.50 (ISBN 0-89083-710-4). Zebra.
Operation Brother's Brother. Cyril E. Bryant. 1970. pap. 0.95 o.p. (N2115). Pyramid Pubns.
Operation Bughouse. Beverley Bowie. LC 47-31034. 1947. Dodd, Mead.
Operation Burning Candle. Blyden Jackson. 1974. pap. 1.50 o.p. (ISBN 0-515-03489-4, A3489). BJ Pub Group.
Operation Burning Candle. Blyden Jackson. 1976. pap. 1.50 o.p. (ISBN 0-515-04093-2). BJ Pub Group.
Operation Burning Candle. Blyden Jackson. 1974. (pbk.) 1.50 (ISBN 0-515-03489-4). Pyramid Books.
Operation Burning Candle: A Novel. Blyden Jackson. LC 73-82639. 1973. 6.95 (ISBN 0-89388-088-4). Third Press.
Operation Cain. Christopher Dickerson. 4.50 o.p. Vantage.
Operation Calpurnia: A Guy Silvestri Mystery. Maggie Rennert. LC 76-7540. 7.95 (ISBN 0-13-637835-8). Prentice-Hall.
Operation Cannibal. Lawrence Cortesi, pseud. 224p. (Orig.). 1982. pap. 2.50 (ISBN 0-8439-1088-7, Leisure Bks). Nordon Pubns.
Operation Chaos. Poul Anderson. LC 74-148602. (Doubleday science fiction). 1971. 4.95. Doubleday.
Operation Che Guevera. Nick Carter. (Nick Carter Ser.). (O.s.i.). (Orig.). 1969. pap. 0.60 o.s.i. (A509X, Award). Univ Pub & Dist.
Operation: Cicero. L. C. Moyzish. 1969. pap. 0.60 o.p. (A536X, Award). Univ Pub & Dist.
Operation Cuttlefish. David R. Mounce. (Orig.). 1972. pap. 0.95 o.p. (N2738). Pyramid Pubns.
Operation Cuttlefish. David R. Mounce. 1974. pap. 1.25 o.p. (ISBN 0-515-03475-4, V3475). Pyramid Pubns.
Operation Dancing Dog. James M. Fox. LC 73-90391. 224p. 1974. 5.95 o.p. (ISBN 0-8027-5292-6). Walker & Co.
Operation Dancing Dog. James M. W. Knipscheer. LC 73-90391. 1974. 5.95 (ISBN 0-8027-5292-6). Walker.
Operation Deathmaker. Dan J Marlowe. (Fawcett gold medal book). 1975. (pbk.) 0.95. Fawcett.
Operation Deep Six. Ken Stanton. (The Aquanauts Ser.: No. 7). 192p. 1972. pap. 0.95 o.p. (ISBN 0-532-95203-0). Woodhill.
Operation Deep Six. Ken Stanton. (The Aquanauts Ser.: No. 7). 192p. 1972. pap. 0.95 o.p. (ISBN 0-532-95203-0). Manor Bks.
Operation Delta. Henry Kane. LC 66-22122. 1966. Trident Press.
Operation Doomsday. Paul Kenyon. (Baroness,#5). 1974. (pbk.) 0.95 (ISBN 0-671-77762-9). Pocket Books.
Operation Firelight. J. L. Kane. 1983. 8.95 (ISBN 0-533-05374-9). Vantage.
Operation Future. Ed. by Groff Conklin. LC 55-8915. (Permabooks, M-4022). 1955. Permabooks; Distributed by Pocket Books.
Operation Goldkill. Bruce Cassiday. (O.s.i.). (Orig.). pap. 0.50 o.s.i. (A211F, Award). Univ Pub & Dist.
Operation Groundhog. William R. Tedvick. 3.00 o.p. Carlton.
Operation Hammerlock. Dan J Marlowe. (Earl Drake,#9). 1974. (pbk.) 0.95. Fawcett.
Operation Hazalah. Gilles Lambert. LC 73-11791. 224p. 1974. 6.95 o.p. (ISBN 0-672-51878-3). Bobbs.
Operation Heartbreak. Duff Cooper. LC 51-9666. 1951. Viking Press.
Operation Heartbreak. Duff Cooper. LC 51-9666. 1951. Viking Press.
Operation Homicide. Elihu Adams. LC 47-17702. (Mill Circle mysteries). 1947. M. S. Mill Co., Inc.
Operation Hong Kong. Peter McCurtin. (Soldier of Fortune Ser.: No. 7). 192p. 1982. pap. 2.25 (ISBN 0-505-51819-8). Tower Bks.
Operation Hooker. Joseph Rosenberger. (Murder Master#3). 1974. (pbk.) 1.25. Manor Books.
Operation Icicle. Peter Buck. (Marc Dean, Mercenary Ser.: No. 4). (Orig.). 1982. pap. 2.50 (ISBN 0-451-11269-5, AE1269, Sig). NAL.
Operation Kuwait. Harry Arvay. 1975. (pbk.) 1.25. Bantam Books.
Operation Lila. Marvin H. Albert. LC 82-72067. 304p. 1983. 14.95 (ISBN 0-87795-411-9). Arbor Hse.
Operation Longlife. E. Hoffmann Price. 320p. 1983. pap. 2.75 (ISBN 0-345-30715-1, Del Rey). Ballantine.
Operation: McMurdo Sound. Nick Carter. (Nick Carter Ser.). (Illus.). 224p. 1982. pap. 2.50 (ISBN 0-441-63400-1, Pub. by Charter Bks). Ace Bks.
Operation Malacca. Joe Poyer, pseud. LC 68-17810. (Doubleday science fiction). 1968. Doubleday.
Operation Mermaid. Ken Stanton. (Aquanaut Ser.: No. 11). 192p. 1974. pap. 0.95 o.p. (ISBN 0-532-95364-9). Woodhill.
Operation Mermaid. Ken Stanton. (Aquanaut Ser.: No. 11). 192p. 1974. pap. 0.95 o.p. (ISBN 0-532-95364-9). Manor Bks.
Operation Midas. Anne O'Grady. LC 72-12105. 1973. 5.95 (ISBN 0-06-013237-X). Harper & Row.
Operation Misfit. E. Hoffmann Price. 288p. 1980. pap. 1.95 (ISBN 0-345-29038-0). Ballantine.
Operation Moon Rocket. Nick Carter. (Nick Carter Espionage Ser). (O.s.i.). (Orig.). 1970. pap. 0.60 o.s.i. (A295X, Award). Univ Pub & Dist.
Operation Nazi-U.S.A. James Gilman, pseud. 176p. (Orig.). 1976. pap. 1.25 (ISBN 0-89041-069-0, 3069). Major Bks.
Operation Neptune. Christopher Nicole. (Laurel Leaf Library). 1973. (pbk) 0.95. Dell.
Operation Nightfall. John Miles & Tom Morris. LC 74-17665. 224p. 1975. 6.95 o.p. (ISBN 0-672-52085-0). Bobbs.
Operation Nightfall. John Miles & Tom Morris. LC 74-17665. 224p. 1975. 6.95 o.p. (ISBN 0-672-52085-0). Bobbs.
Operation Nightfall. John Miles & Tom Morris. (Berkley Medallion Book). 1976. (pbk.) 1.75 (ISBN 0-425-03087-3). Berkley Publishing Corp.
Operation Nightfall: A Novel of Suspense. Jack M Bickham & Tom Morris. LC 74-17665. 6.95 (ISBN 0-672-52085-0). Bobbs-Merrill.
Operation Nuke. Martin Caidin. LC 72-97689. 1973. 6.95 (ISBN 0-87795-041-5). Arbor House.
Operation Nuke. Martin Caidin. (Cyborg#2). 1974. (pbk.) 1.25. Warner Paperback Lib.
Operation Omina. Roland Starr, pseud. Ed. by Alice Sachs. 1970. 3.95 o.p. B Franklin.
Operation Overlord: And Other Stories. Ewald Bash. LC 78-79194. (Perspective series, 8). (Illus.). 1969. 1.25. Concordia Pub. House.
Operation: Perfidia. Leonard Jordan. 1975. (pbk.) 1.25. Warner Paperback Library.
Operation Piracy. 1st American Ed. Paul Somers. LC 59-6342. 1959. Harper.
Operation Prophet. Robert B Asprey. LC 77-72410. 1977. 6.95 (ISBN 0-385-13079-1). Doubleday.
Operation Rat. J. A. Sherrett. 192p. 1973. 6.00 o.p. (ISBN 0-682-47751-6). Exposition.
Operation-Rebel. James Hutchison. LC 67-21092. 1967. T. Gaus' Sons.
Operation Romance. Bennie Caroline Hall. LC 54-990895. 1954. Arcadia House.
Operation S-L. Norman Daniels. (Orig.). 1971. pap. 0.75 o.p. (T2415). Pyramid Pubns.
Operation Scorpio. David Mariner. 1975. (pbk.) 1.25 (ISBN 0-523-00565-2). Pinnacle Books.
Operation Sea Lion. Richard Hubert Francis Cox. LC 77-152396. (Illus.). 1977. 8.95 (ISBN 0-89141-015-5). Presidio Press.
Operation Sea Monster. Ken Stanton. (Aquanaut Ser.: No. 10). 192p. (Orig.). 1974. pap. 0.95 o.p. (ISBN 0-532-95309-6). Woodhill.
Operation Sea Monster. Ken Stanton. (Aquanauts#10). 1974. (pbk.) 0.95. Manor Books.
Operation Skyhook. Joseph Rosenberger. (Death Merchant Ser.: No. 47). 208p. (Orig.). 1981. pap. 1.95 (ISBN 0-523-41328-9). Pinnacle Bks.
Operation Snake. Nick Carter. (Nick Carter Ser). (O.s.i.). (Orig.). 1969. pap. 0.60 o.s.i. (A559, Award). Univ Pub & Dist.
Operation Snake. Nick Carter. (Nick Carter Ser.). (O.s.i.). 1976. pap. 1.50 o.s.i. (AD1624, Award). Univ Pub & Dist.
Operation Splinter Factor. Stewart Steven. 1974. 7.95 o.p. (ISBN 0-397-00982-8). Lippincott.
Operation Springboard. 1st Ed. John Dudley Ball. LC 58-10435. 1958. Duell, Sloan and Pearce.
Operation Stalag. Charles Whiting. 1976. (pbk.) 1.25 (ISBN 0-523-00821-X). Pinnacle Books.
Operation Starvation. Nick Carter. (Nick Carter Ser.). (O.s.i.). (Orig.). 1968. pap. 0.60 o.s.i. (A313X, Award). Univ Pub & Dist.

Operation Steelfish. Ken Stanton. (Aquanauts Ser.: No. 8). 176p. (Orig.). 1972. pap. 0.95 o.p. (ISBN 0-532-95218-9). Woodhill.

Operation Steelfish. Ken Stanton. 1972. 0.95. Manor Books.

Operation: Super Ms. Andrew J Offutt. (Berkley medallion book). 1974. (pbk.) 0.95. Berkley Pub. Co.

Operation Survival Earth. Stefan Denaerde. 1.50 (ISBN 0-671-80840-0). Pocket Books.

Operation Survival Earth. Stefan Denaerde. 1.50 (ISBN 0-671-80840-0). Pocket Books.

Operation Susannah. Dorothy Adelson. LC 82-541. 200p. 1982. 13.95 (ISBN 0-9607830-0-8, AACR2). Pemberley Pr.

Operation Time Search. Alice Mary Norton. LC 67-17156. 1967. Harcourt, Brace & World.

Operation Umanaq. John Rankine. 1973. (pbk) 0.75. Ace Books.

Operation Weatherkill. Paul Edwards. LC 75-24507. (John Eagle - Expeditor#13). 1975. (pbk.) 1.25 (ISBN 0-515-03874-1). Pyramid Books.

Operation Whiplash. Dan J Marlowe. (Fawcett Gold Medal Book)). 1973. (pbk) 0.75. Fawcett.

Operation 10. Hardiman Scott. LC 82-47542. 12.95 (ISBN 0-06-039011-5). Harper & Row.

Operational Necessity. Gwyn Griffin. (Signet Q3526). 1968. New Amer. Lib.

Operational Necessity. Gwyn Griffin. LC 67-23127. 1967. Putnam.

Operative. James W. Covington. (Orig.). 1981. pap. 1.95 (ISBN 0-505-51636-5). Tower Bks.

Operator. Donald Honig. (Orig., Sidewalk Caesar). 1971. pap. 0.95 o.p. (B95-2102). Belmont-Tower.

Operator. Rubens, Robert. LC 66-45371. 1964. M. Joseph.

Operators. Allan Prior. LC 67-73517. 1966. Cassell.

Operators. Allan Prior. LC 67-10899. 1967. Simon and Schuster.

Ophelia. Florence Stevenson. LC 68-20114. 1968. New American Library.

Ophelia the Cat. Jerome Irving Rodale. LC 54-12540. (His 64 series). 1954. Rodale Books.

Ophidian Conspiracy. John F. Carr. LC 75-36119. 176p. (Orig.). 1978. pap. 1.50 (ISBN 0-89041-191-3, 3191). Major Bks.

Ophiuchi Hotline. John Varley. LC 77-1903. (Quantum Science Fiction). 1977. 8.95 (ISBN 0-8037-6120-1). Dial Press/James Wade.

Opinion of the Court. William Woolfolk. (N3610). 1967. Bantam.

Opinion of the Court. William Woolfolk. LC 66-17435. 1966. Doubleday.

Opinions of Jerome Coignard. Anatole France, pseud. lib. bdg. 8.50 o.p. Folcroft.

Opisthophorus: Or, The Man Who Walked Backward; a Book of Modern Life. Caleb Jones & Jones, Julia Anna. LC 9-14218. 1.25. W. B. Conkey Company.

Opium. Rudolph Johnson, Jr. (Novel - Adventure Ser.). 232p. 1981. 11.95 (ISBN 0-938952-00-5). Mona Pub.

Opium & Other Stories. Geza Csath. 208p. 1983. pap. 4.95 (ISBN 0-14-006689-6). Penguin.

Opium Flower. Dan Cushman. LC 63-8931. 1963. Bantam Books.

Opium Hunter. Axel Kilgore. (They Call Me the Mercenary Ser.: No. 4). 1981. pap. 2.25. Zebra.

Opium Murders. Leonard Worswick Clyde. 1930. The Macaulay Company.

Opium Stratagem. Hunton Downs. LC 73-8514. (Illus.). 1973. (pbk.) 1.25. Bantam Books.

Opoponax. Monique Wittig. Tr. by Helen Weaver. LC 76-7818. 1976. 4.50 (ISBN 0-913780-15-4). Daughters.

Opoponax: A Novel. Tr. from French by Helen Weaver. Monique Wittig. LC 66-16157. bds., 4.95. S. & S.

Opovidannia. Bohdan Lepkyi. (Ukrains'ka Kul'turna Skarbnytsia). (Ukrai.). 1975. 10.00 (ISBN 0-918884-26-8). Slavia Lib.

Oppenheim Omnibus: Clowns and Criminals. Edward Phillips Oppenheim. LC 35-6725. 1933. Blue Ribbon Books, Inc.

Oppenheim Secret Service Omnibus: Spies and Intrigues. Edward Phillips Oppenheim. LC 40-3664. Blue Ribbon Books.

Oppermanns. Lion Feuchtwanger. LC 34-5587. 1934. The Viking Press.

Oppidan. Shane Leslie. LC 22-12022. 1922. C. Scribner's Sons.

Opponents: A Novel. Harrison Robertson. LC 2-11136. 1902. C. Scribner's Sons.

Opportunist. 1st Ed. Samuel Youd. LC 56-11106. Harper.

Opportunities of a Night. Claude Crebillon. LC 71-174388. 1971. B. Blom.

Opportunity. A Novel. Anne Moncure Crane Seemuller. LC 8-11248. 1867. Ticknor and Fields.

Opportunity of a Lifetime. Emma Smith. LC 79-7330. 1980. 10.00 (ISBN 0-385-15300-7). Doubleday.

Opposite House; a Novel. Nataly Von Eschstruth & Safford, Mary Joanna, Tr. (choice ser. no. 118). 1894. R. Bonner's Sons.

Opposite House; a Novel. Nataly Von Eschstruth & Safford, Mary Joanna, Tr. (ledger library. no. 413). 1894. R. Bonner's Sons.

Opposites. George W Kite. LC 33-777. 1932. Meador Publishing Company.

Opposition. Nick Caesar. 80p. 1976. 4.00 o.p. (ISBN 0-682-48243-9). Exposition.

Opposition. Selma Adler Gruber. LC 31-319292. 1931.

Optiman. Brian M. Stableford. (Science Fiction Ser.). 1980. pap. 1.95 (ISBN 0-87997-571-7, UJ1571). DAW Bks.

Optimist. Edmee Elizabeth Monica De La Pasture. LC 22-21107. 1922. The Macmillan Company.

Optimist. Susan Taber. LC 17-22703. 1917. 1.30. Duffield & Company.

Optimists Daughter. Eudora Welty. 1973. (pbk) 1.25. Fawcett.

Optimist's Daughter. Eudora Welty. LC 76-39769. 1972. 5.95 (ISBN 0-394-48017-1) (ISBN 0-394-48018-X). Random House.

Optimist's Daughter. Eudora Welty. LC 78-58856. 1978. 1.95 (ISBN 0-394-72667-7). Vintage Books.

Option on Love. lNew York: Avalon Books. Jeanne Judson. LC 57-8743.

Options. Warren Adler. LC 73-94210. 1974. 7.95 (ISBN 0-87426-035-3). Whitmore Pub. Co.

Options. Freda Bright. (Orig.). 1982. pap. 2.95 (ISBN 0-671-41270-1). PB.

Options. William Sydney Porter. LC 9-27747. 1909. Harper & Brothers.

Options. William Sydney Porter. LC 22-16022. 1919. Doubleday, Page & Company, for Review of Reviews Co.

Options. William Sydney Porter. LC 24-27974. 1920. Doubleday, Page & Company.

Options. William Sydney Porter. LC 25-237239. 1925. Doubleday, Page & Company.

Options. William Sydney Porter. LC 9-27747. 1909. Harper & Brothers.

Options. Robert Scheckley. (Orig.). 1975. pap. 1.25 o.p. (ISBN 0-515-03688-9). BJ Pub Group.

Opus One Hundred. Isaac Asimov. 1969. 6.95 o.p. (ISBN 0-395-07351-0). HM.

Opus Posthumous. Wallace Stevens. LC 82-40032. 352p. 1982. pap. 6.95 (ISBN 0-394-71178-5). Random.

Opus Thirty-One, No. 3. Theodore Enslin. 1979. pap. 3.00 (ISBN 0-915316-71-4). Pentagram.

Opus Two Hundred. Isaac Asimov. 1979. 10.95. HM.

Oqua: A Novel. Thomas Blair. LC 79-15861. 1979. 8.95 (ISBN 0-87949-163-9). Ashley Books.

O.R. Barrie Evans. (Orig.). 1982. pap. 2.95 (ISBN 0-440-17623-9). Dell.

Or All the Seas with Oysters. Avram Davidson. (O.s.i.). 1976. pap. 1.50 o.s.i. (ISBN 0-671-80806-0). WSP.

Or All the Seas with Oysters. Avram Davidson. 1.25 (ISBN 0-671-80806-0). Pocket Books.

Or Be He Dead. James Byrom. LC 81-48169. 224p. 1982. pap. 2.84i (ISBN 0-06-080585-4, P585, PL). Har-Row.

Or Be He Dead. James Byrom. 1958. pap. 0.85 o.p. (ISBN 0-14-001609-0, 1609). Penguin.

Or Be He Dead: By Harry Carmichael Pseud. 1st Ed. Leopold Horace Ognall. LC 58-11322. 1958. Published for the Crime Club by Doubleday.

Or Call It Winter. Donald Stevens. LC 51-3278. 1951. Harper.

Or Else, a Park Bench. Edwin Bateman Morris. LC 35-4595. The Penn Publishing Company.

Or Was He Pushed? Richard Lockridge. LC 75-2007. 1975. 7.50 (ISBN 0-397-01080-X). Lippincott.

Or Was He Pushed. Richard Lockridge. LC 81-9986. 1981. 11.95 (ISBN 0-89340-345-8). J. Curley & Associates.

Ora. The Lost Wife. Bella Zilfa Spencer. LC 7-236823. 1863. P. C. Browne.

Oracle. T. L. McDonald. 1978. pap. 4.95 o.s.i. (ISBN 0-8202-5012-0). Sherbourne.

Oracle. Edwin O'Connor. LC 51-10534. 1951. Harper.

Oracle in the Heart. Kathleen Raine. (Orig.). 1980. pap. text ed. cancelled o.p. (ISBN 0-85105-347-5, Dolmen Pr). Humanities.

Oraisons funebres. new ed. Jacques-Benigne Bossuet. (Nouveaux Classiques Larousse Ser.). (Illus.). 168p. (Fr.). 1975. pap. 2.95 (33). Larousse.

Oral Couple. Hal Edwards. 192p. pap. 1.95 o.p. (ISBN 0-87056-164-2, 6164). Brandon.

Oral Daughter. Peggy Swenson, pseud. 224p. pap. 1.95 o.p. (6161). Brandon.

Oral Daughters. Sterling Harkins. 224p. pap. 1.95 o.p. (7136). Barclay Hse.

Oral Family. Hal Edwards. pap. 1.95 o.p. (ISBN 0-87056-209-6, 6209). Brandon.

Oral History. Lee Smith. LC 82-18081. 14.95 (ISBN 0-399-12794-1). Putnam.

Oral Husbands. Charles Richards. 192p. pap. 1.95 o.p. (7160). Barclay Hse.

Oral Lovers. Israel Krupp. 224p. pap. 1.95 o.p. (6141). Brandon.

Oral Mothers. Winters. pap. 1.95 o.p. (ISBN 0-87682-164-6, 7164). Barclay Hse.

Oral Mothers. Deena Winters. 192p. pap. 1.95 o.p. (7164). Barclay Hse.

Oral Orgies. Ward Fulton. pap. 1.95 o.p. (ISBN 0-87682-251-0, 7251). Barclay Hse.

Oral Sex Among Wife Swappers. James L. Brown. pap. 2.45 o.p. (4025). Cameo.

Oral Sisters. Kyle McCambridge. 192p. pap. 1.95 o.p. (7143). Barclay Hse.

Oral Sisters. Carter Sprague. 192p. pap. 1.95 o.p. (6165). Brandon.

Oral Teenagers. John Tanner, pseud. pap. 1.95 o.p. (ISBN 0-87682-243-X, 7243). Barclay Hse.

Oral Twins. Hal Edwards. pap. 1.95 o.p. (ISBN 0-87056-196-0, 6196). Brandon.

Oral Women. Hal Edwards. pap. 1.95 o.p. (ISBN 0-87056-178-2, 6178). Brandon.

Oralism Around the World. Bruno Ogden. 160p. 1974. pap. 1.95 o.p. (ISBN 0-87682-399-1, 7399). Barclay Hse.

Oralism in the Family. Preston Harriman. 192p. pap. 1.95 o.p. (7149). Barclay Hse.

Oram of the Forest. author's ed. Byron E Staley. LC 8-1783. (His The wheel of progress. Book I. Primeval series). 1907. The Tower.

Oramaika. An Indian Story. Elisabeth Brun. LC 6-16704. 1854. E. Dunigan and Brother.

Oran: The Outcast; or, A Season in New-York ... 1833. Peabody & Co.

Orange--Yellow Diamond. Joseph Smith Fletcher. LC 21-260858. 1921. A. A. Knopf.

Orange Balloon. Penny Harter. (Xtras Ser.: No. 8). 36p. (Orig.). 1980. pap. 2.00 (ISBN 0-89120-012-6). From Here.

Orange Blossom Island, the Flowering Valley, the Tideless Sea. Juliet Armstrong. (Harlequin Romances Ser.). 576p. 1982. pap. 3.50 (ISBN 0-373-20066-8). Harlequin Bks.

Orange Blossoms: A Romance. Leslie Lynd. LC 37-11437. Phoenix Press.

Orange Blossoms, a Romance: By Leslie Lynd Pseud. Albert Quandt. LC 37-11437. 1937. Phoenix Press.

Orange Blossoms, Fresh and Faded. Timothy Shay Arthur. 1871. J. M. Stoddart & Co.

Orange Court. Lily Anne Coppard. LC 29-9004. 1929. I. Washburn.

Orange Divan. Valentine Williams. LC 23-11803. 1923. Houghton Mifflin Company.

Orange Envelope. Mario Soldati. LC 69-14848. 1969. Harcourt, Brace & World.

Orange Full of Dreams. Antoni Gronowicz. LC 77-173884. 1972. 6.95 (ISBN 0-396-06424-8). Dodd, Mead.

Orange Girl. Walter Besant. 1899. Dodd, Mead & Company.

Orange Grove: A Tale of the Connecticut... Sarah E. Wall. LC 8-33284. 1866. B. G. Howes.

Orange Power, Black Juice. Maurice Nessen. LC 73-90181. 288p. 1974. 7.95 o.p. (ISBN 0-8129-0429-X). Quadrangle.

Orange Power, Black Juice: A Novel. Maurice Nessen. LC 73-90181. 1974. 7.95 (ISBN 0-8129-0429-X). Quadrangle/New York Times Book Co.

Orange R. John Clagett. 1978. 1.50 (ISBN 0-445-04225-7). Popular Library.

Orange Unicorn. J. B. Herman. 256p. (Orig.). Date not set. pap. cancelled (ISBN 0-505-51796-5). Tower Bks.

Orange Valley. Howard Baker. LC 31-6070. Coward-McCann, Inc.

Orange Wednesday. Leslie Thomas. LC 68-10322. 1968. Delacorte Press.

Orangefield. Agnes Mary Robertson Dunlop. LC 38-30378. The Bobbs-Merrill Company.

Oranges and Lemons. Dolores Charlotte Frederica Harding. LC 16-14280. 1916. Cassell and Company, Ltd.

Oranging of America, and Other Stories. Max Apple. LC 76-23436. 1976. 7.95 (ISBN 0-670-52801-3). Grossman Publishers.

Oranging of America and Other Stories. Max Apple. 1978. 1.95 (ISBN 0-553-10992-8). Bantam Books.

Orbit. Harper & Row.

Orbit Five. Ed. by Damon Francis Knight. 1969. 5.95 o.p. (ISBN 0-399-10604-9). Putnam.

Orbit Fourteen. Ed. by Damon Francis Knight. LC 73-18657. 256p. (YA) 1974. 9.95 o.p. (ISBN 0-06-012438-5, HarpT). Har-Row.

Orbit Nineteen. Ed. by Damon Francis Knight. LC 76-26270. 1977. 9.95 o.p. (ISBN 0-06-012431-8, HarpT). Har-Row.

Orbit One. Mel Jay, pseud. 1970. Repr. pap. 0.60 o.p. (60-447). Manor Bks.

Orbit Seventeen. Ed. by Damon Francis Knight. LC 75-6371. (Illus.). 224p. (YA) 1975. 9.95i (ISBN 0-06-012434-2, HarpT). Har-Row.

Orbit Sixteen. Ed. by Damon Francis Knight. LC 74-15875. (Illus.). 280p. (YA) 1975. 9.95 o.p. (ISBN 0-06-012437-7, HarpT). Har-Row.

Orbit Twenty. Ed. by Damon Francis Knight. LC 77-11784. 1978. 9.95 o.p. (ISBN 0-06-012429-6, HarpT). Har-Row.

Orbit Twenty One. Ed. by Damon Francis Knight. LC 78-20207. 224p. 1980. 12.95i (ISBN 0-06-012426-1, HarpT). Har-Row.

Orbit Unlimited. Poul Anderson. LC 78-560. (Anderson, Paul, 1926-. The Worlds of Paul Anderson). 1978. 8.50 (ISBN 0-8398-2430-0). Gregg Press.

Orbit 15. Ed. by Damon Knight. LC 74-1890. 1974. 7.95 (ISBN 0-06-012439-3). Harper & Row.

Orbit 18. Ed. by Damon Francis Knight. LC 75-25089. 8.95 (ISBN 0-06-012433-4). Harper.

Orbit. 2. 19673. Ed. by Damon Francis Knight. LC 66-15585. 1967. 4.95. Putnam.

Orbit. 3 1968. Ed. by Damon Francis Knight. LC 66-155851. 4.95. Putnam.

Orbitsville. Bob Shaw. 1.95. Ace.

Orchard & a Garden. Dudley Laufman. 1974. pap. 3.95 (ISBN 0-87233-026-5). Bauhan.

Orchard Fence. Mae Foster Jay. LC 36-7572. W. A. Wilde Company.

Orchard Hill. Elizabeth Seifert. LC 73-79146. 1973. 5.95. Aeonian Press.

Orchard Hill. Elizabeth Seifert. LC 45-8595. 1945. Dodd, Mead & Company.

Orchard Keeper. Cormac McCarthy. LC 65-10456. bds., 4.95. Random.

Orchard of Tears. Sax Rohmer, pseud. 1969. 8.50. Bookfinger.

Orchard Princess. Ralph Henry Barbour. LC 3-29103. 1905. J. B. Lippincott Company.

Orchard Upstairs. Penelope Shuttle. 1980. pap. 11.95 (ISBN 0-19-211938-9). Oxford U Pr.

Orchards. Warwick Deeping. LC 22-15202. 1922. Cassell and Company, Ltd.

Orchardscroft: The Story of an Artist. Elsa de'Esterre Keeling. LC 7-11426. Cassell Publishing Company.

Orchestra & Beginners. Frederic Raphael. LC 68-11413. 1968. Viking Press.

Orchestra Mice. cancelled o.p. (ISBN 0-8092-8764-1). Regnery.

Orchid. Robert Grant. LC 68-57527. (Illus.). 1968. Gregg Press.

Orchid. Robert Nathan. LC 31-8637. The Bobbs-Merrill Company.

Orchid Cage. Herbert W. Franke. (Daw sf Books, no. 79). 1973. (pbk.) 0.95. Daw Books.

Orchid House. 1st American Ed. Phyllis Shand Allfrey. LC 54-505743. 1954. Dutton.

Orchid Stories. Kenward Elmslie. LC 70-157586. 1973. 6.95 (ISBN 0-385-07365-8). Doubleday.

Orchids. A Novel. Lelia Hardin Bugg. LC 6-19666. 1894. B. Herder.

Orchids for Mother: A Novel. Aaron Latham. LC 76-30647. 8.95 (ISBN 0-316-51595-7). Little, Brown.

Orchids for Mothers. Peggy Gaddis, pseud. LC 47-18223. 1947. Arcadia House, Inc.

Orchids for the Nurse. Adelaide Humphries. LC 55-14265. 1955. Avalon Books.

Orchids to Murder. Hulbert Footner. LC 45-2146. 1945. Harper & Brothers.

Ordained. Robert Leckie. LC 69-15160. 1969. 6.95. Doubleday.

Ordeal. Vasilii Uladzimiravich Bykau. LC 72-193956. 1972. (ISBN 0-370-01467-7). Bodley Head.

Ordeal. Vasilii Uladzimiravich Bykau. LC 77-179837. 1972. 5.95 (ISBN 0-525-17195-9). E. P. Dutton.

Ordeal. Gordon Gordon & Mildred Gordon. LC 75-40726. 1976. 6.95 (ISBN 0-385-07806-4). Doubleday.

Ordeal. Gordon Gordon & Mildred Gordon. (Berkley Medallion Book). 1977. 1.50 (ISBN 0-425-03496-8). Berkley Pub. Corp.

Ordeal. John London. LC 12-1065. (Orig.). 1969. pap. 1.25 o.p. (B12-1065). Belmont-Tower.

Ordeal. Arkadii A. Perventsev. LC 44-9415. 1944. Harper & Brothers.

Ordeal. Nevil Shute. 1970. pap. 0.75 o.p. (ISBN 0-447-74634-0). Lancer.

Ordeal, 3 vols. A. Tolstoi. 1150p. 1976. Set. 16.50 (ISBN 0-8285-1053-9, Pub. by Progress Pubs USSR). Imported Pubns.

Ordeal: A Mountain Romance of Tenessee. LC 12-242033. 1912. J. B. Lippincott Company.

Ordeal: A Novel. Dale Collins. LC 24-18096. 1924. A. A. Knopf.

Ordeal, a Novel. Nevil Shute Norway. LC 39-293218. 1939. W. Morrow & Company.

Ordeal, a Novel. John Brewster Prescott. LC 58-8058. 1958. Random House.
Ordeal by Glory. James Marshall. LC 27-8784. 1927. R. M. McBride & Company.
Ordeal by Innocence. Agatha Miller Christie. LC 59-6200. (Red badge detective). 1959. Dodd, Mead.
Ordeal by Marriage. Concordia Merrel. LC 26-8387. George H. Doran and Company.
Ordeal by Silence: A Story of Medieval Times. Prudence Andrew. LC 61-15072. 1961. Putnam.
Ordeal for Wives. A Novel. Annie Edwards. LC 6-36565. 1873. Sheldon & Company.
Ordeal in Otherwhere. Andre Norton, pseud. 1980. lib. bdg. 9.95 (ISBN 0-8398-2634-6, Gregg). G K Hall.
Ordeal in Otherwhere. Andre Norton, pseud. 208p. 1982. pap. 2.25 (ISBN 0-441-63825-2, Pub. by Ace Science Fiction). Ace Bks.
Ordeal in Otherwise. Andre Norton. 1973. (pbk) 0.75. Ace Books.
Ordeal in the Forest. Godwin Wachira. 1968. pap. 2.50 o.p. (Pub. by East African Pub Hse). Northwestern U Pr.
Ordeal of Assad Pasha. Ignas Jurkunas. LC 63-19990. Manyland Books.
Ordeal of Brad Ogden, a Romance of the Forest Rangers: By Arthur H. Carhart. Arthur Hawthorne Carthart. LC 29-2378. J. H. Sears & Company, Inc.
Ordeal of Dudley Dean. Richard Scowcroft. LC 69-16164. 1969. 5.95. Lippincott.
Ordeal of Elizabeth. LC 2-175. 1901. J. F. Taylor & Company.
Ordeal of Gilbert Pinfold. Evelyn Waugh. 1979. 10.95 (ISBN 0-316-92624-8); pap. 5.95 (ISBN 0-316-92622-1). Little.
Ordeal of Gilbert Pinfold: A Conversation Piece. 1st Ed. Evelyn Waugh. LC 57-9369. 1957. Little, Brown.
Ordeal of Hogue Bynell. Frank Roderus. LC 82-45303. (Double D Western Ser.). 192p. 1982. 11.95 (ISBN 0-385-18029-2). Doubleday.
Ordeal of Honor. Agnes Russell Weekes. LC 22-26241. 1922. R. M. McBride & Company.
Ordeal of Jason Ord. Lewis B Patten. LC 72-97498. 1973. 4.95 (ISBN 0-385-04486-0). Doubleday.
Ordeal of Jason Ord. Lewis B Patten. (Signet brand western). 1974. (pbk.) 0.95. New American Library.
Ordeal of Jason Ord. Lewis B Patten. LC 78-21985. 1981. 10.50 (ISBN 0-89340-186-2). J. Curley & Associates.
Ordeal of Major Grigsby. John Sherlock. LC 63-20418. 1964. Morrow.
Ordeal of Mansart. William Edward Burghardt Du Bois. LC 57-13796. (His The black flame, a trilogy, book 1). 1957. Mainstream Publishers.
Ordeal of Mansart see Black Flame; a Trilogy.
Ordeal of Minnie Schultz. Helen Reimensnyder Martin. LC 39-249363. 1939. D. Appleton-Century Company, Incorporated.
Ordeal of Richard Feverel. George Meredith. LC 64-11406. (Rinehart editions, 123). 1964. Holt, Rinehart and Winston.
Ordeal of Richard Feverel. George Meredith. LC 75-140997. (Riverside editions, B122). 1971. (ISBN 0-395-11151-X). Houghton Mifflin.
Ordeal of Richard Feverel. George Meredith. LC 28-26469. (Half-title: The Modern library of the world's best books). 1927. The Modern Library.
Ordeal of Richard Feverel: A History of a Father and Son. rev. ed. George Meredith. LC 1-19357. 1896. C. Scribner's Sons.
Ordeal of Richard Feverel: A History of a Father and Son. George Meredith. Ed. by Chandler, Frank Wadleigh. LC 17-11700. (Half-title: The modern student's library, ed. by W. D. Howe). C. Scribner's Sons.
Ordeal of Richard Feverel: A History of a Father and Son. rev. ed. George Meredith. LC 20-19586. 1919. C. Scribner's Sons.
Ordeal of Richard Feverel: A History of a Father and Son. George Meredith. LC 26-26551. (Half-title: The modern readers' series). 1926. The Macmillan Company.
Ordeal of Richard Feverel: A History of a Father and Son. George Meredith. LC 82-19785. 1983. 6.95 (ISBN 0-486-24463-6). Dover Publications.
Ordeal of Richard Feverel: A History of Father and Son. George Meredith. LC 50-13681. (Modern Library college editions, 727). 1950. Modern Library.
Ordeal of Richard Feverel: A History of Father and Son. George Meredith. LC 6-11678. (Half-title: The English Comedie humaine. 2d series). 1906. The Century Co.
Ordeal of Running Standing. Thomas Fall. 1970. 6.95 o.p. (ISBN 0-8415-0047-9). Sat Rev Pr.
Ordeal of Running Standing. Donald Clifford Snow. LC 76-122124. 1970. 6.95 (ISBN 0-8415-0047-9). McCall Pub. Co.
Ordeal of Stanley Stanhope. Richard Bousquet. LC 72-39236. (Illus.). 1972. (ISBN 0-393-08670-4). Norton.
Ordeal of the Falcon. Gosta Larsson. LC 41-3984. The Vanguard Press.
Ordeal of the Rod. R. Bernard Burns. (TC208). 1967. pap., 1.25. Traveller's Companion.
Ordeal of Three Doctors. Elizabeth Seifert. LC 65-22845. bds., 3.75. Dodd.
Ordeal of Willie Brown, a Novel. Arthur Marx. LC 51-2841. 1951. Simon and Schuster.
Ordeal on the Frontier. Sydney Henry Woolf. LC 28-29072. 1928. G. P. Putnam's Sons, Ltd.
Order. Claude Carlos Washburn. LC 20-40144. 1920. Duffield and Company.
Order No. 11: A Tale of the Border. Caroline Abbot Stanley. LC 4-7535. 1904. The Century Co.
Order No. 11: A Tale of the Border. Caroline Abbot Stanley. LC 25-3171. 1921. The Century Co.
Order of Battle. Alfred Coppel. LC 68-24387. 1968. 4.95. Harcourt, Brace & World.
Order of Battle. Ib Melchior. 1973. (pbk.) 1.50. Warner Paperback Library.
Order of Battle. Ib Melchior. LC 72-79710. 1972. 6.95 (ISBN 0-06-012937-9). Harper & Row.
Order of Death. Hugh Fleetwood. LC 76-25899. 6.95 (ISBN 0-671-22357-7). Simon and Schuster.
Order of the Octopus. Sydney Horler. LC 26-4270. George H. Doran Company.
Ordered Steps. Bertha B. Moore McCurry. LC 38-6763. 1937. Wm. B. Eerdmans Pub. Co.
Ordered Steps. Bertha B Moore. LC 38-676340. 1937. Wm. B. Eerdmans Pub. Co.
Orderly Life. Jose Yglesias. LC 68-20893. 1968. 5.95. Pantheon Books.
Orders of Chivalry. Peter Vansittart. LC 59-5353. 1959. Abelard-Schuman.
Ordinary Daylight. Andrew Potok. 256p. 1981. pap. 2.95 (ISBN 0-553-14432-4). Bantam.
Ordinary Families: A Novel. Eileen Arbuthnot Robertson. LC 33-28404. 1933. Doubleday, Doran & Company, Inc.
Ordinary Families: A Novel. Eileen Arbuthnot Robertson. LC 82-25242. (Virago Modern Classic). 1982. 7.95 (ISBN 0-385-27935-3). Dial Press.
Ordinary Girl. Gerald Foster. LC 36-20242. 1936. Godwin.
Ordinary Man. Mel Arrighi. LC 71-114269. 1970. 4.95. P. H. Wyden.
Ordinary People. Judith Guest. LC 76-2368. 1976. 8.95 (ISBN 0-670-52831-5). Viking Press.
Ordways. William Humphrey. LC 64-190892. 1965. 5.95. Knopf.
Ordways. William Humphrey. (Kangaroo Book). 1977. 1.95 (ISBN 0-671-81245-9). Pocket Books.
Orefeo in Paradise. Luigi Santucci. Tr. by Joseph Green. 1969. 4.95 o.p. Knopf.
Oregon Detour. Nard Jones. LC 30-1935. 1930. Payson & Clarke Ltd.
Oregon Girl: A Tale of American Life in the New West. Alfred Ernest Rice. LC 14-6283. 1914. Glass & Prudhomme Co.
Oregon Highroad: By Chuck Stanley Pseud. Charles Stanley Strong. LC 53-704738. 1953. Arcadia House.
Oregon Rifles: By Dwight Bennett Pseud. 1st Ed. Dwight Bennett Newton. LC 62-159184. (Doubled D western). 1962. Doubleday.
Oregon Trail. Francis Parkman. (Hart Illustrated Classics Ser.). (Pap. ed. 3.95 o.p.). (Illus.). 1976. 8.95 o.p. (ISBN 0-8055-0290-4). Hart.
Oregon Trunk. Wayne D Overholser. LC 50-9237. 1950. Bouregy & Curl.
Oregon's First White Men. Daniel Franklin Howard. LC 27-20816. 1927. Rainier Review Press.
Oreo. Fran Ross. LC 74-17264. 1974. 6.95 (ISBN 0-914870-00-9). Greyfalcon House.
Orestes in Progress. Roberta Kalechofsky. LC 76-12977. 4.44 (ISBN 0-916288-02-1). Micah Publications.
ORF. David Meltzer. pap. 1.95 o.p. (0111). Essex Hse.
Org-1. A. D. Winans. LC 77-76620. 1977. pap. 2.00 (ISBN 0-916296-03-2). Poor Souls Pr.
Organ Bank Farm. John Boyd. LC 72-119907. 1970. 5.95 o.p. (ISBN 0-679-40071-0). Weybright.
Organ Bank Farm. Boyd Upchurch. LC 72-119907. 1970. 5.95. Weybright and Talley.
Organdy Cupcakes. Mary Slattery Stolz. 1951. Harper.
Organist's Retrospect: An Autobiography of Ernest Onslow, MUS. D., Illustrating the Development of a Musical Artist ... LC 6-21371. E. T. Clarke.
Organization. David Anthony. LC 75-133919. 1970. 5.95. Coward-McCann.
Organization. Harriet Daimler. 1968. pap. 1.95 o.s.i. (OPS28, Travellers Comp). Olympia.
Organization Baby. Constance Bannister. 1967. pap. 1.00 (ISBN 0-671-10264-8, Fireside). S&S.
Orgasm: Black on White. (Illus.). 4.95 (ISBN 0-910550-75-1). Centurion Pr.
Orgia de Sangre. new ed. John Benteen. Tr. by Jacinto De Torre from Eng. (Compadre Collection, Fargo: No. 7). (Illus.). 160p. (Span.). 1975. pap. 0.95 (ISBN 0-88473-517-6). Fiesta Pub.
Orgiastic Nymphomania. Peter Woodhull. LC 72-186004. (API, 108). 1.95. Nu-Triumph.
Orgy Apprentice. Robinson. pap. 1.95 o.p. (ISBN 0-87977-144-5, DBB144). Dansk Blue Bk.
Orgy at Donna Shannon's. Nikki Marshall. pap. 1.95 o.s.i. (Venus). Grove.
Orgy at Madame Dracula's. F. W. Paul. pap. 0.60 o.p. Lancer.
Orgy Cabin. Sybil Sainte-Claire. pap. 1.95 o.p. (ISBN 0-87056-201-0, 6201). Brandon.
Orgy Campus. Walter Matteo. 176p. pap. 1.95 o.p. (6111). Brandon.
Orgy Lovers. (Illus.). 4.95 (ISBN 0-910550-76-X). Centurion Pr.
Orgy Starts at Nine. Lee Gerald. 1971. pap. 0.75 o.p. (ISBN 0-446-64760-8, 64-760). Paperback Lib.
Oriad Letters. Paul Lester. 192p. (Orig.). 1971. pap. 1.95 o.s.i. (OPH264, Ophelia). Olympia.
Oriana. Valerie Vayle, pseud. 464p. (Orig.). 1981. pap. 3.50 (ISBN 0-440-16779-5). Dell.
Oriane. 1st Ed. Sigrid De Lima. LC 68-12570. 1968. 4.95. Harcourt.
Orient Express. John Dos Passos. 181p. 1976. Repr. of 1927 ed. lib. bdg. 30.00x (ISBN 0-374-92252-7). Octagon.
Orient Express. Graham Greene. 1933. Doubleday, Doran & Company, Inc.
Orient Express. Graham Greene. 1975. (pbk.) 1.95 (ISBN 0-671-80081-7). Pocket Books.
Orient Express: The Life & Times of the World's Most Famous Train. E. H. Cookridge, pseud. LC 78-57119. (Illus.). 1980. pap. 6.95i (ISBN 0-06-090770-3, CN 770, CN). Har-Row.
Orient Express: Uniform Edition. Graham Greene. 272p. 1982. 16.95 (ISBN 0-670-52841-2). Viking Pr.
Oriental Anecdotes: Or, The History of Haroun Alrachid. Marianne Agnes Pillement Fauques. LC 74-19079. (Flowering of the novel). 1974. (ISBN 0-8240-1166-X). Garland Pub.
Oriental Caravan. Ed. by Sirdar Ikbal A. Shah. 1972. pap. 3.65 (ISBN 0-912358-40-8). Omen Pr.
Oriental Constellation. A Romantic Page of Hidden History in the Barbarie Age, Delineating the Fall and Rise of a Peculiar Nation. G Eugene Hartfield. LC 7-2862. 1888. Hewlett & Pierce.
Oriental Division G-2: Captain North's Three Famous Intrigues of the Far East... Francis Van Wyck Mason. LC 42-218964. 1942. Reynal & Hitchcock.
Oriental Pearl: Or, The Catholic Emigrants. Anna Hanson McKenney Dorsey. LC 37-32806. 1857. J. Murphy.
Oriental Philantropist: Or, True Republican... Henry Sherburne. LC 8-11239. 1800. Printed for Wm. Treadwell & Co.
Oriental Pleasure Troves. Martin Ancel. (Illus.). 374p. 1975. lib. bdg. 12.95x. Pleasure Trove.
Oriental Romances. Ed. by Manuel Komroff. LC 30-26831. (Half-title: The modern library of the world's best books). The Modern Library.
Orientale: L'aventure De Therese Beauchamps. Francis De Miomandre & Roeder, Ralph, Tr. LC 29-1961. 1929. Brentano's.
Origen: A Historical Novel. Theodore Vrettos. LC 77-91602. (Illus.). 1978. 10.00 (ISBN 0-89241-079-5). Caratzas Bros.
Origin. Irving Stone. 1981. pap. 8.95 (ISBN 0-452-25284-9, Z5284, Plume). NAL.
Origin of Evil. Ellery Queen, pseud. LC 51-10221. 1951. Little, Brown.
Origin of Life & Death. Ed. by Ulli Beier. (African Writers Ser.: No. 23). (Orig.). pap. text ed. 1.75x o.p. (ISBN 0-435-90323-3, AW23). Humanities.
Origin of the Brunists. Robert Coover. (U7085). 1967. Ballantine.
Origin of the Brunists. Robert Coover. LC 77-21787. 1977. 10.00 (ISBN 0-670-52863-3). Viking Press.
Origin of the Brunists. Robert Coover. 1978. 2.95 (ISBN 0-553-11840-4). Bantam Books.
Origin of the Brunists: A Novel. Robert Coover. LC 66-20270. 6.95. Putnam.
Origin 1: Ed. by Damon Knight. Ed. by Damon Francis Knight. LC 66-155857. 3.50. Putnam.
Original. Larry Smith. LC 71-176366. 1972. 7.95 o.p. (ISBN 0-07-073214-0, GB). McGraw.
Original, a Novel. Larry Smith. 1974. (pbk.) 1.25. Bantam Books.
Original: A Novel. Larry Smith. LC 71-176366. 1972. 7.95 (ISBN 0-665-00007-3). Herder and Herder.
Original Arno Press Anthology Collected Short Stories. Anthony Trollope. Ed. by N. John Hall. LC 80-1909. (Selected Works of Anthony Trollope Ser.). 1981. lib. bdg. 30.00 (ISBN 0-405-14117-3). Ayer Co.
Original Belle. Edward Payson Roe. LC 3-219859. 1885. Dodd, Mead and Company.
Original Belle. Edward Payson Roe. LC 3-24490. (Dodd, Mead & company's Library of fiction, no. 1). 1888. Dodd, Mead & Company.
Original Carcase. Aaron Marc Stein. LC 46-7388. 1946. Pub. for the Crime Club by Doubleday & Company, Inc.
Original Design. Eardley Beswick. LC 33-21275. 1938. Minton, Balch & Comany.
Original Gentleman. Anne Warner French. LC 8-26824. 1908. Little, Brown and Company.
Original Girl. Christine Faber. LC 1-9354. 1901. P. J. Kenedy.
Original Lies and Quaint Conceits. Albert H St. Clair. LC 8-3399. (On cover: Nelson's star library, no. 3). 1891. A. F. Nelson Publishing Co.
Original Mr. Ed. Walter Brooks. LC 63-8615. (Bantam Book). 1963. Bantam Books.
Original Papers. With a Portrait of the Lady. Chester Bailey Fernald. LC 6-38985. 1892. Press of H. S. Crocker Company.
Original Sin. Charles Grayson. LC 33-30567. 1933. A. H. King.
Original Sin. George Tabori. LC 47-3749. 1947. Houghton Mifflin Company.
Original Sin. Translated from the Italian by Ben Johnson. Giose Rimanelli. LC 57-5376. 1957. Random House.
Original Sinner. Linn Boyd Porter. LC 7-377666. (On cover: The albatross novels). 1893. G. W. Dillingham.
Original Sinners. Henry Woodd Nevinson. LC 21-11925. 1921. B. W. Huebsch, Inc.
Original Sins. Lisa Alther. LC 80-22823. 1981. 13.95 (ISBN 0-394-51685-0). Knopf: Distributed by Random House.
Original Stories. Mary Wollstonecraft. 59.95 (ISBN 0-8490-0779-8). Gordon Pr.
Original Stories: With Five Illustrations by William Blake. Mary Wollstonecraft. LC 72-10149. 1973. lib. bdg. 20.00 (ISBN 0-8414-0658-8). Folcroft.
Orioles' Daughter. Jessie Fothergill. LC 6-40017. Tait, Sons & Company.
Orion. Welch D. Everman. 120p. 1975. pap. 4.50 (ISBN 0-87886-055-X, Pub. by Ithaca Hse). SBD.
Orion Line. Nicholas Luard. LC 76-376223. 1976. 3.90 (ISBN 0-436-26901-5). Secker and Werburg.
Orion Shall Rise. Poul Anderson. 480p. 1983. 16.95 (ISBN 0-671-46492-2, Timescape); pap. 7.95 (ISBN 0-671-46495-7, Timescape). PB.
Orion, the Gold Beater: Or, True Hearts and False; a Tale of New York Life. Sylvanus Cobb. LC 6-20719. Cassell & Company.
Orion, the Gold Beater: Or, True Hearts and False. A Tale of New York Life. Sylvanus Cobb. (On cover: Cassell's sunshine series, no. 2). The Cassell Publishing Co.
Orion: The Living Superstar of Song. Gail Brewer. 1981. pap. 3.50 (ISBN 0-671-41503-4). PB.
Orion's Shroud. William Cooke. 1981. pap. 2.75 (ISBN 0-8439-0886-6). Nordon Pubns.
Orissers. Leopold Hamilton Myers. LC 23-7204. 1923. G. P. Putnam's Sons.
Orissers. Leopold Hamilton Myers. LC 23-7318. 1923. C. Scribner's Sons.
Orkney Maid. Amelia Edith Huddleston Barr. LC 18-41532. 1918. 1.50. D. Appleton and Company.
Orko. Dora T. Dombrady. 1977. 10.00 (ISBN 0-918570-06-9). Karpat.
Orlando: A Biography. Virginia Stephen Woolf. LC 73-5729. (Harvest book, HB 266). (Illus.). 1973. 2.95. Harcourt Brace Jovanovich.
Orlando, a Biography. Virginia Stephen Woolf. (Signet classic, CD18). (Illus.). 1960. New American Library.
Orlando: A Biography. Virginia Stephen Woolf. LC 28-24699. 1928. C. Gaige.
Orlando: A Biography. Virginia Stephen Woolf. LC 28-26952. Harcourt, Brace and Company.
Orlando, a Biography by Virginia Woolf. Virginia Stephen Woolf. LC 44-39844. 1942. Penguin Books.
Orlando Furioso: An English Translation with Introductions, Notes & Index by Allan Gilbert, 2 vols. Ludovico Ariosto. 1954. 30.00x set (ISBN 0-913298-31-X). S F Vanni.
Orlando King. Isabel Colegate. LC 69-10694. 1969. 4.95. Knopf.
Orley Farm. Anthony Trollope. LC 50-8190. 1950. Knopf.
Orley Farm. Anthony Trollope. LC 35-27163. (Half-title: The world's classics. 423). 1935. Oxford University Press, H. Milford.
Orley Farm. Anthony Trollope & Thorold, Algar Labouchere, Ed. LC 12-39499. (Half-title: The new pocket library). 1906. John Lane.
Orloff and His Uife: Tales of the Barefoot Brigade. Maksim Gorkii & Hapgood, Isabel Florence, 1850-1928, Tr. LC 1-27062. 1901. C. Scribner's Sons.
Orloff and His Wife: Tales of the Barefoot Brigade. Maksim Gorkii. LC 72-11934. (Short story index reprint series). 1973. (ISBN 0-8369-4232-9). Books for Libraries Press.

Orloff & His Wife: Tales of the Barefoot Brigade. 15th ed. Maksim Gorkii. Tr. by Isabel F. Hapgood from Russian. LC 72-11934. (Short Story Index Reprint Ser). 1973. Repr. of 1901 ed. 26.00 (ISBN 0-8369-4232-9). Ayer Co.

Orme du Mail see Romans et Contes.

Ormerod's Landing. Leslie Thomas. LC 78-21412. 8.95 (ISBN 0-312-58924-7). St. Martin's Press.

Ormond. Charles Brockden Brown & Marchland, Ernest, Ed. LC 37-4089. (Half-title: American fiction series; general editor, H. H. Clark). American Book Company.

Ormond. Maria Edgeworth. (On cover: Seaside library. Pocket ed. no. 708). 1886. G. Munro.

Ormond. Maria Edgeworth. LC 25-2377. (Half-title: The novels of Maria Edgeworth, vol. x). 1893. J. M. Dent & Co.

Ormond: A Tale. Maria Edgeworth & Ritchie, Anne Isabella (Thackeray) Lady, 1837-1919. LC 4-16305. 1895. Macmillan and Co.

Ormond: Or, The Secret Witness. Charles Brockden Brown. LC 63-24272. (His Novels, v. 6). 1963. Kennikat Press.

Ormond: Or, The Secret Witness. Charles Brockden Brown. 1799. Printed by G. Forman, for H. Caritat.

Ormond: Or, The Secret Witness. Charles Brockden Brown. LC 41-34779. 1827. S. G. Goodrich.

Ormond: Or, The Secret Witness. uniform ed. Charles Brockden Brown. LC 6-18970. (On cover: Library of standard romance, no. 2). 1846. W. Taylor & Co.

Ormond: Or, The Secret Witness. Charles Brockden Brown. LC 6-18969. 1857. M. Polock.

Ormond: Or, The Secret Witness. Charles Brockden Brown. 1857. M. Polock.

Ormond: Or, The Secret Witness. Charles Brockden Brown. LC 17-130431. (Half-title: Charles Brockden Brown's novels, vol. vi). 1887. D. McKay.

Ormsteads: A Novel of Three Generations. Nickerson Bangs. LC 39-9402. 1939. H. C. Kinsey & Company, Inc.

Orn. Piers Anthony, pseud. 1975. pap. 2.50 (ISBN 0-380-00266-3, 605902). Avon.

Ornashious. John M. O'Hare. LC 70-90911. 1969. 4.25. Red Dust.

Oro De Panama. new ed. John Benteen. Tr. by Alvaro De Villa from Eng. (Compadre Collection: Fargo Ser., No. 2). Orig. Title: Panama Gold. 160p. (Span.). 1974. pap. 0.75 (ISBN 0-88473-512-5). Fiesta Pub.

Oron. David C. Smith. (Orig.). 1978. pap. 1.95 (ISBN 0-89083-358-3). Zebra.

Oron. David C. Smith. (Oron Ser.). 1982. pap. 1.95 (ISBN 0-89083-994-8). Zebra.

Oron: Mosutha's Magic. David C. Smith. (Oron Ser.). 1982. pap. 2.50 (ISBN 0-89083-986-7). Zebra.

Oron, No. 4: The Valley of Ogrum. David C. Smith. (Orig.). 1982. pap. 2.75 (ISBN 0-8217-1211-X). Zebra.

Oroonoko & Other Prose Narratives. Aphra Amis Behn. Ed. by Montague Summers. LC 67-25151. 1967. B. Blom.

Oroonoko: Or, The Royal Slave. Aphra Amis Behn. LC 73-17252. (Norton library, N702). 1973. 0.95 (ISBN 0-393-00702-2). Norton.

Orphan. Clarence Edward Mulford. LC 73-89647. (Illus.). 1974. 6.95. Aeonian Press.

Orphan. Clarence Edward Mulford. LC 8-6662. 1908. The Outing Publishing Company.

Orphan. Clarence Edward Mulford. LC 24-11654. 1924. A. C. McClurg & Co.

Orphan. Okello Oculi. 1968. pap. 1.80 o.p. (Pub. by East African Publ Hse). Northwestern U Pr.

Orphan. Thomas Otway. 1976. text ed. 8.50x o.s.i. (ISBN 0-8277-3933-8); pap. text ed. 5.95x o.s.i. (ISBN 0-8277-2289-3). British Bk Ctr.

Orphan. John H Shannon. LC 72-79039. 1972. 6.95 (ISBN 0-8415-0201-3). Saturday Review Press.

Orphan. Robert Stallman. (Book of the Beast: No. 1). 1980. pap. 2.25 (ISBN 0-671-82958-0, Timescape). PB.

Orphan, and Other Tales. Samuel Young. LC 15-231142. 1844. Printed by A. A. Anderson.

Orphan Angel. Elinor Hoyt Wylie. LC 26-20062. 1926. A. A. Knopf.

Orphan Ann. Henry Christopher Bailey. LC 41-13492. 1941. Pub. for the Crime Club by Doubleday, Doran & Co., Inc.

Orphan by Choice. Clara Verner. LC 58-59569. 1959. Beacon Hill Press.

Orphan Dinah. Eden Phillpotts. LC 21-937354. 1921. The Macmillan Company.

Orphan Girls; a Tale of Southern Life. James S Peacocke. LC 48-30441. International Book Co.

Orphan in the Sun. T F Vandenberg. LC 69-11214. 1969. 5.95. Houghton Mifflin.

Orphan Island. Rose Macaulay. LC 25-460340. 1925. Boni and Liveright.

Orphan Jim. Lonnie Coleman. 1.50. Dell.

Orphan Jim: A Novel. William Laurence Coleman. LC 75-7253. 1975. 6.95 (ISBN 0-385-11085-5). Doubleday.

Orphan of Eternity: Or, The Katabasis of the Lord Lucifer Satan... Carl Heinrich. LC 30-32139. 1929. L. Carrier & Co.

Orphan of Mars. Joanna Cannan, pseud. LC 30-779666. 1930. The Bobbs-Merrill Company.

Orphan of Moscow, or The Young Governess. A Tale Translated from the French of Madme Woillez. Woillez & Sadlier, Mary Anne (Madden) "Mrs. James Sadlier," 1820-1903, Tr. LC 43-29578. P. J. Kenedy and Sons.

Orphan of the Old Dominion. Her Trials and Travels. Embracing a History of Her Life, Taken Principally from Her Journals and Letters. Harriet Almaria Baker Suddoth. LC 8-16854. 1873. J. B. Lippincott & Co.

Orphan of the Rhine: A Romance. Eleanor Sleath. LC 68-98580. (Northanger Set of Jane Austen Horrid Novels). 1968. 65.00 set.,. Folio Pr.

Orphan Paul. Maksim Gorkii & Turner, Lily, Tr. 1946. Boni and Gaer.

Orphan Sisters; or, The Problem Solved. Mary Jane Hoffman. 1875. D. & J. Sadlier & Co.

Orphan Star. Alan Dean Foster. (Del Rey Book). 1977. 1.50 (ISBN 0-345-25507-0). Ballantine Books.

Orphan Star. Alan Dean Foster. LC 76-30376. 1977. 1.50 (ISBN 0-345-25507-0). Ballantine Books.

Orphan Street. Andre Langevin. LC 76-151467. 10.00 (ISBN 0-397-01204-7). Lippincott.

Orphan Street. Andre Langevin. LC 76-383162. 10.00 (ISBN 0-7710-4682-0). McClelland and Stewart.

Orphan Train. Jim Magnuson & Dorothea G. Petrie. LC 78-26872. 1979. 14.95 (ISBN 0-8161-6666-8). G. K. Hall.

Orphan Train: A Novel. Jim Magnuson & Dorothea G. Petrie. LC 78-6188. 1978. 7.95 (ISBN 0-8037-7375-7). Dial Press.

Orphans. Helen Dawes Brown. LC 11-10950. 1911. Houghton Mifflin Company.

Orphans: A Novel. Barry Spacks. LC 76-181664. 1972. 6.50 (ISBN 0-06-127786-X). Harper's Magazine Press Book.

Orphans and Other Children. Charles Richard Webb. LC 73-93069. 1974. 6.95 (ISBN 0-399-11355-X). Putnam.

Orphans in Gethsemane: A Novel of the Past in the Present. Vardis Fisher. 10.00 o.p. Swallow.

Orphans of Big Swamp. Rose Wyler. LC 75-8438. 5.95 (ISBN 0-8283-1621-X). Branden Press.

Orphans of Coyote Creek. Lewis B Patten. (Signet brand western). 1975. (pbk.) 0.95. New American Library.

Orphans of the Big Swamp. Peter Thayer. LC 75-8438. 80p. 1976. pap. 5.95 o.p. (ISBN 0-8283-1621-X). Branden.

Orphans of the Desert. Leo Papiano. LC 29-24371. 1929. Hollycrofters, Inc. Ltd.

Orphans of the Sky. Robert Anson Heinlein. (Signet bk., D2618). 1965. New Amer. Lib.

Orphans of the Storm: A Complete Novel from D. W. Griffith's Motion Picture Epic on the Immortal Theme of The Two Orphans, Novelized. Henry MacMahon & Griffith, David Wark, 1880- LC 22-948898. Grosset & Dunlap.

Orphan's Tale. Jay Neugeboren. LC 75-24989. 8.95 (ISBN 0-03-015271-2). Holt, Rinehart and Winston.

Orphan's Trials: Or, Alone in a Great City. Emerson Bennett. T. B. Peterson & Brothers.

Orpheus on Top. Edward Stewart. (Medallion bk., N1486). 1967. Berkley.

Orpheus on Top. Edward Stewart. LC 66-12046. 1966. Putnam.

Orrain: A Romance. Sidney Kilner Levett-Yeats. LC 4-22266. 1904. Longmans, Green, and Co.

Orsinian Tales. Ursula K. Le Guin. LC 76-5545. 7.95 (ISBN 0-06-012561-6). Harper & Row.

Orsinian Tales. Ursula K. Le Guin. 1977. pap. 2.25 (ISBN 0-553-10705-4, 13267-9). Bantam.

O'Ruddy: A Romance. Stephen Crane & Barr, Robert. LC 3-27967. 1903. F. A. Stokes Company.

Orvar-Odds Saga. LC 80-1949. Repr. of 1888 ed. 39.00 (ISBN 0-404-18715-3). AMS Pr.

Orville College: A Novel. Ellen Price Henry Wood Wood. (Seaside library, v. 26, no. 508). 1879. G. Munro.

Orwen & Sabina. Ann W. Getty. 1970. 4.50 o.p. Vantage.

Osborne of Arrochar. Amanda Minnie Douglas. LC 6-33471. 1890. Lee and Shepard.

Osbornes. Edward Frederic Benson. LC 10-211007. 1910. Doubleday, Page & Company.

Osborne's Army. John Anthony West. LC 67-25323. (Illus.). 1967. Morrow.

Oscar Montague--Paranoiac. George Lincoln Walton. LC 19-156671. 1919. J. B. Lippincott Company.

Oscar Mooney's Head. 1st Ed. William E Huntsberry. LC 61-8928. (Rinehart suspense novel). 1961. Holt, Rinehart and Winston.

Osceola: Or, Fact and Fiction: a Tale of the Seminole War. James Birchett Ransom. LC 8-233. 1838. Printed by Harper & Brothers.

O'Shaughnessy's Cafe. Henry W. Clune. (O.s.i.). 1969. 6.95 o.s.i. (ISBN 0-02-526370-6). Macmillan.

O'Shaughnessy's Day: A Novel. 1st Ed. Mary Deasy. LC 57-11415. 1957. Doubleday.

Osiris Died in Autumn. Sarah Langley. LC 64-19173. 1961. Published for the Crime Club by Doubleday.

Osprey Dilemma. Steve Hayes. (Orig.). 1983. pap. 3.95 (ISBN 0-440-16159-2). Dell.

Osru: A Tale of Many Incarnations; the History of a Soul. Justin Sterns. LC 10-9515. 1.25. Lenox Publishing Company.

Osterman Weekend. Robert Ludlum. 1973. 1.50. Dell.

Osterman Weekend. Robert Ludlum. LC 76-165262. 1972. 6.95 (ISBN 0-529-04547-8). World Pub.

Ostrekoff Jewels. Edward Phillips Oppenheim. LC 32-144382. 1932. Little, Brown, and Company.

Ostrich Egg. Flora Hill. LC 73-79941. 1973. 6.95 (ISBN 0-8059-1875-2). Dorrance.

Ostrich Egg-Shell Canteen. Musa Nagenda. (Heinemann Secondary Readers Ser.). 1973. pap. text ed. 3.00x (ISBN 0-435-92507-5). Heinemann Ed.

Ostrich Feathers. Barbara Brenner & Vera Williams. LC 77-24284. 5.95. (ISBN 0-8193-0921-4) (ISBN 0-8193-0922-2). Parents' Magazine Press.

Ostrich for the Defence. William H Hile. LC 12-21621. 1912. 1.50. Press of Geo. H. Ellis Co.

Oswald and Matilda. George Lutley. LC 54-118793. Vantage Press.

Oswald Cray: A Novel. Ellen Price Henry Wood Wood. LC 8-37882. T. B. Peterson & Brothers.

Oswald Cray: A Novel. Ellen Price Henry Wood Wood. (Seaside library, v. 19, no. 365). 1878. G. Munro.

Oswald Smith's Short Stories. Oswald J Smith. LC 44-509. Zondervan Publishing House.

Osward Langdon: Or, Pierre and Paul Lanier. A Romance of 1894-1898. Levi Jackson Hamilton. 1900. The Lakeside Press.

Otahki, Trail of Tears Princess. Aileen Dorothy Lorberg. 1967. pap. 1.00 o.p. (ISBN 0-911208-13-5). Ramfre.

Otchainie. Vladimir Nabokov. (Rus.). 1978. 15.00 (ISBN 0-88233-323-2); pap. 7.00 o.p. (ISBN 0-88233-324-0). Ardis Pubs.

Othello: A Novel. Emil Ludwig & Von Hildebrand, Franz, Tr. LC 47-11559. 1947. G. P. Putnam's Sons.

Othello the Second. Frederick William Robinson. LC 8-4783. (On cover: Harper's half-hour series v. 182). 1880. Harper & Brothers.

Other. Thomas Tryon. LC 74-136331. 1971. 6.95 (ISBN 0-394-43608-3). Knopf.

Other Alexander. Translated by Willis and Helle Tzalopoulou Barnstone. Margarita Lymperake. LC 59-15131. (Noonday paperback 153). 1959. Noonday Press.

Other Anne Fletcher. Susanne Jaffe. LC 80-15318. 1980. 8.95 (ISBN 0-453-00386-9). New American Library.

Other Art. Marianne Gray. 1982. pap. 10.00x (ISBN 0-330-26267-X, Pub. by Pan Bks). State Mutual Bk.

Other Basket. Jeanne Judson. LC 52-12538. 1952. Bouregy & Curl.

Other Body in Grant's Tomb. 1st Ed. Richard Starnes. LC 51-11183. (Main line mysteries). 1951. Lippincott.

Other Bond. Dora Russell. LC 8-133857. (On cover: Broadway series, no. 11). 1892. J. A. Taylor and Company.

Other Brother. Clarissa Fairchild Cushman. LC 39-2607. 1939. Little, Brown and Company.

Other Brother. Jessica Steele. (Harlequin Presents Ser.). 192p. 1982. pap. 1.75 (ISBN 0-373-10533-9). PB.

Other Brown. Adele Luehrmann. LC 17-230486. 1917. The Century Co.

Other Bullet. Nancy Barr Mavity. LC 30-16002. 1930. Pub. for The Crime Club, Inc., by Doubleday, Doran & Company, Inc.

Other Caroline: A Novel. Mary Jane Ward. LC 70-108078. 1970. 5.95. Crown Publishers.

Other Cheek. Abraham B. Shiffrin. LC 31-30512. Newland Press.

Other Child. Joanne Fluke. (Orig.). 1983. pap. 2.95 (ISBN 0-440-16767-1). Dell.

Other Children: A Novel. Adeline Rumsey. 1947. Simon and Schuster.

Other Dear Charmer. Peggy Gaddis, pseud. LC 49-214893. 1949. Arcadia House.

Other Dimensions. Clark Ashton Smith. LC 79-117341. 1970. 6.50. Arkham House.

Other Dimensions: Ten Stories of Science Fiction. Ed. by Robert Silverberg. LC 72-7789. 1973. 5.95. Hawthorn Books.

Other Door. Harold Begbie. LC 26-19725. George H. Doran Company.

Other Elizabeth. Jess Gregg. LC 52-5575. 1952. Rinehart.

Other Elizabeth. Jess Gregg. 1973. (pbk.) 0.95. Popular Library.

Other End of the Bridge. Una Troy. LC 60-12300. 1961. Dutton.

Other Father. Laura Keane Zametkin Hobson. LC 50-7123. 1950. Simon and Schuster.

Other Fellow. Francis Hopkinson Smith. LC 77-98595. (Short story index reprint series). (Illus.). 1969. Books for Libraries Press.

Other Fellow. Francis Hopkinson Smith. LC 8-11272. 1899. Houghton, Mifflin and Company.

Other Fellow. special limited ed. Francis Hopkinson Smith. LC 99-5744. 1899. Printed at The Riverside Press.

Other Fires. Maksim Gorkii & Bakshy, Alexander, Tr. LC 33-11071. 1933. D. Appleton and Company.

Other Fires; the Story of Tsali: The Story of Tsali. Nicholas McCabe. Southern Publishers, Inc.

Other Folk. Jennie Maria Drinkwater Conklin. LC 6-304086. 1890. R. Carter and Brothers.

Other Fools and Their Doings: Or, Life Among the Freedmen. Harriet Newell Kneeland Goff. LC 70-38651. (Black Heritage Library Collection). (Illus.). 1972. (ISBN 0-8369-9009-9). Books for Libraries Press.

Other Fools and Their Doings: Or, Life Among the Freedmen. Harriet Newell Kneeland Goff. J. S. Ogilvie & Company.

Other Foot. Damon Francis Knight. (O.s.i.). 1971. pap. 0.75 o.s.i. (532-75433-075). Manor Bks.

Other Gate: And Other Stories. Vere Hutchinson. LC 78-160935. (Short story index reprint series). 1971. (ISBN 0-8369-3914-X). Books for Libraries Press.

Other Gate: And Other Stories. Vere Hutchinson. LC 28-251813. 1928. A. A. Knopf.

Other Gate, & Other Stories. facsimile ed. Vere Hutchinson. LC 78-160935. (Short Story Index Reprint Ser.). Repr. of 1928 ed. 16.00 (ISBN 0-8369-3914-X). Ayer Co.

Other Girl. Marjory Hall, pseud. LC 73-18334. 1974. 5.25 (ISBN 0-664-32542-4). Westminster Press.

Other Girl. Theodora Keogh. pap. 0.60 o.p. (60-289). Manor Bks.

Other Girl, No. 7. Lucy Walker, pseud. 192p. 1981. pap. 1.75 (ISBN 0-345-29422-X). Ballantine.

Other Gods, a Novel. Lew Holston. LC 39-17647. The Oxford Press.

Other Gods: An American Legend. Pearl Sydenstricker Buck. LC 40-27062. The John Day Company.

Other Half. Charles Francis Coe. LC 33-211733. 1930. Cosmopolitan Book Corporation.

Other Half of the Orange. 1st Ed. James Maurice Scott. LC 55-5343. 1955. Dutton.

Other Horizon. 1st Ed. Carl W Lange. LC 56-9674. 1956. AP Books.

Other Horseman. Philip Wylie. LC 42-2249. Farrar & Rinehart, Inc.

Other House. Mary R Higham. (On cover: Sparehour series). A. D. F. Randolph & Company.

Other House. Henry James. LC 75-32756. (Literature of Mystery and Detection). 1976. 22.00 (ISBN 0-405-07880-3). Arno Press.

Other House. Henry James. LC 48-7500. New Directions,

Other House. Henry James. LC 77-17499. 1978. 8.50 (ISBN 0-89244-083-X). Queens House.

Other House: A Novel. Henry James. LC 10-4182. 1896. The Macmillan Company.

Other House: A Study of Human Nature. Kate F. M. Vermilye. Jordan. Lovell, Coryell & Company.

Other Jesus: A Novel. Uell Stanley Andersen. LC 60-139083. 1960. Muhlenberg Press.

Other Kingdom. Victor Price. LC 64-13101. 1964. Doubleday.

Other Lady: A Novel. Leo Loeb. LC 56-12651. (Pan Press fiction library book). 1957. Pan Press.

Other Laws. John Parkinson. LC 11-18193. 1911. 1.25. John Lane.

Other Lips and Other Hearts: A Novel. Joan Sanders. LC 82-9359. 1982. 13.95 (ISBN 0-395-32523-4). Houghton Mifflin.

Other Lives to Live. Herbert Lyons. LC 51-6510. 1951. Dial Press.

Other Log of Phileas Fogg. Philip Jose Farmer. 288p. (Orig.). 1982. pap. 2.50 (ISBN 0-523-48508-5). Pinnacle Bks.

Other Log of Phileas Fogg. Philip Jose Farmer. (Science Fiction Ser.). (Orig.). 1973. pap. 0.95 o.p. (UQ1048). DAW Bks.

Other Love. Adelaide Humphries. LC 64-7421. 1964. Avalon Books.

Other Love. Jeanne Judson. (Fawcett Gold Medal Book). 1974. (pbk.) 0.75. Fawcett.

Other Lovers. Roderick Finlayson. LC 77-350565. 1976. (ISBN 0-908565-09-7). J. McIndoe.

Other Lovers. Margaret Widdemer. LC 34-37830. Farrar & Rinehart, Incorporated.

Other Loves. Barry Devlin. LC 55-195540. 1955. Vixen Press.

Other Magic: A Romance of the Tropics. Elliot Lovegood Grant Watson. LC 21-21698. 1921. A. A. Knopf.

Other Mahoney: A Novel. Ray Wesley Sherman. LC 44-47392. 1944. I. Washburn, Inc.

Other Main-Travelled Roads. Hamlin Garland. Harper & Brothers.

Other Main Travelled Roads see Collected Works.

Other Main-Travelled Roads. Sunset Edition. Hamlin Garland. LC 72-84717. (Illus.). 1974. (lib. ed.) 14.50 (ISBN 0-403-02975-9). Scholarly Press.

Other Man. Francis Durbridge. 192p. 1973. 5.95 o.s.i. (ISBN 0-85617-400-9). White Lion Pubs.

Other Man. Edgar Wallace. LC 11-15860. 1911. Dodd, Mead and Company.

Other Man's Saucer. John Keith Winter. LC 30-32842. 1930. Doubleday, Doran & Company, Inc.

Other Man's Shoes. Abraham Rothberg. LC 69-12095. (O.S.I.). 1969. 6.95 o.s.i. (ISBN 0-671-20188-3). S&S.

Other Man's Wife. Frank Richardson. LC 8-28065. M. Kennerley.

Other Maritha. Constance Leonard. 1973. 0.75. Dell.

Other Maritha. Constance Leonard. LC 74-183001. (Red badge novel of suspense). 1972. 4.95 (ISBN 0-396-06495-7). Dodd, Mead.

Other Mary. Edith T. Spencer. LC 74-19599. 1975. 10.00 (ISBN 0-8059-2103-6). Dorrance.

Other Me. Janet Carter. (Orig.). 1976. pap. 1.50 o.p. (ISBN 0-515-04043-6). BJ Pub Group.

Other Men's Daughters. Richard G. Stern. LC 73-79545. 1973. 6.95 (ISBN 0-525-17245-9). Dutton.

Other Men's Daughters. Richard G. Stern. 1974. (pbk.) 1.25 (ISBN 0-671-78433-1). Pocket Books.

Other Men's Wives. Alan Dubois. LC 33-296413. 1933. W. Godwin, Inc.

Other Men's Wives. Clement Wood. LC 33-29641. 1933. W. Godwin, Inc.

Other Miss Lisle. M. C Martin. LC 6-40586. 1906. Benziger Brothers.

Other Mr. Barclay. Henry Irving Dodge. LC 6-10649. 1906. Consolidated Retail Booksellers.

Other Mrs. Diefenbaker. Simma Holt. LC 80-2860. (Illus.). 384p. 1983. 22.95 (ISBN 0-385-17089-0). Doubleday.

Other Mrs. Wyngate. Anne Long. LC 78-1648. 1978. 3.95 (ISBN 0-89293-047-0). Beta Book Co.

Other Nine. Colleen L Reece. LC 80-20337. 6.95 (ISBN 0-8309-0288-0). Herald Pub. House.

Other One. Sidonie Gabrielle Colette. LC 70-178783. 1972. 8.50 (ISBN 0-8371-6295-5). Greenwood Press.

Other One. Sidonie Gabrielle Colette. Tr. by Garvin, Viola Gerard. LC 31-250509. 1931. Cosmopolitan Book Corporation.

Other One. Julien Green. LC 72-91843. 1973. 6.95 (ISBN 0-15-170445-7). Harcourt Brace Jovanovich.

Other One. Catherine Turney. LC 52-6634. 1952. Holt.

Other Paris: Stories. Mavis Gallant. LC 55-12016. 1956. Houghton Mifflin.

Other Paris: Stories. Mavis Gallant. LC 74-116951. (Short story index reprint series). 1970. Books for Libraries Press.

Other Part. Henry Miller. LC 71-173888. Date not set. price not set o.p. (ISBN 0-8109-0350-4). Abrams.

Other Passenger. John Keir Cross. LC 46-528787. 1946. J. B. Lippincott Company.

Other Passport. Harold MacGrath. LC 31-18592. Doubleday, Doran & Company, Inc.

Other Passport. Harold MacGrath. LC 42-29937. 1932. Grosset & Dunlap.

Other Paths to Glory. Anthony Price. LC 74-22841. 1975. 5.95 (ISBN 0-385-09937-1). Published for the Crime Club by Doubleday.

Other People. Celia Dale. LC 76-86404. 1970. 5.95. Walker.

Other People. G. Y Dryansky. LC 73-76499. 1973. 8.95 (ISBN 0-8415-0276-5). Saturday Review Press.

Other People. Sol Stein. Harcourt Brace Jovanovich.

Other People: A Mystery Story. Martin Amis. LC 80-54195. 1981. 11.95 (ISBN 0-670-52948-6). Viking Press.

Other People's Business: The Romantic Career of the Practical Miss Dale. Harriet Lummis Smith. LC 16-22298. The Bobbs-Merrill Company.

Other People's Children. Sarah Shears. 1978. 8.95 (ISBN 0-236-40117-3, Pub. by Paul Elek). Merrimack Pub Cir.

Other People's Children: Containing a Veracious Account of the Management of Helen's Babies by a Lady Who Knew Just How the Children of Other People Should Be Trained; Also a Statement...of the Success Obtained. John Habberton. LC 6-46676. 1877. G. P. Putnam's Son.

Other People's Houses. Elizabeth Bartol Dewing Kaup. LC 9-28031. 1909. The Macmillan Company.

Other People's Lives. Rosa Nouchette Carey. LC 6-230986. 1898. J. B. Lippincott Company.

Other People's Lives. Joanna Kaplan. LC 74-21322. 1975. 6.95 (ISBN 0-394-47174-1). Knopf: Distributed by Random House.

Other People's Lives. Henry Albert Phillips. LC 24-731679. Boni and Liveright.

Other People's Lives: 34 Short Stories. Ed. by Leonard R. N. Ashley. LC 78-15198. 1970. Houghton Mifflin.

Other People's Money. Jerome Weidman. LC 67-14470. 1967. 6.95. Random.

Other People's Money. From the French of Emile Gaborian... Emile Gaboriau. LC 6-44504. 1875. J. R. Osgood and Company.

Other People's Money: Tr. from the French of Emile Gaboriau. Emile Gaboriau. LC 2823. 1900. C. Scribner's Sons.

Other Peoples's Money. Emile Gaboriau. LC 6-44506. (On cover: Lovell's library. v. 3, no. 120). 1883. J. W. Lovell Company.

Other Persuasion: An Anthology of Short Fiction About Gay Men and Women. Seymour Kleinberg. LC 76-62492. 1977. 3.95 (ISBN 0-394-72237-X). Vintage Books.

Other Place: And Other Stories of the Same Sort. John Boynton Priestley. LC 54-11928. Harper.

Other Place: And Other Stories of the Same Sort. John Boynton Priestley. LC 72-167467. (Short story index reprint series). 1971. (ISBN 0-8369-3993-X). Books for Libraries Press.

Other Room. Worth Tuttle Hedden. LC 47-395135. 1947. Crown Publshers.

Other Sara. Susan Richmond Lee. LC 8-318255. J. Long.

Other Shoe. Mary McMullen. LC 80-2751. 1981. 9.95 (ISBN 0-385-17534-5). Published for the Crime Club by Doubleday.

Other Shoe. Mary McMullen. LC 82-15636. 1982. 7.95 (ISBN 0-8161-3422-7). G.K. Hall.

Other Side. Margaret Storm Jameson. LC 46-25088. 1946. The Macmillan Company.

Other Side: A Fantastic Novel. Alfred Kubin. LC 67-27027. (Illus.). 1967. Crown Publishers.

Other Side. A Social Study Based on Fact. Martin Ambrose Foran. LC 6-41408. 1886. Ingham, Clarke & Co.

Other Side: Being Certain Passages in the Life of a Genius. Horace Annesley Vachell. LC 10-206075. Hodder & Stoughton, George H. Doran Company.

Other Side of Desire. an original timely books ed. Paula Christian. LC 81-50051. 1981. 6.95 (ISBN 0-931328-08-X). Timely Books.

Other Side of Desire. an original timely books ed. Paula Christian. LC 81-50051. 1981. 6.95 (ISBN 0-931328-08-X). Timely Books.

Other Side of Hate. Richard Pierce. 1977. pap. 1.75 (ISBN 0-532-17159-4). Woodhill.

Other Side of Hate. Richard Pierce. pap. 0.60 o.p. Lancer.

Other Side of Love. Denise Robins. (Beagle romance,#40). 1975. (pbk.) 0.95. Ballantine Books.

Other Side of Love: Two Novellas. Howard Charles Brashers. LC 63-11820. (Swallow paperbook). 1963. A. Swallow.

Other Side of Main Street. Wilder Buell. LC 29-7205. 1929. Longmans, Green and Co.

Other Side of Midnight. Sidney Sheldon. LC 73-14778. 1974. 8.95 (ISBN 0-688-00220-X). Morrow.

Other Side of Midnight. Sidney Sheldon. 1975. (pbk.) 1.75. Dell.

Other Side of Silence. Ted Allbeury. LC 81-9119. 10.95 (ISBN 0-684-17306-9). Scribner.

Other Side of Silence. Margaret Perko. 1979. pap. 2.25 o.s.i. (ISBN 0-8439-0698-7, Leisure Bks). Nordon Pubns.

Other Side of the Canyon. Romer Grey. LC 80-21007. 1981. 13.50 (ISBN 0-89340-298-2). J. Curley.

Other Side of the Clock. Ed. by Philip Van Doren Stern. LC 70-90311. 1969. 5.95 o.p. Van Nos Reinhold.

Other Side of the Clock: Stories Out of Time, Out of Place. Ed. by Philip Van Doren Stern. LC 70-90311. 1969. Van Nostrand Reinhold.

Other Side of the Coin. Translated from the French by Richard Howard. Pierre Boulle. LC 58-13675. 1958. Vanguard Press.

Other Side of the Day. 1st Ed. Hilda Sidney Krech. LC 58-967689. 1958. Knopf.

Other Side of the Door. Lucia Chamberlain. 1909. 1.18. The Bobbs-Merrill Company.

Other Side of the Fence: A Novel. Nell Columbia Boyer Martin. LC 29-285093. Rae D. Henkle Co. Inc.

Other Side of the Hill. 1st Ed. Robert Molloy. LC 62-8087. 1962. Doubleday.

Other Side of the Mirror (El Grimorio) Short Stories. Enrique Anderson Imbert. LC 66-11155. (Contemporary Latin American classics). 1966. Southern Illinois University Press.

Other Side of the Moon. Stories. Ed. by August William Derleth. LC 49-2147. 1949. Pellegrini & Cudahy.

Other Side of the Mountain. Michel Bernanos. 1973. 6.95. Norman S. Berg.

Other Side of the Mountain. Michel Bernanos. LC 68-29550. 1968. 4.95. Houghton Mifflin.

Other Side of the Night. Edmund Schiddel. LC 54-36462. 1954. Avon Publications.

Other Side of the Sky. Arthur C. Clarke. LC 58-5477. pap. 0.75 o.p. (ISBN 0-15-670450-1, HPL25, HPL). HarBraceJ.

Other Side of the Sky: Stories. 1st Ed. Arthur Charles Clarke. LC 58-5477. 1958. Harcourt, Brace.

Other Side of the Sky: 24 Short Stories of the Future. Arthur Charles Clarke. (Signet Book, Q5553). 1973. (pbk.) 0.95. New American Lib.

Other Side of the Story: A Novel. Leslie Derville. LC 4-16442. 1904. G. W. Dillingham Company.

Other Side of the Street: A Novel. Sidney Offit. LC 62-20050. 1962. Crown Publishers.

Other Side of the Summer. Translated from the French by Richard Howard. Jean Rene Huguenin. LC 61-12953. 1961. G. Braziller.

Other Side of the Sun. Madeleine L'Engle. LC 73-122824. 1971. 6.95 (ISBN 0-374-22805-1). Farrar, Straus & Giroux.

Other Side of the Tree. 1st Ed. Le Roy Leatherman. LC 54-6395. 1954. Harcourt, Brace.

Other Side of the Universe. Kurt Dreifuss. 3.50 o.p. Twayne.

Other Side of the Wall. Henry Justin Smith. LC 19-15573. 1919. Doubleday, Page & Company.

Other Side of the Wall. Seldon Truss, pseud. LC 54-7021. 1954. Published for the Crime Club by Doubleday.

Other Side of the Wind: A Novel. Thomas L. P Swicegood. LC 74-82257. 1974. Eola Pub. Co.

Other Side of the World. Arlene Hale. LC 75-29303. 6.95 (ISBN 0-316-33855-9). Little, Brown.

Other Side of the World. Arlene Hale. LC 76-19790. 1976. 10.95 (ISBN 0-8161-6406-1). G. K. Hall.

Other Side of Time. Keith Laumer. (Signet Book, Q5255). 1972. New American Library.

Other Side of Time. Keith Laumer. LC 78-142851. 1971. 4.95 (ISBN 0-8027-5537-2). Walker.

Other Side of Tomorrow: Original Science Fiction Stories About Young People of the Future. Ed. by Roger Elwood. LC 73-3046. (Illus.). 1973. (lib. bdg.) 4.95 (ISBN 0-394-82468-7) (ISBN 0-394-92468-1). Random House.

Other Side of Yesterday. Dorothy McKay Martin. LC 77-18069. 2.50 (ISBN 0-8024-6095-X). Moody Press.

Other Stories & the Attack of the Giant Baby. Kit Reed, pseud. (Orig.). 1981. pap. 2.25 (ISBN 0-425-05032-7). Berkley Pub.

Other Story: And Other Stories. Henry Kitchell Webster. LC 23-150294. The Bobbs-Merrill Company.

Other Susan. Jennette Barbour Perry Lee. 1921. C. Scribner's Sons.

Other Than Joy. Rob Eden. LC 46-2401. 1946. Gramercy Publishing Co.

Other Thief. Thomas D. Parks. pap. 0.95 o.p. (ISBN 0-89107-134-2). Good News.

Other Things Being Equal. Emma Wolf. LC 8-37122. 1892. A. C. McClurg and Company.

Other Things Being Equal. Emma Wolf. 1916. A. C. McClurg & Co.

Other Times Other Worlds. John MacDonald. 1978 (ISBN 0-449-14037-7). Fawcett Gold Medal Books.

Other Tomorrow. Octavus Roy Cohen. 1927. D. Appleton and Company.

Other Voices, Other Rooms. Truman Capote. LC 48-513579. 1968. 4.95. Random.

Other Voices, Other Rooms. Truman Capote. LC 55-5729. (Modern library paperbacks, P14). 1955. Random House.

Other Voices, Other Rooms. Truman Capote. LC 48-5135. 1948. Random House.

Other Way Round. Judith Kerr. LC 75-4254. 1975. 7.95 (ISBN 0-698-20335-6). Coward, McCann & Geoghegan.

Other Ways and Other Flesh. Edith Louise Coues O'Shaughnessy. LC 70-150482. (Short story index reprint series). 1971. Books for Libraries Press.

Other Ways and Other Flesh. Edith Louise Coues O'Shaughnessy. LC 29-55971. Harcourt, Brace and Company.

Other Winters, Other Springs. Flora Sandstrom. LC 63-14783. 1963. World Pub. Co.

Other Woman. Octavus Roy Cohen & Gisey, John Ulrich, Joint Author. LC 17-8738. 1917. 1.25. The Macaulay Company.

Other Woman. Sidonie Gabrielle Colette. LC 79-173201. (Signet classic). 1975. (pbk.) 1.25. New American Library.

Other Woman. Norah Davis. LC 20-9140. 1920. 1.75. The Century Co.

Other Woman. Joy Fielding. LC 81-43548. 1982. 14.95 (ISBN 0-385-17811-5). Doubleday.

Other Woman. Rona Jaffe. LC 75-182957. 1972. 5.95. Morrow.

Other Woman. Isabel Moore. LC 42-9307. 1942. Farrar & Rinehart, Inc.

Other Woman: A Life of Violet Trefusis, Including Previously Unpublished Correspondence with Vita Sackville-West. Philippe Jullian & John Phillips. LC 76-25141. (Illus.). 1976. 10.00 (ISBN 0-395-20539-5). Houghton Mifflin.

Other Woman's Husband: An Outline Sketch of Today. Willard Douglas Coxey. LC 6-28854. 1896.

Other Woman's Way. Howard Rockey. The Macaulay Company.

Other Women. Katharine Brush. LC 33-578118. 1933. Farrar & Rinehart, Incorporated.

Other Women's Husbands: A Comedy Based on the Motion Picture Story. E T Lowe. LC 26-132644. (On cover: Popular plays and screen library). Jacobsen-Hodgkinson-Corporation.

Other World. large type ed. Frederic G. Lee. pap. 5.95 (ISBN 0-910122-43-1). Amherst Pr.

Other World. Madelon Lulofs & Pidcock, George Douglas Hammell, 1896- LC 35-164823. 1935. The Viking Press.

Other Worlds. Ed. by Roy Torgeson. (Orig.). 1979. pap. 2.25 (ISBN 0-89083-558-6). Zebra.

Other Worlds: Edited and Introduction by Phil Stong. Ed. by Philip Duffield Stong. LC 41-10142. W. Funk, Inc.

Other Worlds, Other Gods: Adventures in Religious Science Fiction. Mayo A. Moho. LC 76-144282. 1971. 5.95. Doubleday.

Other Worlds, Other Seas: Science-Fiction Stories from Socialist Countries. Ed. by Darko Suvin. LC 69-16412. 1970. 6.95. Random House.

Other Worlds, Other Times. Ed. by Samuel Moskowitz & Roger Elwood. 1969. pap. 0.75 o.p. (75-238). Manor Bks.

Other Worlds, Other Times. 2nd ed. Ed. by Samuel Moskowitz & Roger Elwood. 192p. 1974. pap. 0.95 o.p. (532-95310-095). Manor Bks.

Other Worlds: The Comical History of the States and Empires of the Moon and Sun. Cyrano De Bergerac, Savinien. LC 77-358886. (Science fiction master series). 1976. 0.65 (ISBN 0-450-02995-6). New English Library.

Others. Robert Ferro. LC 77-8702. 7.95 (ISBN 0-684-15137-5). Scribner.

Others. Irving A. Greenfield. (Orig.). 1969. pap. 0.75 o.p. (74-994). Lancer.

Others: A Novel. Ann Aikman, pseud. LC 60-6081. 1960. Simon and Schuster.

Others, Including Morstive Sternbump. Marvin Cohen. LC 76-11615. 1976. 8.95 (ISBN 0-672-52145-8). Bobbs-Merrill.

Others, Including Morstive Sternbump: A Novel. Marvin Cohen. LC 76-11615. 247p. 1976. 15.00 (ISBN 0-672-52145-8). Ultramarine Pub.

Others Who Returned. Fifteen Disturbing Tales. Herbert Russell Wakefield. LC 29-18154. 1929. D. Appleton & Company.

Others Will Come. Harold Jerome Heagney & Pfeiffer, Pankratius, Father, 1872- Father Mary of the Cross Jordan. LC 45-6790. 1945. The Society of the Divine Savior (Salvatorian Seminary.

Otherwise Girl. Keith Claire, pseud. LC 75-29789. 6.95 (ISBN 0-03-016681-0). Holt, Rinehart and Winston.

Otherwise Girl. Keith Claire. (Berkley Medallion Book.). 1977. 1.25 (ISBN 0-425-03386-4). Berkley Pub. Corp.

Otherwise Phyllis. Meredith Nicholson. LC 13-189565. 1913. Houghton Mifflin Company.

Othmar. A Novel. Louise De La Ramee. 1885. J. B. Lippincott Company.

Othmar: A Novel. Louise De La Ramee. (On cover: Lovell's library. v. 16, no. 790). 1886. J. W. Lovell Company.

Othneil Jones. 1st Ed. John Adams Leland. LC 56-11679. 1956. Lippincott.

Otis Dunn, Manhunter. Nat Richards. LC 73-83919. 1974. 6.95 (ISBN 0-87949-018-7). Ashley Books.

Otley. Martin Waddell. LC 66-224836. 3.95. Stein & Day.

Otley. Martin Waddell. (64004). 1968. Pocket Bks.

Otley Forever. Martin Waddell. LC 68-19568. 1968. Stein and Day.

Otley Victorious. Martin Waddell. LC 77-87960. 1969. 4.95. Stein and Day.

O'Toole's Obedient Orb & Other Fanciful Tales. Gaylord B. Castor. 101p. 1975. 5.50 o.p. (ISBN 0-682-48249-8). Exposition.

Otrey Pursued. Martin Waddell. LC 67-157585. 1967. bds., 4.95. Stein & Day.

Ottawa Allegation. Paul Geddes. LC 72-94275. 1973. 6.95 (ISBN 0-698-10511-7). Coward, McCann & Geoghegan.

Ottawa Allegation. Paul Geddes. (Penguin crime fiction)). 1976. 1.95 (ISBN 0-14-004081-1). Penguin.

Otterbrook Parsonage. Sequel to "Otterbrook's Blessing,". Mary Eliza Haines Ireland. LC 18-8320. 1904. United Brethren Publishing House.

Otterbrook's Blessing: A Delightful Story Gleaned from a Girl's Diary. Mary Eliza Haines Ireland. LC 18-17303. 1902. United Brethren Publishing House.

Ottilie: An Eighteenth Century Idyl. Ida Boy-Ed. (On cover: Seaside library. Pocket ed. no. 850). 1886. G. Munro.

Ottilie: An Eighteenth Century Idyl. Violet Paget. (Harper's Franklin square library, no. 542). 1886. Harper & Brothers.

Ottilie Aster's Silence. Ida Boy-Ed & Lowrey, Mrs. D. M., Tr. LC 44-155244. (On cover: Ledger library, no. 23). 1890. R. Bonner's Sons.

Ottilie Aster's Silence. Tr. by Lowrey, D. M. (On cover: The choice series, no. 23). 1890. R. Bonner's Sons.

Otto the Knight: And Other Trans-Mississippi Stories. Alice French. LC 4-15111. 1891. Houghton, Mifflin and Company.

Otto's Inspiration. Mary Hanford Finney Ford. LC 6-41396. 1895. S. C. Griggs & Company.

Ought We to Visit Her? A Novel. Annie Edward. 1871. Sheldon and Company.

Oui, I Am a Soul. Adela L. Holzer. 5.95 o.p. Vantage.

Ounce of Gold. W A Logue. LC 3904. 1900. The Silver Blade Print.

Our Admirable Betty: A Romance. Jeffery Farnol. LC 18-18187. 1918. Little, Brown, and Company.

Our Aunt Auda: A Novel. Humphrey Pakington. LC 42-720217. 1942. W. W. Norton & Company, Inc.

Our Avenue. Ruby Mildred Ayres. LC 37-6531. 1936. Arcadia House.

Our Bed Is Green. Clyde Wilson. LC 34-6044. R. O. Ballou.

Our Best Society: A Novel. John Daniel Barry. LC 5-32923. 1905. G. P. Putnam's Sons.

Our Best Society" and the Rise and Fall of Boomtown: Between the Years 1880 and 1910. L. Jonas L. L. D. Bubblebuster. 1893. Chicago Press.

Our Bethlehem Guests. William Allen Knight. 1944. W. A. Wilde Company.

Our Bible-Class: And the Good That Came of It. Caroline Elizabeth Fairfield Corbin. LC 6-30693. 1860. Derby & Jackson.

Our Brother Red (and His Bull: By Liny Lu (Pseud. Celina LuZanne Boozer. LC 61-18752. 1962. T. Gaus' Sons.

Our Brother the Sun. Basil Beckett Burwell. LC 54-6811. 1954. Hermitage House.

Our Brother's Child: And Other Stories. William Hampton Reynolds. LC 6-23698. 1906. Mayhew Publishing Company.

Our Brother's Child: And Other Stories. 2d rev. ed. William Hampton Reynolds. LC 8-19020. 1908. Mayhew Publishing Company.

Our Burro and Other Animal Friends. Allan Hulsizer & Marian H. Hulsizer. (Illus.). 1974. (pbk.) 3.95. Sunstone Press.

Our Casualty, and Other Stories. James Owen Hannay. LC 74-122713. (Short story index reprint series). 1970. Books for Libraries Press.

Our Casualty, and Other Stories. James Owen Hannay. LC 42-44639. 1919. George H. Doran Company.

Our Chatham Street Uncle: Or, The Three Golden Balls. Julia MacNair Wright. LC 9-52931. H. Hoyt.

Our Child: A Tale of Passion. Clara E Ballou. LC 6-6098. (On cover: Leisure-time series, no. 7). 1891. W. D. Rowland.

Our Children of the Sun: A Suite of Inca Legends from Peru. Abraham Valdelomar. LC 67-10031. (Contemporary Latin American classics). 1968. Southern Illinois University Press.

Our Children's Children. Clifford D. Simak. LC 73-78644. 1974. 5.95 (ISBN 0-399-11185-9). Putnam.

Our Christmas in a Palace: A Traveller's Story. Edward Everett Hale. LC 6-46192. 1883. Funk & Wagnalls.

Our Church & Others. Lewis W. Spitz. text ed. 1.00 o.p. (ISBN 0-570-06336-1); guide 1.50, tests 0.20 o.p. Concordia.

Our Country Then: Tales of Our First Frontier. Dale Van Every. LC 58-6456. 1958. Holt.

Our Cousin Veronica: Or, Scenes and Adventures Over the Blue Ridge. Elizabeth Wormeley Latimer. LC 9-937. 1855. Bunce & Brother.

Our Cousins in Ohio. Mary Botham Howitt. 1849. Collins & Brother.

Our Daily Bread. Enrique Gil Gilbert & Poore, Dudley, Tr. LC 43-6172. 1943. Farrar & Rinehart, Inc.

Our Daily Bread: A Novel. Gosta Larsson. LC 34-153033. 1934. The Vanguard Press.

Our Dancing Daughters: Based on the Photoplay by Josephine Lovett. Winifred Van Duzer & Lovett, Josephine. LC 28-25463. Grosset & Dunlap.

Our Dead Speak: A Novel by E. C. C. Uzodinma. Edmund Chukuemeka Chieke Uzodinma. LC 68-88349. 1967. pap., 1.25. Longmans.

Our Detachment: A Novel. Katharine King. LC 51-548036. 1875. Harper.

Our Distinguished Fellow-Citizen. Carlton McCarthy. LC 7-15277. 1890. J. L. Hill Printing Company.

Our Doctor: A Novel. Mickey Hume. LC 51-14686. 1951. Exposition Press.

Our Doctors: A Novel of to-Day. Maurice Duplay. Tr. by Collins, Joseph. 1926. Harper & Brothers.

Our Doom Is Gone. Richard Harrison. LC 51-7073. 1951. Jarrolds.

Our Ernie. Alice Caldwell Hegan Rice. LC 39-278237. 1939. D. Appleton-Century Company, Incorporated.

Our Erring Brother: Or, Church and Chapel. Frederick William Robinson. LC 7-41987. (On cover: Lovell's international series, no. 57). 1890. F. F. Lovell & Company.

Our Fair Flagellants. Jeremy Hornell. 1972. pap. 1.50 o.s.i. (V1061P, Venus). Grove.

Our Fair Flagellants, Vol. 2. Jeremy Hornell. 1972. pap. 1.95 o.s.i. (V1071T, Venus). Grove.

Our Family: The Church. George B. Scriven. 1946. pap. 2.25 wkbk. o.p. Morehouse.

Our Father. Thomas Hinde. LC 75-43649. (Illus.). 1976. 8.95 (ISBN 0-8076-0821-1). G. Braziller.

Our Father! Pamela Sykes. LC 79-106181. 1970. T. Nelson.

Our Father Our King. Saul Raskin. (O.s.i). (Illus., Heb. & eng). 1966. 15.00 o.s.i. (ISBN 0-8197-0288-9); deluxe ed. 25.00 o.s.i. Bloch.

Our Father, Right or Wrong. Stephen Edward Rose. LC 49-7159. 1948. Dorrance.

Our Father's House. Ed. by Mariella Gable. LC 45-9170. 1945. Sheed & Ward.

Our First Baby: Or, Infelicities of Our Honeymoon. Profusely Illustrated. George G. Small. LC 22-5138. 1887. M. J. Ivers & Co.

Our "First Families," A Novel of Philadelphia Good Society. LC 9-3849. 1855. Whilt & Yost.

Our "First Families," A Novel of Philadelphia Good Society. LC 7-23685. 1857. J. French and Company.

Our First Murder. Marjorie Torrey Hood Chanslor. LC 40-13519. 1940. Frederick A. Stokes Company.

Our First Murder. Torrey Chanslor. LC 40-13519. 1940. Frederick A. Stokes Company.

Our Friend the Charlatan. George Robert Gissing. LC 75-29850. (Society and the Victorians). (Illus.). 1976. 18.50 (ISBN 0-8386-1884-7). Fairleigh Dickinson University Press.

Our Friend the Charlatan. new ed.. ed. George Robert Gissing. LC 77-367265. (Society and the Victorians; No. 28). (Illus.). 1976-1977. 18.50 (ISBN 0-85527-199-X). Harvester Press.

Our Friend the Charlatan: A Novel. George Robert Gissing. LC 78-80631. 1969. AMS Press.

Our Friend the Charlatan: A Novel. George Robert Gissing. LC 1-7296. 1901. H. Holt and Company.

Our Friends from Frolix 8. Philip K Dick. 1977. 1.50 (ISBN 0-441-64401-5). Ace Books.

Our Gang. Philip Roth. 1971. 7.95 (ISBN 0-394-47886-X). Random.

Our Gang (Starring Tricky and His Friends). Philip Roth. LC 76-175015. 1971. 5.95 (ISBN 0-394-47886-X). Random House.

Our Gifted Son. Dorothy Dodds Baker. LC 48-8039. 1948. Houghton Mifflin Co.

Our Glad. Joyce Warren. LC 56-8788. 1957. Harper.

Our Gods Are Not Born: A Book of American Short Stories. Charles Rumford Walker. LC 71-130076. (Short story index reprint series). 1970. Books for Libraries Press.

Our Gods Are Not Born: A Book of American Short Stories. Charles Rumford Walker. LC 31-1513. J. Cape & H. Smith.

Our Gold Mine at Hollyhurst... A Prize Story of Massachusetts. Mary Matthews Bray. LC 6-18277. (Gold mine series, no. 1). American Humane Education Society.

Our Great Indian War. The Miraculous Lives of Mustang Bill (Mr. Wm. Rhodes Decker) and Miss Marion Fannin. The Brave Indian Fighter Among the Hostile Sioux. The Custer Expedition and Massacre ... LC 9-3813. Barclay & Co.

Our Guests Record. 4.95 o.p. Abingdon.

Our Hearts Are Restless. Gladys Baker. LC 55-6996. 1955. Putnam.

Our Heritage: Life on Cape Cod Awhile Ago. Nancy W. Paine. Smith. LC 30-17178. 1930. B. May.

Our Home in the Ozarks. 2nd ed. Fay Noe. 1970. pap. 3.00 (ISBN 0-9600208-5-3). Noe.

Our Homes. Mary Dwinell Chellis. LC 6-23359. (On cover: The Chellis library). 1881. National Temperance Society and Publication House.

Our Homes: Their Cares and Duties, Joys and Sorrows. Ed. by Timothy Shay Arthur. LC 7-3327. T. Bliss & Co.

Our Honor the Mayor. Dave Morrah. LC 64-11283. 1964. Doubleday.

Our Hotel. Georgianna Hamlen. LC 7-9406. 1888. Rand Avery Co.

Our House in the Last World: A Novel. Oscar Hijuelos. LC 82-15092. 12.95 (ISBN 0-89255-069-4). Persea Books.

Our Jo: Or The Chronicle of a Coming Man. Kenneth M. Cameron. LC 73-15145. 1974. 7.95 (ISBN 0-02-521010-6). Macmillan.

Our John Willie. Catherine Cookson. LC 74-32272. 1975. 9.95 (ISBN 0-8161-6267-0). G. K. Hall.

Our Josephine: And Other Tales. Opie Percival Read. LC 2-20824. Street & Smith.

Our Kind of People. John Dillon. LC 58-6915. 1958. Ballantine Books.

Our Kind of People: American Groups & Rituals. Bill Owens. 1975. pap. 7.95 o.p. (ISBN 0-9602462-2-3). Working Pr CA.

Our Lady. Upton Beall Sinclair. LC 38-29532. Rodale Press.

Our Lady, a Parable for Moderns. Upton Beall Sinclair. LC 43-176152. 1943. Murray & Gee, Inc.

Our Lady of Darkenss. Bernard Edward Joseph Capes. LC 99-4527. 1899. Dodd, Mead & Company.

Our Lady of Darkness. Albert Dorrington. LC 11-283694. 1910. The Macaulay Company.

Our Lady of Darkness. Fritz Leiber. (Berkley Medallion Book). 1.75 (ISBN 0-425-03660-X). Berkley Pub. Corp.

Our Lady of Darkness. Fritz Lieber. 1976. pap. 1.75 (ISBN 0-425-03660-X). Berkley Pub.

Our Lady of Darkness. Fritz Lieber. 1976. 7.95 o.p. (ISBN 0-399-11872-1). Putnam.

Our Lady of Guadalupe: And Other Stories. Bertha Belle Baker. LC 41-17064. 1941. Graphic Press.

Our Lady of Litanies. Xavier Donald MacLeod. LC 7-16620. 1861. J. P. Walsh.

Our Lady of Springtime. Mary J. Dorcy. 1953. 1.50 o.p. St Anthony.

Our Lady of the Beeches. Betsey Riddle Hutton Zum Stolzenberg. LC 2-244834. 1902. Houghton, Mifflin & Co.

Our Lady of the Birds. Louis Joseph Alexandre Mercier. 1943. St. Anthony Guild Press.

Our Lady of the Flowers. Jean Genet. LC 61-6715. 1963. Grove Press.

Our Lady of the Flowers. Tr. from French by Bernard Frechtman. Introd. by Jean-Paul Sartre. Jean Genet. (Mod. lib. ML 358). 1965. 2.45. Random.

Our Lady of the Moor. Pat Phillips. (Avalon romances). 1973. 4.50. Avalon Books.

Our Lady Vanity. Ellen Warner Olney Kirk. LC 1-202923. 1901. Houghton, Mifflin and Company.

Our Lady's Lutenist: And Other Stories of the Bright Ages. David Bearne. LC 10-23404. 1910. Benziger Brothers.

Our Last Candle. Wallace Pond. LC 77-365794. 1976. Pioneer Pub.

Our Little Girl". Robert Alfred Simon. LC 23-5951. Boni and Liveright.

Our Little Life: A Novel of to-Day. Jessie Georgina Sime. LC 21-6166. Frederick A. Stokes Company.

Our Lives: American Labor Stories. Ed. by Joseph Gaer. LC 48-8581. 1948. Boni and Gaer.

Our Lives Have Just Begun: A Novel. Henry Myers. LC 39-4483. 1939. Frederick A. Stokes Company.

Our Man from Love. D. M. Gordon. pap. 1.25 o.s.i. (78-674). Lancer.

Our Man in Camelot. Anthony Price. LC 76-2817. 1976. 5.95 (ISBN 0-385-12059-1). Published for the Crime Club by Doubleday.

Our Man in Havana. Graham Greene. 1974. (pbk.). 1.25 (ISBN 0-671-78466-8). Pocket Books.

Our Man in Havans: An Entertainment. Graham Greene. LC 58-117359. 1958. Viking Press.

Our Manifold Nature. Sarah Grand. LC 75-103513. (Short Story Index Reprint Ser.). 1894. 15.00 (ISBN 0-8369-3255-2). Ayer Co.

Our Maniford Nature: Stories from Life. Sarah Grand. LC 6-27662. (Appleton's town and country library, no. 136). 1894. D. Appleton and Company.

Our Master's Church: A Parable. Elmer Allen Bess. The Neely Company.

Our Miss Williams. Tasha Beining. LC 58-5990. (Illus.). 1958. Dodd, Mead.

Our Miss York. Edwin Bateman Morris. LC 16-5581. 1916. The Penn Publishing Company.

Our Mr. Wrenn: The Romantic Adventures of a Gentle Man. Sinclair Lewis. LC 51-13764. 1951. Crowell.

Our Mr. Wrenn: The Romantic Adventures of a Gentle Man. Sinclair Lewis. LC 14-3561. 1914. Harper & Brothers.

Our Mr. Wrenn: The Romantic Adventures of a Gentle Man. Sinclair Lewis. LC 23-9943. 1923. Harcourt, Brace and Company.

Our Mother's House. Julian Gloag. LC 63-10854. 1963. Simon and Schuster.

Our Mrs. Meigs: A Novel. Elizabeth Frances Corbett. LC 54-9424. 1954. Lippincott.

Our Mutual Friend. Charles Dickens. Ed. by Stephen Charles Gill. LC 73-162328. (Penguin English library). (Illus.). 1971. 0.75. Penguin.

Our Mutual Friend. Charles Dickens. LC 52-14816. (New Oxford illustrated Dickens). (Illus.). 1952. Oxford University Press.

Our Mutual Friend. Charles Dickens. LC 4-31644. 1864-65. J. Bradburn.

Our Mutual Friend. Charles Dickens. LC 6-26332. 1865. Harper & Brothers.

Our Mutual Friend. peterson's uniform ed.... ed. Charles Dickens. LC 6-26331. T. B. Peterson & Brothers.

Our Mutual Friend... Charles Dickens. LC 12-19564. (Works of Charles Dickens. Household ed.). 1866. Hurd and Houghton.

Our Mutual Friend. diamond ed. Charles Dickens. LC 6-37249. 1867. Ticknor and Fields.

Our Mutual Friend... Charles Dickens. LC 6-37038. 1867. Hurd and Houghton.

Our Mutual Friend... Charles Dickens. LC 6-26329. 1868. Hurd and Houghton.

Our Mutual Friend... Charles Dickens. LC 15-20302. (Works of Charles Dickens. Globe ed.). 1870. Hurd and Houghton.

Our Mutual Friend. Charles Dickens. LC 9-3007. (Half-title: Works of Charles Dickens. "Carleton's new illutrated ed." xii). 1877. G. W. Carleton & Co.; Etc., Etc.

Our Mutual Friend. Charles Dickens. LC 6-37248. (On cover: Lovell's library, v. 5, no. 228). 1883. J. W. Lovell Company.

Our Mutual Friend. Charles Dickens. Ed. by Whipple, Edwin Percy. LC 16-3380. (Half-title: Works of Charles Dickens. New illustrated library ed. vol. xxii-xxiii). Houghton, Mifflin Company.

Our Mutual Friend. Charles Dickens. Ed. by Dickens, Charles. LC 4-15304. 1895. Macmillan and Co.

Our Mutual Friend. Charles Dickens. (Half-title: Everyman's library, ed. by Ernest Rhys. Fiction). 1907. J. M. Dent & Co.

Our Mutual Friend. Charles Dickens. (Half-title: The centonary edition of the works of Charles Dickens in 36 volumes). 1911. Chapman & Hall, Ltd.

Our Mutual Friend. Charles Dickens. LC 21-27479. (Rittembome classics). 1921. G. W. Jacobs & Company.

Our Mutual Friend. Charles Dickens. LC 43-39951. 1885. Hurst & Co.

Our Mutual Friend. Charles Dickens. LC 78-52996. (Illus.). 1978. 6.95 (ISBN 0-517-25705-X) (ISBN 0-517-25706-8). Bounty Books.

Our Mutual Friend. Charles Dickens & Johnson, Rossiter. LC 12-19563. (Condensed classics). 1876. H. Holt and Company.

Our Mutual Friend. With the Original Illus. by Marcus Stone. New Introd. by J. B. Priestley. Charles Dickens. LC 57-45803. (Macdonald illus. classics, 36). 1957. 3.50. Macdonald.

Our Mutual Friend. With 16 Full-Page Illus., Including Reproductions of Drawings for Early Editions, Together with an Introd. and Captions by Allen Klots, Jr. Charles Dickens. LC 51-13069. (Great illustrated classics). 1951. Dodd, Mead.

Our Nation's Peril. Jacob Marvin Rudy. LC 18-2413. 1918. 1.25. The L. W. Walter Company.

Our Natupski Neighbors. Edith May Dowe Miniter. LC 16-21054. 1916. H. Holt and Company.

Our Neighbor, Martin Luther. Elizabeth Rundle Charles. 1964. pap. 1.35 o.p. (38-9). Moody.

Our Neighbors. Annie Marion MacLean. LC 22-20052. 1922. The Macmillan Company.

Our Neighbors. John Watson. LC 3-6460. 1903. Dodd, Mead & Company.

Our New Crusade. A Temperance Story. Edward Everett Hale. LC 3-54713. 1894. Roberts Brothers.

Our New Mistress: Or, Changes at Brookfield Earl. Charlotte Mary Yonge. (On cover: Seaside library. Pocket ed. no. 1133). 1888. G. Munro.

Our Next-Door Neighbors. Belle Kanaris Maniates. LC 17-745513. 1917. Little, Brown, and Company.

Our Next President: The Incredible Story of What Happened in the 1968 Elections. Russell Baker. LC 68-23262. 1968. Atheneum.

Our Nig: Sketches from the Life of a Free Black. H. E. Wilson. Ed. by Henry L. Gates. LC 82-49197. 192p. 1983. pap. 2.95 (ISBN 0-394-71558-6, Vin). Random.

Our Odyssey Club. A. H. Blaisdell. LC 6-275049. D. Lothrop and Company.

Our of Her Sphere. A Novel. Elizabeth Morrisson Boynton Harbert. LC 7-1920. 1871. Mills & Co.

Our of the Due Season: A Mezzotint. Adeline Sergeant. LC 8-6858. (Half-title: Appletons' town and country library, no. 176). 1895. D. Appleton and Company.

Our Own Kind. Edward McSorley. LC 76-6357. (Irish-Americans). 1976. 18.00 (ISBN 0-405-09350-0). Arno Press.

Our Own Kind. Edward McSorley. LC 46-473782. 1946. Harper & Brothers.

Our Own Pioneers. Florence Grauel Miller. LC 29-29104. The Tribune Publishing Company.

Our Own Set: A Novel. Lula Kirschner. Tr. by Bell. Clara Coutney (Poynton) LC 7-12823. 1884. W. S. Gottsberger.

Our Pariahs Among the Tramps: The Tramps Paradise; Slim Jim's Story; Pat Shorty, the Coal-Digger; Jake Trueheart, the Farmer; Professor Trump. Timothy Gruaz. LC 7-158. (On cover: Household library. v. 4, no. 13). Belford, Clarke & Company; Etc., Etc.

Our Part in the World Wide Church. Lillian W. Shepard & Cranston Clayton. pap. text ed. 0.65 o.p. (ISBN 0-687-29790-7); teachers' ed. 1.75 o.p. (ISBN 0-687-29765-6). Abingdon.

Our Peggotties. Kesiah Shelton. LC 8-5111. (On cover: Satchel series, no. 11). The Authors' Publishing Company.

Our Peter: A Story. George Wilson Slaney. LC 20-8859. E. P. Dutton & Company.

Our Phil, and Other Stories. Katharine Floyd Dana. LC 74-113653. (Short story index reprint series). (Illus.). 1970. Books for Libraries Press.

Our Phil: And Other Stories. Katharine Floyd Dana. 1889. Houghton, Mifflin and Company.

Our Plundered Planet. Fairfield Osborne. 1970. pap. 0.95 o.p. (N2273). Pyramid Pubns.

Our Priceless Heritage. Henry M. Woods. 1957. 3.50 o.p. (ISBN 0-87508-580-6). Chr Lit.

Our Professor. Elizabeth Lynn Linton. LC 7-190068. (Half-title: Harper's half-hour series. v. 87). 1879. Harper & Brothers.

Our Prospects: A Tale of Real Life. Moritz Loth. LC 11-7155. 1870. R. Clarke & Co., Printers.

Our Radicals: A Tale of Love and Politics. Frederick Gustavus Barnaby. LC 6-18651. (Harper's Handy Series, No. 90). 1886. Harper & Brothers.

Our Radicals: A Tale of Love and Politics. Frederick Gustavus Burnaby. LC 6-18285. (Lovell's Library, No. 1828). J. W. Lovell Company.

Our Refugee Household. Louise Clack. LC 6-25380. 1866. Blelock & Co.

Our Revels Now Are Ended, a Novel. 1st Ed. Carl Jonas. LC 57-550359. 1957. Norton.

Our Right to Love. Anna Chase Deppen. LC 6-1374. J. S. Ogilvie Publishing Company.

Our Roman Palace: Or, Hilda and I. Elizabeth Dundas Bedell Benjamin. LC 7-34442. (On cover: Lovell's library, v. 14. no. 748). 1886. J. W. Lovell Company.

Our Russian Neighbors: An International Novel. J. Bryce Murray. LC 61-17972. Greenwich Book Publishers.

Our Saints. A Family Story. Rose Porter. A. D. F. Randolph & Company.

Our Sally: A Novel. William Carl Nolting. LC 54-97558. 1954. Vantage Press.

Our Sea Coast Heroes: Stories of the Wreck & Rescue, Origin, History & Principles of the Construction of the Lightboat. Achilles Daunt. 1977. lib. bdg. 69.95 (ISBN 0-8490-2393-9). Gordon Pr.

Our Search for the Missing Millions: Of Cocos Island) By One of the Searchers. John Chetwood. 1904. The South Sea Bubble Company.

Our Second Murder. Marjorie Torrey Hood Chanslor. LC 41-3902. 1941. Frederick A. Stokes Company.

Our Second Murder. Torrey Chanslor. LC 41-3902. 1941. Frederick A. Stokes Company.

Our Sensation Novel. Justin Huntly McCarthy. LC 7-15173. (Harper's handy series, no. 63). 1886. Harper & Brothers.

Our Sensation Novel. Justin Huntly McCarthy. (On cover: Seaside library. Pocket ed., no. 747). 1886. G. Munro.

Our Sensation Novel. Justin Huntly McCarthy. (On cover: Cassell's "rainbow" series, v. 1, no. 5). 1887. Cassell & Company, Limited.

Our Set: A Collection of Stories. Annie Hall Thomas Cudlip. (Harper's Franklin square library, no. 253). 1882. Harper & Brothers.

Our Snake Is Gone and One of Our Salamanders Is Missing. John J Dalton. LC 77-80982. 2.95 (ISBN 0-89343-027-7). Ermine Publishers.

Our Spanish Journey. Molly Rainey Bishop. LC 42-1099. Bellman Publishing Company, Inc.

Our Spoons Came from Woolworths. Barbara Comyns Carr. LC 51-86. 1951. Holt.

Our Spoons Came from Woolworths. 1st American Ed. Barbara Comyns. LC 51-86. 1951. Holt.

Our Square and the People in It. Samuel Hopkins Adams. LC 78-106241. (Short story index reprint series). (Illus.). 1970. Books for Libraries Press.

Our Square and the People in It. Samuel Hopkins Adams. LC 17-29518. 1917. Houghton Mifflin Company.

Our Story of Atlantis; or, The Three Steps. 1972. 6.95. Philos Pub.

Our Story of Atlantis. Written Down for the Hermetic Brotherhood. William P Phelon. LC 4-70. 1903. Hermetic Book Concern.

Our Story of Atlantis: Written Down for the Hermetic Brotherhood and the Future Rulers of America. William P. Phelon & Clymer, Reuben Swinburne. LC 38-125870. The Philosophical Publishing Co.

Our Story Time. Laurina Havens. LC 40-88218. Fortuny's.

Our Street. Compton Mackenzie. LC 32-9440. 1932. Doubleday, Doran & Company, Inc.

Our Street. Patience Thom. Ed. by John Tedman & Alison Tedman. (Illus.). 48p. 1973. pap. 0.75x o.p. (ISBN 0-19-422379-5, OxC). Oxford U Pr.

Our Time: A Novel. Alexander Edwards. 1974. (pbk.) 1.25. Warner Paperback Library.

Our Town. Thornton Niven Wilder. LC 60-16885. 1960. 12.95i (ISBN 0-06-014645-1, HarpT). Har-Row.

Our Town, U.S.A. Laban Lacy Rice. LC 72-250973. 1965. Cavalier Press.

Our Traveller Returns. David Christie Murray & Herman, Henry. (On cover: Lovell's library, no. 1116). 1888. J. W. Lovell Company.

Our Two Homes: Or, Without and Within the Gates. Sarah Ann Flanders Herbert. LC 7-4302. Congregational Sunday-School and Publishing Society.

Our Two Lives: Or, Graham and I. Eliza A. Warner. LC 8-33714. A. D. F. Randolph & Company.

Our Uncle and Aunt. Amarala Arter Martin. 1888. G. P. Putnam's Sons.

Our Uncle William: Also Nate Sawyer. David Skaats Foster. LC 15-7732. 1.25. The Franklin Book Company.

Our Urban Legacy: Medieval Towns. Clifford B. Moller. LC 77-77127. (Illus.). 1979. 17.50 (ISBN 0-8180-0029-5). Horizon.

Our Valiant Few: Illustrated by John Alan Maxwell. 1st Ed. Francis Van Wyck Mason. LC 56-10640. 1956. Little, Brown.

Our Very Best People. Clifford Samuel Raymond. LC 31-853752. The Bobbs-Merrill Company.

Our Village. Mary Russell Mitford. LC 6-12134. (Half-title: The English Comedie humaine, 2d series). 1906. The Century Co.

Our Village. Mary Russell Mitford & Ritchie, Anne Isabella (Thackeray) Lady, 1837-1919. LC 3-16397. 1902. Macmillan and Co., Limited.

Our Village, Sketches of Rural Character and Scenery. Mary Russell Mitford. LC 7-31096. (On cover: Harper's half-hour series. V. 96). 1879. Harper & Brothers.

Our Village: Sketches of Rural Character and Scenery. Mary Russell Mitford. LC 19-2890. (Half-title: Bohn's standard library). 1892. G. Bell & Sons.

Our Visited Planet. William Justice. 5.95 o.p. Vantage.

Our Wedding Gifts. Amanda Minnie Douglas. LC 6-334703. The Author's Publishing Company.

Our Widow. Three Wayward Girls. Florence Alice Price James. LC 7-7412. The International News Company.

Our Willie: A Folklore Story of the Gunpowder Creek and Hills, Boone County, Kentucky. John Uri Lloyd. LC 34-37241. J. G. Kidd & Son, Inc.

Our Wiser Sons. Ralph Straus. LC 26-20070. H. Holt and Company.

Our Women. Arnold Bennett. 250p. 1980. Repr. of 1920 ed. lib. bdg. 25.00 (ISBN 0-8492-3756-4). R West.

Our Wonderful Selves. Roland Pertwee. LC 19-632937. 1918. Cassell and Company, Ltd.

Our Wonderful Selves. Roland Pertwee. LC 19-104641. 1919. A. A. Knopf.

Our World: Or, The Slaveholder's Daughter. Francis Colburn Adams. LC 78-152927. (Black Heritage Library Collection). (Illus.). 1971. (ISBN 0-8369-8771-3). Books for Libraries Press.

Our World: Or, The Slaveholder's Daughter... Francis Colburn Adams. LC 6-45939. 1855. Miller, Orton & Mulligan.

Our Yankee Heritage: The Making of Greater New Haven. Carleton Beals. LC 58-31565.

Our Yankee Heritage: The Making of Greater New Haven. Carleton Beals. LC 51-6239. 1951.

Our Year Began in April. Meredith Reed. LC 63-11683. 1963. Lothrop, Lee and Shepard Co.

Ouray Jim: And Other Stories. Mary Etta Smith Stickney. LC 4-18778. 1904. The Ledger Publishing Company.

Ourika. Claire De Durfort Duras & John Fowles. LC 77-367861. 1977. W. T. Taylor.

Ourika. Claire de Durfort. Tr. by John Fowles. 1977. signed ed. 110.00x (ISBN 0-935072-01-2). W Thomas Taylor.

Ours for the Love. Margaret Carney. 1975. pap. 2.50 o.p. (ISBN 0-916684-05-9). Rook Pr.

Ours for the Love. Margaret Carney. 1975. pap. 2.50 o.p. (ISBN 0-916684-05-9). Rook Pr.

Ourselves: A Novel. Jonathan Strong. LC 73-152907. 1971. 5.95. Little, Brown.

Ourselves to Know: A Novel. John O'Hara. LC 60-5528. 1960. Random House.

Out. Ronald Sukenick. LC 72-96165. 1973. 7.95 (ISBN 0-8040-0630-X) (ISBN 0-8040-0630-X). Swallow Press.

Out: A Novel. Ronald Sukenick. LC 82-73419. 295p. 1973. 11.95 (ISBN 0-8040-0630-X). Swallow.

Out: A Novel. Ronald Sukenick. LC 72-96165. 1975. pap. 4.95 o.p. (ISBN 0-8040-0631-8). Swallow.

Out Are the Lights. Richard Laymon. 224p. (Orig.). 1983. pap. 2.75 (ISBN 0-446-90519-4). Warner Bks.

Out at Twinnett's: Or, Gnawing a File; a Story of Wall Street Ways and Suburban Mysteries. John Habberton. LC 6-46675. 1891. J. A. Taylor & Co.

Out, Brief Candle. Lee Thayer, pseud. LC 48-7995. (Red badge detective). 1948. Dodd, Mead.

Out by the River. Ludovic Peters. LC 65-15689. 1965. 3.50. Walker.

Out for the Coin. George Vere Hobart. LC 3-18311. 1903. G. W. Dillingham Co.

Out for the Kill: By Anthony Gilbert Pseud. Lucy Beatrice Malleson. LC 60-12157. (Random House mystery). 1960. Random House.

Out from Eden. Victoria Lincoln. LC 51-13628. 1951. Rinehart.

Out from Ganymede. Barry N Malzberg. 1974. (pbk.) 1.25. Warner Paperback Library.

Out from Shanghai. Sydney Muller Parkman. LC 35-12778. 1935. Harper & Brothers.

Out from the Pit: A Story Based on Facts and Experiences. William Henry Hubbard. LC 38-8218. 1938. Meador Publishing Company.

Out from the Shadows: Or, Trial and Triumph. Ella Giles Ruddy. LC 6-44051. 1876. Atwood & Culver.

Out from Tombstone. Albert Butler. LC 66-629. 1966. Arcadia House.

Out from Under Caesar's Frown: Or, The Belle of the Dismal. James Walter Daniel. LC 6-33164. 1891. Printed for the Author.

Out in Society: By Margaret Culkin Banning. Margaret Culkin Banning. LC 40-673873. Harper & Brothers.

Out Loud. Adrian Mitchell. 80p. pap. 2.45 (ISBN 0-904613-33-X). Writers & Readers.

Out of a Blue Sky. Eugene Thomas. LC 33-13756. Sears Publishing Company.

Out of a Clear Sky: A Novel by Maria Thompson Daviess... Maria Thompson Daviess. LC 17-131851. 1917. 1.00. Harper & Brothers.

Out of a Labyrinth. Emma Murdoch Van Deventer. LC 13-2070. 1885. A. T. Loyd & Co.

Out of a Labyrinth. Emma Murdoch Van Deventer. (On cover: The detective and adventure library, no. 8). 1889. A. T. Loyd & Co.

Out of a Labyrinth: A Thrilling American Detective Story. Emma Murdoch Van Deventer. (library of choice fiction no. 55). 1892. Laird & Lee.

Out of a Season. Gabriella Kramer Mautner. LC 68-13591. 1968. T. Y. Crowell Co.

Out of Abaddon: A Novel. 1st Ed. Bart Gelormino. LC 54-13424. 1955. Exposition Press.

Out of Approval: A Story. Mary M Moloney. LC 52-6772. 1952. Exposition Press.

Out of Bohemia. A Story of Paris Student-Life. Gertrude Christian Fosdick. LC 6-40374. 1894. G. H. Richmond & Co.

Out of Bondage: And Other Stories. Rowland Evans Robinson. LC 5-6486. 1905. Houghton, Mifflin and Company.

Out of Bondage and Other Stories. Rowland Evans Robinson. Ed. by Llewellyn Rood Perkins. Perkins, Mrs. Mary (Robinson) LC 38-17092. C. E. Tuttle Company.

Out of Bounds. Lori Boatright. 160p. 1982. pap. 1.95 (ISBN 0-449-70028-3, Juniper). Fawcett.

Out of Bounds. Ralph Cannon. LC 37-351832. 1937. The Reilly & Lee Co.

Out of Bounds. Jon Stallworthy. 1963. 2.40 o.p. (ISBN 0-19-211245-7). Oxford U Pr.

Out of Bounds: Being the Adventures of an Unadventurous Young Man. A Garry. LC 6-40711. (On cover: Beckman ser.). 1896. H. Holt and Company.

Out of Chaos. Ilia Grigorevich Ehrenburg. LC 76-10753. 1976. 16.00 (ISBN 0-374-92504-6). Octagon Books.

Out of Chaos. Ilya Grigorevich Ehrenburg & Bakshy, Aleksandr, Tr. LC 34-27172. H. Holt and Company.

Out of Chaos. Ilia Grigorevich Erenburg & Bakshy, Aleksandr, Tr. LC 34-27172. H. Holt and Company.

Out of Control. Baynard Hardwick Kendrick. LC 45-7087. 1945. W. Morrow & Company.

Out of Control. G. Gordon Liddy. LC 79-16366. 10.95 (ISBN 0-312-59065-2). St. Martin's Press.

Out of Control. Gordon G Liddy. 1980. 2.75 (ISBN 0-425-04695-8). Berkley Books.

Out of Control: A Novel. Daniel F Gerber. LC 73-15506. 1974. 6.95 (ISBN 0-13-645283-3). Prentice-Hall.

Out of Darkness. James McKinley Bryant. LC 78-186378. 1971. 5.00. Rocket Pub. Co.

Out of Darkness. C. Thompson. 2.00 o.p. Carlton.

Out of Darkness: A Drama of Flanders. Kenneth Ingram. LC 27-19201. 1928. Frederick A. Stokes Company.

Out of Darkness into Light: A Story of the Pioneer West. John McArthur Will. LC 18-191395. The Roxburgh Publishing Company, Inc.

Out of Drowning Valley. Susan Carleton Jones. LC 10-24024. 1910. 1.50. H. Holt and Company.

Out of Due Time: A Novel. Josephine Mary Hope-Scott W. P. Ward Ward. 1906. Longmans, Green, and Co.

Out of Eden. Dora Russell. LC 8-1339. (On cover: Lovell's international series, no. 169). 1891. United States Book Company.

Out of Focus. Peter Townend. 1975. (pbk.) 1.25 (ISBN 0-523-00534-2). Pinnacle Books.

Out of Focus. Peter Townend. LC 77-185859. 1972. 5.95. St. Martin's Press.

Out of Focus: A Novella. 2nd ed. Alf MacLochlainin. 1977. 8.95 (ISBN 0-905140-40-0). Irish Bk Ctr.

Out of Gloucester. James Brendan Connolly. LC 70-94712. (Short story index reprint series). (Illus.). 1969. Books for Libraries Press.

Out of Gloucester. James Brendan Connolly. 1902. C. Scribner's Sons.

Out of Hell. Henry Goldring-Goding. LC 55-6607. 1955. Chapman & Grimes.

Out of Hiding. William J Weatherby. LC 67-10976. 1967. Doubleday.

Out of His Head. A Romance...Also, Paul Lynde's Sketch Book. Ed. by Thomas Bailey Aldrich. 1862. Carleton.

Out of His Reckoning. Florence Marryat Church Lean. LC 7-13615. (On cover: Lovell's library. v. 19, no. 954). 1887. J. W. Lovell Company.

Out of Inferno. Nishan Der Hagopian. LC 49-83093. 1949. Dorrance.

Out of It All. Charles Saxby. LC 41-10972. 1941. E. P. Dutton & Co. Inc.

Out of Life. Myron Brinig. LC 34-1823. Farrar & Rinehart, Inc.

Out of Love. Hilma Wolitzer. (Illus.). 1976. 6.95. Farrar, Straus and Giroux.

Out of Many Waters. Louise Mohr. 2.95 o.p. Vantage.

Out of Mulberry Street. Jacob August Riis. LC 74-104550. 1970. Literature House.

Out of Mulberry Street: Stories of Tenement Life in New York City. Jacob August Riis. LC 98-16497. 1898. The Century Co.

Out of Order. Barbara Raskin. LC 79-12061. 8.95 (ISBN 0-671-24281-4). Simon and Schuster.

Out of Order. Phoebe Atwood Taylor. LC 36-273795. W. W. Norton & Company, Inc.

Out of Order. An Asey Mayo Mystery Reissue. Phoebe Atwood Taylor. LC 36-27379. (Asey Mayo mystery). 1965. bds., 3.95. Reissue Norton.

Out of Our Lives: A Selection of Contemporary Black Fiction. Ed. by Quandra Prettyman Stadler. LC 74-7092. 1975. (ISBN 0-88258-027-2). Howard University Press.

Out of Place: A Novel. Joseph Papaleo. LC 72-121430. 1970. 5.95. Little, Brown.

Out of Prison. Mary Andrews Denison. LC 74-164558. (American fiction reprint series). 1971. (ISBN 0-8369-7034-9). Books for Libraries Press.

Out of Prison... Mary Andrews Denison. LC 6-33984. 1864. Graves and Young.

Out of Reach. Barbara Cartland. pap. 1.25 o.p. (ISBN 0-515-03242-5, N3242). BJ Pub Group.

Out of Russia. Crittenden Marriott. LC 11-5378. 1911. 1.25. J. B. Lippincott Company.

Out of Season: A Novel. Ian J Burton. LC 80-22399. 1981. 10.95 (ISBN 0-517-54334-6). Crown Publishers.

Out of Shape. Leonard Greenbaum. LC 72-83637. (Illus.). 1969. 5.95. Harper & Row.

Out of Sight: A Story. Jane Lippitt Patterson, pseud. LC 7-34080. 1883.

Out of Sight: Ten Stories of Victory Over Blindness. Al Sperber. 1976. 7.95 (ISBN 0-316-80700-1). Little.

Out of Soundings. Henry Major Tomlinson. 1931. Repr. 20.00 (ISBN 0-8274-3087-6). R West.

Out of Space and Time. Clark Ashton Smith. LC 42-20807. 1942. Arkham House.

Out of Step: A Novel. Maria Louise Pool. LC 7-38174. 1894. Harper & Brothers.

Out of Such Fires. Jean Crooks Devanny. LC 34-5901. 1934. The Macaulay Company.

Out of That Dream. Katherine Newborg. LC 35-7672. 1935. Doubleday, Doran & Company, Inc.
Out of the Air. Inez Haynes Irwin. LC 21-43183. 1921. Harcourt, Brace and Company.
Out of the Ashes. Ethel Watts Mumford Grant. LC 3-13494. 1913. 1.25. Moffat, Yard and Company.
Out of the Ashes. William W. Johnstone. 1983. pap. 3.50 (ISBN 0-8217-1137-7). Zebra.
Out of the Ashes". Jules Henry Steane. LC 34-220. Dorrance & Company, Inc.
Out of the Ashes: A Possible Solution to the Social Problem of Divorce. Harney Rennolds. LC 6-26069. 1906. The C. M. Clark Publishing Company.
Out of the Blue. Herman Cyril McNeile. LC 25-890719. 1925. George H. Doran Company.
Out of the Blue. Richard O'Connor. LC 63-23223. 1964. Published for the Crime Club by Doubleday.
Out of the Cage. An O'er True Tale. George Washington Owen. LC 7-22778. 1877. G. W. Carleton & Co.; Etc., Etc.
Out of the Clay. Harriet Theresa Smith Comstock. LC 26-23129. 1926. Doubleday, Page & Company.
Out of the Closet into the Light. (Agape Ser.). 1980. pap. 3.50 (ISBN 0-8163-0420-3). Pacific Pr Pub Assn.
Out of the Crate. Crate Jones. LC 79-90650. 1979. 7.95 (ISBN 0-87716-113-5, Pub. by Moore Pub Co). F Apple.
Out of the Dark. Ursula Reilly Curtiss. LC 64-14818. (Red badge detective). 1964. Dodd, Mead.
Out of the Dark. George Fort Gibbs. LC 34-21693. (Tired business man's library of adventure, detective, and mystery novels). 1934. D. Appleton-Century Company, Incorporated.
Out of the Dark. Gertrude Knevels. LC 32-288289. The Penn Publishing Company.
Out of the Dark. Norah Robinson Lofts. LC 71-180087. 1972. 6.95. Doubleday.
Out of the Dark. Norah Robinson Lofts. LC 72-8224. 1972. 10.95 (ISBN 0-8161-6053-8). G. K. Hall.
Out of the Darkness. Charles Judson Dutton. LC 22-56079. 1922. Dodd, Mead & Company.
Out of the Darkness: A Novel. Peg Stokes. LC 51-14054. 1951. Vantage Press.
Out of the Darkness: Or, Diabolism and Destiny. John Wesley Grant. LC 79-39085. (Black Heritage Library Collection). 1972. (ISBN 0-8369-9023-4). Books for Libraries Press.
Out of the Darkness: Or, Diabolism and Destiny. John Wesley Grant. 1909. National Baptist Publishing Board.
Out of the Death Bag in West Hollywood. F. P Tullius. LC 78-155271. 1971. 5.95. Macmillan.
Out of the Deep, a Novel. Jack Calvert Wells. LC 58-6721. 1958. Christopher Pub. House.
Out of the Deep: And Other Stories. James H. Ashabranner. LC 31-32078. Dorrance and Company.
Out of the Deeps: By John Wyndham Pseud. John Wyndham, pseud. LC 53-12491. 1953. Ballantine Books.
Out of the Depths. George Augustus Parker. LC 8-34599. Reid Publishing Company.
Out of the Depths; a Romance of Reclamation. Robert Ames Bennet. LC 13-6773. 1913. 1.35. A. C. McClurg & Co.
Out of the Depths: A Story of Western Love, Religion and Reform. George Reuben Varney. LC 9-16444. The Griffith & Rowland Press.
Out of the Depths: By) Leonard Holton Pseud. Leonard Patrick O'Connor Wibberley. LC 66-175913. (Red badge mystery). bds., 3.50. Dodd.
Out of the Dump. Mary Edna Tobias Marcy. LC 8-37707. 1909. C. H. Kerr & Company.
Out of the Dusk. Elisabeth Stancy Payne. LC 34-34429. 1934. Dodd, Mead & Company.
Out of the Dust. Charles Francis Stocking. LC 39-303698. 1939. The Maestro Company.
Out of the Dust. Helen Waren. LC 51-12002. 1952. Crown Publishers.
Out of the Dust: A Novel. Lars Lawrence. LC 56-6623. (His The seed, v. 2). Putnam.
Out of the Dust: A Novel. Philip Stevenson. LC 56-6623. Putnum.
Out of the Earth. Louis Bromfield. 305p. Repr. of 1950 ed. lib. bdg. 16.30x (ISBN 0-88411-541-0). Amereon Ltd.
Out of the Everywhere. Una Troy. LC 76-382646. 1976. 2.90 (ISBN 0-7091-5071-7). Hale.
Out of the Everywhere & Other Extraordinary Visions. James Tidtree, Jr. 282p. (Orig.). 1981. pap. 2.75 (ISBN 0-345-28485-2, Del Rey). Ballantine.
Out of the Fire. Mary Dwinell Chellis. LC 6-233583. 1869. National Temperance Society and Publication House.
Out of the Foam. A Novel. John Esten Cooke. LC 6-27188. 1871. Carleton; Etc. Etc.
Out of the Foam. A Novel. John Esten Cooke. LC 16-7558. G. W. Dillingham Co.
Out of the Foam. A Novel. John Esten Cooke. LC 34-37764. 1901. G. W. Dillingham Co.
Out of the Fog. Joseph Crosby Lincoln. LC 40-14670. 1940. D. Appleton-Century Company, Incorporated.
Out of the Fog. Clarissa Ross, pseud. (Orig.). 1970. pap. 0.75 o.p. (75-352). Lancer.
Out of the Fog. Clarissa Ross, pseud. (Orig.). 1972. pap. 0.95 o.s.i. (75-352). Lancer.
Out of the Fog: The Story of Peter Parker's Pilgrimage. Claus August Wendell. LC 43-18428. 1943. Augustana Book Concern.
Out of the Frying Pan. Constance Antonina Boyle. LC 23-7545. 1923. T. Seltzer.
Out of the Ground. Norma Patterson & Dalton, Crate. LC 37-38307. Farrar & Rinehart, Inc.
Out of the Jungle. 1st Ed. Josephine Hope Westervelt. LC 56-5510. 1956. Vantage Press.
Out of the Mire,". Charlotte Elvira Gray. LC 11-248235. Jennings and Graham.
Out of the Mist. Robert L Allison. LC 41-360886. 1941. Wm. B. Eerdmans Publishing Co.
Out of the Mist. Ralph Byrne, pseud. LC 69-11344. (Illus.). 1969. 5.95. Branden Press.
Out of the Mist. Gloria Dare. LC 25-108141. California Press.
Out of the Mist. Florence Riddell. LC 26-181654. E. J. Clode, Inc.
Out of the Mouth of the Lion: Or, The Church in the Catacombs. Emma Leslie. LC 7-14492. (Church history stories, v.2). I. Bradley &Co.
Out of the Mouths of Graves. Robert Bloch. LC 78-53503. 1979. 10.00. (ISBN 0-89296-043-4) (ISBN 0-89296-044-2). Mysterious Press.
Out of the Night. authorized ed. Henry Willard French. LC 6-40367. (American Authors' Ser. No. 16). J. W. Lovell Company.
Out of the Night. Michael Horbach. LC 69-11681. 1970. 5.95. F. Fell.
Out of the Night. Gertrude M. Robins Reynolds. LC 10-12779. Hodder & Stoughton, G. H. Doran Company.
Out of the Night. Marion White. LC 38-9299. M. S. Mill Co., Inc.
Out of the Night. Rida Johnson Young. LC 25-20257. W. J. Watt & Co.
Out of the Night; a Nun's Story. Adel Pryor, pseud. LC 63-15727. 1963. Zondervan Pub. House.
Out of the Old Rock. J. Frank Dobie. 247p. 1982. pap. 7.95 (ISBN 0-292-76013-2). U of Tex Pr.
Out of the Ozarks. William Nelson Ruggles. LC 8-23525. 1908. The Neale Publishing Company.
Out of the Past. Eleanor Hooper Coryell. LC 579. Street & Smith.
Out of the Past. Enoch Anson More. LC 7-26205. 1895. Arena Publishing Company.
Out of the Past. 1st Ed. Patricia Wentworth. LC 52-13735. (Her A Silver mystery). 1953. Lippincott.
Out of the Primitive. Robert Ames Bennet. LC 11-266414. 1911. 1.35. A. C. McClurg & Co.
Out of the Red. Caskie Stinnett. LC 60-5614. 1960. Random House.
Out of the Red Brush. Kermit Daugherty. LC 54-5348. 1954. World Pub. Co.
Out of the Roaring Loom. Ethel Hull Miller & Miller, Messenger. LC 36-7624. The Beaver Press.
Out of the Rocks. 1st Ed. Caroline Neilson. LC 68-11934. bds., 5.95. McGraw.
Out of the Rough. Joseph Thompson Shaw. LC 34-9910. Windward House.
Out of the Ruins, and Other Little Novels: By Philip Gibbs. Philip Hamilton Gibbs. LC 28-5873. 1928. Doubleday, Doran & Company, Inc.
Out of the Ruts: A Story for Girls and Their Elders. Julia Willis Kempshall. LC 12-12868. 1.00. Broadway Publishing Co.
Out of the Sand. E. George Lindstrom. LC 43-11745. 1943. High Twelve Publishing Company.
Out of the Shadow. Mary Hubbard Howell. The American Sunday-School Union.
Out of the Shadow: By Alec Glanville Pseud. Alexander Haig Glanville Grieve. LC 58-778486. Roy Publishers.
Out of the Shadows. John Creasey. LC 73-148409. (Falcon's head mystery). 1971. 5.95. World Pub. Co.
Out of the Shadows: A Novel. Milton C Watson. LC 76-189540. 1972. 4.95. Heath Cote Pub. Co.
Out of the Silence. Erle Cox. LC 75-28852. (Classics of science fiction). 1976. 13.95. (ISBN 0-88355-366-X) (ISBN 0-88355-451-8). Hyperion Press.
Out of the Silence: A Novel. Erle Cox. LC 28-22777. Rae D. Henkle Co., Inc.
Out of the Silences. Mary Ella Waller. LC 18-206662. 1918. Little, Brown, and Company.
Out of the Silent North. Harry Sinclair Drago. LC 23-6143. The Macaulay Company.
Out of the Silent Planet. Clive Staples Lewis. LC 67-6858. 6.95. Macmillan.
Out of the Silent Planet see Space Trilogy.
Out of the Silent Plant. Clive Staples Lewis. LC 49-4872. (Avon, 195). 1949. Avon Pub. Co.
Out of the Silent Sky. Lloyd Biggle, Jr. (O.s.i.). 1977. pap. 1.50 o.s.i. (BT51122). Belmont-Tower.
Out of the Square. Peter De Polnay. LC 49-11326. 1949. Creative Age Press.
Out of the Storm. Grace Livingston Hill. 1929. 2.95 o.p. (ISBN 0-448-05247-4). G&D.
Out of the Storm. William Hope Hodgson. (Illus.). 192p. 1980. pap. 4.95 (ISBN 0-87818-016-8). Centaur.
Out of the Streets. Adah M Howard. (On cover: Munro's library, v. 1. no. 83). N. L. Munro.
Out of the Streets: A Story of New York Life. Charles Gayler. LC 6-44261. R. M. De Witt.
Out of the Sun. Benjamin Bova. (Pacesetter series). 1968. Holt, Rinehart and Winston.
Out of the Sunset: A Novel. 1st Ed. Maura McGrath. LC 57-8230. 1957. Pageant Press.
Out of the Sunset Sea. Albion Winegar Tourgee. Merrill & Baker.
Out of the Third. Beverly Dahlen. 3.00x o.p.; signed ed. 15.00x o.p. Momos.
Out of the Time's Abyss. Edgar Rice Burroughs. 144p. 1982. pap. 1.95 (ISBN 0-441-64485-6, Pub. by Ace Science Fiction). Ace Bks.
Out of the Toils. John W Spear. LC 8-15517. 1887. Phillips & Hunt.
Out of the Triangle: A Story of the Far East, and Other Stories. Mary Ellen Bamford. LC 13-17737. (On cover: New Sabbath library, v. 1, no. 4). 1898. D.C. Cook Publishing Co.
Out of the Way.". Annette Lucile Noble. LC 7-33478. American Tract Society.
Out of the West. Elizabeth Higgins Sullivan. LC 2-21488. 1902. Harper & Brothers.
Out of the West. Lu Jones Waite. LC 68-21501. 1968. Deseret Book Co.
Out of the Whirlwind. Audrey Erskine Lindop. LC 52-8831. 1952. Appleton-Century-Crofts.
Out of the Whirlwind: A Novel. William Thomas Walsh. LC 35-7031. R. M. McBride & Company.
Out of the Whirlwind: A West Texas Saga. Maurine Whorton Redway. LC 75-15803. 1975. 12.95 (ISBN 0-8111-0567-9). Naylor Co.
Out of the Wilderness. Jane Dunbar Chaplin. LC 74-38644. (Black Heritage Library Collection). 1972. (ISBN 0-8369-9002-1). Books for Libraries Press.
Out of the Wilderness. Jane Dunbar Chaplin. 1870. H. A. Young & Co.
Out of the Wilderness: Young Abe Lincoln Grows up. Illustrated by Manning De V. Lee. Virginia Louise Snider Eifert. LC 56-5488. 1956. Dodd, Mead.
Out of the Wind. J. Paul Blair. 6.50 o.p. (ISBN 0-533-00689-9). Vantage.
Out of the Woods: A Romance of Camp Life. George P Fisher. LC 6-40748. 1896. A. C. McClurg and Company.
Out of the Wreck I Rise. Beatrice Harraden. LC 12-15746. 1912. T. Nelson and Sons.
Out of the Wreck I Rise. Beatrice Harraden. LC 12-18061. 1912. 1.35. Frederick A. Stokes Company.
Out of the Wreck: Or, Was It a Vicotry? Amanda Minnie Douglas. LC 6-33469. 1885. Lee and Shepard.
Out of Their Minds. Clifford D. Simak. LC 75-97095. 1970. 4.95. Putnam.
Out of These Flames. John Burton Thompson. LC 53-26222. 1953. Woodford Press.
Out of These Roots: A Novel. Boris Todrin. LC 44-8368. 1944. The Caxton Printers, Ltd.
Out of This Furnace. Thomas Bell. LC 76-6657. (Pitt paperback; 120). 1976. 7.95 (ISBN 0-8229-3321-7) (ISBN 0-8229-5273-4). University of Pittsburgh Press.
Out of This Furnace. Thomas Bell. LC 41-51443. 1941. Little, Brown and Company.
Out of This Nettle. Mary Gates. LC 37-1117. 1937. Thomas Y. Crowell Company.
Out of This Nettle. Norah Robinson Lofts. 1976. pap. 1.75 (ISBN 0-532-17127-6). Woodhill.
Out of This Nettle. Norah Robinson Lofts. 1971. pap. 1.25 o.p. (12105). Manor Bks.
Out of This Nettle. 2nd ed. Norah Robinson Lofts. 320p. 1973. pap. 1.25 o.p. (532-12178-125). Manor Bks.
Out of This World: A Collection of Stories. Thomas Asher Fletcher. LC 63-10189. Greenwich Book Publishers.
Out of This World: An Anthology. Ed. by Julius Fast. LC 44-11159. 1944. Penguin Books.
Out of This World: By Murray Leinster Pseud. William Fitzgerald Jenkins. LC 58-7597. 1958. Avalon Books.
Out of Town. Robert Barry Coffin. LC 7-22775. 1896. Harper & Brothers.
Out of Town: A Rural Episode. Robert Barry Coffin. LC 6-267431. 1866. Hurd and Houghton.
Out of Town: A Rural Episode. Robert Barry Coffin. LC 16-25036. 1867. Hurd and Houghton.
Out of Tune. Myra Malinda Johonnot Smith. LC 6-29038. 1906. Mayhew Publishing Company.
Out of Wedlock. William S Henry. LC 32-3908. R. G. Badger.
Out of Wedlock: A Love Story. Linda Lee. (Illus.). 320p. 1982. 15.50 (ISBN 0-316-51951-0). Little.
Out on Any Limb. John Myers Myers. 1942. E. P. Dutton and Company, Inc.
Out on Bail. Raymond Leslie Goldman. LC 37-1007. Coward-McCann, Inc.
Out on Egypt Ridge. George Patterson. LC 59-7129. 1959. Coward-McCann.
Out to Stay. Christopher Stillman. 224p. (Orig.). 1972. pap. 1.95 o.s.i. (TC 3093). Olympia.
Out Went the Candle: A Novel. Harvey Swados. LC 54-11619. 1955. Viking Press.
Out Went the Taper. Rubie Constance Ashby. LC 34-196680. The Macmillan Company.
Out West: An Anthology of Stories. Ed. by Jack Warner Schaefer. LC 54-8386. 1955. Houghton Mifflin.
Out Where the Day Begins. Robert E. Dunton. (Illus.). 200p. 1982. text ed. 10.95 (ISBN 0-9608100-0-5); pap. text ed. 9.95 (ISBN 0-9608100-1-3). Orange Blossom.
Out Where the World Begins: A Story of a Far Country. Abram Edward Cory. LC 21-20113. 1.50. George H. Doran Company.
Out Yonder. Gipsy Clarke. LC 35-4040. 1935. Thomas Y. Crowell Company.
Outback. Aaron Fletcher. (Leisure Books). (Illus.). 1978. 2.25. Nordon Pubns.
Outback Runaway. Dorothy Cork. (Harlequin Romances Ser.). 192p. 1980. pap. 1.25 (ISBN 0-373-02372-3, Pub. by Harlequin). PB.
Outbound Road. Arnold Mulder. LC 19-15728. 1919. 1.65. Houghton Mifflin Company.
Outbreak. Dudley Barker. LC 68-16043. 1968. Stein and Day.
Outbreak. Lionel Black. LC 68-16043. 1968. bds., 4.95. Stein & Day.
Outbreak. Robert De Maria. LC 77-91243. (Jove / HBJ Book). 1978. 1.95 (ISBN 0-515-04433-4). Jove Pubns.
Outbreak. Marianne Ruuth. 1977. pap. 1.50 (ISBN 0-532-15263-8). Woodhill.
Outbreak of Love. Martin Boyd. LC 57-8323. 1957. Reynal.
Outcast. Beverly Byrne. (Griffin Saga Ser.: Vol. I). 512p. (Orig.). 1981. pap. 2.95 (ISBN 0-449-14396-1, GM). Fawcett.
Outcast. Catherine Marye Disch. LC 49-1506. 1948. Story Book Press.
Outcast. Selma Ottiliana Lovisa Lagerlof & Worster, William John Alexander. LC 22-5456. 1922. Doubleday, Page & Company.
Outcast. Winwood Reade. LC 75-1525. (Victorian Fiction: Novels of Faith and Doubt; V. 73). 1975. 35.00 (ISBN 0-8240-1597-5). Garland Pub.
Outcast. Rosemary Sutcliff. (Alpha Books). (Orig.). 1979. pap. text ed. 2.95x (ISBN 0-19-424210-2). Oxford U Pr.
Outcast. rev. ed. Anna Elisabet Weirauch. LC 75-12355. (Homosexuality). 1975. 9.00 (ISBN 0-405-07376-3). Arno Press.
Outcast. rev. ed. Anna Elisabet Weirauch & Endore, S. Guy. LC 48-2646. 1948. Willey Book Co.
Outcast: A Novel. Luigi Pirandello & Ongley, Leo, Tr. LC 25-18350. E. P. Dutton & Company.
Outcast: A Novel. Luigi Pirandello & Ongley, Leo, Tr. LC 35-27059. 1935. E. P. Dutton & Company, Inc.
Outcast. A Tale of the Mountain People. Charles Edward Hewitt. LC 13-17969. 1.00. J. S. Ogilvie Publishing Company.
Outcast Gun. Giles A. Lutz. 160p. 1978. pap. 1.75 (ISBN 0-449-14079-2, GM). Fawcett.
Outcast Gun. Giles A. Lutz. 1970. pap. 0.60 o.p. (R2238, GM). Fawcett World.
Outcast Island: A Novel. 1st Ed. Edward Albalos. LC 54-10973. 1954. Exposition Press.
Outcast Manufacturers. Charles Fort. LC 9-9467. 1909. B. W. Dodge & Company.
Outcast of Lazy S. Eli Colter. LC 33-24082. A. H. King.
Outcast of Milan. A Companion Story to "The Gunmaker of Moscow.". Sylvanus Cobb. (choice series, no. 134). (ledger library, no. 134). 1897. R. Bonner's Sons.
Outcast of the Canyon. Galen C Colin. LC 48-5837. 1948. Phoenix Press.
Outcast of the Family. Charles Garvice. (On cover: Laurel library, no. 23). 1897. G. Munro's Sons.
Outcast of the Island & Almayer's Folly. Joseph Conrad. (Standard Classic Ed). 4.95 o.p. (ISBN 0-00-421457-9, JC457). Collins-World.
Outcast of the Islands. Joseph Conrad. LC 76-372167. (Penguin modern classics). 1975. 2.50 (ISBN 0-14-004054-4). Penguin.
Outcast of the Islands. Joseph Conrad. LC 75-323310. (Illus.). 1975. Printed for the Members of the Limited Editions Club, Avon, Conn., at the Stinehour Press.
Outcast of the Islands. Joseph Conrad. LC 6-30678. (Half-title: Appleton's town and country library, no. 198). 1896. D. Appleton and Company.

Outcast of the Islands. Joseph Conrad. LC 22-10647. 1920. Doubleday, Page & Company.

Outcasts. Al Cody, pseud. 1975. pap. 0.95 (ISBN 0-532-95412-2). Woodhill.

Outcasts. Al Cody, pseud. 1970. 3.95 o.p. Lenox Hill.

Outcasts. Al Cody. 1973. (pbk) 0.75. Manor Books.

Outcasts. Will Cook. 144p. (Orig.). 1981. pap. 1.75 (ISBN 0-553-14740-4). Bantam.

Outcasts. Joe L. Hensley. LC 80-705. 1981. 9.95 (ISBN 0-385-15820-3). Published for the Crime Club by Doubleday.

Outcasts: And Other Stories. Maksim Gorkii. LC 75-113664. (Short story index reprint series). 1970. Books for Libraries Press.

Outcasts & Other Stories. Maksim Gorkii. LC 75-113664. (Short Story Index Reprint Ser.). 1905. 16.00 (ISBN 0-8369-3393-1). Ayer Co.

Outcasts: By Stephen Becker. 1st Ed. Stephen D Becker. LC 67-14325. 1967. 4.95. Atheneum.

Outcasts of Canyon Creek. Henry Wilson Allen. LC 72-8890. 1972. 0.75. Bantam Books.

Outcasts of Foolgarah. Frank J Hardy. LC 72-175524. 1971. 2.50 (ISBN 0-85887-000-2). Allara Publishing.

Outcasts of Heaven Belt. Joan D Vinge. (Signet book). 1978. 1.75 (ISBN 0-451-08407-1). New American Library.

Outcasts of Heavens Belt. Joan D. Vinge. 1982. pap. 2.50 (ISBN 0-451-11653-4, AE1653, Sig). NAL.

Outcasts of Poker Flat. Bret Harte. Ed. by Walter Pauk & Raymond Harris. (Jamestown Classics Ser.). (Illus.). 37p. (gr. 6-12). 1976. pap. text ed. 2.00x (ISBN 0-89061-052-5, 525); tchrs. ed. 3.00 (ISBN 0-89061-053-3, 527). Jamestown Pubs.

Outcasts of Poker Flat & Luck of Roaring Camp. rev. ed. Bret Harte. Ed. by Robert J. Dixson. (American Classics Ser.: Bk. 5). (gr. 9 up). 1973. pap. text ed. 3.25 (ISBN 0-88345-201-4, 18124); cassettes 40.00; 40.00 o.p. tapes. Regents Pub.

Outcasts of Poker Flat & Other Stories. Bret Harte. (American Classics Ser.). (Tchrs. ed. 1.29 o.p.). (gr. 9-12). 1977. pap. text ed. 3.20 (ISBN 0-88343-408-3); tchrs'. manual 1.50 (ISBN 0-88343-409-1). McDougal-Littell.

Outcasts of Poker Flat, and Other Tales. Bret Harte. LC 66-1225. (Signet classic). 1964. New American Library.

Outcasts of Poker Flats, the Luck of Roaring Camp: And Other Sketches. Bret Harte. 1976. Repr. of 1869 ed. lib. bdg. 14.40x (ISBN 0-88411-592-5). Amereon Ltd.

Outcasts of the Islands. Joseph Conrad. (Magnum Easy Eye Classic Ser). 1968. pap. 0.75 o.p. (14-620). Lancer.

Outcross. Roger Longrigg. LC 82-6283. 1982. 14.95 (ISBN 0-688-01334-1). Morrow.

Outcry. Henry James. LC 11-26025. 1911. C. Scribner's Sons.

Outcry. Henry James. LC 80-17012. 1981. 20.00 (ISBN 0-86527-335-9). H. Fertig.

Outdated Man. Ed. by Harry Harrison. 1975. (pbk.) 0.95. Dell.

Outer Dark. Cormac McCarthy. LC 68-14496. 1968. 4.95. Random House.

Outer Darkness. James S. Wallerstein. (Illus.). 1976. 14.00 (ISBN 0-912388-04-8). Aurelon.

Outer Edges. Charles Reginald Jackson. 1973. (pbk.) 1.25. Manor Books.

Outer Fleet. M. Matzkin. 1978. pap. 1.50 (ISBN 0-532-15336-7). Woodhill.

Outer Gate. Octavus Roy Cohen. LC 27-5602. 1927. Little, Brown and Company.

Outer Mongolian. David R. Slavitt. LC 72-89951. 1973. 5.95 (ISBN 0-385-00425-7). Doubleday.

Outer Reaches: Favorite Science-Fiction Tales. Ed. by August William Derleth. LC 51-13540. 1951. Pellegrini & Cudahy.

Outer Ring. Audrey Erskine Lindop. LC 55-5439. 1955. Appleton-Century-Crofts.

Outerworld, No. 3. Isidore Haiblum. 1979. pap. 1.95 (ISBN 0-440-10526-9). Dell.

Outfit. Richard Stark. 1981. lib. bdg. 10.95 (ISBN 0-8398-2710-5, Gregg). G K Hall.

Outfit. Donald E Westlake. LC 80-26554. (Gregg Press Mystery Fiction Series). 1981. 10.95 (ISBN 0-8398-2498-X). Gregg Press.

Outfit: A Cowboy's Primer. J. P. S Brown. LC 71-144384. 1971. 6.95. Dial Press.

Outing with the Queen of Hearts. Albion Winegar Tourgee. LC 8-29843. 1894. Merrill & Baker.

Outland. Mary Hunter Austin. LC 19-198412. 1919. Boni and Liveright.

Outland. Mary Hunter Austin. LC 21-4127. 1920. Boni and Liveright.

Outland. Alan Dean Foster. (Orig.). 1981. pap. 2.75 (ISBN 0-446-95829-8). Warner Bks.

Outlander. Germaine Guevremont. LC 50-6105. 1950. Whittlesey House.

Outlander. Myron David Orr. LC 60-286613. T. Bouregy.

Outlander. Jane Rule. LC 80-84221. (Illus.). 1981. 6.95 (ISBN 0-930044-17-7). Naiad Press.

Outlanders. Dean Anderson. LC 49-7052. 1948. Dorrance.

Outlanders. Blaine Stevens, pseud. (Orig.). 1979. pap. 2.50 (ISBN 0-515-04861-5). Jove Pubns.

Outlaw. Max Brand. LC 33-31149. 1933. Dodd, Mead & Company.

Outlaw. Frederick Faust. LC 33-31149. 1933. Dodd, Mead & Company.

Outlaw. Jackson Gregory. LC 16-474867. 1916. 1.25. Dodd, Mead and Company.

Outlaw. Jackson Gregory. LC 24-25006. 1918. A. L. Burt Company.

Outlaw. Jackson Gregory. LC 24-222216. 1922. A. L. Burt Company.

Outlaw. Frank Gruber. LC 41-14663. Farar & Rinehart, Incorporated.

Outlaw. Ernest Haycox. LC 53-7318. 1953. Little, Brown.

Outlaw. David Hennessey. LC 13-14824. 1913. Hodder and Stoughton.

Outlaw. David Hennessey. LC 13-16340. 1.25. Hodder & Stoughton, George H. Doran Company.

Outlaw. Maurice Henry Hewlett & Gisla Saga Sorssomar. LC 20-43. 1920. 1.75. Dodd, Mead and Company.

Outlaw and Lawmaker: A Novel. Rosa Caroline Murray-Prior Praed. (On cover: Appletons' town and country library, no. 146). 1894. D. Appleton and Company.

Outlaw Blood. Eli Colter. LC 32-4758. A. H. King.

Outlaw Blood. Jake Logan. LC 77-79430. 1977. 1.25. Playboy Press.

Outlaw Brand. William J Craig. LC 40-315193. 1940. Gateway Books.

Outlaw Breed. Frederick Faust. LC 76-24865. 1976. 9.95 (ISBN 0-89340-035-1). J. Curley.

Outlaw Breed. Frederick Faust. 1974. (pbk.) 0.95. Warner.

Outlaw Breed. Lee Floren. Orig. Title: Wild Border Guns. 1977. pap. 1.25 o.s.i. (ISBN 0-8439-0481-X, Leisure Bks). Nordon Pubns.

Outlaw Breed. Oliver Strange. LC 34-23472. 1934. Doubleday, Doran & Company, Inc.

Outlaw Bunch. Lee Floren. (O.s.i.). 1977. pap. 1.25 o.s.i. (BT51135). Belmont-Tower.

Outlaw Canyon. Lewis B Patten. (Berkley medallion book). (Berkley large type western). 1975. (pbk.) 0.95 (ISBN 0-425-02899-2). Berkley Pub. Co.

Outlaw Canyon. Lewis B Patten. (Signet Brand Western, T5798). 1974. (pbk.) 0.75. New American Library.

Outlaw Country. Amos Moore. LC 34-834534. I. Washburn, Inc.

Outlaw Deputy. Peter Field. LC 63-19418. (His A Powder Valley western). 1963. Jefferson House.

Outlaw Doc. David King. (Orig.). 1969. pap. 0.60 o.p. (63-241). Paperback Lib.

Outlaw Express: A Powder Valley Western. Peter Field. 1973. (pbk.) 0.95 (ISBN 0-671-75773-3). Pocket Books.

Outlaw Fury. Burt Arthur, pseud. 1976. pap. 0.95 o.p. (LB385NK, Leisure Bks). Nordon Pubns.

Outlaw Fury. Burt Arthur, pseud. (Western Ser). 1968. pap. 0.50 o.p. (62-032). Paperback Lib.

Outlaw Fury. Burt Arthur. 1976. 0.95 (ISBN 0-8439-0038-5). Leisure Books.

Outlaw Games. Vicki Linder. 304p. 1982. 15.95 (ISBN 0-385-27417-3). Dial.

Outlaw Games. Vicki Lindner. LC 81-17459. 15.95 (ISBN 0-385-27417-3). Dial Press.

Outlaw Guns, a Western Novel. Eugene E. Halleran. LC 47-11463. 1947. Macrae-Smith-Co.

Outlaw Heart. Rosetta Stowe. 1978. pap. 2.25 (ISBN 0-440-08711-2). Dell.

Outlaw Herd. Peter Field. (Powder Valley Western). 1976. (pbk.) 1.25 (ISBN 0-671-80287-9). Pocket Books.

Outlaw in the Saddle. Tom Roan. LC 54-6710. (Silver star westerns). Dodd, Mead.

Outlaw Island. Alec Rowley Hilliard. LC 42-22270. 1942. Farrar & Rinehart, Inc.

Outlaw Josey Wales. Forrest Carter. 1976. 1.50. Dell Publishing Co.

Outlaw Justice. Leigh Carder. LC 35-665883. Covici, Friede.

Outlaw Justice: By Ford Pendleton Pseud. Gifford Paul Cheshire. LC 54-40762. (Graphic western, 88). 1954. Graphic Pub. Co.

Outlaw Loot. Paul Evan Lehman. Orig. Title: Redrock Gold. 1969. pap. 0.50 o.p. (50-492). Manor Bks.

Outlaw Marshall-Wolf Lawman. Ray Hogan. 1982. pap. 2.75 (ISBN 0-451-11744-1, AE1744, Sig). NAL.

Outlaw Moon. Bertha Muzzy Sinclair. LC 52-9999. 1952. Bouregy & Curl.

Outlaw of Antler. Frank Chester Robertson. LC 37-157812. 1937. E. P. Dutton & Co., Inc.

Outlaw of Buffalo Flat. Max Brand. 1974. 4.95 o.p. (ISBN 0-396-06886-3). Dodd.

Outlaw of Buffalo Flat. Max Brand. (Adult Ser.). 1975. lib. bdg. 8.95 o.p. (ISBN 0-8161-6282-4, Large Print Bks). G K Hall.

Outlaw of Buffalo Flat. Frederick Faust. LC 73-15032. (Silver star westerns). 1974. 4.95 (ISBN 0-396-06886-3). Dodd, Mead.

Outlaw of Buffalo Flat. Frederick Faust. LC 75-8637. 1975. 8.95 (ISBN 0-8161-6282-4). G. K. Hall.

Outlaw of Buffalo Flat. Frederick Faust. (Kangaroo Book). 1977. 1.25 (ISBN 0-671-80927-X). Pocket Books.

Outlaw of Camargue. Alexandre De Lamothe. Tr. by Sadlier, Anna Theresa. LC 7-14092. 1896. Benziger Brothers.

Outlaw of Castle Canyon: A Powder Valley Western. Peter Field. LC 55-591698. 1955. Jefferson House.

Outlaw of Eagle's Nest. Peter Field. LC 52-9695. (Triple-A western classic). 1952. Jefferson House.

Outlaw of Eagle's Nest. Peter Field. LC 38-281445. 1938. W. Morrow & Co.

Outlaw of Hidden Valley. William L. Hopson. LC 49-22040. 1949. Phoenix Press.

Outlaw of Longbow. Peter Dawson. 160p. 1981. pap. 1.95 (ISBN 0-553-14997-0). Bantam.

Outlaw of the Red Hills. Lawrence A. Keating. 1969. pap. 0.60 o.p. (0502-06058-060). Curtis.

Outlaw of Torn. Edgar Rice Burroughs. LC 27-3691. 1927. A. C. McClurg & Co.

Outlaw on Horseback. Harry Sinclair Drago. LC 46-6301. 1946. Doubleday & Company, Inc.

Outlaw Posse. Thomas Ernest Mount. LC 36-4199. 1936. W. Morrow & Co.

Outlaw Ranch. Frank Chester Robertson. LC 34-29909. 1934. I. Washburn.

Outlaw Range. Steven Webb. E. J. Clode, Inc.

Outlaw River. Harry Sinclair Drago. LC 45-4853. 1945. Dodd, Mead & Company.

Outlaw River: A Novel of the Frontier West by Dan Temple Pseud. Dwight Bennett Newton. LC 55-328363. (Popular Library eagle book, EB 37). 1955. Popular Library.

Outlaw Sheriff. William Fitzgerald Jenkins. LC 34-10747. A. H. King.

Outlaw Spy. Ford Bowne, pseud. Ed. by Alice Sachs. 1970. 3.95 o.p. Lenox Hill.

Outlaw Thickets. Les Savage. LC 52-10049. (Double D western). 1952. Doubleday.

Outlaw Town. Owen G. Irons. (YA) 1979. 6.95 (Avalon). Bouregy.

Outlaw Trail. Brian Fox. (O.s.i.). (Orig.). pap. 0.75 o.s.i. (AS1006, Award). Univ Pub & Dist.

Outlaw Trail. Eugene E Halleran. LC 49-11522. 1949. Macrae Smith Co.

Outlaw Trail. (Alias Smith & Jones Ser.). (Orig.). 1972. pap. 0.75 o.p. (AS1006, Award). Univ Pub & Dist.

Outlaw Trail. Robert Redford. LC 77-87795. (Illus.). 225p. 1981. 25.00 (ISBN 0-448-14590-1, G&D); pap. 14.95 (ISBN 0-448-12024-0). Putnam Pub Group.

Outlaw Trail. Oscar Schisgall. LC 36-1545. G. H. Watt, Inc.

Outlaw Trail. Ben Thompson. 1978. 1.50 (ISBN 0-8439-0554-9). Leisure Books.

Outlaw Trial. Jackson Cole, pseud. LC 36-1545. G. H. Watt, Inc.

Outlaw Valley. Max Brand. 352p. 1981. pap. 2.25 (ISBN 0-441-64537-2). Ace Bks.

Outlaw Valley. Max Brand. LC 52-11682. 1969. pap. 0.60 o.p. (63-205). Paperback Lib.

Outlaw Valley. Evan Evans, pseud. 253p. 1976. Repr. of 1953 ed. lib. bdg. 14.40x (ISBN 0-89190-205-8). Am Repr-Rivercity Pr.

Outlaw Valley. Frederick Faust. LC 76-6899. 1976. (ISBN 0-89190-205-8). American Reprint Co.

Outlaw Valley: By Evan Evans Pseud. 1st Ed. Frederick Faust. LC 52-11682. 1953. Harper.

Outlaw Vengeance. James D. Sayers. 1973. pap. 0.75 o.s.i. (74-802). Lancer.

Outlawed. Oliver Strange. LC 36-9939. 1936. Lothrop, Lee & Shepard Company.

Outlawed Banner. 1st Ed. Garland Roark. LC 56-596491. 1956. Doubleday.

Outlawed for Love. Hamon. LC 20-856. 1929. The London Publishing Company.

Outlaws. Gary Cartwright. 1976. cancelled o.p. (ISBN 0-06-810719-6). Atheneum.

Outlaws. Dean Owen. (O.s.i.). 160p. (Orig.). 1973. pap. 1.25 o.s.i. (AQ1616, Award). Univ Pub & Dist.

Outlaw's Code. Max Brand. 1970. pap. 0.60 o.p. (63-278). Paperback Lib.

Outlaws Code. Evan Evans, pseud. 210p. 1976. Repr. of 1954 ed. lib. bdg. 12.95x (ISBN 0-89190-206-6). Am Repr-Rivercity Pr.

Outlaw's Code. Frederick Faust. LC 75-40130. 1975. 9.95 (ISBN 0-89190-206-6). American Reprint Co.

Outlaw's Code: By Evan Evans Pseud. 1st Ed. Frederick Faust. LC 53-11835. 1953. Harper.

Outlaws' Gold. Mick Clumpner. 224p. (Orig.). 1981. pap. 1.95 (ISBN 0-89083-712-0). Zebra.

Outlaw's Gold. Frederick Faust. 1976. 1.25 (ISBN 0-446-76302-0). Warner Books.

Outlaw's Gold. Dan Roberts. LC 65-8162. 1965. Arcadia House.

Outlaw's Gold. William Edward Daniel Ross. LC 65-8162. 1965. Arcadia House.

Outlaw's Gold see Tenderfoot.

Outlaws of Boardman's Flat. Llewellyn Perry Holmes. LC 41-135003. Phoenix Press.

Outlaws of Caja Basin. Jackson Cole, pseud. LC 35-3038. G. H. Watt.

Outlaws of Caja Basin. Oscar Schisgall. LC 35-3038. G. H. Watt.

Outlaws of Eden. Peter Bernard Kyne. LC 30-243512. 1930. Cosmopolitan Book Corporation.

Outlaws of Flower-Pot Canyon. Frank Chester Robertson. LC 27-73337. (On cover: A pocket copyright, no. 74). 1926. Garden City Publishing Co., Inc.

Outlaws of Halfaday Creek. James Beardsley Hendryx. LC 35-519882. 1935. Doubleday, Doran & Company, Inc.

Outlaws of Halfaday Creek. James Beardsley Hendryx. LC 44-21951. 1944. Triangle Books.

Outlaws of Lost River. Paul Evan. (Avalon westerns). 1974. 4.50. Avalon Books.

Outlaws of Lost River. Paul Evans. 256p. (YA) 1974. 6.95 (Avalon). Bouregy.

Outlaws of Lost River: By Paul Evan Pseud. Paul Evan Lehman. LC 54-8027. 1954. Avalon Books.

Outlaws of No Man's Land, The Empire of Greer & Other Stories. Louis Maynard. 1976. 2.95 (Barker-Maynard). L Maynard.

Outlaws of Red Canyon. Charles Horace Snow. LC 40-6708. 1940. Macrae-Smith-Company.

Outlaws of Sugar Loaf. Charles Horace Snow. LC 42-21299. 1942. Macrae-Smith-Company.

Outlaws of the Marches. Ernest William Hamilton. LC 7-952. 1897. Dodd, Mead and Company.

Outlaws of the Marsh. Nai-An Shih & Kuan-Chung Lo. LC 80-8665. (Illus.). 37.50 (ISBN 0-253-12574-X). Foreign Languages Press.

Outlaw's Pledge. Ray Hogan. (Orig.). 1981. pap. 1.95 (ISBN 0-451-09778-5, J9778, Sig). NAL.

Outlaws Three. large print ed. Max Brand. 1981. 18.00x o.p. (ISBN 0-89340-072-6, Pub. by Curley Assoc England). State Mutual Bk.

Outlaws Three. Peter Field. LC 34-14549. 1933. W. Morrow & Company.

Outlaws Three. Peter Field. 1974. (pbk.) 0.75 (ISBN 0-671-75813-6). Pocket Books.

Outlaws. Tr. by Raleigh Trevelyan. 1st Ed. Luigi Meneghello. LC 67-11971. 1967. 5.75. Harcourt.

Outlaws' Trap. Tex Holt, pseud. LC 43-13941. 1943. Arcadia House.

Outlaws' Trap. Claude Rister. LC 43-13941. 1943. Arcadia House, Inc.

Outlet. Andy Adams. LC 73-104401. (Illus.). 1970. (ISBN 0-8398-0050-9). Literature House.

Outlet. Andy Adams. LC 5-8678. 1905. Houghton, Mifflin and Company.

Outline of Heaven. Charles Abraham Spickler. LC 33-30835. Horus & Co.

Outlines: A Collection of Brief Imaginative Studies Related to Many Phases of Thought and Feeling, and Representing an Effort to Give an Interpretation to Familiar Human Experiences. John D Barry. LC 14-503. 1.50. P. Elder and Company.

Outlines in Local Color. Brander Matthews. LC 76-98584. (Short story index reprint series). (Illus.). 1969. (ISBN 0-8369-3158-0). Books for Libraries Press.

Outlines in Local Color. Brander Matthews. LC 7-24699. 1898. Harper & Brothers.

Outlyer. James Harrison. (O.S.I.). pap. 2.45 o.s.i. (ISBN 0-671-20853-5, Touchstone-Clarion). S&S.

Outnumbered. Catherine Hutter. LC 44-40048. 1944. Dodd, Mead & Company.

Outpost. Jane Goodwin Austin. LC 6-4496. 1867. J. E. Tilton and Company.

Outpost. Marie Balka. LC 70-180049. 1973. 6.00. Delacorte Press.

Outpost Mars: A Science-Fiction Novel. Cyril Judd. LC 52-10246. 1952. Abelard Press.

Outpost of Arden. Desemea Wilson. LC 30-22753. E. P. Dutton & Co., Inc.

Outpost of Eternity. Cosmo Hamilton. LC 12-23758. 1912. 1.25. D. Appleton and Company.

Outpost of Jupiter. Lester Del Rey. 1982. pap. 1.95 (Del Rey). Ballantine.

Outpost Trail. Archie Joscelyn. LC 48-2105. (Silver star westerns). 1948. Dodd, Mead.

Outposter. Gordon R. Dickenson. 224p. (Orig.). 1976. pap. 1.25 o.p. (ISBN 0-532-12392-1). Woodhill.

Outposter. Gordon R. Dickenson. 224p. (Orig.). 1976. pap. 1.25 o.p. (ISBN 0-532-12392-1). Manor Bks.

Outposter. Gordon R Dickson. 1973. (pbk) 0.95. Manor Books.

Outposter. Gordon R Dickson. LC 75-38324. 1972. (ISBN 0-397-00764-7). Lippincott.

Outposts of Vengeance. Eugene E. Halleran. LC 45-50902. 1945. Macrae-Smith-Company.

Outrage. Annie Vivanti Chartres. LC 18-729499. 1918. A. A. Knopf.

Outrage, a Novel. Henry Denker. LC 81-22551. 1982. 15.00 (ISBN 0-688-01113-6). Morrow.

Outrage in Annapolis. Edward I. Campbell. LC 80-80608. 130p. (Orig.). 1980. pap. 4.95 (ISBN 0-936460-00-8). Camward Hse.

Outraged Orphan. Sherman. pap. 1.95 o.p. (ISBN 0-87977-120-8). Dansk Blue Bk.

Outrageous Fortune. Mary Emblod. 1981. pap. 2.25 (ISBN 0-380-78493-9, 78493, Flare). Avon.

Outrageous Fortune. Claudia Slack. (Signet Book). 1.50 (ISBN 0-451-07894-2). C.

Outrageous Fortune. Patricia Wentworth. LC 33-4543. J. B. Lippincott Company.

Outrageous Fortune see Web of Enchantment.

Outrageous Fortune: A Novel. Edgar Fawcett. LC 6-38784. 1894. C. T. Dillingham & Co.

Outrageous Lady. Barbara Cartland. LC 77-670158. 1977. 6.95 (ISBN 0-87272-072-1). Duron Books.

Outreach: Extending Community Service in Urban Areas. J. J. Bannon. (Illus.). 288p. 1973. 16.25x (ISBN 0-398-02887-7). C C Thomas.

Outrider. Luke Short. LC 73-1150. 1973. 7.95 (ISBN 0-8161-6087-2). G. K. Hall.

Outrun the Constable. Selwyn Jepson. LC 47-12511. 1948. Doubleday.

Outrun the Dark. Cecilia Bartholomew. LC 77-8975. 8.95. Putnam.

Outrun the Dark. Cecilia Bartholomew. (Jove/HBJ Book). 1979. 2.25 (ISBN 0-515-04648-5). Jove Publications.

Outside Eden. Isabel Scott Rorick & Alajalov, Constantin, 1900- Illus. LC 45-101197. 1945. Houghton Mifflin Company.

Outside Eden. John Collings Squire. LC 74-150562. (Short story index reprint series). 1971. (ISBN 0-8369-3860-7). Books for Libraries Press.

Outside Gun. Ray Hogan. 1976. 1.25. Ace.

Outside In. Michael Z. Lewin. 1981. pap. 2.25 (ISBN 0-425-05006-8). Berkley Pub.

Outside in: A Novel. Michael Z Lewin. LC 79-3618. 1980. 8.95 (ISBN 0-394-50006-7). Knopf: Distributed by Random House.

Outside Inn. Ethel May Kelley. LC 20-751946. The Bobbs-Merrill Company.

Outside Man. Richard North Patterson. 216p. 1982. pap. 2.50 (ISBN 0-345-30020-3). Ballantine.

Outside Man: A Novel. Richard North Patterson. LC 80-26123. 11.95 (ISBN 0-316-69362-6). Little, Brown.

Outside Paradise. Louise Rosalie Preysz. LC 40-7919. 1940. Meador Publishing Company.

Outside the Ark. Adelaide Holt. LC 14-1912. 1913. John Lane.

Outside the Law. James Barnes. LC 5-36925. 1906. D. Appleton and Company.

Outside the Law. William Dale. LC 38-35743. The Dodge Publishing Company.

Outside the Radius. William Pett Ridge. LC 690. 1900. Dodd, Mead & Company.

Outside the Walls. Vassilis Vassilikos. LC 72-88795. 1973. 6.95 o.p. (ISBN 0-15-170515-1). HarBraceJ.

Outside There, Somewhere see Gentlemen Prefer Slaves.

Outside There, Somewhere! A Novel. Lucille Kallen. LC 64-19994. 1964. Macmillan.

Outsider. Irene Cleaton. LC 44-1297. 1944. Little, Brown and Company.

Outsider. Giles A. Lutz. 1973. pap. 0.75 o.p. (T2698, GM). Fawcett World.

Outsider. Sheila Scobie Macdonald. LC 33-273980. 1933. Coward-McCann, Inc.

Outsider. Ernesto R Sabato. LC 50-70731. 1950. Knopf.

Outsider. Maurice Samuel. LC 21-19127. 1921. Duffield and Company.

Outsider. Hawley Smart. 1887. G. Munro.

Outsider. Joan Sutherland & Brandon, Dorothy. LC 24-111377. Brentano's.

Outsider. Colin Wilson. LC 81-16702. 1982. 7.95 (ISBN 0-87477-206-0). J.P. Tarcher.

Outsider. Richard Wright. LC 53-5383. 1953. Harper.

Outsider. Richard Wright. LC 72-86655. 1969. 7.50. Harper & Row.

Outsider: A Novel. Maurice Samuel. LC 29-10742. The Stratford Company.

Outsider in Amsterdam. Janwillem Van De Wetering. (Adult Ser.). 1976. lib. bdg. 11.95 o.p. (ISBN 0-8161-6342-1, Large Print Bks). G K Hall.

Outsider in Amsterdam. Janwillem Van de Wetering. LC 75-12579. 256p. 1975. 6.95 (ISBN 0-395-20705-3). HM.

Outsider in Amsterdam. Janwillen Van De Wetering. 1981. pap. 2.50 (ISBN 0-671-43471-3). PB.

Outsider in Amsterdam. Janwillem Van De Wetering. LC 75-12579. 1975. 6.95 (ISBN 0-395-20705-3). Houghton Mifflin.

Outsider in Amsterdam. Janwillem Van De Wetering. LC 75-43628. 1976. 11.95 (ISBN 0-8161-6342-1). G. K. Hall.

Outsider in Amsterdam. Janwillem Van De Wetering. (Kangaroo Book). 1978. 1.95 (ISBN 0-671-81338-2). Pocket Books.

Outsiders. Robert Carson. LC 66-10980. 1966. Little, Brown.

Outsiders. A. E. Martin. 1967. Fawcett.

Outsiders. A. E Martin. LC 45-2947. 1945. Simon and Schuster.

Outsiders: A Novel. Jane Ludlow Drake Abbott. LC 48-6981. 1948. J. B. Lippincott Co.

Outsiders: A Novel. Josephine Bentham. LC 29-11750. Rae D. Henkle Co., Inc.

Outsiders: An Outline. Robert William Chambers. LC 99-2645. F. A. Stokes Company.

Outsiders: An Outline. 2d ed. Robert William Chambers. LC 16-7542. Frederick A. Stokes Company.

Outsiders Inside Vermont: Travelers' Tales of 358 Years. Ed. by T. D. Bassett. LC 67-27301. (Illus.). 1967. 4.95 o.p. (ISBN 0-8289-0067-1). Greene.

Outskirt Episodes... W. G Tittsworth. Success Composition and Printing Co.

Outward Bound. Sutton Vane. LC 30-8781. 1930. Minton, Balch & Company.

Outward Bound from Liverpool. Edouard Peisson. Tr. by Benstead, Charles Richard. LC 35-525. 1935. Frederick A. Stokes Company.

Outward Bound: Or, A Merchant's Adventures. LC 7-7149. 1838. E. L. Carey and A. Hart.

Outward Room. Millen Brand. LC 37-7079. 1937. Simon and Schuster.

Outward Side. James Colton, pseud. pap. 1.95 o.s.i. (TC-506, Travellers Comp). Olympia.

Outwards from Earth. Ed. by Edmund Crispin. (Orig.). Date not set. pap. cancelled o.p. (ISBN 0-571-10489-4). Faber & Faber.

Outwitted at Last. A Novel. S. A Gardner. LC 7-296. 1878. G. W. Carleton & Co.; Etc., Etc.

Outworlder. Lin Carter. 1971. pap. 0.75 o.p. (ISBN 0-447-74722-3). Lancer.

Ova Hamlet Papers. Richard A. Lupoff. (Illus., Orig.). 1979. pap. 5.95 (ISBN 0-930800-11-7). Pennyfarthing.

Oval Lady. Leonora Carrington. Tr. by Rochelle Holt. (Illus.). 1975. pap. 3.75 o.p. (ISBN 0-88496-037-4). Capra Pr.

Oval Lady: Six Surreal Stories. Leonora Carrington. LC 75-19275. 1975. 12.50. (ISBN 0-88496-036-6) (ISBN 0-88496-037-4). Capra Press.

Over Against Green Peak. Zephine Humphrey. LC 8-12764. 1908. H. Holt and Company.

Over and Above. Laura Keane Zametkin Hobson. LC 78-22615. 1979. 8.95 (ISBN 0-385-12912-2). Doubleday.

Over and Out: A Novel. Norman Rosten. LC 72-80735. 1972. 5.95 (ISBN 0-8076-0661-8). G. Braziller.

Over-at-the-Crowleys'. Kathleen Thompson Norris. LC 46-6669. 1946. Doubleday & Company, Inc.

Over Bemerton's: An Easy-Going Chronicle. Edward Verrall Lucas. LC 8-28632. 1908. The Macmillan Company.

Over by the River, and Other Stories. William Maxwell. LC 76-30608. 1977. 8.95 (ISBN 0-394-41384-9). Knopf: Distributed by Random House.

Over Fool's Hill. Mildred I Reid. LC 64-18780. 1964. Bruce Humphries.

Over Grass-Grown Trails. Harry Graves Shedd. LC 5139. 1900. The Kiote Publishing Co.

Over Her Dear Body. Richard S. Prather. (Shell Scott Series). (Orig.). 1968. pap. 0.75 o.p. (T2460, GM). Fawcett World.

Over Here; the Story of a War Bride. Ethel May Kelley. LC 18-7295. 1.50. The Bobbs-Merrill Company.

Over in the Dry Side. Louis L'Amour. 1976. (pbk.) 1.25 (ISBN 0-553-02452-3). Bantam Books.

Over Life's Edge. Vivian Cory. LC 21-16796. Brentano's.

Over Life's Edge. Vivian Cory. LC 22-105473. 1.75. The Macaulay Company.

Over My Dead Body. Rex Stout. LC 82-919. 1982. 13.95 (ISBN 0-8161-3288-7). G.K. Hall.

Over My Dead Body: A Nero Wolfe Mystery. Rex Stout. LC 40-2200. Farrar & Rinehart, Inc.

Over My Dead Body: "a Nero Wolfe Mystery"... Rex Stout. LC 45-16237. (New Avon library. 62). 1945.

Over My Shoulder see Gift from a Stranger.

Over My Shoulder: A Collection of Short Stories. Thomas Spelios. 1982. 8.95 (ISBN 0-533-04976-8). Vantage.

Over-Night: Translated from the German by Guy Endore. Joe Lederer & Endore, S. Guy, 1901- Tr. LC 31-30503. Farrar & Rinehart, Incorporated.

Over on the Dry Side. Louis L'Amour. LC 75-12890. 1975. 6.95 (ISBN 0-8415-0389-3). Saturday Review Press.

Over on the Dry Side. Louis L'Amour. LC 76-42984. 1976. 9.95 (ISBN 0-8161-6410-X). G.K. Hall.

Over Paradise Ridge: A Romance. Maria Thompson Daviess. LC 15-21791. 1915. Harper & Brothers.

Over Seventy. Abigail Wells Cowley. LC 44-9401. 1944. Meador Publishing Company.

Over the Boat-Side. Mathilde Eiker. LC 27-224903. 1927. Doubleday, Page & Company.

Over the Border: A Novel. Herman Whitaker. LC 17-138172. 1917. Harper & Brothers.

Over the Border: A Romance. Robert Barr. LC 3-25727. 1903. F. A. Stokes Company.

Over the Brazier. Robert Graves. 1916. 4.00 o.s.i. Ridgeway Bks.

Over the Counter; a Year in the Village Shop. Sheila Turner. LC 63-18423. 1963. Holt, Rinehart and Winston.

Over the Edge. Arkham House, Sauk City, Wis. Ed. by August William Derleth. LC 64-4189. 1964.

Over the Edge. Michael Butterworth. LC 79-7042. 1979. 7.95 (ISBN 0-385-15289-2). Published for the Crime Club by Doubleday.

Over the Edge. August William Derleth & Arkham House, Sauk City, Wis. LC 77-364507. 1976. 0.60 (ISBN 0-09-912010-0). Arrow Books.

Over the Edge. Harlan Ellison. 1970. pap. 0.75 o.p. (B75-1091). Belmont-Tower.

Over the Edge. Harlan Ellison. 1976. pap. 1.75 o.p. (ISBN 0-515-04050-9). BJ Pub Group.

Over the Edge. Charlie Haas & Tim Hunter. LC 79-51728. (Illus.). 1979. pap. 1.95 o.p. (ISBN 0-394-17088-1, B426, BC). Grove.

Over the Edge. Sarah Kemp. LC 79-7042. (Crime Club Ser.). 1979. 9.95 o.p. (ISBN 0-385-15289-2). Doubleday.

Over the Edge. Lawrence Treat. LC 54-31823. (Ace double novel books, D-51). 1954. Ace Books.

Over the Edge. Lawrence Treat. LC 48-3776. 1948. W. Morrow.

Over the Edge. David Westheimer. LC 72-4413. 1972. 6.95 (ISBN 0-316-93152-7). Little, Brown.

Over the Edge of the World. Clara J Snow. LC 54-12632. 1955. Vantage Press.

Over the Fence. Anges Mary Biddle Dell. LC 48-1585. 1946. Wartburg Press.

Over the Fence. Rosanne K. Pierce. 1973. 4.95 o.p. (ISBN 0-89002-011-6); pap. 2.00 o.p. (ISBN 0-89002-010-8). Northwoods Pr.

Over the Fence. Rick Sterry. LC 68-18779. 1968. Houghton Mifflin.

Over the Frontier. Stevie Smith. 288p. 1982. pap. 3.50 (ISBN 0-523-41685-7). Pinnacle Bks.

Over the Frontier Trail. Archie Joscelyn. LC 45-7780. 1945. Phoenix Press.

Over the Garden Wall. Edith Caroline Rivett. LC 49-4808. 1949. Pub. for the Crime Club by Doubleday.

Over the Gate. Miss Read. 1965. 4.00 o.p. (ISBN 0-395-08117-3). HM.

Over the Gate: By Miss Read Pseud. Illus. by J. S. Goodall 1st Amer. Ed. Dora Jessie Saint. LC 65-15154. 1965. bds., 4.00. Houghton.

Over the High Side. Nicolas Freeling. LC 76-356842. 1975. 0.60 (ISBN 0-14-003599-0). Penguin.

Over the Hills. Jeffery Farnol. LC 30-307733. 1930. Little, Brown, and Company.

Over the Hills. Mary Findlater. 1897. Dodd, Mead and Company.

Over the Hills and Far Away. Edward John Moreton Drax Plunkett Dunsany. (Original adult fantasy). 1974. (pbk.) 1.25 (ISBN 0-345-23886-9). Ballantine Books.

Over the Hills and Far Away. Lavinia Russ. 1968. Harcourt, Brace & World.

Over the Hills and Far Away" An Old Story. Guy Fleming, pseud. 1917. Longmans, Green and Co.

Over the Hookah: The Tales of a Talkative Doctor. George Frank Lydston. LC 9-2487. 1896. F. Klein Company.

Over the Horizon. S. W. Greig. 1964. 5.95 o.p. (ISBN 0-312-59255-8). St Martin.

Over the Line. Alec Coppel. LC 47-12359. 1947. Pub. for the Crime Club by Doubleday.

Over the Mountain. Pamela Frankau. (Frankau, Pamela, 1908-. Clothes of a King's Son: Vol. 3). 1967. 5.95. Random.

Over the Mountain. Ruthven Todd. LC 39-6475. 1939. A. A. Knopf.

Over the Mountain. Ruthven Todd. LC 77-84270. (Lost Race and Adult Fantasy Fiction). 1978. 18.00 (ISBN 0-405-11010-3). Arno Press.

Over the Old Trail: A Novel. Lewis B France. 1895. Arena Publishing Company.

Over the Pass. Frederick Palmer. LC 12-99572. 1912. 1.35. C. Scribner's Sons.

Over the Plum-Pudding. John Kendrick Bangs. LC 70-86136. (Short story index reprint series). (Illus.). 1969. Books for Libraries Press.

Over the Plum-Pudding. John Kendrick Bangs. LC 1-24654. (On cover: Harper's portrait collection of short stories. v. 6). 1901. Harper & Brothers.

Over the Quicksand. Anna Chapin Ray. 1910. 1.50. Little, Brown, and Company.

Over the River Charlie: A Novel. 1st Ed. Lew X Lansworth. LC 56-5587. 1956. Doubleday.

Over the Sea to Death. Gwen Moffat. LC 76-22472. (Illus.). 7.95 (ISBN 0-684-14808-0). Scribner.

Over the Wall. Ed. by Frank Andrews & Al Dickens. (Orig.). 1974. pap. 1.50 o.p. (ISBN 0-515-03513-0). BJ Pub Group.

Over the Wall: By George Irving Pseud. with Conrad Black. George Theodore Waugh. LC 62-21231. (Captain books). 1962. Waugh Pub. Co.

Over There" Chronicles of an English Engineer "Gone West", Dictated to Lura M. Wilkins. Lura M Wilkins. LC 36-2212. Sun Publishing Company.

Over-Time Love. 1944. Phoenix Press.

Over-Time Love. Watkins Eppes Wright. LC 44-6551. 1944. Phoenix Press.

Over to You: Ten Stories of Flyers and Flying. Roald Dahl. LC 74-158082. 1973. 0.25 (ISBN 0-14-003574-5). Penguin.

Over to You: 10 Stories of Flyers and Flying. Roald Dahl. LC 46-894. 1946. Reynal & Hitchcock.

Overboard. Henry Hunt Searls. (Kangaroo Book). 1978. 1.95 (ISBN 0-671-81378-1). Pocket Books.

Overboard. George Frank Worts. LC 43-5528. 1943. H. C. Kinsey & Company, Inc.

Overboard: A Novel. Henry Hunt Searls. LC 76-25519. 8.95. Norton.

Overcoat. Nikolai Vasilevich Gogol. 64p. (Orig.). 1981. pap. 4.50 (ISBN 0-904526-27-5, Pub. by the Journeyman Press, England). Lawrence Hill.

Overcoat. Nikolai Vasilevich Gogol. Tr. by D. Magarshack. 1961. 3.50 o.p. Dufour.

Overcoat see Six Great Modern Short Novels.

Overcoat: And Other Stories. Nikolai Vasilevich Gogol. LC 23-15823. (Added t.-p.: The collected works of Nikolay Gogol, tr. by Constance Garnett). 1923. A. A. Knopf.

Overcoat, and Other Tales of Good and Evil. Nikolai Vasilevich Gogol. LC 79-17318. 1979. 10.00 (ISBN 0-8376-0442-7). R. Bentley.

Overcoat Meeting. George Agnew Chamberlain. LC 49-7955. (Barnes sport novel). 1949. A. S. Barnes.

Overdose of Death. Agatha Miller Christie. 1982. pap. 2.50 (ISBN 0-440-16780-9). Dell.

Overdose of Death. new ed. Dame Agatha Miller Christie. 1975. (pbk.) 1.25. Dell.

Overdraft an Glory: Pseud.1st Ed. Claud Cockburn. LC 55-9155. 1955. Lippincott.

Overdrive. Mike Curtis. (O.s.i.). 1976. pap. 1.50 o.s.i. (BT50968). Belmont-Tower.

Overdrive: A Novel. Michael Francis Gilbert. LC 67-28825. 1967. Harper & Row.

Overdue. Arthur Leonard Bell Thompson. LC 58-5067. 1958. Dutton.

Overdue for Death. Zola Helen Ross. LC 47-12711. 1947. The Bobbs-Merrill Company.

Overhead. Ruby Mildred Ayres. LC 26-7438. George H. Doran Company.

Overheard. Stacy Aumonier. LC 72-3289. (Short Story Index Reprint Ser). 1972. Repr. of 1924 ed. 18.00 (ISBN 0-8369-4142-X). Ayer Co.

Overheard at the Dance. Carol Lynn Pearson. LC 81-67067. 3.95 (ISBN 0-88494-427-1). Bookcraft.

Overheard; Fifteen Tales. Stacy Aumonier. LC 72-3289. (Short story index reprint series). 1972. (ISBN 0-8369-4142-X). Books for Libraries Press.

Overkill. John Benteen. (Sundance Ser.: No. 1). 224p. 1976. pap. 2.25 (ISBN 0-8439-1033-X, Leisure Bks). Nordon Pubns.

Overkill. John Benteen. (Sundance Ser.). (O.s.i.). 1976. pap. 1.25 o.s.i. (LB421ZK, Leisure Bks). Nordon Pubns.

Overkill. John Benteen. 1976. 1.25. Leisure Books.

Overkill. William Garner. LC 66-22217. 3.95. New Amer. Lib.

Overland. John William De Forest. Ed. by Donald Pizer. LC 70-96513. (American Authors Ser). 1970. Repr. of 1871 ed. lib. bdg. 14.25 o.s.i. (ISBN 0-512-00131-6). Garrett Pr.

Overland. A Novel. John William De Forest. LC 6-33387. 1872. Sheldon and Company.

Overland for Gold. Frank Hobart Cheley. LC 20-4892. The Abingdon Press.

Overland Red: A Romance of the Moonstone Canon Trail; with Illustrations by Anton Fischer. Henry Herbert Knibbs. LC 14-504236. 1914. 1.35. Houghton Mifflin Company.

Overland Tales. Josephine McCrakin Clifford. LC 6-20746. 1877. Claxton, Remsen & Haffelfinger.

Overland Tales. Josephine Woempner Clifford McCrackin. LC 6-20746. 1877. Claxton, Remsen & Haffelfinger.

Overload. Arthur Hailey. LC 77-16920. 1979. 10.00 (ISBN 0-385-02104-6). Doubleday.

Overlook Farm: Thrilling Pioneer Stories, the Most Natural, Interesting, Informing Account and Concise Description of the Frontiersmen's Lives and Activities Ever Published... Chauncey F York. LC 16-9780. C. F. York.

Overlook Hospital. Ann Mattews. 1981. pap. 2.95 (ISBN 0-89083-827-5). Zebra.

Overlook House. Will Payne. LC 21-4169. 1921. Dodd, Mead and Company.

Overlooked. Maurice Baring. LC 22-27462. 1929. Houghton Mifflin Company.

Overlord. Susanna Firth. (Harlequin Romances Ser.). 192p. 1982. pap. 1.50 (ISBN 0-373-02493-2). Harlequin Bks.

Overlord. Sue Mildred Lee Johnston. LC 33-7961. 1933. C. Scribner's Sons.

Overlord. Les V Roper. LC 78-66377. (Jove/HBJ Book). 1978. 1.95 (ISBN 0-515-04754-6). Jove Publications.

Overlord: The Story of the Peons of Canada. Allan McIvor. LC 4-28960. 1904. W. Ritchie.

Overlords. William Woolfolk. LC 72-79430. 1972. 6.95 (ISBN 0-385-03988-3). Doubleday.

Overlords. William Woolfolk. (Crest Book, P2008). 1973. (pbk.) 1.25. Fawcett Pubns.

Overlords of War. Gerard Klein. LC 72-84923. 1973. 5.95. Doubleday.

Overlords of War. Gerard Klein. 1974. (pbk.) 0.95. DAW Books.

Overman. Upton Beall Sinclair. LC 7-30837. 1907. Doubleday, Page & Company.

Overman Culture. Edmund Cooper. LC 77-186647. 1972. 5.95. Putnam.

Overnight: A Novel. Matthew Henry Smith. LC 49-118484. 1949. Sheridan House.

Overnight Cabin. Peggy Gaddis, pseud. LC 47-12326. 1947. Phoenix Press.

Overnight Cabins. Peggy Gaddis, pseud. LC 35-2541. W. Godwin, Inc.

Override. Kathryn Anger. LC 79-57122. (Feminist Novels Ser.). 100p. 1976. pap. 4.95 (ISBN 0-935772-03-0). Diotima Bks.

Overseer's Daughter: Or, Love and Life at the Loom. George W Goode. (On cover: New York 10 cent library. no. 9). 1896. Katahdin Publishing Company.

Oversexed. Mona Combs. pap. 1.95 o.p. (8012). Cameo.

Oversexed Teenage Girls. Clark S. Manley. pap. 1.95 o.p. (ISBN 0-87682-257-X). Barclay Hse.

Overshadowed. Sallie Lee Bell. LC 69-19839. 1969. 2.95. Zondervan Pub. House.

Overshadowed. Eugene William Lohrke. LC 29-15289. J. Cape & H. Smith.

Overshadowed: A Novel. Sutton Elbert Griggs. LC 71-144621. 1973. 10.00 (ISBN 0-404-00166-1). AMS Press.

Overshadowed: A Novel. Sutton Elbert Griggs. LC 79-161261. (Black Heritage Library Collection). 1971. (ISBN 0-8369-8820-5). Books for Libraries Press.

Overtaken. Lawrence Rising. LC 27-11033. 1927. Cosmopolitan Book Corporation.

Overture to Death. Ngaio Marsh. LC 39-27602. L. Furman, Inc.

Overture to Death see Ngaio Marsh.

Overture to Passion. James Noble Gifford. LC 40-680233. Phoenix Press.

Ovingdean Grange: A Tale of the South Downs. William Harrison Ainsworth. (Illus.). 1860. 20.00 o.p. R West.

Ovington's Bank. Stanley John Weyman. LC 22-21484. 1922. Longmans, Green and Co.

Owen Glen. Ben Ames Williams. LC 50-13084. 1950. Houghton Mifflin.

Owen Glendower: An Historical Novel... John Cowper Powys. LC 41-51542. Simon and Schuster.

Owen Gwynne's Great Work. Augusta Keppel Noel. LC 18-229. 1875. Macmillan and Co.

Owen Wingrave see Altar of the Dead.

Owen Wister's Medicine Bow. Owen Wister & Tryntje Van Ness Seymour. LC 81-20798. 37.50 (ISBN 0-915998-12-2). Lime Rock Press.

Owl. Herbert Adams. LC 37-197530. J. B. Lippincott Company.

Owl. John Hawkes. LC 77-8227. 1977. 3.95 (ISBN 0-8112-0665-3). New Directions Pub. Corp.

Owl see Goose on the Grave.

Owl: A Thrilling Murder Mystery. Frank King. 1930. G. H. Watt.

Owl & the Nightingale. Intro. by N. R. Ker. (Early English Text Society Ser.). 1963. 10.50x o.p. (ISBN 0-19-722251-X). Oxford U Pr.

Owl & the Nightingale - Cleanness - St. Bernard. Tr. by Brian Stone. (Classics Ser). 1972. pap. 2.95 (ISBN 0-14-044245-6). Penguin.

Owl & the Nightingale: Das Mittelenglische Streigedicht Eule & Nachatigall Nach Beiden Handschriften Neu Herausgegeben. Repr. of 1909 ed. 21.50 (ISBN 0-384-44150-5); pap. 18.50. Johnson Repr.

Owl and the Pussycat. Owen Cameron. LC 49-101540. 1949. Harper.

Owl Hoot Court. Dan T Kelliher. LC 53-112943. 1953. Arcadia House.

Owl Hoot Trail. Bennett Foster. LC 40-6596. 1940. W. Morrow and Company.

Owl Hoots Twice at Catfish Bend. Ben Lucien Burman. (Puffin book). (Illus.). 1974. (ISBN 0-14-030397-9). Penguin Books.

Owl-House. A Posthumous Novel. Eugenie John & Behrens, Bertha. Tr. by Smith, Mary Stuart (Harrison) & Smith, Gesner Harrison. LC 7-9909. (On cover: Seaside library. Pocket ed. no. 1130). G. Munro.

Owl in the Attic: And Other Perplexities. James Thurber. 128p. 1975. pap. 1.25 o.p. (ISBN 0-06-080351-7, P351, PL). Har-Row.

Owl in the Cellar. Margaret Scherf. LC 45-9575. 1945. Pub. for the Crime Club by Doubleday, Doran and Co., Inc.

Owl in the Sun. Leslie Kark. LC 48-8424. 1948. Macmillan Co.

Owl on Every Post. Sanora Babb. 1970. 5.95 o.p. (ISBN 0-8415-0037-1). Sat Rev Pr.

Owl Sacred Pack of the Fox Indians. Truman Michelson. Repr. of 1921 ed. 12.00 o.p. (ISBN 0-403-03677-1). Scholarly.

Owl Sang Three Times. Vera Kelsey. LC 41-59801. 1941. Pub. for the Crime Club by Doubleday, Doran and Company, Inc.

Owl Service. Alan Garner. 192p. 1981. pap. 1.95 (ISBN 0-345-29044-5, Del Rey). Ballantine.

Owl Taxi. Hulbert Footner. LC 21-1679. George H. Doran Company.

Owl Tower: The Story of a Family Feud in Old England. Charles Sleeman Coom. 1906. The C. M. Clark Publishing Co.

Owlhoot Justice. Eugene A. Clancy. 1970. pap. 0.60 o.p. (0502-06119). Curtis.

Owlhoot Trail. Cliff Farrell. LC 72-160868. 1971. 4.95. Doubleday.

Owlhoot Trails. Claude Rister. LC 42-24970. 1942. Gateway Books.

Owls Do Cry. Janet Frame, pseud. LC 79-28167. 211p. 1982. pap. 5.95 (ISBN 0-8076-0956-0). Braziller.

Owls Do Cry. Janet Frame, pseud. 1960. 4.50 o.p. (ISBN 0-8076-0116-0). Braziller.

Owls Don't Blink. A. A. Fair, pseud. LC 42-164543. 1942. W. Morrow and Company.

Owl's Don't Blink. Erle Stanley Gardner. 1974. (pbk.) 0.95. Dell.

Owls Don't Blink. Erle Stanley Gardner. LC 42-16454. 1942. W. Morrow.

Owls Don't Blink. Erle Stanley Gardner. LC 47-3013. 1947. Blakiston Co.

Owls' House. Crosbie Garstin. LC 24-1975. 1924. Frederick A. Stokes Company.

Owl's Nest. Eugenie John & Behrens, Bertha. Tr. by Miller, Hettie E. LC 8-31898. (On cover: Marguerite series. 13). E. A. Weeks and Company.

Owl's Nest. Eugenie John & Bertha Behrens. LC 44-33115. Hurst & Company.

Owls' Nest: A Vacation Among Isms. Anne Gilbert. LC 12-9852. 0.75. Fleming H. Revell Company.

Owls of St. Ursula's: A Story for Girls. Jane Brester Reid. LC 10-7791. 1910. The Baker & Taylor Company.

Owls of the Always Open: A Novel. Richard H Chittenden. 1883. The Author, C. C. Whitney's Steam Print.

Owl's Roost. Helga Sandburg. LC 62-12309. 1962. Dial Press.

Owl's Warning. Herman Landon. LC 32-6526. Liveright, Inc.

Owls' Watch. Ed. by George Brandon Saul. LC 65-23753. (Fawcett Crest book, R886). 1965. Fawcett Publications.

Owlsfane Horror. Duffy Stein. 480p. (Orig.). 1981. pap. 3.50 (ISBN 0-440-16781-7). Dell.

Own Wilderness. Nina Warner Hooke. LC 38-23211. 1938. E. P. Dutton & Co., Inc.

Owner. Frank Deford. LC 76-16797. 1976. 8.95 (ISBN 0-670-53318-1). Viking Press.

Owner Gone Abroad. Ruby Mildred Ayres. LC 37-11439. 1937. Doubleday, Doran & Company, Inc.

Owner Lies Dead. Tyline Perry. LC 30-166040. 1930. Covici-Friede.

Owner of the Lazy D. William Patterson White. LC 19-13366. 1919. Little, Brown, and Company.

Ownley Inn. Joseph Crosby Lincoln & Lincoln, Freeman. Coward-McCann, Inc.

Ox. Piers Anthony, pseud. 1976. pap. 2.95 (ISBN 0-380-00461-5, 82370-5). Avon.

Ox. Jay Brothers. LC 74-17683. 1975. 7.95 (ISBN 0-672-52076-1). Bobbs-Merrill.

Ox & His Herdsman: A Chinese Zen Text. K'Uo-an. (Illus.). 1969. 7.50x o.p. (ISBN 0-8002-1773-X). Intl Pubns Serv.

Ox-Bow Incident. Walter Van Tilburg Clark. (Vintage bk., V146 rebound). 1965. 3.50. P. Smith.

Ox-Bow Incident. Walter Van Tilburg Clark. LC 57-11399. (Modern library paperbacks, P31). 1957. Random House.

Ox-Bow Incident. Walter Van Tilburg Clark. LC 42-332139. Random House.

Ox-Bow Incident. Walter Van Tilburg Clark. LC 42-795126. 1942. The Press of the Readers Club.

Oxbridge Blues. Frederic Raphael. 213p. 13.95 (ISBN 0-224-01871-X, Pub. by Chatto-Bodley-Jonathan). Merrimack Pub Cir.

Oxcart Trail. Herbert Krause. LC 54-6495. (O.s.i.). 1976. Repr. of 1954 ed. 9.95 o.s.i. (ISBN 0-88498-047-2). leatherette 12.95 o.s.i. (ISBN 0-88498-047-2). Brevet Pr.

Oxcart Trail: A Novel. 1st Ed. Herbert Krause. LC 54-6495. 1954. Bobbs-Merrill.

Oxen of the Sun: A Novel of Our Times. Irving Bacheller. LC 35-13902. 1935. Frederick A. Stokes Company.

Oxford Book of Short Stories. Victor Sawdon Pritchett. LC 81-156872. 1981. 19.95 (ISBN 0-19-214116-3). Oxford University Press.

Oxford Chekhov. Anton Chekhov. Ed. & tr. by Ronald Hingley. Incl. Vol. 1. Short Plays. 1968. 32.50x (ISBN 0-19-211349-6); Vol. 2. Platonov, Ivanov, the Seagull. 1967. 32.50x (ISBN 0-19-211347-X); Vol. 5. Stories, 1889-1891. 1970. 27.50x (ISBN 0-19-211353-4); Vol. 6. Stories, 1892-1893. 1971. 32.50x (ISBN 0-19-211363-1); Vol. 8. Stories, 1895-1897. 300p. 1965. 32.50x (ISBN 0-19-211340-2). Oxford U Pr.

Oxford Chekhov, Vol. 4: Stories, 1888-1889. Anton Pavlovich Chekhov. Tr. by Ronald Hingley. 302p. 1980. 39.50x (ISBN 0-19-211389-5). Oxford U Pr.

Oxford Chekhov: Volume Seven Stories 1893-1895. Anton Pavlovich Chekhov. Ed. by Ronald Hingley. (Oxford Chekhov Ser.). 1978. 27.50x (ISBN 0-19-211388-7). Oxford U Pr.

Oxford Gambit. Joseph Hone. 384p. 1981. pap. 2.95 (ISBN 0-449-24436-9, Crest). Fawcett.

Oxford Girls. Barbara Mercer. LC 83-2931. 1983. 11.95 (ISBN 0-312-59366-X). St. Martin's Press.

Oxford Goes to War: A Novel. Henry De Vere Stacpoole. LC 43-17137. 1943. Hutchinson & Co., Ltd.

Oxford Illustrated Jane Austen, 6 vols. 3rd ed. Jane Austen. Ed. by R. W. Chapman. Incl. Sense & Sensibility. 1933. Vol. 1. 16.95x (ISBN 0-19-254701-1); Pride & Prejudice. 1932. Vol. 2. 16.95x (ISBN 0-19-254702-X); Mansfield Park. 1934. Vol. 3. 18.50x (ISBN 0-19-254703-8); Emma. 1933. Vol. 4. 17.95x (ISBN 0-19-254704-6); Northanger Abbey & Persuasion. 1933. Vol. 5. 17.95x (ISBN 0-19-254705-4); Minor Works. (1st ed.). 1954. Vol. 6. 16.95x (ISBN 0-19-254706-2). 16.95. Oxford U Pr.

Oxford Professor Returns. L. Erectus Mentulus. pap. 1.95 o.p. (V1031T, Venus). Grove.

Oxford Short Stories. Ed. by Derek Patmore. 1978. Repr. of 1947 ed. lib. bdg. 17.50 o.s.i. (ISBN 0-89760-700-7, Telegraph). Dynamic Learn Corp.

Oxford Thesis on Love. LC 70-166461. (Venus library). 1971. 1.50. Grove Press.

Oxford Thesis on Love. 1971. pap. 1.50 o.p. (V1028D, Venus). Grove.

Oxley. Reginald Hughes. LC 7-5420. 1873. Scribner, Armstrong & Company.

Oxymoron. Michael Zack. 128p. 1975. 6.95 o.p. (ISBN 0-8059-2184-2). Dorrance.

Ozark Legacy. Amanda Singer. 1975. 4.95. Avalon.

Ozark Nurse. Fern Shepard. 1971. pap. 0.60 o.p. (60-482). Manor Bks.

Ozark Nurse. Florence Stonebraker. LC 65-7327. 1965. Arcadia House.

Ozark Odyssey. 1st Ed. Marion Dickens. LC 55-7176. 1955. Vantage Press.

Ozine Conquest. C. M. Gilbert. 1981. pap. 1.75 (ISBN 0-8439-0891-2, Leisure Bks). Nordon Pubns.

P

P. A. L. A Novel of the American Scene. Felix Riesenberg. LC 25-180632. 1925. R. M. McBride & Company.

P As in Police: 16 Procedural Short Stories. Lawrence Treat. LC 72-99895. (Ellery Queen presents, no. 2). 1970. 1.00. Davis Publications.

P. C. Richardson's First Case: A Tale of Scotland Yard... Basil Home Thomson. LC 33-15239. 1933. Pub. for the Crime Club, Inc., by Doubleday, Doran & Company, Inc.

P. D. F. R. A New Novel. Inez Haynes Irwin. LC 28-21969. 1928. Harper & Brothers.

P. D. Kimerakov. Leslie Epstein. LC 74-34089. 1975. 6.95 (ISBN 0-316-24568-2). Little, Brown.

P. E. N. Short Stories. Ed. by Francisco Arcellana. 1962. wrps. 6.75 o.p. Cellar.

P. J., My Friend. Noel Bertram Gerson. 160p. 1975. pap. 0.95 o.p. (532-95407-95). Manor Bks.

P. Moran, Operative. Percival Wilde. LC 47-1625. 1947. Random House.

P. P. C. Natalie Sumner Lincoln. LC 27-5420. 1927. D. Appleton and Company.

P. S. I Love You. Barbara Conklin. (Teenage Romance Ser.). (Orig.). 1981. pap. 1.95 (ISBN 0-553-20323-1). Bantam.

P. S. What Do You Think of the Market? Messages to Wall Street. new and rev. ed. James L Fraser & A Kustomer. LC 66-29458. 1966. Fraser Pub. Co.

P. S. Wilkinson. Courtlandt Dixon Barnes Bryan. LC 65-11845. 5.95. Harper.

P. S. Wilkinson. Courtlandt Dixon Barnes Bryan. (Crest bk., t891). 1966. Fawcett.

P. S. Your Cat Is Dead. James Kirkwood. 224p. 1973. pap. 3.50 (ISBN 0-446-30705-X). Warner Bks.

P. S. Your Cat Is Dead. James Kirkwood. LC 72-81210. 256p. 1972. 6.95 o.p. (ISBN 0-8128-1511-4). Stein & Day.

P-Town Stories: Or, The Meatrack. R. D. Skillings. 1980. 9.50 (ISBN 0-918222-14-1); pap. 4.50 (ISBN 0-918222-15-X). Apple Wood.

Pa." A History of Comical Adventures. LC 6-30384. (Munro's library. v. 50. no. 733). 1887. N. L. Munro.

Pa: A Novel. Cothburn O'Neal. 1962. Crown Publishers.

Pa and Ma Wilson. Ellsworth Wilson. LC 40-7707. The Book Krafters.

Pa Flickinger's Folks. Bessie Ray Hoover. LC 9-22182. 1909. 1.00. Harper & Brothers.

Pa Gladden: The Story of a Common Man. Elizabeth Cherry Waltz. 1903. The Century Co.

Pa: The Head of the Family. Margaret Eliza Ashmun. LC 27-3686. 1927. The Macmillan Company.

Pablo and the Magi: A Modern Wise Man Finds Ancient Truth on Pablo's Desert. Harold Eldon Dye. LC 67-12168. 1967. Broadman Press.

Pablo De Segovia the Spanish Sharper. Quevedo y Villegas, Francisco Gomez De. Ed. by Watts, Henry Edward. LC 27-10056. (Half-title: Blue jade library). 1926. A. A Knopf.

Pablo, the Bullfighter & Other Stories. Jo Stanchfield. LC 72-92848. (Highway Holidays Ser). 1973. pap. text ed. 3.54 o.p. (ISBN 0-8372-0797-5). Bowmar-Noble.

Pablo's Mountain. Albert Johnston. LC 53-5245. 1953. Crown Publishers.

Pabo: The Priest. Sabine Baring-Gould. LC 99-2916. 1899. Frederick A. Stokes Company.

Pace That Kills. William Hanscom Fuller. (Dell first edition, 105). 1956. Dell Pub. Co.

Pace That Kills; a Chronicle. Edgar Evertson Saltus. LC 79-93535. 1969. AMS Press.

Pacer. Viola Isabel Paradise. LC 17-2536. 1927. E. P. Dutton.

Pacer. Viola Isabel Paradise. LC 27-2536. E. P. Dutton & Company.

Pacha of Many Tales. Frederick Marryat. LC 4-29696. 1834. E. L. Carey & A. Hart.

Pacha of Many Tales. Frederick Marryat. J. B. Smith & Co.

Pacha of Many Tales. Frederick Marryat. LC 7-17574. 1873. D. Appleton and Company.

Pacha of Many Tales. Frederick Marryat. LC 43-40893. (Maryatt's novels. 9). 1840. C. Lane.

Pacha of Many Tales. Frederick Marryat. LC 43-43115. G. Routledge and Sons.

Pachuco. Dennis Rodriguez. 224p. (Orig.). 1980. pap. 1.95 (ISBN 0-87067-651-2, BH651). Holloway.

Pachuco Mark. Rudolph R Melendez. LC 76-28864. 1977. 6.25 (ISBN 0-913182-75-3). Grossmont Press.

Pacific. Robert Carse. LC 32-21188. Farrar & Rinehart, Incorporated.

Pacific. Charles E Mercer. LC 80-22418. 12.95 (ISBN 0-671-25587-8). Simon and Schuster.

Pacific Book of Science Fiction. John Baxter. 1968. pap. 1.60 o.s.i. Tri-Ocean.

Pacific Calvacade. Virginia Coffman. 560p. 1982. pap. 3.50 (ISBN 0-449-20002-7, Crest). Fawcett.

Pacific Cavalcade. Virginia Coffman. LC 80-66502. 1981. 12.95 (ISBN 0-87795-277-9). Arbor Hse.

Pacific Gold. Henry De Vere Stacpoole. LC 31-19687. Sears Publishing Company.

Pacific Hellfire. Jonathan Scofield, pseud. (Freedom Fighters Ser.: No. 13). (Orig.). 1982. pap. 2.95 (ISBN 0-440-06760-X, Bryans). Dell.

Pacific Interlude. Sloan Wilson. LC 81-67221. 256p. 1982. 14.95 (ISBN 0-87795-333-3). Arbor Hse.

Pacific Patrol. Agnes K Halm. LC 53-12138. 1954. Vantage Press.

Pacific Standoff. J. Farragut Jones. (Silent Service Ser.: No. 6). (Orig.). 1982. pap. 2.95 (ISBN 0-440-17170-9, Bryans). Dell.

Pacific Standoff. (Orig.). 1983. pap. 3.25 (ISBN 0-440-06780-4). Dell.

Pacific Tales. Louis Becke. LC 70-98561. (Short story index reprint series). 1969. Books for Libraries Press.

Pacific Tales. Louis Becke. LC 9-2511. 1897. New Amsterdam Book Company; Etc., Etc.

Pacific Tales. Louis Becke. LC 25-26116. 1924. J. B. Lippincott Company.

Pacific Transport: An American Novel. Marguerite Young. 1978. 5.50 (ISBN 0-87164-073-2). William-F.

Pacific Vortex. Clive Cussler. 346p. 1983. pap. 3.50 (ISBN 0-553-22866-8). Bantam.

Pacific War Diary: 1942-1945. James T. Fahey. 432p. 1980. pap. 2.50 (ISBN 0-89083-673-6). Zebra.

Pacifico: A Novel Based on Truth, Fiction and Possibilities. William B Shearer. LC 26-9324. 1926. G. H. Watt.

Pacifist in Trouble. facs. ed. William R. Inge. LC 75-152176. (Essay Index Reprint Ser). 1939. 17.00 (ISBN 0-8369-2192-5). Ayer Co.

Pack. David Fisher. LC 75-45467. 7.95. Putnam.

Pack Mule. Ursula Bloom. LC 32-1752. 1932. E. P. Dutton & Co., Inc.

Pack of Autolycus or Strange & Terrible News of Ghosts. Ed. by Hyder E. Rollins. LC 27-4308. (Illus.). 1969. 14.00x (ISBN 0-674-65125-1). Harvard U Pr.

Pack Rat: A Metaphoric Phantasy. Francis Clement Kelley. LC 42-222963. 1942. The Bruce Publishing Company.

Pack up Your Sins: A Novel. Gene Harvey. LC 35-17235. Phoenix Press.

Package Deal. Willis Todhunter Ballard. LC 56-6255. 1956. Appleton-Century-Crofts.

Package Holiday. Jules Verne. 3.95. Assoc Bk.

Package Included Murder: A Novel of Suspense Featuring the Honourable Constance Morrison-Burke. Joyce Porter. LC 75-30854. 7.95 (ISBN 0-672-52171-7). Bobbs-Merrill.

Package to Spain. Madeleine A Polland. LC 76-167721. 1971. 4.95 (ISBN 0-8027-5241-1). Walker.

Packard Case. William Merrick. LC 61-6255. (Random House mystery). 1961. Random House.

Packard's Mammoth Jimmie Dale: Containing Jimmie Dale and the Phantom Clue. The Further Adventures of Jimmie Dale. Frank Lucius Packard. 1937. A. L. Burt and Company.

Packed for Murder. John Blackburn. LC 64-15477. 1964. M. S. Mill Co.

Pact. Orlando R Petrocelli. LC 72-3919. 1973. 6.95 (ISBN 0-396-06553-8). Dodd, Mead.

Pact with Satan. Leonard Holton, pseud. LC 60-11925. (Red badge detective). 1960. Dodd, Mead.

Pact with Satan. Leonard Patrick O'Connor Wibberley. LC 60-11925. (Red badge detective). 1960. Dodd, Mead.

Pact. 1st Amer. Ed. James Ambrose Brown. LC 66-24100. 1966. 4.50. Putnam.

Pactolus Prime. Albion Winegar Tourgee. LC 68-57555. (American novels of muckraking, propaganda, and social protest). (Illus.). 1968. Gregg Press.

Pactolus Prime. Albion Winegar Tourgee. LC 8-298423. Cassell Publishing Company.

Paddie. Emily Dudley Wright. LC 20-4893. 1920. The Stratford Co.

Paddington Green. Claire Rayner. LC 75-25540. 8.95 (ISBN 0-671-22190-6). Simon and Schuster.

Paddington Green. Claire Rayner. 1977. 1.95 (ISBN 0-449-23265-4). Fawcett Pubns.

Paddington Takes to the Air. Michael Bond. 1974. pap. 1.25 (ISBN 0-440-47321-7, YB). Dell.

Paddle Foot Ann of Old South County. Jennie R Partelow. LC 41-1356. 1940. American Book-Stratford Press, Inc.

Paddlewheels Churning: A Tale of Old Missouri. Anne Tedlock Brooks. LC 42-21003. 1942. Burton Publishing Company.

Paddy. Kelly P Gast. LC 78-18134. 1979. 7.95 (ISBN 0-385-14291-9). Doubleday.

Paddy No More - Modern Irish Short Stories. Juanita Casey et al. LC 77-85604. 1978. 9.95 (ISBN 0-917712-03-X). Longship Pr.

Paddy No More: Modern Irish Short Stories. LC 77-85604. (Illus.). 1978. 9.95 (ISBN 0-917712-03-X). Longship Press.

Paddy on Sundays: A Novel. Edward Caddick. LC 65-21352. 1965. Little, Brown.

Paddy-the-Next-Best-Thing. Gertrude Page. LC 20-189356. 1920. Frederick A. Stokes Company.

Padlocked: A Novel. Rex Ellingwood Beach. LC 26-13794. 1926. Harper & Brothers.

Padma River Boatman. Manik Bandopadhyaya. (Asian & Pacific Writing Ser.). 1973. 14.95x (ISBN 0-7022-0833-7); pap. 8.50x (ISBN 0-7022-0834-5). U of Queensland Pr.

Padre Ignacio: Or, The Song of Temptation. Owen Wister. LC 11-23869. 1911. Harper & Brothers.

Padre Ignacio: Or, The Song of Temptation. Owen Wister. LC 25-17538. 1925. Harper & Brothers.

Padre Must Die. Jack M Bickham. LC 67-11183. (Double D western). 1967. Doubleday.

Padre of the Plains. Alfonso Kieffer & Clark, Henry A., Joint Author. Walter W. Brown Publishing Co.

Paesanos. Jo Pagano & Kredel, Fritz, Illus. LC 40-11892. 1940. Little, Brown and Company.

Pagan. Gordon Arthur Smith. LC 20-5580. 1920. C. Scribner's Sons.

Pagan at the Shrine. Ernest Slater. LC 3-7662. 1903. The Macmillan Company.

Pagan Blessing. Phyllis Gebauer. LC 79-12880. 1979. 8.95 (ISBN 0-670-20972-4). Viking Press.

Pagan Cross, a Romance of Pre-Conquest Yucatan. Benjamin Helprin. LC 39-1301. Raiben Publications.

Pagan Encounter. Charlotte Lamb, pseud. (Harlquin Presents Ser.). (Orig.). 1979. pap. 1.50 (ISBN 0-373-70828-9, Pub. by Harlequin). PB.

Pagan Fire. Norval Richardson. LC 20-21002. 1920. C. Scribner's Sons.

Pagan Interval. Frances Vinciguerra Grebanier. LC 29-11748. The Bobbs-Merrill Company.

Pagan Interval. Frances Winwar. LC 29-11748. 1929. The Bobbs-Merrill Company.

Pagan King. 1st Ed. Edison Marshall. 1959. Doubleday.

Pagan Love. John Murray Gibbon. LC 22-237155. George H. Doran Company.

Pagan Lover. William Vaneer. pap. 0.75 o.p. (75-236). Manor Bks.

Pagan Madonna. Harold MacGrath. LC 21-8310. 1921. Doubleday, Page & Company.

Pagan Music. Dorothy J. Goulding. 1981. 1.00x o.p. (ISBN 0-88020-098-7). Coach Hse.

Pagan of the Alleghanies. Marah Ellis Martin Ryan. LC 43-26670. Grosset & Dunlap.

Pagan of the Alleghanies. Marah Ellis Martin Ryan. LC 8-1357. (On cover: Rialto series, no. 38). 1891. Rand, McNally & Company.

Pagan of the Hills. Charles Neville Buck. LC 19-8010. W. J. Watt & Company.

Pagan Pipings for Those Who Have Ears. Fred W. Renz. 1966. 3.50 o.p. (ISBN 0-682-44040-X). Exposition.

Pagan Place. Edna O'Brien. LC 74-106618. 1970. 5.95. Knopf.

Pagan Place. Edna O'Brien. 1974. (pbk.) 1.50. Bantam.

Pagan Princess: A Story of the Greatest Career Women of Ancient Times, the Vestal Virgins of Rome. Virginia Louise Montgomery. LC 53-12231. 1953. Vantage Press.

Pagan Rabbi, and Other Stories. Cynthia Ozick. LC 75-36498. 1976. 3.45 (ISBN 0-8052-0509-8). Schocken Books.

Pagan Rabbi: And Other Stories. Cynthia Ozick. LC 74-142956. 1971. 6.95 (ISBN 0-394-46970-4). Knopf.

Pagans. Arlo Bates. LC 70-104411. (Series: American Novel Series, No. 2.). 1970. (ISBN 0-8398-0153-X). Literature House.

Pagans. Arlo Bates. (American Novel Series. No. 2). 1884. H. Holt and Company.

Pagans. Arthur Moore. (River of Fortune Ser.: No. 2). 400p. (Orig.). 1980. pap. 2.50 (ISBN 0-89083-608-6). Zebra.

Pagan's Cup. Fergus Hume. LC 2-4952. G. W. Dillingham Company.

Pagan's Progress. Gouverneur Morris. 1904. A. S. Barnes & Company.

Page and the Prince: Or, A Fight for a Throne. Charles Phillips Chipman. LC 8-33780. 1908. The Ball Publishing Co.

Page Mr. Pomeroy. Elizabeth Garver Jordan. LC 34-4565. 1934. D. Appleton-Century Company, Incorporated.

Page Mr. Tutt. Arthur Cheney Train. LC 26-19110. 1926. C. Scribner's Sons.

Page of the Duke of Savoy. Alexandre Dumas. LC 6-43611. 1891. Little, Brown and Company.

Page of the Duke of Savoy. Alexandre Dumas. LC 6-43610. (Half-title: The romances of Alexandre Dumas. Illustrated library ed. vol. iv-v). 1893. Little, Brown, and Company.

Page of the Duke of Savoy. Alexandre Dumas. D. Estes & Company.

Page of the Duke of Savoy: An Historical Romance. Alexandre Dumas. (On cover: Seaside library. Pocket ed., no. 2076). G. Munro.

Pageant. Edith J. Lyttleton. LC 33-27028. The Century Co.

Pageant Faded: A Novel. Richard Karlan. LC 76-173203. 1972. 6.95. Bobbs-Merrill.

Pageant of Life: A Human Drama. Owen Francis Dudley. LC 32-29906. (His Problems of human happiness iv). 1932. Longmans, Green and Co.

Pageant of Murder. Gladys Mitchell. LC 65-20725. 1965. London House & Maxwell.

Pageant of Victory. Jeffery Farnol. LC 36-30062. 1939. Little, Brown, and Company.

Pageant of Youth. Irving Stone. LC 33-11627. A. H. King.

Pageants of Despair. Dennis Hamley. LC 74-10841. 1974. 6.95 (ISBN 0-87599-205-6). S. G. Phillips.

Pageless Air. Ralph L. Kinsey. 1959. 2.75 o.p. (ISBN 0-8233-0053-6). Golden Quill.

Pages. Aram Saroyan. LC 68-28535. 1969. 5.95 o.p. (ISBN 0-394-40405-X); pap. 1.95 o.p. (ISBN 0-394-40421-1). Random.

Pages from a Cold Island. Frederick Exley. LC 74-28321. 1975. 7.95 (ISBN 0-394-49440-7). Random House.

Pages from the Book of Eve: The Fictional Autobiography of Eve Collier. Ora Pate Stewart. LC 46-7942. 1946. The Naylor Company.

Pages from the Life of a Pagan, a Romance of the Real. Cathlyn Pepper Tibbits. LC 21-14803. 1921. G. Routledge & Sons, Ltd.

Pages of Life. John McArthur Will. LC 20-1893. The Roxburgh Publishing Company, Inc.

Paging Cupid. Jean Carew. LC 40-5664. 1939. Arcadia House.

Pagoda. James Atlee Phillips. LC 51-14185. 1951. Macmillan.

Pagoda Tree. Berkely Mather. LC 79-20247. 1979. 8.95 (ISBN 0-684-16313-6). Scribner.

Pagoda Tree. Berkely Mather. LC 79-67069. 1980. 8.95 (ISBN 0-684-16313-6). Scribner.

Paid for! Charles Garvice. (On cover: Laurel library, no. 3). 1892. G. Munro.

Paid in Full. John Hay Beith. LC 25-8667. 1925. Houghton Mifflin Company.

Paid in Full. John William Harding & Walter, Eugene, 1874- LC 8-169493. 1908. G. W. Dillingham Company.

Paid Out. J Percival Bessell. LC 19-14702. 1919. 1.50. The Macaulay Company.

Paige. Jerry B Jenkins. LC 80-39501. 2.50 (ISBN 0-8024-4314-1). Moody Press.

Paige Girls. Elizabeth Frances Corbett. 1973. pap. 0.95 o.p. (95327). Beagle Bks.

Pail of Oysters. Vern J Sneider. LC 52-13648. 1953. Putnam.

Pain, Challenge & Change. Nathaniel Thomas. 80p. 1975. 4.50 o.p. (ISBN 0-682-48255-2). Exposition.

Pain Gain. John F. Carr. 1979. pap. 1.75 (ISBN 0-89041-250-2, 3250). Major Bks.

Pain Lovers. James Kerstetter. pap. 1.95 o.s.i. (OPH-222, Ophelia). Olympia.

Paingod. Harlan Ellison. pap. 0.60 o.p. (X1991). Pyramid Pubns.

Painrock Canyon. Henry Leyford Gates. LC 34-33872. 1934. R. M. McBride & Company.

Painswick Line. Henry Cecil. 1974. Repr. of 1951 ed. 6.95 o.s.i. (ISBN 0-8277-3347-X). British Bk Ctr.

Paint. Thomas Craven. LC 23-3893. Harcourt, Brace and Company.

Paint Me a Million. David L Goodrich. LC 77-16232. 1978. 7.95 (ISBN 0-399-12118-8). Putnam.

Paint Me Rainbows. Fern Michaels. LC 82-2858. (Nightingale Series). 1982. 6.95 (ISBN 0-8161-3391-3). G.K. Hall.

Paint on Their Faces. Jerry Weil. LC 57-8027. (Signet book, 1950). 1957. New American Library.

Paint-Stained Flannels: By Pete Fry Pseud. Clifford King. LC 65-17176. 1966. bds., 2.95. Roy.

Paint the Moon Red. Thomas J. Meinhardt. LC 48-15387. 1947. Vickers Pub. Co.

Paint the Town Black. David Alexander. LC 54-903216. 1954. Random House.

Paint the Town Red. Harold Adams. 224p. 1982. pap. 2.95 (ISBN 0-441-64600-X, Pub. by Charter Bks). Ace Bks.

Paint Your Wagon. George Scullin. (Orig.). 1969. pap. 0.75 o.p. (75-304). Manor Bks.

Painted Bed. Helen De Zglinitzki. LC 38-56023. 1938. Dodd, Mead and Company.

Painted Bird. Jerzy N. Kosinski. LC 65-16949. 4.95. Houghton.

Painted Bird. 2d ed. with a new introd. by the author. ed. Jerzy N. Kosinski. LC 75-35804. 1976. 7.95 (ISBN 0-395-24291-6). Houghton Mifflin.

Painted Bird: By Jerzy Kosinski. Jerzy N. Kosinski. 1966. Pocket Bks.

Painted Bird: By Jerzy Kosinski. Kosinski, Jerzy N. LC 65-16949. 1965. Mifflin.

Painted Buttes. Bar-H Books. Arthur Henry Gooden. LC 41-21280. Carlton House.

Painted Caves. Kate Thompson. 1971. pap. 0.95 o.p. (95166). Beagle Bks.

Painted City: Dry-Points of Washington Life. Mary Badger Wilson. LC 27-253158. 1927. Frederick A. Stokes Company.

Painted Devil. Rachel Billington. LC 75-33027. 1975. 7.95 (ISBN 0-698-10718-7). Coward, McCann & Geoghegan.

Painted Devils: Strange Stories. Robert Aickman. LC 78-23895. 8.95 (ISBN 0-684-15999-6). Scribner.

Painted Dresses. Shelby Hearon. LC 80-69644. 1981. 11.95 (ISBN 0-689-11155-X). Atheneum.

Painted Face. Jean Stubbs. LC 73-93183. 1974. 7.95 (ISBN 0-8128-1696-X). Stein and Day.

Painted Fire. Elliott Pendleton White. LC 52-131014. 1952. Bruce Humphries.

Painted Fires. Nellie Letitia Mooney McClung. LC 25-22638. 1925. Dodd, Mead & Company.

Painted for the Kill. Lucy Michaella Cores. LC 43-9388. 1943. Duell, Sloan and Pearce.

Painted King. 1st Ed. Rhys Davies. 1954. Doubleday.

Painted Lady. Helena Grose. LC 33-15944. The Macaulay Company.

Painted Lady: A Novel. Francoise Sagan, pseud. 448p. 1983. 15.95 (ISBN 0-525-24148-5, 01505-450). Dutton.

Painted Meadows. Sophie Kerr. LC 20-7762. George H. Doran Company.

Painted Minx. Robert William Chambers. LC 30-10984. 1930. D. Appleton & Company.

Painted Mischief. Frank Shay. LC 32-25173. The Macaulay Company.

Painted Ponies. Alan Le May. LC 27-11716. George H. Doran Company.

Painted Ports. Cicely Fox Smith. LC 49-80078. 1948. Oxford Univ. Press.

Painted Post Gunplay. Syl Macdowell. LC 37-39529. J. Messner, Inc.

Painted Post Law. Syl Macdowell. LC 36-121162. J. Messner, Inc.

Painted Post Outlaws. Syl Macdowell. LC 40-261. J. Messner, Inc.

Painted Post Range. Syl Macdowell. LC 37-8763. J. Messner, Inc.

Painted Post Roundup. Syl Macdowell. LC 39-12434. J. Messner, Inc.

Painted Post Rustlers. Syl Macdowell. LC 38-32993. J. Messner, Inc.

Painted Road. Mabel May Morgan Whelen. LC 41-20735. 1941. Wilmarth Publishing Company.

Painted Room. Margaret Wilson. LC 26-149212. 1926. Harper and Brothers.

Painted Scene: And Other Stories of the Theater. Henry Kitchell Webster. LC 79-152962. (Short story index reprint series). (Illus.). 1971. (ISBN 0-8369-3877-1). Books for Libraries Press.

Painted Scene: And Other Stories of the Theater. Henry Kitchell Webster. LC 16-201109. The Bobbs-Merrill Company.

Painted Scene, & Other Stories of the Theater. facsimile ed. Henry Kitchell Webster. LC 79-152962. (Short Story Index Reprint Ser.). (Illus.). Repr. of 1916 ed. 21.00 (ISBN 0-8369-3877-1). Ayer Co.

Painted Shadows. Richard Le Gallienne. LC 77-94738. (Short story index reprint series). 1969. Books for Libraries Press.

Painted Shadows. Richard Le Gallienne. LC 4-28954. 1904. Little, Brown, and Company.

Painted Stallion. Hal George Evarts. LC 26-103139. 1926. Little, Brown, and Company.

Painted Tent. Victor Canning. LC 74-5505. 1974. 6.95 (ISBN 0-688-00270-6). Morrow.

Painted Veil. William Somerset Maugham. LC 75-25362. (Maugham, William Somerset, 1874-1965. Works. 1976). 1977. 15.00. Arno Press.

Painted Veil. William Somerset Maugham. LC 25-708442. George H. Doran Company.

Painted Veils. James Gibbons Huneker. LC 32-19533. (Half-title: The modern library of the world's best books). The Modern Library.

Painted Woman. Frederic Arnold Kummer. 1.35. W. J. Watt & Company.

Painted Women. Chet Cunningham. (Pinkerton Agent Brad Spear Ser.: No. 5). 320p. (Orig.). 1981. pap. 2.25 (ISBN 0-440-06800-2, Banbury). Dell.

Painted Woods. Nevil Gratiot Henshaw. LC 24-7531. The Bobbs Merrill Company.

Painter and the Lady. William James Blech. LC 39-20236. 1939. Simon and Schuster.

Painter Gabriel. Donald Newlove. LC 72-122131. 1970. 6.95. McCall Pub. Co.

Painter of Flowers. Hugh Fleetwood. LC 72-76837. 1972. 4.95 (ISBN 0-670-53565-6). Viking Press.

Painter of Our Time. John Berger. (2334). 1965. Penguin.

Painter of Our Time. John Berger. LC 76-376898. 1976. 2.95 (ISBN 0-904613-12-7). Writers and Readers Pub. Cooperative.

Painter of Our Time. John Berger. LC 59-8044. 1959. Simon and Schuster.

Painter of Parma: Or, The Magic of a Masterpiece; an Italian Story of Love, Mystery, and Adventure. Sylvanus Cobb. Cassell & Company.

Painter of Parma: Or, The Magic of a Masterpiece. An Italian Story of Love, Mystery, and Adventure. Sylvanus Cobb. (On cover: Cassell's sunshine series of choice fiction, v. 1, no. 21). The Cassell Publishing Co.

Painter of Signs. R. K. Narayan. LC 75-43668. 1976. 8.95 (ISBN 0-670-53567-2). Viking Press.

Painters of Dreams. Elisabeth Stancy Payne. LC 28-2386. The Penn Publishing Company.

Painting a Wall. David Lan. 35p. (Orig.). 1981. pap. 3.95 (ISBN 0-86104-215-8). Pluto Pr.

Painting the Roses Red. Michael Malone. LC 74-26907. 1975. 5.95 (ISBN 0-394-49598-5). Random House.

Pair from Space. Incl. Giants in the Earth. James Blish; We, the Marauders. Robert Silverberg. (Orig.). pap. 0.50 o.p. (B50-813). Belmont-Tower.

Pair of Blue Eyes. Thomas Hardy. LC 16-13098. 1895. Harper & Brothers.

Pair of Blue Eyes: A Novel. Thomas Hardy. LC 7-1899. (Leisure hour series, no. 28). 1873. H. Holt and Company.

Pair of Blue Eyes: A Novel. Thomas Hardy. (On cover: Lovell's library, no. 1334). 1889. J. W. Lovell Company.

Pair of Blue Eyes: A Novel. Thomas Hardy. LC 42-43764. Hovendon Company.

Pair of Brown Eyes: A Novel. Bertha N Clay. LC 6-21367. (On cover: The Marguerite ser., no. 11). E. A. Weeks & Company.

Pair of Deuces. John Henry Reese. LC 77-16852. 1978. 7.95 (ISBN 0-385-14007-X). Doubleday.

Pair of Deuces. large print ed. John Henry Reese. LC 81-4463. (Double D western). 1981. 8.95. Thorndike Press.

Pair of Eyes. Reese Williams. 80p. (Orig.). 1983. 12.95 (ISBN 0-934378-31-2); pap. 5.95 (ISBN 0-934378-32-0). Tanam Pr.

Pair of Idols. Stewart Thomas Caven. LC 22-11446. E. P. Dutton & Company.

Pair of Little Patent Leather Boots. Edith Stotesbury Hutchinson. LC 13-733928. 1913. 1.50. J. B. Lippincott Company.

Pair of Patient Lovers. William Dean Howells. LC 78-125219. (Short story index reprint series). (Illus.). 1970. Books for Libraries Press.

Pair of Patient Lovers. William Dean Howells. LC 1-7302. (Publisher's lettering: Harper's portrait collection of short stories v. 1). 1901. Harper & Brothers.

Pair of Ragged Claws. Russell L. McCollom. 1977. pap. 3.95 o.p. (ISBN 0-8059-2384-5). Dorrance.

Pair of Ragged Claws. Russell L. McCollom. 1977. pap. 3.95 o.p. (ISBN 0-8059-2384-5). Dorrance.

Pair of Silk Stockings. Cyril Harcourt. LC 16-2565. 1916. Dodd, Mead and Company.

Pair of Sixes. Lilian Lauferty & Peple, Edward Henry. LC 14-20852. 1914. Moffat, Yard and Company.

Pairing off. Julian Moynahan. LC 70-80909. 1969. 5.95. W. Morrow.

Pairing Off. Julian Moynahan. (Leisure book). 1979. 1.75 (ISBN 0-8439-0642-1). Nordon Pubns.

Paisano My Blood. Nina Miller Elliott. LC 12-23208. 1912. 1.00. The Shakespeare Press.

Paisley Shawl. Frederick John Niven. LC 31-8422. 1931. Dodd, Mead & Company.

Paiute: Novel. Sessions S Wheeler. LC 64-15397. 5.95, 2.75 pap.,. Caxton.

Pajama Story. Lin Ting. 130p. 1980. 6.50 (ISBN 0-89955-161-0, Pub. by Mei Ya China); pap. 4.95 (ISBN 0-89955-190-4). Intl Schol Bk Serv.

Pal Joey. John O'Hara. Popular Library.

Palace, David Guy Compton. LC 69-17631. 1969. 4.95. Norton.

Palace. Claude Simon. LC 63-15829. 1963. G. Braziller.

Palace. Chelsea Quinn Yarbo. 1979. pap. 2.25 (ISBN 0-451-08949-9, E8949, Sig). NAL.

Palace: An Historical Horror Novel. Chelsea Quinn Yarbro. LC 78-3996. 9.95 (ISBN 0-312-59474-7). St. Martin's Press.

Palace and Prison. Ol'Ga Dmitrievna Forsh. LC 75-38498. (Early Soviet Literature in English Translation). (Illus.). 1978. 19.00 (ISBN 0-88355-401-1). Hyperion Press.

Palace Guard. Charlotte MacLeod. LC 80-2750. 1981. 9.95 (ISBN 0-385-17533-7). Published for the Crime Club by Doubleday.

Palace Guard: A Novel. Donald Braider. LC 58-7402. 1958. Viking Press.

Palace of Art. John Innes Mackintosh Stewart. LC 72-170103. 1972. 6.95 (ISBN 0-393-08671-2). Norton.

Palace of Art: A Novel. Johh Innes Mackintosh Stewart. 1970. 6.95 o.p. (ISBN 0-393-08671-2). Norton.

Palace of Danger: A Story of La Pompadour. Mabel Wagnalls. LC 8-27097. 1908. Funk & Wagnalls Company.

Palace of Darkened Windows. Mary Hastings Bradley. LC 14-10074. 1914. 1.30. D. Appleton and Company.

Palace of Dim Night. Edmund Watkins. LC 55-980419. 1955. Comet Press Books.

Palace of Ice. Tarjei Vesaas. LC 68-28673. (Unesco Collection of Contemporary Works). 1968. 4.50. Morrow.

Palace of Intrigue. A. Elsie Rundall Craig. LC 32-34935. 1932. Minton, Balch & Company.

Palace of Love. Jack Vance, pseud. 1979. 1.75 (ISBN 0-87997-442-7). DAW Books.

Palace of Money. William H Manville. LC 66-123282. 4.95. Delacorte.

Palace of Pleasure. Jacques Rochette De La Morliere. LC 49-26760. 1949. Avon Pub. Co.

Palace of Pleasure: An Anthology of the Novella. Maurice Jacques Valency. Ed. by Harry Levtow. (Orig.). 1960. pap. 1.45 o.p. (32, Cap). Putnam.

Palace of Pleasures: An Anthology of the Novella. Ed. by Maurice Jacques Valency & Levtow, Henry. LC 60-6120. (Capricorn books no. 32). 1960. Capricorn Books.

Palace of Shattered Vessels. David Shahar. LC 75-8560. 1975. 7.95 (ISBN 0-395-20550-6). Houghton Mifflin.

Palace of Sin. Olive Dickerson McHugh. LC 40-1420. Gold Seal Publications.

Palace of Strangers. Hilary Masters. LC 70-149424. 1971. 7.95. World Pub. Co.

Palace of the Peacock. Wilson Harris. 152p. (Orig.). 1969. pap. 4.95 (ISBN 0-571-08930-5). Faber & Faber.

Palace of the Princess. Virginia M. Scott. 1978. 7.95 o.p. (ISBN 0-533-03352-7). Vantage.

Palace-Prison: Or, The Past and the Present... LC 7-35785. 1884. Fords, Howard & Hulbert.

Palace Without Chairs. Brigid Brophy. LC 77-18387. 1978. 8.95 (ISBN 0-689-10883-4). Atheneum.

Palace Without Chairs. Brigid Brophy. 1979. 2.25 (ISBN 0-380-46144-7). Avon Books.

Palaces and Prisons. Ann Sophia Winterbotham Stephens. T. B. Peterson & Brothers.

Palaces of Desire. Karen Alexander. LC 78-614. 9.95 (ISBN 0-698-10885-X). Coward, McCann & Geoghegan.

Paladin. Brian Wynne Garfield. 352p. 1981. pap. 2.95 (ISBN 0-553-14261-5). Bantam.

Paladin. Brian Wynne Garfield & Peter Hamilton. 1980. 12.95 o.p. (ISBN 0-671-24704-2). S&S.

Paladin. George Shipway. LC 73-9887. (Illus.). 1973. 7.95 (ISBN 0-15-170740-5). Harcourt Brace Jovanovich.

Paladin: A Novel Based on Fact. Brian Wynne Garfield & Christopher Creighton. LC 79-20290. 12.95 (ISBN 0-671-24704-2). Simon and Schuster.

Paladin: A Novel Based on Facts. Brian Wynne Garfield & Christopher Creighton. LC 80-16922. 1980. 17.95 (ISBN 0-8161-3116-3). G. K. Hall.

Paladin: As Beheld by a Woman of Temperament. Horace Annesley Vachell. LC 9-24959. 1909. Dodd, Mead and Company.

Palais Royal. An Historical Romance. John H Mancur. LC 7-17934. 1845. W. H. Colyer.

Palazzo. Mary Chamberlin. LC 78-134930. 1971. 5.95. Lippincott.

Palazzo. Hans Habe. LC 77-2261. 1977. 9.95 o.p. (ISBN 0-399-11983-3). Putnam Pub Group.

Palazzo: A Novel. Hans Habe. LC 77-2261. 1977. 9.95. Putnam.

Pale Betrayer. Dorothy Salisbury Davis. LC 65-228744. 3.95. Scribners.

Pale Betrayer. Dorothy Salisbury Davis. LC 65-22874. 1965. Scribner.

Pale Blonde of Sands Street. William Chapman White. LC 46-1195. 1946. The Viking Press.

Pale Criminals. Richard Bankowsky. 1967. 7.95 o.p. (ISBN 0-394-44276-8). Random.

Pale Door: By Lee Roberts Pseud. Robert Lee Martin. LC 55-61948. (Red badge detective). 1955. Dodd, Mead.

Pale Fire. Vladimir Vladimirovich Nabokov. LC 79-26742. 1980. 4.95 (ISBN 0-399-50458-3). Perigee Books.

Pale Fire: A Novel. Vladimir Vladimirovich Nabokov. LC 62-7351. 1962. Putnam.

Pale Gray for Guilt. John Dann MacDonald. LC 70-5452. (Fawcett gold metal book). 1968. 0.50. Fawcett Publications.

Pale Gray for Guilt. John Dann MacDonald. LC 70-28985. (His The Travis McGee series). 1971. 5.50. Lippincott.

Pale Hand of Danger. Miriam Lynch. pap. 0.75 o.s.i. (01-338). Lancer.

Pale Horse. Agatha Miller Christie. 224p. 1981. pap. 2.50 (ISBN 0-671-42095-X). PB.

Pale Horse. Boris Viktorovich Savinkov & Vengerova, Zinaida Afanasevna, 1867- Tr. LC 19-27583. 1919. A. A. Knopf.

Pale Horse, Pale Rider. Katherine Anne Porter. LC 67-62420. 12.95 (ISBN 0-15-170750-2). HarBraceJ.

Pale Horse, Pale Rider: Three Short Novels. Katherine Anne Porter. LC 39-27273. Harcourt, Brace and Company.

Pale Moon Rising. Manning O'Brine. LC 77-16739. 1978. 7.95 (ISBN 0-312-59478-X). St. Martin's Press.

Pale Moon: The Story of an Indian Princess. new ed. Pale Moon. 1975. 4.95 o.p. (ISBN 0-8423-4793-3, T-4793). Tyndale.

Pale Moon. 1st Ed. William Riley Burnett. LC 56-576982. 1956. Knopf.

Pale Pink House. Frances Y McHugh. LC 67-5359. 1967. Arcadia House.

Pale Survivor. Mary Louise Mabie. LC 34-36548. The Bobbs-Merrill Company.

Pale View of Hills. Kazuo Ishiguro. LC 81-22713. 1982. 11.95 (ISBN 0-399-12718-6). Putnam.

Pale Warriors: A Novel. David Osborne Hamilton. 1929. C. Scribner's Sons.

Pale Youth: And Other Stories. Zeteo Pseud Tokalon. LC 26-140. The Montmartre Publishers.

Palermo Affair. Colin Forbes, pseud. 1972. 6.95 o.p. (ISBN 0-525-17440-0). Dutton.

Palermo Affair. Raymond H. Sawkins. LC 72-76404. (Illus.). 1972. 6.95 (ISBN 0-525-17440-0). Dutton.

Palestina. Suzanne T. Moore. 1983. 8.95 (ISBN 0-938758-13-6). MTM Pub Co.

Palestra: A Novel. S. D Franklin. LC 78-66682. 3.95 (ISBN 0-9601886-0-6). Herculean Press.

Palgrave Mummy. Florence Mae Pettee. LC 29-10669. 1929. Payson & Clarke Ltd.

Palimpsest. Hilda Doolittle & H. D. LC 68-25566. (Crosscurrents/modern fiction). 1968. Southern Illinois University Press.

Palimpsest. Gilbert Augustin Thierry. LC 8-27054. ("unknown" library v. 24). Cassell Publishing Company.

Palimpset. Margaret Elizabeth Atkins. LC 81-21460. 1982. 11.95 (ISBN 0-312-59485-2). St. Martin's Press.

Paliser Case. Edgar Evertson Saltus. LC 70-113269. 1970. (ISBN 0-404-05543-5). AMS Press.

Paliser Case. Edgar Evertson Saltus. LC 19-61408. 1919. Boni and Liveright.

Palladian. Elizabeth Taylor. LC 47-1073. 1947. A. A. Knopf.

Pallbearers of Justice. Josefa Hoefinger Schwedler. LC 39-2389. New Method Printing Co.

Pallet on the Floor. Ronald Hugh Morrieson. LC 76-382580. (KEA new fiction series; no. 3). 1976. (ISBN 0-908564-15-5). Dunmore Press.

Pallid Giant: A Tale of Yesterday and Tomorrow. Pierrepont B Noyes. LC 27-188448. 1927. Fleming H. Revell Company.

Pallieter, Translated. Felix Timmermans & Bodde, Mrs. Charlotte Beatrice (Hodgkinson) 1867- Tr. LC 24-21076. Harper & Brothers.

Palliser Novels. Anthony Trollope. Incl. Can You Forgive Her; Phineas Finn; The Eustace Diamonds; Phineas Redux; The Prime Minister; The Duke's Children. (Illus.). 1975. pap. 14.95 boxed set (ISBN 0-19-281149-5). Oxford U Pr.

Pallisers. John Garforth. 1.50. Dell.

Pallisers. Anthony Trollope. (Berkley Medallion Book.). 1977. 1.95 (ISBN 0-425-03521-2). Berkley Pub. Corp.

Pallisers. Anthony Trollope & John Michael Drinkrow Hardwick. LC 74-79479. 1975. 8.95. Coward, McCann & Geoghegan.

Pallisers: The Six Famous Parliamentary Novels. abr. ed. Anthony Trollope. Ed. by Michael Hardwick. LC 74-79479. 437p. 1975. 8.95 o.p. (ISBN 0-698-10622-9, Coward). Putnam Pub Group.

Palludia. Anna Robeson Brown Burr. LC 28-24946. 1928. Duffield & Company.

Palm Beach. Cornelius Vanderbilt. LC 31-172282. The Macaulay Company.

Palm Beach Apartment. Peggy Gaddis, pseud. LC 45-2138. 1945. Phoenix Press.

Palm Beach Hotel. Janet Gregory Vermandel. 1978. pap. 1.75 (ISBN 0-532-17187-X). Woodhill.

Palm Beach Nurse. James Noble Gifford. LC 39-33009. 1939. Gramercy Publishing Co.

Palm Beach Nurse. Emily Noble. LC 39-33009. Gramercy Publishing Co.

Palm for Mrs. Pollifax. Dorothy Gilman. LC 72-89947. 1973. 5.95 (ISBN 0-385-09134-6). Doubleday.

Palm for Mrs. Pollifax. Dorothy Gilman. (Fawcett crest book). 1974. (pbk.) 0.95. Fawcett.

Palm for Mrs. Pollifax. large print ed. Dorothy Gilman. LC 83-116. (Nightingale series). 1983. 10.95 (ISBN 0-8161-3369-7). G.K. Hall.

Palm of the Hot Hand. King Phillips. LC 26-17607. 1926. 2.00. A. C. McClurg & Co.

Palm Springs. Tom Ardies. LC 77-92206. 1978. 10.00 (ISBN 0-385-12846-0). Doubleday.

Palm Springs. Tom Ardies. 2.25 (ISBN 0-425-04164-6). Berkley Publishing Corp.,, C.

Palm Sunday. Kurt Vonnegut, Jr. 1981. 13.95 (ISBN 0-440-06593-3, Sey Lawr). Delacorte.

Palm Sunday. Kurt Vonnegut, Jr. 1982. pap. 6.95 (ISBN 0-440-57163-4, Dell Trade Pbks). Dell.

Palm Tree Island: Being the Narrative of Harry Brent Showing How He in Company with William Bobbin of Limehouse Was Left on an Island in the Southern Hemisphere, and the Accidents and Adventures That Sprang Therefrom, the Whole Faithfully Set Forth. Herbert Strang. LC 11-4778. Hodder and Stoughton.

Palm-Wine Drinkard. Amos Tutuola. 1954. pap. 3.95 (ISBN 0-394-17235-3, E328, Ever). Grove.

Palm-Wine Drinkard and His Dead Palm-Wine Tapster in the Dead's Town. Amos Tutuola. LC 53-8397. 1953. Grove Press.

Palm-Wine Drinkard and His Dead Palm-Wine Tapster in the Dead's Town. Amos Tutuola. LC 78-104255. 1970. Greenwood Press.

Palmers Green. Stewart Thomas Caven. LC 12-255343. 1912. 1.35. G. P. Putnam's Sons.

Palmetto Derby, and Other Stories. George Hoyt Smith. LC 26-792. 1925. The Knickerbocker Press.

Palmetto: The Romance of a Louisiana Girl. Stella George Stern Perry. LC 20-15507. Frederick A. Stokes Company.

Palms. Anna Hanson McKenney Dorsey. LC 6-33710. 1887. J. Murphy & Co.

Paloma. Theresa Conway. 672p. (Orig.). 1981. pap. 2.75 (ISBN 0-345-28706-1). Ballantine.

Palominas Pistolero & Smoke Wagon Kid. Nelson Nye. 1978. pap. 1.95 (ISBN 0-89083-418-0). Zebra.

Palomino. Danielle Steel. LC 80-28004. 6.95 (ISBN 0-440-56753-X). Dell Pub. Co.

Palomino. Danielle Steel. LC 81-6782. 1981. 15.95 (ISBN 0-8161-3265-8). G.K. Hall.

Paloverde. Jacqueline Briskin. 1978. 10.95 (ISBN 0-07-007915-3, GB). McGraw.

Pals First: A Romance of Love and Comradery. Francis Perry Elliott. LC 15-711746. 1915. 1.30. Harper & Brothers.

Pam. Betsey Riddle Hutten Zum Stolzenberg. LC 5-6943. 1905. Dodd, Mead and Company.

Pam. Betsey Riddle Hutton Zum Stolzenberg. LC 7-132853. 1906. Dodd, Mead and Company.

Pam at Fifty. Betsey Riddle Hutton Zum Stolzenberg. LC 24-8372. 1923. Cassell and Company, Ltd.

Pam at Fifty. Betsey Riddle Hutton Zum Stolzenberg. LC 24-5803. 2.00. George H. Doran Company.

Pam Decides: A Sequel to "Pam". Betsey Riddle Hutton Zum Stolzenberg. 1906. Dodd, Mead and Company.

Pam Wilson, Registered Nurse. Dorothy Deming. LC 46-1794. (Career books). 1946. Dodd, Mead & Company.

Pamela. Samuel Richardson & Saintsbury, George Edward Bateman, 1845-1933, Ed. (Half-title: Everyman's library, ed. by Ernest Rhys. Fiction no. 683- 684). 1914. J. M. Dent & Sons, Ltd.

Pamela, No. 3. Mary Mackie. (Starlight Romance Ser.). 144p. 1981. pap. cancelled (ISBN 0-553-14365-4). Bantam.

Pamela Anne. David M. Tyler. 31p. 1972. 3.00 o.p. (ISBN 0-682-47563-7). Exposition.

Pamela Congreve: A Novel. Frances Aymar Mathews. LC 4-9962. 1904. Dodd, Mead and Company.

Pamela of Echo Glen. 1st Ed. Jennie McAlpine. Pageant Press.

Pamela: Or, Virtue Rewarded. Samuel Richardson. LC 71-134860. (Riverside editions, B123). 1971. (ISBN 0-395-11155-2). Houghton Mifflin.

Pamela: Or, Virtue Rewarded. Samuel Richardson. LC 74-17290. (Flowering of the Novel). 1974. (ISBN 0-8240-1100-7). Garland Pub. Co.

Pamela: Or, Virtue Rewarded. Samuel Richardson. LC 2-29256. (English Comedie humaine. 1st ser., v. 2). 1902. The Century Co.

Pamela; or, Virtue Rewarded. Introd. by William M. Sale, Jr. Samuel Richardson. LC 59-24418. (Norton library, N12). Norton.

Pamela; or, Virtue Rewarded, 1801, 4 vols. Samuel Richardson. Ed. by Michael F. Shugrue. (Flowering of the Novel, 1740-1775 Ser). (O.s.i.: Vol. 1). 1974. lib. bdg. 50.00 ea. o.s.i. (ISBN 0-8240-1100-7). Garland Pub.

Pamela Pounce: A Tale of Tempestuous Petticoats. Agnes Sweetman Castle & Castle, Egerton. LC 21-18095. 1921. Hodder and Stoughton Ltd.

Pamela Pounce: A Tale of Tempestuous Petticoats. Agnes Sweetman Castle & Castle, Egerton. LC 21-20538. D. Appleton and Company.

Pamela's Palace. 2nd ed. Arlene J. Fitzgerald. (1975 ed. 0.95 o.p.). 192p. 1976. pap. 1.25 o.p. (ISBN 0-532-12480-4). Woodhill.

Pamela's Palace. Arlene J. Fitzgerald. (Orig.). 1971. pap. 0.75 o.p. (75-447). Manor Bks.

Pamela's Palace. 2nd ed. Arlene J. Fitzgerald. (1975 ed. 0.95 o.p.). 192p. 1976. pap. 1.25 o.p. (ISBN 0-532-12480-4). Manor Bks.

Pamela's Palace. Arlene J Fitzgerald. 1975. (pbk.) 0.95. Manor Books.

Pamela's Spring Song. Cecil Roberts. LC 30-169950. 1930. D. Appleton and Company.

Pampa Joe. Charles Elbert Scoggins. LC 56-146203. 1936. D. Appleton-Century Company, Incorporated.

Pampini. Uri Geller. LC 79-57479. 12.95 (ISBN 0-89975-000-1). World Authors.

Pamplona Affair. Nick Carter. (Killmaster series). 1.75 (ISBN 0-441-65085-6). Charter.

Pam's Own Story. Betsey Riddle Hutton Zum Stolzenberg. LC 31-205220. 1931. J. B. Lippincott Company.

Pan. Knut Hamsun & Worster, William John Alexander, 1882-1929, Tr. LC 21-19651. 1921. A. A. Knopf.

Pan. Knut Hamsun & Worster, William W., Tr. LC 24-28526. 1922. A. A. Knopf.

Pan African Short Stories: An Anthology for Schools. Ed. by Neville Denny. (Illus.). 1965. pap. text ed. 3.50x (ISBN 0-17-511099-9). Humanities.

Pan and the Twins. Eden Phillpotts. LC 22-42122. 1922. The Macmillan Company.
Pan: From Lieutenant Thomas Glahn's Papers. Knut Hamsun. LC 56-12295. (Bard book.). 1975. (pbk.) 1.75 (ISBN 0-380-00482-8). Avon.
Pan: From Lieutenant Thomas Glahn's Papers. Translated from the Norwegian by James W. McFarlane. Knut Hamsun. LC 56-12295. 1956. Noonday Press.
Pan in the Parlour. Norman Lindsay. LC 33-300015. Farrar & Rinehart, Incorporated.
Pan Michael, an Historical Novel. Henryk Sienkiewicz. Tr. by Samuel Augustus Binion. LC 5-20918. T. Y. Crowell & Co.
Pan Michael, an Historical Novel. Henryk Sienkiewicz. Tr. by Samuel Augustus Binion. LC 5-20918. T. Y. Crowell & Co.
Pan Michael; an Historical Novel of Poland, the Ukraine, and Turkey. popular ed. Henryk Sienkiewicz. Tr. by Jeremiah Curtin. LC 69-10155. 1968. Greenwood Press.
Pan Michael. An Historical Novel of Poland, the Ukraine, and Turkey. A Sequel to "With Fire and Sword" and "The Deluge". Henryk Sienkiewicz. Tr. by Jeremiah Curtin. LC 9-2516. 1893. Little, Brown & Co.
Pan Michael. An Historical Novel of Poland, the Ukraine, and Turkey; a Sequel to "With Fire and Sword" and "The Deluge." By Henryk Sienkiewicz. Authorized and Unabridged Translation from the Polish by Jeremiah Curtin. Henryk Sienkiewicz. Tr. by Jeremiah Curtin. 1898. Little, Brown, and Company.
Pan Michael (Pan Volodivovski) a Historical Tale. Henryk Sienkiewicz. Tr. by Samuel Augustus Binion. 1898. H. Altemus.
Pan Sagittarius. Ian Wallace. LC 72-94258. 1973. 5.95 (ISBN 0-399-11105-0). Putnam.
Panagyurishte Gold Treasure. I. Venedikov. 1961. 12.50x o.p. (B62). Vanous.
Panama. Ashley Carter, pseud. (Fawcett Gold Medal Book). 2.25 (ISBN 0-449-14025-3). Fawcett Books.
Panama. Thomas McGuane. LC 78-12344. 1978. 7.95 (ISBN 0-374-22942-2). Farrar, Straus, and Giroux.
Panama. Thomas McGuane. LC 79-18016. 1979. 2.95 (ISBN 0-14-005274-7). Penguin Books.
Panama. Earl R. McMillin. 1978. pap. 1.95 (ISBN 0-532-19209-5). Woodhill.
Panama Appassionata. Louis Philip De Saubleaux Warren. LC 51-8636. 1951. Woodford Press.
Panama Canal Bride: A Story of Construction Days. 1st Ed. Elizabeth Kittredge Parker. LC 55-11388. 1955. Exposition Press.
Panama Flame. Mirna Perez-Venero. (Orig.). 1982. pap. 3.50 (ISBN 0-440-16822-8). Dell.
Panama Gold. John Benteen. LC 60-1058. (Orig.). 1969. pap. 0.60 o.p. (B60-1058). Belmont-Tower.
Panama Gold. John Benteen. (Fargo Ser.). (O.s.i.: No. 2). 144p. 1973. pap. 0.95 o.s.i. (BT50533). Belmont-Tower.
Panama Gold see Oro De Panama.
Panama Is Burning. Philip Lindsay. LC 32-13939. Farrar & Rinehart, Incorporated.
Panama Paradox. Michael Wolfe, pseud. LC 77-3808. 8.95 (ISBN 0-06-014717-2). Harper & Row.
Panama Passage. Donald Barr Chidsey. LC 46-1870. 1946. Doubleday & Company, Inc.
Panama Passage. Donald Barr Chidsey. 1947. The Sun Dial Press.
Panama Plot: Pan-American Adventures of Craig Kennedy, Scientific Detective. Arthur Benjamin Reeve. LC 18-94984. 1918. Harper & Brothers.
Panama Red. Stephen Diamond. 1979. pap. 2.75 (ISBN 0-380-45237-5, 45237). Avon.
Panama Story: A Novel. George Vasilou. (Illus.). 1974. 6.50 (ISBN 0-682-47926-8). Exposition Press.
Pancakes for the Queen of Babylon. Peter Levi. 1968. signed ed. 50 copies 12.50 ea. (Pub. by Anvil Pr); pap. 1.50. SBD.
Panchagram: Five Villages. Tarasankar Banerjee. 1973. Manohar Book Service.
Panchita. Gil Procter. LC 60-9212. (Illus.). 1960. Naylor Co.
Pancho McClish. Herbert Coolidge. LC 21-26899. 1912. 1.25. A. C. McClurg & Co.
Panchronicon. Harold Steele MacKaye. LC 4-9632. 1904. C. Scribner's Sons.
Panchronicon Plot. Ron Goulart. (Science Fiction Ser.). 1977. pap. 1.25 o.p. (UY1283). DAW Bks.
Panchronicon Plot. Ron Goulart. 1.25 (ISBN 0-87997-283-1). DAW Books.
Pandemic. Tom Ardies. LC 72-92392. 1973. 5.95 (ISBN 0-385-01521-6). Doubleday.
Pandemic. Geoffrey S. Simmons. LC 79-56017. 1980. 9.95 (ISBN 0-87795-258-2). Arbor Hse.
Pandemonium on the Potomac: A Novel, by William C. Anderson. William C Anderson. LC 66-17329. 1966. Crown Publishers.
Pandora. Arthur Benjamin Reeve. LC 26-17994. 1926. Harper & Brothers.
Pandora, No. 5. Jayge Carr et al. Ed. by Lois Wickstrom. (Illus.). 60p. (Orig.). 1980. pap. 2.50 (ISBN 0-916176-10-X). Sproing.
Pandora, No. 6. Jean Lorrah et al. Ed. by Lois Wickstrom. (Illus.). 60p. (Orig.). 1980. pap. 2.50 (ISBN 0-916176-11-8). Sproing.
Pandora: A Novel. first american ed. Sylvia Fraser. LC 72-7081. (Illus.). 1973. 6.95 (ISBN 0-316-29216-8). Little, Brown.
Pandora: A Novel. Florence Lucie Dickinson Salzscheider. LC 2-186. 1901. The Whitaker & Ray Company (Incorporated.
Pandora, an Original Anthology of Role-Expanding Science Fiction & Fantasy. Lisa Goldstein et al. Ed. by Lois Wickstrom. (Vol. 1, No 3). (Illus.). 1979. pap. 1.50 (ISBN 0-916176-07-X). Sproing.
Pandora La Croix: A Novel. Gene Wright. LC 24-11330. 1924. J. B. Lippincott Company.
Pandora Lifts the Lid. Maysie Greig. LC 32-5592. 1932. L. MacVeagh, Dial Press, Inc.
Pandora Lifts the Lid. Christopher Darlington Morley & Marquis, Don, 1878- Joint Author. George H. Doran Company.
Pandora Man: A Novel. Kerry Newcomb & Frank Schaefer. LC 78-11807. 1979. 8.95 (ISBN 0-688-03420-9). Morrow.
Pandora Plague. Lee A. Matthias. 1981. pap. 2.25 o.s.i. (ISBN 0-8439-0917-X, Leisure Bks). Nordon Pubns.
Pandora Secret: A Captain Justice Story. Anthony Forrest. LC 82-9360. 15.50 (ISBN 0-8090-7504-0). Hill and Wang.
Pandora Seven: Role Expanding Science Fiction & Fantasy. Connie Kidwell et al. Ed. by Lois Wickstrom. (Illus.). 48p. 1981. 2.25 (ISBN 0-916176-12-6). Sproing.
Pandora's Box. Betty Hale Hyatt. (Candlelight Regency). 1977. 0.95 (ISBN 0-440-16920-8). Dell Pub. Co.
Pandora's Box. John Ames Mitchell. LC 14-13335. Grosset & Dunlap.
Pandora's Box. John Ames Mitchell. LC 11-22761. Frederick A. Stokes Company.
Pandora's Box: A Novel. Thomas Chastain. LC 74-76555. 1974. 6.95 (ISBN 0-88405-080-7). Mason & Lipscomb.
Pandora's Box in Sex. F. Rap Gerard. 1972. 5.00 o.p. (ISBN 0-682-47399-5). Exposition.
Pandora's Galley. MacDonald Harris. LC 78-22254. 1979. 10.95 (ISBN 0-15-170802-9). HarBraceJ.
Pandora's Galley. Donald W. Heiney. LC 78-22254. (Illus.). 10.95 (ISBN 0-15-170802-9). Harcourt Brace Jovanovich.
Pandora's Planet. Christopher Anvil. (Daw sf Books, no. 66). (Illus.). 1973. (pbk.) 0.95. Daw Books.
Pandora's Planet. Christopher Anvil. LC 75-182835. (Doubleday science fiction). 1972. 5.95. Doubleday.
Pandurang Hari: Or, Memoirs of a Hindoo (A Novel, 3 vols. William B. Hockley. LC 80-2484. Repr. of 1826 ed. Set. 149.50 (ISBN 0-404-19140-1). AMS Pr.
Panelled Room. Rupert Sargent Holland. LC 21-18470. G. W. Jacobs & Company.
Panglima Muda: A Romance of Malaya. Rounsevelle Wildman. LC 9-1822. 1894. Overland Monthly Publishing Company.
Panglor. Jeffrey A. Carver. (Orig.). 1980. pap. 1.95 (ISBN 0-440-17310-8). Dell.
Pangolin. Peter Driscoll. LC 79-471. 9.95 (ISBN 0-397-01070-2). Lippincott.
Pangs. Rochelle H. Dubois. (Illus., Orig.). 1980. pap. 5.00 (ISBN 0-933044-02-X). Lawton Pr.
Pangs of Venus. Tr. by Paul Anhalt. pap. 1.95 o.p. (6026). Brandon.
Panhandle Brand. Francis Mitchell. LC 64-7360. 1964. Arcadia House.
Panhandle Parson. Charles C Lowther. LC 42-22616. 1942. The Parthenon Press.
Panhandle Pioneer. Leslie Scott. LC 57-3197. 1957. Arcadia House.
Panhandle Pistolero. Ray Hogan. 1977. 1.25. Ace.
Panic! rev. ed. John Creasey. 1973. 0.75. Popular Lib.
Panic. Helen McCloy. LC 44-8487. 1944. W. Morrow & Company.
Panic! Bill Pronzini. LC 72-2900. 1972. 5.95 (ISBN 0-394-47491-0). Random House.
Panic! Bill Pronzini. 1973. (pbk.) 0.95. Pocket Books.
Panic Among Puritans. James Laver. LC 36-12813. Farrar & Rinehart, Inc.
Panic and The Runaway: Two Stories. Takeshi Kaiko. LC 78-309137. (UNESCO Collection of Representative Works: Japanese Series). 9.95 (ISBN 0-86008-196-6). University of Tokyo Press.
Panic Broadcast. Howard Koch. LC 73-121433. (Illus.). 1970. 4.95 o.p. (ISBN 0-316-50060-7). Little.
Panic in Box C. John Dickson Carr. LC 66-21721. 1966. Harper & Row.
Panic in Needle Park. James Mills. LC 66-14153. bds., 4.50. Farrar.
Panic in Paradise: By Alan Amos Pseud. 1st Ed. Kathleen Moore Knight. LC 51-13657. 1951. Published for the Crime Club by Doubleday.
Panic on Page One. Linda Stewart. LC 79-16100. 9.95 (ISBN 0-440-07120-8). Delacorte Press.
Panic Spring. Lawrence Durrell. LC 37-33911. 1937. Covici-Friede.
Panic-Stricken: A Novel of Suspense. Mitchell A Wilson. 1946. Simon and Schuster.
Panic Walks Alone. William L. Rivera. 176p. (Orig.). 1976. pap. 1.50 (ISBN 0-89041-091-7, 3091). Major Bks.
Panjandrum Number One. Ed. by Dennis Koran. (Illus.). 1972. pap. 8.00 (ISBN 0-915572-46-X). Panjandrum.
Panna Maria: Which in English Means "Virgin Mary". Jerome Charyn. LC 81-66960. 320p. 1982. 17.50 (ISBN 0-87795-328-7); pap. 9.50 (ISBN 0-87795-408-9). Arbor Hse.
Panola. A Tale of Louisiana. Sarah Anne Ellis Dorsey. LC 11-17959. T. B. Peterson & Brothers.
Panorama. Leopold Spero. LC 31-6853. Hillman-Curl, Inc.
Panorama Egg. A. E Silas. 1.75 (ISBN 0-87997-395-1). DAW Books.
Panorama of the Short Story. Ed. by Blanche Colton Williams. Lieber, Maxim, Joint Ed. LC 29-17995. (Golden Key Series). D. C. Heath and Company.
Pan's Eyes. Joel Oppenheimer. LC 74-77760. (Haystack Bks.). (Signed ltd. ed. 10.00 o.p.). 64p. 1974. pap. 3.50 (Pub. by Mulch Pr). SBD.
Pan's Garden: A Volume of Nature Stories. Algernon Blackwood. LC 74-157772. (Short story index reprint series). (Illus.). 1971. (ISBN 0-8369-3884-4). Books for Libraries Press.
Pan's Parish. Louise Redfield Peattie. LC 31-280609. 2.00. The Century Co.
Pansy: An Immaterial Romance. Alfred Still. LC 60-12820. Christopher Pub. House.
Pansy Meares: The Story of a London Shop Girl. Horace W. C Newte. LC 12-21771. 1912. John Lane Company.
Pansy Stories. Virge Reese Phelps. LC 7-30577. A. I. Bradley & Co.
Pantechnicon. Lionel Miskin. LC 74-96001. 1970. 4.95 o.p. (ISBN 0-06-012987-5, HarpT). Har-Row.
Pantechnicon. Lionel Miskin. 192p. 1972. pap. 0.95 o.p. (B95-2213). Belmont-Tower.
Panther! Roger A Caras. LC 77-23487. 1977. 1.95 (ISBN 0-14-004576-7). Penguin Books.
Panther! Roger A Caras. LC 79-79371. (Illus.). 1970. 5.95. Little, Brown.
Panther: A Tale of Temptation. Anne Warner French. LC 8-29870. 1908. Small, Maynard & Company.
Panther Genesis. Maurice Scott, Jr. LC 70-148006. 1971. 5.95 o.p. (ISBN 0-87695-130-2). Aurora Pubs.
Panther John. Robert Tralins. (Orig.). 1970. pap. 0.95 o.p. (ISBN 0-447-75116-6). Lancer.
Panther Mountain. 1st Ed. John Brick. LC 58-5931. 1958. Doubleday.
Panther Paradox. rev. ed. Don Schanche. 1971. Repr. pap. 0.95 o.p. (ISBN 0-446-65699-2, 65-699). Paperback Lib.
Panther Rock. Aril Bond Burr. LC 31-29818. Printed for the Author by the Ruter Press.
Panther Throne. Tome Murphy. 1982. pap. 3.95 (ISBN 0-451-11861-8, AE1861, Sig). NAL.
Panther's Cub. Agnes Sweetman Castle & Castle, Egerton. LC 10-12781. 1910. Doubleday, Page & Company.
Panthers' Moon. Victor Canning. LC 48-6160. 1948. M. S. Mill Co.
Panting for Oscar. Scott Arlen. pap. 1.95 o.s.i. (OPS-37). Olympia.
Panting for Pleasure. Sally Barrow. 160p. (Orig.). 1972. pap. 1.95 o.s.i. (TCP 2070). Olympia.
Pantoufle. Frederick Jackson. LC 35-5373. 1935. A. A. Knopf.
Pants for an Octopus. Bert Schierbeek. Tr. by Charles McGeehan from Dutch. 122p. 1973. pap. 2.45 o.s.i. (ISBN 0-912358-44-0). Omen Pr.
Panzer. Harold Calin. 1970. pap. 0.75 o.p. (ISBN 0-447-74693-6). Lancer.
Panzer! Harold Calin. 1975. (pbk.) 1.25. Belmont Tower Books.
Panzer Fort. Robert Newton. (Orig.). 1980. pap. 1.95. Woodhill.
Panzer Grenadiers. Heinrich Muller. 288p. (Orig.). 1980. pap. 2.50 (ISBN 0-89083-697-3). Zebra.
Paola Corletti: The Fair Italian. Alice Howard Hilton. LC 11-16146. (On cover: Neely's popular library, no. 84). F. T. Neely.
Paoli: the Warrior Bishop: Or, The Fall of the Christians. W. C. Kitchin. LC 7-14285. (On cover: The Choice series. no. 39). 1891. R. Bonner's Sons.
Papa Bouchard. Molly Elliot Seawell. LC 1-25452. 1901. C. Scribner's Sons.
Papa Gorski. Catherine B Osborn & Margaret Waterman. LC 69-12043. 1969. Harcourt, Brace & World.
Papa Hemingway: The Ecstasy & Sorrow. A. E. Hotchner. (Illus.). 352p. 1982. pap. 8.95 (ISBN 0-688-02042-9). Quill NY.
Papa, I Can Hardly Wait. Lourdes High. LC 77-85096. 6.95 (ISBN 0-930534-02-6). Brock Pub.
Papa, I Can Hardly Wait. Lourdes High. LC 77-85096. 1977. 6.95 (ISBN 0-930534-02-6). Spilman Pr.
Papa, I Can Hardly Wait: A Novel. Lourdes High. LC 77-85096. 6.95 (ISBN 0-930534-02-6). Brock Pub. Co.
Papa La-Bas. John Dickson Carr. LC 68-28229. 1968. 5.95. Harper & Row.
Papa La Fleur. Zona Gale. LC 33-5483. 1933. D. Appleton and Company.
Papa Married a Mormon. John Dennis Fitzgerald. 1976. Repr. 8.95 (ISBN 0-914740-21-0). Western Epics.
Papa Pasquier. Georges Duhamel. Tr. by Putnam, Samuel. LC 34-28961. 1934. Harper & Brothers.
Papa Pontivy and the Maginot Murder. Bernard Newman. LC 40-13049. H. Holt and Company.
Papa San Files. Henry Henn. 1977. pap. 1.50 (ISBN 0-532-15264-6). Woodhill.
Papa Tango. John Clagett. LC 81-9792. 12.95 (ISBN 0-517-54536-5). Crown Publishers.
Papa, You're Crazy. 1st Ed. William Saroyan. LC 57-7840. 1957. Little, Brown.
Papa's Burlesque House. Bernard Livingston. LC 77-141886. 1971. 5.95 (ISBN 0-87164-116-X). William-F.
Papa's Burlesque House: A Novel. Bernard Livingston. 1972. 0.95 (ISBN 0-515-02789-8). Pyramid Books.
Papa's Burlesque House: A Novel. Bernard Livingston. LC 77-141886. 1971. 5.95. William-Frederick Press.
Papa's Daughter. Thyra Ferre Bjorn. LC 58-6258. 1958. Rinehart.
Papa's Game. Gregory Wallance. 1982. pap. 2.95 (ISBN 0-345-30168-4). Ballantine.
Papa's Gift: A Novel. Bill Erni. LC 63-22627. Citadel Press.
Papa's Own Girl: A Novel. Marie Howland. LC 7-5671. 1874. J. P. Jewett.
Papa's Own Girl: A Novel. Marie Howland. LC 7-5670. (On cover: Lovell's library. v. 10, no. 534). 1885. John W. Lovell Company.
Papa's Own Girl: A Novel. Marie Howland. LC 7-5669. (On cover: American novelists' series. no. 45). 1890. John W. Lovell Company.
Papa's Ugly Duckling. 1st Ed. Olive Van Hyning. LC 56-131220. 1956. Pageant Press.
Papa's Wife. Thyra Ferre Bjorn. LC 55-8009. 1955. Rinehart.
Papa's Wife: Papa's Daughter; Mama's Way; a Trilogy. Thyra Ferre Bjorn. LC 60-11230. 1960. Rinehart.
Papa's Wife: Papa's Daughter; Mama's Way; a Trilogy. 1st Ed. Thyra Ferre Bjorn. LC 61-153573. 1961. Holt, Rinehart and Winston.
Paper Albatross. Croft-Cooke, Rupert. LC 68-14571. (raven book). 1968. 3.95. Abelard-Schuman.
Paper Boats. 1st Ed. Roger Longrigg. LC 63-16525. 1963. Harper & Row.
Paper Bridge: A Novel. Victor Jeremy Jerome. LC 66-24226. 1966. Citadel Press.
Paper Bullet. Otis Carney. LC 66-11662. 1966. bds., 4.95. Morrow.
Paper Cap: A Story of Love and Labor. Amelia Edith Huddleston Barr. LC 48-18888. 1918. 1.50. D. Appleton and Company.
Paper Chase. Oliver Weld Bayer, pseud. LC 43-10420. 1943. Pub. for the Crime Club by Doubleday, Doran & Co., Inc.
Paper Chase. Lesley Egan, pseud. (Harper Novels of Suspense). 256p. 1972. 5.95 o.p. (ISBN 0-06-011158-5, HarpT). Har-Row.
Paper Chase. John Kennedy. LC 56-5912. 1956. Abelard-Schuman.
Paper Chase. Elizabeth Linington. LC 72-76244. 1972. 5.95 (ISBN 0-06-011158-5). Harper & Row.
Paper Chase. John Jay Osborn. LC 78-154337. 1971. 4.95 (ISBN 0-395-12670-3). Houghton Mifflin.
Paper Chase. John Jay Osborn. 224p. 1983. pap. 2.95 (ISBN 0-446-31141-3). Warner Bks.
Paper Chase. Julian Symons. 1971. pap. 0.95 o.p. (95092). Beagle Bks.
Paper Chase: A Novel. Mark Saxton. LC 64-25302. 1964. Bobbs-Merrill.
Paper-Chase Mystery. Archibald E. Fielding. LC 35-2890. 1935. H. C. Kinsey & Company, Inc.
Paper Circle. Bruno Fischer. LC 51-12408. (Red badge detective). 1951. Dodd, Mead.
Paper City. David Ross Locke. LC 68-57539. (American novels of muckraking, propaganda, and social protest). 1968. Gregg Press.
Paper City. David Ross Locke. LC 7-15164. Lothrop, Lee & Shepard Co.
Paper Dolls. Laura Beheler. LC 56-7731. 1956. Houghton Mifflin.
Paper Dolls: 1st Amer. Ed. Leslie Purnell Davies. LC 66-12230. 1966. 3.95. Pub. for Crime Club by Doubleday.

Paper Dragon: A Novel. Evan Hunter. LC 66-123339. 1966. 5.95. Delacorte.
Paper Ghost. Edward Ernest Smith. LC 61-16547. 1961. Morrow.
Paper Gold. Michael Goodkin. LC 81-11823. 12.95 (ISBN 0-02-544660-6). Macmillan.
Paper House. Francoise Mallet-Joris. LC 70-148707. 1972. Curtis Books.
Paper House. Mallet-Joris, Francoise. LC 72-179708. 1971. 2.50. W. H. Allen.
Paper Houses. William Charles Franklyn Plomer. LC 29-13067. 1929. Coward-McCann, Inc.
Paper Mistress. Dorothea Malm. LC 59-130981. 1959. Coward-McCann.
Paper Money. Adam Smith. 1982. pap. 3.95 (ISBN 0-440-16891-0). Dell.
Paper Moon: A Novel. Joe David Brown. (Signet bk., Y5418). 1973. 1.25. New American Lib.
Paper Palace. 1st American Ed. Robert Harling. LC 52-5924. Harper.
Paper Profits, a Novel of Wall Street. Arthur Cheney Train. LC 30-8785. H. Liveright.
Paper Snake. Raymond Johnson. LC 65-15545. (Illus.). 1965. 10.00 (ISBN 0-89366-061-2). Ultramarine Pub.
Paper Thunderbolt. John Innes Mackintosh Stewart. LC 51-13659. 1951. Dodd, Mead.
Paper Tiger. Jack Davies. 1975. (pbk.) 1.50. Dell.
Paper Tiger. Elizabeth N. Walker. (Finding Mr. Right Ser.). 256p. 1983. pap. 2.75 (ISBN 0-380-81620-2, 81620-2). Avon.
Paper Walls of Innocence. Thomas M Livingston. LC 63-12712. 1963. Bantam Books.
Paperback Conspiracy. National Lampoon. 1974. (pbk.) 1.25. Warner Paperback Library.
Paperback Thriller. Lynn Meyer. LC 75-10339. 1975. 6.95 (ISBN 0-394-49767-8). Random House.
Paperback Thriller. Lynn Meyer. 1.50 (ISBN 0-380-00866-1). Avon.
Paperbag. Richard Russell. 1979. pap. 1.75 o.s.i. (ISBN 0-505-51427-3). Tower Bks.
Paperhanger. Suzanne Prou. LC 74-5803. 1974. 5.95 (ISBN 0-06-013444-5). Harper & Row.
Papers of Captain Rufus Lincoln of Wareham, Mass. Ed. by Rufus Lincoln. LC 74-140872. (Eyewitness Accounts of the American Revolution Ser., No. 3). 1970. Repr. of 1904 ed. 15.00 (ISBN 0-405-01220-9). Ayer Co.
Papers of Tony Veitch. William McIlvanney. LC 82-18990. 1983. 12.95 (ISBN 0-394-42437-9). Pantheon Books.
Papillon. Henri Charriere. 1981. pap. 3.50 (ISBN 0-671-41689-8). PB.
Papineau the Terrible. Paul Kurm. 4.95 o.p. Vantage.
Paprika. Erich Von Stroheim. LC 35-3049. The Macaulay Company.
Paquita. Robert Raynolds. 1947. G. P. Putnam's Sons.
Para China con Amor. new ed. Glen Chase, pseud. Tr. by Miguel Sarria from Eng. (Pimienta Collection Ser). Orig. Title: Tong in Cheek. 160p. (Span.). 1974. pap. 1.00 o.p. (ISBN 0-88473-208-8). Fiesta Pub.
Para Handy & Other Tales. Neal Munro. 690p. 20.00x (ISBN 0-85158-138-2, Pub. by Blackwood & Sons England). State Mutual Bk.
Para Ti. Louis Untermeyer. (O.s.i.). (Illus., Span.). 1968. 1.25 o.s.i. Larousse.
Parable: A Story of Jesus, Son of Joseph. Cleta Flynn. LC 79-14062. 1979. 4.95 (ISBN 0-915442-76-0). Donning Co.
Parable & Number. Mariquita Platov. LC 73-89557. pap. 3.50 (ISBN 0-914744-25-9). Inst Byzantine.
Parable of Pilgrims. Ralph A Chalfant. LC 52-8131. 1953. Vantage Press.
Parable of the Virginia. Mary Lapsley Caughey Guest. LC 31-6788. 1931. R. R. Smith, Inc.
Parables. Joseph Miller. LC 66-163092. 2.95. Naylor.
Parables of Peanuts. Robert L. Short. 1978. pap. 1.95 (ISBN 0-449-23677-3, Crest). Fawcett.
Parachute. Ramon Guthrie. LC 28-3430. Harcourt, Brace and Company.
Parachute Murder. Lebbeus Mitchell. LC 33-19081. The Macaulay Company.
Parachutes. Shirley Powell. 1975. pap. 3.00 o.p. (ISBN 0-916266-00-1). A Bifrost.
Parachutists. Edward Klein. LC 81-140298. 1981. 12.95 (ISBN 0-385-12573-9). Doubleday.
Parade: A Novel of New York Society. Emily Price Post. LC 25-168153. 1925. Funk & Wagnalls Company.
Parade Ground. Marion Rolfe Johnson Deitrick. LC 30-23089. 1930. Doubleday, Doran & Company, Inc.
Parade of Cockeyed Creatures: Or, Did Someone Murder Our Wandering Boy? George Baxt. LC 67-22672. 1967. Random House.
Parade of the Empty Boots. Charles Alden Seltzer. LC 74-21536. 1974. (ISBN 0-88411-103-2). Aeonian Press.
Parade of the Empty Boots. Charles Alden Seltzer. LC 38-1031. 1937. Doubleday, Doran and Company, Inc.
Parade of the Empty Boots. Charles Alden Seltzer. LC 39-7933. 1939. The Sun Dial Press, Inc.
Parade on an Empty Street. Margaret Drury Gane. LC 79-2132. 8.95 (ISBN 0-312-59594-8). St. Martin's Press.
Parade on an Empty Street. Margaret Drury Gane. LC 80-177. 1980. 12.95 (ISBN 0-8161-3066-3). G. K. Hall.
Parade to Hell. Allen Robert Taft. LC 36-802018. 1936. Cambridge Press.
Parade's End. Ford Madox Ford. LC 79-2158. 1979. 6.95 (ISBN 0-394-74108-0). Vintage Books.
Parade's End: Consisting of "Some Do Not", "No More Parades", "A Man Could Stand up", & "The Last Post". Ford Madox Ford. LC 79-2158. 1979. pap. 6.95 (ISBN 0-394-74108-0, Vin). Random.
Parade's End. With an Introd. by Robie Macauley. 1st Borzoi Ed. Ford Madox Ford. LC 50-9209. 1950. Knopf.
Paradiddle: A Novel. Gus Weill. LC 73-90946. 1974. 6.95 (ISBN 0-8065-0402-1). Citadel Press.
Paradigm Red: A Novel. Harold King. LC 74-17663. 1975. 7.95 (ISBN 0-672-52051-6). Bobbs-Merrill.
Paradine Case, a Novel. Robert Smythe Hichens. LC 33-199623. 1933. Doubleday, Doran & Company, Inc.
Paradis Desespere: L'Amour, L'Illusion. Jacques Ehrmann. (Yale Romantic Studies). 1963. pap. 37.50x. Elliots Bks.
Paradise. Alice Brown. LC 5-269288. 1905. Houghton, Mifflin and Company.
Paradise. Patrick Dennis, pseud. LC 79-142085. 1971. 7.95 o.p. (ISBN 0-15-170965-3). HarBraceJ.
Paradise. Patrick Dennis, pseud. 1972. pap. 1.25 o.p. (ISBN 0-515-02862-2). Pyramid Pubns.
Paradise. Ken Fishman. LC 78-22466. 1979. 10.95 (ISBN 0-690-01804-5). T. Y. Crowell.
Paradise. Esther Forbes. LC 37-27104. Harcourt, Brace and Company.
Paradise. Cosmo Hamilton. LC 25-3543. 1925. Little, Brown and Company.
Paradise. David Houston. 208p. (Orig.). 1982. pap. 2.50 (ISBN 0-8439-1064-X, Leisure Bks). Nordon Pubns.
Paradise. Edward Everett Tanner. LC 79-142085. 1971. (ISBN 0-15-170965-3). Harcourt Brace Jovanovich.
Paradise: A Novel. Lloyd Stephens Bryce. LC 6-19891. 1887. Funk & Wagnalls.
Paradise: A Novel. Sarah Neilan. LC 82-5729. (Illus.). 13.95 (ISBN 0-312-59596-4). St. Martin's Press.
Paradise Alley. John Desmond Sheridan. LC 47-4513. 1947. The Bruce Publishing Company.
Paradise Alley. Sylvester Stallone. 1978. pap. 1.95 (ISBN 0-425-03811-4, Medallion). Berkley Pub.
Paradise Almost Lost. The First Commercial Trip of an Uninitiated. David B. Shaw. (Fireside series, no. 31). J. S. Ogilvie & Company.
Paradise Auction. Nalbro Isadorah Bartley. 1917. Small, Maynard & Company.
Paradise Bay. John Brodie. LC 53-9423. 1953. A. A. Wyn.
Paradise Below the Stairs: Translated from the French by Herma Briffault. 1st Ed. Andre Brincourt. LC 52-9072. 1952. Duell, Sloan and Pearce.
Paradise Bend. William Patterson White. LC 20-182973. 1920. Doubleday, Page & Company.
Paradise Bird. 1st Ed. Howard Otway. LC 55-10713. 1956. Harper.
Paradise Bit: A Novel by William K. Zinsser. 1st Ed. William Knowlton Zinsser. LC 67-14457. 1967. bds., 5.95. Little.
Paradise Bum. Andrew Sinclair. LC 63-12800. 1963. Atheneum.
Paradise City. Henry Channon. LC 31-1518. E. P. Dutton & Co., Inc.
Paradise County. Roy Sparkia. 1974. (pbk.) 1.25. Dell.
Paradise Court. Joseph Smith Fletcher. LC 29-618727. 1929. Pub. for The Crime Club, Inc., by Doubleday, Doran & Company, Inc.
Paradise Cove: A Novel. Alfred Fullerton Loomis. LC 33-17933. 1933. D. Appleton-Century Company, Incorporated.
Paradise Falls. Don Robertson. LC 68-12109. 1968. Putnam.
Paradise Farm. Katharine Tynan Hinkson, pseud. LC 11-264088. 1911. 1.20. Duffield & Company.
Paradise for Two. 1st Ed. Frank Andrle. LC 57-7792. 1957. Vantage Press.
Paradise Formula. Alan Dipper. LC 74-102189. 1970. 5.95. Morrow.
Paradise Found. Mell. A Neff. LC 14-3565. 1914. The Author.
Paradise Game. Brian M Stableford. 1974. (pbk.) 0.95. DAW Books.
Paradise Garden. by george gibbs... illustrated by william a. hottinger. ed. George Fort Gibbs. LC 16-18563. 1916. 1.35. D. Appleton and Company.
Paradise I: A Novel. Alan Harrington. LC 77-12350. 10.00 (ISBN 0-316-34763-9). Little, Brown.
Paradise in Flames. Joseph Brandon. 1976. (pbk.) 1.95 (ISBN 0-671-80354-9). Pocket Books.
Paradise in Montparnasse. Maurice Dekobra & Hall, Henry Noble, 1872- Tr. LC 46-4805. 1946. B. Ackerman, Inc.
Paradise in Texas. W. B Lewis. LC 34-9209. 1933. The Naylor Company.
Paradise Island: A Love Story. Eleanor Elliott Carroll. LC 33-109833. Chelsea House.
Paradise Island: A Novel of Romance and Adventure. Charles G Cisna. LC 52-5697. 1952. Exposition Press.
Paradise Island: An Interracial Love Story. Christopher George. 52p. 1971. 3.00 o.p. (ISBN 0-682-47380-4). Exposition.
Paradise Isle. Susan Lennox. LC 57-126634. 1957. Avalon Books.
Paradise Loses. George G. Gilman, pseud. (Edge Ser.: No. 15). 160p. 1975. pap. 1.75 (ISBN 0-523-41293-2). Pinnacle Bks.
Paradise Lost. John Milton. Bd. with Paradise Regained; Samson Agonistes. 1962. pap. 0.95 o.s.i. (Collier). Macmillan.
Paradise Lost: Screenplay for Cinema of the Mind. John Collier. 1973. pap. 2.95 o.p. (ISBN 0-394-70964-0). Knopf.
Paradise Man. John Hale. LC 71-84169. 1969. 5.00 o.p. Bobbs.
Paradise Man: A Black and White Farce. John Hale. LC 71-84169. 1969. 5.00. Bobbs-Merrill.
Paradise Mystery. Joseph Smith Fletcher. LC 20-8629. (On verso of half-title: The Borzoi mystery stories. vii). 1920. A.A. Knopf.
Paradise of Birds, When Spring Comes to Texas. Helen G. Cruickshank. 1968. 7.50 o.p. (ISBN 0-396-05695-4). Dodd.
Paradise on Earth. Jeff W. Hayes. LC 42-485923. 1913. F. W. Baltes and Company.
Paradise People. David Lytton. LC 62-16386. 1962. Simon and Schuster.
Paradise Plantation. Henrietta Reid. (Romances Ser.). 192p. (Orig.). 1980. pap. text ed. 1.25 (ISBN 0-373-02345-6, Pub. by Harlequin). PB.
Paradise Plot. Ed Naha. 352p. (Orig.). 1980. pap. 2.25 (ISBN 0-553-13979-7). Bantam.
Paradise Plus: A Selection of Stories from Air Niugini's in-Flight Magazine. Ed. by Gerry Dick. LC 79-89558. (Illus.). 144p. 1980. 12.95 (ISBN 0-85807-044-8, 3028, Pub. by Pacific Pubns Australia). Bks Australia.
Paradise Point. Ethel Lockwood. Ed. by Alice Sachs. 1971. 3.95 o.p. Lenox Hill.
Paradise Prairie. Cecil Brown Williams. LC 53-9559. 1953. J. Day Co.
Paradise Range. George M Johnson. LC 34-243503. E. J. Clode, Inc.
Paradise Reclaimed. Halldor Laxness, pseud. 1962. 8.50 o.p. M McCosh Bkslr.
Paradise Regained see Paradise Lost.
Paradise Rehearsal Club: A Novel. Margaret Cronin Fisk & Alan Fisk. LC 81-16545. 14.95 (ISBN 0-671-40023-1). Summit Books.
Paradise Rezoned. Robert Lieberman. LC 76-350645. (Berkley medallion book). 1974. 1.50 (ISBN 0-425-02681-7). Berkley Pub. Corp.
Paradise Road. David Scott Milton. LC 73-91626. 1974. 7.95 (ISBN 0-689-10597-5). Atheneum.
Paradise Road. David Scott Milton. (pbk.) 1.75. Dell.
Paradise Smith. Ronald Johnston. LC 72-78453. 1972. 5.75 (ISBN 0-15-170967-X). Harcourt Brace Jovanovich.
Paradise Street. Henry Farrand Griffin. LC 43-7756. 1943. D. Appleton-Century Company, Incorporated.
Paradise Trail. William Byron Mowery. LC 36-17724. 1936. Little, Brown, and Company.
Paradise Trap. Robert Crane. (Orig.). pap. 0.50 o.p. (R1603). Pyramid Pubns.
Paradise Valley Girl. Susanna Margaret Davidson Fry. 1899. Woman's Temperance Publishing Association.
Paradise Walk. Boris Todrin. LC 46-215706. 1946. E. P. Dutton & Co., Inc.
Paradise Wild. Johanna Lindsey. 320p. 1981. pap. 2.95 (ISBN 0-380-77651-0, 77651). Avon.
Paradise Wold. Alice V Carey. LC 6-228151. (Dillingham's metropolitan library, no. 12). 1896. G. W. Dillingham.
Paradiso. Jose Lezama-Lima. LC 70-139340. (Illus.). 1974. 12.95 (ISBN 0-374-22984-8). Farrar, Straus and Giroux.
Paradiso. Jose Lezama-Lima. Tr. by Gregory Rabassa from Span. 544p. 1972. 10.00 o.p. (ISBN 0-374-22984-8). FS&G.
Paradiso". Allan Prior. LC 73-2317. 1973. 7.95 (ISBN 0-671-21498-5). Simon and Schuster.
Paradox. Howard Rockey. LC 26-6645. Macrae Smith Company.
Paradox Lost, and Twelve Other Great Science Fiction Stories. Fredric Brown. LC 72-10988. 1973. 5.95 (ISBN 0-394-48448-7). Random House.
Paradox of Purity. A Novel. Edith Darling Garloch. F. T. Neely.
Paradox of the Sets. Brian M. Stableford. (Daw Science Fiction Ser.). 1979. pap. 1.75 o.p. (ISBN 0-87997-493-1, UE1493). Daw Bks.
Paradox Players. Maureen Duffy. LC 68-25745. 1968. 4.95. Simon and Schuster.
Paradoxes. John Hall. LC 56-6812. 1977. Repr. of 1650 ed. 25.00x (ISBN 0-8201-1233-X). Schol Facsimiles.
Paradoxes of Mr. Pond. Gilbert Keith Chesterton. LC 37-5409. 1937. Dodd, Mead & Company.
Paradoxes of Mister Pond. Gilbert Keith Chesterton. 1963. 3.00 o.p. Dufour.
Paragon. John Knowles. (O.s.i.). 1970. 7.95 o.s.i. (ISBN 0-394-43976-7). Random.
Paragon Walk. Anne Perry. LC 80-23186. 9.95 (ISBN 0-312-59598-0). St. Martin's Press.
Paragreens on a Visit to the Paris Universal Exhibition. Giovanni Domenico Ruffini. LC 1-26991. 1857. Dix, Edwards & Co.; Etc., Etc.
Paraja: A Novel of Tribal Life. Gopinath Mohanthy. (Vikas Library of Modern Indian Writing). 288p. 1982. text ed. 22.50x (ISBN 0-7069-1588-7, Pub. by Vikas India). Advent NY.
Parajacker. Jeremiah Jack. 1974. (pbk.) 0.95. Warner Paperback Library.
Parallax: By Vladimir Yurasov. Tr. by Tatiana Balkoff Drowne. 1st Ed. Vladimir Rudolph Shabinsky. LC 65-25943. 1966. bds., 7.95. Norton.
Parallax View. Loren Singer. LC 72-103775. 1970. 4.95. Doubleday.
Parallax View. Loren Singer. 1974. (pbk.) 1.25. Dell.
Paramilitary Plot. Don Pendleton. (Executioner Ser.). 192p. 1982. pap. 1.95 (ISBN 0-373-61045-9, Pub. by Worldwide). Harlequin Bks.
Paramount Right: A Story of New York During the Revolution. Emma Mersereau Newton. LC 27-3098. 1926. F. H. Hitchcock.
Paramours of the Creoles: A Story of New Orleans and the Method of Promiscuous Mating Between White Creole Men and Negro and Colored Slaves and Freewomen. Pierre Paul Ebeyer. LC 44-6748. 1944. Windmill Publishing Company.
Paramours of the Creoles: A Story of New Orleans and the Method of Promiscuous Mating Between White Creole Men and Negro and Colored Slaves and Freewomen. Pierre Paul Ebeyer. LC 46-801. 1945. Windmill Publishing Company.
Parasite. Ramsey Campbell. 1981. pap. 2.95 (ISBN 0-671-41905-6). PB.
Parasite. Arthur Conan Doyle. LC 80-67704. (Conan Doyle Centennial Ser.). (Illus.). 100p. cancelled (ISBN 0-934468-45-1). Gaslight.
Parasite: A Novel. Helen Reimensnyder Martin. LC 13-3763. 1913. 1.25. J. B. Lippincott Company.
Parasite: A Story. Arthur Conan Doyle. LC 6-34238. 1895. Harper & Brothers.
Parasite Person. Celia Fremlin, pseud. LC 82-45394. 1982. 11.95 (ISBN 0-385-18300-3). Published for the Crime Club by Doubleday.
Parasites. Daphne Du Maurier. LC 51-3619. 1951. Garden City Books.
Parasites. Daphne Du Maurier. LC 72-184728. 1971. 8.50 (ISBN 0-8376-0410-9). R. Bentley.
Parasites. 1st American Ed. Daphne Du Maurier. LC 49-50221. 1950. Doubleday.
Parcel of Rogues. Elaine Kidner Dakers. LC 48-3678. 1948. Rinehart.
Parcel of Rogues. Jane Lane. LC 71-21510. (Jane Lane Novels Ser.). 448p. 1967. 10.50x o.p. (ISBN 0-584-31085-4). Intl Pubns Serv.
Parcel of Their Fortunes. Barbara Ninde Byfield. LC 79-7565. 1979. 7.95 (ISBN 0-385-14611-6). Published for the Crime Club by Doubleday.
Parched Earth. Arnold B. Armstrong. LC 34-3284. 1934. The Macmillan Company.
Parchment Key. Stanley Jr. Hopkins. LC 44-3684. 1944. Harcourt, Brace and Company.
Pardemic. Geoffrey S. Simmons. 272p. 1981. pap. 2.75 (ISBN 0-425-05062-9). Berkley Pub.
Pardner of Blossom Range. Frances Asa Charles. LC 6-383971. 1906. Little, Brown, and Company.
Pardners. Rex Ellingwood Beach. LC 74-101792. (Short story index reprint series). 1969. Books for Libraries Press.
Pardners. Rex Ellingwood Beach. LC 5-13199. 1905. McClure, Phillips & Co.
Pardners. Rex Ellingwood Beach. LC 21-146263. 1911. A. L. Burt Company.
Pardners. Edgar Wright. LC 58-3545. 1958. Vantage Press.
Pardners: A Novel of the California Gold Rush. John Weld. LC 41-4023. 1941. C. Scribner's Sons.
Pardners of the Badlands. Harry Sinclair Drago. LC 48-20689. (New Avon library, 156). 1948. Avon Book Co.
Pardners of the Badlands. Harry Sinclair Drago. LC 42-21649. 1942. Doubleday, Doran & Co., Inc.
Pardners of the Dim Trails. 1st Ed. Walt Coburn. LC 51-9339. 1951. Lippincott.

TITLE INDEX PARTING OF THE WAYS

Pardon and Peace. Hilda Vaughan. LC 43-51015. 1943. Duell, Sloan and Pearce.
Pardon Me, You're Stepping on My Eyeball. Paul Zindel. (gr. 8-12). 1977. pap. 2.25 (ISBN 0-553-14836-2). Bantam.
Pardon My Blood. 1st Ed. Paul Whelton. LC 50-10352. (Main line mysteries). 1950. Lippincott.
Pardon My Shadow. Irene M Boord. 1974. 8.95 (ISBN 0-533-00849-2). Vantage Press.
Pardoner's Tale. John Barrington Wain. LC 78-24114. 1979. 10.00 (ISBN 0-670-53825-6). Viking Press.
Pards of Buffalo Bill. Thomas Albert Curry. (Orig.). 1972. pap. 0.60 o.p. (06185). Curtis.
Pards of Buffalo Bill. Tom Curry. 1973. 0.60. Curtis Books.
Parent and Child in Fiction. Robert D Strom. LC 77-24920. 6.95 (ISBN 0-8185-0246-0). Brooks/Cole Pub. Co.
Parentheses: An Autobiographical Journey. Jay Neugeboren. LC 73-95489. 1970. 5.95. Dutton.
Parenthesis. Jacques Lemarchand & Varese, Louise (McCutcheon) Tr. LC 47-16282. 1947. A. A. Knopf.
Parents' Advice. Sam Pallas. LC 53-277876. Vantage Press.
Parents Day, a Novel: Sgraffiti Illus. by Percival Goodman. Paul Goodman. LC 52-42171. 1951-1952. X Press.
Parents Permitting. Anne Wormser. LC 41-41. 1941. Macrae-Smith Company.
Parfit Gentil Knight. Charlton Andrews. LC 1-254202. 1901. A. C. McClurg & Co.
Pariah, 3 vols. in 2. F. Anstey. LC 79-8228. Repr. of 1889 ed. Set. 84.50 (ISBN 0-404-61757-3). AMS Pr.
Pariah: And Other Stories. Joan Williams. LC 83-1002. 1983. 13.45 (ISBN 0-316-94233-2). Little, Brown.
Paris. Nick Carter. (Nick Carter, Killmaster Espionage Ser). (O.s.i.). 1970. pap. 0.75 o.s.i. (A744S, Award). Univ Pub & Dist.
Paris. Sam Dodson. (Kangaroo Book.). 1977. 1.75. (ISBN 0-671-80922-9). Pocket Books.
Paris. Emile Zola. LC 75-20446. 1975. 40.00 (ISBN 0-87968-236-1). Gordon Press.
Paris see Trois Villes.
Paris: A Novel. Anne Green. LC 38-324019. E. P. Dutton & Co., Inc.
Paris: A Novel. Emile Zola & Vizetelly, Ernest Alfred, 1853-1922, Tr. LC 9-131112. 1898. The Macmillan Company.
Paris Bit. Irving Marder. LC 68-16177. 1968. Dodd, Mead.
Paris Blues. Harold Flender. 1974. (pbk.) 1.25. Manor Books.
Paris Drop. Alan Furst. LC 79-7615. 1980. 8.95 (ISBN 0-385-14889-5). Doubleday.
Paris Gazette. Lion Feuchtwanger. Tr. by Willa Muir. Muir, Edwin, 1887- Joint Tr. LC 40-7414. 1940. The Viking Press.
Paris Interlude. Naim Kattan. LC 80-450043. 1979. 12.95 (ISBN 0-7710-4471-2). McClelland and Stewart.
Paris Is for Lovers. Evelyn Herbert. LC 53-6319. 1953. Dodd, Mead.
Paris Is Worth a Mass. Ross Williamson, Hugh. LC 72-93325. 1973. 6.50. St. Martin's Press.
Paris Is Worth a Mass. Hugh R. Williamson. LC 72-93325. 224p. 1973. 6.50 o.p. St Martin.
Paris Kill. Philip Kirk. (Butler Ser.: No. 10). 240p. 1983. pap. 2.50 o.s.i. (ISBN 0-8439-1087-9, Leisure Bks). Dorchester Pub Co.
Paris Love. Nina Wilcox Putnam. LC 32-9031. 1932. R. Long & R. R. Smith, Inc.
Paris Nights. Brad Petersen. 1972. pap. 1.75 o.s.i. (V1093K, Venus). Grove.
Paris Nights: A Chronicle. C. Ross Smith. LC 65-23244. bds., 5.95. S. & S.
Paris of Troy. George Edward Baker. LC 47-11315. 1947. Ziff-Davis Pub. Co.
Paris on the Barricades. George Spiro. LC 29-8009. Workers Library Publishers.
Paris One. James Brady. 1977. 8.95 o.s.i. (ISBN 0-440-06815-0). Delacorte.
Paris Original. Alexandra Orme. LC 54-7088. 1954. Houghton Mifflin.
Paris Pandemonium. Erakine Gwynn. LC 36-138851. R. Speller.
Paris Puzzle: An Inspector Damiot Mystery. Vincent McConnor. 254p. 1981. 12.95 (ISBN 0-02-582950-5). Macmillan.
Paris Summer. April Kihlstron. (Avalon Books). 4.95. Thomas Bouregy.
Parish and the Hill. Mary Doyle Curran. LC 48-8086. Houghton Mifflin Co.
Parish and the Hill. Mary Doyle Curran. LC 48-8086. 1948. Houghton Mifflin Co.
Parish of the Pines: The Story of Frank Higgins, the Lumberjacks' Sky Pilot. Thomas Davis Whittles. LC 13-315. Fleming H. Revell Company.
Parish of Two: Douglas Dayton Letters. percy dashiel letters by price collier (percy collins) ed. Henry Goelet McVickar & Collier, Price, Joint Author. LC 3-26971. 1903. Lothrop Publishing Company.
Parish Picnic: A Story. Jean Reynolds Davis. LC 74-109068. 1970. 4.95. Harper & Row.
Parish Priest-Missionary: A Collection of Best Short Stories from Actual Life. Ed. by Parish Visitors of Mary Immaculate.
Parish-Side. Samuel Hayes Elliot. LC 70-76924. (American fiction reprint series). (Illus.). 1969. Books for Libraries Press.
Parish-Side. Samuel Hayes Elliott. LC 6-37255. 1854. Mason Brothers.
Parish's Fancy. Walter Guest Kellogg. LC 29-8836. The John Day Company.
Parisian Affair. Nick Carter. (Nick Carter Ser.). (Orig.). 1981. pap. 2.50 (ISBN 0-441-65176-3, Pub. by Charter Bks). Ace Bks.
Parisian Pigeon Drop. John P Radford. 1974. (pbk.) 1.50 (ISBN 0-89014-116-9). Canyon Books.
Parisian Points of View. Ludovic Halevy. LC 71-98572. (Short story index reprint series). (Illus.). 1969. Books for Libraries Press.
Parisian Points of View. Ludovic Halevy & Matthews, Edith Virginia Brander, Tr. 1894. Harper & Brothers.
Parisian Romance. Novalized from the Celebrated Play of the Same Name by Octave Feuillet. Downing, Robert L., 1857- Joint Author. LC 7-530. (On cover:Edgemore series, v. 1, no. 2). Street & Smith.
Parisian Romance. Novalized from the Celebrated Play of the Same Name by Octave Feuillet. Arthur D Hall & Feuillet, Octave, 1821-1890. Un Roman Parisien. LC 7-529. (primrose series, no. 8). Street & Smith.
Parisian Romance. Un Roman Parisien.)... Octave Feuillet. LC 12-8763. 1883. T. B. Peterson & Brothers.
Parisian Sultana. Adolphe Belot. (Seaside libraby, v. 50, no. 1021). G. Munro.
Parisians. harper's library ed. Edward George Earle Lytton Bulwer-Lytton Lytton. LC 7-8110. 1874. Harper & Brothers.
Parisians. the lord lytton ed. Edward George Earle Lytton Bulwer-Lytton Lytton. LC 7-8111. 1875. J. B. Lippincott & Co.
Parisians. Edward George Earle Lytton Bulwer-Lytton Lytton. LC 8-266504. G. Routledge and Sons.
Parisians. Edward George Earle Lytton Bulwer-Lytton Lytton. LC 7-8109. (On cover: Lovell's library, v. 5, no. 259). J. W. Lovell Company.
Parisians. Edward George Earle Lytton Bulwer-Lytton Lytton. (Half-title: Novels of Sir Edward Bulwer Lytton. Library ed. Novels of life and manners, vol. XV-XVI). 1893. Little, Brown, and Company.
Parisians. Edward George Earle Lytton Bulwer-Lytton Lytton. LC 43-39494. 1874. Harper & Brothers.
Park. Philippe Sollers. LC 76-90910. 1969. 4.25. Red Dust.
Park: A Novel. Don Gold. LC 76-26268. 8.95 (ISBN 0-06-011556-4). Harper & Row.
Park Avenue. Willis Vernon Cole. LC 28-113977. 1928. The Writer Guild.
Park Avenue. Cornelius Vanderbilt. LC 30-166120. The Macaulay Company.
Park Avenue Doctor. Albert Quandt. LC 40-2390. 1940. Phoenix Press.
Park Avenue Doctor. Charles Thornton. LC 40-23904. 1940. Phoenix Press.
Park Avenue Doctor: A Novel. Jane Winton. LC 51-10772. 1951. F. Fell.
Park Avenue Executioner. David Wilson. (McCloud,#6). 1975. (pbk.) 1.25. Award Books.
Park Avenue Nurse. Adelaide Humphries. LC 56-214923. 1956. Avalon Books.
Park Avenue Poeple: A Novel. Julie Valeria & Young, James, Joint Author. LC 35-35. The Guilford Press.
Park Beat. Reginald Harvey. LC 59-2918. 1959. Castle Books.
Park Circle: A November Song. 1st Ed. Warren Clarkebauer. LC 55-10848. Vantage Press.
Park Is Mine. Stephen Peters. LC 80-2059. (Illus.). 1981. 12.95 (ISBN 0-385-15953-6). Doubleday.
Parke Madison: Or, Fashion the Father of Intemperance, As Shown in the Life of the Senator's Son. Metta Victoria Fuller Victor. LC 8-32793. 1855. Miller, Orton & Mulligan.
Parker's Island. Joan Thompson. LC 78-21413. 8.95 (ISBN 0-312-59669-3). St. Martin's Press.
Parliament of Owls. Patrick Buchanan, pseud. LC 79-151232. 1971. 5.95 (ISBN 0-8128-1383-9). Stein and Day.
Parlor, Bedlam and Bath. Sidney J. Perelman & Reynolds, Quentin J. LC 30-16240. H. Liveright.
Parlor Begat Amos. Arthur Sturges Hildebrand. LC 22-2603. Harcourt, Brace and Company.
Parlor Games. Robert Marasco. LC 79-15599. 8.95 (ISBN 0-440-07060-0). Delacorte Press.
Parlous Times: A Novel of Modern Diplomacy. David Dwight Wells. LC 4-91179. 1900. J. F. Taylor & Company.
Parma Legacy. Dorothy Anne Liot Backer. 1978. 10.95 (ISBN 0-393-08817-0). Norton.
Parma Legacy: A Novel. Dorothy Anne Liot Backer. LC 77-26789. 9.95 (ISBN 0-393-08812-X). Norton.
Parmi Les Meilleurs Contes. Francois Denoeu. (Rinehart Editions). (Fr). 1958. text ed. 6.85 o.p. (ISBN 0-03-015240-2, HoltC). HR&W.
Parnassus on Wheels. Christopher Darlington Morley. LC 55-7994. (Illus.). 1955. Lippincott.
Parnassus on Wheels. Christopher Darlington Morley. LC 17-24508. 1917. Doubleday, Page & Company.
Parnassus on Wheels. Christopher Darlington Morley. LC 25-21765. (The Lambskin library. no. 48). 1925. Doubleday, Page & Company.
Parnassus on Wheels. Christopher Darlington Morley. LC 33-7805. 1931. Doubleday, Doran & Company, Inc.
Parnassus on Wheels: & The Haunted Bookshop. Christopher Darlington Morley. LC 48-5615. 1948. Doubleday.
Parody Party. Ed. by Leonard Russell. Edmund Clerihew Bentley. LC 70-105829. (Illus.). 1970. Kennikat Press.
Parowan Bonanza. Bertha Muzzy Sinclair. LC 23-11706. 1923. Little, Brown, and Company.
Parricide. Belot, Adolphe & Dautin, Jules. Tr. by Sherwood, Mary (Neal) (Seasde library, v, 43, no. 882). G. Munro.
Parricide. A Domestic Romance. Frederic Mansel Reynolds. LC 6-35068. 1836. E. L. Carey & A. Hart.
Parricides: Or, The Doom of the Assassins, the Authors of a Nation's Loss. Edward Zane Carroll Judson. LC 7-11453. (On cover: Ned Buntline's own series). 1865. Hilton & Co.
Parris Mitchell of Kings Row. Henry Bellamann & Bellamann, Katherine. LC 48-6407. 1948. Simon and Schuster.
Parrish, a Novel. Mildred Savage. LC 58-9045. 1958. Simon and Schuster.
Parrish for the Defense. Hillary Waugh. LC 78-186047. 1974. 7.95 (ISBN 0-385-07302-X). Doubleday.
Parrot & Co. Harold MacGrath. LC 13-11964. 1.30. The Bobbs-Merrill Company.
Parrot Dealer. Kurt Wiese. LC 32-32022. Coward-McCann, Inc.
Parrot Man. Robert Middlemiss. (Fawcett Medal Book). 1977. 1.75 (ISBN 0-449-13844-5). Fawcett Pubns.
Parsecs and Parables: Ten Science Fiction Stories. Robert Silverberg. LC 70-89111. 1970. 4.95. Doubleday.
Parsifal Mosaic. Robert Ludlum. LC 81-48276. 15.95 (ISBN 0-394-52111-0). Random House.
Parsival: Or, A Knight's Tale. Richard Monaco. LC 77-22150. 1977. 9.95. (ISBN 0-02-585540-9). Macmillan.
Parsival: Or, A Knights Tale. Richard Monaco. 1978. 2.25 (ISBN 0-671-82225-X). Pocket Books.
Parson: A Novel. Alice Mary Ross Colver. LC 51-9217. 1951. Macrae Smith.
Parson Austen's Daughter: A Novel. Helen Ashton. LC 49-507335. 1949. Dodd, Mead.
Parson Beecher and His Horse. A Humorous Adventure. George G. Small. 1871. Winchell & Small.
Parson Ben. Peggy Martin. LC 57-13915. 1957. W. B. Eerdmans Pub. Co.
Parson Brooks: A Plumb Powerful Hard Shell. A Story of Humble Southern Life. John Montieth. LC 7-31807. 1884. O. H. P. Applegate.
Parson Gay's Three Sermons: Or, Saint Sacrement. Robert Thaxter Edes. LC 8-14518. 1908. Cochrane Publishing Co.
Parson John: A Saga of the Winning of the West. Bernard Alvin Palmer. LC 42-9794. 1942. Wm. B. Eerdmans Publishing Company.
Parson Jones. Florence Marryat Church Lean. LC 7-13616. Cassell Publishing Company.
Parson Kelly. Alfred Edward Woodley Mason & Lang, Andrew, 1844-1912, Joint Author. LC 99-4566. 1899. Longmans, Green, and Co.
Parson McFright; Short Stories for Harried Churchmen. Allen Whitman. LC 67-25370. (Illus.). 1967. Augsburg Pub. House.
Parson O'Dumford: A Story of Lincoln Folk. George Manville Fenn. LC 41-28180. Cassell & Company, Limited.
Parson O'Dumford. A Story of Lincoln Folk. George Manville Fenn. LC 6-39385. (On cover: The seaside library. Pocket ed. no. 587). G. Munro.
Parson of Gunbarrel Basin. Nelson Coral Nye. LC 55-9726. 1955. Dodd, Mead.
Parson of Panamint, and Other Stories. Peter Bernard Kyne. LC 29-5948. 1929. Cosmopolitan Book Corporation.
Parson of the Islands. Adam Wallace. LC 61-17566. (Illus.). 1978. Repr. of 1978 ed. 7.00 (ISBN 0-87033-077-2, Pub. by Tidewater). Cornell Maritime.
Parson Thorne's Trial. A Novel. Emma May Buckingham. LC 6-19653. 1880. G. W. Carleton & Co.; Etc., Etc.
Parson Thring's Secret. Arthur Williams Marchmont. LC 7-20446. The Cassell Publishing Co.
Parson Thring's Secret. Arthur Williams Marchmont. The Mershon Company.
Parsonage Porch: Seven Stories from a Clergyman's Notebook. Bradley Gilman. LC 2617. 1900. Little, Brown and Company.
Parsonage Secret. Annette Lucile Noble. LC 7-33183. (On cover: Crusader series). 1898. J. B. Dunn.
Parson's Daughter. new ed. Theodore Edward Hook. LC 42-318506. 1867. G. Routledge and Sons.
Parson's House. Elizabeth Cadell. LC 77-15561. 1978. 11.95 (ISBN 0-8161-6528-9). G. K. Hall.
Parson's Ladies. Thelma Urban. 1979. 6.75 o.p. (ISBN 0-8062-1129-6). Carlton.
Parson's Mountaineers. Stella Colby Meeker. LC 27-23872. F. H. Hitchcock.
Parson's Nine. Noel Streatfeild. LC 32-331599. 1933. Doubleday, Doran & Company, Inc.
Parson's Progress. Compton Mackenzie. LC 24-8684. 1923. Cassell and Company, Ltd.
Parson's Progress. Compton Mackenzie. LC 24-4511. George H. Doran Company.
Parson's Proxy. Kate Waterman Hamilton. LC 7-949. 1896. Houghton, Mifflin and Company.
Part for a Policeman. John Creasey. LC 73-106528. 1970. 4.50. Scribner.
Part of the Main: Short Stories of the Maine Coast. Edward M Holmes. LC 73-620088. (Maine Studies No. 95). (Illus.). 1973. 4.95. University of Maine.
Part Payment. Elizabeth Gregg. LC 38-11077. 1938. The Pyramid Press.
Part-Time Father. Edith Atkin & Estelle Rubin. LC 75-25146. 1976. 8.95 (ISBN 0-8149-0766-0). Vanguard.
Part Time Girl, Anonymous. 1932. Dodd, Mead and Company.
Part Time Passion. Peggy Gaddis, pseud. LC 40-30575. Phoenix Press.
Part Time Passion. Gail Jordan. LC 40-305754. Phoenix Press.
Part Time Virgin see Virgen Insaciable.
Part-Time Wife. Paul Snow. LC 35-6535. Godwin.
Part 35. John Nicholas Iannuzzi. LC 75-108970. 1970. 6.95. R. W. Baron.
Part 35: John Nicholas Iannuzzi. part thirty-five ed. John Nicholas Iannuzzi. 1979. 2.50 (ISBN 0-671-81963-1). Pocket Books.
Parted at the Altar. A Novel. Laura Jean Libbey. (On cover: The popular series, no. 31). 1893. R. Bonner's Sons.
Parted by Fate. A Novel. Laura Jean Libbey. (choice series, no. 21). 1890. R. Bonner's Sons.
Parted by Fate: A Novel. Laura Jean Libbey. (On cover: The popular series, no. 34). 1893. R. Bonner's Sons.
Parthenia; or, The Last Days of Paganism. Eliza Buckminster Lee. LC 7-12611. 1858. Ticknor and Fields.
Parthian. Victor Hurley. LC 60-7507. 1960. Fleet Pub. Corp.
Parthian Shot. Loyd Little. LC 74-30250. 1975. 8.95 (ISBN 0-670-54063-3). Viking Press.
Parti-Pris Des Choses see Voices of Things.
Partial Magic: The Novel As Self-Conscious Genre. Robert Alter. LC 74-77725. 1975. 24.00x (ISBN 0-520-02755-8); pap. 3.95 (ISBN 0-520-03732-4). U of Cal Pr.
Participation Put On. Anthony Moffett. 1971. 6.95 o.p. (0085-6). Delacorte.
Particles & Fields. L. Lurie. LC 68-22312. (Illus.). 1968. 19.75 o.p. (ISBN 0-470-55642-0, Pub. by Wiley-Interscience). Wiley.
Particular Passions: Talks with Women Who Have Shaped Our Times. Lynn Gilbert & Gaylen Moore. (Illus.). 352p. 1981. 19.95 (ISBN 0-517-54371-0, C N Potter Bks); pap. 10.95 (ISBN 0-517-54594-2). Crown.
Parties. facs. ed. Carl Van Vechten. LC 70-153004. (Select Bibliographies Reprint Ser). 1930. 18.00 (ISBN 0-8369-5758-X). Ayer Co.
Parties, Scenes from Contemporary New York Life. Carl Van Vechten. LC 70-153004. 1971. (ISBN 0-8369-5758-X). Books for Libraries Press.
Parties, Scenes from Contemporary New York Life. Carl Van Vechten. LC 30-213269. 1939. A. A. Knopf.
Parting and a Meeting. William Dean Howells. LC 7-5768. (On cover: Harper's little novels). 1896. Harper & Brothers.
Parting at the Burnside. Lydia L Rouse. LC 8-696. Aemrican Baptist Publication Society.
Parting Breath. Catherine Aird, pseud. LC 77-12836. 1978. 6.95 (ISBN 0-385-13563-7). Published for the Crime Club by Doubleday.
Parting of the Ways. Henry Bordeaux & Houghton, Mrs. Louise (Seymour) 1838- Tr. LC 11-4604. 1911. Duffield & Company.
Parting of the Ways. Florence Gilmore. LC 14-5821. 1914. 0.80. B. Herder.
Parting of the Ways: A Novel. Matilda Barbara Betham- Edwards, pseud. (On cover: Lovell's international ser. no. 86). J. W. Lovell Company.

Partings. Jim Levey. (Orig.). 1974. pap. 1.25 o.p. (ISBN 0-515-03365-0, V3365). Pyramid Pubns.

Partisan. William Gilmore Simms. LC 68-23728. (Americans in Fiction Ser.). lib. bdg. 16.00 (ISBN 0-8398-1859-9); pap. text ed. 4.95x (ISBN 0-89197-878-X). Irvington.

Partisan: A Romance of the Revolution. new and rev. ed. William Gilmore Simms. LC 76-10142. (Simms, William Gilmore, 1806-1870. Simms Revolutionary War Novels). (Simms Revolutionary War novels; v. 2). ((Series: Simms, William Gilmore, 1806-1870.). (Simms Revolutionary War novels; v. 2.: Vol. 2). 1976. 21.00 (ISBN 0-87152-236-5). Reprint Co.

Partisan: A Romance of the Revolution. new and rev. ed. 1st ams ed. chicago, belford, clarke, 1886. ed. William Gilmore Simms. LC 68-55650. 1968. AMS Press.

Partisan; a Romance of the Revolution. new and rev. ed. William Gilmore Simms. 1870. W. J. Widdleton.

Partisan, a Romance of the Revolution. new and rev. ed. William Gilmore Simms. LC 8-11026. 1882. A. C. Armstrong & Son.

Partisan: a Romance of the Revolution. new and rev. ed. William Gilmore Simms. (On cover: Lovell's library, v. 12, no. 640). 1885. J. W. Lovell Company.

Partisan: A Tale of the Revolution. William Gilmore Simms. LC 68-23728. (Americans in fiction). 1968. Gregg Press.

Partisan Captain. Miloslav Zlamal. LC 72-176210. Printed by Circle B. Printing.

Partisan Leader. Nathaniel Beverley Tucker & Bridenbaugh, Carl, Ed. LC 33-10974. 1933. A. A. Knopf.

Partisan Leader: A Key to the Disunion Conspiracy. Nathaniel Beverley Tucker. LC 68-57557. (American novels of muckraking, propaganda, and social protest). 1968. Gregg Press.

Partisan Leader: A Novel, and an Apocalypse of the Origin and Struggles of the Southern Confederacy. Anthaniel Beverley Tucker & Ware, Thomas A., Ed. LC 8-28509. 1862. West & Johnston.

Partisan Leader: A Tale of the Future. Nathaniel Beverley Tucker. LC 78-149477. (Southern literary classics series). 1971. (ISBN 0-8078-1166-1). University of North Carolina Press.

Partisan Leader: A Tale of the Future. Nathaniel Beverley Tucker. LC 8-28511. 1836. Printed by D. Green.

Partisans. Alistair MacLean. LC 82-45836. 1982. 14.95 (ISBN 0-385-18262-7). Doubleday.

Partisans. Lawrence O'Sullivan. LC 77-179853. 1973. 7.95 (ISBN 0-525-17593-8). Dutton.

Partisans. Arnold Rodin. Orig. Title: Woman Soldier. 176p. 1973. pap. 0.95 o.p. (ISBN 0-532-95221-9). Woodhill.

Partisans. Arnold Rodin. Orig. Title: Woman Soldier. 176p. 1973. pap. 0.95 o.p. (ISBN 0-532-95221-9). Manor Bks.

Partisans: A Novel. Peter Matthiessen. LC 55-9639. 1955. Viking Press.

Partisans Against the Nazi War Machine: A Documentary Novel. Hyman Shenkman. LC 78-164516. 1971. 6.95 (ISBN 0-8246-0123-8). J. David.

Partisan's Oath: Or, The Trooper's Revenge. A Tale of the Revolution. Robert F Greeley. Bunce & Brother.

Partizaner. Yitzchok Perlov. Tr. by Nathan Namerovsky. (O.s.i.). (Orig.). 1968. pap. 0.95 o.s.i. (A400N, Award). Univ Pub & Dist.

Partly Cloudy and Cooler. Elizabeth Uhr. LC 68-12602. 1968. Harcourt, Brace & World.

Partners. Louis Auchincloss. LC 73-13633. 1974. 6.95. Houghton Mifflin.

Partners. Louis Auchincloss. LC 74-9782. 1974. (lib. bdg.) 10.95 (ISBN 0-8161-6223-9). G. K. Hall.

Partners. William Harrington. LC 79-67607. 10.95 (ISBN 0-87223-586-6). Seaview Books.

Partners. Louise Platt Hauck. LC 29-20651. The Penn Publishing Company.

Partners. Grace Livingston Hill. LC 40-32080. J. B. Lippincott Company.

Partners. Carol Sturm Smith. (Love & Life Romance Ser.). (Orig.). 1982. pap. 1.95 (ISBN 0-345-29757-1). Ballantine.

Partners: By Margaret Deland: Illustrated by Charles Dana Gibson. Margaret Wade Campbell Deland. LC 13-21019. 1913. 1.00. Harper & Brothers.

Partners in Crime. Agatha Miller Christie. LC 29-17226. Dodd, Mead & Company.

Partners in Crime. Dame Agatha Miller Christie. 1975. (pbk.) 0.95. Dell.

Partners in Sin. Albert Quandt. LC 49-951923. 1949. Phoenix Press.

Partners in Wonder. Harlan Ellison. LC 77-123270. (Illus.). 1971. 8.95 (ISBN 0-8027-5527-5). Walker.

Partners of Chance. Henry Herbert Knibbs. LC 21-193882. 1921. 1.75. Houghton Mifflin Company.

Partners of Providence. Charles David Stewart. LC 7-12008. 1907. The Century Company.

Partners of the Night. Leroy Scott. LC 16-221432. 1916. 1.35. The Century Co.

Partners of the Out-Trail. Harold Bindloss. LC 19-11362. Frederick A. Stokes Company.

Partners of the Saddle. Tevis Miller. LC 39-125818. Phoenix Press.

Partners of the Tide. Joseph Crosby Lincoln. LC 72-98402. (Illus.). 1969. AMS Press.

Partners of the Tide. Joseph Crosby Lincoln. LC 5-13029. 1905. A. S. Barnes & Co.

Partners of the Tide. Joseph Crosby Lincoln. LC 20-18835. 1905. A. L. Burt Company.

Partners Three. Elby Wagner. LC 28-4771. Thomas Y. Crowell Company.

Partners Three: A Novel. Victor Mapes. LC 9-89979. 1.25. F. A. Stokes Company.

Partnership with Death. Clifton Adams. LC 67-11195. (DD western). 1967. Doubleday.

Parton's Island. Illustrated by the Author. Paul Darcy Boles. LC 58-69592. 1958. Macmillan.

Partridge Family, No. 15: The Disappearing Professor. Lee Hays. (Orig.). 1973. pap. 0.60 o.p. (06191). Curtis.

Partridge Family, No. 16. Lee Hays. (Orig.). 1973. pap. 0.75 o.p. (07321). Curtis.

Partridge Family, No. 17. Michael Avallone. (Orig.). 1973. pap. 0.60 o.p. Curtis.

Partridge Kite: A Novel. Michael Nicholson. LC 78-4696. 1978. 8.95 (ISBN 0-03-040301-4). Holt, Rinehart, and Winston.

Parts Men Play. Arthur Beverley Baxter. LC 20-206469. 1920. D. Appleton and Company.

Parts Unknown. Frances Parkinson Wheeler Keyes. LC 42-514927. 1942. Triangle Books.

Parts Unknown. Frances Parkinson Wheeler Keyes. 1.75 (ISBN 0-671-80797-8). Pocket Books.

Parts Unknown: A Novel. Frances Parkinson Wheeler Keyes. J. Messner, Inc.

Party. Renee Auden. pap. 1.95 o.s.i. (OPS-34). Olympia.

Party. Trevor Griffiths. 1974. 8.50 (ISBN 0-571-10629-3); pap. 4.95 (ISBN 0-571-10647-1). Faber & Faber.

Party. Warja Honegger-Lavater. (Folded Story Ser: No. 4). 1964. bds. 3.50x o.p. Wittenborn.

Party: And Other Stories. Anton Pavlovich Chekhov. Tr. by Garnett, Constance (Black) LC 17-23646. (Half-title: The tales of Chekhov, vol. iv). 1917. The Macmillan Company.

Party at Cranton. John W Aldridge. LC 60-9565. 1960. D. McKay Co.

Party at Mrs. Purefoy's. Ward Allison Dorrance. LC 69-11930. 1969. 5.95. Delacorte Press.

Party at No. Five. Shelley Smith. 1979. 11.00x o.p. (ISBN 0-86025-074-1, Pub. by Ian Henry Pubns England). State Mutual Bk.

Party at No. 5. Nancy Bodington. LC 77-361177. (Illus.). 1976. 2.70 (ISBN 0-86025-074-1). I. Henry.

Party at the Penthouse. Arthur Minturn Chase. LC 32-963. 1932. Dodd, Mead & Company.

Party Dress. Joseph Hergesheimer. LC 30-102412. 1930. A. A. Knopf.

Party for Grownups. Babette Rosmond. LC 47-12528. 1948. E. P. Duttton.

Party for Lawty. Maureen Sarsfield. LC 48-6043. (Gargoyle mystery). 1948. Coward-McCann.

Party for the Shooting. Louisa Revell. LC 60-138167. (Cock Robin mystery). 1960. Macmillan.

Party Girl. George Darwin Engel. LC 41-1983. Phoenix Press.

Party Going. Thomas McEvilley. (O.s.i.). pap. 0.60 o.s.i. (A224X, Award). Univ Pub & Dist.

Party Going: A Novel. Henry Green. LC 51-12431. 1951. Viking Press.

Party Going: A Novel. Henry Green. LC 76-122053. (Viking reprint editions). 1970. A. M. Kelley.

Party Husband. James Whittaker. LC 30-24776. A. H. King.

Party of Baccarat. Donn Byrae. 1.25. The Century Co.

Party of Dreamers. Robert James Collas Lowry. LC 62-207004. 1962. Fleet Pub. Corp.

Party of the Year. John Crosby. LC 78-24694. 1979. 9.95 o.s.i. (ISBN 0-8128-2606-X). Stein & Day.

Party of the Year: With Excerpts from the Legend of the Di Castigliones, Annotated. John Crosby. LC 78-24694. 1979. 9.95 (ISBN 0-8128-2606-X). Stein and Day.

Party of the Year: With Excerpts from The Legend of the Di Castigliones, Annotated. John Crosby. LC 79-28633. 1980. 13.95 (ISBN 0-8161-3067-1). G. K. Hall.

Party Party; Girlfriends: Two Short Novels. Ronni Sandroff. LC 74-21337. 1975. 6.95 (ISBN 0-394-49494-6). Knopf: Distributed by Random House.

Party, Party-Girlfriends. Ronni Sandroff. 1975. 6.95 o.p. (ISBN 0-394-49494-6). Knopf.

Party Stewardesses. R. K Kopp. 1974. (pbk.) 1.95. Barclay House.

Party Wire. Bruce Manning. LC 34-126960. Liveright Publishing Corporation.

Party's Over: Four Attempts to Define a Love Story. Juan Goytisolo. LC 66-28733. 1967. Grove Press.

Parvati: A Romance of Present-Day India. Robert Chauvelot. Tr. by Gibbons, Helen Davenport (Brown) LC 19-14907. 1919. 1.50. The Century Co.

Parvin. 1st Ed. Parsegh Der Hagopian. LC 53-7779. 1953. Borden Pub. Co.

Pasang Run. Elleston Trevor. LC 62-15731. 1962. Harper & Row.

Pascal's Mill. Ben Ames Williams. LC 33-12419. 1933. E. P. Dutton & Co., Inc.

Pascarel. Only a Story. Louise De La Ramee. LC 6-33314. 1874. J. B. Lippincott & Co.

Pascarella Family: A Novel. Franz V. Werfel. LC 32-33295. 1932. Simon and Schuster.

Pasghetti & Meat Bulbs! Bil Keane. 128p. 1981. pap. 1.50 (ISBN 0-449-14440-2, GM). Fawcett.

Pasha the Persian. Margaret Linden. LC 37-16728. 1936. C. Kendall, Inc.

Pasha the Persian. Margaret Linden. LC 37-16721. 1936. C. Kendall, Inc.

Pasha's Concubine & Other Tales. Ivo Andric. Tr. by Joseph Hitrec. 1968. 6.95 o.p. (ISBN 0-394-43985-6). Knopf.

Pasha's Web. Howard Bradshaw. LC 21-128552. W. J. Watt & Company.

Pasion y Terror Al Sur Del Rio Grande. new ed. Rod Gray. Tr. by Juan Castellanos from Eng. (Pimienta Collection: La Ninfa De G.O.C.E. Ser., No. 1). 160p. (Span.). 1974. pap. 1.00 o.p. (ISBN 0-88473-216-9). Fiesta Pub.

Pasmore. David Storey. LC 73-15298. 1974. 6.50 (ISBN 0-525-17610-1). Dutton.

Paso Por Aqui. Eugene Manlove Rhodes. LC 72-9273. (Western frontier library). (Illus.). 1973. (pbk.) 2.95 (ISBN 0-8061-1079-1). University of Oklahoma Press.

Pasquier Chronicles. Georges Duhamel. Tr. by Holthoir, Beatrice De. LC 38-27229. H. Holt and Company.

Pass. Thomas Savage. LC 44-40973. 1944. Doubleday, Doran & Co., Inc.

Pass. John Slimming. LC 62-9924. 1962. Harper.

Pass: A Novel. Richard Gibson Hubler. LC 55-6139. 1955. Coward-McCann.

Pass Beyond Kashmir. Berkely Mather. LC 60-12600. 1960. Scribner.

Pass in the Grampians. Nan Shepherd. LC 33-22823. E. P. Dutton & Co., Inc.

Pass It on. Carol Amen. (Uplook Ser.). 1977. pap. 0.75 o.p. (ISBN 0-8163-0310-X, 16027-5). Pacific Pr Pub Assn.

Pass Key to Murder. Blair Reed. LC 48-18945. 1948. Phoenix Press.

Pass the Ammunition. Stan Smith. 144p. 1976. pap. 1.25 (ISBN 0-532-12394-8). Woodhill.

Pass the Body. Christopher St. John Sprigg. LC 33-20977. 1933. L. MacVeagh, Dial Press, Inc.

Pass the Poison Separately: A New Mystery. Oswell Blakeston. LC 76-370316. 1976. 2.95 (ISBN 0-920000-01-0). Catalyst.

Pass Through Manhattan. Richard Edward Wormser. LC 40-14428. 1940. W. Morrow and Company.

Passacaglia. Robert Pinget. Tr. by Barbara Wright from Fr. LC 78-53832. (New French Writing Ser.). 1979. 6.95 (ISBN 0-87376-033-6). Red Dust.

Passage. Victor Wartofsky. (Orig.). 1980. pap. 1.95 o.s.i. (ISBN 0-505-51506-7). Tower Bks.

Passage by Night. Jack Higgins, pseud. 1978. pap. 1.95 (ISBN 0-449-13891-7, GM). Fawcett.

Passage by Night. Henry Patterson. LC 64-13925. (Raven book). 1964. Abelard-Schuman.

Passage from Home. Isaac Rosenfeld. LC 46-4570. 1946. The Dial Press.

Passage in the Night. Shalom Asch. LC 53-8146. 1953. Putnam.

Passage of Arms. 1st American Ed. Eric Ambler. LC 59-15434. 1960. Knopf.

Passage of the Barque Sappho. John Edward Patterson. LC 20-11150. 1919. J. M. Dent & Sons, Ltd.

Passage of Time. Gillian Martin. LC 78-18479. 8.95 (ISBN 0-684-15819-1). Scribner.

Passage Perilous. Rosa Nouchette Carey. 1903. J. B. Lippincott Company.

Passage Through Bohemia: A Novel. Florence Alice Price James. LC 7-7411. Hovendon Company.

Passage Through Fire. Edmond Fleury. LC 65-10135. 1965. Holt, Rinehart and Winston.

Passage Through Fire. Tr. from French by Irene Uribe. Jean Montaurier. LC 65-10135. 5.95. Holt.

Passage Through Gehenna. Madison Jones. LC 77-13724. 8.95 (ISBN 0-8071-0376-4). Louisiana State University Press.

Passage Through the Red Sea. Zofia Romanowicz. 151p. 1962. 2.00. Polish Inst Arts.

Passage Through the Red Sea. Translated by Virgilia Peterson. 1st American Ed. Zofia Romanowiczowa. LC 62-19588. 1962. Harcourt, Brace & World.

Passage to America. Terry Coleman. (Illus.). 137p. 1974. pap. 3.50 (ISBN 0-14-003837-X, Pub. by Penguin England). Irish Bk Ctr.

Passage to Ararat & Exiles. Michael J. Arlen. 1982. pap. 8.95 (ISBN 0-14-006311-0). Penguin.

Passage to Danger. Edwin Moultrie Lanham. 1962. 3.50 o.p. HarBraceJ.

Passage to Dodge City see Lawman for the Slaughter.

Passage to Glory. Robin L. Smith. 400p. Date not set. pap. 3.50 (ISBN 0-441-65219-0). Ace Bks.

Passage to India. Edward Morgan Forster. (Harvest bk. HB85). 1965. pap., 1.65. Harcourt.

Passage to India. Edward Morgan Forster. LC 71-14498. (Harbrace modern classics). 1969. Harcourt, Brace & World.

Passage to India. Edward Morgan Forster. LC 24-19334. Harcourt.

Passage to India. Edward Morgan Forster. LC 40-273411. (Half-title: The modern library of the world's best books). 1940. The Modern Library.

Passage to India. Edward Morgan Forster. LC 78-26692. (Forster, Edward Morgan, 1879-1970. The Abinger Edition of E. M. Forster: Vol. 6). 1979. 40.00 (ISBN 0-8419-0469-3). Meier Publishers.

Passage to India. Walt Whitman. 6.00 o.p. Gordon Pr.

Passage to India: E. M. Forster. William Heppel Mason. LC 65-29613. (Notes on Eng. lit.). Barnes & Noble.

Passage to India: Notes, Including Life of E. M. Forster, the British Raj in India, General Summary, List of Characters...Rev. by Norma Ostrander Consulting, Ed.: James L. Roberts. Norma Ostrander. 1967. pap., 1.00. Cliffs.

Passage to Mutiny. Alexander Kent. LC 76-14819. 1976. 8.95 (ISBN 0-399-11772-5). Putnam.

Passage to Mutiny. Alexander Kent. (Berkley Medallion Book). 1977. 1.75 (ISBN 0-425-03469-0). Berkley Pub. Corp.

Passage to Pontefract. Jean Plaidy. LC 81-148183. (Plantagenet saga). ((Series: Plaidy, Jean, 1906-). (Plantagenet saga.). (Illus.). 1981. 12.95 (ISBN 0-7091-7764-X). Hale.

Passage to Pontefract. Jean Plaidy. (Plantagenet Saga Ser.: Vol. 10). 368p. 1982. 12.95 (ISBN 0-399-12750-X). Putnam Pub Group.

Passage to Terror. Edward Sidney Aarons. 1970. pap. 0.60 o.p. (R2200, GM). Fawcett World.

Passage to the Sky. Howard Coxe. LC 29-29100. 1929. A. and C. Boni.

Passage to Violence. Stetson Kennedy. LC 55-269295. (Lion library, LL9). 1954. Lion Books.

Passage West. Dallas Miller. 1980. 2.75 (ISBN 0-380-50278-X). Avon Books.

Passage West: A Novel. Harry Dallas Miller. LC 79-3982. 10.95 (ISBN 0-06-013034-2). Harper & Row.

Passages. Ann Quin. LC 76-395068. 160p. 1979. pap. 6.95 (ISBN 0-7145-0056-9, Pub. by M Boyars). Merrimack Pub Cir.

Passages from the Diary of a Late Physician. Samuel Warren. LC 26-22293. 1845. Harper & Brothers.

Passages from the Diary of a Late Physician. Samuel Warren. LC 8-22351. (seaside library, v. 14, no. 271). 1878. G. Munro.

Passages from the Diary of a Late Physician. Samuel Warren. 1885. G. Routledge and Sons.

Passages from the History of a Wasted Life. John Ross Dix. LC 6-33870. 1853. B. B. Mussey and Company.

Passages from the History of a Wasted Life. 2d ed. John Ross Dix. LC 6-33869. 1853. B. B. Mussey and Company.

Passages in the Life of Mrs. Margaret Maitland of Sunnyside. Margaret Oliphant Wilson Oliphant. (On cover: Seaside library. Pocket ed., no. 371). 1885. G. Munro.

Passe-muraille. Marcel Ayme. (Illus.). deluxe ed. 61.25. French & Eur.

Passe Rose. Arthur Sherburne Hardy. LC 3-195482. 1889. Houghton, Mifflin and Company.

Passe Rose. Arthur Sherburne Hardy. LC 3-195472. 1890. Houghton, Mifflin and Company.

Passenger. Elizabeth Fenwick. LC 67-14577. 1967. Atheneum.

Passenger. Thomas Keneally. LC 78-22258. 8.95. Harcourt Brace Jovanovich.

Passenger from Calais. Arthur George Frederick Griffiths. LC 6-2340. 1906. L. C. Page and Company.

Passenger from Scotland Yard. H. Freeman Wood. (On cover: Seaside library. Pocket ed. no. 1107). G. Munro.

Passenger from Scotland Yard: A Victorian Detective Novel. H. Freeman Wood. LC 77-76586. (Illus.). 1977. 3.50 (ISBN 0-486-23523-8). Dover Publications.

Passenger on the U. Claude Aveline. LC 69-15188. 1969. 5.95. Doubleday.

Passenger to Folkestone. Joseph Smith Fletcher. LC 27-18558. 1927. A. A. Knopf.
Passenger to Frankfurt. Agatha Miller Christie. 1982. pap. 2.50 (ISBN 0-671-44512-X). PB.
Passenger to Frankfurt. 1980. pap. 2.50 (ISBN 0-671-83047-3). PB.
Passenger to Frankfurt: An Extravaganza. Agatha Miller Christie. LC 76-129953. 1970. 5.95. Dodd, Mead.
Passenger to Nowhere: By Anthony Gilbert Pseud. 1st Amer. Ed. Lucy Beatrice Malleson. LC 66-119987. bds., 3.95. Random.
Passenger to Peking. Frederick Anthony Edwards. LC 35-1209. 1935. Doubleday, Doran and Company, Inc.
Passengers. Thomas G Foxworth & Michael Laurence. LC 82-5032. 1982. 17.95 (ISBN 0-385-12843-6). Doubleday.
Passer-by: An Episode. Pierre Troubetzkoy. 1908. Doubleday, Page & Company.
Passer-by, and Other Stories. Ethel May Dell. LC 72-5867. (Short story index reprint series). 1972. (ISBN 0-8369-4210-8). Books for Libraries Press.
Passer-by and Other Stories. Ethel May Dell. LC 25-8945. 1925. G. P. Putnam's Sons.
Passer-by: And Other Stories. Ethel May Dell. LC 72-5867. (Short Story Index Reprint Ser). Repr. of 1925 ed. 20.00 (ISBN 0-8369-4210-8). Ayer Co.
Passerman's Hollow. Jane Stuart. LC 73-15816. 1974. 7.95 (ISBN 0-07-062202-7). McGraw-Hill.
Passers-by. Edward Phillips Oppenheim. LC 10-1694. 1910. Little, Brown, and Company.
"Passin'-on" Party. Effie Graham. LC 12-21949. 1912. 1.00. A. C. McClurg & Co.
Passing. Nella Larsen. LC 73-82056. 1969. Negro Universities Press.
Passing. Nella Larsen. LC 74-146616. (American Library). 1971. 1.50. Collier Books.
Passing. Nella Larsen. LC 76-92233. (American Negro, His History and Literature). (Afro-American culture series.). 1969. Arno Press.
Passing. Nella Larsen. LC 29-9990. 1929. A. A. Knopf.
Passing Advantage. Mark McGarrity. 288p. 1981. pap. 2.95 (ISBN 0-523-41441-2). Pinnacle Bks.
Passing Advantage. Mark McGarrity. LC 79-67638. 1980. 10.95 (ISBN 0-89256-123-8). Rawson Wade.
Passing Bells. Phillip Rock. LC 78-22109. 9.95 (ISBN 0-87223-518-1). Seaview Books.
Passing by. Elliott Merrick. LC 47-30886. 1947. Macmillan Co.
Passing Ceremony. Helen Weinzweig. LC 72-95751. (Anansi Fiction Ser.: No. 24). 120p. 1973. pap. 4.95 (ISBN 0-88784-325-5, Pub. by Hse Anansi Pr Canada). U of Toronto Pr.
Passing Dream: A Novel. Margaret Gorman Nichols. LC 42-229951. 1942. Macrae-Smith-Company.
Passing Emperor. Robert Shortz. LC 8-7331. (On cover: The welcome series, no. 29). 1897. The Home Publishing Co.
Passing Fancy. Mary Linn Roby. (Orig.). 1980. pap. 1.50 (ISBN 0-440-16770-1). Dell.
Passing for Human. Jody Scott. 1.50 (ISBN 0-87997-330-7). DAW Books.
Passing Go. Ken Schiff. LC 71-180935. 1972. 5.95 (ISBN 0-396-06487-6). Dodd, Mead.
Passing Go: A Novel. Katharine Topkins & Richard Topkins. LC 68-24235. 1968. Little, Brown.
Passing of Alix: A Novel. Marjorie Paul. 1895. Arena Publishing Company.
Passing of Charles Lanson. Louis Tracy. LC 24-239197. E. J. Clode, Inc.
Passing of Prince Rozan: A Romance of the Sea. Charles Henry Cook. LC 99-1519. 1899. G.P. Putnma's Sons.
Passing of the Dragons. Keith Roberts. 1977. pap. 1.75 (ISBN 0-425-03477-1, Medallion). Berkley Pub.
Passing of the Fourteen: Life, Love, and War Among the Brigands and Guerrillas of Mexico. Ransom Sutton. LC 14-12072. 1914. The Devin-Adair Company.
Passing of the Old West: By Hal G. Evarts with Illustrations by Charles Livingston Bull. Hal George Evarts & Bull, Charles Livingston. LC 21-191264. 1921. Little, Brown, and Company.
Passing of the Third Floor Back. Jerome Klapka Jerome. 1908. Dodd, Mead & Company.
Passing of Thomas. Thomas Allibone Janvier. LC 79-94733. (Short Story Index Reprint Ser.). 1900. 15.00 (ISBN 0-8369-3113-0). Ayer Co.
Passing of Thomas: In the St. Peter's Set; At the Grand Hotel Du Paradis; The Fish of Monsieur Quissard; Le Bon Oncle D'Amerique. Five Stories. Thomas Allibone Janvier. LC 79-94733. (Short story index reprint series). (Illus.). 1969. Books for Libraries Press.
Passing of Thomas: In the St. Peter's Set; At the Grand Hotel Du Paradis; The Fish of Monsieur Quissard; Le Bon Oncle D'Amerique. Five Stories. Thomas Allibone Janvier. LC 30472. 1900. Harper & Brothers.
Passing Parade: By Gordon Bennett Pseud. 1st Ed. Russell Bennett. LC 56-632238. 1956. Greenwich Book Publishers.
Passing Shadows. A Novel. Bernard James Reily. LC 9-1204. 1897. Benziger Brothers.
Passing Show. Richard Henry Savage. (On cover: Neely's library of choice literature, no. 14). 1893. F. T. Neely.
Passing Strange. Catherine Aird, pseud. LC 80-1120. 1981. 9.95 (ISBN 0-385-17271-0). Published for the Crime Club by Doubleday.
Passing Strange. John Minahan. LC 65-185166. bds., 3.95. Morrow.
Passing Strange: A Mystery of Birth and Burial. Richard Sale. LC 43-163499. (Handi-book mysteries). 1943. Quinn Publishing Co., Inc.
Passing Strange: A Story of Birth and Burial. Richard Sale. 1942. Simon and Schuster.
Passing Stranger. Morrill Cody. LC 36-18262. (Full name: Edward Morrill Cody). The Macaulay Company.
Passing Stranger. Louise Hoffman. LC 73-87574. 1974. 5.95. St. Martin's Press.
Passing Strangers. Felix Riesenberg. LC 32-263670. Harcourt, Brace and Company.
Passing the Love of Women. Giuseppe Bianco. LC 27-3688. The Bobbs-Merrill Company.
Passing the Love of Women. Elisabeth Stoughton Griffiths. LC 51-593. 1951. Christopher Pub. House.
Passing the Love of Women. Mary Anna Lupton Needell. LC 7-25793. 1892. D. Appleton and Company.
Passing the Portal: Or, A Girl's Struggle. An Autobiography... Metta Victoria Fuller Victor. LC 12-17869. 1876. G. W. Carleton & Co.
Passing Through the Flame. Norman Spinrad. LC 73-93746. 1975. 8.95 (ISBN 0-399-11300-2). Berkley Pub. Corp.: Distributed by Putnam.
Passing Through the Ordeal. Arthur Pratt. LC 7-30128. (sunnyside series, no. 88). 1895. J. S. Ogilvie Publishing Company.
Passing Through: The True Trials and Humor of an Active Playwright from His Youth to Middle Age, and the Reminiscences, Anecdotes, Human Interest Portraits, and Candid Opinions of Those Years, As Felt and Seen from This Hour. Norwood Chamberlin. LC 65-9769. 3.75. Riverton Bks. E. Th St.
Passing Time. Michel Butor. Tr. by Jean Stewart. 1980. pap. 4.95 (ISBN 0-7145-0438-6). Riverrun NY.
Passing Time. Michel Butor. Bd. with Change of Heart. 1969. pap. 3.45 o.s.i. (20229, Touchstone Bks). S&S.
Passing Time & A Change of Heart: Two Novels. Michel Butor. LC 71-5021. (Illus.). 1969. 3.45. Simon and Schuster.
Passing Time. Translated from the French by Jean Stewart. Michel Butor. LC 60-12592. 1960. Simon and Schuster.
Passion. Robert Steiner. Ed. by Michael Peich. (Penmaen Fiction Ser.: No. 2). 1980. 12.00 (ISBN 0-915778-33-5); ltd. signed ed. 40.00x (ISBN 0-915778-32-7). Penmaen Pr.
Passion: A Human Story. Shaw Desmond. LC 20-7288. 1920. C. Scribner's Sons.
Passion and Affect. Laurie Colwin. LC 73-5231. 1974. 6.95 (ISBN 0-670-54137-0). Viking Press.
Passion and Glory. William G Cummings. LC 25-217711. 1925. A. A. Knopf.
Passion & Illusion. Bonnie Drake. (Candlelight Ecstasy Ser.: No. 146). (Orig.). 1983. pap. 1.95 (ISBN 0-440-16816-3). Dell.
Passion and Pain. Stefan Zweig. LC 77-152967. (Short story index reprint series). 1971. (ISBN 0-8369-3882-8). Books for Libraries Press.
Passion and Patience. Janie Prichard Duggan. American Baptist Publication Society.
Passion and Principle. Theodore Edward Hook. LC 44-48082. G. Routledge and Sons.
Passion and Proud Hearts: A Novel. Lydia Lancaster. 2.25 (ISBN 0-446-82548-4). Warner Books.
Passion & Reason. Warja Honegger-Lavater. (Folded Story Ser: No. 7). 1964. bds. 3.75x o.p. Wittenborn.
Passion and the Flower. Barbara Cartland. LC 77-7076. 6.95 (ISBN 0-525-17620-9). E. P. Dutton.
Passion & the Fury. Amanda J. Jarrett. (Southerners Ser.: No. 4). 320p. (Orig.). 1983. pap. 3.50 (ISBN 0-440-06849-5, Emerald). Dell.
Passion & the Pain. Martin Neil. 192p. (Orig.). 1973. pap. 1.95 o.p. (ISBN 0-87977-180-1, DBB180). Dansk Blue Bk.
Passion And The Rage 1. Elizabeth Godwin. 1980. 1.95 (ISBN 0-449-14320-1). Fawcett Gold Medal.
Passion and the Sword. Harald Hornborg & Larsson, Gosta, Tr. LC 41-3906. 1941. D. Appleton-Century Company Incorporated.
Passion Artist. John Hawkes. LC 79-1707. 192p. 1981. pap. 3.95i (ISBN 0-06-090837-8, CN837, CN). Har-Row.
Passion Artist. John Hawkes. LC 79-1707. 1979. 11.49i (ISBN 0-06-011808-3, HarpT). Har-Row.
Passion by the Brook. A Novel About Brook Farm. 1st Ed. Truman John Nelson. LC 53-504293. 1953. Doubleday.
Passion Cargo. Marilyn Ross. 2.25 (ISBN 0-445-04463-2). Popular Library,
Passion Family. Scott Rainey. 224p. pap. 1.95 o.p. (6149). Brandon.
Passion Flower. Bertha M. Clay. LC 6172. (Bertha Clay library, no. 18). 1900. Street & Smith.
Passion Flower. Countess. (On cover: Lovell's library, no. 1347). 1889. J. W. Lovell Company.
Passion Flower. Kathleen Thompson Norris. LC 30-5407. 1930. Doubleday, Doran & Company, Inc.
Passion Flower. Edna Worthley Underwood. LC 24-6733. 1924. Houghton Mifflin Company.
Passion Flower. A Novel. (On cover: Seaside library. Pocket ed. no. 822). 1886. G. Munro.
Passion Flower: A Romance. Ida Stuart Hamilton. LC 18-15376. Printed by the Irving Press.
Passion-Flower Hotel. Rosalind Erskine, pseud. LC 62-16984. 1962. Simon and Schuster.
Passion Flower Hotel. Rosalind Fleming. 1977. 6.80 o.p. State Mutual Bk.
Passion Flower Puzzle. Don Rico. 1968. pap. 0.60 o.p. (73-793). Lancer.
Passion Flowers and the Cross. A Novel. Emma Howard Wight. 1891. Calendar Publishing Co.
Passion Flowers: Or, American Women Abroad; One of a Series. Elizabeth Lloyd Field. LC 6-397270. Field Publishing Company.
Passion for Honor. Louise MacKendrick. (Leisure Books). 1977. 1.75 (ISBN 0-8439-0467-4). Nordon Pubns.
Passion for Life. Diana C Chang. LC 61-624705. 1961. Random House.
Passion for Life: By Joseph Hocking... Joseph Hocking. 1920. Fleming H. Revell Company.
Passion for Privacy. Louis Paul. LC 40-654328. 1940. A. A. Knopf.
Passion for Profit. Peggy Gaddis, pseud. LC 41-2811. Phoenix Press.
Passion for Profit. Gail Jordan. LC 41-281145. Phoenix Press.
Passion for Treason. Robin Nicholson. 384p. (Orig.). 1981. pap. 2.75 (ISBN 0-515-05663-4). Jove Pubns.
Passion for Truth. Abraham J. Heschel. 336p. 1973. 8.95 (ISBN 0-374-22992-9); pap. 6.95 o.p. (ISBN 0-374-51184-5). FS&G.
Passion from the Past. Carole Mortimer. 192p. 1983. pap. 1.75 (ISBN 0-373-10564-9). Harlequin Bks.
Passion in Rome: A Novel. Morley Callaghan. LC 61-12704. 1961. Coward-McCann.
Passion in the Blood. Genevieve Davis. LC 76-57199. 8.95 (ISBN 0-671-22490-5). Simon and Schuster.
Passion in the Desert. Curt Leviant. 160p. 1980. pap. 2.50 (ISBN 0-380-76125-4, 76125). Avon.
Passion in the Desert: An Episode of the Reign of Terror. Honore De Balzac. Tr. by John Rudd. LC 2-21411. 1902. H. M. Caldwell Co.
Passion in the Dust see Hot Triggers.
Passion in the Pantry. Peggy Gaddis, pseud. LC 42-1107. 1942. Phoenix Press.
Passion in the Pantry. Perry Lindsay, pseud. LC 42-1107. Phoenix Press.
Passion in the Pines. Josiah Pitts Woolfolk. LC 51-14061. 1951. Arco Pub. Co.
Passion in the South... Josiah Pitts Woolfolk. LC 35-434. W. Godwin, Inc.
Passion in the Wind. Herman Weiss. 1.95 (ISBN 0-445-08583-5). Popular Library.
Passion Is a Woman. Kate Nickerson. pap. 0.60 o.p. (60-372). Manor Bks.
Passion Is the Gale: By Lewis Lester 3pseud. Louis Lazowick. LC 55-837512. 1955. Woodford Press.
Passion Is the Wind. Bridget Dryden. LC 28-22879. 1928. The John Day Company.
Passion Left Behind. Lewis Masefield. LC 47-5910. 1947. Macmillan Co.
Passion Lighting the World. Maurice Dekobra, pseud. Tr. by Wainwright, Neal. The Macaulay Company.
Passion of Amy Styron. Mona Goodwyn Williams. Orig. Title: Marriage. pap. 0.75 o.p. (54-834). Paperback Lib.
Passion of Gabrielle. Malcolm Stuart Boylan. LC 61-15800. 1961. Crown Publishers.
Passion of Herman: A Story of Oberammergau. Charles Nelson Pace. 1918. The Abingdon Press.
Passion of Loreen Bright Weasel. James Polk. LC 80-26252. 1981. 8.95 (ISBN 0-395-30351-6). Houghton Mifflin.
Passion of New Eve. Angela Carter. LC 76-54629. 7.95 (ISBN 0-15-171285-9). Harcourt Brace Jovanovich.
Passion of Richard Thynne: A Novel. Peter Ritner. LC 75-40193. 1976. 6.95 (ISBN 0-688-03010-6). Morrow.
Passion of Robert Bronson. Juan M. Alonso. LC 78-122111. 1970. 5.95. McCall Pub. Co.
Passion of Rosamund Keith. Augustus Moore. LC 99-1741. 1899. H. S. Stone and Company.
Passion of Sacco and Vanzetti: A New England Legend. Howard Melvin Fast. LC 53-3420. 1953. Blue Heron Press.
Passion of Sacco and Vanzetti: A New England Legend. Howard Melvin Fast. LC 72-138227. 1972. (ISBN 0-8371-5584-3). Greenwood Press.
Passion of Sacco & Vanzetti, a New England Legend. Howard Melvin Fast. LC 72-138227. 254p. 1972. Repr. of 1953 ed. lib. bdg. 15.00x (ISBN 0-8371-5584-3, FASV). Greenwood.
Passion of the Beast. Joseph Lamarre. LC 28-24480. The Stratford Company.
Passion of the Minde. Thomas Wright. Repr. of 1601 ed. 21.85 o.p. Adler.
Passion on the Potomac. Florence Stonebraker. LC 43-6822. 1943. Phoenix Press.
Passion Past a Novel. John A. Slaughter & Slaughter, Daisy Leighton, Joint Author. 1897. Donnally Publishing House.
Passion Pit. Mel Howard. (Orig.). pap. 0.95 o.p. (1135). Brandon.
Passion Play. Jerzy N. Kosinski. LC 79-5035. 11.95 (ISBN 0-312-59783-5). St. Martin's Press.
Passion Play. Jerzy N. Kosinski. 1980. 2.95 (ISBN 0-553-13656-9). Bantam Books.
Passion Players. Edmund P. Murray. 1968. 5.95 o.p. Crown.
Passion Players: A Novel, by Edmund P. Murray. Edmund P Murray. LC 67-27029. 1968. bds., 5.95. Crown.
Passion Pulls the Trigger. Arthur Wallace. LC 36-479. 1936. Valhalla Press.
Passion Road: A Novel. Richard Glendinning. LC 55-338234. (Popular library, 656). 1955. Popular Library.
Passion Scout. James Noble Gifford. LC 41-26003. Phoenix Press.
Passion Season. Joyce E. Bright. LC 78-31894. 1979. 9.95. Ashley Books.
Passion Seekers. Charles Beardsley. ("A Signet Book"). 1975. (pbk.) 1.50. New American Library.
Passion Sisters. Gus Stevens. (Orig.). 1969. pap. 1.25 o.p. (2091). Brandon.
Passion Star. Julia Grice. 1980. pap. 2.50 (ISBN 0-446-91498-3). Warner Bks.
Passion Stone. Harriette DeJarnette. 1980. pap. 2.75 (ISBN 0-8439-0840-8). Nordon Pubns.
Passion Stroke: A Tale of Ancient Masonry. Mary Fairweather. LC 6-21382. 1906. R. G. Badger.
Passion the Plaything: A Novel. R. Murray Gilchrist. (On cover: Lovell's Westminister series, no. 9). 1890. J. W. Lovell Company.
Passion Trap. S. F. Mitchell. 192p. (Orig.). 1973. pap. 1.95 o.p. (ISBN 0-87056-310-6, 6310). Brandon.
Passion Under the Flamboyant. Florence Kerigan. (Avalon romances). 1974. 4.50. Avalon Books.
Passion Under the Flamboyante. Florence Kerigan. (YA) 1974. 4.95 o.p. (Avalon). Bouregy.
Passion Within see Peace Like a River.
Passionate. Rick Nahass. 85p. (Orig.). 1982. pap. 4.75 (ISBN 0-9608422-0-9). R Nahass.
Passionate Adventure. Frank Stayton. LC 24-21508. The Century Co.
Passionate Angel. Ferrin L Fraser. LC 30-1698. Sears Publishing Company, Inc.
Passionate Appeal. Elise Randolph. (Candlelight Ecstasy Ser.: No. 143). (Orig.). 1983. pap. 1.95 (ISBN 0-440-16670-5). Dell.
Passionate Appetite: A Novel. Francine Pinckert. LC 71-95818. 1970. McGraw-Hill.
Passionate Brood. Margaret Campbell Barnes. 300p. 1972. 6.95 (ISBN 0-8255-1542-4). Macrae.
Passionate Brood: A Novel. Margaret Campbell Barnes. LC 45-4146. 1945. Macrae-Smith-Company.
Passionate Captive. Judson Vann. (Orig.). 1969. pap. 1.95 o.p. (6061). Brandon.
Passionate City. Ian Stuart Black. LC 58-7403. 1958. Viking Press.
Passionate Crime: A Tale of Faerie, by E. Temple Thurston... Ernest Temple Thurston. LC 15-19967. 1915. D. Appleton and Company.
Passionate Elopement. Compton Mackenzie. LC 11-5647. 1911. 1.50. John Lane Company.
Passionate Encounter. Flora Kidd. (Harlequin Presents Ser.). 1979. pap. 1.50 (ISBN 0-373-70809-2). Harlequin Bks.
Passionate Enemies. Eleanor Hibbert. LC 76-362424. (Illus.). 1976. 3.25 (ISBN 0-7091-4981-6). Hale.
Passionate Enemies. Eleanor Hibbert. LC 79-12586. (Illus.). 1979. 8.95 (ISBN 0-399-12413-6). Putnam.
Passionate Enemies. Jean Plaidy. 320p. 1981. pap. 2.50 (ISBN 0-449-24390-7, Crest). Fawcett.
Passionate Enemies. Jean Plaidy. LC 79-12586. 1979. 10.00 (ISBN 0-399-12413-6). Putnam Pub Group.

Passionate Follies. Alice Caldwell Hegan Rice & Rice, Cale Young, 1872- LC 36-29008. 1936. D. Appleton-CEntury Company, Incorporated.
Passionate Friends: A Novel. Herbert George Wells. LC 13-22757. 1913. Harper & Brothers.
Passionate Heart. Beatrix Beck. LC 53-10495. 1953. J. Messner.
Passionate Heart. Ursula Bloom. 1978. pap. 1.95 (ISBN 0-89041-186-7, 3186). Major Bks.
Passionate Hearts. Anna MacManus. LC 7-2062. 1904. Funk & Wagnalls Company.
Passionate Impostor. Elizabeth Graham, pseud. (Harlequin Presents Ser.). 192p. 1982. pap. 1.75 (ISBN 0-373-10493-6). Harlequin Bks.
Passionate Invaders. John Clare. LC 65-18393. 1965. Doubleday.
Passionate Jade. Georgianna Bell. 1981. pap. 2.95 (ISBN 0-671-83657-9). PB.
Passionate Journey. Frans Masereel. 1972. pap. 2.00 o.p. (ISBN 0-486-22447-3). Dover.
Passionate Journey. Irving Stone. LC 49-10916. 1949. Doubleday.
Passionate Mind: A Manual for Living Creatively with One's Self. new ed. Joel Kramer. LC 74-6047. (Illus.). 128p. 1974. pap. 5.95 o.p. (ISBN 0-912310-63-4). Celestial Arts.
Passionate North. 1st American Ed. William Sansom. LC 53-10635. 1953. Harcourt, Brace.
Passionate Orphan. Thompson, John Burton. LC 52-10313. 1952. Arco Pub. Co.
Passionate Pagan. Alan Geoffrey Yates. LC 63-3886. (Signet book). 1963. New American Library of World Literature.
Passionate Past of Gloria Gaye. Bernard Kops. LC 71-152664. 1972. 6.95 (ISBN 0-393-08663-1). Norton.
Passionate Persuasion. Jocelyn Day. (Second Chance at Love Ser.: No. 24). 192p. (Orig.). 1982. pap. 1.75 (ISBN 0-515-06147-6). Jove Pubns.
Passionate Pilgrim. Barbara Cartland. 1976. pap. 1.25 o.p. (ISBN 0-515-04063-0). BJ Pub Group.
Passionate Pilgrim. Barbara Cartland. (O.s.i.). 1974. pap. 1.25 o.s.i. (ISBN 0-515-03327-8, V3327). Pyramid Pubns.
Passionate Pilgrim. Mason Gilmore. LC 36-430533. Godwin.
Passionate Pilgrim. Charles Terrot & Terrot, Sarah Anne. LC 49-10572. 1949. Harper.
Passionate Pilgrim. Percy White. LC 11-7148. (Half-title: Appletons' town and country library, no. 235). 1898. D. Appleton and Company.
Passionate Pilgrim: And Other Tales. Henry James. 1875. J. R. Osgood and Company.
Passionate Pilgrim: And Other Tales. Henry James. LC 3-2952. 1903. Houghton, Mifflin and Company.
Passionate Pilgrim: Being the Narrative of an Oddly Dramatic Year in the Life of Henry Calverly, 3rd. Samuel Merwin. LC 19-12719. The Bobbs-Merrill Company.
Passionate Pretenders. Diana Haviland. (Fawcett Gold Medal Book). 1.95 (ISBN 0-449-13810-0). Fawcett Publications,C.
Passionate Princess. Josiah Pitts Woolfolk. LC 48-10606. (Novel library, 4). 1948. Diversey Pub. Corp.
Passionate Prisoners. Will Henry, pseud. pap. 1.95 o.s.i. (Venus). Grove.
Passionate Puritan. Alice Mary Ross Colver. LC 33-29799. 1933. Dodd, Mead & Company.
Passionate Puritan. Jane Mander. LC 21-10174. 1921. John Lane Company.
Passionate Quest. Edward Phillips Oppenheim. LC 24-232887. 1924. Little, Brown, and Company.
Passionate Rebel. Winifred Mary Scott. LC 28-851531. 1928. Doubleday, Doran & Company, Inc.
Passionate Rebel. Frank Gill Slaughter. LC 79-6890. (Illus.). 1979. 12.50 (ISBN 0-385-14336-2). Doubleday.
Passionate Rebel: The Life of Lord Byron. Kasimir Edschmid & Chambers, Whittaker, Tr. 1930. A. & C. Boni.
Passionate Rebel: The Story of Hector Berlioz. Frank Wilson Kenyon. LC 72-185185. 1972. 5.95. Dodd, Mead.
Passionate Savage. Constance Gluyas. (Orig.). 1980. pap. 2.95 (ISBN 0-451-09928-1, E9928, Sig). NAL.
Passionate Shepherd: A Book of Stories. 1st Ed. Samuel Yellen. LC 57-10312. 1957. Knopf.
Passionate Sin. Raymond M Stewart. LC 57-12018. (Milestone book). 1957. Comet Press Books.
Passionate Spectator. Jane Burr. LC 21-3290. 1921. T. Seltzer.
Passionate Stranger. Flora Kidd. (Harlequin Presents Ser.). 192p. 1981. pap. 1.75 (ISBN 0-373-10464-2). Harlequin Bks.
Passionate Tennis Player: And Other Stories. Charles Tekeyan. LC 49-9635. 1949. Pastoral-Universe.
Passionate Tigress. John Saxon. pap. 0.60 o.p. (60-393). Manor Bks.
Passionate Touch. Bonnie Drake. 1981. pap. 1.75 (ISBN 0-440-16776-0). Dell.
Passionate Tree. Beatrice Sheepshanks. LC 27-159702. 1927. Harper & Brothers.
Passionate Victims: By Lange Lewis Pseud. 1st Ed. Jane Beynon. LC 52-8312. 1952. Bobbs-Merrill.
Passionate Witch. Norman Haghejm Matson & Matson, Norman Haghejm, 1893- LC 43-11136. 1942. The Sun Dial Press.
Passionate Witch. Thorne Smith & Matson, Norman Haghejm. LC 41-13943. 1941. Doubleday, Doran & Co., Inc.
Passionate Year. James Hilton. LC 24-237377. 1924. Little, Brown, and Company.
Passionate Year. James Hilton. LC 44-7524. 1944. New Avon Library.
Passionnate Land: A Novel. Geoffrey Atheling Wagner. LC 53-1562. 1953. Simon and Schuster.
Passions. Charlotte Dacre. LC 73-22762. (Gothic Novels II). 1974. (ISBN 0-405-06013-0). Arno Press.
Passions. Barney Leason. 480p. 1982. pap. 3.75 (ISBN 0-523-41207-X). Pinnacle Bks.
Passions. Isaac Bashevis Singer. 1978. pap. 2.95 (ISBN 0-449-24067-3, Crest). Fawcett.
Passion's Acres. Rodney Middleton. 1972. pap. 1.75 o.s.i. (V1113K, Venus). Grove.
Passions, and Other Stories. Isaac Bashevis Singer. LC 75-20267. 1975. 7.95 (ISBN 0-374-22993-7). Farrar, Straus and Giroux.
Passions, and Other Stories. Isaac Bashevis Singer. LC 76-378974. 1976. 3.95 (ISBN 0-224-01249-5). Cape.
Passions & Prejudices. Leo Calvin Rosten. LC 77-16562. 1978. 9.95 (ISBN 0-07-053984-7, GB). McGraw.
Passion's Blossom. Brenna McCartney. 1982. pap. 3.50 (ISBN 0-8217-1109-1). Zebra.
Passion's Child. Fiona Harrowe, pseud. 480p. (Orig.). 1983. pap. 3.50 (ISBN 0-449-12392-8, GM). Fawcett.
Passion's Dark Harvest. Jessica Ward. 320p. (Orig.). 1981. pap. 3.25 (ISBN 0-8439-1001-1, Leisure Bks). Nordon Pubns.
Passion's Domain. Nina Coombs. (Rapture Romance Ser.: No. 6). 192p. 1983. pap. 1.95 (ISBN 0-451-12065-5). NAL.
Passion's Dream. Casey Stuart. 1982. pap. 3.50 (ISBN 0-8217-1086-9). Zebra.
Passion's Flight. Marilyn Mathieu. (Second Chance at Love Ser.: No. 16). 192p. (Orig.). 1981. pap. 1.75 (ISBN 0-515-05978-1). Jove Pubns.
Passion's Fool. Florence Stonebraker. LC 43-18006. 1943. Phoenix Press.
Passion's Fruit: A Novel. Karl Kingshead. LC 98-894. (Dillingham's American authors' library, no. 43). 1898. G. W. Dillingham Co.
Passion's Furnace. Josip Kosor. 3.00 o.p. Branden.
Passion's Fury. Patricia Hagan. 400p. 1981. pap. 2.95 (ISBN 0-380-77727-4, 81497-8). Avon.
Passion's Harvest. Marion Mallasch. 1981. pap. 2.75 (ISBN 0-89083-724-4). Zebra.
Passions in the Sand. Barbara Cartland. (Bantam Barbara Cartland Library#41). 1976. (pbk.) 1.25 (ISBN 0-553-02801-4). Bantam Books.
Passions-Masters. Arnal N. Rafik. 1972. pap. 1.75 o.s.i. (V1103K, Venus). Grove.
Passions of Medora Graeme. Elsie Lee. LC 72-82172. 1972. 6.95 (ISBN 0-87795-047-4). Arbor Hse.
Passions of Medora Graeme. Elsie Lee Sheridan. LC 72-82172. 1972. 6.95 (ISBN 0-87795-047-4). Arbor House.
Passions of the Mind. Irving Stone. LC 75-139064. 1971. 17.95 (ISBN 0-385-02396-0); Limited edition 50.00 (ISBN 0-385-02568-8). Doubleday.
Passions of the Mind. Irving Stone. 816p. 1972. pap. 4.50 (ISBN 0-451-11580-5, AE1580, Sig). NAL.
Passions of the Nightless Night. John B. Alphonso Karkala. 1974. Hind Pocket Books.
Passions of the Ring. Arthur Acred. LC 67-16367. 1967. Morrow.
Passions of Uxport: A Novel. Maxine W Kumin. LC 75-14698. 1975. 19.50 (ISBN 0-8371-8241-7). Greenwood Press.
Passions of Uxport: A Novel. Maxine W Kumin. LC 68-15975. 1968. Harper & Row.
Passion's Paradise. Sonya T. Pelton. 544p. (Orig.). 1981. pap. 3.25 (ISBN 0-89083-765-1). Zebra.
Passion's Pawn. Annabella. 1978. pap. 2.25 (ISBN 0-440-06937-8). Dell.
Passion's Plaything. Tony Trelos, pseud. 176p. pap. 1.95 o.p. (6118). Brandon.
Passion's Pleasure. Valerie Giscard. (Orig.). 1982. pap. 3.50 (ISBN 0-8217-1034-6). Zebra.
Passion's Price. Barbara Bonham. 1977. 1.95. Playboy Press.
Passion's Price. Donna K. Vitek. (Candlelight Ecstacy Ser.: No. 110). (Orig.). 1983. pap. 1.95 (ISBN 0-440-17036-2). Dell.
Passion's Pride. Claudette Williams. 448p. (Orig.). 1980. pap. 2.50 (ISBN 0-449-24278-1, Crest). Fawcett.
Passion's Prisoner. Judith Polley. (Dell Book.). 1978. 1.75 (ISBN 0-440-19357-5). Dell Publishing Co.
Passion's Promise. Paula Fairman. 352p. 1983. pap. 3.25 (ISBN 0-523-41750-0). Pinnacle Bks.
Passion's Promise. Danielle Steel. 1981. pap. 3.75 (ISBN 0-440-12926-5). Dell.
Passion's Promise. Danielle Steele. LC 81-6860. 1981. 16.95 (ISBN 0-8161-3217-8). G.K. Hall.
Passion's Rapture. Penelope Neri. (Orig.). 1982. pap. 3.50 (ISBN 0-89083-912-3). Zebra.
Passion's Reign. Karen Harper. (Orig.). 1983. pap. 3.95 (ISBN 0-8217-1177-6). Zebra.
Passion's Slave. Richard Ashe King. (On cover: Seaside library. Pocket ed. no. 1262). 1889. G. Munro.
Passion's Song. Johanna Phillips. (Second Chance at Love Ser.: No. 88). 1982. pap. 1.75 (ISBN 0-515-06850-0). Jove Pubns.
Passions Spin the Plot. Vardis Fisher. LC 34-117285. 1934. The Caxton Printers, Ltd., and Garden City, N.Y., Doubleday, Doran & Company, Inc.
Passion's Tempest. Nicole Duval. (Orig.). 1982. pap. 3.50 (ISBN 0-8217-1067-2). Zebra.
Passion's Thief. Louise MacKendrick. 1978. pap. 1.95 o.s.i. (ISBN 0-8439-0573-5, Leisure Bks). Nordon Pubns.
Passion's Treasure. Marsha Gibson. 352p. (Orig.). 1982. pap. 3.25 (ISBN 0-505-51805-8). Tower Bks.
Passion's Triumph. Erica Hollis. (Superromances Ser.). 384p. 1982. pap. 2.50 (ISBN 0-373-70037-7, Pub. by Worldwide). Harlequin Bks.
Passion's Wicked Torment. Melissa Hepburne. (Orig.). 1981. pap. 2.75 (ISBN 0-523-41004-2). Pinnacle Bks.
Passive Crime: And Other Stories. Margaret Wolfe Hungerford. LC 7-9059. (On cover: Lovell's library. v. 12, no. 624). 1885. J. W. Lovell Company.
Passover Commando. Irving R Cohen. LC 78-11442. 8.95 (ISBN 0-517-53631-5). Crown Publishers.
Passport. Richard Bagot. LC 5-32390. 1905. Harper & Brothers.
Passport. Emile Voute. LC 15-19071. 1915. M. Kennerley.
Passport for a Girl: A Novel. by mary borden. ed. Mary Borden. LC 39-124396. 1939. Harper & Brothers.
Passport for a Pilgrim. James Leasor. LC 69-15189. 1969. 4.95. Doubleday.
Passport for a Renegade. Kem Bennett. LC 55-5505. 1955. Published for the Crime Club by Doubleday.
Passport for Jennifer. Edward Ellsberg. LC 52-9954. 1952. Dodd, Mead.
Passport Invisible. Perley Poore Sheehan. LC 18-454508. George H. Doran Company.
Passport of Mallam Ilia. Cyprian Ekwensi. 1960. text ed. 3.50x (ISBN 0-521-04883-4). Cambridge U Pr.
Passport to Danger. Jessyca Paull. (Passport to Danger Ser.). (O.s.i.). (Orig.). 1968. pap. 1.25 o.s.i. (AQ1250, Award). Univ Pub & Dist.
Passport to Eden. Eleanor Elliott Carroll. LC 39-10764. The Penn Publishing Company.
Passport to Eternity. Laurence W Foreman. LC 75-264242. 1970. 7.00.
Passport to Life City. Sherwood Wirt. pap. 1.95 o.p. (ISBN 0-89107-127-X). Good News.
Passport to Life City: A Modern Pilgrim's Progress. Sherwood Eliot Wirt. LC 70-85041. 1969. 4.95. Harper & Row.
Passport to Oblivion. James Leasor. LC 65-12598. 1965. bds., 3.95. Lippincott.
Passport to Oblivion. Marion Lee. LC 45-9488. 1945. C. Scribner's Sons.
Passport to Peril. Robert B Parker. LC 50-11153. 1951. Rinehart.
Passport to the Past. Regina Kolitz. LC 49-7401. 1949. H. H. Glanz.
Passport to the Supernatural: An Occult Compendium from All Ages & Many Lands. Bernhardt J. Hurwood. LC 78-164019. 1972. 9.95 (ISBN 0-8008-6261-9). Taplinger.
Past All Dishonor. James Mallahan Cain. LC 46-3855. 1946. A. A. Knopf.
Past and Present of Solomon Sorge. Judith Barnard Papier. LC 67-12903. 1967. Houghton Mifflin.
Past Finding Out. Dan E. L. Patch. LC 39-23859. Bica Press.
Past Folly. Florence Stonebraker. LC 48-586321. 1948. Phoenix Press.
Past Is Ours. Phyllis Gordon Demarest. LC 34-814319. The Macaulay Company.
Past Master. R. A Lafferty. LC 75-416. (Garland Library of Science Fiction). 1975. 11.00 (ISBN 0-8240-1421-9). Garland Pub.
Past Master. R. A Lafferty. (Ace Book). 1977. 1.50 (ISBN 0-441-65301-4). Ace Books.
Past Must Alter. Albert Joseph Guerard. LC 38-277. 1937. Longmans Green and Co.
Past Must Alter. Albert Joseph Guerard. LC 38-6007. H. Holt and Company.
Past Praying for. Sara Woods, pseud. LC 68-28235. (Illus.). 1968. 4.95. Harper & Row.
Past, Present, and Future Perfect: A Text Anthology of Speculative and Science Fiction. Jack Wolf, pseud. LC 73-83186. (Fawcett premier book). 1973. (pbk.) 0.95. Fawcett.
Past, Present, and Murder. Hugh Pentecost. LC 82-9638. (Red badge novel of suspense). 1982. 9.95 (ISBN 0-396-08103-7). Dodd, Mead.
Past? Present? Future? Three Original Short Science Fiction Stories. Greg Kriznik. LC 77-150561. Press of the Good Mountain.
Past Recaptured. Marcel Proust. LC 70-117691. 1970. 7.95. Random House.
Past Recaptured. Marcel Proust. Tr. by Blossom, Frederick Augustus. LC 32-222854. (His Remembrance of things past. pt. ((i. e. 8). 1932. A. & C. Boni.
Past Recaptured. 1st Ed. Translated from the French by Frederick A. Blossom. Marcel Proust. LC 51-13851. (Modern library no. 278). 1951. Modern Library.
Past Sin. James Noble Gifford. LC 45-4605. 1945. Phoenix Press.
Past Tense of Love. Elizabeth Cadell. LC 70-91332. 1970. 5.95. Morrow.
Past the End of the Pavement. Charles Grandison Finney. LC 39-326037. H. Holt and Company.
Past Thirty. Harriet Earhart Monroe. LC 7-31815. 1879. For the Author.
Past Through Tomorrow. Robert Anson Heinlein. 1975. pap. 3.25 (ISBN 0-425-04756-3, Medallion). Berkley Pub.
Past Through Tomorrow: 'Future History' Stories. Robert Anson Heinlein. LC 67-15112. (Berkley medallion book). (His Future history series). 1975. (pbk.) 1.95 (ISBN 0-425-02738-4). Berkley Pub. Co.
Past Through Tomorrow: 'Future History' Stories. Robert Anson Heinlein. (His Future history series). 1967. Putnam.
Past Was a Sleep. Elizabeth Carfrae, pseud. LC 39-174122. G. P. Putnam's Sons.
Paste see Author of Beltraffio.
Paste Jewels. facsimile ed. John Kendrick Bangs. LC 70-96035. (Short Story Index Reprint Ser.). 1897. 15.00 (ISBN 0-8369-3081-9). Ayer Co.
Paste Jewels: Being Seven Tales of Domestic Woe. John Kendrick Bangs. LC 70-96035. (Short story index reprint series). (Illus.). 1969. Books for Libraries Press.
Paste Jewels: Being Seven Tales of Domestic Woe. John Kendrick Bangs. LC 6-6122. 1897. Harper & Brothers.
Paste, or Diamonds? Fontluce. Leon De Tinseau. LC 43-30371. (On cover: Once a week library, vol. XI, no. 12). P. F. Collier.
Paste-Pot Man. Edwin Moultrie Lanham. LC 66-20171. 1967. Farrar, Straus & Giroux.
Pasteboard Crown: A Story of the New York Stage. Clara Morris. LC 2-15353. 1902. C. Scribner's Sons.
Pastel. Georgette Heyer. LC 29-9797. 1929. Longmans, Green and Co.
Pastel City. Mike John Harrison. LC 72-79394. (Doubleday science fiction). 1972. 4.95 (ISBN 0-385-08263-0). Doubleday.
Pastel City. Mike John Harrison. (Avon science fiction). 1974. (pbk.) 0.95 (ISBN 0-380-00057-1). Avon.
Pastels of Men. 1st Series... Paul Charles Joseph Bourget & Wormeley, Katherine Prescott, 1830-1908, Tr. LC 6-14926. 1891. Roberts Brothers.
Pastels of Men. 2d Series... Paul Charles Joseph Bourget & Wormeley, Katherine Prescott, 1830-1908, Tr. 1892. Roberts Brothers.
Pasternak: A Collection of Critical Essays. Ed. by Victor Erlich. LC 77-21223. (Twentieth Century Views Ser.). 1978. 10.95 o.p. (ISBN 0-13-652834-1, Spec); pap. 3.45 o.p. (ISBN 0-13-652826-0, Spec). P-H.
Pastime Stories. Thomas Nelson Page. LC 76-75784. (Short story index reprint series). (Illus.). 1969. Books for Libraries Press.
Pastime Stories. Thomas Nelson Page. LC 15-124791. 1901. C. Scribner's Sons.
Pastime Stories. Thomas Nelson Page. LC 9-250699. 1894. Harper & Brothers.
Pastimes of a Red Summer. Peter Vansittart. 12.95x o.p. (ISBN 0-8464-0704-3). Beekman Pubs.
Paston Carew: Millionaire and Miser. Elizabeth Lynn Linton. (On cover: Seaside library. Pocket ed. no. 886). 1886. G. Munro.
Paston Carew: Millionarie and Miser. A Novel. Elizabeth Lynn Linton. (Harper's Franklin square library. no. 549). 1886. Harper & Brothers.
Pastor. Robert E. Link. 3.95 o.p. Vantage.
Pastor at River Bend. Clark Duncan. LC 55-44312. 1955. Wartburg Press.
Pastor of Poggsee. Gustav Frenssen. Tr. by Potts, Katharine G. LC 31-28017. 1931. Houghton Mifflin Company.
Pastora. Joanna Barnes. LC 77-79533. 1980. 12.95 (ISBN 0-87795-170-5). Arbor Hse.
Pastora. Joanna Barnes. 768p. 1981. pap. 3.50 (ISBN 0-380-56184-0, 56184). Avon.

Pastora: A Novel. Joanna Barnes. LC 80-139206. 12.95 (ISBN 0-87795-170-5). Arbor House.

Pastoral. Eleanor Green. LC 37-17806. 1937. Doubleday, Doran & Co., Inc.

Pastoral. Nevil Shute Norway. LC 73-106690. 1970. Greenwood Press.

Pastoral. Nevil Shute Norway. LC 44-571639. 1944. W. Morrow and Company.

Pastoral Played Out. Mary Lucy Pendered. LC 7-36373. The Cassell Publishing Co.

Pastorale. Nelly Theodorou. LC 61-8105. 1961. Crowell.

Pastorale: Stories. Susan Engberg. LC 82-4730. (Illinois Short Fiction). 11.95 (ISBN 0-252-00993-2) (ISBN 0-252-00994-0). University of Illinois Press.

Pastorals of Dorset. Mary E. Sweetman Blundell. LC 73-160931. (Short story index reprint series). (Illus.). 1971. (ISBN 0-8369-3910-7). Books for Libraries Press.

Pastorals of Dorset. Mary E. Sweetman Blundell. LC 6-39301. 1901. Longmans, Green, and Co.

Pastorate of Martin Wentz: A Segment of a Consistent Life. David Rogers Landis. Greenwood Printing Co.

Pastor's Daughter. Bertha Behrens. Tr. by Mrs. J. W. Davis. LC 6-9432. (On cover: Worthington's international library no. 8). 1890. Worthington Co.

Pastor's Fire-Side, 2 Vols. Jane Porter. LC 75-162887. (Bentley's Standard Novels: Nos. 18 & 19). Repr. of 1832 ed. Set. 25.00 (ISBN 0-404-54560-2); 13.00 ea. Vol. 1 (ISBN 0-404-54418-5). Vol. 2 (ISBN 0-404-54419-3). AMS Pr.

Pastors of Yesterday. A. J McGilvray. LC 72-175796. Spectrum.

Pastor's Son. William Wilfred Walter. LC 7-27617. W. W. Walter.

Pastor's Wife. Mary Annette Beauchamp Russell Russell. LC 14-18806. 1914. Doubleday, Page & Company.

Pasture for Peterkin. Agnes Mary White Sandford. pap. 2.50 (ISBN 0-910924-38-4). Macalester.

Pastures of Heaven. John Steinbeck. LC 32-30511. 1932. Brewer, Warren & Putnam.

Pastures of Heaven. John Steinbeck. LC 45-12226. (On cover: Penguin books. 414). 1942. Penguin Books, Inc.

Pastures of Heaven. John Steinbeck. LC 81-23472. 1982. 3.95 (ISBN 0-14-004998-3). Penguin Books.

Pastures of Heaven: A Novel. John Steinbeck. 1938. Modern Age Books, Inc.

Pat. Katharine Tynan Hinkson, pseud. LC 13-9248. 1913. 1.35. Benzinger Brothers.

Pat Garrett and Billy the Kid. Rudolph Wurlitzer. (Signet Film Series). (Illus.). 1973. (pbk) 1.25. New American Library.

Pat Hobby Stories. Francis Scott Key Fitzgerald. (O.s.i.). 1962. pap. 2.95 (ISBN 0-684-71761-1, SL216, ScribT); 15.00 (ISBN 0-684-16477-9). Scribner.

Pat Whitney, R.N. Lucy Agnes Hancock. LC 42-4611. 1942. Macrae-Smith-Company.

Pat Whitney, R.N. Lucy Agnes Hancock. LC 43-59509. 1943. The Sun Dial Press.

Patapharis Affair: A Novel. Suzanne Prou. LC 79-105117. 1970. 5.95. H. Regnery Co.

Patch. Kathleen Hampton. LC 60-7684. 1960. Random House.

Patch Commission. Frederick C Crews. LC 68-9805. (Illus.). 1968. Dutton.

Patch of Blue. Grace Livingston Hill. LC 32-34233. J. B. Lippincott Company.

Patch of Blue. Elizabeth Kata. 144p. 1975. pap. 2.25 (ISBN 0-445-00303-0). Juniper.

Patch Unit. George G. Bailey. (Orig.). 1981. pap. 1.95 (ISBN 0-505-51624-1). Tower Bks.

Patches: A Montage. David Lawson. LC 75-5087. 7.50 (ISBN 0-911024-17-4). New Voices Pub. Co.

Patchsaddle Drive. Cliff Farrell. LC 72-79386. (Double D western). 1972. 4.95 (ISBN 0-385-08472-2). Doubleday.

Patchsaddle Drive. Cliff Farrell. (Signet brand western). 1973. (pbk.) 0.95. New American Library.

Patchwork. Beverley Nichols. LC 22-4979. 1922. H. Holt and Company.

Patchwork: A Story of "the Plain People,". Anna Balmer Myers. LC 20-5190. G. W. Jacobs & Company.

Patchwork Cat. William Mayne & Nicola Bayley. 9.99 (ISBN 0-394-95021-6). Knopf: Distributed by Random House.

Patchwork Clan. Doris Lund. 272p. 1983. pap. 3.50 (ISBN 0-440-17035-4). Dell.

Patchwork Comedy. Humfrey Robertson Jordan. 1913. 1.30. G. P. Putnam's Sons.

Patchwork Girl. Larry Niven. LC 80-119034. (Illus.). 5.95 (ISBN 0-441-65315-4). Ace Book.

Patchwork Hero: A Novel. Michael Noonan. LC 58-10611. 1958. J. Day Co.

Patchwork Madonna. Harold Weston. LC 29-212083. W. Morrow & Company.

Patchwork Man. David Harper. LC 75-2474. 1975. 6.95 (ISBN 0-396-07135-X). Dodd, Mead.

Patchwork Man. David Harper. LC 75-20339. 1975. 8.95 (ISBN 0-8161-6325-1). G. K. Hall.

Patchwork of Death. Peter Nichols. LC 65-22464. 1965. Holt, Rinehart and Winston.

Patchwork Screen for the Ladies. Jane Barker. Bd. with Prude: A Novel by a Young Lady. LC 74-170553. (Novel in England, 1700-1775 Ser). lib. bdg. 50.00 o.s.i. (ISBN 0-8240-0551-1). Garland Pub.

Patchwork Time. Robert Faucett Gibbons. LC 48-5044. 1948. A. A. Knopf.

Patent Leather Kid and Several Others. Rupert Hughes. LC 27-19898. Grosset & Dunlap.

Paterfamilias. William Budd Trites. 1929. Cosmopolitan Book Corporation.

Paternoster Ruby. Charles Edmonds Walk. LC 10-244838. 1910. A. C. McClurg & Co.

Path. Helena Strassova. LC 79-86122. 1970. 5.95 (ISBN 0-670-54261-X). Orion Press.

Path. David A. Wilson. 1977. pap. 2.00 (ISBN 0-934852-18-9). Lorien Hse.

Path into the Unknown: The Best of Soviet Science Fiction. Ed. by Judith Merril. 1968. 4.95 o.p. Delacorte.

Path into the Unknown: The Best of Soviet Science Fiction. LC 67-20896. 1968. Delacorte Press.

Path of Dalliance. Auberon Waugh. LC 71-875706. 1970 (ISBN 0-14-002562-6). Penguin.

Path of Desire. Ellen Goforth, pseud. 192p. (Orig.). 1980. pap. 1.50 (ISBN 0-671-57005-6). S&S.

Path of Error: And Other Stories. Joseph Moses Meirovitz. LC 18-4150. 1918. The Four Seas Company.

Path of Exoterra. Gordon McBain. LC 80-69897. 1.95 (ISBN 0-380-55434-8). Avon.

Path of Ghosts. Bill Knox. LC 73-146471. 1971. 4.95 (ISBN 0-8415-0110-6). McCall Pub. Co.

Path of Ghosts. Robert MacLeod, pseud. LC 73-146471. 1971. 4.95 o.p. (ISBN 0-8415-0110-6). Sat Rev Pr.

Path of Glory. Paul Leland Haworth. LC 11-9153. 1911. 1.25. Little, Brown, and Company.

Path of Glory: By George Blake. George Blake. LC 29-26894. 1929. Harper & Brothers.

Path of Gold. William Almon Wolff. LC 20-22448. 1920. Reynolds Publishing Company, Inc.

Path of Gold: A Novel. 1st Ed. Maud Miller Hoffmaster. LC 52-6770. 1952. Exposition Press.

Path of Honor: A Tale of the War in the Bocage. Burton Egbert Stevenson. LC 10-22257. 1910. 1.50. J. B. Lippincott Company.

Path of Life. Frank Lateur. Tr. by Teixeira De Mattos, Alexander Louis. LC 15-26767. 1915. Dodd, Mead and Company.

Path of Love: By Warren Howard Pseud. James Noble Gifford. LC 51-14973. 1951. Arcadia House.

Path of Names. Abraham Ben Samuel Abulafia. Tr. by Bruria Finkel & Jack Hirschman. LC 75-22792. pap. 4.00 o.p. Tree Bks.

Path of Peril. Vera Craig. (Candlelight mystery). 1974. (pbk.) 0.75. Dell.

Path of Stars. Margaret Crosby Munn. LC 3-24816. 1903. Dodd, Mead & Company.

Path of the Eclipse: A Historical Horror Novel, Fourth in the Count De Saint-Germain Series. Chelsea Quinn Yarbro. LC 80-53085. 14.95 (ISBN 0-312-59802-5). St. Martin's Press.

Path of the Great. Bitzentzos Kornaros & Gargilis, Stephen. LC 45-13389. 1945. Athena Publishers.

Path of the Hero King. Nigel G Tranter. (Illus.). 1973. (pbk.) 1.25. Ballantine Books.

Path of the King. John Buchan. LC 22-2004. 1921. 1.90. George H. Doran Company.

Path of the Storm. Douglas Reeman. (N1540). 1968. Berkley.

Path of the Storm. Douglas Reeman. LC 67-10961. 1967. Putnam.

Path of the Sun. R. W Alexander. LC 27-6483. 1927. D. Appleton and Company.

Path of Thunder. Peter Abrahams. LC 48-54218. (A Harper "find"). 1948. Harper.

Path of True Love. Margaret Culkin Banning. LC 33-910387. 1933. Harper & Brothers.

Path of Unreason. George Oliver Smith. LC 58-8766. Gnome Press.

Path of Unreason. George Oliver Smith. 1975. (pbk.) 1.50. Ballantine Books.

Path to Paradise. Coningsby William Dawson. LC 32-2462. 1932. A. A. Knopf.

Path to Parnassus. 4th ed. F. Maurice. 1956. pap. 3.00x (ISBN 0-522-83804-9, Pub. by Melbourne U Pr). Intl Schol Bk Serv.

Path to the Nest of Spiders. Italo Calvino. LC 76-5827. 1976. (ISBN 0-912946-31-8). Ecco Press.

Path to the Nest of Spiders. Translated from the Italian by Archibald Colquhoun. Italo Calvino. LC 57-12742. 1957. Beacon Press.

Path to the Peak. Louise Louis. (Illus.). 176p. 1971. pap. 2.50 (ISBN 0-941242-03-X). Pen-Art.

Path to the Silent Country: Charlotte Bronte's Years of Fame. Lynne Reid Banks. LC 77-20290. 8.95 (ISBN 0-440-06985-8). Delacorte Press.

Path. Tr. from Spanish by John and Brita Haycraft. Miguel Delibes, pseud. LC 61-41489. 1966. bds., 3.00. H. Hamilton.

Path Wharton Found. Robert Quillen. LC 24-24346. 1924. The Macmillan Company.

Pather Panchali. Song of the Road: A Bengali Novel. Bibhuti Bhusan Banerjee. LC 68-11277. (UNESCO Collection of Representative Works: Indian Series). 1968. 6.95. Indiana University Press.

Pathetic Snobs. Dolf Wyllarde. LC 18-17240. 1918. John Lane Company.

Pathfinder. James Fenimore Cooper. Ed. by Sharp. Russell Alger. LC 26-2543. (modern readers' series). 1926. The Macmillan Company.

Pathfinder. James Fenimore Cooper. 1928. Minton, Balch & Co.

Pathfinder. James Fenimore Cooper & Robert James Dixson. LC 54-5565. (American Classics, Simplified and Adapted for Greater Reading Pleasure, Book 4). (Illus.). 1973. (pbk.) 1.25. Regents Pub. Co.

Pathfinder: Abridged and Edited. James Fenimore Cooper. Ed. by Knight, Marietta. LC 27-15218. (Academy classics for junior high schools). Allyn and Bacon.

Pathfinder: By James Fenimore Cooper; Illustrated by Donald S. Humphreys... James Fenimore Cooper. LC 26-27489. (Fairmount classic). Macrae Smith Company.

Pathfinder. Introd. by Robert E. Spiller. Illus. by Richard M. Powers. Printed for Members of the Limited Editions Club. James Fenimore Cooper. LC 65-9241. 1965. 6.50. Heritage Dist. Dial.

Pathfinder: Or, The Inland Sea. James Fenimore Cooper. 1840. Lea and Blanchard.

Pathfinder: Or, The Inland Sea. James Fenimore Cooper. 1872. D. Appleton and Company.

Pathfinder: Or, The Inland Sea. James Fenimore Cooper. (On cover: Leather stocking tales household ed.). Houghton, Mifflin and Company.

Pathfinder: Or, The Inland Sea. James Fenimore Cooper. (Seaside library. v. 12 no. 226). 1878. G. Munro.

Pathfinder: Or, The Inland Sea. James Fenimore Cooper. (On cover: Seaside library. Pocket ed. no. 309). 1884. G. Munro.

Pathfinder: Or, the Inland Sea. James Fenimore Cooper. LC 12-195868. T. Y. Crowell & Company.

Pathfinder: Or, The Inland Sea. James Fenimore Cooper. LC 4-19565. 1896. D. Appleton and Company.

Pathfinder: Or, The Inland Sea. James Fenimore Cooper. LC 20-18831. Grosset & Dunlap.

Pathfinder: Or, The Inland Sea. James Fenimore Cooper. LC 28-9849. (Honor books). T. Nelson and Sons.

Pathfinder: Or, The Inland Sea. James Fenimore Cooper. LC 37-3019. (Immortal masterpiece of literature. vol. iii). The Spencer Press.

Pathfinder: Or, The Inland Sea. James Fenimore Cooper. LC 43-48884. The American News Company.

Pathfinder or, The Inland Sea. approved ed. / edited with an historical introduction by richard dilworth rust. ed. James Fenimore Cooper & Richard Dilworth Rust. LC 79-15598. (Writings of James Fenimore Cooper). (Illus.). 24.95 (ISBN 0-87395-365-7). State University of New York Press.

Pathfinder: Or, The Inland Sea, by J. Fenimore Cooper. James Fenimore Cooper. (Half-title: Everyman's library, ed. by Ernest Rhys. Fiction. no. 78). 1906. J. M. Dent &Co.

Pathfinder: Or, The Inland Sea. Introd. by Norman Holmes Pearson. James Fenimore Cooper. LC 52-9772. (Modern library of the world's best books 105). 1952. Modern Library.

Pathfinder: Or,The Inland Sea. James Fenimore Cooper. LC 4-15432. (His leather-stocking tales). 1900. Macmillian and Co., Limited.

Pathfinder: Simplified and Adapted by Robert J. Dixson. Drawings by Syd Browne. With Exercises for Study and Vocabulary Drill. James Fenimore Cooper & Robert James Dixson. LC 54-5565. (American classics, book 4). 1954. Regents Pub. Co.

Pathfinder. With Illus. of the Author and His Encironment and Reproductions of Drawings for Early Editions of the Book Together with an Introd. and Descriptive Captions by Allen Klots, Jr. James Fenimore Cooper. LC 53-4004. (Great illustrated classics). 1953. Dodd, Mead.

Pathfinders. Cecil Lewis. LC 44-4440. 1944. W. Morrow & Company.

Pathfinders of the Revolution: A Story of the Great March into the Wilderness and Lake Region of New York in 1779. William Elliot Griffis. LC 4709. W. A. Wilde Company.

Pathless Trail. Arthur Olney Friel. LC 22-5608. 1922. Harper & Brothers.

Paths and by-Paths. Anna Maria Tolman Pickford. American Tract Society.

Paths Crossing: A Romance of the Plains. Maude Clark Gay. 1908. The C. M. Clark Publishing Company.

Paths of Glory. Humphrey Cobb. LC 35-7808. 1935. The Viking Press.

Paths of Glory. H. E. Danford. 3.50 o.p. Carlton.

Paths of Judgement. Anne Douglas Sedgwick. LC 4-27360. 1904. The Century Co.

Paths of Love: By Vercors. Jean Bruller. LC 61-5682. 1961. Putnam.

Paths of the Sea. Pierre Schoendoerffer. LC 77-18148. 1978. 8.95 (ISBN 0-698-10903-1). Coward, McCann & Geoghegan.

Paths to Conservation. James Sterling Tippett. LC 37-12247. (Our animal books, VI: a series in humane education, ed. by Frances E. Clarke). D. C. Heath and Company.

Pathway. Henry Williamson. LC 29-5958. E. P. Dutton & Co., Inc.

Pathway of Adventure. Ross Tyrrell. LC 20-8517. (On verso of half-title: The Borzoi mystery stories, VI). 1920. A. A. Knopf.

Pathway of Freedom. Edna Nethery. LC 30-22021. The Christopher Publishing House.

Pathway of the Pioneer: Nous Autres) Dolf Wyllarde. LC 12-40178. 1909. John Lane Company.

Pathway to Heaven: Translated by Antonia White. Henry Bordeaux. LC 52-123827. Pellegrini & Cudahy.

Pathway to Paradise. Maysie Greig. LC 42-7338. 1942. Doubleday, Doran & Co., Inc.

Pathway to the Stars. Harnett Thomas Kane. 1973. pap. 0.95 o.p. (09033). Curtis.

Pathway to the Stars: A Novel Based on the Life of John McDonogh of New Orleans and Baltimore. Harnett Thomas Kane. LC 50-10303. 1950. Doubleday.

Pathways East and West. Nell Cramer Woolsey. LC 48-49097. 1948. L. L. Morrison.

Patience. Anna Bartlett Warner. LC 8-33717. 1891. J. B. Lippincott Company.

Patience: A Daughter of the Mayflower. Elizabeth Williams Champney. LC 99-5603. (Her Dames and daughters of colonial days, v. 1). 1899. Dodd, Mead and Company.

Patience: A Novel. John Coates. LC 54-9058. 1954. Macmillan.

Patience & Sarah. Isabel Miller. 1979. pap. 2.50 (ISBN 0-449-23850-4, Crest). Fawcett.

Patience & Sarah. Isabel Miller, pseud. 192p. 1972. 5.95 o.p. (ISBN 0-07-042035-1). McGraw.

Patience and Sarah. Isabel Miller. (Fawcett crest book). 1973. 0.95. Fawcett Publications.

Patience and Sarah. Alma Routsong. LC 73-179714. 1972. (ISBN 0-07-042035-1). McGraw-Hill.

Patience de Maigret. Georges Simenon. pap. 3.95. French & Eur.

Patience of John Morland. Mary C Johnson Dillon. LC 13-20468. 1909. A. L. Burt Company.

Patience of John Morland. Mary C Johnson Dillon. LC 9-16802. 1909. Doubleday, Page & Company.

Patience of Maigret. Georges Simenon & Sainsbury, Geoffrey, Tr. LC 40-4891. Harcourt, Brace and Company.

Patience Pettigrew's Perplexities. Being a Veracious History of the Experiences of Patience Pettigrew, Relict of the Late Lamented Josiah Pettigrew, Esq.... Clara Augusta Jones. LC 7-12142. A. L. Burt.

Patience Preston, M. D. Anna Frances Raffensperger. LC 14-224602. (On cover: The round world series). 1887. D. Lothrop Company.

Patience Sparhawk. Gertrude Franklin Horn Atherton. LC 75-104407. 1970. (ISBN 0-8398-0066-5). Literature House.

Patience Sparhawk and Her Times. Gertrude Franklin Horn Atherton. LC 8-14662. 1913. The Macmillan Company.

Patience Sparhawk and Her Times. Gertrude Franklin Horn Atherton. LC 13-129221. 1897. John Lane.

Patience Strong's Outings. Adeline Dutton Train Whitney. LC 8-36541. 1869. Loring.

Patience Strong's Outings. Adeline Dutton Train Whitney. 1893. Houghton, Mifflin and Company.

Patience Strong's Outings. Adeline Dutton Train Whitney. 1896. Houghton, Mifflin and Company.

Patient. Georges Simenon. LC 68-120199. (B 68-08983). 1968. Penguin.

Patient in Room Eighteen. Mignon Good Eberhart. 1976. Repr. of 1929 ed. lib. bdg. 15.95x (ISBN 0-88411-765-0). Amereon Ltd.

Patient in Room 18. Mignon Good Eberhart. LC 29-9217. 1929. Pub. for The Crime Club, Inc., by Doubleday, Doran & Company, Inc.

Patient Inside the Mayo Clinic. Alan Edward Nourse. 1979. 12.95 o.p. (ISBN 0-07-047493-1, GB). McGraw.

Patira. Marie De Saffron David. LC 6-32172. 1883. J. Murphy & Co.

Paton Street Case. John Bingham. 1965. pap. 0.65 o.p. (ISBN 0-14-002038-1). Penguin.

Patriarch. Chaim I. Bermant. LC 81-510. 14.95 (ISBN 0-312-59804-1). St. Martin's Press.

Patricia. Edith Henrietta Fowler. LC 15-5599. 1915. 1.50. G. P. Putnam's Sons.

Patricia. Grace Livingston Hill. LC 39-149493. J. B. Lippincott Company.

Patricia: A Sequel to "Two Bad Brown Eyes,". Harriet Louise Lynch. LC 8-3402. The Merriam Company.

Patricia at the Inn. John Collis Snaith. LC 6-37964. B. W. Dodge and Company.

Patricia Brent: Spinster. Herbert George Jenkins. LC 18-22829. George H. Doran Company.

Patricia Ellen. Mary Wiltshire. LC 24-21923. 1924. Dodd, Mead & Company.

Patricia Lacked a Lover: A Comedy in Six Days. John North. LC 29-10431. 1929. Duffield and Company.

Patricia Lancaster's Revenge. Olive Katharine Parr. LC 28-11710. 1928. Longmans, Green and Co., Ltd.

Patricia of the Hills: A Novel. Charles Kennett Burrow. LC 2-71274. 1902. G. P. Putnam's Sons.

Patricia Plays a Part. Mabel Sarah Barnes Grundy. 1914. 1.35. Dodd, Mead and Company.

Patricia the Beautiful. Katheryn Kimbrough, pseud. (Saga of the Phenwick Women: Bk 4). 256p. 1975. pap. 1.25 (ISBN 0-445-00294-8). Popular Lib.

Patrician. John Galsworthy. LC 11-5187. 1911. Charles Scribner's Sons.

Patrician. John Galsworthy. LC 20-156108. 1918. C. Scribner's Sons.

Patrician. John Galsworthy. Ed. by Perry, Bliss. LC 26-22413. (modern student's library). C. Scribner's Sons.

Patrician Street. John Gibson. LC 40-8658. 1940. The Vanguard Press.

Patricia's Awakening. Harold James Barrett. LC 24-11555. Thomas Y. Crowell Company.

Patrick Butler for the Defence: A Detective Novel. 1st Ed. John Dickson Carr. LC 56-6045. 1956. Harper.

Patrick Dunbar: Or, What Came of a "Personal in the Times" a Novel. John Pennington Marsden. LC 9-22946. 1909. 1.50. Hallowell Co., Ltd.

Patrick Henry and the Frigate's Keel: And Other Stories of a Young Nation. Howard Melvin Fast. LC 45-35072. 1945. Duell, Sloan and Pearce.

Patrick J. Mc Gillicuddy & the Rabbi. Norman M. Goldburg. LC 77-90818. (Illus.). 1969. 5.95 o.p. (ISBN 0-87672-103-X). Geron-X.

Patrick O'Monighan: Or, The Hidden Treasure of Old Uzarro. George A Kirkland. LC 7-12514. 1880. G. S. Irwin, Printer.

Patrimony (a Horsclans Novel) Robert Adams. (Orig.). 1980. pap. 2.50 (ISBN 0-451-11815-4, AE1815, Sig). NAL.

Patriot. Pearl Sydenstricker Buck. LC 39-27111. The John Day Company.

Patriot. Evan S. Connell, Jr. 1960. 4.95 o.p. (ISBN 0-670-54278-4). Viking Pr.

Patriot. Charles Durbin. LC 70-154785. 1971. 7.95. Coward, McCann & Geoghegan.

Patriot. Thomas Alva Stubbins. 1908. M. A. Donohue & Company.

Patriot. Alexia E Walter & Walter, H. C., Joint Author. LC 28-176391. E. P. Dutton & Company.

Patriot Game. De St. Jorre, John & Brian Shakespeare. LC 73-7532. (Midnight novel of suspense). 1973. 5.95 (ISBN 0-395-17124-5). Houghton Mifflin.

Patriot Game. George V. Higgins. LC 81-18655. 1982. 12.95. Knopf.

Patriot Game. George V. Higgins. LC 82-4687. 1982. 13.95 (ISBN 0-89340-532-9). J. Curley.

Patriot Game. Brian Shakespeare & St. John. 1975. pap. 1.50 o.p. (ISBN 0-515-03793-1). BJ Pub Group.

Patrioteer. Heinrich Mann. LC 75-22422. (Series: The European Library (New York). 1975. H. Fertig.

Patrioteer. Heinrich Mann. Tr. by Ernest Augustus Boyd. LC 21-21695. (Half-title: The European library, ed. by J. E. Spingarn). 1921. Harcourt, Brace and Company.

Patriotic Murders. Agatha Miller Christie. LC 41-33257. 1941. Dodd, Mead & Company.

Patriotism, Inc., and Other Tales. Paul Van Ostayen. LC 79-150314. 1971. 9.50. University of Massachusetts Press.

Patriots. Chet Cunningham. 720p. (Orig.). 1982. pap. 3.95 (ISBN 0-505-51835-X). Tower Bks.

Patriots. Chet Cunningham. (O.s.i.). 1976. pap. 1.75 o.s.i. (BT50988). Belmont-Tower.

Patriots. Joseph Guinan. LC 26-915946. 1928. Benziger Brothers.

Patriots. Robert Emmet Wall. (Canadians Ser.: No. IV). 288p. 1982. pap. 3.50 (ISBN 0-553-22686-X). Bantam.

Patriots and Other Stories. Helen Stuart Colby Haines. LC 29-16825. 1929. Atlantic Coast Printing Corporation.

Patriot's Dream. Barbara Mertz. LC 76-20500. 8.95 (ISBN 0-396-07337-9). Dodd, Mead.

Patriot's Dream. Barbara Michaels. LC 76-20500. 1976. 8.95 o.p. (ISBN 0-396-07337-9). Dodd.

Patriots of Palestine: A Story of the Maccabees. Charlotte Mary Yonge. LC 3-28184. 1896. T. Whitaker.

Patriot's Progress. G. E. Hopkins. LC 61-12330. 1961. Scribner.

Patriot's Progress: Being the Vicissitudes of Pte. John Bullock. Henry Williamson & Kermode, William, Illus. LC 30-18658. E. P. Dutton & Co., Inc.

Patriot's Strategy. A Novel. Thomas F Hargis. LC 7-1908. 1895. C. T. Dearing.

Patriots: The Story of Lee and the Last Hope, by Cyrus Townsend Brady... Cyrus Townsend Brady. 1906. Dodd, Mead & Company.

Patriots. 1st Ed. James Barlow. LC 60-104397. 1960. Harper.

Patrol. Philip MacDonald. LC 28-7868. 1928. Harper & Brothers.

Patrol. Fred Majdalany. LC 53-723522. 1953. Houghton Mifflin.

Patrol of the Mountain. A Tale of the Revolution. Newton Mallory Curtis. 1847. Williams Brothers.

Patrol of the Sun Dance Trail. Charles William Gordon. LC 14-184585. Hodder & Stoughton, George H. Doran Company.

Patrol to Benghazi. Gordon Landsborough. 1978. pap. 1.50 (ISBN 0-532-15315-4). Woodhill.

Patron of the Arts. William Rotsler. LC 74-8318. 1974. 1.25 (ISBN 0-345-24062-6). Ballantine Books.

Patronage. Maria Edgeworth. LC 25-23772. (Half-title: The novels of Maria Edgeworth, vol vii, viii). 1893. J. M. Dent & Co.

Patroon Van Volkenberg: A Tale of Old Manhattan in the Year Sixteen Hundred & Ninety-Nine. Henry Thew Stephenson. LC 5835. The Bowen-Merrill Company.

Patrulla Homicida. new ed. George Fennell. Tr. by Orestes Ramiro from Eng. (Compadre Collection). Orig. Title: Killer Patrol. 160p. (Span.). 1974. pap. 0.75 (ISBN 0-88473-605-9). Fiesta Pub.

Patrulla Sangrienta. new ed. George Fennell. Tr. by Orestes Ramiro from Eng. (Compadre Collection Ser). Orig. Title: Blood Patrol. 160p. (Span.). 1974. pap. 0.75 (ISBN 0-88473-604-0). Fiesta Pub.

Pat's Palace: A Story of Our Country's Curse. Thomas Nield. LC 7-32297. 1892. W. F. Clark.

Patsy. Samuel Rutherford Crockett. LC 13-121. 1912. 1.25. The Macmillan Company.

Patsy: A Story. Henry De Vere Stacpoole. LC 8-23542. 1908. The McClure Company.

Patsy Cline. Ellis Nassour. (Orig.). 1981. pap. 2.95 (ISBN 0-505-51679-9). Tower Bks.

Patsy for Keeps: A Patsy and Patsy Ann Put Together Book. Esther Merriam Ames. LC 32-5309. S. Gabriel Sons & Company.

Patten's Last Days. Jim Stickter. LC 81-80433. (Illus.). 364p. (Orig.). 1981. pap. 15.00 (ISBN 0-930770-18-8). Hemisphere Hse.

Pattern. Mignon Good Eberhart. 1937. Doubleday, Doran and Company, Inc.

Pattern. Mignon Good Eberhart. LC 38-23363. 1938. The Sun Dial Press, Inc.

Pattern. Mignon Good Eberhart. 1975. (pbk.) 0.95. Popular Library.

Pattern. Rose Franken. LC 25-9754. 1925. C. Scribner's Sons.

Pattern for a Heroine: The Life-Story of Rebecca Gratz. Miriam Biskin. LC 67-21067. (Illus.). 1967. Union of American Hebrew Congregations.

Pattern for Conquest: An Interplanetary Adventure. George Oliver Smith. LC 50-3818. 1949. Gnome Press.

Pattern for Destruction. Paul W. Fairman. 1970. pap. 0.75 o.p. (75-308). Manor Bks.

Pattern for Muder. Ione Sandberg Shriber. LC 44-477763. 1944. Farrar & Rinehart, Inc.

Pattern for Panic. Richard S Prather. LC 54-6463. 1954. Abelard-Schuman.

Pattern in Black and Red. Cora Hardy Jarrett. LC 34-30687. 1934. Houghton Mifflin Company.

Pattern of a Man. Seymour Gottlieb. LC 51-11848. 1952. Exposition Press.

Pattern of a Man & Other Stories. James Still. LC 76-45313. 9.50 (ISBN 0-917788-00-1). Gnomon.

Pattern of Chance. Gordon Gardiner. 1930. Houghton Mifflin Company.

Pattern of Love. William Edward Daniel Ross. (Avalon Books). 4.95. Thomas Bouregy.

Pattern of People. Elizabeth Goudge. LC 78-12123. (o.s.i.). 1979. 9.95 o.s.i. (ISBN 0-698-10965-1, Coward). Putnam Pub Group.

Pattern of People: An Anthology. Elizabeth Goudge & Muriel Grainger. LC 78-12123. 1979. 9.95 (ISBN 0-698-10965-1). Coward, McCann & Geoghegan.

Pattern of Perfection, Thirteen Stories. 1st Ed. Nancy Hale. LC 60-11636. 1960. Little, Brown.

Pattern of Three. Mary Hastings Bradley. 1937. D. Appleton-Century Company, Incorporated.

Patternmaster. Octavia E Butler. LC 76-2759. (Doubleday science fiction). 1976. 5.95 (ISBN 0-385-12197-0). Doubleday.

Patternmaster. Octavia E Butler. 1979. 1.75 (ISBN 0-380-41806-1). Avon Books.

Patterns in Glass. Peggy Dunstan. 1968. 3.50 o.s.i. Tri-Ocean.

Patterns of Chaos. Colin Kapp. (O.s.i.). 192p. (Orig.). 1973. pap. 0.95 o.s.i. (AN1118, Award). Univ Pub & Dist.

Patterns of Love. Petrina Crawford. Orig. Title: Lovers Mist. 1972. pap. 0.75 o.p. Belmont-Tower.

Patterns of the Hebrides. Gus Wylie. LC 81-82821. (Illus.). 96p. 1982. 19.95 (ISBN 0-8071-0991-6). La State U Pr.

Patterns of Wolfpen. Harlan Henthorne Hatcher. LC 34-38185. The Bobbs-Merrill Company.

Patti. John Benton. LC 78-14263. (Spire books). 1.95 (ISBN 0-8007-8346-8). Revell.

Patty. Katharine Sarah Gadsden Macquoid. LC 7-16614. 1871. Macmillan & Co.

Patty. A Novel. Katharine Sarah Gadsden Macquoid. (Seaside library, v. 24, no. 478). 1879. G. Munro.

Patty. A Novel. Katharine Sarah Gadsden Macquoid. LC 43-27482. (With Robinson, F. W. A bridge of glass. New York, 1872). 1872. Harper & Brothers.

Patty Cannon Administers Justice. R. W. Messenger. LC 60-15801. 1960. 5.00 (ISBN 0-87033-079-9, Pub. by Tidewater). Cornell Maritime.

Patty Cannon Administers Justice: Or, Joe Johnson's Last Kidnapping Exploit; a Tale of the Del-Mar-Va Peninsula in Its "Dark Ages". R. W. Messenger. LC 26-10919. 1926. J. W. Stowell Printing Co.

Patty Leroy... Amanda Maria Tiernan Kuhn. LC 13-18073. 1.00. R. G. Badger.

Patty of the Palms: A Story of Porto Rico. Adam Christian Haeselbarth. LC 7-40004. The Kenny Publishing Co.

Patty's Perversities. Arlo Bates. LC 6-9085. (Round-Robin Series). 1881. J. R. Osgood and Company.

Patty's Perversities. Arlo Bates. LC 9-175831. Houghton Mifflin Company.

Patty's Suitors. Carolyn Wells. LC 14-157412. 1914. Dodd, Mead and Company.

Patuffa; the Story of an Artist. Beatrice Harraden. LC 23-127852. 1923. Frederick A. Stokes Company.

Paul. Edward Frederic Benson. LC 6-37196. 1906. J. B. Lippincott Company.

Paul, a Herald of the Cross. Florence Morse Kingsley. LC 7-12155. 1897. H. Altemus.

Paul, a Herald of the Cross. Florence Morse Kingsley. LC 7-12156. 1898. H. Altemus.

Paul Adams: A Novel of an American Dentist. S. J Horn. LC 29-19780. 1929. Benedict Publishers, Inc.

Paul and Julia: Or, The Political Mysteries, Hypocrisy, and Cruelty of the Leaders of the Church of Rome. John Claudius Pitrat. LC 7-38200. 1855. E. W. Hinks and Company.

Paul and Persis: Or, The Revolutionary Struggle in the Mohawk Valley. Mary Elizabeth Quackenbush Brush. 1883. Lee and Shepard.

Paul and Virginia. Jacques Henri Bernardin De Saint-Pierre. 1867. Hurd and Houghton.

Paul and Virginia. Jacques Henri Bernardin De Saint-Pierre. (Lovell's library. v. 2, no. 37). 1882. J. W. Lovell Company.

Paul and Virginia. Jacques Henri Bernardin De Saint-Pierre. (On cover: The Franklin library, no. 2). 1887. Franklin News Company.

Paul and Virginia. Jacques Henri Bernardin De Saint-Pierre. LC 41-38133. 1888. Belford, Clarke & Co.

Paul and Virginia of a Northern Zone. Poul Og Virginie Under Nordlig Bredde. Drachmann, Holger Henrik Herholdt. LC 6-34232. 1895. Way & Williams.

Paul and Virginia. With a Memoir and Illustrations. Jacques Henri Bernardin De Saint-Pierre. (On cover: Young folks' series). 1884. D. Lothrop & Co.

Paul Anthony, Christian: A Tale of Truth. Hiram Wallace Hayes. LC 7-42007. 1907. Reid Publishing Company.

Paul Anthony, Christian: A Tale of Truth. 10th thousand ed. Hiram Wallace Hayes. LC 8-19719. 1908. Reid Publishing Company; Etc., Etc.

Paul Ardenheim: The Monk of Wissahikon. George Lippard.

Paul Beaumont. Edward Winslow Gilliam. LC 99-1684. 1899. Press of the Sun Printing Office.

Paul Brewster and Son. Helen E Chapman. LC 79-85681. (American fiction reprint series). 1969. Books for Libraries Press.

Paul Bunyan. James Stevens. (Comstock edition). 1975. (pbk.) 1.75 (ISBN 0-345-24423-0). Ballantine Books.

Paul Clermont's Story and My Own, Following by the Gift of Paul Clermont. Francis Warrington Dawson. LC 29-5226. 1928. The Bernard Publishing Co.

Paul Clifford. Edward George Earle Lytton Bulwer-Lytton Lytton. LC 8-26651. G. Routledge and Sons.

Paul Clifford. Edward George Earle Lytton Bulwer-Lytton Lytton. LC 7-8107. (On cover: Lovell's library, no. 117). 1883. J. W. Lovell Company.

Paul Clifford. Edward George Earle Lytton Bulwer-Lytton Lytton. LC 7-8106. (Half-title: Novels of Sir Edward Bulwer Lytton. Library ed. Novels of life and manners, vol. V-VI). 1893. Little, Brown, and Company.

Paul Clifford. illustrated holiday ed. Edward George Earle Lytton Bulwer-Lytton Lytton. LC 46-37503. 1898. D. Estes & Company.

Paul Crew's Story. Alice Vansittart Strettel Carr. LC 6-24226. (Harper's handy series, no. 21). 1885. Harper & Brothers.

Paul Crew's Story. Alice Vansittart Strettel Carr. (On cover: Seaside library. Pocket ed. no. 571). G. Munro.

Paul Darst: Or, A Conflict Between Love and Infidelity. Daniel R Lucas. LC 7-14755. 1877. Central Book Concern.

Paul Dombey: From Dombey & Son. Charles Dickens. LC 6-37047. (Standard literature series. no. 14). 1896. University Publishing Company.

Paul Douglas--Journalist. Charles Monroe Sheldon. LC 9-30324. 1909. Advance Publishing Company.

Paul Errington and Our Scarlet Prince: A Book for the American People. John McDowell Leavitt. LC 7-18766. F. H. Revell Company.

Paul Faber, Surgeon. George Macdonald. LC 75-1513. (Victorian Fiction: Novels of Faith and Doubt; No. 62). 1975. 35.00 (ISBN 0-8240-1586-X). Garland Pub.

Paul Faber, Surgeon. George MacDonald. LC 51-548015. 1879. Lippincott.

Paul Faber, Surgeon. George Macdonald. (Seaside library. v. 23, no. 435). G. Munro.

Paul Faber, Surgeon. George Macdonald. LC 12-18328. 1911. D. McKay.

Paul Fane: Or, Parts of a Life Else Untold. A Novel. Nathaniel Parker Willis. LC 8-36897. 1857. C. Scribner.

Paul French's Way. Jennie Maria Drinkwater Conklin. A. I. Bradley & Co.

Paul Jones: A Nautical Romance. Alexandre Dumas & Dauzats, Adrien. Tr. by Williams, Henry Llewellyn. LC 6-42320. 1889. F. Warne and Co.

Paul Jones: The Son of the Sea. Alexandre Dumas & Dauzats, Adrien. LC 6-42321. 1853. Garrett & Co.

Paul Judson: A Story of the Kentucky Mountains. Edward Bagby Pollard. LC 5-20776. 1905. The Baptist Argus.

Paul Kelver. Jerome Klapka Jerome. LC 2-21992. 1902. Dodd, Mead & Company.

Paul Knox, Pitman. John Berwick Harwood. (Franklin square library, no. 4). Harper & Brothers.

Paul Patoff. Francis Marion Crawford. LC 6-30891. 1887. Houghton, Mifflin and Company.

Paul Patoff. Francis Marion Crawford. LC 4-15092. 1893. Macmillan and Co.

Paul Perril, the Merchant's Son: Or, The Adventures of a New-England Boy Launched Upon Life. Joseph Holt Ingraham. LC 7-10351. 1847. Williams & Brothers.

Paul Ralston. A Novel. Mary Jane Hawes Holmes. LC 7-6027. 1897. G. W. Dillingham Co.

Paul Redding: A Tale of the Brandywine. 2d ed. Thomas Buchanan Read. LC 11-3207. 1845. E. Ferrett & Co.

Paul Reeves: Or, Life's Mistakes. S G Bowne. LC 6-16099. 1879. Press of Cott & Hann.

Paul Revere Square. Louise Andrews Kent. LC 39-24450. 1939. Houghton Mifflin Company.

Paul Revere's Ride: A Deposition. Esther Forbes. 1976. cancelled o.p. St Onge.

Paul Rundel: A Novel. William Nathaniel Harben. LC 12-22126. 1912. Harper & Brothers.

Paul St. Paul: A Son of the People, a Novel. Ruby Beryl Kyle. LC 7-14175. 1895. C. W. Moulton.

Paul Street Boys. Ferenc Molnar. Tr. by Rittenberg, Louis. LC 27-24009. 1927. Macy-Masius.

Paul; the Christian. By an Unknown Disciple, Author of. LC 31-9376. J. Cape & H. Smith.

Paul: The Christian. LC 31-9376. 1931. J. Cape & H. Smith.

Paul the Jew. By an Unknown Disciple Author of. LC 27-19416. George H. Doran Company.

Paul: the Jew. Cecily Phillimore. LC 27-19416. 1927. George H. Doran Company.

Paul the Minstrel: And Other Stories. Arthur Christopher Benson. LC 70-106247. (Short story index reprint series). 1970. Books for Libraries Press.

Paul, the Smuggler. By the Author of "Dick Clinton, the Masked Highwayman," Etc. Headly. Garrett & Co.

Paul Tiber: Forester. Hertha Gleitsmann. LC 49-11051. 1949. Scribner's Sons.

Paul Vernon, Prisoner. Milton Robinson Scott. LC 4395. 1900. Express Printing Co.

Paul Zwilling: A Novel. Josef Gert Vondra. LC 75-324724. 1974. (ISBN 0-85885-082-6). Wren.

Paula: A Sketch from Life. Vivian Cory. LC 13-2073. (On cover: Seaside library. Pocket ed., no. 2179). 1898. G. Munro's Sons.

Paula: A Sketch from Life. Vivian Cory. LC 42-31598. M. Kennerley.

Paula: A Sketch from Life. Vivian Cory. 1908. Kensington Press.

Paula Ferris. Mary Farley Sanborn Sanborn. LC 8-3755. 1893. Lee and Shepard.

Paula, Go Down to Depravity. Lisa Baxter. pap. 1.95 o.p. (8010). Cameo.

Paulina: A Story of Napoleon and the Fall of Venice. Max Pemberton. LC 22-6028. 1922. Cassell and Company, Ltd.

Paulina 1880. Pierre Jean Jouve. LC 72-89695. 1973. 6.95 (ISBN 0-672-51761-2). Bobbs-Merrill.

Pauline. Isabella Macdonald Alden. LC 1-31810. Lothrop Pub. Co.

Pauline. Freda De Knoop. LC 24-28965. 1924. D. Appleton and Company.

Pauline: A Romance of the Civil War. Arthur Willis Spooner. LC 15-10722. 1915. Sherman, French & Company.

Pauline: Also, Ellice Quentin, and The Countess's Ruby. Julian Hawthorne. LC 7-3884. (American authors' series, no. 25). United States Book Company.

Pauline: Or, A Wife's Revenge. (On cover: Munro's library, popular novels, no. 98). 1884. N. L. Munro.

Pauline Seward. A Tale of Real Life. 7th ed. John Delavan Bryant. LC 6-19894. 1867. J. Murphy & Co.; Etc., Etc.

Pauline's Caprice: Or, A Gay Girl in Gay Paris. Zola, Pseud.? Tr. (On cover: Fox's sensational series, no. 5). R. K. Fox.

Pauline's Trial: A Novel. Lydia L D Courtney. LC 6-28993. 1877. G. W. Carleton & Co.

Paul's Apartment. Hilda Van Siller. LC 48-727869. 1948. Pub. for the Crime Club by Doubleday.

Paul's Offering and Gates Ajar. Charlotte O'Loan. LC 6-16641. 1906. The Angelus Publishing Company.

Paul's Offering and Gates Ajar: Stories. Joseph F Wynne. LC 6-16641. The Angelus Publishing Company.

Paul's Paragon. William Edward Norris. LC 42-437625. 1912. Brentano's.

Paulton Plot. Herbert Adams. LC 31-29190. J. B. Lippincott Comapny.

Paulus Fy: The History of an Esthete, Helene Mullins & Gllegher, Marie, Joint Author. LC 24-29190. 1924. R. M. McBride & Company.

Paumalu: A Story of Modern Hawaii. Rus Calisch. LC 78-78037. 3.95 (ISBN 0-9602354-1-8). Paumalu Press.

Pauper of Park Lane. William Le Queux. LC 8-8090. Cupples & Leon Co.

Pausanius the Spartan. Edward George Earle Lytton Bulwer-Lytton Lytton & Lytton, Edward Robert Bulwer-Lytton, 1st Earl of, 1831-1891, Ed. LC 7-8105. (On cover: Lovell's library, v. 6, no. 317). 1883. J. W. Lovell Company.

Pause for Passion. Florence Stonebraker. 1942. Phoenix Press.

Pause in the Desert: A Collection of Short Stories. Oliver La Farge. LC 57-6381. 1957. Houghton Mifflin.

Pause Under the Sky. Warren Beck. LC 47-335005. 1947. The Swallow Press Etc.

Pavane. Keith Roberts. LC 68-22526. (Doubleday science fiction). 1968. 4.95. Doubleday.

Paved Path: A Novel. Phyllis Hambledon. LC 30-51720. Thomas Y. Crowell Company.

Paved with Gold. Georgia Buchanan. LC 78-63375. 1979. 6.95 (ISBN 0-533-03969-X). Vantage.

Paved with Good Intentions. Dorothy McCleary. LC 38-207969. 1938. Doubleday, Doran and Co., Inc.

Pavement. Louis Second. LC 29-7726. The Stratford Company.

Pavements at Anderby: Tales of "South Riding" and Other Regions. Winifred Holtby & Reid, Hilda Stewart, 1898- Ed. LC 38-37587. 1938. The Macmillan Company.

Pavilion. Hilda Lawrence. LC 46-743012. 1946. Simon and Schuster.

Pavilion. James K. Mugler. 480p. 1982. pap. 3.50 (ISBN 0-515-05523-9). Jove Pubns.

Pavilion by the Lake: A Detective Story. Arthur John Rees. LC 30-24049. 1930. Dodd, Mead & Company.

Pavilion: Of People & Times Remembered of Stories & Places. Stark Young. LC 74-157693. Repr. of 1951 ed. lib. bdg. 11.50x o.p. (ISBN 0-678-02774-9). Kelley.

Pavilion of Women. Pearl Sydenstricker Buck. LC 46-8001. 1946. The John Day Company.

Paving the Way: A Romance of the Australian Bush. Simpson Newland. LC 7-33485. 1899. D. Biddle.

Paw Paw to Ph.D. Randolph E. Spencer. (Orig.). 1977. pap. 3.95 (ISBN 0-917200-16-0). ESPress.

Pawdie. Irene Cory. LC 68-21586. (O.s.i.). 1968. 5.95 o.s.i. (ISBN 0-8149-0047-X). Vanguard.

Pawn. Frances Nichols Hanna. LC 36-29605. 1936. Godwin.

Pawn: A Novel. Bartholomeus Landheer. LC 47-30416. 1947. Querido.

Pawn: A Novel. Arthur R Mather. LC 75-326966. 1975. 5.60 (ISBN 0-85885-155-5). Wren.

Pawn: By Fan Nichols. Frances Nichols Hanna. LC 51-321. 1950. Woodford Press.

Pawn in Danger. Adam Hall, pseud. 1971. pap. 0.75 o.p. (T2578). Pyramid Pubns.

Pawn in Frankincense. Dorothy Dunnett. LC 70-77009. (Illus.). 1969. 6.95. Putnam.

Pawn in Pawn. Hilda Mary Sharp. LC 20-8275. 1920. G. P. Putnam's Sons.

Pawn in the Game. William Henry Fitchett. LC 8-439. Eaton & Mains.

Pawn of Evil. Audrey Leech. (Orig.). 1971. pap. 0.75 o.p. (T2470). Pyramid Pubns.

Pawn of Love. Florence Stonebraker. Orig. Title: Raging Passions. 1967. pap. 0.50 o.p. (B50-800). Belmont-Tower.

Pawn of Prophecy. David Eddings. (Belgariad Ser.: Bk. 1). 256p. (Orig.). 1982. pap. 2.50 (ISBN 0-345-29637-0, Del Rey). Ballantine.

Pawn of the Omphalos. E. C. Tubb. 160p. 1980. pap. 1.95 (ISBN 0-449-14377-5, GM). Fawcett.

Pawn of Time: An Extravaganza. 1st Ed. Robin Carson. LC 57-104145.

Pawn to Infinity. Fred Saberhagon. 256p. 1982. pap. 2.50 (ISBN 0-441-65482-7). Ace Bks.

Pawnbroker. Edward Lewis Wallant. 1973. 1.25. Manor Books.

Pawnbroker. Edward Lewis Wallant. LC 61-11910. 1961. Harcourt, Brace & World.

Pawnbroker. Edward Lewis Wallant. LC 78-7101. (Harvest/HBJ book). 1978. 2.95 (ISBN 0-15-671422-1). Harcourt Brace Jovanovich.

Pawned. Frank Lucius Packard. LC 21-9592. George H. Doran Company.

Pawnee Bill" A Romance of Oklahoma. Herman Edwin Mootz. LC 28-140019. Excelsior Publishing Company.

Pawns. Dale L. Soderberg. (Orig.). 1979. pap. 1.95 (ISBN 0-532-23105-8). Woodhill.

Pawns Count. Edward Phillips Oppenheim. LC 18-645. 1918. Little, Brown, and Company.

Pawn's Count. Edward Phillips Oppenheim. LC 21-137204. 1920. A. L. Burt Company.

Pawns of Destiny: A Romance. John A Devito. LC 31-33069. B. Humphries, Inc.

Pawns of Fate. Paul Eugene Bowers. LC 18-22166. The Cornhill Company.

Pawns of Fate. Meriel Aimie Ross. LC 11-16887. 1911. Harper & Brothers.

Pawns of Fear: A Novel by Jason Manor Pseud. Oakley M Hall. LC 55-587048. 1955. Viking Press.

Pawns of Liberty: A Story of Fighting Yesterdays in the Balkans. Corrinne Stephenson Tsanoff & Tsanoff, Radoslav Andrea, 1887- Joint Author. LC 14-17927. 1914. Outing Publishing Ocmpany.

Pawns of Murder. Nancy Mann Waddel Wilson Woodrow Woodrow. LC 32-208647. 1932. R. Long & R. R. Smith, Inc.

Pax Britannica: The Climax of an Empire. James Morris. LC 79-24725. (Illus.). 544p. 1980. pap. 7.95 (ISBN 0-15-671466-3, Harv). HarBraceJ.

Pax: Peace. Lorenzo Marroquin. Tr. by Isaac Goldberg & W. V. Schierbrand. 1977. lib. bdg. 59.95 (ISBN 0-8490-2417-X). Gordon Pr.

Pax Spheros: A Novel. Caroline E Brooks. 1900. D. Biddle; Etc., Etc.

Paxman Feud. Clement Hardin. (Ace Double). 1973. (pbk) 0.75. Ace Books.

Paxton Pride. Shana Carrol, pseud. (Orig.). 1982. pap. 3.50 (ISBN 0-515-06324-X). Jove Pubns.

Paxton Quigley's Had the Course: A Novel. Stephen H. Yafa. LC 68-10620. 1968. Lippincott.

Pay Attention: A Novel. Nan Thayer Ross. LC 78-78258. 1979. 4.95 (ISBN 0-933568-01-0). Chrysalis Books.

Pay Check. Rob Eden. LC 32-161111. Grosset & Dunlap.

Pay Day. Nathan Asch. LC 30-5938. 1930. Brewer and Warren Inc., Payson and Clarke Ltd.

Pay Dirt: And Other Whispering Sands Stories of Gold Fever & the Western Desert. Erle Stanley Gardner. Ed. by Charles G. Waugh & Martin H. Greenberg. 324p. 1983. 15.95 (ISBN 0-688-01981-1). Morrow.

Pay Envelopes: Tales of the Mill, the Mine and the City Street. James Oppenheim. LC 72-3288. (Short story index reprint series). (Illus.). 1972. (ISBN 0-8369-4158-6). Books for Libraries Press.

Pay Envelopes: Tales of the Mill, the Mine and the City Street. James Oppenheim. LC 11-13523. 1911. 1.25. B. W. Huebsch.

Pay for Your Pleasure. Florenz Branch. LC 37-667800. Phoenix Press.

Pay for Your Pleasure. Florence Stonebraker. LC 37-6678. 1937. Phoenix Press.

Pay Gravel. Hugh Pendexter. LC 28-6141. The Bobbs-Merrill Company.

Pay-off. Joe Barry Lake. LC 43-16522. 1943. Mystery House.

Pay-off at Black Hawk. Harry Sinclair Drago. LC 56-6723. (Permabooks, M-8088. Western, 8). 1956. Permabooks.

Pay-off at Ladron. Bennett Foster. LC 37-5751. 1937. W. Morrow & Co.

Pay-off in Blood. Davis Dresser. LC 62-9977. 1972. Dell.

Pay-off in Switzerland. Bill Knox. LC 77-74271. 1977. 6.95 (ISBN 0-385-13246-8). Published for the Crime Club by Doubleday.

Pay on the Way Out. John Murphy. LC 75-1352. 1975. 6.95 (ISBN 0-684-14212-0). Scribner.

Pay the Doctor. Elizabeth Seifert. LC 66-24269. 1966. bds., 3.95. Dodd.

Pay the Piper: A Novel. Adelyn Bushnell. LC 50-7170. 1950. Coward-McCann.

Pay Thy Pleasure. Elizabeth Inglis-Jones. LC 40-724412. 1940. Doubleday, Doran & Co., Inc.

Paybed. Nicholas Bentley. 1977. 5.00 o.s.i. (ISBN 0-233-96845-8). Transatlantic.

Paying Guest. George Robert Gissing. LC 68-54267. 1968. AMS Press.

Paying Guest. George Robert Gissing. LC 6-439775. 1895. Dodd Mead & Company.

Paying Guest. Natalie Shipman. LC 45-95783. 1945. S. Curl, Inc.

Paying Guests. Edward Frederic Benson. LC 29-14379. 1929. Doubleday, Doran & Company, Inc.

Paying Mother: The Tribute Beautiful. Margaret Hill McCarter. LC 20-16798. Harper & Brothers.

Paying the Penalty and Other Stories. Charles Gibbon et al. LC 43-42710. T. Y. Crowell & Co.

Paying the Piper. Margret Holmes Ernsperger Bates. LC 10-31002. 1910. 1.50. Broadway Publishing Co.

Paying the Price! Anna Johnson. LC 14-22558. 1.00. American Tract Society.

Payment Deferred. Cecil Scott Forester. LC 41-28076. 1942. Little, Brown and Company.

Payment for Silence. Anne Rivers. LC 73-93931. 1975. 5.95 (ISBN 0-8027-5300-0). Walker.

Payment in Full. Elizabeth Carfrae, pseud. 1930. Harper & Brothers.

Payment in Full. Anne Hampson. 192p. (Orig.). 1980. pap. 1.50 (ISBN 0-671-57001-3, Pub. by Silhouette Bks). S&S.

Payment in Lead. Owen G. Irons. 1979. pap. 1.75 (ISBN 0-89041-264-2, 3264). Major Bks.

Payment in Sin. Kay Martin. pap. 0.60 o.p. (60-362). Manor Bks.

Payoff. Don Smith. 192p. (Orig.). 1973. pap. 0.95 o.p. (M2775, GM). Fawcett World.

Payoff. Attilio Veraldi. LC 77-11775. 8.95 (ISBN 0-06-014493-9). Harper & Row.

Payoff at Pawnee. Llewellyn Perry Holmes. 224p. 1981. pap. 1.95 (ISBN 0-445-04671-6). Popular Lib.

Payoff at Piute. Tom West. 1977. 1.50 (ISBN 0-441-65529-7). Ace Books.

Payoff for the Banker... A Mr. and Mrs. North Mystery. Frances Louise Davis Lockridge & Richard Lockridge. LC 45-3115. 1945. J. B. Lippincott Company.

Payoff in Black. William Greenough Schofield. 1947. Macrae-Smith-Company.

Payola Game. Thomas H. Hilton. 192p. (Orig.). 1973. pap. 1.95 o.p. (ISBN 0-87056-350-5, 6350). Brandon.

Paysan Parvenu: Or, the Fortunate Peasant. Pierre C. De Chamblain De Marivaux. LC 78-60836. (Novel 1720-1805 Ser.). (O.s.i.: Vol. 2). 1979. lib. bdg. 45.00 o.s.i. (ISBN 0-8240-3651-4); lib. bdg. 31.00 o.s.i. Garland Pub.

Pea-Pickers. 3d Ed. Eve Langley. LC 66-4088. 1966. bds., 3.75. Angus & Robertson.

Peabody's Mermaid... Guy Pearce Jones & Jones, Constance (Bridges) Joint Author. LC 46-25079. 1946. Random House.

Peace. Arne Garborg & Carleton, Phillips Dean, Tr. LC 29-28182. (Half-title: Scandinavian classics, vol. xxxiii). The American-Scandinavian Foundation, W. W. Norton & Company, Inc.

Peace. Gene Wolfe. LC 74-15896. 1975. 8.95 (ISBN 0-06-014699-0). Harper & Row.

Peace After War. Jose Maria Gironella. LC 69-10714. 1969. 10.00. Knopf.

Peace and Quiet: A Novel. Edwin Milton Royle. LC 16-18488. 1916. 1.35. Harper & Brothers.

Peace and the Vices: A Novel. Anna Alexander Rogers. 1904. C. Scribner's Sons.

Peace at Bowling Green. Alfred Leland Crabb. LC 55-7535. 1955. Bobs-Merrill.

Peace Book. Bernard Benson. 1982. pap. 9.95. Bantam.

Peace Breaks Out. John Knowles. LC 80-19678. 9.95 (ISBN 0-03-056908-7). Holt, Rinehart and Winston.

Peace Breaks Out. John Knowles. LC 81-6355. 12.95 (ISBN 0-8161-3270-4). G.K. Hall.

Peace Breaks Out. Angela Mackail Thirkell. LC 47-3528. 1947. A. A. Knopf.

Peace Campaigns of a Cornet... North Ludlow Beamish. 1829. J. & J. Harper.

Peace Corps Nurse. Rachel C. Payes. 1973. pap. 0.75 o.s.i. (01-366). Lancer.

Peace Eye. Ed Sanders. 84p. (Orig.). 1967. pap. 2.00. Frontier Press Calif.

Peace in Friendship Village. Zona Gale. LC 72-13045. (Short story index reprint series). 1973. (ISBN 0-8369-4244-2). Books for Libraries Press.

Peace in Friendship Village. Zona Gale. LC 19-15971. 1919. The Macmillan Company.

Peace in Nobody's Time. George Borodin. LC 44-20860. Hutchinson & Co. Ltd.

Peace in War: A Novel: Selected Works of Miguel de Unamuno, Vol. 1. Tr. by Anthony Kerrigan & Allen Lacy. LC 82-61390. (Bollingen Ser.: No. LXXXV-1). 300p. 1983. 35.00x (ISBN 0-691-09926-X). Princeton U Pr.

Peace Is Where the Tempests Blow: Translated from the Russian. Valentin Petrovich Kataev. Tr. by Malamuth, Charles. LC 37-461021. Farrar & Rinehart, Inc.

Peace, Its's Wonderful. William Saroyan. LC 39-27391. Modern Age Books.

Peace Keeper. Ray Hogan. LC 77-82446. 1978. 6.95 (ISBN 0-385-13525-4). Doubleday.

Peace Keeper. Ray Hogan. (Signet book). 1979. 1.50 (ISBN 0-451-08522-1). New American Library.

Peace Like a River. Vardis Fisher. Orig. Title: Passion Within. pap. 0.60 o.p. (X777). Pyramid Pubns.

Peace Like a River: A Novel of Christian Asceticism. Vardis Fisher. 3.95 o.p. Swallow.

Peace Marshal. Frank Gruber. LC 39-19011. 1939. W. Morrow & Company.

Peace, My Daughters. Shirley Barker. LC 49-1164. 1949. Crown Publishers.

Peace of Roaring River. George Gray Van Schaick. LC 19-26028. Small, Maynard & Company.

Peace of the Solomon Valley. Margaret Hill McCarter. LC 11-24358. 1911. A. C. McClurg & Co.

Peace of 1975: A Sort of Novel. Richard E Sterne. LC 76-171931. 1972. (ISBN 0-8059-1616-4). Dorrance.

Peace on Earth, Good-Will to Dogs. Eleanor Hallowell Abbott. LC 20-20319. E.P. Dutton & Company.

Peace; or, The Stolen Will. An American Novel. Mary Wolcott Janvrin Ellsworth. LC 7-10337. 1857. J. French and Company.

Peace Pelican, Spinster. A Love Story. Fannie N. Smith. LC 8-8986. 1881. G. W. Carleton & Co.; Etc., Etc.

Peace River Country. 1st Ed. Ralph Allen. LC 57-11407. 1958. Doubleday.

Peace River Justice. Lawrence A Keating. LC 32-869502. E. J. Clode, Inc.

Peace Shall Destroy Many. Rudy Henry Wiebe. (Orig.). pap. 2.95 o.p. (ISBN 0-8028-6023-0). Eerdmans.

Peace with Honour. Hilda Caroline Gregg. LC 3-13625. 1902. L. C. Page & Company.

Peaceable Kingdom. Ardyth Kennelly. LC 49-115839. 1949. Houghton Mifflin Co.

Peaceable Kingdom: An American Saga. Jan De Hartog. (Crest bk., C1773). 1973. 1.95. Fawcett.

Peaceable Kingdom: An American Saga. Jan De Hartog. LC 76-168256. 1972. 10.00. Atheneum.

Peaceable Kingdoms: New England Towns in the 18th Century. Michael Zuckerman. 1970. 7.95 o.p. (ISBN 0-394-44013-7). Knopf.

Peaceable Lane. Keith Wheeler. LC 60-12580. 1960. Simon and Schuster.

Peacemaker: By Richard Poole Pseud. Lee E Wells. LC 53-1359. 1954. Ballantine Books.

Peacemaker of Bourbon: A Tale of the New South. Samuel Josiah Bumstead. LC 6-13684. (Dillingham's metropolitan library, no. 14). 1896. G. W. Dillingham.

Peacemakers. Curtis W. Casewit. 1968. Repr. pap. 0.60 o.p. (60-321). Manor Bks.

Peacemakers. John Thomas Edson. (Orig.). 1982. pap. 1.95 (ISBN 0-425-05311-3). Berkley Pub.

Peacemakers. Henrietta Eliza Vaughan Stannard. LC 8-13400. 1898. J. B. Lippincott Company.

Peacemakers: A Tale of Love. Hiram Wallace Hayes. LC 9-28205. Reid Publishing Company.

Peacemakers. 1st Ed. Marquis William Childs. LC 61-11912. 1961. Harcourt, Brace & World.

Peach Blossom. Gustavo Adolfo Martinez Zuviria. Tr. by Ernest Herman Hespelt. Hespelt, Mrs. Miriam Hasbrouck (Van Dyck) Joint Tr. LC 29-6854. 1929. Longmans, Green and Co.

Peach Blossom see Novels by Hugo Wast.

Peach Groves. Barbara Hanrahan. LC 80-502613. 1980. 12.00 (ISBN 0-7011-2490-3). Chatto & Windus.

Peach Stone: Stories from Four Decades. Paul Horgan. LC 67-13410. 1967. Farrar, Straus and Giroux.

Peach's Progress. Helen Marion Edginton. LC 27-6812. 1927. The Penn Publishing Company.

Peacock. Jon Godden. LC 50-13518. 1950. Rinehart.

Peacock and the Crow: From an Old Chinese Fable. Ann Kirn. LC 70-81693. (Illus.). 1969. 3.95. Four Winds Press.

Peacock & the Phoenix. Richard Shannon. LC 75-28769. 1976. pap. 3.95 o.p. (ISBN 0-89087-153-1). Celestial Arts.

Peacock Bed. Anne Rundle. LC 77-99125. 8.95 (ISBN 0-312-59941-2). St. Martin's Press.

Peacock Bed. Anne Rundle. LC 78-27769. 1979. 11.95 (ISBN 0-8161-6659-5). G. K. Hall.

Peacock Eye. Lewis Lusardi. LC 60-6328. 1960. Scribner.

Peacock Fan: A Mystery Novel. Harry Stephen Keeler. LC 41-1235. 1941. E. P. Dutton & Co., Inc.

Peacock Feather. Anne Tedlock Brooks. LC 56-702463. 1956. Arcadia House.

Peacock Feather: A Romance. Leslie Moore. LC 14-166020. 1914. G. P. Putnam's Sons.

Peacock Feather Murders. John Dickson Carr. LC 37-168095. 1937. W. Morrow & Co.

Peacock Feathers. Temple Bailey. LC 24-187682. 1924. The Penn Publishing Company.

Peacock Feathers. Temple Bailey. LC 29-1966. 1926. Grosset & Dunlap.

Peacock Feathers. Temple Bailey. LC 28-17925. 1927. The Penn Publishing Company.

Peacock House and Other Mysteries. Eden Phillpotts. LC 73-128749. (Short story index reprint series). 1970. Books for Libraries Press.

Peacock in the Jungle. Wynne May. (Harlequin Romances Ser.). 192p. 1983. pap. 1.50 (ISBN 0-373-02532-7). Harlequin Bks.

Peacock Is a Gentleman. Vivian Connell. LC 41-15435. 1941. The Dial Pres.

Peacock of Jewels. Fergus Hume. LC 10-17596. G. W. Dillingham Company.

Peacock Place. Lucy Poate Stebbins. LC 39-4165. The Penn Publishing Company.

Peacock Sheds His Tail. Alice Tisdale Nourse Hobart. LC 45-35157. 1945. The Bobbs-Merrill Company.

Peacock Sheds His Tail. Alice Tisdale Nourse Hobart. LC 47-284535. 1946. The Sun Dial Press.

Peacock Spring. Rumer Godden. LC 75-31701. 1976. 8.95 (ISBN 0-670-54558-9). Viking Press.

Peacock: The Satirical Novels. Ed. by Lorna Sage. 1981. pap. 20.00x (ISBN 0-333-18411-4, Pub. by Macmillan England). State Mutual Bk.

Peacocks and Avaries. Joyce Warren. LC 57-11803. (Illus.). 1957. Harper.

Peacocks and Other Stories of Java. Vennette Herron. LC 27-23505. George H. Doran Company.

Peacock's Feather. George Sidney Hellman. LC 31-247722. The Bobbs-Merrill Company.

Peacock's Feather. George Sidney Hellman. LC 32-1196. The Bobbs-Merrill Company.

Peacocks on the Lawn. Winston David Armstrong Clewes. LC 54-5039. 1954. Dutton.

Peacock's Tail. Katharine Waldo Douglas Fedden. LC 25-19827. 1925. Houghton Mifflin Company.

Peacock's Tail. Edward Hoagland. LC 65-16152. bds., 5.50. McGraw.

Peak & Prairie. Anna Fuller. LC 75-94724. (Short Story Index Reprint Ser.). 1894. 20.00 (ISBN 0-8369-3103-3). Ayer Co.

Peak and Prairie: From a Colorado Sketch-Book. Anna Fuller. LC 75-94724. (Short story index reprint series). (Illus.). 1969. Books for Libraries Press.

Peak and Prairie: From a Colorado Sketch-Book. Anna Fuller. 1894. G. P. Putnam's Sons.

Peak in Darien. Freya Stark. LC 76-365267. 3.50 (ISBN 0-7195-3291-4). J. Murray.

Peak in Darien: A Novel. Roswell Gray Ham. LC 60-114327. 1960. Putnam.

Peak of Success & Other Stories. Iuri Nagibin. Tr. by Helena Goscilo from Rus. 360p. 1983. 25.00 (ISBN 0-88233-800-5); pap. 9.50 (ISBN 0-88233-801-3). Ardis Pubs.

Peak Performance. Ivon Baker. LC 75-34774. 7.95 (ISBN 0-7091-5306-6). St. Martin's Press.

Peak's Island: A Romance of Buccaneer Days. Anna W. Ford Piper. LC 7-39644. 1892. The Author.

Peaks Watch on. Helen Bispham Moore. LC 38-39432. Dorrance and Company.

Peal of Bells. Robert Lynd. LC 78-90660. (Essay Index Reprint Ser). 1925. 16.00 (ISBN 0-8369-1226-8). Ayer Co.

Peal of Bells. Robert Lynd. LC 75-131772. 1971. Repr. of 1925 ed. 13.00 (ISBN 0-403-00659-7). Scholarly.

Peanut Butter or a Soup Sandwich. John J. Baker. 3.75 o.p. Carlton.

Peanut Man. Harry J. Albus. 1948. pap. 1.75 o.p. (ISBN 0-8028-4001-9). Eerdmans.

Peanut Papers. Alan Coren. LC 77-9172. 1978. 6.95 o.p. (ISBN 0-312-59960-9); pap. 2.95 o.p. (ISBN 0-312-59961-7). St Martin.

Peanut" The Story of a Boy. Albert Bigelow Paine. LC 13-22101. 1912. 0.50. Harper & Brothers.

Peanuts in Penang. David Richards. LC 74-157136. 1973. 5.75 (ISBN 0-7022-0826-4) (ISBN 0-7022-0826-4). University of Queensland Press.

Pearce Amerson's Will. Richard Malcolm Johnston. LC 8-11027. 1898. Way and Williams.

Pearl. Ed. by Sara De Ford et al. Tr. by Sara De Ford et al. LC 67-13376. (Crofts Classics Ser.). 1967. pap. text ed. 2.95x (ISBN 0-88295-003-7). Harlan Davidson.

Pearl. Tr. by Israel Gollancz. LC 66-27657. (Medieval Library). (Illus.). Repr. of 1926 ed. 15.00x (ISBN 0-8154-0084-5). Cooper Sq.

Pearl, Vol. II. Ed. by Magazine Editors. 240p. 1982. pap. 2.95 (ISBN 0-441-65788-5, Pub. by Charter Bks). Ace Bks.

Pearl. John Steinbeck. LC 47-12205. 1947. Viking Press.

Pearl see Short Novels of John Steinbeck.

Pearl." A Romance from the German. Marie Bernhard. Tr. by Smith, Mary Stuart (Harrison) LC 6-11324. (On cover: The author's library, no. 6). The International News Company.

Pearl and Plain. Aceituna Griffin. LC 27-7504. 1927. Longmans, Green and Co.

Pearl and the Ruby: Or, The Beautiful Rivals. Alexander McVeigh Miller. (On cover: The library of American authors, no. 44). 1892. G. Munro.

Pearl Bastard. Lillian Halegua. LC 79-308093. 1978. 2.50 (ISBN 0-7043-3828-9). Women's Press.

Pearl Bastard: A Novel. Lillian Hale. LC 58-59915. 1959. G. Braziller.

Pearl Buck, a Biographical Novel. Virginia Veeder Westervelt. LC 79-4063. (Illus.). 8.95 (ISBN 0-525-66627-3). Elsevier/Nelson Books.

Pearl Cleanness, Patience, & Sir Gawain & the Green Knight. Ed. by A. C. Cawley & J. J. Anderson. 1970. 12.95x (ISBN 0-460-00346-1, Evman); pap. 2.95x (ISBN 0-460-11346-1, Evman). Biblio Dist.

Pearl Fishers. Henry De Vere Stacpoole. LC 15-18693. 1915. 1.30. John Lane Company.

Pearl for My Lady: A Novel. Stephen Bartlett. LC 29-3976. 1929. Frederick A. Stokes Company.

Pearl Harbor Periscopes. J. Farragut Jones. (Silent Service Ser.: No. 4). (Orig.). 1981. pap. 3.25 (ISBN 0-440-16711-6, Bryans). Dell.

Pearl-Hunger. Gordon Ray Young. LC 27-3368. George H. Doran Company.

Pearl Island. Henry Cottrell Rowland. LC 19-801228. W. J. Watt & Company.

Pearl Lagoon. Charles Bernard Nordhoff. LC 24-26893. The Atlantic Monthly Press.

Pearl. Large Type Ed. Drawings by Jose Clemente Orozco. John Steinbeck. (Keith Jennison bk.). 1966. 6.95. Watts.

Pearl-Maiden. Henry Rider Haggard. Repr. lib. bdg. 22.15x. Amereon Ltd.

Pearl Maiden. Henry Rider Haggard. (Golden Age of Rome Ser.). 1978. pap. 2.50 (ISBN 0-89083-352-4). Zebra.

Pearl-Maiden: A Tale of the Fall of Jerusalem. Henry Rider Haggard. LC 3-3274. 1903. Longmans, Green and Co.

Pearl of Antioch. A Picture of the East at the End of the Fourth Century. Marc Antoine Bayle. LC 6-10356. 1871. Kelly, Piet and Company.

Pearl of Great Price. Everett A. Doyle. 2.00 o.p. Carlton.

Pearl of Great Price. Marzee King Tew. (YA) 1978. 6.95 (Avalon). Bouregy.

Pearl of Norfolk. Curzon De Courson. LC 22-5157. 1874. Fogarty.

Pearl of Orr's Island. Harriet Elizabeth Beecher Stowe. LC 79-18303. (Stowe, Harriett Elizabeth Beecher, 1811-1896. New England Novels). (Illus.). 1979. 6.95 (ISBN 0-917482-18-2). Stowe-Day Foundation.

Pearl of Orr's Island: A Story of the Coast of Maine. Harriet Elizabeth Beecher Stowe. LC 76-108547. (Illus.). 1970. (ISBN 0-403-00280-X). Scholarly Press.

Pearl of Orr's Island: A Story of the Coast of Maine. Harriet Elizabeth Beecher Stowe. LC 67-29280. (Americans in Fiction). 1967. Gregg Press.

Pearl of Orr's Island: A Story of the Coast of Maine. Harriet Elizabeth Beecher Stowe. LC 8-16118. 1862. Ticknor and Fields.

Pearl of Orr's Island: A Story of the Coast of Maine. 30th ed. Harriet Elizabeth Beecher Stowe. LC 8-16117. 1890. Houghton, Mifflin and Company.

Pearl of the Andes: A Tale of Love and Adventure. Gustave Aimard & St. John, Percy Bolingbroke, 1821-1889, Ed. LC 5-42596. (On cover: Lovell's library, v. 11, no 573). 1885. J. W. Lovell Company.

Pearl of the Realm: A Story of Nonsuch Palace in the Reign of Charles I. Anna L Glyn. LC 3-3612. 1896. Dodd, Mead and Company.

Pearl Pagoda. Susannah Broome. 320p. 1982. pap. 2.95 (ISBN 0-449-24469-5, Crest). Fawcett.

Pearl Pagoda: A Novel. Susannah Broome. LC 80-15143. 12.95 (ISBN 0-671-25535-5). Simon and Schuster.

Pearl Preston and Her Springfield Cousins: A Novel. Allie L Lester. LC 29-2466. Gladney's Print Shop.

Pearl S. Buck. Paul A Doyle. (Twayne's U.S. authors ser., T85). pap., 1.95. Coll. & Univ. Pr.

Pearl S. Buck's Book of Christmas. Ed. by Pearl Sydenstricker Buck. LC 74-11933. 1974. 12.50 (ISBN 0-671-21868-9). Simon and Schuster.

Pearl Ship: A Tale of the Seven Seas. Stanton Davis Kirkham. LC 37-8151. 1937. G. P. Putnam's Sons.

Pearl Summers. Alfred Askin Wright. LC 19-16362. Christopher Publishing House.

Pearl Thief, by Berta Ruck. Berta Ruck. LC 26-888187. 1926. Dodd, Mead and Company.

Pearl Trevelyan: Or, Virtue Reaps Its Own Reward. Rhoby S. Williams. LC 8-36908. 1876. The Whig Book and Job Printing House.

Pearl Wedding. Stephen McKenna. LC 52-722. 1951. Hutchinson.

Pearl Wedding. Anne Wormser. LC 50-9324. 1950. Macrae Smith Co.

Pearls Astray: A Romantic Episode of the Last Democracy. Constance Martha Williams Warren. LC 20-189249. Small, Maynard and Company.

Pearls Before Swine. Margery Allingham. LC 45-35093. 1945. Pub. for the Crime Club by Doubleday, Doran & Co., Inc.

Pearls for a King: Six Short Stories Inspired by Bible Characters. Dorothy Hoyer Scharlemann. LC 76-4101. 5.95 (ISBN 0-570-03260-1). Concordia Pub. House.

Pearls for a King: Six Short Stories Inspired by Bible Characters. Dorothy Hoyer Scharlemann. LC 77-2372. 1977. 10.95 (ISBN 0-8161-6473-8). G. K. Hall.

Pearls of Desire. Austin J Small. LC 25-9293. 1925. Houghton Mifflin Company.

Pearly Essence. Jonathan Quayne. 1970. pap. 1.25 o.p. (ISBN 0-447-78654-7). Lancer.

Peasants. Konrad Bercovici. 1928. Doubleday, Doran & Company, Inc.

Peasants... Wladyslaw Stanislaw Reymont & Dziewicki, Michael Henry, Tr. LC 24-28889. 1924-25. A. A. Knopf.

Peasants: And Other Stories Selected and with a Pref. by Edmund Wilson. Anton Pavlovich Chekhov. LC 56-5969. (Doubleday anchor books, A66). 1956. Doubleday.

Peasants: Autumn, Winter, Spring, Summer: A Tale of Our Own Time. Wladyslaw Stanislaw Reymont & Dziewicki, Michael Henry, Tr. LC 39-175699. 1937. A. A. Knopf.

Peasants in Exile (For Daily Bread.) From the Polish of Henryk Sienkiewicz. Henryk Sienkiewicz & Eccles, C. O'Conor, Tr. LC 99-1754. 1898. The Ave Maria.

Pease Porridge Hot. Nalbro Isadorah Bartley. LC 34-2352. The Bobbs-Merrill Company.

Pease Porridge Hot. Ed. by Katherine Hart. (Illus.). 1967. 4.50 (ISBN 0-88426-020-8). Encino Pr.

Peat-Cutters. Alphonse De Chateabriant. Tr. by Robinson, Frances Mabel. LC 27-654519. 1927. L. MacVeagh. The Dial Press.

Peau de Chagrin. Honore De Balzac. Ed. by Allem. (Coll. Prestige). 8.95 o.p. French & Eur.

Pebble in the Sky. Isaac Asimov. LC 81-15516. 1982. 12.50 (ISBN 0-8376-0462-1). R. Bentley.

Pebble in the Sky. 1st Ed. Isaac Asimov. LC 50-5147. 1950. Doubleday.

Pebblebrook, and the Harding Family. Henry Winsor. LC 8-37044. 1839. B. H. Greene.

Pebbles from the Path of a Pilgrim. Harriet B Hastings. LC 7-2634. (On cover: Faith series). 1881. Scriptural Tract Repostitory.

Pecados En Pandilla. Abel Perez. (Pimienta Collection Ser). (Span.). 1977. pap. 1.00 (ISBN 0-88473-261-4). Fiesta Pub.

Peccadilloes. Cora Hardy Jarrett. LC 72-10770. (Short story index reprint series). 1973. (ISBN 0-8369-4220-5). Books for Libraries Press.

Peccadilloes. Cora Hardy Jarrett. LC 29-29103. The John Day Company.

Peccavi. Ernest William Hornung. LC 6796. 1900. C. Scribner's Sons.

Pecked to Death by Goslings. Jane Trahey. 1969. 4.95 o.p. (ISBN 0-13-655563-2). P-H.

Pecking Order. Mark Kennedy. 1953. Appleton-Century-Crofts.

Pecking Order. Mark Kennedy. LC 73-18561. 1974. (ISBN 0-404-11374-5). Appleton-Century-Crofts; AMS Press.

Peckover. John Davys Beresford. LC 35-1820. G. P. Putnam's Sons.

Peck's Bad Boy, No. 2. The Grocery Man and Peck's Bad Boy. Being a Continuation of Peck's Bad Boy and His Pa. George Wilbur Peck. LC 13-12931. 1883. Belford, Clarke & Co.

Peck's Irish Friend, Phelan Geoheagan. George Wilbur Peck. LC 43-29016. 1888. Belford, Clark & Co.

Peck's Irish Friend: Phelan Geoheagan. George Wilbur Jr Peck. LC 8-28114. (On cover: The White city series, v. 1. no. 8). 1894. W. B. Conkey Company.

Peckster Professorship: An Episode in the History of Physical Research. Josiah Phillips Quincy. LC 7-42422. 1888. Houghton, Mifflin and Company.

Pecos Bill: Junior. Cartoon Illus. by Ace Reid. 1st Ed. Ed Bateman. LC 52-68719. 1952. San Angelo Press.

Pecos Swap. Alex Hawk, pseud. (Orig.). 1969. pap. 0.60 o.p. (63-182). Paperback Lib.

Peculiar: A Hero of the Southern Rebellion. new ed. Epes Sargent. LC 8-1818. (On cover: Good company series, no. 16). 1892. Lee and Shepard.

Peculiar: A Tale of the Great Transition. Epes Sargent. LC 72-2121. (Black Heritage Library Collection). 1972. 18.50 (ISBN 0-8369-9061-7). Books for Libraries Press.

Peculiar: A Tale of the Great Transition. 8th ed. Epes Sargent. LC 8-1817. 1864. Carleton.

Peculiar Exploits of Brigadier Ffellowes. Sterlin E. Lanier. LC 74-188477. 224p. 1972. 5.95 o.p. (ISBN 0-8027-5548-8). Walker & Co.

Peculiar Major: An Almost Incredible Story. John Keble Bell. LC 19-155673. 1.50. George H. Doran Company.

Peculiar Passion. Kenneth Harding. pap. 1.95 o.s.i. (Venus). Grove.

Peculiar People. Samuel Phelps Leland. LC 7-13153. 1891. Aust & Clark.

Peculiar People: Or, Reality in Romance. William Stevens Balch. LC 6-6859. 1881. H. A. Sumner & Company.

Peculiar Treasure. Edna Ferber. LC 60-8865. (Illus., O.s.i.). 1938. 5.95 o.s.i. (ISBN 0-385-00563-6). Doubleday.

Peculiar Truth. Duvie Clark. LC 78-55206. 1978. 9.95 (ISBN 0-689-10909-1). Atheneum.

Pedagogues: A Story of the Harvard Summer School. Arthur Stanwood Pier. LC 99-2589. 1899. Small, Maynard & Company.

Pedant and the Shuffly. John Bellairs. LC 68-15262. (Illus.). 1968. Macmillan.

Pedar Victorious. Ole Edvart Rolvaag. Tr. by Nora Olava Solum. LC 42-12313. 1931. A. L. Burt Company.

Peddler. Mitty Fervar. LC 53-8480. 1953. R. C. Sloane Co.

Peddler. D. Randall Matthews. 1973. 5.95 (ISBN 0-533-00658-9). Vantage Press.

Peddler. William Stevens. 1966. 5.95 o.p. (Pub. by Atlantic Monthly Pr). Little.

Peddler: A Novel. Henry Cottrell Rowland. LC 20-159597. Harper & Brothers.

Peddler: A Novel. 1st Ed. William Stevens. LC 66-20808. 1966. 5.95. Little.

Peddler of Dreams. Peggy Gaddis, pseud. LC 40-104403. 1940. Arcadia House, Inc.

Peddlers. Alan Stratton. LC 82-13546. 1982. 13.95 (ISBN 0-531-09875-3). F. Watts.

Peddler's Girl. Elizabeth Howard, pseud. LC 51-9350. 1951. Morrow.

Peder Victorious. Ole Edvart Rolvaag. Tr. by Nora Olava Solum. LC 20-1081. 1929. Harper & Brothers.

Peder Victorious: A Novel. Ole Edvart Rolvaag. LC 73-11845. 1973. 14.25 (ISBN 0-8371-7067-2). Greenwood Press.

Peder Victorious: A Tale of the Pioneers Twenty Years Later. Ole Edvart Relvaag. Tr. by Nora Olava Solum. LC 66-18853. (Perennial classic). 1966. Harper & Row.

Peder Victorious: A Tale of the Pioneers Twenty Years Later. Ole Edvart Rolvaag. LC 81-16402. 1982. 7.50 (ISBN 0-8032-8906-5). University of Nebraska Press.

Pedestal. 1st Ed. George Lanning. LC 66-15739. 1966. 4.50. Harper.

Pediatric Nurse. Janet Lane Walters. 1973. 4.95 (ISBN 0-517-51418-4). Lenox Hill Press.

Pedigree in Pawn. Arthur Henry Veysey. LC 8-29999. 1898. G. W. Dillingham Co.

Pedigree Lovers. R. Rodgers Kingman. 224p. pap. 1.95 o.p. (7132). Barclay Hse.

Pedigree of Honey. Barbara Webb. LC 34-32937. 1934. Doubleday, Doran & Company, Inc.

Pedigrees: A Novel. Ann Shively. LC 80-7888. 11.95 (ISBN 0-690-02002-3). Lippincott & Crowell.

Pedlar's Pack. Elizabeth Goudge. LC 78-132116. (Short story index reprint series). 1970. (ISBN 0-8369-3673-6). Books for Libraries Press.
Pedlar's Pack. Elizabeth Goudge. LC 37-229745. 1937. Coward-McCann.
Pedlar's Pack. Rowland Kenney. LC 24-26385. 1924. T. Seltzer.
Pedlar's Revenge, and Other Stories. Liam O'Flaherty. LC 77-355599. (Illus.). 3.60. (ISBN 0-905473-00-0) (ISBN 0-905473-01-9). Wolfhound Press.
Pedlar's Revenge: Short Stories. Liam O'Flaherty. 1977. 9.50 (ISBN 0-905473-00-0). Irish Bk Ctr.
Pedlock and Sons. Stephen Longstreet. 1976. (pbk.) 1.75 (ISBN 0-380-00500-X). Avon.
Pedlock & Sons: A Novel. Stephen Longstreet. LC 66-12330. 1966. 5.95. Delacorte.
Pedlock & Sons: A Novel. Stephen Longstreet. (6867). 1967. Dell.
Pedlock at Law. Stephen Longstreet. 1976. 1.75 (ISBN 0-380-00622-7). Avon Books.
Pedlock Inheritance. Stephen Longstreet. LC 76-188263. 1972. 7.95. McKay.
Pedlock Saint Pedlock Sinner. stephen longstreet. ed. Stephen Longstreet. 1.75 (ISBN 0-380-00654-5). Avon Books.
Pedlock Saint, Pedlock Sinner. Stephen Longstreet. LC 76-78794. 1969. 6.95. Delacorte Press.
Pedlocks, a Family: A Novel. Stephen Longstreet. LC 51-1907. 1951. Simon and Schuster.
Pedlocks in Love: A Novel. Stephen Longstreet. LC 78-50882. 1.95 (ISBN 0-380-01890-X). Avon Books.
Pedro Paramo: A Novel of Mexico. Juan Rulfo. Tr. by Lysander Kemp from Spanish. 1959. pap. 2.45 (ISBN 0-394-17446-1, B207, BC). Grove.
Peek into Paradise. John T. Peek. 3.95 o.p. Vantage.
Peel Trait. Joseph Crosby Lincoln. LC 34-29544. 1934. D. Appleton-Century Company, Incorporated.
Peep at New York Society. A Startling Exposition of Facts. LC 21-8676. (On cover: Columbian library, no. 5). 1890. Columbian Publishing Company.
Peep at "Number Five:" Or, A Chapter in the Life of a City Pastor. Elizabeth Steward Phelps. LC 33-779109. 1852. Phillips, Sampson, and Company.
Peep at Number Five; or, a Chapter in the Life of a City Pastor. facsimile ed. Elizabeth Steward Phelps. LC 70-164573. (American Fiction Reprint Ser). Repr. of 1852 ed. 21.00 (ISBN 0-8369-7050-0). Ayer Co.
Peep at the Pilgrims in Sixteen Hundred Thirty-Six. A Tale of Olden Times. Harriet Vaughan Foster Cheney. LC 6-27176. 1824. Wells and Lilly.
Peep at the Pilgrims in Sixteen Hundred Thirty-Six: A Tale of Olden Times, 2 Vols. in 1. Harriet Vaughan Foster Cheney. 1824. 18.00 o.s.i. (ISBN 0-512-00092-1). Garrett Pr.
Peep into the Twentieth Century. Christopher Davis. LC 70-95993. 1971. 5.95 o.p. (ISBN 0-06-010993-9, HarpT). Har-Row.
Peep into the 20th Century. Christopher Davis. LC 70-95993. 1971. 5.95 (ISBN 0-06-010993-9). Harper & Row.
Peep-Show. James E. Doran. pap. 2.25 o.s.i. (Venus). Grove.
Peep Show. Alice Dudeney. LC 29-264924. 1929. G. P. Putnam's Sons.
Peeper. William Brinkley. LC 81-65288. 336p. 1981. 13.95 (ISBN 0-670-69751-6). Viking Pr.
Peeping Tom Patrol. LC 76-150123. 1971. 0.95. Playboy Press.
Peeping Tom Patrol. Playboy Editors. LC 76-150123. (Orig.). 1971. pap. 0.95 o.p. (16125). Playboy.
Peeps from a Belfry. Frederick William Shelton. LC 15-21835. 1856. Dana and Company; Etc., Etc.
Peer and the Woman. Edward Phillips Oppenheim. (On cover: Mayflower library, no. 4). 1892. J. A. Taylor and Company.
Peeress and Player. A Novel. Florence Marryat Church Lean. (On cover: The seaside library. Pocket ed. no. 449). 1885. G. Munro.
Peering Doctors. 6.95 o.p. Vantage.
Peering Doctors: By Doctor Y. Doctor Y. 1973. 6.95 (ISBN 0-533-00444-6). Vantage.
Peerless Kathleen: Or, The Actor's Daughter. Charlotte May Kingsley. 1893. N. L. Munro.
Peerless Theodosia. Rebecca Baldwin. 224p. (Orig.). 1980. pap. 1.75 (ISBN 0-449-50036-5, Coventry). Fawcett.
Peer's Daughters. A Novel. Rosina Doyle Wheeler Bulwer-Lytton Lytton. 1850. Stringer & Townsend.
Peewee. William Briggs MacHarg. LC 22-6025. 1922. The Reilly & Lee Co.
Peg Bunson. A Domestic Story. John W Spear. 1897. G. W. Dillingham Co.
Peg Leg: A Tale of Pioneer Adventure in the Grand River Valley. 1st Ed., Limited. Roy William Adams. LC 50-3564. 1950.
Peg Leg Pete. Mel Ellis. LC 72-78130. 1973. 5.95 o.p. (ISBN 0-03-001366-6). HR&W.
Peg O' My Heart: A Comedy of Youth. John Hartley Manners. LC 13-23200. 1913. Dodd, Mead and Company.
Peg O' My Heart: A Comedy of Youth. John Hartley Manners. LC 16-6829. 1914. Dodd, Mead and Company.
Peg O' the Ring, a Maid of Denewood. Emilie Benson Knipe & Knipe, Alden Arthur. LC 15-19077. 1915. 1.25. The Century Co.
Peg, the Rake. Eliza M. J. Humphreys. LC 15-23100. (On cover: Once a week library, v. 12, no. 16, 17). P. F. Collier.
Peg Woffington: A. Novel. Charles Reade. LC 7-39657. 1858. Ticknor and Fields.
Peg Woffington: A Tale. Charles Reade. LC 51-54806. F. M. Lupton Pub. Co.
Peg Woffington: Also, Clouds and Sunshine, and The Knightsbridge Mystery. Charles Reade. (On cover: The Franklin library, no. 6). 1887. Franklin News Company.
Peg Woffington, & Christie Johnstone. Charles Reade. (Half-title: Everyman's library, ed. by Ernest Rhys. Fiction. no. 299). 1907. J. M. Dent & Co.
Peg Woffington, Christie Johnstone: And Other Stories. household ed. Charles Reade. 1869. Fields, Osgood & Co.
Peg Woffington, Christie Johnstone: And Other Stories. household ed. Charles Reade. LC 42-28088. 1872. J. R. Osgood & Company.
Peganda Sucio y Abajo. W. B. Murphy. (Compadre Collection, Rivera y Razoni: No. 4). 1976. pap. 0.95 (ISBN 0-88473-611-3). Fiesta Pub.
Pegasus. Eleanor A. Cox. 224p. 1981. pap. 1.95 (ISBN 0-449-50195-7, Coventry). Fawcett.
Pegeen. Eleanor Hoyt Brainerd. LC 15-18281. 1915. 1.25. The Century Co.
Pegeen and the Potamus: Or The Sly Giraffe, with Some Account of the Wise Old Man Who Dwells, in Tai-Poo. Lee Wilson Dodd. LC 25-15049. E. P. Dutton & Company.
Peggy: A Country Heroine. Gilbert Ashville Pierce. LC 15-21847. (American library. no. 7). 1883. Donnelley, Loyd & Co.
Peggy and Michael of the Coffee Plantation. Anna Andrews. LC 31-14348. (Her Plantation series). Cupples & Leon Company.
Peggy at Spinster Farm. Helen Maria Winslow. LC 8-337833. 1908. L. C. Page & Company.
Peggy by Request: The Love Story of Noel Adn Peggy, from "The Keeper of the Door". Ethel May Dell. LC 28-317463. 1928. G. P. Putnam's Sons.
Peggy Covers the Clipper: A Story of a Young Newspaper Woman. Emma Bugbee. LC 41-24964. (Dodd, Mead career books). 1941. Dodd, Mead & Company.
Peggy-Elise. Frederic Arnold Kummer & Christian, Mary. LC 19-14906. 1919. 1.60. The Century Co.
Peggy-in-the-Rain. Ralph Henry Barbour. LC 13-9793. 1913. 1.25. D. Appleton and Company.
Peggy Kip: A Novel. Nina Miller Elliott. LC 20-214795. Thos. W. Jackson Publishing Co.
Peggy-Mary. Kay Cleaver Strahan. LC 15-16635.
Peggy of Beacon Hill. Maysie Greig. LC 24-19018. Small, Maynard & Company.
Peggy of the Bartons. Bithia Mary Sheppard Croker. LC 98-226. 1898. R. F. Fenno & Company.
Peggy O'Neal. Alfred Henry Lewis. LC 3-13014. 1903. D. Biddle.
Peggy, the Concerned. Katheryn Kimbrough, pseud. (Saga of the Phenwick Women Ser.: No. 31). (Orig.). 1980. pap. 1.95 (ISBN 0-445-04563-9). Popular Lib.
Peggy: The Daughter. Katharine Tynan Hinkson, pseud. 1909. Cassell and Company, Limited.
Peggy Ware. Milford W. Howard. LC 21-14621. 1921. J. F. Rowny Press.
Pegnitz Junction: A Novella & Five Short Stories. Mavis Gallant. 1973. 5.95 o.p. (ISBN 0-394-48384-7). Random.
Pegsticks. Ada Dudman. LC 12-622. 1.00. H. Lechner.
Peking Agent. James David Horan. LC 81-12652. 13.95 (ISBN 0-517-54338-9). Crown Publishers.
Peking & the Tulip Affair. Nick Carter. (Nick Carter Ser.). (O.s.i.). (Orig.). 1969. pap. 0.60 o.s.i. (A424X, Award). Univ Pub & Dist.
Peking Connection. Don Smith. 1975. (pbk.) 1.25. Award Books.
Peking Dimension. Ned Calmer. LC 76-2760. 1976. 7.95 (ISBN 0-385-11196-7). Doubleday.
Peking Dossier. Nick Carter. (Nick Carter Ser.). (O.s.i.). 192p. (Orig.). 1974. pap. 1.25 o.s.i. (AQ1388, Award). Univ Pub & Dist.
Peking Duck: A Moses Wine Detective Novel. Roger Lichtenberg Simon. LC 78-27839. 8.95 (ISBN 0-671-22880-3). Simon and Schuster.
Peking Incident. George Atcheson. LC 72-10992. 1973. 8.95 (ISBN 0-13-655647-7). Prentice-Hall.
Peking Incident. George Atcheson. 1974. (pbk.) 1.50. Bantam.
Peking Madness. Frederick Anthony Edwards. LC 34-11039. 1934. Doubleday, Doran and Company, Inc.
Peking Man Is Missing. Claire Taschdjian. LC 77-3806. (Illus.). 10.00 (ISBN 0-06-014219-7). Harper & Row.
Peking Mandate. Peter J Siris. LC 82-18621. 1983. 14.95 (ISBN 0-399-12752-6). Putnam.
Peking Payoff. Ian Stewart. LC 74-22226. 1975. 6.95. Macmillan.
Peking Picnic. Mary Dolling Sanders O'Malley. LC 32-22984. 1934. Little, Brown, and Company.
Peking Picnic. Mary Dolling Sanders O'Malley. LC 32-22984. 1932. Little, Brown, and Company.
Peking Pornographer. Mallory T. Knight. (T.O.M.C.A.T. Ser.). (O.s.i.). (Orig.). 1970. pap. 0.60 o.s.i. (A539X, Award). Univ Pub & Dist.
Peking Switch. James J Marsh. LC 72-84209. 1972. 5.95. McKay.
Peking Switch. James J Marsh. 1973. (pbk.) 0.95. Popular Lib.
Peking Target. Adam Hall, pseud. LC 81-82460. 290p. 1982. 13.50 (ISBN 0-87223-755-9, Playboy). Putnam Pub Group.
Peking Target. Elleston Trevor. LC 81-82460. 13.50 (ISBN 0-87223-755-9). Playboy Press.
Pel and the Faceless Corpse. Mark Hebden, pseud. LC 82-60095. 1982. 37.50 (ISBN 0-912004-21-5) (ISBN 0-8027-5473-2). Walker.
Pel Is Puzzled. John Harris. LC 82-143544. 1981. 14.95 (ISBN 0-241-10646-X). H. Hamilton.
Pel Is Puzzled. Mark Hebden, pseud. 224p. 1981. 14.95 o.p. (ISBN 0-241-10646-X, Pub. by Hamish Hamilton England). David & Charles.
Pel Under Pressure. Mark Hebden, pseud. 192p. 1980. 19.95 (ISBN 0-241-10443-2, Pub. by Hamish Hamilton England). David & Charles.
Pelagie. Antoine Maillet. LC 81-43147. 1982. 14.95 (ISBN 0-385-17133-1). Doubleday.
Pelham Affair. Louis Tracy. LC 23-2807. E. J. Clode.
Pelham, Eugene Aram. Edward George Earle Lytton Bulwer-Lytton Lytton. LC 31-32290. (The novels and romances of Edward Bulwer Lytton. v. 11). Aldine Book Publishing Co.
Pelham Murder Case. Monte Barrett. LC 30-17507. The White House.
Pelham: Or, Adventures of a Gentleman. library ed.... ed. Edward George Earle Lytton Bulwer-Lytton Lytton. LC 7-8102. (Half-title: Novels of Sir Edward Bulwer Lytton. Library ed. Novels of life and manners, vol. XXVI-XXVII). 1864. J. B. Lippincott & Co.
Pelham: Or, Adventures of a Gentleman. Edward George Earle Lytton Bulwer-Lytton Lytton. LC 8-26652. G. Routledge and Sons.
Pelham: Or, Adventures of a Gentleman. the lord lytton ed. Edward George Earle Lytton Bulwer-Lytton Lytton. LC 7-8103. 1881. J. B. Lippincott & Co.
Pelham: Or, Adventures of a Gentleman. Edward George Earle Lytton Bulwer-Lytton Lytton. LC 7-8101. (On cover: Lovell's library, v. 4, no. 176). 1883. J. W. Lovell Company.
Pelham: or, Adventures of a Gentleman. a new ed. Edward George Earle Lytton Bulwer-Lytton Lytton. LC 43-42708. G. Routledge & Sons.
Pelham or Adventures of a Gentleman. Edward Robert Bulwer-Lytton Lytton. 1974. (pbk.) 1.50. Popular Library.
Pelham: Or, Adventures of a Gentleman. To Which Is Added, Falkland. Edward George Earle Lytton Bulwer-Lytton Lytton. LC 7-8100. (Half-title: Novels of Sir Edward Bulwer Lytton. Library ed. Novels of life and manners, vol. I-II). 1893. Little, Brown, and Company.
Pelham; or, the Adventures of a Gentleman. Edward G. Bulwer-Lytton. Ed. by Jerome J. McGann. LC 77-88085. xxxvi, 477p. 1972. 26.50x (ISBN 0-8032-0703-4). U of Nebr Pr.
Pelham: Or, The Adventures of a Gentleman. Edward George Earle Lytton Bulwer-Lytton Lytton. LC 77-88085. 1972. 15.00 (ISBN 0-8032-0703-4). University of Nebraska Press.
Pelham: Or, The Adventures of a Gentleman. Edward George Earle Lytton Bulwer-Lytton Lytton. LC 21-153609. (Seaside library, v. 65, no. 1316). 1882. G. Munro.
Pelican Coast. Alan Le May. LC 29-86481. 1929. Doubleday, Doran and Company, Inc.
Pelican Papers. James Watson Gerard. LC 27-18204. 1879. F. B. Patterson.
Pelican Rising. Elizabeth North. LC 79-9884. 1979. 8.95. (ISBN 0-915864-94-0) (ISBN 0-915864-93-2). Academy Chicago.
Pelican Walking. facs. ed. Gladys Bronwyn Stern. LC 78-134981. (Short Story Index Reprint Ser). 1934. 15.00 (ISBN 0-8369-3711-2). Ayer Co.
Pelican Walking: Short Stories. Gladys Bronwyn Stern. LC 78-134981. (Short story index reprint series). 1970. Books for Libraries Press.
Pelicans. Edmee Elizabeth Monica De La Pasture. LC 19-5277. 1919. A. A. Knopf.
Pelican's Clock. Robert Middlemiss. 192p. 1981. pap. 2.50 (ISBN 0-449-14426-7, GM). Fawcett.
Pell of Choti. Anita Allen, pseud. (Berkley Medallion Book). 1977. 1.50 (ISBN 0-425-03362-7). Berkley Pub. Corp.
Pelle the Conqueror. Martin Andersen Nexo & Muir, Jesse, Tr. LC 30-26833. 1930. P. Smith.
Pelle the Conqueror. Martin Andersen Nexo & Muir, Jessie, Tr. LC 23-26503. 1917. H. Holt and Company.
Pelle, the Conqueror: Apprenticeship. Martin Anderson Nexo & Miall, Bernard, Tr. LC 15-2002. 1914. H. Holt and Company.
Pelle, the Conqueror: Boyhood. Martin Andersen Nexo & Muir, Jessie, Tr. 1913. H. Holt and Company.
Pelle, the Conqueror: The Great Struggle. Martin Andersen Nexo & Miall, Bernard, Tr. LC 16-8075. 1915. H. Holt and Company.
Pellucidar. Edgar Rice Burroughs. LC 62-17748. 1962. Canaveral Press.
Pellucidar see Pellucidar Novels.
Pellucidar: A Sequel to "At the Earth's Core", Relating the Further Adventures of David Innes in the Land Underneath the Earth's Crust. Edgar Rice Burroughs. LC 23-124011. 1923. A. C. McClurg & Co.
Pellucidar: A Sequel to "At the Earth's Core", Relating the Further Adventures of David Innes in the Land Underneath the Earth's Crust. Edgar Rice Burroughs. LC 31-236. 1923. Grosset & Dunlap.
Pellucidar Novels. Edgar R. Burroughs. Incl. At the Earth's Core. Repr. of 1922 ed; Pellucidar. Repr. of 1923 ed; Tanar of Pellucidar. Repr. of 1929 ed. (Illus.). pap. 4.50 (ISBN 0-486-21051-0). Dover.
Pelon Drops Out. Celso A. De Casas. LC 79-13385. (Illus.). 1979. pap. 6.00 (ISBN 0-89229-006-4). Tonatiuh-Quinto Sol Intl.
Peloton Detective. H. A. Cartledge. (Illus.). 1937. pap. 1.00 o.p. St Martin.
Pemaquid: A Story of Old Times in New England. Elizabeth Payson Prentiss. LC 7-30127. A. D. F. Randolph & Company.
Pemaquid: A Story of Old Times in New England. Elizabeth Payson Prentiss. LC 98-1636. A. D. F. Randolph Company.
Pemberley Shades. Dorothy Alice Bonavia Hunt. LC 77-23210. 1977. Repr. of 1949 ed. lib. bdg. 25.00 (ISBN 0-8414-9947-0). Folcroft.
Pemberley Shades: A Novel. Dorothy Alice Bonavia Hunt. LC 49-10724. 1949. E.P. Dutton.
Pemberton, Ltd. A Novel by Anthony Glyn. Anthony Geoffrey Leo Simon Glyn. LC 57-12642. 1957. Dial Press.
Pemberton, Ltd. A Novel by Anthony Glyn Pseud. Geoffrey Leo Simon Davson. LC 57-126425. 1957. Dial Press.
Pemberton: Or, One Hundred Years Ago. Henry Peterson. 1873. J. B. Lippincott & Co.
Pemberton: Or, One Hundred Years Ago. Henry Peterson. (On cover: Lovell's library. no. 1015). 1887. J. W. Lovell Company.
Pemberton: Or, One Hundred Years Ago. Henry Peterson. 1900. H. C. Coates & Company.
Pembroke. biographical ed. Mary Eleanor Wilkins Freeman. LC 99-5483. 1899. Harper & Brothers.
Pembroke: A Novel. Mary Eleanor Wilkins Freeman. LC 6-40022. Harper & Brothers.
Pembroke Colors. Stephen Longstreet. LC 80-26276. 12.95 (ISBN 0-399-12582-5). Putnam.
Pembroke Mason Affair: By George Barton... Illustrated by Charles E. Meister. George Barton. LC 20-371242. 1920. The Page Company.
Pembrook Vs. the West. Bob Barrett. LC 77-11773. 1978. 6.95 (ISBN 0-385-13526-2). Doubleday.
Pemex Chart. (Nick Carter Ser.). 288p. (Orig.). 1979. pap. 1.95 (ISBN 0-441-65858-X, Pub. by Charter Bks). Ace Bks.
Pemmican. Vardis Fisher. 341p. Repr. of 1956 ed. lib. bdg. 167.45 (ISBN 0-89190-833-1). Am Repr-Rivercity Pr.
Pemmican. Vardis Fisher. 1977. 8.95 (ISBN 0-918522-54-4). O L Holmes.
Pemmican: A Novel of the Hudson's Bay Company. 1st Ed. Vardis Fisher. Doubleday.
Pen and Ink Passion. Alice Herbert. LC 28-17923. 1928. D. Appleton and Company.
Pen Owen: A Novel... James Hook. LC 7-5391. 1822. Collins & Co. Etc.
Pen Pictures. 3d ed. Beverly Carradine. LC 17-13045. The Christian Witness Co.
Pen Warmed-up in Hell: Mark Twain in Protest. Samuel Langhorne Clemens. Ed. by Frederick Anderson. (Harper Colophon books). 1979. 3.95 (ISBN 0-06-090678-2). Harper & Row.
Pen Warmed up in Hell: Mark Twain in Protest. Mark Twain. Ed. by Frederick Anderson. 224p. 1973. pap. 1.95 o.p. (ISBN 0-06-080279-0, P279, PL). Har-Row.

Penal Colony: Stories & Short Pieces Including The Metamorphosis. Franz Kafka. Tr. by Willa Muir & Edwin Muir. LC 48-9743. (YA) (gr. 9 up). 1961. 9.00x (ISBN 0-8052-3198-6); pap. 5.95 (ISBN 0-8052-0418-0). Schocken.

Penal Colony, Stories and Short Pieces. Franz Kafka. Tr. by Willa Muir. LC 48-9743. 1948. Schocken Books.

Penal Colony: Stories and Short Pieces. Tr. from German by Willa and Edwin Muir. Franz Kafka. (Sb 4). pap., 1.95. Schocken Books.

Penalty. Harold Begbie. LC 7-14251. 1907. Dodd, Mead & Company.

Penalty. Gouverneur Morris. LC 13-6732. 1913. C. Scribner's Sons.

Penalty of Recklessness: Or, Virginia Society Twenty Years Ago; a Thrilling Romance; a Tale of Love, Duelling, and Death As Enacted Among the F. F. V. Charles Evarts Williams. LC 8-36919. 1884. Rand, Avery, & Co.

Penance of John Logan: And A Snow Idyl. William Black. LC 6-12921. (Seaside library. Pocket ed., no. 1227). G. Munro.

Penance of John Logan & Two Other Tales. facsimile ed. William Black. LC 73-106248. (Short Story Index Reprint Ser.). 1893. 16.00 (ISBN 0-8369-3284-6). Ayer Co.

Penance of Portia James. Jessie Catherine Huybers Couvreur. (On cover: Lovell's international series, no. 187). 1891. J. W. Lovell Company.

Penang Appointment. Norman Collins. LC 35-3209. 1935. Doubleday, Doran & Company, Inc.

Pencarnon. Jennifer Rigg. LC 76-45573. 1977. 8.95 (ISBN 0-672-52313-2). Bobbs-Merrill.

Pencil of God. Philippe Thobymarcelin & Marcelin, Pierre. LC 50-583340. 1951. Houghton Mifflin.

Pencil Points to Murder: A Christopher Storm Mystery. Willetta Ann Barber & Rudolph Frederick Schabelitz. LC 41-7855. 1941. Pub. for the Crime Club by Doubleday, Doran & Co., Inc.

Pencil Sketches: Or Outlines of Character and Manners. Eliza Leslie. LC 7-14486. 1833-37. Carey, Lea & Blanchard.

Penciled Frown. James Gray. LC 25-17419. 1925. C. Scribner's Sons.

Pendennis. William Makepeace Thackeray. LC 36-37312. (Half-title: Everyman's library, ed. by Ernest Rhys. Fiction. no. 425-426). 1932. J. M. Dent & Sons, Ltd.

Pender Among the Residents. Forrest Reid, pseud. LC 70-131812. 1971. (ISBN 0-403-00699-6). Scholarly Press.

Pender Among the Residents. Forrest Reid, pseud. LC 23-26342. 1923. Houghton Mifflin Company.

Pending Heaven. William Alexander Gerhardie. LC 30-4861. 1930. Harper & Brothers.

Pending Investigation. Robert T McLaughlin. (Berkley Medallion Book). 1977. 1.50 (ISBN 0-425-03363-5). Berkley Pub. Corp.

Pendragon. Jesse Beers, Jr. 1980. 9.95 (ISBN 0-533-04356-5). Vantage.

Pendragon. Catherine Christian. LC 78-2199. (Illus.). 1979. 10.95 (ISBN 0-394-50105-5). Knopf: Distributed by Random House.

Pendragon. Catherine Christian. (Illus.). 1980. 2.95 (ISBN 0-446-83820-9). Warner Books.

Pendragon... the Montenegran Plot: The Third Adventure of John Hawkdale Pendragon. Forrest-Webb, Robert. LC 78-4391. 1978. 8.95 (ISBN 0-312-54662-9). St. Martin's Press.

Pendragon: An Historical Novel. Douglas Carmichael. LC 77-87959. 9.00 (ISBN 0-682-48905-0). Blackwater Press.

Pendragon: Late of Prince Albert's Own. Robert Trevelyan. LC 75-10083. 224p. 1975. 6.95 o.p. (ISBN 0-8415-0387-7). Dutton.

Pendragon, Late of Prince Albert's Own: A Novel of Adventure. Robert Trevelyan. LC 75-10083. 1975. 6.95 (ISBN 0-8415-0387-7). Saturday Review Press.

Pendulum. John Christopher. LC 68-14835. 1968. Simon and Schuster.

Pendulum. Robert Eastman. LC 78-22250. 8.95 (ISBN 0-15-171652-8). Harcourt Brace Jovanovich.

Pendulum. Theda Kenyon. LC 42-9897. 1942. J. Messner, Inc.

Pendulum. Anna M Lucas. LC 28-528396. Buechler Publishing Co.

Pendulum. Richard Lee Marks. LC 57-12231. 1957. Rinehart.

Pendulum. Elinor Mordaunt, pseud. LC 19-863. 1918. Cassell and Company, Ltd.

Pendulum. Annie S Swan Smith. LC 27-7179. George H. Doran Company.

Pendulum. Alfred Elton Van Vogt. 1982. pap. 2.25 (ISBN 0-87997-698-5, UE1698). Daw Bks.

Pendulum. Alfred Elton Van Vogt. (Science Fiction Ser.). (Orig.). 1978. pap. 1.75 o.p. (ISBN 0-87997-423-0, UE1423). DAW Bks.

Pendulum: A Novel. Cora G Sadler. LC 12-9854. 1912. Sherman, French & Company.

Pendulum: A Novel of Today. Valcour Verne. LC 35-461. 1935. The Mayfair Press.

Pendulum: A Story. Edna Willa Troop. LC 10-26171. 1910. Duffield & Company.

Pendulum Swing. Mary Mitchell. LC 36-10124. C. Kendall and W. Sharp Inc.

Pendulum Swings. Elise S. Tuckerman. 5.95 o.p. Vantage.

Pendy. Ann Kurtz. LC 60-10820. 1960. Heritage House.

Penelope. William C Anderson. LC 63-12061. 1963. Crown Publishers.

Penelope. Ann Fairfax. 176p. (Orig.). 1982. pap. 1.95 (ISBN 0-515-05400-3). Jove Pubns.

Penelope. A Miles Jones. LC 53-251250. 1953. St. Martin's Press.

Penelope: An Entertainment by E. V. Cunningham Pseud. Howard Melvin Fast. LC 65-14009. 3.95. Doubleday.

Penelope and Curlew: By Ann Bullingham Pseud. A Miles Jones. LC 58-14517. 1957-1958. Macmillan.

Penelope Devereux. Sheila Bishop. 1978. Repr. of 1969 ed. pap. 1.75 o.p. (ISBN 0-8439-0551-4, Leisure Bks). Nordon Pubns.

Penelope Devereux. Sheila Bishop. (Inflation Fighter Ser.). 192p. 1982. pap. 1.50 (ISBN 0-8439-1094-1, Leisure Bks). Nordon Pubns.

Penelope Devereux. Sheila Bishop. (Inflation Fighters Ser.). 192p. 1982. pap. 1.50 (ISBN 0-8439-1094-1). Leisure Bks CT.

Penelope Finds Out. Winifred Mary Scott. LC 27-158643. The Macaulay Company.

Penelope Intrudes. Katharine Newlin. LC 12-40661. Cassell and Company, Ltd.

Penelope Now. John Crosby. LC 80-6149. 256p. 1981. 12.95 (ISBN 0-8128-2793-7). Stein & Day.

Penelope Now: A Novel. John Crosby. LC 80-6149. 1981. 12.95 (ISBN 0-8128-2793-7). Syein and Day.

Penelope: The Damp Detective. William C Anderson. LC 73-91506. 1974. 5.95 (ISBN 0-517-51481-8). Crown Publishers.

Penelope's English Experiences. Kate Douglas Smith Wiggin. LC 1-29111. 1900. Houghton, Mifflin & Company.

Penelope's Irish Experiences. Kate Douglas Smith Wiggin. LC 1-31565. 1901. Houghton, Mifflin and Company.

Penelope's Irish Experiences. Kate Douglas Smith Wiggin. 1902. Houghton, Mifflin & Company.

Penelope's Irish Experiences. Kate Douglas Smith Wiggin. LC 2-25605. 1902. Houghton, Mifflin & Company.

Penelope's Man: The Homing Instinct. John Erskine. LC 28-28481. The Bobbs-Merrill Company.

Penelope's Postscripts: Switzerland: Venice: Wales: Devon: Home. Kate Douglas Smith Wiggin. LC 15-16008. 1915. Houghton Mifflin Company.

Penelope's Progress. Kate Douglas Smith Wiggin. LC 6956. (On cover: Penelope's experiences. Scotland. v. 2). 1900. Houghton, Mifflin & Company.

Penelope's Progress: Being Such Extracts from the Commonplace Book of Penelope Hamilton As Relate to Her Experiences in Scotland. Kate Douglas Smith Wiggin. 1898. Houghton, Mifflin and Company.

Penelope's Progress: Being Such Extracts from the Commonplace Book of Penelope Hamilton As Relate to Her Experiences in Scotland. Kate Douglas Smith Wiggin. LC 1-13909. 1898. Houghton, Mifflin and Company.

Penelope's Suitors. Edwin Lassetter Bynner. LC 6-16406. 1887. Ticknor and Company.

Penelope's Web. Harriet Theresa Smith Comstock. LC 26-21583. 1928. Doubleday, Doran & Company, Inc.

Penelope's Web: An Episode of Sorrento. Lucy White Jennison. LC 7-102142. J. G. Cupples Co.

Penelope's Zoo. Robert Leigh James. 1974. (pbk.) 1.25. Dell.

Penelope's Zoo. Robert Leigh James. LC 78-147133. 1971. 6.95 (ISBN 0-396-06332-2). Dodd, Mead.

Penelve: Or, Among the Quakers. An American Story. Richard Henry Thomas. LC 6-28225. 1898. Headley Brothers.

Penetrating. Louis J Lewis. LC 26-14493. Goldray Publishing Co., Incorporated.

Penetrating the Magic Bubble. Pat Hurley. 1978. pap. 3.95 (ISBN 0-88207-183-1). Victor Bks.

Penetrator, No. 4: Hijacking Manhattan. Lionel Derrick, pseud. (Orig.). 1974. pap. 1.50 (ISBN 0-523-40423-9). Pinnacle Bks.

Penetrator, No. 46: Terrorist Torment. Lionel Derrick, pseud. 192p. 1982. pap. 1.95 (ISBN 0-523-41553-2). Pinnacle Bks.

Penetrator, No. 47: Orphan Army. Lionel Derrick, pseud. 208p. (Orig.). 1982. pap. 2.25 (ISBN 0-523-41554-0). Pinnacle Bks.

Penetrator: Showbiz Wipeout, No. 32. Lionel Derrick, pseud. 1979. pap. 1.50 (ISBN 0-523-40514-6). Pinnacle Bks.

Penetrators. Anthony Gray. (6873). 1966. Dell.

Penetrators. Pat Hurley. 1978. pap. 3.95 (ISBN 0-88207-184-X). Victor Bks.

Penetrators: A Novel. Benjamin Gwilliam Aston. LC 64-13021. 1965. Putnam.

Penetrators: A Novel. Anthony Gray. LC 64-13021. 1965. Putnam.

Penfold Adventure. Ralph Delahaye Paine. LC 26-17805. 1926. Houghton Mifflin Company.

Peng Wee's Harvest. Louise Jordan Miln. LC 33-8990. 1933. Frederick A. Stokes Company.

Pengard Awake. Ralph Straus. LC 20-17317. 1920. D. Appleton and Company.

Penguin Book of English Short Stories. Christopher Dolley. LC 67-91405. 1967. Penguin.

Penguin Book of French Short Stories. Ed. by Edward Marielle. LC 68-6132. 1968. 1.25. Penguin Books.

Penguin Book of Italian Short Stories. Ed. by Guido Waldman. LC 70-3703. 1969. 1.45. Penguin Books.

Penguin Book of Italian Short Stories, Vol. 2. Ed. by Dimitri Vittorini. 1972. pap. 1.45 o.p. (ISBN 0-14-002888-9, 3253). Penguin.

Penguin Book of Jewish Short Stories. Emanuel Litvinoff. LC 80-458025. 1979. 2.95 (ISBN 0-14-004728-X). Penguin Books.

Penguin Book of Modern European Short Stories. Ed. by Taubman, Robert. LC 74-445145. 1969. Penguin.

Penguin Book of Russian Short Stories. David Richards. LC 81-170464. 1981. 4.50 (ISBN 0-14-004816-2). Penguin Books.

Penguin Book of Scottish Short Stories. Ed. by J. F. Hendry. LC 78-871548. 1970 (ISBN 0-14-003128-6). Penguin.

Penguin Book of Welsh Short Stories. Alun Richards. LC 76-372041. 1976. 3.95 (ISBN 0-14-004061-7). Penguin.

Penguin Island. Anatole France, pseud. LC 68-55525. (Signet classic, CY425). (Illus.). 1968. 1.25. New American Library.

Penguin Island. Anatole France, pseud. Tr. by Evans, Arthur William. LC 26-7351. (Half-title: The works of Anatole France in an English translation, ed. by Frederic Chapman). 1924. John Lane.

Penguin Island. Anatole France, pseud. Tr. by Evans, Arthur William. 1930. Cornwall, N. Y., The Cornwall Press, Inc.

Penguin Island. Anatole France, pseud. LC 33-2521. (Half-title: The modern library of the world's best books). 1933. The Modern Library.

Penguin Island. Anatole France, pseud. Tr. by Evans, Arthur William. LC 38-200024. For the Members of the Heritage Club.

Penguin Island: Tr. from the French. Anatole France & Evans, Arthur William, Tr. LC 47-5661. 1947. Limited Editions Club.

Penguin Leunig. Michael Leunig. (Illus.). 128p. 1983. pap. 4.95 (ISBN 0-14-004019-6). Penguin.

Penguin Persons & Peppermints. Walter Prichard Eaton. LC 22-15770. W. A. Wilde Company.

Penguin Pool Murder. Stuart Palmer. LC 31-20656. 1931. Brentano's.

Penguin Science Fiction Omnibus: An Anthology. Ed. by Brian Wilson Aldiss. LC 74-176436. 1973. 0.60 (ISBN 0-14-003145-6). Penguin.

Penhallow. Georgette Heyer. LC 76-133595. 1971. 4.95 (ISBN 0-525-17725-6). Dutton.

Penhallow... Georgette Heyer. LC 43-12653. 1943. Doubleday, Doran and Company, Inc.

Penhally. Caroline Gordon. LC 75-164526. 1971. (ISBN 0-8154-0395-X). Cooper Square Publishers.

Penhally. Caroline Gordon. LC 31-25046. 1931. C. Scribner's Sons.

Peninsula Place: Being the Adventures of Ian and Felicity. Denis George Mackail. LC 32-31730. 1932. Doubleday, Doran & Company, Inc.

Peninsulars: A Novel. Linda T. Casper. bds., 4.50. Bookmark.

Penitent. Rene Bazin. Tr. by Mother Mary Reginald. LC 12-40013. 1912. J. B. Lippincott Company.

Penitent. Edna Worthley Underwood. LC 22-19550. 1922. Houghton Mifflin Company.

Penitentes of San Rafael: A Tale of the San Luis Valley. Louis How. LC 5432. 1900. The Bowen-Merrill Company.

Penitentiary Post. Kathrene Sutherland Gedney Pinkerton & Pinkerton, Robert Eugene, 1882- Joint Author. LC 20-10313. 1920. Doubleday, Page & Company.

Penknife in My Heart. Nicholas Blake. (Perennial Library). 1980. 2.25 (ISBN 0-06-080521-8). Harper & Row.

Penknife in My Heart. By Nicholas Blake Pseud. Cecil Day-Lewis. (Crest Book s388). 1960. Fawcett Publications.

Penmarric. Susan Howatch. LC 78-139630. (Illus.). 1971. 8.95 (ISBN 0-671-20823-3). Simon and Schuster.

Penn'a-German Stories. Harvey Monroe Miller. LC 7-15389. The Hawthorne Press.

Pennagan Place. Eleanor Chase. LC 28-1202. J. H. Sears & Co., in.

Pennant Family. Anne Beale. (Franklin square library, no. 124). 1880. Harper & Brothers.

Pennant for the Kremlin. Paul Molloy. LC 64-13864. 1964. Doubleday.

Pennhaven. Helen York. LC 78-52873. 1978. pap. text ed. 1.95 o.s.i. (ISBN 0-89559-052-2). Dale Books Inc.

Pennies from Heaven. Dennis Potter. LC 81-19187. (Illus.). 1981. 5.95 (ISBN 0-7043-3394-5). Quartet Books.

Pennies from Hell. 1st Ed. David Alexander. LC 60-12219. (Main line mysteries). 1960. Lippincott.

Penniless Blues. Melvin Leighton Heimer. LC 55-566582. 1955. Putnam.

Penniless Girl. A Novel. Bertha Behrens. Tr. by Annie Lee Furness Wister. LC 6-9129. 1885. J. B. Lippincott & Co.

Penniless Orphan. Ein Armes Madchen. Bertha Behrens & Benedict, Edwyna, Tr. LC 6-9431. (On cover: Seaside library. Pocket ed. 994). 1887. G. Munro.

Penniless Peer. Barbara Cartland. LC 74-5058. 1974. Bantam Books.

Penningtons. Basil Partridge. LC 52-7257. 1952. Westminster Press.

Pennsylvania Gothic see Blacking Factory.

Pennsylvania Mountain Stories. Henry Wharton Shoemaker. LC 8-11829. Bradford Record Publishing Company.

Pennsylvania Stories. Arthur Hobson Quinn. LC 522. 1899. The Penn Publishing Company.

Penny Box. Dwyer-Joyce, Alice. LC 80-51826. 1981. 8.95 (ISBN 0-312-60002-X). St. Martin's Press.

Penny Dreadful. Malcolm Harrison Ross. LC 29-101785. 1929. Coward-McCann, Inc.

Penny for Charity: Short Stories. Seymour Epstein. LC 65-18135. bds., 4.95. Little.

Penny for the Guy. Jan Roffman. LC 65-225835. 3.50. Pub. for the Crime Club by Doubleday.

Penny for Your Thoughts. J. H Hurley. (Berkley Medallion) (ISBN 0-425-03201-9). Berkley.

Penny Lancaster, Farmer. Elizabeth Whitfield Croom Bellamy. LC 6-11691. (Lovell's international series of modern novels, no. 5). F. F. Lovell & Company.

Penny Lane. Fielding Dawson. 160p. (Orig.). 1977. pap. 4.50 (ISBN 0-87685-314-9). Black Sparrow.

Penny Lane: A Novel. Fielding Dawson. LC 77-11690. 1977. 15.00. (ISBN 0-87685-315-7) (ISBN 0-87685-314-9). Black Sparrow Press.

Penny Links. Ursula Holden. LC 80-27485. 8.95 (ISBN 0-416-00891-7). Methuen.

Penny Links: A Novel. Ursula Golden. 156p. 1981. pap. 8.95 (ISBN 0-416-00891-7, NO. 0213). Methuen Inc.

Penny Marsh Finds Adventure in Public Health Nursing. Dorothy Deming. LC 40-32555. 1940. Dodd, Mead & Company.

Penny Marsh: Public Health Nurse. Dorothy Deming. LC 38-206503. (Career books). 1938. Dodd, Mead & Company.

Penny Marsh: Supervisor of Public Health Nurses. Dorothy Deming. LC 39-21175. (Career books). 1939. Dodd, Mead & Company.

Penny Murders. Lionel Black. 1979. pap. 1.95 (ISBN 0-380-48090-5, 48090). Avon.

Penny Philanthropist: A Story That Could Be True. Clara Elizabeth Laughlin. LC 12-40660. Fleming H. Revell Company.

Penny Plain. Anna Buchan. LC 21-260897. George H. Doran Company.

Penny Saved Is Impossible. Ogden Nash. 1981. 10.95 (ISBN 0-316-59832-1). Little.

Penny Wars. Elliott Baker. LC 68-21516. 1968. Putnam.

Penny Wise. Elizabeth Carfrae, pseud. LC 46-236. 1946. G. P. Putnam's Sons.

Penny Wise. Sarah Carlisle. 224p. 1981. pap. 1.95 (ISBN 0-449-50176-0, Coventry). Fawcett.

Pennycomequicks. A Novel. Sabine Baring-Gould. LC 6-7227. (On cover: Lovell's international series, no. 278). 1889. F. F. Lovell & Company.

Pennycross Murders. 1st American Ed. Maurice Procter. LC 53-5380. 1953. Harper.

Pennyroyal and Mint. Sophia Miriam Swett. LC 22-17341. Estes and Lauriat.

Penobscot Man. Fannie Hardy Eckstorm. LC 74-128733. (Short story index reprint series). 1970. Books for Libraries Press.

Penobscot Man. Fannie Hardy Eckstorm. LC 4-13286. 1904. Houghton, Mifflin and Company.

Penobscot Man. With an Introd. by Edward D. Ives. Fannie Hardy Eckstorm. LC 72-80065. (Illus.). 1972. 7.95 (ISBN 0-912274-16-6). New Hampshire Pub. Co.

Penquin Book of German Stories. Ed. by F. J Lamport. 1975. (pbk.) 2.50. Penquin.

Penrod. Booth Tarkington. LC 14-5820. 1914. Doubleday, Page & Company.

Penrod. Booth Tarkington. 1916. Grosset & Dunlap.

Penrod. Booth Tarkington. LC 22-16015. 1920. Doubleday, Page & Company.

Penrod. Booth Tarkington. LC 24-20477. 1922. Doubleday, Page & Company.

Penrod. one-by-one ed. Booth Tarkington. LC 35-177763. 1935. Doubleday, Doran & Company, Inc.

Penrod. Booth Tarkington & Dickinson, Asa Don, 1876- LC 19-370. 1918. Doubleday, Page & Company.

Penrod. A School Ed., by Lou P. Bunce. Booth Tarkington. LC 54-2676. 1954. Globe Book Co.

Penrod and Sam. Booth Tarkington. LC 16-22263. 1916. Doubleday, Page & Company.

Penrod and Sam. Booth Tarkington. LC 20-15606. 1918. Grosset & Dunlap.

Penrod and Sam. Booth Tarkington. LC 22-16008. 1920. Doubleday, Page & Company.

Penrod: His Complete Story... Booth Tarkington & Grant, Gordon, 1875- Illus. LC 31-28239. 1931. Doubleday, Doran & Company, Inc.

Penrod Jashber. Booth Tarkington. LC 29-18939. 1929. Doubleday, Doran & Company, Inc.

Penrose Mystery. Richard Austin Freeman. LC 36-185731. 1936. Dodd, Mead & Company.

Penruddock of the White Lambs: A Tale of Holland, England and America. Samuel Harden Church. LC 2-25603. 1902. F. A. Stokes Company.

Penser la Bouche Pleine. Judith Schlanger. (Archontes: No. 7). 214p. (Fr.). 1976. pap. text ed. 33.75x (ISBN 90-2797-972-3). Mouton.

Pension Beaurepas see Lady Barbarina.

Pension for Death: A Matthew Coll Mystery. Roy Harley Lewis. LC 83-2888. 1983. 12.95 (ISBN 0-312-60004-6). St. Martin's Press.

Pensionnaires, the Story of an American Girl Who Took a Voice to Europe and Found--Many Things. Albert Richardson Carman. LC 3-24811. 1903. H. B. Turner & Co.

Pent up on a Penthouse. Elliott White Springs. LC 32-323914. E. Springs and Company.

Pentagon. Henry Hunt Searls. LC 75-134218. 1971. 7.95. Bernard Geis Associates.

Pentagon Country: A Novel. Clay Blair. LC 79-167490. 1971. (ISBN 0-07-005602-1). McGraw-Hill.

Pentagon Tapes. Colin Turner. (O.S.I.). Orig. Title: To Rouse a Lion. (Orig.). 1973. pap. 1.25 o.s.i. (ISBN 0-515-03181-X). Pyramid Pubns.

Pentallion. Vanessa Blake. (Ravenswood gothic). 1974. (pbk.) 0.95 (ISBN 0-671-77723-8). Pocket Books.

Pentamerone. Giovanni Basile. 1943. 6.95 (ISBN 0-87140-982-8). Liveright.

Penthouse. Arthur Somers Roche. LC 35-16316. 1935. Dodd, Mead & Company.

Penthouse Love. Alma Sioux Scarberry. LC 34-19028. Grosset & Dunlap.

Penthouse Murders... Raymond Peckham Holden. LC 31-233503. Pub. for the Crime Club, Inc., by Doubleday, Doran & Company, Inc.

Penthouse Mystery. Ellery Queen, pseud. 1968. pap. 0.50 o.p. (R1810). Pyramid Pubns.

Pentowan: Or, The Adventures of Gregory Goulden Esq., and Tobias Penhale. A Cornish Story. William Bentinck Forfar. LC 20-23153. 1859. R. Cunnack; Etc., Etc.

Penumbra, Dawn or Dusk. William Gerard Smith. LC 80-65677. 15.00 (ISBN 0-89754-015-8) (ISBN 0-89754-014-X). Dan River Press.

Penwhistle's Prize. Jack Zovada. 1.75 (ISBN 0-441-65868-7). Ace Books.

Peony. Pearl Sydenstricker Buck. LC 48-19767. 1948. J. Day Co.

Peony. Kenneth Westmacott Lane. LC 46-2895. 1946. The Macmillan Company.

People. Pierre Hamp. LC 74-121558. (Short story index reprint series). 1970. Books for Libraries Press.

People. Pierre Hamp & Whitall, James, 1888- Tr. LC 21-5478. (Half-title: The European library, ed. by J. E. Spingarn). 1921. Harcourt, Brace and Company.

People Against Nancy Preston. John Antonio Moroso. LC 21-16798. 1921. H. Holt and Company.

People Against O'Hara. Eleazar Lipsky. LC 50-10244. 1950. Published for the Crime Club by Doubleday.

People & Animals. Garth Brandtson. 192p. pap. 1.95 o.p. (7152). Barclay Hse.

People & Other Aggravations. Judith Viorst. LC 70-145835. 1971. 5.95 o.p. (ISBN 0-690-00363-3). T Y Crowell.

People Are Fascinating. Sally Benson. LC 36-13043. Covici, Friede.

People Around You Can Make You Fat. Lee Headley. 1979. pap. 2.50 (ISBN 0-445-04341-5). Popular Lib.

People Ask Death. George Dyer. LC 40-6699. 1940. C. Scribner's Sons.

People at Pisgah. Edwin Webster Sanborn. LC 14-22463. 1892. D. Appleton and Company.

People Beyond the Wall. Stephen Tall. (Science Fiction Ser.). 1980. pap. 1.95 (ISBN 0-87997-537-7, UJ1537). DAW Bks.

People Downstairs, and Other City Stories. Rhoda Warner Bacmeister. LC 64-17991. 1964. Coward-McCann.

People Eaters. Hollis Alpert. (O.s.i.). 384p. 1971. 6.95 o.s.i. (ISBN 0-8037-7104-5). Dial.

People Enters. Hollis Alpert. LC 76-163599. 1971. 6.95. Dial Press.

People from Dickens: A Presentation of Leading Characters. Charles Dickens & Field, Rachel Lyman. LC 35-20676. 1935. C. Scribner's Sons.

People from Heaven. John B. Sanford. LC 43-15956. 1943. Harcourt, Brace and Company.

People from the Sea. Velda Johnston. LC 79-12813. 8.95 (ISBN 0-396-07695-5). Dodd, Mead.

People from the Sea. large print ed. Velda Johnston. LC 81-135. 1981. 11.95 (ISBN 0-8161-3187-2). G.K. Hall.

People I Have Met. Beverly Carradine. LC 10-16977. 1.00. The Christian Witness Co.

People I Have Met: Or, Pictures of Society and People of Mark, Drawn Under a Thin Veil of Fiction. Nathaniel Parker Willis. LC 8-36896. 1850. Baker and Scribner.

People Immortal: A Novel. Vasilii Semenovich Grossman. LC 44-21027. 1943. Hutchinson & Co. Ltd.

People in Cages. Helen Ashton. LC 37-4880. 1937. The Macmillan Company.

People in Glass House. June Drummond. LC 70-125773. (Inner sanctum mystery). 1970. 4.95 (ISBN 0-671-20605-2). Simon and Schuster.

People in Glass Houses. Charity Blackstock. LC 74-30597. 256p. 1975. 7.95 o.p. (ISBN 0-698-10652-0, Coward). Putnam Pub Group.

People in Glass Houses. Shirley Hazzard. LC 78-436043. 1967. 2.10. Macmillan of Australia.

People in Glass Houses. Ursula Torday. LC 74-30597. 1975. 7.95 (ISBN 0-698-10652-0). Coward, McCann & Geoghegan.

People in Glass Houses: Portraits from Organization Life. Shirley Hazzard. LC 67-11127. 1967. Knopf.

People in His Life: A Novel. Maia Rodman. LC 79-9661. 1980. 11.95 (ISBN 0-8128-2717-1). Stein and Day.

People in the Summer Night: An Epic Suite. Ihmiset Suviyossa, Tr. from Finnish by Alan Blair. Introd. by Thomas Warburton. Frans Eemil Sillanpaa. LC 66-13807. (Nordic tr. ser.). 1966. 4.00. Univ. of Wis. Pr.

People Like That: A Novel. Kate Lee Langley Bosher. LC 16-10117. 1916. Harper & Brothers.

People Minus X: A Science-Fiction Novel. Raymond Z Gallun. LC 56-992586. 1957. Simon and Schuster.

People: No Different Flesh. Zenna Henderson. 1968. pap. 2.50 (ISBN 0-380-01506-4, 58388). Avon.

People: No Different Flesh. 1st Ed. in the U.S.A. Zenna Henderson. LC 67-11184. 1967. 4.50. Doubleday.

People of a House. William Babington Maxwell. LC 34-10334. 1934. Dodd, Mead & Company.

People of Darkness. Tony Hillerman. LC 80-7605. 9.95 (ISBN 0-06-011907-1). Harper & Row.

People of Hemso. August Strindberg. LC 73-17625. 1974. 10.50 (ISBN 0-8371-7252-7). Greenwood Press.

People of Juvik. Olav Duun. Tr. by Chater, Arthur G. LC 30-654486. A. A. Knopf.

People of My Own: A Novel. Edith Pargeter. LC 42-2245. Reynal & Hitchcock.

People of Our Neighborhood. Mary Eleanor Wilkins Freeman. LC 76-110192. (Short story index reprint series). (Illus.). 1970. Books for Libraries Press.

People of Our Neighborhood. Mary Eleanor Wilkins Freeman. LC 98-426. (Ladies' home journal library of fiction. v. 3). Curtis Publishing Company.

People of Our Neighborhood by Mary E. Wilkins. Mary Eleanor Wilkins Freeman. LC 76-110192. (Short Story Index Reprint Ser.). 1898. 12.50 (ISBN 0-8369-3343-5). Ayer Co.

People of Popham. Mary C. E Wemyss. LC 11-35362. 1911. Houghton Mifflin Company.

People of Position. Stanley Portal Hyatt. LC 10-21158. 1910. 1.20. Wessels & Bissell Co.

People of Providence Street. John Gooding. LC 67-20293. 1967. Viking Press.

People of Seldwyla, and Seven Legends. Gottfried Keller. LC 70-140331. (Short story index reprint series). (Illus.). 1970. Books for Libraries Press.

People of Seldwyla and Seven Legends. Gottfried Keller. Tr. by Hottinger, Marie Donald (Mackie) LC 29-21558. 1929. J. M. Dent & Sons.

People of the Black Circle. Robert E. Howard. LC 78-20392. 1978. 9.95 o.p. (ISBN 0-399-12147-1, Pub. by Berkley). Putnam Pub Group.

People of the Book. David Stacton. LC 65-105646. 5.95. Putnam.

People of the City. Cyprian Ekwensi. 1969. pap. 0.75 o.p. (T455, Prem). Fawcett World.

People of the Comet. Austin Hall. LC 48-9814. 1948. Griffin Pub. House.

People of the Mist. Henry Rider Haggard. LC 6-46149. (On cover: Once a week semi-monthly library. v. 12, no. 8-9). 1894. P. F. Collier.

People of the Mist. Henry Rider Haggard. LC 6-46148. 1894. Longmans, Green, and Co.

People of the Mist. Sir Henry Rider Haggard. 1973. (pbk.) 1.25 (ISBN 0-345-23660-2). Ballantine Books.

People of the Plains. Pal Szabo & Halasz, George, Tr. LC 32-9676. 1932. Little, Brown, and Company.

People of the Planet Clarion. Truman Bethurum. 1975. 6.95 o.p. Saucerian.

People of the Puszta. 2nd ed. Illyes Gyula. LC 68-2212. 308p. 1979. 12.50x (ISBN 963-13-0594-5). Intl Pubns Serv.

People of the Ruins: A Story of the English Revolution and After. Edward Shanks. LC 20-17169. Frederick A. Stokes Company.

People of the Sea. David Thomson. 222p. 1981. pap. 4.95 (ISBN 0-586-08341-3). Academy Chi Ltd.

People of the Sea: A Journey in Search on the Seal Legend. Foreword by Gavin Maxwell. New Rev. Ed. David Thomson. LC 67-14314. 1967. 4.95. World.

People of the Small Arrow. Jack Herbert Driberg. LC 72-3367. (Short story index reprint series). (Illus.). 1972. (ISBN 0-8369-4146-2). Books for Libraries Press.

People of the Valley. Frank Waters. LC 41-39. Farrar & Rinehart, Inc.

People of the Whirlpool: From the Experience Book of a Commuter's Wife; with Eight Full-Page Illustrations. Mabel Wright. LC 3-12000. 1903. The Macmillan Company.

People of the Wind. Poul Anderson. LC 77-4511. (Gregg Press science fiction series). 1977. 9.50 (ISBN 0-8398-2353-3). Gregg Press.

People of the Wind. Poul Anderson. (Signet Book). 1973. (pbk) 0.95. New American Library.

People of the Wind: The Day of Their Return. Poul Anderson. 1982. pap. 2.75 (ISBN 0-451-11849-9, AE1849, Sig). NAL.

People of This Town. Ethel Powelson Hueston. LC 29-20020. The Bobbs-Merrill Company.

People on Other Planets. 2d ed. Richard A Fox. LC 31-173416. 1930. Wetzel Publishing Co., Inc.

People on Our Block. Audrey Lilly Meadows. LC 74-22944. 1975. 5.50. Printing Arts Press.

People on the Earth. Edwin Corle. LC 37-502892. Random House.

People on the Hill. Velda Johnston. LC 71-134320. (Red badge novel of suspense). 1971. 4.95. Dodd, Mead.

People One Knows, a Novel. Boles, Robert. LC 64-17362. 1964. Houghton Mifflin.

People Opposite. Sylvia Thompson. LC 48-10682. 1948. Little, Brown.

People Pieces: A Collection of Mennonite and Amish Stories. Ed. by Merle Good. LC 74-1520. (Illus.). 1974. (ISBN 0-8361-1735-2). Herald Press.

People Round the Corner. Thyra Samter Winslow. LC 27-11715. 1927. A. A. Knopf.

People Speak. Anna L. Arnott. 64p. (Orig.). 1982. pap. 4.50 (ISBN 0-682-49857-2). Exposition.

People Speak, & Other Stories. English Language Services. (Collier-Macmillan English Readers). pap. 1.40 (ISBN 0-02-971350-1). Macmillan.

People That Time Forgot. Edgar Rice Burroughs. 160p. 1982. pap. 2.25 (ISBN 0-441-65945-4, Pub. by Ace Science Fiction). Ace Bks.

People: The Search - the Citadel - the Hill. W. J. Resla. 176p. 1973. 6.00 o.p. (ISBN 0-682-47702-8). Exposition.

People Versus Kirk. Robert Traver. LC 81-8885. 1981. 12.95 (ISBN 0-312-60006-2). St Martin's Press.

People Vs. Baby. Gertrude Samuels. LC 67-10404. 1967. Doubleday.

People Vs. Withers & Malone: Six Inner Sanctum Mystery Novelettes. Stuart Palmer & Craig Rice. LC 63-19285. (An Inner sanctum mystery). 1963. Simon and Schuster.

People We Pass: Stories of Life Among the Masses of New York City. Julian Ralph. 1896. Harper & Brothers.

People Who Have Sex with Animals. S. C. Carew, pseud. 224p. pap. 1.95 o.p. (7138). Barclay Hse.

People Who Pull You Down. Thomas P. Baird. LC 72-95861. 1970. Harcourt, Brace & World.

People Who Pull You Down. Thomas P. Baird. 1979. 1.75 (ISBN 0-380-39339-5). Avon.

People Will Always Be Kind. Wilfrid Sheed. LC 72-97000. 1973. 7.95 (ISBN 0-374-23071-4). Farrar, Straus and Giroux.

People Will Always Be Kind. Wilfrid Sheed. 1974. (pbk.) 1.50. Dell.

People Will Talk. Edith Caroline Rivett. LC 58-5953. 1958. Published for the Crime Club by Doubleday.

People Will Talk. Margaret Lee Runbeck. LC 29-166648. The Reilly & Lee Co.

People with the Dogs. Stead, Christina. LC 52-5004. 1952. Little, Brown.

People You Know. George Ade. LC 3-10200. 1903. R.H. Russell.

Peoples. Robert C. S Downs. LC 73-10704. 1974. 6.95 (ISBN 0-672-51900-3). Bobbs-Merrill.

Peoples. Jerry D. Rose. 1976. pap. 15.00 (ISBN 0-395-30716-3). HM.

People's Man. Edward Phillips Oppenheim. LC 14-915. 1914. Little, Brown, and Company.

People's Martyr: A Legend of Canterbury. Elizabeth M Stewart. LC 33-283510. 1873. D. & J. Sadlier & Co.

People's Program: The Twentieth Century Is Theirs. Henry Lexington Everett. LC 6-38135. Workmen's Publishing Co.

Peoples Reader. Ed. by Marjorie Barrows. LC 49-600427. 1949. Consolidated Book Publishers.

Pepita Jimenez. Valera y Alcala Galiano, Juan. Ed. by Robert E. Lott. LC 74-983. (Pergamon Oxford Spanish series). 1974. (ISBN 0-08-017918-5) (ISBN 0-08-017919-3). Pergamon Press.

Pepita Jimenez. Valera y Alcala Galiano, Juan & Bjornson, Bjornstjerne, 1832-1910. A Happy Boy. LC 17-17424. (Harvard classics shelf of fiction, selected by C. W. Eliot. 20). P. F. Collier & Son.

Pepita Jimenez. Introd., Tr. from Spanish by Harriet De Onis. Valera y Alcala Galiano, Juan. Tr. by Harriet De Onis. LC 64-24870. 1965. pap., 1.25. Barron's.

Pepita Jiminez: By Juan Valera. Valera y Alcala Galiano, Juan. 1966. pap., 1.25. Las Americas.

Pepita Ximenez. Valera y Alcala Galiano, Juan. LC 8-30866. 1886. D. Appleton and Company.

Pepper. Harold Everett Porter. LC 15-555915. 1915. 1.30. The Century Co.

Pepper. Harold Everett Porter. LC 24-20490. 1916. The Century Co.

Pepper Garden: A Novel. John Slimming. LC 68-11376. 1968. Lippincott.

Pepper Potts. Florence B. Diffenderfer. 1969. 4.95 o.p. (ISBN 0-8158-0226-9). Chris Mass.

Pepper Potts: A Novel. Florence B Diffenderfer. LC 73-91806. 1969. 4.95. Christopher Pub. House.

Pepper Tree. John Edward Jennings. 1973. 1.25. Popular Library.

Pepper Tree: A Story of New England and the Spice Islands. John Edward Jennings. LC 50-11659. 1950. Little, Brown.

PepperTide. Jack Weyland. LC 82-25171. 7.95 (ISBN 0-87747-967-4). Deseret Book Co.

Peppertree III. Shyree Latham & Shannon Moore Kincaid Frazier. LC 81-4856. (Illus.). 1981. 15.95 (ISBN 0-86663-601-3) (ISBN 0-86663-600-5). Ide House.

Peppertree Inn. Louise Platt Hauck. LC 41-19313. 1941. Macrae-Smith-Company.

Peppertree Inn. Jean Randall. LC 41-198135. 1941. Macrae-Smith Company.

Pequena En la China - the Little Woman. Gladys Aylward & Christine Hunter. pap. 2.95 (ISBN 0-8024-6466-1). Moody.

Pequeno Vencinito. span. ed. Jim Kelly. (Small Star Stories). (Illus.). 1975. 5.95 o.p. (ISBN 0-02-645500-5, 64550). Glencoe.

Pequinillo: A Tale. George Payne Rainsford James. LC 7-7984. 1852. Harper & Brothers.

Per Hallstrom: Selected Short Stories. Per August Leonard Hallstrom. LC 77-144155. (Short story index reprint series). 1971. (ISBN 0-8369-3770-8). Books for Libraries Press.

Peradventure:; or, The Silence of God. Robert Keable. LC 23-2808. 1923. 2.00. G. P. Putnam's Sons.

Percentage Girl. Wright Williams. LC 40-30895. Phoenix Press.

Percentage Girl. Watkins Eppes Wright. LC 40-30895. 1940. Phoenix Press.

Perception and Pleasure: Stories for Analysis. Ed. by Fred Harold Marcus. LC 68-13131. 1968. Heath.

Perception & Pleasure: Stories for Comparison. Ed. by Fred Harold Marcus. 1967. pap. text ed. 7.95x o.p. (ISBN 0-669-45831-7); teaching suggestions free o.p. (ISBN 0-669-46888-6). Heath.

Perceptions of Beauty & Life. B. Nickerson Vanderbilt. 237p. 1976. 7.50 o.p. (ISBN 0-682-48415-6). Exposition.

Perch of the Devil. Gertrude Franklin Horn Atherton. LC 14-148063. 1914. Frederick A. Stokes Company.

Perchance of Death. Elizabeth Linington. LC 76-52221. 1977. 6.95 (ISBN 0-385-13081-3). Published for the Crime Club by Doubleday.

Perchance to Dream. Ed. by Damon Francis Knight. LC 72-76181. (Doubleday science fiction). 1972. 5.95. Doubleday.

Perchance to Dream. Joyce Lee. (Candlelight Regency Ser.: No. 715). (Orig.). 1982. pap. 2.25 (ISBN 0-440-17497-X). Dell.

Perchance to Dream. Natalie Shipman & Worcester, Gurdon Saltonstall, 1897- Joint Author. LC 46-738559. 1946. Prentice-Hall, Inc.

Perchance to Dream" And Other Stories. Margaret Sutton Briscoe Hopkins. LC 7-52489. 1892. Dodd, Mead and Company.

Percival Keene. Frederick Marryat. LC 1-1767. 1879. D. Appleton and Company.

Percival Keene. Frederick Marryat. LC 36-37169. (Half-title: Everyman's library, ed. by Ernest Rhys. Fiction no. 358). 1926. J. M. Dent & Sons. Ltd.

Percival Keene. A New Novel. Frederick Marryat. LC 1-1764. (Brother Jonathan. Extra, no. 10. Sept. 21, 1842). 1842. Wilson & Company.

Percy. Raymond Hitchcock. LC 70-112900. 1970. 4.95. Dodd, Mead.

Percy and the Prophet: Events in the Lives of a Lady and Her Lovers. Wilkie Collins. (On cover: Harper's half-hour series v. 25). 1877. Harper & Brothers.

Percy Anecdotes. Reuben Percy. 1869. Repr. price not set o.s.i. Finch Pr.

Percy Mallory: A Novel. James Hook. LC 7-5390. 1824. H. C. Carey & I. Lea Etc.

Percy; or, The Four Inseparables. M Lee. LC 99-1144. 1898. The Whitaker & Ray Co. (Incorporated.

Percy Wynn: Or, Making a Boy of Him. 2d ed. Francis James Finn. 1891. Benziger Brothers.

Perdida. A Round Unvarnished Tale Truthfully Delivered. Frederic Werden Pangborn. Wright & Company.

Perdido. Jill Robinson. LC 77-21169. 1978. 9.95 (ISBN 0-394-40893-4). Knopf.

Perdita. Joan Smith. 224p. 1981. pap. 1.95 (ISBN 0-449-50173-6, Coventry). Fawcett.

Perdita, and Other Stories. Ella Wheeler Wilcox. J. S. Ogilvie and Company.

Perdita: Get Lost. Alan R Jackson. LC 64-13344. 1964. Simon and Schuster.

Perdition Express. Brad Lang. (Orig.). 1976. pap. 1.25 o.p. (LB328, Leisure Bks). Nordon Pubns.

Perdition Express. Brad Lang. (Crockett series). 1976. (pbk.) 1.25. Leisure Books.

Perdu: Translated from the Italian. 1st American Ed. Paride Rombi. LC 54-6026. 1954. Harper.

Perdut. Neil Lehrman. LC 78-20558. (Illus.). 1979. 8.95 (ISBN 0-931848-22-9) (ISBN 0-931848-23-7). Dryad Press.

Pere Antoine. Edward Francis Murphy. LC 47-1997. 1947. Doubleday & Company, Inc.

Pere Goriot. Honore De Balzac. LC 63-6851. (Great illustrated classics). 1954. Dodd, Mead.

Pere Goriot. Honore De Balzac. LC 50-5895. (Rinehart editions, 18). 1950. Rinehart.

Pere Goriot. Honore De Balzac. Tr. by Katharine Prescott Wormeley. LC 2-24484. (Half-title: The comedy of human life... Scenes from Parisian life). 1883. Roberts Brothers.

Pere Goriot. tr. from the french by mrs. fred m. dey. ed. Honore De Balzac. Tr. by Frederic M. Dey. (Seaside library. Pocket ed., no. 776). G. Munro.

Pere Goriot. Honore De Balzac. Tr. by Katharine Prescott Wormeley. LC 3-24483. (Half-title: The comedy of human life... Scenes from Parisian life). 1889. Roberts Brothers.

Pere Goriot. Honore De Balzac. Tr. by Katharine Prescott Wormeley. LC 39-17471. 1931. Little, Brown, and Company.

Pere Goriot. Honore De Balzac. Tr. by Katharine Prescott Wormeley. LC 44-32803. 1896. Roberts Brothers.

Pere Goriot. Honore De Balzac. Tr. by Katharine Prescott Wormeley. LC 43-27331. (Jacket library). 1932. National Home Library Foundation.

Pere Goriot. Honore De Balzac. LC 44-12298. (University classics). 1939. Appleby & Company, Incorporated.

Pere Goriot. Honore De Balzac. Ed. by Castex. (Coll. Prestige). 27.95. French & Eur.

Pere Goriot. Honore De Balzac. (Great Il. Classics). (Illus.). 1954. 4.50 o.p. (ISBN 0-396-03645-7). Dodd.

Pere Goriot and Eugenie Grandet. Honore De Balzac. Tr. by Edward Killoran Brown. (Half-title: The Modern library of the world's best books. 245). 1946. The Modern Library.

Pere Goriot: Illustrated by Margot Tomes. Honore De Balzac. LC 51-3398. 1951. Doubleday.

Pere Goriot. Introd. by Horatio Smith. Honore De Balzac. (Mod. Student's lib, French ser.). 1963. pap., 1.50. Scribners.

Pere Goriot. The Marriage Contract. Honore De Balzac. Tr. by Katharine Prescott Wormeley. LC 26-26064. (Half-title: The works of Balzac. Centenary ed. vol. i). Little, Brown and Company.

Pere Goriot. Tr. from French Introd. by Lester G. Crocker. New Crocker. Honore De Balzac. (W149). Washington Sq.

Pere Monnier's Ward. A Novel. William A. McDermott. (American author series of Catholic novels). 1898. Benziger Brothers.

Pereda O la Novela Idilio. Jose Fernandez Montesinos & Jose Maria De Pereda. LC 62-2706. 3.50. Univ. of Calif. Pr.

Peregrinations of Jeremiah Grant, Esq. LC 75-4534. (Flowering of the Novel). 1975. 25.00 (ISBN 0-8240-1163-5). Garland Pub.

Peregrine. William Bayer. LC 81-7762. 13.95 (ISBN 0-86553-024-6). Congdon & Lattes: Distributed by St. Martin's Press.

Peregrine: A Novel, by B. Dyke Acland. Baldwyn Dyke Acland. LC 31-6487. 1931. R. M. McBride & Company.

Peregrine House. Janis Flores. LC 76-42327. 1977. 7.95 (ISBN 0-385-12782-0). Doubleday.

Peregrine House. Janis Flores. (A Candlelight Intrigue Book). 1979. 1.25 (ISBN 0-440-17073-7). Dell Publishing.

Peregrine Pickle... Tobias George Smollett. LC 37-5642. (Half-title: Everyman's library, ed. by Ernest Rhys. Fiction no. 838-839). 1930. J. M. Dent & Sons, Ltd.

Peregrine: Primus. Avram Davidson. LC 75-161122. 1971. 5.95 (ISBN 0-8027-5546-1). Walker.

Peregrine: Secundus. Avram Davidson. (Orig.). 1981. pap. 2.25 (ISBN 0-425-04829-2). Berkley Pub.

Peregrine's Progress. Jeffery Farnol. LC 22-19055. 1922. Little, Brown, and Company.

Perela: The Man of Smoke. Aldo Palazzeschi & Riccio, Peter Michael, 1898- Tr. LC 40-3964. S. F. Vanni, Inc.

Perelandra. Clive Staples Lewis. 1968. 14.95 (ISBN 0-02-570840-6); pap. 2.95 (ISBN 0-02-086900-2). Macmillan.

Perelandra see Space Trilogy.

Perelandra: A Novel. Clive Staples Lewis. LC 79-35. 1968. 4.95. Macmillan.

Perelandra: A Novel. Clive Staples Lewis. LC 44-3319. 1944. The Macmillan Company.

Perella. William John Locke. LC 26-15180. 1926. Dodd, Mead and Company.

Perennial Bachelor. Anne Parrish. LC 25-164923. 1925. Harper & Brothers.

Perennial Boarder: An Asey Mayo Mystery. Phoebe Atwood Taylor. LC 41-7509. 1965. bds., 3.95. Norton.

Perennial Boarder: An Asey Mayo Mystery. Phoebe Atwood Taylor. LC 41-750037. W. W. Norton & Company, Inc.

Perennial Boarder: An Asey Mayo Mystery. Phoebe Atwood Taylor. LC 42-17351. 1942. The Sun Dial Press.

Perfect Adonis... Miriam Coles Harris. LC 12-23260. 1875. G. W. Carleton & Co.; Etc., Etc.

Perfect Age. F. E. Bailey. 1943. Repr. 15.00 (ISBN 0-8274-3121-X). R West.

Perfect Alibi. Christopher St. John Sprigg. LC 34-416023. 1934. Pub. for the Crime Club, Inc., by Doubleday, Doran & Company, Inc.

Perfect Corpse. Laurie R. Wright. 1977. pap. 1.50 (ISBN 0-89041-139-5, 3139). Major Bks.

Perfect Crime. Henry Kane. 1972. pap. 0.75 o.p. (BT40124). Belmont-Tower.

Perfect Crime. Ellery Queen, pseud. LC 42-18364. 1942. Grosset & Dunlap.

Perfect Crime, or Two. Hubert Monteilhet. LC 72-159136. (Inner sanctum mystery special). 1971. 4.95 (ISBN 0-671-21016-5). Simon and Schuster.

Perfect Day. John Gilbert Bohun Lynch. LC 24-6739. 1924. T. Seitzer.

Perfect Day: A Novel. Ira Levin. (Dell book). 1979. 2.25 (ISBN 0-440-18704-4). Dell Pub. Co.

Perfect End. William Leonard Marshall. LC 82-15502. 1983. 13.50 (ISBN 0-03-047481-7). Holt, Rinehart and Winston.

Perfect Fool. Florence Alice Price James. LC 7-7410. The International News Company.

Perfect Fools. Edith Pinero Green. LC 82-1387. 11.50. Dutton.

Perfect Fools: A Dearborn V. Pinch Mystery. Edith Pinero Green. LC 82-1387. 208p. 1982. 11.50 (ISBN 0-525-24122-1, 01117-330). Dutton.

Perfect Frame. William Ard. LC 51-10954. 1951. M. S. Mill Co. and W. Morrow.

Perfect Freedom. Gordon Merrick. 432p. 1982. pap. 3.95 (ISBN 0-380-80127-2, 80127, Flare). Avon.

Perfect Generosity of Price Vessantara: A Buddhist Epic. Ed. by Margaret Cone & Richard Gombrich. (Illus.). 1977. 39.00x (ISBN 0-19-826530-1). Oxford U Pr.

Perfect Gentleman. facs. ed. Ralph Wilhelm Bergengren. LC 67-23177. (Essay Index Reprint Ser). 1919. 10.00 (ISBN 0-8369-0202-5). Ayer Co.

Perfect Invader. Robert Thomas Burns. LC 50-6098. 1950. Bobbs-Merrill.

Perfect Lady: A Novelization of the Channing Pollock-Rennold Wolf Play. Joseph Boardman & Pollock, Channing, 1880- LC 15-12991. E. J. Clode.

Perfect Lady by Mistake & Other Stories. Feng Menglong. 1976. 14.95 (ISBN 0-236-40002-9, Pub. by Paul Elek). Merrimack Pub Cir.

Perfect Lamb. Elisabeth Stancy Payne. 1941. Dodd, Mead & Company.

Perfect Leaf: Being the Confession of Roland Emery. Frank A Fortescue. LC 30-7669. Sears Publishing Company, Inc.

Perfect Love. Diana C. Chang. (Orig.). 1978. pap. 1.95 (ISBN 0-515-04355-9). Jove Pubns.

Perfect Love Casteth Out Fear. Katharine Sedgwick Washburn. 1875. Lee and Shepard.

Perfect Lover. Christopher Priest. LC 77-88506. 7.95 (ISBN 0-684-15140-5). Scribner.

Perfect Lover. Christopher Priest. (Dell book). 1979. 1.75 (ISBN 0-440-16880-5). Dell Pub. Co.

Perfect Marriage. Josephine Henry. 232p. 1975. 8.50 o.p. (ISBN 0-682-48250-1). Exposition.

Perfect Murder. Henry Reymond Fitzwalter Keating. LC 65-11387. 1965. 3.95. Dutton.

Perfect Murder. Shakuntala Devi. LC 76-904484. 5.00. Orient Paperbacks.

Perfect Murder & Other Stories. Doris Parsons. 1981. 5.75 (ISBN 0-8062-1795-2). Carlton.

Perfect Murder Case. Christopher Bush. LC 29-184137. 1929. Pub. for The Crime Club, Inc., by Doubleday, Doran & Company, Inc.

Perfect Pair. Lois Seyster Montross. LC 34-5974. Doubleday, Doran & Company, Inc.

Perfect Partner. Carole Mortimer. (Harlequin Presents Ser.). 192p. 1983. pap. 1.75 (ISBN 0-373-10571-1). Harlequin Bks.

Perfect Plot. Glen Canary. 1974. (pbk.) 0.95 (ISBN 0-523-00302-1). Pinnacle Books.

Perfect Round. Henry Morton Robinson. LC 45-9226. 1945. Harcourt, Brace and Company.

Perfect Score. Robert Emmet Cummins. LC 25-16208. 1925. The Stratford Company.

Perfect Secretary. Peggy O'More, pseud. LC 40-32135. Gramercy Publishing Co.

Perfect Specimen. Samuel Hopkins Adams. LC 36-2218. Liveright Publishing Corporation.

Perfect State of Health. Peter Way. LC 77-18497. 145p. 1972. 6.95 (ISBN 0-89388-039-6). Okpaku Communications.

Perfect State of Health: A Novel. Peter Way. LC 77-184397. 1972. 5.95 (ISBN 0-89388-038-8). Third Press.

Perfect Stenographer. Peggy O'More, pseud. LC 36-7587. Phoenix Press.

Perfect Stranger. Firth Haring. LC 72-90394. 1973. 5.95 (ISBN 0-671-21470-5). Simon and Schuster.

Perfect Stranger. Edward S Hyams. LC 64-12511. 1964. Simon and Schuster.

Perfect Stranger. Danielle Steel. LC 81-22049. 3.50 (ISBN 0-440-17221-7). Dell.

Perfect Stranger. Danielle Steel. LC 82-9170. 1982. 13.95 (ISBN 0-8161-3402-2). G.K. Hall.

Perfect Tribute. Mary Raymond Shipman Andrews. (Illus.). 1906. 4.50 o.p. (ISBN 0-684-10004-5). Scribner.

Perfect Vacuum. Stanislaw Lem. LC 78-14076. 8.95. Harcourt Brace Jovanovich.

Perfect Weapon. Bennett Michelson. (Orig.). 1980. pap. 1.95 o.s.i. (ISBN 0-505-51544-X). Tower Bks.

Perfect Wife. Phyllis Bottome. LC 24-13019. George H. Doran Company.

Perfect Wife. Vida Hurst. LC 47-30775. 1947. Gramercy Pub. Co.

Perfect Wife and Mother. Nicola Thorne, pseud. LC 80-53084. 10.95 (ISBN 0-312-60077-1). St. Martin's Press.

Perfect Woman. Leslie Poles Hartley. LC 55-57325. 1955. H. Hamilton.

Perfect Woman. 1st American Ed. Leslie Poles Hartley. LC 56-5772. 1956. Knopf.

Perfect World: A Romance of Strange People and Strange Places. Ella Scrymsour. LC 22-2315. Frederick A. Stokes Company.

Perfection City. Adela Elizabeth Richards Orpen. LC 3-10903. (Half-title: Appletons' town and country library, no. 212). 1897. D. Appleton and Company.

Perfectionists. Gail Godwin. LC 74-95997. 1970. 5.95. Harper & Row.

Perfectly Natural Act. Dennis Littrell. LC 72-87620. 1973. 6.95. Putnam.

Perfectly Natural Act. Dennis Littrell. 1974. (pbk.) 1.50 (ISBN 0-523-00357-9). Pinnacle Books.

Perfectly Yours. James L. Weil. 1974. wrappers 4.00 o.p. (Pub. by Elizabeth Pr). SBD.

Perfidious Brethren. Bd. with Love in Its Empire: Illustrated in Seven Novels. Paul Chamberlen. (Novel in England, 1700-1775 Ser). 1973. Repr. of 1720 ed. lib. bdg. 50.00 (ISBN 0-8240-0547-3). Garland Pub.

Perfidious Brethren (Anonymous). Love in Its Empire. Paul Chamberlen. LC 78-170546. (Foundations of the Novel). 1973. 22.00 (ISBN 0-8240-0547-3). Garland Pub.

Perfidious P. Bd. with Glorious Life & Actions of St. Whigg; Life & Adventures of Captain John Avery, the Famous English Pirate ... Now in Possession of Madagascar. (Novel in England, 1700-1775 Ser). lib. bdg. 50.00 (ISBN 0-8240-0518-X). Garland Pub.

Perfidious P-- (Anonymous). The Glorious Life and Actions of St. Whigg (Anonymous). The Life and Adventures of Captain John Avery (Anonymous). LC 76-170508. (Foundations of the Novel). 1973. 22.00 ea. (ISBN 0-8240-0518-X). Garland.

Performance. William Hughes. (Orig.). 1970. pap. 0.75 o.p. (A663S, Award). Univ Pub & Dist.

Performer. Heller Toren. 1971. pap. 0.75 o.p. (B75-2139). Belmont-Tower.

Perfume and Poison. Vennette Herron. LC 17-29248. 1.00. R. G. Badger; Etc., Etc.

Perfume of Eros: A Fifth Avenue Incident. Edgar Evertson Saltus. LC 75-182713. 1968. AMS Press.

Perfume of Eros: A Fifth Avenue Incident. Edgar Evertson Saltus. LC 5-36813. 1905. A. Wessels Company.

Perfume of the Lady in Black. Gaston Leroux. LC 9-6576. 1909. Brentano's.

Perfume of the Rainbow: And Other Stories. Lily Moresby Adams Beck. LC 23-17381. 1923. Dodd, Mead and Company.

Perfume of the Violet. Adapted from the French of Dubut De Laforest. Jean Louis Dubut De Laforest. LC 6-34626. (On cover: Idylwild series, v. 1, no. 12). 1892. Morrill, Higgins & Co.

Perfumed Acres. David Jones. LC 70-417280. (Illus.). 1969. Pwllyrheyrn, David Jones.

Perfumed Lure. St. Dennis, Madelon. LC 32-84274. E. J. Clode, Inc.

Perfumes of Arabia. Evelyn Dewar. LC 73-93935. 1974. 5.95 (ISBN 0-8027-5302-7). Walker.

Perhaps a Little Danger. Eileen Helen Clements. LC 42-17220. 1942. E. P. Dutton & Co., Inc.

Perhaps I'll Dream of Darkness. Mary Sheldon. LC 81-40217. 11.95 (ISBN 0-394-51175-1). Random House.

Perhaps It Was in Vail: A Novel. Dan Lewandowski. LC 76-50445. 1977. 7.95 (ISBN 0-672-52306-X). Bobbs-Merrill.

Perhaps It Was Never the Same. Russel Hardin. 1980. write for info.; pap. write for info. Latitudes Pr.

Perhaps Timothy Was. Thomas Broughton. LC 41-4547. Modern Age Books.

Perhaps Tomorrow. Phyllis Yahnke. LC 53-622913. 1953. Arcadia House.

Pericles on 31st Street. Harry Mark Petrakis. LC 65-12778. 1965. Quadrangle Books.

Pericles the Athenian. Rex Warner. LC 63-8311. 1963. Little Brown.

Perico, the Sad; or, The Alvareda Family: And Other Stories. Original, Translated, and Selected. LC 8-33274. 1876. The Catholic Publication Society.

Peril! Sydney Horler. LC 30-31364. 1930. The Mystery League, Inc.

Peril. Lloyd Osbourne. LC 29-12912. 1929. Pub. for the Crime Club, Inc.

Peril. A Novel. Jessie Fothergill. LC 7-30845. (On cover: The seaside library. Pocket ed. no. 314). 1885. G. Munro.

Peril Ahead. John Creasey. 1974. (pbk.) 0.95. Popular Library.

Peril at Dorrough. Juanita Tyree Osborne. 1979. 6.95 (Avalon). Bouregy.

Peril at End House. Agatha Miller Christie. LC 32-26292. 1932. Dodd, Mead & Company.

Peril at End House. Agatha Miller Christie. LC 39-15204. 1938. Modern Age Books, Inc.

Peril at Land's End. Patricia Bird. (Orig.). 1980. pap. 1.75 (ISBN 0-8439-8008-7, Tiara Bks). Nordon Pubns.

Peril at Polvellyn. Marjorie McEvoy. (Orig.). 1973. pap. 0.75 o.p. (ISBN 0-345-20747-5). Beagle Bks.

Peril at Stone Hall. Jane Corby. Ed. by Alice Sachs. 1969. lib. bdg. 3.50 o.p. Arcadia.

Peril at Stone Hall. Jane Corby. 1972. pap. 0.75 o.p. (75-455). Manor Bks.

Peril at the Spy Nest. Arthur Minturn Chase. LC 43-984. 1943. Dodd, Mead & Company.

Peril of Barnabas Collins. Marilyn Ross. (Dark Shadows Ser). (Orig.). 1969. pap. 0.50 o.p. (62-244). Paperback Lib.

Peril of Dionysio. Mary Ellen Mannix. LC 11-31891. 1912. Benziger Brothers.

Peril of Oliver Sargent. Edgar Janes Bliss. LC 6-14216. 1891. C. L. Webster & Co.

Peril of Oliver Sargent. Edgar Janes Bliss. (On cover: Seaside library. Pocket ed., no. 2102). 1895. G. Munro's Sons.

Peril of Richard Pardon: A Novel. Benjamin Leopold Farjeon. LC 6-38647. (On cover: Harper's Franklin square library. no. 635). 1888. Harper & Brothers.

Peril of Silence. Oscar Daniel Meyer. LC 53-116325. Vantage Press.

Peril Rides the Pecos. Jackson Cole. 1973. (pbk) 0.75. Popular Library.

Peril Stalks the Shore. Neal Wakely. 156p. 1978. 5.95 (ISBN 0-8059-2517-1). Dorrance.

Perilous Ascent: Stories of Mountain Climbing. Ed. by Phyllis Reid Fenner. LC 71-124350. (Illus.). 1970. 4.25. W. Morrow.

Perilous Castle. Patricia Laye. (Orig.). 1981. pap. 1.75 (ISBN 0-8439-8027-3, Tiara Bks). Nordon Pubns.

Perilous Country: A Doctor Palfrey Thriller. John Creasey. LC 72-80534. 1973. 5.95 (ISBN 0-8027-5266-7). Walker.

Perilous Dreams. Andre Norton, pseud. (Science Fiction Ser.). pap. 1.75 (ISBN 0-87997-405-2, UE1405). DAW Bks.

Perilous Dreams. Andre Norton. (Daw Science Fiction #196). 1976. 1.25. Daw Books.

TITLE INDEX PERSONS & MASKS OF

Perilous Holiday: A Novel of Suspense. 1st Ed. Don Smith. LC 53-8982. 1953. Holt.
Perilous Homecoming. Shirley A Franklin. 1975. 4.95. Avalon Books.
Perilous Isle: A Story of the San Domingo Uprising Based on an Old Family Journal. Octavia Roberts. 1926. Harper & Brothers.
Perilous Journey: A Tale of the Mississippi River and the Natchez Trace. Clifford MacClellan Sublette & Kroll, Harry Harrison, 1886- Joint Author. LC 43-4309. 1943. The Bobbs-Merrill Company.
Perilous Love. Florence Riddell. LC 32-1752. 1932. J. B. Lippincott Company.
Perilous Night. Burke Boyce. 1972. pap. 1.50 o.p. (ISBN 0-515-02861-4, A2861). Pyramid Pubns.
Perilous Night: A Novel. Burke Boyce. LC 42-1761. 1942. The Viking Press.
Perilous Passage. Arthur Mayse. LC 49-4737. 1949. W. Morrow.
Perilous Passage. Bruce Nicolaysen. LC 75-45356. 1977. pap. 1.95 o.p. (ISBN 0-87223-469-X). Playboy.
Perilous Passage: A Novel. Bruce Nicolaysen. LC 76-45356. 8.95 (ISBN 0-87223-468-1). Playboy Press.
Perilous Path: Or, Apples of Sodom. Kate Davis. LC 1-31850. The Abbey Press.
Perilous Planets. Brian Wilson Aldiss. 1980. pap. 2.50 (ISBN 0-380-47100-0, 47100). Avon.
Perilous Quest. T. A Niccolls. LC 27-6547. 1927. D. Appleton and Company.
Perilous Sanctuary. Donald John Hall. LC 37-273994. 1937. The Macmillan Company.
Perilous Seat. Caroline Dale Parke Snedeker. LC 23-26344. 1923. Doubleday, Page & Company.
Perilous Secret. A Novel. Charles Reade. LC 9-6133. (Harper's Franklin square library, no. 384). 1884. Harper & Brothers.
Perilous Secret: Or, Love and Money. Charles Reade. (On cover: Lovell's library, v. 8, no. 415). 1884. J. W. Lovell Company.
Perilous Spring of Morris Seidman. Elick Moll. LC 72-12514. 1973. 8.95 (ISBN 0-8161-6069-4). G. K. Hall.
Perilous Spring of Morris Seidman. Elick Moll. LC 72-1106. 1972. 5.95 (ISBN 0-395-13949-X). Houghton Mifflin.
Perilous Voyage. Lael Tucker Wertenbaker. LC 75-4511. 1975. (ISBN 0-316-93122-5). Little, Brown.
Perilous Waters. Jane Blackmore. 1981. pap. 1.50 (ISBN 0-440-17309-4). Dell.
Perilous Waters. Jane Blackmore. 1973. (pbk.) 0.95. Dell.
Perils of Josephine. Ernest William Hamilton. 1899. H. S. Stone & Company.
Perils of Pauline: A Motion Picture Novel. Charles William Goddard. LC 15-7360. 1915. Hearst's International Library Co.
Perils of Pearl Street: Including a Taste of the Dangers of Wall Street. Asa Greene. 1834. Betts & Anstice Etc.
Perils of the Jungle: A Tale of Adventure in the Dark Continent. Edward Sylvester Ellis. LC 1-29035. (On cover: Medal library, no. 77). 1900. Street & Smith.
Perimeters. Helena Harlow Worthen. LC 79-3372. 11.95 (ISBN 0-15-572625-0). Harcourt Brace Jovanovich.
Period of Evil. John Creasey. LC 79-148413. (Falcon's head suspense novel). 1971. 5.95. World Pub. Co.
Period of Evil. Kyle Hunt, pseud. LC 79-148413. 1971. 5.95 o.p. World Pub.
Period Piece. Gwen Raverat. (Illus.). 288p. 1976. pap. 3.95 (ISBN 0-393-00822-3). Norton.
Period Pieces. Peggy Morrison, pseud. LC 66-15761. 1966. Chilton Books.
Period Pieces: By March Cost Pseud. Peggy Margaret Mackie Morrison Morrison. LC 66-15761. 4.95. Chilton.
Periodical Lunch, Vol. 7. (Illus.). 1976. pap. 1.50 o.p. (ISBN 0-914908-07-3). Street Fiction.
Periodical Lunch, Vol. 7. (Illus.). 1976. pap. 1.50 o.p. (ISBN 0-914908-07-3). Street Fiction.
Periodical Lunch, Vol. 5. (Illus.). 80p. 1975. pap. 1.50 o.p. (ISBN 0-914908-05-7). Street Fiction.
Peripheral Spy. Bernard Peterson. LC 79-1476. 1980. 8.95 (ISBN 0-698-10979-1). Coward, McCann & Geoghegan.
Peripheral Visions. Gloria Pierce. LC 82-80581. (Illus.). 64p. (Orig.). 1982. pap. 4.95 (ISBN 0-943148-00-6). Nikki Pr.
Periscope Red. Richard Rohmer. 352p. 1980. 12.95 (ISBN 0-8253-0020-7). Beaufort Bks NY.
Perish by the Sword. Poul Anderson. LC 59-10292. (Cock Robin mystery). 1959. Macmillan.
Perish in Their Pride. Henry De Montherlant. Tr. by McGreevy, Thomas. LC 36-1118. 1936. A. A. Knopf.
Perishable Goods. Cecil William Mercer. LC 28-20129. 1928. Minton, Balch & Company.
Perishing Republic. Jerome Bahr. LC 79-129182. (His All good Americans, v. 7). 1971. 5.95. Trempealeau Press.
Perit at Cranbury Hall. Cecil John Charles Street. LC 30-67322. 1930. Dodd, Mead & Company.
Periwinkle: An Autobiography. Arnold Gray. (On cover: Seaside library. Pocket ed., no. 965). 1887. G. Munro.
Periwinkle: An Idyl of the Dunes. William Farquhar Payson. LC 10-21597. 1910. 1.25. Sturgis & Walton Company.
Perjur'd Citizen; or, Female Revenge see Brothers; or, Treachery Punish'd.
Perjured Alibi. Walter S Masterman. LC 35-142346. E. P. Dutton & Co., Inc.
Perkins of Portland: Perkins the Great. Ellis Parker Butler. LC 6-33589. 1906. H. B. Turner & Co.
Perkins Peril: A Novel. George V Wells. (On cover: Pastime series. no. 127). Laird & Lee.
Perkins, the Fakeer: A Travesty on Reincarnation; His Wonderful Workings in the Cases of "When Reginal Was Caroline", "How Chopin Came to Remsen", and "Clarissa's Troublesome Baby". illustrated by hy mayer. ed. Edward Sims Van Zile. 1903. The Smart Set Publishing Co.
Perlycross: A Novel. Richard Doddridge Blackmore. LC 4-15287. 1895. Harper & Brothers.
Perlycross: A Tale of the Western Hills, 3 vols. in 1. Richard Doddridge Blackmore. LC 79-8239. Repr. of 1894 ed. 44.50 (ISBN 0-404-61790-5). AMS Pr.
Perma Book of Ghost Stories. Ed. by West Bob Holland. LC 50-10608. (Permabooks P 94). 1950. Permabooks.
Permanent Eclipse. Conrad Arthur Skinner. LC 26-8006. 1926. Frank-Maurice, Inc.
Permanent Errors. Reynolds Price. LC 70-124974. 1970. 6.50. Atheneum.
Permanent Farewell. Peter De Polnay. LC 73-562844. 1970 (ISBN 0-491-00116-9). W. H. Allen.
Permanent Implosion. John Wood Campbell. 1970. pap. 0.75 o.p. (0502-07064). Curtis.
Permanent Uncle. Douglas Goldring. 1.25. E. P. Dutton & Company.
Permanent Wave. Virginia Sullivan. LC 29-10433. Macrae Smith Company.
Permanente, a Romance. Effie G Sheldon. LC 57-9834. (Nobel book). 1957. Comet Presss Book.
Permata-Permata Di Lumpur. M. Mansur Abdullah. (Karyawan Malaysia Ser.). (Malay.). 1979. pap. text ed. 3.25x o.p. (00354). Heinemann Ed.
Perola. Phyllis Ann Karr. (Coventry Romance Ser.: No. 178). 224p. 1982. pap. 1.50 (ISBN 0-449-50279-1, Coventry). Fawcett.
Perpetua. A Tale of Nimes in A.D. 213, by the Rev. S. Baring-Gould, M.A. Sabine Baring-Gould. LC 6-7288. 1897. E. P. Dutton & Company.
Perpetua Mary. Dion Clayton Calthrop. LC 12-24623. 1912. 1.30. John Lane Company.
Perpetua: Or, The Way to Treat a Woman. Dion Clayton Calthrop. LC 11-11895. 1911. 1.30. John Lane Company.
Perpetual Comedy. Camillo Berg & Hershfield, Harry, 1885- Illus. LC 43-119599. 1943. B. Humphries, Inc.
Perpetual Curate. Margaret Oliphant Wilson Oliphant. LC 75-1544. (Victorian Fiction: Novels of Faith and Doubt; 90). 1975. (ISBN 0-8240-1614-9). Garland Pub.
Perpetual Curate. Margaret Oliphant Wilson Oliphant. (On cover: Seaside library. Pocket ed., no. 568). 1885. G. Munro.
Perpetual Curate. A Novel. Margaret Oliphant Wilson Oliphant. LC 22-4756. (Her Chronicles of Carlingford). 1865. Harper & Brothers.
Perplexed Heart. Angela Du Maurier. LC 39-15268. 1939. Doubleday, Doran & Co., Inc.
Perplexities & Paradoxes. Miguel De Unamuno y Jugo. Tr. by Stuart Gross. Repr. of 1945 ed. lib. bdg. 15.00x (ISBN 0-8371-0253-7, UNPP). Greenwood.
Perri. Felix Salten & Mussey, June Barrows, 1910- Tr. LC 38-27967. The Bobbs-Merrill Company.
Perrine. Dorothy Daniels. 1978. 2.25 (ISBN 0-446-82605-7). Warner Books.
Perris of the Cherry-Trees. Joseph Smith Fletcher. LC 30-8795. 1930. Doubleday, Doran and Company, Inc.
Perry Kimbro, R. N. By Georgia Craig Pseud. Peggy Gaddis, pseud. LC 50-4295. 1950. Arcadia House.
Perry Kimbro, R.N. And Piney Woods Nurse. Georgia Craig. (Manor Books double volume). 1973. (pbk.) 0.95. Manor Books.
Perry Rhodan No. 108: Duel Under the Double Sun. K. H Scheer. (Perry Rhodan series). 1977. 1.25. Ace Books.
Perry Rhodan: The Thrall of Hypno. Clark Darlton. (Illus.). 1973. 0.75. Ace Books.
Perry's Planet. Joe Haldeman, III. 1980. pap. 1.75 (ISBN 0-553-13580-5). Bantam.
Persecutor. Ian Hamilton. LC 65-23206. bds., 4.50. Lippincott.
Persephone of Eleusis: A Romance of Ancient Greece. Clare Winger Harris. LC 23-1439. 1923. The Stratford Company.
Perseverance Island: Or, The Robinson Crusoe of the Nineteenth Century. by douglas frazar... ed. Douglas Frazar. LC 6-43144. 1885. Lee and Shepard.
Persian Boy. Mary Renault, pseud. LC 72-3407. (Illus.). 1972. 7.95 (ISBN 0-394-48191-7). Pantheon Books.
Persian Boy. Mary Renault, pseud. (Illus.). 1974. (pbk.) 1.95. Bantam Books.
Persian Cat: By John Flagg Pseud. John Gearon. LC 50-4300. (Gold medal books, 103). 1950. Fawcett Publications.
Persian Conqueror. George Sidney Hellman. LC 35-13908. 1935. Dodd, Mead & Company.
Persian Journey of the Reverend Ashley Wishard: And His Servant Fathi. Elgin Earl Groseclose. LC 37-143418. The Bobbs-Merrill Company.
Persian Letters. Charles Louis De Secondat Montesquieu. Tr. by John Ozell. LC 73-170550. (Foundations of the Novel). 1972. 22.00 (ISBN 0-8240-0549-X). Garland Pub.
Persian Letters. Charles Louis De Secondat Montesquieu. LC 73-163802. (Penguin classics L281). 1973. (pbk.) 2.65 (ISBN 0-14-044281-2). Penguin Books.
Persian Price. Evelyn Anthony. 1976. Repr. lib. bdg. 12.95 o.p. (ISBN 0-8161-6348-0, Large Print Bks). G K Hall.
Persian Price. Evelyn Anthony. 1976. pap. 1.95 (ISBN 0-451-07254-5, J7254, Sig). NAL.
Persian Price. Eve Stephens, pseud. LC 75-10472. 1975. 8.95 (ISBN 0-698-10694-6). Coward, McCann & Geoghegan.
Persian Price. Eve Stephens, pseud. LC 75-44144. 1976. 12.95 (ISBN 0-8161-6348-0). G. K. Hall.
Persian Tassel. Olivia Smith Cornelius. LC 14-3251. 1914. 1.20. The Neale Publishing Company.
Persians Are Coming. Bruno Frank. Tr. by Lowe-Porter, H. T. LC 29-5601. 1929. A. A. Knopf.
Persimmon: His Story. Paul Stevens. LC 58-14648. 1957. Heritage House.
Persimmons: A Story for Boys and Girls, and Men and Women, Who Have Not Forgotten Their School Days. A. C Butler. LC 6-16678. School News Print.
Persis. A Tale of the White Mountains. Luther Loud Holden. LC 8-211. (On cover: Satchel series, no. 20). 1879. The Author's Publishing Company.
Persis Yorke. M. L. Lord. 1896. Macmillan and Co.
Persistence of Vision. John Varley. LC 78-7874. (Quantum Science Fiction). 9.95 (ISBN 0-8037-6866-4). Dial Press/J. Wade.
Persistent Flame. Linda Turner. (Superromance Ser.). 295p. 1983. pap. 2.95 (ISBN 0-373-70065-2, Pub. by Worldwide). Harlequin Bks.
Persistent Image. Gladys Schmitt. LC 55-7671. 1955. Dial Press.
Persistent Suitor. Peggy Gaddis, pseud. (O.s.i.). 1976. pap. 1.25 o.s.i. (AQ1591, Award). Univ Pub & Dist.
Person Called "Z". Joseph Jefferson Farjeon. LC 29-68590. 1929. L. MacVeagh, The Dial Press.
Person of Quality. Ashton Hilliers. 1913. Desmond FitzGerald, Inc.
Person of Some Importance. Lloyd Osbourne. LC 11-232956. 1.25. The Bobbs-Merrill Company.
Person Shouldn't Die Like That. Arthur D Goldstein. LC 76-9121. 1976. 10.95 (ISBN 0-8161-6376-6). G. K. Hall.
Person Shouldn't Die Like That. Arthur D Goldstein. LC 77-179687. 1972. 4.95 (ISBN 0-394-47230-6). Random House.
Person to Person Call. Josiah Pitts Woolfolk. LC 42-9470. 1942. J. Swift.
Personal Affair. Flora Kidd. (Harlequin Presents Ser.). 192p. 1981. pap. 1.50 (ISBN 0-373-10447-2, Pub. by Harlequin). PB.
Personal Appearance of a Lioness. Virginia Tracy. LC 37-22218. J. B. Lippincott Company.
Personal Combat. Elliott Arnold. LC 36-32115. The Graystone Press.
Personal Conduct of Belinda. Eleanor Hoyt Brainerd. LC 10-7828. 1910. 1.20. Doubleday, Page & Company.
Personal Habits. Shannon Lewis. LC 81-43416. 1982. 15.95 (ISBN 0-385-17279-6). Doubleday.
Personal History and Experience of David Copperfield. Charles Dickens. LC 30-12321. 1910. A. L. Burt Company.
Personal History and Experience of David Copperfield: The Younger. Charles Dickens. Ed. by Buck, Philo Melvin. LC 10-29129. (Standard English classics). Ginn and Company.
Personal History and Experience of David Copperfield: The Younger. Charles Dickens. Ed. by Fairley, Edwin. LC 11-266435. (Macmillan's pocket American and English classics). 1911. The Macmillan Company.
Personal History and Experience of David Copperfield: The Younger. Charles Dickens. Ed. by Buck, Philo Melvin. LC 24-31285. New York Etc.
Personal History and Experience of David Copperfield: The Younger. Charles Dickens & Smith, Edith Freelove. LC 25-206319. 1925. The Macmillan Company.
Personal History of David Copperfield. Charles Dickens. LC 65-7653. 1965. Heritage Press.
Personal History of David Copperfield. Charles Dickens. LC 66-3335. (Penguin English library, EL8). 1966. Enguin Books.
Personal History of David Copperfield. Charles Dickens. Ed. by Trevor Blount. LC 66-71552. (Penguin English library EL8) 8/6). 1966. Penguin.
Personal History of David Copperfield. illustrated household ed. Charles Dickens. LC 11-7157. 1870. Fields, Osgood, & Co.
Personal History of David Copperfield. Charles Dickens. Ed. by Whipple, Edwin Percy. LC 15-231363. (Half-title: Works of Charles Dickens. New illustrated library ed. vol. xiv-xv). Houghton Mifflin Company.
Personal History of David Copperfield. Charles Dickens. (Half-title: Everyman's library, ed. by Ernest Rhys. Fiction). 1908. J. M. Dent & Co.
Personal History of David Copperfield. Charles Dickens. Ed. by Baldwin, Edward Chauncey. LC 10-15597. (Lake English classics). Scott, Foresman and Company.
Personal History of David Copperfield. Charles Dickens. Ed. by Baldwin, Edward Chauncey. LC 20-266. (Half-title: The Lake English classics, general editor, L. T. Damon...). Scott. Foresman and Company.
Personal History of David Copperfield. Charles Dickens. LC 35-27147. 1935. Dodd, Mead and Company.
Personal History of David Copperfield. Charles Dickens. LC 36-39. 1935. The Heritage Press.
Personal History of David Copperfield. Charles Dickens. LC 36-31200. 1936. Dodd, Mead and Company.
Personal History of David Copperfield. Charles Dickens. LC 44-10085. 1884. Hurst & Co.
Personal History of David Copperfield. Charles Dickens & Browne, Hablot Knight, 1815-1882, Illus. LC 48-8979. (Oxford illustrated Dickens). 1947. Oxford Univ. Press.
Personal History of David Copperfield... Edited by Helen Sard Hughes... Charles Dickens. Ed. by Hughes, Helen Sard. LC 36-17944. (Half-title: The Doubleday-Doran series in literature, R. Shafer, general editor). Doubleday, Doran & Company, Inc.
Personal History of David Copperfield: Ed. by Trevor Blount. With 23 of the Orig. Illus. by Hablot K. Browne ('Phiz' Charles Dickens. LC 66-3335. (Penguin Eng. lib., EL8). 1.95. Penguin.
Personal Impressions. Isaiah Berlin. Ed. by Henry Hardy. 1982. pap. 6.95 (ISBN 0-14-006313-7). Penguin.
Personal Justice. Ann Hilborn. 272p. 1982. pap. 2.95 (ISBN 0-380-81109-X, 81109-X). Avon.
Personal Maid. Grace Perkins Oursler. LC 31-7641. 1931. Covici-Friede.
Personal Matter. Kenzaburo Oe. LC 68-22007. 1968. Grove Press.
Personal Matter. Kezaburo Oesm. Tr. by John Natlan. LC 68-22007. 1968. 5.00 o.p. (GP434). Grove.
Personal Passion. Mickey Ross. LC 40-11340. Phoenix Press.
Personal Recollections of Joan of Arc. Samuel Langhorne Clemens. LC 80-23663. 1980. 45.00 (ISBN 0-313-22373-4). Greenwood Press.
Personal Recollections of Joan of Arc. Mark Twain. 1896. 10.95i (ISBN 0-06-014385-1, HarpT). Har-Row.
Personal Touch. Emma Beatrice Kaufman Brunner. LC 22-7924. Brentano's.
Personality Boy. Edward Lowrey. LC 33-14022. A. H. King.
Personality Plus: Some Experiences of Emma McChesney and Her Son, Jock. Edna Ferber. LC 77-150473. (Short story index reprint series). (Illus.). 1971. (ISBN 0-8369-3813-5). Books for Libraries Press.
Personality Plus: Some Experiences of Emma McChesney and Her Son, Jock. Edna Ferber. LC 14-16210. 1914. 1.00. Frederick A. Stokes Company.
Personals. Eleanor De Lamater. LC 31-17274. Farrar & Rinehart, Incorporated.
Personals: Or, Perils of the Period. Joseph Hertford. LC 7-4309. 1870. Printed for the Author.
Persons & Masks of the Law: Cardozo, Holmes, Jefferson & Wythe As Makers of the Masks. John T. Noonan, Jr. LC 75-30991. 1976. 10.00 (ISBN 0-374-23076-5); pap. 3.95 o.p. (ISBN 0-374-51396-1). FS&G.

Persons and Pictures from the Histories of France and England: From the Norman Conquest to the Fall of the Stuarts. Henry William Herbert. LC 7-4293. 1854. Riker, Thorne & Co.

Persons Unknown. Lee Thayer, pseud. LC 41-1985. 1941. Dodd, Mead & Company.

Persons Unknown,". Virginia Tracy. LC 14-18805. 1914. The Century Co.

Persons Unknown, an Exercise in Detection... Philip MacDonald. LC 30-329043. 1931. Pub. for the Crime Club, Inc., by Doubleday, Doran & Company, Inc.

Persuader. Robert Pollock. LC 79-114402. 1970. Putnam.

Persuaders. Geoffrey Kyle. 192p. (Orig.). 1972. pap. 1.95 o.p. (ISBN 0-87056-268-1, 6268). Brandon.

Persuaders. Frederick Smith. 1979. 11.00x o.p. (ISBN 0-86025-060-1, Pub. by Ian Henry Pubns England). State Mutual Bk.

Persuaders. Frederick Smith. 1977. 6.30 o.p. State Mutual Bk.

Persuaders Again. Frederick Smith. 1979. 11.00x o.p. (ISBN 0-86025-063-6, Pub. by Ian Henry Pubns England). State Mutual Bk.

Persuaders Again. Frederick Smith. 1977. 6.45 o.p. State Mutual Bk.

Persuaders at Large. Frederick Smith. 1979. 11.00x o.p. (ISBN 0-86025-012-1, Pub. by Ian Henry Pubns England). State Mutual Bk.

Persuaders at Large. Frederick Smith. 1977. 6.75 o.p. State Mutual Bk.

Persuasion. Jane Austen. (Harcourt library of English and American classics). 1962. Harcourt, Brace & World.

Persuasion. Jane Austen. LC 66-76. (Riverside editions, B95). 1965. Houghton Mifflin.

Persuasion. Jane Austen. LC 7086. 1892. Roberts Brothers.

Persuasion. Jane Austen. LC 43-39948. (Half-title: The World's classics, COCLVI). 1930. Oxford University Press, H. Milford.

Persuasion. Jane Austen & Tony Buonpastore. LC 77-151240. (Illus.). 1977. Printed for the Members of the Limited Editions Club.

Persuasion. Jane Austen & Harding, Denys Clement Wyatt, 1906- Ed. LC 65-29846. (Penguin English library, EL5). 1965. Penguin Books.

Persuasion. Jane Austen & James Kinsley. LC 80-40256. (World's classic). 1980. 2.95 (ISBN 0-19-281546-6). Oxford University Press.

Persuasion. Ed., Introd., Notes, by Andrew Wright. Jane Austen. LC 66-76. (Riverside eds. B95). 3.00, 1.15 pap.,. Houghton.

Persuasion: Introd. by John Dennis Duffy. Jane Austen. (Classics ser., CL107). Airmont.

Persuasion. Introd. by Malcolm Elwin. Illus. by Philip Gough. Jane Austen. LC 66-5492. (Macdonald illus. classics, 41). 1966. 3.50. Macdonald.

Persuasion. The Text Based on Collation of the Early Editions by R. W. Chapman. Introd. by David Daiches. Jane Austen. LC 59-244193. (Norton library, N11). 1958. Norton.

Persuasion: With, A Memoir of Jane Austen, by J. E. Austen-Leigh. Ed., Introd. by D. W. Harding. Jane Austen. (Penguin Eng. lib., 5) Bibl.). Penguin.

Persuasive Peggy. Maravene Thompson. LC 16-1274. 1916. Frederick A. Stokes Company.

Perturbing Spirit. Janet Caird. 1974. (pbk.) 0.95. Ace Books.

Perturbing Spirit. 1st Ed. in the U.S.A. Janet Caird. LC 67-15364. 1967. 3.95. Pub. for the Crime Club by Doubleday.

Peruvian Contracts: A Novel. Frank Fowlkes. LC 75-34217. 8.95 (ISBN 0-399-11710-5). Putnam.

Peruvian Nightmare. Mike Barry. (Lone Wolf). (Berkley medallion book: Vol. 7). 1974. (pbk.) 0.95 (ISBN 0-425-02624-8). Berkley Pub. Co.

Peruvian Nun: Or, The Empress of the Ocean. A Maritime Romance. Harry Halyard. 1848. F. Gleason.

Peruvian Printout. Alec Haig. LC 74-2598. (Red badge novel of suspense). 1974. 4.95 (ISBN 0-396-06960-6). Dodd, Mead.

Perverse Filipina. James I McGovern. LC 74-20312. 1975. 4.00 (ISBN 0-8059-2109-5). Dorrance.

Perversion. William John Conybeare. LC 75-497. (Victorian Fiction: Novels of Faith and Doubt; 48). 1975. 35.00 (ISBN 0-8240-1572-X). Garland Pub.

Perversity. Francis Carco. Tr. by Ford, Ford Madox. LC 28-14556. 1928. P. Covici.

Perverted Triangle. H. R. Kaye, pseud. (Orig.). 1968. pap. 1.95 o.p. (6023). Brandon.

Pervertidos Anonimos. new ed. Javier Lopez. (Pimienta Collection Ser). 160p. (Span.). 1975. pap. 1.00 (ISBN 0-88473-222-3). Fiesta Pub.

Perverts. 2d ed. William Lee Howard. LC 31-233255. 1902. G. W. Dillingham Company.

Perverts: A Novel. William Lee Howard. LC 2-4947. 1901. G. W. Dillingham Co.

Pesquera Bay. La Selle Gilman. LC 57-5852. 1957. W. Sloane Associates.

Pest. William Teignmouth Shore. LC 9-7337. 1909. C. H. Doscher & Co.

Pest. Albert Payson Terhune. LC 23-2472. E. P. Dutton & Company.

Peste. Albert Camus. (Coll. Folio). pap. 3.95. French & Eur.

Pet. Jan Cheux. pap. 1.95 o.p. (8035). Cameo.

Petal of-the-Rose. Charles Pettit. Tr. by Troubridge, Una Elena (Taylor) LC 30-11378. H. Liveright.

Petals from the Dogwood Tree. Elisabeth Offutt Allen. 1977. 4.50 o.p. (ISBN 0-533-02904-X). Vantage.

Petals from the Rose of Sharon. William Todd McLean. LC 42-210. Central Bible, Book and Tract Depot.

Petals of Blood. Wa Thiongo Ngugi. LC 78-60717. 1978. 9.95 (ISBN 0-525-17828-7) (ISBN 0-525-04195-8). Dutton.

Petals of Blood. Ngugi Wa Thiong'O. 1978. pap. 7.75 (ISBN 0-525-04195-8, 0752-230). Dutton.

Petals of the Rose: Poems & Epigrams. facsimile ed. Louis V. Burrell. LC 70-168513. (Black Heritage Library Collection). Repr. of 1917 ed. 9.50 (ISBN 0-8369-8876-0). Ayer Co.

Petals on the Wind. Virginia C Andrews. LC 80-15638. 2.75 (ISBN 0-671-82977-7). Simon and Schuster.

Petals on the Wind. large print ed. Virginia C. Andrews. LC 82-23313. 1983. 19.95 (ISBN 0-8161-3427-8). G.K. Hall.

Pete French, Cattle King: A Biographical Novel. Elizabeth Lambert Wood. LC 52-977. Binfords & Mort.

Pete Maravich: Basketball Whiz. Musemeche & Ellis. 1969. 1.00. Claitors.

Petenera's Daughter. Henry Bellamann. LC 26-15790. Harcourt, Brace and Company.

Peter. Edward Frederic Benson. LC 22-15212. George H. Doran Company.

Peter: A Novel of Which He Is Not the Hero. Francis Hopkinson Smith. 1908. C. Scribner's Sons.

Peter: A Novel of Which He Is Not the Hero. Francis Hopkinson Smith. 1909. C. Scribner's Sons.

Peter: A Novel of Which He Is Not the Hero. 12th impression ed. Francis Hopkinson Smith. LC 11-205832. 1911. C. Scribner's Sons.

Peter Abelard. Helen Jane Waddell. (Illus.). 1976. 1.95 (ISBN 0-14-004254-7). Penguin Books.

Peter Abelard: A Novel. Helen Jane Waddell. LC 33-25684. H. Holt and Company.

Peter Abelard: A Novel. Helen Jane Waddell. LC 47-5136. 1947. H. Holt.

Peter and Alexis. Dmitril Sergieevich Merezhkovskil. Tr. by Guerney, Bernard Guilbert. LC 37-30940. (Half-title: The modern library of the world's best books). The Modern Library.

Peter and Alexis. Dmitril Sergieevich Merezhkovskil. Tr. by Gurney, Bernard Guilbert. LC 31-28463. (Half-title: The modern library of the world's best books). The Modern Library.

Peter and Alexis: The Romance of Peter the Great. Dmitril Sergieevich Merezhkovskil. 1906. G. P. Putnam's Sons.

Peter and Anne. Narena Easterling. LC 42-14123. 1942. Gramercy Publishing Co.

Peter and Jane. Sarah Broom Macnaughton. LC 11-14720. 1911. Dodd, Mead & Company.

Peter and Penny, and Other Stories. Parley E Norseth. (Illus.). 1973. 3.75. Vantage Press.

Peter and the Lovers. Jonathon Clarke. LC 72-169094. 1972. 6.95. Phaedra.

Peter and the Rock. Mary Longstreet Wallace. LC 65-21891. 1965. 4.95. Bruce.

Peter Arbiter: A Novel. Edwin Shrake. LC 75-306307. (Illus.). 1973. 7.95 (ISBN 0-88426-030-5). Encino Press.

Peter Ashley. Du Bose Heyward. LC 32-28018. Farrar & Rinehart, Incorporated.

Peter Binney: A Novel. Archibald Marshall. LC 22-260351. 1921. Dodd, Mead and Company.

Peter Bosten: A Story About Realities. John Preston Buschlen. LC 16-1891. 1.00. Herald Publishing House.

Peter Burling: Pirate. Arthur P Bagby. LC 24-4581. Dorrance.

Peter Called the Great. Maurice Bethell Jones. LC 36-5108. 1936. Frederick A. Stokes Company.

Peter Camenzind. Hermann Hesse. 1975. (pbk.) 1.50. Bantam Books.

Peter Camenzind. Hermann Hesse. LC 74-87213. 1969. 5.50. Farrar, Straus and Giroux.

Peter Carradine: Or, The Martindale Pastoral. Caroline Chesebro' 1863. Sheldon & Company.

Peter Crabtree: A Tale of Two Continents. Oscar Robert Zipf. LC 38-110762. R. F. Seymour.

Peter Domanig in America: Steel. 1st Ed. Victor Francis White. LC 54-6500. 1954. Bobbs-Merrill.

Peter Domanig: Morning in Vienna. new ed. Victor Francis White. LC 78-9247. 1970. 9.95. N. S. Berg.

Peter Domanig; Morning in Vienna. Victor Francis White. LC 44-3822. 1944. The Bobbs-Merrill Company.

Peter Domanig: Morning in Vienna, by Victor White. Victor Francis White. LC 44-3822. 1944. The Bobbs-Merrill Company.

Peter Egge: Hansine Solstad, the History of an Honest Woman, with an Introduction by Henry Goddard Leach, Translated by Jess H. Jackson. Peter Egge & Leach, Henry Goddard, 1880- LC 29-20887. 1929. Doubleday, Doran & Company, Inc.

Peter Francisco, Virginia Giant. Janet Shaffer. LC 76-25334. (Illus.). 7.50 (ISBN 0-87716-068-6). Moore Pub. Co.

Peter Good for Nothing: A Story of the Minnesota Logging Camps. Darragh Aldrich. LC 29-7070. 1929. The Macmillan Company.

Peter Gott: The Cape Ann Fisherman. Joseph Reynolds. 1856. J. P. Jewett & Company.

Peter Homunculus, a Novel. Gilbert Cannan. LC 9-12880. 1909. Duffield and Company.

Peter Ibbetson. George Louis Palmella Busson Du Maurier & Deems Taylor. LC 70-144992. 1973. 19.00 (ISBN 0-403-00920-0). Scholarly Press.

Peter Ibbetson. George Louis Palmella Busson Du Maurier. LC 4-22078. Harper & Brothers.

Peter Ibbetson. George Louis Palmella Busson Du Maurier. LC 4-15307. 1892. Harper & Brothers.

Peter Ibbetson. George Louis Palmella Busson Du Maurier. LC 18-4348. 1893. Harper & Brothers.

Peter Ibbetson. George Louis Palmella Busson Du Maurier & Collier, Constance. LC 17-19504. 1917. Harper & Brothers.

Peter Ibbetson. George Louis Palmella Busson Du Maurier. LC 22-24772. 1919. Harper & Brothers.

Peter Ibbetson. George Louis Palmella Busson Du Maurier & Taylor, Deems. LC 31-3838. 1931. Harper & Brothers.

Peter Ibbetson. George Louis Palmella Busson Du Maurier & Taylor, Deems. LC 32-35808. (Half-title: The modern library of the world's best books). 1932. The Modern Library.

Peter Ibbetson. George Louis Palmella Busson Du Maurier. LC 43-42712. 1900. Harper & Brothers.

Peter Ibbetson with an Introduction by His Cousin Lady ("Madge Plunket") Ed. by George Du Maurier. 1979. Repr. of 1891 ed. lib. bdg. 25.00 (ISBN 0-8495-1044-9). Arden Lib.

Peter in Peril. Victor Bridges. LC 35-7535. The Enn Publishing Company.

Peter Jameson: A Modern Romance. Gilbert Frankau. LC 20-3796. 1920. A. A. Knopf.

Peter Kindred. Robert Nathan. LC 20-1889. 1919. 2.00. Duffield and Company.

Peter Lavelle. John Brophy. LC 30-152214. 1929. E. P. Dutton & Co. Inc.

Peter Marvell. John Hazard Wildman. LC 53-7696. Bruce Humphries.

Peter Middleton. Henry Kingdon Marks. LC 19-707796. R. G. Badger.

Peter of New Amsterdam: A Story of Old New York. James Otis Kaler. LC 10-13921. American Book Company.

Peter Pan Bag. Lee Kingman, pseud. 1971. pap. 1.50 (ISBN 0-440-96822-4, LFL). Dell.

Peter Pan's Daughter. Anita Blackmon Smith. LC 37-23533. 1937. Arcadia House.

Peter Paragon: A Tale of Youth. John Leslie Palmer, pseud. LC 15-209898. 1915. Dodd, Mead & Company.

Peter Pert's Outings. Della Thomas Hughson. LC 7-5412. 1891. H. H. Otis.

Peter-Peter: A Romance Out of Town. Maude Lavinia Radford Warren. LC 9-13914. 1909. Harper & Brothers.

Peter Ploddy: And Other Oddities. Joseph Clay Neal. LC 7-23105. 1844. Carey & Hart.

Peter Porter Reads from His Own Work. Peter Porter. 1974. 9.95x (ISBN 0-7022-0908-2); pap. 2.50. U of Queensland Pr.

Peter Rabbit: Retold by Wallace C. Wadsworth. Illustrated by Anne Sellers Leaf. Beatrix Potter & Wallace Carter Wadsworth. LC 56-6742. (Rand McNally giant book). 1956. Rand McNally.

Peter Ruff and the Double-Four. Edward Phillips Oppenheim. LC 12-1001. 1912. 1.25. Little, Brown, and Company.

Peter Rugg, the Missing Man. William Austin. LC 72-104409. 1970. (ISBN 0-8398-0071-1). Literature House.

Peter Rugg: The Missing Man. William Austin & Higginson, Thomas Wentworth. LC 11-245584. 1910. J. W. Luce & Co.

Peter Salt. James Peter Gardner. LC 48-8772. 1948. B. Humphries.

Peter Sanders: Retired. Gordon Hall Gerould. 1917. 1.50. C. Scribner's Sons.

Peter Schlemihl. Adelbert Von Chamisso. Tr. by Bowring, John. Pogany, Willy. LC 29-21941. D. McKay Co.

Peter Schlemihl in America... George Wood. LC 8-37558. 1848. Carey and Hart.

Peter Schlemilh see Three Great Classics.

Peter Simple. Frederick Marryat. (Half-title: Everyman's library, ed. by Ernest Rhys. Fiction). 1907. J. M. Dent & Co.

Peter Simple. Frederick Marryat. LC 22-5145. (Half-title: Everyman's library, ed. Ernest Rhys. Fiction. no. 232). 1921. J. M. Dent. & Sons, Ltd.

Peter Simple: Or, The Adventures of a Midshipman. Frederick Marryat. (Seaside library, v. 17, no. 340). 1878. G. Munro.

Peter Stories. Gladys Hindmarch. LC 77-362949. Coach House Press.

Peter Strutt: A Novel. Edward Davis. LC 49-4672. Dorrance.

Peter the Brazen: A Mystery Story of Modern China. George Frank Worts. LC 19-15556. 1919. J. B. Lippincott Company.

Peter the Czar. Alfred Henschke & Herman George Schaeffauer. LC 25-23115. 1925. G. P. Putnam's Sons.

Peter the Drunk. Charles Wertenbaker. LC 29-5967. 1929. H. Liveright.

Peter the First. Tolstoi, Aleksei Nikolaevich, Graf. LC 59-11459. 1959. Macmillan.

Peter the Priest. Mor Jokai. Tr. by Waite, S. L. LC 7-11925. R. F. Fenno & Company.

Peter the Second. Bruce Marshall. LC 77-356530. 1976. 2.95 (ISBN 0-09-461150-5). Constable.

Peter, the Whaler. William Henry Giles Kingston. (Lovell's library, v. 5, no. 254). 1883. J. W. Lovell Company.

Peter the Whaler: His Early Life and Adventures in the Arctic Regions. William Henry Giles Kingston. (On cover: Seaside library. Pocket ed., no. 133). 1884. G. Munro.

Peter the Whaler: His Early Life and Adventures in the Arctic Regions. 10th thousand. with illustrations by e. duncan. ed. William Henry Giles Kingston. LC 42-29636. E. P. Dutton & Co.

Peter Ujvari's By Candlelight. Peter Ujvari. LC 76-749. 18.00 (ISBN 0-8386-1895-2). Associated University Presses.

Peter Vacuum. Anthony Gibbs. LC 25-18702. 1925. L. MacVeagh, The Dial Press.

Peter Was Married. Allen Edgar Fletcher. LC 24-20152. 1924. G. P. Putnam's Sons.

Peter Whiffle: His Life and Works. Carl Van Vechten. LC 22-8592. 1922. A. A. Knopf.

Peter Whiffle: His Life and Works. Carl Van Vechten. LC 27-19179. 1927. A. A. Knopf.

Peter Whiffle, His Life and Works. Carl Van Vechten. LC 77-78306. 1981. 29.50 (ISBN 0-404-15126-4). AMS Press.

Peterkin Papers. Lucretia Peabody Hale. LC 31-82277. 1880. J. R. Osgood and Company.

Peter's Mother. New Ed., with Introduction. Elizabeth Bonham De La Pasture. 1906. E. P. Dutton & Company.

Peter's Pence. Jon Cleary. 1975. pap. 1.75 o.p. (ISBN 0-515-03753-2). Pyramid Pubns.

Peter's Pence; a Novel. Jon Cleary. LC 73-20709. 1974. 6.95 (ISBN 0-688-00252-8). Morrow.

Peter's Wife. Vera Murdock Stuart Jervis. LC 44-270355. 1944. Arcadia House, Inc.

Peter's Wife. A Novel. Margaret Wolfe Hamilton Hungerford. LC 7-905864. (On cover: Lippincott's select novels. no. 161). 1894. J. B. Lippincott Company.

Peter's Wife: An "Autobiography.". Rex Miller. LC 75-314. 1968. 5.95. Bible Books.

Petersburg. Andrei Bely, pseud. Tr. by Robert A. Maguire & John E. Malmstad. LC 77-74442. (Midland Bks.: No. 219). 384p. 1978. 22.50x (ISBN 0-253-34410-7); pap. 6.95x (ISBN 0-253-20219-1). Ind U Pr.

Petersburg. Boris Nikolaevich Bugaev. LC 77-74442. (Columbia University. Russian Institute. Sources & Translation Ser.). 17.50 (ISBN 0-253-34410-7). Indiana University Press.

Petersburg-Cannes Express. Hans Koning. LC 74-30413. (Helen & Kurt Wolff Bk.). 234p. 1975. 6.95 o.p. (ISBN 0-15-171715-X). HarBraceJ.

Petersburg-Cannes Express. Hans Koning. 1977. pap. 1.75 o.p. BJ Pub Group.

Petersburg-Cannes Express. 1 ed. Hans Koningsberger. LC 74-30413. 1975. 6.95 (ISBN 0-15-171715-X). Harcourt Brace Jovanovich.

Pete's Devils. Charles Abel Adams. LC 2-20388. 1902. Scroll Publishing Company.

Petey Simmons at Siwash. George Helgeson Fitch. LC 16-162613. 1916. Little, Brown, and Company.

Petit Garcon De l'Ascenseur. Paul Vialar. Ed. by J. R. Miller. (Fr). 1959. pap. text ed. 5.25 o.p. (ISBN 0-395-04897-4, 3-37650). HM.

Petit Prince. Antoine De Saint-Exupery. (Illus., Fr.). pap. 1.95. Schoenhof.

Petite Pallace of Pettie His Pleasure Containing Many Pretie Histories by Him Set Forth in Comely Colours and Most Delightfully Discoursed. George Pettie. LC 72-124763. 1970. AMS Press.

Petite Pallace of Pettie His Pleasure. George Pettie. Ed. by Herbert Weidler Hartman. LC 78-13394. 1970. Barnes & Noble.

Petite Pallace of Pettie His Pleasure. George Pettie. Ed. by Hartman, Herbert Welder. LC 38-34088. 1938. Oxford University Press.

Petites Employees. Maurice D'Apinac. (Black Circle Ser). 1968. 5.00 o.p. (GP449). Grove.

Petitio Principlii: A Free-Wheeling Novel. Kevork Injajikian. 1978. 6.50. William-F.

Petlands... Nard Jones. LC 31-24147. Brewer, Warren & Putnam, Inc.

Petomane. Jean Nohain. 96p. 1967. 2.50 o.p. (ISBN 0-8202-0072-7). Sherbourne.

Petra: "on This Rock I Will Build...". Julie McDonald & Judy LaMotte. LC 78-6753. (Illus.). 1978. 8.95 (ISBN 0-8138-1260-7). Iowa State University Press.

Petrakis Reader. Harry Mark Petrakis. LC 77-15180. 1978. 10.00. (ISBN 0-385-13421-5) (ISBN 0-385-13508-4). Doubleday.

Petrarch, Scipio, & the Africa: The Birth of Humanism's Dream. Aldo S. Bernardo. 1962. 10.00x o.p. (ISBN 0-8018-0069-2). Johns Hopkins.

Petrarch's Secret: Or, The Soul's Conflict with Passion: Three Dialogues Between Himself and S. Augustine. Francesco Petrarca. LC 76-7978. 1976. 20.00 (ISBN 0-8482-0500-6). Norwood Editions.

Petrella at Q. Michael Francis Gilbert. LC 77-3790. 8.95 (ISBN 0-06-011539-4). Harper & Row.

Petrie Estate. Helen Dawes Brown. LC 6-18944. 1893. Houghton, Mifflin and Company.

Petrified Gesture: A Novel. Mary Fanning Wickham, pseud. LC 50-11052. 1951. Lippincott.

Petrified Planet: The Long View, by Fletcher Pratt. Uller Uprising, by H. Beam Piper. Daughters of Earth, by Judith Merril. With an Introd. by John D. Clark. Fletcher Pratt. LC 53-203. (Twayne science fiction triplet). 1952. Twayne Publishers.

Petrodollar Takeover. Peter Tanous & Paul Rubinstein. LC 74-30582. 1975. 7.95 (ISBN 0-399-11510-2). Putnam.

Petrograd Consignment. Owen Sela. LC 78-31309. 9.95 (ISBN 0-8037-6644-0). Dial Press/James Wade.

Petronella's Waterloo. Sally James. 224p. (Orig.). pap. 1.75 (ISBN 0-449-50125-6, Coventry). Fawcett.

Petronilla: And Other Stories. Eleanor Cecilia Donnelly. LC 6-33728. 1896. Benziger Brothers.

Petronilla Heroven. Una Lucy Silberrad. LC 4-69. 1903. Doubleday, Page & Company.

Petronilla. The Sister. Emma Homan Thayer. LC 8-27754. F. T. Neely.

Petrovka Thirty-Eight. Julian Semyonov. LC 65-22271. 205p. 1974. pap. 1.95 (ISBN 0-8128-1745-1). Stein & Day.

Petrovka 38: By Julian Semyonov. Tr. from Russian by Michael Scammel. Julian Semenovich Semenov. LC 65-22271. bds., 4.95. Stein & Day.

Petruck: Prayer-to-God. Frank E Potts. LC 29-4423. Kahoe & Company.

Petter. Beatrice Burton Morgan. LC 27-3687. Grosset & Dunlap.

Pettibone Name: A New England Story. Harriet Mulford Stone Lothrop. LC 7-14770. D. Lothrop and Company.

Pettibone Name: A New England Story. Harriet Mulford Stone Lothrop. (On cover: The household library. no. 1). 1885. D. Lothrop and Company.

Petticoat Court: A Novel. Maud Hart Lovelace. LC 30-269019. The John Day Company.

Petticoat Government. Emmuska Orezy. 1910. Repr. lib. bdg. 20.00 (ISBN 0-8414-9229-8). Folcroft.

Petticoat Government: A Novel. Frances Milton Trollope. LC 52-48514. 1873. Harper.

Petticoat King. Miriam Michelson. LC 29-28885. 1929. R. M. McBride & Company.

Petticoat Rule. Emmuska Orczy. LC 10-18382. Hodder & Stoughton Etc.

Petticoat Town: A Novel. H E Winans. LC 53-7502. 1953. Dorrance.

Petticoat Wagon Train. Wayne C Lee. 1978. 1.75 (ISBN 0-441-66150-5). Ace Books.

Petticoat War in the White House: A Novelized Biography of Peggy O'Neill. Charles Keats. LC 73-173397. 1973. 6.95. Heritage Hall.

Petting Zoo. Brett Singer. LC 79-9299. 9.95 (ISBN 0-671-24942-8). Simon and Schuster.

Pettison Twins. Marion Hill. 1906. McClure, Phillips & Co.

Petty Annoyances of Married Life. From the French of Honore De Balzac; Tr. by O. W. Wight and F. B. Goodrich. Honore De Balzac. Tr. by Orlando Williams Wight. Goodrich, Frank Boott, 1826-1894, Tr. LC 6-6301. (Half-title: Novels of M. Honore de Balzac. Library ed., v. 2). 1861. Rudd & Carleton.

Petty Demon. Fyodor Sologub. Tr. by Sam Cioran from Rus. 400p. 1983. 25.00 (ISBN 0-88233-807-2); pap. 5.95 (ISBN 0-88233-808-0). Ardis Pubs.

Petty Demon. Fyodor Sologub & Samuel D Cioran. LC 83-2723. 1983. 25.95 (ISBN 0-88233-807-2) (ISBN 0-88233-808-0). Ardis.

Petunia, Be Keerful. Anne Christopher & Hogan, Inez, Illus. LC 34-40511. Whitman Publishing Co.

Petunia Pump: A Novel. Irvine Graff. LC 41-5370. M. S. Mill Co., Inc.

Peu de Soleil dans l'Eau Froide. Francoise Sagan, pseud. 14.95. French & Eur.

Peveril of the Peak. Walter Scott. (Seaside library. v. 92, no. 1865). 1884. G. Munro.

Peveril of the Peak. Walter Scott. (Lovell's library, no. 509). 1885. J. W. Lovell Company.

Peveril of the Peak. Walter Scott. (On cover: Seaside library. Pocket ed. no. 392). 1885. G. Munro.

Peveril of the Peak... Walter Scott. Ed. by Lang, Andrew. LC 16-3382. (On cover: Waverley novels). Dana, Estes & Company.

Peveril of the Peak. Walter Scott. (Half-title: Everyman's library, ed. by Ernest Rhys. Fiction). 1907. J. M. Dent & Co.

Peveril of the Peak. Walter Scott. LC 36-37009. (Half-title: Everyman's library, ed. by Ernest Rhys. Fiction. no. 138). 1932. J. M. Dent & Sons, Ltd.

Peveril of the Peak... From the Last Rev. Ed., Containing the Author's Final Corrections, Notes, &C. parker's ed. Walter Scott. (Waverley novels: Library ed. v. 14). 1831. Bazin & Ellsworth.

Pew Group. Anthony Oliver. LC 80-2079. 1981. 9.95 (ISBN 0-385-17412-8). Published for the Crime Club by Doubleday.

Pew Group. Anthony Oliver. LC 80-502622. 1980. 10.95 (ISBN 0-434-54391-8) (ISBN 0-434-54391-8). Heinemann.

Peyton Place. Grace Metalious. LC 56-10450. 1956. Messner.

Peyton Place. Grace Metalious. LC 80-29502. (Fireside book). 1981. 5.95 (ISBN 0-671-42800-4). Simon and Schuster.

Phaedra Complex. Jeannette Eyerly. 1979. 1.50 (ISBN 0-671-29915-8). Pocket Books.

Phaedra Complex: A Novel. Jeannette Eyerly. LC 75-155797. 1971. 1.95. Lippincott.

Phaeton Condition. Douglas R Mason. LC 72-85627. 1973. 5.95 (ISBN 0-399-11048-8). Putnam.

Phaeton Condition. Douglas R Mason. (Berkley medallion book). 1974. (pbk) 0.95 (ISBN 0-425-02499-7). Berkley Pub. Co.

Phamtom in the Rainbow. Slater La Master. LC 29-21210. 1929. A. C. McClurg & Co.

Phantasmagoria. Douglas Alver Menville & R Reginald. LC 75-46292. (Supernatural & Occult Fiction). 1976. 23.00 (ISBN 0-405-08152-9). Arno Press.

Phantasmagoria: An Original Anthology. Ed. by R. Reginald & Douglas Alver Menville. LC 75-46292. (Supernatural & Occult Fiction Ser.). 1976. lib. bdg. 23.00x (ISBN 0-405-08152-9). Ayer Co.

Phantasmagoria: Tales of Fantasy and the Supernatural. Jane Mobley. LC 76-52007. 1977. 3.50. Anchor Books.

Phantasmion: Prince of Palmland... Sata Coleridge. (Coleman's library of romance). 1839. S. Colman.

Phantastes. George MacDonald. LC 74-12128. (Adult fantasy). 1970. 0.95. Ballantine Books.

Phantastes. George Macdonald. LC 37-30962. (Half-title: Everyman's library, ed. by Ernest Rhys. Romance. no. 732). 1923. J. M. Dent & Sons, Ltd.

Phantastes. George MacDonald. LC 82-5249. 1982. 10.95 (ISBN 0-8052-3815-8). Schocken Books.

Phantastes: A Faerie Romance for Men and Women. George Macdonald. (On cover: Seaside library. Pocket ed., no. 326). 1885. G. Munro.

Phantastes: A Faerie Romance for Men and Women. George Macdonald. LC 12-18327. 1911. D. McKay.

Phantastes, and Lilith. George Macdonald & George Macdonald. LC 64-16591. 1964. W. B. Eerdmans Pub. Co.

Phantasy: Zher O'Clok. J. Anthony Salvato. (Orig.). 1982. pap. 3.95 (ISBN 0-943098-00-9). Hearth Pub.

Phantom. Lee Falk. Ed. by Leonard Brown. (Illus.). 1977. pap. 5.95 (ISBN 0-87897-010-X). Nostalgia Pr.

Phantom. Thomas Tessier. LC 82-71058. 1982. 12.95 (ISBN 0-689-11328-5). Atheneum.

Phantom. A Novel. Gerhart Johann Robert Hauptmann & Morgan, Bayard Quincy, 1883-Tr. LC 23-470. 1922. B. W. Huebsch, Inc.

Phantom & Barnabas Collins. Marilyn Ross. (Dark Shadows No. 10). (Orig.). 1969. pap. 0.50 o.p. (62-195). Paperback Lib.

Phantom Army: Being the Story of a Man and a Mystery. Max Pemberton. LC 98-1421. 1898. D. Appleton and Company.

Phantom at Lost Lake. Delphine C. Lyons. (Orig.). 1970. pap. 0.75 o.p. (ISBN 0-447-74654-5). Lancer.

Phantom Bride. Leslie Ames, pseud. 192p. 1972. 3.95 o.p. Lenox Hill.

Phantom Bride. Mary M. Brown. 1976. pap. 1.50 (ISBN 0-89041-124-7, 3124). Major Bks.

Phantom Canoe. William Byron Mowery. LC 35-9329. 1935. Little, Brown, and Company.

Phantom Caravel. Ralph A Emberg. LC 48-905849. 1948. B. Humphries.

Phantom City: A Volcanic Romance. William Westall. (Harper's handy series, no. 97). 1886. Harper & Brothers.

Phantom City. A Volcanic Romance. William Westall. (On cover: Cassell's "rainbow" series, no. 18). 1888. Cassell & Company, Limited.

Phantom City. A Volcanic Romance. William Westall. (On cover: Seaside library. Pocket ed. no. 1163). 1889. G. Munro.

Phantom Clue. Gaston Leroux. LC 26-4066. The Macaulay Company.

Phantom Conspiracy. Michael Barak. LC 80-13591. 324p. 1980. 11.95 (ISBN 0-688-03689-9). Morrow.

Phantom Conspiracy. Michael Bar-Zohar. LC 80-13591. 1980. 10.95 (ISBN 0-688-03689-9). Morrow.

Phantom Corral. Harry Sinclair Drago. LC 46-3354. 1946. Dodd, Mead & Company.

Phantom Cottage. Velda Johnston. LC 78-99185. (Red Badge novel of suspense). 1970. 4.50. Dodd, Mead.

Phantom Days. A Novel. George T Welch. (sunnyside series, no. 58). 1892. J. S. Ogilvie.

Phantom Emperor. Neil Harmon Swanson. LC 34-14539. G. P. Putnam's Sons.

Phantom Emperor: The Romance and Tragedy of Napoleon III. Octave Aubry. LC 29-20594. 1929. Harper & Brothers.

Phantom Empire. Rose McCarthy Sears. 1974. 4.50. Lenox Hill Press.

Phantom-Fighter. Seabury Quinn. 5.00 o.p. Arkham.

Phantom-Fighter: Ten Memoirs of Jules De Grandin, Sometime Member of la Surete General, la Faculte De Medicine Legal De Paris, Etc., Etc. Seabury Quinn. LC 66-4166. 1966. Mycroft & Moran.

Phantom Filly: A Novel. George Agnew Chamberlain. LC 42-256855. The Bobbs-Merrill Company.

Phantom Fingers. Joseph Jefferson Farjeon. LC 31-29201. 1931. L. MacVeagh The Dial Press.

Phantom Fingers. Lyon Mearson. LC 28-17204. The Macaulay Company.

Phantom Flame of Wind House. Katheryn Kimbrough. (Large easy-to-read type.). 1973. (pbk.) 0.95. Popular Library.

Phantom Fleet. Clark Darlton. (Perry Rhodan #97). 1976. Ace Books.

Phantom Fortress. Bruce Lancaster. 1976. 1.75 (ISBN 0-523-00905-4). Pinnacle Books.

Phantom Fortune. Mary Elizabeth Braddon Maxwell. (On cover: Lovell's library, no. 214). 1883. J. W. Lovell Company.

Phantom Fortune. Mary Elizabeth Braddon Maxwell. (Seaside library. v. 85, no. 1715). 1883. G. Munro.

Phantom Fortune. Mary Elizabeth Braddon Maxwell. (On cover: Seaside library. Pocket ed. no. 56). 1883. G. Munro.

Phantom Fortune. A Novel. Mary Elizabeth Braddon Maxwell. (Harper's Franklin square library, no. 336). 1883. Harper & Brothers.

Phantom Future. ... rev. and authorized ed. Hugh Stowell Scott. LC 99-5463. 1899. Dodd, Mead & Co.

Phantom Future: A Novel. Hugh Stowell Scott. LC 3-291520. (On cover: Harper's Franklin square library, no. 644). 1889. Harper & Brothers.

Phantom Gunman. John Benteen. (Fargo Ser). (Orig.). 1971. pap. 0.75 o.p. (B75-2111). Belmont-Tower.

Phantom Gunman. John Benteen. (Fargo Ser.). (O.s.i.). 1972. pap. 0.75 o.s.i. (BT50278). Belmont-Tower.

Phantom Gunman see Pistolero Fantasma.

Phantom Herd. Bertha Muzzy Sinclair. LC 16-8232. 1916. 1.30. Little, Brown, and Company.

Phantom Hill. R. G. Choate, pseud. 1969. pap. 0.60 o.p. (0502-06047-060). Curtis.

Phantom Hill. 1st Ed. R. G. Choate. LC 60-168430. (Double D western). 1960. Doubleday.

Phantom in Red. William Edward Daniel Ross. 1982. pap. 6.95 (Avalon). Bouregy.

Phantom in the Wine. Michealina Marfa-Moya Nugent. LC 29-19597. 1929. Simon and Schuster, Inc.

Phantom Lady. Carter Brown, pseud. (Orig.). 1980. pap. 1.50 (ISBN 0-505-51516-4). Tower Bks.

Phantom Lady. Hopley-Woolrich, Cornell George. LC 67-13688. (Seagull library of mystery and suspense). 1967. Norton.

Phantom Lady. Cornell George Hopley-Woolrich. LC 42-21645. 1942. J. B. Lippincott Company.

Phantom Lady. Cornell Woolrich, pseud. 256p. 1982. pap. 2.50 (ISBN 0-345-30652-X). Ballantine.

Phantom Love. Sonya T. Pelton. (Orig.). 1982. pap. 3.50 (ISBN 0-89083-950-6). Zebra.

Phantom Lover. Ruby Mildred Ayres. LC 22-4238. W. J. Watt & Company.

Phantom Lover. Violet Paget. (On cover: Lovell's library, no 797). 1886. J. W. Lovell Company.

Phantom Lover. A Fantastic Story. Violet Paget. LC 7-3529. 1886. Roberts Brothers.

Phantom Manor. Marilyn Ross. 1970. pap. 0.60 o.p. (63-372). Paperback Lib.

Phantom Marriage. Penny Jordan. (Harlequin Presents Ser.). 192p. 1983. pap. 1.95 (ISBN 0-373-10591-6). Harlequin Bks.

Phantom of Belle Acres. Marilyn Ross. (Empress Gothic). 1973. 0.95. Curtis Books.

Phantom of Edgewater Hall. William Edward Daniel Ross. (YA) 1980. 6.95 (Avalon). Bouregy.

Phantom of Featherford Falls. Marilyn Ezzell. (Susan Sand Mystery: No. 5). 192p. 1983. pap. 1.95 (ISBN 0-523-41744-6). Pinnacle Bks.

Phantom of Fonthill Park. Kay R Vernon. LC 76-10522. 1976. 5.95 (ISBN 0-385-12384-1). Doubleday.

Phantom of Forty-Second Street. Milton Raison & Harvey, Jack. LC 36-3134. The Macaulay Company.

Phantom of Forty-Second Street. Milton Michael Raison & Harvey, Jack, Joint Author. LC 36-3134. 1936. The Macaulay Company.

Phantom of Glencourt. Clarissa Ross, pseud. (Orig.). 1972. pap. 0.95 o.s.i. (75-349). Lancer.

Phantom of Lost Lake Mountain. Jim Shelton. LC 57-54014. 1957. Dorrance.

Phantom of the Caballo Mountains. Viola M. Payne & Rebecca Taggart. 1977. 5.95 o.p. (ISBN 0-533-02921-X). Vantage.

Phantom of the Opera. Gaston Leroux. LC 11-1449. The Bobbs-Merrill Company.

Phantom of the Paradise. Bjarne Rostaing & Brian De Palma. (Illus.). 1975. (pbk.) 1.25. Dell.

Phantom of the Rock Concert. Lee Hays. (Partridge Family #12). 1973. 0.60. Curtis Books.

Phantom of the Sacred Well. Phyllis G Leonard. LC 75-33092. (ISBN 0-679-50551-2). D. McKay Co.

Phantom of the Shore: A Folktale. Lawrence Leeds. LC 28-47705. The Acorn Press.

Phantom of the Swamp. William Edward Daniel Ross. LC 73-189806. (Paperback library gothic). 1972. 0.95 (ISBN 0-446-65829-4). Paperback Library.

Phantom of the Temple. Robert Van Gulik. (Judge Dee Mystery). 1979. pap. 1.95 (ISBN 0-684-16178-8, SL857, ScribT). Scribner.

Phantom of the Temple. Robert Van Gulik. 1967. 3.95 o.p. (ISBN 0-684-10618-3). Scribner.

Phantom of the Temple: A Chinese Detective Story, by Robert Van Gulik. Nine Illus. Drawn by the Author in Chinese Style. Robert Hans Van Gulik, pseud. (His New Judge Dee mysteries). 1967. 3.95. Scribners.

Phantom of the 13th Floor. Marilyn Ross. (Queen-size gothic). 1975. (pbk.) 1.25. Popular Library.

Phantom on Skis. Helen Girvan. LC 39-4494. Farrar & Rinehart, Inc.

Phantom Pass. A Double D Western. William Colt MacDonald. LC 40-33590. 1940. Doubleday, Doran and Co., Inc.

Phantom Passenger. Mansfield Scott. LC 27-13128. E. J. Clode, Inc.

Phantom President. George Frank Worts. LC 32-9883. J. Cape & R. Ballou.

Phantom Reflection. Ann Ashton, pseud. LC 77-82612. 1978. 6.95 o.p. (ISBN 0-385-12200-4). Doubleday.

Phantom Reflection. John M. Kimbro. LC 77-82612. 1978. 6.95 (ISBN 0-385-12200-4). Doubleday.

Phantom Regiment: Or, Stories of "Ours,". James Grant. LC 44-16858. G. Routldege and Sons.

Phantom Rickshaw. Rudyard Kipling. LC 98-499. H. Altemus.

Phantom Rickshaw. Rudyard Kipling. LC 4872. H. M. Caldwell Company.

Phantom Rickshaw and Other Ghost Stories. Rudyard Kipling. LC 39-17499. 1899. R. F. Fenno & Company.

Phantom 'rickshaw, and Other Stories. Rudyard Kipling. LC 27-7336. (American home classics). J. H. Sears & Company, Inc.

Phantom 'rickshaw: And Other Tales. authorized ed. Rudyard Kipling. LC 7-12345. (On cover: Lovell's international series, no. 108). 1890. J. W. Lovell Company.

Phantom 'rickshaw: And Other Tales. Rudyard Kipling. LC 19-725. A. L. Burt Company.

Phantom 'rickshaw: And Other Tales. Rudyard Kipling. LC 42-27484. Hurst and Company.

Phantom 'rickshaw, City of Dreadful Night, and Other Tales. Rudyard Kipling. LC 9-3021. The Lovell Company.

Phantom 'rickshaw. The Works of Rudyard Kipling. Rudyard Kipling. LC 9-16373. 1909. The Nottingham Society.
Phantom Rider. John H. Hamlin. LC 40-8001. Dodge Publishing Company.
Phantom Rider. John Harold Hamlin. LC 40-8001. 1940. Dodge Publishing Company.
Phantom Riders. A. Leslie. LC 45-220547. 1945. Arcadia House, Inc.
Phantom Rubies. Lucile V. Stevens. (YA) 1979. 6.95 (Avalon). Bouregy.
Phantom Rustlers. Jesse Edward Grinstead. Dodge Publishing Company.
Phantom Rustlers. Francis W Hilton. LC 34-308690. 1934. H. C. Kinsey & Company, Inc.
Phantom Setter & Other Stories. Robert Murphy. (Illus.). 1966. 5.50 o.p. (ISBN 0-525-17853-8). Dutton.
Phantom Setter, and Other Stories. By Robert Murphy, Illus. by John Schoenherr. 1st Ed. Robert William Murphy. LC 66-21305. 1966. 4.95. Dutton.
Phantom Sheriff. Walker A Tompkins. LC 41-787020. Phoenix Press.
Phantom Ship. Frederick Marryat. LC 7-24680. (On cover: Seaside library. Pocket ed. no. 1230). G. Munro.
Phantom Spur. Norman A Fox. LC 50-9586. (Silver star westerns). 1950. Dodd, Mead.
Phantom Spy. Max Brand. 1973. 4.95 o.p. (ISBN 0-396-06745-X). Dodd.
Phantom Spy: A Novel of Adventure. Frederick Faust. LC 72-7753. 1973. 4.95 (ISBN 0-396-06745-X). Dodd, Mead.
Phantom Stallions. Robert A. Shaw. (Orig.). 1979. pap. 1.95. Woodhill.
Phantom Victory: The Fourth Reich: 1945-1960. Erwin Christian Lessner. LC 44-8272. 1944. G. P. Putman's Sons.
Phantom Walls. Oliver Lodge. 5.95 o.p. (ISBN 0-8283-1298-2). Branden.
Phantom Warrior. Fred Grove. LC 80-2747. 1981. 9.95 (ISBN 0-385-17044-0). Doubleday.
Phantom Warrior. large print ed. Fred Grove. LC 82-713. 1982. 10.95 (ISBN 0-89621-349-8). Thorndike Press.
Phantom Wedding: Or, The Fall of the House of Flint. Emma Dorothy Eliza Nevitte Southworth & Frances Henshaw Baden. LC 8-10830. T. B. Peterson & Brothers.
Phantom Wife. Metta Victoria Fuller Victor. (select series. no. 12). 1888. Street & Smith.
Phantom Wires. Arthur John Arbuthnott Stringer. LC 23-6146. The Bobbs-Merrill Company.
Phantom Wires: A Novel. Arthur John Arbuthnott Stringer. LC 7-12004. 1907. Little, Brown, and Company.
Phantom with Wings of Gold: A Novel. Vicente Blasco Ibanez & Livingston, Arthur, 1883- Tr. LC 31-480751. E. P. Dutton & Co. Inc.
Phantoms: A Collection of Stories. Barton Midwood. LC 72-108893. 1970. 5.95. Dutton.
Phantoms and Fantasies: 20 Tales. Rudyard Kipling. (Illus.). 1965. Doubleday.
Phantoms and Fugitives: Journeys to the Improbable. Jose Maria Gironella. LC 63-17135. 1964. Sheed and Ward.
Phantoms & Fugitives: Journeys to the Improbable. Jose Maria Gironella. Tr. by Terry B. Fontsere. 1964. 3.95 o.p. (ISBN 0-8362-0011-X, Pub. by Sheed). Twin Circle.
Phantoms, & Other Stories. facsimile ed. Ivan Sergeevich Turgenev. Tr. by I. F. Hapgood from Rus. LC 79-169566. (Short Story Index Reprint Ser.). Repr. of 1904 ed. 18.00 (ISBN 0-8369-4029-6). Ayer Co.
Phantoms of Dixie. Hans Holzer. pap. 1.50 o.p. (6631). Mockingbird Bks.
Phantoms of Fame. Heald Bentley. LC 32-330492. 1932. Meador Publishing Company.
Phantoms of the Foot-Bridge: And Other Stories. Mary Noailles Murfree. 1895. Harper & Brothers.
Phantoms of the Footbridge: And Other Stories. Mary Noailles Murfree. LC 69-11912. (American short story series, v. 71). (Illus.). 1969. Garrett Press.
Phantoms of the Footbridge, and Other Stories. Mary Noailles Murfree. LC 72-8153. (American short story series, v. 71). 1972. (ISBN 0-8422-8100-2). MSS Information Corp.
Pharaoh. Eloise Jarvis McGraw. LC 58-7007. 1958. Coward-McCann.
Pharaoh and the Priest: An Historical Novel of Ancient Egypt, from the Original Polish of Alexander Glovatski. Aleksander Glowacki, pseud. Tr. by Curtin, Jeremiah. 1902. Little, Brown and Company.
Pharaoh's Broker. Ellsworth Douglass. LC 76-9767. (Gregg Press science fiction series). 1976. 15.00 (ISBN 0-8398-2342-8). Gregg Press.
Pharaoh's Chicken. Nicholas Wollaston. LC 74-77870. 1969. 4.95. Lippincott.
Pharaoh's Treasure: An Egyptian Romance. Luman Allen. LC 6-48. (On cover: Dearborn series, no. 47). 1891. Donohue, Henneberry & Co.
Pharisee and the Publican. R. E. Boyns. LC 11-845. 1910. 1.50. Broadway Publishing Co.
Pharisees. Muriel Morgan Gibbon. LC 22-5369. 1922. Doubleday, Page & Company.
Pharisees and Publicans: A Novel. Edward Frederic Benson. George H. Doran Company.
Pharos. Ellery Harding Clark. LC 13-21261. 1.25. R. G. Badger.
Pharos: Or, John Bubb's Jour. George Clary Wing. LC 19-16036.
Pharos, the Egyptian. Guy Newell Boothby. LC 75-46256. (Supernatural and Occult Fiction). 1976. 22.00 (ISBN 0-405-08115-4). Arno Press.
Pharos, the Egyptian: A Romance. Guy Newell Boothby. LC 99-1263. (Half-title: Appleton's town and country library, no. 261). 1899. D. Appleton and Company.
Pharsamond; or, the New Knight-Errant, 1750, 2 vols. in 1. Pierre Corlet de Chamblain de Marivaux. LC 74-17039. (Novel in England, 1700-1775 Ser). 1974. lib. bdg. 50.00 (ISBN 0-8240-1129-5). Garland Pub.
Phase IV. Barry N Malzberg. 1973. (pbk.) 0.95. Pocket Books.
Phase of Darkness: A Novel. Robin Moore & Al Dempsey. LC 73-92799. 1974. 8.95 (ISBN 0-89388-136-8). Third Press.
Phase Three Alert: A Novel. John Dudley Ball. LC 76-56162. 8.95 (ISBN 0-316-07937-5). Little, Brown.
Phases of an Inferior Planet: A Novel. Ellen Anderson Gholson Glasgow. LC 98-479. 1898. Harper & Brothers.
Pheasant-Lined Vest of Charlie Freeman: A Novel of Wall Street. John D Spooner. LC 67-11234. 1967. Little, Brown.
Pheasants Had No Tails: And Other Tales. LC 52-20302. 1950. G. R. Reeve.
Phebe: Or, The Ewings of Killian Hook. Mary Harriott Norris. LC 7-33300. 1890. Hunt & Eaton.
Phelps and His Teachers. 2d ed. Dan Voorhees Stephens. LC 2-17552. 1902. Hammond Bros. & Stephens.
Phemie Frost's Experiences. Ann Sophia Winterbotham Stephens. LC 8-12407. 1874. G. W. Carleton & Co.; Etc., Etc.
Phemie's Temptation. A Novel. Mary Virginia Terhune. LC 8-260592. 1869. Carleton.
Phemie's Temptation. A Novel. Mary Virginia Terhune. LC 8-26060. 1897. G. W. Dillingham Co.
Phenomenal Identity. Chancie De Witt. LC 6-33396. (On cover: Minerva series, no. 32). 1890. The Minerva Publishing Co.
Phi Betta Fanny. Norman Jackson. pap. 1.25 o.p. Lancer.
Phil & Me. Martin Woodhouse. LC 78-123632. 1970. 4.95. Coward-McCann.
Phil Preston: Or, Into the Light... Ella S Birdsell. 1888. Phillips & Hunt.
Phil Scott, the Detective. Judson R Taylor. LC 1-30196. (On cover: Magnet detective library, no. 163). 1900. Street & Smith.
Philadelphia Experiment. William Moore & Charles Berlitz. 224p. 1980. pap. 2.75 (ISBN 0-449-24280-3, Crest). Fawcett.
Philadelphia Murder Story. Zenith Jones Brown. LC 45-3130. 1945. C. Scribner's Sons.
Philadelphian. Richard Pitts Powell. LC 56-12445. 1956. Scribner.
Philadelphian: A Novel. Louis John Jennings. (On cover: Harper's Franklin square library. no. 697). 1891. Harper & Brothers.
Philadelphias. Katharine Bingham. LC 3-2699. (On verso of half-title: Page's commonwealth series, no. 7). 1903. L. C. Page & Company.
Philanderers. Alfred Edward Woodley Mason. LC 41-311192. 1897. Macmillan and Co., Limited.
Philanthropist. Intro. by H. E. Holt. pap. 1.95 o.p. (6032). Brandon.
Philbrick Howell: A Novel. Albert Kinross. LC 1-31552. Frederick A. Stokes Company.
Phileas Fox: Attorney. Anna Theresa Sadlier. The Ave Maria.
Philharmonic. Herbert Russcol & Margalit Banai. LC 70-136441. 1971. 6.95. Coward McCann & Geoghagen.
Philidore & Placentia, or l'Amour Trop Delicat see Four Before Richardson: Selected English Novels, 1720-1727.
Philip and Aurelia: A Novel. John McClelland Work. LC 57-8109. 1957. Comet Press Books.
Philip and His Wife. Margaret Wade Campbell Deland. LC 6-333802. 1894. Houghton, Mifflin and Company.
Philip Desmond. Cora S Day. LC 4326. American Tract Society.
Philip Earnscliffe: Or, The Morals of May Fair. Annie Edwards. (Lovell's library. no. 1371). 1889. J. W. Lovell Company.
Philip Earnscliffe: Or, The Morals of May Fair. A Novel. Annie Edwards. (On cover: Seaside library. Pocket ed. no. 845). 1886. G. Munro.
Philip Gerard, an Individual. Edward Amherst Ott. Drake University, College of Oratory and English.
Philip Harum, the Nihilist Student. Mary Lee Berry. LC 6-103773. 1892. I. H. Brown Publishing Company.
Philip Henson, M.D. A Novel. George Hastings. (On cover: Vanity fair series, no. 1). 1891. E. Brandus & Co.
Philip Jose Farmer: The Complete Riverworld Novels, 5 bks. Philip J. Farmer. Incl. To Your Scattered Bodies Go; Fabulous Riverboat; Dark Design; Riverworld; Magic Labyrinth. 1982. Boxed Set. pap. 13.25 (ISBN 0-425-05835-2). Berkley Pub.
Philip Longstreth: A Novel. Marie Van Vorst. LC 2-11139. 1902. Harper & Bros.
Philip MacGregor: A Novel. William Wilberforce Newton. LC 7-32302. 1895. The Student Publishing Company.
Philip Meyer's Scheme. A Story of Trades Unionism. Archibald McCowan. (sunnyside series, no. 67). 1892. J. S. Ogilvie.
Philip Nolan's Friends. Edward Everett Hale. LC 70-104470. (Illus.). 1970. Literature House.
Philip Nolan's Friends: A Story of the Change of Western Empire. Edward Everett Hale. LC 6-46193. 1877. Scribner, Armstrong, and Company.
Philip Nolan's Friends: A Story of the Change of Western Empire. Edward Everett Hale. LC 4-15114. (Half-title: The works of E. E. Hale. Library ed. vol. V). 1899. Little, Brown, and Company.
Philip Nolan's Friends: A Story of the Change of Western Empire. Edward Everett Hale. LC 16-25052. (Half-title: The works of Edward Everett Hale. Library ed. vol. V). 1915. Little, Brown, and Company.
Philip: Or, The Mollie's Secret. A Tale of the Coal Regions. Patrick Justin McMahon. LC 7-20426. (On cover: Catholic library). H. L. Kilner & Co.
Philip: Or, What May Have Been; a Story of the First Century. Mary C Cutler. LC 6-32237. T. Y. Crowell & Co.
Philip Paternoster. Charles Maurice Davies. LC 75-477. (Victorian Fiction: Novels of Faith and Doubt; V. 31). 1975. 35.00 (ISBN 0-8240-1555-X). Garland Pub.
Philip Paternoster: A Tractarian Love Story, 1858. Charles Maurice Davies. Ed. by Robert L. Wolff. LC 75-477. (Victorian Fiction Ser.). 1975. lib. bdg. 66.00 (ISBN 0-8240-1555-X). Garland Pub.
Philip Roth Reader. Philip Roth. LC 80-19790. 17.50 (ISBN 0-374-23170-2) (ISBN 0-374-51604-9). Farrar, Straus, Giroux.
Philip Segal: Essays & Lectures. Ed. by Marcia Leveson. (Illus.). 223p. 1973. pap. 4.50x (ISBN 0-8476-2402-1). Rowman.
Philip Seymour: Or Pioneer Life in Richland County, Ohio. James Franklin M'Gaw. LC 22-3021. 1858-1908. R. Brickerhoff.
Philip Seymour: Or, Pioneer Life in Richland County, Ohio. 3d ed. James Franklin M'Gaw & Baughman, Abraham J., 1838-1913. LC 22-14569. 1902. A. J. Baughman.
Philip Seymour: Or, Pioneer Life in Richland, County Ohio. 2d ed. James Franklin M'Gaw & Brinkerhoff, Roeliff, 1828-1911. LC 44-24016. 1883. The Herald, G. U. Harn & Bro.
Philip Seymour: Or, Pioneer Life in Richland County, Ohio; Founded on Facts. 3d ed. M'Gaw, James F & Baughman, Abraham J., 1838-1913. LC 22-14569. 1902. A. J. Baughman.
Philip Seymour: Or, Pioneer Life in Richland County, Ohio. Founded on Facts. James F M'Gaw & Baughman, Abraham J., 1838-1913. LC 22-3021. 1858. R. Brickerhoff.
Philip Steele of the Royal Northwest Mounted Police. James Oliver Curwood. LC 11-28360. The Bobbs-Merrill Company.
Philip Thaxter: A Novel. Charles Ames Washburn. LC 79-164578. (American fiction reprint series). 1971. (ISBN 0-8369-7055-1). Books for Libraries Press.
Philip the Draftsman. Francis X. Coleman. LC 74-85113. 1970. 4.95 o.p. (ISBN 0-397-00662-4). Lippincott.
Philip the Forester: A Roman Oif the Valley of Gardens. Daniel Edwards Kennedy. LC 9-14448. 1909. The Queen's Shop.
Philip; the Story of a Boy Violinist. Virginia C. Young & Hungerford, Mary C., Joint Author. LC 98-1715. 1898. Lamson, Wolfe & Company.
Philip Vernon: A Tale in Prose and Verse. Silas Weir Mitchell. LC 7-31093. 1895. The Century Co.
Philip Winwood: A Sketch of the Domestic History of an American Captain in the War of Independence... Written by His Enemy in War. Herbert Russell... Robert Neilson Stephens. LC 2653. 1900. L. C. Page & Company.
Philippa. rainbow romance edition condensed for modern readers. ed. Marion Naismith. (Signet Book, P5453). 1973. 0.60. New American Lib.
Philippa. Anne Douglas Sedgwick. LC 30-29905. 1930. Hougton Mifflin Company.
Philippa: Or, Under a Cloud. Ella Childs Hurlbut. LC 7-9034. ("unknown" libary v. 5). Cassell Publishing Company.
Philippe's Love Story: A Tale of Fashion and Passion in France. Octave Feuillet. 1877. The American News Company.
Philippine. Maurice Bedel. Tr. by Samuel Middlebrook. LC 32-665638. E.P. Dutton & Co., Inc.
Philippine Romance. Lillian Hathaway Mearns. LC 11-468. Aberdeen Publishing Company.
Philippines Is in the Heart: A Collection of Short Stories. Carlos Bulosan, Jr. (Illus.). 1979. pap. 7.00x (Pub. by New Day Pub). Cellar.
Philip's Mother. Ella May Smith. LC 28-297259. The Inskeep Printing Company.
Philistia. A Novel. Grant Allen. LC 6-481. (On cover: Seaside library. Pocket ed. no. 336)). 1884. G. Munro.
Philistia. A Novel. Grant Allen. (Harper's Franklin square library, no. 430)). 1884. Harper & Brothers.
Philistines. Arlo Bates. LC 74-104412. 1970. (ISBN 0-8398-0154-8). Literature House.
Philistines. Arlo Bates. LC 4-9064. 1889. Ticknor and Company.
Phillida. Maud Elliott. LC 6-37780. (On cover: American authors' series, no. 36). 1891. J.W. Lovell Company.
Phillida: Or, The Reluctant Adventurer. H. S Reid. LC 29-238198. 1928. Houghton Mifflin Company.
Phillida's Glad Year: A Story. Grace Blanchard. LC 13-26562. W. A. Wilde Company.
Phillip Andre. Marion McDermott Perkins. LC 30-20633. 1930. Wetzel Publishing Co., Inc.
Phillipia, a Woman's Question. Hannah Maria Conant Tracy Cutler. LC 6-32239. The C. L. Palmer Printing House.
Philly: A Novel. Dan Greenburg. LC 72-75862. 1969. 4.95. Simon and Schuster.
Philly and Kit: Or, Life and Raiment. Caroline Chesebro' 1856. Redfield.
Philo: An Evangeliad. Sylvester Judd. LC 15-20645. 1850. Phillips, Sampson, and Company.
Philo Gubb: Correspondence-School Detective. Ellis Parker Butler. LC 18-185417. 1918. Houghton Mifflin Company.
Philo Vance Murder Cases: The Scarab Murder Case, The Kennel Murder Case, The Dragon Murder Case. Willard Huntington Wright. LC 36-27216. 1936. C. Scribner's Sons.
Philo Vance Week-End: Containing Three Mystery Novels. Willard Huntington Wright. 1937. Grosset & Dunlap.
Philoland. Gilbert Lane Harney. LC 1-31186. F. T. Neely Company.
Philomel Foundation. James Gollin. LC 79-22868. 10.00 (ISBN 0-312-60428-9). St. Martin's Press.
Philomena Leigh. Haze Barleau. LC 41-18040. The Christopher Publishing House.
Philomene's Marriages. A Novel. Alice Marie Celeste Durand. Tr. by Stanley, Helen. LC 6-35688. T. B. Peterson & Brothers.
Philopena. Henry Kitchell Webster. LC 27-3407. The Bobbs-Merrill Company.
Philo's Daughter: The Story of the Daughter of the Thief with Whom Christ Was Crucified. Nellie Grace Robinson. LC 9-7. Press of Jennings and Graham.
Philosopher in Love and in Uniform. William J. Arkell & Worden, A. T., Joint Author. LC 6-20479. (On cover: Judge's novels, no. 2). 1889. The Judge Publishing Co.
Philosopher of Driftwood: A Novel. Annie Jenness Miller. LC 7-25974. 1897. J. Miller Publications.
Philosopher or Dog? Machado De Assis. 288p. 1982. pap. 3.95 (ISBN 0-380-58982-6, 58982, Bard). Avon.
Philosopher's Daughter. Susan Ertz. LC 76-5537. 8.95 (ISBN 0-06-011253-0). Harper & Row.
Philosophers in Trouble: A Volume of Stories. Lawrence Pearsall Jacks. LC 77-125224. (Short Story Index Reprint Ser). 1916. 12.00 (ISBN 0-8369-3591-8). Ayer Co.
Philosopher's Murder Case. Jack Randall Crawford. LC 31-30606. Sears Publishing Company, Inc.
Philosopher's Pupil. Iris Murdoch. 1983. 17.75 (ISBN 0-670-55186-4). Viking Pr.
Philosopher's Stone. Colin Wilson. 320p. 1974. pap. 2.95 (ISBN 0-446-33030-2). Warner Bks.
Philosopher's Stone. Colin Wilson. 1979. pap. 4.95 (ISBN 0-914728-28-8). Wingbow Pr.
Philosopher's Stone: A Novel. Colin Wilson. (rediscovery series). 1974. (pbk.) 1.75. Warner Paperback Lib.
Philosopher's Stone: A Novel. Colin Wilson. LC 77-147331. 1971. 5.95. Crown Publishers.
Philosophy: An Autobiographical Fragment. Ettie Stettheimer. LC 17-5129. 1917. 1.25. Longmans, Green and Co.
Philosophy of Josiah Royce. Josiah Royce. Ed. by John K. Roth. 1971. pap. 2.95 o.p. (ISBN 0-8152-0300-4, A300). Apollo Eds.

Philosophy 4: A Story of Harvard University. Owen Wister. LC 3-12289. (Half-title: Little novels by favourite authors). 1903. The Macmillan Company.

Philosphers in Trouble: A Volume of Stories. Lawrence Pearsall Jacks. LC 77-125224. (Short story index reprint series). 1970. Books for Libraries Press.

Philothea: A Grecian Romance. ... new and cor. ed. Lydia Maria Francis Child. LC 16-339580. 1851. C. S. Francis & Co.

Philothea: A Grecian Romance. ... a new and cor. ed. Lydia Maria Francis Child. LC 6-20979. 1861. T. O. H. P. Burnham.

Philothea: a Romance. Lydia Maria Francis Child. LC 72-85682. (American fiction reprint series). 1969. Books for Libraries Press.

Philothea. A Romance... 2d ed. Lydia Maria Francis Child. LC 7-4425. 1839. Otis, Broaders & Company.

Philothea: Or, Plato Against Epicurus: a Novel of the Transcendental Movement in New England. Lydia Maria Francis Child & Kenneth Walter Cameron. LC 75-327615. (Illus.). Transcendental Books.

Phil's Happy Girlhood: A Story by Grace Blanchard; with Illustrations by William F. Stecher. Grace Blanchard. LC 10-278582. W. A. Wilde Company.

Phineas. John Knowles. LC 68-31536. (OSI). 1968. 4.95 o.s.i. (ISBN 0-394-44039-0). Random.

Phineas Finn. Anthony Trollope. 17.95 o.p. (ISBN 0-19-250447-9, WC447). Oxford U Pr.

Phineas Finn. Anthony Trollope. (Illus.). 1973. pap. 5.95 (ISBN 0-19-281144-4). Oxford U Pr.

Phineas Finn. Anthony Trollope. Ed. by John Sutherland. (English Library). 1978. pap. 4.95 (ISBN 0-14-043085-7). Penguin.

Phineas Finn: The Irish Member. Anthony Trollope. Ed. by John Sutherland. LC 73-159064. (Penguin English library). (Illus.). 1972. 0.65 (ISBN 0-14-043085-7). Penguin.

Phineas Finn: The Irish Member. Anthony Trollope. LC 8-28883. 1868. Harper & Brothers.

Phineas Finn: The Irish Member. Anthony Trollope. LC 4-17598. (On cover: The parliamentary novels. ii). 1893. Dodd, Mead & Company.

Phineas Finn: The Irish Member. Anthony Trollope. LC 37-31197. (Half-title: Everyman's library, ed. by Ernest Rhys. Fiction. no. 832-833). 1929. J. M. Dent & Sons, Ltd.

Phineas Finn: The Irish Member. Anthony Trollope. LC 38-16875. (Half-title: Everyman's library, ed. by Ernest Rhys. Fiction. no. 832, 833). 1929. J. M. Dent & Sons, Ltd.

Phineas Finn: The Irish Member. Anthony Trollope. LC 37-28541. (Half-title: The World's classics, ccxlvii-cdxlviii). 1937. Oxford University Press, H. Milford.

Phineas Finn: The Irish Member. A Novel. Anthony Trollope. (Seaside library. v. 59, no. 1201). 1882. G. Munro.

Phineas Redux. Anthony Trollope. LC 74-162234. (His The Palliser novels). (Illus.). 1973. 3.00 (ISBN 0-19-254614-7) (ISBN 0-19-281146-0). Oxford University Press.

Phineas Redux. Anthony Trollope. LC 37-285427. (Half-title: The world's classics, cdi, cdix). 1937. Oxford University Press, H. Milford.

Phineas Redux. Anthony Trollope & F. S. L Lyons. LC 82-14094. (Centenary edition of Anthony Trollope's Palliser novels). (World's classics). ((Series: Trollope, Anthony, 1815-1882.). (Palliser novels.). 1983. 10.95 (ISBN 0-19-250450-9). Oxford University Press.

Phineas Redux. A Novel. Anthony Trollope & Holl, Frank, 1845-1888, Illus. LC 37-11068. 1874. Harper & Brothers.

Phineas: Six Stories. John Knowles. LC 68-31536. 1968. 4.95. Random House.

Phinease Redux. Anthony Trollope. (On cover: The parliamentary novels (iii). 1893. Dodd, Mead & Company.

Phobia. Thomas Luke. 1980. pap. 2.50. PB.

Phoebe. Patricia Dizenzo. LC 79-126172. 1970. 4.50. McGraw-Hill.

Phoebe: A Novel. Miriam Coles Harris. LC 7-29088. 1884. Houghton, Mifflin and Company.

Phoebe: A Novel. Osmond Young Owings. LC 12-13897. 1912. 1.25. The Cosmopolitan Press.

Phoebe and Ernest. Inez Haynes Irwin. LC 10-24025. 1910. 1.50. H. Holt and Company.

Phoebe Deane. Grace Livingston Hill. LC 9-25180. 1909. J. B. Lippincott Company.

Phoebe Deane. Grace Livingston Hill. LC 22-5527. 1920. Grosset & Dunlap.

Phoebe, Ernest. and Cupid. Inez Haynes Irwin. LC 12-24059. 1912. 1.00. H. Holt and Company.

Phoebe, Junior. Margaret Oliphant Wilson Oliphant. LC 75-1548. (Victorian Fiction: Novels of Faith and Doubt; 92). 1976. 35.00 (ISBN 0-8240-1616-5). Garland Pub.

Phoebe, Junior. A Last Chronicle of Carlingford. Margaret Oliphant Wilson Oliphant. (Seaside library, v. 39, no. 802). 1880. G. Munro.

Phoebe Skibby's Theology. Sarah Lane. LC 7-14091. 1883. H. Gannett.

Phoebe Tilson. Frank Pope Humphrey. LC 7-5786. Rand, McNally & Company.

Phoenician. Bruce Cassiday. (Orig.). 1970. pap. 0.95 o.p. (N2330). Pyramid Pubns.

Phoenix. Amos Aricha & Landau, Eli. (Signet book). 1979. 2.50 (ISBN 0-451-08692-9). New American Library.

Phoenix. Amos Aricha & Eli Landau. LC 79-84368. 1980. 9.95 (ISBN 0-452-00533-7). New American Library.

Phoenix. George E. Samerjan. LC 79-50896. pap. 3.95 o.s.i. (ISBN 0-89516-078-1). Condor Pub Co.

Phoenix: A Novel. Peter J Nicholson. LC 66-4064. (Broadway books, 2). 1966. Knight Publishers.

Phoenix and the Mirror. Avram Davidson. LC 69-10982. (Doubleday science fiction). 1969. 4.95. Doubleday.

Phoenix Assault. John Kerrigan. (Signet Book). 2.50 (ISBN 0-451-09522-7). New American Library.

Phoenix at East Hadley... By Maurice Browning Cramer. Maurice Browning Cramer. LC 41-21275. 1914. Houghton Miffin Company.

Phoenix Birds. Sabin Ryder. 1973. pap. 0.75 o.p. (01-368). Lancer.

Phoenix: By Constance M. Warren; with Frontispiece by Christine Tucke Curtiss. Constance Martha Williams Warren. LC 17-846422. 1917. Houghton Mifflin Company.

Phoenix I. M. K. Wren, pseud. (Orig.). 1981. pap. 2.75 (ISBN 0-425-04746-6). Berkley Pub.

Phoenix Island. Charlotte Paul. 1976. (pbk.) 1.95. New American Library.

Phoenix Island. 1st Ed. Leslie Waller. LC 58-9540. 1958. Lippincott.

Phoenix-Kind. Peter Quennell. LC 31-34775. 1931. The Viking Press.

Phoenix No More. Edwin Gage. LC 77-11787. 8.95 (ISBN 0-06-011403-7). Harper & Row.

Phoenix No More. Edwin Gage. 1980. 1.95 (ISBN 0-380-49957-6). Avon Books.

Phoenix of Megaron. John Rankine. (Space: 1999 series). 1.50 (ISBN 0-671-80764-1). Pocket Books.

Phoenix Over the Galilee. Ka-Tzetnik 135633. LC 75-85045. 1969. 5.95. Harper & Row.

Phoenix Prime. Ted White. Ed. by Hank Stine. LC 82-12872. (Quest of the Wolf Trilogy Ser.: Vol. 1). (Illus.). 168p. 1983. pap. 5.95 (ISBN 0-89865-251-0, Starblaze). Donning Co.

Phoenix Prime. Ted White. 1971. pap. 0.75 o.p. (ISBN 0-447-74593-X). Lancer.

Phoenix Prime. Ted White. LC 74-593. 1969. pap. 0.75 o.p. Lancer.

Phoenix Rising. Jean Evans. LC 76-10552. 1976. 7.95 (ISBN 0-7091-5526-3). St. Martin's Press.

Phoenix Rising. Frances P. Statham. 1983. pap. 5.95 (ISBN 0-449-90010-X, Columbine). Fawcett.

Phoenix Two. D. H. Lawrence. Ed. by Warren Roberts & Harry T. Moore. 1978. pap. 9.95 (ISBN 0-14-004231-8). Penguin.

Phoenix Unbound. Jimmy D. James. 50p. 1982. stapled chapbook 4.00 (ISBN 0-942432-06-1). M O P Pr.

Phoinix. Alan Sims. LC 28-19131. 1928. Little, Brown, and Company.

'phone Booth Mystery. John Ironside. LC 24-27358. 1924. H. Holt and Company.

Phone Call. Jon Messman. 1979. pap. 2.95 (ISBN 0-451-12301-8, AE2301, Sig). NAL.

Phone Calls. Lillian O'Donnell. 1973. (pbk) 0.95. Dell.

Phone Calls. Lillian O'Donnell. LC 77-175251. (Red mask mystery). 1972. 4.95. Putnam.

Phony Hitman. J. R. Pici. 1977. pap. 1.50 (ISBN 0-89041-135-2, 3135). Major Bks.

Photo Finish. Ngaio Marsh. LC 80-16697. 10.95 (ISBN 0-316-54680-1). Little, Brown.

Photo Game. Jack Lang. (Orig., Biter). 1971. pap. 0.95 o.p. (B95-2082). Belmont-Tower.

Photogenic Soprano. Dorothy Dunnett. LC 68-27640. 1968. 4.95. Houghton Mifflin.

Photographer. Pierre Boulle. LC 68-8085. 1968. 4.95. Vanguard Press.

Photographer & the American Landscape. Ed. by John Szarkowski. (Illus., Orig.). 1966. pap. 2.95 o.p. (ISBN 0-87070-523-7, Dist by NYGS). Museum Mod Art.

Photographs. Vassilis Vassilikos. LC 70-139462. 1971. (ISBN 0-15-171800-8). Harcourt Brace Jovanovich.

Photographs Have Been Sent to Your Wife. Philip Loraine. 1973. 0.95. Dell.

Photographs Have Been Sent to Your Wife. Philip Loraine. LC 70-140717. 1971. 5.95 (ISBN 0-394-46761-2). Random House.

Phototropic Woman. Annabel Thomas. LC 81-10469. (Iowa School of Letters Award for Short Fiction). 12.50 (ISBN 0-87745-114-1). University of Iowa Press.

Phra the Phoenician. Edwin Lester Linden Arnold. 1976. lib. bdg. 12.95x (ISBN 0-89968-174-3). Lightyear.

Phra the Phoenician. Edwin Lester Linden Arnold. (Forgotten Fantasy Library: Vol. 11). (Illus.). 1977. pap. 4.95 (ISBN 0-87877-110-7, F-110). Newcastle Pub.

Phreak-Out! Carter Brown, pseud. (Signet Book). 1973. (pbk.) 0.75. New American Lib.

Phroso. buckingham ed. Anthony Hope Hawkins. LC 12-24524. F. A. Stokes Company.

Phroso. Anthony Hope Hawkins. LC 13-12923. 1899. The American News Company.

Phroso. Anthony Hope Hawkins. LC 4-18951. F. A. Stokes Company.

Phrynette. Marthe Troly-Curtin. LC 11-847414. 1911. J. B. Lippincott Company.

Phthor. Piers Anthony, pseud. 208p. 1982. pap. 2.50 (ISBN 0-425-05439-X). Berkley Pub.

Phyllida. Florence Marryat Church Lean. LC 7-13219. (On cover: Lovell's library. v. 19. no. 953). 1887. J. W. Lovell Company.

Phyllida. Irene Northan. (Fawcett Crest Book). 1978. 1.50 (ISBN 0-449-23459-2). Fawcett Books.

Phyllis. Maria Thompson Daviess. LC 14-169441. 1914. 1.25. The Century Co.

Phyllis: A Novel. Howard Melvin Fast. LC 61-12507. 1962. Doubleday.

Phyllis: Also My Lion. Carl Crofton. LC 6-32165. (On cover: The advance library. no. 19). 1892. Springfield Publishing Co.

Phyllis Anne. Florence Jeannette Baier Ward. LC 21-193914. The James A. McCann Company.

Phyllis. Illustrated by Shanks. 1st Ed. Theodore Key. LC 57-699295. 1957. Dutton.

Phyllis in Bohemia. Luther H Bickford & Barbour, Ralph Henry. LC 6-13115. 1897. H. S. Stone & Co.

Phyllis in Middlewych. Margaret Westrup. 1911. John Lane.

Phyllis of Philistia. Frank Frankfort Moore. LC 7-25304. The Cassell Publishing Co.

Phyllis of the Sierras: And A. Drift from Redwood Camp. Bret Harte. LC 7-3646. 1888. Houghton, Mifflin and Company.

Phyllis' Probation. Sophy Beckett. (On cover: Seaside library. Pocket ed. no. 372). 1885. G. Munro.

Physical Education. Bart Browning. pap. 1.95 o.s.i. (Venus). Grove.

Physician Extraordinary: A Novel of the Life and Times of William Harvey. David Weiss. 1976. 1.95. Dell.

Physician Extraordinary: A Novel of the Life and Times of William Harvey. David Weiss. LC 75-6912. 1975. 8.95 (ISBN 0-440-05916-X). Delacorte Press /E. Friede.

Physician of Galilee. Sara Elizabeth Gooselink. LC 44-47313. 1944. Wm. B. Eerdmans Publishing Company.

Physicians. Henry Denker. LC 74-14526. (O.s.i.). 1975. 8.95 o.s.i. (ISBN 0-671-21861-1). S&S.

Physicians: A Novel. Hazel Ai Chun Lin. LC 51-13467. 1951. J. Day Co.

Physicians: A Novel of Malpractice. Henry Denker. 1976. (pbk.) 1.95 (ISBN 0-671-80271-2). Pocket Books.

Physicians: A Novel of Malpractice. Henry Denker. LC 74-14526. 1975. (ISBN 0-671-21861-1). Simon and Schuster.

Physician's Wife. A Novel. Helen King Spangler. LC 8-12381. 1875. J. B. Lippincott & Co.

Physician's Wife and the Things That Pertain to Her Life. Ellen M Firebaugh. LC 6-41216. The F.A. Davis Company.

Physicke Against Fortune. Francesco Petrarca. Tr. by Thomas Twyne. LC 80-22768. 1980. Repr. of 1579 ed. 80.00x (ISBN 0-8201-1359-X). Schol Facsimiles.

Piano Box Mystery. John Russell Coryell. (On cover: Secret service series, no. 59). 1892. Street & Smith.

Piano dans l'Herbe. Francoise Sagan, pseud. 12.95. French & Eur.

Piano for Mrs. Cimino. Robert Oliphant. LC 80-10776. 11.95 (ISBN 0-13-851568-9). Prentice-Hall.

Piano in the Band. Dale Curran. LC 40-11294. Reynal & Hitchcock.

Piano Sport. Don Asher. LC 66-235688. bds., 4.95. Atheneum.

Piazza Boys. Julian Paull. (O.s.i.). (Orig.). 1967. pap. 0.60 o.s.i. (A251X, Award). Univ Pub & Dist.

Piazza of the Decameron. Luigi Fusco. LC 76-56615. 1977. 9.95 (ISBN 0-8076-0862-9). G. Braziller.

Piazza Tales. Herman Melville. Ed. by Egbert Samuel Oliver. LC 48-9243. (His Complete works, v. 9). 1948. Hendricks House.

Piazza Tales. Herman Melville. 1856. Dix & Edwards; Etc., Etc.

Piazza Tales. Herman Melville. LC 29-22539. The Elf Publishers.

Pic. John Kerouac. LC 71-166459. (Zebra books, Z-1090-Z). 1971. 1.25. Grove Press.

Pic: The Weapon-Maker. George Langford. LC 20-135443. Boni and Liveright.

Picaresque. David Osborne Hamilton. LC 30-24055. 1930. C. Scribner's Sons.

Picaro. Rupert Croft-Cooke. LC 34-300379. 1934. Dodd, Mead & Company.

Picaro. Charles Bernard Nordhoff. LC 24-30079. 1924. Harper & Brothers.

Picaro or Me. Arindam Basu. (Writers Workshop Greenbird Ser.). 90p. 1975. 12.00 (ISBN 0-88253-608-7); pap. text ed. 4.80 (ISBN 0-88253-607-9). Ind-US Inc.

Picaroon. Ernest Dudley. LC 53-5846. 1953. Bobbs-Merrill.

Piccadilly, a Fragment of Contemporary Biography. Laurence Oliphant. (On cover: Seaside library. Pocket ed., no. 537). 1885. G. Munro.

Piccadilly: A Novel. Kathleen Coyle. LC 23-119705. E. P. Dutton and Company.

Piccadilly Ghost. Erle Spencer. LC 31-987. 1930. The Macmillan Company.

Piccadilly Jim. Pelham Grenville Wodehouse. LC 73-161923. (Penguin books). 1969. 0.25 (ISBN 0-14-003039-5). Penguin.

Piccadilly Jim. Pelham Grenville Wodehouse. LC 17-6534. 1917. Dodd, Mead and Company.

Piccadilly Jim. Pelham Grenville Wodehouse. LC 35-28589. 1931. A. L Burt Company.

Piccadilly Jim: By P. G. Wodehouse. Pelham Grenville Wodehouse. (Autograph ed.). 1966. bds., 2.75. H. Jenkins Ltd.

Piccadilly Murder... Anthony Berkeley Cox. LC 30-33622. 1930. Pub. for the Crime Club, Inc., by Doubleday, Doran & Company, Inc.

Piccadilly Puzzle. Fergus Hume. (On cover: Seaside library. Pocket ed., no. 1232). 1889. G. Munro.

Piccadilly Puzzle. Fergus Hume. (On cover: The calumet series, no. 19). 1894. G. Munro's Sons.

Piccadilly Puzzle: A Mysterious Story. Fergus Hume. (On cover: Lovell's international series. no. 30). 1889. F. F. Lovell & Company.

Piccadilly Puzzle: A Mysterious Story. Fergus Hume. LC 3017. (Magnet detective library, no. 133). 1900. Street & Smith.

Piccadilly," Story of the Film. Arnold Bennett. LC 74-17299. (Series: The Reader's Library Film Edition.). (Reprint of the ed. published by Readers' Library Pub. Co., London, in series: The Reader's library film edition.). 1974. Repr. (ISBN 0-518-19146-X). Books for Libraries Press.

Picciola. a new ed., rev. by the author, with illustrations by leopold flameng. ed. Joseph Xavier Saintine. LC 8-5789. 1866. Hurd and Houghton.

Picciola. Joseph Xavier Saintine. LC 4-19621. (Riverside classics). Houghton, Mifflin and Company.

Picciola. Joseph Xavier Boniface Saintine & Alger, Abby Langdon, 1850- Ed. and Tr. LC 99-653. (On cover: Home and school library). 1899. Ginn & Company.

Picciola. Joseph Xavier Boniface Known As Saintine & Alger, Abby Langdon, 1850- Ed. and Tr. LC 99-653. (On cover: Home and school library). 1899. Ginn & Company.

Picciola: Or, The Prison Flower. Joseph Xavier Saintine. LC 8-5790. (Lovell's library. v. 14, no. 710). 1886. J. W. Lovell Company.

Picciola. Par X. B. Saintine. Joseph Xavier Boniface Known As Saintine & Masson, Michel, 1800-1883. LC 32-13096. (On cover: Bibliotheque populaire francaise). 1868. D. Appleton et Compagnie.

Picciola. The Prisoner of Fenestrella: or, Captivity Captive. a new ed.... ed. Joseph Xavier Boniface Known As Saintine. LC 8-5788. 1854. Blanchard and Lea.

Picciola. The Prisoner of Fenestrella: or, Captivity Captive. a new ed.... ed. Joseph Xavier Boniface Known As Saintine. LC 31-17949. 1857. Blanchards and Lea.

Picciola: The Prisoner of Fenestrella; or, Captivity Captive. Joseph Xavier Boniface Known As Saintine. LC 8-3730. 1893. D. Appleton and Company.

Pick a Mate. Richard J. Aielli. 3.75 o.p. Carlton.

Pick of the Crop. Doris Mae Murray. LC 37-5835. The Christopher Publishing House.

Pick of Today's Short Stories: 13, Ed. by John Pudney. Ed. by John Pudney. 1965. bds., 3.75. Putnam.

Pick up. Eunice Chapin. LC 31-7406. 1931. Brewer & Warren Inc.

Pick-up. Jerome Darwin Engel. LC 41-239651. Phoenix Press.

Pick up Sticks. Emma Lathen, pseud. LC 72-129191. (Inner sanctum mystery). 1970. Simon and Schuster.

Pick Your Victim. Patricia McGerr. LC 75-44991. (Fifty Classics of Crime Fiction, 1900-1950; 34). 1976. 12.00 (ISBN 0-8240-2383-8). Garland Pub.

Pick Your Victim. Patricia McGerr. LC 46-8485. 1947-1946. Pub. for the Crime Club by Doubleday & Company, Inc.

Pickaninny. Charles Artis. 1973. 5.95 (ISBN 0-533-00520-5). Vantage.

Picked Company: A Novel. Mary Hallock Foote. LC 12-23519. 1912. Houghton Mifflin Company.

Picked up in the Streets: A Romance, from the German of H. Schobert. Hedwig Harnisch Schobert. Tr. by Wister, Annis Lee (Furness) LC 8-2037. 1888. J. B. Lippincott Company.

Picked-up Pieces. John Updike. LC 75-8252. 1975. 12.95 (ISBN 0-394-49849-6). Knopf.

Picked-up Pieces. John Updike. LC 76-376221. 1976. 6.95 (ISBN 0-233-96749-4). Deutsch.

Picketing God: Or, Something to Be God. Eli Siegel. 1959. pap. 0.20 o.p. (ISBN 0-910492-07-7). Definition.

Picking up the Gun. Earl Anthony. 1971. pap. 0.95 o.p. (N2517). Pyramid Pubns.

Picking Winners with Major Miles. L. B Yates. LC 22-17037. The Bobbs-Merrill Company.

Pickings from the Portfolio of the Reporter of the New Orleans "Picayune"... With Original Designs. D Corcoran. 1846. Carey and Hart.

Pickle the Spy. Andrew Lang. LC 72-110132. Repr. of 1897 ed. 10.00 (ISBN 0-404-03853-0). AMS Pr.

Pickled Poodles: A Novel Based on the Characters Created by Craig Rice. Larry M Harris, pseud. LC 60-5559. (Random House mystery). 1960. Random House.

Pickup. Thompson, John Burton. LC 52-13351. 1952. Arco Pub. Co.

Pickup on Noon Street. Raymond Chandler. 1977. pap. 2.25 (ISBN 0-345-28861-0). Ballantine.

Pickwick Ladle and Other Collector's Stories. Winfield Scott Moody. LC 70-37556. (Short story index reprint series). (Illus.). 1972. (ISBN 0-8369-4115-2). Books for Libraries Press.

Pickwick Ladle: And Other Collector's Stories. Winfield Scott Moody. 1907. C. Scribner's Sons.

Pickwick Papers. Charles Dickens. (Penguin English Library). 1975. (pbk.) 3.95 (ISBN 0-14-043078-4). Penguin Books.

Pickwick Papers... Charles Dickens. LC 6-37234. 1868. Hurd and Houghton.

Pickwick Papers... Charles Dickens. LC 6-37232. (Lovell's library. v. 2, no. 91). 1883. J. W. Lovell Company.

Pickwick Papers. Charles Dickens & Crawford, Douglas Gordon. LC 25-8546. (On cover: The Macmillan pocket classics). 1925. The Macmillan Company.

Pickwick Papers. Charles Dickens & Joshua G. M Karton. LC 75-36068. (Illus.). 1977. 8.95. (ISBN 0-8055-1174-1) (ISBN 0-8055-0248-3). Hart Pub. Co.

Picnic. Martin Boyd. LC 37-19005. 1937. G. P. Putnam's Sons.

Picnic and Other Inimitable Stories. Gerald Malcolm Durrell. LC 80-15419. 10.95 (ISBN 0-671-25329-8). Simon and Schuster.

Picnic at Hanging Rock. Joan Weigall Lindsay. LC 67-20059. 1967. aust. 3.75. F. W. Cheshire.

Picnic at Sakkara. 1st American Ed. Percy Howard Newby. LC 55-9264. 1955. Knopf.

Picnic in Babylon: A Jesuit Priest's Journal, 1963-1967. John L'Heureux. 1969. Repr. of 1967 ed. pap. 1.25 o.p. (D262, Im). Doubleday.

Picnic in November: A Novel. 1st Ed. Edward Amshey. LC 56-13115. 1956. Pageant Press.

Picnic on Paradise. Joanna Russ. (Berkley book). 1979. 1.75 (ISBN 0-425-04040-2). Berkley Pub. Corp.

Picnic on Pardise. Joanna Russ. 1974. (pbk.) 0.95. Ace Books.

Picolata Treasure. Ruth Burnett. 192p. (YA) 1974. 6.95 (Avalon). Bouregy.

Picolata Treasure. Ruth Burnett. 1974. 4.50. Avalon.

Pictorial Narratives. LC 7-35910. J. A. Ackley.

Pictorial Tour of Unarius. Unarius. 193p. 1982. pap. 8.95 (ISBN 0-932642-63-2). Unarius.

Pictor's Metamorphoses, and Other Fantasies. Hermann Hesse & Theodore Ziolkowski. LC 81-12616. (Illus.). 1982. 15.00 (ISBN 0-374-23212-1). Farrar, Straus, and Giroux.

Picture see Hunger & Thirst & Other Plays.

Picture Album: By Jeanne Bowman Pseud. Peggy O'More, pseud. 1953. Arcadia House.

Picture Frames. Thyra Samter Winslow. LC 73-145379. 1971. (ISBN 0-403-01282-1). Scholarly Press.

Picture Frames. Thyra Samter Winslow. LC 23-26246. 1923. A. A. Knopf.

Picture. Jack of All Trades. A Matter-of-Fact Romance... Charles Reade. (On cover: Seaside library. Pocket ed., no. 206). 1884. G. Munro.

Picture Miss Seeton. Heron Carvic. LC 68-17039. 1968. Harper & Row.

Picture Mommy Dead. Robert Sherman. pap. 0.50 o.p. Lancer.

Picture of Dorian Gray. Oscar Wilde. LC 66-1256. (airmont classic). 1964. Airmont Pub. Co.

Picture of Dorian Gray. Oscar Wilde. LC 66-2714. (Perennial classic HP6042V). Harper & Row.

Picture of Dorian Gray. Oscar Wilde. LC 74-180250. (Oxford English novels). 1974. 9.75 (ISBN 0-19-255368-2). Oxford University Press.

Picture of Dorian Gray. Oscar Wilde. LC 50-3310. (Illustrated library). Halcyon House.

Picture of Dorian Gray. Oscar Wilde. LC 44-35367. (University classics). 1939. Appleby & Company, Incorporated.

Picture of Dorian Gray. Oscar Wilde. LC 46-8600. (Half-title: The Living library). 1946. The World Publishing Company.

Picture of Dorian Gray. Oscar Wilde & Trugo, Lui, Illus. LC 31-34096. Illustrated Editions Company.

Picture of Dorian Gray & Other Stories. Oscar Wilde. Repr. lib. bdg. 15.95x. Amereon Ltd.

Picture of Dorian Gray & Selected Stories. Oscar Wilde. 1962. pap. 1.95 (ISBN 0-451-51654-0, CJ1654, Sig Classics). NAL.

Picture of Dorian Gray & Thirteen Other Stories. Oscar Wilde. (Standard Classic Ed). 3.95 o.p. (ISBN 0-00-421701-2, JC701). Collins-World.

Picture of Dorian Gray. With an Introd. by Andre Maurois and Illus. by Lucille Corcos. Oscar Wilde. LC 58-94594. 1957. Printed for Members of the Limited Editions Club.

Picture of Dorian Gray. With an Introd. by Andre Maurois, and Illus. by Lucille Corcos. Oscar Wilde. LC 58-4157. 1958. Heritage Press.

Picture of Guilt. Michael Innes, pseud. LC 69-13729. 1969. 3.95 o.p. (ISBN 0-396-05866-3). Dodd.

Picture of Guilt. John Innes Mackintosh Stewart. LC 69-13729. (Red badge mystery). 1969. 3.95. Dodd, Mead.

Picture of Innocence. Hugh Fleetwood. 1979. 1.95 (ISBN 0-671-81788-4). Pocket Books.

Picture of Las Cruces: A Romance of Mexico. Frances Christine Tiernan & Mrs. LC 8-19805. (Half-title: Appletons' town and country library, no. 198). 1896. D. Appleton and Company.

Picture of Millie. Philip Maitland Hubbard. LC 64-8019. (A London House mystery). 1964. London House & Maxwell.

Picture of Success: A Novel. Florence Jane Soman. LC 66-16028. 1966. Bobbs-Merrill.

Picture of the Victim. Dorothy Stockbridge Tillet. LC 40-51933. 1940. Pub. for the Crime Club by Doubleday, Doran & Company, Inc.

Picture on the Wall. John Breckenridge Ellis. LC 21-169333. 1920. Burton Publishing Company.

Picture Ot Hang on the Wall. Hignett, Sean. LC 66-20152. 1965. Coward-McCann.

Picture Palace: A Novel. Paul Theroux. LC 77-18725. 1978. 9.95 (ISBN 0-395-26475-8). Houghton Mifflin.

Picture People. Olga Rosmanith. LC 34-314427. 1934. Doubleday, Doran & Company, Inc.

Picture Play: The Japanese Twins' Lucky Day. Florence Sakade. LC 64-20367. (Illus.). 3.50 o.p. (ISBN 0-8048-0322-6). C E Tuttle.

Picture-Story of Leo Tolstoy's War and Peace: Adapted from the Novel and the Motion Picture. With an Introd. by Arthur I. E. Atwood H. Townsend. Bernard Geis & Lev Nikolaevich Graf. Voina I Mir Tolstol. LC 56-11973. 1956. F. Fell.

Picture the Dawning. Paul F. Page. 1976. pap. 4.96 (ISBN 0-89390-002-8). Resource Pubns.

Picture to Hang on the Wall. Sean Hignett. (6913). 1967. Dell.

Picture Window. Josephine Lawrence. LC 51-5967. 1951. Morrow.

Pictures and Conversations. Elizabeth Bowen. LC 74-7753. 1975. 7.95 (ISBN 0-394-47896-7). Knopf; Distributed by Random House.

Pictures from a Brewery. Asher Barash. LC 73-16802. 352p. 1974. 6.95 o.p. (ISBN 0-672-51916-X). Bobbs.

Pictures from an Exhibition. Giles Gordon. LC 70-116694. 1970. 4.95. Dial Press.

Pictures from an Institution. A Comedy. Randall Jarrell. 1968. 5.95, 2.25 pap.,. Farrar.

Pictures from an Institution: A Comedy. Randall Jarrell. LC 60-6745. (Meridian fiction, MF2). 1960. Meridian Fiction.

Pictures from an Institution: A Comedy. Randall Jarrell. LC 54-5973. 1954. Knopf.

Pictures from Ireland. Henry Arthur Blake. LC 7-257796. (On cover: Leisure hour series. no. 120 5d). 1881. H. Holt and Company.

Pictures from Italy: Sketches by Boz, and American Notes. Charles Dickens. 1877. Harper & Brothers.

Pictures from the Past. Ruth Geller. LC 80-82075. 205p. 1980. pap. 7.95 (ISBN 0-9603008-1-3). Imp Pr.

Pictures from the Past: And Other Stories. Ruth Geller. 203p. 1978. pap. 7.95. Crossing Pr.

Pictures of Death. Kenneth Robeson. (avenger, no. 19). 1973. (pbk) 0.75. Warner Paperback Library.

Pictures of Fear. Lucy Fuchs. (YA) 1981. 6.95 (Avalon). Bouregy.

Pictures of Fidelman: An Exhibition. Bernard Malamud. LC 69-15408. 1975. (pbk.) 1.75 (ISBN 0-671-80147-3). Pocket Books.

Pictures of Hellas: Five Tales of Ancient Greece. Peter Mariager. Tr. by Safford, Mary Joanna. 1888. W. S. Gottsberger.

Pictures of Polly. Mary King Courtney. LC 12-22129. 1912. Harper & Brothers.

Pictures of the Journey Back. Jack Matthews. LC 72-88802. 1973. 5.95 (ISBN 0-15-171920-9). Harcourt Brace Jovanovich.

Pictures of the Olden Time: As Shown in the Fortunes of a Family of the Pilgrims. Edmund Hamilton Sears. LC 8-3376. 1857. Crosby, Nichols and Company.

Pictures That Storm Inside My Head: Poems for the Inner You. Ed. by Richard Peck (ISBN 0-380-00735-5). Avon.

Pidgin Cargo. Alice Tisdale Nourse Hobart. LC 29-19516. 2.50. The Century Co.

Pidgin Island. Harold MacGrath. LC 14-5818. 1.25. The Bobbs-Merrill Company.

Pie and the Pirate. Albert Lee. LC 10-4043. P. F. Collier and Son.

Pie in the Sky. Frederick Hazlitt Brennan. LC 31-24897. 2.50. The Century Co.

Pie in the Sky. Arthur Calder-Marshall. 1937. C. Scribner's Sons.

Piebald, King of Bronchos: The Biography of a Wild Horse. Clarence Hawkes. LC 12-20197. 1912. G. W. Jacobs & Co.

Piece of Blue Heaven. Jacket Designed by Gloria Gentille. 1st Ed. Abraham Margolian. LC 56-8351. New Elizabethan Pub. Co.

Piece of Cake: By Charles Anthony Pseud. Anthony Charles Akerman. LC 57-22164. 1956. W. Blackwood.

Piece of Kitty Hunter's Life. Mary Ellen Bamford. LC 6-6291. 1890. Hunt & Eaton.

Piece of Luck. Stories. Frances Gray Patton. LC 55-104528. 1955. Dodd, Mead.

Piece of Martin Cann. Laurence M. Janifer. (Orig.). 1968. pap. 0.50 o.p. (B50-811). Belmont-Tower.

Piece of My Heart. Richard Ford. LC 76-5536. 8.95 (ISBN 0-06-011362-6). Harper & Row.

Piece of Resistance. Clive Egleton. LC 78-96786. 1970. 5.95. Coward-McCann.

Piece of Something Big. Harry Reed. (Orig.). 1972. pap. 0.95 o.p. Lancer.

Piece of String. George Mendoza. (Illus.). 1965. 7.95 (ISBN 0-8392-1160-0). Astor-Honor.

Piece of the Action. Herb Gardner. (O.S.I.). 1958. 3.95 o.s.i. (57470). S&S.

Piece of the Action. Bill Miles. 1976. 6.95 o.p. (ISBN 0-8059-2338-1). Dorrance.

Piece of the Action. Bill Miles. 1976. 6.95 o.p. (ISBN 0-8059-2338-1). Dorrance.

Piece of the Action. Heather Wyndom. pap. 1.95 o.s.i. (OPH-247, Ophelia). Olympia.

Piece of the Moon. Robert Lambert. LC 74-14817. 1975. 7.95 (ISBN 0-8415-0351-6). Saturday Review Press.

Piece of the Moon. Robert Lambert. 1976. (pbk.) 1.75 (ISBN 0-446-59890-9). Warner Books.

Piece of the Moon Is Missing. James Leonard Johnson. pap. 2.25 (ISBN 0-310-37412-X). Zondervan.

Piece of the Moon Is Missing: A New Code Name Sebastian Novel. James Leonard Johnson. LC 74-8579. 1974. 6.95 (ISBN 0-87981-025-4). A. J. Holman Co.

Piece of the Silence: A Murder Mystery. Jack Livingston. LC 81-21536. 13.95 (ISBN 0-312-61065-3). St. Martin's Press.

Piece of This Country. Thomas Taylor. LC 70-105739. 1970. 4.95. Norton.

Pieces for a Glass Piano. Gerard Majella Lee. LC 78-319164. 1978. 7.25 (ISBN 0-7022-1169-9) (ISBN 0-7022-1175-3). University of Queensland Press.

Pieces from a Small Bomb. George Cuomo. LC 75-23572. 1976. 7.95 (ISBN 0-385-11078-2). Doubleday.

Pieces of a Hero. William Overgard. (Orig.). 1973. pap. 1.25 o.p. (ISBN 0-515-02919-X, V2919). BJ Pub Group.

Pieces of a Hero. William Overgard. 1973. (pbk) 1.25 (ISBN 0-515-02919-X). Pyramid Books.

Pieces of a Woman. Barbara Holley. (Illus.). 12p. 1982. pap. 2.00 (ISBN 0-943696-01-1). Red Key Pr.

Pieces of Cheer: Vignettes of the Real American West and the People Who Made It. Alice H Robinson. LC 76-151288. 7.00 (ISBN 0-682-48697-3). Exposition Press.

Pieces of Eight. Sydney J. Harris. 300p. 1982. 12.95 (ISBN 0-395-32512-9). HM.

Pieces of Eight: Being the Authentic Narrative of a Treasure Discovered in the Bahama Islands, in the Year 1903--Now First Given to the Public. Richard Le Gallienne. LC 18-7990. 1918. Doubleday, Page & Company.

Pieces of Eight: Being the Authentic Narrative of a Treasure Discovered in the Bahama Islands, in the Year 1903--Now First Given to the Public. Richard Le Gallienne. LC 32-26654. 1932. P. Smith.

Pieces of Life. Mark Schorer. LC 77-24293. 10.00 (ISBN 0-374-23280-6). Farrar, Straus and Giroux.

Pieces of Night: A Novel of Childhood. David W. Elliott. LC 72-91576. 1973. 6.95 (ISBN 0-03-007591-2). Holt, Rinehart and Winston.

Pieces of the Game: A Modern Instance. Clara De Longworth Chambrun. LC 15-146695. 1915. 1.35. G. P. Putnam's Sons.

Pied Piper. Nevil Shute Norway. LC 41-22072. 1942-1941. W. Morrow & Company.

Pied Piper. Nevil Shute Norway. LC 42-50437. 1942. The Sun Dial Press.

Pied Piper. Nevil Shute. 1982. 13.95 (ISBN 0-434-69908-X, Pub. by Heinemann). David & Charles.

Pied Piper: A Novel. Robert Paier. LC 78-14408. 9.95 (ISBN 0-07-048091-5). McGraw-Hill.

Pied Piper of Helfenstein. Edward V McCarthy. LC 74-33651. 1975. 5.95 (ISBN 0-385-02018-X). Published for the Crime Club by Doubleday.

Pied Piper of Helfenstein. 1976. 1.50 (ISBN 0-671-80742-0). Pocket Books.

Pied Tendre. Rene de Goscinny. (Lucky Luke Series). (French.). 1976. 5.95x (ISBN 2-205-00305-4). Intl Learn Syst.

Piedouche, a French Detective. Le Coup D'ceil De M. Piedouche). Fortune Du Boisgobey. LC 6-34417. (On cover: Seaside library. Pocket ed. no. 264). G. Munro.

Pier-Glass. Robert Graves. LC 73-11339. Repr. of 1921 ed. lib. bdg. 10.00 (ISBN 0-8414-2047-5). Folcroft.

Pier Glass. Robert Graves. 1921. 4.00 o.s.i. Ridgeway Bks.

Pier Head Crew. Geoffrey Kyle. 192p. (Orig.). 1973. pap. 1.95 o.p. (ISBN 0-87056-281-9, 6281). Brandon.

Pier Head Jump. Donn Pearce. LC 77-173206. 1972. 5.95. Bobbs-Merrill.

Pier 17: A Novel. Walter Havighurst. LC 35-131835. 1935. The Macmillan Company.

Piercing. John Coyne. LC 78-7337. 8.95 (ISBN 0-399-12172-2). Putnam.

Piercing. John Coyne. (Berkley Book). 1980. 2.50 (ISBN 0-425-04563-3). Berkley Pub. Corp.

Pierre and His People. Gilbert Parker. (On cover: Once a week libaryy. v. 11, no. 24). 1894. P. F. Collier.

Pierre and His People: Tales of the Far North. Gilbert Parker. LC 7-34994. 1894. Stone & Kimball.

Pierre and His People: Tales of the Far North. Gilbert Parker. LC 4-18267. 1898. The Macmillan Company.

Pierre and His People: Tales of the Far North. Gilbert Parker. LC 45-25819. 1895. Stone & Kimball.

Pierre and His People: Tales of the Far North. Gilbert Parker. LC 45-25818. 1896. Stone & Kimball.

Pierre and Jean. Guy De Maupassant. LC 76-48441. (Classics of European Literature). (Series: Masterpieces of French romance.). (Hyperion library of world literature). 1977. 12.50. (ISBN 0-88355-578-6) (ISBN 0-88355-579-4). Hyperion Press.

Pierre & Jean. Guy de Maupassant. LC 76-48441. (Library of World Literature Ser.). 1978. Repr. of 1923 ed. lib. bdg. 19.50 (ISBN 0-88355-578-6). Hyperion Conn.

Pierre and Jean: Tr. from the French of Guy De Maupassant. Guy De Maupassant. Tr. by Bell, Clara Courtenay (Poynter) LC 2-29624. (Half-title: A century of French romance. Parisian ed. vol. xix). D. Appleton & Co.

Pierre and Jean: With a Preface by the Author. Guy De Maupassant. Tr. by Hugh Craig. G. Routledge & Son, Limited.

Pierre and Jean: With a Preface by the Author. Guy De Maupassant. Tr. by Hugh Craig. LC 99-2443. 1899. Brentano's.

Pierre & Joseph. Rene Bazin. Tr. by Frank Hunter Potter. LC 20-77228. Harper & Brothers.

Pierre and Luce. Romain Rolland & De Kay, Charles, 1848-1935, Tr. LC 22-9487. 1922. H. Holt and Company.

Pierre Des Voeux. Sara Craven. (Harlequin Collection Ser.). 192p. 1983. pap. 1.95 (ISBN 0-373-49337-1). Harlequin Bks.

Pierre et Jean. Introd., Notes by Aaron Schaffer. Guy De Maupassant. Ed. by Aaron Schaffer. (Mod. student's lib., French ser.). 1963. pap., 1.50. Scribners.

Pierre et Jean (Peter and John) Guy De Maupassant. Tr. by Alexina Loranger. LC 7-25595. (library of choice fiction no. 6). 1890. Laird & Lee.

Pierre et Jean; The Two Brothers. Guy De Maupassant. Tr. by Albert Smith. LC 9-2235. 1889. J. B. Lippincott Company.

Pierre of the Teche. Robert L Olivier. LC 36-5509. Pelican Publishing Company.

Pierre: Or, The Ambiguities. Herman Melville. LC 57-5642. (Evergreen book, E-55). 1957. Grove Press.

Pierre: Or, The Ambiguities. Herman Melville. LC 72-179121. (writings of Herman Melville, v. 7). 1971. (ISBN 0-8101-0266-8) (ISBN 0-8101-0267-6). Northwestern University Press.
Pierre: Or, The Ambiguities. Herman Melville. Ed. by Henry Alexander Murray. LC 49-143448. 1949. Hendrecks House.
Pierre: Or, The Ambiguities. Herman Melville. LC 7-17951. 1852. Harper & Brothers.
Pierre: Or, The Ambiguities. Herman Melville. LC 1-20341. 1855. Harper and Brothers.
Pierre: Or, The Ambiguities. Herman Melville. Ed. by Henry Tomlinson. Moore, John Brooks. LC 29-12403. E. P. Dutton & Co. Inc.
Pierre: Or, The Ambiguities. Herman Melville. Ed. by Forsythe, Robert Stanley. LC 30-10468. (On cover: American deserta). 1930. A. A. Knopf.
Pierre or the Ambiguities. Herman Melville. pap. 3.95 (ISBN 0-451-51707-5, CE1707, Sig Classics). NAL.
Pierre, the Partisan: A Tale of the Mexican Marches. Henry William Herbert. LC 7-4294. 1848. Williams Brothers.
Pierre Vinton; the Adventures of a Superfluous Husband. Edward Carrington Venable. 1914. C. Scribner's Sons.
Pierre Vinton; the Adventures of a Superfluous Husband. Edward Carrington Venable. LC 28-1657. 1924. C. Scribner's Sons.
Pierrette. Marguerite Bouvet. LC 6-22270. 1896. A.C. McClurg and Company.
Pierrette and The Vicar of Tours. Honore De Balzac. Tr. by Katharine Prescott Wormeley. LC 3-23169. (Half-title: The comedy of human life... Scenes from provincial life). 1892. Roberts Brothers.
Pierrot: Dog of Belgium. Walter Alden Dyer. LC 15-7586. 1915. Doubleday, Page & Company.
Piers Plowman. William Langland. 1931. 3.95x o.p. (ISBN 0-460-00571-5, Evman). Dutton.
Piers Plowman: The A Version. William Langland. Ed. by George Kane. 1960. 14.50 o.p. Oxford U Pr.
Pietro Ghisleri. Francis Marion Crawford. LC 4-15093. 1892. Macmillan and Co.
Pietro Ghisleri. Francis Marion Crawford. LC 32-33611. 1893. Macmillan & Co.
Pietro Ghisleri. Francis Marion Crawford. LC 18-4341. 1899. The Macmillan Company.
Piff, Paff, Peuff: Diary of a Young Male Schizophrenic. Aloysius. 1978. 7.50 o.p. (ISBN 0-533-03582-1). Vantage.
Pig. Jeff Nuttall. 1970. 4.50 o.p. (ISBN 0-8180-0608-0, Fulcrum). Horizon.
Pig Earth. John Berger. LC 80-7709. 9.95 (ISBN 0-394-51268-5). Pantheon Books.
Pig in a Poke. Helen M. Strong. 4.95 o.p. Carlton.
Pig in a Poke. Lee Thayer, pseud. LC 48-776. (Red badge detective). 1948. Dodd, Mead.
Pig Iron. Charles Gilman Norris. LC 26-9021. E. P. Dutton & Company.
Pig Iron: Short Stories. Dudres Parker. LC 22-2740. 1921. The Norman, Remington Company.
Pig Is Fat. Lawrence M. Maynard. LC 30-593509. Farrar & Rinehart Incorporated.
Pig Out. Christina Hanley. 1983. pap. 5.95 (ISBN 0-8065-0843-4). Citadel Pr.
Pig Plantagenet. Allen Andrews. LC 80-17226. (Illus.). 208p. 1981. 10.95 (ISBN 0-670-55501-0). Viking Pr.
Pig Plantagent. Allen Andrews & Michael Foreman. LC 80-17226. (Illus.). 1981. 10.95 (ISBN 0-670-55501-0). Viking Press.
Pig World. Charles W. Runyon. LC 73-163093. (Doubleday science fiction). 1971. 4.95. Doubleday.
Pigboats. Edward Ellsberg. 1931. Dodd, Mead & Company.
Pigeon. Jay Bennett. 144p. (YA) 1981. pap. 1.95 (ISBN 0-380-55848-3, 55848, Flare). Avon.
Pigeon. Jay Bennett. LC 79-26270. 1980. 8.95 (ISBN 0-416-30631-4, NO. 0151). Methuen Inc.
Pigeon Among the Cats. Josephine Bell. LC 77-21219. 1977. 7.95 (ISBN 0-8128-2411-3). Stein and Day.
Pigeon Feathers. John Updike. 1978. pap. 2.50 (ISBN 0-449-23951-9, Crest). Fawcett.
Pigeon Feathers, and Other Stories. John Updike. LC 61-17831. 1962. Knopf.
Pigeon Feathers, and Other Stories. John Updike. LC 70-38099. 1971. 8.95 (ISBN 0-8161-6008-2). G. K. Hall.
Pigeon Hill. Ambrose Korn. 1980. pap. 5.00 (ISBN 0-89502-046-7). FEB.
Pigeon Hoo. Franklin Lushington. LC 36-5816. E. P. Dutton & Co., Inc.
Pigeon Irish. Francis Stuart. LC 32-16442. 1932. The Macmillan Company.
Pigeon Lover. George Abbe. LC 81-5417. 5.95 (ISBN 0-89865-163-8). Donning Co.
Pigeon Pair. Elisabeth Ogilvie. Repr. lib. bdg. 11.75x (ISBN 0-88411-336-1). Amereon Ltd.
Pigeon Project. Irving Wallace. LC 78-24352. 10.95 (ISBN 0-671-22622-3). Simon and Schuster.
Pigeons. Coelho Netto. Ed. & tr. by Isaac Goldberg. (International Pocket Library). pap. 3.00. Branden.
Pigmy in the Mist. Thomas Joyner & George Wesley. Ed. by Sylvia Ashton. LC 75-7748. 1976. 7.95 (ISBN 0-87949-041-1). Ashley Bks.
Pignight & Blowjob. Snoo Wilson. 1980. pap. 4.95 (ISBN 0-7145-3509-5). Riverrun NY.
Pigs Have Wings. Pelham Grenville Wodehouse. LC 52-10997. 1952. Doubleday.
Pigs Have Wings. Pelham Grenville Wodehouse. 1977. 1.95 (ISBN 0-345-25516-X). Ballantine Books.
Pigs in Clover: A Novel. Julia Davis Frankau. LC 3-11672. 1903. J. B. Lippincott Company.
Pigs in Love. Revilo. (Illus.). 96p. 1982. pap. 3.95 (ISBN 0-517-54707-4, C N Potter Bks). Crown.
Pigs Is Pigs. Ellis Parker Butler. LC 6-125601. 1906. McClure, Phillips & Co.
Pigs Is Pigs. Ellis Parker Butler. LC 21-4137. 1910. Doubleday, Page & Company.
Pigs Is Pigs. Ellis Parker Butler. LC 32-33617. A. L. Burt Company.
Pigs Is Pigs. Ellis Parker Butler. LC 37-548618. 1937. Doubleday, Doran & Company, Inc.
Pigs Is Pigs, and Other Favorites. Ellis Parker Butler. LC 65-27689. (Illus.). 1966. Dover Publications.
Pigs to Market. George Agnew Chamberlain. LC 20-21187. The Bobbs-Merrill Company.
Pigs with Wings. Lombard Revera. 1980. 8.95 (ISBN 0-531-07407-2). Watts.
Pigskin. Charles Wright Ferguson. LC 29-23875. 1929. Doubleday, Doran and Company, Inc.
Pigskin Bag. Bruno Fischer. LC 46-231365. 1946. Ziff-Davis Publishing Company.
Pigsties with Spires. Georgina Garry. LC 28-18814. E. P. Dutton & Company.
Pigtail of Ah Lee Ben Loo: With Seventeen Other Laughable Tales & 200 COmical Silhouettes. John Bennett. LC 23-256538. 1928. Longmans, Green & Co.
Pigtails, Petticoats & the Old School Tie. Sheila Miller. 1981. pap. 5.95 (ISBN 0-85363-140-9). OMF Bks.
Pigweed and Lilacs. Sara Austin Clark. LC 62-16755. 1962. Dorrance.
Pike. May Dikeman Hoss. LC 54-10705. 1954. Appleton-Century-Crofts.
Pike County Folks. Edward Harold Mott. LC 7-26097. (On cover: Lovell's library, no. 139). J. W. Lovell Company.
Pike's Peak: a Family Saga. Frank Waters. LC 77-150753. 1971. 8.95 (ISBN 0-8040-0503-6). Sage Books.
Pike's Peak Pack see Willis & His Friends Series.
Pike's Peninsula. Leslie A. Davis. LC 74-78667. 1974. 5.95 (ISBN 0-8059-2015-3). Dorrance.
Pilate and Herod: A Tale Illustrative of the Early History of the Church of England, in the Province of Maryland... Harvey Stanley. LC 8-138811. 1853. H. Hooker.
Pilate Gave Sentence. Clarice M Cresswell. LC 20-67103. G. W. Jacobs & Company.
Pilate Plot. Martin Page. LC 78-7711. 1978. 8.95 (ISBN 0-698-10790-X). Coward, McCann & Geoghegan.
Pilate's Query. Susie Champney Clark. 1895. Arena Publishing Company.
Pilditch Puzzle. William Blair Morton Ferguson. Liveright, Inc.
Pile of Stones: Short Stories. Hugh Nissenson. LC 65-12690. 1965. Scribner.
Pile, Petals from St. Klaed's Computer. Brian Wilson Aldiss. LC 79-2260. (Illus.). 36p. 1979. 7.95 (ISBN 0-03-053296-5). HR&W.
Pilebuck. John Hawkins & Hawkins, Ward, Joint Author. LC 43-5576. 1943. E. P. Dutton & Co., Inc.
Pilegesh Be Gib'ah. David Zamoscz. (Heb). 10.00 o.p. AMS Pr.
Pilgermann. Russell Hoban. LC 83-472. 1983. 14.95 (ISBN 0-671-45968-6). Summit Books.
Pilgrim. Ray Hogan. LC 79-7714. 1980. 7.95 (ISBN 0-385-15630-8). Doubleday.
Pilgrim Aflame. Myron S. Augsburger. LC 67-15993. (Illus.). 1967. 5.95 (ISBN 0-8361-1558-9); pap. 2.25 (ISBN 0-8361-1840-5). Herald Pr.
Pilgrim Aflame: By Myron S. Augsburger. Myron S Augsburger. LC 67-159934. 1967. 4.00. Herald Pr.
Pilgrim and the Shrine: Or, Passages from the Life and Correspondence of Herbert Ainslie... Edward Maitland. (On cover: Lovell's occult series, no. 3). J. W. Lovell Company.
Pilgrim at Sea. Par Lagerkvist. LC 81-16076. 1982. 2.95 (ISBN 0-394-70821-0). Vintage Books.
Pilgrim Cottage. Cecil Roberts. LC 33-24913. 1933. D. Appleton-Century Company, Incorporated.
Pilgrim Feet. Margaret Pollock Sherwood. LC 49-1722. 1949. Montrose Press.
Pilgrim Hawk. Glenway Wescott. 1966. 5.95 o.p. (ISBN 0-06-014548-X, HarpT). Har-Row.
Pilgrim Hawk. A Love Story. Glenway Wescott. LC 40-35169. 1966. 4.00. Harper.
Pilgrim Hawks see Six Great Modern Short Novels.
Pilgrim House by the Sea. Robert Merrill Bartlett. LC 72-94709. (Illus.). 1973. 6.95 (ISBN 0-8158-0298-6). Christopher Pub. House.
Pilgrim in Manhattan. Margaret Bell Houston. LC 40-12657. 1940. D. Appleton-Century Company, Incorporated.
Pilgrim of a Smile. Norman Davey. LC 22-2741. George H. Doran Company.
Pilgrim of Passion. T. S. 1972. pap. 1.50 o.s.i. (V1091D, Venus). Grove.
Pilgrim of the Sun and Stars. Sam Toperoff. LC 72-79042. 1972. 6.95 (ISBN 0-8415-0192-0). Saturday Review Press.
Pilgrim; or, a Picture of Life, 1775, 2 vols. in 1. Charles Johnstone. LC 74-16216. (Novel in England, 1700-1775 Ser). 1974. lib. bdg. 50.00 (ISBN 0-8240-1208-9). Garland Pub.
Pilgrim: Or, The Stranger in His Own Country. Vega Carpio, Lope Felix De. LC 71-170598. (Foundations of the Novel). 1973. 22.00 ea. (ISBN 0-8240-0581-3). Garland Pub.
Pilgrim: or the Stranger in His Own Country, Vol. 69. Lope De Vega. LC 71-170598. (Novel in England, 1700-1775 Ser). (O.s.i.). lib. bdg. 50.00 o.s.i. (ISBN 0-8240-0581-3). Garland Pub.
Pilgrim Prince: A Novel Based on the Life of John Bunyan. Gladys Hutchison Barr. LC 63-18430. 1963. Holt, Rinehart and Winston.
Pilgrim Project: A Novel. Henry Hunt Searls. LC 64-17909. 1964. McGraw-Hill.
Pilgrim Son: A Personal Odyssey. John Masters. LC 78-151213. 1971. 6.95. Putnam.
Pilgrim Soul. Anne Miller Downes. LC 52-9539. 1952. Lippincott.
Pilgrim Stories. Margaret Blanche Pumphrey. LC 10-29515. Rand, McNally & Company.
Pilgrim Strangers: A Novel. Charles E Mercer. LC 61-8347. 1961. Putnam.
Pilgrim Street see Jessica's First Prayer.
Pilgrim Thief. Robert W. Burda. LC 76-2758. 1977. 7.95 o.p. (ISBN 0-385-02320-0). Doubleday.
Pilgrim to the Abyss... Axel Eggebrecht & Bozman, Milfred Mary, 1893- Tr. LC 30-5236. 1930. A. H. King.
Pilgrimage. Kathryn Anger. (Feminist Novels Ser.). 1982. write for info. Diotima Bks.
Pilgrimage. Johan Bojer. LC 24-20565. The Century Co.
Pilgrimage. Zenna Henderson. 1970. pap. 1.95 (ISBN 0-380-01507-2, 52597). Avon.
Pilgrimage. Joan Lingard. LC 77-367996. 1976. 2.40 (ISBN 0-241-89399-2). Hamilton.
Pilgrimage. Drew Mendelson. 1981. 2.25 (ISBN 0-87997-612-8). DAW Books.
Pilgrimage. Dorothy Miller Richardson. LC 66-22423. 1967. Knopf.
Pilgrimage. Dorothy Miller Richardson. LC 38-289893. 1938. A. A. Knopf.
Pilgrimage: A Tale of Old Natchez. Louise W. Collier. 424p. (Orig.). 1983. pap. 9.95 (ISBN 0-918518-26-1). St Luke TN.
Pilgrimage of Anglers. Eugene Edward Wilson, pseud. LC 52-671209. 1952.
Pilgrimage of Peter Strong. Paul Francis Geren. LC 48-10241. 1948. Harper.
Pilgrimage of Peter Strong. Paul Francis Green. LC 48-102412. 1948. Harper.
Pilgrimage of Protest. Carolina Foulke Urie. LC 51-14866. 1951. Island Press.
Pilgrimage of the Lyf of the Manhode. Guillaume de Deguilleville. Ed. by W. A. Wright. LC 78-178536. (Eng.). Repr. of 1869 ed. 28.50 (ISBN 0-404-56613-8). AMS Pr.
Pilgrimage: The Book of the People. Zenna Henderson. (Science Fiction Ser.). 12.50 o.p. (ISBN 0-8398-2498-X, Gregg). G K Hall.
Pilgrimage: The Book of the People. 1st Ed. Zenna Henderson. LC 61-7653. 1961. Doubleday.
Pilgrimage to Beethoven. Richard Wagner. Tr. by O. W. Weyer. 1.00x o.p. Open Court.
Pilgrimage to Earth. Robert Sheckley. LC 57-11486. (Bantam books, A1672 2). 1957. Bantam Books.
Pilgrimage to St. Jean. Jerry Carroll. 1978. pap. 1.50 (ISBN 0-532-15364-2). Woodhill.
Pilgrimage to the Kingdom. Vera M. Boyington. 1977. 8.95 o.p. (ISBN 0-533-01985-0). Vantage.
Pilgrims. Ethel Edith Mannin. LC 27-11486. George H. Doran Company.
Pilgrims: A Story of Massachusetts. John Roy Musick. LC 7-33327. (On cover: Columbian historical novels v. 5). 1893. Funk & Wagnalls Company.
Pilgrims Aflame. Myron S Augsburger. LC 78-102311. (Illus.). 2.25 (ISBN 0-8361-1840-5). Herald Press.
Pilgrims All. Ed. by Mary Alice McKenna Curtin. LC 43-15656. 1943. The Bruce Publishing Company.
Pilgrims' Christmas. Cora E Howe. 1899. News Book Print.
Pilgrim's Ford. Muriel Hine Coxon. LC 30-10246. 1930. D. Appleton and Company.
Pilgrims in Paradise, a Novel. Frank Gill Slaughter. LC 60-9491. 1960. Doubleday.
Pilgrims in the Zoo: And Other Stories. Bruce Brooks. LC 60-7397. 1960. Beacon Press.
Pilgrim's Inn. Elizabeth Goudge. LC 48-5845. Coward-McCann,
Pilgrims into Folly: Romantic Excursions. Wallace Irwin. LC 17-16317. 1917. George H. Doran Company.
Pilgrims' March. Henry Howarth Bashford. LC 9-5518. 1909. 1.50. H. Holt and Company.
Pilgrims of Adversity. William McFee. LC 28-25960. 1928. Doubleday, Doran & Company, Inc.
Pilgrims of Fashion. Kinahan Cornwallis. LC 6-287271. 1862. Harper & Brothers.
Pilgrims of the Impossible. Coningsby William Dawson. LC 28-17102. 1928. Doubleday, Doran & Company, Inc.
Pilgrims of the Plains: A Romance of the Santa Fe Trail. Kate Adele Aplington. LC 13-2379. 1913. F.G. Browne & Co.
Pilgrims of the Rhine. Edward George Earle Lytton Bulwer-Lytton Lytton. LC 37-12457. 1834. Harper & Brothers.
Pilgrims of the Rhine. Edward George Earle Lytton Bulwer-Lytton Lytton. LC 7-8097. (On cover: Lovell's library, v. 5, no. 294). 1883. J. W. Lovell Company.
Pilgrims of the Rhine. To Which Is Added, The Ideal World, and Zicci, a Tale. Edward George Earle Lytton Bulwer-Lytton Lytton. LC 7-809684. (Half-title: Novels of Sir Edward Bulwer Lytton. Library ed. Romances, vol. II). 1893. Little, Brown, and Company.
Pilgrims of Walsingham: Or, Talse of the Middle Ages. An Historical Romance. Agnes Strickland. LC 8-16881. 1854. Garrett & Co.
Pilgrims on the Earth. Margaret Marchand. LC 40-742233. 1940. Thomas Y. Crowell Company.
Pilgrim's Pistols. Ford Worth. LC 46-20552. 1946. Phoenix Press.
Pilgrim's Pistols. Ford Worth. LC 46-20552. 1946. Phoenix Press.
Pilgrim's Pride. Marie Chay. LC 61-15630. 1961. Dodd, Mead.
Pilgrim's Progres. John Bunyan & Barnard, Frederick, 1846-1896, Illus. LC 33-33295. The John C. Winston Company.
Pilgrim's Progres: In Words of One Syllable. John Bunyan & Alkin, Lucy, 1781-1864. LC 38-150752. G. Routledge & Sons.
Pilgrim's Progress. John Bunyan. LC 75-321236. (Illus.). 1974. 9.95. Reiner Publications.
Pilgrim's Progress. John Bunyan. LC 65-449483. (Signet classic CD221). 1964. New American Library.
Pilgrim's Progress. John Bunyan. LC 49-484555. (Rinehart editions, 27). 1949. Rinchart.
Pilgrim's Progress. John Bunyan. LC 36-37229. (Half-title: Everyman's library, ed. by Ernest Rhys. Romance. no. 204). 1932. J.M. Dent /& Sons, Ltd.
Pilgrim's Progress. John Bunyan & Aikin, Lucy, 1781-1864. LC 39-23070. 1939. Frederick A Stokes Company.
Pilgrim's Progress. John Bunyan & Blake, William, 1757-1827, Illus. 1941. Printed at the Spiral Press for Members of the Limited Editions Club.
Pilgrim's Progress. John Bunyan & Sharrock, Proger, Ed. LC 65-29888. (Penguin English library,EL4). 1965. Penguin Books.
Pilgrim's Progress. John Bunyan & Venables, Edmund, 1819-1895. LC 35-3492. 1932. Oxford University Press, H. Milford.
Pilgrim's Progress: Arranged for the Modern Reader. John Bunyan & Walters, E. Walter, 1877- LC 40-8855. 1939. Cokesbury Press.
Pilgrim's Progress: By F. R. Leavis. John Bunyan. LC 65-4494. (Signet classic CD221) Bibl.). 1964. New Amer. Lib.
Pilgrim's Progress for Devotional Reading. Simplified by Clara E. Murray. John Bunyan & Clara E Murray. LC 58-124218.
Pilgrim's Progress for Modern Readers. John Bunyan & Ashmore, Laura J. LC 38-6931. Fleming H. Revell Company.
Pilgrim's Progress from the World to That Which Is to Come: Delivered Under the Similitude of a Dream. John Bunyan. LC 48-8978. 1948. Macmillan Co.
Pilgrim's Progress from This World to That Which Is to Come. Illustrated by Leonard Vosburgh. John Bunyan. 1961. Grosset & Dunlap.
Pilgrims Progress: From This World to That Which Is to Come. John Bunyan. LC 67-28719. (Legacy library facsimile). 1967. University Microfilms.
Pilgrim's Progress, from This World, to That Which Is to Come. Delivered Under the Similitude of a Dream. In Two Parts. John Bunyan. LC 30-31341. 1853. T.N. Kurts.
Pilgrim's Progress from This World to That Which Is to Come. John Bunyan. LC 36-29468. 1868. F. Warne and Co.

Pilgrim's Progress from This World to That Which Is to Come. John Bunyan. Ed. by Hugh Reginald Haweis. LC 98-147493. 1898. The Century Co.

Pilgrim's Progress from This World to That Which Is to Come: Delivered Under the Similitude of a Dream. John Bunyan. LC 32-13291. (On cover: Alliance library, no. 13). 1900. Street & Smith.

Pilgrim's Progress from This World to That Which Is to Come. John Bunyan. LC 33-23572. M.A. Donohue & Company.

Pilgrim's Progress from This World to That Which Is to Come: Delivered Under the Similitude of a Dream. John Bunyan. LC 38-21218. (Half-title: The world's classics. xii). 1935. Oxford University Press, H. Milford.

Pilgrim's Progress from This World to That Which Is to Come: Delivered Under the Similitude of a Dream. John Bunyan & Blake, William, 1757-1827, Illus. LC 42-16204. 1942. The Heritage Press.

Pilgrim's Progress from This World to That Which Is to Come. Delivered Under the Similitude of a Dream. John Bunyan & Copping, Harold, Illus. LC 3-25775. 1903. Fleming H. Revell Company.

Pilgrim's Progress from This World to That Which Is to Come. John Bunyan & Walker, Katherine Kent (Child) "Mrs. Edward Ashley Walker.". LC 39-19438. G.A. Leavitt.

Pilgrim's Progress. Illustrated by Frank C. Pape. New Ed. John Bunyan. LC 54-116943. (Children's illustrated classics). 1954. Dent.

Pilgrim's Progress in Modern English. Jean Watson & John Bunyan. LC 79-11036. (Illus.). 1979. 6.95 (ISBN 0-310-38810-4). Zondervan Pub. House.

Pilgrim's Progress in Modern English. Retold by James H. Thomas. Illus. by John M. Cadel. John Bunyan & James Henderson Thomas. LC 64-25255. 3.95. Moody.

Pilgrim's Progress in Other Worlds: Recounting the Wonderful Adventures of Ulysum Storries and His Discovery of the Lost Star "Eden.". Nettie Parrish Martin. LC 8-30616. 1908. Mayhew Publishing Company.

Pilgrim's Progress. Including an Introd. to the Book and a Note on the William Blake Designs by A. K. Adams, Together with an Essay on John Bunyan by Thomas Babington Macaulay. 16 Pages of Illus. Including Reproductions of the Front. and 8 Designs for the 1st Part, by William Blake. John Bunyan. LC 68-16180. (Great illus. classics Titan eds.). 1968. 3.95. Dodd.

Pilgrim's Progress. Introd., Notes by G. B. Harrison. John Bunyan. (Everyman paperback, 1204). 1962. pap., 1.35. Dent Dist. New York, Dutton.

Pilgrim's Progress: John Bunyan's Story Rewritten for Young People by Wade C. Smith; Illustrated by the Little Jetts. John Bunyan & Wade Cothran Smith. LC 50-10654. 1950. Wilde.

Pilgrim's Progress: John Bunyan's Story Rewritten for Young People. John Bunyan & Smith, Wade Cothran, 1869- LC 32-6795. 1932. Harper & Brothers.

Pilgrim's Progress: Most Carefully Collated with the Edition Containing the Author's Last Additions & Corrections, & a Life of the Author, by the Rev. Robert Philip. John Bunyan. 1979. Repr. of 1847 ed. lib. bdg. 65.00 o.p. (ISBN 0-8495-0509-7). Arden Lib.

Pilgrim's Progress; Notes: Including Introduction, Synopses, List of Characters, Summaries and Commentaries, Review Questions and Essay Topics, by George F. Willison. Consulting Ed.: James L. Roberts. George F Willison. 1968. pap., 1.00. Cliff's Notes.

Pilgrim's Progress: With Highlights for a Way of Life. A. Probst. 4.00 o.p. (ISBN 0-8062-0399-4). Carlton.

Pilgrim's Progrss. 4th american ed. John Bunyan & Scott, Thomas, 1747-1821, Ed. LC 40-20511. 1844. Presbyterian Board of Publications.

Pilgrim's Regress. Clive Staples Lewis. (Illus.). 200p. 1981. 13.95 (ISBN 0-8028-6063-X). Eerdmans.

Pilgrim's Regress: An Allegorical Apology for Christianity, Reason, and Romanticism. Clive Staples Lewis. LC 59-6953. 1959. Eerdmans.

Pilgrim's Rest. Francis Brett Young. LC 23-6840. E. P. Dutton & Company.

Pilgrim's Rest. A Miss Silver Mystery. Patricia Wentworth. LC 46-2150. 1946. J. B. Lippincott Company.

Pilgrim's Scrip: Or, Wit and Wisdom of George Meredith: with Selections from His Poetry, and an Introd. George Meredith. LC 78-31730. 1978. 30.00 (ISBN 0-8414-6334-4). Folcroft Library Editions.

Pilgrim's Shell: Or, Fergan the Quarryman, a Tale from the Feudal Times. Eugene Sue & De Leon, Daniel, 1852-1914, Tr. LC 4-16430. 1904. New York Labor News Company.

Pilgrim's Way. John Buchan. 5.00 o.p. (ISBN 0-395-07463-0). HM.

Pilgrims Way. Arthur Thomas Quiller-Couch. Repr. of 1925 ed. 12.50 o.p. Scholars Ref Lib.

Pilgrin's Progress. Afterword by F. R. Leavis. John Bunyan. (Signet classic, CD221). New Amer. Lib.

Pilkington Heir. Anna Theresa Sadlier. LC 3-327750. 1903. Benziger Brothers.

Pilkington's Factory Stories of Last Century. Joseph Barlow Brooks. LC 50-23901. 1950. Oxford.

Pill Versus the Springhill Mine Disaster see Trout Fishing in America.

Pillagers. Max Von Kreisler. LC 79-6180. (Double D Western Ser.). 192p. 1982. 10.95 (ISBN 0-385-15519-0). Doubleday.

Pillar. David Harry Walker. LC 52-6238. 1952. Houghton Mifflin.

Pillar Mountain. Max Brand. 1971. pap. 0.75 o.p. (ISBN 0-446-64509-5, 64-509). Paperback Lib.

Pillar Mountain. Frederick Faust. LC 79-1299. (Max Brand western). 1979. 10.95 (ISBN 0-89340-200-1). J. Curley.

Pillar Mountain: A Western Story. Max Brand. LC 28-21894. 1928. Dodd, Mead & Company.

Pillar Mountain: A Western Story. Frederick Faust. LC 28-21894. 1928. Dodd, Mead & Company.

Pillar of Cloud. Jackson Burgess. LC 57-6721. 1957. Putnam.

Pillar of Cloud. Paddy Kitchen. LC 79-2739. 8.95 (ISBN 0-06-012406-7). Harper & Row.

Pillar of Fire. George Borodin. LC 48-601832. 1948. R. M. McBride.

Pillar of Fire. Naoe Kinoshita. Tr. by Kenneth Strong. (Unesco Asian Fiction Ser). (O.s.i.). 200p. 1972. 12.50x o.s.i. (ISBN 0-8448-0028-7). Crane-Russak Co.

Pillar of Fire: A Novel by Frank Carwin Pseud. 1st Ed. Edwin Keith Schempp. LC 54-12479. 1954. Exposition Press.

Pillar of Fire and Other Plays for Today, Tomorrow, and Beyond Tomorrow. Ray Bradbury. 1975. (pbk.) 0.95. Bantam Books.

Pillar of Fire. Hi No Hashira. Naoe Kinoshita. LC 72-172672. (Unesco Asian Fiction Series, 6). (Unesco collection of representative works: Japanese series). 1972. (ISBN 0-04-823097-9). Allen and Unwin.

Pillar of Fire: Or, Israel I Bondage. Joseph Holt Ingraham. LC 7-10349. 1887. Roberts Brothers.

Pillar of Fire: Or, Israel in Bondage. Joseph Holt Ingraham. LC 7-10348. 1896. Roberts Brothers.

Pillar of Fire: Or, Israel in Bondage. Joseph Holt Ingraham. LC 43-27330. 1859. Pudney & Russell Etc.

Pillar of Fire: Or, Isreal in Bondage. Joseph Holt Ingraham. LC 7-10850. 1866. Roberts Brothers.

Pillar of Iron. Taylor Caldwell. LC 65-12359. 1965. Doubleday.

Pillar of Light a Novel. Louis Tracy. LC 4-15005. 1904. E. J. Clode.

Pillar of Salt. Seymour Epstein. LC 59-14372. 1960. Scribner.

Pillar of Salt. Peter S Gray. LC 34-541018. Minton, Balch & Company.

Pillar of Salt. Jennette Barbour Perry Lee. LC 1-30774. 1901. Houghton, Mifflin and Company.

Pillar of Salt. Albert Memmi. LC 75-331414. 1975. 7.95. (ISBN 0-87955-907-1) (ISBN 0-87955-905-5). J. P. O'Hara.

Pillar of Salt. Catherine Vincent. 1978. pap. 1.95 (ISBN 0-532-19174-9). Woodhill.

Pillar of Salt: A Story of Married Life. Horace W. C Newte. LC 14-184617. 1914. John Lane Company.

Pillar of Salt. Translated by Edouard Roditi. Albert Memmi. LC 55-7841. 1955. Criterion Books.

Pillar of Sand. William Richards Castle. LC 14-4308. 1914. 1.30. Dodd, Mead and Company.

Pillars of Destiny. Theodore Chopourian. LC 30-2695. 1929. Compton Press.

Pillars of Eden: A Novel. Philip Verrill Mighels. LC 9-24235. D. FitzGerald, Inc.

Pillars of Gold. Lucile Selk Edgerton. LC 41-122449. 1941. A. A. Knopf.

Pillars of Hercules. Jeffrey Saltzman. LC 77-93668. (Illus.). 1978. pap. 12.50 (ISBN 0-915346-32-X). A Wofsy Fine Arts.

Pillars of Midnight. Elleston Trevor. LC 58-9385. 1958. W. Morrow.

Pillars of Rehoboth Church: A Glendower Story. Nina Hill Robinson. LC 12-283. 1911. Publishing House of the M. E. Church, South, Smith & Lamar, Agents.

Pillars of Salt. Barbara Paul. (Signet book). 1979. 1.75 (ISBN 0-451-08619-8). New American Library.

Pillars of Smoke ... LC 15-10725. 1915. Sturgis & Walton Company.

Pillars of the House: Or, Under Wode, Under Rode. Charlotte Mary Yonge. LC 4-17554. 1901. Macmillan and Co., Limited.

Pillars to Build. Raymond Smith. 120p. (Orig.). 1973. pap. 5.38 o.p. RHS Bk Assn.

Pillone. From the Danish of Wilhelm Bergsoe. Vilhelm I. E. Jergen Vilhelm Bergsee. Tr. by Hubbard, D. G. LC 7-11679. (Lovell's library. v. 2, no. 77). 1883. J. W. Lovell Company.

Pillow Fight. Nicholas Monsarrat. LC 65-114923. bds., 5.95. W. Sloane Dist. Morrow.

Pillow Fight. Nicholas Monsarrat. LC 65-11492. 1965. W. Sloane Associates.

Pillow Problems & A Tangled Tale. Lewis Carroll. pap. 4.00 (ISBN 0-486-20493-6). Dover.

Pillows. Benny Anderson. 164p. 1983. 7.50 (ISBN 0-915306-37-9). Curbstone.

Pilot. James Fenimore Cooper. LC 6-29703. (Standard literature ser. no. 2-3). 1896. University Publishing Company.

Pilot. James Fenimore Cooper. LC 25-19166. 1925. Minton, Balch & Company.

Pilot. James Fenimore Cooper & John Tracy Winterich. LC 70-1448. (Illus.). 1968. Printed for Members of the Limited Editions Club by Garamond Press.

Pilot. Robert P Davis. LC 75-25860. 1976. 7.95 (ISBN 0-688-02985-X). Morrow.

Pilot: A Tale of the Sea. James Fenimore Cooper. LC 6-29865. 1823. C. Wiley.

Pilot: A Tale of the Sea. 5th ed. James Fenimore Cooper. LC 6-29864. 1833. Carey & Lea.

Pilot: A Tale of the Sea. ... new ed. James Fenimore Cooper. 1852. Stringer and Townsend.

Pilot: A Tale of the Sea. James Fenimore Cooper. LC 26-24687. (Half-title: The choice works of Cooper, Revised and corrected series. v. v. 7). 1856. Stringer & Townsend.

Pilot: A Tale of the Sea. new ed. James Fenimore Cooper. LC 6-29705. 1857. Stringer and Townsend.

Pilot: A Tale of the Sea. James Fenimore Cooper. LC 22-17346. 1859. W. A. Townsend and Company.

Pilot: A Tale of the Sea. James Fenimore Cooper. LC 12-19584. 1873. D. Appleton and Company.

Pilot. A Tale of the Sea. James Fenimore Cooper. (Seaside library. v. 12, no. 233). 1878. G. Munro.

Pilot: A Tale of the Sea. household ed. James Fenimore Cooper. Ed. by Cooper, Susan Fenimore. 1884. Houghton, Mifflin and Company.

Pilot: A Tale of the Sea. James Fenimore Cooper. (On cover: Lovell's library. no. 501). 1885. J. W. Lovell Company.

Pilot: A Tale of the Sea. James Fenimore Cooper. Ed. by Watrous, George Ansel. LC 99-167. (Eclectic English classics). American Book Company.

Pilot: A Tale of the Sea. James Fenimore Cooper. LC 22-17343. (On cover: The home library). A. L. Burt Company.

Pilot: A Tale of the Sea. James Fenimore Cooper. (His Works. Mohawk ed.). G. P. Putnam's Sons.

Pilot: A Tale of the Sea. a new ed. James Fenimore Cooper. LC 42-48370. Carey, Lea, & Blanchard.

Pilot: A Tale of the Sea. James Fenimore Cooper. (On cover: Seaside library, Pocket ed. no. 1170). 1889. G. Munro.

Pilot and His Wife: A Norse Love Story. Jonas Lauritz Idemil Lie. Tr. by Bull. Sara Chapman (Thorp) LC 7-18773. 1876. S. C. Griggs and Company.

Pilot Comes Aboard. Will Levington Comfort. LC 32-16547. E. P. Dutton & Co., Inc.

Pilot Error. Bill Knox. LC 76-50776. 1977. 6.95 (ISBN 0-385-12855-X). Published for the Crime Club by Doubleday.

Pilot Fortune. Marian Calhoun Legare Reeves & Read, Emily, Joint Author. LC 7-30664. 1885. Houghton, Mifflin and Company.

Pilot Judy. Anne Brooks. LC 43-3882. 1943. Gramercy Publishing Company.

Pilots. Richard Frede. LC 77-5997. 10.00 (ISBN 0-394-46232-7). Random House.

Pilots of Pomona: A Story of the Orkney Islands. Robert Leighton. LC 11-16149. 1891. C. Scribner's Sons.

Pimlico Plot. Mary McMullen. LC 75-6272. 1975. 5.95 (ISBN 0-385-11041-3). Published for the Crime Club by Doubleday.

Pimp for the Dead. Ralph Dennis. (Hardman,#4). 1974. (pbk.) 0.95. Popular Library.

Pimpernel and Rosemary. Emmuska Orczy. LC 25-1772. George H. Doran Company.

Pimpernel Sixty. Peter Kinsley. LC 68-17289. 1968. 3.95 o.p. (ISBN 0-525-17955-0). Dutton.

Pimp's Needle. Peter Kevin. 1974. (pbk.) 2.25. Barclay House.

Pin. Andrew Neiderman. 1981. pap. 2.50 (ISBN 0-671-41501-8). PB.

Pin a Rose on Me. 1st Ed. Josephine Blumenfeld. 1958. Doubleday.

Pin Money: A Novel. Catherine Grace Frances Moody Gore. LC 6-27507. 1834. E. L. Carey & A. Hart.

Pin to See the Peepshow. Fryniwyd Tennyson Jesse. LC 73-91726. 1974. 8.95. St. Martin's Press.

Pin to See the Peepshow. Fryniwyd Tennyson Jesse. 1975. (pbk.) 1.95. Avon.

Pin to See the Peepshow. Fryniwyd Tennyson Jesse. LC 34-41601. 1934. Double, Doran & Company, Inc.

Pin-up, Two. LC 79-65531. (Illus.). 1979. pap. 6.95 (ISBN 0-87663-926-0). Universe.

Pinball. Jerzy N. Kosinski. LC 81-15067. 1982. 14.95 (ISBN 0-553-05007-9) (ISBN 0-553-01365-3). Bantam Books.

Pinball Murders. Thomas B Black. LC 47-30901. 1947. Reynal & Hitchcock.

Pinch of Experience. Lucy Bethia Colquhoun Walford. LC 8-32808. (On cover: Lovell's Westminister series. 45). 1891. J. W. Lovell Company.

Pinch of Poison: A Mr. and Mrs. North Mystery. Frances Louise Davis Lockridge & Lockridge, Richard. LC 41-207278. 1941. Frederick A. Stokes Company.

Pinch of Snuff. John Michael Evelyn. LC 73-90897. 1974. 6.95. St. Martin's Press.

Pinch of Snuff. Reginald Hill. LC 78-2067. 10.00 (ISBN 0-06-011876-8). Harper & Row.

Pinch of Snuff. Michael Underwood. LC 73-90897. 1974. 6.95 o.p. St Martin.

Pinchbeck Goddess. Alice Macdonald Fleming. LC 6-39932. (Half-title: Appleton's town and country library, no. 211). 1897. D. Appleton and Company.

Pincher Martin. Gerald Jay Goldberg. LC 57-10059. Orig. Title: Two Deaths of Christopher Martin. 1968. pap. 2.95 (ISBN 0-15-671833-2, Harv). HarBraceJ.

Pincus Hood: By Arthur Hodges... with Illustrations by Frederic R. Gruger. Arthur Hodges. LC 16-18485. 1.40. Small, Maynard & Company.

Pine and Palm: A Novel. Moncure Daniel Conway. LC 6-28055. (Leisure hour series, no. 207). 1887. H. Holt and Company.

Pine Creek Ranch. Harold Bindloss. LC 26-6140. 1926. Frederick A. Stokes Company.

Pine Knot: A Story of Kentucky Life. William Eleazar Barton. LC 3800. 1900. D. Appleton and Company.

Pine Ridge Plantation. facsimile ed. William Drysdale. LC 75-38647. (Black Heritage Library Collection Series). Repr. of 1901 ed. 18.75 (ISBN 0-8369-9005-6). Ayer Co.

Pine Ridge Plantation: Or, The Trials and Successes of a Young Cotton Planter. William Drysdale. LC 75-38647. (Black Heritage Library Collection). (Illus.). 1972. (ISBN 0-8369-9005-6). Books for Libraries Press.

Pine Ridge Plantation: Or, The Trials and Successes of a Young Cotton Planter. William Drysdale. LC 1-24919. T. Y. Crowell & Co.

Pine Tree and the Mole. Ezio Taddei & Putnam, Samuel, 1892- LC 45-6546. 1945. Dial Press.

Pine Valley. Lewis B France. LC 6-43270. T. Y. Crowell & Company.

Pineapple Bay Hotel. Jane Gardam. LC 75-33479. 1976. 5.95 (ISBN 0-688-03014-9). Morrow.

Pineapple White. Jon H Shirota. LC 72-76967. (Illus.). 1972. 5.95. Ohara Publications.

Pinecastle. Ivy Manchester. (empress gothic). 1973. (pbk.) 0.95. Curtis Books.

Pines and Pioneers. Wynifred Staples Smith. LC 66-1051. 1965. House of Falmouth.

Pines of Jaalam. Daniel Chase. LC 29-453756. The Bobbs-Merrill Company.

Pines of Lory. John Ames Mitchell. LC 1-25659. 1901. Life Publishing Company.

Pines of Lory. John Ames Mitchell. LC 21-168842. 1903. Life Publishing Company.

Pines of Lory. John Ames Mitchell. LC 24-112322. The Bobbs-Merrill Company.

Piney: ByZachary Ball Pseud. Kelly R Masters. LC 50-7647.

Piney Ridge Cottage: The Love Story of a "Mormon" Country Girl. Nephi Anderson. LC 12-15149. 1912. 0.75. The Deseret News.

Piney Woods Tavern. Samuel Adams Hammett. LC 71-104473. (Illus.). 1970. (ISBN 0-8398-0758-9). Literature House.

Piney Woods Tavern: Or, Sam Slick in Texas. Samuel Adams Hammett. LC 7-935. T. B. Peterson and Brothers.

Pinfold. Joseph Smith Fletcher. LC 28-29728. 1938. Doubleday, Doran and Company, Inc.

Pingleton: Or, Queer People I Have Met. From the Notes of a New York City Cicerone. William Talbot Burke. LC 6-18654. W. T. Burke & Co.

Pink & White Striped Summer. Hazel Krant. (Caprice Romance Ser.). (Illus.). 192p. 1982. pap. 1.95 (ISBN 0-448-16862-6, Pub. by Tempo). Ace Bks.

Pink and White Tyranny. A Society Novel. Harriet Elizabeth Beecher Stowe. LC 8-16116. 1871. Roberta Brothers.

Pink Camellia. Temple Bailey. LC 42-19130. 1942. Houghton Mifflin Company.

Pink Egg. Polly Chase Boyden. LC 42-12604. 1942. Pamet Press.

Pink for a Lady. Vida Hurst. LC 51-1594. 1951. Gramercy Pub. Co.
Pink Gods and Blue Demons. Cynthia Stockley. LC 20-100576. 1920. Cassell and Company, Ltd.
Pink Gods: And Blue Demons. Cynthia Stockley. LC 20-103038. George H. Doran Company.
Pink Hotel. Dorothy Erskine & Edward Everett Tanner. LC 57-8226. 1957. Putnam.
Pink House. Louise Platt Hauck. LC 33-768518. The Penn Publishing Company.
Pink House. Nelia Gardner White. LC 50-5438. 1950. Viking Press.
Pink Magic. Margaret Lee Runbeck. LC 49-936977. 1949. Houghton Mifflin Co.
Pink Marsh. A Story of the Streets and Town. George Ade. LC 5-42960. 1897. H.S. Stone & Co.
Pink Pants. Ralph Y Hopton & Balliol, Anne, Joint Author. LC 35-23920. The Vanguard Press.
Pink Phaeton. Juliana Davison. (Orig.). 1980. pap. 1.75 (ISBN 0-446-94270-7). Warner Bks.
Pink Pussycat: A Novel. Lee Meredith. LC 73-163315. 1972. 1.95 (ISBN 0-7260-0105-8). Gold Star Publications.
Pink Rose: A Novel of Manners. Elspeth Woodward & Edward Barry Roberts. LC 54-7887. (Illus.). 1955. Lothrop, Lee & Shepard.
Pink Rose of Mexico. A Novel. Nevada McNeil. (Dillingham's metropolitan library, no. 7). 1895. G. W. Dillingham, Successor to G. W. Carleton & Co.
Pink Roses. Gilbert Cannan. LC 19-11942. 1919. 1.75. George H. Doran Company.
Pink Sugar. Anna Buchan. LC 24-189078. 2.00. George H. Doran Company.
Pink; the Travels of an American Revolutionary in Russia: By Charles A. Wells and Elizabeth Boykin; with Illustrations by Charles A. Wells. Charles Arthur Wells & Boykin, Elizabeth. LC 35-7668. 1935. MacArthur Prints.
Pink Typhoon. Harrison Robertson. LC 6-16510. 1906. C. Scribner's Sons.
Pink Umbrella. Frances Kirkwood Crane. LC 43-119511. 1943. J. B. Lippincott Company.
Pink War. Eino Hanski & Eric Sjoquist. LC 81-38459. 1982. 11.95 (ISBN 0-8253-0081-9). Beaufort Books.
Pinkertons Ride Again. August William Derleth. LC 60-12844. 5.95 (ISBN 0-88361-061-2). Stanton & Lee.
Pinkertons Ride Again. August William Derleth. 4.95 o.s.i. (ISBN 0-88451-037-9). Edco-Vis Assoc.
Pinkney's Garden. Neil Bell. 1981. 15.00x (ISBN 0-86025-179-9, Pub. by Ian Henry Pubns England). State Mutual Bk.
Pinkney's Garden: A Novel. Stephen Southwold. LC 37-29935. Doubleday, Doran & Co., Inc.
Pinktoes. Chester B. Himes. 256p. 1975. Repr. of 1965 ed. 8.50x (ISBN 0-911860-58-4). Chatham Bkseller.
Pinktoes: A Novel. Chester B Himes. LC 65-13972. 1965. Putnam.
Pinnacle: A Novel. Edward Havill. LC 51-10112. 1951. Sloane.
Pinnacle of Glory. William Reitzel. LC 35-2188. 1935. The Macmillan Company.
Pinned Man: By George Griswold Pseud. 1st Ed. Robert George Dean. LC 55-7463. 1955. Little, Brown.
Pinocchio's Nose. Jerome Charyn. LC 80-70214. 320p. 1982. 16.95 (ISBN 0-87795-303-1); pap. 8.95. Arbor Hse.
Pinoculus: The Latin Version of Pinocchio, by Enrico Maffacini. English Notes and Vocabulary by Olga Ragusa. Carlo Lorenzini. LC 53-2098. 1953. S. F. Vanni.
Pinon Mesa. Lee Floren. LC 51-14970. 1951. Arcadia House.
Pint of Murder. Alisa Craig. LC 79-6659. 1980. 8.95 (ISBN 0-385-15838-6). Published for the Crime Club by Doubleday.
Pint of Murder. Alisa Craig. LC 80-22948. 9.95 (ISBN 0-89621-255-6). Thorndike Press.
Pinto Ben: And Other Stories. William S Hart & Hart, Mary. LC 19-632728. Britton Publishing Company.
Pinto Blood. Tex Holt, pseud. LC 42-2420. 1941. Arcadia House.
Piojo y la Liendre. Susana Rivera. 1974. pap. 4.95 o.p. (ISBN 0-88412-065-1). Tonatiuh-Quinto Sol Intl.
Pioneer: A Tale of Two States. Geraldine Bonner. LC 5-7898. 1905. The Bobbs-Merrill Company.
Pioneer Breed. Glenn R Vernam. LC 77-157632. (Doubleday western). 1972. 4.95. Doubleday.
Pioneer Church: Or, The Story of a New Parish in the West. Montgomery Schuyler. LC 8-205572. 1867. Hurd and Houghton.
Pioneer Doctor: A Story of the Seventies. Elizabeth Porter Gould. LC 6-17872. 1904. R. G. Badger.
Pioneer from Kentucky: An Idyl of the Raton Range. Henry Inman. LC 98-1979. 1898. Crane & Company.
Pioneer from Missouri. Thomas S Byrd. LC 72-78735. 1972. 3.50 (ISBN 0-8059-1703-9). Dorrance.
Pioneer, Go Home! Richard Pitts Powell. (F2205). 1960. Bantam Books.
Pioneer, Go Home! Richard Pitts Powell. LC 59-5786. 1959. Scribner.
Pioneer Herd. Francis W Hilton. LC 37-197490. 1937. H. C. Kinsey & Company, Inc.
Pioneer Loves. Ernest Haycox. LC 52-5864. 1952. Little, Brown.
Pioneer Mother see Collected Works.
Pioneer Panorama: A Story of St. Anthony and Minnesota in the Turbulent Years of Growth from 1853 to 1866. Mabel Otis Robinson. LC 57-9442. 1957. T. S. Denison.
Pioneer Saga. Wilhelmina G. Hedde. 1978. 8.95 o.p. (ISBN 0-533-03708-5). Vantage.
Pioneer Through Time. Matthias R Heilig. LC 63-11410. American Press.
Pioneer Voices. Thomas G Bond. LC 55-36665. 1955.
Pioneer Youth. Frederic T Cuthbert. LC 35-6651. 1935. Meador Publishing Company.
Pioneering the West and Other Stories. Emanuel Cornella. 4.00 o.p. (ISBN 0-8062-0745-0). Carlton.
Pioneers. Janice N. Bennett. (Orig.). 1979. pap. 1.95 (ISBN 0-532-19237-0). Woodhill.
Pioneers. Terry N. Bonner. (New South Wales Ser.: No. 4). (Orig.). 1983. pap. 3.50 (ISBN 0-440-07166-6). Dell.
Pioneers. Courtney Ryley Cooper. LC 38-1576. 1938. Little, Brown and Company.
Pioneers. James Fenimore Cooper. LC 36-37033. (Half-title: Everyman's library, ed. by Ernest Rhys, Fiction. no. 171). 1929. J. M. Dent & Sons, Ltd.
Pioneers. James Fenimore Cooper & James Franklin Beard. LC 77-21795. (Cooper editions). ((Series: Cooper, James Fenimore, 1789-1851.). (Selected works. 1979.). 1977. 19.00 (ISBN 0-87395-359-2). State University of New York Press.
Pioneers. Katharine Susannah Prichard. LC 15-267792. 1915. Hodder & Stoughton.
Pioneers. ... 2d ed. Katharine Susannah Prichard. LC 16-620499. Hodder and Stoughton.
Pioneers. Jack Warner Schaefer. LC 54-5697. 1954. Houghton Mifflin.
Pioneer's Daughter. Emerson Bennett. (arm chair library. no. 37). 1893. F. M. Lumpton.
Pioneers in Penn's Woods. Errol Vincent Coy. LC 32-14436. Beidel Printing House.
Pioneers: Or, The Sources of the Susquehanna; a Descriptive Tale. James Fenimore Cooper. LC 6-29702. 1832. Carey & Lea.
Pioneers: Or, The Sources of the Susquehanna. A Descriptive Tale. James Fenimore Cooper. LC 26-246956. (Half-title: The choice works of Cooper. Revised and corrected series. v. 5). 1856. Stringer & Townsend.
Pioneers: Or, The Sources of the Susquehanna. A Descriptive Tale. James Fenimore Cooper. 1868. Hurd and Houghton.
Pioneers: Or, The Sources of the Susquehanna. a Descriptive Tale. James Fenimore Cooper. 1872. D. Appleton and Company.
Pioneers: Or, The Sources of the Susquehanna, a Descriptive Tale. James Fenimore Cooper. LC 31-352362. (Lettered on cover: Leather stocking tales. Household ed.). 1876. Houghton, Mifflin and Company.
Pioneers: Or. The Sources of the Susquehanna, a Descriptive Tale. James Fenimore Cooper. (On cover: Lovell's library. no. 471). 1884. J. W. Lovell Company.
Pioneers: Or, The Sources of the Susquehanna. A Descriptive Tale. James Fenimore Cooper. (On cover: Seaside library. Pocket ed. no. 318). 1884. G. Munro.
Pioneers: Or, The Sources of the Susquehanna; a Descriptive Tale. James Fenimore Cooper. LC 6-29699. T. Y. Crowell & Company.
Pioneers: Or. The Sources of the Susquehanna, a Descriptive Tale. James Fenimore Cooper. Ed. by Cooper, Susan Fenimore. LC 6-29398. (Half-title: The Leather stocking tales. Riverside ed.). 1899. Houghton, Mifflin and Company.
Pioneers: Or, The Sources of the Susquehanna, a Descriptive Tale. James Fenimore Cooper. LC 4-15433. (Leather-stocking tales). 1901. Macmillan and Co., Limited.
Pioneers: Or, The Sources of the Susquehanna: a Descriptive Tale. James Fenimore Cooper. LC 28-9839. (Honor books). 1928. T. Nelson and Sons.
Pioneers: Or, The Sources of the Susquehanna; a Descriptive Tale. a new ed. James Fenimore Cooper. LC 42-48365. Carey, Lea, & Blanchard.
Pioneers: Or, The Sources of the Susquehanna. James Fenimore Cooper. LC 27-27812. (Fairmount classics). 1927. Macrae, Smith Company.
Pioneer's Son. Alonzo DeWitte Wilder. LC 40-11822. 1940. Meador Publishing Company.
Pious Agent. John Braine. LC 75-39920. 1976. 7.95 (ISBN 0-689-10706-4). Atheneum.
Pious Pilgrimage. Mary Annette Beauchamp Russell Russell. LC 1-30224. 1901. R. G. Badger & Company, Incorporated.
Pip," a Romance of Youth. John Hay Beith. LC 17-9709. 1917. Houghton Mifflin Company.
Pipe All Hand? Aylward Edward Dingle. LC 35-192803. 1935. J. B. Lippincott Company.
Pipe All Hands! Aylward Edward Dingle. LC 74-101279. (Short story index reprint series). 1969. Books for Libraries Press.
Pipe All Hands. Henry Major Tomlinson. LC 37-6380. 1937. Harper & Brothers.
Pipe Down--Sailor". Charles W Whittemore. LC 28-24482. 1928. Covici, Friede.
Pipe Dream. Julian Symons. LC 59-10624. 1959. Harper.
Pipe Dreams and Twilight Tales. Birdsall Jackson. LC 35-20674. Paumanok Press.
Pipe Line: A Novel. Milt Machlin. LC 76-46183. (Pyramid Book). 1976. 1.95 (ISBN 0-515-03862-8). Pyramid Publications.
Pipe Night. John O'Hara. 1974. (pbk.) 1.25. Popular Library.
Pipe Night. John O'Hara. LC 45-300249. 1945. Duell, Sloan and Peace.
Piper on the Mountain. Ellis Peters. 1979. 15.00x (ISBN 0-86025-071-7, Pub. by Ian Henry Pubns England). State Mutual Bk.
Piper on the Mountain. Ellis Peters. (Orig.). pap. 0.60 o.p. (73-648). Lancer.
Piper on the Mountain. Ellis Peters. 1977. 6.90 o.p. (ISBN 0-86025-071-7). State Mutual Bk.
Piper on the Mountain, by Ellis Peters. Edith Pargeter. LC 66-23349. 1966. bds., 4.50. Morrow.
Piper Spins a Yarn. Hiram E Piper. LC 30-5410. Meador Publishing Company.
Piper Tompkins. Ben Field. LC 46-1629. 1946. Doubleday & Company, Inc.
Pipers and a Dancer. Stella Benson. LC 24-22264. 1924. The Macmillan Company.
Piper's Fee. Samuel Hopkins Adams. LC 26-4584. 1926. Boni & Liveright.
Pipers of the Market Place. Clotilde Inez Mary Graves. LC 24-17904. 2.00. George H. Doran Company.
Piper's Price. Harriet Theresa Smith Comstock. LC 29-22130. Doubleday, Doran and Company, Inc.
Piper's Tune. George Byram. LC 58-692519. 1958. W. Sloane.
Piper's Tune. Joseph McCord. LC 38-12694. 1938. Macrae Smith Company.
Piper's Tune. Margaret Kathleen Avern Maddocks. LC 55-16491. 1954. Hurst & Blackett.
Pipes Are Calling. Carter Brown, pseud. (Signet book). New American Library.
Pipes are Calling: The Early Boyd. Carter Boyd. 304p. 1983. pap. 2.95 (ISBN 0-451-12073-6, Sig). NAL.
Pipes of Margaree. Jacquelyn Aeby. 1978. pap. 1.50 (ISBN 0-532-15348-0). Woodhill.
Pipes of War. Shiona Macpherson. LC 75-8877. 1975. 7.95 (ISBN 0-8128-1813-X). Stein and Day.
Pipes of Yesterday: A Novel. Frederic Arnold Kummer & Christian, Mary. 1921. 1.75. The Century Co.
Piping Down Valleys Wild. Maxine Hart. LC 80-81363 (ISBN 0-89002-145-7) (ISBN 0-89002-146-5). Northwoods Press.
Piping Hot. Emile Zola. LC 48-10916. (New Avon library 167). 1948. Avon Pub. Co.
Piping on the Wind. Brigid Knight. 1971. 6.50x (ISBN 0-7182-0872-2). Intl Pubns Serv.
Pipistrello: And Other Stories. Louise De La Ramee. (seaside library. v. 39, no. 791). 1880. G. Munro.
Pippin. Margaret Shirley McCue. LC 55-10988. 1955. Dorrance.
Pippin. Archibald Marshall. LC 41-311185. 1923. Dodd, Mead and Company.
Pippin. Evelyn Van Buren. LC 13-633641. 1913. The Century Co.
Pippin: A Wandering Flame. Laura Elizabeth Howe Richards. LC 17-9251. 1917. 1.40. D. Appleton and Company.
Pippins and Cheese: Being the Relation of How a Number of Persons Ate a Number of Dinners at Various Times and Places. Elia Wilkinson Peattie. LC 7-33489. 1897. Way and Williams.
Pippin's Journal: Or, Rosemary Is for Remembrance, by Rohan O'Grady. June O'Grady Skinner. LC 62-11925. 1962. Macmillan.
Pique. A Novel. 2d ed. Sarah Ellis. LC 35-33417. 1863. Loring.
Pique. A Novel. 20th ed. Sarah Ellis. LC 6-37843. Loring.
Piracy" A Romantic Chornicle of These Days. Michael Arlen. LC 23-92300. George H. Doran Company.
Piraeus Plot. Harry Arvay. 1975. (pbk.) 1.25. Bantam Books.
Pirate. Harold Robbins. 1978. pap. 3.95 (ISBN 0-671-41714-2). PB.
Pirate. Harold Robbins. (O.s.i.). 384p. 1974. 8.95 o.s.i. (ISBN 0-671-21877-8). S&S.
Pirate. Walter Scott. LC 37-21880. 1822. S. H. Parker.
Pirate. Walter Scott. (On cover: Lovell's library, no. 515). 1885. J. W. Lovell Company.
Pirate. Walter Scott. (On cover: Seaside library. Pocket ed. no. 393). 1885. G. Munro.
Pirate. Walter Scott. Ed. by Lang, Andrew. LC 15-231286. (On cover: Waverley novels). D. Estes & Company.
Pirate. Walter Scott. LC 36-37010. (Half-title: Everyman's library, ed. by Ernest Rhys. Fiction. no. 139). 1925. E. P. Dutton & Co.
Pirate: A Novel. Harold Rubin. LC 74-13407. 1974. 8.95 (ISBN 0-671-21877-8). Simon and Schuster.
Pirate, and The Three Cutters. Frederick Marryat. LC 42-30910. 1878. G. Routledge and Sons.
Pirate, and The Three Cutters. Illustrated with Eight Steel Engravings, from Drawings by Clarkson Stanfield, R. A. Frederick Marryat. LC 9-3033. 1893. G. Bell & Sons.
Pirate Doctor: Or, The Extraordinary Career of a New-York Physician. A Naval Officer, Pseud. LC 7-39632. Garrett & Co.
Pirate from Rome. John Van Duyn Southworth. LC 65-24314. 4.95. Crown.
Pirate... From the Last Rev Ed., Containing the Author's Final Corrections, Notes, &C. parker's ed. Walter Scott. LC 8-5733. (Waverley novels: Library ed. v. 12). Bazin & Ellsworth.
Pirate Gold. Frederic Jesup Stimson. LC 8-15676. 1896. Houghton, Mifflin and Company.
Pirate Island: A Story of the Southern Pacific. William Joseph Cosens Lancaster. LC 5084. (On cover: Medal library. no. 69). 1900. Street & Smith.
Pirate Jean. Reginald Wright Kauffman. LC 30-5176. The Macaulay Company.
Pirate of Barataria. Lawton Bryan Evans & Lafitte, Jean, 1780?-1826?--Fiction. LC 26-146298. Milton Bradley Company.
Pirate of Gramercy Park: The Novel of New York, 1803-1880. Bruce Nicolaysen. 640p. 1983. 3.95 (ISBN 0-380-83014-0). Avon.
Pirate of Hitchfield. Edward Easton, pseud. 1978. pap. 2.25 (ISBN 0-532-22144-3). Woodhill.
Pirate of Jasper Peak. Cornelia Lynde Meigs. LC 18-19512. 1918. 1.35. The Macmillan Company.
Pirate of Panama: A Tale of the Fight for Buried Treasure. William MacLeod Raine. LC 14-9410. 1.25. G. W. Dillingham Company.
Pirate of Parts. Richard Neville. LC 13-21745. 1913. 1.25. The Neale Publishing Company.
Pirate of Pittsburgh. Henry Esmond Oram Whitman. LC 25-6312. 1925. Houghton Mifflin Company.
Pirate of World's End. Lin Carter. 1978. 1.75 (ISBN 0-87997-410-9). DAW Books.
Pirate Plunder: Or, Cap'n Quick. Frank E Potts. LC 27-185396. 1927. Harper & Brothers.
Pirate Queen: The Story of Ireland's Grania O'Malley in the Days of Queen Elizabeth. 1st Ed. Edith Patterson Meyer. LC 61-9287. 1961. Little, Brown.
Pirate Rock. David Harry Walker. 236p. Repr. of 1969 ed. lib. bdg. 11.10x (ISBN 0-88411-870-3). Amereon Ltd.
Pirate Slave. Richard Parker. 1977. 6.95 o.p. (ISBN 0-525-66517-X). Elsevier-Nelson.
Pirate Twins. William Nicholson. LC 50-2564. Coward-McCann.
Pirate Wench. Frank Shay. LC 34-331272. 1934. I. Washburn.
Pirates!! Dorothy J. Goulding. 1981. 1.50x o.p. (ISBN 0-88020-100-2). Coach Hse.
Pirate's Cove: By Cynthia Millburn Pseud. Anne Tedlock Brooks. LC 51-3130. 1951. Arcadia House.
Pirate's Face. Norval Richardson. LC 28-11056. 1928. Little, Brown, and Company.
Pirates' Hope. Francis Lynde. LC 22-9489. 1922. C. Scribner's Sons.
Pirates' Lair. Jane Corrie. (Harlequin Romances Ser.). 192p. 1981. pap. 1.25 (ISBN 0-373-02413-4). Harlequin Bks.
Pirate's Love. Johanna Lindsey. 1978. pap. 3.50 (ISBN 0-380-40048-0, 81638-5). Avon.
Pirate's Mistress. Amanda H. Douglas. (Inflation Fighter Ser.). 192p. 1982. pap. cancelled (ISBN 0-8439-1108-5, Leisure Bks). Nordon Pubns.
Pirate's Mistress. Amanda Hart Douglass. (O.s.i.). 1977. pap. 1.50 o.s.i. (BT51111). Belmont-Tower.
Pirate's Mistress. Amanda Hart Douglass. (Belmont Tower Book). 1.50. Tower Publications.
Pirates of Cape Ann: Or, The Freebooter's Foe. A Tale of Land and Water. Charles E Averill. LC 6-3847. 1848. F. Gleason.
Pirates of Gohar. Jeffrey Lord. (Blade Ser.: No. 32). 1979. pap. 2.25 (ISBN 0-523-41724-1). Pinnacle Bks.
Pirates of Rosinante. Alexis A. Gilliland. 224p. (Orig.). 1982. pap. 2.50 (Del Rey). Ballantine.
Pirates of the Pacific. Arthur Grove Day. 1968. 4.95 o.p. Hawthorn.

Pirates of the Prairies. Gustave Aimard & St. John, Percy Bolingbroke, 1821-1889, Ed. LC 5-42596. (On cover: Lovell's library, no 1011). 1887. J. W. Lovell Company.
Pirates of the Range. Bertha Muzzy Sinclair. LC 37-143993. 1937. Little, Brown and Company.
Pirates of the Sky: A Tale of Modern Adventure. Stephen Gaillard. LC 15-7735. 1.25. Rand McNally & Company.
Pirates of the Spring. Forrest Reid, pseud. LC 76-145255. 1971. (ISBN 0-403-01170-1). Scholarly Press.
Pirates of the Spring. Forrest Reid, pseud. LC 20-26325. 1920. Houghton Mifflin Company.
Pirates of Venus. Edgar Rice Burroughs. LC 62-21735. 1962. Canaveral Press.
Pirates of Venus. Edgar Rice Burroughs. LC 34-48609. E. R. Burroughs, Inc.
Pirates' Purchase. Ben Ames Williams. LC 31-31846. 1931. E. P. Dutton & Company, Inc.
Piri and I. Laurence Vail. LC 23-17989. 1923. Lieber & Lewis.
Pisces' Child. Aletha Caldwell Conner. LC 34-32218. Southwest Press.
Pistol. James Jones. (Signet bk. D1893). 1961. New American Lib.
Pistol. James Jones. LC 59-578501. 1959. Scribner.
Pistol. James Jones. (Dell book). 1979. 2.25 (ISBN 0-440-17068-0). Dell Pub. Co.
Pistol. James Jones. (Dell book). 1973. (pbk) 1.25. Dell.
Pistol Apostle. Dan T Kelliher. LC 45-5487. 1945. Phoenix Press.
Pistol Johnny: By Joseph Wayne Pseud. 1st Ed. Wayne D Overholser. LC 60-10688. 1960. Doubleday.
Pistol Law. Paul Evan Lehman. pap. 0.50 o.p. (50-382). Manor Bks.
Pistol Pardners. William MacLeod Raine. 1975. (pbk.) 0.95. Popular Library.
Pistol Pards. Galen C. Colin. LC 43-104169. 1943. Phoenix Press.
Pistol Passport: A Novel of the Texas Border. Eugene Cunningham. LC 36-597188. 1936. Houghton Mifflin Company.
Pistolero Fantasma. new ed. John Benteen. Tr. by Alvaro De Villa from Eng. (Compadre Collection, Fargo Ser.: No. 3). Orig. Title: Phantom Gunman. 160p. 1974. pap. 0.85 (ISBN 0-88473-513-3). Fiesta Pub.
Pistoleros. John Benteen. (Sundance: No. 5). 1979. pap. 1.75 o.s.i. (ISBN 0-8439-0706-1, Leisure Bks). Nordon Pubns.
Pistols and Pedagogues. Fallon Evans. LC 63-8539. 1963. Sheed and Ward.
Pistols at Potter's Ford: By Chuck Stanley. Charles Stanley Strong. LC 57-4128. 1957. Arcadia House.
Pistols for Hire. Nelson Coral Nye. 1970. pap. 0.60 o.p. (ISBN 0-447-73880-1). Lancer.
Pistols for Hire: A Tale of the Lincoln County War and the West's Most Desperate Outlaw, William (Bill, the Kid) Bonney. Nelson Coral Nye. LC 41-160632. 1941. The Macmillan Company.
Pistols for Two, & Other Short Stories. Georgette Heyer. 1964. 4.95 o.p. (ISBN 0-525-17989-5). Dutton.
Pistols for Two. 1st Ed. Aaron Marc Stein. LC 51-14233. 1951. Published for the Crime Club by Doubleday.
Pistols in the Morning. Donald Barr Chidsey. LC 30-7785. The John Day Company.
Pistols on the Pecos. Paul Evan Lehman. 1971. pap. 0.60 o.p. (60-488). Manor Bks.
Pit. James Hart. (Cloth ed. 7.95 o.p.). 1970. pap. text ed. 2.50x o.p. (ISBN 0-675-09368-6). Merrill.
Pit. Frank Norris. LC 79-105109. (Charles E. Merrill standard editions). (Illus.). 1970. C. E. Merrill.
Pit. Frank Norris. LC 37-30674. 1937. The Sun Dial Press, Inc.
Pit. Owen West. 1982. pap. 2.95 (ISBN 0-515-05696-0). Jove Pubns.
Pit; a Story of Chicago. Frank Norris. LC 56-97476. (His The epic of the wheat). 1956. Grove Press.
Pit: A Story of Chicago. Frank Norris. LC 79-10998. 1969. P. Smith.
Pit: A Story of Chicago. Frank Norris. LC 3-1580. (His The epic of the wheat. 2). 1903. Doubleday, Page & Co.
Pit: A Story of Chicago. Frank Norris. LC 24-27976. (His The epic of the wheat. ii). Grosset & Dunlap.
Pit: A Story of Chicago. Frank Norris. LC 30-26623. 1930. Doubleday, Doran & Company, Inc.
Pit: A Story of Chicago. Frank Norris. LC 34-284253. (Half-title: The modern library of the world's best books). 1934. The Modern Library.
Pit & the Pendulum. Edgar Allan Poe. Ed. by Raymond Harris. (Jamestown Classics Ser.). (Illus.). 48p. (Orig.). 1982. pap. text ed. 2.00x (ISBN 0-89061-265-X, 471); tchr's ed. 3.00x (ISBN 0-89061-266-8, 473). Jamestown Pubs.
Pit and the Pendulum, and Five Other Tales. Edgar Allan Poe. LC 67-11397. (Illus.). 1967. F. Watts.
Pit & the Pendulum & Other Tales of Terror. new ed. Edgar Allan Poe. Ed. by Joseph W. Nash. 1976. pap. 0.95 o.p. (ISBN 0-89319-002-0). Andor Pub.
Pit Bull. Stephen Geller. LC 67-11357. 1967. Dutton.
Pit of Babel. Joseph Zsuffa. LC 75-8097. 1975. 5.95 (ISBN 0-915648-00-8). Orpheus Press.
Pit-Prop Syndicate. Freeman Wills Crofts. LC 65-6773. 1965. Penquin Books.
Pitcairn's Island. Charles Bernard Nordhoff & Hall, James Norman. LC 34-28424. 1934. Little, Brown, and Company.
Pitcher of Romance. Richard Washburn Child. LC 30-7194. Sears Publishing Company, Inc.
Pitcher Who Threw with Both Arms. Joseph J Murphy. LC 74-24257. (Illus.). 1971.
Pitchfork Patrol. Clay Fisher. 1975. (pbk.) 0.95. Bantam Books.
Pitchfork Patrol: By Clay Fisher Pseud. Henry Allen. LC 62-18510. 1962. Macmillan.
Pitchlady. Bob Foreman. (Orig.). 1971. pap. 0.95 o.p. (N2522). Pyramid Pubns.
Pitchman: A Novel. Robert Lowell Moore. LC 56-115210. 1956. Coward-McCann.
Pitchman: A Novel of the Television World. Special Abridged Ed. Robert Lowell Moore. LC 58-116524. (Popular giant, G211). 1958. Popular Library.
Pitchmen. Don James. pap. 0.60 o.p. (60-394). Manor Bks.
Pitfall. Jay Dratler. LC 47-624. 1947. Thomas Y. Crowell Company.
Pitfall in August. 1st Ed. Howard Roman. LC 60-13442. 1960. Harper.
Pitiful Plaything & Other Essays. Li Guangtian. Tr. by Gladys Yang. (Panda Ser.). 154p. (Orig.). 1982. pap. 2.95 (ISBN 0-8351-1024-9). China Bks.
Pitiful Wife. Margaret Storm Jameson. LC 24-866. 1924. A. A. Knopf.
Pitiful Wife. Margaret Storm Jameson. LC 31-6270. 1931. A. A. Knopf.
Pitiless Passion. Ella MacMahon. 1895. Macmillan and Co.
Pittsburg Landing: Or, Adventures of a Young Volunteer. A Thrilling Story of a Western Boy. St. George Rathborne. (War library Pocket ed., v. 1, no. 9). 1883. Novelist Publishing Co.
Pittsburgh Phil: A Novel of a Legend. Frank Mastroly & Heimer, Melvin Leighton. LC 60-5448. 1960. Duell, Sloan and Pearce.
Pity for Pamela, by Mary Fitt Pseud. 1st American Ed. Kathleen Freeman. LC 51-10189. 1951. Harper.
Pity for Women. Helen Anderson. LC 37-12718. 1937. Doubleday, Doran & Company, Inc.
Pity for Women. Henry De Montherlant. Tr. by McGreevy, Thomas & Rodker, John. LC 38-11065. 1938. A. A. Knopf.
Pity Him Afterwards. Donald E Westlake. LC 64-10538. (Random House mystery). 1964. Random House.
Pity Is Not Enough. Josephine Herbst. LC 33-136413. Harcourt, Brace and Company.
Pity My Love. Daoma Winston. (Orig.). 1967. pap. 0.50 o.p. (B50-793). Belmont-Tower.
Pity My Love. Daoma Winston. (Kangaroo Book). 1977. 1.50. Pocket Books.
Pity of God. Beulah Marie Dix. LC 32-11375. 1932. The Viking Press.
Pity of the World. Elinor Mordaunt, pseud. LC 39-8610. The Greystone Press.
Pity the Innocent. Ethel Edith Mannin. LC 57-11141. 1957. Putnam.
Pity the Lover. Gerald Foster. LC 38-14886. 1938. Godwin.
Pity the Poor Blind: A Novel. Henry Howarth Bashford. LC 13-14821. 1913. 1.35. H. Holt and Company.
Pity the Tyrant. Hans Otto Storm. LC 37-24112. 1937. Longmans, Green and Co.
Pity Us All. John Henry Reese. LC 69-16471. 1969. 4.95. Random House.
Pity Youth Does Not Last. Michael O'Guiheen. Tr. by Tim Enright. (Illus.). 1982. pap. 6.95 (ISBN 0-19-281320-X). Oxford U Pr.
Pixie Joe. Virginia Vernard. 1975. pap. 3.00 o.p. (ISBN 0-89105-001-9). AWM Co.
Pixy in Petticoats. Ernest George Henham. LC 13-7885. 1909. Moffat, Yard & Company.
PL Book of Modern American Short Stories. Nicholas Moore. Repr. of 1945 ed. 20.00 (ISBN 0-89987-183-6). Darby Bks.
Place Among People. Rodney Hall. LC 76-356386. 1975. 7.90 (ISBN 0-7022-0962-7) (ISBN 0-7022-0963-5). University of Queensland Press.
Place and Power. Ellen Thorneycroft Fowler. LC 3-20057. 1903. D. Appleton and Company.
Place Apart. Paula Fox. 1982. pap. 1.95 (ISBN 0-451-11283-0, AJ1283, Sig). NAL.
Place at Whitton. Thomas Keneally. LC 65-154231. 1965. 3.50. Walker.
Place Beyond Man. Cary Neeper, pseud. (Dell Book). 1977. 1.50 (ISBN 0-440-16931-3). Dell Pub. Co.
Place Beyond Man. Cary Neeper, pseud. LC 74-12268. 1975. (ISBN 0-684-13888-3). Scribner.
Place by the Sea. Dinah Palmtag. 1977. 1.50 (ISBN 0-440-16784-1). Dell Pub. Co.
Place Called Cavalry. Marcus L. Loane. pap. 1.95 o.p. Zondervan.
Place Called Dagon. Herbert S Gorman. LC 27-23152. George H. Doran Company.
Place Called Empty. Mary Lieber. LC 78-1764. 1978. 2.95 (ISBN 0-89293-067-5). Beta Book Co.
Place Called Estherville. Erskine Caldwell. LC 49-10728. 1949. Duell, Sloan and Pearce.
Place Called Saturday. Mary Astor. LC 68-22677. 1968. 5.95. Delacorte Press.
Place for a Pisoner. Edith Caroline Rivett. LC 50-15994. 1949. Pub. for the Crime Club by Doubleday.
Place for Everyone. Tana Reiff. LC 78-75221. (LifeTimes Ser.). 1979. pap. 3.32 (ISBN 0-8224-4318-X). Pitman Learning.
Place for Human Beings. 2nd. ed. Pam Portugal. (Living on This Planet Ser.). (Illus.). 160p. 1978. pap. 6.95 (ISBN 0-9601088-5-8). Wild Horses.
Place for Love. Peggy O'More, pseud. LC 56-12935. 1956. Arcadia House.
Place for Murder. Emma Lathen, pseud. 1981. pap. 2.50 (ISBN 0-671-83425-8). PB.
Place for My Head. 1st Ed. William Hoffman. 1960. Doubleday.
Place for the Mighty. Henry Denker. LC 73-76561. 1973. 6.95 o.p. (ISBN 0-679-50387-0). McKay.
Place for the Mighty: A Novel About the Superlawyers. Henry Denker. LC 73-76561. 1973. 6.95. McKay.
Place for the Mighty: A Novel About the Super Lawyers. Henry Denker. 1979. 2.50. Pocket Books.
Place for the Supermighty: A Novel About the Superlawyers. Henry Denker. LC 73-76561. 1974. (pbk.) 1.75 (ISBN 0-345-24051-0). Ballantine.
Place for the Wicked. Elleston Trevor. LC 68-14203. 1968. Doubleday.
Place for Us. Alma Routsong. LC 71-97985. 1969. 2.25. Bleecker Street Press.
Place in Colusa. George Benet. LC 76-15308. 2.95 (ISBN 0-917300-00-9). Singlejack Books.
Place in England. Melvyn Bragg. LC 73-142953. 1971. 5.95 (ISBN 0-394-46926-7). Knopf.
Place in the City. Howard Melvin Fast. LC 37-16646. Harcourt, Brace and Company.
Place in the Country. Sarah Gainham. LC 69-11800. 1969. 6.95. Holt, Rinehart and Winston.
Place in the Sun. Frank Fenton. LC 42-21302. 1942. Random House.
Place in the Sun: a Story of the Making of an Ameridan. Emma Henriette Schermeyer Backus. LC 17-12715. 1917. 1.35. The Page Company.
Place in the World. John Hastings Turner. LC 20-3578. 1920. C. Scribner's Sons.
Place Like Dairy-Anne. Sandra Epstein. LC 78-9281. 7.95 (ISBN 0-8037-0139-X). Dial Press.
Place Like Hessberg. Charles Fleet. (Raven House Mysteries Ser.). 224p. 1981. pap. 2.25 (ISBN 0-373-63017-4, Pub. by Worldwide). Harlequin Bks.
Place of Coolness: A Novel. D M Brosia. LC 55-65169. 1955. Kenedy.
Place of Devils. Lucinda Baker. LC 76-3640. 7.95. Putnam.
Place of Devils. Lucinda Baker. (Berkley Medallion Book.). 1977. 1.75 (ISBN 0-425-03498-4). Berkley Pub. Corp.
Place of Hawks. August William Derleth. LC 35-7575. Loring & Mussey.
Place of Honeymoons. Harold MacGrath. LC 12-24562. 1.50. The Bobbs-Merrill Company.
Place of Honor. Frederick G Kelly. LC 73-90102. 1974. 4.95 (ISBN 0-8059-1962-7). Dorrance.
Place of Honor. Mary Verdick. LC 61-9204. 1961. Doubleday.
Place of Jackals. 1st American Ed. Ronald Hardy. LC 55-5593. 1955. Doubleday.
Place of Judgment. Barbara Levy. LC 65-199166. 5.95. Doubleday.
Place of Mists. Robert MacLeod, pseud. 1970. 4.95 o.p. (ISBN 0-8415-0058-4). Sat Rev Pr.
Place of Mists: A Talos Cord Adventure. Bill Knox. LC 78-122146. 1970. 4.95. McCall Pub. Co.
Place of Ravens. Pamela Hill. LC 80-28045. 9.95 (ISBN 0-312-61373-3). St. Martin's Press.
Place of Sapphires. Florence Engel Randall. LC 69-12044. 1969. Harcourt, Brace & World.
Place of Sapphires: A Novel. Laura Owen Miller. LC 56-10215. 1956. J. Day Co.
Place of Shadows. Kage Booton. (Red badge detective). 1959. Dodd, Mead.
Place of Shadows. Kage Booton. pap. 0.50 o.p. (52-893). Paperback Lib.
Place of Stone. Jim Hunter. LC 64-10978. 1964. Pantheon Books.
Place of Stones. Constance Heaven. LC 75-31539. 1975. 11.95 (ISBN 0-8161-6334-0). G. K. Hall.
Place of the Dawn. Gordon Taylor. LC 75-513. 1975. 6.95 (ISBN 0-03-014531-7). Holt, Rinehart and Winston.
Place of the Dawn. Gordon Taylor. 1977. 1.50 (ISBN 0-380-01765-2). Avon Books.
Place of the Lion. Charles Williams. LC 51-9847. 1951. Pellegrini & Cudahy.
Place of the Lion. Charles Walter Stansby Williams. 1965. pap., 1.93. Eerdmans.
Place of the Lion see Novels.
Place of the Trap. William Oliver Turner. LC 73-116908. (Berkley medallion book). 1975. (pbk.) 0.95 (ISBN 0-425-02822-4). Berkley Pub. Co.
Place on Dark Island. Grace Corren, pseud. 1971. pap. 0.75 o.p. (ISBN 0-447-74762-2). Lancer.
Place on Earth. Wendell Berry. LC 67-11965. 1967. Harcourt, Brace & World.
Place on Wishbone Alley: By Nancy Hartwell Pseud. Claire Wallis Callahan. LC 60-6601. 1960. Holt, Rinehart and Winston.
Place to Belong. Wendell Willis. LC 82-80356. (Journey Adult Ser.). 144p. 1982. pap. text ed. 2.95 (ISBN 0-8344-0119-3). Sweet.
Place to Come to. Robert Penn Warren. 1977. 12.95 (ISBN 0-394-41064-5). Random.
Place to Come to: A Novel. Robert Penn Warren. LC 76-50129. 10.00 (ISBN 0-394-41064-5). Random House.
Place to Meet. Mary Orr, pseud. LC 61-131526. 1961. Bobbs-Merrill.
Place to Stand: A Novel by AnnBridge Pseud. Mary Dolling Sanders O'Malley. LC 53-123024. 1953. Macmillan.
Place Where I Am Standing. Theodore Enslin. 1964. pap. 3.00 (Pub. by Elizabeth Pr). SBD.
Place with Two Faces. Josephine Mann. (Ravenswood gothic). 1974. (pbk.) 0.95 (ISBN 0-671-77767-X). Pocket Books.
Place Your Bets. Zeke Masters, pseud. (Faro Blake Ser.: No. 15). 1982. pap. 1.95 (ISBN 0-671-41994-3). PB.
Place Your Bets, Gentlemen. Philip R Carson. LC 39-15201. Printed by Rein Co.
Places. James Morris. LC 72-88806. 1973. 6.95 (ISBN 0-15-172023-1). HarBraceJ.
Places of a Fan. Vincent Sheean. LC 37-284231. 1937. Doubleday, Doran & Company, Inc.
Places of Stones. Constance Heaven. LC 74-30595. 1975. 6.95 (ISBN 0-698-10659-8). Coward, McCann & Geoghegan.
Places Where I've Done Time. William Saroyan. (Delta Book). 1973. (pbk.) 2.25. Dell.
Places Where They Sing. Simon Raven. LC 73-508962. (Alms for Oblivion Ser.: No. 6). 1970. 12.50x (ISBN 0-85634-997-6). Intl Pubns Serv.
Placid Man; or, Memoirs of Sir Charles Beville, 1770, 2 vols. in 1. Charles Jenner. Ed. by Michael F. Shugrue. (Flowering of the Novel, 1740-1775 Ser.: Vol. 91). 1974. lib. bdg. 50.00 (ISBN 0-8240-1190-2). Garland Pub.
Placide, a Spanish Tale... Translated from Les Battuecas, of Madame De Genlis. Stephanie Felicite Ducrest De Saint-Aubin Genlis. Tr. by Jamieson, Alexander, LL. B. LC 6-442513. 1817. Published by Kirk & Mercein. T. & W. Mercein, Printers, Gold-Street....
Plague. Jonathan Black. 1976. (pbk.) 1.50. Belmont Tower Books.
Plague. Albert Camus. (YA) 1948. 10.95 (ISBN 0-394-44061-7). Knopf.
Plague. Albert Camus. Tr. by Stuart Gilbert. 1967. 3.95 o.s.i. (ISBN 0-394-60109-2, M109). Modern Lib.
Plague. Albert Camus. Tr. by Stuart Gilbert. 1965. pap. 1.95 (ISBN 0-394-30969-3, T69, Mod LibC). Modern Lib.
Plague. Gwyneth Cravens & John S. Marr. LC 76-26905. 8.95 (ISBN 0-525-18010-9). Dutton.
Plague. Graham Masterton. 1978. 1.95 (ISBN 0-441-66760-0). Ace Books.
Plague Court Murders. John Dickson Carr. LC 34-179738. 1934. W. Morrow and Company.
Plague Court Murders. Carter Dickson, pseud. 1981. 18.95x (Pub. by Remploy England). State Mutual Bk.
Plague Dogs. Richard Adams. (Illus.). 1978. 2.75 (ISBN 0-449-23904-7). Fawcett Crest Books.
Plague Dogs. Richard George Adams. LC 77-11185. (Illus.). 1978. 10.95 (ISBN 0-394-42247-3). Knopf.
Plague from Space. Harry Harrison. 3.95. Doubleday.
Plague of Demons. John Creasey. LC 76-4733. (Rinehart suspense novel). 1977. 6.95 (ISBN 0-03-017541-0). Holt, Rinehart and Winston.
Plague of Demons. Keith Laumer. 1979. pap. 1.95 (ISBN 0-671-82975-0, Timescape). PB.
Plague of Oblivion. Clark Darlton. (Perry Rhodan, 28). (Illus.). 1973. (pbk.) 0.75. Ace.
Plague of Sailors. Brian Callison. LC 73-151201. 1971. 5.95. Putnam.
Plague of Silence. John Creasey. LC 68-13993. 1968. Walker.

Plague of Spies. Michael Kurland. Orig. Title: Mission: Sneaky Sam. 1969. pap. 0.60 o.p. (X2098). Pyramid Pubns.
Plague of Violence. Hugh Pentecost. (John Jericho Mystery series,#6). 1974. (pbk.) 1.25 (ISBN 0-523-00451-6). Pinnacle Books.
Plague of Violence. Judson Pentecost Philips. LC 73-128860. (Red badge novel of suspense). 1970. 4.50. Dodd, Mead.
Plague of Violence: A John Jericho Mystery Novel. Hugh Pentecost. 1970. 4.50 o.p. (ISBN 0-396-06246-6). Dodd.
Plague on Both Your Causes see Blacklash.
Plague Ship. Andre Norton, pseud. LC 77-25452. (Norton, Andre. the Space Adventure Novels of Andre Norton). 1978. 7.95 (ISBN 0-8398-2416-5). Gregg Press.
Plague Ship. Andre Norton. 1973. (pbk.) 0.95. Ace Books.
Plague Ship. Frank Gill Slaughter. LC 75-36611. 1976. 7.95 (ISBN 0-385-04958-7). Doubleday.
Plague Ship: A Dane Thorson-Solar Queen Adventure, by Andrew North Pseud. 1st Ed. Alice Mary Norton. LC 56-7843. 1956. Gnome Press.
Plague Ship by. Frank Gill Slaughter. (Kangaroo Book). 1977. 1.95 (ISBN 0-671-80938-5). Pocket Books.
Plague: Tr. from the French. Albert Camus. Tr. by Gilbert, Stuart. LC 48-7625. 1948. A. A. Knopf.
Plague. Tr. from the French by Stuart Gilbert. Albert Camus. (Modern lib. coll. ed., T69). 1966. pap., 1.65. Random.
Plagued by the Nightingale. Kay Boyle. LC 31-6593. 1931. J. Cape & H. Smith.
Plagued by the Nightingale: Pref. by Harry T. Moore. Kay Boyle. LC 65-197742. (Crosscurrents: mod. fic.). 5.95. Southern Ill Univ. Pr.
Plain Americans. Mary Helen Fee. LC 26-6811. 1926. A. C. McClurg & Co.
Plain Case of Murder. Lee Thayer, pseud. 1944. Dodd, Mead and Company.
Plain English. Charles Moody. LC 35-6054. 1935. Meador Publishing Company.
Plain Jane Vanilla. Missy McConnell. (Illus.). 48p. 20.00 (ISBN 0-88014-018-6). Mosaic Pr OH.
Plain Man. Julian Symons. LC 62-17130. 1962. Harper and Row.
Plain Mary Smith: A Romance of Red Saunders. Henry Wallace Phillips. 1905. The Century Co.
Plain Murder. Cecil Scott Forester. LC 54-12406. (Dell first edition, 30). 1954. Dell Pub. Co.
Plain Path. Francis Newton Symmes Allen. 1912. Houghton Mifflin Company.
Plain People see Collected Works.
Plain People: A Story of the Western Reserve. Edward P Branch. LC 6-17938. 1892. The Publishers' Printing Co.
Plain Pleasures. Jane Auer Bowles. LC 66-72515. (B 66-11663). 1966. Owen.
Plain Tales from the Hills. authorized ed. Rudyard Kipling. LC 42-29442. United States Book Company.
Plain Tales from the Hills. authorized ed. Rudyard Kipling. LC 14-19346. (On cover: Lovell's international series, no. 59). F. F. Lovell & Company.
Plain Tales from the Hills. Rudyard Kipling. LC 98-500. H. Altemua.
Plain Tales from the Hills. rev. copyright ed. Rudyard Kipling. LC 99-3031. 1899. Doubleday & McClure Co.
Plain Tales from the Hills. Rudyard Kipling. LC 9-3022. 1899. The Lovell Company.
Plain Tales from the Hills. Rudyard Kipling. LC 4873. H. M. Caldwell Company.
Plain Tales from the Hills. Rudyard Kipling. LC 19-724. A. L. Burt Company.
Plain Tales from the Hills. Rudyard Kipling. W. B. Conkey Company.
Plain Tales from the Hills. Rudyard Kipling. LC 28-1666. 1922. Doubleday, Page & Company.
Plain Tales from the Hills. Rudyard Kipling. LC 37-3020. (Immortal masterpieces of literature. vol. iv). The Spencer Press.
Plain Tales from the Hills. The Works of Rudyard Kipling. Rudyard Kipling. LC 9-16446. 1909. The Nottingham Society.
Plain Tales from the Hills. With a Biographical Sketch. by rudyard kipling. ed. Rudyard Kipling & Norton, Charles Eliot, 1827-1908. 1910. Doubleday, Page & Company.
Plain Tales from the Hills: With a Biographical Sketch by Charles Eliot Norton; Rev. Ed. Rudyard Kipling & Norton, Charles Eliot, 1827-1908. LC 16-6652. 1911. Doubleday, Page & Company.
Plain Tales from the Hills. With 11 Original Illus. by Howard Mueller. Rudyard Kipling. LC 50-3268. (World's greatest literature). 1950. Fountain Press.
Plain Tales from the Hills, 1886-1887. Soldiers Three, and Other Stories. Rudyard Kipling. LC 52-491613. (Mandalay edition of the works of Rudyard Kipling). 1925. Doubleday, Page.
Plain Tales of the City. Sonia Ureles. LC 28-7498. Mastermen Printing Co.
Plain Woman's Story. Julia MacNair Wright. LC 9-528. Presbyterian Board of Publication and Sabbath-School Work.
Plains of Abraham. James Oliver Curwood. LC 28-15676. 1928. Doubleday, Doran & Company, Inc.
Plains of Cement. Patrick Hamilton. LC 35-437. 1935. Little, Brown, and Company.
Plains of Silence. Alice J. De C. Leake Askew & Askew, Claude Arthur Cary, Joint Author. LC 8-20350. 1907. Cassell and Company, Limited.
Plains Song. Wright Morris. LC 79-2655. (Illus.). 1980. 11.49i (ISBN 0-06-013047-4, HarpT). Har-Row.
Plains Song for Female Voices. Wright Morris. LC 80-24580. (Penguin contemporary fiction series). 1981. 3.95 (ISBN 0-14-005778-1). Penguin Books.
Plains Woman. Anne Jordan. (Orig.). 1980. pap. 1.75 o.s.i. (ISBN 0-505-51545-8). Tower Bks.
Plaka and Other Stories: Tales of South East Asia, Scandinavia and Greece. Rowan Hewison. LC 76-482898. (Illus.). 1976. Hippo.
Plan for Conquest. A. A. Glyn. Ed. by Alice Sachs. 1969. lib. bdg. 3.50 o.p. Arcadia.
Plan for Escape. Adolfo Bioy-Casares. LC 75-6813. 1975. 7.95 (ISBN 0-525-18015-X). Dutton.
Plan for Escape. Adolfo Bioy-Casares. Tr. by Suzanne J. Levine. LC 75-6813. 160p. 1975. 7.95 o.p. (ISBN 0-525-18015-X). Dutton.
Plan XVI... Garden City, N.Y. 1934. ed. Douglas Gordon Browne. LC 34-23850.
Planchette's Diary. Kate Field. LC 6-41203. 1868. J. S. Redfield.
Plane and Plank: Or, The Mishaps of a Mechanic. William Taylor Adams. (upward and onward series, v. 2). 1898. Lee & Shepard.
Plane Jane. Peggy Gaddis, pseud. Grammercy Publishing Co.
Plane Trees. Monique Lange. Tr. by J. M. Calder. 1980. pap. 2.95 (ISBN 0-7145-0446-7). Riverrun NY.
Plane Trees. Translated from the French by Richard Howard. Monique Lange. LC 62-110851. 1962. Pantheon Books.
Planet Buyer. Cordwainer Smith, pseud. (Orig.). 1969. pap. 0.60 o.p. (X2049). Pyramid Pubns.
Planet Buyer. Cordwainer Smith. 1975. pap. 1.25 o.p. (ISBN 0-515-03969-1). Pyramid Pubns.
Planet Called Treason. Orson Scott Card. LC 78-21420. (Illus.). 8.95 (ISBN 0-312-61395-4). St. Martin's Press.
Planet Called Utopia. J. T. McIntosh. (Orig.). 1979. pap. 1.95 (ISBN 0-89083-503-9). Zebra.
Planet Finders. Vern Dermott. 1977. pap. 1.25 (ISBN 0-532-12499-5). Woodhill.
Planet Finders. Vern Dermott. Ed. by Alice Sachs. 1971. 3.95 o.p. Lenox Hill.
Planet Masters. Allen Wold. LC 78-3997. 8.95 (ISBN 0-312-61398-9). St. Martin's Press.
Planet of Death. Robert Silverberg. LC 67-1721. 1967. Holt, Rinehart and Winston.
Planet of Dread. Gregory Kern. (Cap Kennedy,#10). 1974. (pbk.) 0.95. DAW Books.
Planet of Exile. Ursula K. Le Guin. LC 75-418. (Garland Library of Science Fiction). 1975. 11.00 (ISBN 0-8240-1423-5). Garland Pub.
Planet of Exile. Ursula K. Le Guin. LC 77-3794. 1978. 7.95 (ISBN 0-06-012559-4). Harper & Row.
Planet of No Return. Harry Harrison. LC 81-52094. (Illus.). 6.95 (ISBN 0-671-43138-2). Simon & Schuster.
Planet of Peril. Otis Adelbert Kline. LC 29-206489. 1929. A. C. McClurg & Co.
Planet of Tears. Trish Reinius & Bob Johnson. LC 79-15753. 9.95. (ISBN 0-89742-025-X) (ISBN 0-89742-016-0). Dawne-Leigh Publications.
Planet of the Apes. Pierre Boulle. LC 63-21853. 1963. Vanguard Press.
Planet of the Blind. Paul Corey. 1969. pap. 0.60 o.p. (63-147). Paperback Lib.
Planet of the Blind. Laurence James. (Rack,#4). 1975. (pbk.) 1.25 (ISBN 0-523-00675-6). Pinnacle Books.
Planet of the Damned. Harry Harrison. 256p. 1981. pap. 2.95 (ISBN 0-523-48565-4). Pinnacle Bks.
Planet of the Double Sun. Neil R Jones. LC 75-413. (Garland Library of Science Fiction). 1975. 11.00 (ISBN 0-8240-1418-9). Garland Pub.
Planet of the Gawfs. Steve Vance. (Leisure book). 1.50 (ISBN 0-8439-0545-X). Nordon Pubns.
Planet of the Gods. Kurt Mahr. (Perry Rhodan, #27)). 1973. (pbk) 0.75. Ace Books.
Planet of the Robots. Scott Shirley & Scott Lisetor. (Perspective I Novel Ser.). 48p. 1982. 2.50 (ISBN 0-87879-301-1). Acad Therapy.
Planet of the Voles: A Science Fiction Novel. Charles Platt. LC 72-147058. 1971. 4.95. Putnam.
Planet of Treachery. E. E. Smith & Stephen Goldin. (Orig.). 1982. pap. 2.25 (ISBN 0-425-05301-6). Berkley Pub.
Planet of Youth. Stanton Arthur Coblentz. 1952. 3.50; pap. 1.00. Fantasy Pub Co.
Planet Patrol. Sonya Dorman. LC 78-1566. 6.95 (ISBN 0-698-20435-2). Coward, McCann & Geoghegan.
Planet Probability. Brian N Ball. 1973. 0.95. DAW Books.
Planet Problems: Science Fiction That Could Happen. Henrick Christian Henricksen. LC 57-10170. 1957. William- Frederick Press.
Planet Run. Gordon R. Dickson & Keith Laumer. 288p. 1982. pap. 2.75 (ISBN 0-523-48525-5). Pinnacle Bks.
Planet Run. Keith Laumer & Gordon R. Dickson. LC 67-15365. (Doubleday science fiction). 1967. Doubleday.
Planet Savers. Marion Zimmer Bradley. LC 78-21222. (Gregg Press Science Fiction Series). (Illus.). 1979. 8.00 (ISBN 0-8398-2514-5). Gregg Press.
Planet Savers. Marion Zimmer Bradley. 1.50. Ace.
Planet Story. Harry Harrison & Jim Burns. LC 78-65675. (& W visual library). (Illus.). 1979. 10.95 (ISBN 0-89104-136-2) (ISBN 0-89104-135-4). A & W Publishers.
Planet Toride, Please Reply! Kurt Brand. (Perry Rhodan, 75). (Illus.). 1975. (pbk.) 1.25. Ace Books.
Planet Without a Name. Neil Shapiro. 176p. (Orig.). 1978. pap. 1.50 (ISBN 0-89041-198-0, 3198). Major Bks.
Planeta Fantasma. new ed. Harris Moore, pseud. Tr. by Javier Lopez from Eng. (Compadre Collection). Orig. Title: Slater's Planet. 160p. (Span.). 1974. pap. 0.75 (ISBN 0-88473-603-2). Fiesta Pub.
Planetarium. Nathalie Sarraute. Tr. by Maria Jolas from Fr. 1980. pap. 4.95 (ISBN 0-7145-0444-0). Riverrun NY.
Planetarium: A Novel. Nathalie Sarraute. LC 60-6952. 1960. G. Braziller.
Planetarnoe Soznanie. Mihailo Mihailov. 230p. (Rus.). 1982. 15.00 (ISBN 0-88233-752-1). Ardis Pubs.
Planetary Legion: A Story of War and Peace, 1940-1980, by Romulus Rexner Pseud. Marion Matarisvan. LC 62-160246. 1961. Pantheon Press-G. E.
Planets for Sale. Edna Mayne Hull. LC 54-8076. (Fell's science fiction library). 1954. F. Fell.
Planets of Adventure. Basil Wells. 1949. Fantasy Pub. Co.
Planets of Wonder: A Treasury of Space Opera. Ed. by Terry Carr. LC 76-22506. 6.95 (ISBN 0-8407-6526-6). T. Nelson.
Planets Three. Frederik Pohl. (Orig.). 1982. pap. 2.50 (ISBN 0-425-05224-9). Berkley Pub.
Planned Planethood Caper. F. W. Paul. (Orig.). 1969. pap. 0.75 o.p. (74-531). Lancer.
Planning Women's Banquets. Margaret Wise. 1964. pap. 1.75 o.p. Moody.
Plant-Magic Man. new ed. Lawrence Durrell. (Capra Chapbook Ser.: No. 5). (Illus.). 1973. pap. 4.00 (ISBN 0-912264-51-9). Capra Pr.
Plant Me Now. Miriam Ann Hagen. LC 47-401993. 1947. Pub. for the Crime Club, by Doubleday & Company, Inc.
Plant: The Well; The Angel: a Trilogy. Vassilis Vassilikos. LC 64-13446. 1964. Knopf.
Plantagenet Prelude. Eleanor Hibbert. LC 76-383023. (Illus.). 1976. 3.50 (ISBN 0-7091-5101-2). Hale.
Plantagenet Prelude. Eleanor Hibbert. LC 79-24299. (Illus.). 1980. 10.95 (ISBN 0-399-12448-9). Putnam.
Plantagenet Prelude. Jean Plaidy. 320p. 1981. pap. 2.75 (ISBN 0-449-24422-9, Crest). Fawcett.
Plantagenet Prelude. Jean Plaidy. LC 79-24299. 1980. 10.95 (ISBN 0-399-12448-9). Putnam Pub Group.
Plantain Season. Harriet Hahn. LC 75-19434. 6.95 (ISBN 0-393-08729-8). Norton.
Plantasmion, a Fairy Tale. Sara Coleridge Coleridge. LC 26-749518. 1874. Roberts Brothers.
Plantation. George McNeill. (pbk.) 1.75. Bantam Books.
Plantation. Ovid Williams Pierce. LC 52-13681. 1953. Doubleday.
Plantation Belle and Other Stories. Julia McLemore Dimick. LC 29-93683. The Christopher Publishing House.
Plantation Boy. Jose Lins Do Rego. LC 65-11112. 1966. Knopf.
Plantation Breed. Hugo Paul, pseud. (Orig.). 1969. pap. 0.95 o.p. (75-074). Lancer.
Plantation Murder. Christine Noble Govan. LC 38-5874. 1938. Houghton Mifflin Company.
Plantation Pageants. Joel Chandler Harris. LC 99-4654. 1899. Houghton, Mifflin and Company.
Plantation Patriot: A Biography of Eliza Lucas Pinckney. Frances Leigh Williams. (Illus.). 1967. Harcourt, Brace & World.
Plantation Shadows. Eleanor Fox Ponder. LC 49-3811. 1949. Pelican Pub. Co.
Plantation Trilogy: Deep Summer, The Handsome Road and This Side of Glory. Gwen Bristow. LC 62-9363. 1962. Crowell.
Planteers: The Ultimate Weapon. John Wood Campbell. (ACE double, G-585). Ace.
Planter. David Brown. LC 75-104423. Repr. of 1853 ed. lib. bdg. 15.00 03349986x (ISBN 0-8398-0174-2); pap. text ed. 6.95x (ISBN 0-89197-888-7). Irvington.
Planter: A Novel. Herman Whitaker. 1909. Harper & Brothers.
Planter of the Tree. Ruby Mildred Ayres. LC 27-6909. George H. Doran Company.
Planter's Daughter. A Tale of Louisiana... Eliza Ann Depuy. LC 42-357469. 1858. T. B. Peterson and Brothers.
Planter's Northern Bride. Caroline Lee Whiting Hentz. LC 72-108136. (Southern literary classics series). (Illus.). 1970. 4.25. University of North Carolina Press.
Planter's Northern Bride. A Novel. Caroline Lee Whiting Hentz. LC 14-22449. 1854. Parry & M'Millan.
Planter's Victim: Or, Incidents of American Slavery ... LC 7-38197. 1855. W. W. Smith.
Planting of Chives. Gena Ford. 1964. pap. 3.00 o.p. (Pub. by Elizabeth Pr). SBD.
Plants: A Novel. Kenneth McKenney. LC 75-34725. 7.95 (ISBN 0-399-11627-3). Putnam.
Plashers Mead. Compton Mackenzie. LC 15-21788. 1915. Harper & Brothers.
Plasma Monster. Kurt Mahr. (Perry Rhodan#95). 1976. (pbk.) 1.25. Ace Books.
Plaster Saint: A Novel of Heresy on the Campus. 1st Ed. Martin Alfred Larson. LC 53-51384. 1953. Exposition Press.
Plaster Saints. Frederic Arnold Kummer. LC 22-870822. 1922. The Macaulay Company.
Plaster Sinners. Colin Watson. LC 80-1989. (Crime Club Ser.). 192p. 1981. 10.95 o.p. (ISBN 0-385-17338-5). Doubleday.
Plastic Age. Percy Marks. LC 24-2625. The Century Co.
Plastic Age. Percy Marks. LC 28-17932. 1924. Grosset & Dunlap.
Plastic Age: A Novel. Percy Marks. LC 80-17959. (Lost American Fiction Ser.). 352p. 1980. Repr. of 1924 ed. 12.95 (ISBN 0-8093-0984-X). S Ill U Pr.
Plastic Kind of Death. easy eye ed. Thomas D. Carroll. (Orig.). 1968. pap. 0.60 o.p. (73-787). Lancer.
Plastic Man. David J Gerrity. (Signet Book). 1976. (pbk.) 1.25. New American Library.
Plastic Nightmare. Richard Neely. LC 78-52930. 1978. pap. text ed. 1.75 o.s.i. (ISBN 0-89559-056-5). Dale Books Inc.
Plastics & Rubbers. E. W. Duck. 1972. 10.00 (ISBN 0-8022-2076-2). Philos Lib.
Plate of Red Herrings. Richard Lockridge. LC 68-19830. (Main Line mysteries). 1968. 4.50. Lippincott.
Plateau Pauses. Dorothy D. Harris. 1970. 5.00 o.p. (ISBN 0-8233-0149-4). Golden Quill.
Plated City. Bliss Perry. LC 7-36176. 1895. C. Scribner's Sons.
Platero and I: An Andalusian Elegy; Translated from the Spanish by William H. and Mary M. Roberts. Juan Ramon Jimenez. (Signet classic CD17). New American Library.
Platero and I: An Andalusian Elegy. Translated from the Spanish by William and Mary Roberts. Drawings by Baltasar Lobo. Juan Ramon Jimenez Mantecon. LC 57-14471. 1956. P. C. Duschnes.
Platero and I: Translated by Eloise Roach. Drawings by Jo Alys Downs. Juan Ramon Jimenez Mantecon. LC 57-11131. 1957. University of Texas Press.
Platero y Yo; Elegia Andaluza: 1907-1916. Illustraciones De Zamorano. Juan Ramon Jimenez Mantecon. 1964. pap., 1.50. Taurus Dist. New York, Las Americas.
Platforms. John R Maxim. LC 80-15031. 11.95 (ISBN 0-399-12535-3). Putnam.
Platinum. Myra Cochnar. 352p. (Orig.). 1982. pap. 2.95 (ISBN 0-523-41581-8). Pinnacle Bks.
Platinum Bullet. Richard L Graves. LC 74-78528. 1974. 7.95 (ISBN 0-8128-1710-9). Stein and Day.
Platinum Cat. Miles Burton. LC 38-34141. 1938. Pub. for the Crime Club, Inc., by Doubleday, Doran & Co., Inc.
Platinum Logic. Tony Parsons. 384p. 1982. pap. 8.95 (ISBN 0-933328-13-3). Delilah Bks.
Platinum Rainbow. 2nd ed. Bob Monaco & James Riordan. Ed. by Patricia Monaco. 239p. (Orig.). 1980. pap. 9.95 (ISBN 0-940018-00-4). Swordsman Pr.
Platinum Tower. Jerome Bahr. 1939. C. Scribner's Sons.
Platinum Yoke. McCready Huston. LC 63-15970. 1963. Lippincott.
Plato Paved the Way. Helen Starkey. LC 14-176879. 1913. The Neale Publishing Company.
Platonic Affections. John Smith. LC 8-8170. (On cover: The keynotes series, no. 21). 1896. Roberts Bros.; Etc., Etc.

Platter. Adrianus Michael De Jong & Duym, Alfred Van Ameyden Van, Tr. LC 46-22835. 1946. Querido.

Platypus of Doom and Other Nihilists. Arthur Byron Cover. 1976. (pbk.) 1.50. Warner Books.

Platzo and the Mexican Pony Rider. Theodore Isaac Rubin. LC 65-13106. (Illus.). 1965. Trident Press.

Plautus in the Convent. Conrad F. Meyer. Tr. by William G. Howard. Bd. with Monk's Marriage. LC 64-20048. xiv, 133p. pap. 1.95 (ISBN 0-8044-6503-7). Ungar.

Plautus in the Convent. Two Novellas, with an Introd. Conrad Ferdinand Meyer. LC 64-20048. 1965. F. Ungar Pub. Co.

Plautus: Three Comedies. Tr. by Erich Segal. 1969. pap. 5.95xi o.p. (ISBN 0-06-131932-5, TB1932, Torch). Har-Row.

Play a Lone Hand. Luke Short. LC 76-48101. 1977. 7.95 (ISBN 0-89340-040-8). J. Curley.

Play a Lone Hand. Luke Short. 1974. (pbk.) 0.95. Bantam Books.

Play a Lone Hand: By Luke Short Pseud. Frederick Dilley Glidden. LC 51-6104. 1951. Houghton Mifflin.

Play-Actress. Samuel Rutherford Crockett. LC 6-36174. 1896. G. P. Putnam's Sons.

Play-Actress. Samuel Rutherford Crockett & Crawford, Francis Marion. LC 20-12365. 1901. G. P. Putnam's Sons.

Play-Boy. Elizabeth Garver Jordan. LC 32-6312. 2.00. The Century Co.

Play for Keeps. Harry Whittington. LC 57-132214. Abelard-Schuman.

Play Girl: A Thrilling Romance of a Madcap Gold Digger, Based on the Motion Picture Story. John Stone. LC 29-2472. Jacobsen-Hodgkinson-Corporation.

Play It Again, Charlie Brown. Charles M. Schulz. (O.S.I.). (Illus.). 1971. 2.95 o.s.i. (ISBN 0-529-01327-4, A4179). Random.

Play It As It Lays: A Novel. Joan Didion. LC 79-113779. 1970. 5.95. Farrar, Straus & Giroux.

Play It As It Lays, a Novel. Joan Didion. LC 78-26475. (Touchstone book). 1979. 3.95 (ISBN 0-671-24846-4). Simon and Schuster.

Play it by Heart. Vanessa Valcour. (Second Chance at Love Ser.: No. 121). 1983. pap. 1.75 (ISBN 0-515-07209-5). Jove Pubns.

Play Like You're Dead. Whit Masterson, pseud. LC 67-20776. (Red badge mystery). 1967. Dodd, Mead.

Play Little Victims. Kenneth Cook & Megan Gressor. LC 79-303356. (Illus.). 5.95 (ISBN 0-08-023123-3). Pergamon Press.

Play Misty for Me. Paul Gillette. (Orig.). 1971. pap. 0.75 o.p. (A907S, Award). Univ Pub & Dist.

Play Misty for Me. Paul Gillette. (O.s.i.). (Orig.). pap. 0.75 o.p. (A907S, Award). Univ Pub & Dist.

Play of Darkness. Irving A Greenfield. 1974. (pbk.) 1.50 (ISBN 0-380-00055-5). Avon.

Play on Your Harp. Travis Ingham. LC 36-19835. Farrar & Rinehart Inc.

Play Our Song Again. Lynsey Stevens. (Harlequin Romance Ser.). 192p. 1982. pap. 1.50 (ISBN 0-373-02488-6). Harlequin Bks.

Play the Field Alone: And Other Stories. George Platt. LC 54-835487. 1954. Vantage Press.

Play the Game! Ruth Comfort Mitchell. LC 21-4316. 1921. D. Appleton and Company.

Play This Love with Me. Baird Bryant. pap. 1.25 o.s.i. (203, Travellers Comp). Olympia.

Playback. Raymond Chandler. LC 58-905756. 1958. Houghton Mifflin.

Playboy. Richard Edward Connell. LC 36-7040. 1936. G.P. Putnam's Sons.

Playboy. Deeping Warwick. 1948. Dial Press.

Playboy. Paul W. Fairman. 1970. pap. 0.75 o.p. (75-296). Manor Bks.

Playboy Book of Crime & Suspense. Playboy Editors. 1966. 5.95 o.p. (57793). Trident.

Playboy Book of Crime and Suspense: Selected by the Eds. of Playboy. Playboy Editors. LC 66-12860. 5.95. Playboy Pr.

Playboy Book of Horror & the Supernatural. Playboy Editors. 1967. 5.95 o.p. (57798). Trident.

Playboy Book of Horror and the Supernatural: Selected by the Eds. of Playboy. 1st Ed. LC 67-145529. 1967. 5.95. Playboy Pr.

Playboy Book of Science Fiction and Fantasy. LC 66-12861. 1966. Playboy Press.

Playboy Book of Science Fiction & Fantasy. 1971. 5.95 o.p. (57794). Playboy.

Playboy Book of Science Fiction & Fantasy. Playboy Editors. 1966. 5.95 o.p. (57794). Trident.

Playboy Book of Science Fiction and Fantasy: Selected by the Eds. of Playboy. Playboy Editors. LC 66-12861. 5.95. Trident.

Playboy Riots. James Kilroy. (Irish Theatre Ser.: No. 4). (Orig.). 1971. pap. text ed. 4.00x (ISBN 0-85105-199-5, Dolmen Pr). Humanities.

Playboy The Playboy Book of Crime and Suspense: Selected by the Eds. of Playboy. LC 66-12860. (BA0116). 1968. Playboy.

Playboy The Playboy Book of Science Fiction and Fantasy: Selected by the Eds. of Playboy. LC 66-12861. (BA0115). 1968. Playboy.

Playboy's Girl. Thomas Stone. LC 42-15699. 1942. Phoenix Press.

Playboy's Magnificent Seven. LC 72-90418. 1.25. Playboy Press.

Playboy's Short-Shorts. Playboy Editors. LC 77-89547. (Illus., Orig.). 1970. pap. 0.95 o.p. Playboy.

Playboy's Short-Shorts. LC 77-89547. (Illus.). 1970. 0.95. Playboy Press.

Playboy's Short-Shorts 2. 1st. ed. LC 73-188912. (Illus.). 1972. 0.95. Playboy Press.

Playboy's Stories for Swinging Readers. Playboy Editors. LC 76-78806. 1969. pap. 0.95 o.p. Playboy.

Playboy's Stories for Swinging Readers. LC 76-78806. 1969. 0.95. Playboy Press.

Playboy's Stories of the Sinister & Strange. Playboy Editors. LC 77-78510. 1969. pap. 0.95 o.p. (A00105). Playboy.

Playboy's Stories of the Sinister & Strange. LC 77-78510. 1969. 0.95. Playboy Press.

Player. Warwick Downing. LC 73-22314. 1974. 5.95. Saturday Review Press.

Player King. Earl H Rovit. LC 65-11993. 1965. 5.95. Harcourt.

Player on the Other Side. Ellery Queen, pseud. 1975. (pbk.) 1.25 (ISBN 0-345-24461-3). Ballantine Books.

Player on the Other Side. Ellery Queen, pseud. LC 77-13993. (Ellery Queen mystery). 1978. 9.95 (ISBN 0-89340-107-2). J. Curley.

Player Piano. new ed. Kurt Vonnegut. LC 66-14582. 1966. Holt, Rinehart and Winston.

Player Piano. Kurt Vonnegut. 1974. (pbk.) 1.25. Dell.

Player Piano. Kurt Vonnegut. LC 52-2643. 1952. Scribner.

Players. Gary Brandner. LC 75-10533. 1975. 1.50 (ISBN 0-515-03671-4). Pyramid Books.

Players. Don DeLillo. LC 76-54961. 1977. 7.95 (ISBN 0-394-41260-5). Knopf: Distributed by Random House.

Players. Arnold Schulman. LC 78-69545. 8.95 (ISBN 0-06-014004-6). Harper & Row.

Players and the Game. Julian Symons. LC 72-661. 1975. (pbk.) 1.25 (ISBN 0-380-00376-7). Avon.

Players and Vagabonds. Viola Roseboro' LC 70-101291. (Short story index reprint series). 1969. Books for Libraries Press.

Players & Vagabonds. Viola Roseboro. LC 70-101291. (Short Story Index Reprint Ser.). 1904. 17.00 (ISBN 0-8369-3228-5). Ayer Co.

Players at the Game of People. John Brunner. LC 80-66561. 1980. 2.25 (ISBN 0-345-29235-9). Ballantine Books.

Player's Boy: A Novel. Winifred Bryher. LC 53-613056. 1953. Pantheon Books.

Player's Boy: A Novel. Winifred Bryher. LC 53-6130. 1963. Pantheon Books.

Player's Boy Is Dead. Leonard D Tourney. LC 80-7611. 1980. 9.95 (ISBN 0-06-014341-X). Harper & Row.

Players in a Dark Game. Stephen Coulter. LC 68-31914. 1968. W. Morrow.

Players of London: Written. Louise Isabel Beecher Chancellor. LC 9-28110. 1909. B. W. Dodge Co.

Players of Null-A. Alfred Elton Van Vogt. LC 77-4510. (Gregg Press science fiction series). 1977. 10.00 (ISBN 0-8398-2352-5). Gregg Press.

Playfellow: Containing The Crofton Boys; Feats on the Fiord; The Settlers at Home; The Peasant and the Prince. a new ed., with one hundred and seventy-one illustrations, and eight plates printed in colours from designs by a. w. cooper. ed. Harriet Martineau. LC 4-19742. 1895. G. Routledge and Sons, Limited.

Playgirls in Love. May Christie. LC 32-154319. Grosset & Dunlap.

Playgirls of Yesteryear. Robert Lebeck. (Illus.). 176p. 1981. pap. 6.95 o.p. (ISBN 0-312-61553-1). St Martin.

Playground. John Buell. LC 75-35630. 7.95 (ISBN 0-374-23076-5). Farrar, Straus and Giroux.

Playground. H. V. Elkin. 1979. pap. 2.25 o.s.i. (ISBN 0-505-51423-0). Tower Bks.

Playground. T. M. Wright. 320p. 1982. pap. 2.95 (ISBN 0-523-48046-6). Pinnacle Bks.

Playground of Death. John Buxton Hilton. LC 80-51381. 9.95 (ISBN 0-312-61559-0). St. Martin's Press.

Playground of Satan. Beatrice C Baskerville. LC 19-3703. W. J. Watt & Company.

Playhouse. Elaine Ford. LC 80-10928. 8.95 (ISBN 0-07-021503-0). McGraw-Hill Book Co.

Playing Against Time. Tr. from Czech by Jean Layton. Jiri Fried. LC 65-723. (Artia pocket bks.). pap., 1.10. Artia.

Playing for Change. Bruce Pollock. (O.s.i.). (gr. 7-9). 1978. pap. 1.50 o.s.i. (ISBN 0-671-29877-1). Archway.

Playing for High Stakes. Annie Hall Thomas Cudlp. LC 6-31173. (Seaside library. v. 28, no. 577). 1879. G. Munro.

Playing for Keeps. Lori Copeland. (Candlelight Ecstasy Ser.: No. 134). (Orig.). 1983. pap. 1.95 (ISBN 0-440-17171-7). Dell.

Playing for Keeps. large print ed. Brook Hastings. LC 81-6273. 1981. 11.95 (ISBN 0-8161-3245-3). G.K. Hall.

Playing for Keeps a Novel. Roger Vailland & Hopkins, Gerard, 1892- LC 48-8549. 1948. Houghton Mifflin Co.

Playing from Memory. David Milofsky. 304p. 1982. pap. 2.95 (ISBN 0-380-57166-8, 57166). Avon.

Playing from Memory: A Novel. David Milofsky. LC 80-18600. 12.95 (ISBN 0-671-25252-6). Simon and Schuster.

Playing House. Fredrica Wagman. LC 72-93181. 1973. 5.95 (ISBN 0-03-007746-X). Holt, Rinehart and Winston.

Playing House. Fredrica Wagman. (Fawcett crest book). 1975. (pbk.) 1.25. Fawcett.

Playing Tahoe: A Novel. Sandra Hochman. LC 80-28668. 13.95 (ISBN 0-671-25358-1). Wyndham Books.

Playing the Game. Clarence Fowler Holland. LC 23-5853. Printed by the Democrat Printing & Litho. Co.

Playing the Game. Leslie W Quirk. LC 16-8228. 1.00. M. A. Donohue & Co.

Playing the Game: The Homosexual Novel in America. Roger Austen. LC 76-46228. 8.95 (ISBN 0-672-52287-X) (ISBN 0-672-52318-3). Bobbs-Merrill.

Playing the Game: The Story of a Society Girl. Rita Weiman. LC 10-16094. Cupples & Leon Company.

Playing the Mischief. John William De Forest. Ed. by Donald Pizer. LC 74-96517. (American Authors Ser). 1970. Repr. of 1875 ed. lib. bdg. 13.95 o.s.i. (ISBN 0-512-00135-9). Garrett Pr.

Playing the Mischief. A Novel. John William De Forest. LC 6-400021. (On cover: Library of select novels. no. 442). 1875. Harper & Brothers.

Playing with Fire. Amelia Edith Huddleston Barr. LC 14-7280. 1914. 1.35. D. Appleton and Company.

Playing with Fire: A Novel. Bob Veder. LC 80-17930. 1980. 10.95. Linden Press/Simon & Schuster.

Playing with Fire. A Tale of Love, Sin and Retribution. M. P Green. (On cover: The red cover series, no. 19). 1888. J. S. Ogilvie & Company.

Playing with Love (Liebelei) Arthur Schnitzler & Hofmannsthal, Hugo Hofmann, Edler Von, 1874-1929. LC 44-50642. 1914. A. C. McClurg & Co.

Playing with Murder: By Will U. Lovitt Pseud. Joseph Antoine Paul Levesque. LC 60-11651. 1960. Greenwich Book Publishers.

Playing with Souls: A Novel. Clara De Longworth Chambrun. LC 22-18096. 1922. C. Scribner's Sons.

Playmate. Laura Lou Brookman. LC 28-14241. Grosset & Dunlap.

Playmates. J. N. Williamson. 304p. (Orig.). 1982. pap. 2.95 (ISBN 0-8439-1072-0, Leisure Bks). Nordon Pubns.

Plays & Stories. Barrie. 1975. pap. 2.25 o.p. (ISBN 0-460-01184-7, Evman). Biblio Dist.

Plaything of the Gods. Charles Caldwell Park. LC 12-17204. 1912. 1.25. Sherman, French & Company.

Playthings of Desire. Harry Sinclair Drago. LC 24-23484. The Macaulay Company.

Playthings of Time: Translated from the Germans. Arnold Zweig & Ashton, Emma D., Tr. LC 35-949518. 1935. The Viking Press.

Playtime Is Over. Clyde Brion Davis. LC 49-8192. 1949. J. B. Lippincott Co.

Playwright's Daughter: A Novel. Annie Edwards. (Harper's handy ser. no. 89). 1886. Harper & Brothers.

Playwright's Daughter. A Novel. Annie Edwards. (On cover: Seaside library. Pocket ed. no. 850). 1886. G. Munro.

Playwright's Daughter: A Novel. Annie Edwards. (Lovell's library. no. 1374). 1889. J. W. Lovell Company.

Plaza of Encounters. Ed. by Julio Ortega & Ewing Campbell. LC 79-55315. 1980. pap. 4.00 (ISBN 0-9603476-0-7). Latitudes Pr.

Plea for Old Cap Collier. Irvin Shrewsbury Cobb. LC 21-14551. George H. Doran Company.

Pleading for Justice. William Crawford Burns. LC 20-160936. 1920. Justice Publishing Company.

Pleasant and Grave History of the First Adventures of That Good-Intentioned Gentleman: The Renowned Bartholomew Perigru. LC 7-38194. 1856. Whilt & Yost.

Pleasant Dreams. Robert Bloch. 4.00 o.p. Arkham.

Pleasant Grove Murders. John Holbrook Vance. LC 67-20453. (Illus.). 1967. Bobbs-Merrill.

Pleasant Jim. Max Brand. LC 28-406936. 1928. Dodd, Mead and Company.

Pleasant Jim. Max Brand. 1978. 1.50 (ISBN 0-671-81759-0). Pocket Books.

Pleasant Jim. Frederick Faust. LC 28-4069. 1928. Dodd and Company.

Pleasant Memoirs of the Marquis De Bradomin: Four Sonatas. Valle-Inclan, Ramon Del. LC 76-28508. (Series: The European Library (New York). 1976. 14.00. H. Fertig.

Pleasant Memoirs of the Marquis De Bradomin: Four Sonatas. Ramon Del Valle-Inclan & Broun, May Heywood, Tr. LC 24-257452. (Half-title: The European library, ed.by J. E. Spingarn). Harcourt, Brace and Company.

Pleasant Morning Light. Josephine Lawrence. LC 48-616554. 1948. Whittlesey House.

Pleasant Places. Samuel A Schreiner. 1978. 1.95 (ISBN 0-449-23769-9). Fawcett Crest.

Pleasant Places: A Novel. Samuel Agnew Schreiner. LC 76-8639. 8.95 (ISBN 0-87795-140-3). Arbor House.

Pleasant River. Coman. (Illus.). 1976. pap. 3.95 (ISBN 0-89272-031-X). Down East.

Pleasant Street: By Gay Rutherford Pseud. James Noble Gifford. LC 51-14974.

Pleasant Valley. Louis Bromfield. 1976. Repr. of 1945 ed. lib. bdg. 16.30x (ISBN 0-88411-504-6). Amereon Ltd.

Pleasant Waters: A Story of Southern Life and Character. Graham Claytor. 1888. J. B. Lippincott Company.

Pleasant Ways of St. Medard. Grace Elizabeth King. LC 16-16717. 1916. H. Holt and Company.

Pleasantries of Old Quong. Thomas Burke. LC 72-5861. (Short story index reprint series). 1972. (ISBN 0-8369-4195-0). Books for Libraries Press.

Please Assassinate My Brother. Jane R. Davis. 6.95 o.p. Vantage.

Please Count Your Change: By Peter Towry Pseud. David Piper. 1962. Macmillan.

Please Don't Eat the Daisies. Jean Kerr. LC 57-12467. (Illus.). 1959. 4.95 (ISBN 0-385-04860-2). Doubleday.

Please Don't Eat the Daisies. Jean Kerr. 1979. pap. 1.95 (ISBN 0-449-24099-1, Crest). Fawcett.

Please Don't Leave Me. Louis J Ansbacher. LC 73-93508. 1974. 4.95 (ISBN 0-8059-1988-0). Dorrance.

Please Let Me Die! James D Mackey & I. E. Stanley. LC 76-14099. 1976. 1.95. Damas Pub. Co.

Please Love Me. Keith Miller. 1983. pap. 3.50 (ISBN 0-671-41851-3). PB.

Please, No Paregoric! Ethel Powelson Hueston. LC 46-610575. 1946. The Bobbs-Merrill Company.

Please Omit Funeral. Hildegarde Dolson. LC 74-30007. 1975. 7.95 (ISBN 0-397-01081-8). Lippincott.

Please, One More, Granddaddy; Wild Animal Stories for Young Children. James R. Jennings. 1973. 3.95 (ISBN 0-533-00829-8). Vantage.

Please Pass the Guilt. Rex Stout. (Adult Ser.). 280p. 1974. Repr. lib. bdg. 7.95 o.p. (ISBN 0-8161-6177-1, Large Print Bks). G K Hall.

Please Pass the Guilt: A Nero Wolfe Novel. Rex Stout. LC 73-5112. 1973. 5.95 (ISBN 0-670-55994-6). Viking Press.

Please Pass the Guilt: A Nero Wolfe Novel. Rex Stout. 1974. (pbk.) 1.25. Bantam Books.

Please Stand by. Madeleine Loeb & Schenker, David. LC 31-33379. 1931. Mohawk Press, Inc.

Please Stroll with Me. P. M. Dallas. 1969. 3.95 o.p. (ISBN 0-8059-1385-8). Dorrance.

Pleased to Meet You. Christopher Darlington Morley. LC 27-906633. 1927. Doubleday, Page & Company.

Pleasure After Hours. Florence Stonebraker. LC 47-31407. 1947. Phoenix Press.

Pleasure Before Marriage. Alvin Winston. LC 36-51059. Phoenix Press.

Pleasure-Bent. Jac Lenders. pap. 2.25 o.s.i. (Venus). Grove.

Pleasure Boat. Karl Ashton. LC 35-821985. Godwin.

Pleasure Bond: Diverse Tales from the Edwardian Underground. (Illus.). 1970. pap. 1.75 o.p. (Z1056K, Zebra). Grove.

Pleasure Bound. Florence Riddell. LC 33-4498. J. B. Lippincott Company.

Pleasure Bound see Man-Chaser.

Pleasure Bound: Three Erotic Novels. LC 81-48540. 368p. 1982. pap. 3.95 (ISBN 0-394-17977-3, B-470, BC). Grove.

Pleasure Buyers. Arthur Somers Roche. LC 25-106920. 1925. The Macmillan Company.

Pleasure Campus. Vince Murdoch. pap. 1.95 o.p. (8023). Cameo.

TITLE INDEX PLUNKITT OF TAMMANY HALL.

Pleasure Cruise Mystery. by robin forsythe. ed. Robin Forsythe. LC 34-21692. (Tired business man's library of adventure, detective, and mystery novels). 1934. D. Appleton-Century Company, Incorporated.
Pleasure Dome. Judith Liederman. 1983. pap. 3.75 (ISBN 0-8217-1134-2). Zebra.
Pleasure-Dome: A Novel. David Madden. LC 79-10664. 10.00 (ISBN 0-672-52553-4). Bobbs-Merrill.
Pleasure Factory. Valerii Tarsis. LC 68-13941. 1968. John Day Co.
Pleasure First. Marjorie Fischer. LC 29-17222. The Maccaulay Company.
Pleasure Garden. Leon Garfield. LC 76-905. 1976. 7.95 (ISBN 0-670-56012-X). Viking Press.
Pleasure Garden. Leon Garfield. LC 77-352894. (Illus.). 1976. 2.95 (ISBN 0-7226-5098-1). Kestrel Books.
Pleasure Garden. Oakley M. Hall. 1968. pap. 0.75 o.p. (T1813). Pyramid Pubns.
Pleasure Garden. Oakley M. Hall. 1966. 6.50 o.p. (ISBN 0-670-56011-1). Viking Pr.
Pleasure Garden. Lorna Pegram. 1977. 7.95 (ISBN 0-87645-096-6). Gambit.
Pleasure Garden. Anne Scott-James & Osbert Lancaster. LC 77-84332. 1980. pap. 5.95 (ISBN 0-87645-109-1). Gambit.
Pleasure Garden: By Oakley Hall. Oakley M Hall. LC 66-218036. 1966. 6.50. Viking.
Pleasure House. Cosmo Hamilton. LC 30-11607. 1930. G. P. Putnam's Sons.
Pleasure House. Paul Tabori. 1976. 1.25. Belmont Tower.
Pleasure Hunters. Irving A Greenfield. 1973. (pbk.) 1.25. Dell.
Pleasure Is Our Business. Jack Sandberg. 1977. pap. 1.75 o.p. (Leisure Bks). Nordon Pubns.
Pleasure Island. Nick Carter. (Nick Carter Ser.). 256p. (Orig.). 1981. pap. 2.50 (ISBN 0-441-67081-4). Ace Bks.
Pleasure Lover: Being Some Account of the Early Life and Fortunes of Terence Duke. Edward Harry William Meyerstein. LC 26-12592. George H. Doran Company.
Pleasure Man. Mae West. 1975. (pbk.) 1.50. Dell.
Pleasure Piece. Rose Batterham. LC 35-17234. 1935. Harper & Brothers.
Pleasure Principle. Peter McCurtin. 1974. pap. 1.25 o.s.i. (ISBN 0-8439-0213-2, Leisure Bks). Nordon Pubns.
Pleasure Principle. John O'Mara. LC 95-1063. (Orig.). 1969. pap. 0.95 o.p. (B95-1063). Belmont-Tower.
Pleasure Principle. Jesse Taylor, pseud. LC 74-9987. (Traveller's companion series, TC-454). 1969. 1.95. Olympia Press.
Pleasure Principle: A Novel. Felice Gordon. LC 73-103439. 1970. 5.95. Delacorte Press.
Pleasure Promoter"... S. Jay Bowers. LC 6-16083. 1888.
Pleasure Quest of the R.S.P. Peter Quimme. 1974. (pbk.) 1.50. Dell.
Pleasure Seeker. Jose-Luis De Vilallonga. (O.s.i.). 1962. 3.75 o.s.i. (ISBN 0-671-57890-1). S&S.
Pleasure Seekers. Germaine Detente. 160p. pap. 1.95 o.p. (MP-108). Montmartre.
Pleasure Tube. Robert Onopa. (Berkley book). 1979. 1.75 (ISBN 0-425-03941-2). Berkley Pub. Corp.
Pleasure Was Mine. James Reid Parker. LC 46-25298. 1946. Current Books, Inc., A. A. Wyn.
Pleasures and Days, and Other Writings. Edited and with an Introd. by F. W. Dupee. Translated by Louise Varese, Gerard Hopkins and Barbara Dupee. Marcel Proust. LC 57-676. (Doubleday anchor books, A 97). 1957. Doubleday.
Pleasures and Palaces. Juliet Wilbor Tompkins. LC 12-7619. 1912. Doubleday, Page & Company.
Pleasures and Regrets. Marcel Proust. Tr. by Varese, Louise (McCutcheon) LC 48-7870. 1948. Crown Publishers.
Pleasure's Daughter. Marilyn Ross. 1978. pap. 1.95 (ISBN 0-445-04316-4). Popular Lib.
Pleasures of a Nurse. Peter Kevin. 192p. pap. 1.95 o.p. (ISBN 0-87682-342-8, 7342). Barclay Hse.
Pleasures of Cloris. John Colleton. 176p. 1974. pap. 2.25 (ISBN 0-451-09229-5, E9229, Sig). NAL.
Pleasures of Cloris. John Colleton. 1974. (pbk.) 1.25. New American Library.
Pleasures of Cruelty. 1971. pap. 1.95 o.p. (V1019, Venus). Grove.
Pleasures of Cruelty: Being a Sequel to the Reading of Justine et Juliette by the Marquis De Sade. LC 70-171036. (Venus library, V-1019-T). 1971. 1.95. Grove Press.
Pleasures of Helen. Lawrence Sanders. (Berkley Book). 1979. 1.95 (ISBN 0-425-04064-X). Berkley Publishing Corp.
Pleasures of Helen: A Novel. Lawrence Sanders. LC 79-136788. 1971. 5.95. Putnam.
Pleasures of Manhood: Stories. Robley Wilson. LC 77-24216. (Illinois short fiction series). 1977. 7.50. (ISBN 0-252-00665-8) (ISBN 0-252-00670-4). University of Illinois Press.
Pleasures of Old Age. From the French of Emile Souvestre... Emile Souvestre. LC 8-14262. 1808. G. Routledge and Sons.
Pleasures of Peacock: Comprising in Whole or in Part the Seven Novels of Thomas Love Peacock: Headlong Hall, Melincourt, Nightmare Abbey, Maid Marian, Misfortunes of Elphin, Crotchet Castle, Gryll Grange. Thomas Love Peacock. Ed. by Ben Ray Redman. LC 47-30805. 1947. Farrar, Straus.
Pleasures of Peacock: Comprising in Whole or in Part the Seven Novels of Thomas Love Peacock. Thomas Love Peacock & Ben Ray Redman. LC 78-10740. 1979. 26.75 (ISBN 0-313-20698-8). Greenwood Press.
Pleasures of Penny. Marjorie Postel. 192p. (Orig.). 1973. pap. 1.95 o.p. (ISBN 0-87977-193-3, DBB193). Dansk Blue Bk.
Pleasuring of Rory Malone. Charles Panati. LC 81-16715. 11.95 (ISBN 0-312-61731-3). St. Martin's Press.
Pleasuring of Susan Smith. Helen Maria Winslow. LC 12-14713. 1912. L. C. Page & Company.
Pleasuring Ronnie. Ray Paulten. pap. 1.95 o.s.i. (Venus). Grove.
Plebeian Pestilence: A Small-Pox Interlude. George Wheaton Harrington. LC 22-16145. The Cornhill Publishing Company.
Plebeian's Progress. Frank Tilsley. 1933. Covici, Friede.
Plebiscite: Or, A Miller's Story of the War. Emile Erckmann & Chatrian, Alexandre, 1826-1890, Joint Author. LC 6-38166. (Half-title: Erckmann-Chatrian national novels). 1889. C. Scribner's Sons.
Plebiscite: Or, A Miller's Story of the War. Emile Erckmann & Chatrian, Alexandre, 1826-1890, Joint Author. 1898. C. Scribner's Sons.
Plebiscite: Or, A Miller's Story of the Wary, by One of the 7,500,000 Who Voted "Yes". Emile Erckmann & Chatrian, Alexandre, 1826-1890, Joint Author. LC 46-36239. 1894. C. Scribner's Sons.
Pledge. Friedrich Duerrenmatt. 1959. 4.95 o.p. Knopf.
Pledge. Leonard Slater. LC 79-101883. (O.s.i.). 1970. 6.95 o.s.i. (ISBN 0-671-20465-3). S&S.
Pledge of Love. Jeanne Judson. (Fawcett gold medal book). 1975. (pbk.) 0.75. Fawcett.
Pledge. Translated from the German by Richard and Clara Winston. Friedrich Duerrenmatt. (Signet bk. S1777). 1960. New American Library.
Pledged to the Dead: A Detective Story. Ernest M Poate. LC 25-763. 2.00. Chelsea House.
Pleiads. Arthur De Gobineau. Tr. by J. F. Scanlan from Fr. 359p. 1981. Repr. of 1928 ed. lib. bdg. 30.00 (ISBN 0-89984-234-8). Century Bookbindery.
Pleiads. Arthur De Gobineau. Tr. by J. F. Scanlon from Fr. LC 76-50036. 1978. Repr. of 1928 ed. 21.50x (ISBN 0-86527-332-4). Fertig.
Pleiads. Joseph Arthur Gobineau. LC 76-50036. (Series: Blue Jade Library.). 1976. 14.00. Howard Fertig.
Pleiads. Joseph Arthur Gobineau. Tr. by Scanlan, Jame Fr. LC 28-20339. (Lettered on cover: Blue jade library). 1928. A. A. Knopf.
Plenipotentiaries: A Novel. 1st Ed. Harold J Kaplan. LC 50-7371. 1950. Harper.
Plenty of Love. James Noble Gifford. LC 45-94995. 1945. Phoenix Press.
Plenty of Room & Air. Dan Cushman. 1975. 7.95 (ISBN 0-911436-04-9). Stay Away, Joe Publishers.
Plenty of Sea Room: A Yankee Boyhood. Emery N. Cleaves. 1970. 5.95 o.p. (ISBN 0-395-10933-7). HM.
Plenty, Priscilla: A Novel. 1st Ed. Helen R Mann. LC 56-12964. 1956. Eerdmans.
Plenty Under the Counter. Kathleen Douglas Hewitt. LC 43-11458. 1943. Jarrolds Limited.
Plexus. Henry Miller. (Orig.). 1965. pap. 3.95 (ISBN 0-394-17431-3, B100, BC). Grove.
Plight of Pamela Pollworth. Margaret SeBastian, pseud. 224p. (Orig.). 1980. pap. 1.75 (ISBN 0-449-50119-1, Coventry). Fawcett.
Plodders. Sigurd Jay Simonsen. LC 52-7485. 1952. Vantage Press.
Plodding Toward Terror. Ralph M. Pabst. 5.95 o.p. Vantage.
Plot. Merriam Modell. LC 51-9997. 1951. Simon and Schuster.
Plot. Irving Wallace. 1977. pap. 3.95 (ISBN 0-671-82769-3). PB.
Plot: A Novel. Irving Wallace. LC 67-167231. 1967. bds., 6.95. S. & S.
Plot Against Roger Rider. Julian Symons. LC 73-4161. 1973. 5.95 (ISBN 0-06-014188-3). Harper & Row.
Plot Against Roger Rider. Julian Symons. LC 76-357630. (Penguin crime fiction). 1975. 1.95 (ISBN 0-14-003949-X). Penguin.
Plot Concerns--" The Stories of Twelve Famous Contemporary Plays Told in a New Way. Joseph Kaye & Cook, Burr. LC 25-2281. 1925. G. P. Putnam's Sons.
Plot Counter-Plot. Anna Clarke. LC 74-31918. 1975. 5.95 (ISBN 0-8027-5320-5). Walker.
Plot for Millions: Or, A Game of Cross Purposes. Frederick William Davis. LC 1-29682. (On cover: Magnet detective library, no. 161). 1900. Street & Smith.
Plot for the Fourth Reich. Nick Carter. (Nick Carter Ser). (O.s.i.). 1977. pap. 1.50 o.s.i. (AD1655, Award). Univ Pub & Dist.
Plot It Yourself: A Nero Wolfe Novel. Rex Stout. LC 59-14274. 1959. Viking Press.
Plot of Grass. Lane Kauffmann. LC 77-96838. 1970. 4.95. Lippincott.
Plot of the Short Story: An Exhaustive Study, Both Synthetical and Analytical, with Copious Examples, Making the Work a Practical Treatise. Henry Albert Phillips. LC 73-4412. 1973. 15.00. Folcroft Library Editions.
Plot That Thickened. Pelham Grenville Wodehouse. LC 73-8028. 1973. 6.95 (ISBN 0-671-21572-8). Simon and Schuster.
Plot That Thickened. Pelham Grenville Wodehouse. LC 73-22001. 1974. 8.95 (ISBN 0-8161-6186-0). G. K. Hall.
Plot to Kill the President. Jack Pearl, pseud. LC 72-193007. 1972. 1.50. Pinnacle Books.
Plot to Replace the Constitution. Robert L. Preston. 128p. 1972. pap. 2.00 (ISBN 0-89036-026-X). Hawkes Pub Inc.
Plot. Translated from the Czech by Alice Backer with Bernard Wolfe. 1st Ed. Egon Hostovsky. LC 61-5144. 1961. Doubleday.
Plotkin's Pyramid. Malcolm Kent. LC 73-121389. 1970. 5.95. Laddin Press.
Plots and Characters in the Fiction of Henry James. Robert L Gale. LC 65-16219. 6.50. Archon Dist. Shoe String.
Plots & Counterplots. Louisa May Alcott. 1978. pap. 1.95 (ISBN 0-445-04174-9). Popular Lib.
Plots and Counterplots: More Unknown Thrillers of Louisa May Alcott. Louisa May Alcott & Madeleine Bettina Stern. LC 76-3578. (Illus.). 1976. 8.95 (ISBN 0-688-03046-7). Morrow.
Plotters. Richard Hardwick. LC 65-14008. 1965. Published for the Crime Club by Doubleday.
Plotters: By Alan Caillou Pseud. 1st Ed. Alan Lyle-Smythe. LC 60-7549. 1960. Harper.
Plotting of Frances Ware. James Locke. LC 9-14414. 1909. Moffat, Yard and Company.
Plough and the Cross: A Story of New Ireland. William Patrick O'Ryan. LC 10-19614. 1910. The Aryan Theosophical Press.
Plough & the Stars: Stories from Tamil in English. Ed. by K. Swaminathan et al. 1964. 6.50x o.p. (ISBN 0-210-26880-8). Asia.
Plough and the Stars: Stories from Tamilnad. Ed. by K Swaminathan. M. R. Perumal Mudaliar. (Modern Indian literature). Asia Pub. House.
Plough the Sea. Robert Wilder. LC 61-12747. 1961. Putnam.
Ploughman Poet: A Novel Based Upon the Life of Robert Burns. Bush-Brown, Louise (Carter) LC 72-81637. (Illus.). 1972. 5.95 (ISBN 0-8059-1716-0). Dorrance.
Plow-Woman. Eleanor Gates. LC 6-34690. 1906. McClure, Phillips & Co.
Plowing on Sunday. Sterling North. LC 34-34589. 1934. The Macmillan Company.
Plowing up a Snake. Merle Drown. LC 81-19460. 14.95 (ISBN 0-385-27433-5). Dial Press.
Plowshare and the Sword: A Tale of Empire. Ernest George Henham. LC 15-23126. 1903. Cassell & Company, Limited.
Plowshare in Heaven: Stores. Jesse Stuart. LC 58-11194. 1958. McGraw-Hill.
Pluche or The Love of Art. Jean Dutourd. LC 71-89114. 1970. 5.95. Doubleday.
Pluck: A Novel. Basil King. LC 28-5528. 1928. Harper & Brothers.
Pluck. A Novel. Henrietta Eliza Vaughan Stannard. (On cover: The seaside library. Pocket ed. no. 818). 1886. G. Munro.
Pluck: A Novel, by John Strange Winter Pseud.... Henrietta Eliza Vaughan Stannard. LC 8-27043. (Harper's handy series, no. 79). 1886. Harper & Brothers.
Pluck the Flower. John Brophy. LC 29-2245. E. P. Dutton & Co., Inc.
Plucked Chickens. James Magorian & Adam Laceky. LC 80-68263. (Illus.). 5.00 (ISBN 0-930674-04-9). Black Oak Press.
Plucky One. William Loring Nunez Spencer. LC 8-14078. Cassell & Company, Limited.
Plum-Blossom and Kai Lin: Translated by Joyce Emerson. Hedwig Weiss-Sonnenburg. LC 60-12028. F. Watts, C.
Plum Bun: A Novel Without a Moral. Jessie Redmon Fauset. LC 29-4421. 1929. Frederick A. Stokes Company.
Plum Explosion. John Van Der Zee. LC 67-10772. 1967. Harcourt, Brace & World.
Plum Pie. Pelham Grenville Wodehouse. LC 67-10900. 1967. Simon and Schuster.
Plum Plum Pickers. Raymond Barrio. (Orig.). 1970. 8.50 (ISBN 0-917438-04-3); pap. 3.75 (ISBN 0-917438-05-1). Ventura Pr.
Plum Plum Pickers. Raymond Barrio. LC 78-160604. 1971. Repr. of 1969 ed. 3.95 o.p. (ISBN 0-06-380439-5). Canfield Pr.
Plum Thicket. Janice Holt Giles. LC 54-9122. 1954. Houghton Mifflin.
Plum Tree. Mary Ellen Chase. LC 49-11252. 1949. Macmillan Co.
Plum Tree. David G. Philips. Ed. by Abe C. Ravitz. (American Authors Ser). 1905. 22.75 o.s.i. (ISBN 0-512-00549-4). Garrett Pr.
Plum Tree. David Graham Phillips. LC 68-57547. (American novels of muckraking, propaganda, and social protest). (Illus.). 1968. Gregg Press.
Plum Tree. David Graham Phillips. LC 72-84624. 1976. Scholarly Press.
Plum Tree Lane. Lodwick Charles Hartley. LC 78-53759. 9.95 (ISBN 0-87844-042-9). Sandlapper Store.
Plumb Drillin' David Case. LC 75-11845. 1975. 7.95 (ISBN 0-8128-1835-0). Stein and Day.
Plume of the Arawas. 3d ed. Frank Oswald Victor Acheson. LC 75-324716. (Illus.). 1974. (ISBN 0-589-00862-5). A. H. & A. W. Reed.
Plume Rouge: A Novel of the Pathfinders. John Upton Terrell. LC 42-173573. 1942. The Viking Press.
Plumed Serpent. David H. Lawrence. 1955. pap. 4.95 (ISBN 0-394-70023-6, Vin). Random.
Plumed Serpent. David H. Lawrence. Ed. by William Y. Tindall. (O.s.i.). 1951. 8.95 o.s.i. (ISBN 0-394-44067-6). Knopf.
Plumed Serpent, Quetzalcoatl. David Herbert Lawrence. LC 51-3154. 1951. Knopf.
Plumed Serpent: Quetzalcoatl. David Herbert Lawrence. LC 26-6643. 1926. A. A. Knopf.
Plumed Serpent, Quetzalcoatl. Introd. by William York Tindall. David Herbert Lawrence. LC 55-3818. (Vintage book, K-23). 1955. Vintage Books.
Plumes. Laurence Stallings. LC 24-19532. Harcourt, Brace and Company.
Plummers of Harmony Grove. Edgar Zavitz Palmer. LC 74-8976. (Illus.). 1974. (pbk.) 3.95 (ISBN 0-913408-12-3). Friends United Press.
Plums Hang High. 1st Ed. Gertrude E Bridgeman Finney. LC 55-8307. 1955. Longmans, Green.
Plunder. Ron Goulart. (Orig.). 1972. pap. price not set o.p. (95210). Beagle Bks.
Plunder. Arthur Somers Roche. LC 17-9706. The Bobbs-Merrill Company.
Plunder... Frederic Franklyn Van De Water. LC 33-22213. 1933. Pub. for the Crime Club, Inc., by Doubleday, Doran & Company, Inc.
Plunder: A Novel. Samuel Hopkins Adams. LC 48-6350. 1948. Random House.
Plunder of the Sun. David Dodge. LC 49-2294. 1949. Random House.
Plunder Range. Cover Painting by Frank McCarthy. Homer Hatten. LC 55-38189. (Gold medal books, 492). 1955. Fawcett Publications.
Plunder Squad. Richard Stark. LC 72-2750. 1972. 4.95 o.p. (ISBN 0-394-48102-X). Random.
Plunder Squad. Donald E Westlake. LC 72-5026. 1972. 4.95 (ISBN 0-394-48102-X). Random House.
Plunder Valley. Specially Rev. Ed. Nelson Coral Nye. LC 53-17272. (Ace double novel books, D-6). 1952. Ace Books.
Plundered Host. Fowler Hill. LC 29-5602. E. P. Dutton & Company, Inc.
Plundered Range. Harry Sinclair Drago. LC 36-10350. 1936. W. Morrow & Company.
Plunderer. Roy Norton. W. J. Watt & Company.
Plunderer. Henry Oyen. LC 20-4782. George H. Doran Company.
Plunderer: A Political Story of Maine, Exposing the Piratical System and Explaining the Remedy. George Langtry Crockett. LC 7-23938. 1907. The J. K. Waters Company.
Plunderers. Blond, Georges. LC 51-13407. 1951. Macmillan.
Plunderers. Franklin Coen. LC 79-14289. 9.95 (ISBN 0-698-10998-8). Coward, McCann & Geoghegan.
Plunderers. Llewellyn Perry Holmes. LC 57-6420. (Silver star westerns). 1957. Dodd, Mead.
Plunderers. Llewellyn Perry Holmes. LC 77-14142. 1978. 8.95 (ISBN 0-89340-119-6). J. Curley.
Plunderers: A Novel. Edwin Lefevre. LC 75-152945. (Short story index reprint series). (Illus.). 1971. (ISBN 0-8369-3804-6). Books for Libraries Press.
Plunderers: A Novel. Edwin Lefevre. LC 16-14092. 1916. Harper & Brothers.
Plundering Gun. L. L Foreman. (Ace western). 1974. (pbk.) 0.75. Ace Books.
Plunge into Space. 2d ed. / with a pref. by jules verne. ed. Robert Cromie. LC 75-28853. (Classics of science fiction). (Illus.). 1976. 12.50. (ISBN 0-88355-367-8) (ISBN 0-88355-452-6). Hyperion Press.
Plunger, a Tale of the Wheat Pit. Edward Jerome Dies. LC 74-30627. (American Farmers and the Rise of Agribusiness). (Illus.). 1975. 17.00 (ISBN 0-405-06789-5). Arno Press.
Plunkett's Troubles. Frank M Gilbert. (On cover: Satchel series, no. 39). W. B. Smith & Co.
Plunkitt of Tammany Hall. William Riordan. 98p. 1976. Repr. of 1905 ed. lib. bdg. 14.95x (ISBN 0-89244-088-0). Queens Hse.

Plupy and Old J. Albert. Henry Augustus Shute. LC 24-19217. Dorrance & Company.

Plupy, Beany and Pewt: Contracters. Henry Augustus Shute. LC 26-957247. Dorrance and Company.

Plupy, the Wirst Yet! Henry Augustus Shute. LC 29-20886. Dorrance and Company.

Plural Marriage: the Heart-History of Adele Hersch. Amelie Veronique Petit Child Mathews. LC 7-36077. 1885. E. D. Norton, Printer.

Pluribus. Michael Kurland. LC 74-12695. 1975. 4.95 (ISBN 0-385-02925-X). Doubleday.

Plus. Joseph McElroy. LC 76-13728. 1977. 8.95. (ISBN 0-394-40794-6). Knopf.

Plus and Minus. Frank Harper & Wulff, Derick, Tr. LC 29-16431. 1929. Covici-Friede.

Plus and Minus. Franz Harper. Tr. by Wulff, Derick. LC 29-16431. Covici-Friede.

Plus Ultra. Joseph Glanvill. LC 58-9452. 1978. Repr. of 1668 ed. 30.00x (ISBN 0-8201-1243-7). Schol Facsimiles.

Pluto. Pat Bemis. 1978. pap. 3.50. Macoy Pub.

Plutocracy: Or, American White Slavery; a Politico-Social Novel. Thomas Manson Norwood. LC 7-33276. 1888. The American News Company.

Plutocrat. A Drama in Five Acts. Otto Frederick Schupphaus. 1892. A. Lovell & Co.

Plutocrat: A Novel. Booth Tarkington. LC 27-26113. 1927. Doubleday, Page & Company.

Plutus - the Enemy of the People: Essays on the Vanity of Power. Martha Adams. pap. 3.00 (ISBN 0-87164-019-8). William-F.

Plymouth Adventure: A Chronicle Novel of the Voyage of the Mayflower. 1st Ed. Ernest Gebler. LC 50-7049. 1950. Doubleday.

Plymouth Adventure. Condensed and Simplified for Quick Reading by Evelyn Sibley Lampman. Ernest Gebler. LC 54-6848. (Hanover House headliners). 1954.

Plympton Corner's Folks: A Story of Homey Folks for Homey People. Lucy A Burghardt. LC 28-19287. The Robinson Press.

Pnin. Vladimir Vladimirovich Nabokov. LC 82-1208. 1982. 12.50 (ISBN 0-8376-0465-6). R. Bentley.

Pnin. 1st Ed. Vladimir Vladimirovich Nabokov. LC 57-6299. 1957. Doubleday.

Pnume: Tschai, Planet of Adventure-Four. Jack Vance, pseud. (Daw Science Fiction Ser.). 1979. pap. 1.75 (ISBN 0-87997-484-2, UE1484). Daw Bks.

Poacher. Frederick Marryat. LC 42-30909. G. Routledge and Sons.

Poacher. Frederick Marryat. LC 7-17571. 1873. D. Appleton and Company.

Poacher of Owlhouse Forest. Madison Stahr. LC 36-1309. The Christopher Publishing House.

Poacher's Bag. Douglas Clark. LC 82-48810. 176p. 1983. pap. 2.84i (ISBN 0-06-080643-5, P 643, PL). Har-Row.

Poacher's Pie. Fred Archer. LC 77-355323. (Illus.). 1976. 3.75 (ISBN 0-340-21273-X). Hodder and Stoughton.

Po'buckra. Gertrude Mathews Shelby & Stoney, Samuel Gaillard, Joint Author. LC 30-29257. 1930. The Macmillan Company.

Pocahontas and Captain Smith. Alphonse Maria Grussi. LC 35-121948. The Christopher Publishing House.

Pocahontas: Or, The Nonparell of Virginia. David Garnett. LC 33-3215. Harcourt, Brace and Company.

Pocho. Villarreal, Jose Antonio. LC 59-12654. 1959. Doubleday.

Pochontas: A Story of Virginia. John Roy Musick. LC 8-15728. (On cover: Columbian historical novels. v. 4). 1893. Funk & Wagnalls Company.

Pocket Bible: Or, Christian the Printer, a Tale of the Sixteenth Century. Eugene Sue & De Leon, Daniel, 1852-1914, Tr. LC 10-15598. 1910. New York Labor News Company.

Pocket Book of Adventure Stories... Ed. by Philip Van Doren Stern. LC 45-6216. (On cover: Pocket book. 284). 1945.

Pocket Book of Famous French Short Stories. Ed. by Eric Pierson Swenson. LC 47-25471. (Pocket books, 431). 1947. Pocket Books.

Pocket Book of Father Brown. Gilbert Keith Chesterton. LC 44-7482. 1943. The Blakiston Company, Distributed by Pocket Books Inc., New York, N.Y.

Pocket Book of Great Detectives: Seventeen American and English Masterpieces of Detective Fiction, with an Introduction by Alfred Hitchcock. Ed. by Lee Wright. LC 41-8085. 1941. Pocket Books, Inc.

Pocket Book of Modern American Short Stories. Stendhal. Ed. by Philip V. Stern. (Orig.). 1971. pap. 0.75 o.p. (47189-9). WSP.

Pocket Book of Modern American Short Stories. Ed. by Philip Van Doren Stern. LC 53-352502. (Pocket book 238). 1953. Pocket Books.

Pocket Book of Modern American Short Stories. Ed. by Philip Van Doren Stern. LC 44-994. 1943. The Blakiston Company, Distributed by Pocket Books Inc., New York.

Pocket Book of Mystery Stories: With an Introduction by William Lyon Phelps. Ed. by Lee Wright. LC 41-175531. 1941. Pocket Books, Inc.

Pocket Book of O. Henry. William Sydney Porter. LC 48-9815. (Pocket book 510). 1948. Pocket Books.

Pocket Book of O. Henry Prize Stories. Ed. by Herschel Brickell. LC 47-7232. (Pocket books, 446). 1947. Pocket Books.

Pocket Book of O. Henry Stories. O. Henry. Ed. by Harry Hansen. 256p. pap. 2.95 (ISBN 0-671-45360-2). WSP.

Pocket Book of Science-Fiction. Ed. by Donald A. Wollheim. LC 44-701. 1943. Pocket Books Inc.

Pocket Book of Short Stories. Ed. by Edmund M. Speare. (Orig.). (gr. 9 up). pap. 2.95 (ISBN 0-671-42680-X). WSP.

Pocket Book of Short Stories: American, English and Continental Masterpieces, Edited, with an Introduction. Ed. by Morris Edmund Speare. LC 41-8084. 1941. Pocket Books Inc.

Pocket Book of True Stories. True Story Magazine & Heyn, Ernest V., Ed. LC 49-1246. (Pocket book, 545). 1948. Pocket Books.

Pocket Book of Western Stories... Ed. by Harry Edward Maule. LC 45-8224. 1945.

Pocket Full of Clues. James R Langham. LC 41-5878. 1941. Simon and Schuster.

Pocket Full of Clues. James Richard Langham. LC 41-5878. 1941. Simon and Schuster.

Pocket Full of Dead. John Wyllie. LC 77-89882. 1978. 6.95 (ISBN 0-385-13483-5). Published for the Crime Club by Doubleday.

Pocket Full of Rye. Agatha Miller Christie. LC 53-102561. (Red badge detective). Dodd, Mead.

Pocket Full of Rye. Agatha Miller Christie. 1973. (pbk.) 0.95 (ISBN 0-671-77707-6). Pocket Books.

Pocket Full of Rye. Agatha Miller Christie. LC 81-67345. (Greenway edition). 1981. 8.95 (ISBN 0-396-08019-7). Dodd, Mead.

Pocket Full of Rye see Nursery Rhyme Murders: An Anthology.

Pocket-Handkerchief Park. Rachel Lyman Field. LC 29-21923. 1929. Doubleday, Doran & Company, Inc.

Pocket Hunters. Carter Travis Young. 1974. (pbk.) 0.95. Manor Books.

Pocket Hunters. Carter Travis Young. LC 77-171331. (Double D western). 1972. 4.95. Doubleday.

Pocket Mirror: Poems. Janet Frame, pseud. LC 67-18210. 1967. 4.95 (ISBN 0-8076-0408-9). Braziller.

Pocket Money. J. P. S. Brown. (O.s.i.). Orig. Title: Jim Kane. 1972. pap. 1.25 o.s.i. (AQ1007, Award). Univ Pub & Dist.

Pocket Piece: Short Stories and Sketches by American Authors. Edgar Mayhew Bacon. LC 16-338418. Walbridge & Co.

Pocket Week-End Book. Ed. by Philip Van Doren Stern. LC 49-23212. (Pocket book 586). 1949. Pocket Books.

Pocketful of Poses. Anne Parrish. LC 23-5520. 2.00. George H. Doran Company.

Pocketful of Rye. Archibald Joseph Cronin. LC 70-90272. 1969. 5.95. Little, Brown.

Pocketful of Stars. Ed. by Damon Francis Knight. LC 72-116223. (Doubleday science fiction). 1971. 5.95. Doubleday.

Poco a Poco. William Franklin Johnson. LC 2-195698. 1902. The Saalfield Publishing Co.

Pocock & Pitt. Elliott Baker. LC 78-157059. 1971. 6.95. Putnam.

Pocomoto, Tenderfoot: By Rex Dexon Pseud. Illustrated by Jack Harman. Reginald Alec Martin. LC 53-308753. 1953. Nelson.

Pocono Shot: A Dog Story. John Taintor Foote. LC 24-21356. 1924. D. Appleton and Company.

Pocryphal Stories. Karel Capek. (Penguin modern classics). 1975. (ISBN 0-14-003860-4). Penguin Books.

Pod Bender & Co. George Allan England. LC 16-10469. 1916. R. M. McBride & Company.

Pod Run: By Ada and Anna Chambers. Ada Chambers & Anna Chambers. LC 56-192469. 1955. Falmouth Pub. House.

Poddy: The Story of a Rangeland Orphan. Harry Norman Robb. LC 48-736. 1947. Trail's End Pub. Co.

Podkayne of Mars. Robert Anson Heinlein. 1963. 7.95 (ISBN 0-399-10642-1). Putnam Pub Group.

Podkayne of Mars: Her Life and Times. Robert Anson Heinlein. LC 63-7740. Putnam.

Podvig. Vladimir Vladimirovich Nabokov. (Rus.). 1979. 15.00 (ISBN 0-88233-094-2); pap. 6.00 (ISBN 0-88233-095-0). Ardis Pubs.

Poe Papers: A Tale of Passion. N. L Zaroulis. LC 76-57188. 7.95 (ISBN 0-399-11939-6). Putnam.

Poellenberg Inheritance. Evelyn Anthony. 1973. pap. 1.75 (ISBN 0-451-07838-1, E7838, Sig). NAL.

Poellenberg Inheritance. Evelyn Anthony. 288p. (YA) 1972. 6.95 o.p. (ISBN 0-698-10419-6). Coward.

Poellenberg Inheritance. Eve Stephens, pseud. LC 77-17235. 1973. (pbk) 1.25. New American Library.

Poellenberg Inheritance. Eve Stephens, pseud. LC 77-172635. 1972. 6.95. Coward, McCann & Geoghegan.

Poemes see Oeuvres Completes.

Poemes Saturniens. Paul Verlaine. 1961. pap. 1.25 pocket ed. o.p. French & Eur.

Poems. with a memoir. ed. Clara Bush & Bell, Claude J. LC 21-120833. 1883. Cisco & Hawkins.

Poems. Marcia Nardi. 2.00 o.p. (ISBN 0-8040-0247-9). Swallow.

Poems by a Painter. Joseph N. Paton. LC 73-112941. Repr. of 1861 ed. 16.00 (ISBN 0-404-04905-2). AMS Pr.

Poems by John Wilmot, Earl of Rochester. John Wilmot. Ed. by Vivian De Sola Pinto. (YA) (gr. 7-12). pap. 3.50x o.p. (ISBN 0-674-67850-8). Harvard U Pr.

Poems of Alan Dugan. Alan Dugan. LC 79-144761. (Yale Series of Younger Poets: No. 57). Repr. of 1961 ed. 11.00 (ISBN 0-404-53857-6). AMS Pr.

Poems of Dylan Thomas. rev. ed. Dylan Thomas. Ed. by Daniel Jones. LC 79-145935. 1971. 12.50 (ISBN 0-8112-0398-0). New Directions.

Poems with Drawings. Brenda Chamberlain. 1969. signed ed. 200 copies 10.00 ea. o.p. Enitharmon Pr.

Poe's "Raven" in an Elevator: And Other Tales. being the 3d ed. of more cheerful americans, by charles battell loomis... with illustrations by florence scovel shinn, fanny y. cory, f. r. gruger and may wilson watkins. ed. Charles Battell Loomis. 1907. H. Holt and Company.

Poe's Short Stories. Edgar Allan Poe. Ed. by Killis Campbell. LC 27-205871. (Half-title: American authors series, general editor, Stanley T. Williams). Harcourt, Brace and Company.

Poe's Tales: Selected for Use in Schools. Edgar Allan Poe. Ed. by Eaton, Margaret A. LC 7-8211. (On cover: Ten cent classics). Educational Publishing Company.

Poet. Meredith Nicholson. LC 14-171674. 1914. Houghton Mifflin Company.

Poet and Merchant: A Picture of Life from the Times of Moses Mendelssohn. Berthold Auerbach. Tr. by Brooks, Charles Timothy. (Leisure hour series. v. 89). 1877. H. Holt and Company.

Poet & the Donkey. May Sarton. LC 72-80024. (Illus.). 1969. 4.50 o.p. (ISBN 0-393-08590-2). Norton.

Poet & the Lunatics. Gilbert Keith Chesterton. 1962. 3.00 o.p. Dufour.

Poet and the Lunatics: Episodes in the Life of Gabriel Gale. Gilbert Keith Chesterton. LC 55-9459. (New World Chesterton). 1955. Sheed and Ward.

Poet and the Lunatics: Episodes in the Life of Gabriel Gale. Gilbert Keith Chesterton. LC 29-17227. Dodd, Mead & Company.

Poet and the Parish. Mary Moss. LC 6-34369. 1906. H. Holt and Company.

Poet Assassinated. Guillaume Apollinaire. LC 68-11956. (Illus.). 1968. 9.95. Holt, Rinehart and Winston.

Poet, Miss Kate and I. Margaret Prescott Montague. LC 5-33968. 1905. The Baker & Taylor Co.

Poete Assassine. Guillaume Apollinaire. 12.50. French & Eur.

Poetic Edda. Sturluson Snorri. Tr. by Lee M. Hollander. 1970. Repr. of 1962 ed. 10.00x o.p. (ISBN 0-292-73330-5). U of Tex Pr.

Poetic Justice. Amanda Cross, pseud. 1973. (pbk.) 0.95 (ISBN 0-446-75126-X). Warner Paperback Library.

Poetic Justice. Amanda Cross, pseud. LC 78-106619. 1970. 4.95. Knopf.

Poetic Justice. Amanda Cross, pseud. LC 81-8737. 1981. 9.95 (ISBN 0-89621-291-2). Thorndike Press.

Poetic Memoirs of Lady Daibu. Kenreimonin Ukyo No Daibu & Phillip Tudor Harries. LC 79-65519. 1980. 17.50 (ISBN 0-8047-1077-5). Stanford University Press.

Poetic, Scientific, and Other Forms of Discourse: A New Approach to Greek and Latin Literature. Joshua Whatmough. LC 56-11900. (Sather classical lectures, v. 29). 1956. University of California Press.

Poeticheskii Traktat. Czeslaw Milosz. Tr. by Natalia Gorbanevskaya from Polish. 64p. 1982. pap. text ed. 4.50 (ISBN 0-88233-829-3). Ardis Pubs.

Poetry in Flesh. Josiah Pitts Woolfolk. LC 52-44334. 1952. Signature Press.

Poetry in Painless Birth see Everything Else.

Poets & Murder. Robert Van Gulik. (Judge Dee Mysteries). 1979. pap. 1.95 (ISBN 0-684-16180-X, ScribT). Scribner.

Poets & Murder. Robert Van Gulik. LC 70-161753. 1972. 4.95 o.p. (ISBN 0-684-12560-9). Scribner.

Poets and Murder: A Chinese Detective Story. Robert Hans Van Gulik, pseud. LC 70-161753. (Illus.). 1972. Scribner.

Poet's Pub. Eric Robert Russell Linklater. LC 30-3073. J. Cape & H. Smith.

Poet's Story. Ed. by Howard Moss. LC 73-6058. 1973. 7.95. Macmillan.

Poet's Story. Ed. by Howard Moss. LC 77-8444. (Touchstone book). 1977. 4.95 (ISBN 0-671-23082-4). Simon and Schuster.

Poganuc People. Harriet Elizabeth Beecher Stowe. LC 76-56587. (Stowe, Harriett Elizabeth Beecher, 1811-1896. New England Novels). (Illus.). 1977. 6.95 (ISBN 0-917482-06-9). Stowe-Day Foundation.

Poganuc People: Their Loves and Lives. Harriet Elizabeth Beecher Stowe. 1878. Fords, Howard, & Hulbert.

Poganuc People: Their Loves and Lives. Harriet Elizabeth Beecher Stowe. LC 42-335157. 1888. Houghton, Mifflin and Company.

Poganuc People: Their Loves and Lives, and Pink and White Tyranny; a Society Novel, by Harriet Beecher Stowe. Harriet Elizabeth Beecher Stowe. LC 12-39183. (Half-title: Riverside edition. The writings of Harriet Beecher Stowe... vol. xi). 1899. Houghton, Mifflin and Company.

Poggenpuhls. Theodor Fontane. Ed. by Derrick Barlow. pap. 10.00x o.p. (ISBN 0-631-01640-6, Pub. by Basil Blackwell). Biblio Dist.

Pogo Stepmother Goose. Walt Kelly. (O.S.I.). 1954. 1.25 o.s.i. (ISBN 0-671-59000-6). S&S.

Poignant Interludes: By Theodamus Pseud. 1st Ed. Theodore Glass. LC 50-54900. (Gusto series). 1950. House-Warven.

Poil De Carotte: Ed. by Monique and Anedre Joly. Jules Renard. LC 67-29088. (Twentiethcentury texts). 1968. bds., 2.75. Macmillan.

Poil De Carotte. Original Illus. by Felix Vallotton. Tr. by Ralph Manheim. Jules Renard. LC 67-13224. 1967. 4.95. Walker.

Poilu" A Dog of Roubaix. Eleanor Stackhouse Atkinson. LC 18-20664. 1918. Harper & Brothers.

Poinciana. Phyllis A. Whitney. LC 80-949. 1980. 10.95 (ISBN 0-385-17184-6). Doubleday.

Poinciana. Phyllis A. Whitney. LC 80-27398. 1981. 15.95 (ISBN 0-8161-3148-1). G. K. Hall.

Poinsettia: A Story. Charles Wilder Small. LC 8-6661.

Point Blank. Sonny Grosso & Philip Rosenberg. 1979. pap. 2.75 (ISBN 0-380-45229-4, 45229). Avon.

Point Blank. Philip Rosenberg & Sonny Grosso. LC 77-84860. 10.00 (ISBN 0-448-14547-2). Grosset & Dunlap.

Point Blank. Phillip Rosenberg & Grosso, Sonny. 1979. 2.75 (ISBN 0-380-45229-4). Avon Books.

Point Counter Point. Aldous Leonard Huxley. LC 66-318. (Harper perennial classic). 1965. Harper & Row.

Point Counter Point. Aldous Leonard Huxley. LC 28-251851. 1928. Doubleday, Doran & Company, Inc.

Point Counter Point. Aldous Leonard Huxley. LC 29-523314. 1929. Doubleday, Doran & Company, Inc.

Point Counter Point. Aldous Leonard Huxley. LC 31-26121. (Half-title: The modern library of the world's best books). 1930. The Modern Library.

Point Counter Point. Aldous Leonard Huxley. LC 47-6091. (Harper's modern classics). 1947.

Point Lace & Diamonds. facsimile ed. George A. Baker, Jr. LC 74-103080. (Granger Index Reprint Ser.). 1875. 12.00 (ISBN 0-8369-6095-5). Ayer Co.

Point Noir. Clelie Benton Huggins. LC 37-232345. 1937. Houghton Mifflin Company.

Point of Balance. Barbara Collard. LC 54-973153. 1954. Funk &Wagnalls.

Point of Conscience. Margaret Wolfe Hamilton Hungerford. LC 7-9057. 1896. J. B. Lippincott Company.

Point of Departure: Nineteen Stories of Youth & Discovery. Ed. by Robert S. Gold. (Orig.). 1961. pap. 2.25 (ISBN 0-440-96983-2, LFL). Dell.

Point of Honor. Annie Edwards. LC 6-36506. 1875. Sheldon & Company.

Point of Honor. Annie Edwards. (On cover: Seaside library. Pocket ed. no. 836). 1886. G. Munro.

Point of Honor. Annie Edwards. (Lovell's library. no. 1364). 1889. J. W. Lovell Company.

Point of Honor. Mortimer Raymond Kadish. LC 51-9223. 1951. Random House.

Point of Honor: A Military Tale. Joseph Conrad. LC 8-27098. 1908. The McClure Company.

Point of Honour. Alan Scholefield. LC 79-51250. 1979. 8.95 (ISBN 0-688-03454-3). W. Morrow.

TITLE INDEX POLITE CONVERSATION.

Point of Impact. Robert F Mirvish. LC 61-13542. 1961. W. Sloane Associates.
Point of Lost Souls. Jane Jenke Toombs. 1975. (pbk.) 0.95 (ISBN 0-380-00479-8). Avon.
Point of No Return. a school ed. by lucile d. smith. ed. John Phillips Marquand. LC 52-44814. 1952. Globe Book Co.
Point of No Return. John Phillips Marquand. LC 49-7556. 1949. Little, Brown.
Point of No Return. Carole Mortimer. 192p. 1982. pap. 1.75 (ISBN 0-373-10479-0, Pub. by Harlequin). PB.
Point of Origin. Redmond Wallis. LC 62-16220. 1962. Houghton Mifflin.
Point of Peril. Edward Sidney Aarons. 1969. pap. 0.50 o.p. (50-235). Manor Bks.
Point of Peril: By Edward Ronns Pseud. Edward Sidney Aarons. LC 56-13294. (Mystery house). 1956. Bouregy & Curl.
Point of Reference. Richard Russell. 1979. pap. 1.50 o.s.i. (ISBN 0-505-51394-3). Tower Bks.
Point of Return: Illustrated by Boris Riedel. Merlin L Neff. LC 54-9983. (Stories that win). 1954. Pacific Press Pub. Association.
Point of Sky. John Glassco. 1964. 4.00x o.p. (ISBN 0-19-540035-6). Oxford U Pr.
Point of the Game. Maxwell E. Cox. LC 73-75786. 1969. 5.95. Dodd, Mead.
Point of View. Martha Gilbert Dickinson Bianchi. LC 18-119439. 1918. 1.50. Duffield & Company.
Point of View. Elinor Sutherland Glyn. LC 13-20750. 1913. D. Appleton and Company.
Point of View see Lady Barbarina.
Point of Violence. Lois Duncan. LC 66-23413. 1966. Published for the Crime Club by Doubleday.
Point Prominence: The History of a Church. Y. B. Meredith. 1883. Walden & Stowe.
Point Reyes Poems. Robert Bly. (Orig.). 1974. limited ed. 3.00 o.p. (ISBN 0-914726-11-0); pap. 1.50 o.p. (ISBN 0-914726-10-2). Mudra.
Point-to-Point. Mary Nesta Keane. LC 33-854219. Farrar & Rinehart, Incorporated.
Point-to-Point: By M.J. Farrell Pseud. Mary Nesta Skrine Keane. 1933. Farrar & Rinehart, Incorporated.
Point Ultimate. Jerry Sohl. LC 55-576971. 1955. Rinehart.
Point Venus. Susanne McConnaughey. LC 51-12234. 1951. Little, Brown.
Point Virtue. Anne Tedlock Brooks. 1979. pap. 2.25 o.s.i. (ISBN 0-505-51370-6). Tower Bks.
Point West. Tex Holt, pseud. LC 49-86190. 1949. Phoenix Press.
Pointed Tower: A Novel. Vance Thompson. LC 23-3135. The Bobbs-Merrill Company.
Pointer to a Crime. Archibald E Fielding. LC 45-4855. 1945. Mystery House.
Pointing Man: A Burmese Mystery. Marjorie Douie. LC 20-823935. E. P. Dutton & Company.
Pointing the Way. Sutton Elbert Griggs. LC 75-144622. 1974. 10.00 (ISBN 0-404-00167-X). AMS Press.
Pointing the Way. Sutton Elbert Griggs. 1908. The Orion Publishing Company.
Pointless Knife: A Romantic Novel. Constance Woodbury Dodge. LC 37-296598. Covici, Friede.
Points and Lines. Seicho Matsumoto. LC 72-117385. (Illus.). 1970. 5.95 (ISBN 0-87011-126-4). Kodansha International.
Points of Honor. Thomas Alexander Boyd. LC 72-5859. (Short story index reprint series). 1972. (ISBN 0-8369-4192-6). Books for Libraries Press.
Points of Honor. Thomas Alexander Boyd. LC 25-7673. 1925. C. Scribner's Sons.
Points of View: An Anthology of Short Stories. edited by james moffett and kenneth r. mcelheny. ed. Ed. by James Moffett & McElheny, Kenneth R. LC 66-6263. (Signet classic, CQ307). 1966. New American Library.
Points West. Bertha Muzzy Sinclair. LC 28-562. 1928. Little, Brown, and Company.
Poirot Investigates. Agatha Miller Christie. LC 25-919401. 1925. Dodd, Mead and Company.
Poirot Loses a Client. Agatha Christie. 1.50. Dell.
Poirot Loses a Client. Agatha Miller Christie. LC 37-28593. 1937. Dodd, Mead & Company.
Poirot Loses a Client. Agatha Miller Christie. LC 46-4903. (New Avon library. 70).
Poirot Loses a Client. Agatha Miller Christie. 1974. (pbk.) 0.95. Dell.
Poison. Lee Thayer, pseud. LC 26-4586. 1926. Doubleday, Page & Company.
Poison Arrow. Jefferson Dennis. LC 40-98976. Fortuny's.
Poison Belt. Arthur Conan Doyle. LC 64-17380. (Macmillan's library of science fiction classics). 1964. Macmillan.
Poison Belt: Being an Account of Another Amazing Adventure of Professor Challenger. Arthur Conan Doyle. LC 13-35888. 1913. Hodder and Stoughton, George H. Doran Company.
Poison Case Number 10: A Detective Novel from the Files of the Michael Joyce Agency. Louis Cornell. LC 31-24145. 1931. Brentano's.
Poison Creek Posse. William Frederick Bragg. LC 57-9801. 1957. Arcadia House.
Poison Cross Mystery. Inez Haynes Irwin. LC 36-17371. 1936. H. Smith and R. Haas.
Poison Factory. John Branfield. 1979. pap. 1.50 (ISBN 0-448-17044-2, Pub. by Tempo). Ace Bks.
Poison Flower. Dorothy Daniels. (Kangaroo Book). 1977. 1.75 (ISBN 0-671-81147-9). Pocket Books.
Poison Fly Murder. Harriet Rutland. LC 40-990439. 1940. Harrison-Hilton Books, Inc.
Poison for L. Cecil John Charles Street. LC 34-405120. Dodd, Mead & Company.
Poison for One, "a Doctor Priestly Mystery,". Cecil John Charles Street. LC 44-7476. 1944. New Avon Library.
Poison from a Wealthy Widow. Stephen Longstreet. LC 38-35017. 1938. Hillman-Curl, Inc.
Poison from a Wealthy Widow. Stephen Longstreet. LC 40-11109. 1940. Mystery Book of the Month, Inc.
Poison from a Wealthy Widow. Stephen Longstreet. LC 38-35017. 1938. Hillman-Curl, Inc.
Poison in a Garden Suburb. George Douglas Howard Cole & Margaret Isabel Postgate Cole. LC 29-20652. 1929. Payson & Clarke Ltd.
Poison in Jest. John Dickson Carr. LC 32-24979. 1932. Harper and Brothers.
Poison in Paradise. Anne Hocking. 224p. (O.s.i.). 1973. Repr. of 1955 ed. 5.95 o.s.i. (ISBN 0-85617-764-4). White Lion Pubs.
Poison in Paradise. Mona Naomi Anne Hocking Messer. LC 73-152569. 1972. 5.95 (ISBN 0-85617-764-4). (Baker St., WM FA), White Lion Publishers Ltd.
Poison in Paradise. 1st Ed. Mona Naomi Anne Hocking Messer. LC 55-9500. 1955. Published for the Crime Club by Doubleday.
Poison in the Pen. Patricia Wentworth. 1976. Repr. of 1955 ed. lib. bdg. 15.45x (ISBN 0-88411-739-1). Amereon Ltd.
Poison in the Pen. Patricia Wentworth. 208p. 1980. pap. 1.95 (ISBN 0-553-14237-2). Bantam.
Poison in the Pen. Patricia Wentworth. 1969. pap. 0.60 o.p. (X2029). Pyramid Pubns.
Poison in the Pen. Patricia Wentworth. (O.S.I.). 1973. pap. 0.95 o.s.i. (ISBN 0-515-03176-3). Pyramid Pubns.
Poison in the Pen. 1st Ed. Patricia Wentworth. LC 55-629089. (Her A Miss Silver mystery). 1955. Lippincott.
Poison Is a Bitter Brew. Mona Naomi Anne Hocking Messer. LC 42-9583. 1942. Published for the Crime Club by Doubleday, Doran and Company.
Poison Island. Arthur Thomas Quiller-Couch. LC 7-8212. 1907. C. Scribner's Sons.
Poison Jasmine: A Theocritus Lucius Westborough Story. Clyde B Clason. LC 40-7855. 1940. Pub. for the Crime Club by Doubleday, Doran & Company, Inc.
Poison Ladies, & Other Stories. Herbert Ernest Bates & Mike Poulton. LC 76-373491. (Literature for life series). (Illus.). 1976. 0.90 (ISBN 0-08-020546-1). Wheaton.
Poison of Asps. Florence Marryat Church Lean. LC 7-132208. (On cover: Lovell's library. v. 19. no. 947). 1887. J. W. Lovell Company.
Poison Oracle. Peter Dickinson. LC 73-18716. 1974. 5.95 (ISBN 0-394-49108-4). Pantheon Books.
Poison Oracle. Peter Dickinson. 1977. 1.50 (ISBN 0-380-01662-1). Avon Books.
Poison Oracle. William McIlvanney. (International Crime Ser.). 1982. pap. 2.95 (ISBN 0-394-71023-1). Pantheon.
Poison Orchid. Marie De S Canavarro. LC 30-19630. The Christopher Publishing House.
Poison Party. Margaretta Brucker. LC 38-383323. Phoenix Press.
Poison People. Richard Clayton. LC 78-68540. 1979. 7.95 (ISBN 0-8027-5401-5). Walker.
Poison People. William Haggard. (O.s.i.). 1979. 8.95 o.s.i. (ISBN 0-8027-5401-5). Walker & Co.
Poison Plague. William Levine. LC 29-212025. 1929. R. M. McBride & Company.
Poison, Poker and Pistols. Elisabet M Stone. LC 46-6387. 1946. Sheridan House.
Poison Pussy see Sock It to Me.
Poison Shadows. William Le Queux. LC 27-23154. The Macaulay Company.
Poison Speaks Softly. Dorothy Park Clark. LC 47-12357. 1947. Pub. for the Crime Club by Doubleday.
Poison Springs. Eli Colter. LC 47-31013. 1947. S. Curl.
Poison Summer. Joe L. Hensley. LC 73-83638. 1974. 4.95 (ISBN 0-385-07474-3). Published for the Crime Club by Doubleday.
Poison Tree: And Other Stories. Walter Clemons. LC 58-9058. 1959. Houghton Mifflin.
Poison Unknown: A Detective Story. Charles Judson Dutton. LC 32-9670. 1932. Dodd, Mead and Company.
Poison Valley. Frank Chester Robertson. 1941. E. P. Dutton & Co., Inc.
Poisoned Anemones. Ursula Sanford. 1974. (pbk.) 0.95 (ISBN 0-671-77907-9). Pocket Books.
Poisoned Chocolates Case. Anthony Berkeley, pseud. 1980. pap. 2.25 (ISBN 0-440-16844-9). Dell.
Poisoned Chocolates Case. Anthony Berkeley, pseud. LC 79-83849. (Mystery Library). (O.s.i.: Vol. 12). (Illus.). Repr. 7.95 o.p. (ISBN 0-89163-050-3). Pubs Inc.
Poisoned Chocolates Case. Anthony Berkeley Cox. LC 29-290762. 1929. Pub. for the Crime Club, Inc., by Doubleday, Doran & Company, Inc.
Poisoned Crown: A Novel. Translated from the French by Humphrey Hare. Maurice Druon. LC 57-10564. (His The accursed kings 3). 1957. Scribner.
Poisoned Kiss & Other Portuguese Stories. Joyce Carol Oates. LC 75-385. 196p. 1975. 11.95. Vanguard.
Poisoned Kiss, and Other Stories from the Portuguese. Joyce Carol Oates. LC 75-385. 7.95 (ISBN 0-8149-0761-X). Vanguard Press.
Poisoned Kiss, and Other Stories from the Portugese. Joyce Carol Oates. (Fawcett Crest Book). 1977. 1.95 (ISBN 0-449-23299-9). Fawcett Pubns.
Poisoned Mountain. Mark Channing. LC 35-305673. 1936. J. B. Lippincott Company.
Poisoned Orchard: A Novel of Suspense. Ursula Reilly Curtiss. LC 79-25977. 7.95 (ISBN 0-396-07807-9). Dodd, Mead.
Poisoned Paradise: A Romance of Monte Carlo. Robert William Service. LC 22-20996. 1922. Dodd, Mead and Company.
Poisoned Pen. Arthur Benjamin Reeve. LC 70-150561. (Short story index reprint series). 1971. (ISBN 0-8369-3858-5). Books for Libraries Press.
Poisoned Pen: Further Adventures of Craig Kennedy... Arthur Benjamin Reeve. LC 38-12767. 1911. Harper & Brothers.
Poisoned Pen: Further Adventures of Craig Kennedy. Arthur Benjamin Reeve. LC 13-381767. 1913. Dodd, Mead and Company.
Poisoned Pen: Further Adventures of Craig Kennedy. Arthur Benjamin Reeve. LC 21-13715. 1920. Grosset & Dunlap.
Poisoned Stream. Hans Habe. LC 70-90894. 1969. 6.95. McGraw-Hill.
Poisoned Water. Fernando Benitez. Tr. by Mary E. Ellsworth from Span. LC 74-184549. (Contemporary Latin American Classics Ser.). 160p. 1973. 8.95x (ISBN 0-8093-0634-4). S Ill U Pr.
Poisoned Web. Anna Clarke. LC 82-16772. 1982. 10.95 (ISBN 0-312-61992-8). St. Martin's Press.
Poisoner. Charles Frederick Kenyon. LC 21-16927. Brentano's.
Poisoners. Marjorie Bowen. 1970. pap. 1.25 o.p. (96014). Beagle Bks.
Poisoners. Donald Hamilton. (Matt Helm Ser.). 1979. pap. 2.25 (ISBN 0-449-14163-2, GM). Fawcett.
Poisoner's Base. Elizabeth F. Gresham. 1.50 (ISBN 0-445-04356-3). Popular Library.
Poisons Unknown: A Johnny Liddell Mystery. Frank Kane. 1953. I. Washburn.
Pok O'moonshine. Albert Frederick Wilson. LC 27-13520. 1927. Dodd, Mead and Company.
Poker Jim, Gentleman: And Other Tales and Sketches. George Frank Lydston. LC 8-24453. Monarch Book Company.
Poker King: Or, A Cool Million at Stake. A Story of the Traps and Snares of New York. St. George Rathborne. (secret service series, no. 29). 1890. Street & Smith.
Poker Stories: As Told by Statesmen, Soldiers, Lawyers, Commercial Travelers, Bankers, Actors, Editors, Millionaires, Members of the Ananias Club and the Talent, Embracing the Most Remarkable Games 1845-95. Ed. by John F B Lillard. 1896. F. P. Harper.
Poketown People: Or, Parables in Black. Ella Middleton Tybout. LC 4-32153. 1904. J. B. Lippincott Company.
Pokey Ikey: A Story of a Mountaineer. Marion B Davis. LC 17-14189. 1917. 1.25. Broadway Publishing Company.
Pokjumie: A Story from the Land of Morning Calm. Ellasue Canter Wagner. LC 12-1110. 1911. Publishing House of the M. E. Church, South, Smith & Lamar, Agents.
Poky Clark: A Story of Virginia. N. D. Bagnell. LC 11-10555. 1890. Hunt & Eatopn.
Poland: The Public Inn. Emily Heloise Borne. LC 7-21230. Broadway Publishing Co.
Polaris. Sheldon Perkins. (Belmont Tower books). 1.75 (ISBN 0-505-51386-2). Tower Pubns.
Poldrate Street. Garnett Weston. LC 44-3414. 1944. J. Messner, Inc.
Pole Baker: A Novel. William Nathaniel Harben. LC 5-19414. 1905. Harper & Brothers.
Pole Poppenspaler. Theodor Storm & Reichart, Walter Albert, Ed. LC 33-206692. 1933. Prentice-Hall, Inc.
Pole Poppenspaler: Von Theodor Storm. Theodor Storm & Bernhardt, Wilhelm, D. 1909, Ed. LC 4-12083. (Heath's modern language series). 1904. D. C. Heath & Co.
Pole Poppenspaler: Von Theodor Storm. Theodor Storm & Leser, Eugene, D. 1915, Ed. LC 13-22362. 1913. H. Holt and Company.
Pole Position. Thomas Shire. 192p. (Orig.). 1972. pap. 1.95 o.p. (ISBN 0-87056-272-X, 6272). Brandon.
Pole Shift. John White. 448p. 1982. pap. 3.95 (ISBN 0-425-05390-3). Berkley Pub.
Pole Star. Stewart Edward White & DeVighne, Harry, Joint Author. LC 35-17682. 1935. Doubleday, Doran & Company, Inc.
Polferry Riddle: An Anthony Gethryn Detective Story... Philip MacDonald. LC 31-16134. Pub. for the Crime Club, Inc., by Doubleday, Doran & Company, Inc.
Police!!! Robert William Chambers. LC 15-25467. 1915. 1.30. D. Appleton and Company.
Police at the Funeral... Margery Allingham. LC 32-7609. Pub. for the Crime Club, Inc., by Doubleday, Doran & Company, Inc.
Police Blotter. Robert L Fish. LC 65-17964. 1965. Published for the Crime Club by Doubleday.
Police Blotter: By Robert L. Pike Pseud. Robert L. Fish. LC 65-17964. 3.50. Pub. for the Crime Club by Doubleday.
Police Chief. John Dudley Ball. LC 76-56264. 1977. 6.95 (ISBN 0-385-12883-5). Published for the Crime Club by Doubleday.
Police Know Everything: And Other Maine Stories. Sanford Phippen. Ed. by Constance Hunting. 149p. (Orig.). 1982. pap. 6.95 (ISBN 0-913006-27-0). Puckerbrush.
Police Nurse. William Arthur Neubauer. LC 64-9201. 1964. Arcadia House.
Police Your Planet. Lester Del Rey & Erik Van Lhin. 1975. (pbk.) 1.50 (ISBN 0-345-24465-6). Ballantine Books.
Police Your Planet. Erik Van Lhin. LC 56-13313. Avalon Books.
Policeman at the Door: By Carol Carnac Pseud. 1st American Ed. Edith Caroline Rivett. LC 54-57229. 1954. Published for the Crime Club by Doubleday.
Policeman Flynn. Elliott Flower. LC 2-6284. 1902. The Century Co.
Policeman's Lot. Elizabeth Linington. LC 68-28232. 1968. 4.95. Harper & Row.
Policeman's Nightmare. Marten Cumberland. LC 49-76284. 1949. Pub. for the Crime Club by Doubleday.
Policy King. Lewis A. H Caldwell. LC 46-2017. 1945. New Vistas Publishing House.
Polikouchka. Lev Nikolaevich Tolstoi. (On cover: Lovell's library no. 1113.). 1888. J. W. Lovell Company.
Polikouchka. Lev Nikolaevich Tolstoi. (On cover: Seaside library. Pocket ed., no. 1069). 1888. G. Munro.
Polikushka and Two Hussars. Lev Nikolaevich Tolstoi. LC 56-58631. (Avon, T-133). Avon Publications.
Polish Authors of Today and Yesterday: Bartkiewicz, Falkowski, Gojawiczynska, Morska, Muszal, Olechowski, Orzeszko, Prus, Rey, Reymont, Sienkiewicz, Szymanski and Zeromski. Short Stories. Ed. by Irena Morska. LC 47-7163. 1947. S. F. Vanni.
Polish Blood: A Romance. Nataly Von Eschstruth & Turner, Cora Louise, Tr. LC 6-381522. 1889. J. B. Alden.
Polish Chiefs: An Historical Romance. Porter, John K. Sketches of Character, Author of. LC 7-730. 1832. J. K. Porter.
Polish Complex. Tadeusz. Konwicki. LC 81-5385. 1981. 12.95 (ISBN 0-374-23548-1). Farrar Straus Giroux.
Polish Jew. Emile Erckmann & Chatrian, Alexandre, 1826-1890, Joint Author. (On cover: Seaside library. Pocket ed. no. 329). 1884. G. Munro.
Polish Lad. Isaac Joel Linetzki. LC 74-27601. 7.95 (ISBN 0-8276-0065-8). Jewish Publication Society of America.
Polish Portrait. Michael Tarnowski. 192p. 1972. 6.95 (ISBN 0-89388-044-2). Okpaku Communications.
Polish Princess. Jozef Ignacy Kraszewski. Tr. by De Vere, Meta. LC 7-14167. (On cover: Seaside library. Pocket ed. no. 1174). G. Munro.
Polish Short Story in English: A Guide & Critical Bibliography. Jerzy J. Maciuszko. LC 68-12253. 1968. 17.50x o.p. (ISBN 0-8143-1342-6). Wayne St U Pr.
Polished Ebony. Octavus Roy Cohen. LC 74-128725. (Short story index reprint series). (Illus.). 1970. Books for Libraries Press.
Polished Ebony. Octavus Roy Cohen. LC 19-14475. 1919. 1.60. Dodd, Mead and Company.
Polite Conversation: In Three Dialogues. Jonathan Swift. LC 75-33790. 1975. 15.00 (ISBN 0-8414-7547-4). Folcroft Library Editions.

Polite Conversation in Three Dialogues. Jonathan Swift. LC 76-1019. 1976. 12.50 (ISBN 0-88305-708-5). Norwood Editions.

Political Affair: A Novel. Mickey Ziffren. LC 79-12598. 9.95 (ISBN 0-440-07227-1). Delacorte Press.

Political and Social Ideas of Jules Verne. Jean Chesneaux. LC 72-172427. (Illus.). 1972. (ISBN 0-500-01084-6). Thames and Hudson.

Political Fable. Robert Coover. LC 80-13623. 1980. 5.95 (ISBN 0-670-56309-9). Viking Press.

Political Freshman. Bushrod Washington James. LC 2-7125. 1902. Bushrod Library.

Political Literature of the Progressive Era. Ed., Introd., by George L. Groman. Ed. by George L. Groman. LC 67-154378. 1967. 6.50. Michigan State Univ. Pr.

Political Romance. Laurence Sterne & Cross, Wilbur Lucius. LC 15-2630. 1914. The Club of Odd Volumes.

Political Science Fiction: An Introductory Reader. Ed. by Martin Harry Greenberg. LC 73-22406. 1974. 9.95 (ISBN 0-13-685404-4) (ISBN 0-13-685404-4). Prentice-Hall.

Political Spider: An Anthology of Stories from Black Orpheus. Ed. by Ulli Beier. LC 79-90296. (Illus.). 1969. 1.50 (ISBN 0-8419-0017-5). Africana Pub. Corp.

Politically Mad. Lou Silverstone & Jack Rickard. (Illus.). 1982. pap. 1.95 (ISBN 0-446-30479-4). Warner Bks.

Politician. Antonio Fogazzaro & Mantellini, Gaetano Ettore Raffaele, 1856- Tr. LC 8-4034. 1908. Luce and Company.

Politician. Stephen Longstreet & Ethel Longstreet. (Banner Books). 1968. pap. 0.95 o.p. (95-115). Manor Bks.

Politician. 2d ed. Edith Huntington Mason. LC 10-12776. 1910. A. C. McClurg & Co.

Politician: A Novel by Stephen and Ethel Longstreet. Stephen Longstreet & Ethel Longstreet. LC 59-8636. 1959. Funk & Wagnalls.

Politician and Other Stories. Khamsing Srinawk. LC 73-941411. (Oxford in Asia modern authors). 1973. (pbk.) 4.50. Oxford University Press.

Politician & Other Stories. Khamsing Srinawk. Intro. by Michael Smithies. Tr. by Domnern Garden. 116p. 1973. pap. 6.00x o.p. (ISBN 0-19-638243-2). Oxford U Pr.

Politician: By Stephen and Ethel Longstreet. Stephen Longstreet & Ethel Longstreet. (Popular special SP58). 1960. Popular Library.

Politician's Daughter. Myra Louisa Sawyer Hamlin. LC 7-986. 1886. D. Appleton and Company.

Politicks of Laurence Sterne. Lewis Perry Curtis. LC 76-2382. 1976. 12.50 (ISBN 0-88305-349-7). Norwood Editions.

Politics. Warren, Charles et al. LC 1-25692. (Stories from Mc Clure's). (Half-title: Stories from McClure's). 1901. McClure, Phillips & Co.

Politics Is Murder. Edwin Moultrie Lanham. LC 47-12191. 1947. Harcourt, Brace.

Polkadot Murder. Frances Kirkwood Crane. LC 51-10598. 1951. Random House.

Pollinators of Eden. John Boyd. 1978. pap. 1.95 o.p. (ISBN 0-14-004876-6). Penguin.

Pollinators of Eden. John Boyd. LC 69-19614. 1969. 5.50 o.p. Weybright.

Pollinators of Eden. Boyd Upchurch. LC 69-19614. 1969. 5.50. Weybright and Talley.

Pollinators of Eden. Boyd Upchurch. LC 77-26039. 1978. 1.95 (ISBN 0-14-004876-6). Penguin Books.

Polluters. R. L. Seiffert. 1968. pap. 1.95 o.p. (6006). Brandon.

Polly: A Christmas Recollection. Thomas Nelson Page. 1894. C. Scribner's Sons.

Polly and Dolly: By Mary Frances Blaisdell... Illustrated by Hermann Heyer. Mary Frances Blaisdell. LC 9-30115. 1909. Little, Brown, and Company.

Polly and I: A Novel. Cora M Thrumston. LC 8-19945. Donohue & Henneberry.

Polly; Being a Fairy-Tale of Love: In Which It Is Shown That Men Love Not So Much the Reality, the Substance, As They Do Their Own Ideals. George Van Derveer Morris. LC 6-46773. 1906. The Neale Publishing Company.

Polly Hill. Clifford S. Reynolds. LC 82-5509. (Illus.). 104p. 1982. pap. 4.95 (ISBN 0-89621-067-7). Thorndike Pr.

Polly Kent Rides West in the Days of '49. Robert W McCulloch. LC 40-31182. The John C. Winston Company.

Polly of Lady Gay Cottage. Emma C Dowd. LC 13-9144. 1913. Houghton Mifflin Company.

Polly of the Hospital Staff. Emma C Dowd. LC 12-355521. 1912. Houghton Mifflin Company.

Polly of the Midway-Sunset. Janie Chase Michaels. LC 17-13220. 1917. 1.25. Harr Wagner Publishing Co.

Polly Oliver. facs. ed. Alfred Edgar Coppard. LC 70-132114. (Short Story Index Reprint Ser). 1935. 12.00 (ISBN 0-8369-3671-X). Ayer Co.

Polly Peablossom's Wedding: And Other Tales. Ed. by Thomas A. Burke. LC 7-23668. (On cover: Library of humorous American works). 1851. A. Hart.

Polly Peablossom's Wedding & Other Tales. Ed. by Thomas A. Burke. 1972. Repr. of 1851 ed. lib. bdg. 26.00 (ISBN 0-8422-8157-6). Irvington.

Polly Preferred: A Comedy Romance of Faith and Salesmanship. Guy Reginald Bolton. LC 25-534. The H. K. Fly Company.

Polly State: One of Thirteen. Frances J Delano. LC 2-30050. 1902. The Pilgrim Press.

Polly: The Autobiography of a Parrot. Mollie Lee Clifford. (Illustrated animal autobiographical series). H. M. Caldwell Co.

Polly the Pagan: Her Lost Love Letters. Isabel Weld Perkins Anderson. LC 22-17938. 1922. The Page Company.

Polly to Peggy. Mary Cheseldine Roe. LC 17-11793. 1917. Stewart & Kidd Company.

Polly Tucker, Merchant. Sara Waller Pennoyer. LC 37-21832. 1937. Dodd, Mead & Company.

Polly Valley. Jay Landers. 4.95 o.p. Vantage.

Pollyanna. Eleanor Hodgman Porter. LC 13-38163. 1913. L. C. Page & Company.

Pollyanna. Eleanor Hodgman Porter. LC 16-19173. The Page Company.

Pollyanna. Eleanor Hodgman Porter. LC 18-22740. 1916. The Page Company.

Pollyanna. Eleanor Hodgman Porter. LC 20-15602. 1919. The Page Company.

Pollyanna. Eleanor Hodgman Porter. LC 20-9717. (Glad books). 1920. The Page Company.

Pollyanna. Eleanor Hodgman Porter. LC 16-19173. The Page Company.

Pollyanna. Eleanor Hodgman Porter. LC 43-30368. 1915. The Page Company.

Pollyanna and the Secret Mission. Front. by Harold Cue. Elizabeth Borton, pseud. LC 51-14364. (Pollyanna glad books). 1951. L. C. Page.

Pollyanna and the Secret Mission. Front. by Harold Cue. Elizabeth Borton Trevino. LC 51-14364. (Pollyanna glad books). 1951. L. C. Page.

Pollyanna Grows up. Eleanor Hodgman Porter. LC 15-53810. 1915. 1.25. The Page Company.

Pollyanna Grows up. Eleanor Hodgman Porter. LC 20-15601. 1919. The Page Company.

Pollyanna Grows up. Eleanor Hodgman Porter. LC 20-18390. (Glad books). 1920. The Page Company.

Pollyanna in Hollywood. Elizabeth Borton. LC 32-7833. (The glad books). L. C. Page & Company.

Pollyanna of the Orange Blossoms. illustrated by h. weston taylor. ed. Harriet Lummis Smith. LC 24-12285. 1924. L. C. Page & Company, Inc.

Pollyanna's... Protegee. Margaret Rebecca Piper Chalmers. LC 44-8913. (The Glad books). 1944. L. C. Page & Company.

Pollyanna's Castle in Mexico. Elizabeth Borton. LC 34-34426. (The glad books). L. C. Page & Company.

Pollyanna's Debt of Honor. illustrated by h. weston taylor. ed. Harriet Lummis Smith. LC 27-23755. L. C. Page & Company.

Pollyanna's Door to Happiness. Elizabeth Borton. LC 36-32114. (The glad books). L. C. Page & Company.

Pollyanna's Golden Horseshoe. Elizabeth Borton. LC 39-29730. (The glad books). L. C. Page & Company.

Pollyanna's Jewels. illustrated by h. weston taylor. ed. Harriet Lummis Smith. LC 25-17147. L. C. Page & Comapny.

Pollyanna's Western Adventure. illustrated by h. weston taylor. ed. Harriet Lummis Smith. LC 29-221356. L. C. Page & Company.

Pollyooly: A Romance of Long Felt Wants and the Red Haired Girl Who Filled Them. Edgar Jepson. LC 12-3380. 1.25. The Bobbs-Merrill Company.

Pollyooly Dances. Edgar Jepson. LC 20-3191. 1920. 1.25. Duffield and Company.

Polly's Scheme. George F Jones. D. Lothrop and Company.

Polmarram Tower. Charlotte Massey (ISBN 0-671-80832-X). Pocket Books.

Polonaise. Piers Paul Read. 1977. 11.95 (ISBN 0-380-01714-8). Avon Books.

Polonaise: A Novel. Piers Paul Read. LC 76-15306. 8.95 (ISBN 0-397-01150-4). Lippincott.

Polonaise: A Novel. Piers Paul Read. LC 77-354924. 1976. 3.90 (ISBN 0-436-40976-3). Alison Press.

Poloniaise. Zoe Girling. LC 40-2693. 1940. The Macmillan Company.

Polpetto. A Novel. Frank Mele. LC 72-96673. 1973. 5.95 (ISBN 0-517-50356-5). Crown Publishers.

Polreath Women. Annabella. 1978. pap. 2.50 (ISBN 0-440-07031-7). Dell.

Polutukawa Tree: A Play in Three Acts. 3rd ed. Bruce E. Mason. 98p. 1970. pap. 3.00x o.p. (ISBN 0-7055-0020-9). Intl Pubns Serv.

Polygamist: A Novel. Bernard Harper Friedman. LC 80-24879. 11.95 (ISBN 0-316-29357-1). Little, Brown.

Polygamist: A Novel. Ndabaningi Sithole. LC 79-169156. 1972. 6.95 (ISBN 0-89388-036-1). Third Press.

Polygamy Preferred. Gloria Goddard. LC 33-36075. 1933. W. Godwin, Inc.

Polyglots. rev. definitive collected ed. William Alexander Gerhardie. LC 73-92458. 1974. 7.95. St. Martin's Press.

Polyglots: A Novel. William Alexander Gerhardie. LC 25-11323. 1925. Duffield & Company.

Polygon. Ibrahim Kamil Haddad. LC 38-14373. The Christian Party Press.

Polymath. John Brunner. (Science Fiction Ser). pap. 1.25 o.p. (UY1217). DAW Bks.

Polymath. John Brunner. 1974. (pbk.) 0.95. Daw Books.

Polyphemes: A Story of Strange Adventures Among Strange Beings. Hernaman-Johnson, Francis. LC 74-15981. (Science Fiction). (Illus.). 1975. 18.00 (ISBN 0-405-06297-4). Arno Press.

Polyphemes: Strange Adventures Among Strange Beings. Johnson F. Hernaman. LC 74-15981. (Science Fiction Ser.). 318p. 1975. Repr. of 1906 ed. 18.00x (ISBN 0-405-06297-4). Ayer Co.

Pom-Pom: A Novel of the South Pacific. Carl Raymond McInerney. LC 49-6144. 1949. Stratford House.

Pomander Walk. Louis Napoleon Parker. LC 11-26805. 1911. John Lane Company.

Pomegranate. Walter Adolphe Roberts. LC 41-3985. The Bobbs-Merrill Company.

Pomegranate Seed. A Novel. (Harper's Franklin square library. no. 534). 1886. Harper & Brothers.

Pomegranate Seed. A Novel. (On cover: Seaside library. Pocket ed. no. 831). 1886. G. Munro.

Pomegrante. Jane Bailey. 1976. pap. 3.50 o.p. (Pub. by Black Stone). SBD.

Pomeroy. Gordon M Williams. LC 81-71680. 12.95 (ISBN 0-87795-389-9). Arbor House.

Pomeroy Abbey: A Novel. Ellen Price Henry Wood Wood. (Seaside library, v. 23, no. 443). 1878. G. Munro.

Pomeroy Unleashed. Gordon Williams. LC 82-72072. 304p. 1983. 13.95 (ISBN 0-87795-435-6). Arbor Hse.

Pomfret Mystery, a Novel of Incident. Arthur Dudley Vinton. LC 8-32699. J. S. Ogilvie & Company.

Pomfret Towers. Angela Mackail Thirkell. LC 38-34551. 1938. A. A. Knopf.

Pomona's Travels. Frank Richard Stockton. LC 8-15540. C. Scribner's Sons.

Pomp and Circumstance. Dorothea Gerard Longard De Longgarde. LC 8-309343. 1908. B. W. Dodge & Company.

Pomp & Circumstance: A Novel. Noel Pierce Coward. Ed. by Bill Whitehead. 312p. 1982. pap. 5.95 (ISBN 0-525-48019-6, 0578-170, Obelisk). Dutton.

Pomp of the Lavilettes. Gilbert Parker. LC 7-34993. Lamson, Wolffe, and Company.

Pompadours. Mikhail Evgrafovich Saltykov. Tr. & intro. by David Magarshack. Orig. Title: Pompadury. 300p. 1983. 20.00 (ISBN 0-88233-743-2). Ardis Pubs.

Pompadury see Pompadours.

Pompeii Scroll. Jacqueline La Tourrette. LC 74-17018. 1975. 6.95 (ISBN 0-440-06091-5). Delacorte Press.

Pomp's People. Belle Richardson Harrison. LC 30-430094. 1929. Lewis Copeland Company.

Pond. Robert William Murphy. LC 64-19522. (Illus.). 1964. Dutton.

Pond Hall's Progress. Harold Webber Freeman. LC 33-101565. H. Holt and Company.

Ponder Heart. Eudora Welty. LC 77-92140. (Harvest/HBJ book). (Illus.). 1978. 3.95 (ISBN 0-15-672915-6). Harcourt Brace Jovanovich.

Ponderin' Pete. Lawrence Bradford Saint. LC 45-16236. 1945. Union Gospel Press.

Poniard's Hilt: Or, Karadeucq and Ronan; a Tale of Bagauders and Vagres, by Eugene Sue. Eugene Sue & De Leon, Daniel, 1852-1914, Tr. LC 8-15329. 1907. New York Labor News Company.

Ponjola. Cynthia Stockley. LC 23-65562. 1923. G. P. Putnam's Sons.

Ponkapog Papers. facs. ed. Thomas Bailey Aldrich. LC 70-84293. (Essay Index Reprint Ser). 1903. 10.25 (ISBN 0-8369-1073-7). Ayer Co.

Ponson Case. Freeman Wills Crofts. LC 27-381220. 1927. A. & C. Boni.

Ponsonby Post. Bernice Rubens. LC 78-3998. 1978. 8.95 (ISBN 0-312-62987-7). St. Martin's Press.

Pont Sonore Workbook. Paul Pimsleur. 1974. pap. text ed. 7.95x o.p. (ISBN 0-528-64615-X); 80.00 set, tapes o.p. (ISBN 0-528-64616-8); sample tape free o.p. Rand.

Pontifex Maximus. Mary Raymond Shipman Andrews. LC 25-7087. 1925. C. Scribner's Sons.

Pontifex, Son & Thorndyke. Richard Austin Freeman. LC 31-28118. 1931. Dodd, Mead & Company.

Pontius Pilate. Charles Babb. 1980. 8.95 o.p. (ISBN 0-8062-1477-5). Carlton.

Pontius Pilate. Paul L Maier. LC 68-10585. 1968. 5.95. Doubleday.

Pontius Pilate Papers. Warren Kiefer. LC 75-30352. 8.95 (ISBN 0-06-012367-2). Harper.

Pontius Pilate Papers. Warren Kiefer. LC 77-361969. 1976. 3.75 (ISBN 0-241-89485-9). Hamilton.

Ponty Galler. Frederick Ehrenfried Baume. LC 47-4813. 1947. Dodd, Mead.

Pony Express War. Gary McCarthy. 176p. 1980. pap. 1.75 (ISBN 0-553-14185-6). Bantam.

Pony Lover. Richard Christy. 192p. pap. 1.95 o.p. (6145). Brandon.

Pony Tracks. Frederick Remington. (Golden West Ser.). (Illus.). 1977. pap. 1.25 o.s.i. (ISBN 0-8439-0457-7, Leisure Bks). Nordon Pubns.

Poodle: An Illustrated History of the Reign of Ikus P.Q.R.S. Martha B. Lusk. LC 77-73433. (O.s.i.). (Illus.). 1977. 6.95 o.p. (ISBN 0-8220-1662-1); pap. 3.95 o.p. (ISBN 0-8220-1664-8). Centennial.

Poodles Are People a Petite Histoire. Molli Oliver Mertel. 1974. 3.50 (ISBN 0-682-48003-7). Exposition Press.

Pool. Anthony Bertram. LC 27-4762. 1926. George H. Doran Company.

Pool. Dana Burnet. LC 45-5907. 1945. A. A. Knopf.

Pool. Joseph Hyams. LC 78-13360. 8.95 (ISBN 0-87223-515-7). Seaview Books: Trade Distribution by Simon and Schuster.

Pool in the Desert. Sara Jeannette Duncan Cotes. LC 3-24931. 1903. D. Appleton and Company.

Pool of Death. Keats Patrick. LC 43-12319. (On cover: Best detective selection. No. 5). Select Publications, Inc.

Pool of Fire. John Christopher. LC 68-23062. 1968. Macmillan.

Pool of Flame. Louis Joseph Vance. LC 9-28118. 1909. Dodd, Mead and Company.

Pool of Sacrifice: A Story of Adventure in Central America. Josephine Hope Westervelt. LC 31-13214. Fleming H. Revell Company.

Pool of Tears. John William Wainwright. LC 76-62797. 1977. 7.95 (ISBN 0-312-63008-5). St. Martin's Press.

Pool of Vishnu. Leopold Hamilton Myers. LC 40-301817. Harcourt, Brace and Company.

Pooles' Millions: The Story of a Card House. Julia MacNair Wright. 1896. Congregational Sunday-School and Publishing Society.

Poolroom. William Jourdan Rapp. LC 38-172829. L. Furman, Inc.

Pools of Silence. Henry De Vere Stacpoole. LC 10-16389. 1910. 1.50. Duffield & Company.

Pools of Silence. Henry De Vere Stacpoole. LC 45-450041. 1909. Doubleday, Page & Company.

Poomoto, Pony Express Rider: By Rex Dixon Pseud. Illustrated by Jack Harman. Reginald Alec Martin. LC 53-31294. 1953. Nelson.

Pooped! Lewis Meyer. 96p. 1972. 4.50 o.p. (ISBN 0-8402-1298-4). Nash Pub.

Poor and Proud: Or, The Fortunes of Katy Redburn. William Taylor Adams. LC 457.

Poor Angel. Bennie Caroline Hall. LC 44-3531. 1944. Gramercy Publishing Co.

Poor Caroline. Winifred Holtby. LC 36-7497. 1931. R. M. McBride & Company.

Poor Caroline: The Indiaman's Daughter; or, All's Well That Ends Well. Alexander Lovett Stimson. LC 72-2037. (Black Heritage Library Collection). 1972. 9.00 (ISBN 0-8369-9066-8). Books for Libraries Press.

Poor Caroline: The Indiaman's Daughter. Or, All's Well That Ends Well. A Tale of Boston and Our Own Times. Alexander Lovett Stimson. LC 6-20963. 1845. Pub. by the Author.

Poor Child. Anne Parrish. LC 45-2053. 1945. Harper & Brothers.

Poor Christ of Bomba. Mongo Beti. LC 79-177858. (African writers series). 1971. Heinemann.

Poor Clare. Leslie Poles Hartley. 6.25 o.p. (ISBN 0-241-91338-1). Dufour.

Poor Cousin. A Novel. Ellen Pickering. LC 9-4807. T. B. Peterson.

Poor Cousin Evelyn. James Yaffe. LC 51-9439. 1951. Little, Brown.

Poor Cousins. Ande Manners. 1973. pap. 1.25 o.p. (P1809, Crest). Fawcett World.

Poor Cow. Nell Dunn, pseud. (7041). 1968. Dell.

Poor Cow. Nell Dunn, pseud. LC 67-24336. 1967. Doubleday.

Poor, Dear Margaret Kirby: And Other Stories. Kathleen Thompson Norris. LC 13-1637. 1913. 1.30. The Macmillan Company.

Poor Dear Theodora! Irwin, Florence. LC 20-6636. 1920. G. P. Putnam's Sons.

Poor Devil. Henry Justin Smith. LC 29-16082. 1929. Covici, Friede.

TITLE INDEX PORT OF FRAGRANCE.

Poor Devils. David Ely. LC 70-96844. 1970. 5.95. Houghton Mifflin.
Poor Faun. Charlotte Arthur. LC 30-23187. 1930. G. P. Putnam's Sons.
Poor Fellow. LC 7-38166. 1858. Dick & Fitzgerald.
Poor Fellow My Country. Xavier Herbert. LC 80-51034. 1980. 17.95 (ISBN 0-312-63015-8). St. Martin's.
Poor Fiddler. Franz Grillparzer. LC 66-19471. (Illus.). 1967. F. Ungar Pub. Co.
Poor Folk. Fedor Mikhailovich Dostoevskii. LC 82-16286. 12.50 (ISBN 0-88233-754-8) (ISBN 0-88233-755-6). Ardis.
Poor Folk. Fedor Mikhailovich Dostoevskii & Milman, Lena, Tr. LC 4-16302. (On cover: Keynote series, 8). 1894. Roberts Brothers; Etc., Etc.
Poor Folk & The Gambler. Fedor Mikhailovich Dostoevskii. (Half-title: Everyman's library, ed. by Ernest Rhys. Fiction). J. M. Dent & Sons, Ltd.
Poor Folk & the Gambler. Fodor Dostoyevsky. Tr. by C. J. Hogarth. Bd. with Gambler. 1974. 9.95x (ISBN 0-460-00711-4, Evman); pap. 4.95x (ISBN 0-460-01711-X, Evman). Biblio Dist.
Poor Fool. Erskine Caldwell. LC 30-29662. 1930. Rariora Press.
Poor Gentleman. John Hay Beith. 1928. Houghton Mifflin Company.
Poor Gentleman. Hendrik Conscience. LC 7-32446. 1864. Murphy & Co.
Poor Gentleman. Margaret Oliphant Wilson Oliphant. (On cover: Seaside library. Pocket ed., no. 902). 1886. G. Munro.
Poor Gentleman. Margaret Oliphant Wilson Oliphant. (On cover: Lovell's library, v. 19, no. 925). 1887. J. W. Lovell Company.
Poor George. Paula Fox. LC 67-11966. 1967. Harcourt, Brace & World.
Poor Girl. Bertha Behrens. Tr. by Elise L. Lathrop. LC 6-9428. (On cover: Hurst's library, no. 82). Hurst & Company.
Poor Girl. Bertha Behrens & Lathrop, Elise L., Tr. LC 6-942729. (On cover: Worthington's international library. 26). 1892. Worthington Company.
Poor Girl: Or, The Marchioness and Her Secret. Pierce Egan. (Seaside library, v. 54, no. 1108). 1881. G. Munro.
Poor Governess. Barbara Cartland. (Camfield Romance Ser.: No. 1). 1982. pap. 1.95. Jove Pubns.
Poor Harriet. Elizabeth Fenwick. LC 57-8203. 1957. Harper.
Poor Hater, a Novel. William Bernard Ready. LC 58-12404. 1958. H. Regnery Co.
Poor Human Nature: A Musical Novel. Jessie Bedford. LC 98-1526. 1898. H. Holt and Company.
Poor in Spirit. 1st Ed. Otto Friedrich. LC 52-5021. 1952. Little, Brown.
Poor Jack. Frederick Marryat. LC 42-30908. G. Routledge and Sons.
Poor Little Fool. Fulton Oursler. LC 28-9657. 1928. Harper & Brothers.
Poor Man. Stella Benson. 1923. The Macmillan Company.
Poor Man's Gold. Courtney Ryley Cooper. LC 36-143183. 1936. Little, Brown, and Company.
Poor Man's House. 2d ed. Stephen Sydney Reynolds. LC 9-13969. 1909. John Lane.
Poor Man's Rock. Bertrand William Sinclair. LC 20-17084. 1920. Little, Brown, and Company.
Poor Millie. Thomas P. Baird. LC 77-17727. 8.95 (ISBN 0-06-010202-0). Harper & Row.
Poor Millie. Thomas P. Baird. 1980. 1.95 (ISBN 0-380-46094-7). Avon Books.
Poor Miss Finch: A Domestic Story. Wilkie Collins. LC 8-31170. 1908. C. Scribner's Sons.
Poor Miss Finch: A Novel. Wilkie Collins. LC 77-131672. (Illus.). 1971. (ISBN 0-403-00559-0). Scholarly Press.
Poor Miss Finch. A Novel. Wilkie Collins. LC 6-26938. 1872. Harper & Brothers.
Poor Miss Finch. A Novel. Wilkie Collins. LC 3-27269. 1873. Harper & Brothers.
Poor Mouth: A Bad Story About the Hard Life. Flann O'Brien. Tr. by Patrick Power from Gaelic. LC 80-54558. (Illus.). 128p. 1981. pap. 4.95 (ISBN 0-394-17849-1). Seaver Bks.
Poor Mouth: A Bad Story About the Hard Life. Flann O'Brien. Tr. by Patrick C. Power from Gaelic. LC 74-4797. (Richard Seaver Books). (O.s.i.). (Illus.). 128p. 1974. 7.95 o.s.i. (ISBN 0-670-56441-9). Viking Pr.
Poor Nell. M. B. Smith. (On cover: Munro's library, no. 676). 1886. N. L. Munro.
Poor Nigger. Orio Vergani & Hobson, W. W., Tr. LC 30-13877. The Bobbs-Merrill Company.
Poor No More: A Novel. Robert Chester Ruark. LC 59-13785. 1959. Holt.
Poor Old Lady's Dead. Jack S Scott, pseud. LC 75-25102. 7.95 (ISBN 0-06-013839-4). Harper & Row.
Poor Old Lady's Dead. Jack S Scott, pseud. LC 76-374674. 1976. 2.80 (ISBN 0-7091-5361-9). R. Hale.
Poor Passionate Fool. John Antonio Moroso. LC 32-18950. The Macaulay Company.
Poor People. Fedor Mikhailovich Dostoevskii. LC 18-14991. (Half-title: The modern library of the world's best books). Boni and Liveright, Inc.
Poor People. Fyodor Dostoevsky. Tr. by David Magarshack. Bd. with Little Hero. 5.00 o.p. (ISBN 0-8446-1991-4). Peter Smith.
Poor People: A Novel. Isaac Kahn Friedman. 1900. Houghton, Mifflin and Company.
Poor People, and A Litle Hero: By Fyodor Dostoevsky. Tr., Introd., by David Margarshack. Fedor Mikhailovich Dostoevskii & Fedor Mikhailovich Dostoevskii. (Anchor bk. rebound). 1968. 3.50. Peter Smith.
Poor People, and A Little Hero. Fedor Mikhailovich Dostoevskii. LC 68-10605. 1968. Anchor Books.
Poor People Are People. Elizabeth Richman. 2.75 o.p. Vantage.
Poor Pinney. Marion Chapman. LC 23-4983. Boni and Liveright.
Poor Plutocrats. Mor Jokai. Tr. by Bain, Robert Nisbet. LC 99-5664. 1899. Doubleday & McClure Co.
Poor, Poor, Ophelia. Carolyn Weston. LC 73-179686. 1972. 5.95 (ISBN 0-394-47398-1). Random House.
Poor, Poor Yorick. Frederick Clyde Davis. LC 39-300779. 1939. Pub. for the Crime Club, Inc., by Doubleday, Doran & Company, Inc.
Poor Prisoner's Defense. Richard Sheldon. LC 50-10147. (Inner sanctum mystery). Simon and Schuster.
Poor Relation. Margaret Sebastian, pseud. 1978. 1.75 (ISBN 0-445-04222-2). Popular Library.
Poor Relation. Richard Gilbert Soans. LC 19-18908. 1893. P. F. Collier.
Poor Relations. Compton Mackenzie. LC 19-19599. Harper & Brothers.
Poor Rich Man, and the Rich Poor Man. Catharine Maria Sedgwick. LC 8-11244. Harper & Brothers.
Poor Rich Man, and the Rich Poor Man. Catharine Maria Sedgwick. LC 43-215419. 1837. Harper & Brothers.
Poor Richard's Game. George O'Toole. LC 82-1356. 16.95 (ISBN 0-440-07025-2). Delacorte Press.
Poor Sap by Georges De La Fouchardiere. George De La Fouchardiere. Tr. by Wilson, Forrest. LC 30-28173. 1930. A. A. Knopf.
Poor Shaydullah. Boris Artzybasheff. LC 31-33557. 1931. The Macmillan Company.
Poor Teddy Black. James E Nash. LC 73-106954. 1970. 5.95. Harper & Row.
Poor Theophilus, and the City of Fin. LC 7-38165. (On cover: Satchel series v. 15). The Author's Publishing Company.
Poor White. Sherwood Anderson. LC 26-85911. (Half-title: The Modern library of the world's best books). The Modern Library.
Poor White: A Novel. Sherwood Anderson. LC 20-27471. 1920. B. W. Huebsch, Inc.
Poor White: A Novel. Sherwood Anderson & Rideout, Walter Bates, Ed. LC 66-1691. (Compass books). 1966. Viking Press.
Poor White: Or, The Rebel Conscript. Emily Clemens Pearson. LC 72-1822. (Black Heritage Library Collection). (Illus.). 1972. 15.50 (ISBN 0-8369-9042-0). Books for Libraries Press.
Poor Wise Man. Mary Roberts Rinehart. LC 20-17961. George H. Doran Company.
Poor Women! Norah Hoult. LC 29-11260. 1929. Harper & Brothers.
Poor Young People! Helen Marion Edginton. LC 39-54062. The Macaulay Company.
Poor Zeph! Frederick William Robinson. LC 7-42171. (On cover: Harper's half-hour series. v. 46). 1878. Harper & Brothers.
Poorboy at the Party. Robert Gover. LC 66-16182. 1966. bds., 4.95. Trident.
Poorhouse Fair. new ed. / with a introd. by the author. ed. John Updike. LC 76-21156. 1977. 6.95 (ISBN 0-394-41050-5). Knopf: Distributed by Random House.
Poorhouse Fair. John Updike. LC 59-5431. 1959. Knopf.
Poorhouse Fair. Rabbit, Run. John Updike. LC 65-12450. (Mod. lib. of the world's best bks.). 2.45. Random.
Poorhouse Fair. Rabbit, Run. John Updike. LC 65-12450. (Modern library of the world's best books). 1965. Modern Library.
Pop Goes the Queen: A Mystery Adventure. Bob Wade, pseud. LC 47-30944. 1947. Farrar, Straus.
Popanilla & Other Tales. facsimile ed. Benjamin Disraeli Beaconsfield. LC 79-113649. (Short Story Index Reprint Ser.). 1934. 19.00 (ISBN 0-8369-3378-8). Ayer Co.
Pope and the President: A Novel. William Dick. LC 73-167447. 1972. 1.95 (ISBN 0-7260-0013-2). Gold Star Publications.
Pope Jacynth: & Other Fantastic Tales. 2d ed. Violet Paget. LC 8-9817. 1907. J. Lane.
Pope Joan. Lawrence Durrell. 1974. pap. 1.95 o.p. (ISBN 0-14-003760-8). Penguin.
Pope Joan: An Unorthodox Interlude. Ira Glackens. LC 64-8389. 1965. 3.95. Coleridge Pr., Dist. Taplinger.
Pope, My Brother, and I. Penny Howson. LC 66-14366. bds., 3.95. St. Martin's.
Pope of Greenwich Village. Vincent Patrick. LC 79-12858. 9.95 (ISBN 0-87223-535-1). Seaview Books: Distributed by Harper & Row.
Pope of Greenwich Village. Vincent Patrick. (Illus.). 1980. 2.75 (ISBN 0-671-83229-8). Pocket Books.
Pope of the Sea, an Historical Medley. Vicente Blasco Ibanez & Livingston, Arthur, 1883- Tr. LC 27-3019. E. P. Dutton & Company.
Pope's Divisions. Peter Nichols. 382p. 1983. pap. 6.95 (ISBN 0-14-006368-4). Penguin.
Pope's Favourite. Joseph McCabe. LC 17-14139. 1917. Dodd, Mead and Company.
Popeye Story. Bridget Terry. 1980. pap. 2.75 (ISBN 0-440-06561-5). Dell.
Popeye: The First Fifty Years. Bud Sagendorf. LC 78-65820. (Illus.). 1979. 14.95 o.s.i. (ISBN 0-89480-066-3); pap. 8.95 (ISBN 0-89480-065-5). Workman Pub.
Popeye the Sailor. Ed. by Ron Barlow. LC 79-168727. (Illus.). 1976. 7.95 o.p. Crown.
Poplar Street Park. Frances F. Wright. (Illus.). 1952. 1.50 o.p. Abingdon.
Poplars Across the Moon: The Story of Tula Kruso. Lela Richards. LC 36-30701. L. C. Page & Company.
Poplars: Or, The Good Results of an Evil Deed. Francis Asbury Taulman. LC 9-29632. 1909. Cochrane Publishing Company.
Poplollies & Bellibones. Susan K. Sperling. (Illus.). 1979. pap. 3.95 (ISBN 0-14-005190-2). Penguin.
Popo: A Novel. Rosser Reeves. LC 79-56380. (Illus.). 10.00 (ISBN 0-8149-0838-1). Vanguard Press.
Poppa John. Larry Woiwode. LC 81-6929. 1981. 10.95 (ISBN 0-374-23630-5). Farrar, Straus, and Giroux.
Poppaea. Julie Grinnell Storrow Cruger. LC 6-31583. 1895. J. B. Lippincott Company.
Poppea of the Post-Office. Mabel Osgood Wright. LC 9-189475. 1909. The Macmillan Company.
Poppies & Mandragora. Edgar Evertson Saltus. LC 74-182710. Repr. of 1926 ed. 17.50 (ISBN 0-404-05553-2). AMS Pr.
Poppies in the Wind. Louise O'Flaherty. 448p. (Orig.). 1981. pap. 2.95 (ISBN 0-345-29201-4). Ballantine.
Popping the Question, and Other Tales. Embracing the Best Stories of the Best Authors. Now First Collected. Ed. by George Palmer Putnam. LC 8-59819. 1858. H. C. Peck & T. Bliss.
Poppy. Jean Carew. LC 39-251524. 1939. Arcadia House, Inc.
Poppy. Linda Dubreuil. 1976. pap. 1.50 o.p. (LB357ZK, Leisure Bks). Nordon Pubns.
Poppy. Linda DuBreuil. 1976. (pbk.) 1.50. Leisure Books.
Poppy. True Summers. LC 78-58891. 1978. 2.25 (ISBN 0-380-39446-4). Avon Books.
Poppy Children. E. B Sachem. LC 75-17308. 1975. (pbk.) 3.50. Myrmidon.
Poppy Garden. Emily Malbone Morgan. LC 7-25998. 1892. Belknap & Warfield.
Poppy-Garden. Emily Malbone Morgan. LC 7-25997. A. D. F. Randolph & Co. (Incorporated.
Poppy: The Story of a South African Girl. Cynthia Stockley. LC 12-232533. 1911. G. P. Putnam's Sons.
Poppy Venom. Herbert Stewart Beers. LC 21-15333. Andrew B. Graham Company.
Popular Book of Western Stories: Best Stories of the West. Ed. by Leo Margulies. LC 49-593. (Popular library, 156). 1948. Popular Library.
Popular German Stories... Wilhelm Hauff & Storm, Theodore, 1817-1888.Immensee.
Popular German Stories. Ed. by Frederick William Charles Lieder. (Orig., Ger.). pap. text ed. 2.95x (ISBN 0-89197-351-6). Irvington.
Popular German Stories... Edited, with Notes, Vocabulary, German Questions, and Composition Exercises, Ed. by Frederick William Charles Lieder et al. Hauff, Wilhelm. 1802-1827. Die Geschichte Von Kalif Storch & Storm, Theodor, 1817-1888. Immensee. LC 33-13630. 1933. F. S. Crofts & Co.
Popular Idol. Jessie Hunter Brown Pounds. LC 1-10022. 1901. The Standard Publishing Co.
Popular Novels. Lucy Binetti Cubellis. LC 28-15630. Wetzel Publishing Co.
Popular Opinion: A Novel. E Cecille Cavendish. 1898. The Journal Publishing Co.
Popular Tales. Maria Edgeworth. LC 49-39803. 1895. Macmillan.
Popular Tales. Maria Edgeworth & Edgeworth, Richard Lovell, 1744-1817, Ed. LC 22-10835. 1853. C. G. Henderson & Co.
Popular Tales. Charles Perrault. Ed. by Richard M. Dorson. LC 77-70607. (International Folklore Ser.). 1977. Repr. of 1888 ed. lib. bdg. 15.00 (ISBN 0-405-10118-X). Ayer Co.
Popularity Plan. Rosemary Vernon. (Teenage Romance Ser.). 1981. pap. 1.95. Bantam.
Popularity Summer. Rosemary Vernon. (Sweet Dreams Ser.: No. 20). 160p. 1982. 1.95 (ISBN 0-553-22682-7). Bantam.
Population of One: A Novel. Beresford-Howe, Constance. LC 77-92976. 1978. 8.95 (ISBN 0-312-63150-2). St. Martin's Press.
Por Los Siglos. Sturgis Leavitt & S. Stoudemire. (Rinehart Editions). 1942. 5.20 o.p. (ISBN 0-03-015785-4, HoltC). HR&W.
Porcelain and Clay. Helen Reimensnyder Martin. LC 31-2903. 1931. Dodd, Mead & Company.
Porcelain Fish Mystery. Harriette Russell Campbell. LC 37-599149. 1937. A. A. Knopf.
Porcelain Magician: A Collection of Oriental Fantasies. Frank Owen. LC 49-8344. 1949. Gnome Press.
Porcelain Painter's Son: A Fantasy... Ed. by Samuel Arthur Jones. LC 99-55. 1898. Boericke & Tafel.
Porcelain Tower: Or, Nine Stories of China. Thomas Henry Sealy. 1842. Lea and Blanchard.
Porch. Lee Pennington. 1976. pap. 1.00 (ISBN 0-915216-08-6). Love Street.
Porcupine & Duiker: A Novel of Lebowa. Mapulana Fuller. 1982. 13.95 (ISBN 0-533-05273-4). Vantage.
Porcupine-Man. Sam Toperoff. LC 73-78916. 1974. 7.95 (ISBN 0-8415-0285-4). Saturday Review Press.
Porgy. Du Bose Heyward. LC 68-625. 1967. N. S. Berg.
Porgy. Du Bose Heyward. LC 25-179406. George H. Doran Company.
Porgy. Du Bose Heyward. LC 34-28487. (Half-title: The modern library of the world's best books. 148). 1934. The Modern Library.
Porgy. Foreword by Dorothy Heyward. Du Bose Heyward. LC 53-981471. 1953. Doubleday.
Porius: A Romance of the Dark Ages. John Cowper Powys. LC 52-8709. 1952. Macdonald.
Pork, and Other Stories. Cris Freddi. 1981. 10.95 (ISBN 0-394-51889-6). Knopf.
Pork; or, The Day I Lost the Masters. Thomas J Dulack. LC 68-29343. 1968. 4.95. Dial Press.
Porkchoppers. Thomas Ross. 1973. 1.25 (ISBN 0-671-78289-4). Pocket Books.
Porkchoppers. Ross Thomas. LC 72-170243. 1972. 6.95. Morrow.
P.O.R.N. An Entertainment About the Sexual Counter-Revolution. Howard Liebling. LC 70-110351. 1970. 4.95. P. H. Wyden.
Pornella. Callista McAllister. LC 75-8983. (Capra chapbook series; no. 32). 1975. 10.00. (ISBN 0-88496-034-X) (ISBN 0-88496-033-1). Capra Press.
Porno Girls. Laura Carter & Cathy Stevens. 1974. (pbk.) 1.50. Ace Books.
Pornografia. Witold Gombrowicz. LC 66-29765. 1967. Grove Press.
Pornographer. John McGahern. 256p. 1983. pap. 5.95 (ISBN 0-14-006489-3). Penguin.
Pornographer. Norman Singer. LC 71-219470. 1968. 1.75. Ophelia Press.
Pornographers. Akiyuki Nosaka. LC 68-23962. 1968. 5.95. Knopf.
Pornographers. Aikyuki Nozaka. Tr. by Michael Gallagher from Japanese. 308p. 1968. pap. 6.95 (ISBN 0-8048-1378-7). C E Tuttle.
Pornographers. Aikyuki Nozaka. 1968. 5.95 o.p. Knopf.
Porporino: Or, The Secrets of Naples. Dominique Fernandez. LC 76-3627. 1976. 10.00 (ISBN 0-688-03058-0). Morrow.
Port. Henry Beetle Hough. LC 63-12900. 1963. Atheneum Publishers.
Port Afrique. Bernard Victor Dryer. LC 49-8511. 1949. Harper.
Port Allington Stories. Robert Ernest Vernede. LC 20-21335. George H. Doran Company.
Port Argent: A Novel. Arthur Willis Colton. 1904. H. Holt and Company.
Port Arthur, a Novel: Authorized Translation. Pierre Frondaie. Tr. by Abbott, Elisabeth. LC 38-3731. J. B. Lippincott Company.
Port Arthur Chicken. Tony Chiu. LC 79-13144. 1979. 8.95 (ISBN 0-688-03419-5). Morrow.
Port Eternity. C. J. Cherryh. 192p. 1982. pap. 2.50. DAW Bks.
Port O' Gold: A History-Romance of the San Francisco Argonauts. Louis John Stellman. LC 23-4979. R. G. Badger.
Port O' Heart's Desire. Hampton Del Ruth. LC 26-7903. 1926. H. Del Ruth.
Port O' Heart's Desire. Hampton Del Ruth. LC 26-208895. Barse & Hopkins.
Port of Adventure. Charles Norris Williamson & Alice Muriel Livingston Williamson. LC 13-8761. 1913. Doubleday, Page & Company.
Port of Call. Maxwell Griffith. LC 51-11208. 1952. Lippincott.
Port of Call. Donald Culross Peattie. LC 32-6309. 2.00. The Century Co.
Port of Dreams. Miriam Alexander. LC 12-29472. 1912. G. P. Putnam's Sons.
Port of Fragrance. Bertram Lenox Simpson. LC 30-117163. 1930. Dodd, Mead & Company.

Port of Heaven: A Romance. Thomas Washington Metcalfe. LC 37-14582. 1936. E. P. Dutton & Co., Inc.

Port of London Murders. Josephine Bell. 224p. 1973. 5.95 o.s.i. (ISBN 0-85617-895-0). White Lion Pubs.

Port of London Murders: By Josephine Bell Pseud. Doris Bell Collier Ball. LC 58-12071. (Murder revisited mystery novel, no. 21). 1958. Macmillan.

Port of Missing Men. Meredith Nicholson. LC 7-506219. 1907. The Bobbs-Merrill Company.

Port of Missing Men. Meredith Nicholson. LC 27-136565. Grosset & Dunlap.

Port of Missing Men. Meredith Nicholson. LC 42-47069. 1908. A. Wessels Company.

Port of Missing Men: Strange Tales of the Foreign Legion. Percival Christopher Wren. LC 43-14760. 1943. Macrae-Smith-Company.

Port of Missing Ships: And Other Stories of the Sea. John Randolph Spears. LC 4-15155. 1897. The Macmillan Company.

Port of No Return. Patricia M. Irvine. 176p. (Orig.). 1976. pap. 1.25 (ISBN 0-89041-070-4, 3070). Major Bks.

Port of No Return. Ruth McCarthy Sears. (Orig.). pap. 1.50 (ISBN 0-532-15251-4). Woodhill.

Port of No Return. Ruth McCarthy Sears. 1973. 4.95 (ISBN 0-517-51505-9). Lenox Hill Press.

Port of Saints. William S. Burroughs. LC 80-10309. 1980. 15.95 (ISBN 0-912652-64-0) (ISBN 0-912652-65-9) (ISBN 0-912652-66-7). Blue Wind Press.

Port of Seven Strangers. Kathleen Moore Knight. LC 45-9195. 1945. Pub. for the Crime Club by Doubleday, Doran & Co., Inc.

Port of Storms. Anna McClure Sholl. LC 5-79095. 1905. D. Appleton and Company.

Port-Royal. Henry De Montherlant, pseud. Ed. by Robert Hagspiel. (Illus.). 1967. pap. text ed. 3.50 o.p. (ISBN 0-13-685602-0). P-H.

Port Tarascon: The Last Adventures of the Illustrious Tartarin. Alphonse Daudet. Tr. by James, Henry. LC 6-33040. 1891. Harper & Brothers.

Port Tropique. Barry Gifford. LC 80-15440. (Black Lizard Bks, Fiction Ser.). 200p. 1980. pap. 5.95 (ISBN 0-916870-31-6). Creative Arts Bk.

Port Tropique: A Novel. Barry Gifford. LC 80-15440. (Black lizard book). 1980. 9.95 (ISBN 0-916870-32-4). Creative Arts Book Co.

Port Unknown. Sam Ross. LC 51-10179. 1951. World Pub. Co.

Portable Cervantes. Miguel de Cervantes de Saavedra. LC 51-7568. (Viking portable library 57). 1951. Viking Press.

Portable Cervantes. Miguel de Cervantes de Saavedra & Samuel Putnam. LC 76-44354. 1976. 4.95 (ISBN 0-14-015057-9). Penguin Books.

Portable Charles Dickens. Charles Dickens. Ed. by Angus Wilson. 800p. 1983. pap. 6.95 (ISBN 0-14-015099-4). Penguin.

Portable Conrad. rev. / by frederick r. karl. ed. Joseph Conrad. LC 76-48272. 1976. 4.95 (ISBN 0-14-015033-1). Penguin Books.

Portable Conrad. rev. ed. by frederick r. karl. ed. Joseph Conrad. Ed. by Morton Dauwen Zabel & Frederick Robert Karl. LC 78-4800. (Viking portable library, P33). 1969. 2.45. Viking Press.

Portable Conrad. Joseph Conrad & Zabel, Morton Dauwen, 1901- Ed. LC 47-311957. (Viking portable library). 1947. Viking Press.

Portable Emerson. rev. ed. / edited by carl bode in collaboration with malcolm cowley. ed. Ralph Waldo Emerson & Carl Bode. LC 81-4047. (Viking portable library). 1981. 5.95 (ISBN 0-14-015094-3). Penguin.

Portable F. Scott Fitzgerald. Francis Scott Key Fitzgerald & Parker, Dorothy (Rothschild) 1898- Comp. LC 45-846405. (Half-title: The Viking portable library). 1945. The Viking Press.

Portable Faulkner. rev. and expanded ed. William Faulkner. Ed. by Malcolm Cowley. LC 68-5863. (Viking portable library, P-18). (Illus.). 1968. Viking Press.

Portable Faulkner. rev. and expanded ed. William Faulkner & Malcolm Cowley. LC 77-12068. (Viking Portable library). 1978. 5.95 (ISBN 0-14-015018-8). Penguin Books.

Portable Faulkner. William Faulkner & Cowley, Malcolm, 1898- Ed. LC 46-25133. (On cover: The Viking portable library). 1946. The Viking Press.

Portable Faulkner: Ed. by Malcolm Cowley. William Faulkner. Ed. by Malcolm Cowley. (Viking portable lib., P18). 1961. pap., 1.95. Viking Press.

Portable Hawthorne. rev. and expanded ed. by malcolm cowley. ed. Nathaniel Hawthorne. Ed. by Malcolm Cowley. LC 71-4801. (Viking portable library, P38). 1969. 2.45. Viking Press.

Portable Hawthorne. Nathaniel Hawthorne. Ed. by Malcolm Cowley. LC 48-7869. (Viking portable library, 38). 1948. Viking Press.

Portable Hawthorne. rev. and expanded ed. / edited by malcolm cowley. ed. Nathaniel Hawthorne. Ed. by Malcolm Cowley. LC 48-8215. 1979. 5.95 (ISBN 0-14-015038-2). Penguin Books.

Portable Henry James. Henry James. LC 51-12143. (Viking portable library. 55). 1951. Viking Press.

Portable Henry James. Henry James. Ed. by Morton Dauwen Zabel. LC 75-306. (Viking portable library, P55). 1968. 2.25 (ISBN 0-670-01055-3). Viking Press.

Portable Henry James. rev. in 1968 / by lyall h. p. powers. ed. Henry James & Morton Dauwen Zabel. LC 77-2390. 1977. 4.95 (ISBN 0-14-015055-2). Penguin Books.

Portable Henry James: Edited, and with an Introd., by Morton Dauwen Zabel. Henry James. (Viking portable library. 55). Viking Press.

Portable James Joyce. James Joyce & Levin, Harry, Ed. LC 47-1424. (On cover: The Viking portable library). 1947. The Viking Press.

Portable James Joyce: Rev. Ed. Introd., Notes by Harry Levin. James Augustin Aloysius Joyce. Ed. by Harry Levin. LC 47-1424. (Viking portable lib. P30). 1966. pap., 1.95. Viking.

Portable Maupassant. Guy De Maupassant. Ed. by Lewis Galantiere. LC 47-30167. (On cover: The Viking portable library). 1947. The Viking Press.

Portable Maupassant: Ed., with an Introduction, by Lewis Galantiere, Tr. from French. Guy De Maupassant. Ed. by Lewis Galantiere. 1961. Viking Press.

Portable Melville. Herman Melville. Ed. by Jay Leyda. LC 76-43366. 1976. 4.95 (ISBN 0-14-015058-7). Penguin Books.

Portable Melville. Herman Melville. LC 52-6308. (Viking portable library 58). 1952. Viking Press.

Portable Murder Book. Ed. by Joseph Henry Jackson. LC 45-8414. (Half-title: The Viking portable library). 1945. The Viking Press.

Portable Nabokov. Vladimir Vladimirovich Nabokov & Page Stegner. LC 77-14926. (Viking Portable library). 1978. 5.95 (ISBN 0-14-015071-4). Penguin Books.

Portable Novels of Science. Ed. by Donald A. Wollheim. LC 45-35183. (Half-title: The Viking portable library). 1945. The Viking Press.

Portable Rabelais. Francois Rabelais & Samuel Putnam. LC 77-8018. 1977. 4.95 (ISBN 0-14-015021-8). Penguin Books.

Portable Saul Bellow. Saul Bellow. Ed. by Edith Tarcov. LC 73-11575. (Viking portable library; P79). 1974. 8.95 (ISBN 0-670-15616-7) (ISBN 0-670-01079-0). Viking Press.

Portable Sherwood Anderson. rev. ed. Sherwood Anderson. LC 77-8163. 1977. 4.95 (ISBN 0-14-015076-5). Penguin Books.

Portable Sherwood Anderson. Sherwood Anderson. (Viking portable library). 1949. Viking Press.

Portable Steinbeck. John Steinbeck. Ed. by Pascal Covici. LC 70-149586. 1971. 5.95 (ISBN 0-670-66960-1). Viking Press.

Portable Steinbeck. enl. ed. with an introduction by lewis gannett. ed. John Steinbeck & Covici, Pascal, Comp. LC 46-25068. (Half-title: The Viking portable library). 1946. The Viking Press.

Portable Stephen Crane. Stephen Crane. Ed. by Joseph Katz. LC 69-18738. (Viking portable library, P68). 1969. 2.25. Viking Press.

Portable Stephen Crane. Stephen Crane & Joseph Katz. LC 77-8036. (Viking portable library). 1977. 5.95 (ISBN 0-14-015068-4). Penguin Books.

Portable Thomas Hardy. Thomas Hardy & Julian Moynahan. LC 76-11789. (Viking portable library; 82). (Illus.). 1977. 8.95 (ISBN 0-670-70340-0). Penguin Books.

Portable Thomas Wolfe. Thomas Wolfe & Geismar, Maxwell David, Ed. (On cover: The Viking portable library). 1946. The Viking Press.

Portage to San Cristobal of A.H. George Steiner. LC 82-829. 13.95 (ISBN 0-671-44571-5). Simon and Schuster.

Portal of Dreams. Charles Neville Buck. LC 12-20785. 1.25. W. J. Watt & Company.

Portals. Edward Andrew Mann. LC 73-16879. 1974. 7.95 (ISBN 0-671-21687-2). Simon and Schuster.

Portals of Tomorrow: The Best Tales of Science Fiction, and Other Fantasy. Ed. by August William Derleth. LC 54-6523. 1954. Rinehart.

Portcullis Room. Valentine Williams. LC 34-582419. 1934. Houghton Mifflin Company.

Porte Etroite. Andre Paul Guillaume Gide. 1960. 11.50. French & Eur.

Portent. Marilyn Harris. LC 80-13751. 11.95. Putnam.

Portent: A Story of Second Sight. George MacDonald. LC 79-1768. 1979. 8.95 o.p. (ISBN 0-06-250565-3, HarpR). Har-Row.

Portent. A Story of the Inner Vision of the Highlanders, Commonly Called the Second Sight. George Macdonald. (On cover: Seaside library. Pocket ed., no. 325). 1885. G. Munro.

Portent: A Story of the Inner Vision of the Highlanders Commonly Called the Second Sight. George Macdonald. LC 79-1768. 1979. 7.95 (ISBN 0-06-250565-3). Harper & Row.

Portentous History: A Novel. Alfred Browning Stanley Tennyson. LC 11-208. 1911. Duffield and Company.

Porterfield Legacy. Casey Stephens. (Orig.). 1980. pap. 1.95 (ISBN 0-89083-684-1). Zebra.

Porterhouse Blue. Tom Sharpe. LC 74-7214. 1974. 7.95 (ISBN 0-13-685693-4). Prentice Hall.

Portfino PTA. Gerald Green. Repr. of 1962 ed. lib. bdg. 14.00 o.p. (1135). Am Repr-Rivercity Pr.

Portfolio for Youth. John Frost. LC 15-12472. 1835.

Portia in Distress. Felicia Bryce. (Avalon Books). 4.95. Thomas Bouregy.

Portia Marries. Jeannette Clarke Phillips Gibbs. LC 26-14917. 1926. Little, Brown, and Company.

Portia: Or, "By Passions Rocked.". Margaret Wolfe Hungerford. LC 7-9056. 1883. J. B. Lippincott Co & Co.

Portingale. Alison Macleod. LC 76-377075. 1976. 4.95 (ISBN 0-340-18537-6). Hodder and Stoughton.

Portion for Foxes. Jane McIlvaine McClary. 1973. 1.50. Popular Lib.

Portion for Foxes. Jane McIlvaine McClary. LC 78-185626. 1972. 8.95 (ISBN 0-671-21151-X). Simon and Schuster.

Portion for Foxes. Anthony Thwaite. 1977. pap. 6.95x o.p. (ISBN 0-19-211872-2). Oxford U Pr.

Portion of a Champion. Francis Paul Sullivan. LC 16-8695. 1916. C. Scribner's Sons.

Portion of Labor. Mary Eleanor Wilkins Freeman. LC 67-29267. (Americans in Fiction). (Illus.). 1967. Gregg Press.

Portion of Labor. Mary Eleanor Wilkins Freeman. LC 1-25440. 1901. Harper & Brothers.

Portnoy's Complaint. Philip Roth. LC 69-16414. 1969. 6.95. Random House.

Porto Bello Gold. Arthur Douglas Howden Smith. LC 24-306172. Brentano's.

Portofino PTA. Gerald Green. 1976. Repr. of 1962 ed. lib. bdg. 12.95x (ISBN 0-89190-124-8). Am Repr-Rivercity Pr.

Portrait. R. Q. DeDura. 4.00 o.p. Carlton.

Portrait. A Romance of Cuyahoga Valley. Albert Gallatin Riddle. LC 7-41435. (On cover: American novelist's series, no. 34). 1890. J. W. Lovell Company.

Portrait: A Romance of the Cuyahoga Valley. Albert Gallatin Riddle. LC 7-41434. 1874. Nichols & Hall.

Portrait by Caroline. Sylvia Thompson. LC 31-1384. 1931. Little, Brown, and Company.

Portrait by Kathie. Cateau De Leeuw. LC 51-2358. 1951. Macrae Smith.

Portrait in a Mirror. Charles Morgan. 1957. pap. 0.95 o.p. St Martin.

Portrait in Brownstone. Louis Auchincloss. LC 62-811676. 1962. Houghton Mifflin.

Portrait in Crimsons. A Drama-Novel. Charles Edward Barns. LC 6-7219. 1889. Fracker & Company.

Portrait in Jig-Saw. Fay Grissom. (queen-size gothic). 1975. (pbk.) 1.25. Popular Library.

Portrait in Laughter... Wood Kahler. LC 46-205465. 1946. E. P. Dutton & Co., Inc.

Portrait in Passion. Maggie Osborne. (Orig.). 1981. pap. 3.50 (ISBN 0-451-11107-9, AE1107, Sig). NAL.

Portrait in Pastels. William Arthur Neubauer. LC 50-11863. 1950. Arcadia House.

Portrait in Smoke. 1st Ed. William Sanborn Ballinger. LC 50-8927. 1950. Harper.

Portrait in Smoke. 1st Ed. LC 50-8927. 1950. Harper.

Portrait in the Dark: A Novel. Miriam Wornum. LC 50-14560. 1950. McGraw-Hill.

Portrait Invisible. Joseph Gollomb. LC 28-2808. 1928. The Macmillan Company.

Portrait of a Boy. John G. Fuller. 5.95 o.p. Vantage.

Portrait of a Celibate: By Alec Waugh. Alec Waugh. LC 29-5221. 1929. Doubleday, Doran & Company, Inc.

Portrait of a Courtezan. Charles Caldwell Dobie. LC 34-24863. 1934. D. Appleton-Century Company, Incorporated.

Portrait of a Dead Heiress. Thomas Blanchard Dewey. LC 65-18653. (Inner sanctum mystery). 1965. Simon and Schuster.

Portrait of a Father. Joan Lewisohn Simon. LC 60-11037. 1960. Atheneum Publishers.

Portrait of a Gentleman. Grace Mayhew Putnam. LC 31-35109. Author's Publishing Service.

Portrait of a Judge: And Other Stories. Illus. by Frederick E. Banbery. Henry Cecil. LC 64-18072. 3.95. Harper.

Portrait of a Lady. Henry James. LC 66-20379. (Modern Library college editions, T47). 1966. Modern Library.

Portrait of a Lady. Henry James. LC 72-158782. (Scribner reprint editions). 1975. 13.50 (ISBN 0-678-02803-6). A. M. Kelley.

Portrait of a Lady. Henry James. Limited Editions Club, Inc., New York. LC 67-66242. (Illus.). 1967. Printed for the Members of the Limited Editions Club by the Garamond Press.

Portrait of a Lady. Henry James. LC 74-192911. (Penguin modern classics). 1974. (0.60, 2.50 u.s.) (ISBN 0-14-001921-9). Penguin.

Portrait of a Lady. Henry James. LC 51-22619. (Modern Library college editions, T47). 1951. Modern Library.

Portrait of a Lady. Henry James. LC 20-188418. Houghton, Mifflin and Company.

Portrait of a Lady. Henry James. LC 4-23598. 1882. Houghton, Mifflin and Company.

Portrait of a Lady. 18th ed. Henry James. LC 4-15127. 1897. Houghton, Mifflin and Company.

Portrait of a Lady. Henry James. LC 17-26175. 1916. Houghton Mifflin Company.

Portrait of a Lady. Henry James. LC 17-17432. (Harvard classics shelf of fiction, selected by C. W. Ellot. 11). P. F. Collier & Son.

Portrait of a Lady. Henry James. LC 36-273112. (Half-title: The modern library of the world's best books). 1936. The Modern Library.

Portrait of a Lady. Henry James & Robert James Dixson. LC 54-556856. (American Classics Simplified and Adapted for Greater Reading Pleasure, Book 7). (Illus.). 1973. (pbk.) 1.25. Regents Pub. Co.

Portrait of a Lady. Eleanor Furneaux Smith. LC 37-473645. 1937. Doubleday, Doran & Co., Inc.

Portrait of a Lady see Bodley Head Henry James.

Portrait of a Lady: An Authoritative Text, Henry James and the Novel, Reviews and Criticism. Henry James. Ed. by Robert D. Bamberg. LC 74-19457. (Norton critical edition). 1975. 15.00 (ISBN 0-393-04385-1) (ISBN 0-393-09259-3) (ISBN 0-393-09259-3). Norton.

Portrait of a Lady. Edited with an Introd. by Leon Edel. Henry James. LC 56-13883. (Riverside editions, A7). 1956. Houghton Mifflin.

Portrait of a Lady. Introd. by Quentin Anderson. Henry James. (Collateral classics. CC901). 1966. Washington Sq.

Portrait of a Lady. With a New Introd. by Charles R. Anderson. Henry James. LC 62-13160. (Collier books, AS263. Classic). 1962. Collier Books.

Portrait of a Lady 2 Vols. Henry James. 1908. 7.50 ea. o.p. Scribner.

Portrait of a Lesbian. Samantha Golden. 1968. pap. 1.75 o.p. (3041). Brandon.

Portrait of a Lover. J. Edward Harris. LC 69-10634. 1969. 5.95. L. Stuart.

Portrait of a Man Unknown: A Novel. Pref. by Jean-Paul Sartre. Translated by Maria Jolas. Nathalie Sarraute. LC 58-787360. 1958. G. Braziller.

Portrait of a Man with Red Hair. Hugh Walpole. LC 50-39500. (Avon, 204). 1949. Avon Pub. Co.

Portrait of a Man with Red Hair: A Romantic Macabre. Hugh Walpole. LC 25-21068. George H. Doran Company.

Portrait of a Marriage. Pearl Sydenstricker Buck & Hargens, Charles, 1898- Illus. LC 45-10055. 1945. The John Day Company.

Portrait of a Paladin. Vicente Huidobro & Wells, Warre Bradley, 1892- Tr. LC 32-14448. 1932. H. Liveright, Inc.

Portrait of a Rebel. Netta Syrett. LC 30-12138. 1930. Dodd, Mead & Company.

Portrait of a Romantic. Steven Millhauser. LC 77-4133. 1977. 10.00 (ISBN 0-394-41165-X). Knopf.

Portrait of a Scoundrel. Nathaniel Benchley. LC 78-6361. 1979. 8.95 (ISBN 0-385-12893-2). Doubleday.

Portrait of a Scoundrel. Eden Phillpotts. LC 38-37010. 1938. The Macmillan Company.

Portrait of a Sioux. Robert J. Steelman. LC 76-3124. 1976. 5.95 (ISBN 0-385-11625-X). Doubleday.

Portrait of a Spy, a Novel. Ernest Temple Thurston. LC 29-10171. 1929. Doubleday, Doran & Company, Inc.

Portrait of a Summer Virgin. Edward Lyons. LC 73-77645. 1973. 7.95 (ISBN 0-8180-0615-3). Horizon Press.

Portrait of a Village. Francis Brett Young. LC 68-76134. (Illus.). 1967. Combridge.

Portrait of a Village. Francis Brett Young. LC 73-163050. (Short story index reprint series). (Illus.). 1971. (ISBN 0-8369-3964-6). Books for Libraries Press.

Portrait of a Village. Francis Brett Young. LC 38-8106. Reynal & Hitchcock.

Portrait of a Witch. Dorothy Daniels (ISBN 0-671-80735-8). Pocket Books.

Portrait of a Woman. John Hyde Preston. LC 33-22048. Harcourt, Brace and Company.

Portrait of Alice: A Novel. Evelyn Cowan. LC 77-353889. 1976. 3.30 (ISBN 0-903937-26-3). Canongate.

Portrait of Alice: A Novel. Evelyn Cowan. LC 78-24598. 1979. 8.95 (ISBN 0-8008-6419-0). Taplinger Pub. Co.

Portrait of Alison. Francis Durbridge. 192p. 1973. Repr. of 1962 ed. lib. bdg. 5.95 o.s.i. (ISBN 0-85617-420-3). White Lion Pubs.

Portrait of an Artist with Twenty-Six Horses. William Eastlake. LC 63-9281. 1963. Simon and Schuster.

Portrait of an Artist with Twenty-Six Horses. William Eastlake. LC 80-52282. (Zia book). 1980. 5.95 (ISBN 0-8263-0558-X). University of New Mexico Press.

Portrait of an English Churchman; Charles Lever; Church-Clavering. William Gresley. LC 75-468. (Victorian Fiction: Novels of Faith and Doubt; No. 22). (Series: The Englishman's library; 15.). 1975. 35.00. Garland Pub.

Portrait of an English Churchman, 1838. William Gresley. Ed. by Robert L. Wolff. Bd. with Charles Lever; or, the Man of the Nineteenth Century, 1841; Church Clavering; or, the Schoolmaster, 1843. LC 75-468. (Victorian Fiction Ser). 1975. lib. bdg. 66.00 (ISBN 0-8240-1546-0). Garland Pub.

Portrait of Barbara. Robin Squire. LC 76-28061. 8.95 (ISBN 0-312-63175-8). St. Martin's Press.

Portrait of Bethany. Anne Weale. (Harlequin Presents Ser.). 192p. 1982. pap. 1.75 (ISBN 0-373-10541-X). Harlequin Bks.

Portrait of Caroline. Elizabeth Carfrae, pseud. LC 47-47013. 1947. G. P. Putnam's Sons.

Portrait of Desire. Cassie Edwards. 1982. pap. 3.50 (ISBN 0-8217-1003-6). Zebra.

Portrait of Dorothy. William Arthur Neubauer. LC 48-3915. 1949. Arcadia House.

Portrait of Eden. Margaret Sperry. LC 34-34196. Live-Right Publishing Corporation.

Portrait of Emma. Lillian Cheatham. LC 75-14812. 1975. 5.95 (ISBN 0-385-11241-6). Published for the Crime Club by Doubleday.

Portrait of Evil. Jennifer Hale. 1975. (pbk.) 0.95 (ISBN 0-345-26714-1). Ballantine Books.

Portrait of India: A Selection of Short Stories. Shiv V. Kumar. 122p. 1982. text ed. 13.95x (ISBN 0-7069-1589-5, Pub. by Vikas India). Advent NY.

Portrait of India: A Selection of Short Stories. Ed. by Shiv V. Kumar. 112p. 1982. 36.00x (ISBN 0-7069-1589-5, Pub. by Garlandfold England). State Mutual Bk.

Portrait of Isabelle. Elizabeth Frances Corbett. LC 51-1833. 1951. Lippincott.

Portrait of Jennie. Robert Nathan. LC 40-27011. 1940. A. A. Knopf.

Portrait of Jirjohn Cobb. Harry Stephen Keeler. LC 40-3963. 1940. E. P. Dutton & Co., Inc.

Portrait of Laurel. Kenneth Champion Thomas. LC 43-13709. 1943. D. Appleton-Century Company, Incorporated.

Portrait of Lilith. June Thomson. LC 82-45503. 1983. 11.95 (ISBN 0-385-18335-6). Published for the Crime Club by Doubleday.

Portrait of Love. Barbara Cartland. (Barbara Cartland Ser.: No. 145). 160p. 1981. pap. 1.95 (ISBN 0-553-14922-9). Bantam.

Portrait of Love. Margaret Gorman Nichols. LC 44-2597. 1944. Macrae-Smith-Company.

Portrait of Mellie. Diana Petre. LC 52-9278. 1952. Pantheon Books.

Portrait of Mr. W. H. Oscar Wilde. LC 78-64000. (Gay Experience). Repr. of 1921 ed. 16.50 (ISBN 0-404-61519-8). AMS Pr.

Portrait of Morris. Vern Haddick. LC 78-31684. 1979. 8.95 (ISBN 0-87949-152-3). Ashley Books.

Portrait of My Love. Emily Elliott. (Candlelight Ecstasy Ser.: No. 140). (Orig.). 1983. pap. 1.95 (ISBN 0-440-16719-1). Dell.

Portrait of My Love. Daisy H. Thomson. 1974. pap. 0.95 o.p. (ISBN 0-515-03427-4, N3427). BJ Pub Group.

Portrait of Paula. Hettie Grimstead. (Cameo Romance). (Fawcett gold medal book). 1975. (pbk.) 0.95. Fawcett.

Portrait of Peter West. Suzanne Butler. LC 58-10063. 1958. Little, Brown.

Portrait of Rene: By Harry Davis Pseud. Roberta Hill. LC 56-11387. 1956. Greenberg.

Portrait of Sarah. abr. ed. Veronica Black. Ed. by Alice Sachs. 1970. Repr. of 1969 ed. 3.95 o.p. Lenox Hill.

Portrait of Sex. Laura Patterson. pap. 1.95 o.p. (8043). Cameo.

Portrait of Terry. Phyllis Yahnke. LC 54-114645. 1954. Arcadia House.

Portrait of the Accused. Francis Addington Symonds. LC 52-31004. 1952. T. V. Boardman.

Portrait of the Artist As a Dead Man. Audrey Walz. LC 47-18229. 1947. Duell, Sloan & Pearce.

Portrait of the Artist As a Young Dog. Dylan Thomas. LC 40-34154. 1956. pap. 4.95 (ISBN 0-8112-0207-0, NDP51). New Directions.

Portrait of the Artist As a Young Dog see Collected Prose.

Portrait of the Artist As a Young Man. Joyce James. 1964. pap. 2.95 (ISBN 0-14-004221-0). Penguin.

Portrait of the Artist As a Young Man. James Joyce & Chester G Anderson. LC 77-1609. (Viking critical library). 1977. 1.95 (ISBN 0-14-015505-8). Penguin Books.

Portrait of the Artist As a Young Man. large type ed., complete and unabridged. ed. James Augustine Aloysius Joyce. LC 68-31917. F. Watts.

Portrait of the Artist As a Young Man. James Augustine Aloysius Joyce. Ed. by Chester G Anderson. LC 65-9602. 1962.

Portrait of the Artist As a Young Man. James Augustine Aloysius Joyce. LC 77-11912. 1977. 1.95 (ISBN 0-14-004579-1). Penguin Books.

Portrait of the Artist As a Young Man. James Augustine Aloysius Joyce. LC 64-20678. 1964. Viking Press.

Portrait of the Artist As a Young Man. James Augustine Aloysius Joyce. LC 77-368319. 1977. 0.75 (ISBN 0-586-04475-2). Triad.

Portrait of the Artist As a Young Man. James Augustine Aloysius Joyce. LC 17-4707. 1916. B. W.S Huebsch.

Portrait of the Artist As a Young Man. James Augustine Aloysius Joyce. LC 24-4269. 1922. B. W. Huebsch, Inc.

Portrait of the Artist As a Young Man. James Augustine Aloysius Joyce. LC 25-227635. The Viking Press & B. W. Huebsch.

Portrait of the Artist As a Young Man. James Augustine Aloysius Joyce. LC 28-10873. (Half-title: The modern library of the world's best books). The Modern Library.

Portrait of the Artist As a Young Man: Text, Criticism, and Notes. James Augustine Aloysius Joyce. Ed. by Chester G. Anderson. LC 67-30719. (Viking critical library). (Illus.). 1968. Viking Press.

Portrait of the Artist As a Young Man: With a Commentary by Sean O'Faolain. James Augustine Aloysius Joyce. LC 54-466658. (Signet book, 1150. A Signet giant). 1954. New American Library.

Portrait of the Artist's Children. Edward Charles. LC 35-15049. 1935. Lothrop, Lee and Shepard Company.

Portrait of the Bride. Betty Bergson Spiro Miller. LC 36-8196. 1936. Frederick A. Stokes Company.

Portrait of the Damned. Richard McKaye. LC 54-35686. 1954. Twayne Publishers.

Portrait of the Past. Kate Cameron, pseud. (Holderly Hall Gothic#5). 1975. (pbk.) 1.25. Leisure Books.

Portrait of Two Doctors. John Christopher O'Day. LC 40-5952. Dorrance & Co., Inc.

Portrait Series: Suzanne. Peter Fraser. 176p. 1982. pap. 2.50 (ISBN 0-523-41810-8). Pinnacle Bks.

Portrait: With Love by Joan Sargent Pseud. Sara Lucile Jenkins. LC 55-146313. 1955. Avalon Books.

Portraits. Mark Dunster. 1975. 5.00 o.p. Linden Pubs.

Portraits. Cynthia Freeman. LC 78-73865. 1979. 11.95 (ISBN 0-87795-219-1). Arbor Hse.

Portraits in Moonlight. Carl Jacobi. 1964. 4.00 o.p. (ISBN 0-87054-043-2). Arkham.

Portraits of Mason Stree: A Study on Sociological Problems in Fictional Form. Sarah Alta Schiffman. LC 49-2765. 1949. Highland Press.

Portraits of My Married Friends: Or, A Peep into Hymen's Kingdom. Rhoda Elizabeth Waterman White. LC 8-36612. 1858. D. Appleton & Co.

Portraits of the American Jew: An Anthology of Short Stories by American Jewish Writers. Max Nadel & National Curriculum Research Institute. Commission on Jewish Studies in Public Schools. LC 75-34066. 1975. 2.95 (ISBN 0-8120-0578-3). Barron's Educational Series.

Portraits: Some Contemporary Short Stories. Lewis Howard. LC 39-336766. Appeal Printing Co.

Portreeve. Eden Phillpotts. LC 6-1264. 1906. The Macmillan Company.

Ports of Passion. Paula Fairman. (Orig.). 1980. pap. 2.50 (ISBN 0-523-40697-5). Pinnacle Bks.

Portsmouth Point: The British Navy in Fiction, 1793-1815. Ed. by Cyril Northcote Parkinson. LC 49-49604. 1949. Harvard University Press.

Portugese Fragment. Owen Sela. 1975. pap. 1.50 o.p. (ISBN 0-515-03685-4). Pyramid Pubns.

Portuguese Affair. Anne Betteridge, pseud. 1973. pap. 0.75 o.p. (ISBN 0-345-20730-0). Beagle Bks.

Portuguese Defection. Gerard De Villiers. (Malko, 14) (ISBN 0-523-00966-6). Pinnacle Books.

Portuguese Defection. Gerard De Villiers. (Malko, 14) (ISBN 0-523-00966-6). Pinnacle Books.

Portuguese Escape: A Novel by Ann Bridge Pseud. Mary Dolling Sanders O'Malley. LC 58-101106. 1958. Macmillan.

Portuguese Folk-Tales. Z. Consigliere-Pedroso. LC 68-57186. 1969. Repr. of 1882 ed. 10.00 (ISBN 0-405-08375-0, Blom Pubns). Ayer Co.

Portuguese Fragment. Owen Sela. LC 73-7007. 1973. 5.95 (ISBN 0-394-48824-5). Pantheon Books.

Portuguese Princess. Tibor Dery. 1981. pap. 4.95 (ISBN 0-7145-0486-6). Riverrun NY.

Portuguese Princess, and Other Stories. Tibor Dery. LC 68-26440. 1968. Quadrangle Books.

Portuguese Princess & Other Stories. Tibor Dey. Tr. by Kathleen Szasz. LC 68-26440. 1968. 5.95 o.p. (ISBN 0-8129-0053-7). Quadrangle.

Portulaca. Bernice Kelly. Harris. LC 41-517452. 1941. Doubleday, Doran and Company, Inc.

Portygee: A Novel. Joseph Crosby Lincoln. LC 20-6287. 1920. D. Appleton and Company.

Poseidon Adventure. Paul Gallico. LC 74-81985. 1969. 6.95. Coward-McCann.

Poseidon's Paradise: The Romance of Atlantis. Elizabeth G Birkmaier. LC 11-10545. 1892. The Clemens Publishing Co.

Poseidon's Shadow. A. P Kobryn. LC 78-72896. 8.95 (ISBN 0-89256-087-8). Rawson, Wade.

Posh. Stephanie Gatos. LC 70-149787. (Evergreen black cat book, B-294-N). 1971. 0.95. Grove Press.

Posie Didn't Say. Phyllis Crawford. LC 41-146617. Howell, Soskin.

Position of Peggy. Leonard Merrick. LC 12-685. 1911. 1.20. M. Kennerley.

Position of Peggy Harper. Leonard Merrick. LC 68-12382. (Doughty lib., no. 8). 1968. 5.95. Stein & Day.

Position of Peggy Harper. Leonard Merrick. LC 11-26647. 1911. T. Nelson and Sons.

Position of Peggy Harper. Leonard Merrick. LC 20-5893. (Half-title: The works of Leonard Merrick). 1919. E. P. Dutton and Company.

Position of Ultimate Trust. William Beechcroft. 1982. pap. 2.50 (ISBN 0-451-11551-1, AE1551, Sig). NAL.

Position of Ultimate Trust: A Novel of Suspense. William Beechcroft. LC 80-26561. 8.95 (ISBN 0-396-07933-4). Dodd, Mead.

Position Unknown. Ian Mackersey. LC 56-7726. 1956. Holt.

Positions. Bill Adler. 304p. (Orig.). 1981. pap. 2.75 (ISBN 0-8439-0966-8, LB966). Leisure Bks Ct.

Posse. George Charles Appell. 1961. Macmillan.

Posse Comitatus. Waller A Hurtt. LC 78-14973. 8.95 (ISBN 0-87949-109-4). Ashley Books.

Posse from Hell. Clair Huffaker. 1975. (pbk.) 1.25 (ISBN 0-671-78974-0). Pocket Books.

Posse from Poison Creek. Lewis B Patten. LC 78-78722. (Double D western). 1969. 4.50. Doubleday.

Posse of Crystal Creek. Tevis Miller. LC 36-932. Phoenix Press.

Posse Rider. Strong, Charles Stanley. LC 51-14530. 1951. Arcadia House.

Possesion of Immanuel Wolf and Other Improbable Tales. Marvin Kaye. LC 79-6865. 1981. 9.95 (ISBN 0-385-15862-9). Doubleday.

Possess Me Not. Frances Nichols Hanna. LC 46-17777. 1946. F. Fell Inc.

Possess the Land. Alan White. LC 70-124828. 1970. Harcourt Brace Jovanovich.

Possessed. Fedor Mikhailovich Dostoevskii. LC 66-2051. (Masterworks Ser.: M295). 1966. Fawcett Publications.

Possessed. Fedor Mikhailovich Dostoevskii. Tr. by Constance Black Garnett. LC 49-786. 1948. Macmillan.

Possessed. Fedor Mikhailovich Dostoevskii. Tr. by Constance Black Garnett. Yarmolinsky, Avrahm, 1800- LC 36-3324. (Half-title: The modern library of the world's best books). The Modern Library.

Possessed. Fedor Mikhailovich Dostoevskii. Tr. by Constance Garnett. Ed. by Avraham Yarmolinsky. 7.95 (ISBN 0-394-60441-5). Modern Lib.

Possessed, 2 Vols. Fedor Mikhailovich Dostoevskii. Tr. by Constance Garnett. 3.25x ea. o.p. (Evman, 861, 862). Dutton.

Possessed. Fedor Mikhailovich Dostoevskii. 1936. 3.95 o.p. (ISBN 0-394-60055-X, M55). Modern Lib.

Possessed. Florence Hurd. LC 60-1061. (Orig.). 1969. pap. 0.60 o.p. (B60-1061). Belmont-Tower.

Possessed. Cleveland Moffett. LC 20-2257. 1920. The James A. McCann Company.

Possessed. Catherine Turney. 1971. pap. 0.75 o.p. (ISBN 0-446-64576-1, 64-576). Paperback Lib.

Possessed. C. A Winstone. LC 78-64955. 1979. 7.95 (ISBN 0-312-63193-6). St. Martin's Press.

Possessed. Josiah Pitts Woolfolk. LC 35-436. W. Godwin, Inc.

Possessed. Erika Zastrow. LC 33-322237. H. Holt and Company.

Possessed: A Novel in Three Parts. Fedor Mikhailovich Dostoevskii. Tr. by Constance Black Garnett. LC 14-1911. (Half-title: The novels of Fyodor Dostoevsky. Vol. III). 1913. The Macmillan Company.

Possessed: A Novel in Three Parts. Fedor Mikhailovich Dostoevskii & Garnett, Mrs. Constance (Black) 1862- Tr. (Half-title: Everyman's library, ed. by Ernest Rhys, Fiction. no. 861-882). 1931. J. M. Dent & Sons, Ltd.

Possessed & Other Stories. Arthur C. Clarke. 188p. Repr. lib. bdg. 12.05x (ISBN 0-89190-956-7). Am Repr-Rivercity Pr.

Possessed: Fifteen Days of Bucka Monsterism. Bucka Christopulos. LC 77-150791. 1977. Christopulos.

Possession. Leslie Purnell Davies. LC 75-6155. 1976. 5.95 (ISBN 0-385-11075-8). Published for the Crime Club by Doubleday.

Possession. Mazo De La Roche. LC 23-641933. 1923. The Macmillan Company.

Possession. Nicholas Delbanco. LC 76-27834. 1977. 8.95 (ISBN 0-688-03146-3). Morrow.

Possession. Nicholas Delbanco. LC 81-20994. 1982. 6.95 (ISBN 0-688-00980-8). Quill.

Possession. Celia Fremlin, pseud. LC 76-82665. 1969. 4.95. Lippincott.

Possession. Christopher Starks. (Orig.). 1983. pap. price not set (ISBN 0-449-12547-5, GM). Fawcett.

Possession. Olive Wadsley. LC 17-6113. 1917. Dodd, Mead and Company.

Possession: A Novel. Louis Bromfield. LC 25-19113. 1925. Frederick A. Stokes Company.

Possession: A Novel. Louis Bromfield. LC 26-21493. 1926. Frederick A. Stokes Company.

Possession: A Novel. Louis Bromfield. LC 29-238026. 1927. Grosset & Dunlap.

Possession: A Novel. Ann Rule. LC 82-14377. 15.50 (ISBN 0-393-01641-2). Norton.

Possession: A Novel. Kamala Purnaiya Taylor. LC 63-10224. 1963. John Day Co.

Possession of Amber. Nicholas Jose. LC 81-113315. (Paperback prose). 1980. 13.25 (ISBN 0-7022-1537-6) (ISBN 0-7022-1538-4). University of Queensland Press.

Possession of Elizabeth Calder. Melissa Napier. (Ravenswood gothic). 1973. (pbk.) 0.95 (ISBN 0-671-77681-9). Pocket Books.

Possession of Jessica Young. Russell W. Martin. 320p. (Orig.). 1982. pap. 2.95 (ISBN 0-523-48041-5). Pinnacle Bks.

Possession of Joel Delaney. Ramona Stewart. 1980. pap. 2.25 (ISBN 0-440-17643-3). Dell.

Possession of Joel Delaney: A Novel. Ramona Stewart. LC 75-117036. 1970. 5.95. Little, Brown.

Possession of Tracy Corbin. Dorothy Daniels. 1973. (pbk) 0.95. Warner.

Possessor: By S. Bervl Lush. Samuel Beryl Lush. LC 66-6162. 1966. Heilbronn Bks.

Possessors. John Christopher. LC 65-10387. 1965. 4.50. S. & S.

Possessors & the Possessed. Samuel Agnew Schreiner, Jr. LC 79-54009. 1980. 12.95 (ISBN 0-87795-229-9). Arbor Hse.

Possessors & the Possessed. Samuel Agnew Schreiner, Jr. 512p. 1981. pap. 2.95 (ISBN 0-449-24432-6, Crest). Fawcett.

Possessors and the Possessed: The Saga of the Van Alen Family of New York: a Novel. Samuel Agnew Schreiner. LC 79-54009. 12.95 (ISBN 0-87795-229-9). Arbor House.

Possibilities. Thomas L Baily. LC 6-5011. D. Lothrop Company.

Possibility of an Early Fall. Christine La Belle. 1971. 10.00 o.p. (Pub. by Elizabeth Pr); pap. 5.00 o.p. SBD.

Possible Husbands. Arthur Tuckerman. 1926. Doubleday, Page & Company.

Possible She. Susan Jacoby. 160p. 1980. pap. 2.50 (ISBN 0-345-28735-5). Ballantine.

Possible Worlds of Science Fiction. Ed. by Groff Conklin. LC 51-10781. 1951. Vanguard Press.

Posson Jone & Pere Raphael see Collected Works.

Posson Jone'" and Pere Raphael. With a New Word Setting Forth How and Why the Two Tales Are One. George Washington Cable. LC 72-84536. (Illus.). 1974. 7.50 (ISBN 0-403-02950-3). Scholarly Press.

Posson Jone" and Pere Raphael: With a New Word Setting Forth How and Why the Two Tales Are One. George Washington Cable. LC 75-83931. (Illus.). 1969. Mnemosyne Pub. Co.

Posson Jone'" and Pere Raphael: With a New Word Setting Forth How and Why the Two Tales Are One. George Washington Cable. LC 9-28086. 1909. C. Scribner's Sons.

Possum Creek Poultry Club. by j. h. davis... ed. J H Davis. 1895. The Fanciers' Review.

Possum Hunters: A Story of the Tobacco War in Kentucky. James William Slade. LC 20-13145. Burton Publishing Company.

Possumist: And Other Stories. William Henry Frazer. LC 25-27. 1924. The Murrill Press.

Post-Captain. John Davis & John Moore. LC 77-448. (Garland Library of Narratives of North American Indian Captivities; V. 26). 1977. 25.00 (ISBN 0-8240-1650-5). Garland Pub.
Post Captain. Patrick O'Brian. LC 73-39760. 1972. 7.95 (ISBN 0-397-00804-X). Lippincott.
Post-Captain: Or The Wooden Walls Well Manned: Comprehending a View of Naval Society and Manners; Containing Also a Choice Collection of Sea and Other Songs. 20th american, from the 7th london ed. John Davis & Moore, John. LC 22-8288. 1850. W. A. Leary & Co. Ca.
Post Girl. Edward Charles Booth. LC 8-20677. 1908. The Century Co.
Post-Man Robb'd of His Mail: Or, The Packet Broke Open. Charles Gildon. LC 73-170542. (Foundations of the Novel). 1972. (ISBN 0-8240-0543-0). Garland Pub.
Post Mortem. Anne Edwards. 1971. price not set o.p. Coward.
Post Mortem. Constance Lindsay Taylor. LC 53-8920. (Main Line mysteries). 1953. Lippincott.
Post Mortem: By Harry Carmichael Pseud. Leopold Horace Ognall. LC 66-11724. 1966. 3.50. Pub. for the Crime Club by Doubleday.
Post of Honor. Ronald Frederick Delderfield. LC 74-181501. 1974. (pbk.). 1.50 (ISBN 0-671-78673-3). Pocket Books.
Post of Honor. David Dortort. LC 49-7923. 1949. Whittlesey House.
Post Office. Rabindranath Tagore. Tr. by Devabrata Mukerjee. 48p. 1971. Repr. of 1918 ed. 10.00x (ISBN 0-7165-1347-1, Pub. by Cuala Press Ireland). Biblio Dist.
Post-Office Detective: Or, A Mystery of the Mail. George W Goode. (Secret Service Series. No. 10). 1888. Street & Smith.
Post Reader of Civil War Stories. Edited by Gordon Carroll. With an Introd. by E. B. Long. Illustrated by Ray Houlihan. The Saturday Evening Post. Ed. by Gordon Carroll. LC 58-13291. 1958. Doubleday.
Post Reader of Fantasy and Science Fiction. LC 64-11293. 1964. Doubleday.
Post Stories: Of 1935- Saturday Evening Post. LC 37-272663. Little, Brown, and Company.
Postage Stamp Murder. George Clinton Bestor. LC 35-2534. 1935. The Dial Press.
Postcard Mysteries & Other Stories. Albert Drake. (Illus.). 1976. pap. 2.50 (ISBN 0-936892-10-2). Stone Pr MI.
Posted for Murder. Virginia Rath. LC 42-21958. 1942. Published for the Crime Club by Doubleday, Doran and Company, Inc.
Postern of Fate. Agatha Miller Christie. LC 73-179316. 1973. 6.95 (ISBN 0-396-06881-2). Dodd, Mead.
Postern of Fate. Agatha Miller Christie. LC 74-3050. 1974. 10.95 (ISBN 0-8161-6197-6). G. K. Hall.
Posthumours Papers of the Pickwick Club. people's ed.... ed. Charles Dickens. LC 9-3009. T. B. Peterson & Brothers.
Posthumous Confession. Marcellus Emants. LC 75-9734. (Library of Netherlandic literature; v. 7). 1975. 8.50 (ISBN 0-8057-8152-8). Twayne.
Posthumous Papers of the Pickwick Club. Illustrated by Broom Lynne. Charles Dickens. LC 50-9774. (Macdonald illustrated classics. 2). 1950. Coward-McCann.
Posthumous Papers of the Pickwick Club: Including Three Little-Remembered Chapters from Master Humphrey's Clock, in Which Mr. Pickwick, Sam Weller & Other Pickwickians Reappear. inner sanctum ed. Charles Dickens & Fadiman, Clifton, 1904- Ed. LC 49-500819. 1949. Simon and Schuster.
Posthumous Papers of the Pickwick Club; Some New Bibliographical Discoveries. George William Davis. LC 72-3167. 1972. (ISBN 0-8383-1533-X). Haskell House.
Posthumous Papers of the Pickwick Club. Some New Bibliographical Discoveries. George William Davis. LC 76-2380. 1976. 5.50 (ISBN 0-88305-171-0). Norwood Editions.
Posthumous Papers of the Pickwick Club. Charles Dickens. LC 64-9143. (His The New Oxford illustrated Dickens). 1959. Oxford University Press.
Posthumous Papers of the Pickwick Club. Charles Dickens. Ed. by Robert L. Patten. LC 73-154771. (Penguin English Library). (Illus.). 1972. 3.95 (ISBN 0-14-043078-4). Penguin Books.
Posthumous Papers of the Pickwick Club. Charles Dickens. LC 17-23002. 1838. J. Turney.
Posthumous Papers of the Pickwick Club. 4th ed. Charles Dickens. LC 6-37238. 1840. J. Van Amringe Etc.
Posthumous Papers of the Pickwick Club. a new ed. with numerous illustrations by sam weller, jr. and alfred crowquill, esq. pseud. ed. Charles Dickens. LC 40-18601. 1842. Lea and Blanchard.
Posthumous Papers of the Pickwick Club... Charles Dickens. LC 6-37037. 1867. Hurd and Houghton.
Posthumous Papers of the Pickwick Club. illustrated household ed. Charles Dickens. LC 6-37233. 1870. Fields, Osgood & Co.
Posthumous Papers of the Pickwick Club. Charles Dickens. LC 34-37770. 1873. J. R. Osgood and Company.
Posthumous Papers of the Pickwick Club. Charles Dickens. LC 9-823. Aldine Book Publishing Co.
Posthumous Papers of the Pickwick Club. Charles Dickens. Ed. by Whipple, Edwin Percy. (Half-title: Works of Charles Dickens. New illustrated library ed. vol. i-ii). Houghton Mifflin Company.
Posthumous Papers of the Pickwick Club. Charles Dickens. Ed. by Dickens, Charles. LC 4-15305. 1897. Macmillan and Co., Limited.
Posthumous Papers of the Pickwick Club. Charles Dickens. (Rittenhouse classics). 1920. G. W. Jacobs & Company.
Posthumous Papers of the Pickwick Club. Charles Dickens. LC 32-28171. (Half-title: The modern library of the world's best books). 1932. The Modern Library.
Posthumous Papers of the Pickwick Club. Charles Dickens. LC 36-37120. (Half-title: Everyman's library, ed. by Ernest Rhys. Fiction. no. 235). 1934. J. M. Dent & Sons, Ltd.
Posthumous Papers of the Pickwick Club. Charles Dickens. LC 36-33136. The Heritage Press.
Posthumous Papers of the Pickwick Club. Charles Dickens. LC 42-44640. (On cover: Alta edition). Porter & Coates.
Posthumous Papers of the Pickwick Club. Charles Dickens. LC 43-37796. 1885. Hurst & Co.
Posthumous Papers of the Pickwick Club. Charles Dickens & Brock, Charles Edmund, 1870- Illus. LC 44-401356. (On cover: Great illustrated classics). 1944. Dodd, Mead & Company.
Posthumous Papers of the Pickwick Club. Charles Dickens & Chesterton, Gilbert Keith. (Half-title: Everyman's library, ed. by Ernest Rhys. Fiction. no. 235). 1909. J. M. Dent & Co.
Posthumous Papers of the Pickwick Club. Charles Dickens & McKay, Donald, 1895- Illus. LC 43-51330. 1943. Modern Library.
Posthumous Papers of the Pickwick Club. Charles Dickens & Van Noorden, C. 1909. C. Scribner's Sons.
Postman. Martin Du Gard, Roger. LC 74-130521. 1974-1975. 10.00. H. Fertig.
Postman. Martin Du Gard, Roger. LC 74-13052. 1975. 10.50. H. Fertig.
Postman Always Rings Twice. James Mallahan Cain. LC 34-290654. 1934. A. A. Knopf.
Postman Always Rings Twice. James Mallahan Cain. LC 46-16156. 1945. Grosset & Dunlap.
Postman Always Rings Twice. James Mallahan Cain. LC 77-92633. 1978. 1.65 (ISBN 0-394-72583-2). Vintage Books.
Postman. Translated by John Russell. Martin Du Gard, Roger. LC 55-5866. 1955. Viking Press.
Postmark Murder. Mignon Good Eberhart. 1956. Random House.
Postmark Murder. Mignon Good Eberhart. LC 55-8166. 1974. (pbk.) 0.95. Popular Library.
Postmarked "Colima". Julia Suesserott Alleman. LC 1-29003. (John Rung prize series). Lutheran Publication Society.
Postmaster. Joseph Crosby Lincoln. LC 12-11157. 1912. D. Appleton and Company.
Postmaster-General. Hilaire Belloc. LC 32-23726. 1932. J. B. Lippincott Company.
Postmaster's Daughter. Louis Tracy. LC 16-2214. E. J. Clode.
Postscript for Malpas. Peter Pearson. LC 75-26965. (Red badge novel of suspense). 1976. (ISBN 0-396-07285-2). Dodd, Mead.
Postscript to a Dead Letter. Donald MacKenzie. LC 72-9011. (Midnight novel of suspense). 1973. 5.95 (ISBN 0-395-15472-3). Houghton Mifflin.
Postscript to Nightmare. Dolores Birk Hitchens. (X1462). 1968. Berkley.
Postscript to Nightmare. Dolores Birk Hitchens. LC 67-21730. (Red mask mystery). 1967. Putnam.
Postscript to Wendy. Amram Scheinfeld. LC 48-7689. 1948. Whittlesey House.
Posture of the Eagle: An Anthology of Original Stories. Peter E Besbas & William Vaughan. LC 78-52390. 2.95 (ISBN 0-89260-121-3). Hwong Pub. Co.
Posy Ring. Margaret Raine Hunt. (seaside library, v. 45, no. 917). 1881. G. Munro.
Posy Ring. A Novel. Margaret Raine Hunt. LC 7-227473. (Franklin square library. no. 158). 1881. Harper & Brothers.
"Pot and Kettle". Joellen Ingram. LC 28-2236. The Evangelical Press.
Pot & Pleasure. James Simpson. 1972. pap. 1.75 o.s.i. (V1047K, Venus). Grove.
Pot-Bouille. Emile Zola & Sherwood, Mrs. Mary (Neal) Tr. LC 9-1310. T. B. Peterson & Brothers.
Pot-Bouille (Piping Hot) A Realistic Novel. Emile Zola & Chalmers, Edward Wharton, Ed. LC 9-1309. (pastime series. v. 23). 1889. Laird & Lee.
Pot Luck. Roland Clark. LC 45-3536. 1945. A. S. Barnes and Company.
Pot of Gold. George Clarke Peck. LC 22-24112. The Abingdon Press.
Pot of Gold: A Story of Fire Island Beach. Edward Richard Shaw. LC 8-4805. Belford, Clarke and Co.
Pot of Gold, and Other Stories. Mary Eleanor Wilkins Freeman. LC 74-113661. (Short story index reprint series). (Illus.). 1970. Books for Libraries Press.
Pot of Gold, and Other Stories. Mary Eleanor Wilkins Freeman. LC 6-40028. D. Lothrop Company.
Pot Shot. Lyn Stallworth. LC 68-27377. 1968. 3.95. Walker.
Pot Shots from Pegasus. Keith Preston. LC 20-8738. 1929. Covici, Friede.
Potash and Perlmutter Settle Things. Montague Marsden Glass. LC 19-14943. 1919. Harper & Brothers.
Potash & Perlmutter: Their Copartnership Ventures and Adventures. Montague Marsden Glass. LC 74-27988. (Modern Jewish Experience). (Illus.). 1975. 26.00 (ISBN 0-405-06715-1). Arno Press.
Potash & Perlmutter: Their Copartnership Ventures and Adventures. Montague Marsden Glass. LC 10-13215. 1.50. Henry Altemus Company.
Potash & Perlmutter: Their Copartnership Ventures and Adventures. Montague Marsden Glass. LC 11-18459. 1911. Doubleday, Page & Company.
Potato Child & Others. Lucia Prudence Hall C. J. Woodbury Woodbury. LC 10-15193. P. Elder and Company.
Potato Face. Carl Sandburg. LC 30-9738. Harcourt, Brace and Company.
Potato Peelers. George Zuckerman. 1975. (pbk.) 1.75. Ballantine Books.
Potato Peelers: A Novel. George Zuckerman. LC 74-11796. 1974. 8.95 (ISBN 0-396-07018-3). Dodd, Mead.
Potatoes Are Cheaper. Max Shulman. LC 70-139060. 1971. 5.95. Doubleday.
Potatoes Without Gravy. Hants A. White. 1972. 5.00 o.p. (ISBN 0-682-47419-3). Exposition.
Potbellied Stove. M Lucretia Hayden. LC 53-64620. Vantage Press.
Potent Ash. Leonard Kibera & Samuel Kahiga. 1968. pap. 2.00 o.p. (Pub. by East African Publ Hse). Northwestern U Pr.
Potentate. Frances Forbes-Robertson Harrod. LC 7-2881. The Mershon Company.
Potentate. Frances Forbes-Robertson Harrod. LC 99-4688. 1899. J. F. Taylor & Company.
Potiphar Papers. George William Curtis. LC 72-121280. (Illus.). 1970. (ISBN 0-404-01888-2). AMS Press.
Potiphar Papers. George William Curtis. LC 6-31709. 1858. Harper & Brothers.
Potiphar Papers. George William Curtis. LC 8-30409. 1869. Harper & Brothers.
Potiphar Papers. George William Curtis. LC 9-3004. Harper & Brothers.
Potiphar Papers. George William Curtis. LC 4-13872. 1900. Harper & Brothers.
Potlatch Run. William Price. LC 75-133584. 1971. 6.50 (ISBN 0-525-18200-4). Dutton.
Potomac Conspiracy. D. Lawrence Levy. LC 75-40776. 1976. 1.50 (ISBN 0-89041-062-3). Major Books.
Potomac Poppies. 1st Ed. John Edward Malloy. LC 53-12322. 1953. Pageant Press.
Potpourri. Eunice Loncoske McCloskey. (Illus.). 1966. 5.00 o.p. (ISBN 0-8059-0181-7). Dorrance.
Potpourri. Susan B. Sirkis. (Wish Bklets: Vol. 12). (Illus.). 56p. 1973. pap. 5.50x (ISBN 0-913786-12-8). Wish Bklets.
Potpourri: Number Two Clipbook of Line Artwork. Norman Ludlow, Jr. (Illus.). 1982. pap. 10.95 (ISBN 0-916706-28-1). N H Ludlow.
Potpourri of Tales. Leonard Iljana. 1970. 3.50 o.p. Carlton.
Potrait of a Scoundrel. Nathaniel Benchley. LC 79-22062. 1979. (ISBN 0-8161-3009-4). G. K. Hall.
Pots of Gold. 1st. ed. Edith Marie Beyerle. LC 47-5635. 1946. Loizeaux Bros.
Potted Fiction: Being a Series of Extracts from the World's Best Sellers Put up in Thin Slices for Hurried Consumers. The United States Literary Canning Co. John Kendrick Bangs. LC 70-178436. (Short story index reprint series). 1971. (ISBN 0-8369-4036-9). Books for Libraries Press.
Potted Fiction: Being a Series of Extracts from the World's Best Sellers Put up in Thin Slices for Hurried Consumers. The United States Literary Canning Co. John Kendrick Bangs. 1908. Doubleday, Page & Co.
Potter & His Children. Robert Cole Caples. 6.50 o.p. Carlton.
Potter and His Children: A Stone Age Fable. Robert Cole Caples. LC 75-30787. (Geneva book). (Illus.). 1971. 6.50. Carlton Press.
Potter and the Clay: A Romance of Today, by Maud Howard Peterson Pseud. Illustrated. Mary Howard Hoopes. LC 1-31912. Lothrop Publishing Company.
Potterat and the War. Benjamin Vallotton. LC 18-630831. 1898. Dodd, Mead & Company.
Potterism. Rose Macaulay. LC 20-19045. Boni and Liveright.
Potter's House. Wallace Earle Stegner. LC 39-382. 1938. The Prairie Press.
Potter's House: A Novel. Isabel Constance Clarke. LC 21-62666. 1921. Benziger Brothers.
Potters O' Skunk Hollow. Ivan Blair Anthony. LC 47-6371. 1947. B. Humphries.
Potters O'Skunk Hollow. Ivan Blair Anthony. LC 47-6371. 1946. B. Humphries.
Potter's Thumb: A Novel. Flora Annie Webster Steel. LC 4-15336. 1894. Harper & Brothers.
Pottery: The Moulding of a Love Child. George E Jorgenson & Jorgenson, Nora. LC 34-35878. Authors Publications, Inc.
Pottery, the Moulding of a Love Child: By George and Nora Jorgensen. George Ellington Jorgenson & Nora Jorgenson. LC 34-35878. 1934. Authors Publications.
Pouliuli. Albert Wendt. LC 80-15158. (Pacific Classics; No. 8). 1980. 4.95 (ISBN 0-8248-0728-6). University Press of Hawaii.
Pounamu Pounamu. Witi Chimaera, pseud. LC 73-169580. 132p. 1972. 8.50x o.p. (ISBN 0-8002-0074-8). Intl Pubns Serv.
Pound Foolish. Robert Molloy. LC 50-10386. 1950. Lippincott.
Pound of Cure: A Story of Monte Carlo. William Henry Bishop. LC 6-127110. 1894. C. Scribner's.
Pour Oublier un Reve. Charlotte Lamb, pseud. (Collection Harlequin). 192p. 1983. pap. 1.95 (ISBN 0-373-49321-5). Harlequin Bks.
Pour Sganarelle Recherche d'un Personnage et d'un Roman see Frere Ocean.
Pour the Hemlock. Andrew Joseph Russell. LC 76-14213. 7.95 (ISBN 0-394-49629-9). Random House.
Pour toi. Louis Untermeyer. (Illus., Fr.). 1968. 1.95 o.p. (ISBN 0-88332-128-9, 4420). Larousse.
Pour un Herbier. Sidonie Gabrielle Colette. deluxe ed. 850.00 o.p. French & Eur.
Pour une Seule Valse. Julia Carole. (Collection Colombine). 192p. 1983. pap. 1.95 (ISBN 0-373-48057-1). Harlequin Bks.
Pour Wine for Us: A Novel. Dean Van Clute & Van Clute, Walton, Joint Author. LC 32-30642. 1932. Frederick A. Stokes Company.
Poverina,". Evelyn Mary Buckenham. LC 12-1003. 1912. 0.85. Benziger Brothers.
Poverina. A Story; Tr. from the French of Mme. la Princesse O. Cantacuzene-Altiere. Olga Cantacuzene-Altieri & Ltieri, O Lga. LC 7-1629. (Appletons' new handy-volume series. v. 63). 1881. D. Appleton and Company.
Poverty Corner. "A Little World". A City Story. George Manville Fenn. (On cover: The seaside library. Pocket ed. no. 558). G. Munro.
Poverty Corner. "A Little World.") A City Story. George Manville Fenn. LC 43-26665. 1885. Cassell & Company, Limited.
Poverty Grass. Lillie Buffum Chace Wyman. LC 9-1473. 1886. Houghton, Mifflin and Company.
Poverty Hollow: A True Story. Mary A Post. 1887. T. B. Ventres.
Poverty Knob. Sarah Warner Brooks. LC 3175. 1900. A. Wessels Company.
Powder and Patch: A Comedy of Manners. Georgette Heyer. LC 68-12468. 1968. Dutton.
Powder Barrel. Richard Clayton. LC 65-23221. 1965. I. Washburn.
Powder Barrel. William Haggard. 1965. 3.95 o.p. Washburn.
Powder Burn. William D. Monalbano & Carl Hiaasen. 1983. pap. 2.95 (ISBN 0-441-67573-5, Pub. by Charter Bks). Ace Bks.
Powder Burn. William D Montalbano & Carl Hiaasen. LC 81-65997. 1981. 11.95 (ISBN 0-689-11174-6). Atheneum.
Powder Burner. Frank Chester Robertson. LC 35-16053. 1935. I. Washburn, Inc.
Powder Burns. Al Cody, pseud. 256p. (YA) 1973. 6.95 (Avalon). Bouregy.
Powder Burns. Archie Joscelyn. LC 53-9385. (Avalon Westerns). 1973. 4.50. Avalon Books.
Powder Burns: By Al Cody Pseud. Archie Joscelyn. LC 53-9385. 1953. Bouregy Curl.
Powder Keg. 1st Ed. Frances Marion. LC 53-10242. 1953. Little, Brown.
Powder Mission. Herbert E Stover. LC 51-12111. 1951. Dodd, Mead.
Powder, Patches and Patty. Emilie Benson Knipe & Knipe, Alden Arthur. LC 24-218091. The Century Co.
Powder River. Francis W Hilton. 1935. H. C. Kinsey & Company, Inc.
Powder River Cowman. George Heinzman. LC 62-77911. 1962. Macmillan.

TITLE INDEX PRAIRIE. A TALE.

Powder Smoke on Wandering River. Jackson Gregory. LC 38-5137. 1938. Dodd, Mead & Company.
Powder Train. Warren Tute. 1975. (pbk.) 1.25 (ISBN 0-345-24377-3). Ballantine Books.
Powder Valley Ambush. Peter Field. LC 50-13898. 1950. Jefferson House.
Powder Valley Deadlock. Peter Field. LC 54-7079. 1954. Jefferson House.
Powder Valley Getaway. Peter Field. LC 63-13221. (His A Powder Valley western). 1963. Jefferson House.
Powder Valley Getaway. Peter Field. (Kangaroo Book). 1977. 1.25 (ISBN 0-671-81080-4). Pocket Books.
Powder Valley Holdup. Peter Field. LC 52-5789. 1952. Jefferson House.
Powder Valley Manhunt. Peter Field. LC 57-6937. (His A Powder Valley western). 1957. Jefferson House.
Powder Valley Pay-off. Peter Field. LC 41-193045. 1941. W.Morrow & Company.
Powder Valley Plunder. Peter Field. LC 77-2906. 1977. 3.95 (ISBN 0-89340-073-4). J. Curley.
Powder Valley Ransom. Peter Field. (Kangaroo Book). (Powder Valley Western). 1977. 1.25 (ISBN 0-671-80956-3). Pocket Books.
Powder Valley Renegade. Peter Field. LC 56-532593. (A Powder Valley western). 1956. Jefferson House.
Powder Valley Showdown. Peter Field. LC 45-11147. 1946. Jefferson House.
Powder Valley Stampede. Peter Field. LC 54-11005. (3His A Powder Valley western)). 1954. Jefferson House.
Powder Valley Thunder. Peter Field. (Powder Valley Western). 1973. (pbk.) 0.75. Pocket Books.
Powder Valley Vengeance. Peter Field. LC 77-2915. 1977. 7.95 (ISBN 0-89340-074-2). J. Curley.
Powdered Ashes: A Story of Modern Japan. Theodate Geoffrey, pseud. LC 26-17282. 1926. Houghton Mifflin Company.
Powdered Ashes; a Story of Modern Japan. Dorothy Wayman. LC 26-17282. 1926. Houghton Mifflin Company.
Powdered Eggs. Charles Simmons. (Penguin bk., 3201). 1972. 1.25 (ISBN 0-14-003201-0). Penguin.
Powdered Eggs: A Novel. Charles Simmons. LC 64-19521. 1964. Dutton.
Powderhorn Trail. Tevis Miller. LC 51-17382. 1950. Phoenix Press.
Powdersmoke Canyon: By Lew Smith Pseud. Lee Floren. LC 54-130460. 1954. Arcadia House.
Powdersmoke Fence. A Double D Western. Bennett Foster. LC 40-30399. 1940. Doubleday, Doran & Company, Inc.
Powdersmoke Feud. William MacLeod Raine. (Signet Brand Western, T5574). 1973. (pbk.) 0.75. New American Lib.
Powdersmoke Lawyer. Lee Floren. (Orig.). 1979. pap. 1.50 (ISBN 0-532-15390-1). Woodhill.
Powdersmoke Pass. Archie Joscelyn. LC 38-171. Phoenix Press.
Powdersmoke Pay-off. Fred East. LC 48-2090. 1948. E. P. Dutton.
Powdersmoke Payoff. Al Cody, pseud. 1980. pap. 1.75 (ISBN 0-8439-0834-3). Nordon Pubns.
Powdersmoke Payoff. Archie Joscelyn. 1963. Arcadia House.
Powdersmoke Range. William Colt MacDonald. LC 34-42861. C.
Powdersmoke Trail. Forrest Raymond Brown. LC 38-8108. Greenberg.
Powenz Pack: One Family's Chronicle. Ernst Penzoldt. LC 81-22169. (Illus.). 1982. 13.95 (ISBN 0-88064-002-2). Fromm International Pub. Corp.
Power. Lion Feuchtwanger. Tr. by Willa Muir. Muir, Edwin, 1887- Tr. LC 26-19097. 1926. The Viking Press.
Power. Lion Feuchtwanger. Tr. by Willa Muir. Muir, Edwin, 1887- Joint Tr. LC 32-26894. (Half-title: The modern library of the world's best books). 1932. The Modern Library.
Power. Lion Feuchtwanger & Muir, Willa, Tr. LC 29-252741. 1928. The Viking Press.
Power. Lion Feuchtwanger & Muir, Willa, Tr. LC 31-10352. 1929. Grosset & Dunlap.
Power. Laurence M Janifer. 1974. (pbk.) 0.95. Dell.
Power. Ronald S Joseph. 1979. 2.50 (ISBN 0-446-81468-7). Warner Books.
Power. Frank M Robinson. (Berkley Medallion Book). 1977. 1.75 (ISBN 0-425-03600-6). Berkley Pub. Co.
Power. Richard Martin Stern. LC 74-82991. 1975. 9.95 (ISBN 0-679-50450-8). McKay.
Power. Arthur John Arbuthnott Stringer. LC 25-8591. The Bobbs-Merrill Company.
Power: A Novel. William Harrington. LC 64-25303. 1964. Bobbs-Merrill.
Power and Purity: A Novel. 1st Ed. Francis Minturn Sedgwick. LC 61-131517. 1961. Bobbs-Merrill.
Power and the Glory. Phyllis Eleanor Bentley. LC 40-27202. 1940. The Macmillan Company.
Power and the Glory. Grace MacGowan Cooke. LC 10-16715. 1910. Doubleday, Page & Company.
Power and the Glory. Graham Greene. Ed. by Richard Warrington Baldwin Lewis & Peter J. Conn. LC 79-104160. (Viking critical library). (Illus.). 1970. (pbk) 2.25 (ISBN 0-670-01806-6). Viking Press.
Power and the Glory. Graham Greene. LC 46-1198. 1946. The Viking Press.
Power and the Glory. Graham Greene & Richard Warrington Baldwin Lewis. LC 77-11877. (Viking critical library). 1977. 3.95 (ISBN 0-14-015506-6). Penguin Books.
Power and the Glory: A Romance of the Great La Salle. Gilbert Parker. LC 41-38130. 1925. Harper & Brothers.
Power & the Pain. Charles Platt. 224p. (Orig.). 1971. pap. 1.95 o.s.i. (O*P*H260, Ophelia). Olympia.
Power and the Passion. Christina Nicholson. (Fawcett Crest Book). 1977. 2.25 (ISBN 0-449-23411-8). Fawcett Books.
Power and the Passion. Christopher Nicole. LC 76-56138. 1977. 8.95 (ISBN 0-698-10808-6). Coward, McCann & Geoghegan.
Power and the Passion. Christopher Nicole. (Fawcett Crest Book). 1977. 2.25 (ISBN 0-449-23411-8). Fawcett Books.
Power & the Pride. Robert Vaughan. 1976. pap. 1.95 (ISBN 0-532-19116-1). Woodhill.
Power and the Prize. Chet Cunningham. (Leisure Book). 1977. 1.95 (ISBN 0-8439-0483-6). Nordon Pubns.
Power and the Prize: A Novel. Howard Swiggett. LC 54-6476. 1954. Ballantine Books.
Power & the Wisdom. J. L. McKenzie. 1965. pap. 2.95 o.p. (ISBN 0-02-087730-7). Macmillan.
Power Behind the Throne. A Story of the Modern Maelstrom. Everett W Fish. (On cover: Great West quarterly, no. 1). 1894. The Author.
Power Bent. Flora James Robinson. LC 40-13806. 1940. Carlyle House.
Power Beyond Their Own. Rossie Beaman. LC 59-51393. 1959.
Power Brokers. Thomas Van Dusen. LC 77-358272. 1976. 10.95 (ISBN 0-00-222084-9). Collins.
Power Eaters. Diana Davenport. 320p. 1980. pap. 2.75 (ISBN 0-449-24287-0, Crest). Fawcett.
Power Eaters. Diana Davenport. 1979. 9.95 (ISBN 0-688-03417-9). Morrow.
Power Exchange: A Novel. Alan R Erwin. LC 79-66507. 1979. 9.95 (ISBN 0-932012-08-6). Texas Monthly Press.
Power Failure. James Preston. LC 73-150199. 1971. 3.50 (ISBN 0-09-109080-6). Hutchinson of Australia.
Power for Sale: A Novel. John Knittel. LC 39-258771. 1939. Frederick A. Stokes Company.
Power Forward. Walter Kaylin. LC 78-20438. 1979. 9.95 (ISBN 0-689-10972-5). Atheneum.
Power Grab. Leonard Sanders. Orig. Title: Wooden Horseshoe. pap. 0.75 o.p. (54-832). Paperback Lib.
Power-House. Benjamin Appel. LC 39-6261. 1939. E.P. Dutton & Company, Inc.
Power-House. John Buchan. LC 16-14868. George H. Doran Company.
Power-House. John Buchan. LC 41-52044. 1941. Houghton Mifflin Company.
Power House. Richard Clayton. LC 67-14684. 1967. I. Washburn.
Power House. Alexander Comfort. LC 45-4143. 1945. The Viking Press.
Power House. William Haggard. 1967. 3.95 o.p. Washburn.
Power House: By William Haggard. 1st Amer. Ed. LC 67-14684. 1967. 3.95. I. Washburn.
Power Kill. Charles W. Runyon. (Orig.). 1972. pap. 0.75 o.p. (T2560, GM). Fawcett World.
Power Killers. Judson Pentecost Philips. LC 74-3788. (Red badge novel of suspense). 1974. 5.95 (ISBN 0-396-06979-7). Dodd, Mead.
Power Lot. Sarah Pratt McLean Greene. LC 6-31386. 1906. The Baker & Taylor Co.
Power of a Lie: By Johan Boher: Tr. from the Norwegian by Jessie Muir, with an Introduction by Hall Caine. Johan Bojer & Muir, Jessie, Tr. LC 9-49569. M. Kennerley.
Power of an Eye. Ethel Grimwood. LC 7-289. United States Book Company.
Power of Black: A Novel. M. B. Longman. LC 61-8385. 1961. R. S. Globus.
Power of Blackness. Jack Williamson. LC 75-29508. 6.95 (ISBN 0-399-11467-X). Berkley Pub. Corp.: Distributed by Putnam.
Power of Blackness: Hawthorne, Poe, Melville. Harry Tuchman Levin. (K-90). 1960. pap., 1.25. Vintage Books.
Power of Blackness: Hawthorne, Poe, Melville. Harry Tuchman Levin. LC 58-5826. 1958. Knopf.
Power of Conscience. Lee Barham Davis. LC 11-13731. 1911. 1.00. The Stuyvesant Press.
Power of Darkness. Doris Sutcliffe Adams. LC 68-13995. 1968. Walker.
Power of Gold: A Romance of London, England. Urania Nott Sangster. LC 9-30451. 1909. The Matthews-Northrup Works.
Power of Innocence. Arthur Joseph Westermayr. LC 9-29424. R. F. Fenno & Company.
Power of Joy. Noel Hilliard. LC 66-25840. 1966. 5.95. Regnerv.
Power of Light. Isaac Bashevis Singer. 80p. 1982. pap. 2.25 (ISBN 0-380-60103-6, 60103-6, Camelot). Avon.
Power of Mesmerism see Two Novels of the Victorian Underground.
Power of Nothingness. David-Neel, Alexandra & Albert Arthur Yongden. LC 81-23737. 1982. 10.95 (ISBN 0-395-31557-3). Houghton Mifflin.
Power of Nothingness. large print ed. David-Neel, Alexandra & Albert Arthur Yongden. LC 82-10387. 9.95 (ISBN 0-89621-382-X). Thorndike Press.
Power of Sympathy. William Hill Brown. Ed. by William S. Kable. LC 72-76389. (Illus.). 1970. 7.50. Ohio State University Press.
Power of Sympathy. Critical Introd. by Herbert Brown. William Hill Brown & Sarah Wentworth Apthorp Morton. Ed. by Herbert Roses Brown. LC 62-52425. 1961. New Frontier Press.
Power of the Bug. Ivor Drummond. LC 74-80845. 1974. 7.50. St. Martin's Press.
Power of the Child. John Watson. LC 7-206230. The Sunday School Times Company.
Power of the Dog. Lillian Kate Rowland-Brown. LC 6-45414. 1896. The International News Company.
Power of the Dog. Thomas Savage. LC 67-11220. 1967. Little, Brown.
Power of the Dog. Thomas Savage. LC 82-13705. 1982. 6.95 (ISBN 0-941324-00-1). Van Vactor & Goodheart.
Power of the Gods. Glenn R. Vernam. 1979. pap. 1.95 (ISBN 0-532-19234-6). Woodhill.
Power of the Hills. Laurie York Erskine. LC 28-4072. 1928. D. Appleton and Company.
Power of the Serpent. Peter Valentine Timlett (ISBN 0-553-02370-5). Bantam.
Power of the Sun. Beren Van Slyke. LC 31-8539. 1931. Dodd, Mead & Company.
Power of Ula. Sheldon-Williams, Miles. LC 77-84276. (Lost Race and Adult Fantasy Fiction). (Illus.). 1978. 19.00 (ISBN 0-405-11014-6). Arno Press.
Power of Woman... Archibald Clavering Gunter. LC 7-130. (On cover: The welcome series. nos. 24-25). Home Publishing Co.
Power Play. Kenneth M. Cameron. 2.25 (ISBN 0-445-04348-2). Popular Library.
Power Play. Jayne Castle. (Candlelight Ecstasy Ser.: No. 79). (Orig.). 1982. pap. 1.95 (ISBN 0-440-17067-2). Dell.
Power Play. John Craig. LC 72-9934. 1973. 6.95 (ISBN 0-396-06761-1). Dodd, Mead.
Power Play. John Craig. 1974. (pbk.) 1.25. Warner Paperback Library.
Power Play. Mildred Gordon & Gordon Gordon. 1973. pap. 1.25 o.p. (01062). Curtis.
Power Play. Warren Murphy. (Destroyer: No. 36). 1979. pap. 1.95 (ISBN 0-523-41251-7). Pinnacle Bks.
Power Play: By the Gordons. Mildred Gordon & Gordon Gordon. LC 65-21651. 1965. Doubleday.
Power Players. Arelo Sederberg. 480p. 1981. pap. 2.75 (ISBN 0-553-14141-4). Bantam.
Power Players. Arelo Sederberg. LC 79-15126. 1980. 11.95 o.p. (ISBN 0-688-03514-0). Morrow.
Power Players: A Novel. Arelo Sederberg. LC 79-15126. 1979. 10.95 (ISBN 0-688-03514-0). Morrow.
Power Plays. Collin Wilcox. LC 78-23749. 7.95 (ISBN 0-394-50172-1). Random House.
Power Profane. Robert Calhoun & Schneider, Barry. 2.25 (ISBN 0-449-14113-6). Fawcett Gold Medal.
Power Sellers. Patrick Hall. LC 68-8976. 1969. 5.95. Putnam.
Power Supreme: A Novel of Church and State in South America. Francis Child Nicholas. LC 8-20675. 1908. R. E. Lee Company.
Power That Preserves. Stephen R Donaldson. LC 77-10814. (Donaldson, Stephen R. The Chronicles of Thomas Covenant, the Unbeliever: Bk. 3). 10.00 (ISBN 0-03-022781-X). Holt, Rinehart and Winston.
Power to Kill. Robert Smythe Hichens. LC 34-354693. 1934. Doubleday, Doran & Company, Inc.
Power Trap. Stanton Arthur Coblentz. LC 69-13034. 1970. 3.98 o.p. (ISBN 0-498-06895-1, Encore). A S Barnes.
Power Valley Vengeance. Peter Field. LC 43-1015. 1943. W. Morrow & Company.
Power Within: A Religious Novel. Edited by Margaret E. Woestemeyer. 1st Ed. F O Woestemeyer. LC 55-12364. 1955. Exposition Press.
Power Without Glory. Frank Hardy. pap. 3.95x o.p. (ISBN 0-8464-0740-X). Beekman Pubs.
Power Without Glory. Frank Hardy. 1968. pap. 3.85 o.s.i. Tri-Ocean.
Power. 1st Ed. Frank M Robinson. 1956. Lippincott.
Powerful Long Ladder. Owen Dodson. 103p. 1970. 4.95 o.p. (ISBN 0-374-23668-2); pap. 1.95 o.p. (ISBN 0-374-50880-1, N395). Fs&G.
Powers. William Bailey. LC 82-7601. 14.95 (ISBN 0-399-12753-4). Putnam.
Powers & Dominations: A Novel. Robert Early. LC 74-20575. 1975. 6.95 (ISBN 0-395-20285-X). Houghton Mifflin.
Powers and Maxine. Charles Norris Williamson & Alice Muriel Livingston Williamson. Empire Book Company.
Powers at Play. Bliss Perry. LC 74-110209. (Short story index reprint series). 1970. Books for Libraries Press.
Powers at Play. Bliss Perry. 1899. C. Scribner's Sons.
Powers of Attorney. Louis Auchincloss. 1980. Repr. 3.95 (ISBN 0-395-29846-6). HM.
Powers of Evil. Richard Cavendish. LC 75-7933. 1975. 7.95 o.p. (ISBN 0-399-11484-X). Putnam Pub Group.
Power's Price. Kurt Brand. (Perry Rhodan Series#89). 1976. (pbk.) 1.25. Ace Books.
Powers That Prey. Josiah Flynt Willard & Hodder, Alfred, 1866-1907, Joint Author. LC 6739. 1900. McClure, Phillips & Co.
Powhatan's Daughter. John Clarke Bowman. LC 73-5230. 1973. 7.95 (ISBN 0-670-57040-0). Viking Press.
P.R. Girls. Bernard Glemser. LC 72-7331. 1972. 1.25. Bantam Books.
Practical Heart. Fiona Hill. 1975. pap. 0.95 (ISBN 0-425-02922-0, Medallion). Berkley Pub.
Practice. Alan Edward Nourse. LC 75-25094. 10.95 (ISBN 0-06-013194-2). Harper & Row.
Practice. Alan Edward Nourse. (Dell Book). 1979. 2.50 (ISBN 0-440-17090-7). Dell Pub. Co.
Practice. Stanley Winchester. (7081). 1968. Dell.
Practice: A Novel. Stanley Winchester. LC 67-19974. 1967. Putnam.
Practice of Pleasure. Michael Harris. (Signet Book). 1976. 1.75. New American Library.
Practice to Deceive. Elizabeth Linington. LC 72-123991. (Novel of Suspense Ser). 1971. 5.95 o.p. (ISBN 0-06-012646-9, HarpT). Har-Row.
Practicing of Christopher. Josephine Pauline Eckert. LC 47-302093. 1947. The Dial Press.
Practise to Deceive: A Captain Heimrich Mystery, by Richard and Frances Lockridge. 1st Ed. Richard Lockridge & Frances Louise Davis Lockridge. LC 57-8952. (Main line mysteries). 1957. Lippincott.
Praed Street Dossier. August William Derleth. LC 68-6191. (Illus.). 1968. Mycroft & Moran.
Praed Street Papers. August William Derleth. LC 65-5227. 1965. Candlelight Press.
Praetorius Point. Noel Pierce. LC 77-10064. 8.95 (ISBN 0-698-10858-2). Coward, McCann & Geoghegan.
Prague Diptych: A Novel. Marija Petrovska. LC 80-52476. 6.50 (ISBN 0-87141-069-9). Manyland Books.
Prairie. James Fenimore Cooper. (Half-title: Everyman's library, ed. by Ernest Rhys. Fiction). 1907. J. M. Dent & Co.
Prairie. James Fenimore Cooper. (Fairmount classics). 1928. Macrae, Smith Company.
Prairie. James Fenimore Cooper. LC 36-37034. (Half-title: Everyman's library, ed. by Ernest Rhys. Ficton. no. 172). 1929. J. M. Dent & Sons, Ltd.
Prairie. James Fenimore Cooper. LC 41-1013. 1940. Printed for the Members of the Limited Editions Club.
Prairie. Walter J Muilenburg. LC 25-16658. 1925. The Viking Press.
Prairie: A Tale. James Fenimore Cooper. LC 6-29692. 1833. Carey & Lea.
Prairie: A Tale. new ed. James Fenimore Cooper. LC 6-29690. 1852. Stringer and Townsend.
Prairie: A Tale. new ed. James Fenimore Cooper. LC 6-29697. 1854. Stringer and Townsend.
Prairie: A Tale. James Fenimore Cooper. LC 26-24686. (Half-title: The choice works of Cooper Revised and corrected series. v. 6). 1856. Stringer & Townsend.
Prairie. A Tale. James Fenimore Cooper. 1872. D. Appleton and Company.
Prairie: A Tale. James Fenimore Cooper. LC 31-35232. (Lettered on cover: Leather stocking tales. Household ed.). Houghton, Miffin and Company.
Prairie: A Tale. James Fenimore Cooper. LC 6-29696. 1876. Hurd and Houghton.
Prairie: A Tale. James Fenimore Cooper. (Seaside library. v. 12, no. 231). 1878. G. Munro.
Prairie: A Tale. James Fenimore Cooper. (On cover: Lovell's library. no. 467). 1884. J. W. Lovell Company.
Prairie. A Tale. James Fenimore Cooper. (On cover: Seaside library. Pocket ed. no. 310). 1884. G. Munro.

Prairie: A Tale. James Fenimore Cooper. LC 6-29695. (On cover: Leather stocking tales. Centennial ed). W. L. Allison.
Prairie: A Tale. James Fenimore Cooper. LC 6-29694. T. Y. Crowell & Company.
Prairie: A Tale. James Fenimore Cooper. Ed. by Cooper, Susan Fenimore. (Half-title: The Leather stocking tales. Riverside ed.). 1898. Houghton, Miffin and Company.
Prairie: A Tale. James Fenimore Cooper. LC 4-15434. (His Leather-stocking tales). 1900. Macmillan and Co., Limited.
Prairie. A Tale. James Fenimore Cooper. 1901. D. Appleton and Company.
Prairie: A Tale. a new ed. James Fenimore Cooper. LC 42-47067. 1836. Carey, Lea, & Blanchard.
Prairie, a Tale: Introd. by Henry Nash Smith. James Fenimore Cooper. LC 50-6318. (Rinehart editions, 26). 1950. Rinehart.
Prairie Avenue. Arthur Meeker. LC 49-1455. 1949. A. A. Knopf.
Prairie Boy. 1st Ed. Shannon Bolton. LC 54-13143. 1955. Vantage Press.
Prairie Child. Arthur John Arbuthnott Stringer. LC 22-9192. The Bobbs-Merrill Company.
Prairie Chronicle. Juana Foust. LC 32-16420. 1932. G. P. Putnam's Sons.
Prairie City Pilgrim. Donald S Rowland. 1973. 4.95. Lenox Hill Pr.
Prairie Detective. Leander P. Richardson. LC 7-41219. (secret service series, no. 24). 1889. Street & Smith.
Prairie Dust. James Lyon Rubel. LC 39-521992. Phoenix Press.
Prairie Empire. Clayton Fox. 192p. 1982. pap. 2.25 o.p. (ISBN 0-505-51823-6). Tower Bks.
Prairie Empire: Clayton Fox. Clayton Fox. (Belmont Tower Book). 1977. 1.50 (ISBN 0-505-51215-7). Tower Pubns.
Prairie Fire. Kent White. 200p. (Orig.). 1983. pap. 4.95 (ISBN 0-938936-07-7). Daring Pr.
Prairie Fire. A Double D Western. James Denson Sayers. LC 40-11018. 1940. Doubleday, Doran & Company, Inc.
Prairie Fires. Lorna Doone Beers. LC 25-9292. E. P. Dutton & Company.
Prairie Flame. Jessica Howard, pseud. 320p. 2.95 (ISBN 0-515-04729-5). Jove Pubns.
Prairie Floweer: Or, Adventures in the Far West. Emerson Bennett. LC 7-34099. T. B. Peterson & Brothers.
Prairie Flower. Emerson Bennett. LC 79-104416. 1970. (ISBN 0-8398-0163-7). Literature House.
Prairie Flower. Harry H. Halsell. LC 44-2655. 1943. Wilkinson Printing Co.
Prairie Flower: A Tale. rev. and ed. by percy b. st. john. ed. Gustave Aimard & St. John, Percy Bolingbroke, 1821-1889, Ed. LC 5-42594. (On cover: Lovell's library, no. 1089). 1887. J. W. Lovell Company.
Prairie Flower: A Tale of the Indian Border. Gustave Aimard & Wraxall, Sir Frederick Charles Lascelles, 3d Bart., 1828-1865, Tr. LC 22-17359. (On cover: Indian tales of daring and adventure). Ward, Lock and Co.
Prairie Flower: And Its Sequel, Leni Leoti Being Adventures in the Far West. new ed.... rev. and cor. by the author. ed. Emerson Bennett. LC 7-34100. T. B. Peterson & Brothers.
Prairie Flower: Or, Adventures in the Far West. Emerson Bennett. LC 7-34418. 1849. Stratton & Barnard.
Prairie Flower: Or, Adventures in the Far West. Emerson Bennett. LC 7-34101. 1881. G. W. Carleston & Co.; Etc., Etc.
Prairie Flowers. James Beardsley Hendryx. LC 21-16721. 1920. G. P. Putnam's Sons.
Prairie Folks. Hamlin Garland. LC 6-40718. (On cover: Ariel library, no. 25). 1893. F. J. Schulte & Company.
Prairie Folks. new ed., rev. and enl. ed. Hamlin Garland. LC 99-5835. 1899. The Macmillan Company.
Prairie Folks: Or, Pioneer Life on the Western Prairies. rev. ed. Hamlin Garland. LC 69-11899. (American short story series, v. 57). 1969. Garrett Press.
Prairie Folks: Or, Pioneer Life on the Western Prairies. rev. ed. Hamlin Garland. LC 72-8214. (American short story series, v. 57). 1972. (ISBN 0-8422-8057-X). MSS Information Corp.
Prairie Gold. Harold Bindloss. LC 25-20026. 1925. Frederick A. Stokes Company.
Prairie Gold. Zane Grey. 1982. 18.00x (ISBN 0-86025-185-3, Pub. by Ian Henry Pubns England). State Mutual Bk.
Prairie Gold: By Iowa Authors & Artists. facsimile ed. LC 77-150560. (Short Story Index Reprint Ser.: Vol. 1). Repr. of 1917 ed. 15.00 (ISBN 0-8369-3857-7). Ayer Co.
Prairie Grove Tales. Viola H. Jacobson. 3.00 o.p. Carlton.
Prairie Guide: Or, The Rose of the Rio Grande. Newton Mallory Curtis. Garrett & Co.
Prairie Guns. Eugene E. Halleran. LC 44-7729. 1944. Macrae-Smith-Company.
Prairie Guns. Clarence O Lawson. LC 56-11696. 1956. Arcadia House.
Prairie Guns: A Western Frontier Novel. Will Cook. LC 55-21030. (Popular library, 631). 1954. Popular Library.
Prairie Guns. 1st Ed. Ernest Haycox. LC 54-940912. 1954. Little, Brown.
Prairie Hideout. Hugh D. MacLean. 1968. 1.00 o.p. (ISBN 0-87508-744-2). Chr Lit.
Prairie Is My Garden: The Story of Harvey Dunn. Robert F. Karolevitz. LC 77-83472. (Illus.). 1969. pap. 4.95 (ISBN 0-87970-107-2). North Plains.
Prairie Kid. Charles Stanley Strong. LC 44-9149. 1944. Phoenix Press.
Prairie Marshal. William L Rohde. LC 55-11876. 1955. Arcadia House.
Prairie Marshal. Walker A Tompkins. LC 52-6767. 1952. Macrae Smith.
Prairie Mother. Arthur John Arbuthnott Stringer. LC 20-11073. The Bobbs-Merrill Company.
Prairie Patrol. Harold Bindloss. LC 31-1193. 1931. Frederick A, Stokes Company.
Prairie Peril. Charles Stoddard. LC 47-139486. 1946. Arcadia House, Inc.
Prairie Peril. Charles Stanley Strong. LC 47-1394. 1946. Arcadia House.
Prairie Pinto. Archie Joscelyn. LC 44-236149. 1944. Phoenix Press.
Prairie Pioneers. Charles Francis Horner. LC 67-24774. 1967. Dorrance.
Prairie Pioneers. Archie Joscelyn. LC 45-11424. 1945. Phoenix Press.
Prairie Reckoning. Cover Painting by Stan Galli. Paul Durst. LC 57-209612. (Gold medal books, 619). 1956. Fawcett Publications.
Prairie Schoolma'am. 1st Ed. Emily Eva Mullenger Sloan. LC 56-10540. 1956. Vantage Press.
Prairie Schooner: A Story of the Black Hawk War. William Eleazar Barton. LC 4968. 1900. W. A. Wilde Company.
Prairie-Schooner Princess. Mary Katherine Finigan Maule. LC 20-155080. Lothrop, Lee & Shepard Co.
Prairie Scout: Or, Agatone the Renegade. A Romance of Border Life... Charles Wilkins Webber. LC 7-30294. 1852. Dewitt & Davenport.
Prairie Shrine: A Western Story. Robert J Horton. LC 24-24344. Chelsea House.
Prairie Smoke. Harry Sinclair Drago. LC 36-152621. Green Circle Books.
Prairie Song and Western Story. Hamlin Garland. LC 73-163026. (Short story index reprint series). (Illus.). 1971. (ISBN 0-8369-3940-9). Books for Libraries Press.
Prairie Songs. Hamlin Garland. 1893. lib. bdg. 10.50 o.s.i. (ISBN 0-512-00236-3). Garrett Pr.
Prairie State Blues: Comic Strips & Graphic Tales. Bill Bergeron. LC 73-85174. (Illus.). 64p. 1975. pap. 2.95 o.p. (ISBN 0-914090-02-X). Chicago Review.
Prairie Vengeance. Wayne C Lee. LC 54-9900. 1954. Arcadia House.
Prairie Vengeance. M. L. Warren. (Orig.). 1980. pap. 1.75 o.s.i. (ISBN 0-505-51532-6). Tower Bks.
Prairie Vikings. Peter Henry Pearson. LC 27-19176. K. J. Olson.
Prairie Wife. Arthur Stringer. 1976. lib. bdg. 14.85x (ISBN 0-89968-122-0). Lightyear.
Prairie Wife: A Novel. Arthur John Arbuthnott Stringer. LC 15-18828. The Bobbs-Merrill Company.
Prairie Winter. Belle Owen. LC 3-8906. 1903. The Outlook Company.
Prairie Women: A Novel. by ivan beede. ed. Ivan Beede. LC 30-56896. 1930. Harper & Brothers.
Praise a Fine Day. Sigrid De Lima. LC 59-7837. 1959. Random House.
Praise at Morning. Mildred Masterson McNeilly. LC 47-3746. 1947. W. Morrow and Co.
Praise Be the Walls. W. R. Morgan. 7.75 o.p. Carlton.
Praise Singer. Mary Renault, pseud. LC 78-53495. 8.95 (ISBN 0-394-50273-6). Pantheon Books.
Praise the Human Season. Don Robertson. LC 73-18891. 1974. 8.95 (ISBN 0-525-63013-9). A. Fields Books.
Praise the Lord! A Novel. Dillwyn Parrish. LC 32-6436. 1932. Harper & Brothers.
Praised Be the Name of Jesus. Ora O'Riley. LC 39-126336. 1939. T. B. Williams.
Praisesong for the Widow. Paule Marshall. LC 82-13215. 13.95 (ISBN 0-399-12754-2). Putnam's.
Prancing Nigger. Arthur Annesley Ronald Firbank. LC 24-5944. Brentano's.
Prancing Nigger see Two Novels.
Prankish Pair. Un Petit Menage A Fantasy. Paul Ginisty. Tr. by Davenport, Reuben Briggs. (On cover: The Belford American novel series, no. 31). 1890. Belford Company.
Pranks. Dennis J. Higman. 432p. (Orig.). 1983. pap. 3.50 o.s.i. (ISBN 0-8439-1154-9, Leisure Bks). Dorchester Pub Co.
Prater Violet. Christopher Isherwood. LC 56-7063. (Modern library paperbacks, P19). 1956. Random House.
Prater Violet. Christopher Isherwood. LC 45-97325. 1945. Random House.
Pratfall. T. A. Schock. (Orig.). 1981. pap. 2.25 (ISBN 0-8439-0919-6, Leisure Bks). Nordon Pubns.
Pratidwandi. Sunil Gangopadhyay. Tr. by Enakshi Chatterjee from Bengali. LC 74-900546. 1974. lib. bdg. 4.50x (ISBN 0-8364-0447-5). South Asia Bks.
Pratt Portraits. Anna Fuller. LC 79-94725. (Short Story Index Reprint Ser.). 1897. 17.00 (ISBN 0-8369-3104-1). Ayer Co.
Pratt Portraits: Sketched in a New England Suburb. Anna Fuller. LC 79-94725. (Short story index reprint series). 1969. Books for Libraries Press.
Pratt Portraits: Sketched in a New England Suburb. Anna Fuller. LC 4-16459. 1892. G. P. Putnam's Sons.
Pratt Portraits: Sketched in a New England Suburb. Anna Fuller. 1897. G. P. Putnam's Sons.
Praxis: A Novel. Fay Weldon. LC 78-14376. 9.95 (ISBN 0-671-40061-4). Summit Books.
Pray for a Brave Heart. Helen MacInnes. 1979. pap. 2.50 (ISBN 0-449-24093-2, Crest). Fawcett.
Pray for a Brave Heart. 1st Ed. Helen MacInnes. LC 55-5241. Harcourt, Brace.
Pray for a Miracle. Alan Amos. LC 41-4019. Duell, Sloan and Pearce.
Pray for a Miracle. Kathleen Moore Knight. LC 41-4019. 1941. Duell, Sloan and Pearce.
Pray for a Tomorrow. Anne Parrish. LC 41-519296. Harper & Brothers.
Pray for the Wanderer: A Novel. Kate O'Brien. LC 38-276603. 1938. Doubleday, Doran & Company, Inc.
Pray Love, Remember. Consolata Carroll. LC 47-4644. 1947. Farrar, Straus.
Pray Love, Remember: A Novel. Stephen Wendt. LC 51-10828. 1951. Macmillan.
Pray to the Earth. Evelyn Sybil Mary Eaton. LC 38-24391. 1938. Houghton Mifflin Company.
Pray to the Hustlers' God. Jackson Donahue. LC 77-8382. 1977. 7.95 (ISBN 0-88349-143-5). Reader's Digest Press: Distributed by T. Y. Crowell.
Prayer Answered for Peggy. Dorothy McKay Martin. LC 75-45474. (Peggy Ser.). 128p. 1976. pap. 2.95 (ISBN 0-8024-7610-4). Moody.
Prayer for an Assassin. Translated by Cornelia Schaeffer. Igor Sentjurc. LC 59-8271. 1959. Doubleday.
Prayer for Katerina Horovitzova. Arnost Lustig. LC 73-4153. 1973. 5.95 (ISBN 0-06-012726-0). Harper & Row.
Prayer for My Brethren. Mladen Oljaca. LC 62-17385. 1963. Pantheon Books.
Prayer for My Son: A Novel. Hugh Walpole. LC 36-29835. 1936. Doubleday, Doran & Company, Inc.
Prayer for the Dying. Jack Higgins, pseud. 224p. 1978. pap. 1.75 (ISBN 0-449-23755-9, Crest). Fawcett.
Prayer for the Dying. new ed. Jack Higgins, pseud. LC 73-3749. 224p. 1974. 5.95 o.p. (ISBN 0-03-010806-3). HR&W.
Prayer for the Dying. Jack Higgins. (Fawcett crest book). 1975. (pbk.) 1.25. Fawcett.
Prayer for the Dying. Henry Patterson. LC 73-3749. 1974. 5.95 (ISBN 0-03-010806-3). Holt, Rinehart and Winston.
Prayer for the Living. Bruce Marshall. LC 34-24141. 1934. A. A. Knopf.
Prayer for the Ship. Douglas Reeman. LC 72-96883. 1973. 6.95 (ISBN 0-399-11139-5). Putnam.
Prayer for Tomorrow. John Hyatt Downing. LC 38-8335. 1938. G. P. Putnam's Sons.
Prayer Machine. Hodder-Williams, Christopher. LC 76-28067. 8.95 (ISBN 0-312-63560-5). St. Martin's Press.
Prayer Machine. Hodder-Williams, Christopher. LC 76-364594. 1976. 3.50 (ISBN 0-297-77045-4). Weidenfeld and Nicolson.
Prayer Murders. Mabel A Steed. LC 49-875. (Her A sphinx murder mystery). Wetzel Pub. Co.
Prayers at Midnight. Charles Angoff. 1971. 2.00 (ISBN 0-87141-036-2). Manyland.
Praying Man. Bienvenido N. Santos. 172p. (Orig.). 1982. pap. 9.50x (ISBN 971-10-0002-4, Pub. by New Day Philippines). Cellar.
Praying Mantis. Edgar Johnson. LC 37-35188. Stackpole Sons.
Praying Mantis Kills. Based on the Television Story. Howard Lee. (Kung Fu, #4). 1974. (pbk.) 1.25. Warner Paperback Library.
Praying Mantises. Hubert Monteilhet. (O.S.I.). 1962. 3.50 o.s.i. (ISBN 0-671-59470-2). S&S.
Praying Monkey. Charles Rodda. LC 30-30239. 1930. L. MacVeagh, The Dial Press.
Praying Skipper: And Other Stories. Ralph Delahaye Paine. LC 6-11303. 1906. The Outing Publishing Company.
Pre-Empt: A Novel. John Royal Vorhies. LC 67-28491. 1967. H. Regnery Co.
Pre-War Lady. Margaret Widdemer. LC 32-14327. Farrar & Rinehart, Incorporated.
Preach No More. Richard Lockridge. LC 71-124543. 1971. 4.95. Lippincott.
Preacher. Herbert Ernest Bates. 1935. The Macmillan Company.
Preacher. Garett Holmes. LC 38-9429. Robert Speiler Publishing Corp.
Preacher and the Slave. Wallace Earle Stegner. LC 50-8708. 1950. Houghton Mifflin.
Preacher & the Strumpet: And Other Short Stories. George Bascombe. 1978. 4.50 o.p. (ISBN 0-533-03499-X). Vantage.
Preacher of Cedar Mountain. Ernest Thompson Seton. LC 44-371. 1943. The Seton Village Press.
Preacher of Cedar Mountain: A Tale of the Open Country. Ernest Thompson Seton. LC 17-129571. 1917. Doubleday, Page & Company.
Preacher of Sycamore Valley. Earle Ruskin Bryant. LC 59-692257. 1959. Christopher Pub. House.
Preacher on Horseback. Cecile Hulse Matschat. LC 40-14424. Farrar and Rinehart, Inc.
Preacher's Daughter. A Domestic Romance. Amelia Edith Huddleston Barr. LC 6-7978. Bradley & Woodruff.
Preacher's Son. Wightman Fletcher Melton. LC 7-25851. 1894. Printed for the Author, Publishing House of the Methodist Episcopal Church, South.
Preacher's Son: Parish Baby, Yacht Builder, Sailor. Ralph H. Wiley. 4.95 o.p. Vantage.
Precaution: A Novel. James Fenimore Cooper. LC 73-1898. 1973. AMS Press.
Precaution: A Novel... James Fenimore Cooper. LC 6-29686. 1820. A. T. Goodrich & Co.
Precaution. A Novel. a new ed., rev. by the author... ed. James Fenimore Cooper. LC 6-29689. 1839. Lea & Blanchard, Successors to Carey & Co.
Precaution: A Novel. James Fenimore Cooper. (On cover: Lovell's library. no. 601). 1885. J. W. Lovell Company.
Precaution. A Novel. James Fenimore Cooper. Ed. by Bryant, William Cullen. (On cover: Seaside library. Pocket ed. no. 422). 1885. G. Munro.
Precaution: A Novel, 2 vols. James Fenimore Cooper. LC 73-1898. (BCL Ser.: No. I). Repr. of 1820 ed. Set. 12.50 (ISBN 0-404-01707-X). AMS Pr.
Precaution, a Novel. James Fenimore Cooper. LC 6-29686. Repr. of 1820 ed. 13.50 (ISBN 0-403-00101-3). Scholarly.
Precaution. A Novel. new ed. James Fenimore Cooper & Bryant, William Cullen. LC 13-2072. 1852. Stringer and Townsend.
Precaution: A Novel. With a Discourse on the Life, Genius, and Writings of the Author. James Fenimore Cooper & William Cullen Bryant. LC 72-5189. (Illus.). 1968. Scholarly Press.
Precint Kali & the Gertruce Spicer Story. James Bertolino. LC 81-80548. (Illus.). 108p. 1981. pap. 4.00 (ISBN 0-89823-034-9). New Rivers Pr.
Precious Bane. Mary Gladys Meredith Webb. LC 26-27503. 1926. E. P. Dutton & Company.
Precious Bane. Mary Gladys Meredith Webb. LC 37-18328. 1931. E. P. Dutton & Company, Inc.
Precious Bane. Mary Gladys Meredith Webb. LC 51-54218. 1933. Dutton.
Precious Bane. Mary Gladys Meredith Webb. LC 38-27818. (Half-title: The Modern library of the world's best books). 1938. The Modern Library.
Precious Bane. Mary Gladys Meredith Webb. LC 80-50272. (Illus.). 1980. 12.95 (ISBN 0-268-01538-4). University of Notre Dame Press.
Precious Bane. Mary Gladys Meredith Webb. LC 81-12437. (Virago Modern Classic). 1982. 7.95 (ISBN 0-385-27216-2). Dial Press.
Precious Bane: A Novel. Mary Gladys Meredith Webb. LC 28-17646. 1926. E. P. Dutton & Company.
Precious Jeopardy: A Christmas Story. Lloyd Cassel Douglas. LC 33-334593. 1933. Houghton Mifflin Company.
Precious Legacy. Vida Hurst. LC 48-1979. 1948. Gramercy Pub. Co.
Precious Little. Joseph Whitehill. LC 67-13655. 1967. bds., 4.50. Scribners.
Precious Moments. large print ed. Suzanne Roberts. LC 81-9102. 1981. 9.95 (ISBN 0-89621-310-2). Thorndike Press.
Precious Porcelain. Stephen Southwold. LC 31-240629. 1931. G. P. Putnam's Sons.
Precious Waters. Arthur Murray Chisholm. LC 13-3072. 1913. 1.25. Doubleday, Page & Company.
Precipice. Sergio Galindo. Tr. by John Brushwood & Carolyn Brushwood. (Texas Pan American Series). Orig. Title: El bordo. (Illus.). 199p. 1969. 12.50x (ISBN 0-292-78408-2); pap. 7.95x (ISBN 0-292-76426-X). U of Tex Pr.

TITLE INDEX PRESIDENT'S CONTRACT.

Precipice. Ivan Aleksandrovich Goncharov. LC 73-21714. 1974. 9.50. H. Fertig.
Precipice. Ivan Aleksandrovich Goncharov. LC 76-23879. (Classics of Russian literature). (Hyperion library of world literature). 1977. 4.95 (ISBN 0-88355-487-9). Hyperion Press.
Precipice. Hugh MacLennan. LC 48-8292. 1948. Duell, Sloan and Pearce.
Precipice: A Novel. Elia Wilkinson Peattie. LC 14-310797. 1914. 1.35. Houghton Mifflin Company.
Precipice (El Bordo). Sergio Galindo. LC 74-83762. (Texas pan-American series). (Illus.). 1969. 6.00. University of Texas Press.
Precipitate Choice: Or, The History of Lord Ossory and Miss Rivers. A Novel. In Two Volumes. 1783. Re-Printed and Sold by Benjamin Edes & Sons, in Cornhill.
Predator. Christopher Nicole. LC 68-19834. 1968. Lippincott.
Predator. Denis Pitts. LC 77-4990. 1977. 11.95 (ISBN 0-8161-6485-1). G. K. Hall.
Predator. Andrew York. LC 68-1983. 1968. 4.95g o.p. Lippincott.
Predator: A Novel. Denis Pitts. LC 76-18208. 1976. 8.95 (ISBN 0-88405-357-1). Mason/Charter.
Predator: A Novel. Denis Pitts. 1977. 1.75 (ISBN 0-380-01769-5). Avon Books.
Predecessor. Myrtle Louie Bodle Roe. LC 24-4268. Vail-Ballou Press, Inc.
Predestined: A Novel of New York Life. Stephen French Whitman. LC 74-8672. (Lost American fiction). 1974. (ISBN 0-8093-0701-4). Southern Illinois University Press.
Predestined: A Novel of New York Life. Stephen French Whitman. LC 10-6739. 1910. C. Scribner's Sons.
Predicaments. Louis Evan Shipman. LC 71-142276. (Illus.). 1970. Books for Libraries Press.
Predicaments. Louis Evan Shipman. LC 99-4696. 1899. Life Publishing Company.
Preface to a Killing. Nicholas Ashe. LC 37-16228. 1937. The Macaulay Company.
Preface to a Life. Zona Gale. LC 26-18625. 1926. D. Appleton and Company.
Preface to Death. Fred Rothermell. LC 32-183637. 1932. Little, Brown, and Company.
Preface to Hardy. Merryn Williams. LC 75-28382. (Preface books). (Illus.). 1976. 9.00 (ISBN 0-582-35113-8) (ISBN 0-582-35114-6). Longman.
Preface to Maturity. Jule Brousseau. LC 35-14891. Thomas Y. Crowell Company.
Prefect. P. N. Dedeaux. pap. 1.95 o.p. (V1036T, Venus). Grove.
Preferred Risk: A Science Fiction Novel. Edson McCann. LC 55-100447. 1955. Simon and Schuster.
Pregnant Man. Robert Phillips. LC 77-27727. 1978. pap. 4.95 o.p. (ISBN 0-385-14013-4). Doubleday.
Pregnant Virgin. Weinpie Wongbe. 1974. 3.95 o.s.i. (ISBN 0-8181-0333-7). Pageant-Poseidon.
Prehysterical Pogo. Walt Kelly. (O.S.I.). (1967). pap. 1.50 o.s.i. (ISBN 0-671-59484-2). S&S.
Preisingers: A Novel. S. Apter. LC 78-75296. 9.95. A. S. Barnes.
Prejudice see Willis & His Friends Series.
Prejudice: 20 Tales of Oppression and Liberation. Ed. by Charles R. Larson. LC 77-27458. (Mentor book). 1971. 1.50. New American Library.
Prelate: A Novel. Isaac Henderson. LC 7-4122. 1886. Ticknor and Company.
Preliminaries, and Other Stories. Cornelia Atwood Pratt Comer. LC 78-128726. (Short story index reprint series). 1970. Books for Libraries Press.
Preliminaries: And Other Stoties. Cornelia Atwood Pratt Comer. LC 12-217661. 1912. Houghton Mifflin Company.
Prelude (a Novelette) Donald Jeffries Bear. LC 44-21026. 1943. Pacific Coast Publishing Company.
Prelude and Spring: By Isobel Benedict Pseud. Beatrice Burnell. LC 50-11098. 1950. Exposition Press.
Prelude and the Play. Rufus Mann. LC 1622. 1900. Houghton, Mifflin and Company.
Prelude for War. Leslie Charteris. (Saint Ser.). 294p. 1982. pap. 2.95 (ISBN 0-441-67714-2, Pub. by Charter Bks). Ace Bks.
Prelude for War: A New Saint Story. Leslie Charteris. LC 38-22014. 1938. Pub. for the Crime Club, Inc., by Doubleday, Doran & Co., Inc.
Prelude to a Certain Midnight. Gerald Kersh. LC 47-4017. 1947. Doubleday & Company, Inc.
Prelude to a Rope for Myer. L Steni. LC 28-21222. 1928. L. MacVeagh, The Dial Press.
Prelude to a Song. Margaret Pargeter. (Harlequin Presents Ser.). 192p. 1983. pap. 1.75 (ISBN 0-373-10572-X). Harlequin Bks.
Prelude to Adventure. Hugh Walpole. LC 41-35148. 1912. The Century Co.
Prelude to Battle. Manfred Gottfried. LC 28-111682. 1928. The John Day Company.
Prelude to Blue Mountains. Alan Hyder. LC 36-15572. C. Kendall, Inc.
Prelude to Delilah. Vladimir Evgen'Evich Zhabotinskii. LC 45-8408. 1945. B. Ackerman, Incorporated.
Prelude to Departure. Sylvia Paul Jerman, pseud. LC 33-12238. 1933. Harper & Brothers.
Prelude to Forever: A Novel of the Cape Hatteras Country. 1st Ed. Pat Strawbridge Carson. LC 58-11448. 1958. Greenwich Book Publishers.
Prelude to Glory. William Arthur Neubauer. LC 65-8378. 1965. Arcadia House.
Prelude to Happiness: By Jessica Brown Pseud. Janet Brenner. LC 52-12715. 1952. Arcadia House.
Prelude to Kingship. Jane Lane. 1969. 8.25 o.p. Intl Pubns Serv.
Prelude to Love. Margaret Culkin Banning. LC 30-55398. 1930. Harper & Brothers.
Prelude to Love. Ruth Ben'Ary. LC 42-16956. 1943. Arcadia House, Inc.
Prelude to Love. Elizabeth Renier. 192p. 1981. pap. 1.95 (ISBN 0-441-67698-7). Ace Bks.
Prelude to Love. Shapiro, Irwin, Joint Tr & Shapiro, Irwin, Joint Tr. LC 38-29531. Farrar & Rinehart, Inc.
Prelude to Love. Joan Smith. 192p. (Orig.). 1983. pap. 2.25 (ISBN 0-449-20092-2, Crest). Fawcett.
Prelude to Love. Daisy H. Thomson. 1974. pap. 0.95 o.p. (ISBN 0-515-03266-2, N3266). BJ Pub Group.
Prelude to Mars. Arthur C. Clarke. LC 65-16953. 1965. 8.50x o.p. (ISBN 0-15-173922-6). HarBraceJ.
Prelude to Mars: An Omnibus Containing the Complete Novels Prelude to Space and The Sands of Mars and Sixteen Short Stories. Arthur Charles Clarke. LC 65-16953. 1965. Harcourt, Brace & World.
Prelude to Murder. George Clinton Bestor. LC 36-7119. The Dial Press.
Prelude to Murder see Third Crime Lucky.
Prelude to Murder: By Anthony Gilbert Pseud. Lucy Beatrice Malleson. LC 59-664357. (Random House mystery). 1959. Random House.
Prelude to Night: A Novel. Dayton Stoddard. LC 45-6197. 1945. Coward-McCann, Inc.
Prelude to Paradise. Daphne Hamilton. (Superromances Ser.). 384p. 1983. pap. 2.50 (ISBN 0-373-70048-2, Pub. by Worldwide). Harlequin Bks.
Prelude to Peril. Jerry Sohl. LC 57-556594. 1957. Rinehart.
Prelude to Space. Arthur Charles Clarke. LC 74-100500. 1970. Harcourt, Brace & World.
Prelude to Space see Space Dreamers.
Prelude to Space. 1st Ed. Arthur Charles Clarke. LC 54-7257. 1954. Gnome Press.
Prelude to Summer: By Ann Carter Pseud. Anne Tedlock Brooks. LC 51-12221. 1951. Arcadia House.
Prelude to Terror. Helen MacInnes. LC 78-53888. 10.00 (ISBN 0-15-173926-9). Harcourt Brace Jovanovich.
Prelude to Terror. Helen MacInnes. LC 78-24117. 1980. 18.50 (ISBN 0-8161-6665-X). G. K. Hall.
Prelude to the Long Happy Life of Maximilian Goodman. Gerold Spath. Tr. by Rita Kimber & Robert Kimber. (Eng.). 1975. 10.95 o.p. (ISBN 0-316-80496-7). Little.
Prelude to the Long Happy Life of Maximilian Goodman: A Novel. Gerold Spath. LC 75-20034. 1975. 10.95 (ISBN 0-316-80496-7). Little, Brown.
Preludes. Maurits Ignatius Boas. LC 78-855. 8.95 (ISBN 0-8119-0305-2). F. Fell Publishers.
Prem Masih of Damoh. George Elmer Miller. LC 23-607. Powell & White.
Premar Experiments. Robert H Rimmer. (Signet Book)). 1976. 1.95 (ISBN 0-451-07515-3). New American Library.
Premar Experiments: A Novel. Robert H. Rimmer. LC 75-4540. 1975. 7.95 (ISBN 0-517-52148-2). Crown Publishers.
Premature. Mary Hanner. 1981. pap. 2.75 (ISBN 0-451-11108-7, AE1108, Sig). NAL.
Premature Angel. William Osler. LC 54-8896. 1954. Dorrance.
Prematurely Gay. Jack Iams. LC 48-5364. 1948. W. Morrow.
Premedicated Murder. Douglas Clark. LC 75-39303. 6.95 (ISBN 0-684-14620-7). Scribner.
Premedicated Murder. (Murder Ink Ser.: No. 33). 176p. 1981. pap. 2.25 (ISBN 0-440-17044-3). Dell.
Premeditated Murder: Published Originally Under the Title "A Trap for Bellamy,". Peter Cheyney. LC 44-7591. (Murder mystery monthly, no. 15). Avon Book Company.
Premeditated Virgin. Nalbro Isadorah Bartley. LC 31-507265. Farrar & Rinehart Incorporated.
Premier. Earl Conrad. 1970. pap. 0.95 o.p. (ISBN 0-447-75129-8). Lancer.
Premier and the Painter: A Fantastic Romance. Israel Zangwill & Cowen, Louis, Joint Author. LC 9-2204. Rand, McNally & Company.
Premier and The Train: Two Novels. Georges Simenon. LC 66-16056. 1966. Harcourt, Brace & World.
Premier and The Train: Two Novels. Tr. from the French by Daphne Woodward and Robert Baldick. 1st Amer. Ed. Georges Simenon. LC 66-16056. 1966. 4.95. Harcourt.
Premier De Cordce. Edited by E. Louise Leonard. Frison-Roche, Roger. LC 50-13116. 1950. Harcourt, Brace.
Premonition. J. N. Williamson. 288p. 1981. pap. 2.25 (ISBN 0-8439-0959-5, Leisure Bks). Nordon Pubns.
Prentiss of the Box 8. Archie Joscelyn. 1943. Phoenix Press.
Preparation. A Novel. Mary Lucy Hall. J. S. Ogilvie and Company.
Preparations for the Ascent. Gilbert Rogin. LC 79-5540. 1980. 8.95 (ISBN 0-394-42451-4). Random House.
Prepare Them for Caesar. Mary Louise Mable. LC 49-9503. 1949. Little, Brown.
Prepared for Rage. Mark Saxton. LC 47-3395. 1947. William Sloane Associates.
Preparing for Sabbath. Nessa Rapoport. LC 80-21539. 1981. 10.95 (ISBN 0-688-00294-3). Morrow.
Pres Des Cascades D'Argent. Margaret Way. (Collection Harlequin Ser.). 192p. 1983. pap. 1.95 (ISBN 0-373-49332-0). Harlequin Bks.
Presbyterian Child. Joseph Hergesheimer. LC 23-16996. 1923. A. A. Knopf.
Prescott Chronicles. Albert Fried. LC 76-9116. (Illus.). 8.95 (ISBN 0-399-11711-3). Putnam.
Prescott of Saskatchewan. Harold Bindloss. LC 13-689317. 1913. Frederick A. Stokes Comapany.
Prescription for a Nurse. Alison Bray, pseud. 192p. (OSI). 1973. 4.95 o.s.i. Lenox Hill.
Prescription for a Nurse. Alison Bray. (Illus.). 1973. 4.95. Lenox Hill Press.
Prescription for Love. Helen Murray. (Orig.). 1981. pap. 1.95 (ISBN 0-8439-8039-7, Tiara Bks). Nordon Pubns.
Prescription for Marriage. John Anders. LC 33-33684. J. Messner, Inc.
Prescription for Marriage: A Novel. Mary Brinker Post. LC 52-7408. 1952. J. Messner.
Prescription: Murder. Ann Kurth. (Illus.). 1981. pap. 2.95 (ISBN 0-451-12026-4, AE2026, Sig). NAL.
Prescription: Murder. 1st Ed. Doris Miles Disney. LC 53-9132. 1953. Published for the Crime Club by Doubleday.
Presence. Ethel Charles. LC 27-23637. The Winston-Jordan Publishing Company.
Presence. Rodgers Clemens, pseud. (Fawcett Gold Medal Book). 1977. 1.75 (ISBN 0-449-13890-9). Fawcett Pubns.
Presence. George E. Failing. 32p. pap. 1.00 (ISBN 0-937296-04-X, 221-A). Presence Inc.
Presence. Yvonne MacManus. 288p. (Orig.). 1982. pap. 2.95 (ISBN 0-523-41687-3). Pinnacle Bks.
Presence. Florence Stevenson. 240p. (Orig.). 1982. pap. 2.75 (ISBN 0-515-05814-9). Jove Pubns.
Presence. Alan Williamson. LC 82-47964. (Knopf poetry series; 9). 1982. 11.95 (ISBN 0-394-52850-6) (ISBN 0-394-71259-5). Knopf.
Presence in an Empty Room. Velda Johnston. LC 79-25431. 8.95 (ISBN 0-396-07796-X). Dodd, Mead.
Presence in the House. Marc Lovell, pseud. LC 74-182840. 1972. 4.95. Published for the Crime Club by Doubleday.
Presence of Everett Marsh. Playsted Wood. LC 37-190105. The Bobbs-Merrill Company.
Presence of Grace. James Farl Powers. LC 56-5963. 1956. Doubleday.
Presence of Grace. James Farl Powers. LC 77-85694. (Short story index reprint series). 1969. Books for Libraries Press.
Presence with Secrets. William Mode Spackman. LC 80-11406. 1980. 8.95 (ISBN 0-394-51279-0). A. A. Knopf: Distributed by Random House.
Present and the Past. Ivy Compton-Burnett. LC 53-10500. 1953. J. Messner.
Present-Day American Stories. Hemingway, Ernest. LC 29-207953. 1929. C. Scribner's Sons.
Present-Day Stories. Ed. by John Towner Frederick. LC 41-8083. C. Scribner's Sons.
Present from Peking. David Lampard. LC 65-13097. 1965. Doubleday.
Present Past-Past Present. Eugene Ionesco. Tr. by Helen R. Lane. 1971. 5.95 o.p. (ISBN 0-394-47582-8, GP670). Grove.
Present Problem. A Temeperace Story, Sarah Knowles Bolton. LC 6-14907. 1874. G. P. Putnam's Sons.
Presentation. Henry De Vere Stacpoole. LC 14-15563. 1914. 1.30. John Lane Company.
Presenting Jane McRae. Mark Lee Luther. LC 20-10734. 1920. Little, Brown, and Company.
Presenting Lily Mars. Booth Tarkington. LC 33-21386. 1933. Doubleday, Doran and Company, Inc.
Presenting Lily Mars. Booth Tarkington. LC 43-993027. 1943. Triangle Books.
Presenting Lily Mars... Booth Tarkington. LC 44-51244. (New Avon library. 55). 1944.
Presenting Moonshine... John Collier. LC 41-976. 1941. The Viking Press.
Presenting Mrs. Chase-Lyon. Helen Walker Homan. LC 26-21350. The Devin-Adair Company.
Presently Tomorrow. Joyce Marshall. LC 46-183524. 1946. Little, Brown and Company.
Preservation Hall. Scott Spencer. 1978. pap. 2.50 (ISBN 0-380-01877-2, 52209). Avon.
Preservation Hall. Scott Spencer. (O.s.i.). 1976. 8.95 o.s.i. (ISBN 0-394-49926-3). Knopf.
Preservation Hall: A Novel. Scott Spencer. LC 76-13681. 1976. 8.95 (ISBN 0-394-49926-3). Knopf.
Preservation Hall: A Novel. Scott Spencer. (Kangaroo Book). 1978. 1.75 (ISBN 0-380-01877-2). Avon Books.
Preserve and Protect. Allen Drury. 1974. (pbk.) 1.75. Popular Library.
Preserve and Protect: A Novel. Allen Drury. LC 68-26725. 1968. 6.95. Doubleday.
Preserving Machine. Philip K Dick. 1976. 1.95. Ace Books.
Preshus Child. Belle Travers McCahan. LC 9-6101. 1909. Cochrane Publishing Co.
President. Robert Verlin Cassill. LC 64-14427. 1964. Simon and Schuster.
President. Drew Pearson. LC 73-113074. 1970. 7.95. Doubleday.
President: A Novel by Alfred Henry Lewis... Alfred Henry Lewis. LC 4-22988. 1904. A. S. Barnes and Company.
President Fu Manchu. Sax Rohmer, pseud. 1969. pap. 0.60 o.p. (X2135). Pyramid Pubns.
President Fu Manchu. Rex Stout. 1976. pap. 1.25 o.p. (ISBN 0-515-04056-8). BJ Pub Group.
President Fu Manchu. Arthur Sarsfield Ward. LC 36-10492. 1936. Pub. for the Crime Club, Inc., by Doubleday, Doran & Co., Inc.
President Fu Manchu. Arthur Sarsfield Ward. LC 37-1675. 1936. The Sun Dial Press, Inc.
President Has Been Kidnapped. Paul Richards. (Hotline Ser). (O.s.i.). 160p. 1971. pap. 0.95 o.s.i. (AN1198, Award). Univ Pub & Dist.
President Is a Lot Smarter Than You Think. G. B. Trudeau. (Doonesbury Ser.: No. 1). (Illus.). 1974. pap. 2.25 (ISBN 0-445-00607-2). Popular Lib.
President Is Born. Fannie Hurst. LC 28-2681. 1928. Harper & Brothers.
President John Smith. Frederick Upham Adams. LC 72-154428. (Utopian Literature). (Illus.). 1971. (ISBN 0-405-03511-X). Arno Press.
President Kissinger: A Political Fiction. Monroe Rosenthal & Donald Munson. 1974. (pbk.) 1.75. Free Press.
President McGovern's First Term. Nicholas Max, pseud. LC 72-95745. 1973. 4.95 (ISBN 0-385-04212-4). Doubleday.
President Must Die. Rick Raphael. LC 80-27944. 12.95 (ISBN 0-393-01445-2). Norton.
President of Quex: A Woman's Club Story. Helen Maria Winslow. LC 6-36041. 1906. Lothrop, Lee & Shepard Co.
President Takes a Wife. Joseph Jerry Perling. LC 59-866451. 1959. Denlinger.
President Vanishes. LC 34-30868. Farrar & Rinehart, Incorporated.
President Vanishes. Rex Stout. 272p. 1982. pap. 2.50 (ISBN 0-553-22665-7). Bantam.
President Vanishes. Rex Stout. 1973. pap. 1.25 o.p. (ISBN 0-515-03173-9, N3173). BJ Pub Group.
President Vanishes. Rex Stout. 1977. pap. 1.25 o.p. (ISBN 0-515-04390-7). BJ Pub Group.
Presidential Agent. Upton Beall Sinclair. LC 44-491638. 1944. The Viking Press.
Presidential Agent. Upton Beall Sinclair. (His Lanny Budd Series, No. 5). 1973. 1.50. Curtis Books.
Presidential Campaign of 1896. A Scrap-Book of Chronicle. Catlin, George Lynde. LC 20-16482. 1888. Funk & Wagnalls.
Presidential Diary, Vol. 1. Gerald T. DeFelice. 400p. (Orig.). 1981. pap. 29.95 (ISBN 0-940318-02-4). Une Pub.
Presidential Emergency: A Novel. Walter Stovall. LC 77-7037. 8.95 (ISBN 0-525-18325-6). Dutton.
Presidential Mission. Upton Beall Sinclair. LC 47-30286. 1947. The Viking Press.
Presidential Plot. Stanley Johnson. LC 68-19943. 1968. Simon and Schuster.
Presidential Year: By Frederik Pohl and C. M. Kornbluth. Frederik Pohl & Cyril M. Kornbluth. LC 56-9441. 1956. Ballantine Books.
Presidents. Roland Stone. (Orig.). 1979. pap. 1.95 (ISBN 0-532-23284-4). Woodhill.
President's Child. Fay Weldon. 240p. 1983. 14.95 (ISBN 0-385-18450-6). Doubleday.
President's Contract. Elroy Schwartz. 192p. (Orig.). 1972. pap. 1.95 o.p. (ISBN 0-87056-284-3, 6284). Brandon.

President's Daughter. Eric Ward & Ursula Russell. LC 73-8611. 1973. 1.25. Bantam Books.

President's Daughters. A Narrative of a Governess. Fredrika Bremer. 1843. J. Munroe & Co.

President's Doctor. William Woolfolk. LC 73-91652. 1975. 8.95 (ISBN 0-87223-392-8). Playboy Press.

President's Grass Is Missing. Patricia Breen-Bond. (Orig.). 1980. pap. text ed. 1.75 o.s.i. (ISBN 0-505-51546-6). Tower Bks.

President's Lady. Irving Stone. 1968. pap. 2.50 (ISBN 0-451-09595-2, AE9595, Sig). NAL.

President's Lady: A Novel About Rachel and Andrew Jackson. Irving Stone. LC 51-6885. 1951. Doubleday.

President's Man. Nicholas Guild. LC 81-16690. 14.95 (ISBN 0-312-64128-1). St. Martin's Press.

President's Mistress. Patrick Anderson. (O.s.i.). 1976. 8.95 o.s.i. (ISBN 0-671-22194-9). S&S.

President's Mistress: A Novel. Patrick Anderson. LC 75-37533. 8.95 (ISBN 0-671-22194-9). Simon and Schuster.

President's Mystery Plot. Franklin Delano Roosevelt. LC 67-18930. (Illus.). 1967. Prentice-Hall.

President's Mystery Story. Fulton Oursler et al. LC 36-167. Farrar & Rinehart, Incorporated.

President's Plane Is Missing. Robert J Serling. (7102). 1968. Dell.

President's Plane Is Missing. Robert J Serling. (Dell Book). 1977. 1.95 (ISBN 0-440-17102-4). Dell Pub. Co.

President's Team. Everard Meade. 176p. (Orig.). 1976. pap. 1.50 (ISBN 0-89041-093-3, 3093). Major Bks.

Press Box; the Story of a Young Sports Writer. Robert Fulton Kelley. LC 40-34070. 1940. Dodd, Mead & Company.

Press Lord. James Brady. LC 81-15183. 14.95 (ISBN 0-440-07083-X). Delacorte Press.

Press on Regardless; or, The Confessions of a Sports Car Addict: By Anne Taylor and Fern Most. With Drawings by Paul Bacon. Anne Taylor & Mosk, Fern. LC 56-11184. 1956. Simon and Schuster.

Pressure. Margaret Culkin Banning. LC 27-3547. 1927. Harper & Brothers.

Pressure... Charles Francis Coe. LC 51-12025. 1951. Random House.

Pressure Gauge Murder. Frederick William Berry Von Linsingen. LC 30-7786. E. P. Dutton & Co., Inc.

Pressure Man. Zach Hughes. (Signet Book). 1.95 (ISBN 0-451-09498-0). New American Library.

Pressure of His Hand: A Good Story with an Uplift Appeal. Ima Jewel Woodruff. LC 54-32740. White Wing Pub. House & Press.

Pressure Point. Lucien Agniel. (Orig.). 1970. pap. 0.75 o.p. (64-463). Paperback Lib.

Prester John. John Buchan. LC 75-131650. (Illus.). 1970. Scholarly Press.

Prester John. John Buchan. LC 10-20609. 1910. T. Nelson and Sons.

Prester John. John Buchan. George H. Doran Company.

Prester John. John Buchan. LC 28-26728. 1928. Houghton Mifflin Company.

Prester John. John Buchan. 1973. 0.95. Popular Lib.

Presto! Roberta Smoodin. LC 81-69200. 1982. 12.95 (ISBN 0-689-11273-4). Atheneum.

Prestons. Mary Marvin Heaton Vorse. LC 19-260800. 1918. Boni and Liveright.

Presumed Dead. Jean Larteguy. Tr. by Leonard Mayhew. 1976. 9.95 o.p. (ISBN 0-316-51530-2). Little.

Presumed Dead. Beirne Lay, Jr. (Great Classic Stories of World War II Ser.). Orig. Title: I've Had It. 1980. 8.95 o.p. (ISBN 0-396-07868-0); pap. 5.95 o.p. (ISBN 0-396-07869-9). Dodd.

Presumed Dead: A Novel. Jean Larteguy. LC 76-5209. 9.95 (ISBN 0-316-51530-2). Little, Brown.

Pret a Lire. Gustave W. Andrian & Jane Davies. 1980. pap. 11.95 (ISBN 0-02-303440-8). Macmillan.

Pretender. Lion Feuchtwanger & Muir, Willa, Tr. LC 37-8757. 1937. The Viking Press.

Pretender: A Story of the Latin Quarter. Robert William Service. LC 14-216222. 1914. Dodd, Mead & Company.

Pretender Person. Margaret H. C. Cameron. LC 11-26607. 1911. 1.30. Harper & Brothers.

Pretender: Science Fiction. Piers Anthony & Frances Hall. LC 79-317. (Illus.). 1979. 10.95. (ISBN 0-89370-130-0) (ISBN 0-89370-230-7). Borgo Press.

Pretender to the Throne: The Further Adventures of Private Ivan Chonkin. Vladimir Voinovich. LC 81-3137. 16.95 (ISBN 0-374-23715-8). Farrar, Straus, Giroux.

Pretenders. F. Sionil Jose. 1966. wrps. 6.50x o.p. Cellar.

Pretenders: A Novel. Gwen Davis. LC 69-19630. 1969. 7.95. World Pub. Co.

Prettiest Boy in Dallas. Preston Harriman. 1974. (pbk.) 2.25. Lambda Press.

Prettiest Girl in Town. Snow, Donald Clifford. LC 50-7723. 1950. Harper.

Prettiest of All. John Russell Coryell. LC 44-14383. (Select series...No. 30). 1889. Street & Smith.

Prettiest of All. Julia Edwards, pseud. (select ser. no. 30). 1889. Street & Smith.

Prettiest Woman in Warsaw. Mabel Collins Cook. LC 6-28078. (On cover: Seaside library. Pocket ed. no. 828). G. Munro.

Prettiest Woman in Warsaw. Mabel Collins Cook. LC 6-28075. (On cover: Lovell's library, no. 1272). J. W. Lovell Company.

Pretty As You Please. Minna Bardon. LC 40-182500. Gramercy Publishing Co.

Pretty Bandit. Bailey Millard. LC 7-25975. The Eskdale Press.

Pretty Beggar-Girl: Or, Freaks of Fortune. A Novel, Exemplifying Fortune's Freaks, by the Upper Ten and Lower Million of Metropolitan Life. George Frederick. Winchester & Co.

Pretty Boy: A Novel. William Cunningham. LC 36-185493. 1936. The Vanguard Press.

Pretty Boy Dead. Joseph Hansen. pap. cancelled (ISBN 0-89041-151-4, 3151). Major Bks.

Pretty Creatures. William Alexander Gerhardie. LC 73-93996. 1975. 8.95. St. Martin's Press.

Pretty Creatures. William Alexander Gerhardie. LC 27-906448. 1927. Duffield and Company.

Pretty Enough to Kill. Amanda McAllister. LC 76-14021. 1.50. Playboy Press.

Pretty Governess: And Other Stories. May Agnes Early Fleming. LC 6-39947. (peerless series, no. 32). 1891. J. S. Ogilvie.

Pretty Horse-Breakers. Barbara Cartland. (Hist. Romance Ser.: No. 35). 1975. pap. 1.25 o.p. (ISBN 0-515-03789-3, V3789). Pyramid Pubns.

Pretty Horse-Breakers. Barbara Cartland. 1976. pap. 1.25 o.p. (ISBN 0-515-04088-6). Pyramid Pubns.

Pretty Horsebreakers. Barbara Cartland. pap. 1.50 o.p. (ISBN 0-515-04341-9). BJ Pub Group.

Pretty Imposter. Leonora Dorothy Rivers Cook Mackesy. LC 51-12921. 1951. Arcadia House.

Pretty Jailer. Fortune Du Boisgobey. LC 6-34416. (On cover: Seaside library. Pocket ed. no. 697). G. Munro.

Pretty Kitty Herrick the Horsebreaker: A Romance of Love and Sport. Mary E. Kennard. LC 7-11105. (On cover: Broadway series, no. 3). J. A. Taylor and Company.

Pretty Lady. Arnold Bennett. LC 72-144876. 1971. Scholarly Press.

Pretty Lady. Arnold Bennett. LC 74-17298. (Collected works of Arnold Bennett). 1974. (ISBN 0-518-19148-6). Books for Libraries Press.

Pretty Lady. Arnold Bennett. LC 18-8985. George H. Doran Company.

Pretty Lady. Blanche Howard. LC 76-378992. (Trendsetter edition). 6.95. (ISBN 0-7736-0048-5) (ISBN 0-7737-7117-4). General Publishing Co.

Pretty Leslie. Robert Verlin Cassill. LC 63-9280. 1963. Simon and Schuster.

Pretty Lies. Patricia Hornung & Howard Fish. (Orig.). 1980. pap. 2.50 (ISBN 0-440-15720-X). Dell.

Pretty Little Countess Zina. A Russian Story. Alice Marie Celeste Durand. Tr. by Sherwood, Mary (Neal) LC 6-35687. T. B. Peterson & Brothers.

Pretty Maids All in a Row. Francis Pollini. LC 68-19099. 1968. 5.95. Delacorte Press.

Pretty Michal: A Free Translation of Maurus Jokai's Romance "A Szep Mikhal". Mor Jokai. Tr. by Bain, Robert Nisbet. (On cover: Cassell's sunshine series. no. 92). 1892. Cassell Publishing Company.

Pretty Michal: A Szep Mikhal. Mor Jokai. LC 7-11927. (On cover: Globe library. v. 1, no. 237). 1896. Rand, McNally & Company.

Pretty Miss Neville. A Novel. Bithia Mary Sheppard Croker. (Harper's Franklin square library. no. 363). 1884. Harper & Brothers.

Pretty Miss Neville. A Novel. Bithia Mary Sheppard Croker. LC 13-7651. (On cover: Seaside library. Pocket ed. no. 207). 1887. G. Munro.

Pretty Miss Smith. authorized ed. Florence Alice Price James. LC 7-7409. (On cover: Lovell's Westminister series, no. 30). 1892. United States Book Company.

Pretty Mrs. Gaston: And Other Stories. John Esten Cooke. LC 74-94713. (Short story index reprint series). (Illus.). 1969. Books for Libraries Press.

Pretty Mrs. Gaston: And Other Stories. John Esten Cooke. LC 6-27187. O. Judd Company.

Pretty Mrs. Gaston & Other Stories. facsimile ed. John Esten Cooke. LC 74-94713. (Short Story Index Reprint Ser.). 1874. 16.00 (ISBN 0-8369-3092-4). Ayer Co.

Pretty One. Maysie Greig. LC 38-3423. 1937. Doubleday, Doran & Company, Inc.

Pretty Ones. Dorothy Eden. 238p. pap. 2.25 (ISBN 0-441-67857-2). Ace Bks.

Pretty Peggy O: A Novel. Mary King Elliott. LC 13-24114. 1913. 1.50. Broadway Publishing Co.

Pretty Penny. Joseph L Bonney. LC 49-485043. 1949. Arcadia House.

Pretty Penny. John Dick Scott. LC 64-22672. 1964. Harcourt, Brace and World.

Pretty Pickle. Bellamy Partridge. LC 30-21768. 1930. Brewer and Warren Inc.

Pretty Pink Shroud. E. X Ferrars, pseud. LC 76-56288. 1977. 6.95 (ISBN 0-385-12827-4). Published for the Crime Club by Doubleday.

Pretty Pink Shroud. E. X Ferrars, pseud. LC 79-14570. (Penguin crime fiction). 1979. 1.95 (ISBN 0-14-004994-0). Penguin Books.

Pretty Polly. George Alexis Bankoff. LC 76-380620. 1976. 3.25 (ISBN 0-7091-5392-9). R. Hale.

Pretty Polly. Vida Hurst. LC 43-164407. 1943. Gramercy Publishing Co.

Pretty Polly: And Other Stories. Noel Pierce Coward. LC 65-10642. 1965. 4.50. Doubleday.

Pretty Polly Pemberton. A Love Story. Frances Hodgson Burnett. LC 6-17372. T. B. Peterson & Brothers.

Pretty Redwing. Helen Henslee. LC 82-6052. 13.95 (ISBN 0-03-061372-8). Holt, Rinehart and Winston.

Pretty Sister of Jose. Frances Hodgson Burnett. LC 6-17371. 1889. C. Scribner's Sons.

Pretty Story: Written in the Year of Our Lord 1774. Francis Hopkinson. (American Fiction Ser., American Literature & Culture, 1620-1820 Ser). 1970. Repr. of 1774 ed. lib. bdg. 6.95 o.s.i. (ISBN 0-512-00340-8). Garrett Pr.

Pretty Tales for Tired People. Martha Gellhorn. LC 65-111631. 4.50. S. & S.

Pretty Thing. Robert Turner. LC 71-9280. 1968. 3.95. Olympia Press.

Pretty Tory: Being a Romance of Partisan Warfare During the War of Independence in the Provinces of Georgia and South Carolina Relating to Mistress Geraldine Moncriffe. Jeanie Thomas Gould Lincoln. LC 99-5675. 1899. Houghton, Mifflin and Company.

Pretty Ways O' Providence: Stories. Mark Guy Pearse. LC 6-16305. Jennings and Graham.

Prettybelle: A Lively Tale of Rape and Resurrection. Jean Arnaldi. LC 74-92735. 1970. 4.95. Dial Press.

Prettybelle: A Lively Tale of Rape & Ressurection. Jean Arnold. LC 74-92735. 1970. 4.95 o.p. Dial.

Prevailing Spirits: A Book of Scottish Ghost Stories. Giles Gordon. LC 76-383396. 1976. 3.50 (ISBN 0-241-89403-4). Hamilton.

Prevailing Winds. Margaret Ayer Barnes. LC 26-240846. 1928. Houghton Mifflin Company.

Prevalence of Witches: A Novel. Aubrey Menen. LC 48-5361. 1948. C. Scribner's Sons.

Preventive Man. Gertrude Violet McFadden. 1920. John Lane.

Previous Lady. Jacqueline La Tourrette. (Dell book). 1974. (pbk.) 0.95. Dell.

Prey. Robert Arthur Smith. (Fawcett Gold Medal Book). 1977. 1.95 (ISBN 0-449-13923-9). Fawcett Books.

Prey for Me. Thomas Blanchard Dewey. LC 54-500851. (Inner sanctum mystery). 1954. Simon and Schuster.

Prey of the Eagle. Phyllis G Leonard. LC 74-79295. 1974. 6.95. McKay.

Prey of the Falcon. Robert Charles, pseud. 1976. (pbk.) 1.25 (ISBN 0-523-00835-X). Pinnacle Books.

Preying Mantis. Nancy Rutledge. LC 47-4015. 1947. Pub. for the Crime Club, by Doubleday & Company, Inc.

Preying Streets. Ledru Baker. LC 55-44658. (Ace books, S-122). 1955. Ace Books.

Priam's Daughter. Georgia Sallaska. LC 70-107350. 1970. 7.95. Doubleday.

Price. David Chacko. LC 72-90760. 1973. 6.95. St. Martin's Press.

Price. David Chacko. LC 78-21360. 1979. 3.95 (ISBN 0-312-64211-3). St. Martin's Press.

Price. Francis Lynde. LC 11-12713. 1911. C. Scribner's Sons.

Price. Gertie De S Wentworth-James. LC 11-12265. 1911. 1.35. M. Kennerley.

Price: A Story of to-Day, Founded on the Play of George Broadhurst. Arthur Hornblow & Broadhurst, George H., 1866- LC 14-535239. G. W. Dillingham Company.

Price He Paid. Elisabeth Burstenbinder. (On cover: The primrose series, no. 27). 1891. Street & Smith.

Price Is Love. Barbara Cartland. 1973. pap. 1.25 o.p. (ISBN 0-515-03243-3, V3243). BJ Pub Group.

Price Is Right. Jerome Weidman. 1973. 1.25. Manor Books.

Price Is Right. Jerome Weidman. LC 49-7414. 1949. Harcourt, Brace.

Price of a Coronet: Or, Jeanne Berthout, Countess De Mercoeur. Pierre Sales & Lewis, Mrs. Benjamin, Tr. LC 8-3737. (On verso of half-title: Cassell's blue library v. 5). Cassell Publishing Company.

Price of a Life. A Novel. Rebecca Forbes Sturgis. LC 8-16857. 1881. G. W. Carleton & Co.; Etc., Etc.

Price of a Pearl, a Novel. Eleanor Holmes. LC 7-6114. (On cover: Harper's Franklin square library. no. 744). 1894. Harper & Brothers.

Price of a Wife. Henrietta Eliza Vaughan Stannard. LC 1-24962. 1901. J. B. Lippincott Company.

Price of Admiralty. Howard Barrington. 1942. Hutchinson & Co., Ltd.

Price of Blood. Doris Sutcliffe Adams. LC 66-20540. 1966. Scribner.

Price of Coal. Barry Hines. LC 80-452581. 1979. 9.95 (ISBN 0-7181-1763-8). M. Joseph.

Price of Courage. Curtis Anders. LC 57-124327. 1957. Sagamore Press.

Price of Diamonds. Dan Jacobson. LC 58-582334. 1958. Knopf.

Price of Discontent. Milton Johnson. LC 30-854. 1929. Johnson Publishers.

Price of Freedom, a Tale of to-Day. Creating an Entirely New Literary Form, and an Introduction Thereto. Deane Ballynn. LC 10-23202. 1910. The Walter Scott Publishing Co., Ltd.

Price of Freedom: Or, In the Grip of Hate. Arthur Williams Marchmont. LC 3-12815. 1903. New Amsterdam Book Company.

Price of Gold. Miriam Waddington. 1976. pap. 5.95x o.p. (ISBN 0-19-540265-0). Oxford U Pr.

Price of Happiness: From the Swedish of Betty Pseud. Betty Janson. Tr. by Gustafson, Signhild Victoria. LC 26-95427. The Covenant Book Concern.

Price of Honor. Anne Arrington Tyson. LC 21-21546. 1921. The Four Seas Company.

Price of Liberty. Joseph G. E Hopkins. LC 75-41308. 6.95 (ISBN 0-684-14608-8). Scribner.

Price of Liberty: Stories of the American Revolution. Ed. by Phyllis Reid Fenner. LC 60-5187. (Illus.). 1960. W. Morrow.

Price of Life. Vladimir Germanovich Gomberg. Tr. by Matheson, Helen Chrouschoff. LC 32-535443. 1932. Harper & Brothers.

Price of Life. Vladimir Germanovich Lidin. LC 72-90300. 1973. 14.00 (ISBN 0-88355-011-3). Hyperion Press.

Price of Life. Vladimir Germanovich Lidin & Matheson, Elena Nikolaevna (Krushchova) 1872- Tr. LC 32-5354. 1932. Harper & Brothers.

Price of Lis Doris. Jozua Marius Willen Van Der Poorten Schwartz. 1909. 1.50. D. Appleton and Company.

Price of Love. Arnold Bennett. LC 74-17050. (Collected works of Arnold Bennett). 1974. (ISBN 0-518-19149-4). Books for Libraries Press.

Price of Love. Arnold Bennett. LC 14-10073. 1914. Harper & Brothers.

Price of Murder. John Dann MacDonald. 1979. pap. 1.95 (ISBN 0-449-14242-6, GM). Fawcett.

Price of Murder. John Dann MacDonald. 1970. pap. 0.75 o.p. (T2310, GM). Fawcett World.

Price of Murder: An Original Novel. John Dann MacDonald. LC 57-116243. (Dell first edition, A152). 1957. Dell Pub. Co.

Price of Paradise. Jane Arbor. (Harlequin Romances Ser.). 192p. 1982. pap. 1.50 (ISBN 0-373-02509-2). Harlequin Bks.

Price of Passion. William Arthur Neubauer. LC 47-581077. 1947. Phoenix Press.

Price of Peace. A Story of the Times of Ahab, King of Israel. A. W Ackerman. LC 5-42990. 1894. A. C. McClurg and Company.

Price of Peace & Other Stories. Mary R. Zook. 1975. 7.15. Rod & Staff.

Price of Place. Samuel George Blythe. LC 13-222865. George H. Doran Company.

Price of Salt. Patricia Highsmith. LC 75-12340. (Homosexuality). 1975. 10.00 (ISBN 0-405-07384-4). Arno Press.

Price of Salt. Claire Morgan, pseud. pap. 0.75 o.p. (75-234). Manor Bks.

Price of Salt: By Claire Morgan Pseud. Patricia Highsmith. LC 52-8026. 1952. Coward-McCann.

Price of Silence. Mary Evelyn Moore Davis. 1907. Houghton, Mifflin and Company.

Price of the Graftons. Teignmouth Shore. LC 9-29366. 1909. D. Appleton and Company.

Price of the Prairie: A Story of Kansas. Margaret Hill McCarter. LC 10-22793. 1910. A. C. McClurg & Co.

Price of the Ring. Margret Holmes Ernsperger Bates. LC 6-9074. (On cover: The Ariel library, no. 18). 1892. F. J. Schulte & Company.

Price of Things. Elinor Sutherland Glyn. LC 25-7158. (Authors' press series of the works of Elinor Glyn). 1924. The Authors' Press.

Price of Victory. Maryland Riley Allen. LC 27-7931. 1927. Doubleday, Page & Company.
Price of Wisdom. Marjorie Barkeley McClure. LC 26-185105. 1926. Minton, Balch & Company.
Price of Youth. Margery Williams Bianco. LC 4-5924. 1904. The Macmillan Company.
Price She Paid. David Graham Phillips. Ed. by Abe C. Ravitz. LC 73-96687. (American Authors Ser). 1970. lib. bdg. 20.75 o.s.i. (ISBN 0-512-00562-1). Garrett Pr.
Price She Paid: A Novel. David Graham Phillips. LC 12-14456. 1912. D. Appleton and Company.
Price Tag for Murder: By Spencer Dean Pseud. 1st Ed. Prentice Winchell. LC 59-13962. 1959. Published for the Crime Club by Doubleday.
Price to Be Met. Jessica Steele. (Harlequin Presents). 192p. 1983. pap. text ed. 1.95 (ISBN 0-373-10596-7). Harlequin Bks.
Price Was High: The Last Uncollected Stories of F. Scott Fitzgerald. Francis Scott Key Fitzgerald & Matthew Joseph Bruccoli. LC 78-14074. 19.95. Harcourt Brace Jovanovich.
Price Was High: The Last Uncollected Stories of F. Scott Fitzgerald. Ed. by Matthew J. Bruccoli. LC 78-14074. 832p. 1981. pap. 12.95 (ISBN 0-15-673872-4, Harv). HarBraceJ.
Price You Pay. Peter De Polnay. LC 73-179673. 1973. 2.00 (ISBN 0-491-01381-7). W. H. Allen.
Priceless Passion. Solange Fasquelle. LC 77-6194. 1977. 1.95 (ISBN 0-345-25397-3). Ballantine Books.
Pricking Thumb. Henry C Branson. LC 42-504234. 1942. Simon and Schuster.
Prickly Pear. Hester Pine. LC 40-32623. Farrar & Rinehart, Inc.
Pricksongs & Descants. Robert Coover. 1970. pap. 4.95 (ISBN 0-452-25321-7, Z5321, Plume). NAL.
Pricksongs & Descants: Fictions. Robert Coover. LC 70-87176. 1969. 5.95. Dutton.
Pride and Destiny. Joseph Sheban. LC 45-9769. 1945. The Christopher Publishing House.
Pride and Passion. Fern Michaels. LC 75-19134. 1975. Ballantine Books.
Pride and Passion. A Novel. May Agnes Early Fleming. LC 6-39946. 1882. G. W. Carleton & Co.; Etc., Etc.
Pride and Prejudice. Jane Austen. (Classics ser., CL131). 1967. Airmont.
Pride and Prejudice. Jane Austen. Ed. by A. Walton Litz. LC 67-12360. (Modern Library college editions, T87). 1967. Modern Library.
Pride and Prejudice. Jane Austen. (Harcourt library of English and American classics). 1962. Harcourt, Brace & World.
Pride and Prejudice. Jane Austen. LC 65-6563. 1964. Harper & Row.
Pride and Prejudice. Jane Austen. (Enriched Classics Edition). (Illus.). 1973. 0.95 (ISBN 0-671-47900-8). Pocket Books.
Pride and Prejudice. Jane Austen. Ed. by A. Walton Litz. LC 67-12360. (Modern Library college editions, T87). 1967. Modern Library.
Pride and Prejudice. Jane Austen. LC 71-2815. 1969. 5.95. F. Watts.
Pride and Prejudice. Jane Austen. LC 72-186963. (Penguin English library, EL 72). (Illus.). 1972. (0.30, 1.45 u.s.) (ISBN 0-14-043072-5). Penguin.
Pride and Prejudice. Jane Austen. LC 72-541679. (Oxford English novels). 1970 (ISBN 0-19-255332-1). Oxford U.P.
Pride and Prejudice. Jane Austen. LC 49-427799. (Rinehart editions, 22). 1949. Rinehart.
Pride and Prejudice. Jane Austen. Ed. by Maugham, William Somerset. (Ten Greatest Novels of the World). 1949. J. C. Winston Co.
Pride and Prejudice. Jane Austen. LC 7090. 1899. Roberts Brothers.
Pride and Prejudice. Jane Austen. LC 2-29257. (English Comeddje bussina. 1st series, v. 5). 1902. The Century Co.
Pride and Prejudice. Jane Austen. LC 8-30935. (Macmillan's pocket American and English classics). 1908. The Macmillan Company.
Pride and Prejudice. Jane Austen. Ed. by Sicha, Frank, Jr. LC 18-1223. (Lettered on cover: Standard English classics). Ginn and Company.
Pride and Prejudice. Jane Austen. LC 20-17968. (Lake English classics). Scott, Foresman and Company.
Pride and Prejudice. Jane Austen. (Rittenhouse classics). 1920. G. W. Jacobs & Company.
Pride & Prejudice. Jane Austen. LC 29-1968. (Half-title: Everyman's library; ed. by Ernest Rhys. no. 22). 1926. J. M. Dent & Sons, Ltd.
Pride & Prejudice. Jane Austen. LC 31-18077. (Half-title: Everyman's library; ed. by Ernest Rhys. no. 22). 1929. J. M. Dent & Sons, Ltd.
Pride and Prejudice. Jane Austen. LC 30-26942. 1930. Frederick A. Stokes Company.
Pride and Prejudice. Jane Austen. LC 33-23779. (Half-title: The World's classics. 335). 1933. H. Milford, Oxford Unversity Press.
Pride and Prejudice... Jane Austen. LC 41-3901. 1940. Triangle Books.
Pride and Prejudice. Jane Austen. LC 45-53915. 1940. The Book League of America.
Pride and Prejudice. Jane Austen. LC 80-13177. (Classics in Large Print.). 1980. 13.95 (ISBN 0-8161-3076-0). G. K. Hall.
Pride and Prejudice. Jane Austen & Bailey, John Cann. LC 29-24385. 1928. Dodd, Mead & Company.
Pride and Prejudice. Jane Austen & Ball, Robert, 1890- Illus. LC 45-6105. 1945. Doubleday, Doran & Company, Inc.
Pride and Prejudice. Jane Austen & Cirlin, Edgard, 1913- Illus. LC 46-6883. (Half-title: Rainbow classics). 1946. The World Publishing Company.
Pride and Prejudice. Jane Austen & Dickens, Charles. LC 42-3989. (Prose and poetry individualised program. The novel). 1942. The L. W. Singer Company.
Pride and Prejudice. Jane Austen & Holmes, Mabel Dodge, 1883- LC 46-191974. (CEBCO classics for enjoyment). 1946. College Entrance Book Company.
Pride and Prejudice. Jane Austen & Howells, William Dean. LC 18-729693. (Half-title: The modern student's library, ed. by W. D. Howe). C. Scribner's Sons.
Pride and Prejudice. Jane Austen & Johnson, Reginald Brimley. LC 35-2269. (Half-title: Everyman's library; ed. by Ernest Rhys. 22). 1934. J. M. Dent & Sons, Ltd.
Pride and Prejudice. Jane Austen & Tony Tanner. LC 81-126202. 1980. 1.95 (ISBN 0-14-005774-9). Penguin Books.
Pride & Prejudice see Classics Set.
Pride & Prejudice see Oxford Illustrated Jane Austen.
Pride & Prejudice see Three Nineteenth-Century Novels.
Pride and Prejudice. A Novel. Jane Austen. LC 7088. (Franklin square library, no. 125). 1880. Harper & Brothers.
Pride and Prejudice: A Novel. Jane Austen. LC 7089. (Seaside library, v. 40. no. 819). 1880. G. Munro.
Pride and Prejudice, a Novel. new ed.... ed. Jane Austen. LC 43-43398. (Select library of fiction. 191). Ward, Lock, and Co.
Pride and Prejudice: Adapted by Ollie Depew, Edited by Herbert Spencer Robinson. Jane Austen & Ollie Depew. LC 51-2270. 1951. Globe Book Co.
Pride and Prejudice and Northanger Abbey. Jane Austen. LC 48-41354. 1859. Derby & Jackson.
Pride and Prejudice, and Northanger Abbey. alta ed. Jane Austen. LC 7091. Porter & Coates.
Pride and Prejudice and Sense and Sensibility. Introd. by David Daiches. Jane Austen. LC 50-12233. (Modern Library college editions, T1). 1950. Modern Library.
Pride and Prejudice: Edited with Introduction, Notes and Study Material. Jane Austen. Ed. by Sicha, Frank, Jr. LC 30-188651. Ginn and Company.
Pride and Prejudice. Illustrated by Bernarda Bryson. Afterword by Clifton Fadiman. Jane Austen. LC 62-18385. (Macmillan classics, 4). 1962. Macmillan.
Pride and Prejudice. Introd. by Paul Pickrel. Suggestions for Reading and Discussion by Robert J. Lumsden. Jane Austen. (RLS R22). 1.88, 1.40 pap.,. Houghton.
Pride and Prejudice. Introd. by R. B. Johnson. Jane Austen. LC 50-7332. (Everyman's library. Fiction. 22A). 1950. Dutton.
Pride and Prejudice. Sense and Sensibility. Jane Austen. (Modern library of the world's best books 264). 1949. Modern Library.
Pride & Prejudice: T. V. Tie-in. Jane Austen. Ed. by Tony Tanner. 1981. pap. 1.95 o.p. (ISBN 0-14-005774-9). Penguin.
Pride & Prejudice: Text, Backgrounds, Criticism. Jane Austen. Ed. by Bradford A. Booth. pap. text ed. 3.50 o.p. (ISBN 0-15-571280-2, HC). HarBraceJ.
Pride and Prejudice. With a New Introd. by Elizabeth Stevenson. Jane Austen. LC 61-18550. (Classic Collier books, HS38). 1962. Collier Books.
Pride and Prejudice: With an Introd. by Louis Krouenberger. Jane Austen. LC 50-6142. (Harper's modern classics). 1950. Harper.
Pride and Prejudice. With an Introd. by Mark Schorer. Jane Austen. LC 56-13877. (Riverside editions, B1). 1956. Houghton Mifflin.
Pride and the Anguish. Douglas Reeman. LC 69-11421. 1969. 5.95. Putnam.
Pride & the Anguish: Dark Days in Singapore! Douglas Reeman. 320p. pap. 2.95 (ISBN 0-515-06805-5). Jove Pubns.
Pride & the Poor Princes, No. 134. Barbara Cartland. 160p. (Orig.). 1981. pap. 1.75 (ISBN 0-553-13032-3). Bantam.
Pride of Bear Creek. Robert E. Howard. 7.00 (ISBN 0-937986-20-8). D M Grant.
Pride of Chanur. C. J. Cherryh. 1982. pap. 2.95 (ISBN 0-87997-694-2, UE1694). DAW Bks.
Pride of Dolphins. John Harris. LC 74-26710. 1975. 7.50 (ISBN 0-15-174031-3). Harcourt Brace Jovanovich.
Pride of Felons: Twenty Stories by Members of the Mystery Writers of America. Mystery Writers of America. Ed. by Gordon, Gordon. LC 63-15682. 1963. Macmillan.
Pride of Graystone: A Novel. Gerhard Lewis Wind. LC 27-24575. 1927. Concordia Publishing House.
Pride of Healers. Richard Clark Hirschhorn. LC 76-48130. 1977. 18.95 (ISBN 0-688-03128-5). Morrow.
Pride of Innocence. Maynah Lewis. 1973. pap. 0.75 o.p. (345-26512-2-075). Beagle Bks.
Pride of Innocence. 1st Ed. David Buckley. LC 57-6185. 1957. Holt.
Pride of Jennico. Agnes Sweetman Castle & Castle, Egerton. LC 1-5314. 1897. The Macmillan Company; Etc.,Etc.
Pride of Jennico: Being a Memoir of Captain Basil Jennico. Agnes Sweetman Castle & Castle, Egerton. LC 1-5315. 1898. The Macmillan Company: Etc., Etc.
Pride of Jennico: Being a Memoir of Captain Basil Jennico. Agnes Sweetman Castle & Castle, Egerton. LC 1-623. 1900. The Macmillan Company.
Pride of Jennico: Being a Memoir of Captain Basil Jennico. Agnes Sweetman Castle & Castle, Egerton. LC 41-347854. 1904. The Macmillan Company.
Pride of Jennico: Being a Memoir of Captain Basil Jennico. Agnes Sweetman Castle & Castle, Egerton. LC 41-280741. 1907. The Macmillan Company.
Pride of Lions. 1st Ed. John Nixon Brooks. LC 54-629466. 1954. Harper.
Pride of Lovers. Mary Loos. 432p. 1981. pap. 2.95 (ISBN 0-553-14803-6). Bantam.
Pride of Maura. Nina Larrey Smith Duryea. LC 32-9889. Sears Publishing Company, Inc.
Pride of Monsters. James H. Schmitz. LC 73-159450. 1973. 1.25. Collier Books.
Pride of Monsters. James H. Schmitz. LC 72-85788. 1970. Macmillan.
Pride of Nurse Edna. Dan Ross, pseud. (YA) 1974. 4.95 o.p. (Avalon). Bouregy.
Pride of Nurse Edna. Dan Ross. (Avalon nurse stories). 1974. 4.50. Avalon Books.
Pride of Our Hearts: A Novel. Wilbert L Walker. LC 78-59259. 10.00 (ISBN 0-682-49134-9). Exposition Press.
Pride of Palomar. Peter Bernard Kyne. LC 21-16182. 1921. Cosmopolitan Book Corporation.
Pride of Palomar. Peter Bernard Kyne. LC 24-20459. 1922. Cosmopolitan Book Corporation.
Pride of Palomar. Peter Bernard Kyne. LC 78-54820. (Series: Asian Experience in North America: Chinese and Japanese.). (Illus.). 1978. 17.00 (ISBN 0-405-11276-9). Arno Press.
Pride of Pine Creek. Frank Chester Robertson. LC 38-18601. 1938. E. P. Dutton & Co., Inc.
Pride of Place. William P McGivern. LC 62-17925. 1962. Dodd, Mead.
Pride of Possession: By James Street and Don Tracy. James Howell Street & Tracy, Don. LC 60-7439. 1960. Lippincott.
Pride of Relations: By Richard Charles Pseud. Richard Charles Visger Awdry. LC 58-14920. 1958. Macmillan.
Pride of Royals. Justin Scott. LC 81-71676. 570p. 1983. 15.95 (ISBN 0-87795-382-1). Arbor Hse.
Pride of Summer. John Broderick. LC 77-354811. 1976. 3.25 (ISBN 0-245-52952-7). Harrap.
Pride of Tellfair. Elmore Elliott Peake. LC 3-3273. 1903. Harper & Brothers.
Pride of the Bimbos. John Sayles. LC 74-34177. 1975. 7.95 (ISBN 0-316-77230-5). Little, Brown.
Pride of the Bimbos. John Sayles. (Signet book). 1976. 1.75. New American Library.
Pride of the Chanur. C. J. Cherryh. pap. 2.95. DAW Bks.
Pride of the Forest. Arsinoe Foster Geiger. LC 66-9063. 1966.
Pride of the Mercers. Thomas Cooper De Leon. LC 6-34184. 1898. J. B. Lippincott Company.
Pride of the Mess: A Naval Novel of the Crimean War. William Johnson Neale. LC 44-339304. 1855. G. Routledge and Sons.
Pride of the Moor. 1st Ed. Vian Smith. LC 62-7683. 1962. Doubleday.
Pride of the Paddock: A Novel. Hawley Smart. LC 8-9613. (On cover: Lovell's library, no. 1197). 1888. J. W. Lovell Company.
Pride of the Peacock. Ruth Chatterton. LC 54-8917. 1954. Doubleday.
Pride of the Peacock. Eleanor Hibbert. LC 76-5339. 1976. 7.95 (ISBN 0-385-12281-0). Doubleday.
Pride of the Peacock. Eleanor Hibbert. LC 76-56213. 1977. 14.95 (ISBN 0-8161-6455-X). G. K. Hall.
Pride of the Peacock. Victoria Holt, pseud. LC 76-5339. 1976. 7.95 (ISBN 0-385-12281-0). Doubleday.
Pride of the Peacock. Victoria Holt, pseud. 304p. 1982. pap. 2.95 (ISBN 0-449-24113-0, Crest). Fawcett.
Pride of the Peacock. Victoria Holt, pseud. 1977. lib. bdg. 14.95 o.p. (ISBN 0-8161-6455-X, Large Print Bks). G K Hall.
Pride of the Rancho. Henry E Smith. LC 10-328800. J. S. Ogilvie Publishing Company.
Pride of the Town. Dorothy Walworth. LC 26-7268. 1926. Harper & Brothers.
Pride of the Trevallions. Carola Salisbury. LC 74-9462. 1975. 6.95 (ISBN 0-385-06742-9). Doubleday.
Pride of the Trevallions. Carola Salisbury. (Fawcett Crest Book). 1976. (pbk.) 1.25. Fawcett.
Pride of the West. Walter Robert Cibart. LC 29-10637. The Christopher Publishing House.
Pride of Yosakis. Nat Foster Holmes. LC 40-16019. (Bugbee's popular plays). The Willis N. Bugbee Co.
Pride: Or, The Duchess. Eugene Sue & Oxley, James Macdonald, 1855- Tr. (Seaside library, v. 78, no. 1590). 1883. G. Munro.
Pride's Castle. new ed. Frank Yerby. 1975. (pbk.) 1.75. Dell.
Pride's Castle. Frank Yerby. LC 49-87123. 1949. Dial Press.
Pride's Castle. large print ed. Frank Yerby. LC 82-19224. 1983. 13.95 (ISBN 0-89621-411-7). Thorndike Press.
Pride's Court. Joy Carroll. (Orig.). 1980. pap. 2.50 (ISBN 0-440-17088-5). Dell.
Pride's Fancy. Thomas Head Raddall. LC 46-8244. 1946. Doubleday & Company, Inc.
Pride's Master. Jessica Steele. (Harlequin Romances Ser.). (Orig.). 1980. pap. 1.25 (ISBN 0-373-02309-X, Pub. by Harlequin). PB.
Pride's Way. Robert Molloy. LC 45-35063. 1945. The Macmillan Company.
Priest. Joseph Caruso. LC 77-14629. (American Catholic Tradition). 1978. 16.00 (ISBN 0-405-10821-4). Arno Press.
Priest. Ralph M McInerny. LC 72-9173. 1973. 8.95 (ISBN 0-06-012912-3). Harper & Row.
Priest. William Laurence Sullivan. LC 77-11316. (American Catholic Tradition). 1978. 13.00 (ISBN 0-405-10861-3). Arno Press.
Priest: A Tale of Modernism in New England. William Laurence Sullivan. LC 11-4100. 1911. Sherman, French & Company.
Priest: A Tale of Modernism in New England. 2d ed. William Laurence Sullivan. LC 13-26569. 1914. Sherman, French & Company.
Priest and a Girl. Robert Daley. LC 75-81499. 1969. 6.95. World Pub. Co.
Priest & His Disciples. Hyakuzo Kurata. Tr. by Glenn W. Shaw. 1922. pap. 4.95 o.p. (ISBN 0-89346-037-0, Pub. by Hokuseido Pr). Heian Intl.
Priest and Layman. Ada Carter. LC 11-13728. 1911. 1.20. Wessels & Bissell Co.
Priest and Man: A Story of Love and Duty. Joseph Adelard Rene. LC 5-16518. The Editor Publishing Co.
Priest and Nun. 7th ed. Julia MacNair Wright. LC 9-527933. Western Tract Society.
Priest and Pagan. Herbert Muller Hopkins. 1908. Houghton, Mifflin and Company.
Priest and Puritan. Lorenzo Griswold. LC 7-162. Brentano's.
Priest and the Governor. Tom Luscombe. LC 72-175561. 1970. 5.95 (ISBN 0-7256-0020-9). Hawthorn Press.
Priest and the Hugenot: Or, Persecution in the Age of Louis Xv. Laurence Louis Felix Bungener. LC 6-18673. 1853. Gould and Lincoln.
Priest and the Man: Or, Abelard and Heloisa. A Novel. William Wilberforce Newton & Berington, Joseph, 1746-1827, Tr. LC 7-32301. 1883. Cupples, Upham & Co.
Priest: Fiction. Joseph Caruso. LC 56-11865. 1956. Macmillan.
Priest in the House. Emile Zola. 1957. 13.95 o.p. (ISBN 0-236-30964-1, Pub. by Paul Elek). Merrimack Pub Cir.
Priest in the House. Tr. from French by Brian Rhys. Emile Zola. 1964. 3.95. Elek Bks.
Priest Is at Peace. Davida Brouhard. LC 77-78821. 2.95 (ISBN 0-89343-010-2). Ermine Publishers.
Priest Island. Elliot Lovegood Grant Watson. LC 41-5575. 1941. Smith & Durrell.
Priest of Auvrigny: Or, How a Christian Avenges Himself. And, The King of the Bean. Just Jean Etienne Roy. LC 42-26585. Benziger Brothers, Printers.
Priest of Auvrigny: Or, How a Christian Avenges Himself. And, The King of the Bean. Just Jean Etienne Roy. Tr. by Monroe, Mary C. LC 8-954. 1875. Benziger Brothers.
Priest of the Black Cross. A Tale of the Sea. T Ware Gibson. LC 9-1832. 1848. The "Great West" Office.
Priest of the Ideal. Stephen Graham. LC 17-25855. 1917. 1.60. The Macmillan Company.
Priest or Pagan. John Rathbone Oliver. LC 33-224685. 1933. A. A. Knopf.

Priest or Pretender: A Novel. Frances Berkeley Cunningham. LC 9-10. 1908. The C. M. Clark Publishing Company.
Priest Who Failed and Other Stories. Charles J Mullaly. LC 36-32332. Apostleship of Prayer.
Priest Who Vanished: Or, Murderer at Large. William Wilfrid Whalen & Catholic Literary Guild, Ozone Park, N.Y. LC 42-173581. 1942. Catholic Literary Guild.
Priestess and Queen: A Tale of the White Race of Mexico. Being the Adventures of Ignigene and Her Twenty-Six Fair Maidens. Emily E Reader. LC 7-30960. 1899. Longmans, Green, & Co.
Priestess of Comedy; a Novel. Nataly Von Eschstruth & Lathrop, Elise L., Tr. LC 7-36615. (choice series. no. 90). 1893. R. Bonner's Sons.
Priestess of Comedy: A Novel. Nataly Von Eschstruth & Lathrop, Elise L., Tr. LC 6-38154. (ledger library. no. 90). 1893. R. Bonner's Sons.
Priestess of the Hills. Susan Fontaine Sawyer. LC 28-250227. Meador Publishing Company.
Priests. William Wilfrid Whalen. LC 27-7721. 1927. B. Herder Book Co.
Priests and People: A No-Rent Romance. LC 79-10533. (Ireland, from the Act of Union, 1800, to the Death of Parnell, 1891). 1979. 96.00 (ISBN 0-8240-3526-7). Garland Pub.
Priests & People: A No-Rent Romance. Ed. by Robert L. Wolff. (Ireland-Nineteenth Century Fiction Ser.: Vol. 77). 1979. lib. bdg. 126.00 (ISBN 0-8240-3526-7); lib. bdg. 46.00 ea. Garland Pub.
Priest's Marriage. Nora Vynne. LC 1523. G. P. Putnam's Sons.
Priests of Progress. Gertrude Weaver. LC 9-7569. 1908. B. W. Dodge & Company.
Priests of the Abomination. Ivor Drummond. LC 70-117572. 1971. (ISBN 0-15-174035-6). Harcourt Brace Jovanovich.
Priest's Secretary. Tom McGettrick. 1974. 4.50 (ISBN 0-533-00853-0). Vantage Press.
Priest's Turf-Cutting Day. A Historical Romance. Thomas C Mack. LC 7-16444. 1841. Printed for the Author.
Priglashenie Na Kazn. Vladimir Vladimirovich Nabokov. (Rus.). 1979. 15.00 (ISBN 0-88233-429-8); pap. 7.00 (ISBN 0-88233-430-1). Ardis Pubs.
Prillilgirl: A Fleming Stone Story. Carolyn Wells. LC 24-21149. 1924. J. B. Lippincott Company.
Prima Donna: A Novel. Nancy Mars Freedman. LC 80-21568. 1981. 10.95. W. Morrow.
Prima Donna: A Novel. Nancy Mars Freedman. LC 81-6285. 1981. 16.95 (ISBN 0-8161-3266-6). G.K. Hall.
Prima Donna: A Novel of the Opera. Pitts Sanborn. LC 29-1195. 1929. Longmans, Green and Co.
Prima Donna of the Slums: A Story of Intrigue of the Days of the Third Napoleon. Tr. by McKenna, Stanley. LC 7-30098. (On cover: Idylwild series. v. 1, no. 13). Morrill, Higgins & Co.
Prima Donna's Husband. Fortune Du Boisgobey. (On cover: The Seaside library, Pocket edition. no. 475). G. Munro.
Primacy of Life. Ralph Moreno. 1968. pap. 1.00x o.p. Hartmus Pr.
Primacy of Peter in the Orthodox Church. John Meyendorff & Alexander Schmemann. 1963. 3.50 o.p. Am Orthodox.
Primadonna: A Sequel to "Fair Margaret". Francis Marion Crawford. LC 8-13275. 1908. The Macmillan Company.
Primal Law. Isabel Egenton Ostrander. LC 15-5822. 1915. 1.25. M. Kennerley.
Primal Lure: A Romance of Fort Lu Cerne. Vingie Eve Roe. LC 14-4463. 1914. Dodd, Mead and Company.
Primal Yoke: A Novel. Tom Lea. LC 60-9348. (Illus.). 1960. Little, Brown.
Primary. John LeBoutillier & James C. Humes. (Orig.). 1979. pap. 2.25 (ISBN 0-532-23101-5). Woodhill.
Primary Allegiance. Annie Lyman Sears. LC 25-3550. 1924. B. J. Brimmer Company.
Primavera. Marjorie David. LC 82-286. 1982. 2.50 (ISBN 0-671-45273-8). Poseidon Press.
Prime Cut. Mike Roote. 160p. (Orig.). 1973. pap. 0.75 o.p. (A973S, Award). Univ Pub & Dist.
Prime Cut. Mike Roote. (O.s.i.). 160p. (Orig.). 1973. pap. 0.95 o.s.i. (AN1053, Award). Univ Pub & Dist.
Prime Cut. Mike Roote. 1973. (pbk.) 0.95. Award Books.
Prime Minister. Anthony Trollope. LC 74-196376. (His The Palliser novels). (Illus.). 1973. 3.00. (ISBN 0-19-254615-5) (ISBN 0-19-281147-9). Oxford University Press.
Prime Minister. Anthony Trollope. LC 8-28881. Porter and Coates.
Prime Minister. Anthony Trollope. (International series of new approved novels). 1877. Porter and Coates.
Prime Minister. Anthony Trollope. (On cover: The parliamentary novels. iv). 1893. Dodd, Mead & Company.
Prime Minister... Anthony Trollope. LC 38-27560. (Half-title: The world's classics. 454-455). 1938. Oxford University Press, H. Milford.
Prime Minister Is Dead. Helen De Guerry Simpson. LC 31-26995. 1931. Doubleday, Doran & Company, Inc.
Prime Minister. With a Pref. by L. S. Amery. Illus. by Hector Whistler. Anthony Trollope. LC 52-14549. (Oxford Trollope. Crown ed.). 1952. Oxford University Press.
Prime Minister's Daughter. Maurice Edelman. LC 65-13811. 1965. bds., 4.95. Random House.
Prime Minister's Pencil. Cecil Waye. LC 33-223002. 1933. H. C. Kinsey & Company, Inc.
Prime of Life. Lonnie Laub. LC 78-188285. 1972. 5.95 (ISBN 0-8059-1680-6). Dorrance.
Prime of Miss Jean Brodie. Muriel Spark. LC 62-7182. 1962. Lippincott.
Prime Suspect. R. D. Brown. (Orig.). 1981. pap. 1.95 (ISBN 0-505-51685-3). Tower Bks.
Prime Time. James Kearney. (Leisure Books). 1977. 1.95 (ISBN 0-8439-0499-2). Nordon Pubns.
Prime Time. Rachel Ryan. (Candlelight Ecstasy Ser.: No. 151). (Orig.). 1983. pap. 1.95 (ISBN 0-440-17040-0). Dell.
Prime Time Corpse. Jacqueline Rabbin. (Orig.). 1972. pap. 0.75 o.p. (07225). Curtis.
Primer for Combat: A Novel. Kay Boyle. LC 43-17081. 1942. Simon and Schuster.
Primes and Their Neighbors: Ten Tales of Middle Georgia. Richard Malcolm Johnston. LC 77-101285. (Short story index reprint series). (Illus.). 1969. Books for Libraries Press.
Primes and Their Neighbors: Ten Tales of Middle Georgia. Richard Malcolm Johnston. LC 7-10530. (On cover: Appletons' town and country library, no. 69). 1891. D. Appleton and Company.
Primitive. Chester B Himes. LC 56-6204. (Signet book, 1264). 1955. New American Library.
Primitive. Frederick Feikema Manfred. LC 49-9644. 1949. Doubleday.
Primitive Passions. Joe McDow. pap. 0.75 o.p. (75-239). Manor Bks.
Primitive Splender. Katherine Swinford. (Second Chance at Love Ser.: No. 41). (Orig.). 1982. pap. 1.75 (ISBN 0-515-06401-7). Jove Pubns.
Primitives. Stanley Bennett Hough. LC 54-31246. 1954. Hodder and Stoughton.
Primrose. Joanna Crawford. LC 74-31042. 1975. 6.95 (ISBN 0-15-174220-0). Harcourt Brace Jovanovich.
Primrose. Joanna Crawford. (Signet Book). 1976. (pbk.) 1.25. New American Library.
Primrose Path. Peter Forster. LC 55-12769. 1955. Longmans, Green.
Primrose Path. Claudia Holland. LC 47-4556. 1947. Rinehart.
Primrose Path. A Chapter in the Annals of the Kingdom of Fife. Margaret Oliphant Wilson Oliphant. (Seaside library, v. 20, no. 391). 1878. G. Munro.
Primrose Path of Dalliance: A Story of the Stage. Andrew Carpenter Wheeler. (On cover: Vanderpoole's bimonthly series, no. 2). 1892. L. Vanderpoole & Co.
Primrose Ring. Ruth Sawyer. LC 15-9930. 1915. Harper & Brothers.
Primrose, the Fourth Man. Lou Smith. LC 76-10567. 1976. 7.95 (ISBN 0-7091-5159-4). St. Martin's Press.
Primula and Hyacinth: By Sheila Burns Pseud. Ursula Bloom. LC 50-9001. 1950. Arcadia House.
Primus in India: A Romance. M J Colquhoun. LC 6-31150. (Harper's handy series, no. 33). 1885. Harper & Brothers.
Prince. James Bassett. LC 77-154089. (O.s.i.). 1971. 7.95 o.s.i. (ISBN 0-671-20894-2). S&S.
Prince. R. M. Koster. 1973. (pbk) 1.25. Warner.
Prince. R. M. Koster. LC 78-155996. 1972. 7.95. Morrow.
Prince. Nicolo Machiavelli. 1972. pap. 1.75 o.p. (EP1280). Dutton.
Prince, a Piper, and a Rose. John Scalzo. LC 76-7544. 7.95 (ISBN 0-679-50600-4). McKay.
Prince; a Romance of the Camp and Court of Alexander the Great. The Love Story of Roxana, the Maid of Bactria. Marshall Monroe Kirkman. LC 13-22213. Cropley Phillips Company.
Prince Albrecht of Brandenburg: A Story of the Reformation. Hermann Otto Nietschmann. Tr. by Ireland, Mary Eliza (Haines) (Reformation series, vol. iii). 1907. The German Literary Board.
Prince and Betty. Pelham Grenville Wodehouse. LC 12-292534. W. J. Watt & Company.
Prince and Musician. Max Ring. Tr. by Miller, Hettie E. (On cover: The optimus series. no. 20). 1892. Donohue, Henneberry & Co.
Prince and the Page: A Story of the Last Crusade. Charlotte Mary Yonge. LC 9-2219. D. Lothrop & Company.
Prince and the Page: A Story of the Last Crusade. Charlotte Mary Yonge. 1885. D. Lothrop & Company.
Prince and the Page: A Story of the Last Crusade. Charlotte Mary Yonge. LC 25-16489. 1925. The Macmillan Company.
Prince and the Pauper. Samuel Langhorne Clemens. LC 62-30. 1961. Grosset & Dunlap.
Prince and the Pauper. Samuel Langhorne Clemens. LC 21-663. (Half-title: Harper's modern classics, ed. for educational use by Prof. W. T. Brewster). Harper & Brothers.
Prince and the Pauper. Samuel Langhorne Clemens. LC 46-22269. 1946. Board of Education.
Prince and the Pauper. Samuel Langhorne Clemens & Barry, Mrs. Emily Fanning, Ed. LC 31-28146. (Harper's modern classics). Harper & Brothers.
Prince and the Pauper. Samuel Langhorne Clemens & Lawson, Robert, 1892- Illus. LC 38-1032. The John C. Winston Company.
Prince and the Pauper. Samuel Langhorne Clemens et al. LC 77-91766. (Works of Mark Twain). (works of Mark Twain; v. 6: Vol. 6). (Illus.). 1980. 25.00 (ISBN 0-520-03622-0). Published for the Iowa Center for Textual Studies by the University of California Press.
Prince & the Pauper. Mark Twain. Ed. by John N. Fago. (Now Age Illustrated IV Ser.). (Illus.). (gr. 4-12). 1978. text ed. 5.00 (ISBN 0-88301-329-0); pap. text ed. 1.95 (ISBN 0-88301-317-7); activity bk. 1.25 (ISBN 0-88301-341-X). Pendulum Pr.
Prince & the Pauper. Mark Twain. (Regents Illustrated Classics Ser.). (Illus.). 62p. (gr. 7-12). 1982. pap. text ed. 2.25 (ISBN 0-88345-475-0, 20494). Regents Pub.
Prince & the Pauper. Mark Twain. Ed. by Victor Fischer & Lin Salamo. (Iowa-California Works of Mark Twain). (Illus.). 1980. 27.50 (ISBN 0-520-03622-0). U of Cal Pr.
Prince & the Pauper. Mark Twain. 1982. Repr. lib. bdg. 16.95x (ISBN 0-89966-380-X). Buccaneer Bks.
Prince & the Pauper. Mark Twain. Bd. with Connecticut Yankee. 1982. pap. 3.50 (ISBN 0-451-51628-1, CE1628, Sig Classics). NAL.
Prince & the Pauper. Mark Twain. 256p. 1983. pap. 2.25 (ISBN 0-14-035017-9). Penguin.
Prince & the Pauper. Mark Twain. 3.95 o.p. (ISBN 0-06-014405-X, HarpT). Har-Row.
Prince & the Pauper. abr. ed. Mark Twain. 1958. pap. 0.95 o.p. (ISBN 0-590-03126-0). Schol Bk Serv.
Prince & the Pauper. Mark Twain. (O.s.i.). 1962. pap. 0.95 o.s.i. (04563, Collier). Macmillan.
Prince and the Pauper: A Tale for Young People of All Ages, by Mark Twain Pseud. Illustrated by Peter Spier. Samuel Langhorne Clemens. LC 54-14445. 1954. Junior Deluxe Editions.
Prince and the Pauper: A Tale for Young People of All Ages. Samuel Langhorne Clemens. LC 63-3. Harper & Row.
Prince and the Pauper: A Tale for Young People of All Ages. Samuel Langhorne Clemens. LC 65-6518. (Perennial classic). 1965. Harper & Row.
Prince and the Pauper: A Tale for Young People of All Ages. Samuel Langhorne Clemens. LC 48-11344. 1948. World Pub. Co.
Prince and the Pauper. A Tale for Young People of All Ages. Samuel Langhorne Clemens. LC 3-19550. 1882. J. R. Osgood and Company.
Prince and the Pauper: A Tale for Young People of All Ages. Samuel Langhorne Clemens. LC 3-19551. 1885. C. L. Webster and Company.
Prince and the Pauper: A Tale for Young People of All Ages. Samuel Langhorne Clemens. LC 4-17524. 1903. Harper & Brothers.
Prince and the Pauper: A Tale for Young People of All Ages. Samuel Langhorne Clemens. LC 16-755695. Harper & Brothers.
Prince and the Pauper: A Tale for Young People of All Ages. Samuel Langhorne Clemens. 1909. Harper & Brothers.
Prince and the Pauper: A Tale for Young People of All Ages. Samuel Langhorne Clemens. LC 17-31024. 1917. Harper & Brothers.
Prince and the Pauper: And Other Stories. Portraits of the Author and Scenes from His Book, Together with a Special Introd. by Louis B. Salomon. Samuel Langhorne Clemens. LC 65-27288. (Great illus. classics). 1965. 3.95. Dodd.
Prince and the Pauper: By Mark Twain. Samuel Langhorne Clemens. LC 65-17195. (Companion lib.). 1965. 1.25. Grosset.
Prince and the Pauper: By Mark Twain Pseud. Adapted by Lou P. Bunce; Illustrated by Joseph Low. Samuel Langhorne Clemens & Lou P Bunce. LC 57-950. Scott, Foresman.
Prince and the Pauper: By Mark Twain Pseud. Edited by Marjorie Holmes. Samuel Langhorne Clemens. LC 53-11425. 1953. Globe Book Co.
Prince and the Pauper: By Mark Twain Pseud. Illustrated by Kevin McIntyre. With a New Introd. by DeLancey Ferguson. Samuel Langhorne Clemens. LC 62-20882. 1962. Collier Books.
Prince and the Pekingese. Barbara Cartland. LC 79-153. 1979. 6.95 (ISBN 0-87272-075-6). Duron Books.
Prince and the Princess. Claude Carlos Washburn. LC 25-4341. 1925. A. & C. Boni.
Prince and the Tobacco Lords. Margaret Thomson Davis. LC 76-375929. 1976. 3.50 (ISBN 0-85031-167-5). Allison and Busby.
Prince Arengzeba: A Romance of Lake George. Katherine Tippetts & Tippetts, William Henry, 1850-1909. LC 38-35046. 1892. W. H. Tippetts.
Prince Bart. Jay Richard Kennedy. 1969. pap. 0.95 o.p. (N1948). Pyramid Pubns.
Prince Bart, a Novel of Our Times. Jay Richard Kennedy. LC 53-3953. Farrar, Straus and Young.
Prince Came Riding. Janet Doran. LC 40-238905. Gramercy Publishing Co.
Prince Chap: A Story in Three Curtains and Several Scenes. Edward Henry Peple. LC 4-27985. 1904. G. P. Putnam's Sons.
Prince Charlie's Bluff: A Novel of the Kingdom of Virginia. Donald Thomas. 1974. 7.95 o.p. (ISBN 0-670-57615-8). Viking Pr.
Prince Charlie's Daughter,". Charlotte Mary Brame. (On cover: Lovell's library. v. 17. no. 810). J. W. Lovell Company.
Prince Charlie's Daughter.". Charlotte Mary Brame. LC 44-11265. (On cover: Seaside library. Pocket ed. No. 249). G. Munro.
Prince Charlie's Daughter. Charlotte Mary Brame. LC 4977. (Bertha Clay library, no. 24). 1900. Street & Smith.
Prince Charming... Sophy Beckett. LC 6-9770. (On cover: Seaside library. Pocket edition, no. 1137). 1888. G. Munro.
Prince Cinderella. Alexander, Grace. The Bobbs-Merrill Company.
Prince Commands. Andre Norton, pseud. (Tor Bks.). 1983. pap. 2.95. Pinnacle Bks.
Prince Commands. Andre Norton, pseud. 256p. 1983. pap. 2.95 (ISBN 0-523-48058-X). Tor Bks.
Prince Consort. Godfrey Scheele & Margart Scheele. 1977. 15.95 (ISBN 0-8467-0321-1, Pub. by Two Continents); pap. 9.95 (ISBN 0-8467-0322-X). Hippocrene Bks.
Prince Elmo's Fire. Ernest Lockridge. LC 73-82112. 1974. 8.95 (ISBN 0-8128-1640-4). Stein and Day.
Prince Eugene and His Times. Klara Muller Mundt. Tr. by Chaudron, Adelaide De Vendel. LC 16-1235. (historical romances of Louisa Muhlbach pseud.). D. Appleton and Company.
Prince Eugene and His Times. An Historical Novel. Klara Muller Mundt. Tr. by Chaudron, Adelaide De Vendel. LC 7-39786. 1869. D. Appleton and Company.
Prince Fortunatus. A Novel. William Black. LC 6-12920. (Harper's Franklin square library, no. 664). 1889. Harper & Brothers.
Prince Fortunatus: A Novel. William Black. LC 41-33225. 1890. Harper & Brothers.
Prince Goes Fishing. Elizabeth Duer. LC 6-35453. 1906. D. Appleton and Company.
Prince Goes West. August William Derleth. LC 68-13299. 5.95 (ISBN 0-88361-062-0). Stanton & Lee.
Prince Goes West. August William Derleth. 4.95 o.s.i. (ISBN 0-88451-038-7). Edco-Vis Assoc.
Prince Habib's Iceberg. Edward S Hyams. LC 74-14539. 1975. (ISBN 0-393-08704-2). Norton.
Prince Hagen. Upton Beall Sinclair. LC 77-84267. (Lost Race and Adult Fantasy Fiction). 1978. 15.00 (ISBN 0-405-11008-1). Arno Press.
Prince Hagen: A Phantasy. Upton Beall Sinclair. LC 3-13823. 1903. L. C. Page & Company.
Prince Hal: Or, The Romance of a Rich Young Man. Eliza Frances Andrews. LC 6-2457. 1882. J. B. Lippincott & Co.
Prince Hamlet. Philip Freund. (YA) 1971. 2.75 o.p. (ISBN 0-8057-5731-7). Twayne.
Prince Hermann, Regent (Les Rois En 1900) Tr. from the French of Jules Lemaitre, by Belle M. Sherman. Jules Lemaitre & Sherman, Mrs. Belle M., Tr. (On cover: Cassell's sunshine series. no. 144). Cassell Publishing Company.
Prince Hugo. A Bright Episode. Maria M Grant. LC 6-44841. (Franklin square library. no. 117). 1880. Harper & Brothers.
Prince Hugo. A Bright Episode. Maria M Grant. LC 6-44842. (Seaside library, v. 35, no. 729). G. Munro.
Prince in Petticoats: Or, A King's Folly. Olive Langford. LC 7-14309. Marion Publishing Company.
Prince Incognito. Elizabeth Wormeley Latimer. LC 2-9794. 1902. A. C. McClurg & Co.
Prince Ishmael: A Novel. Marianne Hauser. LC 63-18383. 1963. Stein and Day.

Prince Izon: A Romance of the Grand Canyon. James Paul Kelly. LC 10-8420. 1910. 1.50. A. C. McClurg & Co.

Prince Karl: Novelized from the Play. Archibald Clavering Gunter. 1907. G. W. Dillingham Company.

Prince Lucifer. Etta W Pierce. (American series no. 266). 1892. M. J. Ivers & Co.

Prince of a Fellow. Shelby Hearon. LC 76-56298. 1978. 7.95 (ISBN 0-385-12538-0). Doubleday.

Prince of Abissinia: A Tale, 1759, 2 vols. in 1. Samuel Johnson. Bd. with Candide; or, All for the Best, 1759. Francois M. Voltaire. LC 74-17303. (Novel in England, 1700-1775 Ser). 1974. lib. bdg. 50.00 (ISBN 0-8240-1150-3). Garland Pub.

Prince of Annwn: The First Branch of the Mabinogion. Evangeline Walton. LC 74-195245. 1974. 1.50 (ISBN 0-345-24233-5). Ballantine Books.

Prince of Atlantis. Lillian Elizabeth Becker Roy. The Educational Press.

Prince of Balkistan. Allen Upward. LC 8-32283. (On cover: Lippincott's select novels, no. 170). 1895. J. B. Lippincott Company.

Prince of Berlin. Dan Sherman. 304p. 1983. 15.95 (ISBN 0-87795-480-1). Arbor Hse.

Prince of Breffny. Thomas P May. LC 7-262363. T. B. Peterson & Brothers.

Prince of Carency. Marie Catherine Jumelle De Berneville Aulnoy. LC 70-170541. (Foundations of the Novel). 1973. 22.00 ea. (ISBN 0-8240-0542-2). Garland Pub.

Prince of Central Park. Evan H Rhodes. LC 74-16650. 1975. 7.95 (ISBN 0-698-10643-1). Coward, McCann & Geoghegan.

Prince of Central Park. Evan H Rhodes. 1976. (pbk.) 1.75 (ISBN 0-671-80157-0). Pocket Books.

Prince of Darkness. Susanna Firth. (Romances Ser.). 192p. (Orig.). 1980. pap. text ed. 1.25 (ISBN 0-373-02344-8). Harlequin Bks.

Prince of Darkness. Florence Alice Price James. (On cover: Lovell's library, v. 20, no. 983). 1887. J. W. Lovell Company.

Prince of Darkness. Florence Alice Price James. (On cover: Cassell's "rainbow" series, v. l. no. 9). 1888. Cassell & Company, Limited.

Prince of Darkness. Barbara Mertz. LC 78-91014. 1969. 4.95. Meredith Press.

Prince of Darkness. Jean Plaidy. 320p. 1981. 10.95 (ISBN 0-399-12517-5). Putnam Pub Group.

Prince of Darkness. Jean Plaidy. 320p. 1982. pap. 2.95 (ISBN 0-449-24529-2, Crest). Fawcett.

Prince of Darkness. A Romance of the Blue Ridge. Emma Dorothy Eliza Nevitte Southworth. LC 8-14255. T. B. Peterson & Brothers.

Prince of Darkness & Co., a Novel. Daryl Hine. LC 61-15320. 1961. Abelard-Schuman.

Prince of Darkness: And Other Stories. James Farl Powers. LC 47-5299. 1947. Doubleday.

Prince of Darkness and Other Stories. James Farl Powers. LC 79-7459. 1979. 2.95 (ISBN 0-394-74137-4). Vintage Books.

Prince of Dreamers. Flora Annie Webster Steel. LC 9-4294. 1909. 1.25. Doubleday, Page & Company.

Prince of Eden. Marilyn Harris. LC 77-25420. 12.50. Putnam.

Prince of Eden. Marilyn Harris. 1979. 2.50 (ISBN 0-380-41905-X). Avon Books.

Prince of Egypt. Dorothy Clarke Wilson. LC 49-10839. 1949. Westminster Press.

Prince of Endrevast... John Robinson Pleasants. LC 33-32228. 1933. Meador Publishing Company.

Prince of Foxes. Samuel Shellabarger. (A tale of adventure and romance). 1967. 6.95 o.p. (ISBN 0-316-78467-2). Little.

Prince of Foxes. 1st Ed. Samuel Shellabarger. LC 47-30364. 1947. Little, Brown.

Prince of Georgia and Other Tales. Julian Ralph. LC 74-142274. (Short story index reprint series). (Illus.). 1970. Books for Libraries Press.

Prince of Georgia: And Other Tales. Julian Ralph. LC 99-3834. 1899. Harper & Brothers.

Prince of Good Fellows. Robert Barr. 1902. McClure, Phillips & Co.

Prince of Good Fellows: A Picture from Life. Samuel Humphreys James. The American News Co.

Prince of Graustark. George Barr McCutcheon. LC 14-15791. 1914. Dodd, Mead and Company.

Prince of Gravas. Alfred C Fleckenstein. LC 77-84233. (Lost Race and Adult Fantasy Fiction). 1978. 18.00 (ISBN 0-405-10976-8). Arno Press.

Prince of Gravas: A Story of the Past. Alfred C Fleckenstein. 1898. G. W. Jacobs & Co.

Prince of Hearts. Joan Marsh. (Candlelight Romance). 1972. 0.60. Dell.

Prince of His Race: A College Bred Indian Romance. Oscar Graham. LC 13-179762. 1913. 0.50. W. W. Graves.

Prince of Hungary. Anne Futo Dumont. LC 45-4608. 1945. House of Field-Doubleday, Inc.

Prince of Illusion; "Dolce"; Ein Nix-Nutz; The Honorable Christmas; Gift of Yoshida Aramidzu; "Duzzy Dave": The Horse Trade; "Jane An' Me"; The Dream Woman. John Luther Long. 1901. The Century Co.

Prince of India: Or, Why Constantinople Fell. Lewis Wallace. LC 74-4151. 1974. (ISBN 0-403-03086-2). Scholarly Press.

Prince of India: Or, Why Constantinople Fell. Lewis Wallace. LC 20-15598. Harper & Brothers.

Prince of Israel: A Novel on Bar-Kokba's Uprising Against Rome. 1st Ed. Elias Gilner. LC 52-11665. 1952. Exposition Press.

Prince of Kashna: A West Indian Story. M. C. & Kimball, Richard Burleigh, 1816-1892, Ed. LC 7-19668. 1866. Carleton.

Prince of Malaya. Hugh Charles Clifford. LC 26-21014. 1926. Harper & Brothers.

Prince of Mercuria. Atkinson Kimball. LC 14-20114. 1.25. Hearst's International Library Co.

Prince of Mischance: A Novel. Tom Gallon. LC 6-44485. (Half-title: Appletons' town and country library, no. 234). 1898. D. Appleton and Company.

Prince of Morning Bells. Nancy Kress. (Orig.). 1981. pap. 2.75 (ISBN 0-671-42083-6, Timescape). PB.

Prince of Mount Tahan. Ishak H. Muhammad. Tr. by Harry Aveling from Malay. (Orig.). 1981. pap. text ed. 3.95x (00239). Heinemann Ed.

Prince of Mull: Or, Glimpses of Royal Life. Mary Ellis Smith. 1884. A. N. Marquis & Company.

Prince of My Country. Donald Stuart. LC 75-322251. 1974. 6.95 (ISBN 0-85585-495-2). Georgian House.

Prince of Outlaws: Prince Serebryany. Aleksei Konstantinovich Tolstoi & Manning, Clarence Augustus, 1893- Tr. LC 27-16673. 1927. A. A. Knopf.

Prince of Outlaws Prince Serebryany. Aleksiel Konstantinovich Tolstoi & Manning, Clarence Augustus, 1893- Tr. LC 27-16673. 1927. A. A. Knopf.

Prince of Paradise. Francis Gerard. LC 40-35587. 1941. E. P. Dutton & Co., Inc.

Prince of Passion. Emanuel Milton Baum. W. Neale.

Prince of Peril: The Weird Adventures of Zinlo, Man of Three Worlds, Upon the Mysterious Planet of Venus. Otis Adelbert Kline. LC 30-24768. 1930. A. C. McClurg & Co.

Prince of Plunder. Sydney Horler. LC 34-153104. 1934. Little, Brown, and Company.

Prince of Poisoners: By Ladbroke Black... Ladbroke Lionel Day Black. LC 32-24677. 1932. L. MacVeagh, Dial Press, Inc.

Prince of Raccoon Fork. Baxter Harrison. LC 18-949932. The Roxburgh Publishing Company Inc.

Prince of Romance. by charles b. falls. ed. Stephen Chalmers. 1.20. Small, Maynard and Company.

Prince of Scorpio. Alan Burt Akers. (Science Fiction Ser.). 1974. pap. 1.25 (ISBN 0-87997-251-3, UY1251). DAW Bks.

Prince of Sinners. Edward Phillips Oppenheim. LC 3-13371. 1903. Little, Brown, and Company.

Prince of the Blood. Julius A Lewis. 1899. D. Biddle.

Prince of the Blood. James Payn. (On cover: Lovell's library, no. 1135). 1888. J. W. Lovell Company.

Prince of the Blood: A Novel. Julius A Lewis. LC 7-14365. 1898. Trow Directory, Printing and Book Binding Company.

Prince of the Blood: A Novel. James Payn. LC 42-289002. 1888. Harper & Brothers.

Prince of the Captivity. John Buchan. LC 33-22299. 1933. Houghton Mifflin Company.

Prince of the City. Robert Daley. 352p. 1981. pap. 2.95 (ISBN 0-425-04450-5). Berkley Pub.

Prince of the Ghetto. Maurice Samuel. LC 73-81382. 301p. 1973. pap. 2.45 o.p. (ISBN 0-8052-0401-6). Schocken.

Prince of the House of David. Joseph Holt Ingraham. LC 7-9722. D. C. Cook Publishing Company.

Prince of the House of David. Joseph Holt Ingraham. LC 5746. Rand, McNally & Company.

Prince of the House of David. Joseph Holt Ingraham. LC 5074. W. B. Conkey Company.

Prince of the House of David. Joseph Holt Ingraham. LC 45-48717. H. Altemus.

Prince of the House of David: Or, Three Years in the Holy City. Being a Series of the Letters of Adina... and Relating, As by an Eye Witness, All the Scenes and Wonderful Incidents in the Life of Jesus of Nazareth, from His Baptism in Jordon to His Crucifixion on Calvary. Joseph Holt Ingraham. LC 26-24714. 1855. Pudney & Russell.

Prince of the House of David: Or, Three Years in the Holy City. Being a Series of the Letters of Adina... and Relating, As If by an Eye-Witness, All the Scences and Wonderful Incidents in the Life of Jesus of Nazareth, from His Baptism in Jordon to His Crucifixion of Calvary. carefully revised and corrected by the author, expressly for this new edition. ed. Joseph Holt Ingraham. LC 37-18292. 1859. Pudney & Russell.

Prince of the House of David: Or, Three Years in the Holy City. Being Series of the Letters of Adina... and Relating, As If by an Eye-Witness, All the Scenes and Wonderful Incidents in the Life of Jesus of Nazareth, from His Baptism in Jordon to His Crucifixion on Calvary. carefully rev. and cor. by the author, expressly for this new edition. ed. Joseph Holt Ingraham. LC 7-9726. 1883. Roberts Brothers.

Prince of the House of David: Or, Three Years in the Holy City. Being a Series of the Letters of Adina... and Relating, As If by an Eye-Witness, All the Scenes and Wonderful Incidents in the Life of Jesus of Nazareth, from His Baptism in Jordon to His Crucifixion on Calvary. carefully rev. and cor. by the author, expressly for this new edition. ed. Joseph Holt Ingraham. LC 7-9725. 1887. Roberts Brothers.

Prince of the House of David: Or, Three Years in the Holy City. Being a Series of the Letters of Adina... and Relating, As If by an Eye-Witness, All the Scenes and Wonderful Incidents of the Life of Jesus of Nazareth, from His Baptism in Jordon to His Crucifixion on Calvary. carefully rev. and cor. by the author, expressly for this new edition. ed. Joseph Holt Ingraham. LC 34-37776. 1888. Roberts Brothers.

Prince of the House of David: Or, Three Years in the Holy City. Joseph Holt Ingraham. LC 7-9723. H. Altemus.

Prince of the House of David: Or, Three Years in the Holy City. Being a Series of the Letters of Adina... and Relating, As If by an Eye-Witness, All the Scenes and Wonderful Incidents in the Life of Jesus of Nazareth, from His Baptism in Jordon to His Crucifixion on Calvary. carefully rev. and cor. by the author, expressly for this new ed. Joseph Holt Ingraham. LC 7-9724. 1896. Roberts Brothers.

Prince of the House of David: Or, Three Years in the Holy City... carefully rev. and corrected by the author, expressly for this new ed. Joseph Holt Ingraham. LC 77-28640. 1977. 20.00 (ISBN 0-8414-5076-5). Folcroft Library Editions.

Prince of the Hundred Soups. Violet Paget. (On cover: Lovell's library, no 798). 1886. J. W. Lovell Company.

Prince of the Moon. Louise Platt Hauck. LC 31-23359. The Bobs-Merril Company.

Prince of Ur. Susa Young Gates & Widtsoe, Leah Eudora (Dunford) 1874- Joint Author. LC 46-1768. 1945. Booscraft Company.

Prince of Washington Square: An up-to-the-Minute Story. Harry F Liscomb. LC 25-6703. 1925. Frederick A. Stokes Company.

Prince Ombra. Roderick MacLeish. LC 82-7990. 1982. 13.95 (ISBN 0-86553-050-5) (ISBN 0-312-92658-8). Congdon & Weed.

Prince or Chauffeur? A Story of Newport. Lawrence Perry. LC 11-774491. 1911. 1.35. A. C. McClurg & Co.

Prince or Somebody. Louis Golding. LC 29-964519. 1929. A. A. Knopf.

Prince Otto. Robert Louis Stevenson. LC 33-17517. (Royal blue library). J. H. Sears & Company, Inc.

Prince Otto. A Romance. Robert Louis Stevenson. (Seaside library. Pocket ed. no. 704). 1886. G. Munro.

Prince Otto: A Romance. Robert Louis Stevenson. LC 4-16583. 1902. C. Scribner's Sons.

Prince Otto. A Romance. Robert Louis Stevenson. LC 5-16629. (Half-title: The biographical edition of the works of Robert Louis Stevenson). 1905. C. Scribner's Sons.

Prince Saroni's Wife: And The Pearl-Shell Necklance. Julian Hawthorne. LC 7-38853. (On cover: Standard library, no.129). 1884. Funk & Wagnalls.

Prince Serebryani: An Historical Novel of the Times of Ivan the Terrible and of the Conquest of Siberia. Aleksei Konstantinovich Tolstoi & Curtin, Jeremiah, 1835-1906, Tr. LC 4-8638. 1892. Dodd, Mead & Company.

Prince Serves His Purpose. Alice Duer Miller. LC 29-8721. 1929. Dodd, Mead & Company.

Prince to Order: A Novel. Charles Stokes Wayne. LC 5-8735. 1905. J. Lane.

Prince Valiant Companions in Adventure. Hal Foster, pseud. 160p. 1975. 14.95 o.p. (ISBN 0-517-51583-0). Crown.

Prince Valiant-Companions in Adventure, Vol. 2. LC 74-81371. (Illus.). 1974. 14.95 o.p. (ISBN 0-517-51583-0). Crown.

Prince Valiant in the Days of King Arthur. Hal Foster, pseud. (Illus.). 160p. (YA) 1974. 14.95 o.p. (ISBN 0-517-51584-9). Crown.

Prince Zaleski. Matthew Phipps Shiel. LC 75-32782. (Literature of Mystery and Detection: No. 7). 1976. 10.00 (ISBN 0-405-07898-6). Arno Press.

Prince Zaleski. Matthew Phipps Shiel. LC 8-7343. (On cover: Keynote series. 7). 1895. Roberts Bros.; Etc., Etc.

Prince Zaleski and Cummings King Monk. Matthew Phipps Shiel. LC 76-17993. (Illus.). 7.50 (ISBN 0-87054-007-6). Mycroft & Moran.

Princely Orgies. Olga. 1972. pap. 1.75 o.s.i. (V100K, Venus). Grove.

Princes. Manohar Malgonkar. pap. 0.95 o.p. (95-117). Manor Bks.

Prince's Darling. George Preedy, pseud. LC 30-5169. 1930. Dodd, Mead & Company.

Princes' Favors: A Study of Love, War and Politics. Wilson J Vance. LC 8-30231. 1880. The American News Company.

Prince's Love Affair. Alice Horlock Bennett. LC 26-15429. 1926. Longmans, Green and Co., Ltd.

Princes of Earth. Michael Kurland. LC 78-803. 6.95 (ISBN 0-8407-6602-5). T. Nelson.

Princes of Jade. Capon. 1973. 8.95 o.p. (ISBN 0-525-18349-3). Dutton.

Princes of Naragpur: Or, A Daughter of Allah. E Elliot Durant & Roach, Cuthbert M. LC 29-698. The Grafton Press.

Princes of Peele. William Westall. LC 8-36228. (On cover: The Canterbury series, no. 6). Lovell, Gestefeld & Company.

Princes of the Night. Joseph Kessel & Kahane, Jack, Tr. LC 28-28964. The Macaulay Company.

Prince's Shadow. Margaret Elsie Crowther Baillie-Saunders. LC 13-20485. Hodder and Stoughton.

Prince's Story Book: Being Historical Stories Collected Out of English Romantic Literature, in Illustration of the Reigns of English Monarchs, from the Conquest to Victoria. Ed. by George Laurence Gomme. LC 6-437365. 1900. A. Constable & Co.

Princess. Mary Greenway McClelland. LC 7-15431. (Leisure season series. No. 3). 1886. H. Holt and Company.

Princess. Margaret Horton Potter. LC 7-9844. 1907. Harper & Brothers.

Princess. Philip Duffield Stong. LC 41-8360. Farrar & Rinehart, Inc.

Princess: A Novel. Diana Carter. LC 77-151202. 1971. 6.95. Putnam.

Princess: A Novel. Margaret Greenway McClelland. LC 7-15431. (On cover: Leisure season series, no. 3). 1886. H. Holt and Company.

Princess Ahmedee: A Romance of Heidelberg. James Leonard Groning. LC 5005. 1900. G. A. S. Wieners.

Princess Aline. Richard Harding Davis. LC 6-32264. 1895. Harper & Brothers.

Princess Aline. biographical ed. Richard Harding Davis. LC 99-4898. 1899. Harper & Brothers.

Princess Amelia. Carola Mary Anima Oman Lenanton, pseud. LC 25-2657. 1924. Duffield & Company.

Princess Amelie. A Fragment of Autobiography. Elizabeth Wormeley Latimer. LC 7-13861. (No name series. 3d series, v. 17). 1883. Roberts Brothers.

Princess and a Woman: A Romance of Carpathia. Robert MacDonald. LC 7-18789. 1897. F. A. Munsey.

Princess and Another. Stephen Jenkins. LC 7-38268. 1907. B. W. Huebsch.

Princess, and Other Stories. David Herbert Lawrence. LC 73-161878. 1971. 0.35 (ISBN 0-14-003263-0). Penguin.

Princess and the Clowns. Jean Jose Frappa. Tr. by Swinburne, Marie Louise. LC 24-27748. 1924. Duffield and Company.

Princess & the Goblin. Paul Rosner. 1978. 6.95 o.s.i. Sherbourne.

Princess & the Goblin. Paul Rosner. 606p. 1966. 6.95 o.p. Sherbourne.

Princess and the Goblin: A Novel. Paul Rosner. LC 66-23910. 1966. 6.95. Sherbourne.

Princess and the Jew. Jozef Ignacy Kraszewski. Tr. by De Vere, Meta. LC 7-14168. (On cover: Seaside library. Pocket ed. no. 1207). G. Munro.

Princess and the Ploughman. Florence Morse Kingsley. LC 7-18593. 1907. Harper & Brothers.

Princess Anne, a Story of the Dismal Swamp: And Other Sketches. Albert Reid Ledoux. LC 7-12783. 1896. The Lookeron Publishing Co.

Princess Athura: A Romance of Iran. Samuel W Odell. LC 13-4611. 1913. Thomas Y. Crowell Company.

Princess Bride. William Goldman. 1977. pap. 2.50 (ISBN 0-345-29412-2). Ballantine.

Princess Bride: S. Morgenstern's Classic Tale of True Love and High Adventure. The "Good Parts" Version, Abridged. William Goldman. LC 73-6812. 1973. 7.95 (ISBN 0-15-173085-7). Harcourt Brace Jovanovich.

Princess by Proxy. Roland Pertwee. LC 34-121729. 1934. Houghton Mifflin Company.

Princess Casamassima. Henry James. LC 59-13842. (Harper torchbooks, TB1005. The Academy library). 1959. Harper.

Princess Casamassima. Henry James. LC 48-6136. 1948. Macmillan Co.

Princess Casamassima. Henry James. LC 77-373551. (Penguin modern classics). 1977. 2.95 (ISBN 0-14-004102-8). Penguin Books.

Princess Casamassima see Bodley Head Henry James.

Princess Casamassima: A Novel. Henry James. LC 75-27312. (Apollo editions; A-395). 1976. 5.95 (ISBN 0-8152-0395-0). Crowell.

Princess Casamassima: A Novel. Henry James. 1886. Macmillan and Co.

Princess Casamissima, Vol. 1. Henry James. LC 70-158784. (Novels & Tales of Henry James: Vol. 5). Repr. of 1908 ed. lib. bdg. 22.50x (ISBN 0-678-02805-2). Kelley.

Princess Cecilia. Elmer Holmes Davis. LC 15-8940. 1915. 1.30. D. Appleton and Company.

Princess Charming: A Romance. Wilbur Finley Fauley. LC 27-75127. The Macaulay Company.

Princess Daisy. Judith Krantz. LC 79-26254. 12.95 (ISBN 0-517-53606-4). Crown Publishers.

Princess Daphne. A Novel... Edward Heron-Allen & Delaro, Selian. LC 6-478. 1888. Belford, Clarke & Co.

Princess Dehra. 2d ed. John Reed Scott. 1908. J. B. Lippincott Company.

Princess Elopes. Harold MacGrath. LC 5-11072. (On cover: The pocket books). 1905. The Bobbs-Merrill Company.

Princess Flower Hat: A Comedy from the Perplexity Book of Barbara, the Commuter's Wife. Mabel Osgood Wright. LC 10-236669. 1910. The Macmillan Company.

Princess Ilse. Marie Petersen. Tr. by Cronise, Florence M. LC 7-36169. 1891. Albert, Scott & Company.

Princess Ilse: A Story of the Harz Mountains. And The Will-O'-the-Wisps. Marie Petersen. LC 6-35181. 1868. J. E. Etilton and Company.

Princess Ilse: A Story of the Harz Mountain. Marie Petersen. LC 7-35801. 1867. Gould and Lincoln.

Princess in Berlin. R. G. Solmssen. 1981. pap. 2.75 (ISBN 0-345-29807-1). Ballantine.

Princess in Berlin: A Novel. Arthur R. G Solmssen. LC 80-19250. (Illus.). 12.95 (ISBN 0-316-80369-3). Little, Brown.

Princess in Distress. Barbara Cartland. LC 78-13321. 1978. 6.95 (ISBN 0-87272-043-8). Duron Books.

Princess in England. Michael Campbell. LC 64-129795. 1964. Orion Press.

Princess Katharine. Katharine Tynan Hinkson, pseud. LC 11-1964. 1911. 1.20. Duffield & Company.

Princess Laura: A Story True to Life. Stephanie Marie Bridge. LC 34-34596. 1934. Reynolds Printing.

Princess" Mae: A Romance. Louise Wellons Kernodle. LC 15-1696. 1914. Central Publishing Co., Inc.

Princess Malah. John H Hill. LC 70-144637. 1972. 15.00 (ISBN 0-404-00171-8). AMS Press.

Princess Malah. John H Hill. LC 33-3600. The Associated Publishers, Inc.

Princess Maritza. Percy James Brebner. LC 31-195027. 1906. Grossett & Dunlap.

Princess Maritza. Percy James Brebner. 1906. T. J. McBride & Son.

Princess Mary of Maryland. Nan H. Agle. LC 70-12561. (Illus.). viii, 109p. 1967. Repr. 30.00x (ISBN 0-8103-5029-7). Gale.

Princess Mary's Locked Book. Anon. Alice Muriel Williamson. LC 13-3303. 1913. Cassell and Company.

Princess Mazaroff: A Romance of the Day. Joseph Hatton. LC 7-2201. J. W. Lovell Company.

Princess Nadine. Frances Christine Tierman. LC 7-42008. 1908. G. P. Putnam's Sons.

Princess Naida. Brewer Corcoran. LC 21-12359. 1921. The Page Company.

Princess Napraxine: A Novel. Louise De La Ramee. LC 6-33313. (On cover: Lovell's library. v. 7. no. 387). 1884. J. W. Lovell Company.

Princess Nourmahal. George Sand & Vanderpoole, Lew, 1855- LC 6-34633. 1888. G. W. Dillingham.

Princess of Alaska: A Tale of Two Countries. A Novel, by Richard Henry Savage... Richard Henry Savage. (On cover: Neely's library of choice literature, no. 33). 1894. F. T. Neely.

Princess of All Lands. Russell Kirk. LC 78-67063. 8.95 (ISBN 0-87054-084-X). Arkham House Publishers.

Princess of Aragon see Katherine of Aragon.

Princess of Arcady. Arthur Henry. LC 6232. 1900. Doubleday, Page & Co.

Princess of Cleves. Marie Madeleine Pioche De La Vergne La Fayette. LC 77-22941. 1977. 16.50 (ISBN 0-8371-9729-5). Greenwood Press.

Princess of Cleves. Marie Madeleine Pioche De La Vergne La Fayette. Tr. by Jean Regnauld De Segrais. Francois La Rochefoucauld. LC 51-10612. (New classics series 31). 1951. New Directions.

Princess of Cleves. Marie Madeleine Pioche De La Vergne La Fayette. LC 77-22941. 1977. Repr. of 1951 ed. lib. bdg. 19.25x (ISBN 0-8371-9729-5, LAFPC). Greenwood.

Princess of Copper: A Novel. Archibald Clavering Gunter. LC 3340. (On cover: The Welcome series. No. 57). The Home Publishing Company.

Princess of Fiji. William Churchill. LC 6-25382. Dodd, Mead & Company.

Princess of Forge. George Clifford Shedd. LC 10-12785. 1910. The Macaulay Company.

Princess of Gan-Sar (Mary Magdalen) Andrew Francis Klarmann. LC 7-25166. 1907. F. Pustet & Co.

Princess of Glendale: A Story of the South. Maia Pettus. LC 3-1574. 1902. The Neale Publishing Company.

Princess of Gramfalon. Edwin Carlile Litsey. LC 98-1337. 1898. The Editor Publishing Co.

Princess of Hearts. Charles Stuart Welles. LC 16-22940. 1917. C. S. Welles.

Princess of Java, a Tale of the Far East. Sarah Jane Hatfield Higginson. LC 7-4773. 1887. Houghton, Mifflin and Company.

Princess of Mars. Edgar Rice Burroughs. LC 71-14778. (Illus.). 1970. N. Doubleday.

Princess of Mars. Edgar Rice Burroughs. LC 17-28074. 1917. A. C. McClurg & Co.

Princess of Mars. Edgar Rice Burroughs. LC 21-8170. 1918. Grosset & Dunlap.

Princess of Montserrat: A Strange Narrative of Adventure and Peril on Land and Sea. William Drysdale. LC 6-34215. 1890. Albany Book Company.

Princess of Moonlight. William Arthur Neubauer. 1949. Arcadia House.

Princess of New York. Cosmo Hamilton. LC 38-11643. The William Caslon Company, Inc.

Princess of Paradise Island. Lorin Andrews Lathrop. LC 25-8905. 2.00. George H. Doran Company.

Princess of Paris: A Novel. Archibald Clavering Gunter. LC 7-131. 1894. The Home Publishing Co.

Princess of Powder River. Lee D. Willoughby. (Women Who Won the West Ser.: Vol. 8). 368p. 1982. pap. 3.25 (ISBN 0-440-06326-4, Bryans). Dell.

Princess of Seventy Second Street. Elaine Kraf. LC 79-12784. 1979. 9.95 (ISBN 0-8112-0749-8); pap. 4.95 (ISBN 0-8112-0748-X, NDP494). New Directions.

Princess of Sorry Valley. John Fleming Wilson. LC 13-14820. 1913. Sturgis & Walton Company.

Princess of the Atom. Ray Cummings. LC 50-34021. (Avon fantasy novels, no. 1). 1950. Avon Pub. Corp.

Princess of the Gutter. Elizabeth Thomasina Meade Smith. LC 8-865256. G. P. Putnam's Sons.

Princess of the Hills: An Italian Romance. Constance Cary Harrison. LC 1-13980. Lothrop Publishing Company.

Princess of the Indies: A Tale of the Sea. Wilbur Daniel Spencer. LC 37-6525. 1937. Falmouth Book House.

Princess of the Moor. Eugenie John. LC 7-9910. (On cover: Seaside library. Pocket ed. no. 1136). G. Munro.

Princess of the Night Rides. John D. Holt. LC 76-12962. 1977. 7.95 (ISBN 0-914916-21-1); pap. 3.50 (ISBN 0-914916-22-X). Topgallant.

Princess of the Night Rides and Other Tales. John Dominis Holt. LC 76-12962. 10.00 (ISBN 0-914916-21-1) (ISBN 0-914916-22-X). TopGallant Pub. Co.

Princess of the Old Dominion: A Historical Novel of the First Virginia Colony. 1st Ed. Margaret Collins Denny Dixon. LC 53-6713. 1953. Exposition Press.

Princess of the Orient. Ethel Black Kealing. LC 19-368. 1.50. The Christopher Press.

Princess of the Stage. A Novel. Nataly Von Eschstruth & Lathrop, Elise L., Tr. LC 6-38149. (choice ser. no. 103). 1894. R. Bonner's Sons.

Princess of the Stage. A Novel. Nataly Von Eschstruth & Lathrop, Elise L., Tr. LC 6-38150. (ledger library. no. 105). 1894. R. Bonner's Sons.

Princess of the Two Lands. Lois M. Parker. (Crown Ser.). 128p. 1975. pap. 3.50 o.p. Review & Herald.

Princess of the Two Lands. Lois M. Parker. (Crown Ser.). 128p. 1975. pap. 3.50 o.p. Southern Pub.

Princess of Thule. William Black. (Seaside library, v. 1, no. 13). G. Munro.

Princess of Thule. William Black. LC 11-10516. (Lovell's library v. 1, no. 48). J. W. Lovell Company.

Princess of Thule. William Black. (Seaside library. Pocket ed. no. 23). G. Munro.

Princess of Thule. William Black. LC 11-106157. 1894. J. Knight Company.

Princess of Thule. A Novel. William Black. LC 41-4546. (Harper's library of select novels). 1874. Harper & Brothers.

Princess of Thule. A Novel. William Black. LC 4-15286. 1877. Harper & Brothers.

Princess of Vascovy: Her Trials and Troubles, Her Adventures and Misadventures, and Where They Brought Her. John Oxenham, pseud. LC 99-2451. 1899. G. W. Dillingham Co.

Princess Ogherof. A Russian Love Story. Alice Marie Celeste Durand. Tr. by Sherwood, Mary (Neal) LC 11-82127. T. B. Peterson & Brothers.

Princess Pamela. Ed. by Ray Russell. 1979. 11.95 (ISBN 0-395-28210-1). HM.

Princess Pamela: Being the Personal Journal of Miss Pamela Summerfield of Berkeley Square, Mayfair, London. Ray Russell. LC 79-9242. 1979. 12.95 (ISBN 0-395-28210-1). Houghton Mifflin.

Princess Passes: A Romance of a Motor-Car. Charles Norris Williamson & Alice Muriel Livingston Williamson. LC 5-5442. 1905. H. Holt and Company.

Princess Pourquoi. Margaret Pollock Sherwood. LC 73-178461. (Short story index reprint series). (Illus.). 1971. (ISBN 0-8369-4062-8). Books for Libraries Press.

Princess Pourquoi. Margaret Pollock Sherwood. LC 7-31285. 1907. Houghton, Mifflin & Company.

Princess Priscilla's Fortnight. Elizabeth. 1973. pap. 0.95 o.p. (09180). Curtis.

Princess Priscilla's Fortnight. Elizabeth. 1973. (pbk) 0.95. Curtis Books.

Princess Priscilla's Fortnight. Mary Annette Beauchamp Russell Russell. LC 5-361191. 1905. C. Scribner's Sons.

Princess Pro Tem. Arthur Cheney Train. LC 32-182462. 1932. C. Scribner's Sons.

Princess Roubine. A Russian Story. Alice Marie Celeste Durand. Tr. by Cox, George D. LC 6-35686. T. B. Peterson & Brothers.

Princess Russalka. Frank Wedekind & Eisemann, Frederick, Tr. LC 20-12338. 1919. J. W. Luce & Company.

Princess Salome: A Tale of the Days of Camel-Bells. Burris Atkins Jenkins. LC 21-6801. 1921. J. B. Lippincott Company.

Princess Sarah. Henrietta Eliza Vaughan Stannard. (On cover: Seaside library. Pocket ed. no. 1117). 1888. G. Munro.

Princess Sayrane: A Romance of the Days of Prester John. by harold h. betts. ed. Edith Ogden Carter H. Harrison Harrison. LC 10-23314. 1910. 1.35. A. C. McClurg & Co.

Princess Scargo: An Indian Legend. 4.50 o.p. Vantage.

Princess Sonia. Julia Magruder. LC 9-24949. 1895. The Century Co.

Princess Sophia. Edison Marshall. LC 58-8103. 1958. Doubleday.

Princess Sophia: A Novel. Edward Frederic Benson. LC 2056. 1900. Harper & Brothers.

Princess Splendour and Other Stories. Helen Jane Waddell. Ed. by Eileen Colwell. (Puffin bks., PS548). (Illus.). 1972. 1.25. Penguin Bks.

Princess Stakes Murder. Kin Platt. LC 72-10095. 1973. 4.95 (ISBN 0-394-48147-X). Random House.

Princess Sunshine. ...authorized ed. Charlotte Eliza Lawson Cowan Riddell. (On cover: Lovell's international series, no. 116). 1890. J. W. Lovell Company.

Princess Tarakanova. A Dark Chapter of Russian History. Tr. from the Russian of G. P. Danilevski. Grigovii Petrovich Danilevskii. Tr. by Monchanoff, Ida De. LC 7-46652. Macmillan & Co.; Etc., Etc.,

Princess Thora. Burland Harris. Ed. by R. Reginald & Douglas Melville. LC 77-92408. (Lost Race & Adult Fantasy Ser.). (Illus.). 1978. Repr. of 1904 ed. lib. bdg. 23.00x (ISBN 0-405-10961-X). Ayer Co.

Princess Thora. John Burland Harris-Burland. LC 4-18893. 1904. Little, Brown, and Company.

Princess Thora. Harris-Burland, John Burland. LC 77-92408. (Lost Race and Adult Fantasy Fiction). (Illus.). 1978. 23.00 (ISBN 0-405-10961-X). Arno Press.

Princess Vic. James Brough. LC 65-18128. bds., 4.95. Little.

Princess Virginia. Charles Norris Williamson & Alice Muriel Livingston Williamson. LC 7-15121. 1907. McClure, Phillips & Co.

Princess' Wedding Feast: Or, The Wind Spirit of Woenfels. A Romance. Helen Watson Beck. LC 99-885. (On cover: Neely's popular library. no. 131). 1899. F. T. Neely.

Princess with Love. Terri Lees. 3.00 o.p. Carlton.

Princess Xenia: A Romance. Henry Brereton Marriott Watson. LC 99-556039. 1899. Harper & Brothers.

Princess Zara. Ross Beeckman. LC 9-6276. 1909. W. J. Watt & Company.

Princesse De Cleves. Marie Lafayette. Ed. by K. B. Kettle. (Fr). 1967. 2.95x o.p. St Martin.

Princesse De Cleves. Marie Madeleine Pioche de La Vergne La Fayette, pseud. Tr. by Nancy Mitford. LC 79-345806. (Penguin classics). 1978. 2.95 (ISBN 0-14-044337-1). Penguin Books.

Princesse De Cleves: Tr. from French by Nancy Mitford. Marie Madeleine Pioche De La Vergne La Fayette. Tr. by Jean Regnauld De Segrais. Francois Duc De La Rochefoucauld. (1846). 1963. Penguin.

Princeton Stories. Jesse Lynch Williams. LC 73-101292. (Short story index reprint series). 1969. Books for Libraries Press.

Princeton Stories. Jesse Lynch Williams. LC 8-34352. 1895. C. Scribner's Sons.

Principal Girl. John Collis Snaith. LC 12-580456. 1912. Moffat, Yard and Company.

Principato. Tom McHale. LC 71-104134. 1970. 6.95. Viking Press.

Principia Discordia. Malaclypse the Younger. 1978. pap. 4.95. Loompanics.

Principia Martindale: A Comedy in Three Acts. Edward Swift. LC 82-48150. 12.95 (ISBN 0-06-015110-2). Harper & Row.

Print of a Hare's Foot. Rhys Davies. 1969. 4.95 o.p. (ISBN 0-396-06002-1). Dodd.

Print of a Hare's Foot: An Autobiographical Beginning. Rhys Davies. LC 72-91278. 1969. 4.95. Dodd, Mead.

Print-Out. Robert B Gillespie. LC 82-9413. 1982. 9.95 (ISBN 0-396-08100-2). Dodd, Mead.

Printer of Malgudi. R. K. Narayan. LC 57-5845. 1957. Michigan State University Press.

Printer's Measure see Marty.

Prinzessin Brambilla. E. T. Hoffman. Ed. by M. Raraty. (Blackwell's German Text Ser.). 1972. pap. 9.95x (ISBN 0-631-01880-8, Pub. by Basil Blackwell). Biblio Dist.

Prior Betrothal. Elsie Lee. LC 73-82183. 1973. 6.95 (ISBN 0-87795-066-0). Arbor House.

Priorsford. Anna Buchan. LC 32-25837. 1932. H. C. Kinsey & Company, Inc.

Priory. Dorothy Whipple. LC 39-196956. 1939. The Macmillan Company.

Priory of St. Bernard: An Old English Tale. M Harley. LC 77-2039. (Gothic Novels). 1977. 35.00 (ISBN 0-405-10138-4). Arno Press.

Prisca of Patmos: A Tale of the Days of St. John. Henry Christopher McCook. LC 11-243601. 1911. The Westminster Press.

Priscilla. Jan Laing. LC 51-10282. 1951. Putnam.

Priscilla Devens. Elisabeth Stoughton Griffiths. LC 37-288. King-Richardson Company.

Priscilla Falls in Love. Winifred Mary Scott. LC 35-23329. 1935. Doubleday, Doran & Company, Inc.

Priscilla of the Good Intent: A Romance of the Grey Fells. Halliwell Sutcliffe. LC 9-263199. 1909. Little, Brown, and Company.

Priscilla: Or, Trials for the Truth. An Historic Tale of the Puritans and the Baptists. Joseph Banvard. LC 6-8629. 1854. Heath and Graves.

Priscilla Won't. Louise Platt Hauck. LC 39-31682. 1939. Macrae-Smith-Company.

Priscilla Won't. Jean Randall. LC 39-316825. 1939. Macrae Smith Company.

Priscilla's Love-Story. Harriet Elizabeth Prescott Spofford. 1898. H. S. Stone & Company.

Priscilla's Spies. James Owen Hannay. LC 12-14397. 1912. Hodder & Stoughton, Geroge H. Doran Company.

Prisling. Susan Eastwood. 1977. pap. 1.00 o.p. (ISBN 0-931832-07-1). No Dead Lines.

Prism. Maria E. Guerra. 3.95 o.p. (ISBN 0-8111-0325-0). Naylor.

Prism. Valerie Taylor. LC 81-80019. 1981. 6.95 (ISBN 0-930044-18-5). Naiad Press.

Prism One. Ed. by Cecil Hemley. 1962. 1.25x o.p. Twayne.

Prisms. Marianne Mackay. LC 80-52415. 11.95 (ISBN 0-87223-655-2). Seaview Books.

Prison. Georges Simenon. LC 69-12048. 1969. Harcourt, Brace & World.

Prison at Obregon. Bill Adkins. 1976. (pbk.) 1.25. Popular Library.

Prison Doctor. Louis Berg. LC 32-5306. Brentano's.

Prison-Flower: A Romance of the Consulate and Empire. Romaine Callender. LC 12-10266. 1.50. R. G. Badger.

Prison Life in Siberia... Fedor Mikhailovich Dostoevskii & Edwards, Henry Sutherland, 1828- Tr. LC 8-1112. (Harper's Franklin square library, no. 501). 1887. Harper & Brothers.

TITLE INDEX PRIVATE LIFE OF HELEN

Prison Life of Harris Filmore. Jack Richardson. LC 63-8626. 1963. New York Graphic Society.
Prison Nurse. Louis Berg. The Macaulay Company.
Prison Nurses. William Arthur Neubauer. LC 62-5809. 1962. Arcadia House.
Prison of Ice. Dean Koontz. LC 76-26514. 8.95 (ISBN 0-397-01182-2). Lippincott.
Prison of Ice. Dean Koontz. (Fawcett Crest Book). 1977. 1.75 (ISBN 0-449-23345-6). Fawcett Books.
Prison of Love. Diego de San Pedro. Tr. by Keith Whinnom from Span. 148p. 1979. pap. 8.00x (ISBN 0-85224-380-4, Pub. by Edinburgh U Pr Scotland). Columbia U Pr.
Prison of Love, 1492: Together with the Continuation by Nicolas Nunez, 1496. San Pedro, Diego De & Nicolas Nunez. LC 80-473761. (Illus.). 8.00 (ISBN 0-85224-380-4). Edinburgh University Press.
Prison of Night: Dumarest No. 7. E. C. Tubb. (Science Fiction Ser). (Orig.). 1977. pap. 1.50 o.p. (ISBN 0-87997-346-3, UW1346). DAW Bks.
Prison Satellite. Leo P. Kelley. LC 79-51075. (Space Police Bks.). 1979. pap. 4.24 (ISBN 0-8224-6377-6). Pitman Learning.
Prison Wall. Ethel May Dell. LC 33-1848. 1933. G. P. Putnam's Sons.
Prison Without a Wall. Ralph Straus. LC 12-813631. 1912. H. Holt and Company.
Prisoner. John Davys Beresford. LC 47-205842. 1946. Hutchinson & Co. Ltd.
Prisoner. Alice Brown. LC 16-265451. 1916. The Macmillan Company.
Prisoner: A Novel. Ernst Lothar & Galston, James Austin, 1881- LC 45-350803. 1945. Doubleday, Doran and Company, Inc.
Prisoner: A Novel by Ernst Lothar. Ernst Lothar. LC 45-35080. 1945. Doubleday, Doran.
Prisoner at the Bar. Roderic Jeffries. LC 69-15719. 1969. 4.50. Walker.
Prisoner Ate a Hearty Breakfast, a Novel. Earl Jerome Ellison. LC 39-10760. Random House.
Prisoner Born. Claude Aveline. LC 70-157622. 1971. 4.95. Doubleday.
Prisoner: Cell Block H. Murray Sinclair. 224p. (Orig.). 1980. pap. 2.25 (ISBN 0-523-41113-8). Pinnacle Bks.
Prisoner, Cell Block H: Number 4, The Frustrations of Vera. Robert Hoskins. 224p. (Orig.). 1981. pap. 2.25 (ISBN 0-523-41215-0). Pinnacle Bks.
Prisoner-Cell Block H: The Karen Travers Story, No. 3. Maggie O'Shell. 224p. (Orig.). 1981. pap. 2.25 (ISBN 0-523-41176-6). Pinnacle Bks.
Prisoner Cell Block H: Trials of Erica. Mary Carter. (Prisoner Cell Block H Ser.: No. 6). 224p. (Orig.). 1981. pap. 2.25 (ISBN 0-523-41404-8). Pinnacle Bks.
Prisoner Cellblock H: The Reign of Queen Bea, No. 5. Angela Michaels. 224p. (Orig.). 1981. pap. 2.25 (ISBN 0-523-41403-X). Pinnacle Bks.
Prisoner Halm. Karl Wilke. LC 37-341791. 1931. The Bobbs-Merrill Company.
Prisoner in Babylon. Madeleine D Strain. LC 30-15341. 1930. The Macaulay Company.
Prisoner in Fairyland: The Book That "Uncle Paul" Wrote. Algernon Blackwood. LC 13-15686. 1913. The Macmillan Company.
Prisoner in Paradise. Marjorie Lewty. (Harlequin Romances Ser.). 192p. (Orig.). 1981. pap. 1.25 (ISBN 0-373-02382-0, Pub. by Harlequin). PB.
Prisoner in Paradise. Garet Rogers. LC 54-10489. 1954. Putnam.
Prisoner in the Opal. Alfred Edward Woodley Mason. LC 28-259624. 1928. Pub. for The Crime Club, Inc., by Doubleday, Doran & Company, Inc.
Prisoner in the Skull. Charles Dye, pseud. LC 75-9076. (O.s.i.). 192p. (Orig.). 1975. pap. 1.25 o.s.i. (ISBN 0-89041-027-5, 3027). Major Bks.
Prisoner in the Skull: A Science-Fiction Novel. Charles Dye, pseud. LC 52-13707. 1952. Abelard Press.
Prisoner in the Square. Dorothy Quentin. 1972. pap. 0.95 o.p. (ISBN 0-515-02830-4, N2830). Pyramid Pubns.
Prisoner of Evil. Diana Tower, pseud. LC 75-32271. 176p. 1976. pap. 1.25 (ISBN 0-89041-057-7, 3057). Major Bks.
Prisoner of Fire. Edmund Cooper. 192p. 1976. 6.95 o.p. (ISBN 0-8027-5334-5). Walker & Co.
Prisoner of Garve. Sandra Shulman. (Gothic Ser). (Orig.). 1970. pap. 0.60 o.p. (ISBN 0-446-63202-3, 63-202). Paperback Lib.
Prisoner of Grace. Joyce Cary. (Grosset's universal library, UL125). 1962. Grosset & Dunlap.
Prisoner of Grace: A Novel. Joyce Cary. LC 78-3593. 1978. 9.95 (ISBN 0-89244-072-4). Queens House.
Prisoner of Grace: A Novel. 1st Ed. Joyce Cary. LC 52-7281. 1952. Harper.
Prisoner of Love. Barbara Cartland. LC 79-13513. 1980. 6.95 (ISBN 0-87272-080-2). Duron Books.
Prisoner of Love. Tr. from French by Richard Howard. Hubert Monteilhet. LC 65-22265. 3.50. S. &S.
Prisoner of Mademoiselle: A Love Story. Charles George Douglas Roberts. LC 4-26863. 1904. L. C. Page & Company.
Prisoner of Mother England. Douglas Hayes. LC 61-17187. 1961. Abelard-Schuman.
Prisoner of Ornith Farm. Frances Powell Case. LC 6-777508. 1906. C. Scribner's Sons.
Prisoner of Passion. Nancy John. 192p. 1981. pap. 1.50 (ISBN 0-671-57057-9). S&S.
Prisoner of Perote. A Tale of American Valor and Mexican Love. John E Tuel. 1848. F. Gleason.
Prisoner of Power. Arkadii Natanovich Strugatskii & Boris Natanovich Strugatskii. Tr. by Helen S. Jacobson. 1977. 9.95 o.s.i. (ISBN 0-02-615160-X). Macmillan.
Prisoner of the Devil. Michael Hardwick. 307p. 1981. pap. 5.95 (ISBN 0-86276-007-0). Proteus Pub NY.
Prisoner of the Queen. Alison Macleod. LC 72-9077. 1973. 5.95 (ISBN 0-395-14010-2). Houghton Mifflin.
Prisoner of the Sky. C. C. Macapp. LC 74-587. (Orig.). 1969. pap. 0.75 o.p. Lancer.
Prisoner of Tordesillas. 1st Ed. Lawrence L Schoonover. LC 59-733734. 1959. Little, Brown.
Prisoner of Zenda. Anthony Hope Hawkins. LC 61-132002. (Looking glass library, 25). 1961. Looking Glass Library; Distributed by Random House.
Prisoner of Zenda. Anthony Hope Hawkins. pap. 1.95x (ISBN 0-460-01637-7, Pub. by Evman England). Biblio Dist.
Prisoner of Zenda. Anthony Hope. lib. bdg. 16.95x (ISBN 0-89966-226-9). Buccaneer Bks.
Prisoner of Zenda. Anthony Hope. (O.s.i.). 1962. pap. 0.95 o.s.i. (ISBN 0-02-043710-2, Collier). Macmillan.
Prisoner of Zenda. Anthony Hope. Ed. by John C. Fago. (Now Age Illustrated IV Ser.). (Illus.). (gr. 4-12). 1978. text ed. 5.00 (ISBN 0-88301-330-4); pap. text ed. 1.95 (ISBN 0-88301-318-5); activity bk. 1.25 (ISBN 0-88301-342-8). Pendulum Pr.
Prisoner of Zenda. Anthony Hope. (Magnum Easy Eye Classic Ser). 1968. pap. 0.60 o.p. (13-432). Lancer.
Prisoner of Zenda: Abridgment Illustrated by Emil Weiss. Anthony Hope Hawkins. LC 60-8672. (World-famous book, 201). 1960. Hart Pub. Co.
Prisoner of Zenda and Rupert of Hentzau: Ruritainia Complete. Anthony Hope Hawkins & Anthony Hope. (Illus.). 1961. Dover Publications.
Prisoner of Zenda & Rupert of Hentzau. Anthony Hope. (Illus.). 7.95x (ISBN 0-460-00637-1, Evman). Biblio Dist.
Prisoner of Zenda: Being the History of Three Months in the Life of an English Gentleman. Hawkins, Anthony Hope. LC 64-9511. (Children's illustrated classics). 1962. Dent.
Prisoner of Zenda: Being the History of Three Months in the Life of an English Gentleman. Hawkins, Anthony Hope. LC 62-21797. 1962. Collier Books.
Prisoner of Zenda: Being the History of Three Months in the Life of an English Gentleman. Anthony Hope Hawkins. LC 7-12339. 1894. H. Holt and Company.
Prisoner of Zenda: Being the History of Three Months in the Life of an English Gentleman. Anthony Hope Hawkins. (Buckram series). 1896. H. Holt and Company.
Prisoner of Zenda: Being the History of Three Months in the Life of an English Gentleman. Anthony Hope Hawkins. LC 4-15314. 1898. H. Holt and Company.
Prisoner of Zenda: Being the History of Three Months in the Life of an English Gentleman. Anthony Hope Hawkins. LC 4-8621. 1899. The American News Company.
Prisoner of Zenda: Being the History of Three Months in the Life of an English Gentleman. Anthony Hope Hawkins. (Half-title: Author's edition. Works of Anthony Hope...). D. Appleton and Company.
Prisoner of Zenda: Being the History of Three Months in the Life of an English Gentleman. Anthony Hope Hawkins. LC 12-31380. 1909. H. Holt and Company.
Prisoner of Zenda: Being the History of Three Months in the Life of an English Gentleman. Anthony Hope Hawkins. LC 22-24755. Grosset & Dunlap.
Prisoner of Zhamanak. Lyon Sprague De Camp. 2.50 (ISBN 0-441-67937-4, Pub. by Ace Science Fiction). Ace Bks.
Prisoner Pleads 'Not Guilty.' Lee Thayer, pseud. LC 53-753241. (Red badge detective). 1953. Dodd, Mead.
Prisoner Who Sang. Johan Bojer. LC 24-26380. The Century Co.
Prisoners. Dorothy Bryant. LC 79-55170. (Orig.). 1980. 10.00 (ISBN 0-931688-04-3); pap. 6.00 (ISBN 0-931688-05-1). Ata Bks.
Prisoners. George G. Gilman, pseud. (Edge Ser.: No. 39). 192p. 1982. pap. 1.95 (ISBN 0-523-41450-1). Pinnacle Bks.
Prisoners. Aleksandr Isaevich Solzhenitsyn. LC 83-1651. 1983. 10.50 (ISBN 0-374-23739-5). Farrar, Straus, and Giroux.
Prisoners: A Novel. Ferenc Molnar. Tr. by Szebenyei, Joseph. LC 25-5962. The Bobbs-Merrill Company.
Prisoners All. Oskar Maria Graf. Tr. by Green, Margaret M. LC 28-19960. 1928. A. A. Knopf.
Prisoners All. Oskar Maria Graf & Green, Margaret Minna, 1886- Tr. LC 44-4114. 1943. O. M. Graf.
Prisoners and Captives. rev. and authorized ed. Hugh Stowell Scott. LC 99-5464. 1899. Dodd, Mead and Company.
Prisoners and Captives. Hugh Stowell Scott. LC 99-189942. 1899. R. F. Fenno & Company.
Prisoner's Base. Celia Fremlin, pseud. LC 67-18818. 1967. bds., 3.50. Lippincott.
Prisoner's Base: A Nero Wolfe Novel. Rex Stout. LC 52-13719. 1952. Viking Press.
Prisoner's Face: And Other Tales. Ella Waldron Winston. LC 39-32042. The Valiant Printing Company.
Prisoners, Fast Bound in Misery and Iron. Mary Cholmondeley. 1906. Dodd, Mead & Company.
Prisoner's Friend. Paul Winterton. LC 62-11226. 1962. Harper.
Prisoners in Paradise. Wal Watkins. LC 73-163288. 1972. 1.65 (ISBN 0-7260-0000-0). Gold Star Publications.
Prisoners in the Riff: A Novel. 1st Ed. Garet Fairchild. LC 56-12284. 1956. Exposition Press.
Prisoners of Chance: The Story of What Befell Geoffrey Benteen, Borderman, Through His Love of a Lady of France. Randall Parrish. 1908. A. C. McClurg & Co.
Prisoners of Combine D. Len Giovannitti. LC 57-10420. 1957. Holt.
Prisoners of Conscience. Amelia Edith Huddleston Barr. LC 6-7977. 1897. The Century Co.
Prisoners of Fate. Lillian R Fuller. LC 31-10520. Sears Publishing Company, Inc.
Prisoners of Fortune: A Tale of the Massachusetts Bay Colony. Ruel Perley Smith. 1907. L. C. Page & Company.
Prisoners of Hartling. John Davys Beresford. LC 22-3895.
Prisoners of Hope: A Tale of Colonial Virginia. Mary Johnston. LC 98-498. 1898. Houghton, Mifflin and Company.
Prisoners of Hope: A Tale of Colonial Virginia. Mary Johnston. LC 7-10800. 1899. Houghton, Mifflin and Company.
Prisoners of Hope: A Tale of Colonial Virginia. Mary Johnston. LC 20-18833. 1900. Houghton, Mifflin and Company.
Prisoners of Hope: A Tale of Colonial Virginia. Mary Johnston. LC 24-279646. Grosset & Dunlap.
Prisoners of Malville Hall. Dorothy Daniels. (Warner paperback library gothic). 1973. (pbk.) 0.95. Warner Paperback Lib.
Prisoners of Power. Arkady Strugatsky & Arkadii Natanovich Strugatskii. 1978. pap. 2.45 o.s.i. (ISBN 0-02-025580-2, Collier). Macmillan.
Prisoners of Quai Dong. Victor Kolpacoff. LC 67-25937. (Signet bk., T3500). 1968. New Amer. Lib.
Prisoners of St. Lazare. Ed. by Pauline De Grandpre. Tr. by McCarthy, E. M. LC 6-27664. 1872. D. Appleton & Company.
Prisoners of September. Leon Garfield. LC 74-32285. 1975. 8.95 (ISBN 0-670-57843-6). Viking Press.
Prisoners of the Forest. Hugh Charles Clifford. LC 29-27485. 1929. Harper & Brothers.
Prisoners of the Sea: A Romance of the Seventeenth Century. Florence Morse Kingsley. 1897. D. McKay.
Prisoners of the Stars: The Collected Fiction of Isaac Asimov, Vol. 2. Isaac Asimov. LC 77-25576. 1979. 12.95 (ISBN 0-385-13270-0). Doubleday.
Prisoners of This World: Stories. Bernard Kaplan. LC 70-106298. 1970. 5.95. Grossman.
Prisoners of War: A Reminiscence of the Rebellion. Archibald McCowan. LC 1-23653. The Abbey Press.
Prisoners Under the Sun. Norbert Bauer. Tr. by Dixey, Annie Coath. LC 31-30508. 1832. Frederick A. Stokes Company.
Prisoner's Wife. Jack Holland. LC 81-3208. 8.95 (ISBN 0-396-07988-1). Dodd, Mead.
Prisoners' Years. Isabel Constance Clarke. LC 12-228135. 1917. Benziger Brothers.
Prisoners. 1st Ed. Evans Harrington. LC 55-10709. 1956. Harper.
Prisons. Mary Lee Settle. LC 73-78614. (Illus.). 1973. 6.95 (ISBN 0-399-11164-6). Putnam.
Prisons of Air. Moncure Daniel Conway. LC 6-28054. (American authors' series, no. 35). J. W. Lovell Company.
Pritcher Mass. Gordon R Dickson. LC 72-76151. (Doubleday science fiction). 1972. 4.95 (ISBN 0-385-05669-9). Doubleday.
Private. Frank Daniel Gilroy. LC 79-124833. (Illus.). 1970. Harcourt Brace Jovanovich.
Private Adventure of Captain Shaw. Edith Foley Shay & Dos Passos, Katharine (Smith) LC 45-2272. 1945. Houghton Mifflin Company.
Private and Bizarre. C S Vanek. LC 78-28510. (Traveller's companion series, TC-503). 1971. 1.95. Traveller's Companion.
Private Angelo. Eric Robert Russell Linklater. LC 46-8554. 1946. The Macmillan Company.
Private Angelo Ferraro, U.S.N.G. Mary Agnes Sullivan. LC 19-6407. 1919. Pittsburgh Printing Company.
Private Anger: And Flight and Pursuit. Frank O'Rourke. LC 63-17682. 1963. W. Morrow.
Private Clinic. Jamie O'Crossen. 1975. (pbk.) 1.50 (ISBN 0-523-00575-X). Pinnacle Books.
Private Companion. James Noble Gifford. LC 39-207282. Phoenix Press.
Private Cosmos. Philip Jose Farmer. 288p. 1981. pap. 2.50 (ISBN 0-441-67954-4). Ace Bks.
Private Demons. Macdonald Harris. LC 61-11953. 1961. Houghton Mifflin.
Private Detective, No. 39: Or, The Mysterious Client. John W Postgate. (peerless series, no. 59). 1892. J. S. Ogilvie.
Private Detective: The Marvelous Career of a Notorious Criminal. John D Shea. (Pinkerton detective series, v. 32). 1889. Laird & Lee.
Private Duty. Faith Cuthrell Baldwin, pseud. 1973. (pbk.) 0.95. Warner Paperback Library.
Private Duty. Faith Baldwin Cuthrell. LC 36-9857. Farrar & Rinehart, Incorporated.
Private Enterprise. Angela Mackail Thirkell. LC 48-513785. 1948. A. A. Knopf.
Private Eye. Cleve Franklin Adams. LC 42-21434. 1942. Reynal & Hitchcock.
Private Face of Murder: By John and Emery Bonett. Pseud. 1st Ed. in the U.S.A. John Coulson & Felicity Winifred Carter. LC 66-17400. 3.50. Pub. for the Crime Club by Doubleday.
Private Gaspard: A Soldier of France. Rene Benjamin. Tr. by Fougner, Selmer. LC 16-140501. 1916. Brentano's.
Private Gollantz. Naomi Ellington Jacob. LC 43-10503. 1943. Hutchinson & Co., Ltd.
Private Hell. H. G. Gunther. (Gunther Romance Ser.: No. 5). 208p. (Orig.). 1981. pap. 1.95 (ISBN 0-515-05677-4). Jove Pubns.
Private Hospital. Margaret Littell. LC 39-120002. 1939. Gramercy Publishing Co.
Private I. Jimmy Sangster. 1968. pap. 0.60 o.p. (73-741). Lancer.
Private I: A Novel. Jimmy Sangster. LC 67-15459. 1967. 4.50. Norton.
Private I, and Other Stories. Phyllis Reynolds Naylor. LC 78-83676. (Illus.). 1969. 1.75. Fortress Press.
Private Inquiries: A Novel. Dorothy Johnson. LC 32-104505. 1932. Longmans, Green and Co.
Private Interests. Nigel Balchin. LC 53-7075. 1953. Houghton Mifflin.
Private Investigation. Karl Alexander. LC 80-16647. 9.95 (ISBN 0-440-06834-7). Delacorte Press.
Private Killing. James Walker Benet. LC 49-728313. 1949. Harper.
Private Lessons. Ann Lawrence. LC 33-23680. 1933. W. Godwin, Inc.
Private Letters from Phyllis to Marie: Or, The Art of Child Love; or, The Adventures and Experiences of a Little Girl Showing How Pretty Little Maidens Indulge Those Secret Passions, Alone and with Others, Which but Too Often Lead to Their Seduction at an Early Age. Phyllis Norroy. LC 71-149790. (Zebra books, Z-1065-X). 1971. 1.75. Grove Press.
Private Letters of Luke. Roger Bradshaigh Lloyd. LC 57-120352. 1958. Channel Press.
Private Lies. Mae Klein Cooper. LC 79-1134. 8.95 (ISBN 0-671-24738-7). Simon and Schuster.
Private Lies. Mae Klein Cooper. 1980. 2.25. Popular Library.
Private Life. large print ed. Cynthia Propper Seton. LC 82-13987. 1983. 12.95 (ISBN 0-89340-536-1). J. Curley.
Private Life see Altar of the Dead.
Private Life: A Novel. Cynthia Propper Seton. LC 81-11335. 10.95 (ISBN 0-393-01515-7). Norton.
Private Life, Lord Beaupre, The Visits. Henry James. LC 7-7438. 1893. Harper & Brothers.
Private Life of Doctor Kelso: A Novel. Joseph Noel. LC 44-53451. 1944. Gansevoort Square Pub. Co., Reg.
Private Life of Florence Nightingale. Gordon Ostlere. LC 78-56342. 1978. 8.95 (ISBN 0-689-10929-6). Atheneum.
Private Life of Helen of Troy. John Erskine. LC 25-21590. The Bobbs-Merrill Company.
Private Life of Helen of Troy. 20th anniversary ed. John Erskine. LC 47-3783. 1947. The Bobbs-Merrill Company.

Private Life of Henry Perkins. John Murray Reynolds. LC 47-1833. 1947. Thomas Y.Crowell Company.
Private Life of Mona Lisa. Pierre La Mure. LC 76-16811. 8.95 (ISBN 0-316-51300-8). Little, Brown.
Private Matter. Mary R. Myers. (Love & Life Romance Ser.). 176p. (Orig.). 1983. pap. 1.75 (ISBN 0-345-30845-X). Ballantine.
Private Matter: Or, An Adventurer's Narrative. Louis Paul Kirby. (On cover: Nelson's star library, no. 1). 1890. A. F. Nelson Publishing Company.
Private Memoirs and Confessions of a Justified Sinner. James Hogg. LC 75-14882. (Norton library, N515). (Illus.). 1970. 1.85. Norton.
Private Memoirs and Confessions of a Justified Sinner. With an Introd. by Andre Gide. James Hogg. LC 59-6253. 1959. Grove Press.
Private Memoirs and Confessions of a Justified Sinner: Written by Himself, with a Detail of Curious Traditionary Facts and Other Evidence by the Editor. James Hogg. Ed. by John Carey. LC 74-382669. (Oxford English novels). (Illus.). 1969. Oxford U.P.
Private Office. Peggy Gaddis, pseud. LC 40-8136. Phoenix Press.
Private Office. Gail Jordan. LC 40-8136. Phoenix Press.
Private Papers of Henry Ryecroft. George Robert Gissing. LC 3-17566. 1903. E. P. Dutton & Co.
Private Papers of Henry Ryecroft. George Robert Gissing. (wayfarer's library). 1915. E. P. Dutton & Co.
Private Papers of Henry Ryecroft. George Robert Gissing. (Half-title: Everyman's library, ed. by Ernest Rhys. Fiction). 1927. E. P. Dutton & Co.
Private Parlor. Peggy Gaddis. LC 46-18487. 1946. Phoenix Press.
Private Parts in Public Places. Robin Cook. LC 69-14957. 1969. 4.95. Atheneum.
Private Party. William Ard. LC 53-8113. (Murray Hill mystery). 1953. Rinehart.
Private Passion. Carlotta Baker. LC 36-195598. Phoenix Press.
Private Passion. Leona Slottman. LC 36-19559. 1936. Phoenix Press.
Private Pavilion. James William MacQueen. LC 35-34918. 1935. Pub. for the Crime Club, Inc. by Doubleday, Doran & Company, Inc.
Private Pieces. Tom Johnson. LC 76-14367. 1976. pap. 2.95 (ISBN 0-938690-01-9). Two Eighteen.
Private Practice. Matthew Benn. LC 74-16631. 1975. 7.95 (ISBN 0-698-10641-5). Coward, McCann & Geoghegan.
Private Practice. Matthew Benn. (Berkley Medallion Book). 1976. 1.75 (ISBN 0-425-03166-7). Berkley.
Private Practice. Abraham Loew Furman. LC 33-776. 1933. The Macaulay Company.
Private Practice. Nolan Jagger. 1972. pap. 1.95 o.s.i. (V1094T, Venus). Grove.
Private Practice. Linda Pubreuil. 1976. pap. 1.50 o.p. (LB366DK, Leisure Bks). Nordon Pubns.
Private Practice of Michael Shayne. Davis Dresser. LC 40-4981. H. Holt and Company.
Private Practices. Linda Wolfe. LC 79-17100. 9.95 (ISBN 0-671-22858-7). Simon and Schuster.
Private Props. Gertrude Ethel Mallette. LC 37-17352. 1937. Doubleday, Doran & Company, Inc.
Private Reports: A Novel. Katharine Roberts. LC 43-11849. 1943. Doubleday, Doran and Company, Inc.
Private Revolt of Merton Burton: A Story for Children to Read to Their Parents. Samuel N Antupit. LC 57-22170.
Private Secretary. Alan Brener Schultz. LC 29-14909. 1929. Simon and Schuster.
Private Secretary. A Novel. George Tomkyns Chesney. LC 27-7346. (Seaside library, v. 53, no. 1084). 1881. G. Munro.
Private Sector. Joseph Hone. 1973. (pbk) 1.25. New American Lib.
Private Sector. Joseph Hone. LC 70-179843. 1972. 7.95 (ISBN 0-525-18469-4). E. P. Dutton.
Private Sector. Jeff Millar. LC 79-17493. 9.95 (ISBN 0-8037-6965-2). Dial Press.
Private Sins. Millicent Kent. LC 36-6317. Godwin.
Private Stair. David Culberson Loughlin. LC 50-13803. 1950. Harper.
Private T. Pigeon's Tale. Jaimy Gordon. (Story Ser.: No. 5). (Illus.). 36p. 1979. signed 8.00 (ISBN 0-914232-19-3); pap. 2.50 (ISBN 0-914232-18-5). McPherson & Co.
Private Tinker: And Other Stories. Henrietta Eliza Vaughan Stannard. LC 12-14353. F. A. Stokes Company.
Private Truce. Anthony Lawman. 1982. pap. 3.25 (ISBN 0-440-17321-3). Dell.
Private Truce. Anthony Lawman. 1981. 12.95 o.p. (ISBN 0-671-25408-1). S&S.
Private Truce: A Novel. Tony Lawman. LC 80-19283. (Illus.). 12.95 (ISBN 0-671-25408-1). Simon and Schuster.
Private Tutor. Gamaliel Bradford. LC 4-25103. 1904. Houghton, Mifflin and Company.
Private Undertaking. Hildegarde Tolman Teilhet. LC 52-11702. 1952. Coward-McCann.
Private Undre Luneville of Harlem. 131p. 1976. pap. 3.95 o.p. E L Harris.
Private Vendetta. Roderick Grant. 1980. pap. 2.25 (ISBN 0-425-04506-4). Berkley Pub.
Private Vendetta: A Novel of Suspense. Roderick Grant. LC 78-14574. 8.95 (ISBN 0-684-15801-9). Scribner.
Private View. Beryl Cook. 64p. (Orig.). 1981. pap. 6.95 (ISBN 0-14-005654-8). Penguin.
Private War: Being the Truth About Gordon Traill; His Personal Statement. Louis Joseph Vance. LC 6-14748. 1906. D. Appleton and Company.
Private War of Dr. Yamada. Lee Ruttle. LC 77-4577. 1978. 9.95 (ISBN 0-913374-79-2). San Francisco Book Co.
Private Weapon. Franz T Hansell. LC 75-28598. (Traveller's companion series, TC-501). 1971. 1.95. Traveller's Companion, Inc.
Private Weapon. Joe Stonebridge. pap. 1.95 o.s.i. (TC-501, Travellers Comp). Olympia.
Private Wire to Washington: The Inside Story of the Great Long Island Spy Mystery That Baffled the Secret Service. Harold MacGrath. LC 19-3996. 1919. Harper & Brothers.
Private World of Cully Powers. 1st Ed. George Bluestone. LC 60-10665. 1960. Doubleday.
Private World of Jean Giono. W. D Redfern. LC 67-20396. 1967. Duke University Press.
Private Worlds. Phyllis Bottome. LC 34-68359. 1934. Houghton Mifflin Company.
Private Worlds. Sarah Gainham. LC 73-117258. 1971. 6.95 (ISBN 0-03-085062-2). Holt, Rinehart and Winston.
Private Wound. Nicholas Blake. LC 68-15980. 224p. 1981. pap. 2.25i (ISBN 0-06-080531-5, P 531, PL). Har-Row.
Privateer. Elizabeth Mackintosh. LC 52-12235. 1952. Macmillan.
Privateer. Jon Williams. (Orig.). 1981. pap. 2.75 (ISBN 0-440-16811-2). Dell.
Privateer, a Tale ... LC 7-30089. 1821. Hickman and Hazzard.
Privateers. Henry Brereton Marriott Watson. LC 7-2061. 1907. Doubleday, Page & Company.
Privateersman. Frederick Marryat. Ed. by Finger, Charles J. (Pocket series, no. 483, ed. by E. Haldeman-Julius). Haldeman-Julius Company.
Privateersman: Adventures by Sea and Land, and Savage Life, One Hundred Years Ago. Frederick Marryat. LC 42-29445. G. Routledge and Sons.
Privateersman. Adventures by Sea and Land, in Civil and Savage Life, One Hundred Years Ago. Frederick Marryat. LC 7-17569. (On cover: Lovell's library, v. 5, no. 212). J. W. Lovell Company.
Privateersman. Adventures by Sea and Land, in Civil and Savage Life, One Hundred Years Ago. Frederick Marryat. LC 7-24679. (On cover: Seaside library. Pocket ed. no. 88). G. Munro.
Privateersman's Legacy. Le Pignon Maudit. Fortune Du Boisgobey & Kendall, Laura E., Tr. (Seaside library, v. 72, no. 1465). G. Munro.
Privet Hedge. Annie Edith Foster Jameson. LC 22-7755. 1.75. George H. Doran Company.
Privilege: A Novel of the Transition. Michael Sadleir. LC 21-18415. G. P. Putnam's Sons.
Privileged Character. Jean Laborde. LC 63-8737. 1963. Doubleday.
Prize. Stanley R Reilly. LC 79-13143. (Spire books). 2.25 (ISBN 0-8007-8371-9). Revell.
Prize. Irving Wallace. pap. 2.95 (ISBN 0-451-09455-7, E9455, Sig). NAL.
Prize. Irving Wallace. (O.s.i.). 1962. 5.95 o.s.i. (ISBN 0-671-59890-2). S&S.
Prize Baby. Victor Norman. LC 34-21302. The Christopher Publishing House.
Prize Essay: And The Mitherless Bairn, Originally Published in the Missouri Republican. Augusta R Nelson. LC 8-308893. 1857. G. Knapp & Co.
Prize Loser: With the Theory of the Ascendency of Man. Harry Ellsworth Winters. LC 32-10339. 1932. Meador Publishing Co.
Prize Master. 1st Ed. Harvey Haislip. LC 59-6358. 1959. Doubleday.
Prize of Fear. Anne Nash. (Orig.). 1980. pap. 1.75 (ISBN 0-8439-8006-0, Tiara Bks). Nordon Pubns.
Prize Paradise. Oliver Pritchett. LC 79-3114. 1979. 8.95 (ISBN 0-312-64720-4). St. Martin's Press.
Prize Science Fiction. 1st-Ed. Ed. by Donald A. Wollheim. LC 53-1807. McBride.
Prize Stories from Collier's. Collier's, The National Weekly. LC 17-47. (Half-title: The Collier classics; literature, science, history, contemporary belles-letters, ed. by W. A. Nilson). P. F. Collier & Son.
Prize Stories from Latin America: Winners of the Life on Espanol Literary Contest. LC 62-15886. 1968. Doubleday.
Prize Stories, Nineteen Eighty: The O. Henry Awards. Ed. by William Miller Abrahams. LC 21-9372. 456p. 1980. 12.95 o.p. (ISBN 0-385-15106-3). Doubleday.
Prize Stories of the Seventies from O. Henry Awards. Ed. by William Miller Abrahams. LC 80-22790. 408p. 1981. 12.95 (ISBN 0-385-17158-7). Doubleday.
Prize Stories: The O. Henry Awards. Doubleday.
Prize Stories. The O. Henry Awards. 1919- Ed. by Williams, Blanche Colton & Hansen, Harry. Society of Arts and Sciences, New York. LC 21-9372. Doubleday Etc.
Prize Stories 1960: The O'Henry Awards. Ed. by Blanche Colton Williams et al. LC 21-9372. 3.95. Doubleday.
Prize Stories, 1961: The O. Henry Awards. Ed. by Richard Poirier. Ed. by Richard Poirier. LC 21-9372. 3.95. Doubleday.
Prize Stories, 1979: The O. Henry Awards. Doubleday.
Prize to the Hardy. Alice Ames Winter. 1905. The Bobbs-Merrill Company.
Prize-Winning Stories from China (1978-1979) Liu Xinwu & Wang Meng. (Illus.). 535p. 1981. pap. 9.95 (ISBN 0-8351-1032-X). China Bks.
Prized Possession. Debbie Hayes. 192p. (Orig.). Date not set. pap. cancelled o.p. (ISBN 0-505-51828-7). Tower Bks.
Prizzi's Honor. Richard Condon. LC 81-17366. 13.95 (ISBN 0-698-11143-5). Coward, McCann & Geoghegan.
Pro. Gordon R Dickson. (Ace Book.). (Illus.). 1978. 1.95 (ISBN 0-441-68023-2). Ace Books.
Pro. Bob Packard. (Leisure books). 2.25 (ISBN 0-8439-0647-2). Nordon Pubns.
Pro-Am Murders. Patrick Cake, pseud. LC 78-70580. (Illus.). 1979. 8.95. Proteus Press.
Pro Patria. Max Pemberton. LC 1-3499. 1901. Dodd, Mead & Company.
Pro Patria. Ramon Jose Sender & Cleugh, James, Tr. LC 35-16592. 1935. Houghton Mifflin Company.
Pro Quarterback. Donal Hamilton Haines. LC 40-31626. Farrar & Rinehart, Incorporated.
Probability: A Novel. L. Neil Smith. ("A Del Rey Book"). 2.25. Ballantine Books.
Probability Corner. Walt Richmond & Leigh Richmond. 1977. 1.50 (ISBN 0-441-37088-8). Ace Books.
Probability Factor. Walter Kempley. LC 78-139535. 1972. 5.95 (ISBN 0-8415-0094-0). Saturday Review Press.
Probability Man. Brian N. Ball. (Science Fiction Ser.). 176p. (Orig.). 1972. pap. 0.95 o.p. (UQ1003). DAW Bks.
Probability Pad. T. A. Waters. (Orig.). 1970. pap. 0.75 o.p. (T2206). Pyramid Pubns.
Probation... Jessie Fothergill. (seaside library. no. 661). 1879. G. Munro.
Probation. Maria Longworth Storer. LC 16-3307. 1916. B. Herder.
Probation: A Novel. Jessie Fothergill. LC 4-16525. R. F. Fenno & Company.
Probationer. Mary Denny Phillips. LC 32-23425. 1932. W. Godwin, Inc.
Probationer and Other Stories. Herman Whitaker. LC 5-69451. 1905. Harper & Brothers.
Problem. Anna Adelia Robertson. LC 13-6900. 1.25. R. G. Badger.
Problem: A Military Novel. F. Grant Gilmore. LC 78-76109. (Illus.). 1969. McGrath Pub. Co.
Problem," A Military Novel. F. Grant Gilmore. LC 15-20988. 0.75. Press of H. Conolly Co.
Problem Girl. Thomas Stone. Phoenix Press.
Problem Girl. Florence Stonebraker. LC 40-4506. 1940. Phoenix Press.
Problem Heart. By Norma Newcomb Pseud. William Arthur Neubauer. LC 56-116983. 1956. Arcadia House.
Problem in Angels. Leonard Holton, pseud. Orig. Title: Father Bredder Mystery Story. 1970. 4.50 o.p. (ISBN 0-396-06044-7). Dodd.
Problem in Angels: A Father Bredder Mystery Novel. Leonard Patrick O'Connor Wibberley. LC 73-105291. (Red badge novel of suspense). 1970. 4.50. Dodd, Mead.
Problem in Prague. Noah Webster. LC 81-43398. 1982. 10.95 (ISBN 0-385-17944-8). Published for the Crime Club by Doubleday.
Problem Island. Francis Clement Kelley. LC 37-3825. 1937. St. Anthony Guild Press.
Problem of the Green Capsule. John Dickson Carr. (O.s.i.). 224p. 1976. pap. 1.50 o.s.i. (AD1565, Award). Univ Pub & Dist.
Problem of the Green Capsule. John Dickson Carr. 1976. (pbk.) 1.50. Award Books.
Problem of the Green Capsule: Being: the Psychologists' Murder Case. John Dickson Carr. LC 39-12586. 1939. Harper & Brothers.
Problem of the Wire Cage. [New York and London: Harper & Brothers. John Dickson Carr. LC 39-30765. 1939. Harper & Borthers.
Problem Wife. Louise Holmes. LC 42-14122. 1942. Arcadia House, Inc.
Problematic Characters: A Novel. author's ed. Friedrich Spielhagen. LC 76-28509. 1976. 17.00. H. Fertig.
Problematic Characters: A Novel. author's ed.... ed. Friedrich Spielhagen. Tr. by Maximilian Schele De Vere. LC 3-4380. 1869. Leypoldt & Holt.
Problematic Characters: A Novel. author's ed.... ed. Friedrich Spielhagen. Tr. by Maximilian Schele De Vere. 1870. Leypoldt & Holt.
Problems and Other Stories. John Updike. LC 79-1480. 1979. 10.00 (ISBN 0-394-50705-3). Knopf: Distributed by Random House.
Problems of Dr. A. Elizabeth Seifert. LC 79-11017. 7.95 (ISBN 0-396-07686-6). Dodd, Mead.
Problems of Dr. A. Elizabeth Seifert. LC 80-27324. 1981. 12.50 (ISBN 0-89340-296-6). J. Curley & Associates.
Problems of Love. Barbara Cartland. LC 78-992912. 1978. 6.95 (ISBN 0-87272-037-3, Duron Bks). Brodart.
Procane Chronicle. Oliver Bleeck. 1972. 5.95 o.p. (ISBN 0-688-00118-1). Morrow.
Procane Chronicle. Oliver Bleeck. LC 82-48808. 224p. 1983. pap. 2.84i (ISBN 0-06-080647-8, P 647, PL). Har-Row.
Procane Chronicle. Ross Thomas. 1973. (pbk.) 1.25 (ISBN 0-671-78319-X). Pocket Books.
Procane Chronicle. Ross Thomas. LC 74-163447. 1972. 5.95. Morrow.
Proceed at Will. Novel. Burke Wilkinson. LC 48-1892. 1948. Little, Brown.
Proceed, Sergeant Lamb. Robert Graves. LC 41-17321. Random House.
Proceed to Judgement. Sara Woods, pseud. LC 79-22854. 1980. 8.95 (ISBN 0-312-64776-X). St. Martin's Press.
Proceed to Judgment. Sara Woods, pseud. 1979. 8.95 o.p. (ISBN 0-312-64776-X). St Martin.
Process. Brion Gysin. LC 69-12207. 1969. 5.95 o.p. Doubleday.
Process: A Novel. Brion Gysin. LC 69-12207. 1969. 5.95. Doubleday.
Process Server & Other Stories. Dorothy LaPell. 3.95 o.p. Vantage.
Process Server and Other Stories. first ed. Dorothy LaPell. 1973. 3.95 (ISBN 0-533-00838-7). Vantage Press.
Procession. Fannie Hurst. LC 29-1806. 1929. Harper & Brothers.
Procession Moves on. 1st Ed. Mattie Abney Hartzog. LC 57-8224. 1957. Pageant Press.
Procession of Life: A Novel. Horace Annesley Vachell. LC 99-1003. 1899. D. Appleton and Company.
Procession of Lovers. Lloyd R. Morris. LC 29-5700. Harcourt, Brace and Company.
Procession of the Damned. Wilson Tucker. LC 65-106870. 3.50. Pub. for Crime Club by Doubleday.
Proclaiming Harmony. William O. Hennessey. LC 81-18143. (Michigan Papers in Chinese Studies; No. 41). 1981. 6.00 (ISBN 0-89264-041-3). Center for Chinese Studies, University of Michigan.
Prodical Daughter. Mary Nantz McCrae Culter. 1908. Monfort & Co.
Prodical Virgin. Homer G. Thomas. pap. 1.75 o.p. (6001). Brandon.
Prodigal. Abboth. LC 20-19242. Eerdmans-Sevensma Co.
Prodigal. Mary Hallock Foote. LC 6627. 1900. Houghton, Mifflin and Company.
Prodigal Bandit. Randolph Hale. LC 40-30884. Dodge Publishing Company.
Prodigal Brother. McCready Huston. LC 51-11209. 1952-1951. Lippincott.
Prodigal: By Mary Wallace Brooks. Mary Wallace Brooks. LC 7-22410. 1907. R. G. Badger.
Prodigal Daughter. Jeffrey Archer. 1982. 15.95 (ISBN 0-671-42229-4, Linden Pr). S&S.
Prodigal Daughter. Jeffrey Archer. (General Ser.). 1983. lib. bdg. 21.50 (ISBN 0-8161-3499-5, Large Print Bks). G K Hall.
Prodigal Daughter. A Story of Female Prison Life. Eustace Clare Grenville Murray. (Seaside library. v. 43, no. 877). 1880. G. Munro.
Prodigal Daughters. Joseph Hocking. LC 21-21366. Fleming H. Revell Company.
Prodigal Duke. Richard Hoffmann. LC 33-152421. Farrar & Rinehart, Incorporated.
Prodigal Father. George Steele Bearden. LC 21-871. 1920. The Stratford Company.
Prodigal Father. Joseph Storer Clouston. LC 9-25631. 1909. 1.50. The Century Co.
Prodigal Father. Una Troy. LC 64-11088. 1965. Dutton.
Prodigal Genius: The Life and Times of Honore De Balzac. Noel Bertram Gerson. LC 78-175376. (Illus.). 1972. 8.95. Doubleday.
Prodigal Girl. Grace Livingston Hill. LC 29-24589. 1929. J. B. Lippincott Company.
Prodigal Gunfighter. Lewis B Patten. (Signet book). 1.25. New American Library.
Prodigal Heart. Susan Ertz. LC 50-4868. 1950. Harper.
Prodigal in Love: A Novel. Emma Wolf. LC 8-37121. 1894. Harper & Brothers.

TITLE INDEX PROLOGUE, THE KNIGHT'S TALE

Prodigal Judge. Vaughan Kester. LC 11-477472. The Bobbs-Merrill Company.
Prodigal Judge. Vaughan Kester. LC 24-25307. 1913. Grosset & Dunlap.
Prodigal Lover. Dorothy Yost. LC 37-4386. The Greystone Press.
Prodigal Moll. Sara Christy. LC 37-529923. J. H. Hopkins & Sons, Inc.
Prodigal Nurse. Teresa Hyde Phillips. LC 37-28292. J. B. Lippincott Company.
Prodigal Parents. Sinclair Lewis. LC 39-11083. (A Mercury book, no. 17). The American Mercury, Inc.
Prodigal Parents: A Novel. Sinclair Lewis. LC 38-27043. 1938. Doubleday, Doran & Company, Inc.
Prodigal Pedagogue: A Novel. Terrel Howard Bell. LC 55-9395. 1955. Exposition Press.
Prodigal Pro Tem. Frederick Orin Bartlett. LC 10-26226. 1.50. Small, Maynard and Company.
Prodigal Returns. by roy l. smith... ed. Harold Garnet Black. LC 41-20857. Fleming H. Revel Company.
Prodigal Son. Hall Caine. LC 4-31325. 1904. D. Appleton and Company.
Prodigal Village. Irving Bacheller. LC 23-4361. Grosset & Dunlap.
Prodigal Village: A Christmas Tale. Irving Bacheller. LC 20-21481. The Bobbs-Merrill Company.
Prodigal Virgin. Homer G. Thomas. pap. 1.95 o.p. (V1059T, Venus). Grove.
Prodigal Women. Nancy Hale. LC 42-21901. 1942. C. Scribner's Sons.
Prodigal. 1st Ed. Josephine Lawrence. LC 57-100664. 1957. Harcourt, Brace.
Prodigals: and Their Inheritance. Margaret Oliphant Wilson Oliphant. (On cover: Seaside library. Pocket ed., no. 321). 1885. G. Munro.
Prodigal's Daughter: And Other Tales. Lelia Hardin Bugg. LC 6-19665. 1898. Benziger Brothers.
Prodigals of Monte Carlo. Edward Phillips Oppenheim. LC 26-12242. 1926. Little, Brown, and Company.
Prodigious Adventures of Tartarin of Tarascon. Alphonse Daudet. Tr. by Minot, Robert S. LC 6-33039. (On cover: Lovell's library. v. 9, no. 478). J. W. Lovell Company.
Prodigious Adventures of Tartarin of Tarascon. by robert s. minot. ed. Alphonse Daudet & Minot, Robert S. LC 12-19589. 1880. Lee and Shepard.
Prodigious Fool. John Calvin Wallis. LC 8-33263. 1881. J. C. Lippincott & Co.
Prodigious Hickey: A Lawrenceville Story. Owen McMahon Johnson. LC 11-9943. 1910. 1.50. The Baker and Taylor Company.
Prodigy. M. Jay Livingston. LC 78-17370. 8.95 (ISBN 0-698-10926-0). Coward, McCann & Geoghegan.
Prodigy. Pepita Riera. LC 56-8402. 1956. Pageant Press.
Producer. Edward Seaman. LC 77-185422. (Venus library). 1972. 1.95. Grove Press.
Producer: A Novel. Richard Brooks. LC 51-7129. 1951. Simon and Schuster.
Product of the Mills: A Romance. Thomas Littlefield Marble. LC 35-19686. B. Humphries, Inc.
Production. Daniel Broun. 1971. pap. 1.25 o.p. (ISBN 0-446-66581-9, 66-581). Paperback Lib.
Production: A Novel of the Broadway Theater. Daniel Broun. LC 75-103434. 1970. 6.95. Dial Press.
Productions of Time. John Brunner. (Science Fiction Ser.). 1977. pap. 1.50 o.p. (ISBN 0-87997-329-3, UW1329). DAW Bks.
Prof. Slagg, of London. Dwight Edwards Marvin. Broadway Publishing Company.
Profane. William Arthur Neubauer. LC 48-142687. 1947. Phoenix Press.
Profane Earth. Holger Cahill. LC 27-194097. The Macaulay Company.
Profane Junction. Leslie Turner White. LC 58-10201. 1958. W. Morrow.
Profession. Albert Mol. (O.s.i.). (Orig.). 1970. pap. 0.75 o.s.i. (A562, Award). Univ Pub & Dist.
Profession of Marie Simone. Beth Brown. 1968. pap. 0.60 o.p. (B60-089). Belmont-Tower.
Professional. James David Buchanan. 1974. (pbk.) 1.25 (ISBN 0-523-00330-7). Pinnacle Books.
Professional. James David Buchanan. LC 72-77936. 1972. 5.95 (ISBN 0-698-10477-3). Coward, McCann & Geoghegan.
Professional. Joseph Chadwick. (O.s.i.). 1972. pap. 0.75 o.s.i. (BT50240). Belmont-Tower.
Professional. Edwin Fadiman. LC 73-84052. 1973. 6.95 (ISBN 0-679-50406-0). McKay Co.
Professional Aunt. Mary C. E Wemyss. LC 10-35337. 1910. Houghton Mifflin Company.
Professional Escort. Wright Williams. LC 40-654967. Phoenix Press.
Professional Guest. William A Garrett. LC 28-214222. 1928. D. Appleton & Company.
Professional Hero. Maysie Greig. LC 43-7892. 1943. Doubleday, Doran & Company, Inc.
Professional Lover. Maysie Greig. LC 34-215. 1933. Doubleday, Doran & Co., Inc.
Professional Lover. Maysie Greig. LC 43-18242. 1943. Triangle Books.
Professional Lover. By Gyp. Pseud.... Tr. by Mrs. Edward Lees Coffey. Sibylle Gabrielle Marie Antoinette De Riquetti De Mirabeau Martel De Janville. Tr. by Coffey, Edward Lees. LC 7-24382. 1896. F. T. Neely.
Professional Model. Charles Stanley Strong. LC 40-12361. Phoenix Press.
Professional Passion. Leona Slottman. LC 47-19149. 1947. Phoenix Press.
Professional Prince. Edgar Jepson. LC 17-3154. 1917. 1.00. P. R. Reynolds.
Professional Virgin. Frank Owen. LC 31-18066. The Lantern Press, Inc.
Professional. 1st Ed. Wilfred Charles Heinz. LC 57-11798. 1958. Harper.
Professionals. Frank O'Rourke. 1982. pap. 1.95 (ISBN 0-451-11352-7, AE1352, Sig). NAL.
Professionals. Frank O'Rourke. (O.s.i.). 192p. (Orig.). 1974. pap. 0.95 o.s.i. (AN1339, Award). Univ Pub & Dist.
Professionals: A Novel. Derwent May. LC 68-25735. 1968. 4.95. D. White.
Professor. Charlotte Bronte. (World's classics, 78). 1959. Oxford University Press.
Professor. Charlotte Bronte. LC 73-3131. (Bronte, Charlotte, 1816-1855. Life & Works of the Sisters Bronte: Vol. 4). (Illus.). 1973. 25.00 (ISBN 0-404-08834-1). AMS Press.
Professor. Charlotte Bronte. LC 6-17952. (On cover: Fitch's popular library, no. 8). 1878. G. W. Fitch.
Professor. Charlotte Bronte. LC 1697. (Half-title: Life and works of the sisters Bronte... vol. iv). 1900. Harper & Brothers.
Professor. Charlotte Bronte. (Half-title: Everyman's library, ed. by Ernest Rhys. Fiction). 1910. J. M. Dent & Sons, Ltd.
Professor. Charlotte Bronte. LC 45-40840. (Half-title: The novels of Charlotte, Emily, & Anne Bronte). 1922. J. M. Dent & Sons Ltd.
Professor. Stanley Johnson. LC 25-8787. Harcourt, Brace and Company.
Professor. Rex Warner. LC 39-5898. 1939. A. A. Knopf.
Professor. A Late. Charlotte Bronte. LC 7-3545. 1857. Harper & Brothers.
Professor. A Novel. Charlotte Bronte. (Harper's Franklin square library, no. 471). 1885. Harper & Brothers.
Professor. A Novel. Charlotte Bronte. (On cover: Seaside library. Pocket ed., no. 944). 1887. G. Munro.
Professor & Emma. Charlotte Bronte. (Fragment Ser.). 1975. 9.95x (ISBN 0-460-00417-4, Evman); pap. 3.75x (ISBN 0-460-01417-X, Evman). Biblio Dist.
Professor and His Favorites. Emilia Smith Flygare Carlen. LC 6-20143. 1843. Stjernefeldt & Broadmeadow.
Professor and the Coed: A Novel. Edward Semple Le Comte. LC 79-63192. 8.95 (ISBN 0-87949-141-8). Ashley Books.
Professor and the Petticoat. Alvin Saunders Johnson. LC 14-679574. 1914. 1.30. Dodd, Mead and Company.
Professor Bernhardi: A Comedy. Arthur Schnitzler & Pohli, Kate A. (Jacoby) LC 13-20509. P. Elder and Company.
Professor Descending: A Novel. Ramona Stewart. LC 64-11284. 1964. Doubleday.
Professor Dowell's Head. Aleksandr Romanovich Beliaev. LC 79-28200. (Macmillan's Best of Soviet Science Fiction). 7.95 (ISBN 0-02-508370-8). Macmillan.
Professor Dowell's Head. Aleksandr Romanovich Beliaev. LC 80-36764. (Series: Macmillan's Best of Soviet Science Fiction.). 1980. 7.95 (ISBN 0-02-508370-8). Collier Books.
Professor, Emma and Poems. Charlotte Bronte. Estes and Lauriat.
Professor How Could You! A Novel. Harry Leon Wilson. LC 24-23599. 1924. Cosmopolitan Book Corporation.
Professor Huskins. Lettie M Cummings. LC 16-103441. 1.50. R. G. Badger; Etc., Etc.
Professor Knits a Shroud: By Wirt Van Arsdale Pseud. 1st Ed. Martha W Davis. LC 51-9945. 1951. Published for the Crime Club by Doubleday.
Professor Latimer's Progress: A Novel of Contemporaneous Adventure; with Illustrations by J. Ormsbee. Simeon Strunsky. LC 18-9290. 1918. H. Holt and Company.
Professor Lovdahl. Alexander Lange Kielland & Flandrau, Rebecca Blair McClure, D. 1911, Tr. LC 4-26874. 1904. H. B. Turner.
Professor MMAA's Lecture. Stefan Themerson. LC 74-21585. 226p. 1975. 14.95 (ISBN 0-87951-029-3). Overlook Pr.
Professor of Desire. Philip Roth. LC 77-24032. 8.95. Farrar, Straus and Giroux.
Professor on Paws. Anthony Berkeley Cox. LC 27-6054. 1927. L. MacVeagh, The Dial Press.
Professor on the Case. Jacques Futrelle. LC 47-347658. (On cover: Nelson's library). T. Nelson and Sons.
Professor Pressensee: Materialist and Inventor: a Story. John Esten Cooke. LC 6-27186. (On cover: half-hour series, v. 78). 1878. Harper & Brothers.
Professor Preston at Home. 1st Ed. Elizabeth Frances Corbett. LC 57-9187. 1957. Lippincott.
Professor Wilmess Must Die: A Novel. Paul Rader. LC 76-79085. 1969. 4.95. Dial Press.
Professors. Edwin Diamond. 1970. price not set o.p. Atheneum.
Professor's Daughter. Anna Farquhar Bergengren. LC 99-1679. 1899. Doubleday & McClure Co.
Professor's Daughter. Piers Paul Read. LC 79-156369. 1971. 6.95. Lippincott.
Professor's Daughter. Piers Paul Read. 1980. 2.25 (ISBN 0-380-49981-9). Avon Books.
Professor's Dilemma. Annette Lucile Noble. LC 7-33477. (The Hudson library, no. 21). 1897. G. P. Putnam's Sons.
Professor's Experiment. Margaret Wolfe Hamilton Hungerford. R. F. Fenno & Company.
Professor's House. Willa Sibert Cather. LC 72-10470. 1973. (pbk.) 2.45 (ISBN 0-394-71913-1). Vintage Books.
Professor's House. Willa Sibert Cather. LC 25-17276. 1925. A. A. Knopf.
Professor's Legacy. Cecily Ullmann Sidgwick. LC 5-33937. 1905. H. Holt and Company.
Professors Like Vodka. Harold Loeb. LC 73-16121. (Lost American fiction). 1974. 7.95 (ISBN 0-8093-0664-6). Southern Illinois University Press.
Professors Like Vodka. Harold A Loeb. LC 27-18323. 1927. Boni & Liveright.
Professors Like Vodka: A Novel. Harold Loeb. LC 73-16121. (Lost American Fiction Ser.). 267p. 1974. Repr. of 1927 ed. 7.95 (ISBN 0-8093-0664-6). S Ill U Pr.
Professor's Mystery. Wells Southworth Hastings & Hooker, Brian I.E. William Brian, 1880- Joint Author. LC 11-5370. 1.25. The Bobbs-Merrill Company.
Professor's Poison. Archibald Gordon Macdonnell. LC 28-3432. Harcourt, Brace & Company.
Professor's Sister: A Romance. Julian Hawthorne. LC 7-3886. Belford, Clarke & Co.
Professor's Umbrella: A Novel. Mary Jane Ward. LC 48-348. 1948. Random House.
Professor's Wife. Sue Hartman. pap. 1.95 o.p. (8094). Cameo.
Professor's Wife. Bravig Imbs. LC 28-29078. 1928. L. MacVeagh, The Dial Press.
Professor's Wife: Or, It Might Have Been. Annie Lyndsay MacGregor. LC 7-16458. 1870. J. B. Lippincott & Co.
Profile in Gilt. Jeannette Covert Nolan. LC 41-3122. W. Funk, Inc.
Profile of a Murder: A New Valcour Mystery. Rufus King. LC 35-4596. Harcourt, Brace and Company.
Profit & Loss. Amelia Edith Huddleston Barr. LC 16-170718. 1916. 1.30. D. Appleton and Company.
Profit and Loss. Mary Dwinell Chellis. LC 6-23357. (On cover: The Chellis library). 1884. National Temperance Society and Publication House.
Profit and Loss: A Story of the Life of the Genteel Irish-American, Illustrative of Godless Education. Hugh Quigley. LC 7-42417. 1873. T. O'Kane.
Profit and the Loss: A Novel by Thomas Fall Pseud. Donald Clifford Snow. LC 65-24491. bds., 5.95. McKay.
Profit Motive. Warren Murphy. (Destroyer Ser.: No. 48). 256p. (Orig.). 1982. pap. 2.75 (ISBN 0-523-41558-3). Pinnacle Bks.
Profiteers. Edward Phillips Oppenheim. LC 21-11495. 1921. Little, Brown, and Company.
Profligate: A Novel. Arthur Hornblow. LC 8-16713. 1908. G. W. Dillingham Company.
Profundis. Richard Cowper, pseud. 2.25 (ISBN 0-671-83502-5). Pocket Books.
Progeny of the Adder. Leslie H Whitten. LC 65-12360. 1965. Published for the Crime Club by Doubleday.
Program for a Puppet. Roland Perry. LC 79-23840. 1980. 10.95. Crown Publishers.
Program for Passion. Florence Stonebraker. LC 48-113637. 1948. Phoenix Press.
Programmed Man. William D Blankenship. LC 72-96502. 1973. 5.95 (ISBN 0-8027-5279-9). Walker.
Programmed to Live. Rene Noorbergen. LC 75-18267. 1975. pap. 1.95 o.p. (ISBN 0-8163-0189-1, 16590-2). Pacific Pr Pub Assn.
Programmer. Bruce Jackson. 224p. 1981. pap. 2.25 (ISBN 0-345-29079-8). Ballantine.
Programmer: A Novel. Bruce Jackson. LC 78-20078. 1979. 8.95 (ISBN 0-385-14868-2). Doubleday.
Progreso Del Peregrino. Juan Bunyan & L. P. Leavell. Tr. by Hiram F. Duffer, Jr. from Eng. (Span.). 1980. pap. 2.20 (ISBN 0-311-37006-3). Casa Bautista.
Progress and Prejudice. Catherine Grace Frances Moody Gore. LC 6-27509. De Witt & Davenport.
Progress of a Crime: 1st Ed. Julian Symons. LC 60-104525. (Harper novel of suspense.). 1960. Harper.
Progress of an Affair. Felice Gordon. LC 74-150737. 1972. 2.50 (ISBN 0-491-00823-6). W. H. Allen.
Progress of an Affair. Felice Gordon. 1973. (pbk) 1.25. Dell.
Progress of Julius. Daphne Du Maurier. LC 33-205174. 1933. Doubleday, Doran & Company, Inc.
Progress of Julius. Daphne Du Maurier. LC 42-21084. 1939. The Sun Dial Press, Inc.
Progress of Mrs. Cripps-Middlemore. Gerard Bendall. LC 12-117142. 1912. 1.25. John Lane.
Progress of Pauline Kessler. Frederic Carrel. 1900. L. C. Page & Company.
Progress of Stories. Laura Riding Jackson. LC 70-167469. (Short story index reprint series). 1971. (ISBN 0-8369-3995-6). Books for Libraries Press.
Progress of Stories. a new, enl. ed. / with new material, including other early stories and a new preface by laura (riding) jackson. ed. Laura Riding Jackson. LC 81-12571. 15.95 (ISBN 0-385-27212-X). Dial Press.
Progress of Stories. facsimile ed. Laura Riding, pseud. LC 70-167469. (Short Story Index Reprint Ser.). Repr. of 1935 ed. 18.00 (ISBN 0-8369-3995-6). Ayer Co.
Progress of the Pilgrim Good Intent: In Jacobinical Times... 2d american, from the 5th english ed. Mary Anne Burges. LC 10-4176. 1801. Printed and Sold by Samuel Etheridge.
Progress, U S A: A Novel. Guy Daniels. LC 68-22819. 1968. Macmillan.
Progress, U. S. A. Guy Daniels. (Timothy Abbott Ser.: Bk. 1). 1968. 4.95 o.p. (ISBN 0-02-529460-1). Macmillan.
Progress, U. S. A. Guy Daniels. (Timothy Abbott Ser.: Bk. 1). 1968. 4.95 o.p. (ISBN 0-02-529460-1). Macmillan.
Progressionists, and Angels: Tr. from the German of Conrad Von Bolanden Pseud. Josef Eduard Konrad Bischoff. LC 11-105121.
Progressive Petticoats: Or, Dressed to Death. An Autobiography of a Married Man. Robert Barnwell Roosevelt. LC 7-40764. 1874. G. W. Carleton & Co.; Etc., Etc.
Progressive Teacher. James Alonzo Adams. LC 17-24694. 1917. The Goodspeed Press.
Prohibition and Man: A Drama of Saloon Days, and a Romance of Prohibition Days Combined. A Gripping Story Dealing with the Underworld and the Forces of Prohibition, Who Are Combatting This Lawlessness. Anne Kidwell Webb. LC 32-13680. Wallace-Homestead Co., Printers.
Project. Andrew Sinclair. LC 60-10992. 1960. Simon and Schuster.
Project, and Other Short Pieces. Michael Brodsky & Michael Hafftka. LC 82-1017. (Illus.). 10.95 (ISBN 0-941062-02-3) (ISBN 0-941062-03-1) (ISBN 0-941062-04-X). Guignol Books.
Project & Other Short Pieces by Michael Brodsky. Michael Brodsky. (Illus.). 224p. 1982. 11.95 (ISBN 0-941062-02-3); pap. 7.95 (ISBN 0-941062-03-1); signed ed. 85.00 (ISBN 0-941062-04-X). Guignol Bks.
Project Cheers. Tom Follett et al. 1969. text ed. 7.50x o.p. Humanities.
Project: Earthsave. Kurt Brand. (Perry Rhodan,#38). 1974. (pbk.) 0.75. Ace Books.
Project for a Revolution in New York: A Novel. Robbe-Grillet, Alain. LC 77-187581. 1972. 5.95 (ISBN 0-394-48020-1). Grove Press.
Project Lambda. Paul O'M. Welles. LC 78-11353. 9.95 (ISBN 0-87949-146-9). Ashley Books.
Project Midas. Eugenia Macer-Story. 1979. pap. 2.95 (ISBN 0-89185-210-7). Anthelion Pr.
Project Norouz. Rebecca Swift. 512p. (Orig.). 1982. pap. 3.50 (ISBN 0-505-51834-1). Tower Bks.
Project: Passion. Geoffrey Kyle. 192p. (Orig.). 1972. pap. 1.95 o.p. (ISBN 0-87056-258-4, 6258). Brandon.
Project Pope. Clifford D. Simak. LC 80-21365. 1981. 10.95 (ISBN 0-345-29138-7). Ballantine Books.
Project Sunlight. June Strong. LC 80-13011. 2.95 (ISBN 0-8127-0289-1). Southern Pub. Association.
Project Web. Barbara Rogers. LC 79-25673. 8.95 (ISBN 0-396-07795-1). Dodd, Mead.
Prologue. Phyllis Duganne. LC 20-14598. 1920. Harcourt, Brace and Howe.
Prologue of the Seed of the Love Apple. Harry Barba. LC 68-8606. 1968. Harian Press.
Prologue, The Knight's Tale, & The Nun's Priest's Tale. Geoffrey Chaucer. Ed. by Frank J. Mather. LC 72-969. lxxxii, 61p. 1975. Repr. of 1899 ed. 9.50 o.p. (ISBN 0-404-04257-0). AMS Pr.

Prologue to Analog. Edited by John W. Campbell. 1st Ed. Astounding Science Fiction. Ed. by John Wood Campbell. LC 62-7608. 1962. Doubleday.
Prologue to Love. Taylor Caldwell. 768p. 1980. pap. 2.95 (ISBN 0-553-14238-0). Bantam.
Prologue to Love. Taylor Caldwell. LC 61-12500. 1961. 5.95 (ISBN 0-385-03269-2). Doubleday.
Prologue to Love. Martha Ostenso. LC 32-245511. 1932. Dodd, Mead & Company.
Prologue to Love: Novel About a Woman Financial Genius. Taylor Caldwell. LC 61-12500. (O.s.i.). 5.95 o.s.i. (ISBN 0-385-03269-2). Doubleday.
Prologue to Love. 1st Ed. Taylor Cadwell. LC 61-12500. 1961. Doubleday.
Prolong Your Pleasure. Robert Zeiss & Antoinette Zeiss. 1978. pap. 1.95 (ISBN 0-671-82041-9). PB.
Promenade. Edith J. Lyttleton. LC 33-273482. Reynal & Hitchcock.
Promenade Au Soleil. Harry Peter M'Nab Brown. (Overseas edition. French translations 18). 1945.
Promenade Deck. Ishbel Ross. LC 32-171498. 1932. Harper & Brothers.
Promenade En Ville. Warja Honegger-Lavater. (Folded Story Ser: No. 5). 1964. bds. 3.50 o.p. Wittenborn.
Promessi Sponsi. Alessandro Manzoni. 1969. 5.00 o.p. (T584). Chilton.
Prometheam Pilgraimage. 1st Ed. Oather Houghton Carpenter. LC 56-6839. 1956. Vantage Press.
Promethee Mal Enchaine: Nouvelles. Andre Paul Guillaume Gide. pap. 7.95. French & Eur.
Prometheus Crisis. Thomas N. Scortia & Frank M. Robinson. LC 74-33689. 1975. 8.95 (ISBN 0-385-09653-4). Doubleday.
Prometheus Crisis. Thomas N. Scortia & Frank M. Robinson. 1976. 1.95 (ISBN 0-553-02770-0). Bantam Books.
Prometheus' Diarial Account, While on the Inspection Tour with Gabriel and Mephistopheles. A Novelistic Extravaganza... William Busch. LC 7-30059. 1869.
Prometheus Man. Ray F. Nelson. Ed. by Hank Stine. LC 82-5025. 174p. 1982. pap. 6.95. Donning Co.
Prometheus Man: A Nrobook. Ray Faraday Nelson & Hank Stine. LC 82-5025. (Starblaze editions). (Illus.). 6.95 (ISBN 0-89865-192-1). Donning.
Prometheus Misbound see Marshland.
Prometheus Operation. Mark Elder. LC 80-14577. 11.95 (ISBN 0-07-019191-3). McGraw-Hill.
Prometheus Outnumbered. Glen Roberts. LC 75-153043. 1971. 5.95 (ISBN 0-8059-1561-3). Dorrance.
Prometheus: The Fall of the House of Limon, Sunday Sunlight (Poetic Novels of Spanish Life) Ramon P. De Ayala. Tr. by Alice P. Hubbard & Grace Hazard. 1978. Repr. of 1920 ed. lib. bdg. 25.00 (ISBN 0-8414-1855-1). Folcroft.
Prometheus: The Fall of the House of Limon: Sunday Sunlight: Poetic Novels of Spanish Life. Ramon Perez De Ayala. Tr. by Hubbard, Alice P. F. & Conkling, Grace Walcott (Hazard) LC 20-12561. E. P. Dutton & Co.
Prometheus Trap. Vivian Connolly. LC 82-80839. 288p. (Orig.). 1982. pap. 2.95 (ISBN 0-86721-176-8). Playboy Pbks.
Prominent Among the Mourners. Carolyn Thomas. LC 46-20794. 1946. J. B. Lippincott Company.
Promiscuous. Grace Perkins Oursler. LC 31-31666. 1931. Brentano's.
Promiscuous Doll. Clayton Matthews. 1969. pap. 0.75 o.p. (75-275). Manor Bks.
Promise. Sallie Lee Bell. LC 66-25445. 1966. Zondervan Pub. House.
Promise. Pearl Sydenstricker Buck. LC 43-15073. 1943. The John Day Company.
Promise. Mildred Cram. LC 49-109322. 1949. Knopf.
Promise. Esther Kellner. LC 56-5430. Westminster Press.
Promise. Chaim Potok. LC 71-88744. 1969. 6.95. Knopf.
Promise. Danielle Steel. 1983. pap. 3.50 (ISBN 0-440-17079-6). Dell.
Promise. Ann L. Wilson. LC 72-88939. 1972. 6.50 (ISBN 0-910750-26-2). Yucca Books.
Promise: A Tale of the Great Northwest. James Beardsley Hendryx. LC 28-4851. 1915. A. L. Burt Company.
Promise: A Tale of the Great Northwest. James Beardsley Hendryx. LC 15-19193. 1915. G. P. Putnam's Sons.
Promise, & Other Stories. Elva D. Codrington. 1979. 4.95 o.p. (ISBN 0-533-03647-X). Vantage.
Promise & Other Stories. Ed. by Winifred Roderman. (Read on! Write on! Ser.). (Illus.). (gr. 7 up). 1980. pap. text ed. 3.10 (ISBN 0-915510-40-5). Janus Bks.
Promise at Midnight. Lilian Peake. (Harlequin Romances Ser.). 192p. 1981. pap. 1.25 (ISBN 0-373-02404-5). Harlequin Bks.
Promise for Death. Jon Messman. (Revenger). (Signet Book: Vol. 6). 1975. (pbk.) 1.25. New American Library.
Promise Is for Ever. Denise Robins. 1973. pap. 0.75 o.p. (94356-075). Beagle Bks.
Promise Me Love. Lynn M. Bartlett. pap. 3.50 (ISBN 0-380-60418-3). Avon.
Promise Me Romance. Jeannie Sakol. 1979. pap. 1.95 o.s.i. (ISBN 0-8439-0607-3, Leisure Bks). Nordon Pubns.
Promise Me Tomorrow. Jennifer Lee. 224p. pap. 2.25 (ISBN 0-449-14444-5, GM). Fawcett.
Promise Me You'll Sing Mud. Ian Wallace. 1982. 15.00 (ISBN 0-7145-3500-1); pap. 7.95 (ISBN 0-7145-3594-X). Riverrun NY.
Promise Morning. Charles E Mercer. LC 65-20681. 1966. Putnam.
Promise of Air. Algernon Blackwood. LC 18-10696. E. P. Dutton & Company.
Promise of Delight. Mary Howard, pseud. LC 52-10197. 1952. Arcadia House.
Promise of Diamonds. John Creasey. LC 64-20206. (Red badge detective). 1964. Dodd Mead.
Promise of Joy. Allen Drury. LC 74-18774. 1975. 10.00 (ISBN 0-385-04396-1). Doubleday.
Promise of Joy. Allen Drury. 1976. (pbk.) 1.95. Avon.
Promise of Love. Mary Renault, pseud. LC 39-5769. 1939. W. Morrow & Company.
Promise of Love. Mary Renault, pseud. LC 78-3853. 1978. 11.95 (ISBN 0-89244-079-1). Queens House.
Promise of Marriage. Emile Gaboriau. LC 6-44502. (On cover: Lovell's library. v. 4, no. 161). 1883. J. W. Lovell Company.
Promise of Summer. Charles Gnaegy. (Orig.). 1979. pap. 2.25 (ISBN 0-532-22172-9). Woodhill.
Promise of Tomorrow. Arlene Hale. LC 72-6671. 1973. 6.95 (ISBN 0-316-33858-3). Little, Brown.
Promise of Tomorrow. Arlene Hale. 1975. (pbk.) 0.95. Bantam Books.
Promise of Tomorrow. Arlene Hale. LC 76-45203. 1977. 7.95 (ISBN 0-89340-048-3). J. Curley & Associates.
Promise the Earth. Clive Irving. LC 82-47789. (Illus.). 15.34 (ISBN 0-06-015063-7). Harper & Row.
Promise to Cherish. LaVyrle Spencer. (Second Chance at Love Ser.: No. 100). 1983. pap. 1.75 (ISBN 0-515-06864-0). Jove Pubns.
Promise to Keep. Lois A. Sunagel. (Orig.). 1980. pap. 1.95 (ISBN 0-532-23133-3). Woodhill.
Promise to Pay. Daphne Clair. (Harlequin Presents Ser.). 192p. 1982. pap. 1.75 (ISBN 0-373-10481-2). Harlequin Bks.
Promise to Possess. Jessica Logan. (Superromances Ser.). 384p. 1982. pap. 2.50 (ISBN 0-373-70027-X, Pub. by Worldwide). Harlequin Bks.
Promise Unto Death. Grace Cash. LC 67-15992. 1967. Herald Press.
Promise You Won't Marry Me: A Novel. Rosita Torr Forbes. LC 32-107443. 1932. Frederick A. Stokes Company.
Promised Isle. Laurids Valdemar Bruun. LC 22-15475. 1922. A. A. Knopf.
Promised Land. Cedric Belfrage. LC 76-52089. (Garland Classics of Film Literature). 1978. 16.00 (ISBN 0-8240-2865-1). Garland Pub.
Promised Land. Ralph Hayes. (Orig.). 1980. pap. text ed. 2.25 o.s.i. (ISBN 0-505-51577-6). Tower Bks.
Promised Land. Gilbert Lubin. LC 30-22020. The Christopher Publishing House.
Promised Land. Robert B. Parker. LC 76-20527. 1976. 7.95 (ISBN 0-395-24771-3). Houghton Mifflin.
Promised Land. Robert B. Parker. LC 76-55717. 1977. 9.95 (ISBN 0-8161-6450-9). G. K. Hall.
Promised Land. Robert B. Parker. (Berkley Medallion Book). 1978. 1.75 (ISBN 0-425-03614-6). Berkley Pub. Corp.
Promised Land. Brian M Stableford. 1974. (pbk.) 0.95. Daw Books.
Promised Land, Vol. 2. Stewart Holbrook. 1974. pap. 1.50 o.p. (23800-150). Comstock Edns.
Promised Land: A Novel Karel Schoeman; Translated by Marion V. Friedmann. Karel Schoeman. LC 78-6788. 8.95 (ISBN 0-671-40031-2). Summit Books.
Promised Land, a Story of David in Israel. Gilbert Parker. LC 29-1678. 1929. Frederick A. Stokes Company.
Promised Land, and Other Tales. Charles Elmer Waterman. 1897. Ledger Publishing Company.
Promised Land: The Story of the Palatine Emigration from the Rhineland Homes to the Hudson and Schoharie Valleys. John J Vrooman. LC 59-141. 1958. Baronet Litho Co.
Promised Land: Translated from the Polish of Ladislas Reymont. Wladyslaw Stanislaw Reymont & Dziewicki, Michael Henry, Tr. LC 27-18535. 1927. A. A. Knopf.
Promised Portrait. Kathleen Daley. LC 81-71629. (Serenade Romance; 7). 2.95 (ISBN 0-671-44827-7). Simon & Schuster: Distributed by Pocket Books.
Promised Spring. Dolores Warwick. LC 60-6025. 1960. Dodd, Mead.
Promisekeeper: A Tephramancy. Charles Hamilton Newman. LC 76-139651. 1971. 7.95 (ISBN 0-671-20822-5). Simon and Schuster.
Promises. Charlotte Vale Allen. LC 79-25499. 10.95 (ISBN 0-525-18540-2). Dutton.
Promises for Tomorrow. Claire Clement. (Dear Miss Lonely hearts romance series,#6). 1975. (pbk.) 1.25 (ISBN 0-523-00563-6). Pinnacle Books.
Promises from the Past. Donna K. Vitek. 192p. 1981. pap. 1.50 (ISBN 0-671-57066-8). S&S.
Promises of Alice: The Romance of a New England Parsonage. Margaret Wade Campbell Deland. LC 19-13646. 1919. Harper & Brothers.
Promises of Marriage. Emile Gaboriau. Tr. by Garnett, F. E. LC 6-445010. (On cover: The seaside library. Pocket ed. no. 144). 1884. G. Munro.
Promises to Keep. Hy Brett & Barbara Brett. LC 81-47247. 10.95 (ISBN 0-06-014881-0). Harper & Row.
Promises to Keep. Valerie Ferris. (Candlelight Ecstasy Ser.: No. 30). 192p. (Orig.). 1981. pap. 1.75 (ISBN 0-440-17159-8). Dell.
Promises to Keep. Thomas J. Fleming. LC 77-16915. 1978. 10.00 o.p. (ISBN 0-385-13555-6). Doubleday.
Promises to Keep. Thomas J. Fleming. 400p. 1980. pap. 2.50 (ISBN 0-446-91192-5). Warner Bks.
Promises to Myself: Ziggy's Thirty-Day Ledger of I Owe Me's. Tom Wilson. (Alligator Bks). 1975. pap. 2.50 (ISBN 0-8362-0643-6). Andrews & McMeel.
Promising Affair. Glenna Finley, pseud. (Orig.). 1974. pap. 1.50 (ISBN 0-451-07917-5, W7917, Sig). NAL.
Promising Career. Christy Brown. 248p. 1983. 16.95 (ISBN 0-436-07097-9, Pub. by Secker & Warburg England). David & Charles.
Promising Young Men. George Sklar. LC 51-10487. 1951. Crown Publishers.
Promoters: A Novel Without a Woman. William Hawley Smith. LC 4-11533. 1904. Rand, McNally & Company.
Promotion: A Story of the Philippine War. John Marvin Dean. LC 6-32355. 1906. The Griffith and Rowland Press.
Prompter's Box. Eleanor Hinman. LC 45-2359. 1945. Dorrance & Company.
Proof of the Pudding. Meredith Nicholson. LC 16-11043. 1916. Houghton Mifflin Company.
Proof of the Pudding. Phoebe Atwood Taylor. (Foul Play Press Bks.). 1979. pap. 4.95 (ISBN 0-914378-55-4). Countryman.
Proof of the Pudding. Phoebe Atwood Taylor. 1969. pap. 0.60 o.p. (X2132). Pyramid Pubns.
Proof of the Pudding: An Asey Mayo Mystery. Phoebe Atwood Taylor. LC 45-35103. 1945. W. W. Norton & Company, Inc.
Proofs of Affection. Rosemary Friedman. LC 81-22450. 1982. 12.00 (ISBN 0-688-01106-3). Morrow.
Proofs of Holy Writ. Rudyard Kipling. LC 34-7445. 1934. Doubleday, Doran & Company, Inc.
Propeller Island. Jules Verne. LC 61-44196. (Fitzroy edition of Jules Verne). 1961. Associated Booksellers.
Proper Bohemians: A Novel. Edith Templeton. LC 51-8852. 1952-1951. Houghton Mifflin.
Proper Gods. Virginia Eggertsen Sorensen. LC 51-9941. 1951. Harcourt, Bruce.
Proper Marriage: A Complete Novel from Doris Lessing's Masterwork, Children of Violence. Doris May Lessing. 1970. pap. 3.95 (ISBN 0-452-25093-5, Z5093, Plume). NAL.
Proper Place. Anna Buchan. LC 26-18505. George H. Doran Company.
Proper Price. William Groninger. LC 66-24429. 1966. 5.50. New American Lib.
Property of a Gentleman. Catherine Gaskin. LC 73-15341. 1974. 7.95 (ISBN 0-385-03934-4). Doubleday.
Property of a Gentleman. Catherine Gaskin. (Fawcett crest book). 1975. (pbk.) 1.75. Fawcett.
Property of a Gentleman. Richard Ullmann. LC 39-3292. E. P. Dutton & Co., Inc.
Property of: A Novel. Alice Hoffman. LC 77-3036. 1977. 8.95. Farrar, Straus and Giroux.
Property of: A Novel. Alice Hoffman. 1978. 1.95 (ISBN 0-449-23579-3). Fawcett Crest Books.
Property of Don Gilbar. Henri Black Wall. LC 8-33286. (On cover: United authors' library, no. 20). Authors' Publishing Association.
Prophecy. David Seltzer. 1979. 2.25 (ISBN 0-345-28034-2). Ballantine Books.
Prophecy. Patricia Young. (AS-252). 1966. All Saints, Dist. Guild.
Prophecy. Patricia Young. LC 65-14699. 1965. Bruce Pub. Co.
Prophecy & the Parasites. John Symonds. LC 75-10910. 403p. 1975. 9.95o.s.i. (ISBN 0-8076-0786-X). Braziller.
Prophecy and the Parasites: A Novel. John Symonds. LC 75-7916. 1975. 9.95 (ISBN 0-8076-0786-X). G. Braziller.
Prophet: A Novel. H. E. Newman. LC 12-15564. Broadway Publishing Co.
Prophet and the King. 1st Ed. Shirley Watkins. LC 56-8097. 1956. Doubleday.
Prophet and the Miracle, and Other Stories. Stephen G Prokopoff. LC 55-9075. 1955. Vantage Press.
Prophet by Experience. Jack Iams. LC 43-1150. 1943. W. Morrow and Company.
Prophet in Babylon: A Story of Social Service. William James Dawson. LC 7-31420. F. H. Revell Company.
Prophet of Berkeley Square. Robert Smythe Hichens. LC 1-24845. 1901. Dodd, Mead and Company.
Prophet of Fire. John Creasey. 1982. 15.00x (ISBN 0-86025-177-2, Pub. by Ian Henry Pubns England). State Mutual Bk.
Prophet of Fire. John Creasey. (O.s.i.). 1978. 7.95 o.s.i. (ISBN 0-8027-5394-9). Walker & Co.
Prophet of Lamath. Robert D. Hughes. 1982. pap. 1.95 (ISBN 0-345-26232-8, Del Rey). Ballantine.
Prophet of Martinique: A Love Story Embracing a Vivid Account of the Historic Destruction by Mont Pelee. Lydia Whitaker. J. S. Barcus Company.
Prophet of Peace. Asenath Carver Coolidge. LC 8-8302. 1907. Hungerford-Holbrook Company.
Prophet of the Great Smoky Mountains. Mary Noailles Murfree. LC 76-110350. 1970. AMS Press.
Prophet of the Great Smoky Mountains. Mary Noailles Murfree. LC 4-15142. 1885. Houghton, Mifflin and Company.
Prophet of the Great Smoky Mountains. Mary Noailles Murfree. LC 16-25045. Houghton Mifflin Company.
Prophet of the Ruined Abbey: Or, A Glance of the Future of Ireland: a Narrative Founded on the Ancient "Prophecies of Culmkill", and on Other Predictions and Popular Traditions Among the Irish. Hugh Quigley. LC 7-42419. 1855. E. Dunigan and Brothers.
Prophet of the Wind. Barbara Rees. LC 73-6946. 1973. 6.95 (ISBN 0-15-175100-5). Harcourt Brace Jovanovich.
Prophet. Translated by Arthur Saul Super. Shalom Asch. LC 55-10089. 1955. Putnam.
Prophet Without Honour. Russell Green. LC 35-3431. 1934. T. Nelson and Sons, Ltd.
Prophetess. Janet Kidde. LC 78-50759. (Jove/HBJ Book). 1978. 1.95 (ISBN 0-515-04456-3). Jove Pubns.
Prophetic Marriage. Warwick Deeping. LC 20-11501. 1920. Cassell and Company, Ltd.
Prophetic Romance Mars to Earth. John McCoy. LC 7-15305. 1896. Arena Publishing Company.
Prophet's Chamber: A Novel. Joseph Chamberlain Furnas. LC 35-185635. 1935. W. Morrow and Company.
Prophet's Landing: A Novel. Edwin Asa Dix. LC 7-12634. 1907. C. Scribner's Sons.
Prophet's Mantle. Fabian Bland. (On cover: The household library, v. 4, no. 29). Belford, Clarke & Co.; Etc., Etc.
Prophet's People. Lee D. Willoughby. (Making of America Ser.: No. 39). (Orig.). 1983. pap. 3.25 (ISBN 0-440-06858-4). Dell.
Prophet's Raven. Mark Guy Pearse. LC 8-27802. Eaton & Mains.
Prophet's Wife. Anna Cecilla Browne. LC 14-17993. 1914. 1.25. Benziger Brothers.
Prophet's Wife. Richard Orton Prowse. LC 30-10813. 1929. Houghton Mifflin Company.
Proposal. Karen Ray. LC 80-29311. 9.95 (ISBN 0-440-07047-3). Delacorte Press /E. Friede.
Proposal. Anne Stretton. LC 36-561. 1936. W. Morrow & Co.
Proposal. Henry Sutton, pseud. 320p. (Orig.). 1980. pap. 2.50 (ISBN 0-441-68342-8, Pub. by Charter Bks). Ace Bks.
Proposals to Kathleen. Lucy Lane Clifford. LC 8-7894. 1908. A. S. Barnes & Company.
Proposition Thirty-One. Robert H. Rimmer. LC 68-57495. 1968. 5.95. New American Library.
Props: Tales of the Pawnshop and Other Stories. J. Bernard Lynch. LC 32-164373. 1932. Meador Publishing Company.
Prose Bowl. Bill Pronzini & Barry N. Malzberg. LC 80-14208. 1980. 9.95 (ISBN 0-312-65194-5). St. Martin's Press.
Prose Fictions. Written for the Illustration of True Principles, in Their Bearing Upon Every-Day Life. Timothy Shay Arthur. LC 45-42405. 1844. G. B. Zieber & Co.
Prose Poem: An International Anthology. Ed. by Michael Benedikt. (Laurel original). Dell.
Prose Romances of Edgar A. Poe... Uniform Serial Ed.... No. 1. Containing The Murders in the Rue Morgue, and The Man That Was Used up. Edgar Allan Poe. LC 7-35800. 1843. W. H. Graham.

Prose Romances: The Murders in the Rue Morgue and The Man That Was Used up. Edgar Allan Poe. LC 68-54551. 1968. St. John's University Press.

Prose Tales. facsimile ed. Aleksandr Sergeevich Pushkin. Tr. by T. Keane from Rus. LC 78-150484. (Short Story Index Reprint Ser.). Repr. of 1914 ed. 22.00 (ISBN 0-8369-3825-9). Ayer Co.

Prose Tales of Alexander Poushkin. Aleksandr Sergeevich Pushkin. Tr. by T. Keane. LC 78-150484. (Short story index reprint series). 1971. (ISBN 0-8369-3825-9). Books for Libraries Press.

Prose Tales of Edgar Allan Poe. Second Series. Edgar Allan Poe. 1889. A. C. Armstrong & Co.

Prose Tales of Edgar Allan Poe. 1st Ser. Edgar Allan Poe. LC 15-23119. 1878. W. J. Widdleton.

Prose Works of Jonathan Swift, 14 vols. shakespearan head ed. Jonathan Swift. Ed. by Herbert Davis. 1964-68. Repr. of 1939 ed. Set. 475.00x (ISBN 0-06-496661-5). B&N Imports.

Prosecutor. James Mills. 256p. 1969. 5.95 o.p. (ISBN 0-374-23836-7). FS&G.

Prosecutor. P. R Van Zyl. LC 73-93752. 1974. 6.95. Berkley Pub. Corp.; Distributed by Putnam.

Prosecutor: A Novel. Bernard Botein. LC 56-9917. 1956. Simon and Schuster.

Proselyte. Susan Ertz. LC 33-256877. 1933. D. Appleton-Century Company, Incorporated.

Proselytes of the Ghetto. Amos Isaac Dushaw. J. Heidingsgeld.

Proselytizer. D. Keith Mano. LC 75-171127. 1972. 6.95 (ISBN 0-394-46658-6). Knopf.

Prospect Before Us. Herbert Gold. (O.s.i.). Orig. Title: Room Service. 1964. pap. 0.60 o.s.i. (A106X, Award). Univ Pub & Dist.

Prospect Before Us. 1st Ed. Herbert Gold. LC 54-533634. World Pub. Co.

Prospector: A Tale of the Crow's Nest Pass. special limited ed. Charles William Gordon. LC 9-32303. Grosset & Dunlap.

Prospector: A Tale of the Crow's Nest Pass. Charles William Gordon. 1904. F. H. Revell Company.

Prospects Are Pleasing. Honor Lilbush Wingfield Tracy. LC 75-319697. 1973. 1.80 (ISBN 0-85617-684-2). White Lion Publishers.

Prospects Are Pleasing: A Novel. Honor Lilbush Wingfield Tracy. LC 58-9866. 1958. Random House.

Prospects of Love. William Camp. LC 57-2750. 1957. Longmans, Green.

Prosper, a Novel. Victor Cherbuliez & Bristed, Charles Astor, 1820-1874, Tr. (Leisure hour series. v. 26). 1874. H. Holt and Company.

Prosper: By Pati Hill. Patricia Hill. LC 60-122493. 1960. Houghton Mifflin.

Prosper Merimee. Prosper Merimee. Tr. by Ives, George Burnham. LC 3-26366. (Little French masterpieces... i). 1903. G. P. Putnam's Sons.

Prospering. Elizabeth George Speare. LC 67-16482. 1967. 5.95. Houghton.

Prosperity Street. Collin Brooks. LC 30-24773. 1930. Minton, Balch & Company.

Prostitute. (Illus.). pap. 5.00 (ISBN 0-910550-78-6). Centurion Pr.

Protagonists. James Barlow. LC 57-11793. Harper.

Protect Our Schools. A Story with a Ring to It. Peter M Hannibal. LC 1-27102. 1901. P. M. Hannibal.

Protecting Margot. Alice Grant Rosman. LC 33-16586. 1933. Minton, Balch & Company.

Protective Footwear: Stories and Fables by George Bowering. George Bowering. LC 78-314480. 6.95 (ISBN 0-7710-1595-X). McClelland and Stewart.

Protector. Larry M Harris. LC 61-12147. (Random House mystery). 1961. Random House.

Protector. Larry Niven. 224p. (Orig.). 1981. pap. 2.25 (ISBN 0-345-29302-9, Del Rey). Ballantine.

Protector. Larry Niven. 1973. (pbk.) 1.25 (ISBN 0-345-23486-3). Ballantine.

Protector Conclusion. Jon Burmeister. LC 76-62750. 1977. 7.95 o.p. (ISBN 0-312-65222-4). St Martin.

Protector, No. 1: Venus Underground. Rich Rainey. 208p. (Orig.). 1982. pap. 2.25 (ISBN 0-523-41849-3). Pinnacle Bks.

Protectors. Richard Clayton. LC 72-80530. 1972. 5.95 (ISBN 0-8027-5262-4). Walker.

Protectors. William Haggard. Ed. by Lois D. Cole. LC 72-80530. 208p. 1972. 5.95 o.p. (ISBN 0-8027-5262-4). Walker & Co.

Protege. Charlotte Armstrong. LC 76-92619. 1970. 4.95. Coward McCann.

Protege. Malcolm MacPherson. 256p. 1981. pap. 2.75 (ISBN 0-553-14706-4). Bantam.

Protege. Malcolm MacPherson. (F). 1980. 11.95 o.p. (ISBN 0-525-18560-7). Dutton.

Protege, a Novel. Malcolm MacPherson. LC 79-28279. 10.95 (ISBN 0-525-18560-7). Dutton.

Protegee of Jack Hamlin's: And Other Stories. Bret Harte. LC 7-3647. 1894. Houghton, Mifflin and Company.

Protest Ball. Ann Griffin. pap. 1.95 o.p. (8058). Cameo.

Protestant. Ezekiel Harry Miller. LC 33-2940. Christopher Publishing House.

Proteus. Morris L. West. 382p. 1980. pap. 2.95 (ISBN 0-553-13201-6). Bantam.

Proteus: A Novel. Morris L. West. LC 78-11949. 1979. 9.95 (ISBN 0-688-03404-7). Morrow.

Proteus Pact. Geoffrey St. George. 1975. 7.95 o.p. (ISBN 0-316-76670-4). Little.

Proteus Pact: A Novel. St. George, Geoffrey. LC 74-26561. 1975. 6.95. (ISBN 0-316-76670-4). Little, Brown.

Proteus: Voices for the Eighties. Ed. by Richard S. McEnroe. (Destinies Ser.). 288p. (Orig.). 1981. pap. 2.50 (ISBN 0-441-68697-4). Ace Bks.

Prothalamium, a Cycle of the Holy Grail: A Novel. Philip Toynbee. LC 75-110839. 1970. Greenwood Press.

Prothalamium: A Cycle of the Holy Graal; a Novel. Philip Toynbee. LC 47-30486. 1947. Doubleday.

Protocol. Sarah Allan Borisch. LC 81-13557. 15.50 (ISBN 0-671-42926-4). Simon and Schuster.

Protocol for a Kidnapping. Oliver Bleeck. LC 82-48807. 256p. 1983. pap. 2.84i (ISBN 0-06-080646-X, P 646, PL). Har-Row.

Protocol for a Kidnapping. Oliver Bleeck. 1972. 5.95 o.p. (ISBN 0-688-02341-X). Morrow.

Protocol for a Kidnapping. Ross Thomas. LC 75-133288. 1971. 5.95. Morrow.

Protocol of a Damnation: A Novel. Peter L Berger. LC 75-9594. 1975. 7.95 (ISBN 0-8164-0280-9). Seabury Press.

Proud. Arthur Moore. (River of Fortune Ser.). 400p. (Orig.). 1980. pap. 2.50 (ISBN 0-89083-665-5). Zebra.

Proud and the Free. 1st Ed. Howard Melvin Fast. LC 50-10024. 1950. Little, Brown.

Proud Beggars. Albert Cossery. LC 81-1095. 1981. 14.00 (ISBN 0-87685-451-X) (ISBN 0-87685-450-1) (ISBN 0-87685-452-8). Black Sparrow Press.

Proud Blood. Joy Carroll. (Dell Book). 1978. 1.95 (ISBN 0-440-11562-0). Dell Pub. Co.

Proud Breed. Celeste De Blasis. LC 77-20282. 12.50 (ISBN 0-698-10870-1). Coward, McCann & Geoghegan.

Proud Breed: A Novel. Celeste De Blasis. 1978. 2.75 (ISBN 0-449-23905-5). Fawcett Crest.

Proud Canaries. David Johnson. LC 59-11474. 1959. W. Sloane Associates.

Proud Castle. 1st Ed. Eleanor Mercein Kelly. LC 51-1166. 1951. Bobbs-Merrill.

Proud Citadel. 1st Ed. Dorothy Evelyn Smith. LC 53-60979. 1953. Dutton.

Proud Destiny: A Novel. Lion Fauchtwanger & Rose, William, 1894- Tr. LC 47-30905. 1947. Viking Rpess.

Proud Diggers. William Oliver Turner. LC 54-5699. 1954. Houghton Mifflin.

Proud Diggers. William Oliver Turner. 1980. 1.75 (ISBN 0-425-04498-X). Berkley Publishing Corp.

Proud Dishonor. A Novel. Genie Holtzmeyer Johnson Rosenfeld. (Added t.-p.: The Manhattan series, no. 15). A. L. Burt.

Proud Dishonor. A Novel. Genie Holtzmeyer Johnson Rosenfeld. (select series, no. 76). 1891. Street & Smith.

Proud Flesh. William Humphrey. LC 72-11017. 1973. 6.95 (ISBN 0-394-46637-3). Knopf; Distributed by Random House.

Proud Flesh. Lawrence Rising. LC 24-152914. Boni and Liveright.

Proud Gun. Gordon D Shirreffs. (Belmont Tower Book). 1977. 1.25 (ISBN 0-505-51197-5). Tower Pubns.

Proud Heritage. Salie Elizabeth Robinson. LC 49-506611. United-International Pub. Co.

Proud Heritage: A Novel Based on the Life of Gilbert Stuart. Ilse Bischoff. LC 49-11691. 1949. Coward-McCann.

Proud House. Esty, Annette. LC 32-4562. 1932. Harper & Brothers.

Proud Hunter. Marianne Harvey. (Orig.). 1981. pap. 3.50 (ISBN 0-440-17098-2). Dell.

Proud Journey. LC 63-20516. (Double D western). 1963. Doubleday.

Proud Journey. Joseph Wayne. 1969. pap. 0.60 o.p. (0502-06009-060). Curtis.

Proud Lady. Neith Boyce. LC 23-288169. 1923. A. A. Knopf.

Proud Land. Logan Forster. LC 54-5391. 1954. Random House.

Proud Lover. Marsha Manning. (Cameo Romance). (Fawcett gold medal book). 1975. (pbk.) 0.95. Fawcett.

Proud Man. R. E. Harrington. 400p. 1983. pap. 3.50 (ISBN 0-345-30032-7). Ballantine.

Proud Man. R. E. Harrington. 416p. 1983. 17.95 (ISBN 0-436-19113-X, Pub. by Secker & Warburg England). David & Charles.

Proud Man: A Novel. Elizabeth Linington. LC 55-964153. 1955. Viking Press.

Proud New Flags. Francis Van Wyck Mason. (Berkley Medallion Book). 1975. (pbk.) 1.95 (ISBN 0-425-02966-2). Berkley Pub. Co.

Proud New Flags. Francis Van Wyck Mason. LC 51-10079. 1951. Lippincott.

Proud Old Name. Charles Elbert Scoggins. LC 25-152666. The Bobbs Merrill Company.

Proud Ones. Verne Athanas. LC 52-8109. (Essandess western). 1952. Simon and Schuster.

Proud Paladin. Iris Morley. LC 70-144164. (Short story index reprint series). 1971. (ISBN 0-8369-3779-1). Books for Libraries Press.

Proud Paladin. Iris Morley. LC 36-21823. 1936. W. Morrow and Company.

Proud People. Kyle Samuel Crichton. LC 44-2101. 1944. C. Scribner's Sons.

Proud Peter. William Edward Norris. LC 17-5135. 1916. Brentano's.

Proud Prince. Justin Huntly McCarthy. LC 3-25721. 1903. R. H. Russell.

Proud Rachel. James Whitfield Ellison. LC 75-8880. 1975. 8.95 (ISBN 0-8128-1814-8). Stein and Day.

Proud Retreat: A Novel of the Lost Confederate Treasure. 1st Ed. Clifford Dowdey. LC 53-5039. 1953. Doubleday.

Proud Revelry. Amber Lee, pseud. LC 26-7014. 1926. T. Seltzer.

Proud Servant: The Story of Montrose. Margaret Emma Faith Irwin. LC 34-374307. Harcourt, Brace and Company.

Proud Sheriff. new ed. Eugene Manlove Rhodes & Henry Herbert Knibbs. LC 68-31368. (Western frontier library, no. 42). (Illus.). 1968. University of Oklahoma Press.

Proud Sheriff. Eugene Manlove Rhodes & Knibbs, Henry Herbert, 1874- LC 35-2488. 1935. Houghton Mifflin Company.

Proud Surrender. Casey Douglas. (Super Romances Ser.). 384p. 1983. pap. 2.95 (ISBN 0-373-70056-3, Pub. by Worldwide). Harlequin Bks.

Proud Surrender. Diana Haviland. 384p. (Orig.). 1983. pap. 3.50 (ISBN 0-449-12406-1, GM). Fawcett.

Proud Taste for Scarlet and Miniver. E. L Konigsburg. (Illus.). 1973. (lib. ed.) 5.95. Atheneum.

Proud Thistle: A Romantic Chronicle. Helen A F Penniman. LC 51-5486. 1951. Vantage Press.

Proud Tower. Barbara Tuchman. (Illus.). 1972. pap. 4.50 (ISBN 0-553-20314-2, 13074-9). Bantam.

Proud Walk. Nancy Moore. LC 60-11434. 1960. Putnam.

Proud Waters. Ewart Brookes. LC 54-3486. 1954. Jarrolds.

Proud Waters. Lon Riley Woodrum. LC 58-33035. 1958. Zondervan Pub. House.

Proud Way. Shirley Seifert. 1976. Repr. of 1948 ed. lib. bdg. 7.95 (ISBN 0-89190-138-8). Am Repr-Rivercity Pr.

Proud Young Thing. Helen Topping Miller. LC 52-7522. 1952. Appleton-Century-Crofts.

Proud Youth. Alexander Eliot. LC 53-9121. 1953. Farrar, Straus and Young.

Proudest Day. C. Muller. 1972. pap. 1.25 o.p. (01025). Curtis.

Proudly They Die. Lewis B Patten. LC 64-11300. (Double D western). 1964. Doubleday.

Proust's Way: An Essay in Descriptive Criticism. Translated from the French by Gerard Hopkins. Georges Piroue. LC 58-2990. 1958. Essential Books.

Prove It, Mr. Tolefree. Robert Alfred John Walling. LC 33-17937. 1933. W. Morrow & Company.

Proved by Trial. James Hearst. 1979. 10.00; pap. 4.50. Juniper Pr WI.

Proved Unworthy. Emily Sharp H. Cameron. LC 1577. (Arrow library, no. 110). 1900. Street & Smith.

Provenance. Frank McDonald. LC 79-16535. 11.95 (ISBN 0-316-55552-5). Little, Brown.

Provenance House. Elizabeth St. Clair. (Signet Book). 1976. (pbk.) 1.25. New American Library.

Provenance of Death. Kenneth Giles. (O.S.I.). 1967. 3.95 o.s.i. (60206). S&S.

Provence Puzzle. Vincent McConnor. 208p. 1981. pap. 1.95 (ISBN 0-553-14596-7). Bantam.

Provence Puzzle. Vincent McConnor. 1980. 9.95 (ISBN 0-02-582920-3). Macmillan.

Provence Puzzle: An Inspector Damiot Mystery. Vincent McConnor. LC 79-26897. 9.95 (ISBN 0-02-582920-3). Macmillan.

Provence Rose. Louise De La Ramee. LC 9-2496. ("Cozy corner series"). 1894. J. Knight Company.

Proverb & Other Stories. Marcel Ayme. 1961. 4.50 o.p. Atheneum.

Proverb: And Other Stories. Translated from the French by Norman Denny. 1st American Ed. Marcel Ayme. 1961. Atheneum.

Providence Island. Jacquetta Hopkins Hawkes. LC 59-7980. 1959. Random House.

Providence Island. Calder Willingham. LC 68-8088. (Illus.). 1969. 6.95. Vanguard Press.

Province, Port, and Pirate. Lloyd E Griscom. LC 65-4062. 1964. South Jersey Publications.

Provincetown. Burt Hirschfeld. LC 77-670162. 1977. 8.95 (ISBN 0-87272-068-3). Brodart.

Provincetown: A Story (for the Most Part True. Fitzgerald Sale Parker. LC 25-3198. 1924. Cokesbury Press.

Provincial Lady in America. Edmee Elizabeth Monica De La Pasture. LC 34-271473. 1934. Harper & Brothers.

Provincial Lady in London. Edmee Elizabeth Monica De La Pasture. LC 33-27024. 1933. Harper & Brothers.

Provincial Lady in Wartime. Edmee Elizabeth Monica De La Pasture. LC 40-27382. Harper & Brothers.

Provincials. John Cornish. LC 51-3440. 1951. W. Sloane Associates.

Proving Flight. David Beaty. LC 56-8408. 1957. Morrow.

Proving Ground. Elliott Arnold. LC 72-11123. 320p. 1973. 6.95 o.p. (ISBN 0-684-13301-6). Scribner.

Proving Ground. Elizabeth R. Edwards, pseud. LC 73-2665. 1973. 4.95. Zondervan Pub. House.

Proving Ground. Mack Morriss. LC 51-9607. 1951. Duell, Sloan and Pearce.

Proving Ground: A Novel of Civil War Days in the West. Leone Lowden. LC 46-3288. 1946. R. M. McBride & Comapny.

Proving Gun. Ray Hogan. LC 75-9224. 1975. 5.95 (ISBN 0-385-11177-0). Doubleday.

Proving Gun. Ray Hogan. (Signet brand western). 1976. 1.25 (ISBN 0-451-07223-5). New American Library.

Proving Gun. Ray Hogan. LC 80-21890. 1980. 10.95 (ISBN 0-8161-3172-4). G. K. Hall.

Proving of Virginia. Daisy Rhodes Campbell. LC 15-7111. 1915. 1.25. The Page Company.

Proving Trail. Louis L'Amour. LC 79-27829. 1980. 12.95 (ISBN 0-8161-3061-2). G. K. Hall.

Provocateur: A Historical Novel of the Russian Terror. Roman Borisovich Gul' Tr. by Zarine, Leonide. Ed. by Grahan, Stephen. LC 31-4806. Harcourt, Brace and Company.

Provocateur: A Novel. Rene Victor Pilhes. LC 76-5555. 8.95 (ISBN 0-06-013337-6). Harper & Row.

Provocative Merchant of Venice. Daniel Banes. LC 75-28622. 1975. 9.99. Malcolm Hse.

Provost. John Galt. Ed. by Ian Alistair Gordon. LC 73-179679. (Oxford English novels). 1973. (ISBN 0-19-255357-7). Oxford University Press.

Provost. John Galt. LC 72-172253. (His Works, v. 10). (Illus.). 1968. AMS Press.

Provost. John Galt & Ian Alistair Gordon. LC 82-8026. (World's classics). 1982. 4.94 (ISBN 0-19-281629-2). Oxford University Press.

Provost: And The Last of the Lairds. John Galt. Ed. by Meldrum, David Storrar. LC 17-486. (Works of John Galt. Ed. by D. Storrar Meldrum). 1896. Roberts Brothers.

Prowl Cop. Gregory Jones. LC 56-26713. (Ace double novel books, D-147). 1956. Ace Books.

Prowler. Frances Rickett. LC 63-9283. (Inner sanctum mystery). 1963. Simon and Schuster.

Prowler. Hugh Wiley. LC 24-31905. 1924. A. A. Knopf.

Proxy. Violette Newton. 4.50 o.p. Eakin Pubns.

Proxy. Jane White. LC 68-12606. 1968. Harcourt, Brace & World.

Proxy Princess. Josiah Pitts Woolfolk. LC 37-5033. 1937. Godwin.

Prude: A Novel by a Young Lady. Ma. A & Ma A. LC 74-170553. (Foundations of the Novel). 1973. 22.00 ea. (ISBN 0-8240-0551-1). Garland Pub.

Prude: A Novel by a Young Lady see Patchwork Screen for the Ladies.

Prude & the Prodigal. Barbara Cartland. 160p. (Orig.). 1980. pap. 1.75 (ISBN 0-553-14133-3). Bantam.

Prudence. Jilly Cooper. LC 80-13008. 1980. 9.95 (ISBN 0-531-09556-8). D. Elliott: Distributed by Watts.

Prudence. Jilly Cooper. LC 81-3111. 1981. 11.95 (ISBN 0-89340-350-4). J. Curley & Associates.

Prudence: A Story of Aesthetic London. Lucy Cecil White Lillie. LC 7-187989. 1882. Harpe & Brothers.

Prudence and the Pill. Hugh Mills. LC 66-133652. 1966. bds., 2.95. Lippincott.

Prudence Be Damned. Mary McMullen. LC 77-83938. 1978. 6.95 (ISBN 0-385-13187-9). Published for the Crime Club by Doubleday.

Prudence Be Damned. large print ed. Mary McMullen. LC 81-18252. 1981. 9.95 (ISBN 0-89621-326-9). Thorndike Press.

Prudence, Indeed. Anne Bernays. LC 66-26230. 1966. 4.95. Trident.

Prudence, Indeed. Anne Bernays. (75268). 1968. Pocket Bks.

Prudence of the Parsonage. Ethel Powelson Hueston. LC 15-16774. The Bobbs-Merrill Company.

Prudence Palfrey. A Novel. Thomas Bailey Aldrich. LC 6-50162. 1874. J. R. Osgood and Company.
Prudence Palfrey: A Novel. 13th ed. Thomas Bailey Aldrich. LC 41-30711. 1886. Houghton, Mifflin and Company.
Prudence Palfrey: A Novel. Thomas Bailey Aldrich. 1902. Houghton, Mifflin and Company.
Prudence Says So. Ethel Powelson Hueston. LC 16-16688. 1916. The Bobbs-Merrill Company.
Prudence's Daughter. Ethel Powelson Hueston. LC 24-9667. The Bobbs-Merrill Company.
Prudence's Omnibus... Ethel Powelson Hueston. 1936. Grosset & Dunlap.
Prudent Angle. Anne Tedlock Brooks. LC 48-4399. 1948. Arcadia House.
Prudent Priscilla. Mary C. E. Wemyss. LC 12-24055. 1912. Houghton Mifflin Company.
Prue and I. George William Curtis. LC 6-31708. 1856. Dix, Edwards & Co.
Prue and I. George William Curtis. 1857. Dix, Edwards & Co.
Prue and I. George William Curtis. LC 8-30412. 1870. Harper & Brothers.
Prue and I. George William Curtis. LC 9-30053. Harper & Brother.
Prue and I. George William Curtis. LC 13-177413. 1892. Harper & Brothers.
Prue and I. George William Curtis. LC 99-3341. T. Y. Crowell & Company.
Prue & I. George William Curtis. LC 4-19009. 1899. Harper & Brothers.
Prue and I. George William Curtis. LC 4560. 1900. W. B. Conkey Company.
Prue and I. George William Curtis. LC 31-35219. 1902. The Marshon Company.
Prue and I: And The Public Duty of Educated Men. George William Curtis. Ed. by Brecht, Vincent B. LC 19-9476. (Macmillan's pocket American and English classics). 1919. The Macmillan Company.
Prue and I, and The Public Duty of Educated Men. George William Curtis & Brecht, Vincent Bean, 1874- Ed. LC 19-9476. (Macmillan's pocket American and English classics). 1919. The Macmillan Company.
Prue & I: Lotus Eating. George William Curtis & Mable, Hamilton Wright. (Half-title: Everyman's library, ed. by Ernest Rhys. Essays and belles lettres. no. 418). 1910. J. M. Dent & Sons, Ltd.
Prusias: A Romance of Ancient Rome Under the Republic. authorized ed. rev. and corrected in the united states. ed. Ernst Eckstein & Bell, Mrs. Clara Courtney (Poynter) 1834- Tr. LC 6-3618. 1884. W. S. Gottsberger.
Prussian Officer, and Other Stories. David Herbert Lawrence. LC 72-160939. (Short story index reprint series). 1971. (ISBN 0-8369-3918-2). Books for Libraries Press.
P's Progress. Frank O'Rourke. LC 66-24559. 1966. bds., 3.95. Morrow.
P.S. Your Cat Is Dead! A Novel. James Kirkwood. LC 72-81210. 1972. 6.95 (ISBN 0-8128-1511-4). Stein and Day.
P.S. Your Shrink Is Dead. John Reisan. 1979. pap. 1.95 o.s.i. (ISBN 0-8439-0687-1, Leisure Bks). Nordon Pubns.
P.S. Your Shrink Is Dead. John Reisman. (Leisure Book). 1.95 (ISBN 0-8439-0687-1). Norda Publications, Inc.
Psalm of Sodomy. George Anthony. (Orig.). 1969. pap. 1.25 o.p. (2096). Brandon.
Pseudo One. Clark Darlton. (Perry Rhodan#44). 1974. (pbk.) 0.75. Ace Books.
Pseudo People. William F. Nolan. 1978. pap. 4.95 o.s.i. (ISBN 0-8202-5021-X). Sherbourne.
Pseudo-People: Androids in Science Fiction, Ed. by William F. Nolan. Introd. by A.E. Van Vogt. Ed. by William F. Nolan. (S1437). 1967. Berkley.
Pseudo-People: Androids in Science Fiction. Introd. by A. E. Van Vogt. Ed. by William F. Nolan. LC 65-23703. 4.50. Sherbourne.
Psi High, and Others: By Alan E. Nourse. Alan Edward Nourse. LC 67-17527. 1967. 3.95. McKay.
Psicologo Perverso. new ed. Juan Castellanos. (Pimienta Collection Ser). 160p. 1974. pap. 1.00 (ISBN 0-88473-194-4). Fiesta Pub.
Psionics War. Joseph Rosenberger. (Death Merchant Ser.: No. 48). 192p. (Orig.). 1982. pap. 1.95 (ISBN 0-523-41644-X). Pinnacle Bks.
Psmith in the City. Pelham Grenville Wodehouse. LC 74-22918. 1970. 0.25 (ISBN 0-14-003207-X). Penguin.
Psmith: Journalist. P. G. Wodehouse. 187p. 1981. pap. 2.95 (ISBN 0-14-003214-2). Penguin.
Psmith, Journalist. Pelham Grenville Wodehouse. LC 78-22919. 1970. 0.30 (ISBN 0-14-003214-2). Penguin.
Pstalemate. Lester Del Rey. LC 78-172410. 1971. 4.95. Putnam.
Psy-Fi One: An Anthology of Psychology in Science Fiction. Kenneth B. Melvin & Stanley L. Brodsky. LC 76-56825. 5.95 (ISBN 0-394-30576-0). Random House.
Psyche. Pierre Louys. LC 48-10776. ((New Avon library 166). 1948. Avon Pub. Co.
Psyche. Pierre Louys & Farrere, Claude. LC 28-22361. 1928. Covici, Friede.
Psyche: A Novel. Phyllis Brett Young. LC 60-52108. 1959. Longmans, Green.
Psyche, Novelle: Von Theodor Storm. Theodor Storm & Eiserhardt, Ewald, Ed. LC 13-20277. (Oxford German series). 1913. Oxford University Press, American Branch; Etc., Etc.
Psychedelic Spy. T. A. Waters. (Orig.). 1967. pap. 0.60 o.p. (73-656). Lancer.
Psyche's Art. Louisa May Alcott. 1976. Repr. of 1868 ed. 25.00 o.p. (ISBN 0-403-05872-4, Regency). Scholarly.
Psychiatric Exam & Other Tales. Richard Baldasty. 118p. (Orig.). 1975. pap. 2.25 (ISBN 0-915112-07-8). Seattle Bk.
Psychiatric Murders. Milton Scott Michel. LC 46-1780. 1946. Mystery House.
Psychiatric Novels of Oliver Wendell Holmes. 2d ed., rev. and enl. ed. Oliver Wendell Holmes & Oberndorf, Clarence Paul, 1882- Ed. 1946. Columbia University Press.
Psychiatric Novels of Oliver Wendell Holms: Abridgment, Introduction, and Psychiatric Annotations. 2d ed., rev. and enl. ed. Oliver Wendell Holmes. Ed. by Clarence Paul Oberndorf. LC 72-156193. 1971. (ISBN 0-8371-6142-8). Greenwood Press.
Psychiatric Novels of Oliver Wendell Holmes: Abridgment, Introduction and Annotations by Clarence P. Oberndorf... Oliver Wendell Holmes & Oberndorf, Clarence Paul, 1882- Ed. LC 48-15139. 1943. Columbia University Press.
Psychiatric Nurse. Dan Ross, pseud. 1971. 3.95 o.p. (Avalon). Bouregy.
Psychiatric Nurse. Florence Stonebraker. LC 67-2439. 1967. Arcadia House.
Psychiatrist: A Novel. George Victor Bishop. LC 68-57141. 1968. 4.95. Sherbourne Press.
Psychiatrist, and Other Stories. Machado De Assis, Joaquim Maria. LC 63-9407. 1963. University of California Press.
Psychiatrist Says Murder. Lucy Freeman. LC 73-82190. 1973. 6.95 (ISBN 0-87795-073-3). Arbor House.
Psychiatrists. Wolf Wallace. 1976. (pbk.) 1.25. Award Books.
Psychic and the Swamp Man. Kathleen Martell Gordon. LC 80-52855. 1981. 12.95 (ISBN 0-670-58188-7). Viking Press.
Psychic Detective No. 1. Hans Holzer. 192p. 1976. pap. 1.25 (ISBN 0-532-12374-3). Woodhill.
Psychic Stories Strange but True. Linda Atkinson. (Hi Lo Ser.). 96p. 1981. pap. 1.50 (ISBN 0-553-14823-0). Bantam.
Psychic Trio: Or, Nations Reconciled. Charles Edmund De Land. LC 19-13973. R. G. Badger.
Psychical Stories. John Adams. 1978. 6.95 o.p. (ISBN 0-533-03224-5). Vantage.
Psycho. Robert Bloch. LC 59-2155. (Inner sanctum mystery). 1959. Simon and Schuster.
Psycho II. Robert Bloch. 320p. (Orig.). 1982. pap. 3.50 (ISBN 0-446-90804-5). Warner Bks.
Psycho Sex Camp. Jason Harper. pap. 1.95 o.p. (8044). Cameo.
Psychoanalysis of a Poet. Ambrose Brierty. LC 40-111833. Fortuny's.
Psychogeist. Leslie Purnell Davies. LC 67-12839. 1967. Doubleday.
Psychological Fiction. Ed. by Morris Beja. LC 73-134874. 1971. Scott, Foresman.
Psychological Kingdom... William Earl Harvey. LC 27-23259. 1927. Review Publishing Company.
Psychologist. Putnam P Bishop. LC 6-12719. 1886. G. P. Putnam's Sons.
Psychology of the Observer. Richard Rose. 1979. pap. 5.00. Pyramid WV.
Psychomorph. Michael Butterworth. (Space:1999). (Illus.). 1977. 1.50 (ISBN 0-446-88344-1). Warner Books.
Psychopath Plague. Steven G Spruill. LC 77-77661. 1978. 6.95 (ISBN 0-385-13147-X). Doubleday.
Psychotron Plot see Complot del Psicotron.
P'tit Homme." Little Man. Adolphe Belot. Tr. by Miller, Hettie E. LC 6-11352. (On cover: The optimus series. no. 23). 1892. Donohue, Henneberry & O.
Ptolia, Bk. 1. Fred Baker. LC 82-81453. 175p. (Orig.). 1982. pap. 4.95 (ISBN 0-914766-83-X, 0197). IWP Pub.
Ptomaine Kid: A Hamburger Western. Conger Beasley. LC 81-12736. 6.95 (ISBN 0-8362-6115-1). Andrews and McMeel.
Ptomaine Street: A Tale of Warble Petticoat. Carolyn Wells. LC 21-21552. 1921. J. B. Lippincott Company.
Pu der Bar. Illus. Von Ernest H. Shepard. Ubers. Von E. L. Schiffer. Alan Alexander Milne. LC 68-134151. 1968. 3.95. Dutton.
Pub Crawler. Maurice Procter. LC 81-47386. (Fifty Classics of Crime Fiction, 1950-1975). 1982. 14.95 (ISBN 0-8240-4997-7). Garland Pub.
Pub Crawler. 1st American Ed. Maurice Procter. LC 57-615341. 1957. Harper.
Public Affaires. Barbara Worsley-Gough. LC 32-24664. 1932. L. MacVeagh, Dial Press, Inc.
Public Burning. Robert Coover. LC 77-4923. 1977. 10.00 (ISBN 0-670-58200-X). Viking Press.
Public Burning: A Novel. Robert Coover. 1978. 2.95 (ISBN 0-553-11828-5). Bantam Books.
Public Enemy. Kubec Glasmon & Bright, John. LC 31-113847. Grosset & Dunlap.
Public Faces. Harold George Nicolson. LC 33-144618. 1933. Houghton Mifflin Company.
Public Faces: A Novel... Harold George Nicolson. LC 45-3438. (Penguin books. 489). 1944. Penguin Books.
Public Faces in Private Places. Joseph Rosner. LC 66-127695. 4.95. Delacorte Dist. Dial.
Public Image. Muriel Spark. LC 68-23954. 1968. 4.50. Knopf.
Public Life of Sherlock Holmes. Michael Pointer. LC 74-12785. (Illus.). 1975. 7.95 (ISBN 0-87749-725-7). Drake Publishers.
Public Readings. Charles Dickens & Philip Arthur William Collins. LC 76-354076. (Illus.). 1975. 39.00 (ISBN 0-19-812501-1). Clarendon Press.
Public Relations: A Novel of the Utilities Field. Louis Lefko. LC 36-19094. Dorrance and Company.
Public School Murder. Ralph Carter Woodthorpe. (On cover: Penguin books. 285). 1940. Middlesex, Eng.
Public Smiles, Private Tears. Helen Van Slyke & James Elward. LC 81-47794. 13.95 (ISBN 0-06-014961-2). Harper & Row.
Public Smiles, Private Tears. large print ed. Helen Van Slyke & James Elward. LC 82-10341. 13.95 (ISBN 0-89621-376-5). Thorndike Press.
Public Smiles, Private Tears: The Last Novel. Helen Van Slyke & James Elward. LC 81-47794. 256p. 1982. 13.41i (ISBN 0-06-014961-2, HarpT). Har-Row.
Public Square. Will Levington Comfort. LC 23-8243. 1923. D. Appleton and Company.
Public Sweetheart No. 1. Grace Perkins Oursler. LC 35-15902. Farrar & Rinehart, Incorporated.
Publicans and Sinners; or, Lucius Davoren. A Novel. Mary Elizabeth Braddon Maxwell. LC 6-1248. (On cover: Library of select novels. no. 408). 1874. Harper & Brothers.
Publicans and Sinners: Or, Lucius Davoren. Mary Elizabeth Braddon Maxwell. (Seaside library. v. 31, no. 649). 1879. G. Munro.
Publicans and Sinners: Or, Lucius Davoren. Mary Elizabeth Braddon Maxwell. (On cover: Seaside library. Pocket ed. no. 947). 1887. G. Munro.
Publicity Girl. Paula Gould. LC 40-900927. House of Field Inc.
Publish and Perish. Francis M Nevins. LC 75-20156. (Red mask mystery). 1975. 6.95 (ISBN 0-399-11604-4). Putnam.
Publisher. Alexander Fullerton. LC 75-136787. 1971. 5.95. Putnam.
Publishers Choice. Scribner Editors. 1967. 4.95 o.p. Scribner.
Publisher's Choice. Richard Yates et al. 1967. 6.95 o.p. Scribner.
Publisher's Choice: Ten Short Story Discoveries by the Eds. of Scribners. Scribner, Firm, Publishers, New York. LC 67-24056. 1967. 4.95. Scribners.
Publit. Ferdinand Kriwet. (Illus.). 96p. (Orig.). 1971. pap. 4.50 (ISBN 0-89366-018-3). Ultramarine Pub.
Puck: His Vicissitudes, Adventures, Observations, Conclusions, Friendships, and Philosophies. Related by Himself, and. Louise De La Ramee. LC 3-10901. 1870. J. B. Lippincott & Co.
Puck: His Vicissitudes, Adventures, Observations, Conclusions, Friendships, and Philosophies. Related by Himself, and. Louise De La Ramee. LC 3-10900. (seaside library. v. 17, no. 334). 1878. G. Munro.
Puck: His Vicissitudes, Adventures, Observations, Conclusions, Friendships, and Philosophies. Related by Himself, and. Louise De La Ramee. LC 3-10899. (Seaside library. Pocket ed. no. 1000). 1887. G. Munro.
Puck: His Vicissitudes, Adventures, Observations, Conclusions, Friendships, and Philosophies. Related by Himself, and. Louise De La Ramee. LC 3-10902. 1896. J. B. Lippincott Company.
Puck of Pook's Hill. Rudyard Kipling. LC 67-24221. (Illus.). 1968. Dover Publications.
Puck of Pook's Hill. Rudyard Kipling. LC 6-35734. 1906. Doubleday, Page & Company.
Puck of Pook's Hill. Rudyard Kipling. LC 18-21688. 1914. Doubleday, Page & Company for Review of Reviews Co.
Puck of Pook's Hill. Rudyard Kipling. LC 20-22087. 1920. Doubleday, Page & Company.
Puck of Pook's Hill. Rudyard Kipling. LC 28-1671. 1923. Doubleday, Page & Company.
Puck of Pook's Hill. Rudyard Kipling. LC 41-252581. 1925. Doubleday, Page & Company.
Puck of Pook's Hill. Rudyard Kipling. LC 46-20642. Doubleday & Company, Inc.
Puck of Pook's Hill. Illus. by Arthur Rackham. Rudyard Kipling. (Dover bk., T1880 rebound). 1968. 4.00. Peter Smith.
Puddenhead Wilson with "Those Extraordinary Twins". Mark Twain. Repr. of 1894 ed. 10.00 o.p. (ISBN 0-06-014415-7, HarpT). Har-Row.
Puddleford, and Its People. Henry Hiram Riley. LC 7-41646. 1854. S. Hueston.
Puddleford Papers: Or, Humors of the West. Henry Hiram Riley. LC 15-12482. 1857. Derby & Jackson.
Puddleford Papers: Or Humors of the West. Henry Hiram Riley. LC 24-29460. (On cover: Library of wit and humor). 1860. Derby & Jackson.
Puddleford Papers: Or, Humors of the West. Henry Hiram Riley. LC 7-41647. (On cover: Wild life series). 1875. Lee and Shepard.
Pudd'nhead Wilson. Samuel Langhorne Clemens. Limited Editions Club. LC 74-196082. (Illus.). 1974. Limited Editions Club.
Pudd'nhead Wilson. Mark Twain. (Bantam Classics Ser.). 1981. pap. 1.75 (ISBN 0-553-21004-1). Bantam.
Pudd'nhead Wilson. Mark Twain. pap. 1.75 (ISBN 0-451-51743-1, CE1743, Sig Classics). NAL.
Pudd'nhead Wilson. Mark Twain. (YA) (gr. 9 up). 1955. pap. 1.95 o.p. (ISBN 0-394-17202-7, E25, Ever). Grove.
Pudd'nhead Wilson. Mark Twain. pap. 1.48 o.p. (HP6043, PL). Har-Row.
Pudd'nhead Wilson. Mark Twain. (Library of English & American Classics). 1962. 3.95 o.p. (ISBN 0-15-175295-8). HarBraceJ.
Pudd'nhead Wilson: A Tale by Mark Twain Pseud. With an Introd. by F. R. Leavis. Samuel Langhorne Clemens. LC 56-361. (Evergreen books, 25). 1955. Grove Press.
Pudd'nhead Wilson, and The Man That Corrupted Hadleyburg. Samuel Langhorne Clemens. LC 65-5828. 1964. Harper & Row.
Pudd'nhead Wilson, and Those Extraordinary Twins. Samuel Langhorne Clemens. LC 68-10821. (Chandler facsimile editions in American literature). (Illus.). 1968. Chandler Pub. Co.; Science Research Associates, Distributors, Chicago.
Pudd'nhead Wilson: And, Those Extraordinary Twins. Samuel Langhorne Clemens. LC 71-424786. (Penguin English library). (Illus.). 1969. Penguin.
Pudd'nhead Wilson and Those Extraordinary Twins. Samuel Langhorne Clemens. LC 4-15439. 1903. Harper & Brothers.
Pudd'nhead Wilson and Those Extraordinary Twins. Samuel Langhorne Clemens. LC 20-12306. Harper and Brothers.
Pudd'nhead Wilson and Those Extraordinary Twins. Samuel Langhorne Clemens. Harper & Brothers.
Pudd'nhead Wilson: Facsimile Ed. Mark Twain. Ed. by Hamlin Hill. LC 68-10821. (Facsimile Series in American Literature). (Illus.). 1968. pap. 2.25x o.p. (ISBN 0-8102-0228-X, 23-10534). Chandler Pub.
Pudney and Walp. Fannie Bean. LC 6-10270. (On cover: American authors' series, no. 40). J.W. Lovell Company.
Pudney & Walp: Two Millionaires of Maine. A Novel. Fannie Bean. LC 6-10355. (On cover: The Waldorf series, no. 1). 1893. Saalfield & Fitch.
Pudoria. Tom Pease. LC 61-11367. L. Stuart.
Pueblo Boy: A Story of Coronados' Search for the Seven Cities of Cibola. Cornelia James Cannon. 1926. lib. bdg. 15.00 o.s.i. (ISBN 0-512-00823-X). Garrett Pr.
Puffball: A Novel. Fay Weldon. LC 80-14585. 10.95 (ISBN 0-671-44809-9). Summit Books.
Pug: A Novel. Albert E Idell. LC 41-7692. The Greystone Press.
Pugilist & Other Short Stories. Charles Tortorello. 1978. 5.95 (ISBN 0-533-03233-4). Vantage.
Pulaski Place. Ruth M. Tabrah. LC 50-5054. 1950. Harper.
Pulitzer Prize Murders. Dorothy Hartzell Kuhns Heyward. LC 32-10753. Farrar & Rinehart, Incorporated.
Pulitzer Prize Winner. Ted Lloyd. LC 34-15302. Empire Publishing Company.
Pull Down to New Orleans. Zachary Ball, pseud. LC 46-7569. 1946. Crown Publishers.
Pull Down to New Orleans. Kelly R. Master & Frankie Lee Weed. LC 46-7569. 1946. Crown Publishers.
Pulled Down. Phyllis Paul. LC 64-18752. 4.50. Norton.
Pulling Through. Dean Ing. 1983. pap. 2.95 (ISBN 0-441-69050-5, Pub. by Ace Science Fiction). Ace Bks.
Pullman Car Detective. George P. Farley. LC 6-38760. (On cover: Pinkerton detective series. no. 17). 1894. Laird & Lee.

Pulp Jungle. Frank Gruber. 192p. 1967. 3.95 o.p. (ISBN 0-8202-0048-4). Sherbourne.
Pulp Jungle. Frank Gruber. LC 67-21873. 1967. 6.95x o.p. Boulevard.
Pulpit Germs. William W. Wythe. 1.50 o.p. (ISBN 0-8170-0156-5). Judson.
Pulpit in the Grill Room. Edward Phillips Oppenheim. LC 39-11255. 1939. Little, Brown and Company.
Pulps: Fifty Years of American Pop Culture. Ed. by Tony Goodstone. LC 71-127013. (Illus.). 1970. 15.00. Chelsea House.
Pulse. J. M. Henegan. 1980. 11.95 (ISBN 0-7145-3667-9); pap. 6.95 (ISBN 0-7145-3618-0). Riverrun NY.
Pulse of Danger: A Novel. Jon Cleary. LC 66-11664. bds., 4.50. Morrow.
Pulse of Darkness: A Tale of Eastern Seas... Edward Noble. 1929. Houghton Mifflin Company.
Pulse of Death. Peter Kaufman. 3.95 o.p. Vantage.
Pulse of Life: A Story of a Passing World. Marie Adelaide Belloc Lowndes. LC 9-2771. 1909. Dodd, Mead & Company.
Pulsebeat: A Novel. Frank Smith. LC 54-212353. 1954. Woodford Press.
Puma. Ulf Miehe. LC 77-10285. 10.00 (ISBN 0-312-65573-8). St. Martin's Press.
Puma Pistoleers. Lee Floren. (Orig.). 1981. pap. 1.95 (ISBN 0-8439-0920-X, Leisure Bks). Nordon Pubns.
Puma Pistoleers: By Dave Wilson Pseud. Lee Floren. LC 51-14989. 1951. Arcadia House.
Pumkin Shell. Estelle Thomson. LC 28-12299. 1928. The Canterbury Company.
Pump Dont Work. Doug Kermode. 1978. pap. 3.00 o.p. (ISBN 0-9602202-1-6). D Kermode.
Pumpkin Coach. Louis Paul. LC 35-526354. 1935. Doubleday, Doran & Company.
Pumpkin Eater. Penelope Mortimer. LC 75-16509. 1975. pap. 4.00 (ISBN 0-913780-36-7). Daughters.
Pumpman & Other Stories. E. L. Sherrill. 1980. 5.95 (ISBN 0-533-03416-7). Vantage.
Punch, a Novel of Negro Life: By George Barksdale, M. D. George Barksdale. LC 4-14367. 1904. The Neale Publishing Company.
Punch and Judy Murders. John Dickson Carr. LC 37-1012. 1937. W. Morrow & Company.
Punch Book of Short Stories II. Ed. by Alan Coren. 192p. 1981. 9.95 (ISBN 0-312-65577-0). St Martin.
Punch, Brothers, Punch. And Other Sketches. Samuel Langhorne Clemens.
Punch Goes the Judy. William Sonzski. 1971. 5.95 o.p. (7128-6). Delacorte.
Punch Goes the Judy: A Novel. William Sonzski. LC 70-142593. 1972. (440-07225-125) 1.25. Dell.
Punch with Care: An Asey Mayo Mystery. Phoebe Atwood Taylor. LC 46-7999. 1946. Farrar, Straus and Company.
Puncher Pards. C. William Harrison. LC 42-158213. 1942. Phoenix Press.
Punching the Clock for Freedom. Strader Westfall. LC 44-20100. 1944. The Franklin Press.
Punch's Boy: A Romance of the Nineteenth Century. Carmel Goldsmid Guest. LC 43-3707. 1942. Hutchinson & Co. Ltd.
Punctual Rape. Campbell Black. LC 78-141909. 1971. 4.95. Lippincott.
Punish Me with Kisses. William Bayer. 1981. pap. 2.95 (ISBN 0-671-41991-9). PB.
Punish Me with Kisses. William Bayer. 256p. 1980. 10.95 (ISBN 0-312-92664-2). St Martin.
Punish the Sinners. John Saul. (Dell Book). 1978. 2.25 (ISBN 0-440-17084-2). Dell Pub. Co.
Punishment. Doris Shannon. 320p. 1981. 12.95 (ISBN 0-312-65584-3). St Martin.
Punishment: A Novel. Lawrence Highland. LC 28-7327. The Four Seas Company.
Punishment: A Novel of Terror. Doris Shannon. LC 80-14997. 12.95 (ISBN 0-312-65584-3). St. Martin's Press.
Punishment Master. Tom Young. 192p. (Orig.). 1973. pap. 1.95 o.p. (ISBN 0-87977-184-4, DBB184). Dansk Blue Bk.
Punishment of a Vixen. Barbara Cartland. LC 77-670161. 1977. 6.95 (ISBN 0-87272-071-3). Duron Books.
Punishment of the Stingy: And Other Indian Stories. George Bird Grinnell. LC 1-25669. (Half-title: Harper's portrait collection of short stories, v. 5). 1901. Harper & Brothers.
Punishment of the Stingy and Other Indian Stories. George Bird Grinnell. LC 81-21922. (Illus.). 17.50 (ISBN 0-8032-2113-4) (ISBN 0-8032-7008-9). University of Nebraska Press.
Punishment Pawn. Robert F. Slatzer. 192p. (Orig.). 1972. pap. 1.95 o.p. (ISBN 0-87977-176-3, DBB-176). Dansk Blue Bk.
Punishment Without Crime. L. H. Green. 1977. 7.50 o.p. (ISBN 0-533-02345-9). Vantage.
Punjabi Short Stories: An Anthology. G. S. Khosla. 119p. 1982. 32.00x (ISBN 0-7069-1311-6, Pub. by Garlandfold England). State Mutual Bk.
Punjabi Short Stories-an Anthology. Ed. by G. S. Khosla. 140p. 1981. text ed. 15.95x (ISBN 0-7069-1311-6, Pub. by Vikas India). Advent NY.
Punk Novel. Bad Al. 1980. 6.95 o.s.i. (ISBN 0-02-504630-6); prepack 83.40 o.s.i. (ISBN 0-02-504640-3). Macmillan.
Punks. Eugenia Woods. LC 45-35400. House of Field-Doubleday, Inc.
Pup Called Cinderella. Esther Watson Reno. LC 39-21778. The Bobbs-Merrill Company.
Pupil of Pleasure: Exhibiting, the Adventures of a Man of Birth, Rank, Figure, Fortune, and Character, Ardent in the Pursuit of Pleasure, Much Delighted with, Attracted by, and Formed Upon the Chesterfieldean System... Samuel Jackson Pratt. LC 7-302893. Printed by Robert Bell, in Third-Street.
Pupil of the Legion of Honor. Louis Enault & Tutt, Mrs. Rebecca L., Tr. LC 6-37822. Porter and Coates.
Puppet Booth see Collected Works.
Puppet Crown. Harold MacGrath. LC 2-5224. The Bowen-Merrill Company.
Puppet Crown. Harold MacGrath. LC 17-9710. 1916. The Bobbs-Merrill Company.
Puppet for a Corpse: A Luke Thanet Mystery. Dorothy Simpson. 192p. 1983. 12.95 (ISBN 0-684-17909-1, ScribT). Scribner.
Puppet Master. Nick Carter. (Nick Carter Ser.). (Illus.). 224p. 1982. pap. 2.50 (ISBN 0-441-69148-X, Pub. by Charter Bks). Ace Bks.
Puppet Master. Robert Nathan. LC 23-14805. 1923. R. M. McBride & Company.
Puppet Masters. Robert Anson Heinlein. (Signet book). 1975. (pbk.) 0.95. New American Library.
Puppet Masters. Robert Anson Heinlein. LC 51-13249. (Doubleday science fiction). 1951. Doubleday.
Puppet Masters. Robert Anson Heinlein. LC 79-14086. (Gregg Press science fiction series). (Illus.). 1979. 11.00 (ISBN 0-8398-2508-0). Gregg Press.
Puppet on a Chain. Alistair MacLean. LC 71-91110. 1969. 5.95. Doubleday.
Puppet Show. Martin Donisthorpe Armstrong. LC 71-163020. (Short story index reprint series). 1971. (ISBN 0-8369-3934-4). Books for Libraries Press.
Puppet Show. Pauline Follansbee. LC 32-25726. Dorrance & Company, Inc.
Puppet-Show: A Sketch. 2d ed. The Abbey Press.
Puppet-Show: A Sketch. Leonidas Westervelt. LC 8-36224. F. T. Neely.
Puppet Show of Memory. Maurice Baring. 1922. 25.00 (ISBN 0-8274-3227-5). R West.
Puppets: A Work-a-Day Philosophy. George Forbes. LC 11-23410. 1911. The Macmillan Company.
Puppets of Chance. Robert Portner Koehler. LC 33-16728. Sears Publishing Company, Inc.
Puppies. John Valentine. LC 79-51411. 5.95 (ISBN 0-9601428-3-5). Entwhistle Books.
Puppies of Terra. Thomas M. Disch. 1980. 1.75 (ISBN 0-671-82839-8). Pocket Books.
Puppy Love: A Hollywood Romance... Alma Sioux Scarberry. LC 33-29345. Grosset & Dunlap.
Pups and Pies. Ellis Parker Butler. LC 38-6351. 1938. The Sun Dial Press, Inc.
Purcell Papers. Joseph Sheridan Le Fanu. LC 71-148813. 57.50 (ISBN 0-404-08880-5). AMS Press.
Purcell Papers. Joseph Sheridan Le Fanu. LC 75-2524. 1975. 7.00 (ISBN 0-87054-072-6). Arkham House.
Purcell Papers. Joseph Sheridan Le Fanu. LC 76-5274. (Le Fann, Joseph Sheridan, 1814-1873. Works. 1976). 1976. (3 vols.) 53.00 (ISBN 0-405-09225-3). Arno Press.
Purcell Papers. Joseph Sheridan Le Fanu. LC 78-12574. (Ireland, from the Act of Union, 1800, to the Death of Parnell, 1891). 1979. (ISBN 0-8240-3507-0). Garland Pub.
Purchase of the North Pole. Jules Verne. 3.95. Assoc Bk.
Purchase Price: Or, The Cause of Compromise. Emerson Hough. LC 10-27881. The Bobbs-Merrill Company.
Pure and Simple. Bellamy Partridge. LC 34-36547. W. Godwin, Inc.
Pure and the Impure: A Case-Book of Love. Sidonie Gabrielle Colette. Tr. by Dally, Edith. Farrar & Rinehart, Inc.
Pure and Untouched. Barbara Cartland. LC 81-3082. 10.95 (ISBN 0-89696-138-9). Everest House.
Pure As the Lily. Catherine Cookson. LC 72-86550. 1973. 6.95. Bobbs-Merrill.
Pure As the Lily. Catherine Cookson. 1974. (pbk.) 1.25. Bantam Books.
Pure Gamble. Neal Metcalf. LC 73-85213. (Illus.). 1974. 3.25 (ISBN 0-913700-00-2). Word Wheel Books.
Pure Girl. James Noble Gifford. LC 33-738167. 1933. W. Godwin, Inc.
Pure Gold. Emily Sharp H. Cameron. LC 6-21849. (On cover: Lovell's library, v. 19, no. 927). J. W. Lovell.
Pure Gold. Ole Edvart Rolvaag. LC 73-11846. 1973. 13.50 (ISBN 0-8371-7070-2). Greenwood Press.
Pure Gold. Ole Edvart Rolvaag & Erhahl, Silvert, Tr. LC 30-429912. 1930. Harper & Brothers.
Pure Gold. A Novel. Emily Sharp H. Carmeron. LC 6-21850. (On cover: Seaside library. Pocket ed., no. 912). G. Munro.
Pure in Heart. Jack Kahane. LC 28-15168. 1928. Brentanos, Ltd.
Pure in Heart. Franz V. Werfel. Tr. by Geoffrey Dunlop. LC 31-26884. 1931. Simon and Schuster.
Pure in Heart: Translated from the French... Joseph Kessel. LC 29-948827. 1928. Dodd, Mead and Company.
Pure Land. Lonnie C. Mings. LC 79-20094. 4.95 (ISBN 0-8024-2636-0). Moody Press.
Pure Poison. Hillary Waugh. LC 66-197516. 3.50. Pub. for Crime Club by Doubleday.
Pure Souled Liar: By ... LC 7-42395. 1888. C. H. Kerr & Company.
Purely Academic: A Novel. Stringfellow Barr. LC 57-12400. 1958. Simon and Schuster.
Purgatory of the Conquered: A Novel. 1st Ed. Joseph L Whatley. LC 56-12584. Greenwich Book Publishers.
Purgatory Street. Roman McDougald. 1946. Simon and Schuster.
Purgatory Zone. Arsen Darney. 288p. (Orig.). 1981. pap. 2.25 (ISBN 0-441-69168-4). Ace Bks.
Puritan. Liam O'Flaherty. LC 32-4344. Harcourt, Brace and Company.
Puritan and His Daughter. LC 7-34066. 1849. Baker and Scribner.
Puritan and Pagan. Elizabeth Frances Corbett. LC 20-201885. 1920. 1.75. H. Holt and Company.
Puritan and the Quaker: A Story of Colonial Times... Rebecca Beach. 1879. G. P. Putnam's Sons.
Puritan Bohemia. Margaret Pollock Sherwood. LC 8-7349. 1896. The Macmillan Company.
Puritan Captain. Emanuel C Charlton. 1908. Christian Publishing Association.
Puritan Fairy Tales: Short Stories & Poems, for Young and Old. Stephanie Marie Bridge. LC 34-36070. 1934. Reynolds Printing.
Puritan Image. Barbara Gilman. LC 47-326484. 1947. Doubleday & Company, Inc.
Puritan Lover. Laura Dayton Fessenden. LC 6-38979. (With her A colonial dam. Chicago and New York, Rand, McNally & company c1897).
Puritan Pagan: A Novel. Julie Grinnell Storrow Cruger. 1891. D. Appleton and Company.
Puritan Strain. Faith Baldwin Cuthrell. LC 35-9288. Farrar & Rinehart, Incorporated.
Puritan Wooing: A Tale of the Great Awakening in New England. Frank Samuel Child. LC 99-2887. 1898. The Baker & Taylor Co.
Puritan 5. Roger R Larson. LC 82-8713. 1983. 14.95 (ISBN 0-87949-220-1). Ashley Books.
Puritans. Arlo Bates. LC 68-20005. (Americans in Fiction). 1968. Gregg Press.
Puritans. Arlo Bates. LC 98-43931. 1898. Houghton, Mifflin and Company.
Puritan's Daughter: Sequel to "Creole and Puritan." A Character Romance of Two Sections. Thomas Cooper De Leon. LC 6-34183. 1891. The Gossip Printing Company.
Puritan's Wife. Max Pemberton. LC 3-21934. 1896. Dodd, Mead and Company.
Purity League. Alan Williams. LC 76-77632. 1969. 5.95. Putnam.
Purity's Passion. Janette Seymour. (Kangaroo Book). 1977. 1.95 (ISBN 0-671-81036-7). Pocket Books.
Purloined Letter. The Murders in the Rue Morgue. Illus. by Rick Schreiter. Edgar Allan Poe. LC 66-105787. 2.65, 1.98 lib. ed.,. Watts.
Purloined Letter: The Murders in the Rue Morgue. Edgar Allan Poe. LC 66-10578. 1966. F. Watts.
Purloined Paperweight: By P. G. Wodehouse. Pelham Grenville Wodehouse. LC 67-16724. 1967. 4.50. S.&S.
Purloined Prince. Ian Wallace. LC 72-154251. (Illus.). 1971. 5.95 (ISBN 0-8415-0134-3). McCall Books.
Purloining Tiny. John Franklin Bardin. LC 77-10192. 8.95 (ISBN 0-06-010227-6). Harper & Row.
Purple & Fine Linen. Emily Price Post. LC 5-33650. 1905. D. Appleton and Company.
Purple and Fine Linen. A Novel. Edgar Fawcett. LC 6-38783. 1873. G. W. Carleton & Co.; Etc., Etc.
Purple and Fine Women. Edgar Evertson Saltus. LC 79-182714. 1968. AMS Press.
Purple and Fine Women. Edgar Evertson Saltus. LC 25-8944. 1925. P. Covici.
Purple and Homespun: A Novel. Samuel Major Gardenhire. LC 8-12767. 1908. Harper & Brothers.
Purple Ball. Frank Lucius Packard. LC 33-33270. 1933. Pub. for the Crime Club, Inc., by Doubleday Doran & Company, Inc.
Purple Book. Philip Jose Farmer. 288p. (Orig.). 1982. pap. 2.95 (ISBN 0-523-48529-8). Pinnacle Bks.
Purple Butterfly. Louise Coddington Denio. LC 7-22114. Broadway Publishing Co.
Purple Cloud. Matthew Phipps Shiel. LC 77-8905. (Gregg Press science fiction series). 1977. 20.00 (ISBN 0-8398-2381-9). Gregg Press.
Purple Cloud. Matthew Phipps Shiel. LC 30-9244. The Vanguard Press.
Purple Cloud see Empress of the Earth.
Purple Dawson, Rancher. William L Hawkins. LC 34-35690. Phoenix Press.
Purple Dragon. Kenneth Robeson, pseud. (Doc Savage; no. 91). 1978. 1.25 (ISBN 0-553-11116-7). Bantam Books.
Purple Hat. James F Deffet. LC 72-86216. 2.50 (ISBN 0-8059-1740-3). Dorrance.
Purple Hearts: A Tale of the World War. Sam H Elliott & Tepper, Louis, Joint Author. LC 38-31057. Allied Publishing Company.
Purple Heights. Marie Conway Oemler. LC 20-17411. 1920. The Century Co.
Purple Land. William Henry Hudson. LC 27-6056. The Modern Library.
Purple Land: Being the Narrative of One Richard Lamb's Adventures in the Banda Oriental in South America. William Henry Hudson. LC 72-182049. (collected works of W. H. Hudson). (Illus.). 1968. AMS Press.
Purple Land: Being the Narrative of One Richard Lamb's Adventures in the Banda Oriental, in South America, As Told by Himself. A Novel. William Henry Hudson. 1906. E. P. Dutton & Co.
Purple Land: Being the Narrative of One Richard Lamb's Aventures in the Banda Oriental, in South America, As Told by Himseld. William Henry Hudson. LC 17-1333. 1916. E. P. Dutton and Company.
Purple Land: Being the Narrative of One Richard Lamb's Adventures in the Banda Oriental in South America As Told by Himself. William Henry Hudson & Roosevelt, Theodore, Pres. U.S., 1858-1919. (Half-title: Everyman's library, edited by Ernest Rhys. Fiction. no. 800B(). 1927. E. P. Dutton & Co.
Purple Light of Love. Henry Goelet McVickar. LC 7-20277. 1894. D. Appleton and Company.
Purple Mask: Adapted from the Play "Le Chevalier Au Masque" of Mm. Pual Armont and Jean Manoussi. Louise Jordan Miln & Armont, Paul. Le Chevalier Au Masque. LC 21-4512. 1921. Frederick A. Stokes Company.
Purple Mist. Gladys Edson Locke. LC 24-172505. 1924. L. C. Page & Company, Inc.
Purple Mists. Florence Ethel Mills Young. LC 14-5476. 1914. John Lane.
Purple Onion Mystery. Harriette Ashbrook. LC 41-13224. Coward-McCann Inc.
Purple Parasol. George Barr McCutcheon. LC 5-11906. 1905. Dodd, Mead and Company.
Purple Parrot. Clyde B Clason. LC 37-11248. 1937. Pub. for the Crime Club, Inc., by Doubleday, Doran & Co., Inc.
Purple Parrot. Clyde B Clason. LC 38-23548. 1938. The Sun Dial Press, Inc.
Purple Passage: A Novel About a Lady Both Famous and Fantastic. Emily Hahn. LC 50-9525. 1950. Doubleday.
Purple Peaks. Peggy O'More, pseud. LC 54-5844. Arcadia House.
Purple Pearl. Agnes Russell Weekes & Weekes, Rose Kirkpatrick, 1874- Joint Author. LC 22-443286. 1922. Dodd, Mead and Company.
Purple Pirate. Talbot Mundy. LC 35-19981. 1935. D. Appleton-Century Company, Incorporated.
Purple Place for Dying. John Dann MacDonald. LC 76-4096. 1976. 7.95 (ISBN 0-397-01166-0). Lippincott.
Purple Plain. Herbert Ernest Bates. LC 47-123508. 1947. Little, Brown.
Purple Private. Talbot Mundy. Repr. lib. bdg. 19.40x (ISBN 0-89190-489-1). Am Repr-Rivercity Pr.
Purple Prophet. William Everett Cox. LC 53-13226. 1953. Bruce Humphries.
Purple Pterodactyls. Lyon Sprague De Camp. Ed. by Jim Baen. 1980. pap. 2.25 (ISBN 0-441-69190-0). Ace Bks.
Purple Pterodactyls: The Adventures of W. Wilson Newbury, Ensorcelled Financier. Lyon Sprague De Camp. (W. Wilson Newbury Ser.). 1979. 15.00 (ISBN 0-932096-02-6). Phantasia Pr.
Purple Pugassus and His Bravery Trips. Garven Dalglish. (Illus.). 1972. 1.95. Argus Communications.
Purple Pugassus Do-It-Yourself Cooking School. Garven Dalglish. (Illus.). 1972. 1.95. Argus Communications.
Purple Quest: A Novel of Seafaring Adventure in the Ancient World. Frank Gill Slaughter. LC 65-10637. 4.95. Doubleday.

Purple Quest: A Novel of Seafaring Adventure in the Ancient World. Frank Gill Slaughter. (50275). 1966. Pocket Bks.
Purple Rhododendron, and Other Stories. John Fox. LC 67-5416. 1967. Young Publications.
Purple Rim: And Six Other Tales for Summer Reading. Hamilton Ormsbee. (On verso of t.-p.: Brooklyn daily eagle library. v. 11, no. 3). 1896. Brooklyn Daily Eagle.
Purple Sapphire. Eric Temple Bell. LC 24-23174. E. P. Dutton & Company.
Purple Sapphire see Three Science-Fiction Novels.
Purple Sapphire see Time Stream.
Purple Sash. A. Nunez Alonso. Orig. Title: Lazo De Purpura. 1969. 7.50 o.p. McKay.
Purple Sash: A Historical Novel. Nunez Alonso, Alejandro. LC 72-79506. (Illus.). 1969. D. McKay Co.
Purple Sea: More Splashes of Chinese Color. Frank Owen. 1930. The Lantern Press.
Purple Shells. Raymond Leslie Goldman. LC 47-6382. 1947. Ziff-Davis Pub. Co.
Purple Sickle Murders: An Inspector French Detective Story. Freeman Wills Crofts. 1929. Harper & Brothers.
Purple Springs. Nellie Letitia Mooney McClung. LC 22-133212. 1922. Houghton Mifflin Company.
Purple Stockings. Edward Salisbury Field. LC 11-255581. 1.25. W. J. Watt & Company.
Purple Was the Robe: The Divine Truth. Mary Cashion. 1970. 5.50 o.p. (ISBN 0-682-47150-X). Exposition.
Purple-6. Henry Brinton. LC 62-18733. 1962. Walker.
Purse. Elma E Karki. LC 72-7987. (Geneva book). 1969. 2.00. Carlton Press.
Purse of Coppers: Short Stories. Sean O'Faolain. LC 38-7458. 1938. The Viking Press.
Purse Strings. Edith Mendel Stern. LC 27-18846. 1927. Boni and Liveright.
Purslane. Bernice Kelly Harris. LC 39-273761. The University of North Carolina Press.
Pursue the Wind. Richards Leslie. 240p. (Orig.). 1975. pap. 1.25 o.p. (ISBN 0-532-12353-0, 12353). Woodhill.
Pursue the Wind. Lestie Richards. 240p. (Orig.). 1975. pap. 1.25 o.p. (ISBN 0-532-12353-0, 12353). Manor Bks.
Pursued. Robert Friedman. LC 72-77800. 1972. pap. 1.95 o.p. (ISBN 0-8307-0153-2, 50-059-06). Regal.
Pursued by the Law. James MacLaren Cobban. LC 99-1806. (Half-title: Appletons' town and country library, no. 263). 1899. D. Appleton and Company.
Pursuer. Louis Golding. LC 36-491. Farrar & Rinehart, Inc.
Pursuit. Robert L. Fish. 1979. pap. 2.50 (ISBN 0-425-04258-8). Berkley Pub.
Pursuit. Rosita Torr Forbes. LC 28-11399. The Macaulay Company.
Pursuit. Berry Morgan. LC 66-11221. 1966. 4.95. Houghton.
Pursuit. Berry Morgan. Pocket Bks.
Pursuit. Lewis B Patten. LC 57-11179. (Perma books, M-3088. Western 8). 1957. Permabooks.
Pursuit. Lewis B Patten. LC 81-2895. 1981. 7.95 (ISBN 0-89621-292-0). Thorndike Press.
Pursuit. Roland Pertwee. LC 30-25304. 1930. Houghton Mifflin Company.
Pursuit. Frank Mackenzie Savile. LC 10-13479. 1910. Little, Brown, and Company.
Pursuit: A Novel. Robert L Fish. LC 77-27700. 1978. 10.00 (ISBN 0-385-13398-7). Doubleday.
Pursuit in Peru. Mary Violet Herberden. 1946. Pub. for the Crime Club by Doubleday & Company, Inc.
Pursuit of a Parcel. Patricia Wentworth. LC 42-123124. 1942. J. B. Lippincott Company.
Pursuit of D. B. Cooper. D. B. Cooper. 1981. pap. 2.50 (ISBN 0-440-17167-9). Dell.
Pursuit of Furies. Janice Davis Warnke. LC 66-10401. 5.95. Random.
Pursuit of Gentlemen: Illustrated by Jack Long. Kathryn Cravens. LC 51-6910. 1951. Coward-McCann.
Pursuit of Happiness. Mervyn Jones. LC 76-4069. 1976. 7.95 (ISBN 0-88405-146-3). Mason/Charter.
Pursuit of Happiness. Mervyn Jones. 1977. 1.75 (ISBN 0-380-01660-5). Avon Books.
Pursuit of Happiness. Roy Monroe Micklethwait. LC 50-366422. 1949. Malo Pub. Co.
Pursuit of Happiness. Thomas H. Rogers. LC 68-201132. 1968. 5.50. New Amer. Lib.
Pursuit of Love. Nancy Mitford. LC 57-6497. (Modern library paperbacks, P27). 1957. Random House.
Pursuit of Love. Nancy Mitford. LC 46-3949. 1946. Random House.
Pursuit of Love: A Novel. Nancy Mitford. LC 47-6423. 1947. Sun Dial Press.
Pursuit of Love & Love in a Cold Climate. Nancy Mitford. 6.95 (ISBN 0-394-60481-4). Modern Lib.
Pursuit of Love & Love in a Cold Climate. Nancy Mitford. 1975. (pbk.) 1.95. Popular Library.
Pursuit of Phyllis. John Harwood Bacon. 1904. H. Holt and Company.
Pursuit of the House-Boat. John Kendrick Bangs. LC 79-89550. Repr. of 1897 ed. 6.00 (ISBN 0-404-00497-0). AMS Pr.
Pursuit of the House-Boat. John Kendrick Bangs. Repr. of 1900 ed. lib. bdg. 12.50 (ISBN 0-8414-1671-0). Folcroft.
Pursuit of the House-Boat: Being Some Further Account of the Divers Doings of the Associated Shades, Under the Leadership of Sherlock Holmes, Esq. John Kendrick Bangs. LC 70-115228. (Illus.). 1970. Scholarly Press.
Pursuit of the House-Boat: Being Some Further Account of the Divers Doings of the Associated Shades, Under the Leadership of Sherlock Holmes, Esq. John Kendrick Bangs. LC 79-89550. (Illus.). 1969. AMS Press.
Pursuit of the House-Boat: Being Some Further Account of the Divers Doings of the Associated Shades, Under the Leadership of Sherlock Holmes, Esq. John Kendrick Bangs. LC 6-6121. 1897. Harper & Brothers.
Pursuit of the Houseboat. John Kendrick Bangs. Repr. lib. bdg. 12.70x (ISBN 0-89190-626-6). Am Repr-Rivercity Pr.
Pursuit of the Houseboat. John Kendrick Bangs. (O.s.i.). 204p. 1976. Repr. of 1897 ed. lib. bdg. 7.95x o.s.i. Queens Hse.
Pursuit of the Houseboat. John Kendrick Bangs. 1897. 6.00 (ISBN 0-403-00474-8). Scholarly.
Pursuit of the Prodigal. Louis Auchincloss. LC 59-9633. 1959. Houghton Mifflin.
Pursuit of the Screamer. Ansen Dibell, pseud. 1978. 1.95 (ISBN 0-87997-386-2). DAW Books.
Pursuit on Ganymede. Michael D. Resnick. (Science Fantasy Series). (Orig.). 1968. pap. 0.50 o.p. (52-760). Paperback Lib.
Pursuit till Morning, a Novel. Alan Wykes. LC 47-4530. 1947. Random House.
Pururu, Novela. Juan P Cartosio. LC 57-23143. 1955.
Push Boat. Glen Ford Mott. LC 41-18615. 1941. Franklin Printing Co.
Push-Button Spy. Leigh James. LC 72-101257. 1970. 6.95. Prentice-Hall.
Pushbutton Butterfly. Kin Platt. LC 75-101334. (Random House mystery). 1970. 4.95. Random House.
Pushcart Prize IV: Best of the Small Presses. Ed. by Bill Henderson. 600p. 1976. pap. 7.95 (ISBN 0-380-48827-2, 48827). Avon.
Pushcarts & Dreamers. Ed. by Max Rosenfeld. (Illus.). 1969. 4.95 o.p. (ISBN 0-498-06984-2, Yoseloff). A S Barnes.
Pushcarts and Dreamers: Stories of Jewish Life in America. Ed. by Max Rosenfeld. Shalom Asch. LC 69-18106. (Illus.). 1969. 4.95. T. Yoseloff.
Pusher. Ed McBain. (Signet Book). 1974. (pbk.) 0.95. New American Library.
Pusher. F. C. A McBain. LC 56-10591. (Permabooks. Mystery, 3062). 1956. Permabooks.
Pushkinskill Dom. Andrei Bitov. (Rus.). 1978. 15.00 o.p. (ISBN 0-88233-350-X); pap. 8.50 (ISBN 0-88233-351-8). Ardis Pubs.
Pushmataha: An Historical Novel. 1st Ed. Edwin Isherwood Reeser. LC 54-10075. 1954. Exposition Press.
Pushover. Kenneth Harding. pap. 1.95 o.s.i. (Venus). Grove.
Pushover Mom. Carter Sprague. 192p. 1973. pap. 1.95 o.p. (ISBN 0-87682-332-0, 7332). Barclay Hse.
Puss in the Penthouse: The Cat That Struck It Rich. Photos. by Ken Foster. 1st Ed. Marcia Nobel. LC 57-59551. 1957. Exposition Press.
Pussy in Boots. Keith Kerner. (Orig., Pap). 1969. pap. 1.95 o.s.i. (OPH166, Ophelia). Olympia.
Pussycat Man. Victor Bannis. LC 75-83564. (O.s.i.). 1970. pap. 0.75 o.s.i. (A665S, Award). Univ Pub & Dist.
Pussycat, Pussycat. Ted Mark, pseud. (Orig.). 1976. pap. 1.50 o.p. (ISBN 0-532-15193-3). Woodhill.
Pussycat, Pussycat. 3rd ed. Ted Mark, pseud. (Orig.). 1968. pap. 0.75 o.p. (73-461). Lancer.
Pussycat, Pussycat. Ted Mark, pseud. (Orig.). 1976. pap. 1.50 o.p. (ISBN 0-532-15193-3). Manor Bks.
Pussycat, Pussycat, I Love You. Norman Jackson. (O.s.i.). (Orig.). 1970. pap. 0.75 o.s.i. (A658S, Award). Univ Pub & Dist.
Pussywillow. Mama S. Rampa. 1976. pap. 2.95. Weiser.
Pusuit of Love & Love in Cold Climate. Nancy Mitford. LC 81-70282. 560p. 1982. pap. 2.95 (ISBN 0-394-70817-2, Vin). Random.
Put Asunder. A Novel. Charlotte Mary Brame. (On cover: The primrose series. no. 16). Street & Smith.
Put Back the Clock. Denise Robins. 1972. pap. 0.75 o.p. (T2653). Pyramid Pubns.
Put Back the Clock. Denise Robins. 1977. pap. 1.25 o.p. (ISBN 0-515-04272-2). BJ Pub Group.
Put off Thy Shoes. Ethel Lillian Boole Voynich. LC 45-4308. 1945. The Macmillan Company.
Put-On. Jacob Brackman. LC 73-143847. 1971. 4.95 o.p. Regnery.
Put on the Spot. Jack Lait. LC 30-29554. Grosset & Dunlap.
Put Out More Flags. Evelyn Waugh. LC 42-11453. 1942. Little, Brown and Company.
Put Out the Light. Elinore Denniston. LC 76-26512. (Red badge novel of suspense). 1976. 6.95 (ISBN 0-396-07352-2). Dodd, Mead.
Put Out the Light. Ethel Lina White. LC 33-195620. 1933. L. MacVeagh, Dial Press, Inc.
Put Out the Light. Ethel Lina White. LC 43-11291. 1943. Harper & Brothers.
Put Out the Light see Sinister Light.
Put to a Test: A Novel. Mary Elizabeth Braddon Maxwell. (On cover: Seaside library. Pocket ed. no. 487). 1885. G. Munro.
Put to the Test: A Novel. Charles Chamberlain. LC 6-23423. 1874. H. L. Hinton.
Put Yourself in His Place. Charles Reade. LC 49-37130. (works of Charles Reade. Library ed.). 1895. Metropolitan Pub. Co.
Put Yourself in His Place. Charles Reade. (Seaside library, v. 5, no. 86). 1877. G. Munro.
Put Yourself in His Place. Charles Reade. (On cover: Lovell's library, v. 16, no. 773). 1886. J. W. Lovell Company.
Put Yourself in His Place. A Novel. Charles Reade. (On cover: Seaside library. Pocket ed. no. 214). 1884. G. Munro.
Put Yourself in My Shoes. Raymond Carver. LC 75-316457. (Yes! Capra chapbook series; no. 21). (Illus.). 1974. 2.50 (ISBN 0-88496-006-4) (ISBN 0-88496-005-6). Capra Press.
Putter Perkins. Kenneth H. Brown. LC 23-4981. 1923. 1.50. Houghton Mifflin Company.
Puttering Round. MacGregor Jenkins. LC 27-20603. 1927. Little, Brown, and Company.
Putting into Harbor. Margie Fusco. 1978. pap. 1.00 (ISBN 0-931122-11-2). West End.
Putting It Over. Ellery Harding Clark. LC 23-9849. 1923. The Cornhill Publishing Company.
Putting on the Screws. Gouverneur Morris. 1909. Doubleday, Page & Company.
Puzzle for Fiends. Patrick Quentin. LC 46-18161. 1946. Simon and Schuster.
Puzzle for Fools. Patrick Quentin. LC 36-20440. 1936. Simon and Schuster.
Puzzle for Friends. Patrick Quentin. 1979. pap. 2.25 (ISBN 0-380-45518-8, 45518). Avon.
Puzzle for Pilgrims. Patrick Quentin. LC 47-18228. 1947. Simon and Schuster.
Puzzle for Players. Patrick Quentin. LC 38-38823. 1938. Simon and Schuster.
Puzzle for Players: A Mystery Novel. abridged ed. Patrick Quentin. LC 47-25468. 1946. Quinn Pub. Co.
Puzzle for Puppets. Patrick Quentin. LC 44-940046. 1944. Simon and Schuster.
Puzzle for Wantons. Patrick Quentin. LC 45-7645. 1945. Simon and Schuster.
Puzzle in Paint... Samuel Melvin Kootz. LC 43-173152. 1943. Crown.
Puzzle in Paisley. Elizabeth F. Gresham. (Orig.). 1972. pap. 0.75 o.p. (07260). Curtis.
Puzzle in Paisley. Elizabeth F. Gresham. 1972. 0.75. Curtis Books.
Puzzle in Parchment. Elizabeth F. Gresham. 1973. pap. 0.95 o.p. (09228). Curtis.
Puzzle in Parquet. Elizabeth F. Gresham. (Orig.). 1973. pap. 0.75 o.p. (07297). Curtis.
Puzzle in Parquet. Elizabeth F. Gresham. 1973. (pbk) 0.75. Curtis Books.
Puzzle in Patchwork. Elizabeth F. Gresham. (Orig.). 1973. pap. 0.75 o.p. (07304). Curtis.
Puzzle in Petticoats. Samuel Melvin Kootz. LC 44-502531. 1944. Crown.
Puzzle in Pewter. Elizabeth F. Gresham. LC 47-805. 1947. Duell, Sloan and Pearce.
Puzzle in Pewter. Elizabeth F. Gresham. (Orig.). 1972. pap. 0.75 o.p. (07251). Curtis.
Puzzle in Poison. Anthony Berkeley Cox. LC 38-337403. 1938. Pub. for the Crime Club, Inc., by Doubleday, Doran & Company, Inc.
Puzzle in Poison. Anthony Berkeley Cox. LC 39-32050. 1939. The Sun Dial Press, Inc.
Puzzle in Porcelain. Elizabeth F. Gresham. LC 45-9822. 1945. Duell, Sloan and Pearce.
Puzzle in Porcelain. Elizabeth F. Gresham. LC 47-16267. (On cover: A Bart house mystery, 29). 1946.
Puzzle in Porcelain. Elizabeth F. Gresham. LC 47-16267. (On cover: A Bart house mystery, 29). 1946.
Puzzle in Porcelain. Elizabeth F. Gresham. 1973. 0.75. Curtis Books.
Puzzle Lock. Richard Austin Freeman. LC 26-7269. 1926. Dodd, Mead and Company.
Puzzle of Five Pistols: The Strange Fate of Lawyer Deems; The Eye of Fire: Three Complete Stories of the Exploits of Nicholas Carter, America's Greatest Detective. John Russell Coryell. LC 99-43841. (On cover: Magnet detective library, no. 97). 1899. Street & Smith.
Puzzle of the Blue Banderilla: A Hildegarde Withers Story. Stuart Palmer. LC 37-13865. 1937. Pub. for the Crime Club, Inc., by Doubleday, Doran & Co., Inc.
Puzzle of the Blue Banderilla: A Hildegarde Withers Story. Stuart Palmer. LC 38-24916. 1938. The Sun Dial Press, Inc.
Puzzle of the Happy Hooligan: A Hildegarde Withers Mystery Novel. Stuart Palmer. LC 41-5113. 1941. Pub. for the Crime Club by Doubleday, Doran & Co., Inc.
Puzzle of the Pepper Tree... Stuart Palmer. LC 33-253771. 1933. Pub. for the Crime Club, Inc., by Doubleday, Doran & Company, Inc.
Puzzle of the Red Stallion. Stuart Palmer. LC 36-759411. 1936. Pub. for the Crime Club, Inc., by Doubleday, Doran and Company, Inc.
Puzzle of the Red Stallion. Stuart Palmer. LC 36-32344. 1936. The Sun Dial Press.
Puzzle of the Silver Persian. Stuart Palmer. LC 34-10748. 1934. Pub. for the Crime Club, Inc., by Doubleday, Doran & Company, Inc.
Puzzle of the Space Pyramids. Eando Binder, pseud. (Orig.). 1971. pap. 0.75 o.p. (07134). Curtis.
Puzzled Picture. Archibald Henderson. 56p. 1971. pap. 8.00 (ISBN 0-913030-00-7). St le Macs Pr.
Puzzleheaded Girl. G. Stead. 1967. 6.95 o.p. (ISBN 0-03-064915-3). HR&W.
Puzzleheaded Girl: Four Novellas, 1st Ed. Christina Stead. LC 67-179926. 1967. 6.95. Holt.
Py Jap Cot", and Other Tales. J. H Le Coeur. LC 7-12781. Excelsior Publishing House.
Pylon. William Faulkner. 1965. 4.95. Random.
Pylon. William Faulkner. LC 65-8629. (Modern Lib., 380). 1967. 2.45. Random.
Pylon. William Faulkner. LC 35-4415. 1935. H. Smith and R. Haas, Inc.
Pylon. Introd. by Reynolds Price. William Faulkner. (Signet modern classic, CQ415). 1968. New Amer. Lib.
Pynnshurst: His Wanderings and Ways of Thinking. Xavier Donald MacLeod. LC 7-16619. 1852. C. Scribner.
Pyramid. William Gerald Golding. LC 67-19198. 1967. Harcourt, Brace & World.
Pyramid. William Gerald Golding. LC 80-28718. (Harvest/HBJ book). 1981. 3.95 (ISBN 0-15-674703-0). Harcourt Brace Jovanovich.
Pyramid: A Novel. Robert Smythe Hichens. 1936. Doubleday, Doran & Company, Inc.
Pyramid: A Novel. Robert Smythe Hichens. LC 36-35242. 1936. The Sun Dial Press.
Pyramid of Lead. Bertram Atkey. LC 25-147160. 1925. D. Appleton and Company.
Pyramid Power. Max Toth & Greg Nielsen. 272p. 1976. pap. 2.95 (ISBN 0-446-30508-1). Warner Bks.
Pyramids from Space. Jack Bertin. LC 76-9700. 1977. pap. 1.25 (ISBN 0-532-12502-9). Woodhill.
Pyramids from Space. Jack Bertin. 1971. pap. 0.75 o.p. (75-440). Manor Bks.
Pyramids from Space. Jack Bertin. Ed. by Alice Sachs. 1970. 3.95 o.p. Lenox Hill.
Pyrencan: Being the Adventures of Miles Walker on His Journey from the Mediterranean to the Atlantic. John Bingham Morton. 1938. Longmans, Green and Co.
Pyrrha: A Story of Two Crimes. Pauline Grayson. LC 6-45541. 1889. The American News Company.
Python Project. Victor Canning. LC 68-19427. 1968. Morrow.
Python Project. Victor Canning. LC 79-436062. 1967. 2.85. Readers Book Club in Association with Companion Book Club, London.
Pyx: A Novel. John Buell. LC 59-13710. 1959. Farrar, Straus & Cudahy.

Q

Q". Katharine Newlin Burt. LC 22-8939. 1922. 2.00. Houghton Mifflin Company.
Q & A. Edwin Torres. LC 77-4775. 1977. 7.95 (ISBN 0-8037-7312-9). Dial Press.
Q & A. Edwin Torres. 1978. 1.95 (ISBN 0-380-01862-4). Avon Books.
Q As in Quicksand. Lawrence Treat. LC 47-4528. 1947. Duell, Sloan and Pearce.
Q Document. James Hall Roberts. LC 64-15166. 1964. W. Morrow.
Q. E. D. Lee Thayer, pseud. LC 22-660318. 1922. Doubleday, Page & Company.
Q. E. D: Queen's Experiments in Detection. Ellery Queen, pseud. LC 68-23847. 1968. 5.95 o.p. (HO239, NAL). Norton.
Q 39. Michael Banner. LC 37-216390. 1937. A. A. Knopf.
QB Seven. Leon M. Uris. 1972. pap. 3.50 (ISBN 0-553-14693-9). Bantam.
QB VII. Leon M. Uris. LC 70-129894. 1970. 7.95. Doubleday.

Q.B.I. Queen's Bureau of Investigation). Ellery Queen. 1973. (pbk) 0.75. New American Library.

QE Two Is Missing. Harry Harrison. 1982. pap. 2.95. Dell.

QE Two Is Missing. Harry Harrison. 352p. 1982. pap. 2.95 (ISBN 0-523-48031-8). Pinnacle Bks.

Q.E.D.: Queen's Experiments in Detection. Ellery Queen, pseud. LC 68-23847. 1968. 5.50. World Pub. Co.

QMP Stories... Quentin Morrow Phillip & The Grail. LC 44-5587. The Grail.

QR: The Quieting Reflex. Charles F. Stroebel. 208p. 1983. pap. 2.95 (ISBN 0-425-05867-0). Berkley Pub.

Qua: a Romance of the Revolution. Joel Chandler Harris & English, Thomas Hopkins, 1856- Ed. LC 46-6906. (Half-title: Emory university publications. Sources & reprints. Ser. III). 1946. The Library, Emory University.

Quack!" The Portrait of an Experimentalist. Robert Elson. LC 25-10058. Small, Maynard and Company.

Quadraphonic Homicide. John Weisman & Brian Boyer. (Headhunters#4). 1975. (pbk.) 1.25 (ISBN 0-523-00731-0). Pinnacle Books.

Quadratus. A Tale of the World in the Church. Emma Leslie. LC 7-14493. (Church history stories. v. 9). Nelson & Phillips.

Quadrifariam. Frank Samperi. (Mushinsha Books). 1973. 15.00 o.p. (ISBN 0-670-58373-1, Grossman). Viking Pr.

Quadrille. Marion Chesney. 224p. 1981. pap. 1.95 (ISBN 0-449-50174-4, Coventry). Fawcett.

Quadrille. Frank Arthur Swinnerton. 1978. 1.95 (ISBN 0-523-40250-3). Pinnacle Books.

Quadrille Court. Evelyn Everett Green. LC 29-19454. International Fiction Library.

Quadrille: 1st Amer. Ed. Frank Arthur Swinnerton. LC 65-15372. 4.50. Doubleday.

Quadroom: Or Adventures in the Far West. With Twelve Illus. by Wm. Harvey, Engraved by Evans. Thomas Mayne Reid. LC 67-29278. (Americans in Fic.). 1967. Gregg Pr.

Quadroon. Thomas Mayne Reid. LC 67-29278. (Americans in Fiction Ser.). (Illus.). lib. bdg. 16.00 (ISBN 0-8398-1751-7); pap. text ed. 4.95x (ISBN 0-89197-912-3). Irvington.

Quadroon Ball. Mattie Payne Blank. LC 53-365105. 1953.

Quadroon: Or, A Lover's Adventures in Louisiana. Thomas Mayne Reid. LC 51-48708. (Capt. Mayne Reid's works). 1897. G. W. Dillingham.

Quadroone: Or, St. Michael's Day. Joseph Holt Ingraham. LC 7-9721. 1841. Harper & Brothers.

Quag Keep. Andre Norton, pseud. (Daw Science Fiction Ser.). 1979. pap. 1.95 (ISBN 0-87997-487-7, UJ1487). Daw Bks.

Quail. Dorothy Hamilton. LC 73-7634. 160p. 1973. 5.95 (ISBN 0-8361-1716-6). Herald Pr.

Quail in Aspic: The Life Story of Count Charles Korsetz As Tape-Recorded to Cecil Beaton. Cecil Walter Hardy Beaton. LC 63-11639. 1963. Bobbs-Merrill.

Quaint Companions. Leonard Merrick. LC 18-23231. (Half-title: The works of Leonard Merrick). 1918. Hodder & Stoughton.

Quaint Companions. Leonard Merrick. LC 24-30084. (Half-title: The works of Leonard Merrick). 1924. E. P. Dutton and Company.

Quaint Courtships... Ed. by William Dean Howells and Henry Mills Alden. Ed. by William Dean Howells. Alden, Henry Mills, 1836-1919, Joint Ed. LC 6-28455. (Harper's novelettes). 1906. Harper & Brothers.

Quaint Crippen, Commercial Traveler. Alwyn M Thurber. LC 8-19943. 1896. A. C. McClurg and Company.

Quaint Locality. Watkins Eppes Wright. LC 35-15155. 1935. Arcadia House.

Quaint Spinster. Frances E Russell. LC 8-1341. 1895. Roberts Brothers.

Quake: A Novel. Rudolph Wurlitzer. 1974. (pbk.) 1.25. Bantam Books.

Quake: A Novel. Rudolph Wurlitzer. LC 72-82696. 1972. 4.95 (ISBN 0-525-18660-3). Dutton.

Quaker Ben: A Tale of Colonial Pennsylvania in the Days of Thomas Penn. Henry Christopher McCook. LC 11-12263. 1911. G. W. Jacobs & Co.

Quaker-Born: A Romance of the Great War. Ian Campbell Hannah. LC 16-205531. 1916. G. A. Shaw.

Quaker Boy: A Tale of the Outgoing Generation As It Appears Chronicled in the Autobiography of Robert Barclay Dillingham Pseud. William Dudley Foulke. LC 10-18877. 1910. Cochrane Publishing Company.

Quaker Bride. 1st Ed. Janet Payne Whitney. LC 54-8676. 1954. Little, Brown.

Quaker City, Or, the Monks of Monk Hall. George Lippard. LC 77-93635. (American Fiction Ser). 1970. lib. bdg. 22.75 o.s.i. (ISBN 0-512-00504-4). Garrett Pr.

Quaker City: Or, The Monks on Monk-Hall. A Romance of Philadelphia Life, Mystery, and Crime. 16th ed. George Lippard. LC 7-16039. (Illus.). Pub. by the Author,

Quaker Cross: A Story of the Old Bowne House. Cornelia Mitchell Parsons. LC 11-25993. 1911. 1.50. National Americana Society.

Quaker Girl of Nantucket. Mary Catherine Jenkins Lee. LC 4-23595. 1889. Houghton, Mifflin and Company.

Quaker Girl of Nantucket. Mary Catherine Jenkins Lee. LC 4-1513. Houghton, Mifflin and Company.

Quaker Girl of Nantucket. Mary Catherine Jenkins Lee. LC 25-107700. 1925. Houghton Mifflin Company.

Quaker Home. George Fox Tucker. LC 8-282792. 1891. G. B. Reed.

Quaker Idyls. Sarah M. H Gardner. LC 70-110193. (Short story index reprint series). 1970. Books for Libraries Press.

Quaker Idyls. Sarah M. H Gardner. LC 7-294. (On cover: Buckram series). 1894. H. Holt and Company.

Quaker Idyls. enl. ed., containing two new idyls... ed. Sarah M. H Gardner. LC 10-8336. 1910. H. Holt and Company.

Quaker Jim. Richard Albert Kelty. 1.50. Broadway Publishing Company.

Quaker Schoolmarm. Phillip A Gifford. LC 98-1519. The Mershon Company.

Quaker Scout: A Story. Nicholas Patterson Runyan. The Abbey Press.

Quaker Soldier: Or, The British in Philadelphia. An Historical Novel... John Richter Jones. LC 7-12848. T. B. Peterson and Brothers.

Quakeress. Charles Heber Clark. LC 5-10050. 1905. The J.C. Winston Co.

Quakeress Versus Priest: Or, A Peep Behind the Veil. Mary Bell Mallory. 1895. Methodist Book Concern.

Quakers: A Tale. Elizabeth B Lester. LC 7-32445. 1818. J. Eastburn & Co.

Quakers Courageous: A Wartime Novel of a Friends Family. 1st Ed. Ruth Taber Whittlesey. LC 55-113915. 1955. Exposition Press.

Quaking Terror. Lionel Derrick, pseud. (Penetrator Ser.: No. 45). 208p. (Orig.). 1982. pap. 1.95 (ISBN 0-523-41398-X). Pinnacle Bks.

Qualified Adventurer: A Novel. Selwyn Jepson. LC 22-8238. Harcourt, Brace and Company.

Quality. Cid Ricketts Sumner. LC 46-578817. 1946. The Bobbs-Merrill Company.

Quality Corner: A Study of Remorse. C. L Antrobus. LC 2-23998. 1902. G.P. Putnam's Sons.

Quality House. Celeste Dunbar Lindsay. LC 35-38318. The Dial Press.

Quality of Fear. Bruce Cassiday. (Bold Ones Ser.: No. 2). 192p. (Orig.). 1973. pap. 0.95 o.p. (532-95296-095). Manor Bks.

Quality of Mercy. Margaret Culkin Banning. 1972. pap. 0.95 o.p. (532-95184-095). Manor Bks.

Quality of Mercy. William Dean Howells & James Paul Elliott. LC 78-20655. (selected edition of W. D. Howells; v. 18). (Illus.). 1979. 20.00 (ISBN 0-253-35789-6). Indiana University Press.

Quality of Mercy. Allen Jacobs. LC 24-7322. 1924. The Torch Press.

Quality of Mercy. Mercedes McCambridge. 304p. 1982. pap. 2.95 (ISBN 0-425-05389-X). Berkley Pub.

Quality of Mercy: A Novel. Margaret Culkin Banning. LC 62-20119. Harper & Row.

Quality of Mercy: A Novel. William Dean Howells. LC 7-5767. (On cover: Harper's Franklin square library. New ser. no. 726). 1892. Harper & Brothers.

Quality of Mercy. 1st Ed. Robert Carson. LC 54-544300. 1954. Holt.

Quality of Quiros. 1st Ed. Robert Raynolds. LC 55-6821. 1955. Bobbs-Merrill.

Quality of Youth. Louis Evan Shipman. LC 4-104781. 1904. Scott-Thaw Co.

Quanah, the Serpent Eagle. Paul Foreman. LC 82-62545. (Illus.). 144p. text ed. 15.95 (ISBN 0-87358-329-9); pap. 8.95 (ISBN 0-87358-324-8); 60.00 (ISBN 0-87358-330-2). Northland.

Quand L'Amour est une Guerre. Charlotte Lamb, pseud. (Harlequin Romantique Ser.). 192p. 1983. pap. 1.95 (ISBN 0-373-41177-4). Harlequin Bks.

Quantrell's Raiders. Frank Gruber. 1981. pap. 1.95 (ISBN 0-451-09735-1, J9735, Sig). NAL.

Quarante-Cinq, 3 tomes. Alexandre Dumas, Sr. 1962. Set. pap. 3.50 o.p. French & Eur.

Quarantine: A Novel. Nicholas P Hasluck. LC 78-14160. 1979. 8.95 (ISBN 0-03-044201-X). Holt, Rinehart and Winston.

Quare Women: A Story of the Kentucky Mountains. Lucy Furman. LC 23-26338. The Atlantic Monthly Press.

Quark, No. 2. Ed. by Samuel R. Delany & Marilyn Hacker. (Anthologies Ser). (Illus.). 1971. pap. 1.25 o.p. (66-530). Paperback Lib.

Quark, No. 3. Ed. by Samuel R. Delany & Marilyn Hacker. (Quark Speculative Fiction Quarterlies Ser). (Illus., Orig.). 1971. pap. 1.25 o.p. (66-593). Paperback Lib.

Quark, No. 4. Ed. by Samuel R. Delany. (Illus., Orig.). 1971. pap. 1.25 o.p. (66-658). Paperback Lib.

Quark Maneuver. Mike Jahn. LC 76-18076. 1.50 (ISBN 0-345-25171-7). Ballantine Books.

Quarrel: A Novel. Otto Reising. LC 47-30759. 1947. Duell, Sloan and Pearce.

Quarrel with the Moon. J. C. Conaway. 320p. (Orig.). 1982. pap. 2.95 (ISBN 0-523-48033-4). Pinnacle Bks.

Quarries of Sicily. Thomas Doulis. LC 72-75077. 1969. 5.95. Crown Publishers.

Quarry. 2nd ed. Friedrich Durrenmatt, pseud. Bd. with Judge & His Hangman. (Double Detective Ser.: No. 2). 256p. 1983. pap. 7.95 (ISBN 0-87923-408-3). Godine.

Quarry. Robert L Fish. LC 64-11404. 1964. Published for the Crime Club by Doubleday.

Quarry. John Antonio Moroso. LC 13-9242. 1913. Little, Brown, and Company.

Quarry. Mildred Walker, pseud. LC 47-30059. 1947. Harcourt, Brace and Company.

Quarry. Jane White. (75-203). 1968. Macfadden.

Quarry. Jane White. LC 67-10773. 1967. Harcourt, Brace & World.

Quarry for Middlemarch: By George Eliot Pseud. Edited, with an Introd. and Notes, by Anna Theresa Kitchel. Eliot, George, Pseud., I. E. Marian Evans, Afterwards Cross. Ed. by Anna Theresa Kitchel. LC 50-62923. 1950. University of California Press.

Quarry Ghost. Mildred Benson. (Willow Bks). 1971. pap. 0.75 o.p. (JT48). Pyramid Pubns.

Quarry House. Judith Ware. 1970. pap. 0.60 o.p. (63-315). Paperback Lib.

Quarry Road. A. R. Dispaldo. 1969. pap. 0.60 o.p. (60-426). Manor Bks.

Quarry Wood. Nan Shepherd. LC 28-23274. E. P. Dutton & Company.

Quarrytown. Douglas Dobbins. LC 15-11995. 1.00. American Issue Publishing Company.

Quarter-Back's Pluck: A Story of College Football. Lester Chadwick. (His The college sports series). 1.00. Cupples & Leon Company.

Quarter Horse. Gordon Ray Young. LC 48-5047. (Double D western). 1948. Doubleday.

Quarter Race in Kentucky: And Other Sketches, Illustrative of Scenes, Characters, and Incidents, Throughout "the Universal Yankee Nation.". Ed. by William Trotter Porter. LC 78-174281. (Series: Carey & Hart's Library of Humorous American Works, V. 5.). (Illus.). 1973. 10.00 (ISBN 0-404-05088-3). AMS Press.

Quarter Race in Kentucky: And Other Sketches, Illustrative of Scenes, Characters, and Incidents, Throughout "The Universal Yankee Nation.". Ed. by William Trotter Porter. LC 7-37392. (On cover: Carey & Hart's library of humorous American works. v. 5). 1847. Cary and Hart.

Quarter to Four: Or, The Secret of Fortune Island. William Wallace Cook. LC 9-106478. G. W. Dillingham Company.

Quarter to Six: A Novel. Translated from the Spanish by Emil G. Beavers. 1st Ed. Robert H Ayala. LC 55-121226. 1955. Exposition Press.

Quarterback: A Novel. Hamilton Maule. LC 62-18961. 1962. D. McKay Co.

Quarterbreed. Robert Ames Bennet. LC 14-9278. 1914. 1.25. Browne & Howell Company.

Quartet. Raymond Barrio. 1968. 4.00 o.p. Ventura.

Quartet. Vladimir Vladimirovich Nabokov. LC 66-28101. 1966. Phaedra.

Quartet. Eden Phillpotts. Hutchinson & Co. Ltd.

Quartet. Jean Rhys. LC 74-165837. 1973. 0.25 (ISBN 0-14-003610-5). Penguin.

Quartet. Jean Rhys. LC 77-138795. 1971. 4.95 (ISBN 0-06-013537-9). Harper & Row.

Quartet. Jean Rhys. LC 74-8114. 1974. (ISBN 0-394-71319-2). Vintage Books.

Quartet: A Novel. Jean Rhys. LC 29-14910. Simon & Schuster, Inc.,

Quartet in Autumn. american ed. Barbara Pym. LC 78-58498. 1978. 7.95 (ISBN 0-525-18665-4). Dutton.

Quartet in Autumn. Barbara Pym. LC 78-26794. 1979. 10.95 (ISBN 0-8161-6661-7). G. K. Hall.

Quartet in Autumn: Barbara Pym. Barbara Pym. 1980. Perennial Library.

Quartet in Farewell Time. Mary B Durant. LC 63-13503. 1963. Harcourt, Brace & World.

Quartet in 'H' Original Title: Second Ending. Evan Hunter. LC 57-1150. (Cardinal edition, C-236. Fiction, 6). 1957. Pocket Books.

Quartet: New Voices from South Africa; Alex La Guma, James Matthews, Alf Wannenburgh, Richard Rive. Ed. by Richard Rive. LC 63-21108. 1963. Crown Publishers.

Quartet-Stories. Ed. by Harold P. Simonson. 1973. pap. text ed. 5.95x o.p. (ISBN 0-06-046175-6, HarpC). Har-Row.

Quartet: Translated by Ernest Boyd. Emil Ludwig & Boyd, Ernest Augustus, 1887- LC 39-193537. Alliance Book Corporation.

Quartz Eye: A Mystery in Ultra Violet. Henry Kitchell Webster. LC 28-18757. The Bobbs-Merrill Company.

Quartzsite Trip. William Hogan. LC 79-55601. 1980. 11.95. Atheneum.

Quarup. Antonio Callado. 1970. 8.95 o.p. (ISBN 0-394-44203-2). Knopf.

Quarup: A Novel. american 1st ed. Antonio Callado. LC 75-98644. 1970. 8.95. Knopf.

Quas Starbrite. James R. Berry. 224p. 1981. pap. 1.95 (ISBN 0-553-14820-6). Bantam.

Quatemass. Nigel Kneale. 288p. (Orig.). 1981. pap. 2.50. Bantam.

Quater Mass. Nigel Kneale. 1981. pap. 2.50. Bantam.

Quatre Evangiles, 3 pts. Emile Zola. Incl. Fecondite; Travail; Verite. 7.50 ea. French & Eur.

Quatre-Vingt-Treize. Victor Marie Hugo. Ed. by Boudout. (Coll. Prestige). 9.95 o.p. French & Eur.

Quatrefoil. James Barr. 1982. pap. 6.95 (ISBN 0-932870-16-3). Alyson Pubns.

Quatrefoil. James Barr. pap. 0.75 o.p. (54-871). Paperback Lib.

Quatrefoil. James Barr. 6.95 o.p. Wehman.

Quatrefoil, a Modern Novel. James Barr. LC 50-9145. 1950. Greenberg.

Quayle's Invention. Eric Temple Bell. LC 27-7724. E. P. Dutton & Company.

Que Faire. Guillaume Apollinaire. 13.90 o.p. French & Eur.

Que Ma Joie Demeure see Oeuvres Romanesques.

Queechy. Susan Warner. 1852. G. P. Putnam.

Queechy. 30th thousand. ed. Susan Warner. 1880. J. B. Lippincott & Co.

Queechy. Susan Warner. LC 8-336986. 1894. J. B. Lippincott Company.

Queed: A Novel. Henry Sydnor Harrison. LC 11-10951. 1911. Houghton Mifflin Company.

Queed: A Novel. Henry Sydnor Harrison. LC 42-289794. 1914. Grossett & Dunlap.

Queen. Morton Cooper. LC 74-3341. 1974. 7.95 (ISBN 0-13-748202-7). Prentice-Hall.

Queen. Morton Cooper. 1975. (pbk.) 1.75. Bantam Books.

Queen After Death. William Harman Black. Real Book Company.

Queen Against Defoe & Other Stories. Stefan Heym. LC 73-20380. (Illus.). 128p. 1974. 6.95 o.p. (ISBN 0-88208-041-5). Lawrence Hill.

Queen Amongst Women. Charlotte Mary Brame. LC 44-116786. (On cover: Seaside library. Pocket ed. No. 68). G. Munro.

Queen Amongst Women. Charlotte Mary Brame. LC 44-11653. (On cover: Lovell's library, v. 14, no. 733). J. W. Lovell Company.

Queen & I. Ray C. Stedman. LC 77-75471. (Discovery Bks.). 1977. 4.95 (ISBN 0-8499-0015-8); pap. 2.95 (ISBN 0-8499-2807-9). Word Bks.

Queen and Lord M. Eleanor Hibbert. LC 77-3644. 1977. 7.95. Putnam.

Queen and Lord M. Eleanor Hibbert. (Her The Queen Victoria series). (Illus.). 1978. 1.75 (ISBN 0-449-23605-6). Fawcett Crest Books.

Queen & Lord M. Jean Plaidy. 268p. Repr. of 1973 ed. lib. bdg. 12.00x (ISBN 0-88411-895-9). Amereon Ltd.

Queen & Lord M. Jean Plaidy. LC 77-3644. 1977. 7.95 (ISBN 0-399-11994-9). Putnam Pub Group.

Queen and the Corpse. Max Murray. LC 49-9512. 1949. Farrar, Straus.

Queen and the Gypsy. Constance Heaven. LC 76-44004. 1977. 8.95 (ISBN 0-698-10794-2). Coward, McCann & Geoghegan.

Queen Anne Boleyn, a Novel. Francis Hackett. LC 39-27888. 1939. Doubleday, Doran & Company, Inc.

Queen Anne's Gate Mystery: A Novel, 2 vols. in 1. Richard Arkwright. LC 75-32733. (Literature of Mystery & Detection). 1976. Repr. of 1889 ed. 28.00x (ISBN 0-405-07863-3). Ayer Co.

Queen Anne's Lace. Frances Parkinson Wheeler Keyes. LC 30-23897. H. Liveright.

Queen Anne's Lace. Frances Parkinson Wheeler Keyes. LC 31-4334. 1931. H. Liveright.

Queen Bee. Edna L. Mooney Lee. LC 49-4526. 1949. Appleton-Century-Crofts.

Queen Bess: Or, What's in a Name? Marian Shaw. LC 8-4809. 1885. G. P. Putnam's Sons.

Queen Calafia. Vicente Blasco Ibanez. LC 24-28342. E. P. Dutton & Company.

Queen City Murder Case: A Johnny Saxon Mystery. William Bogart. LC 46-18492. 1946. Mystery House.

Queen Cleopatra: A Novel. Talbot Mundy. LC 29-4296. The Bobbs-Merrill Company.

Queen Cophetua. Robert Edward Francillon. (Seaside library, v. 44, no. 904). G. Munro.

Queen Dick. Nalbro Isadorah Bartley. LC 29-679250. 1929. Doubleday, Doran & Company, Inc.

Queen Elfreda: A Historic Romance of British Life. E. W. Warne. LC 8-33722. 1884. Printed for the Author.
Queen Emma of the South Seas. Geoffrey Dutton. LC 77-71162. 1977. 7.95 (ISBN 0-312-65992-X). St. Martin's Press.
Queen Emma of the South Seas: A Novel by Geoffrey Dutton. Geoffrey Dutton. LC 76-367435. 1976. (ISBN 0-333-21038-7). Macmillan.
Queen Esther. Effie Lawrence Marshall. LC 51-431. 1950. Falmouth Pub. House.
Queen Hildegarde: A Story for Girls. Laura Elizabeth Howe Richards. D. Estes and Company.
Queen Hortense. Klara Muller Mundt. Tr. by Coleman, Chapman. LC 16-1234. (historical romances of Louisa Muhlbach pseud.). D. Appleton and Company.
Queen Hortense. A Life Picture of the Napoleonic Era. An Historical Novel. Klara Muller Mundt. Tr. by Coleman, Chapman. LC 4-25604. 1870. D. Appleton and Company.
Queen in Danger. Adam Hall, pseud. 1971. pap. 0.75 o.p. (T2502). Pyramid Pubns.
Queen in Danger: A Hugo Bishop Story by Simon Rattray Pseud. Elleston Trevor. LC 52-67772. 1952. T. V. Boardman.
Queen Is Dead. Glenn Kezer. LC 78-70790. 1979. 1.75 (ISBN 0-515-04856-9). Jove/HBJ.
Queen Is in the Garbage. Lila Karp. LC 72-89665. 1969. 4.95. Vanguard Press.
Queen Jezabel. Eleanor Hibbert. (Berkley Medallion Book). 1977. 1.95 (ISBN 0-425-03546-8). Putnam.
Queen Jezebel. Eleanor Hibbert. LC 76-10751. 1976. 8.95 (ISBN 0-399-11787-3). Putnam.
Queen Jezebel. Jean Plaidy. 1977. pap. 1.95 (ISBN 0-425-03546-8, Medallion). Berkley Pub.
Queen Jezebel. Jean Plaidy. LC 76-10751. 1976. 8.95 o.p. (ISBN 0-399-11787-3). Putnam Pub Group.
Queen Jezebel: By Jean Plaidy Pseud. Eleanor Hibbert. LC 53-870112. 1953. Appleton-Century -Crofts.
Queen Kate. Charles Garvice. (On cover: Laurel library, no. 24). 1896. G. Munro's Sons.
Queen Krinaleen's Plagues: Or, How a Simple People Were Destroyed. A Discourse in the Twenty-Second Century, by "Jonquil" Pseud.... J. L. Collins. LC 6-25420. 1874. American News Company.
Queen Lucia,". Edward Frederic Benson. LC 20-15389. George H. Doran Company.
Queen Money. Ellen Warner Olney Kirk. LC 7-123613. 1888. Ticknor and Company.
Queen of a Day. Joseph Smith Fletcher. LC 29-24389. 1929. Doubleday, Doran & Company,Inc.
Queen of a Distant Country. John Braine. LC 72-94277. 1973. 6.95 (ISBN 0-698-10512-5). Coward, McCann & Geoghegan.
Queen of a Lonely Country. Megan Castell. 240p. 1980. pap. 2.50 (ISBN 0-671-82732-4). PB.
Queen of Air and Darkness. Poul Anderson. LC 78-574. (Worlds of Paul Anderson). ((His). 1978. 8.50 (ISBN 0-8398-2433-5). Gregg Press.
Queen of Air & Darkness see Winter of the World.
Queen of Air and Darkness and Other Stories. Poul Anderson. 1973. (pbk.) 0.95. New American Library.
Queen of America. Russell H Greenan. 1973. (pbk) 1.25. Warner Paperback Library.
Queen of America. Russell H Greenan. LC 70-37043. 1972. 5.95 (ISBN 0-394-47208-X). Random House.
Queen of Atlantis: A Romance of the Caribbean Sea. Frank Aubrey. LC 74-15949. (Science Fiction). (Illus.). 1975. 22.00 (ISBN 0-405-06275-3). Arno Press.
Queen of Barefoot. Ina Bradford. LC 58-7385. 1958. Dorrance.
Queen of Caper: A Selection from the Heptameron. With Traditional Illus. by Freudenberg, Dunker and Flameng, and New Illus. by Wong Shui. Marguerite D'angouleme. LC 59-468852. 1959. Plaza Book Co.
Queen of Clubs. Hulbert Footner. LC 27-24946. George H. Doran Company.
Queen of Curds and Cream. Dorothea Gerard Longard De Longgarde. LC 7-15159. (On cover: Appletons' town and country library. no. 94). 1892. D. Appleton and Company.
Queen of Darkness. Harry Preston. 1976. pap. 1.95 (ISBN 0-532-19121-8). Woodhill.
Queen of Death. John Milne. (Heinemann Guided Readers). 1979. pap. text ed. 2.00x (ISBN 0-435-27049-4). Heinemann Ed.
Queen of Ecuador: A Novel. R. M Manley. LC 7-20461. (On cover: The traveler's library, no. 1). 1894. The H. W. Hagemann Publishing Company.
Queen of Egypt. Susan Fromberg Schaeffer. 1980. 9.95 o.p. (ISBN 0-525-18667-0). Dutton.
Queen of Egypt: Short Fiction. Susan Fromberg Schaeffer. LC 79-54205. 9.95 (ISBN 0-525-18667-0). Dutton.
Queen of Farrandale: A Novel. Clara Louise Root Burnham. LC 23-13725. 1923. Houghton Mifflin Company.
Queen of Hearts. Wilkie Collins. LC 75-32740. (Literature of Mystery and Detection). 1976. 26.00 (ISBN 0-405-07868-4). Arno Press.
Queen of Hearts. Kaye Dobkin. 1982. pap. 3.50 (Banbury). Dell.
Queen of Hearts, No. 87. Lucia Curzon, pseud. 1982. pap. 1.75 (ISBN 0-515-06698-2). Jove Pubns.
Queen of Hearts. A Novel. Wilkie Collins. 1874. Harper & Brothers.
Queen of Heat. Michael Perkins. pap. 1.95 o.p. (0114). Essex Hse.
Queen of Hell. J. N. Williamson. 288p. (Orig.). 1981. pap. 2.50 (ISBN 0-8439-0995-1, Leisure Bks). Nordon Pubns.
Queen of Love. A Novel. Sabine Baring-Gould. LC 6-7225. 1894. J. B. Lippincott Company.
Queen of Naples. Elizabeth Mayhew. 1976. (pbk.) 1.95 (ISBN 0-671-80457-X). Pocket Books.
Queen of Nineveh: A Tale of the Wickedest City. Algernon Crofton. LC 29-616232. 1929. Covici, Friede.
Queen of Quelparte. Archer Butler Hulbert. LC 2-22174. 1902. Little, Brown, and Company.
Queen of Sheba. Thomas Bailey Aldrich. 1877. J. R. Osgood and Company.
Queen of Sheba. Thomas Bailey Aldrich. 1886. Houghton, Mifflin and Company.
Queen of Sheba. Thomas Bailey Aldrich. LC 9-269318. 1889. Houghton, Mifflin and Company.
Queen of Sheba. Thomas Bailey Aldrich. LC 5-339698. Houghton, Mifflin and Company.
Queen of Sheba: Her Life and Times. Phinneas A. Crutch. LC 22-136005. 1922. 2.50. G. P. Putnam's Sons.
Queen of Sinners: A Novel. Winfield F Mott. LC 98-511. (On cover: Dillingham's American authors' library. no. 42). 1898. G. W. Dillingham Co.
Queen of Sorcery: Book Two of the Belgariad. David Eddings. (Orig.). 1982. pap. 2.95 (ISBN 0-345-30079-3, Del Rey). Ballantine.
Queen of Spades. Harold Henderson. LC 82-83127. 208p. 1983. 12.95 (ISBN 0-932966-27-6). Permanent Pr.
Queen of Spades. Marjorie McEvoy. 1975. (pbk.) 0.95 (ISBN 0-345-26710-9). Ballantine Books.
Queen of Spades. Aleksandr Sergeevich Pushkin. Ed. by D. Bondar. (Rus). pap. 1.50x o.p. (ISBN 0-273-00490-5, 490). Pitman.
Queen of Spades: A Joshua Clunk Mystery. Henry Christopher Bailey. LC 44-31571. 1944. Pub. for the Crime Club by Doubleday, Doran and Company, Inc.
Queen of Spades & Other Stories. Aleksandr Sergeevich Pushkin. Tr. by Rosemary Edmonds from Rus. (Classics Ser.). 1978. pap. 2.95 (ISBN 0-14-044119-0). Penguin.
Queen of Spades: And Other Tales. Translated by Ivy and Tatiana Litvinov. With a Foreword by George Steiner. Aleksandr Sergeevich Pushkin. LC 61-597446. (Signet classic, CP70). 1961. New American Library.
Queen of Spades. The Negro of Peter the Great. Dubrovsky. The Captain's Daughter. Translated with an Introd. by Rosemary Edmonds. Aleksandr Sergeevich Pushkin. LC 62-229176. (Penguin classics, L119). 1962. Penguin Books.
Queen of Swords. Anne Eliot Crompton. LC 79-26496. 1980. 8.95 (ISBN 0-416-30611-X, NO. 0165). Methuen Inc.
Queen of the Black Coast. Robert E. Howard. 15.00 (ISBN 0-937986-21-6). D M Grant.
Queen of the Block. Alexander L Kinkead. LC 7-12529. (On cover: The household library, v. 4, no. 23). 1888. Belford, Clarke and Company; Etc., Etc.
Queen of the City. Eugene C Kennedy. LC 81-43918. 1982. 17.95 (ISBN 0-385-17509-4). Doubleday.
Queen of the County... Julia Cecilia Collinson Stretton. (Seaside library, v. 63, no. 1272). 1882. G. Munro.
Queen of the County. Julia Cecilia Collinson Stretton. (Lovell's library, v. 2 no. 72). 1883. J. W. Lovell Company.
Queen of the Dawn: A Love Tale of Old Egypt. Henry Rider Haggard. LC 25-8118. 1925. Doubleday, Page & Company.
Queen of the East. Alexander Baron. LC 56-141484. 1956. Washburn.
Queen of the Guarded Mounts. John Oxenham, pseud. LC 12-12871. 1912. John Lane.
Queen of the Isle. A Novel. May Agnes Early Fleming. LC 6-39945. 1886. G. W. Dillingham; Etc., Etc.
Queen of the Jesters: And Her Strange Adventures in Old Paris. Max Pemberton. LC 76-101818. (Short story index reprint series). (Illus.). 1969. Books for Libraries Press.
Queen of the Jesters: And Her Strange Adventures in Old Paris. Max Pemberton. 1897. Dodd, Mead and Company.
Queen of the Jesters & Her Strange Adventures in Old Paris. Max Pemberton. LC 76-101818. (Short Story Index Reprint Ser.). 1897. 17.00 (ISBN 0-8369-3206-4). Ayer Co.
Queen of the Legion. Jack Williamson. 304p. 1983. pap. 2.95 (ISBN 0-671-82509-7, Timescape). PB.
Queen of the Looking-Glass. Annie Laurie McAllister. (Berkley Medallion Book). 1.50 (ISBN 0-425-03617-0). Berkley Pub. Corp.
Queen of the Meadow. A Novel. Charles Gibbon. (Franklin square library. no. 103). 1880. Harper & Brothers.
Queen of the Meadow. A Novel. Charles Gibbon. (Seaside library, v. 33, no. 682). 1880. G. Munro.
Queen of the Night. Marc Behm. LC 77-8434. 1977. 8.95 (ISBN 0-395-25779-4). Houghton Mifflin.
Queen of the Night. Marc Behm. 1978. 1.95 (ISBN 0-380-39958-X). Avon Books.
Queen of the Night. Kenneth Perkins. LC 25-8788. 1925. 2.00. A. C. McClurg & Co.
Queen of the North Parlor. Roz Young. 198p. 1976. pap. 4.95 (ISBN 0-913428-23-X). Landfall Pr.
Queen of the Pirate Isle. Bret Harte. LC 31-28120. 1931. F. Warne & Co., Ltd.
Queen of the Rushes: A Tale of the Welsh Country. Beynon Puddicombe. LC 6-35940. G. W. Jacobs & Co.
Queen of the Savannah. A Story. rev. and ed. by percy b. st. john. ed. Gustave Aimard & St. John, Percy Bolingbroke, 1821-1889, Ed. LC 5-42979. (On cover: Lovell's library, no 1112). 1888. J. W. Lovell Company.
Queen of the Swamp and Other Plain Americans. Mary Hartwell Catherwood. LC 69-11882. (American short story series, v. 40). 1969. Garrett Press.
Queen of the Swamp and Other Plain Americans. Mary Hartwell Catherwood. LC 72-8308. (American short story series, v. 40). 1972. (ISBN 0-8422-8024-3). MSS Information Corp.
Queen of the Swamp: And Other Plain Americans. Mary Hartwell Catherwood. LC 99-2077. 1899. Houghton, Mifflin and Company.
Queen of the What Ifs. Norma Klein. 224p. 1982. pap. 2.25 (ISBN 0-449-70026-7, Juniper). Fawcett.
Queen of the Woods. Andre Theuriet & Miller, Henrietta E., Tr. (library of choice fiction no. 19). 1891. Laird & Lee.
Queen of the World. George Weston. LC 23-56227. 1923. Dodd, Mead & Company.
Queen of Zamba. Lyon Sprague De Camp. (Krishna Ser.). 224p. 1982. pap. 2.50 (ISBN 0-441-69658-9). Ace Bks.
Queen of Zamba. L. Sprague de Camp. LC 77-82627. 1977. pap. 1.50 o.s.i. (ISBN 0-89559-006-9). Davis Pubns.
Queen Pedauque. national home library edition, complete and unabridged ed. Anatole France, pseud. LC 43-27328. (On cover: National home library). 1935. National Home Library Foundation.
Queen Sends for Mrs. Chadwick. David Sanders. LC 79-29745. 1980. 10.95 (ISBN 0-312-66000-6). St. Martin's Press.
Queen Sheba's Ring. illustrated by sigurd schou. ed. Henry Rider Haggard. LC 10-21159. 1910. Doubleday, Page & Company.
Queen Tempest. Jane Goodwin Austin. LC 6-38586. (American series, no. 271). M. J. Ivers & Co.
Queen Titania. Hjalmar Hjorth Boyesen. LC 77-122691. (Short story index reprint series). 1970. Books for Libraries Press.
Queen Titania. Hjalmar Hjorth Boyesen. LC 6-152176. 1881. C. Scribner's Sons.
Queen Versus Billy: And Other Stories. Lloyd Osbourne. LC 70-101286. (Short story index reprint series). 1969. Books for Libraries Press.
Queen Versus Billy: And Other Stories. Lloyd Osbourne. LC 6827. 1900. C. Scribner's Sons.
Queen Versus Billy & Other Stories. Lloyd Osbourne. LC 70-101286. (Short Story Index Reprint Ser.). 1900. 16.00 (ISBN 0-8369-3223-4). Ayer Co.
Queen Victoria's Bomb; the Disclosures of Professor Franklin Huxtable, M.A., Cantab: A Novel. Ronald William Clark. LC 68-12148. 1968. W. Morrow.
Queen Victoria's Revenge. Harry Harrison. LC 73-81435. 1974. 5.95 (ISBN 0-385-07802-1). Published for the Crime Club by Doubleday.
Queen Was in the Kitchen. Daphne Alloway McVicker. LC 44-2991. 1944. Whittlesey House, McGraw-Hill Book Company, Inc.
Queen Zix of Ix: The Story of the Magic Cloak. Lyman Frank Baum. (Illus.). 8.50 (ISBN 0-8446-0026-1). Peter Smith.
Queenie: A Novel. Hortense Calisher. LC 70-141640. 1971. 6.95. Arbor House.
Queenie Hetherton. Mary Jane Hawes Holmes. LC 8-15722. G. W. Dillingham Company.
Queenie Hetherton. A Novel. Mary Jane Hawes Holmes. LC 7-6028. 1883. G. W. Carleton & Co.
Queenie: The Adventures of a Nice Young Lady. Wilbur Finley Fauley. LC 21-7331. The Macaulay Company.
Queenie's Brood. 1st Ed. Edgar Neil Rogers. LC 56-12871. 1957. Vantage Press.
Queenie's Terrible Secret, and The Rose and the Lily. Alexander McVeigh Miller. (On cover: Clover series, no. 121). 1896. Street & Smith.
Queenie's Terrible Secret: Or, A Young Girl's Strange Fate. Alexander McVeigh Miller. (On cover: Munro's library, v. 1, no. 4). N. L. Munro.
Queenie's Whim. A Novel. Rosa Nouchette Carey. (On cover: Seaside library. Pocket ed. no. 932). Munro.
Queens. E. B Emery. LC 6-37829. Estes & Lauriat.
Queen's Advocate. Arthur Williams Marchmont. LC 4-25676. 1904. F. A. Stokes Company.
Queen's Affair. Ursula Bloom. 1979. pap. 1.95 (ISBN 0-89041-247-2, 3247). Major Bks.
Queen's Awards... The Winners of the... Annual Detective Short-Story Contest, Sponsored by Ellery Queen's Mystery Magazine... 1st- Ed. by Ellery Queen, pseud. LC 46-8129. Little, Brown and Company.
Queen's Bedfellow. Roger Bowdler. 1975. 11.95x (ISBN 0-8464-0775-2). Beekman Pubs.
Queen's Cadet: And Other Tales. James Grant. LC 44-20553. 1874. G. Routledge and Sons.
Queen's Caprice. Marjorie Bowen. 1970. pap. 1.25 o.p. (96013). Beagle Bks.
Queen's Caprice: A Novel of Mary, Queen of Scots. George Preedy, pseud. LC 34-12974. 1934. A. H. King.
Queen's Confession. Eleanor Hibbert. LC 68-10586. 1968. Doubleday.
Queen's Confession. Victoria Holt, pseud. 498p. 1981. pap. 2.95 (ISBN 0-449-23213-1, Crest). Fawcett.
Queen's Confession: A Biography of Marie Antoinette. Victoria Holt, pseud. LC 68-10586. 1968. 14.95 (ISBN 0-385-08276-2). Doubleday.
Queen's Consent. 1st. amer. ed. Rose Meadows. 1974. (pbk.) 0.95 (ISBN 0-671-77695-9). Pocket Books.
Queen's Cross: A Biographical Romance of Queen Isabella of Spain. Lawrence L Schoonover. LC 55-102323. 1955. W. Sloane Associates.
Queen's Crossing. Bill Granger. 288p. (Orig.). 1982. pap. 2.95 (ISBN 0-449-14483-6, GM). Fawcett.
Queen's Doctor: Being the Strange Story of the Rise and Fall of Struensee, Dictator, Lover, and Doctor of Medicine. Robert Neumann. Tr. by Muir, Edwin. LC 36-33403. 1936. A. A. Knopf.
Queen's Falcon... Ernest E Blau. LC 47-206294. 1947. David McKay Company.
Queens Favorite. Constance Heaven. pap. 1.50 (ISBN 0-440-17192-X). Dell.
Queen's Favourites. Eleanor Hibbert. LC 78-1752. 1978. 10.00. Putnam.
Queen's Favourites. Jean Plaidy. LC 78-1752. 1978. 10.00 (ISBN 0-399-12236-2). Putnam Pub Group.
Queen's Fillet. Patrick Augustine Sheehan. LC 11-19988. 1911. Longmans, Green, and Co.
Queens Folly. Elswyth Thane. 310p. 1974. Repr. of 1941 ed. lib. bdg. 15.95x (ISBN 0-88411-955-6). Amereon Ltd.
Queen's Folly. Stanley John Weyman. LC 25-179364. 1925. Longmans, Green and Co.
Queen's Folly: A Romance. Elswyth Thane. LC 74-4543. (Illus.). 1974. 6.95. Aeonian Press.
Queen's Folly: A Romance. Elswyth Thane. LC 37-4763. Harcourt, Brace and Company.
Queens Full: 3 Novelets and a Pair of Short Shorts. Ellery Queen, pseud. LC 65-10460. 3.95. Random.
Queen's Garden. Mary Evelyn Moore Davis. LC 2072. 1900. Houghton, Mifflin and Company.
Queen's Gate Mystery. Herbert Adams. LC 27-183087. 1927. J. B. Lippincott Company.
Queens Gate Reckoning. Lewis Perdue. 384p. (Orig.). 1982. pap. 3.50 (ISBN 0-523-41436-6). Pinnacle Bks.
Queen's Gift. Inglis Clark Fletcher. LC 78-5778. 1978. 13.50 (ISBN 0-89244-005-8). Queens House.
Queen's Gift. 1st Ed. Inglis Clark Fletcher. LC 52-10694. 1952. Bobbs-Merrill.
Queen's Grace. Jan Vlachos Westcott. LC 59-14029. 1959. Crown Publishers.
Queen's Harem. James Gerald Dunton. LC 33-25376. Sears Publishing Company.
Queen's Heart. J H Hildreth. LC 18-16018. 1918. 1.50. Marshall Jones Company.
Queen's Holiday. Elizabeth Frances Corbett. LC 40-5184. 1940. D. Appleton-Century Company, Incorporated.

TITLE INDEX QUEST OF LEDGAR DUNSTAN.

Queen's Hostage. Harriet Theresa Smith Comstock. LC 6-30464. 1906. Little, Brown, and Company.
Queen's Husband. Noel Bertram Gerson. LC 60-8830. 1960. McGraw-Hill.
Queen's Husband. Eleanor Hibbert. LC 77-21161. (Illus.). 1978. 8.95. Putnam.
Queen's Husband. Jean Plaidy. 1979. pap. 1.95 (ISBN 0-449-23896-2, Crest). Fawcett.
Queen's Husband. Jean Plaidy. LC 77-21161. 1978. 8.95 (ISBN 0-399-12128-5). Putnam Pub Group.
Queen's in the Parlor. Helen Rosen Woodward. LC 33-24535. The Bobbs-Merrill Company.
Queen's Jest. Sallie Lee Bell. (Hearth Ser.). 1979. pap. 1.95 o.p. (ISBN 0-310-21102-6). Zondervan.
Queen's Jest: A Romance of the Time of Louis Xvi. Sallie Lee Bell. LC 52-9882. 1952. Zondervan Pub. House.
Queen's Knight. Marvin Borowsky. LC 55-5805. 1955. Random House.
Queen's Lady. Patricia Parkes. LC 80-28054. 12.95 (ISBN 0-312-66008-1). St. Martin's Press.
Queen's Maries. A Romance of Holyrood. George John Whyte-Melville. (seaside library. v. 81, no. 1650). 1883. G. Munro.
Queen's Mate. Herbert Adams. LC 31-134868. 1931. J. B. Lippincott Company.
Queen's Mate. Philip MacDonald. LC 27-6432. 1927. L. MacVeagh, The Dial Press.
Queen's Messenger. W. R Duncan. LC 81-15300. 14.95 (ISBN 0-440-07212-3). Delacorte Press.
Queen's Necklace... Alexandre Dumas. LC 4-17498. (Half-title: The romances of Alexandre Dumas. Handy library edition. The Marie Antoinette romances...). 1893. Little, Brown and Company.
Queen's Necklace. Alexandre Dumas & Maquet, Auguste. LC 6-42319. 1890. Little, Brown and Company.
Queen's Necklace. Alexandre Dumas & Maquet, Auguste. LC 4-21712. Little, Brown, & Company.
Queen's Necklace. Alexandre Dumas & Maquet, Auguste. LC 6-41704. (Half-title: The romances of Alexandre Dumas. Illustrated library ed. vol. 30-31). 1893. Little, Brown, and Company.
Queen's Necklace. Alexandre Dumas & Maquet, Auguste. LC 6-41703. (American series. no. 314). M. J. Ivers & Co.
Queen's Necklace. Alexandre Dumas & Maquet, Auguste. LC 8-26659. 1894. Little, Brown, and Company.
Queen's Necklace. Alexandre Dumas & Maquet, Auguste. LC 6-41702. (On cover: Seaside library. Pocket ed. no. 2120). G. Munro's Sons.
Queen's Necklace: A Sequel to "Memoirs of a Physician". Alexandre Dumas & Maquet, Auguste. G. Routledge and Sons, Limited.
Queen's Necklace. With an Introd. by Henri Peyre and Illus. by Cyril Arnstam. Alexandre Dumas & Auguste Maquet. LC 73-168391. (Illus.). 1973. Printed for the Members of the Limited Editions Club.
Queens of the Road. Jack Milton, pseud. 176p. pap. 1.95 o.p. (6096). Brandon.
Queen's Own: An Original Novel. George Charles Appell. LC 55-120294. (Dell first edition 74). 1955. Dell Pub. Co.
Queen's Page. A Story of the Days of Charles I. of England. Katharine Tynan Hinkson, pseud. LC 1-29326. 1900. Benzinger Brothers.
Queen's Panetelas. Crosby George. LC 35-9323. 1935. D. Appleton-Century Company, Incorporated.
Queen's Pawn. Victor Canning. 1973. 1.25. Dell.
Queen's Pawn. Victor Canning. LC 75-111619. 1970. 5.95. Morrow.
Queen's Physician. Edgar Maass. LC 50-3385. 1950. Sun Dial Press.
Queen's Physician. Edgar Maass. LC 48-5262. 1948. C. Scribner's Sons.
Queen's Play. Dorothy Dunnett. (E125). 1965. Popular Lib.
Queen's Play. Dorothy Dunnett. LC 64-13015. 1964. Putnam.
Queen's Quadrille. Georgina Grey, pseud. 224p. 1981. pap. 1.50 (ISBN 0-449-50212-0, Crest). Fawcett.
Queen's Quair: Or; The Six Years' Tragedy. Hewlett, Maurice Henry. LC 78-145084. 1971. (ISBN 0-403-01023-3). Scholarly Press.
Queen's Quair: Or, The Six Years' Tragedy. Maurice Henry Hewlett. LC 4-12092. 1904. The Macmillan Company.
Queen's Quorum. Ellery Queen, pseud. LC 68-56450. 146p. 1951. 15.00x (ISBN 0-8196-0229-9). Biblo.
Queen's Revenge. A Novel. Sylvanus Cobb. (On cover: The idle hours series, no. 17). The F. M. Lupton Publishing Company.
Queen's Rings: The True Romance of Elizabeth, Queen of England. Anne Hughston Meeker. LC 38-21313. D. Ryerson, Inc.
Queen's Rival. Shannon Clare. 1978. pap. 1.95 o.s.i. (ISBN 0-8439-0590-5, Leisure Bks). Nordon Pubns.
Queen's Royal. John Quigley. LC 76-45786. 10.95 (ISBN 0-698-10756-X). Coward, McCann & Geoghegan.
Queen's Royal. John Quigley. 1978. 2.25 (ISBN 0-449-23574-2). Fawcett Crest Books.
Queen's Sailors. A Nautical Novel. Edward Greey. LC 6-44865. 1870. E. Greey & Co.
Queen's Sister. Sandra Wilson. LC 74-81468. 1974. 6.95. St. Martin's Press.
Queen's Sister. Sandra Wilson. LC 77-3661. 1977. 7.95 (ISBN 0-89340-067-X). J. Curley.
Queen's Stairway. William Edward Daniel Ross. (YA) 1978. 6.95 (Avalon). Bouregy.
Queen's Treasure. Clifford Ashdown. LC 76-352201. 1975. Train.
Queen's Treasure. first ed. Richard Austin Freeman & John J Pitcairn. 1975. 7.50. Oswald Train.
Queen's Twin and Other Stories. Sarah Orne Jewett. LC 69-11907. (American short story series, v. 66). 1969. Garrett Press.
Queen's Twin and Other Stories. Sarah Orne Jewett. LC 76-178443. (Short story index reprint series). 1971. (ISBN 0-8369-4044-X). Books for Libraries Press.
Queen's Twin: And Other Stories. Sarah Orne Jewett. LC 57. 1899. Houghton, Mifflin and Company.
Queen's Twin and Other Stories. Sarah Orne Jewett. LC 79-10815. 1979. 20.00 (ISBN 0-403-03180-X). Scholarly Press.
Queen's Twin & Other Stories see Collected Works.
Queens Walk in the Dusk. Thomas Burnett Swann. LC 77-22295. (Illus.). 1977. 15.00 (ISBN 0-930068-00-9). Heritage Press.
Queens Walk in the Dust. Thomas Burnett Swann. LC 77-79742. (Illus.). 1977. 15.00 o.s.i. (ISBN 0-930068-02-5). Heritage Pr.
Queen's Ward. Hebe Elsna. 1971. pap. 0.95 o.p. (95177). Beagle Bks.
Queen's Wigs. Naomi Gwladys Royde-Smith. LC 34-28460. 1934. The Macmillan Company.
Queenshite: A Novel. Henrietta Gould Rowe. LC 8-936. 1895. C. W. Moulton.
"Queer" Case. John Russell Coryell. LC 99-5052. (On cover: Magnet detective library, no. 103). 1899. Street & Smith.
Queer Dutchman. Peter Agnos. Ed. by Cy Adler. (Illus.). 1979. 4.50 (ISBN 0-914018-03-5). Green Eagle Pr.
Queer Free. Alabama Birdstone. (Illus.). 200p. (Orig.). 1980. pap. 6.00 (ISBN 0-930762-04-5). Calamus Bks.
Queer Judson. Joseph Crosby Lincoln. LC 25-19433. 1925. D. Appleton and Company.
Queer Kind of Death. George Baxt. LC 66-16148. (Inner sanctum mystery). 1966. Simon and Schuster.
Queer Kind of Death. George Baxt. LC 78-19248. 1979. 10.00. (ISBN 0-312-66021-9) (ISBN 0-312-66022-7). St. Martin's Press.
Queer Letters. Kym Allyson, pseud. 192p. pap. 1.95 o.p. (6119). Brandon.
Queer Letters see His Male Lover.
Queer Little People. Harriet Elizabeth Beecher Stowe. LC 12-39190. Houghton, Miffin and Company.
Queer Mr. Quell. William James Makin. LC 38-5745. 1938. R. M. McBride and Company.
Queer People. Carroll Graham & Graham, Garrett. LC 30-17096. The Vanguard Press.
Queer People: A Novel. Carroll Graham & Garrett Graham. LC 76-3478. (Lost American Fiction Ser.). 285p. 1976. Repr. of 1930 ed. 7.95 (ISBN 0-8093-0784-7). S Ill U Pr.
Queer Race: A Story of a Strange People. William Westall. LC 2665. (On cover: Columbia library. v. 2, no. 23). 1900. Street & Smith.
Queer Race: the Story of a Strange People. William Westall. LC 41-42514. 1887. Cassell & Company, Limited.
Queer Race: the Story of a Strange People. William Westall. (On cover: Lovell's library, no. 1157). 1888. J. W. Lovell Company.
Queer Race: the Story of a Strange People. William Westall. (On cover: Seaside library. Pocket ed. no. 1061). 1888. G. Munro.
Queer Street. Edward Shanks. LC 33-6704. The Bobbs-Merrill Company.
Queer Street: The Story of Some Native New Yorkers. John Wiley. LC 28-9655. 1928. C. Scribner's Sons.
Queerest Man Alive, and Other Stories. George Hughes Hepworth. LC 7-4276. R. F. Fenno & Company.
Quelques Nouvelles Histoires. Helene Gobel. LC 36-8426. (Fr). 1964. 3.12 o.p. (ISBN 0-395-02677-6). HM.
Quelques Textes Naturalistes. Jean A. Bede. (Fr). 1937. text ed. 3.80 o.p. (ISBN 0-03-014955-X). HR&W.
Quemado; a Western Story. William West Winter. LC 23-10468. Chelsea House.
Quench the Moon. Walter Macken. LC 48-5852. 1948. Viking Press.
Quenchless Light. Agnes Christina Laut. LC 24-16809. 1924. D. Appleton and Company.
Quentin Durward. Walter Scott. Ed. by Yonge, Charlotte, Mary. LC 8-3024. (Classics for children. v. 2). 1884. Ginn, Heath & Co.
Quentin Durward. Walter Scott. (On cover: Lovell's library, no. 575). 1885. J. W. Lovell Company.
Quentin Durward. Walter Scott. LC 8-3025. 1887. Worthington Co.
Quentin Durward. Walter Scott. Ed. by Lang, Andrew. LC 16-3383. (On cover: Waverley novels). Dana, Estes & Company.
Quentin Durward... Walter Scott. Ed. by Norris, Mary Harriot. LC 16-3381. (Eclectic school readings). 1900. American Book Co.
Quentin Durward. Walter Scott. Ed. by Eno, Arthur Llewellyn. LC 5-9715. (Macmillan's pocket American and English classics). 1905. The Macmillan Company.
Quentin Durward. Walter Scott. Ed. by Bruere, Robert Walter. LC 7-7196. (Standard English classics). Ginn & Company.
Quentin Durward. Walter Scott. Ed. by Munger, L. M. Francis, Susan M. (Riverside literature series). Houghton, Mifflin and Company.
Quentin Durward. Walter Scott. Ed. by Brewster, William Tenney. LC 10-30890. (belles-lettres series. Section vii--The English novel). 0.50. D. C. Heath & Co.
Quentin Durward. Walter Scott. Ed. by Simonds, William Edward. LC 10-8929. (lake English classics). 0.45. Scott, Foresman and Company.
Quentin Durward. Walter Scott. Ed. by Colby, June Rose. LC 12-9565. (Half-title: Twentieth contury text-books). 1912. D. Appleton and Company.
Quentin Durward. Walter Scott. Ed. by Herzberg, Max John. LC 18-20167. (Merrill's English texts). Charles E. Merrill Company.
Quentin Durward. Walter Scott. Ed. by Simonds, William Edward. LC 19-66059. (Half-title: The Lake English classics. General editor: L. T. Damon). Scott, Foresman and Company.
Quentin Durward. Walter Scott. LC 23-26862. 1923. Dodd, Mead and Company.
Quentin Durward. Walter Scott. LC 23-16047. 1923. C. Scribner's Sons.
Quentin Durward. Walter Scott. Ed. by Bessey, Mabel Abbot. LC 27-12291. (Academy classics for junior high schools). Allyn and Bacon.
Quentin Durward. Walter Scott. Ed. by Bruere, Robert Walter. LC 29-2467. (Standard English classics). Ginn and Company.
Quentin Durward. Walter Scott. LC 36-37011. (Half-title: Everyman's library, ed. by Ernest Rhys. Friction. no. 140). 1933. J. M. Dent & Sons, Ltd.
Quentin Durward. Walter Scott. LC 45-48715. (His Waverley novels). De Wolfe, Fiske, & Co.
Quentin Durward. Walter Scott. LC 44-5772. (On cover: Great illustrated classics). 1944. Dodd, Mead & Company.
Quentin Durward. Walter Scott. (Seaside library, v. 50, no. 1607). 1881. G. Munro.
Quentin Durward; a Romance. From the Last Rev. Ed., Containing the Author's Final Corrections, Notes, &C. parker's ed. Walter Scott. LC 8-5781. (Waverley novels: Library ed. v. 15). Sanborn, Carter, Bazin & Co.
Quentin Durward: Introd. by C. L. Bennet. Walter Scott. (Classics ser., CL132). 1967. Airmont.
Quentin Durward: Ivanhoe, Kenilworth. Walter Scott. LC 33-27351. (Half-title: The modern library of the world's best books). 1933. The Modern Library.
Quentin Durward, the Loser and the Winner. William Henry Bogart & Bogart, Miss, Joint Author. LC 6-14189. 1869. J. Munsell.
Querelle. Jean Genet. LC 73-17693. 1974. 7.95 (ISBN 0-8021-0010-4). Grove Press: Distributed by Random House.
Querrils. Stacy Aumonier. LC 19-13965. 1919. 1.60. The Century Co.
Querschnitt. Ed. by Ian C. Loram & Leland R. Phelps. (Orig., Ger.). 1962. pap. 6.95x (ISBN 0-393-09575-4, NortonC). Norton.
Quest. tr. from the spanish, by issac goldberg. ed. Baroja y Nessi, Pio. Tr. by Goldberg, Issac. LC 22-21802. 1922. A. A. Knopf.
Quest. Miles Lanier Colean. LC 23-120037. E. P. Dutton & Company.
Quest. Nelson De Mille. 224p. (Orig.). 1975. pap. 1.50 (ISBN 0-532-15183-6). Woodhill.
Quest. Frederik Van Eeden & C. L. W., Tr. LC 7-15321. 1907. J. W. Luce & Company.
Quest. Frederik Willem Van Eeden & Cole, Laura (Ward) 1847- Tr. LC 7-15321. 1907. J. W. Luce & Company.
Quest. Helen Rose Hull. LC 22-204237. 1922. The Macmillan Company.
Quest. Elsie Frances Wilson Mack. 1953. Bouregy & Curl.
Quest,". Thomas A Stoddard. LC 10-4589. 1909. 1.50. Cochrane Publishing Company.
Quest. Octave Frederick Ursenbach. LC 45-11433. 1945. Bookcraft.
Quest: A Novel. Katharine Newlin Burt. LC 25-212574. 1925. Houghton Mifflin Company.
Quest. A Novel of Religious Revolution. Lawrence Wilson Neff. LC 53-542. 1953. Banner Press.
Quest: A Story of the Pursuit of the Ideal of Love. 1st Ed. Jean Pierre Le Coq. LC 60-15734. 1960. American Press.
Quest, an Agelong Romance: By Williston Merrick Pseud. 1st Ed. Williston Merrick Ford. LC 53-5144. 1953. Exposition Press.
Quest and Conquest. Vane Erskine Bannisdale. LC 29-9494. 1929. Longmans, Green and Co.
Quest Crosstime. Andre Norton, pseud. 256p. 1981. pap. 2.50 (ISBN 0-441-69684-8). Ace Bks.
Quest Eternal. William Otis Lillibridge. LC 8-22346. 1908. Dodd, Mead and Company.
Quest for Alexis. Nancy Buckingham. LC 72-7733. 1973. 5.95. Hawthorn Books.
Quest for Bowie's Blade. John Thomas Edson. 192p. 1982. pap. 2.25 (ISBN 0-425-05654-6). Berkley Pub.
Quest for Christa T. Christa Wolf. LC 78-133199. 1971. 5.95. Farrar, Straus & Giroux.
Quest for Corvo: An Experiment in Autobiography. A. J. A Symons. (Penguin 291). 1967. pap., 1.45. Penguin.
Quest for Fire. J. H. Rosny. 128p. 1982. pap. 2.50 (ISBN 0-345-30067-X). Ballantine.
Quest for Karla. John Le Carre. LC 82-47961. 1982. 10.95 (ISBN 0-394-52848-4). Knopf.
Quest for Love. Jacquetta Hawkes. 1981. 10.95 (ISBN 0-8076-1003-8). Braziller.
Quest for Love. Emily Coddington Williams. LC 29-280558. 1929. The Macaulay Company.
Quest for Love of Lao Lee. Ch'ing Ch'un Shu. Tr. by Kuo, Ching-Ch'lu. LC 48-92362. Reynal & Hitchcock.
Quest for Meaning: Modern Short Stories. Glenn O Carey. LC 74-27168. 1975. 3.95 (ISBN 0-679-30273-5). D. McKay Co.
Quest for Simbilis. Michael Shea. (Science Fiction Ser.). 1974. pap. 0.95 o.p. (UQ1092). DAW Bks.
Quest for Tanelorn. Michael Moorcock. 1.25. Dell.
Quest for the Faradawn. Richard Ford. LC 82-1495. (Illus.). 14.95 (ISBN 0-440-07196-8). Delacorte Press/Eleanor Friede.
Quest for the Future. Alfred Elton Van Vogt. 1973. 0.95. Ace.
Quest for the Red Prince. Michael Bar-Zohar & Eitan Haber. (Illus.). 320p. 1983. 15.95 (ISBN 0-688-02043-7). Morrow.
Quest for the Rose of Sharon. Burton Egbert Stevenson. LC 9-12275. 1909. L. C. Page & Company.
Quest for the Three World's. Cordwainer Smith, pseud. (Dell Rey book). 1978. 1.75 (ISBN 0-345-27715-5). Ballantine Books.
Quest for the White Witch. Tanith Lee. 1.95 (ISBN 0-87997-357-9). DAW Books.
Quest for Tomorrow. Virginia M Owens. LC 57-163775. 1956. Zondervan Pub. House.
Quest for Youth. E. T. Cooper. LC 76-45863. 7.95 (ISBN 0-8111-0634-9). Naylor Co.
Quest Illusive: Truth Vs. Fiction. Frances McCall Lewis. LC 17-43858. 1916. The Howell Company.
Quest in the Desert. Roy Chapman Andrews. (Illus.). 1950. Viking Press.
Quest: Novelization. G S Madden. 1977. 1.50 (ISBN 0-441-69670-8). Ace Books.
Quest of a Pearl. Annie McKnight Young. LC 26-1060. 1925. F. L. Rowe.
Quest of Alistair. Robert Allison Hood. LC 21-17814. 1.90. George H. Doran Company.
Quest of Coronado: An Historical Romance of the Spanish Cavaliers in Nebraska. Denis Gerald Fitzgerald. LC 1-11780. J. Murphy Company.
Quest of Dirk & Honey. Roland De Forrest. 256p. 1983. pap. 2.75 (ISBN 0-446-30297-X). Warner Bks.
Quest of Enlightenment. Edward J. Thomas. (Wisdom of the East Ser). 1.75 o.p. (ISBN 0-7195-1405-3). Paragon.
Quest of Excalibur. Leonard Patrick O'Connor Wibberley. LC 59-12007. 1959. Putnam.
Quest of Excalibur. Leonard Patrick O'Connor Wibberley. LC 79-192. 1979. 10.95. (ISBN 0-89370-131-9) (ISBN 0-89370-231-5). Borgo Press.
Quest of Flowers. Harold Fletcher. 1975. 30.00x (ISBN 0-85224-278-6, Pub. by Edinburgh Pr Scotland). Columbia U Pr.
Quest of John Chapman: The Story of a Forgotten Hero. Newell Dwight Hillis. LC 4-33221. 1904. The Macmillan Company.
Quest of Juror Nineteen. David Davidson. 1971. 5.95 o.p. (ISBN 0-385-05637-0). Doubleday.
Quest of Juror 19. David Albert Davidson. LC 72-154050. 1971. 5.95. Doubleday.
Quest of Kadji. Lin Carter. (O.s.i.). (Orig.). 1971. pap. 0.95 o.s.i. (B95-2416). Belmont-Tower.
Quest of Ledgar Dunstan. Alfred Tresidder Sheppard. LC 17-21976. 1917. D. Appleton and Company.

Quest of "Little Blessing,". Anna Taggart Clark. LC 17-394. W. T. Potter.
Quest of Polly Locke. Zoe Anderson Norris. LC 2-21413. 1902. J. S. Ogilvie Publishing Company.
Quest of Qui. A Superhero Adventure. Kenneth Robeson. (His The fantastic adventures of Doc Savage, 4). (Illus.). 1975. 1.75. (ISBN 0-307-02378-8). Western Publishing Company.
Quest of the Absolute. Honore De Balzac. Tr. by Ellen Marriage. LC 36-37130. (Half-title: Everyman's library, ed. by Ernest Rhys. Fiction. no. 286). 1927. J. M. Dent & Sons, Ltd.
Quest of the Absolute. Honore De Balzac. Tr. by Ellen Marriage. (Half-title: Everyman's library, ed. by Ernest Rhys. Fiction). 1908. J. M. Dent & Co.
Quest of the Bogeyman: By Frances and Richard Lockridge. Frances Louise Davis Lockridge & Lockridge, Richard. LC 64-10873. (Main line mysteries). 1964. Lippincott.
Quest of the Dark Lady. Quinn Reade. 1976. pap. 1.25 o.s.i. (ISBN 0-505-51101-0). Tower Bks.
Quest of the Dark Lady. Quinn Reade. LC 60-1067. (Orig.). 1969. pap. 0.60 o.p. (B60-1067). Belmont-Tower.
Quest of the Dream. Edna Kingsley Wallace. LC 13-208229. 1913. G. P. Putnam's Sons.
Quest of the Four-Leaved Clover: A Story of Arabia: Adapted from the French Laboulaye's "Abdallah". Edouard Rene Lefebvre De Laboulaye. Tr. by Field, Walter Taylor. LC 11-775. 1910. Ginn and Company.
Quest of the Four: Story of the Comanches and Buena Vista. Joseph Alexander Altsheler. LC 11-23845. 1911. D. Appleton and Company.
Quest of the Gilt-Edged Girl. Richard De Lyrienne. (Bodley booklets, no. 2). 1897. J. Lane.
Quest of the Golden Girl: A Romance. Richard Le Gallienne. LC 9-2492. 1896. J. Lane.
Quest of the Golden Girl: A Romance. Richard Le Gallienne. 1897. J. Lane.
Quest of the Golden Girl: A Romance. Richard Le Gallienne. LC 24-22211. 1920. John Lane Company.
Quest of the Golden Stairs: A Mystery of Kinghood in Faerie. Arthur Edward Waite. LC 74-6440. (Newcastle occult book X-28). 1974. (pbk.) 2.95 (ISBN 0-87877-028-3). Newcastle Pub. Co.
Quest of the Golden Stairs: A Mystery of Kinghood in Faerie. Arthur Edward Waite. LC 80-19659. 1980. 9.95 (ISBN 0-87877-328-2). Borgo Press.
Quest of the Sacred Slipper. Arthur Sarsfield Ward. LC 19-16373. 1919. Doubleday, Page & Company.
Quest of the Sacred Slipper. Arthur Sarsfield Ward. LC 24-20464. 1922. Doubleday, Page & Company.
Quest of the Sacred Slipper. Arthur Sarsfield Ward. (On cover: Masterpieces of Oriental mystery). McKinlay, Stone & Mackenzie.
Quest of the: Sea Eagle. Sheila Brathwaite. LC 68-132706. 1967. bds., 4.50. Bell.
Quest of the Sea Otter. Sabra Conner. LC 27-10953. The Reilly & Lee Co.
Quest of the Silver Fleece. W. E. B. Du Bois. LC 74-7364. 451p. 1975. Repr. of 1911 ed. lib. bdg. 18.00 (ISBN 0-527-25325-1). Kraus Intl.
Quest of the Silver Fleece. William Edward Burghardt Du Bois. pap. 3.95 (N261P). Mnemosyne.
Quest of the Silver Fleece. William Edward Burghardt Du Bois. LC 72-76102. 1969. Repr. of 1911 ed. 21.00x o.p. (ISBN 0-8434-0005-6). Consortium Pr.
Quest of the Silver Fleece: A Novel. William Edward Burghardt Du Bois. LC 74-7364. (Illus.). 1974. 15.00 (ISBN 0-527-25325-1). Kraus-Thomson Organization.
Quest of the Silver Fleece: A Novel. William Edward Burghardt Du Bois. LC 70-92742. (Illus.). 1969. Negro Universities Press.
Quest of the Silver Fleece: A Novel. William Edward Burghardt Du Bois. LC 71-83922. (Illus.). 1969. Mnemosyne Pub. Co.
Quest of the Silver Fleece: A Novel. William Edward Burghardt Du Bois. LC 72-76102. (Illus.). 1969. 15.00. McGrath Pub. Co.
Quest of the Silver Fleece: A Novel. William Edward Burghardt Du Bois. LC 73-144599. 1972. (ISBN 0-404-00154-8). AMS Press.
Quest of the Silver Fleece: A Novel. William Edward Burghardt Du Bois. LC 11-279123. 1911. A. C. McClurg & Co.
Quest of the Snow Leopard. Roy Chapman Andrews. LC 55-2896. (Illus.). 1955. Viking Press.
Quest of Youth. Jeffery Farnol. LC 27-22947. 1927. Little, Brown, and Company.
Quest: The Story of Anne, Three Men, and Some Arabs. Rosita Torr Forbes. LC 24-14457. 1922. Cassell and Company, Ltd.
Quest: The Story of the Shepherds of Bethlehem. Ludwig Bauer. LC 46-12921. 1945. Concordia Publishing House.
Quest: Translated from the German by Jane Bannard Greene. 1st American Ed. Elisabeth Langgasser. LC 52-121764. 1953. Knopf.
Questing Beast. Jane Lane. 1970. 6.50 o.p. Intl Pubns Serv.
Questing Heart. Nelma Haynes. (Orig.). 1980. pap. 1.75 (ISBN 0-8439-8011-7, Tiara Bks). Nordon Pubns.
Questing Heart. Deborah Joyce. (Super Romances Ser.). 384p. 1983. pap. 2.95 (ISBN 0-373-70061-X, Pub. by Worldwide). Harlequin Bks.
Questing Heart: A Romantic Novel About George Sand, by F. W. Kenyon. Frank Wilson Kenyon. LC 64-18741. 1964. Dodd, Mead.
Question: A Novel. Franklin Pierce Ramsay. LC 9-18057. 1909. The Neale Publishing Company.
Question Mark. Muriel Jaeger. LC 26-6262. 1926. The Macmillan Company.
Question of Character. Translated from the French by Mervyn Savill. Jean Hougron. LC 58-10543. 1958. Farrar, Straus and Cudahy.
Question of Choice. 1st American Ed. Prudence Andrew. LC 62-182457. 1962. Putnam.
Question of Color. Francis Charles Philips. LC 7-36067. F. A. Stokes Company.
Question of Damages. John Townsend Trowbridge. LC 28-16605. (The hearthstone series). 1897. Lee and Shepard, Publishers.
Question of Dolly. Sara Lippincott Richards. LC 27-330. R. G. Badger.
Question of Faith. Lily Dougall. LC 6-33693. 1895. Houghton, Mifflin and Company.
Question of Gregory. Elizabeth Janeway. LC 49-103123. 1949. Doubleday.
Question of Guilt. Richard Posner. (Lucas Tanner Ser.: No. 1). (Orig.). 1975. pap. 1.25 o.p. (ISBN 0-515-03709-5, V3777). Pyramid Pubns.
Question of Guilt: The Curious Case of Dr. Crippen. Richard Gordon. LC 81-66026. 1981. 9.95 (ISBN 0-689-11192-4). Atheneum.
Question of Harmony. Gretchen Sprague. LC 65-13511. 1965. Dodd, Mead.
Question of Honor. A Novel. Frances Christine Tiernan. LC 12-16797. 1875. D. Appleton and Company.
Question of Honour. Mary Louise Parmelee Peebles. LC 7-36471. Dodd, Mead & Company.
Question of Identity. Louise Dodge. LC 13-9395. (Half-title: No name series). 1887. Roberts Brothers.
Question of Identity. June Thomson. LC 77-15749. 1977. 6.95 (ISBN 0-385-13245-X). Published for the Crime Club by Doubleday.
Question of Inheritance. Josephine Bell. LC 80-54819. 1981. 9.95 (ISBN 0-8027-5438-4). Walker.
Question of Innocence. Donald Winks. LC 60-8576. 1960. Macmillan.
Question of Judgment. Phyllis Brett Young. LC 78-85287. 1969. 5.95. Putnam.
Question of Judgment: Robert Shogan. Robert Shogan. LC 74-173224. 1972. 10.00 o.p. (ISBN 0-672-55268-X). Bobbs.
Question of Latitude. Laura Bogue Luffman. LC 12-35103. 1912. John Lane.
Question of Law. Montague Jon. LC 81-21444. 9.95 (ISBN 0-312-66031-6). St. Martin's Press.
Question of Love. Hilary March, pseud. LC 67-13032. 1967. Simon and Schuster.
Question of Love. Marianne Ruuth. 1974. 4.50. Avalon.
Question of Love: A Story of Switzerland. Adele Huguenin & Ramsey, Annie R., Tr. LC 7-5851. 1891. Roberts Brothers.
Question of Loving. Marjorie H. Gardner. 1982. pap. 6.95 (Avalon). Bouregy.
Question of Marriage. Jessie Bell Vaizey. LC 11-18978. 1911. G. P. Putnam's Sons.
Question of Max. Amanda Cross, pseud. LC 76-2561. 1976. 7.95. Knopf.
Question of Max. Amanda Cross, pseud. 1977. 1.75 (ISBN 0-380-01770-9). Avon.
Question of Max. Carolyn G. Heilbrun. LC 76-56158. 1977. 6.95 (ISBN 0-394-48223-9). G. K. Hall.
Question of Murder: By Anthony Gilbert Pseud. Lucy Beatrice Malleson. LC 55-5816. 1955. Random House.
Question of Negligence. Hugh McLeave. LC 73-124837. 1970. 5.95. Harcourt, Brace, Jovanovich.
Question of Power. Bessie Head. (African Writers Ser.: No. 149). 1974. pap. text ed. 1.50x o.p. (ISBN 0-435-90149-4). Humanities.
Question of Power: A Novel. Bessie Head. LC 73-18011. 1974. 6.95 (ISBN 0-394-49155-6). Pantheon Books.
Question of Proof. Nicholas Blake. LC 35-9334. 1979. pap. 1.95i (ISBN 0-06-080494-7, P 494, PL). Har-Row.
Question of Proof. Cecil Day-Lewis. LC 35-9334. 1935. Harper & Brothers.
Question of Quarry. large print ed. George Bagby, pseud. LC 81-9031. 9.95 (ISBN 0-89621-300-5). Thorndike Press.
Question of Quarry. Aaron Marc Stein. LC 80-1668. 1981. 9.95 (ISBN 0-385-17294-X). Published for the Crime Club by Doubleday.
Question of Queens: By Michael Innes Pseud. John Innes Mackintosh Stewart. LC 56-6870. (Red badge mysteries). 1956. Dodd, Mead.
Question of Reality: A Novel of Poland. Kazimierz Brandys. Tr. by Isabel Barzun. 1980. 8.95 o.p. (ISBN 0-684-16599-6). Scribner.
Question of Silence. Amanda Minnie Douglas. LC 1-30973. 1901. Dodd, Mead & Company.
Question of Taste. Jozua Marius Willen Van Der Poorten Schwartz. (On cover: Lovell's Westminster series, no. 67). Lovell, Coryell & Company.
Question of Taste. Jozua Marius Willen Van Der Poorten Schwartz. LC 8-2927. (On cover: Lovell's Westminister series, no. 67). Lovell, Coryell & Company.
Question of Time. Helen McCloy. LC 75-163072. (Red badge novel of suspense). 1971. 4.95 (ISBN 0-396-06387-X). Dodd, Mead.
Question of Time. Helen McCloy. LC 72-37948. (Red badge novel of suspense). 1971. 7.95 (ISBN 0-8161-6000-7). G. K. Hall.
Question of Trust. Dorothy A. Bernard. (Candlelight Ecstasy Ser.: No. 53). (Orig.). 1982. pap. 1.75 (ISBN 0-440-17315-9). Dell.
Question of Upbringing: A Dance to the Music of Time. Anthony Dymoke Powell. (Medallion bk., S1123). 1965. Berkley.
Question of Upbringing: A Novel. Anthony Dymoke Powell. LC 51-3026. 1951. Scribner.
Question of Values. Martin Shepard. LC 76-13855. 7.95 (ISBN 0-8415-0449-0). Saturday Review Press.
Question: The Idyl of a Picture by His Friend Alma Tadema. authorized ed. Georg Moritz Ebers. Tr. by Mary Joanne Stafford. LC 41-31315. 1883. W. S. Gottsberger.
Question: The Idyl of a Picture by His Friend, Alma Tadema. authorized ed. Georg Moritz Ebers. Tr. by Mary Joanne Stafford. LC 42-320986. 1889. W. S. Gottsberger & Co.
Question: The Idyl of a Picture by His Friend Alma Tadema. Georg Moritz Ebers. Tr. by Mary Joanne Stafford. 1881. W. S. Gottsberger.
Question the Night. Mary Kennedy. LC 38-25877. 1938. Dodd, Mead & Company.
Questionable Practices. Ruth Karen. LC 79-2650. 10.95 (ISBN 0-06-012293-5). Harper & Row.
Questionable Shapes. William Dean Howells. LC 74-86145. (Short story index reprint series). (Illus.). 1969. Books for Libraries Press.
Questionable Shapes. William Dean Howells. LC 3-12810. 1903. Harper & Brothers.
Questionnaire, or, Prayer for a Town & a Friend. Jiri Grusa. LC 82-5042. (Illus.). 15.95 (ISBN 0-374-24010-8). Farrar, Straus & Giroux.
Questions of Precedence (Preseances) Translated by Gerard Hopkins. Francois Mauriac. LC 59-9959. 1959. Farrar, Straus and Cudahy.
Questor Tapes. D C Fontana & Gene Roddenberry. LC 75-35857. 1975. (ISBN 0-88411-091-5). Onian Press.
Quests Beyond the Mirror: A Trio of Tales. Elbert Rynberg. LC 81-65301. 15.00 (ISBN 0-682-49735-5). Exposition Press.
Quetzalcoatl. Jose Lopez-Portillo Y Pacheco. Tr. by Eliot Weinberger & Diana S. Goodrich. LC 76-25163. 1976. 8.95 (ISBN 0-8264-0145-7). Continuum.
Quetzalcoatl: A Novel. Lopez-Portillo y Pacheco, Jose. LC 76-25163. 8.95 (ISBN 0-8164-9303-0). Seabury Press.
Quex. Douglas Jerrold. LC 28-8588. 1928. Cosmopolitan Book Corporation.
Quianta; Candius: A Romance of Imperial Rome. Ernst Eckstein & Bell, Mrs. Clara Courney, (Poynter) Tr. 1834-1927. LC 6-34439. 1882. W. S. Gottsberger.
Quiberon Touch: A Romance of the Days When "the Great Lord Hawke" Was King of the Sea. Cyrus Townsend Brady. LC 1-24234. 1901. D. Appleton and Company.
Quick. Leigh Ellis. 208p. 1982. pap. 2.25 (ISBN 0-380-79640-6, 79640). Avon.
Quick Action. Robert William Chambers. LC 14-5428. 1914. 1.30. D. Appleton and Company.
Quick & the Dead. Harlan Cole. 3.75 o.p. Vantage.
Quick and the Dead. Judy Gardiner. LC 81-18213. 1982. 10.95 (ISBN 0-312-66050-2). St Martin's Press.
Quick and the Dead. Louis L'Amour. LC 74-5015. 1974. (lib. bdg.) 8.95 (ISBN 0-8161-6206-9). G. K. Hall.
Quick and the Dead. Claire Spencer. LC 32-183624. 1932. H. Smith.
Quick and the Dead. Vincent Starrett. LC 65-289724. 3.50. Arkham.
Quick and the Dead. Thomas Wiseman. LC 69-12252. 1969. 6.95. Viking Press.
Quick and the Dead: A Novel. Gerald William Bullett. LC 34-451. 1933. A. A. Knopf.
Quick Badge. Martin Ryerson. 1981. pap. 1.95 (ISBN 0-8439-0863-7, Leisure Bks). Nordon Pubns.
Quick, Before It Melts. Philip Benjamin. 1964. 4.95 o.p. (ISBN 0-394-44201-6). Random.
Quick Brown Fox. William Riley Burnett. LC 42-1762. 1942. A. A. Knopf.
Quick Brown Fox. Richard L Schoonover. LC 52-12146. 1952. Macmillan.
Quick Change. Jay Cronley. LC 80-5450. 1981. 10.95 (ISBN 0-385-15180-2). Doubleday.
Quick-Fire Hombre. Nelson Coral Nye. LC 37-16221. Greenberg.
Quick, Mr. Bunnifeel! William Emmet Deaton. LC 35-310221. R. Speller, Inc.
Quick on the Shoot. George Charles Appell. LC 55-6195. (Silver star westerns). 1955. Dodd, Mead.
Quick Red Fox. John Dann MacDonald. LC 64-55123. (Gold medal books). 1964. Fawcett Publications.
Quick Red Fox. John Dann MacDonald. LC 82-6044. 1982. 12.95 (ISBN 0-8161-3382-4). G.K. Hall.
Quick Rich Fox. Isabella Taves. LC 59-10816. 1959. Random House.
Quick Service. Pelham Grenville Wodehouse. LC 40-36106. 1940. Doubleday, Doran & Co., Inc.
Quick Service. Pelham Grenville Wodehouse. LC 42-242822. 1941. The Sun Dial Press.
Quick to Passion. William Arthur Neubauer. 1948. Phoenix Press.
Quick Trigger. Charles Stanley Strong. LC 45-6722. 1945. Phoenix Press.
Quick-Trigger Country: By Clem Colt Pseud. Nelson Coral Nye. LC 55-6206. (Silver star westerns). 1955. Dodd, Mead.
Quick Triggers. Eugene Cunningham. LC 35-12764. 1935. Houghton Mifflin Company.
Quick Tunes & Good Times. Newton F. Tolman. LC 72-781117. (Illus.). 112p. 1972. 5.50 o.s.i. (ISBN 0-87233-018-4). Bauhan.
Quick Years. Jean Ariss. LC 58-6167. 1958. Harper.
Quickened. Anna Chapin Ray. 1908. Little, Brown, and Company.
Quickening. Francis Lynde. LC 6-5140. 1906. The Bobbs-Merrill Company.
Quickening of Caliban: A Modern Story of Evolution. Joseph Compton-Rickett. LC 7-41415. The Cassell Publishing Co.
Quickie Suckers. Cynthia Boomis. 224p. pap. 1.95 o.p. (6140). Brandon.
Quickie Thrillers. Ed. by Arthur Liebman. (O.s.i.). (Orig.). 1975. pap. 1.50 o.s.i. (ISBN 0-671-48517-2). WSP.
Quickie Thrillers: 25 Mini-Mysteries. Arthur Liebman. LC 75-327002. (Illus.). 1975. 1.50 (ISBN 0-671-48517-2). Washington Square Press.
Quickies. Joe Goldberg. (Dell book). 1974. (pbk.) 1.25. Dell.
Quicksand. John Brunner. LC 67-22466. (Doubleday science fiction). 1967. Doubleday.
Quicksand. John Brunner. (Daw Science Fiction 3). 1976. 1.50. Daw Books.
Quicksand. Myrick Land. LC 68-29575. 1969. 4.95. Harper & Row.
Quicksand. Nella Larsen. LC 70-146615. (American Library). 1971. 1.50. Collier Books.
Quicksand. Nella Larsen. LC 74-75553. 1969. Negro Universities Press.
Quicksand. Nella Larsen. LC 28-97400. 1928. A. A. Knopf.
Quicksand. Noel Pierce. LC 40-32089. R. M. McBride & Company.
Quicksand. Hervey White. LC 6734. 1900. Small, Maynard & Company.
Quicksand, a Novel. William W Brinkley. LC 48-7801. 1948. E. P. Dutton.
Quicksand: A Novel of the City. Elliott Arnold. LC 77-3955. 9.95 (ISBN 0-671-22459-X). Simon and Schuster.
Quicksand: A Novel of the City. Elliott Arnold. 1978. 1.95 (ISBN 0-671-82120-2). Pocket Books.
Quicksands. Fannie Heaslip Lea. LC 11-6717. 1911. Sturgis & Walton Company.
Quicksands: From the German of Adolph Streckfuss. Adolf Streckfuss & Wister, Mrs. Annie Lee (Furness) 1830-1908, Tr. LC 4-35655. 1902. J. B. Lippincott Company.
Quicksands of Pactolus: A Novel. Horace Annesley Vachell. (The Protean series). 1896. H. Holt and Company.
Quicksilver. Fitzroy Davis. LC 42-221432. 1942. Harcourt, Brace and Company.
Quicksilver. Mary Gallagher. LC 82-585. 12.95 (ISBN 0-399-12697-X). Putnam.
Quicksilver. Richard L Graves. LC 75-35864. 1976. 8.95. Stein and Day.
Quicksilver. Norman Hartley. LC 78-73070. 1979. 8.95 (ISBN 0-689-10958-X). Atheneum.
Quicksilver. Robert Pohle. 1978. pap. 1.25 (ISBN 0-532-12570-3). Woodhill.
Quicksilver Horse. Anne Digby. LC 82-16830. 1982. 8.95 (ISBN 0-312-66083-9). St. Martin's Press.
Quicksilver Lady. Barbara Whitehead. LC 79-7457. 1980. 8.95 (ISBN 0-385-12779-0). Doubleday.

Quicksilver Love. Rose Flynn. (YA) 1980. 6.95 (Avalon). Bouregy.
Quicksilver Pool. Phyllis A Whitney. LC 55-6547. 1955. Appleton-Century-Crofts.
Quickthorn. Lanora Miller. 1975. (pbk.) 0.95. Ace Books.
Quidnunc: A Novel. Bartley, Robert F. LC 63-4306. (Comet book). 1963. Carlton Press.
Quiet American. Graham Greene. LC 56-6281. 1956. Viking Press.
Quiet As a Nun. Antonia Fraser. LC 77-9063. 1977. 7.95 (ISBN 0-670-58556-4). Viking Press.
Quiet As a Nun. Antonia Fraser. 1978. 1.95. Ace Books.
Quiet Birdman. Louis W. Klappich. 3.95 o.p. Vantage.
Quiet Cities. Joseph Hergesheimer. LC 28-13911. 1928. A. A. Knopf.
Quiet Corner. William Arthur Neubauer. LC 65-8248. 1965. Arcadia House.
Quiet Days in Clichy. Henry Miller. LC 65-23309. (Evergreen black cat book, BC-98). 1965. Grove Press.
Quiet Drink. Deborah Moggach. LC 80-51380. 12.50 (ISBN 0-312-66106-1). St. Martin's Press.
Quiet End of Evening. Honor Lilibush Wingfield Tracy. 1972. 6.95 o.p. (ISBN 0-394-47188-1). Random.
Quiet Enemy, & Other Stories. Cecil Dawkins. 1963. 4.50 o.p. Atheneum.
Quiet Fear. John Creasey. LC 68-16767. (Cock Robin mystery). 1968. Macmillan.
Quiet Fear. Jeremy York. 1968. 4.50 o.p. (63325). Macmillan.
Quiet Game of Bambu. Roger Gouze. LC 64-23222. 1964. Published for the Crime Club by Doubleday.
Quiet Gentleman. Georgette Heyer. LC 77-186359. 1972. 6.95. Putnam.
Quiet Gentleman. Georgette Heyer. LC 52-5266. 1952. Putnam.
Quiet Gun. Leo Brady. 1972. pap. 0.95 o.p. (09158). Curtis.
Quiet Hills. Iris Bromige. 1971. pap. 0.75 o.p. (94121). Beagle Bks.
Quiet House. Marjorie Warby. 1971. pap. 0.75 o.p. (94102). Beagle Bks.
Quiet Husband. Ellen Pickering. LC 43-357772. 1840. Carey & Hart.
Quiet Husband. A Novel. Ellen Pickering. G. B. Zieber & Co.
Quiet Interior. Emily Beatrix Coursolles Jones. LC 21-17276. 1921. Boni and Liveright.
Quiet Killer: A Novel. Donald MacKenzie. LC 68-15608. 1968. Houghton Mifflin.
Quiet King: A Story of Christ. Caroline Atwater Mason. 1896. American Baptist Publication Society.
Quiet Kingdom. Richard Gibson Hubler. LC 48-5384. 1948. Rinehart.
Quiet Lady. Norman Collins. LC 42-51126. 1942. Harper & Brothers.
Quiet Lady. Agnes Mure Mackenzie. LC 27-2819. 1926. Doubleday, Page & Company.
Quiet Life. Beryl Bainbridge. LC 76-55837. 208p. 1977. 7.95 (ISBN 0-8076-0846-7). Braziller.
Quiet Life of Mrs. General Lane. 1st Ed. Victoria Case. LC 52-8753. 1952. Doubleday.
Quiet Light, a Novel. 1st American Ed. Louis De Wohl. LC 50-8449. 1950. Lippincott.
Quiet Man. Leonard London Foreman. (O.s.i.). 1977. pap. 1.25 o.s.i. (BT51114). Belmont-Tower.
Quiet Man. Leonard London Foreman. (Belmont Tower Book). 1977. 1.25. Tower Publications.
Quiet Man. Patrick Purcell. LC 46-4355. 1946. G. P. Putnam's Sons.
Quiet Miracle. Jo Skelton Montgomery. LC 62-105006. 1962. Herald House.
Quiet Miss Godolphin. and, a chance ed. Isabella Fyvie Mayo. LC 7-18487. 1871. J. B. Lippincott & Co.
Quiet! Mommy's Asleep! Bil Keane. (Family Circus Ser.). (Illus.). 1978. pap. 1.75 (ISBN 0-449-13930-1, GM). Fawcett.
Quiet Murder. Virginia Reynolds Muzzey. LC 72-95572. 1973. 5.95 (ISBN 0-8059-1802-7). Dorrance.
Quiet Neighborhood. Anne Goodwin Winslow. LC 47-31452. 1947. A. A. Knopf.
Quiet Night of Fear. Charles L. Grant. (Orig.). 1981. pap. 2.25 (ISBN 0-425-04844-6). Berkley Pub.
Quiet Passion. Louise Hoffman. LC 74-18894. 1975. 6.95. St. Martin's Press.
Quiet Passion. William Arthur Neubauer. LC 49-953098. 1949. Phoenix Press.
Quiet Pilgrimage. Elizabeth Gray Vining. LC 73-129675. (Illus.). 1970. 8.95. Lippincott.
Quiet Place. Peter Burchard. 128p. 1982. pap. 1.75 (ISBN 0-441-17328-4, Pub. by Tempo). Ace Bks.
Quiet Place. Elisabeth Stancy Payne. LC 32-28020. 1932. Dodd, Mead & Company.
Quiet Place to Work: By Harry Brown. 1st Ed. Harry Peter M'Nab Brown. LC 67-18597. 1968. 6.95. Knopf.
Quiet, Please. James B. Cabell. 1952. 4.50 (ISBN 0-8130-0040-8). U Presses Fla.
Quiet River. Philip Maitland Hubbard. LC 77-27709. 1978. 7.95 (ISBN 0-385-14244-7). Published for the Crime Club by Doubleday.
Quiet Shore. Walter Havighurst. LC 37-2830. 1937. The Macmillan Company.
Quiet Sound of Fear. Lois Paxton, pseud. LC 79-158016. 1971. 5.95. Hawthorn Books.
Quiet Street. James Noble Gifford. LC 45-8641. 1945. Gramercy Publishing Co.
Quiet Street. Mikhail Andreevich Il'In. Tr. by Helstein, Nadia. LC 30-25618. 1930. L. MacVeagh, The Dial Press.
Quiet Street: A Novel. Zelda Popkin. LC 51-3210. 1951. Lippincott.
Quiet Town. John Thomas Edson. 192p. 1982. pap. 2.25 (ISBN 0-425-05818-2). Berkley Pub.
Quiet, Under the Sun. 1st American Ed. Kevin FitzGerald. LC 54-5143. 1954. Little, Brown.
Quiet Voice. Peter Graham. 1966. 5.00 o.p. (ISBN 0-8059-0107-8). Dorrance.
Quiet Voice: By Peter Graham. Peter L Abraham. LC 65-26149. 1966. Dorrance.
Quiet Voyage Home: A Novel. Richard Jessup. LC 78-105567. 1970. 5.95. Little, Brown.
Quiet Way. Manly P. Hall. pap. 2.00 (ISBN 0-89314-348-0). Philos Res.
Quiet Woman. Harry Carmichael. LC 72-82843. 192p. 1972. 5.95 o.p. (ISBN 0-8415-0212-9). Sat Rev Pr.
Quiet Woman. Agnes Adams Fisher. LC 54-6358. 1954. Funk & Wagnalls.
Quiet Woman. Leopold Horace Ognall. LC 72-82843. 1972. 5.95 (ISBN 0-8415-0212-9). Saturday Review Press.
Quiet Youth: Or, Just Like His Uncle. George G. Small. LC 21-205900. M. J. Ivers & Co.
Quietly Crush the Lizard. Earle Hill. LC 79-155668. 1972. 6.95 (ISBN 0-8149-0698-2). Vanguard Press.
Quietly My Captain Waits. Evelyn Sybil Mary Eaton. LC 40-6339. Harper & Brothers.
Quietly She Lies. E. M. D. Hawthorn. LC 52-7285. 1953. Harper.
Quietness of Dick. Robert Ernest Vernede. LC 11-11743. 1911. H. Holt and Company.
Quill. David Deihl. 1980. pap. 1.75 o.s.i. (ISBN 0-505-51472-9). Tower Bks.
Quill. Robert Steiner. LC 70-181665. 1973. 7.95 (ISBN 0-06-014081-X). Harper & Row.
Quill-Driver. Elisabeth Burstenbinder. Tr. by Miller, Hettle E. (On cover: The Marguerite series, no. 54). 1895. E. A. Weeks & Company.
Quiller Memorandum. Adam Hall, pseud. LC 65-125897. 4.50. S.&S.
Quiller Memorandum. Adam Hall, pseud. (Jove). 1979. 1.75 (ISBN 0-515-05211-6). Jove Publications.
Quiller Memorandum: By Adam Hall. Elleston Trevor. LC 65-12589. 1965. Simon and Schuster.
Quillian Sector: Dumarest of Terra No. 19. E. C. Tubb. (Science Fiction Ser.). (Orig.). 1978. pap. 1.50 (ISBN 0-87997-426-5, UW1426). DAW Bks.
Quill's Window. George Barr McCutcheon. LC 21-15954. 1921. Dodd, Mead and Company.
Quilocho and the Dancing Stars. Frances De Brundige. LC 72-80670. (Illus.). 1973. 8.95 (ISBN 0-8059-1715-2). Dorrance.
Quilocho & the Dancing Stars: A Historical Novel of Mexico. Frances De Brundige. (Illus., Limited Deluxe First Ed. with 20 photos). 1973. 8.95 o.p. (ISBN 0-8059-1715-2). Dorrance.
Quilt & Other Stories. Tayama Katai. Tr. by Kenneth G. Henshall from Japanese. 210p. 1981. 14.50x (ISBN 0-86008-279-2, Pub. by U of Tokyo Japan). Columbia U Pr.
Quilt and Other Stories. Katai Tayama & Kenneth G Henshall. LC 81-188871. 14.50 (ISBN 0-86008-279-2). University of Tokyo Press.
Quimby and Son. Marian Mira Grosberg Champagne. LC 62-12980. 1962. Bobbs-Merrill.
Quin. Alice Caldwell Hegan Rice. LC 21-14705. 1921. The Century Co.
Quince Bush. Marian Bower. LC 27-23254. The Bobbs Merrill Company.
Quince Cuentos De las Espanas. Doris K. Arjona & Carlos V. Arjona. LC 71-135971. 1971. pap. text ed. 8.50x (ISBN 0-684-41153-9, ScribC). Scribner.
Quince Cuentos Populares. Bernard Levy. (Rinehart Editions). 1939. text ed. 5.25 o.p. (ISBN 0-03-015850-8, HoltC). HR&W.
Quincie Bolliver. Mary Paula King. LC 41-13060. 1941. Houghton Mifflin Company.
Quincie Bolliver. Mary Paula King O'Donnell. LC 41-13060. 1941. Houghton Mifflin Company.
Quincunx Case. William Dent Pitman. LC 4-26121. 1904. H. B. Turner & Co.
Quincunx of Time. James Blish. 1973. (pbk.) 0.95. Dell.
Quincy Adams Sawyer and Mason's Corner Folks: A Novel; a Picture of New England Home Life. Charles Felton Pidgin. LC 5807. 1900. C. M. Clark Publishing Company.
Quincy Adams Sawyer and Mason's Corner Folks: A Picture of New England Home Life. rev. ed. Charles Felton Pidgin. LC 2-25602. 1902. C. M. Clark Publishing Company.
Quinn. Sally Mandel. LC 81-15269. 13.95 (ISBN 0-440-07205-0). Delacorte Press.
Quinneys' Horace Annesley Vachell. LC 14-18460. George H. Doran Company.
Quinneys' A Comedy in Four Acts. Horace Annesley Vachell. 1916. G. H. Doran Company.
Quinneys' Adventures. Horace Annesley Vachell. LC 24-18266. George H. Doran Company.
Quin's Hide. Margaret Summerton. LC 65-11393. 1965. 3.95. Dutton.
Quin's Shanghai Circus. Edward Whittemore. LC 73-8248. 1974. 7.95. Holt, Rinehart and Winston.
Quin's Shanghai Circus. Edward Wittemore. 304p. 1982. pap. 3.50 (ISBN 0-380-61200-3, 61200-3, Bard). Avon.
Quintain. R. E. Harrington. 224p. 1979. pap. 1.95 (ISBN 0-441-69985-5, Pub. by Charter Bks). Ace Bks.
Quintain: A Novel. R. E Harrington. LC 77-4598. 7.95 (ISBN 0-399-11908-6). Putnam.
Quintet: A Novel. Peter Vansittart. LC 76-380787. 1976. 4.50 (ISBN 0-7206-0344-7). Owen.
Quintin Chivas: By Barnaby Ross Pseud. Ellery Queen, pseud. LC 61-12292. 1961. Simon and Schuster.
Quintin Matsys: Or, The Blacksmith of Antwerp. Pierce Egan. (Seaside library, v. 22, no. 430). 1878. G. Munro.
Quintin's Man. David Rees. LC 76-365326. 1976. 1.95 (ISBN 0-234-77433-9). Dobson.
Quintin's Man. David Rees. LC 78-26308. 1979. 6.95 (ISBN 0-8407-6593-2). Elsevier/Nelson Books.
Quintus Oakes: A Detective Story. Charles Ross Jackson. LC 4-6740. 1904. G. W. Dillingham Company.
Quips & Bits, Bk. 2. Howard G. Tumolillo. 3.00 o.p. Carlton.
Quirinal Hill Affair. Barbara Hambly. LC 82-17051. 1983. 15.95 (ISBN 0-312-66123-1). St. Martin's Press.
Quirk. Gordon Merrick. 1978. pap. 2.95 (ISBN 0-380-38992-4, 79228). Avon.
Quirt. Bertha Muzzy Sinclair. LC 20-8857. 1920. Little, Brown, and Company.
Quisante: A Novel. 5th ed. Anthony Hope Hawkins. LC 26-22326. Frederick A. Stokes Company.
Quisante: A Novel. Anthony Hope Hawkins. LC 3-24935. (Half-title: Author's edition. Works of Anthony Hope...). D. Appleton and Company.
Quisisana: Or, Rest at Last. Friedrich Spielhagen & Goldschmidt, H. E., Tr. LC 8-14063. (On cover: Lovell's library. v. 8, no. 449). 1884. J. W. Lovell Company.
Quit for the Next. Anthony March. LC 45-4018. 1945. C. Scribner's Sons.
Quite Another Story. authorized ed. Jean Ingelow. (On cover: Lovell's international series. 119). 1890. J. W. Lovell Company.
Quite by Accident. Kage Booton. LC 72-76126. 1972. 4.95 (ISBN 0-385-07476-X). Published for the Crime Club by Doubleday.
Quite Contrary: The Mary and Newt Story. Stephen Dixon. LC 78-20202. 8.95 (ISBN 0-06-011072-4). Harper & Row.
Quite Early One Morning. Dylan Thomas. LC 54-12907. pap. 4.95 (ISBN 0-8112-0208-9, NDP90). New Directions.
Quite Early One Morning see Collected Prose.
Quite True. A Novel. Dora Russell. (Seaside library, v. 48, no. 985). 1881. G. Munro.
Quits: A Novel. Jemima Montgomery Tautphoeus. LC 8-20132. 1857. J. B. Lippincott & Co.
Quits: A Novel. Jemima Montgomery Tautphoeus. LC 8-20131. 1861. J. B. Lippincott & Co.
Quits. A Novel. Jemima Montgomery Tautphoeus. (Seaside library. v. 25, no. 517). 1879. G. Munro.
Quitter. Harrie Victor Schieren. LC 24-19017. Small, Maynard and Company.
Quitter: A Novel. Sabine W. Wood. LC 14-15743. The John C. Winston Company.
Quitters. Lincoln Hamlin Beyerle. LC 10-17987. 1.50. W. B. Conkey Company.
Quitting Time: A Novel. Leonard Kriegel. LC 81-16941. 15.50 (ISBN 0-394-50893-9). Pantheon Books.
Quiver Full of Arrows. Jeffrey Archer. LC 82-12707. 1982. 10.00 (ISBN 0-671-42602-8). Linden Press/Simon & Schuster.
Quivering Earth: A Novel of the Everglades. Wilma Russ. LC 52-6432. 1952. McKay.
Quivering Rose. Gene North. pap. 1.95 o.s.i. (OPH-210, Ophelia). Olympia.
Quixote Anthology. Ed. by Jean Rikhoff. (Orig.). 1962. pap. 2.45 o.p. (ISBN 0-448-00120-9, UL). G&D.
Quixote Anthology: Edited by Jean Rikhoff, in Collaboration with Kam and Richard Tiernan. Ed. by Jean Rikhoff. LC 62-2011. (Universal library, UL120). Grosset & Dunlap.
Quizma. Millie Sherman. LC 8-6417. 1878. Godfrey & Crandall, Printers.
Quo Vadis. altemus' ed. Henryk Sienkiewicz. Tr. by Samuel Augustus Binion. Malevsky, S., Joint Tr. LC 8-7311. H. Altemus.
Quo Vadis." A Narrative of the Time of Nero. Henryk Sienkiewicz. Tr. by Jeremiah Curtin. 1896. Little, Brown, and Company.
Quo Vadis." A Narrative of the Time of Nero. popular ed. Henryk Sienkiewicz. Tr. by Jeremiah Curtin. LC 4-16893. 1897. Little, Brown and Company.
Quo Vadis." A Narrative of the Time of Nero. souvenir ed. Henryk Sienkiewicz. Tr. by Jeremiah Curtin. LC 2330. 1900. Little, Brown, and Company.
Quo Vadis: A Narrative of the Time of Nero. Henryk Sienkiewicz. Tr. by Jeremiah Curtin. LC 43-156501. 1943. Little, Brown and Company.
Quo Vadis: A Narrative of the Time of Nero. Henryk Sienkiewicz. Tr. by Jeremiah Curtin. LC 43-18237. 1943. Garden City Publishing Co., Inc.
Quo Vadis' A Narrative of the Time of Nero. Authorized Unabridged Translation from the Polish, by Jeremiah Curtin.Illustrated by Howard Pyle and Other Artists. Souvenir Ed. Henryk Sienkiewicz. LC 2330. 1900. Little, Brown.
Quo Vadis." A Narrative of the Time of Nero: By Henryk Sienkiewicz; Tr. from the Polish by Jeremiah Curtin. New Ed. With Maps of Ancient Rome, and Photograuvres from Pictures by Howard Pyle, Edmund H. Garrett, Van Muyden, and from Ancient Sculptures... Henryk Sienkiewicz. Tr. by Jeremiah Curtin. LC 8-7310. 1897. Little, Brown and Company.
Quo Vadis." A Story of the Time of Nero. Henryk Seinkiewicz & Smith, William E., Tr. LC 8-11270. (sunny side series. no. 101). J. S. Ogilvie Publishing Company.
Quo Vadis" A Story of the Time of Nero. Henryk Sienkiewicz & Smith, William E., Tr. (On cover: Eagle series. no. 183). 1900. Street & Smith.
Quo Vadis: A Tale of the Time of Nero. Henryk Sienkiewicz. Tr. by Samuel Augustus Binion. Malevsky, S., Joint Tr. T. Y. Crowell & Co.
Quo Vadis: A Tale of the Time of Nero. new large type ed. with biographical introduction. ed. Henryk Sienkiewicz. Tr. by Samuel Augustus Binion. Malevsky, S., Joint Tr. LC 24-22816. Thomas Y. Crowell Company.
Quo Vadis: Adapted by C. Y. Stark. Henryk Sienkiewicz & Crandall Y. Stark. LC 53-11431. 1953. Globe Book Co.
Quo Warranto: A Story of Psychic Phenomena. Henry Goodacre. The Abbey Press.
Quodlibet. John Pendleton Kennedy. LC 75-104502. 1970. (ISBN 0-8398-1052-0). Literature House.
Quodlibet: Containing Some Annals Thereof... John Pendleton Kennedy. LC 7-19670. 1840. Lea & Blanchard.
Quodlibet: Containing Some Annals Thereof... 2d ed. John Pendleton Kennedy. LC 7-10955. 1860. J. B. Lippincott & Co.
Quonsett. James F. Murphy. LC 77-92074. 8.95 (ISBN 0-89256-050-9). Rawson Associates Publishers.
Quorndon Hounds: Or, A Virginian at Melton Mowbray. Henry William Herbert. T. B. Peterson.
Quorum. Phyllis Eleanor Bentley. LC 51-9157. 1951. Macmillan.
Quota: A Novel. by Vercors Pseud. Tr. from French by Rita Barisse. Jean Bruller. LC 66-14461. 4.95. Putnam.
Quotations from Other Lives. Penelope Gilliatt. LC 81-19544. 12.95 (ISBN 0-698-11135-4). Coward, McCann & Geoghegan.
Quotations of J. R. Ewing. (Orig.). 1980. pap. 1.50 (ISBN 0-553-14440-5). Bantam.
Quoth the Raven. Bruno Fischer. LC 44-9574. 1944. Pub. for the Crime Club by Doubleday, Doran and Co., Inc.

R

R Document. Irving Wallace. LC 76-26663. 1976. 14.95 (ISBN 0-8161-6404-5). G. K. Hall.
R Document: A Novel. Irving Wallace. LC 75-41329. 8.95 (ISBN 0-671-22229-5). Simon and Schuster.
R. F. D. No. 3. Homer Croy. LC 24-23172. 1924. Harper & Brothers.

R. HOLMES & CO. FICTION 1876 - 1983

R. Holmes & Co. John Kendrick Bangs. LC 78-91073. (American humorists series). (Illus.). 1969. Literature House.

R. Holmes & Co. Being the Remarkable Adventures of Raffles Holmes, Esq., Detective and Amateur Cracksman by Birth. John Kendrick Bangs. LC 6-20855. 1906. Harper & Brothers.

R. Holmes & Co. Being the Remarkable Adventure of Raffles Holmes. John Kendrick Bangs. LC 78-91073. (American Humorists Ser.). Repr. of 1906 ed. lib. bdg. 18.50 (ISBN 0-8398-0151-3). Irvington.

R. Holmes & Co. Being the Remarkable Adventures of Raffles Holmes. John Kendrick Bangs. (American Humorists Ser: Vol. 2). 1969. Repr. of 1906 ed. lib. bdg. 11.50x o.p. (ISBN 0-8398-0151-3). Gregg.

R Is for Rocket. Ray Bradbury. (gr. 9-12). 1969. pap. 1.95 (ISBN 0-553-14303-4). Bantam.

R. J.'s Mother: And Some Other People. Margaret Wade Campbell Deland. LC 3-15300. 1908. Harper & Brothers.

R-Master. Gordon R Dickson. LC 73-13837. 1973. 6.95 (ISBN 0-397-00920-8). Lippincott.

R. S. V. P. Murder. Mignon Good Eberhart. LC 65-11578. 3.95. Random.

Ra-Ta-Plan-! Dorothy Ogburn. LC 30-46574. 1930. Little, Brown, and Company.

Rab and His Friends. John Brown. LC 6-18937. 1890. J.B. Lippincott Company.

Rab and His Friends. John Brown. LC 6-18938. (On cover: Cosy corner series). 1894. J. Knight Company.

Rab and His Friends. John Brown. LC 6-32113. McLoughlin Brothers.

Rab and His Friends. John Brown. LC 10-1695. (Golden classics). Rand, McNally & Company.

Rab and His Friends. John Brown. LC 9-22940. 1909. H. Altemus Company.

Rab and His Friends. John Brown. LC 23-26589. (On cover: Cosy corner series). The Page Company.

Rab and His Friends. John Brown & Blaisdell, Albert Franklin, 1847- Ed. LC 6-18936. (On cover: English classic series, no. 52). 1884. Clark & Maynard.

Rab and His Friends: And Other Dog Stories. John Brown & French, Charles Wallace, 1858- Ed. LC 2-10735. (Canterbury classics). 1902. Rand, McNally & Co.

Rab and His Friends and Other Dogs and Men. John Brown. LC 4-17296. 1900. Houghton, Mifflin and Company.

Rab & His Friends & Other Papers. John Brown. 1970. 7.95x (ISBN 0-460-00116-7, Evman); pap. 2.95x (ISBN 0-460-01116-2, Evman). Biblio Dist.

Rab & His Friends, & Other Papers & Essays. John Brown. LC 72-5910. (Short story index reprint series). 1972. (ISBN 0-8369-4193-4). Books for Libraries Press.

Rab and His Friends: And Other Papers and Essays. John Brown. (Half-title: Everyman's library, ed. by Ernest Rhys. Essays). 1907. J.M. Dent & Co.

Rab and His Friends: And Other Sketches. John Brown. LC 4830. W.B. Conkey Company.

Rab and His Friends: And Other Stories of Dogs. John Brown. LC 1-12802. (Lettered on cover: Heath's home and school classics. The young reader's series). 1901. D.C. Heath & Co.

Rab and Marjorie Fleming. John Leech. Thackeray's Literary Career. John Brown. LC 7-731. (Modern classics. no. 9). 1881. Houghton, Mifflin and Company.

Rabbi. Noah Gordon. (Fawcett crest bk., m954). 1966. Fawcett.

Rabbi. Noah Gordon. LC 65-21583. 1965. McGraw-Hill.

Rabbi and Priest. A Story. Milton Goldsmith. 1891. Jewish Publication Society of America.

Rabbi Burns: A Novel. Aben Kandel. 1931. Covici, Friede.

Rabbi Eizik: Hasidic Stories About the Zaddik of Kallo. Ed. & tr. by Andrew Handler. LC 75-5245. 195p. 1976. 16.50 (ISBN 0-8386-1739-5). Fairleigh Dickinson.

Rabbi of Bacherach: A Fragment. Heinrich Heine & Loewenthal, Erich, 1894- LC 48-5121. (Schocken library, 4). 1947.

Rabbis and Wives. Chaim Grade. LC 82-14. 1982. 15.95 (ISBN 0-394-50979-X). A.A. Knopf: Distributed by Random House.

Rabbi's Life Contract. Marilyn Greenberg. LC 82-45834. 1983. 15.95 (ISBN 0-385-19003-4). Doubleday.

Rabbi's Spell. Stuart C Cumberland. (Lovell's library. no. 1338). 1889. J. W. Lovell Company.

Rabbi's Spell. A Russo-Jewish Romance. Stuart C Cumberland & Stuart C Cumberland. (On cover: Seaside library Pocket ed. no. 641). 1885. G. Munro.

Rabbi's Wife. David Benedictus. LC 76-364064. 1976. 3.50 (ISBN 0-85634-046-4). Blond and Briggs.

Rabbit Boss. Thomas Sanchez. LC 72-11028. 1973. 7.95 (ISBN 0-394-48187-9). Knopf; Distributed by Random House.

Rabbit Habit; a Novel. Jay Ingram. 1974. (pbk.) 1.25. Warner Paperback Library.

Rabbit Is Rich. John Updike. LC 81-1287. 1981. 13.95 (ISBN 0-394-52087-4) (ISBN 0-394-52064-5). Knopf: Distributed by Random House.

Rabbit Redux. John Updike. LC 70-154927. 1972. (449-01753-150) 1.50. Fawcett Publications.

Rabbit Redux. John Updike. LC 74-185849. 1973. 0.45 (ISBN 0-14-003497-8). Penguin.

Rabbit, Run. John Updike. LC 60-12552. 1960. Knopf.

Rabbitfoot. Arthur W Grahame. LC 67-27421. 1967. Dorrance.

Rabbits by the Acre. Louis Enard Abrams. LC 54-7380. 1954. McBride Co.

Rabbits, Crabs, Etc. Stories by Japanese Women. Phyllis Birnbaum. LC 82-8365. 1982. 15.00 (ISBN 0-8248-0777-4). University of Hawaii Press.

Rabbit's Foot in Her Pocket: A Novel. Dorothy Soule Boehm. LC 51-2679. 1951. Exposition Press.

Rabbit's New Rug. Judy Delton & Marc Tolon Brown. 1979. 4.99 (ISBN 0-8193-1010-7). Parents' Magazine Press.

Rabbits Rafferty. Gerald Dumas. (Camelot Book). (Illus.). 1981. 1.95 (ISBN 0-380-53348-0). Avon Books.

Rabble in Arms. Kenneth Lewis Roberts. LC 62-5137. 1958. Doubleday.

Rabble in Arms. Kenneth Lewis Roberts. LC 47-11831. 1947. Doubleday.

Rabble in Arms: A Chronicle of Arundel and the Burgoyne Invasion. Kenneth Lewis Roberts. LC 33-33263. 1933. Doubleday, Doran & Company, Inc.

Rabble in Arms: A Chronicle of Arundel and the Burgoyne Invasion. Kenneth Lewis Roberts. LC 47-1746. 1946. Doubleday & Company, Inc.

Rabble of Rebels. Gordon Ashe. LC 76-158838. (Rinehart Suspense Novel Ser.). 1972. 4.95 o.p. (ISBN 0-03-091404-3). HR&W.

Rabble of Rebels. John Creasey. LC 76-158838. (Rinehart suspense novel). 1972. 4.95 (ISBN 0-03-091404-3). Holt, Rinehart and Winston.

Rabble Rouser. Charles Morrow Wilson. LC 36-7827. 1936. Longmans, Green and Co.

Rabble's Curse. Catherine Ann Fought. LC 79-27305. 10.00 (ISBN 0-453-00381-8). New American Library.

Raccoon John Smith: A Novel Based on the Life of the Famous Pioneer Kentucky Preacher. Louis Cochran. LC 63-16818. 1963. Duell, Sloan and Pearce.

Race. William McFee. LC 24-9265. 1924. Doubleday, Page & Company.

Race. Eunice Walkup & Oscar Otis. LC 72-93511. 1973. 8.95 (ISBN 0-671-21504-3). Simon and Schuster.

Race: A Novel of Marriage. Mary Grace Ashton. LC 28-208408. 1928. Frederick A. Stokes Company.

Race: A Novel of Polar Exploration. Kare Holt. LC 76-21752. 8.95 (ISBN 0-440-07198-4). Delacorte Press.

Race: A Novel of Wives and Others. A. L Samms. LC 24-1495. 1923. Covici-McGee.

Race Against Love. Sally Wentworth. (Harlequin Presents Ser.). 192p. (Orig.). 1981. pap. 1.50 (ISBN 0-373-10414-6, Pub. by Harlequin). PB.

Race Against Time. Piers Anthony, pseud. 224p. 1973. 5.95 o.p. Hawthorn.

Race Between the Flags. Priscilla D. Willis. 1955. 2.75 o.p. McKay.

Race Car Woman. Laurie Simons. 1977. pap. 1.50 o.s.i. (ISBN 0-8439-0445-3, LB445, Leisure Bks). Nordon Pubns.

Race for Copper Island. Henry Stanislaus Spalding. LC 5-149648. 1905. Benziger Brothers.

Race for Home. J. P. Miller. LC 68-16420. 1968. 5.95 o.p. (71973). Dial.

Race for Home: A Novel. James Pinckney Miller. LC 68-16420. 1968. Dial Press.

Race for Life (Dyke Darrel) A. Frank Pinkerton. (On cover: Pinkerton detective series, no. 5). 1898. Laird & Lee.

Race for Love. Barbara Cartland. LC 78-13322. 6.95 (ISBN 0-87272-047-0). Duron Books.

Race for Love. Faye Wildman. 192p. (Orig.). 1980. pap. 1.50 (ISBN 0-671-57048-X, Pub. by Silouette Bks). S&S.

Race for Revenge. Lynsey Stevens. (Harlequin Romances Ser.). 192p. 1982. pap. 1.50 (ISBN 0-373-02495-9). Harlequin Bks.

Race of Death. Nick Carter. (Nick Carter Ser.). 224p. (Orig.). 1978. pap. 1.75 o.p. (ISBN 0-441-70270-8). Charter Bks.

Race of Life. Guy Newell Boothby. LC 6-15428. 1906. F. M. Buckles and Company.

Race of Rebels. Andrew Tully. LC 60-6098. 1960. Simon and Schuster.

Race Rock: A Novel. Peter Matthiessen. LC 54-6020. 1954. Harper.

Race the Lazy River. Wal Watkins. LC 73-163289. 1972. 1.65. Gold Star Publications.

Race the Sun. Dale Collins. LC 37-9475. Metro-Goldwyn-Mayer Corporation.

Race to Happiness. Edward Van Fossan. LC 73-153415. 1971. 5.95 (ISBN 0-8059-1563-X). Dorrance.

Race to the Moon. G. C. Richardson. (Illus.). 1958. 2.50 o.p. Wehman.

Race Track Girls. Ken Robertson. 192p. (Orig.). 1974. pap. 1.95 o.p. (ISBN 0-87056-392-0, 6392). Brandon.

Race Track Girls. Ken Robertson. 1974. (pbk.) 1.95 (ISBN 0-87056-392-0). Brandon Books.

Race with a Hurricane: And Other Stories. Alice Miriam Roundy. LC 1-29967. The Abbey Press.

Race with Fate: Or, A Double Crime. Emma May Quick King. LC 13-19936. 1913. The Shakespeare Press.

Race with the Sun. Granville Church. LC 44-47771. (On cover: Circle Mill mysteries). 1944. M. S. Mill Co., Inc.

Race with Time & the Devil. Paul J. Petrie. 1965. 3.00 o.p. (ISBN 0-8233-0081-1). Golden Quill.

Racer. Hans Ruesch. LC 53-6124. 1953. Ballantine Books.

Racer of Illinois. Mary Gay Humphreys. LC 2-22849. 1902. McClure, Phillips & Co.

Racers to the Sun: A Novel. James B Hall. LC 60-9042. 1960. I. Obolensky.

Races of Mankind: With Travels in Grubland. Allen W. Gazlay. LC 6-442595. 1856. Longley Brothers Etc.

Rachel. Jane Helen Findlater. LC 4-19010. 1899. Doubleday & McClure Company.

Rachel: A Romance. Josephine Franklin. LC 6-43161. 1860. Thayer & Eldridge.

Rachel: A Story of the Great Deluge; with an Introduction Giving the Results of the Author's Investigations into the Question of the Location of the Lands of Eden and Nod, and Incidentally Explaining the Origin of the American Indians. Ernest Urial Smith. LC 4-29363. 1904. The Grafton Press.

Rachel and Leah: A Tale of the Jewish Pale in Russia. 2d and rev. ed. John Legum. LC 12-23069. Press of City Mission Publ. Co.

Rachel Cade. Charles E Mercer. LC 56-10239. 1956. Putnam.

Rachel Craig. A Novel, Connected with the Valley of Wyoming. Caleb Earl Wright. 1888. R. Baur & Son.

Rachel Dene: A Tale of the Deepdale Mills. Robert Williams Buchanan. LC 6-19878. 1894. F. T. Neely.

Rachel Dyer: A North American Story. John Neal. LC 7-33170. 1828. Shirley and Hyde.

Rachel Fitzpatrick. Ida Margaret Graves Poore. LC 20-11899. 1920. John Lane.

Rachel Kell. John Mitchell. 1853. M. W. Dodd.

Rachel Lorian. Alice Dudeney. LC 9-7038. 1909. Duffield & Company.

Rachel Marr. Morley Roberts. LC 4-16432. 1904. L. C. Page & Company.

Rachel Moon. Lorna Rea. LC 31-528. 1931. Harper & Brothers.

Rachel Papers. Martin Amis. LC 73-19848. 1974. 5.95 (ISBN 0-394-49143-2). Knopf.

Rachel, Rachel, or, A Jest of God. Margaret Laurence. (60-8076). 1968. Popular Lib.

Rachel Ray. Anthony Trollope. LC 51-11975. (Borzol Trollope). 1952. Knopf.

Rachel Ray. Anthony Trollope. LC 25-26589. (Half-title: The World's classics. cclxxix). 1924. H. Milford.

Rachel Ray. Anthony Trollope. LC 79-56319. 1980. 5.00 (ISBN 0-486-23930-6). Dover Publications.

Rachel Ray. Anthony Trollope & Thorold, Algar Labouchere, Ed. LC 12-394507. (Half-title: The new pocket library). 1906. John Lane.

Rachel Ray. A Novel. Anthony Trollope. (On cover: The seaside library. Pocket ed. no. 147). 1884. G. Munro.

Rachel Rosing. Howard Spring. LC 36-1048. Hillman-Curl, Inc.

Rachel Sylvestre: A Story of the Pioneers. Jessie Hunter Brown Pounds. LC 5-10176. The Standard Publishing Company.

Rachel, the Possessed. Katheryn Kimbrough, pseud. (Saga of the Phenwick Women: Bk 5). 256p. 1975. pap. 1.50 (ISBN 0-445-00304-9). Popular Lib.

Rachel, the Rabbi's Wife. Silvia Tennenbaum. LC 77-22578. 1978. 9.95 (ISBN 0-688-03243-5). Morrow.

Rachel Trevellyan. Anne Mather. (Presents Ser.). 1975. pap. 1.25 (ISBN 0-373-70586-7, 70586, Pub. by Harlequin). PB.

Rachel Weeping: A Triptych by Shelley Smith Pseud. 1st American Ed. Nancy Bodington. LC 58-6174. Harper.

Rachel Weeping for Her Children Uncomforted. Hazel Ai Chun Lin. LC 76-365399. 7.95 (ISBN 0-8283-1619-8). Branden Press.

Rachel's Children. Harriet Hassell. LC 38-996989. 1938. Harper & Brothers.

Rachel's Hope. Carol G. Page. LC 79-84168. 202p. 1979. pap. 2.25 o.p. (ISBN 0-89877-004-1). Jeremy Bks.

Rachel's Inheritance; or, Damocles. A Novel. Margaret Veley. (Harper's Franklin square library, no. 278). 1882. Harper & Brothers.

Rachel's Share of the Road... Kate Waterman Hamilton. LC 13-2079. (Round-Robin series). 1882. J. R. Osgood and Company.

Racherl: The Possessed. Katheryn Kimbrough. (Saga of the Phenwick Women: No. 5). 1975. (pbk.) 1.25. Popular Library.

Racing and 'chasing: A Collection of Sporting Stories. Alfred Edward Thomas Watson. LC 1-22391. 1897. Longmans, Green and Co.

Racing Bits: A Story of the Oil-Fields of Texas. Jesse Crawford Rickman. LC 26-11487. R. G. Badger.

Racing Game (Odds Against) Dick Francis. pap. 2.95 (ISBN 0-671-83350-2). PB.

Racing Start. Stewart Beach. LC 41-21537. 1941. Little, Brown and Company.

Racing Tides. Martin Kevan. LC 82-20560. 16.95 (ISBN 0-8253-0121-1). Beaufort Books.

Rack. A. E Ellis. LC 59-11882. 1959. Little, Brown.

Racket Hall. Frances Stickney Nott. LC 61-14272. 1961. Dorrance.

Rackety Rax. Joel Sayre & Dunn, Alan, 1900- Illus. LC 32-4563. 1932. A. A. Knopf.

Rackham's Fairy Tale Coloring Book. Arthur Rackham. (Illus.). pap. 2.00 (ISBN 0-486-23844-X). Dover.

Rackhouse: A Novel. George Agnew Chamberlain. LC 22-202785. 1922. Harper & Brothers.

Radcliff, No. Four: New Jersey Showdown. Roosevelt Mallory. (Orig.). 1976. pap. 1.50 (ISBN 0-87067-472-2, BH472). Holloway.

Radcliff, No. One: Harlem Hit. Roosevelt Mallory. (Orig.). 1973. pap. 1.50 (ISBN 0-87067-435-8, BH435). Holloway.

Radcliff, No. Three: Double Trouble. Roosevelt Mallory. (Orig.). 1975. pap. 1.50 (ISBN 0-87067-455-2, BH455). Holloway.

Radcliff, No. Two: San Francisco Vendetta. Roosevelt Mallory. (Orig.). 1974. pap. 1.50 (ISBN 0-87067-436-6, BH436). Holloway.

Radetzky March. Joseph Roth. LC 72-97581. 1974. 8.95 (ISBN 0-87951-015-3). Overlook Press.

Radetzky March. Joseph Roth. Tr. by Dunlop, Geoffrey. LC 33-29997. 1933. The Viking Press.

Radiana: A Novel. Edward Harold Crosby. LC 6-42923. 1906. The Ivy Press.

Radiance. Anne Maybury. LC 78-57129. 8.95 (ISBN 0-394-50334-1). Random House.

Radiance of the King. Camara Laye. LC 70-123141. (American Library). 1971. 1.50. Collier Books.

Radiance of the Morning Club. Clara Viola Fleharty. LC 11-32250. R. G. Badger.

Radiant Cross: World War Two Experiences. Herbert Hirschfield. pap. 4.00 (ISBN 0-87164-031-7). William-F.

Radiant Dove. Annabel Jones. LC 74-76712. 1974. 6.95. St. Martin's Press.

Radiant Hills. P. Zaphiriou. 2.95 o.p. Vantage.

Radiant Mountain. Translated from the German by ElinorCastendyk Briefs. Heinz Von Homeyer. LC 57-8242. 1957. H. Regnery Co.

Radiant Tree, and Other Stories. Temple Bailey. LC 73-116932. (Short story index reprint series). 1970. Books for Libraries Press.

Radiant Tree and Other Stories. Temple Bailey. LC 34-35703. The Penn Publishing Company.

Radiant Years. Elizabeth Carfrae, pseud. LC 32-17526. 1932. G. P. Putnam's Sons.

Radical. Isaac Kahn Friedman. LC 78-38629. (Illus.). 1971. Johnson Reprint Corp.

Radical. Isaac Kahn Friedman. LC 7-30992. 1907. D. Appleton and Company.

Radical Millionaire. Leah C Shear. LC 23-957818. 1923. The Stratford Company.

Radigan. Louis L'Amour. LC 58-117788. (Bantam book, 1853. Western, 3). 1958. Bantam Books.

Radio Beasts. Ralph Milne Farley. 1976. lib. bdg. 10.95x (ISBN 0-89968-030-5). Lightyear.

Radio City. Hartzell Spence. LC 41-22519. 1941. Dial.

Radio Detective. Arthur Benjamin Reeve. LC 26-12323. Grosset & Dunlap.

Radio Gunner... Alexander Forbes. LC 24-27881. 1924. Houghton Mifflin Company.

Radio Man. Roger Sherman Hoar. LC 49-196. (His Myles Cabot on Venus). 1948. Fantasy Pub. Co.

Radio Man: Miles Cabot on Venus. Farley. 5.00; pap. 2.00. Fantasy Pub Co.

Radio Planet. Ralph Milne Farley. 1976. 1.50. Ace.

Radio Studio Murder. Carolyn Wells. LC 37-6303. J. B. Lippincott Company.

Radio Sweetheart. Vida Hurst. LC 36-43008. J. H. Hopkins & Son, Inc.

Radiobuster: Being Some of the Adventures of Samuel Jones, Deep Sea Wireless Operator. Volney G Mathison. LC 24-4679. 1924. Frederick A. Stokes Company.
Radish River Caper. Ross H. Spencer. 144p. 1981. pap. 1.95 (ISBN 0-380-77248-5, 77248). Avon.
Raditzer: Novel. Peter Matthiessen. LC 61-6034. 1961. Viking Press.
Radium: A Novel by Rudolf Brunngraber. Rudolf Brunngraber. Tr. by Paul, Eden. LC 37-218233. Random House.
Radium Pool. Edward Earl Repp. LC 49-49237. 1949. Fantasy Pub. Co.
Radium Terrors. Albert Dorrington. LC 12-3552. 1912. Doubleday, Page & Company.
Radkin Revenge. Will Davis Roberts. (Black Pearl series; V). 1979. 1.75 (ISBN 0-445-04401-2). Popular Library.
Radnitz. Joseph Nathenson. (Orig.). 1979. pap. 1.95 (ISBN 0-532-19251-6). Woodhill.
Rafael: A Story of Nueva California. Charles Franklin Carter. LC 23-17347. 1923. Grafton Publishing Corporation.
Rafe. Peter Gentry. 304p. (Orig.). 1982. pap. 2.95 (ISBN 0-449-12362-6, GM). Fawcett.
Rafe. Gentry, Peter. (Fawcett Gold Medal Book). 1976. (pbk.) 1.95. Fawcett.
Rafe. Nelson Nye. (Ace western). 1974. (pbk.) 0.75. Ace Books.
Rafe. LC 66-10934. bds., 4.95. McKay.
Rafe: By Weldon Hill. Weldon Hill, pseud. LC 66-10934. 1966. D. McKay Co.
Rafe: Modern Sioux Rebel. Bob Stuart McKnight. LC 74-113200. 1970. T. Gaus' Sons.
Rafferty: A Novel. 1st Ed. Lionel White. LC 59-696525. 1959. Dutton.
Rafferty & Co. Betty Wahl. 1970. pap. 0.95 o.p. (ISBN 0-447-75139-5). Lancer.
Rafferty & Co. A Novel. Betty Wahl. LC 69-15406. 1969. 5.95. Farrar, Straus & Giroux.
Rafferty and the Gold Dust Twins: A Novel. Lillian Roberts & John Kaye. 1975. (pbk.) 1.25 (ISBN 0-446-76604-6). Warner Paperback Library.
Rafferty by Willard Wiener. Willard Wiener. LC 31-11091. Farrar & Rinehart, Incorporated.
Rafferty. 1st Ed. William Sanborn Ballinger. LC 53-5360. 1953. Harper.
Raffles. David Fletcher, pseud. LC 76-54939. 8.95. Putnam.
Raffles. Ernest William Hornung. (Crime Ser.). 1976. pap. 1.95 o.p. (ISBN 0-14-000063-1). Penguin.
Raffles. Ernest William Hornung. 3.00 o.p. (556). Collins-World.
Raffles and the Key Man. Barry Perowne. LC 40-7250. J. B. Lippincott Company.
Raffles: Further Adventures of the Amateur Cracksman. Ernest William Hornung. LC 1-23638. 1901. C. Scribner's Sons.
Raffles: Further Adventures of the Amateur Cracksman. Ernest William Hornung. LC 36-29321. 1908. C. Scribner's Sons.
Raffles of the Albany: Footprints of a Famous Gentleman Crook in the Times of a Great Detective. Barry Perowne. LC 76-28049. 8.95 (ISBN 0-312-66220-3). Saint Martin's Press.
Raffles of the M. C. C. Barry Perowne. LC 78-3999. 7.95 (ISBN 0-312-66222-X). St. Martin's Press.
Raffles Revisited; New Adventures of a Famous Gentleman Crook. Barry Perowne. LC 73-14321. (Illus.). 1974. 7.95 (ISBN 0-06-013314-7). Harper & Row.
Raffles, the Amateur Cracksman. Ernest William Hornung. (Illus.). 3.25. University of Nebraska Press.
Rafnaland: The Story of John Heath Howard. William Huntington Wilson. LC 6138. 1900. Harper & Brothers.
Raft. Coningsby William Dawson. LC 14-169173. 1914. 1.35. H. Holt and Company.
Raft of Swords. Duncan Kyle. 1974. 6.95 o.p. St Martin.
Raft of the Medusa. Jean Bruller. LC 70-122152. 1971. 6.50 (ISBN 0-8415-0074-6). McCall Pub. Co.
Raft of the Medusa. Vercors. LC 70-122152. 1971. 6.50 o.p. (ISBN 0-8415-0074-6). Sat Rev Pr.
Rafter Romance. John Wells. LC 32-4756. Brentano's.
Rag and a Bone... Hillary Waugh. LC 54-6253. 1954. Published for the Crime Club by Doubleday.
Rag Bag Clan. Richard Barth. 1979. pap. 1.95 (ISBN 0-380-46078-5, 46078). Avon.
Rag Bag Clan: A Novel. Richard Barth. LC 78-6072. 6.95. Dial Press.
Rag Dolls. Simon Cooper. LC 69-18522. 1969. 5.95. World Pub. Co.
Rag Fair and May Fair. The Story of "Me and Benje.". Julia MacNair Wright. Presbyterian Board of Publication and Sabbath-School Work.
Rag Opera. Harlan Ware & Prindle, James, Joint Author. LC 29-596676. The Bobbs-Merrill Company.
Rag-Picker of Paris. Aime Felix Pyat. Tr. by Tucker, Benjamin Ricketson. LC 18-10679. 1890. B. R. Tucker.
Rag Pickers. Harry Vernor Dixon. LC 66-19260. 1966. D. McKay Co.
Rag Rug. Martha Reishus. LC 54-13136. 1955. Vantage Press.
Rag Trade. Lewis Orde. LC 77-16737. 10.95 (ISBN 0-312-66241-6). St. Martin's Press.
Raga Six. Frank Lauria. LC 72-8932. 1972. 1.25. Bantam Books.
Ragan's Law. Ray Hogan. LC 79-6653. 1980. 8.95 (ISBN 0-385-15959-5). Doubleday.
Ragazzi. P. Pasolini. Tr. by Emile Capouya. 1968. 5.95 o.p. (GP399). Grove.
Rage. Richard Bachman. (Signet Book). 1977. 1.50. New American Library.
Rage. Philip Friedman. 1973. (pbk) 1.25. Warner.
Rage. Philip Friedman. LC 72-84261. 1972. 6.95. Atheneum.
Rage. L. V. Roper. (Orig.). 1973. pap. 0.95 o.p. Curtis.
Rage, a Novel. Tr. from Italian by Isabel Quigly. Lorenza Mazzetti. LC 65-116415. bds., 3.95. McKay.
Rage Against Heaven. Fred Mustard Stewart. LC 77-28369. 1978. 12.95 (ISBN 0-670-58910-1). Viking Press.
Rage & Desire. Leslie Arlen. (Borodins Bk.: No. V). 336p. 1982. pap. 3.50 (ISBN 0-515-05852-1). Jove Pubns.
Rage in Harlem. Chester B Himes. LC 65-6642. 1965. Avon Books.
Rage in Heaven. James Hilton. New Avon Library.
Rage in Paradise. Gary Brandner. LC 81-80080. 304p. (Orig.). 1981. pap. 2.95 (ISBN 0-87216-872-7). Playboy Pbks.
Rage in Silence: A Novel Based on the Life of Goya. Donald Braider. LC 69-11457. 1969. 6.95. Putnam.
Rage of Angels. Sidney Sheldon. LC 80-13328. 1980. 12.95 (ISBN 0-688-03687-2). W. Morrow.
Rage of Desire. Clayton Matthews. 1969. pap. 0.75 o.p. (75-260). Manor Bks.
Rage of Heaven: A Charlie Rope Mystery. John Eller. 160p. 1982. 10.95 (ISBN 0-312-66246-7). St Martin.
Rage of Honor. Denne Bart Petitclerc. LC 65-19921. 1966. Doubleday.
Rage of McAllister. Matt Chisholm, pseud. 1970. pap. 0.75 o.p. (94023). Beagle Bks.
Rage of the Age: A Story. Alice Huntley Payne. LC 7-33765. 1883. O. Dryer.
Rage of the Soul. Vincent Sheean. LC 52-5168. 1952. Random House.
Rage of the Vulture. Barry Unsworth. LC 82-23249. 1983. 15.95 (ISBN 0-395-32526-9). Houghton Mifflin Co.
Rage of the Vulture: A Novel. Alan Moorehead. LC 48-9095. 1948. C. Scribner's Sons.
Rage on the Bar. Wagner, Geoffrey Atheling. LC 57-8033. 1957. Noonday Press.
Rage on the Range. David King. LC 77-73332. 1977. 6.95 (ISBN 0-385-12807-X). Doubleday.
Rage to Live. John O'Hara. 1974. (pbk.) 1.50. Popular Library.
Rage to Possess. Abra Taylor. (Superromances Ser.). 384p. 1982. pap. 2.50 (ISBN 0-373-70038-5, Pub. by Worldwide). Harlequin Bks.
Rage Under the Arctic. Basil Jackson. LC 73-8991. (Illus.). 1974. 6.95 (ISBN 0-393-08379-9). Norton.
Ragged Banners: A Novel with an Index. Ethel Edith Mannin. LC 31-18271. 1931. A. A. Knopf.
Ragged Edge. John Christopher. LC 66-11062. 1966. 4.50. S. & S.
Ragged Edge. Jack Karney. LC 46-1631. 1946. W. Morrow & Company.
Ragged Edge. Harold MacGrath. LC 22-3190. 1922. Doubleday, Page & Company.
Ragged Edge: A Tale of Ward Life & Politics. John Thomas McIntyre. LC 2-22663. (Lettered on cover: First novel series)). 1902. McClure, Phillips & Co.
Ragged Edge Rambles. Marcus Lafayette Byrn. (Ratttlehead's humorous series, no. 4). M. L. Byrn.
Ragged Inlet Guards: A Story of Adventure in Labrador. Dillon Wallace. LC 20-226251. Fleming H. Revell Company.
Ragged Lady: A Novel. William Dean Howells. LC 99-5577. 1899. Harper & Bros.
Ragged Messenger. William Babington Maxwell. LC 4-31058. 1904. G. P. Putnam's Sons.
Ragged Messenger. William Babington Maxwell. LC 15-26150. The Bobbs-Merrill Company.
Ragged Ones. Burke Davis. LC 51-3028. 1951. Rinehart.
Ragged Plot. Richard Barth. LC 80-25878. 9.95 (ISBN 0-8037-0053-9). Dial Press.
Ragged Regiment. George Marion. 256p. (Orig.). 1981. pap. 2.25 (ISBN 0-505-51745-0). Tower Bks.
Ragged Roads. William Solon Porter. LC 51-36135.
Ragged Robin. Warren Howard. LC 37-153443. 1937. Arcadia House.
Ragged Staff. C. M. Edmondston & Hyde, M. L. F., Joint Author. LC 32-281396. 1932. Longmans, Green and Co.
Ragged-Trousered Philanthropists. Robert Tressell. LC 14-11528. 1914. Frederick A. Stokes Company.
Ragged Trousered Philanthropists. Robert Tressell. LC 62-11421. (Leo Huberman People's Library). 1978. pap. 7.50 (ISBN 0-85345-457-4, PB 457-4). Monthly Rev.
Raggedy Ann and the Golden Ring. John B Gruelle. LC 61-15552. 1961. Bobbs-Merrill.
Raggedy Man. William Wittliff & Sara Clark. 1979. pap. 2.75 (ISBN 0-523-41702-0). Pinnacle Bks.
Raging Flood. R. T Larkin. 1975. (pbk.) 1.50. Belmont Tower Books.
Raging Hearts. Patricia Hagan. 480p. 1982. pap. 3.50 (ISBN 0-380-46201-X, 80085). Avon.
Raging Moon: A Novel. Peter Marshall. LC 66-15952. 4.50. Bobbs.
Raging Passions. Thomas Stone. 1971. pap. 0.75 o.p. (75-385). Manor Bks.
Raging Passions see Pawn of Love.
Raging River-Lonely Trail: Tales Told by the Campfires Glow. Vaughn T. Short. LC 77-95548. (Illus.). 1978. 7.95 (ISBN 0-9607760-1-X); pap. 4.95. Two Horses.
Raging Waters. Dorothy Daniels. (Orig.). 1970. pap. 0.75 o.p. (T2346). Pyramid Pubns.
Raging Waters. Mary E Morse. LC 31-5759. 1931. Cumberland Presbyterian Publishing House.
Raging Winds of Heaven. June Lund Shiplett. (Signet Book). 1978. 1.95 (ISBN 0-451-08213-3). New American Library.
Ragland. John Van Orsdell. LC 71-178833. 1975. (pbk.) 1.25 (ISBN 0-671-78411-0). Pocket Books.
Ragman's Daughter, & Other Stories. Alan Sillitoe. 1964. 4.95 o.p. Knopf.
Ragna: A Novel. Anna Costantini. LC 10-103201. 1910. 1.50. Sturgis & Walton Company.
Rags. Edith Barnard Delano. LC 15-5742. 1915. 1.30. D. Appleton and Company.
Rags & Riches. Joanne Kaye. LC 81-47262. (Garment Center Ser.). 224p. (Orig.). 1981. pap. 2.25 (ISBN 0-87216-895-6). Playboy Pbks.
Rags in Heaven. James Hilton. LC 34-340195. 1932. A. H. King, Inc.
Rags of Glory. Stuart Cloete. LC 63-12972. 1963. Doubleday.
Rags to Riches. Alice Vosper. 240p. pap. 2.25 (ISBN 0-380-83873-7, Flare). Avon.
Ragtime. E. L. Doctorow. LC 75-9613. 1975. 8.95 (ISBN 0-394-46901-1). Random House.
Ragtime. E. L. Doctorow. LC 75-26969. 1975. 12.95 (ISBN 0-8161-6306-5). G. K. Hall.
Ragtime. E. L. Doctorow. 1976. 2.25 (ISBN 0-553-02600-3). Bantam Books.
Ragweed; a West-World Story. Julia MacNair Wright. LC 9-524. 1894. Presbyterian Board of Publication and Sabbath-School Work.
Ragweed the Pixie, the Pixies & the Great Flood: Ragweed & the Coldest Winter. F. F. Foss. (Illus.). 48p. 1982. pap. 4.00 (ISBN 0-682-49923-4). Exposition.
Rahab. Waldo David Frank. LC 22-4977. Boni and Liveright.
Rahab Link. J. Alexander McKenzie. LC 79-55750. (Canaan Trilogy Ser.). 240p. (Orig.). 1980. pap. 2.95 (ISBN 0-87123-492-0, 200492). Bethany Hse.
Rahne. Susan Coon. 1979. pap. 1.95 (ISBN 0-380-75044-9, 75044). Avon.
Raid. John Brick. LC 51-9985. 1951. Farrar, Straus & Young.
Raid. Victor Kolpacoff. LC 75-162966. 1971. 5.95. Atheneum.
Raid. Mark Sufrin. 240p. 1982. pap. 2.25 (ISBN 0-8439-0949-8). Leisure Bks CT.
Raid, and Other Stories. Lev Nikolaevich Tolstoi & Louise Shanks Maude. LC 81-16982. (World's Classics). 1982. 4.95 (ISBN 0-19-281584-9). Oxford University Press.
Raid from Beausejour and How the Carter Boys Lifted the Mortgage: Two Stories of Acadie. Charles George Douglas Roberts. LC 7-41027. 1894. Hunt & Eaton.
Raid of the Guerilla: And Other Stories. Mary Noailles Murfree. LC 71-150556. (Short story index reprint series). (Illus.). 1971. (ISBN 0-8369-3853-4). Books for Libraries Press.
Raid of the Guerilla, & Other Stories. facsimile ed. Mary Noailles Murfree. LC 71-150556. (Short Story Index Reprint Ser.). (Illus.). Repr. of 1912 ed. 18.00 (ISBN 0-8369-3853-4). Ayer Co.
Raid on Reichswald Fortress. J. M. Flynn. (O.s.i.). 208p. (Orig.). 1974. pap. 1.25 o.s.i. (AQ1367, Award). Univ Pub & Dist.
Raid on the Bremerton. Irv Eachus. LC 80-14635. 1980. 12.95 (ISBN 0-670-58912-8). Viking Press.
Raid on the Gila. A. A. Baker. (YA) 1973. 4.50 o.p. (Avalon). Bouregy.
Raid on the Villa Joyosa. Robert S. Hopkins. LC 72-97310. (Red mask mystery). 1973. 4.95 (ISBN 0-399-11111-5). Putnam.
Raid the Icebox with Andy Warhol. Daniel Robbins & David Bourdon. (Illus.). 104p. 1970. pap. 4.00 o.p. (ISBN 0-913456-94-2). Interbk Inc.
Raid: Tr. from French by J. F. Newcombe. Roger Frison-Roche. LC 64-25126. 1965. 3.95. Harper.
Raider. Jesse Hill Ford. LC 75-17563. 1975. 10.00 (ISBN 0-316-28891-8). Little, Brown.
Raider. Charles Alden Seltzer. LC 76-39973. 1976. 6.95 (ISBN 0-88411-115-6). Aeonian Press.
Raider. Charles Alden Seltzer. LC 29-11671. 1929. Doubleday, Doran & Company, Inc.
Raider. Jon Williams. (Privateers & Gentlemen Ser.: No. 3). (Orig.). 1981. pap. 2.95 (ISBN 0-440-17357-4). Dell.
Raider: A Novel of World War I; the Chronicle of a Gallant Ship. John Edward Jennings. LC 63-22814. 1963. Morrow.
Raider Battalion. Edwin P. Hoyt. (Orig.). 1980. pap. 1.95 (ISBN 0-523-41590-7). Pinnacle Bks.
Raider Sixteen. Edwin P. Hoyt. 1971. pap. 0.95 o.p. (ISBN 0-447-75179-4). Lancer.
Raiders. S. R. Crockett. Bd. with Lilac Sunbonnet. 3.00 o.p. (ISBN 0-00-422463-9). Collins-World.
Raiders. Will Henry. 1974. (pbk.) 0.95. Bantam Books.
Raiders. William Edward Wilson. LC 55-6426. 1955. Rinehart.
Raiders: A Novel of the Civil War at Sea. Willard Mosher Wallace. LC 77-99899. (Illus.). 1970. 6.95. Little, Brown.
Raiders at Medicine Bow. Peter Field. LC 57-109325. (His A Powder Valley western). 1957. Jefferson House.
Raiders: Being Some Passages in the Life of John Fualord and Earl. by s. r. crockett. ed. Samuel Rutherford Crockett. LC 4-16513. 1894. Macmillan and Co.
Raiders Gold. J. D. Hardin. LC 80-85105. (J.D.Hardin Ser.). 256p. 1981. pap. 1.95 (ISBN 0-87216-861-1). Playboy Pbks.
Raider's Hell. J. D. Hardin. LC 80-82214. (J.D. Hardin Ser.). 224p. 1980. pap. 1.95 (ISBN 0-87216-883-2). Playboy Pbks.
Raider's Moon. Alexander Knox. LC 76-5375. 8.95. St. Martin's Press.
Raiders of Concho Basin. Eli Albert Chappe. LC 45-3747. 1945. Phoenix Press.
Raiders of Lost River. Clee Woods. LC 36-169345. The Macaulay Company.
Raiders of Spanish Peaks. Zane Grey. LC 88-129567. 1938. Harper & Brothers.
Raiders of the Cherokee Strip. George Brydges Rodney. LC 40-337896. Phoenix Press.
Raiders of the Lost Ark: A Novelization Adapted from the Screenplay by Lawrence Kasden. Campbell Clark. 192p. 1981. 6.95 (ISBN 0-345-28480-1); pap. 2.50 (ISBN 0-345-29490-4). Ballantine.
Raiders of the Lost Ark: Novel. Campbell Black & Lawrence Kasdan. LC 80-69250. 1981. 2.50 (ISBN 0-345-29548-X). Ballantine Books.
Raiders of the Rimrock. Frederick Dilley Glidden. LC 39-30680. 1939. Doubleday, Doran & Company, Inc.
Raiders of the Rimrock. Stephen Payne. LC 56-345422. 1956. Avalon Books.
Raiders of the Rimrock. Luke Short. LC 39-30630. 1939. Doubleday, Doran & Company, Inc.
Raiders of the Tonto Rim. Charles Horace Snow. LC 35-153206. 1935. The Hartney Press.
Raiders of White Pine: By Lew Smith Pseud. Lee Floren. LC 53-7220. 1953. Arcadia House.
Raider's Revenge. J. D. Hardin. LC 80-82851. (J. D. Hardin). 256p. (Orig.). 1981. pap. 1.95 (ISBN 0-87216-767-4). Playboy Pbks.
Raids and Romance of Morgan and His Men. Sallie Rochester Ford. LC 6-41226. 1864. C. B. Richardson.
Rail Fiction Classics. Ed. by William C. Jones. National Railway Historical Society. Intermountain Chapter. LC 74-84237. (Illus.). 1974. Intermountain Chapter, National Railway Historical Society.
Rail-Road Forger and the Detectives. Allan Pinkerton. LC 12-37632. 1881. G. W. Carleton & Co.
Rail Rogues. Glebe Morgan. (Orig.). 1980. pap. 1.75 o.s.i. (ISBN 0-505-51490-7). Tower Bks.
Railroad. Peake, Elmore Elliott et al. LC 2-17482. 1901. McClure, Phillips & Co.
Railroad Battalion. James Bob Miller. LC 51-8227. 1951. Story Book Press.
Railroad King. Paul R. Rothweiler. (Westward Rails Ser.: No. 1). 320p. (Orig.). 1981. pap. 2.75 (ISBN 0-440-07392-8, Banbury). Dell.
Railroad Murder Case. R M Laurenson. LC 48-4475. 1948. Phoenix Press.
Railroad Street. Bruce Hunsberger. LC 70-113802. 1970. 5.95. L. Stuart.
Railroad Waif. C. B Sargent. LC 8-1815. 1885. Cranston and Stowe.
Railroad West: A Novel. Cornelia Lynde Meigs. LC 37-16075. 1937. Little, Brown and Company.

Railroaded. Rufe Jefferson. 176p. (Orig.). 1981. pap. 1.95 (ISBN 0-8439-0955-2). Leisure Bks CT.
Railroadin, Etc. A Novel. J J Grienbrier. LC 77-75651. (Illus.). 6.95. Burnt-River House.
Rails West to Glory. Lee Floren. 1978. pap. 1.25 (ISBN 0-532-12559-2). Woodhill.
Railtown Sheriff: By Stuart Brock Pseud. Louis Trimble. LC 57-875055. 1957. Avalon Books.
Railway Guns. John Earl Lewis. 1983. 6.95 (Avalon). Bouregy.
Railway King. Margaret Mayhew. LC 78-18553. 1979. 8.95 (ISBN 0-385-14603-5). Doubleday.
Railway Man and His Children. Margaret Oliphant Wilson Oliphant. LC 7-325044. (On cover: Lovell's international series, no. 177). 1891. J. W. Lovell Company.
Railway Police, and The Last Trolley Ride. Hortense Calisher. LC 66-16561. 5.00. Little.
Rain Across the Moon. Dorothy Lester Chadwick. LC 38-464608. 1938. Arcadia House.
Rain and the Fire and the Will of God. Donald Wetzel. LC 57-646065. 1957. Random House.
Rain Before Seven. Margaret Emerson Bailey. 1939. Dodd, Mead & Company.
Rain Before Seven. Bernard Augustine De Voto. LC 40-13623. 1940. Little, Brown and Company.
Rain Before Seven. Jessie Douglas Fox. LC 29-104817. 1929. Payson & Clarke Ltd.
Rain Before Seven. Eric Leadbitter. LC 20-9473. G. W. Jacobs & Company.
Rain Before Seven: A Low Fantasy. Marcus Beresford. LC 45-8513. 1945. Harper & Brothers.
Rain Check: A Novel by Arlo Wayne Pseud. Wayne Arlo Forde. LC 52-40862. 1952. Woodford Press.
Rain-Coat Girl. Jennette Barbour Perry Lee. LC 19-15562. 1919. C. Scribner's Sons.
Rain Every Day. Eileen Helen Clements. LC 41-146595. 1941. E. P. Dutton & Co., Inc.
Rain Forest: From Palms to Evergreens. Elizabeth Marston. LC 69-11334. 1969. 6.95. Branden Press.
Rain-Girl: A Romance of Today. Herbert George Jenkins. LC 19-14626. George H. Doran Company.
Rain Harbor. Rebecca Merrick. LC 47-3351. 1947. The Bobbs-Merrill Company.
Rain in the Doorway. Thorne Smith. LC 33-968320. 1933. Doubleday, Doran and Company, Inc.
Rain Lady. Faye Wildman. 192p. (Orig.). 1980. pap. 1.50 (ISBN 0-671-57029-3, Pub. by Silhouette Bks). S&S.
Rain of Ashes. James Neugass. LC 49-9440. 1949. Harper.
Rain of Diamonds. Anne Weale. (Harlequin Romances Ser.). 192p. 1981. pap. 1.50 (ISBN 0-373-02436-3, Pub. by Harlequin). PB.
Rain of Scorpions. Estela P. Trambley. LC 75-37178. 1975. pap. 6.50 (ISBN 0-89229-001-3). Tonatiuh-Quinto Sol Intl.
Rain of Terror: By Malcolm Douglas Pseud. Cover Painting by James Meese. Douglas Sanderson. LC 56-230682. (Gold medal books, 539). 1955. Fawcett Publications.
Rain on Her Face: A Novel. John Paddy Carstairs. LC 43-6823. 1943. Hurst & Blackett, Ltd.
Rain on the Just. Kathleen Moore Morehouse. LC 36-8617. L. Furman, Inc.
Rain on the Just: A Novel. Kathleen Moore Morehouse. LC 79-18762. (Lost American fiction). 12.95 (ISBN 0-8093-0945-9). Southern Illinois University Press.
Rain on the Mountain. Green Peyton Wertenbaker. LC 34-2905. 1934. Little, Brown, and Company.
Rain on the Rolls: A Whopping Tarradiddle. Morgan Cunnington. LC 32-20530. The Vanguard Press.
Rain on the Roof. Kay Lipke. LC 32-3496. L. MacVeagh, The Dial Press.
Rain on the Wind. Walter Macken. LC 51-10559. 1951. Macmillan.
Rain Through the Night. Buddhadeva Bose. 1973. Hind Pocket Books.
Rain with Violence. Elizabeth Linington. LC 67-25319. 1967. W. Morrow.
Rain with Violence. Dell Shannon. (Raven House Mysteries Ser.). 224p. 1981. pap. 2.25 (ISBN 0-373-63015-8, Pub. by Worldwide). Harlequin Bks.
Rain with Violence. Dell Shannon. 1971. pap. 0.75 o.p. (T2427). Pyramid Pubns.
Rainbird Pattern. Victor Canning. LC 72-12854. 1973. 6.95 (ISBN 0-688-00155-6). Morrow.
Rainbow. Pearl Sydenstricker Buck. 1976. (pbk.) 1.75 (ISBN 0-671-80319-0). Pocket Books.
Rainbow. D. H Lawrence & John Worthen. LC 82-173043. (Penguin English Library). 1982. 4.50 (ISBN 0-14-043155-1). Penguin Books.
Rainbow. David Herbert Lawrence. 1976. 2.50 (ISBN 0-14-004266-0). Penguin.
Rainbow. David Herbert Lawrence. LC 15-27933. 1916. B. W. Huebsch.
Rainbow. David Herbert Lawrence. LC 27-266274. (Half-title: The modern library of the world's best books). 1927. The Modern Library.
Rainbow. David Herbert Lawrence. LC 77-367182. 1976. 2.50 (ISBN 0-14-000692-3). Penguin.
Rainbow. Howard Phillips Lovecraft. 1.95. Necronomicon.
Rainbow. Wanda Wasilewska & Bone, Edith, Tr. LC 44-3237. 1944. Simon and Schuster.
Rainbow: A Novel. Pearl Sydenstricker Buck. LC 74-8696. 1974. 8.95 (ISBN 0-381-98273-4). John Day Co.
Rainbow: A Novel. William Harry Harding. LC 79-1245. 10.00 (ISBN 0-03-050396-5). Holt, Rinehart, and Winston.
Rainbow & the Rose. Nevil Shute. 1958. 4.95 o.p. Morrow.
Rainbow and the Rose: By Nevil Shute Pseud. Nevil Shute Norway. LC 58-111336. 1958. Morrow.
Rainbow at Dusk. Emilie Baker Loring. LC 76-40434. 1976. 6.95 (ISBN 0-88411-360-4). Aeonian Press.
Rainbow at Dusk. Emilie Baker Loring. LC 42-216914. 1942. Little, Brown, and Company.
Rainbow at Night. Mary Graham Bonner. LC 36-6662. L. Eurman, Inc.
Rainbow at Noon. Dorothy Walworth. LC 35-19932. R. M. McBride & Company.
Rainbow Bird. Margaret Way. (Presents Ser.). 1975. pap. 1.25 (ISBN 0-373-70602-2, 70602, Pub. by Harlequin). PB.
Rainbow by the Bayou. Ken Kraft. LC 65-139229. 4.95. Chilton.
Rainbow by the Bayou. Ken Kraft. LC 65-13922. 1965. Chilton Books.
Rainbow Cadenza: A Novel in Logosta Form. Neil J. Schulman. 320p. 1983. 15.95 (ISBN 0-671-42003-8). S&S.
Rainbow Chasers. a rainbow romance edition. ed. Marion Naismith. 1973. (pbk.) 0.60. New American Library.
Rainbow Chasers: A Story of the Plains. John Harvey Whitson. LC 4-6884. 1904. Little, Brown, and Company.
Rainbow City & the Inner Earth People. Michael X. 1969. pap. 6.95. G Barker Bks.
Rainbow Colored Shroud. Joseph Hedges. (Stark Ser.: No. 5). 1975. pap. 1.25 o.p. (ISBN 0-515-03811-3). Pyramid Pubns.
Rainbow Conspiracy. Dan Lees. LC 75-179614. 1972. 4.95 (ISBN 0-8027-5243-8). Walker.
Rainbow Cottage. Grace Livingston Hill. LC 34-41919. J. B. Lippincott Company.
Rainbow Feather. Fergus Hume. LC 98-1558. 1898. G. W. Dillingham Co.
Rainbow for a Dying Old Man. Martin Haley. Date not set. 3.95 o.p. Vantage.
Rainbow for Clari. Claire Blackburn, pseud. 1973. 4.50 o.p. (Avalon). Bouregy.
Rainbow for the Christian West. Tr. by Jack Hirschman. 1972. pap. 2.50 (Pub. by Red Hill). SBD.
Rainbow Glass. Alice Dwyer-Joyce. LC 73-21888. 1974. (lib. bdg.). 7.95 (ISBN 0-8161-6181-X). G. K. Hall.
Rainbow Glass. Dwyer-Joyce, Alice. LC 73-78858. 1973. 6.95. St. Martin's Press.
Rainbow Glass. Alice Dwyer-Joyce. (Bantam gothic novel). 1974. (pbk.) 1.25. Bantam Books.
Rainbow Glory. Louise Platt Hauck. LC 35-2536. The Penn Publishing Company.
Rainbow Goblins. Ul De Rico. (Illus.). 1978. 24.95 (ISBN 0-500-95005-9). Thames Hudson.
Rainbow Goblins. Ul de Rico. (Illus.). 1979. pap. 9.95 (ISBN 0-446-87942-8). Warner Bks.
Rainbow Gold. A Novel. David Christie Murray. (Harper's Franklin square library, no. 509). 1886. Harper & Brothers.
Rainbow Gypsy. Sandra Lynn Eirls. 1980. 2.75 (ISBN 0-671-82836-3). Pocket Books.
Rainbow Has Seven Colors: A Novel. Nadia Legrand. LC 58-8737. 1958. St. Martin's Press.
Rainbow in the Royals. Garland Roark. LC 50-10311. 1950. Doubleday.
Rainbow in the Sky. Peggy O'More, pseud. 1948. Arcadia House.
Rainbow in the Spray. Winifred Mary Scott. LC 29-23794. 1929. Doubleday, Doran & Company, Inc.
Rainbow in the Spray. Pamela Wynne. (Barbara Cartland's Library of Love: Vol. 13). 218p. 1980. 12.95x (ISBN 0-7156-1473-8, Pub. by Duckworth England). Biblio Dist.
Rainbow: Introd. by Richard Aldington. David Herbert Lawrence. (Compass bk. C77). 1961. pap., 1.85. Viking.
Rainbow Island. Mark Caywood. LC 27-13794. 1927. The Viking Press.
Rainbow Jordan. Alice Childress. 128p. 1982. pap. 2.25 (ISBN 0-380-58974-5, 58974, Flare). Avon.
Rainbow Love. Joan W. Anglund. LC 82-70028. (Illus.). 1982. 5.95 (ISBN 0-915696-51-7). Determined Prods.
Rainbow Man. Theodore Marvin Pollock. LC 78-26250. 9.95 (ISBN 0-07-050390-7). McGraw-Hill.
Rainbow Men. Douglas Sheldon. LC 74-9466. 1975. 10.00. (ISBN 0-385-01288-8). Doubleday.
Rainbow of Gold. Joseph Alexander Altsheler. LC 6-63. 1898. Continental Publishing Company.
Rainbow on the Road. Esther Forbes. LC 53-9248. 1954. Houghton Mifflin.
Rainbow Over Broadway. Alma Sioux Scarberry. LC 36-31240. J. H. Hopkins & Son, Inc.
Rainbow Riddle. Margaret Sutton. (Judy Bolton Mysteries). 1976. Repr. of 1946 ed. lib. bdg. 12.35x (ISBN 0-88411-711-1). Amereon Ltd.
Rainbow Road. Davenport Steward. LC 53-1509. 1953. Tupper & Love.
Rainbow Saga. Chet Cunningham. (Leisure book). 1.95 (ISBN 0-8439-0622-7). Nordon Pubns.
Rainbow Season. Lisa Gregory, pseud. (Orig.). 1979. pap. 2.25 (ISBN 0-515-05350-3). Jove Pubns.
Rainbow to Heaven. Barbara Cartland. 1976. pap. 1.25 o.p. (ISBN 0-515-03988-8). BJ Pub Group.
Rainbow Trail. Zane Grey. 1982. 18.00x (ISBN 0-86025-195-0, Pub. by Ian Henry Pubns England). State Mutual Bk.
Rainbow Trail: A Romance. Zane Grey. LC 41-32215. Grosset & Dunlap.
Rainbow Trail: A Romance. Zane Grey. LC 15-16338. 1915. 1.35. Harper & Brothers.
Rainbow Trail: A Romance. Zane Grey. LC 21-137222. 1920. Grosset & Dunlap.
Rainbow Trail: A Romance. Zane Grey. LC 40-1226. 1939. T. Nelson and Sons Ltd.
Rainbowland. William Hegner. LC 77-4777. 8.95. Playboy Press.
Rainbowland: A Novel. William Hegner. 1978. 1.95 (ISBN 0-87216-499-3). Playboy Press.
Rainbows. Edith Marie Beyerle. LC 40-884231. Zondervan Publishing House.
Rainbow's and. Vivian Radcliffe. LC 36-9613. Phoenix Press.
Rainbows and Echoes from Fairyland. Dorothy Whipple Fry. LC 28-5424. The Four Seas Company.
Rainbow's End. James Mallahan Cain. LC 74-28336. 1975. 7.95 (ISBN 0-88405-092-0). Mason/Charter.
Rainbow's End. James Mallahan Cain. (Berkley Medallion Book). 1976. (pbk.) 1.50 (ISBN 0-425-03054-7). Berkley Publishing Corp.
Rainbow's End. Sara Lucile Jenkins. LC 56-13298. 1956. Avalon Books.
Rainbow's End. Edith Pargeter. LC 79-87538. 1979. 8.95 (ISBN 0-688-03518-3). Morrow.
Rainbow's End. Ellis Peters. LC 79-87538. 1979. 8.95 o.p. (ISBN 0-688-03518-3). Morrow.
Rainbow's End: A Novel. Rex Ellingwood Beach. LC 16-204412. 1916. Harper & Brothers.
Rainbow's End: Edited by Albert Nani. 1st Ed. Kathleen Nani. LC 53-8100. 1953. Pageant Press.
Rainbow's Ends. Ona Mahitta Rounds. LC 33-36230. 1933. Overland-Outwest Publications.
Rainbows of Song. Georgiana L. Lahr. 3.95 (ISBN 0-533-01774-2). Vantage.
Rainbow's Pot O' Gold. Marie Merceret & Clark, Helen Whitney. LC 26-21492. 1926. B. Herder Book Co.
Raincrow. Jane Gilmore Rushing. LC 76-52223. 1977. 8.50 (ISBN 0-385-13059-7). Doubleday.
Raincrow. Jane Gilmore Rushing. LC 78-6885. 1978. 11.95 (ISBN 0-8161-6587-4). G. K. Hall.
Raincrow. Jane Gilmore Rushing. 1979. 1.95 (ISBN 0-380-41749-9). Avon Books.
Rainer Maria Rilke. Eliza Marian Butler. 437p. 1973. Repr. of 1941 ed. lib. bdg. 25.00x (ISBN 0-374-91129-0). Octagon.
Rainier of the Last Frontier. John Marvin Dean. LC 11-19986. 1911. 1.20. Thomas Y. Crowell Company.
Rainmaker. Jan Ostergren. LC 82-24554. 13.95 (ISBN 0-8214-0745-7) (ISBN 0-8214-0746-5). Ohio University Press.
Rainmaker. Jan Ostergren. Tr. by John Matthais & Goran Printz-Pahlson. 56p. 1983. 13.95x (ISBN 0-8214-0745-7, 82-85140); pap. 7.95 (ISBN 0-8214-0746-5, 82-85157). Ohio U Pr.
Rainproof Invention: Or, Some Tangled Threads. Emily Poynton Weaver. LC 8-36750. Congregational Sunday-School and Publishing Society.
Rains Came. Louis Bromfield. 1976. Repr. of 1937 ed. lib. bdg. 26.65x (ISBN 0-88411-505-4). Amereon Ltd.
Rains Came. Louis Bromfield. 528p. 1974. pap. 1.75 (ISBN 0-532-17101-2). Woodhill.
Rains Came: A Novel of Modern India. Louis Bromfield. LC 76-6525. 1976. (ISBN 0-88411-505-4). Onian Press.
Rains Came: A Novel of Modern India. Louis Bromfield. 1937. Harper & Brothers.
Rains in the Jungle: Lao Short Stories. 1967. pap. 0.50 o.p. China Bks.
Rainsplitter in the Zodiac Garden. Penelope Shuttle. LC 78-66699. 1978. 9.95 (ISBN 0-917712-05-6). Longship Press.
Raintree County... Which Had No Boundaries in Time and Space: Where Lurked Musical and Strange Names and Mythical and Lost Peoples, and Which Was Itself Only a Name Musical and Strange. Abridgment by Edmund Fuller. Ross Franklin Lockridge. LC 57-7479. (Dell book, F58). 1957. Dell Pub. Co.
Raintree County:... Which Had No Boundaries in Time and Space, Where Lurked Musical and Strange Names and Mythical and Lost Peoples, and Which Was Itself Only a Name Musical and Strange. Ross Franklin Lockridge. 1948. Houghton Mifflin Co.
Raintree County:...Which Had No Boundaries in Time and Space: Where Lurked Musical and Strange Names and Mythical and Lost Peoples, and Which Was Itself Only a Name Musical and Strange. Abridgment by Edmund Fuller. Ross Franklin Lockridge. LC 57-74792. (Dell book, F58). 1957. Dell Pub. Co.
Raintree Valley, Black Douglas: The Pagan Island. Violet Winspear. (Harlequin Romances Ser.). 576p. 1981. pap. 3.50 (ISBN 0-373-20052-8). Harlequin Bks.
Rainy June. Louise De La Ramee. LC 6-33310. (Lovell's library. v. 12, no. 675). 1885. J. W. Lovell Company.
Rainy Week. Eleanor Hallowell Abbott. LC 21-12704. E.P. Dutton & Company.
Raise High the Roof Beam, Carpenters. J. D. Salinger. Bd. with Seymour - An Introduction. 1963. 9.95 (ISBN 0-316-76957-6). Little.
Raise High the Roof Beam, Carpenters, and Seymour, an Introduction: Stories. J. D. Salinger. LC 63-8969. 1963. Little, Brown.
Raise the Dark Gambler. Mary Sellers. (Berkley Medallion Book). 1977. 1.50 (ISBN 0-425-03409-7). Berkley Pub. Corp.
Raise the Titanic! Clive Cussler. LC 76-25871. 1976. 8.95 (ISBN 0-670-58933-0). Viking Press.
Raised a Communist: Life in a Religious Commune. Duke Farson. LC 36-102372. 1936. Farson Studio Publications.
Raisin in the Sun. Lorraine Hansberry. Bd. with Sign in Sidney Brustein's Window. pap. 3.50 (ISBN 0-451-11303-9, AE1303, Sig). NAL.
Raisin Valley. Rebecca Newman Porter. LC 53-121509. Vantage Press.
Raising Cain. Carolyn Elizabeth Hosmer & Hocking, Lorena Winchell, Joint Author. LC 13-952. 1912. The W. H. Kistler Stationery Co.
Raising Demons see Magic of Shirley Jackson.
Raising Hell: A Contemporary Novel of Modern Juvenile Delinquency Told from the Standpoint of the Deliquents Themselves. Dave Jay. LC 63-24301. 1963. Vantage Press.
Raiz India. Nunez Rosario Beltran. Odyssey Press.
Raj. Donald Hannibal Robinson. LC 73-137466. 1971. 7.95 (ISBN 0-395-12104-3). Houghton Mifflin.
Raj Quartet. Paul Scott. LC 76-13249. 1976. 22.50 (ISBN 0-688-03065-3). Morrow.
Raj Quartet. Paul Scott. LC 77-368313. 1976. 7.50 (ISBN 0-434-68112-1). Heinemann.
Rajac: A Story. Stanley Spain & Eric Mache. LC 82-7325. (Illus.). 11.50. Macmillan.
Rajah's Honour. Pearl Weymouth. LC 25-20708. 1925. T. Seltzer.
Rajah's Sapphire. Matthew Phipps Shiel. (Nautilus Ser.). (Illus.). 163p. 1981. pap. 6.00. Highflyer Pr.
Rajan. Tim Lukeman. LC 78-20083. 1979. 7.95 (ISBN 0-385-14936-0). Doubleday.
Rake and the Hussy. Robert William Chambers. LC 30-20597. 1930. D. Appleton and Company.
Rake and the Rebel. Ira J Morris. LC 67-21132. 1967. Morrow.
Rakehell. Deirdre Stiles. (Leisure Book.). 1978. 1.95 (ISBN 0-8439-0541-7). Nordon Pubns.
Rakehell Dynasty. Michael W. Scott. 544p. (Orig.). 1980. pap. 3.50 (ISBN 0-446-30308-9). Warner Bks.
Rakehell Dynasty: China Bride, No. 2. Michael W. Scott. 544p. (Orig.). 1981. pap. 3.50 (ISBN 0-446-30309-7). Warner Bks.
Rakehell Dynasty: No. 3, Orient Affair. Michael W. Scott. 512p. (Orig.). 1982. pap. 3.95 (ISBN 0-446-30771-8). Warner Bks.
Rakehells of Heaven. John Boyd. 1978. pap. 1.95 (ISBN 0-14-004877-4). Penguin.
Rakehells of Heaven. John Boyd. LC 79-87067. 1969. 5.50 o.p. Weybright.
Rakehells of Heaven. Boyd Upchurch. LC 79-87067. 1969. 5.50. Weybright and Talley.
Rakehells of Heaven. Boyd Upchurch. LC 78-928. 1978. 1.95 (ISBN 0-14-004877-4). Penguin Books.
Raker. Andrew Sinclair. LC 64-22097. 1964. Atheneum.
Raker, No. 1. Don Scott. 192p. (Orig.). 1982. pap. 2.25 (ISBN 0-523-41689-X). Pinnacle Bks.
Raker: Tijuana Traffic, No. 2. Don Scott. 208p. (Orig.). 1982. pap. 2.25 (ISBN 0-523-41733-0). Pinnacle Bks.

Rake's Junction. Peter Kanto. 1970. pap. 0.75 o.p. (ISBN 0-447-74673-1). Lancer.
Rake's Progress. Philip Lindsay. LC 50-9396. 1950. Sheridan House.
Rake's Reward. Madelaine Gibson. 176p. (Orig.). 1981. pap. 1.95 (ISBN 0-553-13191-5). Bantam.
Rakish Halo. Harriet Henry, pseud. LC 32-15434. 1932. W. Morrow & Co.
Rakossy. Cecelia Holland. LC 67-13037. 1967. Atheneum.
Ralegh's Fair Bess. Judy Turner, pseud. LC 73-91344. 1974. 5.95. St. Martin's Press.
Raleigh: A Romance of Elizabeth's Court. William Devereux & Lovell, Stephen. LC 10-1693. 1910. J. B. Lippincott Company.
Raleigh Rivers: A Tale of the New South. O. O'B Strayer. (On cover: Globe library, no. 87). 1889. Rand, McNally & Company.
Raleigh Westgate: Or, Epimenides in Maine; a Romance. Helen Kendrick Johnson. LC 7-10543. (On cover: Appletons' town and country library, no. 21). 1889. D. Appleton and Company.
Raleigh's Eden. Inglis Clark Fletcher. LC 76-6105. 1976. 11.50 (ISBN 0-89244-006-6). Queens House.
Raleigh's Eden: A Novel. Inglis Clark Fletcher. LC 52-975. 1951. Garden City Books.
Raleigh's Eden, a Novel. Inglis Clark Fletcher. LC 40-301009. The Bobbs-Merrill Company.
Raleigh's Eden: A Novel. Inglis Clark Fletcher. LC 40-30100. The Bobbs-Merrill Company.
Raliegh's Eden. Inglis Clark Fletcher. 608p. 1980. pap. 2.95 (ISBN 0-553-13395-0). Bantam.
Rally Round the Flag, Boys: 1st Ed. Max Shulman. LC 57-9513. 1957. Doubleday.
Rally to Kill. Bill Knox. LC 74-22840. 1975. 5.95 (ISBN 0-385-02690-0). Published for the Crime Club by Doubleday.
Ralph. Bruce D. Price. LC 77-122135. 1970. 5.95. McCall Pub. Co.
Ralph Dacre. Anne Stevenson, pseud. LC 67-23644. 1967. Walker.
Ralph Herne. William Henry Hudson. LC 25-26037. (Borsoi pocket books). 1924. A. A. Knopf.
Ralph Herne. William Henry Hudson & Rogers, Bruce, 1870- LC 23-238. 1923. A. A. Knopf.
Ralph Makes Good: By Wally Cox. Wallace Cox. LC 65-262546. 1966. bds., 2.50. S. & S.
Ralph Marlowe: A Novel. James Ball Naylor. LC 1-31209. 1901. The Saalfield Publishing Company.
Ralph Norbreck's Trust. William Westall. LC 44-432635. 1885. Cassell & Company, Limited.
Ralph: Or, What's Eating the Folks in Fatchakulla County? Ned Crabb. LC 78-13370. 1979. 8.95 (ISBN 0-688-03403-9). Morrow.
Ralph Ranscomb, Banker. Theodore W Nevin. LC 8-33907. 1908. The Neale Publishing Company.
Ralph Rashleigh see Australian Classics.
Ralph Raymond's Heir. Horatio Alger. 125p. 1974. Repr. of 1892 ed. lib. bdg. 14.65x (ISBN 0-88411-805-3). Amereon Ltd.
Ralph Ryder of Brent: A Novel. Florence Alice Price James. LC 7-7408. J. W. Lovell Company.
Ralph Somerby at Panama. Francis Raleigh. LC 13-213590. 1913. 1.50. L. C. Page & Company.
Ralph the Heir. Anthony Trollope. LC 39-27838. (Half-title: The World's classics. CDLXXV-CDLXXVI). 1939. Oxford University Press, H. Milford.
Ralph the Heir. Anthony Trollope. LC 78-51956. (Illus.). 1978. 4.50 (ISBN 0-486-23642-0). Dover Publications.
Ralph Wilton's Weird: A Novel. Annie French Hector. (On cover: Leisure hour series. no. 47). 1875. H. Holt and Company.
Ralph Wilton's Weird. A Novel. Annie French Hector. (On cover: Seaside library. Pocked ed., no. 815). 1886. G. Munro.
Ralph 124 C41t; a Romance of the Year 2660, by Hugo Gernsback... Hugo Gernsback. LC 25-23817. 1925. The Stratford Company.
Ralph 124C 41. 2d ed. Hugo Gernsback. LC 50-13967. (Fell's science fiction library). (Illus.). 1950. Fell.
Ralphton: Or, The Young Carolinian of 1776. A Romance on the Philosophy of Politics. Abbott Hall Brisbane. LC 6-18252. 1848. Burges and James, Printers.
Ralstons. Francis Marion Crawford. 1895. Macmillan and Co.
Ram: Being the Tale of One Ramillies Anstruther, 1704-55... Winchcombe Taylor. LC 60-8771. 1960. St. Martins Press.
Ram on the Rampage. Toller Cranston. (O.s.i). 1977. pap. 4.95 o.s.i. Vanguard.
Rama, the Hero of India: Valmiki's "Ramayana" Done into a Short English Version for Boys and Girls. Dhan Gopal Mukerji & Valmiki. Ramayana. LC 30-232462. E. P. Dutton & Co., Inc.
Ramacaritamanasa see Ramayana of Tulasidasa.
Ramage: A Novel. Dudley Pope. LC 65-15252. (Illus.). 1965. Lippincott.
Ramage & the Guillotine. Dudley Pope. 256p. 1981. pap. 2.50 (ISBN 0-380-55491-7, 55491). Avon.
Ramage & the Renegades. Dudley Pope. 288p. 1982. pap. 2.75 (ISBN 0-380-60137-0, 60137-0). Avon.
Ramage's Diamond. Dudley Pope. 288p. 1982. pap. 2.50 (ISBN 0-380-57828-X, 57828). Avon.
Ramage's Prize. Dudley Pope. LC 74-6542. (Illus.). 1975. 8.95 (ISBN 0-671-21860-3). Simon and Schuster.
Ramakien: The Thai Epic. J. M. Cadet & Valmiki. LC 70-128685. (Illus.). 1971. (u.s.) 14.50 (ISBN 0-87011-134-5). Kodansha International.
Ramalalup. Warja Honegger-Lavater. (Folded Story Ser: No. 18). 5.75x o.p. Wittenborn.
Ramayana. Aubrey Menen & Valmiki. LC 72-598. 1972. (ISBN 0-8371-6181-9). Greenwood Press.
Ramayana. R. K. Narayan. (Illus.). 1977. pap. 3.95 (ISBN 0-14-004428-0). Penguin.
Ramayana: A Shortened Modern Prose Version of the Indian Epic (Suggested by the Tamil Version of Kamban. R. K. Narayan & Kampar. LC 79-189514. (Illus.). 1972. 7.95 (ISBN 0-670-58950-0). Viking Press.
Ramayana: A Shortened Modern Prose Version of the Indian Epic: (Suggested by the Tamil Version of Kamban) R. K. Narayan & Th Cent Kampar. LC 77-1986. (Illus.). 1977. 2.95 (ISBN 0-14-004428-0). Penguin Books.
Ramayana: As Told by Aubrey Menen. Aubrey Menen & Valmiki. LC 54-5919. 1954. Scribner.
Ramayana at a Glance. Keshavadas & Valmiki. LC 76-47423. (Illus.). 3.95. Temple of Cosmic Religion.
Ramayana: King Rama's Way. William Buck & Valmiki. LC 78-153549. (Illus.). 14.95 (ISBN 0-520-02016-2). University of California Press.
Ramayana of Tulasidasa. Ed. by R. C. Prasad. Tr. by F. S. Growse from Hindi. Orig. Title: Ramacaritamanasa. 1978. 22.50 (ISBN 0-89684-067-0); pap. 13.50_o.s.i. Orient Bk Dist.
Ramayana of Tulasidasa. Tulasidas. Tr. by F. S. Growse. 1979. 24.00x (ISBN 0-8364-0363-0). South Asia Bks.
Rambler. Samuel Johnson. 1953. 5.00x o.p. (ISBN 0-460-00994-X, Evman). Dutton.
Rambler Club in the Mountains. William Henry Crispin Sheppard. LC 10-301444. 1910. The Penn Publishing Company.
Rambler Club's Winter Camp. William Henry Crispin Sheppard. LC 10-30143. 1910. The Penn Publishing Company.
Rambles in Brazil: Or, A Peep at the Aztecs, by One Who Has Seen Them. 2d ed.... ed. A. R. Middletoun Payne. LC 9-8964. 1854. C. B. Norton.
Rambles of Fudge Fumble: Or The Love Scrapes of a Lifetime. Marcus Lafayette Byrn. 1860. F. A. Brady.
Rambleton: A Romance of Fashionable Life in New-York During the Great Speculation of 1836. Charles Sealsfield. LC 5-41080. J. Winchester.
Ramblin' Kid. Earl Wayland Bowman. LC 20-7723. The Bobbs-Merrill Company.
Ramblin' Kid. Oscar Schisgall. LC 34-42177. 1933. G. H. Watt.
Rambling Rose. Calder Willingham. 1973. (pbk) 1.50. Dell.
Rambling Rose. Calder Willingham. LC 72-83351. 1972. 6.95. Delacorte Press.
Rambling Top Hand. William L Hopson. LC 46-223504. 1946. Phoenix Press.
Rambunctious Lady Royston. Kasey Michaels. 224p. 1982. pap. 2.50 (ISBN 0-380-81448-X, 81444-X). Avon.
Rameau's Nephew & D'Alembert's Dream. Denis Diderot. Tr. & intro. by L. W. Tancock. lib. bdg. 3.70x o.p. (ISBN 0-88307-078-2). Gannon.
Ramera Fogoza. Abel Castano. (Pimienta Collection Ser.). 1977. pap. 1.00 (ISBN 0-88473-268-1). Fiesta Pub.
Ramey. Jack Farris. LC 52-13741. 1953. Lippincott.
Ramon J. Sender. Charles L King. LC 73-19612. (Twayne's world authors series, TWAS 307. Spain). (Illus.). 1974. 5.95 (ISBN 0-8057-2815-5). Twayne Publishers.
Ramon, the Rover of Cuba: And Other Tales. LC 8-214. 1843. Nafis & Cornish.
Ramona. Helen H. Jackson. 1970. pap. 3.50 (ISBN 0-380-00383-X, 59303-1). Avon.
Ramona. Helen H. Jackson. 1976. lib. bdg. 20.10x (ISBN 0-89968-051-8). Lightyear.
Ramona. Helen H. Jackson. 384p. 1981. pap. 2.75 (ISBN 0-523-41440-4). Pinnacle Bks.
Ramona, a Story. Helen Jackson. 490p. 1981. Repr. of 1884 ed. lib. bdg. 25.00 (ISBN 0-89760-411-3). Telegraph Bks.
Ramona: A Story. Helen Maria Fiske Hunt Jackson. LC 1-1275. 1884. Roberts Brothers.
Ramona. A Story. Helen Maria Fiske Hunt Jackson. LC 7-9471. 1885. Roberts Brothers.
Ramona. A Story. Helen Maria Fiske Hunt Jackson. LC 4-15459. 1903. Little, Brown, and Company.
Ramona: A Story. Helen Maria Fiske Hunt Jackson. LC 13-21255. 1913. Little, Brown, and Company.
Ramona: A Story. Helen Maria Fiske Hunt Jackson. LC 18-5413. 1915. Little, Brown and Company.
Ramona: A Story. Helen Maria Fiske Hunt Jackson. LC 16-7002. 1916. Little, Brown, and Company.
Ramona: A Story. Helen Maria Fiske Hunt Jackson. LC 23-9031. 1922. Little, Brown, and Company.
Ramona: A Story. Helen Maria Fiske Hunt Jackson. LC 42-26741. 1925. Little, Brown, and Company.
Ramona: A Story. Helen Maria Fiske Hunt Jackson. LC 32-269571. 1932. Little, Brown, and Company.
Ramona. A Story. Helen Maria Fiske Hunt Jackson. LC 39-27379. 1939. Little, Brown and Company.
Ramona: A Story by Helen Hunt Jackson (H. H. Helen Maria Fiske Hunt Jackson. LC 6249. 1900. Little, Brown and Company.
Ramona, a Story. With an Introd. by J. Frank Dobie and Illus. by Everett Gee Jackson. Helen Maria Fiske Hunt Jackson. LC 59-419830. 1959. Printed for the Members of the Limited Editions Club at the Plantin Press.
Ramona: Adapted by Olive Eckerson. Helen Maria Fiske Hunt Jackson & Olive Eckerson. LC 52-11660. 1952. Globe Book Co.
Ramona's Daughter. Virginia Myers. 384p. (Orig.). 1981. pap. 2.75 (ISBN 0-523-40964-8). Pinnacle Bks.
Rampage. Bob Haning, pseud. (O.s.i.). 1975. pap. 0.95 o.s.i. (BT50831). Belmont-Tower.
Rampage: By Alan Caillou Pseud. Alan Lyle-Smythe. LC 61-15645. Appleton-Century-
Rampage in Rio. Lionel Derrick, pseud. (Penetrator Ser.: No. 43). 208p. (Orig.). 1981. pap. 1.95 (ISBN 0-523-41157-X). Pinnacle Bks.
Rampage in the Rockies. Shoshone Green. LC 44-5022. 1944. Phoenix Press.
Rampant Age. Robert Spencer Carr. LC 28-7956. 1928. Doubleday, Doran & Company, Inc.
Rampart Street. Everett Webber & Webber, Olga. LC 48-8723. 1948. E. P. Dutton.
Rampole Place. Isabella Holt. LC 52-10278. 1952. Bobbs-Merrill.
Ramrod. George Charles Appell. LC 56-264643. (Lion library edition, 57). 1955. Lion Books.
Ramrod. Frederick Dilley Glidden. LC 43-13840. 1943. The Macmillan Company.
Ramrod. Luke Short. 224p. 1981. pap. 1.95 (ISBN 0-553-20008-9). Bantam.
Ramrod Jones, Hunter and Patriot: A Tale of the Texas Revolution Against Mexico. Clinton Giddings Brown. LC 5-32729. The Saalfield Publishing Co.
Ramrod of the K Bar. Galen C Colin. LC 40-358846. Phoenix Press.
Ramrod Rebel. Dean Owen. 1974. (pbk.) 0.95. Manor Books.
Ramrod Vengeance. William L. Hopson. 1978. pap. 1.25 o.s.i. (ISBN 0-8439-0564-6, Leisure Bks). Nordon Pubns.
Ramrod Vengeance. Nelson Coral Nye. LC 81-17299. 1982. 12.95 (ISBN 0-89340-378-4). J. Curley & Associates.
Ramrodders: A Novel. Holman Francis Day. LC 10-10187. 1910. Harper & Brothers.
Ram's Tales of the Past: Given Clair Audiently Verbatim et Literatim Through E. B. Wait. E. B Wait. LC 34-16290. Advanced Thought Publishing Co.
Ramsay, Andrew Michael: To Which Is Annexed, A Discourse Upon the Theology and Mythology of the Pagans. the 10th ed.--1st american. ed. LC 9-2226. 1793. Printed by I. Neale.
Ramsden Case: A Novel. David Chandler. LC 67-16725. 1967. Simon and Schuster.
Ramsey Milholland. Booth Tarkington. LC 19-13300. 1919. Doubleday, Page & Company.
Ramsey Milholland. Booth Tarkington. LC 22-16007. 1920. Doubleday, Page & Company.
Ramsey the Detective: Or, The Weirdest of Weird Tales. Harlan Page Halsey. (Old Sletuh's own, no. 119). 1898. The Parlor Car Publishing Co.
Ramsgate Paradox. Stephen Tall. (Berkley Medallion). Berkley.
Ramshackle House. Hulbert Footner. LC 23-110873. George H. Doran Company.
Ramspeed. 1980. pap. text ed. write for info. (ISBN 0-88074-161-9). Metagam.
Ramuntcho. Julien Viaud & Pene Du Bois, Henri, 1858-1906, Tr. LC 8-29993. 1897. R. F. Fenno & Company.
Ran Away from the Dutch: Or, Borneo from South to North. Michael Theophile Hubert Perelaer. Tr. by Block; Maurice. Mendes, Abraham Pereira. LC 7-36357. Dodd, Mead & Company.
Ranch at Powder River. Al Cody, pseud. 1976. pap. 1.25 (ISBN 0-532-12436-7). Woodhill.
Ranch at Powder River. Al Cody, pseud. Ed. by Alice Sachs. 192p. 1972. 3.95 o.p. Lenox Hill.
Ranch at the Wolverine. Bertha Muzzy Sinclair. LC 14-16915. 1914. Little, Brown, and Company.
Ranch by the Sea. Richard Edward Wormser. LC 71-105620. 1970. 4.50. Doubleday.
Ranch of the Raven. Hamilton Craigie. LC 35-170933. Phoenix Press.
Ranch of the Rio. Francis Mitchell. LC 58-367. 1958. Arcadia House.
Ranch of the Thorn: An Adventure Story. William Henry Hamby. LC 24-3167. Chelsea House.
Ranch of the Two Thumbs. Archie Joscelyn. LC 39-258781. Phoenix Press.
Ranch on the Beaver: A Sequeal to "Wells Brothers; the Young Cattle Kings". Andy Adams. LC 27-23003. 1927. Houghton Mifflin Company.
Ranch on the Laramie. Ted Olson. LC 72-8985. 1973. 6.95 (ISBN 0-316-65052-8). Little, Brown.
Ranch Stealers. Ford Bowne, pseud. LC 65-8380. 1965. Arcadia House.
Ranch Tales of the Rockies. author's ed. Harry Ellard. LC 281. 1899.
Rancher Jim. Harold Bindloss. LC 30-20589. 1930. Frederick A. Stokes Company.
Ranchero. Thomas Wakefield Blackburn. (Dell book). 1979. 1.25 (ISBN 0-440-17317-5). Dell Pub. Co.
Ranchero. Stewart Edward White. LC 33-7093. 1933. Doubleday, Doran & Company, Inc.
Ranchero. Stewart Edward White. LC 39-24455. 1939. The Sun Dial Press, Inc.
Ranchero. Stewart Edward White. LC 43-15353. 1943. Triangle Books.
Rancher's Gold, a New Western: By Pete Danvers Pseud. James Maddock Henderson. LC 52-66413. 1952. Hammond, Hammond.
Rancher's Revenge. Max Brand. LC 34-16899. 1934. Dodd, Mead & Company.
Rancher's Revenge. Frederick Faust. LC 34-16899. 1934. Dodd, Mead & Company.
Ranching for Sylvia. Harold Bindloss. LC 12-248232. 1913. 1.25. Frederick A. Stokes Company.
Ranching on Eagle Eye. Sarah Lindsay Schmidt. LC 36-29838. R. M. McBride & Company.
Ranchman. Charles Alden Seltzer. LC 19-15321. 1919. A. C. McClurg & Co.
Rancho Bonita. James Denson Sayers. LC 36-29304. 1936. Godwin.
Rancho Bonita. James Denson Sayers. LC 41-6799. 1940. Western Novel of the Month, Inc.
Rancho Del Muerto. Charles King et al. LC 7-12832. (Outing Library). (Outing library. v. 1, no. 3: Vol. 1, No. 3). 1894. Outing Publishing Company.
Rancho of the Little Loves. Robert Nathan. LC 56-10905. (Illus.). 1956. Knopf.
Rancho of the Twelve Apostles: A Story of New Mexican Life. Gorbes Heermans. LC 28-6927. 1928. The Stratford Company.
Rancho Paradise. John N. Deck. LC 72-174506. 1972. 8.50 o.p. HarBraceJ.
Rancho Villa and the Revolutionist. Santiago Reachi. LC 76-372825. 8.50 (ISBN 0-682-48552-7). Exposition Press.
Rancy Cottem's Courtship. Detailed, with Other Humorous Sketches and Adventures. William Tappan Thompson. LC 8-37111. T. B. Peterson & Brothers.
Randall and the River of Time. Cecil Scott Forester. LC 50-10441. 1950. Little, Brown.
Randall Household. C Tennant Copeland. LC 50-4108. 1950. Christopher Pub. House.
Randiana. pap. 1.95 o.p. (ISBN 0-87056-242-8, 6242). Brandon.
Randiana or Excitable Tales. rev. ed. Ed. by Brian Kirby. pap. 1.25 o.p. (2019). Brandon.
Randolph. John Neal. Ed. by J. V. Ridgely. LC 70-93652. (American Fiction Ser). 1970. lib. bdg. 22.50 o.s.i. (ISBN 0-512-00533-8). Garrett Pr.
Randolph: A Novel... John Neal. LC 13-33854. 1823.
Randolph Gordon and Other Stories. ... second series. ed. Louise De La Ramee. LC 42-26164. 1867. J. B. Lippincott & Co.
Randolph Gordon: And Other Stories. Louise De La Ramee. (Seaside library. v. 11, no. 211). 1878. G. Munro.
Randolph Honor. Marian Calhoun Legare Reeves. 1868. Richardson and Company.
Randolph Mason: Corrector of Destinies. Melville Davisson Post. LC 72-150559. (Short story index reprint series). 1971. (ISBN 0-8369-3856-9). Books for Libraries Press.

Randolph Mason: The Clients. Melville Davisson Post. LC 73-3469. (Short story index reprint series). 1973. (ISBN 0-8369-4259-0). Books for Libraries Press.
Randolph Mason: The Strange Schemes. Melville Davisson Post. LC 29-6460. 1922. G. P. Putnam's Sons.
Randolphs. Isabella Alden. LC 32-19538. D. Lothrop & Co.
Randolphs. Isabella Alden. LC 5-7479. 1904. Lothrop Publishing Company.
Random. Lance Jensen. 1975. pap. 1.25 o.p. (ISBN 0-515-03861-X). Pyramid Pubns.
Random. Milar Larson. LC 75-24868. 1975. (pbk.) 1.25 (ISBN 0-515-03861-X). Pyramid Books.
Random Death. large print ed. Lesley Egan, pseud. LC 82-9208. 1982. 8.95 (ISBN 0-8161-3408-1). G.K. Hall.
Random Factor. Linda J. LaRosa & Barry Tanenbaum. LC 77-82764. 1978. 8.95 (ISBN 0-385-13282-4). Doubleday.
Random Factor. Linda J. LaRosa & Tanenbaum, Barry. 1979. 2.25 (ISBN 0-515-05166-7). Jove Publications.
Random Gentleman. Elizabeth Chater. 224p. 1981. pap. 1.95 (ISBN 0-449-50210-4, Crest). Fawcett.
Random Harvest. James Hilton. LC 41-51508. 1941. Little, Brown and Company.
Random Harvest... James Hilton. LC 45-157880. 1944.
Random Killer. Hugh Pentecost. LC 79-271. (Pierre Chambrun Mystery & Red Badge Novel of Suspense Ser.). 1979. 7.95 o.p. (ISBN 0-396-07654-8). Dodd.
Random Killer. Judson Pentecost Philips. LC 79-271. (Red badge novel of suspense). 7.95. Dodd, Mead.
Random Measures. Olav Kallenberg. 1976. pap. 15.65. Adler.
Random Shaft... James Marion Miller. LC 8-17787. 1908. The C. M. Clark Publishing Co.
Random Shots. Charles Heber Clark. LC 70-164557. (American fiction reprint series). (Illus.). 1971. (ISBN 0-8369-7033-0). Books for Libraries Press.
Random Shots. Charles Heber Clark. LC 6-25360. (On cover: Lovell's library, v. 5 no. 295). 1883. J. W. Lovell Company.
Random Shots from a Rifleman. John Kincaid. LC 7-12238. 1835. E. L. Carey & A. Hart.
Random Skits. Edwin W Hale. LC 7-25993. 1896. The Brooks Company.
Random Track to Peking: A Novel. Austin Ferguson. LC 78-21258. 1979. 8.95 (ISBN 0-688-03466-7). Morrow.
Random Winds. Belva Plain. LC 79-26845. 9.95 (ISBN 0-440-07124-0). Delacorte Press.
Random Winds. Belva Plain. LC 81-95. 1981. 18.95 (ISBN 0-8161-3178-3). G.K. Hall.
Randy Roy Persnazznur. David B. Creps. LC 80-930830. (Orig.). 1980. pap. 4.95 (ISBN 0-930830-32-6). Great Basin.
Raneslough. Monica Heath. (Signet Book). 1976. 1.25. New American Library.
Rangatira, the High-Born: A Polynesian Saga, by Norman B. Tindale and Harold A. Lindsay. Illustrated by Douglas E. Maxted. Norman Barnett Tindale & Harold Arthur Lindsay. LC 59-16350. 1959. F. Watts.
Range Beyond the Law. William MacLeod Raine. 1974. (pbk.) 0.95. Popular Library.
Range Boss. Dwight Bennett Newton. LC 49-16461. (Pocket Book 563). 1949. Pocket Books.
Range Boss. Charles Alden Seltzer. LC 16-201053. 1916. A. C. McClurg & Co.
Range Buster: Cover Painting by Frank McCarthy. William Heuman. LC 54-42476. (Gold medal books, 429). 1954. Fawcett Publications.
Range Camp. William Frederick Bragg. LC 50-8448. 1950. Phoenix Press.
Range Cavalier. Johnston McCulley. LC 34-421763. 1933. G. H. Watt.
Range Doctor. Oscar Jerome Friend. LC 50-19177. (Handi-book western, 101). 1950. Handi-Book Editions.
Range Drifter. Thomas Thompson. 192p. 1981. pap. 1.95 (ISBN 0-553-14541-X). Bantam.
Range Dwellers. Bertha Muzzy Sinclair. LC 7-6407. 1907. G. W. Dillingham Company.
Range Feud. Buck Billings. LC 40-8930. 1940. Gateway Books.
Range Feud. Claude Rister. LC 40-8930. 1940. Gateway Books.
Range Hawk. Stetson Cody. LC 73-152520. 1972. 4.95 (ISBN 0-7075-0013-3). Gold Lion Books.
Range Hawk. Arthur Henry Gooden. LC 40-32132. Carlton House.
Range Kid. William Colt MacDonald. LC 56-38432. (Pyramid books, 172). 1955. Pyramid Books.
Range-Land Avenger: A Western Story. George Owen Baxter. LC 24-23488. Chelsea House.
Range-Land Avenger: A Western Story. Frederick Raust. LC 24-23488. 1924. Chelsea House.
Range Law. Gene Thompson. 1962. Avalon Books.
Range Maverick. Oscar Jerome Friend. LC 31-30963. 1931. G. H. Watt.
Range of Golden Hoofs. John Trace. LC 41-20929. 1941. Doubleday, Doran and Company, Inc.
Range of No Return. Archie Joscelyn. LC 39-7776. Phoenix Press.
Range Rebel. Gordon D. Shirreffs. 1978. pap. 1.50 o.s.i. (ISBN 0-505-51226-2). Tower Bks.
Range Rebellion. W. D. Hoffman. LC 45-46063. 1945. Phoenix Press.
Range Reckoning. Dan T Kelliher. LC 53-7225. 1953. Arcadia House.
Range Rider. William H. B Kent. LC 43-10067. 1943. The Macmillan Company.
Range Rider. Bradford Scott. LC 45-4663. 1945. Arcadia House, Inc.
Range Riders. Charles Alden Seltzer. LC 11-730110. 1911. Outing Publishing Company.
Range Robbers. Oliver Strange. LC 32-785. 1931. L. MacVeagh, Dial Press Inc.
Range the Mountains High. Judith Wright. (Illus.). 10.00x o.p. (ISBN 0-392-04330-0, ABC). Soccer.
Range Town Renegade. T. W. Ford. LC 50-7355. 1950. Phoenix Press.
Range Trouble. Clay Allen, pseud. LC 81-71190. 1982. 10.95 (ISBN 0-8027-4010-3). Walker.
Range Trouble: By Dean Jennings Pseud. Steve Frazee. LC 51-11738. 1951. Phoenix Press.
Range War. Lee Floren. (O.s.i.). 1975. pap. 0.95 o.s.i. (50842). Belmont-Tower.
Range War. Philip Morgan. LC 56-8977. 1956. Arcadia House.
Range War in Squaw Valley. Stuart Adams. LC 40-100092. 1939. Hillman-Curl, Inc.
Range War West. George Cassidy. LC 50-14689. 1950. Phoenix Press.
Rangeland Hercules. J. T Edson. 1981. 1.95 (ISBN 0-425-04626-5). Berkley Books.
Rangeland Hercules. John Thomas Edson. 1981. 1.95 (ISBN 0-425-04625-7). Berkley Books.
Rangeland Justice. Johnston McCulley. LC 35-304288. G. H. Watt.
Rangeland Marshal. Ford Bowne, pseud. 1972. 4.95. Lenox Hill Pr.
Rangeland Marshall. Ford Bowne, pseud. (Orig.). 1977. pap. 1.25 (ISBN 0-532-12509-6). Woodhill.
Ranger. Harry H. Halsell. LC 43-11295. 1942. The Seton Village Press.
Ranger: And Other Stories. Zane Grey. LC 61-17806. Grosset & Dunlap.
Ranger: And Other Stories. 1st Ed. Zane Grey. LC 60-13714. 1960. Harper.
Ranger Bill. Clement Yore. LC 31-601948. The Macaulay Company.
Ranger Called Solitary. Peter Germano. 1966. Arcadia House.
Ranger Daring. Bradford Scott. (Orig.). 1971. pap. 0.60 o.p. (X2402). Pyramid Pubns.
Ranger District Number Five. Hunter Stephen Moles. LC 24-354. The Spencerian Press.
Ranger Man. William Colt MacDonald. LC 51-13257. (Double D western). 1951. Doubleday.
Ranger of Ravenstream. A Tale of the Revolution. Newton Mallory Curtis. 1847. Boston, Williams Brothers.
Ranger: Or, The Fugitives of the Border. Edward Sylvester Ellis. LC 11-13616. 0.50. Hurst & Company.
Ranger Rides Alone. Amos Moore. LC 36-208472. I. Washburn, Inc.
Ranger Rides the Death Trail. Bradford Scott. pap. 0.75 o.p. (T2881). Pyramid Pubns.
Ranger Two-Rifles. Dane Coolidge. LC 37-184341. 1937. E. P. Dutton & Co., Inc.
Ranger Way. Eugene Cunningham. LC 37-8762. 1937. Houghton Mifflin Company.
Ranger Wins. Bradford Scott. (Walt Slade Original Westerns Ser). (Orig.). 1971. pap. 0.60 o.p. (X2526). Pyramid Pubns.
Rangers and Regulators. A Novel. Alfred W. Arrington. LC 12-37959. 1892. G. W. Dillingham.
Rangers and Regulators of the Tanaha: Or, Life Among the Lawless. A Tale of the Republic of Texas. Alfred W. Arrington. LC 6-2429. R. M. De Witt.
Rangers' Code. Johnston McCulley. LC 30-123327. Grosset & Dunlap.
Ranger's Code. Johnston McCulley. LC 24-194683. 1924. G. H. Watt.
Rangers Is Powerful Hard to Kill. Caddo Cameron. LC 37-173614. 1937. The Sun Dial Press, Inc.
Ranger's Luck. William MacLeod Raine. LC 50-43. 1950. Houghton Mifflin.
Rangers of Bloody Silver. Van Cort. LC 41-140461. Phoenix Press.
Rangers of the Shield: A Collection of Stories Written by Men of the National Forests of the West, Edited. Ed. by Ovid McOuat Butler. LC 34-34591. 1934. The American Forestry Association.
Rangers: Or, The Tory's Daughter. A Tale, Illustrative of the Revolutionary History of Vermont, and the Northern Campaign of 1777. 4th ed. Daniel Pierce Thompson. LC 8-26631. 1856. Sanborn, Carter & Bazin.
Rangers: Or, The Tory's Dauther. A Tale, Illustrative of the Revolutionary History of Vermont, and the Northern Campaign of 1777... Daniel Pierce Thompson. 1851. B. B. Mussey and Company.
Ranger's Ransom: A Story of Ticonderoga. Herbert Best. LC 53-12166. (American heritage). (Illus.). 1953. Aladdin Books.
Ranger's Round-up. Amos Moore. LC 40-311837. I. Washburn, Inc.
Rangers Roundup. Bradford Scott. (Orig.). 1970. pap. 0.60 o.p. (X2321). Pyramid Pubns.
Ranging Heart. Arthur Moore. Date not set. pap. price not set. Pinnacle Bks.
Rangoon. Frederick Barthelme. LC 74-118570. (Illus.). 1970. 7.95. Winter House.
Rangy Pete. Guy Eugene Morton. LC 22-3188. Small, Maynard & Company.
Ranhild. Neve Conklin. LC 52-25667. 1952. Dorrance.
Rania. Dane Rudhyar. 200p. (Orig.). 1972. pap. 3.45 o.p. (ISBN 0-913300-11-X). Orenda-Unity.
Rania: An Epic Narrative. Dane Rudhyar. LC 73-161390. 1973. 3.45 (ISBN 0-913300-11-X). Unity Press.
Rank Vs. Merit: A Novel. Victoria Worthington. (On cover: Modern novelists' series, no. 9). 1893. Home Book Company.
Ranka. Apostolos N. Athanassakis. LC 78-60634. 1978. pap. 4.00 (ISBN 0-918618-14-2). Pella Pub.
Rankell's Remains: An American Novel. Barrett Wendell. LC 8-36240. 1887. Ticknor and Company.
Rankell's Remains: An American Novel. Barrett Wendell. 1896. C. Scribner's Sons.
Ranleigh Court. Marjorie Shoebridge. LC 79-7610. 1980. 7.95 (ISBN 0-385-15452-6). Doubleday.
Ranny, Otherwise Randolph Harrington Dukes: A Tale of Those Activities Which Made Him an Important Figure in His Town, in His Family--and in Other Families. Howard Brubaker. LC 17-20177. 1917. 1.40. Harper & Brothers.
Ransack. Mike Henson. LC 80-53807. (Illus.). 151p. (Orig.). 1980. pap. 3.00 (ISBN 0-931122-18-X). West End.
Ransom. Jon Cleary. LC 72-10378. 1973. 6.95 (ISBN 0-688-00028-2). Morrow.
Ransom. Charles Francis Coe. LC 34-19026. J. B. Lippincott Company.
Ransom. Grace Livingston Hill. LC 33-910119. J. B. Lippincott Company.
Ransom. Anthony Richardson. LC 25-121759. Small, Maynard & Company.
Ransom! Arthur Somers Roche. LC 18-119445. George H. Doran Company.
Ransom. Arthur Somers Roche. LC 24-26524. 1920. A. L. Burt Company.
Ransom. Robert Kimmel Smith. LC 72-152281. 1971. 6.95. D. McKay Co.
Ransom for a Nude. Dudley Barker. LC 72-81209. 1972. 5.95 (ISBN 0-8128-1491-6). Stein and Day.
Ransom for a Nude. Lionel Black. 190p. 1982. pap. 2.50 (ISBN 0-8128-7050-6). Stein & Day.
Ransom for a Nude. Lionel Black. LC 72-81209. 1972. 5.95 o.p. (ISBN 0-8128-1491-6). Stein & Day.
Ransom! Jefferson Boone. Jon Messman. (Handyman Ser.: No. 5). (Orig.). 1975. pap. 1.25 o.p. (ISBN 0-515-03516-5, V3516). BJ Pub Group.
Ransom of King Tut. Thomas P. Hanna. LC 79-50894. pap. 2.25 o.s.i. (ISBN 0-89516-079-X). Condor Pub Co.
Ransom Racket. Lee Thayer, pseud. LC 38-6239. 1938. Dodd, Mead & Company.
Ransom Run. Martin Dibner. LC 76-18341. 1977. 7.95 (ISBN 0-385-12242-X). Doubleday.
Ransom Run. Martin Dibner. 1978. 1.95 (ISBN 0-345-27172-6). Ballantine Books.
Ransom Town. Peter Alding. LC 79-63635. 1979. 7.95 (ISBN 0-8027-5409-0). Walker.
Ransomed Heart. Sparky Ascani. 208p. pap. 2.95 (ISBN 0-380-83287-9). Avon.
Ransome's Army. Kyle Hollingshead. (Ace Western). 1974. (pbk.) 0.75. Ace Books.
Ransome's Debt. Kyle Hollingshead. 288p. 1981. pap. 2.25 (ISBN 0-441-70461-1). Ace Bks.
Ranson's Folly. Richard Harding Davis. LC 79-152938. (Short story index reprint series). (Illus.). 1971. (ISBN 0-8369-3797-X). Books for Libraries Press.
Ranson's Folly. Richard Harding Davis. 1910. C. Scribner's Sons.
Ransons's Folly. Richard Harding Davis. LC 2-17864. 1902. C. Scribner's Sons.
Ranthorpe. George Henry Lewes. LC 74-82496. 1974. 12.00 (ISBN 0-8214-0167-X). Ohio University Press.
Ranthorpe. George Henry Lewes. LC 42-30193. 1881. W. S. Gottsberger.
Ranthorpe. George Henry Lewes. (On cover: Seaside library. Pocket ed., no. 442). 1885. G. Munro.
Raoul and Iron Hand: Or, Winning the Golden Spurs, a Tale of the 14th Century. May Halsey Miller. 1898. E. P. Dutton & Company.
Rap. Ernest Brawley. LC 73-91631. 1974. 10.00 (ISBN 0-689-10563-0). Atheneum.
Rapaho. Jamie Lee Cooper. LC 67-25170. 1967. bds., 4.50. Bobbs.
Rape. Robert Lamb. 1974. (pbk.) 1.50. Bantam Books.
Rape. Leslie Trevor. (Police Woman Ser.). (O.s.i.). (Orig.). 1975. pap. 1.25 o.s.i. (AQ1438, Award). Univ Pub & Dist.
Rape. Leslie Trevor. (Police Woman,#1). 1975. (pbk.) 1.25. Award Books.
Rape. Marcus Van Heller, pseud. pap. 1.75 o.p. (3009). Brandon.
Rape Conspiracy. Robert Moore, pseud. pap. 1.95 o.s.i. (OPH-225, Ophelia). Olympia.
Rape Machine. Ann Taylor. 192p. pap. 1.95 o.p. (6120). Brandon.
Rape Machine see Sex Machine.
Rape Observed: An Edition of Alexander Pope's "The Rape of the Lock". Ed. by Clarence Tracy. LC 73-85091. (Illus.). 1974. 17.50x (ISBN 0-8020-5298-3). U of Toronto Pr.
Rape of a Quiet Town. Dan Lees. LC 72-96693. 1973. 5.95 (ISBN 0-8027-5280-2). Walker.
Rape of Berlin. W. Howard Baker. pap. 0.60 o.p. (73-628). Lancer.
Rape of Glory: A Romance of the Volga. Val Lewton. LC 31-21750. The Mohawk Press.
Rape of Honor. Translated from the German by Sigrid Rock. Willi Heinrich. LC 60-146928. 1961. Dial Press.
Rape of Tamar. Dan Jacobson. Ed. by Robert Markel. LC 78-119134. (O.s.i). 1970. 5.95 o.s.i. (ISBN 0-02-558570-3). Macmillan.
Rape of Tamar: A Novel. Dan Jacobson. LC 78-119134. 1970. Macmillan.
Rape of the Blindfolded Lady. Carole Raft. 1979. pap. 2.25 (ISBN 0-933664-00-1). Motiv Methods.
Rape of the Gamp. A Novel. Charles Welsh Mason. LC 7-25575. 1875. Harper & Brothers.
Rape of the Nicollet Mall Mannequin. Steve Hall. LC 78-64893. 1978. pap. 2.50 (ISBN 0-9602068-0-9). Con Brio.
Rape of the Sabines. Warja Honegger-Lavater. (Folded Story Ser: No. 6). 1964. bds. 3.75 o.p. Wittenborn.
Rape of the Statue. Marjorie Cartwright. Orig. Title: Lessons in Love. 1968. pap. 1.75 o.s.i. (104, Ophelia). Olympia.
Rape of the Sun. Ian Wallace. 1982. pap. 2.95 (ISBN 0-87997-704-3, UE1704). DAW Bks.
Rape of the Virgin Butterfly: A Novel. Valerie Kohler Smith. LC 73-7767. 1973. 6.95. Dial Press.
Rape One. Frederick C Canavor. LC 81-14263. 1982. 13.95 (ISBN 0-914842-75-7). Madrona Publishers.
Rape Squad. Simon Wolf. 192p. (Orig.). 1975. pap. 1.25 o.p. (ISBN 0-532-12322-0). Woodhill.
Rape Squad. Simon Wolf. 192p. (Orig.). 1975. pap. 1.25 o.p. (ISBN 0-532-12322-0). Manor Bks.
Rapes of Wrath. Robert Moore, pseud. (Orig.). 1970. pap. 1.95 o.s.i. (OPH-174, Ophelia). Olympia.
Raphael... Alphonse Marie Louis De Lamartine. Tr. by Walton, William. (Roman contemporain. Romancists. v. 6). Printed Only for Subscribers by G. Barrie & Son.
Raphael Inglesse: Or, The Jew of Milan! A Thrilling Tale of the Victories of Virtue, and the Punishments of Vice. Mary Andrews Denison. LC 9-1836. (On cover: American popular tales. no. 1). 1848. J. E. Farwell & Co.
Raphael: Or, Pages of the Book of Life at Twenty. Alphonse Marie Louis De Lamartine. LC 1-10454. 1849. Harper & Brothers.
Raphael: Or, Pages of the Book of Life at Twenty. Alphonse Marie Louis De Lamartine. LC 1-16455. 1859. Harper & Brothers.
Raphael: Or, Pages of the Book of Life at Twenty. connoisseur ed. Alphonse Marie Louis De Lamartine. LC 5-32478. (Added t.-p.: Comedie d'amour series). 1905. Societe Des Beaux-Arts.
Raphael: Or, Pages of the Book of Life at Twenty, from the French of Alphonse De Lamartine. new american ed. Alphonse Marie Louis De Lamartine. LC 7-3526. (Half-title: Laurel crowned tales). 1891. A. C. McClurg and Company.
Rapids. Alan Sullivan. LC 20-11223. 1920. D. Appleton and Company.
Rapids: A Novel. Basil Davidson. LC 57-5571. 1957. Houghton Mifflin.
Rapin. Henry De Vere Stacpoole. LC 99-852. 1899. H. Holt and Company.
Rapist. Daniel Dorbes. 1982. pap. 2.95 (ISBN 0-440-17294-2). Dell.

Rapist. Michael Kenyon. LC 76-42219. 7.95 (ISBN 0-698-10803-5). Coward, McCann & Geoghegan.

Rappaport. Morris Lurie. LC 67-22749. 1967. Morrow.

Raptors. Ray Hogan. LC 78-14680. 1979. 7.95 (ISBN 0-385-14823-2). Doubleday.

Rapture. Richmond Brooks Barrett. LC 24-289592. Boni and Liveright.

Rapture. Hal Lindsey. 1983. 7.95. Bantam.

Rapture. Rosamond Royal. 2.50 (ISBN 0-445-04359-8). Popular Library.

Rapture & the Marx. D. R. Smith. 3.50 o.p. Carlton.

Rapture Beyond. Katharine Newlin Burt. LC 35-13186. 1935. C. Scribner's Sons.

Rapture for Three. Vivian Elmore. (Orig.). 1968. pap. 0.75 o.p. (74-937). Lancer.

Rapture in My Rags. Phyllis Hastings. LC 54-8119. 1954. Dutton.

Rapture! Is It for Real? Ralph Blodgett. LC 75-275618. (Stories That Win Ser.). 1975. pap. 0.95 (ISBN 0-8163-0183-2, 18033-1). Pacific Pr Pub Assn.

Rapture of the Deep. Margaret Rome. (Harlequin Romances Ser.). 192p. 1983. pap. 1.75 (ISBN 0-373-02553-X). Harlequin Bks.

Rapture Regained. (Second Chance at Love, Contemporary Ser.: No. 8). 192p. (Orig.). 1981. pap. 1.75 (ISBN 0-515-05776-2). Jove Pubns.

Rapture Yet to Come. Mabel Dana Lyon. LC 39-80196. Gramercy Publishing Co.

Raptured. 2d Ed. Ernest W Angley. LC 52-20981. 1950. Carolina Press.

Rapture's Angel. Sylvie F. Sommerfield. 1982. pap. 2.75 (ISBN 0-89083-750-3). Zebra.

Rapture's Bounty. Wanda Owen. 1982. pap. 3.50 (ISBN 0-8217-1002-8). Zebra.

Rapture's Rage. Bobbi Smith. 1983. pap. 3.50 (ISBN 0-8217-1121-0). Zebra.

Rapture's Reign. Dorothy MacCarthy. 304p. (Orig.). 1982. pap. 2.95 (ISBN 0-523-41632-6). Pinnacle Bks.

Rapture's Rendezvous. Cassie Edwards. (Orig.). 1982. pap. 3.50 (ISBN 0-8217-1049-4). Zebra.

Raquel, the Jewess of Toledo. Translated from the German by Ernst Kaiser and Eithne Wilkins. Lion Feuchtwanger. LC 55-726031. 1956. Messner.

Rarahu: Or, The Marriage of Loti. Julien Viaud. Tr. by Bell, Clara. 1890. W. S. Gottsberger & Co.; Etc., Etc.

Rare Adventure. Bernard Fergusson. LC 55-8414. 1955. Rinehart.

Rare & Undone Saints. Phyllis Demong. 96p. 1983. pap. 3.95 (ISBN 0-380-63081-8, 63081-8). Avon.

Rare Earth. Frank Owen. LC 31-8538. 1931. The Lantern Press.

Rare Pale Margaret. A Novel ... (Franklin square library, no. 27). 1878. Harper & Brothers.

Rare Pale Margaret. A Novel. (On cover: Seaside library. Pocket ed. no. 780). 1886. G. Munro.

Ras Bravado. John Walter Paisley. LC 38-12835. The Christopher Publishing House.

Rascal Club. Julius Chambers. LC 13-7654. (On cover: Neely's continental library, no. 2). 1897. F. T. Neely.

Rascal, Oh No! Mabel E. Jones. 4.95 o.p. Vantage.

Rascals Heaven. F. Van Wyck Mason. 1976. Repr. of 1964 ed. lib. bdg. 23.60x (ISBN 0-89190-351-8). Am Repr-Rivercity Pr.

Rascals in Paradise. James A. Michener. 1979. pap. 2.95 (ISBN 0-449-24022-3, Crest). Fawcett.

Rascals in the Rectory. Ann L Marks. LC 72-78737. 1972. 2.95 (ISBN 0-8059-1701-2). Dorrance.

Rash Act: A Novel. Ford Madox Ford. LC 33-4724. 1933. R. Long & R. R. Smith, Inc.

Rash Act: A Novel. Ford Madox Ford. LC 82-128021. 1982. 14.95 (ISBN 0-85635-399-X) (ISBN 0-85635-399-X). Carcanet New Press.

Rash, Reckless Love. Valerie Sherwood. 576p. (Orig.). 1983. pap. 3.95 (ISBN 0-446-30701-7). Warner Bks.

Rash Resolve; or, the Untimely Discovery. Eliza Fowler Haywood. Bd. with Life & Adventures of the Lady Lucy. Penelope Aubin. LC 74-170561. (Foundations of the Novel Ser.: Vol. 43). lib. bdg. 50.00 (ISBN 0-8240-0555-4). Garland Pub.

Rash Romance. Laura Lou Brookman. LC 30-138714. Grosset & Dunlap.

Rashanyn Dark. William Tedford. (Timequest Ser.: No. 1). 1981. pap. 2.25 (ISBN 0-8439-0869-6, Leisure Bks). Nordon Pubns.

Rashomon, and Other Stories. Ryunosuke Akutagawa. LC 60-17194. (Bantam classic, AC42). (Illus.). 1959. Bantam Books.

Rashomon: And Other Stories. Translated by Takashi Kojima Introd. by Howard Hibbet. Ryunosuke Akutagawa. LC 60-20216. 1952. C. E. Tuttle.

Rashomon, and Other Stories: Translated by Takashi Kojima. Introd. by Howard Hibbett. Illus. by M. Kuwata. Ryunosuke Akutagawa. LC 52-9665. 1952. Liveright Pub. Corp.

Rashomon: And Other Stories Translated by Takashi Kojima, with an Introd. by Osamu Shimizu. Ryunosuke Akutagawa. LC 60-171946. (Bantam classic, AC42). 1959. Bantam Books.

Rasmussen Disasters. James Leigh. LC 71-83634. 1969. 5.95. Harper & Row.

Rasp. Philip MacDonald. (S. S. Van Dine detective library). 1928. C. Scribner's Sons.

Rasp. Philip MacDonald. LC 79-52526. (Illus.). 1979. 3.50 (ISBN 0-486-23864-4). Dover Publications.

Rasp: A Detective Story. Philip MacDonald. LC 26-152. 1925. The Dial Press.

Raspberry Jam. Carolyn Wells. LC 20-7522. 1920. J. B. Lippincott Company.

Raspberry Tart Affair: A Gourmet's Guide to Dining Out. Fred Halliday (ISBN 0-523-00725-6). Pinnacle Books.

Rasputin and the Empress. Val Lewton & MacArthur, Charles G., 1897- LC 33-2627. Grosset & Dunlap.

Rasputin: Translated from the Russian. Ivan Fedorovich Nazhivin. Tr. by Hogarth, C. J. LC 29-189417. 1929. A. A. Knopf.

Rasselas. Samuel Johnson. LC 36-36437. (Half-title: The new universal library). G. Routledge & Sons, Limited.

Rasselas, Prince of Abissinia: A Tale. first american edition. ed. Samuel Johnson. LC 7-10547. 1803. Printed for and Sold by Oliver D. Cooke. Lincoln & Gleason, Printers.

Rasselas, Prince of Abissinia: A Tale. Samuel Johnson. LC 17-22996. 1810. Printed at the "Herald" Press by and for John P. Thomson.

Rasselas, Prince of Abyssinia. new american ed. Samuel Johnson. LC 4-17541. (Half-title: Laurel crowned tales). 1901. A. C. McClurg and Company.

Rasselas, Prince of Abyssinia. Samuel Johnson. LC 40-37530. G. P. Putnam's Sons.

Rasselas: Prince of Abyssinia. new american ed. 9th ed. Samuel Johnson. LC 14-169238. (Half-title: Laurel-crowned tales). 1913. A. C. McClurg and Company.

Rasselas, Prince of Abyssinia. Samuel Johnson & West, William. LC 41-38129. 1906. J. Pott and Co.

Rasselas, Prince of Abyssinia: A Tale. Samuel Johnson. LC 7-10548. 1810. Lyman Hall & Co.

Rasselas, Prince of Abyssinia: Being a Facsimile Reproduction of the First Edition Published in 1759. Samuel Johnson. LC 76-11793. 1976. 45.00 (ISBN 0-8414-5346-2). Folcroft Library Editions.

Rasskazy Nazara Il'icha, Gospodina Sinebriukhova. Mikhail M. Zoshchenko. (Rus.). 1978. pap. 3.00 o.p. (ISBN 0-933884-02-8). Berkeley Slavic.

Rasskazy: Stories. Fyodor Sologeib. Ed. by Evelyn Bristol. LC 79-25535. (Rus.). 1979. 22.50 (ISBN 0-933884-11-7); pap. 12.50 (ISBN 0-933884-10-9). Berkeley Slavic.

Rat. Phyllis Bottome & Novello, Ivor, 1893- LC 27-1234. George H. Doran Company.

Rat Began to Gnaw the Rope. C. W. Grafton. LC 82-48243. 256p. 1983. pap. 2.84i (ISBN 0-06-080639-7, P 639, PL). Har-Row.

Rat Factory. J. M Ryan. LC 79-139956. 1971. 6.95 (ISBN 0-13-753079-X). Prentice-Hall.

Rat on Fire. George V Higgins. LC 80-22713. 1981. 10.95 (ISBN 0-394-42409-3). Knopf: Distributed by Random House.

Rat Pack. Shane Stevens. LC 74-10614. (Continuum book). 1974. 7.95 (ISBN 0-8164-3118-3). Seabury Press.

Rat Patrol No. 1. Norman Daniels. (Orig.). pap. 0.60 o.p. (53-387). Paperback Lib.

Rat Patrol No. 2: In Desert Danger. David King. (Orig.). pap. 0.60 o.p. (53-411). Paperback Lib.

Rat Patrol No. 3: In the Trojan Tank Affair. David King. (Orig.). pap. 0.60 o.p. (53-477). Paperback Lib.

Rat Patrol No. 4: In the Two-Faced Enemy. David King. (Orig.). 1967. pap. 0.60 o.p. (53-566). Paperback Lib.

Rat Patrol No. 6: In Desert Masquerade. David King. (Orig.). 1968. pap. 0.60 o.p. (53-696). Paperback Lib.

Rat-Pit. Patrick MacGill. LC 15-9699. George H. Doran Company.

Rat Race. Dick Francis. LC 71-135186. 1971. 5.95. Harper & Row.

Rat Race. Dick Francis. 1978. 1.95 (ISBN 0-671-82158-X). Pocket Books.

Rat Race. Franklin. 5.00; pap. 2.00. Fantasy Pub Co.

Rat Race. Edward Rager. LC 52-13302. 1952. Vantage Press.

Rat Race: By Jay Franklin Pseud. 1st Ed. John Franklin Carter. LC 50-8121. 1950. Fantasy Pub. Co.

Rat Trap. William Le Queux. LC 30-21776. 1930. The Macaulay Company.

Rat Trap. Craig Thomas. 1978. pap. 2.75 (ISBN 0-553-14048-5). Bantam.

Rat Trap. Craig Thomas. 237p. 1976. 10.95 o.p. (ISBN 0-7181-1497-3, Pub. by Michael Joseph). Merrimack Pub Cir.

Rat-Trap. Dolf Wyllarde. LC 4-8585. 1904. J. Lane.

Rat-Trap. Dolf Wyllarde. LC 20-18822. 1914. John Lane Company.

Rated PG. Virginia Euwer Wolff. LC 80-14382. 1980. 10.95 (ISBN 0-312-66400-1). St. Martin's Press.

Rather a Common Sort of Crime. Joyce Porter. 1970. 4.95 o.p. (ISBN 0-8415-0064-9). Sat Rev Pr.

Rather a Common Sort of Crime: A Novel. Joyce Porter. LC 70-122133. 1970. 4.50 (ISBN 0-8415-0064-9). McCall Pub. Co.

Rather Cool for Mayhem. 1st Ed. Lawrence Goldtree Blochman. LC 50-11099. (Mainline mysteries). 1951. Lippincott.

Rather Simple Fellow. Charles Samuels. LC 31-787219. 1931. Coward-McCann, Inc.

Rathina. Mairin Cregan. LC 42-22993. 1942. The Macmillan Company.

Rational Hind. Ben Ames Williams. LC 25-11001. 1925. E. P. Dutton & Company.

Rational Marriage. Florence Marryat Church Lean. 1899. F. M. Buckles & Company; Etc., Etc.

Rationalist Narrative in Some Works of Arno Schmidt. Tony Phelan. LC 73-158815. (Occasional Papers in German Studies, No. 2). 1972. (ISBN 0-903426-01-3). University of Warwick, Department of German Studies.

Ratman's Notebook. Stephen Gilbert. 1970. pap. 0.95 o.p. (ISBN 0-447-75142-5). Lancer.

Ratman's Notebooks. Stephen Gilbert. LC 69-18797. 1969. 4.95. Viking Press.

Ratner's Star. Don DeLillo. LC 75-36808. (Illus.). 1976. 10.00 (ISBN 0-394-40083-6). Knopf.

Ratner's Star. Don DeLillo. LC 80-10927. 1980. 3.95 (ISBN 0-394-74495-0). Vintage Books.

Raton Pass. Thomas Wakefield Blackburn. LC 50-11081. (Double D western). 1950. Doubleday.

Ratoon. Christopher Nicole. LC 62-11111. 1962. St. Martin's Press.

Ratoons. Daphne Rooke. LC 53-9250. 1953. Houghton Mifflin.

Rats. James Herbert. (Signet book). 1975. (pbk.) 1.50. New American Library.

Rats' Castle. Roy Bridges. LC 24-205672. 1924. D. Appleton and Company.

Rats of Norway. John Keith Winter. LC 32-807005. 1932. Doubleday, Doran & Company, Inc.

Rats of Rutland Grange. Edmund Wilson. (Illus.). 1974. pap. 6.50 o.p. (ISBN 0-910664-35-8). Gotham.

Ratsel Vom Waldsee: Reader 2. Rita M. Walbruck. LC 80-22126. (Auf Heisser Spur Ser.). (gr. 9-12). 1981. pap. 1.95 (ISBN 0-88436-851-3). EMC.

Rattle His Bones. Julian Shore. LC 41-15456. 1941. W. Morrow and Company.

Rattle His Bones. Julian Shore. LC 44-6008. 1944. London Publishing Corp.

Rattle of His Chains: A Novel. Walter Clarence Hanscome. LC 6-2342. Eastern Publishing Co.

Rattlehead's Travels: Or, The Recollections of a Backwoodsman, That Has Travelled Many Thousand Miles on the Highway of Human Destiny; Brought About a Revolution in Domestic Happiness; and Affected a General Shake up of Creation. Marcus Lafayette Byrn. LC 6-16400. 1852. Lippincott, Grambo, & Co.

Rattlehead's Travels: Or, The Recollections of a Backwoodsman, Who Has Traveled Many Thousand Miles on the Highways of Human Destiny: Brought About a Revolution in Domestic Happiness, and Effected a General Shake-up. Marcus Lafayette Byrn. (Phudge Phumble's humorous series no. 2). 1880. M. L. Byrn.

Rattler Gang. (Klaw Ser.: No. 3). (Orig.). 1981. pap. 1.95 (ISBN 0-505-51689-6). Tower Bks.

Rattlers. Joseph L Gilmore. (Signet Book). 1979. 1.95 (ISBN 0-451-08464-0). New American Library.

Rattlesnake. Theodore V. Olsen. LC 78-7763. 1979. 7.95 (ISBN 0-385-14290-0). Doubleday.

Rattlesnake. Theodore V. Olsen. LC 78-7763. 1979. 7.95 o.p. (ISBN 0-385-14290-0). Doubleday.

Rattlesnake. Theodore V. Olsen. 1980. pap. 1.75 (ISBN 0-671-83305-7). PB.

Rattlesnake Dick: A Novel. Robert Baker Elder. LC 53-8827. 1954. Chapman & Grimes.

Rattlesnake Dick, a Novel of Gold Rush Days. Robert Baker Elder. LC 81-187803. 8.95 (ISBN 0-934878-14-5). Dembner Books: Distributed by W.W. Norton.

Rattlesnake Range. Peter Field. LC 60-10777. (Powder Valley Western). 1974. (pbk.) 0.75 (ISBN 0-671-75832-2). Pocket Books.

Rattlesnake Ridge. Robert Claiborne Pitzer. LC 55-11869. 1955. Arcadia House.

Rattlesnakes. J. Frank Dobie. 207p. 1982. pap. 6.95 (ISBN 0-292-77023-5). U of Tex Pr.

Rattlesnakes. Venetia Gleason. 1977. pap. 1.00 o.p. (ISBN 0-931832-08-X). No Dead Lines.

Rattlin the Reefer. Edward Howard. LC 73-882081. (Oxford English novels). 1971. 3.25. Oxford University Press.

Rattling of Old Bones. Jonathan Ross. LC 81-14478. 1982. 10.95 (ISBN 0-684-17335-2). Scribner.

Rature's Dream. Carol Finch. (Orig.). 1982. pap. 3.50 (ISBN 0-8217-1037-0). Zebra.

Raum. Carl Sherrell. LC 77-72119. 1977. 1.50 (ISBN 0-380-01646-X). Avon Books.

Ravaged Range. Peter Field. LC 46-18720. 1946. Jefferson House.

Ravager. David Lord. LC 47-2410. 1947. F. Fell, Inc.

Ravanels: A Novel. Harris Dickson. LC 5-8074. 1905. J. B. Lippincott Company.

Ravellings from the Web of Life. Charles James Cannon. LC 6-21476. 1855. D. & J. Sadler & Co.

Raven. Shana Carrol, pseud. (Orig.). 1982. pap. 3.50 (ISBN 0-515-06325-8). Jove Pubns.

Raven. Shana Carrol, pseud. (Orig.). pap. 2.25 (ISBN 0-515-04439-3). Jove Pubns.

Raven. William Kinsolving. LC 82-13238. 15.95. G.P. Putnam's Sons.

Raven. Chancellor Williams. LC 73-18611. 1975. 28.00 (ISBN 0-404-11421-0). AMS Press.

Raven. Chancellor Williams. LC 43-17566. 1943. Dorrance and Company.

Raven After Dark. Donald MacKenzie. LC 79-13932. 1979. 7.95 (ISBN 0-395-28209-8). Houghton Mifflin.

Raven and the Dove. Kathleen Kinder, pseud. LC 80-14398. 1980. 8.95 (ISBN 0-312-66405-2). St. Martin's Press.

Raven and the Kamikaze: A Novel. Donald MacKenzie. LC 77-5143. 1977. 7.95 (ISBN 0-395-25695-X). Houghton Mifflin.

Raven and the Paperhangers. Donald MacKenzie. LC 80-14239. 8.95 (ISBN 0-395-29450-9). Houghton Mifflin.

Raven and the Phantom. Dana Fuller Ross. 1976. (pbk.) 1.95 (ISBN 0-671-80463-4). Pocket Books.

Raven and the Ratcatcher: A Novel. Donald MacKenzie. LC 76-41286. 1977. 7.95 (ISBN 0-395-24902-3). Houghton Mifflin.

Raven Feathers His Nest. Donald MacKenzie. 1982. 15.00x (ISBN 0-333-26292-1, Pub. by Macmillan England). State Mutual Bk.

Raven in Flight. Donald MacKenzie. LC 75-34220. 1976. 6.95 (ISBN 0-395-24292-4). Houghton Mifflin.

Raven McCord. Emily Austin. 1980. pap. 2.75 (ISBN 0-8439-0837-8). Nordon Pubns.

Raven Rough. John Cecil Moore. LC 31-28034. 1931. Houghton Mifflin Company.

Raven Settles a Score. Donald MacKenzie. LC 78-19204. 1978. 7.95 (ISBN 0-395-27100-2). Houghton Mifflin.

Raven Settles a Score. Donald MacKenzie. 1981. 1.95 (ISBN 0-425-04717-2). Berkley Publishing Corporation.

Raven Sisters. Dorothy Mack. (Candlelight Regency Special). 1977. 1.25 (ISBN 0-440-17255-1). Dell Pyb. Co.

Raven: The Love Story of Edgar Allan Poe. (Twixt Fact and Fancy. George Cochrane Hazelton. 1909. D. Appleton and Company.

Ravenburn. Laura Black. LC 77-15917. 1978. 10.00 (ISBN 0-312-66408-7). St. Martin's Press.

Ravenburn. Laura Black. LC 80-19300. 1980. 16.95 (ISBN 0-8161-3129-5). G. K. Hall.

Ravenburn. Laura Black. 1980. 2.50 (ISBN 0-446-91155-0). Warner Books.

Ravenelle Riddle: A Peter Strangely Mystery. Elizabeth Best Black. LC 33-249142. Loring and Mussey.

Ravenhurst. Marilyn Ross. (Queen-size gothic). 1975. (pbk.) 1.25. Popular Library.

Ravenia: Or, The Outcast Redeemed. Annie Hamilton Nelles Dumond. LC 6-35873. 1872. Commonwealth Printing Company's Press.

Ravens. O'Philip Bonn. LC 31-35110. 1931. California Graphic Press.

Raven's Brood. E. F Benson. (Queen-size gothic). 1975. (pbk.) 1.25. Popular Library.

Raven's Brood. Edward Frederic Benson. LC 34-34011. 1934. Doubleday, Doran & Company, Inc.

Raven's Forge. Jennie Melville, pseud. LC 74-25724. 1975. 7.95 (ISBN 0-679-50480-X). McKay.

Raven's Forge. Jennie Melville, pseud. (A Fawcett Crest Book). 1977. 1.50 (ISBN 0-449-23171-2). Fawcett Pubns.

Ravens of the Moon. Charles L Grant. LC 77-82758. 1978. 6.95 (ISBN 0-385-12969-6). Doubleday.

Raven's Revenge. Donald MacKenzie. LC 81-20018. 1982. 10.95 (ISBN 0-395-32050-X). Houghton Mifflin Co.

Raven's Wing. Elizabeth Sprigge. LC 40-33598. 1940. The Macmillan Company.

Ravens-Wood. Janet Louise Roberts. (Kangaroo Book). 1978. 1.50. Pocket Books.

Ravenscroft. Dorothy Eden. 1978. pap. 1.95 (ISBN 0-449-23760-5, Crest). Fawcett.

Ravenscroft Affair. Cyril Arthur Edward Ranger Gull. E. J. Clode, in.
Ravenscroft: 1st Amer. Ed. Dorothy Eden. LC 64-25029. 1965. 4.50. Coward.
Ravensdale Mystery. Gladys Edson Locke. LC 35-18239. L. C. Page & Company.
Ravensdene Court. Joseph Smith Fletcher. LC 22-156753. 1922. A. A. Knopf.
Ravensgate. Deirdre Rowan. (Gold Medal Book) (ISBN 0-449-13588-8). Fawcett.
Ravenshoe. Henry Kingsley. Ed. by William H. Scheuerle. LC 67-12117. (Bison book, BB365). 1967. University of Nebraska Press.
Ravenshoe. author's ed. Henry Kingsley. LC 7-12522. 1862. Ticknor and Fields.
Ravenshoe. Henry Kingsley. LC 4-16540. 1903. Longmans, Green & Co.
Ravenshoe. Henry Kingsley. (Half-title: The world's classics. CCLXVII). 1925. H. Milford, Oxford University Press.
Ravenshoe. Ed., Introd. by William H. Scheuerle. Henry Kingsley. Ed. by William H. Scheuerle. (Bison bk., BB365 rebound). 1967. 4.25. P. Smith.
Ravensley Manor. Cecily Clark. 1976. 1.75 (ISBN 0-671-80777-3). Pocket Books.
Ravensley Touch. Constance Heaven. LC 82-7247. (Illus.). 1982. 13.95 (ISBN 0-698-11109-5). Coward, McCann & Geoghegan.
Ravensmount. Marjorie McEvoy. (Orig.). 1974. pap. 0.95 o.p. (26565-095). Beagle Bks.
Ravensnest. Caroline Farr. (Signet Book). 1977. 1.25 (ISBN 0-451-07437-8). New American Library.
Ravenstor. Elizabeth Renier. (Orig.). 1981. pap. 2.50 (ISBN 0-441-70809-9). Ace Bks.
Ravenswood. Edward Winslow Gilliam. LC 8-18573. 1908. The Neale Publishing Company.
Ravenswood: A Story of the Impact of a Family and an Industry on a Great Lakes Town. Mary Frances Doner. LC 48-8042. 1948. Doubleday.
Ravenswood Hall. Angela Gray, pseud. 1973. pap. 0.95 o.s.i. (75-456). Lancer.
Ravenswyke. Alan White. LC 79-18862. 1980. 11.95 (ISBN 0-395-28589-5). Houghton Mifflin.
Raventree. Sarah Sloan. 1972. 4.95. Lenox Hill Pr.
Ravi Lancers: A Novel. John Masters. LC 73-182095. 1972. 7.95 (ISBN 0-385-09028-5). Doubleday.
Ravi Lancers: A Novel. John Masters. 1973. (pbk.) 1.50 (ISBN 0-671-78625-3). Pocket Books.
Raving Monarchist. Julian Rathbone. LC 77-9127. 1978. 7.95 (ISBN 0-312-66412-5). St. Martin's Press.
Ravished. Richard E. Geis. pap. 1.95 o.p. (0113). Essex Hse.
Ravished. Andrew Laird. pap. 1.95 o.s.i. (OPH-208, Ophelia). Olympia.
Ravishers. Merle L. Brown. 1970. 5.95 o.p. Bartholomew.
Ravishers. Merle Lynn Browne. LC 75-110741. 1970. 5.95. Bartholomew House.
Ravishers: A Novel of White Slavery in Its Heyday. By Anthony Kirkor Pseud Translated from the Polish. Antoni Marczynski. LC 55-321773. 1955. Ignis Co.
Ravishing Doctor. H. G. Gunther. (Gunther Ser.). pap. 1.95 (ISBN 0-515-05676-6). Jove Pubns.
Ravishing of Lol Stein. Marguerite Duras. LC 79-21724. 1979. 13.75 (ISBN 0-8357-0471-8). University Microfilms International.
Ravishing of Lol Stein. Tr. by Richard Seaver. Marguerite Duras. LC 65-14200. 1967. 3.95. Grove.
Ravola of Thunder Mountain. Royal Rosamond. LC 47-5501. 1947. Gem Pub. Co.
Raw Country. Lauran Paine. LC 67-8971. 1967. Arcadia House.
Raw Edge. Benjamin Appel. LC 58-52636. 1958. Random House.
Raw Edge. Edward Sefton Porter. LC 33-17931. 1933. D. Appleton-Century Company, Incorporated.
Raw Gold. James Beardsley Hendryx. LC 33-4992. 1933. Doubleday, Doran & Company, Inc.
Raw Gold. James Beardsley Hendryx. LC 43-4734. 1943. The Sun Dial Press.
Raw Gold. Clement Yore. LC 26-223077. (On cover: A pocket copyright. no. 68). 1926. Garden City Publishing Co., Inc.
Raw Gold, a Novel. Bertrand William Sinclair. 1908. G. W. Dillingham Company.
Raw Material. Dorothea Frances Canfield Fisher. LC 23-120046. Harcourt, Brace and Company.
Raw Material. Alan Sillitoe. 1973. 6.95 o.p. (ISBN 0-684-13385-7). Scribner.
Raw Passion. Charles Martin. 1979. pap. 1.75 (ISBN 0-8439-0695-2, Leisure Bks). Nordon Pubns.
Raw Silk: Janet Burroway. Janet Burroway. 1979. 2.50 (ISBN 0-671-82252-7). Pocket Books.
Raw Summer. Jane Blackmore. 1972. Dell.
Raw Youth. Fedor Mikhailovich Dostoevskii. Tr. by Constance Black Garnett. LC 47-2415. (Permanent library series). 1947. The Dial Press.
Raw Youth: A Novel in Three Parts. Fedor Mikhailovich Dostoevskii. Tr. by Constance Black Garnett. (Half-title: Novels of Fyodor Dostoevsky, vol. VII). 1916. The Macmillan Company.
Raw Youth: A Novel in Three Parts. Fedor Mikhailovich Dostoevskii & Garnett, Mrs. Constance (Black) 1862- Tr. LC 30-19636. (Half-title: The novels of Fyodor Dostoevsky. Vol. VII). 1923. The Macmillan Company.
Rawhide. Lucien Waldo Emerson. LC 36-100536. 1936. W. Morrow & Co.
Rawhide. Lee Floren. (O.s.i.). Orig. Title: Rawhide Summons. 1975. pap. 0.95 o.s.i. (BT50863). Belmont-Tower.
Rawhide Bound. Incidental Western Silhouettes by Ace Reid, Jr. 1st Ed. Ed Bateman. LC 50-56414. 1950. C. K. Wilson Co., Exclusive Distributors.
Rawhide Country. Farris Fletcher. (Texans Ser.: No. 1). 1982. pap. 2.95 (ISBN 0-440-07242-5). Dell.
Rawhide Gunman: A Western Novel. Willis Todhunter Ballard. LC 54-443616. (Popular library, 617). 1954. Popular Library.
Rawhide Guns. Frank Bonham. (Berkley Book). 1978. 1.50 (ISBN 0-425-03817-3). Berkley Pub. Corp.
Rawhide Johnny. Dane Coolidge. LC 36-3325. 1936. E. P. Dutton & Co., Inc.
Rawhide Justice. Max Brand. 186p. 1975. 5.95 o.p. (ISBN 0-396-07198-8). Dodd.
Rawhide Justice. Frederick Faust. (Kangaroo Book). 1977. 1.50 (ISBN 0-671-81055-3). Pocket Books.
Rawhide Justice. Frederick Faust. LC 75-31967. (Silver star westerns). 1976. (ISBN 0-396-07198-6). Dodd, Mead.
Rawhide Killer see Vengeance Rider.
Rawhide Knot and Other Stories. Conrad Richter. LC 78-1637. 1978. 8.95 (ISBN 0-394-50208-6). Knopf.
Rawhide Men. Lee Floren. (Orig.). 1979. pap. 1.50 (ISBN 0-532-15399-5). Woodhill.
Rawhide Men: By Members of the Western Writers of America. Ed. by Kenneth Fowler. Western Writers of America. Ed. by Kenneth Fowler. LC 65-110601. 3.95. Doubleday.
Rawhide Range. Wade Hamilton, pseud. 1978. pap. 1.25 (ISBN 0-532-12586-X). Woodhill.
Rawhide Range. Ernest Haycox. LC 52-65926. (Popular Library, 460). 1952. Popular Library.
Rawhide Rawlins Stories. Charles Marion Russell. LC 21-20539. 1921. Printed by Montana Newspaper Association.
Rawhide Rawlins Stories. Charles Marion Russell. LC 46-217833. 1946. Trail's End Publishing Co., Inc.
Rawhide Rider: A Powder Valley Western. Peter Field. LC 55-7122. 1955. Jefferson House.
Rawhide Roundup. William Frederick Bragg. LC 57-4127. 1957. Arcadia House.
Rawhide Roundup. William Frederick Bragg. LC 81-15187. (Atlantic large print). (Atlantic series). 1982. 11.95 (ISBN 0-89340-406-3). Chivers Press.
Rawhide Summons. Lee Floren. LC 47-24089. 1947. Phoenix Press.
Rawhide Summons see Rawhide.
Rawhide War. Frank Roderus. 1981. pap. 1.95 (ISBN 0-440-17284-5). Dell.
Rawhide Years. Norman A Fox. LC 53-840333. (Silver star westerns). 1953. Dodd, Mead.
Rawhider. Charles N Heckelmann. LC 52-6223. (Holt western). 1952. Holt.
Rawhider. Charles N. Heckelmann. 1979. 1.75 (ISBN 0-445-04340-7). Popular Library.
Rawhiders of the Brasada. Leonard London Foreman. 1977. 1.25. Ace Books.
Rawlins. Ron McClure. LC 76-37441. 1972. 6.95. Dial Press.
Rax. Michael G Coney. (DAW Books no. 170.). 1975. (pbk.) 1.25. DAW Books.
Ray. Barry Hannah. LC 81-10577. (Penguin Contemporary American Fiction Series). 1941. 3.95 (ISBN 0-14-005945-8). Penguin Books.
Ray: A Novel with the Original Characters of Spira, and Intended As Further Inspiration Toward Divine Life. Monroe E Miller. LC 41-27319. Press of H. L. & J. B. McQueen, Inc.
Ray Burton. A Chicago Tale. M Train. 1895.
Ray of Darkness: By Margiad Evans Pseud. Peggy Eileen Arabella Williams. LC 53-978064. 1953. Roy Publishers.
Raya. Frank King. 272p. 1981. pap. 2.95 (ISBN 0-441-70566-9). Ace Bks.
Raya: A Novel. Frank King. LC 79-26869. 10.95 (ISBN 0-399-90078-0). R. Marek.
Raymond and Agnes: Or, The Bleeding Nun. Matthew Gregory Lewis. LC 7-5029. (romancist and novelist's library. new ser., v. 4). 1841. J. Clements.
Raymond and Me That Summer. Dick Perry. LC 64-22670. 1964. Harcourt, Brace & World.
Raymond Chandler Omnibus: Four Famous Classics. Raymond Chandler. LC 64-14417. 1964. Knopf; Distributed by Random House.
Raymond Kershaw: A Story of Deserved Success. Maria McIntosh Cox. LC 6-28857. 1888. Roberts Brothers.
Raymonde. A Tale. Andre Theuriet. LC 8-277362. (Appletons' new handy-volume series v. 21). 1878. D. Appleton and Company.
Raymond's Atonement. Elisabeth Burstenbinder. Tr. by Tyrrell. Christina. (On cover: Seaside library. Pocket ed., no. 327). 1884. G. Munro.
Rayner--Slade Amalagamation. Joseph Smith Fletcher. LC 22-7438. 1922. A. A. Knopf.
Raynor-Moland Feud. Howard Ray Allgood. LC 18-20935. 1918. Saulsbury Publishing Company.
Rayo Que No Cesa. Miguel Hernandez. Bd. with Viento Del Pueblo; Silbo Vulnerado; Imagen De Tu Huella. pap. 1.50 o.s.i. French & Eur.
Ray's Daughter: A Story of Manila. Charles King. LC 6805. 1901. J. B. Lippincott Company.
Ray's Recruit. Charles King. LC 7-12214. 1898. J. B. Lippincott Company.
Rayton: A Backwoods Mystery. Roberts Theodore Goodridge. LC 12-2239. 1912. 1.25. L. C. Page & Company.
Razorback. Peter Brennan. 384p. (Orig.). 1981. pap. 2.95 (ISBN 0-515-05392-9). Jove Pubns.
Razor's Edge. William Somerset Maugham. LC 47-2347. 1946. Triangle Books, the Blakiston Company.
Razor's Edge: A Novel. William Somerset Maugham. LC 48-40654. 1945. Blakiston Co.
Razor's Edge: A Novel. William Somerset Maugham. LC 44-6503. 1944. Doubleday, Doran & Co., Inc.
Razor's Edge: A Novel. William Somerset Maugham. LC 44-40090. 1944. Doubleday, Doran & Co., Inc.
Razzle-Dazzle. Francis Wallace. LC 38-249084. M. S. Mill Co., Inc.
Razzmatazz: A Novel. Philip Wheaton. LC 80-12978. 12.95 (ISBN 0-89696-097-8). Everest House.
Re-Birth. John Beynon Harris. LC 70-107003. 1970. 4.95. Walker.
Re-Birth. John Wyndham, pseud. LC 70-107003. (Science Fiction Ser). 1970. Repr. 4.95 o.p. Oxford U Pr.
Re-Birth: By John Wyndham Pseud. John Beynon Harris. LC 55-9098. 1955. Ballantine Books.
Re: Colonized Planet 5-Shikasta. Doris May Lessing. LC 81-40194. 384p. 1981. pap. 5.95 (ISBN 0-394-74977-4, Vin). Random.
Re-Creation of Brian Kent: A Novel. Harold Bell Wright. LC 19-133702. 1919. The Book Supply Company.
Re-Creations. Grace Livingston Hill. LC 24-111411. 1924. J. B. Lippincott Company.
Re-Echo Club. Carolyn Wells. LC 13-21045. (Her Onyx series) $1.00.). Franklin Bigelow Corporation.
Re-Enter Sir John. Winifred Ashton & Simpson, Helen De Guerry, 1897- Joint Author. LC 32-19829. Farrar and Rinehart, Incorporated.
Re-Entry. Paul Preuss. (Orig.). 1981. pap. 2.25 (ISBN 0-553-14834-6). Bantam.
Re Joyce. Anthony Burgess. 1968. pap. 4.95 (ISBN 0-393-00445-7, Norton Lib). Norton.
Re-Told Tales of the Hills and Shores of Maine. Henrietta Gould Rowe. LC 8-935. 1892. D. Bugbee & Co.
Reach for Glory. Betty Ferm. (Fawcett Gold Medal Book). 1.75 (ISBN 0-449-13791-0). Fawcett Publications.
Reach for the Ground. Fernandez De la Reguera, Ricardo. LC 64-13927. 1964. Abelard-Schuman.
Reach for the Moon. Royce Brier. LC 34-31646. 1934. D. Appleton-Century Company, Incorporated.
Reach for the Shadows. Dwyer-Joyce, Alice. LC 73-84332. 1973. 6.95. St. Martin's Press.
Reach for the Shadows. Alice Dwyer-Joyce. 1975. (pbk.) 1.25. Bantam Books.
Reach for Tomorrow. Arthur Charles Clarke. LC 71-95869. 1970. Harcourt, Brace & World.
Reach for Tomorrow: Stories. Arthur Charles Clarke. LC 56-8164. 1956. Ballantine Books.
Reach of Fear. D. L. Mathews. LC 58-62553. 1958. Rinehart.
Reach Out for a Star & Grab the Devil: Two Tales of the World Beyond. Fred J. Edwards, Jr. 54p. 1975. 4.00 o.p. (ISBN 0-682-48227-7). Exposition.
Reach to Eternity. Dobrica Cosic. LC 79-2234. 14.95 (ISBN 0-15-175961-8). Harcourt Brace Jovanovich.
Reach to the Stars. Calder Willingham. LC 51-14302. 1951. Vanguard Press.
Reaching Hand. Andrew MacKenzie. LC 57-453560. (British bloodhound, no. 159). 1957. T. V. Boardman.
Read with Me. Ed. by Thomas Bertram Costain. LC 65-162634. 5.95. Doubleday.
Reader: I Married Him. Anne Green. LC 31-263591. 1931. E. P. Dutton & Co., Inc.
Reader in the Dickens World: Style and Response. Susan R Horton. LC 80-53031. 1981. 29.95 (ISBN 0-8229-1140-X). University of Pittsburgh Press.
Reader Is Warned. John Dickson Carr. LC 39-230411. 1939. W. Morrow and Company.
Reader's Choice Treasury. Together & Leland Davidson Case. LC 64-13817. 1964. Doubleday.
Reader's Digest Great True Stories of Crime & Detection. Readers Digest Editors. 5.95 o.p. (440180). Funk & W.
Reader's Digest Modern Short Story Classics of Suspense. LC 68-9449. (Illus.). 1968. Reader's Digest.
Reader's Digest Murder Case. Fulton Oursler. 1962. pap. 0.95 o.p. (02327, Collier). Macmillan.
Reader's Guide to Fritz Leiber. Jeff Frane. Ed. by Roger C. Scholbin. LC 80-22107. (Starmont Reader's Guides to Contemporary Science Fiction & Fantasy Authors Ser.: Vol. 8). (Illus., Orig.). 1980. 10.95x (ISBN 0-916732-02-9); pap. text ed. 4.95x (ISBN 0-916732-10-X). Starmont Hse.
Readiana. Charles Reade. LC 28-5193. (On cover: Lovell's library. v. 19, no. 919). 1887. J. W. Lovell Company.
Readiana: Comments on Current Events. Charles Reade. LC 28-5194. (On cover: The Seaside library. Pocket edition. no. 210). G. Munro.
Reading Modern Fiction: Thirty-One Stories with Critical Aids. 4th ed. Ed. by Winifred C. Lynskey. 1968. pap. text ed. 11.95x (ISBN 0-684-41341-8, ScribC). Scribner.
Reading Modern Fiction: 29 Stories with Study Aids. Rev. Ed. Ed. by Winifred C. Lynskey. LC 57-7588. 1957. Scribner.
Reading Modern Fiction: 31 Stories with Critical Aids. 4th ed. Ed. by Winifred C. Lynskey. LC 67-23690. 1968. Scribner.
Reading Modern Fiction: 31 Stories with Critical Aids, Edited by Winifred Lynskey. 4th Ed. Ed. by Winifred C. Lynskey. LC 67-23690. 1968. pap., 2.95. Scribners.
Reading Modern Fiction: 31 Stories with Critical Aids. 3d Ed. Ed. by Winifred C. Lynskey. LC 62-14023. 1962. Scribner.
Reading Modern Short Stories. Ed. by Jarvis A. Thurston. LC 55-697. (Key editions, 5F). 1955. Scott, Foresman.
Reading of Jane Austen. Barbara Nathan Hardy. LC 75-39852. (Gotham library). 1979. (ISBN 0-8147-3397-2). New York University Press.
Reading of Mr. Charles Dickens: As Condensed by Himself. David Copperfield and Mr. Bob Sawyer's Party (from Pickwick. Charles Dickens. LC 14-22451. 1868. Ticknor and Fields.
Reading the Novel: From Austen to E.M. Forster. Elizabeth Jean Higgins & Richard A. Long. LC 81-51490. 12.95 (ISBN 0-533-05072-3). Vantage Press.
Reading the Novel: The Adventures of Tom Sawyer, The Call of the Wild, Treasure Island Edited by Edward J. Gordon and Virginia T. Willinson. Ed. by Edward J. Gordon & Virginia T. Wilkinson. Clemens, Samuel Langborne, 1835-1916. The Adventures of Tom Sawyer et al. LC 67-13469. (Bulfinch edition). 1967. Ginn.
Reading the Short Story. Ed. by Harry Shaw. Bement, Douglas, 1898- Joint Ed. LC 41-51727. Harper & Brothers.
Reading the Short Story: By Harry Shaw and the Late Douglas Bement. 2d Ed. by Harry Shaw. Ed. by Harry Shaw & Douglas Bement. Harper.
Readings and Scenes from David Copperfield: Sixteen Readings and Twelve Scenes for Twelve Girls. Charles Dickens. Ed. by Selman, James Ella. LC 6-37049. 1898. E. S. Werner.
Readings for the Young at Heart. Laura M. Hawkes. 1978. pap. 3.50 (ISBN 0-89036-017-0). Hawkes Pub Inc.
Readings from the Waverley Novels. Walter Scott. Ed. by Blaisdell, Albert, Franklin. (On cover: Cambridge series of English classics). 1889. Lee and Shepard.
Readjustment. William Henry Irwin. LC 11-316. 1910. B. W. Huebsch.
Ready Blade: A Medieval Tapestry. A. Edwards Chapman. LC 34-24858. (Tired business man's library of adventure, detective, and mystery novels). 1934. D. Appleton-Century Company, Incorporated.
Ready for Death. Helen Joan Hultman. LC 39-31534. Phoenix Press.
Ready for Love. James Noble Gifford. LC 38-537293. Phoenix Press.
Ready for the Tiger. Sam Ross. LC 64-20234. 1964. Farrar, Straus.
Ready-Money Mortiboy: A Matter-of-Fact Story. Walter Besant & Rice, James. (Seaside library, v. 35, no. 726). 1880. G. Munro.
Ready-Money Mortiboy: A Matter-of-Fact Story. library ed.... ed. Walter Besant & Rice, James. LC 3-28170. 1888. Dodd, Mead & Co.
Ready or Not. Frank Scannell. 1968. 5.95 o.p. Crown.

Ready or Not. Mary Slattery Stolz. 1953. Harper.
Ready or Not: A Novel. Frank Scannell. LC 68-9087. 1968. 5.95. Crown Publishers.
Ready to Die. Jocko Fredericks. 1971. pap. 0.60 o.p. (06129). Curtis.
Ready to Love. Jeanne Bowman, pseud. (O.s.i.). 1976. pap. 0.95 o.s.i. (BT50931). Belmont-Tower.
Ready to Love. Peggy O'More, pseud. LC 65-7723. 1965. Arcadia House.
Ready-to-Use Floral Designs. Ed Sibbett, Jr. pap. 2.50 (ISBN 0-486-23976-4). Dover.
Ready to Wear. Claudia Cranston. LC 32-294993. 1932. Dodd, Mead & Company.
Real Adventure: A Novel. Henry Kitchell Webster. LC 16-26125. The Bobbs-Merrill Company.
Real Adventures of Robinson Crusoe. Francis Cowley Burnand. United States Book Company.
Real Agatha: The Unusual Adventures of Two Young Men and an Heiress. Edith Huntington Mason. LC 7-39194. 1907. A. C. McClurg & Co.
Real America in Romance. John Roy Musick. LC 8-5880. W. H. Wise & Company.
Real America in Romance... John Roy Musick & Markham, Edwin. LC 7-7521. 1907. W. H. Wise.
Real Charlotte. Edith Anna CEnone Somerville & Violet Florence Martin. LC 33-17488. 1911. Longmans, Green, and Co.
Real Charlotte. Edith Anne CEnone Somerville & Violet Florence Martin. LC 4-890. 1901. Longmans, Green, and Co.
Real Cool Killers. Chester B. Himes. (Coffin Ed and Grave Digger Jones series,#2). 1975. (pbk.) 1.25. New American Library.
Real Diary of the Worst Farmer. Henry Augustus Shute. LC 20-7300. 1920. Houghton Mifflin Company.
Real Duke: An Unauthorized Biography. Jackson Stanley. LC 69-17949. 1969. 5.95. Stein and Day.
Real Endings. Gene Duris. 1978. pap. 1.95 (ISBN 0-532-19186-2). Woodhill.
Real Gone Girls. Ted Mark, pseud. LC 75-101. (Man from O.R.G.Y. Ser). 1969. pap. 0.95 o.p. Lancer.
Real Gone Girls. Ted Mark. (man from ORGY). 1973. (pbk.) 1.25. Dell.
Real Gone Goose. Aaron Marc Stein. LC 59-9143. 1959. Published for the Crime Club by Doubleday.
Real Gone Guy. Frank Kane. LC 56-10179. 1956. Rinehart.
Real Issue. William Allen White. LC 72-98603. (Short Story Index Reprint Ser.). 1896. 15.00 (ISBN 0-8369-3177-7). Ayer Co.
Real Issue: A Book of Kansas Stories. William Allen White. LC 72-98603. (Short story index reprint series). 1969. Books for Libraries Press.
Real Issue: A Novel. William Allen White. LC 8-36565. 1896. Way and Williams.
Real Killing: A Novel. William Keegan. LC 76-28041. 1977. 7.95 (ISBN 0-312-66517-2). St. Martin's Press.
Real Lady Hilda: A Sketch. Bithia Mary Sheppard Croker. LC 99-1668. 1899. F. M. Buckles & Company; Etc., Etc.
Real Life. Mathilde Lippens Bourdon & Newlin, Miss, Tr. 1876. Kelly. Piet & Company.
Real Life. Deborah Pease. LC 78-139385. 1971. 5.95 (ISBN 0-393-08629-1). Norton.
Real Life: Into Which Miss Leda Swan of Hollywood Makes an Adventurous Excursion. Henry Kitchell Webster. LC 21-13059. The Bobbs-Merrill Company.
Real Life of Sebastian Knight. Vladimir Vladimirovich Nabokov. LC 59-94893. 1959. New Directions.
Real Life of Sebastian Knight. Vladimir Vladimirovich Nabokov. LC 42-2424. New Directions.
Real Life Sketches from Devon and Cornwall: Historical and Personal Reminiscences. Frank L Vosper. LC 3-9626. 1903. Jennings & Pye.
Real Losses, Imaginary Gains. Wright Morris. LC 75-33473. 8.95 (ISBN 0-06-013098-9). Harper & Row.
Real Man. Francis Lynde. LC 15-26505. 1915. C. Scribner's Sons.
Real Men Don't Eat Quiche. Bruce Feirstein. (Illus., Orig.). 1982. pap. 3.95 (ISBN 0-671-44831-5). PB.
Real Motive. Dorothea Frances Canfield Fisher. LC 16-119671. 1916. H. Holt and Company.
Real People. Alison Lurie. LC 69-16426. 1969. 4.95. Random House.
Real People. Marrion Wilcox. LC 8-37050. 1886. White, Stokes & Allen.
Real Presence: A Novel. Richard Bausch. LC 79-27136. 9.95 (ISBN 0-8037-7779-5). Dial Press.
Real Queen. Robert Edward Francillon. (On cover: Lovell's library, v. 6, no. 319). J. W. Lovell Company.
Real Queen. A Novel. Robert Edward Francillon. LC 6-43252. (Harper's Franklin square library, no. 368). Harper & Brothers.
Real Right Thing see Altar of the Dead.
Real Serendipitous Kill. Aaron Marc Stein. LC 64-22413. (Inner sanctum mystery). 1964. Simon and Schuster.
Real Serendiptitous Kill. Hampton Stone, pseud. (Hampton Stone Mystery Ser). 1971. pap. 0.75 o.p. (ISBN 0-446-64504-4, 64-504). Paperback Lib.
Real Silvestri. Mario Soldati. LC 60-53010. 1961. Knopf.
Real Spiro Agnew: Commonsense Quotations of a Household Word. Ed. by James Calhoun. 1970. 5.95 o.p. (ISBN 0-911116-29-X). Pelican.
Real Stuff. Katharine Haviland Taylor. LC 21-16316. 1921. Harcourt, Brace and Company.
Real Thing. Kurt Andersen. LC 81-7043. 192p. (Orig.). 1982. pap. 5.25 (ISBN 0-03-060037-5, Owl Bks). HR&W.
Real Thing. William Carney. LC 68-15502. 1968. Putnam.
Real Thing, and Other Tales. Henry James. LC 70-167453. (Short story index reprint series). 1971. (ISBN 0-8369-3979-4). Books for Libraries Press.
Real Thing: And Other Tales. Henry James. LC 7-7437. 1893. Macmillan and Co.
Real Thing, Man Out of Reach, Gone Before Morning. Mervyn Laurence Peake. (Harlequin Romances Ser.). 576p. 1982. pap. 3.50 (ISBN 0-373-20064-1). Harlequin Bks.
Real Time. Eve Sonneman. LC 76-48873. 1976. pap. text ed. 9.50 o.p. (ISBN 0-89439-008-2). Printed Matter.
Real World. Robert Herrick. LC 1-28214. 1901. The Macmillan Company.
Real World see Collected Works.
Realism. Damian Grant. (Critical Idiom Ser., Vol. 9). 1970. pap. 3.75x o.p. (ISBN 0-416-17820-0). B&N.
Realism & Romanticism in Fiction: An Approach to the Novel. Ed. by Eugene Current-Garcia & Walton R. Patrick. 1962. pap. 6.95x o.p. (ISBN 0-673-05400-4). Scott F.
Realistic American Short Fiction. Ed. by George B. Perkins. LC 73-175924. 1972. Scott, Foresman.
Realists. Chauncey Bradley Ives. LC 47-31046. 1947. Dodd, Mead.
Realite et Fantaisie: Neuf Nouvelles Modernes. Ed. by Anthony M. Nazzaro & Frank W. Lindsay. LC 73-138979. (Orig., Fr). 1971. pap. 6.95x o.p. (ISBN 0-471-00392-1). Wiley.
Realities. Marie Sofle Birath Schwartz. LC 81-8849. 1981. 13.95 (ISBN 0-312-66526-1). St. Martin's Press.
Realities of Life: Sketches Designed for the Improvement of the Head and Heart. By a Philanthropist. LC 7-30959. 1839. S. Babcock.
Reality. Paul Arnold Peterson. LC 67-13053. 1967. Dorrance.
Reality. Lilian L. Schalet. 70p. (Orig.). 1983. pap. 5.00 (ISBN 0-682-49940-4). Exposition.
Reality Doll. Clifford D. Simak. 1971. 4.95 o.p. Putnam.
Reality: Or, A History of Human Life.A Novel. Marie Louise Hankins. LC 7-1935. 1858. M. L. Hankins & Co.
Reality; or, The Millionaire's Daughter. A Book for Young Men and Young Women. Louisa Caroline Huggins Tuthill. LC 8-32318. 1856. C. Scribner.
Realization: A Novel. Edwina Sedgebury. LC 34-387152. 1934. Benziger Brothers.
Realized Ideal. Julia Magruder. LC 7-20129. 1898. H. S. Stone & Company.
Really, Frau Blum Would Very Much Like to Get to Know the Milkman. Peter Bischel. 1969. 4.75 o.p. (Sey Lawr). Delacorte.
Really Romantic Age. Lizzie Allen Harker. LC 23-48109. 1923. C. Scribner's Sons.
Really Sincere Guy. Robert Van Riper. LC 58-9804. 1958. D. McKay Co.
Realm of Fiction: Sixty Five Short Stories. 2nd ed. James B. Hall. 1970. pap. 7.50 o.p. (ISBN 0-07-025592-X, C). McGraw.
Realm of Fiction: Sixty-One Short Stories. Ed. by James B. Hall. (gr. 11 up). 1965. text ed. 4.50, s.p. 3.38 o.p.; teachers' manual 1.25, s.p. 1.00 o.p. McGraw.
Realm of Fiction: 61 Short Stories. Ed. by James B. Hall. LC 64-66022. 1965. McGraw-Hill.
Realm of Fiction: 74 Short Stories. 3d ed. Ed. by James B. Hall. Elizabeth C Hall. LC 76-53745. (Illus.). 7.95 (ISBN 0-07-025594-6). McGraw-Hill.
Realm of Light. Frank Hatfield. 1908. Reid Publishing Company; Etc., Etc.,
Realm of Numbers. Isaac Asimov. 144p. 1981. pap. 2.50 (ISBN 0-449-24399-0, Crest). Fawcett.
Realm of the Tri-Planets. K. H Scheer. (Perry Rhodan #31). 1973. (pbk.) 0.75. Ace Books.
Realms of Enchantment. Lorice F. Mulhern. 1970. 3.95 o.p. (ISBN 0-8059-1319-X). Dorrance.
Realms of Gold. Margaret Drabble. LC 75-8229. 1975. 8.95 (ISBN 0-394-49877-1). Knopf.
Realms of Gold. Margaret Drabble. 1.95 (ISBN 0-445-08554-1). Popular Library.
Realms of Tartarus. Brian M Stableford. 1977. 1.95 (ISBN 0-87997-309-9). DAW Books.
Realms of Wizardry. Ed. by Lin Carter. LC 76-2761. 7.95 (ISBN 0-385-11393-5). Doubleday.
Reamer Lou. Louis Forgione. LC 25-759. E. P. Dutton & Company.
Reap the Bitter Winds. June Shiplett. 1979. pap. 2.95 (ISBN 0-451-11690-9, AE1690, Sig). NAL.
Reap the Savage Wind. Ellen T. Marsh. 1982. pap. 4.95. Ace Bks.
Reap the Whirlwind. Edith Kneipple Roberts. LC 38-10193. 1938. The Bobbs-Merrill Company.
Reap the Whirlwind: Translated from the French by Elizabeth Abbott. Jean Hougron. LC 53-7615. 1953. Farrar, Straus and Young.
Reap the Wild Harvest. Elizabeth Bright. 2.75 (ISBN 0-671-83233-6). Pocket Books.
Reap the Wild Wind. Thelma Strabel. LC 42-575. 1941. Triangle Books.
Reaper. Martha Edith Rickert. LC 4-21725. 1904. Houghton, Mifflin and Company.
Reapers of the Storm: By Elizabeth Lyttleton and Herbert Sturz. Elizabeth Lyttleton & Herbert Sturz. LC 58-9718. 1958. Crowell.
Reaping. Edward Frederic Benson. LC 9-35805. 1909. Doubleday, Page and Company.
Reaping. Mary Imlay Taylor. LC 8-178119. 1908. Little, Brown and Company.
Reaping: A Novel. Bernard Taylor. LC 80-51898. 10.95 (ISBN 0-312-66528-8). St. Martin's Press.
Reaping the Whirlwind. Mary Cecil Hay. LC 7-375622. (On cover: Harper's half-hour series no. 66). 1878. Harper & Brothers.
Reaping the Whirlwind. Mamie A Roussel. LC 26-1450. 1924. Gem Publishing Company.
Reaping the Whirlwind: A Story of to-Day. Christine Faber. LC 6-3512. 1905. P. J. Kenedy & Sons.
Rear-View Mirror. Caroline B Cooney. LC 79-5544. 8.95 (ISBN 0-394-51054-2). Random House.
Reardon. Robert L. Pike, pseud. 1972. pap. 0.75 o.p. (07186). Curtis.
Reardon: A Police Procedural Novel. Robert L Fish. LC 79-97680. 1970. 4.95. Doubleday.
Rearguard. Thomas Compton Pakenham. LC 30-27754. 1930. A. A. Knopf.
Reason for Gladness. Mary Wallace. LC 65-219386. 4.95. Funk & Wagnalls.
Reason for Madness. Theodore S Drachman. LC 68-15223. (Raven book). 1970. Abelard-Schuman.
Reason for Roses. Babs H Deal. LC 73-81428. 1974. 6.95 (ISBN 0-385-05883-7). Doubleday.
Reason Why. Barbara Cartland & Elinor Sutherland Glyn. LC 80-146418. (Cartland, Barbara, 1902- Barbara Cartland's Library of Love: 6). 1979. 12.95 (ISBN 0-7156-1382-0). Duckworth.
Reason Why. Ethel M. Dell. 402p. Repr. of 1925 ed. lib. bdg. 19.70x (ISBN 0-88411-293-4). Amereon Ltd.
Reason Why. Elinor Sutherland Glyn. LC 11-23055. 1911. 1.30. D. Appleton and Company.
Reason Why: A Story of Fact and Fiction. Ernest E Russell. LC 8-1340. 1896. E. E. Russell.
Reason Why: A Story of Fact and Fiction. Ernest Emory Russell. LC 8-1340. 1896. E. E. Russell.
Reasonable Doubt. Edgar Smith. LC 74-119902. 1970. 6.95. Coward-McCann.
Reasonable Doubt. Dorothy Stockbridge Tillet. LC 51-10320. 1951. Published for the Crime Club by Doubleday.
Reasonable Shores. Gladys Bronwyn Stern. LC 46-25171. 1946. The Macmillan Company.
Reasons of State. Alejo Carpentier. LC 75-36816. 1976. 10.00 (ISBN 0-394-49909-3). Knopf.
Reat Los Angeles Blizzard: Thom Racina. 1978. 2.25 (ISBN 0-515-04718-X). Jove /HBJ.
Reata: Or, What's in a Name. Emily Gerard & Longard De Longgarde, Dorothea (Gerard) (Seaside library, v. 36, no. 747). 1880. G. Munro.
Reata Vengeance. Everal R Vaughn. 2.95. Arcadia House.
Reata: What's in a Name. A Novel. Emily Gerard & Longard De Longgarde, Dorothea (Gerard) (Franklin square library, no. 122). 1880. Harper & Brothers.
Reavers of Skaith. Leigh Brackett. LC 76-7345. 1976. 1.50. Ballantine Books.
Rebecca. Daphne Du Maurier. LC 38-27778. 1938. Doubleday, Doran and Company, Inc.
Rebecca. Daphne Du Maurier. LC 39-24230. 1939. Doubleday, Doran and Company Inc.
Rebecca. Daphne Du Maurier. 1940. Garden City Publishing Co., Inc.
Rebecca. Daphne Du Maurier. LC 42-7629. 1941. The Sun Dial Press.
Rebecca. Daphne Du Maurier. (Half-title: The Modern library of the world's best books). 1943. The Modern Library.
Rebecca McGregor. Kim Hansen. (Orig.). 1980. pap. text ed. 2.25 o.s.i. (ISBN 0-505-51582-2). Tower Bks.
Rebecca Mary. Annie Hamilton Donnell. LC 72-4455. (Short story index reprint series). (Illus.). 1972. (ISBN 0-8369-4173-X). Books for Libraries Press.
Rebecca Mary. Annie Hamilton Donnell. 1905. Harper & Brothers.
Rebecca Notebook and Other Memories. Daphne Du Maurier. LC 80-652. 1980. 12.50 (ISBN 0-385-15885-8). Doubleday.
Rebecca of Sunnybrook Farm. Kate Douglas Smith Wiggin. LC 3-23481. 1903. Houghton, Mifflin and Company.
Rebecca of Sunnybrook Farm. illustrated holiday ed. Kate Douglas Smith Wiggin. LC 10-23401. 1910. Houghton Mifflin Company.
Rebecca: Or, A Woman's Secret. Caroline Elizabeth Fairfield Corbin. LC 41-40968. 1868. Clarke and Company.
Rebecca: Or, A Woman's Secret. Caroline Elizabeth Fairfield Corbin. 1877. Jansen, McClurg & Co.
Rebecca: Rev. Ed. Daphne Du Maurier. (Reader's enrichment ser., RE316). Washington Sq.
Rebecca, the Mysterious. Katheryn Kimbrough, pseud. (Saga of the Phenwick Women: No. 7). 1975. pap. 1.75 (ISBN 0-445-00320-0). Popular Lib.
Rebecca the Wise. Josef Israels. LC 30-32337. 1930. Doubleday, Doran & Company, Inc.
Rebecca West: A Celebration. Rebecca West. 1978. pap. 5.95 (ISBN 0-14-004912-6). Penguin.
Rebecca's Daughters. Dylan Thomas. LC 82-7986. (Illus.). 160p. 1982. Repr. 8.50 (ISBN 0-8112-0852-4). New Directions.
Rebecca's Mother, Patricia. Russell Smith. pap. 1.95 o.s.i. (Venus). Grove.
Rebecca's Pride. Donald McNutt Douglass. LC 56-8778. 1956. Harper.
Rebecca's Promise. Frances Roberta Sterrett. LC 19-11712. 1919. D. Appleton and Company.
Rebekah: A Tale of Three Cities. M. P Jones. 1889. J. B. Alden.
Rebekka Moon. Michelle Spence. (Orig.). 1983. pap. 3.25 (ISBN 0-440-17099-0). Dell.
Rebel. Philip Merrill Marsh. LC 38-32861. 1938. Falmouth Book House.
Rebel Against Love. Elizabeth Ashton. (Harlequin Romances Ser.). 192p. 1981. pap. 1.50 (ISBN 0-373-02444-4). Harlequin Bks.
Rebel Against the Light. Alexander Ramati. LC 60-126963. 1960. Page.
Rebel Agent. James Lawrence. (Fawcett gold medal book). 1976. 1.75. Fawcett Publications, Inc.
Rebel Angel. Myrtle Smith. LC 47-19426. Moon-Hart Publishing Co.
Rebel Angels. William Robertson Davies. LC 81-51907. 1982. 13.95 (ISBN 0-670-59063-0). Viking Press.
Rebel Angels. William Robertson Davies. LC 82-15071. 1983. 3.95 (ISBN 0-14-006271-8). Penguin Books.
Rebel: Being a Memoir of Anthony, Fourth Earl of Cherwell; Including an Account of the Rising at Taunton in 1684. Ed. by Henry Brereton Marriott Watson. LC 1204. 1900. Harper & Brothers.
Rebel Bird. Desemea Wilson. LC 27-819. E. P. Dutton & Company.
Rebel Blood: A Novel. 1st Ed. V Ray Foster. LC 54-116875. 1954. New Exposition Press.
Rebel Bride. rev. ed. May Christie. Grosset & Dunlap.
Rebel Bride. Catherine Coulter. (Orig.). 1979. pap. 2.25 (ISBN 0-451-11719-0, AE1719, Sig). NAL.
Rebel Chief: A Tale. rev. and ed. by percy b. st. john. ed. Gustave Aimard & St. John, Percy Bolingbroke, 1821-1889, Ed. LC 5-42593. (On cover: Lovell's library, no. 1121). 1888. J. W. Lovell Company.
Rebel Doctor. Elizabeth Seifert. LC 78-6457. 7.95 (ISBN 0-396-07553-3). Dodd, Mead.
Rebel Doctor. Elizabeth Seifert. LC 79-957. 1981. 11.50 (ISBN 0-89340-202-8). J. Curley & Associates.
Rebel Drums. Nancy Faulkner, pseud. LC 52-5751. (Illus.). 1952. Doubleday.
Rebel General's Loyal Bride: A True Picture of Scenes in the Late Civil War. M A Avery. LC 6-3848. 1873. W. J. Holland and Company.
Rebel Generation. Jo Van Ammers-Kuller. Tr. by Hoper, M. W. LC 29-196510. E. P. Dutton & Co., Inc.
Rebel Gun. Arthur Steuer. LC 56-13166. (Dell first edition, A124). 1956. Dell Pub. Co.
Rebel Guns. A. A Baker. 1975. 4.95. Avalon Books.
Rebel Hawke. James Lawrence. (Fawcett Gold Medal Book). 1976. (pbk.) 1.50. Fawcett.
Rebel Heiress. Jane Aiken Hodge. LC 75-10474. 1975. 7.95 (ISBN 0-698-10690-3). Coward, McCann & Geoghegan.
Rebel Heiress. Robert Neill. LC 54-5165. 1954. Doubleday.
Rebel in Blue. Herman Toepperwein. LC 63-17681. 378p. 1973. pap. 1.95. Adm Nimitz Foun.

Rebel in Blue: A Novel of the Southwest Frontier, 1861-1864. Herman Toepperwein. LC 72-192983. (Illus.). 1972. Admiral Nimitz Foundation.
Rebel in His Arms. Francine Rivers. 380p. 1982. pap. 3.50 (ISBN 0-441-70885-4). Ace Bks.
Rebel in Love. Rochel Denore. (Americana Romance). 1978. 1.25 (ISBN 0-441-70886-2). Ace Books.
Rebel in Time. Harry Harrison. 320p. 1983. pap. 3.50 (ISBN 0-523-48554-9). Pinnacle Bks.
Rebel Lover. Paula Allardyce, pseud. LC 79-89490. 1979. pap. 1.75 (ISBN 0-87216-568-X). Playboy Pbks.
Rebel Loyalist. Charles William Gordon. LC 35-32772. 1935. Dodd, Mead & Company.
Rebel of Antares. Dray Prescot. 1980. 1.95 (ISBN 0-87997-582-2). DAW Books.
Rebel of Ronde Valley. Charles Horace Snow. LC 43-126872. 1943. Macrae-Smith Company.
Rebel of the Family. A Novel. Elizabeth Lynn Linton. (Franklin square library. no. 154). 1880. Harper & Brothers.
Rebel on the Range. Charles Horace Snow. LC 38-31282. The Greystone Press.
Rebel Outlaw: Josey Wales. Forrest Carter. LC 74-154369. 1973. 4.95. Whipporwill Publishers.
Rebel Passion. Katharine Burdekin. LC 29-184177. 1929. W. Morrow & Company.
Rebel Preacher. Ruby A. Newman. LC 78-70488. 1979. pap. 2.00 (ISBN 0-932964-02-8). MN Pubs.
Rebel Pride. Sylvie F. Sommerfield. 512p. (Orig.). 1980. pap. 2.75 (ISBN 0-89083-691-4). Zebra.
Rebel Princess. Eve Stephens, pseud. (Signet book, Y5801). 1974. (pbk.) 1.25. New American Library.
Rebel Princess: By Evelyn Anthony Pseud. Eve Stephens, pseud. LC 53-8428. 1953. Crowell.
Rebel Queen. Walter Besant. LC 74-27964. (Modern Jewish Experience). (Illus.). 1975. 27.00. Arno Press.
Rebel Queen: A Novel. Walter Besant. LC 6-12388. 1893. Harper & Brothers.
Rebel Raider. Cover Painting by Leslie Ross. Joseph Chadwick. LC 55-205358. (Gold medal books, 442). 1954. Fawcett Publications.
Rebel Ramrod. Dean Owen. 160p. 1974. pap. 0.95 (ISBN 0-532-12466-9). Woodhill.
Rebel Ranger. William Colt MacDonald. LC 43-51174. 1943. Doubleday, Doran & Co., Inc.
Rebel Ranger. Sidney Edgerton Whitman. LC 57-9985. 1957. Houghton Mifflin.
Rebel Rapture. Anne Gaynor. 1983. pap. 3.50 (ISBN 0-8217-1136-9). Zebra.
Rebel Rose. Ishbel Ross. LC 54-8986. 1981. pap. 2.25 (ISBN 0-89176-026-1). Mockingbird Bks.
Rebel Rose: A Novel... Justin McCarthy & Praed, Rosa Caroline (Murray-Prior) "Mrs. Campbell Praed," 1851- Joint Author. LC 7-15287. (On cover: Harper's Franklin square library, no. 627). 1888. Harper & Brothers.
Rebel Saints. Mary A. Best. 333p. 1980. Repr. lib. bdg. 17.50 o.p. (ISBN 0-89984-053-1). Century Bookbindery.
Rebel Seige. James Arthur Kjelgaard. LC 43-51297. 1943. Holiday House.
Rebel Spy: Or, The King's Volunteers. A Romance of the Siege of Boston. John Hovey Robinson. LC 7-421651. 1852. F. Gleason's Publishing Hall.
Rebel to Judgement. Anthony C. West. 1963. pap. 0.60 o.p. (60-279). Manor Bks.
Rebel to Judgment: A Novel. Anthony C West. LC 62-108073. 1962. I. Obolensky.
Rebel Town. Jack Zavada. 240p. 1981. pap. 1.95 (ISBN 0-441-71066-2). Ace Bks.
Rebel Town. Jack Zavada. 1976. 1.50. Ace Books.
Rebel Trail. Newton, Dwight Bennett. LC 63-20506. (Double D western). 1963. Doubleday.
Rebel Wench. Cover Painting by Walter Baumhofer. Gardner F Fox. LC 55-37191. (Gold medal books, 484). Fawcett Publications.
Rebel Women. Evelyn Sharp. LC 1-277408. 1910. John Lane Company.
Rebel Worlds. Poul Anderson. LC 79-12730. (Gregg Press science fiction series). (Illus.). 1979. 12.50 (ISBN 0-8398-2525-0). Gregg Press.
Rebel Yell. Leslie Charles Ernenwein. LC 48-3504. 1948. E. P. Dutton.
Rebel Yell. Leslie Charles Ernenwein. 1979. pap. 1.25 o.s.i. (ISBN 0-505-51358-7). Tower Bks.
Rebelled Against Love. E. J. Barnes. 4.75 o.p. (ISBN 0-8062-0981-X). Carlton.
Rebellion. Mateel Howe Farnham. LC 27-24008. 1927. Dodd, Mead and Company.
Rebellion. Joseph Medill Patterson. LC 11-259922. 1911. 1.25. The Reilly & Britton Co.
Rebellion at Cripple Creek. Jack Ehrlich, pseud. 1979. 1.75 (ISBN 0-671-81942-9). Pocket Books.
Rebellion of Lennie Barlow. Philip Duffield Stong. LC 37-28476. Farrar & Rinehart, Inc.
Rebellion of Leo McGuire. Clyde Brion Davis. LC 44-487589. 1944. Farrar & Rinehart, Inc.
Rebellion of the Hanged. B Traven. LC 51-11974. 1952. Knopf.
Rebellion of the Hanged. B Traven. LC 74-185432. 1972. 6.95 (ISBN 0-8090-8046-X). Hill and Wang.
Rebellion of the Lost. Henry Jaeger. LC 69-15276. 1970. 6.95 o.p. (ISBN 0-06-012168-8, HarpT). Har-Row.
Rebellion of the Princess. Mary Imlay Taylor. LC 3-7160. 1903. McClure, Phillips & Co.
Rebellion of Yale Marratt. Robert H Rimmer. LC 64-16411. 1964. Challenge Press.
Rebellion Road: By Helen Topping Miller and John Dewey Topping. 1st Ed. Helen Topping Miller & John Dewey Topping. LC 54-6497. 1954. Bobbs--Merrill.
Rebellious Heroine. John Kendrick Bangs. 1973. Repr. of 1896 ed. 12.50 (ISBN 0-8274-1491-9). R West.
Rebellious Heroine. A Story. John Kendrick Bangs. LC 6-6120. 1896. Harper & Brothers.
Rebellious Love. Maura Seger. 1983. pap. 2.50. PB.
Rebellious Rapture. Jane Archer. 448p. (Orig.). 1980. pap. 2.50 (ISBN 0-345-28262-0). Ballantine.
Rebellious Stars. Original Title. The Stars, Like Dust. Isaac Asimov. LC 55-188206. (Ace double novel books. D-84). 1954. Ace Books.
Rebels. book club ed.. ed. John W. Jakes. LC 78-105283. (Jakes, John W., 1932-. The American Bicentennial Ser.). (HIS The Kent chronicles; v. 2: Vol. 2). (Illus.). 1977. 3.99. N. Doubleday.
Rebels. Alfred Neumann. Tr. by Paterson, Huntley. LC 29-152859. 1929. A. A. Knopf.
Rebels and Assassins Die Hard. George G Gilman. (Adam Steele,#1). 1975. (pbk.) 1.25 (ISBN 0-523-00558-X). Pinnacle Books.
Rebels & Redcoats. George F. Scheer & Hugh F. Rankin. LC 56-9263. 1972. 6.95 o.p. (ISBN 0-690-00364-1). T Y Crowell.
Rebels and Tories: Or, The Blood of the Mohawk! A Tale of the American Revolution... Lawrence Labree. LC 7-14769. Dewitt & Davenport.
Rebel's Daughter: A Story of Love, Politics and War. John Gabriel Woerner. LC 211. 1899. Little, Brown & Co.
Rebel's Daughter. 1st Ed. Florence Mary Bennett Anderson. LC 57-8831. 1957. Vantage Press.
Rebels in the Shadows. Robert T Reilly. LC 62-200185. 1962. Bruce Pub. Co.
Rebels of Sabrehill. Raymond Giles. 1977. pap. 2.75 (ISBN 0-449-13695-7, GM). Fawcett.
Rebels of Sabrehill. Raymond Giles. (Gold Medal) (ISBN 0-449-13695-7). Fawcett.
Rebels of the New South. Walter Marion Raymond. LC 72-2027. (Black Heritage Library Collection). (Illus.). 1972. 13.50 (ISBN 0-8369-9055-2). Books for Libraries Press.
Rebels of the New South. Walter Marion Raymond. LC 4-35725. 1905. C. H. Kerr & Company.
Rebels: Or, Boston Before the Revolution. Lydia Maria Francis Child. 1825. Cummings, Hilliard, and Company.
Rebels: Or, Boston Before the Revolution. Lydia Maria Francis Child. 1850. Phillips, Sampson & Company.
Rebels Passion. Andrea Layton, pseud. LC 81-83260. 320p. (Orig.). 1982. pap. 2.95 (ISBN 0-87216-994-4). Playboy Pbks.
Rebels Rapture. Pamela Windsor. (Berkely Medallion book). 1979. 1.95 (ISBN 0-425-04129-8). Berkely Pub. Corp.
Rebels' Rendezvous. Lee Forest, pseud. LC 37-5403. 1937. D. Appleton-Century Company, Incorporated.
Rebel's Return. Edwin Booth. LC 81-17261. (Atlantic series). 1982. 11.95 (ISBN 0-89340-416-0). J. Curley & Associates.
Rebels Ride Proudly. Leslie Charles Ernenwein. LC 49-7615. (Dutton Diamond D Western). 1949. E. P. Dutton.
Rebels Roundup: A Texas Western of the Post-Confederacy. William Edmunds Claussen. LC 52-10720. 1959. Abelard Press.
Rebirth of Venkata Reddi. A Story of India. Pearl Dorr Longley. LC 39-14796. The Judson Press.
Rebirth: When Everyone Forgot. Thomas Calvert McClary. LC 75-28860. (Classics of science fiction). 1976. 10.50. (ISBN 0-88355-373-2) (ISBN 0-88355-459-3). Hyperion Press.
Rebirth, When Everyone Forgot. Thomas Calvert McClary. LC 44-9793. 1944. Bartholomew House, Inc.
Reborn. Leonard Simon. 256p. 1980. pap. 2.50 (ISBN 0-425-04507-2). Berkley Pub.
Reborn: A Novel. Leonard Simon. LC 78-57333. 9.95 (ISBN 0-87795-202-7). Arbor House.
Rebound. Freeman Lincoln. LC 36-1007. Coward-McCann.
Recall. Thomas Page. LC 79-4881. 9.95 (ISBN 0-87223-542-4). Seaview Books.
Recall. Thomas Walker. 320p. 1982. pap. 3.25 (ISBN 0-445-04725-9). Popular Lib.
Recalled to Life. Grant Allen. LC 6-482. (Leisure hour series)). 1891. Holt and Company.
Recalled to Life. Robert Silverberg. 1.75. Ace Books.
Recalled to Life. Robert Silverberg. LC 70-186042. (Doubleday science fiction). 1972. 4.95. Doubleday.
Recapitulation. Wallace Earle Stegner. 1980. 2.50 (ISBN 0-449-24263-3). Fawcett Crest Books.
Recapitulation. Wallace Earle Stegner. LC 78-8203. 1979. 8.95 (ISBN 0-385-11580-6). Doubleday.
Recapture a Dream. Ellen Harris. (Orig.). Date not set. pap. 1.75 (ISBN 0-440-17403-1). Dell.
Recapture the Moon. Sylvia Thompson. LC 37-17233. 1937. Little, Brown and Company.
Recaptured. Sidonie Gabrielle Colette. Tr. by Garvin, Viola Gerard. LC 32-965. 1932. Doubleday, Doran & Company, Inc.
Receive the Gale. Frances Gillespy Wickes. LC 46-4804. 1946. D. Appleton-Century Company, Inc.
Receiver. Hamilton Maule. LC 68-29631. 1968. 4.50. D. McKay Co.
Recent Remarkable Discoveries in Central Africa. LC 7-30957. Barclay & Co.
Recent Stories for Enjoyment. Ed. by Howard Francis Seely. Roling, Margaret, Joint Ed. LC 37-5108. Silver, Burdett Company.
Reception. Margaret Pargeter. (Harlequin Romances Ser.). 192p. 1981. pap. 1.25 (ISBN 0-373-02416-9, Pub. by Harlequin). PB.
Receptionist. James Noble Gifford. LC 37-18256. Phoenix Press.
Recess for the Teacher. Jeanne Bowman, pseud. 1972. pap. 0.75 o.s.i. (01-359). Lancer.
Recess, or, a Tale of Other Times, 3 Vols. Sophia Lee. LC 77-131325. (Gothic Novels Ser). 1971. Repr. of 1783 ed. Set. 38.00 (ISBN 0-405-00806-6). Ayer Co.
Recipe for Diamonds. Charles John Cutcliffe Wright Hyne. LC 7-8850. (On cover: Appletons' town and country library, 129). 1893. D. Appleton and Company.
Recipe for Homicide. Lawrence Goldtree Blochman. LC 52-5633. (Main line mysteries). 1952. Lippincott.
Recipe for Murder. Jeffrey Ashford, pseud. 152p. 1980. 8.95 (ISBN 0-8027-5423-6). Walker & Co.
Reciprocity: A Story of Love and Mining. Asenath Carver Coolidge. LC 11-261783. 1911. 1.00. Hungerford-Holbrook Company.
Reckless. Helen Marion Edginton. The Macaulay Company.
Reckless. Jeanette M. Ryan. 176p. 1983. pap. 2.25 (ISBN 0-380-83717-X, Flare). Avon.
Reckless Angel. Marie Adelaide Belloc Lowndes. LC 39-316847. 1939. Longmans, Green and Co.
Reckless Character: And Other Stories. Ivan Sergeevich Turgenev. Tr. by Isabel Florence Hapgood. LC 78-178465. (His Novels and stories). (Short story index reprint series). (Illus.). 1971. (ISBN 0-8369-4066-0). Books for Libraries Press.
Reckless Company. Frederick W De Valda. LC 35-867460. 1934. T. Nelson and Sons, Ltd.
Reckless Era. James McKinley Bryant. 1968. pap. 5.50. J M Bryant.
Reckless Era. James McKinley Bryant. LC 69-17330. pap. 5.50. Rocket Pub Co.
Reckless Fires. Kaye Wilson Klein. (Fawcett Gold Medal Book). 1.95 (ISBN 0-449-13939-5). Fawcett Books.
Reckless Heart. Katherine G Pollock. LC 51-11770. 1951. Doubleday.
Reckless Hollywood. Haynes Lubou. LC 33-3216. Amour Press, Inc.
Reckless Lady. Elinore Denniston. LC 73-7493. (Red badge novel of suspense). 1973. 4.95 (ISBN 0-396-06853-7). Dodd, Mead.
Reckless Lady. Rae Foley. 216p. 1973. 4.95 o.p. (ISBN 0-396-06853-7). Dodd.
Reckless Lady. Rae Foley. 1975. (pbk.) 0.95. Dell.
Reckless Lady. Philip Hamilton Gibbs. LC 25-26330. George H. Doran Company.
Reckless Lady. Philip Hamilton Gibbs. LC 42-28980. 1925. Grosset & Dunlap.
Reckless Lady. Mira Stables. 1974. pap. 0.95 o.p. (26572-095). Beagle Bks.
Reckless Longing. Daisy Logan. (Second Chance at Love Ser.: No. 50). (Orig.). 1982. pap. 1.75 (ISBN 0-515-06544-7). Jove Pubns.
Reckless Lovers. Barry Caldwell. LC 35-15323. Godwin.
Reckless Men. 1st Ed. Clifton Adams. LC 62-15919. (Double D western). 1962. Doubleday.
Reckless, Pride of the Marines. Introd. by R. McC. Pate; Foreword by E. A. Pollock. 1st Ed. Andrew Clare Geer. LC 55-5642. 1955. Dutton.
Reckless Puritan. Jessie Louisa Moore Rickard. LC 21-2590. G. H. Doran Co.
Reckless Puritan. Jessie Louisa Moore Rickard. LC 21-2590. George H. Doran Company.
Reckless Range. Johnston McCulley. The Dodge Publishing Company.
Reckless Rapture. Gayle O'Brian. 1983. pap. 3.50 (ISBN 0-8217-1157-1). Zebra.
Reckless Wager. Nella J. Benson. 160p. (Orig.). 1980. pap. 2.25 (ISBN 0-553-13973-8). Bantam.
Reckless Wedding. Maria Flook. 1982. 12.95 (ISBN 0-395-32507-2); pap. 5.95 (ISBN 0-395-32508-0). HM.
Reckon with the River. Clark McMeekin. LC 41-51702. 1941. D. Appleton-Century Company, Incorporated.
Reckoning. Hugh Atkinson. LC 70-190279. 1972. 4.95. D. McKay Co.
Reckoning. Robert William Chambers. LC 5-32684. 1905. D. Appleton and Company.
Reckoning. Robert William Chambers. 1907. A. Wessels Company.
Reckoning. Joan Conquest. The Macaulay Company.
Reckoning. Charles H Downing. LC 27-18432. 1927. Calif., Gem Publishing Company.
Reckoning. Aaron Fletcher. 192p. 1981. pap. 1.95 (ISBN 0-8439-0963-3, Leisure Bks). Nordon Pubns.
Reckoning. May Sarton. 256p. 1981. pap. 3.95 (ISBN 0-393-00075-3). Norton.
Reckoning. Leane Zugsmith. LC 34-568919. 1934. H. Smith & R. Hass.
Reckoning, a Novel. Charles E Mercer. LC 62-129541. 1962. Putnam.
Reckoning: A Novel. May Sarton. LC 78-9691. 9.95. Norton.
Reckoning at Yankee Flat: By Will Henry Pseud. Henry Allen. LC 58-5278. 1958. Random House.
Reckoning Frontier. 1st Ed. Nellie B Noyce. LC 57-7818. 1957. Vantage Press.
Reckoning: The Daily Ledgers of Newman Yagodah, Advokat Sic and Factor. Richard M Elman. LC 70-81370. 1969. 5.95. Scribner.
Reclaimed: Or, The Mountain Castle Mystery; an International Romance. J J Gray. LC 8-2609. Broadway Publishing Company.
Reclaimed: The Story of a Parish, Rendered from the Swedish of Hillis Grane Pseud. J. J. Gray & Olson, Ernst Wilheim, 1870- Tr. LC 20-14760. Augustana Book Concern.
Reclaimers. Margaret Hill McCarter. LC 18-20781. 1918. Harper & Brothers.
Reclamation: A Novel. Edward Thomas Glover. LC 30-13801. Dorrance & Company.
Reclamation of Wales: A Patriotic Romance Founded of Facts; a Sequel to "Dear Old Wales". Ivan Morgan Merlinjones. LC 13-469. 1912. 0.50. E. S. Gorham.
Reclamation of Wales: A Patriotic Romance Founded on Facts; a Sequel to "Dear Old Wales". Ivan Morgan Merlinjones. LC 13-3814. 1913. 0.75. E. S. Gorham.
Reclining Figure: By Marco Page Pseud. Harry Kurnitz. LC 52-5145. 1952. Random House.
Reclining Nude. Claudia Riess. LC 82-10589. 1982. 14.95 (ISBN 0-8128-2869-0). Stein and Day.
Recluse of Fifth Avenue. Wyndham Martyn. LC 29-5228. 1929. R. M. McBride & Company.
Recluse of Norway. Anna Maria Porter. LC 25-23768. 1815. Printed.
Recluse of Rambouillet. Just Jean Etienne Roy. LC 8-955. 1873. D. & J. Sadlier & Co.
Recluse of the Conewaga: Or, The Little Valley of the Blue Spring. A Legend of Adams County. William Tell Barnitz. 1853. E. Cornman, Printer.
Recognitions: A Novel. 1st Ed. William Gaddis. LC 55-524711. 1955. Harcourt, Brace.
Recoil. Brian Wynne Garfield. LC 76-45211. 1977. 8.95 (ISBN 0-688-03158-7). Morrow.
Recoil. Jocelyn Lee Hardy. 1936. Doubleday, Doran & Company, Inc.
Recoiling Vengeance. Frank Barrett. LC 26-3676. (On cover: Appleton's town and country library, no. 24). 1888. D. Appleton and Company.
Recoiling Vengeance. Frank Barrett. LC 6-8663. (On cover: Seaside library. Pocket ed. no. 112). 1888. G. Munro.
Recoiling Vengeance. Frank Barrett. LC 7-22755. United States Book Company.
Recollection Creek. 1st Ed. Frederick Benjamin Gipson. LC 54-12177. Harper.
Recollection of a Journey: A Novel. Ray Coryton Hutchinson. LC 74-180646. 1973. 1.95 (ISBN 0-85617-756-3). White Lion Publishers.
Recollections of a New England Bride: And of a Southern Matron. new ed., rev. ed. Caroline Howard Gilman. LC 6-44035. 1852. G. P. Putnam & Co.
Recollections of a Night. Kizhakkethalakkal Mathan Tharakan Tharakan. LC 76-905848. 1976. 3.00. Christian Literature Society.
Recollections of a Policeman. William Russell. LC 32-19523. 1861. Thayer and Eldridge.
Recollections of a Rotten Kid: A Novel. Joan Dim. LC 74-6530. 6.95 (ISBN 0-672-52024-9). Bobbs-Merrill.
Recollections of a Southern Matron. Caroline Howard Gilman. LC 6-44035. 1838. Harper & Brothers.
Recollections of a Southern Matron. Caroline Howard Gilman. LC 17-23017. 1839. Harper & Brothers.

TITLE INDEX RED BELLS.

Recollections of a Southern Matron. Caroline Howard Gilman. LC 34-28853. 1852. Walker, Richards and Co.
Recollections of Auton House... 8th impression ed. Augustus Hoppin. LC 5-18473. Houghton, Mifflin and Company.
Recollections of Geoffry Hamlyn. Henry Kingsley. (On cover: Lovell's library, v. 14, no. 736). 1886. J. W. Lovell Company.
Recollections of Geoffry Hamlyn. Henry Kingsley. LC 7-12523. 1894. C. Scribner's Sons.
Recollections of Geoffry Hamlyn. Henry Kingsley. LC 36-37187. (Half-title: Everyman's library, ed. by Ernest Rhys. Fiction. no. 416). 1924. J. M. Dent & Sons, Ltd.
Recollections of Geoffry Hamlyn. Henry Kingsley. LC 25-26581. (Half-title: The World's classics. CCLXXI). 1924. H. Milford.
Recollections of Geoffry Hamlyn. Henry Kingsley & Shorter, Clement King, 1857-1926. LC 4-16541. 1899. Longmans, Green & Co.
Recollections of James Clinton. James Clinton. 1972. pap. 1.75 o.p. (V1081K, Venus). Grove.
Recollections of Roderic Fyfe. John Oxenham, pseud. LC 27-10055. 1927. Longmans, Green, and Co., Ltd.
Recollections of the Old Quarter. William Clair Gordon. LC 75-39084. (Black Heritage Library Collection). (Illus.). 1972. (ISBN 0-8369-9022-6). Books for Libraries Press.
Recollections of the Old Quarter. William St. Clair Gordon. LC 2-30266. 1902. Moose Bros. Company.
Recollections of the United States Army. A Series of Thrilling Tales and Sketches. LC 7-30955. 1845. J. Munroe and Company.
Recollections of Things to Come. Elena Garro. LC 76-93099. (Texas pan American series). 1969. 6.50. University of Texas Press.
Recompense, a Sequel to "Simon Called Peter". Robert Keable. LC 24-7674. 1924. 2.00. G. P. Putnam's Sons.
Reconciled: A Story of Common Life. Martha Penman. LC 946. (On cover: The Quarterly economist. v. 1, no. 3). 1900. F. Vierth.
Reconciliations. Elizabeth Klein. LC 81-19192. 1982. 14.95 (ISBN 0-395-32048-8). Houghton Mifflin.
Reconnaissance. Gordon Gardiner. LC 14-3288. 1914. The Macmillan Company.
Reconstructed Marriage. Amelia Edith Huddleston Barr. LC 10-22057. 1910. 1.25. Dodd, Mead and Company.
Reconstructing Eden. Howard Louis Conard. LC 9-74362. 1909. New Eden Publishing Co.
Reconstruction. De Witt C Hill. LC 26-135347. 1926. Printed by Chicago Legal News Co.
Reconstruction of Elinore Wood. Florenz S Merrow. LC 11-726425. 1.50. Broadway Publishing Co.
Record Apart. Richard Heron. 1974. 12.50x (ISBN 0-7073-0147-5, Pub. by Scottish Academic Pr Scotland). Columbia U Pr.
Record No. 33. Ida Clyde Gallagher Clarke. LC 15-18111. 1915. 1.30. D. Appleton and Company.
Record of a Ministering Angel. Mary J Clark. LC 6-21464. 1885. Belford, Clarke & Co.
Record of a Silent Life. Anna Preston. LC 13-1488. 1912. 1.25. B. W. Huebsch.
Record of an Abscure Man... Mary Traill Spence Lowell Putnam. LC 7-42402. 1861. Ticknor and Fields.
Record of an Obscure Man. Mary Lowell Putnam. LC 70-82213. (Anti-Slavery Crusade in America). 1969. Arno Press.
Recording Angel. Corra May White Harris. LC 12-117106. 1912. 1.25. Doubleday, Page & Company.
Recording Angel. Corra May White Harris. LC 26-16263. (The Lambskin library, 52). 1926. Doubleday, Page & Company.
Recording Angel: A Novel. Edwin Arnold Brenholtz. LC 5-11350. 1905. C. H. Kerr & Company.
Records of a Good Man's Life. 2d ed. Charles Benjamin Tayler. LC 8-20124. (On cover: C. B. Tayler's works). 1851. Stanford and Swords.
Records of a Good Man's Life. By the Rev. Charles B. Tayler... Charles Benjamin Tayler. LC 14-22453. 1832. W. Van Norden.
Records of the Bubbleton Parish: Or, Papers from the Experience of an American Minister. With Illustrations by Billings... Elhanan Winchester Reynolds. LC 7-30599. 1854. A Tompkins and B. B. Mussey & Co.
Recovered Continent: A Tale of the Chinese Invasion. Oto Mundo. LC 98-1416. 1898. The Harper-Osgood Co.
Recovery. John Berryman. LC 72-84779. 1973. 6.95 (ISBN 0-374-24817-6). Farrar, Straus and Giroux.
Recovery. warner books ed. Steven L Thompson. LC 80-12706. (Illus.). 8.95 (ISBN 0-446-51207-9). Warner Books.
Recovery: A Story of Kentucky. Joseph Alexander Altsheler. LC 9-113. F. F. Lovell Company.
Recreation Hall: A Novel. Richard Jessup. LC 67-23833. 1967. Little, Brown.
Recreations of a Psychologist. Granville Stanley Hall. LC 20-20441. 1920. D. Appleton and Company.
Recruit for Abe Lincoln. Maribelle Cormack. LC 42-24741. 1942. D. Appleton-Century Company, Incorporated.
Recruits for Arkon. Clark Darlton. (Perry Rhodan#76). (Illus.). 1975. (pbk.) 1.25. Ace Books.
Rector. Virginia Gay. LC 79-7110. 1980. 8.95 (ISBN 0-385-15218-3). Doubleday.
Rector. Virginia Gay. LC 80-24539. 1981. 11.50 (ISBN 0-89340-305-9). J. Curley & Associates.
Rector and the Doctor's Family. Margaret Oliphant Wilson Oliphant. LC 75-1543. (Victorian Fiction: Novels of Faith and Doubt; V. 89). 1975. 35.00 (ISBN 0-8240-1613-0). Garland Pub.
Rector of Justin. Louis Auchincloss. LC 67-31846. (Modern Library book, 383). 1967. Modern Library.
Rector of Justin. Louis Auchincloss. 1974. (pbk.) 1.25. Avon.
Rector of Justin. Louis Auchincloss. LC 64-14523. 1964. Houghton Mifflin.
Rector of Justin. Louis Auchincloss. LC 79-25874. 1980. 3.95 (ISBN 0-395-29179-8). Houghton Mifflin.
Rector of St. Bardolph's: Or, Superannuated. Frederick William Shelton. LC 8-5106. 1853. C. Scribner.
Rector of St. Bardolph's, or, Superannuated. Frederick William Shelton. LC 8-5107. 1856. Dana and Company; Etc., Etc.
Rector of St. Bardolph's, or, Superannuated. Frederick William Shelton. LC 8-11234. 1882. T. Whittaker.
Rector of Wyck. May Sinclair. LC 25-561601. 1925. The Macmillan Company.
Rector's Daughter: A Novel. Flora Macdonald Mayor. LC 31-26108. 1930. Coward-McCann, Inc.
Rector's Secret: Or, Love Conquers All. A Study from Life. Jacob Ralph Abarbanell. LC 5-42188. (peerless series. no. 61). J.S. Ogilvie.
Rectory of Moreland: Or, My Duty... Clara M. Thompson. LC 6-38138. 1860. J. E. Tilton and Company.
Rectory Umbrella & Mischmasch. Lewis Carroll. (Illus.). 1932. pap. 2.50 (ISBN 0-486-21345-5). Dover.
Recueil De Petits Contes Francais. Ed. by Harold W. Streeter. 1956. 4.95 o.p. Xerox College.
Recuerdos. Andres Rivero. LC 80-66235. (Series: Cuentos En Espanol; V. 1, No. 3.). (Short stories in Spanish; v. 1, no. 3). 4.00 (ISBN 0-933648-02-2). Cruzada Spanish Publications.
Recycled Souls. Ian Ross. (Signet book). New American Library.
Red. Richard Vincent. LC 57-111804. (Permabooks, M-3008. Western, 8). 1957. Permabooks.
Red Aces. Edgar Wallace. 192p. 1973. Repr. of 1931 ed. 5.95 o.s.i. (ISBN 0-85617-953-1). White Lion Pubs.
Red Aces, Being Three Cases of Mr. Reeder. Edgar Wallace. LC 30-546. 1930. Pub. for The Crime Club, Inc., by Doubleday, Doran & Company, Inc.
Red Adam's Lady. Grace Ingram. LC 72-95910. 1973. 7.95 (ISBN 0-8128-1564-5). Stein and Day.
Red Adam's Lady. Grace Ingram. (Fawcett crest book). 1974. (pbk.) 1.25. Fawcett.
Red Alley. Charles J Bready. LC 38-34796. The Torch Press.
Red and Black. Grace Louise Smith Richmond. LC 19-18301. 1919. Doubleday, Page & Company.
Red and Black. Grace Louise Smith Richmond. LC 22-5159. 1921. A. L. Burt Company.
Red and Black: A Chronicle of the Nineteenth Century. Marie Henri Beyle. Tr. by Robins, E. P. 1898. G. H. Richmond & Son.
Red and Black: A New Translation, Backgrounds and Sources, Criticism. Marie Henri Beyle. Ed. by Robert Martin Adams. LC 67-16619. (Norton critical edition). 1969. 6.47. Norton.
Red and the Black. Marie Henri Beyle. Tr. by Scott-Moncrieff, Charles Kenneth. LC 26-18392. 1954. Liveright.
Red and the Black. Marie Henri Beyle. Tr. by Scott-Moncrieff, Charles Kenneth. LC 26-18392. 1926. Boni & Liveright.
Red and the Black. Marie Henri Beyle. Tr. by Scott-Moncrieff, Charles Kenneth. LC 29-26912. (Half-title: The modern library of the world's best books). 1929. The Modern Library.
Red and the Black. Marie Henri Beyle. Tr. by Scott-Moncrieff, Charles Kenneth. LC 39-1757. 1937. Liveright Publishing Corp.
Red and the Black. Marie Henri Beyle & Charles Kenneth Scott-Moncrieff. LC 47-5736. 1947.
Red & the Black. Stendhal. Ed. by Charles Tergie. (O.s.i.). 1961. pap. 0.95 o.s.i. (ISBN 0-02-054080-9, Collier). Macmillan.
Red & the Black. Stendhal. Tr. by Lloyd C. Parks. (Orig.). 1970. pap. 3.95 (ISBN 0-451-51793-8, CE1793, Sig Classics). NAL.
Red and the Black: A Chronicle of the Nineteenth Century. Marie Henri Beyle. Tr. by Lloyd C. Parks. LC 79-120771. (Signet classic, CQ492). 1970. 0.95. New American Library.
Red and the Black: A Chronicle of 1830. 3d impression. ed. Marie Henri Beyle. Tr. by Samuel, Horace Barnett. LC 26-26986. 1922. K. Paul. Trench. Trubner & Co., Ltd.
Red and the Black: By Stendhal Pseud. A New and Complete Translation by Lowell Bair. With an Introd. by Clifton Fadiman. Marie Henri Beyle. LC 58-599264. (Bantam book, S1734). 1958. Bantam Books.
Red and the Black (The) Chapter Notes and Criticism. (Study master pubn. 221). pap., 1.00. Amer. R. D. M. Corp.
Red and the Green. Iris Murdoch. LC 65-20778. bds., 5.00. Viking.
Red and the White. Translated from the French by Anthony Hinton. Henri Troyat. LC 57-924456. Crowell.
Red Angel. fifth thousand. ed. D. Guy Adams. 1943. Hutchinson & Co., Ltd.
Red Anger. Geoffrey Household. LC 75-5626. 1975. 7.95 (ISBN 0-316-37435-0). Little, Brown.
Red Anvil: A Romance of Fifty Years Ago. Charles Reginald Sherlock. LC 2-15212. 1902. F. A. Stokes Company.
Red Apache Sun. Robert E. Mills. (Kansan Ser.: No. 3). 1981. pap. 1.95 (ISBN 0-8439-0877-7, Leisure Bks). Nordon Pubns.
Red Arrows: By Chuck Stanley. Charles Stanley Strong. LC 56-8984. 1956. Arcadia House.
Red As a Rose Is She. Rhoda Broughton. (On cover: Lovell's library, no. 1023). 1887. J. W. Lovell Company.
Red As a Rose Is She. A Novel. Rhoda Broughton. (On cover: Seaside library. Pocket ed., no. 768). 1886. G. Munro.
Red as Blood. Tanith Lee. 208p. 1983. pap. 2.50. NAL.
Red Ascent. Esther Waggaman Neill. 1914. 1.00. P. J. Kenedy & Sons.
Red Ashes. Margaret Bass Pedler. LC 25-8121. George H. Doran Company.
Red Ashes. Margaret Bass Pedler. LC 32-19521. 1925. Grosset & Dunlap.
Red Axe. Samuel Rutherford Crockett. LC 98-1115. 1899. Harper & Brothers.
Red Badge of Courage. Stephen Crane. (Riverside lit. ser., R27). Houghton.
Red Badge of Courage. unabridged. illustrated by harvey kidder. ed. Stephen Crane. (Golden press classics library). (Illus.). 1968. Golden Press.
Red Badge of Courage. Stephen Crane. LC 68-56086. (Cambridge classics library). (Illus.). 1968. Cambridge Book Co.
Red Badge of Courage. Stephen Crane. LC 76-76032. (Facsimile first edition American classics). 1969. Fleet Press Corp.
Red Badge of Courage. Stephen Crane. LC 25-18277. 1925. D. Appleton and Company.
Red Badge of Courage. Stephen Crane. Ed. by Herzberg. Max John. LC 26-20523. (Half-title: Appleton modern literature series). D. Appleton and Company.
Red Badge of Courage. Stephen Crane. LC 80-13182. (Classics in Large Print). 1980. 8.95 (ISBN 0-8161-3078-7). G. K. Hall.
Red Badge of Courage. Stephen Crane & Robert James Dixson. LC 54-5571. (American Classics, Simplified and Adapted for Greater Reading Pleasure, Book 10). (Illus.). 1973. (pbk.) 1.25. Regents Pub. Co.
Red Badge of Courage. Stephen Crane & Herzberg, Max John. LC 42-36053. (Half-title: The Modern library of the world's best books 130). 1942. The Modern Library.
Red Badge of Courage see Classics Set.
Red Badge of Courage see Four Classic American Novels.
Red Badge of Courage: A Facsimile Edition of the Manuscript. Stephen Crane & Fredson Thayer Bowers. LC 72-84751. (Illus.). 1973. NCR/Microcard Editions.
Red Badge of Courage: A Facsimile of the Manuscript. Ed. by Fredson Bowers. 1973. deluxe ed. 150.00 boxed (ISBN 0-89723-035-3). Bruccoli.
Red Badge of Courage. A Facsimile Reprod. of the New York Press Appearance of December 9, 1894, with Introd., Textual Notes by Joseph Katz. Stephen Crane. LC 67-26616. 1967. 6.00. Scholars' Facsimiles.
Red Badge of Courage. A School Ed., by Frederick Houk Law. Stephen Crane. LC 53-2063. 1953. Globe Book Co.
Red Badge of Courage: An Annotated Text, Backgrounds and Sources, Essays in Criticism. Ed. by Sculley Bradley, Richmond Croom Beatty, E. Hudson Long. Stephen Crane. Ed. by Edward Sculley Bradley. LC 62-9572. (Norton critical eds.) Bibl.). 1965. 4.10, 1.95 pap.,. Norton.
Red Badge of Courage: An Annotated Text, Backgrounds and Sources, Essays in Criticism. Stephen Crane. Ed. by Edward Sculley Bradley. LC 62-9572. (Norton critical editions, N305). 1962. Norton.
Red Badge of Courage: An Authoritative Text, Backgrounds and Sources, Criticism. 2d ed. / rev. by donald pizer. ed. Stephen Crane & Edward Sculley Bradley. LC 76-18237. (Norton critical edition). 1977. 12.50 (ISBN 0-393-04435-1) (ISBN 0-393-09182-1). Norton.
Red Badge of Courage: An Episode of the American Civil War. Stephen Crane. LC 63-16938. (Library of literature). 1964. Bobbs-Merrill.
Red Badge of Courage: An Episode of the American Civil War. Stephen Crane. Ed. by Fredson Thayer Bowers. (works of Stephen Crane, v. 11). 1975. 17.50 (ISBN 0-8139-0514-1). University of Virginia Press.
Red Badge of Courage: An Episode of the American Civil War. Stephen Crane. LC 69-13318. (Charles E. Merrill program in American literature). (Charles E. Merrill standard editions.). 1969. C. E. Merrill Pub. Co.
Red Badge of Courage: An Episode of the American Civil War. new ed., with portrait and preface. ed. Stephen Crane. LC 3652. 1900. D. Appleton and Company.
Red Badge of Courage: An Episode of the American Civil War. Stephen Crane. LC 82-24532. (Penguin American Library). 1983. 2.95 (ISBN 0-14-039021-9). Penguin Books.
Red Badge of Courage: An Episode of the American Civil War. Stephen Crane & Henry Binder. LC 81-22419. 14.95 (ISBN 0-393-01345-6). Norton.
Red Badge of Courage: An Episode of the American Civil War. Introd. by Robert Wooster Stallman. Stephen Crane. LC 51-2278. (Modern Library college editions, T45). 1951. Modern Library.
Red Badge of Courage, & Other Stories. Stephen Crane. (World's Classics). 1.75 o.p. (ISBN 0-19-250579-3). Oxford U Pr.
Red Badge of Courage: And Other Stories. With an Introd. by Daniel G. Hoffman. Stephen Crane. LC 56-12644. (Harper's modern classics). 1957. Harper.
Red Badge of Courage, and Selected Prose and Poetry. 3d ed. Stephen Crane. Ed. by William Merriam Gibson. LC 69-10874. (Rinehart editions). 1968. Holt, Rinehart and Winston.
Red Badge of Courage: And Selected Prose and Poetry. Edited with an Introd. by William M. Gilbeon. Stephen Crane. LC 56-7831. (Rinehart editions, 47). 1956. Rinehart.
Red Badge of Courage: Illustrated by John Steuart Curry. Stephen Crane & Curry, John Steuart, 1897- Illus. LC 44-621605. 1944. The Heritage Press.
Red Badge of Courage. Introd. by Kenneth S. Lynn. Suggestions for Reading and Discussion by Kirby E. Judd Sch. Ed. Stephen Crane. (Riverside Lit. Ser., R27). Houghton.
Red Badge of Courage. Introd. by William Targ and Illustrated with Wood Engravings from Drawings by Winslow Homer, from the Collection of the Cooper Union Museum. Stephen Crane. LC 51-14132. (Living library). 1951. Cleveland, World Pub. Co.
Red Badge of Courage: Simplified and Adapted by Robert J. Dixson. Drawings by Syd Browne. With Exercises for Study and Vocabulary Drill. Stephen Crane & Robert James Dixson. (American classics, book 10). 1955. Regents Pub. Co.
Red Badge of Courage. Unabridged. Stephen Crane. LC 68-19471. (Golden press classics library). (Illus.). 1968. 1.25. Golden Press.
Red Band. The Adventures of a Young Girl During the Siege of Paris. Fortune Du Boisgobey. LC 6-34414. (On cover: Seaside library. Pocket ed. no. 918). G. Munro.
Red Barbara and Other Stories: The Mountain Tavern, Prey, The Oar. Liam O'Flaherty. LC 28-20131. 1928. C. Gaige.
Red Barn Mystery. Donald McCormick. LC 68-27192. (Illus.). 1968. 4.95 o.p. (ISBN 0-498-06869-2). A S Barnes.
Red Beacon. Espina De Serna, Concha. LC 24-12524. 1924. D. Appleton and Company.
Red Bean Row. Robert Emmet Kennedy. LC 29-221458. 1929. Dodd, Mead & Company.
Red Beard of Virginia. Rupert Sargent Holland. LC 27-22052. 1927. J. B. Lippincott Company.
Red Beauty, a Story of the Pawnee Trail. William Osborn Stoddard. LC 8-16301. 1887. J. B. Lippincott Company.
Red Bells. Hugh Pendexter. LC 20-226128. 1920. Doubleday, Page & Company.

Red Berets. Tom Biracree. 352p. 1983. pap. cancelled (ISBN 0-523-41704-7). Pinnacle Bks.

Red Bill. Arthur Murray Chisholm. ("Published serially in Popular magazine under the title of Red."). 1930. Frederick A. Stokes Company.

Red Bishop: By Howard Mason Pseud. Jennifer Ramage. LC 54-5077. 1954. M. S. Mill Co. and W. Morrow.

Red Blades of Black Cathay. Robert E. Howard & Tevis Clyde Smith. LC 70-31208. (Illus.). 1971. 4.00. D. M. Grant.

Red Blizzard. Clay Fisher. 160p. 1981. pap. 1.75 (ISBN 0-553-14542-8). Bantam.

Red Blizzard: A Novel of the North Plains Sioux, by Clay Fisher Pseud. Henry Allen. LC 51-11348. (Essandess western). 1951. Simon and Schuster.

Red-Blood: A Novel. Harold Hunter Armstrong. LC 23-12450. Harper & Brothers.

Red Blood and Blue. Harrison Robertson. LC 2135. 1900. C. Scribner's Sons.

Red Blood & Blue: The Romance of Nelly Custis. Hope Dahle Jordan. LC 37-2382. Chapman & Grimes.

Red Blood at White River. Ed Will. (Orig.). 1980. pap. 1.75 (ISBN 0-532-23143-0). Woodhill.

Red Blossoms: A Story of Western India. Isabel Brown Rose. LC 25-201437. Fleming H. Revell Company.

Red Boat. Gwen Kelly. 1969. pap. 9.50x (ISBN 0-392-04361-0, ABC). Sportshelf.

Red Bone Woman, a Novel. Tillery, Carlyle. LC 50-6056. 1950. J. Day.

Red Boomerang: A Novel of 1956. Walter Oliver Jerome. LC 56-2612. 1956. Excelsior International Publications.

Red Box. Rex Stout. LC 80-29555. 1981. 13.50 (ISBN 0-8161-3223-2). G. K. Hall.

Red Box: A Nero Wolfe Mystery. Rex Stout. LC 37-536300. Farrar & Rinehart, Incorporated.

Red Box: A Nero Wolfe Mystery. Rex Stout. LC 44-8523. (Murder mystery monthly. No. 9). 1943. Avon Book Company.

Red Branch. Charles McMorris Purdy. LC 28-24476. 1928. R. M. McBride & Company.

Red Brand. Charles Alden Seltzer. LC 76-40939. 1976. 6.95 (ISBN 0-88411-116-4). Aeonian Press.

Red Brand. Charles Alden Seltzer. LC 29-221298. 1929. Doubleday, Doran & Company, Inc.

Red-Bridge Neighborhood: A Novel. Maria Louise Pool. LC 7-38173. 1898. Harper & Brothers.

Red Button. William Henry Irwin. LC 12-24246. The Bobbs-Merrill Company.

Red Canvas. Marcel H Wallenstein. LC 46-1797. 1946. Creative Age Press, Inc.

Red Cardinal. A Romance. Frances Minto Dickinson Elliot. (On cover: Seaside library. Pocket ed., no. 381). 1885. G. Munro.

Red Carl: Tr. from the German of J. J. Messmer. John J Messmer. Tr. by Ireland, Mary Eliaz (Haine) LC 7-25876. T. Y. Crowell & Co.

Red Carnation. V. Morazova. 232p. 1981. 7.00 (ISBN 0-8285-2024-0, Pub. by Progress Pubs USSR). Imported Pubns.

Red Carnation. Elio Vittorini. LC 52-11063. 1952.

Red Carnation. Elio Vittorini. LC 75-152614. 1972. (ISBN 0-8371-6049-9). Greenwood Press.

Red Carnation: An Antony Bigelow Story. Burton Egbert Stevenson. LC 39-27932. 1939. Dodd, Mead & Company.

Red Carpet. Dan Wickenden. LC 51-26055. 1952. Morrow.

Red Carpet for the Shah. Peter Ritner. LC 75-15806. 1975. 6.95 (ISBN 0-688-02957-4). Morrow.

Red Castle Mystery. Henry Christopher Bailey. LC 32-22714. 1932. Pub. for the Crime Club, Inc., by Doubleday, Doran & Company, Inc.

Red Castle Women. Margaret Widdemer. LC 68-17811. 1968. 4.95. Doubleday.

Red Cavalier: Or, The Twin Turrets Mystery. Gladys Edson Locke. LC 22-9573. 1922. The Page Company.

Red Cavalry. Isaak Emmanuilovich Babel. Tr. by Helestein, Nadia. LC 29-17889. 1929. A. A. Knopf.

Red Chair Waits. Alice Margaret Huggins & Ballou, Earle Holt, 1892- LC 48-7963. 1948. Westminster Press.

Red Chancellor: A Romance. William Magnay. LC 1-256873. 1901. Brentano's.

Red Chief. Ion Idriess. 1967. Repr. pap. 1.25 o.s.i. Tri-Ocean.

Red Chindvit Conspiracy. Hans Holaer. 1976. pap. 1.25 (ISBN 0-532-12441-3, 532-12441-125). Woodhill.

Red Chindvit Conspiracy. Hans Holzer. (O.s.i.). 160p. 1973. pap. 0.95 o.s.i. (AN1193, Award). Univ Pub & Dist.

Red Christmas. Patrick Ruell. 176p. 1974. pap. 1.25 (ISBN 0-532-12249-6). Woodhill.

Red Circle. Gerard A Reynolds. LC 16-557. P. J. Kenedy & Sons.

Red City: A Novel of the Second Administration of President Washington. Silas Weir Mitchell. LC 8-30709. 1908. The Century Co.

Red City: A Novel of the Second Administration of President Washington. Silas Weir Mitchell. LC 16-6650. 1914. The Century Co.

Red Clark at the Showdown. Gordon Ray Young. LC 47-773. 1947. Doubleday & Company, Inc.

Red Clark for Luck. A Double D Western. Gordon Ray Young. LC 40-7861. 1940. Doubleday, Doran & Company, Inc.

Red Clark in Paradise. Gordon Ray Young. LC 47-5249. 1947. Doubleday.

Red Clark O' Tulluco. Gordon Ray Young. LC 33-10966. 1933. Doubleday, Doran & Company, Inc.

Red Clark of the Arrowhead. Gordon Ray Young. LC 35-665266. 1935. Doubleday, Doran & Company, Inc.

Red Clark on the Border. Gordon Ray Young. LC 37-112466. 1937. Doubleday, Doran & Company, Inc.

Red Clark, Range Boss. Gordon Ray Young. LC 38-19934. 1938. Doubleday, Doran & Company, Inc.

Red Clark: Range Boss. Gordon Ray Young. LC 40-908019. 1940. The Sun Dial Press.

Red Clark Rides Alone. Gordon Ray Young. LC 34-903. 1933. Doubleday, Doran & Company, Inc.

Red Clark Takes a Hand. A DD Western Selection. Gordon Ray Young. LC 41-8925. 1941. Doubleday, Doran & Co., Inc.

Red Clark to the Rescue. Gordon Ray Young. LC 48-8225. (Double D western). 1949. Doubleday.

Red Clark, Two-Gun Man. Gordon Ray Young. LC 39-27345. 1939. Doubleday, Doran & Company, Inc.

Red Clay. Frederic Arnold Kummer. LC 33-25380. Sears Publishing Company.

Red Clay Country. Margaret Cabell Self. LC 36-22620. 1936. Harper & Brothers.

Red Cloak Flying. 1st Ed. Margaret Widdemer. LC 50-5013. 1950. Doubleday.

Red Coats: Or, The Sack of Unquowa. A Tale of the Revolution. Charles F Sterling. 1848. Williams Brothers.

Red Cock Crows. Frances Ormond Jones Gaither. LC 44-4612. 1944. The Macmillan Company.

Red Cock Flies to Heaven. Translated by E. D. Goy. Miodrag Bulatovic. LC 62-15126. 1962. B. Geis Associates; Distributed by Random House.

Red Cockade: A Novel. Stanley John Weyman. LC 4-16592. 1896. Harper & Brothers.

Red Colonel. George Edgar. LC 13-20124. 1913. 1.30. D. Appleton and Company.

Red Colonel. Graham Seton Hutchinson. LC 47-20100. Hutchinson & Co. Ltd.

Red Commissar: Including Further Adventures of the Good Soldier Svejk and Other Stories. Jaroslav Hasek & Josef Lada. LC 81-179427. (Illus.). 14.95 (ISBN 0-385-27237-5). The Dial Press.

Red Confessor: The Adventures of Guido, Lord of Fiorano and of His Friend and Patron, Benvenuto Cellini. Nathan Gallizier. LC 26-11030. L. C. Page & Company.

Red Cord: A Romance of China. Thomas Grant Springer. LC 25-172775. Brentano's.

Red Court Farm. Ellen Price Henry Wood Wood. (Seaside library, v. 18, no. 357). 1878. G. Munro.

Red Court Farm: A New Novel. Ellen Price Wood. LC 52-52925. T. B. Peterson.

Red Court, Last Seat of National Government of the United States of America: The Story of the Revolution to Come Through Communism... Rena Marie Vale. LC 53-200319. 1952. Nelson Pub. Co.

Red Cross Girl. Richard Harding Davis. LC 12-21148. 1912. C. Scribner's Sons.

Red Damask: A Story of Nurture and Nature. Emanie Louise Nahm Sachs. LC 27-5837. 1927. Harper & Brothers.

Red Dancer of Moscow. Henry Leyford Gates. LC 28-21418. 1928. Barse & Co.

Red Daniel. Duncan MacNeil. 1977. pap. 1.50 o.s.i. (ISBN 0-8439-0477-1, Leisure Bks). Nordon Pubns.

Red Daniel. Duncan Macneil. LC 73-77056. 1974. 6.95 o.p. (ISBN 0-312-66640-3). St Martin.

Red Daniel: An "Ogilvie" Novel. Philip McCutchan. LC 73-77056. 1974. 6.95. St. Martin's Press.

Red Dawn: A Novel. Adele Blonden. LC 29-12491. The Four Seas Company.

Red Death. Gilbert Collins. LC 32-30925. H. Holt and Company.

Red Debt: Echoes from Kentucky. Everett MacDonald. LC 16-250958. 1916. G. W. Dillingham Co.

Red Demon: A Dramatic Novel. Albert Jay Wright. LC 33-36947. 1933. G. P. Putnam's Sons.

Red Devil of the Range. George Owen Baxter. LC 34-362299. The Macaulay Company.

Red Devil of the Range. Frederick Faust. LC 34-36229. 1934. The Macaulay Company.

Red Devils: Story of the British Airborne Forces. G. C. Norton. 1971. 7.50 o.p. (ISBN 0-8117-1405-5). Stackpole.

Red Diamond: Private Eye. Mark Schorr. 256p. 1983. 12.95 (ISBN 0-312-66645-4). St Martin.

Red Diamonds: A Novel. Justin McCarthy. LC 7-15285. (On cover: Appletons' town and country library, no. 144). 1894. D. Appleton and Company.

Red Dick: The Tiger of California. Edward Zane Carroll Judson. LC 7-11455. (sea and shore series--no. 26). 1890. Street & Smith.

Red-Dirt Marijuana, and Other Tastes. Terry Southern. LC 67-28231. 1967. New American Library.

Red Doe: By Drayton Mayrant Pseud. Katherine Drayton Mayrant Simons. LC 53-10670. 1953. Appleton-Century-Crofts.

Red Dove. Derek Lambert. LC 82-42837. 270p. 1983. 14.95 (ISBN 0-8128-2913-1). Stein & Day.

Red Dragon. Thomas Harris. LC 81-8674. 13.95 (ISBN 0-399-12442-X). Putnam.

Red Dragon: A China Story of to-Day. Lewis Stanton Palen. LC 27-20084. 1927. Houghton Mifflin Company.

Red Dress: A Novel. John Cherry Watson. LC 49-9313. 1949. Harper.

Red Drums: A Novel. Edward Alexander Powell. LC 35-16056. 1935. I. Washburn.

Red Dusk. Celeste Dunbar Lindsay. LC 32-5038. 1932. L. MacVeagh, The Dial Press.

Red Dust. David Houston. (Tales of Tomorrow Ser.: No. 2). (Illus.). 208p. (Orig.). 1981. pap. 2.25 (ISBN 0-8439-0921-8, Leisure Bks). Nordon Pubns.

Red Dust Three: New Writing. Thomas Fallon et al. LC 72-12794. 1979. 8.95 (ISBN 0-87376-026-3). Red Dust.

Red Eagle; a Tale of the Frontier. Edward Sylvester Ellis. LC 1-17670. (War chief series, no. 3). 1901. H. T. Coates & Co.

Red Eagle of the Medicine-Way. Marion Reid-Girardot. LC 22-22777. 1922. The Cornhill Publishing Company.

Red Earth. Tom Gill. LC 37-649. Farrar & Rinehart, Incorporated.

Red Earth. Vera Murdock Stuart Jervis. LC 26-17293. 1926. Cassell and Company, Ltd.

Red Earth. Vera Murdock Stuart Jervis. LC 26-17294. George H. Doran Company.

Red Earth. David Mitchell. LC 56-5516. 1956. Vantage Press.

Red Emerald. John Reed Scott. LC 14-324791. 1914. 1.25. J. B. Lippincott Company.

Red Ending. Harry Hervey. LC 29-212174. 1929. H. Liveright, Inc.

Red Eve. illustrations by arthur c. michael. ed. Henry Rider Haggard. LC 11-27105. 1911. Doubleday, Page & Company.

Red Eve. Henry Rider Haggard. LC 11-25053. Hodder and Stoughton.

Red Eye Blues. Joyce Elbert. 1982. pap. 3.50 (ISBN 0-451-11505-8, AE1505, Sig). NAL.

Red Eye of Betelgeuse. Clark Darlton. (Perry Rhodan, #40). 1974. (pbk.) 0.75. Ace Books.

Red Feather Love. Suzanna Lynne. (Harlequin Presents Ser.). 1975. pap. 1.25 (ISBN 0-373-70588-3, 70588). Harlequin Bks.

Red File for Callan. James Mitchell. LC 79-159135. (Inner sanctum mystery). 1971. 4.95 (ISBN 0-671-21020-3). Simon and Schuster.

Red File for Callan. James Mitchell. 1974. (pbk.) 1.25. Dell.

Red Flag. facsimile ed. Frederick Britten Austin. LC 72-37258. (Short Story Index Reprint Ser.). Repr. of 1934 ed. 19.50 (ISBN 0-8369-4069-5). Ayer Co.

Red Flag. Georges Ohnet. LC 10-9075. G. W. Dillingham Company.

Red Fleece. Will Levington Comfort. LC 15-4856. George H. Doran Company.

Red Flower. Henry Van Dyke. 1920. Repr. 8.50 o.p. (ISBN 0-8274-3258-5). R West.

Red Flower Kill. Walter Sheldon. (Orig.). 1971. pap. 0.75 o.p. (T2387, GM). Fawcett World.

Red Flowers. Francis Haffkine Snow. LC 21-8309. Boni and Liveright.

Red Fog. Bruce Harper. LC 30-29556. 1930. Caxton.

Red Fog Over America. William G. Carr. 280p. pap. 4.00 (ISBN 0-913022-35-7). Angriff Pr.

Red for Danger. new ed. Lionel Thomas Caswell Rolt. LC 76-28618. (Illus.). 192p. 1982. 16.95 (ISBN 0-7153-8362-0). David & Charles.

Red for Passion. Florence Stonebraker. LC 48-404348. 1948. Phoenix Press.

Red for Terror. Richard Crighton. LC 82-1368. 9.95 (ISBN 0-396-08066-9). Dodd, Mead.

Red Fountain. Janine Montupet. LC 61-9060. 1961. St. Martin's Press.

Red Fox of the Kinapoo: A Tale of the Nez Perce Indians. William Marshall Rush. LC 49-9794. 1949. Longmans, Green.

Red Fox's Son: A Romance of Bharbazonia. Edgar Meck Dilley. LC 11-170994. 1911. 1.50. L. C. Page & Company.

Red Friday. George Kibbe Turner. LC 19-9477. 1919. Little, Brown, and Company.

Red Fruit. Temple Bailey. LC 45-1222. 1945. Houghton Mifflin Comapny.

Red Fury. George G. Gilman, pseud. (Edge Ser.: No. 33). 160p. 1980. pap. 1.95 (ISBN 0-523-42033-1). Pinnacle Bks.

Red Gardenias. Jonathan Latimer. LC 39-25445. 1939. Pub. for the Crime Club, Inc., by Doubleday, Doran & Company, Inc.

Red Gash Outlaws. Charles Horace Snow. LC 40-450515. The Greystone Press.

Red Gate. Richard Burke. LC 47-116949. (fingerprint mystery). 1947. Ziff-Davis Pub. Co.

Red Gate. La Selle Gilman. LC 52-14044. 1953. Ballantine Books.

Red Geranium: Together with My Son and The Case of Mathews. Frederick Orin Bartlett. LC 15-164442. 1.35. Small, Maynard and Company.

Red Ginger Blossom, Wife to Sim: The Pool of Pink Lilies. Joyce Dingwell. (Harlequin Romances Ser.). 576p. 1982. pap. 3.50 (ISBN 0-373-20057-9). Harlequin Bks.

Red Gods. Donald Lindquist. (O.s.i.). 1981. 11.95 o.s.i. (ISBN 0-440-07349-9). Delacorte.

Red Gods Call. Charles Elbert Scoggins. LC 26-10565. The Bobbs-Merrill Company.

Red Gods (Les Dieux Rouges) A Romance. Jean D'Esmenard & Acklom, George Moreby, 1870- Tr. LC 24-5505. E. P. Dutton & Company.

Red Grass. Carter Travis Young. LC 75-41678. 1976. 5.95 (ISBN 0-385-11151-7). Doubleday.

Red Grass. Carter Travis Young. LC 81-5340. 1981. 8.95 (ISBN 0-89621-275-0). Thorndike Press.

Red Guard. Nick Carter. (Nick Carter Ser.). (O.s.i.). (Orig.). 1967. pap. 0.95 o.s.i. (AN1089, Award). Univ Pub & Dist.

Red Gun. Archie Joscelyn. 1965. Arcadia House.

Red Hair and Blue Sea. Stanley R Osborn. LC 25-10417. 1925. C. Scribner's Sons.

Red-Haired Alibi. Wilson Collison. LC 32-137771. 1932. R. M. McBride & Company.

Red-Haired Bitch. Clifford Hanley. LC 69-15014. 1969. 4.95. Houghton Mifflin.

Red-Haired Brat. Joanna Dessau. LC 78-19821. 1979. 7.95 (ISBN 0-312-66720-5). St. Martin's Press.

Red-Haired Girl: A Fleming Stone Story. Carolyn Wells. LC 26-21899. 1926. J. B. Lippincott Company.

Red-Haired Lady. Elizabeth Frances Corbett. LC 45-5094. 1945. Doubleday, Doran & Company, Inc.

Red Hand. Sylvanus Cobb. (On cover: The pastime series, no. 106). Laird & Lee.

Red Hand of Ulster. James Owen Hannay. LC 12-22594. Hodder & Stoughton, George H. Doran Company.

Red Hands, Blue Hands. William Dady. 1967. 3.50 o.p.; pap. 1.45 o.p. (ISBN 0-87637-502-6). Hse of Collectibles.

Red Hart Magic. Andre Norton, pseud. 192p. 1982. pap. 1.95 (ISBN 0-441-71101-4). Ace Bks.

Red Harvest. Dashiell Hammett. LC 72-1756. 1972. 1.25 (ISBN 0-394-71828-3). Vintage Books.

Red Harvest. Dashiell Hammett. LC 29-90974. 1929. A. A. Knopf.

Red Harvest. Olav Nordra. LC 78-5381. (Library of Scandinavian Literature; V. 32). (Twayne's international studies and translations program). 9.50 (ISBN 0-8057-8162-5). Twayne Publishers.

Red Hawk. A. G. Hales. LC 19-4410. Hodder and Stoughton.

Red Head. John Uri Lloyd. 1903. Dodd, Mead and Company.

Red Head and Whistle Breeches. Ellis Parker Butler. LC 15-267757. 0.50. The Bancroft Company.

Red Head: Anonymous. Herman Alfred Kasen. LC 42-2570. G. H. Watt.

Red Head from Sun Dog. Wilbur C Tuttle. LC 30-4658. 1930. Houghton Mifflin Company.

Red-Headed Gal. Charles Stanley Strong. LC 40-2316. Phoenix Press.

Red-Headed Goddess. Alice Mary Ross Colver. LC 29-19776. 1929. Dodd, Mead & Company.

Red-Headed Kids: An Adventure Story. Arthur Murray Chisholm. Chelsea House.

Red-Headed League. Arthur Conan Doyle. Ed. by Walter Pauk & Raymond Harris. (Jamestown Classics Ser.). (Illus.). 47p. (gr. 6-12). 1976. pap. text ed. 2.00x (ISBN 0-89061-060-6, 541); tchrs. ed. 3.00 (ISBN 0-89061-061-4, 543). Jamestown Pubs.

Red-Headed League: And The Adventure of the Speckled Band. Arthur Conan Doyle & Arthur Conan Doyle. 1968. F. Watts.

Red Headed School Ma'am. Darragh Aldrich. LC 35-27027. The Penn Publishing Company.

Red-Headed Woman. Katharine Brush. LC 31-28227. Farrar & Rinehart, Incorporated.

Red-Headed Woman. Katharine Brush. LC 43-7379. (Avon pocket-size books). 1942. Avon Book Company.

Red Heat. William Katz. 320p. (Orig.). 1982. pap. 3.50 (ISBN 0-440-17558-5). Dell.

Red Heifer: A Story of Men and Cattle. Frank Dalby Davison. LC 34-39746. 1934. Coward-McCann.

Red Hen Conspiracy. Kenneth Benton. 1982. 15.00x (ISBN 0-333-21940-6, Pub. by Macmillan England). State Mutual Bk.

Red Herring. Edward Acheson. LC 32-22289. 1939. W. Morrow & Co.

Red Herring. Wilson Tucker. LC 51-11446. (Murray Hill mystery). 1951. Rinehart.

Red Herring Murder. Perry D Westbrook. LC 49-4127. 1949. Phoenix Press.

Red Hibiscus. Padmini Sathianadhan Sengupta. LC 62-5371. 1962. Asia Pub. House.

Red Hill Tragedy. Emma Dorothy Eliza Nevitte Southworth. (arm chair library. no. 48). 1893. F. M. Lupton.

Red Hill Tragedy. A Novel. Emma Dorothy Eliza Nevitte Southworth. LC 8-10831. 1897. T. B. Peterson & Brothers.

Red Hills. Rhys Davies. LC 33-1629. 1932. Putnam.

Red Hills. Rhys Davies. LC 33-262919. 1933. Covici, Friede.

Red Horizon. Patrick MacGill. LC 16-7234. George H. Doran Company.

Red Horse. C. C. L Browne. LC 67-27303. (Illus.). 1967. Stephen Greene Press.

Red Horse Hill. Mary Fenollosa. LC 9-12084. 1909. Little, Brown, and Company.

Red Horses. Felix Riesenberg. LC 28-5533. 1928. R. M. McBride & Company.

Red Hot. Roy Booth. LC 37-2063. 1937. Goodwin.

Red Hot & Blue: An X-Rated History of the American Revolution. Hugh Best. LC 75-40061. (Illus.). 1.75 (ISBN 0-915460-13-0). New Hope Pub. Co.

Red Hot & Dangerous. Michael Geller. (Bud Dugan Ser.: No. 4). 192p. (Orig.). 1982. pap. 2.25 (ISBN 0-505-51773-6). Tower Bks.

Red-Hot Dollar: And Other Stories from the Black Cat. Herman Daniel Umbstaetter. LC 11-18461. 1911. L. C. Page & Company.

Red Hot Ice: A Johnny Liddell Mystery. Frank Kane. LC 55-359415. 1955. I. Washburn.

Red Hot Trip in the Sunny South: Or, The Experiences of a Commercial Traveler. David B Shaw. (peerless series, no. 26). J. S. Ogilvie.

Red House. George Agnew Chamberlain. LC 45-405243. 1945. The Bobbs-Merrill Company.

Red House. Margaret Wolfe Hungerford. LC 7-9054. (On cover: Rialto series. no. 62). 1894. Rand, McNally & Company.

Red House. Else Kotanyi Jerusalem. Tr. by Colbron, Grace Isabel. LC 32-1643. The Macaulay Company.

Red House. Derek Lambert. LC 74-172637. 1972. 6.95. Coward, McCann and Geoghegan.

Red House: A Novel. Edith Nesbit Bland. LC 2-25517. 1902. Harper & Brothers.

Red House Mystery. Alan Alexander Milne. LC 75-44994. (Fifty Classics of Crime Fiction, 1900-1950; 37). 1976. 12.00 (ISBN 0-8240-2386-2). Garland Pub.

Red House Mystery. Alan Alexander Milne. LC 22-7879. E. P. Dutton & Company.

Red House Mystery. Alan Alexander Milne. LC 42-47280. 1936. E. P. Dutton & Co., Inc.

Red House on Rowan Street. Lily Augusta Long. LC 10-7954. 1910. 1.50. Little, Brown, and Company.

Red Hunters and the Animal People. Charles Alexander Eastman. LC 4-310555. 1904. Harper & Brothers.

Red Ice. Mary J. Hutchinson. 224p. (Orig.). 1981. pap. 2.25 (ISBN 0-380-78725-3, 78725). Avon.

Red in the Morning. Edith P Begner. LC 63-7717. 1963. Doubleday.

Red Indians of Newfoundland. Charles Augustus Murray. LC 9-3816. T. B. Peterson.

Red Inn of Saint Lyphar. Anna Theresa Sadlier. LC 5-6279. Benziger Brothers.

Red Iron! The Story of a Young Civil Engineer. by courtney parmly brown. ed. Courtney Parmly Brown. LC 40-31870. 1940. Dodd, Mead & Company.

Red Is for Killing. George A Bagby, pseud. 1941. Pub. for the Crime Club by Doubleday, Doran & Co., Inc.

Red Is for Killing. Aaron Marc Stein. LC 42-937. 1941. Pub. for the Crime Club by Doubleday, Doran & Co., Inc.

Red Is for Murder. Phyllis A Whitney. LC 43-16386. 1943. Ziff-Davis Publishing Company.

Red is for Shrouds. Mary Ann Taylor. (Raven House Mysteries Ser.). 224p. 1981. pap. 2.25 (ISBN 0-373-63006-9, Pub. by Worldwide). Harlequin Bks.

Red Is the River. Theodore V. Olsen. 416p. (Orig.). 1983. pap. 3.50 (ISBN 0-449-12407-X, GM). Fawcett.

Red Is the Valley: By Joseph Wayne. 1st Ed. Wayne D. Overholser. LC 67-16901. 1967. 3.95. Doubleday.

Red Ivory. Walton Hall Smith. LC 28-18756. 1928. Houghton Mifflin Company.

Red Jaguar. Nelle McFather. (Ace gothic). 1974. (pbk.) 0.95. Ace Books.

Red Jaguar: A Novel by Jason Manor Pseud. Oakley M Hall. LC 54-522558. 1954. Viking Press.

Red Jasmine. Inglis Clark Fletcher. 320p. 1976. Repr. of 1932 ed. lib. bdg. 16.95x (ISBN 0-89244-012-0). Queens Hse.

Red Jasmine: A Novel of Africa. Inglis Clark Fletcher. LC 32-11115. The Bobbs-Merrill Company.

Red-Keggers. Eugene Thwing. LC 3-22099. 1903. The Book-Lover Press.

Red King, the Corsair Chieftain. A Romance of the Ocean. Justin Jones. LC 7-12845. H. Long & Brother.

Red Kite Clue. Oscar Jerome Friend. LC 26-29079. E. J. Clode, Inc.

Red Klover. Klarenc Wade Mak. LC 22-13451. Dr. Mak & Himself.

Red Knight: A Romance. Francis Brett Young. LC 22-17150. E. P. Dutton & Company.

Red Lacquer Case. H Raymond Jorgensen. LC 33-28932. The World Syndicate Publishing Company.

Red Lacquer Case. Patricia Wentworth. LC 24-27646. Small, Maynard & Company.

Red Lacquer Case. Patricia Wentworth. LC 24-18761. 1924. A. Melrose Ltd.

Red Lady. Katharine Newlin Burt. LC 20-670925. 1920. 1.75. Houghton Mifflin Company.

Red Lady. Katharine Newlin Burt. 1973. (pbk) 0.75. New American Library.

Red Lady. Robert McNair Wilson. LC 35-170923. 1. B. Lippincott Company.

Red Lamp. Mary Roberts Rinehart. George H. Doran Company.

Red Lances. Uslar Pietri, Arturo. LC 62-15566. 1963. Knopf.

Red Lane: A Romance of the Border. Holman Francis Day. LC 12-172961. 1912. Harper & Brothers.

Red Lantern. 1972. 3.00 o.p. (ISBN 0-8351-0293-9); pap. 1.50 o.p. (ISBN 0-8351-0294-7). China Bks.

Red Lantern: Being the Story of the Goddess of the Red Lantern Light. Edith Wherry. LC 11-9902. 1911. John Lane Company.

Red Lanterns on St. Michael's. Thornwell Jacobs. 1940. E. P. Dutton & Co., Inc.

Red Law. Jackson Gregory. LC 41-21724. 1941. Dodd, Mead & Company.

Red Ledger. Frank Lucius Packard. LC 26-12291. George H. Doran Company.

Red Legion. George Brydges Rodney. LC 36-99353. Greenberg.

Red-Light Victim. Lawrence Kinsley. (Orig.). 1981. pap. 2.50 (ISBN 0-505-51649-7). Tower Bks.

Red Lights. Georges Simenon. LC 76-358393. 1975. 2.50 (ISBN 0-7274-0019-3). White Lion Publishers.

Red Like Crimson. Jane Paradine. LC 81-218892. 1931. G. P. Putnam's Sons.

Red Like Mine. Yvonne Lehman. LC 78-121358. 1970. 3.50. Zondervan.

Red Like Mine. Yvonne Lehman. LC 78-121358. 1970. 3.50 o.p. (10000). Zondervan.

Red Likker. Irvin Shrewsbury Cobb. LC 29-16557. 1929. Cosmopolitan Book Corporation.

Red Lily. 6th ed. Anatole France, pseud. LC 62-57451. (His Works). 1922. Bodley Head; New York, Dodd, Mead.

Red Lily. Anatole France, pseud. LC 6-43277. Brentano's.

Red Lily. Anatole France, pseud. Tr. by Whale, Winifred (Stephens) LC 14-3908. 1914. John Lane.

Red Lily and Chinese Jade: Three Chapters in the Chinatown Life of Donald Martin, M.D. Louise Jordan Miln. LC 28-11051. 1928. Frederick A. Stokes Company.

Red Limit: The Search for the Edge of the Universe. Timothy Ferris. 1979. pap. 2.95 (ISBN 0-553-20192-1). Bantam.

Red Lion: A Tale of Ancient Persia. Diane Wolkstein & Ed Young. 1977. 8.95 (ISBN 0-690-01347-7). Crowell.

Red Lion and Gold Dragon: A Novel of the Norman Conquest. Rosemary Sprague. LC 67-14018. 1967. Chilton Books.

Red Lion Inn. Pierre Stephen Robert Payne. LC 51-6192. 1951. Prentice-Hall.

Red Lock: A Tale of the Flatwoods. David Wulf Anderson. LC 22-19914. The Bobbs-Merrill Company.

Red Lodge: A Mystery of Campden Hill. Victor Bridges. LC 24-7946. 1924. Doubleday, Page & Company.

Red Lottery Ticket. Fortune Du Boisgobey. LC 6-34415. (On cover: Lovell's library. no. 1148). J. W. Lovell Company.

Red Love. Aleksandra Mikhailovna Kollontai. LC 72-90296. 1973. (ISBN 0-88355-007-5). Hyperion Press.

Red Love. Aleksandra Mikhailovna Kollontai. LC 27-6908. Seven Arts Publishing Company.

Red Macaw. Phoebe Haggard. LC 34-20806. 1934. C. Scribner's Sons.

Red Machines. Franklin D. Reeve. LC 68-18105. 1968. W. Morrow.

Red Mack Truck Massacre. Luana Luther. (Illus.). 64p. (Orig.). 1981. pap. 4.75 (ISBN 0-939470-00-4). Syder Pr.

Red Magician. Lisa Goldstein. (Orig.). 1982. pap. 2.25 (ISBN 0-671-41161-6, Timescape). PB.

Red Man, White Man. 1st Ed. Designed and Decorated by Don Perceval. Harry Clebourne James. LC 58-10424. 1958. Naylor Co.

Red Man's Trail. Leon W Dean. LC 48-106497. 1948. Rinehart.

Red Mark, and Other Stories. John Russell. LC 73-3470. (Short story index reprint series). 1973. (ISBN 0-8369-4256-6). Books for Libraries Press.

Red Mark: And Other Stories. John Russell. LC 19-15745. 1919. A. A. Knopf.

Red Marshal. Gordon Casserly. LC 23-29756. E. J. Clode.

Red Marten. Translated from the Swedish by Naomi Walford. 1st American Ed. Peter William Nisser. LC 57-5657. 1957. Knopf.

Red Masquerade: Being the Story of the Lone Wolf's Daughter. Louis Joseph Vance. LC 21-9710. 1921. Doubleday, Page & Company.

Red Mass. Valentine Williams. LC 25-2349. 1925. Houghton Mifflin Company.

Red Mata Hari: A Novel Based on Actual Events InYugoslavia During World War II. 1st Ed. Milan D Shijachki. LC 57-10670. 1957. Exposition Press.

Red Meekins. William Alexander Fraser. LC 72-125212. (Short story index reprint series). 1970. Books for Libraries Press.

Red Meekins. William Alexander Fraser. LC 21-17192. 1.90. George H. Doran Company.

Red Men and White. Owen Wister. LC 68-55691. (American short story series, v. 31). (Illus.). 1969. Garrett Press.

Red Men and White. Owen Wister. LC 72-8176. (American short story series, v. 31). 1972. (ISBN 0-8422-8128-2). MSS Information Corp.

Red Men and White. Owen Wister. LC 4-15184. 1896. Harper & Brothers.

Red Mesabi. George Ryland Bailey. LC 30-8902. 1930. Houghton Mifflin Company.

Red Mist. Johan Borgen. 1981. 9.95 (ISBN 0-7145-0896-9). Riverrun NY.

Red Mist: A Tale of Civic Strife. Randall Parrish. LC 14-17088. 1914. A. C. McClurg & Co.

Red Moccasins: A Story. Morrison Heady. LC 8-51857. 1901. Courier-Journal Job Print. Co.

Red Money. Fergus Hume. LC 11-27108. G. W. Dillingham Company.

Red Moon. Warren Murphy. 320p. (Orig.). 1982. pap. 2.95 (ISBN 0-449-14491-7, GM). Fawcett.

Red Moon. Kenneth Robeson. (Avenger,#26). 1974. (pbk.) 0.95. Warner Paperback Library.

Red Morning. Ruby Frazier Parsons Frey. LC 46-6088. 1946. G. P. Putnam's Sons.

Red Morton: Waterboy. Alan Drady. LC 32-22564. 1932. D. Appleton and Company.

Red Mountain. Laura Nelson Baker. LC 46-8460. 1946. The Webb Publishing Company.

Red Mountain. Will Comstock. (Orig.). 1981. pap. 1.95 (ISBN 0-505-51688-8). Tower Bks.

Red Mountain. David Sievert Lavender. LC 63-7704. 1963. Doubleday.

Red Mouse: A Mystery Romance. William Hamilton Osborne. LC 9-559816. 1909. Dodd, Mead & Company.

Red Mutiny: A Diary. John Wingate. LC 77-14717. 1978. 7.95 (ISBN 0-312-66661-6). St. Martin's Press.

Red Nails. authorized ed. Robert E. Howard & Karl Edward Wagner. LC 78-27086. (Illus.). 1979. 9.95 (ISBN 0-399-12333-4). Berkley Pub. Corp.: Distributed by Putnam.

Red Napoleon. Floyd Phillips Gibbons. (Lost American fiction). 1977. 1.95 (ISBN 0-445-04016-5). Popula Library.

Red Napoleon. Floyd Phillips Gibbons. LC 29-17091. 1929. J. Cape & H. Smith.

Red Napoleon. Floyd Phillips Gibbons. LC 33-175111. 1931. Grosset & Dunlap.

Red Napoleon: A Novel. Floyd P. Gibbons. LC 75-26975. (Lost American Fiction Ser.). 494p. 1976. Repr. of 1929 ed. 9.85 (ISBN 0-8093-0764-2). S Ill U Pr.

Red Neck. McAlister Coleman & Hilmar Stephen Raushenbush. LC 74-22772. (Labor Movement in Fiction and Non-Fiction). 1976. 21.50 (ISBN 0-404-58412-8). AMS Press.

Red Neck. McAlister Coleman & Hilmar Stephen Raushenbush. LC 36-7599. H. Smith & R. Haas.

Red Nights of Paris: From the "Coup Double" and "Policiers et Rastas,". Marie Francois Goron. Tr. by Crewe-Jones, Florence. LC 12-101369. 1.25. G. W. Dillingham Company.

Red of Surley: A Novel. Clarence Aaron Robbins. LC 19-6661. 1919. Harper & Brothers.

Red of the Redfields. Grace Louise Smith Richmond. LC 24-29828. 1924. Doubleday, Page & Company.

Red Omega. John Kruse. LC 81-40230. 14.50 (ISBN 0-394-52141-2). Random House.

Red on Black. Eben G Weed. LC 63-50137. 1963. Weed Publishers.

Red on Wight. Diana Winsor. LC 77-18072. (Jubilee mystery). 1978. 7.95 (ISBN 0-8128-2426-1). Stein and Day.

Red One. Jack London. LC 22-5156. 1918. Grosset & Dunlap.

Red One. Jack London. LC 18-20098. 1918. The Macmillan Company.

Red Orm. Frans Gunnar Bengtsson. Tr. by June Barrows Mussey. LC 43-723108. 1943. C. Scribner's Sons.

Red Over Green: A Novel. Robert David Quixano Henriques. LC 56-6282. 1956. Viking Press.

Red Owl. Rida Johnson Young. LC 27-17810. The Curtiss Press.

Red Pants and Other Stories. John William Thomason. LC 27-10467. 1927. C. Scribner's Sons.

Red Paper. Chauncey Crafts Hotchkiss. LC 12-207840. W. J. Watt & Company.

Red Pavilion. John Gunther. LC 27-110058. 1926. Harper & Brothers.

Red Pavilion... Pauline Stiles. LC 36-39606. 1936. Doubleday, Doran & Company, Inc.

Red Pavilion: A Chinese Detective Story. Robert Hans Van Gulik, pseud. LC 68-12494. (His New Judge Dee mysteries). (Illus.). 1968. Scribner.

Red Pawns: By George Griswold Pseud. 1st Ed. Robert George Dean. LC 54-8863. (Guilt edged mystery). 1954. Dutton.

Red Peony. Lin Yutang. 400p. 1980. 6.95 (ISBN 0-89955-165-3, Pub. by Mei Ya China); pap. 5.95 (ISBN 0-89955-194-7). Intl Schol Bk Serv.

Red Peony. 1st Ed. Lin Yutang. LC 61-12018. 1961. World Pub. Co.

Red Pepper Burns. Grace Louise Smith Richmond. LC 10-23742. 1910. Doubleday, Page & Company.

Red Pepper Burns. Grace Louise Smith Richmond. LC 16-936400. 1910. A. L. Burt Company.

Red Pepper Burns. Grace Louise Smith Richmond. LC 40-11449. 1940. Triangle Books.

Red Pepper Returns. Grace Louise Smith Richmond. LC 31-17129. 1931. Doubleday, Doran & Company, Inc.

Red Pepper's Patients: With an Account of Anne Linton's Case in Particular. Grace Louise Smith Richmond. LC 17-244032. 1917. Doubleday, Page & Company.

Red Pepper's Patients: With an Account of Anne Linton's Case in Particular. Grace Louise Smith Richmond. LC 18-588124. 1918. Doubleday, Page & Company.

Red Peri. Stanley Grauman Weinbaum. LC 52-41135. (FP science fiction.). 1952. Fantasy Press.

Red Petticoat: And Other Stories. Bryan MacMahon. LC 54-11699. 1955. Dutton.

Red Pioneer. Michael Marku. LC 55-12198. 1955. Comet Press Books.

Red Pioneers: Romance of Early Indian Life in the West. author's ed. Jacob Calvin Cooper. LC 28-302653. 1928.

Red Planet. Robert Anson Heinlein. (Del Rey Book). 1977. 1.75 (ISBN 0-345-26069-4). Ballantine Books.

Red Planet. William John Locke. LC 17-26481. 1917. John Lane Company.

Red Plush: The Story of the Moorhouse Family. Guy McCrone. LC 47-11838. 1947. Farrar, Straus.

Red Pony. John Steinbeck. LC 62-3607. 1962. Viking Press.

Red Pony... John Steinbeck. LC 37-226745. 1937. Covici-Friede.

Red Pony. John Steinbeck & Dennis, Wesley, Illus. LC 45-8597. 1945. The Viking Press.

Red Pony see Short Novels of John Steinbeck.

Red Pony and the Pearl: A Critical Commentary. Text by Frederick D. Highland. Highland, Frederick D. (Study master pubn., 421). pap., 1.00. Amer. R.D.M.

Red Pony and the Pearl: Notes by Armand Schwerner. (Monarch notes and study guides, 694-0). pap., 1.00. Monarch Pr.

Red Poocher. Seumas MacManus. LC 3-21772. 1903. Funk & Wagnalls Company.

Red Poppies: A Novel. Margarete Anna Adelheid Munsterberg. LC 15-28469. 1915. 1.25. D. Appleton and Company.

Red Pottage. Mary Cholmondeley. LC 99-5200. 1899. Harper & Brothers.

Red Pottage. Mary Cholmondeley. LC 41-311014. 1900. Harper & Brothers.

Red Quare. Samuel Andrew Wood. LC 34-2563. 1934. E. P. Dutton & Co., Inc.

Red Queen, White Queen. Henry Treece. LC 58-9871. 1958. Random House.

Red Rackham's Treasure. Georges Remy. LC 73-21253. (Adventures of Tintin). (Atlantic Monthly Press book). (Illus.). 1974. (pbk.) 2.50 (ISBN 0-316-35834-7). Little, Brown.

Red Rage & China Shops. Ronald Beatson. 1977. 6.95 o.p. (ISBN 0-533-02670-9). Vantage.
Red Rain. Leslie Kark. LC 46-1076. 1946. The Macmillan Company.
Red Range. Eugene Cunningham. LC 39-30545. 1939. Houghton Mifflin Company.
Red Range: By Roy Manning Pseud. Fred East. LC 50-5786. 1950. Macrae Smith Co.
Red Raskall. Clark McMeekin. LC 43-14365. 1943. D. Appleton-Century Company, Incorporated.
Red Ravage: A Novel of the Experiences of an American in the Philippines. Jesse Buel Ralston. LC 53-6477. 1953. Vantage Press.
Red Raven: A Novel. Lilli Palmer. LC 79-16516. 1979. 13.95 (ISBN 0-8161-6750-8). G. K. Hall.
Red Rays. Nick Carter. (Nick Carter Ser.). 160p. 1981. pap. 2.25 (ISBN 0-441-71114-6). Ace Bks.
Red Rays. Nick Carter. (Nick Carter Ser.). (O.s.i.). (Orig.). 1969. pap. 0.60 o.s.i. (A423X, Award). Univ Pub & Dist.
Red Rebellion. Nick Carter. (Nick Carter Ser.). (O.s.i.). 1970. pap. 0.60 o.s.i. (A584X, Award). Univ Pub & Dist.
Red Redmaynes. Eden Phillpotts. LC 22-23718. 1922. The Macmillan Company.
Red Redmaynes. Eden Phillpotts. LC 81-19499. 1982. 6.00 (ISBN 0-486-24255-2). Dover.
Red Republic: A Romance of the Commune. Robert William Chambers. LC 4-16821. 1895. G. P. Putnam's Sons.
Red Revenge. Gilbert Ralston. (Dakota series,#2). 1974. (pbk.) 0.95 (ISBN 0-523-00319-6). Pinnacle Books.
Red Rhapsody. Cortland Fitzsimmons. LC 33-31886. 1933. Frederick A. Stokes Company.
Red Riders. Thomas Nelson Page. LC 24-21999. 1924. C. Scribner's Sons.
Red Riding Hood: A Novel. Elizabeth Garver Jordan. LC 25-6700. The Century Co.
Red Riding-Hood. A Novel. Frances Eliza Millett Notley. (Harper's Franklin square library, no. 364). 1884. Harper & Brothers.
Red Right Hand. Joel Townsley Rogers. LC 45-4234. 1945. Simon and Schuster.
Red River. George G. Gilman, pseud. (Edge Ser.: No. 6). 192p. 1973. pap. 1.95 (ISBN 0-523-41770-5). Pinnacle Bks.
Red River Crossing. Charles Stanley Strong. LC 47-11533. 1947. Phoenix Press.
Red River Gunman. Claude Rister. LC 41-20164. Dodge Publishing Company.
Red River Half Breed: A Tale of the Wild Northwest. Gustave Aimard. LC 5-42592. (On cover: Lovell's library, no. 1150). 1888. J. W. Lovell Company.
Red River Road. Allan K. Echols. pap. 0.50 o.p. (50-460). Manor Bks.
Red River Road. Alvin Ogren. LC 56-13210. 1956. Comet Press Books.
Red River Sheriff. Peter Germano. LC 65-7721. 1965. Arcadia House.
Red Road. Simon Harvester. 1968. pap. 0.60 o.p. (60-311). Manor Bks.
Red Road: A Romance of Braddock's Defeat. Hugh Pendexter. LC 27-8782. The Bobbs-Merrill Company.
Red Robins. Kenneth Koch. LC 74-29155. 1975. 5.95 (ISBN 0-394-71467-9). Vintage Books.
Red Rock. Thomas Nelson Page. LC 67-29275. (Americans in Fiction Ser.). (Illus.). Repr. of 1898 ed. lib. bdg. 15.00 (ISBN 0-8398-1551-4). Irvington.
Red Rock: A Chronicle of Reconstruction. Thomas Nelson Page. LC 67-29275. (Americans in Fiction). (Illus.). 1967. Gregg Press.
Red Rock: A Chronicle of Reconstruction. Thomas Nelson Page. LC 98-1252. 1898. C. Scribner's Sons.
Red Rock: A Chronicle of Reconstruction. Thomas Nelson Page. LC 8-2115. 1899. C. Scribner's Sons.
Red Rock Wilderness. Elspeth Joscelin Grant Huxley. LC 57-8938. 1957. Morrow.
Red Rods... Ronal Kayser. LC 46-8609. 1946. Julian Messner, Inc.
Red Romance. Catulle Mendes. Tr. by Dingman, Marie B. (On cover: Neely's universal library no. 70). F. T. Neely.
Red Room. Geoffery Pomeroy Dennis. LC 32-126058. 1932. Simon and Schuster.
Red Room. William Le Queux. LC 11-13730. 1911. Little, Brown, and Company.
Red Room: Scenes of Artistic and Literary Life; Tr. by Elizabeth Sprigge. August Strindberg. LC 67-109337. (Everyman's Lib., No. 348). 1967. pap., 2.45. Dent.
Red Room. Translated from the French by Herma Briffault. Francoise Mallet-Joris. LC 56-6154. 1956. Farrar, Straus & Cudahy.
Red Rope. Francis Gerard. LC 39-22736. 1939. E. P. Dutton & Co., Inc.
Red Rose for Love. Carole Mortimer. (Harlequin Presents Ser.). 192p. 1982. pap. 1.75 (ISBN 0-373-10522-3). Harlequin Bks.
Red Rose Inn. Edith Tunis Sale. LC 11-11739. 1911. 1.00. J. B. Lippincott Company.
Red Rose of Love. Margaret Peterson. LC 33-17677. 1933. Doubleday, Doran & Company, Inc.
Red Rose of Savannah. A Novel. Nevada McNeill. LC 7-20297. G. W. Dillingham.
Red Roses for Jim. Lillian R Fuller. LC 32-9669. Sears Publishing Company, Inc.
Red Roses Forever. Amanda J. Jarrett. (Southerners Ser.: No. 5). (Orig.). 1983. pap. 3.50 (ISBN 0-440-07456-8). Dell.
Red Route. A Novel. William Sime. (On cover: Seaside library. Pocket ed., no. 580). 1885. G. Munro.
Red Rover. James Fenimore Cooper. LC 4-15435. (His Works. Mohawk ed.). 1896. G. P. Putnam's Sons.
Red Rover. A Tale. ... new ed. James Fenimore Cooper. LC 6-29083. 1852. Stringer and Townsend.
Red Rover. A Tale. ... new ed. James Fenimore Cooper. 1854. Stringer and Townsend.
Red Rover: A Tale. James Fenimore Cooper. LC 8-30410. 1872. Hurd and Houghton.
Red Rover: A Tale. James Fenimore Cooper. 1873. D. Appleton and Company.
Red Rover: A Tale. ... household ed. James Fenimore Cooper. Ed. by Cooper, Susan Fenimore. LC 6-29685. Houghton, Mifflion and Company.
Red Rover: A Tale. James Fenimore Cooper. LC 4-19566. 1896. D. Appleton and Company.
Red Rover, a Tale. a new ed. Charles Stanley Strong. LC 42-48371. 1836. Carey, Lea, & Blanchard.
Red Rover. A Tale of the Sea. James Fenimore Cooper. (Seaside library. v. 30, no. 615). 1879. G. Munro.
Red Rover. A Tale of the Sea. James Fenimore Cooper. (On cover: Seaside library. Pocket ed. no. 361). 1885. G. Munro.
Red Rowan Berry. Frances Murray. LC 76-22940. 1977. 8.95. St. Martin's Press.
Red Rowans: A Love Story. Flora Annie Webster Steel. LC 8-13431. 1895. Macmillan and Co.
Red Runs the Earth. 2nd ed. Joe E. Pierce. LC 70-93459. 1977. pap. 5.95 (ISBN 0-913244-06-6). Hapi Pr.
Red Runs the Earth. Joe E. Pierce. 6.00 o.s.i. (ISBN 0-8181-0169-5). Pageant-Poseidon.
Red Runs the River. Lewis B Patten. LC 78-103771. (Double D western). 1970. 4.50. Doubleday.
Red Rupert, the American Bucanier. A Tale of the Spanish Indies. Maturin Murray Ballou. LC 6-26929. 1845. Gleason's Publishing Hall.
Red Rupert, the American Buccaneer. A Tale of the Spanish Indies. Maturin Myrray Ballou. LC 9-1817. 1848. F. Gleason.
Red Rust. Cornelia James Cannon. LC 28-5165. 1928. Little, Brown, and Company.
Red Rust. Cornelia James Cannon. LC 43-4559. 1943. The Sun Dial Press.
Red Ruth: The Birth of Universal Brotherhood. Anna Ratner Shapiro. LC 17-29332. 1917. Arc Publishing Co.
Red Ryvington. William Westall. LC 42-27136. 1885. Cassell & Company, Limited.
Red Sabbath. Lewis B Patten. LC 68-18086. (DD western). 1968. Doubleday.
Red Saint. 5th impression. ed. Warwick Deeping. LC 9-31027. 1909. Cassell and Company, Limited.
Red Saint. Warwick Deeping. LC 40-34190. 1940. R. M. McBride and Company.
Red Sand. Thomas Sigismund Stribling. LC 24-8567. Harcourt, Brace and Company.
Red Sands of Santa Maria. Bill Murphy. LC 56-10063. 1956. Dodd, Mead.
Red Sap. John Easton. LC 30-974127. 1930. G. P. Putnam's Sons.
Red Saunders: His Adventures West & East. Henry Wallace Phillips. LC 2-9443. 1902. McClure, Phillips & Co.
Red Scar. Robert McNair Wilson. LC 28-24470. 1928. J. B. Lippincott.
Red Scarf. Gil Brewer. LC 58-351533. 1958. Mystery House.
Red Scarf. Grace Perry. 3.50 o.s.i. Tri-Ocean.
Red Seal. Natalie Sumner Lincoln. LC 20-42669. 1920. D. Appleton and Company.
Red Shadow. Patricia Wentworth. LC 32-231354. 1932. J. B. Lippincott Company.
Red Shadows see Hand of Kane.
Red Shadows see Moon of Skulls.
Red Shadows see Solomon Kane.
Red Shirts: A Tale of "The Terror,". new ed., with a frontispiece by stanley l. wood. ed. Paul Gaulot & De Villiers, Sir John Abraham Jacob, 1863-1961, Tr. LC 1-201922. 1899. The New Amsterdam Book Company; Etc.,Etc.
Red Shoes. Michael Powell. LC 78-58854. 1978. 1.95 (ISBN 0-380-37812-4). Avon Books.
Red Signal. Grace Livingston Hill. LC 19-105249. 1919. J. B. Lippincott Company.
Red Silence. Kathleen Thompson Norris. LC 29-17223. 1929. Doubleday, Doran & Company, Incorporated.
Red Skeleton in Your Closet: Ghost Gay and Grim, Selected, Ed. by Red Skelton. Ed. by Richard Bernard Skelton. LC 65-21855. bds., 4.95. Grosset.
Red Skel'ton in Your Closet. Red Skelton. 4.95 o.p. G&D.
Red Skull. Fergus Hume. LC 8-12806. Dodge Publishing Company.
Red Sky. Theodore Acland Harper. LC 35-19989. 1935. The Viking Press.
Red Sky at Dawn... Philip Rooney. LC 39-146141. 1939. P. J. Kenedy & Sons.
Red Sky at Midnight. Robert F Mirvish. LC 55-8851. 1955. W. Sloane Associates.
Red Sky at Morning. Richard Bradford. LC 68-11272. 1968. 12.45i (ISBN 0-397-00549-0). Har-Row.
Red Sky at Morning. Richard Bradford. 1974. pap. 2.25 (ISBN 0-671-83695-1). PB.
Red Sky at Morning. Richard Bradford. 1974. pap. 2.25 (ISBN 0-671-83695-1). WSP.
Red Sky at Morning. Margaret Kennedy. LC 27-27695. 1927. Doubleday, Page & Co.
Red Sky at Morning: A Novel. Richard Bradford. LC 68-11373. 1968. Lippincott.
Red Sky at Night. Hugh McCutcheon. LC 72-80529. 1972. 4.95 (ISBN 0-8027-5261-6). Walker.
Red Sky at Night: Lovers' Delight? Jane Aiken Hodge. LC 77-6351. 1977. 8.95 (ISBN 0-698-10841-8). Coward, McCann & Geoghegan.
Red Sky at Night, Lovers' Delight. Jane Aiken Hodge & Jane Aiken Hodge. 1978. pap. 1.95 (ISBN 0-449-23745-1, Crest). Fawcett.
Red Sky in the Morning. Robert Peter Tristram Coffin. LC 35-17494. 1935. The Macmillan Company.
Red Sky's Annie: A Story of the Bad Lands. Jessie Hollis Beebe. LC 12-324763. The Roxburgh Publishing Company, Inc.
Red Snow. Oliver Lange. LC 77-25310. 8.95 (ISBN 0-87223-481-9). Seaview Books: Trade Distribution by Simon and Schuster.
Red Snow. Frank Wright Moxley. LC 30-198341. 1930. Simon and Schuster.
Red Snow: A Novel. Oliver Lange. (Jove / HBJ Book). 1979. 2.25 (ISBN 0-515-04703-1). Jove Publications.
Red Snow: A Novel About Peace and War and People. William Peter. 208p. 1976. 8.00 o.p. (ISBN 0-682-48495-4). Exposition.
Red Soil. Rajendra Awasthi. (Vikas Library of Modern Indian Writing: No.27). 136p. 1982. text ed. 20.00x (ISBN 0-7069-1961-0, Pub. by Vikas India). Advent NY.
Red Soil. L E Gielgud. LC 27-3692. 1926. Doubleday, Page & Company.
Red Sombrero. Nelson Coral Nye. LC 54-8503. (Silver star westerns). 1954. Dodd, Mead.
Red Sonja, No. 1: The Ring of Ikribu. David C. Smith & Richard L. Tierney. (Red Sonja Ser.). 224p. (Orig.). 1981. pap. 2.25 (ISBN 0-441-71156-1). Ace Bks.
Red Sonja, No. 2: The Demon Knight. David C. Smith & Richard L. Tierney. (Red Sonja Ser.). 224p. 1982. pap. 2.50 (ISBN 0-441-71157-X). Ace Bks.
Red Sonja, No. 3: When Hell Laughs. David C. Smith & Richard L. Tierney. (Red Sonja Ser.). 192p. 1982. pap. 2.25 (ISBN 0-441-71158-8). Ace Bks.
Red Sonja, No. 4: Endithor's Daughter. David C. Smith & Richard L. Tierney. 1982. pap. 2.50 (ISBN 0-441-71159-6, Pub. by Ace Science Fiction). Ace Bks.
Red Sonja, No. 6: Star of Doom. David C. Smith & Richard L. Tierney. 1983. pap. 2.50 (ISBN 0-441-71162-6, Pub. by Ace Science Fiction). Ace Bks.
Red Spell. Francis Henry Gribble. F. A. Stokes Company.
Red Spider, 2 vols. in 1. Sabine Baring-Gould. LC 79-8232. Repr. of 1887 ed. 44.50 (ISBN 0-404-61772-7). AMS Pr.
Red Spider. A Novel. Sabine Baring-Gould. (On cover: Lovell's library, no. 1061). J. W. Lovell Company.
Red Stain. Achmed Abdullah. LC 15-199668. 1915. 1.25. Hearst's International Library Co.
Red Stain. John George Haslette Vahey. LC 32-9374. 1932. W. Morrow & Company.
Red Staircase. Gwendoline Butler. LC 78-31665. 11.95 (ISBN 0-698-10981-3). Coward, McCann & Geoghegan.
Red Star. L MacManus. LC 7-20425. (Half-title: The autonym library, no. v). 1895. G. P. Putnam's Sons.
Red Stefan. Patricia Wentworth. LC 35-131861. 1935. J. B. Lippincott Company.
Red Stockings: By Pete Fry Pseud. Clifford King. LC 62-15487. 1962. Roy Publishers.
Red Strangers: A Novel. Elspeth Joscelin Grant Huxley. LC 39-279128. 1939. Harper & Brothers.
Red Sultan: The Remarkable Adventures in Western Barbary of Sir Cosmo MacLaurin, Bart., of Monzie in the County of Perth. James Maclaren Cobban. LC 6-26757. (On cover: Rialto series, no. 64). 1894. Rand, McNally & Company.
Red Sun. Ola Harris Beaubien. LC 38-31829. 1938. The Naylor Company.
Red Sun and Harvest Moon. Adelaide Champneys. LC 47-1391. 1947. The Bobbs-Merrill Company.
Red Sun of Nippon. Herbert Osborn Yardley. LC 34-362372. 1934. Longmans, Green and Co.
Red Sun South: A Novel. Oswald Wynd. LC 48-767449. 1948. Doubleday.
Red Sunset. John Stockwell. LC 81-16811. 1982. 12.95 (ISBN 0-688-00782-1). Morrow.
Red Swan's Neck: A Tale of the North Carolina Mountains. David Reed Miller. LC 11-25742. 1911. Sherman, French & Company.
Red Symbol. John Ironside. LC 10-992164. 1910. Little, Brown, and Company.
Red Tape and Broken Hearts: Tragedy in Veterans Hospitals. Anne M Hanson. LC 75-307500. 1975. 7.50 (ISBN 0-682-48218-8). Exposition Press.
Red Tassel. David Dodge. LC 50-9902. 1950. Random House.
Red Tavern. Charles Raymond Macauley. LC 14-5198. 1914. D. Appleton and Company.
Red Threads. Rex Stout. 192p. 1982. pap. 2.50 (ISBN 0-553-22530-8). Bantam.
Red Threads. Rex Stout. 1973. pap. 1.25 o.p. (ISBN 0-515-03071-6, N3071). BJ Pub Group.
Red Thumb Mark. Richard Austin Freeman. LC 67-8739. (Seagull library of mystery and suspense). 1967. Norton.
Red Thumb Mark. Richard Austin Freeman. LC 24-26925. 1924. Dodd, Mead & Company.
Red Tide. D. D Chapman & Deloris Lehman Tarzan. (Ace science fiction special 2). 1975. (pbk.) 1.25. Ace Books.
Red Tiger. Don Skene. LC 34-23655. 1934. D. Appleton-Century Company, Incorporated.
Red Track: A Story of Social Life in Mexico. rev. and ed. by percy b. st. john. ed. Gustave Aimard & St. John, Percy Bolingbroke, 1821-1889, Ed. LC 5-42591. (On cover: Lovell's library, no. 1138). 1888. J. W. Lovell Company.
Red Triangle. Arthur Morrison. LC 75-116962. (Short Story Index Reprint Ser). 1903. 17.00 (ISBN 0-8369-3466-0). Ayer Co.
Red Triangle: Being Some Further Chronicles of Martin Hewett, Investigator. Arthur Morrison. LC 75-116962. (Short story index reprint series). (Illus.). 1970. Books for Libraries Press.
Red Triangle: Being Some Further Chronicles of Martin Hewitt, Investigator. Arthur Morrison. LC 3-18747. 1903. L. C. Page & Company.
Red Turban. Irene Wilde. LC 43-17346. 1943. Liveright Publishing Corporation.
Red Turrets of Orne. Candice Connell. LC 78-1191. 1979. 7.95 (ISBN 0-385-12683-2). Doubleday.
Red Umbrellas. Kelvin Lindemann. LC 55-11352. 1955. Appleton-Century-Croft.
Red Umbrellas. Kelvin Lindemann. LC 74-30367. 1975. 12.25 (ISBN 0-8371-7521-6). Greenwood Press.
Red Velvet. Johanna Phillips. (Second Chance at Love Ser.: No. 30). 192p. (Orig.). 1982. pap. 1.75 (ISBN 0-515-06280-4). Jove Pubns.
Red Velvet Mansion. Margaret Egerton. 1979. 6.00 o.p. (ISBN 0-682-49226-4). Exposition.
Red Velvet-the Sexy Italian Aristocrat. Jacqueline Borghese. (Illus.). 5.00 o.s.i. (ISBN 0-8181-0059-1). Pageant-Poseidon.
Red Virgin: Or, The Interregnum. George Frederic Turner. LC 14-10526. 1914. Hodder and Stoughton.
Red Vulture. Frederick Sleath. LC 23-7982. 1923. Houghton Mifflin Company.
Red Wagon. Eleanor Furneaux Smith. LC 30-166154. The Bobbs-Merrill Company.
Red Wallflower. Susan Warner. LC 8-33696. 1884. R. Carter & Brothers.
Red War. Judson Pentecost Philips & Johnson, Thomas Marvin. LC 36-10716. 1936. Doubleday, Doran & Company, Inc.
Red Warning: Written by the Detective "Gaillard". Englished and Rearranged with New Punctuation. Virgil Markham. LC 33-25223. Farrar & Rinehart, Incorporated.
Red, White and Black: Twelve Stories of the South. Murrell Edmunds. LC 45-8456. 1945. B. Ackerman, Incorporated.
Red, White and Blue in the Face. Bob Clisco Cox. 1974. 4.95. Vantage Press.
Red Wilderness. Frank J Tate. LC 39-17807. 1938. Oxford University Press.
Red Willows. Constance Lindsay Skinner. LC 29-23130. 1929. Coward-McCann, Inc.
Red Wind: A Collection of Short Stories. Raymond Chandler. LC 46-472174. 1946. The World Publishing Company.
Red Wind of Wyoming. 3rd ed. Peggy Simson Curry. 2.00 o.p. Swallow.
Red Window. Fergus Hume. LC 4-12977. 1904. G. W. Dillingham Company.
Red Window Murders. John Dickson Carr. LC 35-66552. 1935. W. Morrow and Company.
Red Wine First. Nedra Tyre. LC 47-11698. 1947. Simon and Schuster.

Red Wing: Or The Weird Cruiser of Van Dieman's Land. George S Raymond. LC 6-20750. Stringer & Townsend.

Red Wing: Or, The Weird Cruiser of Vau Dieman's Land. Charley Clewline. LC 6-20750. Stringer & Townsend.

Red Wrath. John Oxenham, pseud. LC 14-824219. 1914. John Lane Company.

Red Year: A Story of the Indian Mutiny. Louis Tracy. LC 8-979. E. J. Clode.

Redbeard. Michael Resnick. (Orig.). 1969. pap. 0.75 o.p. (74-579). Lancer.

Redburn. Henry Ochiltree. 1896. Dodd, Mead and Company.

Redburn, His First Voyage; White-Jacket, or, The World in a Man-of-War; Moby-Dick, or, The Whale. Herman Melville. Ed. by G. Thomas Tanselle. LC 82-18677. (Library of America). 27.50 (ISBN 0-940450-09-7). Literary Classics of the United States, Inc.: Distributed to the Trade by the Viking Press.

Redburn, His First Voyage: Being the Sailor Boy Confessions and Reminiscences of the Son-of-a-Gentleman in the Merchant Service. Herman Melville. LC 57-3890. (Doubleday anchor books, A118). 1957. Doubleday.

Redburn: His First Voyage: Being the Sailor Boy Confessions and Reminiscences of the Son-of-a-Gentleman in the Merchant Service. Herman Melville. LC 57-3390. (Doubleday anchor books, A118). 1957. Doubleday.

Redburn, His First Voyage: Being the Sailor-Boy Confessions and Reminiscences of the Son-of-a-Gentleman, in the Merchant Service. Herman Melville. LC 67-21601. (writings of Herman Melville, v. 4). 1969. Northwestern University Press.

Redburn, His First Voyage: Being the Sailor-Boy Confessions and Reminiscences of the Son-of-a-Gentleman, in the Merchant Service. Herman Melville. LC 79-177917. (Rinehart editions). 1971. (ISBN 0-03-082862-7). Holt, Rinehart and Winston.

Redburn, His First Voyage. Being the Sailor-Boy Confessions and Reminiscences of the Son-of-Gentleman, in the Merchant Service. Herman Melville. LC 7-17950. 1849. Harper & Brothers.

Redburn: His First Voyage. Being the Sailor-Boy Confessions and Reminiscences of the Son-of-a-Gentleman, in the Merchant Service. Herman Melville. LC 22-51420. 1850. Harper & Brothers.

Redburn: His First Voyage. Being the Sailor-Boy Confessions and Reminiscences of the Son-of-a-Gentleman, in the Merchant Service. Herman Melville. LC 7-179490. 1855. Harper & Brothers.

Redburn, His First Voyage: Being the Sailor Boy Confessions and Reminiscences of the Son-of-a-Gentleman in the Merchant Service. Herman Melville. LC 24-1493. 1924. The St. Botolph Society.

Redburn, His First Voyage: Being the Sailorboy Confessions and Reminiscences of the Son-of-a-Gentleman in the Merchant Service. Herman Melville. Ed. by Harold Lowther Beaver. LC 77-369556. (Penguin English library). (Illus.). 1977. 3.95 (ISBN 0-14-043105-5). Penguin.

Redburn, His First Voyage: By Herman Melville. Herman Melville. Ed. by Weaver, Raymond Melbourne. LC 24-23605. (Half-title: The Pequod edition of Herman Melville's collected works). 1924. A. & C. Boni.

Redcliff. Eden Phillpotts. LC 24-22272. 1924. The Macmillan Company.

Redcloud of the Lakes: A Novel. Frederick Russell Burton. LC 9-14513. G. W. Dillingham Company.

Redcoat and Minuteman. Bernard G Marshall. LC 24-24807. 1924. D. Appleton and Company.

Redcoat Captain: A Story of That Country. Alfred Ollivant. LC 7-29092. 1907. The Macmillan Company.

Redder Blood: A Novel. William Mobile Ashby. LC 73-18570. 1975. 12.50 (ISBN 0-404-11380-X). AMS Press.

Redder Blood: A Novel. William Mobile Ashby. LC 15-15866. 1915. The Cosmopolitan Press.

Reddy Brant, His Adventures. illustrated by clyde forsythe. ed. Wilbur Tuttle. LC 20-18257. 1920. The Century Co.

Redeema: A Novel. 1st Ed. Manja H Knoll. LC 54-12352. 1954. Pageant Press.

Redeemed. Sarah Elizabeth Forbush G. S. Downs Downs. LC 11-22325. G. W. Dillingham Company.

Redeemed: A Novel. Charles Hull, pseud. LC 7-5852. 1894. G. W. Dillingham.

Redeemed by Love. Charlotte Mary Brame. (On cover: Lovell's library. no. 1007). J. W. Lovell Company.

Redeemed by Love. Charlotte Mary Brame. LC 44-39936. (On cover: Seaside library. Pocket ed. No. 73). G. Munro.

Redeemed by Love: Or, Love's Conflict. Charlotte Mary Brame. LC 6507. (Bertha Clay library, no. 31). 1900. Street & Smith.

Redeemer. Hugh Fleetwood. LC 79-55598. 1980. 6.95 (ISBN 0-689-11037-5). Atheneum.

Redemption: A Novel. Beckles Willson. LC 24-19917. 1924. G. P. Putnam & Sons.

Redemption ("De Toute Son Ime") Rene Bazin. Tr. by Angelo Solomon Rappoport. LC 8-30021. 1908. C. Scribner's Sons.

Redemption Island. Charles Maynard Hale & Simpson, Evan John, 1901- Joint Author. LC 28-16621. 1928. W. Morrow & Company.

Redemption of Arthur True: A Rural School Story. Arno Bratten. LC 9-191865. 1909. The Stafford Publishing Company.

Redemption of Black Rock Ranch. Clyde W Hightower. LC 24-6639. Dorrance & Company.

Redemption: Of Charley Phillips. Etta Florence Stock. LC 19-5845. 1919. The Four Seas Company.

Redemption of David Corson. Charles Frederic Goss. LC 43-36864. 1900. The Bowen-Merrill Company.

Redemption of Edward Strahan: A Social Story. William James Dawson. LC 6-32248. F. H. Revell Company.

Redemption of Freetown. Charles Monroe Sheldon. United Society of Christian Endeavor.

Redemption of Grace Milroy. William Carlton Lanyon Dawe. LC 16-20502. 1916. 1.25. John Lane.

Redemption of Howard Gray. Charles Wesley Naylor. LC 25-22640. Gospel Trumpet Company.

Redemption of Kenneth Galt. William Nathaniel Harben. LC 9-25184. 1909. Harper & Brothers.

Redemption of Morley Darville. Stephen McKenna. LC 30-48500. 1930. Dodd, Mead & Company.

Redemption of Preacher Bull. Harry M Denton. LC 63-12529. B. Humphries.

Redemption of Richard Livingston. 1st Ed. Peggy Ballard. LC 53-8800. 1953. Pageant Press.

Redemption of the Brahman: A Novel. Richard Von Garbe. LC 7-1522. 1894. The Open Court Publishing Company.

Redemption of Tycho Brahe. Max Brod & Crosse, Felix Warren, Tr. LC 28-13908. 1928. A. A. Knopf.

Redemptioner. Isaac Rusling Pennypacker. LC 75-151503. (Illus.). 1972. (ISBN 0-87106-113-9). Pequot Press.

Redfern's Miracle. Trevor, Elleston. LC 52-25666. 1951. T. V. Boardman.

Redfields Succession: A Novel. Henry Burnham Boone. LC 3-118179. 1903. Harper & Brothers.

Redgate Gold. Jack Slade, pseud. (Lassiter Ser.: No. 28). (Orig.). 1981. pap. 1.95 (ISBN 0-505-51724-8). Tower Bks.

Redgauntlet. A Tale of the Eighteenth Century. Walter Scott. LC 8-3367. 1824. H. C. Carey and I. Lea.

Redgauntlet. A Tale of the Eighteenth Century. Walter Scott. (On cover: Lovell's library, no. 544). 1885. J. W. Lovell Company.

Redgauntlet. A Tale of the Eighteenth Century. Walter Scott. (On cover: Seaside library. Pocket ed. no. 463). 1885. G. Munro.

Redhead"... Vera Brown. LC 33-8144. Grosset & Dunlap.

Redhead. William Arthur Neubauer. LC 48-4960. 1948. Phoenix Press.

Redhead for Mike Shayne: Michael Shayne's 48th Case. Davis Dresser. LC 64-12573. (Torquil book). 1964. Distributed by Dodd, Mead.

Redhead from Chicago: Translated from the French by Lawrence Blochman. Louis Charles Royer. LC 54-3128. (Pyramid books, 110). 1954. Pyramid Books.

Redheaded Outfield: And Other Baseball Stories. Zane Grey. LC 20-129569. Grosset & Dunlap.

Redhouse on the Hill. Joseph McCord. LC 38-29162. 1938. Macrae Smith Company.

Rediscovery: Three Hundred Years of Stories by & about Women. Ed. by Betzy Dinesen. 272p. 1982. pap. 3.50 (ISBN 0-380-60756-5, 60756-5, Bard). Avon.

Redlakes. Francis Brett Young. LC 30-28398. 1930. Harper & Brothers.

Redlander. Sigman Byrd. LC 39-16518. 1939. E. P. Dutton & Company, Inc.

Redman Cave Murder. Elsa Barker. LC 30-19278. Sears Publishing Company, Inc.

Redman in White Moccasins. Glenn R Vernam. LC 72-84950. (DD western). 1973. 4.95 (ISBN 0-385-01550-X). Doubleday.

Redmaynes. Gladys Edson Locke. LC 28-18239. L. C. Page & Company.

Redneck Way of Knowledge: Down-Home Tales. Blanche M. Boyd. LC 82-160. 1982. 10.95 (ISBN 0-394-51050-X). Knopf.

Redolmo Affair. Nick Carter. (Nick Carter Ser.). 192p. (Orig.). 1979. pap. 1.95 (ISBN 0-441-71133-2, Pub. by Charter Bks). Ace Bks.

Redrock Gold see Outlaw Loot.

Reds of the Midi: An Episode of the French Revolution. 6th ed. Felix Gras. Tr. by Janvier, Catharine Ann (Drinker) LC 1-18500. 1899. D. Appleton and Company.

Reds of the Midi: An Episode of the French Revolution. Felix Gras. Tr. by Janvier, Catharine Ann (Drinker) Ed. by Ward, Bertha Evans. LC 30-24953. (Half-title: Appleton modern literature series). D. Appleton and Company.

Reds of the Midi: An Episode of the French Revolution. Felix Gras. Tr. by Janvier, Catharine Ann (Drinker) Janvier, Thomas Allibone. 1938. D. Appleton-Century Company Incorporated.

Reds of the Midi: An Episode of the French Revolution; Tr. from the Provencal of Felix Gras. Felix Gras. Tr. by Janvier, Catharine Ann (Drinker) Janvier, Thomas Allibone. LC 11-150807. 1896. D. Appleton and Company.

Reds of the Midi: An Episode of the French Revolution, Tr. from the Provencal of Felix Gras. Felix Gras. Tr. by Janvier, Catharine Ann (Drinker) Janvier, Thomas Allibone. LC 16-9352. 1912. D. Appleton and Company.

Redskin. Elizabeth Pickett Chevalier. LC 29-3966. Grosset & Dunlap.

Redskin. Lewis B. Patten. Bd. with Two For Vengeance. 1982. pap. 2.75 (ISBN 0-451-11929-0, AE1929, Sig). NAL.

Redskins: Or, Indian and Injin: Being the Conclusion of The Littlepage Manuscript. new ed. James Fenimore Cooper. LC 6-29681. 1852. Stringer and Townsend.

Redskins: Or, Indian and Injin. Being the Conclusion of The Littlepage Manuscripts. James Fenimore Cooper. (On cover: Seaside library. Pocket ed. no. 421). 1885. G. Munro.

Redskins: Or, Indian and Injin: Being the Conclusion of the Littlepage Manuscripts. James Fenimore Cooper. LC 6-29680. 1846. Burgess & Stringer.

Redskins: Or, Indian and Injin: Being the Conclusion of The Littlepage Manuscripts. James Fenimore Cooper. (On cover: Lovell's library no. 603). 1885. J. W. Lovell Company.

Redskins: Or, Indian and Injin. Being the Conclusion of the Littlepage Manuscripts. James Fenimore Cooper. LC 4-19558. 1888. D. Appleton and Company.

Redstick: Or, Scenes in the South. B. R. Montesano. LC 7-26083. 1856. U. P. James.

Redward Edward Papers. Avram Davidson. LC 74-27578. (Doubleday science fiction). 1978. 7.95 (ISBN 0-385-02058-9). Doubleday.

Redwood: A Tale. Catherine Maria Sedgwick. LC 70-93660. 1969. Garrett Press.

Redwood: A Tale. Catherine Maria Sedgwick. LC 72-8147. 1972. (ISBN 0-8422-8108-8). MSS Information Corp.

Redwood; a Tale. Catherine Maria Sedgwick. LC 8-11246. 1824. E. Bliss and E. White.

Redwood and Gold. Jackson Gregory. LC 28-21970. 1928. Dodd, Mead & Company.

Redwood Valley Romance. William Arthur Neubauer. LC 67-5181. 1967. Arcadia House.

Redwoods & Other Stories. Lavinia T. Bentley. 2.95 o.p. Vantage.

Redwoods, Iron Horses, & the Pacific: The Story of the California Western "Skunk" Railroad. 4th rev. ed. Spencer Crump. LC 74-84821. (Illus.). 1975. 15.00 (ISBN 0-87046-012-9, Pub. by Trans-Anglo). Interurban.

Reed Anthony: Cowman; an Autobiography. Andy Adams. LC 7-16751. 1907. Houghton, Mifflin and Company.

Reed Shaken with the Wind: A Love Story. Emily Faithfull. LC 6-38427. Adams, Victor & Co.

Reeds and Med. Vicente Blasco Ibanez & Beberfall, Lester, 1911- LC 66-19236. 1966. Bruce Humphries.

Reeds and Mud: "Canas y Barro". Isaac Goldberg & Goldberg, Isaac, 1887-1938, Tr. LC 28-9158. E. P. Dutton & Company.

Reeds in Shifting Sand: Illustrated by D. Karsell. Alban Maurice Emley. LC 50-57057. (Gusto classics). 1950. House-Warven.

Reef. Edith Newbold Jones Wharton. LC 65-21879. 5.95. Scribners.

Reef: A Novel. Edith Newbold Jones Wharton. LC 12-25996. 1912. D. Appleton and Company.

Reef, a Novel. 1st Ed. Keith Wheeler. LC 51-9396. 1951. Dutton.

Reef Girl. Zane Grey. LC 77-3791. 8.95 (ISBN 0-06-011624-2). Harper & Row.

Reefs of Earth. R. A. Lafferty. 1977. pap. 1.50 (ISBN 0-425-03565-4, Medallion). Berkley Pub.

Reefs of Eden. Conn Maguire. 1971. pap. 0.95 o.p. (N2571). Pyramid Pubns.

Reefs: The Journeys of McGill Feligham, Book II. Kevin O'Donnell, Jr. 224p. (Orig.). 1981. pap. 2.50 (ISBN 0-425-05059-9). Berkley Pub.

Reenter Fu Manchu. Sax Rohmer, pseud. 1976. pap. 1.25 o.p. (ISBN 0-515-03944-6). Pyramid Pubns.

Reference to Death. 1st Ed. Lavinia Riker Davis. LC 50-11183. 1950. Published for the Crime Club by Doubleday.

Refiner's Fire. Martha Caroly Davis. LC 6-32473. 1896. J. Pott and Company.

Refiner's Fire: The Life and Adventures of Marshall Pearl, a Foundling. Mark Helprin. LC 77-2575. 1977. 10.00 (ISBN 0-394-41273-7). Knopf: Distributed by Random House.

Refiner's Fire: The Life and Adventures of Marshall Pearl, a Foundling. Mark Helprin. LC 81-5379. 6.95 (ISBN 0-440-57486-2). Dell Pub.

Refining Fires: A Novel. Alice Dease. LC 17-7456. 0.75. P. J. Kenedy & Sons.

Reflection of Evil. Jan Roffman. 1976. (pbk.) 0.95. Ace Books.

Reflections. Alice Lent Covert. 1981. pap. 2.75 (ISBN 0-89083-779-1). Zebra.

Reflections. Susan Hufford. LC 81-50318. 13.50 (ISBN 0-87223-713-3). Seaview Books.

Reflections. Mark Insingel. LC 72-82381. 1972. 4.95 (ISBN 0-87376-021-2). Red Dust.

Reflections. L. H. Maack. 3.75 o.p. Carlton.

Reflections in a Glass Eye, a Novel. Don Prince. LC 60-16574. Hesperian House.

Reflections in a Golden Eye. Carson Smith McCullers. LC 50-6225. (New Classics Series). 1950. New Directions.

Reflections in a Golden Eye. Carson Smith McCullers. LC 41-2706. 1941. Houghton Mifflin Company.

Reflections in a Mirage. Leonard Daventry. 1970. pap. 0.75 o.p. (0502-07061). Curtis.

Reflections in a Mirage: And The Ticking Is in Your Head. Leonard Daventry. LC 69-10992. (Doubleday science fiction). 1969. 5.95. Doubleday.

Reflections in the Dark. B. A. Uronovitz. 1961. pap. 3.00 o.p. (Pub. by Elizabeth Pr). SBD.

Reflections in Thought. Reed L. Hart. 3.75 o.p. Carlton.

Reflections of a Mountain Summer. Joanna M Glass. LC 74-7221. 1974. (ISBN 0-394-48919-5). Knopf.

Reflections of Ambrosine. Elinor Sutherland Glyn. 1972. pap. 0.95 o.p. (09109). Curtis.

Reflections of Ambrosine: A Novel. Elinor Sutherland Glyn. LC 2-26863. 1902. Harper & Brothers.

Reflections Upon a Sinking Ship. Gore Vidal. LC 68-30880. (A collection of essays). 1969. 6.95 o.p. (ISBN 0-316-90259-4). Little.

Reflex. Dick Francis. LC 80-23234. 11.95 (ISBN 0-399-12598-1). Putnam.

Reflex. large print ed. Dick Francis. LC 81-6235. 14.95 (ISBN 0-8161-3255-0). G.K. Hall.

Reflex Action. Christopher Fitzsimons. LC 77-55615. 10.95 (ISBN 0-689-11036-7). Atheneum.

Reflex and Bone Structure. Clarence Major. LC 75-10746. 8.95. (ISBN 0-914590-16-2) (ISBN 0-914590-17-0). Fiction Collective: Distributed by G. Braziller.

Reflexes. Emily White Sandford. LC 39-2489. The Christopher Publishing House.

Reform'd Coquet. Mary Davys. Bd. with Familiar Letters Betwixt a Gentleman & a Lady; Mercenary Lover: or the Unfortunate Heiresses. Eliza Haywood. LC 72-170558. (Foundations of the Novel Ser.: Vol. 42). lib. bdg. 50.00 (ISBN 0-8240-0553-8). Garland Pub.

Reform'd Coquet and Familiar Letters Betwixt a Gentleman and a Lady. Mary Davys. LC 72-170558. (Foundations of the Novel). 1973. 22.00 ea. Garland Pub.

Reformed Gun. Marvin H. Albert. 1970. pap. 0.60 o.p. (R2348, GM). Fawcett World.

Reformed Woman: Or, Passages from the Life of Mrs. Anna Cooley. With Brief Sketches of Her Mission, and a Plea for the Fallen. Edith Rivers. LC 7-41014. 1859. For the Author.

Reformer. Charles Monroe Sheldon. LC 2-27421. 1902. Advance Publishing Co.

Reformers & Their Step-Children. Leonard Verduin. 1964. 5.75 o.p. (ISBN 0-8028-3284-9). Eerdmans.

Refracted Light. Grace Helen Davies Yerbury. LC 59-12467. 1959. Pageant Press.

Refractions. Leon Fleischman. LC 29-21804. 1929. H. Liveright.

Refractory Husbands. Mary Stewart Doubleday Cutting. LC 79-128729. (Short story index reprint series). (Illus.). 1970. Books for Libraries Press.

Refractory Husbands. Mary Stewart Doubleday Cutting. LC 13-201258. 1913. Doubleday, Page & Company.

Refuge. Kenneth Mackenzie. 1969. pap. 2.75 o.s.i. Tri-Ocean.

Refuge in Avalon: A Novel. Marguerite Steedman. LC 61-12585. 1962. Doubleday.

Refuge in Terror. Wal Watkins. LC 73-163290. 1972. 1.65 (ISBN 0-7260-0026-4). Gold Star Publications.

Refugee. Herman Melville. LC 7-17948. T. B. Peterson & Brothers.

Refugee. Linda Shah & Khalid Shah. LC 74-8820. (Illus.). 1974. 7.95 (ISBN 0-690-00556-3). Crowell.
Refugee Centaur. Antonio Robles. LC 52-12880. 1952. Twayne Publsihers.
Refugee from Judea: And Other Jewish Tales. William Zukerman. LC 60-53162. 1961. Philosophical Library.
Refugee in America: A Novel. Frances Milton Trollope. LC 8-28504. 1833. Whittaker, Treacher, and Co.
Refugee River. Stephen Edward Rose. LC 44-8558. 1944. Margent Press.
Refugee: The Strange Story of Nether Hall. Charles James Louis Gilson. LC 10-21595. 1910. 1.25. The Century Co.
Refugees: A Sequel to "Uncle Tom's Cabin". Annie Jefferson Holland. LC 7-6130. 1892. Pub. for the Author.
Refugees: A Tale of Two Continents. Arthur Conan Doyle. LC 4-16304. 1893. Harper & Brothers.
Refugees: A Tale of Two Continents. Arthur Conan Doyle. LC 25-15492. Harper & Brothers.
Refugees: A Tale of Two Continents. Arthur Conan Doyle. 8.95. Transatlantic.
Refugiados. Angel Castro. 1969. pap. 1.25. Lectorum Corp.
Refusal. Jane West. LC 1-17894. 1810. Printed for M. Carey, No., Market-Street. Sold in Philadelphia by Birch & Small, Bradford & Inskeep, Edward Earle, J. & A. Y. Humphreys, W. W. Woodward in New-York, by Inskeep & Bradfrod, M. & W. Ward and D. Longworth.
Refusers: An Epic of the Jews: a Trilogy of Novels Based on Three Heroic Lives. Stanley Burnshaw. LC 81-82840. (Illus.). 14.95 (ISBN 0-8180-0630-7). Horizon Press.
Regain see Oeuvres Romanesques.
Regan. Ian Kennedy Martin, pseud. LC 75-940. 1975. 6.95 (ISBN 0-03-014541-4). Holt, Rinehart and Winston.
Regarding Electra. Maurice Valency. 55p. 1976. pap. 2.95x. Dramatists Play.
Regards to Broadway. Donald Henderson Clarke. LC 35-143876. 1935. The Vanguard Press.
Regards to Broadway. Donald Henderson Clarke. LC 47-197822. 1947. Triangle Books, the Blakiston Company.
Regatta. Douglass Wallop. LC 80-15077. (Illus.). 11.95 (ISBN 0-393-01364-2). Norton.
Regatta Moon. Anne Stewart. LC 37-24835. Phoenix Press.
Regatta Mystery. Agatha Miller Christie. 1983. pap. 2.95 (ISBN 0-440-17336-1). Dell.
Regatta Mystery. Agatha Miller Christie. 1973. (pbk) 0.75. Dell.
Regatta Mystery: And Other Stories. Agatha Miller Christie. LC 39-16743. 1939. Dodd, Mead & Company.
Regency: A Quadruple Portrait. David Leslie Murray. LC 36-17127. 1936. A. A. Knopf.
Regency Buck. Georgette Heyer. (SB4055). 1967. Bantam.
Regency Buck. Georgette Heyer. LC 66-25131. 1966. Dutton.
Regency Charade. Elizabeth Mansfield, pseud. 224p. 1981. pap. 2.25 (ISBN 0-425-04835-7). Berkley Pub.
Regency Frost, No. 69. Anne Devon. Date not set. pap. 1.75 (ISBN 0-515-06680-X). Jove Pubns.
Regency Galatea. Elizabeth Mansfield, pseud. 1981. pap. 2.25 (ISBN 0-425-04739-3). Berkley Pub.
Regency Gold. Marion Chesney. 1980. pap. 1.75 (ISBN 0-449-50002-0, Coventry). Fawcett.
Regency Match. Elizabeth Mansfield, pseud. 1980. pap. 2.25 (ISBN 0-425-04514-5). Berkley Pub.
Regency Rogue. Helen Ashfield. LC 81-23177. 9.95 (ISBN 0-312-66900-3). St Martin's Press.
Regency Rose. Miriam Lynch. 1980. pap. 1.75 (ISBN 0-449-50031-4, Coventry). Fawcett.
Regency Row. Blanche Chenier. (Fawcett Crest Book). 1.50 (ISBN 0-449-23419-3). Fawcett Books.
Regency Royal. John Michael Drinkrow Hardwick. LC 78-5554. 1978. 9.95 (ISBN 0-698-10895-7). Coward, McCann & Geoghegan.
Regency Wager. Elizabeth Mansfield, pseud. 208p. (Orig.). 1981. pap. 2.25 (ISBN 0-425-05088-2). Berkley Pub.
Regency Windows. David Emerson. 1930. Little, Brown, and Company.
Regeneration: A Novel. Herbert Baird Stimpson. LC 8-15683. 1896. W. Neale.
Regenesis: A Novel. Robert Granat. LC 72-83899. 1972. 7.95 (ISBN 0-671-21362-8). Simon and Schuster.
Regensburg Legacy. Jack M Bickham. LC 79-7801. 1980. 10.95 (ISBN 0-385-15546-8). Doubleday.
Regent. Arnold Bennett. LC 74-17073. (Collected Works of Arnold Bennett: Vol. 70). 1976. Repr. of 1913 ed. 21.00 (ISBN 0-518-19151-6). Ayer Co.
Regent: A Five Towns Story of Adventure in London. Arnold Bennett. LC 74-17073. (Collected works of Arnold Bennett). 1974. (ISBN 0-518-19151-6). Books for Libraries Press.
Regent Square. Forbes Bramble. LC 77-5746. 1977. 9.95 (ISBN 0-698-10836-1). Coward, McCann & Geoghegan.
Regent Square. Forbes Bramble. 1980. 2.50 (ISBN 0-671-82185-7). Pocket Books.
Regenta. Leopoldo Alas. 1983. pap. 5.95 (ISBN 0-14-044346-0). Penguin.
Regent's Daughter. Alexandre Dumas & Louis Couailhac. (Half-title: The regency romances). 1891. Little, Brown and Company.
Regent's Daughter. Alexandre Dumas & Louis Couailhac. LC 6-43632. (Half-title: The romances of Alexandre Dumas. Illustrated library ed. v. 24). 1893. Little, Brown, and Company.
Regent's Daughter. Alexandre Dumas & Louis Couailhac. LC 8-7672. 1894. Little, Brown, and Company.
Regent's Daughter: A Sequel to "The Conspirators. Alexandre Dumas & Louis Couailhac. G. Routledge and Sons.
Regent's Daughter. An Historical Romance. (Sequel to "The Conspirators.". Alexandre Dumas & Louis Couailhac. LC 6-43631. (American series. no. 337). M. J. Ivers & Co.
Regent's Daughter. An Historical Romance. (Sequel to "The Conspirators"). Alexandre Dumas & Louis Couailhac. LC 6-43630. (On cover: Seaside library. pocket ed, no. 2114). G. Munro's Sons.
Regent's Daughter. Translated from the French of Alexandre Dumas. Alexandre Dumas & Louis Couailhac. LC 6-43629. 1845. Harper & Brothers.
Reggie: A Portrait of Reginald Turner. Stanley Weintraub. LC 65-19321. 6.00. Braziller, Park Ave.
Reggis Arms Caper. Ross H. Spencer. 1979. pap. 1.95 (ISBN 0-380-47092-6, 47092). Avon.
Regicides. A Tale of Early Colonial Times. Frederick Hull Cogswell. LC 6-27174. 1896. Colonial Publishing Co.
Regiment. Clement Lister Skelton. LC 78-11789. (His The regiment quartet; v. 2). 9.95 (ISBN 0-8037-7372-2). Dial Press.
Regiment of Women. Winifred Ashton. LC 17-3574. 1917. The Macmillan Company.
Regiment of Women. Winifred Ashton. LC 78-17055. 1978. 19.75 (ISBN 0-313-20582-5). Greenwood Press.
Regiment of Women. Thomas Berger. (Orig.). 1982. pap. 7.95 (ISBN 0-440-57261-4, Delta). Dell.
Regiment of Women: A Novel. Thomas Berger. LC 72-93503. 1973. 8.95 (ISBN 0-671-21492-6). Simon and Schuster.
Regimental Legends. Henrietta Eliza Vaughan Stannard. LC 8-27042. (Harper's handy series, no. 114). 1887. Harper & Brothers.
Regiments of Night. Brian N. Ball. (Science Fiction Ser.). 192p. (Orig.). 1972. pap. 0.95 o.p. (UQ1019). DAW Bks.
Regina. Clare Darcy. LC 76-13812. 8.95. Walker.
Regina. Clare Darcy. LC 77-15544. 1977. 11.95 (ISBN 0-8161-6529-7). G. K. Hall.
Regina. Clare Darcy. (Signet Book). 1978. 1.75 (ISBN 0-451-07878-0). New American Library.
Regina. Leslie Epstein. 288p. 1982. 13.95 (ISBN 0-698-11203-2, Coward). Putnam Pub Group.
Regina: Or, The Sins of the Fathers. Hermann Sudermann & Marshall, Beatrice, Tr. LC 6-69333. 1905. J. Lane.
Regina: Or, The Sins of the Fathers. Hermann Sudermann & Marshall, Beatrice, Tr. LC 13-93613. 1910. John Lane Company.
Reginald and Reginald in Russia. Hector Hugh Munro. LC 29-8994. (Half-title: The works of "Saki" (H. H. Munro). 1928. The Viking Press.
Reginald Archer. A Novel. Anne Moncure Crane Seemuller. LC 8-6445. 1871. J. R. Osgood & Company.
Reginald Dalton. John Gibson Lockhart. LC 7-15170. 1823. E. Duyckinck Etc.
Reginald: The Story of an Idle Young Man. Fanny Derington Green. LC 28-11700. 1928. Brentano's Ltd.
Regine. Hermann Sudermann & Miller, Hettie E., Tr. (On cover: The Marguerite series, no. 23). 1894. E. A. Weeks & Company.
Region Cloud. Percy Lubbock. LC 26-26285. 1925. C. Scribner's Sons.
Region of the Summer Stars. Charles Williams. 1944. 3.50x o.p. (ISBN 0-19-812410-4). Oxford U Pr.
Regional Sketches: New England and Florida. Harriet Elizabeth Beecher Stowe. LC 76-142864. (Masterworks of literature series). 1972. 6.50, 2.95 (pbk.). College & University Press.
Regions of Courage. Hartney Myers. LC 60-4344. (Milestone book). 1959. Comet Press Books.
Registrator. Filipp Berman. 140p. (Rus.). 1983. 16.00 (ISBN 0-88233-729-7); pap. 8.00 (ISBN 0-88233-730-0). Ardis Pubs.
Regret of Spring: A Love Episode. Pitts Harrison Burt. LC 6-19656. 1898. G. W. Dillingham Co.
Regular Fellows I Have Met. Ring W. Lardner. 1919. Repr. 10.00 o.s.i. Finch Pr.
Regulars. Stephen Lewis. (Orig.). 1980. pap. 2.50 o.s.i. (ISBN 0-8439-0735-5, Leisure Bks). Nordon Pubns.
Regulation Guy. Eugene Cunningham. LC 22-23261. 1922. The Cornhill Publishing Company.
Regulator: The Life and Death of William Thompson. Ray Hogan. (Signet book). New American Library.
Regulators. William Degenhard. 600p. 1981. pap. 11.95 (ISBN 0-933256-23-X). Second Chance.
Regulators. William Degenhard. 1981. 22.50 (ISBN 0-531-07318-1, Pub. by Second Chance Pr); pap. 11.95 (ISBN 0-531-07336-X). Watts.
Regulators: Being an Account of the Late Insurrections in Massachusetts Known As the Shays' Rebellion As Witnessed by Warren Hascott, Esq. Also Conveying Some Idea of the Interior Circumstances of Massachusetts and Other Sections of the Newly Founded United States of America. William Degenhard. LC 43-7380. 1943. The Dial Press.
Regulators of Arkansas: A Thrilling Tale of Border Adventure. Friedrich Wilhelm Christian Gerstacker. LC 5-41088. 1857. Dick & Fitzgerald.
Rehabilitation Nurse. Neubauer, William Arthur. LC 66-4731. 1966. Arcadia House.
Rehearsal. Terence Brady. LC 73-164282. 1973. 2.10 (ISBN 0-491-00564-4). W. H. Allen.
Rehearsal. Fredericka Faxon. LC 40-12031. Coward-McCann, Inc.
Rehearsal for Love. Faith Baldwin. 1976. Repr. of 1940 ed. lib. bdg. 16.30x (ISBN 0-88411-612-3). Amereon Ltd.
Rehearsal for Love. Faith Baldwin Cuthrell. LC 74-82152. 1975. (ISBN 0-88411-612-3). Aeonian Press.
Rehearsal for Love. Faith Baldwin Cuthrell. LC 40-6297. Farrar & Rinehart, Inc.
Rehearsal for Love: By Kathleen Harris Pseud. Adelaide Humphries. LC 53-722114. 1953. Arcadia House.
Rehearsal for Murder. Frank Bunce. pap. 0.95 o.p. (01807, Collier). Macmillan.
Rehearsal for Murder: A Crime Novel. Frank Buce. LC 56-5913. 1956. Abelard-Schuman.
Rehearsal for the Funeral. Eli Colter. LC 53-11304. 1953. Arcadia House.
Rehearsal of Love. Arthur Shumway. LC 33-305613. A. H. King.
Rehearsals for Armageddon, No. 2. David C. Hon. Ed. by Arthur L. Zapel. LC 79-84744. (Illus.). 1976. pap. text ed. 4.95 (ISBN 0-916260-02-X). Meriwether Pub.
Rehearsals for Murder. Morna Doris MacTaggart Brown. LC 41-6692. 1941. Published for the Crime Club by Doubleday, Doran.
Rehearsals for Murder. E. X. Ferrars, pseud. 1971. pap. 0.75 o.p. (07177). Curtis.
Rehearsals for Murder. Elizabeth Ferrars. LC 41-669222. 1941. Pub. for the Crime Club Doubleday, Doran and Co., Inc.
Rehearsal's off! George Booth. (Illus.). 1977. pap. 5.95 (ISBN 0-380-01719-9, 60574). Avon.
Reich Four. Nick Carter. 192p. (Orig.). 1979. pap. 1.95 (ISBN 0-441-71228-2, Pub. by Charter Bks). Ace Bks.
Reign of Gilt. David Graham Phillips. Ed. by Donald Pizer. LC 79-96675. (American Authors Ser). 1970. lib. bdg. 16.95 o.s.i. (ISBN 0-512-00550-8). Garrett Pr.
Reign of Guilt. David Graham Phillips. (American Author Ser.). 1981. Repr. lib. bdg. 29.00. Scholarly.
Reign of Law. James Lane Allen. Repr. of 1900 ed. lib. bdg. 15.00 (ISBN 0-8414-3070-5). Folcroft.
Reign of Law: A Tale of the Kentucky Hemp Fields. James Lane Allen. LC 77-164556. (American fiction reprint series). (Illus.). 1971. (ISBN 0-8369-7032-2). Books for Libraries Press.
Reign of Law: A Tale of the Kentucky Hemp Fields. James Lane Allen. LC 3311. 1900. The Macmillan Company.
Reign of Quantity. Rene Guenon. (Metaphysical Library). 1972. pap. 2.65 o.p. (ISBN 0-14-003537-0). Penguin.
Reign of Queen Isyl. Gelett Burgess & Irwin, William Henry, 1873- Joint Author. LC 3-29838. 1903. McClure, Phillips & Company.
Reign of Selfishness. A Story of Concentrated Wealth. Samuel Walker. LC 8-33288. M. K.Pelletreau.
Reign of Terror: The 1st Corgi Book of Great Victorian Horror Stories. Michel Parry. LC 77-364069. 1976. 0.65 (ISBN 0-552-10335-7). Corgi.
Reign of the Evil One. Charles Ferdinand Ramuz. Tr. by Whitall, James. LC 22-23117. (Half-title: The European library, ed. by J. E. Spingarn). Harcourt, Brace and Company.
Reign of the Great Elector. Klara Muller Mundt. Tr. by Smith, Mary Stuart (Harrison) LC 12-36992. (Half-title: The historical romances of Louise Muhlbach pseud.). D. Appleton and Company.
Reign of the Madman: The Birdcatcher: a Novel. Walter J Schenck. LC 80-81523. 15.95. Pheasant Run Publications.
Reign of the Nightriders. Elizabeth Levin. LC 32-334191. The Christopher Publishing House.
Reign of Wizardry. Jack Williamson. 1979. Repr. of 1964 ed. 15.00 (ISBN 0-932096-01-8). Phantasia Pr.
Reign of Wizardry. easy eye ed. Jack Williamson. (Orig.). 1968. pap. 0.60 o.p. (73-748). Lancer.
Reign of Wizardry. Jack Williamson. 1973. pap. 0.95 o.s.i. (75-431). Lancer.
Reigning Belle. Ann Sophia Winterbotham Stephens. LC 8-14266. T. B. Peterson & Brother.
Reigning Belle. A Society Novel. Ann Sophia Winterbotham Stephens. LC 8-142641. T. B. Peterson & Brothers.
Reigning Cats & Dogs. Sonia Levitin. LC 77-15811. 1978. 7.95 (ISBN 0-689-10868-0). Atheneum.
Reigning Passions: A Novel. Kathrin Perutz. LC 77-20701. 10.00 (ISBN 0-397-01247-0). Lippincott.
Reilly's Luck. Louis L'Amour. 224p. (Orig.). 1982. pap. 2.50 (ISBN 0-553-22674-6, Y13589-9). Bantam.
Reimann Curse. Jean DeWeese. 1975. (pbk.) 0.95 (ISBN 0-345-26688-9). Ballantine Books.
Reina de Placer. new ed. Regina Valdes. (Pimienta Collection). 160p. (Span.). 1974. pap. 1.00 o.p. (ISBN 0-88473-200-2). Fiesta Pub.
Reina del Amor. Wilson Ferranti. (Pimienta Collection Ser). (Orig., Span.). 1977. pap. 1.00 (ISBN 0-88473-269-X). Fiesta Pub.
Reincarnation in the Twentieth Century. Martin Ebon. pap. 1.50 (ISBN 0-451-08479-9, W8479, Sig). NAL.
Reincarnation in Venice. Max Simon Ehrlich. LC 78-15241. 9.95 (ISBN 0-671-22689-4). Simon and Schuster.
Reincarnation of Peter Proud. Max Simon Ehrlich. LC 73-22665. 1974. 6.95 (ISBN 0-672-52001-X). Bobbs-Merrill.
Reincarnation of Robert Macready. Robert Macready. 336p. (Orig.). 1981. pap. 2.75 (ISBN 0-89083-703-1). Zebra.
Reincarnation: The Best Short Stories of R. B. Cunninghame Graham. Robert Bontine Cunninghame Graham. LC 79-28208. 1980. 10.00 (ISBN 0-89919-004-9). Ticknor & Fields.
Reindeer Trek. Allen Roy Evans. LC 36-4992. 1935. Coward-McCann, Inc.
Reinhard Action: A Novel. Hershey Eisenberg. LC 79-19446. 1980. 8.95 (ISBN 0-688-03583-3). Morrow.
Reinhart in Love. Thomas Berger. LC 62-9631. 1962. Scribner.
Reinhart in Love: A Novel. Thomas Berger. LC 82-5147. 1982. 15.95 (ISBN 0-440-07343-X). Delacorte Press/S. Lawrence.
Reinhart's Women. Thomas Berger. 1982. pap. 7.95 (ISBN 0-440-57408-0, Delta). Dell.
Reinhart's Women: A Novel. Thomas Berger. LC 81-3271. 12.95 (ISBN 0-440-07408-8). Delacorte Press/S. Lawrence.
Reinhart's Women: A Novel. Thomas Berger. LC 82-10000. 1982. 7.95 (ISBN 0-440-57408-0). Delta/S. Lawrence.
Reini Kugel: Lover of This Earth. Herman Fetzer. LC 29-5960. 1929. Doubleday, Doran and Company, Inc.
Reivers. William Faulkner. 1962. 13.95 (ISBN 0-394-44229-6). Random.
Reivers: A Reminiscence. William Faulkner. LC 62-10335. 1962. Random House.
Rejected Apostle: And Other Stories. Helen Wainright et al. LC 24-4586. The Vincentian Press.
Rejected Bride: "Only a Girl's Heart." 2d Series. Emma Dorothy Eliza Nevitte Southworth. LC 8-14256. (Ledger library, no. 100). 1894. R. Bonner's Sons.
Rejected Lovers. William Steig. (Illus.). 153p. 1973. pap. 1.50 (ISBN 0-486-22956-4). Dover.
Rejected Messiah. Solomon L'Vovich Poliakov. LC 28-19755. 1928. A. & C. Boni.
Rejected of Men: A Story of to-Day. Howard Pyle. LC 3-14989. 1903. Harper & Brothers.
Rejected Wife. Ann Sophia Winterbotham Stephens. LC 8-14265. T. B. Peterson & Brothers.
Rejected Wife: Or, The Ruling Passion. Ann Sophia Winterbotham Stephens. LC 8-14263. T. B. Peterson & Brothers.
Rejections of 1927- Baker, Charles Henry, 1895- Ed. LC 20-20572. Doubleday, Doran and Company, Inc.
Rejoice. Samuel Astrachan. LC 77-101364. 1970. 4.95. Dial Press.
Rejuvenated. Effie Woodward Merriman. LC 28-20916. The Midwest Company.

Rejuvenation of Aunt Mary. Anne Warner French. 1905. Little, Brown, and Company.

Rejuvenation of Aunt Mary. Anne Warner French. 1907. Little, Brown, and Company.

Rejuvenation of Aunt Mary. Anne Warner French. LC 7-42009. 1908. Little, Brown, and Company.

Rejuvenation of Miss Semaphore: A Farcical Novel. Hal Godfrey. LC 98-150. 1898. L. C. Page and Company.

Rejuvenation of Siegfried Immerselbe: A Novel. Ignas Jurkunas. LC 65-17034. 1965. Manyland Books.

Rekill. Ian Kennedy Martin, pseud. LC 77-7646. 7.95 (ISBN 0-399-11986-8). Putnam.

Rekindle the Dreams. Kyra P. Wayne. LC 78-50824. 1978. pap. 1.50 o.s.i. (ISBN 0-89559-021-2). Dale Books Inc.

Rekindled Fires. Joseph Anthony. LC 18-10175. 1918. H. Holt and Company.

Rekindled Fires. Mary Crosbie. LC 29-170433. J. H. Sears & Company, Inc.

Rekindled Flame. Elizabeth Ashton. (Harlequin Romances Ser.). 192p. 1980. pap. 1.25 (ISBN 0-373-02347-2, Pub. by Harlequin). PB.

Related to Caesar. Harold E. Wagner. 1968. 6.95 o.p. Vantage.

Relations. Johannes Allen. LC 70-115807. 1970. 5.95. World Pub. Co.

Relations. Harry Hamilton Johnston. LC 26-4587. 1926. Harper & Brothers.

Relations. Carolyn Salughter. 1978. 1.95 (ISBN 0-671-82060-5). Pocket Books.

Relations. Carolyn Slaughter. LC 77-8704. 1977. 8.95 (ISBN 0-88405-549-3). Mason/Charter.

Relative Stranger. Anne Stevenson, pseud. LC 71-105592. 1970. 5.95. Putnam.

Relative to Death. Stanton Forbes, pseud. LC 65-18392. 1965. Published for the Crime Club by Doubleday.

Relative to Poison. Edith Caroline Rivett. LC 48-2169. 1948. Pub. for the Crime Club of Doubleday.

Relatives. George Alec Effinger. LC 73-4147. 224p. 1973. 6.95 o.p. (ISBN 0-06-011149-6, HarpT). Har-Row.

Relatives. Russell Neale. LC 29-20107. 1929. Harper & Brothers.

Relatives: A Novel. George Alec Effinger. LC 73-4147. 1973. 6.95 (ISBN 0-06-011149-6). Harper & Row.

Relatos Escogidos. Konstantin Georgievich Paustovskii. 335p. (Span.). 1975. 6.45 (ISBN 0-8285-1326-0, Pub. by Progress Pubs USSR). Imported Pubns.

Relatos Humoristicos. Ed. by Homero Castillo. (Illus.). (YA) (gr. 9 up). 1956. 3.95 o.p. (ISBN 0-19-500847-2, OxfordC). Oxford U Pr.

Release: Or, Caroline's French Kindred. Charlotte Mary Yonge. LC 9-1210. 1896. Macmillan and Co.

Release the Lions. Rupert Croft-Cooke. LC 34-4678. 1934. Dodd, Mead & Company.

Release Your Cosmic Powers. Michael X. 1969. pap. 6.95. G Barker Bks.

Relentless. Brian Wynne Garfield. LC 71-159586. 1972. 5.95 (ISBN 0-529-04549-4). World Pub.

Relentless. Myrtle Johnston. LC 30-20599. 1930. D. Appleton and Company.

Relentless Adversary. Jayne Castle. (Candlelight Ecstasy Ser.: No. 45). (Orig.). 1982. pap. 1.75 (ISBN 0-440-17290-X). Dell.

Relentless City. Edward Frederic Benson. LC 3-24536. 1903. Harper & Brothers.

Relentless Current. M. E. Charlesworth. LC 12-4355. 1912. 1.25. G. P. Putnam's Sons.

Relentless Desire. Sandra Brown. (Second Chance at Love Ser.: No. 106). 1.75 (ISBN 0-515-06870-5). Jove Pubns.

Relentless Gun. Giles A. Lutz. 144p. 1981. pap. 1.75 (ISBN 0-449-13996-4, GM). Fawcett.

Relentless Love. Hayton Monteith. (Candlelight Ecstasy Ser.: No. 80). (Orig.). 1982. pap. 1.95 (ISBN 0-440-17188-1). Dell.

Relentless Storm. Claire Lorrimer. 224p. 1981. pap. 2.25 (ISBN 0-553-13658-5). Bantam.

Relentless Storm. Claire Lorrimer. 1975. (pbk.) 0.95 (ISBN 0-380-00417-8). Avon.

Relentless Strangers. Edward W Warner. LC 58-5746. 1958. Muhlenberg Press.

Relentless Tide. 1st Ed. Dorothy Alice Bonavia Hunt. LC 51-9680. 1951. Dutton.

Reliable Source. Robert Elverman. LC 76-28929. (Exposition-banner book). 7.00 (ISBN 0-682-48658-2). Exposition Press.

Relic. Jose Maria de. Eca de Queiros & Bell, Aubrey Fitz Gerald, 1882- Tr. LC 25-16206. 1925. A. A. Knopf.

Relic, a Novel: Translated from the Portuguese by Aubrey F. G. Bell. With an Introd. by Francis Steegmuller. Jose Maria De Eca De Queiroz. LC 54-1659. 1954. Noonday.

Relics. Agnes Fraser. LC 7-20301. (On cover: Appleton's town and country library, no. 125). 1893. D. Appleton and Company.

Relics and Angels. Hamilton Basso. LC 29-17261. 1929. The Macaulay Company.

Relief from Depression. Helen D. Wright. (Illus., Orig.). 1978. pap. 2.95 o.p. (ISBN 0-8431-0430-9). Price Stern.

Relief Pitcher. Russell Guy Emery. LC 52-14003. 1953. Macrae Smith.

Religion. Nicholas Conde. LC 82-2166. 13.95 (ISBN 0-453-00412-1). New American Library.

Religion at Home: A Story, Founded on Facts... 2d ed. Catherine Read Arnold Williams. LC 8-36920. 1837. Printed by B. Cranston & Co.

Religious Body. Catherine Aird, pseud. 1981. 15.00x (ISBN 0-86025-167-5, Pub. by Ian Henry Pubns England). State Mutual Bk.

Religious Body: 1st Ed. Catherine Aird, pseud. LC 66-24332. 1966. 3.50. Pub. for the Crime Club by Doubleday.

Religious Forms and Faith in the Volksbuch. Siegfried Berthold Puknat. (California. University. University of California Publications in Modern Philology: Vol. 36, No. 11). 1952. University of California Press.

Religious Sentiments of Charles Dickens. Charles Dickens. Ed. by Charles H. McKenzie. LC 73-7504. 1973. 9.95 (ISBN 0-8383-1697-2). Haskell House.

Reluctant Abbess: Angelique Arnauld of Port-Royal: 1591-1661. Margaret Lahey Trouncer. LC 57-6047. 1957. Sheed and Ward.

Reluctant Adam. Sidney Williams. LC 15-634175. 1915. Houghton Mifflin Company.

Reluctant Admiral: Yamamoto and the Imperial Navy. Hiroyuki Agawa. LC 79-84652. 1979. 14.95 (ISBN 0-87011-355-0). Kodansha International.

Reluctant Adventuress. June Sylvia Thimblethorpe. (Fawcett crest book, M2055). 1974. (pbk.) 0.95. Fawcett Publications.

Reluctant Adventuress. Sylvia Thorpe. 224p. 1977. pap. 1.50 (ISBN 0-449-23426-6, Crest). Fawcett.

Reluctant Angel. Edna Constance. LC 67-95581. 1967. aust. 3.00. Macmillan.

Reluctant Angel. Ennen Reaves Hall. LC 51-3091. 1951. Morrow.

Reluctant Bachelor: An Original Japanese Story. Translated by Kuni Sasaki and Jiro C. Araki. 1st Ed. Kuni Sasaki. LC 62-4878. 1962. Vantage Press.

Reluctant Bride. Barbara Cartland. (Orig.). 1982. pap. 1.95 (ISBN 0-515-06382-7). Jove Pubns.

Reluctant Bride. Barbara Cartland. 1972. pap. 1.25 o.p. (ISBN 0-515-04133-5). BJ Pub Group.

Reluctant Bride. Joan Smith. (Coventry Romance Ser.: No. 171). 224p. 1982. pap. 1.50 (ISBN 0-449-50272-4, Coventry). Fawcett.

Reluctant Bride see Mistress of Tara.

Reluctant Cavalier. Jeanne Judson. LC 55-3088. 1955. Avalon Books.

Reluctant Cavalier: A Novel. Donald Barr Chidsey. LC 60-862866. 1960. Crown Publishers.

Reluctant Cinderella. Jennifer Ames, pseud. 1974. 4.50. Avalon Books.

Reluctant Cinderella: By Jennifer Ames Pseud. Maysie Greig. LC 52-10652. 1952. Bouregy & Curl.

Reluctant Couple. Doug Buck. (Orig.). pap. 0.95 o.p. (1142). Brandon.

Reluctant Dragon. Kenneth Grahame. LC 38-28954. Holiday House.

Reluctant Duchess. Alice Duer Miller. LC 25-17122. 1925. Dodd, Mead & Company.

Reluctant Goddess. Oleda Baker. 480p. (Orig.). 1981. pap. 2.75 (ISBN 0-515-05869-6). Jove Pubns.

Reluctant Gunman. William MacLeod Raine. LC 54-6821. 1954. Houghton Mifflin.

Reluctant Hangman and Other Stories of Crime: Those Being the Two Criminous Tales from Ivan Greet's Masterpiece, Etc. With the Original Illus. from the Strand Magazine. Grant Allen. LC 74-175887. (Illus.). 1973. 4.50. Aspen Press.

Reluctant Hangman & Other Stories of Crime. Grant Allan. Ed. by Tom Schantz & Enid Schantz. (Illus.). 56p. 1975. pap. 4.50 o.p. (ISBN 0-915230-00-3). Rue Morgue.

Reluctant Hangman & Other Stories of Crime. Grant Allan. Ed. by Tom Schantz & Enid Schantz. (Illus.). 56p. 1975. pap. 4.50 o.p. (ISBN 0-915230-00-3). Aspen Pr.

Reluctant Heiress. George Harmon Coxe. LC 65-20521. 1965. Knopf.

Reluctant Heiress. Annabel Laine. LC 77-14895. 1978. 7.95 (ISBN 0-385-13455-X). Doubleday.

Reluctant Hussy. Richard Burke. LC 46-4852. 1946. S. Curl, Inc.

Reluctant Impostor. Muriel Hine Coxon. LC 25-226372. 1925. Dodd, Mead and Company.

Reluctant Landlord: Illustrated by Paul Galdone. Scott Corbett. LC 50-7335. 1950. Crowell.

Reluctant Lesbian. Rex Weldon, pseud. (Orig.). 1969. pap. 1.25 o.p. (2089). Brandon.

Reluctant Lover. Amber Fitzgerald. LC 80-2321. 1982. 10.95 (ISBN 0-385-17458-6). Doubleday.

Reluctant Lover. Stephen McKenna. LC 13-442319. 1913. 1.20. The John C. Winston Company.

Reluctant Madonna: A Novel. Marguerite Steen. LC 30-5175. 1930. Frederick A. Stokes Company.

Reluctant Maiden. Glenna Finley, pseud. (Orig.). 1975. pap. 1.75 (ISBN 0-451-09863-3, E9863, Sig). NAL.

Reluctant Medium. Leslie Purnell Davies. LC 67-22468. 1967. Published for the Crime Club by Doubleday.

Reluctant Millionaire. Maysie Greig. 1972. pap. 0.75 o.p. (94229). Beagle Bks.

Reluctant Millionaire: A Romance. Maysie Greig. LC 45-9492. 1945. Random House.

Reluctant Murderer. 1st. ed. Bernice Carey. LC 49-10141. 1949. Pub. for the Crime Club by Doubleday.

Reluctant Paragon. Sarah Farrant. LC 75-34423. 1976. 1.25 (ISBN 0-345-24818-X). Ballantine Books.

Reluctant Paragon. Catherine George. (Harlequin Romances Ser.). 192p. 1983. pap. 1.75 (ISBN 0-373-02535-1). Harlequin Bks.

Reluctant Partner. John Durham, pseud. 1979. 1.50 (ISBN 0-440-17770-7). Dell Book.

Reluctant Partner. Lauran Paine. LC 77-16732. 1978. 7.95. (ISBN 0-312-67146-6) (ISBN 0-312-67147-4). St. Martin's Press.

Reluctant Prophet. Harald Tandrup & Chater, Arthur G., Tr. LC 39-5288. 1939. A. A. Knopf.

Reluctant Protegee. Maggie Gladstone, pseud. 1980. 1.75 (ISBN 0-87216-654-6). Playboy Press.

Reluctant Queen. 1st Ed. Molly Costain Haycraft. LC 62-11333. 1962. Lippincott.

Reluctant Rapist. Ed Bullins. LC 73-4143. 1973. 6.95 (ISBN 0-06-010579-8). Harper & Row.

Reluctant Rebel. Frederic Franklyn Van De Water. LC 48-194042. 1948. Duell, Sloan and Pearce.

Reluctant Shaman & Other Fantastic Tales. L. Sprague de Camp. (Orig.). 1970. pap. 0.75 o.p. (T2347). Pyramid Pubns.

Reluctant Sinners. Sidney Herbert Daukes. LC 35-2775. 1935. H. C. Kinsey & Company, Inc.

Reluctant Soil. George Stewart. LC 36-25552. 1936. The Caxton Printers, Ltd.

Reluctant Spy. John Blackburn. Orig. Title: Scent of New Mown Hay. pap. 0.60 o.p. (73-509). Lancer.

Reluctant Spy. E. D. Calnan. (Orig.). 1973. pap. 0.95 o.p. (09226). Curtis.

Reluctant Star. Margaret Elizabeth Sangster. LC 40-6706. 1940. Macraw-Smith-Company.

Reluctant Suitor. Megan Daniel. (Orig.). 1981. pap. 1.95 (ISBN 0-451-09671-1, J9671, Sig). NAL.

Reluctant Tease. Amy Irwin. (Orig.). pap. 0.95 o.p. (1153). Brandon.

Reluctant Viscountess. Jasmine Cresswell. 192p. 1982. pap. 1.50 (ISBN 0-449-50313-5, Coventry). Fawcett.

Reluctant Ward. Rosalind Foxx. (Coventry Romance Ser.: No. 194). 192p. 1982. pap. 1.50 (ISBN 0-449-50296-1, Coventry). Fawcett.

Reluctant Widow. 2d american ed. Georgette Heyer. LC 78-30576. 1971. 6.95. Putnam.

Reluctant Widow. Georgette Heyer. LC 47-15519. 1946. G. P. Putnam's Sons.

Reluctant Wizard. Neil K. Newell. (Orig.). 1980. pap. 1.95 (ISBN 0-532-23315-8). Woodhill.

Reluctant Worker-Priest. Eugene P Heideman. LC 67-13981. 1967. Eerdmans.

Relunctant Queen. Molly Costain Haycraft. (Signet book). 1974. (pbk.) 1.25. New American Library.

Remainder Biscuit. Robert Hartman. 6.75 o.p. Transatlantic.

Remains of a Father. Michael Ramsbotham. LC 68-27657. 1969. 4.95. Atheneum.

Remains to Be Seen. Michael Butterworth. LC 75-21214. 1976. 5.95 (ISBN 0-385-11152-5). Published for the Crime Club by Doubleday.

Remarkable Adventures of Christopher Poe. Robert Carlton Brown. LC 13-21104. 1913. F.G. Browne & Co.

Remarkable Andrew: Being the Chronicle of a Literal Man. Dalton Trumbo. LC 41-51551. J. B. Lippincott Company.

Remarkable Case of Burglary. Henry Reymond Fitzwalter Keating. LC 75-21232. 1976. 5.95 (ISBN 0-385-11387-0). Published for the Crime Club by Doubleday.

Remarkable Case of Burglary. Henry Reymond Fitzwalter Keating. 1977. 1.50 (ISBN 0-380-00983-8). Avon Books.

Remarkable Cure of Solomon Sunshine. William A Block. LC 73-18493. 1974. 7.95 (ISBN 0-13-773234-1). Prentice-Hall.

Remarkable Exploits of Lancelot Biggs: Spaceman. 1st Ed. Nelson Slade Bond. LC 50-9028. (Doubleday science fiction). 1950. Doubleday.

Remarkable Feat: Or, Jack and Gil's Great Detective Work. Harlan Page Halsey. (Old Sleuth's own, no. 106). The Parlor Car Publishing Co.

Remarkable History of Sir Thomas Upmore: Bart., M.P., Formerly Known As "Tommy Upmore.". Richard Doddridge Blackmore. LC 6-13131. (Harper's Franklin square library, no. 378). Harper & Brothers.

Remarkable History of Sir Thomas Upmore, Bart., MF., Formerly Known As "Tommy Upmore.". Richard Doddridge Blackmore. LC 6-13828. (On cover: Seaside library. Pocket ed., no. 427). G. Munro.

Remarkable History of Sir Thomas Upmore. Richard Doddridge Blackmore. LC 6-13141. (On cover: Lovell's library, no. 1039). J. W. Lovell Company.

Remarkable Rocket. Oscar Wilde. LC 74-196025. (Illus.). 1974. (ISBN 0-914182-04-8). Graham-Johnston.

Remarkable "Shadow" Or, Detective Payne's Tragic Quest. Harlan Page Halsey. LC 12-32987. (Old Sleuth's own, no. 93). 1897. The Parlor Car Publishing Co.

Remarkable Young Man. Cecil Roberts. LC 54-11649. 1954. Macmillan.

Remating Time. Jesse Lynch Williams. LC 16-11226. 1916. C. Scribner's Sons.

Rembrandt: A Novel. Gladys Schmitt. LC 61-9641. 1961. Random House.

Rembrandt: A Romance of Divine Love and Art. Sandor Brody & Rittenberg, Louis, Tr. LC 28-148290. Globus Press.

Rembrandt: A Romance of Holland. Walter Cranston Larned. LC 98-1987. 1898. C. Scribner's Sons.

Rembrandt Decisions. Anne V Badgley. LC 78-13159. 8.95 (ISBN 0-396-07622-X). Dodd, Mead.

Rembrandt Murder. Henry James Forman. LC 31-3863. 1931. R. R. Smith, Inc.

Rembrandt Panel. Oliver T. Banks. 1980. 11.95 (ISBN 0-316-08021-7). Little.

Rembrandt Panel. Oliver T. Banks. 288p. 1982. pap. 2.95 (ISBN 0-523-41621-0). Pinnacle Bks.

Rembrandt Panel: A Novel. Oliver T Banks. LC 80-11964. 10.95 (ISBN 0-316-08021-7). Little, Brown.

Rembrandt Panel: A Novel. Oliver T Banks. LC 80-27955. 1981. 11.95 (ISBN 0-89621-264-5). Thorndike Press.

Rembrandt's Hat. Bernard Malamud. LC 72-96998. 1973. 6.95 (ISBN 0-374-24909-1). Farrar-Straus-Giroux.

Remedy for Love. Ellen Warner Olney Kirk. LC 2-14138. 1902. Houghton, Mifflin and Company.

Remember. Taube, Herman & Taube, Suzanne. LC 51-37088. 1951. Gossmann Pub. Co.

Remember Caroline Mary. Dorothy Wakely. 1982. pap. 2.25 (ISBN 0-441-71324-6). Ace Bks.

Remember Jack Hoxie. Jon Cleary. LC 69-18945. 1969. 5.95. Morrow.

Remember John Marshall: A Biography of the Great Chief Justice. 1st Ed. Joe Cunningham. LC 56-58191. 1956. Biographic Press.

Remember Matt Boyer. Helen Huntington. LC 44-9742. 1944. Crown Publishers.

Remember Maybelle? Carter Brown, pseud. (Signet Book). 1976. (pbk.) 1.25. New American Library.

Remember Me. Barbara Collard. LC 54-635467. 1954. Funk &Wagnalls.

Remember Me. Virginia Nielsen, pseud. 1973. pap. 0.75 o.s.i. (01-394). Lancer.

Remember Me. Fay Weldon. LC 76-14165. 7.95 (ISBN 0-394-40554-4). Random House.

Remember Me. Fay Weldon. LC 77-365410. 1976. 4.25 (ISBN 0-340-21204-7). Hodder and Stoughton.

Remember Me to God. 1st Ed. Myron S Kaufmann. LC 57-895187. 1957. Lippincott.

Remember Me to Marcie. Martin Yoseloff. LC 79-124214. 1972. 6.95 (ISBN 0-498-07696-2). A. S. Barnes.

Remember Me When I Am Dead. Carol B. York. 112p. 1981. pap. 1.75 (ISBN 0-553-20213-8). Bantam.

Remember No More. Ann Seidel Armstrong. LC 63-21346. Bruce Pub. Co.

Remember Ruben. Mongo Beti. LC 81-116773. (African Writers Series). 1980. 7.00 (ISBN 0-89410-241-9). Heinemann.

Remember the Alamo. Amelia Edith Huddleston Barr. LC 4-17489. 1898. Dodd, Mead and Company.

Remember the Alamo. Amelia Edith Huddleston Barr. LC 79-14303. (Series: Gregg Press Western Fiction Series.). 1979. 9.95 (ISBN 0-8398-2579-X). Gregg Press.

Remember the Days: A Novel. Kenneth Walter Sollitt. LC 75-165306. 1971. Douglas-West, Inc.

Remember the End: A Novel by Agnes Sligh Turnbull. Agnes Sligh Turnbull. 1938. The Macmillan Company.

Remember the House. Santha Rama Rau. LC 55-10715. 1956. Harper.

Remember the Shadows. Davis Duncan. LC 44-4336. 1944. R. M. McBride & Company.

Remember the Summer We Lived at the Pad. Antonia Lamb. 1973. pap. 1.25 o.s.i. (78-715). Lancer.
Remember to Forget. Maude Williamson. LC 40-316381. Farrar & Rinehart, Inc.
Remember to Love Me. Elsie B. Webster. 5.95 o.p. Carlton.
Remember Today: Leaves from a Guardian Angel's Notebook. Elswyth Thane. LC 41-1057. Duell, Sloan and Pearce.
Remember Valerie March. Katherine Albert. LC 39-16111. 1939. Simon and Schuster.
Remember When We Had a Doorman? Lawrence, Josephine. LC 71-134580. 1971. 5.95 (ISBN 0-15-176665-7). Harcourt Brace Jovanovich.
Remember William Kite? A Novel by Stephen Longstreet, J. J. Godoff. Stephen Longstreet & J. J. Godoff. LC 65-262528. 1966. bds., 5.95. S. & S.
Remember Without Wanting. Margaret Gorman Nichols. LC 42-11708. The Bell Syndicate, Inc.
Remember Without Wanting. Margaret Gorman Nichols. LC 42-14359. 1942. Macrae-Smith-Company.
Rememberance of Love. Cathie Linz. (Candlelight Ecstasy Ser.: No. 52). (Orig.). 1982. pap. 1.75 (ISBN 0-440-17297-7). Dell.
Remembered Anger. Martha Albrand. (O.s.i.). 1967. pap. 0.60 o.s.i. (A256X, Award). Univ Pub & Dist.
Remembered Anger. Heidi Huberta Loewengard. LC 46-25045. 1946. Little, Brown and Company.
Remembered April. Stewart Vanderveer. LC 41-230675. Gramercy Publishing Company.
Remembered Darkness. John Ratti. LC 69-18798. 1969. 4.50 o.p. (ISBN 0-670-59368-0). Viking Pr.
Remembered Death... Agatha Miller Christie. LC 45-18711. 1945. Dodd, Mead & Company.
Remembered Heritage. William Arthur Neubauer. LC 63-6670. 1963. Arcadia House.
Remembered Kiss. Heather Sinclair. (Signet Book). 1976. 1.25. New American Library.
Remembered Melody. Jeanne Judson. 1964. Avalon Books.
Remembered Moment. Norman Bligh. 1970. pap. 0.75 o.p. (75-382). Manor Bks.
Remembered Visit. Edward Gorey. (O.S.I.). (Illus.). 1965. 2.50 o.s.i. S&S.
Remembering Laughter. Wallace Earle Stegner. LC 37-28646. 1937. Little, Brown and Company.
Remembering Louise. Anna Gilbert. LC 78-4387. 1978. 8.95 (ISBN 0-312-67153-9). St. Martin's Press.
Remembering the Yellow Journal. Hal Z. Bennett. (Orig.). 1978. pap. 3.95. Hal Z Bennett.
Remembrance. Rosalind Austenssen. LC 41-91681. B. Humphries, Inc.
Remembrance. Danielle Steel. LC 81-5579. 13.95 (ISBN 0-440-07347-2). Delacorte Press.
Remembrance Day. Gerhard Zwerenz. LC 66-6633. 1966. Dutton.
Remembrance of Miranda 1. Mary Ingate. (Dell Book). 1977. 1.25 (ISBN 0-440-18145-3). Dell Pub. Co.
Remembrance of Things Past. Marcel Proust. LC 79-5542. (per vol.) 20.00 (ISBN 0-394-50644-8) (ISBN 0-394-50645-6) (ISBN 0-394-50646-4). Random House.
Remembrance of Things Past. Marcel Proust. LC 82-40052. 1982. 40.00 (ISBN 0-394-71243-9). Vintage Books.
Remembrance Rock. Carl Sandburg. LC 48-28125. 1948. Harcourt, Brace.
Remembrance Rock. Carl Sandburg. LC 48-8509. 1948. Harcourt, Brace.
Remembrance Way: A Novel. Jessie C Rehder. LC 56-10241. 1956. Putnam.
Remind Me to Forget. Carolyn Byrd Dawson. LC 42-36152. 1942. Pub. for the Crime Club by Doubleday, Doran & Company, Inc.
Reminiscences of a Preacher. A Theological Romance. William McDonnell. LC 7-20106. 1887. J. P. Mendum.
Reminiscences of a Pullman Conductor: Or, Character Sketches of Life in a Pullman Car. Herbert Owen Holderness. LC 1-255437. 1901.
Reminiscences of a Virginia Physician. P. S Ruter. 1849. B. Casseday & Co.
Reminiscences of an Old Westchester Homestead. Charles Pryer. LC 7-300830. 1897. G. P. Putnam's Sons.
Reminiscences of Court and Diplomatic Life Under Queen Victoria. Georgiana Liddell Bloomfield Bloomfield. LC 21-153662. (Seaside library, v. 73, no. 1483). 1882. G. Munro.
Reminiscences of Lonely Hours: Or, The Bachelor's Sketch Book. William White. 1845. T. K. & P. G. Collins.
Reminiscences of Solar Pons. August William Derleth. LC 61-19886. 1961. Mycroft & Moran.
Reminiscences of Virginia Life a Century Ago. Mary Elizabeth Bennett. 1924. Thomas & Evans Printing Company.
Remittance-Woman. Achmed Abdullah. LC 24-7115. (Famous authors series. no. 42). 1924. Garden City Publishing Co., Inc.
Remittance Woman. Wright Williams. LC 41-1592. Phoenix Press.
Remittance Woman. Watkins Eppes Wright. LC 41-1592. 1941. Phoenix Press.
Remnant. Mary LaCroix. 1981. pap. 4.95 (ISBN 0-380-77107-1, 77107). Avon.
Remnant. Stephen C Shadegg. LC 68-13315. 1968. Arlington House.
Remnants of Glory. Teresa Miller. LC 80-52413. 12.95 (ISBN 0-87223-657-9). Seaview Books.
Remnants of Glory. Teresa Miller. 1982. Berkley Publishing Corp.
Remorse. Cspedes Alba De. LC 67-10390. 1967. Doubleday.
Remorse: A Novel from the French. Marie Therese Blanc. LC 14-19340. (Half-title: Collection of foreign authors, no. xiii). 1878. D. Appleton and Company.
Remorse: And Other Tales. George Payne Rainsford James. LC 7-798033. 1852. Bunce & Brother.
Remorse: Il Remorso. Alba De Cespedes. LC 78-14003. 1979. 22.50 (ISBN 0-313-20731-3). Greenwood Press.
Remote Control. Harry Carmichael. LC 74-134483. 1971. 4.50 o.p. (ISBN 0-8415-0081-9). Sat Rev Pr.
Remote Control. Leopold Horace Ognall. LC 74-134483. 1971. 4.50. McCall Pub. Co.
Removers. Donald Hamilton. (Matt Helm Ser.). 1978. pap. 1.95 (ISBN 0-449-14157-8, GM). Fawcett.
Remy St. Remy: Or, The Boy in Blue. Abby Buchanan Longstreet. LC 6-44055. 1866. J. O'Kane.
Renagade No. 3: Fear Merchant. Ramsay Thorne, pseud. (Orig.). 1980. pap. 2.25 (ISBN 0-446-30774-2). Warner Bks.
Renagade No. 4: Death Hunter. Ramsay Thorne, pseud. (Orig.). 1980. pap. 1.95 (ISBN 0-446-90902-5). Warner Bks.
Renaissance. Alfred Elton Van Vogt. 1979. 1.95 (ISBN 0-671-81859-7). Pocket Books.
Renaissance, a Science Fiction Novel of Two Human Worlds. 1st Ed. Raymond F Jones. LC 51-10436. 1951. Gnome Press.
Renaissance Storybook. Ed. by Morris Bishop. LC 79-129332. (Illus.). 1971. 14.50 o.p. (ISBN 0-8014-0592-0). Cornell U Pr.
Renald the Adventurer. Robert Duc. LC 77-70428. 7.95 (ISBN 0-87949-069-1). Ashley Books.
Rena's Experiment. Mary Jane Hawes Holmes. LC 4-19869. 1904. G. W. Dillingham Company.
Renatus: A Man Reborn. Mary Hornibrook Cummins. LC 14-16920. 1.00. Davis & Bond.
Render Unto Caesar. Nancy Fairweather. 1978. pap. 1.95 o.s.i. (ISBN 0-8439-0515-8, Leisure Bks). Nordon Pubns.
Rendevous with Danger. Lynn Williams. (Candlelight Mystery). 1973. (pbk) 0.60. Dell.
Rendevous with Fear. Anne Worboys. (Illus.). 1977. 1.75 (ISBN 0-441-71362-9). Ace Books.
Rendevous with Rama. Arthur Charles Clarke. 1974. (pbk.) 1.75. Ballantine Books.
Rendezuous at the Hallows. Juanita Tyree Osborne. 1974. 4.50. Avalon.
Rendezvous. Evelyn Anthony. (YA) 1968. 4.95 o.p. (ISBN 0-698-10315-7). Coward.
Rendezvous. Wilfred Jay Holmes. LC 42-36023. 1942. The Macmillan Company.
Rendezvous. Eve Stephens, pseud. 1977. 1.95 (ISBN 0-425-03573-5). Berkley Pub. Corp.
Rendezvous. Eve Stephens, pseud. LC 68-11874. 1968. Coward-McCann.
Rendezvous. Elisabeth Finley Thomas. The Bobbs-Merrill Company.
Rendezvous: And Other Long & Short Stories About Our Navy in Action. Wilfred Jay Holmes. LC 43-17321. 1943. The Press of the Readers Club.
Rendezvous at Bitter Wells. Peter Germano. LC 66-4980. 1966. Arcadia House.
Rendezvous at Bruges. Armand Lanoux. LC 61-5695. 1961. Putnam.
Rendezvous at Live Oaks. Elsie W. Strother. 192p. (YA) 1975. 4.95 o.p. (Avalon). Bouregy.
Rendezvous at the Hallows. Juanita Tyree Osborne. 192p. (YA) 1975. 6.95 (Avalon). Bouregy.
Rendezvous in a Landscape. August William Derleth. 3.50 o.s.i. (ISBN 0-88451-014-X). Edco-Vis Assoc.
Rendezvous in Black. Cornell George Hopley-Woolrich. LC 48-2414. (Murray Hill mystery). 1948. Rinehart.
Rendezvous in Black. Hopley-Woolrich, Cornell George. LC 79-10251. (Series: Gregg Press Mystery Fiction Series.). (Illus.). 1979. 9.95 (ISBN 0-8398-2537-4). Gregg Press.
Rendezvous in Black. Cornell Woolrich, pseud. 1979. lib. bdg. 9.95 (ISBN 0-8398-2537-4, Gregg). G K Hall.
Rendezvous in Black. Cornell Woolrich, pseud. 224p. 1982. pap. 2.25 (ISBN 0-345-30489-6). Ballantine.
Rendezvous in Veracruz. Carolyn G Hart. LC 76-106593. 1970. 4.95. M. Evans; Distributed in Association with Lippincott, Philadelphia.
Rendezvous of Mysteries. Karl S Nakagawa. LC 28-11317. Dorrance and Company.
Rendezvous off Newport. Howard R. Simpson. 1973. pap. 0.75 o.p. (07279). Curtis.
Rendezvous-South Atlantic. Douglas Reeman. LC 71-175271. 1972. 6.95. Putnam.
Rendezvous with Danger. Margaret Pemberton. (Berkley large type edition). 1975. (pbk.) 1.25. Berkley Pub. Co.
Rendezvous with Rama. Arthur Charles Clarke. LC 73-3497. 1973. 6.95 (ISBN 0-15-176835-8). Harcourt Brace Jovanovich.
Rendezvous with Rama. Arthur Charles Clarke. LC 80-17641. 1980. 15.90 (ISBN 0-8161-3038-8). G. K. Hall.
Rendezvous with the Past. Kathleen Moore Knight. LC 40-30403. 1940. Pub. for the Crime Club by Doubleday, Doran & Company, Inc.
Rendezvous with the Sea. Robert Olmsted. (Illus.). 1976. 9.00 o.p. (ISBN 0-89002-064-7); pap. 4.00 o.p. (ISBN 0-89002-063-9). Northwoods Pr.
Rendezvous with the Unknown. Adolph H. Parr. pap. 0.95 (ISBN 0-8198-0133-X). Dghtrs St Paul.
Rendezvous with Victory. Ella M Noller. LC 43-13677. 1943. Wm. B. Eerdmans Publishing Company.
Rendezvous. 1st Ed. Rose Franken. LC 54-625099. 1954. Doubleday.
Rene. Francois August Rene de Chateaubriand. Ed. by R. D. Finch & C. R. Parsons. LC 58-4314. 1957. 2.50x o.p. (ISBN 0-8020-2015-1). U of Toronto Pr.
Rene Leys. Victor Segalen. LC 72-13317. 1974. 6.95 (ISBN 0-87955-901-2). J. P. O'Hara.
Renee. Herself. (Dreams & Fantasies Ser.: No. 5). (Orig.). 1983. pap. 2.95 (ISBN 0-440-07476-2). Dell.
Renee: A Romance. Marian Calvert Wilson. 1888. C. T. Dillingham.
Renee and Colette: From the French of Debut Laforest; Adapted by Mrs. Banjamin Lewis... Jean Louis Dubut De Laforest & Lewis, Mrs. Benjamin, Tr. LC 7-22754. Cassell Publishing Company.
Renee and Franz: Le Bleuet. Wilhelmine Josephine Simonin Fould. LC 6-43599. (Half-title: Collection of foreign authors. no. vii). 1878. D. Appleton and Company.
Renee la Vagabonde. Sidonie Gabrielle Colette. Tr. by Remfry-Kidd, Charlotte. LC 31-11277. 1931. Doubleday, Doran & Company, Inc.
Renee Mauperin. Edmond Louis Antoine Huot De Goncourt & Goncourt, Jules Alfred Huot De. Tr. by Ward, Alice Hall. LC 3-3280. (Half-title: A century of French romance. Parisian ed. vol. xii). D. Appleton & Co.
Renee Mauperin. Edmond Louis Antoine Huot De Goncourt & Goncourt, Jules Alfred Huot De. LC 28-28134. (Half-title: The modern library of the world's best books). 1919. The Modern Library.
Renee: Translated from the French by Frances Frenaye. Henri Rene Lenormand. LC 51-2609. 1951. Creative Age Press.
Renee's Marriage. Marthe Lachese. Tr. by S., P. P. LC 7-14176. (On cover: Catholic library). H. L. Kilner & Co.
Renegade. Charles Victor Prevot Arlincourt. LC 6-2036. 1822. H. C. Carey & I. Lea.
Renegade. Andre Armandy & Le Clercq, Frederic, Tr. LC 30-24047. 1930. Brentano's.
Renegade. Walt Coburn. LC 60-1053. 1969. pap. 0.60 o.p. (B60-1053). Belmont-Tower.
Renegade. Al Cody, pseud. 1972. pap. 0.60 o.p. (532-00498-060). Manor Bks.
Renegade. John Thomas Edson. 1978. 1.50 (ISBN 0-425-03845-9). Berkley.
Renegade. Cliff Farrell. LC 74-116202. (DD western). 1970. 4.50. Doubleday.
Renegade. John Finnemore & Stewart, Allan, Illus. LC 18-187494. 1917. The Macmillan Company.
Renegade. Leonard London Foreman. LC 42-7958. 1942. E. P. Dutton & Co., Inc.
Renegade. Arthur Olney Friel. LC 26-14623. 1926. The Penn Publishing Company.
Renegade. Ludwig Lewisohn. LC 42-628519. 1942. The Dial Press.
Renegade. Donald Clayton Porter. LC 83-170. (White Indian series; bk. 2). ((Series: Porter, Donald Clayton.). (Colonization of America series; bk. 2.). 1983. 19.95 (ISBN 0-8161-3447-2). G.K. Hall.
Renegade. Donald Clayton Porter. (Colonization of America Ser.: No. 2). (Orig.). 1980. pap. 2.95 (ISBN 0-553-14968-7). Bantam.
Renegade. Jack Slade, pseud. (Sundance Ser.: No. 12). 192p. 1982. pap. 2.25 o.s.i. (ISBN 0-8439-1146-8, Leisure Bks). Dorchester Pub Co.
Renegade. Jack Slade. (Sundance, #12). 1974. (pbk.) 0.95. Leisure Books.
Renegade see Gunhand.
Renegade. A Historical Romance of Border Life. Emerson Bennett. LC 7-36492. 1848. Robinson & Jones.
Renegade: A Novel of Cornwall, 1783-1787. Winston Graham. LC 51-13530. 1951. Doubleday.
Renegade. A Tale of Real Life. J. B. Coppinger. LC 9-3865. 1855. Sherman & Co.
Renegade Agent. Don Pendleton. (Executioner Ser.). 192p. 1982. pap. 1.95 (ISBN 0-373-61047-5, Pub. by Worldwide). Harlequin Bks.
Renegade, and Other Tales. Martha Wolfenstein. LC 79-101824. (Short story index reprint series). 1969. Books for Libraries Press.
Renegade: And Other Tales. Martha Wolfenstein. LC 5-416383. 1905. The Jewish Publication Society of American.
Renegade & the Comancheros. Jack Slade, pseud. (Sundance Ser.). 1978. pap. 2.25 o.s.i. (ISBN 0-8439-0569-7, Leisure Bks). Nordon Pubns.
Renegade at Drumfork. Dale London. Ed. by Alice Sachs. 1970. 3.95 o.p. Lenox Hill.
Renegade Brand. Richard Brister. LC 81-15185. (Atlantic large print). (Atlantic series). 1982. 11.95 (ISBN 0-89340-401-2). J. Curley & Associates.
Renegade Cowboy. Nelson Coral Nye. LC 44-6548. 1944. N.Y., Phoenix Press.
Renegade Gambler. Lee Floren. LC 79-11611. 1979. 10.95 (ISBN 0-8161-6708-7). G. K. Hall.
Renegade Girl. Mary Ann Gibbs. 224p. 1981. pap. 1.95 (ISBN 0-449-50198-1, Crest). Fawcett.
Renegade Gun. Ray Hogan. LC 82-45095. 1982. 10.95 (ISBN 0-385-18042-X). Doubleday.
Renegade Guns. Robert J Hogan. LC 52-12458. (Silver star westerns). 1952. Dodd, Mead.
Renegade Guns. James Lyon Rubel. LC 36-19256. Phoenix Press.
Renegade Hills. Allan K. Echols. 1963. pap. 0.50 o.p. (50-349). Manor Bks.
Renegade Kid. T. W. Ford. LC 49-49622. 1949. Phoenix Press.
Renegade Lady. Kathryn Atwood. 352p. 1982. pap. 3.25 (ISBN 0-515-06045-3). Jove Pubns.
Renegade No. Nine: Hell Raider. Ramsay Thorne, pseud. 208p. (Orig.). 1981. pap. 2.25 (ISBN 0-446-30777-7). Warner Bks.
Renegade No. 1. Ramsay Thorne, pseud. (Orig.). 1979. pap. 1.95 (ISBN 0-446-90976-9). Warner Bks.
Renegade No. 10: The Great Game. Ramsay Thorne, pseud. 192p. (Orig.). 1981. pap. 1.95 (ISBN 0-446-90737-5). Warner Bks.
Renegade No. 11: Citadel of Death. Ramsay Thorne, pseud. 192p. (Orig.). 1981. pap. 2.25 (ISBN 0-446-30778-5). Warner Bks.
Renegade, No. 14: Harvest of Death. Ramsay Thorne, pseud. 192p. 1982. pap. 1.95 (ISBN 0-446-30124-8). Warner Bks.
Renegade, No. 15: Terror Trail. Ramsay Thorne, pseud. 192p. 1982. pap. 2.25 (ISBN 0-446-30125-6). Warner Bks.
Renegade, No. 16: Mexican Marauder. Ramsay Thorne, pseud. 192p. (Orig.). 1983. pap. 2.25 (ISBN 0-446-30255-4). Warner Bks.
Renegade, No. 17: Slaughter in Sinaloa. Ramsay Thorne, pseud. 192p. (Orig.). 1983. pap. 2.25 (ISBN 0-446-30257-0). Warner Bks.
Renegade, No. 18: Cavern of Doom. Ramsay Thorne, pseud. 192p. (Orig.). 1983. pap. 2.25 (ISBN 0-446-30258-9). Warner Bks.
Renegade, No. 19: Hellfire in Honduras. Ramsay Thorne, pseud. 224p. (Orig.). 1983. pap. 2.25 (ISBN 0-446-30630-4). Warner Bks.
Renegade No. 2: Blood Runner. Ramsay Thorne, pseud. (Orig.). 1979. pap. 2.25 (ISBN 0-446-30780-7). Warner Bks.
Renegade No. 5: Macumba Killer. Ramsay Thorne, pseud. 224p. (Orig.). 1980. pap. 2.25 (ISBN 0-446-30775-0). Warner Bks.
Renegade No. 6: Panama Gunner. Ramsay Thorne, pseud. 256p. (Orig.). 1980. pap. 1.95 (ISBN 0-446-90235-7). Warner Bks.
Renegade No. 7: Death in High Places. Ramsay Thorne, pseud. 192p. (Orig.). 1981. pap. 2.25 (ISBN 0-446-30776-9). Warner Bks.
Renegade No. 8: Over the Andes to Hell. Ramsay Thorne, pseud. 192p. (Orig.). 1981. pap. 2.25 (ISBN 0-446-30781-5). Warner Bks.
Renegade Number Thirteen: Mahogany Pirates. Ramsay Thorne, pseud. (Orig.). 1982. pap. 1.95 (ISBN 0-446-30123-X). Warner Bks.
Renegade N0. 12: Badlands Brigade. Ramsay Thorne, pseud. 224p. (Orig.). 1982. pap. 2.25 (ISBN 0-446-30779-3). Warner Bks.
Renegade of Callisto. Lin Carter. 1978. 1.50 (ISBN 0-440-14377-2). Dell Pub. Co.
Renegade of Kregen. Alan Burt Akers. (Daw Science Fiction Ser.). 1976. pap. 1.25 o.p. (ISBN 0-87997-271-8, UY1271). DAW Bks.
Renegade Ramrod. Leslie Charles Ernenwein. 1976. pap. 0.95 o.p. (LB345, Leisure Bks). Nordon Pubns.
Renegade Ramrod. Lessie Charles Ernenwein. 1976. (pbk.) 0.95. Leisure Books.

TITLE INDEX RESCUE.

Renegade Ramrod: A New Western Novel. Leslie Charles Ernenwein. LC 50-31778. (Handi-book western, 111). 1950. Quinn Pub. Co.
Renegade Ranch. Fred East. LC 48-8351. 1948. Macrae-Smith-Co.
Renegade Rancher. Lee Floren. 1978. pap. 1.25 (ISBN 0-532-12575-4). Woodhill.
Renegade Range. Fred East. LC 46-205474. 1946. E. P. Dutton & Co., Inc.
Renegade Ranger. Charles Horace Snow. 1943. Macrae-Smith-Company.
Renegade Rider. Ben Smith. LC 58-8908. 1958. Macmillan.
Renegade Riders. Donald McGregor. (Orig.). 1980. pap. 1.75 (ISBN 0-505-51549-0). Tower Bks.
Renegade Riders. Claude Rister. LC 34-32754. E. J. Clode.
Renegade River: A Western Novel. Ray Townsend. LC 55-17014. (Popular library, 623). 1954. Popular Library.
Renegade Roundup. A Double D Western. William Colt MacDonald. LC 40-6300. 1940. Doubleday, Doran & Company, Inc.
Renegade Scout. Al Cody, pseud. pap. 0.50 o.p. (50-316). Manor Bks.
Renegade Scout. Archie Joscelyn. LC 54-12957. 1954. Avalon Books.
Renegade Sheriff. Wilbur C. Tuttle. LC 53-8452. 1953. Bouregy & Curl.
Renegade Ship: A Novel of Adventure at Sea. 1st Ed. Reece London Joines. LC 52-9240. 1952. Exposition Press.
Renegades. Mary Canon. (O'Hara Dynasty Ser.). 1982. pap. 2.95 (ISBN 0-373-89003-6). Harlequin Bks.
Renegades. Jackson Flynn, pseud. (Gunsmoke Ser.). (O.s.i.: No. 1). 160p. (Orig.). 1974. pap. 0.95 o.s.i. (AN1283, Award). Univ Pub & Dist.
Renegades. Ray Hogan. 1982. pap. 2.25 (ISBN 0-451-11928-2, AE1928, Sig). NAL.
Renegades of the Future. Kurt Mahr. (Perry Rhodan#65). 1975. (pbk.) 1.25. Ace Books.
Renegade's Trail. T. W. Ford. LC 49-11962. 1949. Phoenix Press.
Renegade's Trail. Gordon D Shirreffs. (Gold medal book, M2953). 1974. (pbk.) 0.95. Fawcett Pubns.
Renewal. Carol Sturm Smith. LC 81-22892. (Love & Life). 1982. 1.75 (ISBN 0-345-29755-5). Ballantine Books.
Renewed from Without. Charles Edmund De Land. LC 26-15709. The Torch Press.
Renfrew Flies Again. Laurie York Erskine. LC 41-5108. 1941. D. Appleton-Century Company, Incorporated.
Renfrew Rides the Range. Laurie York Erskine. LC 35-272108. 1935. D. Appleton-Century Company, Incorporated.
Renni the Rescuer: A Dog of the Battlefield. Felix Salten & Kaufman, Kenneth Carlyle, 1887- Tr. LC 40-34599. The Bobbs-Merrill Company.
Rennlaufer. Nina Galen. LC 67-11383. 1967. Dutton.
Renno. Donald Clayton Porter. LC 83-167. (White Indian series; 5). ((Series: Porter, Donald Clayton.). (Colonization of America; 5.). 1983. 17.95 (ISBN 0-8161-3450-2). G.K. Hall.
Renno. Donald Clayton Porter. (Orig.). 1981. pap. 3.25 (ISBN 0-553-20028-3). Bantam.
Renny's Daughter. Mazo De La Roche. (Jalna Ser, Whiteoak ed). 1951. 8.95 o.p. (ISBN 0-316-18004-1, Pub. by Atlantic Monthly Pr). Little.
Renny's Daughter. 1st Ed. Mazo De La Roche. LC 51-12443. 1951. Little, Brown.
Reno. Cornelius Vanderbilt. LC 29-463982. The Macualay Company.
Reno Crescent. Zola Helen Ross. LC 51-1195. 1951. Bobbs-Merrill.
Reno Fever. Dorothy Walworth. LC 32-6523. 1932. R. Long & R. R. Smith, Inc.
Reno Rendezvous. Zenith Bown. LC 39-105230. Farrar & Rinehart, Inc.
Renown. Frank Olney Hough. LC 88-27212. Carrick & Evans, Inc.
Renshawe. A Novel. Ellen Peck. LC 7-30322. 1867. G. W. Carleton & Co.; Etc., Etc.
Rent a Wife. Rachel Lindsay. (Harlequin Presents Ser.). 192p. 1980. pap. 1.50 (ISBN 0-373-10375-1, Pub. by Harlequin). PB.
Rented a Husband. Clara Collins. LC 11-10551. Cassell & Company, Limited.
Rented Earl. Edward Salisbury Field. LC 12-244664. 1.00. W. J. Watt & Company.
Rented Wife. Josiah Pitts Woolfolk. LC 33-24093. 1933. W. Godwin, Inc.
Repair My House. Glen Williamson. LC 73-81984. 1973. 4.95 (ISBN 0-88419-042-0). Creation House.
Repairment of Cyclops. John Brunner. (Science Fiction Ser.). 1981. pap. 2.25 (ISBN 0-87997-638-1, UE1638). DAW Bks.
Repealers. A Novel. Marguerite Power Farmer Gardiner Blessington. LC 43-26890. 1833. Carey, Lea & Blanchard.
Repeat Performance. William O'Farrell. LC 42-252308. 1942. Houghton Mifflin Company.
Repeat the Instructions. R. Vernon Beste. LC 67-25255. 1967. Harper & Row.
Repent at Leisure. Anne Duffield. LC 46-177759. 1946. Arcadia House, Inc.
Repent at Leisure. Rae Foley. 1975. (pbk.) 0.95. Dell.
Repent in Haste. John Phillips Marquand. LC 45-9462. 1945. Little, Brown and Company.
Repent, Lanny Merkel. Faith Sullivan. LC 80-26132. 9.95 (ISBN 0-07-062347-3). McGraw-Hill.
Repentance at Leisure. Olive Moore. LC 30-251569. 1930. Harper & Brothers.
Repentance of Lorraine. Ames Claire. 1976. 1.75 (ISBN 0-671-80577-0). Pocket Books.
Repentant Magdalen: And Other Stories. May Isabel Fisk. (Zimmerman's pocket library). 1900. Zimmerman's.
Repentant Rebel. Florence E. Kyle. 2.75 o.p. Vantage.
Repented at Leisure. Charlotte Mary Brame. LC 44-12250. (On cover: Lovell's library, v. 8, no. 423). J. W. Lovell Company.
Repented at Leisure. Charlotte Mary Brame. LC 44-378284. (On cover: Seaside library. Pocket ed. No. 237). G. Munro.
Repented at Leisure. Charlotte Mary Brame. LC 44-11136. (On cover: Seaside library. Pocket ed. No. 967). G. Munro.
Repented at Leisure. A Novel. Charlotte Mary Brame. LC 44-37827. (On cover: The Primrose series, no. 30). Street & Smith.
Replacement. Richard L Husted. LC 48-525549. 1948. Meador Pub. Co.
Replacing Miss Raymond. Marjorie Deans. LC 47-31467. 1947. Arcadia House.
Replay. Michael Curtin. LC 81-15536. 1982. 9.95 (ISBN 0-8076-1027-5). Braziller.
Replenishing Jennifer. John Colleton. (Orig.). 1975. pap. 2.50 (ISBN 0-451-11585-6, AE1585, Sig). NAL.
Replenishing Jessica. Maxwell Bodenheim. LC 73-18548. 1974. 16.50 (ISBN 0-404-11363-X). AMS Press.
Replenishing Jessica. Maxwell Bodenheim. (Avon, 191). 1949. Avon Pub. Co.
Replenishing Jessics. Maxwell Bodenheim. LC 25-11487. Boni and Liveright.
Reply Paid: A Mystery. Gerald Heard. 1942. The Vanguard Press.
Report for a Corpse and Divers Other Reports on Dames, Deaths, and Desperadoes, with Shenanigans and Solutions. Henry Kane. LC 48-7176. (Inner sanctum mystery). 1948. Simon and Schuster.
Report from Argyll. Allan Mackinnon. LC 64-11301. 1964. Doubleday.
Report from Beau Harbor. Oakley M Hall. LC 70-151925. 1971. 6.95. Morrow.
Report from Group Seventeen. Robert C. O'Brien, pseud. LC 76-175291. (YA) 1972. 5.95 (ISBN 0-689-10445-6). Atheneum.
Report from Group 17. Robert C O'Brien, pseud. 1973. 1.25. Warner Paperback Lib.
Report from Group 17. Robert C O'Brien, pseud. LC 76-175291. 1972. 5.95. Atheneum.
Report from the Red Windmill: By Hiram Haydn. 1st Ed. Hiram Collins Haydn. LC 67-16087. 1967. 5.95. Harcourt.
Report on Bruno. Josef Breitbach. LC 64-12300. 1964. Knopf.
Report on Probability A. Brian Wilson Aldiss. LC 78-84385. (Doubleday science fiction). 1969. 4.50. Doubleday.
Report on Probability A. Brian Wilson Aldiss. 1980. 1.95 (ISBN 0-380-52498-8). Avon Books.
Report on the Death of Rosenkavalier. Jan Drabek. LC 77-368006. 10.00 (ISBN 0-7710-2880-6). McClelland and Stewart.
Report on the Status Quo. Terence Roberts. LC 55-12135. 1955. Merlin Press.
Report to the Commissioner. James Mills. 1973. (pbk.) 1.75 (ISBN 0-671-78605-9). Pocket Books.
Report to the Commissioner. James Mills. LC 79-165402. 1972. 6.95 (ISBN 0-374-24940-7). Farrar, Straus and Giroux.
Reported Safe Arrival: The Journal of a Voyage to Port "X,". Michael Harrison. LC 43-15328. 1943. Rich & Cowan.
Reporter. Jess Stearn. LC 70-103777. 1970. 5.95. Doubleday.
Reporter: A Novel. Meyer Levin. The John Day Company.
Reporter Detective. Donald J McKenzie. LC 1620. (On cover: Magnet detective library. no. 119). 1900. Street & Smith.
Reporter Detective's Triumph: Or, The Mystery of the Missing Bride. Frederick William Davis. LC 1-30644. (On cover: Magnet detective library, no. 164). 1900. Street & Smith.
Reporters. Larry Spencer. LC 76-17732. 1.75. Playboy Press.
Reporter's Romance. Arthur Rees Kimball. (On cover: Globe library, v. 1, no. 166). 1892. Rand, McNally & Company.
Representative American Short Stories. Ed. by Alexander Jessup. LC 23-852837. Allyn and Bacon.
Representative Irish Tales. William Butler Yeats. LC 79-4503. 1979. 23.50 (ISBN 0-391-00987-7) (ISBN 0-391-00988-5). Humanities Press.
Representative Modern Short Stories. Ed. by Alexander Jessup. LC 29-1675. 1929. The Macmillan Company.
Representative Selections: With Introduction, Bibliography, and Notes. James Fenimore Cooper. Ed. by Spiller, Robert Ernest. LC 36-10603. (Half-title: American writers series). American Book Company.
Representative Selections, with Introduction, Bibliography, and Notes. James Fenimore Cooper & Robert Ernest Spiller. LC 76-48040. (Illus.). 1976. 23.50 (ISBN 0-8371-9317-6). Greenwood Press.
Representative Selections: With Introduction, Bibliography, and Notes. Nathaniel Hawthorne. LC 78-145076. (American writers series). 1970. (ISBN 0-403-01017-9). Scholarly Press.
Representative Selections: With Introduction, Bibliography, and Notes. Nathaniel Hawthorne & Warren Austin, 1869- LC 34-10889. (Half-title: American writers series). American Book Company.
Representative Selections: With Introduction, Bibliography, and Notes. Henry James. Ed. by Richardson, Lyon Norman. LC 41-19830. (Half-title: American writers series; H. H. Clark, general editor). American Book Company.
Representative Selections, with Introduction, Bibliography, and Notes. Herman Melville. Ed. by Thorp, Willard. LC 38-18635. (Half-title: American writers series:H. H. Clark, general editor). American Book Company.
Representative Selections: With Introd., Bibliography and Notes, by Clara Marburg Kirk and Rudolf Kirk. William Dean Howells. LC 50-136807. (American writers series). 1950. American Book Co.
Representative Short-Stories. Ed. by Amanda Mae Ellis. LC 28-30261. (Half-title: Nelson's English series). 1928. T. Nelson and Sons.
Representative Short Stories. Ed. by Nina Hart. (On verso of half-title: Macmillan's pocket American and English classics). 1917. The Macmillan Company.
Representative Short Stories. Ed. by Nina Hart. Ed. by Moffett. Harold Young. LC 30-23553. (Half-title: New pocket classics). The Macmillan Company.
Representative Short-Stories: And a Brief Discussion of the Development of the Short Story. rev. ed. Ed. by Amanda Mae Ellis. LC 38-7063. (Half-title: Nelson's English series, general editor, E. Bernbaum). 1938. T. Nelson and Sons.
Repression: Plowing Time and Other Stories. Carmea L Kesting. LC 32-32120. Burton Publishing Company.
Reprieve. Warwick Deeping. LC 45-6317. 1945. Dial Press.
Reprieve. Agnes De Mille, pseud. 1982. pap. 2.95 (ISBN 0-451-11914-2, AE1914, Sig). NAL.
Reprieve. Jean Paul Sartre. LC 68-574. (His The roads to freedom, 2). 1967. Modern Library.
Reprieve. Jean Paul Sartre. LC 72-4475. 1973. 1.95. Vintage Books.
Reprieve. Tr. by Eric Sutton. Sutton, Eric, Tr. LC 47-11584. (His The roads to freedom, 2). 1947. A. A. Knopf.
Reprieve: A Christmas Story of 1863. Ralph Bradford. LC 41-8523. 1940. R. H. Darby.
Reprieve from Paradise. Harry Chandler Elliott. LC 55-5465. 1955. Gnome Press.
Reprieve of Roger Maine. Gordon McDonell. LC 61-10983. 1961. Prentice-Hall.
Reprieve: Trans. from the French by Eric Sutton. Jean Paul Sartre. Tr. by Eric Sutton. (His The roads to freedom, 2). (Bantam classic SC69). 1960. Bantam Books.
Reprinted Pieces. Charles Dickens. LC 6-37231. (Lovell's library, v. 5, no. 298). 1883. J. W. Lovell Company.
Reprinted Pieces, and Others. Charles Dickens. LC 37-30969. (Half-title: Everyman's library, ed. by Ernest Rhys. Fiction. no. 744). 1928. J. M. Dent & Sons, Ltd.
Reprinted Pieces: And The Lazy Tour of Two Idle Apprentices. Charles Dickens. Ed. by Dickens, Charles. Collins, Wilkie I. E. William Wilkie. LC 6-26416. 1896. The Macmillan Company.
Reprinted Pieces, Etc. Also, The Lamplighter to Be Read at Dusk, and Sunday Under Three Heads. Charles Dickens. (Half-title: Everyman's library, ed. by Ernest Rhys. Fiction). 1909. J. M. Dent & Co.
Reprints of Modern Negro American Fiction, 24 Vols. Set. 225.00 o.p. McGrath.
Reprisal. Arthur Gordon. LC 50-7121. 1950. Simon and Schuster.
Reprisal. William Harold Hull. LC 24-182676. Dorrance & Company.
Reprisal! Giles A Lutz. 1976. (pbk.) 1.25. Ace Books.
Reprisal. William P McGivern. LC 72-12538. 1973. 6.95 (ISBN 0-396-06750-6). Dodd, Mead.
Reprisal. Grace Zaring Stone. LC 42-36381. 1942. Little, Brown and Company.
Reprise. Joan Smith. (Coventry Romance Ser.: No. 182). 224p. 1982. pap. 1.50 (ISBN 0-449-50284-8, Coventry). Fawcett.
Reproach of Annesley. Mary Gleed Tuttiett. (On cover: Seaside library. Pocket ed. no. 1182). 1889. G. Munro.
Reptiles: A Novel. Harry Whitney McVickar. LC 5-37785. 1905. D. Appleton & Co.
Republic of the Southern Cross, and Other Stories. Valerii Iakovlevich Briusov. LC 76-23873. (Classics of Russian literature). (Hyperion library of world literature). 1977. 9.50. (ISBN 0-88355-477-1) (ISBN 0-88355-478-X). Hyperion Press.
Republic Without a President, and Other Stories. Herbert Dickinson Ward. LC 8-36030. Tait, Sons & Company.
Republican Marriage: A Novel. Leslie J Swabacker. LC 27-23869. Argus Books, Inc.
Reputation. Elinor Mordaunt, pseud. LC 24-11554. Small, Maynard & Company.
Reputation: A Story of April Low, Known As "the Wickedest Woman in Hollywood,". Anne Gardner, pseud. LC 29-12486. A. L. Burt Company.
Reputation for a Song. 1st American Ed. Edward Grierson. LC 52-11754. 1953-1952. Knopf.
Request for Sherwood Anderson: And Other Stories. Frank Brookhouser. LC 47-11465. 1947. A. Swallow.
Requiem: A Novel. Edward Fisher. LC 33-23362. The John Day Company.
Requiem for a Black American Capitalist. Wms-Forde, Bily. LC 75-27371. 8.95. Troisieme Canadian.
Requiem for a Blonde. Kelley Roos. LC 58-131000. (Red badge detective). 1958. Dodd, Mead.
Requiem for a Dream. Hubert Selby. LC 78-15251. 9.95 (ISBN 0-87223-510-6). Playboy Press: Trade Distribution by Simon and Schuster.
Requiem for a Dream. Hubert Selby. 1979. 2.25 (ISBN 0-87216-567-1). Playboy Press.
Requiem for a Nun. William Faulkner. LC 74-17145. 1975. (pbk.) 2.45 (ISBN 0-394-71412-1). Vintage Books.
Requiem for a Nun. William Faulkner. LC 51-12731. 1951. Random House.
Requiem for a Redhead. Lindsay Hardy. LC 53-118105. 1953. Appleton-Century-Crofts.
Requiem for a Schoolgirl. Ivan T Ross, pseud. LC 61-5847. (Inner sanctum mystery). 1961. Simon and Schuster.
Requiem for a Spanish Village. Barbara Norman Makanowitzky. LC 72-82853. 1972. 6.95 (ISBN 0-8128-1522-X). Stein and Day.
Requiem for a Wren. Nevil Shute. 1982. 13.95 (ISBN 0-434-69916-0, Pub. by Heinemann). David & Charles.
Requiem for Idols. Norah Robinson Lofts. LC 38-16224. 1938. A. A. Knopf.
Requiem for Idols; and, You're Best Alone. Norah Robinson Lofts. LC 78-22817. 1981. 12.95 (ISBN 0-385-01768-5). Doubleday.
Requiem for Mignon. Catherine Malberbe. (Berkley Medallion Book). 1975. (pbk.) 1.25. Berkeley Pub Co.
Requiem for Naaman. Benjamin Tammuz. LC 81-22382. 11.95 (ISBN 0-453-00417-2). New American Library.
Requiem for Sharks. Patrick Buchanan, pseud. 1975. pap. 0.95 o.p. (ISBN 0-515-03540-8). BJ Pub Group.
Requiem in Utopia. Richard Starnes. LC 67-17362. 1967. 4.95. Trident.
Requiem in Utopia. Richard Starnes. 1968. Pocket Bks.
Requiem of Sharks: A Novel of Suspense. Patrick Buchanan, pseud. LC 73-7488. 1973. 5.95 (ISBN 0-396-06841-3). Dodd, Mead.
Requiem Por un Campesino Espanol. Requiem for a Spanish Peasant: Novel. Pref. by Mair Jose Benardete. English Translation by Elinor Randall. Ramon Jose Sender. (Cypress book). 3.00. Las Americas Pub. Co.
Requim for a Cop. Victor B Miller. 1974. (pbk.) 1.25 (ISBN 0-671-78488-9). Pocket Books.
Rerun: A Novel. Neil Crichton. LC 76-380230. 5.95. (ISBN 0-7737-0026-9) (ISBN 0-7737-7130-1). Musson Book Co.
Reruns. Jonathan Baumbach. LC 74-77780. 1974. 7.95 (ISBN 0-914590-00-6); pap. 3.95 (ISBN 0-914590-01-4). Fiction Coll.
Reruns. Sabina Thorne. LC 80-52008. 1981. 11.95 (ISBN 0-670-59526-8). Viking Press.
Reruns. Sabina Thorne. 1982. 2.75. Avon Books.
Rescue. Joseph Conrad. 1968. pap. 1.95 o.p. (ISBN 0-393-00457-0, Norton Lib). Norton.
Rescue. Anne Douglas Sedgwick. LC 2-12294. 1902. The Century Co.

Rescue: A Romance of the Shallows. Joseph Conrad. LC 20-10316. 1920. Doubleday, Page & Company.
Rescue from the Rose. John Buxton Hilton. LC 75-34775. 1976. 7.95. St. Martin's.
Rescue in Denmark. Harold Flender. 224p. 1974. pap. 1.50 o.p. (ISBN 0-532-15128-3). Woodhill.
Rescue in Denmark. Harold Flender. 224p. 1974. pap. 1.50 o.p. (ISBN 0-532-15128-3). Manor Bks.
Rescue Mission. John Ball. LC 66-13854. 1966. 8.95 o.p. (ISBN 0-06-010196-2, HarpT). Har-Row.
Rescue of Broken Arrow. Evan Evans, pseud. 249p. 1976. Repr. of 1948 ed. lib. bdg. 12.05x (ISBN 0-89190-207-4). Am Repr-Rivercity Pr.
Rescue of Broken Arrow. Frederick Faust. LC 75-42193. 1975. 5.95 (ISBN 0-89190-207-4). American Reprint Co.
Rescue of Captain Leggatt. William Townend. LC 39-330045. 1939. W. Morrow & Co.
Rescue of Charlie Kalu. J. V. Clinton. (Heinemann Secondary Readers Ser.). 1971. pap. text ed. 3.00x (ISBN 0-435-92502-4). Heinemann Ed.
Rescue Operation. Penny Jordan. (Harlequin Presents Ser.). 192p. 1983. pap. 1.95 (ISBN 0-373-10602-5). Harlequin Bks.
Rescue; or, the Villain Unmasked. Rinaldo D'Elville. 1977. Repr. 15.00 o.p. (ISBN 0-403-08082-7). Scholarly.
Rescued from Fiery Death: A Powerful Narrative of the Iroquois Theater Disaster. Wesley Allen Stanger. LC 4-5918. 1904. Laird & Lee.
Rescued Madonna. Harriet Anna Cheever. Congregational Sunday-School and Publishing Society.
Rescuers. Margery Sharp. 160p. 1974. pap. 1.50 (ISBN 0-440-47378-0, YB). Dell.
Rescuers. Granville Trace. LC 9-18366. 1909. The Sentinel Company.
Rescuing the Czar. James P Smythe. LC 20-15962. 1920. California Printing Co.
Research Magnificent. Herbert George Wells. LC 15-18282. 1915. The Macmillan Company.
Research Magnificent. Herbert George Wells. LC 43-260020. 1922. The Macmillan Company.
Research Nurse. Florence Stonebraker. LC 67-6621. 1967. Arcadia House.
Resemblance: And Other Stories. Clare Benedict. LC 9-5526. 1909. 1.50. G. P. Putnam's Sons.
Resentment. Mary Etta Spencer. LC 21-20882. 1921. Printed by A. M. E. Book Concern.
Reservation. Lila Marie Platt. LC 55-9090. 1956. Chapman & Grimes.
Reservation: A Romance of the Pioneer Days of Minnesota and of the Indian Massacre of 1862. Asa Passavant Brooks. LC 7-36914.
Reservation Nurse. Ethel E. Bangert. 1973. pap. 0.75 o.s.i. (01-387). Lancer.
Reservations for Death. Baynard Hardwick Kendrick. LC 57-5160. (His A Duncan Maclain mystery). 1957. Morrow.
Reservoir. Murrell Edmunds. LC 75-38452. (ISBN 0-498-01910-1). A. S. Barnes.
Reservoir, Stories and Sketches. Janet Frame, pseud. LC 63-15827. 1963. G. Brazilier.
Resident. Warren Tute. 1975. (pbk.) 1.25 (ISBN 0-345-24412-5). Ballantine Books.
Resident Nurse. Lucy Agnes Hancock. LC 47-774. 1947. Macrae-Smith Company.
Residuary Legatee: Or, The Posthumous Jest of the Late John Austin. Frederic Jesup Stimson. LC 8-15677. 1888. C. Scribner's Sons.
Resignation. An American Novel. Evans. LC 6-38140. 1825. Printed for the Author by J. B. Russell.
Resistance, No. 1: Night & Fog. Gregory St. Germain. 192p. Date not set. pap. 2.50 (ISBN 0-451-11827-8, Sig). NAL.
Resistance, No. 2: Magyar Massacre. Gregory St. Germain. 192p. Date not set. pap. 2.50 (ISBN 0-451-11828-6, Sig). NAL.
Resisting Arrest. Steven Phillips. LC 79-8939. 1980. 11.95 (ISBN 0-385-14757-0). Doubleday.
Resnick's Odyssey: A Novel. Morton Cooper. LC 78-14008. 1978. 9.95 (ISBN 0-688-03379-2). Morrow.
Resolution: Or, The Soul of Power. Azel Stevens Roe. 1871. G. W. Carleton & Co.; Etc., Etc.
Resolved to Be Rich: A Novel. Edward Herbert Cooper. LC 99-4636. 1899. H. S. Stone and Company.
Resort. Sol Stein. LC 79-21781. 1980. 10.95 (ISBN 0-688-03541-8). Morrow.
Resort Doctor. Charles Stanley Strong. LC 38-16093. Phoenix Press.
Resort Hotel. Celia Page. LC 42-21646. 1942. Doubleday, Doran and Company, Inc.
Resort M.D. Dorothy Dawes. 1975. (pbk.) 1.50. Ace Books.
Resort Nurse. Rose Dana, pseud. Ed. by Alice Sachs. 1969. lib. bdg. 3.50 o.p. Arcadia.
Resort Nurse. Rose Dana, pseud. 1970. pap. 0.60 o.p. (ISBN 0-447-73878-X). Lancer.
Resort Secretary. Arnold English. pap. 0.60 o.p. (60-385). Manor Bks.
Resort to Sin. William Manners. LC 52-2333. 1952. Arco Pub. Co.
Resort to War. George Revelli. LC 65-111024. 1971. 5.95 o.p. (ISBN 0-394-47571-2, GP629). Grove.
Resort to War: A Novel. George Revelli. LC 75-111024. 1971. 5.95. Grove Press.
Resources of Mycroft Holmes, Solver of Historical Mysteries. Charlton Andrews & Tom Schantz. LC 74-178240. (Illus.). 1973. 4.00. Aspen Press.
Respectability. John Gilbert Bohun Lynch. LC 27-155226. 1927. Little, Brown, and Company.
Respectable? Peggy Gaddis, pseud. LC 36-430469. Godwin.
Respectable Lady. Katharine Tynan Hinkson, pseud. LC 28-128820. 1928. D. Appleton and Company.
Respectable Sinners. a new ed. Mary Imbella Irwin Brotherton. LC 41-40503. 1865. G. Routledge and Sons.
Respectable Woman. David Fletcher, pseud. LC 75-10471. 1975. 6.95 (ISBN 0-698-10687-3). Coward, McCann & Geoghegan.
Respectable Woman. David Fletcher, pseud. 1976. 1.50 (ISBN 0-671-80769-2). Pocket Books.
Respectable Women. Gilbert Rees. LC 54-7795. 1954. Random House.
Respite. Kimon Lolos. LC 61-6183. 1961. Harper.
Responsibility. James Evershed Agate. 1943. Hutchinson & Co., Ltd.
Responsibility: A Novel. James Evershed Agate. LC 20-76516. 1920. George H. Doran Company.
Responsibility of Ruffles. Margery Watson Hall. LC 13-22873. 1.00. The Pilgrim Press.
Rest And Be Thankful. Helen MacInnes Highet. LC 40-10088. 1949. Little, Brown.
Rest & Be Thankful. Helen MacInnes. 1978. pap. 2.95 (ISBN 0-449-23621-8, Crest). Fawcett.
Rest Cure: A Novel. William Babington Maxwell. LC 10-23402. 1910. D. Appleton and Company.
Rest Harrow: A Comedy of Resolution. Maurice Henry Hewlett. LC 16-10878. 1910. C. Scribner's Sons.
Rest Hollow Mystery. Rebecca Newman Porter. LC 22-17726. 1922. 1.75. The Century Co.
Rest House. Isabel Constance Clarke. LC 17-133185. 1917. Benziger Brothers.
Rest in Agony. easy eye ed. Paul W. Fairman. pap. 0.75 o.p. Lancer.
Rest in the Church, 1848 see From Oxford to Rome, & How It Fared with Some Who Lately Made the Journey, 1847.
Rest Is Done with Mirrors: A Novel. Carolyn See. LC 70-105356. 1970. 6.95. Little, Brown.
Rest Is Silence. easy eye ed. Virginia Coffman. (Orig.). 1968. pap. 0.75 o.p. (74-973). Lancer.
Rest Is Silence. Virginia Coffman. 1973. pap. 0.95 o.s.i. (75-225). Lancer.
Rest Is Silence. Virginia Coffman. (Signet book). 1.50. New American Library.
Rest Is Silence. Erico Verissimo. LC 74-88994. 1969. Greenwood Press.
Rest Is Silence. Erico Verissimo & Kaplan, Lewis C., 1911- Tr. LC 46-4246. 1946. The Macmillan Company.
Rest Is Silence: And Other Stories. Warren Beck. LC 63-12585. (Swallow paperbook). 1963. A. Swallow.
Rest Is Silence & Other Stories. Warren Beck. LC 82-71835. 132p. (Orig.). 1963. pap. 5.95 (ISBN 0-8040-0261-4). Swallow.
Rest of My Life with You. Faith Baldwin Cuthrell. LC 42-24441. 1942. Farrar & Rinehart, Inc.
Rest of the Afternoon Was Watermelon. Mary Santomauro. LC 78-53081. 1979. 8.95 (ISBN 0-87949-120-5). Ashley Books.
Rest of the Robots. Isaac Asimov. LC 64-22323. (Doubleday science fiction). 1964. Doubleday.
Rest of the Week. Kenneth J. Roberts. LC 73-87984. 1973. 3.95 (ISBN 0-87973-879-0). Our Sunday Visitor.
Rest They Need. Herbert Lyons. LC 50-9823. 1950. Dial Press.
Rest Without Peace. Elizabeth Byrd. 1975. (pbk.) 1.50 (ISBN 0-380-00427-5). Avon.
Rest You Merry. Charlotte MacLeod. LC 77-27713. 1978. 7.95 (ISBN 0-385-14245-5). Published for the Crime Club by Doubleday.
Rest You Merry. Charlotte MacLeod. LC 79-22210. 1979. 7.95 (ISBN 0-8161-3000-0). G. K. Hall.
Rest You Merry. Charlotte Macleod. 1979. 1.95 (ISBN 0-380-47530-8). Avon Books.
Restaurant: A Novel of Suspense. Parley J Cooper. LC 79-17971. 9.95 (ISBN 0-02-528050-3). Macmillan.
Restaurant at the End of the Universe. Douglas Adams. LC 81-6563. 1981. 7.95 (ISBN 0-517-54535-7). Harmony Books.
Restdale. Julia Eliza Shotland. Burre Publishing Company.
Restless: A Novel. Jean Boley. 1946. E. P. Dutton & Company, Inc.
Restless Age. John Tinney McCutcheon. LC 21-202675. The Bobbs-Merrill Company.
Restless Are the Sails. Evelyn Sybil Mary Eaton. LC 41-10770. Harper & Brothers.
Restless Border. 1st Ed. Dick Pearce, pseud. LC 52-13733. 1953. Lippincott.
Restless Breed. 1st Ed. J. William Terry. LC 56-10428. 1956. World Pub. Co.
Restless City & Christmas Gold. Cyprian Ekwensi. (African Writers Ser.). 1975. pap. text ed. 4.00x (ISBN 0-435-90172-9). Heinemann Ed.
Restless City and Christmas Gold, with Other Stories. Cyprian Ekwensi. LC 76-363137. (African writers series). (H.E.B. paperback). 1975. 2.75 (ISBN 0-435-90172-9). Heinemann.
Restless City & Christmas Gold: With Other Stories. Cyprian Ekwensi. (African Writers Ser: No.172). 100p. 1975. pap. text ed. 2.50x o.p. (ISBN 0-435-90172-9). Humanities.
Restless Corpse. Alvin Emanuel Rose. LC 47-3656. 1947. Ziff-Davis Publishing Company.
Restless Flame: A Novel. 1st Ed. Louis De Wohl. LC 51-11193. 1951. Lippincott.
Restless Frontier: A 'James Ogilvie' Novel. Philip McCutchan. LC 79-22790. 8.95 (ISBN 0-312-67782-0). St. Martin's Press.
Restless Ghosts of Ladye Place & Other True Hauntings. Harry Ludlam. LC 68-31250. 1968. 6.95 (ISBN 0-8008-6775-0). Taplinger.
Restless Hands. Bruno Fischer. LC 49-102754. (Red badge mystery). 1949. Dodd, Mead.
Restless Heart. Robert C. Harvey. 192p. 1973. pap. 3.95 o.p. (ISBN 0-8028-1507-3). Eerdmans.
Restless Heart. Sergei Maximov. LC 51-10216.
Restless Heart. Denise Robins. LC 42-242752. 1940. Arcadia House, Inc.
Restless Heart. Translated by Barney Blackley. Genevieve Gennari. LC 56-13534. 1955. Abelard-Schuman.
Restless House. Emile Zola. 1971. 13.95 (ISBN 0-236-30967-6, Pub. by Paul Elek). Merrimack Pub Cir.
Restless House. With Illus. by Philip Gough, Introd. by Angus Wilson. Translated from the French 'Pot-Bouille' by Percy Pinkerton. Emile Zola. LC 53-9913. (Illustrated Noval Library). 1953. Farrar, Straus & Young.
Restless Is the River. August William Derleth. LC 39-27856. 1939. C. Scribner's Sons.
Restless Lady, and Other Stories. Frances Parkinson Wheeler Keyes. LC 63-8972. Liveright Pub. Corp.
Restless Land & Other Stories. Frances Parkinson Wheeler Keyes. 1982. pap. 2.95 (ISBN 0-451-11416-7, AE1416, Sig). NAL.
Restless Men. Peter Pinney. (Illus.). 1967. pap. 1.80 o.s.i. Tri-Ocean.
Restless Nights. Dino Buzzati. Tr. & intro. by Lawrence Venuti. LC 82-73713. 176p. 1983. pap. 12.00 (ISBN 0-86547-100-2). N Point Pr.
Restless Ones. M. Vincent Guarino & James F Collier. LC 72-82676. (Word paperback, 90030). 1972. 1.25. Word Books.
Restless Passion. LC 48-153152. 1947. Avon Book Co.
Restless River. Jerry E. Mueller. LC 74-80107. 1975. 8.00 o.p. (ISBN 0-87404-050-7); pap. 5.00 o.p. Tex Western.
Restless Road. Bert R Ferris. LC 46-6986. 1946. Houghton Mifflin Company.
Restless Sands. Marcel Prevost. Tr. by Kahane, Jack. LC 31-4331. Sears Publishing Company, Inc.
Restless Sex. Robert William Chambers. 1918. 1.50. D. Appleton and Company.
Restless Sex. Robert William Chambers. LC 21-20586. 1920. A. L. Burt Company.
Restless Soul Finds Mrs. Crusoe. Illus. by Evelyn F. Haines. Martha Groves McKelvie. LC 67-16060. 1967. 3.95. Franklin Pub.
Restless Spurs. Archie Joscelyn. 1974. 4.95. Lenox Hill Press.
Restless Voyage. Stanley David Porteus & Campbell, Archibald, B. 1787. A Voyage Round the World, from 1806-1812. LC 48-9100. 1948. Prentice-Hall.
Restlessness of Shanti Andia: And Other Writings. Baroja y Nessi, Pio. LC 59-5063. (Illus.). 1959. University of Michigan Press.
Restlessness of Shanti Andia: And Selected Writings. Tr. by Anthony and Elaine Kerrigan. Foreword by Anthony Kerrigan. Baroja y Nessi, Pio. (Signet classic, CT149). New Amer. Lib.
Restoration & the Cat. Edward Bond. 128p. 1982. pap. 7.95 (ISBN 0-413-49920-0, NO. 3638). Methuen Inc.
Restoration Comedy: Being a Brief & True Account of the Adventures of David Carter Pencible, Esq. in Kingsburg, Virginia, During National Restoration Week in May. Robert Manson Myers. LC 61-3384. 1961. Printed by the Dietz Press.
Restoration: The Fairy-Tale of a Farm. Ethel Sidgwick. LC 23-7990. Small, Maynard and Company.
Restoree. Anne McCaffrey. LC 77-357696. 1976. 0.65 (ISBN 0-552-10161-3). Corgi.
Resume for Murder. Claire McCormick. LC 81-71189. 1982. 11.95 (ISBN 0-8027-5462-7). Walker.
Resurrected Christ: A Novel. 1st Ed. Gourgen Yanikian. LC 55-821843. 1955. Exposition Press.
Resurrection. John Gardner. LC 66-19514. 1974. (pbk.) 1.50 (ISBN 0-345-23881-8). Ballantine Books.
Resurrection. William Alexander Gerhardie. LC 34-338679. Harcourt, Brace and Company.
Resurrection. William Alexander Gerhardie. 1975. 7.95 o.p. St Martin.
Resurrection. Lev Nikolaevich Tolstoi. LC 63-3763. 1963. Washington Square Press; Distributed in the U.S. by Affiliated Publishers, a Division of Pocket Books, Inc.
Resurrection. Lev Nikolaevich Tolstoi. Tr. by Rosemay Edmonds. LC 67-3041. 1966. Penguin Books.
Resurrection. Lev Nikolaevich Tolstoi. 585p. 1972. 6.95 (ISBN 0-8285-1060-1, Pub. by Progress Pubs USSR). Imported Pubns.
Resurrection. Lev Nikolaevich Tolstoi. Ed. by John W. Strahan. Tr. by Louise Maude. pap. 0.60 o.p. (W720). WSP.
Resurrection. Lev Nikolaevich Tolstoi & Delano, Mrs. Aline P. (Kus'michova) 1845- Tr. LC 11-5643. T. Y. Crowell & Co.
Resurrection. Lev Nikolaevich Tolstoi & Maude, Mrs. Louise (Shanks) 1855-1939, Tr. LC 33-229392. (Half-title: The world's classics, XXIX). 1928. Oxford University Press.
Resurrection. Lev Nikolaevich Tolstoi & Musacchia, John B., Illus. LC 42-10429. Illustrated Editions Company.
Resurrection. Lev Nilolaevich Tolstoi. LC 3-100309. 1903. Dodd, Mead & Company.
Resurrection: A Novel. John Champlin Gardner. LC 66-19514. 1966. New American Library.
Resurrection, a Novel. Lev Nikolaevich Tolstoi. LC 3-26188. 1900. Dodd, Mead & Company.
Resurrection; a Novel. Lev Nikolaevich Tolstoi & Maude, Mrs. Louise, Tr. LC 24-279820. 1901. Dodd, Mead and Company.
Resurrection: By L. N. Tolstoy; Tr. Introd. by Rosemary Edmonds. Lev Nikolaevich Tolstoi. LC 67-760533. (Penguin classics L184). 1966. pap., 2.45. Penguin.
Resurrection Days. Wilson Tucker. (Orig.). 1981. pap. 2.25 (ISBN 0-671-83242-5, Timescape). PB.
Resurrection Man. Thomas Walsh. LC 66-12353. (Inner sanctum mystery). 1966. Simon and Schuster.
Resurrection Murder Case. Stanley Hart Page. LC 32-29681. 1932. A. A. Knopf.
Resurrection of a Heart. E. W. Westerfield. LC 13-18070. 1913. Broadway Publishing Co.
Resurrection of Candy Sterling. Russell W. Martin. LC 81-85179. 288p. (Orig.). 1982. pap. 2.95 (ISBN 0-86721-094-X). Playboy Pbks.
Resurrection of Frank Borchard. Jerry Sohl. LC 72-89250. 1973. 7.95 (ISBN 0-671-21463-2). Simon and Schuster.
Resurrection of Miss Cynthia. Florence Morse Kingsley. LC 5-29102. 1905. Dodd, Mead & Company.
Resurrection of Peter;' A Reply to Olive Schreiner. Ekaterina Rzewiska Radziwill. LC 6063. 1900. G. P. Putnam's Sons.
Resurrection of the R. K. 7 Ranch. Lee Albert Rademaker. LC 43-12651. 1943. Meador Publishing Company.
Resurrection River. William Byron Mowery. LC 35-442. 1935. Little, Brown, and Company.
Resurrection Rock. Edwin Balmer. LC 20-15536. 1920. Little, Brown, and Company.
Resurrection Row. Anne Perry. LC 81-8846. 1981. 9.95 (ISBN 0-312-67797-9). St. Martin's Press.
Resurrection Shuffle. Angus W. Murray. 190p. 1982. 14.95 (ISBN 0-7206-0519-9, Pub. by Peter Owen). Merrimack Pub Cir.
Resurrection. (The Awakening.) Lev Nikolaevich Tolstoi & Britoff, Henry, Tr. LC 3583. 1900. J. S. Ogilvie Publishing Company.
Resurrectionist. Gary K Wolf. LC 77-12894. 1979. 7.95 (ISBN 0-385-13141-0). Doubleday.
Resurrections. Gloria Oden. (Illus.). 1978. pap. 15.00x (ISBN 0-87956-071-1). Olivant.
Retaliation, Love's Kickback. Mabel Dana Lyon. LC 34-35879. Author Publications, Inc.
Retaliators. Donald Hamilton. (Matt Helm Ser.). 1978. pap. 1.75 (ISBN 0-449-13984-0, GM). Fawcett.
Retaliators. Donald Hamilton. (Fawcett Gold medal book). 1976. 1.50. Fawcett Publications, Inc.
Retarded Genius. R. J Meaddough. LC 78-70673. 9.95 (ISBN 0-932938-01-9). Troisieme Canadian.
Retief: Ambassador to Space: Seven Incidents of the Corps Diplomatique Terrestrienne. Keith Laumer. LC 69-12230. (Doubleday science fiction). 1969. 4.95. Doubleday.
Retief and the Warlords. Keith Laumer. LC 68-27128. (Doubleday science fiction). 1968. 4.50. Doubleday.

Retief and the Warlords. Keith Laumer. (Kangaroo Book). 1978. 1.75 (ISBN 0-671-81864-3). Pocket Books.
Retief: Diplomat at Arms. Keith Laumer. 1982. pap. 2.75 (ISBN 0-671-44029-2, Timescape). PB.
Retief: Emissary to the Stars. Keith Laumer. 1979. pap. 2.50 (ISBN 0-671-82918-1). PB.
Retief of the CDT. Keith Laumer. LC 73-150902. (Doubleday science fiction). 1971. 4.95. Doubleday.
Retief of the CDT. Keith Laumer. (Kangaroo Book). 1978. 1.75 (ISBN 0-671-81865-1). Pocket Books.
Retief's Ransom: A Science Fiction Novel. Keith Laumer. LC 74-154789. 1971. 4.95. Putnam.
Retief's War. Keith Laumer. 1978. 1.75 (ISBN 0-671-81863-5). Pocket Books.
Retief's War. Illus. by John B. Gaughan. Keith Laumer. LC 66-17436. 1966. 3.95. Doubleday.
Retour a Roissy see Story of O: Part Two, Return to the Chateau.
Retraite Sentimentale. Sidonie Gabrielle Colette. 12.95; pap. 3.95. French & Eur.
Retreat. Constance Leonie Caroline Borgstrom Aminoff. LC 38-6237. (Her Torchlight series of Napoleonic romances. x). E. P. Dutton & Co., Inc.
Retreat: A Novel of 1918. Charles Richard Benstead. LC 30-5240. The Century Co.
Retreat and Recall. G. E. Hopkins. LC 66-16690. 1966. Scribner.
Retreat, As It Was: A Fantasy. Donna J Young. LC 79-52900. (Illus.). 1979. 5.00 (ISBN 0-930044-12-6). Naiad Press.
Retreat from Love. Sidonie Gabrielle Colette. LC 73-16804. 1974. 7.95 (ISBN 0-672-51767-1). Bobbs-Merrill.
Retreat from Love. Sidonie Gabrielle Colette. LC 79-19831. (Harvest HBJ/book). 1980. 3.95 (ISBN 0-15-676588-8). Harcourt Brace Jovanovich.
Retreat from Love. Maysie Greig. LC 38-97. 1937. Doubleday, Doran and Company, Inc.
Retreat from Love. Maysie Greig. 1973. pap. 0.75 o.p. (94325). Beagle Bks.
Retreat from Oblivion. David Goodis. LC 39-20247. 1939. E. P. Dutton & Company, Inc.
Retreat from Rostov: A Novel. Paul Hughes. LC 43-147593. 1943. Random House.
Retreat from the Dolphin. Darwin Le Ora Teilhet. LC 43-15771. 1943. Little, Brown and Company.
Retreat, Hell! William Martin Camp. LC 43-15845. 1943. D. Appleton-Century Company, Incorporated.
Retreat in Good Order. Jane White. LC 77-134579. 1971. Harcourt Brace Jovanovich.
Retreat into Night. Cover Painting by Barye Phillips. Richard Glendinning. LC 54-26997. (Gold medal books, 889). 1954. Fawcett Publications.
Retreat of a Frontier. Kathryn Fingado O'Neil. LC 50-11507. 1950. Westernlore Press.
Retreat with Honor. Josephine Lawrence. LC 73-4626. 1973. 6.95 (ISBN 0-15-177081-6). Harcourt Brace Jovanovich.
Retreat with Honor. Josephine Lawrence. LC 73-16110. 1973. 8.95 (ISBN 0-8161-6164-X). G. K. Hall.
Retreat. 1st American Ed. Percy Howard Newby. LC 52-12202. 1953. Knopf.
Retribution. Charlotte Lamb, pseud. (Harlequin Presents Ser.). 192p. 1981. pap. 1.50 (ISBN 0-373-10442-1, Pub. by Harlequin). PB.
Retribution. A Border Mystery. Joshua Rhodes Forrest. LC 6-40588. J. S. Ogilivie Publishing Company.
Retribution at Last. A Mormon Tragedy of the Rockies. Charles Louis Brewer. LC 99-2882. 1899. The Editor Publishing Co.
Retrospection. Mary Wilson Little. Broadway Publishing Company.
Retrospection: A Tale. Ann Martin Taylor. LC 8-25970. 1822. Collins and Croft.
Return. Evelyn Anthony. LC 78-19118. 1978. 9.95 (ISBN 0-698-10938-4). Coward, McCann & Geoghegan.
Return. Evelyn Anthony. (Signet Book). 1979. 2.50 (ISBN 0-451-08843-3). New American Library.
Return. Wes Brown. LC 73-80760. 1973. 4.95 (ISBN 0-8059-1881-7). Dorrance.
Return. Walter John De La Mare. LC 75-46266. (Supernatural and Occult Fiction). 1976. 17.00 (ISBN 0-405-08124-3). Arno Press.
Return. Walter John De La Mare. 1911. G. P. Putnam's Sons.
Return. Walter John De La Mare. LC 22-19482. 1922. A. A. Knopf.
Return. Isidore Haiblum. (Dell book). 1973. (pbk.) 0.95. Dell.
Return. Michael Home, pseud. LC 33-27331. 1933. W. Morroe and Company.
Return. K. S. Maniam. (Writing in Asia Ser.). 185p. (Orig.). 1981. pap. text ed. 7.00x (00263). Heinemann Ed.
Return. Herbert Mitgang. LC 59-7266. 1959. Simon and Schuster.
Return. Margaret Rhodes Peattie. LC 44-664. 1944. W. Morrow and Company.
Return. Neilma Sidney. LC 76-376961. 1976. (ISBN 0-17-005082-3). Thomas Nelson (Australia)
Return. Thomas Wolfe. LC 76-25606. (Illus.). Thomas Wolfe Memorial.
Return: A Novel. Yaw M Boateng. LC 77-5018. 6.95 (ISBN 0-394-41724-0). Pantheon Books.
Return: A Story of the Sea Islands in 1739. Alice MacGowan & Cooke, Mrs. Grace (MacGowan) 1863- Joint Author. LC 5-8709. 1905. L. C. Page & Company, Inc.
Return Engagement. Gwen Davenport. LC 46-557092. 1946. The Bobbs-Merrill Company.
Return Engagement. Glenna Finley, pseud. 1981. pap. 2.25 (ISBN 0-451-12323-9, AE2323, Sig). NAL.
Return Engagement, No. 73. Kay Robbins. 1982. pap. 1.75 (ISBN 0-515-06684-2). Jove Pubns.
Return Fare: Translated from the French by Humphrey Hare. Jean M Kolar. LC 60-13812. 1960. half cloth, 3.95. Macmillan.
Return from Hell. Lucy W McKellup. LC 72-92738. 1973. 4.95 (ISBN 0-8059-1789-6). Dorrance.
Return from No-Return. Dane Rudhyar. 175p. (Orig.). 1974. pap. 5.00 (ISBN 0-916108-03-1). Seed Center.
Return from No-Return: A Paraphysical Novel. Dane Rudhyar. LC 74-166384. 1973. 3.00. Seed Center.
Return from Parnassus: Or, The Scourge of Simony. Ed. by Edward Arber. LC 72-194942. (English Scholar's Library of Old and Modern Works V. 1 No. 6). 1967. AMS Press.
Return from the Ashes. Hubert Monteilhet. (O.s.i.). 1963. 3.50 o.s.i. (ISBN 0-671-61995-0). S&S.
Return from the Deep. Hugh J Trimble. LC 59-16077. McHew Pub. Co.
Return from the Grave. Hugh Lamb. LC 76-381405. 1976. 3.50 (ISBN 0-491-01937-8). Allen.
Return from the Stars. Stanislaw Lem. LC 79-3358. 9.95 (ISBN 0-15-177082-4). Harcourt Brace Jovanovich.
Return from the Void. Kurt Mahr. (Perry Rhodan#51). (Illus.). 1974. (pbk.) 0.95. Ace Books.
Return from Witch Mountain. Alexander Key. (Orig.). (gr. 5-7). 1978. pap. 1.75 (ISBN 0-671-56073-5). Archway.
Return I Dare Not. Margaret Kennedy. LC 31-28309. 1931. Doubleday, Doran & Company, Inc.
Return in August. 1st Ed. Philip Duffield Stong. LC 53-5284. 1953. Doubleday.
Return in December. Cora Hardy Jarrett. LC 51-3562. 1951. Rinehart.
Return Journey. Ruby Mildred Ayres. LC 38-38070. 1938. Doubleday, Doran and Company, Inc.
Return Journey. Ronald Frederick Delderfield. LC 73-21471. 1974. 8.95 (ISBN 0-671-21786-0). Simon and Schuster.
Return Journey. Ronald Frederick Delderfield. LC 74-18282. 1974. (ISBN 0-8161-6252-2). G. K. Hall.
Return Journey. Beatrice Kean Stapleton Seymour. LC 43-1379. 1943. The Macmillan Company.
Return Load. James Douglas Rutherford McConnell. LC 77-80632. 1977. 7.95 (ISBN 0-8027-5373-6). Walker.
Return Match. Elizabeth Cadell. LC 78-27084. 1979. 8.95 (ISBN 0-688-03473-X). W. Morrow.
Return Match. Elizabeth Cadell. LC 79-16934. 1979. 13.95 (ISBN 0-8161-6757-5). G. K. Hall.
Return Not Again. Annette Heard. LC 37-3287. The Bobbs-Merrill Company.
Return of a Fighter. Ernest Haycox. LC 77-22458. 1977. 7.95 (ISBN 0-8161-6504-1). G. K. Hall.
Return of a Heroine. Marguerite Steen. LC 36-210973. The Bobbs-Merrill Company.
Return of A. J. Raffles. Graham Greene. (O.s.i.). 1976. 5.95 o.s.i. (ISBN 0-671-22297-X). S&S.
Return of Agatha Crumm. Bill Hoest, pseud. 1982. pap. 1.75 (ISBN 0-451-11526-0, AE1526, Sig). NAL.
Return of Alfred. Herbert George Jenkins. LC 22-15473. George H. Doran Company.
Return of Angela. Jean Blanche. LC 56-264724. 1956. Castle Books.
Return of Another Spring. 1st Ed. Columbia Anne Botticello. LC 55-12400. Pageant Press.
Return of Ansel Gibbs. 1st Ed. Frederick Buechner. LC 57-10302. 1958. Knopf.
Return of Anthony Trent. Wyndham Martyn. LC 25-147182. Barse & Hopkins.
Return of Arsene Lupin. Maurice Leblanc. LC 34-339. The Macaulay Company.
Return of Blackshirt. Graham Montague Jeffries. LC 27-13519. 1927. Dodd, Mead and Company.
Return of Blue Mask. John Creasey. LC 37-34176. 1937. J. B. Lippincott Co.
Return of Blue Mask. Anthony Morton, pseud. LC 37-341762. J. B. Lippincott Company.
Return of Blue Pete. Lacey Amy. LC 23-19159. 1922. George H. Doran Company.
Return of Caroline. Florence Morse Kingsley. LC 11-12060. 1911. Funk & Wagnalls Company.
Return of Christopher: A Novel. Margaret Echard. LC 51-10933. 1951. Doubleday.
Return of Conan: By Bjorn Nyberg with the Collaboration of L. Sprague De Camp. Based Upon and Continuing the Conan Stories, by Robert E. Howard. Bjorn Nyberg & Lyon Sprague De Camp. LC 57-7113. 1957. Gnome Press.
Return of Dr. Fu Manchu. Sax Rohmer, pseud. 1976. lib. bdg. 13.95x (ISBN 0-89968-141-7). Lightyear.
Return of Dr. Fu Manchu. Sax Rohmer, pseud. 1970. pap. 0.60 o.p. (X2225). Pyramid Pubns.
Return of Dr. Fu Manchu. Sax Rohmer, pseud. 1970. pap. 0.60 o.p. (X2225). Pyramid Pubns.
Return of Dr. Fu-Manchu. Arthur Sarsfield Ward. LC 24-28553. 1919. A. L. Burt Company.
Return of Dr. Fu-Manchu. Arthur Sarsfield Ward. LC 25-7162. 1920. A. L. Burt Company.
Return of Dr. Fu-Manchu. Arthur Sarsfield Ward. LC 22-16038. 1922. R. M. McBride & Company.
Return of Don Quixote. Gilbert Keith Chesterton. LC 26-14755. 1926. Dodd, Mead & Company.
Return of Don Quixote. Gilbert Keith Chesterton. LC 27-962509. 1927. Dodd, Mead & Company.
Return of Eva Peron with the Killings in Trinidad. Vidiadhar Surajprasad Naipaul. LC 79-22148. 1980. 10.00 (ISBN 0-394-50968-4). Knopf.
Return of Frank Clamart. Henry Cottrell Rowland. LC 23-8939. Harper & Brothers.
Return of Gerard. Arthur Conan Doyle. 192p. (Orig.). 1982. pap. 2.25 (ISBN 0-515-05531-X). Jove Pubns.
Return of Gunner Asch. Hans Hellmut Kirst. 1968. pap. 0.75 o.p. (T1871). Pyramid Pubns.
Return of Gunner Asch. Translated from the German by Robert Kee. 1st American Ed. Hans Hellmut Kirst. LC 57-9368. 1957. Little, Brown.
Return of Gunner Ashe. Hans Hellmut Kirst. 1976. pap. 1.50 o.p. (ISBN 0-515-04087-8). BJ Pub Group.
Return of HYMAN KAPLAN. Large Type Ed. Leo Calvin Rosten. 1966. 5.11. Harper.
Return of HYMANKAPLAN. 1st Ed. Leo Calvin Rosten. LC 59-10617. 1959. Harper.
Return of Jack the Ripper. Mark Andrews. 1977. pap. 1.75 o.s.i. (ISBN 0-8439-0476-3, Leisure Bks). Nordon Pubns.
Return of Jeeves. Pelham Grenville Wodehouse. LC 54-5469. 1954. Simon and Schuster.
Return of Jennifer. Helen Upshaw. LC 64-17773. 1964. Dodd, Mead.
Return of Jenny Weaver. Margaret Turnbull. LC 32-690197. 1932. J. B. Lippincott Company.
Return of Kai Lung. Ernest Bramah Smith. LC 38-1976. 1937. Sheridan House.
Return of Kavin. David Mason. 1972. pap. 0.95 o.s.i. (75-361). Lancer.
Return of Lady Brace. Nancy Wilson Ross. LC 57-10029. 1957. Random House.
Return of Lance Tennis. Laurence Snelling. LC 65-22444. 1965. Holt, Rinehart and Winston.
Return of Lanny Budd. Upton Beall Sinclair. LC 53-5202. 1953. Viking Press.
Return of Lono. Oswald A. Bushnell. (Pacific Classics Ser.: No. 1). 1971. pap. 4.95 (ISBN 0-87022-931-1). UH Pr.
Return of Lono: A Novel of Captain Cook's Last Voyage. Oswald A Bushnell. LC 72-149793. (Pacific Classics, 1). 1971. (ISBN 0-87022-931-1). University of Hawaii Press.
Return of Lono: A Novel of Captain Cook's Last Voyage. Oswald A Bushnell. LC 56-5936. (Atlantic Monthly Press book). 1956. Little, Brown.
Return of Morality. John Gardner. 304p. 1981. pap. 2.25 (ISBN 0-425-05093-9). Berkley Pub.
Return of Moriarity. John E Gardner. (Berkley Medallion Book). 1976. (pbk.) 1.95 (ISBN 0-425-03095-4). Berkley Publishing Corp.
Return of Moriarty. John E Gardner. LC 74-79646. 1974. 7.95 (ISBN 0-399-11382-7). Putnam.
Return of O'Mahony see Collected Works.
Return of Peter Grimm: Novelised from the Play. David Belasco. LC 12-23210. 1912. Dodd, Mead and Company.
Return of Philo T. McGiffen: A Novel of Annapolis. David Poyer. 288p. 1983. 13.95 (ISBN 0-312-67907-6). St Martin.
Return of Pierre. Donal Hamilton Haines. LC 12-3792. 1912. 1.25. H. Holt and Company.
Return of Raffles: Further Adventures of the Amateur Cracksman. Barry Perowne. LC 34-449. 1933. The John Day Company.
Return of Sabata. Brian Fox. (O.s.i.). 160p. (Orig.). 1972. pap. 0.75 o.s.i. (AS1064, Award). Univ Pub & Dist.
Return of Sanders of the River. Francis Gerard & Wallace, Edgar. LC 39-9649. 1939. E. P. Dutton & Co., Inc.
Return of Sappho. Mary Stephenson Barnes. LC 49-54146. 1949. De Vorss.
Return of Service. Jonathan Baumbach. LC 79-18102. (Illinois Short Fiction Ser.). 1979. 11.95 (ISBN 0-252-00784-0); pap. 4.95 (ISBN 0-252-00785-9). U of Ill Pr.
Return of Sgt. Hawk. Patrick Clay. (Sgt. Hawk Ser.: No. 2). 1980. pap. 1.95 (ISBN 0-8439-0845-9). Nordon Pubns.
Return of She: Ayesha. Henry Rider Haggard. (Orig.). 1968. pap. 0.75 o.p. (74-899). Lancer.
Return of Sherlock Holmes. Arthur Conan Doyle. LC 36-29320. 1907. A. Wessels Company.
Return of Sherlock Holmes. Arthur Conan Doyle. LC 12-24109. 1910. Doubleday, Page & Company.
Return of Sherlock Holmes. Arthur Conan Doyle. LC 37-4944. 1937. The Sun Dial Press, Inc.
Return of Sherlock Holmes. Arthur Conan Doyle. LC 41-13228. 1941. Triangle Books.
Return of Sherlock Holmes. Arthur Conan Doyle. 1982. pap. 2.95 (ISBN 0-14-005708-0). Penguin.
Return of Sherlock Holmes. Arthur Conan Doyle & Macauley, Charles Raymond, 1871- Illus. LC 16-137472. 1915. N.Y., Doubleday, Page & Company.
Return of Sherlock Holmes. Arthur Conan Doyle & Macauley, Charles Raymond, 1871- Illus. 1917. Doubleday, Page & Company.
Return of Sherlock Holmes. Sir Arthur Conan Doyle. 1975. (pbk.) 1.25. Belmont Tower Books.
Return of Sherlock Holmes: A Facsmile of the Stories As They Were First Published in the Strand Magazine, London. Arthur Conan Doyle. LC 75-24567. (Illus.). 1975. 5.95 (ISBN 0-8052-3603-1) (ISBN 0-8052-0506-3). Schocken Books.
Return of Sherlock Holmes: Facsimile of the First Publication with All the Original Sidney Paget Illustrations. Arthur Conan Doyle. LC 75-24567. (Illus.). 1975. 5.95 o.p. (ISBN 0-8052-3603-1); pap. 2.95 o.p. (ISBN 0-8052-0506-3). Schocken.
Return of Skull-Face. Robert E. Howard & Richard Lupoff. LC 77-89158. 1977. 9.95x (ISBN 0-913960-17-9). Fax Collect.
Return of Solar Pons. August William Derleth. (Solar Pons Series#6). (Illus.). 1975. (pbk.) 1.50 (ISBN 0-523-00650-0). Pinnacle Books.
Return of Solar Pons. August William Derleth. LC 58-59473. 1958. Mycroft & Moran.
Return of Spring: A Romance. Henry De Vere Stacpoole. LC 28-103977. 1928. Doubleday, Doran & Company, Inc.
Return of Sumuru: By Sax Rohmer Pseud. Cover Painting by James Meese. Arthur Sarsfield Ward. LC 54-33272. (Gold medal books, 408). 1954. Fawcett Publications.
Return of Tarzan. Edgar Rice Burroughs. LC 15-555370. 1915. A. C. McClurg & Co.
Return of Tarzan. Edgar Rice Burroughs. LC 17-303494. 1915. A. L. Burt Company.
Return of Tarzan. Edgar Rice Burroughs. LC 37-328094. 1915. Grosset & Dunlap.
Return of Tarzan, No. 2. Edgar Rice Burroughs. 224p. 1975. pap. 1.95 (ISBN 0-345-28996-X). Ballantine.
Return of the Assassin. Alfred Tack. LC 73-87211. 1974. 6.95 (ISBN 0-399-11272-3). Putnam.
Return of the Brute. Liam O'Flaherty. LC 30-4656. 1930. Harcourt, Brace and Company.
Return of the Eagle. Nancy Dorer & Frances Dorer. (Orig.). 1979. pap. 1.95 (ISBN 0-532-23267-4). Woodhill.
Return of the Half Moon. Kenneth Bruce. LC 9-27267. 1909. 1.00. Broadway Publishing Co.
Return of the Hero. Darrell Figgis & Stephens, James, 1882- LC 30-15105. 1930. C. Boni.
Return of the Jedi: Illustrated Edition. James Kahn. 224p. (Orig.). 1983. pap. 5.95 (ISBN 0-345-30960-X). Ballantine.
Return of the Jedi Portfolio. Ralph McQuarrie. (Orig.). 1983. pap. 9.95 (ISBN 0-345-30961-8). Ballantine.
Return of the Kid: By Joseph Wayne Pseud. 1st Ed. Wayne D Overholser. LC 55-8343. (Dutton Diamond D western). 1955. Dutton.
Return of the King. John Ronald Reuel Tolkien. 1976. pap. 2.95 (ISBN 0-345-29608-7). Ballantine.
Return of the King. John Ronald Reuel Tolkien. 1967. 11.95 (ISBN 0-395-08256-0). HM.
Return of the King: Being the Third Part of The Lord of the Rings. silver anniversary ed. John Ronald Reuel Tolkien. LC 81-166154. (Tolkien, John Ronald Reuel, 1892-1973. Lord of the Rings: Pt. 3). 1981. 11.95 (ISBN 0-395-31268-X). Houghton Mifflin.
Return of the Living Dead. John Russo. LC 78-60737. 1978. pap. 1.95 o.s.i. (ISBN 0-89559-062-X). Dale Books Inc.

Return of the Long Riders. Cliff Farrell. LC 64-13853. (Double D western). 1964. Doubleday.
Return of the Long Riders. Cliff Farrell. LC 64-13853. (Signet book). 1975. (pbk.) 0.95. New American Library.
Return of the Mucker. Edgar Rice Burroughs. (pbk.) 0.95. Ace Books.
Return of the Native. Thomas Hardy. Dolphin Books.
Return of the Native. Thomas Hardy. LC 62-21185. 1962. Collier Books.
Return of the Native. standard ed. Thomas Hardy. LC 66-12788. (Perennial classic, P3064D). Harper & Row.
Return of the Native. Thomas Hardy. (Signet classic, CT625). 1973. (pbk.) 0.75. New American Lib.
Return of the Native. Thomas Hardy. Ed. by A. Walton Litz. LC 67-5356. (Illus.). 1967. Houghton Mifflin.
Return of the Native. Thomas Hardy. LC 68-56082. (Cambridge classics library). (Illus.). 1968. Cambridge Book Co.
Return of the Native. Thomas Hardy. LC 75-2796. 1969. 5.95. F. Watts.
Return of the Native. Thomas Hardy. LC 50-697811. (Great Illustrated Classics). (Illus.). 1950. Dodd, Mead.
Return of the Native. author's ed. Thomas Hardy. LC 7-1900. (On cover: Leisure hour series. no. 103). 1878. H. Holt and Company.
Return of the Native. Thomas Hardy. LC 16-13097. 1895. Harper & Brothers.
Return of the Native. Thomas Hardy. Ed. by Cunliffe, John William. LC 17-11699. (Half-title: The modern student's library, ed. by W. D. Howe). C. Scribner's Sons.
Return of the Native. Thomas Hardy. (Harper's modern classics). Harper & Brothers.
Return of the Native. Thomas Hardy. LC 27-266253. (Half-title: The modern library of the world's best books). 1927. The Modern Library.
Return of the Native. Thomas Hardy. LC 33-7783. (Half-title: The modern library of the world's best books). The Modern Library.
Return of the Native. Thomas Hardy. LC 42-15421. 1942. The Heritage Press.
Return of the Native. Thomas Hardy. 1943. Pocket Books, Inc.
Return of the Native. Thomas Hardy & Baugh, Albert Croll. LC 28-23924. (modern readers' series). 1928. The Macmillan Company.
Return of the Native. Thomas Hardy & Brownsword, Walter. LC 65-1806. 1956. Scribner.
Return of the Native. Karl Meyer. (Orig.). 1980. pap. 1.75 (ISBN 0-532-23184-8). Woodhill.
Return of the Native. Abridged and Edited by Verds Evans; Illustrated by Thomas G. Fraumeni. Thomas Hardy. LC 54-1532. 1953. Globe Book Co.
Return of the Native: An Authoritative Text, Background and Criticism. Thomas Hardy. Ed. by James Jack Gindin. LC 68-12184. (Norton critical editions). 1969. 5.97. Norton.
Return of the Native. Ed., Introd., Notes by John Paterson. Thomas Hardy. LC 64-7106. (Perennial classic). 1.95, .75 pap.,. Harper.
Return of the Native. Edited with an Introd. by Albert J. Guerard. Thomas Hardy. LC 50-122807. (Rinehart editions, 39). 1950. Rinehart.
Return of the Night Wind: A Sequel to "Alias the Night Wind". Frederic Van Rensselaer Dey. LC 14-2477. 1.25. G. W. Dillingham Company.
Return of the O'Mahony: A Novel. Harold Frederic. LC 7-752. (Ledger library, no. 71). R. Bonner's Sons.
Return of the Outlaw: By Michael Carder Pseud. Vernon L Fluharty. LC 54-10360. (Bull's-eye western). 1954. Macrae Smith.
Return of the Pink Panther. Frank Waldman. LC 76-56397. 1977. 1.50. Ballantine Books.
Return of the Princess. Angele Dussaud Bary d'Arnex. LC 8-19786. (Appletons' new handy volume series v. 51). 1880. D. Appleton and Company.
Return of the Prodigal. May Sinclair. LC 14-10423. 1914. 1.35. The Macmillan Company.
Return of the Rancher. Frank Austin. LC 33-19968. 1933. Dodd, Mead & Company.
Return of the Rancher. Max Brand. 240p. 1972. pap. 1.95 (ISBN 0-446-90309-4). Warner Bks.
Return of the Rebel. Jeanette W Lockerbie. LC 68-22173. 1968. 2.95. Zondervan Pub. House.
Return of the Rio Kid. Davis Dresser. LC 48-10778. (Triple-A western classic).
Return of the Rio Kid. Davis Dresser. LC 40-27286. 1940. W. Morrow & Company.
Return of the Snow-White Puritan. John Paolitti. LC 63-16527. 1963. Harper & Row.
Return of the Soldier. Rebecca West. LC 18-651796. 1918. The Century Co.
Return of the Soldier. rev. ed. Rebecca West. LC 81-15240. (Virago modern classics). 1982. 6.95 (ISBN 0-385-27226-X). Dial Press.
Return of the Sphinx. Hugh MacLennan. LC 67-21221. 1967. 5.95. Scribners.
Return of the Stranger. Dorothy James Roberts. LC 58-12101. 1958. Appleton-Century-Crofts.
Return of the Swallows. Blanche Chenier. (Orig.). 1975. pap. 1.50 o.p. (ISBN 0-515-03684-6). Pyramid Pubns.
Return of the Texan. Burt Arthur, pseud. 1975. pap. 0.95 o.p. (LB321, Leisure Bks). Nordon Pubns.
Return of the Texan. 1st Ed. Herbert Arthur, pseud. LC 56-113265. (Signet books. 1339). 1956. New American Library.
Return of the Tide. Zenobia Bird. LC 32-23722. Fleming H. Revell Company.
Return of the Tide. Zenobia Bird. LC 32-23722. 1932. Fleming H. Revell Company.
Return of the Time Machine. Egon Friedell. (Orig.). 1972. pap. 0.95 o.p. (UQ1022). Daw Bks.
Return of the Traveller. Rex Warner. LC 44-3948. 1944. J. B. Lippincott Company.
Return of the Virginian. Harry Allen Smith. LC 73-15367. 1974. 6.95 (ISBN 0-385-03405-9). Doubleday.
Return of the Weed. Paul Horgan. LC 36-32103. 1936. Harper & Brothers.
Return of the Whistler. Blossom Elfman. LC 80-27681. 1981. 8.95 (ISBN 0-395-29464-9). Houghton Mifflin.
Return of the Wise Man. Winifred Margaretta Kirkland. LC 35-17679. Fleming H. Revell Company.
Return of William Shakespeare. Hugh Kingsmill Lunn. LC 29-20647. The Bobbs-Merrill Company.
Return of William Shakespeare. Hugh Kingsmill Lunn. LC 77-84240. (Lost Race and Adult Fantasy Fiction). 1978. 20.00 (ISBN 0-405-10988-1). Arno Press.
Return Ticket. Frederick James Howard. LC 29-6462. 1929. Longmans, Green and Co.
Return to Aylforth. Anne Eliot, pseud. 1967. 4.95 o.p. (ISBN 0-696-77108-X). Hawthorn.
Return to Aylforth: A Novel of Suspense. Lois Dwight Cole. LC 67-12636. 1967. Meredith Press.
Return to Bondage. Barbara Blackburn, pseud. LC 26-16329. 1926. L. MacVeagh, The Dial Press.
Return to Broken Crossing. Lee Hoffman. 1974. (pbk.) 0.75. Ace Books.
Return to Cheltenham. Helen Ashton. 1981. 18.95x (Pub. by Remploy England). State Mutual Bk.
Return to Coolami: By Elanor Dark. Eleanor O'Reilly Dark. LC 36-11550. 1936. The Macmillan Company.
Return to Cottington. Francis Bamford. LC 46-21055. 1946. Longmans, Green and Co.
Return to Darkness. easy eye ed. Willo Davis Roberts. pap. 0.95 o.s.i. (75-293). Lancer.
Return to Dreams. Lawrence Nelson. LC 35-4593. An Arcadia House Publication.
Return to Dust. Alice Lent Covert. LC 39-20479. 1939. H. C. Kinsey & Company, Inc.
Return to Eden. 1st Ed. Edgar Cary Markham. LC 55-116612. 1956. Vantage Press.
Return to Elkhorne. Lester Wayne Merha. (Avalon Books). 4.95. Thomas Bouregy.
Return to Fort Yavapa. Al Cody, pseud. (YA) 1975. 6.95 (Avalon). Bouregy.
Return to Fort Yavapa. Al Cody. 1975. 4.95. Avalon Books.
Return to Hawkeston Hall. Leo Whitaker. LC 75-13497. 1.25 (ISBN 0-89041-010-0). Major Books.
Return to Innocent Earth. Wilma Dykeman. LC 72-84401. 1973. 8.95 (ISBN 0-03-066640-6). Holt, Rinehart and Winston.
Return to Innocent Earth. Wilma Dykeman. (Signet book). 1974. (pbk.) 1.75. New American Library.
Return to Ithaca, the Odyssey Retold As a Modern Novel: With a Pref. by Mark Van Doren. Eyvind Johnson. LC 52-13394. New York.
Return to Jalna. whiteoak ed. Mazo De La Roche. LC 46-7090. 1946. Little, Brown, and Company.
Return to Kaldak. Jeffrey Lord. (Blade Ser.: No. 36). 224p. (Orig.). 1983. pap. 2.25 (ISBN 0-523-41210-X). Pinnacle Bks.
Return to Kingsessing: By William Leech Pseud. William L Crothers. LC 52-6932. 1952. Vantage Press.
Return to Life. Erich Ebermayer & Goldsmith, Margaret Leland, 1894- Tr. LC 37-5030. R. M. McBride & Company.
Return to Love. Peggy Gaddis, pseud. LC 40-318750. 1940. Arcadia House, Inc.
Return to Love. Mary Howard, pseud. LC 46-2679. 1946. Arcadia House, Inc.
Return to Love. Virginia K. Smiley. (Silver Bell). 192p. 1982. pap. 1.95 o.s.i. (ISBN 0-8439-1156-5, Leisure Bks). Nordon Pubns.
Return to Love. Beverly Sommers. (Candlelight Romance Ser.: No. 693). (Orig.). 1982. pap. 1.75 (ISBN 0-440-17543-7). Dell.
Return to Moon Bay. Lee Belvedere, pseud. 192p. (YA) 1973. 4.95 o.p. (Avalon). Bouregy.
Return to Murder. Mary Ann Taylor. (Raven House Mysteries Ser.). 224p. 1981. pap. 2.25 (ISBN 0-373-63012-3, Pub. by Worldwide). Harlequin Bks.
Return to Night... Mary Renault, pseud. LC 47-191531. 1947. W. Morrow & Company.
Return to Night. Mary Renault, pseud. LC 78-3855. 1978. 9.95 (ISBN 0-89244-082-1). Queens House.
Return to Octavia. Daria Macomber, pseud. (Signet bk., P3530). 1968. New Amer. Lib.
Return to Octavia. Daria Macomber, pseud. LC 67-26235. 1967. New American Library.
Return to Paradise. James A. Michener. 416p. 1978. pap. 2.95 (ISBN 0-449-23831-8, Crest). Fawcett.
Return to Peyton Place. Grace Metalious. LC 59-15580. 1959. J. Messner.
Return to Powder Valley: A Powder Valley Western. Peter Field. LC 48-7984. 1948. Jefferson House.
Return to Ramos. Leo Cardenas. LC 77-126788. (Challenger book. La raza series). (Illus.). 1970. (ISBN 0-394-02018-9). Hill and Wang.
Return to Rapture. John Gorman. LC 41-462567. Phoenix Press.
Return to Rapture. Meg Hudson. (Superromances Ser.). 384p. 1983. pap. 2.50 (ISBN 0-373-70053-9, Pub. by Worldwide). Harlequin Bks.
Return to Red Castle. Dorothy M. Keddington. 200p. 1981. 8.95 (ISBN 0-913420-93-X). Olympus Pub Co.
Return to Romance: By Warren Howard Pseud. James Noble Gifford. LC 53-129253. 1953. Arcadia House.
Return to Sender. Raymond Mungo. 1975. 4.95 (Pub. by Montana Bks). Madrona Pubs.
Return to Sender. Audrie M. Tucker, pseud. Ed. by Gene DeRoin. (Aston Hall Presents Ser.). (Orig.). 1980. pap. 1.50 (ISBN 0-89936-021-1). Aston Hall.
Return to Spring. Elinor Mordaunt, pseud. LC 40-7595. The Greystone Press.
Return to Spring, Moment of Decision, Adam's Daughter. Jean S. MacLeod. (Harlequin Romances Ser.). 576p. 1982. pap. 3.50 (ISBN 0-373-20067-6). Harlequin Bks.
Return to Terror. Sally T. Smith. 1982. 6.95 (Avalon). Bouregy.
Return to Texas. Al Cody, pseud. 1978. pap. 1.25 (ISBN 0-532-12571-1). Woodhill.
Return to the Ardennes. Harold Calin. (Orig.). pap. 0.60 o.p. (73-724). Lancer.
Return to the Chateau: Preceded by A Girl in Love. Pauline Reage. LC 77-155130. 1971. (ISBN 0-394-47589-5). Grove Press.
Return to the Chateau: Story of O, Part II: Preceded by A Girl in Love. Pauline Reage. LC 79-28728. 1980. 2.95 (ISBN 0-394-17812-2). Grove Press.
Return to the Chateau: Story of O, Part 2. Pauline Reage. Tr. by Sabine D'Estree. 1971. 5.00 o.p. (ISBN 0-394-47589-5, GP689). Grove.
Return to the Elm. Ann Eric. 112p. 1975. 5.50 o.p. (ISBN 0-682-48398-2). Exposition.
Return to the Gate. William Corlett. LC 76-57889. 1977. 6.95 (ISBN 0-87888-112-3). Bradbury Press.
Return to the Range. Archie Joscelyn. 1945. Phoenix Press.
Return to the Scene. Q. Patrick, pseud. LC 41-15449. 1941. Simon and Schuster.
Return to the Shadows. Robert Serumaga. LC 76-108819. 1970. 4.95. Atheneum.
Return to the Source. Lanzo Del Vasto. 1973. pap. 2.95 o.p. (ISBN 0-671-21684-8, Touchstone Bks). S&S.
Return to the Vineyard. Mary Loos & Duranty, Walter, 1884- Joint Author. LC 45-35014. 1945. Doubleday, Doran and Company, Inc.
Return to the Wood: A Novel. James Lansdale Hodson. LC 55-9476. 1955. Morrow.
Return to Thebes. Allen Drury. LC 76-23757. (Illus.). 1977. 8.95 (ISBN 0-385-04199-3). Doubleday.
Return to Thrush Green. Read. LC 79-858. 1979. 8.95 (ISBN 0-395-27627-6). HM.
Return to Thrush Green. LC 79-858. (Illus.). 1979. 8.95 (ISBN 0-395-27627-6). Houghton Mifflin.
Return to Timberlake. Mary Collins Dunne. (YA) 1981. 6.95 (Avalon). Bouregy.
Return to Tomorrow. La Fayette Ronald Hubbard. LC 75-412. (Garland Library of Science Fiction). 1975. 11.00 (ISBN 0-8240-1417-0). Garland Pub.
Return to Treasure Island. Denis Judd. LC 78-61014. 1979. 8.95 (ISBN 0-312-67912-2). St Martin.
Return to Vienna. 1st Ed. Ernst Lothar. LC 49-7927.
Return to Vietnam. Don Pendleton. (Executioner Ser.). 192p. 1982. pap. 1.95 (ISBN 0-373-61043-2, Pub. by Worldwide). Harlequin Bks.
Return to Walden West. August William Derleth. LC 75-125927. (Illus.). 1970. 6.00. Candlelight Press.
Return to Warbow, an Original Western. Les Savage. LC 55-11055. (Dell first edition, 65). 1955. Dell Pub. Co.
Return to Windhaven. Marie De Jourlet. (Windhaven). 1978. pap. 3.50 (ISBN 0-523-41858-2). Pinnacle Bks.
Return Trip. Elaine Evain. (Orig.). 1974. pap. 1.25 o.p. (ISBN 0-515-03512-2, V3512). Pyramid Pubns.
Returned Empty. Florence Louisa Charlesworth Barclay. LC 20-10737. 1920. G. P. Putnam's Sons.
Returning. Catherine D. Solis. 224p. 1982. pap. 2.75 (ISBN 0-445-04734-8). Popular Lib.
Returning Home. Dorthea Dahl. LC 21-1677. 1920. Augsburg Publishing House.
Returning Hunter. Mario J Azevedo. LC 77-94643. (Africa Sketches Series). (Illus.). 1.65 (ISBN 0-89253-108-8). InterCulture Associates.
Returning to the Body. Robley Wilson. 1979. 3.00. Juniper Pr WI.
Retz. Van Zo Post. LC 8-16717. 1908. The McClure Company.
Reube Dare's Shad Boat: A Tale of the Tide Country. Charles George Douglas Roberts. LC 7-41028. 1895. Hunt & Eaton.
Reuben & Rachel. Susanna Haswell Rowson. LC 72-78815. 1798. Repr. 25.00 o.p. (ISBN 0-403-01952-4). Somerset Pub.
Reuben & Rachel. Susanna Haswell Rowson. LC 72-93658. (American Fiction Ser). 1970. lib. bdg. 18.00 o.s.i. (ISBN 0-512-00661-X). Garrett Pr.
Reuben and Rachel: Or, Tales of Old Times. A Novel. Susanna Haswell Rowson. LC 8-945. 1798. Printed by Manning & Loring, for D. West.
Reuben & Rachel; or, Tales of Old Times, 2 vols. in one. Susanna Haswell Rowson. LC 78-64089. Repr. of 1798 ed. 37.50 (ISBN 0-404-17074-9). AMS Pr.
Reuben Foreman, the Village Blacksmith. A Novel. Francesca Maria Steele. (Ledger library, no. 72). 1892. R. Bonner's Sons.
Reuben Larkmead. Edward Waterman Townsend. LC 5-8075. 1905. G. W. Dillingham Company.
Reuben, Reuben. Peter De Vries. LC 64-10471. 1964. Little Brown.
Reuben, Reuben. Peter De Vries. LC 64-10471. 1974. (pbk.) 1.50. Popular Library.
Reuben Sachs: A Sketch. Amy Levy. LC 78-37699. 1973. 13.50 (ISBN 0-404-56758-4). AMS Press.
Reuben Sachs: A Sketch. 2d ed. Amy Levy. LC 1-11868. 1889. Macmillan and Co.
Reubeni: Prince of the Jews; a Tale of the Renaissance. Max Brod & Waller, Hannah, Tr. 1928. A.A. Knopf.
Reunion. Lester V. Roper. (Orig.). 1981. pap. 2.75 (ISBN 0-440-18087-2). Dell.
Reunion. Richard Russell. (Belmont Tower Book). (Illus.). 1.50 (ISBN 0-505-51364-1). Tower Publications.
Reunion. Laurence Dwight Smith. LC 46-18818. 1946. S. Curl, Inc.
Reunion. Fred Uhlman. LC 76-50514. 1977. 6.95 (ISBN 0-374-24951-2). Farrar, Straus and Giroux.
Reunion. Fred Uhlman. LC 77-28224. 1978. 1.95 (ISBN 0-14-004790-5). Penguin Books.
Reunion. Jack Weyland. LC 81-19595. 1982. 7.95 (ISBN 0-87747-892-9). Deseret Book Co.
Reunion: A Novel. William Kuhns. LC 72-10472. 1973. 6.95 (ISBN 0-688-00146-7). W. Morrow.
Reunion: A Novel. Merle Miller. LC 54-9880. 1954. Viking Press.
Reunion & Other Stories. Tr. by Ly Singko from Chinese. (Writing in Asia Ser.). (Orig.). 1981. pap. text ed. 6.50x (ISBN 9-97164-019-8, 00231). Heinemann Ed.
Reunion at Chattanooga. Alfred Leland Crabb. LC 50-14370. 1950. Bobbs-Merrill.
Reunion at Meads: A Novel of Time and Many Women. Kathleen Wallace. LC 47-7150. 1948. G. P. Putnam's Sons.
Reunion at Pitereeka. Kerry Allyne. (Harlequin Romances Ser.). 192p. 1981. pap. 1.25 (ISBN 0-373-02407-X, Pub. by Harlequin). PB.
Reunion in Renfrew. William Edward Daniel Ross. (YA) 1972. 4.50 o.p. (Avalon). Bouregy.
Reunion in Reno. Maysie Greig. LC 41-13237. 1941. Carlton House.
Reunion in Reno. Mary Douglas Warren, pseud. LC 41-132376. Carlton House.
Reunion of the 108th. Donald Gilbert Taggart. LC 67-10425. 1967. Doubleday.
Reunion of the 108th: By Donald Taggart. Donald Gilbert Taggart. (N166). 1968. Avon.
Reunion on Strawberry Hill. Berenice Du Rae Thorpe. LC 44-1340. 1944. A. A. Knopf.
Reunion on the Wabash. Sterling North. LC 52-10403. 1952. Doubleday.
Reunion with Murder. Timothy Fuller. LC 41-114960. 1941. Little, Brown, and Company.
Reunion with Murder. Timothy Fuller. LC 43-10070. 1943. Triangle Books.
Reunion. 1st Ed. Robert Molloy. LC 59-6368. 1959. Doubleday.

Reunited. A Story of the Civil War. Alfred Rochefort Calhoun. (choice series, no. 30). 1891. R. Bonner's Sons.

Rev. Adonijah and His Wife's Relations. L A B Steele. LC 8-13426. The Authors' Publishing Company.

Rev. John Henry: Incidents Which Deeply Concerned One Life, and Were Not Without Their Bearing Upon Others. Percival R Benson. LC 6-11336. 1895. A. S. Barnes & Co.

Rev. Josiah Hilton: The Apostle of the New Age. George Farnell. LC 98-863. 1898. Journal of Commerce Company.

Rev. Mr. Dashwell: The New Minister at Hampton. E P Buffett. LC 6-19648. J. E. Potter and Company.

Revanche De Bozambo see Bozambo's Revenge.

Revealed by Fire. G. W Millican. LC 13-1640. 1912. Broadway Publishing Co.

Reveille for Romance. Ethel Hamill, pseud. LC 46-80222. 1946. Arcadia House, Inc.

Reveille for Romance. Jean Francis Webb. LC 46-802. 1946. Arcadia House.

Revelation. Andre Birabeau & Troubridge, Una Elena (Taylor) LC 30-19277. 1930. The Viking Press.

Revelation of Herself. Mary Farley Sanborn Sanborn. LC 4-21995. 1904. Dodd, Mead and Company.

Revelations. Olive Amanda McGrew. LC 32-20147. 1932. Printed by Shenandoah Publishing House, Inc.

Revelations. 1972. pap. 0.75 o.p. Paperback Lib.

Revelations: A Novel. Phyllis Reynolds Naylor. LC 79-16340. 10.95 (ISBN 0-312-67928-9). St. Martin's Press.

Revelations in Black. Carl Jacobi. LC 47-114482. 1947. Arkham House.

Revelations in Politics. A Story; Illustrating Thirty Years of American Political History... Dwight S. Prentice. 1885. Populist Publishing Co.

Revelations of a Disappearing Man. Charles Tekeyan. LC 76-116259. 1971. 6.95. Doubleday.

Revelations of Dr. Modesto. Alan Harrington. (SP403). 1965. Popular Lib.

Revelations of Dr. Modesto. 1st Ed. Alan Harrington. LC 55-9261. 1955. Knopf.

Revelations of Inspector Morgan. Oswald John Frederick Crawfurd. LC 7-25506. 1907. Dodd, Mead & Company.

Revellers. Louis Tracy. LC 18-652019. E. J. Clode.

Revellers: The Choruses of the Bacchai of Euripides, and the Third Book of Lucretius. Tr. by Robert Ekin McBride. Euripides. Bacchae & Lucretius Carus, Titus. LC 9-16557. 1909. Broadway Publishing Co.

Revelry. Samuel Hopkins Adams. LC 26-213081. 1926. Boni & Liveright.

Revelry by Night. John Lawrence Barnard. LC 41-14541. 1941. Doubleday, Doran & Co., Inc.

Revelry Manor. Elisabeth Barr. (Candlelight Regency). 0.95 (ISBN 0-440-19610-8). Dell.

Revels Are Ended. Robert Carson. LC 36-85055. 1936. Doubleday, Doran & Company, Inc.

Revenant. Sarah C. Liby. 3.00 o.p. Carlton.

Revenant. Brana Lobel. LC 78-18140. 1979. 8.95 (ISBN 0-385-14598-5). Doubleday.

Revenant. Remi Tremblay. (Novels by Franco-Americans in New England 1850-1940 Ser.). 348p. (Fr.). (gr. 10 up). 1980. pap. 4.50x (ISBN 0-911409-21-1). Natl Mat Dev.

Revenge. Justin Cartwright. LC 77-23691. 7.95 (ISBN 0-8092-7765-4). Contemporary Books.

Revenge. Noel Hynd. LC 75-34127. 1976. 8.95 (ISBN 0-8037-7384-6). Dial Press.

Revenge. Noel Hynd. (Dell Book). 1978. 1.95 (ISBN 0-440-17442-2). Dell Pub. Co.

Revenge. James Magorian. 1979. pap. 1.00 o.p. Samisdat.

Revenge: A Novelization. Joseph Warren & Bercovici, Konrad, 1882- LC 28-289631. Grosset & Dunlap.

Revenge Can Wait. Irene Alexander. LC 41-106751. G. P. Putnam's Sons.

Revenge for Love. Wyndham Lewis. LC 52-12706. 1952. H. Regnery Co.

Revenge for Love. Wyndham Lewis. LC 73-331167. (Penguin modern classics). 1972. 0.60 (ISBN 0-14-003368-8). Penguin.

Revenge Game. Gerald Hammond. LC 81-8903. 1981. 9.95 (ISBN 0-312-67930-0). St Martin's Press.

Revenge in Peace Valley. Gene Tuttle. 1982. pap. 6.95 (Avalon). Bouregy.

Revenge in 'The Convent' A Novel of Suspense and Mystery. 1st Ed. Catherine Bradshaw Boyd. LC 54-131704. 1955. Expositiion Press.

Revenge Is Sweet. Thomas Hardy & Weber, Carl Jefferson. LC 40-11990. 1940. Colby College Library.

Revenge of Annie Charlie. Alan Fry. LC 73-79666. 1973. 5.95 o.p. (ISBN 0-385-06257-5). Doubleday.

Revenge of Broken Arrow. Max Brand. 288p. 1981. pap. 1.95 (ISBN 0-441-71828-0). Ace Bks.

Revenge of Coil Collins. Chalmer Chastain, Jr. 3.00 o.p. Carlton.

Revenge of Dracula. Peter Tremayne, pseud. LC 79-64722. 1979. 8.95 (ISBN 0-8027-0634-7). Walker.

Revenge of Fantomas. Marcel Allain & Allinson, Alfred Richard, Tr. LC 27-24346. (Fantomas detective novels). David McKay Company.

Revenge of Increase Sewall. Heinrich Graat. LC 75-1066. (Orig.). 1969. pap. 0.75 o.p. (B75-1066). Belmont-Tower.

Revenge of Lucas Helm. Auguste Blondel. LC 6-14905. 1898. D. Biddle.

Revenge of Moriarty. John E Gardner. LC 75-34799. 1975. 8.95 (ISBN 0-399-11664-8). Putnam.

Revenge of Moriarty. John E Gardner. (Berkley Medallion Book). 1978. 1.95 (ISBN 0-425-03673-1). Berkley Pub. Corp.

Revenge of Taurus. Robert Lory. (Horrorscope,#2). 1974. (pbk.) 0.95 (ISBN 0-523-00347-1). Pinnacle Books.

Revenge of the Gambler. Spencer Knight. (Orig.). 1979. pap. 1.50 (ISBN 0-532-15394-4). Woodhill.

Revenge of the Generals. Nick Carter. 1.75 (ISBN 0-441-71834-5). Charter.

Revenge of the Horseclans. Robert Adams. 1982. pap. 2.50 (ISBN 0-451-11431-0, AE1431, Sig). NAL.

Revenge of the Lawn. Richard Brautigan. (gr. 10 up). pap. 2.95 (ISBN 0-671-41852-1). PB.

Revenge of the Lawn: Stories, 1962-1970. Richard Brautigan. LC 76-154094. 1971. 5.95 (ISBN 0-671-20960-4). Simon and Schuster.

Revenge of the Manitou. Graham Masterton. 1979. pap. 2.95 (ISBN 0-523-48071-7). Pinnacle Bks.

Revenge of the Pink Panther. Ed. by Fotonovel Publications Staff. (Illus., Orig.). 1979. pap. 2.75. Fotonovel.

Revenge: Or, The Robber of Guatemala. F Lindo. LC 7-160491. 1848. Robinson & Jones.

Revenge Returned. Joan Wills. 4.75 o.p. Carlton.

Revenge Rider. Jim Wilmeth. 192p. (Orig.). 1981. pap. 1.95 (ISBN 0-505-51738-8). Tower Bks.

Revenge Rides High. G. L. Guthridge. 208p. 1982. pap. 2.25 o.s.i. (ISBN 0-8439-1159-X, Leisure Bks). Nordon Pubns.

Revenger. Jon Messmann. 1973. (pbk.) 0.95. New American Library.

Revengers. Donald Hamilton. 352p. (Orig.). 1982. pap. 2.95 (ISBN 0-449-14487-9). Fawcett.

Revenue Detective. William H. Van Orden. (secret service series, no. 27). 1890. Street & Smith.

Reverberator. Thomas Hardy. Repr. lib. bdg. 12.70x (ISBN 0-88411-562-3). Amereon Ltd.

Reverberator. Henry James. LC 79-108255. (Black Cat book). 1979. 2.25 (ISBN 0-394-17079-2). Grove Press.

Reverberator: A Novel. Henry James. LC 7-7436. 1888. Macmillan and Co.

Reverberator & Other Stories. Henry James. 1908. 7.50 o.p. Scribner.

Reverberator. With an Introductory Note by Simon Nowell-Smith. Henry James. 1957. Grove Press.

Revere Estate. Mary Dwinell Chellis. LC 6-23356. 1883. Fairbanks, Palmer & Company.

Reverend Ben Pool: A Novel. Louis Paul. LC 41-892363. Duell, Sloan and Pearce.

Reverend Gentleman. James Maclaren Cobban. LC 6-267624. (On cover: Lovell's international series, no. 107). 1890. J. W. Lovell Company.

Reverend Green Willingwood: Or, Life Among the Clergy. A Novel. Robert Fisher. 1877. The Authors' Publishing Company.

Reverend Idol. A Novel. Lucretia Gray Noble. LC 12-37531. 1882. J. R. Osgood and Company.

Reverend Mama. Parley J Cooper. 1975. (pbk.) 1.25 (ISBN 0-671-80168-6). Pocket Books.

Reverend Melancthon Poundex: A Novel. Donn Piatt. LC 7-35928. (On cover: The Valentin series, no. 1). 1893. R. J. Belford.

Reverend Mister "Red.". Ethel Powelson Hueston. LC 49-109726. 1949. Bobbs-Merrill Co.

Reverend Randollph and the Avenging Angel. Charles Merrill Smith. LC 77-6617. 7.95. Putnum.

Reverend Randollph and the Fall From Grace, Inc. Charles Merrill Smith. LC 78-19097. 8.95. Putnam.

Reverend Randollph and the Holy Terror. Charles Merrill Smith. LC 80-17849. 10.95 (ISBN 0-399-12461-6). Putnam.

Reverend Randollph and the Wages of Sin. Charles Merrill Smith. LC 74-16619. 1974. 6.95 (ISBN 0-399-11461-0). Putnam.

Reverend Randolph & the Avenging Angel. Charles Merrill Smith. 192p. 1982. pap. 2.50 (ISBN 0-380-58933-8, 58933). Avon.

Reverend Randolph & the Fall from Grace, Inc. Charles Merrill Smith. 224p. 1982. pap. 2.50 (ISBN 0-380-59832-9, 59832). Avon.

Reverend Randolph & the Wages of Sin. Charles Merrill Smith. 208p. 1982. pap. 2.50 (ISBN 0-380-57174-9, 57174). Avon.

Reverie; or, a Flight to the Paradise of Fools, 1763, 2 vols. in 1. Charles Johnstone. LC 74-16307. (Novel in England, 1700-1775 Ser). 1974. lib. bdg. 50.00 (ISBN 0-8240-1162-7). Garland Pub.

Reveries of a Bachelor. Donald Grant Mitchell. LC 43-40894. A. L. Burt Company.

Reveries of a Bachelor: Or, A Book of the Heart. Donald Grant Mitchell. LC 4-8631. 1850. Baker & Scribner.

Reveries of a Bachelor: Or, A Book of the Heart. Donald Grant Mitchell. LC 7-31108. 1858. C. Scribner.

Reveries of a Bachelor: Or, A Book of the Heart. a new ed. Donald Grant Mitchell. LC 8-2127. 1877. Scribner, Armstrong & Co.

Reveries of a Bachelor: Or, A Book of the Heart. new ed. Donald Grant Mitchell. LC 7-31106. 1878. Scribner, Armstrong & Company.

Reveries of a Bachelor: Or, A Book of the Heart. new and rev. ed. Donald Grant Mitchell. LC 4-23818. 1892. C. Scribner's Sons.

Reveries of a Bachelor: Or, A Book of the Heart. Donald Grant Mitchell. LC 32-33621. (The Altemus library. 20). 1893. H. Altemus.

Reveries of a Bachelor: Or, A Book of the Heart. Donald Grant Mitchell. LC 7-31105. (On cover: Seaside library. Pocket ed. no. 2108). C. Munro's Sons.

Reveries of a Bachelor: Or, A Book of the Heart. Donald Grant Mitchell. LC 4757. W. B. Conkey Company.

Reveries of a Bachelor: Or, A Book of the Heart. Donald Grant Mitchell. LC 4342. T. Y. Crowell & Co.

Reveries of a Bachelor: Or, A Book of the Heart. Donald Grant Mitchell. LC 6-38354. The Bobbs-Merrill Company.

Reveries of a Bachelor: Or, A Book of the Heart. Donald Grant Mitchell. LC 6-29090. R. F. Fenno & Company.

Reveries of a Bachelor: Or, A Book of the Heart. Donald Grant Mithcell. LC 7-311075. 1889. C. Scribner's Sons.

Reveries of a Widow. Teresa H Dean. LC 99-785. 1899. Town Topics Publishing Co.

Reveries of a Young Man in Quest of a Wife. T Hood Stevens. LC 8-20118. 1888. Sherman & Co.

Reverse Negative: A Novel of Suspense. Andre Jute. LC 79-13293. 9.95 (ISBN 0-393-01216-6). Norton.

Reversible Santa Claus. Meredith Nicholson. LC 17-28188. 1917. Houghton and Mifflin Company.

Reversion of Form, and Other Horse Stories. George Wheaton Harrington. LC 11-18194. 1911. 1.20. Sherman, French & Company.

Reversion to Type. Edmee Elizabeth Monica De La Pasture. LC 23-13191. 1923. The Macmillan Company.

Revi-Lona: A Romance of Love in a Marvelous Land. Frank Cowan. LC 77-84216. (Lost Race and Adult Fantasy Fiction). 1978. 16.00 (ISBN 0-405-10971-7). Arno Press.

Revival and Other Short Stories. Roxylea Melas. LC 34-405929. 1934. The Naylor Company.

Revival in Tin Town. Effie M. Williams. 84p. pap. 0.75. Faith Pub Hse.

Revoke. Willem De Veer. LC 18-3023. 1917. John Lane.

Revolt. Don Pendleton. (Orig.). pap. 0.95 o.s.i. (313N, Travellers Comp). Olympia.

Revolt Along the Rio Grande. J Clyde Ryan. LC 64-17020. 1964. Naylor Co.

Revolt: An American Novel. William Henry McMasters. LC 19-18647. D. D. Nickerson & Company.

Revolt at Roskelly's. William Caine. LC 11-35690. 1911. G. P. Putnam's Sons.

Revolt in April. Charles E Mercer. LC 78-142137. 1971. 6.95. World Pub. Co.

Revolt in Arcadia. Gosta Larsson. LC 42-18358. 1942. American Publishers.

Revolt in San Marcos. Robert Carver North. LC 49-971821. 1949. Houghton Mifflin Co.

Revolt in Switzerland. Cyril Chessex. LC 53-121297. Vantage Press.

Revolt in Two Thousand One-Hundred. Robert Anson Heinlein. pap. 2.50 (ISBN 0-451-11148-6, AE1148, Sig). NAL.

Revolt in 2100: The Prophets and the Triumph of Reason Over Superstition. Robert Anson Heinlein. LC 53-12529. (His Future history series). 1953. Shasta Publishers.

Revolt of a Daughter. Ellen Warner Olney Kirk. LC 7-12362. 1897. Houghton, Mifflin and Company.

Revolt of Anne Royle. Helen Reimensnyder Martin. LC 8-25996. 1908. The Century Co.

Revolt of Cinderella. Peggy O'More, pseud. (Starlight Romance Ser.). 160p. 1973. pap. 0.75 o.p. (532-75492-075). Manor Bks.

Revolt of Gunnar Asch. 1st American Ed. Translated from the German by Robert Kee. Hans Hellmut Kirst. LC 56-504414. Little, Brown.

Revolt of Gunner Asch. Hans H. Kirst. 1956. 5.95 o.p. Little.

Revolt of Gunner Asch. Hans H. Kirst. 1968. pap. 0.75 o.p. (T1840). Pyramid Pubns.

Revolt of Gunner Ashe. Hans H. Kirst. 1975. pap. 1.50 o.p. (ISBN 0-515-03929-2). BJ Pub Group.

Revolt of Henry. Frederick Hugh Herbert. LC 39-21786. G. P. Putnam's Sons.

Revolt of Mamie Stover. William Bradford Huie. LC 51-12073. 1951. Duell, Sloan and Pearce.

Revolt of Man. Walter Besant. LC 6-123371. (On cover: Leisure hour series. no. 136). 1882. H. Holt and Company.

Revolt of Mother and Other Stories. Mary Eleanor Wilkins Freeman. LC 74-16322. 1974. Feminist Press.

Revolt of Sarah Perkins. Marian Cockrell. LC 65-19078. 1965. D. McKay Co.

Revolt of the Angels. Anatole France, pseud. LC 76-222313. (Illus.). 1953. For the Members of the Limited Editions Club.

Revolt of the Angels. Anatole France, pseud. Tr. by Jackson, Emilie. LC 14-17990. (Half-title: The works of Anatole France in an English translation, ed. by F. Chapman. Popular ed.). John Lane Company.

Revolt of the Angels. Anatole France, pseud. LC 31-30702. (Half-title: The modern library of the world's best books). The Modern Library.

Revolt of the Angels. Anatole France, pseud. Tr. by Jackson, Emille. LC 31-2525. 1927. Dodd, Mead & Company.

Revolt of the Birds. Melville Davisson Post. LC 27-18257. 1927. D. Appleton & Company.

Revolt of the Cockroach People. Oscar Zeta Acosta. (Illus.). 1974. (pbk.) 1.95. Bantam Books.

Revolt of the Cockroach People. Oscar Zeta Acosta. LC 73-79837. (Illus.). 1973. 7.95 (ISBN 0-87932-060-5). Straight Arrow Books; Distributed by Quick Fox, New York.

Revolt of the Eaglets. Jean Plaidy. 320p. 1981. pap. 2.75 (ISBN 0-449-24460-1, Columbine). Fawcett.

Revolt of the Eaglets. Jean Plaidy. 1980. 10.95 (ISBN 0-399-12495-0). Putnam Pub Group.

Revolt of the Fisherman. Anna Seghers & Goldsmith, Margaret Leland, 1894- Tr. LC 30-4855. 1930. Longmans, Green and Co.

Revolt of the Fishermen. Netty Reiling Radvanyi. Tr. by Goldsmith, Margaret Leland. LC 30-4855. 1930. Longmans, Green.

Revolt of the Idiots: A Story. burton blatt. ed. Burton Blatt. (Illus.). 10.95. Exceptional Press.

Revolt of the Micronauts. Gordon Williams. 192p. 1981. pap. 1.95 (ISBN 0-553-20107-7). Bantam.

Revolt of the Perverts (Gay Short Stories) Daniel Curzon. LC 77-83394. (Orig.). 1978. pap. 4.50 (ISBN 0-930650-01-8). D Brown Bks.

Revolt of the Saints. Lilie Strongin & Boris S. Holmstock. LC 65-28502. 1966. Living Books.

Revolt of the Scapegoats. Norman Linker. LC 78-7486. 1969. 5.00. House of Falmouth.

Revolt of the Sinners: Translated from the Italian by Marianne Ceconi. Ugo Zatterin. LC 54-120296. Appleton-Century-Crofts.

Revolt of the Unemployable. Ray Nelson, pseud. 1978. 7.95 (ISBN 0-89185-095-3); pap. 2.95 (ISBN 0-89185-094-5). Anthelion Pr.

Revolt of Zengo Takakuwa: A Novel. Richard M Baker, Jr. LC 62-10502. 1962. Farrar, Straus and Cudahy.

Revolt on Jupiter. John Martin. 1978. pap. 1.50 (ISBN 0-532-15356-1). Woodhill.

Revolt on the Border. Stanley Vestal. LC 38-7727. 1938. Houghton Mifflin Company.

Revolt on the Painted Desert. Earl Haley. LC 52-124874. 1952. House-Warven.

Revolution: A Novel. Adolph Gillis. LC 34-255997. Duffield & Green.

Revolution; a Story of the Near Future in England. John Davys Beresford. LC 21-8833. 1921. 2.00. G. P. Putnam's Sons.

Revolution & Roses: 1st American Ed. Percy Howard Newby. LC 57-8720. 1957. Knopf.

Revolution from Rosinante. Alexis A. Gilliland. 192p. (Orig.). 1981. pap. 2.25 (ISBN 0-345-29265-0, Del Rey). Ballantine.

Revolution in Tanner's Lane. William Hall White & Shapcott, Reuben, Ed. LC 38-10856. 1936. Oxford University Press, H. Milford.

Revolution in Tanner's Lane; Miriam's Schooling. William Hale White. LC 75-1515. (Victorian Fiction: Novels of Faith and Doubt; No. 64). 1975. (ISBN 0-8240-1588-6). Garland Pub.

Revolution in Tanner's Lane, 1887. William H. White. Ed. by Robert L. Wolff. Bd. with Miriam's Schooling, Eighteen Ninety. LC 75-1515. (Victorian Fiction Ser.). 1975. lib. bdg. 66.00 (ISBN 0-8240-1588-6). Garland Pub.

Revolution Island. Julian Fane. 352p. 1980. 17.95 (ISBN 0-241-10319-3, Pub. by Hamish Hamilton England). David & Charles.
Revolution of the Dead. Chris Powell. 1974. 6.50 o.p. (ISBN 0-682-47953-5). Exposition.
Revolutionary. Hans Koningsberger. 212p. 1967. 4.95 (ISBN 0-374-24984-9). FS&G.
Revolutionary. Lawrence L Schoonover. LC 58-7849. 1958. Little, Brown.
Revolutionary Love-Story: And The High Steeple of St. Chrysostom's. Ellen Warner Olney Kirk. LC 7-12363. 1898. H. S. Stone & Company.
Revolutionary Petunias. Alice Walker. LC 72-88796. 1973. 6.95 o.p. (ISBN 0-15-177090-5). HarBraceJ.
Revolutionary Road. Richard Yates. LC 70-163123. 1971. (ISBN 0-8371-6221-1). Greenwood Press.
Revolutionary Road. Richard Yates. LC 61-5740. 1961. Little, Brown.
Revolving Boy. Gertrude Friedberg. LC 66-20976. 1966. Doubleday.
Revue. Beverley Nichols. LC 39-14792. 1939. Doubleday, Doran & Company, Inc.
Revulsion: A Novel. Tr. from Hungarian by Kathleen Szasz. Laszlo Nemeth. LC 65-19789. 1966. 7.95. Grove.
Reward. Michael Barrett. LC 55-2885. 1955. Longmans, Green.
Reward. Michael Barrett. LC 56-5761. 1956. Farrar, Straus, and Cudahy.
Reward. Max Brand. 1977. pap. 1.75 (ISBN 0-671-82892-4). PB.
Reward for a Defector. John Michael Evelyn. LC 73-84677. 1974. 6.95. St. Martin's Press.
Reward for a Defector. Michael Underwood. LC 73-84677. 221p. 1973. 6.95 o.p. St Martin.
Reward Game. Gerald Hammond. LC 80-51897. 9.95 (ISBN 0-312-68078-3). St. Martin's Press.
Reward of Faith: Illustrated by Nora Unwin. Elizabeth Goudge. LC 51-7747. 1951. Coward-McCann.
Rewarding Short Stories. David A. Weems. 1977. 4.95 o.p. (ISBN 0-533-03103-6). Vantage.
Rewards and Fairies. Rudyard Kipling. LC 49-7702. 1949. Doubleday.
Rewards and Fairies. Rudyard Kipling. LC 10-22932. 1910. Doubleday, Page & Company.
Rewards and Fairies. Rudyard Kipling. LC 15-20033. 1911. Doubleday, Page & Company.
Rewards and Fairies. Rudyard Kipling. LC 22-145372. 1920. Doubleday, Page & Company.
Rewards and Fairies. Rudyard Kipling. LC 28-167003. 1922. Doubleday, Page & Company.
Rewards and Fairies. Rudyard Kipling. LC 43-36307. 1922. Doubleday, Page & Company.
Rewards for a P. O. W. O. R. Bassett. 192p. (Orig.). 1973. pap. 1.95 o.p. (ISBN 0-87056-318-1). Brandon.
Rex. Edward Frederic Benson. LC 25-15637. George H. Doran Company.
Rex. Joyce Stranger, pseud. 1972. pap. 0.95 o.p. (95264). Beagle Bks.
Rex: A Novel. Joyce Stranger, pseud. 1968. Viking Press.
Rex Amoris (The King of Love) A Romance of the Time of Christ. Gerhard Lewis Wind. LC 28-30709. 1928. Concordia Publishing House.
Rex Lardner Selects the Best of Sports Fiction. Ed. by Rex Lardner. LC 66-11845. 1966. Grosset & Dunlap.
Rex Lee, Night Flyer. LC 29-18705. (His Rex Lee flying stories). Grosset & Dunlap.
Rex Wayland's Fortune: Or, The Secret of the Thunderbird. Hiram Alonzo Stanley. Laird & Lee.
Rexworth Mystery. Scott Cummings. LC 11-144072. 1.50. Philadelphia Suburban Publishing Company.
Rezanov. Gertrude Franklin Horn Atherton. LC 78-96873. (Illus.). 1969. Literature House.
Rezanov. Gertrude Franklin Horn Atherton. 1906. The Authors and Newspapers Association.
Rezanov. with an introduction by william marion reedy. ed. Gertrude Franklin Horn Atherton. LC 20-7825. (Half-title: The modern library of the world's best books). 1919. Boni and Liveright, Inc.
Rezanov. Gertrude Franklin Horn Atherton. LC 35-271451. 1934. Frederick A. Stokes Company.
Rezanov. Gertrude Franklin Horn Atherton. LC 6-42373. 1906. The Authors and Newspapers Association.
Rezanov and Dona Concha: Previously Published Under the Title Concha Arguello, Sister Dominica. Gertrude Franklin Horn Atherton. LC 37-27275. 1937. Frederick A. Stokes Company.
Rezo Strange: A Novel of the Old West. Dan Dakota. LC 81-81863. 155p. (Orig.). 1981. pap. 5.95 (ISBN 0-940360-00-4). Leaf Pr.
Rhapsodist & Other Uncollected Writings. Charles Brockden Brown. LC 43-9591. 1977. Repr. of 1943 ed. 25.00x (ISBN 0-8201-1203-8). Schol Facsimiles.
Rhapsody. Dorothy Edwards. LC 28-3334. 1928. A. A. Knoph.
Rhapsody: A Dream Novel. Arthur Schnitzler. LC 70-175442. 1971. 9.00 (ISBN 0-404-05614-8). AMS Press.
Rhapsody: A Dream Novel. Arthur Schnitzler. Tr. by Schinnerer, Otto Paul. LC 27-4328. 1927. Simon and Schuster.
Rhapsody, a Dream Novel. Arthur Schnitzler. Tr. by Otto P. Schinnerer. 1979. Repr. of 1927 ed. lib. bdg. 12.50 (ISBN 0-8495-4919-1). Arden Lib.
Rhapsody in Andros: A Tale of the Shallows of Andros, Bahamas. Nelson Hayes. LC 53-7979. 1953. Doubleday.
Rhapsody in Black. Brian M. Stableford. (Science Fiction Ser.). (Orig.). 1973. pap. 0.95 o.p. (UQ1059). DAW Bks.
Rhapsody in Death. John Francis Mauro. LC 41-1127. Fortuny's.
Rhapsody in Gold. Russell Long. LC 32-22986. Missouri Valley Press.
Rhapsody in Gold. Arthur Somers Roche. LC 31-22581. Sears Publishing Company, Inc.
Rhapsody in Green. Elizabeth Carfrae, pseud. LC 41-120226. G. P. Putnam's Sons.
Rhapsody of a Hermit & Other Tales. Michael Rothschild. 192p. 1973. 7.50 o.p. (ISBN 0-670-59725-2). Viking Pr.
Rhapsody of a Hermit, and Three Tales. Michael Rothschild. LC 72-9924. 1973. 7.50 (ISBN 0-670-59725-2). Viking Press.
Rhea. Russell W. Martin. LC 78-52800. 8.95 (ISBN 0-89343-048-X). Ermine Publishers.
Rhea. Russell W. Martin. (Playboy Press paperback). 1980. 2.50. Playboy Press.
Rhea: Or, The Case of Dr. Plemen. Leon Rene Delmas. LC 7-37418. (On cover: Globe library. no. 110). 1889. Rand, McNally & Company.
Rheingold Route. Arthur Maling. LC 78-69506. 8.95 (ISBN 0-06-012843-7). Harper & Row.
Rheingrafenstein. A Romance of the Eleventh Century. S. A. Brown. 1893. G.W. Dillingham.
Rhesa: A Romance of Babylon. Walter Bliss Newgeon. LC 22-139612. The Raymond Publishing Company.
Rhiannon. Roberta Gellis. LC 81-82368. 384p. (Orig.). 1982. pap. 3.50 (ISBN 0-87216-933-2). Playboy Pbks.
Rhine Journey. Ann Schlee. 1983. pap. 3.95 (ISBN 0-14-006215-7). Penguin.
Rhine Journey: A Novel. Ann Schlee. LC 80-12265. (Illus.). 1981. 10.95 (ISBN 0-03-056894-3). Holt, Rinehart and Winston.
Rhine Madens. Carolyn See. 304p. 1981. 13.95 (ISBN 0-698-11105-2, Coward). Putnam Pub Group.
Rhine Replica. Martha Albrand. LC 70-85597. 1969. 5.95. Random House.
Rhinelander Center. Barbara Harrison. 464p. (Orig.). 1981. pap. 2.75 (ISBN 0-89083-704-X). Zebra.
Rhinelander Pavilion. Barbara Harrison. (Orig.). 1980. pap. 2.50 (ISBN 0-89083-572-1). Zebra.
Rhinemann Exchange. Robert Ludlum. LC 74-9789. 1974. 8.95 (ISBN 0-8037-7532-6). Dial Press.
Rhinemann Exchange. Robert Ludlum. 1975. (pbk.) 1.95. Dell.
Rhinestone As Big As the Ritz. Alan Coren. LC 79-83524. 1979. 8.95 o.p. (ISBN 0-312-68091-0). St Martin.
Rhinestone Sharecropping. Bill Gunn. LC 81-52032. 194p. (Orig.). 1981. pap. 5.95 (ISBN 0-918408-19-9). Reed & Cannon.
Rhinestone Sharecropping: A Novel. Bill Gunn. LC 81-52032. 5.95 (ISBN 0-918408-19-9). I. Reed Books.
Rhinestones, a Romance. Margaret Widdemer. LC 29-9220. Harcourt, Brace and Company.
Rhino Ritz: An American Mystery. Keith Abbott. LC 78-23542. 1979. 10.95 (ISBN 0-912652-42-X, Dynamite Bks); pap. 5.95 (ISBN 0-912652-43-8); signed ed. 25.00x (ISBN 0-912652-44-6). Blue Wind.
Rhoda Fair. Clarence Budington Kelland. LC 26-1953. 1926. Harper & Brothers.
Rhoda Fleming. A Story. George Meredith. LC 1-19359. (On cover: Seaside library. Pocket ed. no. 1146). 1888. G. Munro.
Rhoda of the Underground. Florence Finch Kelly. LC 9-29503. 1909. Sturgis & Walton Company.
Rhoda Fleming: A Story. rev. ed. George Meredith. LC 1-19361. 1897. C. Scribner's Sons.
Rhode-Island Tales. By a Friend to Youth, of New-Port, R.I. Avis C. Howland. LC 48-304383. 1829. M. Day.
Rhode Island Tales: Depicting Social Life During the Colonial, Revolutionary and Post-Revolutionary Era. Ed. by Henrietta Raymer Palmer. Williams, Mrs. Catherine R. (Arnold) 1790-1872. LC 28-30262. 1928. The Purdy Press.
Rhodes Reader: Stories of Virgins, Villians, and Varmints. 2d ed. Eugene Manlove Rhodes. LC 74-15904. 1975. 9.95. (ISBN 0-8061-1260-3) (ISBN 0-8061-1290-5). University of Oklahoma Press.
Rhodes Reader: Stories of Virgins, Villians, and Varmints. Eugene Manlove Rhodes. LC 57-11196. 1957. University of Oklahoma Press.
Rhodesia. Nick Carter. (Nick Carter Ser.). (O.s.i.). (Orig.). 1970. pap. 0.95 o.s.i. (AN1097, Award). Univ Pub & Dist.
Rhodesians: Sketches of English South-African Life. Stracey Chambers. LC 5676. 1900. John Lane.
Rhododendron Man. John Aubrey Tyson. LC 30-175052. E. P. Dutton & Co., Inc.
Rhododendron Pie. Margery Sharp. LC 30-17094. 1930. D. Appleton and Company.
Rhody. Frances Stanton Brewster. LC 12-21731. 1912. 1.00. G. W. Jacobs & Company.
Rhomelle. Leila Stephens. LC 71-149443. 1971. 5.95 (ISBN 0-8059-1554-0). Dorrance.
Rhona. Mrs. Bridges. (On cover: Lovell's library, v. 18, no. 863). 1887. J. W. Lovell Company.
Rhona. A Novel. Mrs. Bridges. (Seaside library, v. 26, no. 504). 1879. G. Munro.
Rhona. A Novel. Mrs. Bridges. (On cover: Seaside library. Pocket ed., no. 740). 1886. G. Munro.
Rhubarb. Harry Allen Smith. LC 46-5945. 1946. Doubleday & Co., Inc.
Rhubarb," The Diary of a Gentleman's Hunter. J. Stanley Reeve. LC 9-2041. 1908. Press of J. B. Lippincott Company.
Rhyme and the Reason. 1st Ed. Richard Percival Lister. LC 63-8093. 1963. Harcourt, Brace & World.
Rhymer. Charlotte Stewart. LC 2271. 1900. C. Scribner's Sons.
Rhymes and Stories. Mary Carral Loughlin. LC 22-5686.
Rhymes Here and There: By the Merry Rhymster of the A. G. O. Copyright... Mildred Emma Walton. LC 20-131919. Columbian Printing Company.
Rhymes of Our Valley. Anthony Henderson Euwer. LC 16-17087. 1916. 1.00. J. B. Pond.
Rhyming Message. W. W. Colbert. 2.00 o.p. Carlton.
Rhythm for Rain. John Louw Nelson. LC 37-6121. 1937. Houghton Mifflin Company.
Rhythms. Michael French. LC 79-6650. 1980. 11.95 (ISBN 0-385-14358-3). Doubleday.
Rhythms. Michael French. 1981. 2.75 (ISBN 0-425-05023-8). Berkley Publishing Corp.
Riallaro: The Archipelago of Exiles. John Macmillan Brown. LC 1-31063. 1901. G.P. Putnam's Sons.
Riallaro: The Archipelago of Exiles. 2d ed. John Macmillan Brown. LC 31-28163. 1931. H. Milford, Oxford University Press.
Rib of The Hawk. Rosamond Van Der Zee Marshall. LC 56-103394. 1956. Appleton-Century. Crofts.
Ribbons in Her Hair. Lucy Walker, pseud. 1980. pap. 1.75 (ISBN 0-345-29278-2). Ballantine.
Ribstone Pippins; a Country Tale. Mary Gleed Tuttiett. LC 8-32312. 1898. Harper & Brothers.
Ric Harper: A Novel. 1st Ed. Anthony Carlozzi. LC 59-65160. 1959. Pageant Press.
Rice: A Novel. Louise Jordan Miln. LC 30-2726. 1930. Frederick A. Stokes Company.
Rice-Cake Rabbit. Lifton. 3.75 o.p. (21192). G&D.
Rice in Silver Bowls: A Novel. Ekert-Rotholz, Alice Maria. LC 81-22174. 15.95 (ISBN 0-88064-003-0). Fromm International Pub. Corp.
Rice in Silver Bowls: A Novel. Ekert-Rotholz, Alice Maria. LC 81-22174. 15.95 (ISBN 0-88064-003-0). Fromm International Pub. Corp.
Rice in the Wind. Kathleen Wallace. LC 43-1687. 1943. G. P. Putnam's Sons.
Rice Mills of Port Mystery. Benjamin Franklin Heuston. LC 7-18778. (On cover: Unity library, no. 8). 1891. C. H. Kerr & Company.
Rice Papers. Hugh Leigh Norris. LC 5-40806. 1905. Longmans, Green, and Co.
Rice Powder: Polvos De Arroz: a Novella. Sergio Galindo. LC 78-51332. (Perivale translation series). 3.00 (ISBN 0-912288-12-4). Perivale Press.
Rice-Sprout Song. Eileen Chang. LC 55-7192. 1955. Scribner.
Riceyman Steps. Arnold Bennett. LC 23-17269. 1923. Cassell and Company, Ltd.
Riceyman Steps: 11th Ed. Arnold Bennett. LC 65-29942. 1966. bds., 3.95. Cassell.
Rich. Graham Masterton. LC 78-9917. 12.95 (ISBN 0-671-24673-9). Simon and Schuster.
Rich. Graham Masterton. 1980. 2.75 (ISBN 0-671-81768-X). Pocket Books.
Rich and Dangerous Game. Lionel White. LC 74-82992. 1974. 7.95 (ISBN 0-679-50476-1). D. McKay Co.
Rich & Famous. Eileen Lottman. 160p. (Orig.). 1981. pap. text ed. 2.50 (ISBN 0-553-14991-1). Bantam.
Rich and Strange: A Novel. Dale Collins. 1931. Houghton Mifflin Company.
Rich and the Beautiful. Ruth Harris. LC 78-9137. 9.95 (ISBN 0-671-24211-3). Simon and Schuster.
Rich and the Lonely. G. Christopher Morgan. LC 80-27486. 10.95 (ISBN 0-8253-0043-6). Beaufort Books.
Rich and the Righteous. Helen Van Slyke. 1977. 1.95 (ISBN 0-445-08585-1). Popular Library.
Rich and the Righteous. Helen Van Slyke. LC 78-150922. 1971. 6.95. Doubleday.
Rich Are Always with Us. Ethel Pettit. LC 31-10519. Sears Publishing Company.
Rich Are Different. Susan Howatch. LC 76-51432. 1977. 11.50 (ISBN 0-671-22669-X). Simon & Schuster.
Rich Are Different: Susan Howatch. Susan Howatch. 1978. 2.50 (ISBN 0-449-23480-0). Fawcett Books.
Rich Are Not Proud. Maysie Greig. LC 42-11246. 1942. Carlton House.
Rich Are with You Always. Malcolm Macdonald. LC 76-13702. (Illus.). 1976. 10.00 (ISBN 0-394-49850-X). Knopf.
Rich Are with You Always. Malcolm Macdonald. (Signet Book). 1977. 2.25 (ISBN 0-451-07682-6). New American Library.
Rich As the Wine: An Autobiographical Novel. 1st Ed. Alan Arthur. LC 57-8240. 1957. Pageant Press.
Rich Boy from Chicago. Derek Marlowe. LC 79-16325. 1979. 12.95 (ISBN 0-312-68097-X). St. Martin's Press.
Rich Brat: A Novel of Paris. Robert Forrest Wilson. LC 29-22136. The Bobbs-Merrill Company.
Rich Crowd. Alexander Fedoroff. Orig. Title: Swords & Scepters, Coins & Cups. 480p. 1972. pap. 1.25 o.p. (P1730, Crest). Fawcett World.
Rich Crowd see Swords & Scepters, Coins & Cups.
Rich Die Hard. Beverley Nichols. LC 58-5224. 1958. Dutton.
Rich Dreams. Ben Barzman & Norma Barzman. 528p. 1982. pap. 3.50 (ISBN 0-446-90034-6). Warner Bks.
Rich Enough: A Tale of the Times. Hannah Farnham Sawyer Lee. LC 49-10696. 1837. Whipple & Damrell.
Rich Friends. Jacqueline Briskin. 1983. pap. 3.95 (ISBN 0-440-17380-9). Dell.
Rich Friends: A Novel. Jacqueline Briskin. LC 75-29469. 8.95 (ISBN 0-440-07367-7). Delacorte Press.
Rich Get It All. Fran Huston. LC 72-92223. 1973. 5.95 (ISBN 0-385-03544-6). Published for the Crime Club by Doubleday.
Rich Get It All. Fran Huston. LC 74-5033. 1974. 10.95 (ISBN 0-8161-6208-5). G. K. Hall.
Rich Girl. Margaretta Brucker. LC 42-51785. 1942. Gramercy Publishing Co.
Rich Girl. Elizabeth Villars, pseud. LC 77-5347. 9.95 (ISBN 0-698-10786-1). Coward, McCann & Geoghegan.
Rich Girl. Elizabeth Villars, pseud. 1978. 2.50 (ISBN 0-671-81838-4). Pocket Books.
Rich Girl--Poor Girl. Ruth Dewey Groves. LC 30-554. Grosset & Dunlap.
Rich Girl, Poor Girl. Faith Baldwin Cuthrell. LC 38-14001. Farrar & Rinehart, Inc.
Rich Girl, Poor Girl. Faith Baldwin Cuthrell. 1974. (pbk.) 0.95. Warner Paperback Library.
Rich Girl, Poor Girl: A Novel. Mary Orr, pseud. LC 75-20487. 1975. 8.95 (ISBN 0-8037-6042-6). Dial Press.
Rich Have Secrets. Unity Hall. (Orig.). 1982. pap. 3.25 (ISBN 0-440-16786-8). Dell.
Rich, Hip & Deadly. Hugo Paul, pseud. 1968. pap. 0.60 o.p. (73-730). Lancer.
Rich House. Stella Gibbons. LC 42-40087. 1941. Longmans, Green and Co.
Rich Husband. A Novel. Charlotte Eliza Lawson Cowan Riddell. LC 42-27301. T. B. Peterson & Brothers.
Rich Irish. James Mandeville Neville. LC 31-21308. Coward-McCann, Inc.
Rich Is Better, a Novel. Max Wilk. LC 62-7513. 1962. Macmillan.
Rich Man. Alexander Brinchmann & Birkeland, Joran, Tr. LC 39-22586. E. P. Dutton & Co., Inc.
Rich Man. Georges Simenon. LC 76-151139. 1971. 5.95 (ISBN 0-15-177162-6). Harcourt Brace Jovanovich.
Rich Man and the Poor Man. From the German of Gustav Nieritz. Karl Gustav Nieritz. Tr. by Gotwald, William H. LC 12-37241. (Added t.-p.: The fatherland series). 1875. Lutheran Board of Publication.
Rich Man, Dead Man... Hillary Waugh. LC 56-7650. 1956. Published for the Crime Club by Doubleday.
Rich Man, Poor Girl. Maysie Greig. LC 35-18995. 1935. Doubleday, Doran and Co., Inc.
Rich Man, Poor Girl. Maysie Greig. LC 37-12766. 1937. The Sun Dial Press, Inc.
Rich Man, Poor Girl. Maysie Greig. LC 42-255889. 1942. The Sun Dial Press.
Rich Man, Poor Man. Janet Ayer Fairbank. LC 36-35990. 1936. Houghton Mifflin Company.

Rich Man, Poor Man. Maximilian Foster. LC 16-2215. 1916. 1.30. D. Appleton and Company.
Rich Man, Poor Man. Irwin Shaw. LC 74-120463. 1970. 7.95. Delacorte Press.
Rich Man's Daughter. Ralph Hale Mottram. LC 30-25153. 1930. Harper & Brothers.
Rich Man's Daughter: A Novel. Charlotte Eliza Lawson Cowan Riddell. LC 7-41427. The International News Company.
Rich Man's Fool: A Novel. Robert C Givins. LC 6-43971. (library of choice fiction). 1890. Laird & Lee.
Rich Men's Children. Geraldine Bonner. LC 6-37925. 1906. The Bobbs-Merrill Company.
Rich Miss Riddell. Dorothea Gerard Longard De Longgarde. (On cover: Appletons' town and country library. no. 142). 1894. D. Appleton and Company.
Rich Mrs. Burgoyne. Kathleen Thompson Norris. 1912. The Macmillan Company.
Rich Pay Late. Simon Raven. (Alms for Oblivion Ser.: No. 1). 1964. pap. 8.50x o.p. (ISBN 0-85634-992-5). Intl Pubns Serv.
Rich Pay Late: A Novel. 1st Amer. Ed. Simon Raven. LC 65-13295. 1965. 4.50. Putnam.
Rich People. Morton Cooper. LC 76-51785. 1977. 8.95 (ISBN 0-87131-235-2). M. Evans.
Rich People. Morton Cooper. (Bantam Book). 1978. 2.25 (ISBN 0-553-11339-9). Bantam Books.
Rich People: And Other Stories. Betty S Tigay. LC 42-25357. 1942. L. M. Stein.
Rich Radiant Love. Valerie Sherwood. 576p. 1983. pap. 3.95 (ISBN 0-446-30555-3). Warner Bks.
Rich Relations. Besse Sprague. LC 34-287710. A. L. Burt Company.
Rich Relations. William Wright. LC 80-15418. 12.95 (ISBN 0-399-12462-4). Putnam.
Rich Relatives. Compton Mackenzie. LC 21-20043. Harper & Brothers.
Rich Rewards. Alice Boyd Adams. LC 81-2809. 1981. 4.95 (ISBN 0-14-005918-0). Penguin Books.
Rich Twin, Poor Twin. Jennifer Ames, pseud. 1971. pap. 0.75 o.p. (94135). Beagle Bks.
Rich Twin, Poor Twin. Maysie Greig. LC 40-31452. 1940. Doubleday, Doran and Company, Inc.
Rich Uncle. Keith Robertson. LC 63-16624. 1963. Published for the Crime Club by Doubleday.
Rich Woman. Lucy Beatrice Malleson. LC 47-4069. 1947. Random House.
Rich Young Man: A Comedy with Digressions. by g. m. attenborough. ed. Gladys Mary Attenborough. LC 29-21218. 1929. Frederick A. Stokes Company.
Richard. Marguerite Bryant. LC 22-17066. 1922. 2.00. Duffield and Company.
Richard A. Sol Yurick. 480p. pap. 3.50 (ISBN 0-380-62430-3). Avon.
Richard A. A Novel. Sol Yurick. LC 80-66497. 1982. 14.95 (ISBN 0-87795-272-8). Arbor House.
Richard A. A Novel about Genius Rampant Sol Yurick. LC 80-66497. 446p. 1982. 14.95 (ISBN 0-87795-272-8). Arbor Hse.
Richard and the Knights of God. Pamela Bennetts. LC 73-76756. 1973. 5.95. St. Martin's Press.
Richard and the Knights of God. Pamela Bennetts. LC 77-3682. 1977. 9.95 (ISBN 0-89340-069-6). J. Curley.
Richard Baldock: An Account of Some Episodes in His Childhood, Youth, and Early Manhood, and of the Advice That Was Freely Offered to Him. Archibald Marshall. LC 18-26920. 1918. Dodd, Mead and Company.
Richard Baxter: A Story of New England Life of 1830 to 1840. Edward Franc Jones. LC 3-28592. 1903. The Grafton Press.
Richard Bruce: Or, The Life That Now Is. Charles Monroe Sheldon. LC 8-5094. Congregational Sunday-School and Publishing Society.
Richard Carvel. Winston Churchill. LC 99-2646. 1899. The Macmillan Company.
Richard Carvel. Winston Churchill. LC 41-80729. 1900. The Macmillan Company.
Richard Carvel. Winston Churchill. LC 13-12941. 1911. The Macmillan Company.
Richard Carvel. Winston Churchill. LC 20-15606. 1917. Grosset & Dunlap.
Richard Carvel. Winston Churchill. LC 23-130658. (Macmillan's pocket American and English classics). 1923. The Macmillan Company.
Richard Carvel. new ed., with a preface. ed. Winston Churchill. LC 14-16757. 1914. The Macmillan Company.
Richard Chatterton, V. C. Ruby M Ayres. LC 20-137180. W. J. Watt & Company.
Richard Edney and the Governor's Family. A Rusurban Tale... of Morals, Sentiment, and Life... Containing, Also, Hints on Being Good and Doing Good. Sylvester Judd. LC 7-11435. 1850. Phillips, Sampson & Company.
Richard Elliott: Financier. George Frederick Stratton. LC 6-34796. 1906. L. C. Page & Company.
Richard Escott. Edward Herbert Cooper. LC 6-30188. 1893. Macmillan & Co.
Richard Forrest, Bachelor.". Clement R Marley. LC 7-24690. (On cover: The primrose series, no. 39). Street & Smith.
Richard Furlong. Ernest Temple Thurston. LC 13-20753. 1913. D. Appleton and Company.
Richard Gordon. Alexander Black. LC 2-23835. 1902. Lothrop Publishing Company.
Richard Haddon; a Romance of Old Fort Crawford. William Stanislaus Hoffman. LC 20-230219. 1920. The Stratford Co.
Richard Hurdis. William Gilmore Simms. 1974. Repr. of 1890 ed. lib. bdg. 30.00 (ISBN 0-8414-8066-4). Folcroft.
Richard Hurdis: a Tale of Alabama. new and rev. ed. William Gilmore Simms. LC 70-176021. 1971. (ISBN 0-404-06035-8). AMS Press.
Richard Hurdis; a Tale of Alabama. new and rev. ed. William Gilmore Simms. LC 8-13054. (Half-title: Border novels and romances of the South. II). 1855. Redfield.
Richard Hurdis, a Tale of Alabama. new and rev. ed. William Gilmore Simms. LC 8-11018. (With his Guy Rivers. New York, 1882). 1882. A. A. Armstrong & Son.
Richard Hurdis: a Tale of Alabama. new and rev. ed. William Gilmore Simms. (On cover: Lovell's library, v. 13, no. 687). 1885. J. W. Lovell Company.
Richard III: The Last Plantagenet. Tyler-Whittle, Michael Sidney. LC 73-116916. 1970. Chilton Book Co.
Richard Judkins' Wooing: A Tale of Virginia in the Revolution. Thornton Jenkins Hains. LC 6-46161. 1898. F. T. Neely.
Richard, Myrtle, and I. Stephen Hudson. LC 26-12244. 1926. A. A. Knopf.
Richard: Myrtle, and I. Sydney Schiff. LC 62-720129. 1962. University of Pennsylvania Press.
Richard of York: Or, "The White Rose of England.". Norton, Hon. Mrs. Caroline (Sheridan) 1808-1877 & Warren, Samuel, 1807-1877. LC 7-41209. 1835. Wallis & Newell.
Richard: Or, Devotion to the Stuarts. A. C Leclerc. Tr. by Murphy, Blanche Elizabeth Mary Annunciata (Noel) LC 7-12780. 1882. Benziger Brothers.
Richard Pryne: A Novel of the American Revolution. Cyril Harris. LC 41-3119. 1941. C. Scribner's Sons.
Richard Raynal, Solitary. Robert Hugh Benson. LC 56-13847. (Thomas More book to live). 1956. H. Regnery Co.
Richard Richard. Hughes Mearns. LC 16-13971. 1916. The Penn Publishing Company.
Richard Rogers, Christian. Alive Barber McConnell. LC 7-152926. Presbyterian Board of Publication and Sabbath-School Work.
Richard Rosny. Mary Gleed Tuttiett. 1903. D. Appleton and Company.
Richard Said No:... By Peter Towry Pseud. David Piper. LC 53-8296. 1953. Morrow.
Richard Savage. Gwyn Jones. LC 35-15153. 1935. The Viking Press.
Richard the Brazen. Cyrus Townsend Brady & Peple, Edward Henry. LC 6-28452. 1906. Moffat, Yard & Company.
Richard the Fearless: Or, The Little Duke. Charlotte Mary Yonge. LC 9-2217. 1856. D. Appleton and Company.
Richard Vandermarck. Miriam Coles Harris. LC 99-2921. Houghton, Mifflin and Company.
Richard Vandermarck. A Novel. Miriam Coles Harris. 1871. C. Scribner & Company.
Richard Walden's Wife. 1st Ed. Eleanor Mercein Kelly. LC 50-6113. 1950. Bobbs-Merrill.
Richard Wyndham: A Novel. Frances Gordon Fane. LC 2-28517. 1902. G. W. Dillingham Company.
Richard's Things. Frederic Raphael. LC 75-6399. 208p. 1975. 6.95 o.p. (ISBN 0-672-52167-9). Bobbs.
Richard's Way. Kate Thompson. 1971. pap. 0.95 o.p. (95167). Beagle Bks.
Richardsoniana. Samuel Richardson. LC 74-16012. (Life & times of seven major British writers). 22.00. Garland Pub.
Richardson's Familiar Letters: And the Domestic Conduct Books; Richardson's AEsop. Katherine Gee Hornbeak. LC 38-10739. (Smith college studies in modern languages. vol. xix, no. 2. January, 1938). 1937. Smith College, Departments of Modern Languages of Smith College.
Richardson's Second Case: A Tale of Scotland Yard... Basil Home Thomson. LC 34-2564. 1934. Pub. for the Crime Club, Inc., by Doubleday, Doran & Company, Inc.
Richards's Crown: How He Won and Wore It. Anna D Weaver. LC 8-36751. 1882. B. S. Heath.
Richelieu: A Tale of France. George Payne Rainsford James. LC 4-16534. 1895. G. P. Putnam's Sons.
Richelieu: A Tale of France. George Payne Rainsford James. (Half-title: Everyman's library, ed. by Ernest Rhys. Fiction. no. 357). 1909. J. M. Dent & Co.
Richer--the Poorer. Ira L Jones. LC 2-27941. 1902. The Fiction Publishing Company.
Richer Dust... Margaret Storm Jameson. LC 31-8217. 1931. A. A. Knopf.
Richer Dust. Storm Jameson. (Berkley Medallion Book). 1975. (pbk.) 1.50. Berkley Publishing Corp.
Richer Harvest. 1st Ed. Elizabeth Frances Corbett. LC 52-5090. 1952. Lippincott.
Richer Than All His Tribe. Nicholas Monsarrat. LC 69-19284. (Illus.). 1969. 6.95. Morrow.
Riches. Emery Bemsley Pottle. LC 26-3731. (Half-title: Appleton short plays. no. 15). 1926. D. Appleton and Company.
Riches and Fame and the Pleasures of Sense. Kathy Black. LC 76-154934. 1971. 3.50 (ISBN 0-394-47145-8). Knopf.
Riches for Caroline: By Edwin Bateman Morris. Edwin Bateman Morris. LC 34-5277. The Penn Publishing Company.
Riches Have Wings: A Tale for the Rich & Poor. facs. ed. Timothy Shay Arthur. LC 77-137720. (American Fiction Reprint Ser). Repr. of 1847 ed. 15.00 (ISBN 0-8369-7019-5). Ayer Co.
Riches Have Wings; or, A Tale for the Rich and Poor. Timothy Shay Arthur. LC 77-137720. (American fiction reprint series). 1970. Books for Libraries Press.
Riches of Life. Jane Geniesse. LC 75-36623. 1976. 6.95 (ISBN 0-385-11287-4). Doubleday.
Riches Untold. Lete Belle Moriarty. LC 33-12645. Herald Publishing House.
Riches Without Wings: Or, The Cleveland Family. Elizabeth Oakes Prince Smith. LC 8-8640. 1838. G. W. Light.
Richest Girl in the World. Virginia Coffman. (Orig.). 1968. pap. 0.75 o.p. (74-954). Lancer.
Richest Girl in the World: An American Odyssey. Nona Coxhead. LC 77-82619. 1978. 10.00 (ISBN 0-385-13380-4). Doubleday.
Richest Man. Edward Shanks. LC 24-15677. 1924. A. A. Knopf.
Richest Man in Kansas. Charles Monroe Sheldon. LC 21-13505. The Christian Herald.
Richest Man in the World. J. P. 1969. 6.95 o.p. Bartholomew.
Richest Man in the World: A Novel. J. P & J P. LC 72-97062. 1969. 6.95. Bartholomew House.
Richest Man on Earth. Test Dalton. LC 31-19273. L. Shearon.
Richest Poor Folks. Leland Frederick Cooley. LC 77-1267. 1977. 8.95 (ISBN 0-312-68225-5). St. Martin's Press.
Richest Poor Folks. Leland Frederick Cooley. LC 63-18219. 1963. Doubleday.
Richest Woman in Town. Henry Bellamann. LC 32-4906. 2.00. The Century Co.
Richlands. Agnes Sligh Turnbull. LC 74-9955. 1974. 6.95 (ISBN 0-395-19428-8). Houghton Mifflin.
Richlands. Agnes Sligh Turnbull. (Fawcett Crest Book). 1976. (pbk.) 1.50. Fawcett.
Richmond Raid: A Novel. John Brick. LC 63-20509. 1963. Doubleday.
Richmond, Scenes in the Life of a Bow Street Runner, Drawn up from His Private Memoranda. Richmond. Ed. by E. F. Bleiler. LC 74-28942. 320p. 1976. pap. 4.50 (ISBN 0-486-23279-4). Dover.
Richmond: Scenes in the Life of a Bow Street Runner, Drawn up Form His Private Memoranda. Thomas Skinner Surr. LC 74-28942. (Illus.). 4.50 (ISBN 0-486-23279-4). Dover Publications.
Richmond, Vol. 1: The Flame. Elizabeth Fritch. 480p. (Orig.). 1980. pap. 2.75 (ISBN 0-89083-654-X). Zebra.
Richmond Vol. 3: The Embers. Elizabeth Fritch. 1981. pap. 2.75 (ISBN 0-89083-716-3). Zebra.
Richmond, Vol. 5: The Blaze. (Orig.). 1982. pap. 3.50 (ISBN 0-8217-1054-0). Zebra.
Richmond Vol.2: The Fire. Elizabeth Fritch. 1980. pap. 2.75 (ISBN 0-89083-679-5). Zebra.
Rich's Farewell to Military Profession, 1581. Barnabe Rich. Ed. by Thomas M. Cranfill. 1959. 12.00x o.p. (ISBN 0-292-73353-4). U of Tex Pr.
Rickey: A Novel. Charles J Calitri. LC 52-11386. 1952. Scribner.
Rickshaw Boy. Ch'ing Ch'un Shu. Tr. by Ward, Robert Spencer. LC 45-7026. 1945. Reynal & Hitchcock.
Rickshaw Boy. Shu, Ch'ing-Ch'un & King, Evan, Tr. LC 45-7026. 1945. Reynal & Hitchcock.
Rickshaw Boy. Ch'Ing-Ch'Un Shu & King, Evan, Tr. LC 45-8206. 1945. Reynals & Hitchcock.
Rickshaw Boy. Ch'Ng-Ch'Un Shu & King, Evan, Tr. LC 47-284. 1946. The Sun Dial Press.
Rickshaw: The Novel Lo-to Hsiang Tzu. Ch'ing Ch'un Shu. LC 79-10658. (Illus.). 10.95 (ISBN 0-8248-0616-6) (ISBN 0-8248-0655-7). University Press of Hawaii.
Rico, Bandit and Dictator. Antonio De Fierro Blanco. LC 34-22375. 1934. Houghton Mifflin Company.
Ricochets: Miniature Tales of Human Life. Andre Maurois. LC 73-150551. (Short story index reprint series). 1971. (ISBN 0-8369-3848-8). Books for Libraries Press.
Ricochets: Miniature Tales of Human Life. Andre' Maurois. Tr. by Miles Hamish. 1935. Harper & Brothers.
Ricroft of Withens. Halliwell Sutcliffe. LC 99-583. (Half-title: Appletons' town and country library, no. 258). 1899. D. Appleton and Company.
Riddarasogur. Ed. by Eugen Kolbing. LC 80-1948. Repr. of 1872 ed. 38.00 (ISBN 0-404-18716-1). AMS Pr.
Riddle. Dan Sherman. LC 77-79527. 7.95 (ISBN 0-87795-164-0). Arbor House.
Riddle: And Other Tales. Walter John De La Mare. LC 23-9575. 1923. A. A. Knopf.
Riddle-Master of Hed. Patricia A. McKillip. (Del Rey Bk.). 1978. pap. 2.25 (ISBN 0-345-28881-5). Ballantine.
Riddle Me This: By Mike Roscoe Pseud. John Roscoe & Michael Ruso. LC 52-10764. 1952. Crown Publishers.
Riddle of a Lady. Anthony Gilbert, pseud. 1978. 9.95 o.p. (ISBN 0-86025-130-6). State Mutual Bk.
Riddle of a Lady: By Anthony Gilbert Pseud. Lucy Beatrice Malleson. LC 56-8801. 1956. Random House.
Riddle of Cruelty. G. Rothman. 1971. 7.50 (ISBN 0-8022-2345-1). Philos Lib.
Riddle of Hangar Eighteen. Timothy G. Beckley. (Illus.). 72p. (Orig.). 1981. pap. write for info. (ISBN 0-938294-03-2). Global Comm.
Riddle of Life: A Novel. James Wesley Johnston. LC 2-5870. Jennings & Pye.
Riddle of Luck. Mary E. Stone Bassett. LC 6-90941. 1893. J. B. Lippincott Company.
Riddle of Ramrod Ridge. William Colt MacDonald. LC 42-10311. 1942. Doubleday, Doran and Company, Inc.
Riddle of Ramrod Ridge. William Colt MacDonald. LC 43-4982. 1943. The Sun Dial Press.
Riddle of Samson. Andrew Garve. 1978. pap. 1.95i (ISBN 0-06-080450-5, P 450, PL). Har-Row.
Riddle of Samson. Paul Winterton. (Perennial Library). 1978. 1.95 (ISBN 0-06-080450-5). Harper & Row.
Riddle of Samson: By Andrew Garve Pseud. 1st American Ed. Paul Winterton. LC 55-8042. Harper.
Riddle of the Ages. Frank Allen Peake. LC 29-9538. The Christopher Publishing House.
Riddle of the Amber Ship. Mary E Hanshew & Hansbew, Thomas W., 1897-1914, Joint Author. LC 24-943571. 1924. Doubleday, Page & Company.
Riddle of the Eighth Guest. Benson Wheeler & Purdy, Claire Lee, Joint Author. LC 36-102341. R. Speller.
Riddle of the Florentine Folio: A Case for Peggy Fairfield. Eloise S Liddon. 1935. Published for the Crime Club, Inc., by Doubleday, Doran & Company, Inc.
Riddle of the Fly: & Other Stories. Elizabeth Enright. LC 70-121538. (Short story index reprint series). 1970. Books for Libraries Press.
Riddle of the Fly & Other Stories. facsimile ed. Elizabeth Enright. LC 70-121538. (Short Story Index Reprint Ser.). Repr. of 1959 ed. 15.00 (ISBN 0-8369-3494-6). Ayer Co.
Riddle of the Frozen Flame. Mary E Hanshew & Hanshew, Thomas W., 1857-1914, Joint Author. LC 20-9476. 1920. Doubleday, Page & Company.
Riddle of the Mysterious Light. Mary E Hanshew & Hanshew, Thomas W., 1857-1914, Joint Author. LC 21-1283. 1921. Doubleday, Page & Company.
Riddle of the Night: Being the Record of a Singular Adventure of That Remarkable Detective Genius, Hamilton Cleek, the Man of the Forty Faces, Ones Known to the Police As "the Vanishing Cracksman.". Thomas W Hanshew. LC 15-185722. 1915. Doubleday, Page & Company.
Riddle of the Purple Emperor. Thomas W Hanshew & Hanshew, Mary E., Joint Author. LC 19-4790. 1919. Doubleday, Page & Company.
Riddle of the Red Devil Costume. Thomas J. Saunders. 4.95 o.p. Vantage.
Riddle of the Rose. William Blair Morton Ferguson. LC 29-20437. 1929. R. M. McBride & Company.
Riddle of the Rovers. Arthur B Maurice. LC 42-1553. 1942. Dodd, Mead and Company.
Riddle of the Russian Princess. Eloise S Liddon. LC 34-120346. 1934. Pub. for the Crime Club, Inc., by Doubleday, Doran & Company, Inc.
Riddle of the Sand. Erskine Childers. 1976. Repr. of 1913 ed. lib. bdg. 17.95x (ISBN 0-89190-240-6). Am Repr-Rivercity Pr.
Riddle of the Sands. Erskine Childers. 352p. 1976. pap. 3.95 (ISBN 0-486-23280-8). Dover.

Riddle of the Sands. Erskine Childers. (Crime Ser.). 1978. pap. 2.95 (ISBN 0-14-000905-1). Penguin.

Riddle of the Sands. Erskine Childers. (Illus.). 304p. 1971. Repr. of 1903 ed. 35.00 o.p. (ISBN 0-87636-016-9). Barre-Westover.

Riddle of the Sands: A Record of Secret Service. Erskine Childers. LC 75-36077. (Illus.). 1976. 3.50 (ISBN 0-486-23280-8). Dover Publications.

Riddle of the Sands: A Record of Secret Service Recently Achieved. Erskine Childers. LC 71-142580. (Illus.). 1971. (ISBN 0-87636-016-9). Imprint Society.

Riddle of the Sands: A Record of Secret Service Recently Achieved. Erskine Childers. LC 77-78725. (Illus.). 1977. 12.50 (ISBN 0-679-50772-8). D. McKay Co.

Riddle of the Spinning Wheel: Being an Exploit in the Career of Hamilton Cleek, Detective. Mary E Hanshew & Hanshew, Thomas W., 1857-1914, Joint Author. LC 22-22655. 1922. Doubleday, Page & Company.

Riddle of the Traveling Skull. Harry Stephen Keeler. LC 34-25936. E. P. Dutton & Co., Inc.

Riddle of the Veiled Song. 1st Ed. Charles B MacDonald. LC 54-12694. 1954. Pageant Press.

Riddle of the Yellow Zuri: A Mystery Novel. Harry Stephen Keeler. LC 30-307134. E. P. Dutton & Co., Inc.

Riddle of Three-Way Creek. Ridgwell Cullum. LC 25-7077. 2.00. George H. Doran Company.

Riddle Ring. Justin McCarthy. LC 7-15284. (Half-title: Appletons' town and country library, no. 195). 1896. D. Appleton and Company.

Riddley Walker. Russell Hoban. LC 80-25859. 1981. 13.95 (ISBN 0-671-42147-6). Summit Bks.

Riddley Walker. Russell Hoban. 240p. 1982. pap. 5.95 (ISBN 0-671-45118-9). WSP.

Ride. Kip Crosby. 1973. (pbk.) 0.95. Popular Lib.

Ride. Kip Crosby. LC 74-184478. 1972. 8.95 (ISBN 0-670-61085-2). Grossman Publishers.

Ride a Cock-Horse. Lela Seftali. pap. 1.95 o.s.i. (OPS-4). Olympia.

Ride a Cock Horse. Elma Williams. 1972. 8.95 (ISBN 0-7181-0930-9). Transatlantic.

Ride a Crooked a Trail. Paul Winchester. LC 75-13495. 0.95 (ISBN 0-89041-008-9). Major Books.

Ride a Crooked Trail. Burt Arthur & Budd Arthur. 1979. pap. 1.25 o.s.i. (ISBN 0-505-51389-7). Tower Bks.

Ride a Crooked Trail. Lewis B Patten. (Signet Book). 1976. 1.25. New American Library.

Ride a Paper Tiger. William Ash. LC 69-15712. 1969. 4.50. Walker.

Ride a Tall Horse. Lewis B Patten. LC 79-7844. 1980. 8.95 (ISBN 0-385-15714-2). Doubleday.

Ride a Tiger. Douglas Orgill. 1977. 6.70 o.p. (ISBN 0-86025-092-X). State Mutual Bk.

Ride a White Dolphin. Anne Maybury. LC 78-140719. 1971. 6.95 (ISBN 0-394-46245-9). Random House.

Ride Against the Rifles. Wade Hamilton, pseud. 1978. pap. 1.25 (ISBN 0-532-12574-6). Woodhill.

Ride Down the Wind. Wayne Barton. LC 80-2950. (Double D western). 1981. 10.95 (ISBN 0-385-17525-6). Doubleday.

Ride East, Ride West. Anne Powers, pseud. 1978. pap. 1.95 o.s.i. (ISBN 0-505-51300-5). Tower Bks.

Ride East! Ride West! A Romance of the Hundred Years' War. Anne Powers, pseud. LC 47-30848. 1947. Bobbs-Merrill Co.

Ride 'em Montana. Pete Jones. LC 36-7588. Phoenix Press.

Ride for a Fall: A Novel. Val Henry Gielgud. LC 53-9313. 1953. Morrow.

Ride for Hell. A. A. Baker. 160p. (Orig.). 1978. pap. 1.50 (ISBN 0-89041-205-7, 3205). Major Bks.

Ride for Revenge. Jake Logan. LC 76-57342. (Jake Logan Ser.). 160p. (Orig.). 1977. pap. 1.95 (ISBN 0-86721-159-8). Playboy Pbks.

Ride for Texas. Cover Painting by Frank McCarthy. William Heuman. LC 54-430964. (Gold medal books, 414). 1954. Fawcett Publications.

Ride for Trinidad: A Powder Valley Western. Peter Field. LC 54-5523. 1954. Jefferson House.

Ride Him, Cowboy. Kenneth Perkins. LC 23-13888. The Macaulay Company.

Ride Home. Sallie Burrow. 32p. (Orig.). 1982. pap. 3.75 (ISBN 0-9608706-0-1). Waterford Pr.

Ride Home Tomorrow: The Chronicle of a Crusader Newly Set Forth by Evan John Pseud. Evan John Simpson. LC 51-9681. 1951. Putnam.

Ride in the Sun. George G. Gilman, pseud. (Edge Ser.: No. 34). 160p. 1980. pap. 1.95 (ISBN 0-523-41987-2). Pinnacle Bks.

Ride into Gunsmoke. Llewellyn Perry Holmes. 1972. pap. 0.75 o.p. (74-789). Lancer.

Ride into Hell. Jack Slade. (Lassiter,#16). 1974. (pbk.) 0.95. Belmont Tower Books.

Ride on a Cyclone. William Hosea Ballou. LC 6-6090. (On cover: The household library, v. 4, no. 37). Belford, Clarke & Company; Etc., Etc.

Ride on, Cowboy! William Frederick Bragg. LC 56-129326. Arcadia House.

Ride on Stranger. Kylie Tennant, pseud. LC 43-130054. 1943. The Macmillan Company.

Ride on the Milky Way: A Novel. Marguerite Dorian. LC 66-26189. 1967. Crown Publishers.

Ride Out Singing. Alice F Loomis. LC 51-2606. 1951. Whittlessy House.

Ride Out the Storm. Aleen Malcom. (Orig.). 1981. pap. 2.95 (ISBN 0-440-17399-X). Dell.

Ride Out the Storm. Roger Vercel. LC 52-13646. 1953. Putnam.

Ride, Slocum, Ride. Jake Logan. LC 75-14619. 1.25. Playboy Press.

Ride the Blue Riband. Rosalind Laker. LC 76-29791. 1977. 7.95 o.p. (ISBN 0-385-12416-3). Doubleday.

Ride the Blue Riband. Barbara Ovstedal. (Signet Book). 1978. New American Library.

Ride the Blue Riband. Barbara Vstedal. LC 76-29791. 1977. 7.95 (ISBN 0-385-12416-3). Doubleday.

Ride the Dark Hills. William Edmunds Claussen. LC 54-61260. (Silver star westerns). 1954. Dodd, Mead.

Ride the Dark Storm. Nard Jones. LC 55-43682. (Gold medal books, 512). 1955. Fawcett Publications.

Ride the Dark Trail. Ford Bowne, pseud. LC 65-7555. 1965. Arcadia House.

Ride the Dark Trail. Louis L'Amour. LC 72-8138. 1972. 7.95 (ISBN 0-8161-6052-X). G. K. Hall.

Ride the Golden Tiger. new ed. Jonathan Black. LC 75-30828. 312p. 1976. 8.95 o.p. (ISBN 0-688-03001-7). Morrow.

Ride the Golden Tiger. B. W Von Block. LC 75-30828. 1976. 8.95 (ISBN 0-688-03001-7). Morrow.

Ride the Gray Planet. 2nd ed. Blake Savage, pseud. (Griffon Ser). 1969. pap. 0.50 o.p. (Golden Pr). Western Pub.

Ride the High Places. Muriel Naomi Evans. LC 54-11340. 1954. Little, Brown.

Ride the Hot Wind. Mark Fackler. LC 77-78850. 1978. pap. 2.95 (ISBN 0-88419-126-5). Creation Hse.

Ride the Lonely Country. B. Griffin. 3.00 o.p. Carlton.

Ride the Long Night. E A Alman. LC 58-13666. 1959. Macmillan.

Ride the Man Down. John Benteen. (Leisure Books). 1977. 1.50 (ISBN 0-8439-0488-7). Nordon Pubns.

Ride the Man Down. Frederick Dilley Glidden. LC 42-25553. 1942. Doubleday, Doran & Company, Inc.

Ride the Man Down. large print ed. Luke Short. LC 81-4809. 1981. 9.95 (ISBN 0-89621-277-7). Thorndike Press.

Ride the Nightmare. Ward Greene. LC 30-217694. J. Cape & H. Smith.

Ride the Nightmare. Richard Matheson. LC 59-9212. (Ballantine suspense novel, 301K). 1959. Ballantine Books.

Ride the Pink Horse. Dorothy Belle Flanagan Hughes. LC 46-7903. 1946. Duell, Sloan and Pearce.

Ride the Rattler to Romance. Paul P. Northcutt. 4.50 o.p. Vantage.

Ride the Rattler to Romance. Paul P Northcutt. 1974. 4.50. (ISBN 0-533-01107-8). Vantage Press.

Ride the Red Earth. Paul Iselin Wellman. 1971. pap. 1.25 o.p. (01005). Curtis.

Ride the Red Earth: A Novel. Paul Iselin Wellman. LC 58-5959. 1958. Doubleday.

Ride the River. William MacLeod Raine. 1973. 0.75. Popular Lib.

Ride the Roller Coaster. Carter Brown, pseud. (Signet Book). 1975. (pbk.) 1.25. New American Library.

Ride the Thunder. Janet Dailey. 1981. pap. 2.95 (ISBN 0-671-43667-8). PB.

Ride the Tiger. Robert Emmott. (American Avenger Ser.: No. 2). (Orig.). 1982. pap. 2.50 (ISBN 0-451-11268-7, AE1268, Sig). NAL.

Ride the Vengeance Trail. William Oliver Turner. 192p. (Orig.). 1982. pap. 2.25 (ISBN 0-425-05755-0). Berkley Pub.

Ride the Vengeance Trail. William Oliver Turner. (Berkley medallion). 1974. (pbk.) 0.95 (ISBN 0-425-02728-7). Berkley Pub. Co.

Ride the Whirlwind. Richard David. 1973. 7.95 (ISBN 0-533-00522-1). Vantage.

Ride the Wild Country. Wade Hamilton, pseud. (Belmont Tower Books). 1977. 1.50 (ISBN 0-505-51205-X). Tower Pubns.

Ride the Wild Plains. Nelson Nye. 1975. (pbk.) 0.95. Belmont Tower Books.

Ride the Wild Trail. Max Brand. 1981. pap. 1.75 (ISBN 0-671-41556-5). PB.

Ride the Wild Trail. Max Brand. (General Ser.). 1983. lib. bdg. 13.95 (ISBN 0-8161-3435-9, Large Print Bks). G K Hall.

Ride the Wild Trail. Cliff Farrell. (Signet book). 1974. (pbk.) 0.95. New American Library.

Ride the Wild Trail: By Max Brand Pseud. Frederick Faust. LC 66-116036. (Silver star westerns). 1966. bds., 3.50. Dodd.

Ride the Wind. Lucia St. Clair Robson. (Orig.). 1982. pap. 6.95 (ISBN 0-345-29145-X). Ballantine.

Ride the Wind South: By John Hunter Pseud. Willis Todhunter Ballard. LC 57-9606. (Perma books. Western. M3092 2). 1957. Permabooks.

Ride the Wind: The Story of Cynthia Ann Parker and the Last Days of the Comanche. Lucia St. Clair Robson. LC 82-90215. (Illus.). 1982. 6.95 (ISBN 0-345-29145-X). Ballantine.

Ride This Night! Vilhelm Moberg & Alexander, Henry, 1890- LC 43-9539. 1943. Doubleday, Doran and Company, Inc.

Ride to Blizzard. Archie Joscelyn. LC 53-6603. 1953. Bouregy & Curl.

Ride to Hell. Frank Gruber. (Signet Book). 1977. 1.25 (ISBN 0-451-07656-7). New American Library.

Ride to Hell. Ben Thompson. (Belmont Tower Book.). 1978. 1.50 (ISBN 0-505-51287-4). Tower Pubns.

Ride to Panmunjom. Duane Thorin. LC 56-13423. 1956. H. Regnery Co.

Ride to Revenge. Eric Allen. (Orig.). 1979. pap. 1.95 (ISBN 0-89083-551-9). Zebra.

Ride to Sundown. W. C Rawford. 1976. (pbk.) 1.25. Pinnacle Books.

Ride to Violence. Johanas L. Bouma. 1978. pap. 1.50 o.s.i. (ISBN 0-8439-0596-4, Leisure Bks). Nordon Pubns.

Ride West. Frank O'Rourke. LC 53-127341. 1953. Ballantine Books.

Ride with Me. Thomas B Costain. 1974. (pbk.) 1.50 (ISBN 0-380-00032-6). Avon.

Ride with Me. Thomas Bertram Costain. LC 51-4954. 1951. Doubleday.

Ride with Me. Thomas Bertram Costain. LC 44-7411. 1944. Doubleday, Doran and Company, Inc.

Rider. Edgar Rice Burroughs. 1974. (pbk.) 1.25. Ace Books.

Rider from Texas, a Ranchland Novel. Philip Ketchum. LC 55-40524. (Popular library, 673). 1955. Popular Library.

Rider from Yonder. Norman A Fox. LC 47-16291. 1947. Dodd, Mead and Company.

Rider in Khaki: A Novel. Nathaniel Gould. LC 18-6696. Frederick A. Stokes Company.

Rider in the Rain. Scott Siegel. (Orig.). 1979. pap. 1.50 (ISBN 0-532-15403-7). Woodhill.

Rider in the Sun. Edmund Ware Smith. LC 35-7599. 1935. Lothrop, Lee and Shepard Company.

Rider in the Sun. Edmund Ware. LC 35-7599. 1935. Lothrop, Lee and Shepard Company.

Rider O' the Stars: A Western Story. Robert J Horton. LC 24-580124. Chelsea House.

Rider of Distant Trails. Zane Grey. 1982. 18.00x (ISBN 0-86025-180-2, Pub. by Ian Henry Pubns England). State Mutual Bk.

Rider of Golden Bar. William Patterson White. LC 22-8543. 1922. Little, Brown, and Company.

Rider of Lost Creek. Louis L'Amour. 160p. (gr. 8-12). 1976. pap. 2.25 (ISBN 0-553-20139-5). Bantam.

Rider of San Felipe. Charles Horace Snow. LC 30-315937. Hale, Cushman & Flint.

Rider of the Dim Trails. Buck Billings. LC 38-5291. The William Caslon Company, Inc.

Rider of the Dim Trails. Claude Rister. LC 38-5291. The William Caslon Company, Inc.

Rider of the High Hill. Max Brand. 240p. 1983. pap. 1.95 (ISBN 0-446-30607-X). Warner Bks.

Rider of the High Hills. Max Brand. 1977. 6.95 o.p. (ISBN 0-396-07499-5). Dodd.

Rider of the High Hills. Frederick Faust. LC 77-14593. (Silver star western). 6.95 (ISBN 0-396-07499-5). Dodd, Mead.

Rider of the High Hills. Frederick Faust. LC 77-27944. 1978. 11.95 (ISBN 0-8161-6545-9). G. K. Hall.

Rider of the High Mesa. Ernest Haycox. LC 78-7816. 1978. 7.95 (ISBN 0-8161-6578-5). G. K. Hall.

Rider of the King Log: A Romance of the Northeast Border. Holman Francis Day. LC 19-14698. 1919. Harper & Brothers.

Rider of the Mesquite Trail. Bradford Scott. (Orig.). 1969. pap. 0.50 o.p. (R2067). Pyramid Pubns.

Rider of the Midnight Range. Harry Sinclair Drago. 1940. W. Morrow & Company.

Rider of the Midnight Range: By Will Ermine Pseud. Harry Sinclair Drago. LC 51-4871. (Triple-A western classic). 1951. Jefferson House.

Rider of the Mohave: A Western Story. James Fellom. LC 24-27745. Chelsea House.

Rider of the Night. Hanns Heinz Ewers. Tr. by Halasz, George. LC 32-30512. The John Day Company.

Rider of the Red Ranges. Clement Yore. LC 33-778. The Macaulay Company.

Rider of the Rifle Rock. Bennett Foster. LC 39-23530. 1939. W. Morrow & Co.

Rider of the Tetons. Ben Smith. LC 54-12715. 1954. Avalon Books.

Rider on a White Horse. Rosemary Sutcliff & Fairfax, Thomas Fairfax. LC 59-11454. 1959. Coward-McCann.

Rider on Rattlesnake Hill. Lester W. Merha. 1982. pap. 6.95 (Avalon). Bouregy.

Rider on the Bronze Horse. Harry Harrison Kroll. LC 42-19938. 1942. The Bobbs-Merrill Company.

Rider on the Mountains. Elisabeth Carleton Hubbard Lansing. LC 49-11720. 1949. Crowell.

Rider on the White Horse: And Selected Stories. Theodor Storm. LC 64-6489. (Signet classic). 1964. New American Library.

Riders Across the Border. Jackson Gregory. 1932. Dodd, Mead & Company.

Riders Against the Moon. Johnston McCulley. LC 36-154426. G. H. Watt, Inc.

Riders by Night. Nelson Coral Nye. LC 50-6180. (Silver star westerns). 1950. Dodd, Mead.

Riders in the Chariot. Patrick White. LC 61-137284. 1961. Viking Press.

Riders in the Chariot. Patrick White. 1975. (pbk.) 2.25 (ISBN 0-380-00467-4). Avon.

Riders in the Night. Lee Floren. LC 50-8451. 1950. Phoenix Press.

Riders in the Storm. Lee Floren. LC 55-12492. 1955. Arcadia House.

Riders of Buck River. William MacLeod Raine. LC 40-1856. 1940. Houghton Mifflin Company.

Riders of Buck River. William MacLeod Raine. 1973. (pbk) 0.75. Popular Library.

Riders of Judgment. Frederick Feikema Manfred. LC 57-538735. 1957. Random House.

Riders of Judgment. Frederick Feikema Manfred. (Signet Book). 1973. (pbk) 1.25. New American Lib.

Riders of Judgment. Frederick Feikema Manfred. LC 80-19032. (Series: Gregg Press Western Fiction Series.). 1980. 15.95 (ISBN 0-8398-2593-5). Gregg Press.

Riders of Judgment. Frederick Feikema Manfred. LC 82-8631. 1982. 6.95 (ISBN 0-8032-8117-X). University of Nebraska Press.

Riders of Lobo Valley: A Novel of the Transition West. Robert Claiborne Pitzer. LC 52-3490. 1952. Abelard Press.

Riders of Red Butte. Roe Richmond. LC 51-3124. 1951. Phoenix Press.

Riders of Steel. Thomas Albert Curry. (Orig.). 1973. pap. 0.75 o.p. (07288). Curtis.

Riders of the Broken Circle. Tevis Miller. LC 38-11895. Phoenix Press.

Riders of the Buffalo Grass: By Bliss Lomax Pseud. Harry Sinclair Drago. LC 52-10159. (Silver star westerns). 1952. Dodd, Mead.

Riders of the Chaparral. George Brydges Rodney. LC 35-27216. Greenberg.

Riders of the Desert Trail. John Ulrich Giesy. LC 42-155523. 1942. Dodge Publishing Company.

Riders of the Flood. W. E. Blackhurst. LC 53-102850. 1954. Vantage Press.

Riders of the Grande Ronde. Robert Ormond Case. LC 28-156254. 1928. Doubleday & Company, Inc.

Riders of the Mesquite Trail. Jackson Cole. 1972. Popular Lib.

Riders of the Night: A Novel of Cattle-Land. Eugene Cunningham. LC 32-297663. 1932. Houghton Mifflin Company.

Riders of the Night: A Novel of Cattle-Land. Eugene Cunningham. LC 43-3870. 1943. The Sun Dial Press.

Riders of the North Star. Esther A. Albrecht. 1970. 4.00 o.p. Carlton.

Riders of the Oregon. Charles Wesley Sanders. LC 32-18247. A. H. King, Inc.

Riders of the Outlaw Trail: A Powder Valley Western. Peter Field. LC 52-10780. 1952. Jefferson House.

Riders of the Plains. Max Brand. LC 40-32553. 1940. Dodd, Mead & Company.

Riders of the Plains. Max Brand. LC 40-32553. 1940. Dodd, Mead & Company.

Riders of the Plains. Max Brand. 1978. 1.50 (ISBN 0-671-81760-4). Pocket Books.

Riders of the Purple Sage. Zane Grey. 1980. pap. 2.50 (ISBN 0-671-83422-3). PB.

Riders of the Purple Sage: A Novel. Zane Grey. LC 12-1131. 1912. 1.30. Harper & Brothers.

Riders of the Purple Sage: A Novel. Zane Grey. LC 16-131212. 1913. Harper & Brothers.

Riders of the Purple Sage: A Novel. Zane Grey. LC 21-10259. 1914. Grosset & Dunlap.

Riders of the Purple Sage: A Novel. Zane Grey. LC 21-136926. 1920. Grosset & Dunlap.

Riders of the Purple Sage: A Novel. Zane Grey. 3.00. Harper & Brothers.

Riders of the Range. Charles Horace Snow. LC 39-316783. 1939. Macrae Smith Company.
Riders of the Rio Grande: A Cattle-Rustling Mystery Story. Glenn Balch. LC 37-4589. Thomas Y. Crowell Company.
Riders of the Rocker K. Stephen Payne. LC 35-13187. 1935. The Dial Press, Inc.
Riders of the Shadows. Joseph Archibald. LC 38-5287. The Dodge Publishing Company.
Riders of the Sierra Madre. Clee Woods. LC 35-6881. The Macaulay Company.
Riders of the Trail. George M Johnson. LC 32-222040. E. J. Clode, Inc.
Riders of the Valley Range. Lawrence A Keating. LC 33-4387. E. J. Clode, Inc.
Riders of the Whistling Skull. William Colt MacDonald. LC 34-7029. Covici, Friede.
Riders of the Wind. Elswyth Thane. 1976. Repr. of 1926 ed. lib. bdg. 16.30x (ISBN 0-88411-968-8). Amereon Ltd.
Riders of the Wind: A Romance. Elswyth Thane. LC 26-3375. 1926. Frederick A. Stokes Company.
Riders of Vengeance. Zane Grey. 1982. 18.00x (ISBN 0-86025-190-X, Pub. by Ian Henry Pubns England). State Mutual Bk.
Rider's Revenge. Roger McDonald. 1978. pap. 1.25 (ISBN 0-532-12573-8). Woodhill.
Riders to Cibola. Norman Zollinger. (Illus.). 416p. 1982. pap. 3.50 (ISBN 0-441-72356-X, Pub. by Charter Bks). Ace Bks.
Riders to Cibola: A Novel. Norman Zollinger. LC 77-18491. 1978. 10.95 (ISBN 0-89013-101-5). Museum of New Mexico Press.
Riders to the Dust. Henry Leyford Gates. LC 36-4154. 1935. R. M. McBride & Company.
Riders to the Stars: Novelization by Robert Smith Based Upon the Screenplay by Curt Siodmark. Robert Smith & Curt Siodmark. LC 53-13081. (Ballantine books,). Ballantine Books.
Riders up! Gerald Beaumont. LC 22-192151. 1922. D. Appleton and Company.
Riders West. Ernest Haycox. LC 34-14768. 1934. Doubleday, Doran & Company, Inc.
Riders West: With Stories and Articles by Luke Short Pseud., and Others. Frederick Dilley Gildden. LC 56-58360. (Dell first edition, A110). 1956. Dell Pub. Co.
Ridgway of Montana: A Story of to-Day, in Which the Hero Is Also the Villain. William MacLeod Raine. LC 9-11151. 1.50. G. W. Dillingham Company.
Ridgway of Montana: A Story of Today, in Which the Hero Is Also the Villain. William MacLeod Raine. LC 38-561235. Grosset & Dunlap.
Ridgway Women. Richard Neely. LC 74-34347. 1975. 6.95 (ISBN 0-690-00748-5). Crowell.
Ridgway Women. Richard Neely. (Signet Book). 1976. 1.50. New American Library.
Ridiculous Courting: And Other Stories of French Canada. George Moore Fairchild. LC 2227. 1900. R. R. Donnelley & Sons Company.
Ridin' Kid from Powder River. Henry Herbert Knibbs. LC 19-15555. 1919. Houghton Mifflin Company.
Ridin' Kid from Powder River. Henry Herbert Knibbs. LC 25-15512. 1921. Grosset & Dunlap.
Riding Devils. Archie Joscelyn. LC 40-12264. Phoenix Press.
Riding for Custer. Thomas Albert Curry. (Orig.). 1972. pap. 0.60 o.p. (06183). Curtis.
Riding for Custer: A "Captain Mesquite" Novel. Thomas Albert Curry. LC 47-31062. 1947. Arcadia House.
Riding Gun: A Buscadero Novel. Eugene Cunningham. LC 55-11725. 1956. Houghton Mifflin.
Riding High. Hank Madison, pseud. 1979. pap. 1.50 (ISBN 0-505-51430-3). Tower Bks.
Riding High. Grace Perkins Oursler. LC 36-33404. Farrar & Rinehart, Inc.
Riding Master. Dolf Wyllarde. LC 11-493720. 1911. John Lane Company.
Riding Shotgun. John Benteen. (Sundance Ser.: No. 20). 160p. 1981. pap. 1.75 (ISBN 0-8439-1051-8, Leisure Bks). Nordon Pubns.
Riding the Range. Lawrence A Keating. LC 32-22205. E. J. Clode, Inc.
Riding the Rim. Lillian Mayer Marvin. 1950. Como Heights, Publishers.
Riding to the Moon. Barbara Cartland. LC 82-10198. 10.95 (ISBN 0-89696-174-5). Everest House.
Riding Tough. Jim Busbee. 1981. pap. 1.95 (ISBN 0-8439-0912-9, Leisure Bks). Nordon Pubns.
Ridolfo, the Coming of the Dawn: A Tale of the Renaissance. Egerton Ryerson Williams. LC 6-36880. 1906. A. C. McClurg & Co.
Rienzi. Edward George Earle Lytton Bulwer-Lytton Lytton. (Half-title: Everyman's library, ed. by Ernest Rhys. Fiction). 1911. J. M. Dent & Sons, Ltd.
Rienzi, the Last of the Roman Tribunes. Edward George Earle Lytton Bulwer-Lytton Lytton. LC 70-145150. (Illus.). 1971. (ISBN 0-403-01079-9). Scholarly Press.
Rienzi, the Last of the Roman Tribunes. Edward George Earle Lytton Bulwer-Lytton Lytton. LC 8-11032. G. Routledge and Sons.
Rienzi, the Last of the Roman Tribunes. the lord lytton ed. Edward George Earle Lytton Bulwer-Lytton Lytton. LC 7-80942. 1882. J. B. Lippincott & Co.
Rienzi, the Last of the Roman Tribunes. Edward George Earle Lytton Bulwer-Lytton Lytton. LC 35-33411. 1891. J. B. Lippincott Company.
Rienzi, the Last of the Roman Tribunes. Edward George Earle Lytton Bulwer-Lytton Lytton. LC 4-16552. 1893. Little, Brown, & Company.
Rienzi, the Last of the Roman Tribunes. Edward George Earle Lytton Bulwer-Lytton Lytton. LC 2-20035. 1902. C. Scribner's Sons.
Rienzi, the Last of the Tribunes. Edward George Earle Lytton Bulwer-Lytton Lytton. LC 7-8095. (On cover: Seaside library. Pocket ed. no. 1144). G. Munro.
Rievaulx Abbey. Norma Davison. (Ace gothic#11). 1975. (pbk.) 0.95. Ace Books.
Riffian. Carleton Stevens Coon. LC 33-23511. 1933. Little, Brown, and Company.
Rififi in New York. Auguste Le Breton, pseud. LC 68-31519. 1968. 5.95. Stein and Day.
Rifle Pass: A Western Novel by Dean Owen Pseud. Dudley Dean McGaughy. LC 54-31860. (Popular library, 583). 1954. Popular Library.
Rifle River. Roy LeBeau. (Buckskin Ser.: No. 1). 240p. (Orig.). 1982. pap. (ISBN 0-505-51801-5). Tower Bks.
Rifle River. Roy LeBeau. (Buckskin Ser.: No. 1). 240p. (Orig.). 1982. pap. 2.25 o.s.i. (ISBN 0-8439-1158-1, Leisure Bks). Nordon Pubns.
Rifled Gold. Wilbur C Tuttle. LC 34-2422. 1934. Houghton Mifflin Company.
Rifleman: A Novel. 1st Ed. John Brick. LC 53-5293. 1953. Doubleday.
Rifleman Dodd, and The Gun: Two Novels of the Peninsular Campaigns. Cecil Scott Forester. LC 43-51140. 1943. Little, Brown and Company.
Rifleman Dodd, and The Gun, Two Novels of the Peninsular Wars. with a foreword by carl van doren. ed. Cecil Scott Forester. LC 42-14077. 1942. The Press of the Readers Club.
Riflemen of the Miami. Edward Sylvester Ellis. LC 12-14458. 0.50. Hurst & Company.
Rifles for Watie. Harold Keith. LC 57-10280. (Illus.). 1957. Crowell.
Rifles of Revenge. Lewis B. Patten. 1979. pap. 1.95 (ISBN 0-89083-568-3). Zebra.
Rifles on the Range. Lee Floren. 1978. pap. 1.25 o.s.i. (ISBN 0-8439-0531-X, Leisure Bks). Nordon Pubns.
Rifles on the Rattlesnake. Lee Floren. LC 54-10724. 1954. Arcadia House.
Rifles on the Rimrock. Lee Floren. 1976. (pbk.) 0.95. Belmont Towers.
Rifles on the Rimrock. LC 52-9318. 1952. Arcadia House.
Rift and the Spray: A Tale of the Smugglers of the English Channel. Malcolm J Errym. 1863. F.A. Brady.
Rift in the Lute. Drawings by Regina Tor. Noel Langley. LC 52-13995. 1953. Coward-McCann.
Rig. Ronald Wilcox. 1978. pap. 1.95 o.s.i. (ISBN 0-8439-0593-X, Leisure Bks). Nordon Pubns.
Rigadoon. Louis-Ferdinand Celine, pseud. 273p. 1974. 8.95 o.p. (ISBN 0-440-07364-2, Sey Lawr). Delacorte.
Rigadoon. Louis-Ferdinand Celine, pseud. Tr. by Ralph Manheim from Fr. 304p. 1975. pap. 3.95 (ISBN 0-14-004083-8). Penguin.
Rigadoon. Louis Ferdinand Destouches. LC 73-19906. 1974. 8.95. Delacorte Press.
Rigadoon. Louis Ferdinand Destouches. LC 75-318145. 1975. 2.95 (ISBN 0-14-004083-8). Penguin Books.
Right. Bob Sang. LC 80-117763. 2.50 (ISBN 0-932844-02-2). R. H. Sang.
Right and Left. A Novel. Emma Barry Newby. (On cover: Turners' select novels, no. 6). Turner Brothers & Co.
Right at Last, and Other Tales. Elizabeth Cleghorn Stevenson Gaskell. LC 2-29918. 1860. Harper & Brothers.
Right Bank: A Novel of Paris. Elaine W Neal. LC 58-5726. 1958. Morrow.
Right Burgee. Henry Walsh Lee. LC 64-18689. 1964. Trident Press.
Right Fuse. Barry Cuff, pseud. (Orig.). 1969. pap. 1.75 (ISBN 0-87067-179-0, BH179). Holloway.
Right Hand of Dextra. David J. Kake. (Science Fiction Ser.). 1977. pap. 1.50 o.p. (UW1290). DAW Bks.
Right-Handed Wilderness. Robert Wells. 1973. (pbk.) 1.25 (ISBN 0-345-03355-8). Ballantine Books.
Right Ho, Jeeves. P. G. Wodehouse. 1957. 11.95 o.s.i. (ISBN 0-8277-0228-0). British Bk Ctr.
Right Honorable Corpse. Max Murray. LC 51-9933. 1951. Farrar, Straus and Young.
Right Honourable," A Romance of Society and Politics. Justin McCarthy. LC 46-44336. 1887. D. Appleton and Company.
Right Image. James David Horan. 1975. (pbk.) 1.75 (ISBN 0-380-00220-5). Avon.
Right Image: A Novel of the Men Who Make Candidates for the Presidency. James David Horan. LC 66-26187. 1967. Crown Publishers.
Right Image: By James D. Horan. James David Horan. (7456). 1968. pap., 1.25. Dell.
Right Knock. A Story. Helen Van Metre Van-Anderson Gordon. 1889. The Author.
Right Knock. A Story. 3d ed. Helen Van Metre Van-Anderson Gordon. LC 7-1633. 1890. New Era Publishing Co.
Right Knock: A Story. th ed. Helen Van Metre Van-Anderson Gordon. LC 9-8353. 1892. New Era Publishing Co.
Right Knock: A Study. 8th ed. Helen Van Metre Van-Anderson Gordon. 1908. The New York Magazine of Mysteries.
Right Line of Cerdic. Alfred Leo Duggan. LC 61-14772. 1961. Pantheon Books.
Right Man. Brian Hooker. LC 8-29648. 1908. The Bobbs-Merrill Company.
Right Man for Julie. Renee Shann. Orig. Title: Tread Softly in Love. pap. 0.45 o.p. (56-965). Paperback Lib.
Right Murder. Craig Rice. LC 41-4718. 1941. Simon and Schuster.
Right of Dextra. David J Lake. 1977. 1.50 (ISBN 0-87997-290-4). DAW Books.
Right of Possession. Jayne Castle. (Candlelight Ecstasy Ser.: No. 23). (Orig.). 1981. pap. 1.75 (ISBN 0-440-17441-4). Dell.
Right of Reply. John Harris. LC 68-14309. 1968. Coward-McCann.
Right of the Strongest. Frances Nimmo Greene. LC 13-784721. 1913. C. Scribner's Sons.
Right of Way. Harold Bindloss. LC 32-5305. 1932. Frederick A. Stokes Company.
Right of Way. Gilbert Parker. 1976. lib. bdg. 16.25x (ISBN 0-89968-079-8). Lightyear.
Right of Way: A Novel. Gilbert Parker. LC 1-23068. 1901. Harper & Brothers.
Right off the Map: A Novel. Charles Edward Montague. LC 27-21621. 1927. Doubleday, Page & Co.
Right on Cue, Andy Capp. Smythe. (Andy Capp Ser.). (Illus.). 128p. 1978. pap. 1.25 (ISBN 0-449-13589-6, GM). Fawcett.
Right on Time Andy Capp. Smythe. (Andy Capp Ser.). (Illus.). 1978. pap. 1.25 (ISBN 0-449-14076-8, GM). Fawcett.
Right on with Love: Hearth Ser. Lon Riley Woodrum. 1979. pap. 1.75 (ISBN 0-310-34792-0). Zondervan.
Right One. Marie Sofle Birath Schwartz. Tr. by Borg, Selma & Shipley, Marie Adelaide (Brown) LC 8-2064. 1871. Lee and Shepard.
Right People. McCready Huston. LC 49-100024. 1949. J. B. Lippincott.
Right Place at the Right Time. Alison Miller. (Orig.). 1979. pap. 1.95 (ISBN 0-532-23339-5). Woodhill.
Right Place for Love. Charlotte Edwards. LC 53-9012. 1953. McGraw-Hill.
Right Princess. Clara Louise Root Burnham. LC 2-206523. 1902. Houghton, Mifflin and Company.
Right Side of the Car. John Uri Lloyd. LC 7-193973. 1897. R. G. Badger & Company.
Right Spirit. Lizzie D Cottier. LC 6-29015. 1885. The Courier Company.
Right Stuff. John Hay Beith. LC 10-11643. 1910. Houghton Mifflin Company.
Right Stuff. Tom Wolfe. 384p. 1980. pap. 3.50 (ISBN 0-553-13828-6). Bantam.
Right Time. Carol Sturm Smith. LC 82-6668. 1982. 1.75 (ISBN 0-345-29756-3). Ballantine Books.
Right Time, the Right Place. Joseph S. Salzburg. 1978. 7.00 (ISBN 0-682-49039-3). Exposition.
Right to an Answer. John Anthony Burgess Wilson. LC 61-5617. 1961. W. W. Norton.
Right to Be Wrong. John P Goring. LC 41-5369. Liveright Publishing Corporation.
Right to Die. Julie Davis. (O.s.i.). 1976. pap. 1.50 o.s.i. (BT50937). Belmont-Tower.
Right to Die: A Nero Wolfe Novel. Rex Stout. LC 64-22621. 1964. Viking Press.
Right to Happiness. Mabel Goode Frantz. LC 42-2418. Fleming H. Revell Company.
Right to Kill. Scott Jansen. 192p. (Orig.). Date not set. pap. (ISBN 0-505-51711-6). Tower Bks.
Right to Kill. Scott Jansen. 192p. (Orig.). 1982. pap. 2.25 (ISBN 0-8439-1112-3, Leisure Bks). Nordon Pubns.
Right to Love: By Markoosha Fischer. 1st Ed. Bertha Mark Fischer. LC 54-12228. Harper.
Right to Reign: A Romance of the Kingdom of Drecq. Adele Ferguson Knight. LC 12-21400. 1912. 1.25. G. W. Jacobs & Company.
Right to Solo: A Collection of the Best Airplane Stories for Boys and Girls. Ed. by Ramon Wilke Kessler. LC 31-232006. 1931. E. P. Dutton & Co.,Inc.
Right Track. Clara Louise Root Burnham. LC 14-15181. 1914. 1.25. Houghton Mifflin Company.
Right True End. Stan Barstow. LC 77-352235. 1976. 3.95 (ISBN 0-7181-1511-2). Joseph.
Right Trumpet. John Roberts. LC 68-11936. 1967. McGraw-Hill.
Righteous Apostate. Clara Lanza. LC 7-13836. 1883. G. P. Putnam's Sons.
Rightful Inheritance. Gerald Zeigerman. LC 67-14576. 1967. Atheneum.
Rights of a Man. Lysander D Childs. LC 19-2712. Enquirer Printing and Publishing Co.
Riley Hoosier Stories. James Whitcomb Riley. LC 17-310223. The Bobbs-Merrill Company.
Riley McCullough. 1st Ed. Carl Jonas. LC 54-688259. 1954. Little, Brown.
Rilkes Werke in Drei Baenden: Gedicht-Zyklen, Vol. 1. Rainer Maria Rilke. xxxii, 563p. 1966. 6.40 o.p. Schoenhof.
Rilla of Ingleside. Lucy Maud Montgomery. LC 21-14703. Frederick A. Stokes Company.
Rillbourne: By Sydney Malcolm Pseud. Gertrude Sydney Perrin. LC 52-68395. 1952. Staples Press.
Rim. Francis Minturn Sedgwick. LC 45-4375. 1945. Coward-McCann, Inc.
Rim Gods: The Ship from Outer Space. A. Bertram Chandler. 412p. 1981. pap. 2.75 (ISBN 0-441-72403-5). Ace Bks.
Rim O' the World. Bertha Muzzy Sinclair. LC 19-16662. 1919. Little, Brown, and Company.
Rim of Forever. Ann Boyle. 1973. 4.50 o.p. (Avalon). Bouregy.
Rim of Space. A. Bertram Chandler. LC 82-155109. (Rim World Series; V. 1). 1981. (5.95, 12.95 u.s.) (ISBN 0-85031-360-0). Allison & Busby.
Rim of Space. A. Bertram Chandler. 192p. 1981. 12.95 (ISBN 0-8052-8090-1, Pub. by Allison & Busby England). Schocken.
Rim of Space: The Ship from Outside. A. Bertram Chandler. 320p. 1981. pap. 2.75 (ISBN 0-441-72404-3). Ace Bks.
Rim of Terror. Hildegarde Tolman Teilhet. LC 50-5067. 1950. Coward-McCann.
Rim of the Caprock. Noel M. Loomis. LC 52-8266. 1952. Macmillan.
Rim of the Desert. Ada Woodruff Anderson. LC 15-84290. 1915. 1.35. Little, Brown, and Company.
Rim of the Desert. Ernest Haycox. LC 75-35628. 1975. 9.95 (ISBN 0-89190-974-5). Rivercity Press.
Rim of the Desert. Ernest Haycox. LC 40-337131. 1941-1940. Little, Brown and Company.
Rim of the Desert. Ernest Haycox. LC 42-51490. 1942. The Sun Dial Press.
Rim of the Desert. Ernest Haycox. LC 45-13283. 1944. Triangle Books, the Blakiston Company.
Rim of the Pit: A Rogan Kincaid Story. Henning Nelms. LC 44-6374. 1944. Simon and Schuster.
Rim of the Prairie. Bess Streeter Aldrich. LC 25-19624. 1925. D. Appleton and Company.
Rim of the Prairie. Bess Streeter Aldrich. LC 31-963296. 1930. A. L. Burt Company.
Rim of the Prairie. Bess Streeter Aldrich. LC 45-13286. 1944. The Blakiston Company.
Rim of the Prairie: By Bess Streeter Aldrich. Bess Streeter Aldrich. 1966. pap., 1.75. Univ. of Neb. Pr.
Rim of the Range. Al Cody, pseud. 1980. pap. 1.75 (ISBN 0-8439-0822-X). Nordon Pubns.
Rim of the Tub. Elizabeth A Scott. LC 74-113740. 1970. 5.95. Morrow.
Rim of the Unknown. Frank Belknap Long. LC 72-88123. 1972. 7.50. Arkham House.
Rimless Wheel. Roger W Eddy. LC 47-2666. 1947. The Macmillan Company.
Rimrock. Frederick Dilley Glidden. 1974. (pbk.) 0.75. Bantam Books.
Rimrock. Don P. Jenison. (Orig.). 1980. pap. 1.95 (ISBN 0-89083-576-4). Zebra.
Rimrock. Luke Short. 1974. (pbk.) 0.75. Bantam Books.
Rimrock: A Story of the West. T. C Hoyt. LC 24-18908. The Four Seas Company.
Rimrock: By Luke Short Pseud. Frederick Dilley Glidden. 1955. Random House.
Rimrock Colt. F. W. Parker. 3.50 o.p. Carlton.
Rimrock Jones. Dane Coolidge. LC 17-13184. 1.35. W. J. Watt & Company.
Rimrock Raiders: By Lew Smith Pseud. Lee Floren. LC 54-990553. 1954. Arcadia House.
Rimrock Renegade. Lee Floren. 1978. pap. 1.25 o.s.i. (ISBN 0-505-51247-5). Tower Bks.
Rimrock Renegade: By Wade Hamilton Pseud. Lee Floren. LC 51-11735. 1951. Phoenix Press.
Rimrock Rider. Walker A Tompkins. LC 50-7409. 1950. Macrae Smith.
Rimrock Riders. Peter Field. 1976. 1.25 (ISBN 0-671-80579-7). Pocket Books.
Rimrock Town. William Heuman. LC 55-12491. 1955. Arcadia House.
Rimrock Trail. Joseph Allan Elphinstone Dunn. LC 22-6604. The Bobbs-Merrill Company.
Rimrock Vengeance. Al Cody, pseud. 1981. pap. 1.75 (ISBN 0-8439-0879-3, Leisure Bks). Nordon Pubns.
Rimrock Vengeance. Archie Joscelyn. 1965. Arcadia House.

Rimshot. Ted Perry. (Illus.). 140p. 1982. 9.95 (ISBN 0-87754-357-7). Chelsea Hse.
Rinconete and Cortadillo. Miguel de Cervantes de Saavedra. Tr. by Lorente, Mariano J. LC 18-2054. 1917. 1.50. The Four Seas Company.
Rind and All, Fifty Poems: 1st Ed. Joseph Tusiani. LC 61-16947. 1962. Monastine Press.
Rinehart Book of Short Stories. alternate ed. Ed. by Clarence Lee Cline. LC 64-22616. (Rinehart editions, 129). 1964. Holt, Rinehart and Winston.
Rinehart Book of Short Stories: Edited with Notes by C. L. Cline. Ed. by Clarence Lee Cline. LC 52-5605. (Rinehart editions, 59). 1952. Rinehart.
Ring. Danielle Steel. LC 80-17175. 9.95 (ISBN 0-440-07622-6). Delacorte Press.
Ring. Danielle Steel. LC 81-6784. 1981. 16.95 (ISBN 0-8161-3218-6). G.K. Hall.
Ring. Marcus Van Heller, pseud. (Orig.). 1968. pap. 1.95 o.s.i. (OPH-245, Ophelia). Olympia.
Ring and Diamond. William Henry Greenfield. LC 21-10017. 1921. The Cook Publishing Company.
Ring and the Cross: A Novel. Robert Rylee. LC 47-5698. 1947. A. A. Knopf.
Ring and the Dream. Margaret Grant La Farge Osborn. 1947. Harper & Brothers.
Ring and the Lamp. William Rollins. LC 47-30447. 1947. Simon and Schuster.
Ring and the Man, with Some Incidental Relation to the Woman. Cyrus Townsend Brady. LC 9-5701. 1909. Moffat, Yard and Company.
Ring & the River. Winthrop Neilson & Frances Fullerton Neilson. LC 78-27372. 8.95. Putnam.
Ring & Walk In. Miriam Borgenicht. 1967. pap. 0.60 o.p. Lancer.
Ring and Walk in. 1st Ed. Miriam Borgenicht. LC 52-5422. 1952. Harper.
Ring Around a Murder. George A Bagby, pseud. LC 36-21821. Covici, Friede.
Ring Around a Murder. Aaron Marc Stein. LC 36-21821. 1936. Covici, Friede.
Ring Around Rosa. William Campbell Gault. LC 55-6978. (Guilt edged mystery). 1955. Dutton.
Ring Around the Moon. Vere Hobart. LC 35-9324. R. Speller, Inc.
Ring Around the Sun: A Story of Tomorrow. Clifford D Simak. LC 53-782853. 1953. Simon and Schuster.
Ring Around the Sun: A Story of Tomorrow. Clifford D Simak. LC 54-32741. (Ace double novel books, D-61). 1954. Ace Books.
Ring Buster: A Story of the Erie Canal. James Monroe Fitch. LC 41-978. Fleming H. Revell Company.
Ring Cost a Dime. Rob Eden. LC 39-33014. Gramercy Publishing Col.
Ring Cycle. Melvin Gorham. LC 79-64509. (Orig.). 1979. 8.95 (ISBN 0-914752-11-1); pap. 5.00 (ISBN 0-914752-10-3). Sovereign Pr.
Ring Down the Curtain- A Novel. Margel Holst. LC 54-12638. Vantage Press.
Ring Fence. Eden Phillpotts. LC 28-172747. 1928. The Macmillan Company.
Ring Finger. Louise Redfield Peattie. LC 43-3409. 1943. E. P. Dutton and Company, Incorporated.
Ring for a Fortune. Lilian Peake. (Harlequin Presents Ser.). 192p. 1980. pap. 1.50 (ISBN 0-373-10384-0, Pub. by Harlequin). PB.
Ring for Jeeves. P. G. Wodehouse. 1963. 11.95 o.s.i. (ISBN 0-8277-0229-9). British Bk Ctr.
Ring for Nancy: A Sheer Comedy. Ford Madox Ford. LC 13-21819. The Bobbs-Merrill Company.
Ring Has No End. Thomas Armstrong. LC 58-10309. 1958. W. Sloane Associates.
Ring Horse: A Novel. Thomas William Duncan. LC 40-7857. 1940. Doubleday, Doran & Company, Inc.
Ring Horse. New Ed. Thomas William Duncan. LC 52-10862. 1952. Lippincott.
Ring in Meiji: A Novel. William Butler. LC 65-13971. 6.95. Putnam.
Ring in the Grass. Maude Hill Beaton. LC 47-15858. 1946. Margent Press.
Ring in the New. Laura B Harris. LC 50-9265. 1950. Morrow.
Ring in the New. Richard Whiteing. LC 6-348013. 1906. The Century Co.
Ring Is Closed. Knut Hamsun & Gay-Tifft, Eugene, Tr. LC 37-8397. Coward-McCann, Inc.
Ring Lardner Reader. Ring Wilmer Lardner. LC 63-8675. 1963. Scribner.
Ring Lardner's Best Stories: Including, Haircut, Alibi Ike, The Golden Honeymoon, and All the Other Brilliant Stories Originally Collected in Round-up--Together with His Inimitable Novel of Not-So-Dumb Mid-Westerner in the Wilds of New York, Entitled, The Big Town. de luxe ed. Ring Wilmer Lardner. Garden City Publishing Co., Inc.
Ring Lardner's "You Know Me Al" The Comic Strip Adventures of Jack Keefe. Ring Lardner. LC 78-20641. (Orig.). 1979. pap. 6.95 (ISBN 0-15-676696-5, Harv). HarBraceJ.
Ring of Ages: A Modern Novel of the Romance of Reincarnation. Sophie Mann Klimbach. LC 53-8949. 1953. William-Frederick Press.
Ring of Allaire. Susan Dexter. 224p. 1981. pap. 2.50 (ISBN 0-345-29273-1, Del Rey). Ballantine.
Ring of Amasis. From the Papers of a German Physician. Edward Robert Bulwer-Lytton Lytton. LC 7-23203. 1863. Harper & Brothers.
Ring of Darkness. Kate Ostrander. (Berkley medallion book). 1974. (pbk.) 1.25 (ISBN 0-425-02712-0). Berkley Pub Co.
Ring of Eyes. Hulbert Footner. LC 33-10598. 1933. Harper & Brothers.
Ring of Gold. Eloise R Weld. LC 78-3543. 8.95 (ISBN 0-399-12137-4). Putnam.
Ring of Mischief. Margaret Summerton. LC 65-19950. 3.95. Dutton.
Ring of Mischief. Margaret Summerton. (Ace Gothic). 1974. (pbk.) 0.95. Ace Books.
Ring of the Lowenskolds... Selma Ottiliana Lovisa Lagerlof. Tr. by Martin, Francesca & Howard, Velma (Swanston) LC 31-985. 1931. Doubleday, Doran & Company, Inc.
Ring of the Swamis: And Other Stories. Elizabeth Beachley. LC 28-13498. 1928. The Canterbury Company.
Ring of Truth. Josephine Lawrence. LC 58-108954. 1958. Harcourt, Brace.
Ring of Truth. 1st Ed. George Harmon Coxe. LC 66-12392. 1966. 3.95. Knopf.
Ring on the Bar Is Mine. J. D. Kent. 3.50 o.p. Carlton.
Ring She Rejected. Milton Ogburn. 201p. (YA) 1972. 7.00 o.p. (ISBN 0-682-47520-3). Exposition.
Ring Tailed Roarers: Tall Tales of the American Frontier, 1830-60. Ed. by Victor Lovitt Oakes Chittick. LC 41-3987. 1941. The Caxton Printers, Ltd.
Ring the Bell at Zero. Hugh Lawrence Nelson. (Murray Hill mystery). 1949. Rinehart.
Ring the Bell Softly. Pamela Bennetts. LC 78-4001. 1978. 7.95 (ISBN 0-312-68239-5). St. Martin's Press.
Ring the Bell Softly. Margaret James. LC 78-4001. 1978. 7.95 o.p. (ISBN 0-312-68239-5). St Martin.
Ring Without Romance. Maysie Greig. LC 41-243231. 1941. Doubleday, Doran Ad Co., Inc.
Ring Without Romance. Maysie Greig. LC 42-17481. 1942. The Sun Dial Press.
Ringan Gilhaize: Or, The Covenanters. John Galt. LC 72-172057. (His Works, v. 7-8). (Illus.). 1968. AMS Press.
Ringby Lass & Other Stories. Mary Beaumont. LC 6-10282. (Half-title: Iris series). 1895. Macmillan and Co.
Ringed Castle. Dorothy Dunnett. 1973. (pbk) 1.25. Popular Library.
Ringed Castle. Dorothy Dunnett. LC 70-185056. 1972. 7.95. Putnam.
Ringed Horizon. Edmund Gilligan. LC 43-14974. 1943. C. Scriber's Sons.
Ringed with Fire. Alice Ormond Campbell. 1942. Random House.
Ringer. Elizabeth Linington. LC 70-142420. 1971. 5.95. Morrow.
Ringer. Dell Shannon. 1971. 5.95 o.p. Morrow.
Ringer. David R. Slavitt. LC 82-5103. 1982. 12.95 (ISBN 0-525-24139-6). E.P. Dutton.
Ringer. Edgar Wallace. LC 26-22965. 1926. Doubleday, Page & Company.
Ringer Returns... Edgar Wallace. LC 31-26169. Pub. for the Crime Club, Inc., by Doubleday, Doran & Company, Inc.
Ringer Returns see Again the Ringer.
Ringing Bells. Reese Rockwell. LC 7-39796. 1890. Hunt & Eaton.
Ringing of the Glass. Preston Schoyer. LC 50-13931. 1950. Dodd, Mead.
Ringleader. Lee Dunne. LC 79-23397. 9.95 (ISBN 0-671-24887-1). Simon and Schuster.
Ringmaster. Darryl Ponicsan. LC 77-24467. 8.95 (ISBN 0-440-07579-3). Delacorte Press.
Ringold Griffitt: Or, The Raftsman of the Susquehannah. A Tale of Pennsylvania. Joseph Holt Ingraham. LC 7-9719. 1847. F. Gleason.
Ringo's Tombstone. W. R Garwood. LC 81-67729. (Diamond back westerns). 11.95 (ISBN 0-937618-01-2). Bath Street Press.
Rings of Dhone. Joseph Michael Martin. LC 81-154028. (Illus.). 9.95 (ISBN 0-86666-000-3). Great Western Pub. Co.
Rings of Glass. Translated from the German by Richard and Clara Winston. Luise Rinser. LC 58-10535. 1958. H. Regnery Co.
Rings of Ice. Piers Anthony, pseud. (Avon science fiction). 1974. (pbk.) 0.95. Avon.
Rings of Tantalus. Richard Avery. (Expendables). (Fawcett gold medal book: Vol. 2). 1975. (pbk.) 1.25. Fawcett.
Rings on Her Finger: A Novel. Eric Andrew Simpson. LC 36-8549. 1936. Doubleday, Doran & Company, Inc.
Rings on Her Fingers- Rhys Davies. LC 30-18867. Harcourt, Brace and Company.
Ringside Jezebel. Kate Nickerson. 1969. pap. 0.75 o.p. (75-255). Manor Bks.
Ringstones and Other Curious Tales. John W Wall. LC 75-46312. (Supernatural and Occult Fiction). 1976. 16.00 (ISBN 0-405-08174-X). Arno Press.
Ringtailed Rannyhans. Walt Coburn. LC 27-22760. IN The Century Co.
Ringtime. Thomas M Disch. LC 82-19279. (Singularities; 1st). 1982. 35.00 (ISBN 0-915124-70-X) (ISBN 0-915124-71-8). Toothpaste Press.
Ringway Virus. Russell Foreman. LC 77-6244. 1977. 8.95 (ISBN 0-316-28920-5). Little, Brown.
Ringworld. Larry Niven. 352p. (Orig.). 1981. pap. 2.50 (ISBN 0-345-29301-0, Del Rey). Ballantine.
Ringworld: A Novel. Larry Niven. LC 76-45284. 1977. 8.95 (ISBN 0-03-020656-1). Holt, Rinehart and Winston.
Ringworld Engineers. Larry Niven. LC 79-18992. (Illus.). 9.95 (ISBN 0-03-021376-2). Holt, Rinehart, and Winston.
Rio Bravo: A Romance of the Texas Frontier. Edwin Legrand Sabin. LC 26-9913. 1926. Macrae Smith Company.
Rio Bravo: Based on the Screenplay by Jules Furthman and Leigh Brackett. Leigh Brackett. LC 58-13077. (Bantam books, 1896. Western 3). 1959. Bantam Books.
Rio Casino Intrigue: A Major North Intrigue Novel. Francis Van Wyck Mason. LC 41-22959. Reynal & Hitchcock.
Rio Chama. Bennett Garland. (O.s.i.). 1967. pap. 0.75 o.s.i. (AS1159, Award). Univ Pub & Dist.
Rio Grande Deadline. 1st Ed. Allan Vaughan Elston. LC 57-9188. 1957. Lippincott.
Rio Grande Death Ride. Terrell L. Bowers. (YA) 1980. 6.95 (Avalon). Bouregy.
Rio Grande Echoes. Kate Klingeman. LC 50-2507. 1950. Klingeman Publication.
Rio Grande Riptide. Roe Richmond. (Orig.). 1980. pap. 1.75 o.p. (Leisure Bks). Nordon Pubns.
Rio Grande Robert. James V. McDowell. 1948. Naylor Co.
Rio Hondo Kid. John Thomas Edson. 192p. (Orig.). 1983. pap. 2.25 (ISBN 0-425-05939-1). Berkley Pub.
Rio Kid. Tom Roan. LC 35-5306. Godwin.
Rio Kid Justice. Davis Dresser. LC 41-8167. 1941. W. Morrow & Company.
Rio Kid Justice: By Don Davis Pseud. Davis Dresser. LC 50-6894. (Triple-A western classic). 1950. Jefferson House.
Rio Kid Rides Again. Thomas Albert Curry. (Orig.). 1971. pap. 0.60 o.p. (06144). Curtis.
Rio Loja Ringmaster. Lamar Herrin. LC 76-41747. 1977. 10.00 (ISBN 0-670-59896-8). Viking Press.
Rio Patrol. Strong, Charles Stanley. LC 51-1625. 1951. Phoenix Press.
Rio Red. Galen C. Colin. 1944. Phoenix Press.
Rio Renegade. Leslie Erenwein. 1975. pap. 0.95 o.p. (LB296NK, Leisure Bks). Nordon Pubns.
Rio Renegade. Leslie Charles Ernenwein. LC 46-3220. 1946. R. M. McBride & Company.
Rio Rita: Novelized. Harry Sinclair Drago. LC 29-18945. A. L. Burt Company.
Rio Rustlers. James French Dorrance. LC 28-3331. The Macaulay Company.
Riogeways. Frances Barton Fox. LC 33-27472. 1934. Frederick A. Stokes Company.
Riordan Rides the Range. James P Olsen. LC 42-12608. 1942. Dodge Publishing Company.
Riot. Frank Elli. (N169). 1968. Avon.
Riot. William Ernst Trautmann & Hagboldt, Peter, Joint Author. LC 22-11085. 1922. Chicago Labor Printing Co.
Riot: A Novel. Frank Elli. LC 66-25542. 1967. Coward-McCann.
Riot at Gravesend: A Novel of Wat Tyler's Rebellion. William Howard Woods. LC 52-9076. 1952. Duell, Sloan and Pearce.
Riot. St American Ed. John Wyllie. LC 57-532994. 1957. Dutton.
Riot '71. Ludovic Peters. LC 67-14563. 1967. Walker.
Riotous Assembly. Tom Sharpe. LC 74-170675. 1971. 5.95 (ISBN 0-670-59907-7). Viking Press.
R.I.P. Five Stories of the Supernatural. R. Reginald & Douglas Alver Menville. LC 76-1539. (Supernatural & Occult Fiction). (Illus.). 1976. 18.00 (ISBN 0-405-08425-0). Arno Press.
Rip-Off. Carter Brown, pseud. 1979. pap. 1.50 (ISBN 0-505-51425-7). Tower Bks.
Rip-off. Bernhardt J. Hurwood. (Orig.). 1972. pap. 0.75 o.p. (T2606, GM). Fawcett World.
Rip-off. Wayne C Ulsh. LC 75-15082. 1975. 1.50 (ISBN 0-515-03687-0). Pyramid Books.
Rip Roarin' Rincon. Frank Chester Robertson. LC 39-157991. 1939. E. P. Dutton & Company, Inc.
Rip Tide, and Other Stories. Elsie Kendrick. LC 25-15050. 1925. The Stratford Company.
Rip Van Winkle. Sanford Friedman. LC 80-66016. 1980. 12.95 (ISBN 0-689-11099-5). Atheneum.
Rip Van Winkle. Washington Irving. (Half-title: Stories we love). T. C. & E. C. Jack.
Rip Van Winkle. Washington Irving & Merrill, Frank T., Illus. LC 11-15068. J. Knight Company.
Rip Van Winkle. Washington Irving & Perard, Victor Semon, 1870- Illus. LC 33-33485. 1933. Frederick A. Stokes Company.
Rip Van Winkle. Joseph Jefferson. LC 71-131755. 199p. 1895. Repr. 7.50 o.p. (ISBN 0-403-00642-2). Scholarly.
Rip Van Winkle: A Posthumous Writing of Diedrich Knickerbocker Pseud. Washington Irving & Limited Editions Club, Inc., New York. LC 30-174478. 1930. The Limited Editions Club.
Rip Van Winkle & The Legend of Sleepy Hollow. 2d ed. Washington Irving & Felix Octavius Carr Darley. LC 80-36844. 1980. 14.95 (ISBN 0-912882-42-5). Sleepy Hollow Press.
Rip Van Winkle. Drawings by Arthur Rackham. Washington Irving. LC 67-19272. 1967. 4.95. Lippincott.
Ripe Breadfruit. Armine Von Tempski. LC 35-13559. 1935. Dodd, Mead & Company.
Ripe for Love. Brownie Greaton Col. LC 47-11515. 1947. Phoenix Press.
Ripe for Mischief. Renee Shann. LC 37-144043. G. P. Putnam's Sons.
Ripe Young Bodies. Richard Orth, pseud. (O.s.i.). 1969. pap. 0.75 o.s.i. (A499S, Award). Univ Pub & Dist.
Ripened Hopes: A Novel. Otto Chester Brodhay. LC 51-13051. 1951. Exposition Press.
Ripeness Is All. Eric Robert Russell Linklater. LC 35-6656. Farrar & Rinehart, Inc.
Ripening. Sidonie Gabrielle Colette. Tr. by Zeitlin, Ida. LC 32-21436. Farrar & Rinehart, Incorporated.
Ripening Seed. Sidonie Gabrielle Colette. LC 73-178784. 1972. 8.25 (ISBN 0-8371-6292-0). Greenwood Press.
Ripening Seed. Le Ble En Herbe. Sidonie Gabrielle Colette. LC 56-7282. 1956. Farrar, Straus and Cudahy.
Ripening: Selected Work, 1927-1980. Meridel Le Sueur & Elaine Hedges. LC 81-22063. (Illus.). 14.95 (ISBN 0-912670-98-3) (ISBN 0-912670-99-1). Feminist Press.
Ripley Under Ground. Patricia Highsmith. LC 73-124557. 1970. 5.95. Doubleday.
Ripley's Game. Patricia Highsmith. LC 73-20739. 1974. 5.95 (ISBN 0-394-49005-3). Knopf; Distributed by Random House.
Ripoff. Arthur Maling. LC 75-25091. 7.95 (ISBN 0-06-012809-7). Harper & Row.
Ripoff. Arthur Maling. LC 76-18929. 1976. 12.95 (ISBN 0-8161-6394-4). G. K. Hall.
Ripoff. Arthur Maling. (Perennial library). 1979. 1.95 (ISBN 0-06-080483-1). Harper & Row.
Ripper from Rawhide. Dan Cushman. LC 52-9496. 1952. Macmillan.
Ripper. 1st Ed. Maurice Procter. LC 56-6916. 1956. Harper.
Ripple. Miriam Alexander. LC 13-18002. 1913. G. P. Putnam's Sons.
Ripple from the Storm: A Complete Novel from Doris Lessing's Masterwork, Children of Violence. Doris May Lessing. 1970. pap. 3.95 (ISBN 0-452-25137-0, Z5137, Plume). NAL.
Ripple of Murders. John William Wainwright. LC 78-66406. 1979. 7.95 (ISBN 0-312-68243-3). St. Martin's.
Rippling Ruby. Joseph Smith Fletcher. LC 23-141163. 1923. G. P. Putman's Sons.
Rippon Rides Double. Frederick Faust. LC 68-13596. (Silver star westerns). 1968. Dodd, Mead.
Rise & Fall of a Teen Age Wacko. Mary Anderson. 1982. pap. 1.95 (ISBN 0-553-20532-3). Bantam.
Rise and Fall of Carol Banks. Elliott White Springs. LC 31-19626. 1931. Doubleday, Doran & Company, Inc.
Rise and Fall of Cesar Birotteau: Grandeur et Decadence De Cesar Birotteau. Honore De Balzac. Tr. by Ellen Marriage. LC 4-21347. (Half-title:... Comedie humaine...). 1896. J. M. Dent and Co.
Rise and Fall of Cesar Birotteau. Nucingen and Co., Bankers. Another Study of Woman. Illustrated by P. G. Jeanniot. Honore De Balzac. Tr. by Katharine Prescott Wormeley. LC 26-269853. (Half-title: The works of Balzac, Centenary ed. vol xv). Little, Brown, and Company,
Rise and Fall of Jake Sullivan. Hunter Davies. LC 74-117033. 1970. 6.95. Little, Brown.
Rise & Fall of the City of Mahagonny. Bertolt Brecht. Tr. by W. H. Auden & Chester Kallman. LC 75-11466. 1976. 12.95 (ISBN 0-87923-149-1); pap. 6.95 (ISBN 0-87923-205-6). Godine.

Rise & Fall of the Mustache. Robert J. Burdette. LC 71-91074. (American Humorists Ser.). 1878. Repr. of 1878 ed. lib. bdg. 18.50 (ISBN 0-8398-0179-3). Irvington.

Rise and Progress of the Kingdoms of Light Darkness: Or, The Reign of Kings Alpha and Abadon. Lorenzo D. Blackson. LC 72-78568. (Illus.). 1968. Gregg Press.

Rise at Dawn. Norman Fisher. LC 76-182199. 1971. 5.95 (ISBN 0-8027-5248-9). Walker.

Rise in the World: A Novel. Adeline Sergeant. LC 3-3375. 1900. F. M. Buckles & Company; Etc., Etc.

Rise of a Star. Edith Ayrton Zangwill. LC 18-21170. 1918. The Macmillan Company.

Rise of American Jewish Literature: An Anthology of Selections from the Major Novels. Ed. by Charles Angoff. LC 74-101863. 1970. 15.00 (ISBN 0-671-20369-X). Simon and Schuster.

Rise of Daniel Cavour. E S Evens. LC 42-17384. 1942. G. P. Putnam's Sons.

Rise of David Levinsky. Abraham Cahan. pap. 6.95xi (ISBN 0-06-131912-0, TB1912, Torch). Har-Row.

Rise of David Levinsky: A Novel, by Abraham Cahan. Abraham Cahan. LC 17-23760. 1917. 1.60. Harper & Brothers.

Rise of David Levinsky. Introd. by John Higham. Abraham Cahan. LC 60-52282. (Harper torchbooks, TB1028. The Academy library). 1960. Harper.

Rise of Elsa Potter. Alan Brener Schultz. LC 32-214302. 1932. Simon and Schuster.

Rise of Gerry Logan. Brian Glanville. LC 65-19374. 1965. 3.95. Delacorte Pr. Dist. Dial.

Rise of Henry Morcar. Phyllis Eleanor Bentley. LC 46-8522. 1946. The Macmillan Company.

Rise of Jennie Cushing. Mary Stanbery Watts. LC 14-17486. 1914. The Macmillan Company.

Rise of Ledgar Dunstan. Alfred Tresidder Sheppard. LC 16-228509. 1916. D. Appleton and Company.

Rise of Mrs. Simpson. A True Story. Roman Ivanovitch Zubof. LC 8-37858. (Dillingham's American authors library, no. 1). 1895. G. W. Dillingham.

Rise of Roscoe Paine. Joseph Crosby Lincoln. LC 12-248243. 1912. D. Appleton and Company.

Rise of Ruderick Clowd. Josiah Flynt Willard. LC 3-9629. 1903. Dodd, Mead & Company.

Rise of Silas Lapham. William Dean Howells. (Collateral Classic, CC705). 1966. Washington Sq.

Rise of Silas Lapham. William Dean Howells. (CL165). 1968. Airmont.

Rise of Silas Lapham. William Dean Howells. LC 66-1226. (Signet classic). New American Library of World Literature.

Rise of Silas Lapham. William Dean Howells. LC 65-29806. (Perennial classic). 1965. Harper & Row.

Rise of Silas Lapham. William Dean Howells. LC 54-5569. (American Classics Simplified and Adapted for Greater Reading Pleasure, Book 8). (Illus.). 1973. (pbk.) 1.25. Regents Pub. Co.

Rise of Silas Lapham. William Dean Howells. Ed. by Walter J. Meserve. LC 70-92321. (His A selected edition, v. 12). (Illus.). 1971. 12.50 (ISBN 0-253-35016-6). Indiana University Press.

Rise of Silas Lapham. William Dean Howells. LC 49-4871. (Rinehart editions, 19). 1949. Rinehart.

Rise of Silas Lapham. William Dean Howells. LC 4-15125. 1885. Ticknor and Company.

Rise of Silas Lapham. William Dean Howells. LC 18-3840. Houghton Mifflin Company.

Rise of Silas Lapham. centenary ed. with introduction by booth tarkington. ed. William Dean Howells. LC 37-9254. 1937. Houghton Mifflin Company.

Rise of Silas Lapham. William Dean Howells. LC 47-35488. Houghton, Mifflin and Company.

Rise of Silas Lapham. William Dean Howells. LC 82-24038. (Penguin American Library). 1983. 4.95 (ISBN 0-14-039030-8). Penguin Books.

Rise of Silas Lapham. William Dean Howells & Cooper, James Fenimore, 1789-1851. LC 42-3995. (Prose and poetry individualized program. The novel). 1942. The L. W. Singer Company.

Rise of Silas Lapham. new ed., with notes, questions, topics for themes and suggestions for dramatization, by james m. spinning... ed. William Dean Howells & Spinning, James Martin, 1892- Ed. LC 28-813628. (Riverside literature series). Houghton Mifflin Company.

Rise of Silas Lapham. Edited with an Introd. by Edwin H. Cady. William Dean Howells. LC 58-430. (Riverside editions, A28). 1957. Houghton Mifflin.

Rise of Silas Lapham: Introd. by Everett Carter. William Dean Howells. (Perennial classic, HP6057K). 1966. 1.75. Harper.

Rise of Silas Lapham: Introd. by Harry Hayden Clark. William Dean Howells. LC 51-5402. (Modern Library college editions, T56). 1951. Modern Library.

Rise of Silas Lapham: Simplified and Adapted by Robert J. Dixson in Collaboration with Lewis T. Davis. Drawings by Syd Browne With Exercises for Study and Vocabulary Drill. William Dean Howells & Robert James Dixson. LC 54-5569. (American classics, book 8). 1954. Regents Pub. Co.

Rise of Silas Lapham (The) Notes by Randal Keenan. Edit. Bd. of Consultants: Stanley Cooperman, Charles Leavitt, Unicio J. Violi. (Monarch notes and study guides, 675-99). pap., 1.00. Monarch Pr.

Rise of Silas Lapham. With a New Introd. by Rudolf and Clara Marburg Kirk. William Dean Howells. LC 62-12076. (Classic Collier books, HS29V). 1962. Collier Books.

Rise of Silas Lapham. With an Introd. by Everett Carter. William Dean Howells. (Harper's modern classics). 1958. Harper.

Rise of Silas Lapham. With an Introd. by Henry Steele Commager, and Illus. by Mimi Korach. William Dean Howells. LC 61-19149. 1961. Printed for the Members of the Limited Editions Club.

Rise of Silas Laphan. William Dean Howells. Repr. lib. bdg. 18.80x (ISBN 0-89190-456-5). Am Repr-Rivercity Pr.

Rise of Simon Lachaume: Translated from the French by Edward Fitzgerald. 1st American Ed. Maurice Druon. LC 52-7796. 1952. Dutton.

Rise of Terry Schuman: A Novel. Bruce Carpenter. LC 42-4002. 1942. Macrae-Smith-Company.

Rise of the Goldbergs. Gertrude Berg. LC 31-10354. Barse & Co.

Rise of Young Shakespeare: A Biographic Novel. Denton Jaques Snider. LC 25-8743. 1925. The William Harvey Miner Co., Inc.

Rise up in Anger: A Novel. Reinhart Stalmann. LC 63-9668. 1963. Putnam.

Rise up, My Love. Phyllis Speshock. LC 56-250109. 1956. Zondervan Pub. House.

Rise with the Wind. Alfred Coppel. LC 69-14850. 1969. Harcourt, Brace & World.

Rise with the Wind. A. C. Marin. LC 69-14850. 1969. 4.95 o.p. (ISBN 0-15-177652-0). HarBraceJ.

Risen Dead. authorized ed. Florence Marryat Church Lean. LC 7-13222. (Lovell's international series, no. 148). 1891. United States Book Company.

Rising. Myrtle Johnston. LC 39-9646. 1939. D. Appleton-Century Company.

Rising, a Novel: Translated from the French by Lothian Small. Henri Rene Lenormand. LC 52-3414. 1952. Thames and Hudson.

Rising Dawn: A Tale Which Tells the Adventures, Journeys and Love Story of Andrew Mallet, Sometime Squire to the Duke of Lancaster. Harold Begbie. LC 13-12874. Hodder and Stoughton.

Rising Fortunes: The Story of a Man's Beginnings. John Oxenham, pseud. LC 99-5529. 1899. G. W. Dillingham Co.

Rising Gorge. Sidney J. Perelman. LC 61-12861. 1969. pap. 1.95 (ISBN 0-671-20234-0, Fireside). S&S.

Rising Higher. Robert Stuart Nathan. LC 80-22827. 11.95 (ISBN 0-8037-7251-3). Dial Press.

Rising in Love. Alan Cohen. 150p. (Orig.). 1982. pap. 5.95 (ISBN 0-910367-31-0). Eden Co.

Rising in the World: Or, A Tale for the Rich and Poor. Timothy Shay Arthur. LC 34-4937. 1848. Baker & Scribner.

Rising of the Lark. Ann Moray. LC 64-11270. 1964. Morrow.

Rising of the Lark. Ann Moray. 1977. 1.75 (ISBN 0-380-01648-6). Avon.

Rising of the Lark. Berta Ruck. LC 51-11622. 1951. Dodd, Mead.

Rising of the Tide: The Story of Sabinsport. Ida Minerva Tarbell. LC 19-527802. 1919. The Macmillan Company.

Rising Out of the Flint Hills. Robert Killoren. 1972. 1.00 (ISBN 0-933532-24-5). BkMk.

Rising River. Agnes Mary White Sanford. LC 68-17501. 1968. Lippincott.

Rising Star. Alice Duer Miller. LC 37-27106. 1937. Dodd, Mead & Company.

Rising Star. David Christie Murray. LC 7-31826. (On cover: Once a week library, v. 12, no. 6). P. F. Collier.

Rising Star. Brenda Treet. 192p. 1981. pap. 1.50 (ISBN 0-671-57056-0). S&S.

Rising Storm: A Novel. Marguerite Allis. LC 55-10088. 1955. Putnam.

Rising Tide. Margaret Wade Campbell Deland. LC 16-165203. 1916. Harper & Brothers.

Rising Tide. Mary Nesta Skrine Keane. LC 38-27034. 1938. The Macmillan Company.

Rising Tide. Mary Lesta Skrine. LC 33-27034. 1938. The Macmillan Company.

Rising Tide: A Novel Dealing with the Spread of Bolshevism and Atheism Throughout America. Elizabeth Knauss. LC 27-20343. The Christian Alliance Pubishing Company.

Rising Wind. Virginia Moore. LC 28-21224. E. P. Dutton & Company.

Rising Young Men, and Other Tales. 4th ed. Louise Elemjay. LC 6-87589. 1859. J. F. Trow, Printer.

Risk. Dick Francis. LC 77-11786. 8.95 (ISBN 0-06-011302-2). Harper & Row.

Risk. Risk Francis. 1979. 1.95 (ISBN 0-671-82226-8). Pocket Books.

Risk. Rachel Mackenzie. (O.s.i). 1971. 3.95 o.s.i. (ISBN 0-670-59931-X). Viking Pr.

Risk Business. Michael Blakstad. 144p. 1979. pap. 11.95x (ISBN 0-85072-098-2, Pub. by Design Council England). Intl Schol Bk Serv.

Risk. 1st Ed. Cecilia Bartholomew. LC 58-139047. 1958. Doubleday.

Risks. Katherine Ryna. (Orig.). 1982. pap. 3.95 (ISBN 0-440-17345-0). Dell.

Risky Rustling. Frederick J Jackson. LC 33-222825. 1933. L. MacVeagh, Dial Press, Inc.

Risky Way to Kill: An Inspector Heimrich Mystery. Richard Lockridge. LC 76-75173. 1969. 4.95. Lippincott.

Rissa Kerguelen. F. M. Busby. (Orig.). 1977. pap. 2.75 (ISBN 0-425-03739-8, Medallion). Berkley Pub.

Rissa Kerguelen: Book One Is the Saga of Rissa. F. M Busby. LC 76-10199. 9.95 (ISBN 0-399-11791-1). Berkley Pub. Co.: Distributed by Putnam.

Rita & Marian. Peggy Swenson, pseud. (Orig.). pap. 1.25 o.p. (2501). Brandon.

Rita Coventry. Julian Leonard Street. LC 22-19913. 1922. Doubleday, Page & Company.

Rita Regina,I: By Beatrice Grimshaw... Beatrice Ethel Grimshaw. LC 40-81180. 1940. Arcadia House, Inc.

Rite. Gregory Douglas. (Orig.). 1979. pap. 2.50 (ISBN 0-89083-529-2). Zebra.

Rite of Expiation. Dick Riley. LC 76-10210. 8.95 (ISBN 0-399-11807-1). Putnam.

Rite of Love. Lucy Lee. (Superromances Ser.). 384p. 1982. pap. 2.50 (ISBN 0-373-70044-X, Pub. by Worldwide). Harlequin Bks.

Rite of Passage. Gunnard Landers. LC 79-56014. 1980. 10.95 (ISBN 0-87795-248-5). Arbor Hse.

Rite of Passage. Alexei Panshin. LC 76-10808. (Gregg Press science fiction series). 1976. 12.00 (ISBN 0-8398-2336-3). Gregg Press.

Rite of Passage. Alexei Panshin. 1982. pap. 2.50 (ISBN 0-671-44068-3, Timescape). PB.

Rite of Passage: A Novel. Sheila Fugard. LC 77-352457. 1976. (ISBN 0-949937-26-6). Ad. Donker.

Rite of the Dragon. Janet Gluckman. LC 81-5094. 9.95 (ISBN 0-89865-101-8). Donning Co.

Rites. George McKenna. 240p. 1981. pap. 2.25 (ISBN 0-8439-0979-X, Leisure Bks). Nordon Pubns.

Rites of Passage. William Gerald Golding. 1982. 2.95. Playboy Paperbacks.

Rites of Passage. Joanne Greenberg. (Avon Bard Books). 1973. (pbk.) 1.25. Avon.

Rites of Passage. Joanne Greenberg. LC 79-155511. 1972. 6.95 (ISBN 0-03-086617-0). Holt, Rinehart and Winston.

Rites of Passage. Jean Rikhoff. LC 66-13469. 5.75. Viking.

Rites of Passage: A Brief History. Edward Dorn. LC 66-5997. Frontier Press.

Rites of Passages. William Gerald Golding. LC 80-16809. 1980. 10.95 (ISBN 0-374-25086-3). Farrar, Straus, Giroux.

Rites of Summer. Robert P Hansen. LC 61-87929. 1961. Morrow.

Rithian Terror. Damon Francis Knight. (O.s.i.). 160p. 1973. pap. 0.95 o.s.i. (AN1253, Award). Univ Pub & Dist.

Rittenhouse Square: A Novel. Arthur R. G Solmssen. LC 68-17265. 1968. Little, Brown.

Ritter Double Cross. Frederick W. Nolan. LC 74-21768. 1975. 5.95 (ISBN 0-688-02892-6). Morrow.

Ritual. J. N. Williamson. 1979. pap. 2.25 o.s.i. (ISBN 0-8439-0673-1, Leisure Bks). Nordon Pubns.

Ritual. J. N. Williamson. 320p. 1982. pap. 3.25 o.s.i. (ISBN 0-8439-1168-9, Leisure Bks). Nordon Pubns.

Ritual in the Dark. Colin Wilson. LC 60-8119. 1960. Houghton Mifflin.

Ritual Murder. S. T Haymon. LC 82-5781. 1982. 11.95 (ISBN 0-312-68478-9). St. Martin's Press.

Ritual of the Hearth. R. Sickler. (O.s.i.). 1973. pap. 3.95 o.s.i. (ISBN 0-02-010350-6, Collier). Macmillan.

Rituals. Linda Gray Sexton. LC 81-9839. 1982. 15.95 (ISBN 0-385-17301-6). Doubleday.

Rituals: A Novel Pegasus Prize for Literature. LC 82-17278. 152p. 1983. 12.95 (ISBN 0-8071-1081-7). La State U Pr.

Rituals of Infinity. Michael Moorcock. 1978. 1.50 (ISBN 0-87997-404-4). DAW Books.

Rituals of Surgery. Richard Selzer. LC 73-16668. 224p. 1974. 8.95 o.p. (ISBN 0-06-127760-6). Har-Row.

Rituals of Surgery. Richard Selzer. 1980. pap. 3.95 o.s.i. (ISBN 0-671-25340-9, Touchstone Bks). S&S.

Rituals of Surgery: Short Stories. Richard Selzer. LC 73-16668. 1974. 6.95 (ISBN 0-06-127760-6). Harper's Magazine Press.

Rituals of Surgery: Short Stories. Richard Selzer. LC 79-24093. (Touchstone book). 1980. 3.95 (ISBN 0-671-25340-9). Simon and Schuster.

Ritz Carltons. Fillmore Hyde. LC 27-21469. 1927. Macy-Masius.

Rival Beauties: Or, Love and Treachery. Evalena Praed. (sunnyside series, no. 77). 1893. J. S. Ogilvie.

Rival Belles: Or, Life in Washington. John Beauchamp Jones. LC 11-8221. T. B. Peterson & Brothers.

Rival Campers: Or, The Adventures of Henry Burns. Ruel Perley Smith. LC 5-24189. 1905. L. C. Page & Company.

Rival Charms. A Novel... Annie Edwards. LC 6-36567. 1884. G. W. Carleton & Co.: Etc., Etc.

Rival Chieftains: Or, The Brigands of Mexico. A Tale of Santa Anna and His Times. Justin Jones. 1847. F. Gleason.

Rival Doctors. Elizabeth Seifert. LC 67-13367. 1967. bds., 4.95. Dodd.

Rival Doctors: From the French of A. Lapointe. Armand Lapointe. Tr. by Van Laun, Henri. LC 7-13840. (On cover: Lovell's library. v. 8. no. 445). 1884. J. W. MLovell Company.

Rival Lovers: A Story of the War Between the States. William Ferguson Smith & Harriet Stovall Kelley. LC 80-50677. (Illus.). 9.95 (ISBN 0-931948-04-5). Peachtree Publishers.

Rival Pitchers: A Story of College Baseball. Lester Chadwick. LC 10-7822. 1.00. Cupples & Leon Company.

Rival Princess. Justin McCarthy & Praed, Rosa Caroline (Murray-Prior) "Mrs. Campbell Praed," 1851- Joint Author. LC 7-15286. (On cover: Lovell's international series, no. 84). 1890. J. W. Lovell Co.

Rival Rigelians and Planetary Agent X. Mack Reynolds. (Ace science fiction double). 1974. (pbk.) 0.95. Ace Books.

Rival Shores. Arthur Raymond Beverley-Giddings. LC 56-10007. 1956. Morrow.

Rival Temples: What God Did in Pine Valley. Claus August Wendell. LC 49-7498. 1948. Augustana Book Concern.

Rival Volunteers: Or, The Black Plume Rifles. Mary A Howe. LC 7-6623. 1864. J. Bradburn.

Rivalries of Long and Short Codiac. George Wharton Edwards. 1895. The Century Co.

Rivalry. Sarah Warder MacConnell. LC 27-3810. The Macaulay Company.

Rivals. Francois Coppee. LC 6-30862. (On cover: Harper's black & white ser.). 1893. Harper & Brothers.

Rivals. Joseph W Feldman. LC 76-11732. 1976. Ballantine Books.

Rivals. Adam Ulam. (O.s.i.). 10.95 o.s.i. (ISBN 0-670-59959-X). Viking Pr.

Rivals; Tracy's Ambition. Gerald Griffin. LC 78-24143. (Ireland, from the Act of Union, 1800, to the Death of Parnell, 1891; 29). 1979. 42.00 (ISBN 0-8240-3478-3). Garland Pub.

Rivals. A Chickahominy Story. Mary Jane Haw. LC 7-2616. 1864. Ayres & Wads.

Rivals: A Tale of the Times of Aaron Burr and Alexander Hamilton. Jeremiah Clemens. LC 1-18049. 1860. J. B. Lippincott & Co.

Rivals: And Other Folklore Tales. Eva Josephine Beede Odell. LC 24-30619. 1924. The Meredith News Press.

Rivals for Love. Carrie Jordan. LC 81-81979. 192p. (Orig.). 1981. pap. 1.95 (ISBN 0-87216-942-1). Playboy Pbks.

Rivals of Acadia: An Old Story of the New World. Harriet Vaughan Foster Cheney. 1827. Wells and Lilly.

Rivals of Frankenstein. Michel Parry. 224p. 1980. pap. 1.95 o.p. (ISBN 0-06-465105-3, PBN-5000). Har-Row.

Rivals of Sherlock Holmes. Ed. by Hugh Greene. (O.S.I.). 1970. 6.95 o.s.i. (ISBN 0-394-41330-X). Pantheon.

Rivals of Sherlock Holmes: Early Detective Stories. Ed. by Hugh Greene. LC 72-182694. 1971. (0.40, 0.95 u.s.) (ISBN 0-14-003311-4). Penguin.

Rivals of Sherlock Holmes: Early Detective Stories. Ed. by Hugh Greene. LC 73-130039. (Illus.). 1970. 6.95. Pantheon Books.

Rivals on the Ridge. Ferdinand Hoorman. LC 30-30228. Frederick Puslet Co. (Inc.

Rivals. Tracy's Ambition. Gerald Griffin. LC 6-45427. 1830. Printed by J. & J. Harper.

Rivard House. F. Edwin Lamberth. 1980. pap. 2.25 (ISBN 0-8439-0830-0). Nordon Pubns.

Riven Fetters: A Romance of the Early Christian Era. Sallie Lee Bell. LC 53-36689. 1953. Zondervan Pub. House.

Riven Heart. Genevieve Gennari. LC 56-14297. 1956. McKay.

River. Rumer Godden. LC 46-6854. 1946. Little, Brown and Company.

River. Rumer Godden. LC 46-6854. 1975. (pbk.) 1.25 (ISBN 0-380-00451-8). Avon.

River. Jefferson Sutton. 192p. 1982. pap. 2.25 o.p. (ISBN 0-505-51864-3). Tower Bks.

River. Tristram Tupper. LC 28-20921. 1928. J. B. Lippincott Company.

River: A Novel by Eden Phillpotts... Eden Phillpotts. LC 2-23307. 1902. F. A. Stokes Company.

River and Empty Sea: A Novel. Louis Charles Vaczek. LC 50-8506. 1950. Houghton Mifflin.

River and the Road. rev. ed. Judith Wright. LC 73-150455. (Illus.). 1971. 2.95 (ISBN 0-7018-0152-2). Lansdowne.

River & the Stone: Moses' Early Years in Egypt. Kathleen Jenks. (Illus.). 1977. 9.95 o.p. (ISBN 0-525-19260-3). Dutton.

River and the Wilderness. 1st Ed. Don Robertson. 1962. Doubleday.

River Bend Feud. William MacLeod Raine. LC 39-23191. 1939. Houghton Mifflin Company.

River Between. Louis Forgione. LC 74-17927. (Italian American Experience). 1975. 13.00 (ISBN 0-405-06400-4). Arno Press.

River Between. Louis Forgione. LC 28-9652. E. P. Dutton & Company.

River Between. Ngugi. (African Writers Ser.). 1965. pap. text ed. 2.50x (ISBN 0-435-90017-X). Heinemann Ed.

River Between. James Ngugi. (African Writers Ser: No. 17). 1965. pap. text ed. 2.00x o.p. (ISBN 0-435-90317-9). Humanities.

River Between. Lawrence Clark Powell. LC 79-15594. 112p. 1979. 10.00 (ISBN 0-88496-141-9). Capra Pr.

River-Bottom Boy. Harold Matthews. LC 42-25232. 1942. Thomas Y. Crowell Company.

River Breaks Up. Israel Joshua Singer. Tr. by Maurice Samuel from Yiddish. LC 70-155671. 368p. 1976. Repr. 10.00 (ISBN 0-8149-0703-2). Vanguard.

River Breaks up: A Volume of Stories Translated from the Yiddish. Israel Joshua Singer & Samuel, Maurice, 1895- LC 38-24910. 1938. A. A. Knopf.

River: By Ednah Aiken. Ednah Robinson Aiken. LC 14-20737. The Bobbs-Merrill Company.

River Devils. Noel Bertram Gerson. LC 68-17812. 1968. Doubleday.

River Devils. Noel Bertram Gerson. LC 80-28166. 1981. 10.95 (ISBN 0-89621-266-1). Thorndike Press.

River Devils. large print ed. Carter A. Vaughan. LC 80-28166. 1981. Repr. of 1969 ed. 10.95 (ISBN 0-89621-266-1). Thorndike Pr.

River Devils. Carter A. Vaughan, pseud. LC 68-17812. 1968. 4.95 o.p. Doubleday.

River Enchantment. Emma Bennett. (Candlelight Ecstasy Ser.: No. 139). (Orig.). 1983. pap. 1.95 (ISBN 0-440-17470-8). Dell.

River Flows. Frank Laurence Lucas. LC 28-282236. 1926. The Macmillan Company.

River Garden of Pure Repose. Grace Morrison Boynton. LC 52-9450. (Illus.). 1952. McGraw-Hill.

River George. George Washington Lee. LC 73-18590. 1975. 18.00 (ISBN 0-404-11401-6). AMS Press.

River George. George Washington Lee. LC 37-612790. The Macaulay Company.

River Gets Wider. Richard Laurence Gordon. LC 73-15761. 1974. 6.95 (ISBN 0-690-00006-5). T. Y. Crowell.

River Girl. Vivien Grey. LC 43-8954. 1943. Arcadia House, Inc.

River Girl: A Realistic Romance of the High Days of Mississippi Steamboating. Homer Croy. LC 31-2158. 1931. Harper & Brothers.

River God. Evans Wall. LC 34-1463. The Macaulay Company.

River Goes with Heaven. Howell Vines. LC 30-29555. 1930. Little, Brown, and Company.

River Horsemen. David Williams. (Anansi Fiction Ser.: No. 43). 224p. (Orig.). 1981. pap. 9.95 (ISBN 0-88784-086-8, Pub. by Hse Anansi Pr Canada). U of Toronto Pr.

River House. Florance Barrett Willoughby. LC 36-7258. 1936. Little, Brown, and Company.

River House. Stark Young. 1929. C. Scribner's Sons.

River in the Sun. Elizabeth Beatty. LC 58-9119. 1958. Avalon Books.

River Is Home. Pat Smith. LC 53-5256. 1953. Little, Brown.

River Journey. Robert Nathan. LC 49-10410. 1949. A. A. Knopf.

River Ki. Sawako Ariyoshi. LC 79-66240. (Illus.). 1980. 9.95 (ISBN 0-87011-385-2). Kodansha International.

River Lady. Houston Branch & Walters, Frank. LC 42-762593. 1942. Farrar & Rinehart, Inc.

River Line. Charles Morgan. 1949. Macmillan Co.

River Man. Leonard Lupton. LC 30-24350. 1930. L. MacVeagh, The Dial Press.

River Mystery. Arthur John Rees. LC 32-8078. 1932. Dodd, Mead & Company.

River Notes: The Dance of Herons. Barry Holstun Lopez. LC 79-17192. 6.95 (ISBN 0-8362-6106-2). Andrews and McMeel.

River Notes: The Dance of Herons. Barry Holstun Lopez. (Bard Book). 1980. 2.25 (ISBN 0-380-52514-3). Avon Books.

River of Blood: A Novel. Indira Parthasarthy. 1980. text ed. 10.50x (ISBN 0-7069-0715-9, Pub. by Vikas India). Advent NY.

River of Death. Alistair MacLean. LC 81-43305. 1982. 14.95 (ISBN 0-385-17205-2). Doubleday.

River of Death. Alistair MacLean. LC 82-9196. 1982. 14.95 (ISBN 0-8161-3401-4). G.K. Hall.

River of Desire. Abra Taylor. pap. price not set. Harlequin Bks.

River of Diamonds. Geoffrey Jenkins. LC 64-20854. 1964. Viking Press.

River of Earth. James Still. LC 40-27120. 1940. The Viking Press.

River of Earth. James Still. LC 77-92928. 1978. 4.95 (ISBN 0-8131-1372-5). University Press of Kentucky.

River of Fate. Michael Hastings. LC 76-378395. 1976. 3.25 (ISBN 0-356-08388-8). Macdonald and Jane's.

River of Fire; a Novel. 1st Ed. Grace Jamison Breckling. LC 58-59567. 1959. Pageant Press.

River of Fortune: The Passion. Arthur Moore. (Orig.). 1979. pap. 2.50 (ISBN 0-89083-561-6). Zebra.

River of Glass. Wilfred Martens. LC 79-23122. (Illus.). 1980. 6.95 (ISBN 0-8361-1913-4). Herald Press.

River of Gold: A Novel. Harry Sinclair Drago. LC 45-10362. 1945. Dodd, Mead & Company.

River of Ice. Kenneth Robeson. (Avenger #11). 1973. (pbk) 0.75. Warner Paperback Library.

River of Life. Rutherford Platt. 1962. pap. 1.75 o.p. (ISBN 0-671-62451-2, Touchstone Bks). S&S.

River of Life: And Other Stories. Aleksandr Ivanovich Kuprin. LC 75-75781. (Short story index reprint series). 1969. Books for Libraries Press.

River of Life, and Other Stories. Aleksandr Ivanovich Kuprin. Tr. by Kotellansky, Samuel Solomonovitch. LC 16-6478. 1916. J. W. Luce and Company.

River of Light. Brenda Peterson. LC 77-11868. 1978. 8.95 (ISBN 0-394-41894-8). Knopf.

River of Love. (Rapture Romance Ser.: No. 2). 1982. pap. 1.95 (ISBN 0-451-12004-3, AJ2004). NAL.

River of Love, No. 146. Barbara Cartland. (Cartland Ser.). 160p. (Orig.). 1981. pap. text ed. 1.95 (ISBN 0-553-20013-5). Bantam.

River of No Return. Cort Conley & John Carrey. LC 78-52373. 1978. pap. 10.95 (ISBN 0-9603566-2-2). Backeddy Bks.

River of No Return. Leslie Turner White. LC 41-7663. 1941. Macrae-Smith-Company.

River of Rogues: A Novel. Arthur Raymond Beverley-Giddings. LC 48-6408. 1948. W. Morrow.

River of Skulls. George Tracy Marsh. LC 36-30321. The Penn Publishing Company.

River of Strangers. Frank Parker Day. LC 26-207620. 1926. Doubleday, Page & Company.

River of the Sun. James Ramsey Ullman. LC 50-10995. 1951. Lippincott.

River of the Wind. Kenn Smith. (Orig.). 1980. pap. text ed. 2.25 o.s.i. (ISBN 0-505-51534-2). Tower Bks.

River Out of Eden. Shirley Seifert. LC 40-7598. M. S. Mill Co., Inc.

River People. Lee D. Willoughby. 1981. pap. 2.75 (ISBN 0-440-07248-4). Dell.

River Pirate. Charles Francis Coe. LC 28-965604. 1928. G. P. Putnam's Sons.

River Pirates: A Tale of New York. LC 7-41013. H. Long & Brother.

River Prophet. Raymond Smiley Spears. LC 20-10310. 1920. Doubleday, Page & Company.

River Raiders. Bradford Scott. 1973. pap. 0.75 o.p. (ISBN 0-515-03066-X, T3066). Pyramid Pubns.

River Ran Out of Eden. Donald Gordon Payne. LC 63-11749. (Illus.). 1963. Morrow.

River Ranch. Doris Gates. LC 49-11227. 1949. Viking Press.

River Rat. Hollis C Powell. LC 82-90279. (Exposition-banner book). 10.50 (ISBN 0-682-49891-2). Exposition Press.

River Rat: An Extravaganza of the 'teens. Daniel Lundberg. LC 41-62309. Reynal & Hitchcock.

River Riders. Walter William Liggett. LC 28-7751. The Macaulay Company.

River Rises. Helen Raymond Abbott Beals. 1941. The Macmillan Company.

River Rising. Jessica North. LC 75-10289. 1975. 7.95 (ISBN 0-394-49001-0). Random House.

River Rising. Jessica North. (Signet Book). 1977. 1.75 (ISBN 0-451-07391-6). New American Library.

River Road. Frances Parkinson Wheeler Keyes. LC 45-10546. 1945. J. Messner, Inc.

River Road: A Novel of New England Seacoast Folk. Hamilton Thompson. LC 23-9860. 1923. W. J. Watt & Company.

River Rogue. Brainard Cheney. LC 42-19135. 1942. Houghton Mifflin Company.

River Running by. Charles Gidley. LC 81-8926. 1981. 14.95 (ISBN 0-312-68509-2). St. Martin's Press.

River Runs Through It, and Other Stories. Norman F Maclean. LC 75-20895. (Illus.). 1976. 7.95 (ISBN 0-226-50055-1). University of Chicago Press.

River Runs Through It, and Other Stories. Norman F Maclean. LC 76-20484. (Illus.). 1976. 10.95 (ISBN 0-8161-6398-7). G. K. Hall.

River Song. Harry Hamilton. LC 45-2564. 1945. The Bobbs-Merrill Company.

River Supreme. Alice Tisdale Nourse Hobart. LC 34-27185. The Bobbs-Merrill Company.

River Supreme. Alice Tisdale Nourse Hobart. LC 43-3708. 1943. Triangle Books.

River Syndicate and Other Stories. Charles Edward Carryl. LC 70-106258. (Short story index reprint series). (Illus.). 1970. Books for Libraries Press.

River Syndicate and Other Stories: By Charles E. Carryl... Charles Edward Carryl. LC 99-1096. 1899. Harper & Brothers.

River That God Forgot: The Story of the Amazon Rubber Boom. Richard Collier. LC 68-12451. 1968. 7.95 o.p. (ISBN 0-525-19264-6). Dutton.

River to Pickle Beach. Doris Betts. LC 77-138779. 1972. 7.95 (ISBN 0-06-120365-3). Harper & Row.

River to River. Gladys L'Ashley Hoover. LC 74-79472. (Illus.). 1974. Pennsylvania Record Press.

River to the Sea. George Agnew Chamberlain. LC 31-2437. 1930. Brewer & Warren Inc.

River to the West: A Novel of the Astor Adventure. John Edward Jennings. LC 52-31438. (Permabooks, P 157). 1952. Permabooks.

River to the West: A Novel of the Astor Adventure. John Edward Jennings. LC 48-8883. 1948. Doubleday.

River Trail: Romance of the Royal Mounted. Laurie York Erskine. LC 23-11976. 1923. D. Appleton and Company.

River Why: A Novel. David James Duncan. LC 82-5508. 14.95 (ISBN 0-87156-321-5). Sierra Club Books.

River Witch. Marjorie McIntyre. LC 55-7232. 1955. Crown Publishers.

River World & Other Explorations. Berton Roueche. LC 78-4738. 1978. 9.95 o.p. (ISBN 0-06-013686-3, HarpT). Har-Row.

Riverboat Showdown. Zeke Masters, pseud. (Orig.). 1980. pap. 1.95 (ISBN 0-671-83516-5). PB.

Riveresco. William Cherry Henson. LC 38-30795. The Christopher Publishing House.

Riverfinger Women. Elana Nachman. LC 74-79916. 1974. 3.50 (ISBN 0-913780-31-6). Daughters, Inc.

Rivergate House. Elissa Grandower, pseud. LC 79-6036. 288p. 1980. 10.95 (ISBN 0-385-15420-8). Doubleday.

Rivergate House. Hillary Waugh. LC 79-6036. 1980. 10.95 (ISBN 0-385-15420-8). Doubleday.

Rivergate House. Hillary Waugh. LC 80-29028. 1980. 11.95 (ISBN 0-89621-268-8). Thorndike Press.

Riverhead. Robert Silliman Hillyer. LC 32-30518. 1932. A. A. Knopf.

Riverlisp; Black Memories. Frederick Ward. LC 73-76299. 1974. 5.95. Tundra Books.

Riverman. Stewart Edward White. 1908. The McClure Company.

River's Children: An Idyl of the Mississippi. Ruth McEnery Stuart. LC 4-27873. 1904. The Century Co.

River's End. James Oliver Curwood. LC 46-22503. 1946. Triangle Books, the Blakiston Company.

River's End: A New Story of God's Country. James Oliver Curwood. LC 19-15317. 1919. Cosmopolitan Book Corporation.

River's End: A New Story of God's Country. James Oliver Curwood. LC 24-27992. 1922. Grosset & Dunlap.

River's End, and Other Stories. Anthony C West. LC 58-8703. 1958. McDowell, Obolensky.

Rivers Glide on. Arthur Hamilton Gibbs. LC 34-191785. 1934. Little, Brown, and Company.

Rivers into Wilderness. Arthur J. Burks. LC 33-24729. 1932. The Mohawk Press, Inc.

Rivers of Damascus and Other Stories. Donn Byrae. LC 31-225759. 2.00. The Century Co.

Rivers of Damascus: And Other Stories. Donn Byrne. LC 72-106253. (Short story index reprint series). 1970. Books for Libraries Press.

Rivers of Darkness. Ronald Hardy. LC 78-11788. 10.95 (ISBN 0-399-12266-4). Putnam.

Rivers of Darkness. Ronald Hardy. 1981. 3.50 (ISBN 0-425-05147-1). Berkley Publishing Corp.

Rivers of Eros. Cyrus Colter. LC 73-189191. 1972. 6.95 (ISBN 0-8040-0563-X). Swallow Press.

Rivers of Eros: A Novel. Cyrus Colter. LC 82-72965. 219p. 1972. 10.95 (ISBN 0-8040-0563-X). Swallow.

Rivers of Glory. Francis Van Wyck Mason. LC 42-25679. 1942. J. B. Lippincott Company.

Rivers of Glory. Francis Van Wyck Mason. (Berkley Medallion). 1.95 (ISBN 0-425-03177-2). Berkley.

Rivers of Rain: Being a Fictional Accounting of the Adventures and Misadventures of John Rodgers Jewitt, Captive of the Indians at Friendly Cove on Nootka Island in Northwest America. Thomas M Aumack. LC 48-9057. 1948. Binfords & Mort.

Rivers of Time. Jean Barlow Hudson. LC 79-21751. 1980. 10.95 (ISBN 0-89340-232-X). J. Curley.

Rivers Parting: A Novel. Shirley Barker. LC 50-14406. 1950. Crown Publishers.

River's Rim, a Novel. 1st Ed. Jane Ludlow Drake Abbott. LC 50-6057. 1950. Lippincott.

Rivers Run Together. James Sherburne. LC 74-6242. 1974. 6.95 (ISBN 0-395-19425-3). Houghton Mifflin Co.

Rivers to Cross. Roland Pertwee. LC 27-583972. 1927. Houghton Mifflin Company.

Rivers to Cross: A Collection of Stories by Members of Western Writers of Amer. Ed. by William R. Cox. Western Writers of America. Ed. by William Robert Cox. LC 66-125756. 1966. bds., 3.50. Dodd.

Rivers to the Sea: An American Story. Lucien Hubbard. LC 42-11118. Simon and Schuster.

Rivers West. Louis L'Amour. LC 74-23313. 1975. 6.95 (ISBN 0-8415-0370-2). Saturday Review Press.

Rivers West. Louis L'Amour. LC 75-8640. 1975. 8.95 (ISBN 0-8161-6288-3). G. K. Hall.

Rivers West. Louis L'Amour. 1975. (pbk.) 1.25. Bantam Books.

Rivers Westward. James Denson Sayers. LC 40-1858. 1939. Hillman-Curl, Inc.

Riverside. Patrick Hamilton. LC 47-5253. 1947. Random House.

Riverside Drive. Beth Brown. LC 36-31574. 1936. E. P. Dutton & Company, Inc.

Riverside Drive. Louis Aston Marantz Simpson. LC 62-11686. 1962. Atheneum.

Riverside Villas Murder. Kingsley Amis. LC 73-5946. 1973. 6.95 (ISBN 0-15-177720-9). Harcourt Brace Jovanovich.

Riverside 90. Douglas Enefer. LC 70-103718. 1970. 3.95. Roy Publishers.

Riversons: A Novel. Samuel Josiah Bumstead. LC 6-18682. 1890. Welch, Fracker Company.

Riversons. A Novel. Samuel Josiah Bumstead. LC 6-18683. (American series, no. 269). M. J. Ivers & Co.

Riverton Minister. Martin Post. LC 7-30318. 1897. American Publishing and Engraving Co.

Rivertown Risk. Joe L. Hensley. LC 75-38164. 1977. 5.95 (ISBN 0-385-11224-6). Published for the Crime Club by Doubleday.

Riverwitch. Felicia Andrews. (O.s.i). (Orig.). 1979. pap. 2.75 (ISBN 0-515-05861-0). Jove Pubns.

Riverwood. Jane Irenita Corby. LC 68-1542. 1968. Arcadia House.

Riverwood. Miriam Lynch. 1971. pap. 0.75 o.p. (ISBN 0-447-74747-9). Lancer.

Riverworld see Philip Jose Farmer: The Complete Riverworld Novels.

Riverworld and Other Stories. Philip Jose Farmer. LC 80-24826. (Series: Gregg Press Science Fiction Series.). 1981. 15.95 (ISBN 0-8398-2618-4). Gregg Press.

Riverworld War: The Suppressed Fiction of Philip Jose Farmer. Philip Jose Farmer. LC 81-159091. (Philip Jose Farmer Society Series; 1). 1980. (11.95 signed and numbered) 6.95 (ISBN 0-933180-13-6). Ellis Press.

Rivet in Grandfather's Neck. James B. Cabell. 1929. 9.00 o.p. (ISBN 0-404-01353-8). AMS Pr.

Rivet in Grandfather's Neck. Bruce Elliott. (Orig.). 1970. pap. 0.75 o.p. (0502-07101). Curtis.

Rivet in Grandfather's Neck: A Comedy in Limitations. James Branch Cabell. LC 22-614. 1921. R. M. McBride & Company.

Rivet in Grandfather's Neck, a Comedy of Limitations. James B. Cabell. LC 70-144930. Repr. of 1929 ed. 39.00 (ISBN 0-403-00892-1). Scholarly.

Rivet in Grandfather's Neck: A Comedy of Limitations. James Branch Cabell. LC 70-144930. 1972. (ISBN 0-403-00892-1). Scholarly Press.

Rivet in Grandfather's Neck: A Comedy of Limitations. James Branch Cabell. LC 15-29589. 1915. R. M. McBride & Company.

Rivet in Grandfather's Neck: A Comedy of Limitations. branch cabell... ed. James Branch Cabell. LC 37-32804. 1928. R. M. McBride & Company.

Rivets. 1977. pap. write for info. (ISBN 0-88074-005-1). Metagam.

Rivev Cowboy. LC 56-169758. 1956. Arcadia House.

Riviera. Robert S. Hopkins. 288p. 1981. pap. 2.75 (ISBN 0-445-04657-0). Popular Lib.

Riviera: A Novel About the Cannes Film Festival. Robert S Hopkins. LC 79-26825. 1980. 10.95 (ISBN 0-688-03618-X). W. Morrow.

TITLE INDEX ROADS OF DESTINY.

Riviera Puzzle: An Inspector Damiot Mystery. Vincent McConnor. 236p. 1981. 10.95 (ISBN 0-02-582930-0). Macmillan.
Rivington Street. Meredith Tax. LC 81-22587. 1982. 15.50 (ISBN 0-688-01135-7). Morrow.
Rizpah. Charles E. Israel. pap. 1.25 o.p. (78-606). Lancer.
Rizpah: A Novel. Charles E Israel. LC 61-5850. 1961. Simon and Schuster.
Rizpah's Heritage. Jennie Maria Drinkwater Conklin. R. Carter and Brothers.
Rm. 205 & Beyond. Ernel A. Henry. 1978. 5.95 o.p. (ISBN 0-533-03037-4). Vantage.
R.N. Sharon Webb. (Orig.). 1982. pap. 2.95 (ISBN 0-89083-915-8). Zebra.
Roach & Co.-- Pirates, and Other Stories. Hector Fuller & Ridpath, John Clark. LC 6-44583. 1898. The Bowen-Merrill Company.
Roach & Co.-Pirates, and Other Stories. Hector Fuller. LC 78-113662. (Short story index reprint series). 1970. Books for Libraries Press.
Roach & Company - Pirates & Other Stories. Hector Fuller. LC 78-113662. (Short Story Index Reprint Ser.). 1897. 15.00 (ISBN 0-8369-3391-5). Ayer Co.
Road. Mulk Raj Anand. 110p. 1974. 3.50 o.p. (ISBN 0-88253-471-8); pap. 2.40 o.p. (ISBN 0-88253-916-7). InterCulture.
Road. Andre Chamson. Tr. by Brooks, Van Wyck. LC 29-26491. 1929. C. Scribner's Sons.
Road. John Ehle. LC 67-11334. 1967. Harper & Row.
Road. Henry Beetle Hough. LC 73-95872. 1970. 5.95. Harcourt, Brace & World.
Road. Herman Petersen. LC 52-8849. 1952. Crowell.
Road. Elias Tobenkin. LC 22-2346. Harcourt, Brace and Company.
Road: A Modern Romance. Frank Mackenzie Savile. LC 11-2969. 1911. Little, Brown, and Company.
Road: A Romance of the Proletarian Revolution. George Spiro. LC 32-1751. 1932. Red Star Press.
Road and the Star. Berkely Mather. LC 65-13659. 4.95. Scribners.
Road Back. Erich Maria Remarque & Wheen, Arthur Wesley, Tr. LC 31-11921. 1931. Little, Brown, and Company.
Road Between. James Thomas Farrell. LC 49-8444. 1949. Vanguard Press.
Road Beyond. Harriet Theresa Smith Comstock. LC 39-18658. 1939. Doubleday, Doran & Company, Inc.
Road Beyond the Town: And Other Little Verses. Michael Earls. LC 12-26822. 1912. Benziger Brothers.
Road Block. 1st Ed. Hillary Waugh. LC 60-8688. 1960. Published for the Crime Club by Doubleday.
Road-Builders. Samuel Merwin. LC 5-32832. The Macmillan Company.
Road End. Woods Morrison. LC 27-10459. 1927. G. P. Putnam's Sons.
Road from Echo: A Tale of the Virginia Mountains. Lillian K Craig. LC 30-20868. L. C. Page & Company.
Road from Olivet. Edward Francis Murphy. LC 46-4659. 1946. The Bruce Publishing Company.
Road from Remo. Peggy O'More, pseud. LC 37-380978. 1937. Hillman-Curl, Inc.
Road from the Monument. Margaret Storm Jameson. LC 62-4089. 1962. Macmillan.
Road from the Monument. 1st Ed. Margaret Storm Jameson. LC 62-114783. 1962. Harper.
Road from Toomi. Leonard Patrick O'Connor Wibberley. LC 68-14806. 1967-1968. W. Morrow.
Road Goes Ever on. 2nd, rev. ed. John Ronald Reuel Tolkien & Donald Swann. 1978. 10.00 (ISBN 0-395-24758-6). HM.
Road Grows Strange. Glady Hasty Carroll. (60-2344). 1968. Popular Lib.
Road Grows Strange. Gladys Hasty Carroll. LC 65-213545. 4.95. Little.
Road Grows Strange. Gladys Hasty Carroll. LC 65-21354. 1965. Little, Brown.
Road House Murders. Robert Portner Koehler. LC 46-8055. 1946. Phoenix Press.
Road into Sunrise: A Narrative of the Eternal Verities. William Dudley Pelley. LC 51-16693.
Road Is Long. Mary Mabel Cabana Wirries. LC 40-32102. The Ave Maria Press.
Road Leading Somewhere. Katherine Ursula Parrott. LC 41-4020. 1941. Dodd, Mead & Company.
Road Leads on. Knut Hamsun & Gay-Tifit, Eugene, Tr. LC 34-27173. 1934. Coward-McCann, Inc.
Road Less Traveled. Richard Belair. LC 65-11801. 1965. Doubleday.
Road Lies West. Elizabeth Howard, pseud. LC 55-6745. 1955. Morrow.
Road of Ages. Robert Nathan. LC 35-1939. 1935. A. A. Knopf.
Road of Ambition. Elaine Sterne. LC 17-13078. 1917. 1.35. Britton Publishing Company.
Road of Azrael. Robert E. Howard. 192p. 1980. pap. 2.25 (ISBN 0-553-13326-8). Bantam.
Road of Azrael. Robert E. Howard. 20.00 (ISBN 0-937986-23-2); deluxe ed. 35.00 (ISBN 0-937986-24-0). D M Grant.
Road of Desperation. Mary Hastings Bradley. LC 32-21190. 1932. D. Appleton and Company.
Road of Destiny: A Romance of the Eighteenth Century. Ellis Middleton. LC 23-11082. 1923. Frederick A. Stokes Company.
Road of Kings: Conan. Karl Edward Wagner. (No. 4). 1979. pap. 2.25 (ISBN 0-553-14321-2). Bantam.
Road of Living Men: A Novel. Will Levington Comfort. LC 13-677412. 1913. 1.25. J. B. Lippincott Company.
Road of No Regrets: A Novel of the Homosexual in Our Culture. 1st Ed. Joseph De Pelissero. LC 56-9748. 1956. Greenwich Book Publishers.
Road of the Gods. Isabel Bowler Paterson. LC 30-8168. 1930. H. Liveright.
Road of the Rough: A Simple Story of Life in New York City. Maurice Meyer Minton. LC 7-32458. (On cover: The Illustrated American series, no. 1). The Illustrated American Publishing Company.
Road of the Rough: A Simple Story of Life in New York City. Maurice Meyer Minton. LC 3519. (On cover: Eagle library, no. 165). 1900. Street & Smith.
Road of the Sea Horse. Poul Anderson. (Last Viking Ser.: No. 2). 400p. (Orig.). 1980. pap. 2.50 (ISBN 0-89083-610-8). Zebra.
Road Past Altamont. Gabrielle Carbotte Roy. LC 66-22286. 1966. Harcourt, Brace & World.
Road Past Altamont. Gabrielle Carbotte Roy. LC 76-370663. (New Canadian library; no. 129). McClelland and Stewart.
Road Past Altmont. Tr. from French by Joyce Marshall. Gabrielle Carbotte Roy. LC 66-22286. 3.95. Harcourt.
Road Racer. William E Butterworth. 1967. Norton.
Road Returns. Paul Corey. LC 40-31517. The Bobbs-Merrill Company.
Road Show. Eric Hatch. LC 34-12029. 1934. Little, Brown, and Company.
Road Show: A Novel. John Haase. LC 60-6734. 1960. Simon and Schuster.
Road That Bends. Ruby M Ayres. LC 16-6765. 1916. Cassell and Company, Ltd.
Road That Led Home: A Romance of Plow-Land; with Some Passages from the Lives of Henry Nicol, Philosopher of Islay; Ernie Bedford, Pedagogue; Jim Dover, of the Everlasting Thirst; and Sioux Ben Sun Cloud, the Scotch-Talking Indian; As Well As Others, Not Excluding Charlie Tinker of the Continuous Speech and Ida Bethune of the Pale-Green Smile; Jim Is Dead. Will E Ingersoll. LC 18-6803. 1918. Harper & Brothers.
Road, the Eye. Michael Anderson. 1978. pap. 4.00 o.s.i. Tex Ctr Writers.
Road Through the Wall. Shirley Jackson. LC 48-5523. 1948. Farrar, Straus.
Road to Avalon. Coningsby William Dawson. LC 11-59943. 1.20. Hodder & Stoughton, George H. Doran Company.
Road to Bagdad. George Fort Gibbs. LC 38-16534. 1938. D. Appleton-Century Company, Incorporated.
Road to Baltimore. Robert S Harper. LC 42-17218. 1942. M. S. Mill Co., Inc.
Road to Bithynia: A Novel of Luke, the Beloved Physician. Slaughter, Frank Gill. LC 51-12110. 1951. Doubleday.
Road to Bithynia: A Novel of Luke, the Beloved Physician. Frank Gill Slaughter. (Kangaroo Book). 1977. 1.95 (ISBN 0-671-81051-0). Pocket Books.
Road to Black Mountain. Joseph Bruchac. LC 76-28248. (Orig.). 1976. pap. 4.00x (ISBN 0-914476-45-9). Thorp Springs.
Road to Calvary. Aleksei Nikolaevich Tolstoi & Bone, Edith, Tr. LC 46-3966. 1946. A. A. Knopf.
Road to Calvary. Aleksei Nikolaevich Tolstoi & Townsend, Mrs. R. S., Tr. LC 23-6951. Boni and Liveright.
Road to Canaan. Pernet Patterson. LC 72-8555. (Black Heritage Library Collection). 1972. (ISBN 0-8369-9193-1). Books for Libraries Press.
Road to Canaan. Pernet Patterson. LC 31-84170. 1931. Minton, Balch & Company.
Road to Corlay. Richard Cowper, pseud. 1979. pap. 1.95 (ISBN 0-671-82917-3, Timescape). PB.
Road to Damascus. Hersilia A. Mitchell Copp Keays. LC 7-31480. 1907. Small, Maynard & Company.
Road to Damascus. August Strindberg. 1958. 3.50 o.p. Verry.
Road to Destiny. Temple Ann Ellis. LC 39-20478. 1939. The Naylor Company.
Road to Destiny. 1st Ed. Gertrude Potter. LC 60-303. 1960. Vantage Press.
Road to En-Dor: A Novel. Louis Joseph Vance. LC 25-7675. E. P. Dutton & Company.
Road to Endor. Esther Barstow Hammand. LC 40-822952. Farrar & Rinehart.
Road to Folly. Zenith Jones Brown. LC 40-272951. 1940. C. Scribner's Sons.
Road to Fortune. Frederic Arnold Kummer. LC 26-112572. George H. Doran Company.
Road to Frontenac. Samuel Merwin. LC 1-24840. 1901. Doubleday, Page & Co.
Road to Gandolfo. Robert Ludlum. (General Ser.). 1983. lib. bdg. 15.95 (ISBN 0-8161-3506-1, Large Print Bks). G K Hall.
Road to Gandolfo: A Novel. Michael Shepherd. LC 75-1113. 1975. 7.95 (ISBN 0-8037-5920-7). Dial Press.
Road to Glenfairlie. David Garth. LC 40-87456. 1940. H. C. Kinsey & Company, Inc.
Road to Glory. Robert French. 1979. pap. 1.50 (ISBN 0-532-15386-3). Woodhill.
Road to Glory. Darwin Le Ora Teilhet. LC 56-77718. 1956. Funk & Wagnalls.
Road to Glory: A Biographical Novel of Napoleon. Frederick Britten Austin & Ustin. LC 35-170917. 1935. Frederick A. Stokes Company.
Road to Glory: Story of the Third Purple Heart. Thompson, Arthur Ripley. LC 52-10362. (Americana). 1952. Library Publishers.
Road to Heaven: A Romance of Morals. Thomas Beer. LC 28-12656. 1928. A. A. Knopf.
Road to Hell... Hubert Monteilhet. LC 64-17502. (Inner sanctum mystery). 1964. Simon and Schuster.
Road to Infinity. Isaac Asimov. LC 78-22362. 1979. 10.95 (ISBN 0-385-14962-X). Doubleday.
Road to Jericho. Josephine Powell Beaty. LC 65-24254. 4.00. Dorrance.
Road to Laramie: A New Powder Valley Western. Peter Field. LC 45-19537. 1945. Jefferson House.
Road to Le Reve. Breiver Corcoran. LC 16-21397. 1916. The Page Company.
Road to Leenane. Angela Du Maurier. LC 64-22662. 1964. Appleton-Century.
Road to Life. 1st Ed. Byllee Pugh Golsan Masters. LC 55-10866. 1956. Vantage Press.
Road to London. David Skaats Foster. LC 14-9408. 1.25. The Franklin Book Company.
Road to Many a Wonder. David Wagoner. LC 76-93. 1976. 9.95 (ISBN 0-8161-6354-5). G. K. Hall.
Road to Many a Wonder: A Novel. David Wagoner. LC 73-87690. 1974. 6.95 (ISBN 0-374-25127-4). Farrar, Straus, Giroux.
Road to Mecca. Florence Irwin. LC 16-108777. 1916. G. P. Putnam's Sons.
Road to Miltown. Sidney J. Perelman. (O.s.i.). 1960. pap. 2.95 o.s.i. (ISBN 0-671-21117-X, Fireside). S&S.
Road to Monterey. George Washington Ogden. LC 25-238193. 1925. A. C. McClurg & Co.
Road to Needles. Dorothy Speare. LC 37-205923. 1937. Houghton Mifflin Company.
Road to Nowhere. Eric Leadbitter. LC 21-16709. G. W. Jacobs & Company.
Road to Nowhere. Elizabeth Ogilvie. 288p. 1983. 14.95 (ISBN 0-07-047700-0, GB). McGraw.
Road to Nowhere: A Novel. Maurice Walsh. LC 34-19657. 1934. Frederick A. Stokes Company.
Road to Oobliadooh. Fritz Rudolf Fries. LC 68-54935. 1968. 6.95. McGraw-Hill.
Road to Paris: A Story of Adventure. Robert Neilson Stephens. LC 98-1088. 1898. L. C. Page and Company.
Road to Paris: A Story of Adventure. Robert Neilson Stephens. LC 6-24360. (Fleur le lis library, no. 9). 1901. L. C. Page & Company.
Road to Providence. Maria Thompson Daviess. LC 10-25214. 1.50. The Bobbs-Merrill Company.
Road to Rhuine. Simon Troy. LC 52-7352. (Red badge detective). 1952. Dodd, Mead.
Road to Rhuine: By Simon Troy Pseud. Thurman Warriner. LC 52-7352. (Red badge detective). 1952. Dodd, Mead.
Road to Ridgeby's. Frank Burlingame Harris. LC 1-16998. 1901. Small, Maynard & Company.
Road to Romance. Anne Allison. LC 50-11199. 1950. Gramercy Pub. Co.
Road to Romance. Hope Jordan. 1982. pap. 6.95 (Avalon). Bouregy.
Road to Rouen. Gene Markey. LC 30-30770. The John Day Company.
Road to San Jacinto. James Francis Davis. LC 36-8770. The Bobbs-Merrill Company.
Road to San Jacinto. L. L Foreman. (Belmont Tower Book). 1977. 1.25. Tower Publications.
Road to San Jacinto. Leonard London Foreman. LC 43-384947. 1943. E. P. Dutton & Co., Inc.
Road to San Jancinto. Leonard London Foreman. 1977. pap. 1.25 o.s.i. (ISBN 0-505-51117-7). Tower Bks.
Road to San Luis Rey. Thelma Hester Jones. LC 73-87882. (Illus.). 1974. (ISBN 0-912472-18-9). Miller Books.
Road to Santa Fe. Edwin Bateman Morris. LC 30-719977. The Penn Publishing Company.
Road to Santa Fe. Gunhild Nordling Tegen. Tr. by Jones, Llewellyn. 1947. Dierkes Press.
Road to Science Fiction, No. 3. Ed. by James Gunn. (Orig.). 1979. pap. 3.50 (ISBN 0-451-61910-2, ME1910, Ment). NAL.
Road to Science Fiction, No. 4. James E. Gunn. 1982. pap. 4.95 (ME2136, Ment). NAL.
Road to Sixty. Thomas, Howard. LC 67-1585. 1966. Prospect Books.
Road to Sodom: A Novel. Jean A Rees. LC 61-14891. 1961. Random House.
Road to Spain: A Novel. by Ira Morris. Ira Victor Morris. LC 65-24571. 1966. bds., 4.95. Monthly Review.
Road to Tamazunchale. Ron Arias. 110p. 1978. pap. 5.00 (ISBN 0-915596-12-1). West Coast.
Road to the City: Two Novelettes Tr. from the Italian. Natalia Ginzburg. LC 49-10245. 1949. Doubleday.
Road to the Coast. John Harris. LC 73-155561. 1972. 5.95 (ISBN 0-85617-901-9). White Lion Publishers.
Road to the Land of TH. Cameron W. Garbutt. (Illus.). 48p. 1971. pap. text ed. 1.25x (ISBN 0-8134-1324-9, 1324). Interstate.
Road to the Left. Clara Wallace Overton. LC 35-1086. Farrar & Rinehart, Incorporated.
Road to the Middle Islands. Niel Hancock. (Wilderness of Four Ser.: Vol. 4). (Orig.). 1982. pap. 2.95 (ISBN 0-445-04743-7). Popular Lib.
Road to the Ocean. Leonid Maksimovich Leonov & Guterman, Norbert, 1900- Tr. LC 44-473099. 1944. L. B. Fischer.
Road to the Open. Arthur Schnitzler. Tr. by Samuel, Horace Barnett. LC 26-3554. 1923. A. A. Knopf.
Road to the River. Lon Riley Woodrum. LC 57-17516. 1956. Zondervan Pub. House.
Road to the Shore, and Other Stories. Michael McLaverty. LC 77-350664. 1976. 0.99. Poolbeg Press.
Road to the Snail. William P McGivern. LC 61-8180. 1961. Dodd, Mead.
Road to the Stars. Ruth Tracy Millard. LC 40-104451. The Penn Publishing Company.
Road to the Sun. Marjory Stoneman Douglas. LC 51-14824. 1951. Rinehart.
Road to the Valley: A Novel for Young Adults. Virginia Nielsen, pseud. LC 61-6107. (Illus.). 1961. D. McKay Co.
Road to the World. Webb Waldron. LC 22-6315. 1922. The Century Co.
Road to Understanding. Eleanor Hodgman Porter. LC 17-9250. 1917. 1.40. Houghton Mifflin Company.
Road to Utopia. Ada Nate McIntosh. LC 40-7248. Modern Printing Service Co.
Road to Victory: Twelve Tales of the Red Army. Bek, A. A. 1945. Hutchinson & Co. Ltd.
Road to Winesburg: A Mosaic of the Imaginative Life of Sherwood Anderson. William Alfred Sutton. LC 73-181997. (Illus.). 1972. (ISBN 0-8108-0312-7). Scarecrow Press.
Road to Xanadu. John L. Lowes. (O.s.i.). 7.95 o.s.i. (ISBN 0-395-07935-7). HM.
Road: Translated from the Swedish by M. A. Michael. Harry Martinson. LC 56-7599. 1956. Reyal.
Road Unconventional. 1st Ed. Louis Gilmore. LC 55-736095. Pageant Press.
Road up to the Rim: The Hard Way up. A. Bertram Chandler. 352p. 1981. pap. 2.75 (ISBN 0-441-73102-3). Ace Bks.
Road Winds on. Francena Harriet Arnold. LC 55-589544. 1955. Moody Press.
Road with No End. Mochtar Lubis. LC 72-105118. 1970. 4.95. H. Regnery Co.
Road. 1st Ed. Austin Coates. 1959. Harper.
Roadblock. Miriam Borgenicht. LC 73-1747. (Black bat mystery). 1973. 5.95 (ISBN 0-672-51851-1). Bobbs-Merrill.
Roadhouse. Roy Booth. W. Godwin, Inc.
Roadmarks. Roger Zelazny. LC 79-2280. 1979. 2.25 (ISBN 0-345-28530-1). Ballantine Books.
Roadmender. Michael Fairless. (Illus.). 1.75 o.p. (ISBN 0-525-19281-6). Dutton.
Roads. Seabury Quinn. LC 49-316. 1948. Arkham House.
Roads from Home. Daniel Marcus Davin. LC 77-358992. (New Zealand fiction). (Illus.). 1976. 11.50 (ISBN 0-19-647948-7). Auckland University Press.
Roads from the Fort. Arvid Shulenberger. LC 54-9717. 1954. Harcourt, Brace.
Roads Going South. Robert Luther Duffus. LC 21-15817. 1921. The Macmillan Company.
Roads Lead Home. William Arthur Neubauer. LC 49-597989. 1948. Arcadia House.
Roads of Destiny. William Sydney Porter. LC 25-71684. 1913. Doubleday, Page & Company, for Review of Reviews Co.
Roads of Destiny. William Sydney Porter. LC 15-174130. 1914. Doubleday, Page & Company.
Roads of Destiny. William Sydney Porter. LC 19-135241. 1918. Doubleday, Page & Company.
Roads of Destiny. William Sydney Porter. LC 22-160217. 1919. Doubleday, Page & Company, for Review of Reviews Company.
Roads of Destiny. William Sydney Porter. LC 20-19324. 1920. Doubleday, Page & Company.

Roads of Destiny. William Sydney Porter. LC 25-716993. 1922. Doubleday, Page & Company.
Roads of Destiny. William Sydney Porter. LC 25-237252. 1925. Doubleday, Page & Company.
Roads of Destiny. William Sydney Porter. LC 9-11539. 1909. Doubleday, Page & Company.
Roads of Doubt. William MacLeod Raine. LC 25-8117. 1925. Doubleday, Page & Company.
Roads: the First Movement: I Am Your Christ. first ed. Taylore. 1972. 4.95 (ISBN 0-533-00401-2). Vantage.
Roads to Dawn Lake. John O. Simon. 1968. pap. 2.00 (Pub. by Oyez). SBD.
Roads to Glory. Richard Aldington. LC 71-132109. (Short story index reprint series). 1970. Books for Libraries Press.
Roads to Glory. Richard Aldington. LC 31-1276. 1931. Doubleday, Doran & Company, Inc.
Roads to Liberty. Francis Van Wyck Mason. LC 72-5353. (Illus.). 1972. 12.95 (ISBN 0-316-54930-4). Little, Brown.
Roadside and Fireside: Irish Folk Tales. William Love. LC 38-157273. 1938. Meador Publishing Company.
Roadside Meetings see Collected Works.
Roadside Picnic. Arkady Strugatsky & Arkadii Natanovich Strugatskii. 1982. pap. 2.25 (ISBN 0-671-45842-6, Timescape). PB.
Roadside Picnic - Tale of the Troika. Arkadii Natanovich Strugatskii & Boris Natanovich Strugatskii. 1978. pap. 2.25 (ISBN 0-671-81976-3, Timescape). PB.
Roadside Picnic; Tale of the Troika. Arkadii Natanovich Strugatskii & Boris Natanovich Strugatskii. LC 77-543. 8.95 (ISBN 0-02-615170-7). Macmillan.
Roadside Picnic & Tale of the Troika. Arkady Strugatsky & Arkadii Natanovich Strugatskii. Tr. by Antonina W. Bouis. 1977. 10.95 o.s.i. (ISBN 0-02-615170-7, 61517). Macmillan.
Roadside Picnic: Tale of the Troika. Arkadii Natanovich Strugatskii & Boris Natanovich Strugatskii. (Kangaroo Book). 1978. 1.95 (ISBN 0-671-81976-3). Pocket Books.
Roadside Rest. Ann Eric. 1970. 2.95 o.p. Vantage.
Roadwork. Robert Bell. 1979. pap. 2.25 o.s.i. (ISBN 0-8439-0697-9, Leisure Bks). Nordon Pubns.
Roald Dahl's Tales of the Unexpected. Roald Dahl. LC 79-5079. 1979. 2.95 (ISBN 0-394-74081-5). Vintage Books.
Roamer. Joseph N. Gagnon. 3.50 o.p. Carlton.
Roamin' in the Gloamin' Harry Lauder. 1977. Repr. of 1928 ed. text ed. 15.95x o.s.i. (ISBN 0-8277-5125-7). British Bk Ctr.
Roamin' with the Roamin' Man of the Smoking Mountains. Wiley Oakley. LC 40-32506. The Little Pigeon Press of the Galinburg News.
Roanoke Hundred. Inglis Clark Fletcher. 501p. 1976. Repr. of 1948 ed. lib. bdg. 18.95x (ISBN 0-89244-007-4). Queens Hse.
Roanoke Hundred: A Novel. Inglis Clark Fletcher. LC 52-31009. (Permabooks, P151). 1952. Permabooks.
Roanoke Hundred: A Novel. Inglis Clark Fletcher. LC 77-21357. 1977-1976. 14.95 (ISBN 0-89244-007-4). Queens House.
Roanoke Hundred: A Novel. Inglis Clark Fletcher. LC 48-8702. 1948. Bobbs-Merrill Co.
Roanoke of Roanoke Hall. Malcolm Bell. LC 1-29997. (On cover: Columbia library, vol. ii, no. 32). 1900. Street & Smith.
Roanoke of Roanoke Hall. A Romance. Malcolm Bell. LC 6-11704. (On cover: Belford American novel series, no. 18). Belford, Clarke and Company; Etc., Etc.
Roanoke Renegade. Don Tracy. LC 54-10534. 1954. Dial Press.
Roanoke Warrior. Carter A. Vaughan, pseud. (Hall of Fame Historical Novels). 1980. pap. 2.25 (ISBN 0-441-73112-0). Ace Bks.
Roanoke Warrior: By Carter A. Vaughan Pseud. Noel Bertram Gerson. LC 65-148331. 4.50. Doubleday.
Roar Lion Roar. Irvin Faust. 1965. 5.95 o.p. (ISBN 0-394-44340-3). Random.
Roar Lion Roar, and Other Stories. Irvin Faust. LC 64-20026. 1965. bds., 3.95. Random.
Roar of the Dragon. B. William Max. LC 75-130582. 1971. 5.95. Dorrance.
Roar of Thunder. Wilbur A Smith. LC 66-24030. 1966. Simon and Schuster.
Roar of Thunder. Wilbur A. Smith. (Dell Book.). 1977. 1.95 (ISBN 0-440-18146-1). Dell Pub. Co.
Roarin' Lead. William Colt MacDonald. LC 35-114974. Covici, Friede.
Roarin' Rinconada. W. D Hoffman. LC 30-15647. 1930. A. C. McClurg & Co.
Roaring Bones. Wilhelm & Freeburg, Victor Oscar, 1882- Tr. LC 27-22160. E. P. Dutton & Company.
Roaring Dove. Elizabeth Burton. LC 48-6122. 1948. Dodd, Mead.
Roaring in the Wind: Being a History of Alder Gulch, Montana, in Its Great and Its Shameful Days. Robert Lewis Taylor. LC 77-16509. 10.00 (ISBN 0-399-12089-0). Putnam.
Roaring Kleinschmids. Ramsey Yelvington. LC 50-11744. 1950. Highland Press.
Roaring Lion. Russ Johnson. LC 69-19901. 1971. 3.00. Dorrance.
Roaring Queen. Wyndham Lewis. LC 73-80783. 1973. 10.00 (ISBN 0-87140-576-8). Liveright.
Roaring Range. Llewellyn Perry Holmes. LC 35-335844. Greenberg.
Roaring River. Bill Brown, pseud. LC 52-13422. Coward-McCann.
Roaring River. William MacLeod Raine. LC 34-13505. 1934. Houghton Mifflin Company.
Roaring River Range. Arthur Henry Gooden. LC 42-36125. 1942. Houghton Mifflin Company.
Roaring Road. Byron Morgan. LC 20-9273. George H. Doran Comapny.
Roaring Road: A Sports Car Novel. Gene Olson. LC 62-122051. 1962. Dodd, Mead.
Roaring Shock Test. Eunice Luccock Corfman. LC 67-28817. 1968. Harper & Row.
Roaring Sword. Oscar Turning. LC 66-29255. 1967. Dorrance.
Roaring Tower: And Other Short Stories. Stella Gibbons. LC 37-230873. 1937. Longmans, Green and Co.
Roaring Waters. Cornelius Kuipers. LC 38-1084. Zondervan Publishing House.
Roast Beef Medium: The Business Adventures of Emma McChesney. Edna Ferber. LC 70-169550. (Short story index reprint series). (Illus.). 1971. (ISBN 0-8369-4012-1). Books for Libraries Press.
Roast Beef, Medium: The Business Adventures of Enna McChesney. Edna Ferber. LC 13-6546. 1913. Frederick A. Stokes Company.
Roast Eggs. Douglas Clark. LC 81-7850. (Red badge novel of suspense). 8.95 (ISBN 0-396-08004-9). Dodd, Mead.
Rob of the Bowl. John Pendleton Kennedy. Ed. by William S. Osborne. (Masterworks of Literature Ser). 1965. 7.50x (ISBN 0-8084-0263-3); pap. 4.45x (ISBN 0-8084-0264-1, M12). Coll & U Pr.
Rob of the Bowl: A Legend of St. Inigoe's. Ed. for Modern Reader by William S. Osborne. John Pendleton Kennedy. LC 65-25630. (Masterworks of lit. ser.). 1966. 5.00. Coll. & Univ. Pr.
Rob of the Bowl: A Legend of St. Inigoe's. Ed. for the Mod. Reader by William S. Osborne. John Pendleton Kennedy. LC 65-25630. (Masterworks of lit. ser., M-12). pap., 2.95. Conn.
Rob of the Bowl. A Legend of St. Inigoe's. rev. ed. John Pendleton Kennedy. LC 7-10956. 1860. J. B. Lippincott & Co.
Rob Rockafellow. A Boston Society Man's Diary. Nevada McNeill. LC 7-25588. 1894. G. W. Dillingham, Successor to G. W. Carleton & Co.
Rob Roy. Walter Scott. Ed. by Johnson, Rossiter I. E. Edwin Rossiter. LC 12-37845. (Condensed classics v. 3). 1877. H. Holt and Company.
Rob Roy. Walter Scott. (Seaside library. v. 45, no. 920). 1881. G. Munro.
Rob Roy. Walter Scott. (On cover: Lovell's library, no. 632). 1885. J. W. Lovell Company.
Rob Roy. Walter Scott. LC 8-30523. (Classics for children). 1887. Ginn and Company.
Rob Roy. Walter Scott. (On cover: Seaside library. Pocket ed. no. 1164). 1889. G. Munro.
Rob Roy. Walter Scott. LC 8-3050. (Standard literature series, no. 3). 1896. University Publishing Company.
Rob Roy. Walter Scott. (Half-title: Everyman's library, ed. by Ernest Rhys. Fiction. no. 142). 1908. J. M. Dent & Co.
Rob Roy. Walter Scott. Ed. by Lang, Andrew. LC 12-24350. (On cover: Waverley novels). D. Estes & Company.
Rob Roy. Walter Scott. Ed. by Musgrove, Eugene Richard. LC 19-15733. (Macmillan's pocket American and English classics). 1919. The Macmillan Company.
Rob Roy. Walter Scott. LC 96-37013. (Half-title: Everyman's library, ed. by Ernest Rhys. Fiction. no. 142). 1931. J. M. Dent & Sons, Ltd.
Rob Roy: Edited with an Introd. and Notes by Edgar Johnson. Walter Scott. LC 56-3901. (Riverside editions, B12). 1956. Houghton Mifflin.
Rob Roy... From the Last Rev. Ed., Containing the Author's Final Corrections, Notes, &C. parker's ed. Walter Scott. (Waverley novels: Library ed. v. 4). 1817. Bazin & Ellsworth.
Rob. Roy... From the Last Revised Ed., Containing the Author's Final Corrections, Notes, &C. parker's ed. Walter Scott. LC 12-23265. (Waverley novels. Library edition. vol. iv). Bazin & Ellsworth.
Robbed Heart. Clifton Cuthbert. LC 45-10155. 1945. L. B. Fischer.
Robben Island. D. M. Zwelonke. (African Writers Ser: No. 128). 151p. 1974. pap. text ed. 1.75x o.p. Humanities.
Robber. A Tale. George Payne Rainsford James. LC 22-4754. 1855. Harper & Brothers.
Robber: A Tale of the Time of the Herods. 1st ed. Bertram Brooker. LC 49-497819. 1949. Duell, Sloan and Pearce.
Robber Baroness. William Kendall Clarke. LC 78-21417. 10.95 (ISBN 0-312-68549-1). St. Martin's Press.
Robber Bridegroom. Eudora Welty. LC 48-827654. 1948. Harcourt, Brace.
Robber Bridegroom. Eudora Welty. LC 42-23596. 1942. Doubleday, Doran & Company, Inc.
Robber Bridegroom. Eudora Welty. LC 78-6660. (Harvest/HBJ book). 1978. 2.95 (ISBN 0-15-676807-0). Harcourt Brace Jovanovich.
Robber Count: A Story of the Hartz Country. Julius Wolff & Harz Mountains--Descr. & Trav. LC 8-36564. T. Y. Crowell & Co.
Robber Countess: A Novel. Sylvanus Cobb. (On cover: The popular series, no. 11). 1891. R. Bonner's Sons.
Robber King: Thrilling Episodes in a Career of Crime. Patrick Tyrell. (On cover: Pinkerton detective series, v. 33). 1889. Laird & Lee.
Robberies Company, Ltd. Nelson McAllister Lloyd. LC 6-34042. 1906. C. Scribner's Sons.
Robbers and Soldiers. Albert Ehrenstein & Dunlop, Geoffrey, Tr. LC 29-11285. 1929. A. A. Knopf.
Robber's Cook. 1st ed. David Hoag. 50p. 1973. pap. 1.95x o.p. SF Arts & Letters.
Robbers' Roost. Zane Grey. LC 32-18431. 1932. Harper & Brothers.
Robber's Wife. A Domestic Romance. LC 7-41021. 1853. Stringer & Townsend.
Robbery at Portage Bend: A Story of the Royal North-West Mounted Police. T Lund. LC 34-8350. C. Kendall.
Robbery at Rudwick House. Victor Lorenzo Whitechurch. 1929. Duffield and Company.
Robbery at Three Wells. Fred N Kimmel. LC 62-7365. 1962. Macmillan.
Robbery Under Arms see Australian Classics.
Robbery Under Arms: A Story of Life and Adventure in the Bush and in the Goldfields of Australia. Thomas Alexander Browne. LC 63-22990. (World's classics, 510). 1957. Oxford University Press.
Robbery Under Arms: A Story of Life and Adventure in the Bush and in the Goldfields of Australia. Thomas Alexander Browne. LC 6-17227. 1897. Macmillan and Co.
Robbery with Violence: By John Rhode Pseud. Cecil John Charles Street. LC 57-10166. (Red badge detective). 1957. Dodd, Mead.
Robbie. Bettina Bird. LC 68-28964. (Trend books). (Illus.). 1968. 0.90. Cheshire.
Robbing Paul to Pay Peter. William Neuss. LC 28-8702. G. J. Roberts & Sons, Inc.
Robbing Peter to Pay Paul: A Novel. John Saunders. (Seaside library, v. 88, no. 1780). 1884. G. Munro.
Robb's Island Wreck: And Other Stories. Lynn Roby Meekins. 1894. Stone and Kimball.
Robbut: A Tale of Tails. Robert Lawson. 1981. lib. bdg. 7.95 (ISBN 0-8398-2728-8, Gregg). G K Hall.
Robby Walton's Christmas Eve. Edward Harold Mott. 1886. Hackett, Carhart & Co.
Robe. Lloyd Cassel Douglas. LC 57-33754. 1953. Houghton Mifflin.
Robe. Lloyd Cassel Douglas. LC 42-24099. 1942. Houghton Mifflin Company.
Robe. Lloyd Cassel Douglas. LC 43-15179. 1943. Houghton Mifflin Company.
Robe. Lloyd Cassel Douglas. LC 47-12175. 1947. Houghton Mifflin Co.
Robe of Nessus: An Historical Romance. Duffield Osborne. LC 7-23178. (On cover: The Belford American novel series, v. 2, no. 4). 1890. Belford Company.
Robert Ainsleigh. copyright ed.... ed. Mary Elizabeth Braddon Maxwell. LC 7-17831. 1872. A. Asher & Col.
Robert Andrew Parker's Illustrated Frankenstein. Mary Wollstonecraft Godwin Shelley. 1976. pap. 5.95 o.p. (ISBN 0-517-51697-7, Dist by Crown). Potter.
Robert Annys: Poor Priest; a Tale of the Great Uprising. Annie Nathan Meyer. LC 1-312059. 1901. The Macmillan Company.
Robert Atterbury: A Study of Love and Life. John R Jarboe. LC 7-10340. ("unknown" library). The Cassell Publishing Co.
Robert Bage's Hermsprong, or, Man As He Is Not. Robert Bage & Stuart M Tave. LC 81-83149. 20.00 (ISBN 0-271-00298-0). Pennsylvania State University Press.
Robert Cavelier: The Romance of the Sicue De La Salle and His Discovery of the Mississippi River. William Dana Orcutt. LC 4-9501. 1904. A. C. McClurg & Co.
Robert Cordon: M.D. Adelaide Humphries. LC 46-3805. 1946. Arcadia House.
Robert Devoy, a Tale of the Palmyra Massacre. Frank Hanley Sosey. LC 3-17014. 1903. Press of Sosey Bros.
Robert E. Howard's The Incredible Adventures of Dennis Dorgan. Robert E. Howard. LC 74-83075. (Illus.). FAX Collector's Editions.
Robert Elsemer. Mary Augusta Arnold Humphry Ward Ward. LC 41-35149. 1888. Hurst & Company.
Robert Elsmere. Mary Augusta Arnold Humphry Ward Ward. LC 75-1534. (Victorian Fiction: Novels of Faith and Doubt; V. 82). 1975. 35.00. Garland Pub.
Robert Elsmere. Mary Augusta Arnold Humphry Ward Ward. LC 7-3070. (On cover: Macmillan's summer reading library. no. 16). 1888. Macmillan and Co.
Robert Elsmere. Mary Augusta Arnold Humphry Ward Ward. (On cover: Lovell's library, no. 1186). 1888. J. W. Lovell Company.
Robert Elsmere. Mary Augusta Arnold Humphry Ward Ward. (On cover: Seaside library. Pocket ed. no. 1116). 1888. G. Munro.
Robert Elsmere: By Mrs. Humphry Ward. Ed., Introd. by Clyde De L. Ryals. Mary Augusta Arnold Ward. (Univ. of Neb. Pr. Bison bk. rebound). 1968. 5.00. P. Smith.
Robert Elsmere: By Mrs. Humphry Ward. Ed., Introd. by Clyde De L. Ryals. Mary Augusta Arnold Humphry Ward Ward. Ed. by Clyde De L. Ryals. LC 67-12116. (Bison bk.). 1967. pap., 2.85. Univ. of Neb. Pr.
Robert Emmet: Or, True Irish Hearts. Dennis O'Sullivan. (On cover: Munro's library, popular novels, v. 1, no. 504). N. L. Munro.
Robert Emmet's Wooing. Edgar C Blum. LC 10-7172. 1910. Cochrane Publishing Company.
Robert Falconer. George Macdonald. LC 75-1510. (Victorian Fiction: Novels of Faith and Doubt; V. 60). 1975. 35.00 (ISBN 0-8240-1584-3). Garland Pub.
Robert Falconer. George Macdonald. LC 22-10834. 1876. Loring.
Robert Falconer. George Macdonald. LC 9-3851. G. Routledge and Sons, Limited.
Robert Falconer. George Macdonald. LC 12-18324. 1911. D. McKay.
Robert Fulton: An Historical Novel. Johannes Carsten Hauch & Sinding, Paul Christian, 1812-1887, Tr. LC 7-2598. 1868. Printed by Macdonald & Palmer.
Robert Gordon, M.D. Kathleen Harris, pseud. LC 46-380530. 1946. Arcadia House, Inc.
Robert Graham. A Novel. Caroline Lee Whiting Hentz. LC 7-4139. 1855. Parry & McMillan.
Robert Greathouse. An American Novel. John Franklin Swift. LC 8-25631. 1870. Carleton; Etc., Etc.
Robert Gregory: The History of a Little Soul. John Owen. LC 24-300338. E. P. Dutton & Company.
Robert Grossetete Carmina Anglo-Normannica. Ed. by M. Cooke. 1966. Repr. of 1852 ed. 18.00 o.p. B Franklin.
Robert Hardy's Seven Days: A Dream and Its Consequences. Charles Monroe Sheldon. LC 90-1841. (On cover: Alliance library, no. 2). Street & Smith.
Robert Hardy's Seven Days. A Dream and Its Consequences. rev. and authorized ed. Charles Monroe Sheldon. LC 29-8260. 1900. D. C. Cook Publishing Company.
Robert Kimberly. Frank Hamilton Spearman. 1911. C. Scribner's Sons.
Robert Louis Stevenson's Kidnapped: Followed by Who Killed the Red Fox? Being the True Account of the Famous Murder Mystery in "Kidnapped", Based on the Records of the Trail, Together with the Solution of the Murder Now Revealed for the First Time. Robert Louis Stevenson & Hersey, Frank Wilson Cheney. LC 38-20761. Ginn and Company.
Robert Louis Stevenson's The Black Arrow. Robert Louis Stevenson. Ed. by Schwelkert, Harry Christian. LC 31-10172. (Modern literature series). Ginn and Company.
Robert Louis Stevenson's Treasure Island. Robert Louis Stevenson. Ed. by Hamilton, Clayton Meeker. LC 10-114663. (Half-title: Longmans' English classics...). 1910. 0.25. Longmans' Green, and Co.
Robert Louis Stevenson's Treasure Island. Robert Louis Stevenson & Dunshee, Truman E. LC 36-18564. D. C. Heath and Company.
Robert Louis Stevenson's Treasure Island. Robert Louis Stevenson & Packer, Eleanor Lewis. (On cover: The big little books). Whitman Publishing Company.
Robert Martin's Lesson. american ed. Annie S Swan Smith. LC 8-8620. 1890. Cranston and Stowe.
Robert or, The Influence of a Good Mother: And Other Stories, Original and Translated. 1876. The Catholic Publication Society.
Robert Orange: By John Oliver Hobbes Pseud.... Pearl Mary Teresa Richards Craigie. LC 3651. Frederick A. Stokes Company.
Robert Ord's Atonement. Rosa Nouchette Carey. (On cover: Lovell's library, v. 19. no. 912). J. W. Lovell Company.

Robert Ord's Atonement. A Novel. Rosa Nouchette Carey. (On cover: Seaside library. Pocket ed. no. 396). G. Munro.

Robert Peckham. Maurice Baring. LC 30-22760. 1930. A. A. Knopf.

Robert Penn Warren: The Dark and Bloody Ground. Leonard Casper. LC 71-90479. 1969. (ISBN 0-8371-2131-0). Greenwood Press.

Robert Penn Warren's All the King's Men: A Critical Handbook. Ed. by Maurice Beebe, Leslie A. Field. Ed. by Beebe, Maurice & Leslie A. Field. LC 66-12643. (Wadsworth guides to lit. study). 3.00, text ed., pap., 2.25. Wadsworth.

Robert Reid: Cotton-Spinner. A Novel. Alice O'Hanlon. (Harper's Franklin square library, no. 328). 1883. Harper & Brothers.

Robert Sanders: Or, Light Out of Darkness. A Romance of Greenville and of the Pee Dee Section of South Carolina. T. W Hart. LC 7-2870. 1897. The Irving Co.

Robert Severne: His Friends and His Enemies. A Novel. William Alexander Hammond. LC 7-557. 1867. J. B. Lippincott & Co.

Robert Shenstone; a Novel. William James Dawson. LC 17-242100. 1917. John Lane Company.

Robert Silverberg Omnibus. Robert Silverberg. LC 80-8232. 12.95 (ISBN 0-06-014047-X). Harper & Row.

Robert Silverberg Omnibus: Downward to Earth, the Man in the Maze, & Nightwings. Robert Silverberg. LC 80-8232. 540p. 1981. 16.30i (ISBN 0-06-014047-X, HarpT). Har-Row.

Robert Taylor. Jane E. Wayne. 1976. pap. 1.95 (ISBN 0-532-19122-6, 0-532-19122). Woodhill.

Robert the Bruce: The Price of the King's Peace. Nigel G Tranter. LC 72-88427. (Illus.). 1972-1973. 7.50. St. Martin's Press.

Robert the Bruce: the Steps to the Empty Throne: The First of a Trilogy of Novels. Nigel G Tranter. LC 71-182057. (Illus.). 1971. 6.95. St. Martin's Press.

Robert Tournay: A Romance of the French Revolution. William Sage. LC 2140. 1900. Houghton, Mifflin and Company.

Robert Urquhart. Thomas Nicoll Hepburn. LC 7-4145. 1898. F. Warne & Co.

Robert Warren, the Texas Refugee. A Thrilling Story of Field and Camp Life During the Late Civil War. LC 43-26889. 1890. The Keystone Publishing Co.

Roberta: A Novel. Lilian Blanche Fearing. LC 6-38975. 1895. C. H. Kerr & Company.

Roberta, Lab Secretary: By Frances Dean Hancock Pseud. Jeanne Judson. LC 55-14470. 1955. Avalon Books.

Roberta of Roseberry Gardens. Frances Duncan. LC 16-9062. 1916. 1.25. Doubleday, Page & Company.

Roberte Ce Soir: And The Revocation of the Edict of Nantes. Pierre Klossowski. LC 69-18124. (Illus.). 1969. 6.00. Grove Press.

Robespierre Serial. Nicholas Luard. LC 74-22081. 1975. 6.95 (ISBN 0-15-178319-5). Harcourt Brace Jovanovich.

Robespierre: The Story of Victorien Sardon's Play, Adapted and Novelized Under His Authority. Ange Galdemar & Sardon, Victorien. LC 99-2238. 1899. Dodd, Mead and Company.

Robin. Frances Hodgson Burnett. LC 22-14719. Frederick A. Stokes Company.

Robin. Peggy Gaddis, pseud. pap. 0.50 o.p. (B50-678). Belmont-Tower.

Robin. Louisa Taylor Parr. LC 7-347148. (Leisure hour series, no. 140). 1882. H. Holt and Company.

Robin. Louisa Taylor Parr. (Lovell's library, no. 42). 1882. John W. Lovell Company.

Robin and Marian. James Goldman. (Illus.). 1976. (pbk.) 1.50. Bantam Books.

Robin Aroon: A Comedy of Manners. Armistead Churchill Gordon. LC 8-289890. 1908. The Neale Publishing Company.

Robin Blake: By Bette Allan Pseud. Elizabeth Ashbey. LC 51-2277. 1951. Gramercy Pub. Co.

Robin Gray. A Novel. Charles Gibbon. (Seaside library, v. 33, 690). 1880. G. Munro.

Robin Hill. Lida Larrimore Thomas. LC 32-28974. 1932. Macrae Smith Company.

Robin Hood. J. C. Holt. LC 81-53059. (Illus.). 208p. 1982. 17.95 (ISBN 0-500-25081-2). Thames Hudson.

Robin Hood: Prince of Outlaws. Alexandre Dumas. LC 66-5749. 1965. Dell Pub. Co.

Robin Hood's Barn. Alice Brown. LC 13-203478. 1913. The Macmillan Company.

Robin Linnet. Edward Frederic Benson. LC 19-19852. 1.75. George H. Doran Company.

Robin Must Be Fed. James Anthony Lemon. LC 55-8781. 1955. Comet Press Books.

Robin Redbreast in a Cage. Myrtle Johnston. LC 51-13317. 1951. Houghton Mifflin.

Robin the Bobbin. Vale Downie. LC 15-18967. 1915. Harper & Brothers.

Robin. 1st Ed. Doris Hedges. LC 57-10256. 1957. Vantage Press.

Robina. E. V. Timms. 1967. Repr. pap. 1.60 o.s.i. Tri-Ocean.

Robina Goes Modern. Jean Carew. LC 37-35650. 1937. Arcadia House.

Robineau Look. Kathleen Moore Knight. 1976. pap. 1.25 o.p. (ISBN 0-515-04150-5). Pyramid Pubns.

Robineau Look. 1st Ed. Kathleen Moore Knight. LC 55-7159. 1955. Published for the Crime Club by Doubleday.

Robinetta. Kate Douglas Smith Wiggin & Findlater, Mary, 1865- Joint Author. LC 11-4934. 1911. Houghton Mifflin Company.

Robino and Other Stories. Umberto Fracchia. Tr. by Scott, Sir Samuel Hasiam. LC 34-2908. 1933. R. O. Ballou.

Robinsheugh. Eileen Dunlop. LC 76-356204. (Illus.). 1975. 2.50 (ISBN 0-19-271371-X). Oxford University Press.

Robinson Christopher. Sherman A Noyes. LC 74-98187. 1970. Dorrance.

Robinson Crousoe: Travels and Adventures. by daniel defoe... ed. Daniel Defoe. LC 37-8148. (Immortal masterpieces of literatur. vol. ix). The Spencer Press.

Robinson Crusoe. Daniel Defoe. Ed. by Michael Shinagel. LC 74-34116. (Norton critical edition). 1975. 12.50 (ISBN 0-393-04407-6) (ISBN 0-393-09231-3). Norton.

Robinson Crusoe. Daniel Defoe. (Macmillan classics, 15). (Illus.). 1962. Macmillan.

Robinson Crusoe. Daniel Defoe. LC 67-350. (Legacy library facsimile). (Illus.). 1966. University Microfilms.

Robinson Crusoe. Daniel Defoe. Ed. by Goodrich Samuel Griswold. LC 6-32882. (On cover: Maynard's English classics series, Special no.). Maynard, Merrill & Co.

Robinson Crusoe. Daniel Defoe. Ed. by Shaw, Edward Richard. (On cover: Standard literature seriesd. no. 25). 1897. University Publishing Company.

Robinson Crusoe. Daniel Defoe. LC 4687. 1899. G. H. McKibbin.

Robinson Crusoe. Daniel Defoe. LC 6379. 1900. Dodd, Mead and Company.

Robinson Crusoe. Daniel Defoe. LC 13-20580. (On cover: The Washington square classics). 1913. G. W. Jacobs and Company.

Robinson Crusoe. Daniel Defoe. LC 20-20191. 1920. Cosmopolitan Book Corporation.

Robinson Crusoe. Daniel Defoe. Ed. by Peck, Lora B. LC 25-252806. The John C. Winston Company.

Robinson Crusoe. Daniel Defoe. LC 26-14343. (Sears illustrated juveniles). J. H. Sears & Company, Inc.

Robinson Crusoe. Daniel Defoe. Ed. by Hutchins, Henry Clinton. LC 30-15337. (modern readers' series). 1930. The Macmillan Company.

Robinson Crusoe. Daniel Defoe. LC 42-2565. (On cover: Classics club library). Pub. for the Classics Club by W. J. Black.

Robinson Crusoe. Daniel Defoe & Welsh, Charles. LC 3-17903. (Added t.-p.: Library for young people. vol. x). 1903. P. F. Collier & Son.

Robinson Crusoe: A New Adaptation of the Famous Old Story by Daniel Defoe. Ronald Telfer & Defoe, Daniel, 1661?-1731. Robinson Crusoe. LC 39-13911. Banner Play Bureau, Inc.

Robinson Crusoe: Adapted by Glenn Holder, Edited by Maurice Lapman. Daniel Defoe & Glenn Holder. LC 51-10984. 1951. Globe Book Co.

Robinson Crusoe: And A Journal of the Plague Year. Daniel Defoe. LC 48-11364. (Modern library of the world's best books). 1948. Modern Library.

Robinson Crusoe & Other Writings. Daniel Defoe. Ed. by James Sutherland. (YA) (gr. 9 up). 1968. pap. 1.75x o.p. (3-47737, RivEd, B103). HM.

Robinson Crusoe and Other Writings. Ed., Introd., Notes by James Sutherland. Daniel Defoe. Ed. by James Sutherland. (Riverside eds., B103). 1968. pap., 1.75. Houghton.

Robinson Crusoe & the Farther Adventures of Robinson Crusoe. Daniel Defoe. 320p. 1968. pap. 2.25 (ISBN 0-671-48953-4). WSP.

Robinson Crusoe for Young Readers. Daniel Defoe & Chappell, Louise A. LC 6-14754. A. Flanagan Company.

Robinson Crusoe, His Life on a Desert Island: Following the Language of the Original Text by Daniel De Foe (1661-1731. Daniel Defoe. Ed. by Lang, Ossian. LC 7-15548. 1907. A. S. Barnes & Company.

Robinson Crusoe in Words of One Syllable. Daniel Defoe. Ed. by Aikin, Lucy. 1882. McLoughlin Brothers.

Robinson Crusoe: In Words of One Syllable. Daniel Defoe. LC 99-3915. (Altemus' illustrated one syllable series. v. 4). H. Altemus.

Robinson Crusoe. Introd. by Charles Angoff. Daniel Defoe. LC 57-4960. 1957. Fine Editions Press.

Robinson Crusoe Reader. Daniel Defoe & Cowles, Julia (Darrow) LC 7-26458. A. Flanagan Company.

Robinson Crusoe: The Life and Strange Surprising Adventures of Robinson Crusoe, of York, Mariner: Who Lived Eight and Twenty Years All Alone in an Uninhabited Island on the Coast of America, Near the Mouth of the Great River of Orinoco; Having Been Cast on Shore by Shipwreck, Wherein All the Men Perished but Himself. With an Account How He Was at Last As Strangely Delivered by Pirates. Daniel Defoe & Kredel, Fritz, 1900- Illus. LC 45-4861. 1945. Doubleday, Doran and Company, Inc.

Robinson Crusoe's Return. Eric Odell. Ed. by R. Reginald & Douglas Menville. LC 75-46298. (Supernatural & Occult Fiction Ser.). 1976. Repr. of 1907 ed. lib. bdg. 10.00x (ISBN 0-405-08158-8). Ayer Co.

Robinson Crusoe's Return. Barry Eric Odell Pain & Daniel Defoe. LC 75-46298. (Supernatural and Occult Fiction). 1976. 10.00 (ISBN 0-405-08158-8). Arno Press.

Robinson of England. John Drinkwater. LC 37-19452. 1937. The Macmillan Company.

Robot and the Man: By John D. MacDonald and Others. 1st Ed. Ed. by Martin Greenberg. LC 53-9363. (Adventures in science fiction series). 1953. Gnome Press.

Robot Brains. Sydney J Bounds. LC 67-8605. 1967. Arcadia House.

Robot Failure. Lennart Bruce. 1.50 o.p. (Pub. by Cloud Marauder Pr). Panjandrum Pr.

Robot in the Closet. Ron Goulart. (Science Fiction Ser.). 160p. 1981. pap. 1.95 (ISBN 0-87997-626-8, UJ1626). DAW Bks.

Robot Rulers. George E. Shirley. 2.50 o.p. Vantage.

Robot Who Looks Like Me. Robert Sheckley. 192p. 1982. pap. 2.50 (ISBN 0-553-13031-5). Bantam.

Robots Have No Tails. Henry Kuttner. 1973. pap. 0.95 o.s.i. (75-464). Lancer.

Robots Have No Tails: By Lewis Padgett Pseud. 1st Ed. Henry Kuttner. LC 52-10383. 1952. Gnome Press.

Robsart Affair. Jennette Dowling Letton & Francis Letton. LC 78-3604. 1978. 9.95 (ISBN 0-89244-015-5). Queens House.

Robsart Affair: By Jennette and Francis Letton. Jennette Dowling Letton & Francis Letton. LC 56-6048. 1956. Harper.

Robthorne Mystery. Cecil John Charles Street. LC 34-17245. 1934. Dodd, Mead & Company.

Robur the Conqueror and Master of the World. Introd. by Major Alexander P. De Seversky, Internationally Known Aeronautical Expert. Jules Verne. 1951. Didier.

Rocannon's World. Ursula K. Le Guin. LC 75-419. (Garland Library of Science Fiction). 1975. 11.00 (ISBN 0-8240-1424-3). Garland Pub.

Rocannon's World. Ursula K. Le Guin. LC 76-47250. 1977. 6.95 (ISBN 0-06-012568-3). Harper & Row.

Rocannon's World. Ursula K. Le Guin. 144p. (Orig.). 1976. pap. 2.25 (ISBN 0-441-73295-X). Ace Bks.

Rocannon's World. Ursula K. Le Guin. Ed. by Lester Del Rey. LC 75-419. (Library of Science Fiction). 1975. lib. bdg. 17.50 (ISBN 0-8240-1424-3). Garland Pub.

Rocannon's World. Ursula K. Le Guin. 1974. (pbk.) 1.25. Ace Books.

Rochelle: Or, Virtue Rewarded. David R. Slavitt. (7585). 1968. Dell.

Rochelle: Or, Virtue Rewarded. David R. Slavitt. LC 67-20251. 1967. Delacorte Press.

Rochemer Hag. Louise W King. LC 67-20919. 1967. Published for the Crime Club by Doubleday.

Rocher Fendu: The Story of a Twain Parted from Kin and Country. John Lovell Rice. LC 15-21419. R. G. Badger; Etc., Etc.

Rochester's Wife. Dorothy Emily Stevenson. LC 40-12360. Farrar & Rinehart, Inc.

Rochester's Wife. Dorothy Emily Stevenson. LC 77-26134. 1978. 8.95 (ISBN 0-03-042616-2). Holt, Rinehart and Winston.

Rock. Hal Ellson. LC 55-8270. (Originals, 103). 1955. Ballantine Books.

Rock. Warren Tute. LC 59-7410. 1959. W. Sloane Associates.

Rock. Warren Tute. 1973. (pbk.) 1.50 (ISBN 0-345-23601-7). Ballantine Books.

Rock: A Novel. John Masters. LC 70-124094. 1970. 6.95. Putnam.

Rock: A Novel. David Wagoner. LC 58-9240. 1958. Viking Press.

Rock; a Story of the War. Bradfute Warwick. LC 13-11963. Broadway Publishing Company.

Rock & Other Stories. Siegfried Lenz. Ed. by C. A. Russ. 168p. (Orig.). 1967. pap. text ed. 4.50x (ISBN 0-435-38536-4). Heinemann Ed.

Rock and Roll Retreat Blues. Douglas Kent Hall. (Illus.). 1974. (pbk.) 1.50 (ISBN 0-380-00159-4). Avon.

Rock and Sand. John Rathbone Oliver. LC 30-259044. 1930. The Macmillan Company.

Rock and the River: A Romance of Quebec. Charles William Gordon. LC 31-32950. 1931. Dodd, Mead & Company.

Rock and the Sand. Gladys Zehnpfennig. LC 54-8416. 1954. Webb Pub. Co.

Rock and the Wind. Vivien R Bretherton. LC 42-762628. 1942. E. P. Dutton and Company, Inc.

Rock-Art Files. David T. Shore & Rosina M. Shore. (Illus.). 1978. pap. 5.95 (ISBN 0-9601804-1-9). Rock Pub.

Rock Cried Out. Ellen Douglas, pseud. LC 79-87474. 10.95 (ISBN 0-15-178322-5). Harcourt Brace Jovanovich.

Rock Cried Out. Edward Stanley. LC 49-4281. 1949. Duell, Sloan and Pearce.

Rock Crystal: A Christmas Tale. Adalbert Stifter & Mayer, Elizabeth, Tr. LC 45-10418. 1945. Pantheon Books.

Rock Crystal: A Christmas Tale. Tr. from German by Elizabeth Mayer, Marianne Moore. Illus. by Josef Scharl. Rev. Ed. Adalbert Stifter & Josef Scharl. LC 65-20663. 3.50, 3.39 lib. ed.,. Pantheon.

Rock Garden. Nikos Kazantzakis. 1969. pap. 3.95 o.p. (ISBN 0-671-20340-1, Touchstone Bks). S&S.

Rock Haven. Adelyn Bushnell. 1948. Coward-McCann.

Rock in Lingayen Beach & Other Stories. Gonzalo Quiogue. (Illus.). 1964. wrps. 3.50 o.p. Cellar.

Rock in the Baltic. Robert Barr. LC 6-16737. 1906. The Authors and Newspapers Association.

Rock Island Line. David Rhodes. LC 74-15888. 1975. 8.95 (ISBN 0-06-013559-X). Harper & Row.

Rock Nations. George W. Rae. (Orig.). 1971. pap. 0.95 o.p. (ISBN 0-446-65613-5, 65-613). Paperback Lib.

Rock Oak. Peggy O'More, pseud. LC 52-9343. 1952. Arcadia House.

Rock of Chickamauga. Charles King. LC 7-22113. 1907. G, W. Dillingham Company.

Rock of Chickamauga: A Story of the Western Crisis. Joseph Alexander Altsheler. LC 15-187263. (His The civil was series). 1915. D. Appleton and Company.

Rock of Decision. Bertha B. Moore McCurry. LC 31-15087. 1931. Wm. B. Eerdmans Publishing Co.

Rock of Decision. Bertha B Moore. LC 31-150874. Wm. B. Eerdmans Publishing Co.

Rock of Diamonds. James Quartermain, pseud. LC 79-150286. 1972. 4.95. Doubleday.

Rock of Life. Etienne Goddard Bolly. LC 45-820113. 1945. Wm. B. Eerdmans Publishing Company.

Rock of Refuge. Betty S Tigay. LC 53-12161. Vantage Press.

Rock Pool. Cyril Connolly. LC 68-55799. 1968. 3.95. Atheneum.

Rock Pool. Cyril Connolly. LC 37-1452. 1936. C. Scribner's Sons.

Rock Pool. Cyril Connolly. LC 49-11070. (Direction, 12). 1948. New Directions.

Rock Rude. Edward Stewart. LC 75-107267. 1970. 6.95. Simon and Schuster.

Rock Wagram: A Novel. William Saroyan. LC 51-9937. 1951. Doubleday.

Rock Wars. Rock Wars Company. 1979. pap. 6.95 o.p. (ISBN 0-385-15402-X, Dolp). Doubleday.

Rock Was Free. Paul Moss. LC 45-6676. 1945. Dorrance & Company.

Rockabye. Laird Koenig. LC 81-16568. 1981. (pbk.) 11.95 (ISBN 0-312-68793-1). St. Martin's Press.

Rockabye Contract. Philip Atlee. (Joe Gall Contract Ser). 1970. pap. 0.60 o.p. (R2228, GM). Fawcett World.

Rockafella. Les Scott et al. 1981. script 15.00x (ISBN 0-237-75054-6, Pub. by Evans Bros); script 15.00x. State Mutual Bk.

Rockbound. Frank Parker Day. LC 73-81763. (Literature of Canada: poetry and prose in reprint). 1973. 12.50 (ISBN 0-8020-1995-1) (ISBN 0-8020-1995-1). University of Toronto Press.

Rockbound. Frank Parker Day. LC 28-256336. 1928. Doubleday, Doran & Company, Inc.

Rockburg Railroad Murder. K. C. Constantine. 1982. pap. 6.95 (Nonpareil Bks). Godine.

Rockefeller Gift. Pauline Glen Winslow. LC 81-8588. 1980. 12.95 (ISBN 0-312-68795-8). St. Martin's Press.

Rocket. Jeffery Eardley Marston. LC 36-182671. 1936. Dodd, Mead & Company.

Rocket in the Night. Frances Clippinger. LC 53-9717. 1954. Random House.

Rocket Jockey. Lester Del Rey. 1982. pap. 1.95 (ISBN 0-345-30655-4, Del Rey). Ballantine.

Rocket Ship Galileo. Robert Anson Heinlein. 1975. (pbk.) 1.25. Ace Books.

Rocket to Luna. Richard Marsten. LC 52-12899. (Science fiction novel). 1953. Winston.

Rocket to the Moon. Thea Von Harbou. LC 77-5956. (Gregg Press science fiction series). 1977. 12.00 (ISBN 0-8398-2378-9). Gregg Press.

Rocket to the Moon: From the Novel. "The Girl in the Moon". Thea Von Harbou & Hutten Xum Stolzenburg, Betsey (Riddle) Freifrau Von, 1874- Tr. LC 30-10094. World Wide Publishing Co., Inc.

Rocket to the Morgue. Anthony Boucher. 1975. pap. 0.95 o.p. (ISBN 0-515-03567-X, N3567). BJ Pub Group.

Rocket to the Morgue. William Anthony Parker White. LC 42-51486. 1942. Duell, Sloan and Pearce.

Rockets in Ursa Major. Fred Hoyle & Geoffrey Hoyle. LC 77-110329. 1970. 4.95 o.p. (ISBN 0-06-011977-2, HarpT). Har-Row.

Rocketship. Robert Malone & J. C. Suares. LC 77-261. (Illus.). 1977. pap. 6.95i o.p. (ISBN 0-06-012851-8, TD-288, HarpT). Har-Row.

Rockford: A Romance. A B Seals. LC 6-24362. 1861. Franklin Printing House.

Rockford; or, Sunshine and Storm. Lillie Devereux Blake. LC 8-819118. 1863. Carleton.

Rockford Parish: Or, The Fortunes of Mr. Mason's Successors. John Nicholas Norton. 1856. Dana and Company; Etc., Etc.

Rockhaven. Charles Clark Munn. LC 2-8243. 1902. Lee and Shepard.

Rocking. Rosalind Wright. LC 74-15897. 1975. 6.95 (ISBN 0-06-014752-0). Harper & Row.

Rocking Arrow. Bertha Muzzy Sinclair. LC 32-17908. 1932. Little, Brown, and Company.

Rocking Horse: Children's Stories. Douglas Young. Ed. by Constance Hunting. (Illus.). 88p. (Orig.). 1982. pap. 5.95 (ISBN 0-913006-26-2). Puckerbrush.

Rocking-Horse Winner. David Herbert Lawrence. Ed. by Dominick Peter Consolo. LC 76-92599. (Merrill literary casebook series). 1969. C. E. Merrill Pub. Co.

Rocking Moon: A Romance of Alaska. Florance Barrett Willoughby. LC 25-8268. 1925. G. P. Putnam's Sons.

Rockinghorse. Yoram Kaniuk. LC 76-5546. 10.00 (ISBN 0-06-012245-5). Harper & Row.

Rocks and Romance. A Story. F Barrett Johnson. J. S. Ogilvie.

Rocks and Roses. Florence Derby. LC 57-1988. 1957. Eerdmans.

Rocks and Ruin. Hal Jason Calin. LC 54-5987. 1954. Vanguard Press.

Rocks and Shoals in the River of Life. A Novel. Bella French Swisher. 1889. G. W. Dillingham, Successor to G. W. Carleton & Co.

Rocks in the White Field. Temperance L. Thornton. 2.95 o.p. Vantage.

Rocks of Valpre. Ethel May Dell. LC 13-26183. 1913. 1.35. G. P. Putnam's Sons.

Rocks of Valpre. Ethel May Dell. LC 21-868692. A. L. Burt Company.

Rocksburg Railroad Murders. K. C. Constantine. 1973. 5.95 o.p. (ISBN 0-8415-0180-7). Dutton.

Rocksburg Railroad Murders; The Blank Page. K. C. Constantine. LC 81-47322. (Godine Double Detective). 1982. 6.95 (ISBN 0-87923-408-3). David R. Godine.

Rockspring. R. G. Vliet. LC 73-17787. 1974. 6.95 (ISBN 0-670-60247-7). Viking Press.

Rockton. A Story of Springtime Recreation. James O Knowles. LC 7-14187. 1891. Cranston & Stowe.

Rocktown, Arkansas: An Ozark Novel. 1st Ed. Otis Welton Coan. 1953. Exposition Press.

Rockwell Case. A Novel. O P Caylor. (Dillingham's metropolitan library, no. 18). 1896. G. W. Dillingham Co.

Rocky. Julia Sorel. 1977. pap. 1.95 (ISBN 0-345-27198-X). Ballantine.

Rocky. Sylvester Stallone. 1982. pap. 1.95 (ISBN 0-345-26236-0). Ballantine.

Rocky Bend. Jackson Gregory. LC 39-271662. 1939. Dodd, Mead & Company.

Rocky II. Sylvester Stallone. 1982. pap. 1.95 (ISBN 0-345-26237-9). Ballantine.

Rocky III. Sylvester Stallone. LC 82-1643. 1982. 2.75 (ISBN 0-345-30126-9). Ballantine Books.

Rocky Libido in San Francisco. Louis Felder. LC 62-15386. Contact Editions.

Rocky Mountain Feud. Hattie Horner Louthan. LC 11-192813. 1.25. The C. M. Clark Publishing Company.

Rocky Mountain Sam. Nathan D. Urner. (On cover: Sea and shore series, no. 21). 1890. Street & Smith.

Rocky Mountain Stories. Ed. by Ray Benedict West. LC 42-5129. (Sage Books). 1941. Swallow and Critchlow.

Rocky Mountain Vamp. Dirk Fletcher. (Spur Ser.: No. 4). 224p. (Orig.). 1982. pap. 2.50 o.s.i. (ISBN 0-8439-1180-8, Leisure Bks). Nordon Pubns.

Rocky Road to Jericho. Frank Chester Robertson. LC 35-16060. Hillman-Curl, Inc.

Rocky's Yarns. Rocky Reagan. LC 72-13476. (Illus.). 1973. 7.95 (ISBN 0-8111-0482-6). Naylor Co.

Rod and the Staff: A Novel. Marcus Beresford. LC 47-1460. 1947. Harper & Brothers.

Rod of Anger. Derrick Nabarro. LC 53-9732. 1953. W. Sloane Associates.

Rod of the Snake. Vere Dawson Shortt & Mathews, Mrs. Frances H. (Shortt) Joint Author. LC 18-5884. 1917. John Lane.

Rod Serling's Triple W: Witches, Warlocks, and Werewolves, a Collection. Ed. by Rod Serling. LC 63-14177. (Bantam book). 1963. Bantam Books.

Roden's Corner. Hugh Stowell Scott. LC 98-532426. 1898. Harper & Brothers.

Rodeo. Red Mitchell. (Rodeo Ser.: No. 1). 208p. (Orig.). 1981. pap. 2.25 (ISBN 0-523-41652-0). Pinnacle Bks.

Rodeo. Bertha Muzzy Sinclair. LC 29-138913. 1929. Little, Brown, and Company.

Rodeo. Bertha Muzzy Sinclair. LC 43-13635. 1943. Triangle Books.

Rodeo. Thomas Grant Springer. LC 37-813. Greenberg.

Rodeo: A Collection of the Tales and Sketches of R. B. Cunninghame Graham. Robert Bontine Cunninghame Graham & Tschiffely, Aime Felix. LC 36-35025. 1936. Doubleday, Doran and Company, Inc.

Rodeo Cowboy. Gene Lamb. LC 58-59730. 1959. Naylor Co.

Rodeo Cowboy. Charles Morris Martin. 1979. pap. 1.75 o.s.i. (ISBN 0-8439-0696-0, Leisure Bks). Nordon Pubns.

Rodeo Drive. Barney Leason. 416p. (Orig.). 1981. pap. 3.75 (ISBN 0-523-42054-4). Pinnacle Bks.

Rodeo, Number Two: Slayride. Red Mitchell. 208p. (Orig.). 1982. pap. 2.25 (ISBN 0-523-41653-9). Pinnacle Bks.

Rodeo Playboy. Scott Rainey. 1974. (pbk.) 1.95 (ISBN 0-87056-387-4). Brandon Books.

Rodeo Whirl: A Behind the Scenes Novel of America's Most Thrilling Spectacle, the Rodeo. Nina Fields Rippeteau. LC 51-4407. 1951. Naylor Co.

Roderick Hudson. Henry James. LC 77-1082. (Sentry edition; 85). 1977. 4.95 (ISBN 0-395-25353-5). Houghton Mifflin.

Roderick Hudson. Henry James. LC 7-7435. 1876. J. R. Osgood and Company.

Roderick Hudson. rev. ed. Henry James. LC 4-15128. 1882. Houghton, Mifflin and Company.

Roderick Hudson. Henry James. LC 46-30079. 1917. Houghton Mifflin Company.

Roderick Hudson. Henry James. LC 80-40626. (World's classics). 1980. 4.95 (ISBN 0-19-281547-4). Oxford University Press.

Roderick Hudson. Introd. by Leon Edel. Henry James. LC 60-2661. (Harper torchbooks. TB1016. The Academy library). 1960. Harper.

Roderick Hume: The Story of a New York Teacher. Charles William Bardeen. LC 6-7212. (On cover: School bulletin publications). 1878. Davis, Bardeen & Co.

Roderick Hume: The Story of a New York Teacher. 2d ed., from new plates. ed. Charles William Bardeen. LC 8-5760. (On cover: Standard teachers' library, no. 6). 1894. C. W. Bardeen.

Roderick Hume: The Story of a New York Teacher. 3d ed., with 26 full-page illustrations by miss l. a. shrimpton. ed. Charles William Bardeen. LC 5-4091. 1905. C. W. Bardeen.

Roderick of Kildare. A Novel. Sylvanus Cobb. (On cover: The popular series, no. 15). 1891. R. Bonner's Sons.

Roderick Random. Tobias George Smollett. (Half-title: Everyman's library, ed. by Ernest Rhys. Fiction. no. 790). 1927. J. M. Dent & Sons, Ltd.

Roderick Random. Tobias George Smollett. LC 36-37484. (Half-title: Everyman's library, ed. by Ernest Rhys. Fiction. no. 790). 1931. J. M. Dent & Sons, Ltd.

Roderick Talisferro: A Story of Maxmillian's Empire. George Cram Cook. 1903. The Macmillan Companyl Etc., Etc.

Roderick: The Education of a Young Machine, Vol. I. John Thomas Sladek. (Orig.). 1982. pap. 2.75 (Timescape). PB.

Roderick Wayne. Jessie Hunter Brown. LC 6-18934. 1889. Standard Publishing Company.

Roderick Wayne. Jessie Hunter Brown Pounds. LC 6-18934. 1889. Standard Publishing Company.

Rodger Latimer's Mistake: A Novel. Katharine Donelson. Laird & Lee.

Rodman the Boat-Steerer: And Other Stories. Louis Becke. LC 25-82168. 1924. J. B. Lippincott Company.

Rodman the Boat-Steerer, & Other Stories. facs. ed. Louis Becke. LC 70-125206. (Short Story Index Reprint Ser). 1924. 17.00 (ISBN 0-8369-3573-X). Ayer Co.

Rodman the Keeper: Southern Sketcher. Constance Fenimore Woolson. LC 8-37226. 1880. D. Appleton and Company.

Rodman the Keeper: Southern Sketches. Constance Fenimore Woolson. LC 69-11928. (American short story series, v. 87). 1969. (ISBN 0-512-00745-4). Garrett Press.

Rodman the Keeper: Southern Sketches. Constance Fenimore Woolson. LC 72-8166. (American short story series, v. 87). 1972. (ISBN 0-8422-8130-4). MSS Information Corp.

Rodman the Keeper: Southern Sketches. Constance Fenimore Woolson. LC 77-137310. 1971. 8.75 (ISBN 0-404-07038-8). AMS Press.

Rodman the Keeper: Southern Sketches. Constance Fenimore Woolson. 1886. Harper & Brothers.

Rodmoor: A Romance. a new ed. with a pref. by g. wilson knight. ed. John Cowper Powys. LC 73-77361. 1973. Cólgate University Press.

Rodmoor: A Romance. John Cowper Powys. LC 16-20552. 1916. 1.50. G. A. Shaw.

Rodney McGraw: A Story of the Big Show and the Cheerful Spirit. Arthur Emerson McFarlane. LC 9-28951. 1909. Little, Brown, and Company.

Rodney Stone. Arthur Conan Doyle. LC 6-34237. 1896. D. Appleton and Company.

Rodney Stone. Arthur Conan Doyle. LC 16-6991. 1911. D. Appleton and Company.

Rodney Stone. Arthur Conan Doyle. LC 16-1803. 1914. D. Appleton and Company.

Rodney Stone. Arthur Conan Doyle. LC 25-154930. 1924. D. Appleton and Company.

Rodney Stone. Arthur Conan Doyle. 6.75 o.p. Transatlantic.

Rodomont: A Romance of Mont St Michel in the Days of Louis Xiv. Henry Bedford-Jones. LC 26-21013. 1926. G.P. Putnam's Sons.

Rod's Salvation. Annie Eliot Trumbull. LC 98-195. 1898. A. S. Barnes and Company.

Roe Deer of Cranborne Chase: An Ecological Survey. Richard Prior & A. McDiarmid. LC 68-135026. (Illus.). 1968. 7.00x o.p. (ISBN 0-19-217620-X). Oxford U Pr.

Roebuck: a Novel. Charles Wells Russell. LC 8-1333. 1866. M. Doolady.

Roebuck: A Novel. Charles Wells Russell & Bledsoe, Albert Taylor. LC 41-42351. 1868. H. Taylor & Co.

Rogan. Hugh Marlowe. Orig. Title: Candle for the Dead. 224p. Date not set. pap. 0.75 o.p. (A985S, Award). Univ Pub & Dist.

Rogano: A Novel. Stephen Knight. LC 78-22335. 1979. 10.00 (ISBN 0-385-14763-5). Doubelday.

Roger Berkeley's Probation. A Story. Helen Stuart Campbell. 1888. Roberts Brothers.

Roger Camerden. A Strange Story. Samuel Hayes Elliot. LC 6-611996. 1887. G. J. Coombes.

Roger Casement. Brian Inglis. LC 73-15422. 1974. 8.95 (ISBN 0-15-178327-6). HarBraceJ.

Roger Drake, Captain of Industry: A Novel. Henry Kitchell Webster. LC 2-25600. 1902. The Macmillan Company.

Roger Hunt a Novel. Celia Parker Woolley. LC 8-37235. 1892. Houghton, Mifflin and Company.

Roger Martin Du Gard. Denis Boak. LC 63-5172. 5.60. Clarendon Pr. Dist. New York, Oxford.

Roger Martin Du Gard. Robert Donald Davidson Gibson. LC 62-295255. (Studies in modern European lit. and thought). 1962. bds., 12.00. Hillary.

Roger Martin Du Gard. Catharine H Savage, pseud. LC 67-30721. (Twayne's world authors series, 42). 1968. 4.50. Twayne Publishers.

Roger of Fairfield. Virginia Carter Castleman. LC 6-30468. 1906. The Neale Publishing Company.

Roger Sudden. Thomas Head Raddall. LC 45-3238. 1945. Doubleday, Doran and Company, Inc.

Roger, the Lodger. Elizabeth R Roberts. LC 47-31150. 1947. Greenberg.

Rogers' Folly. 1st Ed. Albert Edward Idell. LC 57-11425. 1957. Doubleday.

Rogerson at Bay: A Novel. Ralph M McInerny. LC 76-5108. 8.95 (ISBN 0-06-012944-1). Harper & Row.

Rogue. Janet Dailey. 1981. pap. 2.95 (ISBN 0-671-43665-1). PB.

Rogue. William Edward Norris. (On cover: Lovell's library, no. 1275). 1888. J. W. Lovell Company.

Rogue. William Edward Norris. (On cover: Seaside library. Pocket ed. no. 1141). 1888. G. Munro.

Rogue and the Witch. John Edward Newton. LC 55-5654. 1955. Abelard-Schuman.

Rogue Black. Raymond Giles. 208p. 1978. pap. 2.25 (ISBN 0-449-13809-7, GM). Fawcett.

Rogue Black. Raymond Giles. (Gold medal, M2824). 1973. (pbk.) 0.95. Fawcett.

Rogue by Compulsion: An Affair of the Secret Service. Victor Bridges. LC 15-18569. 1915. G. P. Putnam's Sons.

Rogue Cavalier. 1st Ed. Rosamond Van Der Zee Marshall. LC 55-7659. 1955. Doubleday.

Rogue Cop. William P McGivern. LC 54-598653. (Red badge detective). 1954. Dodd, Mead.

Rogue Country. John R Brannen. LC 51-2301. 1950. Chapman & Grimes.

Rogue Diamond. James Broom Lynne. LC 79-55621. 1980. 11.95 (ISBN 0-689-11048-0). Atheneum.

Rogue Eagle. James McClure. LC 76-9211. 8.95 (ISBN 0-06-012949-2). Harper & Row.

Rogue Eagle. James McClure. LC 77-353487. (Illus.). 1976. 3.50 (ISBN 0-333-19698-8). Macmillan.

Rogue Eagle. James McClure. 1979. (ISBN 0-380-42267-0). Avon Books.

Rogue Elephant. Walter Ernest Allen. LC 46-73465. 1946. W. Morrow & Co.

Rogue Errant. Michael Leigh. LC 51-13091. 1951. Crowell.

Rogue from Padus. Jay Williams. LC 52-5525. 1952. Little, Brown.

Rogue Hercules. Denis Pitts. LC 77-88904. 1978. 6.95. Atheneum Publishers.

Rogue Herries. Hugh Walpole. LC 30-265645. 1930. Doubleday, Doran & Company, Inc.

Rogue Herries: A Novel. Hugh Walpole. 1930. 9.00 o.p. (ISBN 0-312-68915-2). St Martin.

Rogue in Space. Fredric Brown. LC 57-5347. 1957. Dutton.

Rogue Justice. Geoffrey Household. 192p. 1983. 14.00i (ISBN 0-316-37440-7, Pub. by Atlantic Monthly Pr). Little.

Rogue Male. Geoffrey Household. LC 39-27659. 1939. Little, Brown and Company.

Rogue Moon. Algis Budrys, pseud. LC 77-4497. (Gregg Press science fiction series; 3). 1977. 11.00 (ISBN 0-8398-2369-X). Gregg Press.

Rogue of Falconhurst. Ashley Carter, pseud. 384p. 1983. pap. 3.50 (ISBN 0-449-12514-9, GM). Fawcett.

Rogue of Gor. John Norman. (Science Fiction Ser.). 1981. pap. 2.50 (ISBN 0-87997-602-0, UE1602). Daw Bks.

Rogue of the African Night. Harold Lowther Beaver. LC 66-23219. (Illus.). 1966. Dodd, Mead.

Rogue: Or, The Life of Guzman De Alfarache. Mateo Aleman. Tr. by James Mabbe. LC 73-159349. (Series: The Tudor Translations, 2d Ser., V. 2-5.). (Illus.). 1967. AMS Press.

Rogue Planet. Dan Dare. (Illus.). 112p. 1981. pap. 9.95 (Quick Fox). Putnam Pub Group.

Rogue Planet. Frank Hampson & Don Harley. (Dan Dare Ser.: Vol. 2). 104p. 1981. pap. 9.95 (ISBN 0-8256-9553-8, Pub. by Dragon's Dream Holland). Music Sales.

Rogue Planet. E. C Tubb. (Space: 1999 series). 1.50 (ISBN 0-671-80710-2). Pocket Books.

Rogue Queen. Lyon Sprague De Camp. LC 51-11464. 1972. New Amer. Lib.

Rogue Rancher. Will Travers, pseud. (Orig.). 1980. pap. 1.75 (ISBN 0-505-51602-0). Tower Bks.

Rogue River Cowboy. Lauran Paine. LC 56-11697. 1956. Arcadia House.

Rogue River Feud. Zane Grey. 1975. (pbk.) 1.25 (ISBN 0-671-68015-3). Pocket Books.

Rogue River Feud. Zane Grey. LC 48-3221. 1948. Harper.

Rogue Roman. Lance Horner. 1978. pap. 2.25 (ISBN 0-449-13968-9, GM). Fawcett.

Rogue Running. Maurice Procter. LC 67-10494. 1966. Harper & Row.

Rogue Sergeant. Lawrence Cortesi, pseud. 224p. 1982. pap. 2.50 o.p. (ISBN 0-505-51854-6). Tower Bks.

Rogue Sergeant. Lawrence Cortesi, pseud. 208p. 1983. pap. 2.50 (ISBN 0-8439-2016-5, Leisure Bks). Dorchester Pub Co.

Rogue Sheriff. James Wyckoff. (Dell Book). 1977. 1.25 (ISBN 0-440-14138-9). Dell Pub. Co.

Rogue Ship. Alfred Elton Van Vogt. LC 65-19922. 4.50. Doubleday.

Rogue Ship. Alfred Elton Van Vogt. 1980. 1.95 (ISBN 0-87997-536-9). DAW Books.

Rogue Slave. Lionel Webb. 1977. pap. 1.75 (ISBN 0-532-17161-6). Woodhill.

Rogue Slave. Lionel Webb. (Orig.). 1969. pap. 0.95 o.p. (75-061). Lancer.

Rogue Song. Val Lewton. LC 30-7429. A. L. Burt Company.

Rogue Sword. Poul Anderson. 256p. (Orig.). 1980. pap. 2.25 (ISBN 0-89083-638-8). Zebra.

Rogue Valley: A Novel. Verne Athanas. LC 53-7680. 1953. Simon and Schuster.

Rogue Wind: Translated from the Italian by Giuseppina T. Salvadori and Bernice L. Lewis. Ugo Moretti. LC 53-962812. 1953. Prentice-Hall.

Rogue Worth Trapping: Or, Nick Carter's King of Crooks. Nick Carter & Dey, Frederic Van Rensselaer. LC 34-382743. (On cover: New magnet library. no. 867). Street & Smith.

Rogue Yates. 1st American Ed. Tom Ronan. LC 57-673619. 1957. Putnam.

Rogues. George Smith. LC 80-81006. (American Freedom: No. 2). 400p. (Orig.). 1980. pap. 2.75 (ISBN 0-87216-630-9). Playboy Pbks.

Rogues & Company. Ida Alexa Ross Wylie. LC 21-11025. 1921. John Lane Company.

Rogues and Diamonds. Selwyn Jepson. LC 25-9297. 1925. L. Macveagh, The Dial Press.

Rogues and Riches. Rick Lucas. LC 54-2279. 1954. Vixen Press.

Rogues and Vagabonds. Compton Mackenzie. LC 27-84594. George H. Doran Company.

Rogues and Vagabonds. George Robert Sims. (On cover: Seaside library. Pocket ed. no. 816). 1886. G. Munro.

Rogue's Badge. Charles Neville Buck. LC 24-22270. 1924. Doubleday, Page & Company.

Rogue's Castle. Sandra Stanley. (Ravenswood gothic). 1974. (pbk.) 0.95 (ISBN 0-671-77930-3). Pocket Books.

Rogue's Coat. Theodora McCormick Du Bois. LC 49-89623. 1949. Pub. for the Crime Club by Doubleday.

Rogues' Company: A Novel of John Murrell. Harry Harrison Kroll. LC 43-162181. 1943. The Bobbs-Merrill Company.

Rogue's Conscience. David Christie Murray. 1899. F. M. Buckles & Company; Etc., Etc.

Rogue's Covenant. Sylvia Thorpe. LC 78-3754. 1978. 9.95 (ISBN 0-89340-149-8). J. Curley.

Rogues' Covenant. Sylvia Thorpe. 1976. 1.50 (ISBN 0-449-23041-4). Fawcett Crest.

Rogue's Daughter: By Adeline Sergeant... Adeline Sergeant. LC 8-6859. F. A. Stokes Company.

Rogues Fall Out. Herbert Adams. LC 26-65189. 1928. J. B. Lippincott Company.

Rogues' Gallery: A Variety of Mystery Stories. Ed. by Walter Brown Gibson. LC 68-22469. (Illus.). 1969. 5.95. Doubleday.

Rogues' Gallery: The Great Criminals of Modern Fiction. Ed. by Ellery Queen, pseud. LC 45-8207. 1945. Little, Brown and Company.

Rogues' Gallery: The Great Criminals of Modern Fiction. Ed. by Ellery Queen, pseud. LC 47-6082. 1947. Sun Dial Press.

Rogue's Harbor. Inglis Clark Fletcher. LC 63-23359. 1964. Bobbs-Merrill.

Rogues' Haven. Roy Bridges. LC 22-149942. 1922. D. Appleton and Company.

Rogue's Heiress: A Novel. Tom Gallon. LC 10-30147. 1.50. G. W. Dillingham Company.

Rogue's Holiday... Maxwell March. LC 35-13816. 1935. Pub. for the Crime Club, Inc., by Doubleday, Doran & Company, Inc.

Rogue's Holiday: A Novel. Hamilton Cochran. LC 47-209863. 1947. The Bobbs-Merrill Company.

Rogues in Clover. Percival Wilde. LC 29-1674. 1929. D. Appleton & Company.

Rogues in the House. Robert E. Howard. 15.00 (ISBN 0-937986-25-9). D M Grant.

Rogue's Island. Barry Perowne. LC 50-5368. 1950. Mill.

Rogues' Kingdom. John Brick. LC 65-13100. 1965. Doubleday.

Rogue's Lady. Paula Allardyce, pseud. LC 78-61744. 1978. 1.50 (ISBN 0-87216-500-0). Playboy Press.

Rogue's Lady. Anne Devon. 192p. 1982. pap. 1.75. Jove Pubns.

Rogue's Legacy. Leonard London Foreman. 1974. (pbk.) 0.95. Ace Books.

Rogue's Legacy. Leonard London Foreman. LC 68-17814. (Double D western). 1968. Doubleday.

Rogue's Legacy: A Novel About Francois Villon. Babette Deutsch. LC 42-2906. Coward-McCann, Inc.

Rogue's March. Maristan Chapman. LC 49-6827. 1949. J. B. Lippincott Co.

Rogues' March. Ivan Obolensky. LC 56-6350. 1956. Random House.

Rogues' March. Margaret Turnbull. LC 28-20463. 1928. J. B. Lippincott Company.

Rogue's March: A Novel. W. T Tyler. LC 82-47544. 14.95 (ISBN 0-06-015048-3). Harper & Row.

Rogue's March: A Romance. Ernest William Hornung. LC 7-5192. 1896. C. Scribner's Sons.

Rogue's Mistress. Constance Gluyas. (Orig.). 1977. pap. 2.95 (ISBN 0-451-11099-4, AE1099, Sig). NAL.

Rogue's Moon. Robert William Chambers. LC 28-19239. 1928. D. Appleton and Company.

Rogue's Moon. Robert William Chambers. 1929. D. Appleton & Company.

Rogues of the North. Albert M Treynor. LC 22-792857. 1922. Chelsea House.

Rogue's Range. Archie Joscelyn. LC 68-3387. 1968. Arcadia House.

Rogue's Rendezvous. Nelson Nye. 128p. (Orig.). 1976. pap. 1.95 (ISBN 0-441-73425-1). Ace Bks.

Rogue's Rendezvous. Nelson Nye. 128p. 1982. pap. 1.95 (ISBN 0-441-73426-X, Pub. by Charter Bks). Ace Bks.

Rogues' Road: Seven Turbulent Days in the Lives of Francis Talbot, His Wife Dorothy, and the Scamp--Risks and Rescues Which Befell in the Summer of 1726. Virgil Markham. LC 30-30779. 1930. The Macmillan Company.

Rogue's Yarn. John Edward Jennings. LC 53-6452. 1953. Little, Brown.

Rokudan: A Tale of Love in Six Movements. Pat Burch. LC 80-29375. 8.95 (ISBN 0-8008-6818-8). Taplinger Pub. Co.

Roland Blake. Silas Weir Mitchell. LC 7-31092. 1886. Houghton, Mifflin and Company.

Roland Blake. 9th ed. Silas Weir Mitchell. LC 16-250466. 1901. The Century Co.

Roland Cashel. Charles James Lever. LC 12-24353. (On cover: Novels of adventure). 1907. Little, Brown, and Company.

Roland Graeme; Knight: A Novel of Our Time. Agnes Maule Machar. LC 7-19999. Fords, Howard & Hulbert.

Roland Oliver: A Novel. Justin McCarthy. LC 3-22378. (On cover: Lovell's international series, no. 37). 1889. F. F. Lovell & Company.

Roland, the Warrior. Virginia MacMakin Collier & Eaton, Jeanette. LC 34-27292. Harcourt, Brace and Company.

Roland Whately: A Novel. Alec Waugh. LC 22-18782. 1922. The Macmillan Company.

Roland Yorke. A Sequel to "The Channings". Ellen Price Henry Wood Wood. T. B. Peterson & Brothers.

Roland Yorke. A Sequel to "The Channings.". Ellen Price Henry Wood Wood. (Seaside library, v. 16, no. 310). 1878. G. Munro.

Rolande. Clare Darcy. 1979. lib. bdg. 10.95 o.p. (ISBN 0-8161-6670-6, Large Print Bks). G K Hall.

Rolande. Clare Darcy. 1979. pap. 1.95 (ISBN 0-451-08552-3, J8552, Sig). NAL.

Rolande. Clare Darcy. LC 77-85242. 1978. 8.95 (ISBN 0-8027-0588-X). Walker & Co.

Roland's Daughter: A Nineteenth-Century Maiden. Julia MacNair Wright. LC 9-52324. Presbyterian Board of Publication.

Role in Manila: Fifteen Tales of War. Postwar, Peace. and Adventure. Eugene Burdick. LC 66-251138. 1966. 4.95. New Amer. Lib.

Role of the Unconquered. Test Dalton. LC 2-3447. 1901. G. W. Dillingham Co.

Roles. Elizabeth Alexander. LC 24-7479. 1924. Little, Brown, and Company.

Rolinda: A Tale of the Mississinewa. Rolland Lewis Whitson. The Champlin Press.

Roll Back the Sea: A Novel by A. Den Doolaard Pseud. C Spoelstra. Tr. by Mussey, June Barrows. LC 48-3298. 1948. Simon and Schuster.

Roll Back the Sky: A Novel. Ward Taylor. LC 56-6463. 1956. Holt.

Roll-Call. Arnold Bennett. LC 74-17047. (Collected works of Arnold Bennett). 1974. (ISBN 0-518-19152-4). Books for Libraries Press.

Roll-Call. Arnold Bennett. LC 19-138. George H. Doran Company.

Roll Call of Death. Param Jit Kumar. LC 76-153369. 1971. 6.95 (ISBN 0-87141-033-8). Manyland Books.

Roll, Jordan, Roll. Dorothy Park Clark. LC 47-631. 1947. Pub. for the Crime Club by Doubleday & Company, Inc.

Roll of Honor. authorized ed. Annie Hall Thomas Cudlip. LC 6-31160. (Lovell's international ser. no. 149). United States Book Company, Successors to J. W. Lovell Company.

Roll of Thunder, Hear My Cry. Mildred Taylor. (gr. 8-12). 1978. pap. 2.25 (ISBN 0-553-20444-0). Bantam.

Roll on: Pioneers. Fred Lape. LC 35-8037. Godwin.

Roll River. James Boyd. LC 25-27166. 1935. C. Scribner's Sons.

Roll, Shenandoah. Bruce Lancaster. LC 56-106524. 1956. Little, Brown.

Roll the Wagons. William Heuman. LC 51-22487. (Gold Medal book, 146). 1951. Gold Medal Books.

Roll the Wagons: By Brett Austin Pseud. Lee Floren. LC 56-701572. 1956. Arcadia House.

Roll-Top Desk Mystery: A Fleming Stone Story. Carolyn Wells. LC 32-843091. 1932. J. B. Lippincott Company.

Roll up the Wallpaper, We're Moving! How to Rip up Family Roots and Plant Them in a Brave New Green World with Unbelievable Shock to the Nerve Endings and the Pocketbook. William C Anderson. LC 70-108075. 1970. 5.95. Crown Publishers.

Rolled Away. Lydia L Rouse. LC 8-697. American Baptist Publication Society.

Roller Ball Murder. William Harrison. LC 73-20052. 1974. 5.95 (ISBN 0-688-00265-X). Morrow.

Roller Derby Girl. Frederick Colson, pseud. (Orig.). pap. 0.95 o.p. (1114). Brandon.

Rollicking Rogue. Johnston McCulley. LC 42-242276. 1941. Arcadia House, Inc.

Rollicking Shore. E R Karr. LC 60-109447. 1960. McDowell, Obolensky.

Rolling Acres. Bessie Ray Hoover. LC 22-18401. Small, Maynard & Company.

Rolling All the Time (Stories) James Ballard. LC 76-13475. (Illinois Short Fiction Ser). 1976. 11.95 (ISBN 0-252-00613-5); pap. 4.95 (ISBN 0-252-00614-3). U of Ill Pr.

Rolling Heads. Aaron Marc Stein. LC 78-69671. 1979. 7.95 (ISBN 0-385-14643-4). Published for the Crime Club by Doubleday.

Rolling Ridge: Or, The Book of Four and Twenty Chapters... Samuel Hayes Elliot. LC 7-1243. 1838. Crocker and Brewster.

Rolling River Range. Lee Floren. LC 50-12636. 1950. Phoenix Press.

Rolling Road. 3d ed. Ernest Andrew Ewart. LC 73-110186. (Short story index reprint series). 1970. Books for Libraries Press.

Rolling Stone. Bithia Mary Sheppard Croker. LC 12-16966. 1912. Brentano's.

Rolling Stone. Westmoreland Gray. LC 32-24131. The Bobbs-Merrill Company.

Rolling Stone. George Sand & Owen, Carroll. LC 15-6310. 1871. J. R. Osgood and Company.

Rolling Stone: A Mystery Novel. Patricia Wentworth. LC 40-4197. J. B. Lippincott Company.

Rolling Stone: A Novel. Catharine Amy Dawson Scott. LC 20-13696. 1920. A. A. Knopf.

Rolling Stone; or, the Adventures of Wanderer. Horatio Alger. 294p. 1974. Repr. of 1902 ed. lib. bdg. 15.95x (ISBN 0-88411-806-1). Amereon Ltd.

Rolling Stones. Robert Anson Heinlein. (Del Rey Book). 1977. 1.50 (ISBN 0-345-26067-8). Ballantine Books.

Rolling Stones. William Sydney Porter. LC 13-117. 1912. Doubleday, Page & Company.

Rolling Stones. William Sydney Porter. Ed. by Steger, Harry Peyton. LC 15-174122. 1913. Doubleday, Page & Company.

Rolling Stones. William Sydney Porter. LC 22-16020. 1919. Doubleday, Page & Company, for Review of Reviews Co.

Rolling Stones. William Sydney Porter. LC 33-17508. 1926. Doubleday, Page & Company.

Rolling Stones. Ferdinand Anthony Stahl. LC 28-29241. 1829.

Rolling Thunder. Doug Boyd. 1976. pap. 6.95 (ISBN 0-440-57435-8, Delta). Dell.

Rolling Thunder. Richard L Graves. (Kangaroo Book.). 1977. 1.75 (ISBN 0-671-81201-7). Pocket Books.

Rolling Westward: Illustrated by Louis Macouillard. Fern Row Casebeer. LC 54-752856. 1954. Pacific Press Pub. Association.

Rolling Years. Agnes Sligh Turnbull. LC 36-3326. 1936. The Macmillan Company.

Rollo in Hawaii. Max Nodaway. 1908. Thompson & Thomas.

Rollo of Normandy: A Novel. Sylvanus Cobb. (On cover: The popular series, no. 2). 1891. R. Bonner's Sons.

Rollo of Normandy. A Novel. Sylvanus Cobb. (On cover: The choice series, no. 135). (On cover: Ledger library, no. 135). 1897. R. Bonner's Sons.

Rolltown. Reynolds, Mack. 1976. 1.50. Ace Books.

Roma. Tr. from Italian by Mihaly Csikszentmihalyi. Aldo Palazzeschi. 4.50. Regnery.

Romain Kalbris. His Adventures by Sea and Shore. Hectory Henri Malot & Wright, Mrs. Julia (MacNair) 1840-1903, Tr. LC 7-24300. Porter & Coates.

Romain Kalbris: The Adventures of a Runaway by Land and Sea. Hector Henri Malot & Serrano, Mrs. Mary Jane (Christie) Tr. LC 7-16804. (On cover: Harper's Franklin square library. no. 705). 1891. Harper & Brothers.

Romain Rolland's Jean-Christophe. Romain Rolland. Tr. by Gilbert Canaan. LC 27-27822. 1927. H. Holt and Company.

Roman. Mika Toimi Waltari. pap. 1.95 (ISBN 0-425-03107-1, Medallion). Berkley Pub.

Roman Affair. Translated from the Italian by Constantine Fitzgibbon. Ercole Patti. LC 57-11893. 1957. W. Sloane Associates.

Roman and a Jew: A Tale of Jerusalem. Nick B Williams. LC 42-2248. Broadman Press.

Roman Biznet. Georgia Wood Pangborn. LC 2-12215. 1902. Houghton, Mifflin and Company.

Roman Candle. Glen Chase, pseud. (Cherry Delight Ser.). (Orig.). 1975. pap. 1.25 o.p. (LB2932K, Leisure Bks). Nordon Pubns.

Roman Comedy: An Impolite Extravaganza. Whitfield Cook. LC 51-11670. 1951. Coward-McCann.

Roman de la Monie. Theophile Gautier. Ed. by Boschot. (Coll. Prestige). 17.95. French & Eur.

Roman de Rose: Par Guillaume De Lorris. Roman De la Rose & II. Guiliaume De Lorris. Ed. by Stephen G. Nichols. LC 67-251142. (Series in Medieval French Literature). 1967. Appleton-Century-Crofts.

Roman Enigma. Walter F. Murphy. LC 81-11792. 12.95 (ISBN 0-02-588250-3). Macmillan.

Roman Fever, and Other Stories. Edith Newbold Jones Wharton. LC 64-11254. (Scribner library books). 1964. Scribner.

Roman Folly. Alice Leone Moats. LC 65-14709. 1965. Harcourt, Brace & World.

Roman Go Home. Adam Fergusson. LC 77-81644. (Illus.). 1969. 5.95. Putnam.

Roman Gold. Michael Arthur Lewis. LC 29-65. 1928. Houghton Mifflin Company.

Roman Hat Mystery. Ellery Queen. 325p. 1976. lib. bdg. 15.95x (ISBN 0-89966-147-5). Buccaneer Bks.

Roman Hat Mystery. Ellery Queen, pseud. LC 78-64323. 1979. Repr. of 1929 ed. 10.00 (ISBN 0-89296-045-0). Mysterious Pr.

Roman Hat Mystery. Ellery Queen, pseud. pap. 2.50 (ISBN 0-451-11836-7, AE1836, Sig). NAL.

Roman Hat Mystery: A Problem in Deduction. Ellery Queen, pseud. LC 29-26789. 1929. Frederick A. Stokes Company.

Roman Hat Mystery: A Problem in Deduction. Ellery Queen, pseud. LC 42-23860. 1942. Triangle Books.

Roman Hat Mystery, a Problem in Deduction. Ellery Queen, pseud. LC 78-64323. (Illus.). 1979. 10.00 (ISBN 0-89296-045-0). Mysterious Press.

Roman Holiday. Don Ryan. LC 30-3356. 1930. The Macaulay Company.

Roman Holiday. Upton Beall Sinclair. LC 31-119816. Farrar & Rinehart, Incorporated.

Roman Holiday: The Catholic Novels of Evelyn Waugh. A. A. De Vitis. LC 56-4435. 1956. Bookman Associates.

Roman Holiday: The Catholic Novels of Evelyn Waugh. A. A De Vitis. LC 71-153314. 1971. (ISBN 0-404-02119-0). AMS Press.

Roman Hookers. Aretino, Jr. (Orig.). 1973. pap. 0.95 o.p. (09181). Curtis.

Roman Joy. Edward Carl Stephens. LC 65-12372. 4.95. Doubleday.

Roman Magic. Hugh Fleetwood. LC 77-12547. 1978. 7.95 (ISBN 0-689-10839-7). Atheneum.

Roman Maiden: Or, The Story of the Lost Vestal. Emma Martin Marshall. G. W. Jacobs & Co.

Roman Marriage. Brian Glanville. LC 67-15276. 1967. Coward-McCann.

Roman Nights: Or, The Tomb of the Scipios. Alessandro Verri. LC 8-30004. 1825-26. E. Bliss & E. White.

Roman Nights: Or, The Tomb of the Scipios. Alessandro Verri. 1850. J. Ball.

Roman Novel. The 'Satyricon' of Petronius and the 'Metamorphoses' of Apuleius. Patrick Gerard Walsh. LC 70-98700. 1970. University Press.

Roman Orgy. Marcus Van Heller, pseud. pap. 1.95 o.p. (ISBN 0-87056-232-0). Brandon.

Roman Pictures. Percy Lubbock. LC 46-36491. 1923. C. Scribner's Sons.

Roman Policier. Pierre Boileau & Thomas Narcejac. 1964. pap. 1.60 o.s.i. Paris Pubns.

Roman Road. Gwendoline Keats. LC 71-157782. (Short story index reprint series). 1971. (ISBN 0-8369-3894-1). Books for Libraries Press.

Roman Road. Gwendoline Keats. LC 3-11161. 1903. C. Scribner's Sons.

Roman Scandal: The Story of Beatrice Cenci: a Novel. Susanne Kircher. LC 76-20526. 1976. 8.95 (ISBN 0-88405-362-8). Mason/Charter.

Roman Singer. Francis Marion Crawford. LC 6-30887. 1884. Houghton, Mifflin and Company.

Roman Singer. Francis Marion Crawford. 1893. Macmillan & Co.

Roman Singer. Francis Marion Crawford. LC 13-20466. (On cover: The works of F. Marion Crawford). 1910. The Macmillan Company; Etc., Etc.

Roman Spring of Mrs. Stone. Tennessee Williams. LC 50-9067. 1950. New Directions.

Roman Summer. Ludwig Lewisohn. LC 27-3550. 1927. Harper & Brothers.

Roman Tales. Alberto Moravia. 1974. (pbk.) 1.50. Manor Books.

Roman Tales. Alberto Moravia. LC 75-26219. 1975. 12.75 (ISBN 0-8371-8412-6). Greenwood Press.

Roman Tales. Alberto Moravia. LC 75-26219. 1975. (ISBN 0-8371-8412-6). Greenwood Press.

Roman Tales: By Alberto Moravia Pseud. Selected and Translated by Angus Davidson. Alberto Pimcherle. LC 57-8717. 1957. Farrar, Straus and Cudahy.

Roman: The Memoirs of Minus Lausus Manilianus, Who Has Won the Insignia of a Triumph, Who Has the Rank of Consul, Who Is Chairman of the Priests' Collegium of the God Vespasian and a Member of the Roman Senate. Mika Toimi Waltari. LC 66-15593. 1966. G. P. Putnam's Sons.

Roman: The Memoirs of Minutus Lausus Manilianus, Who Has Won the Insignia of a Triumph, Who Has the Rank of Consul, Who Is Chairman of the Priests' Collegium of the God Vespasian and a Member of the Roman Senate. English Version by Joan Tate. Abridged Ed. Mika Toimi Waltari. (Medallion bk., N1434). 1967. Berkley.

Roman Traitor: Or, The Days of Cicero, Cato and Cataline. A True Tale of the Republic. Henry William Herbert. LC 11-150897. T. B. Peterson & Brothers.

Roman Traitor: Or, The Days of Ciecro, Cato and Cataline. A True Tale of the Republic. Henry William Herbert. LC 22-14557. T. B. Peterson and Brothers.

Roman Vergil. Revised Ed. William Francis Jackson Knight. LC 66-74262. (Peregrine books) 15/-). 1966. Penguin.

Roman Wall: A Novel. Winifred Bryher. 1965. pap., 1.95. Pantheon.

Roman Wall: A Novel. Winifred Bryher. LC 54-7067. 1954. Pantheon Books.

Roman Year. Isabel Constance Clarke. LC 37-885. 1936. Longmans, Green and Co.

Romance. Joseph Conrad & Ford Madox Ford. LC 4-10852. 1901. McClure, Phillips & Co.

Romance. Joseph Conrad & Ford Madox Ford. LC 22-164810. 1920. Doubleday, Page & Company.

Romance. Gwen Davis. 1983. 14.50 (ISBN 0-87795-497-6). Arbor Hse.

Romance. LC 82-463262. (No-Frills Book). 1981. 1.50 (ISBN 0-515-06246-4). Jove Publications.

Romance. Natalie Anderson Scott. LC 51-14033. 1951. Dutton.

Romance: A Novel. Acton Davies & Sheldon, Edward Brewster. LC 13-10542. 1913. The Macaulay Company.

Romance Along the Bayou. Sallie Lee Bell. LC 64-22833. 1964. Zondervan Pub. House.

Romance and Jane Weston. Richard Pryce. LC 24-25744. 1924. Houghton Mifflin Company.

Romance & Reality. Holbrook Jackson. 1911. Repr. 15.00 o.p. (ISBN 0-8274-3912-1). R West.

Romance and Reality. Martin Sindell. LC 19-16154. 1919. Paramount Publishing Company.

Romance and Revolution. Martin Sindell. LC 18-22894. 1918. Paramount Publishing Company.

Romance and Rome. Historical. Almus Hugh Edwards. LC 1-29475. The Abbey Press.

Romance and Tragedy in Joseph Conrad. Walter Francis Wright. LC 49-9417. 1949. Univ. of Nebraska Press.

Romance at Red Pines: A Novel. Elizabeth Rice Handford. LC 60-2642. 1960. Zondervan Pub. House.

Romance at Redhaven. Kathleen Yapp. (Chime Romance Ser.: No. 101). 1980. pap. 2.50 (ISBN 0-89191-292-4). Cook.

Romance at Redhaven. Kathleen Yapp. (Chime Ser.). 1982. pap. 2.50 o.p. Caroline Hse.

Romance at the Antipodes. R. Dun. Douglass. LC 6-35880. 1890. G. P. Putnam's Sons.

Romance: By Joseph Conrad and F. M. Hueffer. Joseph Conrad & Ford Madox Ford. LC 50-14824. 1950. Doubleday.

Romance by Request. Steuart MacKie Emery. LC 30-104655. Macrae Smith Company.

Romance Comes Riding. Joyce Berggren. LC 53-27308. 1953. Zondervan Pub. House.

Romance De Carnaval. Maria J. Santiago. (Romance Real Ser.). 192p. 1981. pap. 1.50 (ISBN 0-88025-000-3). Roca Pub.

Romance Dust from the Historic Placer. William Starbuck Mayo. LC 7-18478. 1851. G. P. Putnam; Etc., Etc.

Romance for Julie. Davis Dresser. LC 38-14887. 1938. Hillman-Curl, Inc.

Romance for Sale. Maysie Greig. LC 34-23466. 1934. Doubleday, Doran & Company, Inc.

Romance for Sale. Maysie Greig. LC 42-207978. 1942. Triangle Books.

Romance Goes Sailing. Portia Maxwell. LC 39-25868. Gramercy Publishing Co.

Romance in Crimson. Octavus Roy Cohen. LC 40-7350. 1940. D. Appleton Century Company, Incorporated.

Romance in Glenmore Street. Ivy Preston. 1978. 1.75 (ISBN 0-441-73455-3). Ace Books.

Romance in Lavender. Neil Bell. 1977. 6.00 o.p. State Mutual Bk.

Romance in Meditation. Elaine L Field. LC 1-31616. The Abbey Press.

Romance in Starland: A Scientific Novel. Kate Elizabeth Perkins Glass. 1.00. J. F. McElheney Printing Company.

Romance in the Headlines. Mary Ann Taylor. Bd. with Bon Voyage, My Darling. 1980. pap. 1.95 (ISBN 0-451-09175-2, J9175, Sig). NAL.

Romance in the Headlines. Mary Ann Taylor. (Signet Book). 1977. 1.50 (ISBN 0-451-07439-4). New American Library.

Romance in the Jungle. Ethel Matson. LC 50-11793. 1950. Zondervan Pub. House.

Romance in the Rain. Ethel Owen. LC 37-22961. Green Circle Books.

Romance in the Rockies: A Novel. 1st Ed. George Currie. LC 54-13421. 1955. Exposition Press.

Romance in the Sky. Anne Tedlock Brooks. LC 40-10289. Gramercy Publishing Co.

Romance in Transit. Francis Lynde. LC 7-14719. (The ivory series). 1897. C. Scribner's Sons.

Romance in Two Keys. Berta Ruck. LC 55-9925. 1955. Dodd, Mead.

Romance Island. Zona Gale. LC 6-38393. 1906. The Bobbs-Merrill Company.

Romance Island. Frances Shelley Wees. LC 33-13638. 1933. Macrae Smith Company.

Romance of a Back Street. Frederick William Robinson. (On cover: Harper's half-hour series. v. 79). 1878. Harper & Brothers.

Romance of a Black Veil. Charlotte Mary Brame. LC 7253. (On cover: Lovell's library, v. 17, no. 801). 1886. J. W. Lovell Company.

Romance of a Black Veil. Charlotte Mary Brame. LC 6508. (Bertha Clay library, no. 30). 1900. Street & Smith.

Romance of a Chalet. A Story. Rosa Caroline Murray-Prior Praed. (On cover: Lippincott's copyright foreign novels). 1892. J. B. Lippincott Company.

Romance of a Child. Julien Viaud. Tr. by Watkins, Mary Lindsay. (On cover: Globe library, no. 157). 1891. Rand, McNally & Company.

Romance of a Christmas Card. Kate Douglas Smith Wiggin. LC 16-21128. 1916. Houghton Mifflin Company.

Romance of a Dictator. George E Slocombe. LC 32-12198. 1932. Houghton Mifflin Company.

Romance of a Dry Goods Drummer. Marie Walsh. (On cover: Mascot library, no. 1). 1893. The Mascot Publishing Co.

Romance of a French Parsonage. Matilda Barbara Betham- Edwards, pseud. LC 6-36591. J. U. Lovell Company.

Romance of a Guardsman. Ethel Roads. LC 17-21876. 1.00. Press of Reading Eagle.

Romance of a Jesuit Mission: A Historical Novel. Mary Bourchier Sanford. LC 8-1812. The Baker & Taylor Company.

Romance of a Midshipman. William Clark Russell. LC 98-939. 1898. R. F. Fenno & Company; Etc., Etc.

Romance of a Million Dollars. Elizabeth Dejeans. LC 22-17035. The Bobbs-Merrill Company.

Romance of a Missionary: A Story of English Life and Missionary Experiences. Nephi Anderson. LC 20-2. 1919. Zion's Printing and Publishing Company.

Romance of a Monk. Alix King. LC 10-29133. 1910. 1.20. The Metropolitan Press.

Romance of a Mummy. Tr. from the French of Theophile Gautier. Theophile Gautier & Wright, Augusta McC., Tr. LC 6-44268. 1882. J. B. Lippincott & Co.

Romance of a Plain Man. Ellen Anderson Gholson Glasgow. LC 9-12083. 1909. The Macmillan Company.

Romance of a Plain Man. Ellen Anderson Gholson Glasgow. LC 24-27993. 1922. Doubleday, Page & Company.

Romance of a Plain Man. Ellen Anderson Gholson Glasgow. LC 26-19255. (The Lambskin library, no. 51). 1926. Doubleday, Page & Company.

Romance of a Playwright. Henri De Bornier & McMahon, Mary, Tr. LC 6-15017. Cincinnati Etc.

Romance of a Poor Man. Octave Feuillet & Compton, C. G., Tr. LC 2-19996. (Half-title: A century of French romance...Parisian ed. v.9). 1902. D. Appleton & Co.

Romance of a Poor Young Man. Octave Feuillet. (On cover: Seaside library. Pocket ed., no. 66). 1883. G. Munro.

Romance of a Poor Young Man. Octave Feuillet. (On Cover: Sea and Shore Series, No. 34). 1891. Street & Smith.

Romance of a Poor Young Man. Octave Feuillet. LC 42-26576. The F. M. Lupton Publishing Company.

Romance of a Poor Young Man. Octave Feuillet. LC 6-39539. (On cover: Round table library.). 1897. L. C. Page and Company.

Romance of a Poor Young Man. Octave Feuillet & Hager, J. Henry, Tr. LC 6-39540. 1887. W. S. Gottsberger.

Romance of a Pretty Girl: A Novel. Leon Rene Delmas. LC 7-37417. (On cover: Mayfair series, no. 1). 1891. E. Brandus & Co.

Romance of a Quiet Watering-Place (Being the Unpremeditated Confessions of a Not Altogether Frivolous Girl). Extracted from the Private Correspondence of Miss Evelyn L. Dwyer. Nora Helen Warddel. LC 8-37109. 1888. Belford, Clarke & Co.

Romance of a Rogue. Ruby Mildred Ayres. LC 23-162692. 1.75. George H. Doran Company.

Romance of a Rogue. Joseph William Sharts. LC 2-100185. 1902. H. S. Stone & Co.

Romance of a Schoolboy. Mary Andrews Denison. LC 6-33983. The Price-McGill Company.

Romance of a Shop. Amy Levy. LC 42-261741. 1889. Cupples and Hurd.

Romance of a Spahi. Julien Viaud & Watkins, Mary Linsay, Tr. LC 8-299921. (On cover: Rialto series, no. 29). 1890. Rand, McNally & Company.

Romance of a Spanish Nun. Alice Montgomery Baldy. LC 6-63309. (On cover: American novels). 1891. J. B. Lippincott Company.

Romance of a Trained Nurse. Francina Scott. 1901. Cooke & Fry.

Romance of a Young Girl: Or, The Heiress of Hilldrop. Charlotte Mary Brame. LC 6585. (On cover: Bertha Clay library, no. 34). 1900. Street & Smith.

Romance of a Young Girl: Or, The Heiress of Hilldrop. Charlotte Mary Brame. LC 7254. (On cover: Lovell's library, v. 14, no. 730). F. W. Lovell Company.

Romance of Alexander and Roxana: Being One of the Alexandrian Romances, "Alexander the Prince," "Alexander the King" & "Alexander and Roxana,". Marshall Monroe Kirkman. 1.50. Cropley Phillips Company.

Romance of Alexander the King: Being One of the Alexandrian Romances, "Alexander the Prince," "Alexander the King" & "Alexander and Roxana,". Marshall Monroe Kirkman. 1.50. Etc. Cropley Phillips Company.

Romance of Alexander the Prince: Being One of the Alexandrian Romances, "Alexander the Prince," "Alexander the King" & "Alexander and Roxana,". Marshall Monroe Kirkman. LC 9-27993. 1.50. Cropley Phillips Company.

Romance of Ali. Eleanor Stuart Childs. LC 13-15855. 1913. 1.25. Harper & Brothers.

Romance of an Alter Ego. Lloyd Stephens Bryce. LC 6-19890. Brentano's.

Romance of an Honest Woman. Victor Cherbuliez & Robbins, Mrs. Mary Caroline (Pike) 1842-1912, Tr. LC 6-27164. (On cover: Gill's home novels). 1874. W. F. Gill and Company.

Romance of an Old-Fashioned Gentleman. Francis Hopkinson Smith. LC 7-31210. 1907. C. Scribner's Sons.

Romance of Arlington House. Sarah Ann Reed. LC 9-2765. The Chapple Publishing Co., Ltd.

Romance of Atlantis. Taylor Caldwell. LC 74-17399. 1975. 6.95 (ISBN 0-688-00334-6). Morrow.

Romance of Barnstable. Mary Matthews Bray. 1909. R. G. Badger.

Romance of Beauseincourt. An Episode Extracted from the Retrospect of Miriam Monfort. Catherine Ann Ware Warfield. LC 8-34832. 1867. G. W. Carleton & Co.; Etc., Etc.

Romance of Billy-Goat Hill. Alice Caldwell Hegan Rice. LC 12-217691. 1912. The Century Co.

Romance of California Life: Illustrated by Pacific Slope Stories, Thrilling, Pathetic and Humorous. John Habberton. LC 2-3034. 1880. Baker, Pratt & Co.

Romance of Casanova: A Novel. Richard Aldington. LC 46-5236. 1946. Duell, Sloan and Pearce.

Romance of Cyrano De Bergerac. Raymond Fuller Ayers. LC 99-2490. F. T. Neely.

Romance of Dollard. Mary Hartwell Catherwood. LC 75-137725. (American fiction reprint series). (Illus.). 1970. Books for Libraries Press.

Romance of Dollard. Mary Hartwell Catherwood. 1889. The Century Co.

Romance of Elaine: Sequel to "Exploits of Elaine". Arthur Benjamin Reeve. LC 16-6819. 1916. Hearst's International Library Co.

Romance of Evangeline. Finis Fox & Longfellow, Henry Wadsworth, Evangeline. LC 29-163962. A. L. Burt Company.

Romance of Fiddler's Green. Clara Endicott Sears. LC 22-4439. 1922. Houghton Mifflin Company.

Romance of Fire. Paul Hutchens. LC 34-41288. The Bible Institute Colportage Ass'n.

Romance of Gilbert Holmes: An Historical Novel. Marshall Monroe Kirkman. LC 4879. 1900. The World Railway Publishing Company.

Romance of Glenwood Springs. A. M Book. LC 6-752933. Colorado Book Company.

Romance of Golden Star... George Chetwynd Griffith. LC 77-84234. (Lost Race and Adult Fantasy Fiction). (Illus.). 1978. 18.00 (ISBN 0-405-10982-2). Arno Press.

Romance of Graylock Manor. Louise Frances Paine Hamilton. LC 99-3783. Rand, McNally & Company.

Romance of Guardamonte. Arline E Davis. LC 6-32496. J. S. Tait & Son.

Romance of His Life, and Other Romances. Mary Cholmondeley. LC 70-37540. (Short story index reprint series). 1972. (ISBN 0-8369-4099-7). Books for Libraries Press.

Romance of History. England. Henry Neele. LC 7-26121. 1828. Carey, Lea & Carey.

Romance of History. France. Leitch Ritchie. LC 17-13017. F. Warne and Co.

Romance of History. France. Leitch Ritchie. ("Chandos classics"). 1872. F. Warner and Co.

Romance of History. India. John Hobart Caunter. LC 16-1247. F. Warne and Co.

Romance of History. Italy. Charles Macfarlane. LC 7-16460. 1832. J. & J. Harper.

Romance of History. Italy. Charles Macfarlane. LC 15-21851. 1872. F. Warne and Co.

Romance of History. Spain. Trueba y Cosio, Joaquin Telesforo. LC 12-39647. 1830. Printed by J. & J. Harper, Sold by Collins and Hannay Etc.

Romance of History. Spain. Trueba y Cosio, Joaquin Telesforo. LC 15-21850. 1872. F. Warne and Co.

Romance of I'Aiglon. authorized ed. Charles Peale Didier. Tr. by Wilson, John Paul. LC 6521. 1901. Brentano's.

Romance of Indian Life. Mary Henderson Eastman. LC 74-104447. (Illus.). 1971. Repr. of 1852 ed. lib. bdg. 11.50x o.p. (ISBN 0-8398-0451-2). Gregg.

Romance of Jessamine Place: And Other Stories. Ella Miller Cheshire. LC 24-7808. The Christopher Publishing House.

Romance of John Bainbridge. Henry Jr. George. LC 6-37965. 1906. The Macmillan Company.

Romance of King Arthur and His Knights of the Round Table: Abridged from Malory's Morte D'Arthur. Thomas Malory & Pollard, Alfred William, 1859-Ed. LC 17-28655. 1917. The Macmillan Company.

Romance of Lace. Mary E. Jones. (Illus.). 15.00x o.p. (ISBN 0-87556-500-X). Saifer.

Romance of Lake Conneaut: Or, All Is Well That Ends Well. Inez A. Ellison Hall. LC 32-222833. The Christopher Publishing House.

Romance of Leonardo Da Vinci. Dmitrii Sergeevich Merezhkovskii & Guerney, Bernard Guilbert, Tr. LC 35-5266. 1931. Random House.

Romance of Leonardo Da Vinci. Dmitrii Sergeevich Merezhkovskii & Herbert Trench. LC 75-36063. (Merezhkovskii, Dmitrii Sergeevich, 1865-1941. Christ & Anti-Christ: Vol. 2). (Illus.). 8.95. (ISBN 0-8055-1178-4) (ISBN 0-8055-0265-3). Hart Pub. Co.

Romance of Leonardo Da Vinci. Dmitrii Sergeevich Merezhkovskii & Trench, Herbert, 1856-1923, Tr. LC 25-4779. G. P. Putnam's Sons.

Romance of Leonardo Da Vinci. Dmitrii Sergeevich Merezhkovskii & Trench, Herbert, 1865-1923, Tr. LC 34-38286. G. P. Putnam's Sons.

Romance of Leonardo Da Vinci. Dmitril Sergieevich Merezhkovskii. Tr. by Guerney, Bernard Guilbert. LC 34-425761. 1934. Garden City Publishing Company, Inc.

Romance of Leonardo Da Vinci. Dmitril Sergieevich Merezhkovskil. Tr. by Guerney, Bernard Guilbert. LC 29-18338. (Half-title: The modern library of the world's best books). 1928. The Modern Library.

Romance of Leonardo Da Vinci. Dmitril Sergieevich Merezhkovskil. Tr. by Guerney, Bernard Guilbert. LC 28-11059. (Half-title: The modern library of the world's best books). The Modern Library.

Romance of Leonardo Da Vinci. Dmitril Sergieevich Merezhkovskil. Tr. by Trench, Herbert. LC 34-382862. G. P. Putnam's Sons.

Romance of Leonardo Da Vinci. Dimitri Merezhkovsky. pap. 0.90 o.p. (W1074). WSP.

Romance of Leonardo Da Vinci: The Forerunner. Dmitril Sergieevich Merezhkovskil. Tr. by Trench, Herbert. LC 2-24103. (His Christ and Antichrist. 2d division). 1902. G. P. Putnam's Sons.

Romance of Leonardo Da Vinci: The Godsresurgent) Tr. from Russian by Bernard Guilbert Guerney. 3d Rev. with Additional Material Newly Tr. Dmitrii Sergeevich Merezhkovskii. Tr. by Bernard Guilbert Guerney. (Signet bk. Q2482). New Amer. Lib.

Romance of Leonardo Da Vinci: Translated from the Original Russian of Dmitri Merejkowski. Dmitrii Sergeevich Merezhkovskii & Guerney, Bernard Guilbert, Tr. LC 28-11059. (Half-title: The modern library of the world's best books). The Modern Library.

Romance of Lilies. Charles Howard Montague. LC 7-4443. 1886. W. I. Harris & Co.

Romance of Louis XVII of France. The Romance of Louis Xvii of France. translated from the french. ed. Octave Aubry. LC 27-13599. 1927. Frederick A. Stokes Company.

Romance of Lust. 1969. 10.00 o.p. (GP509). Grove.

Romance of Lust. 1969. pap. 1.95 o.p. (Z1028T, Zebra). Grove.

Romance of Lust: Or, Early Experiences. Edward Sellon. LC 68-58141. 1968. 10.00. Grove Press.

Romance of Lust: Or, Early Experiences. Edward Sellon. LC 78-73427. (Black cat book). 2.95 (ISBN 0-394-17086-5). Grove Press: Distributed by Random House.

Romance of Marriage. Lev Nikolaevich Tolstoi & Donovan, Mrs. Alexina (Loranger) Tr. (On cover: The pastime series, no. 45). 1890. Laird & Lee.

Romance of Mary Maiden: Or, How the Farm Mortgage Was Lifted. Walter R. Nursey. 1898. C. I. Hood & Co.

Romance of Mary W. Shelley, John Howard Payne and Washington Irving. Mary Wollstonecraft Godwin Shelley & John Howard Payne. LC 72-7323. (Illus.). 1972. (ISBN 0-8414-0324-4). Folcroft Library Editions.

Romance of Old Cape May. Matilda Butler Hand. LC 28-31013. Dorrance and Company.

Romance of Old Fort Hall. Minerva Kohlhepp Teichert. LC 32-23284. 1932. Metropolitan Press.

Romance of Old Jerusalem. Florence Gilmore. LC 11-3151. 1911. 0.50. B. Herder.

TITLE INDEX ROMANTIC PASSION OF DON

Romance of Old New Orleans. Anna Margaret Denbo. LC 49-49117. 1949. Pelican Pub. Co.
Romance of Old New York. Edgar Fawcett. LC 6-38782. 1897. J. B. Lippincott Company.
Romance of Old Wars. Valentina Hawtrey. LC 7-8220. 1906. H. Holt and Company.
Romance of Perfume Lands, or, The Search for Capt. Jacob Cole. With Interesting Facts About Perfumes and Articles Used in the Toilet... Frank S Clifford. 1875. Clifford.
Romance of Piscator. Henry Wysham Lanier. LC 4-109256. 1904. H. Holt and Company.
Romance of Poverty Hollow. O B King. LC 36-8547. Southern Library Association.
Romance of Providence. Effie Spencer. LC 29-17657. The Four Seas Company.
Romance of Reality. Margaret Le Boutillier O'Connell & O'Connell, Lilian Margaret, Ed. LC 12-22318. 1912. Press of the New Era Printing Company.
Romance of Rhoda: A New Testament Love Story. William Eleazar Barton. LC 17-12139. 1917. Advance Publishing Company.
Romance of Rosy Ridge. MacKinlay Kantor. LC 37-28597. Coward-McCann, Inc.
Romance of Runnibede. Steele Rudd. (O.s.i.). 1975. 2.75x o.s.i. (ISBN 0-7022-0912-0). U of Queensland Pr.
Romance of St. Sacrement: A Story of New France and the Iroquois. Grayson N. Sherwen. LC 16-10841. 1912. Free Press Printing Company.
Romance of Second Avenue. Joel Sayre. (O.s.i.). 16p. 1933. pap. 1.50 o.s.i. (ISBN 0-8466-0231-8, SJS231). Shorey.
Romance of Silk. 1st Ed. Sallie H Gunnell. LC 56-112052. 1956. Vantage Press.
Romance of Sorcery. Sax Rohmer, pseud. 1976. Repr. of 1914 ed. lib. bdg. 16.60x (ISBN 0-89190-808-0). Am Repr-Rivercity Pr.
Romance of Student Life Abroad. Richard Burleigh Kimball. LC 33-374055. 1853. G. P. Putnam & Co.
Romance of Summer Seas: By Varina Anne Jefferson--Davis... Varina Anne Jefferson Davis. 1898. Harper & Brothers.
Romance of Swedenborg's Life. Anna Cronhjelm Wallberg. LC 8-332653. 1890. C. A. Murdock & Co.
Romance of the Caribbean Sea. Herbert Weeks. LC 25-17537. 1925. Printed by J. J. Little and Ives Company.
Romance of the Charter Oak: A Picture of Colonial Times. William Seton. LC 8-687228. P. O'Shea.
Romance of the Floridas. Michael Kenny. LC 70-120573. (Illus.). Repr. of 1934 ed. 15.00 (ISBN 0-404-03656-2). AMS Pr.
Romance of the Forest. Ann Ward Radcliffe. LC 73-22770. (Gothic Novels II). 1974. (ISBN 0-405-06020-3). Arno Press.
Romance of the Forest. Ann Ward Radcliffe. LC 30-123151. 1872. Claxton, Remsen & Haffelfinger.
Romance of the Forest, Interspersed with Some Pieces of Poetry. 4th ed. london, printed for t. hookham and j. carpenter, 1794. ed. Ann Ward Radcliffe. LC 76-135896. (Belles lettres in English). 1970. Johnson Reprint Corp.
Romance of the Forest: Interspersed with Some Pieces of Poetry. Ann Ward Radcliffe. LC 7-42431. 1835. G. Clark.
Romance of the Green Seal. Catherine Ann Ware Warfield. LC 8-34831. Beadle and Company.
Romance of the Hamilton Estate: A Novel. Loo B Van Fossen. LC 15-27762. Burton Publishing Company.
Romance of the Harem. Anna H. Leonowens. Repr. of 1873 ed. 15.00 o.s.i. Finch Pr.
Romance of the Harem. Julia Pardoe. LC 7-35603. 1839. E. L. Carey and A. Hart.
Romance of the Jersey Pines. Bessie B Warwick. LC 22-23713. R. G. Badger.
Romance of the Martin Connor. Oswald Kendall. LC 16-189129. 1916. 1.25. Houghton Mifflin Company.
Romance of the Mighty Deep. Agnes Giberne. 1905. Repr. 16.00 o.s.i. Finch Pr.
Romance of the Milky Way and Other Studies and Stories. Lafcadio Hearn. LC 73-184818. 1974. (pbk.) 3.25 (ISBN 0-8048-1040-0). Charles E. Tuttle.
Romance of the Milky Way: And Other Studies & Stories. Lafcadio Hearn. LC 77-75779. (Short story index reprint series). 1969. Books for Libraries Press.
Romance of the Milky Way: And Other Studies & Stories. Lafcadio Hearn. LC 5-33310. 1905. Houghton, Mifflin and Company.
Romance of the Milling Revolution: Or, The History of a Typical Modern Mill. Louis Henry Gibson. 1886. C. F. Hall.
Romance of the Moors. Mona Alison Caird. (On cover: Leisure moment series. 2d group, no. 17). 1891. H. Holt and Company.
Romance of the New Bethesda. Jane Lippitt Patterson, pseud. 1888. Universalist Publishing House.
Romance of the New Virginia. Martha Frye Boggs. LC 6-14188. 1896. Arena Publishing Company.
Romance of the Nineteenth Century. William Hurrell Mallock. LC 75-1528. (Victorian Fiction: Novels of Faith and Doubt). 1976. 35.00 (ISBN 0-8240-1600-9). Garland Pub.
Romance of the Nineteenth Century. William Hurrell Mallock. LC 7-16805. (On cover: Trans-Atlantic novels. v. 6). 1881. G. P. Putnam's Sons.
Romance of the Nursery. rev. and enl. ed. Lizzie Allen Harker. LC 9-25979. 1909. 1.25. C. Scribner's Sons.
Romance of the Ocean: A Narrative of the Voyage of the Wildfire to California. by fanny foley... ed. Fanny Foley. LC 6-41425. 1850. Lindsay and Blakiston.
Romance of the Old Cave Mill. A Study in Ethics. Walter L Jenkins. LC 7-10207. 1897. F. B. & F. P. Gos.
Romance of the Queen Pedauque. With Illus. by Alexander King. Anatole France, pseud. LC 50-3333. (Illustrated library). Halcyon House.
Romance of the Republic. Lydia Maria Francis Child. LC 76-83926. 1969. Mnemosyne Pub. Co.
Romance of the Republic. Lydia Maria Francis Child. LC 13-177462. 1867. Ticknor and Fields.
Romance of the Road: Making Love and a Living. Alice Curtice Moyer. LC 12-14400. 1.00. Laird & Lee.
Romance of the Rose, 3 Vols. Guillaume de Lorris & J. Clopinel. Tr. by Frederick S. Ellis. LC 74-154119. Repr. of 1928 ed. Set. 64.50 (ISBN 0-404-09640-9). AMS Pr.
Romance of the Sawtooth. F. G. Mock. LC 17-18359. The Author.
Romance of the Sea Serpent, or, The Ichthyosaurus. Eugene Batchelder. LC 6-909394. 1849. J. Bartlett.
Romance of the Siege of Vicksburg. Jane Frances Swallow. LC 26-2449. 1925. The Chapple Publishing Company, Ltd.
Romance of the Sword: A Napoleonic Novel. Georges Duval. Tr. by Safford, Mary Joanna. LC 6-36398. The Merriam Company.
Romance of the Table. In Three Parts. I. Breakfast, II Dinner, III Tea. Jehiel Keeler Hoyt. LC 7-39810. 1872. Times Publishing Co.
Romance of the Ten Thousand Islands (a Florida Story) Albert Edwin Philips. LC 10-1226. 1.50. Broadway Publishing Co.
Romance of the West. H. H Halsell. LC 39-20477. 1939. The Naylor Comapny.
Romance of the West. Harry H. Halsell. LC 39-20477. 1939. The Naylor Company.
Romance of the West Indies. Eugene Sue & O'Donoghue, Mrs. Marian Adele (Longfellow) 1849- LC 98-1089. (On cover: Neely's universal library, no. 27). 1898. F. T. Neely.
Romance of the Western Chamber. S. I. Hsiung. LC 68-22412. (Translations from the Oriental Classics Series). (Illus.). 1968. 24.00x (ISBN 0-231-02996-9); pap. 9.00x (ISBN 0-231-08615-6). Columbia U Pr.
Romance of the Western Chamber. T. C. Lai & Ed Gamarekian. (Writing in Asia Ser). 135p. 1974. pap. text ed. 2.50x o.p. (ISBN 0-435-90152-4). Humanities.
Romance of the Wire. Matilda Barbara Betham-Edwards, pseud. LC 6-365926. (On cover: Lovell's Westminster ser. no. 11). J. W. Lovell Company.
Romance of Toronto (Founded on Fact) A Novel. Annie G Savigny. LC 74-166777. (Toronto reprint library of Canadian prose and poetry). (ISBN 0-8020-7527-4). University of Toronto Press.
Romance of Travel. Comprising Tales of Five Lands. Nathaniel Parker Willis. LC 8-36895. 1840. S. Colman.
Romance of Tristan. Beroul. Tr. by Alan S. Fredrik. (Classics Ser.). 1978. pap. 3.95 (ISBN 0-14-044230-8). Penguin.
Romance of Trouville: A Novel. Alfred Guezenec. Tr. by De Vere, Meta. LC 7-140. (choice series. no.69). 1892. R. Bonner's Sons.
Romance of Two Centuries: A Tale of the Year 2025. Kenneth Sylvan Guthrie. LC 19-6138. The Platonist Press.
Romance of Two Worlds. Marie Corelli. LC 75-484. (Victorian Fiction: Novels of Faith and Doubt). 1976. 35.00 (ISBN 0-8240-1561-4). Garland Pub.
Romance of Two Worlds. Marie Corelli. LC 72-81601. (Steinerbooks). 1973. 2.45 (ISBN 0-8334-1737-1). Rudolf Steiner Publications.
Romance of Two Worlds. Marie Corelli. LC 9-3340. Rand. McNally & Company.
Romance of Two Worlds. Marie Corelli. LC 16-90703. Rand, McNally & Company.
Romance of Two Worlds. A Novel. new ed. Marie Corelli. (On cover: American series, no. 73 (extra). M. J. Ivers & Co.
Romance of Two Worlds. A Novel. Marie Corelli. (On cover: Seaside library. Pocket ed., no. 2136). 1895. G. Munro's Sons.
Romance of Vienna. Frances Milton Trollope. LC 8-28503. 1838. E. L. Carey & A. Hart.
Romance of Villon. Francis Carco. Tr. by Miles, Hamish. LC 27-18716. 1927. A. A. Knopf.
Romance of Wilson Creek. Sam Clay Pilkington. LC 61-165172. 1961. Dorrance.
Romance of Zion Chapel. 3d ed. Richard Le Gallienne. LC 3-195370. 1898. J. Lane.
Romance on a Cruise. Maysie Greig. LC 35-3210. 1935. Doubleday, Doran & Co., Inc.
Romance on Capri. Nell M. Dean. (YA) 1973. 4.95 o.p. (Avalon). Bouregy.
Romance on Capri. Nell Marr Dean. (Avalon romances). 1973. 4.50. Avalon Books.
Romance on El Camino Real: Reminiscences and Romances Where the Footsteps on the Padres Fall. Jarrett Thomas Richards. LC 14-2275. 1914. B. Herder.
Romance Prescribed. Eric Hatch. LC 30-21170. Farrar & Rinehart.
Romance Recaptured. Janet Doran. LC 38-146969. Gramercy Publishing Co.
Romance Round the Corner. Portia Maxwell. LC 38-379218. Gramercy Publishing Co.
Romance Royal. Berta Ruck. LC 37-198357. 1937. Dodd, Mead & Company.
Romance That Linked Heaven to Earth: A Short Story: Love in the Humble Cottage. L. Florence Fleming. LC 28-16161. Press of Judd & Detweiler, Inc.
Romance: The Loveliest Thing. Dorothy Black. LC 25-176992. 1925. H. Holt and Company.
Romance to the Rescue. Denis George Mackail. LC 21-19386. 1921. 1.90. Houghton Mifflin Company.
Romance, When and Where You Find It: A Novel of Romance in the Ozarks. Edgar E Hulse. LC 76-3175. S.N.
Romances and Narratives. Daniel Defoe. Ed. by George Atherton Aitken. LC 75-163691. 1973. (16 vol. set) 175.00 (ISBN 0-404-07910-5). AMS Press.
Romances and Realities: Tales of Truth Anc Fancy. Amelia Edith Huddleston Barr. 1876. J. B. Ford and Company.
Romances of Alexandre Dumas... Alexandre Dumas. LC 6-42303. 1896. G. D. Sproul.
Romances of Blanche la Mare. R. H. Davis. 1972. pap. 1.95 o.s.i. (V1090T, Venus). Grove.
Romances of Chivalry. John Ashton. 1978. Repr. of 1887 ed. lib. bdg. 65.00 (ISBN 0-8482-0122-1). Norwood Edns.
Romances of Colonial Days. Geraldine Brooks. LC 3-19176. 1903. T. Y. Crowell & Company.
Romances of Herman Melville: Typee, Omoo, Mardi, Moby-Dick, White Jacket, Israel Potter, Redburn. Herman Melville. LC 28-5399. 1928. The Pickwick Publishers, Inc.
Romances of Matilda. Joseph Carleton Beal. LC 29-1670. 1928. Wright & Potter Printing Company.
Romances of New Orleans. 2d ed. George Augustin. LC 6-3862. 1891. L. Graham & Son.
Romances of Old Berkshire. Willard Douglas Coxey. LC 31-15933. 1931. The Berkshire Courier.
Romances of Old France. Richard Le Gallienne. LC 75-81271. (Short story index reprint series). (Illus.). 1969. Books for Libraries Press.
Romances of Old France. Richard Le Gallienne. LC 5-33976. 1905. The Baker & Taylor Co.
Romances of the East. Joseph Arthur Gobineau. LC 73-6282. (Middle East Collection). (Series: Collection of foreign authors, no. 6.). 1973. 17.00 (ISBN 0-405-05340-1). Arno Press.
Romances of the Law. Robert Edward Francillon. LC 6-43251. 1889. Gebbie & Co.
Romances of the Rockies. Lelah Palmer Morath. LC 7-24765. The Gowdy-Simmons Printing Company.
Romances of the Rugged Road. Henry B Rutledge. LC 23-11085.
Romances of Victor Hugo. the sidney library ed.... ed. Victor Marie Hugo. LC 7-5881. 1896. G. D. Sproul.
Romanian Short Stories. Ed. by Olivia Manning. (World's Classics). 1971. 7.95 (ISBN 0-19-250615-3). Oxford U Pr.
Romanian Short Stories. LC 72-179308. (World's classics, 615). 1971. 1.50 (ISBN 0-19-250615-3). Oxford University Press.
Romanoff. Leonid Sergeevich Sobolev. LC 74-10091. 1975. 17.50 (ISBN 0-88355-177-2). Hyperion Press.
Romanoff. Leonid Sergeevich Sobolev. Tr. by Fremantle, Alfred. LC 35-163131. 1935. Longmans, Green and Co.
Romanoff Jewels. Maxwell Grant, pseud. (Shadow Ser.: No. 9). 1975. pap. 0.95 o.p. (ISBN 0-515-03877-6). BJ Pub Group.
Romanoff Jewels: From the Shadow's Private Annals. Maxwell Grant. (Shadow#9). 1975. (pbk.) 0.95 (ISBN 0-515-03877-6). Pyramid Books.
Romanov Ransom. Anne Armstrong Thompson. LC 77-24530. 1978. 8.95 (ISBN 0-671-22926-5). Simon and Schuster.
Romanov Ransom. Anne Armstrong Thompson. (Jove/HBJ Book). 1978. 1.95 (ISBN 0-515-04723-6). Jove Pubns.
Romanov Succession. Brian Wynne Garfield. LC 73-918863. (Fawcett Crest Book). 1975. (pbk.) 1.75. Fawcett.
Romans, Countrymen, Lovers. Thomas J Fleming. LC 72-82289. 1969. 5.95. Morrow.
Romans et Contes, 10 tomes. Anatole France, pseud. Set. 1194.40. French & Eur.
Romans et Contes, 10 tomes. Anatole France, pseud. Incl. Tome I. Thais; Tome II. Lys Rouge; Tome III. Dieux Ont Soif; Tome IV. Crime de Sylvestre Bonnard; Tome V. Rotisserie de la Reine Pedauque; Tome VI. Contes de Jacques Tournebroche, Histoire Contemporaine; Tome VII. Orme du Mail; Tome VIII. Mannequin d'Osier; Tome IX. Anneau d'Amethyste; Tome X. Monsieur Bergeret a Paris. Set. lea. 1623.15. French & Eur.
Romans Et Nouvelles, 2 tomes. Prosper Merimee. Ed. by Parturier. 1934. pap. 22.50. French & Eur.
Romantic. May Sinclair. LC 20-18389. 1920. The Macmillan Company.
Romantic... I Call It. Ethel Harriman. LC 26-18315. 1926. Boni & Liveright.
Romantic Adventure of Mr. Darby and of Sarah His Wife. Martin Donisthorpe Armstrong. LC 31-286999. Harcourt, Brace and Company.
Romantic Adventurers: The Maurice Walsh Big Three: "The Key Above the Door", "While Rivers Run", "The Small Dark Man". Maurice Walsh. LC 34-27008. 1933. Frederick A. Stokes Company.
Romantic Adventures of a Milkmaid. A Novel. Thomas Hardy. (On cover: Seaside library. Pocket ed., no. 139). 1884. G. Munro.
Romantic Adventures of Rosy, the Octoroon: With Some Account of the Persecution of the Southern Negroes During the Reconstruction Period. Albert Evander Coleman. LC 29-29522. Meador Publishing Company.
Romantic Afterthought. Berta Ruck. LC 59-6190. 1959. Dodd, Mead.
Romantic Blues. Janet Doran. LC 42-460505. 1942. Gramercy Publishing Co.
Romantic Comedians. Ellen Anderson Gholson Glasgow. LC 76-51668. (Recovered Fiction by American Women). 1977. 22.00 (ISBN 0-405-10047-7). Arno Press.
Romantic Comedians. Ellen Anderson Gholson Glasgow. LC 26-16199. 1926. Doubleday, Page & Co.
Romantic Detour. Edith Austin Holton. LC 42-50912. 1942. H. C. Kinsey & Company, Inc.
Romantic Education. Mary Richie. LC 77-104942. 1970. 5.95. McCall Pub. Co.
Romantic Egoists. Louis Auchincloss. LC 73-106666. 1970. Greenwood Press.
Romantic Englishwoman. Thomas Wiseman. LC 74-163420. 1972. 6.95. Putnam.
Romantic Frenchman. Mary Ann Gibbs. 1973. pap. 0.95 o.p. (95351-095). Beagle Bks.
Romantic Frenchman. Mary Ann Gibbs. (Fawcett Crest Book). 1976. 1.25. Fawcett Publications.
Romantic Fugitive. Ursula Bloom. LC 44-4536. 1944. Arcadia House, Inc.
Romantic Fugitive. Sheila Burns. LC 44-4536. 1944. Arcadia House, Inc.
Romantic Gothic Tales Seventeen Ninety-Eight to Eighteen Forty. Ed. by G. Richard Thompson. LC 78-19817. (Orig.). 1979. pap. 2.95i (ISBN 0-06-080343-6, P-343, PL). Harper & Row.
Romantic Gothic Tales, 1790-1840. Gary Richard Thompson. LC 78-19817. (Perennial library). 3.95 (ISBN 0-06-080343-6). Harper & Row.
Romantic Interlude. Janet Ford. LC 39-11571. Gramercy Publishing Co.
Romantic Journey. Anne Tedlock Brooks. LC 48-11769. 1948. Arcadia House.
Romantic Lady. Michael Arlen. LC 21-21093. 1921. Dodd, Mead and Company.
Romantic Lady. Sylvia Thorpe. 224p. 1977. pap. 1.75 (ISBN 0-449-50057-8, Coventry). Fawcett.
Romantic Lady. Sylvia Thorpe. (Fawcett crest book, M2047). 1974. (pbk.) 0.95. Fawcett Publications.
Romantic Lady. 1st Ed. Alice Walworth Graham. LC 52-5880. 1952. Doubleday.
Romantic Legends of Spain. Gustavo Adolfo Becquer. Tr. by Cornelia Frances Bates & Katharine Lee Bates. LC 78-169539. (Short story index reprint series). (Illus.). 1971. (ISBN 0-8369-4000-8). Books for Libraries Press.
Romantic Legends of Spain. Gustavo Adolfo Becquer & Bates, Mrs. Cornelia Frances, 1826-1908, Tr. LC 9-237308. 1909. T.Y. Crowell & Co.
Romantic Liar. Lawrence Perry. LC 19-6567. 1919. 1.50. C. Scribner's Sons.
Romantic Mardi Gras. Bertie Freret & Virginia Freret. 2.50 o.p. Vantage.
Romantic Passion of Don Luis. Henri Malo & Preston, Ellen, Tr. LC 25-19526. 1925. L. MacVeagh, The Dial Press.

Romantic Prince. Rafael Sabatini. LC 29-8985. 1929. Houghton Mifflin Company.
Romantic Rivals. Caroline Courtney. LC 81-20069. 1982. 13.95 (ISBN 0-8161-3198-8). G.K. Hall.
Romantic Spirit. Glenna Finley, pseud. 1973. pap. 1.95 (ISBN 0-451-11493-0, AJ1493, Sig). NAL.
Romantic Story of David Robertson: Among the Islands, off and on the Coast of Maine. John Pendleton Farrow. LC 42-43707. 1898. Press of Belfast Age Publishing Company.
Romantic Story of Wickly's Woods. Henry William Taylor. LC 8-25663. 1888. T. S. Denison.
Romantic Storybook. Ed. by Morris Bishop. LC 70-155821. (Illus.). 1971. 7.50 (ISBN 0-8014-0658-7). Cornell University Press.
Romantic Widow. Mollie Chappell. 1979. pap. 1.75 (ISBN 0-449-50013-6, Coventry). Fawcett.
Romantic Woman. Mary Borden. LC 20-15390.
Romantic Young Man. Achmed Abdullah. LC 32-18614. Farrar & Rinehart, Incorporated.
Romantics. Mary Roberts Rinehart. LC 29-224202. Farrar & Rinehart, Incorporated.
Romany. Eleanor Furneaux Smith. LC 35-210153. The Bobbs-Merrill Company.
Romany Curse. Suzanne Somers, pseud. (Orig.). 1971. pap. 0.75 o.p. (B75-2097). Belmont-Tower.
Romany Free. Robert Vavra & Fleur Cowles. LC 77-77315. (Illus.). 1977. 8.95 (ISBN 0-688-61193-1). Morrow.
Romany of the Snows: Second Series of An Adventurer of the North; Being a Continuation of Pierre and His People, and the Latest Existing Records of Pretty Pierre. Gilbert Parker. LC 79-94741. (Short story index reprint series). 1969. Books for Libraries Press.
Romany of the Snows. Second Series of An Adventurer of the North; Being a Continuation of Pierre and His People and the Latest Existing Records of Pretty Pierre. Gilbert Parker. 1898. The Macmillan Company.
Romany Passions. Alexandra Ellis. (Berkley Medallion Book). 1.95 (ISBN 0-425-03672-3). Berkley Pub. Corp.
Romany Rebel. Zabrina Faire, pseud. 1979. pap. 1.75 (ISBN 0-446-94206-5). Warner Bks.
Romany Rebel. Florence Stevenson. LC 80-10829. 1981. 10.50 (ISBN 0-89340-255-9). J. Curley.
Romany Rye. George Henry Borrow. 1961. 8.95x o.p. (ISBN 0-460-00120-5, Evman); pap. 3.95x o.p. (ISBN 0-460-01120-0). Biblio Dist.
Romany Rye. George Henry Borrow. 1948. 7.00 o.p. (ISBN 0-248-98251-6). Dufour.
Romany Rye. George Henry Borrow. 3.50 o.p. (ISBN 0-460-00120-5, E120, Evman). Dutton.
Romany Rye: A Sequel to "Lavengro.". George Henry Borrow. LC 7-3541. 1857. Harper & Brothers.
Romany Rye: A Sequel to "Lavengro". George Henry Borrow. Ed. by William Ireland Knapp. LC 4-17815. 1900. G. P. Putnam's Sons.
Romany Rye. Introd. by Walter Starkie. George Henry Borrow. (Cresset Lib.). 1965. 3.95. Cresset Pr.
Rombella Shuttle. Bill Convertito. (Orig.). 1977. pap. 1.50 (ISBN 0-89041-160-3, 3160). Major Bks.
Rome. Emile Zola & Vizetelly, Ernest Alfred, 1853-1922, Tr. LC 9-1306. 1896. Macmillan and Co.
Rome. Emile Zola & Vizetelly, Ernest Alfred, 1853-1922, Tr. LC 47-34768. 1907. The Macmillan Company.
Rome see Trois Villes.
Rome & a Villa. Eleanor Clark. LC 74-5979. 1975. 10.00 o.p. (ISBN 0-394-49446-6); pap. 4.95 o.p. (ISBN 0-394-70940-3). Pantheon.
Rome and the Abbey: A Tale of Conscience. Emily C. Agnew. LC 21-13963. 1885. D. & J. Sadlier & Co.
Rome Express. Bertrand Collins. LC 28-25815. 1928. Harper & Brothers.
Rome Express. Arthur George Frederick Griffiths. LC 75-35443. (Literature of Mystery and Detection). 1976. 14.00 (ISBN 0-405-07874-9). Arno Press.
Rome Express. Arthur George Frederick Griffiths. LC 7-9550. 1907. L. C. Page and Company.
Rome for Sale, Jack Lindsay. LC 34-17654. (Illus.). 1934. Harper & Brothers.
Rome Haul. Walter Dumaux Edmonds. LC 29-5703. 1929. Little, Brown, and Company.
Rome Haul. Walter Dumaux Edmonds. LC 38-4884. (Half title: The modern library of the world's best books). 1938. The Modern Library.
Rome in the Rain: Untitled Autobiographical Novel. Anthony Burgess. LC 76-10439. (ISBN 0-07-008960-4). McGraw-Hill.
Rome Is the World. Katharine Hill. LC 51-13722. 1951. Putnam.
Rome, My Love. Nonna Osipova. (Illus.). 25p. (Orig.). 1979. pap. 2.00 (ISBN 0-935500-25-1). Am Samizdat.
Rome, 12 Noon. Kenneth Macpherson. LC 64-17975. 1964. Coward-McCann.
Romelle... William Riley Burnett. LC 46-6627. 1946. A. A. Knopf.
Romeo & Juliet & West Side Story. Ed. by Houghton. (YA) 1965. pap. 2.50 (ISBN 0-440-97483-6, LFL). Dell.
Romeo & Juliet of Another Century. Michael Bertone. LC 78-50635. 1979. 8.95 (ISBN 0-87949-118-3). Ashley Bks.
Romeo in Moon Village. George Barr McCutcheon. LC 25-18357. 1925. Dodd, Mead and Company.
Romeo und Julia Auf Dem Dorfe. Gottfried Keller. Ed. by Adams, Warren Austin. LC 3082. (Heath's modern language series). 1900. D. C. Heath & Co.
Romeo und Julia Auf Dem Dorfe: Erzahlung. Gottfried Keller. Ed. by Corwin, Robert Nelson. LC 12-24639. 1912. H. Holt and Company.
Rommany. Florence Hurd. 1976. 1.75. Avon.
Rommany Stone. 2d impression. ed. James Henry Yoxall. LC 3-1277. 1902. Longmans, Green, and Co.
Rommel Drives on Deep into Egypt. Richard Brautigan. 1970. 5.95 o.p. (ISBN 0-440-07495-9, Sey Lawr). Delacorte.
Rommel Plot. Clive Egleton. LC 77-5731. 8.95 (ISBN 0-397-01235-7). Lippincott.
Rommel's Gold. Maggie Hill Davis. LC 74-141908. (Illus.). 1971. 7.95. Lippincott.
Rommel's Panzers. 1980. pap. text ed. write for info. Metagam.
Romola. harper's library ed. George Eliot. LC 7-40743. (Added t.-p.: Novels of George Eliot, v. 5). 1877. Harper & Brothers.
Romola. George Eliot. (Seaside, library, v. 1, no. 15). 1877. G. Munro.
Romola... George Eliot. (Lovell's library, v. 2, no. 79). 1883. J. W. Lovell Company.
Romola. George Eliot. LC 6-10746. Estes and Lauriat.
Romola. George Eliot. LC 6-40747. T. Y. Crowell & Co.
Romola. George Eliot. (Half-title: Everyman's library, ed. by Ernest Rhys. Fiction. no. 231). 1909. J. M. Dent & Co.
Romola. George Eliot & Biagi, Guido, 1855-1925, Ed. LC 6-42367. 1906. A. C. McClurg & Co.
Romola. George Eliot & Blind, Mathilde, 1841-1898. LC 1-29690. (Half-title: The works of George Eliot. Foleshill ed. v. 1-2). 1900. Little, Brown, and Company.
Romola. harper's library ed. George Eliot & Romola. LC 6-40745. (Added t-p.: Novels of George Eliot, v.5). 1881. Harper & Brothers.
Romola. A Novel. George Eliot. LC 25-23767. 1863. Harper & Brothers.
Romola: An Historical Novel... George Eliot. LC 98-581. Rand, McNally & Company.
Romola...Biographical Introduction: By Esther Wood. George Eliot. LC 1-31173. (personal edition of George Eliot's works. v. 10-11). Doubleday, Page & Co.
Romona: A Story. Helen Maria Fiske Hunt Jackson. LC 18-541246. 1916. Little, Brown and Company.
Romula, the Dedicated. Katheryn Kimbrough. (Saga of the Phenwick Women: No. 37). 224p. 1981. pap. 2.25 (ISBN 0-445-04665-1). Popular Lib.
Ron. Carl Tiktin. LC 78-57328. 9.95 (ISBN 0-87795-198-5). Arbor House.
Ronald Bannerman's Boyhood. George Macdonald. LC 41-31116. 1879. J. B. Lippincott & Co.
Ronald O' the Moors. Gladys Edson Locke. LC 20-943. 1919. The Four Seas Company.
Ronald Rabbit Is a Dirty Old Man. Lawrence Block. 1971. 5.95 o.p. (ISBN 0-87035-027-7). Geis.
Ronald Rabit Is a Dirty Old Man. Lawrence Block. 176p. 1974. pap. 1.25 (ISBN 0-532-12241-0). Woodhill.
Ronald's Mission. Henriette Eugenie Delamare. LC 13-163451. 0.60. H. L. Kilner & Co.
Ronaldsha: A Romance... Hugh Doherty. LC 6-33856. 1809. Hastings, Etheridge & Bliss.
Ronbar: A Counterfeit Presentment. Richmond Sheffield Dement. LC 6-340082. 1895. G. W. Dillingham, Successor to G. W. Carleton & Co.
Rondah: Or, Thirty-Three Years in a Star. Florence Lucinda Carpenter Dieudonne. LC 6-39432. T. B. Peterson & Brothers.
Ronde. Arthur Schnitzler. Tr. by Frank Marcus. 50p. 1982. pap. 6.95 (ISBN 0-413-49530-2, NO. 3635). Methuen Inc.
Rondo. Cyril Norman. 1898. G. W. Dillingham Co.; Etc., Etc.
Rongataurian Renaissance: A Fantasy & a Philosophy. Philanthus Shavius. LC 81-40799. (Illus.). 64p. 1981. pap. 4.95 (ISBN 0-941006-00-X). Rongataur.
Ronin: A Novel Based on a Zen Myth. William Dale Jennings. LC 68-25890. (Signet book). 1975. (pbk.) 1.25. New American Library.
Ronin: A Novel Based on a Zen Myth. William Dale Jennings. LC 68-25890. 1968. 3.75. C. E. Tuttle Co.
Roof Against the Rain. Elizabeth Higgins Sullivan. LC 38-882745. 1938. Lothrop, Lee & Shepard Company.
Roof Over Their Heads. Ethel Powelson Hueston. LC 37-1372. The Bobbs-Merrill Company.
Roof Tile of Tempyo. Yasushi Inoue. LC 76-365325. (UNESCO Collection of Representative Works: Japanese Series). 1975. 6.95 (ISBN 0-86008-145-1).
Roof Tree. Charles Neville Buck. LC 21-4167. 1921. Doubleday, Page & Company.
Roofs of Elm Street: A Tale of the Middle West. William James McNally. LC 36-8048. G. P. Putnam's Sons.
Roofs Over Strawtown. Sara Elizabeth Gosselink. LC 45-4378. 1945. Wm. B. Eerdmans Publishing Co.
Rooftops. Tom Lewis. 1982. pap. 2.95 (ISBN 0-451-11735-2, AE1735, Sig). NAL.
Rooftops: A Novel. Tom Lewis. LC 81-7372. 11.95 (ISBN 0-87131-345-6). M. Evans.
Rook Takes Knight. Stuart Palmer. LC 68-28577. 1968. 4.50. Random House.
Rookery. Hugh C. Rae. LC 74-14404. 256p. 1975. 7.95 o.p. (ISBN 0-312-69265-X). St Martin.
Rookie: By Tex Maule. 1st Ed. Hamilton Maule. LC 61-17445. 1961. D. McKay Co.
Rookie Leadfoot: A Season on Dirt. Herb Anastor. LC 72-92739. 1973. 4.95 (ISBN 0-8059-1788-8). Dorrance.
Rookie Running Back. Cliff Hankin. LC 68-57466. (Illus.). 1968. 3.95. Vanguard Press.
Rookies: A Novel, Adapted from the T.V. Series. Claire Parker. LC 72-12807. 1973. 1.95. Bantam Books.
Rook's Gambit. Adam Hall, pseud. Orig. Title: Dead Circuit. 1972. pap. 0.75 o.p. Pyramid Pubns.
Rookwood. William Harrison Ainsworth. LC 87-5594. (Half-title: Everyman's library, ed. by Ernest Rhys. Fiction. no. 870). 1931. J. M. Dent & Sons, Ltd.
Rookwood: A Romance, 3 vols. in 2. William Harrison Ainsworth. LC 79-8225. (Illus.). Repr. of 1850 ed. Set. 84.50 (ISBN 0-404-61758-1). AMS Pr.
Room. Hubert Selby. LC 72-155129. 1971. 5.95 (ISBN 0-394-47588-7). Grove Press.
Room. Gladys Bronwyn Stern. LC 22-22772. 1922. A. A. Knopf.
Room at the Hotel Ambre. Anthony Armstrong. 1969. pap. 0.60 o.p. (0502-06013-060). Curtis.
Room at the Hotel Ambre: By Anthony Armstrong Pseud. 1st Ed. Anthony Armstrong Willis. LC 56-5599. 1956. Published for the Crime Club by Doubleday.
Room at the Inn. Clark McMeekin. LC 53-8152. 1953. Putnam.
Room at the Top. John Braine. LC 79-24813. 9.95. Methuen.
Room at the Top: A Novel. John Braine. LC 57-11710. 1957. Houghton Mifflin.
Room at the Topless. Ted Mark, pseud. pap. 0.60 o.p. Lancer.
Room at the Topless. Ted Mark. (Man from O.R.G.Y.). 1973. (pbk.) 1.25. Dell.
Room Beneath the Stairs. T. E Huff. LC 75-6394. 1975. 7.95. Bobbs-Merrill.
Room Beneath the Stairs. T. E Huff. (Berkley Medallion Book). 1977. 1.50 (ISBN 0-425-03465-8). Berkley Pub. Corp.
Room Beneath the Stairs. Katherine St. Clair, pseud. (Berkley Medallion Book). 1977. 1.50 (ISBN 0-425-03465-8). Berkley Pub. Corp.
Room Beneath the Stairs: A Novel of Romantic Suspense. Katherine St. Clair, pseud. LC 75-6394. 224p. 1975. 7.95 o.p. (ISBN 0-672-52164-4). Bobbs.
Room Beyond. Robert Spencer Carr. LC 48-4616. 1948. Appleton-Century-Crofts.
Room Downtown. Elizabeth Carden Brown. LC 37-3286. 1937. Godwin.
Room for a Son: A Novel. Robert David Abrahams. LC 51-6675. 1951. Jewish Publication Society of America.
Room for Love. James Noble Gifford. LC 44-5023. 1944. Phoenix Press.
Room for Mr. Roosevelt. Ambrose Flack. LC 51-2725. 1951. Crowell.
Room for Murder. Doris Miles Disney. 1971. pap. 0.75 o.p. (75-448). Manor Bks.
Room for Murder. 1st Ed. Doris Miles Disney. 1955. Published for the Crime Club by Doubleday.
Room for the Night. Pauline Leader. LC 46-3292. 1946. The Vanguard Press.
Room in Berlin. Gunther Birkenfeld. Tr. by Sutton, Eric. LC 30-29015. H. Liveright.
Room in Our Hearts, Room in Our Home. Monroe Ballard et al. LC 79-90249. 1979. pap. 3.95 o.p. (ISBN 0-914850-80-6). Impact Tenn.
Room in Paris. 1st Ed. Peggy Mann. LC 55-5574. 1955. Doubleday.
Room in Peking see Hostage in Peking.
Room No. 879. Andrew Newton Hollabaugh. LC 25-20405. 1925. Cokesbury Press.
Room of Secrets. Caroline Farr. 1979. pap. 1.75 (ISBN 0-451-08965-0, E8965, Sig). NAL.
Room of the Rose: And Other Stories. Sara Trainer Smith. LC 1659. 1900. J. J. McVey.
Room on the Roof. Ruskin Bond. LC 56-12492. 1957. Coward-McCann.
Room on the Route: A Novel. Godfrey Blunden. LC 47-491. 1947-1946. J. B. Lippincott Company.
Room Opposite: And Other Tales of Mystery and Imagination. Flora Macdonald Mayor. LC 35-11501. 1935. Longmans, Green and Co.
Room Service. Alan Williams. LC 36-930. Godwin.
Room Service see Prospect Before Us.
Room to Die in. Ellery Queen, pseud. LC 67-233. Pocket Books.
Room to Die in. Ellery Queen. 1975. (pbk.) 0.95. New American Library.
Room to Swing. Ed Lacy. 1971. pap. 0.75 o.p. (T2543). Pyramid Pubns.
Room to Swing: A Novel. 1st Ed. Ed Lacy. LC 57-850811. 1957. Harper.
Room Under the Stairs. Herman Landon. LC 23-168183. 1923. G. H. Watt.
Room Upstairs. Mildred Davis. 1974. (pbk.) 1.25. Dell.
Room Upstairs. Monica Dickens. LC 66-16932. 4.50. Doubleday.
Room with a View. Edward Morgan Forster. LC 43-51346. (New classics series). 1943. New Directions.
Room with a View. abinger ed. Edward Morgan Forster. LC 78-324406. (Forster, Edward Morgan. 1879-1970 The Abinger Edition of E. M. Forster). (Illus.). 1977. 17.50 (ISBN 0-7131-5946-4). Edward Arnold.
Room with Dark Mirrors. Velda Johnston. LC 75-43605. 1976. 9.95 (ISBN 0-8161-6344-8). G. K. Hall.
Room with Dark Mirrors. Velda Johnston. (Signet book). 1976. 1.50. New American Library.
Room with Dark Mirrors: A Novel of Suspense. Velda Johnston. LC 75-11938. 1975. 6.95 (ISBN 0-396-07150-3). Dodd, Mead.
Room with No Number: A Novel. Frank Shingle. LC 78-69783. (Exposition-Banner book). 8.00 (ISBN 0-682-49182-9). Exposition Press.
Room with the Iron Shutters. Robert McNair Wilson. LC 30-8779. 1930. J. B. Lippincott Company.
Room with the Tassels. Carolyn Wells. LC 18-183392. George H. Doran Company.
Room with the Tassels. Carolyn Wells. LC 24-22213. 1920. Grosset & Dunlap.
Rooming House. Wright Williams. Phoenix Press.
Rooming House. Watkins Eppes Wright. LC 38-22013. 1938. Phoenix Press.
Roommate. Jacqueline Wein. 1980. pap. 2.25 (ISBN 0-451-09160-4, E9160, Sig). NAL.
Roommate: A Novel. Jacqueline Wein. LC 78-26006. 7.95 (ISBN 0-517-53682-X). Crown.
Rooms at the Top. Thomas H Hilton. 1974. (pbk.) 1.95. Brandon Books.
Rooms of Paradise. Lee John Harding. LC 79-5106. 1979. 8.95 (ISBN 0-312-69306-0). St. Martin's Press.
Roon. Herbert Asquith. LC 29-11647. 1929. C. Scribner's Sons.
Roosevelt After Inauguration. William S. Burroughs. LC 79-21111. 1979. pap. 3.00 (ISBN 0-87286-115-5). City Lights.
Rooster Cogburn. Martin Julien. (Signet Film Series). (Illus.). 1975. (pbk.) 1.50. New American Library.
Rooster Crows for Day. Ben Lucien Burman. LC 45-605011. 1945. E. P. Dutton & Company, Inc.
Roosters Crow in Town. Henry Beetle Hough. LC 45-294616. 1945. D. Appleton-Century Company, Incorporated.
Roosters Loud in Africa. Irmgard Muske. LC 68-13894. (Illus.). 1968. Concordia Pub. House.
Root and Branch: A Novel. Hugo Wolfram. LC 73-86824. 1969. 6.50. Hill & Wang.
Root and the Bough. Francine Findley. LC 33-1839. 1933. A. H. King.
Root and the Flower. Josephine Dodge Daskam Bacon. LC 39-20170. 1939. D. Appleton-Century Company, Incorporated.
Root and the Flower. new ed. Leopold Hamilton Myers. LC 47-30337. 1947. Harcourt, Brace.
Root-Bound. Rose Terry Cooke. LC 68-23719. (Americans in Fiction Ser.). (Illus.). lib. bdg. 14.00x (ISBN 0-8398-0275-7); pap. text ed. 4.95x (ISBN 0-89197-924-7). Irvington.
Root-Bound. Rose Terry Cooke. LC 68-23719. (Americans in Fiction Ser). 1968. Repr. of 1885 ed. lib. bdg. 8.00x o.p. (ISBN 0-8398-0275-7). Gregg.

Root-Bound: And Other Sketches. Rose Terry Cooke. LC 6-27182. 1885. Congregational Sunday-School and Publishing Society.
Root, Hog, and Die. George Dixon Snell. LC 36-20996. 1936. The Caxton Printers, Ltd.
Root in the Rock: An Indian Saga, 1876-1936. Dora Hilda Southgate. LC 38-27106. 1938. A. A. Knopf.
Root of All Evil. Del Kimbel. 2.50 o.p. Carlton.
Root of All Evil. Florence Marryat Church Lean. (On cover: Lovell's library. v. 19. no. 940). 1887. J. W. Lovell Company.
Root of All Evil. Elizabeth Linington. LC 64-10736. 1964. Morrow.
Root of All Evil. Alice Owen. LC 9-27257. 1.25. Broadway Publishing Co.
Root of All Evil. St. John, Adela Rogers. LC 40-9316. 1940. E. P. Dutton & Co., Inc.
Root of All Evil. Dell Shannon. 1964. 4.50 o.p. Morrow.
Root of All Evil. Dell Shannon. 1970. pap. 0.75 o.p. (T2228). Pyramid Pubns.
Root of Evil. Eaton K Goldthwaite. LC 48-5176. (Bloodhound mystery). 1948. Duell, Sloan and Pearce.
Root of Evil. Frances McHugh. pap. 0.75 o.s.i. (01-328). Lancer.
Root of Evil: A Novel. Thomas Dixon. LC 11-143324. 1911. Doubleday, Page & Company.
Root of Evil: By James Cross Pseud. Hugh Jones Parry. LC 57-76695. 1957. J. Messner.
Root of His Evil. William Ard. LC 57-102116. 1957. Rinehart.
Root of the Lotus. Mary Louise Mabie. LC 38-21322. 1938. C. Scribner's Sons.
Root Out of Dry Ground. Argye M Briggs. LC 48-9176. 1948. W. B. Eerdmans Pub. Co.
Rooted Sorrow. Philip Maitland Hubbard. LC 72-95906. 1973. 5.95 (ISBN 0-689-10559-2). Atheneum.
Rootless. 1st Ed. Waters Edward Turpin. LC 56-12795. 1957. Vantage Press.
Roots. Eduardo Zamacois. LC 29-22807. The Viking Press.
Roots: A Novel of the Dutch East Indies. Marie Therese Colette Boecop-Malye. LC 42-18462. 1942. Doubleday, Doran & Company, Inc.
Roots & Wings. Jakub Herzig & Lena Allen-Shore. LC 82-60602. 152p. 1982. pap. 3.95 (ISBN 0-88400-085-0); 8.95 (ISBN 0-88400-087-7). Shengold.
Roots in Adobe. Dorothy L. Pillsbury. LC 59-13409. (Illus.). 240p. 1974. pap. 2.95 o.p. (ISBN 0-8263-0327-7). U of NM Pr.
Roots in the Sky. Sidney Meller. LC 38-21545. 1938. The Macmillan Company.
Roots of a Revolution: Scenes from Zimbabwe's Struggle. Ndabaningi Sithole. LC 77-30074. 1977. 9.50 (ISBN 0-19-215672-1). Oxford University Press.
Roots of Coincidence. Arthur Koestler. 1973. pap. 2.95 (ISBN 0-394-71934-4, Vin). Random.
Roots of Evil: Weird Stories of Supernatural Plants. Michel Parry. LC 75-29661. 1976. 7.95 (ISBN 0-8008-6837-4). Taplinger Pub. Co.
Roots of Heaven. Romain Gary, pseud. LC 75-304756. 1973. 1.95 (ISBN 0-85617-892-6). White Lion Publishers.
Roots of Heaven. Annabel Murray. (Harlequin Romance Ser.). 192p. 1983. pap. 1.75 (ISBN 0-373-02549-1). Harlequin Bks.
Roots of Mankind. John Napier. pap. 2.95x o.p. (ISBN 0-06-131726-8, TB1726, Torch). Har-Row.
Roots of the Mountains. William Morris. (Forgotten Fantasy Library: Vol. 19). 1979. pap. 5.95 (ISBN 0-87877-118-2). Newcastle Pub.
Roots of the Mountains: Wherein Is Told Somewhat of the Lives of the Men of Burgdale, Their Friends, Their Neighbours, Their Foemen, and Their Fellows in Arms. William Morris. LC 80-19676. (Newcastle Forgotten Fantasy library; v. 19). 1980. 11.95. Borgo Press.
Roots of the Tree. Helen Todd. LC 44-8100. 1944. Houghton Mifflin Company.
Rope. Harold Everett Porter. LC 22-19906. 1922. 1.75. Dodd, Mead and Company.
Rope Bridge. Leslie, Cecilie. LC 64-17730. 1964. Doubleday.
Rope Crazy. Frank Chester Robertson. LC 48-10422. 1948. E. P. Dutton.
Rope-Dancer. Victor Marchetti. LC 73-158742. 1971. 6.95 (ISBN 0-448-02460-8). Grosset & Dunlap.
Rope Dances. David Porush. LC 78-68135. 1979. 8.95 (ISBN 0-914590-50-2); pap. 3.95 (ISBN 0-914590-51-0). Fiction Coll.
Rope Enough. Dorothy Stockbridge Tillet. LC 38-20480. 1938. Pub. for the Crime Club, Inc. by Doubleday, Doran & Co., Inc.
Rope Enough... Dorothy Stockbridge Tillet. LC 40-33069. 1940. The Sun Dial Press.
Rope for a Convict. Ralph Carter Woodthorpe. LC 40-4892. 1940. Pub. for the Crime Club by Doubleday, Doran & Company, Inc.
Rope for an Ape. Albert Leffingwell. LC 47-234852. 1947. The Dial Press.
Rope for Dr. Webster. James Gould Cozzens. 1976. boxed 35.00 (ISBN 0-89723-010-8). Bruccoli.
Rope for General Dietz. John Rossiter. LC 77-188475. 192p. 1972. 4.95 o.p. (ISBN 0-8027-5253-5). Walker & Co.
Rope for the Baron. John Creasey. LC 49-7340. 1949. Duel Sloan and Pearce.
Rope for the Hanging: A Mrs. Pym Story. Nigel Morland. LC 39-2928. Farrar & Rinehart, Incorporated.
Rope Law see Drift Fence.
Rope Neckties. John Wilstach. LC 39-13748. Dodge Publishing Company.
Rope of Gold. Josephine Herbst. LC 39-5403. Harcourt, Brace and Company.
Rope of Sand: By Francis Bonnamy Pseud. Audrey Walz. LC 44-8095. 1944. Duell, Sloan and Pearce.
Rope of Wind. Henry Dumas. 1979. 8.95 o.p. (ISBN 0-394-50529-8). Random.
Rope of Wind and Other Stories. Henry Dumas & Eugene Redmond. LC 78-21815. 7.95 (ISBN 0-394-50529-8). Random House.
Rope Skips Max. Illus. by Hanne Turk. (Max the Mouse Bk.). (Illus.). 28p. 1980. pap. 2.95 (ISBN 0-907234-20-8). Neugebauer Pr.
Rope: The Strange Story of a Strange Murder. Alfred Hitchcock. LC 49-428523. 1948. Dell Pub. Co.
Rope the Wild Wind. Lee Floren. (Orig.). 1979. pap. 1.75 (ISBN 0-532-23149-X). Woodhill.
Rope the Wind. Norman A. Fox. 160p. 1979. pap. 1.25 (ISBN 0-440-17494-5). Dell.
Rope the Wind. Norman A Fox. 1973. (pbk) 0.75. Dell.
Rope to Spare: An Anthony Gethryn Detective Story... Philip MacDonald. LC 32-28089. Pub. for the Crime Club, Inc., by Doubleday, Doran & Company, Inc.
Roped Wolf. Robert Ames Bennet. LC 31-3097. 1931. G. H. Watt.
Roper's Row. Warwick Deeping. LC 29-17320. 1929. A. A. Knopf.
Ropes of Sand. Rose Lucile Ellerbe. LC 26-11636. 1925. David Graham Fischer Corporation.
Ropes of Sand. Robert Edward Francillon. LC 6-43249. (On cover: Seaside library. Pocket ed. no. 360). G. Munro.
Ropes of Sand: And Other Stories. Cecilia Viets Dakin Jamison. LC 7-10327. 1873. J. R. Osgood and Company.
Roque Sergeant. Lawrence Cortesi, pseud. (Belmont Tower book). 1.75 (ISBN 0-505-51352-8). Tower Pubns.
Roquefort Gang. Sandy Clifford. 1982. pap. write for info. Bantam.
Roque's Mistress. Constance Gluyas. (Signet Book). 1977. 1.95 (ISBN 0-451-07533-1). New American Library.
Rork! Avram Davidson. 142p. 1968. 14.00 o.p. (ISBN 0-89366-121-X). Ultramarine Pub.
Rory and Bran. Edward John Moreton Drax Plunkett Dunsany. LC 37-844524. G. P. Putnam's Sons.
Rory O'More. Samuel Lover. LC 7-15835. (On cover: Lovell's library v. 14. no. 719). 1886. J. W. Lovell Company.
Rory O'More. Samuel Lover. LC 4-16549. 1901. Little, Brown, & Company.
Rory O'More: A National Romance. Samuel Lover. Repr. of 1839 ed. 16.00 o.p. (ISBN 0-404-54476-2). AMS Pr.
Rosa. L. De Stefani. Tr. by C. Barford & S. Hodges. 1963. 4.50x o.p. Verry.
Rosa. Knut Hamsun & Chater, Arthur G., Tr. LC 26-66411. 1926. A. A. Knopf.
Rosa. Brian Stanford Morgan. LC 49-118304. 1949. Little Brown.
Rosa. Maurice Pons. LC 70-37450. 1972. 5.95. Dial Press.
Rosa. Margery Sharp. LC 74-97908. 1970. 5.95. Little, Brown.
Rosa at Ten O'clock. Marco Denevi. LC 64-14369. 1964. Holt, Rinehart and Winston.
Rosa Emerson: Or, A Young Woman's Influence; a Story of the Lodge, the Church and the School. John Augustus Williams. LC 8-36912. 1897. Christian Publishing Company.
Rosa Fielding, or the Victim of Lust. Intro. by H. E. Holt. 1968. pap. 1.95 o.p. (6010). Brandon.
Rosa, la Flauta. Sergio Elizondo. 1980. pap. 3.95 (ISBN 0-915808-37-4). Editorial Justa.
Rosa Mundi, and Other Stories. Ethel May Dell. LC 79-121535. (Short story index reprint series). 1970. (ISBN 0-8369-3491-1). Books for Libraries Press.
Rosa Mundi: And Other Stories. Ethel May Dell. LC 21-7337. 1921. G. P. Putnam's Sons.
Rosa: Or, The Parisian Girl. Elise Francoise Louise De Plessis-Gouret De Pressense. Tr. by Fletcher, Henrietta (Malan) LC 12-37756. 1860. Harper & Brothers.
Rosa. Tr. from Italian by Carla Barford, Sheila Hodges. Livia De Stefani. LC 65-295592. 1965. bds., 4.00. Eyre & Spottiswoode.
Rosabel. Esther Miller. LC 4-31050. 1904. J. B. Lippincott Company.
Rosalba. Sheila Bishop. 192p. (Orig.). 1982. pap. 1.50 (ISBN 0-449-50312-7, Coventry). Fawcett.
Rosalba: The Story of Her Development. Grant Allen. LC 4816. (Hudson library, no 30)). 1899. G. P. Putnam's Sons.
Rosaleen. Louise Platt Hauck. LC 30-7196. The Penn Publishing Company.
Rosaleen Among the Artists. Elisabeth Sanxay Holding. LC 21-14543. George H. Doran Company.
Rosalie. Charles Major. LC 25-10882. 1925. The Macmillan Company.
Rosalie Du Pont: Or, Treason in the Camp. A Sequel to the Female Spy. Emerson Bennett. LC 7-36491. L. Stratton.
Rosalie's Career. Faith Baldwin Cuthrell. LC 28-4772. E. J. Clode, Inc.
Rosalind. A Novel. by thomas lodge. ed. Thomas Lodge. LC 7-3044. (Cassell's national library. v. 2, no. 62). 1887. Cassell & Company, Limited.
Rosalind. A Novel. Thomas Lodge. LC 7-14799. (Cassell's national library. v. 2, no. 62). The Cassell Publishing Co.
Rosalind at Red Gate. Meredith Nicholson. LC 7-38599. 1907. The Bobbs-Merrill Company.
Rosalind Morton: Or, The Mystery of Ivy Crown. A Kentucky Story. Alice Kate Roland. LC 98-280. 1898. C. T. Dearing.
Rosalind Passes: A Novel. Frank Arthur Swinnerton. LC 73-10820. 1974. 6.95 (ISBN 0-385-02629-3). Doubleday.
Rosalita. Stacey B Day. LC 68-24049. 1968. Cultural and Educational Productions.
Rosalynde. Thomas Lodge. 1976. text ed. 8.50x o.s.i. (ISBN 0-8277-0474-7); pap. text ed. 5.95x o.s.i. (ISBN 0-8277-3896-X). British Bk Ctr.
Rosalynde, or Euphues Golden Legacie. Thomas Lodge. LC 2-24060. 1902. Elston Press.
Rosalynde: Or, Euphues' Golden Legacy. Thomas Lodge. Ed. by Baldwin, Edward Chauncey. LC 10-27304. (On cover: Standard English classics). Ginn and Company.
Rosalynde's Lovers. Maurice Thompson. LC 1-241881. The Bowen-Merrill Company.
Rosamond Howard. Katie R Lovelace. LC 7-14782. (On cover: Satchel series. no. 5). The Authors' Publishing Company.
Rosamond of Monterre: A Canadian Pastoral. Elizabeth Bruce R. Winslow. LC 23-15826. 1923. The Four Seas Company.
Rosamond: or, Sundered Hearts. Alexander McVeigh Miller. (On cover: The select series, no. 18). 1889. Street & Smith.
Rosamond the Second: Being the True Record of the Unparalleled Romance of One Claudius Fuller. Mary Martha Mears. LC 10-11299. 1910. Frederick A. Stokes Company.
Rosamund of the Snow. Agnes Theresa Holliday. LC 11-297282. 1911. Chochrane Publishing Company.
Rosamunda. Marjory Hall. 1974. (pbk.) 0.95. Dell.
Rosaria. Susan Thaler. LC 67-23575. 1967. D. McKay Co.
Rosary. Florence Louisa Charlesworth Barclay. LC 50-4795. 1950. Grosset & Dunlap.
Rosary. Florence Louisa Charlesworth Barclay. 1909. G. P. Putnam's Sons.
Rosary. Florence Louisa Charlesworth Barclay. LC 10-305807. 1910. G. P. Putnam's Sons.
Rosary. Florence Louisa Charlesworth Barclay. LC 20-123713. 1915. Grosset & Dunlap.
Rosary. Florence Louisa Charlesworth Barclay. LC 29-252840. Grosset & Dunlap.
Rosary Murders. William X Kienzle. LC 78-31833. 9.95 (ISBN 0-8362-6101-1). Andrews and McMeel.
Rosa's Confession: A Realistic Romance of Love and Adventure. Paul James Duff. The Morgan Publishing Co.
Rosaura a las Diez. Ed., Introd. by Donald A. Yates. Marco Denevi. Ed. by Donald A. Yates. LC 64-172123. (Scribner Spanish ser.). 1965. pap., 2.95. Scribners.
Rose. Marilyn Hoff. LC 69-12036. 1969. Harcourt, Brace & World.
Rose--the Dancer. Winifred Carter. LC 29-22922. 1929. Thomas Y. Crowell Company.
Rose a Charlitte: An Acadien Romance. Marshall Saunders. LC 8-1834. 1898. L. C. Page and Company.
Rose, a Color of Darkness. Amon Liner. LC 80-24458. 1980. 5.00. Carolina Wren Press.
Rose-A-Down Dilly. Judi Beckley & Randy West. (Illus.). 32p. (Orig.). 1981. pap. 2.50x (ISBN 0-942478-01-0). Photopia Pr.
Rose: A Novel. Leonore Fleischer. 2.25 (ISBN 0-446-82996-X). Warner Books.
Rose and Elza. Songs and Stories of Bygone Days in Fayette County and Elsewhere. By E. C--. Elizabeth Custead. Printed by E. O. Jenkins' Sons.
Rose and Millie... Mary Ellen Atkinson. LC 6-38391. (On cover: The young folks' library, no. 19). D. Lothrop & Co.
Rose and Ninette: A Story of the Morals and Manners of the Day. Alphonse Daudet. Tr. by Serrano, Mary Jane. LC 6-33042. (On cover: Cassell's sunshine series, no. 100). Cassell Publishing Company.
Rose and Rose: A Story. Edward Verrall Lucas. LC 23-26031. 1.90. George H. Doran Company.
Rose and the Flame. Jonreed Lauritzen. LC 51-10191. 1951. Doubleday.
Rose and the Key. Joseph Sheridan Le Fanu. LC 76-5275. (Le Fann, Joseph Sheridan, 1814-1873. Works. 1976). 1976. (3 vols.) 59.00 (ISBN 0-405-09229-6). Arno Press.
Rose and the Key. Joseph Sheridan Le Fanu. LC 82-9569. 1982. 6.50 (ISBN 0-486-24377-X). Dover Publications.
Rose & the Key. Joseph Sheridan Le Fanu. (Mystery Ser.). 448p. 1983. pap. 6.95 (ISBN 0-486-24377-X). Dover.
Rose & the Lily. Frances Parkinson Wheeler Keyes. pap. 0.60 o.p. (53-460). Paperback Lib.
Rose and the Lily. Alexander McVeigh Miller. (Lovell's library, no. 1251). 1888. J. W. Lovell Company.
Rose and the Lily: Or, Love Wins Love. Alexander McVeigh Miller. (On cover: Munro's library, v. 1, no. 7). N. L. Munro.
Rose and the Ogre. Fredrika Shumway Smith. LC 48-3287. 1948. Christopher Pub. House.
Rose & the Ring. William M. Thackeray. (Illus.). 1947. 30.00 o.p. (ISBN 0-87598-006-6). Pierpont Morgan.
Rose and the Ring; or, The History of Prince Giglio and Prince Bulbo: A Fireside Pantomime for Great and Small Children. William Makepeace Thackeray. LC 58-59972. 1958. Macmillan.
Rose and the Ring: Or, The History of Prince Giglio and Prince Bulbo; a Fire-Side Pantomime for Great and Small Children. William Makepeace Thackeray. LC 67-28169. (Legacy library facsimile). (Illus.). 1967. University Microfilms.
Rose and the Ring: Or, The History of Prince Giglio and Prince Bulbo. A Fireside Pantomime for Great and Small Children. William Makepeace Thackeray. LC 42-273762. 1883. Estes and Lauriat.
Rose and the Ring: Or, The History of Prince Giglio and Prince Bulbo; a Fireside Pantomime of Great and Small Children. William Makepeace Thackeray. (On cover: Lovell's library, v. 6, no. 320). 1883. J. W. Lovell Company.
Rose and the Ring: Or, The History of Prince Giglio and Prince Bulbo; a Fireside Pantomime for Great and Small Children. William Makepeace Thackeray. (On cover: Heath's home and school classics. The story book series, no. 34). 1901. D. C. Heath & Co.
Rose and the Ring: Or, The History of Prince Giglio and Prince Bulbo, a Fireside Pantomime for Great and Small Children. William Makepeace Thackeray. LC 7-41580. 1907. A. Wessels Company.
Rose and the Ring: Or, The History of Prince Giglio and Prince Bulbo, a Fireside Pantomime for Great and Small Children. William Makepeace Thackeray. LC 23-26864. (On verso of half-title: The Little library). 1923. The Macmillan Company.
Rose and the Ring: Reproduced in Facsimile from the Author's Original Illustrated Manuscript in the Pierpont Morgan Library. William Makepeace Thackeray & Pierpont Morgan Library, New York. LC 48-249. 1947. Pierpont Morgan Library.
Rose and the Sheepskin. Joseph Gordian Daley. LC 2-30410. 1902. W. H. Young and Company.
Rose & the Sword. Joan Mattingly. 352p. (Orig.). 1981. pap. 2.75 (ISBN 0-8439-0994-3, Leisure Bks). Nordon Pubns.
Rose and the Sword. Sandra Paretti. LC 68-14313. 1969. 6.95. Coward-McCann.
Rose & the Sword. Katherine Sargent. 256p. (Orig.). 1983. pap. 2.75 (ISBN 0-449-12379-0, GM). Fawcett.
Rose and the Thorn: A Tale of Modern Life. Charles Jaques Goodwin. LC 1-29317. The Neely Company.
Rose and the Yew Tree. Agatha Miller Christie. 1975. (pbk.) 0.95. Dell.
Rose and the Yew Tree. Agatha Miller Christie. LC 48-5803. 1948. Rinehart.
Rose & the Yew Tree. Mary Westmacott. LC 77-150378. 256p. 1981. pap. 6.95 (ISBN 0-87795-351-1). Arbor Hse.
Rose & the Yew Tree. Mary Westmacott. LC 77-150378. 1971. 5.95 (ISBN 0-87795-014-8). Arbor Hse.
Rose & the Yew Tree. Mary Westmacott. 192p. 1982. pap. 2.50 (ISBN 0-440-17503-8). Dell.
Rose and the Yew Tree: A Novel of Romance and Suspense. Agatha Miller Christie. LC 77-150378. 1971. 5.95. Arbor House.
Rose at Harvest End. Eleanor M. Fairburn. 224p. 1975. 6.95 o.p. (ISBN 0-88349-068-4). Readers Digest Pr.

Rose Bath Riddle. Anthony M Rud. LC 34-8990. The Macaulay Company.
Rose Bowl. William H Meincke. LC 36-138787. R. Speller.
Rose-Bush of a Thousand Years. Mabel Wagnalls. LC 13-10840. 1918. Funk & Wagnalls Company.
Rose by Any Other Name. Ora Lewis Bradley. LC 46-22638. 1946. The Christopher Publishing House.
Rose Clark. Sara Payson Willis Parton. LC 7-34089. 1856. Mason Brothers.
Rose-Colored World: And Other Fantasies. Ethel Mary Brodie. LC 10-236342. 1910. The Metropolitan Press.
Rose Cottingham. Netta Syrett. LC 77-16345. 1977. 5.00. (ISBN 0-915864-21-5) (ISBN 0-915864-20-7). Cassandra Editions.
Rose Cottingham: A Novel. Netta Syrett. LC 15-25938. 1915. 1.35. G. P. Putnam's Sons.
Rose Croix. David Tod Gilliam. LC 6-22858. The Saalfield Publishing Company.
Rose Dawn. Stewart Edward White. LC 20-212903. 1920. Doubleday, Page & Company.
Rose-De-Noel. Being the Continuation of "Conrad De Valgeneuse.". Alexandre Dumas. Tr. by Sherwood, Mary Neal. LC 3662. (On cover: Seaside library. Pocket ed., no. 2045). G. Munro's Sons.
Rose Deeprose. Sheila Kaye-Smith. LC 37-287. 1936. Harper & Brothers.
Rose Domino. Sheila Walsh. (Orig.). 1981. pap. 2.25 (ISBN 0-451-11077-3, AE1077, Sig). NAL.
Rose Door. Estelle Baker. LC 11-12127. 1911. 1.00. C. H. Kerr & Company.
Rose Door. Estelle Baker. LC 18-191437. 1913. C. H. Kerr & Company.
Rose Exterminator: A Novel; by William Carney. William Carney. LC 82-9260. 13.95 (ISBN 0-89696-177-X). Everest House.
Rose Fleming: The Story of an Heiress. Dora Russell. (On cover: Seaside library. Pocket ed., no. 103). 1883. G. Munro.
Rose for Ana Maria: A Novel. Frank Yerby. LC 75-45143. 1976. 7.95 (ISBN 0-8037-7248-3). Dial Press.
Rose for Armageddon. Hilbert Schenck. (Orig.). 1982. pap. 2.25 (ISBN 0-671-44311-9, Timescape). PB.
Rose for Carlie. Venita Mastin. 1981. pap. 6.95 (Avalon). Bouregy.
Rose for Marianne. 1st American Ed. Francis Treseder Giles. LC 56-10635. Little, Brown.
Rose for Virtue. Norah Robinson Lofts. 320p. 1977. pap. 1.95 (ISBN 0-449-23435-5, Crest). Fawcett.
Rose for Virtue: The Very Private Life of Hortense, Stepdaughter of Napoleon I, Mother of Napoleon III. Norah Robinson Lofts. LC 77-150903. 1971. 6.95. Doubleday.
Rose for Virtue: The Very Private Life of Hortense, Stepdaughter of Napoleon I, Mother of Napoleon III. Norah Robinson Lofts. LC 77-38930. 1972. (ISBN 0-8161-6021-X). G. K. Hall.
Rose from Brier. Amy Carmichael. 1972. 4.50 (ISBN 0-87508-078-2); pap. 2.95 (ISBN 0-87508-077-4). Chr Lit.
Rose from Lucifer. Anne Hampson. (Harlequin Presents Ser.). 192p. 1982. pap. 1.75 (ISBN 0-373-10483-9). Harlequin Bks.
Rose Galbraith. Grace Livingston Hill. LC 40-98994. J. B. Lippincott Company.
Rose-Garden Husband. Margaret Widdemer. LC 15-4583. 1915. J. B. Lippincott Company.
Rose Gay, Wanted! Alex Campbell. LC 33-208245. The Macaulay Company.
Rose Geranium. A Tragedy. Patience Stapleton. (On cover: Idylwild series, v. 1, no. 8). 1892. Morrill, Higgins & Co.
Rose-Gorwer. Jean Sutbbs. LC 63-9420. 1963. St. Martin's Press.
Rose in December. Edwin Ritchie. LC 67-29226. 1967. Courthouse Square Enterprises.
Rose in the Banyan Tree. Richard Hilsop. 256p. 1980. pap. cancelled (ISBN 0-553-13662-3). Bantam.
Rose in the Heart. Edna O'Brien. LC 78-18563. 1979. 8.95 (ISBN 0-385-14349-4). Doubleday.
Rose in the Ring. George Barr McCutcheon. LC 10-20295. 1910. Dodd, Mead and Company.
Rose in Thorns. Charlotte Mary Brame. (On cover: Seaside library. Pocket ed. no. 296). G. Munro.
Rose Island: The Strange Story of a Love Adventure at Sea. William Clark Russell. 1899. H. S. Stone and Company.
Rose Leblanc. Georgiana Charlotte Leveson-Gower Fullerton. LC 6-44735. D. & J. Sadlier & Co.
Rose-Lit Street. Rosamund Nugent. LC 26-157350. 1926. D. Appleton and Company.
Rose MacLeod. Alice Brown. LC 8-122255. 1908. Houghton, Mifflin and Company.
Rose Mather: A Novel. Mary Jane Hawes Holmes. LC 1-29058. 1897. G. W. Dillingham Co.
Rose Mather; a Tale of the War. Mary Jane Hawes Holmes. LC 1-1179. 1868. G. W. Carleton & Co.
Rose Mather: a Tale of the War. Mary Jane Hawes Holmes. LC 1-1180. 1896. G. W. Dillingham.
Rose Mervyn, of Whitelake. A Novel. Anne Beale. LC 6-102773. (Franklin square library, no. 76). 1879. Harper & Brothers.
Rose Milton. A Romance ... LC 7-40769. 1855. Parry and McMillan, Successors to A. Hart, Late Carey and Hart.
Rose O' the River. Kate Douglas Smith Wiggin. LC 5-20445. 1905. Houghton, Mifflin & Company.
Rose O' the Sea: A Romance. Marguerite Florence Helene Evans. LC 20-17652. 1920. Houghton Mifflin Company.
Rose of a Hundred Leaves: A Love-Story. Amelia Edith Huddleston Barr. LC 6-7973. 1891. Dodd, Mead and Company.
Rose of Alhama: Or, The Conquest of Granada. An Episode of the Moorish Wars in Spain. Charles Warren Currier. LC 6-31703. 1897. Christian Press Association Publishing Company.
Rose of Auzeburg. Mary Franklyn Latham Norton. LC 12-3601. 1.50. Broadway Publishing Co.
Rose of Auzenburg; an Historical Romance: The Balkan War Scare of 1907 and Forces Which Led to the World War of 1914. 2d ed. Mary Franklyn Latham Norton. LC 47-38838. 1947. Mercury Press.
Rose of Calnevaria. Mack L Townsend. LC 64-3268. 1964. Exposition Press.
Rose of Dawn. Ethel May Dell. LC 17-24287. 1917. G. P. Putnam's Sons.
Rose of Disentis. A Novel. Heinrich I. E. Johann Heinrich Daniel Zschokke & Trenor, James J. D., Tr. LC 8-37798. 1873. Sheldon & Company.
Rose of Dutcher's Coolly. Hamlin Garland. LC 74-90103. (Illus.). 1969. AMS Press.
Rose of Dutcher's Coolly. sunset ed. new york, harper. ed. Hamlin Garland. LC 76-108484. 1970. Scholarly Press.
Rose of Dutcher's Coolly. Hamlin Garland. LC 79-82509. 1969. 3.00. University of Nebraska Press.
Rose of Dutcher's Coolly. Hamlin Garland. LC 6-407179. 1895. Stone & Kimball.
Rose of Dutcher's Coolly. Hamlin Garland. LC 99-1832. 1899. The Macmillan Company.
Rose of Flesh. Jan Wolkers. LC 67-12383. 1967. G. Braziller.
Rose of Fury, Rose of Flame. Jeanne Sommers. (Orig.). 1980. pap. 2.50 (ISBN 0-440-17589-5). Dell.
Rose of God. Raymond Johnson. LC 77-74864. 6.95. Libra Publishers.
Rose of Hever. Maureen Peters. 1971. pap. 0.95 o.p. (95099). Beagle Bks.
Rose of Jericho. Ruth Holt Boucicault. LC 20-67079. 1920. 1.90. G.P. Putnam's Sons.
Rose of Jericho: And Other Stories. Tage Aurell. LC 68-14036. (Nordic translation series). 1968. University of Wisconsin Press.
Rose of Jericho & Other Stories. Tage Aurell. Tr. by Martin S. Allwood from Swedish. (Nordic Translation Ser). Orig. Title: Smarre besattelser & Nya bersattelser. 152p. 1968. 15.00 (ISBN 0-299-04701-6); pap. 6.00 (ISBN 0-299-04704-0). U of Wis Pr.
Rose of Los Angeles: The Love Story of a City. John B. T Campbell. LC 29-12651. Tribune Press, Inc.
Rose of Love. Angeline Teal. LC 8-260321. 1893. Dodd, Mead & Company.
Rose of Magdala. Charles Edward Hewitt. LC 52-6731. B. Humphries.
Rose of Normandy. William Robert Anthony Wilson. LC 3-9628. 1903. Little, Brown, and Company.
Rose of Old Harpeth. Maria Thompson Daviess. LC 11-241160. The Bobbs-Merrill Company.
Rose of Old Quebec. Anne Hollingsworth Wharton. LC 13-22756. 1913. J. B. Lippincott Company.
Rose of Old St. Louis. Mary C Johnson Dillon. LC 4-17219. 1904. The Century Co.
Rose of Old St. Louis. Mary C Johnson Dillon. LC 13-20469. 1910. The Century Co.
Rose of Old Viginia: A Romance of the Old South & the War Between the States. Charles Ervine Clarkson. 59p. 1927. 6.00 (ISBN 0-937130-11-7). Burke's Bk Store.
Rose of Old Virginia" A Romance of the Old South and the War Between the States. Charles Ervine Clarkson. Calvert-McBride Printing Co.
Rose of Paradise: Being a Detailed Account of Certain Adventures That Happended to Captain John Mackra, in Connection with the Famous Pirate, Edward England, in the Year 1720, off the Island of Juanna in the Mozambique Channel. Howard Pyle. LC 7-42406. 1888. Harper & Brothers.
Rose of Paradise: Being a Detailed Account of Certain Adventures That Happended to Captain John Mackra, in Connection with the Famous Pirate, Edward England, in the Year 1720, off the Island of Juanna in the Mozambique Channel. Howard Pyle. LC 7-42407. (On cover: Harper's quarterly, no. 4). 1894. Harper & Brothers.
Rose of Passion Rose of Love. Jeanne Sommers. (Dell-James a Bryans Bk.). (Dell Publishing Co.). 2.25 (ISBN 0-440-07515-7). Dell Publishing Co.
Rose of Persia: Or, Giafar Al Barmeki. A Tale of the East. 2d ed. Samuel Spring & Spring, Gardiner, Jr., Supposed Author. LC 8-14044. 1847. Harper & Brothers.
Rose of Remembrance. Donald G. Lane. 3.50 o.p. Carlton.
Rose of Santa Fe. Edwin Legrand Sabin. LC 23-7543. G. W. Jacobs & Company.
Rose of Sharon. Mae Van Norman Long. LC 37-25342. DeVorss & Co.
Rose of Sharon. Andrew Sheffield. LC 8-30932. 1908. The C. M. Clark Publishing Co.
Rose of Sharon: By Harley Rosso Pseud. Harvey Ross McClure. LC 54-77162. Comet Press Books.
Rose of Sharon: The Story of the Shulammite Maiden. Everett Hollingsworth Sperow. LC 18-6027. (Lettered on cover: Library of religious thought) $1.00.). The Gorham Press; Etc., Etc.
Rose of the Garden: The Romance of Lady Sarah Lennox; a Novel. Katharine Tynan Hinkson, pseud. LC 13-22288. 1.35. The Bobbs-Merrill Company.
Rose of the Parsonage: An Idyll of Our Own Times. Robert Giseke. LC 6-43990. 1854. Parry and M'Millan.
Rose of the Sea. Paul Vialar. Tr. by Wells, Warre Bradley. LC 40-13811. 1940. Carrick & Evans, Inc.
Rose of the Wilderness: Or, Washington's First Love, Taken and Rev. from Authentic Sources. Walter Scott Browne. LC 2-1780. 1901.
Rose of the World. Agnes Sweetman Castle & Castle, Egerton. LC 5-10920. 1905. F. A. Stokes Company.
Rose of the World. M. C Martin. LC 7-39998. 1907. Benziger Brothers.
Rose of the World. Kathleen Thompson Norris. LC 24-20379. 1924. Doubleday, Page & Company.
Rose of the World. Kathleen Thompson Norris. LC 29-190292. 1926. A. L. Burt Company.
Rose of Tibet. Lionel Davidson. 1977. pap. 1.95 o.p. (ISBN 0-14-002137-X). Penguin.
Rose of Tibet. Lionel Davidson. LC 82-47558. 288p. 1982. pap. 2.84i (ISBN 0-06-080593-5, P593, PL). Har-Row.
Rose of Typhaines: A Tale of the Commune in the Twelfth Century. Joseph Arthur Gobineau. Tr. by Meigs, Charles Delucena. LC 6-43751. 1872. Claxton, Remsen & Haffelfinger.
Rose of Wissahikon: Or, The Fourth of July, 1776. A Romance, Embracing the Secret History of the Declaration of Independence. George Lippard. LC 7-16038. 1847. G. B. Zieber & Co.
Rose of Yesterday. Francis Marion Crawford. LC 6-30888. 1897. The Macmillan Company.
Rose of Youth. Elinor Mordaunt, pseud. LC 15-21424. 1915. 1.35. John Lane Company.
Rose on the Summit. Catharine Plummer. LC 51-5600. 1951. Putnam.
Rose O'paradise. Grace Miller White. LC 15-19965. 1915. The H. K. Fly Company.
Rose Parnell: The Flower of Avondale. A Tale of the Rebellion, '98. David Power Conyngham. LC 6-30211. 1883. D. & J. Sadlier & Co.
Rose Petal Murders. Charles G Givens. LC 35-12186. The Bobbs-Merrill Company.
Rose Petal Murders. Charles G Givens. LC 43-12457. (On cover: Prize mystery novels. No. 1). 1943. Crestwood Publishing Co., Inc.
Rose Rabbi. Daniel Stern. LC 75-161847. 1971. 6.95 (ISBN 0-07-061203-X). McGraw-Hill.
Rose Raymond's Wards. Margaret Thomson Janvier. LC 7-10330. Porter & Coates.
Rose, Red & White. Betty Alice Martin King. (shadow of the tower series). 1974. (pbk.) 0.95 (ISBN 0-523-00305-6). Pinnacle Books.
Rose, Rose... Where Are You? Rosemary Ellerbeck. LC 77-12133. 8.95 (ISBN 0-698-10869-8). Coward, McCann & Geoghegan.
Rose Royal. Edith Nesbit Bland. LC 11-28738. 1912. Dodd, Mead & Company.
Rose-White Youth. Dolf Wyllarde. LC 8-29001. 1908. J. Lane Company.
Rose Window. Suzanne Blanc. LC 67-10981. 1967. Published for the Crime Club by Doubleday.
Rose Window: A Novel. 1st Ed. Frances Beckler Rubley. LC 53-12645. Exposition Press.
Rose with a Thorn. Teignmouth Shore. LC 11-11740. 1911. D. Appleton and Company.
Roseanna. Maj Sjowall & Per Wahloo. LC 75-34370. (Sjowall, Maj, 1935-, Wahloo, per, 1926-1975. Martin Beck Police Mystery). 1976. 1.65. Vintage Books.
Roseanna. Maj Sjowall & Per Wahloo. LC 67-23963. 1967. Pantheon Books.
Roseanna McCoy. Alberta Pierson Hannum. LC 47-11489. 1947. H. Holt.
Rosebud. Paul Bonnecarrere & Joan Hemingway. LC 74-740. 1974. 7.95 (ISBN 0-688-00253-6). Morrow.
Rosebud. Joan Hemingway & Paul Bonnecarrere. LC 74-740. 288p. 1974. 6.95 o.p. (ISBN 0-688-00253-6). Morrow.
Rosebush: Or, Life in California. A Story of Astrology. William Bradford. LC 6-15202. (On cover: Satchel series, no. 34). W. B. Smith & Co.
Rosecrest Cell. Vera Caspary. (95-198). 1968. Popular Lib.
Rosecrest Cell. Vera Caspary. LC 67-23120. 1967. Putnam.
Rosecroft; a Story of Common Places and Common People. William Marshall Fitts Round. LC 8-688. 1881. Lee and Shepard.
Rosedale: A Story of Self-Denial. H. C. Gardner. LC 7-306. 1863. Poe & Hitchcock.
Rosedale Hoax. Rachel Wyatt. (Anansi Fiction Ser.: No. 37). 136p. (Orig.). 1977. pap. 6.95 (ISBN 0-88784-061-2, Pub. by Hse Anansi Pr Canada). U of Toronto Pr.
Roseheath. Anne Maybury. LC 78-80473. 1969. 4.95. D. McKay Co.
Roseheath. Katherine Troy. 1969. 4.95 o.p. McKay.
Rosehurst: Or, The Step-Daughter. A Novel. Annie Somers Gilchrist. LC 6-44058. 1884. J. B. Lippincott & Co.
Roselin: Or, A Ruby Necklace. Freda Virginia Metz. LC 13-25941. 1913. 1.00. W. B. Conkey Company.
Roselynde. Roberta Gellis. LC 77-72968. 512p. 1978. pap. 2.95 (ISBN 0-86721-141-5). Playboy Pbks.
Rosemarie. Erich Kuby. LC 59-15319. 1960. Knopf.
Rosemary--for Remembrance. Norma Bright Carson. LC 14-18304. 0.75. George H. Doran Company.
Rosemary and Rue. Elizabeth Williams Champney. LC 6-23324. (Round-robin series. v. 7). 1881. J. R. Osgood and Company.
Rosemary and Rue. Martha Everts Holden. LC 12-34372. 1896. Rand, McNally & Company.
Rosemary for Remembrance. Helen Sherman Griffith. LC 11-248206. 1911. 1.20. The Penn Publishing Company.
Rosemary in Search of a Father. Charles Norris Williamson & Alice Muriel Livingston Williamson. LC 6-40214. 1906. McClure, Phillips & Co.
Rosemary Leigh: A Story of the South. Annie H Smith. LC 6-5142. 1905. The Neale Publishing Company.
Rosemary Touch. Lois Wyse. LC 73-19315. 1974. 6.95 (ISBN 0-385-04391-0). Doubleday.
Rosemary Tree. Elizabeth Goudge. LC 56-5950. 1956. Coward-McCann.
Rosemary's Baby. Ira Levin. (Dell Book). 1979. 2.25 (ISBN 0-440-17541-0). Dell Pub. Co.
Rosemary's Baby: A Novel. Ira Levin. LC 67-14767. 1967. 4.95. Random.
Rosery Folk. George Manville Fenn. LC 6-39387. (On cover: The seaside library. Pocket ed. no. 193). G. Munro.
Roses Are Red: By Emily Noble Pseud. James Noble Gifford. 1955. Arcadia House.
Roses De Septembre. Andre Maurois. 1968. pap. 0.75 o.s.i. Paris Pubns.
Roses for Breakfast. Hettie Grimstead. (Cameo Romance). (Fawcett gold medal book). 1975. (pbk.) 0.95. Fawcett.
Roses for Paula. Teresa Holloway. 192p. 1974. pap. 0.95 o.p. (ISBN 0-532-95297-9). Woodhill.
Roses for Paula. Teresa Holloway. 192p. 1974. pap. 0.95 o.p. (ISBN 0-532-95297-9). Manor Bks.
Roses for Paula. Theresa Holloway. 1974. (pbk.) 0.95. Manor Books.
Roses from a Haunted Garden. Jean Francis Webb. (Dell gothic, 7528). 1972. Dell.
Roses from a Haunted Garden. Jean Francis Webb. LC 77-151158. 1971. 6.95. D. McKay Co.
Roses from the South. 1st Ed. Perceval Reniers. LC 59-6272. 1959. Doubleday.
Roses from Yesterday. Sharon Wagner. (Ace gothic). 1975. (pbk.) 0.95. Ace Books.
Roses in December. Peggy Gaddis, pseud. LC 55-11885. 1955. Arcadia House.
Roses in Iron. William Bryant. LC 67-22954. 1967. McGraw-Hill.
Roses in the Snow. Jane McCarthy. (YA) 1973. 4.95 o.p. (Avalon). Bouregy.
Roses in the Snow. Jane McCarthy. (Avalon romances). 1973. 4.50. Avalon Books.
Roses In Winter. Joan Dial. (Orig.). 1982. pap. 3.50 (ISBN 0-671-41983-8). PB.

Rose's Last Summer. Margaret Millar. LC 52-7152. 1952. Radom House.
Roses of Crein. Beryl Symons. LC 12-17203. 1912. D. Appleton and Company.
Roses of Goose Bay. William Arthur Neubauer. LC 65-8173. 1965. Arcadia House.
Roses of Lovewell. Edgar Lawrence Fixler. LC 43-14321. 1943. The Hobson Press, Incorporated.
Roses of Malmaison: The Turbulent Life of the Beautiful Josephine. Tr. from German by Therese Pol. 1st Amer. Ed. Gaby Von Schonthan. LC 68-2206. 1968. bds., 5.95. Meredith.
Roses of Shadow: A Novel. Thomas Russell Sullivan. LC 8-176625. 1885. C. Scribner's Sons.
Roses Out of Reach. Marjorie Vernon. Ed. by Gene DeRoin. (Aston Hall Presents Ser.). (Orig.). 1979. pap. 1.50 (ISBN 0-89936-010-6). Aston Hall.
Roses Round the Door. Elisabeth Beresford. pap. 0.50 o.p. (52-889). Paperback Lib.
Rose's Story. Terence Brady & Charlotte Bingham. 1975. (pbk.) 1.50 (ISBN 0-671-78791-8). Pocket Books.
Roses Will Bloom Again. Goodloe Elkins. LC 76-2553. 3.95 (ISBN 0-8111-0617-9). Naylor Co.
Rosevean. Iris Bromige. LC 63-937. 1963. Chilton Books.
Rosewood. Petra Leigh. 1979. 2.50. Pocket Books.
Rosicrucian's Story: The Wonderful Things That Happened to Mr. Thomas W., and His Wife. Embracing the Celebrated "Miranda Theory.". Paschal Beverley Randolph. LC 8-226. 1863. M. J. Randolph.
Rosie. M. M Costantin. LC 74-11008. 1974. 6.95 (ISBN 0-395-19420-2). Houghton Mifflin.
Rosie World. Parker Hoysted Fillmore. 1914. H. Holt and Company.
Rosiebelle Lee Wildcat Tennessee: A Novel. Raymond Andrews. LC 79-28705. (Illus.). 8.95 (ISBN 0-8037-8336-1). Dial Press.
Rosina Copper, Mystery Mare. Kitty Barne. (Illus.). 3.25 o.p. Dutton.
Rosine. new ed. George John Whyte-Melville. Ward, Lock, & Co.
Rosine Laval: A Novel. Ralph Ingersoll Lockwood. LC 7-15161. 1833. Carey, Lea & Blanchard.
Roslyn's Fortune. A Novel. Frances Christine Tiernan. 1885. D. Appleton and Company.
Roslyn's Trust. A Novel. Lucy Cecil White Lillie. (On cover: The ideal series of American copyright novels). A. L. Burt.
Roslyn's Trust. A Novel. Lucy Cecil White Lillie. (select series. no. 68). Street & Smith.
Ross & Tom: Two American Tragedies. John Leggett. 464p. 1975. pap. 2.95 o.p. (ISBN 0-14-004051-X). Penguin.
Ross Forgery. William H Hallahan. LC 73-3780. 1975. (pbk.) 1.50 (ISBN 0-380-00296-5). Avon.
Ross Grant, Tenderfoot. John Garland. LC 15-118708. 1915. 1.25. The Penn Publishing Company.
Ross Macdonald's Lew Archer, Private Investigator. Ross Macdonald. LC 77-81870. 1977. 25.00 (ISBN 0-89296-033-7). Mysterious Press.
Ross Poldark: A Novel of Cornwall, 1783-1787. Winston Graham. LC 78-26790. 1979. 16.95 (ISBN 0-8161-6676-5). G. K. Hall.
Ross-Shire Buffs. James Grant. LC 44-31630. G. Routledge and Sons.
Rosscommon. Charles Allen Smart. LC 40-14190. Random House.
Rossellini: The War Trilogy. Roberto Rossellini. LC 72-94917. (Library of Film Classics). (Illus.). 544p. 1973. 12.50 o.p. (ISBN 0-670-60835-1, Grossman). Penguin.
Rossenal. Ernest Raymond. LC 22-20736. 1922. 7.60. Cassell and Company, Ltd.
Rosshalde. Hermann Hesse. LC 75-97612. 1970. 5.50. Farrar, Straus, and Giroux.
Rosshalde. Tr. by Ralph Manheim. 213p. 1970. pap. 1.95 o.p. (ISBN 0-374-50896-8, Noonda). FS&G.
Rossmoyne. Margaret Wolfe Hungerford. (On cover: The seaside library. Pocket ed., no. 129). 1884. G. Munro.
Roswell Heritage. Mary F. Ford. 1972. pap. 0.75 o.s.i. (01-351). Lancer.
Rosy. Louis Dodge. LC 19-707819. 1919. 1.60. C. Scribner's Sons.
Rosy Crucifixion. Henry Miller. LC 65-23919. Gorve Press.
Rosy Is My Relative. Gerald Malcolm Durrell. LC 68-11416. 1968. Viking Press.
Rosy Path: A Dickens Birthday Book... With 12 Colored Illustrations. Charles Dickens. LC 25-2839. De Wolfe, Fiske & Co.
Rot-World. Thomas Burnett Swann. 1975. (pbk.) 1.25. DAW Books.
Rotation, a Novel. 1st Ed. Alexander Massian. LC 55-8685. 1955. Exposition Press.
Rotchfords: Or The Friendly Counsellor: Designed for the Instruction and Amusement of the Youth of Both Sexes. Dorothy Kilner. 1801. Printed and Sold by J. Humphreys.
Rothermal: A Story of Lost Identity. Louis Reeves Harrison. The American News Company.
Rothhaven. William Edward Daniel Ross. (1974 ed. 0.95 o.p.). 192p. (Orig.). 1977. pap. 1.25 o.p. (ISBN 0-532-12467-7). Woodhill.
Rothhaven. William Edward Daniel Ross. (1974 ed. 0.95 o.p.). 192p. (Orig.). 1977. pap. 1.25 o.p. (ISBN 0-532-12467-7). Manor Bks.
Rothhaven. William Edward Daniel Ross. 1974. (pbk.) 0.95. Manor Books.
Rothmell. Mary Andrews Denison. 1878. Lee and Shepard.
Rothschild Conversion. Peter Buckman. LC 79-9108. 10.95 (ISBN 0-07-008795-4). McGraw-Hill.
Rothschild's Fiddle: And Other Stories. Anton Pavlovich Chekhov. LC 72-121528. (Short Story index reprint series). 1970. Books for Libraries Press.
Rothschild's Fiddle: And Other Stories. Anton Pavlovich Chekhov. LC 19-9663. (Half-title: The modern library of the world's best books). 1917. Boni and Liveright, Inc.
Rothschild's Fiddle, & Other Stories. Anton Pavlovich Chekhov. LC 72-121528. (Short Story Index Reprint Ser). 1917. 16.00 (ISBN 0-8369-3484-9). Ayer Co.
Rothschild's Lapwing. John Temple. 1968. signed 9.00 o.p.; pap. 5.00 o.p. Ferry Pr.
Rotisserie De la Reine Pedauque. Anatole France, pseud. (Coll. Bleue). 1959. pap. 8.50. French & Eur.
Rotisserie de la Reine Pedauque see Romans et Contes.
Rotten Apples. Edith Pinero Green. LC 77-7090. 7.95 (ISBN 0-525-19415-0). E. P. Dutton.
Rotten Apples. Edith Pinero Green. LC 80-12816. 1981. 11.50. J. Curley.
Rotten with Honour. Derek Robinson. LC 73-2337. 1973. 6.95 (ISBN 0-670-60858-0). Viking Press.
Rotten Years. Maia Wojciechowska. 1973. pap. 0.95 o.p. (ISBN 0-515-02928-9). Pyramid Pubns.
Rotterdam Delivery. Edward A O'Neill. LC 75-10461. 1975. 7.95 (ISBN 0-698-10678-4). Coward, McCann & Geoghegan.
Rotting Hill. Wyndham Lewis. LC 52-8209. 1952. H. Regnery Co.
Rotunda. Robert R. Siegrist. LC 77-83871. 1977. pap. 2.25 o.s.i. (ISBN 0-89516-009-9). Condor Pub Co.
Rotwang: Or, The Delirious Precision of Dreams: a Novel. Tim Hildebrand. LC 75-9979. 1975. 8.95. (ISBN 0-912652-13-6) (ISBN 0-912652-14-4). Blue Wind Press.
Roua Pass: Or, Englishmen in the Highlands. 6th american ed. Mercy Grogan. (On cover: Loring's select novels). 1867. Loring.
Roue the Fourth. Harold Shumate. LC 34-120353. The Macaulay Company.
Rouge with Ease: A Novel by M. K. Argus Pseud. 1st Ed. Mikhail K. Jeleznov. LC 53-7737. 1953. Harper.
Rough Air. Ernest Haycox. LC 34-34012. 1934. Doubleday, Doran & Company, Inc.
Rough and the Smooth. Tr. by Ian Raeside. 1966. Asia Pub. House.
Rough and the Smooth, a Novel. Robert Cecil Romer Maugham. LC 51-12092. 1951. Harcourt, Brace.
Rough and the Smooth: Short Stories Translated from Marathi. Tr. by Ian Raeside. LC 67-1973. 1966. Asia Pub. House.
Rough Country. Lee Floren. 1976. pap. 0.95 o.p. (LB362NK, Leisure Bks). Nordon Pubns.
Rough Cut. Andrew McCullough. (Kangaroo Book). 1977. 1.95 (ISBN 0-671-81197-5). Pocket Books.
Rough Cut: A Novel. Andrew McCullough. LC 76-10725. 1976. 7.95 (ISBN 0-688-03066-1). Morrow.
Rough Diamond. Robert L Fish. LC 80-2855. 1981. 13.95 (ISBN 0-385-15648-0). Doubleday.
Rough Diamond. Brooke Hastings. (Nightingale Ser.). 1983. pap. 10.95 (ISBN 0-8161-3523-1, Large Print Bks). G K Hall.
Rough Field. John Montague. 1972. pap. text ed. 4.50x o.p. (ISBN 0-85105-264-9, Dolmen Pr). Humanities.
Rough-Hewn. Dorothea Frances Canfield Fisher. Harcourt, Brace and Company.
Rough Justice. Janine Ellis. (Harlequin Romance Ser.). (Orig.). 1980. pap. 1.25 (ISBN 0-373-02330-8). Harlequin Bks.
Rough Justice. Ernest Haycox. LC 75-35640. 1975. 9.95 (ISBN 0-89190-978-8). Rivercity Press.
Rough Justice. Ernest Haycox. LC 50-6199. 1950. Little, Brown.
Rough Justice. Mary Elizabeth Braddon Maxwell. LC 79-50482. (Maxwell, Mary Elizabeth Braddon, 1837-1915. The Fiction of Mary Elizabeth Braddon: Vol. 12). 1979. 32.00 (ISBN 0-8240-4361-8). Garland Pub.
Rough Justice. Charles Edward Montague. LC 26-10202. 1926. Doubleday, Page & Company.
Rough Life on the Frontier. Scott Van Gorden. LC 21-20576. 1904. Rhodes & McClure Publishing Company.
Rough Mesa. A Double D Western. John Trace. LC 40-7922. 1940. Doubleday, Doran and Company, Inc.
Rough Music. Barbara Bennett. LC 80-15000. 1980. 11.95 (ISBN 0-312-69355-9). St. Martin's Press.
Rough on Rats. William Francis. 1942. W. Morrow and Company.
Rough Rapids Ahead. Renken, Aleda. LC 74-38. (Haley adventure book). (Illus.). 1974. (pbk.) 1.00 (ISBN 0-570-03605-4). Concordia.
Rough Rider. Robert Ames Bennet. LC 25-7071. 1925. 2.00. A. C. McClurg & Co.
Rough Rider. Jake Logan. LC 80-81630. (Jake Logan Ser.). 224p. 1980. pap. 1.95 (ISBN 0-87216-935-9). Playboy Pbks.
Rough Riders: A Romance. Hermann Hagedorn. LC 27-28006. 1927. Harper & Brothers.
Rough Road. William John Locke. LC 18-152631. 1918. John Lane Company.
Rough Road in the Rockies. Hermina G. Kilgore. 2.75 o.p. (SB). Swallow.
Rough Shoot. Geoffrey Household. LC 51-11032. 1951. Little, Brown.
Rough Shooting: True Tales & Strange Stories. Percival Christopher Wren. LC 44-67444. 1944. Macrae-Smith-Company.
Rough Sketch. Robert Sylvester. LC 48-5156. 1948. Dial Press.
Rough Strife. Lynne Sharon Schwartz. LC 79-2740. 10.00 (ISBN 0-06-014024-0). Harper & Row.
Rough Strife. Lynne Sharon Schwartz. LC 81-15125. 1981. 11.95 (ISBN 0-89340-389-X). J. Curley.
Rough-Stuff and Moonlight: Of Deeper Love Hath None. Harry Buhro. LC 48-8474. 1948. Dorrance.
Rough Trade. Hogan, Lou Rand. LC 65-4613. Argyle Books.
Rough Trade. Lou Rand. pap. 0.75 o.p. (54-821). Paperback Lib.
Rough Trail to the Pulpit. C. C. Rouse. (Daybreak Ser.). 1981. pap. 4.95 (ISBN 0-8163-0434-3). Pacific Pr Pub Assn.
Rough Weather. Iris Bromige. Ed. by Gene DeRoin. (Aston Hall Presents Ser.). (Orig.). 1980. pap. 1.50 (ISBN 0-89936-016-5). Aston Hall.
Rough Winds of May. 1st Ed. Nancy Hallinan. LC 54-12182. 1955. Harper.
Roughest Trail. Alonzo DeMoines Snyder. LC 36-969356. Wetzel Publishing Co., Inc.
Roughing It. Mark Twain & Hamlin Lewis Hill. LC 81-10593. (Penguin American Library). 1981. 3.95 (ISBN 0-14-039010-3). Penguin.
Roughly Speaking. Harry Charles Witwer. LC 26-4708. 1926. G. P. Putnam's Sons.
Roughneck. Robert William Service. LC 23-176523. Barse & Hopkins.
Roughneck. James Myers Thompson. LC 54-28810. (Lion book, 201). 1954. Lion Books by Arrangement with Atlas News Co.
Roughrider. Jack Pollard. (Illus.). 12.50x o.p. (ISBN 0-392-04442-0, ABC). Soccer.
Roughshod. Norman A Fox. LC 51-12088. (Silver star westerns). 1951. Dodd, Mead.
Roughshod. Norman A Fox. (Dell book). 1979. 1.25 (ISBN 0-440-17518-6). Dell Pub. Co.
Roughshod. Thomas Shaw. 208p. (Orig.). 1982. pap. 2.25 (ISBN 0-449-14503-4, GM). Fawcett.
Roughshod Posse. Lester W. Merha. 1981. pap. 6.95 (Avalon). Bouregy.
Rougon-Macquart Family. (La Fortune Des Rougon.) Emile Zola & Sherwood, Mary (Neal) Tr. LC 9-1305. (His Rougon-Macquart series, v. 1). T. B. Peterson & Brothers.
Rougon-Macquart Family. La Fortune Des Rougon. Emile Zola & Sherwood, Mrs. Mary (Neal) Tr. T. B. Peterson & Brothers.
Roumanian Stories. Lucy Bying. 1979. Repr. of 1921 ed. lib. bdg. 35.00 (ISBN 0-8495-0517-8). Arden Lib.
Roumanian Stories. Ed. by Lucy Margaret Greenly Schomberg Byng. LC 73-169543. (Short story index reprint series). 1971. (ISBN 0-8369-4004-0). Books for Libraries Press.
Roumanian Stories: Tr. from the Original Roumanian. Lucy Margaret Greenly Schomberg Byng. 1921. John Lane.
Round-About. Annie Edith Foster Jameson. LC 16-8073. 1916. Hodder and Stoughton.
Round-About. Annie Edith Foster Jameson. LC 16-9063. 1.25. George H. Doran Company.
Round About a Great Estate. Richard Jefferies. LC 7-101901. 1880. Roberts Brothers.
Round Anvil Rock: A Romance. Nancy Huston Banks. 1903. The Macmillan Company.
Round Corners. Harold Charles Le Baron Jackson. LC 45-21019. 1945. Arnold-Powers, Inc.
Round Dozen. Elizabeth Cadell. LC 77-27363. 1978. 7.95. Morrow.
Round Dozen. Elizabeth Cadell. LC 78-16175. 1978. 10.95 (ISBN 0-8161-6616-1). G. K. Hall.
Round Hill Farm. Mary Annette Stillamn Miner. LC 12-6703. The C. M. Clark Publishing Company.
Round House. Illustrated by J. S. Goodall. Reginald Arkell. LC 58-813506. 1958. Reynal.
Round of Tales from Washington Irving to Algernon Blackwood. Compiled by N. Henry. 192p. 1981. Repr. of 1924 ed. lib. bdg. 20.00 (ISBN 0-89987-049-X). Darby Bks.
Round Robin. Graham Ward Bain. LC 37-13861. J. B. Lippincott Company.
Round Shape. Alma Routsong. LC 58-907258. 1959. Houghton Mifflin.
Round Table Murders. Leonard Worswick Clyde. LC 31-14781. The Macaulay Company.
Round Table Murders. Amelia Reynolds Long. LC 52-10203. 1952. Phoenix Press.
Round Table of the Representative American Catholic Novelists: At Which Is Served a Feast of Excellent Stories. Eleanor Cecilia Donnelly et al. LC 4-15063. 1897. Benziger Brothers.
Round Table of the Representative French Catholic Novelists ... With Portraits, Biographical Sketches, and Bibliography. LC 400. 1899. Benziger Brothers.
Round Table of the Representative German Catholic Novelists: At Which Is Served a Feast of Excellent Stories... with Portraits, Biographical Sketches, and Bibliography. Jungst, Antonie et al. LC 2-24327. 1902. Benziger Brothers.
Round Table of the Representative Irish and English Catholic Novelists: At Which Is Served a Feast of Excellent Stories... with Portraits, Biographical Sketches, and Bibliography. Dobree, Louisa Emily et al. 1897. Benziger Brothers.
Round the Bend. Nevil Shute Norway. LC 77-106691. 1970. (ISBN 0-8371-3364-5). Greenwood Press.
Round the Bend. Nevil Shute. 1977. Repr. of 1951 ed. lib. bdg. 16.95x (ISBN 0-89244-053-8). Queens Hse.
Round the Bend: a Novel. Nevil Shute. Repr. of 1951 ed. lib. bdg. 17.00 (ISBN 0-8371-3364-5, NORB). Greenwood.
Round the Bend: A Novel by Nevil Shute Pseud. Nevil Shute Norway. LC 51-9629. 1951. Morrow.
Round the Block. An American Novel... John Bell Bouton. LC 6-14916. 1864. D. Appleton and Company.
Round the Clock. Lees-Milne James. LC 78-54022. 7.95 (ISBN 0-684-15882-5). Scribner.
Round the Corner in Gay Street. Grace Louise Smith Richmond. LC 8-23930. 1908. Doubleday, Page & Company.
Round the Fire Stories. Arthur Conan Doyle. LC 8-28056. 1908. The McClure Company.
Round the Galley Fire. William Clark Russell. (On cover: Seaside library. Pocket ed., no. 180). 1884. G. Munro.
Round the Moon. Jules Verne. LC 1-9778. (Seaside library. Pocket ed., no. 1153). 1889. G. Munro.
Round the Red Lamp. facsimile ed. Arthur Conan Doyle. LC 77-101802. (Short Story Index Reprint Ser.). 1894. 16.00 (ISBN 0-8369-3190-4). Ayer Co.
Round the Red Lamp: Being Facts and Fancies of Medical Life. Arthur Conan Doyle. LC 77-101802. (Short story index reprint series). 1969. Books for Libraries Press.
Round the Red Lamp: Being Facts and Fancies of Medical Life. Arthur Conan Doyle. LC 8-34236. 1894. D. Appleton and Company.
Round the Red Lamp: Being Facts and Fancies of Medical Life. Arthur Conan Doyle. LC 12-23262. 1910. D. Appleton and Company.
Round the Red Lamp: Being Facts and Fancies of Medical Life. Arthur Conan Doyle. LC 15-20313. 1913. D. Appleton and Company.
Round the Red Lamp: Being Facts and Fancies of Medical Life. Arthur Conan Doyle. LC 24-20488. 1921. D. Appleton and Company.
Round the Words in Seven Days. Herbert Strang. LC 10-27189. Hodder & Stoughton, George H. Doran Company.
Round the World. A Tale. William Henry Giles Kingston. (On cover: Lovell's library, v. 6, no. 324). 1883. J. W. Lovell Company.
Round the World in Eighty Days. Jules Verne. LC 50-4472. Didier.
Round the World in Eighty Days. Jules Verne & Magee, Katherine E., Ed. LC 98-961. (Standard literature series, no. 34). University Pub. Co.
Round Tower. Catherine Cookson. (Orig.). 1975. pap. 1.50 (ISBN 0-451-06310-4, W6310, Sig). NAL.
Round Tower. Catherine Cookson. (Signet book). 1975. (pbk.) 1.50. New American Library.
Round Tower. Catherine Marchant, pseud. 1971. pap. 0.95 o.p. (95051). Beagle Bks.
Round Trip. Don Tracy. LC 34-14234. 1934. The Vanguard Press.
Round Trip to Hell in a Flying Saucer. Cecil Michael. LC 54-11898. 1955. Vantage Press.

Round Trip to Nowhere. J. T. MacCargo. (Mannix Ser). (O.s.i.: No. 4). (Orig.). 1975. pap. 1.25 o.s.i. (BT50834). Belmont-Tower.

Round Trip to the Year Two Thousand. William Wallace Cook. LC 75-13250. (Classics of Science Fiction Ser.). 318p. 1974. 12.50 o.s.i. (ISBN 0-88355-106-3); pap. 3.85 (ISBN 0-88355-135-7). Hyperion Conn.

Round Trip to the Year 2000: Or, A Flight Through Time. William Wallace Cook. LC 73-13250. (Classics of science fiction). 1974. 9.50 (ISBN 0-88355-106-3) (ISBN 0-88355-106-3). Hyperion Press.

Round, Unvarnished Tale. Dunbar Maury Hinrichs. LC 65-27766. 5.00. Dorrance.

Round-up. Zane Grey. 192p. (Orig.). 1976. pap. text ed. 1.50 (ISBN 0-532-15189-5). Woodhill.

Round-up. Clarence Edward Mulford. LC 73-89657. 1973. 5.95. Aeonian Press.

Round-up. Clarence Edward Mulford. LC 33-2220. 1933. Doubleday, Doran & Company, Inc.

Round-up: A Romance of Arizona Novelized from Edmund Day's Melodrama. John Murray & Miller, Marion Mills. LC 8-11703. 1908. G. W. Dillingham Company.

Round-up: A Story of Ranchmen, Cowboys, Rustlers, and Bad-Men Happening in the Days When the Great Southwest Was Becivilization. Oscar J Friend. LC 24-4699. 1924. 2.00. A. C. McClurg & Co.

Round-up at Tiger Gap. Jesse Edward Grinstead. LC 40-6538. Phoenix Press.

Round-up Guns. Thomas Albert Curry. LC 40-8742. 1939. Gateway Books.

Round-up in the River. Frank Chester Robertson. LC 45-7349. 1945. E. P. Dutton & Company.

Round up: The Stories of Ring W. Lardner. Ring Wilmer Lardner. LC 29-9877. 1929. C. Scribner's Sons.

Round Voyage: A Novel. 1st Ed. John Rowan Wilson. LC 57-6292. 1957. Doubleday.

Roundabout. Nancy Hoyt. LC 26-9826. A. A. Knopf,

Roundabout Papers. William Makepeace Thackeray. LC 37-30951. (Half-title: Everyman's library, ed. by Ernest Rhys. Fiction. no. 687). 1922. J. M. Dent & Sons, Ltd.

Roundabout Way. Louis McNeice. LC 33-3294. 1932. Putnam.

Roundelay. Edwa Moser. LC 48-6482. 1948. Duell, Sloan and Pearce.

Rounders. Max Evans. LC 79-28632. (Gregg Press Western Fiction Series). 1980. 10.95 (ISBN 0-8398-2686-9). Gregg Press.

Roundhouse, Paradise, and Mr. Pickering. Dick Perry. LC 66-12235. 1966. Doubleday.

Rounding Cape Horn: And Other Sea Stories. Walter McRoberts. 1895. H. S. Hill Printing Company.

Rounding Third and Heading Home. Victor C Strasburger. LC 73-87410. 1974. 7.95. St. Martin's Press.

Rounds. Frederick Busch. LC 79-19470. 1979. 10.95 (ISBN 0-374-25258-0). Farrar, Straus, and Giroux.

Roundtable in Poictesme. James Branch Cabell. 69.95 (ISBN 0-87968-234-5). Gordon Pr.

Roundtree Women. Margaret Lewerth. 2.50 (ISBN 0-440-11255-9). Dell Publishing Co.

Roundup. Stephen Overholser. LC 81-43728. (Illus.). 1982. 11.95 (ISBN 0-385-17947-2). Doubleday.

Roundup. Western Writers of America. Ed. by Steven Overholser. LC 81-43728. (Double D Western Ser.). 192p. 1982. 11.95 (ISBN 0-385-17947-2). Doubleday.

Roundup on the Picketwire. 1st Ed. Allan Vaughan Elston. LC 52-5092. 1952. Lippincott.

Rouse the Demon. Carolyn Weston. LC 76-6895. 6.95. Random House.

Rousing of Mrs. Potter: And Other Stories. Gertrude Smith. LC 4-22073. 1894. Houghton, Mifflin and Company.

Rout of the Foreigner. Gulielma Zollinger. LC 10-233185. 1910. A. C. McClurg & Co.

Route Obscure and Lonely. Scott Hart. LC 67-29094. 1967. National Press.

Route of Entry. Scott Simeon. 160p. (Orig.). 1971. pap. 1.95 o.s.i. (0*P*H263, Ophelia). Olympia.

Route One. Agnes Mary White Sandford. LC 74-25139. 1976. pap. 3.95 o.p. (ISBN 0-88270-155-X, Pub. by Logos). Bridge Pub.

Route 13. Len Zinberg. LC 54-2924. (Illus.). 1954. Funk & Wagnalls Co.

Route 28. Ward Greene. LC 40-33583. 1940. Doubleday, Doran & Co.

Routledge Rides Alone. Will Levington Comfort. LC 10-853474. 1910. J. B. Lippincott Company.

Roux the Bandit. Andre Chamson. Tr. by Brooks, Van Wyck. LC 29-18556. 1929. C. Scribner's Sons.

Rover. Joseph Conrad. LC 24-632. 1923. Doubleday, Page & Company.

Rover Boys at College: Or, The Right Road and the Wrong. Edward Stratemeyer. (On cover: The Rover boys' series for young Americans). Grosset & Dunlap.

Rover of the Reef: Or The Nymph of the Nightingale. A Romance of Massachusetts Bay. Harry Halyard. F. Gleason.

Rover Youngblood: An American Fable. Thomas McAfee. LC 76-89954. 1969. 4.95. R. W. Baron.

Roving Eye. Humphrey Pakington. LC 32-23880. W. W. Norton & Company, Inc.

Roving Heart. Marcia Miller. (Starlight romance). 1973. (pbk.) 0.75. Manor Books.

Roving Red Rangers: Or Laura Lamar, of the Susquehanna. A Thrilling Romance of the Old Colonial Days. Charles Asbury Robinson. LC 2-8338. The Author.

Roving River. Clair Willard Perry. LC 21-18887. The Bobbs-Merrill Company.

Rovings on Land and Sea. Henry E Davenport. LC 11-15060. 1860. Thayer and Eldridge.

Row of Plums. Irma Dunn. (Illus.). 1960. bds. 3.50 o.p. Vantage.

Row of Tigers. Barbara Corcoran. LC 69-13523. 1969. 4.25 o.p. (ISBN 0-689-20070-6). Atheneum.

Rowan Head. Elisabeth Ogilvie. LC 75-38998. 1976. 6.95 (ISBN 0-88411-181-4). Aeonian Press.

Rowan Head. Elisabeth Ogilvie. LC 49-10325. 1949. Whittlesey House.

Rowdyman: A Novel. Gordon Pinsent. LC 73-14395. 1973. 6.95 (ISBN 0-07-077663-6). McGraw-Hill Ryerson.

Rowena Rides the Rumble. Ethel Powelson Hueston. LC 31-9624. The Bobbs-Merrill Company.

Rowforest. Agnes Russell Weekes. LC 27-11490. 1927. Dodd, Mead & Company.

Rowney in Boston: A Novel. Maria Louise Pool. LC 7-38172. 1892. Harper & Brothers.

Row's End. 1st Ed. Louis Cochran. LC 54-6887. Duell, Sloan and Pearce.

Roxana. Marian Castle. LC 55-10262. 1955. Morrow.

Roxana. Daniel Defoe. Ed. by Jane Jack. (World's Classics Ser.). 1982. pap. 3.95 (ISBN 0-19-281563-6). Oxford U Pr.

Roxana. Clarence Budington Kelland. LC 36-6809. 1936. Harper & Brothers.

Roxana: Or, The Fortunate Mistress. Daniel Defoe. LC 46-7998. (Half-title: The Living library). 1946. The World Publishing Company.

Roxana: The Fortunate Mistress; or, A History of the Life and Vast Variety of Fortunes of Mademoiselle De Beleau, Afterwards Called the Countess De Wintselsheim in Germany, Being the Person Known by the Name of the Lady Roxana in the Time of Charles II. Ed., Introd., by Jane Jack. Daniel Defoe. LC 64-56215. (Oxford Eng. novels). 1965. pap., 1.35. Oxford.

Roxana, the Fortunate Mistress: Or A History of the Life of Mademoiselle De Beleau Known by the Name of the Lady Roxana. Daniel Defoe. (SP139). Popular Lib.

Roxia: A Biographical Novel. Vernon Franklin Kelly. LC 49-119856. 1949. Exposition Press.

Roxie Raker. Ray Hogan. 1975. (pbk.) 0.95. Ace Books.

Roxobel. Mary Martha Butt Sherwood. LC 8-7345. Harper & Brothers.

Roxy. Edward Eggleston. LC 68-20010. (Americans in Fic.). 1968. 10.00. Gregg Pr.

Roxy. Edward Eggleston. LC 4-22067. 1878. C. Scribner's Sons.

Roxy. Edward Eggleston. LC 6-27714. 1906. C. Scribner's Sons.

Roxy Hastings: Or, A Raffle for Life. Peter Hamilton Myers. (select series. no. 55). 1890. Street & Smith.

Roy and Viola. Mrs. Bridges. (On cover: Lovell's library, v. 18, no. 864). 1887. J. W. Lovell Company.

Roy and Viola. A Novel. Mrs. Bridges. (Seaside library, v. 42, no. 858). 1880. G. Munro.

Roy and Viola. A Novel. Mrs. Bridges. (On cover: Seaside library. Pocket ed., no. 736). 1886. G. Munro.

Roy Rogers and the Ghost of Mystery Rancho: An Original Story Featuring Roy Rogers, Famous Motion Picture Star, As the Hero. authorized ed. Walker A Tompkins. LC 50-12508. 1950. Whitman.

Roy Rogers and the Raiders of Sawtooth Ridge: An Original Story Featuring Roy Rogers, Famous Motion Picture Star, As the Hero. authorized ed. Snowden Miller. LC 46-7937. 1946. Whitman Publishing Company.

Roy Rogers and the Rimrod Renegades: An Original Story Featuring Roy Rogers, Famous Motion Picture, Radio and Television Star As the Hero. authorized ed. Snowden Miller. LC 52-4207. 1952. Whitman Pub. Co.

Royal Adventure. Gino Vanzillotta. 4.50 o.p. Vantage.

Royal Americans. Mary Hallock Foote. LC 10-9693. 1910. Houghton Mifflin Company.

Royal Anne Tree. Patricia Campbell. LC 56-13658. 1956. Macmillan.

Royal Bed for a Corpse. Max Murray. LC 56-680. 1955. Washburn.

Royal Blood. Alissa Channing. 96p. 1981. pap. 1.95 (ISBN 0-380-77743-6, 77743). Avon.

Royal Box. Frances Parkinson Wheeler Keyes. LC 54-6770. 1954. J. Messner.

Royal Box. Frances Parkinson Wheeler Keyes. LC 54-6770. 1975. (pbk.) 1.75 (ISBN 0-671-78897-3). Pocket Books.

Royal Captive. Patricia Phillips. 1977. pap. 1.95 o.p. (ISBN 0-515-04173-4). BJ Pub Group.

Royal Captive. Patricia Phillips. 1977. 1.95 (ISBN 0-515-04173-4). Pyramid Publicati Ons.

Royal Captives: A Fragment of Secret History Copied from an Old Manuscript. Ann Yearsley. LC 73-22211. (Feminist Controversy in England, 1788-1810). 1974. (ea. 4 vols.) 22.00 (ISBN 0-8240-0892-8). Garland Pub.

Royal Captives: A Fragment of Secret History. Ann Yearsley. LC 9-1226. 1795. Printed by William W. Woodward, Franklin's Head, No., Chesnut Street.

Royal Captives, A Fragment of Secret History. Ann Yearsley. LC 9-1227. Printed for Robert Campbell.

Royal Caravan. C. Savery. 1971. pap. 1.50 (ISBN 0-87508-751-5). Chr Lit.

Royal Chase: An Historical Romance. Tr. by William Hale. Hale, William, Tr. M. J. Ivers & Co.

Royal City. Les Savage. LC 56-940426. 1956. Hanover House.

Royal Cravatts. Lillian Rogers. LC 27-18960. 1927. I. Washburn.

Royal Dirk. John Louis Beatty & Beatty, Patricia, Joint Author. LC 66-11233. 1966. Morrow.

Royal Dragoons Immortal Love. Marian Helm-Pirgo. 314p. 1976. 10.00. Polish Inst Arts.

Royal Dragoons: Immortal Love: a Historical Novel of the Seventeenth Century. Helm-Pirgo, Marian. LC 76-374090. (Illus.). 1976. 9.95. Bicentennial Pub. Corp.

Royal Enchantress: The Romance of the Last Queen of the Berbers. Leo Charles Dessar. LC 4273. 1900. Continental Publishing Co.

Royal End: A Romance. Henry Harland. LC 9-5217. 1909. Dodd, Mead & Company.

Royal Escape. Georgette Heyer. LC 67-20553. 1967. Dutton.

Royal Escape. Georgette Heyer. LC 39-328767. 1939. Doubleday, Doran & Company, Inc.

Royal Flash, from the Flashman Papers, 1842-3 and 1847-8. George MacDonald Fraser. LC 75-126293. (Illus.). 1970. 5.95. Knopf.

Royal Flush. William Dryden. 1971. pap. 0.95 o.p. (95-152). Manor Bks.

Royal Flush. William Dryden. 1964. 4.95 o.p. (ISBN 0-374-25264-5). FS&G.

Royal Flush. William Dryden. (O.s.i.). pap. 0.95 o.s.i. (532-95152-095). Manor Bks.

Royal Flush. Margaret Irwin. 368p. 1983. 13.95 (ISBN 0-312-69471-7). St Martin.

Royal Flush. Margaret Irwin. 1959. Repr. of 1932 ed. 8.95 o.p. (ISBN 0-7011-0844-4). Dufour.

Royal Flush: A Nero Wolfe Omnibus. Rex Stout. Bd. with Fer-De-Lance; Murder by the Book; Next Witness; When a Man Murders; Die Like a Dog. 448p. 1965. 3.95 o.p. (ISBN 0-670-60934-X). Viking Pr.

Royal Flush: A Nero Wolfe Omnibus. Rex Stout. 1965. 3.95 o.p. (ISBN 0-670-60934-X). Viking Pr.

Royal Flush: A Novel. William Dryden. LC 64-11454. 1964. Farrar, Straus.

Royal Flush: The Fourth Nero Wolfe Omnibus. Rex Stout. LC 65-19269. 1965. 3.95. Viking.

Royal Flush: The Story of Minette. Margaret Emma Faith Irwin. LC 32-22287. 1966. 3.95. Chatto & Windus.

Royal Flush: The Story of Minette. Margaret Emma Faith Irwin. LC 32-25849. Harcourt, Brace and Company.

Royal Gamble. Jane Aiken Hodge & Jane Aiken Hodge. Orig. Title: Adventurers. 1971. pap. 0.75 o.p. (T2468). Pyramid Pubns.

Royal Game. Amok. Letter from an Unknown Woman. Stefan Zweig & Huebsch, Benjamin W., Tr. LC 44-3264. 1944. The Viking Press.

Royal Game and Other Stories. Stefan Zweig. LC 81-6331. 12.95 (ISBN 0-517-54553-5). Harmony Books.

Royal Gentleman. Albion Winegar Tourgee. LC 8-29841. Fords, Howard & Hulbert.

Royal Gentleman: A Novel. Albion Winegar Tourgee. LC 67-29281. (American in Fic.). 1967. Gregg Pr.

Royal George. Jonathan H Glidden. LC 48-8398. (Silver star westerns). 1948. Dodd, Mead.

Royal Good Fellow. Hiram Wallace Hayes. LC 10-206058. The Howerton Press.

Royal Guest, and Other Classical Danish Narrative. Phillip Marshall Mitchell & Kenneth H Ober. LC 77-78070. 1977. 12.50 (ISBN 0-226-53213-5). University of Chicago Press.

Royal Gypsies. Wesley Sylvester Thompson. LC 61-880. 1960. Pareil Press.

Royal Heiress: Or, A Youthful Error. Emilie Edwards. (On cover: Lucile ser. no. 2). E. A. Weeks & Company.

Royal Heritage. Roland Pertwee. LC 31-21428. 1931. Houghton Mifflin Company.

Royal Highlanders: Or, The Black Watch in Egypt. James Grant. LC 6-27678. (Harper's Franklin square library, no. 487). Harper & Brothers.

Royal Highlanders: Or, The Black Watch in Egypt. A Novel. James Grant. LC 6-27677. (On cover: Seaside library. Pocket ed. no. 566). G. Munro.

Royal Highness. Thomas Mann. Tr. by A. Cecil Curtis. LC 48-34213. Grosset & Dunlap.

Royal Highness. Thomas Mann & Curtis, A. Cecil, Tr. LC 40-27007. 1939. A. A. Knopf.

Royal Highness: A Novel of German Court Life. Thomas Mann & Curtis, A. Cecil, Tr. LC 26-26514. 1926. A. A. Knopf.

Royal Hunt: Translated from the French by Ralph Manheim. 1st Ed. Pierre Moinot. LC 55-5605. 1955. Knopf.

Royal Intrigue. Evelyn Anthony. LC 54-8716. 1974. (pbk.) 1.25. New American Library.

Royal Intrigue. Deborah Chester. (Candlelight Regency Ser.: No. 712). (Orig.). 1982. pap. 2.25 (ISBN 0-440-17065-6). Dell.

Royal Intrigue: By Evelyn Anthony Pseud. Eve Stephens, pseud. LC 54-8716. 1954. Crowell.

Royal Marine: An Idyl of Narragansett Pier. Brander Matthews. LC 7-24698. (On cover: Harper's little novels). 1894. Harper & Brothers.

Royal Master. Stuart Jason. 1976. pap. 1.50 (ISBN 0-532-15191-7). Woodhill.

Royal Merry-Go-Round. Frank Wilson Kenyon. LC 54-5528. 1954. Crowell.

Royal Mistress. Patricia Campbell Horton. LC 77-82087. 1977. 1.95 (ISBN 0-380-01713-X). Avon Books.

Royal Mistress. Rose Meadows. 1975. (pbk.) 1.25 (ISBN 0-671-80051-5). Pocket Books.

Royal Outlaw. A Novel. Sylvanus Cobb. (On cover: The popular series, no. 13). 1891. R. Bonner's Sons.

Royal Outlaw. A Novel. Sylvanus Cobb. (choice series, no. 133). (On cover: Ledger library, no. 133). 1897. R. Bonner's Sons.

Royal Outlaw: A Novel. Charles B. Hudson. LC 17-17619. E. P. Dutton & Co.

Royal Physician: A Historical Episode... Frederick Hunt. LC 46-8614. 1946. Rich & Cowan.

Royal Physician: An Historical Novel. Frederick Hunt. LC 47-274146. 1947. Roy Publishers.

Royal Pledge. Barbara Cartland. Orig. Title: Captive Heart. 1970. pap. 0.95 o.p. (N2377). Pyramid Pubns.

Royal Pledge. Barbara Cartland. 1974. pap. 1.25 o.p. (ISBN 0-515-03518-1, V3518). BJ Pub Group.

Royal Prisoner. Pierre Souvestre & Allain, Marcel, Joint Author. LC 18-14992. (Their The Fantomas detective novels). 1918. Brentano's.

Royal Purple: The Story of Alexander and Draga of Serbia. Bertita Leonarz Harding. LC 35-20302. The Bobbs-Merrill Company.

Royal Regiment: A Novel of Contemporary Behaviours. Gilbert Frankau. LC 38-29011. 1939. E. P. Dutton & Co.

Royal Regiment: And Other Novelettes. James Grant. LC 41-38287. G. Routledge and Sons.

Royal Road. Arthur Kuhl. LC 41-19416. 1941. Sheed & Ward.

Royal Road: Being the Story of the Life, Death, and Resurrection of Edward Hankey of London. Alfred Ollivant. LC 12-24060. 1912. 1.25. Doubleday, Page & Company.

Royal Road: Or, Taking Him at His Word. Mary Virginia Terhune. LC 8-26061. 1894. A. D. F. Randolph, and Company.

Royal Road to Fotheringay. Eleanor Hibbert. LC 68-31841. 1968. 5.95. Putnam.

Royal Road to Fotheringay: A Novel of Mary Queen of Scots. Jean Plaidy. 1968. 6.95 o.p. (ISBN 0-399-10711-8). Putnam Pub Group.

Royal Robbert. Herbert Rau. Tr. by Blake, Agnes A. E. LC 8-595. (On cover: Idylwild series. v. 1, no. 40). Morrill, Higgins & Co.

Royal Rogues. Alberta Bancroft. 1901. G. P. Putnam's Sons.

Royal Southern Family: A Biographical Novel of Facts. Arthur Talmage Abernethy. LC 34-9915. Printed for the Author, The Parthenon Press.

Royal Street. Francis Swann. (Orig.). pap. 0.60 o.p. (73-472). Lancer.

Royal Street. Francis Swann. (73-472). Lancer.

Royal Street: A Novel of Old New Orleans. Walter Adolphe Roberts. LC 73-18605. 1974. (ISBN 0-404-11415-6). AMS Press.

Royal Street: A Novel of Old New Orleans. Walter Adolphe Roberts. LC 44-8366. 1944. The Bobbs-Merrill Company.

Royal Summons. Elizabeth Cadell. LC 73-2724. 1973. 8.95 (ISBN 0-8161-6092-9). G. K. Hall.

Royal Summons. Elizabeth Cadell. LC 72-109. 1973. 5.95 (ISBN 0-688-00008-8). Morrow.

Royal Sword at Agincourt. Pamela Bennetts. LC 77-3875. 1977. 9.95 (ISBN 0-89340-070-X). J. Curley.
Royal Sword at Agincourt: A Novel. Pamela Bennetts. 1973. (pbk.) 0.95. Popular Lib.
Royal Twilight, a Historical Episode. Frederick Hunt. LC 46-22553. 1945. Rich & Cowan.
Royal Twilight: A Historical Romance. Frederick Hunt. LC 46-6953. 1946. Roy Publishers.
Royal Ward, by Percy Brebner... Illustrated by Harry C. Edwards. Percy James Brebner. 1909. 1.50. Little, Brown, and Company.
Royal Way. Andre Malraux & Gilbert, Stuart, Tr. LC 35-2723. 1935. H. Smith and R. Haas.
Royal Way: "Via Crucis, Via Lucis.". Isabel Graham Eaton. LC 6-36810. 1891. The Young Churchman Co.
Royal Wedding. Florence Riddell. LC 36-8685. J. B. Lippincott Company.
Royal Widow see Katherine Parr.
Royal William: The Story of a Democrat. Doris Leslie. LC 41-2813. 1941. The Macmillan Company.
Royal Woman. Tr. by Heinrich Mann. Ashton, Arthur Jacob, 1855- Tr. LC 30-14098. The Macaulay Company.
Royalists and Republicans: Or, The Victims of the Revolution: a Historical Novel. Henrik Af Trolle & Lagervall, Charles G. C., Tr. LC 8-29713. 1883. W. W. Williams.
Royalists and Roundheads: A Tale of the Youth of King Charles II After the Battle of Worcester, How He Evaded Capture Through the Aid of a Virginia Lad, and His Final Escape to France. Oliver Vernon Caine. LC 3-253977. 1903. G. W. Jacobs & Co.
Royalized. Reese Rockwell. LC 7-39797. 1887. Phillips & Hunt.
Royce of the Royal Mounted. Amos Moore. LC 32-16435. The Macaulay Company.
Royo County. Robert Roper. LC 73-8042. 1973. 4.95 (ISBN 0-688-00181-5). Morrow.
Roy's Wife. A Novel. George John Whyte-Melville. (On cover: The seaside library. Pocket ed. no. 409). 1885. G. Munro.
Royston Affair. Dominic Devine. LC 65-11694. (Red badge mystery). 1965. Dodd, Mead.
Royton Manor. Caroline Atwater Mason. LC 28-24274. Fleming H. Revell Company.
Rpince of the Captivity. Hilda Caroline Gregg. LC 2-13110. 1902. L. C. Page & Company.
RSVP Cycles. Lawrence Halprin. (O.s.i.). 1970. 15.00 o.s.i. (ISBN 0-8076-0557-3); pap. 13.95 (ISBN 0-8076-0628-6). Braziller.
Ru, the Conqueror. Jackson Gregory. LC 83-296405. 1933. C. Scribner's Sons.
Ruan. Winifred Bryher. LC 60-13199. 1960. Pantheon Books.
Rub-a-Dub-Dub. Robert L Fish. LC 78-154065. (Inner sanctum mystery). 1971. 4.95 (ISBN 0-671-20895-0). Simon and Schuster.
Rub-A-Dub-Dub. Hamilton Maule. 1969. Repr. of 1968 ed. pap. 0.75 o.p. (ISBN 0-446-64196-0, 64-196). Paperback Lib.
Rub-a-Dub-Dub: A Novel. Hamilton Maule. LC 68-20459. 1968. Crown Publishers.
Rubber Band. Rex Stout. LC 44-2186. 1943. Pocket Books Inc.
Rubber Band. Rex Stout. LC 80-29550. 1981. 12.95 (ISBN 0-8161-3224-0). G. K. Hall.
Rubber Band: A Nero Wolfe Mystery. Rex Stout. LC 36-8385. Farrar & Rinehart, Incorporated.
Rubbish Heap. Eliza M. J. Humphreys. LC 17-131827. 1917. G. P. Putnam's Sons.
Rube. Giuseppe Antonio Borgese & Goldberg, Isaac, 1887-1938, Tr. LC 23-34455. (Half-title: The European library, ed. by J. E. Spingaro). Harcourt, Brace and Company.
Rube Burrows' League: Or, The Swamp Angels of Alabama. St. George Rathborne. (secret service series, no. 40). 1891. Street & Smith.
Ruben and Ivy Sen. Louise Jordan Miln. LC 25-172727. 1925. Frederick A. Stokes Company.
Rubicon. Edward Frederic Benson. LC 6-11338. (On cover: Appletons' town and country library, no. 140). 1894. D. Appleton and Company.
Rubicon. Agnar Mykle. LC 66-21314. 1967. Dutton.
Rubies. Lily Moresby Adams Beck. LC 27-27943. George H. Doran Company.
Rubout at the Onyx. H. Paul Jeffers. LC 81-5709. 1981. 10.95 (ISBN 0-89919-046-4). Ticknor & Fields.
Ruby. Jack Siegel, pseud. (Orig.). 1972. pap. 0.75 o.p. (ISBN 0-515-02825-8, T2825). Pyramid Pubns.
Ruby. Kerry Stuart. 1978. pap. 1.75 (ISBN 0-425-03640-5, Medallion). Berkley Pub.
Ruby: A Novel. Rosa Guy. LC 76-2019. 8.95 (ISBN 0-670-20628-8). Viking Press.
Ruby Beyond Price. Gilbert Edward Campbell. LC 6-21493. (On cover: Romantic series, no. 6). The Minerva Publishing Co.
Ruby Cross: A Novel. Mary Wallace. 1917. Benziger Brothers.
Ruby Cross, a Novel by Mary Wallace Pseud. Grace Doonan. LC 17-29182. 1917. Benziger Brothers.
Ruby Dana. A Novel. Mary Marsh Baker. LC 6-6875. 1890. J. B. Alden.
Ruby Duke. H. K. Potwin. LC 11-7142. 1872. Lee and Shepard.
Ruby Floyd's Temptation: And Other Stories About Schools. Charles William Bardeen. LC 16-127619. C. W. Bardeen.
Ruby Heart of Kishgar. Arthur Williams Marchmont. LC 12-5158. Hodder and Stoughton.
Ruby Maclaine. John Roeburt. 1970. pap. 0.60 o.p. (60-439). Manor Bks.
Ruby of Kishmoor. Howard Pyle. LC 8-31166. 1908. Harper & Brothers.
Ruby Red. William Price Fox. 1973. (pbk.) 1.25. Bantam Books.
Ruby Red. William Price Fox. LC 75-146686. 1971. 6.95. Lippincott.
Ruby Ring: Or, Truth Will Prevail. Emily Nonnen. Tr. by Olson, E W. LC 8-37184. 1908. The Engberg-Holmberg Pub. Co.
Ruby Sweetwater and the Ringo Kid. Sheldon Bart. LC 80-14683. 11.95 (ISBN 0-07-003872-4). McGraw-Hill.
Rubyfruit Jungle. Rita Mae Brown. LC 73-86276. 1973. 3.00 (ISBN 0-913780-02-2). Daughters, Inc.
Rubyiat of a Freshman. Harry Charles Witwer. LC 22-194733. The Collegiate World Publishing Company.
Ruby's Husband. Mary Virginia Terhune. 1869. Sheldon and Company.
Ruby's Husband. Mary Virginia Terhune. LC 3-19528. 1896. G. W. Dillingham Co.
Ruckus at Roaring Gap. Amos Moore. LC 41-196472. I. Washburn, Inc.
Rudard Kipling Storybook. Rudyard Kipling. LC 51-7576. (Thrushwood book). 1951. Grosset & Dunlap.
Rudder: A Novel with Several Heroes. Mary Stanbery Watts. LC 16-6609. 1916. The Macmillan Company.
Rudder Grange. Frank Richard Stockton. LC 8-15539. 1879. C. Scribner's Sons.
Rudder Grange. Frank Richard Stockton. LC 4-15161. 1885. C. Scribner's Sons.
Rudder Grange. Frank Richard Stockton. LC 8-2382. 1907. C. Scribner's Sons.
Rudder Grange. Frank Richard Stockton. LC 34-36299. C. Scribner's Sons.
Rudder Grange. Frank Richard Stockton. LC 43-36303. 1887. C. Scribner's Sons.
Rudder Grangers Abroad: And Other Stories. Frank Richard Stockton. LC 79-90592. (Short story index reprint series). 1969. Books for Libraries Press.
Rudder Grangers: Abroad and Other Stories. Frank Richard Stockton. LC 8-15538. 1891. C. Scribner's Sons.
Rudder Grangers Abroad, & Other Stories. facs. ed. Frank Richard Stockton. LC 79-90592. (Short Story Index Reprint Ser.). 1891. 13.00 (ISBN 0-8369-3075-4). Ayer Co.
Rudderless: A University Chronicle. William Hummel Stockwell. LC 30-5237. The Norwood Press.
Rude Awakening. Brian Wilson Aldiss. LC 78-10854. 8.95 (ISBN 0-394-50425-9). Random House.
Rude Awakening. Jean Sarment. 3.00 o.p. Branden.
Rudelstein Affair: A Novel. Michael Marsh. LC 80-29323. 9.95 (ISBN 0-918056-02-0). Ariadne Press.
Rudeness of the Honourable Mr. Leatherhead. Charles Walston. LC 51-50184. (His The ethics of the surface series, no. 1). 1896. M. Manges.
Rudge. J. B Masterson. LC 78-22341. 1979. 7.95 (ISBN 0-385-14449-0). Doubleday.
Rudin. Ivan Sergeevich Turgenev. LC 75-323307. (Penguin classics). 1975. 2.25 (ISBN 0-14-044304-5). Penguin Books.
Rudin: A Novel. Ivan Sergeevich Turgenev. LC 78-10317. (His Novels, v. 1). 1970. AMS Press.
Rudolf Martin: A Story of Nebraska. Berndt Emil Bengtson. LC 34-12973. The Progress Printing Company.
Rudolph and Amina: Or, The Black Crook. Christopher Darlington Morley. LC 30-28640. The John Day Company.
Rudolph of Rosenfeldt: Or, The Leaven of the Reformation. A Story of the Times of William the Silent. John W Spear. LC 8-15515. The American Sunday-School Union.
Rudra: a Romance of Ancient India. Arthur Joseph Westermayr. LC 12-7303. G. W. Dillingham Company.
Rue and Roses. Angela Langer. LC 13-13960. 1.25. George H. Doran Company.
Rue Morgue No. 1. Ed. by Rex Stout. Greenfield, Louis, Joint Ed. LC 46-231144. 1946. Creative Age Press, Inc.
Rue Notre Dame: With an Introd. by Bruce Marshall. Translation by A. Gordon Smith. Daniel Pezeril. LC 53-9798. 1953. Sheed and Ward.
Rue Pigalle: Translated from the French by Frances Frenaye. Francis Carco. LC 54-312861. (Avon 555). 1954. Avon Publications.
Rue the Day. Marjorie Alan. LC 46-852734. 1946. M. S. Mill Co., Inc.
Rue the Reservoir: A Mystery Novel. Annabelle McConnell Melville. LC 56-9646. 1956. Bruce Pub. Co.
Rue with a Difference. Rosa Nouchette Carey. LC 6366. 1901. J. B. Lippincott Company.
Rue with a Difference. Charles Recht. LC 24-234864. 1924. Boni and Liveright.
Rueben Sachs: A Sketch. Amy Levy. LC 42-30875. 1888. Macmillan and Co.
Rueful Mating. Gladys Bronwyn Stern. LC 32-266702. 1932. A. A. Knopf.
Ruel Durkee: Master of Men. George Waldo Browne. LC 10-22721. 1910. 1.50. R. G. Badger.
Ruff Justice, No. 6: The Spirit Woman War. Warren T. Longtree. 1982. pap. 2.50 (ISBN 0-451-11783-2, AE1783, Sig). NAL.
Ruffian, International Champion. Kurt Unkelbach. LC 67-23316. 1967. Prentice-Hall.
Ruffino: And Other Stories. ... authorized ed. Louise De La Ramee. LC 6-33311. (Lovell's international series, no. 131). 1890. United States Book Company.
Ruffino, and Other Stories. authorized ed. Louise De La Ramee. LC 6-33311. (Lovell's international series, no. 131). 1890. United States Book Company.
Rufus. Grace Louise Smith Richmond. LC 23-14199. 1923. Doubleday, Page & Company.
Rufus. Grace Louise Smith Richmond. LC 30-12310. 1925. A. L. Burt Company.
Rufus Starbuck's Wife. Catherine Drinker Bowen. LC 32-8697. 1932. G. P. Putnam's Sons.
Rugged Trail. R. H. Floyd. LC 49-938648. 1949. B. Humphries.
Rugged Water. Joseph Crosby Lincoln. LC 24-23068. 1924. D. Appleton and Company.
Rugged Way. Harold Morton Kramer. LC 11-18974. 1911. 1.35. Lothrop, Lee & Shepard Co.
Ruggles, Bunker & Merton: Three Masterpieces of Humor. Harry Leon Wilson. LC 35-27245. 1935. Doubleday, Doran & Company, Inc.
Ruggles of Red Gap. Harry Leon Wilson. LC 15-7367. 1915. Doubleday, Page & Company.
Ruggles of Red Gap. Harry Leon Wilson. LC 18-21380. 1917. Doubleday, Page & Company.
Ruggles of Red Gap. Harry Leon Wilson. LC 35-132014. Grosset & Dunlap.
Ruggles of Red Gap. Harry Leon Wilson. LC 40-11453. 1940. Triangle Books.
Rugue Herries. Hugh Walpole. LC 37-276023. 1937. The Sun Dial Press, Inc.
Ruhainah; a Story of Afghan Life. Thomas Patrick Hughes. LC 7-5416. Cassell & Company, Limited.
Ruhainah, the Maid of Herat: A Story of Afghan Life. 2d ed. Thomas Patrick Hughes. LC 7-5414. 1896. T. Whittaker.
Ruin: A Gothic Novel. Edward Sackville-West. LC 27-951. 1927. A. A. Knopf.
Ruined Abbeys. Peter Levi. 1968. pap. 0.60 o.p. Anvil Pr.
Ruined Cities of Mashonaland. facsimile ed. James T. Bent. LC 70-161256. (Black Heritage Library Collection). Repr. of 1892 ed. 30.50 (ISBN 0-8369-8528-1). Ayer Co.
Ruined City. Clay Putman. LC 59-8558. 1959. McGraw-Hill Book Co.
Ruined City. Nevil Shute. 1982. 13.95 (ISBN 0-434-69904-7, Pub. by Heinemann). David & Charles.
Ruined Map. Kobo Abe. LC 69-10703. 1969. 5.95. Knopf.
Ruined Map. Kobo Abe. LC 80-14780. (Illus.). 1980. 4.95 (ISBN 0-399-50470-2). Perigee Books.
Ruins in Jungles. Stella Snead. 1964. 14.95 o.s.i. (ISBN 0-8277-0110-1). British Bk Ctr.
Ruins of Earth: An Anthology of Stories of the Immediate Future. Ed. by Thomas M. Disch. (YA) 1971. 6.95 o.p. (ISBN 0-399-10712-6). Putnam.
Ruins of Isis. Marion Zimmer Bradley & Polly Freas. LC 78-14268. (Starblaze editions). (Illus.). 1978. 4.95 (ISBN 0-915442-60-4). Donning.
Ruke Anehm. Georgina Houldsworth Parks. LC 38-38712. Dorrance and Company.
Rule Britannia. Daphne Du Maurier. LC 72-86230. 1973. 6.95 (ISBN 0-385-02038-4). Doubleday.
Rule Britannia. Daphne Du Maurier. LC 73-5997. 1973. 11.95 (ISBN 0-8161-6110-0). G. K. Hall.
Rule by Proxy. Bruce Ducker. LC 76-10217. 8.95 (ISBN 0-517-52662-X). Crown Publishers.
Rule of Folly. rev ed. James R. Newman. (O.S.I.). 1962. pap. 1.25 o.s.i. (ISBN 0-671-63095-4). S&S.
Rule of Hate. George F Trost. LC 73-150171. 1972. 1.65 (ISBN 0-7260-0027-2). Gold Star Publications.
Rule of Might: A Romance of Napoleon at Schonbrunn. John Adam Cramb. LC 18-20777. 1918. 1.60. G. P. Putnam's Sons.
Rule of the Door. Lloyd Biggle, Jr. 1969. pap. 0.75 o.p. (0502-07024-075). Curtis.
Rule of the Door: And Other Fanciful Regulations by Lloyd Biggle, Jr. 1st Ed. Lloyd Biggle, Jr. LC 67-22469. (Doubleday sci. fiction). 1967. 3.95. Doubleday.
Rule of Three: A Story of Pike's Peak. Alma Martin Estabrook. Small, Maynard and Company.
Rule Three: Pretend to Be Nice: 1st Amer. Ed. Annabel Mary Dilke. LC 65-15944. 1965. bds., 3.50. McKay.
Ruled by a Woman; or, The Heir of Croylands. A Novel of Intense Interest. Michael Angelo Holmes. LC 11-16154. G. W. Ogilvie.
Ruler of the Kingdom and Other Phases of Life and Character. Grace Wallace Doonan. LC 4-33222. 1904. Benziger Brothers.
Ruler of the Range: By Peter Dawson Pseud. Jonathan H Glidden. LC 52-6720. Dodd, Mead.
Rulers' Morning, and Other Stories. Joseph George Hitrec. LC 46-248938. 1946. Harper & Brothers.
Rulers of Darkness. Frederick J Lipp. LC 66-13957. 6.95. World.
Rulers of Kings. Gertrude Franklin Horn Atherton. LC 4-9508. 1904. Harper & Brother.
Rulers of Men. Ethel Winifred Savi. LC 24-11478. 1922. G. P. Putnam's Sons.
Rulers of the City. Thomas J Fleming. LC 76-50765. 1977. 10.00 (ISBN 0-385-04472-0). Doubleday.
Rulers of the Lakes: A Story of George and Champlain. Joseph Alexander Altsheler. LC 17-24207. (His The French and Indian war series). 1917. D. Appleton and Company.
Rulers of the South. Stanley G. Crawford. 1900. 35.00 o.p. Norwood Edns.
Rulers of the Surf: A Story of the Mysteries and Perils of the Sea. Julius Washington Muller. LC 10-23124. 1910. 1.50. D. Appleton and Company.
Rules of Chaos: Or, Why Tomorrow Doesn't Work. Stephen Vizinczey. LC 75-107894. (Illus.). 1970. 6.95. McCall Pub. Co.
Rules of Marriage. Sheila Bishop. 1978. 1.75 (ISBN 0-449-23819-9). Fawcett Crest Books.
Rules of the Game. Elaine Chase. (Orig.). 1980. pap. 1.25 (ISBN 0-440-17340-X). Dell.
Rules of the Game. Roy Doliner. LC 70-94945. 1970. 5.95. Doubleday.
Rules of the Game. Susan Morrow. LC 64-16252. 1964. Published for the Crime Club by Doubleday.
Rules of the Game. Stewart Edward White. LC 10-10512. 1910. Doubleday, Page & Company.
Rules of the Game: A Novel. 1st Ed. James Chace. LC 60-5916. 1960. Doubleday.
Rules of the Game: Translated from the Italian by Robert Rietty The Life I Gave You and Lazarus Translated by Frederick May Introduced and Edited by E. Martin Browne. Luigi Pirandello. LC 60-4255. (Penguin plays, PL34). Penguin Books.
Rules of the Heart. Charlotte Tranbarger. 1982. pap. 6.95 (Avalon). Bouregy.
Ruling Machine. Jack Vance, pseud. (Science Fiction Ser.). 1978. pap. 1.75 o.p. (ISBN 0-87997-409-5, UE1409). DAW Bks.
Ruling Passion. Henry Dyke. 1901. Repr. 15.00 (ISBN 0-8274-3313-1). R West.
Ruling Passion. Shaun Herron. (Signet Book). 1978. 2.25 (ISBN 0-451-08042-4). New American Library.
Ruling Passion. Reginald Hill. LC 76-47258. 1977. 8.95 (ISBN 0-06-011888-1). Harper & Row.
Ruling Passion. Anne Acland-Troyte Marreco, pseud. LC 76-378938. 1976. 3.50 (ISBN 0-432-00412-2). P. Davies.
Ruling Passion: Tales of Nature and Human Nature. Henry Van Dyke. LC 71-38725. (Short story index reprint series). 1972. (ISBN 0-8369-4138-1). Books for Libraries Press.
Ruling Passion: Tales of Nature and Human Nature. Henry Van Dyke. LC 1-24184. 1901. C. Scribner's Sons.
Ruling the Planets: A Novel. Mina E Burton. LC 6-16694. (On cover: Harper's Franklin square library, no. 717). 1892. Harper & Brothers.
Rum and Roosters. Manuel Rodriguez. LC 57-6622. 1957. Crowell.
Rum and Ruin: The Story of Dr. Caldwell; a Thrilling Romance. Edward Reynolds Roe. Laird & Lee.
Rum Colony. Terry N. Bonner. 352p. 1982. pap. 3.50 (ISBN 0-440-07469-X, Emerald). Dell.
Rum Row Murders. Charles Reed Jones. LC 31-11728. The Macaulay Company.
Rumbin Galleries. Booth Tarkington. LC 37-28787. 1937. Doubleday, Doran & Co., Inc.
Rumble Murders. Henry Ware Eliot. LC 32-10752. 1932. Houghton, Mifflin Company.
Rumble on the Docks. By Frank Paley Pseud. Frank Palescandolo. LC 53-99703. 1953. Crown Publishers.

Rumblefish. S. E. Hinton. 1976. pap. 1.75 (ISBN 0-440-97534-4, LFL). Dell.
Rumbo Al Infierno. new ed. Rogelio A. Rios. (Pimienta Collection Ser). 160p. (Span.). 1974. pap. 1.00 (ISBN 0-88473-203-7). Fiesta Pub.
Rumelheart Must Roam. Maude Smith Delavan. LC 39-27077. 1939. Frederick A. Stokes Company.
Rumelhearts of Rampler Avenue. Maude Smith Delavan. LC 37-22640. 1937. Frederick A. Stokes Company.
Rummage Man. Kingsley Douthwaite. LC 67-17398. 1967. Dorrance.
Rummage Sale: Collections and Recollections. Donald R. Marshall. LC 75-4759. (Illus.). 1975. 3.45 (ISBN 0-87905-041-1). Peregrine Smith.
Rummy Kid Goes Home, and Other Stories of the Southwest. Ross Santee. LC 65-26671. 1965. Hastings House.
Rummyniscences. Frederick P Kafka. LC 22-1068. The Cornhill Publishing Co.
Rumor Hath It. Frances Moyer Ross Stevens. LC 46-893769. 1945. Pub. for the Crime Club by Doubleday, Doran & Company, Inc.
Rumor of Angels. Peter L. Berger. LC 68-27103. pap. 3.95 (ISBN 0-385-06630-9, Anch). Doubleday.
Rumors of Peace. Ella Leffland. LC 78-20209. 10.00 (ISBN 0-06-012572-1). Harper & Row.
Rumour. Elizabeth Sara Sheppard & Spofford, Mrs. Harriet Elizabeth (Prescott) 1835- Ed. LC 8-5118. 1893. A. C. McClurg and Company.
Rumour at Nightfall. Graham Greene. LC 32-223271. 1932. Doubleday, Doran & Company, Inc.
Rumour of Heaven. Beatrix Lehmann. 1934. W. Morrow & Co.
Rumours of Rain: A Novel. Andre Philippus Brink. LC 78-60693. 1978. 10.95 (ISBN 0-688-03367-9). Morrow.
Rumpelstiltskin. Evan Hunter. LC 80-54086. 1981. 12.95 (ISBN 0-670-61059-3). Viking Press.
Rumpelstiltskin. Ed McBain. (Matthew Hope Mystery Ser.). 1981. 12.95 (ISBN 0-670-61059-3). Viking Pr.
Rumpole of the Bailey. John Clifford Mortimer. LC 78-319398. 1980. 2.50 (ISBN 0-14-004670-4). Penguin Books.
Rumpole's Return. John Clifford Mortimer. 1982. pap. 2.95 (ISBN 0-14-005571-1). Penguin.
Rumrunner & Other Stories. Mary A. Armstrong. 1979. 5.00 o.p. (ISBN 0-682-49334-1). Exposition.
Run! Patricia Wentworth. LC 38-5361. J. B. Lippincott Company.
Run Around the Block. Veta Griggs. 1967. 5.00 o.p. (ISBN 0-682-45785-X). Exposition.
Run Away Home, a Novel. 1st Ed. Charles Christopher Mark. LC 60-12839. 1960. Duell, Sloan and Pearce.
Run Away, Love: By Rutherford Pseud. James Noble Gifford. 1953. Arcadia House.
Run Away to Murder. John Creasey. LC 71-89934. (Cock Robin mystery). 1970. Macmillan.
Run Before Midnight. Anne Maguire, pseud. 1981. pap. 6.95 (Avalon). Bouregy.
Run Before the Wind. Joellyn Carroll. (Candlelight Ecstasy Ser.: No. 131). (Orig.). 1983. pap. 1.95 (ISBN 0-440-17880-0). Dell.
Run Before the Wind. Mary Moore. (Harlequin Romances Ser.). 192p. 1982. pap. 1.50 (ISBN 0-373-02512-2). Harlequin Bks.
Run Before the Wind: A Novel. Stuart Woods. LC 82-14266. 1983. 16.50 (ISBN 0-393-01651-X). Norton.
Run Come See Jerusalem. David Coxhead. LC 72-79628. (O.s.i.). 1969. 4.95 o.s.i. (ISBN 0-671-20322-3). S&S.
Run, Come See Jerusalem! Richard C Meredith. LC 75-45061. 1976. 1.50 (ISBN 0-345-25066-4). Ballantine Books.
Run Come See Jerusalem: A Novel. David Coxhead. LC 72-79628. 1969. 4.95. Simon and Schuster.
Run, Don't Walk. Harriet M. Savitz. 1980. pap. 1.75 (ISBN 0-451-11488-4, AE1488, Sig). NAL.
Run Down; the World of Alan Brett. Robert Garrett. LC 72-185043. 1972. 4.95. Atheneum.
Run, Ellen, Run. Elaine F. Wells. (YA) 1978. 6.95 (Avalon). Bouregy.
Run Far, Run Fast. Lawrence Arthur Goldstone. LC 37-24572. The Greystone Press.
Run Far, Run Fast. Lawrence Treat. LC 37-24572. 1937. The Greystone Press.
Run, Fool, Run. Frank Gruber. LC 66-21293. 3.95. Dutton.
Run for Cover. John Benteen. (Sundance Ser.: No. 16). 176p. 1983. pap. 2.25 o.s.i. (ISBN 0-8439-1172-7, Leisure Bks). Dorchester Pub Co.
Run for Cover. John Benteen. (Orig.). 1976. pap. 1.25 o.p. (LB324ZK, Leisure Bks). Nordon Pubns.
Run for Cover. John Benteen. (Sundance series). 1976. (pbk.) 1.25. Leisure Books.
Run for Cover. John Brennan. LC 72-170106. (Harrow books, HW7027). 1972. 0.95 (ISBN 0-06-087027-3). Harper & Row.
Run for Cover. John Welcome, pseud. 1972. pap. 0.95 o.p. (ISBN 0-06-087027-3, HW). Harper & Row.
Run for Cover: By John Welcome Pseud. 1st American Ed. John Brennan. LC 59-9258. 1959. Knopf.
Run for the Elbertas. James Still. LC 80-51019. 12.50 (ISBN 0-8131-1414-4) (ISBN 0-8131-0151-4). University Press of Kentucky.
Run for the Trees. James S Rand, pseud. LC 67-12335. 1967. Putnam.
Run for Your Life. Elinore Denniston. 1973. (pbk.) 0.75. Dell.
Run for Your Life. Bruno Fischer. LC 54-19838. (Gold medal books, 543). 1953. Fawcett Publications.
Run for Your Life! Michael Stark. LC 46-6671. 1946. Crown Publishers.
Run for Your Life, a Novel. James Whittaker. LC 50-13853. 1950. Simon & Schuster.
Run for Your Life: By Rae Foley Pseud. Elinore Denniston. LC 57-587012. (Red badge detective). Dodd, Mead.
Run for Your Love. Lilian Peake. (Harlequin Presents Ser.). (Orig.). 1980. pap. 1.50 (ISBN 0-373-10341-7, Pub. by Harlequin). PB.
Run from Death. James P Duff. LC 57-126652. 1957. Mystery House.
Run from Nightmare. Maxine O'Callaghan. (Raven House Mysteries Ser.). 224p. 1982. pap. cancelled (ISBN 0-373-63047-6, Pub. by Worldwide). Harlequin Bks.
Run from the Mountain, a Novel. William Groninger. LC 59-6572. 1959. Rinehart.
Run from the Sheep. Capit Van Eykereh, Eline. LC 55-118682. 1955. Arcadia House.
Run, Heart, Run. William Arthur Neubauer. LC 67-9486. 1967. Arcadia House.
Run If You Can. Joyce Madison, pseud. 192p. (Orig.). 1981. pap. 2.25 (ISBN 0-523-41171-5). Pinnacle Bks.
Run If You're Guilty. James McKimmey. LC 63-15971. 1963. Lippincott.
Run in Diamonds. Alex Saxon. 1973. (pbk.) 0.95 (ISBN 0-671-77657-6). Pocket Books.
Run, Killer, Run. William Campbell Gault. LC 54-5049. (Guilt edged mystery). 1954. Dutton.
Run Like a Thief. Howard Breslin. LC 62-19412. 1962. M. S. Mill Co. and Morrow.
Run, Little Leather Boy. Larry Townsend. LC 79-28564. (Other traveller, TC-505). 1971. 1.95. Traveller's Companion.
Run Man Run. Chester B. Himes. 192p. 1975. Repr. of 1966 ed. 8.50x (ISBN 0-911860-56-8). Chatham Bkseller.
Run Man. Run: By Chester Himes. Chester B Himes. LC 66-20282. 1966. 4.95. Putnam.
Run, Mann, Run! James Keenan. LC 75-27345. 192p. (Orig.). 1975. pap. 1.25 (ISBN 0-89041-035-6, 3035). Major Bks.
Run Masked. Robb White. LC 38-729. 1938. A. A. Knopf.
Run Me a River. Janice Holt Giles. 1.75 (ISBN 0-380-00875-0). Avon.
Run, Mongoose: 1st Ed. Burke Wilkinson. LC 50-9979. 1950. Little, Brown.
Run, Nigger, Run. Zach Carver. (Orig.). 1970. pap. 0.95 o.p. (ISBN 0-447-75118-2). Lancer.
Run of the Brush. William MacLeod Raine. LC 36-4030. 1936. Houghton Mifflin Company.
Run of the Brush. William MacLeod Raine. 1975. (pbk.) 0.95. Popular Library.
Run of the Bush. William MacLeod Raine. 1976. Repr. of 1936 ed. lib. bdg. 15.45x (ISBN 0-88411-554-2). Amereon Ltd.
Run of the Stars. Dora Aydelotte. 1940. D. Appleton-Century Company, Incorporated.
Run on the Wind. Jenifer Dalton. 368p. (Orig.). 1983. pap. 3.50 (ISBN 0-440-01977-X, Emerald). Dell.
Run Out of Time. Matthew Carney. LC 81-68605. 334p. 1982. 14.95 (ISBN 0-937444-02-2); pap. 9.95 (ISBN 0-937444-03-0). Caislan Pr.
Run River. Joan Didion. 1961. 12.00 (ISBN 0-8392-1094-9). Astor-Honor.
Run, Run, Run. Frank Taubes. LC 55-5977. 1955. Crowell.
Run, Sara, Run. Anne Worboys. LC 80-27151. 10.95 (ISBN 0-684-16818-9). Scribner.
Run Scared. Mignon Good Eberhart. LC 63-8340. (Random House mystery). 1963. Random House.
Run Scared. Mignon Good Eberhart. LC 63-8340. 1974. (pbk.) 0.95. Popular Library.
Run, Sheep, Run. Gordon Sager. LC 50-5860. 1950. Vanguard Press.
Run, Sheep, Run. June Pat Wetherell. LC 47-31389. 1947. E. P. Dutton.
Run, Sheep, Run. Thames Ross Williamson. LC 26-188. Small, Maynard & Company.
Run, Sheep, Run, a Novel. Maxwell Bodenheim. LC 32-3184. 1932. Liveright, Inc.
Run Silent, Run Deep. Edward Latimer Beach. LC 55-6416. (Illus.). 1955. Holt.
Run Silent, Run Deep. Edward Latimer Beach. 1979. 2.50 (ISBN 0-440-17829-0). Dell Publishing.
Run Spy Run. Nick Carter. (Nick Carter Espionage Ser). (O.s.i.). (Orig.). 1969. pap. 0.60 o.s.i. (A622X, Award). Univ Pub & Dist.
Run to Daylight. Vince Lombardi & W. C. Heinz. (Illus.). 304p. 1982. pap. 8.95 (ISBN 0-13-783845-X). P-H.
Run to Death: A Peter Duluth Story. Patrick Quentin. LC 48-2893. (Inner sanctum mystery). 1948. Simon and Schuster.
Run to Evil: By Lesley Egan Pseud. 1st Ed. Elizabeth Linington. LC 63-16529. 1963. Harper & Row.
Run to Morning. James Graham, pseud. LC 74-79425. 216p. 1974. 6.95 o.p. (ISBN 0-8128-1736-2). Stein & Day.
Run to Morning. Jack Higgins, pseud. 1981. pap. 2.95 (ISBN 0-8128-7062-X). Stein & Day.
Run to Morning. Henry Patterson. LC 74-79425. 1974. 6.95 (ISBN 0-8128-1736-2). Stein and Day.
Run to Morning. Henry Patterson. LC 74-79425. 1975. (pbk.) 1.25. Fawcett.
Run to the Mountain. Theodore V. Olsen. (Fawcett gold medal). 1974. (pbk.) 0.95. Fawcett.
Run to the Waterfall. Arturo Vivante. LC 79-15448. 8.95 (ISBN 0-684-16276-8). Scribner.
Run, Traitor, Run. Richard Pierce. 1977. pap. 1.25 o.p. (ISBN 0-532-12514-2). Woodhill.
Run Traitor Run. Richard Pierce. (Orig.). pap. 0.60 o.p. (73-717). Lancer.
Run, Traitor, Run. Richard Pierce. 1977. pap. 1.25 o.p. (ISBN 0-532-12514-2). Manor Bks.
Run When I Say Go. Hillary Waugh. LC 69-12358. 1969. 5.95. Doubleday.
Run with the Hare. Abbey, Kieran. LC 41-14657. 1941. C. Scribner's Sons.
Run with the Horsemen. Ferrol Sams. LC 81-22671. 1982. 12.95 (ISBN 0-931948-32-0). Peachtree Publishers.
Run with the Pack. Patricia Frame. LC 42-239508. 1942. Arcadia House, Inc.
Run. 1st Ed. Margaret Cochran Shedd. LC 55-10516. 1956. Doubleday.
Runagate Courage. Hans Jacob Christoffel Von Grimmelshausen. LC 64-19854. 1965. University of Nebraska Press.
Runagates Club. John Buchan. LC 28-172022. 1928. Houghton Mifflin Company.
Runaround. Benjamin Appel. LC 37-17244. 1937. E.P. Dutton & Company, Inc.
Runaway. John Creasey. (A Falcon's Head Mystery). 5.95 o.p. (ISBN 0-529-01152-2, A3957). World Pub.
Runaway. Richard Hubbard. (Adam 12 Ser.). (O.s.i.). 160p. (Orig.). 1972. pap. 0.95 o.s.i. (AN1002, Award). Univ Pub & Dist.
Runaway. Gloria Miklowitz. 1977. pap. 1.95 (ISBN 0-448-17247-X, Pub. by Tempo). Ace Bks.
Runaway. Kathleen Thompson Norris. LC 39-11256. 1939. Doubleday, Doran & Co., Inc.
Runaway. John Desmond Peter. LC 69-12232. 1969. 5.95. Doubleday.
Runaway. Albertine Sarrazin. LC 67-20340. 1967. Grove Press.
Runaway: A Novel. Floyd Dell. LC 25-19120. George H. Doran Company.
Runaway Bag. Albert Payson Terhune. LC 25-21493. George H. Doran Company.
Runaway Black. Ed McBain. (Signet book). 1978. 1.50. New American Library.
Runaway Black: By Richard Marsten Pseud. Cover Painting by Lu Kimmel. Evan Hunter. LC 55-22307. (Gold medal books, 415). 1954. Fawcett Publications.
Runaway Browns: A Story of Small Stories. Henry Cuyler Bunner & Taylor, Charles Jay, 1855-1929, Illus. LC 44-15484. 1892. Keppler & Schwarzmann.
Runaway Countess. Eva McDonald. 1973. pap. 0.75 o.p. (07306). Curtis.
Runaway Couple: A Story of New York Society. Oliver Lowrey. LC 98-261. 1898. F. T. Neely.
Runaway Desire. Sara Orwig. 1979. pap. 1.95 (ISBN 0-89041-233-2, 3233). Major Bks.
Runaway Flying-Machine: And Other Stories of Outdoor Adventure. Richard Hayes Barry. LC 10-23201. 1910. 0.60. Harper & Brothers.
Runaway Girl. Lucy Walker, pseud. LC 75-22202. 1975. 1.25 (ISBN 0-345-26744-3). Ballantine Books.
Runaway Heart. Barbara Cartland. 1974. pap. 1.25 o.p. (ISBN 0-515-03428-2, V3428). BJ Pub Group.
Runaway Heart. Arlene Hale. LC 76-45197. 1977. 8.95 (ISBN 0-89340-051-3). John Curley & Associates.
Runaway Heart. Arlene Hale. LC 71-175480. 1972. 5.95. Little, Brown.
Runaway Heart, No. 69. Barbara Cartland. 224p. 1983. pap. 2.25 (ISBN 0-515-06389-4). Jove Pubns.
Runaway Home! 1st Ed. Kage Booton. LC 67-10977. 1967. 3.95. Pub. for the Crime Club by Doubleday.
Runaway Horse. Martin Walser. Tr. by Leila Vennewitz from Ger. LC 79-22749. 128p. 1980. 9.95 (ISBN 0-03-046501-X). HR&W.
Runaway Horses. Yukio Mishima, pseud. LC 72-11039. (His The sea of fertility 2). 1973. 7.95 (ISBN 0-394-46618-7). Knopf; Distributed by Random House.
Runaway June. George Randolph Chester & Chester, Lillian, Joint Author. LC 15-12881. 0.50. Hearst's International Library Co.
Runaway Love. Jasmine Craig. (Second Chance at Love Ser.: No. 46). (Orig.). 1982. pap. 1.75 (ISBN 0-515-06547-1). Jove Pubns.
Runaway Marriage. Mary Wibberley. (Harlequin Romance). 1979. pap. 1.25 (ISBN 0-373-02298-0, Pub. by Harlequin). PB.
Runaway Nurse. Florence Stonebraker. LC 63-6666. 1963. Arcadia House.
Runaway Nurse. Florence Stuart. pap. 0.50 o.p. (50-473). Manor Bks.
Runaway Nurse: By Ethel Hamill Pseud. Jean Francis Webb. LC 55-14478. 1955. Avalon Books.
Runaway Pigeon. 1st Ed. Leslie Edgley. LC 52-13370. 1953. Published for the Crime Club by Doubleday.
Runaway Place: A May Idyl of Manhattan. Walter Prichard Eaton & Underhill, Elise Morris, Joint Author. LC 9-14514. 1909. 1.25. H. Holt and Company.
Runaway Slave. Robert Tralins. pap. 0.95 o.p. (75-083). Lancer.
Runaway Star. Barbara Cartland. LC 78-19107. 6.95 (ISBN 0-87272-042-X). Duron Books.
Runaway Sweetheart. Allen Eppes. LC 41-11976. Gramercy Publishing Co.
Runaway Sweetheart. Watkins Eppes Wright. LC 41-11976. 1941. Gramercy Pub. Co.
Runaway. Tr. by Charles Lam Markmann. Albertine Sarrazin. LC 67-203408. 1967. 7.50. Grove.
Runaway Trail. Albert M Treynor. LC 27-23029. 1927. Dodd, Mead & Company.
Runaway Turns at Blackfish. Janie M. Woodard. 3.50 o.p. (ISBN 0-8062-0669-1). Carlton.
Runaway West. H. A. Everts. 1979. pap. 6.00 (ISBN 0-682-49379-1, Lochinvar). Exposition.
Runaway Wife. Vernie E Connelly. LC 32-7124. Grosset & Dunlap.
Runaway Wife: Or, Love and Vengeance. Simon O'Donnell. (On cover: Pinkerton detective series, v. 25). 1889. Laird & Lee.
Runaway Woman. Louis Dodge. LC 18-193983. 1918. 1.50. C. Scribner's Sons.
Runaways. Victor Canning. LC 77-181352. 1972. 5.95. Morrow.
Runaways. James Owen Hannay. LC 28-215858. The Bobbs-Merrill Company.
Runaways. John R. Townsend. Ed. by David Fickling. (Australian Bibliographies Ser.). (Orig.). 1979. pap. text ed. 2.95x (ISBN 0-19-424211-0). Oxford U Pr.
Rundown. James Magnuson. LC 77-11144. 1979. 1.75 (ISBN 0-515-04725-2). Jove/HBJ.
Rundown. Jim Magnuson. LC 77-11144. 7.95. Dial Press.
Runes. R. W. Elliott. 1959. pap. 6.50 (ISBN 0-7190-0787-9). Manchester.
Runes are Cast. R. P. Back. 1981. 15.00x (ISBN 0-7223-1368-3, Pub. by Stockwell). State Mutual BK.
Runestaff. Michael Moorcock. 1977. 1.25 (ISBN 0-87997-324-2). D.A.W. Books.
Runestaff No. 4. Michael Moorcock. (Science Fiction Ser). 1977. pap. 1.75 (ISBN 0-87997-616-0, UE1616). DAW Bks.
Runestruck. Calvin Trillin. LC 76-45610. 1977. 7.95 (ISBN 0-316-85275-9). Little, Brown.
Rung Ho! Talbot Mundy. LC 14-5473. 1914. C. Scribner's Sons.
Rungs of the Ladder. Sivasankara Pillai, Thakazhi. LC 76-901281. 1976. 10.00. Arnold-Heinemann (India)
Runner. Charles William Gordon. LC 40-5394. 1939. Triangle Books.
Runner. Lance Jensen. (Orig.). 1975. pap. 1.50 o.p. (ISBN 0-515-03751-6). BJ Pub Group.
Runner. Brian Swann. LC 79-9366. (Illus.). 5.00 (ISBN 0-914140-07-8). Carpenter Press.
Runner: A Romance of the Niagaras. Charles William Gordon. LC 29-23128. 1929. Doubleday, Doran & Company, Inc.
Runner Mack. Barry Beckham. LC 75-170225. 1972. 6.95. Morrow.
Runner of the Trail: A Mystery of the Hudson Bay Country. Maribelle Cormack. LC 35-13170. 1935. D. Appleton-Century Company, Incorporated.
Runnin' Gal Outa Bath. Charles Philip Moody. LC 68-18464. 1968. Dorrance.
Running. George Bower. LC 81-82837. 12.02 (ISBN 0-87223-745-1). Seaview Books.
Running. Robin Shaw. LC 72-87629. (Red mask mystery). 1973. 4.95. Putnam.
Running Against the Wind: A Novel. Lewis Christopher Warden. LC 80-69177. 9.75 (ISBN 0-8158-0401-6). Christopher Pub. House.
Running Away. Allen, Charlotte Vale. (Signet Book). 1977. 1.75. New American Library.

TITLE INDEX RUSTLER'S BLOOD.

Running Back. William Cox. (Bantam Pathfinder editions). 1974. (pbk.) 0.95. Bantam Books.
Running Back: A Novel of Professional Football. Hamilton Maule. LC 66-24422. 1966. D. McKay Co.
Running Blind. Desmond Bagley. LC 71-135711. 1971. 5.95. Doubleday.
Running Dog. Don DeLillo. LC 77-26674. 1978. 8.95 (ISBN 0-394-50143-8). Knopf.
Running Dog. Don DeLillo. LC 79-2159. 1979. 2.95 (ISBN 0-394-74121-8). Vintage Books.
Running Dog. Ding Fai Lee. LC 82-161581. 1980. 7.50. Heinemann Asia.
Running Fight. William Hamilton Osborne. LC 10-11137. 1910. 1.50. Dodd, Mead and Company.
Running Footman: Or, The Sentimental Servant. John Owen. LC 32-7343. 1932. The Macmillan Company.
Running for the Exit. H. W Wright. LC 79-12275. 6.95 (ISBN 0-89407-035-5). Strawberry Hill Press.
Running Foxes. Joyce Stranger. (Illus.). 1966. 3.95 o.p. (ISBN 0-670-61103-4). Viking Pr.
Running Foxes. Joyce Stranger, pseud. 1972. pap. 0.95 o.p. (95266). Beagle Bks.
Running Foxes: A Novel. Illus. by David Rook. Joyce Stranger, pseud. LC 66-16066. 1966. 3.95. Viking.
Running Free. James Brendan Connolly. LC 17-242723. 1917. C. Scribner's Sons.
Running Gun. Robert Macleod, pseud. 1979. pap. 1.75 (ISBN 0-449-14302-3, GM). Fawcett.
Running Gun. Robert MacLeod, pseud. 176p. 1973. pap. 0.75 o.p. (T2682, GM). Fawcett World.
Running Horse Inn. Alfred Tresidder Sheppard. LC 7-18182. 1907. J. B. Lippincott Company.
Running Horses. Fred Grove. LC 79-7625. 1980. 10.95 (ISBN 0-385-14741-4). Doubleday.
Running in Place. Winston J. Churchill. LC 72-92832. 1973. 5.95 (ISBN 0-8076-0662-6). G. Braziller.
Running Iron. Rachel Ann Fish. LC 56-11836. 1957. Coward-McCann.
Running M. W. D. Hoffman. LC 44-803176. 1944. Phoenix Press.
Running Man. Richard Bachman. 1982. pap. 2.50 (ISBN 0-451-11508-2, AE1508, Sig). NAL.
Running Man. W. A. Harbinson. (O.s.i.). 1970. pap. 0.60 o.s.i. (A603X, Award). Univ Pub & Dist.
Running Man. Jon Ruddy. LC 77-358592. (Trendsetter edition). 1976. 6.95. (ISBN 0-7736-0047-7) (ISBN 0-7737-7116-6). General Pub. Co.
Running Man: A Ralph Lindsey Mystery. Ben Benson. LC 57-10400. 1957. M. S. Mill Co., and W. Morrow.
Running of Beasts. Bill Pronzini & Barry N. Malzberg. LC 75-26767. 8.95 (ISBN 0-399-11647-8). Putnam.
Running of Beasts. Bill Pronzini & Barry N. Malzberg. 1.75 (ISBN 0-449-23061-9). Fawcett Crest.
Running of the Deer. Ewan Clarkson. LC 71-179849. (Illus.). 1972. 5.95 (ISBN 0-525-19473-8). Dutton.
Running of the Deer. Dan Wickenden. LC 37-28697. 1937. W. Morrow and Company.
Running of the Tide. Esther Forbes. LC 48-4573. 1948. Houghton Mifflin Co.
Running Out. Christopher Brookhouse. LC 79-105350. 1970. 5.95. Little, Brown.
Running Sands. Reginald Wright Kauffman. LC 13-5414. 1913. 1.35. Dodd, Mead and Company.
Running Scared. Jon Burmeister. LC 73-86257. 1973. 6.95. St. Martin's Press.
Running Scared. Gregory McDonald. (Signet, Q5596). 1973. (pbk.) 0.95. New American Lib.
Running Special. Frank Lucius Packard. LC 25-7085. George H. Doran Company.
Running Spy. Joseph Milton. Orig. Title: Assignment: Assassination. pap. 0.75 o.p. (74-881). Lancer.
Running the Blockade: Or, U.S. Secret Service Adventures. William Henry Thomes. LC 12-16796. 1875. Lee and Shepard.
Running the Blockade: Or, U.S. Secret Service Adventures. William Henry Thomes. LC 12-164261. (Half-title: Ocean-life series). 1884. A. T. Loyd & Co.
Running the Blockade: Or, U.S. Secret Service Adventures. William Henry Thomes. (On cover: The detective and adventure library, no. 9). 1889. A. T. Loyd & Co.
Running the Blockade: Or, U.S. Secret Service Adventures. William Henry Thomes. (On cover: The library of choice fiction, no. 32). 1891. Laird & Lee.
Running the Cuban Blockade: Captain Jack; The Boy Wreckers. William Osborn Stoddard. 1900. H. S. Stone and Company.
Running the Gantlet: The Daring Exploits of Lieutenant Cushing, U. S. N. Jessie Peabody Frothingham. LC 6-32669. 1906. D. Appleton & Company.
Running the Gauntlet. A Novel. Edmund Hodgson Yates. LC 9-1463. 1866. Loring.
Running the Gauntlet. A Novel. 5th ed. Edmund Hodgson Yates. (On cover: Lovell's library, no. 723). J. W. Lovell Company.
Running Thread. Katherine Drayton Mayrant Simons. LC 49-3883. 1949. Appleton-Century-Crofts.
Running Tide. Irina Aleksander & Guerney, Bernard Guilbert, Tr. LC 43-18554. 1943. Duell, Sloan and Pearce.
Running Time. Gavin Lambert. LC 82-21676. 15.95. Macmillan.
Running to Paradise. John Lodwick. LC 43-5438. 1943. Dodd, Mead & Company.
Running to Waste. The Story of a Tomboy. George Melville Baker. LC 6-6884. (maidenhood series). 1875. Lee and Shepard.
Running Water. Alfred Edward Woodley Mason. LC 7-7196. 1907. The Century Co.
Running Wild. Arnold Hano. 1973. (pbk) 0.95. Popular Lib.
Running Wild. Shirley Powell. 192p. 1981. pap. 2.25 (ISBN 0-380-78170-0, 78170). Avon.
Running Wild. Joy Thorne. pap. 1.95 o.s.i. (OPH-212, Ophelia). Olympia.
Running Wild. Antony Trew. LC 82-17021. 1983. 13.95 (ISBN 0-312-69601-9). St. Martin's Press.
Runnymede and Lincoln Fair: A Story of the Great Charter. John George Edgar. (Half-title: Everyman's library, ed. by Ernest Rhys. Fiction). J. M. Dent & Co.
Runts of Sixty-One Cygni C. James A. Grazier. (Orig.). 1970. pap. 0.75 o.p. (B75-2062). Belmont-Tower.
Runway to Death. Macartney-Filgate Terence. LC 80-52080. 1980. 9.95 (ISBN 0-8027-5428-7). Walker.
Runway Zero-Eight. Arthur Hailey & John Castle. LC 73-166423. 1973. 6.95 (ISBN 0-385-04862-9). Doubleday.
Runway Zero-Eight, Doubleday: 1959 C1958. Arthur Hailey & John Castle. LC 59-6993.
Runyon a la Carte. Damon Runyon. LC 44-9749. 1944. J.B. Lippincott Company.
Runyon First and Last. Damon Runyon. LC 49-9949. 1948. J. B. Lippincott Co.
Ruodlieb. Ed. by Gordon B. Ford, Jr. Facsimile Ed. Ed. by Gordon B. Ford. LC 66-4677. 1965. 20.00. Pyramid Pr.
Ruodlieb: The Earliest Courtly Novel After 1050. Ed. & tr. by Edwin H. Zeydel. LC 59-63490. (North Carolina University. Studies in the Germanic Languages & Literatures: N0. 23). 1959. 18.50 (ISBN 0-404-50923-1). AMS Pr.
Rupavati see Beauty.
Rupert Aubrey of Aubrey Chase. An Historical Tale of 1681. Thomas Joseph Potter. LC 44-27429. 1873. P. Donahoe.
Rupert Godwin. Mary Elizabeth Braddon Maxwell. (Lovell's Library: No. 879). 1887. J. W. Lovell Company.
Rupert Godwin. A Novel. Mary Elizabeth Braddon Maxwell. (Seaside library. v. 24, no. 469). 1879. G. Munro.
Rupert Godwin. A Novel. Mary Elizabeth Braddon Maxwell. (On cover: Seaside library. Pocket ed. no. 489). 1885. G. Munro.
Rupert of Hentzau: From the Memoirs of Fritz Von Tarlenheim. Anthony Hope Hawkins. LC 4-18952. 1898. H. Holt and Company.
Rupert of Hentzau: From the Memoirs of Fritz Von Tarlenheim. Anthony Hope Hawkins. LC 12-313703. 1906. H. Holt and Company.
Rupert of Hentzau: From the Memoirs of Fritz Von Tarlenheim. Anthony Hope Hawkins. LC 23-19915. H. Holt and Company.
Rupert of Hentzau (Sequel to Prisoner of Zenda) Anthony Hope. lib. bdg. 16.95x (ISBN 0-89966-227-7). Buccaneer Bks.
Rural Life in New England. A Domestic Romance. LC 8-968967. (On cover: New world library of fiction, no. 20). J. Winchester.
Rural School-Teacher: Or, A Double West Virginia Love Story. Buchanan White. LC 9-13037. Broadway Publishing Company.
Rurality. Original Desultory Tales. Mary Elizabeth Talbot. LC 5-4153. 1830. Marshall and Hammond, Printers.
Ruse of the Vanished Women. Val Henry Gielgud. LC 34-17246. 1934. Pub. For the Crime Club, Inc., by Doubleday, Doran & Company, Inc.
Rush Against the Wind. Richard L. Ten Eyck. 1970. 2.50 o.p. (ISBN 0-8059-1494-3). Dorrance.
Rush Hour, a Novel. James Cleugh. LC 33-213915. 1933. H. C. Kinsey & Company, Inc.
Rush-Light Stories. Maud Louise Hudnut Chapin. LC 18-227360. 1918. 1.35. Duffield & Company.
Rush of Eagle Wings. Richard C. Folta. 1983. 14.95 (ISBN 0-87949-219-8). Ashley Bks.
Rush on the Ultimate. Henry Reymond Fitzwalter Keating. LC 82-45074. (Crime Club Ser.). 192p. 1982. 10.95 (ISBN 0-385-18170-1). Doubleday.
Rush to the Sun. William Brown Meloney. LC 37-22935. Farrar & Rinehart, Inc.
Rushers. John Thomas Edson. 192p. 1982. pap. 2.25 (ISBN 0-425-05638-4). Berkley Pub.
Rushes. John Rechy. LC 79-2302. 1979. 10.00 (ISBN 0-394-50861-0, GP831). Grove.
Rushes. John Rechy. LC 79-2302. 288p. 1981. pap. 3.95 (ISBN 0-394-17883-1, B-455, BC). Grove.
Russell. A Tale of the Reign of Charles Ii. George Payne Rainsford James. LC 7-7570. 1847. Harper & Brothers.
Russell, Alexandra, & John. Ed. by Joseph R. Simonetta. LC 81-90481. 144p. (Orig.). 1981. pap. 7.95 (ISBN 0-941594-00-9). Simonetta Pr.
Russell Millions and The Call. Charles Melvin Van Curen. LC 27-18265. The Christopher Publishing House.
Russells in Chicago. Emily Wheaton. LC 2-15862. (Page's commonwealth series, no. 5). 1902. L. C. Page & Company.
Russia and the Woman: A Novel of the Virgin Mary, Mother of Jesus. Clarence P Milligan. LC 53-11548. 1953. Vantage Press.
Russia Laughs. Mikhail Mikhailovich Zoshchenko & Clayton, Mrs. Helena, Tr. LC 35-27440. 1935. Lothrop, Lee and Shepard Company.
Russian America. Hector Chevigny. 1973. pap. 1.65 o.p. (345-23575-4-165). Comstock Edns.
Russian Ballet Girl. Intro. by A. D. Warner. pap. 1.75 o.p. (3021). Brandon.
Russian Beauty and Other Stories. Vladimir Vladimirovich Nabokov. LC 72-10094. 1973. 7.95 (ISBN 0-07-045735-2). McGraw-Hill.
Russian Chaps. Marjorie Colt Byrne Lethbridge. LC 19-856710. 1916. John Lane.
Russian Comic Fiction. Ed. by Guy Daniels. LC 75-125856. (Signet classic, CY 505). 1970. 1.25. New American Library.
Russian Enigma: A Novel. Clive Egleton. LC 82-45170. 1982. 11.95 (ISBN 0-689-11303-X). Atheneum.
Russian Gypsy. Alexandre Dumas. LC 6-417015. (O, cover: Seaside library. Pocket ed. no. 2063). 1896. G. Munro's Sons.
Russian Humorous Stories. Ed. by Janko Lavrin. 208p. 1982. Repr. of 1946 ed. lib. bdg. 30.00 (ISBN 0-89760-745-7). Telegraph Bks.
Russian Interpreter. Michael Frayn. LC 66-23823. 1966. 4.50. Viking.
Russian Leave. Anthony Stuart, pseud. LC 81-66967. 208p. 1981. 12.50 (ISBN 0-87795-336-8). Arbor Hse.
Russian Nights. Vladimir Fedorovich Odoevskii. LC 65-2339. 1965. E. P. Dutton.
Russian Nights. Tr. from Russian by Olga Koshansky-Olienikov, Ralph E. Matlaw. Introd. by Dr. Matlaw. Vladimir Fedorovich Odoevskii. LC 65-233945. (Dutton paperback, D163). pap., 1.95. Dutton.
Russian Portraits. Eugene Marie Melchior Vogue & Cary, Elisabeth Luther, 1867- Tr. LC 8-32695. (On cover: Autonym library v. 6). 1895. G. P. Putnam's Sons.
Russian Priest. Ignatii Nikolaevich Potapenko. Ed. by Gaussen, William Frederick Armytage. LC 7-30052. Cassell Publishing Company.
Russian Primer. Agnes Jacques. 1959. pap. 3.45 (ISBN 0-87532-159-3). Hendricks House.
Russian Princess. A Love Story. Emmanuel Gonzales. Tr. by Cox, George D. LC 6-43731. T. B. Peterson & Brothers.
Russian Proprietor: And Other Stories. Lev Nikolaevich Tolstoi. LC 71-110219. (Short story index reprint series). 1970. (ISBN 0-8369-3371-0). Books for Libraries Press.
Russian Proprietor & Other Stories. Lev Nikolaevich Tolstoi. Tr. by Nathan H. Dole. LC 77-110219. (Short Story Index Reprint Ser.). 1887. 19.00 (ISBN 0-8369-3371-0). Ayer Co.
Russian Proprietor, and Other Stories. Lev Nikolaevich Tolstoi & Dole, Nathan Haskell, 1852-1935, Tr. T. G. Crowell & Co.
Russian Refuge: A Tale of the Blue Ridge. Henry R Wilson. LC 8-37099. 1887. T. R. Knox & Co.
Russian Refuge: A Tale of the Blue Ridge. Henry R Wilson. LC 8-37098. (On cover: Library of progress, no. 7). 1893. C. H. Kerr & Company.
Russian Romance Is Different. Nellie Marguerite Seeds Nearing. LC 47-19016. 1946. Island Press.
Russian Romantic Prose: An Anthology: Containing Tales by Alexander Pushkin, Nikolai Gogol, Orest Somov, Vladimir Odoevsky, Alexander Veltman, Mikhail Lermontov, Count Vladimir Sollogub, Alexander Bestuzhev-Marlinsky. Ed. by Carl R. Proffer. LC 78-68670. (Illus.). 1979. 15.00 (ISBN 0-931556-00-7). Translation Press.
Russian Rose. Randall Wallace. LC 80-13495. 11.95 (ISBN 0-399-12536-1). Putnam.
Russian Roulette. James Mitchell. LC 73-9841. 1973. 5.95 (ISBN 0-688-00201-3). W. Morrow.
Russian Roulette. 1st American Ed. Anthony Bloomfield. LC 56-8528. 1956. Harcourt, Brace.
Russian Schoolboy. Sergey Aksakov. Tr. by J. D. Duff from Rus. 216p. 1981. pap. write for info. (ISBN 0-86649-074-4). Twentieth Century.
Russian Science Fiction: Eleven Short Stories. Ed. by Robert Magidoff. Tr. by Doris Johnson. 1964. 6.95 o.p. (ISBN 0-8147-0278-3). NYU Pr.
Russian Science Fiction 1968. Ed. by Robert Magidoff. Tr. by Helen Jacobson. 1968. 6.95x o.p. (ISBN 0-8147-0279-1). NYU Pr.
Russian Science Fiction, 1968: An Anthology. Ed. by Robert Magidoff. LC 68-16804. 1968. New York University Press.
Russian Science Fiction, 1969: An Anthology. Ed. by Robert Magidoff. LC 75-88134. 1969. 6.95. New York University Press.
Russian Short Stories. Ed. by John Iwanik. 1962. pap. text ed. 9.95x (ISBN 0-669-30692-4). Heath.
Russian Short Stories. Ed. by Harry Christian Schweikert. LC 72-3278. (Series: The Lake English Classics.). (Short story index reprint series). 1972. 14.50 (ISBN 0-8369-4160-8). Books for Libraries Press.
Russian Short Stories. Tr. by Rochelle Townsend. 288p. 1982. Repr. of 1924 ed. pap. text ed. 4.50x (ISBN 0-460-01758-6, Pub by Evwan). Biblio Dist.
Russian Short Stories: A Bilingual Collection, 2 vols, Vol. 1. Ed. by Maurice Freidberg. (Eng. & Rus.). 1964. 6.95 o.p. (ISBN 0-394-44352-7). Random.
Russian Short Stories: A Bilingual Collection, 2 vols, Vol. 2. Ed. by Maurice Friedberg & Robert Maguire. (Eng. & Rus.). 1965. 6.95 o.p. (ISBN 0-394-44312-8). Random.
Russian Silhouettes. facs. ed. Anton Pavlovich Chekhov. Tr. by Marian Fell. LC 72-142260. (Short Story Index Reprint Ser). 1915. 19.00 (ISBN 0-8369-3744-9). Ayer Co.
Russian Silhouettes: More Stories of Russian Life. Anton Pavlovich Chekhov. LC 72-142260. (Short story index reprint series). 1970. Books for Libraries Press.
Russian Silhouettes: More Stories of Russian Life. Anton Pavlovich Chekhov. Tr. by Fell, Marian. LC 15-205953. 1915. C. Scribner's Sons.
Russian Stories and Legends. Tr. from Russian by Louise and Aylmer Maude Illus. by Alexander Alexeieff. Lev Nikolaevich Tolstoi. Tr. by Aylmer Maude. LC 67-142252. 1967. 3.95. Pantheon.
Russian Tales. Aylmer Maude. 25.00 (ISBN 0-89987-091-0). Darby Bks.
Russian Windfall. Theodore Safine & London, Meyer, Tr. LC 47-1195. 1946. B. Humprhies, Inc.
Russian Woman. Vernon Tom Hyman. LC 83-2923. 1983. 16.95 (ISBN 0-312-69614-0). St. Martin's/Marek.
Russians. Stephan Strogoff. LC 61-6240. 1961. Random House.
Russians Abroad: And Other Stories. Margery Mayo. LC 22-11287. 1922. The Stratford Co.
Russia's Other Writers: Selections from Samizdat Literature. Ed. by Michael Scammell. LC 74-83344. 1971. 6.95. Praeger.
Russia's Vortex. Gregory Aleksis Ptitsin. LC 32-211930. 1932. Wetzel Publishing Co., Inc.
Russkaia Literaturnaia Parodiia. (Rus.). 1981. pap. 6.50 (ISBN 0-88233-604-5). Ardis Pubs.
Russko-Anglijsky Razgovornik. Natalia Ozernoy. (Eng. & Rus.). 1982. pap. 9.50 (ISBN 0-938920-21-9). Hermitage MI.
Rust. R. C. Calif. (Orig.). 1980. pap. 1.95 (ISBN 0-532-23198-8). Woodhill.
Rust of Rome. Warwick Deeping. LC 10-20388. 1910. Cassell and Company, Ltd.
Rusticus. Lonnie C. Mings. LC 77-29098. 2.50 (ISBN 0-8024-8684-3). Moody Press.
Rustle of Petticoats. Renee De Fontarce McCormick & McCormick, Leander James, 1888- Tr. LC 46-7818. 1946. Houghton Mifflin Company.
Rustle of Silk. Cosmo Hamilton. LC 22-9186. 1922. 1.90. Litte, Brown, and Company.
Rustle of Spring: Simple Annals of a London Girl. Winifred Wells Burke. LC 28-28026. 1927. George H. Doran Company.
Rustle of Wings. Charles H Holding. LC 64-16587. 1964. Eerdmans.
Rustler of the Owlhorns: By Jim O'Mara Pseud. 1st Ed. Vernon L Fluharty. LC 52-10435. (Dutton Diamond D western). 1952. Dutton.
Rustler of Wind River. George Washington Ogden. LC 17-101606. 1917. 1.30. A. C. McClurg & Co.
Rustler on the Beach. Frank Mulville. LC 82-1155. 12.95 (ISBN 0-89182-047-7). Charles River Books.
Rustler Passage. Walt Santee. Ed. by Alice Sachs. 1970. 3.95 o.p. Lenox Hill.
Rustlers' Bend. Harry Sinclair Drago. LC 49-9742. (Double D western). 1949. Doubleday.
Rustler's Blood. David Everett. 1979. pap. 1.75 o.s.i. (ISBN 0-8439-0702-9, Leisure Bks). Nordon Pubns.

Rustlers' Canyon, a Western Novel. Eugene E Halleran. LC 49-71531. 1949. Macrae-Smith Co.

Rustlers' Hill: A Thrilling Narrative of the Texas Frontier. Vincent Frank Taylor. LC 53-8257. 1953. Naylor Co.

Rustlers' Justice. Ladell J. Futch. 1978. pap. 1.75 (ISBN 0-89041-217-0, 3217). Major Bks.

Rustlers' Moon. Harry Sinclair Drago. LC 49-988842. (Triple-A western classic).

Rustlers' Moon. Harry Sinclair Drago. LC 39-2059. 1939. W. Morrow & Co.

Rustlers of Beacon Creek. Max Brand. 1.25. Warner Books.

Rustlers of Beacon Creek. Frederick Faust. LC 35-19984. 1935. Dodd, Mead & Company.

Rustlers of Hidden Valley. Clinton Dangerfield. 1932. G. H. Watt.

Rustlers of Pecos County. Zane Grey. (Belmont Tower book). 1.95 (ISBN 0-505-51355-2). Tower Pubns.

Rustlers of Pecos County. Zane Grey. LC 80-11525. 1980. 12.95 (ISBN 0-8161-3085-X). G. K. Hall.

Rustlers of Silver River. Zane Grey. 226p. Repr. of 1920 ed. lib. bdg. 13.55x (ISBN 0-89190-765-3). Am Repr-Rivercity Pr.

Rustlers of Slabrock. William Edmunds Claussen. LC 46-178423. 1946. Phoenix Press.

Rustlers of Table Butte. Ernie Phillips. LC 36-23000. Phoenix Press.

Rustlers of the Bar T. Del Morrow. LC 39-20474. Phoenix Press.

Rustlers of the Basin. George Clifford Shedd. LC 40-725250. The Penn Publishing Company.

Rustlers of the Rio Grande. Paul Evan Lehman. 1968. pap. 0.50 o.p. (62-014). Paperback Lib.

Rustlers on the High Range. Montgomery Meigs Atwater. LC 52-7217. 1952. Random House.

Rustlers on the Smoky Trail. James Denson Sayers. LC 36-4301. Godwin.

Rustlers' Paradise. William Colt Macdonald. LC 32-195000. Covici, Friede.

Rustlers' Ranch. George Parker Milne. LC 36-19255. E. J. Clode, Inc.

Rustlers' Roost. Nelson Coral Nye. LC 43-23505. 1943. Phoenix Press.

Rustlers' Round-up: A "Whistler" Story. Edward Beverly Mann. LC 35-185681. 1935. W. Morrow & Company.

Rustlers Three. Claude Rister. LC 43-16879. 1943. Arcadia House, Inc.

Rustler's Trail. James D. Sayers. 1969. pap. 0.60 o.p. (73-856). Lancer.

Rustlers' Valley. Clarence Edward Mulford. LC 73-89658. (Illus.). 1973. 6.95. Aeonian Press.

Rustlers' Valley. Clarence Edward Mulford. LC 24-1643. 1924. Doubleday, Page & Company.

Rustler's Warning. Ford Worth. LC 51-13777. 1951. Phoenix Press.

Rustlin' Along the Brazos. Al Klement. 1980. 7.95 (ISBN 0-533-04161-9). Vantage.

Rustling of the Wind. Barbara Paradise. 2.00 o.p. Carlton.

Rusty. Peggy O'More, pseud. LC 43-14762. 1943. Grammercy Publishing Co.

Rusty, a Cowboy of the Old West. Ross Santee. LC 50-10313. (Illus.). 1950. Scribner.

Rusty Carrousel. Francis Sylvin, pseud. LC 43-14773. 1943. E. P. Dutton & Company, Inc.

Rusty Colt of the Cross L. Gene Tuttle. 192p. (YA) 1975. 6.95 (Avalon). Bouregy.

Rusty Colt of the Cross L. Gene Tuttle. 1975. 4.95. Avalon Books.

Rusty Guns. Harry Sinclair Drago. LC 44-8364. 1944. Dodd, Mead & Company.

Rusty Mallory. Archie Joscelyn. LC 45-843773. 1945. Phoenix Press.

Rusty: The Adventures of a Little Dog. Nason Henry Arnold. LC 30-24233. Lothrop, Lee & Shepard Co.

Rut. John A. Ryan. 1966. pap. 1.50. White Rabbit.

Ruta Sixty-Nine. new ed. Rogelio Rios. (Pimienta Collection Ser). (Illus.). 160p. (Span.). 1975. pap. 1.25 o.p. (ISBN 0-88473-230-4). Fiesta Pub.

Rute and the Glove. Eyre, Katherine Wigmore. LC 55-10907. 1955. Appleton-Century--Crofts.

Ruth. Irving Fineman. LC 49-10898. 1949. Harper.

Ruth. Elizabeth Cleghorn Stevenson Gaskell. LC 33-34498. (Half-title: The novels and tales of Mrs. Gaskell--ii). H. Frowde, Oxford University Press.

Ruth. Elizabeth Cleghorn Stevenson Gaskell. Ed. by Adolphus William Ward. LC 6-36050. (Half-title: The works of Mrs. Gaskell... Knutsford ed. v. 3). 1906. G. P. Putnam's Sons; Etc., Etc.

Ruth: A Biography of the Future. Alan Winslow. LC 77-92156. 8.95 (ISBN 0-87949-047-0). Ashley Books.

Ruth: A Novel. Elizabeth Cleghorn Stevenson Gaskell. LC 75-1507. (Victorian Fiction: Novels of Faith and Doubt; V. 57). 1975. 35.00 (ISBN 0-8240-1581-9). Garland Pub.

Ruth: A Novel. Lois T Henderson. LC 81-65722. 8.95 (ISBN 0-915684-91-8). Christian Herald Books.

Ruth: A Novel. Lois T Henderson. LC 82-48400. 6.68 (ISBN 0-06-063864-8). Harper & Row.

Ruth: A Romance of the Civil War. Howell Lake Piner. LC 7-35807. 1895. Leader Publishing House.

Ruth: An Unusual Novel. Thomas George Mayberry. LC 40-35098. 1940. Savoy Book Publishers.

Ruth and Marie. A Fascinating Story of the Nineteenth Century. Emma Pow Bauder. LC 6-10344. 1895. American Biblie House.

Ruth Anne. Rose Cullen Bryant. LC 13-21016. 1913. 1.25. J. B. Lippincott Company.

Ruth Bergen's Limitations: A Modern Auto-Da-Fe. Mary Virginia Terhune. LC 8-260620. 1897. F. H. Revell Company.

Ruth Crane. Alison Morgan. LC 74-9075. 1974. 5.95. (ISBN 0-06-024347-3). Harper and Row.

Ruth Emsley, the Betrothed Maiden. A Tale of the Virginia Massacre. William Henry Carpenter. LC 6-21346. 1850. A Hart.

Ruth Endicott's Way: Or, Halgrave's Mission. Lucy Cecil White Lillie. LC 7-19026. (On cover: Honest endeavor series). H. T. Coates & Co.

Ruth Erskine's Son. Isabella Macdonald Ablen. LC 8-3521. 1907. Lothrop, Lee & Shepard Co.

Ruth Farmer: A Story. Agnes Marchbank. The Cassell Publishing Co.

Ruth Hall: A Domestic Tale of the Present Time. Sara Payson Willis Parton. LC 7-34088. 1855. Mason Brothers.

Ruth Irving, M.D. Alice A Barber. LC 6-7217. Presbyterian Board of Publication.

Ruth Marsh. A Little Story of the Aroostook. Fannie Bean. (On cover: The Waldorf series no. 5). 1893. Saalfield & Fitch.

Ruth Marsh: A Story of the Aroostook. Fannie Bean. LC 6-10269. United States Book Company.

Ruth Middleton. Louis Zara. LC 46-4176. 1946. Creative Age Press.

Ruth of the U.S.A. Edwin Balmer. LC 19-5429. 1919. A. C. McClurg & Co.

Ruth Sawyer: 1st Amer. Ed. Virginia Haviland. LC 65-241759. 2.75. Walck.

Ruth the Outcast. Mary Edwards Bryan. (On cover: The library of American authors, no. 30). 1891. G. Munro.

Ruth, the Unsuspecting. Katheryn Kimbrough, pseud. (Saga of the Phenwick Women: No. 17). 1977. pap. 1.75 (ISBN 0-445-04037-8). Popular Lib.

Ruth. To Which Have Been Added: Cumberland Sheep-Shearers, Bessy's Troubles at Home, Modern Greek Songs, Company Manners, Hand and Heart. Elizabeth Cleghorn Stevenson Gaskell. LC 72-186542. (works of Mrs. Gaskell, v. 3). (Illus.). 1972. 24.00 (ISBN 0-404-07253-4). AMS Press.

Ruth Trent. Ethel Matson. LC 55-14960. 1955. Zondervan Pub. House.

Ruth Whalley: Or, The Fair Puritan. A Romance of the Bay Province. by henry uilliam herbert... ed. Henry William Herbert. LC 7-429519. 1845. H. L. Williams.

Rutherford. Edgar Fawcett. LC 6-38781. (On cover: Standard library. no. 121). 1884. Funk & Wagnalls.

Ruthless Breed. Clement Hardin. (G-584 Ace double reader). Ace.

Ruthless Gun. T. C. Lewellen. 1969. pap. 0.60 o.p. (R2130, GM). Fawcett World.

Ruthless Rake. Barbara Cartland. 1974. (pbk.) 0.95. Bantam Books.

Ruthless Range. Lewis B. Patten. 1978. pap. 1.25 (ISBN 0-425-03748-7, Medallion). Berkley Pub.

Ruthless Range. Lewis B Patten. (Berkley large-type western). 1975. (pbk.) 0.95 (ISBN 0-425-02994-8). Berkley Pub. Co.

Ruth's Marriage in Mars: A Scientific Novel. Kate Elizabeth Perkins Glass. LC 13-949. J. F. McElheney.

Ruth's Rebellion. Achmed Abdullah. LC 27-507961. George H. Doran Company.

Ruth's Sacrifice: Or, Life of the Rappahannock. Emily Clemens Pearson. LC 7-33496. 1863. C. H. Pearson Etc.

Rutland Mystery. Cecil Freeman Gregg. LC 3-135982. 1931. L. MacVeagh, The Dial Press.

Rutledge. Miriam Coles Harris. LC 42-26740. The Mershon Company.

Rutledge. Miriam Coles Harris. LC 7-2912. 1860. Derby & Jackson.

Rutledge. Miriam Coles Harris. LC 7-2914. 1888. Houghton, Mifflin and Company.

Rutledge. Miriam Coles Harris. 1893. Houghton, Mifflin and Company.

Rutledge. 21st ed. Miriam Coles Harris. LC 7-2913. 1872. C. Scribner & Co.

Rutledge Trails the Ace of Spades. William MacLeod Raine. LC 30-196400. 1930. Doubleday, Doran & Company, Inc.

Rutting Ground. C. B. Vanek. pap. 1.75 o.p. Lancer.

RX, Prescription for Murder. Elizabeth Head Fetter. LC 42-102. Random House.

Rx: Take Two Joints & Go to Bed. Bob Marx. LC 81-86204. 208p. 1983. pap. 5.95 (ISBN 0-86666-077-1). GWP.

Ryan's Return. Lynsey Stevens. (Harlequin Presents Ser.). 192p. 1982. pap. 1.75 (ISBN 0-373-10497-9). Harlequin Bks.

Ryder. Djuna Barnes. LC 28-21480. 1928. H. Liveright.

Ryder. Djuna Barnes. LC 79-21604. (Illus.). 1979. 10.95 (ISBN 0-312-69640-X). St. Martin's Press.

Ryder. Djuna Barnes. LC 80-23258. 1980. 10.00 (ISBN 0-312-69640-X) (ISBN 0-312-69641-8). St. Martin's Press.

Ryhoves of Antwerp. An Historical Tale. Annette Lucile Noble. Presbyterian Board of Publication and Sabbath-School Work.

Ryle's Open Gate. Susan Teacklee Moore. 1891. Houghton, Mifflin and Company.

Rynox Murder Mystery. Philip MacDonald. LC 31-12256. Pub. for the Crime Club, Inc., by Doubleday, Doran & Company, Inc.

Rynox Murder Mystery. Philip MacDonald. (Superior reprint. M 642). 1944. The Military Service Publishing Co.

S

S-Com, No. 3: Battle in Botswana. Steve White. (Men of Action Ser.). 160p. (Orig.). 1982. pap. 1.95 (ISBN 0-446-30134-5). Warner Bks.

S-Com, No. 4: Fighting Irish. Steve White. (Men of Action Ser.). 160p. (Orig.). 1982. pap. 1.95 (ISBN 0-446-30141-8). Warner Bks.

S-Com: No. 5, King of Kingston. Steve White. (Men of Action Ser.). 192p. (Orig.). 1982. pap. 1.95 (ISBN 0-446-30133-7). Warner Bks.

S-COM, No. 6: Sierra Death Dealers. Steve White. (Men of Action Ser.). 192p. (Orig.). 1982. pap. 1.95 (ISBN 0-446-30142-6). Warner Bks.

S. D. Treasure Trove: A Tale. Samuel Lover. LC 10-14255. 1844. D. Appleton & Company.

S-E-X in the Living Room? Alfred Augustus Burrell. LC 66-28613. 1966. Exposition Press.

S. F. The Best of the Best. Ed. by Judith Merril. 1967. 6.50 o.p. Delacorte.

S-F, the Year's Greatest Science-Fiction and Fantasy: Stories and Novelettes. Introd. by Orson Welles. Ed. by Judith Merril. LC 56-8938. (Dell first edition, B106). 1956. Dell Pub. Co.

S-F Twelve. Ed. by Judith Merril. 5.95 o.p. Delacorte.

S Is for Space. Ray Bradbury. LC 66-616411. 3.50, 4.25 lib. ed.,. Doubleday.

S. O. B. Jack M. Oppenheim. (O.s.i.). 224p. (Orig.). 1973. pap. 1.25 o.s.i. (AQ1077, Award). Univ Pub & Dist.

S. O. P. H I. A. Pierre Boulle. LC 59-12392. 1959. Vanguard Press.

S, Portrait of a Spy. Ian Adams. LC 82-731. 1982. 11.95 (ISBN 0-89919-087-1). Ticknor & Fields.

S, Portrait of a Spy: RCMP Intelligence - the Inside Story. Ian Adams. (O.s.i.). 1978. 8.95 o.s.i. (Pub. by Gage). Vanguard.

S. S. Glory. Frederick John Niven. LC 16-1888. George H. Doran Company.

S. S. Murder. Q. Patrick, pseud. LC 33-28731. Farrar & Rinehart, Incorporated.

S. S. San Pedro. James Gould Cozzens. LC 67-19206. (Harvest bk., HB 135). 1968. pap., 1.15. Harcourt.

S. S. San Pedro. James Gould Cozzens. LC 67-19206. 1967. Harcourt, Brace & World.

S. S. San Pedro. James Gould Cozzens. LC 31-28013. Harcourt, Brace and Company.

S. S. San Pedro, and Castaway. James Gould Cozzens. LC 56-7061. (Modern library paperbacks, P17). 1956. Random House.

S. S. Silverspray: A Novel. Franklin Coasten Langdon. LC 58-8906. 1958. Macmillan.

S-W-O-O-P. Don Prince. LC 41-3912. J. Messner, Inc.

S. Y. Agnon and Ivo Andric. Samuel Joseph Agnon. LC 73-29758. (Nobel Prize Library). (Illus.). 1971. A Gregory.

S-54, Stories of the Sea. Edward Ellsberg. LC 32-5749. 1932. Dodd, Mead, & Company.

Saba's Treasure. Donald Douglas. 1965. pap. 0.95 o.p. (01956, Collier). Macmillan.

Sabattic Leave: A Novel. Sherman Peer. LC 47-6417. 1947. B. Humphries.

Sabbath Guest. Iris Foster, pseud. 1973. pap. 0.95 o.s.i. (75-467). Lancer.

Sabbath Has No End: A Novel of Negro Slavery. John Weld. LC 42-5133. 1942. C. Scribner's Sons.

Sabbath Quest. Iris Foster. 1973. (pbk) 1.50. Lancer Books.

Sabbatical: A Romance. John Barth. LC 81-22660. 14.95 (ISBN 0-399-12717-8). Putnam.

Sabbatical Year. George Shively. LC 26-16532. Harcourt, Brace and Company.

Sabella, or The Blood Stone. Lee Tanith. (Science Fiction Ser.). 1980. pap. 1.75 (ISBN 0-87997-529-6, UE1529). Daw Bks.

Saber-Tooth Curriculum: Including Other Lectures in the History of Paleolithic Education. Harold Benjamin. LC 39-4058. 1939. McGraw-Hill Book Company, Inc.

Saberlegs. Eric Pace. LC 73-112436. 1970. 6.95. World Pub. Co.

Sabers in the Wind. Duane Schultz. 448p. 1981. pap. 2.50 (ISBN 0-449-14380-5, GM). Fawcett.

Sabertooth: A Romance of Put-in-Bay. Stephen Kinder. LC 2-11150. Laird & Lee.

Sabina, a Story of the Amish. Helen Reimensnyder Martin. LC 5-21464. 1905. The Century Co.

Sabina Zembra. William Black. LC 6-12918. (Lovell's library. v. 20, no. 958). J. W. Lovell Company.

Sabina Zembra: A Novel. William Black. LC 42-27476. 1887. Harper & Brothers.

Sabina Zembra. A Novel. William Black. (Harper's Franklin square library, no. 573). 1887. Harper & Brothers.

Sabina Zembra. A Novel. William Black. (Seaside library. Pocket ed. no. 962). 1887. G. Munro.

Sabine. Nicolas Freeling. LC 74-15871. 1978. 7.95 (ISBN 0-06-011356-1). Harper & Row.

Sabine. Nicolas Freeling. LC 79-23077. 1980. 1.95 (ISBN 0-394-74553-1). Vintage Books.

Sabine's Deception: A Novel from the French of the Princess Olga Cantacuzene-Altieri. Olga Cantacuzene-Altieri & Nute, E., Tr. LC 6-21473. (Harper's handy series, no. 158). 1887. Harper & Brothers.

Sabine's Falsehood. Le Mensonge De Sabine.) A Love Story. Olga Cantacuzene-Altieri & Sherwood, Mrs. Mary (Neal) Tr. 1881. T.B. Peterson & Brothers.

Sable Cloud. Harriet Verona Cadwalader Ogden. LC 23-13945. 1923. The Penn Publishing Company.

Sable Cloud: A Southern Tale with Northern Comments. Nehemiah Adams. LC 78-138329. (Black Heritage Library Collection). 1971. (ISBN 0-8369-8721-7). Books for Libraries Press.

Sable Cloud: A Southern Tale, with Northern Comments. Nehemiah Adams. LC 70-109312. 1970. (ISBN 0-8371-3563-X). Negro Universities Press.

Sable Cloud: A Southern Tale, with Northern Comments. Nehemiah Adams. LC 5-42973. 1861. Ticknor and Fields.

Sable Flanagan. Betty Layman Receveur. 1979. pap. 2.50 (ISBN 0-380-41046-X, 41046). Avon.

Sable in the Rain. William Edward Daniel Ross. 3.95 o.p. Lenox Hill.

Sable in the Rain. William Edward Daniel Ross. 1970. 3.95 o.p. B Franklin.

Sable Lion: By Jan Van Dorp Pseud. Translated by Clarissa B. Cooper. Oscar Van Godtsenhoven. LC 54-8704. 1954. Putnam.

Sable Lorcha. Charles Stokes Wayne. LC 12-3376. 1912. A. C. McClurg.

Sable Moon. Nancy Springer. (Pocket fantasy.). 1981. 2.50 (ISBN 0-671-83157-7). Pocket Books.

Sable Night. Archie Roy. 1973. 4.95 (ISBN 0-09-116820-1, Pub. by Hutchinson). Merrimack Pub Cir.

Sabotage. Cleve Franklin Adams. LC 40-7586. 1940. E. P. Dutton & Co., Inc.

Sabotage. Owen John. LC 72-94694. 1973. 6.95 (ISBN 0-525-19590-4). Dutton.

Sabotage Murder Mystery: Traitor's Curse I.E. Purse) "An Albert Campion Thriller,". Margery Allingham. LC 44-8412. 1943. New Avon Library.

Saboteurs. June Drummond. LC 69-11803. (Rinehart suspense novel). 1969. 3.95. Holt, Rinehart and Winston.

Sabre Squadron. Simon Raven. LC 67-13697. 1967. Harper & Row.

Sabre-Tooth: 1st U.S.A. Ed. Peter O'Donnell. LC 66-16325. 4.95. Doubleday.

Sabrehill. Raymond Giles. 1978. pap. 2.50 (ISBN 0-449-13956-5, GM). Fawcett.

Sabres on the Sand. And Other Stories. 1st Amer. Ed. Geoffrey Household. LC 66-10977. bds., 4.95. Atlantic-Little.

Sabrina. Joseph Chadwick. (Orig.). 1970. pap. 0.95 o.p. (65-397). Paperback Lib.

Sabrina. Madelina Pollard. 1980. pap. 2.50 (ISBN 0-440-17633-6). Dell.

Sabrina: A Novel. Madeleine A Polland. LC 78-14437 (ISBN 0-440-07893-8). Delacorte Press.

Sabrina Kane. Will Cook. 288p. 1982. pap. 2.95 (ISBN 0-441-74554-7). Ace Bks.

Sabrina Kane: A Novel of Frontier Illinois. Will Cook. LC 56-7421. 1956. Dodd, Mead.

Sabrina Warham: The Story of Her Youth. Laurence Housman. LC 4-21731. 1904. The Macmillan Company.

Sac Prairie People. August William Derleth. LC 48-7762. 1948. Stanton & Lee.

Sacajawea. Anna Lee Waldo. 1979. pap. 3.95 (ISBN 0-380-75606-4, 75606). Avon.

Sachem. Donald Clayton Porter. LC 83-168. (White Indian series; bk. 4). ((Series: Porter, Donald Clayton.). (Colonization of America series; bk. 4.). 1983. 19.95 (ISBN 0-8161-3449-9). G.K. Hall.
Sachem. Donald Clayton Porter. 352p. 1981. pap. 2.95 (ISBN 0-553-13681-X). Bantam.
Sack and Sugar. Cecily Ullmann Sidgwick. LC 27-8282. 1927. Doubleday, Page & Company.
Sack of Monte Carlo: An Adventure of to-Day As Narrated by Vincent Blacker, Esq., Lieutenant H. M.'s East -- Shire Militia; by Walter Frith... Walter Frith. LC 6-44721. 1898. Harper & Brothers.
Sackcloth and Ashes. Ethel Winifred Savi. LC 27-246731. The Curtiss Press.
Sackcloth and Scarlet. George Fort Gibbs. LC 24-21510. Etc.
Sackcloth for Susan: A Light-Hearted Romance. Rosemary Frances Rees. LC 46-38953. 1941. Arcadia House, Inc.
Sackett. Louis L'Amour. LC 74-18281. 1974. (ISBN 0-8161-6243-3). G. K. Hall.
Sackett Brand. Louis L'Amour. (Orig.). 1971. pap. 2.25 (ISBN 0-553-12829-9, Y13780-3). Bantam.
Sackett Novels of Louis L'Amour, 4 vols. 1982. pap. 39.95 boxed set (ISBN 0-553-01379-3). Bantam.
Sacketts: Beginnings of a Dynasty. Louis L'Amour. LC 76-5243. 9.95 (ISBN 0-8415-0436-9). Saturday Review Press.
Sackett's Land. Louis L'Amour. LC 74-6320. 1974. 5.95. Saturday Review Press.
Sacrament of Silence. Frances Margaret Mary Comper. LC 24-22273. 1924. The Macmillan Company.
Sacramento Walts. 1st Ed. Elva Williams. LC 57-11875. 1957. McGraw-Hill.
Sacred Affair. 1982. 2.98 (ISBN 0-938574-02-7). Cherubim.
Sacred and Profane. Margaret Maitland, pseud. (Belmont Tower Book.). 1978. 1.75 (ISBN 0-505-51241-6). Tower Pubns.
Sacred and Profane: A Novel of the Life and Times of Mozart. David Weiss. LC 68-58298. 1968. 7.95. W. Morrow.
Sacred and Profane Love Machine. Iris Murdoch. LC 73-22649. 1974. 8.95 (ISBN 0-670-61433-5). Viking Press.
Sacred Bullock: And Other Stories. Mazo De La Roche. LC 76-101798. (Short story index reprint series). 1969. Books for Libraries Press.
Sacred Bullock: And Other Stories. by mazo de la roche. ed. Mazo De La Roche. LC 39-243056. 1939. Little, Brown and Company.
Sacred Bullock & Other Stories. facsimile ed. Mazo De La Roche. LC 76-101798. (Short Story Index Reprint Ser.). 1939. 12.00 (ISBN 0-8369-3186-6). Ayer Co.
Sacred Cup. Vincent Brown. 1906. G.P. Putnam's Sons.
Sacred Falls: A Novel of India. Mark Channing. LC 39-16109. J. B. Lippincott Company.
Sacred Families: Three Novellas. Jose Donoso. LC 76-45455. 1977. 7.95 (ISBN 0-394-40222-7). Knopf.
Sacred Fount. Henry James. LC 53-6867. 1979. pap. 4.95 (ISBN 0-394-17081-4, B418, BC). Grove.
Sacred Fount. Henry James. 1959. 7.95 o.p. (ISBN 0-246-63733-1). Dufour.
Sacred Ground. Victor Briggs. (Ace Book.). 1978. 1.95 (ISBN 0-441-74600-4). Ace Books.
Sacred Herb. Fergus Hume. LC 8-1405. 1908. G. W. Dillingham Company.
Sacred Hill La Colline Inspiree. Maurice Barres. Tr. by Cowley, Malcolm. LC 29-20105. (Transatlantic library). 1929. The Macaulay Company.
Sacred Hoop and the Flowering Tree: A Fable of Earth and Humankind. Bill Broder. LC 79-13286. 12.95. (ISBN 0-87156-260-X). Sierra Club Books.
Sacred Legion. Lucien Price. LC 51-8305. 1951. University Press.
Sacred Locomotive Flies. Richard Lupoff. 1971. pap. 0.95 o.p. (95143). Beagle Bks.
Sacred Mushroom: Key to the Door of Eternity. Andrija Puharich. LC 73-111140. 240p. 1974. pap. 2.95 o.p. (ISBN 0-385-08593-1, Anch). Doubleday.
Sacred Nugget: A Novel. Benjamin Leopold Farjeon. LC 6-38656. (Harper's handy series. no. 32). 1885. Harper & Brothers.
Sacred Nugget: A Novel. Benjamin Leopold Farjeon. (On cover: Lovell's library. no. 1376). 1889. J. W. Lovell Company.
Sacred Refuge. Ralph H Romig. LC 80-14984. 1981. 10.95 (ISBN 0-87949-189-2). Ashley Books.
Sacred Shroud. rev. ed. Thomas Humber. (gr. 11 up). 1978. pap. 2.50 (ISBN 0-671-81872-4). PB.
Sacred Sin. Harry A. Keller. LC 32-6898. The Macaulay Company.
Sacred Sin. Daniel Panger. 352p. (Orig.). 1981. pap. 2.75 (ISBN 0-523-41269-X). Pinnacle Bks.
Sacred Stories from Byzantium. Eva C. Topping. LC 77-16696. (Illus.). 79p. 1977. 5.95 (ISBN 0-916586-15-4); pap. 3.95 (ISBN 0-916586-16-2). Holy Cross Orthodox.
Sacrifice. Herman Irving Bloom. LC 36-8689. Godwin.
Sacrifice. Pamela Ferguson. LC 79-55619. 1980. 12.95 (ISBN 0-689-11035-9). Atheneum.
Sacrifice. Norah C James. LC 34-5177. Covici-Friede.
Sacrifice. Owen McMahon Johnson. LC 29-18261. 1929. Longmans, Green and Co.
Sacrifice. Mary Larrimer. LC 27-11714. 1926. H. Vinal.
Sacrifice. Henry Sutton, pseud. 320p. 1979. pap. 2.25 (ISBN 0-441-74610-1, Pub. by Charter Bks). Ace Bks.
Sacrifice. Stephen French Whitman. 1922. D. Appleton and Company.
Sacrifice, a Novel. Adele Wiseman. LC 56-8566. 1956. Viking Press.
Sacrifice: A Novel of the Occult. David R. Slavitt. LC 78-52902. 10.00 (ISBN 0-448-14719-X). Grosset & Dunlap.
Sacrifice: A True Story. Weston J Le Moine. LC 19-115654. Cox Printing and Publishing Co., Inc.
Sacrifice for Love. Harriet Theresa Smith Comstock. LC 36-10528. 1936. Doubleday, Doran & Company, Inc.
Sacrifice of Fools. Richard Manifold Craig. F. A. Stokes Company.
Sacrifice of the Shannon. William Albert Hickman. LC 3-14269. 1903. F. A. Stokes Company.
Sacrifice Play. John Bishop Ballem. 256p. 1981. pap. 2.25 (ISBN 0-449-14381-3, GM). Fawcett.
Sacrifice to the Graces. Arthur Meeker. LC 37-1375. 1937. D. Appleton-Century Company, Incorporated.
Sacrifice Years. Kathleen Thompson Norris. 1970. pap. 0.75 o.p. (ISBN 0-446-64434-X, 64-434). Paperback Lib.
Sacrificed Love. L'evangeliste. Alphonse Daudet. LC 2-14810. F. T. Neely.
Sacrificial Goat. Ernita Lascelles. LC 23-15476. Boni and Liveright.
Sacrificial Pawn. Francis Ryck. LC 73-79799. 1973. 5.95 (ISBN 0-8128-1641-2). Stein and Day.
Sacrilege of Alan Kent. Erskine Caldwell. LC 36-35967. 1936. Falmouth Book House.
Sacrilege of Alan Kent: A Novella with Two Complete Novels. Erskine Caldwell. LC 58-3374. (Signet books, S1497). 1958. New American Library.
Sacrilegious Hands. William Henry Warner. LC 25-8908. 1925. Greenberg, Inc.
Sacristan's Household. A Story of Lippe-Detmold. Frances Eleanor Trollope. LC 8-28514. 1869. Harper & Brothers.
Sad Adventurers: A Novel. Marice Rutledge Hale. LC 24-20380. 1924. Frederick A. Stokes Company.
Sad Cypress. Agatha Miller Christie. LC 40-30880. 1940. Dodd, Mead & Company.
Sad Cypress. Dame Agatha Miller Christie. 1973. (pbk) 0.75. Dell.
Sad Cypress. Agatha Miller Dame Christie. 1976. 1.50. Dell.
Sad-Eyed Seductress. Carter Brown, pseud. Bd. with Ever-Loving Blues. 1982. pap. 2.50 (ISBN 0-451-11520-1, AE1520, Sig). NAL.
Sad Fortunes of the Rev. Amos Barton. George Eliot. LC 6-40732. (On cover:Harper's half-hour series, v. 29). 1877. Harper & Brothers.
Sad Indian: A Novel About Mexico. Thames Ross Williamson. LC 32-23282. Harcourt, Brace and Company.
Sad, Sad Lovers. Daniel Carson Goodman. LC 31-6380. 1931. Duffield & Company.
Sad Shepherd: A Christmas Story. Henry Van Dyke. LC 11-23057. 1911. C. Scribner's Sons.
Sad Song Singing. Thomas Blanchard Dewey. LC 63-19272. (Inner sanctum mystery). 1963. Simon and Schuster.
Sad Song Singing. Thomas Blanchard Dewey. LC 81-47377. (Fifty Classics of Crime Fiction, 1950-1975). 1982. 14.95 (ISBN 0-8240-4980-2). Garland.
Sad Sontag Plays His Hunch. Wilbur Tuttle. LC 26-204165. 1926. Garden City Publishing Co., Inc.
Sad, Sudden Death of My Fair Lady. Stanton Forbes, pseud. LC 71-139020. 1971. 4.50. Published for the Crime Club by Doubleday.
Sad Tales and Glad Tales. Grenville Mellen. LC 7-18470. 1828. S. G. Goodrich.
Sad Tender Flesh. Stephen Frances. (John Gail Ser., Bk. 2). (O.s.i.). 1970. pap. 0.60 o.s.i. (A570, Award). Univ Pub & Dist.
Sad Variety. Nicholas Blake. (Perennial library). 1979. 1.95 (ISBN 0-06-080495-5). Harper & Row.
Sad Variety. Cecil Day-Lewis. LC 64-18086. 1964. Harper & Row.
Saddest of All Is Loving. Louise Montgomery Sale. LC 8-37341. The Authors' Publishing Company.
Saddest Summer of Samuel S. James Patrick Donleavy. LC 66-111161. (Seymour Lawrence bk.). bds., 3.95. Delacorte Dist. Dial.
Saddle and Ride. Ernest Haycox. LC 40-7594. 1940. Little, Brown and Company.
Saddle and Ride. Ernest Haycox. 1976. (pbk.) 1.25. New American Library.
Saddle & Ride - The Feudists. Ernest Haycox. 1980. pap. 1.95 (ISBN 0-451-09467-0, J9467, Sig). NAL.
Saddle and Sabre. Hawley Smart. (On cover: Lovell's library, no. 1103). 1887. J. W. Lovell Company.
Saddle and the Plow: An Historical Novel of Texas. Ross McLaury Taylor. LC 42-22453. 1942. The Bobbs-Merrill Company.
Saddle Bow Slim. Nelson Coral Nye. LC 81-12653. 1982. 11.95 (ISBN 0-89340-372-5). J. Curley.
Saddle Bum. George Metcalf. LC 36-9349. E. J. Clode, Inc.
Saddle by Starlight. Luke Short. LC 76-48106. 1977. 7.95 (ISBN 0-89340-038-6). J. Curley.
Saddle by Starlight: By Luke Short Pseud. Frederick Dilley Glidden. LC 52-9595. 1952. Houghton Mifflin.
Saddle Hawks. Harry Sinclair Drago. LC 44-666. 1944. Doubleday, Doran & Co., Inc.
Saddle Men of the C Bit Brand. Arthur Hawthorne Carhart. LC 37-5480. 1937. Dodd, Mead & Company.
Saddle on a Cloud. Frank Chester Robertson. LC 52-10426. (Dutton Diamond D western). 1952. Dutton.
Saddle Pals. Lee Floren. LC 47-218379. 1947. Phoenix Press.
Saddle River Spread. Archie Joscelyn. LC 42-19942. 1942. Phoenix Press.
Saddle Tramp: A Western Story. Arthur Preston. LC 28-8371. 1927. Chelsea House.
Saddle Tramps. Lee Floren. 1977. pap. 1.25 (ISBN 0-532-12520-7). Woodhill.
Saddle up for Steamboat. Allan Vaughan Elston. 1972. pap. 0.75 o.p. (07262). Curtis.
Saddle up for Steamboat. Allan Vaughan Elston. 1973. 0.75. Curtis Books.
Saddle up for Sunlight. 1st Ed. Allan Vaughan Elston. LC 52-8786. 1952. Lippincott.
Saddle Wolf. W. D Hoffman. LC 28-292324. 1928. A. C. McClurg & Co.
Saddle Wolves. Allan Echols. Bd. with Killers Two. Orig. Title: Keep off My Ranch. 256p. 1973. pap. 0.95 (ISBN 0-532-50410-0, 532-95226-095). Woodhill.
Saddle Wolves. Lee Floren. 1971. pap. 0.60 o.p. (ISBN 0-447-73215-3). Lancer.
Saddlebag of Tales: A Collection of Stories by Members of the Western Writers of America. facsimile ed. Western Writers of America. Ed. by Rutherford Montgomery. LC 79-38727. (Short Story Index Reprint Ser.). (Illus.). Repr. of 1959 ed. 16.00 o.p. (ISBN 0-8369-4140-3). Ayer Co.
Saddlebag Parson. Sara Lucile Jenkins. LC 56-5695. 1956. Crowell.
Saddlebum. William MacLeod Raine. LC 51-11703. 1951. Houghton Mifflin.
Saddleroom Murder. Neil Kenneth McKechnie. LC 37-4016. The Penn Publishing Company.
Saddles and Lariats: The Largely True Story of the Bar-Circle Outfit, and of Their Attempt to Take a Big Drove of Longhonrs from Texas to California, in the Days When the Gold Fever Raged. Lewis Bennett Miller. LC 12-23928. D. Estes & Company.
Saddletramp. Michael Hammonds. 1975. (pbk.) 0.95. Belmont Tower Books.
Sade-Fourier-Loyola. Roland Barthes. Tr. by Richard Miller. 184p. 1976. 8.95 (ISBN 0-8090-8380-9); pap. 5.95 (ISBN 0-8090-1381-9). Hill & Wang.
Sadeq Chubak, an Anthology. Sadiq Chubak & F. R. C Bagley. LC 81-17970. (Modern Persian Literature Series; No. 3). 1981 (ISBN 0-88206-048-1). Caravan Books.
Sadeq Hedayat, an Anthology. Sadegh Heydayat. LC 79-5100. (Bibliotheca Persica: Modern Persian Literature Ser.: No. 2). 1979. 20.00 (ISBN 0-89158-386-6). Westview Press.
Sadhu on the Mountain Peak: An "Ogilvie" Novel. Duncan MacNeil. LC 72-96137. (Illus.). 1973. 6.95. St. Martin's Press.
Sadia the Rosebud. John Russell Coryell. LC 44-39230. (Select series. No. 47). 1890. Street & Smith.
Sadie Love. Avery Hopwood. LC 15-26845. 1915. 1.25. John Lane Company.
Sadie: Or, Happy at Last. May F Shepherd. LC 11-7870. Broadway Publishing Co.
Sadie Shapiro in Miami. Robert Kimmel Smith. LC 77-19067. 1978. 9.95 (ISBN 0-8161-6551-3). G. K. Hall.
Sadie Shapiro in Miami: A Novel. Robert Kimmel Smith. LC 77-3667. 7.95 (ISBN 0-671-22607-X). Simon and Schuster.
Sadie Shapiro in Miami: A Novel. Robert Kimmel Smith. 1978. 1.95 (ISBN 0-449-23764-8). Fawcett Crest Books.
Sadie Shapiro, Matchmaker. Robert Kimmel Smith. LC 79-20784. 9.95 (ISBN 0-671-24014-5). Simon and Schuster.
Sadie Shapiro, Matchmaker. Robert Kimmel Smith. LC 80-16733. 1980. 10.95 (ISBN 0-8161-3108-2). G. K. Hall.
Sadie Shapiro's Knitting Book: A Novel. Robert Kimmel Smith. LC 72-90796. 1973. 5.95 (ISBN 0-671-21485-3). Simon and Schuster.
Sadie Shapiro's Knitting Book: A Novel. Robert Kimmel Smith. LC 73-8962. 1973. 7.95 (ISBN 0-8161-6123-2). G. K. Hall.
Sadie: The Story of a Girl, Some Men, and the Eternal Fitness of Things. Karl Edwin Harriman. LC 7-36087. 1907. D. Appleton and Company.
Sadie When She Died. Evan Hunter. (Signet, Q5570). 1973. (pbk.) 0.95. New American Lib.
Sadie When She Died. Evan Hunter. LC 78-186039. 1972. 5.95. Doubleday.
Sadie When She Died. Ed McBain. LC 78-186039. 216p. 1972. 5.95 o.p. (ISBN 0-385-01307-8). Doubleday.
Sadist. by edson t. hamill. ed. Edson T Hamill. (Ryker Series#6). 1975. (pbk.) 1.25. Leisure Books.
Sadist. (Ryker Ser). 1975. pap. 1.25 o.p. (LB309ZK, Leisure Bks). Nordon Pubns.
Sadist in Satin. Evelyn Astin. LC 77-180146. (Venus library, V-1040-T). 1971. 1.95. Venus Library.
Sadler's Birthday. Rose Tremain. LC 76-28062. 8.95 (ISBN 0-312-69650-7). St. Martin's Press.
Sadness. Donald Barthelme. LC 72-84774. (Illus.). 1972. 5.95 (ISBN 0-374-25333-1). Farrar, Straus and Giroux.
Sadness. Donald Barthelme. (Illus.). 1974. (pbk.) 1.65. Bantam Books.
Sadness at Leaving: A Novel of Espionage. Erje Ayden. 110p. (Orig.). 1972. pap. 7.50 (ISBN 0-89366-005-1). Ultramarine Pub.
Sadness in Lexington Avenue. Myron Brinig. LC 51-13511. 1951. Rinehart.
Sado-Ship. Marus Van Heller. pap. 1.95 o.s.i. (OPH-221, Ophelia). Olympia.
Sadopaideia: Being the Experiences of Cecil Prendergast, Undergraduate of the University of Oxford, Shewing How He Was Led Through the Pleasant Paths of Masochism to the Supreme Joys of Sadism. LC 67-26442. 1968. pap., 1.50. Grove.
Safar-Hadgi: Or, Russ and Turcoman. From the French of Prince Lubomirski. Jozef Lubomirski. LC 7-14753. (Half-title: Collection of foreign authors. no. 11). 1878. D. Appleton and Company.
Safari. Frank Dorn. (Orig.). 1979. pap. 1.95 (ISBN 0-532-23175-9). Woodhill.
Safari. Evan Rhodes. 272p. 1979. pap. 1.95 (ISBN 0-441-74750-7, Pub. by Charter Bks). Ace Bks.
Safari Encounter. Rosemary Carter. (Harlequin Presents Ser.). 192p. 1981. pap. 1.50 (ISBN 0-373-10439-1). Harlequin Bks.
Safari for Spies. Nick Carter. (Nick Carter Espionage Ser). (O.s.i.). (Orig.). 1970. pap. 0.60 o.s.i. (A623X, Award). Univ Pub & Dist.
Safari into Danger. Elsie W. Strother. LC 81-67799. 211p. (Orig.). 1981. pap. 2.95x (ISBN 0-935774-02-5). Elgen Pub Co.
Safari to Dishonor. Edmund Schiddel. (O.s.i.). 1977. pap. 1.50 o.s.i. (AD1663, Award). Univ Pub & Dist.
Safari to Love. Elyeen Harrold. pap. 0.45 o.p. (56-978). Paperback Lib.
Safari Women. Frank Anvic, pseud. 192p. (Orig.). 1974. pap. 1.95 o.p. (ISBN 0-87056-358-0, 6358). Brandon.
Safe Bridge. Frances Parkinson Wheeler Keyes. LC 34-37433. 1934. J. Messner, Inc.
Safe Bridge. Frances Parkinson Wheeler Keyes. LC 42-51491. 1942. The Sun Dial Press.
Safe Bridge. Frances Parkinson Wheeler Keyes. 1976. (pbk.) 1.75 (ISBN 0-671-80441-3). Pocket Books.
Safe Conduct. Boris Leonidovich Pasternak. LC 58-12799. 1958. pap. 6.25 (ISBN 0-8112-0135-X, NDP77). New Directions.
Safe Custody. Cecil William Mercer. 1932. Minton, Balch & Company.
Safe Harbor: Jenifer Blair. Cecil Blair. 0.95 (ISBN 0-440-17573-9). Dell Pub. Co.
Safe House. Jon Cleary. LC 74-34360. 1975. 7.95 (ISBN 0-688-02902-7). Morrow.
Safe Place. Anne Rider. LC 73-22656. 6.95 (ISBN 0-672-51992-5). Bobbs-Merrill.
Safe Road. Katharine Newlin Burt. LC 38-5744. 1938. Macrae Smith Company.
Safe Secret. Leopold Horace Ognall. LC 64-3636. 1964. Published for The Crime Club by Collins.
Safe Secret: By Harry Carmichael Pseud. 1st Amer. Ed. Leopold Horace Ognall. LC 65-10666. (Cock Robin mystery). 1965. bds., 3.95. Macmillan.
Safe Valley. Lewis A. Young. 5.95 o.p. Vantage.
Safety Candle. Ethel Stefana Stevens Drower. LC 17-24291. 1917. Cassell and Company, Ltd.

Safety Curtain: And Other Stories. Ethel May Dell. LC 17-29862. 1917. 1.50. G. P. Putnam's Sons.
Safety Curtain: And Other Stories. Ethel May Dell. LC 22-24773. 1921. Grosset & Dunlap.
Safety First. Margot Neville. LC 24-21919. 1924. Houghton Mifflin Company.
Safety Match. John Hay Beith. LC 11-269529. 1911. Houghton Mifflin Company.
Safety Match. Barbara Cartland & John Hay Beith. LC 80-146450. (Cartland, Barbara, 1902- Barbara Cartland's Library of Love: 4). 1979. 12.95 (ISBN 0-7156-1380-4). Duckworth.
Safety Match. Ian Hay. (Barbara Cartland's Library of Love: Vol. 4). 181p. 1979. 12.95x (ISBN 0-7156-1380-4, Pub. by Duckworth England). Biblio Dist.
Safety Matches: A Novel. Robert Sabatier. LC 75-133592. 1972. 6.95 (ISBN 0-525-19595-5). E. P. Dutton.
Safety Net. Heinrich Boll. LC 81-47513. 1982. 13.95 (ISBN 0-394-51404-1). Knopf: Distributed by Random House.
Safety Net. Heinrich Boll. LC 82-16485. 1983. 3.50 (ISBN 0-14-006468-0). Penguin.
Safety Pin. Joseph Smith Fletcher. LC 24-4505. 1924. G. P. Putnam's Sons.
Saffron Summer. Margaret Summerton. LC 74-9468. 1975. 5.95 (ISBN 0-385-01451-1). Published for the Crime Club by Doubleday.
Saffron Veil: By Pundit Acharya Pseud. 1st Ed. Basudeb Bhattacharya. LC 53-36511. 1953. Prana Press.
Saga Af Tristram Ok Isond Samt Mottuls Saga. Ed. by Gisli Brynjulfsson. LC 80-1941. Repr. of 1878 ed. 54.00 (ISBN 0-404-18724-2). AMS Pr.
Saga Behind Hamlet, Prince of Denmark. Percy MacKaye. 1969. 7.50 o.p. Wheelwright.
Saga in Green. Mabel Gregory Walker. LC 67-20524. 1967. Dorrance.
Saga of a Hillbilly. H. L. Rowland. 1978. pap. 3.95 (ISBN 0-89185-186-0). Anthelion Pr.
Saga of an Ego Trip. Jeannette V. Durlach. 1976. pap. 1.95 (ISBN 0-87844-038-0). Sandlapper Pub Co.
Saga of Andy Burnett. Illustrated by Albert Orbaan. Stewart Edward White. LC 58-6890. 1958. Garden City Books.
Saga of Andy Burnett: With an Introduction. Stewart Edward White. LC 47-1723. 1947. Doubleday & Company, Inc.
Saga of Denny Maccune. Budd Arthur & Burt Arthur. (Orig.). 1968. pap. 0.50 o.p. (52-688). Paperback Lib.
Saga of Denny McCune. Burt Arthur & Budd Arthur. 1979. pap. 1.25 o.s.i. (ISBN 0-505-51397-8). Tower Bks.
Saga of Frank Dover. Johannes Buchholtz. Tr. by Gay-Tifft, Eugene. LC 38-33407. 1938. G. P. Putnam's Sons.
Saga of Gisli the Outlaw. Tr. by George Johnston. LC 67-207. (Illus.). 1963. pap. 6.50 (ISBN 0-8020-6219-9). U of Toronto Pr.
Saga of Grettir the Strong. Tr. by G. A. Hight. 1978. Repr. of 1972 ed. 9.95x (ISBN 0-460-00699-1, Evman); pap. 6.95x (ISBN 0-460-01699-7). Biblio Dist.
Saga of Halfaday Creek. James Beardsley Hendryx. LC 47-5909. 1947. Doubleday.
Saga of Hrafn Sveinbjarnarson. Hrafns Saga Sveinbjarnarsonar. Tr. by Anne Tjomsland. (Islandica Ser.: Vol. 35). 1951. pap. 8.00 (ISBN 0-527-00365-4). Kraus Repr.
Saga of Hrafn Sveinbjarnarson. Anne Tjomsland. 1951. pap. 6.00 o.p. Kraus Repr.
Saga of King Olaf Tryggwason. Tr. by J. Sephton. LC 80-1950. Repr. of 1895 ed. 60.00 (ISBN 0-404-18714-5). AMS Pr.
Saga of Leif Ericsson: Discoverer of America. 1st Ed. Carl Stearns Clancy. LC 56-11347. 1956. Pageant Press.
Saga of Lost Earths. Emil Petaja. (Science Fiction Ser.). 1979. pap. 1.95 o.p. (ISBN 0-87997-462-1, UJ1462). DAW Bks.
Saga of Polecat Ridge. Gordon Mackey. LC 50-28130. 1949. Anson Jones Press.
Saga of the Black Swamp. Peter Myerholtz. LC 36-6665. Dorrance & Company.
Saga of the Corn Country. John Dudley Spencer. LC 36-19445. Wetzel Publishing Co., Inc.
Saga of the Hocking. Charles H Byron. LC 62-53321. (Prestige book). 1962. Godlen-Bell Press.
Saga of the Phenwick Women: Letitia, the Dreamer, Vol. 35. Katheryn Kimbrough. 1981. pap. 2.25 (ISBN 0-445-04638-4). Popular Lib.
Saga of the Phenwick Women: Ursala the Proud, No. 34. Katheryn Kimbrough. 256p. 1980. pap. 1.95 (ISBN 0-445-04627-9). Popular Lib.
Saga of the Prairies. Herbert Perry Wright. LC 45-8765. 1945. Brown, White, Lowell Press.
Saga of the Red Hills of Oregon: A Historical Novel. John Aubrey Kramien. Exposition Press.
Saga of the Sea. Frederick Britten Austin. LC 76-116930. (Short story index reprint series). 1970. Books for Libraries Press.
Saga of the Sea. Frederick Britten Austin. LC 29-9878. The Macmillan Company.
Saga of the Sergeant. Vsevolod Ivanov. Ed. by G. A. Birkett. LC 66-25016. (Rus.). 1966. pap. text ed. 1.75x (ISBN 0-89197-489-X). Irvington.
Saga of the Sword. Frederick Britten Austin. LC 75-106243. (Short story index reprint series). 1970. (ISBN 0-8369-3279-X). Books for Libraries Press.
Saga of the Volsungs. Tr. by Margaret Schlauch from Norse. 1930. 12.50x (ISBN 0-89067-006-4). Am Scandinavian.
Saga of the Volsungs, Together with Excerpts from the Nornageststhattr and Three Chapters from the Prose Edda. LC 81-14833. 29.50 (ISBN 0-87413-172-3). University of Delaware Press.
Saga of Thorgils & Haflidi. Halldor Hermannsson. LC 35-15601. 1945. pap. 6.00 (ISBN 0-527-00362-X). Kraus Repr.
Sagacity. Janet Hamilton. (Anansi Fiction Ser.: No. 44). 135p. (Orig.). 1981. pap. 7.95 (ISBN 0-88784-087-6, Pub. by Hse Anansi Pr Canada). U of Toronto Pr.
Sagamore of Old Orchard. Alas Ellis Auger. LC 43-5429. 1943. The Christopher Publishing House.
Sagarana. Tr. from Portuguese by Harriet De Onis. Introd. by Franklin De Oliveira. 1st Amer. Ed. Joao Guimaraes Rosa. LC 66-11341. 1966. 5.95. Knopf.
Sagas of Kormak & the Sworn Brothers. L. M. Hollander. LC 49-11928. Repr. of 1949 ed. 16.00 o.p. (ISBN 0-527-41900-1). Kraus Repr.
Sagas of the Mounted Police: Illustrated by Carl Kidwell. William Byron Mowery. LC 53-1773. 1953. Bouregy & Curl.
Sage and the Olive. Florence Whitfield Barton. LC 53-10109. 1953. Muhlenberg Press.
Sage Brush Bandit. Harry Sinclair Drago. LC 49-9667. (Silver star westerns). 1949. Dodd, Mead.
Sage Brush Parson. Alice Ward Bailey. LC 6-3122. 1906. Little, Brown, & Company.
Sage, Father of Generations to Come: A Novel of the Crucial Years 38-60 A.D. Woodcut Illus. by Jakob Steinhardt. Leon Kolb. LC 65-11198. 6.95. Genuart Pubrs. Pacific Ave.
Sage: Father of Generations to Come; a Novel of Thecrucial Years 38-60 A. D. Leon Kolb. LC 65-11198. Genuart Publishers.
Sage Hen. Frederic Robert Buckley. LC 25-8374. The Bobbs-Merrill Company.
Sage of Canudos: A Novel. Translated from the French by Charles Duff. 1st American Ed. Lucien Marchal. LC 54-8849. 1954. Dutton.
Sage of Halfaday Creek. James Beardsley Hendryx. 1976. Repr. of 1947 ed. lib. bdg. 12.05x (ISBN 0-88411-837-1). Amereon Ltd.
Sage of the Sacred Mountain: A Gospel of Tranquility. Stanwood Cobb. LC 58-33834. 1953. Avalon Press.
Sage Quarter. Bernice Kelly Harris. LC 45-3928. 1945. Doubleday, Doran and Company, Inc.
Sagebrush Bandit. Ford Bowne, pseud. LC 65-7070. Arcadia House.
Sagebrush Buckaroo. Thomas Grant Springer. LC 33-137. 1932. G. H. Watt.
Sagebrush: By Wade Hamilton Pseud. Lee Floren. LC 52-11389. 1952. Arcadia House.
Sagebrush Kid: By Barry Cord Pseud. Peter Germano. LC 54-749382. 1954. Arcadia House.
Sagebrush Lawman. William Frederick Bragg. LC 51-12277. 1951. Phoenix Press.
Sagebrush Showdown. Tom West. (Orig.). 1979. pap. 1.95 (ISBN 0-89083-520-9). Zebra.
Sagebrusher: A Story of the West. Emerson Hough. LC 19-5273. 1919. D. Appleton and Company.
Sagittal Section: Poems, New and Selected. Miroslav Holub & Stuart Friebert. LC 79-92784. (Field Translation Series; 3). 9.95 (ISBN 0-932440-04-5). Oberlin College.
Sagittarius. Ray Russell. LC 78-155831. (Playboy science fiction). 1971. 0.75. Playboy Press.
Sagittarius in Warsaw. Richard Lourie. LC 73-83036. 1973. 6.95 (ISBN 0-8149-0729-6). Vanguard Press.
Sagomi Gambit. Jonathan Evans. (Tor Bks.). 416p. (Orig.). 1983. pap. 3.95 (ISBN 0-523-48064-4). Pinnacle Bks.
Saguaro. Doris Evans. LC 80-50647. (Popular Ser.: No. 28). (Illus.). 1980. pap. 4.95 (ISBN 0-911408-55-X). SW Pks Mnmts.
Sagusto. Cecil Roberts. LC 28-7944. 1928. Doubleday, Doran & Company, Inc.
Sahara Road. Henry Gibbs. LC 72-186189. 1972. 5.95 (ISBN 0-8027-5250-0). Walker.
Sahara Road. Simon Harvester. LC 72-186189. 224p. 1973. pap. 1.25 (ISBN 0-532-12197-X). Woodhill.
Sahara Road. Simon Harvester. LC 72-186189. 224p. 1972. 5.95 o.p. (ISBN 0-8027-5250-0). Walker & Co.
Sahara Survival: A Novel. Burt Cole. LC 72-12098. 1973. 6.95 (ISBN 0-06-121550-3). Harper's Magazine Press.
Said the Fisherman. 4th ed. Marmaduke William Pickthall. LC 4-14551. 1904. M'Clure, Phillips & Co.
Said the Fisherman. Marmaduke William Pickthall. LC 25-19906. (Half-title: Blue jade library). 1925. A. A. Knopf.
Said the Spider to the Fly. Lois Barth. LC 77-154494. 4.95. Avalon Books.
Said the Spider to the Fly. Dora Richards Shattuck. LC 44-4726. 1944. Simon and Schuster.
Said with Flowers... Anne Nash. LC 46-21108. (On cover: Bart house mystery. 19). 1945.
Said with Flowers: A Mystery Novel. Anne Nash. LC 43-6909. 1943. Pub. for the Crime Club by Doubleday, Doran & Co., Inc.
Saigon. Nick Carter. (Nick Carter Espionage Ser). (O.s.i.). (Orig.). 1970. pap. 0.60 o.s.i. (A625X, Award). Univ Pub & Dist.
Saigon. Anthony Grey. LC 82-14025. 1982. 19.95 (ISBN 0-316-32822-7). Little, Brown.
Saigon Sex Trap. Gus Murdoch. (Orig.). pap. 0.95 o.p. (1134). Brandon.
Saigon Singer. Francis Van Wyck Mason. LC 75-32514. 1975. 9.95 (ISBN 0-89190-352-6). American Reprint Co.
Saigon Singer. Francis Van Wyck Mason. LC 46-8056. 1946. Doubleday & Company, Inc.
Saigon Singer. F. Van Wyck Mason. 1976. Repr. of 1946 ed. lib. bdg. 16.60x (ISBN 0-89190-352-6). Am Repr-Rivercity Pr.
Sail a Crooked Ship. 1st Ed. Nathaniel Benchley. LC 60-10593. 1960. McGraw-Hill.
Sail into Silence. Dana Marble. LC 58-12512. 1958. Mystery House.
Sail the Dark Tide. Davenport Steward. LC 54-9657. 1954. Tupper & Love.
Sail Your Own Seas. George E. Vandeman. (Stories That Win Ser.). 1975. pap. 0.95 (ISBN 0-8163-0191-3, 19124-7). Pacific Pr Pub Assn.
Sailcloth Shroud. Charles Williams. LC 82-48819. 192p. 1983. pap. 2.84i (ISBN 0-06-080654-0, P 654, PL). Har-Row.
Sailing into Night. John Digby. 1978. pap. 3.00. Kayak.
Sailing Out. Julie McDonald. LC 82-10065. 1982. 12.95 (ISBN 0-8138-1624-6). Iowa State University Press.
Sailing Under Bare Poles. Marjorie Dudley. 1968. 3.95 o.p. Vantage.
Sailor. John Collis Snaith. LC 16-15317. 1916. D. Appleton and Company.
Sailor: A Novel of the Sea. Richard Jessup. LC 69-12639. 1969. 6.95. Little, Brown.
Sailor and the Fox. Brian Burland. LC 72-81288. 1973. 5.95 (ISBN 0-8090-8385-X). Hill and Wang.
Sailor Comes Home. Howard Clewes. LC 38-37578. 1938. Longmans, Green and Co.
Sailor Comes Home. Howard Clewes. LC 39-120025. W. W. Norton & Company.
Sailor from Gibraltar. Marguerite Duras. LC 67-20345. 1967. Grove Press.
Sailor Girl. Frederick Ferdinand Moore. LC 20-5774. 1920. D. Appleton and Company.
Sailor Girl. Watkins Eppes Wright. LC 43-6824. 1943. Gramercy Pub. Co.
Sailor in the Bottle. Tr. from German by James Clark. Manfred Bieler. LC 65-19956. 1966. bds., 4.50. Dutton.
Sailor Named Jones: A Novel of America's Greatest Captain. 1st Ed. Harvey Haislip. LC 57-6708. 1957. Doubleday.
Sailor off the Bremen: And Other Stories. Irwin Shaw. LC 39-23638. Random House.
Sailor on the Seas of Fate. Michael Moorcock. LC 77-356744. 1976. 3.95 (ISBN 0-7043-2110-6). Quartet Books.
Sailor on the Seas of Fate. Michael Moorcock (ISBN 0-87997-270-X). Daw Books.
Sailor: Sense of Humour, and Other Stories. Victor Sawdon Pritchett. LC 56-5775. 1956. Knopf.
Sailor, Take Warning!... Kelley Roos. LC 44-1337. 1944. Dodd, Mead & Company.
Sailor Town. Paul Hervey Fox. LC 35-5372. 1935. Little, Brown, and Company.
Sailor Who Fell from Grace with the Sea. Yukio Mishima, pseud. LC 80-14789. 1980. 3.95 (ISBN 0-399-50489-3). Perigee Books.
Sailor Who Fell from Grace with the Sea. Tr. from Japanese by John Nathan. 1st Amer. Ed. Yukio Mishima, pseud. LC 66-10032. bds., 3.95. Knopf.
Sailor with a Gun. 1st Ed. Hjalmar Rutzebeck. LC 58-14509. 1957. Pageant Press.
Sailors and Saints: Or, Matrimonial Manaeuvers. William Nugent Glascock. LC 6-43966. 1829. Printed by J. & J. Harper.
Sailors Are Gobs of Fun, Hattie: The Salty Letters of a Sailor to His Girl Friend. Johnny Viney. LC 43-119461. 1943. M. S. Mill Co., Inc.
Sailor's Bane. William McFee. LC 77-10446. 1977-1978. 9.95 (ISBN 0-8383-2209-3). Haskell House.
Sailor's Blood. Adam Hardy. (Fox series,#5). 1974. (pbk.) 0.95 (ISBN 0-523-00341-2). Pinnacle Books.
Sailor's Choice. Carl Huntington Bottume. LC 51-4763. 1951. Little, Brown.
Sailors Don't Care. Edwin Moultrie Lanham. LC 30-20355. J. Cape and H. Smith.
Sailors Have More Fun. Mercedes M. Griffin. 1977. 5.00 o.p. (ISBN 0-8059-2425-6). Dorrance.
Sailor's Holiday. Eric Robert Russell Linklater. LC 38-281230. Farrar & Rinehart, Incorporated.
Sailor's Home: And Other Stories. Clotilde Inez Mary Graves. LC 77-122711. (Short story index reprint series). 1970. Books for Libraries Press.
Sailor's Homes: And Other Stories. Clotilde Inez Mary Graves. LC 19-13972. George H. Doran Company.
Sailors' Knots. William Wymark Jacobs. LC 9-28396. 1909. C. Scribner's Sons.
Sailors' Life and Sailors' Yarns. John Codman. LC 6-26752. 1847. C. S. Francis & Co.
Sailors of Fortune. William McFee. LC 29-28645. 1929. Doubleday, Doran & Company, Inc.
Sailors' Rendezvous: A Maigret Mystery. Georges Simenon. LC 70-19361. 1970. Penguin.
Sailor's Return. David Garnett. LC 25-18585. 1925. A. A. Knopf.
Sailor's Star. Fannie Heaslip Lea. LC 44-4735. 1944. Dodd, Mead & Company.
Sailors, Subs & Senoritas. William Minarik. 1967. 6.95 o.p. (ISBN 0-8283-1115-3). Branden.
Sailor's Sweetheart. William Clark Russell. LC 4-16577. 1897. New Amsterdam Book Company.
Sailor's Sweetheart. An Account of the Wreck of the Sailing Ship "Waldershare," from the Narrative of Mr. William Lee, Second Mate. William Clark Russell. (Franklin's square library. no. 142). 1880. Harper & Brothers.
Sailor's Sweetheart. An Account of the Wreck of the Sailing Ship "Waldershare," from the Narrative of Mr. William Lee, Second Mate. William Clark Russell. (Seaside library, v. 41, no. 848). 1880. G. Munro.
Sailor's Sweetheart. An Account of the Wreck of the Sailing Ship "Waldershare," from the Narrative of Mr. William Lee, Second Mate. William Clark Russell. (On cover: Seaside library. Pocket ed., no. 223). 1884. G. Munro.
Sailor's Sweetheart. An Account of the Wreck of the Sailing Ship "Waldershare," from the Narrative of Mr. William Lee, Second Mate. William Clark Russell. (On cover: Lovell's library, v. 17, no. 835). 1886. J. W. Lovell Company.
Sailor's Sweetheart: Or, Fighting for Love and Country. St. George Rathborne. (On cover: Eagle series, no. 196). 1901. Street & Smith.
Sailor's Wife. 2nd ed. Lucy G. Wright. LC 61-18487. (Illus.). 1967. pap. 1.95 o.p. (ISBN 0-87021-588-4). Naval Inst Pr.
Sailors' Wives. Warner Fabian. LC 24-21814. Boni and Liveright.
Sails of Sunset: A Novel. Cecil Roberts. LC 24-22459. 1924. Frederick A. Stokes Company.
Sainclair, or The Victim to the Arts and Sciences; and Hortense, or The Victim to Novels and Travel. A Novel, in Two Volumes. Translated from the French of Madame De Genlis. Stephanie Felicite Ducrest De Saint-Aubin Genlis & Haralson, Archibald. LC 7-1500. D. of C., Published by Richards and Mallory, for M. Carey, M. Thomas, E. Earle, A. Finley, and J. Delaplaine.
Saint. Paul Charles Joseph Bourget. Tr. by Katherine Prescott Normeley. LC 6-14924. 1895. Roberts Brothers.
Saint. Conrad Ferdinand Meyer. Tr. by Edward Franklin Hauch. LC 75-1104. 1975. 11.50. H. Fertig.
Saint. Conrad Ferdinand Meyer. Tr. by Hauch, Edward Franklin. LC 30-10710. 1930. Simon and Schuster.
Saint--Wanted for Murder: The Further Adventures of Simon Templar. Leslie Charteris. LC 43-6642. 1943. The Sun Dial Press.
Saint: A Fictional Biography of Thomas Becket. Conrad Ferdinand Meyer. LC 77-7038. 7.50 (ISBN 0-87057-149-4). Brown University Press.
Saint Abigail of the Pines. William Allen Knight. LC 5-33939. 1905. The Pilgrim Press.
Saint Abroad. Leslie Charteris. LC 69-15193. (Crime Club Novel). 1969. 4.50 o.p. Doubleday.
Saint Abroad. Leslie Charteris. 1973. pap. 0.75 o.p. (07137). Curtis.
Saint and Mary Kate. Frank O'Connor, pseud. LC 32-22557. 1932. The Macmillan Company.
Saint and Mary Kate. Michael O'Donovan. LC 32-22557. 1932. The Macmillan Company.
Saint and Mr. Teal. Leslie Charteris. LC 33-13054. 1933. Pub. for the Crime Club, Inc., by Doubleday, Doran & Company, Inc.
Saint and Siren. Rob Eden. LC 39-4169. M. S. Mill Co., Inc.

Saint & the Brighter Buccaneer. Leslie Charteris. (Saint Ser.). 160p. 1981. pap. 2.25 (ISBN 0-441-74884-8). Ace Bks.

Saint & the Fiction Makers. Leslie Charteris. LC 68-27111. 1968. 4.50 o.p. Doubleday.

Saint and the Fiction Makers. Fleming Lee & Leslie Charteris. LC 68-27111. (Saint series). 1968. 4.50. Published for the Crime Club by Doubleday.

Saint & the Happy Highwayman. Leslie Charteris. (Saint Ser.). 224p. 1981. pap. 2.50 (ISBN 0-441-74891-0, Pub. by Charter Bks). Ace Bks.

Saint & the Hapsburg Necklace. Leslie Charteris. LC 75-14811. (Crime Club Ser.). 192p. 1976. 5.95 o.p. (ISBN 0-385-11226-2). Doubleday.

Saint and the Hunchback. Donald Alfred Stauffer. LC 46-7306. 1946. Simon and Schuster.

Saint and the People Importers. Leslie Charteris. LC 79-171282. 1972. 4.95. Published for the Crime Club by Doubleday.

Saint and the Sinner. Barbara Cartland. LC 77-25521. (ISBN 0-87272-034-9). Duron Books.

Saint and the Templar Treasure. Leslie Charteris & Charles Nicolae Aurel King. LC 78-22154. 7.95 (ISBN 0-385-15097-0). Published for the Crime Club by Doubleday.

St. Ann's. William Edward Norris. LC 7-33284. The Cassell Publishing Co.

St. Antholin's: Milford Malvoisin. Francis Edward Paget. LC 75-469. (Victorian Fiction: Novels of Faith and Doubt; 23). 1975. 35.00. Garland Pub.

Saint Anthony, and Other Stories. Guy De Maupassant. LC 79-150479. (Short story index reprint series). 1971. (ISBN 0-8369-3820-8). Books for Libraries Press.

Saint Anthony, and Other Stories. Guy De Maupassant. Tr. by Lefcadio Hearn. Mordell, Albert, 1885- Ed. LC 25-2967. 1924. A. & C. Boni.

Saint Around the World. Leslie Charteris. 1966. pap. 0.60 o.p. (60-260). Manor Bks.

Saint Around the World. 1st Ed. Leslie Charteris. LC 56-114996. 1956. Published for the Crime Club by Doubleday.

Saint at Large: The Best Short Stories of the Adventures of Simon Templar from The Brighter Buccaneer, The Happy Highwayman and The Saint Intervenes. Leslie Charteris. LC 43-15363. 1943. The Sun Dial Press.

Saint Augustine: A Story of the Huguenots in America. John Roy Musick. LC 7-33326. (On cover: Columbian historical novels. v. 3). 1892. Funk & Wagnalls Company.

St. Augustine's Pigeon: The Selected Stories of Evan S. Connell. Evan S. Connell & Gus Blaisdell. LC 80-18186. 1980. 12.50 (ISBN 0-86547-013-8). North Point Press.

Saint Bids Diamonds. Leslie Charteris. LC 42-15693. (Triangle books). 1942. Triangle Books.

Saint Camber. Katherine Kurtz. LC 78-16702. (Her The Legends of Camber of Culdi; v. 2). (Illus.). 1978. 9.95 (ISBN 0-345-27750-3). Ballantine Books.

Saint Cecilia. A Modern Tale from Real Life. G. Manigault. LC 7-16801.

Saint Cecilia. A Modern Tale from Real Life. Part First. Adversity... G. Manigault. LC 7-16801. 1871. J. B. Lippincott & Co.

St. Clair: Or, The Heiress of Desmond. Sydney Owenson Morgan. LC 7-18742. 1807. S. F. Bradford.

St. Clair, or The Protege: A Tale of the Federal City. John E. Tuel. LC 8-28272. 1846. W. Taylor & Co.

St. Clair Summer. Marvin Werlin & Mark Werlin. 1981. pap. 3.50 (ISBN 0-451-11201-6, AE1201, Sig). NAL.

St. Clair Summer: A Novel. Marvin Werlin & Mark Werlin. LC 80-26214. 13.95 (ISBN 0-453-00395-8). New American Library.

Saint Closes the Case. Leslie Charteris. Orig. Title: Last Hero. 192p. (O.S.I.). 1973. Repr. of 1930 ed. lib. bdg. 5.95 o.s.i. White Lion Pubs.

Saint Cuthbert's. John Edwin Copus. 1903. Benziger Brothers.

St. Cuthbert's: A Novel. Robert Edward Knowles. LC 5-32322. F. H. Revell Company.

St. Cuthbert's Tower: A Novel. Florence Alice Price James. (Lovell's international series, no. 9). F. F. Lovell & Company.

St. Cutherbert's Tower: A Novel. Florence Alice Price James. (On cover: Seaside library. Pocket ed., no. 1178). 1889. G. Munro.

St. Dingan's Bones: By Julian Callender Pseud. Austin Lee. LC 58-9250. 1958. Vanguard Press.

St. Elizabeth's Square. Tr. by Margot Schierl. Rudolf Jasik. LC 65-355023. (Artia pocket bks.). 1965. pap., 1.20. Artia.

St. Elmo: A Novel. Augusta J. Evans. LC 74-15736. (Popular Culture in America Ser.). 576p. 1975. Repr. 32.00x (ISBN 0-405-06371-7). Ayer Co.

St. Elmo: A Novel. Augusta Jane Evans Wilson. LC 74-15736. (Popular Culture in America). 1974. 32.00 (ISBN 0-405-06371-7). Arno Press.

St. Elmo: A Novel. magnolia ed. Augusta Jane Evans Wilson. LC 8-37114. G. W. Dillingham Co.

St. Elmo: A Novel. illustrated ed. for theatre patrons ed. Augusta Jane Evans Wilson. LC 10-2145. Hurst & Company.

Saint Errant. Leslie Charteris. (Saint Ser.). 224p. 1981. pap. 2.25 (ISBN 0-441-74888-0, Pub. by Charter Bks). Ace Bks.

Saint Errant. Leslie Charteris. 1973. (pbk.) 0.95. Manor Books.

Saint Eva: A Novel. Amelia Lehmann Pain. LC 7-35790. 1897. Harper & Brothers.

Saint Francis: A Novel. Nikos Kazantzakis. LC 62-9606. 1962. Simon and Schuster.

St. Francis Effect. Zachary Hughes. (Berkley Medallion Book). 1976. (pbk.) 1.75 (ISBN 0-425-03111-X). Berkley Publishing Corp.

Saint Francis of Assisi. Helen Constance White. 1962. pap. 0.95 o.p. (Collier). Macmillan.

Saint Game. Cicely Louise Evans. LC 73-11631. 1975. 5.95 (ISBN 0-385-04241-8). Doubleday.

St. George and St. Michael. A Novel. George Macdonald. LC 8-2121. J. B. Ford and Company.

St. George and St. Michael. A Novel. George Macdonald. (Seaside library, v. 33, no. 677). 1880. G. Munro.

St. George and St. Michael: A Novel. George Macdonald. LC 4-16560. G. Routledge & Sons, Limited.

St. George and St. Michael. A Novel. George Macdonald. LC 12-18280. 1911. D. McKay.

St. George Manor. Ruth McCarthy Sears. (O.s.i.). 1975. pap. 1.25 o.s.i. (LB311ZK, Leisure Bks). Nordon Pubns.

St. George Manor. Ruth McCarthy Sears. 1973. 4.95. Lenox Hill Pr.

St. George of Weldon. Robert Rylee. LC 37-4269. Farrar & Rinehart, Incorporated.

Saint-Germain Chronicles. Chelsea Quinn Yarbo. 256p. (Orig.). 1983. pap. 2.95 (ISBN 0-671-45903-1, Timescape). PB.

Saint Goes on. Leslie Charteris. LC 35-702994. 1935. Pub. for the Crime Club, Inc., by Doubleday, Doran & Company, Inc.

Saint Goes on. Leslie Charteris. LC 40-114899. 1940. Triangle Books.

Saint Goes Wes: Some Further Exploits of Simon Templar. Leslie Charteris. LC 42-18494. 1942. Published for the Crime Club by Doubleday, Doran and Company, Inc.

Saint Goes West. Leslie Charteris. LC 48-10747. (New Avon library 130). 1948. Avon Pub. Co.

Saint Guido. Richard Jefferies & Brown, John. LC 2-25941. (The brocade series, xxv). 1901. T. B. Mosher.

Saint Helena, Little Island. Mark Aleksandrovich Aldanov. Tr. by Chamot, Alfred Edward. LC 24-4863. 1924. A. A. Knopf.

St. Helios. Anna Robeson Brown Burr. LC 25-17620. 1925. Duffield & Company.

Saint: Il Santo. Antonio Fogazzaro. LC 76-48422. (Classics of European Literature). (Hyperion library of world literature). 1977. 15.50. (ISBN 0-88355-540-9) (ISBN 0-88355-541-7). Hyperion Press.

Saint (Il Santo) Antonio Fogazzaro & Agnetti, Mary Prichard, Tr. LC 6-309243. 1906. G. P. Putnam's Sons.

Saint in Action. Leslie Charteris. LC 47-24088. (New Avon library. 118). 1947. Avon Book Co.

Saint in Europe. Leslie Charteris. LC 75-46555. 1975. 9.95 (ISBN 0-89190-387-9). American Reprint Co.

Saint in Europe. Leslie Charteris. LC 53-11654. 1953. Published for the Crime Club by Doubleday.

Saint in Ivory: The Story of Genevieve of Paris and Nanterrc. Lorine Pruette. LC 27-10645. 1927. D. Appleton and Company.

Saint in Miami. Leslie Charteris. LC 40-32320. 1940. Pub. for the Crime Club by Doubleday, Doran & Co., Inc.

Saint in Miami... Leslie Charteris. LC 45-2332. 1944. Triangle Books, the Blakiston Company.

Saint in New York. Leslie Charteris. LC 35-1203. 1935. Pub. for the Crime Club, Inc., by Doubleday, Doran & Company, Inc.

Saint in New York. Leslie Charteris. LC 38-32643. 1938. The Sun Dial Press, Inc.

Saint in New York. Leslie Charteris. LC 44-7575. New Avon Library.

Saint in Pursuit. Leslie Charteris. LC 71-123684. 1970. 4.50. Published for the Crime Club by Doubleday.

Saint in the Sun. Charteris, Leslie. LC 63-20517. (His The Saint series). 1963. Published for the Crime Club by Doubleday.

Saint Intervenes. Leslie Charteris. LC 34-372425. 1934. Pub. for the Crime Club, Inc., by Doubleday, Doran & Company, Inc.

Saint Intervenes. Leslie Charteris. LC 40-9137. 1940. Triangle Books.

St. Ives. Robert Louis Stevenson. LC 37-31205. (Half-title: Everyman's library, ed. by Ernest Rhys. Fiction. no. 904). 1934. J. M. Dent & Sons, Ltd.

Saint Ives. Robert Louis Stevenson. 1968. 3.50 o.p. (ISBN 0-460-00904-4, Evman). Dutton.

St. Ives: Being the Adventures of a French Prisoner in England. Robert Louis Stevenson & Quiler-Couch, Arthur Thomas. Ed. by Colvin, Sidney. LC 14-19356. (Novels and tales of Robert Louis Stevenson, vol. xxi). 1897. C. Scribner's Sons.

St. Ives Murders. Richard Wincor. LC 58-12357. 1958. Oceana Publications.

Saint Jack: A Novel. Paul Theroux. LC 72-12400. 1973. 5.95 (ISBN 0-395-17118-0). Houghton Mifflin.

St. James Quest. Stephen Notar. LC 76-381299. 1.95 (ISBN 0-671-80374-3). Simon & Schuster of Canada.

St. John of Honeylea. G. I Whitham. LC 20-75265. 1919. John Lane.

St. John's Eve & Other Stories. facsimile ed. Nikolai Vasilevich Gogol. Tr. by Isabelf. Hapgood from Rus. LC 70-152941. (Short Story Index Reprint Ser.). (From Evenings at the Farm - St. Petersburg Stories). Repr. of 1886 ed. 17.00 (ISBN 0-8369-3800-3). Ayer Co.

St. John's Eve: And Other Stories from "Evenings at the Farm" and "St. Petersburg Stories,". Nikolai Vasilevich Gogol. LC 70-152941. 1971. (ISBN 0-8369-3800-3). Books for Libraries Press.

St. John's Eve: And Other Stories, from "Evenings at the Farm" and "St. Petersburg Stories". Nikolai Vasilevich Gogol. Tr. by Hapgood, Isabel Florence. LC 6-43746. T. Y. Crowell & Co.

St. John's Wood. Nancy Fitzgerald. LC 76-42326. 1977. 6.95 (ISBN 0-385-12684-0). Doubleday.

St. John's Wooing: A Story. Margaret Greenway McClelland. LC 7-15432. (On cover: Harper's little novels). 1895. Harper & Brothers.

Saint Johnson. William Riley Burnett. LC 30-249499. 1930. L. MacVeagh, The Dial Press.

Saint Josephine. Forest Blake. LC 9-28268. Jennings and Graham.

St. Jude's. John Watson. LC 7-21223. 1907. The Sunday School Times Company.

St. Katherine's by the Tower: A Novel. Walter Besant. (On cover: Harper's Franklin square library, no. 702). 1891. Harper & Brothers.

St. Lawrence Blues. Marie Claire Blais. Tr. by Ralph Manheim. 229p. 1974. 7.95 (ISBN 0-374-25350-1). FS&G.

St. Lawrence Blues: A Novel. Marie Claire Blais. LC 74-4318. 1974. 7.95 (ISBN 0-374-26945-9). Farrar, Straus and Giroux.

Saint Leger: Or, The Threads of Life. Richard Burleigh Kimball. LC 7-12244. 1854. G. P. Putnam & Co.

Saint Leger: Or, The Threads of Life. 3d ed. Richard Burleigh Kimball. LC 34-37779. 1850. G. P. Putnam.

Saint Leger: Or, The Threads of Life. 6th ed. Richard Burleigh Kimball. 1852. G. P. Putnam.

St. Leon: A Tale of the Sixteenth Century. William Godwin. LC 74-8070. (Feminist Controversy in England, 1788-1810). 1974. 22.00 (ISBN 0-8240-0862-6). Garland Pub. Inc.

St. Leon, a Tale of the Sixteenth Century. William Godwin. LC 74-162884. (Illus.). 1975. 18.50 (ISBN 0-404-54405-3). AMS Press.

St. Leon: A Tale of the Sixteenth Century. William Godwin. LC 70-131318. (Gothic novels). (Illus.). 1972. (ISBN 0-405-00802-3). Arno Press.

St. Louis Jezebel. Dirk Fletcher. (Spur Ser.: No. 3). 208p. (Orig.). 1983. pap. 2.50 o.s.i. (ISBN 0-8439-1157-3, Leisure Bks). Dorchester Pub Co.

St. Louis Showdown. Don Pendleton. (Executioner Ser.: No. 23). 192p. (Orig.). 1975. pap. 2.25 (ISBN 0-523-42036-6). Pinnacle Bks.

St. Luke of the Nineteenth Century: Contrasts an Oldfashioned Story About a Few Gentlemen and Gentlewomen, and Some Others, Who Lived During the Reign of Queen Victoria. Emilie Isabel Wilson Barrington. LC 22-20883. 1922. Longmans, Green and Co.

Saint Magazine Reader. Ed. by Leslie Charteris. The Saint Magazine. LC 66-24333. 1966. Published for the Crime Club by Doubleday.

Saint Maker. Leonard Patrick O'Connor Wibberley. LC 59-6179. (Red badge detective). 1959. Dodd, Mead.

Saint Mammon: A Novel of American Society. William Neely Freeman. LC 8-31163. 1908. The Broadway Publishing Co.

St. Margaret's Cave: Or, the Nun's Story, 4 vols. Elizabeth Helme. Ed. by Devendra P. Varma. LC 77-2040. (Gothic Novels Ser. III). 1977. Set. lib. bdg. 70.00x (ISBN 0-405-10139-2). Ayer Co.

St. Martin's Eve: A Novel. Ellen Price Henry Wood Wood. (Seaside library, v.19, no. 373). 1878. G. Munro.

Saint Martin's Summer. Rafael Sabatini. LC 24-25419. 1924. Houghton Mifflin Company.

Saint Martin's Summer: Or, The Romance of the Cliff. Rose Porter. LC 7-37427. F. H. Revell Company.

Saint Mawr. David H. Lawrence. Bd. with Man Who Died. 1959. pap. 3.95 (ISBN 0-394-70071-6, Vin). Random.

St. Mawr. David Herbert Lawrence. LC 25-11588. 1925. A. A. Knopf.

St. Mawr & Other Stories: Letters & Works of D. H. Lawrence. D. H. Lawrence. Ed. by Brian Finney. LC 82-14584. 400p. Date not set. price not set (ISBN 0-521-22265-6). Cambridge U Pr.

St. Mawr, and The Man Who Died. David Herbert Lawrence. LC 59-549. 1959. Vintage Books.

Saint Michael. Elisabeth Burstenbinder. Tr. by Smith, Mary Stuart (Harrison) (On cover: Seaside library. Pocket ed., no. 1067). 1888. G. Munro.

Saint Michael: A Romance. Elisabeth Burstenbinder. Tr. by Wister. Annis Lee (Furness) LC 6-19403. 1887. J. B. Lippincott Company.

Saint Michael: A Romance. Elisabeth Burstenbinder. Tr. by Wister, Annis Lee (Furness) LC 24-22224. 1910. J. B. Lippincott Company.

Saint Michael's Gold. Henry Bedford-Jones. LC 26-19726. 1926. G.P. Putnam's Sons.

St. Nazarius. A. C Farquharson. LC 1-26206. 1901. The Macmillan Company.

Saint of Montparnasse: A Novel Based on the Life of Constantin Brancusi. Peter Neagoe. LC 65-13921. 1965. Chilton Books.

Saint of the Atom Bomb: Translated from the German by David Heimann. Josef Schilliger. LC 55-7051. 1955. Newman Press.

Saint of the Dragon's Dale: A Fantastic Tale. William Stearns Davis. (Half-title: Little novels by favorite authors). 1903. The Macmillan Company.

Saint of the Speedway. Ridgwell Cullum. LC 24-18099. George H. Doran Company.

Saint of the Twentieth Century. Fannie Bond Rice. LC 10-11364. 1910. R. G. Badger.

Saint of the Wilderness. Jess Carr. LC 74-77781. 441p. 1974. 8.95 (ISBN 0-89227-008-X); pap. 4.95 (ISBN 0-89227-026-8). Commonwealth Pr.

Saint of the Wilderness: A Biographical Novel Depicting the Life and Works of Robert Sayers Sheffey. Jess Carr. LC 74-77781. (Illus.). 1974. 8.95. Commonwealth Press.

St. Olave's. Eliza Tabor Stephenson. (Seaside library, v. 39, no. 797). 1880. G. Munro.

Saint on Guard. Leslie Charteris. LC 44-3677. 1944. Pub. for the Crime Club by Doubleday, Doran and Co., Inc.

Saint on the Spanish Main. Leslie Charteris. 1966. pap. 0.60 o.p. (60-252). Manor Bks.

Saint on the Spanish Main. Stories. Leslie Charteris. LC 55-5270. (Illus.). 1955. Published for the Crime Club by Doubleday.

Saint on TV. Fleming Lee & Leslie Charteris. LC 68-11192. 1968. Published for the Crime Club by Doubleday.

Saint Overboard. Leslie Charteris. LC 36-748. 1936. Pub. for the Crime Club, Inc., by Doubleday, Doran & Company, Inc.

Saint Overboard. Leslie Charteris. LC 36-33419. 1936. The Sun Dial Press.

Saint Overboard: A Saint Story. Leslie Charteris. LC 75-46554. 1975. 7.95 (ISBN 0-89190-381-X). American Reprint Co.

St. Patrick Told the Shoemaker: A Novel. Gerard G O'Kane. LC 49-715725. 1948. Dorrance.

Saint Patrick's Battalion. Carl Krueger. 1960. 3.95 o.p. Dutton.

Saint Patrick's Battalion: An Historical Novel. 1st Ed. Carl Krueger. LC 60-13376. 1960. Dutton.

St. Patrick's Eve; or, Three Eras in the Life of an Irish Peasant. Charles James Lever. LC 79-8151. (Illus.). Repr. of 1845 ed. 44.50 (ISBN 0-404-61970-3). AMS Pr.

Saint Paul: A Historical Novel of His Life. Leon Poirier. LC 61-137105. 1961. B. Herder Book Co.

St. Paul's of I Am, the Father of Jesus Christ: A Novel. Lloyd Champlain. LC 47-5795. 1947. Meador Pub. Co.

St. Peter and the Profile. John North. LC 30-230884. 1930. Duffield and Company.

St. Peter Asks the Questions. Frances Kaltenborn. LC 55-32691. 1955. Standard Publishers.

Saint Peter's Day & Other Tales. Anton Pavlovich Chekhov. Tr. by Frances H. Jones. (Orig.). 1959. pap. 1.25 o.p. (15, Cap). Putnam.

St. Peter's Day: And Other Tales. Translated, with an Introd., by Frances H. Jones. Anton Pavlovich Chekhov. LC 59-65276. 1959. Capricorn Books.

Saint Peter's Fair: The Fourth Chronicle of Brother Cadfael. Ellis Peters. LC 81-11020. 1981. 9.95 (ISBN 0-688-00667-1). Morrow.

St. Petersburg. Boris Nikolaevich Bugaev. LC 59-5417. 1959. Grove Press.

St. Petersburg Affair: A Novel. Olga Ilyin. LC 81-17130. 13.95. Holt, Rinehart, and Winston.

St. Philip's. Miriam Coles Harris. LC 70-164399. (American fiction reprint series). 1971. (ISBN 0-8369-7042-X). Books for Libraries Press.

St. Philip's. Miriam Coles Harris. LC 7-3344. 1865. Carleton.

St. Philip's. Miriam Coles Harris. LC 7-3343. Houghton, Mifflin and Company.

St. Phillip's. Miriam Coles Harris. LC 12-37860. 1871. C. Scribner & Company.

Saint Plays with Fire. Leslie Charteris. LC 42-23859. 1942. Triangle Books.

St. Quin. Dion Clayton Calthrop. LC 13-628. 1943. 1.30. John Lane Company.

Saint Returns: In Two New Adventures from Television: The Dizzy Daughter and The Gadget Lovers. Leslie Charteris. LC 68-14206. 1968. Published for the Crime Club by Doubleday.

St. Rockwells' Little Brother. Harriet Anna Cheever. LC 6-23427. Congregational Sunday-School and Publishing Society.

St. Ronan's Well. Walter Scott. (On cover: Lovell's library, v. 11, no. 586). 1885. J. W. Lovell Company.

St. Ronan's Well. Walter Scott. LC 36-37014. (Half-title: Everyman's library, ed. by Ernest Rhys. Fiction. no. 143). 1921. J. M. Dent & Sons, Ltd.

St. Ronan's Well. Walter Scott. LC 45-29156. (His Waverley novels). 1885. Dodd, Mead, and Company.

St. Ronan's Well: A Romance. Walter Scott. (On cover: Seaside library. Pocket ed. no. 418). 1885. G. Munro.

St. Ronan's Well... From the Last Rev. Ed., Containing the Author's Final Corrections, Notes, &C. parker's ed. Walter Scott. (Waverly novels: Library ed. v. 16). 1832. Bazin & Ellsworth.

Saint Saturnin. Jean Schlumberger. Tr. by Bussy, Dorothy (Strachey) LC 32-19825. 1932. Dodd, Mead & Company.

Saint Sees It Through. Leslie Charteris. LC 75-46607. 1975. (ISBN 0-89190-389-5). American Reprint Co.

Saint Sees It Through. Leslie Charteris. LC 46-7995. 1946. Pub. for the Crime Club by Doubleday & Company, Inc.

St. Solifer: With Other Worthies and Unworthies. James Vila Blake. LC 6-13850. 1891. C. H. Kerr and Company.

Saint Steps in. Leslie Charteris. LC 43-15862. 1943. Pub. for the Crime Club, by Doubleday, Doran and Co., Inc.

Saint Steps in. Leslie Charteris. LC 47-20002. 1947. Triangle Books, the Blakiston Company.

Saint Street. Ron Renauld. 256p. (Orig.). 1982. pap. 2.50 (ISBN 0-523-41634-2). Pinnacle Bks.

Saint Teresa: A Novel. Henry Sydnor Harrison. LC 22-8242. 1922. Houghton Mifflin Company.

St. Thomas's Eve. Eleanor Hibbert. LC 74-132107. 1970. 5.95. Putnam.

St. Thomas's Eve. Jean Plaidy. 1970. 6.95 (ISBN 0-399-10717-7). Putnam Pub Group.

Saint to the Rescue. Leslie Charteris. 1973. (pbk) 0.95. Manor Books.

Saint to the Rescue. 1st Ed. Leslie Charteris. LC 59-149994. 1959. Published for the Crime Club by Doubleday.

Saint: Two in One. Leslie Charteris. LC 42-28949. 1942. The Sun Dial Press.

Saint Udo: How, by a Mortal Sin, He Balked a Duke, Pleased a Prince, and Saved a Lady's Life. Richard L Masten. LC 30-7960. 1930. Houghton Mifflin Company.

Saint Urbain's Horseman. Mordecai Richler. 448p. 1972. pap. 2.50 (ISBN 0-553-11078-0, 01536-9). Bantam.

St. Urbain's Horseman: A Novel. Mordecai Richler. LC 76-136329. 1971. 7.95 (ISBN 0-394-44473-6). Knopf.

St. Valentine's Day: Or, The Fair Maid of Perth. Walter Scott. (Half-title: Everyman's library, ed. by Ernest Rhys. Fiction). 1908. J. M. Dent & Co.

St. Vitus Day. Stephen Graham. LC 31-1918. 1931. D. Appleton and Company.

Saint Vs. Scotland Yard. Leslie Charteris. LC 75-45466. 1976. 9.95 (ISBN 0-89190-390-9). American Reprint Co.

Saint Vs. Scotland Yard. Leslie Charteris. LC 32-242816. Pub. for the Crime Club, Inc., by Doubleday, Doran & Company, Inc.

Saint Vs. Scotland Yard. Leslie Charteris. LC 36-13197. 1935. A. L. Burt & Company.

Saint Vs. Scotland Yard. LC 53-11400. (Twenty-fifth anniversary Crime Club classic). 1953. Published for the Crime Club by Doubleday.

Saintmaker's Christmas Eve. Paul Horgan. LC 55-12208. (Illus.). 1955. Farrar, Straus and Cudahy.

Saintmakers's Christmas Eve. Paul Horgan. LC 78-72887. 1978. Repr. of 1955 ed. 15.00 (ISBN 0-88307-567-9). Gannon.

Saints and Innocents. Barbara Rex. LC 70-169045. 1972. 6.95 (ISBN 0-393-08664-X). Norton.

Saints and Sinners. Marian Ackerman. LC 79-90323. (Illus.). 4.50 (ISBN 0-932906-07-9) (ISBN 0-932906-06-0). Pan-American Pub.

Saints and Sinners. A Romance of Life. Lillie Dyett. LC 6-36393. 1878. The American News Company.

Saints and Sinners. Noirs et Rouges.) From the French of Victor Cherbuliez... Victor Cherbuliez & Sherwood, Mrs. Mary (Neal) Tr. LC 6-26968. 1882. D. Appleton and Company.

Saints and Sinners: Or, The Minister's Daughter. Marie Walsh. (On cover: The library of American authors, no. 9). 1889. G. Munro.

Saints and Tomahawks. Jacob John Sessler. LC 40-33707. The Pyramid Press.

Saint's Choice of Hollywood Crime. Ed. by Leslie Charteris. LC 46-21217. (On cover: The Saint's choice, v. 6). 1946. Saint Enterprises, Inc.

Saint's Choice of Humorous Crime. Ed. by Leslie Charteris. LC 46-1318. (On cover: The Saint's choice. Vol. 4). 1945. The Shaw Press.

Saint's Getaway. Leslie Charteris. LC 75-46606. 1976. 9.95 (ISBN 0-89190-388-7). American Reprint Co.

Saint's Getaway. Leslie Charteris. LC 43-5030. 1943. The Sun Dial Press.

Saints in Buckskins: A Novella. Gordan E Wick. 1974. 3.50 (ISBN 0-682-47848-2). Exposition Press.

Saints in Hell: Translated from the French by John Russell. 1st American Ed. Gilbert Cesbron. LC 54-6246. 1954. Doubleday.

Saints in Secret: Short Stories and Poems by Dulcie M. Oakley Hill... With a Foreword by Colonel Herbert J. Shirley... Dulcie M. Oakley Hill. The Faith Press, Ltd.

Saints in Society. Margaret Elsie Crowther Baillie-Saunders. LC 6-9624. 1906. G. P. Putnam's Sons.

Saints in Summertime. Brinckerhoff Jackson. LC 38-18390. W. W. Norton & Co., Inc.

Saints of St. Charles. Pilar Rich. 1970. 5.00 o.p. Exposition.

Saint's Progress. John Galsworthy. LC 19-10834. 1919. C. Scribner's Sons.

Saints' Rest. Sadie Fuller Seagrave. LC 18-7605. 1918. 1.00. C. V. Mosby Company.

Saints, Sinners and Queer People: Novelettes and Short Stories. Marie Edith Beynon. LC 6-12915. 1897. Authors Publishing Association.

Saints, the Devil & the King. Mary Louise Mabie. LC 30-767954. The Bobbs-Merrill Co.

Saint's Theatre. Horace Fish. LC 23-13341. 1923. Cassell and Company, ltd.

Saint's Theatre: A Novel. Horace Fish. LC 24-7953. 1924. B. W. Huebsch, Inc. Etc.

Saintsbury Affair. Lily Augusta Long. LC 12-2462. 1912. 1.25. Little, Brown, and Company.

Sakuran: A Novel of Medieval Japan. Edward Tolosko. LC 78-6560. (Illus.). 1978. 8.95 (ISBN 0-374-25367-6). Farrar Straus Giroux.

Salad Days. Theodora Benson. LC 29-26490. 1929. Harper & Brothers.

Saladin! A Novel. Andrew Osmond. LC 75-21239. (Illus.). 1976. 7.95 (ISBN 0-385-11138-X). Doubleday.

Salamanca Drum. Dorothy Eden. LC 77-9634. 1977. 13.95 (ISBN 0-8161-6501-7). G. K. Hall.

Salamanca Drum. Dorothy Eden. (Fawcett Crest Book). 1978. 1.95. Fawcett Pub.

Salamander. Owen McMahon Johnson. The Bobbs-Merrill Company.

Salamander. Morris L. West. LC 72-124. 1973. 7.95 (ISBN 0-688-00194-7). Morrow.

Salamander. Morris L. West. 1974. (pbk.) 1.75 (ISBN 0-671-78683-0). Pocket Books.

Salamander. A Naval Romance. Eugene Sue & Herbert, Henry William, 1807-1858, Tr. LC 8-17672. J. Winchester.

Salamander and Other Stories. Masuji Ibuse. LC 80-84421. 1981. 4.25 (ISBN 0-87011-458-1). Kodansha International.

Salamander: Found Amongst the Papers of the Late Ernest Helfenstein Pseud.... 2d ed. Elizabeth Oakes Prince Smith. LC 8-8641. 1849. G. P. Putnam.

Salamander Touch. Ivan Roe. LC 52-2805. New York.

Salambo. Gustave Flaubert. LC 76-372137. (Illus.). 3.95 (ISBN 0-8055-0247-5). Hart Pub. Co.

Salammbo. Gustave Flaubert. LC 72-9208. (Illus.). 1960. Printed at the University Press for Members of the Limited Editions Club.

Salammbo. Gustave Flaubert. LC 29-26371. (Half-title: The Modern library of the world's best books). 1929. The Modern Library.

Salammbo. Gustave Flaubert. LC 43-34447. (On cover: National home library). 1935. National Home Library Foundation.

Salammbo. Gustave Flaubert. LC 77-569876. (Penguin classics). 1977. 2.95 (ISBN 0-14-044328-2). Penguin.

Salammbo. Gustave Flaubert & Chartres, J. S., Tr. (Half-title: Everyman's library, ed. by Ernest Rhys. Fiction. no. 869). 1931. J. M. Dent & Sons, Ltd.

Salammbo. Gustave Flaubert & Lauvriere, Emile, 1866- Ed. LC 36-28499. (Oxford higher French series, ed. by Leon Delbos). 1925. The Clarendon Press.

Salammbo: A Story of Ancient Carthage. Gustave Flaubert & Ranous, Mrs. Dora Knowlton (Thompson) 1859-1916, Ed. LC 21-21697. (On cover: The lotus library). 1919. Brentano's.

Salammbo of Gustave Flaubert. Gustave Flaubert & King, Edward, 1848-1896. LC 15-231. Lovell, Coryell & Company.

Salammbo of Gustave Flaubert. Englished by M. French Sheldon. Translation Authorized by the Heirs of Gustave Flaubert. Gustave Flaubert & Sheldon, Mrs. Mary (French) 1846-Tr. 1886. Saxon & Co.

Salammbo, the Maid of Carthage: Re-Told from the French of Gustave Flaubert. Gustave Flaubert & Ragozin, Mme. Zenaide Alexeieuna, 1885-1924. (Tales of the heroic ages. no. iii). 1900. G. P. Putnam's Sons.

Salammbo: Translated from the French of Gustave Flaubert with an Introduction by Ben Ray Redman, Illustrated & Decorated by Mahlon Blaine. Gustave Flaubert & Redman, Ben Ray, 1896-Tr. LC 27-24857. The John Day Company.

Salander and the Dragon: A Romance of the Hartz Prison. Frederick William Shelton. LC 8-5108. 1850. S. Hueston, G.P. Putnam.

Salar the Salmon. Henry Williamson. (Illus.). 210p. (Orig.). 1973. pap. 6.95 (ISBN 0-571-04811-0). Faber & Faber.

Salathiel: A Story of the Past, the Present, and the Future. George Croly. LC 9-3448. 1847. J. A. & U. P. James.

Salavin. Georges Duhamel. Tr. by Billings, Gladys. LC 36-24406. 1936. G. P. Putnam's Sons.

Salazar Grant. E L Withers, pseud. LC 59-6450. 1959. Rinehart.

Saldo Trench and Others: Stories of Americans in Italy. Henry Blake Fuller. LC 8-23926. 1908. C. Scribner's Sons.

Sale. Joan Conquest. 1930. The Macaulay Company.

Sale of a Soul. Frank Frankfort Moore. LC 7-253033. F. A. Stokes Company.

Sale of an Appetite. Paul Lafargue. Tr. by Kerr, Charles H. LC 3-32403. 1904. C. H. Kerr & Company.

Sale of Mrs. Adral. A Novel. F. H. Costellow. LC 6-29025. 1889. G. W. Dillingham.

Salekov Kill. Guy Richards. 256p. (Orig.). 1981. pap. 2.50 (ISBN 0-449-14405-4, GM). Fawcett.

Salem. M. Paskra Chelvam. LC 77-358704. 6.50 (ISBN 0-533-02575-3). Vantage Press.

Salem: A Tale of the Seventeenth Century. Caroline Rosina Derby. LC 6-33972. 1874. Harper & Brothers.

Salem Belle: A Tale of Love and Witchcraft in the Year 1692. LC 8-3735. 1847. J. M. Whittemore.

Salem Chapel. Margaret Oliphant Wilson Oliphant. LC 75-1508. (Victorian Fiction: Novels of Faith and Doubt). 1976. 35.00 (ISBN 0-8240-1582-7). Garland Pub.

Salem Chapel. Margaret Oliphant Wilson Oliphant. (On cover: Seaside library. Pocket ed., no. 177). 1884. G. Munro.

Salem Frigate. John Edward Jennings. LC 46-617619. 1946. Doubleday & Company, Inc.

Salem Frigate. John Edward Jennings. LC 47-643601. 1947. Sun Dial Press.

Salem Frigate. John Edward Jennings. 1973. (pbk.) 1.25. Popular Lib.

Salem Kittredge, and Other Stories. Bliss Perry. LC 71-133165. (Short story index reprint series). 1970. (ISBN 0-8369-3689-2). Books for Libraries Press.

Salem Kittredge: And Other Stories. Bliss Perry. LC 7-36175. 1894. C. Scribner's Sons.

Salem's Children. Mary Leader. LC 78-24115. 9.95 (ISBN 0-698-10724-1). Coward, McCann & Geoghegan.

Salem's Daughter. Maggie Osborne. (Orig.). 1981. pap. 2.75 (ISBN 0-451-09602-9, E9602, Sig). NAL.

Salem's Lot. Stephen King. LC 73-22804. 1975. 7.95 (ISBN 0-385-00751-5). Doubleday.

Salem's Lot. Stephen King. (Signet book). 1976. 1.95. New American Library.

Saleslady: A Novel of Department Store Life. Honore McCue Willsie Morrow. LC 32-253206. Grosset & Dunlap.

Salesman, a Novel. John Herrmann. LC 39-14382. 1939. Simon and Schuster.

Salesmen Never Complain. 1st Ed. Donald McGraw. LC 53-12694. 1953. Pageant Press.

Saleswoman: A Guide to Career Success. Barbara Fletcher. (gr. 12). 1980. pap. 2.95 (ISBN 0-671-82895-9). PB.

Saline Solution. Marco Vassi. 192p. 1976. pap. 2.25 (ISBN 0-532-22102-8). Woodhill.

Saline Solution. Marco Vassi. pap. 1.95 o.s.i. (OPS-27). Olympia.

Salisbury Manuscript. William M. Green. LC 73-3779. 1974. 5.95 o.p. (ISBN 0-672-51855-4). Bobbs.

Salisbury Plain. Henry C Branson. LC 65-15243. 4.95. Dutton.

Saliva Tree. Brian Wilson Aldiss. LC 79-28703. (Gregg Press science fiction series). 1981. 16.95 (ISBN 0-8398-2566-8). Gregg Press.

Salka Valka. Halldor K. Laxness. Tr. by F. H. Lyon. 1965. Repr. of 1963 ed. 6.75 o.p. Verry.

Salka Valka: A Novel of Iceland. Halldor Kiljan Laxness. Tr. by Lyon, Francis Hamilton. LC 36-17734. 1936. Houghton Mifflin Company.

Salka Valka. Tr. from Danish by F. H. Lyon. Halldor Kiljan Laxness. Tr. by Francis Hamilton Lyon. LC 65-6288. 1965. 5.00. Allen & Unwin.

Sallie Blue Bonnet. W. Rockwood Conover. LC 12-6586. The C.M. Clark Publishing Co.

Sallie Seull on the Texas Frontier: Phantoms on Rio Turbio. Tennessee Virginia Bradford. LC 52-11250. 1952. Naylor Co.

Sallie's Newspaper: A Novel. Edwin Herbert Lewis. LC 24-17883. 1924. Hyman-McGee Co.

Sally. E. V. Cunningham, pseud. 1967. 4.50 o.p. Morrow.

Sally. Jennie Tremaine. (Candlelight Edwardian Ser.: No. 709). (Orig.). 1982. pap. 2.25 (ISBN 0-440-17523-2). Dell.

Sally, No. 156. Leonora Blythe. 224p. 1981. pap. 1.50 (ISBN 0-449-50229-5, Coventry). Fawcett.

Sally, a Doll Story. Mabel Kohler Holbrock. (Illus.). 1974. 3.50 (ISBN 0-533-01036-5). Vantage.

Sally: A Novel, by E. V. Cunningham. Howard Melvin. Fast. LC 67-151562. 1967. 4.50. Morrow.

Sally & Joe. Bob Sang. 288p. (Orig.). 1981. pap. 2.75 (ISBN 0-932844-04-9). R H Sang & Son.

Sally Ann's Experience. Eliza Caroline Calvert Obenchain. LC 10-20611. 1910. 1.00. Little, Brown, and Company.

Sally Bishop: A Romance. Ernest Temple Thurston. LC 10-73055. M. Kennerley.

Sally Castleton: Southerner. 2d ed. Crittenden Marriott. LC 13-3766. 1913. 1.25. J. B. Lippincott Company.

Sally Dows. Bret Harte. Repr. lib. bdg. 20.00 (ISBN 0-8414-5011-0). Folcroft.

Sally Dows, and Other Stories. Bret Harte. LC 79-113673. (Short story index reprint series). 1970. Books for Libraries Press.

Sally Dows: And Other Stories. Bret Harte. LC 7-3648. 1893. Houghton, Mifflin and Company.

Sally, Heir of the Ages. Lucie Corner Dysart. LC 42-5683. 1942. Meador Publishing Company.

Sally Hemings. Barbara Chase-Riboud. 1980. 2.75 (ISBN 0-670-61605-2). Avon Publishers.

Sally Hemings: A Novel. Barbara Chase-Riboud. LC 78-12682. 1979. 12.95 (ISBN 0-670-61605-2). Viking Press.

Sally Jo. Laura Zenobia Le Fevre. LC 34-34423. 1934. Fleming H. Revell Company.

Sally Lunn. Leo Walmsley. LC 37-18107. 1937. The Macmillan Company.

Sally, Mrs. Tubbs. Harriet Mulford Stone Lothrop. LC 3-20898. 1903. Lothrop Publishing Company.

Sally of Missouri. Rose Emmet Young. LC 3-25396. 1903. McClure, Phillips & Co.

Sally of Show Alley. Homer King Gordon. LC 28-5398. Thomas Y. Crowell Company.

Sally on the Rocks. Winifred Boggs. LC 15-15608. 1915. Brentano's.

Sally Salt. Nancy Mann Waddel Wilson Woodrow Woodrow. LC 12-5842. The Bobbs-Merrill Company.

Sally Seal. Gant Gaither. (Illus.). 1964. 3.00 o.p. (ISBN 0-8392-1096-5). Astor-Honor.

Sally Seal: The Unexpurgated Love Life of Her Imperial Highness the Grand Duchess of Cod-Sardinska. Gant Gaither. LC 63-20871. 1964. L. Obolensky.

Sally: The Story of a Foster-Girl. John Metcalfe. LC 36-12812. 1936. C. Scribner's Sons.

Sally Townsend: Patriot. Dorothy Horton McGee. LC 52-7214. Dodd, Mead.

Sally's in the Alley. Norbert Davis. LC 43-13571. 1943. W. Morrow & Company.

Sally's Shoulders. Beatrice Burton Morgan. LC 27-24889. Grosset & Dunlap.

Salmagundi: Second Series, 2 Vols. in 1. James Kirke Paulding. LC 70-144669. Repr. of 1835 ed. 32.00 (ISBN 0-404-04944-3). AMS Pr.

Salmon People. Hugh W. McKervill. 1967. 7.25 o.p. Superior Pub.

Salome; Notes for a New Novel & Don Giovanni: Notes for a Revised Opera. Gaia Servadio. LC 69-15410. 1969. 5.50. Farrar, Straus & Giroux.

TITLE INDEX SAMANTHA AMONG THE COLORED

Salome of the Tenements. Anzia Yezierska. LC 23-2031. Boni and Liveright.
Salome: Princess of Galilee. Henry Denker. LC 52-7035. 1952. Crowell.
Salome, the Wandering Jewess: My First Two Thousand Years of Love. George Sylvester Viereck & Eldridge, Paul, 1888- Joint Author. LC 30-29014. 1930. H. Liveright.
Salomy Jane. Bret Harte. LC 10-23748. 1910. Houghton Mifflin Company.
Salomy Jane's Kiss. photo-play ed. revised and elaborated version of the famous story by bret harte... ed. Bret I. E. Francis Bret Harte. LC 15-14446. 0.50. Grosset & Dunlap.
Salon of Madame Necker. Gabriel Paul Othenin De Cleron Haussonville & Trollope, Henry Merivale, 1846- Tr. LC 21-15365. (Seaside library, v. 73, no. 1472). 1882. G. Munro.
Salt: A Novel. Herbert Gold. LC 68-2381. 5.95. Random.
Salt Air. Louise Breckenridge. LC 36-212. Alliance Press.
Salt and the Savor: A Novel. Howard William Troyer. LC 50-9840. 1950. Wyn.
Salt Doll: A Novel on India. Shouri Daniels. 1977. 6.50x o.p. (ISBN 0-8364-0055-0). South Asia Bks.
Salt Eaters. Toni Cade Bambara. LC 79-4806. 1980. 9.95 (ISBN 0-394-50712-6). Random House.
Salt Eaters. Toni Cade Bambara. LC 81-3434. 1981. 3.95 (ISBN 0-394-75050-0). Vintage Books.
Salt for the Tiger. Wilbur C. Tuttle. LC 52-12540. ("Avalon books."). 1952. Bouregy & Curl.
Salt Harbor: By Mary Douglas Warren Pseud. Maysie Greig. LC 53-112956. 1953. Arcadia House.
Salt House: A Novel. Hazel Hawthorne. LC 34-418834. 1934. Frederick A. Stokes Company.
Salt in Our Wounds. Jack Harvey. LC 54-5044. 1954. Dutton.
Salt in the Wound. Leonardo Sciascia. 1969. 6.00 o.p. (ISBN 0-670-61630-3, Orion Pr). Grossman.
Salt in the Wound: Followed by The Death of the Inquisitor. Leonardo Sciascia. LC 69-19663. 1969. 6.00. Orion Press.
Salt Is Leaving. John Boynoton Priestley. LC 81-47381. (Fifty Classics of Crime Fiction, 1950-1975). 1982. 14.95 (ISBN 0-8240-4988-8). Garland Pub.
Salt Is Leaving. John Boynton Priestley. LC 66-67790. 1966. Pan, by Arrangement with Heinemann.
Salt Is Leaving. John Boynton Priestley. LC 74-15886. 1975. 6.95 (ISBN 0-06-013427-5). Harper & Row.
Salt Is Leaving. John Boynton Priestley. LC 75-17982. 1975. 12.95 (ISBN 0-8161-6310-3). G. K. Hall & Co.
Salt Lake. Lucile Bogue. 352p. (Orig.). 1982. pap. 2.95 (ISBN 0-523-41319-X). Pinnacle Bks.
Salt Lake: A Novel by Pierre Benoit. Pierre Benoit. Tr. by Llona, Florence. LC 22-5458. 1922. A. A. Knopf.
Salt-Lake Fruit: A Latter-Day Romance. William Loring Spencer. LC 8-14077. 1884. Rand, Avery, and Company.
Salt Master of Luneburg. Julius Wolff & Windlow W. Henry, Tr. T. Y. Crowell & Co.
Salt Mine. David Lippincott. LC 78-26870. 1979. 9.95 (ISBN 0-670-61634-6). Viking Press.
Salt O' Life. Howard Murry. LC 61-16638. (Illus.). 1966. 3.25 o.p. (ISBN 0-910244-25-1). Blair.
Salt of the Earth. Rose Istad. 5.95 o.p. (ISBN 0-8062-1050-8). Carlton.
Salt of the Earth. Marguerite Mooers Marshall. LC 35-4413. 1935. Doubleday, Doran & Company, Inc.
Salt of the Earth. Carlo Monterosso. LC 67-22021. 1967. Prentice-Hall.
Salt of the Earth. Cecily Ullmann Sidgwick. LC 17-20666. W. J. Watt & Company.
Salt of the Earth. Frances Wright Turner. LC 41-1477. House of Field, Inc.
Salt of the Earth. Joseph Wittlin. Tr. by Pauline De Chary. LC 71-102381. (Great Novels & Memoirs of World War I Ser). 1970. 6.95 o.p. (ISBN 0-8117-1504-3). Stackpole.
Salt of the Earth: A Novel. Jozef Wittlin. LC 71-102381. (Great Novels and Memoirs of World War I). 1970. 6.50. Stackpole Books.
Salt of the Earth: A Novel. Jozef Wittlin & De Chary, Pauline, Tr. 1941. Sheridan House.
Salt of the Sea, Red Saunders: The Chronicle of a Genial Outcast. Aylward Edward Dingle. LC 34-32946. 1934. J. B. Lippincott. Company.
Salt O'life. With Reproductions of the Author's Water Colors. Howard Murry. LC 61-16638. 1961. J. F. Blair.
Salt: Or, The Education of Griffith Adams. Charles Gilman Norris. LC 18-11362. E. P. Dutton and Company.
Salt: Or, The Education of Griffith Adams. Charles Gilman Norris. LC 22-17224. 1921. E. P. Dutton and Company.
Salt: Or, The Education of Griffith Adams. Charles Gilman Norris. LC 22-18654. 1922. E. P. Dutton and Company.
Salt: Or, The Education of Griffith Adams. Charles Gilman Norris. LC 80-25152. (Lost American fiction). 1981. 19.95 (ISBN 0-8093-1011-2). Southern Illinois University Press.
Salt or the Education of Griffith Adams: A Novel. Charles Gilman Norris. LC 80-25152. (Lost American Fiction Ser.). 394p. 1981. Repr. of 1918 ed. 19.95x (ISBN 0-8093-1011-2). S Ill U Pr.
Salt Pork. Ruth Hesse Artist. LC 38-9973. Burney Brothers Publishing Co.
Salt River Ranny. Nelson Coral Nye. LC 42-363442. 1943. The Macmillan Company.
Salt-Sea Mastodon: A Reading of Moby-Dick. Robert Zoellner. LC 72-89793. (Illus.). 1973. 10.00 (ISBN 0-520-02339-0). University of California Press.
Salt Streak. Florance Walton Taylor. LC 39-23742. Fleming H. Revell Company.
Salt Water Bubbles: Or, Life on the Wave. John Sherburne Sleeper. LC 8-960076. 1854. W. J. Reynolds & Co.
Salt Water Daffy. Philip Wylie. LC 41-1948. Farrar and Rinehart, Inc.
Salt Water, Fresh Water, and Fire Water. 1st Ed. Louis Woodbury Eaton. LC 56-13153. 1956. Blackmore Press.
Salt Water: Or, The Sea Life and Adventure of Neil D'Arcy, the Midshipman. William Henry Giles Kingston. (On cover: Lovell's library, v. 7, no. 337). 1884. J. W. Lovell Company.
Salt Winds and Gobi Dust. John William Thomason. LC 34-11257. 1934. C. Scribner's Sons.
Saltacres. Leslie Reid. LC 27-5682. E. P. Dutton & Company.
Salted with Fire. Reb Cameron. LC 6-21498. 1872. E. J. Hale & Son.
Salted with Fire: A Story of a Minister. George Macdonald. LC 7-18784. 1897. Dodd, Mead and Company.
Salthaven. William Wymark Jacobs. LC 8-30011. 1908. C. Scribner's Sons.
Saltmarsh Murders. Gladys Mitchell. LC 33-11097. 1933. Macrae Smith Company.
Salutation. Sylvia Townsend Warner. LC 32-25845. 1932. The Viking Press.
Salutations see Hunger & Thirst & Other Plays.
Salute Blue Mask. John Creasey. LC 38-18757. 1938. J. B. Lippincott Co.
Salute for the Baron. John Creasey. LC 72-95795. 1973. 5.95 (ISBN 0-8027-5277-2). Walker.
Salute for the Baron. Anthony Morris, pseud. 192p. 1973. 5.95 o.p. (ISBN 0-8027-5277-2). Walker & Co.
Salute from a Dead Man. Donald MacKenzie. LC 66-10213. 3.95. Houghton.
Salute the Colonel. Warren Thomas. LC 35-860. The Beaver Press.
Salute the Toff. John Creasey. 1971. 4.95 o.p. Walker & Co.
Salute the Toff. John Creasey. (O.s.i.). 160p. 1974. pap. 0.95 o.s.i. (AN1212, Award). Univ Pub & Dist.
Salute to Adventurers. John Buchan. George H. Doran Company.
Salute to Adventurers. John Buchan. LC 18-564672. George H. Doran Company.
Salute to Adventurers. John Buchan. LC 36-15169. 1930. Houghton Mifflin Company.
Salute to Aphrodite: A Novel by Rearden Conner. Rearden Conner, pseud. LC 35-2969. The Bobbs-Merrill Company.
Salute to Bazarada & Other Stories. Sax Rohmer, pseud. 311p. 1972. 8.50. Bookfinger.
Salute to Cyrano: The Further Adventures of D'Artagnan and Cyrano, by Paul Fevel. Paul Feval & Chase, Cleveland Bruce, 1903-Tr. LC 31-263821. 1931. Longmans, Green and Co.
Salute to Freedom: A Novel. Eric Lowe. LC 39-21192. Reynal & Hitchcock.
Salute to Glory. William Arthur Neubauer. LC 65-7900. 1965. Arcadia House.
Salute to Heaven. Manfred Hausmann & Fredrick, Caroline, Tr. LC 31-11274. 1931. A. A. Knopf.
Salute to Murder. Robert Portner Koehler. LC 44-410455. 1944. Phoenix Press.
Salute to Spring. Meridel Le Sueur. LC 75-38588. 1977. 1.95 (ISBN 0-7178-0463-1). International Publishers.
Salute to Spring. Meridel Le Sueur. LC 40-10297. International Publishers.
Salute to the Brave: Stories of World War II. Ed. by Albert B Tibbets. LC 60-9341. 1960. Little, Brown.
Salute to the Gods. Malcolm Campbell. LC 35-1693. G. P. Putnam's Sons.
Salute to the Great McCarthy: A Novel. Barry Oakley. LC 71-533006. 1970. 3.95 (ISBN 0-85561-008-5). Heinemann.
Salute to the Hero. Constance Noyes Robertson. LC 42-1114. Farrar & Rinehart, Inc.
Salute to the Marines. Randall M White & Bruce, George, 1898- LC 43-150629. 1943. Grosset & Dunlap.
Salute to Yesterday. Gene Fowler, pseud. LC 37-237821. Random House.
Salvage. Jacky Gillott. LC 69-12233. 1969. 4.95. Doubleday.
Salvage. Aquila Kempster. LC 6-39730. 1906. D. Appleton and Company.
Salvage... Elizabeth Wormeley Latimer. LC 7-13862. (No name series. 2d series. v. 5). 1880. Roberts Brothers.
Salvage. Roger Vercel & Wells, Warre Bradley, 1892- Tr. LC 36-35047. 1936. Harper & Brothers.
Salvage All. Grace Jones Morgan. LC 28-6766. Thomas Y. Crowell Company.
Salvage Job. Bill Knox. LC 78-8198. 1979. 7.95 (ISBN 0-385-14601-9). Published for the Crime Club by Doubleday.
Salvage of the Cynthia. Jules Verne. 3.95. Assoc Bk.
Salvation. 2d ed. Shalom Asch. LC 68-25867. 1968. 7.50. Schocken Books.
Salvation. Shalom Asch & Muir, Mrs. Willa, Tr. LC 34-30866. 1934. G. P. Putnam's Sons.
Salvation Johnny. 1st Ed. Natalie Anderson Scott. 1958. Doubleday.
Salvation of Pisco Gabar: And Other Stories. Geoffrey Household. LC 40-27447. 1940. Little, Brown and Company.
Salvation of Zachary Baumkletterer. George Mavrodes. 1976. pap. 0.50 (ISBN 0-87784-160-8). Inter-Varsity.
Salvation on a String: And Other Tales of the South. Paul Green. LC 46-695619. 1946. Harper & Brothers.
Salvation: Translated by Willa and Edwin Muir. Rev. and Enl. Ed. Shalom Asch. LC 51-98493. 1951. Putnam.
Salvator. Perceval Gibbon. 1909. 1.50. Double-Day, Page & Company.
Salvator: Being the Continuation and Conclusion of "The Mohicans of Paris.". Alexandre Dumas & Bocage, Paul Touses, Called. LC 21-13965. (Seaside library, v. 72, no. 1452). 1882. G. Munro.
Salzburg Affair. Stanley White. LC 78-304116. 1977. 8.95 (ISBN 0-09-128430-9). Hutchinson.
Salzburg Comedy. Translated from the German by Cyrus Brooks. Illustrated by Walter Trier. American Ed. Erich Kastner. LC 57-10986. 1957. F. Ungar Pub. Co.
Salzburg Connection. Helen MacInnes. LC 68-24394. 1968. Harcourt, Brace & World.
Salzburg Tales. Christina Stead. LC 34-20399. 1934. D. Appleton-Century Company, Incorporated.
Sam. Freeman Lincoln. LC 31-7414. Coward-McCann, Inc.
Sam. E. J. Rath. LC 16-721. 1.25. W. J. Watt & Company.
Sam. John Selby. LC 39-27879. Farrar & Rinehart, Inc.
Sam. Jack Weyland. LC 81-682. 1981. 6.95 (ISBN 0-87747-854-6). Deseret Book Co.
Sam: A Novel in Verse. Francis Hartman Markoe. LC 44-1334. (His: Shelmar editions, no. II). 1943.
Sam Blick's Diary. Stephen C Noland. 1922. Harper & Brothers.
Sam Campbell: Gentleman. Edison Marshall. LC 35-15467. 1935. H. C. Kinsey & Company, Inc.
Sam Casanova. Max Catto. (Signet Book). 1977. 1.75 (ISBN 0-451-07790-3). New American Library.
Sam Chance. Benjamin Capps. (Gold Medal bk., d1907). 1968. Fawcett.
Sam Chance. Benjamin Capps. 1976. (pbk.) 1.25. Ace Books.
Sam Chance: A Novel. Benjamin Capps. LC 65-12604. bds., 4.95. Duell Dist. Meredith.
Sam Chard. Don Bannister. LC 79-2030. 1979. 8.95 (ISBN 0-394-50679-0). Knopf.
Sam Clemens of Hannibal. Dixon Wecter & Samuel Langhorne Clemens. (Sentry ed.). 1961. pap., 1.85. Houghton.
Sam Durell Assignment Thirteenth Princess. Will B Aarons. (Assignment series). (Fawcett Gold Medal Book). 1.75 (ISBN 0-449-13919-0). Fawcett Books.
Sam Houston: A Biographical Novel. Noel Bertram Gerson. LC 68-11796. 1968. 5.95. Doubleday.
Sam Houston Story: A Swashbuckling Account of the Man Whose Daring Exploits Altered the Course of Texan History by Dean Owen Pseud. Dudley Dean McGaughy. LC 61-247558. (Monarch Americana series, MA308). 1961. Monarch Books.
Sam in Schnabelweide: Eine Lustige Kleinstadtgeschichte, Von Will Vesper. Will Vesper. Ed. by Goodloe, Jane Faulkner. LC 36-5649. 1936. F. S. Crofts & Co.
Sam in the Suburbs. Pelham Grenville Wodehouse. LC 26-26140. George H. Doran Company.
Sam in the Suburbs. Pelham Grenville Wodehouse. LC 35-285874. 1927. A. L. Burt Company.
Sam Lawson's Oldstown Fireside Stories. Harriet Elizabeth Beecher Stowe. LC 67-29279. (Americans in Fiction Ser.). (Illus.). lib. bdg. 16.50 (ISBN 0-8398-1874-2); pap. text ed. 5.95x (ISBN 0-89197-928-X). Irvington.
Sam Lawson's Oldtown Fireside Stories. Harriet Elizabeth Beecher Stowe. LC 67-29279. (Americans in Fic.). 1967. Gregg Pr.
Sam Lawson's Oldtown Fireside Stories. Harriet Elizabeth Beecher Stowe. LC 701. 1899. Houghton, Mifflin and Company.
Sam Lovel's Boy. Rowland Evans Robinson. LC 1-30628. 1901. Houghton, Mifflin and Company.
Sam Lovel's Boy & Forest & Stream Fables. Roland E. Robinson. Ed. by Llewellyn E. Perkins. (Works of Rowland Robinson). (Illus.). 255p. 1936. 10.00 (ISBN 0-8048-0634-9). C E Tuttle.
Sam Lovel's Boy: With Forest & Stream Fables. Rowland Evans Robinson. LC 70-160949. (Short story index reprint series). (Illus.). 1971. (ISBN 0-8369-3928-X). Books for Libraries Press.
Sam Lovel's Boy, with Forest & Stream Fables. facsimile ed. Rowland Evans Robinson. Ed. by Llewellyn R. Perkins. LC 70-160949. (Short Story Index Reprint Ser.). Repr. of 1901 ed. 16.00 (ISBN 0-8369-3928-X). Ayer Co.
Sam Lovel's Boy: With Forest & Stream Fables. Rowland Evans Robinson & Perkins, Liewellyn Rood, Ed. LC 36-12314. Chas. E. Tuttle Company.
Sam Lovel's Camp: And Other Stories Including In the Green Wood. Rowland Evans Robinson & Perkins, Liewellyn Rood, Ed. LC 35-676961. The Tuttle Company.
Sam Lovel's Camps: & Other Stories, Including 'In the Green Wood' facsimile ed. Rowland Evans Robinson. Ed. by Llewellyn R. Perkins. LC 77-37558. (Short Story Index Reprint Ser.). Repr. of 1934 ed. 17.00 (ISBN 0-8369-4117-9). Ayer Co.
Sam Lovel's Camps. Uncle Lisha's Friends Under Bark and Canvas. A Sequel to Uncle Lisha's Shop. Rowland Evans Robinson. LC 7-42178. 1889. Forest and Stream Publishing Co.
Sam McGoo and Texas Too. Paul Patterson. LC 47-5200. 1947. Mathis, Van Nort.
Sam Seven. Richard Hubert Francis Cox. LC 76-51429. 1977. 8.95 (ISBN 0-88349-118-4). Reader's Digest Press: Distributed by Crowell.
Sam Shirk: A Tale of the Woods of Maine. George Humphrey Devereux. LC 6-33402. 1871. Hurd and Houghton.
Sam Simple's First Trip to New Orleans. George T. Wilburn. 1870. Hancock, Graham & Reilly.
Sam Simple's First Trip to New Orleans. 3d ed. revised by e. walters.. ed. George T. Wilburn. 1899. The J. W. Burke Co.
Sam Slick in Search of a Wife: Or, Wise Saws. Thomas Chandler Haliburton. (seaside library, v. 60, no. 1219). 1882. G. Munro.
Sam Slick, the Clockmaker. The Sayings and Doings of Samuel Slick, of Slickville. Thomas Chandler Haliburton. LC 17-13021. 1887. J. B. Alden.
Sam Small Flies Again: The Amazing Adventures of the Flying Yorkshireman. Eric Mowbray Knight. LC 42-5832. 1942. Harper & Brothers.
Sam Weskit on the Planet Framingham. William Johnston. LC 79-106331. (Tempo books, 5335). 1970. 0.75. Grosset & Dunlap.
Sam Wiggins' Excursion into Society. Wilfred T Jennings. LC 19-1033. 1918. Saulsbury Publishing Company.
Sam Williams; a Tale of the Old South. W. S Harrison. LC 70-39088. (Black Heritage Library Collection). 1972. (ISBN 0-8369-9026-9). Books for Libraries Press.
Sam Williams: A Tale of the Old South. W. S Harrison. LC 7-288037. 1892. Publishing House of the M. E. Church, South.
Samadhi: A Novel. Will Levington Comfort. LC 27-20254. 1927. Houghton Mifflin Company.
Samain. Margaret Elizabeth Atkins. LC 76-9204. 7.95 (ISBN 0-06-010161-X). Harper & Row.
Samantha. Jean Carew. 1969. Repr. pap. 0.60 o.p. (60-373). Manor Bks.
Samantha. E. V. Cunningham, pseud. 1967. 4.50 o.p. Morrow.
Samantha. Hazel Gerland. 4.50 o.s.i. (ISBN 0-8181-0200-4). Pageant-Poseidon.
Samantha. Clarice Peters. (Regency Romance Ser.). 224p. (Orig.). 1983. pap. 2.25 (ISBN 0-449-20217-8, Crest). Fawcett.
Samantha: A Novel. Howard Melvin Fast. LC 67-25317. 1967. W. Morrow.
Samantha Among the Brethren- Marietta Holley. LC 7-6034. 1890. Funk & Wagnalls.
Samantha Among the Brethren. Marietta Holley. LC 7-6035. (On cover: Farm and fireside library. no. 152). Mast, Crowell & Kirkpatrick.
Samantha Among the Colored Folks. "My Ideas on the Race Problem,". Marietta Holley & Kremble, Edward Windsor, 1861-1963, Illus. LC 12-34246. 1894. Dodd, Mead and Company.

Samantha at Coney Island and a Thousand Other Islands. Marietta Holley. LC 11-27297. The Christian Herald.
Samantha at Coney Island and a Thousand Other Islands. Marietta Holley. LC 14-138843. 1914. The Christian Herald.
Samantha at Saratoga; or, "Flirtin' with Fashion,". Marietta Holley. LC 1-1175. 1887. Hubbard Bros., San Francisco, The History Co.
Samantha at Saratoga; or, "Racin' After Fashion.". Marietta Holley. LC 41-32222. F. M. Lupton Publishing Company.
Samantha at Saratoga; or, Racing After Fashion. Marietta Holley. LC 1-293281. (On cover: The pastime series no. 94). Laird & Leo.
Samantha at the St. Louis Exposition. Marietta Holley. LC 4-30955. 1904. G. W. Dillingham Company.
Samantha at the World's Fair. Marietta Holley. LC 7-6086. 1893. Funk & Wagnalls Company.
Samantha in Europe. Marietta Holley. LC 7-6037. 1896. Funk & Wagnalls Company.
Samantha on Children's Rights. Marietta Holley. G. W. Dillingham Company.
Samantha on the Race Problem. Marietta Holley. LC 71-91082. (American humorists series). (Illus.). 1969. Literature House.
Samantha on the Race Problem. Marietta Holley. LC 7-6038. Dodd, Mead & Company.
Samantha on the Woman Question. Marietta Holley. Fleming H. Revell Company.
Samantha Vs. Josiah: Being the Story of a Borrowed Automobile and What Came of It. Marietta Holley. LC 6-18589. 1906. Funk & Wagnalls Company.
Samanthy Billins of Hangin '-Dog. Georgia Elizabeth Duncan. LC 6-2339. 1905. Mutual Publishing Company.
Samaritan. Philippe Van Rjndt. LC 82-9695. 416p. 1983. 15.95 (ISBN 0-385-27221-9). Dial.
Samaritan Mary. Sumner Locke. LC 16-5619. 1916. 1.25. H. Holt and Company.
Samaritan Scheme. David Christopher. (Orig.). 1978. pap. 2.25 (ISBN 0-89083-413-X). Zebra.
Samaritans. Anton Gross. LC 49-2536. 1948. B. Humphries.
Samarkand. Graham Diamond. LC 79-92150. 1980. 2.25 (ISBN 0-87216-631-7). Playboy Press.
Samarkand Dawn. Graham Diamond. LC 80-82850. 256p. (Orig.). 1981. pap. 2.25 (ISBN 0-87216-781-X). Playboy Pbks.
Sambatyon-2: A Documentary Novel. Meir Simha Ostrinsky. LC 77-116870. 1970. 7.95. Bloch Pub. Co.
Same Clay: A Novel. Joseph Kling. LC 45-3236. Harbinger House.
Same Door. John Updike. (YA) 1959. 11.95 (ISBN 0-394-44361-6). Knopf.
Same Door. John Updike. 1971. pap. 0.95 o.p. (M520, Prem). Fawcett World.
Same Door: Short Stories. John Updike. LC 59-9776. 1959. Knopf.
Same Door: Short Stories. John Updike. LC 81-40079. 1981. 4.95 (ISBN 0-394-74763-1). Vintage Books.
Same Last Name. Kathleen G. Seidel. (American Romance Ser.). 192p. 1983. pap. 2.25. Harlequin Bks.
Same Old Grind: A Novel. Judy Roe. LC 75-10578. 1975. 8.95. (ISBN 0-89087-985-0) (ISBN 0-89087-900-1). Les Femmes Pub.
Same Person. Anna Robeson Brown Burr. LC 31-11002. 1931. Duffield & Company.
Same River Twice. Corinne Demas Bliss. LC 82-45169. 1982. 12.95 (ISBN 0-689-11306-4). Atheneum.
Same Scourge. 1st American Ed. John Goldthorpe. LC 56-6489. 1956. Patnam.
Same Thing Happened Over & Over see Novella Box.
Same Thing Happening Over and Over. Leonard Chabrowe. LC 76-3359. (Illus.). 1976. 3.00 (ISBN 0-912292-40-7). The Smith.
Same Way Home. Rupert Croft-Cooke. LC 40-12262. 1940. The Macmillan Company.
Saml. Pepys, Listener. Robert Massie Freeman & Drinkwater, John. LC 32-55996. 1931. E. P. Dutton & Co., Inc.
Sammy Bo Everett. M. S. Webber. 3.00 o.p. Carlton.
Sammy's Service Star: The Story of a Christmas Angel. Georgene Faulkner. LC 18-3016. R. F. Seymour.
Samoubiitsa. Nikolai Erdman. (Rus.). 1980. 12.00 (ISBN 0-88233-402-6); pap. 3.50 (ISBN 0-88233-403-4). Ardis Pubs.
Samovar Girl. Frederick Ferdinand Moore. LC 21-103353. 1921. D. Appleton and Company.
Samples: A Collection of Short Stories. The Community Workers of the New York Guild for the Jewish Blind. Ed. by Ryttenberg, Lillie. Ade, George. LC 27-208275. Boni & Liveright.
Sampson Rideout, Quaker. Una Lucy Silberrad. LC 11-8100. 1911. T. Nelson and Sons.
Sampson Rock, of Wall Street: A Novel. Edwin Lefevre. LC 7-821692. 1907. Harper & Brothers.
Sam's Kid. Florence Ethel Mills Young. LC 11-12452. 1911. John Lane.
Sam's Legacy. Jay Mengebower. LC 73-8249. 320p. 1974. 8.95 o.p. (ISBN 0-03-011436-5, HoltC). HR&W.
Sam's Legacy: A Novel. Jay Neugeboren. LC 73-8249. 1974. 8.95 (ISBN 0-03-011436-5). Holt, Rinehart and Winston.
Sam's Song. Shirley Schoonover. LC 69-11061. 1969. 4.95. Coward-McCann.
Sam's Sweetheart, by Helen B. Mathers... Helen Buckingham Mathers Reeves. LC 7-30675. (On cover: Lovell's library. no. 1047). 1887. J. W. Lovell Company.
Sams Wang's College: Or, China Won. Charles Buttz Titus. LC 25-6704. The Christopher Publishing House.
Samskara: A Rite for a Dead Man. Anantha Murthy, U. R. LC 76-902708. 1976. 3.00 (ISBN 0-19-560687-6). Oxford University Press.
Samskara: A Rite for a Dead Man. U. R. Murthy. Tr. by A. K. Ramnujan. (Three Crowns Books). 1976. pap. 3.00x (ISBN 0-19-561079-2). Oxford U Pr.
Samson. David Langstone Bolt. LC 80-14715. 1980. 12.95 (ISBN 0-312-69848-8). St. Martin's Press.
Samson. Thomas E Roach. LC 53-11333. Meador Pub. Co.
Samson. Robert Collyer Washburn. LC 28-22059. J. H. Sears & Company, Inc.
Samson Agonistes see Paradise Lost.
Samson and Delilah: A Novel. Felix Salten & Chambers, Whittaker, Tr. LC 31-9300. 1931. Simon and Schuster.
Samson Catches a Mystery. Le Grand, pseud. (Illus.). 1962. 3.50 o.p. (ISBN 0-395-06884-3). HM.
Samson Duke: A Novel. Seymour Kern. LC 75-182520. 1972. 7.95 (ISBN 0-8202-0096-4). Sherbourne Press.
Samson Riddle. Mankowitz. 8.95 (ISBN 0-87677-102-9). Hartmore.
Samson Strike. Tony Williamson. LC 79-55593. 1980. 8.95 (ISBN 0-689-11061-8). Atheneum.
Samson Touch. Charles Whited. (Signet Book). 1975. (pbk.) 1.75. New American Library.
Samson's Deal. Rochelle Singer. LC 83-2901. 1983. 11.95 (ISBN 0-312-69849-6). St. Martin's Press.
Samuel Beckett: a Study of His Novels. Eugene Webb. LC 73-103289. 1970. 6.95. University of Washington Press.
Samuel Beckett Reader. Ed. by Richard Seaver. 1971. pap. 1.95 o.p. (B277, BC). Grove.
Samuel Brannan and the Golden Fleece: A Biography. Reva Lucile Holdaway Scott. LC 44-4871. 1944. The Macmillan Company.
Samuel Brohl and Company. Victor Cherbuliez. LC 18-4339. (Half-title: Collection of foreign authors, no. 1). 1878. D. Appleton and Company.
Samuel Brohl and Company. Victor Cherbuliez & Moore, Mrs. Annie Aubertine (Woodward) 1841- Tr. LC 6-26966. (On cover: Collection of foreign authors, no. 1). 1877. D. Appleton and Company.
Samuel Brohl and Partner. Victor Cherbuliez. LC 6-26965. (On cover: Lovell's library. v. 5, no. 242). 1883. J. W. Lovell Company.
Samuel Drummond. Thomas Alexander Boyd. LC 25-16486. 1925. C. Scribner's Sons.
Samuel Lyle, Criminologist. Arthur Crabb. LC 74-121531. (Short story index reprint series). (Illus.). 1970. Books for Libraries Press.
Samuel Lyle: Criminologist. illustrated by s. c. coll. ed. Arthur Crabb. LC 20-17409. 1920. 1.90. The Century Co.
Samuel Pepys of the Navy: A Biographical Novel. Kay McKemy. LC 77-85217. (Illus.). 1970. 4.95. F. Warne.
Samuel Richardson: By A. M. Kearney. A. M Kearney & Samuel Richardson. LC 68-104412. (Profiles in lit. ser.). 1968. 2.75, 1.45 pap.,. Routledge & K. Paul.
Samuel the Seeker. Upton Beall Sinclair. LC 10-8163. 1910. B. W. Dodge & Company.
Samurai. Shusaku Endo. Tr. by Van C. Gessel from Japanese. LC 82-57851. 272p. 1982. 12.45i (ISBN 0-06-859852-1, HarpT). Har-Row.
Samurai. George MacBeth. LC 75-2234. 1975. 6.95 (ISBN 0-15-179270-4). Harcourt, Brace, Jovanovich.
Samurai. George MacBeth. (Signet Book). 1976. 1.95. New American Library.
Samurai. Hisako Matsubara. LC 79-51443. 9.95 (ISBN 0-8129-0852-X). Times Books.
Samurai: A Novel. Shusaku Endo. LC 82-47851. 12.95. Harper & Row: Kodansha International.
San Celestino. Francis Browning Drew Bickerstaffe-Drew. LC 9-27446. 1909. G. P. Putnam's Sons.
San Diego Lightfoot Sue and Other Stories. Tom Reamy. LC 79-54396. 1979. 14.95 (ISBN 0-935128-00-X) (ISBN 0-935128-01-8). Earth Light Publishers.
San Diego: Plaza Sitiada. Don Pendleton. Tr. by Osvaldo J. Blanco. (Compadre Collection, El Verdugo Ser: No. 14). 1976. pap. 0.95 (ISBN 0-88473-314-9). Fiesta Pub.
San Diego Sailor. Tony Barron. LC 73-8664. 1969. 1.75. Monkey Publication.
San Fairy Ann, Ca Ne Fait Rien: A Love Story of the Great War. Hugh Kimber. LC 27-23255. J. H. Sears & Company, Inc.
San Felipians. Roger Cowles. LC 32-20149. 1932. C. Scribner's Sons.
San Franciscans: A Novel. Niven Busch. LC 61-583259. 1962. Simon and Schuster.
San Francisco. Parley J Cooper. (Kangaroo Book.). 1977. 1.95. (ISBN 0-671-80964-4). Pocket Books.
San Francisco. John Haase. 544p. 1983. pap. 3.50 (ISBN 0-523-41866-3). Pinnacle Bks.
San Francisco Adventures. Charles Caldwell Dobie. LC 70-101800. (Short story index reprint series). 1969. Books for Libraries Press.
San Francisco Adventures. Charles Caldwell Dobie. LC 37-20193. 1937. D. Appleton-Century Company, Incorporated.
San Francisco Tales. Charles Caldwell Dobie. LC 35-151575. 1935. D. Appleton-Century Company Incorporated.
San Gabriel Days. Margaret Price McConnell. 1913. Publishing House of the Pentecostal Church of the Nazarene.
San Isidro. Mary Bradford Crowinshield. LC 99-5615. 1900. H. S. Stone & Company.
San Isidro. Mary Bradford Crowninshield. LC 41-32204. 1906. Duffield & Company.
San Juan. John Houghton Allen & Bugbee, Harold Dow, 1900- Illus. LC 45-11124. 1945.
San Juan Hill: By Will Henry Pseud. Henry Allen. LC 62-8447. 1962. Random House.
San Juan: Or, The Fall of the Tyrant. St. Justin Beale. LC 99-2494. (On cover: Neely's universal library. no. 61). F. T. Neely.
San Luis of Apalache: A Tale of Early American Life. Mary Bethell Alfriend. LC 39-29732. Chapman & Grimes.
San Pasqual: A Tale of Old Pasadena. Charlotte Bronto Herr. LC 24-19330. The Post Printing and Binding Co.
San Patricios. Ralph Hayes. 1982. pap. price not set o.p. (ISBN 0-8439-1106-9, LB427KK, Leisure Bks). Nordon Pubns.
San Patricios. Ralph Hayes. (Leisure Book). 1.75. Nordon Publications.
San Rosario Ranch. Maud Howe Elliott. LC 6-37779. 1884. Roberts Brothers.
San Salvador. Mary Agnes Tincker. LC 77-11319. (American Catholic Tradition). 1978. 20.00 (ISBN 0-405-10864-8). Arno Press.
San Salvador a Novel. Mary Agnes Tincker. LC 8-27018. 1892. Houghton, Mifflin and Company.
Sanatorium. Paul Dufualt. (Novels by Franco-Americans in New England 1850-1940 Ser.). 153p. (Fr.). (gr. 10 up). 1982. pap. 4.50x (ISBN 0-911409-23-8). Natl Mat Dev.
Sanatorium: A Novel. Donald Stewart. LC 30-332641. 1930. Harper & Brothers.
Sanatorium Under the Sign of the Hourglass. Bruno Schulz. LC 79-17564. (Writers from the Other Europe). (Illus.). 1979. Penguin Books.
Sanchez, and Other Stories. Richard Dokey. LC 80-154986. (Gusto Press Regional Series). 4.75 (ISBN 0-933906-14-5). Gusto.
Sancho, or. The Proverbialist. John William Cunningham. LC 6-31728. 1817. Published by Wells and Lilly. Sold by Van Winkle & Wiley, New York--and M. Carey and Son, Philadelphia.
S'Ancrer. Ibbie Raymond. LC 6-44371. 1906.
Sancroft Sisters: A Novel of the Nineteen-Twenties. Beatrice Curtis Brown, pseud. LC 34-35307. G. P. Putnam's Sons.
Sanction. William W. Johnstone. 1981. pap. 2.95 (ISBN 0-89083-775-9). Zebra.
Sanctity. Dennis Selby. pap. 1.25 o.s.i. (78-672). Lancer.
Sanctity: Or, There's No Such Thing As a Naked Sailor. Dennis Selby. LC 69-14285. 1969. 4.95. Simon and Schuster.
Sanctuary. William Faulkner. LC 32-26345. (Half-title: The modern library of the world's best books). The Modern Library.
Sanctuary. Mary Howard Hoopes. LC 12-17513. 1.25. Lothrop, Lee, & Shepard Co.
Sanctuary. Frank Arthur Swinnerton. LC 67-16793. 1967. Doubleday.
Sanctuary. Edith Newbold Jones Wharton. LC 70-104592. (Illus.). 1970. (ISBN 0-8398-2160-3). Literature House.
Sanctuary. Edith Newbold Jones Wharton. LC 3-26865. 1903. C. Scribner's Sons.
Sanctuary, a Novel. Heber Sensenig. LC 41-9502. Dorrance and Company.
Sanctuary: A Story of the Civil War. George Ward Nichols. 1866. Harper & Brothers.
Sanctuary Five. Budd Schulberg. LC 71-93470. 1970. 6.95 o.p. (HO321, NAL). Norton.
Sanctuary in Love. Lawrence Howard. LC 78-66221. 1979. 5.95 o.p. (ISBN 0-533-04153-8). Vantage.
Sanctuary. Introd. by Allen Tate. William Faulkner. (Signet modern classic, CQ413). 1968. New Amer. Lib.
Sanctuary: The Original Text. William Faulkner & Noel Polk. LC 80-23475. 14.95 (ISBN 0-394-51278-2). Random House.
Sanctury. William Faulkner. LC 31-418296. J. Cape & H. Smith.
Sanctus Spiritus and Company. Edward Alfred Steiner. LC 19-16663. George H. Doran Company.
Sand. Olive Wadsley. LC 22-19219. 1922. Cassell and Company, Ltd.
Sand. Olive Wadsley. LC 22-186732. 1922. Dodd, Mead and Company.
Sand Against the Wind: By Lewis Arnold Pseud. 1st Ed. David Evans. LC 54-503151. 1954. Dutton.
Sand and Cactus. Wolcott Le Clear Beard. LC 99-4154. 1899. C. Scribner's Sons.
Sand & Satin. Sax Rohmer, pseud. 1978. 6.50. Bookfinger.
Sand and Shells. Nautical Sketches. James Hannay. 1854. G. Routledge and Co.
Sand and Water. Frank Longenecker. LC 33-38688. The Best Sellers Co.
Sand Castle. Walter Millis. LC 29-4535. 1929. Houghton Mifflin Company.
Sand Castle: A Novel. Janet Beith. LC 36-312347. 1936. Frederick A. Stokes Company.
Sand Castles. Louise Montague Athearn. LC 74-16573. 1975. 7.95 (ISBN 0-399-11468-8). Putnam.
Sand Castles. Louise Montague Athearn. (Berkley Medallion Book). 1976. (pbk.) 1.95 (ISBN 0-425-03130-6). Berkley Publishing Corp.
Sand Castles. Frank Camper. (Orig.). 1980. pap. 2.25 (ISBN 0-532-23132-5). Woodhill.
Sand Castles. Louise M. Montague. LC 74-16573. 320p. 1975. 7.95 o.p. (ISBN 0-399-11468-8). Putnam.
Sand Doctor. Arnold Mulder. LC 21-275572. 1921. 2.00. Houghton Mifflin Company.
Sand Dollars. Robert Terrall. LC 77-18367. 8.95 (ISBN 0-312-69908-5). St. Martin's Press.
Sand Dollars. Robert Terrall. 1979. 2.25 (ISBN 0-440-17529-1). Dell Pub. Co., Inc.
Sand Fortress. John Coriolan. (O.s.i.). (Orig.). 1968. pap. 0.95 o.s.i. (A363N, Award). Univ Pub. & Dist.
Sand Fortress. John Coriolan. (O.s.i.). 1976. pap. 1.75 o.s.i. (AR1646, Award). Univ Pub & Dist.
Sand Hiller. John Coleman. LC 44-5092. 1944. B. Humphries, Inc.
Sand-Hills of Jutland. Hans Christian Andersen. 1860. Ticknor and Fields.
Sand Holler. Belle Kanaris Maniates. LC 20-17656. The Reilly & Lee Co.
Sand in the Wind. Robert Roth. LC 73-8768. (Illus.). 1973. 8.95 (ISBN 0-316-75765-9). Little, Brown.
Sand 'n' Bushes. Maria Louise Pool. LC 99-1057. 1899. H. S. Stone & Company.
Sand of Saturn. Robert French. (Orig.). 1979. pap. 1.95 (ISBN 0-532-23334-4). Woodhill.
Sand Pebbles. Richard McKenna. LC 62-15726. 1963. 11.95 o.p. (ISBN 0-06-012910-7, HarpT). Har-Row.
Sand Rose. Margaret Summerton. LC 71-84386. 1969. 4.50. Published for the Crime Club by Doubleday.
Sanda Mala. Maurice Collis. LC 40-27140. Carrick & Evans, Inc.
Sandals: A Tale of Palestine. Zelotes Grenel. LC 2-8806. (The hour-glass stories, 2). 1902. Funk & Wagnalls Company.
Sandalwood. Fulton Oursler. LC 25-8372.
Sandalwood Fan. Diana Brown. LC 83-2894. 1983. 13.95 (ISBN 0-312-69909-3). St. Martin's.
Sandalwood Fan. Thomas McMorrow. LC 28-20417. J. H. Sears & Company, Inc.
Sandalwood Fan: A Novel of Suspense. Katherine Wigmore Eyre. LC 68-28723. 1968. 4.95. Meredith Press.
Sandalwood Mountains: Readings & Stories of the Early Chinese in Hawaii. Ed. by Tin-Yuke Char. LC 74-76375. 400p. 1975. 14.95 (ISBN 0-8248-0305-1). UH Pr.
Sandalwood Slipper: Or, Nick Carter's Isle of Safety. Nick Carter & Dey, Frederic Van Rensselaer. LC 34-382754. (On cover: New magnet library. no. 846). Street & Smith.
Sandbar Sinister. Phoebe Atwood Taylor. 1971. pap. 0.75 o.p. (T2529). Pyramid Pubns.
Sandbar Sinister. Phoebe Atwood Taylor. 1968. 4.95 o.p. (ISBN 0-393-08523-6). Norton.
Sandbar Sinister: An Asey Mayo Mystery. Phoebe Atwood Taylor. LC 34-21695. W. W. Norton & Company, Inc.
Sandbox Tree. Thomas J Fleming. LC 70-118341. 1970. 7.95. Morrow.
Sandburrs. Alfred Henry Lewis. LC 72-90585. (Short story index reprint series). (Illus.). 1969. Books for Libraries Press.
Sandburrs. Alfred Henry Lewis. LC 72-104512. (Illus.). 1970. Literature House.

Sandburrs Short Stories. Alfred Henry Lewis. LC 1955. F. A. Stokes Company.
Sandcastle. Iris Murdoch. 1978. pap. 3.95 (ISBN 0-14-001474-8). Penguin.
Sandcastle: A Novel. Iris Murdoch. 1973. 1.25. Warner Paperback Library.
Sandcastle: A Novel. Iris Murdoch. LC 57-7554. 1957. Viking Press.
Sandcastle Murder. Elizabeth St. Clair. (Mystery Puzzler: No. 24). (Illus., Orig.). 1979. pap. 1.95 (ISBN 0-89083-478-4). Zebra.
Sandcatcher. Stuart Brooke Jackman. LC 79-23239. 1980. 8.95 (ISBN 0-689-11026-X). Atheneum.
Sandcats of Rhyl. Robert E. Vardeman. 1978. pap. 1.50 (ISBN 0-89041-209-X, 3209). Major Bks.
Sanders of the River. Edgar Wallace. 1930. Doubleday, Doran & Company, Inc.
Sandhill Sundays and Other Recollections. Mari Sandoz. LC 78-82707. 1970. 5.00. University of Nebraska Press.
Sandhog: By Borden Chase. Borden Chase. LC 39-178095. The Penn Publishing Company.
Sanditon. Jane Austen & Anne Telscombe. (Signet Book). 1976. (pbk.) 1.95. New American Library.
Sanditon. Jane Austen & Anne Telscombe. LC 74-20584. 1975. (ISBN 0-395-20284-1). Houghton Mifflin.
Sanditon: An Unfinished Novel. Jane Austen & B. C Southam. LC 76-353971. 1975. 14.75 (ISBN 0-19-812556-9). Clarendon Press.
Sandkings. George R. R. Martin. (Orig.). 1981. pap. 2.75 (ISBN 0-671-42663-X, Timescape). PB.
Sandler Inquiry. Noel Hynd. LC 77-10184. 8.95 (ISBN 0-8037-7545-8). Dial Press.
Sandler Inquiry. Noel Hynd. (Dell Book). 1979. 2.50 (ISBN 0-440-17958-0). Dell Publishing Co.
Sandling Case. Louis Tracy. LC 31-3506. E. J. Clode, Inc.
Sandman. Robert Ward. LC 78-54040. 7.95 (ISBN 0-89256-064-9). Rawson Associates.
Sandman. Robert Ward. 1979. 2.50 (ISBN 0-440-16064-2). Dell Publishing Co.
Sandollar. Charles Neville Buck. LC 27-14967. Chelsea House.
Sandoval: A Romance of Bad Manners. Thomas Beer. LC 24-12286. 1924. A. A. Knopf.
Sandoval: Or, The Freemason. A Spanish Tale. Valentin Llanos Gutierrez. LC 7-25457. 1826. E. Bliss & E. White Etc.
Sandpeep. Sara Elisabeth Siegrist Boggs. LC 6-14752. 1906. Little, Brown, and Company.
Sandra. Pearl Doles Bell. LC 24-401158. W. J. Watt & Co.
Sandra. Vida Hurst. LC 33-785. Grosset & Dunlap.
Sandra Belloni: Originally Emilia in England. rev. ed. George Meredith. LC 1-20260. 1897. C. Scribner's Sons.
Sandra Effect. James Lumpp. 1978. pap. 1.75 (ISBN 0-532-17183-7). Woodhill.
Sandra Mitchell Stands by. Elisabeth Carleton Lansing. LC 44-433041. 1944. Thomas Y. Crowell Company.
Sandra Rifkin's Jewels. Roy Doliner. (Signet bk., P3108). 1968. New Amer. Lib.
Sandra Rifkin's Jewels. Roy Doliner. LC 66-13372. 1966. New American Library.
Sandra Street & Other Stories. Michael Anthony. (Heinemann Secondary Readers Ser.). 1973. pap. text ed. 3.00x (ISBN 0-435-92512-1). Heinemann Ed.
Sandro Iz Chegema: Sandro from Chegem. Fazil Iskander. 1979. 20.00 o.p. (ISBN 0-88233-392-5); pap. 10.00 o.p. (ISBN 0-88233-394-1). Ardis Pubs.
Sandro of Chegem. Fazil Iskander. Tr. by Susan Brownsberger from Russian. LC 82-13219. 416p. (Orig.). 1983. pap. 8.95 (ISBN 0-394-71516-0, Vin). Random.
Sands of Destiny. Ethel Lockwood. 192p. (OSI). 1972. 3.95 o.s.i. Lenox Hill.
Sands of Fortune. Alan Sullivan. LC 28-151573. 1928. E. P. Dutton & Company.
Sands of Gold. Kathlyn Rhodes. LC 19-12251. 1919. Duffield & Company.
Sands of Kalahari: A Novel. William Mulvihill, pseud. LC 60-8479. 1960. Putnam.
Sands of Karakorum. James Ramsey Ullman. LC 53-8929. 1953. Lippincott.
Sands of Malibu. Alice Morgan. (Candlelight Ecstasy Ser.: No. 54). (Orig.). 1982. pap. 1.75 (ISBN 0-440-18112-7). Dell.
Sands of Mars. Arthur Charles Clarke. LC 52-10185. 1952. Gnome Press.
Sands of Mars. Arthur Charles Clarke. LC 67-2596. 1967. Harcourt, Brace & World.
Sands of Oro. Beatrice Ethel Grimshaw. LC 24-1646. 1924. Doubleday, Page & Company.
Sands of Pleasure. Filson Young. LC 16-13104. D. Estes & Co.
Sands of Summer: A Novel. David Pryce-Jones. LC 64-21919. 1964. Holt, Rinehart and Winston.
Sands of Sylt: An Episode of the North Sea Before the War. Maurice Griffiths. LC 46-2253. 1945. Rich & Cowan.
Sands of the Desert. Helen A Carey. House of Field, Inc.
Sands of Time. Peter Dagmar. LC 67-5179. 1967. Arcadia House.
Sands of Valor. Geoffrey Atheling Wagner. LC 67-11134. 1967. Knopf.
Sands of Windee. Arthur William Upfield. 1968. 4.50 o.p. (ISBN 0-8277-0128-4). British Bk Ctr.
Sands of Windee. Arthur William Upfield. 1967. Repr. pap. 1.60 o.s.i. Tri-Ocean.
Sands of Xapa. Tom Walters. LC 67-29490. 1968. Dorrance.
Sands Run Red. C. J. Floyd. (Assault Ser.). (O.s.i.). (Orig.). 1976. pap. 1.25 o.s.i. (AQ1504, Award). Univ Pub & Dist.
Sands Run Red. C. J Floyd. (Assault Series # 3). 1976. (pbk.) 1.25. Award Books.
Sands Street. William Bogart. LC 42-15006. 1942. J. Swift.
Sandsong. Alex Cord. 1976. (pbk.) 1.75. Warner Books.
Sandstone. Robert Rhode. LC 82-60150. 11.95 (ISBN 0-8027-4015-4). Walker.
Sandstorm. Anne Mather. (Harlequin Presents Ser.). 192p. 1980. pap. 1.50 (ISBN 0-373-10382-4, Pub. by Harlequin). PB.
Sandworld. Richard A Lupoff. (Berkley Medallion Book). 1976. (pbk.) 1.25 (ISBN 0-425-03116-0). Berkley Publishing Corp.
Sandy. Samuel Rutherford Crockett. LC 14-221220. 1914. 1.35. The Macmillan Company.
Sandy". Elenore Meherin. LC 26-12465. Grosset & Dunlap.
Sandy. Alice Caldwell Hegan Rice. LC 5-10054. 1905. The Century Co.
Sandy. Alice Caldwell Hegan Rice. LC 16-250214. 1911. The Century Co.
Sandy. Della A Ricker. LC 47-19082. 1947. Meador Publishing Company.
Sandy: A Novel. John Burton Thompson. LC 53-242922. 1953. Woodford Press.
Sandy & Alex & Daphnis & Leonie. pap. 1.95 o.p. (V1044T, Venus). Grove.
Sandy and the Lavender Tub. Nell Marr Dean. LC 63-6705. 1963. Avalon Books.
Sandy from the Sierras. Richard Hayes Barry. LC 7-7190. 1906. Moffat, Yard & Company.
Sandy Joe. Mary Teresa Waggaman. LC 17-6993. 1916. Benziger Brothers.
Sandy MacDonald's Man: A Tale of the Mackinaw Fur Trade. Richard Clyde Ford. LC 29-14143. Michigan School Service, Inc.
Sandy of Skyline. Amos Moore. LC 35-75335. 1935. I. Washburn.
Sandy Trails. Clara Holton Ulseth. LC 47-669794. 1947. House of Field-Doubleday.
Sandy Was a Soldier's Boy: A Fable. Illustrated by Dobson Broadhead. David Harry Walker. LC 57-9024. 1957. Houghton Mifflin.
Sane Lunatic. Clara Louise Root Burnham. LC 6-19673. ("Hammock series." no. 4). 1882. H. A. Sumner and Company.
Sanfelice: A Novel. Vincent Sheean. LC 36-12313. Doubleday, Doran & Co., Inc.
Sanfield Scandal. Clifford James Wheeler Hosken. LC 29-17315. 1929. Harper & Brothers.
Sangaree. Frank Gill Slaughter. LC 75-31890. 1975. 9.95 (ISBN 0-89190-283-X). American Reprint Co.
Sangaree. Frank Gill Slaughter. LC 48-8734. 1948. Doubleday.
Sanglorians Run. Peter Vincent. LC 75-131922. (Illus.). 1971. 5.95. Delacorte Press.
Sanguman. 3.95 o.p. Brown Bk.
Sanhedrin Papers, Including the Gospel of Judas. Charles A Schafer. 1973. 5.95 (ISBN 0-533-00537-X). Vantage.
Sanine. Mikhail Petrovich Artsybashev & Pinkerton, Percy E., Tr. LC 15-4668. 1915. B. W. Huebsch.
Sanine. 19th impression. ed. Mikhail Petrovich Artsybashev & Pinkerton, Percy E., Tr. LC 24-20485. 1922. B. W. Huebsch, Inc.
Sanine. Mikhail Petrovich Artsybashev & Pinkerton, Percy E., Tr. LC 26-4061. 1926. The Viking Press.
Sanine. Mikhail Petrovich Artsybashev & Pinkerton, Percy E., Tr. LC 31-30268. (Half-title: The modern library of the world's best books). 1931. The Modern Library.
Sanine: A Russian Love Novel. Mikhail Petrovich Artsybashev & Wright, Cameron, Illus. LC 32-19267. Illustrated Editions Company.
Sanitary Mary. Jewel Montreu. LC 34-23654. 1934. Meador Publishing Company.
Sanity Inspectors: By Friedrich Deich Pseud. Translated by Robert Kee. Friedrich August Weeren. LC 57-5688. 1957. Rinehart.
Sanjo. Evelyn Wilde Mayerson. LC 78-27300. 5.95 (ISBN 0-397-01348-5). Lippincott.
Sanna: A Novel. Mary Ella Waller. LC 5-12391. 1905. Harper & Brothers.
Sanna of the Island Town. new ed. Mary Ella Waller. LC 12-8412. 1912. Little, Brown, and Company.
Sanpriel: The Promised Land. Alvilde Prydz. Tr. by Coddington, Hester. LC 14-10523. 1.25. R. G. Badger; Etc., Etc.
Sans Famille. Hector Henri Malot & Meade, Ruth Elizabeth, Ed. LC 31-5544. (Half-title: The Chicago French series. O. F. Bond, editor). The University of Chicago Press.
Sans Famille. rev. ed. Hector Henri Malot & Meade, Ruth Elizabeth, Ed. LC 32-15184. (Half-title: The Chicago French series, O. F. Bond, editor). The University of Chicago Press.
Sans Famille. Hector Henri Malot & Thieme, Hugo Paul, 1870- Ed. LC 2-20021. 1902. H. Holt and Company.
Sans Famille. Hector Henry Malot & Storer, Walter Henry, 1898- Ed. LC 31-306421. American Book Company.
Sans Merci: Or, Kestrels and Falcons. George Alfred Lawrence. LC 24-14919. 1892. G. Routledge and Sons.
Sanshiro. Natsume Soseki. Tr. by Jay Rubin from Japanese. (Perigee Japanese Library). 248p. 1982. pap. 5.95 (ISBN 0-399-50613-6, Perige). Putnam Pub Group.
Sanshiro: A Novel. Soseki Natsume & Jay Rubin. LC 77-3680. 14.95 (ISBN 0-295-95558-9). University of Washington Press.
Sanshiro: A Novel. Soseki Natsume & Jay Rubin. LC 81-15428. 1982. 4.95 (ISBN 0-399-50613-6). Putnam.
Sanshiro: A Novel. Natsume Soseki. Tr. by Jay Rubin from Japanese. LC 77-3680. 258p. 1977. 14.95 o.p. (ISBN 0-295-95558-9). U of Wash Pr.
Sansho-Dayu & Other Short Stories. Tr. by Tsutomu Fukuda. 1970. pap. 5.95 (ISBN 0-89346-038-9, Pub. by Hokuseido Pr). Heian Intl.
Sant' Ilarid. Francis Marion Crawford. LC 3-22370. 1889. Macmillan and Co.
Sant' Ilario. Francis Marion Crawford. LC 42-891. 1897. The Macmillan Company.
Sant' Ilario. Francis Marion Crawford. LC 29-222077. 1926. The Macmillan Company.
Sant' Illario. Francis Marion Crawford. LC 33-17490. 1893. Macmillan and Co.
Santa Ana Wind. Sharon Ashton. LC 74-2787. 1974. 4.95 (ISBN 0-385-08214-2). Published for Crime Club by Doubleday.
Santa Ana Wind. Helen Van Slyke. LC 82-6065. 1982. 11.95 (ISBN 0-8161-3388-3). G.K. Hall.
Santa Ana Wind. Helen Van Slyke. 224p. 1981. pap. 2.95 (ISBN 0-445-04687-2). Popular Lib.
Santa-Baby. Vesle Fenstermaker. LC 75-11329. 1975. 6.95 (ISBN 0-385-09652-6). Doubleday.
Santa Barbara: And Other Stories. Louise De La Ramee. LC 6-33312. United States Book Company.
Santa Barbara: And Other Stories. Louise De La Ramee. 1901. Street & Smith.
Santa Barbara and Other Stories. Louise De La Ramee. LC 6-33312. United States Book Company.
Santa Claus Killer. A. H Garnet. LC 81-1255. 1981. 12.95 (ISBN 0-89919-029-4). Ticknor & Fields.
Santa Claus's Baby, and Other Christmas Stories: By John Coleman Adams. John Coleman Adams. LC 11-316351. 1911. The Murray Press.
Santa Dolores Stage: A Story of Hashknife Hartley. Wilbur C Tuttle. LC 34-220318. 1934. Houghton Mifflin Company.
Santa Fe. Jonathan Richards. 288p. 1982. pap. 2.95 (ISBN 0-445-04704-6). Popular Lib.
Santa Fe Passage: By Clay Fisher Pseud. Henry Allen. LC 52-5254. 1952. Houghton Mifflin.
Santa Fe Passage: By Clay Fisher Pseud. Henry Allen. LC 57-4091. (Pocket book 1186. Western 6). 1957. Pocket Books.
Santa Fe's Partner: Being Some Memorials of Events in a New-Mexican Track-End Town. Thomas Allibone Janvier. LC 7-29432. 1907. Harper & Brothers.
Santa Lucia: A Common Story. Mary Hunter Austin. 1908. Harper & Brothers.
Santa Rogelia. Palacio Valdes, Armando & Schug, Howard Lesher, Ed. LC 41-8099. 1941. F. S. Crofts & Co.
Santal. Arthur Annesley Ronald Firbank. LC 55-6323. Bonacio &Saul.
Santana Enslaved. John Cleve, pseud. LC 81-85828. (Spaceways Ser.: No. 4). 224p. (Orig.). 1982. pap. 2.50 (ISBN 0-86721-111-3). Playboy Pbks.
Santana, the Hero Dog of France. Ernest Thompson Seton. LC 45-6213. 1945. The Phoenix Press.
Santanic Condition. David Thoreau. LC 80-66499. 1981. 13.95 (ISBN 0-87795-274-4). Arbor Hse.
Santan's Realm. Edgar C Blum. LC 99-4368. 1899. Rand, McNally & Company.
Santaroga Barrier. Frank Herbert. LC 77-49. 1977. 7.95 (ISBN 0-399-11944-2). Berkley Pub. Corp.: Distributed by Putnam.
Santee Massacre. Robert J. Steelman. (Orig.). 1982. pap. 1.95 (ISBN 0-440-17967-X). Dell.
Santi: The Brief Career of a Modern Young Criminal. Roy Alvin Baldwin. LC 29-993273. Meador Publishing Company.
Santone, a Story of the Texas Rangers. W. D Hoffman. LC 29-11404. 1920. A. C. McClurg & Co.
Sao Bernardo: A Novel. Graciliano Ramos. LC 78-27169. 1979. 7.95 (ISBN 0-8008-6991-5). Taplinger Pub. Co.
Sapbucket Genius, a Novel. 1st Ed. Sichel, Pierre. LC 60-7849. 1960. Lippincott.
Saphira and the Slave Girl. Willa Sibert Cather. LC 74-20797. 1975. 2.95 (ISBN 0-394-71434-2). Vintage Books.
Sapho. Alphonse Daudet. 1966. 4.95 o.p. French & Eur.
Sapho: Moeurs Parisiennes. Alphonse Daudet. 1949. 10.25 o.p. (ISBN 0-8371-4087-0). Greenwood.
Sapho: Parisian Customs... Alphonse Daudet. Tr. by Rogerson, T. F. (Roman contemporain. Realists. v. 5). 1897. G. Barrie & Son.
Saplin Ridge Letters. Harry Price Sturm. LC 64-891. 1963. Education Foundation.
Saplings: A Novel. Irene Stiles. 1929. Rae D. Henkle Co., Inc.
Sapphira and the Slave Girl. Willa Sibert Cather. 1940. A. A. Knopf.
Sapphira and the Slave Girl. Willa Sibert Cather. LC 41-19126. 1941. Houghton Mifflin Company.
Sapphire. Alfred Edward Woodley Mason. LC 33-4988. 1933. Doubleday, Doran & Company, Inc.
Sapphire and the Pearl. Audrey Curling. 1973. (pbk.) 0.75. Ace.
Sapphire Bracelet: By Edward Salisburgy Field; Illustrations by Will Grefe. Edward Salisbury Field. LC 10-22931. 1.25. W. J. Watt & Company.
Sapphire Conference. Peter Graaf, pseud. LC 59-9370. (Chantecler mystery novel). 1959. Washburn.
Sapphire Legacy. Rachel Cosgrove Payes. (Berkley Medallion) (ISBN 0-425-03185-3). Berkley.
Sapphire Lotus. Betty Hale Hyatt. LC 82-45640. (Starlight Romance Ser.). 192p. 1983. 11.95 (ISBN 0-385-17909-X). Doubleday.
Sapphire Ring. Marjorie Warby. 1972. pap. 0.75 o.p. (94222). Beagle Bks.
Sapphires. Vernon Knowles. LC 77-84243. (Lost Race and Adult Fantasy Fiction). (Illus.). 1978. 30.00 (ISBN 0-405-10989-X). Arno Press.
Sapphires: Here & Otherwhere & Silver Nutmegs, 2 vols. in 1. Vernon Knowles. Ed. by R. Reginald & Douglas Melville. LC 77-84243. (Lost Race & Adult Fantasy Ser.). (Illus.). 1978. Repr. of 1927 ed. lib. bdg. 30.00x (ISBN 0-405-10989-X). Ayer Co.
Sapphires on Wednesday. 1st Ed. Malcolm Gair. LC 57-630458. 1957. Published for the Crime Club by Doubleday.
Sappho. Alphonse Daudet. LC 51-27397. (Avon pocket-size books, 294). Avon Pub. Co.
Sappho. Alphonse Daudet. LC 30-14832. 1930. The Golden Bough Press.
Sappho: A Picture of Life in Paris. Translated from the French by Eithne Wilkins. Alphonse Daudet. LC 51-141338. (Novel library 39). New York.
Sappho: A Realistic Novel. Alphonse Daudet. LC 22-4765. (On cover: The universal library. no. 43). 1892. Hurst and Company.
Sappho in Boston... Roland Alexander Wood-Seys. 1908. Moffat, Yard & Company.
Sappho of Green Springs: And Other Stories. Bret Harte. LC 7-3649. 1891. Houghton, Mifflin and Company.
Sappho of Lesbos. Jefferson Cooper, pseud. pap. 0.60 o.p. (53-920). Paperback Lib.
Sappho; Parisian Manners. Alphonse Daudet. LC 43-20446. G. Routledge and Sons, Limited.
Sappho's Island: A Novel. Byron Sorel. LC 64-1826. 1964. Adelphi Press.
Sar. John Robert Russell. 1974. (pbk.) 0.95 (ISBN 0-671-77726-2). Pocket Books.
Sara. Brian Talbot Cleeve. 1977. 1.95 (ISBN 0-446-89261-0). Warner Books.
Sara: A Princess. Fannie E Newberry. LC 7-17283. Bradley & Woodruff.
Sara: A Romance of the Early Nineteenth Century. Frances Stocker Hopkins. LC 12-27199. 1912. The Neale Publishing Company.
Sara Alone; a Novel. Nancie Stansfield Wilson Leitch. LC 34-10275. 1934. Doubleday, Doran & Company, Inc.
Sara Becomes a Witch. Rosalee Daughton. 80p. 1982. 7.95 (ISBN 0-89962-283-6). Todd & Honeywell.
Sara Dane. Catherine Gaskin. LC 55-62932. 1955. Lippincott.
Sara of Upper Dam. Jose Bergin King Burmeister. LC 25-762. George H. Doran Company.

Sara Videbeck and The Chapel. Carl Jonas Love Almquist & Benson, Adolph Burnett, 1881- Tr. LC 20-1696. (Half-title: Scandinavian classics, vol. xii). 1919. The American-Scandinavian Foundation; Etc., Etc.

Sara Videbeck. The Chapel. Carl Jonas Love Almquist. LC 77-185449. (Library of Scandinavian Literature, V. 13). 1972. 5.50. Twayne Publishers.

Saraband. Eliot Bliss. LC 81-30594. 1931. W. Morrow & Company.

Saraband for Dead Lovers. Helen De Guerry Simpson. LC 35-7015. 1935. Doubleday, Doran & Company, Inc.

Saraband for Two Sisters. Philippa Carr, pseud. 1977. pap. 2.25 (ISBN 0-449-23207-7, Crest). Fawcett.

Saraband for Two Sisters. Philippa Carr, pseud. LC 75-45062. 384p. 1976. 8.95 o.p. (ISBN 0-399-11746-6). Putnam Pub Group.

Saraband for Two Sisters. Philippa Carr. LC 75-45062. 384p. 1976. 8.95 o.p. (ISBN 0-399-11746-6). Putnam.

Saraband for Two Sisters. Eleanor Hibbert. (Fawcett Crest Book). 1977. 1.95 (ISBN 0-449-23207-7). Fawcett Pubns.

Sarabande: Authorized Adaptation from the Original Dutch by Lee Marlino. Mary Noothoven Van Goor & Lee Marlino. LC 50-14611. 1950. Exposition Press.

Sarabande for a Bitch. Mickey Dikes. pap. 1.75 o.p. (3011). Brandon.

Sarabande for a Bitch. Mickey Dikes. 207p. 1972. pap. 1.95 o.p. (ISBN 0-87056-265-7, 6265). Brandon.

Saracen Blade. Frank Yerby. 1973. (pbk.) 1.50. Dell.

Saracen Blade: A Novel. Frank Yerby. LC 52-5616. 1952. Dial Press.

Saracen Gardens. Mary Kay Simmons. (Dell book). 1974. (pbk.) 0.95. Dell.

Saracen: Or, Maltida and Malek Adel, a Crusade Romance, from the French of Madame Cottin, with an Historical Introduction. Marie Risteau Called Sophie Cottin & Michaud, Joseph Francois. LC 4-22091. 1810. Printed and Published by Isaac Riley.

Saracen's Head: Or, The Reluctant Crusader. Osbert Lancaster. LC 49-9963. 1949. Houghton Mifflin Co.

Saracinesca. Francis Marion Crawford. LC 12-19587. 1887. Macmillan and Co.

Saracinesca. Francis Marion Crawford. LC 33-17491. 1893. Macmillan and Co.

Saracinesca. Francis Marion Crawford. LC 21-21459. 1894. Macmillan and Co.

Saracinesca. Francis Marion Crawford. LC 4-15443. 1902. The Macmillan Company.

Saracinesca. Francis Marion Crawford. LC 99-5818. 1899. The Macmillan Company.

Saragossa: A Story of Spanish Valor. Galdos Benito Perez & Smith, Minna Caroline, 1860- Tr. LC 99-5314. 1899. Little, Brown, and Company.

Saragossa Manuscript: A Collection of Weird Tales. Edited and with Pref. by Roger Caillois. Translated from the French by Elisabeth Abbott. Jan Potocki. Ed. by Roger Caillois. LC 60-8360. 5.00. Orion Press.

Sarah. Margueritte Harmon Bro. LC 49-10405. 1949. Doubleday.

Sarah. Winifred Carter. LC 44-865954. 1943. Selwyn & Blount Ltd.

Sarah. Alycia De Dallas. 128p. 1976. 5.50 o.p. (ISBN 0-682-48541-1). Exposition.

Sarah. Gamelia. 1975. pap. 3.50 (ISBN 0-913054-09-7). Poet Gal Pr.

Sarah. Diane Pearson. LC 74-155439. 1971. 6.95. Lippincott.

Sarah: A Survival; a Novel. M. L. Lord. (On cover: Harper's Franklin square library, no. 751). 1894. Harper & Brothers.

Sarah and After: Five Women Who Founded a Nation. Lynne Reid Banks. LC 76-16250. 6.95. (ISBN 0-385-11456-7) (ISBN 0-385-11455-9). Doubleday.

Sarah and Her Daughter. Bertha Pearl Moore. LC 20-11892. 1920. T. Seltzer.

Sarah and Son. Alden Arthur Knipe. LC 29-15478. 1929. Dodd, Mead & Company.

Sarah Ann. Mabel Nelson Thurston. LC 17-23979. 1917. Dodd, Mead and Company.

Sarah Bernhardt Brown and What She Did in a Country Town: A Dramatic Novel. Charles Felton Pidgin. LC 6-1265. 1906. The J. K. Waters Company.

Sarah Dakota: A Novel. Mary Elizabeth Quackenbush Brush. LC 6-16413. 1894. Hunt & Eaton.

Sarah De Berenger. A Novel. Jean Ingelow. LC 7-8855. 1879. Roberts Brothers.

Sarah Defiant: A Novel. Mary Borden. LC 31-33333. 1931. Doubleday, Doran & Company, Inc.

Sarah Eden. Ethel Stefana Stevens Drower. LC 14-4585. 1914. Dodd, Mead and Company.

Sarah Hall's Sea God. Theodora McCormick Du Bois. 1970. pap. 0.75 o.p. (0502-07097). Curtis.

Sarah Hall's Sea God: A Novel, 1st Ed. Theodora McCormick Du Bois. LC 52-5124. 1952. Doubleday.

Sarah Mandrake. Maggie Jeanne Melody Wadelton. 1946. The Bobbs-Merrill Company.

Sarah Martha in Paris: A Novel. Saidee Bourgoin. LC 6-14921. The Merriam Company.

Sarah Mason: Call Girl. Jack Michlin. LC 56-13215. 1956. Comet Press Books.

Sarah Morris Remembers. Dorothy Emily Stevenson. LC 67-19047. 1967. Holt, Rinehart and Winston.

Sarah: Or The Exemplary Wife. Susanna Haswell Rowson. LC 8-946. 1813. C. Williams.

Sarah, or the Exemplary Wife. Susanna Haswell Rowson. LC 78-64090. Repr. of 1813 ed. 37.50 (ISBN 0-404-17165-6). AMS Pr.

Sarah T.-Portrait of a Teen-Age Alcoholic. Robin S Wagner & Richard Shapiro. 1975. (pbk.) 1.25 (ISBN 0-345-24720-5). Ballantine Books.

Sarah Thornton. Margaret Weymouth Jackson. LC 33-5183. The Bobbs-Merrill Company.

Sarah Walked Over the Mountain: A Novel. Ruth Moore. LC 79-14331. 1979. 8.95 (ISBN 0-688-03523-X). Morrow.

Sarah's Awakening. Susan V. Billings. (Orig.). 1979. pap. 2.50 (ISBN 0-89083-536-5). Zebra.

Sarah's Choice: Or, The Norton Family... Emma F Altgeld. Laird & Lee.

Sarah's Cottage. Dorothy Emily Stevenson. LC 68-24754. 1968. 5.95. Holt, Rinehart, and Winston.

Sarah's Story. Mollie Hardwick. 1975. (pbk.) 1.50 (ISBN 0-671-78792-6). Pocket Books.

Sarang: the Story of a Bengal Tiger and of Two Children in Search of a Miracle: A Novel. Roger A Caras. LC 68-30869. 1968. Little, Brown.

Saranoff Murder. Mark Lee Lurther & Ford, Mrs. Lilliam Cummings, 1881- Joint Author. LC 30-23195. The Bobbs-Merrill Company.

Saraswattee: A Novel of India. Kit Puran Singh. LC 82-7175. 1982. 14.95 (ISBN 0-914842-88-9). Madrona Publishers.

Saratoga. Dorothy Daniels. 320p. (Orig.). 1982. pap. 2.75 (ISBN 0-8439-0942-0). Leisure Bks CT.

Saratoga. A Story of 1787. Daniel Shepherd. LC 8-511578. 1856. W. P. Fetridge & Co.

Saratoga: A Tale of the Revolution... Eliza Lanesford Foster Cushing. LC 3-10894. 1824. Cummings. Hilliard & Co.

Saratoga Lady. Frances Y. McHugh. 3.95 o.p. Lenox Hill.

Saratoga Lady. Frances Y. McHugh. Ed. by Alice Sachs. 1970. 3.95 o.p. B Franklin.

Saratoga Longshot. Stephen Dobyns. 1976. 8.95 (ISBN 0-689-10707-2). Atheneum.

Saratoga Season. large print ed. MacWilliams, Margaret. LC 81-9200. 1981. 9.95 (ISBN 0-89621-307-2). Thorndike Press.

Saratoga Season. Margaret MacWilliams. (Orig.). 1980. pap. 1.50 (ISBN 0-440-18081-3). Dell.

Saratoga Swimmer. Stephen Dobyns. LC 81-66003. 1981. 12.95 (ISBN 0-689-11193-2). Atheneum.

Saratoga Trunk. Edna Ferber. LC 41-24504. 1941. Doubleday, Doran & Company, Inc.

Saratoga Trunk. Edna Ferber. LC 81-2112. 1981. 16.50 (ISBN 0-8161-3194-5). G.K. Hall.

Sarcasm of Destiny: Or, Nina's Experience. A Novel. Mary Elizabeth Wilson Sherwood. 1878. D. Appleton and Company.

Sarchedon. A Legned of the Great Queen. new ed. George John Whyte-Melville. LC 44-29545. (On cover: Select library of fiction). Ward, Lock and Co.

Sard Harker. John Masefield. LC 24-256437. 1924. The Macmillan Company.

Sard Harker: A Novel. John Masefield. LC 73-8870. 1973. Scholarly Press.

Sardinian Brigade. Emilio Lussu. Tr. by Marion Rawson. (Great Novels & Memoirs of World War 1 Ser.: Vol. 3). 1967. 5.95 o.p. (ISBN 0-8117-1508-6). Stackpole.

Sardinian Smile. Petru Dumitriu. LC 68-24752. 1968. 4.50. Holt, Rinehart, and Winston.

Sardis and the Spirit-Guest: The Story of a Dream. Josephine Rand. 1897. E. P. Dutton & Company.

Sardonic Smile: Being the Authorized Translation of Ahasuerus. Ludwig Diehl. Tr. by Willcox, Louise (Collier) LC 26-17292. 1926. Houghton Mifflin Company.

Sardonics; Sixteen Sketches. Harris Merton Lyon. LC 9-288. Metropolitan Syndicate, Inc.

Sardonics; Sixteen Sketches. Harris Merton Lyon. LC 9-12878. 1909. The Stuyvesant Press.

Sardonyx Net. Elizabeth A Lynn. LC 81-8648. 14.95 (ISBN 0-399-12588-4). Putnam.

Sardonyx Seal: A Romance of Normandy. Belle Gray Taylor. LC 8-25658. 1891. G. P. Putnam's Sons.

Sardou's Cleopatra. A Novelization of the Celebrated Play. Arthur D Hall & Sardou. Victorien, 1831-1898 Cleopatre. (On cover: The sea and shore series, no. 4). 1892. Street & Smith.

Sardou's Cleopatra. A Novelization of the Celebrated Play. Victorien Sardou & Sardou, Victorian, 1831- Cleopatre. LC 7-931. (primrose series. no. 4). Street & Smith.

Sareel. Edith Dart. LC 22-12018. Boui and Liveright.

Sargasso. Edwin Corley. LC 76-18337. 1977. 7.95 (ISBN 0-385-11401-X). Doubleday.

Sargasso of Space. Andre Norton, pseud. LC 77-26135. (Norton, Andre. The Space Adventure Novels of Andre Norton). 1978. 7.95 (ISBN 0-8398-2415-7). Gregg Press.

Sargasso of Space: By Andrew North Pseud. 1st Ed. Alice Mary Norton. LC 55-5464. (Dane Thorson-Solar Queen adventures). 1955. Gnome Press.

Sargasso Ogre. A Superhero Adventure. Kenneth Robeson. (His the fantastic adventures of Doc Savage, 5). (Illus.). 1975. 1.75. (ISBN 0-307-02380-X). Western Publishing Company.

Sargasso Sea. Donn B. Byrne. LC 72-3275. (Short Story Index Reprint Ser). 1972. Repr. of 1932 ed. 19.00 o.p. (ISBN 0-8369-4144-6). Arno.

Sargasso Sea and Other Stories. Donn Byrne. LC 72-3275. (Short story index reprint series). 1972. (ISBN 0-8369-4144-6). Books for Libraries Press.

Sargasso Secret. Ken Stanton. (Aquanauts Ser.). (Orig.). 1971. pap. 0.75 o.p. (532-75431-075). Manor Bks.

Sargeant Von; or, Along Chase. From the Diary of Inspector Byrnes. William Henry Bishop & Byrnes Thomas F., 1844?-1910. LC 6-11720. C.

Sari Bron. Luella Reed. LC 45-26903. 1945. The Christopher Publishing House.

Sari: By Bette Allan Pseud. Elizabeth Ashbey. LC 50-5961. 1950. Gramercy Pub. Co.

Sariband for Two Sisters. Eleanor Hibbert. LC 75-45062. 8.95 (ISBN 0-399-11746-6). Putnam.

Sarita, the Carlist. Arthur Williams Marchmont. F. A. Stokes Company.

Sarits. A Tale of the Pack Saddle District. Allen Smith. LC 13-17747. (On cover: Neely's popular library, no. 109). 1898. F. T. Neely.

Sarjint Larry An' Frinds. Chauncey M'Govern. LC 10-14587. 1906. The Escolta Press.

Sarkhan. William J. Lederer & Eugene Burdick. LC 65-26481. 1965. McGraw-Hill.

Sarkhan: By William J. Lederer, Eugene Burdick. William J. Lederer & Eugene Burdick. (Crest bk., m976). 1966. Fawcett.

Sarnia. Hilary Ford, pseud. LC 73-15339. 1974. 6.95 (ISBN 0-385-02804-0). Doubleday.

Saroyan Special. facs. ed. William Saroyan. LC 70-134979. (Short Story Index Reprint Ser). 1948. 22.00 (ISBN 0-8369-3709-0). Ayer Co.

Saroyan Special: Selected Short Stories. William Saroyan. LC 70-134979. (Short story index reprint series). (Illus.). 1970. Books for Libraries Press.

Saroyan Special: Selected Short Stories. William Saroyan. LC 48-9565. 1948. Harcourt, Brace.

Saroyan's Fables. William Saroyan & Chappell, Warren, Illus. LC 41-245054. 1941. Harcourt, Brace and Company.

Sarrasine: Translated by G. B. Ives. Honore De Balzac. Tr. by George Burnham Ives. LC 99-3456. 1899. Croscup & Sterling Co.

Sarsen Place. Gwendoline Butler. LC 73-86855. 1974. 6.95 (ISBN 0-698-10570-2). Coward, McCann & Geoghegan.

Sarsfield: Or, The Last Struggle for Ireland. David Power Conyngham. LC 6-302009. 1871. P. Donahoe.

Sarton Kell. Kate Mallory. LC 76-56398. 1977. 8.95 (ISBN 0-688-03092-0). Morrow.

Sarton Kell. Kate Mallory. 1978. 1.95 (ISBN 0-445-04273-7). Popular Library.

Sartor Resartus. Thomas Carlyle. 1977. Repr. 29.00 o.p. (ISBN 0-403-07182-8). Scholarly.

Sartoris. William Faulkner. LC 29-3496. Harcoure, Brace and Company.

Sasha. Aleksandr Ivanovich Kuprin. Tr. by Ashby, Douglas. LC 29-13479. 1928. S. Paul & Co., Ltd.

Sassafras. Mary Vann Hunter. LC 79-26716. 10.95 (ISBN 0-453-00376-1). New American Library.

Sassafras Hill. Charles Allen Smart. LC 47-2905. 1947. Random House.

Sassafrass. Ntozake Shange. (Illus.). 40p. 1976. pap. 1.95 o.p. (ISBN 0-915288-14-1). Shameless Hussy.

Sassafrass, Cypress & Indigo: A Novel. Ntozake Shange. LC 82-5565. 10.95 (ISBN 0-312-69971-9). St. Martin's Press.

Satan: A Romance of the Bahamas. Henry De Vere Stacpoole. LC 21-26422. 1921. R. M. McBride & Company.

Satan and Cardinal Campbell. Bruce Marshall. LC 59-7219. 1959. Houghton Mifflin.

Satan As Lightning: A Novel. Basil King. LC 29-14145. 1929. Harper & Brothers.

Satan Black & Cargo Unknown. Kenneth Robeson, pseud. (Doc Savage Ser.: Nos. 97 & 98). 224p. 1980. pap. 1.95 (ISBN 0-553-13421-3). Bantam.

Satan Bug. Alistair MacLean. 224p. 1978. pap. 2.95 (ISBN 0-449-14212-4, GM). Fawcett.

Satan Bug: By Ian Stuart Pseud. Alistair MacLean. LC 62-15837. 1962. Scribner.

Satan Came Also. Dorothy Carle Pierce Walker. LC 41-24633. Liveright Publishing Corporation.

Satan, Demons & Dildoes. Eugene Richards. 160p. 1974. pap. 1.95 o.p. (ISBN 0-87682-406-8, 7406). Barclay Hse.

Satan Had a Daughter. Francis M Fitzpatrick. LC 55-7168. 1955. Vantage Press.

Satan Has Six Fingers. Vera Kelsey. LC 43-2941. 1943. Pub. for the Crime Club by Doubleday, Doran and Company, Inc.

Satan, His Psychotherapy and Cure by the Unfortunate Dr. Kassler, J.S.P.S. Jeremy Leven. LC 81-48107. 13.95 (ISBN 0-394-52370-9). Knopf: Distributed by Random House.

Satan: His Psychotherapy & Cure by the Unfortunate Dr. Kassler, J.S.P.S. Jeremy Leven. 576p. 1983. pap. 3.95 (ISBN 0-345-30265-6). Ballantine.

Satan in Goray. Isaac Bashevis Singer. LC 55-10731. 1955. Noonday Press.

Satan in the Suburbs, and Other Stories: Illustrated by Asgeir Scott. Bertrand Russell Russell. LC 53-11006. 1953. Simon and Schuster.

Satan Is a Woman. Gil Brewer. LC 51-31787. (Gold medal books, 169). 1951. Fawcett Publications.

Satan Never Sleeps. Pearl Sydenstricker Buck. LC 62-1055. (Cardinal edition, C-429). 1962. Pocket Books.

Satan of the Wild Herd. Ernest W. Schultz. 6.95 o.p. Vantage.

Satan Rules the Night. Davis Dresser. LC 38-7790. Godwin.

Satan Sampler. Victor Canning. LC 79-27310. 1980. 8.95 (ISBN 0-688-03612-0). Morrow.

Satan Sanderson. Hallie Erminie Rives. LC 7-26018. 1907. The Bobbs-Merrill Company.

Satan Strike see Atague Diabolico.

Satan Trap. Nick Carter. (Nick Carter Ser.). 224p. (Orig.). 1979. pap. 1.95 (ISBN 0-441-75035-4, Pub. by Charter Bks). Ace Bks.

Satan Underfoot. Don Hughes. (O.s.i.). 48p. (Orig.). 1974. pap. 1.25 o.s.i. (ISBN 0-89274-008-6). Harrison Hse.

Satan Was a Man: A Novel of Murder. Edward Hale Bierstadt. LC 35-7177. 1935. Doubleday, Dorna & Company, Inc.

Satan Whispers. William Edward Daniel Ross. 1981. pap. 2.50 (ISBN 0-8439-0913-7, Leisure Bks). Nordon Pubns.

Satan Will Never Die:: a Socio-Religious Novel. George C Ebbert. 1974. 7.50 (ISBN 0-682-48072-X). Exposition Press.

Satanella: A Story of Punchestown. George John Whyte-Melville. LC 7-25847. 1899. Longmans, Green & Co.

Satanella; a Story of Punchestown. new ed. George John Whyte-Melville. LC 41-42361. (On cover: Select library of fiction. 125). Ward, Lock, and Co.

Satanic Omnibus. Kurt D. Singer. LC 74-150035. 1973. 2.50. W. E. Allen.

Satanic Sex. Arlene J. Fitzgerald. 192p. (Orig.). 1973. pap. 1.25 o.p. (532-12194-125). Manor Bks.

Satanist. Dennis Yates Wheatley. (Black magic ser.). 1972. 1.50. Ballantine.

Satanists. Ed. by Peter Haining. LC 78-102068. 1970. 5.95. Taplinger Pub. Co.

Satan's Acres. Sharon Wagner. (Ace gothic). 1974. (pbk.) 0.95. Ace Books.

Satan's Back Yard. Sam J Slate. LC 73-17771. 1974. 6.95 (ISBN 0-385-00501-6). Doubleday.

Satan's Bushel. Garet Garrett. LC 24-127642. E. P. Dutton & Company.

Satan's Chance. Alan R. Shrader. 400p. 1982. pap. 3.25 (ISBN 0-441-75018-4). Ace Bks.

Satan's Child. Peter Saxon. (Orig.). 1968. pap. 0.60 o.p. (73-784). Lancer.

Satan's Children. 1983. 10.00 (ISBN 0-89023-017-X). Forrest Printing.

Satan's Children: 2 Novels: I Take This Woman and Four Days in a Lifetime. Translated from the French by Louise Varese. 1st American Ed. Georges Simenon. LC 52-135813. Prentice-Hall.

Satan's Circus. Eleanor Furneaux Smith. LC 34-16710. The Bobbs-Merrill Company.

Satan's Coach: L'equipage Du Diable. Fortune Du Boisgobey. Tr. by Caroline A. Merighi. (Seaside library, v. 76, no. 1534). 1883. G. Munro.

Satan's Coast. Elsie Lee. 1971. pap. 0.75 o.p. (ISBN 0-447-74548-4). Lancer.

Satan's Coast. easy eye ed. Elsie Lee. pap. 0.75 o.p. Lancer.

Satan's Coast. Elsie Lee. (Orig.). 1972. pap. 0.95 o.s.i. (75-368). Lancer.

Satan's Daughters. George G. Gilman, pseud. (Steele Ser.: No. 17). 160p. 1980. pap. 1.50 (ISBN 0-523-40527-8). Pinnacle Bks.

Satan's Gal: By Carolina Lee Pseud. Peggy Gaddis, pseud. LC 50-1515. (Handi-book romance, 102). 1950. Quinn Pub. Co.

Satan's Harvest. Sanford Aday. LC 53-12326. Vantage Press.

Satan's Hoof and the Two Witches. Eugenie R Eliscu. LC 99-1676. 1899. Banner of Light Publishing Co.

Satan's Island. Marilyn Ross. 1975. (pbk.) 1.25. Warner Books.

Satan's Manor. Mark Andrews. (Leisure books). 1.75 (ISBN 0-8439-0460-7). Nordon Pubns.

Satan's Master. Carole Mortimer. (Harlequin Presents Ser.). 192p. 1981. pap. 1.75 (ISBN 0-373-10452-9). Harlequin Bks.

Satan's Mules. Gil Martin. (Berkley medallion book). 1974. (pbk.) 0.75 (ISBN 0-425-02533-0). Berkley Pub. Co.

Satan's Pets. Ed. by Vic Ghidalia. (O.s.i.). 192p. 1972. pap. 0.75 o.s.i. (532-00478-095). Manor Bks.

Satan's Playground: A Novel. Charles Drummond Woodyatt. LC 34-24864. 1934. Dodd, Mead & Company.

Satan's Range. Archie Joscelyn. LC 42-249734. 1942. Phoenix Press.

Satan's Rock. Carl D Burton. LC 54-9283. 1954. Appleton-Century-Crofts.

Satan's Rock. Marilyn Ross. 1970. pap. 0.60 o.p. (63-404). Paperback Lib.

Satan's Sabbath. Don Pendleton. (Executioner Ser.: No. 38). (Orig.). 1980. pap. 2.25 (ISBN 0-523-41796-9). Pinnacle Bks.

Satan's Saint. Guy Endore. (O.s.i.). 1967. pap. 0.95 o.s.i. (A268N, Award). Univ Pub & Dist.

Satan's Saint: A Novel About the Marquis De Sade. S. Guy Endore. LC 65-158381. 4.95. Crown.

Satan's Seal. Patricia Rose. 1978. pap. 1.50 (ISBN 0-532-15360-X). Woodhill.

Satan's Seed. Jory Sherman. 1978. 1.50 (ISBN 0-523-40220-1). Pinnacle Books.

Satan's Sergeants. Josephine Herbst. 1941. C. Scribner's Sons.

Satan's Sister. Ruby Jean Jensen. 1979. pap. 1.75 (ISBN 0-89041-223-5, 3223). Major Bks.

Satan's Spring. Sarah Nichols. (Queen-size gothic). 1974. (pbk.) 1.25. Popular Library.

Satan's Swarm. Lionel Derrick, pseud. (The Penetrator Ser.: No. 49). 192p. (Orig.). 1983. pap. 2.25 (ISBN 0-523-41681-4). Pinnacle Bks.

Satan's World. Poul Anderson. (Berley Medallion Book). 1977. 1.50 (ISBN 0-425-03361-9). Berkley Pub. Corp.

Satan's World. Poul Anderson. LC 79-89786. (Doubleday science fiction). 1969. 4.95. Doubleday.

Satanstoe. James Fenimore Cooper. Ed. by Spiller, Robert Ernest & Coppock, Joseph D. LC 37-4084. (Half-title: American fiction series; general editor, H. H. Clark). American Book Company.

Satanstoe. Introd. by Robert L. Hough. James Fenimore Cooper. Ed. by Robert Lee Hough. (Bison bk., BB138 rebound). 1968. 4.00. Peter Smith.

Satanstoe: Or, The Littlepage Manuscripts. A Tale of the Colony. James Fenimore Cooper. LC 6-29679. 1845. Burgess, Stringer & Co.

Satanstoe: Or, The Littlepage Manuscripts. A Tale of the Colony. new ed. James Fenimore Cooper. 1852. Stringer and Townsend.

Satanstoe: Or, The Littlepage Manuscripts. A Tale of the Colony. new edition. ed. James Fenimore Cooper. LC 26-36616. 1855. Stringer and Townsend.

Satanstoe: Or, The Littlepage Manuscripts; a Tale of the Colony. James Fenimore Cooper. (On cover: Lovell's library. no. 570). 1885. J. W. Lovell Company.

Satanstoe: Or, The Littlepage Manuscripts. A Tale of the Colony. James Fenimore Cooper. 1888. D. Appleton and Company.

Satellite. Frances Clippinger. LC 51-12516. 1951. Random House.

Satellite City. Mack Reynolds. 1975. (pbk.) 1.25. Ace.

Satellite E One. Jeffery Lloyd Castle. LC 54-11231. 1954. Dodd, Mead.

Satellite Slaughter. Lionel Derrick, pseud. (Penetrator Ser.: No. 33). 1979. pap. 1.50 (ISBN 0-523-40513-8). Pinnacle Bks.

Satiated Passion. Royal A Couey. (On cover: Algoma library, no. 1). 1897. The Author.

Satin & Stars. Joanne Kaye. LC 81-82364. (Garment Center Ser.). 224p. (Orig.). 1982. pap. 2.50 (ISBN 0-87216-982-0). Playboy Pbks.

Satin & Steele, No. 71. Jaelyn Conlee. 1982. pap. 1.75 (ISBN 0-515-06682-6). Jove Pubns.

Satin Palms. Elizabeth Inness-Brown. LC 81-71001. 119p. (Orig.). 1981. pap. 6.95 (ISBN 0-931362-04-0). Fiction Intl.

Satin Straps. Maysie Greig. LC 29-9796. 1929. L. MacVeagh, The Dial Press.

Satin Tie: Being a Story of the Inner Life of the Civil War, Based Upon Incidents Which Occurred During the Great Strife. Burton W Dix. LC 6-34597. 1889.

Satire see Insight: English Literature.

Satirical Stories. Nikolai Semenovich Leskov. Ed. by William Benbow Edgerton. LC 68-27987. 1969. 7.50. Pegasus.

Satiricon. annotated ed. by evan t. sage. rev. and expanded by brady b. gilleland. ed. Petronius Arbiter. Ed. by Evan Taylor Sage & Brady B. Gilleland. LC 72-87112. 1969. Appleton-Century-Crofts.

Satiro, Ninfas, y Cia. Leon Calvino. (Pimienta Collection Ser). 160p. (Span.). 1974. pap. 1.00 (ISBN 0-88473-211-8). Fiesta Pub.

Satisfaction Guaranteed. 1972. pap. 1.75 o.s.i. (V1098K, Venus). Grove.

Satori. Dennis Schmidt. (Orig.). 1981. pap. 2.75 (ISBN 0-441-75058-3). Ace Bks.

Satsang with Baba, 2 vols. Swami Muktananda. LC 76-670008. Vol. 1 1974. pap. 5.95 (ISBN 0-914602-30-6); Vol. 2 1976. pap. 5.95 (ISBN 0-914602-31-4). SYDA Found.

Saturday: A Novel. Jeb Rosebrook. LC 65-22706. 1965. Dutton.

Saturday at Hazeldines. Vera Wheatley. LC 36-7582. E. P. Dutton & Co., Inc.

Saturday City. Jan Webster. LC 78-21203. (Illus.). 10.95 (ISBN 0-312-69974-3). St. Martin's Press.

Saturday Epic. Hugh C Rae. LC 74-113523. 1970. 4.95. Coward-McCann.

Saturday Evening Post Book of the Sea and Ships. LC 78-61519. (Illus.). 11.95 (ISBN 0-89387-023-4). Curtis Pub. Co.

Saturday Evening Post Reader of Sea Stories: Edited by Day Edgar. 1st Ed. The Saturday Evening Post. Ed. by Day Edgar. LC 62-15885. 1962. Doubleday.

Saturday Evening Post Reader of Western Stories: Edited by E. N. Brandt. The Saturday Evening Post. LC 60-11390. 1960. Doubleday.

Saturday Evening Post Stories, 1950. The Saturday Evening Post. LC 51-2440. 1951. Random House.

Saturday Evening Post (The) Best Short Stories: Selected from the Saturday Evening Post. LC 65-20463. 5.95. Curtis Bks.; Dist. Doubleday.

Saturday Evening Post. (The) The Saturday Evening Post Reader of Western Stories. Ed. by E. N. Brandt. (Western heritage bk., M2066). 1965. Popular Lib.

Saturday Evening Post Western Stories: Compiled by Barthold Fles. Stories by Bill Gulick and Others. Avon Reprint Ed. The Saturday Evening Post. Ed. by Fles, Barthold. LC 52-22902. 1951. Avon Pub. Co.

Saturday Games. Brown Meggs. LC 73-18460. 1974. 5.95 (ISBN 0-394-48846-6). Random House.

Saturday Games. Brown Meggs. (Fawcett Crest Book). 1976. (pbk.) 1.50. Fawcett.

Saturday Heroes. Curtis Kent Bishop. LC 51-12419. 1951. Steck Co.

Saturday Island. Hugh Brooke. LC 35-135494. 1935. Doubleday, Doran & Company, Inc.

Saturday Nation: A Novel. John Hermansen. LC 72-77855. 1972. 4.95 (ISBN 0-87141-045-1). Manyland Books.

Saturday Night. Guy Berne. LC 36-933. Godwin.

Saturday Night. Marjorie Holmes. 1982. pap. 1.95 (ISBN 0-440-97645-6, LFL). Dell.

Saturday Night. Thomas Moult. LC 31-22897. 1931. Doubleday, Doran & Company, Inc.

Saturday Night and Sunday Morning. Alan Sillitoe. 1973. (pbk) 0.75. New American Lib.

Saturday Night and Sunday Morning. Alan Sillitoe. LC 59-9260. 1959. Knopf.

Saturday Night at Daisy's. Jeffrey Cohn. LC 77-92055. 8.95 (ISBN 0-15-179412-X). Harcourt Brace Jovanovich.

Saturday Night at the Greyhound. Simpson John Frederick Norman Hampson. LC 31-15287. 1931. A. A. Knopf.

Saturday Night in los Angeles. Owen Elliott. (Orig.). 1973. pap. 1.25 o.p. (01046). Curtis.

Saturday Night in Los Angeles. Owen Elliott. 1973. 1.25. Curtis Books.

Saturday Night in Milwaukee. Gary Brandner. (Orig.). 1973. pap. 1.25 o.p. (01052). Curtis.

Saturday Night in San Francisco. Charles Beardsley. (Orig.). 1973. pap. 1.25 o.p. (01047). Curtis.

Saturday Night in San Francisco. Charles Beardsley. 1973. 1.25. Curtis Books.

Saturday Night Is My Delight: A Novel by Torrey Hood. Marjorie Torrey Hood Chanslor. LC 52-9837. 1952. Putnam.

Saturday Night Knife & Gun Club. B. P. Reiter. LC 76-51437. 8.95 (ISBN 0-397-01141-5). Lippincott.

Saturday Night Town. A Crest 1st Ed. Novel. Harry Whittington. LC 57-23987. (Crest book, 151). 1956. Fawcett Publications.

Saturday Nights. Earl G Curtis. LC 22-6164. The Reilly & Lee Co.

Saturday of Glory. David Serafin. LC 81-16711. 1982. 9.95 (ISBN 0-312-69975-1). St. Martin's Press.

Saturday, Sunday & Salvation. Dwight Herbert. (Stories That Win Ser.). 1980. pap. 0.95 (ISBN 0-8163-0355-X). Pacific Pr Pub Assn.

Saturday the Rabbi Went Hungry. Harry Kemelman. LC 66-15114. 3.95. Crown.

Saturday to Monday. Patrick Carleton. LC 36-8262. E. P. Dutton & Co., Inc.

Saturday to Monday. Translated from the German by Catherine Hutter. Ruth Rehmann. LC 61-10443. 1961. Viking Press.

Saturday Waiting. Jerome Nilssen. LC 77-99462. (Illus.). 1970. 5.95. Fortress Press.

Saturday's Child. Clell Edgar Bowman. 1976. 10.00 o.p. (ISBN 0-682-48520-9). Exposition.

Saturday's Child. Mary Lieber. LC 76-56151. 2.95 (ISBN 0-88494-307-0) (ISBN 0-89293-066-7). Beta Books.

Saturday's Child. Kathleen Thompson Norris. LC 14-14457. 1914. The Macmillan Company.

Saturday's Child. Charlie May Hogue Simon. LC 50-8890. (Illus.). 1950. Dutton.

Saturdays: Written and Illustrated by Elizabeth Enright. Elizabeth Enright. LC 41-17880. Farrar & Rinehart, Inc.

Saturn Over the Water: An Account of His Adventures in London, New York, South America and Australia, by Tim Bedford, Painter; Edited, with Some Preliminary and Concluding Remarks, by Henry Sulgrave; and Here Presented to the Reading Public. 1st American Ed. John Boynton Priestley. LC 61-13133. 1961. Doubleday.

Saturn's Child. LC 75-42206. 1976. 7.95 o.p. (ISBN 0-8415-0423-7). Dutton.

Saturn's Child. Irving Shulman. LC 75-42206. 7.95 (ISBN 0-8415-0423-7). Saturday Review Press.

Satyr. Robert De Maria. 176p. (Orig.). 1973. pap. 1.25 o.p. (ISBN 0-532-12171-6). Woodhill.

Satyr. Robert De Maria. LC 72-80800. 1972. 5.95 o.p. (ISBN 0-672-51712-4). Bobbs.

Satyr. Robert De Maria. 176p. (Orig.). 1973. pap. 1.25 o.p. (ISBN 0-532-12171-6). Manor Bks.

Satyr. Hugh Knox. (Orig.). 1970. pap. 1.25 (ISBN 0-87067-305-X, BH305). Holloway.

Satyr; a Novel of Love and Passion. Reflecting Modern Social Organization. Mina Holt. LC 99-3948. 1899. F. T. Neely.

Satyr and the Saint. Leonardo Bercovici. LC 64-20051. 1964. Scribner.

Satyr Trek. Ray Kainen. pap. 1.95 o.s.i. (OPS-13). Olympia.

Satyrday, a Fable. Steven Bauer. LC 80-13534. (Illus.). 11.95 (ISBN 0-399-12533-7). Berkley Pub. Corp.: Distributed by Putnam.

Satyrday: A Fable. Steven Bauer. LC 80-13534. (Illus.). 1982. 4.95 (ISBN 0-425-05317-2). Berkley Books.

Satyriasis: The Male Nymphomania. Walter P. Jay. (Orig.). 1973. pap. 1.95 o.p. (ISBN 0-87682-319-3, 7319). Barclay Hse.

Satyricon. Petronius Arbiter. Tr. by William Arrowsmith from Lat. LC 59-6026. 1959. 24.00x o.p. (ISBN 0-472-72935-7). Irvington.

Satyricon of Petronius Arbiter. Complete, Unexpurgated Tr. by W. C. Firebaugh, in Which Are Incorporated the Forgeries of Nodot and Marchena, and the Readings Introd. into the Text by De Salas. Illus. by Norman Lindsay. Petronius Arbiter. Tr. by W. C. Firebaugh. (W922). 1966. Washington Sq.

Sauce and Sensuality. Elisabeth Ayrton. LC 57-8968. (Illus.). 1957. Dutton.

Sauce for the Goose. Peter De Vries. LC 81-8124. 11.95 (ISBN 0-316-18202-8). Little, Brown.

Sauce for the Goose. Peter De Vries. LC 82-5367. 1982. 11.95 (ISBN 0-14-006281-5). Penguin Books.

Sauce for the Goose. Peter De Vries. LC 81-8124. 235p. 1981. 11.95 (ISBN 0-316-18202-8). Little.

Saucelito: Sausalito: Legends and Tales of a Changing Town. George Cleborn Hoffman. LC 76-716. (Illus.). 5.00 (ISBN 0-916028-02-X). Woodward Books.

Saucer People. Ronald G Garver. LC 57-9477. 1957. Meador Pub. Co.

Saucy Arethusa. A Naval Story. Frederick Chamier. LC 6-20164. 1867. F. Warne and Co.

Saul. William Jonathan Calvert. LC 73-166988. Printed by Blue & Gray Press.

Saul. Corinne Martin Lowe. LC 19-10684. 1919. The James A. McCann Company.

Saul and Morris, Worlds Apart: A Novel. James Yaffe. LC 81-13304. 15.50. Holt, Rinehart, and Winston.

Saul of Tarsus: A Tale of the Early Christians. Elizabeth Jane Miller. LC 6-36043. 1906. The Bobbs-Merrill Company.

Saul's Book. Paul T. Rogers. 350p. 1982. 15.95 (ISBN 0-916366-04-9); pap. 14.95 o.p. (ISBN 0-916366-13-8). Godine.

Saunders Oak. Robert Raynolds. LC 33-2857. 1933. Harper & Brothers.

Saurus. Eden Phillpotts. LC 75-10667. (Classics of science fiction). 1976. 11.95. (ISBN 0-88355-358-9) (ISBN 0-88355-461-5). Hyperion Press.

Sausalito. Sam Dodson. (Fawcett Gold Medal Book). (Illus.). 1978. 1.95 (ISBN 0-449-13940-9). Fawcett Books.

Sauvagine: A Novel. Nicole Bressy. LC 78-157982. 1972. 5.95 (ISBN 0-200-71832-0). Abelard-Schuman.

Sauve Qui Peut. Lawrence Durrell. LC 66-21312. (Illus.). 1967. Dutton.

Savage. Mikhail Petrovich Artsybashev & Cannan, Gilbert, 1884, Tr. LC 24-11138. Boni and Liveright.

Savage. Paul Boorstin. LC 79-28636. 12.95 (ISBN 0-399-90037-3). R. Marek.

Savage. Paul Boorstin. 1981. 2.95 (ISBN 0-425-04938-8). Berkley, Publishing Corp.

Savage. Noel Clad. LC 59-215. (Inner sanctum mystery). 1958. Simon and Schuster.

Savage. Frances Casey Kerns. 576p. (Orig.). 1981. pap. 2.75 (ISBN 0-446-95603-1). Warner Bks.

Savage. Peter McCurtin. (Sundance Ser.: No. 28). 1979. pap. 1.75 o.s.i. (ISBN 0-8439-0678-2, Leisure Bks). Nordon Pubns.

Savage. Tom Ryan. 1979. pap. 2.95 (ISBN 0-451-11981-9, AE1981, Sig). NAL.

Savage Affair. 1st Ed. Virgil Scott. LC 58-5475. 1958. Harcourt, Brace.

Savage Ally. Helen H. Jacobs. 1977. pap. 1.95 (ISBN 0-532-19154-4). Woodhill.

Savage Aristocrat. Roberta Leigh. 1979. pap. 1.75 (ISBN 0-449-14246-9, GM). Fawcett.

Savage Beauty: A Satirical Allegorical Novel... P. W Sproat. LC 8-14040. 1822. Printed by S. Roberts.

Savage Body. Neil Martin. 192p. (Orig.). 1973. pap. 1.95 o.p. (ISBN 0-87056-296-7, 6296). Brandon.

Savage Breast. John Trinian. 1968. pap. 0.60 o.p. (60-330). Manor Bks.

Savage Bride: By Cornell Woolrich Pseud. Hopley-Woolrich, Cornell George. LC 51-17381. (Gold medal book, 136). 1950. Fawcett Publications.

Savage Brood. Martha Rofheart. LC 78-403. 10.95 (ISBN 0-690-01484-8). Crowell.

Savage City. Jean Paradise. LC 55-10164. 1955. Crown Publishers.

Savage Crows. Robert Drewe. LC 77-361821. 1976. (ISBN 0-00-221589-6). Collins.

Savage Dawn. George G. Gilman, pseud. (Edge Ser.: No. 26). 1978. pap. 1.95 (ISBN 0-523-41837-X). Pinnacle Bks.

Savage Dawn. Ralph Hayes. (Orig.). 1979. write for info. (ISBN 0-515-05075-X). Jove Pubns.

Savage Day. Jack Higgins, pseud. 1972. 5.95 o.p. (ISBN 0-03-001036-5). HR&W.

Savage Day. Jack Higgins. (Fawcett crest book). 1974. (pbk.) 0.95. Fawcett.

Savage Day. Henry Patterson. LC 72-78101. 1972. 5.95 (ISBN 0-03-001036-5). Holt, Rinehart and Winston.

Savage Day. Thomas Wiseman. LC 81-3273. 13.95 (ISBN 0-440-09070-9). Delacorte Press.

Savage Delinquents. Alan Bennett. 1968. pap. 0.60 o.p. (60-360). Manor Bks.

Savage Desire. Constance O'Banyon. 1983. pap. 3.50 (ISBN 0-8217-1120-2). Zebra.

Savage Earth. Helga Moray. 1973. (pbk.) 1.25 (ISBN 0-671-78323-8). Pocket Books.

Savage Ecstasy. Janelle Taylor. (Orig.). 1981. pap. 3.50 (ISBN 0-89083-824-0). Zebra.

Savage Eden. Constance Gluyas. 1976. pap. 2.50 (ISBN 0-451-09285-6, E9285, Sig). NAL.

Savage Eden. Constance Gluyas. (Signet book). New American Library.

Savage Eden, No. 79. Diane Crawford. 1982. pap. 1.75 (ISBN 0-515-06690-7). Jove Pubns.

Savage Embrace. Alexis Boyard. (Orig.). 1982. pap. 3.50 (ISBN 0-8217-1069-9). Zebra.

Savage Embrace. Jessica Howard, pseud. 1978. 2.25 (ISBN 0-446-82322-8). Warner Books.

Savage Empire. Jean Lorrah. LC 80-83592. 224p. (Orig.). 1981. pap. 2.25 (ISBN 0-87216-794-1). Playboy Pbks.

Savage Enchantment. Parris Afton Bonds. 320p. 1982. pap. 2.95 (ISBN 0-445-04332-6). Popular Lib.

Savage Game. James Trevor. (O.s.i.). 1967. pap. 0.75 o.s.i. (A279S, Award). Univ Pub & Dist.

Savage Gentleman. Noel Bertram Gerson. LC 60-7981. 1950. Doubleday.

Savage Gentleman. Philip Wylie. LC 32-32262. Farrar & Rinehart, Incorporated.

Savage Gunlaw. Bradford Scott. (Orig.). 1971. pap. 0.60 o.p. (X2465). Pyramid Pubns.

Savage Guns. Matt Stuart. 1972. pap. 0.75 o.s.i. (74-793). Lancer.

Savage Heart. Norman Daniels. (Orig.). 1970. pap. 0.75 o.p. (ISBN 0-447-74651-0). Lancer.

Savage Heart. Aurora Moore. 384p. (Orig.). 1982. pap. 2.95 (ISBN 0-523-41145-6). Pinnacle Bks.

Savage Heart: A Novel. 1st Ed. Denton Whitson. LC 59-7278. 1959. Chilton Co., Book Division.

Savage Height. James Trevor. (O.s.i.). 1969. pap. 0.60 o.s.i. (A476, Award). Univ Pub & Dist.

Savage Heroes: Tales of Magical Fantasy. Michel Parry. LC 79-66645. 1980. 4.95 (ISBN 0-8008-6997-4). Taplinger Pub. Co.

Savage Holiday. Richard Wright. 220p. 1975. Repr. of 1954 ed. 8.50x (ISBN 0-911860-54-1). Chatham Bkseller.

Savage Holiday. Richard Wright. (O.s.i.). 1969. pap. 0.95 o.s.i. (A558N, Award). Univ Pub & Dist.
Savage Hours. L. P Holmes. 1974. (pbk.) 0.75. Ace Books.
Savage in Silk. Donna Comeaux Zide. 1978. 2.25 (ISBN 0-446-82702-9). Warner Books.
Savage Interlude. Carole Mortimer. (Harlequin Presents Ser.). (Orig.). 1980. pap. 1.50 (ISBN 0-373-10340-9, Pub. by Harlequin). PB.
Savage Is Loose. Max Simon Ehrlich. 1974. (pbk.) 1.50. Bantam Books.
Savage Journey. Allan W. Eckert. LC 79-13646. 1979. 9.95 (ISBN 0-316-20876-0). Little.
Savage Journey. Allan W. Eckert. 256p. pap. 1.95 (ISBN 0-445-04614-7). Popular Lib.
Savage Journey: A Novel. Allan W Eckert. LC 79-13646. (Illus.). 9.95 (ISBN 0-316-20876-0). Little, Brown.
Savage Kingdom. Zane Grey. 1978. pap. 1.50 (ISBN 0-505-51293-9). Tower Bks.
Savage Kingdom. Zane Grey. 1982. 18.00x (ISBN 0-86025-147-0, Pub. by Ian Henry Pubns England). State Mutual Bk.
Savage Land. Ann Ahlswede. 1972. pap. 1.25 o.p. (ISBN 0-345-02622-5). Comstock.
Savage Land. Matthew Braun. 1978. 1.95 (ISBN 0-671-82030-3). Pocket Books.
Savage Land: A Novel. Matthew Braun. 1973. (pbk) 0.95. Popular Library.
Savage Mountains: A Horseclans Science Fiction Novel. Robert Adams. (Orig.). 1980. pap. 2.50 (ISBN 0-451-12316-6, AE2316, Sig). NAL.
Savage Oaks. Julie Ellis. LC 77-8997. 8.95 (ISBN 0-671-22874-9). Simon and Schuster.
Savage of Civilization. LC 8-2014. 1895. J. S. Tait & Sons.
Savage Passage. Gardner F. Fox. 1978. pap. 1.95 o.s.i. (ISBN 0-505-51270-X). Tower Bks.
Savage Passion. Barbara A. Cooper. 400p. (Orig.). Date not set. pap. cancelled (ISBN 0-89083-707-4). Zebra.
Savage Pellucidar. Edgar Rice Burroughs. LC 63-21733. 1963. Canaveral Press.
Savage Pelucidar. Edgar Rice Burroughs. (Pellucidar Ser.). 256p. 1982. pap. 2.25 (ISBN 0-441-75136-9). Ace Bks.
Savage Place. Robert B. Parker. 1981. 14.95 (ISBN 0-440-09070-9, Sey Lawr). Delacorte.
Savage Place. Robert B. Parker. 1982. pap. 2.95 (ISBN 0-440-18095-3). Dell.
Savage Place: A Novel. Leon Arden. LC 57-12821. 1957. Crown.
Savage Place: A Novel. Frank Gill Slaughter. LC 64-11693. 1964. Doubleday.
Savage Place: A Spenser Novel. Robert B. Parker. LC 80-29370. 10.95 (ISBN 0-440-08094-0). Delacorte Press/S. Lawrence.
Savage Place: A Spenser Novel. large print ed. Robert B. Parker. LC 81-21446. 10.95 (ISBN 0-89621-343-9). Thorndike Press.
Savage Play: Translated from the French by Alfred Van Ameyden Van Duym. 1st Ed. Paul Colin. LC 52-10428. 1953. Dutton.
Savage Possession. Margaret Pargeter. (Harlequin Presents Ser.). (Orig.). 1980. pap. text ed. 1.50 (ISBN 0-373-10366-2, Pub. by Harlequin). PB.
Savage Prodigal. Konrad Bercovici. LC 48-6968. 1948. Beechhurst. Press.
Savage Range. Luke Short. 1974. (pbk.) 0.75. Bantam Books.
Savage Range. Luke Short. 1976. 0.95. Dell.
Savage Ransom. David Lippincott. LC 78-3114. 8.95 (ISBN 0-89256-061-4). Rawson Associates.
Savage Ransom. David Lippincott. (Signet book.). 1979. 2.25 (ISBN 0-451-08749-6). New American Library.
Savage Rapture. Paula Moore. 1978. pap. 2.25 (ISBN 0-440-07743-5). Dell.
Savage Rapture. Sylvie F. Sommerfield. 1982. pap. 3.50 (ISBN 0-8217-1085-0). Zebra.
Savage Rebel. Robert J Hogan. LC 53-631861. (Silver star westerns). 1953. Dodd, Mead.
Savage Rite. Eric Corder. 1976. (pbk.) 1.50 (ISBN 0-671-80307-7). Pocket Books.
Savage Sanctuary. Jane Donnelly. (Harlequin Romance). 1979. pap. 1.25 (ISBN 0-373-02293-X, Pub. by Harlequin). PB.
Savage Sanctuary. Richard Lionel Spittel. LC 42-16499. 1942. Liveright Publishing Corporation.
Savage Sands. Christina Nicholson. 1978. 2.25 (ISBN 0-449-23762-1). Fawcett Crest.
Savage Sands. Christopher Nicole. LC 77-15983. 1978. 9.95 (ISBN 0-698-10898-1). Coward, McCann & Geoghegan.
Savage Scalpel. Alain Rothstein. (Orig.). 1968. pap. 0.75 o.p. (74-964). Lancer.
Savage Scalpel. x ed. Alain Rothstein. 1972. pap. 0.95 o.s.i. (75-274). Lancer.
Savage Scorpio. Alan Burt Akers. (Illus.). 1978. 1.50 (ISBN 0-87997-372-2). DAW Books.
Savage Scorpio: Dray Prescott No. 16. Alan Burt Akers. (Science Fiction Ser). (Orig.). 1978. pap. 1.50 (ISBN 0-87997-372-2, UW1372). DAW Bks.
Savage Sierra. Theodore V. Olsen. 1970. pap. 0.60 o.p. (R2237, GM). Fawcett World.
Savage Sisters. Carter Brown, pseud. (Signet Book). 1976. (pbk.) 1.25. New American Library.
Savage Slaughter. Bruno Rossi, pseud. (Sharpshooter Ser). (O.s.i.: No. 13). 1975. pap. 1.25 o.s.i. (LB244ZK, Leisure Bks). Nordon Pubns.
Savage Sleep: A Novel. Millen Brand. LC 68-9094. 1968. 6.95. Crown Publishers.
Savage Spirits of Seahedge Manor. Dianne Price. (Orig.). 1982. pap. 2.95 (ISBN 0-89083-940-9). Zebra.
Savage Stars. Richard Reinsmith. (Orig.). 1981. pap. 1.95 (ISBN 0-505-51712-4). Tower Bks.
Savage State. Georges Conchon. LC 65-22450. 1965. Holt, Rinehart and Winston.
Savage State: Tr. by Peter Freyer. Georges Conchon. LC 66-73393. 1966. 4.95. Colins.
Savage State. Tr. from French by Peter Fryer. Georges Conchon. LC 65-22450. bds., 4.50. Holt.
Savage State: Translated by Peter Fryer. London, Collins. Georges Conchon. LC 66-73393. (B 66-3474). 1966. Holt, Rinehart & Winston.
Savage Streets. William P McGivern. 1959. Dodd, Mead.
Savage Sundown. Elizabeth Forbush. 256p. (Orig.). 1980. pap. 2.50 (ISBN 0-523-40664-9). Pinnacle Bks.
Savage Surrender. Charlotte Lamb, pseud. (Harlequin Presents Ser.). 192p. 1980. pap. 1.50 (ISBN 0-373-10401-4, Pub. by Harlequin). PB.
Savage Surrender. Natasha Peters. 600p. 1982. pap. 3.50 (ISBN 0-441-75160-1). Ace Bks.
Savage Touch. Helen Bianchin. (Harlequin Presents Ser.). 192p. 1981. pap. 1.75 (ISBN 0-373-10457-X). Harlequin Bks.
Savage Triangle: Translated from the French by Lawrence G. Blochman. Louis Charles Royer. LC 54-41715. (Pyramid books, 134). 1954. Pyramid Books.
Savage Women. Mike Curtis. 1976. pap. 1.50 o.p. (LB379DK, Leisure Bks). Nordon Pubns.
Savage Women. Mike Curtis. Leisure Books.
Savages. Christopher Hampton. 86p. 1974. pap. 5.95 (ISBN 0-571-10348-0). Faber & Faber.
Savages. Ronald Hardy. (Signet bk., Q3440). 1968. New Amer. Lib.
Savages. Ronald Hardy. LC 66-20279. 1967. Putnam.
Savages. Gordon Ray Young. 1921. Doubleday, Page & Company.
Savages and Saints. Cora Miranda Baggerly Older. LC 36-8263. E. P. Dutton & Co., Inc.
Savages of Gor. John Norman. 1982. pap. 3.50. Daw Bks.
Savanna. Janice Holt Giles. 1977. 1.75 (ISBN 0-380-01643-5). Avon Books.
Savannah. Helen J. Burn. LC 81-47260. 320p. pap. 2.95 (ISBN 0-87216-908-1). Playboy Pbks.
Savannah. John T. Foster. (Orig.). 1982. pap. 3.50 (ISBN 0-89083-953-0). Zebra.
Savannah. Eugenia Price. LC 82-45572. 1983. 19.95 (ISBN 0-385-15274-4). Doubleday.
Savannah: A Novel. Nancy Faulkner. 1.95 (ISBN 0-445-04291-5). Popular Library.
Savannah Blue. William Harrison. LC 80-15436. 9.95 (ISBN 0-399-90081-0). R. Marek.
Savannah Grey. Georgia York. 288p. 1981. pap. 2.75 (ISBN 0-449-14442-9, GM). Fawcett.
Savannah Purchase. Jane Aiken Hodge. LC 73-139034. 1971. 5.95. Doubleday.
Savannah Sayre. Winifred Wadell. LC 52-7517. 1952. Austin-Phelps.
Savata: My Fair Sister. William Goyen. 1970. 13.50 (ISBN 0-7206-7695-9). Dufour.
Save a Lady. Wilson Collison. LC 36-220820. C. Kendall & W. Sharp, Inc.
Save a Rope. Henry Christopher Bailey. LC 48-7744. 1948. Pub. for the Crime Club by Doubleday.
Save Johanna! Francine Pascal. LC 81-1281. 1981. 10.95 (ISBN 0-688-00448-2). Morrow.
Save Johanna! Francine Pascal. 2.95 (ISBN 0-425-05300-8). Berkley Books,, C.
Save Me a Seat. Rhea Kohan. 320p. 1980. pap. 2.25 (ISBN 0-449-24281-1, Crest). Fawcett.
Save Me a Seat. Rhea Kohan. LC 78-69503. 1979. 9.95i (ISBN 0-06-012428-8, HarpT). Har-Row.
Save Me the Sun. Hassoldt Davis. LC 39-30544. H. Holt and Company.
Save Me the Waltz. Zelda Sayre Fitzgerald. LC 67-5363. (Crosscurrents: modern fiction). 1967. Southern Illinois University Press.
Save Me the Waltz. Zelda Sayre Fitzgerald. LC 32-30021. 1932. C. Scribner's Sons.
Save Me the Waltz. Pref. by Harry T. Moore, Afterword by Matthew J. Bruccoli. Zelda Sayre Fitzgerald. (Signet bk., Q3485). 1968. New Amer. Lib.
Save Queen of Sheba. Louise Moeri. 112p. 1982. pap. 1.95 (ISBN 0-380-58529-4, 58529, Flare). Avon.
Save the Tiger. Steve Shagan. (Dell Book, 7559). 1973. 1.25. Dell.
Save the Tiger. Steve Shagan. LC 72-3674. 1972. Dial Press.
Save the Whale: A Novel. Michael Koepf. LC 77-26677. 7.95 (ISBN 0-07-035280-1). McGraw-Hill.
Save the Witness. Patricia McGerr. LC 49-116786. 1949. Published for the Crime Club by Doubleday.
Saved As by Fire. A Story Illustrating How One of Nature's Noblemen Was Saved from the Demon of Drink. Timothy Shay Arthur. (On cover: Cottage library). Cottage Library Publishing House.
Saved at Last from Among the Mormons. Cornelia Paddock. (On cover: Farm and fireside library, v. 1. no. 4). 1881. Farm and Fireside Company.
Saved by a Dream. Anna Cyrene Reifsnider. (library of choice fiction no. 30). 1891. Laird & Lee.
Saved by a Woman: Or, The Hidden Romance. A Story of the Late War. Whitemarsh B. Seabrook. LC 3-3396. 1884. J. P. Harrison & Co., Printers.
Saved by the Enemy. Upton Beall Sinclair. LC 99-369. (On cover: Columbia library, vol. 1, no 8). 1898. Street & Smith.
Saved by the Sword: A Novel. Robert Rexdale. LC 7-30931. 1889. Winthrop Publishing Company.
Saved by the Sword: A Novel. Robert Rexdale. LC 7-30930. (On cover: American novelists' series, no. 39). 1890. J. W. Lovell Company.
Saved for a Purpose. Mary Morrison Chitwood. LC 21-21548. The Chirstopher Publishing House.
Saved for Service. 2d ed.... ed. Emma Fox Puthuff & American Baptist Association. Baptist Sunday School Committee. LC 43-171393. 1943. Baptist Sunday School Committee.
Saved from the Sea: Or, The Loss of the "Viper," and the Adventures of Her Crew in the Great Sahara. William Henry Giles Kingston. LC 44-23379. 1884. T. Nelson and Sons.
Saved to Serve. Harriet Cecil Magee. (On cover: The crown series). 1895. American Baptist Publication Society.
Saveli's Expiation. A Russian Story. Alice Marie Celeste Durand. Tr. by Sherwood, Mary (Neal) LC 6-35685. T. B. Peterson & Brothers.
Saveli's Expiation. A Russian Story. Alice Marie Celeste Durand. Tr. by Sherwood, Mary (Neal) T. B. Peterson & Brothers.
Savignys. Edith J. Lyttleton. LC 19-862. 1918. Hodder and Stoughton.
Saville. David Storey. LC 76-379889. 1976. 4.50 (ISBN 0-224-01273-8). Cape.
Saville. David Storey. LC 76-50169. 1978. 2.25 (ISBN 0-380-01889-6). Avon.
Savinelli. John Chartres Molony. LC 30-27686. 1930. L.MacVeagh, The Dail Press.
Saving Grace. Celia Gittelson. LC 81-47520. 1981. 10.95 (ISBN 0-394-51776-8). Knopf: Distributed by Random House.
Saving Grace. McCready Huston. LC 53-11115. 1954-1953. Lippincott.
Saving Graces. Rhoda Tagliacozzo. LC 79-16343. 1979. 9.95 (ISBN 0-312-69988-3). St. Martin's Press.
Saving Pride. Yvette Prost. Tr. by Dearborn, Frank Alvah. LC 12-22137. 1912. 1.25. Dodd, Mead and Company.
Saving Sence. Wesley B. Kerr. LC 29-228024. 1929. The Acorn Press.
Saving the Queen. William Frank Buckley. LC 75-17405. 1976. 7.95 (ISBN 0-385-03800-3). Doubleday.
Saving the Queen. William Frank Buckley. 1.95 (ISBN 0-446-89164-9). Warner.
Saving Worlds: A Collection of Original Science Fiction Stories. Ed. by Roger Elwood. LC 72-84910. 1973. 6.95 (ISBN 0-385-05409-2). Doubleday.
Savior. Marvin Werlin & Mark Werlin. LC 78-17878. 9.95 (ISBN 0-671-24013-7). Simon and Schuster.
Saviors of God. Nikos Kazantzakis. Tr. by Kimor Friar. 1969. pap. 4.95 (ISBN 0-671-20232-4, Touchstone Bks). S&S.
Saviours of Society: Being the First Part of The Realists. Stephen McKenna. LC 26-16327. 1926. Little, Brown, and Company.
Savoy Stories. Evelyn Gatliff. 1950. 7.50x o.p. (ISBN 0-522-83611-9, Pub. by Melbourne U Pr); pap. 3.00 o.p. (ISBN 0-522-83795-6, Pub. by Melbourne U Pr). Intl Schol Bk Serv.
Saw. Steve Katz. LC 74-178961. 1972. 3.50 (ISBN 0-394-47930-0). Knopf.
Saw-Ge-Mah (Medicine Man) 1st Ed. Louis J Gariepy. LC 50-23479. 1950. Northland Press.
Saw the House in Half: A Novel. Oliver Jackman. LC 73-88971. 1974. (ISBN 0-88258-010-8). Howard University Press.
Sawabas-Black Africa's Mafia. Chidi Onyekwelu. LC 78-62147. 6.95 (ISBN 0-533-03878-2). Vantage Press.
Sawbones of Desolate Range. Archie Joscelyn. LC 41-78646. Phoenix Press.
Sawdust. Mary L Vissing. LC 46-1438. 1945. Meador Publishing Company.
Sawdust: A Romance of the Timberlands. Dorothea Gerard Longard De Longgarde. LC 5-17281. (The Griffin series of new fiction). 1905. The J. C. Winston Co.
Sawdust & Sixguns. Evan Evans, pseud. 246p. 1976. Repr. of 1950 ed. lib. bdg. 14.10x (ISBN 0-89190-208-2). Am Repr-Rivercity Pr.
Sawdust and Sixguns. Frederick Faust. LC 76-41326. 1976. 6.95 (ISBN 0-89190-208-2). American Reprint Co.
Sawdust and Sixguns: By Evan Evans Pseud. 1st Ed. Frederick Faust. LC 50-8578. 1950. Harper.
Sawdust Doll. Anna Farwell De Koven. LC 6-33182. (Half-title: The peacock library). 1895. Stone and Kimball.
Sawdust in Your Eyes. W. E. Blackhurst. 1963. 10.00 (ISBN 0-87012-006-9). McClain.
Sawdust Season. Day Thorpe. 192p. 1972. pap. 0.60 o.p. S&S.
Saxby: A Tale of Old and New England. Emma Leslie. LC 7-14494. (Church history stories, 2d ser. v 4). 1880. Phillips & Hunt.
Saxby for God. Richard Haley. 1974. 6.95 o.p. (ISBN 0-698-10589-3). Coward.
Saxe Holm's Stories. Helen Maria Fiske Hunt Jackson. LC 69-11903. (American short story series, v. 61-62). 1969. Garrett Press.
Saxe Holm's Stories. Helen Maria Fiske Hunt Jackson. LC 74-110225. (Short story index reprint series). Books for Libraries Press.
Saxe Holm's Stories. Helen Maria Fiske Hunt Jackson. LC 72-8140. (American short story series, v. 61-62). 1972. (ISBN 0-8422-8079-0). MSS Information Corp.
Saxe Holm's Stories. Helen Maria Fiske Hunt Jackson. LC 7-25586. 1874-78. Scribner, Armstrong, & Company.
Saxe Holm's Stories... Helen Maria Fiske Hunt Jackson. LC 16-9374. 1906-08. C. Scribner's Sons.
Saxe Holm's Stories, First Series. Helen Maria Fiske Hunt Jackson. LC 74-110225. (Short Story Index Reprint Ser.). 1873. 17.00 (ISBN 0-8369-3375-3). Ayer Co.
Saxe Holm's Stories, Second Series. facsimile ed. Helen H. Jackson. LC 74-110225. (Short Story Index Reprint Ser.). Repr. of 1878 ed. 16.00 (ISBN 0-8369-3817-8). Ayer Co.
Saxe Holm's Stories, Ser. 1. Helen H. Jackson. Ed. by Clarence Gohdes. LC 69-11903. (American Short Story Ser., Vol. 61). 1969. Repr. of 1874 ed. lib. bdg. 17.95 o.s.i. (ISBN 0-512-00362-9). Garrett Pr.
Saxe Holm's Stories, Ser. 2. Helen H. Jackson. Ed. by Clarence Gohdes. LC 69-11903. (American Short Story Ser., Vol. 62). 1969. Repr. of 1878 ed. lib. bdg. 17.95 o.s.i. (ISBN 0-512-00363-7). Garrett Pr.
Saxenhurst: A Story of the Old World and New. Daniel Clarke Eddy. LC 6-26316. American Baptist Publication Society.
Saxon Ashe, Secret Agent. LC 42-10428. 1942. Alliance Book Corporation.
Saxon Charm. Frederic Wakeman. LC 47-5596. 1947. Rinehart.
Saxon Sheep: A Novel Based on the Activities of the Templeton and Forlang Families in the Early Days of Australian Settlement. Nancy Mitchell Adams. LC 66-5624. 1966. 8.75. Cheshire- Lansdowne Pr.
Saxon's Folly. Hebe Elsna. 1971. pap. 0.95 o.p. (95073). Beagle Bks.
Saxon's Ghost. Stephen Gould Fisher. LC 76-83559. 1969. 4.95. Sherbourne Press.
Say and Seal. Susan Warner & Anna Bartlett Warner. LC 8-33695. 1860. J. B. Lippincott & Co.
Say and Seal. Susan Warner & Anna Bartlett Warner. LC 25-15521. 1887. J. B. Lippincott Company.
Say, Darling: A New Novel. 1st Ed. Richard Pike Bissell. LC 56-9071. 1957. Little, Brown.
Say Good-Bye to Katharine. Allene Soule Corliss. LC 43-983. 1943. Farrar & Rinehart, Inc.
Say Hello to Yesterday. William Hughes. (O.s.i.). (Orig.). 1971. pap. 0.75 o.s.i. (A815S, Award). Univ Pub & Dist.
Say Hello to Yesterday. Sally Wentworth. (Harlequin Presents Ser.). 192p. 1981. pap. 1.50 (ISBN 0-373-10426-X, Pub. by Harlequin). PB.
Say It Ain't So, Gordon Littlefield. Eliot Asinof. LC 77-1608. 1977. 7.95 o.p. (ISBN 0-525-19610-2). Dutton.
Say It Ain't So, Gordon Littlefield: A Novel. Eliot Asinof. LC 77-1608. 7.95 (ISBN 0-525-19610-2). E. P. Dutton.
Say It My Way. Willard Espy. 220p. 1981. pap. 5.95 (ISBN 0-14-005733-1). Penguin.
Say It with Bullets. Richard Pitts Powell. LC 53-108158. (Inner sanctum mystery). 1953. Simon and Schuster.
Say It with Love: By Emily Noble Pseud. James Noble Gifford. LC 52-10859. 1952. Arcadia House.

Say It with Murder. 3rd ed. Edward Sidney Aarons. 1971. pap. 0.95 o.p. (532-75405-075). Manor Bks.
Say It with Songs. Arline De Haas & Zanuck, Darryl Francis. LC 29-22046. Grosset & Dunlap.
Say Nothing. James Hanley. LC 62-15296. 1962. Horizon Press.
Say Uncle. Dorothy A Burgess. LC 45-7199. 1944. Murray & Gee, Inc.
Say Yes! Ralph Caplan. LC 64-13856. 4.95. Doubleday.
Say Yes, Samantha. Barbara Cartland. (Barbara Cartland library, 27). 1975. (pbk.) 1.25. Bantam.
Say Yes to Murder. Willis Todhunter Ballard. LC 42-22990. 1942. G. P. Putnam's Sons.
Say You Never Saw Me. Arthur Nesbitt. LC 57-8933. 1957. Scribner.
Sayage Chase: By Frederick Lorenz Pseud. Lorenz Heller. LC 54-44357. (Lion book, 223). 1954. Lion Books by Arrangement with Medalion Pub. Corp.
Sayanara. James A Michener. LC 54-5953. 1974. (pbk.) 1.25. Fawcett.
Sayings and Doings: Or, Sketches from Life. 2d series... ed. Theodore Edward Hook. LC 7-5270. 1825. H. C. Carey and I. Lea.
Sayings of Buddha: The Iti-Vuttaka. Buddha. Tr. by Justin H. More. 1908. 10.00 o.p. AMS Pr.
Sayings of Lao Tzu. Lionel Giles. (Wisdom of the East Ser). 4.50 o.p. (ISBN 0-7195-0485-6). Paragon.
Sayonara. James A Michener. LC 81-7024. 1981. 13.95 (ISBN 0-8161-3260-7). G.K. Hall.
Sayonara. James Albert Michener. LC 54-5953. Random House.
Sayonara: Good-Bye. John Paris, pseud. LC 24-8162. Boni and Liveright.
Says Mrs. Crowley: Says She! Doran Hurley. LC 41-462686. 1941. Longmans, Green and Co.
Scabby Dichson. Richard Blaker. LC 28-7946. Doubleday, Doran & Company, Inc.
Scaffold. Adam Kennedy. 1971. 7.95 o.p. (27078). Trident.
Scaffold: A Novel. Adam Kennedy. LC 75-147387. 1973. (pbk) 1.25 (ISBN 0-671-78305-X). Pocket Books.
Scaffold: A Novel. Adam Kennedy. LC 75-147387. 1971. 7.95 (ISBN 0-671-27078-8). Trident Press.
Scala Dei: A Novel. Daniel Boone Dodson. LC 75-1419. 1975. 7.95 (ISBN 0-88405-103-X). Mason/Charter.
Scalawags. James Ball Naylor. LC 7-11210. 1907. B. W. Dodge and Company.
Scales of Justice. George Leonard Knapp. LC 10-22133. 1910. 1.50. J. B. Lippincott Company.
Scales of Justice. Ngaio Marsh. 1976. Repr. of 1955 ed. lib. bdg. 16.60x (ISBN 0-88411-493-7). Amereon Ltd.
Scales of Justice. Ngaio Marsh. 1977. pap. 1.50 (ISBN 0-425-03551-4, Medallion). Berkley Pub.
Scales of Justice. Ngaio Marsh. 256p. 1980. pap. 2.50 (ISBN 0-515-06497-1). Jove Pubns.
Scales of Justice. 1st Ed. Ngaio Marsh. LC 55-7471. 1955. Little, Brown.
Scally: The Story of a Perfect Gentleman. John Hay Beith. LC 15-24880. 1915. Houghton Mifflin Company.
Scallywag. Grant Allen. LC 12-10050. 1893. Cassell Publishing Company.
Scalp-Lock. Dane Coolidge. LC 24-2621. E. P. Dutton & Company.
Scalpel. Horace McCoy. LC 52-10495. 1952. Appleton-Century-Crofts.
Scalpel of Honor. Dolores Craig. 1969. pap. 0.60 o.p. (73-850). Lancer.
Scalpel's Edge. Alfred A. Weinstein. 1970. pap. 0.95 o.p. (ISBN 0-447-75147-6). Lancer.
Scalpel's Edge. Alfred A. Weinstein. 4.50 o.s.i. (ISBN 0-8181-0279-9). Pageant-Poseidon.
Scalphunters. Ed Friend. 128p. 1981. pap. 1.75 (ISBN 0-449-12351-0, GM). Fawcett.
Scalphunters. Ed Friend. 1970. pap. 0.60 o.p. (R2351, GM). Fawcett World.
Scalps: A Murder Mystery. William Fitzgerald Jenkins. LC 30-20811. 1930. Brewer & Warren Inc.
Scamp: The Fortunes of Francis Talbot and His Friends During the Reign of His Majesty George the First. Virgil Markham. LC 26-11633. 1926. The Macmillan Company.
Scandal. Pedro Antonio De Alarcon & Riley, Philip Henry, 1898- Tr. LC 45-4133. 1945. A. A. Knopf.
Scandal. Frances Nichols Hanna. LC 37-8282. 1937. Godwin.
Scandal. Violette Newton. 1980. 4.95 (ISBN 0-89015-290-X). Eakin Pubns.
Scandal. Fan Nichols. 1970. pap. 0.75 o.p. (75-316). Manor Bks.
Scandal! Janet Street-Porter. 224p. (Orig.). 1983. pap. 8.95 (ISBN 0-440-58260-1). Dell.
Scandal: A Novel. Cosmo Hamilton. LC 17-239822. 1917. 1.50. Little, Brown, and Company.
Scandal at Daybreak. 1st Ed. Elizabeth West Wallace. LC 54-123421. 1954. Pageant Press.
Scandal at High Chimneys: A Victorian Melodrama. 1st Ed. John Dickson Carr. LC 59-11155. 1959. Harper.
Scandal Bride. Louise Holmes. LC 40-315233. 1940. Gateway Books.
Scandal Goddess. William Hegner. LC 75-96997. 1975. (pbk.) 1.50 (ISBN 0-671-80057-4). Pocket Books.
Scandal Goddess. William Hegner. LC 75-96997. 1970. 5.95. Delacorte Press.
Scandal Has Two Faces. Mary Elizabeth Campbell. LC 43-15843. 1943. Pub. for the Crime Club by Doubleday, Doran and Co., Inc.
Scandal House. Madeline Woods. LC 33-31758. J. Messner, Inc.
Scandal in Bohemia. Arthur Conan Doyle. (On cover: Seaside library. Pocket ed, no. 2093). 1895. G. Munro's Sons.
Scandal in Eden: A Novel. Garet Rogers. LC 63-10561. 1963. Dial Press.
Scandal in the Chancery. John Franklin Carter. LC 31-21896. J. Cape & H. Smith.
Scandal in Troy. Translated by Dorothy F. Grimm and Sven O. Karell. Eva Hemmer Hansen. LC 56-8795. 1956. Random House.
Scandal Monger. Emile Henry Gauvreau. LC 32-22716. The Macaulay Company.
Scandal of Falconhurst. Ashley Carter, pseud. (Orig.). 1980. pap. 2.50 (ISBN 0-449-14334-1, GM). Fawcett.
Scandal of Father Brown. Gilbert Keith Chesterton. LC 35-163186. 1935. Dodd, Mead & Company.
Scandal of Father Brown. Gilbert Keith Chesterton. LC 82-125631. (Penguin crime fiction). 1982. 2.95 (ISBN 0-14-004739-5). Penguin Books.
Scandal on the Hill. Gabrielle Vincent. (O.s.i.). (Orig.). pap. 0.60 o.s.i. (A218, Award). Univ Pub & Dist.
Scandal Rag. Joseph Harrington. LC 42-22994. 1942. Smith & Durrell, Inc.
Scandal Sheets: A Novel Based on the Life of Pietro Arentino, the First Yellow Journalist. E. R Conde. 1930. G. H. Watt.
Scandalous. Manley M Bannister. LC 39-7586. 1939. Godwin.
Scandalous. William Arthur Neubauer. LC 45-6683. 1945. Phoenix Press.
Scandalous Affair. Clarissa Ross, pseud. 1977. pap. 1.50 o.s.i. (ISBN 0-505-51213-0). Tower Bks.
Scandalous Affair: Clarissa Ross. Clarissa Ross, pseud. (Belmont Tower Book). 1977. 1.50 (ISBN 0-505-51213-0). Tower Pubns.
Scandalous Bequest. April Kihlstrom. 1982. pap. 2.25 (ISBN 0-451-11774-3). NAL.
Scandalous French Doctor. Jean Calvet. 1969. pap. 0.75 o.p. (75-269). Manor Bks.
Scandalous John: An Authentic History of the Life and Exploits of the Last of the Great Trail Bosses, Together with Elucidation of His Mission, Descriptions of His Friends and Antagonists, and Including a Detailed Account of His Timely and Bloody End. Richard M Gardner. LC 63-11246. 1963. Doubleday.
Scandalous Lady. Maggie Gladstone, pseud. LC 78-54990. 192p. 1978. pap. 1.50 (ISBN 0-87216-473-X). Playboy Pbks.
Scandalous Lady Robin: A Romantic Comedy. June Sylvia Thimblethorpe. (Georgian romance). (Fawcett crest book). 1975. (pbk.) 1.25. Fawcett.
Scandalous Life of King Carol. Barbara Cartland. 1977. pap. 1.25 o.p. (ISBN 0-515-04318-4). BJ Pub Group.
Scandalous Mrs. Blackford. Harnett Thomas Kane. LC 51-10943. 1951. J. Messner.
Scandalous Widow. Monette Cummings. 192p. (Orig.). 1982. pap. 2.25 (ISBN 0-8439-1102-6, Leisure Bks). Nordon Pubns.
Scandalous Widow: A Novel. Sylvester B Yapp. LC 59-63. Exposition Press.
Scandalous Woman, and Other Stories. Edna O'Brien. LC 74-7366. 1974. 6.95 (ISBN 0-15-179558-4). Harcourt Brace Jovanovich.
Scandalous Woman: And Other Stories. Edna O'Brien. 1976. (pbk.) 1.75 (ISBN 0-345-24805-8). Ballantine Books.
Scandals. Barney Leason. 448p. 1982. pap. 3.50 (ISBN 0-523-41596-6). Pinnacle Bks.
Scandals at the Country Club see Sinful.
Scandals of Clochemerle. Gabriel Chevallier & Godefroi, Jocelyn, Tr. LC 37-9867. 1937. Simon and Schuster.
Scandaroon. Henry Williamson. 1973. 5.95 o.p. (ISBN 0-8415-0240-4). Sat Rev Pr.
Scanner Darkly. Philip K Dick. LC 73-11630. 1977. 6.95 (ISBN 0-385-01613-1). Doubleday.
Scanners. Leon Whiteson. (Orig.). 1981. pap. 2.25 (ISBN 0-505-51675-6). Tower Bks.
Scapa Flow. Malcolm Brown & Patricia Meehan. 1968. 7.50 o.p. (ISBN 0-7139-0070-9, AL70). Allen Lane.
Scapegoat. 1stamerican ed. Jocelyn Brooke. LC 49-50342. 1950. Harper.
Scapegoat. Daphne Du Maurier. LC 57-5902. 1957. Doubleday.
Scapegoat. Poul Orum. Tr. by Kenneth Barclay from Danish. LC 75-4964. Orig. Title: The Whipping Boy. 264p. 1975. Repr. 6.95 o.p. (ISBN 0-394-49055-X). Pantheon.
Scapegoat. large print ed. Mary Lee Settle. LC 81-5636. 1981. 12.95 (ISBN 0-89621-285-8). Thorndike Press.
Scapegoat. August Strindberg. Tr. by Arvid Paulson. LC 66-26646. 1967. P. S. Eriksson.
Scapegoat: A Mystery. Poul Rum. LC 75-4964. 1975. 6.95 (ISBN 0-394-49055-X). Pantheon Books.
Scapegoat: A Novel. Mary Lee Settle. LC 80-5266. 11.95 (ISBN 0-394-50477-1). Random House.
Scapegoat for a Stuart. Kate Kirby. LC 76-28074. 1976. 7.95. St. Martin's Press.
Scapegoats: A Novel. George Mandel. LC 73-110502. 1970. 5.95. Delacorte Press.
Scapegrace. Janet Templeton. LC 81-43150. 10.95 (ISBN 0-385-17630-9). Doubleday.
Scapegrace. Sylvia Thorpe. 1978. pap. 1.50 (ISBN 0-449-23478-9, Crest). Fawcett.
Scapgraces. P. J. Wade. (Orig.). 1975. pap. price not set o.p. (ISBN 0-515-03669-2). Pyramid Pubns.
Scar. Ruby Mildred Ayres. LC 21-712207. W. J. Watt & Company.
Scar. Sallie Lee Bell. LC 64-8836. bds., 2.50. Zondervan.
Scar. Francis Warrington Dawson. LC 10-8158. 1910. Small, Maynard & Company.
Scar. Charles H Holding. LC 46-17838. 1946. Wm. B. Eerdmans Publishing Company.
Scar. William Michael Robison. LC 11-133571. 1911. The Cumberland Press.
Scar. Derek Vane. LC 25-185802. E. J. Clode, Inc.
Scar Mirror. Derek Pell. (Illus.). 1979. signed ed. cancelled (ISBN 0-916866-06-8); pap. 2.50 (ISBN 0-916866-05-X). Cats Pajamas.
Scar. 1st Ed. Eric Rhodin. LC 61-6466. 1961. Harper.
Scarab Murder Case. S. S. Van Dine. 1980. lib. bdg. 10.95 (ISBN 0-8398-2556-0, Gregg). G K Hall.
Scarab Murder Case. Willard Huntington Wright. LC 79-22852. (Series: Philo Vance Series.). (Gregg Press mystery fiction series). (Illus.). 1980. 10.95 (ISBN 0-8398-2556-0). Gregg Press.
Scarab Murder Case: A Philo Vance Story. Willard Huntington Wright. LC 30-26602. (Half-title: The Philo Vance series). 1930. C. Scribner's Sons.
Scarabaeus: The Story of an African Beetle. Clara Hammond Lanza & Harvey, James Clarence. LC 7-13837. Lovell Coryell & Company.
Scaramouche. Rafael Sabatini. 10.95 (ISBN 0-395-08142-4). HM.
Scaramouche: A Romance of the French Revolution. Rafael Sabatini. LC 21-10172. 1921. Houghton Mifflin Company.
Scaramouche: A Romance of the French Revolution. Rafael Sabatini. LC 24-1977. 1923. Grosset & Dunlap.
Scaramouche the King-Maker. Rafael Sabatini. LC 31-25044. 1931. Houghton Mifflin Company.
Scarborough Hall. Boyd Upchurch. (Berkley Medallion) (ISBN 0-425-03256-6). Berkley.
Scarborough House. Sharon Anne Salvato. LC 74-27000. 1975. 8.95 (ISBN 0-8128-1772-9). Stein and Day.
Scarcity of Love: A Novel. Helen Woods Edmonds. LC 74-181007. 1972. 5.95. Herder and Herder.
Scarcity of Love: A Novel. Anna Kavan. LC 74-181007. (Orig.). 5.95 o.p. (ISBN 0-07-073262-0). McGraw.
Scarecrow. Archibald E. Fielding. LC 37-13111. 1937. H. C. Kinsey & Company, Inc.
Scarecrow. Eaton K Goldthwaite. LC 45-5489. 1945. Duell, Sloan and Pearce.
Scarecrow. Calvin C Hernton. LC 73-14049. 1974. 6.95. Doubleday.
Scarecrow: And Other Stories. Gwendolyn Ranger Wormser. LC 18-19926. E. P. Dutton & Company.
Scarecrow Man. Christopher Bray. LC 68-29053. 1968. 3.95. Viking Press.
Scarecrow Murders. Frederic Arnold Kummer. LC 38-5597. 1938. Dodd, Mead & Company.
Scarecrow Rides. Arthur Russell Thorndike. LC 35-38102. The Dial Press.
Scarecrow Soldiers. Shepherd Welsh. 384p. (Orig.). 1981. pap. 2.95 (ISBN 0-523-48007-5). Pinnacle Bks.
Scarecrows of Saint-Emmanuel. Andre Major. LC 77-377702. 12.95 (ISBN 0-7710-5471-8). McClelland and Stewart.
Scared to Death. Anne Morice. LC 77-4601. 7.95 (ISBN 0-312-70043-1). St. Martin's Press.
Scared to Death. Anne Morice. LC 78-7521. 1978. 9.95 (ISBN 0-8161-6584-X). G. K. Hall.
Scared to Death: By George Bagby Pseud. Aaron Marc Stein. LC 52-5239. 1952. Published for the Crime Club by Doubleday.
Scared to Death: By Rae Foley. Elinore Denniston. LC 66-21752. (Red badge mystery). 1966. 3.50. Dodd.
Scarel: Only a Story. a new ed. Louise Pela Ramee. LC 42-35201. 1888. Chatto and Windus.
Scarf. Robert Bloch. LC 47-30429. 1947. Dial Press.
Scarf. Francis Durbridge. Orig. Title: Case of the Twisted Scarf. 192p. 1973. Repr. of 1961 ed. 5.95 o.s.i. (ISBN 0-85617-992-2). White Lion Pubs.
Scarf Cloud. Robert Lloyd Pruett. LC 47-24594. 1947. Printed by the Nevada Printing & Pub. Co.
Scarf on the Scarecrow. Martin Joseph Freeman. LC 38-11471. 1938. E. P. Dutton & Co., Inc.
Scarface. Armitage Trail. LC 30-81625. E. J. Clode, Inc.
Scarfaced Killer. Bruno Rossi, pseud. (Sharpshooter Ser). (O.s.i.: No. 12). (Orig.). 1975. pap. 1.25 o.s.i. (LB235ZK, Leisure Bks). Nordon Pubns.
Scarhaven Keep. Joseph Smith Fletcher. LC 22-1723. 1922. A. A. Knopf.
Scarlatti Inheritance: A Novel. Robert Ludlum. LC 77-133476. 1971. 6.95. World Pub. Co.
Scarlet & Black. Stendhal. Tr. by M. R. Shaw. (Classics Ser.). (Orig.). 1953. pap. 3.95 (ISBN 0-14-044030-5). Penguin.
Scarlet and Black: A Chronicle of the Nineteenth Century by Stendhal Pseud. Translated and with an Introd. by Margaret R. B. Shaw. Marie Henri Beyle. LC 56-376225. (Penguin classics, L30). 1955. Penguin Books.
Scarlet and Hyssop: A Novel. Edward Frederic Benson. 1902. D. Appleton and Co.
Scarlet and Purple: A Study of Souls and "Signs". Sydney Watson. LC 33-32919. Fleming H. Revell Company.
Scarlet and White. Olive Wadsley. LC 36-784321. 1938. Dodd, Mead & Company.
Scarlet Angel. Manning Lee Stokes. LC 51-9300. 1950. Phoenix Press.
Scarlet Angel: A Novel. Dorene Clark. LC 54-24971. 1954. Woodford Press.
Scarlet Arena 30303. Silas Moore. LC 74-190272. (Illus.). 1972. 5.95. Oddo Pub.
Scarlet Banner. Felix Ludwig Sophus Dahn. LC 3-28841. 1903. A. C. McClurg & Co.
Scarlet Banners of Love. Sacha Carnegie, pseud. LC 68-54453. 1968. 6.95. Dodd, Mead.
Scarlet Boy. 1st Ed. Arthur Calder-Marshall. LC 62-7899. 1962. Harper.
Scarlet Button. Lucy Beatrice Malleson. LC 45-9071. 1945. Smith & Durrell.
Scarlet Car. Richard Harding Davis. LC 7-22818. 1907. C. Scribner's Sons.
Scarlet Car: The Princess Aline. Richard Harding Davis. LC 10-19386. 1910. C. Scribner's Sons.
Scarlet Charm: A Romance of Alaska. A. Warren West. LC 30-852. 1929. Chapple Publishing Company, Limited.
Scarlet Children. Etheldra Kaye. LC 35-19002. Alliance Press.
Scarlet Circle. Jonathan Stagge, pseud. LC 43-8698. 1943. Pub. for the Crime Club by Doubleday, Doran & Co., Inc.
Scarlet Cockerel. Clifford MacClellan Sublette. LC 31-21885. (Beacon hill bookshelf). 1931. Little, Brown, and Company.
Scarlet Cockerel: A Novel. Garald Lagard. LC 48-8680. 1948. W. Morrow.
Scarlet Cockerel: A Tale Wherein Is Set Down a Record of the Strange and Exceptional Adventures of Blaise De Breault and Martin Belcastel in the New World, As Members of Expeditions Sent Out by the Great Coligny. Clifford MacClellan Sublette. LC 25-7832. The Atlantic Monthly Press.
Scarlet Cord. Lewis W. Sullivan. 1977. pap. 1.75 (ISBN 0-89041-137-9, 3137). Major Bks.
Scarlet Cord: A Novel of the Woman of Jericho. 1st Ed. Frank Gill Slaughter. LC 56-5595. 1956. Doubleday.
Scarlet Dog Collage. Merle G. Snider. 1978. pap. 2.95 (ISBN 0-89185-181-X). Anthelion Pr.
Scarlet Domino. Sylvia Thorpe. LC 79-25386. 1980. 10.95 (ISBN 0-89340-247-8). J. Curley.
Scarlet Empire. David Maclean Parry. LC 6-92753. The Bobbs-Merrill Company.
Scarlet Empire. David Maclean Parry. LC 43-39054. Grosset & Dunlap.
Scarlet Fan. Henry Leyford Gates. LC 32-6897. 1932. The Macaulay Company.
Scarlet Feather. Joan Marshall Grant. LC 78-20228. (Grant, Joan Marshall, 1907-. Works.). (Illus.). 1980. 20.00 (ISBN 0-405-11789-2). Arno Press.
Scarlet Feather. Houghton Townley. LC 9-16440. 1909. W. J. Watt & Company.
Scarlet Feather. Dale Van Every. LC 59-5760. 1959. Holt.
Scarlet Feather: A Johnny Fletcher Mystery. Frank Gruber. LC 48-1847. (Murray Hill mystery). 1948. Rinehart.
Scarlet Flower. Daniel Joseph Clinton. LC 33-31428. 1933. Farrar & Rinehart, Incorporated.

Scarlet Flower: Or, The Token of Love, Faith, and Death. Pierce Egan. (Seaside library, v. 63, no. 1271). 1882. G. Munro.
Scarlet Flush. Alan Geoffrey Yates. LC 64-1103. (N. A. L. Signet books). 1963. New American Library of World Literature.
Scarlet Fox: A Novel of Mystery. Eustace Hale Ball. LC 28-677. Grosset & Dunlap.
Scarlet Frontier. Edward Vivian Timms. LC 54-19813. 1953. Angus and Robertson.
Scarlet Guidon. Toepfer, Ray Grant. LC 58-13327. 1958. Coward-McCann.
Scarlet Handkerchief. Symmes M Jelley. LC 7-10194. (Pinkerton detective series, v. 30). Laird & Lee.
Scarlet Heels. Netta Muskett. 1975. pap. 1.25 o.p. (ISBN 0-515-03707-9, V3707). BJ Pub Group.
Scarlet Heels. Edith Mendel Stern. LC 28-20918. H. Liveright.
Scarlet Hill. Frank Owen. LC 41-7800. 1941. Carlyle House.
Scarlet Hills. Harry Beck. 160p. 1982. 9.95 (ISBN 0-8027-4005-7). Walker & Co.
Scarlet Hills. Betty Hale Hyatt. (Candlelight Regency, 118). 1973. (pbk.) 0.75. Dell.
Scarlet Hills. Lauran Paine. LC 81-69103. 9.95 (ISBN 0-8027-4005-7). Walker.
Scarlet Imposter. Dennis Yates Wheatley, pseud. 1973. (pbk.) 1.50. Ballantine.
Scarlet Iris. Vance Thompson. The Bobbs-Merrill Company.
Scarlet Josephine". Marjorie Muir Worthington. LC 33-25192. 1933. A. A. Knopf.
Scarlet Kisses. Stephanie Blake. LC 81-80079. 368p. (Orig.). 1981. pap. 2.95 (ISBN 0-87216-847-6). Playboy Pbks.
Scarlet Letter. Nathaniel Hawthorne. (Large type ed. Keith Jennison bk.). 6.95. Watts.
Scarlet Letter. Nathaniel Hawthorne. Ed. by Spector, Robert Donald. LC 65-17435. (Bantam pathfinder editions, FP91). 1965. Bantam Books.
Scarlet Letter. Hawthorne, Nathaniel. LC 65-6533. (Perennial classic). 1965. Harper & Row.
Scarlet Letter. large type ed., complete and unabridged ed. Hawthorne, Nathaniel. LC 66-31944. 1966. F. Watts.
Scarlet Letter. Nathaniel Hawthorne. LC 68-56080. (Cambridge classics library). (Illus.). 1968. Cambridge Book Co.
Scarlet Letter. Nathaniel Hawthorne. LC 48-1188. (Rinehart editions, 1). 1947. Rinehart.
Scarlet Letter. Nathaniel Hawthorne. LC 48-8215. (Great Illustrated Classics). 1948. Dodd, Mead.
Scarlet Letter. Nathaniel Hawthorne. LC 9-2678. Truslove and Combs.
Scarlet Letter. Nathaniel Hawthorne. LC 9-19674. 1885. Houghton, Mifflin and Co.
Scarlet Letter. universal ed. Nathaniel Hawthorne. 1892. Houghton, Mifflin and Company.
Scarlet Letter. salem ed. Nathaniel Hawthorne. LC 42-27365. 1892. Houghton, Mifflin and Company.
Scarlet Letter. large paper ed. Nathaniel Hawthorne. LC 1-1055. 1892. Printed at the Riverside Press.
Scarlet Letter. Nathaniel Hawthorne. LC 4716. W. B. Conkey Company.
Scarlet Letter. Nathaniel Hawthorne. 1900. Dodd, Mead and Company.
Scarlet Letter. Nathaniel Hawthorne. LC 36-37110. (Half-title: Everyman's library, ed. by Ernest Rhys. Fiction. no. 122). 1927. J. M. Dent & Sons, Ltd.
Scarlet Letter. Nathaniel Hawthorne. LC 27-6055. (Half-title: The modern library of the world's best books). The Modern Library.
Scarlet Letter. Nathaniel Hawthorne. LC 36-40. 1935. The Heritage Press.
Scarlet Letter. Nathaniel Hawthorne. (Half-title: The Living library). 1946. The World Publishing Company.
Scarlet Letter. Nathaniel Hawthorne. LC 50-5575. (World's greatest literature). 1950. Fountain Press.
Scarlet Letter. Nathaniel Hawthorne. LC 80-13327. 1980. 11.95 (ISBN 0-8161-3073-6). G. K. Hall.
Scarlet Letter. Nathaniel Hawthorne & Boughton, George Henry, 1834-1905, Illus. 1908. The Grolier Club.
Scarlet Letter. Nathaniel Hawthorne & Harrison, Elizabeth Deering, 1865- Ed. LC 27-13523. (Half-title: The modern readers' series). 1927. The Macmillan Company.
Scarlet Letter. Hawthorne, Nathaniel & James, Henry. LC 64-6120. (Literary perspectives, no. 2). 1964. Asia Pub. House.
Scarlet Letter. Nathaniel Hawthorne & Littledale, Clara (Savage) 1891- Ed. LC 45-22131. (Keep-worthy book. 2). 1945. The Parents' Institute, Inc.
Scarlet Letter. Nathaniel Hawthorne & A Robaudi. LC 76-6689. (Illus.). 8.95. (ISBN 0-8055-1199-7) (ISBN 0-8055-0285-8). Hart Pub. Co.
Scarlet Letter. Nathaniel Hawthorne & Seay, Claire Soule, Ed. LC 20-1284. (Macmillan's pocket American and English classics). 1920. The Macmillan Company.
Scarlet Letter. Nathaniel Hawthorne & Angelo Valenti. LC 44-18239. 1928. Printed by E. And R. Grabhorn for Random House Inc.
Scarlet Letter see Best Known Works.
Scarlet Letter see Classics Set.
Scarlet Letter see Four Classic American Novels.
Scarlet Letter: A Romance. Nathaniel Hawthorne. LC 66-1434. Dolphin Books.
Scarlet Letter: A Romance. Nathaniel Hawthorne. S. E. Cassino.
Scarlet Letter: A Romance. vignette ed, with... illustrations by frederick c. gordon. ed. Nathaniel Hawthorne. LC 1-1056. F. A. Stokes Company.
Scarlet Letter: A Romance. Nathaniel Hawthorne. (Half-title: Everyman's library, ed. by Ernest Rhys. Fiction). 1907. J. M. Dent & Co.
Scarlet Letter: A Romance. Nathaniel Hawthorne. LC 31-20771. 1931. Cheshire House.
Scarlet Letter: A Romance. Nathaniel Hawthorne. LC 1-1048. 1850. Ticknor, Reed and Fields.
Scarlet Letter: A Romance. Nathaniel Hawthorne & Burnham, Phillip Edward1913- LC 62-129407. 1962. S/R Books.
Scarlet Letter: A Romance. Nathaniel Hawthorne & Hyatt Howe Waggoner. LC 68-10822. (Chandler facsimile editions in American literature). 1968. Chandler Pub. Co.
Scarlet Letter: A Romance. Ed., Introd., by Terence Martin. Nathaniel Hawthorne & Terence Martin. LC 67-12077. (New World writers ser.). 1967. 1.95. World.
Scarlet Letter, a Romance: Introd. by John C. Gerber. Nathaniel Hawthorne. LC 50-12245. (Modern Library college editions, T21). 1950. Modern Library.
Scarlet Letter, a Romance. With a Foreword by Louise Bogan. Drawings by Jacob Landau. Nathaniel Hawthorne. LC 60-14435. (Libra collection). 1960. Libra.
Scarlet Letter: Adapted and Edited by Herbert Spencer Robinson. Nathaniel Hawthorne & Herbert Spencer Robinson. LC 54-1385. 1954. Globe Book Co.
Scarlet Letter: An Annotated Text, Backgrounds and Sources, Essays in Criticism. Nathaniel Hawthorne. Ed. by Edward Sculley Bradley. LC 62-9570. (Norton critical editions, N303). (Illus.). 1962. Norton.
Scarlet Letter: An Authoritative Text, Backgrounds and Sources, Criticism. 2d ed. Nathaniel Hawthorne & Edward Sculley Bradley. LC 77-24583. (Norton critical edition). 12.95 (ISBN 0-393-04495-5). Norton.
Scarlet Letter & Other Tales of the Puritans. Nathaniel Hawthorne. Ed. by Harry Levin. LC 61-2662. pap. 4.50 (ISBN 0-395-05153-3, 3-47690, RivEd, A56). HM.
Scarlet Letter: And Other Tales of the Puritans. 2d. Ed. Ed., Introd., Notes by Harry Levin. Nathaniel Hawthorne. LC 60-266255. (Riverside eds., A45). pap., 1.25. Houghton.
Scarlet Letter, and Other Writings. Ed. by H. Bruce Franklin. Nathaniel Hawthorne. Ed. by Howard Bruce Franklin. LC 67-155111. (Contrasts in lit. ser.) Lippincott coll. English ser. Preceptor, P. 22.). 1967. pap., 1.95. Lippincott.
Scarlet Letter: And Selected Prose Works. Nathaniel Hawthorne & Roper, Gordon Herbert, 1911- Ed. LC 49-7470. 1949. Hendricks House.
Scarlet Letter, and Selected Tales. Nathaniel Hawthorne. Ed. by Thomas Edmund Connolly. LC 71-30203. (Pengiun English library). (Illus.). 1970 (ISBN 0-14-043052-0). Pengiun.
Scarlet Letter and the Blithedale Romance. Nathaniel Hawthorne. LC 1-1052. (In his works. Illustrated library ed.). 1879. Houghton, Osgood and Company.
Scarlet Letter: And The Blithedale Romance. Nathaniel Hawthorne & Lathrop, George Parsons, 1851-1898, Ed. LC 4-21137. (Half-title: Riverside edition. The complete works... vol. v). 1883. Houghton, Mifflin and Company.
Scarlet Letter, and Young Goodman Brown. Nathaniel Hawthorne. LC 71-107353. 1970. 1.45. Anchor Books.
Scarlet Letter. Fredson Bowers, Textual Ed. Nathaniel Hawthorne. Ed. by Fredson Thayer Bowers. LC 63-694. (His The Centenary Ed. of the Works of Nathaniel Hawthorne, V. 1). 1963. 6.75. Ohio State Univ. Pr.
Scarlet Letter. Introd. by William Charvat. Suggestions for Reading and Discussion by Hubert Anderson. Nathaniel Hawthorne. (RLS R21). 1.76, 1.32 pap.,. Houghton.
Scarlet Letter. School Ed. Advisory Ed. Bd., Dora V. Smith, Joseph Mersand, James Squire. Nathaniel Hawthorne. Ed. by Dora V. Smith. (Literary heritage: Macmillan paperback ser.). Macmillan.
Scarlet Letter. Special Aids Prep. by Robert Donald Spector. Nathaniel Hawthorne. Ed. by Robert Donald Spector. LC 65-17435. (Bantam pathfinder edns., FP91). Bantam.
Scarlet Letter: Text, Sources, Criticism by Kenneth S. Lynn. Nathaniel Hawthorne. Ed. by Kenneth Schuyler Lynn. LC 61-98873. (Harbrace sourcebooks). 1961. Harcourt, Brace & World.
Scarlet Letter: With an Introd. by Newton Arvin. Nathaniel Hawthorne. LC 50-6269. (Harper's modern classics). 1950. Harper.
Scarlet Letter with Reader's Guide. Nathaniel Hawthorne. (AMSCO Literature Program). (gr. 10-12). 1970. pap. text ed. 5.25 (ISBN 0-87720-808-5); tchr's ed. 3.35 (ISBN 0-87720-908-1). AMSCO Sch.
Scarlet Letters. Ellery Queen, pseud. LC 53-6449. 1953. Little, Brown.
Scarlet Lily. Edward Francis Murphy. LC 44-47780. 1944. The Bruce Publishing Company.
Scarlet Macaw. Gladys Edson Locke. LC 23-11806. 1923. L. C. Page & Company (Inc.
Scarlet Messenger, Inspector Silver's Eighth Case... Henry Holt. LC 34-375. 1938. Pub. for the Crime Club, Inc., by Doubleday, Doran & Company, Inc.
Scarlet Night. Dorothy Salisbury Davis. LC 79-28467. 1980. 8.95 (ISBN 0-684-16492-2). Scribner's.
Scarlet Night. Dorothy Salisbury Davis. 1981. 2.25 (ISBN 0-380-55129-2). Avon Books.
Scarlet Patch. Bruce Lancaster. LC 76-41411. 1976. 6.95 (ISBN 0-88411-682-4). Aeonian Press.
Scarlet Patch. Bruce Lancaster. LC 47-2060. 1947. Little, Brown and Company.
Scarlet Patch: The Story of a Patriot Boy in the Mohawk Valley. Mary Elizabeth Quackenbush Brush. LC 5-24191. 1905. Lee and Shepard.
Scarlet Patrol: My Story. Dorine Manners. LC 37-14280. 1936. Godwin.
Scarlet Petticoat. Nard Jones. LC 41-23672. 1941. Dodd, Mead & Company.
Scarlet Pimpernel. Emmuska Orczy. LC 64-14820. 1964. Dodd, Mead.
Scarlet Pimpernel. Emmuska Orczy. 1905. G. P. Putnam's Sons.
Scarlet Pimpernel. Emmuska Orczy. LC 8-15153. 1908. G. P. Putnam's Sons.
Scarlet Pimpernel. Emmuska Orczy. LC 21-8674. G. P. Putnam's Sons.
Scarlet Pimpernel. Emmuska Orczy. LC 44-11968. 1944. Triangle Books.
Scarlet Pimpernel. Emmuska Orczy. LC 80-13184. (Classics in Large Print.). 1980. 12.95 (ISBN 0-8161-3077-9). G. K. Hall.
Scarlet Pimpernel see Classics Set.
Scarlet Plague. Jack London. LC 74-16506. (Science Fiction). (Illus.). 1975. 10.00 (ISBN 0-405-06304-0). Arno Press.
Scarlet Plague. Jack London. LC 15-9313. 1915. 1.00. The Macmillan Company.
Scarlet Plague. Jack London. LC 20-15624. (With his The call of the wild. New York, 1919). 1919. The Macmillan Company.
Scarlet Plume. Frederick Feikema Manfred. (Signet, Y5567). 1973. (pbk.) 1.25. New American Lib.
Scarlet Plume. Frederick Feikema Manfred. LC 80-19048. (Series: Gregg Press Western Fiction Series.). 1980. 15.95 (ISBN 0-8398-2594-3). Gregg Press.
Scarlet Poppies. Janet Louise Roberts. 480p. 1983. pap. 3.50 (ISBN 0-446-30211-2). Warner Bks.
Scarlet Poppy: And Other Stories. Harriet Elizabeth Prescott Spofford. LC 69-11917. (American short story series, v. 76). 1969. Garrett Press.
Scarlet Poppy, and Other Stories. Harriet Elizabeth Prescott Spofford. LC 72-8167. (American short story series, v. 76). 1972. (ISBN 0-8422-8111-8). MSS Information Corp.
Scarlet Poppy: And Other Stories. Harriet Elizabeth Prescott Spofford. LC 8-14053. 1894. Harper & Brothers.
Scarlet Ribbon. Flora M Searles. LC 1-29234. J. H. Earle.
Scarlet Rider. Bertha Runkle. LC 13-11302. 1913. 1.35. The Century Co.
Scarlet Riders. Edith Ogden Carter H. Harrison Harrison. LC 31-31224. R. F. Seymour.
Scarlet Riders: A Story of the Royal Canadian Mounted Police. William Campbell. The Bruce Publishing Company.
Scarlet Royal. Anne Emery. LC 76-23407. 1976. 6.50 o.s.i. (ISBN 0-664-32604-8). Westminster.
Scarlet Ruse. John Dann MacDonald. LC 79-24843. 1980. 9.95 (ISBN 0-690-01887-8). Lippincott & Crowell.
Scarlet Ruse. John Dann MacDonald. LC 80-17732. 1980. 13.95 (ISBN 0-8161-3118-X). G. K. Hall.
Scarlet Ruse. John Dann MacDonald. (Travis McGee Series, #14). 1973. (pbk.) 1.25. Fawcett.
Scarlet Sails. Aleksandr Stepanovich Grinevskii & Nesbitt, Esta, Illus. LC 67-15481. (Romanized: Alye parusa). 1967. Scribner.
Scarlet Scourge. Johnston McCully. Repr. lib. bdg. 14.40x (ISBN 0-89190-998-2). Am Repr-Rivercity Pr.
Scarlet Secrets. Janette Radcliffe. (Candlelight Regnecy). Dell.
Scarlet Shadow: A Story of the Great Colorado Conspiracy. Walter Hurt. 1907. The Appeal to Reason.
Scarlet Shadows. Emma Drummond. 1978. pap. 2.25 (ISBN 0-440-17812-6). Dell.
Scarlet Sin. James Noble Gifford. LC 46-2501. 1946. Phoenix Press.
Scarlet Sin: A Novel. Florence Marryat Church Lean. (On cover: Lovell's international series. 77). 1890. J. W. Lovell Company.
Scarlet Sister Mary. Julia Mood Peterkin. LC 66-31348. 1966. 5.95, 4.98 lib. ed.,. N. S. Berg.
Scarlet Sister Mary. Julia Mood Peterkin. LC 28-21177. The Bobbs-Merrill Company.
Scarlet Sister Mary. Julia Mood Peterkin. LC 43-36615. Grosset & Dunlap.
Scarlet Sketches. Max Ehrmann. LC 25-18596. (On cover: Scarlet women series). Indiana Publishing Company.
Scarlet Skull. C. E. Owston. (Orig.). 1979. pap. 1.75 (ISBN 0-532-17239-6). Woodhill.
Scarlet Slippers: By James M. Fox Pseud. 1st Ed. James M. W. Knipscheer. LC 52-5522. 1952. Little, Brown.
Scarlet Sofa see Amorous Adventures of Margot.
Scarlet Spade. Eaton K Goldthwaite. LC 53-172733. (Ace double novel books, D-5). 1952. Ace Books.
Scarlet Storm. Marguerite DeMoss. 272p. (Orig.). 1981. pap. 2.50 (ISBN 0-8439-0971-4, Leisure Bks). Nordon Pubns.
Scarlet Strain. Valborg C. Bogstad. LC 38-38825. Dorrance and Company.
Scarlet Surf at Makaha. Patrick Morgan. (Operation Hang Ten Ser). 1970. pap. 0.75 o.p. (75-348). Manor Bks.
Scarlet Sword. Herbert Ernest Bates. LC 50-11401. 1951. Little, Brown.
Scarlet Tanager. John Aubrey Tyson. LC 22-7758. 1922. The Macmillan Company.
Scarlet Thread. Doris Betts. LC 62-14552. 1965. 5.95. Harper.
Scarlet Thread. Doris Betts. 1973. 1.25. Curtis Books.
Scarlet Thread. Margaret Page Hood. LC 56-5951. Coward-McCann.
Scarlet Thread. Mary Virginia Wulff. LC 24-31283. 1924. J. P. Morton & Company, Incorporated.
Scarlet Thread Through the Bible. W. A. Criswell. (O.S.I.). 1973. pap. 0.95 o.s.i. (ISBN 0-515-02935-1, FN2935). Pyramid Pubns.
Scarlet Thumb. Dorothy Anna Maria Webb. LC 29-6178. Rae D. Henkle Co., Inc.
Scarlet Tree. Osbert Sitwell. 4.95 (ISBN 0-7043-3157-8, Pub. by Quartet England). Charles River Bks.
Scarlet Wagon. Claude Monica Girard. LC 14-17284. 1914. 1.25. H. Holt and Company.
Scarlet Woman. Octavus Roy Cohen. LC 34-19472. 1934. D. Appleton Century Company, Incorporated.
Scarlet Woman. Julia Fitzgerald, pseud. 352p. 1981. pap. 2.75 (ISBN 0-8439-0967-6, Leisure Bks). Nordon Pubns.
Scarlet Woman: A Novel. Joseph Hocking. G. Routledge & Sons, Limited.
Scarlet X. Harvey Wickham. LC 22-5606. E. J. Clode.
Scarlett Domino. Sylvia Thorpe. 1975. (pbk.) 1.25. Fawcett.
Scarlett of the Mounted. Marguerite Merington. LC 6-28757. 1906. Moffat, Yard & Company.
Scarlett O'Hara's Younger Sister. Evelyn Keyes. 1978. pap. 2.25 (ISBN 0-449-23656-0, Crest). Fawcett.
Scarperer. Brendan Behan. LC 64-15773. 1964. Doubleday.
Scarperer. Brendan Behan. LC 66-66439. 1966. Hutchinson.
Scarred. Bruce Lowery. LC 61-15476. 1961. Vanguard Press.
Scarred Chin. Will Payne. LC 20-3574. 1920. 1.75. Dodd, Mead and Company.
Scarred Hand: A Story of Unusual Complications, Coincidences and Consequences. Eliot Harlow Robinson. LC 31-25641. L. C. Page & Company.
Scarred Jungle. Hulbert Footner. LC 35-12780. 1935. Harper & Brothers.
Scarred Man. Basil Heatter. (Gold medal, T2736). 1973. (pbk.) 0.75. Fawcett.
Scars Make Your Body More Interesting. Sherril Jaffe. LC 74-23281. 1974. 15.00. (ISBN 0-87685-221-5) (ISBN 0-87685-220-7). Black Sparrow Press.

Scars Make Your Body More Interesting. Sherril Jaffe. LC 74-23281. (Illus.). 1975. 15.00. (ISBN 0-87685-221-5) (ISBN 0-87685-220-7). Black Sparrow Press.
Scars of Dracula. Angus Hall. (Orig.). 1971. pap. 0.75 o.p. (94071). Beagle Bks.
Scars of the Cross. F. X. Muttoo. 4.95 o.p. Vantage.
Scars on the Soul. Francoise Sagan, pseud. Tr. by Joanna Kilmartin from Fr. LC 73-19755. 156p. 1974. 6.95 o.p. (ISBN 0-07-054415-8). McGraw.
Scars on the Soul: A Novel. Francoise Quoirez. LC 73-19755. 1974. 6.95 (ISBN 0-07-054415-8). McGraw-Hill.
Scars on the Southern Seas: A Romance. George Fitzalan Bronson Howard. LC 7-40047. 1907. B. W. Dodge & Company.
Scarsdale Murder. Jay David, pseud. 1981. pap. 2.50 (ISBN 0-8439-0866-1). Nordon Pubns.
Scattered Death. Ivan Somerville. LC 32-6434. The Alexandrian Society.
Scattered Leaves from a Physician's Diary. Albert Abrams. LC 5-42584. 1900. Fortnightly Press Co.
Scattered Seed. Stuart David Engstrand. LC 53-757021. 1953. J. Messner.
Scattergood Baines. Clarence Budington Kelland. LC 21-3632. Harper & Brothers.
Scattergood Baines Pulls the Strings. Clarence Budington Kelland. LC 41-516338. 1941. Harper & Brothers.
Scattergood Baines Returns. Clarence Budington Kelland. LC 40-27091. 1940. Harper & Brothers.
Scattergun Ranch. 1st Ed. Tom J Hopkins. LC 50-9528. (Double D western). 1950. Doubleday.
Scattershot: A "Nameless Detective" Mystery. Bill Pronzini. LC 81-21445. 1982. 10.95 (ISBN 0-312-70046-6). St. Martin's Press.
Scavenger. Scott Rainey. 1973. (pbk.) 1.95. Barclay House.
Scavenger Kill. Ralph Hayes. (Hunter#1). 1975. (pbk.) 1.25. Leisure Books.
Scavenger. Translated into English and with an Introd. by Hugh A. Harter. Francisco Gomez De Quevedo Y Villegas. LC 62-422110. 1962. Las Americas Pub. Co.
Scavenger's Son. Thakazhi S. Pillai. Tr. by R. E. Asher from Malayalam. 143p. 1975. pap. 2.50 (ISBN 0-89253-025-1). Ind-US Inc.
Scavenger's Son. .translated by r. e. asher. ed. Swasankara Pillai, T. (UNESCO collection of representative work Indian series). 1975. (ISBN 0-89253-025-1). Orient.
Scavengers. 1st Ed. Bill Knox. LC 64-15771. 1964. Published for the Crime Club by Doubleday.
Scence in the Ice-Blue Eyes. Percy Winner. LC 47-11011. 1947. Harcourt, Brace.
Scene. Mike Jahn. LC 71-97591. 1970. 5.95. Bernard Geis Associates; Distributed by World Pub. Co.
Scene-Four. Ed. by Stanley Nelson. LC 77-70415. (Illus.). 1977. pap. 5.00 (ISBN 0-912292-42-3). The Smith.
Scenes & Portraits. Frederic Manning. LC 31-11623. 1931. C. Scribner's Sons.
Scenes and Songs of Social Life. by isaac fitzgerald shepard... ed. Isaac Fitzgerald Shepard. LC 8-5114. 1846. Saxton & Kelt.
Scenes at Washington: A Story of the Last Generation. LC 8-2024. 1848. Harper & Brothers.
Scenes from a Marriage. Ingmar Bergman. Tr. by Alan Blair. LC 74-4753. (O.s.i.). 1974. 6.95 o.s.i. (ISBN 0-394-49305-2). Pantheon.
Scenes from a Receding Past. Aidan Higgins. 1979. 9.95 (ISBN 0-7145-3556-7); pap. 5.95 (ISBN 0-7145-3753-5). Riverrun NY.
Scenes from Adam Bede. George Eliot. LC 6-40733. (On cover: English classic series, no. 67). 1888. Clark & Maynard.
Scenes from American Life; Contemporary Short Fiction. Ed. by Joyce Carol Oates. LC 72-4721. 1973. 3.95 (ISBN 0-394-31683-5). Random House.
Scenes from American Life: Contemporary Short Fiction. Ed. by Joyce Carol Oates. LC 73-83040. 1973. 6.95 (ISBN 0-8149-0750-4). Vanguard Press.
Scenes from Life: By William Cooper Pseud. Harry Summerfield Hoff. LC 61-6962. 1961. Scribner.
Scenes from Real Life. An American Tale. Johnson Jones Hooper. LC 7-25774. 1840. J. P. Giffing.
Scenes from the Bathhouse: And Other Stories of Communist Russia. Mikhail Zoshchenko. Tr. by Sidney Monas. 1961. pap. 5.95 (ISBN 0-472-06070-8, 70, AA). U of Mich Pr.
Scenes from the Bathhouse, and Other Stories of Communist Russia. Translated, with an Introd., by Sidney Monas. Stories Selected by Marc Slonim. Mikhail Mikhallovich Zoshchenko. LC 61-13499. 1961. University of Michigan Press.
Scenes from the "George Eliot" Country. S Parkinson. LC 77-9386. 1977. 20.00 (ISBN 0-8414-6833-8). Folcroft Library Editions.
Scenes from the Heart. Marle Charles. (Second Chance at Love Ser.: No. 107). 1.75 (ISBN 0-515-06871-3). Jove Pubns.
Scenes from the Life of Cleopatra. Mary Butts. LC 74-11648. 1974. 7.95 (ISBN 0-912946-14-8). Ecco Press.
Scenes in Georgia. Isabel Drysdale. LC 4-19538. 1827. American Sunday School Union.
Scenes in Our Parish. Elizabeth Emra Holmes. LC 7-6116. 1851. Stanford and Swords.
Scenes in Our Parish. Elizabeth Erma Holmes. 1833. Harper & Brothers.
Scenes in the Life of Joanna of Sicily. Elizabeth Fries Lummis Ellet. LC 3-26203. 1840. Marsh, Capen, Lyon and Webb.
Scenes in the Practice of a New York Surgeon. Edward H Dixon. LC 6-33868. DeWitt & Davenport.
Scenes of Childhood. Sylvia Townsend Warner. LC 81-51529. 192p. 1982. 10.95 (ISBN 0-670-62043-2). Viking Pr.
Scenes of Clerical Life. George Eliot. Ed. by David Lodge. LC 74-155459. (Penguin English library, EL 87). 1973. (u.s.) 3.60 (ISBN 0-14-043087-3). Penguin Books.
Scenes of Clerical Life. George Eliot. LC 75-491. (Victorian Fiction: Novels of Faith and Doubt). 1975. (ISBN 0-8240-1567-3). Garland Pub.
Scenes of Clerical Life. George Eliot. LC 41-88238. John W. Lovell Co.
Scenes of Clerical Life. George Eliot. LC 36-37323. (Half-title: Everyman's library, ed. by Ernest Rhys. Fiction. no. 468)). 1932. J. M. Dent & Sons, Ltd.
Scenes of Clerical Life: Biographical Introduction. George Eliot. LC 1-31179. (personal edition of George Eliot's works). Doubleday, Page & Co.
Scenes of Crime. Lesley Egan, pseud. (Crime Club Ser.). 192p. 1976. 5.95 o.p. (ISBN 0-385-11468-0). Doubleday.
Scenes of Crime. Elizabeth Linington. LC 75-36590. 1976. 5.95 (ISBN 0-385-11468-0). Published for the Crime Club by Doubleday.
Scent of Apples: A Collection of Stories. Bienvenido N Santos. LC 79-4857. 1979. 12.95 (ISBN 0-295-95683-6) (ISBN 0-295-95695-X). University of Washington Press.
Scent of Apples: Stories. Olivia Davis. LC 72-4129. 1972. 5.95 (ISBN 0-395-14009-9). Houghton Mifflin.
Scent of Cloves. 1st Ed. Norah Robinson Lofts. LC 57-11430. 1957. Doubleday.
Scent of Danger. Agnes Mary Robertson Dunlop. LC 71-182755. 1972. 5.95 (ISBN 0-03-091351-9). Holt, Rinehart and Winston.
Scent of Danger. Elisabeth Kyle, pseud. 1972. 5.95 o.p. HR&W.
Scent of Danger. Donald MacKenzie. LC 58-9069. 1958. Houghton Mifflin.
Scent of Fear. Margaret Yorke. LC 80-28442. 1981. 9.95 (ISBN 0-312-70048-2). St. Martin's Press.
Scent of Lilies. Claire Gallois. LC 74-159517. 1971. 5.95 (ISBN 0-8128-1396-0). Stein and Day.
Scent of New-Mown Hay. John Blackburn. LC 58-13530. 1958. M. S. Mill Co., and W. Morrow.
Scent of New Mown Hay see Reluctant Spy.
Scent of Pepper Trees: A Novel of Old California. 1st Ed. Gertrude Henderson. LC 56-9034. 1956. Vantage Press.
Scent of Rosemary. Lorna Hill. Ed. by Gene DeRoin. (Aston Hall Presents Ser.). (Orig.). pap. 1.50 (ISBN 0-89936-008-4). Aston Hall.
Scent of Roses. Hester Bourne. 1975. pap. 1.25 o.p. (ISBN 0-515-03608-0, V3608). BJ Pub Group.
Scent of Sandalwood. easy eye ed. Clara Coleman. (Orig.). 1968. pap. 0.60 o.p. (73-744). Lancer.
Scent of the Roses: A Novel. Leslie, Aleen. LC 63-10933. 1963. Viking Press.
Scent of Violets. Ruth Fabian. (queen-size gothic). 1974. (pbk.) 0.95. Popular Library.
Scent of Water. Elizabeth Goudge. LC 63-8212. 1963. Coward-McCann.
Scent of White Poppies. John Christopher. LC 59-804959. 1959. Simon and Schuster.
Scented Flesh. Milton K Ozaki. LC 51-20413. (Handi-book mystery, 124). 1950. Quinn Pub. Co.
Scented Gardens for the Blind. Janet Frame, pseud. LC 64-10786. 1980. pap. 4.95 o.p. (ISBN 0-8076-0985-4). Braziller.
Scented Gardens for the Blind: A Novel. Janet Frame, pseud. LC 64-10786. 1964. G. Braziller.
Schack Job. Henry Kane. (Peter Chambers Ser.). 1972. pap. 0.95 o.s.i. (75-407). Lancer.
Schatten Affair. Frederic Morton. LC 65-21706. 1965. Atheneum.
Scheherazade: A London Night's Entertainment. Florence Alice Price James. (On cover: Lovell's library, no. 1073). 1887. J. W. Lovell Company.
Scheherazade: A London Night's Entertainment. Florence Alice Price James. (On cover: Seaside library. Pocket ed., no. 1037). 1887. G. Munro.
Scheme of Things. Allen Wheelis. LC 80-7949. 9.95 (ISBN 0-15-179573-8). Harcourt Brace Jovanovich.
Schemer of Gracewood Hall. James F Humphreys. LC 7-5878.
Schemers. D Torbett. LC 8-10856. C. H. Doscher & Co.
Schemers. 1st Ed. Ruth Fenisong. 1957. Published for the Crime Club by Doubleday.
Scherz and Schabernack: Hundert Deutsche Kurzgeschichten, Edited with Notes and Vocabulary. Ed. by Wolfgang Stendel & Kremer, Edmund Philipp. LC 38-17205. J. B. Lippincott Company.
Schindler's List. Thomas Keneally. LC 82-10489. (Illus.). 16.95 (ISBN 0-671-44977-X). Simon and Schuster.
Schirmer Inheritance. 1st American Ed. Eric Ambler. LC 52-12175. 1953. Knopf.
Schism. Bill Granger. 1982. pap. 3.50 (ISBN 0-671-45274-6). PB.
Schism: A Novel. Bill Granger. LC 81-38478. 12.95 (ISBN 0-517-54491-1). Crown.
Schleppenwolf. John Morressy. (Orig.). 1973. pap. 0.95 o.p. (09223). Curtis.
Schlomo Raven. Ed. by Byron Preiss. (Orig.). 1976. pap. 1.00 o.p. (ISBN 0-515-04076-2). BJ Pub Group.
Schoene 27. September. Thomas Brasch. 100p. (Ger.). 1980. pap. 6.50 (ISBN 3-518-02264-4, Pub. by Suhrkamp Verlag Germany). Suhrkamp.
Scholar and the Sprout. Stoddard Benham Colby. LC 46-4510. 1946. Whittlesey House, McGraw-Hill Book Company, Inc.
Scholars. Ching-Tzu Wu. LC 73-151941. (Grosset's universal library, UL 263). (Illus.). 1972. 3.95 (ISBN 0-448-00263-9). Grosset and Dunlap.
Scholar's Daughter. Beatrice Harraden. LC 6-12138. 1906. Dodd, Mead and Company.
School and Society Through Science Fiction. Joseph D Olander & Martin Harry Greenberg. LC 74-12644. 5.95 (ISBN 0-528-61240-9). Rand McNally College Pub. Co.
School and Society Through Science Fiction. Joseph D Olander & Martin Harry Greenberg. LC 81-40587. 1982. 23.75 (ISBN 0-8191-1996-2) (ISBN 0-8191-1997-0). University Press of America.
School at the Frontier. Geza Ottlik. LC 66-15018. Harcourt, Brace & World.
School Book. Anne Bernays. LC 79-2643. 1980. 12.45i (ISBN 0-06-010332-9, HarpT). Harrow.
School for Eternity. Harry Hervey. LC 41-13937. G. P. Putnam's Sons.
School for Fathers. An Old English Story. Josepha Heath Galston. LC 6-46692. 1852. Harper & Brothers.
School for Fools. Sasha Sokolov. LC 76-57545. 10.00. (ISBN 0-88233-248-1) (ISBN 0-88233-249-X). Ardis.
School for Girls. Michel Mellot. Tr. by Mary Glavin. (Orig.). 1970. pap. 1.50 (ISBN 0-87067-413-7, BH413). Holloway.
School for Girls. pap. 1.95 o.p. (ISBN 0-87056-267-3, 6267). Brandon.
School for Hope. Michael McLaverty. LC 54-109969. 1954. Macmillan.
School for Love. Arthur Barton. LC 77-359676. 1976. 3.95 (ISBN 0-09-126410-3). Hutchinson.
School for Love. Lorine Pruette. LC 36-106043. 1936. Doubleday, Doran & Company, Inc.
School for Lust. Wallace Williams. pap. 1.95 o.p. (ISBN 0-87056-200-2, 6200). Brandon.
School for Saints. Pearl Mary Teresa Richards Craigie. LC 6-31097.
School for Saints; Robert Orange. Pearl Mary Teresa Richards Craigie. LC 75-463. (Victorian Fiction: Novels of Faith and Doubt). 1975. (ISBN 0-8240-1541-X). Garland Pub.
School for Sex. Arnold English. pap. 0.75 o.p. (75-235). Manor Bks.
School for Wives. rev. ed. Alexander Trocchi. (Orig.). pap. 1.25 o.p. (2032). Brandon.
School for Wives; Robert; Genevieve: Or, The Unfinished Confidence. Andre Paul Guillaume Gide. LC 79-23993. 1981. 10.00 (ISBN 0-8376-0454-0). R. Bentley.
School for Wives: By Andre Gide. Andre Paul Guillaume Gide. Tr. by Bussy, Dorothy. LC 29-189491. 1929. A. A. Knopf.
School Grammar of the Latin Language. Karl Gottlob Zumpt & Anthon, Charles, 1797-1867, Ed. LC 11-11857. 1847. Harper and Brothers.
School in the Country: The Adventures of a Small Town Superintendent. Chalmer Orin Richardson. LC 40-32003. Greenberg.
School Life in Paris. pap. 1.75 o.p. (V1011K, Venus). Grove.
School-Marm Tree: A Novel. Howard O'Wagan. LC 78-314425. 1979. 5.95 (ISBN 0-88922-129-4). Talonbooks.
School Nurse. Arlene Hale. (Ace nurse novel). 1974. (pbk.) 0.75. Ace Books.
School Nurse. Arlene Hale. 1976. 1.25. Ace.
School of God. Peggy Arbogast. LC 43-20002. 1943. Wm. B. Eerdmans Publishing Co.
School of Life. Anna Mary Howitt Watts. LC 17-13016. 1855. Ticknor and Fields.
School of Soft Knocks. William George Wiegand. LC 68-24139. 1968. 5.95. Lippincott.
School of Venus. Michel Millot & Jean L'Ange. LC 71-26470. (Signet book Q4483). 1971. 0.95. New American Library.
School on One Hundred Third Street. 2nd ed. Roland S. Jefferson. Ed. by Saul Burnstein. 1980. pap. 2.25 (ISBN 0-931656-01-X, Bedpress Bks). New Bedford.
School on the Range. Elmer Ellsworth Rush. LC 45-3528. 1945. The Hobson Book Press.
School Principal: A Novel. LC 75-300709. (Studies in Middle Eastern Literatures ; No. 4). 1974. 5.00 (ISBN 0-88297-008-9). Bibliotheca Islamica.
School Spirit: A Novel. Tom McHale. LC 75-14830. 1976. 7.95 (ISBN 0-385-01466-X). Doubleday.
Schoolboy Johnson. John Roberts Tunis. LC 58-5728. (Morrow junior books). 1958. W. Morrow.
Schoolboy with Satchel. G. Anderson. 3.90 o.p. (ISBN 0-8062-1075-3). Carlton.
Schoolcraft's Indian Legends. Henry R. Schoolcraft. Ed. by Mentor L. Williams. 1956. 7.50 o.p. (ISBN 0-87013-069-2). Mich St U Pr.
Schooled to Kill. Elizabeth Linington. LC 69-13398. 1969. 5.50. Morrow.
Schooled to Kill. Dell Shannon. 1971. pap. 0.75 o.p. (T2447). Pyramid Pubns.
Schooled to Kill. Dell Shannon. 1969. 5.50 o.p. Morrow.
Schoolgirl. Carman Dee Barnes. LC 29-11282. 1929. H. Liveright.
Schoolgirl Murder Case. Colin Wilson. LC 73-91525. 1974. 5.95 (ISBN 0-517-51482-6). Crown Publishers.
Schoolgirl Sex. Ed. by John W. Fitzgerald. pap. 2.95 o.p. (ISBN 0-87964-102-9). Academy-Parliament.
Schoolmaster. Earl Lovelace. LC 68-31462. 1968. 4.95. H. Regnery Co.
Schoolmaster: A Novel. William John Burley. LC 76-52297. 1977. 6.95 (ISBN 0-8027-5367-1). Walker.
Schoolmaster and His Son: A Narrative of the Thirty Years' War. Karl Heinrich Caspari. LC 17-13221. 1916. The Lutheran Publication Society.
Schoolmaster: And Other Stories. Anton Pavlovich Chekhov. Tr. by Garnett, Constance (Black) LC 21-18808. (Half-title: The tales of Chekhov. Vol. xi). 1921. The Macmillan Company.
Schoolmaster of Abbach: And Other Stories. Wilhelm Oertel. LC 7-32636. 1870. Claxton, Remsen & Haffelfinger.
Schoolmaster of Hessville. Helen Reimensnyder Martin. LC 20-16342. 1920. Doubleday, Page & Company.
Schoolmaster with the Blackfeet Indians. Douglas Gold. LC 63-7444. Caxton Printers.
Schoolmaster's Trial: Or, Old School and New. A Perry. LC 7-361823. 1881. C. Scribner's Sons.
Schoolmistress: And Other Stories. Anton Pavlovich Chekhov. Tr. by Garnett, Constance (Black) LC 21-1275. (Half-title: The tales of Chekhov, vol. ix). 1921. The Macmillan Company.
Schools and Schoolmasters. From the Writings of Charles Dickens. Charles Dickens. Ed. by Chapman, Thomas Jefferson. LC 6-37230. A. S. Barnes & Company.
Schools Are People: An Anthology of Stories Highlighting the Human Drama of Teaching and Learning. LC 70-150904. 1971. 3.50. National Education Association.
Schoolteachers. Alvin Granowsky. LC 67-12666. 1967. 5.00. Fell.
Schooner Bay. Jack Neilson. 1977. 7.50 (ISBN 0-682-48930-1). Exposition.
Schooner California. Henry Burgess Drake. LC 27-263714. 1927. Harper & Brothers.
Schooners That Bump on the Bar: An Automatic Tow from "Ships That Pass in the Night.". Thomas Cooper De Leon. LC 6-34181. 1894. Gossip Printing Company.
Schooners That Pass in the Dark. Robert Jones Burdette. LC 5-18665. 1894. G.W. Dillingham.
Schrodinger's Cat I. Robert A. Wilson. (Orig.). 1979. pap. 2.50 (ISBN 0-671-82114-8). PB.
Schrodinger's Cat III: The Homing Pigeons. Robert Anton Wilson. (Orig.). 1981. pap. 2.50 (ISBN 0-671-82119-9, Timescape). PB.
Schrodinger's Cat: The Universe Next Door. Robert Anton Wilson. 2.50 (ISBN 0-671-82114-8). Pocket Books.

Schroeder's Game. Arthur Maling. LC 76-5547. 8.95 (ISBN 0-06-012811-9). Harper & Row.

Schroeder's Game. Arthur Maling. (Perennial library). 1979. 1.95 (ISBN 0-06-080484-X). Harper & Row.

Schubert Fantasies Adapted from the German of Ottfried: Pseud. Gottfried Jolsdorf. Tr. by Ferguson, Arthur Foxton. LC 14-9389. 1914. The Four Seas Company.

Schudders: A Story of to-Day. Irving Bacheller. LC 23-8184. 1923. The Macmillan Company.

Schuld: And Other Stories. Ilse Leskien & Morgan, Bayard Quincy, 1883- Ed. LC 15-24918. (Oxford German series, by American scholars. General editor, J. Goebel) $0.40). 1916. Oxford University Press, American Branch; Etc., Etc.,

Schultz. James Patrick Donleavy. LC 79-15756. 10.95 (ISBN 0-440-07957-8). Delacorte Press/Seymour Lawrence.

Schultz Money. Malcolm Gair. LC 60-8867. 1960. Published for the Crime Club by Doubleday.

Schwester Anna: A Tale of German Home Life. Felicia Buttz Clark. LC 6-25349. Eaton & Mains.

Sci-Fi: A Yellowthread Street Mystery. William Leonard Marshall. LC 80-27267. (Rinehart suspense novel). 10.95 (ISBN 0-03-047486-8). Holt, Rinehart and Winston.

Science & Sorcery, an Anthology. pap. 1.75 o.p. Fantasy Pub Co.

Science and Sorcery: Illustrated by Arnold and Lorraine Walter. Ed. by Garret Ford. LC 54-17738. 1953. Fantasy Pub. Co.

Science Book of Machines. George Ten Broeck. LC 63-6878. 1963. McLoughlin Bros.

Science Book of Magnets. George Ten Broeck. LC 63-6879. 1963. McLoughlin Bros.

Science Book of Rocks. George Ten Broeck. LC 63-6880. 1963. McLoughlin Bros.

Science Book of Seeds. George Ten Broeck. LC 63-6881. 1963. McLoughlin Bros.

Science Book of Time and Space. George Ten Broeck. LC 63-6882. 1963. McLoughlin Bros.

Science Book of Weather. George Ten Broeck. LC 63-6877. 1963. McLoughlin Bros.

Science Fiction. LC 82-463264. (No-Frills Book). 1981. 1.50 (ISBN 0-515-06247-2). Jove Publications.

Science Fiction, 61 vols. (Illus.). 1975. 1038.00 set (ISBN 0-405-06270-2). Ayer Co.

Science Fiction. Ed. by Jim Villani & Rose Sayre. (Pig Iron Ser.: No. 10). (Illus.). 96p. (Orig.). 1982. pap. 5.95 (ISBN 0-917530-18-7). Pig Iron Pr.

Science Fiction: A Historical Anthology. Eric S Rabkin. LC 82-14363. 1983. 25.00 (ISBN 0-19-503272-1) (ISBN 0-19-503272-1). Oxford University Press.

Science-Fiction Adventures in Dimension. Ed. by Groff Conklin. LC 53-6899. 1953. Vanguard Press.

Science-Fiction Adventures in Mutation. Ed. by Groff Conklin. LC 55-10482. 1955. Vanguard Press.

Science Fiction: An Historical Anthology. Ed. by Eric S. Rabkin. 496p. 1983. 19.95 (ISBN 0-19-503271-3); pap. 9.95 (ISBN 0-19-503272-1). Oxford U Pr.

Science Fiction Anthology. Mark Savee & Ken Savee. (Fantasy Ser.). (Illus.). 32p. (Coloring book). 1974. pap. 3.50 o.p. (ISBN 0-912300-52-3, 52-3). Troubador Pr.

Science Fiction Argosy. Ed. by Damon Francis Knight. LC 73-165473. 1972. 9.95 (ISBN 0-671-21126-9). Simon and Schuster.

Science Fiction Bestiary: Nine Stories of Science Fiction. Ed. by Robert Silverberg. (Laurel-leaf library). 1974. (pbk.) 0.95. Dell.

Science Fiction Bestiary: Nine Stories of Science Fiction. Ed. by Robert Silverberg. LC 70-160148. 1971. (ISBN 0-8407-6172-4). T. Nelson.

Science Fiction by Gaslight. Ed. by Samuel Moskowitz. LC 73-15074. (Classics of Science Fiction Ser.). (Illus.). 364p. 1974. 13.95 o.s.i. (ISBN 0-88355-128-4); pap. 4.25 (ISBN 0-88355-157-8). Hyperion Conn.

Science Fiction by Gaslight. Ed. by Samuel Moskowitz. LC 67-24481. (Illus.). 1968. 7.95 o.p. (A1372). World Pub.

Science Fiction by Gaslight: A History and Anthology of Science Fiction in the Popular Magazines, 1891-1911. hyperion reprint ed. Ed. by Samuel Moskowitz. LC 73-15074. (Classics of science fiction). (Illus.). 1974. (ISBN 0-88355-128-4) (ISBN 0-88355-157-8). Hyperion Press.

Science-Fiction Carnival: Fun in Science-Fiction. Edited, and with Introductions by Fredric Brown and Mack Reynolds. 1st Ed. Ed. by Frederic Brown & Mack Reynolds. LC 53-12530. 1953. Shasta Publishers.

Science Fiction Classics, 6 Vol. Set. 1950. pap. 1.50x. Wehman.

Science-Fiction Collections: Fantasy, Supernatural & Weird Tales. Ed. by Hal W. Hall. LC 82-21355. (Special Collection Ser.: Vol. 2, Nos. 1 & 2). 1983. 29.95 (ISBN 0-917724-49-6, B49). Haworth Pr.

Science Fiction: Contemporary Mythology: the SFWA-SFRA Anthology. Patricia S Warrick & Martin Harry Greenberg. LC 76-26232. 10.95 (ISBN 0-06-011626-9). Harper & Row.

Science Fiction Diet Book. George R. R. Martin & Martin Harry Greenberg. LC 82-19811. 1983. 12.95 (ISBN 0-517-54978-6). Crown.

Science Fiction Digest. V. 1, No. 1-2. LC 66-97327. 1954. Specific Fiction Corp.

Science Fiction Emphasis: 1. Ed. by David Gerrold. 1974. (pbk.) 1.25 (ISBN 0-345-23962-8). Ballantine Books.

Science Fiction Film: Focus on. W. Johnson. 1972. pap. 2.95 o.p. (ISBN 0-13-795161-2). P-H.

Science Fiction for People Who Hate Science Fiction. Ed. by Terry Carr. LC 66-24334. (Doubleday science fiction). 1966. Doubleday.

Science Fiction Galaxy. Ed. by Groff Conklin. LC 50-6028. (Permabooks, 67). 1950. Permabooks.

Science Fiction Hall of Fame. Ed. by Robert Silverberg & Benjamin Bova. Science Fiction Writers of America. LC 70-97691. (v. 1) 7.95 (ISBN 0-385-04576-X). Doubleday.

Science Fiction Hall of Fame, Vol. 2A. Ed. by Ben Bova & Benjamin Bova. 1974. pap. 3.95 (ISBN 0-380-00038-5, 58750). Avon.

Science Fiction Hall of Fame, Vol. 2B. Ed. by Ben Bova & Benjamin Bova. 1974. pap. 3.95 (ISBN 0-380-00054-7, 60194-X). Avon.

Science Fiction Hall of Fame, Vol. 2B. Ed. by Ben Bova & Benjamin Bova. LC 70-97691. 432p. 1973. 9.95 o.p. (ISBN 0-385-05788-1). Doubleday.

Science Fiction Hall of Fame, Vol. 3: The Nebula Winners. Ed. by Arthur Charles Clarke & George Proctor. 688p. 1982. pap. 3.95 (ISBN 0-380-79335-0, 79335). Avon.

Science Fiction Handbook: For Readers & Writers. George Elrick. LC 78-59828. (Illus.). 1978. pap. 8.95 (ISBN 0-914090-52-6). Chicago Review.

Science Fiction Inventions. Damon Francis Knight. (Orig.). 1968. pap. 0.60 o.p. (73-691). Lancer.

Science Fiction, Masters of Today. Arthur Liebman. LC 80-22203. 1981. 7.97 (ISBN 0-8239-0537-3). Richards Rosen Press.

Science Fiction Novel. Basil Davenport. 1959. 12.50 o.s.i. Ridgeway Bks.

Science Fiction Novellas. Ed. by Harry Harrison. LC 74-13151. (Scribner student paperbacks). 1975. (pbk.) 4.00 (ISBN 0-684-13847-6). Scribner.

Science Fiction of Edgar Allan Poe. Edgar Allan Poe. LC 77-355093. (Penguin English library). 1976. 1.95 (ISBN 0-14-043106-3). Penguin.

Science Fiction of Frank R. Stockton: An Anthology. Frank Richard Stockton. LC 76-10724. (Gregg Press science fiction series). 1976. 15.00 (ISBN 0-8398-2344-4). Gregg Press.

Science Fiction of Jack London: An Anthology. Jack London. LC 75-11937. (Gregg Press science fiction series). 1975. 15.00 (ISBN 0-8398-2307-X). Gregg Press.

Science Fiction of Mark Clifton. Mark Clifton & Barry N Malzberg. LC 80-20977. (Alternatives). 15.00 (ISBN 0-8093-0985-8). Southern Illinois University Press.

Science Fiction of Mark Clifton. Barry N. Malzberg. Ed. by Martin Harry Greenberg. LC 80-20877. (Alternatives Ser.). 318p. 1980. 15.00 (ISBN 0-8093-0985-8). S Ill U Pr.

Science Fiction of Samuel R. Delany. Samuel R. Delany. 1977. 110.00 o.p. (Gregg). G K Hall.

Science Fiction of the Fifties. Martin Harry Greenberg & Joseph D Olander. LC 79-51349. 4.95 (ISBN 0-380-46409-8). Avon.

Science Fiction of the Forties. Frederik Pohl & Martin Harry Greenberg. LC 78-57654. 1978. 4.95 (ISBN 0-380-40097-9). Avon.

Science Fiction of the Thirties. Ed. by Damon Francis Knight. 1977. 4.95 (ISBN 0-380-00904-8). Avon Books.

Science Fiction Omnibus: The Best Science Fiction Stories, 1949,1950. Ed. by Everett Franklin Bleiler. The Best Science Fiction Stories. LC 52-545. 1952. Garden City Books.

Science Fiction Origins. Ed. by William Noland & Martin Greenberg. 288p. 1980. pap. 2.25 (ISBN 0-445-04626-0). Popular Lib.

Science Fiction Reader. Ed. by Harry Harrison. LC 72-2210. (Scribner student paperbacks, SSP 31). 1973. 2.65 (ISBN 0-684-13023-8). Scribner.

Science Fiction Reader's Guide. L. David Allen. (O.s.i.). 1974. pap. 1.50 o.p. (ISBN 0-8220-1611-7). Centennial.

Science Fiction Roll of Honor: An Anthology of Fiction and Nonfiction by Guests of Honor at World Science Fiction Conventions. Frederik Pohl. LC 75-10340. 1975. 8.95 (ISBN 0-394-48677-3). Random House.

Science Fiction Showcase. Ed. by Mary Kornbluth. 1969. pap. 0.60 o.p. (0502-06068-060). Curtis.

Science Fiction Showcase, an Anthology: 1st Ed. Ed. by Mary Cornbluth. LC 59-11601. 1959. Doubleday.

Science Fiction Stories of Walter M. Miller, Jr. Walter M. Miller, Jr. 15.00 (ISBN 0-8398-2496-3, Gregg). G K Hall.

Science Fiction Story Index. Fred Siemon. LC 70-162470. 1971. pap. 5.00 o.p. (ISBN 0-8389-0107-7). ALA.

Science-Fiction Subtreasury. Wilson Tucker. LC 54-8255. 1954. Rinehart.

Science Fiction Terror Tales. Ed. by Groff Conklin. LC 56-28390. (Pocket book, 1045. Science fiction, 5). 1955. Pocket Books.

Science Fiction Terror Tales: By Isaac Asimov and Others. 1st Ed. Ed. by Groff Conklin. Isaac - Asimov. LC 55-6842. 1955. Gnome Press.

Science Fiction: The Academic Awakening. Willis Everett McNally. LC 75-306795. (College English Association. A CEA Chapbook). 1974. 2.00. College English Association.

Science Fiction: The Best of Yesterday. Arthur Liebman. (Science Fiction Ser.). 140p. 1980. lib. bdg. 7.97 (ISBN 0-8239-0510-1). Rosen Group.

Science Fiction: the Future. Ed. by Richard Stanley Allen. LC 78-152576. 1971. (ISBN 0-15-578650-4). Harcourt Brace Jovanovich.

Science-Fiction Thinking Machines: Robots, Androids, Computers. Ed. by Groff Conklin. LC 54-6995. 1954. Vanguard Press.

Science Fictional Dinosaur. Ed. by Martin Harry Greenberg et al. 224p. (Orig.). 1982. pap. 2.25 (ISBN 0-380-77974-9, 77974, Flare). Avon.

Science-Fictional Sherlock Holmes. LC 61-30557. 1960. Council of Four.

Science of Herondale. Joan Aiken. (Star bk., K-219). 1965. Ace.

Scientific Proof of the Existence of God Will Soon Be Announced by the White House! John Da Free. LC 80-81175. 1980. pap. 12.95 (ISBN 0-913922-48-X). Dawn Horse Pr.

Scientific Research in Underpants. Domingo De Guzman. LC 72-77980. (Geneva book). (Illus.). 1972. 7.95. Carlton Press.

Scientific Sprague. Francis Lynde. LC 12-23516. 1912. C. Scribner's Sons.

Scientist: A Novel Autobiography. John C. Lilly. 224p. 1981. pap. 2.95 (ISBN 0-553-12813-2). Bantam.

Scientists and Engineers: The Professionals Who Are Not. Louis V McIntire & Marion Bayard McIntire. LC 75-27243. (Illus.). 1971. Arcola Communications Co.

Scimitar. Rick DeMarinis. 1978. 1.75 (ISBN 0-380-01873-X). Avon.

Scimitar. Noel Bertram Gerson. LC 55-8755. 1955. Farrar, Straus and Cudahy.

Scimitar: A Novel. Rick De Marinis. LC 76-41228. 8.95 (ISBN 0-525-19805-9). Dutton.

Scimitars Over Ukraine. Peter Hrycenko. (Orig.). 1979. pap. 2.25 (ISBN 0-532-22153-2). Woodhill.

Scintillations from the Prose Works of Heinrich Heine. I. Florentine Nights. Ii. Excerpts. Heinrich Heine & Stern, Simon Adler, 1838- Tr. LC 7-4106. (Leisure hour series v. 14). 1873. Holt & Williams.

Scirocco. Romulado Romano. LC 51-7522. 1951. Farrar, Straus and Young.

Scissorbills. Belvina Bertino. 5.95 (ISBN 0-533-01964-8). Vantage.

Scissors: A Novel of Youth. Cecil Roberts. LC 23-6841. 1923. Frederick A. Stokes Company.

Scissors, Paper, Stone: A Novel. Marcus Boggs. LC 81-7536. 1981. 11.95 (ISBN 0-531-09860-5). F. Watts.

Scobie: A Novel. George Reginald Turner. LC 59-13137. 1959. Simon and Schuster.

Scofield Diagnosis. Henry Denker. LC 77-22599. 9.95 (ISBN 0-671-22892-7). Simon and Schuster.

Scofield Diagnosis. Henry Denker. 1978. 2.50 (ISBN 0-671-81645-4). Pocket Books.

Scola. Ann Eliza Brainerd Smith. LC 8-8645. 1878. Lee and Shepard.

Scollay Square. Pearl Schiff. LC 52-8781. 1952. Rinehart.

Scoop. James S Hart & Byrnes, Garrett D. LC 30-48470. 1930. Little, Brown, and Company.

Scoop. Evelyn Waugh. LC 77-88212. 1977. 8.95 (ISBN 0-316-92617-5). Little, Brown.

Scop. Barry N. Malzberg. (Orig.). 1976. pap. 1.25 o.p. (ISBN 0-515-03895-4). BJ Pub Group.

Scorched-Wood People: A Novel. Rudy Henry Wiebe. LC 78-303296. 12.95 (ISBN 0-7710-8979-1). McClelland and Stewart.

Scorching Wind. Walter Macken. 304p. 1966. pap. 3.75 (ISBN 0-330-02113-3, Pub. by Pan Bks England). Irish Bk Ctr.

Score. Mary St. Leger Kingsley Harrison. LC 9-19190. 1909. E. P. Dutton & Company.

Score. Richard Stark. 1981. lib. bdg. 10.95 (ISBN 0-8398-2711-3, Gregg). G K Hall.

Score. Donald E Westlake. LC 80-39927. (Gregg Press Mystery Fiction Series). 1981. 10.95 (ISBN 0-8398-2711-3). Gregg Press.

Score by Innings. Charles Emmett Van Loan. LC 19-5196. George H. Doran Company.

Score for the Toff. John Creasey. 1972. pap. 0.95 o.p. (75-331). Lancer.

Scorn Her Own Image. Stuart Hamill. LC 44-453443. 1944. S. Curl, Inc.

Scornful Corpse. Milward Rodon Kennedy Burge. LC 36-16195. 1936. Dodd, Mead & Company.

Scorpio. Steve Lawson, pseud. (Orig.). 1975. pap. 1.50 o.p. (ISBN 0-515-03825-3). Pyramid Pubns.

Scorpio Cipher. Ralph Hayes. 320p. (Orig.). 1983. pap. 3.25 (ISBN 0-8439-1060-7, Leisure Bks). Dorchester Pub Co.

Scorpio Letter. Victor Canning. 272p. 1981. pap. 2.50 (ISBN 0-441-75519-4, Pub. by Charter Bks). Ace Bks.

Scorpio Letters. Victor Canning. LC 64-24637. 1964. W. Sloane Associates.

Scorpio Summer. Jacqueline Gilbert. (Harlequin Romances Ser.). (Orig.). 1980. pap. 1.25 (ISBN 0-373-02308-1, Pub. by Harlequin). PB.

Scorpio 5. William Harrington. LC 74-16637. 1975. 8.95 (ISBN 0-698-10637-7). Coward, McCann & Geoghegan.

Scorpion. Mildred B Davis. LC 77-1642. 6.95 (ISBN 0-394-41082-3). Random House.

Scorpion. Mildred B Davis. 1979. 1.95 (ISBN 0-671-82113-X). Pocket Books.

Scorpion. Christopher Hill. LC 73-78870. 1974. 6.95. St. Martin's Press.

Scorpion. Peter McCurtin. (Sundance Ser.: No. 32). 1980. pap. 1.75 o.s.i. (ISBN 0-8439-0756-8, Leisure Bks). Nordon Pubns.

Scorpion. 2nd ed. Albert Memmi. LC 79-114950. 242p. (Eng.). 1975. 8.95 (ISBN 0-87955-908-X); pap. 5.95 (ISBN 0-87955-906-3). O'Hara.

Scorpion. Albert Memmi. LC 79-114950. (Orion Ser). (O.s.i.). 1971. 8.95 o.s.i. (ISBN 0-670-62271-0). Grossman.

Scorpion. Anna Elisabet Weirauch. LC 75-12357. (Homosexuality). 1975. 10.00 (ISBN 0-405-07375-5). Arno Press.

Scorpion. rev. ed. Anna Elisabet Weirauch. Tr. by Whittaker Chambers. LC 48-2543. 1948. Willey Book Co.

Scorpion. Anna Elisabet Weirauch. Tr. by Whittaker Chambers. LC 32-7601. Greenberg.

Scorpion. Anna Elisabet Weirauch. Tr. by Whittaker Chambers. LC 34-183528. 1933. Greenberg.

Scorpion, a Good Bad Horse. Will James. LC 75-311791. (Illus.). 1975. 3.25 (ISBN 0-8032-5822-4). University of Nebraska Press.

Scorpion East. Jerrold Morgulas. LC 80-52417. 14.50 (ISBN 0-87223-653-6). Seaview Books.

Scorpion Field. J L Nusser. LC 57-114836. 1957. Appleton-Century-Crofts.

Scorpion God. Gerald Jay Goldberg. LC 70-174508. 178p. 1971. 5.95 o.p. (ISBN 0-15-136410-9). HarBraceJ.

Scorpion God: Three Short Novels. William Gerald Golding. LC 70-174508. 1972. 5.95 (ISBN 0-15-136410-9). Harcourt Brace Jovanovich.

Scorpion Killers. Ray Hogan. (Shawn Starbuck). (Signet brand western). 1974. (pbk.) 0.75. New American Library.

Scorpion of Chateau Laverria. Mary M. Fletcher. (Orig.). 1970. pap. 0.75 o.p. (94020). Beagle Bks.

Scorpion on a Stone. Gwyn Griffin. LC 65-13409. 1965. Holt, Rinehart and Winston.

Scorpion on a Stone: Six Stories of Loyalty & Betrayal Modern Africa. Gwyn Griffin. 1965. 4.95 o.p. HR&W.

Scorpion: Or the Imaginary Confession. Albert Memmi. Tr. by Eleanor Levieux. 1975. 7.95 (ISBN 0-87955-908-X). J. Philip O'Hara, Inc.

Scorpion: Or, The Imaginary Confession. Albert Memmi. LC 79-114950. (Orion Press book). (Illus.). 1971. 8.95 (ISBN 0-670-62271-0). Grossman.

Scorpion Orchid. Lloyd Fernando. (Writing in Asia Ser.). 1976. pap. text ed. 4.50x (00233). Heinemann Ed.

Scorpion Reef. Charles Williams. LC 55-13576. 1955. Macmillan.

Scorpion Sanction. Gordon Pape & Tony Aspler. LC 79-56262. 1980. 13.95 (ISBN 0-670-19965-6). Viking Press.

Scorpion Signal. Adam Hall, pseud. LC 79-8284. 1980. 10.00 o.p. (ISBN 0-385-12277-2). Doubleday.

Scorpion Signal. Adam Hall, pseud. LC 80-85103. 288p. 1981. pap. 2.95 (ISBN 0-87216-831-X). Playboy Pbks.

Scorpion Signal. Elleston Trevor. LC 79-8284. 1980. 10.00 (ISBN 0-385-12277-2). Doubleday.

Scorpion Summer. Elaine Booth Selig. (Kangaroo Book.). 1977. 1.75 (ISBN 0-671-81039-1). Pocket Books.

Scorpions. Robert Kelly. LC 66-20978. 1967. Doubleday.

Scorpion's Sting. Edward A. Pollitz. (Orig.). 1983. pap. 3.50 (ISBN 0-440-17872-X). Dell.

Scorpion's Tail. Richard Clayton. LC 74-31924. 1975. 5.95 (ISBN 0-8027-5323-X). Walker.

Scorpion's Trail. T. C. H Jacobs, pseud. LC 35-1695. 1934. The Macaulay Company.

Scorpius Equation. Larry Townsend. 256p. (Orig.). 1971. pap. 1.95 o.s.i. (T*C513, Travellers Comp). Olympia.

Scorpus the Moor. Leslie Turner White. 1969. pap. 0.95 o.p. (0502-09026-095). Curtis.

Scorpus the Moor. 1st Ed. Leslie Turner White. LC 62-15944. 1962. Doubleday.

Scot Free: A Novel. Ivy Strick. LC 78-66809. 1978. 8.95 (ISBN 0-8008-7012-3). Taplinger Pub. Co.

Scotch and Water. Guy Gilpatric. LC 37-10638. 1931. Dodd, Mead & Company.

Scotch Love. Heddy Chapman. 3.75 o.p. Carlton.

Scotch Valley. Mildred Cram. LC 28-97363. 1928. Doubleday, Doran & Company, Inc.

Scotch Verdict. Lillian Faderman. (Illus.). 388p. 1983. pap. 8.95 (ISBN 0-688-02054-2). Quill NY.

Scotchman's Incentive. Albert Leslie. 2.75 o.p. Carlton.

Scotia Jones. Lee Karr. 1979. pap. 1.95 (ISBN 0-532-19216-8). Woodhill.

Scotia Westward: A Novel. 1sr ed. Katherine Whittet Weeks. LC 56-12381. 1956. Exposition Press.

Scotish Chiefs. Jane Porter. LC 21-12946. (On cover: The home library). A. L. Burt Company.

Scotland Yard Book of Edgar Wallace: An Omnibus of Wallace's Most Exciting Work...Two Complete Novels--Ten Stories. Edgar Wallace. LC 32-26960. Pub. for the Crime Club, Inc., by Doubleday, Doran & Company, Inc.

Scotland Yard Book of Edgar Wallace: An Omnibus of Wallace's Most Exciting Works--Over Nine Hundred Pages--Two Complete Novels--Seven Stories. Edgar Wallace. A. L. Burt Co.

Scotland Yard Can Wait. Zenith Jones Brown. LC 33-34616. Farrar & Rinehart, Incorporated.

Scotland's Burning. 1st Ed. Nathaniel Burt. LC 54-51089. 1953. Little, Brown.

Scots Brigade: And Other Tales. James Grant. LC 43-29584. 1882. G. Routledge and Sons.

Scots Quair: A Trilogy of Novels. James Leslie Mitchell. LC 77-4988. 1977. 10.95 (ISBN 0-8052-3661-9). Schocken Books.

Scots Quair: A Trilogy of Sunset Song, Cloud Howe, & Grey Granite. Lewis G. Gibbon. LC 77-75288. 496p. 1982. 16.95 (ISBN 0-8052-3661-9); pap. 9.95 (ISBN 0-8052-0710-4). Schocken.

Scotswoman. Inglis Clark Fletch. 1974. (pbk.) 1.50. Bantam Books.

Scotswoman. Inglis Clark Fletcher. LC 78-3544. 1978. 12.95 (ISBN 0-89244-008-2). Queens House.

Scotswoman. 1st Ed. Inglis Clark Fletcher. LC 54-119412. 1955. Bobbs-Merrill.

Scott-Dunlap Ring. George La Fountaine. LC 77-20112. 8.95 (ISBN 0-698-10871-X). Coward, McCann & Geoghegan.

Scott-King's Modern Europe. Evelyn Waugh. LC 49-419. 1949. Little, Brown.

Scott on Himself: A Selection of the Autobiographical Writings of Sir Walter Scott. Walter Scott & David Hewitt. LC 81-164641. (Association for Scottish Literary Studies; no. 10). (Illus.). 1981. 15.00 (ISBN 0-7073-0283-8). Scottish Academic Press.

Scott Was Here. Elaine Ipswitch. 1979. 8.95 o.p. (ISBN 0-440-07665-X). Delacorte.

Scottie and His Lady. Margaret Fessenden Morse. LC 10-291301. 1910. Houghton Mifflin Company.

Scottish Adventures: Or, The Way to Rise; an Historical Tale. Hector Macneill. LC 7-16617. 1812. Printed for B. Chapman.

Scottish Cavalier: Or, The First Royal Scots. James Grant. LC 43-26606. 1850. G. Routledge and Sons Pref.

Scottish Chiefs. Jane Porter. LC 4-7541. T. Y. Crowell & Company.

Scottish Chiefs. Jane Porter. LC 20-23135. T. Y. Crowell Company.

Scottish Chiefs. Jane Porter. Ed. by Wiggin, Kate Douglas (Smith) & Smith, Nora Archibald. LC 21-17817. 1921. C. Scribner's Sons.

Scottish Chiefs: A Romance. Jane Porter. 1899. A. C. McClurg and Company.

Scottish Chiefs (Abridged) Jane Porter. Ed. by Smith, Robert Metcalf. LC 27-2556. (Modern readers' series). 1927. The Macmillan Company.

Scottish Chiefs: Or, The Life of Sir William Wallace. Jane Porter. LC 41-31386. The F. M. Lupton Publishing Company.

Scottish Decision. Alan Hunter. LC 81-51982. 1981. 9.95 (ISBN 0-8027-5456-2). Walker.

Scottish Exiles, Rendered into Prose: From Sir Walter Scott's Lady of the Lake. Walter Scott. LC 8-3048. 1828. J. Field.

Scottish Lord. Joan Wolf. 1982. pap. 2.25 (ISBN 0-451-11273-3, AE1273, Sig). NAL.

Scottish Marriage. Karen Lynn. LC 81-43294. 1982. 10.95 (ISBN 0-385-17684-8). Doubleday.

Scottish Poetry: Drummond of Hawthornden to Fergusson. George Douglas. LC 74-13044. 1973. lib. bdg. 22.50 (ISBN 0-8414-3777-7). Folcroft.

Scottish Short Stories. Ed. by John Macnair Reid. LC 63-25061. (World's classics, 595). 1963. Oxford University Press.

Scottish Short Stories, Eighteen Hundred to Nineteen Hundred. Ed. by Douglas Gifford. (Scottish Library Ser.). 347p. 1971. text ed. 14.50x (ISBN 0-7145-0656-7). Humanities.

Scottish Short Stories 1800-1900. Ed. by Douglas Gifford. LC 71-573595. (Scottish library). 1976. 9.50 (ISBN 0-7145-0656-7). Calder and Boyars.

Scottish Sketches. Amelia Edith Huddleston Barr. LC 70-157771. (Short story index reprint series). 1971. (ISBN 0-8369-3883-6). Books for Libraries Press.

Scottish Sketches. Amelia Edith Huddleston Barr. LC 6-7974. American Tract Society.

Scott's Ivanhoe. Walter Scott. LC 8-2932. (Longman's English classics). 1897. Longmans, Green and Co.

Scott's Ivanhoe. Walter Scott. Ed. by May, Alfred Arundel. (Half-title: English readings for schools). 1911. 0.50. H. Holt and Company.

Scott's Ivanhoe. Walter Scott. Ed. by Merrill, A. Marion. LC 16-19221. (academy classics). Allyn and Bacon.

Scott's Ivanhoe. Walter Scott. Ed. by Dudley, Luther Edwin. LC 29-18157. (Golden key series). D. C. Heath and Company.

Scott's Ivanhoe. Walter Scott & Timm, Carolyn (Pulcifer) LC 36-19024. (Golden key series). D. C. Heath and Company.

Scott's Ivanhoe: A Romance. Walter Scott. Ed. by Lewis, William Dodge. LC 6-37931. (Standard English classics). Ginn & Company.

Scott's Ivanhoe: A Romance. Walter Scott. LC 16-220521. (Standard English classics). Ginn and Company.

Scott's Lady of the Lake. Albert E. Cornetti. LC 74-76333. 1969. 1.75. W. Murray.

Scott's Quentin Durward. Walter Scott. Ed. by Briggs, Thomas Henry. LC 12-16362. (Half-title: English readings for schools. General editor: W. L. Cross). 1912. 0.45. H. Holt and Company.

Scoundrel Time. Lillian Hellman. 1977. lib. bdg. 8.95 o.p. (ISBN 0-8161-6446-0, Large Print Bks). G K Hall.

Scoundrel's Brigade. Noel Bertram Gerson. LC 62-7692. 1962. Doubleday.

Scourge. Francis Warrington Dawson. LC 10-26227. 1910. 1.50. Small, Maynard & Company.

Scourge. Thomas L Dunne. LC 78-597. 9.95 (ISBN 0-698-10893-0). Coward, McCann & Geoghegan.

Scourge of Damascus. Sylvanus Cobb. (On cover: The popular series, no. 5). 1891. R. Bonner's Sons.

Scourge of Damascus: A Novel. Sylvanus Cobb. LC 99-1411. (On cover: Ledger library, no. 141). 1899. R. Bonner's Sons.

Scourge of God: A Romance of Religious Persecution. John Edward Bloundelle-Burton. (Appletons' town and country library, no 251.). 1898. D. Appleton & Co.

Scourge of Scapa Flow. J. Farragut Jones. (Orig.). 1981. pap. 2.75 (ISBN 0-440-17701-4). Dell.

Scourge of the Little "C". J. E. Grinstead. LC 26-22308. (On cover: A pocket copy-right. no. 65). Garden City Publishing Co.

Scourge of the Ocean: A Story of the Atlantic. Robert Burts. LC 6-16692. 1847. Carey and Hart.

Scout. R. M. Roberts. LC 56-12122. 1956. Ballantine Books.

Scout. William Gilmore Simms. 1974. Repr. of 1890 ed. lib. bdg. 30.00 (ISBN 0-8414-8067-2). Folcroft.

Scout. William Gilmore Simms. LC 68-20021. (Americans in Fiction Ser.). Repr. of 1854 ed. lib. bdg. 16.00 (ISBN 0-8398-1860-2). Irvington.

Scout. A Legend of Old Thornbury Township. Edward H Williamson. LC 8-36905. 1886.

Scout; a Tale of the Civil War. Charles Waller Tyler. LC 12-1128. 1911. The Cumberland Press.

Scout Commander. Sidney Edgerton Whitman. LC 55-996599. 1955. Houghton Mifflin.

Scout, No. 1: Rowan's Raiders. Buck Gentry. 1981. pap. 2.50 (ISBN 0-89083-754-6). Zebra.

Scout, No. 10: Traitor's Gold. Buck Gentry. (Orig.). 1983. pap. 2.50 (ISBN 0-8217-1209-8). Zebra.

Scout, No. 2: Dakota Massacre. Buck Gentry. 1981. pap. 2.50 (ISBN 0-89083-794-5). Zebra.

Scout, No. 3. Buck Gentry. (Orig.). 1982. pap. 2.50 (ISBN 0-89083-853-4). Zebra.

Scout, No. 4: Cheyenne Vengeance. Buck Gentry. (Orig.). 1982. pap. 2.50 (ISBN 0-89083-969-7). Zebra.

Scout, No. 5: Sioux Slaughter. Buck Gentry. (Orig.). 1982. pap. 2.50 (ISBN 0-8217-1024-9). Zebra.

Scout, No. 6: Bandit Fury. Buck Gentry. (Orig.). 1982. pap. 2.50 (ISBN 0-8217-1075-3). Zebra.

Scout, No. 7: Prairie Bush. Buck Gentry. 1982. pap. 2.50 (ISBN 0-8217-1110-5). Zebra.

Scout, No. 8: Pawnee Rampage. Buck Gentry. 1983. pap. 2.50 (ISBN 0-8217-1161-X). Zebra.

Scout, No. 9: Apache Ambush. Buck Gentry. (Orig.). 1983. pap. 2.50 (ISBN 0-8217-1193-8). Zebra.

Scout of Buckhannon" An Historical Romance of Western Virginia Border, 1764-1782. John Camillus McWhorter. LC 24-18762.

Scout of Terror Trail. Walker A Tompkins. LC 44-8097. 1944. Phoenix Press.

Scout of the Buckongehanon: An Historical Romance of the Western Virginia Border, 1764-1782. John Camillus McWhorter. LC 27-8283. The Christopher Publishing House.

Scout of the Silver Pond. Newton Mallory Curtis. LC 43-26804. 1849. W. F. Burgess.

Scout: Or, The Black Riders of Congaree. William Gilmore Simms. LC 68-200210. (Americans in Fic.). 1968. 10.00. Gregg Pr.

Scout: Or, The Black Riders of Congaree. new and rev. ed. William Gilmore Simms. LC 76-10143. (Simms, William Gilmore, 1806-1870. Simms Revolutionary War Novels). (Simms Revolutionary War novels; v. 5). ((Series: Simms, William Gilmore, 1806-1870.). (Simms Revolutionary War novels; v. 5.: Vols. 5). 1976. 21.00 (ISBN 0-87152-239-X). Reprint Co.

Scout: Or, The Black Riders of Congaree. new and rev. ed. William Gilmore Simms. LC 48-322536. (His Border romances). Lovell, Coryell.

Scout; or, The Black Riders of Congaree. new and rev. ed. William Gilmore Simms. LC 8-13053. 1854. Redfield.

Scout; or, The Black Riders of Congaree. new and rev. ed. William Gilmore Simms. LC 8-11010. (With his Katharine Walton. New York, 1882). 1882. A. A. Armstrong & Son.

Scout: or, The Black Riders of Congaree. new and rev. ed. William Gilmore Simms. (On cover: Lovell's library. v. 12, no. 671). 1885. J. W. Lovell Company.

Scout; or, The Black Riders of Congaree. new and rev. ed. William Gilmore Simms. LC 41-26010. 1887. Belford, Clarke & Co.

Scout: Or, The Fast of Saint Nicholas. A Tale of the Seventeenth Century. John Linnaeus Edward Whitridge Shecut. LC 8-5089. 1844. C. L. Stickney.

Scouting for Washington: A Story of the Days of Sumter and Tarleton. John Preston True. LC 5172. 1900. Little, Brown & Company.

Scouts of Seventy Six. Richard S. Baldwin. 1979. 5.75 o.p. (ISBN 0-8062-1388-4). Carlton.

Scouts of Stonewall. Joseph Alexander Altsheler. 1976. lib. bdg. 15.80x (ISBN 0-89968-004-6). Lightyear.

Scouts of the Valley. Joseph Alexander Altsheler. 345p. 1981. Repr. lib. bdg. 14.95 (ISBN 0-89968-227-8). Lightyear.

Scouts of the Valley: A Story of Wyoming and the Chemung. Joseph Alexander Altsheler. LC 11-23844. 1911. D. Appleton and Company.

Scrabble of the Fairchilds. Arthur Warren Hamilton. LC 7-1222. J. H. Earle.

Scramble Six Hurricanes. 1st Ed. Donald Moore. LC 58-7363. 1958. Doubleday.

Scramble: Sunshine, Rainfall, Sunshine-Such Is Life. Trena T. Nelson. 1979. pap. 4.00 o.p. (ISBN 0-682-49231-0). Exposition.

Scrambled Eggs and Bedposts. Robert A. O Andreson. LC 67-20526. 1967. Dorrance.

Scrambled Yeggs. Octavus Roy Cohen. LC 34-21306. (Tired business man's library of adventure, detective and mystery novels). 1934. D. Appleton Century Company, Incorporated.

Scramouche: A Romance of the French Revolution, by Rafael Sabatini; Edited with an Introduction, Notes, Questions for Study and Exercises. Rafael Sabatini & Herzberg, Max John, 1886- Ed. LC 27-21615. (Riverside literature series). Houghton Mifflin Company.

Scraphita; with an Introduction by George Frederic Parsons. Honore De Balzac. Tr. by Katharine Prescott Wormeley. Parsons, George Frederic. LC 9-2704. 1893. Roberts Brothers.

Scrapped. Meta Schoepp. Tr. by Tavsiq, Louise. 1929. Covici-Friede.

Scraps. George W Wear. LC 34-31286. 1934. Meador Publishing Company.

Scratch a Lover. Janet Gregory Vermandel. LC 69-17600. (Red badge mystery). 1969. 3.95. Dodd, Mead.

Scratch One. John Lange. 1974. (pbk.) 1.25. Bantam Books.

Scratch One Dreamer. David Lewis Stein. LC 67-18410. 1967. Bobbs-Merrill.

Scratch the Surface. Edmund Schiddel. LC 39-212933. Harcourt, Brace and Company.

Scratch the Surface. Edmund Schiddel. 1974. (pbk.) 1.25. Manor Books.

Scratches: A Picaresque Autobiography. Hilscher-Wittgenstein, Herta. LC 77-93741. 8.95. Nautilus Books.

Scratchproof. Michael Maguire. LC 76-381294. 1976. 3.50 (ISBN 0-491-01697-2). Allen.

Scratchproof. Michael Maguire. LC 76-45771. 1977. 7.95. St. Martin's Press.

Screaker Murders: A Novel. Philip Dorian. 1976. 5.95 (ISBN 0-8059-2298-9). Dorrance.

Scream Along with Me. Alfred Hitchcock. 1981. pap. 2.25 (ISBN 0-440-13633-4). Dell.

Scream & Scream Again. Peter Saxon. Orig. Title: Disoriented Man. 1970. pap. 0.60 o.p. (63-273). Paperback Lib.

Scream at Midnight. Joseph Payne Brennan. LC 63-24895. 1963. Macabre House.

Scream at the Sea. Christopher Murphy. LC 81-23179. 10.95 (ISBN 0-312-70587-5). St. Martin's Press.

Scream Away. Andrea Harris. LC 78-62017. 1979. 1.50 (ISBN 0-87216-510-8). Playboy Press.

Scream in a Cave. Edwin Denby. 6.95 o.p. (ISBN 0-8180-0614-5). Horizon.

Scream in a Cave. Edwin Denby. 1973. pap. 0.95 o.p. (09244). Curtis.

Scream in the Dark: Or, Nat Ridley's Crimson Clue. Nat Jr Ridley. LC 26-176344. (On cover: Nat Ridley series--9). 1926. Garden City Publishing Co.

Scream in the Storm. Caroline Farr. (Signet Book). 1975. (pbk.) 1.25. New American Library.

Scream, My Darling, Scream. Angela Pearson. pap. 1.75 o.s.i. (OPH-135, Ophelia). Olympia.

Scream of Murder. Gordon Ashe. LC 73-80331. (Suspense Novels Ser). 1970. 4.50 o.p. (ISBN 0-03-084512-2). HR&W.

Scream of Murder. John Creasey. LC 76-117280. (Rinehart suspense novel). 1970. 4.50. Holt, Rinehart and Winston.

Scream of the Doll: A Mystery in Reverse. Stanley Kidder Wilson. LC 31-6486. 1931. Duffield & Company.

Scream of the Dove. Robert Charles, pseud. 1975. (pbk.) 1.25 (ISBN 0-523-00723-X). Pinnacle Books.

Screaming Dead Balloons: A Commander Shaw Novel. Philip McCutchan. LC 68-24146. 1968. John Day Co.

Screaming Face. John Lymington, pseud. 1978. pap. 1.50 (ISBN 0-532-15312-X). Woodhill.

Screaming Face. John Lymington, pseud. 1970. pap. 0.60 o.p. (60-436). Manor Bks.

Screaming Ghost: And Other Stories, Collected and Told by Carl Carmer. Illustrated by Irv Docktor. 1st Ed. Carl Lamson Carmer. LC 55-8953. 1956. Knopf.

Screaming Mimi. Fredric Brown. LC 49-49010. (Dutton guilt edged mystery). 1949. Dutton.

Screaming on the Wire. Peter McCurtin. (Carmody Ser., No. 6). 1974. pap. 0.95 o.p. (LB153NK). Leisure Bks.

Screaming on the Wire. Peter McCurtin. (Orig., Osi). 1972. pap. 0.75 o.s.i. (BT50232). Belmont-Tower.

Screaming Portrait. Ferrin L Fraser. LC 28-896916. J. H. Sears & Company, Inc.

Screaming Rabbit. Harry Carmichael. (O.S.I.). 1955. 2.75 o.s.i. (63750). S&S.

Screaming Rabbit: By Harry Carmichael Pseud. Leopold Horace Ognall. LC 55-33860. (Inner sanctum mystery). 1955. Simon and Schuster.

Screaming Skulls, and Other Ghost Stories: The Collected True Tales and Legends of Elliott O'Donnell. Elliot O'Donnell. LC 69-18114. 1969. 4.95. Taplinger Pub. Co.

Screed. Jack Saunders. (ISBN 0-912824-24-7). Vagabond Press,C.

Screen. Barry N. Malzberg. pap. 1.95 o.s.i. (OPS-8). Olympia.

Screen a Novel. Paul Charles Joseph Bourget. LC 1-27448. 1901. J. F. Taylor & Company.

Screen for Murder. Albert Jeffers. LC 41-7299. 1941. Mystery House.

Screen for Murder. Edith Caroline Rivett. LC 48-8714. 1948. Pub. for the Crime Club by Doubleday.

Screen Lover. Julia Grice. 1971. pap. 0.75 o.p. (94168). Beagle Bks.

Screen Star. John Preston Buschlen. LC 32-1273. 1932. Doubleday, Doran and Company, Inc.

Screen Test. Sara George. 1982. 15.00x (ISBN 0-333-24149-5, Pub. by Macmillan England). State Mutual Bk.

Screenplay. MacDonald Harris. LC 82-45175. 1982. 12.95 (ISBN 0-689-11306-4). Atheneum.

Screwball King Murder. Kin Platt. LC 77-90262. 6.95 (ISBN 0-394-41249-4). Random House.

Screwballs. Jay Cronley. LC 79-7796. 1980. 10.00 (ISBN 0-385-15179-9). Doubleday.

Screwge. Bob Tramonte. Ed. by Barbara Paturick. (Illus.). 44p. (Orig.). 1982. pap. 2.25 (ISBN 0-939602-01-6). Blue Star.

Screwtape Letters. Clive Staples Lewis. LC 80-70554. (Illus.). 160p. 1981. pap. 5.95 (ISBN 0-385-17594-9, Im). Doubleday.

Scribble-Foolers. Bernard Hamber. LC 79-92052. 175p. (Orig.). 1980. pap. 6.95 (ISBN 0-9604896-8-1). BH Ent.

Scribble, Scribble, Scribble... Don Hendrie, Jr. LC 76-27963. 1976. pap. 3.00 (ISBN 0-89924-007-0). Lynx Hse.

Scribes and Pharisees: A Story of Literary London. William Le Queux. LC 7-128560. 1898. Dodd, Mead and Company.

Scribner Treasury (The) 22 Classic Tales by Mary Raymond, Shipman Andrew Others Introd., Notes by J. G. E. Hopkins. LC 53-11026. (Scribner lib. omnibus vol. SL133). 1966. pap., 2.95. Scribners.

Scribner Treasury: 22 Classic Tales by Mary Raymond Shipman Andrews and Others Introd. and Notes by J. G. E. Hopkins. LC 53-11026. 1953. Scribner.

Scrimshaw Millions. LC 32-22555. Sears Publishing Company, Inc.

Scripture Club of Valley Rest: Or, Sketches of Everybody's Neighbours. John Habberton. LC 75-165172. (American fiction reprint series). (Illus.). 1971. (ISBN 0-8369-7038-1). Books for Libraries Press.

Scripture Club of Valley Rest: Or, Sketches of Everybody's Neighbours. John Habberton. LC 6-46674. 1877. G. P. Putnam's Sons.

Scripture Club of Valley Rest; or, Sketches of Everybody's Neighbours. facsimile ed. John Habberton. LC 75-165172. (American Fiction Reprint Ser). Repr. of 1877 ed. 18.00 (ISBN 0-8369-7038-1). Ayer Co.

Scripture of the Blind. Giannes Ritsos, pseud. LC 78-14319. 20.00 (ISBN 0-8142-0298-5). Ohio State University Press.

Scripture Reader of St. Mark's. Katherine Douglas King. LC 7-127866. (On cover: The Waldorf series. no. 26). The Merriam Company.

Scroggins. John Uri Lloyd. 1904. Dodd, Mead & Company.

Scrolls of Lysis. Ellery Queen, pseud. LC 62-21295. 1962. Simon and Schuster.

Scrope & the Spinster. David Emerson. 1981. 18.95x (Pub. by Remploy England). State Mutual Bk.

Scrope; or, The Lost Library. A Novel of New York and Hartford. Frederic Beecher Perkins. LC 1-22392. 1874. Roberts Brothers.

Scrub Oak. Michael Oppenheimer. LC 76-368570. (Illus.). Lone Mountain Press.

Scruffy. Paul Gallico. 4.95 o.p. (ISBN 0-385-02369-3). Doubleday.

Scruffy Scoundrels (Gli Straccioni) Annibal Caro. Tr. by M. Ciavolella & Donald Beecher. 95p. 1980. pap. text ed. 3.50x (ISBN 0-88920-103-X, Pub. by Wilfred Laurier U Pr Canada). Humanities.

Scruples. Judith Krantz. 1978. 10.00 (ISBN 0-517-53253-0). Crown.

Scruples. Judith Krantz. 1979. pap. 3.95 (ISBN 0-446-30531-6). Warner Bks.

Scruples: A Novel. Judith Krantz. LC 77-27648. 10.00 (ISBN 0-517-53253-0). Crown.

Scruples: A Novel. Jeannette Ritchie Hadermann Walworth. LC 8-33130. (On cover: Cassell's "rainbow" series, no. 10). Cassell & Company, Limited.

Scrut. George Roberts. LC 82-81349. 72p. 1983. pap. 4.00 (ISBN 0-930100-10-7). Holy Cow.

Scuba Duba. Bruce Jay Friedman. (O.S.I.). 1968. 3.95 o.s.i. (ISBN 0-671-20001-1). S&S.

Scudamores: A Novel. Francis Charles Philips & Wills, Charles James. (On cover: Lovell's international series, no. 110). J. W. Lovell Company.

Scudda-Hoo! Scudda Hay! George Agnew Chamberlain. LC 46-125123. 1946. The Bobbs-Merrill Company.

Scuffler. Harvey Orkin. LC 74-12270. 1974. 6.95 (ISBN 0-15-179700-5). Harcourt Brace Jovanovich.

Scuffles. Sally Nelson Robins. LC 12-20304. 1912. 1.00. The Alice Harriman Company.

Sculptor's Daughter. Margot la Balafree. Fortune Du Boisgobey. Tr. by Laura E. Kendall. (Seaside library, vol. XCII, no. 1885). 1884. G. Munro.

Sculptor's Daughter.(Margot la Balafree.) By F. Du Boisgobey. Tr. from the French by Laura E. Kendall... Fortune Du Boisgobey & Kendall, Mrs. Laura E., Tr. (On cover: Seaside library. Pocket ed., no. 699). 1886. G. Munro.

Scum. authorized ed. Palacio Valdes, Armando. (On cover: Lovell's series of foreign literature, no. 9). 1890. United States Book Company.

Scum of the Earth. Henry Dahnke. LC 74-194742. 1974. 3.95 (ISBN 0-533-01189-2). Vantage Press.

Scurry County Style: Stories from Below the Cap Rock and Beyond, by Viola M. Payne. Introd. by Thomas B. Whitbread. Viola M Payne. LC 67-27371. 1967. Univ. of Tex. Pr.

Scutari. Mladin Zarubica. LC 67-15016. 1969. pap. 0.75 o.p. (64-067). Paperback Lib.

Scutari: A Novel. Mladin Zarubica. LC 67-15016. 1967. Farrar, Straus, and Giroux.

Scuttlers. Clyde C Westover. LC 14-317812. 1914. 1.20. The Neale Publishing Company.

Scylla or Charybdia! A Novel. Rhoda Broughton. LC 6-18950. (Half-title: Appleton's town and country library, no. 177). 1895. D. Appleton and Company.

Scylla or Charybdis! Rhoda Broughton. LC 18-11270. (Macmillan's two shilling library, no. 16). 1899. Macmillan and Co., Limited.

Sea. Bernhard Kellermann. Tr. by Best, Sasha. LC 24-5829. 1924. R. M. McBride & Company.

Sea Above Them. John Wingate. LC 75-24661. 1976. 7.95. St. Martin's Press.

Sea Adventure. Ed. by Raymond McFarland. LC 38-33208. 1938. Harper & Brothers.

Sea and Poison: A Novel. Shusaku Endo. LC 80-16867. 1980. 8.95 (ISBN 0-8008-7021-2). Taplinger Publishing Co.

Sea & Sardinia. D. H. Lawrence. 1981. pap. 3.95 (ISBN 0-14-000465-3). Penguin.

Sea and Shore. A Sequel to "Miriam's Memoirs.". Catherine Ann Ware Warfield. LC 8-34830. T. B. Peterson & Brothers.

Sea and the Gallows. Monica Mugan. (Signet book). 1975. (pbk.) 1.25. New American Library.

Sea and the Jungle. Henry Major Tomlinson. LC 76-142576. (Illus.). 1971. (ISBN 0-87636-011-8). Imprint Society.

Sea and the Land. Josef Israels. LC 31-22909. 1931. Doubleday, Doran & Company, Inc.

Sea and the Shore. Frank Leslie Hower. LC 54-8142. 1954. Pageant Press.

Sea and the Shore. Jacland Marmur. LC 41-236744. H. Holt and Company.

Sea and the Stars. Robert Wilder. (N3686). 1968. Bantam.

Sea and the Stars. Robert Wilder. LC 67-10964. 1967. Putnam.

Sea and the Stone: By Charmian Clift and George Johnston. Charmian Clift & George Henry Johnston. LC 55-10906. 1955. Bobbs-Merrill.

Sea and the Wedding. 1st American Ed. Pamela Hansford Johnson. LC 57-13633. 1957. Harcourt, Brace.

Sea Beasts. A. Bertram Chandler. (Orig.). 1971. pap. 0.75 o.p. (07135). Curtis.

Sea Beggars. Cecelia Holland. LC 81-48115. 1982. 13.95 (ISBN 0-394-50406-2). Knopf: Distributed by Random House.

Sea Birds Are Still Alive. Toni Cade Bambara. 1977. 7.95 o.p. (ISBN 0-394-48143-7). Random.

Sea Birds Are Still Alive: Stories. Toni Cade Bambara. LC 82-4845. 1982. 3.95 (ISBN 0-394-71176-9). Vintage Books.

Sea Boots. Robert C. Du Soe. LC 49-7592. 1949. Longmans, Green.

Sea Bride. Ben Ames Williams. LC 19-15548. 1919. The Macmillan Company.

Sea Captain. Henry Christopher Bailey. LC 13-21264. 1.25. Hodder & Stoughton, George H. Doran Company.

Sea Change. Nigel Forbes Dennis. LC 49-483049. 1949. Houghton Mifflin Co.

Sea-Change. Lois Gould. LC 76-13579. 6.95 (ISBN 0-671-22326-7). Simon and Schuster.

Sea Change. Elizabeth Jane Howard. LC 60-5958. 1960. Harper.

Sea Change. Barbara Hunt. LC 46-47993. 1946. Rinehart & Company, Inc.

Sea Change. Eleanor Mercein Kelly. LC 31-28149. 1931. Harper & Brothers.

Sea-Change. Muna Lee de Munoz-Marin. 1977. lib. bdg. 59.95 (ISBN 0-8490-2580-X). Gordon Pr.

Sea-Change. Philip Loraine. LC 82-17063. 1982. 10.95 (ISBN 0-312-70811-4). St. Martin's Press.

Sea Change. Flora Louise Shaw Lugard. (On cover: The seaside library. Pocket ed. no 441). 1885. G. Munro.

Sea Change. J. R. Salamanca. LC 76-79330. 1969. 6.95. Knopf.

Sea-Change: An Anthology of Short Stories. Ralph E. West. 228p. (Orig.). (gr. 11-12). 1980. pap. text ed. 4.95x (ISBN 0-88334-126-3). Ind Sch Pr.

Sea Change of Angela Lewes: A Novel. Cynthia Propper Seton. LC 75-152673. 1971. 5.95 (ISBN 0-393-08641-0). W. W. Norton.

Sea Chase. Andrew Clare Geer. LC 48-8517. 1948. Harper.

Sea Demons. Victor Rousseau Emanuel. LC 75-28861. (Classics of science fiction). 1976. 12.50. (ISBN 0-88355-375-9) (ISBN 0-88355-462-3). Hyperion Press.

Sea Demons. Victor Rousseau. LC 75-28861. (Classics of Science Fiction Ser.). 254p. 1976. 12.50 (ISBN 0-88355-375-9); pap. 3.95 (ISBN 0-88355-462-3). Hyperion Conn.

Sea Dust. Vera Andrus. (Illus.). 1955. 5.00 o.p. (ISBN 0-87482-009-X). Wake-Brook.

Sea Duty: And Other Stories of Naval Action. Jacland Marmur. LC 44-8302. 1944. H. Holt and Company.

Sea Eagle. James Aldridge. LC 73-153559. 1971. 5.95 (ISBN 0-85617-570-6). White Lion Publishers.

Sea Eagle. James Aldridge. LC 44-1736. 1944. Little, Brown and Company.

Sea Eagles: A Story of the American Navy During the Revolution; of the Men Who Fought and the Ships They Sailed and the Women Who Stood Behind Them. John Edward Jennings. LC 50-5839. 1950. Doubleday.

Sea Fever. Antony Trew. LC 80-53083. 10.95 (ISBN 0-312-70813-0). St. Martin's Press.

Sea Fighters: Navy Yarns of the Great War. Warren Hastings Miller. LC 20-212911. 1920. The Macmillan Company.

Sea File. Jack Denton Scott. 288p. 1981. 10.95 o.p. (ISBN 0-07-056110-9, GB). McGraw.

Sea File. large print ed. Jack Denton Scott. LC 81-9089. 371p. 1981. Repr. of 1981 ed. 11.95x (ISBN 0-89621-306-4). Thorndike Pr.

Sea File: A Novel of Suspense. Jack Denton Scott. LC 80-17701. 10.95 (ISBN 0-07-056110-9). McGraw-Hill.

Sea File: A Novel of Suspense. large print ed. Jack Denton Scott. LC 81-9089. 11.95 (ISBN 0-89621-307-2). Thorndike Press.

Sea Flower. Ruth Moore. LC 64-757678. 1965. bds., 4.50. Morrow.

Sea Fog. Joseph Smith Fletcher. LC 26-16353. 1926. A. A. Knopf.

Sea for Breakfast. Lillian Beckwith. (Illus.). 4.95 o.p. (ISBN 0-525-19825-3). Dutton.

Sea Gate. Jacquelyn Aeby. (Leisure Books). 1977. 1.75 (ISBN 0-8439-0509-3). Nordon Pubns.

Sea-Gift. A Novel. Edwin Wiley Fuller. LC 6-44584. 1873. E. J. Hale & Son.

Sea Girl. Ray Cummings. LC 30-28181. 1930. A. C. McClurg & Co.

Sea Gods: A Japanese Fantasy in Five Parts. Isidor Baumgartl. LC 37-360381. Kroch's Bookstores, Inc.

Sea-Grape Tree. Rosamond Lehmann. LC 77-73058. 7.95 (ISBN 0-15-179720-X). Harcourt Brace Jovanovich.

Sea-Grape Tree. Rosamond Lehmann. LC 76-382616. 1976. 3.50 (ISBN 0-00-222447-X). Collins.

Sea-Green Horse: A Collection of Short Stories. Ed. by Barbara Howes. LC 73-89589. 1970. Macmillan.

Sea Guerrillas. Dean W. Ballenger. 1982. pap. 1.95 (ISBN 0-451-11413-2, AJ1413, Sig). NAL.

Sea Gull. Kathleen Thompson Norris. LC 27-7185. 1927. Doubleday, Page & Company.

Sea-Gull Cry. Robert Nathan. LC 42-13731. 1942. A. A. Knopf.

Sea Gull: La Gaviota. Fernan Caballero. Tr. by Joan MacLean from Span. LC 65-18177. (Text ed. 4.75 o.p.). (Orig.). (YA) 1965. pap. text ed. 2.95 (ISBN 0-8120-0124-9). Barron.

Sea Gull. Tr. from Spanish, Introd. by Joan Maclean. Fernan Cabellero. LC 65-18177. 1965. pap., 1.75. Barron's.

Sea Gulls Don't Fly at Night. Alvin J. Hunter. Date not set. 6.95 o.p. (ISBN 0-533-04098-1). Vantage.

Sea Gypsy. Fern Michaels. LC 81-4768. 1981. 10.95 (ISBN 0-8161-3194-5). G.K. Hall.

Sea-Harrower. Abigail Clements. (Orig.). 1980. pap. 2.25 (ISBN 0-449-14326-0, GM). Fawcett.

Sea Hawk. Manohar Malgonkar. (Orient Paperbacks Ser.). 293p. 1980. pap. 4.95 (ISBN 0-86578-069-2); 9.95 (ISBN 0-86578-136-2). Ind-US Inc.

Sea Hawk. Bailey Millard. LC 10-23126. 1910. Wessels & Bissell Co.

Sea-Hawk. Rafael Sabatini. 1923. Houghton Mifflin Company.

Sea-Hawk. Rafael Sabatini. LC 24-24984. 1924. Grosset & Dunlap.

Sea-Hawk. Rafael Sabatini. LC 80-23696. 1980. 15.00 (ISBN 0-89783-012-1). Larlin Corp.

Sea-Horse in the Sky. Edmund Cooper. 1978. 1.75 (ISBN 0-441-75655-7). Ace Books.

Sea Horse in the Sky: A Science Fiction Novel. Edmund Cooper. LC 78-113165. 1970. 4.95. Putnam.

Sea Horses. Francis Brett Young. 1925. A. A. Knopf.

Sea House. Margaret Summerton. LC 61-10460. (Rinehart suspense novel). 1961. Holt, Rinehart and Winston.

Sea Hunters. Frank Robb. LC 54-1207. 1953. Longmans, Green.

Sea Is Red: A Novel. 1st Ed.,54. Scott O'Dell. LC 58-14131. 1958. Holt.

Sea Is So Wide. Evelyn Sybil Mary Eaton. LC 43-3610. 1943. Harper & Brothers.

Sea Is Wide. Evelyn Sybil Mary Eaton. 1967. pap. 0.95 o.p. Lancer.

Sea Is Woman. Albert Edward Idell. LC 47-177943. 1947. H. Holt and Company.

Sea Island Lady. Francis Griswold. LC 39-30688. 1939. W. Morrow & Co.

Sea-Island Romance. A Story of South Carolina After the War. William Perry Brown. 1888. J.R. Alden.

Sea Jade. Phyllis A. Whitney. LC 65-12605. bds., 4.95. Appleton-Century Dist. Meredith.

Sea-King. Frederick Marryat. LC 7-17568. (On cover: Seaside library. Pocket ed. no. 1165). 1889. G. Munro.

Sea King of Barnegat. Russell Duryee Smith. LC 18-18532. 1918. Duffield & Company.

Sea King's Daughter. Barbara Mertz. LC 75-28200. 1975. 7.95. (ISBN 0-396-07208-9). Dodd, Mead.

Sea King's Daughter. Barbara Mertz. LC 76-10197. 1976. 11.95 (ISBN 0-8161-6381-2). G. K. Hall.

Sea King's Daughter. barbara michaels. ed. Barbara Mertz. 1976. 1.75 (ISBN 0-449-23023-6). Fawcett Crest.

Sea King's Daughter. Barbara Michaels. LC 75-28200. 1975. 7.95 o.p. (ISBN 0-396-07208-9). Dodd.

Sea Lady. Herbert George Wells. LC 2-23406. 1902. D. Appleton and Company.

Sea Lady: A Tissue of Moonshine. Herbert George Wells. LC 75-28862. (Classics of science fiction). 1976. 11.95. (ISBN 0-88355-376-7) (ISBN 0-88355-465-8). Hyperion Press.

Sea Lady; a Tissue of Moonshine. Herbert George Wells. LC 75-28862. (Classics of Science Fiction Ser.). (Illus.). vii, 300p. 1976. 12.50 (ISBN 0-88355-376-7); pap. 3.95 (ISBN 0-88355-465-8). Hyperion Conn.

Sea Lavender. Sidney Floyd Gowing. LC 25-17701. 1925. H. Holt and Company.

Sea Leopard. Craig Thomas. LC 81-65277. 1981. 13.95 (ISBN 0-670-62622-8). Viking Press.

Sea Lepers. Gerald F Lieberman. LC 70-139041. 1971. 6.95. Doubleday.

Sea Level. Anne Parrish. LC 34-87579. 1934. Harper & Brothers.

Sea-Life Sixty Years Ago. A Record of Adventures Which Led up to the Discovery of the Relics of the Long Missing Expedition Commanded by the Comte De La Perouse. George Bayly. (Harper's handy series, no. 67.). 1886. Harper & Brothers.

Sea Lion: Or, The Privateer of the Penobscot. A Story of Ocean Life and the Heart's Love. Sylvanus Cobb. LC 6-20717. 1853. S. French.

Sea Lions. James Fenimore Cooper. Ed. by Warren S. Walker. LC 65-18416. (Illus.). 1965. pap. 2.45x o.p. (ISBN 0-8032-5037-1, BB 306, Bison). U of Nebr Pr.

Sea Lions. James Fenimore Cooper. Ed. by Warren S. Walker. 4.50 o.p. (ISBN 0-8446-1899-3). Peter Smith.

Sea Lions. Ed., Introd. by Warren S. Walker. James Fenimore Cooper. Ed. by Warren S. Walker. (Bison bk., BB306 rebound). 4.00. P. Smith.

Sea Lions. Ed. Introd. by Warren S. Walker. James Fenimore Cooper. Ed. by Warren S. Walker. LC 65-18416. (Bison bk., BB306). pap., 1.85. Univ. of Neb. Pr.

Sea Lions: Or, The Lost Sealers. James Fenimore Cooper. LC 6-29672. 1849. Stringer & Townsend.

Sea Lions: Or, The Lost Sealers. new ed. James Fenimore Cooper. LC 6-29677. 1852. Stringer and Townsend.

Sea Lions: Or, The Lost Sealers. James Fenimore Cooper. LC 26-24685. (Half-title: The choice works of Cooper. Revised and corrected series. v. 20). 1856. Stringer & Townsend.

Sea Lions: Or, The Lost Sealers. household ed. James Fenimore Cooper. Ed. by Cooper, Susan Fenimore. LC 11-10562. Houghton, Mifflin and Company.

Sea-Lions: Or, The Lost Sealers. James Fenimore Cooper. (On cover: Lovell's library. no. 553). 1885. J. W. Lovell Company.

Sea-Lions: Or, The Lost Sealers. James Fenimore Cooper. (On cover: Seaside library. Pocket ed. no. 423). 1885. G. Munro.

Sea Loot. Arthur Durham Divine. LC 31-11911. 1931. R. M. McBride & Company.

Sea Magic. Sara Ware Bassett. LC 42-156006. 1942. Doubleday, Doran & Company, Inc.

Sea Maid. Ronald Macdonald. LC 6-3656. 1906. H. Holt and Company.

Sea-Mary. Oliver Ramsay Pilat. LC 36-7121. 1936. C. Scribner's Sons.

Sea Master. Sally Wentworth. (Harlequin Presents Ser.). 192p. 1982. pap. 1.75 (ISBN 0-373-10512-6). Harlequin Bks.

Sea Mey Abbey: A Novel. Florence Alice Price James. LC 7-7978. J. W. Lovell Company.

Sea Monks. Andrew Garve. pap. 0.50 o.p. (72-759). Lancer.

Sea Monks. Paul Winterton. LC 63-16531. 1963. Harper & Row.

Sea Mystery. Freeman W. Crofts. pap. 0.75 o.p. (ISBN 0-14-001395-4, 1395). Penguin.

Sea Mystery: An Inspector French Case. Freeman Wills Crofts. LC 65-5023. (Penguin crime, 1895). 1965. Penquin Books.

Sea Mystery: An Inspector French Dective Story. Freeman Wills Crofts. LC 28-19241. 1928. Harper & Brothers.

Sea Nymphs by the Hour. L. J Schneiderman. LC 72-76926. 1972. 6.50. Bobbs-Merrill.

Sea of Darkness. Roland Huntford. LC 75-17690. 1975. 7.95 (ISBN 0-684-14418-2). Scribner.

Sea of Dreams. Alfred Gordon Bennett. LC 26-14987. The Macaulay Company.

Sea of Fertility: A Cycle of Four Novels. Yukio Mishima, pseud. LC 72-755. (UNESCO Collection of Representative Works: Japanese Series). 1972-74. (ISBN 0-394-46613-6). Knopf.

Sea of Gold. Adam Hardy. (Fox,#6). 1974. (pbk.) 0.95 (ISBN 0-523-00400-1). Pinnacle Books.

Sea of Grass. Conrad Richter. LC 37-27107. 1937. A. A. Knopf.

Sea of Grass. Large Type Ed. Conrad Richter. LC 66-6177. 1966. 6.95. Watts.

Sea of Ice: Or, The Arctic Adventurers. St. John, Percy Bollingbroke. LC 44-42705. 1859. Mayhew and Baker.

Sea of Matrimony: A Novel. Jessie Dow Hopkins Childs. LC 9-31478. 1.50. Broadway Publishing Company.

Sea of Process. Alexander Steinmetz. 1975. 5.00 o.p. (ISBN 0-87482-043-X). Wake-Brook.

Sea of Thighs. Ray Kainen. LC 78-9882. (Traveller's companion series). 1968. 1.75. Traveller's Companion, Inc.

Sea of Troubles. Marguerite Duras. LC 76-599106. 1969 (ISBN 0-14-002661-4). Penguin.

Sea Officer. Showell Styles. LC 62-779056. 1962. Macmillan.

Sea on Fire. Rory Brennan. (Orig.). 1980. pap. text ed. 8.00x (ISBN 0-85105-308-4, Dolmen Pr). Humanities.

Sea Panther. Raymond McFarland. LC 28-2000. 1928. Frederick A. Stokes Company.

Sea Panther: A Novel About the Commander of the U.S.S. Constitution. Philip Vail. LC 62-16791. 1962. Dodd, Mead.

Sea People. Jorg. Steiner. LC 82-5488. 1982. 14.95 (ISBN 0-8052-3813-1). Schocken Books.

Sea People: A Fantasy. Julius C Sizemore & Wilkie G Sizemore. LC 57-9224. 1957. Exposition Press.

Sea Plander. Patrick Casey, pseud. LC 25-6856. Small, Maynard & Company.

Sea Plunder: By H. De Vere Stacpoole... Henry De Vere Stacpoole. LC 17-11465. 1917. John Lane Company.

Sea Queen. C. Savery. 1971. pap. 1.50 (ISBN 0-87508-755-8). Chr Lit.

Sea Queen. A Novel. William Clark Russell. (Harper's Franklin square library, no. 314). 1883. Harper & Brothers.

Sea Queen. A Novel. William Clark Russell. (Seaside library, v. 82, no. 1653). 1883. G. Munro.

Sea Queen. A Novel. William Clark Russell. (On cover: Seaside library. Pocket ed., no. 85). 1883. G. Munro.

Sea Ringed with Visions. Translated from Spur Im Treibsand by Eithne Wilkins and Ernst Kaiser. 1st American Ed. Oskar Kokoschka. LC 62-13969. 1962. Horizon Press.

Sea Road to Yorktown. 1st Ed. Harvey Haislip. LC 60-13736. 1960. Doubleday.

Sea Runners. Ivan Doig. LC 82-45174. (Illus.). 1982. 13.95 (ISBN 0-689-11302-1). Atheneum.

Sea Runners. Ralph Hayes. (Orig.). 1981. pap. 2.50 (ISBN 0-505-51647-0). Tower Bks.

Sea Scamps: Three Adventurers of the East. Henry Cottrell Rowland. LC 3-23896. 1903. McClure, Phillips & Co.

Sea Scorpion. George Brydges Rodney. Greenberg.

Sea Serpent. Herbert Luther Kneen. LC 34-18840. H. L. Kneen.

Sea Serpent: Or, The Queen of the Coral Cave. A Romance of the Ocean. By B. Barker... Benjamin Barker. LC 9-1845. 1847. F. Gleason.

Sea Serpent: The Yarns of Jean-Marie Cabidoulin. Jules Verne. 3.95. Assoc Bk.

Sea Siege. Andre Norton, pseud. 224p. 1980. pap. 2.25 (ISBN 0-449-24293-5, Crest). Fawcett.

Sea Siege: By Andre Norton Pseud. 1st Ed. Alice Mary Norton. LC 57-8586. 1957. Harcourt, Brace.

Sea Spell. Caroline Fox. LC 80-19604. 10.95 (ISBN 0-698-11060-9). Coward, McCann & Geoghegan.

Sea-Spray: A Long Island Village. Cornelia Huntington. LC 17-6112. 1857. Derby & Jackson.

Sea, Spray and Spindrift, Naval Yarns. Henry Taprell Dorling, pseud. LC 19-5431. 1917. J. B. Lippincott Company.

Sea-Spray: Or, Facts and Fancies of a Yachtsman. Samuel Greene Wheeler Benjamin. LC 7-34439. 1887. Benjami & Bell.

Sea Sprite & the Shooting Star. Jack London. 1975. pap. 1.00 o.p. (ISBN 0-915046-18-0). Wolf Hse.

Sea Star: The Private Life of Anne Bonny, Pirate Queen. Pamela Jekel. LC 82-21232. 5.95 (ISBN 0-517-54946-8). Harmony Books.

Sea Star: The Private Life of Anne Bonny, Pirate Queen. Pamela Jekel. 1983. pap. 5.95 (ISBN 0-517-54946-8, Harmony). Crown.

Sea Stories. Ed. by Brady, Cyrus Townsend. LC 3-8563. (Young folks' library. 3d ed. vol. xiii). Hall and Locke Company.

Sea Stories. Joseph Conrad. 200p. 1980. 14.95x (ISBN 0-8464-1240-3). Beekman Pubs.

Sea Stories. Joseph Conrad. (Mariners Lib). 4.25 o.p. Fernhill.

Sea Story. Ronald Johnston. LC 79-55622. 1980. 10.95 (ISBN 0-689-11046-4). Atheneum.

Sea Story. Ronald Johnston. LC 81-1485. 1981. 13.95 (ISBN 0-89340-336-9). J. Curley & Associates.

Sea Story Annual. 1943- LC 45-5366. Street & Smith Publications, Inc.

Sea Story Anthology. 1943- LC 45-5366. Street & Smith Publications.

Sea Struck. Stanley Bennett Hough. LC 53-8439. 1953. Crowell.

Sea Tales. Joseph Conrad. LC 30-26973. (windmill books). 1930. Doubleday, Doran & Company, Inc.

Sea Tales. Joseph Conrad. LC 39-18162. (Young moderns books). 1937. Doubleday, Doran & Company, Inc.

Sea Texas and Die. Jake Logan. LC 77-93129. 1.25 (ISBN 0-87216-458-6). Playboy Press.

Sea, the Sea. Iris Murdoch. LC 78-13516. 1978. 10.95 (ISBN 0-670-62651-1). Viking Press.

Sea, the Sea. Iris Murdoch. LC 80-11380. 1980. 4.95 (ISBN 0-14-005199-6). Penguin Books.

Sea-Time. Frances Snyder. LC 72-80313. 1972. 2.95 (ISBN 0-8059-1714-4). Dorrance.

Sea Tower. Kate Ostrander. (Queen-size gothic). 1974. (pbk.) 0.95. Popular Library.

Sea Tower. Hugh Walpole. LC 39-27885. 1939. Doubleday, Doran and Company, Inc.

Sea Trap. Nick Carter. (Nick Carter Ser.). (O.s.i.). (Orig.). 1972. pap. 0.95 o.s.i. (AN1314, Award). Univ Pub & Dist.

Sea Treasure. Elisabeth Barr. LC 77-12835. 1979. 7.95 (ISBN 0-385-13323-5). Doubleday.

Sea Trial. Frank De Felitta. LC 80-66147. 4.95 (ISBN 0-380-76042-8). Avon.

Sea Troll. Suzanne Blanc. LC 68-22531. 1969. 3.95. Published for the Crime Club by Doubleday.

Sea Turn: And Other Matters. Thomas Bailey Aldrich. LC 76-81258. (Short story index reprint series). 1969. Books for Libraries Press.

Sea Turn and Other Matters. Thomas Bailey Aldrich. LC 2-21986. 1902. Houghton, Mifflin and Company.

Sea Turtle & the Shark. M. B. Tolson. (Broadside Ser., No. 5). broadsheet. 0.50 o.p. Broadside.

Sea Tyrant. Peter Freuchen. Tr. by Bjorkman, Edwin August. LC 32-216721. Liveright, Inc.

Sea Urchins. Mary Ann Gibbs. 1973. pap. 0.95 o.p. (345-26503-3-095). Beagle Bks.

Sea Venture. F. Van Wyck Mason. 1976. Repr. of 1961 ed. lib. bdg. 17.70x (ISBN 0-89190-353-4). Am Repr-Rivercity Pr.

Sea Wall. Marguerite Duras. LC 67-3360. 1967. Farrar, Straus and Giroux.

Sea Wall: By L. A. G. Strong. Leonard Alfred George Strong. LC 33-32230. 1933. A. A. Knopf.

Sea Wall. Tr. by Herma Briffault, Pref. by Germaine Bree. 1967. 4.95. Farrar.

Sea Wall: Translated by Herma Briffault. Marguerite Duras. LC 51-10420. 1953. Pellegrini &Cudahy.

Sea Whispers. William Wymark Jacobs. LC 26-22062. 1926. C. Scribner's Sons.

Sea Wind. Maeva Park Dobner. Dell.

Sea Wind: By Gay Rutherford Pseud. James Noble Gifford. LC 55-101923. 1955. Arcadia House.

Sea Witch: A Narrative of the Experiences of Capt. Roger Murray and Others in an American Clipper Ship During the Years 1846 to 1856. Shorter Ed. Alexander Kinnan Laing. LC 58-6762. (Clipper-Ship). 1958. Duell, Sloan and Pearce.

Sea Witch: A Narrative of the Experiences of Capt. Roger Murray and Others in an American Clipper Ship During the Year 1843 to 1856. Alexander Kinnan Laing. LC 33-3289. 1933. Farrar & Rinehart, Inc.

Sea Witch: A Narrative of the Experience of Capt. Roger Murray and Others in an American Clipper Ship During the Years 1846 to 1856. new ed., illustrated by gordon grant. ed. Alexander Kinnan Laing. LC 44-9148. 1944. Murray Hill Books, Inc.

Sea Witch: A Novel. Laurence Yep. LC 77-3809. 8.95 (ISBN 0-06-014771-7). Harper & Row.

Sea Wolf. Jack London. (Collateral classic, CC517). 1967. Washington Sq.

Sea-Wolf. Jack London. LC 59-1892. 1958. Macmillan.

Sea-Wolf. Jack London. LC 67-7675. 1967. Macmillan.

Sea-Wolf. Jack London. LC 69-12445. (Horizon edition of the works of Jack London). 1969. 3.95. Horizon Press.

Sea-Wolf. Jack London. LC 4-30593. 1904. The Macmillan Company.

Sea-Wolf. Jack London. LC 24-28523. Grosset & Dunlop.

Sea-Wolf. Jack London. LC 18-4338. The Macmillan Company.

Sea-Wolf. Jack London. LC 20-16458. 1919. The Macmillan Company.

Sea-Wolf. Jack London. LC 24-222276. 1922. Grosset & Dunlap.

Sea-Wolf: And Selected Stories. Jack London. LC 64-4818. (Signet classic, CP217). 1964. New American Library.

Sea Wolf, No. 2: Shark North. Bruno Krauss. 1981. pap. 2.25 (ISBN 0-89083-782-1). Zebra.

Sea Wolf: Shark Raid, No. 6. Bruno Krauss. (Sea Wolf Ser.). 1982. pap. 2.25 (ISBN 0-8217-1043-5). Zebra.

Sea-Wolf. With Illus. by Fletcher Martin, and an Introd. by Edmund Gilligan. Jack London. LC 61-65445. 1961. Printed for the Members of the Limited Editions Club, by Connecticut Printers.

Sea-Wolf. With Illus. by Fletcher Martin and an Introd. by Edmund Gilligan. Jack London. LC 62-52460. 1962. Heritage Press.

Sea Wolves. Wolfgang Frank. 224p. 1981. pap. 2.50 (ISBN 0-345-29504-8). Ballantine.

Sea Wolves: A Novel. Max Pemberton. LC 7-363760. (On cover: Harper's Franklin square library. no. 754). 1894. Harper & Brothers.

Sea World, No. 4: Shark Hunt. Bruno Krauss. pap. 2.25 (ISBN 0-89083-833-X). Zebra.

Sea Wrack. Vere Hutchinson. LC 22-16476. 1922. 1.75. The Century Co.

Sea-Wyf & Biscuit. J. M. Scott. 1979. 11.00x o.p. (ISBN 0-86025-043-1, Pub. by Ian Henry Pubns England). State Mutual Bk.

Sea-Wyf & Biscuit. J. M. Scott. 1977. 6.20 o.p. State Mutual Bk.

Sea-Wyf. 1st American Ed. James Maurice Scott. LC 56-5257. 1956. Dutton.

Seabird Nine. James McVean, pseud. LC 81-1285. 1981. 11.95 (ISBN 0-698-11063-3). Coward, McCann & Geoghegan.

Seaboard Parish. A Sequel to "Annals of a Quiet Neighborhood.". George Macdonald. (Seaside library, v. 29, no. 606). 1879. G. Munro.

Seaboard Parish: A Sequel to "Annals of a Quiet Neighborhood". George Macdonald. G. Routledge & Sons, Limited.

Seaboard Parish: A Sequel to "Annals of a Quiet Neighborhood,". George Macdonald. LC 12-18329. 1911. D. McKay.

Seabury Castle: A Novel. Cecil Hope. LC 7-52592. 1869. J. B. Lippincott & Co.

Seacage: A Romance for Another Time in Three Voices. Lolah Burford. LC 79-13147. 9.95 (ISBN 0-02-518180-7). Macmillan.

Seacliff. John William De Forest. Ed. by Donald Pizer. LC 72-96511. (American Authors Ser). 1970. Repr. of 1859 ed. lib. bdg. 22.95 o.s.i. (ISBN 0-512-00129-4). Garrett Pr.

Seacliff Nurse. Peggy O'More, pseud. LC 66-1867. 1966. Arcadia House.

Seacliff: Or, The Mystery of the Westervelts. John William De Forest. 1859. Phillips. Sampson and Company.

Seacliff; or, the Mystery of the Westervelts. John William De Forest. 1978. Repr. of 1859 ed. lib. bdg. 50.00 (ISBN 0-8414-1897-7). Folcroft.

Seacoast of Bohemia. Louis Golding. LC 24-9783. 1924. A. A. Knopf.

Seacoast of Bohemia. Arona McHugh. LC 64-19300. 6.95. Doubleday.

Seademons: A Novel. Laurence Yep. (Perennial library). 1979. 1.95 (ISBN 0-06-080477-7). Harper & Row.

Seadon Fortune. St. Clair, Leonard. LC 76-27373. 9.95 (ISBN 0-671-22369-0). Simon and Schuster.

Seadon Fortune. Leonard St. Clair. (Berkley Book). 1979. 2.25 (ISBN 0-425-03865-3). Berkley Pub. Corp.

Seadrift House. Clare Hamilton, pseud. 256p. (Orig.). 1981. pap. 2.25 (ISBN 0-505-51746-9). Tower Bks.

Seafarer. Olive San Louis Anderson. 1978. Repr. lib. bdg. 10.00 (ISBN 0-8495-0110-5). Arden Lib.

Seafarer. Ed. by L. I. Gordon. LC 79-55530. (Old & Middle English Texts Ser.). 70p. 1979. pap. text ed. 6.75x (ISBN 0-06-492491-2). B&N Imports.

Seafarers: A Modern Romance. John Edward Bloundelle-Burton. (Half-title: Appletons' town and country library no. 285). 1900. D Appleton and Company.

Seafire. Bill Knox. LC 70-157606. 1971. 4.95. Published for the Crime Club by Doubleday.

Seafire. Karen Robards. 416p. (Orig.). 1982. pap. 3.75 (ISBN 0-8439-1084-4, Leisure Bks). Nordon Pubns.

Seaflame. Valerie Vayle, pseud. (Orig.). 1980. pap. 2.75 (ISBN 0-440-17693-X). Dell.

Seaforth. Florence Montgomery. LC 18-20855. 1878. J. B. Lippincott & Co.

Rainbow/Seagreen Case. P. K Palmer. (Killinger series,#2). 1974. (pbk.) 1.25 (ISBN 0-523-00300-5). Pinnacle Books.

Seagull. Yashar Kemal. 1981. 11.95 (ISBN 0-394-51856-X). Pantheon.

Seagull. Charles Gilman Norris. LC 80-8650. 1981. 11.95 (ISBN 0-394-51856-X). Pantheon Books.

Seagull Crag. Elisabeth Welles. (Kangaroo Book). 1977. 1.50 (ISBN 0-671-80952-0). Pocket Books.

Seagull on the Step. 1st Ed. Kay Boyle. LC 55-5604. 1955. Knopf.

Seagulls Over Sorrento. John D. Drummond. Ed. by Hugh Hastings. 223p. Date not set. Repr. of 1956 ed. 6.95 o.s.i. (ISBN 0-85617-273-1). White Lion Pubs.

Seagulls Under Glass, and Other Stories. Peter Tate. LC 74-12717. 1975. 5.95 (ISBN 0-385-01827-4). Doubleday.

Seahorse: 1st Amer. Ed. Anthony Masters. LC 66-23387. bds., 5.75. Atheneum.

Seal. W. H. Canaway. 1978. 9.95 (ISBN 0-86025-018-0). State Mutual Bk.

Seal Called Andre. Harry Goodridge & Lew Dietz. (Adult Ser.). 1976. Repr. lib. bdg. 8.95 o.p. (ISBN 0-8161-6341-3, Large Print Bks). G K Hall.

Seal of Dracula. Barrie Pattison. (Illus.). 128p. 1975. pap. 2.95 o.p. (ISBN 0-517-52153-9). Crown.

Seal of Silence: A Novel. Arthur Reignier Conder. 1901. D. Appleton and Company.

Seal-Woman. Ronald Mathias Lockley. LC 76-352028. 1975. 6.95 (ISBN 0-87888-087-9). Bradbury Press.

Seal-Woman. Ronald Mathias Lockley. 1977. 1.25. Avon Books.

Sealed Book. Alice Livingston. LC 7-5060. R. F. Fenno & Company.

Sealed Door of Love. Winifred Mary Scott. LC 33-6257. 1933. Doubleday, Doran & Company, Inc.

Sealed Knot. Jane Lane. 1971. pap. 0.95 o.p. (95130). Beagle Bks.

Sealed Lips. Marcel Ernest Bechu & Hartigan, Margaret, Tr. LC 30-8786. 1930. Doubleday, Doran and Company, Inc.

Sealed Lips. Fortune Du Boisgobey. (On cover: Seaside library. Pocket ed. no. 82). G. Munro.

Sealed Lips. (Bouche Close.) Tr. from the French of Leon De Tinseau. Leon De Tinseau & Page, Anna Dyer, Tr. (On cover: The primrose series, no. 19). 1891. Street & Smith.

Sealed Message. Fergus Hume. LC 7-39190. G. W. Dillingham Company.

Sealed Orders. Sidney Floyd Gowing. LC 29-16772. 1929. G. P. Putnam's Sons.

Sealed Orders. Elizabeth Stuart Phelps Ward. LC 69-11926. (American short story series, v. 85). 1969. Garrett Press.

Sealed Orders. Elizabeth Stuart Phelps Ward. LC 8-36035. 1879. Houghton, Osgood and Company.

Sealed Orders. Elizabeth Stuart Phelps H. D. Ward Ward. LC 7-23460. Houghton, Mifflin and Company.

Sealed Trunk. Henry Kitchell Webster. LC 29-3265. The Bobbs-Merrill Company.

Sealed Valley. Hulbert Footner. LC 14-17986. 1914. Doubleday, Page & Company.

Sealed Verdict. 1st Ed. Lionel S. B Shapiro. LC 47-11086. 1947. Doubleday.

Sealers. Peter Tutein. LC 79-22105. (Seafaring Men, Their Ships and Times Series). 1979. 22.50 (ISBN 0-930576-28-4). E. M. Coleman.

Sealers. Peter Tutein & Gay-Tifft, Eugene, Tr. LC 38-27328. 1938. G. P. Putnam's Sons.

Seamless Robe. Ada Carter. LC 9-28093. 1909. A. Wessles.

Seamstress of Stettin. Adapted from the German. Adelheid Katharina Mathilde Rothenburg. Tr. by Nicholl, Cornelia (Mather) 1889. Cranston & Stowe.

Seamy Side. A Novel. Walter Besant & Rice, James. (Seaside library, v. 34, no. 700). 1880. G. Munro.

Seamy Side: A Story of the True Condition of Things Theatrical. Percy Ives. LC 7-12981. Percy Ives Publishing Co.

Sean O'Faolain: A Critical Introduction. Maurice Harmon. LC 67-12124. 1966. University of Notre Dame Press.

Seance. Isaac Bashevis Singer. 256p. 1981. pap. 2.75 (ISBN 0-449-24364-8, Crest). Fawcett.

Seance, and Other Stories. Isaac Bashevis Singer. LC 68-23742. 1968. 5.95. Farrar, Straus & Giroux.

Seance for the Dead. Florence Hurd. 1972. pap. 0.75 o.p. (75-459). Manor Bks.

Seance for Two. Mark McShane. LC 72-79407. 1972. 4.95. Published for the Crime Club by Doubleday.

Seance. 1st Ed. in the U. S. A. Mark McShane. LC 62-11750. 1962. Published for the Crime Club by Doubleday.

Seaports in the Moon: A Fantasia on Romantic Themes. Vincent Starrett. LC 28-10628. 1928. Doubleday, Doran & Company, Inc.

Search. John E. Briggs. 3.50 o.p. Carlton.

Search. Grace Livingston Hill. LC 19-18374. 1919. J. B. Lippincott Company.

Search. Grace Livingston Hill. 1974. (pbk.) 0.95. Bantam Books.

Search. Carol F. Olvera. LC 79-84347. (Illus.). 191p. 1979. pap. 2.25 o.p. (ISBN 0-89877-006-8). Jeremy Bks.

Search. Carol Lynn Pearson. LC 74-28895. 64p. 1975. 5.95 (ISBN 0-385-07758-0). Doubleday.

Search. Charles Percy Snow. LC 35-2968. 1935. Bobbs-Merrill.

Search. Charles Percy Snow. LC 59-6070. 1950. Scribner.
Search. Charles Percy Snow. LC 59-6070. 1959. Scribner.
Search. Charles Percy Snow. LC 35-2968. The Bobbs-Merrill Company.
Search. Margaret Rivers Larminie Tragett. LC 22-8711. 1922. G. P. Putnam's Sons.
Search. Robert Weverka. LC 72-10854. 1973. 0.75. Bantam Books.
Search After Hapiness Sic: A Tale. Charlotte Bronte. LC 79-91305. (Illus.). 1969. 3.50 (ISBN 0-671-20423-8). Simon & Schuster.
Search After Happiness. Charlotte Bronte. (O.s.i.). 1969. 3.50 o.s.i. (ISBN 0-671-20423-8). S&S.
Search After Happiness: A Pastoral Drama. To Which Is Added, Joseph Made Known to His Brethren: a Sacred Drama... Hannah More. LC 1-5499. 1811. Printed for Johnson and Warner, No., Market Street. Lydia R. Bailey, Printer, No., North Alley.
Search and Destroy. Irwin R Blacker. (7687). 1967. Dell.
Search and Destroy. Irwin R Blacker. LC 66-21492. 1966. Random House.
Search & Destroy. Robin Moore, pseud. 352p. 1980. pap. 2.50 (ISBN 0-441-75691-3, Pub. by Charter Bks). Ace Bks.
Search & Destroy. Robin Moore, pseud. LC 78-68007. 1978. pap. 2.25 o.s.i. (ISBN 0-89516-048-X). Condor Pub Co.
Search for a Hero. Thomas Hal Phillips. LC 52-6805. 1952. Rinehart.
Search for a Key. Walter Duranty. LC 43-3710. 1943. Simon and Schuster.
Search for a Missing Lady. Neill Graham. 1976. 4.95 (ISBN 0-09-126360-3, Pub. by Hutchinson). Merrimack Pub Cir.
Search for a Scientist. Mary Violet Herberden. LC 47-31137. 1947. Pub. for the Crime Club by Doubleday.
Search for a Sultan. Manning Coles, pseud. 224p. 1973. Repr. of 1961 ed. lib. bdg. 5.95 o.s.i. (ISBN 0-85617-991-4). White Lion Pubs.
Search for Amelia. David K Findlay. LC 58-11130. 1958. Lippincott.
Search for Anderson. I. I Magdalen. LC 81-21456. 1982. 11.95 (ISBN 0-312-70815-7). St. Martin's Press.
Search for Andrew Field; a Story of the Times of 1812. Everett Titsworth Tomlinson. LC 4-16472. (On cover: War of 1812 series, v. 1). 1894. Lee and Shepard.
Search for Basil Lyndhurst. Rosa Nouchette Carey. (On cover: Lovell's international series, no. 16). F. F. Lovell & Company.
Search for Basil Lyndhurst. Rosa Nouchette Carey. (On cover: Seaside library. Pocket ed., no. 1194). G. Munro.
Search for Basil Lyndhurst. Rosa Nouchette Carey. LC 16-19138. 1908. J. B. Lippincott Company.
Search for Bruno Heidler: By Stephen Marlowe. Pseud. Milton Lesser. LC 66-11435. 4.95. Macmillan.
Search for Bruno Heidler: By Stephen Marlowe. Milton Lesser. (V2226). 1968. Avon.
Search for Eden. Gladys Zehnpfennig. LC 55-11066. T. S. Denison.
Search for Elisabeth Brandt. William Harrington. LC 68-9782. 1968. 6.95. D. McKay Co.
Search for Franklin. L. H. Neatby. 1970. 7.50 o.p. (ISBN 0-8027-0317-8). Walker & Co.
Search for Freedom. Caroline Ballin. LC 66-24221. 1966. Citadel Press.
Search for Goodbye-to-Rains. Paul McHugh. LC 79-28565. 192p. 1980. pap. 7.50 (ISBN 0-933280-07-6). Island CA.
Search for Happiness. David Ritz. LC 79-24221. 1980. 11.95 (ISBN 0-671-25349-2). Simon and Schuster.
Search for Home. Sasthi Brata. 1975. (ISBN 0-88253-771-7). Orient.
Search for Intimacy. Walter J. LaCentra. 3.95 o.p. Vantage.
Search for Joseph Tully: A Novel. William H Hallahan. LC 74-1901. (Illus.). 1974. 6.95 (ISBN 0-672-51997-6). Bobbs-Merrill.
Search for Life on Mars. Henry S. Cooper, Jr. LC 81-2440. 264p. 1981. pap. 6.95 (ISBN 0-03-059818-4, Owl Bk). HR&W.
Search for Lost Cities. James Howard Wellard. 1981. 24.00x (ISBN 0-09-463140-9, Pub. by Constable Pubs). State Mutual Bk.
Search for Love. Matthew O. Emiohe. 224p. 1983. 11.00 (ISBN 0-682-49954-4). Exposition.
Search for Love. Benjamin Friedman. 172p. 1975. 4.95 o.s.i. (ISBN 0-8181-0347-7). Pageant-Poseidon.
Search for Love. John G. Horton. 5.00 o.p. Carlton.
Search for Maggie Hare. Elizabeth Byrd. LC 76-376517. 1976. 3.95 (ISBN 0-333-17748-7). Macmillan.
Search for Meaning. Richard P Dennis & Edwin P Moldof. LC 76-151286. Great Books Foundation.
Search for My Great-Uncle's Head: The Seasons Most Startling and Diverting Mystery Story. Peter Pseud Coffin. LC 38-5022. 1937. Pub. for the Crime Club, Inc., by Doubleday, Doran & Company, Inc.
Search for Rachel: A Stirring Account of the Capture of Rachel Plummer from Ft. Parker and Her Husband's Search for Her. Zula Plummer. LC 76-14516. Z. Plummer.
Search for Tabatha Carr. Richard Martin Stern. LC 60-7344. 1960. Scribner.
Search for the King. Gore Vidal. 1973. pap. 0.95 o.p. (ISBN 0-515-02883-5, N2883). Pyramid Pubns.
Search for the King: A 12th Century Legend. Gore Vidal. LC 49-50412. 1950. Dutton.
Search for the Red River Heiress. Vincent Charles Sweeney. LC 54-28553. 1954.
Search for the Sun. 1st Ed. Charles Furcolowe. LC 53-6649. 1953. World Pub. Co.
Search in Gomorrah: A Novel. Daniel Panger. LC 81-17248. 13.95 (ISBN 0-934878-11-0). Dembner Books: Distributed by Norton.
Search in the Shadows. Paulette Warren. (Berkley Medallion Book). 1976. (pbk.) 1.25 (ISBN 0-425-03113-6). Berkley Publishing Corp.
Search Relentless. Constance Lindsay Skinner. LC 29-10744. 1928. Coward McCann Inc.
Search the Dark Woods. Myrick Land. LC 55-758840. 1955. Funk & Wagnalls.
Search the Sky: By Frederik Pohl and C. M. Kornbluth. Frederik Pohl & Cyril M. Kornbluth. LC 54-647859. 1954. Ballantine Books.
Search Through the Mist. Lucile V. Stevens. pap. 0.75 o.s.i. (01-327). Lancer.
Search to Belong. Christmas Carol Miller Kauffman. 1967. pap., 1.29. Moody.
Search to Belong. Christmas Carol Miller Kauffman. LC 63-7538. 1963. Herald Press.
Searchers. John Foster. LC 20-26880. 1.90. George H. Doran Company.
Searchers. Alan Le May. LC 78-14521. (Gregg Press Western Fiction Series). 1978. 9.95 (ISBN 0-8398-2464-5). Gregg Press.
Searchers. Alan Le May. Repr. lib. bdg. 12.35x (ISBN 0-88411-179-2). Amereon Ltd.
Searchers. Alan Le May. 352p. 1982. pap. 2.95 (ISBN 0-441-75693-X, Pub. by Charter Bks). Ace Bks.
Searchers. Stephen Korwin Szymanowski. LC 8-16466. 1908. Southern California Printing Co.
Searchers at the Gulf. Franklin Russell. LC 66-18087. 1970. 5.95. Norton.
Searchers. 1st Ed. Alan Le May. LC 54-10711. 1954. Harper.
Searches and Seizures. Stanley Elkin. LC 73-3989. 1973. 6.95 (ISBN 0-394-48329-4) (ISBN 0-394-48329-4). Random House.
Searching. Jessie Ford. (Love & Life Romance Ser.). 176p. (Orig.). 1982. pap. 1.75 (ISBN 0-345-30696-1). Ballantine.
Searching. Philip Freund. LC 74-30859. 1975. 6.95 (ISBN 0-8397-7552-0). P. S. Eriksson.
Searching. Philip Freund. LC 72-172703. 1972. 2.10 (ISBN 0-491-00652-7). W. H. Allen.
Searching for Caleb. Anne Tyler. LC 75-8251. 1976. 8.95 (ISBN 0-394-49848-8). Knopf.
Searching for Caleb. Anne Tyler. 1977. 1.95 (ISBN 0-445-08565-7). Popular Library.
Searching for Fifth Mesa. Juana Foust. Ed. by James C. Smith, Jr. LC 78-31284. (Orig.). 1979. pap. text ed. 4.95 (ISBN 0-913270-81-4). Sunstone Pr.
Searching for Fifth Mesa: A Novella of the Southwest. Juana Foust. LC 78-31284. 1979. 4.95 (ISBN 0-913270-81-4). Sunstone Press.
Searching for Gethsemane (the Streetgod & Other Unlikely Tales) Barbara Stock. LC 73-91535. 244p. 1974. 8.95 o.p. (ISBN 0-8059-1975-9). Dorrance.
Searching for Gethsemane (the Streetgod & Other Unlikely Tales) Barbara Stock. LC 73-91535. 244p: 1974. 8.95 o.p. (ISBN 0-8059-1975-9). Dorrance.
Searching for My Brother. Tr. by Jan Feidel. (Illus.). 1973. pap. 5.95 (Pub. by Mushinsha Bks). SBD.
Searching for Survivors. Russell Banks. LC 74-24911. 1975. 7.95. (ISBN 0-914590-07-3) (ISBN 0-914590-06-5). Fiction Collective.
Searching for the White Elephant in New York. A Humorous Record of Many Adventures. Office of "Wild Oats.
Searching for You. Cecelia Barth. 1978. 5.95 o.p. (ISBN 0-533-03533-3). Vantage.
Searching Guns and The Hangman of San Sabal. Ray Hogan. (Signet Book). 1977. 1.75 (ISBN 0-451-07657-5). New American Library.
Searching Heart. Virginia C. Holmgren. 1970. pap. 0.60 o.p. (ISBN 0-447-73883-6). Lancer.
Searching Heart. Ralph Webster Neighbour. LC 64-15561. 1964. Zondervan Pub. House.
Searching Heart. Anne Shore. LC 82-23340. (Candlelight romance). 1983. 7.95 (ISBN 0-8161-3472-3). G.K. Hall.
Searching Light. 1st Ed. Martha Dodd. LC 55-6799. 1955. Citadel Press.
Searching Years. Lee Bryan. 1981. pap. 2.25 (ISBN 0-8439-0871-8, Leisure Bks). Nordon Pubns.
Searing. John Coyne. 1981. 2.95. (ISBN 0-425-04924-8). Berkley Publishing Corp.
Sea's a Thief: A Novel. Ronald Mathias Lockley. LC 36-27490. 1936. Etc. Longmans, Green and Co.
Seas of God: A Novel... Anne Armstrong. LC 15-9929. Hearst's International Library Co.
Seas of God: Great Stories of the Human Spirit. Ed. by Whit Burnett. LC 44-28105. 1944. J. B. Lippincott Company.
Seas Stand Watch. Helen Parker Mudgett. LC 44-2896. 1944. A. A. Knopf.
Seascape. Elizabeth Carfrae, pseud. LC 38-367391. G. P. Putnam's Sons.
Seaside Kisses. Margaret M. Jensen. 1982. pap. 6.95 (Avalon). Bouregy.
Season. Patricia Hornung & Robin Moore. 1976. 1.95 (ISBN 0-523-00973-9). Pinnacle Books, Inc.
Season. David Walden. LC 42-15039. 1942. The Greystone Press.
Season Abroad. Rebecca Baldwin. 224p. 1981. pap. 1.50 (ISBN 0-449-50215-5, Crest). Fawcett.
Season at Coole. Michael Gregory Stephens. LC 74-179839. 1972. 5.95 (ISBN 0-525-19863-6). Dutton.
Season for Change. Margaret Way. (Harlequin Romances Ser.). 192p. 1981. pap. 1.50 (ISBN 0-373-02448-7). Harlequin Bks.
Season For Love. Heather Graham. (Candlelight Ecstasy Ser.: No. 154). (Orig.). 1983. pap. 1.95 (ISBN 0-440-18041-4). Dell.
Season for Murder. Hugh Lawrence Nelson. LC 52-5561. (Murray Hill mystery). 1952. Rinehart.
Season for Passion. Manning Lee Stokes. LC 50-14783. 1950. Phoenix Press.
Season for Unnatural Causes. Philip F. O'Connor. LC 75-2289. (Short Fiction Ser). 140p. 1975. pap. 4.95 (ISBN 0-252-00531-7). U of Ill Pr.
Season for Unnatural Causes: Stories. Philip F O'Connor. LC 75-2289. (Illinois short fiction). 1975. 6.95. (ISBN 0-252-00518-X) (ISBN 0-252-00531-7). University of Illinois Press.
Season In-Between. Jan Greenberg. 1981. 1.75 (ISBN 0-440-97710-X, LFL). Dell.
Season in England. Percy Howard Newby. LC 51-11972. 1952. Knopf.
Season in Monte Carlo. Edwin Gilbert. LC 75-40512. 1976. 8.95 (ISBN 0-87795-131-4). Arbor Hse.
Season in Paradise: By Gay Rutherford Pseud. James Noble Gifford. LC 52-10893. 1952. Arcadia House.
Season in Purgatory. Thomas Keneally. LC 76-24458. 8.95 (ISBN 0-15-179922-9). Harcourt Brace Jovanovich.
Season in the Life of Emmanuel. Marie Claire Blais. LC 66-14420. 1966. Farrar, Straus and Giroux.
Season in the Life of Emmanuel. Marie Claire Blais. Tr. by Derek Coltman et al from Fr. 145p. 1980. 10.95; pap. 5.95 (ISBN 0-374-51616-2). FS&G.
Season in the Life of Emmanuel. Marie Claire Blais. Tr. by D. Coltman. 1966. 4.50 o.p. FS&G.
Season in the Life of Emmanuel. Marie Claire Blais. 1969. pap. 1.95 o.p. (ISBN 0-448-00234-5, UL). G&D.
Season of Adventure. George Lamming. 368p. 14.95 (ISBN 0-8052-8012-X, Pub. by Allison & Busby England); pap. 6.95 (ISBN 0-8052-8035-9). Schocken.
Season of Assassins. Geoffrey Atheling Wagner. 1980. pap. 1.75 o.s.i. (ISBN 0-505-51457-5). Tower Bks.
Season of Change. Lois Battle. LC 80-21832. 10.95 (ISBN 0-312-70818-1). St. Martin's Press.
Season of Comfort. Gore Vidal. LC 49-7028. 1949. E. P. Dutton.
Season of Danger. Rosemary Gatenby. LC 74-10008. (Red badge novel of suspense). 1974. 5.95 (ISBN 0-396-06998-3). Dodd, Mead.
Season of Deception. Florence Faulkner. 1981. pap. 6.95 (Avalon). Bouregy.
Season of Delight. Joanne Greenberg. LC 80-20421. 12.95. Holt, Rinehart and Winston.
Season of Dishonor. Helen Tucker. 192p. (Orig.). 1982. pap. 1.50 (ISBN 0-449-50310-0, Coventry). Fawcett.
Season of Doubt. Jon Cleary. LC 68-19465. 1968. Morrow.
Season of Evil. easy eye ed. Jane Gordon. pap. 0.75 o.p. Lancer.
Season of Evil. Susan Morrow. LC 75-84387. 1969. 4.50. Published for the Crime Club by Doubleday.
Season of Evil. Elsie Lee Sheridan. (Dell Book). 1977. 1.50 (ISBN 0-440-17599-2). Dell Pub. Co.
Season of Fear. Guy Owen. LC 60-12125. 1960. Random House.
Season of Fear. 1st Ed. Abraham Polonsky. LC 57-8080. 1956. Cameron Associates.
Season of Grace: a Novel. N. V. Gonzalez. 1975. wrps. 5.75x. Cellar.
Season of Hunger-Cry of Rain. E. Ethelbert Miller. LC 81-82660. 67p. 1982. pap. 4.50 perfect bdg. (ISBN 0-916418-35-9). Lotus.
Season of Love. Arlene Hale. LC 76-44852. 1977. 8.95 (ISBN 0-89340-050-5). J. Curley.
Season of Love. Arlene Hale. LC 71-150059. 1971. 5.95. Little, Brown.
Season of Love: By Colin Ross Pseud. Harry Roskolenko. LC 54-26083. 1954. Woodford Press.
Season of Migration to the North. Tayeb Salih. Tr. by Denys Johnson-Davies from Arabic. 168p. 1978. 10.00 (ISBN 0-89410-198-6); pap. 5.00 (ISBN 0-89410-199-4). Three Continents.
Season of Mists. Charles Angoff. LC 76-132208. 1971. 6.95 (ISBN 0-498-07778-0). Yoseloff.
Season of Mists. Anne Mather. (Harlequin Presents Ser.). 192p. 1982. pap. 1.75 (ISBN 0-373-10546-0). Harlequin Bks.
Season of Mists: A Novel. Honor Lilbush Wingfield Tracy. LC 61-12144. 1961. Random House.
Season of Passion. Danielle Steel. (Dell book). 1979. 2.50 (ISBN 0-440-17703-0). Dell Pub. Co.
Season of Passion. Danielle Steel. LC 81-20121. 1982. 15.95 (ISBN 0-8161-3331-X). G.K. Hall.
Season of Power. Sam Tanenhaus & Gregory Tobin. (Orig.). 1981. pap. 2.95 (ISBN 0-505-51717-5). Tower Bks.
Season of Shadows. Yvonne Whittal. (Harlequin Romances Ser.). 192p. 1981. pap. 1.50 (ISBN 0-373-02430-4). Harlequin Bks.
Season of Snows and Sins. Patricia Moyes. LC 74-155526. (Rinehart suspense novel). 1971. 4.95 (ISBN 0-03-086615-4). Holt, Rinehart and Winston.
Season of Snows and Sins. Patricia Moyes. LC 82-23258. (Inspector Henry Tibbett mystery). ((Series: Moyes, Patricia.). (Inspector Henry Tibbett mystery.). 1983. 3.95 (ISBN 0-03-063542-X). Holt, Rinehart, and Winston.
Season of Surprises. Rebecca Ashley. (Orig.). 1981. pap. 1.50 (ISBN 0-440-18281-6). Dell.
Season of the Briar. Hesba Fay Brinsmead. 1967. Coward-McCann.
Season of the Heart. Clare Barroll. LC 76-28797. 1976. 8.95 (ISBN 0-684-14811-0). Scribner.
Season of the Machete. James Patterson. LC 77-1641. 1977. 1.95. Ballantine Books.
Season of the Owl: A Novel. Miles Wolff. LC 80-51607. 1980. 10.95 (ISBN 0-8128-2744-9). Stein and Day.
Season of the Stranger. 1st Ed. Stephen D Becker. LC 51-2842. 1951. Harper.
Season of the Strangler. Madison Jones. LC 81-43108. 1981. 12.95 (ISBN 0-385-17292-3). Doubleday.
Season of the Witch. James Leo Herlihy. LC 73-151496. 1971. 6.95 (ISBN 0-671-20905-1). Simon and Schuster.
Season of the Witch. Hank Stine. pap. 1.95 o.p. (0112). Essex Hse.
Season of Vengeance. W. W Southard. LC 82-15462. 1982. 12.95 (ISBN 0-8161-3360-3). G.K. Hall.
Season of Violence. The Punishment Room. The Yacht and the Boy. Shintaro Ishihara & Shintaro Ishihara. LC 65-23712. (Library of Japanese literature). 1966. C. E. Tuttle Co.
Season on the Coast. John Grindley. LC 73-80496. 1969. 5.95. Dial Press.
Season Ticket. Margaret Iles. LC 35-2532. 1935. Harper & Brothers.
Season to Be Born. Suzanne Arms & John Arms. 1973. pap. 4.50 o.p. (ISBN 0-06-090323-6, CN323, CN). Har-Row.
Season to Be Deadly. Richard Hardwick. LC 66-11725. 1966. Published for the Crime Club by Doubleday.
Season to Be Wary. Rod Serling. LC 67-18110. 1967. Little, Brown.
Season to Beware. William Edward Burghardt Du Bois. LC 56-7204. 1956. Putnam.
Seasoned Timber. Dorothea Frances Canfield Fisher. LC 39-27079. Harcourt, Brace and Company.
Seasons. Marguerite Dorian. LC 76-54819. 7.95 (ISBN 0-02-532190-0). Macmillan.
Seasons. Ellin Pollachek. (Orig.). 1980. pap. 2.50 (ISBN 0-89083-578-0). Zebra.
Seasons and Moments. John Haase. LC 78-156149. 1971. 5.95 (ISBN 0-671-20971-X). Simon and Schuster.
Seasons Change. James Noble Gifford. LC 37-35645. 1937. Arcadia House.
Season's Edge. Edith Hodgkinson. 1980. pap. 2.00 (ISBN 0-914610-22-8). Hanging Loose.
Season's Greetings: A Novel. Herbert Clyde Lewis. LC 41-223597. 1941. The Dial Press.
Seasons Hereafter. Elisabeth Ogilvie. LC 66-16773. 1966. McGraw-Hill.
Seasons of Celebration. Thomas Merton. 256p. 1978. pap. 5.95 (ISBN 0-374-51419-4). FS&G.

TITLE INDEX SECOND HONEYMOON.

Seasons of Death. M. K Wren, pseud. LC 80-2082. 1981. 9.95 (ISBN 0-385-17413-6). Published for the Crime Club by Doubleday.
Seasons of God: A Novel. Edythe Latham. LC 63-18208. 1963. Doubleday.
Seasons of Heroes: A Novel. Paxton Davis. LC 67-21731. 1967. Morrow.
Seasons of Jupiter: A Novel of India. Anand Lall. LC 58-61714. 1958. Harper.
Seasons of Jupiter, a Novel of India. Anand Lall. Repr. of 1958 ed. lib. bdg. 15.00x (ISBN 0-8371-3837-X, LASJ). Greenwood.
Seasons of Jupiter: A Novel of India. Arthur Samuel Lall. LC 78-109294. 1971. (ISBN 0-8371-3837-X). Greenwood Press.
Seasons of Love. Gene Conlon. 3.95 o.p. Vantage.
Seasons of Love. Genevieve Dormann. (O.s.i.). 1960. 4.50 o.s.i. (ISBN 0-8076-0120-9). Braziller.
Seasons of Love: A Novel. 1st Ed. Nora Harvey Leonard. LC 58-59814. 1958. Greenwich Book Publishers.
Seasons of Our Joy: A Handbook of Jewish Festivals. Arthur Waskow. 1982. pap. 8.95 (ISBN 0-553-01369-6). Bantam.
Seasons of the Heart. Ramona Stewart. LC 77-15066. 8.95. Putnam.
Seasons of the Heart: A Novel. Margaret Abrams. LC 64-11619. 1964. Houghton Mifflin.
Seasons of the Mind. Arlene Zekowski. LC 69-20441. (Archives of Post-Modern Literature). (Illus.). 1969. pap. 7.00 (ISBN 0-913844-06-3). Am Canadian.
Seasons of the Mind. Arlene Zekowski. 304p. 1973. pap. 3.75 (ISBN 0-8180-0617-X). Horizon.
Seasons of the Mind. With the Correspondence of Sir Herbert Read. Arlene Zekowski & Herbert Edward Read. LC 69-20441. (Archives of modern literature series). (Illus.). 1969. G. Wittenborn.
Seasons of the Ram: A Novel. Maurice Pons. LC 76-28052. 7.95 (ISBN 0-312-70822-X). St. Martin's Press.
Season's Passion. Iain Davidson. 1980. 7.95 (ISBN 0-533-04305-0). Vantage.
Seasons Past. Damon Rice. LC 74-1739. 1976. 9.95 o.p. (ISBN 0-275-05890-5). Praeger.
Seasons Such As These: Two Novels, New Letters. Natalie L. M. Petesch. LC 82-75935. 163p. 1978. 15.95 (ISBN 0-8040-0803-5). Swallow.
Seaswept. Maureen Norris. 192p. 1983. pap. 1.75. Jove Pubns.
Seat of Power. James David Horan. LC 65-15846. 5.95. Crown.
Seat of the Scornful. John Dickson Carr. 1981. 18.95x (Pub. by Remploy England). State Mutual Bk.
Seats of the Mighty. Gilbert Parker. 1976. lib. bdg. 16.75x (ISBN 0-89968-077-1). Lightyear.
Seats of the Mighty: A Novel of James Stuart, Borther of Mary, Queen of Scots. Alice Harwood. LC 56-13270.
Seats of the Mighty: Being the Memoirs of Captain Robert Moray, Sometime an Officer in the Virginia Regiment, and Afterwards, of Amherst's Regiment. Gilbert Parker. LC 7-39308. 1897. D. Appleton and Company.
Seats of the Mighty: Being the Memoirs of Captain Robert Moray, Sometime an Officer in the Virginia Regiment and Afterwards of Amherst's Regiment. Gilbert Parker. LC 4-15149. 1898. D. Appleton and Company.
Seats of the Mighty: Being the Memoirs of Captain Robert Moray, Sometime an Officer in the Virginia Regiment, and Afterwards of Amherst's Regiment. Gilbert Parker. LC 8-7702. 1899. D. Appleton and Company.
Seats of the Mighty: Being the Memoirs of Captain Robert Moray, Sometine an Officer in the Virginia Regiment, and Afterwards of Amherst's Regiment. Gilbert Parker. LC 4-35650. 1901. D. Appleton and Company.
Seats of the Mighty: Being the Memoirs of Captain Robert Moray, Sometime an Officer in the Virginia Regiment, and Afterwards of Amherst's Regiment. Gilbert Parker. LC 5-33629. 1905. D. Appleton and Company.
Seats of the Mighty: Being the Memoirs of Captain Robert Moray, Sometime an Officer in the Virginia Regiment, and Afterwards of Amherst's Regiment. Gilbert Parker. LC 16-19141. A. L. Burt Company.
Seats of the Mighty: Being the Memoirs of Captain Robert Moray, Sometime an Officer in the Virginia Regiment and Afterwards of Amherst's Regiment. Gilbert Parker. LC 15-20311. 1913. D. Appleton and Company.
Seats of the Mighty: Being the Memoirs of Captain Robert Moray, Sometime an Officer in the Virginia Regiment, and Afterwards of Amherst's Regiment. Gilbert Parker. Ed. by Otto, William Nalli. LC 27-4324. (Half-title: Appleton modern literature series). D. Appleton and Company.
Seavesta: A Story. Dee-Dee Williams. LC 51-12824. 1951. Exposition Press.
Seaview. Toby Olson. LC 88-22359. 288p. 1982. 15.95 (ISBN 0-8112-0828-1); pap. 6.95 (ISBN 0-8112-0829-X, NDP532). New Directions.
Seaview: A Novel. Toby Olson. LC 81-22359. 1982. 15.95 (ISBN 0-8112-0828-1) (ISBN 0-8112-0829-X). New Directions.
Seaview Manor. Elissa Grandower, pseud. LC 75-26445. 1976. 7.95 (ISBN 0-385-11046-4). Doubleday.
Seaways. psued. ed. Lewis Awselm da Costa Ritchie. LC 23-10233. 1923. Cassell and Company, Ltd.
Seawitch. Alistair MacLean. LC 76-47825. 1977. 7.95 (ISBN 0-385-12852-5). Doubleday.
Seawitch. Alistair MacLean. LC 77-15536. 1978. 11.95 (ISBN 0-8161-6538-6). G. K. Hall.
Seaworthy. Aylward Edward Dingle. LC 31-9393. 1930. Houghton Mifflin Company.
Sebastian. Flora Armytage. LC 46-6624. 1946. Doubleday & Company, Inc.
Sebastian. Julia Davis Frankau. LC 9-9253. 1909. The Macmillan Company.
Sebastian. Lionel Webb. (Orig.). 1970. pap. 0.75 o.p. (B75-2061). Belmont-Tower.
Sebastian Strome. A Novel. Julian Hawthorne. LC 7-388717. (On cover: Appletons' library of American fiction. no. 22). 1880. D. Appleton and Company.
Sebastopol. Lev Nikolaevich Tolstoi. LC 61-65401. (Ann Arbor paperbacks, AA58). 1961. University of Michigan Press.
Sebastopol. Lev Nikolaevich Tolstoi & Kendall, Mrs. Laura E., Tr. (On cover: Seaside library. Pocket ed. no. 1108). 1888. G. Munro.
Sebastopol. Lev Nikolaevich Tolstoi & Millet, Frank Davis, 1846-1912, Tr. LC 8-25985. 1887. Harper & Brothers.
Secession, Coercion, and Civil War. The Story of 1861... John Beauchamp Jones. LC 7-11916. T. B. Peterson and Brothers.
Seclusion Room. Fredric Neuman. LC 78-6142. 1978. 8.95 (ISBN 0-670-62742-9). Viking Press.
Seco Bonanza. George Brydges Rodney. LC 42-24971. 1942. Phoenix Press.
Second Agreement With Hell. Chancellor Williams. 1979. 8.95 o.p. (ISBN 0-8062-1356-6). Carlton.
Second Amendment. Henry Clay Hansbrough. LC 11-11446. 1911. The Hudson Publishing Company.
Second April. Edna S. Millay. Bd. with Buck in the Snow. (Harper's Modern Classics Ser.). (gr. 9-12). text ed. 2.00, s.p. 1.50 o.p. (ISBN 0-06-534042-6). Har-Row.
Second Awakening. 1st Ed. Cranford, E Wade. LC 56-7516. 1956. Vantage Press.
Second Best. Jennie Maria Drinkwater Conklin. LC 6-30412. Bradley & Woodruff.
Second Best. Denise Robins. LC 34-42415. G. H. Watt.
Second Best: A Novel. Jeannette Covert Nolan. LC 33-22040. 1933. R. M. McBride & Company.
Second-Best Bride. Margaret Rome. (Harlequin Presents Ser.). 192p. 1981. pap. 1.50 (ISBN 0-373-10438-3, Pub. by Harlequin). PB.
Second Best Lady. Elizabeth Mansfield, pseud. 192p. 1983. pap. 2.25 (ISBN 0-425-05501-9). Berkley Pub.
Second Best Wife. Isobel Chace. (Romances Ser.). 1978. pap. 0.95 (ISBN 0-373-02176-3, 52176, Pub by Harlequin). PB.
Second Blooming. Walter Lionel George. LC 14-22556. 1915. 1.35. Little, Brown, and Company.
Second Body. Sue Payer. 1979. pap. 1.95 o.s.i. (ISBN 0-505-51381-1). Tower Bks.
Second Book of Fritz Leiber. Fritz Leiber. (Science Fiction Ser). 1975. pap. 1.25 o.p. (UY1195). DAW Bks.
Second Book of Fritz Leiber. Fritz Leiber. 1975. (pbk.) 1.25. DAW Books.
Second Book of Robert E. Howard. Ed. by Glenn Lord. (Orig.). 1980. pap. 1.95 (ISBN 0-425-04455-6). Berkley Pub.
Second Breath. Jan Benes. Tr. by Michael Montgomery. LC 72-86123. 1969. 5.95 o.p. (ISBN 0-670-62759-3, Orion Pr). Grossman.
Second Bullet. Charles Judson Dutton. LC 25-775170. 1925. 2.00. Dodd, Mead and Company.
Second Bullet. Isabel Egenton Ostrander. 1919. R. M. McBride & Company.
Second Bullet. Lee Thayer, pseud. LC 34-370. Sears Publishing Company, Inc.
Second Cabin. Mary Marvin Heaton Vorse. LC 28-25816. H. Liveright.
Second Chance. Khalid Ali. 1982. 7.95 (ISBN 0-533-05102-9). Vantage.
Second Chance. Beatrice Tolman Gardner. LC 73-167293. 1971. 4.95 (ISBN 0-8059-1601-6). Dorrance.
Second Chance. David Hanna. (O.s.i.). 1976. pap. 1.50 o.s.i. (BT50989). Belmont-Tower.
Second Chance. Nellie Letitia Mooney McClung. LC 10-22799. 1910. Doubleday, Page & Company.
Second Chance. Nancy B. Peck. 1981. pap. 2.50 (ISBN 0-89083-745-7). Zebra.
Second Chance. Marcia Rose, pseud. 440p. 1982. pap. 2.75 (ISBN 0-345-28670-7). Ballantine.
Second Chance. Alan Sillitoe. 1981. 12.95 (ISBN 0-671-42761-X). S&S.
Second Chance. Nancy Mann Waddel Wilson Woodrow Woodrow. LC 24-794925. W. J. Watt & Co.
Second Chance. Hugh Zachary. 1976. pap. 1.50 (ISBN 0-89041-115-8, 3115). Major Bks.
Second Chance: Tales of Two Generations. Louis Auchincloss. LC 77-108306. 1970. 5.95. Houghton Mifflin.
Second Chance. 1st Ed. Almet Jenks. LC 58-12278. 1959. Lippincott.
Second Choice. Rob Pseud Eden. LC 32-86989. Grosset & Dunlap.
Second Choice. Gloria Goddard. LC 37-543. 1937. Godwin.
Second Choice. Marcia Miller. (Adventures in Love Ser.: No. 36). 1982. pap. 1.95 (ISBN 0-451-11876-6, AJ1876, Sig). NAL.
Second Choice: A Novel. Elizabeth Alexander. LC 28-204. J. H. Sears & Company, Inc.
Second Choice: A Romance. William Nathaniel Harben. LC 16-174944. Harper & Brothers.
Second Circle. Winston Brebner. LC 51-13927. 1951. Viking Press.
Second-Class Citizen. Buchi Emecheta. LC 75-10909. 1975. 6.95 (ISBN 0-8076-0801-7). G. Braziller.
Second Coming. Thom Keyes. LC 73-162695. 1972. 2.00 (ISBN 0-491-00693-4). W. H. Allen.
Second Coming. Richard Marsh. 1900. J. Lane.
Second Coming. Walker Percy. LC 80-12899. 12.95 (ISBN 0-374-25674-8). Farrar, Straus, Giroux.
Second Coming: A Vision. Frederic Arnold Kummer & Janes, Henry P. LC 16-9961. 1916. 0.50. Dodd, Mead and Company.
Second Coming of Lucas Brokaw. Matthew Braun. (Dell / Bernard Geis Associates Book). 1977. 1.95 (ISBN 0-440-18091-0). Dell Pub Co.
Second Confession. Rex Stout. 1975. (pbk.) 1.25. Bantam Books.
Second Confession. Rex Stout. LC 49-10527. 1949. Viking Press.
Second Conquest: A Novel. 1st Ed. Louis De Wohl. LC 54-5595. 1954. Lippincott.
Second-Cousin Sarah. A Novel. Frederick William Robinson. (seaside library. v. 37, no. 757). 1880. G. Munro.
Second-Cousin Sarah. A Novel. Frederick William Robinson. LC 43-31957. (With Farjeon, B. L. At the sign of the Silver flagon. New York, 1875). 1874. Harper & Brothers.
Second Crash. Charles D Ellis. LC 72-93508. 1973. 5.95 (ISBN 0-671-21474-8). Simon and Schuster.
Second Crossing: A Novel. N. A Diaman. LC 82-7564. 9.95 (ISBN 0-931906-03-2). Persona Press.
Second Crucifixion. Maurice Samuel. LC 60-8995. 1960. Knopf.
Second Curtain. Roy Fuller. LC 56-2626. (Cock Robin mystery). 1956. Macmillan.
Second Curtain. Roy Fuller. (Penguin crime fiction). 1976. 1.95 (ISBN 0-14-001760-7). Penguin.
Second Dandy Chater. Tom Gallon. LC 1-30743. 1901. Dodd, Mead & Company.
Second Deadly Sin. Lawrence Sanders. LC 77-3652. 9.95 (ISBN 0-399-12023-8). Putnam.
Second Deadly Sin. Lawrence Sanders. (Berkley Medallion Book). 1978. 2.50 (ISBN 0-425-03923-4). Berkley Pub. Corp.
Second Death of Ramon Mercader. Jorge Semprun. LC 73-3665. 1973. 7.95 (ISBN 0-394-48801-6). Grove Press.
Second Death of Samuel Auer. Bernard Packer. LC 78-10728. 10.95 (ISBN 0-15-179955-5). Harcourt Brace Jovanovich.
Second Deluge. Garrett Putman Serviss. LC 73-13266. (Classics of science fiction.). (Illus.). 1974. 10.95 (ISBN 0-88355-120-9) (ISBN 0-88355-120-9). Hyperion Press.
Second Deluge: By Garrett P. Serviss... Garrett Putman Serviss. LC 12-8802. 1912. McBride, Nast & Company.
Second Dune. Shelby Hearon. LC 73-7261. 1973. 5.95 (ISBN 0-394-48600-5). Knopf; Distributed by Random House.
Second Eden. Florence Jeannette Baier Ward. LC 28-244723. 1928. Macrae Smith Company.
Second Eden: A Romance. Cobie Muyskens De Lespinasse. LC 51-8742. 1951. Christopher Pub. House.
Second Ending. evan hunter. ed. Evan Hunter. 1.75 (ISBN 0-380-00787-8). Avon Books.
Second Ending: A Novel. Evan Hunter. LC 55-110444. 1956. Simon and Schuster.
Second Ewings. John O'Hara. LC 77-152438. (Illus.). 1977. Bruccoli Clark.
Second Exodus. Ada Aharoni. LC 82-90872. 136p. 1983. 10.95 (ISBN 0-8059-2862-6). Dorrance.
Second Experiment. J. O Jeppson. LC 74-7110. 1974. 5.95 (ISBN 0-395-19504-7). Houghton Mifflin.
Second Experiment. J. O Jeppson. 1976. 1.25 (ISBN 0-449-23005-8). Fawcett Crest.
Second Face of Valor. Ray Grant Toepfer. LC 66-23064. 4.50. Chilton.
Second Face: Translated from the French by Norman Denny. 1st American Ed. Marcel Ayme. LC 52-5416. 1952. Harper.
Second Fiddle. Phyllis Bottome. LC 17-288040. 1917. The Century Co.
Second Fiddle. Peggy Finner. 1974. 6.95 (ISBN 0-533-00848-4). Vantage Press.
Second Fiddle. Henry Harrison & Cliff Dudley. LC 77-81362. (O.s.i.). 1977. 5.95 o.s.i. (ISBN 0-89221-039-7). New Leaf.
Second Fiddle: A Novel. Margie Ingram Mills. LC 51-11858. 1951. Exposition Press.
Second Flight. Nalbro Isadorah Bartley. LC 32-149502. Farrar & Rinehart, Incorporated.
Second Flight of the Starfire. Edwin Mumford. 1972. 4.00 (ISBN 0-682-47462-2). Exposition.
Second Flowering. Samuel Gordon. LC 22-19607. The Macaulay Company.
Second Flowering of Emily Mountjoy. Joan Lingard. LC 79-22791. (est.) 8.95 (ISBN 0-312-70833-5). St. Martin's Press.
Second Fontana Book of Great Ghost Stories. Ed. by Christine Bernard. 1971. pap. 0.95 o.p. (95160). Beagle Bks.
Second Foundation. Isaac Asimov. LC 53-10530. 1953. Gnome Press.
Second Foundation. Isaac Asimov. LC 79-10901. 1979. 10.95 (ISBN 0-89340-211-7). J. Curley.
Second Frutes. John Florio. LC 53-11448. 1977. Repr. of 1591 ed. 25.00x (ISBN 0-8201-1222-4). Schol Facsimiles.
Second Game. Charles De Vet & Katherine MacLean. (Science Fiction Ser.). 1981. pap. 2.25 (ISBN 0-87997-620-9, UE1620). DAW Bks.
Second Generation. Howard Melvin Fast. LC 78-5540. 1978. 9.95 (ISBN 0-395-26483-9). Houghton Mifflin.
Second Generation. Howard Melvin Fast. LC 79-10580. 1979. 19.95 (ISBN 0-8161-6715-X). G. K. Hall.
Second Generation. James Weber Linn. LC 2-2764. 1902. The Macmillan Company.
Second Generation. David Graham Phillips. LC 72-84630. 1974. 13.50 (ISBN 0-403-02971-6). Scholarly Press.
Second Generation. David Graham Phillips. LC 7-4160. 1907. D. Appleton and Company.
Second Generation. David Graham Phillips. 1909. D. Appleton and Company.
Second Generation. David Graham Phillips. LC 16-9354. 1916. D. Appleton and Company.
Second Generation. David Graham Phillips. LC 20-16461. 1919. D. Appleton and Company.
Second Generation. Anthony M Rud. LC 23-16271. 1923. Doubleday, Page & Company.
Second Generation: A Novel. Raymond Williams. LC 65-11739. 1965. Horizon Press.
Second Generation: A Professional Program for Producing Perpetual Profits. Louis A. Wilhelm. 210p. 1971. 6.50 o.p. (ISBN 0-682-47379-0). Exposition.
Second Ghost Book. Ed. by Cynthia Mary Evelyn Charteris Asquith. 1970. pap. 0.95 o.p. (95018). Beagle Bks.
Second Glencannon Omnibus: Including Mr. Glencannon, The Gentleman with the Walrus Mustache and Glencannon Afloat, by Guy Gilpatric. Guy Gilpatric. LC 42-36111. 1942. Dodd, Mead & Company.
Second Growth. Leta Zoe Adams. LC 51-13074. 1951. Macrae Smith.
Second Growth. Ruth Moore. LC 62-10655. 1962. Morrow.
Second Growth. Wallace Earle Stegner. LC 47-43983. 1947. Houghton Mifflin Co.
Second Growth: A Novel. Arthur Pound. LC 35-10858. Reynal & Hitchcock.
Second Hand: A Story of Mission Work in Japan. Emma Gerberding Lippard. LC 34-12885. (John Rung prize series). The United Lutheran Publication House.
Second-Hand Life. C. Jackson. 1967. 5.95 o.p. (55825). Macmillan.
Second-Hand Life: By Charles Jackson. Charles Reginald Jackson. LC 67-21250. 1967. 5.95. Macmillan.
Second Hand Persons. William Vincent Burgess. LC 68-18090. 1969. 4.95. Doubleday.
Second Hand Wife. Kathleen Thompson Norris. LC 32-26291. 1932. Doubleday, Doran & Company, Inc.
Second Happiest Day: By John Phillips Pseud. 1st Ed. John Phillips Marquand. 1953. Harper.
Second Heaven. Judith Guest. LC 82-70124. 1982. 14.95 (ISBN 0-670-62830-1). Viking Press.
Second Hoeing. Hope Williams Sykes. LC 35-7171. G. P. Putnam's Sons.
Second Hoeing. Hope Williams Sykes. LC 82-8424. 1982. (ISBN 0-8032-4136-4) (ISBN 0-8032-9129-9). University of Nebraska Press.
Second Home. Brian Glanville. LC 66-15470. 1966. 4.95. Delacorte Dist. Dial.
Second Honeymoon. Ruby Mildred Ayres. LC 22-3959. 1921. W. J. Watt & Company.

Second House. Jan Alexander, pseud. 1971. pap. 0.75 o.p. (94157). Beagle Bks.
Second House from the Corner. Max Miller. LC 34-256957. 1934. E. P. Dutton & Co., Inc.
Second If Reader of Science Fiction. Ed. by Frederik Pohl. LC 68-27132. 1968. 4.95 o.p. Doubleday.
Second Inheritance. Melvyn Bragg. LC 67-16212. 1967. 4.95. Dodd.
Second Jungle Book. Rudyard Kipling. 1895. The Century Co.
Second Jungle Book. Rudyard Kipling. LC 7-41591. 1899. The Century Co.
Second Key. Marie Adelaide Belloc Lowndes. LC 36-9464. 1936. Longmans, Green and Co.
Second Kiss. Gayle Rogers. LC 72-186556. 1972. 6.95. McKay.
Second Lady. Irving Wallace. LC 80-16655. 11.95 (ISBN 0-453-00388-5). New American Library.
Second Lady Cameron. Frieda Thomas. (Belmont Tower Book). 1977. 1.50. Tower Pubns.
Second Lady Cameron. Frieda Thomsen. 1977. pap. 1.50 o.s.i. (ISBN 0-505-51204-1). Tower Bks.
Second Latchkey. Charles Norris Williamson & Alice Muriel Livingston Williamson. LC 20-7290. 1920. Doubleday, Page & Company.
Second Life. Annie French Hector. (On cover: Lovell's library, v. 16, no. 777). 1886. J. W. Lovell Company.
Second Life. A Novel. Annie French Hector. (On cover: Seaside library. Pocket ed., no. 490). 1885. G. Munro.
Second Love. Hortense Lion. LC 66-17352. 1966. Liveright Pub. Corp.
Second Love. Martha Martell. LC 7-16815. 1851. G. P. Putnam.
Second Love. Martin Solow. 1973. (pbk.) 1.25. Dell.
Second Man. Edward Grierson. LC 56-6249. 1956. Knopf.
Second Man. Edward Grierson. LC 81-47400. (Fifty Classics of Crime Fiction, 1950-1975). 1982. 14.95 (ISBN 0-8240-4969-1). Garland Pub.
Second Man. Charles Blanton Roberts. LC 39-7579. Fleming H. Revell Company.
Second Man. Mae Urbanek. 182p. 3.50x (ISBN 0-940514-06-0). Urbanek.
Second Marriage. Viola Meynell. LC 19-161618. 1919. George H. Doran Company.
Second Marriage: Or, A Daughter's Trials. A Domestic Tale of New York. Charles Burdett. LC 6-18668. 1856. C. Scribner.
Second Meeting. Lucian Cary. LC 38-38827. 1938. Doubleday, Doran & Co., Inc.
Second Mercury Story Book. facsimile ed. London Mercury. LC 79-37553. (Short Story Index Reprint Ser.). Repr. of 1931 ed. 21.00 (ISBN 0-8369-4112-8). Ayer Co.
Second Mercury Story Book. LC 79-37553. (Short story index reprint series). 1972. (ISBN 0-8369-4112-8). Books for Libraries Press.
Second Mercury Story Book. The London Mercury. LC 31-243081. 1931. Longmans, Green and Co.
Second Mile. Harry E. Fosdick. 1912. 10.00 o.p. Folcroft.
Second Mrs. Clay. Katharine Haviland Taylor. LC 21-8516. 1921. Doubleday, Page & Company.
Second Mrs. Draper. Noel Pierce. LC 37-37589. R. M. McBride and Company.
Second Mrs. Jim. Stephen Conrad Stuntz. LC 4-14153. 1904. L. C. Page & Company.
Second Mrs. Locke: By John Cassells Pseud. William Murdoch Duncan. LC 52-3671. 1952. A. Melrose.
Second Mrs. Lynton. Wilson Collison. LC 35-188483. C. Kendall & W. Sharp, Inc.
Second Mrs. Whitberg. Chaim I Bermant. LC 77-1537. 1977. 9.95 (ISBN 0-8161-6478-9). G. K. Hall.
Second Mrs Whitberg: A Novel. Chaim I Bermant. LC 75-40783. 8.95. St. Martin's Press.
Second Mrs. Wu. Agnes Mary White Sanford. LC 65-15253. bds., 3.95. Lippincott.
Second Mystery Book: One Full-Length Novel, One Story and Four Novelettes. LC 40-348686. Farrar & Rinehart, Inc.
Second Mystery Companion. Ed. by Abraham Louis Furman. LC 44-47148. 1944. Gold Label Books.
Second Nature. Gordon Glasco. LC 81-8860. 1981. 13.95 (ISBN 0-312-70844-0). St. Martin's Press.
Second Nature. Cherry Wilder, pseud. (Orig.). 1982. pap. 2.75 (ISBN 0-671-83482-7, Timescape). PB.
Second Novel: Becoming a Writer. Norbert Blei. LC 77-91291. (Illus.). 6.00 (ISBN 0-913204-09-9). December Press.
Second Odd Number: Thirteen Tales. Guy De Maupassant. Tr. by Charles Henry White. Watson, Virginia Cruse, 1872- Tr. LC 17-13186. Harper & Brothers.
Second Oldest Profession. Robert Sylvester. LC 49-50312. 1950. Dial Press.
Second Omnibus of Crime: The World's Great Crime Stories. Ed. by Dorothy Leigh Sayers. LC 36-28488. 1936. Blue Ribbon Books, Inc.
Second Opinion. Isadore Rosenfeld. 1981. pap. write for info. Bantam.
Second Opinion see Dark Shadow.
Second Opportunity of Mr. Staplehurst: A Novel. William Pett Ridge. LC 7-41641. 1896. Harper & Brothers.
Second Pan Book of Horror Stories. Ed. by H. Van Thal. 1982. pap. 10.00x (ISBN 0-330-10067-X, Pub. by Pan Bks). State Mutual Bk.
Second Possession. Ann Lawrence. LC 37-7127. 1937. Godwin.
Second Prince. Thomas Bell. LC 35-3928. G. P. Putnam's Sons.
Second Red Dragon. Voss Bark, Conrad. LC 68-27386. 1968. 3.95. Walker.
Second Romance. Rosemary Frances Rees. LC 41-312387. 1940. Arcadia House, Inc.
Second Saint Omnibus. 1st Ed. Leslie Charteris. LC 51-13646. 1951. Published for the Crime Club by Doubleday.
Second Saladin. Stephen Hunter. LC 81-18930. 1982. 14.50 (ISBN 0-688-00639-6). Morrow.
Second Season. Pauline D. Marrs. 1979. pap. 1.75 (ISBN 0-449-50012-8, Coventry). Fawcett.
Second Season. Elsie Lee Sheridan. (Dell book). 1973. (pbk) 0.95. Dell Publishing Co.
Second Seroll. 1st Ed. Abraham Moses Klein. LC 51-11078. 1951. Knopf.
Second Shot... Anthony Berkeley Cox. LC 31-12258. Pub. for the Crime Club, Inc., by Doubleday, Doran & Company, Inc.
Second Sickle. Ursula Reilly Curtiss. LC 50-6194. (Red badge mystery). 1950. Dodd, Mead.
Second Sickle. Ursula Reilly Curtiss. 1977. 1.50 (ISBN 0-671-80951-2). Pocket Books.
Second Sight. Cecilia Bartholomew. LC 79-22463. 10.95 (ISBN 0-399-12346-6). Putnam.
Second Sight. Clifton Cuthbert. LC 34-11660. W. Godwin, Inc.
Second Sight: A Novel. Sidney Bigman. LC 59-12273. 1959. D. McKay Co.
Second Sight: A Novel. David Williams. LC 77-22292. 7.95 (ISBN 0-671-22626-6). Simon & Schuster.
Second Skin. John Hawkes. LC 64-10674. 1964. pap. 4.95 (ISBN 0-8112-0067-1, NDP146). New Directions.
Second Son. Dominique Dunois. Tr. by Billings, Gladys. LC 32-30927. The Macaulay Company.
Second Son. Margaret Oliphant Wilson Oliphant & Aldrich, Thomas Bailey. LC 42-26496. 1888. Macmillan and Co.
Second Son: A Novel. Margaret Oliphant Wilson Oliphant & Aldrich, Thomas Bailey. 1888. Houghton, Mifflin and Company.
Second Son: A Novel. 1st Ed. Winfred B Senior. LC 54-12890. 1955. Exposition Press.
Second Spring: A Modern Love Story. 1st Ed. Marsha Allen. LC 56-13139. 1957. Greenwich Book Publishers.
Second Stage Lensman. Edward Elmer Smith. 1970. pap. 0.95 o.p. (N2169). Pyramid Pubns.
Second Stage Lensmen: Illustrated by Ric Binkley. 1st Ed. Edward Elmer Smith. LC 53-99398. (His The 'Lensman' series, 5). 1953. Fantasy Press.
Second Star to the Right. Deborah Hautzig. 160p. 1982. pap. 1.95 (ISBN 0-380-60343-8, 60343-8, Flare). Avon.
Second Start. Paul Salsini. LC 79-92442. 168p. (Orig.). 1980. pap. 4.95 (ISBN 0-87973-525-2, 525). Our Sunday Visitor.
Second Story Man. Mimi Albert. LC 75-10743. 106p. 1975. 8.95 (ISBN 0-914590-12-X); pap. 3.95 (ISBN 0-914590-13-8). Fiction Coll.
Second Story Man: A Novel. Mimi Albert. LC 75-10743. 8.95. Fiction Collective.
Second String. Anthony Hope Hawkins. LC 10-24710. 1910. 1.50. Doubleday, Page & Company.
Second String. Anthony Hope Hawkins. LC 12-252091. 1910. T. Nelson and Sons.
Second Sunrise. Francesca Greer, pseud. (Illus.). 2.50 (ISBN 0-446-91214-X). Warner Books.
Second Tale of a Tub, or, the History of Robert Powel the Puppet-Show-Man. Thomas Burnet & George Duckett. Ed. by Michael Shugrue. LC 71-170539. (Foundations of the Novel Ser). (O.s.i.: Vol. 26). iv, 219p. 1973. Repr. of 1715 ed. lib. bdg. 50.00 o.s.i. (ISBN 0-8240-0538-4). Garland Pub.
Second Thoughts. Rhoda Broughton. LC 6-18949. (Lovell's library, no. 23). 1882. J. W. Lovell Company.
Second Thoughts. Rhoda Broughton. LC 18-11266. (Macmillan's two shilling library. no. 17). 1899. Macmillan and Co., Limited.
Second Thoughts: A Novel. Rhoda Broughton. (Seaside library, v. 37, no. 762). 1880. G. Munro.
Second Thoughts. A Novel. Rhoda Broughton. (On cover: Seaside library. Pocket ed., no. 101). 1883. G. Munro.
Second Time. large print ed. Janet Dailey. LC 83-114. (Nightingale series). 1983. 7.95 (ISBN 0-8161-3517-7). G.K. Hall.
Second Time Around. Sally Biskin. (Orig.). 1981. pap. 2.75 (ISBN 0-440-17629-8). Dell.
Second Time Around. Otty Lippi. LC 81-85177. 240p. 1982. pap. 2.95 (ISBN 0-86721-099-0). Playboy Pbks.
Second Time Around. Hugh McLeave. LC 81-50546. 1981. 9.95 (ISBN 0-8027-5439-2). Walker.
Second Time Round. Clifford Hanley. LC 64-11935. 1964. Houghton Mifflin.
Second to None, "Royal Scots Greys" A Military Romance. James Grant. LC 43-26607. G. Routledge and Sons.
Second Tomorrow. Anne Hampson. 192p. (Orig.). 1980. pap. 1.50 (ISBN 0-671-57016-1, Pub. by Silhouete Bks). S&S.
Second Treasury of the Familiar. R. L. Woods. (O.s.i.). 1950. 9.95 o.s.i. (ISBN 0-02-631430-4). Macmillan.
Second Triangle. William Utterback. LC 32-227112. R. G. Badger.
Second Trip. Robert Silverberg. 192p. 1981. pap. 2.25 (ISBN 0-380-54874-7, 54874). Avon.
Second Vanetti Affair. Marc Lovell, pseud. LC 76-50778. 1977. 5.95 (ISBN 0-385-12828-2). Published for the Crime Club by Doubleday.
Second Vespers. Ralph M McInerny. LC 81-273. 1981. 10.95 (ISBN 0-89621-272-6). Thorndike Press.
Second Vespers: A Father Dowling Mystery. Ralph M McInerny. LC 79-56379. 9.95 (ISBN 0-8149-0837-3). Vanguard Press.
Second War of the Worlds. George H. Smith. (Science Fiction Ser.). 1976. pap. 1.75 (ISBN 0-87997-512-1, UE1512). DAW Bks.
Second War of the Worlds. George H Smith. Daw Books.
Second Wedding. Delsa Walton. (Orig.). 1981. pap. 1.75 (ISBN 0-8439-8019-2, Tiara Bks). Nordon Pubns.
Second Wife. Thompson Buchanan. LC 11-2978. 1.50. W. J. Watt & Company.
Second Wife. Lewis Meyer. LC 63-13276. 1963. Prentice-Hall.
Second Wife: A Romance, from the German of E. Marlitt Pseud.... Eugenie John. Tr. by Wister, Annis Lee (Furness) LC 7-9911. 1874. J. B. Lippincott & Co.
Second Wife: A Romance from the German of E. Marlitt Pseud.... Eugenie John. Tr. by Wister, Annis Lee (Furness) LC 2-10109. 1902. J. B. Lippincott Co.
Second Window: A Novel. Robin Maugham. LC 68-20055. 1968. McGraw-Hill.
Second Wooing of Salina Sue: And Other Stories. Ruth McEnery Stuart. LC 69-11920. (American short story series, v. 79). (Illus.). 1969. Garrett Press.
Second Wooing of Salina Sue, and Other Stories. Ruth McEnery Stuart. LC 72-8196. (American short story series, v. 79). 1972. (ISBN 0-8422-8114-2). MSS Information Corp.
Second Wooing of Salina Sue: And Other Stories. Ruth McEnery Stuart. LC 5-10921. 1905. Harper & Brothers.
Second Year Ashore. Jules Verne. 3.95. Assoc Bk.
Second Year Latin. rev. ed. Robert J Henle. LC 46-20775. 1946. Loyola University Press.
Second Youth. Warwick Deeping. LC 20-963041. 1919. Cassell and Company, Ltd.
Second Youth: Being, in the Main, Some Account of the Middle Comedy in the Life of a New York Bachelor; a Novel. Allan Eugene Updegraff. LC 17-12137. 1917. Harper & Brothers.
Seconde. Sidonie Gabrielle Colette. 1955. pap. 3.95. French & Eur.
Secondhand Lovers. Vida Hurst. LC 33-213902. Grosset & Dunlap.
Secondhand Tomb. Reginald James White. LC 70-160661. (Illus.). 1971. 5.95 (ISBN 0-06-014613-3). Harper & Row.
Seconds. Nick Wayte. 1969. pap. 3.00 (Pub. by Ferry Pr); pap. 9.00 signed ed. SBD.
Secresy: Or, The Ruin on the Rock. Eliza Fenwick. LC 73-22070. (Feminist Controversy in England, 1788-1810). 1974. (3 vols.) 66.00 (ISBN 0-8240-0859-6). Garland Pub.
Secret. Linda DuBreuil. 1972. pap. 0.95 o.s.i. (75-391). Lancer.
Secret. Byron Preiss. 208p. 1982. pap. 9.95 (ISBN 0-553-01408-0). Bantam.
Secret. Margaret Lee Runbeck. LC 46-3700. 1946. D. Appleton-Century Company, Inc.
Secret: A Novel. Michael Amrine. LC 50-8771. 1950. Houghton Mifflin.
Secret, a Novel. James Drought. LC 63-14894. 1963.
Secret Adversary. Agatha Miller Christie. LC 22-6608. 1922. John Lane, Ltd.
Secret Adversary. Agatha Miller Christie. LC 22-12469. 1922. Dodd, Mead and Company.
Secret Adversary. Agatha Miller Christie. LC 34-10756. 1931. Grosset & Dunlap.
Secret Affair. Lilian Peake. (Harlequin Presents Ser.). 192p. (Orig.). 1981. pap. 1.50 (ISBN 0-373-10407-3, Pub. by Harlequin). PB.
Secret Agent. Joseph Conrad. lib. bdg. 12.95x (ISBN 0-89966-058-4). Buccaneer Bks.
Secret Agent. Joseph Conrad. 1953. pap. 4.95 (ISBN 0-385-09352-7, Anch). Doubleday.
Secret Agent. Joseph Conrad. 1982. pap. 10.00x (ISBN 0-330-24129-X, Pub.by Pan Bks). State Mutual Bk.
Secret Agent,". Campbell Dixon & Maugham, William Somerset, 1874- Ashenden. LC 46-38417.
Secret Agent. Sydney Horler. LC 34-5287. 1934. Little, Brown, and Company.
Secret Agent: A Simple Tale. Joseph Conrad. LC 54-3596. (Doubleday anchor books, A8). 1953. Doubleday.
Secret Agent: A Simple Tale. Joseph Conrad. LC 7-29428. 1907. Harper & Brothers.
Secret Agent in Africa: A New Gunston Cotton Story. Rupert Grayson. LC 39-12108. 1939. E. P. Dutton and Company, Inc.
Secret Agent Nine. Alex Raymond & Dashiell Hammett. Ed. by Woody Gelman. LC 76-19616. (Illus.). 176p. 1976. pap. 8.95. Nostalgia Pr.
Secret Agent Number One. Frederick Frost. LC 36-8769. 1936. Macrae Smith Company.
Secret Agent X-Nine. Alex Raymond & Dashiell Hammett. LC 76-19616. (Illus.). pap. 8.95 o.p. (ISBN 0-517-20797-4). Crown.
Secret Agent X-9. Dashiel Hammett & Raymond, Alex, 1909- Illus. David McKay Company.
Secret & Lily Hart: Two Tales. Charlotte Bronte & William V Holtz. LC 78-19645. (Illus.). 1979. 5.95 (ISBN 0-8262-0268-3). University of Missouri Press.
Secret and Other Stories. Alan Alexander Milne. LC 29-14244. 1929. The Fountain Press.
Secret Annie Oakley. Marcy Heidish. LC 82-22498. 14.95. New American Library.
Secret at Ravenswood. Caroline Farr. (Orig.). 1980. pap. 1.75 (ISBN 0-451-09181-7, E9181, Sig). NAL.
Secret Battle. Alan Patrick Herbert. LC 20-6283. 1920. A. A. Knopf.
Secret Battle. Alan Patrick Herbert. LC 81-66448. 1981. 8.95 (ISBN 0-689-11156-8). Atheneum.
Secret Bequest. Frances Christine Tiernan. LC 15-246679. The Ave Maria.
Secret Beyond the Door. Rufus King. LC 48-737. 1947. Triangle Books.
Secret Book. George Wemyss. LC 11-12059. 1911. Sturgis & Walton Company.
Secret Book, Vol. 1. Edmund Lester Pearson. LC 72-3419. (Short Story Index Reprint Ser). Repr. of 1914 ed. 16.00 (ISBN 0-8369-4159-4). Ayer Co.
Secret Brand. 1st Ed. Gene Austin. LC 52-13384. (Double D western). 1953. Doubleday.
Secret Bread. Fryniwyd Tennyson Jesse. LC 17-20670. 1.50. George H. Doran Company.
Secret Brotherhood. John Gordon Brandon. LC 28-203452. 1928. L. MacVeagh, The Dial Press.
Secret Brotherhood. Karl May. 1979. 12.95 (ISBN 0-8264-0152-X). Continuum.
Secret Brotherhood: A Novel. Karl Friedrich May. LC 79-1359. (Collected works of Karl May; ser 3, v. 3). (Continuum book). 1979. 12.95 (ISBN 0-8164-9360-X). Seabury Press.
Secret Cards. John Joy Bell. LC 22-191711. 1922. Hodder and Stoughton, Limited.
Secret Challenge. Annie L Gelsthorpe. (Candlelight romance.). 1974. (pbk.) 0.75. Dell.
Secret Circle: Cuban Expedition. Gary Null. (Orig.). 1974. pap. 1.25 o.p. (ISBN 0-515-03288-3, V3288). Pyramid Pubns.
Secret Circle: Operation Royal Family. Gary Null. LC 73-21128. (Secret circle#2). 1974. (pbk.) 1.25 (ISBN 0-515-03379-0). Pyramid Books.
Secret Circus. Richard Frede. LC 67-127301. 1967. 4.95. Random.
Secret Citadel. Isabel Constance Clarke. LC 14-5350. 1914. Benziger Brothers.
Secret Citadel. Monica Heath. 1975. (pbk.) 0.95. New American Library.
Secret City: A Novel in Three Parts. Hugh Walpole. LC 19-2710. George H. Doran Company.
Secret Code of the Odyssey: Did the Greeks Sail the Atlantic? Gilbert Pillot. LC 77-141555. (Illus.). 1972. 7.95 (ISBN 0-200-71773-1). Abelard-Schuman.
Secret Deed. Julia Cleft Addams. LC 26-19674. 1926. R. M. McBride & Company.
Secret Delights of Love. 1.95 o.p. (ISBN 0-442-82394-0). Peter Pauper.
Secret Despatch. James Grant. LC 6-44852. (Lovell's library. v. 2 no. 49). J. W. Lovell Company.
Secret Diary of Ho Chi Minh's Daughter. Ed. by Lanh Ba. 1970. pap. 1.25 o.p. Lancer.
Secret Directory. A Romance of Hidden History. Madeleine Vinton Dahlgren. LC 6-32179. H. L. Kilner & Co.
Secret Dispatch. James Grant. LC 6-44853. (On cover: Seaside library. Pocket ed. no. 781). G. Munro.

Secret Door. Grethe Grammer. (Orig.). 1977. pap. 6.50 (ISBN 0-89351-009-2). Western Her Texas.
Secret Doorways. John Pleasant McCoy. LC 74-116525. 1971. 6.95. Weybright and Talley.
Secret Dragnet. Bruce Sanders. LC 57-7192. 1957. Roy Publishers.
Secret Drama. Constance I. Smith. LC 23-5625. Harcourt, Brace and Company.
Secret Duel: Or, The Soldier's Dream. A Story of the Late War. Sarah Ann Wright. LC 1-20910. 1869. New York Publishing Company.
Secret Envoy. Maude Parker. LC 30-8790. The Bobbs-Merrill Company.
Secret Errand. John Creasey. LC 74-12943. (MW suspense). 1974. 5.95 (ISBN 0-679-50484-2). McKay.
Secret Fathers. Mildred Seydell. LC 30-28174. The Macaulay Company.
Secret Fear. Barbara Cartland. 1973. pap. 0.95 o.p. (ISBN 0-515-03020-1). Pyramid Pubns.
Secret Fear, No. 23. Barbara Cartland. 1975. pap. 1.25 o.p. (ISBN 0-515-03832-6, V3832). BJ Pub Group.
Secret Fire. Clayton Moore. (River Falls Ser.). (Berkley medallion book). 1975. (pbk.) 1.25 (ISBN 0-425-02651-5). Berkley Pub. Co.
Secret Flower of Ranatan. Herbert L. McClelland. (Illus.). 60p. pap. 2.95x (ISBN 0-943864-10-0). MD Bks.
Secret Foe. Gertrude Warden. LC 8-34842. (On cover: The authors' library, no. 15). 1896. The International News Company.
Secret Fool. Victor MacClure. LC 27-13385. 1927. Brentano's.
Secret Front. Paul Gallico. LC 40-31626. 1940. A. A. Knopf.
Secret Galactics. Alfred Elton Van Vogt. LC 73-17427. (Reward book science-fiction original, no. 1). 1974. (pbk.) 2.45 (ISBN 0-13-797902-9). Prentice-Hall.
Secret Game. Francois Boyer. LC 50-8587. 1950. Harcourt, Brace.
Secret Garden. Mahmud Shabistari. 1974. pap. 2.25 o.p. (ISBN 0-525-47375-0). Dutton.
Secret Gift: A Novel. 1st Ed. in the U. S. A. E. Johnson. 1961. Doubleday.
Secret Girl-Watchers. Robert Earliton. 192p. (Orig.). 1973. pap. 1.95 o.p. (ISBN 0-87682-387-8, 7387). Barclay Hse.
Secret Glass. Beryl Bainbridge. LC 73-93608. 1974. 5.95 (ISBN 0-8076-0746-0). G. Braziller.
Secret Glory. Arthur Machen. LC 22-21804. 1922. A.A. Knopf.
Secret Gold. Alice Muriel Livingston Williamson. LC 25-3846. 1925. Doubleday, Page & Company.
Secret Harbour. Stewart Edward White. LC 26-97529. 1926. Doubleday, Page & Company.
Secret Heart. Barbara Cartland. Orig. Title: Cupid Rides Pillion. 1972. pap. 0.95 o.p. (ISBN 0-515-02796-0). Pyramid Pubns.
Secret Heart. Barbara Cartland. 1975. pap. 1.25 o.p. (ISBN 0-515-03565-3, V3565). BJ Pub Group.
Secret Heart. Vida Hurst. 1948. Gramercy Pub. Co.
Secret Heart. Aurora Moore. 352p. (Orig.). 1982. pap. 2.95 (ISBN 0-523-41146-4). Pinnacle Bks.
Secret Heart see Brownstone Gothic.
Secret Heiress. Lillian Shelley. LC 81-43534. 1982. 10.95 (ISBN 0-385-17836-0). Doubleday.
Secret History of Mama Oella, Princess Royal of Peru see Finished Rake: or Gallantry in Perfection.
Secret History of Queen Zarah and the Zarazians. Mary De La Riviere Manley. LC 79-170514. (Foundations of the Novel). 1972. 22.00 (ISBN 0-8240-0522-8). Garland Pub.
Secret History of the Lord of Musashi; and, Arrowroot. first ed. Junichiro Tanizaki. LC 81-48257. 1982. 12.95 (ISBN 0-394-52454-3). Knopf.
Secret History of the Lord of Musashi & Arrowroot: Two Novellas. Junichiro Tanizaki. 1982. 12.95 (ISBN 0-394-52454-3). Knopf.
Secret History of the Present Intrigues of the Court of Caramania. Eliza Fowler Haywood. LC 71-170571. (Foundations of the Novel). 1972. (part of 71 vol. series). 22.00 ea. (ISBN 0-8240-0562-7). Garland Pub.
Secret History of Time to Come. Robie Macauley. LC 79-2087. 1979. 9.95 (ISBN 0-394-50166-7). Knopf.
Secret History Revealed by Lady Peggy O'Malley. Charles Norris Williamson & Alice Muriel Livingston Williamson. LC 15-21423. 1915. Doubleday, Page & Company.
Secret Hole. Jim Kelly. (Small Star Stories). (Illus.). 1975. 5.95 o.p. (ISBN 0-02-645740-7, 64574); cassette 6.95 o.p. (ISBN 0-02-645750-4, 64575). Glencoe.
Secret Honeymoon. Peggy Gaddis, pseud. LC 47-18111. 1947. Arcadia House.
Secret Honeymoon. Peggy Gaddis. (rainbow romance edition). 1973. (pbk.) 0.60. New Amer. Lib.
Secret Hope. Constance Robinson. 1976. pap. 1.50 o.p. (ISBN 0-8007-8263-1, Spire). Revell.
Secret House. Edgar Wallace. LC 19-13296. Small, Maynard & Company.
Secret House of Death. Ruth Rendell. LC 76-17325. 1976. 8.95 (ISBN 0-89340-018-1). J. Curley & Associates.
Secret House of Death. Ruth Rendell. LC 74-79414. 1969. 4.50. Published for the Crime Club by Doubleday.
Secret Identity. Joanna Campbell. 1982. pap. 1.95 (ISBN 0-553-22683-5). Bantam.
Secret Image. Laurence Oliver Brown. LC 31-5215. 1931. Simon and Schuster.
Secret in the Cave. Jennie Brown Rawlins. LC 67-21350. 1967. Deseret.
Secret in the Daisy. Carol Grace. LC 55-10629. 1955. Random House.
Secret in the Sky. Superhero Adventure. Kenneth Robeson. (His the fantastic adventures of Doc Savage, 6). (Illus.). 1975. 1.75. (ISBN 0-307-02375-3). Western Publishing Company.
Secret Information. Robert Smythe Hichens. LC 33-12841. 1938. Doubleday, Doran & Company, Inc.
Secret Ingredients. Patrick Skene Catling. LC 76-365302. 1976. 3.50 (ISBN 0-246-10852-5). Hart-Davis MacGibbon.
Secret Isaac. Jerome Charyn. 240p. 1980. pap. 2.75 (ISBN 0-380-47126-4, 47126, Bard). Avon.
Secret Isaac: A Novel. Jerome Charyn. LC 78-57326. 9.95 (ISBN 0-87795-196-9). Arbor House.
Secret Islands. Franklin Russell. (O.s.i.). 1970. pap. 2.45 o.s.i. (ISBN 0-671-20507-2, Touchstone Bks). S&S.
Secret Journey. James Hanley. LC 36-29005. 1936. The Macmillan Company.
Secret Keeper. Shirley Eskapa. LC 83-3045. 272p. 1983. 10.95 (ISBN 0-312-70849-1). St Martin.
Secret Lemonade Drinker. Guy Bellamy. LC 77-2254. 6.95 (ISBN 0-03-020906-4). Holt Rinehart and Winston.
Secret Life of Algernon Pendleton. Russell H Greenan. LC 72-10990. 1973. 5.95 (ISBN 0-394-48283-2). Random House.
Secret Life of Algernon Pendleton. Russell H Greenan. 1976. 1.75 (ISBN 0-449-23038-4). Fawcett Crest.
Secret Life of Mother Wonderful. Myra Chanin. LC 80-22904. 9.95 (ISBN 0-8253-0021-5). Beaufort Books.
Secret Life of Our Times: New Fiction from Esquire. Ed. by Gordon Lish. Esquire. LC 73-80734. 1973. 12.95 (ISBN 0-385-06215-X). Doubleday.
Secret Life of Our Times: New Fiction from Esquire. Ed. by Gordon Lish. LC 73-80734. 648p. 1973. 12.95 o.p. (ISBN 0-385-06215-X). Doubleday.
Secret Life of Queen Victoria: Her Majesty's Missing Diaries: Being an Account of Her Hitherto Unknown Travels Through the Island of Jamaica in the Year 1871. Jonathan Routh. LC 79-7320. (Illus.). 1980. 20.00 (ISBN 0-385-15353-8). Doubleday.
Secret List of Heinrich Roehm. Michael Barak. LC 75-28316. 1976. 6.95 (ISBN 0-688-02991-4). Morrow.
Secret List of Heinrich Roehm. Michael Barak. (Signet Book). 1977. 1.75 (ISBN 0-451-07352-5). New American Library.
Secret List of Heinrich Roehm. Michael Bar-Zohar. 1976. G. K. Hall.
Secret Listeners of the East. Dhan Gopal Mukerji. LC 26-8614. E. P. Dutton & Company.
Secret Lives. Edward Frederic Benson. LC 32-240634. 1932. Doubleday, Doran & Company, Inc.
Secret Lives. D. J. McKinney. 432p. (Orig.). 1982. pap. 3.25 (ISBN 0-441-75730-8). Ace Bks.
Secret Lives and Other Stories. Wa Thiongo Ngugi. LC 75-23931. 1975. 6.95 (ISBN 0-88208-061-X). L. Hill.
Secret Lives: And Other Stories. Ngugi Wa Thiong O, pseud. LC 75-23931. 160p. 1975. 6.95 (ISBN 0-88208-058-X). Lawrence Hill.
Secret Love. Rachael Borne. LC 66-30569. 1967. Zondervan Pub. House.
Secret Love. Louise Gerard. LC 33-2635. The Macaulay Company.
Secret Love House. Maravene Thompson. LC 26-13138. The Macaulay Company.
Secret Lover. Ursula Bloom. 1979. pap. 1.95 (ISBN 0-89041-242-1, 3242). Major Bks.
Secret Lover: By Ursula Bloom. Ursula Bloom. LC 31-29313. E. P. Dutton & Co., Inc.
Secret Lovers. Charles McCarry. LC 76-5244. 1977. 8.95. Dutton.
Secret Lovers. Charles McCarry. 1978. 1.95 (ISBN 0-449-23549-1). Fawcett Crest Book.
Secret Marriage. Carol Brown. LC 33-5930. A. L. Burt Company.
Secret Marriage. Kathleen Thompson Norris. LC 36-5514. 1936. Doubleday, Doran and Company, Inc.
Secret Masters. Gerald Kersh. LC 53-8523. 1953. Ballantine Books.
Secret Meeting. Cecil John Charles Street. LC 52-6504. Dodd, Mead.
Secret Memoirs from the New Atalantis. Mary De La Riviere Manley. LC 71-170520. (Foundations of the Novel). 1972. 22.00 (ISBN 0-8240-0527-9). Garland Pub.
Secret Memoirs of Bertha Krupp: From the Papers and Diaries of Chief Gouvernante Baroness D'Alteville. Henry William Hubert Fischer. LC 16-3765. 1916. Cassell and Company, Ltd.
Secret Memoirs of Lord Byron: A Novel. Christopher Nicole. LC 78-14395. 10.95 (ISBN 0-397-01290-X). Lippincott.
Secret Memoranda of Stanley J. Fairweather: As Purloined from the Files of the Law Firm of Fairweather, Winters & Sommers. Arnold B. Kanter. LC 80-53532. 15.00 (ISBN 0-8040-0419-6). Swallow Press.
Secret Mission. Canfield Cook. LC 43-234239. 1943. Grosset & Dunlap.
Secret Mission. Margit Strom Heppenstall. LC 72-91358. (Illus.). 1972. 1.95 (ISBN 0-8127-0055-4). Southern Pub. Association.
Secret Mission: A Novel. Emily Gerard. LC 6-44240. (On cover: Harper's Franklin square library, no. 690). 1891. Harper & Brothers.
Secret Mission: Africa. Don Smith. (Orig.). 1970. pap. 0.60 o.p. (A697, Award). Univ Pub & Dist.
Secret Mission: Angola. Don Smith. (Secret Mission Ser.). (O.s.i.). (Orig.). 1970. pap. 0.95 o.s.i. (AN1153, Award). Univ Pub & Dist.
Secret Mission: Athens. Don Smith. (Secret Mission Ser.). (O.s.i.). (Orig.). 1971. pap. 0.75 o.s.i. (A801S, Award). Univ Pub & Dist.
Secret Mission: Cairo. Don Smith. (Secret Mission Ser.). (O.s.i.). 160p. 1970. pap. 0.95 o.s.i. (AN1207, Award). Univ Pub & Dist.
Secret Mission: Corsica. Don Smith. (Secret Mission Ser.). (O.s.i.). 148p. (Orig.). 1968. pap. 0.95 o.s.i. (AN1162, Award). Univ Pub & Dist.
Secret Mission: Haiti. Don Smith. (Secret Mission Ser). 160p. (Orig.). 1972. pap. 0.75 o.p. (A9545, Award). Univ Pub & Dist.
Secret Mission: Istanbul. Don Smith. (Secret Mission Ser). (O.s.i.). 160p. 1975. pap. 1.25 o.s.i. (AQ1498, Award). Univ Pub & Dist.
Secret Mission: Moluk. William Voltz. (Perry Rhodan #84). 1975. (pbk.) 1.25. Ace Books.
Secret Mission: Morocco. Don Smith. (Secret Mission Ser). (O.s.i.). 160p. 1974. pap. 0.95 o.s.i. (AN1260, Award). Univ Pub & Dist.
Secret Mission: Munich. Don Smith. (Secret Mission Ser.). (O.s.i.). 192p. 1975. pap. 1.25 o.s.i. (AQ1408, Award). Univ Pub & Dist.
Secret Mission: North Korea. Don Smith. (Secret Mission Ser.). (O.s.i.). (Orig.). 1970. pap. 0.60 o.s.i. (A616X, Award). Univ Pub & Dist.
Secret Mission: Peking. Don Smith. (Secret Mission Ser). (O.s.i.). 160p. 1968. pap. 0.95 o.s.i. (AN1209, Award). Univ Pub & Dist.
Secret Mission: Prague. Don Smith. (Secret Mission Ser.). (O.s.i.). 160p. 1968. pap. 0.95 o.s.i. (AN1221, Award). Univ Pub & Dist.
Secret Mission to Bangkok. Francis Van Wyck Mason. LC 60-5938. 1960. Doubleday.
Secret Mountains. John Appleby. LC 56-12824. 1957. Washburn.
Secret No More. Janina Marecka. LC 66-146747. 1966. 4.00. Dorrance.
Secret Notebooks. 160p. pap. 1.95 o.p. (MP-109). Montmartre.
Secret of a Birth. Charlotte M. Stanley McKenna & Stanley, J. LC 8-28180. (On cover: Munro's library, v. 1, no. 114). 1884. N. L. Munro.
Secret of a Letter. Gertrude Warden. LC 8-34841. The International News Company.
Secret of Apache Canyon. Richard Telfair. 1970. pap. 0.60 o.p. (R2362, GM). Fawcett World.
Secret of Awen Castle. Florence Hurd. (Avon gothic original). 1974. (pbk.) 0.95. Avon.
Secret of Barnabas Collins. Marilyn Ross. (Orig.). 1969. pap. 0.60 o.p. (ISBN 0-446-63413-1, 63-413). Paperback Lib.
Secret of Benjamin Square. Jennifer Plum. (Orig.). 1972. pap. 0.95 o.s.i. (75-417). Lancer.
Secret of Benjamin Square. Jennifer Plum. (O.s.i.). 1976. pap. 1.25 o.s.i. (BT50921). Belmont-Tower.
Secret of Big Foot Pass. Mike Jahn. (Berkley Medallion) (ISBN 0-425-03307-4). Berkley.
Secret of Blackoaks. Ashley Carter, pseud. (Fawcett Gold Medal Book). 1978. 1.95 (ISBN 0-449-13960-3). Fawcett Books.
Secret of Bogey House. Herbert Adams. LC 25-242752. 1925. J. B. Lippincott Company.
Secret of Bourke's Mansion. Caroline Moyer. (Avalon Books). 1977. 4.95. Thomas Bouregy.
Secret of Canfield House. Florence Hurd. 1971. pap. 0.75 o.p. (T2442, GM). Fawcett World.
Secret of Castle Montebello. Liz Varga. 3.00 o.p. Carlton.
Secret of Chapultepec Castle. Henrietta Bell. Date not set. pap. 4.95 (ISBN 0-89741-013-0). Roadrunner Tech.
Secret of Chateau Kendell. Susan Richard. 1971. pap. 0.60 o.p. (ISBN 0-446-63518-9, 63-518). Paperback Lib.
Secret of Chimneys. Agatha Miller Christie. LC 25-17145. 1925. Dodd, Mead and Company.
Secret of Chimneys. Agatha Miller Christie. LC 30-12329. 1927. Grosset & Dunlap.
Secret of Chimneys. Dame Agatha Miller Christie. 1975. (pbk.) 1.25. Dell.
Secret of Crane's Castle. Eleanor H. Spaak. 1973. pap. 0.95 o.p. (09161). Curtis.
Secret of Cypress Manor. Phyllis Luxem. 192p. (YA) 1974. 4.95 o.p. (Avalon). Bouregy.
Secret of Cypress Manor. Phyllis Luxem. (Avalon romances). 1974. 4.50. Avalon Books.
Secret of Devil's Cave. Jennifer Hale. 1973. pap. 0.95 o.s.i. (75-468). Lancer.
Secret of Dr. Kildare. Max Brand. LC 40-7412. 1940. Dodd, Mead & Company.
Secret of Dr. Kildare. Frederick Faust. LC 40-7413. 1940. Dodd, Mead & Company.
Secret of Dr. Kildare. Frederick Faust. LC 43-130122. 1943. The Sun Dial Press.
Secret of Dresden Farm. Genevieve St. John. 1971. pap. 0.75 o.p. (B75-2088). Belmont-Tower.
Secret of Estcourt. Dora Delmar. (On cover: Library of American authors. no. 54). 1894. G. Munro's Sons.
Secret of Father Brown. Gilbert Keith Chesterton. LC 27-191202. 1927. Harper & Brothers.
Secret of Fire Five. Jack Olsen, pseud. 1977. 8.95 o.p. (ISBN 0-394-41174-9). Random.
Secret of Fire 5. Jack Olsen, pseud. LC 76-48306. 8.95 (ISBN 0-394-41174-9). Random House.
Secret of Fontaine-La-Croix. Margaret Field. LC 6-41202. (On cover: Appletons' town and country library, no. 15). 1888. D. Appleton and Company.
Secret of Fougereuse: A Romance of the Fifteenth Century. Louis Marvan & Guiney, Louise Imogen, 1861-1920, Tr. LC 96-2305. 1898. Marlier, Callanan & Co.
Secret of Frontellac. Frank Kimball Scribner. LC 12-22587. 1.25. Small, Maynard and Company.
Secret of Giltham Hall. Jeanne Cheyney. (Chime Gothic Ser.: No. 201). (Orig.). 1980. pap. 2.50 (ISBN 0-89191-326-2). Cook.
Secret of Giltham Hall. Jeanne Cheyney. (Chime Ser.). 1982. pap. 2.50 o.p. Caroline Hse.
Secret of Gold. Tr. from French by Anne Carter. 1st Amer. Ed. Madeleine Raillon. LC 65-12615. 3.25. Harcourt.
Secret of Greenwillows. abr ed. Marjorie Harte, pseud. Ed. by Alice Sachs. Orig. Title: Masquerade for a Nurse. 1970. Repr. of 1964 ed. 3.95 o.p. Lenox Hill.
Secret of Harbor House. Claudette Nicole. (Orig.). 1975. pap. 1.25 o.p. (ISBN 0-515-03722-2). BJ Pub Group.
Secret of Hayworth Hall. Florence Hurd. 1975. (pbk.) 0.95 (ISBN 0-380-00387-2). Avon.
Secret of Hedges Hall. Lynn Williams. (candlelight mystery.). 1973. (pbk). 0.75. Dell Pub. Co.,
Secret of Her Life. Edward Jenkins. (On cover: Seaside library. Pocket ed. no. 810). G. Munro.
Secret of Hidden Valley. Loring Hutchinson. LC 56-8811. 1956. Random House.
Secret of High Eldersham. Miles Burton. LC 75-44961. (Fifty Classics of Crime Fiction, 1900-1950; 8). 1976. 12.00 (ISBN 0-8240-2357-9). Garland Pub.
Secret of High Eldersham. Miles Burton. LC 31-12125. 1931. The Mystery League, Inc.
Secret of His Presence: A Novel. Anna L Schroeder. LC 68-12952. 1968. Zondervan Pub. House.
Secret of Killer Mountain Inn. Kate Brooks. 1978. pap. 1.50 (ISBN 0-532-15375-8). Woodhill.
Secret of Klosterholm: From the Swedish of Betty Pseud. Betty Janson. Tr. by Gustafson, Signhild Victoria. LC 25-3948. The Covenant Book Concern.
Secret of Life. Roy Masters. LC 77-9148. 1972. pap. 6.50 (ISBN 0-933900-02-3). Foun Human Under.
Secret of Lonesome Cove. Samuel Hopkins Adams. LC 12-21395. The Bobbs-Merrill Company.
Secret of Luca. Ignazio Secondo Tranquilli Siline. LC 57-821267.
Secret of Luca. Tr. from Italian by Darina Silone. Ignazio Silone. (Dolphin bk., C251). 1961. Doubleday.
Secret of Major Thompson. Pierre Daninos. (Illus.). 1957. 5.95 o.p. Knopf.
Secret of Major Thompson. Translated from the French by W. Marmaduke Thompson. Translated by Don Cortes Illustrated by Walter Goetz. 1st American Ed. Pierre Daninos. LC 57-12575. 1957. Knopf.
Secret of Mallet Castle. William Edward Daniel Ross. LC 66-5426. 1966. Arcadia House.

Secret of Mankind. With Some Singular Hints Gathered in the Elsewheres or After-Life from Certain Eminent Personages; As Also Some Brief Account of the Planet Mercury and of Its Institutions... Willis Brewer. 1895. G. P. Putnam's Sons.
Secret of Mary Celeste. Gershom Bradford. (Illus.). 1967. 7.95 o.p. (ISBN 0-8271-6702-4). Barre.
Secret of Mary Magdalene. Paul Ilton. LC 56-8993. (Signet book, 1301). 1956. New American Library.
Secret of Mirror House. Patricia Maxwell. (Orig.). 1970. pap. 0.60 o.p. (R2570, GM). Fawcett World.
Secret of MI6. Lou Smith. LC 77-17639. 1978. 7.95 (ISBN 0-312-70859-9). St. Martin's Press.
Secret of Mohawk Pond. Natalie Sumner Lincoln. LC 28-17816. 1928. D. Appleton & Company.
Secret of Montoya Mission. Dorothy Baughman. (YA) 1981. 6.95 (Avalon). Bouregy.
Secret of Musterton House. George Granby. LC 20-7428. E. P. Dutton & Co., Inc.
Secret of M1 6. Lou Smith. LC 80-83570. 1981. 2.50 (ISBN 0-87216-800-X). Playboy Press.
Secret of Narcisse: A Romance. Edmund William Gosse. LC 6-27515. United States Book Company.
Secret of Pettinggill Farm. Dorothy Dearborn. (YA) 1972. 4.95 o.p. (Avalon). Bouregy.
Secret of Pocomoke. Mary Teresa Waggaman. LC 14-756414. The Ave Maria Press.
Secret of Quarry House. Claire Lorrimer. 1976. (pbk.) 1.25 (ISBN 0-380-00497-6). Avon Books.
Secret of Runestaff. Michael Moorcock. (Orig.). 1969. pap. 0.60 o.p. (73824). Lancer.
Secret of Sam Marlow: The Further Adventures of the Man with Bogart's Face. Andrew J Fenady. LC 80-19031. 9.95 (ISBN 0-8092-5989-3). Contemporary Books.
Secret of San Felipe. Peter Buck. (Mercenary Ser.: No. 2). (Orig.). 1981. pap. 2.25 (ISBN 0-451-09894-3, E9894, Sig). NAL.
Secret of Santa Vittoria. Robert Crichton. (7710). 1967. Dell.
Secret of Santa Vittoria: A Novel. Robert Crichton. LC 66-20256. 1966. Simon and Schuster.
Secret of Saramount. Lillian Cheatham. LC 76-56275. 1978. 6.95 (ISBN 0-385-12720-0). Doubleday.
Secret of Sarek. Maurice Leblanc. Tr. by Teixeira De Mattos, Alexander Louis. LC 20-5586. The Macaulay Company.
Secret of Sea-Dream House: A Novel. Albert Payson Terhune. LC 29-4640. 1932. Harper & Brothers.
Secret of Secrets. Joseph Smith Fletcher. LC 29-3597. E. J. Clode, Inc.
Secret of Sheen. John Laurence. LC 29-194533. International Fiction Library.
Secret of Shower Tree. Virginia Coffman. 1968. pap. 0.60 o.p. (73-760). Lancer.
Secret of Somerset Place. Carol Marsh. (History Mystery Ser.). (Illus.). 160p. (Orig.). 1980. pap. 3.95 (ISBN 0-935326-02-2). Gallopade Pub Group.
Secret of Stonehenge: A New Thought Story. J W Rowe. LC 13-12499. 1913. 1.00. Broadway Publishing Co.
Secret of Strangeways. Joyce Bentley. 1976. 1.50. Pocket Books.
Secret of Success: Or, Family Affairs, a Memoir, in One Volume. John P Darden. 1853. W. Scott.
Secret of Sulphur Creek. Ralph Hayes. (Orig.). 1970. pap. 0.60 o.p. (B60-2031). Belmont-Tower.
Secret of Tangles: Another Case for Anthony Slade and Department X2. Leonard Reginald Gribble. LC 34-18691. J. B. Lippincott Company.
Secret of Tarn-End House. Christine Randell. (Paperback Library Gothic). (Orig.). 1969. pap. 0.60 o.p. (ISBN 0-446-63207-4, 63-207). Paperback Lib.
Secret of Tate's Beach. Augusta Huiell Seaman. LC 26-18166. 1.75. The Century Co.
Secret of the Andes: A Romance. Friedrich Hassaurek. LC 7-33389. 1879. R. Clarke & Co.
Secret of the Barbican: And Other Stories. Joseph Smith Fletcher. LC 79-121543. (Short story index reprint series). 1970. Books for Libraries Press.
Secret of the Barbican and Other Stories. Joseph Smith Fletcher. LC 25-27965. 1925. George H. Doran Company.
Secret of the Bastille. Paul Feval & M. Lassez. LC 29-34313. (His The years between: adventures of D'Artagnan and Cyrano de Bergerac. III). 1929. Longmans, Green and Co.
Secret of the Bungalow. Robert Joseph Casey. LC 30-22019. The Bobbs-Merrill Company.
Secret of the Canon. Adam Stump. (On cover: The John Rung prize series). Lutheran Publication Society.
Secret of the Chateau see House of Dark Illusions.
Secret of the Clan. Alice Brown. LC 12-239273. 1912. The Macmillan Company.
Secret of the Cliffs. Charlotte French. (On cover: Seaside library. Pocket ed. no. 387). 1885. G. Munro.
Secret of the Crater: A Mountain Moloch. Duffield Osborne. 1900. G. P. Putnam's Sons.
Secret of the Doubting Saint. Leonard Patrick O'Connor Wibberley. LC 61-12916. (Red badge detective). 1961. Dodd, Mead.
Secret of the Downs. Walter S Masterman. LC 39-1038. E. P. Dutton & Co., Inc.
Secret of the Earth. Charles Willing Beale. LC 74-15950. (Science Fiction). 1975. 14.00 (ISBN 0-405-06276-1). Arno Press.
Secret of the Elms. Daniel Pratt Mannix. 1977. pap. 1.50 (ISBN 0-425-03359-7, Medallion). Berkley Pub.
Secret of the Flames. William North. LC 29-20007. 1929. L. MacVeagh, The Dial Press.
Secret of the Flying T. Charles E. Wheeler. (YA) 1979. 6.95 (Avalon). Bouregy.
Secret of the Forest. Jeanne Bowman. (Contemporary Teens Ser.). 224p. (Orig.). 1981. pap. 2.25 (ISBN 0-89531-146-1, 0146-96). Sharon Pubns.
Secret of the Ghostly Shroud. Nancy Buckingham. pap. 0.75 o.p. Lancer.
Secret of the Green Vase. Frances Cooke. LC 7-386043. 1907. Benziger Brothers.
Secret of the Island. Being the Conclusion of "The Abandoned.". Jules Verne. LC 15-124714. (On cover: Seaside library. Pocket ed. no. 2146). 1895. G. Munro's Sons.
Secret of the Kingdom. Mika Toimi Waltari. LC 61-5714. 1961. Putnam.
Secret of the Lake House. Cecil John Charles Street. LC 46-1347. 1946. Dodd, Mead & Company.
Secret of the Lamas: A Tale of Thibet. (On cover: Cassell's sunshine series, no. 30). 1889. Cassell & Company, Limited.
Secret of the Lodge. Noel Streatfeild & Flothe, Richard, Illus. LC 40-13522. Random House.
Secret of the Lost Race. Andre Norton, pseud. LC 77-25542. (Norton, Andre. The Space Adventure Novels of Andre Norton). 1978. 7.95 (ISBN 0-8398-2419-X). Gregg Press.
Secret of the Marionettes: A Romance. Ernest De Lancey Pierson. (On cover: The railway series, no. 1). National Book Company.
Secret of the Marne: How Sergeant Fritsch Saved France. Marcel Berger & Berger, Maude. LC 18-8489. 1918. 1.50. G. P. Putnam's Sons.
Secret of the Marsh. Oliver Warner. LC 27-12373. 1927. E. P. Dutton & Company.
Secret of the Marshbanks. Kathleen Thompson Norris. LC 40-301821. 1940. Doubleday, Doran & Co., Inc.
Secret of the Martian Moons. Donald A. Wollheim. 1956. 2.95 o.p. (ISBN 0-03-034520-0). HR&W.
Secret of the Moor Cottage. Bryan Mary Angell. LC 6-40587. 1906. Small, Maynard & Company.
Secret of the Morgue. Frederick George Eberhard. LC 32-189514. The Macaulay Company.
Secret of the Mountain. Ethel Van Pelt. (Avalon Books). 4.95. Thomas Bouregy.
Secret of the Mouse Gray Room. Tibor Varady. Tr. by Alan Duff. 1982. pap. 4.95 (ISBN 0-7145-3843-4). Riverrun NY.
Secret of the Night: Further Adventures of Rouletablulle. Gaston Leroux. LC 14-3901. 1914. The Macaulay Company.
Secret of the Pale Lover. Clarissa Ross, pseud. 1969. pap. 0.75 o.p. (75-350). Lancer.
Secret of the Pale Lover. Clarissa Ross, pseud. (Orig.). 1972. pap. 0.95 o.p. (75-350). Lancer.
Secret of the Peony Vase. Ethel E. Bangert. 1975. 4.95. Avalon Books.
Secret of the Priory. Sofi O'Bryan. (candlelight gothic). 1975. (pbk.) 0.95. Dell.
Secret of the Red Spot. Eando Binder, pseud. 1971. pap. 0.75 o.p. (07163). Curtis.
Secret of the Reef. Harold Bindloss. LC 14-19168. 1.30. Frederick A. Stokes Company.
Secret of the Satin Doll. Jean Sprouse. (YA) 1978. 6.95 (Avalon). Bouregy.
Secret of the Sea. William Allison. LC 20-642821. 1920. Doubleday, Page & Company.
Secret of the Sea. Cornelia Mitchell Parsons. LC 7-34094. J. S. Ogilvie Publishing Company.
Secret of the Sea, &C. Brander Matthews. LC 74-160942. (Short story index reprint series). 1971. (ISBN 0-8369-3921-2). Books for Libraries Press.
Secret of the Sea: &C. Brander Matthews. LC 7-24697. 1886. C. Scribner's Sons.
Secret of the Silver Car: Further Adventures of Anthony Trent, Master Criminal. Wyndham Martyn. LC 20-5579. 1920. Moffat, Yard and Company.
Secret of the Spa. Mary Violet Heberden. LC 44-5300. 1944. Pub. for the Crime Club by Doubleday, Doran and Co., Inc.
Secret of the Sphinx. Hans P Dreyer. LC 30-19341. Burton Publishing Company.
Secret of the Spring Tower. Euatt. 3.25 o.p. Bobbs.
Secret of the Stone Face. Phyllis A. Whitney. (Signet Book). 1978. 1.25 (ISBN 0-451-08054-8). New American Library.
Secret of the Tower. Anthony Hope Hawkins. LC 19-12254. 1919. 1.60. D. Appleton and Company.
Secret of the Unicorn. Georges Remy. LC 73-21250. (Adventures of Tintin). (Atlantic Monthly Press book). (Illus.). 1974. (pbk.) 2.50 (ISBN 0-316-35832-0). Little, Brown.
Secret of the Villa Como. easy eye ed. Susan Marvin. pap. 0.75 o.p. Lancer.
Secret of the Wastelands. Harry Sinclair Drago. LC 40-442. 1940. Doubleday, Doran & Co., Inc.
Secret of the Willows. Elna Stone. (O.s.i.). 1976. pap. 1.25 o.s.i. (BT50984). Belmont-Tower.
Secret of the Wooden Lady. Carolyn Keene, pseud. LC 50-5633. (Her Nancy Drew mystery stories). 1950. Grosset & Dunlap.
Secret of the Yew Tree: Or, A Christian Woman. Pardo Bazan, Emilia. Tr. by Springer, Mary. LC 2296. (On cover: Holly library, no. 175). 1900. The Mershon Company.
Secret of Thundermyer House. Ruth Burnett. 1976. 4.95. Avalon Books.
Secret of Toni. Molly Elliot Seawell. LC 7-56873. 1907. D. Appleton and Company.
Secret of Villa Nova. 2nd ed. Susan Marvin. 1969. pap. 0.75 o.p. (74-991). Lancer.
Secret of Wilhelm Storitz. Jules Verne. 1964. 3.95. Assoc Bk.
Secret of 37 Hardy Street. Robert Joseph Casey. LC 29-23795. The Bobbs-Merrill Company.
Secret Orchard. Agnes Sweetman Castle & Castle, Egerton. 1901. F. A. Stokes Company.
Secret Partner. Elizabeth Frazer. LC 22-11514. 1922. H. Holt and Company.
Secret Passage. Fergus Hume. LC 5-10179. 1905. G. W. Dillingham Company.
Secret People. John B. Harris. pap. 0.50 o.p. (72-155). Lancer.
Secret People. Raymond F Jones. LC 56-13307. 1956. Avalon Books.
Secret People. John Wyndham, pseud. 208p. (Orig.). 1973. pap. 0.95 o.p. (M2890, GM). Fawcett World.
Secret Pilgrim. Edward Kimbrough. LC 49-6776. 1949. Rinehart.
Secret Place. Orig. Title: The Man Who Looked Like the Prince of Wales. Frederick Feikema Manfred. (75190). 1967. Pocket Bks.
Secret Places. Robert De Maria. (Orig.). 1980. pap. 2.25 (ISBN 0-515-05160-8). Jove Pubns.
Secret Places. Janice Elliott. LC 81-16740. 9.95 (ISBN 0-312-70871-8). St. Martin's Press.
Secret Places. Joan Sutherland. LC 30-13872. 1930. Harper & Brothers.
Secret Places of the Heart. Herbert George Wells. LC 22-26494. 1922. The Macmillan Company.
Secret Power. 2d ed. Marie Corelli. LC 22-116. 1921. Doubleday, Page & Company.
Secret Power of Pyramids. Bil Schul & Ed Pettit. 1977. pap. 2.50 (ISBN 0-449-13986-7, GM). Fawcett.
Secret Project of Sigurd O'Leary. Martin Peter Quigley. LC 59-5401. 1959. Lippincott.
Secret Quest. George Manville Fenn. (On cover: Broadway series, no. 20). 1893. J. A. Taylor and Company.
Secret Rendezvous. Kobo Abe. LC 79-9875. 1979. 8.95 (ISBN 0-394-50372-4). Knopf: Distributed by Random House.
Secret Road. John Alexander Ferguson. LC 25-15388. 1925. Dodd, Mead and Company.
Secret Road. Bruce Lancaster. 1976. 1.75 (ISBN 0-523-00889-9). Pinnacle Books.
Secret Room. Agnes Russell Weekes. LC 29-9939. 1929. Dodd, Mead and Company.
Secret Room of Morgate House. Elissa Grandower, pseud. LC 77-788879. 1977. 8.95 (ISBN 0-385-12452-X). Doubleday.
Secret Room of Morgate House. Hillary Waugh. LC 77-19075. 1978. 12.95 (ISBN 0-8161-6558-0). G. K. Hall.
Secret Rose: Stories. a variorum ed. William Butler Yeats & Phillip L. Marcus. LC 80-25824. 1981. 28.50 (ISBN 0-8014-1194-7). Cornell University Press.
Secret Runner & Other Stories. Linda T. Casper. 1974. wrps. 5.00 o.p. Cellar.
Secret Sanctuary: Or, The Saving of John Stretton. Warwick Deeping. LC 23-7037. 1923. Cassell and Company, Ltd.
Secret Sceptre. Francis Gerard. 1939. E. P. Dutton & Co., Inc.
Secret Scorpio: Dray Prescott No. 15. Alan Burt Akers. (Science Fiction Ser). (Illus.). 1977. pap. 1.50 (ISBN 0-87997-344-7, UW1344). DAW Bks.
Secret Sea. Thomas F Monteleone. 1979. 1.75 (ISBN 0-445-04404-7). Popular Library.
Secret Servant. Gavin Lyall. LC 80-14712. 1980. 9.95 (ISBN 0-670-46337-X). Viking Press.
Secret Service Man. Sydney Horler. LC 30-26923. 1930. A. A. Knopf.
Secret Service Operator 13. Robert William Chambers. LC 34-5174. 1934. D. Appleton-Century Company, Incorporated.
Secret Service Smith: Wanderings of an American Detective. Reginald Thomas Maitland Scott. LC 23-13893. E. P. Dutton & Company.
Secret Sex Curse of Bertha T. Jackson Short. 1973. (pbk.) 1.25. Dell.
Secret Sharer see Stories of the Double.
Secret Sharer & Other Great Stories. Ed. by Abraham Lass & Norma Tasman. (Orig.). 1969. pap. 2.25 (ISBN 0-451-62084-4, ME2084, Ment). NAL.
Secret Sharer: And Other Great Stories. Ed. by Abraham Harold Lass. LC 69-17924. (Mentor book). 1969. 0.95. New American Library.
Secret Sharer: Conrad see Heart of Darkness: Conrad.
Secret Sign. Gladys Malvern. LC 61-7147. 1961. Abelard-Schuman.
Secret Sins. Stephanie Blake. LC 80-80982. (Stephanie Blake Ser.). 400p. (Orig.). 1980. pap. 2.75 (ISBN 0-87216-719-4). Playboy Pbks.
Secret Six. Frances Marion. LC 31-10978. Grosset & Dunlap.
Secret Soldier. John Ouigley. LC 66-13825. bds., 4.95. New Amer. Lib.
Secret Son. Sheila Kaye-Smith. LC 42-395133. 1942. Harper & Brothers.
Secret Sorrow. May Agnes Early Fleming. LC 6-39944. (On cover: Ogilvie's popular library, v. 1. no. 1). 1883. J. S. Ogilvie & Company.
Secret Sorrow. Karen Van Der Zee. (Harlequin Presents Ser.). 192p. 1981. pap. 1.50 (ISBN 0-373-10433-2, Pub. by Harlequin). PB.
Secret Speech: The Failure of Comrade Khrushchev's Leadership. 1st Ed. John Robinson Beal. LC 61-10387. 1961. Duell, Sloan and Pearce.
Secret Spring. Pierre Benoit. LC 20-7919. 1920. 1.75. Dodd, Mead and Company.
Secret Stair. 1st American Ed. Phyllis Bottome. LC 54-6391. 1954. Harcourt, Brace.
Secret Stream: Translated from the French by Norman Denny. Marcel Ayme. LC 53-11828. Harper.
Secret Stud. Marcia Marcoux. 176p. pap. 1.95 o.p. (6097). Brandon.
Secret Swinger. Alan Harrington. (Signet bk., T3217). 1967. New Amer. Lib.
Secret Swinger: 1st Ed. Alan Harrington. LC 66-12393. 1966. bds., 4.95. Knopf.
Secret Table. Mark Mirsky. LC 74-24914. 1975. 7.95. (ISBN 0-914590-10-3) (ISBN 0-914590-11-1). Fiction Collective: Distributed by G. Braziller.
Secret Talents. Borgia. 1972. pap. 2.25 o.s.i. (V1096R, Venus). Grove.
Secret Telephone. William Le Queux. LC 23-6289. The James A. McCann Company.
Secret That Was Kept: A Study in Fear. Elizabeth Robins. LC 26-149231. 1926. Harper & Brothers.
Secret the Song. Elizabeth Kjellberg. LC 47-173. 1946. Ziff-Davis Publishing Company.
Secret Thread. Grace Zaring Stone. LC 48-8230. 1948. Harper.
Secret Toll. Paul Thorne & Thorne, Mabel, Joint Author. LC 22-12467. 1922. Dodd, Mead and Company.
Secret Tomb. Maurice Leblanc. LC 23-16386. The Macaulay Company.
Secret Trail. Anthony Armstrong Willis. LC 29-2247. 1929. Macrae Smith Company.
Secret Trail. Anthony Armstrong Willis. LC 30-16620. 1930. The White House.
Secret. Translated by Isabel Quigly. Alba De Cespedes. LC 58-11810. 1958. Simon and Schuster.
Secret Treasure at Tentenbury Manor. Alan Hunter. 1973. pap. 0.75 o.p. (ISBN 0-8024-3830-X). Moody.
Secret Trees. Luci Shaw. LC 76-1342. (Wheaton Literary Ser.). (Illus.). 80p. 1976. cloth 5.95 (ISBN 0-87788-909-0). Shaw Pubs.
Secret Understanding. easy eye ed. Merle Miller. 1968. pap. 0.75 o.p. (74-939). Lancer.
Secret Understanding: A Novel of Suspense. Merle Miller. LC 56-5649. 1956. Viking Press.
Secret Understandings. abr. ed. Morris H. Philipson. 384p. 1983. 16.95 (ISBN 0-671-46619-4). S&S.
Secret Valley. Jackson Gregory. LC 39-17414. 1939. Dodd, Mead & Company.
Secret Valleys. John Cousins. LC 49-10216. 1949. A. A. Knopf.
Secret Vanguard. Michael Innes, pseud. LC 81-48200. 288p. 1982. pap. 2.84i (ISBN 0-06-080584-6, P-584, PL). Har-Row.
Secret Vanguard. John Innes Mackintosh Stewart. LC 41-1360. 1941. Dodd, Mead & Company.
Secret Vanguard see Appleby Intervenes.

Secret Victory. Stephen McKenna. LC 22-10776. (His The sensationalists, III). George H. Doran Company.
Secret Voyage. Basil Carey. A. H. King.
Secret Way. Joseph Smith Fletcher. LC 25-19119. Small, Maynard & Company.
Secret Ways. Alistair MacLean. LC 75-31751. 1975. 9.95 (ISBN 0-89190-172-8). American Reprint Co.
Secret Ways. Andrew Soutar. LC 34-23657. C. Kendall.
Secret Ways. 1st Ed. Alistair MacLean. LC 59-636737. 1959. Doubleday.
Secret Weapon, By Francis Beeding. Francis Beeding. LC 40-13260. 1940. Harper & Brothers.
Secret Wife. Alice Acland. LC 75-26170. 204p. 1976. 7.95 o.p. (ISBN 0-312-70910-2). St Martin.
Secret Wife. Anne Acland-Troyte Marreco. LC 75-26170. 7.95. St. Martin's Press.
Secret Wind. Lewis Sherman. LC 78-68515. 4.95 (ISBN 0-912760-85-0). Freedom Press.
Secret Witness. George Fort Gibbs. LC 17-222963. 1917. D. Appleton and Company.
Secret Woman. Eleanor Hibbert. LC 75-103757. 1970. 5.95. Doubleday.
Secret Woman. Victoria Holt, pseud. LC 75-103757. 1970. 6.95 (ISBN 0-385-03601-9). Doubleday.
Secret Woman. Victoria Holt, pseud. 352p. 1981. pap. 2.50 (ISBN 0-449-23283-2, Crest). Fawcett.
Secret Woman. Eden Phillpotts. LC 5-2438. 1905. The Macmillan Company.
Secret World, No. 21. Peter Deriabin. (Espionage-Intelligence Library). 416p. 1982. pap. 3.50 (ISBN 0-345-30416-0). Ballantine.
Secret Year. Betty Evelyn Davies. LC 31-2171. 1930. L. MacVeagh, The Dial Press.
Secretary: A Novel. Vivian Ringer. LC 74-1471. 1974. 6.95 (ISBN 0-440-08235-8). Delacorte Press.
Secretary: A Novel. Vivian Ringer. (Dellbook). 1977. 1.50 (ISBN 0-440-17920-3). Dell Pub.Co.
Secretary of Firvolous Affairs. May Peel Futrelle. LC 11-20823. 1.25. The Bobbs-Merrill Company.
Secretary of State: Being the Second Part of The Realists. Stephen McKenna. LC 27-122996. 1927. Little, Brown and Company.
Secretary to Bayne, M. P. A Novel. William Pett Ridge. 1898. Harper & Brothers.
Secreto De Sonia: Pimienta Collection Ser. new ed. Jairo Ibero. (Illus.). 160p. (Span.). 1975. pap. 1.25 (ISBN 0-88473-243-6). Fiesta Pub.
Secrets. Francis Lee Bailey. LC 78-7500. 1978. 9.95 (ISBN 0-8128-2527-6). Stein and Day.
Secrets. Nancy Hale. LC 71-145460. 1971. 4.95. Coward, McCann & Geoghegan.
Secrets. Burt Hirschfeld. LC 75-15691. 1975. 7.95 (ISBN 0-671-22101-9). Simon and Schuster.
Secrets. Burt Hirschfeld. 1976. (pbk.) 1.95 (ISBN 0-671-80445-6). Pocket Books.
Secrets. L. T. Lorimer. 192p. 1982. pap. 2.25 (ISBN 0-441-05691-1, Pub. by Tempo). Ace Bks.
Secrets. Michael A. Smith. LC 80-23266. (Illus.). 10.95 (ISBN 0-312-70913-7). St. Martin's Press.
Secrets. Unity Hall. 1982. pap. 10.00x (ISBN 0-330-26339-0, Pub. by Pan Bks). State Mutual Bk.
Secrets. Sharon Wagner. 416p. (Orig.). 1980. pap. 2.50 (ISBN 0-89083-641-8). Zebra.
Secrets. Frances Wilshire. 1976. pap. 1.50 o.p. Willing Pub.
Secrets: A Siboney Romance in Cuba. Frederic Vernon Bouic. 3.50 o.p. (ISBN 0-8181-0029-X). Pageant-Poseidon.
Secrets, Adapted from the Norma Talmadge Picture. Roger Batchelder & Besier, Rudolf. LC 24-21666. Grosset & Dunlap.
Secrets & Suprises. Ann Beattie. 320p. 1983. pap. 3.50 (ISBN 0-446-31114-6). Warner Bks.
Secrets & Surprises. Ann Beattie. 1980. pap. 2.95. Popular Lib.
Secrets & Surprises. Ann Beattie. 1979. 8.95 o.p. (ISBN 0-394-50314-7). Random.
Secrets and Surprises: Short Stories. Ann Beattie. LC 78-57098. 8.95 (ISBN 0-394-50314-7). Random House.
Secrets and Surprises: Short Stories. Ann Beattie. 1980. 2.50 (ISBN 0-445-04534-5). Fawcett Popular Library.
Secrets Beneath the Sea. Robert F. Marx. (O.s.i.). 1975. pap. 1.25 o.s.i. (BT50839). Belmont-Tower.
Secrets Can't Be Kept. Ernest Robertson Punshon. LC 46-444. 1946. The Macmillan Company.
Secrets for Sale: By Charles L. Leonard Pseud. 1st Ed. Mary Violet Heberden. LC 50-9137. 1950. Published for the Crime Club by Doubleday.
Secrets from a Stargazer's Notebook. Debbi K. Smith. 512p. 1982. pap. 3.50 (ISBN 0-553-22587-1). Bantam.
Secrets Not Shared. Aimee Martel. 1981. pap. 2.25 (ISBN 0-8439-0874-2, Leisure Bks). Nordon Pubns.
Secrets of a Superthief. Jack MacLean. 192p. (Orig.). 1983. pap. 5.95 (ISBN 0-425-05645-7). Berkley Pub.
Secrets of Caroline Cherie: Translated from the French by Coburn Gilman. Jacques Laurent. LC 56-7185. 1956. Crown Publishers.
Secrets of Cromwell Crossing. Daoma Winston. 1.50 (ISBN 0-671-80693-9). Pocket Books.
Secrets of Doc Savage. William Murray. (Illus.). pap. 2.95x (ISBN 0-933752-23-7). Odyssey MA.
Secrets of Dr. Taverner. 3d ed., rev. and enl. ed. Violet Mary Firth. LC 79-114320. (Illus.). 1978-1979. 3.95. Llewellyn Publications.
Secrets of Higher Contact. Michael X. 1969. pap. 6.95. G Barker Bks.
Secrets of Hillyard House. Kathleen Thompson Norris. LC 50-3302. 1949. N. Y., Sun Dial Press.
Secrets of Hillyard House. Kathleen Thompson Norris. LC 47-5251. 1947. Doubleday.
Secrets of Mabel Eastlake. Donald Olson. LC 82-11347. 1983. 13.95 (ISBN 0-89479-119-2). A & W Publishers.
Secrets of Sedbury Manor. Marilyn Ross. 1973. (pbk) 0.95. Curtis Books.
Secrets of Stardeep-Time Gate. John Jakes. 1982. pap. 2.50 (ISBN 0-451-11794-8). NAL.
Secrets of the Blood. Felix Jackson. LC 80-14389. 1980. (ISBN 0-689-11076-6). Atheneum.
Secrets of the Children of Og, 1st Part. Rikki. (Story of Og & Man Ser.). (Illus.). 220p. (Orig.). 1982. pap. 10.00 (ISBN 0-910149-01-1). Missing Link.
Secrets of the Convent. Hudson Tuttle. (On cover: The portrait series, no. 1). 1892. The Carter Publishing Company.
Secrets of the Convent and Confessional: An Exhibition of the Influence and Workings of Papacy Upon Society and Republican Institutions. Julia MacNair Wright. LC 9-522. 1872. National Publishing Company.
Secrets of the Heart. Pearl Sydenstricker Buck. LC 76-6550. (John Day Bk.). 1965. 14.37i (ISBN 0-381-98287-4). T Y Crowell.
Secrets of the Heart. Cassie Edwards. 400p. (Orig.). 1982. pap. 3.50 o.s.i. (ISBN 0-8439-1142-5, Leisure Bks). Nordon Pubns.
Secrets of the Heart. Kahlil Gibran. Tr. by Anthony R. Ferris from Arabic. 1978. pap. 4.95 (ISBN 0-8065-0062-X). Citadel Pr.
Secrets of the Heart: Stories. Pearl Sydenstricker Buck. LC 76-6550. 7.95 (ISBN 0-381-98287-4). John Day Co.
Secrets of the Past. Ed. by Reader's Digest Editors. (Orig.). 1980. pap. 2.50 (ISBN 0-425-04551-X). Berkley Pub.
Secrets of the Police. A Thrilling Story. Founded Upon the Play of the Same Name. Grace Miller White & Woods, Albert Herman. LC 33-28362. (On cover: Play book series. no. 95). 1906. J.S. Ogilvie Publishing Company.
Secrets of the Rain Forest. Betty Frost. (Perspectives II Ser.). (Illus.). 48p. (Orig.). (gr. 7-12). 1982. pap. 2.50 (ISBN 0-87879-321-6). Acad Therapy.
Section G: United Planets. Mack Reynolds. 1976. (pbk.) 1.25. Ace Books.
Section 558: Or, The Fatal Letter, from the Diary of Inspector Byrnes. Julian Hawthorne. LC 73-164563. (American fiction reprint series). 1971. (ISBN 0-8369-7040-3). Books for Libraries Press.
Section 558: Or, The Fatal Letter; from the Diary of Inspector Byrnes. Julian Hawthorne. LC 9-2212. Cassell & Company, Limited.
Sector General. James White. 208p. (Orig.). 1983. pap. 2.75 (ISBN 0-345-30851-4, Del Rey). Ballantine.
Security. Esme Wynne-Tyson. LC 27-15393. George H. Doran Company.
Sedgewick Manor: 1st Ed. Ellen V Brown. LC 51-14927. 1951. Pageant Press.
Sedona. Joan Farmer. LC 78-21418. 8.95 (ISBN 0-312-70917-X). St. Martin's Press.
Seduce and Destroy. James Eastwood. (7718). 1968. Dell.
Seduce the Unwary Mind: A Novel by Harry D. Northrop. Harry D Northrop. LC 67-17189. 1967. 4.95. William-Frederick.
Seduce the Unwary Mind: A Reactionary Novel. Harry D. Northrop. 1973. 4.95 (ISBN 0-87164-069-4). William-F.
Seducer. Jule Lange. LC 60-5532. 1960. Random House.
Seducers. Martin Shepard. LC 80-80408. 218p. 1981. Repr. of 1976 ed. 11.95 (ISBN 0-932966-12-8). Permanent Pr.
Seducers in Ecuador. Victoria Mary Sackville-West. LC 25-12986. 1925. George H. Doran Company.
Seduction. David Houston. (Illus.). 208p. (Orig.). 1982. pap. 2.50 (ISBN 0-505-51780-9). Tower Bks.
Seduction. Charlotte Lamb, pseud. (Harlequin Presents Ser.). 192p. 1981. pap. 1.50 (ISBN 0-373-10428-6, Pub. by Harlequin). PB.
Seduction & Other Stories. Joyce Carol Oates. LC 75-4541. (Illus.). 1975. 9.95. (ISBN 0-87685-229-0) (ISBN 0-87685-228-2) (ISBN 0-87685-230-4). Black Sparrow Press.
Seduction & Other Stories. Joyce Carol Oates. 1980. 2.75 (ISBN 0-449-24284-6). Fawcett Crest Books.
Seduction: By Susan Yorke Pseud. Suzette Telenga. LC 60-14398. 1960. Farrar, Straus & Cudahy.
Seduction of Inga. Jon Maas. (Orig.). 1971. pap. 0.95 o.p. (A707N, Award). Univ Pub & Dist.
Seduction of Joe Tynan. Richard Cohen. 1979. pap. 2.25 (ISBN 0-440-17610-7). Dell.
Seduction of Lucy Mattson. Dell McLaren. (Belmont Tower Books). 1977. 1.50 (ISBN 0-505-51179-7). Tower Pubns.
Seduction of Marianna. John Colleton. (Orig.). 1980. pap. 2.95 (ISBN 0-451-12167-8, AE2167, Sig). NAL.
Seduction of the Minotaur. Anais Nin. LC 61-17529. (Illus.). 1961. A. Swallow.
Seductive Babysitters. Ward Fulton. pap. 1.95 o.p. (ISBN 0-87682-241-3, 7241). Barclay Hse.
Seductor Irresistible. new ed. Fernando Rivera. (Pimienta Collection Ser). 160p. (Span.). 1974. pap. 1.00 (ISBN 0-88473-217-7). Fiesta Pub.
See How She Runs. Julia Sorel. LC 77-26784. (Illus.). 1978. 1.95 (ISBN 0-345-27432-6). Ballantine Books.
See How They Run. Helen Grace Carlisle. LC 29-14149. J. Cape and H. Smith.
See How They Run. William M Green. (Kangaroo Book). 1977. 1.75 (ISBN 0-671-80963-6). Pocket Books.
See How They Run. Don M. Mankiewicz. LC 51-9557. 1951. Knopf.
See How They Run. Jerrard Tickell. LC 36-7793. 320p. 1975. Repr. of 1936 ed. 7.50x o.p. (ISBN 0-7182-0903-6). Intl Pubns Serv.
See How They Run: A Novel of Suspense. William M. Green. LC 75-8639. 256p. 1976. 7.95 o.p. (ISBN 0-672-52163-6). Bobbs.
See If He Wins. Richard Spong. LC 49-11514. 1949. Sloane Associates.
See It Again, Sam. Carter Brown, pseud. 1979. pap. 1.50 (ISBN 0-505-51415-X). Tower Bks.
See My Shining Palace! Desemea Wilson. LC 29-1192. E. P. Dutton & Co., Inc.
See Naples & Die. Joseph Nathenson. (Orig.). 1979. pap. 1.95 (ISBN 0-532-23250-X). Woodhill.
See No Evil. William Hughes. 1971. pap. 0.75 o.p. (A895S, Award). Univ Pub & Dist.
See No Evil. Finlay McDermid. LC 59-1493. (Inner sanctum mystery). 1959. Simon and Schuster.
See No Evil. John A. Vizzard. 1970. 6.95 o.p. (20479). S&S.
See Rome and Die. Louisa Revell. LC 57-6758. (Cock Robin mystery). 1957. Macmillan.
See-Saw: A Story of to-Day. Sophie Kerr. LC 19-4968. 1919. Doubleday, Page & Company.
See-Saw, or Civil Service in the Departments. Cynthia Eloise Cleveland. LC 6-20953. 1887. F. B. Dickerson & Co.
See-Saw War. Donald Kurlander & Stephen Tarantal. LC 76-134438. (Illus.). 1970. 1.00. Printed by Noble Offset Printers.
See Texas & Die. Jake Logan. LC 80-82218. 192p. (Orig.). 1978. pap. 1.95 (ISBN 0-86721-160-1). Playboy Pbks.
See the Forest: A Novel. 1st Ed. Shirley E Pfoutz. LC 59-11336. 1959. W. W. Norton.
See the Kid Run. Bob Ottum. 1980. 2.75 (ISBN 0-446-95123-4). Warner Books.
See the Kid Run: A Novel. Bob Ottum. LC 78-9174. 8.95 (ISBN 0-671-23095-6). Simon and Schuster.
See the Living Crocodiles. Voss Bark, Conrad. LC 68-13997. 1968. Walker.
See the Old Lady Decently. Bryan Stanley Johnson. LC 74-4804. 1975. 6.95 (ISBN 0-670-63173-6). Viking Press.
See the Woman. Dallas Barnes. (Signet, Y5529). 1973. (pbk.) 1.25. New American Lib.
See Them Die: An Inner Sanctum 87th Precinct Mystery, by Ed McBain Pseud. Evan Hunter. LC 60-13407. 1960. Simon and Schuster.
See Them Die: An 87th Precinct Mystery. Evan Hunter. (Signet Book). 1976. 1.25. New American Library.
See-Through Revolver. Craig McGregor. LC 78-313030. 1977. 8.75 (ISBN 0-7022-1005-6) (ISBN 0-7022-1006-4). University of Queensland Press.
See What I Mean? Lewis Browne. LC 43-15350. 1943. Random House.
See What I Mean: A Novel... Lewis Browne. LC 44-51248. (New Avon library. 54). C.
See You at the Morgue. Lawrence Goldtree Blochman. LC 62-21186. (Collier mystery classic). 1962. Collier Books.
See You at the Morgue. Lawrence Goldtree Blochman. LC 41-5491. Duell, Sloan and Pearce.
See You in Yasukuni. Gerald Hanley. LC 78-101237. 1970. 6.95. World Pub. Co.
Seed. Peter Cowan. LC 66-74239. 1966. bds., 4.95. Angus & Robertson.
Seed. Charles Gilman Norris. LC 31-33071. 1931. Doubleday, Doran & Company, Inc.
Seed: A Novel of Birth Control. Charles Gilman Norris. LC 30-21871. 1930. Doubleday, Doran & Company, Inc.
Seed and the Fruit. Henri Troyat. LC 56-7494. Simon and Schuster.
Seed & the Sower. Laurens Van Der Post. 1963. 4.50 o.p. Morrow.
Seed Beneath the Snow. Ignazio Silone & Frenaye, Frances, Tr. LC 42-20277. 1942. Harper & Brothers.
Seed Beneath the Snow: New Version Tr. from Italian by Harvey Fergusson II. Ignazio Silone. LC 65-15922. 1965. 6.50. Atheneum.
Seed from the Ukraine. Katharine Nickel. LC 53-8059. 1953. Pageant Press.
Seed in the Wind. Leon Odell Griffith. LC 60-121193. 1960. Random House.
Seed Is Blown. Illus. by Joan Berg. Alice Virginia Wright & Joan Illus Berg. LC 65-20334. 3.95. Rand McNally.
Seed Is Sown: A Historical Novel of Life in Revolutionary South America a Century Ago. 1st Ed. Ottilie Gertrude Boetzkes & Pedro II, Emperor of Brazil. LC 56-112899. Greenwich Book Publishers.
Seed Must First Fall: By Felicia Bond Pseud. 1st Ed. Lanette S Hanson. LC 52-3342. 1952. De Vorss.
Seed of a Woman. Ruth Geller. LC 79-53219. 5.95 (ISBN 0-9603008-0-5). Imp Press.
Seed of Adam. Violet Campbell. LC 34-302460. E. P. Dutton & Co., Inc.
Seed of Desire. Jean Blanche. LC 56-365827. 1956. Castle Books.
Seed of Doubt: A Novel. Day Keene. LC 61-12858. 1961. Simon and Schuster.
Seed of Earth. Robert Silverberg. 1977. 1.50. Ace Books.
Seed of Evil. Barrington J. Bayley. 176p. 1980. 11.95 (ISBN 0-8052-8013-8, Pub. by Allison & Busby England); pap. 4.95 (ISBN 0-8052-8014-6, Pub. by Allison & Busby England). Schocken.
Seed of Evil. Petrina Crawford. 1976. pap. 1.25 o.p. (LB410, Leisure Bks). Nordon Pubns.
Seed of Evil. easy eye ed. Petrina Crawford. pap. 0.60 o.p. Lancer.
Seed of Evil. Petrina Crawford. 1973. pap. 0.95 o.s.i. (75-458). Lancer.
Seed of Evil. Petrina Crawford. 1976. 1.25. Leisure Books.
Seed of Mischief. Willa Gibbs. 1953. Farrar, Straus and Young.
Seed of the Falcon. Catherine Darby, pseud. (falcon saga-10). 1.75 (ISBN 0-445-04253-2). Popular Library.
Seed of the Gods. Zachary Hughes. (Berkley medallion book). 1974. (pbk.) 0.95 (ISBN 0-425-02642-6). Berkley Pub. Co.
Seed of the Land. Isabel Stewart Way. LC 35-10854. 1935. D. Appleton-Century Company, Incorporated.
Seed of the Puritan. Elizabeth Bartol Dewing Kaup. LC 44-2897. 1944. The Dial Press.
Seed of the Righteous. Frank Thomas Bullen. LC 8-29867. Eaton & Mains.
Seed of the Righteous. Juliet Wilbor Tompkins. LC 16-10121. The Bobbs-Merrill Company.
Seed of the Serpent. Esme Davis. LC 47-11572. 1947. Bobbs-Merrill Co.
Seed of the Sun. Wallace Irwin. LC 21-928. George H. Doran Company.
Seed of the Sun. Wallace Irwin. LC 78-54842. (Series: Asian Experience in North America: Chinese and Japanese.). 1978. 21.00 (ISBN 0-405-11308-0). Arno Press.
Seed on the Wind. Rex Stout. LC 30-22905. 1930. The Vanguard Press.
Seed. Spring Night. Two Novels. Tarjei Vesaas & Tarjei Vesaas. LC 65-5918. 1964. American-Scandinavian Foundation.
Seed Thought. Sara Lee Young. LC 14-617916. 1913. Monfort & Company.
Seed-Time and Harvest: Or, "During My Apprenticeship". Fritz Reuter. LC 7-30645. 1871. J. B. Lippincott & Co.
Seed-Time & Harvest; or, During My Apprenticeship. Fritz Reuter. 292p. 1976. Repr. of 1871 ed. 16.50x (ISBN 0-86527-301-4). Fertig.
Seed-Time and Harvest: Or, During My Apprenticeship Translated from the Ut Mine Stromtid of Fritz Reuter. Fritz Reuter. LC 75-5548. 1975. 13.00. H. Fertig.
Seed-Time and Harvest: Or, Whatsoever a Man Soweth, That Shall He Also Reap. Timothy Shay Arthur. LC 6-3417. (On cover: Lovell's library, v. 11, no. 563). J. W. Lovell Company.
Seed Was Sown. Robert Clancy. (Illus.). 124p. 1952. pap. 1.00 (ISBN 0-911312-41-2). Schalkenbach.
Seed Was Sown. Buel W Dunham. LC 49-449147. 1948. L. L. Morrison.

Seed Was Sown. 1st Ed. Maysie Brooks. LC 57-7817. 1957. Vantage Press.
Seedbearers. Peter Valentine Timlett. 1976. (pbk.) 1.50. Bantam Books.
Seedling Stars. 1st Ed. James Blish. LC 57-7109. 1957. Gnome Press.
Seedlings' Harvest. Lillian Elizabeth Becker Roy. LC 10-23740. 1910. 1.25. Wessels & Bissell Co.
Seeds & Other Stories. 193p. 1972. 1.95 o.p. (ISBN 0-8351-0319-6); pap. 1.00 o.p. China Bks.
Seeds Beneath the Snow: Vignettes from the South. Arthenia J. Bates. LC 69-18851. 146p. 1975. 6.95 (ISBN 0-88258-046-9). Howard U Pr.
Seeds in the Passes: Special Issue 25 - The Smith. Robert Summers. pap. 1.00 o.p. The Smith.
Seeds in the Wind. Translated by Adrienne Foulke. Francesco Jovine & Foulke, Adrienne W., 1915- LC 46-7691. 1946. Roy Publishers.
Seeds of Change. Kerry Livgren & Kenneth Boa. 180p. 1983. pap. 7.95 (ISBN 0-89107-265-9, Crossway Bks). Good News.
Seeds of Change. limited collector's ed. Thomas F Monteleone. 1975. (ISBN 0-88950-900-X). Laser Books.
Seeds of Corruption. Sabri Musa. LC 79-24666. 1980. 7.95 (ISBN 0-395-28541-0). Houghton Mifflin.
Seeds of Destruction. Thomas Merton. 328p. 1964. pap. 6.95 (ISBN 0-374-51586-7). FS&G.
Seeds of Enchantment: Being Some Attempt to Narrate the Curious Discoveries of Doctor Cyprian Beamish, M. D., Glasgow; Commandant Rene De Gys, Annamite Army, and the Honourable Richard Assheton Smith, in the Golden Land of Indo-China. Gilbert Frankau. LC 21-93672. 1921. Doubleday, Page & Company.
Seeds of Fire. Kenneth M. Cameron. (Arms Ser.: Vol. II). 288p. 1981. pap. 2.95 (ISBN 0-445-04672-4). Popular Lib.
Seeds of Fury. Lynn Westland, pseud. (Orig.). 1980. pap. text ed. 1.75 (ISBN 0-505-51568-7). Tower Bks.
Seeds of Hiroshima. Edita Morris. LC 66-15753. 1966. 4.00. Braziller.
Seeds of Life. John Taine, pseud. Bd. with White Lilly. 364p. pap. 2.50 o.p. (ISBN 0-486-21626-8). Dover.
Seeds of Life, and White Lily. Eric Temple Bell. LC 66-20328. 1966. Dover Publications.
Seeds of Life, and White Lily: Two Science Fiction Novels, by John Taine (Eric Temple Bell. Eric Temple Bell. (Dover bk. rebound). 1967. 4.00. P. Smith.
Seeds of Life: By John Taine Pseud. Decorations by Ric Binkley. 1st Ed. Eric Temple Bell. LC 51-5874. 1951. Fantasy Press.
Seeds of Murder... Francis Van Wyck Mason. LC 30-208172. 1930. Pub. for The Crime Club, Inc., by Doubleday, Doran & Company, Inc.
Seeds of Rebellion. Chet Cunningham. (Patriots Bicentennial Ser.). 1977. pap. 1.75 o.s.i. (ISBN 0-505-51129-0). Tower Bks.
Seeds of Rebellion. Chet Cunningham. (Belmont Tower Book.). 1977. 1.75. (ISBN 0-505-51129-0). Tower Publications.
Seeds of Singing. Kay McGrath. (Orig.). 1983. pap. 3.95 (ISBN 0-440-19120-3). Dell.
Seeds of Survival. Patrick King. LC 77-77042. 1977. pap. 2.50 o.p. (ISBN 0-912760-52-4). Valkyrie Pr.
Seeds of the Nation: A Novel of Texas and the Oklahoma Territory. 1st Ed. Miriam Richardson Du Mars. LC 54-12884. Exposition Press.
Seeds of Time. Arden G Anthony. LC 40-14678. Dorrance and Company.
Seeds of Time. Ethel Doherty & Long, Louise. LC 38-676020. 1938. E. P. Dutton & Co., Inc.
Seeds of Tomorrow. Mikhail Aleksandrovich Sholokhov & Garry, Stephen, Tr. LC 35-21574. 1935. A. A. Knopf.
Seeds of Turmoil: A Novel of American PW's Brainwashed in Korea. 1st Ed. Freeman Pollard. LC 59-655011. 1959. Exposition Press.
Seedtime. Leo Katz & Follett, Wilson, 1887- Tr. LC 47-45025. 1947. A. A. Knopf.
Seedtime. Vance Palmer. 208p. 1973. 15.00x (ISBN 0-7022-0816-7); pap. 7.95x (ISBN 0-7022-0817-5). U of Queensland Pr.
Seedtime & Harvest. Neville. 3.50 o.p. (ISBN 0-87516-077-8). De Vorss.
Seedtime and Harvest. Mary Emily Pearce. LC 82-5616. 1982. 11.95 (ISBN 0-312-70922-6). St. Martin's Press.
Seedtime and Harvest. Eleanor Blake Atkinson Pratt. LC 35-27258. G. P. Putnam's Sons.
Seedy Gentleman. Peter Robertson. LC 2-30149. 1903. A. M. Robertson.
Seeing. William P. McGivern. (Orig.). 1980. pap. 2.50 (ISBN 0-505-51493-1). Tower Bks.
Seeing. Kate Miller. LC 74-451463. (Inside and outside books, 8). (Illus.). 1969. Oxford U.P.
Seeing Double: By E. X. Ferrars Pseud. 1st Ed. Morna Doris MacTaggart Brown. LC 62-7628. 1962. Published for the Crime Club by Doubleday.
Seeing England with Uncle John. Anne Warner French. LC 8-8098. 1908. The Century Co.
Seeing Eye. Genevieve Knapp McConnell. LC 25-251241. The Cornhill Publishing Company.
Seeing Eye Girl. Barbara Westphall. (Panda Ser.). 1980. pap. 4.95 (ISBN 0-8163-0359-2). Pacific Pr Pub Assn.
Seeing France with Uncle John. Anne Warner French. LC 6-34808. 1906. The Century Co.
Seeing Is Believing. John Dickson Carr. LC 41-12687. 1941. W. Morrow & Co.
Seeing Is Perceiving. Julia Atkinson. 1978. 5.00 (ISBN 0-931040-02-7). Independence Unlimited.
Seeing Red. 1st Ed. Theodora McCormick Du Bois. LC 54-767265. 1954. Published for the Crime Club by Doubleday.
Seeing the Multitudes Delayed. Lissa McLaughlin. (Burning Deck Fiction Ser.). (Illus.). 1979. 15.00 (ISBN 0-930900-75-8); pap. 4.00 (ISBN 0-930900-76-6). Burning Deck.
Seeing Things. Charlotte Painter. LC 75-31501. (Illus.). 8.95 (ISBN 0-394-49739-2). Random House.
Seeing Things. Charlotte Painter. LC 81-1288. 1981. 6.95 (ISBN 0-932654-02-9). Context Publications.
Seeing's Believing. Gerard Hopkins. LC 29-14375. E. P. Dutton & Company, Inc.
Seek-a-Word, No. 1. 128p. 1982. pap. 1.50 (ISBN 0-505-51777-9). Tower Bks.
Seek-a-Word, No. 2. Ed. by Anita Pfouts. 128p. 1982. pap. 1.50 (ISBN 0-505-51792-2). Tower Bks.
Seek-a-Word, No. 3. 128p. 1982. pap. 1.50 (ISBN 0-505-51811-2). Tower Bks.
Seek No Tomorrow. Bernard Alvin Palmer. LC 79-143468. 1971. 3.95. Moody Press.
Seek Out and Destroy. James David Horan. LC 58-128787. 1958. Crown Publishers.
Seek, Strike, & Destroy. Ken Stanton. 1978. pap. 1.25 o.p. (ISBN 0-532-12536-3). Woodhill.
Seek, Strike & Destroy. Ken Stanton. (Aquanauts Ser.). (Orig.). 1971. pap. 0.75 o.p. (532-75406-075). Manor Bks.
Seek, Strike, & Destroy. Ken Stanton. 1978. pap. 1.25 o.p. (ISBN 0-532-12536-3). Manor Bks.
Seek the Fair Land. Walter Macken. 300p. 1962. pap. 3.75 (ISBN 0-330-02062-5, Pub. by Pan Bks England). Irish Bk Ctr.
Seek the North Star. Robert C Wright. LC 72-79873. 1972. 4.95 (ISBN 0-8059-1705-5). Dorrance.
Seeker. Anna Appleby. LC 30-19511. 1930. The Christopher Publishing House.
Seeker. William Alan Bales. LC 75-34415. 6.95 (ISBN 0-07-003557-1). McGraw-Hill.
Seeker. Pierre V. Daigle. 126p. 1973. pap. 3.95 o.p. (ISBN 0-914216-08-2). Acadian Pub.
Seeker and the Sought. Marie Baumer. LC 49-5881. 1949. C. Scribner's Sons.
Seeker of the Gentle Heart. Blaine M. Yorgason & Brenton G. Yorgason. 156p. 1982. 6.95 (ISBN 0-88494-456-5). Bookcraft Inc.
Seekers. Irwin M Herzig. LC 26-144. Press of J. J. Little & Ives Company.
Seekers. John W. Jakes. LC 75-21695. (His The American bicentennial series; v. 3). 1975. 1.75 (ISBN 0-515-03794-X). Pyramid Books.
Seekers. book club ed.. ed. John W. Jakes. LC 78-105286. (Jakes, John W., 1932-. The American Bicentennial Ser.). (His The Kent chronicles; v. 3: Vol. 3). (Illus.). 1977. 3.99. N. Doubleday.
Seekers. Doris Shannon. (Fawcett gold medal). 1975. (pbk.) 0.95. Fawcett.
Seekers. Stanley Waterloo. LC 714. 1900. H. S. Stone & Company.
Seekers of Shar-Nuhn. Ardath Mayhar. LC 79-7887. (Doubleday sciene fiction). 1980. 8.95 (ISBN 0-385-15623-5). Doubleday.
Seekers of the Sky. Richard H. Curtis. (Skymasters Ser.). 1982. pap. 3.25 (ISBN 0-440-07868-7). Dell.
Seekers of Tomorrow. Ed. by Samuel Moskowitz. LC 73-15073. (Classics of Science Fiction Ser.). 441p. 1974. 16.50 o.s.i. (ISBN 0-88355-129-2); pap. 5.95 (ISBN 0-88355-158-6). Hyperion Conn.
Seekers of Tomorrow: Masters of Modern Science Fiction. Ed. by Samuel Moskowitz. (U7083). 1967. Ballantine.
Seeking. Walter E. Adams. 145p. (Orig.). 1981. pap. 3.50 (ISBN 0-937408-04-2). Gospel Pubns FL.
Seeking. Robert S Elegant. LC 68-56457. (Illus.). 1969. 6.95. Funk & Wagnalls.
Seeking a City, a Novel Based on the Biblical Story of Abraham; an Interpretative Account of the Old Testament Patriarch's Prophetic Role; a Modern Portrait of the Ancient Nomad, His Wife Sarah, and Son Isaac. John R. Rice. LC 57-14223. 1957. W. B. Eerdmans Pub. Co.
Seeking Air: A Novel. Barbara Guest. LC 77-17340. 1977. 17.50. (ISBN 0-87685-352-1) (ISBN 0-87685-327-0). Black Sparrow Press.
Seeking Sword. Jaan Kangilaski. 352p. (Orig.). 1981. pap. 2.25 (ISBN 0-345-29073-9, Del Rey). Ballantine.
Seeking Swork. Jaan Kangilaski. LC 76-13215. 1976. 1.95 (ISBN 0-345-25650-6). Ballantine Books.
Seeley-Bohn at School. Donald Gilchrist. LC 40-122340. 1937. Longmans, Green and Co.
Seems Like Time. Kevin Urick. LC 76-62813. (Illus.). 3.00 (ISBN 0-917976-00-2). White Ewe Press.
Seen and Heard Before and After 1914. Mary Findlater & Findlater, Jane Helen, Joint Author. LC 17-26479. 1916. E. P. Dutton and Compnay.
Seen & Heard, Selections from Seen and Heard. Henry W Clune. LC 33-37431. The Democrat and Chronicle.
Seen Dimly Before Dawn. Nigel Balchin. LC 62-14628. 1962. Simon and Schuster.
Seen from the Saddle. Isa Carrington Cabell. LC 12-19582. (On cover: Harper's black & white series). 1893. Harper & Brothers.
Seer. Perley Poore Sheehan. LC 12-237622. 1912. Moffat, Yard and Company.
Seersucker Whipsaw. Ross Thomas. LC 67-19248. 1967. Morrow.
Seesaw. Ira Miller. LC 82-16907. 1982. 12.95 (ISBN 0-312-70935-8). St. Martin's Press.
Seesaw. Ira Miller. 224p. 1983. 12.95 (ISBN 0-312-70935-8, Pub. by Mareu). St Martin.
Seesaw Sunday: A Novel. Leon Arden. LC 65-15833. 4.95. Crown.
Seetee Alert! A "Cap Kennedy" Novel. Gregory Kern. (Secret agent of the spaceways,#6). 1974. (pbk.) 0.95. DAW Books.
Seetee Ship. Jack Williamson. LC 51-11667. 1931. Gnome Press.
Seetee Shock. Jack Williamson. LC 50-7396. 1950. Simon and Schuster.
Seffy, a Little Comedy of Country Manners. John Luther Long. LC 5-40409. 1905. The Bobbs-Merrill Company.
Segaki. David Stacton. LC 59-11954. 1959. Pantheon Books.
Segar a los Muertos. M. M. Huidobro. LC 79-51343. (Coleccion Caniqui). (Illus.). 82p. (Orig., Span.). 1980. pap. 5.95 (ISBN 0-89729-227-8). Ediciones.
Segelfoss Town. Knut Hamsun & Scott, J. S., Tr. LC 25-4775. 1925. A. A. Knopf.
Segunda Parte De la Vida De Lazarillo De Tormes, Sacada De las Cronicas Antiguas De Toledo, Por H. De Luna. Ed. by Elmer R. Sims. xxviii, 138p. 1928. 6.00x o.p. (ISBN 0-292-73368-2). U of Tex Pr.
Segundo. Frank O'Rourke. (Dell first edition, 108). 1956. Dell Pub. Co.
Seibert of the Island. Gordon Ray Young. LC 25-20979. 1925. George H. Doran Company.
Seidman and Son. Elick Moll. LC 58-8062. 1958. Putnam.
Seige of Buckingham Palace: A Novel. Walter Henry Nelson. LC 79-25072. 10.95 (ISBN 0-316-60313-9). Little, Brown.
Seige Perilous. Lester Del Rey. (Orig.). pap. 0.60 o.p. (73-468). Lancer.
Seigneur De Beaufoy. Hamilton Drummond. LC 2-13618. 1902. L. C. Page & Company.
Seigneurs of La Saulaye: Gentlemen Adventurers of New France Two Centuries Ago. Johnston Abbott. LC 28-18896. 1928. The Macmillan Company.
Sein and Schein: A Collection of Ten German Stories. Ed. by Wayne Wonderley. LC 66-15616. 1966. Harcourt, Brace & World.
Seine Mystery. Cleveland Moffett. LC 26-7273. 1925. Dodd, Mead & Company.
Seiners. James Brendan Connolly. LC 4-13284. 1904. C. Scribner's Sons.
Seis Relatos Americanos. Ed. by Donald Walsh. (Span). 1943. pap. 2.25x o.p. (ISBN 0-393-09460-X, NortonC). Norton.
Seize the Dawn. Vanessa Royall. (Orig.). 1983. pap. 3.50 (ISBN 0-440-17335-3). Dell.
Seize the Day. Saul Bellow. 1976. pap. 3.95 (ISBN 0-14-004311-X). Penguin.
Seize the Day. Saul Bellow. 1956. 3.95 o.p. (ISBN 0-670-63176-0). Viking Pr.
Seize the Day: With Three Short Stories and a One-Act Play. Saul Bellow. LC 56-10686. 1956. Viking Press.
Seized by Love. Susan M Johnson. 1979. 1.95 (ISBN 0-87216-503-5). Playboy Press.
Seizer of Eagles. James Willard Schultz. LC 22-12392. 1922. Houghton Mifflin Company.
Seizure of Power. Czeslaw Milosz. LC 55-7838. 1955. Criterion Books.
Seizure of Power. Czes Aw Mi Osz. LC 82-9297. 12.95 (ISBN 0-374-25788-4) (ISBN 0-374-51697-9). Farrar, Straus, Giroux.
Sejanus: The Secret Ruler of Rome. John W. Graham. (Golden Age of Rome Ser.). 1978. pap. 2.50 (ISBN 0-89083-353-2). Zebra.
Sekani's Solution. Tito Banda. (Malawian Writers Ser.). (Illus.). 112p. (Orig.). (gr. 9-12). 1979. pap. 5.00x. Three Continents.
Sekhet. Irene Miller. LC 12-3604. 1912. John Lane.
Selah Harrison. Sarah Broom Macnaughton. LC 6-237065. 1899. Macmillan and Co., Limited.
Selbys. Anne Green. LC 30-11718. E. P. Dutton & Co., Inc.
Seldens in Chicago: A Domestic Tale. Sarah Davieson. LC 6-324995. 1889. Brentano's.
Seldom Without Love: A Mock Mock Epic, by Josephine Curtsinger and E. C. Curtsinger, Jr. Josephine Curtsinger & Eugene Cleveland Curtsinger. LC 65-201949. 4.95. Macmillan.
Seldwyla Folks: Three Singular Tales. Gottfried Keller. LC 70-150545. (Short story index reprint series). 1971. (ISBN 0-8369-3842-9). Books for Libraries Press.
Seldwyla Folks: Three Singular Tales by the Swiss Poet. facsimile ed. Gottfried Keller. Tr. by Wolf Von Schierbrand from Ger. LC 70-150545. (Short Story Index Reprint Ser.). Repr. of 1919 ed. 17.00 (ISBN 0-8369-3842-9). Ayer Co.
Select Conversations with an Uncle... Herbert George Wells. J. Lane.
Select Fables of Esop and Other Fabulists. a new ed. Robert Dodsley. LC 70-161796. (Illus.). 1976. 15.00 set (ISBN 0-404-54101-1). AMS Press.
Select Tales of Tchehov. Anton Pavlovich Chekhov & Constance Black Garnett. LC 64-1685. Barnes & Noble.
Select Tales of Tchehov. Tr. by Constance Garnett from Rus. 1979. Repr. of 1899 ed. lib. bdg. 27.50 (ISBN 0-8495-2002-9). Arden Lib.
Select Tales of Tchehov, 2 vols. Anton Tchehov. Tr. by Constance Garnett. 1961-1963. Repr. of 1949 ed. 8.50 ea. o.p. Vol. 1 (ISBN 0-06-496785-9). Vol. 2 (ISBN 0-06-496786-7). B&N.
Select Translations and Imitations from the French of Marmontell ! and Gresset. Jean Francois Marmontel & Gresset, Jean Baptiste, Louis. LC 7-34698. 1801. Printed for S. Campbell.
Select Works of Robert Rollock, 2 Vols. Robert Rollock. Ed. by William Gunn. 1844. Set. lib. bdg. 48.00 o.p. (ISBN 0-404-05394-7); lib. bdg. 24.25 ea. o.p. (ISBN 0-404-05395-5) (ISBN 0-404-05396-3). AMS Pr.
Selected Austrian Short Stories. Tr. by Marie Busch. LC 70-37260. (Short story index reprint series). 1971. (ISBN 0-8369-4071-7). Books for Libraries Press.
Selected Austrian Short Stories. Tr. by Marie Busch. LC 30-8414. (Half-title: The world's classics, cccxxxvii). 1929. H. Milford, Oxford University Press.
Selected Czech Tales. Tr. by Marie Busch. LC 73-132112. (Short story index reprint series). 1970. Books for Libraries Press.
Selected Czech Tales. facs. ed. (Short Story Index Reprint Ser). 1925. 8.50 o.p. (ISBN 0-8369-3669-8). Bks for Libs.
Selected English Short Stories. Hugh Walker. Repr. of 1914 ed. 10.00 (ISBN 0-89987-093-7). Darby Bks.
Selected English Short Stories. Hugh Walker. 1914. 10.00. Havertown Bks.
Selected English Short Stories (Nineteenth Century) Walker, Hugh, 1855- Comp. LC 22-13968. (Half-title: The world's classics. CXCIII). 1920. H. Milford.
Selected English Short Stories (XIX and XX Centuries) LC 22-5702. (Half-title: The world's classics, CCXXVIII). 1921. H. Milford.
Selected English Short Stories: XIX & XX Centuries. (Third Series)... LC 29-11581. (Half-title: The World's classics. CCCXV). 1927. H. Milford, Oxford University Press.
Selected English Short Stories, 19th & 20th Centuries, 2nd Ser. (World's Classics Ser.: No. 228). 6.95 o.p. (ISBN 0-19-250228-X). Oxford U Pr.
Selected English Short Stories, 19th & 20th Centuries, 2nd Ser. (World's Classics Ser.: No. 228). 6.95 o.p. (ISBN 0-19-250228-X). Oxford U Pr.
Selected English Short Stories: 19th Century. Intro. by Hugh Walker. (World's Classics Ser). 7.95 o.p. (ISBN 0-19-250193-3). Oxford U Pr.
Selected English Short Stories: 19th Century. Intro. by Hugh Walker. (World's Classics Ser). 7.95 o.p. (ISBN 0-19-250193-3). Oxford U Pr.
Selected Essays of Henry Fielding. Henry Fielding & Gerould, Gordon Hall, 1879- Ed. LC 5-21794. (Athenseum press series). Ginn & Company.
Selected Fables. Jean De La Fontaine. LC 68-15259. 1968. 9.50x (ISBN 0-88307-654-3). Gannon.
Selected Fiction. Henry James. 1960. 3.25 o.p. (Evman). Dutton.
Selected French Short Stories of the Nineteenth and Twentieth Centuries. Ed. by James Llewellyn Cattell & Fotos, John Theodore. LC 39-5881. 1939. Thomas Y. Crowell Company.

Selected French Stories of the Nineteenth & Twentieth. Ed. by John Theodore Fotos. J. Fotos. 20.00 (ISBN 0-89987-094-5). Darby Bks.

Selected Lithuanian Short Stores. 2d, rev. and enl. ed. Ed. by Stepas Zobarskas. LC 60-52253. 1960. Voyages Press.

Selected Lithuanian Short Stories. Ed. by Stepas Zobarskas. LC 59-15934. 1959. Voyages Press.

Selected Novels of G. Bernard Shaw. George Bernard Shaw. LC 46-738921. (Half-title: The Caxton library of the world's greatest literature). 1946. Caxton House, Inc.

Selected Novels of Henry James. Henry James. LC 46-7632. (Half-title: The Caxton library of the world's greatest literature). 1946. Caxton House, Inc.

Selected Poems by Ai Qing. Ching Ai & Eugene Eoyang Chen. LC 82-47956. 1981. 20.00 (ISBN 0-253-34519-7) (ISBN 0-253-20302-3). Indiana University Press.

Selected Poetry. William Blake. LC 75-29627. (Signet Classic Poetry). (Signet book). New American Library.

Selected Polish Tales. Tr. by Else Cecilia Mendelssohn Benecke. LC 22-11595. (Half title: The world's classics. cxxx). (Illus.). 1921. H. Milford, Oxford University Press.

Selected Prose & Poetry of Rudyard Kipling. authorized ed. Rudyard Kipling. LC 37-27112. 1937. Garden City Publishing Co., Inc.

Selected Readings. Wolfgang Borchert. Ed. by Anna Otten. LC 72-84089. (Holt series in German literature). 1973. (pbk.) 4.25 (ISBN 0-03-080277-6). Holt.

Selected Readings. Heinz Risse. Ed. by Valentine C. Hubbs. LC 72-84091. (Holt series in German literature). 1973. (pbk.) 4.25 (ISBN 0-03-085978-6). Holt.

Selected Readings from the Most Popular Novels: For the Use of Public Readers and for the Department of English Literature and Public Speaking in Schools and Colleges. Ed. by William Mather Lewis. 1903. Hinds & Noble.

Selected Russian Short Stories. Tr. by Alfred Edward Chamot. 2.75 o.p. (WC287). Oxford U Pr.

Selected Russian Short Stories: Chosen and Translated. Ed. by Alfred Edward Chamot. LC 26-18393. (Half-title: The world's classics. cclxxxvii). 1925. H. Milford. Oxford University Press.

Selected Science Fiction & Fantasy Stories. Jack London. LC 76-52712. (Illus.). 1979. 8.50 (ISBN 0-934882-03-7). Fictioneer Bks.

Selected Short Fiction. Charles Dickens & Deborah A Thomas. LC 76-368436. (Penguin English library). (Illus.). 1976. 2.95 (ISBN 0-14-043103-9). Penguin.

Selected Short Stories. Wolfgang Borchert. Ed. by A. W. Hornsey. 1964. 3.35 (ISBN 0-08-010714-1); pap. 3.00 (ISBN 0-08-010713-3). Pergamon.

Selected Short Stories. Anton Pavlovich Chekhov. Ed. by G. A. Birkett & Gleb Struve. 1951. 8.25x o.p. (ISBN 0-19-872004-1, OxC). Oxford U Pr.

Selected Short Stories. William Faulkner. 1962. 3.95 o.s.i. (ISBN 0-394-60324-9, M324). Modern Lib.

Selected Short Stories. Ed. by Claude Moore Fuess. LC 14-5754. (Merrill's English texts). Charles E. Merrill Company.

Selected Short Stories. Maksim Gorkii. LC 58-8959. 1959. F. Ungar Pub. Co.

Selected Short Stories. Maksim Gorkii. 410p. 1975. 12.95x (ISBN 0-8464-0834-1). Beekman Pubs.

Selected Short Stories. Maksim Gorkii. 410p. 1974. 4.95 (ISBN 0-8285-0981-6, Pub. by Progress Pubs USSR). Imported Pubns.

Selected Short Stories. Maksim Gorkii. LC 58-8959. 1959. 8.00 o.p. (ISBN 0-8044-2276-1). Ungar.

Selected Short Stories. Alexander Grin. Ed. & tr. by Nicholas Luker. 250p. 1983. 17.50 (ISBN 0-88233-684-3); pap. 6.00. Ardis Pubs.

Selected Short Stories. facsimile ed. Per Hallstrom. Tr. by F. J. Fielden from Swedish. LC 77-144155. (Short Story Index Reprint Ser.). Repr. of 1922 ed. 16.00 (ISBN 0-8369-3770-8). Ayer Co.

Selected Short Stories. Thomas Handy. LC 48-18948. (Story Cavalcade, No. 1). 1948. Rodale Press.

Selected Short Stories. Nathaniel Hawthorne. Ed. by Alfred Kazin. LC 67-133. (Fawcett premier book). (Masterworks series). 1966. Fawcett Publications.

Selected Short Stories. Henry James. LC 63-2761. (Penguin modern classics, 1919). 1963. Penguin Books.

Selected Short Stories. Gwyn Jones. LC 74-175073. (Oxford paperbacks 323). 1974. (u.s.) 3.95 (ISBN 0-19-281162-2). Oxford University Press.

Selected Short Stories. Franz Kafka. LC 52-9771. (Modern library of the world's best books 283). 1952. Modern Library.

Selected Short Stories. Norman Lavers. (Juniper Bks: No. 28). 1979. pap. 3.00. Juniper Pr Wi.

Selected Short Stories. Guy De Maupassant. LC 77-24815. (Penguin classics). 1971. 0.50 (ISBN 0-14-044243-X). Penguin.

Selected Short Stories. Guy de Maupassant. Tr. by Roger Colet. (Classics Ser). 1971. pap. 3.95 (ISBN 0-14-044243-X). Penguin.

Selected Short Stories. John O'Hara. LC 56-8834. (Modern library of the world's best books 211). 1956. Modern Library.

Selected Short Stories. Edgar Allan Poe & Edgar Allan Poe. LC 51-2534. 1952. Fine Editions Press.

Selected Short Stories. Irwin Shaw. LC 61-10674. (Modern library of the world's best books, 319). 1961. Modern Library.

Selected Short Stories. Hjalmar Emil Fredrik Soderberg. LC 35-249064. 1935. Princeton University Press.

Selected Short Stories. Herbert George Wells. 1979. pap. 3.95 (ISBN 0-14-001310-5). Penguin.

Selected Short Stories. Ed. Introd. by Irving Howe. Isaac Bashevis Singer. LC 66-13012. (Mod. lib. of the world's best bks.). 2.45. Random.

Selected Short Stories. Edited with an Introd. by Quentin Anderson. Rev. Henry James. LC 57-963. (Rinehart editions, 31). 1957. Rinehart.

Selected Short Stories: Edited with an Introd. by Quentin Anderson. Henry James. LC 50-14135. 1950. Rinehart.

Selected Short Stories. Edited with an Introd. by QuentinAnderson. Rev. Henry James. LC 57-9639. (Rinehart editions, 31). 1957. Rinehart.

Selected Short Stories. Introd. and Notes by A. W. Hornsey. Wolfgang Borchert. LC 64-7680. (Commonwealth & intl. lib. of sci., tech., engin. and liberal studies. Pergamon Oxford German ser. v.1, no.283) Bibl.). 1965. Pergamon.

Selected Short Stories of Honore De Balzac. Honore De Balzac. Tr. by Sylvia Raphael. LC 77-366318. (Penguin classics). 1977. 2.95 (ISBN 0-14-044325-8). Penguin.

Selected Short Stories of John O'Hara. Lionel Trilling. LC 56-8834. Date not set. 6.95 (ISBN 0-394-60494-6). Modern Lib.

Selected Short Stories of Nathaniel Hawthorne. Ed. by Alfred Kazin. 1977. pap. 2.25 (ISBN 0-449-30846-4, Prem). Fawcett.

Selected Short Stories of Sinclair Lewis. Sinclair Lewis. LC 35-9053. 1935. Doubleday, Doran & Company, Inc.

Selected Short Stories of Sinclair Lewis. Sinclair Lewis. LC 38-31836. 1937. Doubleday, Doran & Company, Inc.

Selected Short Stories of Thein Pe Myint. Tr. by Patricia M. Milne. 105p. 1973. 4.00 (ISBN 0-87727-091-0, DP 91). Cornell SE Asia.

Selected Short Stories of Thein Pe Myint. Thein Pe Myint & Patricia M Milne. LC 75-9882. (Cornell University. Southeast Asia Program.). (Data paper no. 91). 1973. 4.00. Southeast Asia Program, Cornell University.

Selected Short Stories of Thomas Hardy. Thomas Hardy. LC 48-682. 1948. Story Classics.

Selected Short Stories of Today. Ed. by Dorothy Scarborough. LC 35-6197. Farrar & Rinehart, Incorporated.

Selected Short Stories of William Faulkner. William Faulkner. 5.95 (ISBN 0-394-60456-3). Modern Lib.

Selected Short Stories of 1939. LC 40-1417. 1939. The Pyramid Press.

Selected Short Stories. With an Introd. by L. E. Fredman. Nathan Frederick Spielvogel. LC 57-48328. 1956. Hawthorn Press.

Selected Silvae, with Introd. and Notes by Joseph Henry Howard. Publius Papinius Statius. Ed. by Howard, Joseph Henry. LC 52-17027. 1911-1950.

Selected Spanish Short Stories. Robert R. Ashburg. Ed. by F. Herrera Y Sanchez & R. R. Ashburn. 1957. 3.50 ea. o.p. T Y Crowell.

Selected Spanish Stories of the Nineteenth & Twentieth Centuries. Robert R. Ashburn. Repr. of 1943 ed. 25.00 (ISBN 0-89987-095-3). Darby Bks.

Selected Stories. Sholom Aleichem. 2.95 o.p. (ISBN 0-394-60145-9, 145). Modern Lib.

Selected Stories. Benny Andersen. 120p. 1983. pap. 6.00 (ISBN 0-915306-25-5). Curbstone.

Selected Stories. Anton Pavlovich Chekhov. LC 63-25063. (World's classics, 599). 1963. Oxford University Press.

Selected Stories. Gilbert Keith Chesterton. Ed. by Kingsley Amis. 282p. 1972. 9.95 (ISBN 0-571-09914-9). Faber & Faber.

Selected Stories. Roald Dahl. 1968. 3.95 o.s.i. (ISBN 0-394-60242-0, 242). Modern Lib.

Selected Stories. N. V. Gonzalez. 1964. 4.95 o.p. (ISBN 0-8040-0270-3). Swallow.

Selected Stories. Nadine Gordimer. LC 75-29460. 1976. 10.00 (ISBN 0-670-63197-3). Viking Press.

Selected Stories. Vladimir Galaktionovich Korolenko. 391p. 1978. 5.45 (Pub. by Progress Pubs USSR). Imported Pubns.

Selected Stories. Mary Lavin. LC 59-6293. 1959. Macmillan.

Selected Stories. 3rd ed. Lu Hsun. 1972. 6.95 (ISBN 0-8351-0326-9); pap. 5.50 (ISBN 0-8351-0327-7). China Bks.

Selected Stories. Guy De Maupassant. Tr. by James Lewis May. LC 26-26503. (International library). S. Paul & Co., Ltd.

Selected Stories. Osman Edward Middleton. LC 76-376960. (ISBN 0-908565-01-1) (ISBN 0-908565-02-X). J. McIndoe.

Selected Stories. Konstantin Georgievich Paustovskii. 335p. 1974. 5.45 (ISBN 0-8285-1020-2, Pub. by Progress Pubs USSR). Imported Pubns.

Selected Stories. Isaac Loeb Peretz. LC 73-91342. (Illus.). 1974. 6.95 (ISBN 0-8052-3541-8). Schocken Books.

Selected Stories. Victor Sawden Pritchett. LC 78-23587. 1979. 4.95 (ISBN 0-394-72859-9). Vintage Books.

Selected Stories. Victor Sawdon Pritchett. LC 77-90244. 10.00 (ISBN 0-394-50128-4). Random House.

Selected Stories. Arthur Thomas Quiller-Couch. LC 24-6157. (Half-title: The King's treasuries of literature). 1921. J. M. Dent & Sons, Ltd.

Selected Stories. Opie Percival Read. LC 7-36498. F. J. Schulte & Company.

Selected Stories. Robert Walser. LC 82-9257. 13.95 (ISBN 0-374-25901-1). Farrar, Straus, Giroux.

Selected Stories. Eudora Welty. 6.95 (ISBN 0-394-60445-8). Modern Lib.

Selected Stories. Pelham Grenville Wodehouse. LC 58-11472. (Modern library of the world's best books 126). 1958. Modern Library.

Selected Stories, Containing All of A Curtain of Green, and Other Stories, and The Wide Net, and Other Stories. Eudora Welty. LC 54-9969. (Modern library of the world's best books 290). 1954. Modern Library.

Selected Stories from Gujarat. Ed. by Sarla Jagmohan. (Jaico Paperback Ser). pap. 1.75 o.p. (ISBN 0-87902-091-1). Orientalia.

Selected Stories from Gujarat. Ed. & tr. by Sarla Jagmohan. 212p. 1961. pap. 1.00 o.p. (ISBN 0-88253-041-0). InterCulture.

Selected Stories from Guy De Maupassant: Edited with Introductions in English and French, Notes, Exercises and Vocabulary. Guy De Maupassant. Ed. by Moore, Olin Harris & Havens, George Remington. LC 28-21170. (International modern language series). Ginn and Company.

Selected Stories from Kipling. Rudyard Kipling & Phelps, William Lyon, 1865- Ed. LC 21-217592. 1921. Doubleday, Page & Company.

Selected Stories from O. Henry Pseud. William Sydney Porter. Ed. by Smith, Charles Alphonso. LC 22-11515. 1922. Doubleday, Page & Company.

Selected Stories of Alphonse Daudet. Alphonse Daudet. pap. 3.95 o.p. (ISBN 0-498-04011-9, Prpta). A S Barnes.

Selected Stories of Bret Harte. Bret Harte. Repr. lib. bdg. 20.00 (ISBN 0-8414-5012-9). Folcroft.

Selected Stories of Bret Harte: The Luck of Roaring Camp, The Outcasts of Poker Flat Tennessees Partner Miles and Other Tales. Bret Harte. LC 46-1319. (Half-title: The Caxton library of the world's greatest literature). 1946. Caxton House, Inc.

Selected Stories of Jack London. Jack London. LC 34-382854. 1930. Pub. for Three Pay Sales Corporation, by The World Syndicate Publishing Company, Cleveland, New York.

Selected Stories of Katherine Mansfield. Katherine Mansfield & Daniel Marcus Davin. LC 70-529960. (Oxford paperbacks, 183). 1969 (ISBN 0-19-281044-8). Oxford U.P.

Selected Stories of Lu Hsun. Shu-Jen Chou. LC 72-92717. (Illus.). 1972-1973. 8.50 (ISBN 0-88211-042-X). Oriole Editions.

Selected Stories of Lu Hsun. Lu Hsun. Tr. by Yang Hsien-Yi & Gladys Yang. 1977. pap. 4.95 (ISBN 0-393-00848-7, Norton Lib). Norton.

Selected Stories of Lu Hsun I.E. S. Chou. Shu-Jen Chou. LC 77-931. (Norton library; N848). 1977. 3.95 (ISBN 0-393-00848-7). Norton.

Selected Stories of Mary E. Wilkins Freeman. Mary Eleanor Wilkins Freeman & Marjorie Pryse. LC 82-21179. 25.95 (ISBN 0-393-01726-5) (ISBN 0-393-30106-0). W.W. Norton.

Selected Stories of Mary E. Wilkins Freeman. Ed. by Marjorie Pryse. 1983. 27.50 (ISBN 0-393-01726-5); pap. 5.95 (ISBN 0-393-30106-0). Norton.

Selected Stories of Sean O'Faolain. Sean O'Faolain. LC 78-5780. 1978. 9.95 (ISBN 0-316-63285-6). Little, Brown.

Selected Stories of Sholom Aleichem: Pseud. With an Introd. by Alfred Kazin. Shalom Rabinowitz. LC 56-88365. (Modern library of the world's best books 145). 1956. Modern Library.

Selected Stories of Thomas Hardy. John Barrington Wain. (Orig.). 1966. pap. 1.95 o.p. (ISBN 0-312-71120-4, Papermac). St Martin.

Selected Stories of Xiao Hong. Xiao Hong. Tr. by Howard Goldbratt from Chinese. 220p. 1982. pap. 3.50 (ISBN 0-8351-1049-4). China Bks.

Selected Stories: Readings and Poems. Persis Guffy. LC 38-17819. Persis Guffy.

Selected Stories, Reminiscences, and Essays. Mikhail Osorgin & Donald M Fiene. LC 81-20618. 22.50 (ISBN 0-88233-445-X). Ardis Publishers.

Selected Stories: The Luck of Roaring Camp, The Outcasts of Poker Flat, Tennessee's Partner, Mliss, and Other Tales. Bret Harte. LC 47-6520. 1947. Sun Dial Press.

Selected Stories: With Illus. by Jacob Getlar Smith. Alphonse Daudet. Ed. by Jerome Irving Rodale. LC 52-18689. 1951. Story Classics.

Selected Tales. Algernon Blackwood. 381p. 1971. Repr. of 1970 ed. 6.50x o.p. (ISBN 0-8426-1167-3). Verry.

Selected Tales. Algernon Blackwood. (Illus.). 1964. 7.95 o.p. (ISBN 0-212-35910-X). Dufour.

Selected Tales. Henry James. 1956. 8.95 o.p. (ISBN 0-212-35902-9). Dufour.

Selected Tales. Rudyard Kipling & Mittell, Sherman Fabian, 1902- Ed. LC 43-273084. 1935. National Home Library Foundation.

Selected Tales. Nikolai Semenovich Leskov. Tr. by David Magarshack. 1962. price not set o.p. FS&G.

Selected Tales. Nikolai Semenovich Leskov. Tr. by David Magarshack from Rus. 1961. pap. 3.45 o.p. (ISBN 0-374-50208-0, N220, Noonday). FS&G.

Selected Tales. Guy De Maupassant. Ed. by Saxe Commins. LC 50-6135. (Illus.). 1950. Random House.

Selected Tales. new paperback ed. Edgar Allan Poe. Ed. by Julian Symons. LC 79-41696. (World's classics). 1980. 4.95 (ISBN 0-19-281522-9). Oxford University Press.

Selected Tales and Poems: Edited with an Introd. by Richard Chase. Herman Melville. LC 51-244. (Rinehart editions, 36). 1950. Rinehart.

Selected Tales and Sketches. 3d ed. with introductions by hyatt h. waggoner. ed. Nathaniel Hawthorne. LC 74-94894. (Rinehart editions, 33). 1970. Holt, Rinehart and Winston.

Selected Tales and Sketches: Introd. by Hyatt H. Waggoner. Nathaniel Hawthorne. LC 50-142232. (Rinehart editions, 33). 1950. Rinehart.

Selected Tales: Edited with an Introd., by Saxe Commins. Guy De Maupassant. Ed. by Saxe Commins. LC 50-6135. 1950. Random House.

Selected Tales from Conrad. Joseph Conrad & Nigel Stewart. LC 77-377818. (Faber paperbacks). 1977. 5.95 (ISBN 0-571-10763-X). Faber.

Selected Tales from Conrad. Ed. by Nigel Stewart. 224p. 1977. pap. 5.95 (ISBN 0-571-10763-X). Faber & Faber.

Selected Tales from the Don. Mikhail Aleksandrovich Sholokhov. Ed. by C. G. Bearne. 1967. 7.75 o.p. (ISBN 0-08-012157-8); pap. 4.00 o.p. (ISBN 0-08-012156-X). Pergamon.

Selected Tales. Newly Translated with an Introd. by David Magarshack. 1st Ed. Turgenev, Ivan Sergeevich. LC 60-10685. (Anchor books, A203). 1960. Doubleday.

Selected Tales of Algernon Blackwood: Stories of the Supernatural and the Uncanny. Algernon Blackwood. LC 44-4359. 1942. Penguin Books.

Selected Tales of Ivan Turgenev see First Love & Other Tales.

Selected Tales of Laiozhai. Pu Songling. (Panda Bks.). 151p. (Orig.). 1981. pap. 2.95 (ISBN 0-8351-0943-7). China Bks.

Selected Tales. Translated by David Magarshack. With an Introd. by V. S. Pritchett. Nikolai Semenovich Leskov. LC 61-109591. 1961. Farrar, Straus and Cudahy.

Selected Tales; with an Introduction by Kenneth Graham. Edgar Allan Poe. LC 67-95291. (Classic American texts). 1967. Oxford U.P.

Selected Works. Jack London. LC 64-15718. (Classics to grow on). 1966. Parents' Magazine's Cultural Institute.

Selected Works. Vera Fedorovna Panova. LC 77-357336. (Progress Soviet authors library). 1976. Progress.

Selected Works of Djuna Barnes. Djuna Barnes. 366p. 1962. 12.95 (ISBN 0-374-25936-4). FS&G.

Selected Works of Israel Zangwill. Israel Zangwill. LC 72-38728. (Short story index reprint series). 1972. (ISBN 0-8369-4141-1). Books for Libraries Press.

Selected Works of Israel Zangwill: Children of the Ghetto, Ghetto Comedies, Ghetto Tragedies; a Golden Jubilee Volume. Israel Zangwill. LC 38-36267. 1938. The Jewish Publication Society of America.

Selected Works of Zinaida Hippius. Zinaida Nikolaevna Gippius. LC 72-188447. 1972. 10.00 (ISBN 0-252-00260-1). University of Illinois Press.

Selected Works. Translated from the Italian and with an Introd. by R. W. Flint. Cesare Pavese. LC 68-14914. 1968. Farrar, Straus and Giroux.

Selected Writings. Truman Capote. LC 63-8334. 1963. Random House.

Selected Writings. Lafcadio Hearn & Goodman, Henry, 1893- Ed. LC 49-11635. 1949. Citadel Press.

Selected Writings. James Albert Michener. LC 57-6493. (Modern library of the world's best books, 296). 1957. Modern Library.

Selected Writings: Edited, with an Introd., by Henry Steele Commager. William Dean Howells. LC 50-9450. 1950. Random House.

Selected Writings of Blaise Cendrars. Blaise Cendrars & Walter Albert. LC 78-14223. 1978. 19.75 (ISBN 0-313-21020-9). Greenwood Press.

Selected Writings of E. T. A. Hoffmann. Ernst Theodor Amadeus Hoffmann. Ed. by Leonard J. Kent & Elizabeth C. Knight. LC 73-88790. (Illus.). 1969. University of Chicago Press.

Selected Writings of Herman Melville: Complete Short Stories, Typee and Billy Budd, Foretopman. Herman Melville. LC 51-14537. (Modern library of the world's best books). 1952. Modern Library.

Selected Writings of Joaquin Miller. Joaquin Miller. LC 76-25508. (Illus.). 1977. 9.95 (ISBN 0-913522-05-8). Urion Press.

Selected Writings of the Ingenious Mrs. Aphra Behn... Together with a Critical Portrait by Robert Phelps by Way of Introduction. Aphra Amis Behn. LC 50-81461. 1950. Grove Press.

Selected Writings of William Goyen. William Goyen. LC 73-20592. (Illus.). 1974. 8.95, 2.95 (pbk.). (ISBN 0-394-49284-6) (ISBN 0-394-49284-6). Random House.

Selection from the World's Greatest Short Stories. facsimile ed. Ed. by Sherwin Cody. LC 74-106267. (Short Story Index Reprint Ser.). 1902. 20.00 o.p. (ISBN 0-8369-3304-4). Ayer Co.

Selection from the World's Greatest Short Stories. facsimile ed. Ed. by Sherwin Cody. LC 74-106267. (Short Story Index Reprint Ser.). 1902. 20.00 o.p. (ISBN 0-8369-3304-4). Arno.

Selection from the World's Greatest Short Stories: Illustrative of the History of Short Story Writing, with Critical and Historical Comments. Sherwin Cody. LC 74-106267. (Short story index reprint series). 1970. (ISBN 0-8369-3304-4). Books for Libraries Press.

Selection from the World's Greatest Short Stories, Illustrative of the History of Short-Story Writing, with Critical and Historical Comments. 10th ed. Ed. by Sherwin Cody. (The "world's best" series, ed. by S. Cody). 1912. A. C. McClurg & Company.

Selection from the World's Greatest Short Stories: Illustrative of the History of Short Story Writing, with Critical and Historical Comment. re-edited ed. Ed. by Sherwin Cody. LC 40-13735. A. C. McClurg & Co.

Selection of Letters of C. F. W. Walther. Carl F. Walther. Ed. by Carl S. Meyer. (Seminar Editions Ser). (Orig.). 1969. pap. 2.95x o.p. (1-1995). Fortress.

Selection of Short Stories. Peter Neagoe. Ed. by J. S. Mayfield. 1969. 6.50x o.p. (ISBN 0-8156-8050-3); pap. 2.50x o.p. (ISBN 0-8156-8051-1). Syracuse U Pr.

Selection of Stories. Peter Neagoe. LC 78-4346. (Illus.). 1969. 2.50. Syracuse University.

Selection Stories. Paul Johann Von Heyse. LC 7-6609. (Overland library no. 4). L. Schick.

Selections from British Fiction: 1880-1900. Ed. by Ian Fletcher. LC 72-88055. (Signet classic, CJ606). 1972. (pbk) 1.95. New American Library.

Selections from Don Quijote. Miguel de Cervantes de Saavedra. Ed. by J. D. Fords. 1908. text ed. 3.75 o.p. (ISBN 0-669-31369-6). Heath.

Selections from Don Quixote. Miguel de Cervantes de Saavedra. Tr. by Florence Fishman from Span. (gr. 9 up). 1950. pap. text ed. 0.95 o.p. (ISBN 0-8120-0326-8). Barron.

Selections from Gavin Douglas. Gawin Douglas & Publius. Aeneis Virgilius Maro. LC 64-5751. (Clarendon med'eval and Tudor series). 1964. Clarendon Press.

Selections from Gavin Douglas. Maro Publius Vergilius & David F. C Coldwell. LC 64-5751. (Clarendon med'eval and Tudor series). 1964. Clarendon Press.

Selections from Guy De Maupassant: Ten Short Stories, Ed. with an Introduction, Linguistic and Literary Notes, and a Vocabulary. Guy De Maupassant. LC 6-10322. (International modern language series). Ginn & Company.

Selections from Guy De Maupassant: Ten Short Stories, Ed. with an Introduction, Linguistic and Literary Notes, Exercises, and a Vocabulary. Guy De Maupassant. LC 20-5139. (International modern language series). Ginn and Company.

Selections from Homer's Iliad. Homer. Ed. by Allen R. Benner. (Gr.). 1976. Repr. of 1931 ed. text ed. 18.95x (ISBN 0-89197-636-1). Irvington.

Selections from Homer's Iliad. Homerus & Allen Rogers Benner. LC 79-18756. (Series: Twentieth Century Text Books.). 1979. 14.95 (ISBN 0-89197-636-1). Irvington Publishers.

Selections from London Labour & the London Poor. Henry Mayhew. pap. 2.50 o.p. (ISBN 0-19-250607-2). Oxford U Pr.

Selections from Marcel Proust. Marcel Proust & Payen-Payne, James Bertrand De Vinchdls. LC 36-28465. 1930. Oxford University Press, H. Milford.

Selections from P. K. Rosegger's Waldheimat: With Introduction and Explanatory Notes. Peter Rosegger. Ed. by Fossler, Laurence. LC 32-30595. 1895. Ginn & Company.

Selections from Perez De Ayala. Ramon Perez De Ayala. Ed. by Adams, Nicholson Barney & Stoudemire, Sterling Aubrey. LC 34-148875. (Norton Spanish series. vol. iv). W. W. Norton & Company, Inc.

Selections from "The Deerslayer," "The Last of the Mohicans," "The Pilot," "The Red Rover," "The Spy" and "A Naval History of the United States.". James Fenimore Cooper. (S&S little classics). 1902. Street and Smith.

Selections from the Greek Lyric Poets. Tr. by Francis Joseph McCool. (Collection of Greek and Latin classics. P. Collin, S.J., 3d.). 1939. H. Dessain.

Selections from the Prose Tales of Edgar Allan Poe: With Notes and Introduction. Edgar Allan Poe. LC 1-30926. (Macmillan's pocket American and English classics). 1901. The Macmillan Company.

Selections from the Prose Tales of Edgar Allan Poe: With Notes and Introduction. Edgar Allan Poe. LC 15-20312. (Macmillan's pocket American and English classics). 1914. The Macmillan Company.

Selections from the Sketch Book. Washington Irving & Smith, Lewis Worthington, 1866- Ed. LC 9-29771. 0.25. A. Flanagan Company.

Selections from the Tatler & the Spectator. Angus Ross. 1982. pap. 6.95 (ISBN 0-14-043130-6). Penguin.

Selections from the World's Greatest Short Stories, Illustrative of the History of Short Story Writing: With Critical and Historical Comments. by sherwin cody... ed. Ed. by Sherwin Cody. LC 2-16453. 1902. A. C. McClurg and Company.

Selections from the Writings of Eleanor C. Donnelly: With Notes and Questions. Eleanor Cecilia Donnelly. LC 27-7265. (Lakeside series of English readings. no. 101.). 1904. Ainsworth & Company.

Selections from the Writings of John J. Ingalls. John James Ingalls. LC 3-302. Hudson Press.

Selections from Twice-Told Tales. Nathaniel Hawthorne & Gaston, Charles Robert, Ed. LC 1-24973. (Macmillan's pocket American and English classics). 1901. The Macmillan Company.

Selections from William Caxton. William Caxton & Norman Francis Blake. LC 73-163858. (Clarendon medieval and Tudor series). (Illus.). 1973. (ISBN 0-19-871081-X). Clarendon Press.

Selena. Ernest Brawley. LC 78-65199. 1979. 9.95 (ISBN 0-689-10951-2). Atheneum.

Selena. Ernest Brawley. (Signet Book). 1980. 2.75 (ISBN 0-451-09242-2). New American Library.

Selene: A Story. Kenneth Young. LC 9-1198. The Daily Herald Job Office.

Selesai Sudah. Shahnon Ahmad. (Karyawan Malaysia Ser.). (Malay.). 1979. pap. text ed. 3.25x o.p. (00352). Heinemann Ed.

Selestor's Men of Atlantis. Clara Iza Tibbetts Von Ravn. LC 37-8402. The Christopher Publishing House.

Self. Beverley Nichols. LC 41-6177. (On cover: Penguin books, 138). 1938. Penguin Books Limited.

Self. Rebecca Ruter Springer. LC 8-14041. 1861. J. B. Lippincott & Co.

Self- Starting Wheel. 1st Ed. William Murray. LC 60-599994. 1960. Dutton.

Self-Accused. Frank Morton. 1893. G. W. Dillingham, Successor to G. W. Carleton & Co.

Self and the Other. Vivian Cory. LC 11-34727. 1911. 1.50. Press of W. G. Hewitt.

Self-Appointed Saint. Audrey Erskine Lindop. LC 74-25114. 1975. 7.95 (ISBN 0-385-03050-9). Doubleday.

Self-Betrayed: A Novel. 1st Ed. Joseph Wechsberg. LC 54-12041. 1955. Knopf.

Self Condemned. Wyndham Lewis. (Illus.). 420p. 1983. 20.00 (ISBN 0-87685-576-1); deluxe ed. 30.00 (ISBN 0-87685-577-X); pap. 12.50 (ISBN 0-87685-575-3). Black Sparrow.

Self-Condemned. A Romance. Thomas Gaspey. LC 44-297794. 1836. Harper & Brothers.

Self-Control: A Novel. Mary Balfour Brunton. LC 73-22009. (Feminist Controversy in England, 1788-1810). 1974. (2 vols.) 44.00 (ISBN 0-8240-0852-9). Garland Pub.

Self-Denying Ordinance. M Hamilton. LC 7-944. (Half-title: Appletons' town and country library, no. 183). 1895. D. Appleton and Company.

Self-Devoted Friend. Marvin Cohen. LC 67-30102. (New Directions book). 1968. New Directions.

Self-Discovery. Vladimir Ivanovich Savchenko. LC 78-31292. (Macmillan's Best of Soviet Science Fiction). 11.95 (ISBN 0-02-606840-0). McMillan.

Self-Discovery. Vladimir Ivanovich Savchenko. LC 79-21125. 1980. 3.95. Collier Books.

Self-Doomed: A Novel. Benjamin Leopold Farjeon. LC 6-38767. (Harper's handy series. no. 27). 1885. Harper & Brothers.

Self-Effacement of Malachi Joseph. Everett Titsworth Tomlinson. LC 7-25164. 1906. The Griffith & Rowland Press.

Self-Giving: A Story of Christian Missions. William Folwell Bainbridge. LC 6-5012. D. Lothrop.

Self-Made Countess: The Justification of a Husband. Henrietta Eliza Vaughan Stannard. LC 5148. 1901. J. B. Lippincott Company.

Self-Made Mad. (Mad Ser.). (Illus.). 192p. 1977. pap. 1.50 (ISBN 0-446-88862-1). Warner Bks.

Self-Made Man's Wife: Her Letters to Her Son Being the Woman's View of Certain Famous Correspondence. Charles Eustace Merriman. LC 5-8339. 1905. G. P. Putnam's Sons.

Self-Made: Or, Living for Those We Love. E. A. Welty. 1868. Sheldon and Company.

Self-Made Thief. Hulbert Footner. LC 29-3662. 1929. Pub. for the Crime Club, Inc., by Doubleday, Doran & Company, Inc.

Self-Made Woman. Faith Baldwin Cuthrell. LC 32-23564. Farrar & Rinehart, Incorporated.

Self-Made Woman: A Novel. Ruth Harris. LC 82-12752. 14.38 (ISBN 0-02-548280-7). Macmillan.

Self-Made Woman: Or, Mary Idyl's Trials and Triumphs. Emma May Buckingham. LC 6-196526. 1873. S. R. Wells.

Self or Bearer.". Walter Besant. (On cover: Seaside library. Pocket ed., no. 651). 1885. G. Munro.

Self or Bearer.". Walter Besant. (On cover: Lovell's library, v. 13, no. 699). 1886. J. W. Lovell Company.

Self-Portrait: A Story. Nicolai Rabeneck. LC 73-177603. 1973. Society for the Study of Human Being.

Self-Portrait in a Convex Mirror: Poems. John Ashbery. LC 75-1095. 1975. 6.95 (ISBN 0-670-63283-X). Viking Press.

Self-Raised: Or, From the Depths. Emma Dorothy Eliza Nevitte Southworth. LC 4-21502. 1904. R. F. Fenno & Company.

Self-Raised; or, From the Depths. A Sequel to Ishmael; or, In the Depths. Emma Dorothy Eliza Nevitte Southworth. LC 8-10833. 1876. T. B. Peterson & Brothers.

Self-Raised: Or From the Depths. Originally Published in the "New York Ledger," Under the Name of "Self-Made; or, Out of the Depths". Emma Dorothy Eliza Nevitte Southworth. LC 8-10834. 1884. T. B. Peterson & Brothers.

Self-Renunciation: By the Author of "Nuggets of Gold.". Bruce Hughes. 1902.

Selfish and the Storng. Richard Schuster. LC 58-5272. 1958. Random House.

Selfish Giant. Oscar Wilde. LC 54-10070. (Illus.). P. J. Kenedy.

Selichoth Night. Gershon Kranzler, pseud. saddle-stitched 3.00 (ISBN 0-87559-132-9). Shalom.

Selina: A Romantic Novel. Holmes Moss Alexander. LC 42-40683. 1942. Harper & Brothers.

Selina: Her Hopeful Efforts and Her Livelier Failures. George Madden Martin. LC 14-18501. 1914. 1.30. D. Appleton and Company.

Selkie. Charles Sheffield & David Bischoff. LC 81-18617. (Illus.). 12.95 (ISBN 0-02-610080-0). Macmillan.

Selkirks. Eden Hughes. 1982. pap. 2.95 (ISBN 0-451-11506-6, AE1506, Sig). NAL.

Sell Not Thyself: A Novel. Winnifred Kent. LC 7-10963. Laird & Lee.

Seller of Talismans: Liberius Gaius. Josef Ciger. LC 78-20357. (Illus.). 2.50 (ISBN 0-9602084-0-2). Kester.

Selling of the President. Joe McGinniss. 288p. 1980. pap. 2.95 (ISBN 0-671-42681-8). WSP.

Selling the Bear's Hide" and Other Tales. Charles Stewart Davison. 1902. The Nassau Press.

Selma. Ann Eliza Brainerd Smith. (Lovell's library. v. 2, no. 65). 1883. J. W. Lovell Company.

Selma: A Novel. Isabel Constance Clarke. LC 26-6263. 1926. Benziger Brothers.

Selma Lagerloef. Hanna A. Larsen. LC 36-27415. 1975. Repr. of 1936 ed. 13.00 (ISBN 0-527-54880-4). Kraus Repr.

Selmans. Victor Rousseau Emanuel. LC 25-19431. 1925. L. MacVeagh, The Dial Press.

Seluang Menodak Baung. Shahnon Ahmad. (Karyawan Malaysia Ser.). (Malay.). 1979. pap. text ed. 5.50x o.p. (00355). Heinemann Ed.

Selves of Quinte. Marcel J Moreau. LC 65-14604. 1965. G. Braziller.

Selves of Quinte. Tr. from French by Bernard Frechtman. Marcel J Moreau. LC 65-14604. 5.00. Braziller.

Selwood of Sleepy Cat. Frank Hamilton Spearman. LC 25-6314. 1925. C. Scribner's Sons.

Semaine De Boite: A Surrealistic Novel in Collage. Max Ernst. 10.00 (ISBN 0-8446-5454-X). Peter Smith.

Sembal. Gilbert Cannan. LC 24-9263. 1924. T. Seltzer.

Semi-Attached. Anne Parrish. 2.00. George H. Doran Company.

Semi-Attached Couple. 2d. ed. Emily Eden. LC 6-263153. 1861. T. O. H. P. Burnham.

Semi-Attached Couple. Emily Eden. LC 47-3425. 1947. Houghton Mifflin Company.

Semi-Attached Couple; &, The Semi-Detached House. Emily Eden. LC 81-12450. (Virago Modern Classics). 1982. 7.95 (ISBN 0-385-27217-0). Dial Press.

Semi-Detached House. Emily Eden. LC 38-103424. (Halfititle: The rescue series. iv"*d). 1939. Frederick A. Stokes Company.

Semi-Detached House. Emily Eden. LC 48-8700. 1948. Houghton Mifflin Co.

Semi-Detached House. Emily Eden & Lewis, Lady Maria Theresa (Villers) Lister, 1808-1865, Ed. LC 41-40508. 1860. Ticknor and Fields.

Semi-Detached Marriage. Sally Wentworth. (Harlequin Presents Ser.). 192p. 1982. pap. 1.75 (ISBN 0-373-10542-8). Harlequin Bks.

Semi-Detached Wife. Alan Dubois. LC 35-7315. Phoenix Press.

Semi-Detached Wife. Clement Wood. LC 35-7315. Phoenix Press.

Semi-Precious Stones. Aleksandra Ivanovna Voinova & Snow, Valentine, Tr. LC 31-33678. J. Cape & H. Smith.

Semi-Tough. Dan Jenkins. LC 72-78289. 1972. 7.95. Atheneum.

Semi-Tough: Movie Edition. Dan Jenkins. (Illus.). 1977. pap. 1.95 (ISBN 0-451-08184-6, J8184, Sig). NAL.

Seminar in Evil. Daoma Winston. 1972. pap. 0.95 o.s.i. (75-392). Lancer.

Seminarian. Michel Del Castillo. LC 69-10232. 1970. 4.95. Holt, Rinehart and Winston.

Semiranis: A Tale of Battle and of Love. Edward Henry Peple. LC 7-26347. 1907. Moffat, Yard & Company.

Semonov Impulse. James Meldrum. LC 76-5378. 7.95. St. Martin's Press.

Semper Fi! The Story of the Ninth Marines. 1st Ed. Gene Hendryx. LC 59-12682. 1959. Pageant Press.

Sempinski Affair. W. S. Kuniczak. LC 69-15196. 1969. 5.95. Doubleday.

Sem's Morroccan ! Love. Arthur Kay. LC 29-19249. International Fiction Library.

Senator. Drew Pearson. LC 68-18091. 1968. 6.95. Doubleday.

Senator at Sea. A Story of Mine and Thine. George F Duysters. LC 6-36394. 1894. G. W. Dillingham.

Senator Cashdollar, of Washington. Lewis Levy. LC 99-2807. (On cover: The Phoenix series, no. 13). 1899. E. A. Weeks Company.

Senator from Alabama: A Romance Treating of the Disfranchisement of the Negro and Including a Scathing Arraignment of the White House Social-Equality Policy. John H. Wallace. LC 4-23714. 1904. The Neale Publishing Company.

Senator from Slaughter County. Harry M. Caudill. LC 73-9888. 1973. 6.95 (ISBN 0-316-13215-2). Little, Brown.

Senator Intrigue and Inspector Noseby: A Tale of Spoils. Frances Campbell Sparhawk. LC 8-12384. 1895. Red-Letter Publishing Company.

Senator Lars Erikson: A Story of Love and Politics. Franklyn Warner Lee. (On cover: Idle moments series. no. 9). 1891. The Price-McGill Company.

Senator Licinius. William Patrick Kelly. LC 25-3167. 1909. G. Routledge and Sons, Limited.
Senator Marlowe's Daughter. Frances Parkinson Wheeler Keyes. LC 33-31430. 1933. J. Messner, Inc.
Senator Marlowe's Daughter. Francis Parkinson Wheeler Keyes. 1976. 1.95 (ISBN 0-671-80275-5). Pocket Books.
Senator North. Gertrude Franklin Horn Atherton. LC 67-29258. (Americans in Fic.). 1967. Gregg Pr.
Senator North. Gertrude Franklin Horn Atherton. LC 6-4530. 1900. J. Lane.
Senator North. 13th ed. Gertrude Franklin Horn Atherton. LC 9-2700. 1900. J. Lane.
Senator North. 14th ed. Gertrude Franklin Horn Atherton. LC 6-4521. 1900. J. Lane.
Senator North. 18th ed. Gertrude Franklin Horn Atherton. LC 6-4522. 1900. J. Lane.
Senator North. 22d ed. Gertrude Franklin Horn Atherton. LC 4-7540. 1908. R. F. Fenno & Company.
Senator North. Gertrude Franklin Horan Therton. LC 16-6726. (Half-title: Lane's Indians and colonial library). 1914. John Lane Company.
Senator Silverthorn. Stephen Longstreet. LC 68-3967. 1968. Dell Pub. Co.
Senator Solomon Spiffledink. Louis Ludlow. LC 27-119571. Pioneer Book Company.
Senator's Bride. Alexander McVeigh Miller. (On cover: Street & Smith's select series, no. 1). 1887. Street & Smith.
Senator's Lady. Shirley Seifert. LC 67-16921. 1967. Lippincott.
Senator's Lady, a Novel. Mathilde Eiker. LC 32-26237. 1932. Doubleday, Doran & Company, Inc.
Senator's Last Night. Francis Hackett. LC 43-11549. 1943. Doubleday, Doran & Co., Inc.
Senator's Nude. William F. Goodykoontz. LC 47-3659. 1947. Ziff-Davis Publishing Company.
Senator's Ransom. Ken Bernstein. LC 79-172622. 1971. 5.95. Coward, McCann & Geoghegan.
Senator's Secret. Phyllis Pieratos. 2.75 o.p. Vantage.
Senator's Son, or, The Maine Law: A Last Refuge; a Story Dedicated to the Law-Makers. Metta Victoria Fuller Victor. LC 43-26797. 1853. Tooker and Gatchel.
Senator's Whore. Cindy Kallmer. (Orig.). 1976. pap. 1.50 (ISBN 0-87067-810-8, BH810). Holloway.
Senator's Wife: Being a Tale of Washington Life. Melville Philips. LC 7-36064. F. T. Neely.
Send Another Coffin: A Mystery. Frank G Presnell. LC 39-12105. 1939. W. Morrow and Company.
Send Another Hearse. Harold Q Masur. LC 60-5538. (Random House mystery). 1960. Random House.
Send Down a Dove. Charles MacHardy. LC 68-23370. 1968. 5.95. Coward-McCann.
Send for Miss Cora. Charley Robertson. LC 48-5623. 1948. Reynal & Hitchcock.
Send for Mr. Robinson! Jon Manchip White. 1975. (pbk.) 1.25 (ISBN 0-523-00649-7). Pinnacle Books.
Send Him Victorious. Douglas Hurd & Andrew Osmond. LC 69-12650. 1969. Macmillan.
Send in the Lions. Eric Clark. LC 80-69371. 1981. 9.95 (ISBN 0-689-11125-8). Atheneum.
Send Me an Angel. Alice Nisbet. LC 47-884. 1946. The University of North Carolina Press.
Send Me Down. Henry Steig. LC 41-8082. 1941. A. A. Knopf.
Send No Flowers. Charles Rodda. LC 47-210439. 1947. Howell, Soskin.
Send-off. Christopher Leach. LC 73-16732. 1974. 4.95 (ISBN 0-684-13710-0). Scribner.
Send Somebody Nice: Stories and Sketches. Noel Hilliard. LC 77-366284. 1976. 3.10 (ISBN 0-7091-5477-1). Hale.
Send Superintendent West. John Creasey. LC 76-11735. 1976. 6.95 (ISBN 0-684-14730-0). Scribner.
Send the Wise Wind. Kate Bigelow Montague. LC 52-5372. 1952. J. Day Co.
Send Them Summer. Hansford Martin. LC 46-3774. 1946. Harcourt, Brace and Company.
Sendai. William Woolfolk. 288p. 1981. pap. 2.75 (ISBN 0-445-04628-7). Popular Lib.
Sending. Geoffrey Household. LC 79-24664. 9.95 (ISBN 0-316-37438-5). Little, Brown.
Sending. Geoffrey Household. LC 80-25171. 1981. 2.95 (ISBN 0-14-005780-3). Penguin Books.
Seneca Hostage. Noel Bertram Gerson. LC 71-90251. 1969. 4.95. Doubleday.
Seneca, U.S.A. John Roeburt. LC 47-30334. 1947. S. Curl, Inc.
Seneca World of Ga-No-Say-Yeh (Peter Crouse, White Captive) Joseph A. Francello. LC 80-1358. 227p. 1980. pap. text ed. 10.50 (ISBN 0-8191-1141-4). U Pr of Amer.
Senior Lieutenant's Wager: And Other Stories. LC 5-16119. (Stories by the foremost Catholic writers). 1905. Benziger Brothers.
Senior Partner. A Novel. Charlotte Eliza Lawson Cowan Riddell. (Harper's Franklin square library, no. 223). 1882. Harper & Brothers.
Senior Quarter-Back. Thomas Truxtum Hare. LC 10-24477. 1910. 1.25. The Penn Publishing Company.
Senior Songman. A Novel. Eliza Tabor Stephenson. (Harper's Franklin square library, no. 324). 1883. Harper & Brothers.
Senior Spring: A Novel. Charles G Lumbard. LC 54-546491. 1954. Simon and Schuster.
Senor Avalanche. Johnston McCulley. LC 46-267742. 1946. Arcadia House, Inc.
Senor Hurricane. Ben Thrash. LC 46-17222. 1946. Dorrance & Company.
Senor Presidente. Miguel Angel Asturias. LC 64-10908. 1964. 6.95 o.p. (ISBN 0-689-10016-7). Atheneum.
Senor Presidente. Miguel Angel Asturias & Frances Partridge. LC 64-10908. 1975. pap. text ed. 4.95x (ISBN 0-689-70521-2, 211). Atheneum.
Senor Saint. Leslie Charteris. 1968. pap. 0.60 o.p. (60-315). Manor Bks.
Senor Saint: Short Stories. 1st Ed. Leslie Charteris. LC 58-132754. 1958. Published for the Crime Club by Doubleday.
Senora Villena and Gray: An Oldhaven Romance... Marrion Wilcox. LC 8-37026. 1887. White, Stokes & Allen.
Senora's Granddaughters: A Tale of Modern Mexico, by Janie Prichard Duggan... Janie Prichard Duggan. LC 98-722. 1898. American Baptist Publication Society.
Senorita from Chicago. Vida Hurst. LC 41-7860. Gramercy Publishing Co.
Senorita Montenar. Archer Philip Crouch. LC 6-32869. 1898. Harper & Brothers.
Sens-Plastique. 2nd, rev. ed. Malcolm De Chazal. Ed. by Irving Weiss. LC 79-25078. 163p. (Orig.). 1980. pap. 6.00 (ISBN 0-915342-29-4). SUN.
Sensation. Norman Keifetz. LC 74-11612. 1975. 8.95 (ISBN 0-689-10644-0). Atheneum.
Sensation. Norman Keifetz. (Signet Book). 1976. (pbk.) 1.50. New American Library.
Sensation. Charlotte Lamb, pseud. (Harlequin Presents Ser.). (Orig.). 1980. pap. text ed. 1.50 (ISBN 0-373-10364-6, Pub. by Harlequin). PB.
Sensational Case. Florence Alice Price James. LC 7-7977. The International News Company.
Sense and Sensibility. Jane Austen. (Harcourt library of English and American classics). 1962. Harcourt, Brace & World.
Sense and Sensibility. Jane Austen. LC 75-541981. (Oxford English novels). 1970 (ISBN 0-19-255335-6). Oxford U.P.
Sense and Sensibility. Jane Austen. LC 78-11582. (Penguin English library). (Illus.). 1969. (pbk) 1.45. Penguin Books.
Sense and Sensibility. Jane Austen. LC 6-3868. 1892. Roberts Brothers.
Sense and Sensibility. Jane Austen. LC 4-15275. 1897. Macmillan and Co., Limited.
Sense & Sensibility. Jane Austen. (Half-title: Everyman's library, ed. by Ernest Rhys. Fiction). 1908. J. M. Dent & Co.
Sense and Sensibility. Jane Austen. Ed. by Miller, Edwin Lillie. LC 13-34797. (Macmillan's pocket American and English classics). 1913. The Macmillan Company.
Sense and Sensibility. Jane Austen. LC 33-16598. (Half-title: The World's classics. 369). 1931. H. Milford, Oxford University Press.
Sense & Sensibility. Jane Austen. LC 36-37053. (Half-title: Everyman's library. ed. by Ernest Rhys. Fiction. no. 21). 1931. M. Dent & Sons, Ltd.
Sense and Sensibility. Jane Austen. LC 34-28480. (Half-title: The works of Jane Austen). 1933. E. P. Dutton & Co., Inc.
Sense and Sensibility. Jane Austen & Bailey, John Cann. LC 29-24286. 1928. Dodd, Mead & Company.
Sense & Sensibility see Oxford Illustrated Jane Austen.
Sense and Sensibility: A Novel. Jane Austen. LC 6-3867. 1838. Carey & Lea.
Sense and Sensibility. A Novel. Jane Austen. LC 21-13959. (Seaside library, v. 41, no. 836). 1880. G. Munro.
Sense and Sensibility. Afterword by Caroline G. Mercer. Jane Austen. (Signet classic). 1961. New American Lib.
Sense and Sensibility. Introd. by Duke Schirmer. Jane Austen. (Collateral Classic, CC510). 1966. Washington Sq.
Sense and Sensibility. With a New Introd. by Louis Kronenberger. Jane Austen. LC 62-19929. (Collier books, HS26). 1962. Collier Books.
Sense and Sensibility. With a New Introd. by Stella Gibbons and Illus. by Helen Sewell. Jane Austen. LC 57-591733. 1957. Heritage Press.
Sense and Sensibility. With a New Introd. by Stella Gibbons and Illus. by Helen Sewell. Jane Austen. LC 57-23989. 1957. Printed at the Spiral Press for the Members of the Limited Editions Club.
Sense and Sensibility. With Illus. Reproducing Drawings for Early Editions and Photos. of Historical Scenes Together with an Introductory Biographical Sketch of the Author and Anecdotal Captions. Jane Austen & Davenport, Basil. LC 49-818625. (Great Illustrated Classics). 1949. Dodd, Mead.
Sense & Sensibility with Lady Susan & the Watsons. Jane Austen. (Macdonald Classics Ser.). (O.s.i.). 528p. 1974. 12.95x o.p. (ISBN 0-8464-0837-6). Beekman Pubs.
Sense and Sensibility. With Lady Susan and The Watsons. Introd. by Q. D. Leavis. Illus. by Philip Gough. Jane Austen. LC 66-5545. (Macdonald illus. classics, 37). 1966. 3.50. Macdonald.
Sense & Sensibilty. Jane Austen. 1982. pap. 10.00x (ISBN 0-330-02949-5, Pub. by Pan Bks). State Mutual Bk.
Sense and Sensuality. Coralie Hobson. LC 29-17276. Payson & Clarke Ltd.
Sense of Dark. William Malliol. LC 68-23512. 1968. Atheneum.
Sense of Detachment. John Jay Osborn. 1973. 5.95 o.p. (ISBN 0-571-10211-5, Pub. by Faber & Faber). Merrimack Pub Cir.
Sense of Honor. James H Webb, Jr. LC 81-25852. (Illus.). 10.95 (ISBN 0-13-806646-9). Prentice-Hall.
Sense of Reality. Graham Greene. LC 63-13352. 1963. Viking Press.
Sense of Reality. Graham Greene. LC 70-367255. 1968. Penguin.
Sense of Shadow. Kate Wilhelm. LC 80-25747. 1981. 9.95 (ISBN 0-395-30545-4). Houghton Mifflin Co.
Sense of Slavery. Phil Hruskocy. 1978. pap. 5.00 (ISBN 0-910122-51-2). Amherst Pr.
Sense of the Past. Henry James. LC 73-158805. (Scribner reprint editions). 1975. 12.50 (ISBN 0-678-02826-5). A. M. Kelley.
Sense of the Past. Henry James. Ed. by Lubbock, Percy. LC 17-28794. 1917. C. Scribner's Sons.
Sense of Values. 1st Ed. Sloan Wilson. LC 60-10449. 1960. Harper.
Sense of Warning. Barry N. Kaufman. 1983. 15.95 (ISBN 0-440-07782-6, E Friede). Delacorte.
Sense, Symbol and Suggestion in Selected Novels of Vicente Blasco Ibanez. Janet E King. LC 72-188487. 1972.
Sensei. David Charney. 448p. Date not set. pap. 3.25 (ISBN 0-441-75887-8). Ace Bks.
Senseless. J. Douglas Burtt. (Orig.). 1981. pap. 1.95 (ISBN 0-505-51637-3). Tower Bks.
Sensible Cecily. Margaret Sommerville. (Orig.). 1980. pap. 1.50 (ISBN 0-440-17908-4). Dell.
Sensible Courtship. Megan Daniel. (Signet Book). ("A Regency Romance.). 2.25 (ISBN 0-451-11739-5). New American Library.
Sensitive Encounter. Canella Lewis. (Berkley Medallion Book). 1977. 1.50 (ISBN 0-425-03593-X). Berkley Pub Corp.
Sensitive Woman. Sandra Chandler. LC 75-178885. pap. 1.75 o.p. (ISBN 0-89081-037-0, 0370). Harvest Hse.
Sensualid Ad per Vertida, 2 vols. Pio Baroja y Nessi. 3.50 o.s.i. French & Eur.
Sensualist: A Novel of the Life and Times of Oscar Wilde. Clement Wood. LC 42-8911. 1942. J. Swift.
Sensualists. Ben Hecht. LC 59-8834. 1959. Messner.
Sensualists. Frank Mace. 1972. pap. 1.95 o.s.i. (V1054T, Venus). Grove.
Sensuous Burgundy. Bonnie Drake. (Candlelight Ecstasy Ser.: No. 32). 224p. (Orig.). 1981. pap. 1.75 (ISBN 0-440-18427-4). Dell.
Sensuous Child Bride. Marsha Alexander. 192p. (Orig.). 1973. pap. 1.95 o.p. (ISBN 0-87056-301-7, 6301). Brandon.
Sensuous Golfer. Mark Oman. LC 76-19347. (Illus.). pap. 4.95 (ISBN 0-917346-01-7). Oman Ent.
Sensuous Group. S. V. 192p. 1971. pap. 1.95 o.p. (ISBN 0-87056-213-4, 6213). Brandon.
Sensuous Man. M, pseud. 1982. pap. 3.25 (ISBN 0-440-17916-5). Dell.
Sensuous Orphan Child. Carl Schubbe. 192p. (Orig.). 1973. pap. 1.95 o.p. (ISBN 0-87682-317-7, 7317). Barclay Hse.
Sensuous Side of Mass Media. Donna Ogcrigh. 1974. (pbk.) 1.95 (ISBN 0-87056-394-7). Brandon Books.
Sensuous Southpaw. Paul R. Rothweiler. 1978. pap. 1.95 (ISBN 0-425-03758-4, Medallion). Berkley Pub.
Sensuous Southpaw: A Novel. Paul R. Rothweiler. LC 76-11731. 7.95. Putnam.
Sensuous Stepfather. Mark S. Wolin. 192p. (Orig.). 1973. pap. 1.95 o.p. (ISBN 0-87682-302-9, 7302). Barclay Hse.
Sensuous Summer. William Bostock. (Berkley medallion book). 1975. (pbk.) 1.50 (ISBN 0-425-02897-6). Berkley Pub. Co.
Sensuous Woman. J, pseud. 1982. pap. 3.25 (ISBN 0-440-17859-2). Dell.
Sensuously Yours. Fred Hoffman. (Illus.). pap. 4.75 o.p. (ISBN 0-87964-567-9). Academy-Parliament.
Sent for You Yesterday. John Edgar Wideman. 208p. 1983. pap. 3.50 (ISBN 0-380-82644-5, Bard). Avon.
Sent to His Account. Eilis Dillon. LC 69-13203. 1969. 4.50. Walker.
Sentence Deferred: A Judge Peck Mystery. August William Derleth. LC 39-5475. 1939. C. Scribner's Sons.
Sentence of Death. John Creasey. LC 64-8021. (Cock Robin mystery). 1964. Macmillan.
Sentence of Death see Up.
Sentence of Life. Julian Gloag. (95077). 1968. Pocket Bks.
Sentence of Life: A Novel. Julian Gloag. LC 66-13844. 1966. Simon and Schuster.
Sentence of Silence. Reginald Wright Kauffman. LC 12-7963. 1912. 1.35. Moffat, Yard and Company.
Sentence of the Six-Gun: By Anthony M. Rud. Anthony M Rud. LC 26-24289. (On cover: A pocket copyright. no. 73). 1926. Garden City Publishing Co., Inc.
Sentence of Youth. Nancy Pope. LC 36-19218. 1936. Doubleday, Doran & Co., Inc.
Sentenced & Other Stories. Vladimir Soloukhin. Tr. by D. W. Martin from Rus. 200p. 20.00 (ISBN 0-88233-802-1); pap. 6.50 (ISBN 0-88233-803-X). Ardis Pubs.
Sentenced to Life. Mary Agnes Adamson Hamilton. LC 35-16903. 1935. Houghton Mifflin Company.
Sentiment. Vincent O'Sullivan. LC 17-29624. 1.50. Small, Maynard & Company.
Sentiment and Story. Robert Jesse Gresham. LC 8-4035. 1908. The Neale Publishing Company.
Sentimental Adventures of Jimmy Bulstrode. Marie Van Vorst. LC 8-10276. 1908. C. Scribner's Sons.
Sentimental Agents in the Volyen Empire. Doris May Lessing. LC 82-25172. (Canopus in Argos-archives; 5). ((Series: Lessing, Doris May, 1919-). (Canopus in Argos-archives; 5.). 1983. 12.95 (ISBN 0-394-52968-5). Knopf.
Sentimental Calendar. facsimile ed. J. S. Of Dale Stimson. LC 70-98596. (Short Story Index Reprint Ser.). 1886. 16.00 (ISBN 0-8369-3171-8). Ayer Co.
Sentimental Calendar: Being Twelve Funny Stories. Frederic Jesup Stimson. LC 70-98596. (Short story index reprint series). (Illus.). 1969. Books for Libraries Press.
Sentimental Calendar: Being Twelve Funny Stories. Frederic Jesup Stimson. LC 3-15675. 1886. C. Scribner's Sons.
Sentimental Dragon. Nina Larrey Smith Duryea. LC 16-9544. 1.25. George H. Doran Company.
Sentimental Education. Gustave Flaubert. LC 64-55756. (Penguin classics, L141) Title.). 1964. Penguin Books.
Sentimental Education. Gustave Flaubert. Tr. by Perdita Burlingame. LC 78-184428. 1972. 1.50. New American Library.
Sentimental Education. Gustave Flaubert & Goldsmith, Anthony, Tr. LC 42-36001. (Half-title: Everyman's library, ed. by Ernest Rhys. Fiction No. 9695d). 1941. J. M. Dent & Sons Ltd.
Sentimental Education: Stories. Joyce Carol Oates. LC 80-36767. 11.95 (ISBN 0-525-19950-0). Dutton.
Sentimental Education: The Story of a Young Man. Gustave Flaubert & Ranous, Mrs. Dora Knowlton (Thompson) 1859-1916, Ed. LC 22-9358. (On cover: The lotus library). Brentano's.
Sentimental Education. Tr. from French Introd., Notes by Anthony Goldsmith. Gustave Flaubert. Tr. by Anthony Goldsmith. (Everyman paperback, 1969). 1962. pap., 1.55. Dutton.
Sentimental Journey. Laurence Sterne. Ed. by Ian Jack. (Oxford English Novels Ser.). (Illus.). 1968. 6.50x o.p. (ISBN 0-19-255316-X). Oxford U Pr.
Sentimental Romance & Other Stories. Aleksandr Ivanovich Kuprin. Tr. by S. E. Berkenblit. 5.95 o.s.i. (ISBN 0-8181-0046-X). Pageant-Poseidon.
Sentimental Spy. Alice Chetwynd Ley. LC 78-12833. 1979. 9.95 (ISBN 0-89340-175-7). J. Curley.
Sentimental Studies: And A Set of Village Tales. Hubert Montague Crackanthorpe. LC 6-31148. 1895. G. P. Putnam's Sons.
Sentimental Talk see Sentimental Talks.
Sentimental Talks. Daniel Castelain. Tr. by Patrick Bowles from Fr. Incl. Unlikely Meeting; Sentimental Talk. LC 79-131217. 128p. (Orig.). 1971. 4.95 (ISBN 0-87376-014-X). Red Dust.
Sentimental Tommy. peter pan ed. James Matthew Barrie. LC 74-30185. 1975. 24.50 (ISBN 0-404-08785-X). AMS Press.
Sentimental Tommy. James Matthew Barrie. LC 20-18816. 1919. C. Scribner's Sons.
Sentimental Tommy: The Story of His Boyhood. James Matthew Barrie. LC 4-15279. 1896. C. Scribner's Sons.

Sentimental Tommy: The Story of His Boyhood. James Matthew Barrie. LC 38-7780. (people's library). The American News Company.
Sentimental Vagabond. Albert T'Serstevens & Chambers, Whittaker, Tr. LC 30-25306. Farrar & Rinehart, Incorporated.
Sentimental Venture. Elza Ivan Edwards. LC 76-21423. (Illus.). 10.00 (ISBN 0-914224-06-9). Tales of the Mojave Road Pub. Co.
Sentimental Yankee. John De Meyer. LC 41-26739. Random House.
Sentimentalist: A Novel. Frances Winwar. LC 43-15972. 1943. Harper & Brothers.
Sentimentalists. Dale Collins. LC 27-19193. 1927. Little, Brown, and Company.
Sentimentalists: A Novel. Arthur Stanwood Pier. 1901. Harper & Brothers.
Sentinel. Jeffrey Konvitz. LC 74-8984. 1974. 7.95 (ISBN 0-671-21834-4). Simon and Schuster.
Sentinel. Jeffrey Konvitz. 1976. (pbk.) 1.75 (ISBN 0-345-24600-4). Ballantine Books.
Sentinel of the Desert. Jackson Gregory. LC 29-4210. 1929. Dodd, Mead and Company.
Sentinel Point. Nancy Dorer. 1978. pap. 1.50 (ISBN 0-532-15346-4). Woodhill.
Sentinel Stars: A Novel of the Future. Louis H Charbonneau. LC 63-19052. 1963. Bantam Books.
Sentinels from Space. eric frank russell. ed. Eric Frank Russell. 1976. 1.50. Ace Books.
Sentinels from Space. Eric Frank Russell. LC 52-14743. 1953. Bouregy and Curl.
Sentries. Ed McBain. 1965. 4.95 o.p. S&S.
Sentries: A Novel by Ed. McBain Pseud. Evan Hunter. LC 65-11973. bds., 4.95. S. & S.
Sentry. Heyward Emerson Canney. LC 28-23041. 1928. Harper & Brothers.
Sentry, and Other Stories. Nikolai Semenovich Leskov. LC 76-23888. (Classics of Russian literature). (Hyperion library of world literature). 1977. 12.50. (ISBN 0-88355-501-8) (ISBN 0-88355-502-6). Hyperion Press.
Sentry: And Other Stories. Nikolai Semenovich Leskov. Tr. by Alfred Edward Chamot. LC 23-10908. 1923. A. A. Knopf.
Sentry: And Other Stories. by nicolai lyeskov; translated by a. e. chamot, with an introduction by edward garnett. ed. Nikolai Semenovich Leskov. Tr. by Alfred Edward Chamot. LC 23-10908. 1923. A. A. Knopf.
Sepang Loca & Others. Amelia Lapena-Bonifacio. 296p. 1982. text ed. 13.50x (ISBN 0-8248-0768-5, Pub by U of Philippines Pr); pap. text ed. 9.50x (ISBN 0-8248-0769-3). UH Pr.
Separate Development. Christopher Hope. LC 81-9341. 1981. 10.95 (ISBN 0-684-17308-5). Scribner.
Separate from His Brethren. Pierre Lambert. LC 37-798717. 1937. Meador Publishing Company.
Separate Peace. John Knowles. LC 67-7047. 1967. Macmillan.
Separate Peace. John Knowles. LC 76-367933. 1968. 0.95. Cassell Australia.
Separate Peace: A Novel. John Knowles. LC 60-5312. 1960. Macmillan.
Separate Star. Mary Badger Wilson. LC 32-3417. The Penn Publishing Company.
Separate Ways. Hester Mundis. LC 77-21544. 8.95 (ISBN 0-698-10864-7). Coward, McCann & Geoghegan.
Separate Ways. Hester Mundis. 1979. 1.95 (ISBN 0-380-44750-9). Avon Books.
Separated by Mountains. Samuel Hoffman Davis. LC 33-28592. Dorrance & Company, Inc.
Separation. Richard H Rohmer. LC 76-382528. 9.95 (ISBN 0-7710-7704-1). McClelland and Stewart.
Separation. A Novel. Charlotte Campbell Bury. LC 6-16384. 1830. Printed by J. & J. Harper.
Sepastian Agente Secreto. James Leonard Johnson. Tr. by Francisco Lievano. 200p. 1977. pap. 3.95 (ISBN 0-311-37021-7). Casa Bautista.
Sepia. Owen Rutter. LC 26-13345. George H. Doran Company.
Sept Aventures Completes. Rene de Goscinny. (Lucky Luke Series). (French.). 1976. 5.95x. Intl Learn Syst.
Septameron... Williams Francis Howard, 1844-1922 & Morris, Harrison Smith, 1856- LC 8-11259. 1888. D. McKay.
September. Shelby Foote. 1979. 2.25 (ISBN 0-345-26027-9). Ballantine Books.
September. Frank Arthur Swinnerton. LC 19-18833. George H. Doran Company.
September Can Be Dangerous in Edinburgh. Bill Craig. LC 70-161118. 1971. 4.95 (ISBN 0-8027-5240-3). Walker.
September in Quinze: A New Novel. Vivian Connell. LC 52-5949. 1952. Dial Press.
September Moon. John Cecil Moore. LC 58-6902. 1958. Lippincott.
September Remember. Eliot Taintor. 1945. Prentice-Hall, Inc.
September Roses. Translated from the French, by Gerard Hopkins. Andre Maurois. LC 58-8890. 1958. Harper.
September, September. Shelby Foote. LC 77-12523. 8.95 (ISBN 0-394-40721-0). Random House.
Septimius Felton see Dolliver Romance.
Septimus. William John Locke. LC 9-562. 1909. J. Lane Company.
Septimus. William John Locke. LC 12-31343. 1910. John Lane Company.
Septimus. William John Locke. LC 29-252713. 1927. Dodd, Mead and Company.
Septimus and the Minster Ghost Mystery. Stephen Chance. LC 73-20355. (Illus.). 1974. 4.95. T. Nelson.
Septimus Felton: Or, The Elixir of Life. Nathaniel Hawthorne. LC 99-2923. Houghton, Mifflin and Company.
Sequel of a Wasted Life: Comprising a Story Founded on Facts. Helen Marian Weeks. LC 8-36631. 1896. Murphy & Nichols, Printers.
Sequel to a Tragedy: A Story of the Far West. Henry C Dibble. 1901. J. B. Lippincott Company.
Sequel to Old Jolliffe: Written in the Same Spirit, by the Same Spirit. Matilda Anne Mackarness. 1850. J. Munroe and Company.
Sequel to Rolling Ridge. By the Author of the Latter; Assisted by the Worthy Mr. Fory... Samuel Hayes Elliot. LC 6-39371.
Sequel to Sonia. Vida Hurst. LC 27-18717. Grosset & Dunlap.
Sequel to The Neighbors' Children. From the German. Myers, Sarah Ann (Irwin) 1800-1876, Tr. LC 45-53922. 1854. Lindsay & Blakiston.
Sequels of the Manifest Destiny. Manuel Lavandero. 4.95 o.p. Vantage.
Sequence. Elinor Sutherland Glyn. (Barbara Cartland's Library of Love: Vol. 17). 213p. 1980. 12.95x (ISBN 0-7156-1477-0, Pub. by Duckworth England). Biblio Dist.
Sequence in Hearts. Mary Moss. LC 3-22516. 1903. J. B. Lippincott Company.
Sequin Syndicate. Olga Hesky. LC 69-16205. (Red badge mystery). 1969. 3.95. Dodd, Mead.
Sequoia Shootout. John Henry Reese. LC 76-29792. 1977. 5.95 (ISBN 0-385-12693-X). Doubleday.
Sequoyah: A Romance Under Western Skies. Louisa Haynes Moorer. LC 12-289. 1.50. Broadway Publishing Co.
Ser un Hombre (to Be a Man see Willis & His Friends Series.
Seraglio. 1st Ed. James Ingram Merrill. LC 57-56538. 1957. Knopf.
Seraltha. Abel M Rawson. LC 8-597. 1893. The Author's Association.
Seraph--or Mortal? A Romance. Celia Emmeline Gardner. LC 7-313. 1890. G. W. Dillingham, Successor to G. W. Carleton & Co
Seraph on the Suwanee: A Novel. Zora Neale Hurston. LC 73-18580. 1974. 18.50 (ISBN 0-404-11391-5). AMS Press.
Seraph on the Suwanee: A Novel. Zora Neale Hurston. LC 74-18580. 1974. (ISBN 0-404-11391-5). AMS Press.
Seraph on the Suwanee: A Novel. Zora Neale Hurston. LC 48-8745. 1948. C. Scribner's Sons.
Seraphica: A Romance. Justin Huntly McCarthy. 1908. Harper & Brothers.
Seraphim Grosse Pointe. Oswald De Andrade. LC 78-70340. 8.95 (ISBN 0-918722-08-X). New Latin Quarter Editions.
Seraphim Grosse Pointe. Oswald De Andrade. Tr. by Kenneth D. Jackson & Albert Bork. LC 78-70340. 1979. 8.95 (ISBN 0-918722-08-X); pap. cancelled (ISBN 0-918722-09-8). Nefertiti.
Seraphina. Jean Merrill. 224p. (Orig.). 1980. pap. 1.75 (ISBN 0-449-50124-8, Coventry). Fawcett.
Seraphita. Honore De Balzac. LC 76-12203. 2.50 (ISBN 0-8334-1757-6). Steinerbooks.
Seraphita. Honore De Balzac. LC 73-134961. (Short story index reprint series). 1970. Books for Libraries Press.
Seraphita: A Daughter of Eve, and Other Stories. saintsbury ed. Honore De Balzac. Tr. by Clara Courtenay Poynter Bell. Scott, R. S., Joint Tr. Lou's Lambert. The Sceaux Ball. The Unconscious Mummbers. A Daughter of Eve. Letterrs of Two Bride. (At head of title: H. de Balzac.). 1899. The Gebbie Publishing Co., Ltd.
Seraphita. With an Introduction by George Frederic Parsons. Honore De Balzac. Wormeley, Katharine Prescott, 1830-Tr. Jesus Christ in Flanders. The Exile. LC 3-23165. (Half-title: The comedy of human life... Philosophical studies). 1889. Roberts Brothers.
Serapis. popular uniform ed. Georg Moritz Ebers. Tr. by Clara Courtenay Bell. LC 16-157121. (historical romances of Georg Ebers. vol. vii). 1915. D. Appleton and Company.
Serapis: A Romance. authorized ed., rev. and cor. in the united states. ed. Georg Moritz Ebers. Tr. by Clara Courtenay Bell. LC 6-43636. 1885. W. S. Gottsberger.
Serapis: A Romance. Georg Moritz Ebers. Tr. by Clara Courtenay Bell. LC 16-230568. 1886. W. S. Gottsberger.
Serapis. An Historical Novel. Georg Moritz Ebers & Smith, Mrs. Mary Stuart (Harrison) 1834- Tr. (On cover: Seaside library. Pocket ed., no. 474). 1885. G. Munro.
Serena. Janine Fitzpatrick. 1976. (pbk.) 1.25. Warner Books.
Serena: A Novel. Virginia Frazer Boyle. LC 5-13026. 1905. A. S. Barnes & Company.
Serena and Samantha: Being a Chronicle of Events at the Torbolton Home. Rosa Kellen Hallett. LC 12-239232. 1912. Sherman, French & Company.
Serena Blandish. Enid Bagnold. 1972. pap. 0.75 o.p. (07214). Curtis.
Serena Blandish: Or, The Difficulty of Getting Married. Enid Bagnold. LC 25-11075. George H. Doran Company.
Serena Blandish: Or, The Difficulty of Getting Married. Enid Bagnold. LC 46-22118. 1946. W. Morrow & Company.
Serena Fair. Thomas Andrew Broadus. LC 7-4429. 1906. The Baptist Argus.
Serenade. James Mallahan Cain. LC 37-395321. 1937. A. A. Knopf.
Serenade. James Mallahan Cain. LC 77-92634. 1978. 1.65 (ISBN 0-394-72585-9). Vintage Books.
Serenade. Olive Wadsley. 1932. Dodd, Mead & Company.
Serenade for a Lost Love. Jocelyn Haley. (Super Romances Ser.). 384p. 1983. pap. 2.95 (ISBN 0-373-70054-7, Pub. by Worldwide). Harlequin Bks.
Serenade for a Shylock. Henry A Zeiger. LC 76-8882. 7.95 (ISBN 0-399-11780-6). Putnam.
Serenade Pour Anne. Flora Kidd. (Collection Harlequin Ser.). 192p. 1983. pap. 1.95 (ISBN 0-373-49324-X). Harlequin Bks.
Serenity in Storm. 1966. 5.00. Allied Pubs.
Serf Lovers of Siberia. A Novel. Leon Lewis. (On cover: The popular series, no. 16). 1891. R. Bonner's Sons.
Sergeant. Dennis Murphy. LC 58-5965. 1958. Viking Press.
Sergeant Atkins. A Tale of Adventure. Founded on Fact. James Lowry Donaldson. 1871. J. B. Lippincott & Co.
Sergeant Back Again: A Novel. Charles Coleman. LC 80-7601. 12.95 (ISBN 0-06-010864-9). Harper & Row.
Sergeant Chung Ming: A Novel of the Red Earth of China. Translated from the German by Oliver Coburn. 1st Ed. Hans Maeter. LC 61-138089. 1961. Dutton.
Sergeant Death. Stephen Coulter. LC 68-25485. 1968. 4.95. Morrow.
Sergeant Death. James Mayo. LC 68-25485. Orig. Title: Once in a Lifetime. 1968. 4.50 o.p. Morrow.
Sergeant Eadie. Leonard Hastings Nason. LC 28-8412. 1928. Doubleday, Doran & Company, Inc.
Sergeant Getulio. Joao Ubaldo Ribeiro. LC 77-10799. 1978. 7.95 (ISBN 0-395-25705-0). Houghton Mifflin.
Sergeant: Hawk Under Attack. Patrick Clay. (Sergeant Hawk: No. 3). 256p. 1981. pap. 2.25 (ISBN 0-8439-0962-5, Leisure Bks). Nordon Pubns.
Sergeant Lamb's America. Robert Graves. LC 40-27841. Random House.
Sergeant Major's Daughter. Sheila Walsh. (Signet Book). 1978. 1.75 (ISBN 0-451-08220-6). New American Library.
Sergeant Michael Cassidy. Herman Cyril McNeile. LC 16-16392. 1916. Hodder and Stoughton.
Sergeant Nelson of the Guards. Gerald Kersh. LC 45-3352. 1945. The John C. Winston Company.
Sergeant Nikola: A Novel of the Chetnik Brigades. Istvan Tamas. LC 42-50211. 1942. L. B. Fischer Publishing Corp.
Sergeant of Fort Toronto. George F Millner. LC 14-17929. R. G. Badger; Etc., Etc.
Sergeant Ritchie's Conscience: A Novel. Frank Branston. LC 77-9171. 1978. (ISBN 0-312-71307-X). St. Martin's Press.
Sergeant Series, No. 5. Gordon Davis, pseud. 192p. (Orig.). 1981. pap. 2.25 (ISBN 0-553-14721-8). Bantam.
Sergeant Series, No. 7. Gordon Davis, pseud. 192p. (Orig.). 1981. pap. 2.25 (ISBN 0-553-14895-8). Bantam.
Sergeant Series, No. 8. Gordon Davis, pseud. 192p. (Orig.). 1981. pap. 2.25 (ISBN 0-553-20034-8). Bantam.
Sergeant Sir Peter... Edgar Wallace. LC 33-9678. 1933. Pub. for the Crime Club, Inc., by Doubleday, Doran & Company, Inc.
Sergeant Sue. Peggy O'More, pseud. LC 42-10813. 1942. Gramercy Publishing Company.
Sergeant Sutton. Robert E Ford. LC 78-121776. 1970. 7.95. Hawthorn.
Sergeant Verity and the Blood Royal. Francis Selwyn. LC 78-20670. 1979. 8.95 (ISBN 0-8128-2608-6). Stein and Day.
Sergeant Verity and the Imperial Diamond. Francis Selwyn. LC 75-34219. 1976. 7.95 (ISBN 0-8128-1917-9). Stein and Day.
Sergeant Verity and the Swell Mob. Francis Selwyn. LC 80-5402. 1980. 10.95 (ISBN 0-8128-2727-9). Stein and Day.
Sergeant Verity Presents His Compliments. Francis Selwyn. LC 76-41724. 1977. 7.95. Stein and Day.
Sergeant's Legacy. Elie Bertrand Berthet. Tr. by Venables, Gilbert. (On cover: Lovell's library, v. 7, no. 366). J. W. Lovell Company.
Sergent Death. Frank P Grady. LC 36-25380. B. Mussey.
Serial. Cyra McFadden. 1978. pap. 2.50 (ISBN 0-451-09267-8, E9267, Sig). NAL.
Serial: A Year in the Life of Marin County. Cyra McFadden. LC 76-47946. (Illus.). 1977. 4.95 (ISBN 0-394-73361-4). Knopf.
Serial: A Year in the Life of Marin County. Cyra McFadden. (Signet Book). 1978. 1.95 (ISBN 0-451-08080-7). New American Library.
Serial Biography. Tom Raworth. LC 77-82307. (New World Writing Ser.). 1977. pap. 4.95 (ISBN 0-913666-16-5). Turtle Isl Foun.
Serious Complications. Mary Frances Hanford Delanoy. LC 1-30047. The Abbey Press.
Serious Investigation. Lesley Egan, pseud. 1968. 4.95 o.p. (ISBN 0-06-011154-2, HarpT). Har-Row.
Serious Investigation. Elizabeth Linington. LC 67-22517. 1968. Harper & Row.
Serious Morning. Andrei Codrescu. (Capra Chapbook Ser.). (Cloth ed. 10.00 o.p.: No. 9). pap. 2.50 o.p. (ISBN 0-912264-60-8). Capra Pr.
Serious Reflections During the Life and Surprising Adventures of Robinson Crusoe: With His Vision of the Angelic World. Daniel Defoe. LC 74-13445. (Illus.). 1974. (ISBN 0-404-07913-X). AMS Press.
Serious Unconventionalities. Philena Ricker Maxwell Peabody-Lloyd. LC 28-10996. The Christopher Publishing House.
Serious Wooing: A Heart's History. Pearl Mary Teresa Richards Craigie. LC 1-13967. F. A. Stokes Company.
Sermons and Soda-Water. John O'Hara. LC 60-16572. 1960. Random House.
Sermons from the Ammunition Hatch of the Ship of Fools. Hans Juergensen. (Illus.). 1968. 2.00 o.p. Vagabond.
Sermons in Stone: Inspirational Fables for Today. Melvin Richard Ellis. LC 74-5096. (Illus.). 1975. 5.95 (ISBN 0-03-089589-8). Holt, Rinehart and Winston.
Sermons of Jean Harlow & the Curses of Billy the Kid. Michael McClure. 1968. 15.00 o.p. Serendipity.
Sern Charter. Francis Ryck. LC 75-45249. 1976. 7.95 (ISBN 0-698-10740-3). Coward, McCann & Geoghegan.
Serowe: Village of the Rain-Wind. Bessie Head. (African Writers Ser.: No. 220). (Orig.). 1981. pap. text ed. 6.00x (ISBN 0-435-90220-2). Heinemann Ed.
Serpent. Jane Gaskell. LC 76-62771. (Gaskell, Jane, 1941-. The Atlan Ser.: No. 1). 1977. 7.95 (ISBN 0-312-71312-6). St. Martin's Press.
Serpent. Luigi Malerba. LC 68-14915. 1968. Farrar, Straus and Giroux.
Serpent. David Wiltse. 320p. 1983. 14.95 (ISBN 0-440-07590-4). Delacorte.
Serpent & Lily: A Novella, with a Manifesto: The Sickness of the Age. Nikos Kazantzakis. Tr. by Theodora Vasils from Gr. LC 78-68832. 1980. 9.95 (ISBN 0-520-03885-1). U of Cal Pr.
Serpent and Lily: A Novella, with a Manifesto, The Sickness of the Age. Nikos Kazantzakis & Theodora Vasils. LC 78-68832. 9.95 (ISBN 0-520-03885-1). University of California Press.
Serpent & the Messenger. Wilma Williamson. 3.00 o.p. Carlton.
Serpent & the Rope. Rao Raja. LC 75-32512. 407p. 1976. Repr. of 1963 ed. lib. bdg. 22.75x (ISBN 0-8371-8437-1, RASR). Greenwood.
Serpent & the Rope. Raja Rao. 408p. 1968. pap. 4.75 (ISBN 0-88253-766-0). Ind-US Inc.
Serpent and the Staff. Frank Yerby. LC 58-12773. 1958. Dial Press.
Serpent-Charmer. Louis Rousselet. Tr. by Hauteville, Mary De. LC 8-93336. 1879. C. Scribner's Sons.
Serpent-Headed Stick. John Hawk. LC 27-7926. George H. Doran Company.
Serpent Heart. Mary Ann Taylor. (Orig.). 1971. pap. 0.75 o.p. (T2449). Pyramid Pubns.
Serpent in the Garden. Ethel May Dell. 1938. Doubleday, Doran & Company, Inc.
Serpent in the Sky. Irwin Rose. LC 58-7222. 1958. Associated Booksellers.
Serpent of Lilith. Margot Villiers. 1976. (pbk.) 1.50 (ISBN 0-671-80284-4). Pocket Books.
Serpent of Paradise: The Story of an Indian Pilgrimage. Miguel Serrano. LC 70-188031. (Harper colophon books, CN 284). 1972. 2.95 (ISBN 0-06-090284-1). Harper & Row.

Serpent of Satan. Barbara Cartland. LC 79-13514. 1980. 6.95 (ISBN 0-87272-077-2). Duron Books.
Serpent of Venice. Cesare Lanzol. LC 76-96224. 1970. 4.25. Roy.
Serpent Tempted Her: A Novel. Saqui Smith. LC 8-9627. (On cover: The household library. v. 4, no. 4). Belford, Clarke & Co.
Serpent under It: A Novel. Edith Taylor. 256p. 1973. 5.95 (ISBN 0-393-08673-9). Norton.
Serpent-Wreathed Staff. Alice Tisdale Nourse Hobart. LC 51-13794. 1951. Bobbs-Merrill.
Serpentine. Thomas Thompson. 1981. pap. 3.50 (ISBN 0-440-17611-5). Dell.
Serpentine Murder. Leonard Reginald Gribble. LC 33-1255. 1932. Dodd, Mead & Company.
Serpentine Track. Carl Malone. LC 79-90666. 1980. 9.95 (ISBN 0-533-04459-6). Vantage.
Serpents Coil. Farley Mowat. 224p. 1982. pap. 2.95 (ISBN 0-553-20377-0). Bantam.
Serpent's Delight. 1st Ed. in the U. S. A. Ruth Park. LC 62-11299. 1962. Doubleday.
Serpent's Egg. David Duncan. LC 49-49687. 1950. Macmillan.
Serpents in Paradise. Nancy Creagh Phelan. LC 68-107504. 1967. Macmillan.
Serpent's Reach. C. J Cherryh. LC 81-101763. 2.25. Nelson Doubleday.
Serpent's Smile. Hesky, Olga. LC 67-16214. (Red badge mystery). 1967. Dodd, Mead.
Serpent's Tooth. Marthedith Furnas. LC 46-2115. 1946. Harper & Brothers.
Serpent's Tooth. Sara Woods, pseud. LC 72-91588. (Rinehart suspense novel). 1973. 4.95 (ISBN 0-03-007766-4). Holt, Rinehart and Winston.
Serpent's Trail: Or, Memoirs of Harold Bagote, Physician; a Tale of the South and of Cuba. Frederic Bacon Cullen. LC 10-9923. 1.00.
Serra, California Conquistador: A Narrative History. E. B Waterhouse. LC 68-21310. (Illus.). 1968. Parker.
Serum 2000. Stephen Fredd. 1976. (pbk.) 1.50. Dell.
Servant. Robert Cecil Romer Maugham. LC 49-1452. 1949. Harcourt, Brace.
Servant-Girl of the Period the Greeatest Plague of Life. What Mr. and Mrs. Honeydew Learned of Housekeeping. Charles Chamberlain. LC 6-23422. 1873. J. S. Redfield.
Servant of Death. James Harold Wallis. LC 32-19499. 1932. E. P. Dutton & Co., Inc.
Servant of Reality. Phyllis Bottome. LC 19-150802. 1919. The Century Co.
Servant of Satan. Romatic Career of Prado the Assassin. Louis Berard. (Far near series.no. 8). 1889. Street & Smith.
Servant of Slaves: A Biographical Novel of John Newton. Grace Lillian Irwin. LC 61-173894. 1961. Eerdmans.
Servant of the Public. Anthony Hope Hawkins. LC 5-29100. 1905. F. A. Stokes Company.
Servants & the Snow see Three Arrows.
Servants and Their Masters: A Novel. Fergus Reid Buckley. LC 72-76128. 1973. 10.00 (ISBN 0-385-04160-8). Doubleday.
Servants Entrance. Sigrid Holmesland Boo & Walford, Naomi, Tr. LC 33-7089. 1933. Simon and Schuster.
Servants of Corruption. Al Dewlen. LC 79-123686. 1971. 6.95. Doubleday.
Servants of the Wankh: Tschai, Planet of Adventure, No. 2. Jack Vance, pseud. (Science Fiction Ser.). 1979. pap. 1.75 (ISBN 0-87997-467-2, UE1467). DAW Bks.
Servant's Problem. Veronica Parker Johns. pap. 0.95 o.p. (02175, Collier). Macmillan.
Servant's Problem. 1st Ed. Veronica Parker Johns. LC 58-10312. 1958. Published for the Crime Club by Doubleday.
Servers: Or, "In Business for Christ, Why Not?". Joseph Erwin Wilson. LC 19-188347. Mercules Printing & Book Co.
Service Entrance. O. R. Bassett. pap. 1.95 o.p. (ISBN 0-87682-264-2, 7264). Barclay Hse.
Service of All the Dead. Colin Dexter. LC 79-65919. 1980. 9.95 (ISBN 0-312-71316-9). St. Martin's.
Service of the Heart. Evelyn Garfiel. pap. 4.00 (ISBN 0-87980-140-9). Wilshire.
Service Wife. Anonymous. LC 33-7385. The Macaulay Company.
Service with a Smile. Pelham Grenville Wodehouse. LC 61-12864. 1961. Simon and Schuster.
Services Rendered. pap. 2.25 o.s.i. (Venus). Grove.
Servitude. Irene Osgood. 1908. The Trow Press.
Servitude Et Grandeur Militaires. Alfred De Vigny. Ed. by Germain. 1965. pap. 6.95. French & Eur.
Servitude et Grandeur Militaires see Oeuvres Completes.
Servius and His Sources in the Commentary on the Georgica. Louis Frederick Hackemann. LC 41-14080.
Session: A Novel. Al Dewlen. LC 81-43051. 1981. 14.95 (ISBN 0-385-13474-6). Doubleday.
Sestrina: A Romance of the South Seas. Arnold Safroni-Middleton. LC 21-6909. 1921. Doran.
Set a Thief. Lee Thayer, pseud. LC 31-19568. Sears Publishing Company, Inc.
Set All Afire: A Novel of St. Francis Xavier. 1st Ed. Louis De Wohl. LC 53-8933. 1953. Lippincott.
Set Free. Jennie Maria Drinkwater Conklin & Drinkwater, Ella A., Joint Author. LC 6-30413. Ward & Drummond.
Set Free. Sylvia Paul Jerman, pseud. LC 34-46897. 1934. H. Smith & R. Haas.
Set Free Barabbas. Ivan Roe. LC 50-5142. 1950. Harper.
Set in Authority. Sara Jeannette Duncan Cotes. LC 6-32107. 1906. Doubleday, Page & Company.
Set in Diamonds. Charlotte Mary Brame. (Seaside library, v. 103, no. 2072). 1886. G. Munro.
Set in Diamonds. Charlotte Mary Brame. LC 6586. (On cover: Bertha Clay library. no. 33). Street & Smith.
Set in Motion. Valerie Martin. LC 78-3822. 1978. 7.95 (ISBN 0-374-26140-7). Farrar, Straus and Giroux.
Set in Motion. Valerie Martin. 1979. 1.95 (ISBN 0-380-44578-6). Avon Books.
Set in Silver. Charles Norris Williamson & Alice Muriel Livingston Williamson. LC 9-10033. 1909. Doubleday, Page & Company.
Set Love in Order. Renee Shann. 1971. pap. 0.75 o.p. (94179). Beagle Bks.
Set of Rouges: Namely Christopher Sutton, John Dawson, the Senor Don Sanchez Del Castello De Castelana and Moll Dawson... Frank Barrett. LC 6-8662. 1895. Macmillan and Co.
Set of Six. Joseph Conrad. 1915. Doubleday, Page & Company.
Set of Variations. Frank O'Connor, pseud. 1969. 10.00 o.p. (ISBN 0-394-44486-8). Knopf.
Set of Variations: Twenty-Seven Stories. Michael O'Donovan. LC 69-11479. 1969. 6.95. Knopf; Distributed by Random House.
Set of Wheels. Robert Thurston. 288p. (Orig.). 1983. pap. 2.50 (ISBN 0-425-05820-4). Berkley Pub.
Set Piece. Barbara Willard, pseud. LC 39-252. 1938. T. Nelson and Sons, Ltd.
Set the Stars on Fire. Sally Wentworth. (Harlequin Presents Ser.). 192p. 1980 (ISBN 0-373-10389-1, Pub. by Harlequin). pap. 1.50. PB.
Set This House on Fire. William Styron. LC 60-556822. 1960. Random House.
Set up. Lou Corradi. (Fawcett Gold Medal book). 1.75 (ISBN 0-449-14151-9). Fawcett Pubns.
Set-up. Leonard S. Goldberg. (Orig.). 1979. pap. 1.95 (ISBN 0-89041-262-6, 3262). Major Bks.
Set-up. Edmund G Love. LC 78-22737. 1980. 8.95 (ISBN 0-385-02729-X). Doubleday.
Set up. Robin Moore & Milt Machlin. 1975. pap. 1.75 o.p. (ISBN 0-515-03747-8). BJ Pub Group.
Set up. Robin Moore & Milt Machlin. 1975. (pbk.) 1.75. Pyramid Books.
Seth. David Brynley. LC 54-791820. 1954. Scribner.
Seth & Belle & Mr. Quarles and Me: The Bloody Affray at Lakeside Drive. William Rayner. LC 72-93510. 1973. 5.95 (ISBN 0-671-21497-7). Simon and Schuster.
Seth Bond: Or, A Lost Treasure Mystery. A Startling Detective Narrative. Harlan Page Halsey. (Old Sleuth's own, no. 105). 1898. The Parlor Car Publishing Co.
Seth Jones. Edward Sylvester Ellis & Edward Lytton. Deadwood Dick On Deck Wheeler. Ed. by Philip Durham. LC 66-23255. 1966. Odyssey Press.
Seth Jones: By Edward S. Ellis, and Deadwood Dick on Deck by Edward L. Wheeler; Dime Novels, Ed. by Philip Durham. Edward Sylvester Ellis. Ed. by Philip Durham. LC 66-232256. (Popular Amer. fic.). 1966. pap., 1.50. Odyssey.
Seth Jones: Or, The Captives of the Frontier. Edward Sylvester Ellis. LC 43-47579. (Beadle's dime novels. No. 8). 1860. I. P. Beadle and Company.
Seth Jones: Or, The Captives of the Frontier. Edward Sylvester Ellis. LC 78-11084. (Garland Library of Narratives of North American Indian Captivities; V. 77). 1978. 29.50 (ISBN 0-8240-1701-3). Garland Pub.
Seth Parker and His Jonesport Folks, Way Back Home. Phillips Haynes Lord, pseud. LC 32-5026. The John C. Winston Company.
Seth Speaks. Jane Roberts. 552p. 1981. pap. 5.95 (ISBN 0-13-807222-1). P-H.
Seth Speaks. Jane Roberts. LC 78-38925. (Illus.). 552p. 1972. 9.95 (ISBN 0-13-807206-X). P-H.
Seth Way: A Romance of the New Harmony Community. Caroline Dale Parke Snedeker. LC 17-31029. 1917. Houghton Mifflin Company.
Seth's Brother's Wife. Harold Frederic. LC 68-23720. (Americans in Fiction Ser.). lib. bdg. 14.50 (ISBN 0-8398-0565-9); pap. text ed. 6.50x (ISBN 0-89197-934-4). Irvington.
Seth's Brother's Wife see Collected Works.
Seth's Brother's Wife: A Study of Life in the Greater New York. Harold Frederic. LC 68-23720. (Illus.). 1968. Gregg Press.
Seth's Brother's Wife: A Study of Life in the Greater New York. Harold Frederic. LC 72-3263. 1968. Scholarly Press.
Seth's Brother's Wife. A Study of Life in the Greater New York. Harold Frederic. LC 6-43130. 1887. C. Scribner's Sons.
Seth's Work Is Done; or, The Phantom of the Belfry. John H Kelson. LC 7-10979. 1883. J. H. Parry.
Setting Free the Bears. John Irving. 1974. (pbk.) 1.95. Avon Books.
Setting Free the Bears. John Irving. LC 68-28537. 1969. 5.95. Random House.
Setting Sun. Translated by Donald Keena. Osamu Dazai. LC 56-133509. (New Directions book). 1956. J. Laughlin.
Setting the Golden Egg: Being the Prayer of a Woman for the Union and Growth of Science and Art in This Day of Human Upheaval. Lelia Mary Tinsley Tinsley. LC 16-243197. The Tinsley Company.
Setting the World on Fire. Angus Wilson. LC 80-14785. 1980. 9.95 (ISBN 0-670-63502-2). Viking Press.
Settled Furrows. Dorothy Hamilton. LC 77-186446. (Illus.). 1972. 3.95 (ISBN 0-8361-1669-0). Herald Press.
Settled in Chambers. Honor Lilibush Wingfield Tracy. (O.S.I.). 1968. 6.95 o.s.i. (ISBN 0-394-44485-X). Random.
Settled in Chambers: A Novel, by Honor Tracy. 1st Amer. Ed. Honor Lilbush Wingfield Tracy. LC 67-226712. 1968. bds., 4.95. Random.
Settled Out of Court. Ronald Arbuthnott Knox. LC 34-7023. E. P. Dutton & Co., Inc.
Settled Out of Court. 1st American Ed. Henry Cecil. LC 59-111543. 1959. Harper.
Settler. William Oliver Turner. 1956. Houghton Mifflin.
Settler. William Oliver Turner. (Berkley Medallion Book). 1977. 1.25 (ISBN 0-425-03297-3). Berkley Pub. Co.: Distributed by Putnam.
Settler: A Novel. Herman Whitaker. LC 7-32564. 1907. Harper & Brothers.
Settler Mac and the Charmed Quarter-Section. Hal Russell. LC 56-14257. 1956. Sage Books.
Settlers. William Stuart Long. LC 80-131723. (Long, William Stuart. Australians). 2.95 (ISBN 0-440-15923-7). Dell Pub. Col.
Settlers. Vilhelm Moberg. (Emigrants Saga Ser.: No. 3). 480p. 1982. pap. 2.95 (ISBN 0-445-04290-7). Popular Lib.
Settlers, a Novel. Meyer Levin. 1973. 1.75 (ISBN 0-671-78582-6). Pocket Books.
Settlers: A Novel. Meyer Levin. LC 74-179591. 1972. 10.00 (ISBN 0-671-21154-4). Simon and Schuster.
Settlers at Home. Harriet Martineau. LC 7-17817. 1864. Routledge, Warne and Routledge.
Settlers in Canada. Frederick Marryat. (Half-title: Everyman's library, ed. by Ernest Rhys. For young people). 1909. J. M. Dent & Co.
Settlers in Space. Steven Caldwell. LC 79-52772. 3.98 (ISBN 0-517-29226-2). Crescent Books.
Settlers of the Marsh. Frederick Philip Grove, pseud. LC 25-21065. George H. Doran Company.
Settling Down. Jane V. Barker & Sybil Downing. (Colorado Heritage Ser.: Bk. 8). (Illus.). 59p. (gr. 3-4). 1979. pap. text ed. 3.50x (ISBN 0-87108-227-6). Pruett.
Settling of Accounts. Carolyn G Hart. LC 76-2776. 1976. 5.95 (ISBN 0-385-12153-9). Published for the Crime Club by Doubleday.
Settling of the Sage. Hal George Evarts. LC 22-2102. 1922. 1.75. Little, Brown, and Company.
Settling of the Sage. Hal George Evarts. 1973. (pbk) 0.75. Pocket Books.
Settling Price. William Edward Hingston. LC 20-5582. The Cornhill Company.
Seule Sans Lui. Anne Hampson. (Harlequin Romantique Ser.). 192p. pap. 1.95 (ISBN 0-373-41178-2). Harlequin Bks.
Sevastopol. Lev Nikolaevich Tolstoi & Hapgood, Isabel Florence, 1850-1928, Tr. LC 8-25984. T. Y. Crowell & Co.
Seven. John Dann MacDonald. LC 78-27111. (Fawcett gold medal book). 1971. 0.75. Fawcett Publications.
Seven Against Greece. Nick Carter. (Nick Carter Ser). (O.s.i.). 160p. 1974. pap. 1.25 o.p. (AQ1393, Award). Univ Pub & Dist.
Seven Against Reeves: A Comedy-Farce. Richard Aldington. 1938. Doubleday, Doran & Company, Inc.
Seven Against the Years. Sterling North. LC 39-257028. 1939. The Macmillan Company.
Seven Ages of Woman. Compton Mackenzie. LC 23-1446. Frederick A. Stokes Company.
Seven Altars of Dusarra. Lawrence Watt-Evans. 240p. 1981. pap. 2.50 (ISBN 0-345-29264-2, Del Rey). Ballantine.
Seven Arms. Leonard Alfred George Strong. LC 35-18423. 1935. A. A. Knopf.
Seven Arrows. Hyemeyohsts Storm. LC 77-184216. (Illus.). 1972. 9.95 (ISBN 0-06-014134-4). Harper & Row.
Seven Bar Seven Ranch. Jay Lucas. The Macaulay Company.
Seven Black Chessmen. Gerald William Phillips. LC 28-18579. H. Holt and Company.
Seven Blue Diamonds. Charles B. Stilson. LC 27-221561. 1927. G. H. Watt.
Seven Brave Men. Brian Wynne Garfield. 1970. pap. 0.60 o.p. (ISBN 0-447-73897-6). Lancer.
Seven Brothers. Aleksis Kivi. LC 76-48428. (Classics of European Literature). 1977. 14.50. (ISBN 0-88355-552-2) (ISBN 0-88355-553-0). Hyperion Press.
Seven Brothers. Aleksis Stenvall. Tr. by Matson, Alex. LC 29-2731. 1929. Coward-McCann, Inc.
Seven Brothers of Wyoming: Or, The Brigands of the Revolution. LC 8-6873. H. Long & Brother.
Seven by Colette. Sidonie Gabrielle Colette. LC 55-11186. 1955. Farrar, Straus and Cudahy.
Seven by Seven: A Novel. Hans Duffy. LC 33-19077. 1933. W. Morrow and Company.
Seven Cardinal Virtues of Science Fiction. Ed. by Isaac Asimov et al. 1981. pap. 2.50 (ISBN 0-449-24440-7, Crest). Fawcett.
Seven Chinese Stories. T. J. Sheridan. (Oxford Progressive English Readers Ser.). (Illus.). 1975. pap. 3.50x (ISBN 0-19-638230-0). Oxford U Pr.
Seven Cities of Gold. Virginia Davis Hersch. LC 46-6850. 1946. Duell, Sloan and Pearce.
Seven Conquests. Poul Anderson. 1970. pap. 0.95 o.p. (00907, Collier). Macmillan.
Seven Conquests; an Adventure in Science Fiction. Poul Anderson. LC 69-12644. 1969. Macmillan.
Seven Contemporary Short Novels. 2d ed. Ed. by Charles Clerc. LC 74-83538. 1975. 5.95 (ISBN 0-673-07971-6). Scott, Foresman.
Seven Contemporary Short Novels. 2d ed. Ed. by Charles Clerc. LC 74-83538. 1975. (ISBN 0-673-07971-6). Scott, Foresman.
Seven Conundrums. Edward Phillips Oppenheim. LC 78-134973. (Short story index reprint series). (Illus.). 1970. Books for Libraries Press.
Seven Conundrums. Edward Phillips Oppenheim. LC 23-4986. 1923. Little, Brown, and Company.
Seven Darlings. Gouverneur Morris. LC 15-560027. 1915. C. Scribner's Sons.
Seven Daughters. Mabel Margaret Clark. LC 31-7079. Farrar & Rinehart, Incorporated.
Seven Daughters. Henry Lieferant & Sylvia Saltzberg Lieferant. LC 47-30222. 1947. Coward-McCann, Inc.
Seven Day Soldiers. Tony Kenrick. LC 75-32971. 224p. 1976. 7.95 o.p. (ISBN 0-8092-8127-9). Contemp Bks.
Seven Day Soldiers: A Novel. Tony Kenrick. LC 75-32971. 7.95 (ISBN 0-8092-8127-9). H. Regnery.
Seven Day Soldiers: A Novel. Tony Kenrick. 1977. 1.95 (ISBN 0-446-79979-3). Warner Books.
Seven Days. Adolf Andreas Latzko. Tr. by Sutton, Eric. LC 31-19572. 1931. The Viking Press.
Seven Days at the Silbersteins. Etienne Leroux. LC 67-21719. 1967. Houghton Mifflin.
Seven Days' Darkness. Gunnar Gunnarsson. Tr. by Tapley, Roberts. LC 30-29253. 1930. The Macmillan Company.
Seven Days in a Pullman Car. Ausburn Towner. LC 8-29830. J. S. Ogilvie & Company.
Seven Days in May. Fletcher Knebel & Charles Waldo Bailey. LC 62-14555. 1962. Harper & Row.
Seven Days' Mystery. Frederick Russell Burton. LC 4266. (On cover: Magnet detective library, no. 142). Street & Smith.
Seven Days of Creation. Vladimir Emelianovich Maksimov, pseud. LC 73-20781. 1975. 10.00 (ISBN 0-394-48522-X). Knopf: Distributed by Random House.
Seven Days of Creation. Vladimir Maximov. LC 73-20781. 448p. 1975. 10.00 o.p. (ISBN 0-394-48522-X). Knopf.
Seven Days of Mourning. L S Simckes. LC 63-16151. 1963. Random House.
Seven Days of Our Life: By Andrei Goulyashki. Tr. by Zdravko Stankov. Andrei Guliashki. LC 66-9482. (Rila lib.). 1966. bds., 2.50. Foreign Langs. Pr.
Seven Days' Secret. Joseph Smith Fletcher. LC 30-278162. 1930. E. J. Clode, Inc.
Seven Days to a Killing. Clive Egleton. LC 72-87586. 1973. 6.95 (ISBN 0-698-10495-1). Coward, McCann & Geoghegan.
Seven Days to Disaster. Jonas Flagg & Geoffrey Graves. 176p. (Orig.). 1976. pap. 1.50 (ISBN 0-89041-075-5, 3075). Major Bks.
Seven Days to Glory. Richard Newhafer. (Orig.). 1973. pap. 1.50 o.p. (ISBN 0-515-03201-8, A3073). Pyramid Pubns.
Seven Days Whipping. John Biggs. LC 28-173861. 1928. C. Scribner's Sons.

Seven Dead. Joseph Jefferson Farjeon. LC 40-4860. The Bobbs-Merrill Company.

Seven Deadly Sins of London, Drawn in Seven Several Coaches, Through the Seven Several Gates of the City: Bringing the Plague with Them. October 1606. Thomas Dekker. LC 72-194943. (English Scholar's Library of Old and Modern Works V. 1 No. 7). 1967. AMS Press.

Seven Deadly Sins of Science Fiction. Ed. by Isaac Asimov et al. 1980. pap. 2.50 (ISBN 0-449-24349-4, Crest). Fawcett.

Seven Deadly Sisters. Patricia McGerr. LC 47-30477. 1947. Pub. for the Crime Club by Doubleday.

Seven Dials Mystery. Agatha Miller Christie. LC 29-70699. 1929. Dodd, Mead & Company.

Seven Doors to Sin. Nicholas A Dunaev. LC 53-5691. 1953. Vantage Press.

Seven Dreamers. Bernard St. James, pseud. LC 81-43282. (Crime Club Ser.). 192p. 1982. 10.95 (ISBN 0-385-17860-3). Doubleday.

Seven Dreamers. Annie Trumbull Slosson. LC 79-98602. (Short story index reprint series). (Illus.). 1969. Books for Libraries Press.

Seven Dreamers. Annie Trumbull Slosson. LC 4-15153. 1891. Harper & Brothers.

Seven Eight - One Eight Seven Eight Eight Zero. Ira Einhorn. LC 78-187880. (Illus.). pap. 2.95 o.p. (ISBN 0-385-06392-X, Anch). Doubleday.

Seven Eleven Officer Needs Help. Whit Masterson. LC 65-23535. (Red badge detective). bds., 3.50. Dodd.

Seven Famous Novels. Herbert George Wells. LC 34-27157. 1934. A. A. Knopf.

Seven File. William P McGivern. LC 56-683124. (Red badge detective). 1956. Dodd, Mead.

Seven Footprints to Satan. Abraham Merritt. LC 28-10390. 1928. Boni and Liveright.

Seven Footprints to Satan. Abraham Merritt. LC 43-12321. (Murder of the month. No. 1). 1942. The Avon Book Company.

Seven Footprints to Satan and Burn, Witch, Burn! Complete and Unabridged. Abraham Merritt. LC 52-9663. 1952. Liveright Pub. Corp.

Seven for a Secret: A Love Story. Mary Gladys Meredith Webb. LC 23-9231. George H. Doran Company.

Seven for a Secret: A Love Story. Mary Gladys Meredith Webb. LC 29-16671. 1929. E. P. Dutton & Co., Inc.

Seven for Cordelia. Catherine Macdonald MacLean. LC 42-36024. 1942. The Macmillan Company.

Seven Frozen Sailors. George Manville Fenn & Reade, Compton, Joint Author. LC 6-39389. New Amsterdam Book Company.

Seven Games in October. Charles Brady. LC 79-14345. 9.95 (ISBN 0-316-10594-5). Little, Brown.

Seven Gothic Tales. Karen Blixen. LC 72-662. 1972. 1.95 (ISBN 0-394-71807-0). Vintage Books.

Seven Gothic Tales. with an introduction by dorothy canfield. ed. Karen Blixen & Fisher, Mrs. Dorothea Frances (Canfield) 1879- LC 34-120408. 1934. H. Smith and R. Haas.

Seven Gothic Tales. Karen Blixen & Fisher, Mrs. Dorothea Frances (Canfield) 1879- LC 39-27353. (Half-title: The modern library of the world's best books). 1939. The Modern Library.

Seven Gothic Tales. Isak Dinesen, pseud. 6.95 (ISBN 0-394-60496-2). Modern Lib.

Seven Gothic Tales. Isak Dinesen, pseud. 2.95 o.p. (54). Modern Lib.

Seven Gray Pilgrims. A Personal Romance. By a Subaltern of Artillery. Frederic Robinson. LC 8-28098. 1874. A. Williams and Company.

Seven Great British Short Novels: Ed., Introd. by Philip Rahv. Ed. by Philip Rahv. (DQ1554). 1968. pap., 1.25. Berkeley.

Seven Great Detective Stories. Ed. by William Herbert Larson. LC 68-25323. (Whitman classics). 1968. 0.69. Whitman Pub. Division, Western Pub. Co.

Seven Hills. Leonard Wibberley. 1977. pap. 1.95 (ISBN 0-89041-138-7, 3138). Major Bks.

Seven Hills: A Novel. Meade Minnigerode. LC 23-12398. 1923. G. P. Putnam's Sons.

Seven Hills Away. N. V. Gonzalez. LC 47-31351. 1947. A. Swallow.

Seven Hills of Paradise. Rosemary Simpson. LC 79-8439. (Illus.). 1980. 12.95 (ISBN 0-385-15775-4). Doubleday.

Seven Hills of the Dove. Scharmen Iris. 3.00 o.p. (ISBN 0-8283-1391-1). Branden.

Seven Icelandic Short Stories. 2nd ed. 1961. 4.95x (ISBN 0-89067-037-4). Am Scandinavian.

Seven in One House. Vitalii Nikolaevich Semin. LC 68-22673. 1968. Dutton.

Seven in One House. Vitaly Syomin. Tr. by Michael Glenny. LC 68-22673. 1968. 4.95 o.p. Dutton.

Seven Islands. 1st American Ed. Jon Godden. LC 56-577073. 1956. Knopf.

Seven Japanese Tales. Junichiro Tanizaki. LC 62-15574. (Illus.). 1963. Knopf.

Seven Japanese Tales. Junichiro Tanizaki. LC 80-39965. 1981. 5.95 (ISBN 0-399-50523-7). Perigee Books.

Seven Keys to Baldpate. Earl Derr Biggers. LC 13-376220. The Bobbs-Merrill Company.

Seven Keys to Baldpate. Earl Derr Biggers. LC 33-17497. 1914. Grossett & Dunlap.

Seven Last Years. Carol Balizet. LC 78-27012. 10.95 (ISBN 0-912376-36-8). Chosen Books.

Seven Letters to Counsel: Or, The Irritable Codicils of A. S. Cory. Charles Nagel. LC 65-8991. 1965. Vantage Press.

Seven Little Lanes. Chaim Grade. LC 76-186506. (Remembrance award library). 1972. Bergen Belsen Memorial Press.

Seven Lovers: And Other Stories. Muriel Hine Coxon. LC 28-267397. 1928. D. Appleton & Company.

Seven Make a Honeymoon. Lois Bull. LC 35-526. The Macaulay Company.

Seven Masterpieces of Gothic Horror. Ed. by Robert Donald Spector. LC 63-8941. (Bantam classic). 1963. Bantam Books.

Seven Men. Max Beerbohm. LC 20-19582. 1920. A. A. Knopf.

Seven Men and Two Others. Max Beerbohm. (Vintage book, K80). 1959. Vintage Books.

Seven Men and Two Others. Max Beerbohm. LC 79-42711. (World's classics). 1980. 4.95 (ISBN 0-19-281512-1). Oxford University Press.

Seven Men, and Two Others: Introd. by Lord David Cecil. Max Beerbohm. LC 66-73997. (World's classics, 610). 1966. 2.75. Oxford Univ. Pr.

Seven Men Are Murdered. Robert Wallace. LC 30-344102. 1930. The Fiction League.

Seven Men at Mimbres Springs: By Will Henry Pseud. Henry Allen. LC 58-9870. 1958. Random House.

Seven Men Came Back. Warwick Deeping. LC 34-139023. 1934. A. A. Knopf.

Seven Men for Nelda: By Joan Sargent Pseud. Sara Lucile Jenkins. LC 54-134445. 1954. Avalon Books.

Seven Men in the Barracks Room. Bruce Kilnsbay. LC 79-63926. 139p. 1980. 7.95 (ISBN 0-533-04288-7). Vantage.

Seven Men of Gascony. Ronald Frederick Delderfeld. 1976. 1.95 (ISBN 0-671-80723-4). Pocket Books.

Seven Men of Gascony. Ronald Frederick Delderfield. LC 74-4315. 1974-1975. 8.95 (ISBN 0-671-21794-1). Simon and Schuster.

Seven Men of Gascony: A Novel. Ronald Frederick Delderfield. LC 49-7543. 1949. Bobbs-Merrill Co.

Seven Miles to Arden. Ruth Sawyer. LC 16-103049. 1916. Harper & Brothers.

Seven Minutes. Irving Wallace. pap. 3.95 (ISBN 0-671-41668-5). PB.

Seven Minutes: A Novel. Irving Wallace. LC 72-75870. 1969. 7.50. Simon and Schuster.

Seven Minutes Past Midnight. Walter Winward. LC 79-26613. (Illus.). 12.95 (ISBN 0-671-24932-0). Simon and Schuster.

Seven Miracles of Gubbio and the Eighth: A Parable. Raymond Leopold Bruckberger. LC 48-9327. 1948. Whittlesey House.

Seven Months of Sin: A Novel of Intrigue, Love, and Deceit. Ned Elvin Wick. LC 74-78891. 1974. 3.50. Fenwynn Press.

Seven More Short Stories. M. Schrader. 2.00 o.p. Carlton.

Seven Murders. Robert Harold May. LC 32-107472. The Macaulay Company.

Seven Must Die. James Warner Bellah. LC 38-4428. 1938. D. Appleton-Century Company, Incorporated.

Seven: Navy Subchaser. William Edward Syers. LC 60-7105. 1960. Duell, Sloan and Pearce.

Seven Novellas. Marsden Dillenback & John Schweitzer. 1966. pap. text ed. 4.45 o.p. (ISBN 0-684-51510-5, ScribC). Scribner.

Seven Novellas. Marsden Dillenback & John Schweitzer. 1966. pap. text ed. 4.45 o.p. (ISBN 0-684-51510-5, ScribC). Scribner.

Seven Novellas. edited by marsden v. dillenbeck and john c. schweitzer. ed. Ed. by Marsden V Dillenbeck & John C. Schweitzer. LC 66-11375. 1966. Scribner.

Seven Novellas: Ed by Marsden V. Dillenbeck, John C. Schweitzer. Ed. by Marsden V Dillenbeck & John C. Schweitzer. LC 66-11375. 3.60, 2.40 pap.,. Scribners.

Seven Oaks. Charlotte York. 1978. 1.95 (ISBN 0-8439-0549-2). Nordon Pubns.

Seven Occasions. Hollis Spurgeon Summers. 1965. 6.50 o.p. (ISBN 0-8135-0469-4). Rutgers U Pr.

Seven of Diamonds. Max Brand. LC 35-440. 1935. Dodd, Mead & Company.

Seven of Diamonds. Frederick Faust. LC 35-440. 1935. Dodd, Mead & Company.

Seven of Swords: A Novel. R. E Harrington. LC 75-37436. 7.95 (ISBN 0-399-11624-9). Putnam.

Seven on the Highway. Blanche Willis Howard Von Teuffel. LC 77-37566. (Short story index reprint series). 1972. (ISBN 0-8369-4125-X). Books for Libraries Press.

Seven on the Highway. Blanche Willis Howard Von Teuffel. LC 8-25950. 1897. Houghton, Mifflin, and Company.

Seven Out of Time. Arthur Leo Zagat. LC 49-5461. 1949. Fantasy Press.

Seven Peas in Pod... Margery Bailey. LC 19-14799. 1919. Little, Brown, & Company.

Seven-per-Cent Solution: Being a Reprint from the Reminiscences of John H. Watson, M.D. Nicholas Meyer. LC 74-4018. 1974. 6.95. Dutton.

Seven Pillars to Hell. Henry Patterson. LC 63-10430. (Raven book). 1963. Abelard-Schuman.

Seven Pilots. Charles Graves. LC 43-7556. 1943. Hutchinson & Co. Ltd.

Seven Poor Men of Sydney. Christina Stead. LC 65-28396. 1966. 4.85. Angus & Robertson.

Seven Poor Men of Sydney. Christina Stead. LC 35-304806. 1935. D. Appleton-Century Company, Incorporated.

Seven Red Sundays. Ramon Jose Sender & Mitchell, Sir Peter Chalmers, 1864- Tr. LC 36-18554. Liveright Publishing Corporation.

Seven Rivers. Eli Fackler. (Orig.). 1982. pap. 1.95 (ISBN 0-440-17986-6). Dell.

Seven Russian Short Novel Masterpieces. Ed. by Leo Hamalian. LC 67-27812. (Popular living classics library). 1967. Popular Library.

Seven Science Fiction Novels. Herbert George Wells. LC 51-2132. 1950. Dover Publications.

Seven Scots Stories. Jane Helen Findlater. LC 75-121542. (Short story index reprint series). 1970. Books for Libraries Press.

Seven Seas Murders: Four Cases in the Career of Captain North. Francis Van Wyck Mason. LC 36-179489. 1936. Pub. for the Crime Club, Inc., by Doubleday, Doran & Company, Inc.

Seven Seas Murders: Four Cases in the Career of Captain North. Francis Van Wyck Mason. LC 37-383113. 1937. The Sun Dial Press, Inc.

Seven Seasons. Peter Forbath. LC 77-139307. 1971. 7.95. Atheneum.

Seven Seats to the Moon. Charlotte Armstrong. LC 69-15735. 1969. 5.95. Coward-McCann.

Seven Selected Short Stories. Sinclair Lewis. LC 44-7528. (Avon modern short story monthly, no. 6). 1943. Avon Book Company.

Seven Serpents & Seven Moons. Demetrio Aguilera-Malta. Tr. by Gregory Rabassa. 320p. 1981. pap. 3.50 (ISBN 0-380-54767-8, 54767, Bard). Avon.

Seven Serpents & Seven Moons. Demetrio Aguilera-Malta. Tr. by Gregory Rabassa from Sp. LC 79-10516. (Texas Pan American Ser.). 315p. 1979. 12.95 (ISBN 0-292-77552-0); pap. cancelled (ISBN 0-292-77555-5). U of Tex Pr.

Seven Serpents and Seven Moons. Aguilera-Matta Demetrio. (Illus.). 1981. 3.50. Avon.

Seven Sexes. William Tenn. 240p. 1980. pap. 2.25 (ISBN 0-345-28956-0). Ballantine.

Seven Short Novel Masterpieces. Ed. by Leo Hamalian & Edmond L. Volpe. Incl. Daughters of the Vicar. D. H. Lawrence; Metamorphosis. Franz Kafka; Candide. Voltaire; Lesson of the Master. Henry James; First Love. Ivan Turgenev; Benito Cereno. Herman Melville; Master & Man. Leo Tolstoy. (YA) (gr. 7up). pap. 2.50 (ISBN 0-445-08504-5). Popular Lib.

Seven Short Novel Masterpieces: Edited by Leo Hamalian and Edmond L. Volpe. With an Introd. by Mark Schorer. Ed. by Leo Hamalian & Edmond Loris Volpe. LC 61-9790. (Popular special W1103). 1961. Popular Living Classics Library.

Seven Short Novels. Anton Pavlovich Chekhov. LC 63-8936. (Bantam classic). 1963. Bantam Books.

Seven Short Novels from the Woman's Home Companion. Woman's Home Companion. Ed. by Fles, Barthold. LC 49-27390. 1949. Pocket Books.

Seven Short Stories. Anton Pavlovich Chekhov. Tr. & intro. by Ronald Hingley. (Oxford Paperbacks Ser). 1974. 5.95x (ISBN 0-19-281159-2). Oxford U Pr.

Seven Silent Men. Noel Behn. 356p. 1983. 15.50 (ISBN 0-87795-499-2). Arbor Hse.

Seven Sins. Arthur Sarsfield Ward. LC 43-14777. 1943. R. M. McBride & Co.

Seven Sisters. Jean Lilly. LC 28-16719. E. P. Dutton & Company.

Seven Sisters. Frederic Prokosch. LC 62-18414. 1962. Farrar, Straus and Cudahy.

Seven Sisters. Frederic Prokosch. LC 73-178792. 1972. 15.25 (ISBN 0-8371-6286-6). Greenwood Press.

Seven Six-Gunners. Nelson Nye. 1976. 1.25. Ace.

Seven Sixes Are Forty-Three. Kiran Nagarkar & Shubha Slee. LC 81-113322. (Asian and Pacific Writing; 14). 1980. 15.75 (ISBN 0-7022-1503-1). University of Queensland Press.

Seven Sixes Are Forty-Three: A Novel. Kiran Nagarkar. Tr. by Shubha Slee from Marathi. (Vikas Library of Modern Indian Writing: No. 15). 175p. 1981. text ed. 15.95x (ISBN 0-7069-1346-9, Pub. by Vikas India). Advent NY.

Seven Slash Range. Bennett Foster. LC 36-201439. 1936. W. Morrow & Co.

Seven Slayers. Paul Cain. LC 47-24599. (On cover: A Chartered collection. 21). 1946. Saint Enterprises Inc.

Seven Sleepers. Francis Beeding. LC 25-754. 1925. Little, Brown, and Company.

Seven Sleepers. Morna Doris MacTaggart Brown. LC 76-103382. 1970. 4.50. Walker.

Seven Sleepers. E. X. Ferrars, pseud. LC 76-103382. (Mystery Ser). 1970. 4.50 o.p. (ISBN 0-8027-5152-0). Walker & Co.

Seven Smiles and a Few Fibs. Thomas Jondrie Vivian. LC 8-32696. (On verso of t.-p.: Neely's prismatic library). F. T. Neely.

Seven Sons. Angela Simon. (Berkley Medallion Book). 1977. 1.75 (ISBN 0-425-03543-3). Berkley Pub. Corp.

Seven Sons of Ballyhack. Thomas Sawyer Spivey. LC 11-32252. 1911. The Cosmopolitan Press.

Seven Sons of Mammon. George Augustus Henry Sala. LC 8-5791. 1862. T. O. H. P. Burnham.

Seven Stabs. Archibald Gordon Macdonnell. LC 30-7793. 1930. Pub. for The Crime Club, Inc., by Doubleday, Doran & Company, Inc.

Seven Stars. Andre Malvil & Lucas, Mrs. Elizabeth, Tr. LC 32-4341. 1932. The Macmillan Company.

Seven Stars: A Novel. Tou Matsumoto. LC 49-8142. 1949. Friendship Press.

Seven Steps East: A Ralph Lindsey Mystery. Ben Benson. LC 59-7927. 1959. M. S. Mill Co. and W. Morrow.

Seven Steps to the Arbiter. La Fayette Ronald Hubbard. LC 75-13442. 1.25 (ISBN 0-89041-018-6). Major Books.

Seven Steps to the Sun. Fred Hoyle & Geoffrey Hoyle. (Crest bk., T1778). 1973. Fawcett.

Seven Storey Mountain. Thomas Merton. pap. 1.95 (ISBN 0-451-61393-7, MJ1393, Ment). NAL.

Seven Stories. Anton Pavlovich Chekhov. Tr. by Ronald Hingley. LC 74-175888. (OXford paperbacks, 315). 1974. (1.25, 3.95 u.s.) (ISBN 0-19-281159-2). Oxford University Press.

Seven Stories. James Hall. Ed. by Mary Burtschi. LC 75-23549. 1975. 5.95 (ISBN 0-9601642-1-9). Little Brick Hse.

Seven Stories. Nathaniel Hawthorne. Ed. by Carl Clinton Van Doren. LC 20-146029. 1920. Harcourt, Brace and Howe.

Seven Stories from Spanish America. Ed. by Gordon Brotherston. LC 67-31497. (Commonwealth and international library). 1968. New York, Pergamon Press.

Seven Stories, with Basement and Attic. Donald Grant Mitchell. LC 69-11911. (American short story series, v. 70). 1969. (ISBN 0-512-00519-2). Garrett Press.

Seven Stories with Basement and Attic. Donald Grant Mitchell. LC 72-8317. (American short story series, v. 70). 1972. (ISBN 0-8422-8096-0). MSS Information Corp.

Seven Stories: With Basement and Attic. Donald Grant Mitchell. LC 7-25323. 1864. C. Scribner.

Seven Stories: With Basement and Attic. Donald Grant Mitchell. 1884. C. Scribner's Sons.

Seven Suspects. Florence Ryerson & Clements, Colin Campbell, 1894- Joint Author. LC 30-7682. 1930. D. Appleton and Company.

Seven Suspects. John Innes Mackintosh Stewart. LC 37-2028. 1937. Dodd, Mead & Company.

Seven Sweethearts. Emilie Johnson. LC 28-223102. Hollywood Print Shop.

Seven Tales. Edgar Allan Poe & Charles Pierre Baudelaire. LC 78-148839. (Illus.). 1971. 10.00 (ISBN 0-8052-3401-2). Schocken Books.

Seven Tales and Alexander. Herbert Ernest Bates. LC 31-26025. 1930. The Viking Press.

Seven Tears for Apollo. Phyllis A. Whitney. 1977. pap. 2.50 (ISBN 0-449-23428-2, Crest). Fawcett.

Seven Tempest. William Vaughan Wilkins. 1942. The Macmillan Company.

Seven That Were Hanged: And Other Stories. Leonid Nikolaevich Andreev. LC 58-6369. (Modern library paperbacks, P40). 1958. Random House.

Seven Thunders. Rupert Croft-Cooke. LC 55-9816. 1955. St. Martin's Press.

Seven Tickets to Singapore. Ared White. LC 39-9056. 1939. Houghton Mifflin Company.

Seven Tides. Virginia McCall. LC 72-3013. (Red rose romance #129). 1972. 0.75. Bantam Books.

Seven Times the Leading Man. Egon Hostovsky. LC 45-9240. 1945. L. B. Fischer.

Seven to Twelve: A Detective Story. Anna Katharine Green Rohlfs. LC 11-821940. 1887. G. P. Putnam's Sons.

Seven Trails. Max Brand. 1982. 18.00x (ISBN 0-86025-208-6, Pub. by Ian Henry Pubns England). State Mutual Bk.

Seven Vagabonds. Nathaniel Hawthorne. LC 16-194531. 1916. 1.00. Houghton, Mifflin Company.

Seven Vices: A Novel of Italy in Our Own Times. Guglielmo Ferrero & Livingston, Arthur, 1888- Tr. LC 29-14295. Harcourt, Brace and Company.

Seven Wagons West. Jon Sharpe. (Trailsmen Ser.: No. 1). (Orig.). 1980. pap. 2.25 (ISBN 0-451-11052-8, AE1052, Sig). NAL.

Seven Was the Padre's Number. Henry James. 1973. 6.00 (ISBN 0-682-47784-2). Exposition.

Seven Was the Padre's Number: A Novel. Henry James. 1973. 5.00 (ISBN 0-682-47784-2). Exposition Pr.

Seven Ways from Sundown. Clair Huffaker. LC 82-838. 1982. 9.95 (ISBN 0-89621-350-1). Thorndike Press.

Seven Ways from Sundown. Clair Huffaker. 1975. (pbk.) 1.25 (ISBN 0-671-78895-7). Pocket Books.

Seven Ways to Sunday. John Coriolan. (Orig.). 1972. pap. 1.95 o.s.i. (TC3232). Olympia.

Seven Were Veiled. Kathleen Moore Knight. LC 37-4078. 1937. Pub. for the Crime Club, Inc., by Doubleday, Doran & Company, Inc.

Seven Were Veiled. Kathleen Moore Knight. LC 38-9430. 1938. The Sun Dial Press, Inc.

Seven Who Fled. Frederic Prokosch. LC 37-18251. 1937. Harper & Brothers.

Seven Who Waited. August William Derleth. LC 43-13713. 1943. C. Scribner's Sons.

Seven Windows. Russell Fischer. LC 48-908102. 1948. Christopher Pub. House.

Seven Winters. Elizabeth Bowen. 72p. 1971. Repr. of 1942 ed. 10.00x (ISBN 0-7165-1397-8, Pub. by Cuala Press Ireland). Biblio Dist.

Seven Wise Owls. Ellen J. Macleod. 1958. 1.50 o.p. (ISBN 0-87508-754-X). Chr Lit.

Seven Witches. George MacBeth. LC 77-92539. 8.95 (ISBN 0-15-181370-1). Harcourt Brace Jovanovich.

Seven Witches. George Macbeth. (Signet Book). 1979. 2.50 (ISBN 0-451-08597-3). New American Library.

Seven Wives of Bluebeard. Anatole France, pseud. LC 73-144154. (Short story index reprint series). 1971. (ISBN 0-8369-3769-4). Books for Libraries Press.

Seven Women. William Mestrezat John. LC 29-21924. J. H. Sears & Company.

Seven Years and Mair. Anna Theresa Sadlier. LC 8-4786. (On cover: Harper's half-hour series v. 62). 1878. Harper & Brothers.

Seven Years, and Other Tales. Julia Kavanagh. LC 29-30776. 1860. D. Appleton and Company.

Seven Years Dead. Seldon Truss, pseud. LC 61-6523. 1961. Published for the Crime Club by Doubleday.

Seven Years of My Life. Fritz Reuter. Tr. by Carl F. Bayerschmidt. (International Studies & Translations). 1975. lib. bdg. 12.95 (ISBN 0-8057-5740-6, Twayne). G K Hall.

Seven Yesterdays. Paul Hoffman. LC 33-21387. 1933. Harper & Brothers.

Sevenoaks. Josiah Gilbert Holland. LC 68-57531. (Muckrakers Ser.). Repr. of 1875 ed. lib. bdg. 14.00 (ISBN 0-8398-0785-6). Irvington.

Sevenoaks: A Story of Today. Josiah Gilbert Holland. LC 68-57531. (American novels of muckraking, propaganda, and social protest). 1968. Gregg Press.

Sevenoaks, a Story of Today. Josiah Gilbert Holland. LC 7-6142. 1875. Scribner, Armstrong & Co.

Sevenoaks; a Story of Today. Josiah Gilbert Holland. LC 7-6141. 1882. C. Scribner's Sons.

Seventeen. Carl Erik Soya. LC 61-15216. 1961. P. S. Eriksson.

Seventeen. Booth Tarkington. (Perennial classic, P3078). 1968. Harper.

Seventeen: A Tale of Youth and Summer Time and the Baxter Family, Especially William. Booth Tarkington. LC 16-6604. 1916. Harper & Brothers.

Seventeen: A Tale of Youth and Summer Time and the Baxter Family, Especially William. Booth Tarkington. LC 21-13948. 1918. Grosset & Dunlap.

Seventeen: A Tale of Youth and Summer Time and the Baxter Family, Especially William. Booth Tarkington & Holmes, Mabel Dodge, 1883- Ed. LC 32-11118. (Harper's modern classics). 1932. Harper & Brothers.

Seventeen: A Tale of Youth and Summer Time and the Baxter Family, Especially William. Booth Tarkington & Tunis, Edwin, 1897- Illus. LC 32-25850. 1932. Harper & Brothers.

Seventeen and Black: A Novel. Jack Waer. LC 54-9879. 1954. Viking Press.

Seventeen Ben Gurion: A Novel. Jack Hoffenberg. LC 76-28471. 10.00 (ISBN 0-399-11878-0). Putnam.

Seventeen Ben Gurion: A Novel. Jack Hoffenberg. (Berkley Medallion Book). 1978. 2.25 (ISBN 0-425-03762-2). Berkley Pub. Corp.

Seventeen Blocks from the River. Vonder Marylou Brink. Ed. by Sylvia Ashton. LC 75-16568. 1976. 8.95 o.p. (ISBN 0-87949-046-2). Ashley Bks.

Seventeen Blocks from the River. Vonder Brink, Marylou. LC 77-16568. 7.95 (ISBN 0-87949-046-2). Ashley Books.

Seventeen Chimneys. Theodore Acland Harper. LC 38-21854. 1938. The Viking Press.

Seventeen from Seventeen: An Anthology of Stories, Selected by Babette Rosmond. Ed. by Babette Rosmond. Seventeen. LC 67-179182. 1967. 4.95. Macmillan.

Seventeen Lost Stories. William Somerset Maugham. LC 75-26137. (Maugham, William Somerset, 1874-1965. Works. 1976). (Works. 1976.). 1977. 15.00 (ISBN 0-405-07858-7). Arno Press.

Seventeen Lost Stories. William Somerset Maugham. Ed. by Craig V. Showalter. LC 69-12234. 1969. 5.95. Doubleday.

Seventeen Modern German Stories. Ed. by Richard Hinton Thomas. (Clarendon German ser.). 1966. pap., 1.25. Oxford.

Seventeen Modern German Stories. Ed. by Thomas, Richard Hinton. LC 66-9408. 1965. Oxford University Press.

Seventeen Ninety-One: A Tale of San Domingo. Edward Winslow Gilliam. LC 6-44046. 1890. J. Murphy & Co.

Seventeen of Leyden: A Frolic Through This Vale of Tears. John James. LC 70-163454. 1972. 7.50. St. Martin's Press.

Seventeen Seventy-Nine: General Sullivan's Great War Trail. Thomas Kelly. LC 13-6074. 1913. 1.50. Pub. at Mt. Pleasant Farm.

Seventeen Seventy-Six & All That: Being a True and Detailed Account of a Celestial Visitation to the White House in Connection with the Bicentenary of the United States of America, 1776-1976) Leonard Patrick O'Connor Wibberley. LC 75-20061. 1975. 6.95 (ISBN 0-688-02969-8). Morrow.

Seventeen Steps to 221B: A Collection of Sherlockian Pieces by English Writers. Ed. by James E. Holroyd. 1967. text ed. 6.50x o.p. Humanities.

Seventeen Widows of Sans Souci. Charlotte Armstrong. LC 59-11000. 1959. Coward-McCann.

Seventeen's Stories. Ed. by Babette Rosmond. 1958. 3.95 o.p. Lippincott.

Seventeenth Stair. Barbara Paul. LC 74-25219. (Troubadour). 1975. 7.95. St. Martin's Press.

Seventeenth Stair. Barbara Vstedal. LC 76-772. 1976. 10.95 (ISBN 0-8161-6352-9). G. K. Hall.

Seventeenth Summer. Maureen Daly, pseud. LC 42-12642. 1942. Dodd, Mead & Company.

Seventeeth Summer. Maureen Daly, pseud. LC 48-10238. 1948. Dodd Mead.

Seventh. Richard Stark. 1981. lib. bdg. 10.95 (ISBN 0-8398-2737-7, Gregg). G K Hall.

Seventh. Donald E Westlake. LC 80-39928. (Gregg Press Mystery Fiction Series). 1981. 10.95 (ISBN 0-8398-2737-7). Gregg Press.

Seventh All Hallows' Eve. Ruby Jean Jensen. (Warner gothic). 1974. (pbk.) 1.25. Warner Paperback Library.

Seventh Angel. Alexander Black. LC 21-2591. Harper & Brothers.

Seventh Angel. Lorol E. Toy. 197p. 1970. 6.00 o.s.i. (ISBN 0-910348-06-5). Channel Pub.

Seventh Assembling. Richard Kostelanetz & Henry J. Korn. (Illus.). 1977. pap. 6.95. Assembling Pr.

Seventh Avenue. Norman Bogner. (7810). 1968. Dell.

Seventh Avenue. Norman Bogner. LC 66-26527. 1967. Coward-McCann.

Seventh Avenue. Dorothy Meyersburg. LC 40-35994. 1941. E. P. Dutton & Co., Inc.

Seventh Babe. Jerome Charyn. 352p. 1980. pap. 2.95 (ISBN 0-380-51540-7, 51540). Avon.

Seventh Babe: A Novel. Jerome Charyn. LC 78-73866. 9.95 (ISBN 0-87795-220-5). Arbor House.

Seventh Chasm. Oliver Gard. LC 53-12424. (Red badge detective). 1953. Dodd, Mead.

Seventh Child. Henrietta Eliza Vaughan Stannard. J. S. Tait & Sons.

Seventh Child. Brooks Stanwood, pseud. LC 81-15604. 1981. 13.50 (ISBN 0-671-43637-6). Linden Press/Simon & Schuster.

Seventh Christmas. Coningsby William Dawson. LC 17-291805. 1917. H. Holt and Company.

Seventh City of Cibola. Red Landho. LC 68-2472. 1968. Vantage Press.

Seventh Commandment. Sarah Shears. 1973. 7.95 (ISBN 0-236-15485-0, Pub. by Paul Elek). Merrimack Pub Cir.

Seventh Commandment: Anonymous. Herman Alfred Kasen. LC 32-10940. 1932. G. H. Watt.

Seventh Cross. 3531st ed. Netty Reiling Radvanyi. Tr. by Galston, James Austin. LC 42-20567. 1942. Little, Brown.

Seventh Cross. Anna Seghers & Galston, James Austin, 1861- Tr. LC 42-20567. 1942. Little, Brown and Comapny.

Seventh Day. Hans H. Kirst. 1968. pap. 0.75 o.p. (T1887). Pyramid Pubns.

Seventh Day. Ed. by Avrahim Shapira. 1971. 6.95 o.p. (ISBN 0-684-12345-2). Scribner.

Seventh Day. Translated by Richard Graves. Hans Hellmut Kirst. LC 59-8267. 1959. Doubleday.

Seventh Dream. Eliza M. J. Humphreys. (On cover: Seaside library. Pocket ed., no. 1252). 1889. G. Munro.

Seventh Earl: A Dramatized Biography. Grace Lillian Irwin. LC 76-3649. (Illus.). 7.95 (ISBN 0-8028-6059-1). Eerdmans.

Seventh Escape. Jan Doward. LC 68-54399. (Destiny Ser.). 1979. pap. 4.95 o.p. (ISBN 0-8163-0385-1, 19295-5). Pacific Pr Pub Assn.

Seventh Game. Roger Kahn. LC 82-2214. 13.95 (ISBN 0-453-00420-2). New American Library.

Seventh Gate. Carlin Aden. 1973. pap. 3.00. Goliards Pr.

Seventh Gate. Muriel Harris. LC 30-8166. 1930. Harper & Brothers.

Seventh Girl. Tom Pendleton. 1970. 6.95 o.p. (ISBN 0-07-049257-3). McGraw.

Seventh Girl: A Romantic Tale of Civil War Texas. Edmund Van Zandt. LC 76-107294. 1970. 6.95. McGraw-Hill.

Seventh Heaven. Hal Z. Bennett. LC 75-36579. 1976. 7.95 (ISBN 0-385-06659-7). Doubleday.

Seventh Heaven. John Golden & Strong, Austin. LC 25-213. The H. K. Fly Company.

Seventh Hexagram: A Novel. Ian McLachlan. LC 76-25602. 1976. 8.95. Dial Press.

Seventh Hour. Grace Livingston Hill. LC 39-2163. J. B. Lippincott Company.

Seventh Level: A Sexual Progress. William Nicholson. LC 79-65114. 1979. 10.95 (ISBN 0-8128-2683-3). Stein and Day.

Seventh Man. Wilson Barclay. LC 35-8287. 1935. Dial Press, Inc.

Seventh Man. Max Brand. LC 21-18472. 1921. 1.90. G. P. Putnam's Sons.

Seventh Man. Max Brand. 1974. (pbk.) 0.95. Warner Paperback Library.

Seventh Man. Frederick Faust. LC 21-18472. 1921. G. P. Putnam's Sons.

Seventh Man. Jay Scotland. LC 58-125069. 1958. Mystery House.

Seventh Miracle. Bruce Cassiday. (Orig.). 1968. pap. 0.75 o.p. (T1811). Pyramid Pubns.

Seventh Month. Frank Miceli. LC 69-20389. 1970. 5.95. F. Fell.

Seventh Noon. Frederick Orin Bartlett. LC 10-4591. 1910. Small, Maynard and Company.

Seventh Pan Book of Horror Stories. Ed. by H. Van Thal. 1982. pap. 10.00x (ISBN 0-330-10555-8, Pub. by Pan Bks). State Mutual Bk.

Seventh Passenger. Alice MacGowan & Newberry, Perry, 1870- Joint Author. LC 26-1062. 1926. Frederick A. Stokes Company.

Seventh Person. Benjamin Brace. LC 6-346869. 1906. Dodd, Mead and Company.

Seventh Plank. William McDowell. LC 39-17650. G. P. Putnam's Sons.

Seventh Power. James Mills. LC 76-18957. 8.95 (ISBN 0-525-20050-9). E. P. Dutton.

Seventh Saracen. Ben Morreale. LC 58-9704. 1958. Coward-McCann.

Seventh Sense. Harrison R. Thompson. (Orig.). 1979. pap. 2.25 (ISBN 0-532-23275-5). Woodhill.

Seventh Shot: A Detective Story. Harry Coverdale. LC 24-19417. 2.00. Chelsea House.

Seventh Simenon Omnibus. Georges Simenon. LC 75-306334. (Penguin crime). 1974. 0.60 (ISBN 0-14-003838-8). Penguin.

Seventh Sin. Jessie Joy Baines. LC 31-32340. Sears Publishing Company, Inc.

Seventh Sinner. Elizabeth Peters, pseud. (Dell book). 1973. (pbk.) 0.95 (ISBN 0-396-06520-1). Dell.

Seventh Sinner. Elizabeth Peters, pseud. LC 78-38523. 1972. 5.95 (ISBN 0-396-06520-1). Dodd, Mead.

Seventh Station. Ralph M. McInerny. (Father McDowling Ser.). 224p. 1979. pap. 1.95 (ISBN 0-441-75947-5, Pub. by Charter Bks). Ace Bks.

Seventh Station: A Father Dowling Mystery. Ralph M McInerny. LC 77-77417. 7.95 (ISBN 0-8149-0787-3). Vanguard Press.

Seventh Suitor. Laura Matthews. 208p. (Orig.). 1979. pap. 1.75 (ISBN 0-446-94340-1). Warner Bks.

Seventh Summer. Hadrian Keene. (O.s.i.). (Orig.). 1969. pap. 0.75 o.s.i. (A474S, Award). Univ Pub & Dist.

Seventh Summer. Hadrian Keene. (O.s.i.). 1977. pap. 1.75 o.s.i. (AR1657, Award). Univ Pub & Dist.

Seventh Trumpet. Ferenc Kormendi. LC 53-5848. 1953. Bobbs-Merrill.

Seventh Trumpet. 1st Ed. Peter Julian. LC 53-5848. 1953. Bobbs-Merrill.

Seventh Wave. Marietta Minnigerode Andrews. LC 30-9241. 1930. A. & C. Boni.

Seventh Wave. Eugene L Pearce. LC 21-21095. 1921. Moffat, Yard & Company.

Seventh Wave. Olive Wadsley. LC 38-5023. 1938. Dodd, Mead & Company.

Seventh Well. Fred Wander. LC 75-45392. 1.95 (ISBN 0-7178-0466-6). International Publishers.

Seventh Well. Fred Wander. LC 77-471015. (Seven Seas Books). 1976. Seven Seas Publishers.

Seventh Winter. Hal Glen Borland. 1960. 3.95 o.p. (ISBN 0-397-00144-4). Lippincott.

Seventrees. Janice Y. Brooks. (Orig.). 1981. pap. 3.50 (ISBN 0-451-11068-4, AE1068, Sig). NAL.

Seventy-Five Short Masterpieces: Stories from the World's Literature. Ed. by Roger B. Goodman. (Orig.). (gr. 10-12). pap. 2.75 (ISBN 0-553-14669-6, 13052-8). Bantam.

Seventy-Nine Park Avenue. Harold Robbins. 1981. pap. 3.95. PB.

Seventy-Nine Park Avenue: By Harold Robbins Pseud. 1st Ed. Harold Rubin. LC 55-9267. 1955. Knopf.

Seventy Ninety-One: A Tale of San Domingo. facsimile ed. Edward Winslow Gilliam. LC 70-37591. (Black Heritage Library Collection). Repr. of 1890 ed. 17.25 (ISBN 0-8369-8967-8). Ayer Co.

Seventy-One Hours. Michael Mason. LC 77-185406. 1972. 5.95. Coward, McCann & Geoghegan.

Seventy-Seven Rue Paradis: Cover Painting by James Meese. Gil Brewer. LC 55-24551. (Gold medal book, 448). 1954. Fawcett Publications.

Seventy-Seven Willow Pond. Helen Douglas-Irvine. LC 45-455684. 1945. Doubleday, Doran and Company, Inc.

Seventy-Six. John Neal. LC 7-33169. 1823. J. Robinson.

Seventy-Six Hours: The Invasion of Tarawa. Eric Hammel & John Lane. 1980. pap. 2.25 (ISBN 0-505-51464-8). Tower Bks.

Seventy-Six Short Stories. Saki. 1.95 o.p. (ISBN 0-00-422609-7). W Collins.

Seventy Sutton Place. Joseph DiMona. LC 79-183005. 1972. 6.95 (ISBN 0-396-06500-7). Dodd, Mead.

Seventy Sutton Place. Joseph DiMona. 1973. 1.50. Dell.

Seventy Thousand Witness: A Football Mystery. Cortland Fitzsimmons. LC 31-31667. 1931. R. M. McBride & Company.

Seventy Times Seven. Jennie Comrie Brown. LC 14-1658. 1914. 1.50. Broadway Publishing Co.

Seventy Times Seven. Carl Christian Jensen. LC 35-196755. 1935. Lothrop, Lee and Shepard Company.

Seventy Times Seven: A Novel. John B Sanford. LC 39-5849. 1939. A. A. Knopf.

Seventy Times Seven: A Novel. Gladys Bronwyn Stern. LC 57-11229. 1957. Macmillan.

Seventy Weeks & the Great Tribulation. Philip Mauro. 285p. 1975. pap. 5.95. Reiner.

Severa: A Novel from the German of E. Hartner Pseud. Emma Eva Henriette Von Twardowska & Wister, Mrs. Annis Lee (Furness) 1830-1908, Tr. 1882. J. B. Lippincott & Co.

Severance: A Novel. Thomas Cobb. LC 2-2468. 1901. J. Lane.

Severance Pay. Philip Whalen. LC 74-114626. (Writing Ser: No. 24). 84p. (Orig.). 1970. pap. 2.50 (ISBN 0-87704-012-5). Four Seasons Foun.

Severed at Gettysburg. Martha Caroline Keller. LC 7-10968. (Ogilvie, J. S., & co.'s fireside series). J. S. Ogilvie & Company.

Severed Crown. Elaine Kidner Dakers. LC 73-1127. 1973. 6.95 (ISBN 0-671-21567-1). Simon and Schuster.

Severed Crown. Jane Lane. (O.s.i.). 224p. 1973. 6.95 o.s.i. (ISBN 0-671-21567-1). S&S.

Severed Hand. Fortune Du Boisgobey. LC 6-34412. (On cover: Lovell's library. no. 1156). J. W. Lovell Company.

Severed Hand see Mano Cercenada.

Severed Hand. La Main Coupee. Fortune Du Boisgobey. LC 6-34411. (On cover: Seaside library. Pocket ed. no. 1082). 1888. G. Munro.

Severed Head. Iris Murdoch. 1976. 1.95 (ISBN 0-14-002003-9). Penguin.

Severed Head: A Novel. Iris Murdoch. LC 61-7278. 1961. Viking Press.

Severed Mantle. William Lindsey. LC 9-27996. 1909. Houghton Mifflin Company.

Severed Ties. George Simpson & Neal Burger. (Orig.). 1983. pap. 3.50 (ISBN 0-440-17705-7). Dell.

Severed Wasp. Madeleine L'Engle. LC 82-15694. 15.50 (ISBN 0-374-26131-8). Farrar, Straus, Giroux.

Severing Line. Sara Cardiff. LC 74-4317. 1974. 5.95 (ISBN 0-394-49071-1). Random House.

Severing Line. Sara Cardiff. LC 74-32269. 1975. 11.95 (ISBN 0-8161-6266-2). G. K. Hall.

Severing Line. Sara Cardiff. (Fawcett crest book). 1975. (pbk.) 1.25. Fawcett.
Severith Style. Donald Honig. LC 79-37194. 1972. 6.95 (ISBN 0-684-12824-1). Scribner.
Severn Tunnel. Thomas Walker. 10.00 o.p. (ISBN 0-87556-400-3). Saifer.
Severn Woods. Martha Edith Rickert. LC 30-710621. Harcourt, Brace and Company.
Sevier Secrets. Dorothy Daniels. 1970. pap. 0.75 o.p. (ISBN 0-447-74619-7). Lancer.
Seward's Folly. Edison Marshall. LC 24-15290. 1924. 2.00. Little, Brown and Company.
Sewers of Warsaw. Tadeusz Rogala. (Illus.). 1973. 6.50 (ISBN 0-533-00636-8). Vantage.
Sex Alarm. Olga Woller & Galston, James Austin, 1881- Tr. LC 46-16346. 1946. Margent Press.
Sex & Her Flowered Box. John O'Donnel. pap. 1.95 o.p. (8070). Cameo.
Sex & Hypnosis. Joseph R. Rosenfeld. (Orig.). 1969. pap. 1.95 o.p. (6046). Brandon.
Sex & Julia Swane. Marion Saunders. pap. 1.95 o.s.i. (Venus). Grove.
Sex and Rage. Eve Babitz. 1981. 2.50 (ISBN 0-380-53009-0). Avon Books.
Sex and Rage: Advice to Young Ladies Eager for a Good Time: a Novel. Eve Babitz. LC 79-2088. 1979. 8.95 (ISBN 0-394-42581-2). Knopf: Distributed by Random House.
Sex & the High Command. John Boyd. 1970. 5.50 o.p. Weybright.
Sex and the High Command. Boyd Upchurch. LC 74-99003. 1970. 5.50. Weybright and Talley.
Sex & the Leather Lovers. Henry Wilcox. 192p. (Orig.). 1973. pap. 1.95 o.p. (ISBN 0-87682-368-1, 7368). Barclay Hse.
Sex & the Single Tourist. Carl Stanton. 192p. 1974. pap. 1.95 o.p. (ISBN 0-87056-380-7, 6380). Brandon.
Sex & the Swinging Secretary. Dana Bunty. 224p. pap. 1.95 o.p. (7134). Barclay Hse.
Sex Appeal. Photos by Jurgen Vollmer. (Illus.). pap. 12.95 o.p. (ISBN 0-89237-005-X). Modernismo.
Sex Arena. Carl Driver. pap. 1.95 o.p. (8014). Cameo.
Sex As a Family Affair. Cynthia Marshall. pap. 1.95 o.p. (ISBN 0-87682-247-2, 7247). Barclay Hse.
Sex Avengers. Evan Burke. 176p. pap. 1.95 o.p. (6106). Brandon.
Sex Broker. Ginger Craig. 1974. (pbk.) 1.50 (ISBN 0-523-00450-8). Pinnacle Books.
Sex Bum. Tony Trelos, pseud. 176p. pap. 1.95 o.p. (6091). Brandon.
Sex Cage. Ilonka. 1970. pap. 0.75 o.p. (75-345). Manor Bks.
Sex Castle see Shoot It Again.
Sex Clinic. Linda Dubreuil. 1975. pap. 1.50 o.p. (LB307DK, Leisure Bks). Nordon Pubns.
Sex Connection. Richard B. Long. pap. 1.95 o.p. (ISBN 0-87977-164-X, DBB164). Dansk Blue Bk.
Sex-Crazed Teacher. Mark S. Woling. 192p. pap. 1.95 o.p. (2015). Intimate Lib.
Sex-Crazy World of Ted Trogdon. Ted Trogdon. pap. 1.95 o.p. (ISBN 0-87056-305-X, 6305). Brandon.
Sex Cure. Dana Lloyd. 192p. (Orig.). 1981. pap. 2.50 (ISBN 0-380-78477-7, 78477). Avon.
Sex Cycle Gang. Rod Hibbs. pap. 1.95 o.p. (8026). Cameo.
Sex Devices. Richard Glasser. pap. 1.75 o.p. (V1052K, Venus). Grove.
Sex Diary of Gerald Sorme. Colin Wilson. LC 63-10555. 1963. Dial Press.
Sex Doctors in the Bedroom see Bedroom Sex Doctors.
Sex Dreams '70. Gerald Summers. pap. 1.95 o.p. (ISBN 0-87682-108-5, 7108). Barclay Hse.
Sex Family. Neil. pap. 1.95 o.p. (ISBN 0-87056-153-7, 6153). Brandon.
Sex Family. Martin Neil. 192p. pap. 1.95 o.p. (6153). Brandon.
Sex Fantasies of the Housewife. Diane Laughlin. 160p. 1974. pap. 1.95 o.p. (ISBN 0-87682-396-7, 7396). Barclay Hse.
Sex for Pennies. Anne Saddens. 1974. (pbk.) 2.25 (ISBN 0-87682-430-0). Barclay House.
Sex Goddess. Martin Ryerson. (O.s.i.). Orig. Title: Actresses. 160p. 1974. pap. 0.95 o.s.i. (AN1334, Award). Univ Pub & Dist.
Sex Happening of Margo Turner. Tony Trelos, pseud. 1968. pap. 1.25 o.p. (2066). Brandon.
Sex Hypocrites. Carl Stanton. 192p. pap. 1.95 o.p. (ISBN 0-87056-317-3, 6317). Brandon.
Sex in Sin. Zelota M Garner. LC 6-40714. 1884. Gage, De Vos & Company.
Sex Is Such Fun. James William MacQueen. LC 37-2324. 1937. Godwin.
Sex Life: A Novel. Bruce Cook. LC 78-13487. 1979. 9.95 (ISBN 0-87131-263-8). M. Evans.
Sex Machine. Troy Conway, pseud. (Coxeman Ser). (Orig.). 1970. pap. 0.60 o.p. (63-251). Paperback Lib.
Sex Machine. D. Royal. Orig. Title: Rape Machine. 1969. pap. 1.25 o.p. (B12-1022). Belmont-Tower.
Sex of Angels. K. K. Klein, pseud. (Orig.). 1969. pap. 1.75 o.s.i. (437, Travellers Comp). Olympia.
Sex of Angels. Robert Turner. LC 75-9884. (Traveller's companion series). 1969. 1.75. Traveller's Companion, Inc.
Sex Picnic. Robert H. Sheldon. pap. 1.95 o.p. (8024). Cameo.
Sex Power. Hal Edwards. 192p. pap. 1.95 o.p. (7109). Barclay Hse.
Sex Probers. Joseph Smyth. (O.s.i.). 192p. 1975. pap. 1.25 o.s.i. (AQ1497, Award). Univ Pub & Dist.
Sex Rampage. Guy Palmer. (Illus.). 1976. pap. 2.00 o.s.i. Fedora Bks.
Sex Substitute. Russell Trainer. (Orig.). pap. 1.25 o.p. (2045). Brandon.
Sex Surrogates. Michael Davidson. (Signet Book, Y5410). 1973. 1.25. New American Lib.
Sex Surrogates. Michael Davidson & David M. Rorvick. 1972. 6.95 o.p. (ISBN 0-87035-030-7). Geis.
Sex Swappers. Hal Edwards. 192p. pap. 1.95 o.p. (7144). Barclay Hse.
Sex Talk. Myron Brenton. 192p. 1973. pap. 1.25 o.p. (P1925, Crest). Fawcett World.
Sex Target. Matt Lee. 192p. (Orig.). 1974. pap. 1.95 o.p. (ISBN 0-87682-378-9, 7378). Barclay Hse.
Sex Tax: A Political Fantasy. W. E. Dunn. 1979. 6.00 (ISBN 0-682-49463-1). Exposition.
Sex Tenants at the Three Hundred & Twenty-Seven Venable Street. John Vining. pap. 1.25 o.p. (2070). Brandon.
Sex Theme from a Couch. Mac James. 1968. pap. 1.25 o.p. (2065). Brandon.
Sex Token. James Shreeve. (Treacle Story Ser.: No. 3). (Illus.). 48p. 1976. signed ed. 8.00 (ISBN 0-914232-11-8); pap. 2.50 (ISBN 0-914232-10-X). McPherson & Co.
Sex Trap. Carter Brown, pseud. 1975. (pbk.) 0.95. New American Library.
Sex Trip. John Sontago. LC 72-186125. (API, 107). 1.95. Nu-Triumph.
Sex Uproar. Jock Pearson. pap. 1.95 o.p. (8031). Cameo.
Sex Witches & Warlocks. Stan O'Dair. (Orig.). pap. 0.95 o.p. (1050). Brandon.
Sex with Animals. Preston Harriman. 192p. pap. 1.95 o.p. (7157). Barclay Hse.
Sex with Animals. Preston Harriman. pap. 1.95 o.p. (ISBN 0-87682-157-3). Barclay Hse.
Sex with Strangers. Ed. by John W. Fitzgerald. pap. 2.95 o.p. (ISBN 0-87964-106-1). Academy-Parliament.
Sex Without Sentiment. Thyra Samter Winslow. LC 54-8778. 1954. Abelard-Schuman.
Sexational Eve. Wilson Collison. LC 33-30454. 1933. R. M. McBride & Company.
Sexless Dynasty. William Worden Bolton. LC 60-855482. 1960. Dorrance.
Sexmax. Hughes Cooper. (Orig.). 1969. pap. 0.75 o.p. (ISBN 0-446-64174-X, 64-174). Paperback Lib.
Sexo, Dinero y Balas. new ed. Glen Chase. Tr. by Danilo Cesto from Eng. (Cereza Delicias: No.7). Orig. Title: Chuck You Farley! (Illus.). 160p. (Span.). 1975. pap. 1.25 (ISBN 0-88473-241-X). Fiesta Pub.
Sexpo '69. Winston Smith. (Orig.). 1969. pap. 1.25 o.p. (2088). Brandon.
Sextet. Henry Miller. LC 77-20795. 1977. 3.95 (ISBN 0-88496-119-2). Capra Press.
Sextet. J. Hume Parkinson. pap. 1.95 o.s.i. (TC-464, Travellers Comp). Olympia.
Sextet in A Minor: A Novella & Thirteen Stories. Norma Klein. 224p. 1983. 12.95 (ISBN 0-312-71348-7, Pub. bt Mareu). St Martin.
Sextet: Six Story Discoveries in the Novella Form. First Publication of Domhnall O'Conaill, Charles Mohler, Tom Bair, Gilbert Rees, George Moffet and John Eichrodt. Edited by Whit Burnett and Hallie Burnett. Ed. by Whit Burnett. LC 51-13446. 1951. McKay.
Sextet: Six Story Discoveries in the Novella Form. Ed. by Hallie Burnett & Whit Burnett. LC 51-13446. 1968. Repr. of 1951 ed. 12.00 (ISBN 0-527-13700-6). Kraus Repr.
Sexton Blake's Early Cases. Union Jack. LC 76-381095. (Illus.). 1976. 3.75 (ISBN 0-213-16593-7). Barker.
Sexton Women. Richard Neely. LC 72-86878. 1972. 5.95 (ISBN 0-399-11077-1). Putnam.
Sexton Women. Richard Neely. (Berkeley medallion book). 1974. (pbk) 0.95 (ISBN 0-425-02514-4). Berkley Pub. Co.
Sextuplets of Loqmaria: Tr. by Eric Harmsworth. Michel Labry. LC 65-2854. 1965. bds., 4.50. Allen & Unwin.
Sexual Adventures of Sherlock Holmes. J. Watson. pap. 1.95 o.s.i. (TC-511, Travellers Comp). Olympia.
Sexual Bond. Francois Duyckaerts. 1970. 6.95 o.p. (ISBN 0-440-07847-4). Delacorte.
Sexual Exhibitionists. S. P. Blake. 192p. (Orig.). 1973. pap. 1.95 o.p. (ISBN 0-87056-263-0, 6263). Brandon.
Sexual Fix. Ed. by A. Norman Jeffares. 192p. 1982. 39.00x (ISBN 0-333-32750-0, Pub. by Macmillan England); pap. 25.00x (ISBN 0-333-32751-9). Humanities.
Sexual Love of Children. Dean Challot. 192p. (Orig.). 1972. pap. 1.95 o.p. (ISBN 0-87056-260-6, 6260). Brandon.
Sexual Outlaw. John Rechy. pap. 2.25 (ISBN 0-440-17667-0). Dell.
Sexual Relationship and Other Stories. Gillman Noonan. LC 76-368809. 1976. 0.99 (ISBN 0-905169-01-8). Poolbeg Press.
Sexus. Henry Miller. (Orig.). 1965. pap. 4.95 (ISBN 0-394-17430-5, B325, BC). Grove.
Sexy Egg Love-In. Jay Martin. (Orig.). 1969. pap. 0.75 o.p. (74-522). Lancer.
Seymour - An Introduction see Raise High the Roof Beam, Carpenters.
Seymour Charlton: A Novel. W. B Maxwell. 1909. D. Appleton and Company.
Sezz Who? John Lomax. LC 73-83916. 1974. 5.95 (ISBN 0-87949-021-7). Ashley Bks.
SF; the Best of the Best. Ed. by Judith Merril. LC 68-2517. 1967. Delacorte Press.
Sforza: A Story of Milan. William Waldorf Astor Astor. LC 9-2699. 1889. C. Scribner's Sons.
Sgt. Hawk. Patrick Clay. (Leisure book). 1.75. Nordon Pubns.
Shabby Genteel Story. William Makepeace Thackeray. LC 72-165541. (Illus.). 1971. (ISBN 0-8147-8154-3). New York University Press.
Shabby Glory. Peggy Gaddis, pseud. LC 42-203277. 1942. Arcadia House, Inc.
Shabby Street. Orrie Hitt. LC 55-32180. (Beacon book original, no. 104). 1954. Beacon Publications Corp.
Shabby Tiger: A Novel. Howard Spring. LC 35-2339. Covici, Friede.
Shabot. Wayne Wallace. 1977. 5.95 o.p. (ISBN 0-533-02359-9). Vantage.
Shack by the River. Edward Woodward Johnson. LC 38-35016. The Christopher Publishing House.
Shack Job. Henry Kane. pap. 0.60 o.p. Lancer.
Shackle. Sidonie Gabrielle Colette. 1982. pap. 2.95 (ISBN 0-345-30058-0). Ballantine.
Shackle. Sidonie Gabrielle Colette. Tr. by Antonia White from Fr. 224p. 1976. 7.95 (ISBN 0-374-26184-9); pap. 3.95 (ISBN 0-374-51311-2). FS&G.
Shackle. Sidonie Gabrielle Colette. 1976. pap. 2.95 o.p. (ISBN 0-374-51311-2, N520). FS&G.
Shackled. Achmed Abdullah. LC 24-22269. Brentano's.
Shackled. Bruce Clay. LC 37-33669. 1937. Hillman-Curl, Inc.
Shackled Cinderella. Edward Joseph Doherty. LC 32-16438. Covici, Friede.
Shackled Souls. Elenore Meherin. LC 28-21972. Grosset & Dunlap.
Shackles. Madge Hamilton Lyons Macbeth. LC 27-11621. 1927. Henry Waterson Company.
Shackles of Flesh. Leslie J. Swabacker. LC 30-5692. The Macaulay Company.
Shackles of Flesh. Leslie J. Swabacker. LC 30-5692. The Macaulay Company.
Shackles of the Free. Mary Grace Ashton. LC 29-570484. 1929. Frederick A. Stokes Company.
Shacklett. The Evolution of a Statesman. Walter Barr. LC 1-21945. 1901. D. Appleton and Co.
Shacks Under the River Bank. LC 56-13690. 1956. Meador Pub. Co.
Shad and Shed: Or, The Remarkable Adventures of the Puritan Brothers. Elisha Jay Edwards. (On cover: United service library. v. 1, no. 3). 1889. The United Service Publishing Company.
Shad Are Running. St. George, Judith & Richard Cuffari. 1977. 5.29. Putnam.
Shad Run. Howard Breslin. LC 55-11104. 1955. Crowell.
Shad Treatment. Garrett Epps. LC 76-20493. 1977. 9.95 o.p. (ISBN 0-399-11829-2). Putnam Pub Group.
Shad Treatment: A Novel. Garrett Epps. LC 76-20493. 9.95 (ISBN 0-399-11829-2). Putnam.
Shade of Difference. Allen Drury. LC 62-8838. 1962. 15.95 (ISBN 0-385-02389-8). Doubleday.
Shade of Difference: A Novel. Allen Drury. LC 62-15897. 1962. Doubleday.
Shade of Scarlet. Ed. by Julian Ocean, pseud. (O.s.i.). 1974. 5.50 o.s.i.; pap. 2.00 o.s.i. Northwoods Pr.
Shade of Sycamore. Percy Marks. LC 44-961. 1944. Reynal and Hitchcock, Inc.
Shade of Time. David Duncan. LC 46-7496. 1946. Random House.
Shade of Time. Davis Duncan. LC 46-7496. 1946. Random House.
Shade Too Dark. B. E. Kowalik. 5.75 o.p. Carlton.
Shades and Shadows. Luanna Churchill. 1973. 4.95 (ISBN 0-517-51395-1). Lenox Hill Press.
Shades of Gray. Mark Denning. LC 76-275 (ISBN 0-515-03891-1). Pyramid Books.
Shades of Greene. Graham Greene. 1977. pap. 3.50 (ISBN 0-14-004023-4). Penguin.
Shades of Greene: The Televised Stories of Graham Greene. Graham Greene. LC 77-23985. 1977. 1.95 (ISBN 0-14-004023-4). Penguin Books.
Shades of Grey. Ward Jouve, Nicole. LC 82-141339. 1981. 5.95 (ISBN 0-86068-229-3). Virago.
Shades of Hades. Frederic Arnold Kummer. LC 77-84242. (Lost Race and Adult Fantasy Fiction). (Illus.). 1978. 33.00 (ISBN 0-405-10990-3). Arno Press.
Shades of Jade. Val Colebrook. LC 80-52170. (Illus.). 52p. (Orig.). 1980. pap. 3.50 (ISBN 0-932384-11-0). Tashmoo.
Shades of Minos. Joe E Pierce. LC 74-176087. 3.50 (ISBN 0-913244-04-X). HaPi Press.
Shades of Peril. Melissa Cordell. 1977. pap. 1.50 (ISBN 0-532-15280-8). Woodhill.
Shades of the Past; or, Indiscreet Tales of Japan. Harold S. Williams. LC 63-19394. (Illus.). 352p. 1972. pap. 2.95 (ISBN 0-8048-1050-8). C E Tuttle.
Shades of the Wilderness: A Story of Lee's Great Stand. Joseph Alexander Altsheler. 312p. Repr. of 1916 ed. lib. bdg. 13.20x (ISBN 0-88411-940-8). Amereon Ltd.
Shades of Time: A Science-Fiction Novella. William A. Darity. LC 68-19721. 1969. 2.25. William-Frederick Press.
Shades of Time: A Science-Fiction Novella. William A. Darrity, Jr. 1975. pap. 3.00 (ISBN 0-87164-101-1). William-F.
Shadow. Henry Bedford-Jones. LC 30-29252. 1930. The Fiction League.
Shadow. Blaise Cendrars & Marcia Brown. LC 81-9424. (Illus.). 12.95 (ISBN 0-684-17226-7). Scribner's.
Shadow. Walter Brown Gibson. LC 74-18800. 1975. 5.95 (ISBN 0-385-03712-0). Published for the Crime Club by Doubleday.
Shadow. Walter Brown Gibson. LC 77-82757. 1978. 6.95 (ISBN 0-385-13413-4). Published for the Crime Club by Doubleday.
Shadow. Maxwell Grant, pseud. 1975. pap. 0.95 o.p. (ISBN 0-515-03876-8). BJ Pub Group.
Shadow. Mary White Ovington. LC 72-4736. (Black Heritage Library Collection). 1972. 14.25 (ISBN 0-8369-9118-4). Books for Libraries Press.
Shadow. Mary White Ovington. LC 20-5123. 1920. Harcourt, Brace and Howe.
Shadow. Perez Galdos, Benito. LC 80-10549. 1980. 5.95 (ISBN 0-8214-0553-5). Ohio University Press.
Shadow. Lillian Rogers. LC 28-229619. 1928. I. Washburn.
Shadow. Arthur John Arbuthnott Stringer. LC 13-1899. 1913. The Century Co.
Shadow: A Quarter of Eight & the Freak Show Murders. Walter Gibson. LC 77-82757. 1978. 10.95 (ISBN 0-385-13413-4). Doubleday.
Shadow Across My Heart: By Mary Douglas Warren Pseud. Maysie Greig. LC 52-6507. 1952. Arcadia House.
Shadow Across the Sun. Betty Swinford. 1966. 2.95 o.p. Moody.
Shadow: And Other Stories. Jeffery Farnol. LC 75-122696. (Short story index reprint series). 1970. Books for Libraries Press.
Shadow: And Other Stories. Jeffery Farnol. LC 29-167898. 1929. Little, Brown, and Company.
Shadow, & Other Stories. Jeffery Farnol. LC 75-122696. (Short Story Index Reprint Ser). 1929. 15.00 (ISBN 0-8369-3529-2). Ayer Co.
Shadow and Sunshine. Adna H Lightner. LC 7-19388. 1884. Wrightson & Company.
Shadow and Sunshine: Or, Goldie Ransom's Triumph. Adna H Lightner. (On cover: Library of American authors, no. 3). 1889. G. Munro.
Shadow and the Fear. Jane Corby. (Belmont Tower Book). 1977. 1.50 (ISBN 0-505-51174-6). Tower Pubns.
Shadow and the Glory. John Edward Jennings. LC 43-18432. 1943. Reynal & Hitchcock.
Shadow & the Light. Elizabeth Jenkins. (Illus.). 352p. 1983. 32.95 (ISBN 0-241-10892-6, Pub. By Hamish Hamilton England). David & Charles.
Shadow and the Stone. Laurence Walter Meynell. LC 29-17550. 1929. D. Appleton & Company.
Shadow and the Web. Mary Allerton, pseud. LC 40-33358. The Bobbs-Merrill Company.
Shadow Before. Leslie Purnell Davies. LC 76-111157. 1970. 4.50. Published for the Crime Club by Doubleday.
Shadow Before. William Rollins. LC 34-857858. R. M. McBride & Company.
Shadow Between. Ruth Abbey. (Ace gothic). 1974. (pbk.) 0.95. Ace Books.
Shadow Between His Shoulder-Blades. Joel Chandler Harris. LC 9-28150. Small Maynard and Company.
Shadow Box. easy eye ed. Virginia Coffman. (Orig.). 1968. pap. 0.75 o.p. (75-226). Lancer.
Shadow Box. Virginia Coffman. 1973. pap. 0.95 o.p. (75-226). Lancer.
Shadow Box. Virginia Coffman. (Signet Book). 1976. (pbk.) 1.25. New American Library.

Shadow Boxers. Edith Heal. LC 56-7125. 1956. Scribner.

Shadow Boxers: By Edith Heal. Edith Heal Berrien. LC 56-7125. 1956. Scribner.

Shadow Captain: An Account of the Activities of One Christopher Rousby in the Town of New Yorke During Several Months of the Year of Our Lord 1703... Emilie Benson Knipe & Knipe, Alden Arthur. LC 25-6389. 1925. 2.00. Dodd, Mead and Company.

Shadow Catcher. James David Horan. LC 61-15801. 1961. Crown Publishers.

Shadow Dance. Margaret Way. (Harlequin Romances Ser.). 192p. 1981. pap. 1.50 (ISBN 0-373-02435-5). Harlequin Bks.

Shadow Destination: Moon. Maxwell Grant, pseud. 1967. pap. 0.50 o.p. (B50-737). Belmont-Tower.

Shadow Detective: Or, The Mysteries of a Night. Harlan Page Halsey. (On cover: The calument series, no. 1). G. Munro.

Shadow Falls. Claire Lorrimer. 1974. (pbk.) 0.95 (ISBN 0-380-00185-3). Avon.

Shadow Falls. Georges Simenon & Gilbert, Stuart, Tr. LC 45-8454. 1945. Harcourt, Brace and Company.

Shadow Flies. Rose Macaulay. LC 70-145153. 1971. (ISBN 0-403-01082-9). Scholarly Press.

Shadow Flies. Rose Macaulay. LC 32-29684. 1932. Harper & Brothers.

Shadow for a Lady. Alex Watkins. LC 47-19422. 1947. M. S. Mill Co.

Shadow from Ladakh. Bhabani Bhattacharya. 359p. 1969. pap. 3.00 (ISBN 0-88253-018-6). Ind-US Inc.

Shadow from Ladakh: A Novel. Bhabani Bhattacharya. LC 66-151115. 4.95. Crown.

Shadow from the Bogue. Clement Wood. LC 28-6758. 1928. E. P.Dutton & Company.

Shadow Game. Dorinda Kamm. (Orig.). 1979. pap. 1.95 (ISBN 0-89083-492-X). Zebra.

Shadow Game. Michael Underwood. 1982. 15.00x (ISBN 0-86025-166-7, Pub. by Ian Henry Pubns England). State Mutual Bk.

Shadow, Go Mad. Maxwell Grant, pseud. (Orig.). pap. 0.50 o.p. (B50-709). Belmont-Tower.

Shadow Guest. Hillary Waugh. LC 78-139070. 1971. 5.95. Doubleday.

Shadow Guns: By Dan James Pseud. James D. Sayers. LC 53-13090. 1953. Avalon Books.

Shadow Hunter. Pat Murphy. 224p. 1982. pap. 2.75 (ISBN 0-445-04730-5). Popular Lib.

Shadow in Scarlet. Scott Stone. LC 54-31287. 1954. Vixen Press.

Shadow in the Courtyard see Maigret Mystified.

Shadow in the Courtyard and The Crime at Lock 14. Georges Simenon. LC 34-498489. Covici, Friede.

Shadow in the Glass. August William Derleth. LC 62-8520. 1963. Duell, Sloan and Pearce.

Shadow in the Glen: By Gyle Cullen Pseud. Winifred Rooney McConville. LC 59-10924. 1959. Crowell.

Shadow in the House. Sinclair Gluck. LC 29-17086. 1929. Dodd, Mead & Company.

Shadow in the House. Maxwell March. LC 36-19167. 1936. Doubleday, Doran & Company, Inc.

Shadow in the House. A Novel. John Saunders. LC 8-18328. 1861. M. Doolady.

Shadow in the Sea. Owen John. LC 72-82709. 1972. 6.95 (ISBN 0-525-20125-4). E. P. Dutton.

Shadow in the Sun: A Novel About the Virgin Queen Elizabeth I. Frank Wilson Kenyon. LC 58-10087. 1958. Crowell.

Shadow in the Wild. Whit Masterson, pseud. LC 57-67888. (Red badge detective). 1957. Dodd, Mead.

Shadow in the Wind. Larayne Whalen Webb. LC 77-151733. (Illus.). 5.95 (ISBN 0-533-02681-4). Vantage Press.

Shadow: Jade Dragon & House of Ghosts. Walter Gibson. LC 81-43260. (Crime Club Ser.). (Illus.). 216p. 1981. 11.95 (ISBN 0-385-17823-9). Doubleday.

Shadow: Jade Dragon & House of Ghosts. Walter Gibson. LC 81-43260. 205p. 1981. Repr. of 1943 ed. limited ed. 45.00 (ISBN 0-89296-056-6). Mysterious Pr.

Shadow Knows. Diane Johnson. LC 74-9155. 1974. (ISBN 0-394-48035-X). Knopf; Distributed by Random House.

Shadow Knows. Diane Johnson. LC 82-40027. 1982. 3.50 (ISBN 0-394-71193-9). Vintage Books.

Shadow Knows: Stories. David Madden. LC 78-108593. 1970. 5.95. Louisiana State University Press.

Shadow Land; Stories of the South. Florence Royall Henderson Robertson. LC 72-3188. (Black Heritage Library Collection). (Illus.). 1972. 9.50 (ISBN 0-8369-9077-3). Books for Libraries Press.

Shadow Land: Stories of the South. Florence Royall Henderson Robertson. LC 6-16733. 1906. R. G. Badger.

Shadow Line. Joseph Conrad. 1973. pap. 2.55 o.p. (ISBN 0-460-01190-1, EP1190, Evman). Dutton.

Shadow Line. Laura Furman. LC 81-24089. 1982. 14.95 (ISBN 0-670-63764-5). Viking Press.

Shadow Line: A Confession. Joseph Conrad. LC 17-12955. 1917. Doubleday, Page & Company.

Shadow-Line: A Confession. Joseph Conrad. LC 30-25911. 1928. Doubleday, Doran & Company, Inc.

Shadow-Line & Two Other Tales. Joseph Conrad. Ed. by Morton D. Zabel. 1970. pap. 1.45 o.p. (ISBN 0-385-09416-7, Anch). Doubleday.

Shadow Love. Olive Wadsley. LC 35-530343. 1935. Dodd, Mead & Company.

Shadow Maker. Edwin R. Papin. 3.95 o.p. Vantage.

Shadow Man. Sidney Floyd Gowing. LC 32-190477. 1932. Putnam.

Shadow Man. Sidney Floyd Gowing. LC 32-19191. Sears Publishing Company.

Shadow Man. John Lutz. LC 80-27157. 1981. 10.95 (ISBN 0-688-00459-8). Morrow.

Shadow Mansion. Wilma Forrest. 176p. 1973. pap. 0.95 o.p. (M2863, GM). Fawcett World.

Shadow Market. Netta Muskett. 1975. pap. 1.25 o.p. (ISBN 0-515-03758-3). Pyramid Pubns.

Shadow Marriage. Kathleen Thompson Norris. 1971. pap. 0.75 o.p. (ISBN 0-446-64536-2, 64-536). Paperback Lib.

Shadow Masque. Iris Tracy Comfort. LC 80-495. 1980. 8.95 (ISBN 0-385-17088-2). Doubleday.

Shadow Master. Elaine Feinstein. LC 79-14140. 1979. 9.95 (ISBN 0-671-22884-6). Simon and Schuster.

Shadow Men. Donald Randall Richberg. LC 11-261773. 1911. Forbes & Company.

Shadow Mountain. Dane Coolidge. LC 19-801177. W. J. Watt & Company.

Shadow Mountain. Harry Sinclair Drago. LC 48-557296. (Silver star westerns). 1948. Dodd, Mead.

Shadow Mountain. Bliss Lomax. 1974. (pbk.) 0.75. Dell.

Shadow Mountain. Bertha Muzzy Sinclair. LC 36-155719. 1936. Little, Brown, and Company.

Shadow Mountain. Bertha Muzzy Sinclair. LC 42-17353. 1942. Triangle Books.

Shadow of a Broken Man. George C Chesbro. LC 76-55716. 7.95 (ISBN 0-671-22696-7). Simon and Schuster.

Shadow of a Cat. Poppy Nottingham. (Ace gothic). 1974. (pbk.) 0.95. Ace Books.

Shadow of a Cloud. Charley Robertson. LC 50-8822. 1950. Harcourt, Brace.

Shadow of a Cloud. Granville Toogood. LC 32-4338. 1932. Brewe, Warren & Putnam.

Shadow of a Crime. Hall Caine. (On cover: Seaside library. Pocket ed. no. 445). 1885. G. Munro.

Shadow of a Crime. Hall Caine. (Harper's Franklin square library, no. 460). 1885. Harper & Brothers.

Shadow of a Crime. Cecil John Charles Street. LC 45-6686. 1945. Dodd, Mead & Company.

Shadow of a Crime. A Cumbrian Romance. Hall Caine. LC 6-21867. 1895. J. Knight Company.

Shadow of a Crime. A Novel. Hall Caine. LC 16-9875. A. L. Burt Company.

Shadow of a Crime: Based on the German "Seile der Liebe" of Alfred Ira Pseud. Albert Friedrich Wilhelm Grimm. Tr. by Ireland, Mary Eliza (Haines) LC 17-31883. 1916. Concordia Publishing House.

Shadow of a Curse: Or, Under the Lilac Bush. Sara Rebecca Emrick. LC 13-152653. 1913. 1.50. Broadway Publishing Co.

Shadow of a Doubt. June Thomson. LC 81-43621. 1982. 10.95 (ISBN 0-385-18054-3). Published for the Crime Club by Doubleday.

Shadow of a Dream. Charlotte Franken Haldane. LC 53-7435. Roy Publishers.

Shadow of a Dream. William Dean Howells. Ed. by Edwin H. Cady. Bd. with Imperative Duty. (Masterworks of Literature Ser.). 1962. 6.50x (ISBN 0-8084-0339-7); pap. 3.95x (ISBN 0-8084-0340-0, M2). Coll & U Pr.

Shadow of a Dream. William Dean Howells. 1973. lib. bdg. 25.00 (ISBN 0-8414-5176-1). Folcroft.

Shadow of a Dream: A Story. William Dean Howells. LC 7-5765. (On cover: Harper's Franklin square library. new ser. no. 672). 1890. Harper & Brothers.

Shadow of a Dream: And An Imperative Duty. Edited with Notes and Introd. by Edwin H. Cady. William Dean Howells. LC 61-15674. (Twayne's United States classics series). 1962. Twayne Publishers.

Shadow of a Dream & an Imperative Duty. William Dean Howells. LC 71-79475. (Selected Edition of W. D. Howells: Center for Editions of American Authors: Vol. 17). 272p. 1969. 15.00x (ISBN 0-253-35190-1). Ind U Pr.

Shadow of a Great Rock. Murrell Edmunds. LC 68-14408. 1968. 4.50 o.p. (ISBN 0-498-06721-1). A S Barnes.

Shadow of a Great Rock. William Rheem Lighton. 1907. G. P. Putnam's Sons.

Shadow of a Hawk. Anne Bonner Glasscock. LC 63-17458. (Double D western). 1963. Doubleday.

Shadow of a Hero. Allan Chase. LC 49-214515. 1949. Little, Town.

Shadow of a Lady. Jane Aiken Hodge. LC 73-78746. 1973. 7.95 (ISBN 0-698-10537-0). Coward, McCann & Geoghegan.

Shadow of a Lady. Jane Aiken Hodge. (Fawcett crest book). 1974. (pbk.) 1.25. Fawcett.

Shadow of a Lady. Holly Roth. LC 57-13690. (Inner sanctum mystery). 1957. Simon and Schuster.

Shadow of a Lion. Anne Edwards. LC 72-146077. 1971. 7.95. Coward, McCann & Geoghegan.

Shadow of a Love. Jessyca R. Gaver. 1977. pap. 1.75 (ISBN 0-532-17160-8). Woodhill.

Shadow of a Man. Dorothy Daniels. (Queen-size gothic). 1975. (pbk.) 1.25. Popular Library.

Shadow of a Man. Doris Miles Disney. LC 65-190472. 3.50. Pub. for the Crime Club by Doubleday.

Shadow of a Man. Ernest William Hornung. LC 1-30997. 1901. C. Scribner's Sons.

Shadow of a Man. May Sarton. LC 50-7235. 1950. Rinehart.

Shadow of a Past Love. Willo Davis Roberts. (Orig.). 1970. pap. 0.75 o.p. (ISBN 0-447-74620-0). Lancer.

Shadow of a Sin. Cahrlotte M. Stanley McKenna. LC 8-28177. (On cover: Munro's library, v. 1, no. 111). 1884. N. L. Munro.

Shadow of a Sin. A Romance. Charlotte Mary Brame. LC 7258. (On cover: Seaside library. Pocket ed. no. 948). G. Munro.

Shadow of a Sin: A Romance. Charlotte Mary Brame. LC 7257. (On cover: Lovell's library, v. 13, no. 694). J. W. Lovell Company.

Shadow of a Spy. Andrew MacKenzie. (British bloodhound no. 190). T. V. Boardman.

Shadow of a Star. Jamie Lee Cooper. LC 65-21403. 4.50. Bobbs.

Shadow of a Star. Elmer Kelton. LC 59-921313. (Ballantine books, 304K). 1959. Ballantine Books.

Shadow of a Sun: A Novel. Antonia Susan Drabble Byatt. LC 64-19942. 1964. Harcourt, Brace.

Shadow of a Tiger. Michael Collins, pseud. (Dan Fortune Detective Ser.). 208p. 1979. pap. 2.25 (ISBN 0-87216-915-4). Playboy Pbks.

Shadow of a Tiger. Michael Collins, pseud. LC 72-874. 189p. 1972. 4.95 o.p. (ISBN 0-396-06597-X). Dodd.

Shadow of a Tiger. Clyde Brion Davis. LC 63-15907. 1963. John Day Co.

Shadow of a Tiger. Dennis Lynds. LC 72-874. (Red badge novel of suspense). 1972. 4.95 (ISBN 0-396-06597-X). Dodd, Mead.

Shadow of a Tiger. Dennis Lynds. (Dan Fortune novel of suspense). 1978. 1.50 (ISBN 0-87216-506-X). Playboy Press.

Shadow of a Titan. A. F Wedgwood. LC 11-4940. 1910. John Lane Company.

Shadow of All Night Falling. Glen Cook. 1979. pap. 1.95 (ISBN 0-425-04260-X). Berkley Pub.

Shadow of Alpha. Charles L. Grant. 1976. 1.25 (ISBN 0-425-03143-8). Berkley Publishing Corp.

Shadow of an Agony. Oswald Chambers. 1965. pap. 1.95 (ISBN 0-87508-128-2). Chr Lit.

Shadow of an Alibi. Cecil John Charles Street. LC 49-7652. (Red badge mystery). 1948-1949. Dodd, Mead.

Shadow of an Eagle. Sue Peters. (Harlequin Romances Ser.). 192p. 1980. pap. 1.25 (ISBN 0-373-02351-0). Harlequin Bks.

Shadow of an Unknown Woman. Daoma Winston. pap. 0.60 o.p. Lancer.

Shadow of an Unknown Woman. Daoma Winston. 1976. (pbk.) 1.50 (ISBN 0-671-80311-5). Pocket Books.

Shadow of Apollo. Anne Hampson. 192p. 1981. pap. 1.50 (ISBN 0-671-57064-1, Pub. by Silhouette Bks). S&S.

Shadow of Ashlydyat. Ellen Price Henry Wood Wood. (Seaside library, v. 17, no. 328). 1878. G. Munro.

Shadow of Cain. Edith Sitwell. LC 77-7598. 1977. Repr. of 1947 ed. lib. bdg. 8.50 (ISBN 0-8414-7755-8). Folcroft.

Shadow of Christine. Evelyn Charles H Vivian. LC 10-8936. 1910. R. F. Fenno & Company.

Shadow of Chu-Sheng. Eugene Thomas. LC 33-25383. Sears Publishing Company, Inc.

Shadow of Danger. Mary Ford. pap. 0.75 o.s.i. (01-335). Lancer.

Shadow of Death. John Creasey. LC 75-21494. (Rinehart suspense novel). 1976. 6.95 (ISBN 0-03-017446-5). Holt, Rinehart and Winston.

Shadow of Death. William X. Kienzle. 264p. 1983. 10.95 (ISBN 0-8362-6119-4). Andrews & McMeel.

Shadow of Desire. Sara Craven. (Harlequin Presents Ser.). 192p. 1980. pap. 1.50 (ISBN 0-373-10398-0). Harlequin Bks.

Shadow of Desire: A Novel. Irene Osgood. LC 7-23176. 1893. The Cleveland Publishing Company.

Shadow of Don Pedro. R. Rivera Correa. 1970. 2.95 o.p. Vantage.

Shadow of Doubt. Arthur Somers Roche. LC 35-4591. 1935. Dodd, Mead & Company.

Shadow of Eagles. Jane Barry. LC 64-21910. 1964. Doubleday.

Shadow of Earth. Phyllis Eisenstein. 1979. pap. 2.25 (ISBN 0-440-18032-5). Dell.

Shadow of Eversleigh. Jane Lansdowne. LC 8-289877. 1908. Benziger Brothers.

Shadow of Evil. Greye La Spina. Orig. Title: Invaders from the Dark. pap. 0.50 o.p. (52-334). Paperback Lib.

Shadow of Evil. Dallas Romaine. (Berkley Medallion Book). 1976. (pbk.) 1.25 (ISBN 0-425-30381-0). Berkley Publishing Corp.

Shadow of Evil. Frank Gill Slaughter. LC 59-13042. 1975. (pbk.) 1.75 (ISBN 0-671-78877-9). Pocket Books.

Shadow of Evil: A Detective Story. Charles Judson Dutton. LC 30-10254. Dodd, Mead & Co.

Shadow of Fu Manchu. Sax Rohmer, pseud. 1976. pap. 1.25 o.p. (ISBN 0-515-04053-3). BJ Pub Group.

Shadow of Fu Manchu. Arthur Sarsfield Ward. LC 48-791649. 1948. Pub. for the Crime Club by Doubleday.

Shadow of God. Aileen Crawley. LC 83-2874. 12.95 (ISBN 0-312-71406-8). St. Martin's Press.

Shadow of God. Frank Rooney. LC 67-25069. 1967. Harcourt, Brace & World.

Shadow of Guilt. Leslie Edgley. LC 47-3658. 1947. Pub. for the Crime Club by Doubleday & Company, Inc.

Shadow of Guilt. Patrick Quentin. LC 59-5721. (Random House mystery). 1959. Random House.

Shadow of Gulls. Patricia Finney. LC 77-5733. 7.95 (ISBN 0-399-11979-5). Putnam.

Shadow of Guy Denver. Stephen McKenna. LC 29-929. 1929. Dodd, Mead & Company.

Shadow of Hampton Mead. Elizabeth Van Loon. LC 12-176683.

Shadow of Heaven, a Novel. Alfred Hayes. LC 47-111393. 1947. Howell, Soskin.

Shadow of Hilton Fernbrook. A Romance of Maoriland. Atha Westbury. LC 3-19526. 1896. New Amsterdam Book Company.

Shadow of Himself. Michael Delving, pseud. LC 76-162768. 1972. 4.95 o.p. (ISBN 0-684-12585-4). Scribner.

Shadow of Himself. Jay Williams. LC 76-162768. 1972. 4.95 (ISBN 0-684-12585-4). Scribner.

Shadow of John Wallace: A Novel. Louise Clarkson Whitelock. LC 8-36553. 1884. White, Stokes, & Allen.

Shadow of Life. Anne Douglas Sedgwick. LC 6-2544. 1906. The Century Co.

Shadow of Love. Rahal F Rahal. 3.75 o.p. Vantage.

Shadow of Love. Sondra Stanford. 192p. (Orig.). 1980. pap. 1.50 (ISBN 0-671-57025-0, Pub. by Silhouette Bks). S&S.

Shadow of Love. Marcelle Tinayre & Allinson, Alfred, Tr. LC 11-11220. 1911. John Lane.

Shadow of Love see Voyage to Love.

Shadow of Malreward. John Burland Harris-Burland. LC 19-127229. 1919. A. A. Knopf.

Shadow of Me. Paul Olsen. LC 66-13105. 5.95 o.p. (ISBN 0-03-065560-9). HR&W.

Shadow of Me: A Novel. Paul Olsen. LC 68-10054. 1968. Holt, Rinehart, and Winston.

Shadow of Moloch Mountain. Jane Goodwin Austin. LC 9-18476. 1870. Sheldon & Company.

Shadow of Murder. Amelia Reynolds Long. LC 47-200138. 1947. Phoenix Press.

Shadow of My Brother. Davis Grubb. LC 66-13204. 1966. Holt, Rinehart and Winston.

Shadow of My Gun. Lee Floren. LC 53-11305. 1953. Arcadia House.

Shadow of My Gun. Lee Floren. 1976. (pbk.) 0.95. Belmont Tower Books.

Shadow of My Hand. 1st Ed. Holger Cahill. LC 56-5332. 1956. Harcourt, Brace.

Shadow of Night. August William Derleth. LC 43-153225. 1943. C. Scribner's Sons.

Shadow of Our Own. Charles O Locke. LC 51-1293. 1951. Scribner.

Shadow of Peril. John Alvin Davis. LC 63-18033. 1963. Doubleday.

Shadow of Peril. Aleksandr Ivanovich Zhdanov. LC 63-18033. 1963. Doubleday.

Shadow of Power. Paul Bertram. LC 12-111662. 1912. 1.25. John Lane.

Shadow of Quong Lung. Charles William Doyle. LC 39-5626. 1900. J. B. Lippincott Company.

Shadow of Ravenscliffe. Joseph Smith Fletcher. LC 28-218902. E. J. Clode, Inc.

Shadow of Roger Laroque. Jules Mary. Cassell Publishing Company.

Shadow of Rosalie Byrnes. Grace Sartwell Mason. LC 19-149187. 1919. D. Appleton and Company.

Shadow of Shadows. Ted Allbeury. LC 82-10338. 1982. 12.95 (ISBN 0-684-17628-9). Scribner.

Shadow of Shame. Granville, Austyn. (On cover: Sergel's international library, v. l., no. 14). 1891. C. H. Sergel & Company.

Shadow of Sheila Ann. Ruth Wissmann. (Paperback Library gothic). 1974. (pbk.) 0.95. Warner Paperback Library.

Shadow of Spanish Swamp. Genevieve St. John. (Orig.). pap. 0.75 o.p. (B75-2014). Belmont-Tower.

Shadow of Sunrise: Selected Stories of Japan and the War. Selection, Introd. by Shoichi Saeki. 1st Ed. Shoichi Saeki. LC 66-25757. 1966. 3.95. Kodansha Intl.

Shadow of Suspicion. Emilie Baker Loring. 1957. Grosset & Dunlap.

Shadow of Suspicion. Emilie Baker Loring. LC 82-6075. 1982. 12.95 (ISBN 0-8161-6550-5). G.K. Hall.

Shadow of Suspicion. 1st Ed. Emilie Baker Loring. LC 55-10753. 1955. Little, Brown.

Shadow of Swords. Robert Henry Hill. LC 35-7810. 1935. D. Appleton-Century Company, Incorporated.

Shadow of the Astral: A Mystic Narrative. Louis Plante. LC 21-13413. The Austin Publishing Co.

Shadow of the Badlands. Eugene E. Halleran. LC 46-143777. 1946. Macrae-Smith-Company.

Shadow of the Bars: A Novel. Ernest De Lancey Pierson. (On cover: The household library. v. 4, no. 6). Belford, Clarke & Co.

Shadow of the Big Horn. Eugene E. Halleran. 160p. 1981. pap. text ed. 1.75 (ISBN 0-345-29430-0). Ballantine.

Shadow of the Bridge. Betsey Barton. LC 50-6932. 1950. Duell, Sloan and Pearce.

Shadow of the Butte. Thomas Thompson. LC 52-6356. (Double D western). 1952. Doubleday.

Shadow of the Caravan. Saliee O'Brien. (Kangaroo Book). 1978. 1.50 (ISBN 0-671-81876-7). Pocket Books.

Shadow of the Carovan. Saliee O'Brien. (Berkley medallion book). 1974. (pbk.) 0.95 (ISBN 0-425-02686-8). Berkley Pub. Co.

Shadow of the Cathedral: A Novel. Vicente Blasco Ibanez & Gillespie, Mrs. W. A., Tr. LC 19-440618. E. P. Dutton & Company.

Shadow of the Cliff. Nancy Macdougall Kennedy. 144p. 1972. pap. 0.75 (ISBN 0-532-75469-7). Woodhill.

Shadow of the Condor. James Grady. LC 75-16365. 1975. 7.95 (ISBN 0-399-11596-X). Putnam.

Shadow of the Crescent. Edward Bedinger Mitchell. LC 9-17586. 1909. F. A. Stokes Company.

Shadow of the Crooked Tree. Helen Clark Fernald. LC 65-22566. 4.50. McKay.

Shadow of the Crooked Tree. Helen Clark Fernald. LC 65-22566. 1965. D. McKay Co.

Shadow of the Cross. Jean Tharaud & Tharaud, Jerome, 1874- Joint Author. LC 24-26196. 1924. A. A. Knopf.

Shadow of the Czar. John R Carling. LC 2-21487. 1902. Little, Brown, and Company.

Shadow of the Czar. John R Carling. LC 16-69947. 1903. Little, Brown and Company.

Shadow of the Eagle. Roy Smith. LC 67-24480. 1967. World Pub. Co.

Shadow of the East. Edith Maude Hull. LC 21-16800. Small, Maynard & Company.

Shadow of the East. Edith Maude Hull. LC 42-29014. A. L. Burt Company.

Shadow of the Guillotine: A Story of the Reign of Terror; a Novel Also, Gertrude, the Amazon; a Romance of the First Crusade. Sylvanus Cobb. (On cover: The choice series, no. 115). 1894. R. Bonner's Sons.

Shadow of the Gun. Wayne C. Lee. 1981. pap. 1.95 (ISBN 0-89083-758-9). Zebra.

Shadow of the Hawk. Evelyn Scott. LC 41-7659. 1941. C. Scribner's Sons.

Shadow of the House. tr. from the french by emma a. clinton. ed. Anna Mitrofanovna Avinova Anichkova & Clinton, Emma A., Tr. 1906. McClure, Phillips & Co.

Shadow of the Iroquois: In Which I, Blaise Lafond, Tell the Tale of Those Strange and Terrible Happenings, Through Which, I, a Humble French Lad, Became Acquainted with That English by Everett McNeil... Everett McNeil. LC 28-17383. E. P. Dutton and Company.

Shadow of the Knife. Kenneth R. McKay. LC 78-58395. 304p. 1978. pap. 2.95 (ISBN 0-86721-048-6). Playboy Pbks.

Shadow of the Long Knives: A Novel. Thomas Alexander Boyd. LC 28-151626. 1928. C. Scribner's Sons.

Shadow of the Lynx. Eleanor Hibbert. LC 72-144273. 1971. 6.95. Doubleday.

Shadow of the Lynx. Eleanor Hibbert. LC 77-38981. 1972. (ISBN 0-8161-6020-1). G. K. Hall.

Shadow of the Lynx. Victoria Holt, pseud. LC 72-144273. 1971. 13.95 (ISBN 0-385-05427-0). Doubleday.

Shadow of the Lynx. Victoria Holt, pseud. 320p. 1981. pap. 2.50 (ISBN 0-449-23278-6, Crest). Fawcett.

Shadow of the Lynx. Victoria Holt, pseud. 1972. Repr. lib. bdg. 12.95 o.p. (ISBN 0-8161-6020-1, Large Print Bks). G K Hall.

Shadow of the Millionaire: Or, The Now Ideal; a Novel. P Gerome. LC 6-44237. (On cover: The Belford American novel series, no. 13). 1890. Belford Company.

Shadow of the Monsoon. 1st Ed. William Raymond Manchester. 1956. Doubleday.

Shadow of the Moon. Mary Margaret Kaye. LC 57-5084. 1957. J. Meesner.

Shadow of the Moon. rev. ed. Mary Margaret Kaye. LC 79-5033. 1979. 12.95 (ISBN 0-312-71410-6). St. Martin's Press.

Shadow of the Moth: A Novel of Espionage with Virginia Woolf. Ellen Hawkes & Peter Manso. LC 82-17058. 12.95 (ISBN 0-312-71414-9). St. Martin's/Marek.

Shadow of the Moth: A Novel of Espionage with Virginia Woolf. Ellen Hawkes & Peter Manso. 272p. 1983. 12.95 (ISBN 0-312-71414-9, Pub. by Mareu). St Martin.

Shadow of the Mountain. Sylvia Wilkinson. 1978. 1.75 (ISBN 0-671-82039-7). Pocket Books.

Shadow of the Mountain: A Novel. Sylvia Wilkinson. LC 76-57742. 1977. 8.95 (ISBN 0-395-25170-2). Houghton Mifflin.

Shadow of the Mutant Master. Kurt Brand. (Perry Rhodan, #47). 1974. (pbk.) 0.95. Ace Books.

Shadow of the Needle. Lois A Sunagel. (Avalon Books). 4.95. Thomas Bouregy.

Shadow of the Ninja. Toda Katsumi. LC 82-71143. (Illus.). 118p. (Orig.). 1982. pap. 5.95 (ISBN 0-86568-036-1, 513, Pub. by Dragon Bks Ltd). Unique Pubns.

Shadow of the North. Joseph Alexander Altsheler. 357p. 1976. Repr. of 1917 ed. lib. bdg. 14.60x (ISBN 0-88411-944-0). Amereon Ltd.

Shadow of the Palms. Janice Law, pseud. LC 79-17096. 1980. 8.95 (ISBN 0-395-28591-7). Houghton Mifflin.

Shadow of the Past. Florence Ethel Mills Young. LC 19-8075. George H. Doran Company.

Shadow of the Potrock. Paul Moss. LC 32-30923. Southwest Press.

Shadow of the Rim. Llewellyn Perry Holmes. 192p. 1982. pap. 2.25 (ISBN 0-445-04723-2). Popular Lib.

Shadow of the Rock. Patricia Wright. LC 78-2050. (Illus.). 1979. 10.00 (ISBN 0-385-14231-5). Doubleday.

Shadow of the Rock. Patricia Wright. 1980. 2.50 (ISBN 0-380-49064-1). Avon Books.

Shadow of the Rock: A Novel. Gina Norgaard. LC 56-5644. 1956. Muhlenberg Press.

Shadow of the Rope. Ray Gaulden. LC 57-8438. (Permabooks, M-3095. Western, 5). 1957. Permabooks.

Shadow of the Rope. Ernest William Hornung. LC 2-21093. 1902. C. Scribner's Sons.

Shadow of the Scarlet Sin: A Novel of "Real Life,". Marion Curtis. LC 11-31844. 1.50. Broadway Publishing Co.

Shadow of the Ship. Robert W. Franson. 288p. (Orig.). 1983. pap. 2.75 (ISBN 0-345-30688-0, Del Rey). Ballantine.

Shadow of the Sun. Sylvia Pell. LC 77-17877. 1978. 9.95 (ISBN 0-698-10849-3). Coward McCann & Geoghegan.

Shadow of the Sun. Sylvia Pell. 1981. 2.50 (ISBN 0-698-10849-3). Avon Books.

Shadow of the Swan. Gene Todd. 3.95 o.p. Vantage.

Shadow of the Swan. M. K Wren, pseud. (Phoenix Legacy). 1981. 2.75 (ISBN 0-425-04747-4). Berkley Publishing Corporation.

Shadow of the Swan: A Story of the Revolutionary War in Georgia. Gene Todd. LC 75-315878. (Illus.). 1975. 3.95 (ISBN 0-533-01379-8). Vantage Press.

Shadow of the Sword. A Romance. Robert Williams Buchanan. (Seaside library, v. 56, no. 1135). 1881. G. Munro.

Shadow of the Torturer. Gene Wolfe. LC 79-22371. (Wolfe, Gene. Book of the New Sun: Vol. 1). 10.95 (ISBN 0-671-25325-5). Simon and Schuster.

Shadow of the Tower. Florence Mary Bennett Anderson. LC 55-14438. 1955. Christopher Pub. House.

Shadow of the Truth. Helen Arvonen. (O.S.I.). 208p. (Orig.). 1973. pap. 0.95 o.s.i. (ISBN 0-446-75140-5). Paperback Lib.

Shadow of the Truth. Helen Arvouen. 1973. 0.95. Warner Paperback Library.

Shadow of the Volcano. Deirdre Rowan. (Fawcett gold medal book). 1975. (pbk.) 0.95. Fawcett.

Shadow of the Walls. Lucy Fuchs. 1980. 6.95 (Avalon). Bouregy.

Shadow of the War: A Story of the South in Reconstruction Times. LC 7-42183. 1884. Jansen, McClurg, & Company.

Shadow of the Wolf. James Barwick. 1981. pap. 2.75 (ISBN 0-345-28316-3). Ballantine.

Shadow of the Wolf. James Barwick. LC 78-31203. 1979. 9.95 o.p. (ISBN 0-698-10966-X, Coward). Putnam Pub Group.

Shadow of the Wolf. Richard Austin Freeman. LC 25-183519. 1925. Dodd, Mead and Company.

Shadow of the Wolf. Donald James & Tony Barwick. LC 78-31203. 1979. 9.95 (ISBN 0-698-10966-X). Coward, McCann & Geoghegan.

Shadow of Theale. Frances Cowen. (Ace gothic). 1974. (pbk.) 0.95. Ace Books.

Shadow of Thunder. Max Evans. LC 69-20469. (Illus.). 1969. 5.00. Swallow Press.

Shadow of Truth. Alice Lent Covert. LC 53-9376. 1953. Bouregy & Curl.

Shadow of Tyburn Tree. Dennis Yates Wheatley. (Roger Brook spy adventure). 1973. 1.50. Ballantine.

Shadow of Victory: A Romance of Fort Dearborn. Myrtle Reed. LC 3-20451. 1903. G. P. Putnam's Sons.

Shadow of Wings. Stella Morton. LC 41-14055. Harper & Brothers.

Shadow on Mercer Mountain. easy eye ed. Daoma Winston. pap. 0.60 o.p. Lancer.

Shadow on Mercer Mountain. Daoma Winston. 1976. 1.50 (ISBN 0-671-80547-9). Pocket Books.

Shadow on Summer. Christy Brown. LC 74-79420. 1975. 7.95 (ISBN 0-8128-1735-4). Stein and Day.

Shadow on Summer. Christy Brown. LC 76-376541. 1976. 0.75 (ISBN 0-330-24647-X). Pan Books.

Shadow on the Border. George Charles Appell. LC 57-7711. (Ballantine books, 185). 1957. Ballantine Books.

Shadow on the Brook. Elisabeth Stancy Payne. LC 35-19985. 1935. Dodd, Mead & Company.

Shadow on the Cliff. Miles Burton. LC 44-4922. 1944. Pub. for the Crime Club by Doubleday, Doran & Co., Inc.

Shadow on the Downs. Ralph Carter Woodthorpe. LC 36-489. 1935. Pub. for the Crime Club, Inc., by Doubleday, Doran & Company, Inc.

Shadow on the Earth: A Tale of Tradgedy and Triumph. Owen Francis Dudley. LC 26-18124. (His Problems of human happiness. ii). 1926. Longmans, Green and Co., Ltd.

Shadow on the Glass. Charles Judson Dutton. LC 23-1445. 1923. Dodd, Mead and Company.

Shadow on the Hearth. Forrest Halsey. LC 15-5993. The American Issue Publishing Company.

Shadow on the Hearth. Judith Merril. LC 50-8437. 1950. Doubleday.

Shadow on the House. Florence Stevenson. 1975. (pbk.) 1.25. New American Library.

Shadow on the Left. Augustus Muir. LC 28-209263. The Bobbs-Merrill Company.

Shadow on the Mesa. Jackson Gregory. 1933. Dodd, Mead & Company.

Shadow on the Moon. Luanna Churchill. 1974. 4.50 (ISBN 0-517-51639-X). Lenox Hill Press.

Shadow on the Plains. Alice Wheeler Greve. LC 44-41890. 1944. Binfords & Mort.

Shadow on the Range. Norman A. Fox. LC 49-113073. (Silver star westerns). 1949. Dodd, Mead.

Shadow on the Snow. Teresa Gerbers. (Avalon romances). 1974. 4.50. Avalon Books.

Shadow on the Snow. Nancy MacDougall Kennedy. 1973. (pbk) 0.75. Dell.

Shadow on the Stone. Marguerite Bryant. LC 17-295169. 1917. 1.35. Duffield and Company.

Shadow on the Stones. Moyra Caldecott. LC 78-24035. (Caldecott, Moyra. The Sacred Stones). 1979. 8.95 (ISBN 0-8090-8599-2). Hill and Wang.

Shadow on the Sun. Wynwode Reid. LC 67-10183. 1967. Rigby.

Shadow on the Sun. Lily Jay Silver. LC 57-11055. 1958. Duell, Sloan and Pearce.

Shadow on the Sun. Sharon Wagner. 1973. pap. 0.95 o.s.i. (75-448). Lancer.

Shadow on the Threshold. Mary Cecil Hay. LC 7-3755. (On cover: Harper's half-hour series no. 53). 1878. Harper & Brothers.

Shadow on the Trail. Grey, Zane. LC 63-6980. (Great western edition, 82). 1963. Grosset & Dunlap.

Shadow on the Trail. Zane Grey. LC 46-16263. 1946. Harper & Brothers.

Shadow on the Wall. Henry Christopher Bailey. LC 34-16182. 1934. Pub. for the Crime Club, Inc., by Doran & Company, Inc.

Shadow on the Wall. Henry Christopher Bailey. LC 42-44992. Grosset & Dunlap.

Shadow on the Waters. Drawings by Dianne Weiss. 1st Ed. Jack Thomas Leahy. LC 60-8350. 1960. Knopf.

Shadow on the Wind. Anne Lowing. 1977. pap. 1.25 o.p. (ISBN 0-515-04248-X). BJ Pub Group.

Shadow over Beauclaire. Sylva Miles, pseud. 192p. (YA) 1975. 6.95 (Avalon). Bouregy.

Shadow Over Beauclaire. Sylva Miles. 1975. 4.95. Avalon Books.

Shadow Over Elveron. Michael Kingsley. LC 63-7646. 1963. Random House.

Shadow Over Emerald Castle. Marilyn Ross. (Beagle book). 1975. (pbk.) 0.95 (ISBN 0-345-26708-7). Ballantine Books.

Shadow Over Grove House. Mary Linn Roby. (Signet book, T5477). 1973. (pbk) 0.75. New American Library.

Shadow over Hawkhaven. J. H. Rodes. 1982. 6.95 (Avalon). Bouregy.

Shadow Over Heldon Hall. Nan Herbert. 1978. pap. 1.95 (ISBN 0-89083-407-5). Zebra.

Shadow Over Innsmouth. Howard Phillips Lovecraft. LC 37-14575. 1936. Visionary Publishing Co.

Shadow Over Mt Sharon. Frances McHugh. (O.s.i.). 1976. pap. 1.25 o.s.i. (BT50942). Belmont-Tower.

Shadow Over Pheasant Heath. Katheryn Kimbrough. (queen-size gothic). 1974. (pbk.) 0.95. Popular Library.

Shadow Over the Earth. Philip Wilding. LC 58-1996. 1956. Philosophical Library.

Shadow Over the Garden. Clarissa Ross. Leisure Books.

Shadow Over the Garden. 1976. pap. 1.25 o.p. (LB402, Leisure Bks). Nordon Pubns.

Shadow Over the Island: By Mary Douglas Waren Pseud. Maysie Greig. LC 55-102042. 1955. Arcadia House.

Shadow Over the Land. Charles Dwoskin. LC 46-20994. 1946. The Beechhurst Press.

Shadow Over Wide Ruin. Florence Crannell Means. LC 42-22718. 1942. Houghton Mifflin Company.

Shadow Over Wyndham Hall. Juanita Tyree Osborne. 1976. 4.95. Avalon Books.

Shadow Passes. Eden Phillpotts. LC 34-1476. 1934. The Macmillan Company.

Shadow People. Kenneth Laing. LC 56-9516. Roy Publishers.

Shadow Play. Marvin Werlin. LC 75-23338. 1976. 7.95 (ISBN 0-688-02980-9). Morrow.

Shadow Play. Marvin Werlin. LC 75-23338. (Kangaroo Book). 1977. 1.50 (ISBN 0-671-80853-2). Pocket Books.

Shadow President. Shelley Katz. (Orig.). 1982. pap. 3.50 (ISBN 0-440-17875-4). Dell.

Shadow Range. Curtis Kent Bishop. LC 47-17970. 1947. The Macmillan Company.

Shadow Rider. Double D Western. William Colt MacDonald. LC 42-36039. 1942. Doubleday, Doran and Company, Inc.

Shadow Riders. Louis L'Amour. 192p. 1982. pap. 2.95 (ISBN 0-553-23132-4). Bantam.

Shadow Riders. Isabel Bowler Paterson. LC 16-519198. 1916. 1.35. John Lane Company.

Shadow Riders of the Yellowstone. Les Savage. LC 51-9435. (Double D western). 1951. Doubleday.

Shadow River. Walton Hall Smith. LC 27-15202. 1927. Houghton Mifflin Company.

Shadow-Shapes. Maude Annesley. LC 11-17102. 1911. John Lane Company.

Shadow Shapes. Edwin Carlile Litsey. LC 29-287877. 1929. R. Packard & Company.

Shadow Show. Pat Flower. LC 77-17990. (Jubilee mystery). 1978. 7.95 (ISBN 0-8128-2412-1). Stein and Day.

Shadow Slithering in. Helen Snyder. (Orig.). 1980. pap. 2.25 (ISBN 0-937172-01-4). JLJ Pubs.

Shadow Spy. Nicholas Luard. LC 78-22264. 7.95 (ISBN 0-15-125712-4). Harcourt Brace Jovanovich.

Shadow Syndicate. Clifford James Wheeler Hosken. LC 30-12524. 1930. L. MacVeagh, The Dial Press.

Shadow That Caught Fire. Hamilton Jobson. LC 75-38223. 1976. 6.95 (ISBN 0-684-14566-9). Scribner.

Shadow: The Mask of Mephisto & Murder by Magic. Walter Gibson. LC 74-18800. 192p. 1975. 5.95 o.p. (ISBN 0-385-03712-0). Doubleday.

Shadow: The Red Menace, No. 7. Maxwell Grant, pseud. 1975. pap. 0.95 o.p. (ISBN 0-515-03875-X). BJ Pub Group.

Shadow: The Silent Seven, No. 10. Maxwell Grant, pseud. 1975. Repr. pap. 0.95 o.p. (ISBN 0-515-03966-7). BJ Pub Group.

Shadow Trade. Alan Furst. 288p. 1983. 14.95 (ISBN 0-440-07698-6). Delacorte.

Shadow Valley. Barry Cord. 1978. pap. 1.25 o.s.i. (ISBN 0-505-51329-3). Tower Bks.

Shadow Valley: By Barry Cord Pseud. Peter Germano. LC 51-10904. 1951. Phoenix Press.

Shadow Wife. Dorothy Eden. LC 68-11882. 1968. Coward-McCann.

Shadow Without Light: A Novel. Sarah Louise Mende Richards. LC 47-31362. 1947. Dial Press.

Shadow World. Hamlin Garland. Ed. by Donald Pizer. (American Authors Ser). 1908. 16.95 o.s.i. (ISBN 0-512-00254-1). Garrett Pr.

Shadow World see Collected Works.

Shadow 81. Lucien Nahum. LC 74-17770. 1975. 7.95 (ISBN 0-385-08467-6). Doubleday.

Shadowbox. Stanley Noyes. LC 78-97759. 1970. Macmillan.

Shadowboxer. Noel Behn. LC 77-75858. (O.S.I.). 1969. 5.95 o.s.i. (ISBN 0-671-20193-X). S&S.

Shadowboxer. Mark A. Calde. LC 76-8278. 7.95 (ISBN 0-399-11799-7). Putnam.

Shadowed! Hilaire Belloc. LC 29-1803. 1929. Harper & Brothers.

Shadowed by a Detective: Or, The Woman in Wax. By Virginia Chaplin Psued. Grace Virginia Lord. J. S. Ogilvie & Company.

Shadowed by Three. Emma Murdoch Van Deventer. (On cover: The detective and adventure library. no. 5). 1889. A. T. Loyd & Company.

Shadowed by Three. Emma Murdoch Van Deventer. (library of choice fiction no. 4). 1890. Laird & Lee.

Shadowed Faith. Jack M Bickham. LC 68-18092. 1968. Doubleday.

Shadowed Love. Ursula Torday. (Dell Book). 1977. 1.50 (ISBN 0-440-12925-7). Dell Pub. Co.

Shadowed Millions. Maxwell Grant, pseud. (Shadow Ser.: No. 3). 1976. pap. 0.95 o.p. (ISBN 0-515-03968-3). BJ Pub Group.

Shadowed Perils. A Novel. M A Avery. LC 6-3849. 1876. Authors' Publishing Co.

Shadowed Porch. Emily Moor. (Orig.). 1972. pap. 0.75 o.p. (94292). Beagle Bks.

Shadowed Reunion. Lillian Cheatham. 1981. pap. 1.75 (ISBN 0-440-18247-6). Dell.

Shadowed Spring. Michael Butterworth. LC 79-7808. 1980. 10.00 (ISBN 0-385-14958-1). Doubleday.

Shadowed Spring. Carola Salisbury. LC 79-7807. 1980. 10.00 (ISBN 0-385-14958-1). Doubleday.

Shadowed Spring. Carola Salisbury. 288p. 1981. pap. 2.50 (ISBN 0-449-24412-1, Crest). Fawcett.

Shadowed Stranger. Carole Mortimer. (Harlequin Presents Ser.). 192p. 1982. pap. 1.75 (ISBN 0-373-10531-2). Harlequin Bks.

Shadowed Three. Emma Murdoch Van Deventer. LC 13-2067. (On cover: D. G. & L. series). Donnelley, Gassette & Loyd.

Shadowed to Europe: A Chicago Detective on Two Continents. Symmes M Jelley. LC 13-2069. (Mooney & Boland detective series). 1885. Belford, Clarke & Co.

Shadowed Trail. Arthur Henry Gooden. LC 46-719310. 1946. Houghton Mifflin Company.

Shadowers. Donald Hamilton. 144p. 1981. pap. 1.95 (ISBN 0-449-14006-7, GM). Fawcett.

Shadowgraphs. Susan Austin Arnold McCausland. LC 25-1287. Authors & Publishers Corporation.

Shadowgraphs. A Novel. Judson Chubbuck. Pub. by the Author; Chicago, Atwell & Goodall, Printers.

Shadowland. Elaine Evans. 1970. pap. 0.75 o.p. (ISBN 0-447-74705-3). Lancer.

Shadowland. Peter Straub. LC 80-23691. 1980. 13.95 (ISBN 0-698-30715-1). Coward, McCann & Geoghegan.

Shadowland. Peter Straub. 1981. 2.50 (ISBN 0-425-05056-4). Berkley, Publishing Corp.

Shadowline. Glen Cook. 352p. (Orig.). 1982. pap. 2.95 (ISBN 0-446-30578-2). Warner Bks.

Shadowman. George W. Proctor. 256p. 1980. pap. 1.95 (ISBN 0-449-14350-3, GM). Fawcett.

ShadowPlay. Norman Hartley. LC 81-69237. 288p. 1982. 12.95 (ISBN 0-689-11249-1). Atheneum.

Shadows. Jan Alexander, pseud. (Orig.). 1970. pap. 0.75 o.p. (ISBN 0-447-74670-7). Lancer.

Shadows. Jan Alexander. Bd. with Wolves of Craywood; Blood Moon. 1973. pap. 1.65 o.s.i. (70-409). Lancer.

Shadows. Edwin Corley. LC 75-11832. 1975. 8.95 (ISBN 0-8128-1741-9). Stein and Day.

Shadows. Charles L Grant. LC 77-12856. 1978. 7.95 (ISBN 0-385-12937-8). Doubleday.

Shadows. Alma Newton. LC 21-490781. 1921. John Lane Company.

Shadows. Florence Ryerson & Clements, Colin Campbell, 1894- Joint Author. LC 34-21307. (Tired business man's library of adventure, detective, and mystery novels). 1934. D. Appleton-Century Company, Incorporated.

Shadows. Herman August Schroeder. LC 27-9311. 1927. Concordia Publishing House.

Shadows. Will Scott. 1928. Macrae Smith Company.

Shadows Across the Bayou. Sue L. Anderson. 1977. pap. 1.50 (ISBN 0-532-15298-0). Woodhill.

Shadows and Images. Meriol Trevor. LC 62-3875. 1960. Macmillan.

Shadows and Images: A Novel. Meriol Trevor. LC 62-1578. 1962. D. McKay Co.

Shadows and Light: Nine Stories by Anton Chekhov. Selected, Tr. by Miriam Morton. Illus. by Ann Grifalconi. 1st Ed. Anton Pavlovich Chekhov. LC 68-11575. 1968. 2.95, 3.70 lib. ed.,. Doubleday.

Shadows and Wolves: A Novel. William Herrick. LC 79-20726. 1980. 9.95 (ISBN 0-8112-0758-7). New Directions.

Shadows Around the Lake. Guy De Pourtales. Tr. by Sainsbury, Geoffrey. LC 38-34143. 1938. A. A. Knopf.

Shadows at Noon... Martin M Goldsmith. LC 43-10498. 1943. Ziff-Davis Publishing Company.

Shadows at Noon. Kamelle Hess. 1978. pap. 1.50 (ISBN 0-532-15339-1). Woodhill.

Shadows Before. Dorothy Bowers. LC 39-32827. 1940. Pub. for the Crime Club by Doubleday, Doran & Company, Inc.

Shadows Before: Or, A Century Onward. Fayette Stratton Giles. (On cover: Twentieth century library, no. 57). 1894. The Humboldt Publishing Company.

Shadows by the Sea. Joseph Jefferson Farjeon. LC 28-639420. 1928. L. MacVeagh, The Dial Press.

Shadows Cast. N. T. Leonard. 3.75 o.p. (ISBN 0-8062-0614-4). Carlton.

Shadows Five. Charles L. Grant. LC 81-43740. (Science Fiction Ser.). 192p. 1982. 11.95 (ISBN 0-385-17756-9). Doubleday.

Shadows Flying. Howard Browne. LC 36-8134. 1936. A. A. Knopf.

Shadows Flying. John Evans, pseud. LC 36-8134. 1836. A. A. Knopf.

Shadows Four. Charles L. Grant. LC 80-3005. (Double D Science Fiction Ser.). 192p. 1981. 10.95 (ISBN 0-385-17187-0). Doubleday.

Shadows from the Past. Dorothy Daniels. (Dorothy Daniels Ser). 192p. 1972. pap. 0.95 o.p. (ISBN 0-446-65877-4). Paperback Lib.

Shadows II. Charles L Grant. LC 79-7056. 1979. 8.95 (ISBN 0-385-14320-6). Doubleday.

Shadows in a Hidden Land: By Simon Harvester. Henry Gibbs. LC 66-22496. 1966. bds., 3.50. Walker.

Shadows in Ecstasy. John R. Tapia. 2.95 o.p. Vantage.

Shadows in Go-Yeu. James Carver. LC 79-142838. 1971. 6.95 (ISBN 0-8027-0337-2). Walker.

Shadows in Paradise. Erich Maria Remarque. LC 79-174513. 1972. (ISBN 0-15-181480-5). Harcourt Brace Jovanovich.

Shadows in Succession. Elma K. Lobaugh. LC 46-574346. 1946. Pub. for the Crime Club by Doubleday & Company, Inc.

Shadows in the Dusk. 1st Ed. John Edward Jennings. LC 55-5530. Little, Brown.

Shadows in the Sun. R. Rabindranath Menon. 1976. 8.00 (ISBN 0-89253-813-9); flexible cloth 4.80 (ISBN 0-89253-814-7). Ind-US Inc.

Shadows in the Sun. Chad Oliver. LC 54-12509. Ballantine Books.

Shadows in the Sun. Symmes Chadwick Oliver. LC 54-12509. 1954. Ballentine Books.

Shadows in the Sun. Ronald Payne. LC 73-83484. 1973. 7.95 (ISBN 0-8059-1893-0). Dorrance.

Shadows in Umbria. Jacqueline La Tourrette. LC 78-23798. 8.95 (ISBN 0-399-12182-X). Putnam.

Shadows Lifted: A Sequel to Saint Cuthbert's. John Edwin Copus. LC 4-35724. 1904. Benziger Brothers.

Shadows Move Among Them. Edgar Mittelholzer. LC 51-11185. 1951. P. Nevill.

Shadows Move Among Them. Edgar Mittelholzer. LC 51-8454. 1951. Lippincott.

Shadows of Castle Fosse. Jill Tattersall. LC 76-10194. 1976. 7.95 (ISBN 0-688-03077-7). Morrow.

Shadows of Castle Fosse. Jill Tattersall. (Fawcett Crest Book). 1977. 1.50 (ISBN 0-449-23296-4). Fawcett Pubns.

Shadows of Castle Fosse. Jill Tattersall. LC 78-14017. 1981. 11.50 (ISBN 0-89340-177-3). J. Curley.

Shadows of Cliffside. Bonnie Lee. LC 74-31247. 1975. 4.95 (ISBN 0-517-52118-0). Lenox Hill Press.

Shadows of Death. Gregory St. Germaine. (Resistance: No. 3). 192p. 1983. pap. 2.50 (ISBN 0-451-11999-1, Sig). NAL.

Shadows of Ecstacy see Novels.

Shadows of Ecstasy. Charles Williams. LC 50-14559. 1950. Pellegrini & Cudahy.

Shadows of Ecstasy. Charles Williams. LC 75-306783. 1973. 2.45 (ISBN 0-8028-1223-6). Eerdmans.

Shadows of Ecstasy. Charles Walter Stansby Williams. 1965. pap., 1.95. Eerdmans.

Shadows of Fear. Kamelle Hess. (Orig.). 1979. pap. 1.95 (ISBN 0-532-23251-8). Woodhill.

Shadows of Fieldcrest Manor. Casey Stephens. 224p. (Orig.). 1980. pap. 1.95 (ISBN 0-89083-698-1). Zebra.

Shadows of Forgotten Ancestors. Mykhailo Kotsiubynskyi & Bohdan Rubchak. LC 81-432. (Ukrainian Classics in Translation; No. 4). (Illus.). 1981. 9.50 (ISBN 0-87287-205-X). Published for the Canadian Institute of Ukrainian Studies by Ukrainian Academic Press.

Shadows of Lust. William Arthur Neubauer. LC 46-20368. 1946. Phoenix Press.

Shadows of Men. Jim Tully. LC 30-3652. 1930. Doubleday, Doran and Company, Incorporated.

Shadows of Moonsong. Jessica Stuart. (Moonsong Chronicles Ser.). 352p. (Orig.). 1983. pap. 2.95 (ISBN 0-523-41966-X). Pinnacle Bks.

Shadows of Passion. Patricia Gallagher. 1976. pap. 1.75 (ISBN 0-380-00928-5, 31906). Avon.

Shadows of Reddoch's Landing. Melissa Lee. (O.s.i.). 1976. pap. 1.25 o.s.i. Belmont-Tower.

Shadows of Reddoch's Landing. Melissa Lee. 1976. 1.25. Leisure Books.

Shadows of Sanctuary. Robert L. Asprin. 320p. (Orig.). 1981. pap. 2.75 (ISBN 0-441-76028-7, Pub. by Ace Science Fiction). Ace Bks.

Shadows of Shasta. Joaquin Miller. LC 7-25967. 1881. Jansen, McClurg & Company.

Shadows of Summers Past. Mildred Ames. 192p. (YA) 1974. 4.95 o.p. (Avalon). Bouregy.

Shadows of Summers Past. Mildred Ames. (Avalon romances). 1974. 4.50. Avalon Books.

Shadows of the Clouds. James Anthony Froude. 1971. Repr. of 1847 ed. 12.00 o.s.i.; pre-Jan 9.00 o.s.i. Gregg Intl.

Shadows of the Clouds, 1847 see Nemesis of Faith, 1849.

Shadows of the Half Moon. John W. Kisselburgh. 5.95 o.p. Vantage.

Shadows of the House. Margaret Elizabeth Atkins. LC 69-17625. 1969. 5.95. Viking Press.

Shadows of the Images. William Edmund Barrett. LC 52-13562. 1953. Doubleday.

Shadows of the Past. Kate Cameron, pseud. (Holderly Hall Ser.). (O.s.i.: No. 2). 1974. pap. 0.95 o.s.i. (LB209NK, Leisure Bks). Nordon Pubns.

Shadows of the Past. Mary Craig. 224p. 1976. pap. 1.25 (ISBN 0-532-12408-1). Woodhill.

Shadows of the Sun. Perez Lugin, Alejandro & Franklin, Sidney. LC 34-325691. 1934. C. Scribner's Sons.

Shadows of Tomorrow. Dorothy Daniels. (Gothic Ser). (Orig.). 1969. pap. 0.60 o.p. (63-156). Paperback Lib.

Shadows of Yesterday: Stories from an Old Catalogue. Marjorie Bowen. LC 16-24323. 1916. E. P. Dutton and Company.

Shadows on a Throne. Juliet Dymoke. LC 77-350217. 1976. 3.50 (ISBN 0-85523-074-6). Wingate.

Shadows on a Wall: A Novel. Charles E Israel. LC 65-12590. bds., 5.95. S. &S.

Shadows on Cassiopeia. Robert W. Olmsted. LC 76-528. (Illus.). 1976. 14.95 (ISBN 0-89002-073-6); pap. 5.00 (ISBN 0-89002-072-8). Northwoods Pr.

Shadows on Our Skin. Jennifer Johnston. LC 77-72415. 1978. 7.95 (ISBN 0-385-13125-9). Doubleday.

Shadows on Our Skin. Jennifer Johnston. (Bard book). 1979. 2.50 (ISBN 0-380-44347-3). Avon Books.

Shadows on the Fields. Ludovic Masse. Tr. by Katherine Woods. LC 48-8485. 1948. Ziff-Davis Pub. Co.

Shadows on the Hill. Marjorie Chalmers Carleton. 1973. pap. 0.95 o.p. (ISBN 0-515-02927-0, N2927). Pyramid Pubns.

Shadows on the Left Bank. Gertrude Schweitzer. 1973. (pbk.) 0.95. Dell.

Shadows on the Moon. Kate Cameron, pseud. (Whispering Hills gothic,#3). 1974. (pbk.) 0.95. Leisure Books.

Shadows on the Moon. Nancy Fairweather. (Belmont Tower Book). 1978. 1.50 (ISBN 0-505-51234-3). Tower Pubns.

Shadows on the Moon. David Houston. (Inflation Fighters Ser.). 192p. 1982. pap. 1.50 (ISBN 0-8439-1081-X, Leisure Bks). Nordon Pubns.

Shadows on the Praire. Lydia Leeds. 3.50 o.p. Carlton.

Shadows on the Rock. Willa Sibert Cather. LC 31-272121. 1931. A. A. Knopf.

Shadows on the Sand. Rona Randall. 1973. (pbk) 0.95. Ace Books.

Shadows on the Sceptered Isle. JoAnne Stang. LC 79-19433. 8.95 (ISBN 0-517-53958-6). Crown Publishers.

Shadows on the Tor. Susan Brand, pseud. LC 77-3712. 7.95 (ISBN 0-671-22748-3). Simon and Schuster.

Shadows on the Tor. Susan Brand, pseud. LC 78-6958. 1978. 11.95 (ISBN 0-8161-6589-0). G. K. Hall.

Shadows on the Valley. Barbara Webster. LC 40-8389. 1940. C. Scribner's Sons.

Shadows on the Wall. Joan O'Donovan. LC 60-3496. 1960. Morrow.

Shadows on the Wall. Mary Reisner. LC 43-12152. 1943. Dodd, Mead & Company.

Shadows on the Water. Elizabeth Cadell. LC 58-6674. 1958. Morrow.

Shadows on the Water. Dorothy Fletcher. 1972. pap. 0.75 o.p. (94223). Beagle Bks.

Shadows on the Wind. Rita Gallagher. (Orig.). 1982. pap. 2.95 (ISBN 0-440-18042-2). Dell.

Shadows Out of Hell. Andrew J Offutt. 1.95 (ISBN 0-425-04447-5). Berkley Publishing Corp.

Shadows Over Castle Rising. Fanny Craddock. 1978. pap. 2.25 (ISBN 0-345-27352-4). Ballantine.

Shadows Over Castle Rising. Phyllis Cradock. LC 76-11893. 1977. 8.95 (ISBN 0-525-20128-9). Dutton.

Shadows Over Castle Rising. Phyllis Cradock. LC 76-382519. (Illus.). 1976. 4.50. W. H. Allen.

Shadows Over Silver Sands. Margaret Pemberton. (Berkley Medallion Book). 1976. (pbk.) 1.25. Berkley Publishing Corp.

Shadow's Shadow. Lulah Ragsdale. 1893. J. B. Lippincott Company.

Shadow's Shadow. 1977. pap. 1.25 o.p. (ISBN 0-515-04278-1). BJ Pub Group.

Shadows Slant North. Mary Bledsoe. 1937. Lothrop, Lee & Shepard Co.

Shadows That Pass: By Otto Rung; Translated from the Danish by Grace Isabel Colbron. Otto Rung. Tr. by Colbron, Grace Isabel. 1924. D. Appleton and Company.

Shadows Three. Charles L. Grant. LC 80-651. (DD Science Fiction Ser.). 224p. 1980. 10.95 (ISBN 0-385-15777-0). Doubleday.

Shadows Two. Charles L. Grant. LC 79-7056. (Science Fiction Ser.). 1979. 9.95 o.p. (ISBN 0-385-14320-6). Doubleday.

Shadows Under the Midnight Sun. Kenneth Anderson. LC 43-10298. 1943. Zondervan Publishing House.

Shadows Under the Stars. Dorothy Black. LC 45-2143. 1945. Macrae-Smith-Company.

Shadows Under Whiteface: A Novel. 1st Ed. Aya Heald. LC 55-10858. Vantage Press.

Shadows Waiting. Lois Dwight Cole. LC 69-19044. 1969. 4.95. Meredith Press.

Shadows Waiting: A Novel in Three Parts. Eleanor Carroll Chilton. LC 27-3101. 1927. The John Day Company.

Shadows 5. Charles L Grant. LC 81-43740. 1982. 11.95 (ISBN 0-385-17756-9). Doubleday.

Shadowy Thing. Henry Burgess Drake. LC 28-228781. 1928. Macy Masius.

Shadowy Third. Harry Kurnitz. LC 75-44997. (Fifty Classics of Crime Fiction, 1900-1950; 40). 1976. 12.00 (ISBN 0-8240-2389-7). Garland Pub.

Shadowy Third. Harry Kurnitz. LC 46-8486. 1946. Dodd, Mead & Company.

Shadowy Third. Marco Page. LC 75-44997. (Crime Fiction Ser). 1976. Repr. of 1946 ed. lib. bdg. 17.50 (ISBN 0-8240-2389-7). Garland Pub.

Shadowy Third: And Other Stories. Ellen Anderson Gholson Glasgow. LC 23-17163. 1923. Doubleday, Page & Company.

Shadrach in the Furnace. Robert Silverberg. LC 75-31608. 8.95 (ISBN 0-672-51993-3). Bobbs-Merrill.

Shadrach in the Furnace. Robert Silverberg. (Kangaroo Book). 1978. 1.75 (ISBN 0-671-81273-4). Pocket Books.

Shadrin: The Spy Who Never Came Back. Henry Hurt. 304p. 1981. 13.95 (ISBN 0-07-031478-0). Readers Digest Pr.

Shady Doings. Veronica Parker Johns. LC 41-260040. Duell, Sloan and Pearce.

Shady Doings. Veronica Parker Johns. LC 45-13591. 1944. Select Publications Inc.

Shady Grove: A Novel. Janice Holt Giles. LC 68-11108. 1968. Houghton Mifflin.

Shady Grove: A Novel. Janice Holt Giles. LC 78-12454. 1978. 12.00 (ISBN 0-89783-002-4). Larlin Corp.

Shady Lady. Peggy Gaddis, pseud. LC 41-9499. 1941. Phoenix Press.

Shady Lady. Ruth Gordon. 1983. pap. 3.25 (ISBN 0-8217-1187-3). Zebra.

Shady Lady. Perry Lindsay, pseud. Phoenix Press.

Shady Lady: A Novel. Ruth Gordon. LC 81-70029. 12.95 (ISBN 0-87795-364-3). Arbor House.

Shady Place to Die. John Savage. LC 57-84478. (Dell first edition, A137). 1957. Dell Pub. Co.

Shady Secrets. Edgar Hart. LC 34-128809. The Christopher Publishing House.

Shady Side: Or, Life in a Country Parsonage. Martha Hubbell. LC 7-5658. 1853. Jewett, Proctor & Worthington.

Shaft. Ernest Tidyman. LC 70-96450. 1970. Macmillan.

Shaft Among the Jews. Ernest Tidyman. LC 74-37454. 1972. 5.95. Dial Press.

Shaft Has a Ball. Ernest Tidyman. LC 73-958. 1973. 0.95. Bantam Books.

Shaft in the Sky. John Temple Jr. Graves. LC 23-55165. 1.75. George H. Doran Company.

Shaft of Sunlight. Barbara Cartland. (Cartland Ser.: No, 149). (Orig.). 1981. pap. text ed. 1.95 (ISBN 0-553-20234-0). Bantam.

Shafted Sunlight. Paul Hutchens. LC 39-33747. 1939. Wm. B. Eerdmans Publishing Co.

Shaft's Carnival of Killers. Ernest Tidyman. 1974. (pbk.) 0.95. Bantam Books.

Shag Bag: More Stuff from Maine. John Gould. 1972. 5.95 o.p. (ISBN 0-316-32179-6). Little.

Shagbark Hill. Elizabeth Roget. LC 72-112843. 1970. 7.95. McGraw-Hill.

Shaggy D.A. Vic Crume. 1978. pap. 1.75 (ISBN 0-449-13642-6, GM). Fawcett.

Shaggy Dog, and Other Murders. Fredric Brown. LC 63-9856. 1963. Dutton.

Shaggy Legion. Hal George Evarts. LC 30-7299. 1930. Little, Brown, and Company.

Shaggy Planet. Ron Goulart. 1973. pap. 0.95 o.s.i. (75-420). Lancer.

Shah-Mak. Alan Williams. LC 76-26087. 1976. 8.95 (ISBN 0-698-10773-X). Coward, McCann & Geoghegan.
Shah-Mak. Alan Williams. LC 77-354927. 1976. 4.50 (ISBN 0-85634-048-0). Blond and Briggs.
Shaihu Umar: A Novel. Abubakar Tafawa Balewa. (Orig.). 1967. pap. text ed. 1.75x o.p. Humanities.
Shaihu Umar: A Novel by Alhaji Sir Abubakar Tafawa Balewa; Tr., with an Introd., Notes by Mervyn Hiskett. Abubakar Tafawa Balewa. LC 67-113524. 1967. pap., 1.00. Longmans.
Shaitan. Max Simon Ehrlich. LC 80-66498. 320p. 1982. 13.95 (ISBN 0-87795-273-6). Arbor Hse.
Shaitan. Max Simon Ehrlich. (Tor Bks.). 384p. 1983. pap. 3.95 (ISBN 0-523-48075-X). Pinnacle Bks.
Shake Down the Stars. Harriet Henry, pseud. LC 39-939952. E. P. Dutton & Co., Inc.
Shake Hands Forever. Ruth Rendell. LC 74-25121. 1975. 5.95 (ISBN 0-385-09939-8). Published for the Crime Club by Doubleday.
Shake Hands Forever. Ruth Rendell. LC 78-3820. 1978. 9.98 (ISBN 0-89340-143-9). J. Curley.
Shake Hands with the Devil. Rearden Conner, pseud. LC 34-2274. 1934. W. Morrow and Company.
Shake Him till He Rattles. Malcolm Braly. 1.50 (ISBN 0-671-80741-2). Pocket Books.
Shake-Speares Sweetheart. Sara Hawks Sterling. LC 5-35597. 1905. G. W. Jacobs & Co.
Shake This Town. Robert V Williams. LC 60-14647. 1960. Viking Press.
Shake Your Head, Darling. Jose Eber. LC 82-50639. (Illus.). 208p. (Orig.). 1983. 17.50 (ISBN 0-446-51250-8). Warner Bks.
Shakedown. Johnathan Kwitny Kwitny. LC 76-51436. 8.95. Putnam.
Shakedown. Jonathan Kwitny Kwitny. 1978. 1.95 (ISBN 0-380-01957-4). Avon Books.
Shakedown: By Ben Kerr Pseud. 1st Ed. William Ard. LC 52-6629. (Holt mystery). 1952. Holt.
Shakedown Kid. Norman Singer. 224p. (Orig.). 1975. pap. 1.25 (ISBN 0-532-12331-X). Woodhill.
Shakedown. 1st Ed. Ben. Kerr. LC 52-6629. (Holt mystery). 1952. Holt.
Shaken by the Wind: A Story of Fanaticism. Rachel Costelloe Strachey. LC 28-4067. 1928. The Macmillan Company.
Shaken Down. Alice MacGowan & Newberry, Perry, 1870- Joint Author. LC 25-354510. 1925. Frederick A. Stokes Company.
Shaken with the Wind. Miriam Allen De Ford. LC 42-18659. 1942. Doubleday, Doran and Company, Inc.
Shakespeare & Son, a Novel. Edward Fisher. LC 62-15060. 1962. Abelard-Schuman.
Shakespeare & Son: A Novel. Edward Fisher. LC 62-15060. (His The Silver Falcon, 1). 1962. Abelard-Schuman.
Shakespeare Curse. John Boland. LC 77-109188. 1970. 4.50. Walker.
Shakespeare Murders. Amelia Reynolds Long. LC 39-20476. Phoenix Press.
Shakespeare Murders. Archibald Gordon Macdonnell. LC 33-23181. H. Holt and Company.
Shakespeare Never Did This. Charles Bukowski. LC 79-21877. (Illus.). 12.95. City Lights Books.
Shakespeare's Christmas: And Other Stories. Arthur Thomas Quiller-Couch. LC 5-22359. 1905. Longmans, Green, and Co.
Shakespeare's Dog: A Novel. Leon Rooke. LC 82-48889. 1983. 12.95 (ISBN 0-394-53031-4). Knopf: Distributed by Random House.
Shakespeare's Planet. Clifford D. Simak. LC 75-43651. 6.95 (ISBN 0-399-11729-6). Berkley Pub. Corp.: Distributed by Putnam.
Shakespeare's Planet. Clifford D. Simak. 1977. 1.25 (ISBN 0-425-03394-5). Berkley Pub. Corp.
Shaking the Apple Tree: Or, Education Vs. Common Sense. A Novel. William A. Sturdy. LC 8-16866. 1886. The Author, H. Partridge & Co., Printers.
Shakwa. Gene March. (Orig.). 1979. pap. 1.95 (ISBN 0-89083-482-2). Zebra.
Shalako. Louis L'Amour. 176p. (Orig.). 1980. pap. 2.25 (ISBN 0-553-14762-5). Bantam.
Shale Creek Showdown. Lewis Brant, pseud. 1974. 4.95. Lenox Hill Press.
Shalimar Pavilion. Betty Hale Hyatt. LC 81-43449. 1982. 10.95 (ISBN 0-385-17908-1). Doubleday.
Shall Do No Murder. Holmes Moss Alexander. LC 59-9054. 1959. H. Regnery Co.
Shall Love Be Lost? Iris Bromige. 1974. pap. 0.75 o.p. (26577-7-075). Beagle Bks.
Shall We Tell the President? Jeffrey Archer. LC 77-9087. 1977. 7.95 (ISBN 0-670-63934-6). Viking Press.
Shallow End. John Hay Beith. LC 25-320326. 1924. Houghton Mifflin Company.
Shallow Grass: A Novel of Texas. Tom Horn. LC 68-12930. 1968. Macmillan.
Shallow Grave. Jack S Scott, pseud. LC 77-11546. 8.95 (ISBN 0-06-013791-6). Harper & Row.
Shallow Soil. Knut Hamsun & Hyllested, Carl Christian, Tr. LC 14-474019. 1914. C. Scribner's Sons.
Shallows. Frederick Watson. 1913. E. P. Dutton & Company.
Shallows of Night. Eric Van Lustbader. LC 77-12884. 1978. 7.95 (ISBN 0-385-12968-8). Doubleday.
Shallows of Night. Eric Van Lustbader. 1980. pap. 2.50 (ISBN 0-425-04453-X). Berkley Pub.
Shallows of Night. Eric Van Lustbader. LC 77-12884. 1978. 7.95 o.p. (ISBN 0-385-12968-8). Doubleday.
Shalom. Dean Brelis. LC 59-13731. 1959. Little, Brown.
Shalom, Aviva! Christine Arnothy. LC 73-113764. 1970. 4.95. McKay.
Shalom My Beloved. Loret D. C Mullins. 1973. 6.95. Bell-Dell Co.
Shalom, My Love. Ida Hills. LC 82-10668. 9.95 (ISBN 0-89621-387-0). Thorndike Press.
Sham: A Story of Today. Joseph Hocking. LC 29-184142. F. H. Revell Company.
Shaman. Frank Coffey. LC 79-26900. 10.95 (ISBN 0-312-71615-X). St. Martin's Press.
Shaman from Elko. Sandner & Oakes. Ed. & frwd. by Gareth Hill. 272p. 1978. pap. 12.00 (ISBN 0-932630-00-6). C G Jung Frisco.
Shaman's Daughter. Nan F. Salerno & Rosamond M. Vanderburgh. LC 79-20280. 12.50 (ISBN 0-13-807768-1). Prentice-Hall.
Shaman's Revenge. Violet Mary Irwin. LC 25-16606. 1925. The Macmillan Company.
Shaman's Secret. Larry D Names. LC 78-20088. 1979. 7.95 (ISBN 0-385-14625-6). Doubleday.
Shamba la Wanyama. George Orwell. 1967. 1.75 o.p. Northwestern U Pr.
Shamballah. John F Rossman. (Mind Masters). (Signet book: Vol. 2). 1975. (pbk.) 1.25. New American Library.
Shambleau, and Others. 1st Ed. Catherine L Moore. LC 53-12604. 1953. Gnome Press.
Shame. Gerald Foster. LC 38-38062. 1938. Godwin.
Shame and Glory. Eric M. Corder. (Kangaroo Book). 2.50 (ISBN 0-671-81970-4). Pocket Books.
Shame: Confessions of a Wanton. Tr. by E. LaBan & L. E. Laban. (Orig.). pap. 1.75 o.p. (3010). Brandon.
Shame Dance: And Other Stories. Wilbur Daniel Steele. LC 23-894114. Harper & Brothers.
Shame Girl. Elliot Storm. LC 36-14931. 1936. Godwin.
Shame (La Honte) Translated by Lee Marcourt Pseud. Emile Zola. LC 55-180854. (Ace books, S 76). 1954. Ace Books.
Shame of Jenny. John Carver, pseud. LC 63-21022. (Beacon-signal books). Universal Pub. and Distributing Corp.
Shame of Motley: Being the Memoir of Certain Transactions in the Life of Lazzaro Biancomonte, of Biancomonte, Sometime Fool of the Court of Pesaro. Rafael Sabatini. LC 26-15376. 1926. Houghton Mifflin Company.
Shame of Our Wounds. Arthur J Roth. LC 61-9418. 1961. Crowell.
Shame, Shame on the Johnson Boys! Joel Oliansky. LC 66-115409. bds., 4.95. Dutton.
Shame the Devil. Philip Appleman. Ed. by Herbert Michaelman. 160p. 1981. 10.00 o.p. (ISBN 0-517-54286-2, Michelman Books). Crown.
Shame the Devil. Nancy Moore. LC 64-13295. (Torquill book). 1964. Distributed by Dodd, Mead.
Shame the Devil: A Novel. Philip Appleman. LC 80-22966. 10.00 (ISBN 0-517-54286-2). Crown Publishers.
Shameful Acts. Hamlin Gage. 1972. pap. 1.95 o.s.i. (V1089T, Venus). Grove.
Shamelady. Stephen Coulter. LC 66-28740. 1966. W. Morrow.
Shameless. Peggy Gaddis, pseud. LC 34-1579. 1934. W. Godwin, Inc.
Shameless. Jim Gustafson. 1979. pap. 4.00 o.p. (ISBN 0-939180-07-3). Tombouctou.
Shameless Innocent. Maxwell Laurie. LC 24-21146. 1924. 2.00. Duffield and Company.
Shameless Wayne: A Romance of the Last Feud of Wayne and Ratcliffe. Halliwell Sutcliffe. LC 99-5751. 1899. Dodd, Mead & Company.
Shaming of Broken Horn: And Other Stories, by Bill Gulick. 1st Ed. Grover C Gulick. LC 61-14465. (Double D western). 1961. Doubleday.
Shamir of Dachau. Christopher Davis. LC 66-244286. bds., 4.50. New Amer. Lib.
Shamp of the City-Solo. rev. ed. Jaimy Gordon. LC 79-24979. 131p. 1980. 12.50 (ISBN 0-914232-38-X); pap. 3.95 (ISBN 0-914232-37-1). McPherson & Co.
Shamp of the City-Solo: A Novel. Jaimy Gordon. LC 73-89556. (Illus.). 1974. 2.95 (ISBN 0-914232-01-0) (ISBN 0-914232-01-0). Treacle Press.
Shamrock in the Sun. Patricia Bird. (YA) 1980. 6.95 (Avalon). Bouregy.
Shamrock Season. Jennifer Rose, pseud. (Second Chance at Love Ser.: No. 35). 192p. (Orig.). 1982. pap. 1.75 (ISBN 0-515-06195-6). Jove Pubns.
Shamrock Smash. Joseph Rosenberger. (Death Merchant Ser.: No. 41). 192p. (Orig.). 1980. pap. 1.75 (ISBN 0-523-41019-0). Pinnacle Bks.
Shams; or, Uncle Ben's Experience with Hyprocrites. A Story of Simple Country Life Giving a Humorous and Entertaining Picture of Every Day Life and Incidents in the Rural Districts, with Uncle Ben's Trip to the City of Chicago and to California, and His Experience with the Shams and Sharpers of the Metropolitan World. John Smith Draper. LC 71-166712. (Illus.). 1971. (ISBN 0-403-01430-1). Scholarly Press.
Shams: Or, Uncle Ben's Experience with Hyprocrites. A Story of Simple Country Life Giving a Humorous and Entertaining Picture of Every Day Life and Incidents in the Rural Districts, with Uncle Ben's Trip to the City of Chicago and to California, and His Experience with the Shams and Sharpers of the Metropolitan World. John Smith Draper. LC 52-48515. Thompson & Thomas.
Shams: Or, Uncle Ben's Experience with Hypocrites. John Smith Draper. The Lewis Publishing Company.
Shamus. Raymond Giles. (Illus.). 1973. 0.95. Lancer Books.
Shamus: A True Tale of Thiefdom and an Expose of the Real System in Crime. Harry J Loose. LC 20-12959. 2.00. Christopher Publishing House.
Shanadu; Collection of Fantasy, by Brian J. McNaughton and Others Front. by Ralph Rayburn Phillips; Map of Shanadu by Robert E. Briney. 1st Ed. Ed. by Robert E Briney. LC 53-12280. 1953. SSR Publications.
Shandon Bells: A Novel. William Black. 1883. Harper & Brothers.
Shandon Bells. A Novel. William Black. (Harper's Franklin square library. no. 257). 1883. Harper & Brothers.
Shandon Bells: A Novel. William Black. LC 6-12917. (Lovell's library, v. 3. no. 85). J. W. Lovell Company.
Shandon Bells. A Novel. William Black. (Seaside library. Pocket ed. no. 18). G. Munro.
Shandon Bells. A Novel. William Black. LC 26-247089. (Seaside library, v. 77, no. 1556). 1883. G. Munro.
Shandon Bells. A Novel. William Black. LC 9-2708. A. L. Burt.
Shandon Bells: A Novel. library ed. William Black. 1899. Harper & Brothers.
Shane. Jack Warner Schaefer. LC 49-11299. 1949. Houghton Mifflin Co.
Shane. Ed., Introd., Reading Aids by Margaret Early. Sch. Ed. Jack Warner Schaefer. (Riverside Reading Ser., G1). pap., 1.24. Houghton.
Shanghai: A Novel. William Leonard Marshall. LC 78-14178. 1979. 8.95 (ISBN 0-03-048966-0). Holt, Rinehart and Winston.
Shanghai Bund Murders... Francis Van Wyck Mason. LC 33-20521. 1933. Pub. for the Crime Club, Inc., by Doubleday, Doran & Company, Inc.
Shanghai Deadline: A Novel. La Selle Gilman. LC 36-23908. Dodge Publishing Company.
Shanghai Flame. Albert Sidney Fleischman. LC 55-44655. (Gold medal books, 514). 1955. Fawcett Publications.
Shanghai Honeymoon. Maurice Dekobra, pseud. LC 46-6886. 1946. Philosophical Library.
Shanghai Inciedent: By Steve Dodge Pseud. Cover Painting by Lu Kimmel. Stephen D Becker. LC 55-25860. (Gold medal books, 456). 1955. Fawcett Publications.
Shanghai Jim. Frank Lucius Packard. LC 28-12309. 1928. Pub. for the Crime Club, Inc., by Doubleday, Doran & Company, Inc.
Shanghai Lady: Novelized. Karen Brown & Colton, John, 1889- Drifting. LC 30-117. Efrus & Bennett, Inc.
Shanghai Romance. Henry Francis Misselwitz. LC 43-5795. 1943. Harbinger House.
Shangrila & Linda. Alesia Kunz. LC 81-182834. 6.95 (ISBN 0-9605794-0-0). Prickly Pear Press.
Shaniko: From Wool Capital to Ghost Town. Helen G. Rees. LC 81-70285. (Illus.). 1982. 8.95 (ISBN 0-8323-0398-4); pap. 6.50 (ISBN 0-8323-0399-2). Binford.
Shankill Road Contract. Philip Atlee. (Joe Gall). (Gold medal, T2819: Vol. 17). 1973. (pbk.) 0.75. Fawcett.
Shanklin. Webb Waldron. LC 25-204100. The Bobbs-Merrill Company.
Shanna. Kathleen E Woodiwiss. LC 77-72117. 3.95 (ISBN 0-380-00898-X). Avon.
Shannahan's Feud. Al Cody, pseud. 176p. 1975. pap. 0.95 (ISBN 0-532-95395-9). Woodhill.
Shannahan's Feud. Al Cody, pseud. 1970. pap. 0.50 o.p. (50-494). Manor Bks.
Shannahan's Feud: A New Western Novel. Archie Joscelyn. LC 50-4106. (Handi-book western, 109). 1950. Quinn Pub. Co.
Shannon. Bob Haning. 1974. 4.95 (ISBN 0-517-51565-2). Lenox Hill Press.
Shannon. Jerry B Jenkins. LC 82-8070. (Jenkins, Jerry B. A Margo Mystery: 7). 2.95 (ISBN 0-8024-4317-6). Moody Press.
Shannon. Gordon Parks. LC 81-3713. 14.95 (ISBN 0-316-69249-2). Little, Brown.
Shannon Terror: A Novel of Suspense. Theodora McCormick Du Bois. LC 64-12371. 1964. I. Washburn.
Shannon's Way. Archibald Joseph Cronin. LC 50-9012. 1950. Grosset & Dunlap.
Shannon's Way. j. cronin. ed. Archibald Joseph Cronin. 1979. 2.50 (ISBN 0-671-82107-5). Pocket Books.
Shanty Boat Girl. Kirk Westley. 1969. pap. 0.60 o.p. (60-429). Manor Bks.
Shanty Boy. John W Fitzmaurice. LC 70-104451. 1970. (ISBN 0-8398-0557-8). Literature House.
Shanty Boy," or, Life in a Lumber Camp. Being Pictures of the Pine Woods in Discriptions !, Tales, Songs and Adventures in the Lumbering Shanties of Michigan and Wisconsin. John W Fitzmaurice. LC 6-41118. 1889. Democrat Steam Print.
Shanty Irish. Jim Tully. LC 32-33997. (star book). 1930. Garden City Publishing Co., Inc.
Shanty Paradise. Katherine Moore Kingsbury. LC 47-30765. 1947. Caxton Printers.
Shanty Sled. Hulbert Footner. LC 26-673519. George H. Doran Company.
Shantytown Sketches. Anthony Joseph Drexel Biddle. LC 6-13105. 1897. D. Biddle.
Shape Changer. Keith Laumer. 256p. 1981. pap. 2.50 (ISBN 0-441-76088-0). Ace Bks.
Shape Changer: A Science Fiction Novel. Keith Laumer. LC 71-171473. 1972. 4.95. Putnam.
Shape-Cropper. Charlie May Hogue Simon. LC 37-28526. E. P. Dutton & Company, Inc.
Shape of a Stain. Morna Doris MacTaggart Brown. LC 42-16839. 1942. Published for the Crime Club by Doubleday, Doran.
Shape of a Stain. Elizabeth Ferrara. LC 42-16839. 1942. Published for the Crime Club by Doubleday, Doran & Company, Inc.
Shape of Danger: Translated from the Swedish Text and the Original Norwegian Manuscript. Axel Kielland & Hannay, Carolyn, Tr. LC 45-18706. 1945. Little, Brown and Company.
Shape of Desire. Terence FitzBancroft. LC 70-28559. (Traveller's companion series, TC-500). 1971. 1.95. Traveller's Companion, Inc.
Shape of Fear. Lyda B. Long. (Orig.). 1971. pap. 0.75 o.p. (94106). Beagle Bks.
Shape of Fear. Hugh Pentecost. 1972. pap. 0.75 o.p. (ISBN 0-515-02827-4). Pyramid Pubns.
Shape of Fear. Judson Pentecost Philips. LC 64-10324. (Red badge detective).
Shape of Fear: And Other Ghostly Tales. Elia Wilkinson Peattie. LC 72-98591. (Short story index reprint series). 1969. Books for Libraries Press.
Shape of Fear: And Other Ghostly Tales. Elia Wilkinson Peattie. 1898. The Macmillan Company.
Shape of Fiction. 2d ed. Ed. by Alan Casty. LC 74-17740. 1975. 5.95 (ISBN 0-669-91066-X). Heath.
Shape of Fiction: British and American Short Stories. Leo Hamalian & Frederick Robert Karl. LC 67-12624. 1967. McGraw-Hill.
Shape of Fiction: British and American Short Stories. 2d ed. Leo Hamalian & Frederick Robert Karl. LC 77-5839. 6.95 (ISBN 0-07-025699-3). McGraw-Hill.
Shape of Fiction: Stories for Comparison. Ed. by Alan Casty. LC 67-20848. 1967. pap., 3.95. Heath.
Shape of Further Things. Brian Wilson Aldiss. LC 70-139001. (Science Fiction Ser). 1971. 4.95 o.p. (ISBN 0-385-06576-0). Doubleday.
Shape of Illusion. William Edmund Barrett. LC 78-184917. 1972. 5.95. Doubleday.
Shape of the World. Evelyn S Leger Savile Randolph. LC 12-287. 1911. 1.25. G. P. Putnam's Sons.
Shape of Waters. David Swanger. LC 78-17237. 3.50 (ISBN 0-87886-096-7). Ithaca House.
Shape Up. Harold Albert. 1975. 4.40 (ISBN 0-89536-212-0). CSS Pub.
Shapes for the Deep Unrest. Carlton Culmsee. 22p. 1970. pap. 3.00 (ISBN 0-87421-038-0). Utah St U Pr.
Shapes in the Fire. Matthew Phipps Shiel. LC 76-20072. (Decadent Consciousness). (Series: The Keynotes series; 29.). 1977-1978. 26.00 (ISBN 0-8240-2771-X). Garland Pub.
Shapes in the Fire: Being a Mid-Winter-Night's Entertainment in Two Parts and an Interlude. Matthew Phipps Shiel. LC 8-7342. (Keynotes series. 29). 1896. Roberts Bros.; Etc., Etc.
Shapes of Clay. Dinah Haller. LC 62-10145. 1962. Dodd, Mead.
Shapes of Fiction: Open and Closed. Ed. by Beverly Gross. LC 70-127096. 1970. (ISBN 0-03-081389-1). Holt, Rinehart and Winston.
Shapes of Midnight. Joseph Payne Brennan. (Orig.). 1980. pap. 2.25 (ISBN 0-425-04567-6). Berkley Pub.

Shapes of Sleep: A Topical Tale. 1st Ed. John Boynton Priestley. LC 62-11749. 1962. Doubleday.
Shapes of the Supernatural. Ed. by Seon Manley. LC 69-15199. (Illus.). 1969. 5.95. Doubleday.
Shapes That Creep. Margerie Bonner. LC 46-1550. 1946. C Scribner's Sons.
Shapes That Haunt the Dusk... Ed. by William Dean Howells. Alden, Henry Mills, 1837-1919, Joint Ed. LC 7-21368. (Harper's novelettes). 1907. Harper & Brothers.
Shaping of Fiction. Ed. by Robert M. Bender. LC 77-20430. 1970. (pbk.) 0.95 (ISBN 0-671-47802-8). Washington Square Press.
Shar Burbank: Her Love Story. Jennie Maria Drinkwater Conklin. A. J. Rowland.
Shard. Heidi Jorgensen. LC 81-86420. 256p. 1983. pap. 8.95 (ISBN 0-86666-048-8). GWP.
Shard. Daphne Lambart. LC 30-9810. 1930. G. P. Putnam's Sons.
Shardik. Richard George Adams. LC 74-32031. (Illus.). 1975. 9.95 (ISBN 0-671-22015-2). Simon and Schuster.
Shardik. Richard George Adams. 1976. (pbk.) 1.95 (ISBN 0-380-00516-6). Avon.
Shards of God. Ed Sanders. LC 74-111021. 1970. 5.00. Grove Press.
Shards of Light: Fables, Essays, Sonnets & Humor. Neil Millar. LC 81-68095. 208p. 1981. cloth 14.00 (ISBN 0-930616-04-9); pap. 9.00 sewn (ISBN 0-930616-03-0). Foursquare Pr.
Share My Sister. Robert F. Slatzer. 192p. (Orig.). 1973. pap. 1.95 o.p. (ISBN 0-87682-352-5, 7352). Barclay Hse.
Share of Danger. Isabel Cabot. (YA) 1980. 6.95 (Avalon). Bouregy.
Share of Earth & Glory. Katherine Giles. 528p. 1982. 3.50 (ISBN 0-515-04756-2). Jove Pubns.
Share of Honor. Scott C. S. Stone. LC 69-14497. 1969. 4.95. Lippincott.
Share of the World. Newman, Andrea. LC 64-20058. (NAL-World book). 1964. New American Library.
Share the Warm Flesh. Gracie Amber. pap. 1.95 o.p. (8054). Cameo.
Share Your Heart. Arlene Hale. (Candlelight Romance, 209). 0.95. Dell.
Shared Tomorrows. Barry N. Malzberg & Bill Pronzini. 1979. 10.00 o.p. (ISBN 0-312-71637-0). St Martin.
Shared Tomorrows: Science Fiction in Collaboration. Bill Pronzini & Barry N Malzberg. LC 79-16344. 10.00 (ISBN 0-312-71637-0). St. Martin's Press.
Shared Woman. Harold S Kahm. LC 34-698. The Macaulay Company.
Shareworld. Morris Hershman. LC 71-177915. 1972. 5.95 (ISBN 0-8027-5543-7). Walker.
Sharing. M. M. Faraday. 304p. 1982. pap. 3.50 (ISBN 0-553-22579-0). Bantam.
Sharing: A Novel. Roslyn Rosen Lund. LC 77-15519. 1978. 8.95. Morrow.
Sharing Her Crime. A Novel. May Agnes Early Fleming. LC 36-29332. 1883. G. W. Carleton & Co.
Sharing the Vision: The Church Teaching Series Reader. Ed. by Ruth G. Cheney. 112p. (Orig.). 1980. pap. 3.95 (ISBN 0-8164-2044-0). Seabury.
Shark. Thomas Monroe Helm. 1963. pap. 1.95 (ISBN 0-02-063000-X, Collier). Macmillan.
Shark Africa. Bruno Krauss. (Sea Wolf Ser.: No. 5). (Orig.). 1981. pap. 2.25 (ISBN 0-89083-871-2). Zebra.
Shark Fighter. Nicholas Brady, pseud. (O.s.i.). 1976. pap. 1.25 o.s.i. (BT50969). Belmont-Tower.
Shark Fighter. Nicholas Brady. 1976. 1.25. Belmont Tower.
Shark Hunter. Trevor Housby. LC 76-21193. 1977. 8.95 o.p. (ISBN 0-312-71645-1). St Martin.
Shark Hunter. William E. Young. Orig. Title: Shark! Shark! 1978. pap. 1.50 o.s.i. (ISBN 0-8439-0563-8, Leisure Bks). Nordon Pubns.
Shark-Infested Rice Pudding. Sylvia Wright. LC 69-10983. 1969. 4.95. Doubleday.
Shark Island. Maurice Edelman. (75-1277). 1968. Popular Lib.
Shark Island. Maurice Edelman. LC 67-14468. 1967. Random House.
Shark Pack. Bruno Krauss. (Sea Wolf Ser.: No. 3). 1981. pap. 2.25 (ISBN 0-89083-817-8). Zebra.
Shark! Shark! see Shark Hunter.
Shark! Zane Grey's Tales of Man-Eating Sharks. Zane Grey. (Illus.). 1976. (pbk.) 1.50. Belmont Tower Books.
Shark! 1st American Ed. Patrick Fitzgerald O'Connor. LC 54-7556. 1954. Norton.
Sharkey. James Wyckoff. LC 77-76273. 1980. 8.95 (ISBN 0-385-11564-4). Doubleday.
Sharks and Little Fish. Translation by Ralph Manheim. Wolfgang Ott. LC 57-10236. 1957. Pantheon Books.
Sharks and Little Fish. Translation by Ralph Manheim. Wolfgang Ott. LC 58-1762. 1958. Pantheon Books.
Sharkskin Book: A Mystery Novel. Harry Stephen Keeler. LC 41-7865. 1941. E. P. Dutton and Company, Inc.
Sharky's Machine. William Diehl. LC 78-7814. 8.95 (ISBN 0-440-07591-2). Delacorte Press.
Sharky's Machine. William Diehl. 1979. 2.50 (ISBN 0-440-18292-1). Dell Publishing Co.
Sharon. Helen Topping Miller. LC 31-247786. The Penn Publishing Company.
Sharon. (Dreams & Fantasies Ser.: No. 4). (Orig.). 1983. pap. 2.95 (ISBN 0-440-08085-1, Emerald). Dell.
Sharon, a Novel. Margaret Mackprang Mackay. LC 48-5527. 1948. J. Day Co.
Sharon Garrison, Clinic Nurse. Phyllis Taylor Pianka. LC 78-300010. (Avalon nurse stories). 4.95. Avalon Books.
Sharon James: Free-Lance Photographer by Elizabeth Wesley Pseud. Adeline McElfresh. LC 56-13309. Avalon Books.
Sharon of Glencoe. Fran P. Yariv. (Orig.). 1980. write for info. (ISBN 0-515-05192-6). Jove Pubns.
Sharon Valley. Sophia Edith Igo. LC 47-5833. C. & S. Pub. Co.
Sharp Edges of Facts. Alice Naylor. 2.75 o.p. Carlton.
Sharp Practice. John Farris. 1982. pap. 2.95 (ISBN 0-440-17760-X). Dell.
Sharp Practice. John Farris. (O.s.i.). 256p. 1974. 7.95 o.s.i. (ISBN 0-671-21832-8). S&S.
Sharp Practice: A Novel. John Farris. LC 74-8991. 1974. 6.95 (ISBN 0-671-21832-8). Simon and Schuster.
Sharp Practice: A Novel. John Farris. 1975. (pbk.) 1.75 (ISBN 0-671-80098-1). Pocket Books.
Sharp Rise in Crime. John Creasey. LC 78-11132. 1979. 8.95 (ISBN 0-684-14921-4). Scribner.
Sharpe's Company: Richard Sharpe and the Siege of Badajoz, January to April 1812. Bernard Cornwell. LC 81-69930. (Illus.). 1982. 14.95 (ISBN 0-670-63942-7). Viking Press.
Sharpe's Eagle. Bernard Cornwell. (Illus.). 352p. 1982. pap. 3.25 (ISBN 0-441-76091-0, Pub. by Charter Bks). Ace Bks.
Sharpe's Eagle: Richard Sharpe and the Talavera Campaign July 1809. Bernard Cornwell. LC 80-54081. 1981. 12.95 (ISBN 0-670-63944-3). Viking Press.
Sharpe's Gold. Bernard Cornwell. 352p. Date not set. pap. 3.25 (ISBN 0-441-76089-9). Ace Bks.
Sharpe's Gold: Richard Sharpe and the Destruction of Almeida, August 1810. Bernard Cornwell. LC 81-51908. 1982. 13.95 (ISBN 0-670-63943-5). Viking Press.
Sharpe's Sword. Bernard Cornwell. LC 82-40371. 1983. 15.75 (ISBN 0-670-63941-9). Viking Press.
Sharpie Sanderling. Leonard Hill. 6.95 o.p. (ISBN 0-8283-1282-6). Branden.
Sharpshooter. John Benteen. (Fargo Ser). (O.s.i.). 1972. pap. 0.75 o.s.i. (BT50263). Belmont-Tower.
Sharpshooter. Norman Jackson. 1969. pap. 0.95 o.p. (75-092). Lancer.
Sharpshooter. John Henry Reese. (Leisure Book). 1977. 1.25. Nordon Publications.
Sharpshooter. John Henry Reese. LC 73-9045. 1974. (ISBN 0-385-08549-4). Doubleday.
Sharpshooters. John Benteen. (Fargo Ser.: No.9). 160p. 1982. pap. 1.75 (ISBN 0-505-51790-6). Tower Bks.
Sharpshooters. John Benteen. (Fargo Ser). (Orig., Osi). 1970. pap. 0.75 o.s.i. (B75-2074). Belmont-Tower.
Sharra's Exile. Marion Zimmer Bradley. (A dark over novel). 1981. DAW Books, Inc.
Sharrow. Betsey Riddle Hutton Zum Stolzenberg. LC 12-117069. 1912. 1.30. D. Appleton and Company.
Shatter the Dream. Norah C James. LC 31-524. 1931. W. Morrow & Company.
Shatter the Rainbow. Nina Bowyer. LC 46-3689. 1946. Arcadia House, Inc.
Shatter the Rainbow. Nina Conarain. LC 46-3689. 1946. Arcadia House, Inc.
Shatter the Sky. Denise Robins. 1972. pap. 0.75 o.p. (94289). Beagle Bks.
Shatterday. Harlan Ellison. LC 80-20406. 1980. 11.95 (ISBN 0-395-28587-9). Houghton Mifflin.
Shattered. Dean Koontz. LC 73-5054. 1973. 5.95 (ISBN 0-394-48529-7). Random House.
Shattered Chain. Marion Zimmer Bradley. LC 78-21227. (Gregg Press science fiction series). (Illus.). 1979. 12.00 (ISBN 0-8398-2502-1). Gregg Press.
Shattered Chain: A Darkover Novel. Marion Zimmer Bradley. (DAW Science Fiction#191). 1976. (pbk.) 1.50. DAW Books.
Shattered Dream. Louis A. Wilhelm. 6.95 o.p. Vantage.
Shattered Dream. Louis A. Wilhelm. 1974. 6.95 (ISBN 0-533-01094-2). Vantage.
Shattered Dreams. Howard Rockey. LC 33-179329. A. L. Burt Company.
Shattered Eye. Bill Granger. LC 82-10043. 12.95 (ISBN 0-517-54742-2). Crown Publishers.
Shattered Glass. 1st Ed. Jean Ariss. LC 62-8689. 1962. Knopf.
Shattered Goddess. Darrell Schweitzer. LC 82-5012. 5.95 (ISBN 0-89865-197-2). Donning Co.
Shattered Goddess. Darrell Schweitzer. Ed. by Hank Stine. LC 82-5012. (Illus.). 186p. 1983. pap. 5.95 (ISBN 0-89865-197-2, AACR2, Starblaze). Donning Co.
Shattered Halo. Adeline McElfresh. LC 56-3581. 1956. Avalon Books.
Shattered Halo: And Other Stories About Schools. Charles William Bardeen. LC 13-752323. C. W. Bardeen.
Shattered Idol. Charlotte Mary Brame. (On cover: Lovell's library. no. 1031). J. W. Lovell Company.
Shattered Idol. Bertha M. Clay. LC 44-11662. (On cover: Lovell's library, no. 1081). J. W. Lovell Company.
Shattered Idol and Letty Leigh. Charlotte Mary Brame. (On cover: Seaside library. Pocket ed. no. 988). G. Munro.
Shattered Idol and Letty Leigh. Charlotte Mary Brame. LC 44-11675. (On cover: Seaside library. Pocket ed. No. 968). G. Munro.
Shattered Lamp: A Novel. Robert Archibald Jelliffe. LC 35-20270. (Half-title: University club novels. no. 1). Marshall Jones Company.
Shattered People. Robert Hoskins. LC 74-24487. 1975. 5.95 (ISBN 0-385-09934-7). Doubleday.
Shattered Raven. Edward D. Hoch. LC 77-93940. 1978. pap. text ed. 1.75 o.s.i. (ISBN 0-89559-012-3). Dale Books Inc.
Shattered Raven. Edward D. Hoch. (Orig.). 1969. pap. 0.75 o.p. (74-525). Lancer.
Shattered Sexes, a Novel. Translated by Denise Folliot and Mildred Shapiro. Loys Masson. LC 61-17216. 1961. Channel Press.
Shattered Visage Lies. Richard E. Baker. 130p. (Orig.). (YA) 1981. pap. 3.95 (ISBN 0-939066-03-3). Rapier Pr.
Shattering of the Image. 1st Ed. Richard Gibson Hubler. LC 59-555419. 1959. Duell, Sloan and Pearce.
Shaughnessy Eighty. Emmay Dee. LC 73-77519. 1973.
Shaver Mystery & the Inner Earth. Timothy G. Beckley. (Illus.). 1967. pap. 4.95 o.p. Saucerian.
Shaving. Joseph Crosby Lincoln. LC 21-13931. 1920. A. L. Burt Company.
Shaving of Shagpat: An Arabian Entertainment. rev. ed. George Meredith. LC 1-19364. 1898. C. Scribner's Sons.
Shaving of Shagpat. With a Pref. by Sir Francis Meredith Meynell and Illus. by Honore Guilbeau. The Centenary Ed. for the Members of the Limited Editions Club. George Meredith. LC 56-813. 1955. Limited Editions Club.
Shawnee Dawn. Paul J. Lederer. (Indian Heritage Ser.: No. 2). 288p. 1983. pap. 2.95 (ISBN 0-451-12000-0, Sig). NAL.
Shawnie Wade. Sarah Johnson Prichard. LC 9-29772. 1909. 1.00. R. G. Badger.
Shay Scally and Manny Wagstaff: A Novel. Sean Treacy. LC 76-375702. 1976. 3.75 (ISBN 0-7206-0274-2). Owen.
She. Henry Rider Haggard. (Harper's Franklin square library. no. 558). 1886. Harper & Brothers.
She, a History of Adventure. Henry Rider Haggard. LC 6-46151. (On cover: Lovell's library. v. 17. no. 848). 1887. J. W. Lovell Company.
She, a History of Adventure. Henry Rider Haggard. LC 18-17317. 1918. Longmans, Green, and Co.
She: A History of Adventure. new impression. ed. Henry Rider Haggard. LC 24-204742. (Half-title: The Silver library). 1921. Longmans, Green, and Co.
She: A History of Adventure. Henry Rider Haggard. LC 26-8590. Grosset & Dunlap.
She: A History of Adventure. Introd. by Malcolm Elwin. Illus. by Hookway Cowles. Henry Rider Haggard. LC 66-5453. 1966. bds., 2.95. Macdonald.
She: A Novel. Herbert Gold. LC 79-57079. 10.00 (ISBN 0-87795-264-7). Arbor House.
She" A Novel of Innocence Awakened. Robert Couste. LC 35-6468. 1935. River Publishing Co.
She and Allan. Henry Rider Haggard. LC 75-23088. (Forgotten fantasy classic series; F-105). 1975. (ISBN 0-87877-105-0). Newcastle Pub. Co.
She and Allan. Henry Rider Haggard. LC 20-12377. 1920. Longmans, Green and Co.
She and Allan. Henry Rider Haggard. LC 80-19461. (Newcastle Forgotten Fantasy library; v. 6). 1980. 10.95 (ISBN 0-87877-505-6). Borgo Press.
She and Allan. Illus. by Hookway Cowles. Henry Rider Haggard. 1966. bds., 2.95. MacDonald.
She & Ayesha: The Return of She. Henry Rider Haggard. 1972. pap. 1.25 o.p. Lancer.
She & He. George Sand. LC 78-14444. (Sand, George, Pseud. of Mme. Dudlevant, 1804-1876. The Masterpieces of George Sand). 1978. 11.95 (ISBN 0-915864-84-3) (ISBN 0-915864-83-5). Cassandra Editions.
She and I. Pamela Frankau. LC 31-3408. 1931. Doubleday, Doran & Company, Inc.
She, & King Solomon's Mines. With an Introd. by Orville Prescott. 1st Modern Library Ed. Henry Rider Haggard. LC 57-6491. (Modern library of the world's best books 163). 1957. Modern Library.
She Asked for It. Evelyn Berckman. LC 70-81034. 1969. 4.95. Doubleday.
She Ate Her Cake. Blair Treynor. 1946. W. Morrow & Company.
She-Beast. Hunter Adams. (man from Planet X). 1975. (pbk.) 1.50 (ISBN 0-523-00544-X). Pinnacle Books.
She Boss: A Western Story. Arthur Preston Hankins. LC 23-16433. Chelsea House.
She Buildeth Her House. Will Levington Comfort. LC 11-135206. 1911. 1.25. J. B. Lippincott Company.
She Came Back. Patricia Wentworth. 208p. 1981. pap. 2.25 (ISBN 0-553-14434-0). Bantam.
She Came Back. Patricia Wentworth. 1969. pap. 0.75 o.p. (T2131). Pyramid Pubns.
She Came Back. Patricia Wentworth. (O.s.i.). 1973. pap. 0.95 o.s.i. (ISBN 0-515-03026-0, N3026). Pyramid Pubns.
She Came Back: A Miss Silver Mystery. Patricia Wentworth. LC 45-10154. 1945. J. B. Lippincott Company.
She Came to Stay: A Novel. Simone De Beauvoir. LC 54-5344. 1954. World Pub. Co.
She Came to the Valley. Cleo Dawson. LC 43-14464. 1943. W. Morrow & Company.
She Child. Mardiningsih Arquette. (Illus.). 32p. (Orig.). 1982. pap. 4.00 (ISBN 0-9605594-1-8). Monkey Man.
She Comes When You're Leaving & Other Stories. Bruce Boston. LC 82-208377. 1982. 3.95 (ISBN 0-917658-14-0). Berkeley Poets' Workshop & Press.
She Danced in the Ballet. Berta Ruck. LC 48-7769. 1948. Dodd, Mead.
She Dared to Win... William Lee Popham. LC 10-236678. 0.50. Printed by Westerfield-Bonte Co.
She-Devil. Renee Foxton. 160p. pap. 1.95 o.p. (MP-111). Montmartre.
She Devil. James Noble Gifford. LC 38-22131. Phoenix Press.
She Devil. John Saxon. LC 38-22131. Phoenix Press.
She-Devil: A Romance of the Spanish-American War. Montmorency Hill Le Burke. LC 10-236281. 1910. 1.50. C. E. Apgar.
She-Devils (Les Diaboliques) Jules Amedee Barbey D'Aurevilly. LC 64-57125. (Oxford library of French classics). 1964. Oxford University Press.
She Did Take It with Her: Illustrated by Nora Zuver. 1st Ed. Dudley Zuver. LC 54-5846. 1954. Harper.
She Didn't Care. William Arthur Neubauer. 1944. Phoenix Press.
She Died a Lady. John Dickson Carr. LC 43-348. 1943. W. Morrow and Co.
She Died on the Stairway. Knight Rhoades. LC 47-18225. 1947. Arcadia House.
She Faded into Air. Ethel Lina White. LC 41-147598. Harper & Brothers.
She Fell Among Actors. James Warren. LC 44-51276. 1944. Pub. for the Crime Club by Doubleday, Doran & Company, Inc.
She Fell Among Thieves. Cecil William Mercer. LC 35-4911. Minton, Balch & Company.
She Fell Among Thieves. Gretchen Travis. LC 63-10516. (Crime Club selection). 1963. Published for the Crime Club by Doubleday.
She Goes to War, and Other Stories. Rupert Hughes. LC 29-3427. Grosset & Dunlap.
She Got What She Asked for: A Mystery Novel. James Ronald. LC 43-2266. (Handi-book mysteries). 1942. Quinn Publishing Co., Inc.
She Got What She Wanted. Orrie Hitt. LC 55-32179. (Beacon book original, no. 101). 1954. Beacon Publications Corp.
She Has What They Wanted. Florence Stonebraker. 1946. Phoenix Press.
She Kept Men Standing. Ruth Black Aten. LC 67-26107. (Illus.). 1967. Adams Press.
She Knew No Evil. Ethel Nishua Arnold. LC 52-11888. Vantage Press.
She Knew She Was Right. Ivy Low Litvinova. LC 75-104135. 1971. 6.95 (ISBN 0-670-63947-8). Viking Press.
She Knew She Was Right. Jesse Lynch Williams. LC 30-11847. 1930. C. Scribner's Sons.
She Knew Three Brothers. Margaret Widdemer. LC 39-211779. Farrar & Rinehart, Inc.
She Learned About Love. Peggy Gaddis, pseud. LC 43-18008. 1943. Phoenix Press.
She Left a Silver Slipper: A Mystery Novel. Frank Stevens. LC 54-10207. 1954. M. S. Mill Co., and W. Morrow.
She Let Him Continue. Stephen Geller. LC 66-13655. bds., 3.50. Dutton.

She Let Him Continue. Stephen Geller. (U5093). 1967. Ballantine.
She Liked the Man: A Novel. Josiah Pitts Woolfolk. LC 36-984. Godwin.
She Lived in New York: A Novel. Stinson Jarvis. LC 7-10177. 1894. The Judge Publishing Company.
She Lives! Paul G Neimark. LC 74-167533. 1972. 6.95 (ISBN 0-8402-1219-4). Nash Pub.
She Loved Him. Annie Hall Thomas Cudlip. (On cover: Seaside library. Pocket ed. no. 141). 1884. G. Munro.
She Loved Him. Charles Garvice. (On cover: Laurel library, no. 20). 1895. G. Munro's Sons.
She Loves Me. Norman Klein. LC 33-577767. Farrar & Rinehart, Incorporated.
She Loves Me Not. Edward Hope Coffey. LC 33-11628. The Bobbs-Merrill Company.
She Made Her Bed. Sally Chayes. LC 36-929. Phoenix Press.
She Made It Pay: A New Novel. Leslie Scott. LC 52-2731. (Arco sophisticate). 1952. Arco Pub. Co.
She Made the Big Town! And Other Stories. Frank Brookhouser. LC 52-8666. 1952. University of Kansas City Press; Twayne Publishers.
She Married a Doctor. Dorothy Carle Pierce Walker. LC 39-23855. Liveright Publishing Corporation.
She Married a Doctor. Dorothy Carle Pierce Walker. LC 47-200070. 1946. Triangle Books, the Blakiston Company.
She Married a Hero. Nina Kaye. LC 40-32297. Gramercy Publishing Co.
She Married the Doctor. Jessie G Gilbert. LC 36-6812. B. Humphries, Inc.
She, Me & Murder. Robert Lee Martin. 1971. pap. 0.75 o.p. (07162). Curtis.
She Never Grew Old. Garland Lord, pseud. LC 42-186623. 1942. Published for the Crime Club by Doubleday, Doran & Co., Inc.
She Never Reached the Top. Elma K Lobaugh. LC 45-7800. 1945. Pub. for the Crime Club by Doubleday, Doran & Co., Inc.
She of the Holy Light. Donna Brooks Beaumont. LC 6-10352. 1893. Western Authors' Publishing Association.
She Painted Her Face. Cecil William Mercer. 1937. G. P. Putnam's Sons.
She Passed This Way. Kingsley Douthwaite. 2.75 o.p. Carlton.
She Rode a White Horse. Evelyn Tyler. LC 52-8848. 1952. Crowell.
She Rode a Yellow Stallion. Warren Reed. LC 50-10529. 1950. Bobbs-Merrill.
She Saw Them Go by. Hester W Chapman. LC 33-27400. 1933. Houghton Mifflin Company.
She Shall Have Murder. Delano L Ames. LC 49-10952. (Murray Hill mystery). 1949. Rinehart.
She Shall Have Murder. Delano L. Ames. LC 82-48240. (Perennial library; P638). 1983. 2.84 (ISBN 0-06-080638-9). Harper & Row.
She Shall Have Music. Alyse Gregory. LC 26-15184. Harcourt, Brace and Company.
She Shall Have Music. Raya Keen. LC 46-3589. 1946. J. B. Lippincott Company.
She Should Have Cried on Monday. Enid S Russell. LC 68-22628. 1968. 3.95. Published for the Crime Club by Doubleday.
She-Slaves of Cinta Vincente. Lon Beam. pap. 1.95 o.s.i. (Venus). Grove.
She Stands Alone: The Story of Pilate's Wife. Mark Ashton. LC 1-13958. 1901. L. C. Page & Company.
She Takes a Lover. Anthony Thorne. LC 32-9032. 1932. The Macmillan Company.
She That Hesitates. Harris Dickson. LC 3-25723. 1903. The Bobbs-Merrill Company.
She Waited Patiently. Mary Diuguid Davis. LC 1-30045. 1900. J.P. Bell Company, Printers.
She Waits. Henry Clement. 1975. (pbk.) 1.25. Popular Library.
She Walks Alone. Helen McCloy. LC 48-2086. 1948. Random House.
She Walks in Beauty. Stephen Longstreet. LC 77-81017. 1970. 6.95 (ISBN 0-87795-004-0). Arbor Hse.
She Walks in Beauty. Stephen Longstreet. 1972. pap. 1.25 o.p. (V2628). Pyramid Pubns.
She Walks in Beauty. Dawn Powell. LC 28-81412. 1928. Brentano's.
She Walks in Beauty. Joel Augustus Rogers. LC 62-22256. 1963. Western Publishers.
She Walks in Shadow. Leslie Paige. (O.s.i.). (Orig.). 1974. pap. 0.95 o.s.i. (BT50685). Belmont-Tower.
She Walks in Shadow. Leslie Paige. 1974. (pbk.) 0.95. Belmont Tower Books.
She Walks with Grace. Jennie Dethloffs Klein. LC 46-31448. 1946. Dorrance & Company.
She Wanted More. Ann Lawrence. LC 33-13042. 1933. W. Godwin, Inc.
She Was a Lady. Elisabeth Cobb Chapman. LC 34-18243. The Bobbs-Merrill Company.
She Was Carrie Eaton. Elizabeth Frances Corbett. 1973. pap. 0.95 o.p. (95372). Beagle Bks.
She Was Carrie Eaton: A Novel About the Young Mrs. Meigs. Elizabeth Frances Corbett. LC 38-23358. 1938. D. Appleton-Century Company, Incorporated.
She Was Doomed,". Lillian D. Morsbach. 1894. Veronee Publishing Co.
She Was His Secretary. Florence Demarest Bond. LC 30-330013. Gramercy Publishing Company.
She Was My Mother. Daniel L Reedy. LC 40-792985. C.
She Was Only the Sheriff's Daughter. Stanton Forbes, pseud. LC 74-89120. 1970. 4.50. Published for the Crime Club by Doubleday.
She Who Hesitated. Eula Lankford Brooks. LC 36-195605. 1936. Meador Publishing Company.
She Who Is Alive: A Novel. Robert A. Harris. LC 76-40944. 1977. 7.95. (ISBN 0-912652-29-2) (ISBN 0-912652-28-4). Blue Wind Press.
She Who Sleeps, a Romance of New York and the Nile. Arthur Sarsfield Ward. LC 28-28681. 1928. Doubleday, Doran & Company, Inc.
She Who Was Helena Cass. Lawrence Rising. LC 20-176490. George H. Doran Company.
She Who Was King. Wendy Lozano. 384p. 1980. pap. 2.50 (ISBN 0-345-28638-3). Ballantine.
She Who Will Not When She May. Eleanor Going Walton. LC 6-13418. 1898. H. Altemus.
She. With a New Introd. by Morton N. Cohen. Henry Rider Haggard. LC 62-17415. (Collier bolks, HS13V. Classic). 1962. Collier Books.
She Woke to Darkness: By Brett Halliday Pseud. Davis Dresser. LC 54-8250. 1954. Torquil.
She-Wolf. Pamela Bennetts. LC 75-15376. 205p. 1976. 7.95 o.p. (ISBN 0-312-71680-X). St Martin.
She-Wolf: And Other Stories. Giovanni Verga. LC 58-6524. 1958. University of California Press.
She-Wolf, and Other Stories. 2d ed., rev. and enl. translated, with an introd. by giovanni cecchetti. ed. Giovanni Verga. LC 79-181437. (Illus.). 1973. 10.00 (ISBN 0-520-02153-3). University of California Press.
She Wolves of Machecoul. Alexandre Dumas. LC 13-2075. (On cover: Seaside library. Pocket ed., no. 2127). 1898. G. Munro's Sons.
She-Wolves of Machecoul. To Which Is Added The Corsican Brothers. Alexandre Dumas. LC 6-436021. 1894. Little, Brown and Company.
She-Wolves of Machecoul. To Which Is Added, The Corsican Brothers. Alexandre Dumas. (Half-title: The romances of Alexandre Dumas. Illustrated library ed. vol. xlvii-xlviii). 1894. Little, Brown and Company.
She Would and She Wouldn't: By Helen Eliat; Translated by Bernard Miall. Helene Eliat & Miall, Bernard, Tr. LC 33-4546. 1933. The Viking Press.
She Wouldn't Say Who. Delano L Ames. LC 57-110435. (Jane and Dagobert Brown mystery). 1958. I. Washburn.
Shea of the Irish Brigade: A Soldier's Story. Randall Parrish. LC 14-5425. 1914. 1.30. A. C. McClurg & Co.
Sheaf of Bluebells. Emmuska Orczy. LC 17-17973. 1.35. George H. Doran Company.
Sheaf of Oatstraw. Elliott A. White. 3.00 o.s.i. (ISBN 0-8181-0129-6). Pageant-Poseidon.
Shears of Delilah: Stories of Married Life. Virginia Belle Terhune Van De Water. LC 14-32485. 1914. G. P. Putnam's Sons.
Shears of Destiny. Leroy Scott. LC 10-202962. 1910. 1.20. Doubleday, Page & Company.
Sheaves. Edward Frederic Benson. LC 7-20434. 1907. Doubleday, Page & Company.
Sheaves: A Comedy of Manners. Marie Conway Oemler. LC 28-108664. The Century Co.
Sheba. Eliza M. J. Humphreys. LC 75-1535. (Victorian fiction: Novels of faith and doubt; 83). 1975. 35.00 (ISBN 0-8240-1607-6). Garland Pub.
Sheba,". Eliza M. J. Humphreys. (On cover: Lovell's international series, no. 38). F. F. Lovell & Company.
Sheba: A Story of Girlhood. Desmond Humphreys. Ed. by Robert L. Wolff. LC 75-1535. (Victorian Fiction Ser.). 1975. lib. bdg. 66.00 (ISBN 0-8240-1607-6). Garland Pub.
Sheba" A Study of Girlhood. Eliza M. J. Humphreys. (On cover: Seaside library., Pocket ed., no. 1229). 1889. G. Munro.
Sheba on Trampled Grass. Tom Powers. LC 46-1386. 1946. The Bobbs-Merrill Company.
Sheba Visits Solomon: A Novel. Helene Eliat & Zablodowski, David, Tr. LC 32-16663. 1932. The Viking Press.
Sheba's Landing. Thomas P. Baird. 1964. 4.95 o.p. HarBraceJ.
Shed a Bitter Tear. Harry F S Moore. LC 44-5992. 1944. Pub. for the Crime Club by Doubleday, Doran and Company, Inc.
Shedding. Verena Stefan. Tr. by Beth Weckmueller & Johanna Moore. LC 77-94979. 1978. pap. 5.00 (ISBN 0-913780-22-7). Daughters.
Shedding Skin. Robert Ward. LC 78-156567. 1971. 6.95 (ISBN 0-06-014527-7). Harper & Row.
Shedding the Years. James Clark Bennett. LC 25-106858. 1925. Capitol Book Company.
Shedevils. Barbara Sheen. 80p. 1978. 3.50 (ISBN 0-934816-01-8). Metis Pr Inc.
Sheehan's Mill. John Henry Reese. LC 43-15774. 1943. Doubleday, Doran and Co., Inc.
Sheep in Wolf's Clothing. From the French of C. Debans. Camille I. E. Jean Baptiste Camille Debans. Tr. by Jerrold, Evelyn Douglas. (On cover: Lovell's library, v. 9, no. 475). 1884. J. W. Lovell Company.
Sheep in Wolf's Clothing" Ruses De Guerre) from the French of Albert Rhodes. Albert Rhodes & Wade, Stuart Charles, Tr. LC 7-30589. (On cover: Globe library, v. 1, no. 182). 1893. Rand, McNally & Co.
Sheep Limit. George Washington Ogden. LC 28-206063. 1928. Dodd, Mead & Company.
Sheep Look up. John Brunner. 1973. (pbk.) 1.65 (ISBN 0-345-23612-2). Ballantine Books.
Sheep Look up. John Brunner. LC 72-79705. 1972. 6.95 (ISBN 0-06-010558-5). Harper & Row.
Sheep, Moors, and Sea. Alice Cary Williams. LC 66-30701. 1967. Vantage Press.
Sheep of the Shepherd: Little Idyls of a Sheep Farm. Lillian A North. LC 23-13321. E. P. Dutton and Company.
Sheep Rock: A Novel. George Rippey Stewart. LC 51-1695. 1951. Random House.
Sheep-Skin Coat & an Absolutely Happy Village. Boris Vakhtin. Tr. by Robert Dessaix & Michael Ulman. 15.00; pap. 6.00. Ardis Pubs.
Sheep-Stealers. Violet Jacob. LC 2-21412. 1902. G. P. Putnam's Sons.
Sheeper. Irving Rosenthal. 1968. pap. 1.25 o.p. (B192, BC). Grove.
Sheeper: "the Poet! the Crooked! the Extrafingered!". Irving Rosenthal. LC 67-20342. 1967. 5.95. Grove.
Sheepherding Man. Frank Roderus. LC 80-10387. 1980. 8.95 (ISBN 0-385-15570-0). Doubleday.
Sheepman's Gold. Robert Ames Bennet. LC 39-299684. I. Washburn.
Sheep's Clothing. Louis Joseph Vance. LC 15-3968. 1915. Little, Brown, and Company.
Sheepshead Point. Mary Mellon McClung. LC 47-15516. 1946. Dorrance & Company.
Sheepskins & Grey Russet. Ernest Temple Thruston. LC 20-121273. 1920. G. P. Putnam's Sons.
Sheepskins and Grey Russet. Ernest Temple Thurston. LC 20-1973. 1919. Cassell & Company, Ltd.
Sheets in the Wind. Ridgwell Cullum. LC 32-299053. J. B. Lippincott Company.
Sheik. Maggie Hill Davis. LC 76-30366. 1977. 8.95 (ISBN 0-688-03179-X). Morrow.
Sheik. Edith Maude Hull. 1976. Repr. of 1921 ed. lib. bdg. 15.95x (ISBN 0-89190-734-3). Am Repr-Rivercity Pr.
Sheik. Edith Maude Hull. (Barbara Cartland's Library of Love: Vol. 1). 216p. 1979. 12.95x (ISBN 0-7156-1377-4, Pub. by Duckworth England). Biblio Dist.
Sheik. Edith Maude Hull. pap. 0.50 o.p. (52-979). Paperback Lib.
Sheik: A Novel. Edith Maude Hull. LC 21-975. Small, Maynard & Company.
Sheik: A Novel. Edith Maude Hull. LC 25-15516. A. L. Burt.
Sheiks & Adders: A Sir John Appleby Mystery Novel. Michael Innes, pseud. LC 82-9694. (Red Badge Novel of Suspense Ser.). 196p. 1982. 10.95 (ISBN 0-396-08063-4). Dodd.
Sheik's Captive. Harlan Page Halsey. (On cover: The calumet series, no. 30). G. Munro's Sons.
Sheila. Pamela Kaye. (Orig.). pap. 1.25 o.p. (2504). Brandon.
Sheila. St. Clair, Robert. LC 47-221. 1946. The Gagnon Company, Inc.
Sheila and Others: The Simple Annals of an Unromantic Household. Winifred Cotter. LC 20-18386. E. P. Dutton & Company.
Sheila Bolingbrook: A Novel. Talbot, Edna Betts. LC 52-7350. 1952. B. Humphries.
Sheila Both-Ways. Joanna Cannan, pseud. LC 29-6791. 1929. Frederick A. Stokes Company.
Sheila Goes to Reno. Latifa Johnson. LC 52-11895. Vantage Press.
Sheila Lacey. Eileen Jeanette Lyttle Garrett. LC 45-579. 1944. Creative Age Press, Inc.
Sheila Levine Is Dead and Living in New York. Gail Parent. LC 72-75028. 1972. 6.95 (ISBN 0-399-11018-6). Putnam.
Sheila of Big Wreck Cove: A Story of Cape Cod. James A Cooper, pseud. LC 22-631268. G. Sully & Company.
Sheila Vedder. Amelia Edith Huddleston Barr. LC 11-518920. 1911. 1.25. Dodd, Mead and Company.
Sheilah McLeod: A Heroine of the Back Blocks. Guy Newell Boothby. LC 6-15030. F. A. Stokes Company.
Sheila's Dilemma. Ivy Valdes. (Signet Book, P5406: Rainbow romance edition). 1973. 0.60. New American Lib.
Shekinah. Evelyn Whitell. LC 37-15345. DeVorss & Co.
SheLa, a Satire. Aubrey Menen. LC 62-8471. 1962. Random House.
Shelby. William C. Kautz, Jr. LC 79-89272. 192p. (Orig.). 1979. pap. 2.75 (ISBN 0-934620-00-8). Brady Pr.
Sheldon's Way. Wynard Browne. 1936. D. Appleton-Century Company, Incorporated.
Shelf Full of Dreams. Florence Stonebraker. LC 50-5201. 1949. Arcadia House.
Shelia. Annie S Swan Smith. LC 8-8621. 1891. Cranston and Stowe.
Shelia. Gunard Solberg. LC 79-80425. 1969. 4.95. Houghton Mifflin.
Shelia Intervenes. Stephen McKenna. LC 20-263138. 1920. George H. Doran Company.
Shell. Mae Foster Jay. LC 34-2343. W. A. Wilde Company.
She'll Be Dead by Morning! A New Jim Steele Mystery. Albert Leffingwell. LC 40-30531. 1940. The Dial Press.
She'll Do Me. Mark Vizzers. LC 61-34026. 1960. Jacaranda Press.
Shell Fish. Emile Zola. Repr. lib. bdg. 5.95x (ISBN 0-88411-290-X). Amereon Ltd.
Shell Game. Richard Pitts Powell. LC 50-5174. (Inner sanctum mystery). 1950. Simon and Schuster.
She'll Never Get off the Ground. Robert J Serling. LC 72-131104. 1971. 6.95. Doubleday.
Shell of Death. Cecil Day-Lewis. LC 36-969442. 1936. Harper & Brothers.
Shell Scott's Murder Mix. Richard S Prather. LC 74-101244. 1970. 7.95. Trident Press.
Shellback. Alexander J Boyd. Ed. by Campbell, Archie. LC 99-5179. 1899. Brentano's.
Shellbreak. J. W. Groves. 1970. pap. 0.60 o.p. (63-293). Paperback Lib.
Shelley Lasrozzi: Self-Revelation of a Neurotic. Eustace Chesser & Percy Bysshe Shelley. LC 67-2851. 1966. 6.95. Gregg/Achive.
Shelley's Elopement: A Study of the Most Romantic Episode in Literary History. Alexander Harvey. LC 18-18189. 1918. A. A. Knopf.
Shelleys of Georgia. Beatrice York Houghton. LC 17-236492. 1917. Lothrop, Lee & Shepard Co.
Shellfire on the Bay. Jonathan Scofield, pseud. (Freedom Fighters Ser.: No. 8). 352p. (Orig.). 1981. pap. 2.95 (ISBN 0-440-07830-X, Bryans). Dell.
Shelter. Dan Ljoka. (1973 ed. 0.95 o.p.). 1977. pap. 1.25 (ISBN 0-532-12474-X). Woodhill.
Shelter. Dan Ljoka. 1973. (pbk) 0.95. Manor Books.
Shelter. Charles Fielding Marsh. LC 25-20832. 1925. D. Appleton and Company.
Shelter. Jane Nicholson. LC 41-11975. 1941. The Viking Press.
Shelter: A Novel. Marguerite Steen. LC 41-11975. 1941. The Viking Press.
Shelter from the Wind. Marion Dane Bauer. 1978. pap. 1.25 (ISBN 0-440-97969-2, LE). Dell.
Shelter Island: Or, The Power of God. Benjamin Hiram Pelton. LC 13-174162. 1.50. The Pelton Publishing Company.
Shelter, No. 1: Prisoner of Revenge. Paul Ledd. 224p. (Orig.). 1980. pap. 1.95 (ISBN 0-89083-598-5). Zebra.
Shelter, No. 10: Massacre Mountain. Paul Ledd. (Orig.). 1982. pap. 2.25 (ISBN 0-89083-972-7). Zebra.
Shelter, No. 11: Rio Rampage. Paul Ledd. 1983. pap. 2.25 (ISBN 0-8217-1141-5). Zebra.
Shelter, No. 12: Blood Mesa. Paul Ledd. 1983. pap. 3.50 (ISBN 0-8217-1181-4). Zebra.
Shelter, No. 2: Hanging Moon. Paul Ledd. 256p. (Orig.). 1980. pap. 1.95 (ISBN 0-89083-637-X). Zebra.
Shelter, No. 3: Chain Gang Kill. Paul Ledd. 256p. (Orig.). 1980. pap. 1.95 (ISBN 0-89083-658-2). Zebra.
Shelter, No. 4: China Doll. Paul Ledd. 1980. pap. 1.95 (ISBN 0-89083-682-5). Zebra.
Shelter, No. 5: The Lazarus Guns. Paul Ledd. 256p. (Orig.). 1980. pap. 1.95 (ISBN 0-89083-694-9). Zebra.
Shelter, No. 6: Circus of Death. Paul Ledd. (Orig.). 1981. pap. 1.95 (ISBN 0-89083-723-6). Zebra.
Shelter, No. 7: Lookout Mountain. Paul Ledd. 1981. pap. 1.95 (ISBN 0-89083-756-2). Zebra.
Shelter, No. 8: The Bandit Queen. Paul Ledd. (Orig.). 1981. pap. 2.25 (ISBN 0-89083-869-0). Zebra.
Shelter, No. 9: Apache Trail. Paul Ledd. (Orig.). 1982. pap. 2.25 (ISBN 0-89083-956-5). Zebra.
Shelter Without Walls. Ann Katherine Gilliland Ritner. LC 42-500784. 1942. M. S. Mill Co., Inc.
Sheltered Life. Ellen Glascow. 320p. 1979. 12.95 (ISBN 0-8090-8652-2, AmCen); pap. 5.95 (ISBN 0-8090-0138-1). Hill & Wang.
Sheltered Life. Ellen Anderson Gholson Glasgow. LC 32-26955. 1932. Doubleday, Doran & Company, Inc.
Sheltered Life. Ellen Anderson Gholson Glasgow. LC 36-83142. The Sun Dial Press.

Sheltered Life. Ellen Anderson Gholson Glasgow. LC 78-27534. (American century series). 1979. 12.50 (ISBN 0-8090-8652-2) (ISBN 0-8090-0138-1). Hill and Wang.

Sheltered Lives. Mary Hazzard. LC 79-25492. 1980. 10.95 (ISBN 0-914842-43-9). Madrona Publishers.

Sheltered Sex. Madge Mears. LC 16-16528. 1916. John Lane Company.

Sheltering Sky. Paul Frederic Bowles. LC 49-11888. 1949. New Directions.

Sheltering Sky. Paul Frederic Bowles. LC 77-22233. (Neglected Books of the Twentieth Century). 1978. 4.95 (ISBN 0-912946-43-1). Ecco Press.

Sheltering Tree. Iris Bromige. 1973. pap. 0.75 o.p. (94316). Beagle Bks.

Sheltern: A Novel. Christopher Coningsby. 1868. Blelock & Co.

Shelton Conspiracy. Elinore Denniston. (Dell bk., 7930). 1972. Dell.

Shelton Conspiracy. Elinore Denniston. LC 67-19227. (Red badge mystery). 1967. Dodd, Mead.

Shenandoah. A Story of Sheridan's Great Ride. A Novel. J. Perkins Tracy. (On cover: The war series, no. 1). Novelist Publishing Co.

Shenandoah. A Story of Sheridan's Great Ride. A Novel. J. Perkins Tracy. (On cover: Clover series, no. 67). Street & Smith.

Shenandoah, Love and War in the Valley of Virginia 1861-5: Based Upon the Famous Play by Bronson Howard. Henry Tyrrell. LC 12-22595. 1912. G. P. Putnam's Sons.

Shenandoah: Or, The Horizon's Bar. A Story of the War. Frederick G Gedney. (On cover: The fireside series, no. 108). J. S. Ogilvie.

Shenanigan. Howard J. Chesshire. LC 75-5226. (Illus.). pap. 2.75 (ISBN 0-9603226-0-4). Mandala Bks.

Shep: A Reminiscence. Charles Barth. LC 68-8347. 1969. 4.00 o.p. (ISBN 0-87426-009-4). Whitmore.

Shepherd. Frederick Forsyth. LC 76-18075. (Illus.). 1976. 4.95 (ISBN 0-670-63969-9). Viking Press.

Shepherd. Pierre Stephen Robert Payne. LC 59-14698. 1959. Horizon Press.

Shepherd File. 1st Ed. Conrad Voss Bark. LC 66-25125. 1966. bds., 3.95. Dutton.

Shepherd Is My Lord. Dimitri V. Gat. LC 76-131077. (Doubleday science fiction). 1971. 4.95. Doubleday.

Shepherd King: A Romance of Abraham and the Ancient Near East. John Clover Monsma. LC 35-199921. 1935. Zondervan Publishing House.

Shepherd Kings. Peter Danielson. 448p. (Orig.). 1981. pap. 2.95 (ISBN 0-553-14653-X). Bantam.

Shepherd Market & Other Stories. Tim Aldridge. 7.95 o.p. Carlton.

Shepherd of Beth. Albert Davis Porter. LC 22-481. N. H. Smith & Co.

Shepherd of Beth: And Other Stories. Albert Davis Porter. LC 25-3940. Cokesbury Press.

Shepherd of Guadaloupe. Zane Grey. LC 30-14881. 1930. Harper & Brothers.

Shepherd of Israel. Margaret Leonora Pitcairn Eyles. LC 29-18173. Harcourt, Brace and Company.

Shepherd of Jerusalem: The Story of Reuel the Strong. Morris Howland Turk. LC 29-19244. 1929. Minton, Balch & Company.

Shepherd of Kensington. Baillie Saunders. 1907. P. R. Reynolds.

Shepherd of Salisbury Plain: And Other Tales. Hannah More. LC 17-7993. 1857. Derby & Jackson.

Shepherd of the East. Louis Greene. LC 24-128. The Roxburgh Publishing Company, Inc.

Shepherd of the Hills. Harold Bell Wright. LC 81-21274. 1982. 11.95 (ISBN 0-89621-331-5). Thorndike Press.

Shepherd of the Hills: A Novel. Harold Bell Wright. LC 7-26339. 1907. The Book Supply Company.

Shepherd of the Hills: A Novel. Harold Bell Wright. LC 19-13372. 1907. A. L. Burt Company.

Shepherd of the Hills: A Novel. Harold Bell Wright. LC 13-23592. 1909. The Book Supply Company.

Shepherd of the Hills: A Novel. Harold Bell Wright. LC 24-20457. 1922. A. L. Burt Company.

Shepherd of the North. Richard Aumerle Maher. LC 16-5616. 1916. The Macmillan Company.

Shepherd of the Sea. Henry Leverage. LC 20-26194. 1920. Doubleday, Page & Company.

Shepherd of the Valley. Evelyn Voss Wise. LC 49-8008. 1949. Bruce Pub. Co.

Shepherd. Pictures by Gilvert Riswodl. Heywood Campbell Broun & Riswold, Gilbert, Illus. LC 67-21129. 1967. Prentice Hall.

Shepherd Who Did Not Go to Bethlem. Susan Alice Ranlett. LC 9-10490. 1909. R. G. Badger.

Shepherd Who Missed the Manger. Rufus Matthew Jones. LC 49-26761. 1948. Friends Book Store.

Shepherd Who Missed the Manger. Rufus Matthew Jones. LC 42-25684. 1942. Doubleday, Doran and Company, Inc.

Shepherdess of Sheep. Noel Streatfeild. LC 35-3541. Reynal & Hitchcock.

Shepherdess of the Alps. A Moral Tale. 2d american ed. Jean Francois Marmontel. LC 36-213783. 1797. Printed by John Hayes, for George Keating's Wholesale and Retail Book-Store.

Shepherds All and Maidens Fair. Walter Besant & Rice, James. (On cover: Harper's half-hour series. v. 47). 1878. Harper & Brother.

Shepherds: By Marie Conway Oemler... Marie Conway Oemler. LC 26-4944. 2.00. The Century Co.

Shepherd's Crook. Paul Frischauer. LC 51-12444. 1951. Scribner.

Shepherd's Crook: By E. C. R. Lorac Pseud. 1st Ed. Edith Caroline Rivett. LC 53-10646. 1953. Published for the Crime Club by Doubleday.

Shepherds in Sackcloth. Sheila Kaye-Smith. LC 30-16250. 1930. Harper & Brothers.

Shepherds of the Night. Jorge Amado. LC 66-19366. 1967. Knopf.

Shepherds of the Wild. Edison Marshall. LC 22-4084. 1922. 1.75. Little, Brown, and Company.

Shepherds on the Move. Joseph A Young. LC 32-14952. 1932. Benziger Brothers.

Shepherd's Pipe, and Other Stories. Arthur Schnitzler. LC 74-140340. (Short story index reprint series). 1970. Books for Libraries Press.

Shepherd's Pipe: And Other Stories. Arthur Schnitzler. Tr. by Theis, Otto Frederick. LC 22-11591. (On verso of half-title: The sea gull library, by O. F. Theis, vol. iii). 1922. N. L. Brown.

Shepherd's Purse. Renee Shann. LC 53-8574. 1953. Arcadia House.

Shepherd's Staff". Fletcher M Sisson. LC 31-2175. 1930. Print. by De Vinne-Hallenbeck Company.

Shepherd's Warning. Eric Leadbitter. LC 21-176216. G. W. Jacobs & Company.

Sheppard Lee. Robert Montgomery Bird. LC 6-12725. 1836. Harper & Brothers.

Sherbert & Sodomy. I. V. Ebbing. pap. 1.95 o.s.i. (TC-509, Travellers Comp). Olympia.

Sherborne. Edward Heneage Dering. LC 75-457. (Victorian Fiction: Novels of Faith and Doubt). 1976. 35.00 (ISBN 0-8240-1536-3). Garland Pub.

Sherborne; or, the House at the Four Ways, 1875. Edward Meneage Dering. Ed. by Robert L. Wolff. LC 75-457. (Victorian Fiction Ser.). 1975. lib. bdg. 66.00 (ISBN 0-8240-1536-3). Garland Pub.

Sherborne Sapphires. Sandra Heath. 1982. pap. 2.25 (ISBN 0-451-11513-9, AE1513, Sig). NAL.

Sherbourne's Folly. Nora Barry. LC 77-76220. 1978. 10.95 o.p. (ISBN 0-385-12882-7). Doubleday.

Sherbrookes. Nicholas Delbanco. LC 78-11141. 1978. 8.95 (ISBN 0-688-03406-3). Morrow.

Sherbrookes. Nicholas Delbanco. LC 81-20995. 1982. 6.95 (ISBN 0-688-00979-4). Quill.

Sherburne Cousins. Amanda Minnie Douglas. LC 6-33468. (The Sherburne series). 1894. Dodd, Mead & Company.

Sherburne Girls. Amanda Minnie Douglas. (The Sherburne series). Dodd, Mead and Company.

Sherburne House. Amanda Minnie Douglas. LC 6-33467. (The Sherburne series). Dodd, Mead & Company.

Sherburne Inheritance. Amanda Minnie Douglas. LC 1-24572. (Sherburne series). 1901. Dodd, Mead & Company.

Sherburne Quest. Amanda Minnie Douglas. LC 2-28288. (The Sherburne series). Dodd, Mead & Company.

Sherburne Romance. Amanda Minnie Douglas. LC 6-33465. (The Sherburne series). 1895. Dodd, Mead and Company.

Sherel. J. Jenelle Tuttle. 4.95 o.p. Vantage.

Sheridan La I.E. Le Fanu: The Diabolical Genius. Joseph Sheridan Le Fanu. LC 63-1138. (Forgotten classics of mystery, v. 3). 1959. Juniper Press.

Sheridan Road. Helen Topping Miller. LC 42-18365. 1942. D. Appleton-Century Company, Incorporated.

Sheridan Road Mystery. Paul Thorne & Thorne, Mabel, Joint Author. LC 21-187965. 1921. Dodd, Mead and Company.

Sheriff. James Perrigo. LC 11-4214. 0.15. The Franklin Printing Company.

Sheriff & the Gambler. Gene Tuttle. (YA) 1972. 4.50 o.p. (Avalon). Bouregy.

Sheriff for All the People. John Henry Reese. LC 75-14839. 1976. 5.95 (ISBN 0-385-11011-1). Doubleday.

Sheriff Hater, a Western: By Pete Danvers Pseud. James Maddock Henderson. 1953. Hammond, Hammond.

Sheriff Killer. Dane Coolidge. LC 32-2125. 1932. E. P. Dutton & Co., Inc.

Sheriff of Badger: A Tale of the Southwest Borderland. George Pattullo. LC 12-16963. 1912. 1.25. D. Appleton and Company.

Sheriff of Big Hat: By Barry Cord Pseud. Peter Germano. LC 57-590352. 1957. Arcadia House.

Sheriff of Chispa Loma. Charles Horace Snow. LC 31-29189. 1931. Macrae Smith Company.

Sheriff of Durango. Bob Haning, pseud. 192p. 1973. pap. 0.75 o.p. (532-75494-075). Manor Bks.

Sheriff of Dyke Hole: The Story of a Legacy. Ridgwell Cullum. 1.50. G. W. Jacobs & Company.

Sheriff of Elk Ridge. James Lyon Ruble. LC 36-485. E. J. Clode, Inc.

Sheriff of Jack Hollow. Lee Hoffman. (Dell Book). 1977. 1.25 (ISBN 0-440-17712-X). Dell Pub Co.

Sheriff of Lonesome. Herbert Arthur, pseud. LC 48-20697. 1948. Phoenix Press.

Sheriff of Mad River. Dan Roberts. (Orig.). 1980. pap. text ed. 1.75 o.s.i. (ISBN 0-505-51571-7). Tower Bks.

Sheriff of Mad River. Dan Roberts. 1970. 3.95 o.p. Lenox Hill.

Sheriff of Painted Post. Syl MacDowell. LC 35-36178. J. Messner, Inc.

Sheriff of Purgatory. Jim Morris. LC 78-22342. 1979. 8.95 (ISBN 0-385-14615-9). Doubleday.

Sheriff of Red Wolf. Archie Joscelyn. 1963. Arcadia House.

Sheriff of San Miquel. Allan Vaughan Elston. LC 49-10157. 1949. J. B. Lippincott Co.

Sheriff of Silver Bow. Berton Braley. LC 21-157132. The Bobbs-Merrill Company.

Sheriff of Singing River. Al Cody, pseud. 1981. pap. 1.75 (ISBN 0-8439-0862-9, Leisure Bks). Nordon Pubns.

Sheriff of Singing River. Archie Joscelyn. 1965. Arcadia House.

Sheriff of Sycamore Flat. Robert Baker Elder. LC 52-11936. 1952. Dorrance.

Sheriff of the Beech Fork: A Story of Kentucky. Henry Stanislaus Spalding. 1903. Benziger Brothers.

Sheriff of Tombstone. Willis Todhunter Ballard. LC 76-53410. 1977. 6.95 (ISBN 0-385-12694-8). Doubleday.

Sheriff of Wasco. Charles Ross Jackson. LC 7-16754. 1907. G. W. Dillingham Company.

Sheriff of Yavisa. Charles Horace Snow. LC 41-35. 1941. Macrae-Smith Company.

Sheriff Olson. Mary Grace Chute. LC 42-2415. 1942. D. Appleton-Century Company, Incorporated.

Sheriff on the Spot: "a Powder Valley Western,". Peter Field. LC 43-7759. 1943. W. Morrow & Company.

Sheriff Rides. Frank Austin. 1934. Dodd, Mead & Company.

Sheriff Rides. Max Brand. 240p. 1973. pap. 1.95 (ISBN 0-446-90310-8). Warner Bks.

Sheriff Rides. Frederick Faust. 1973. 0.75. Warner.

Sheriff Wanted. Peter Field. LC 49-70079. 1949. Jefferson House.

Sheriff Without a Gun. Martin Ryerson. 1979. pap. 1.75 (ISBN 0-89041-231-6, 3231). Major Bks.

Sheriff's Son. William MacLeod Raine. LC 18-10961. 1918. Houghton Mifflin Company.

Sheriff's Son. William MacLeod Raine. LC 22-4738. 1918. Grosset & Dunlap.

Sherlock Bones. John Keane. 240p. 1980. pap. 2.25 (ISBN 0-380-50641-6, 50641). Avon.

Sherlock Holmes. Arthur Conan Doyle. Ed. by Charles Verral. (Illus.). 1957. 1.00 o.p. (10723, Golden Pr). Western Pub.

Sherlock Holmes. LC 76-372824. (E-GO collectors series ; no. 3). (Illus.). 1976. 1.00. E-GO Enterprises.

Sherlock Holmes. A Definitive Text, Corr. and Edited by Edgar W. Smith, with an Introd. by Vincent Starrett, and Illustrated with a Selective Collation of the Original Illus. by Frederic Dorr Steele and Others. Arthur Conan Doyle. LC 57-14107. 1957. Heritage Press.

Sherlock Holmes and Dr. Watson: A Textbook of Friendship. Arthur Conan Doyle & Morley, Christopher Darlington, 1890- Ed. LC 44-3528. 1944. Harcourt, Brace and Company.

Sherlock Holmes and Dr. Watson: The Chronology of Their Adventures. New Ed. Harold Wilmerding Bell. LC 53-12548. 1953. Baker Street Irregulars.

Sherlock Holmes and His Creator. Trevor H Hall & Charles O Ellison. LC 77-18322. 1978. 8.95 (ISBN 0-312-71718-0). St. Martin's Press.

Sherlock Holmes: And Other Detective Stories... Arthur Conan Doyle & Musacchia, John B., Illus. LC 42-9804. Illustrated Editions Company.

Sherlock Holmes and the Drood Mystery. Edmund Lester Pearson. LC 74-178273. (Illus.). 1973. Aspen Press.

Sherlock Holmes & the Golden Bird. Frank Thomas. 1979. pap. 2.25 (ISBN 0-523-40616-9). Pinnacle Bks.

Sherlock Holmes & the Sacred Sword. Frank Thomas. 256p. (Orig.). 1980. pap. 2.50 (ISBN 0-523-41013-1). Pinnacle Bks.

Sherlock Holmes Book of Quotations: Being a Compilation of the Words of Wit and Wisdom Spoken by the World's First Consulting Detective: and Including the Observations of His Friend and Biographer, John H. Watson, M.D.: with a Selection of the More Memorable Remarks Made by Their Intimates and Acquaintances. Arthur Conan Doyle & Bruce R Beaman. LC 79-55659. (Sherlock Holmes Reference Series). 1980. 8.95 (ISBN 0-934468-02-8). Gaslight Publications.

Sherlock Holmes Companion: By Michael and Mollie Hardwick. Illus. by Sidney Paget. John Michael Drinkrow Hardwick & Mollie Hardwick. LC 63-120836. 1963. bds., 4.95. Doubleday.

Sherlock Holmes, Esq., and John H. Watson, M.D. An Encyclopaedia of Their Affairs. Orlando Park. LC 62-17805. 10.00. Northwestern Univ. Pr.

Sherlock Holmes: Fact or Fiction New Ed. Thomas S Blakeney. LC 54-9261. 1954. Baker Street Irregulars.

Sherlock Holmes File. Ed. by Michael Pointer. LC 76-17464. 10.00 (ISBN 0-517-52560-7). C. N. Potter: Distributed by Crown Publishers.

Sherlock Holmes' Greatest Cases. large type ed. complete and unabridged. ed. Arthur Conan Doyle. LC 67-4076. Watts.

Sherlock Holmes' Greatest Cases. large type ed. complete and unabridged. ed. LC 67-4076. Watts.

Sherlock Holmes: His Most Famous Mysteries. Arthur Conan Doyle. LC 74-27722. 1975. 4.95 (ISBN 0-448-11982-X). Grosset Dunlap.

Sherlock Holmes: His Most Famous Mysteries. Arthur Conan Doyle. (O.s.i.). 384p. (Orig.). 1975. pap. 1.50 o.s.i. (ISBN 0-448-07484-2, Tempo). G&D.

Sherlock Holmes Illustrated Omnibus: The Complete Text and Original Drawings of The Adventures of Sherlock Holmes, The Memoirs of Sherlock Holmes, The Hound of the Baskervilles, The Return of Sherlock Holmes: a Facsimile of the Stories and the Novel As They Were First Published in the Strand Magazine, London. Arthur Conan Doyle. LC 75-37293. 1976. 9.95 (ISBN 0-8052-0507-1). Schocken Books.

Sherlock Holmes Illustrated Omnibus: The Complete Texts & Original Drawings of The Adventures of Sherlock Holmes, Memoirs of Sherlock Holmes, The Hound of the Baskervilles, & The Return of Sherlock Holmes. Arthur Conan Doyle. LC 75-37293. (Illus.). 704p. 1976. pap. 9.95 o.p. (ISBN 0-8052-0507-1). Schocken.

Sherlock Holmes in Dallas. Edmund Aubrey. LC 80-15980. 240p. 1980. 9.95 o.p. (ISBN 0-396-07904-0). Dodd.

Sherlock Holmes in Dallas. Edmund S Ions. LC 80-15980. (Illus.). 9.95 (ISBN 0-396-07904-0). Dodd, Mead.

Sherlock Holmes in Modern Times: An Anthology of Original Short Stories. Ira Bernard Dworkin. LC 80-81295. 1980. 6.50 (ISBN 0-87164-088-0). William-Frederick Press.

Sherlock Holmes in Portrait and Profile. Walter Klinefelter. LC 75-10715. (Illus.). 1975. 3.95 (ISBN 0-8052-0498-9). Schocken Books.

Sherlock Holmes in Portrait and Profile. With an Introd. by Vincent Starrett. Walter Klinefelter. LC 63-19727. 1963. Syracuse University Press.

Sherlock Holmes in Tibet. Richard Wincor. LC 68-12872. 1968. Weybright and Talley.

Sherlock Holmes Investigates: Stories. Arthur Conan Doyle. LC 66-14610. (Illus.). 1967. Lothrop, Lee & Shepard Co.

Sherlock Holmes, Master Detective. Arthur Conan Doyle. LC 80-54136. (Silver Classic). (Illus.). 1981. 2.95 (ISBN 0-382-03442-2). Silver Burdett.

Sherlock Holmes Reader. Arthur Conan Doyle. 1975. pap. 3.95 (ISBN 0-425-03010-5, Windhover). Berkley Pub.

Sherlock Holmes Scrapbook: Fifty Years of Occasional Articles, Newspaper Cuttings, Letters, Memoirs, Anecdotes, Pictures, Photographs and Drawings Relating to the Great Detective. Peter Haining. LC 74-81590. (Illus.). 1974. 10.00 (ISBN 0-517-51756-6). C. N. Potter: Distributed by Crown Publishers.

Sherlock Holmes: Selected Stories. Arthur Conan Doyle. (World's Classics Ser.). 1980. pap. 3.95 (ISBN 0-19-281530-X). Oxford U Pr.

Sherlock Holmes: Selected Stories, With an Introd. by S. C. Roberts. Arthur Conan Doyle. LC 51-12288. (World's classics, 528). 1951. Oxford University Press.

Sherlock Holmes: Ten Literary Studies. Trevor H Hall. LC 76-373432. (Illus.). 1976. 3.95. St. Martin's Press.

Sherlock Holmes, the Published Apocrypha. Arthur Conan Doyle & Jack Tracy. LC 80-16328. (Illus.). 1980. 11.95 (ISBN 0-395-29454-1). Houghton Mifflin.
Sherlock Holmes Versus Arsene Lupin: The Case of the Golden Blonde. Maurice Leblanc & B. J. LC 46-19793. 1946. Atomic Books, Inc.
Sherlock Holmes Vs. Dracula: Or, The Adventure of the Sanguinary Count. Loren D Estleman. LC 77-11392. 1978. 7.95 (ISBN 0-385-14051-7). Doubleday.
Sherlock Holmes Vs. Dracula: Or, The Adventure of the Sanguinary Count. Loren D Estleman. LC 79-11661. 1979. 2.50 (ISBN 0-14-005262-3). Penguin Books.
Sherlock Holmes vs. Dracula or the Adventure of the Sanguinary Court. John H. Watson. Ed. by Loren D. Estleman. 1979. pap. 2.75 (ISBN 0-14-005262-3). Penguin.
Sherlock Holmes's War of the Worlds. Manly Wade Wellman. LC 75-326051. (Warner science fantasy). 1975. 1.25 (ISBN 0-446-76982-7). Warner Books.
Sherlocks. A Novel. John Saunders. (Franklin square library, no. 51). 1879. Harper & Brothers.
Sherluck Bones Mystery Detective. Jim Razzi & Mary Razzi. 1982. pap. write for info. Bantam.
Sherman Hale and the Stapleton Mystery. George Hart Rand. LC 12-22597. 0.75. R. F. Fenno & Company.
Shermans of Mannerville. Jack Ansell. LC 77-139295. 1971. 6.95 (ISBN 0-87795-008-3). Arbor Hse.
Shermans of Mannerville. Jack Ansell. 1972. pap. 1.25 o.p. (ISBN 0-446-66801-X, 64-810). Paperback Lib.
Sherrill Blandon's Call. Zenobia Bird. LC 39-245785. Fleming H. Revell Company.
Sherrill Blandon's Call. Zenobia Bird. LC 39-24578. 1939. Fleming H. Revell Company.
Sherrods. George Barr McCutcheon. LC 3-20892. 1903. Dodd, Mead and Company.
Sherry. George Barr McCutcheon. LC 19-14354. 1919. Dodd, Mead and Company.
Sherston's Progress. Siegfried Sassoon. 152p. 1983. pap. 4.95 (ISBN 0-571-13033-X). Faber & Faber.
Sherwood Anderson. Sherwood Anderson. Ed. by Rosenfield, Paul. LC 47-11718. 1947. Houghton Mifflin Co.
Sherwood Anderson: Short Stories. Sherwood Anderson. Ed. by Maxwell Geismar. (Orig.). 1962. pap. 3.95 o.p. (ISBN 0-8090-0052-0, AmCen). Hill & Wang.
Sheryl. Ralph Hayes. 1980. pap. 2.25 o.s.i. (ISBN 0-505-51452-4). Tower Bks.
She's a Cop, Isn't She? A Documentary Novel. Irene King & Caryl Thurman. LC 74-34202. 1975. 7.95 (ISBN 0-8037-4534-6). Dial Press.
She's All the World to Me. Hall Caine. (On cover: Seaside library. Pocket ed. no. 520). 1885. G. Munro.
She's All the World to Me. Hall Caine. LC 6-19898. (Harper's handy series, no. 13). 1885. Harper & Brothers.
She's All the World to Me. A Novel. Hall Caine. LC 16-19155. 1895. H. Altemus.
Shete Ha'Qesawot: The Two Extremes Novel. 2nd ed. R A Braudes. (Literaria Judaica Section 2 Ser.: No. 5). Repr. of 1888 ed. 29.50 (ISBN 0-404-13861-6). AMS Pr.
Shetland Summer. Audrie Manley-Tucker. Ed. by Gene DeRoin. (Aston Hall Presents Ser.). (Orig.). pap. 1.50 (ISBN 0-89936-006-8). Aston Hall.
Shiatsu. T. Namikoshi. (Illus.). 1974. pap. 7.95x (Pub. by Japan Pubns). Wehman.
Shibboleth: A Novel. S. Ella Wood. W. B. Conkey Company.
Shibumi. Trevanian. LC 78-20950. 10.95 (ISBN 0-517-53243-3). Crown Publishers.
Shibusawa: Or, The Passing of Old Japan. I. William Adams. LC 6-41721. 1906. G. P. Putnam's Sons.
Shield. Poul Anderson. (Orig.). 1982. pap. 2.50 (ISBN 0-425-04704-0). Berkley Pub.
Shield for Murder. William P McGivern. LC 51-9866. (Red badge detective). 1951. Dodd, Mead.
Shield Lies Over. Elizabeth Perdix. LC 43-3705. 1943. Creative Age Press, Inc.
Shield Mares. Ben K Green. LC 68-2394. (Illus.). 1967. Encino Press.
Shield of His Honor: A Novel. Richard Henry Savage. (On cover: The welcome series, no. 53). 1900. The Home Publishing Company.
Shield of Honor. 1st Ed. Alice Walworth Graham. LC 57-104546. 1957. Doubleday.
Shield of Love. Warwick Deeping. LC 41-26419. 1940. R. M. McBride & Company.
Shield of Love. Benjamin Leopold Farjeon. LC 6-38766. (Leisure hour series). 1891. H. Holt and Company.
Shield of Silence. Edwin Balmer & Philip Wylie. LC 36-7260. 1936. Frederick A. Stokes Company.
Shield of Silence. Harriet Theresa Smith Comstock. LC 21-6908. 1921. Doubleday, Page & Company.
Shield of Silence. Margaret Ellen Henry Ruffin. LC 14-6567. 1914. 1.35. Benziger Brothers.
Shield of the Valiant. August William Derleth. LC 45-9494. 1945. C. Scribner's Sons.
Shield Project. David R. Mounce. 1971. pap. 0.75 o.p. (T2451). Pyramid Pubns.
Shielding Wing. Will Levington Comfort. LC 19-563. 1.50. Small, Maynard & Company.
Shifting Change. Dorothy Grant. LC 73-76217. 1973. 5.95 (ISBN 0-8059-1846-9). Dorrance.
Shifting Sands. Margaret W. Baender. 276p. 1981. 10.00 (ISBN 0-8059-2792-1). Dorrance.
Shifting Sands. Sara Ware Bassett. LC 33-20282. 1933. The Penn Publishing Company.
Shifting Sands. Clarence E. Bessick. 1978. 6.95 o.p. (ISBN 0-533-03482-5). Vantage.
Shifting Sands. Frederick Russell Burton. Rand, McNally & Company.
Shifting Sands. Katharine Waldo Douglas Fedden. 1914. 1.35. Houghton Mifflin Company.
Shifting Sands. Lorine Proctor. 1969. 3.00 o.p. (ISBN 0-8059-1415-3). Dorrance.
Shifting Shadows; a Tale of Real Life. S. E Simmonds. LC 8-89918. 1889. Standard Publishing Co.
Shifting Spell. Leslie Probyn. LC 17-701. 1.35. Duffield & Co.
Shifting Winds. Kathryn Cotten. LC 39-37273. Mathis, Van Nort & Co.
Shiftless Folks. An Undiluted Love Story. Fannie N. Smith. LC 8-8987. 1875. G. W. Carleton & Co.; Etc., Etc.
Shikasta: Re, Colonised Planet 5: Personal, Psychological, Historical Documents Relating to Visit by Johor (George Sherban) Emissary (Grade 9) 87th of the Period of the Last Days. Doris May Lessing. LC 79-11295. (Canopus in argos archives). 1979. 10.95 (ISBN 0-394-50732-0). Knopf: Distributed by Random House.
Shikasta: Re, Colonised Planet 5: Personal, Psychological, Historical Documents Relating to Visit by Johor (George Sherban) Emissary (Grade 9) 87th of the Period of the Last Days. Doris May Lessing. LC 81-40194. (Canopus in argos archives). 1981. 4.95 (ISBN 0-394-74977-4). Vintage Books.
Shike: Book 1: Time of the Dragons. Robert Shea. 1981. pap. 3.50. Jove Pubns.
Shilling for Candles. Josephine Tey. 1981. pap. 2.50 (ISBN 0-671-80974-1). PB.
Shilling for Candles. Josephine Tey. 1972. pap. 1.25 (ISBN 0-425-03221-3, Medallion). Berkley Pub.
Shilling for Candles: By Josephine Tey Pseud. Elizabeth Mackintosh. LC 54-8661. (Murder revisited mystery novel, no. 4). 1954. Macmillan.
Shilling Shockers of the Gothic School: A Study of Chapbook Gothic Romances. William Whyte Watt. LC 32-340947. (Half-title: Harvard honors theses in English. no. 5). 1932. Harvard University Press.
Shilling Shockers: Stories of Terror from the Gothic Bluebooks. Peter Haining. LC 77-9184. (Illus.). 1979. 8.95 (ISBN 0-312-71734-2). St. Martin's Press.
Shilling Soldiers. Denis Norman Garstin. LC 19-6663. Hodder and Stoughton.
Shiloh: A Novel. Shelby Foote. LC 52-5614. 1952. Dial Press.
Shiloh: A Novel. Shelby Foote. LC 76-13221. (Illus.). 1976. 8.95. (ISBN 0-394-40873-X) (ISBN 0-394-73261-8). Random House.
Shiloh and Other Stories. Bobbie Ann Mason. LC 82-47541. 12.45 (ISBN 0-06-015062-9). Harper & Row.
Shiloh: Or, Without and Within. Julia Louise Matilda Woodruff. E. P. Dutton and Co.
Shiloh Project. David C. Poyer. 256p. (Orig.). 1981. pap. 2.50 (ISBN 0-380-78733-4, 78733). Avon.
Shiloh, the Man of Nazareth. New Rev. Ed. Avery-Stuttle, Lilla Dale. LC 51-3098. Pacific Press Pub. Association.
Shim. 1st Ed. Reuben Davis. LC 53-10553. 1953. Bobbs-Merrill.
Shimmering Stones. Maryann Young. (Candlelight romances, 119). 1973. (pbk.) 0.75. Dell.
Shindano-Swahili Essays & Other Stories. Alice Grant et al. (Foreign & Comparative Studies-African Special Publications Ser.: No.6). 55p. 1971. pap. 3.50x. Syracuse U Foreign Comp.
Shine on, Bright & Dangerous Object. Laurie Colwin. LC 75-1255. 1975. 7.95 (ISBN 0-670-63970-2). Viking Press.
Shinega's Village: Scenes of Ethiopian Life. Berhane Marian Sahle Sellassie. Tr. by Wolf Leslau. LC 64-12607. 1964. University of California Press.
Shining. Stephen King. LC 76-24212. 1977. 7.95 (ISBN 0-385-12167-9). Doubleday.
Shining. Stephen King. (Signet Book). 1978. 2.50 (ISBN 0-451-07872-1). New American Library.
Shining Adventure. Dana Burnet. LC 16-22049. 1916. Harper & Brothers.
Shining After Rain. Louise Harrison McCraw. LC 40-11553. Zondervan Publishing House.
Shining & Free. Gladys Bronwyn Stern. 1969. pap. 0.95 o.p. (N2089). Pyramid Pubns.
Shining and Free: A Day in the Life of the Matriarch... Gladys Bronwyn Stern. LC 35-3663. 1935. A. A. Knopf.
Shining Armor. Louise E Dew. LC 35-837319. J. H. Hopkins & Son.
Shining Chance. Berta Ruck. LC 44-12969. 1944. Dodd, Mead & Company.
Shining Cloud... Margaret Bass Pedler. LC 36-1300. 1936. Doubleday, Doran & Company, Inc.
Shining Cloud... Margaret Bass Pedler. LC 36-32116. 1936. The Sun Dial Press.
Shining Cloud... Margaret Bass Pedler. LC 40-11447. 1940. Triangle Books.
Shining Day. Frank Ross. LC 80-69394. 1981. 13.95 (ISBN 0-689-11111-8). Atheneum.
Shining Ferry. Arthur Thomas Quiller-Couch. LC 5-9058. 1905. C. Scribner's Sons.
Shining Harvest. E. V. Timms. 1977. pap. 1.50 o.p. (ISBN 0-515-04397-4). BJ Pub Group.
Shining Harvest. E. V. Timms. (Historical Adventure Novels). pap. 1.80 o.s.i. Tri-Ocean.
Shining Headlands. Sara Ware Bassett. LC 37-20202. 1937. Doubleday, Doran & Company, Inc.
Shining Heights. Ida Alexa Ross Wylie. LC 17-30354. 1917. John Lane Company.
Shining Light. Effie E. Sanders. 1969. 3.50 o.p. (ISBN 0-682-47079-1). Exposition.
Shining Mischief. Barbara Levy. LC 74-150274. 1971. 5.95. Putnam.
Shining Mountain. Peter Boardman & Joe Tasker. (Illus.). 192p. 1983. 14.95 (ISBN 0-525-24186-8, 01451-440); pap. 7.95 (ISBN 0-525-48053-6, 0772-230). Dutton.
Shining Mountains. Steve Frazee. LC 51-10257. 1951. Rinehart.
Shining Mountains. Arlene Hale. LC 81-3173. 1981. 10.95 (ISBN 0-89340-341-5). J. Curley & Associates.
Shining Mountains. Dale Van Every & Julian Messner. 320p. 1982. pap. 3.25 (ISBN 0-553-20671-0). Bantam.
Shining: Movie Edition. Stephen King. 1980. pap. 2.95 (ISBN 0-451-09216-3, E9432, Sig). NAL.
Shining Palace. Christine Whiting Paramenter. LC 33-3286. Thomas Y. Crowell Company.
Shining River. Francis Carey Slater. LC 25-23373. 1925. 2.25. Longmans, Green and Co.
Shining River. Joan Sutherland. LC 36-24680. Coward-McCann, Inc.
Shining Road: A Novel. Bernice Brown. LC 23-400881. 1923. G. P. Putnam's Sons.
Shining Scabbard. Ray Coryton Hutchinson. LC 37-109. Farrar & Rinehart, Incorporated.
Shining Sea, Translated from the Swedish by Barrows Mussey. Kjerstin Gertrud Elisabeth Goransson-Ljungman & Mussey, June Barrows, 1910- Tr. LC 43-10496. 1943. Sheridan House.
Shining Shield. Kenneth Anderson. LC 44-4113. 1944. Zondervan Publishing House.
Shining Spirit. Louise Jones. LC 41-5373. 1937. Phoenix Press.
Shining Tides: A Novel. Win Brooks. LC 52-5785. 1952. Morrow.
Shining Trail. Iola Fuller, pseud. LC 43-51208. 1943. Duell, Sloan and Pearce.
Shining Trail. Iola Fuller, pseud. LC 46-4403. 1946. The Sun Dial Press.
Shining Trail: Illustrated by Dale Nichols. Iola Fuller, pseud. LC 51-10401. 1951. Duell, Sloan and Pearce.
Shining Trails. Florence E Gerber. LC 30-18661. Dorrance & Company, Inc.
Shining Tree & Other Christmas Stories. LC 40-32979. 1940. A. A. Knopf.
Shining Way. Norma Norris. LC 48-99115. 1948. Review and Herald Pub. Assn.
Shining Windows. Kathleen Thompson Norris. LC 35-191521. 1935. Doubleday, Doran & Company, Inc.
Shining Years. Emilie Baker Loring. LC 72-7482. 1972. 9.95 (ISBN 0-8161-6051-1). G. K. Hall.
Shining Years. Emilie Baker Loring. 1974. (pbk.) 0.95. Bantam.
Shining Years. Emilie Baker Loring. LC 72-4473. 1972. 5.95 (ISBN 0-316-53285-1). Little, Brown.
Shinning Day. Frank Ross. LC 80-69394. 1981. 12.95 (ISBN 0-689-11111-8). Atheneum.
Shiny Night. Beatrice Tunstall. LC 33-11794. 1933. Garden City Publishing Company, Inc.
Shiny Night. Beatrice Tunstall. LC 31-26997. 1931. Doubleday, Doran & Company, Inc.
Shiny Objects. Dianne Benedict. LC 82-10853. (Iowa School of Letters Award for Short Fiction). 12.95 (ISBN 0-87745-116-8) (ISBN 0-87745-117-6). University of Iowa Press.
Shiokari Pass. Ayako Miura. LC 76-6868. 1976. 5.95 (ISBN 0-8007-0796-6). F. H. Revell Co.
Ship. Cecil Scott Forester. LC 43-5899. 1943. Little, Brown and Company.
Ship. Arnold Sherman. 1980. pap. 2.25 (ISBN 0-8439-0809-2). Nordon Pubns.
Ship and the Flame. Jerre Gerlando Mangione. LC 48-6858. 1948. Current Books.
Ship Ashore. Sydney Muller Parkman. LC 37-4381. 1937. Harper & Brothers.
Ship Ashore. 3rd ed. Jeannette E. Rattray. 1968. 9.95 o.p. (ISBN 0-911660-00-3); pap. 5.95 o.p. (ISBN 0-911660-01-1). Yankee Peddler.
Ship Beautiful: A Two-Fold Tale. 2d impression. ed. C. R Allen. LC 26-18105. 1925. F. Warne & Co., Ltd.
Ship-Carpenter's Family. A Story for the Times. William Edward Seaver Whitman. LC 8-36551. H. Long and Brother.
Ship Is Dying. Brian Callison. LC 76-11887. 1976. 7.95 (ISBN 0-8415-0450-4). Dutton.
Ship Island: And Other Stories. Elizabeth Spencer. LC 68-22767. 1968. McGraw-Hill.
Ship Must Die. Douglas Reeman. LC 79-66009. 1979. 9.95 (ISBN 0-688-03555-8). W. Morrow.
Ship of Coral. Henry De Vere Stacpoole. LC 11-8609. 1911. 1.20. Duffield & Company.
Ship of Death. Edward Stilgebauer & Sadler, M. T. H., Tr. LC 18-19924. 1918. Brentano's.
Ship of Destiny. Marshall N Goold. LC 24-24695. 1924. Houghton Mifflin Company.
Ship of Dreams: A Novel. Mary Louise Foster. LC 2-22672. 1902. Harper & Brothers.
Ship of Dreams: By Warren Howard Pseud. James Noble Gifford. LC 55-118832. 1955. Arcadia House.
Ship of Fools. Sebastian Brant. Tr. by E. H. Zeydel. (Illus.). 5.00 o.p. (ISBN 0-8446-1731-8). Peter Smith.
Ship of Fools. Katherine Anne Porter. LC 62-9557. 1962. Little, Brown.
Ship of Gold. Thomas Allen. LC 81-48027. 256p. 1982. write for info. o.p. (ISBN 0-06-038017-9, HarpT). Har-Row.
Ship of Hate. Rebecca Danton, pseud. (Dell Book). 1977. 1.50 (ISBN 0-440-17852-5). Dell Pub. Co.
Ship of Hope. Ruben Rothgiesser. Tr. by Gerson, Felix Napoleon. Jewish Publication Society of America. LC 39-14380. 1939. The Jewish Publication Society of America.
Ship of Ishtar. Abraham Merritt. LC 26-4777. 1926. G. P. Putnam's Sons.
Ship of Ishtar... Abraham Merritt. LC 46-15531. (Murder mystery monthly, no. 34). 1945.
Ship of Solace. Elinor Mordaunt, pseud. LC 11-18065. 1911. 1.00. Sturgis & Walton Company.
Ship of Souls. Emerson Hough. LC 25-4862. 1925. D. Appleton and Company.
Ship of Spies. Gerald Sinstadt. pap. 0.60 o.p. Lancer.
Ship of Stars. Arthur Thomas Quiller-Couch. LC 99-505322. 1899. C. Scribner's Sons.
Ship of the Damned. Joseph Hilton. (Orig.). 1972. pap. 0.95 o.s.i. (75-398). Lancer.
Ship of the Line. Cecil Scott Forester. (Hornblower Saga,#6). 1975. (pbk) 1.25. Pinnacle Books.
Ship of the Line. Cecil Scott Forester. LC 38-6962. 1938. Little, Brown, and Company.
Ship of Truth. Lettice Ulpha Cooper. LC 30-10089. 1930. Little, Brown, and Company.
Ship Ride Down the Spring Branch and Other Stories. Jess Carr. LC 78-60480. 8.95 (ISBN 0-87716-092-9). Moore Pub. Co.
Ship Sails on. Nordahl Grieg. Tr. by Chater, Arthur G. LC 27-16676. 1927. A. A. Knopf.
Ship That Died of Shame: And Other Stories. Nicholas Monsarrat. LC 59-13587. 1959. W. Sloane Associates.
Ship That Died of Shame, and Other Stories. Nicholas Monsarrat. LC 70-163044. (Short story index reprint series). 1971. (ISBN 0-8369-3958-1). Books for Libraries Press.
Ship That Sailed the Time Stream. G. C Edmondson. 1978. 1.95 (ISBN 0-441-76092-9). Ace Books.
Ship They Called the Fat Lady. William M Hardy. LC 77-96034. 1969. 4.50. Dodd, Mead.
Ship to Shore. William McFee. LC 44-7126. 1944. Random House.
Ship. Translated by Catherine Hutter. Hans Henny Jahnn. LC 61-7207. 1961. Scribner.
Ship Who Sang. Anne McCaffrey. LC 79-86390. 1969. 4.95. Walker.
Ship Window Murders. John George Haslette Vahey. LC 30-14007. 1930. W. Morrow & Company.
Ship with the Flat Tire. Todd Hunt. LC 64-19303. 1964. Doubleday.
Ship Without Sails. Barbara Barclay Carter. LC 34-5896. E. P. Dutton & Co., Inc.
Ship Wrecked. Graham Greene. Orig. Title: England Made Me. Repr. of 1935 ed. 3.00 o.p. (ISBN 0-670-64038-7). Viking Pr.
Shipbuilders. George Blake. LC 37-27054. J.B. Lippincott Company.
Shipkiller. Justin Scott. 1979. pap. 2.50 (ISBN 0-449-24036-3, Crest). Fawcett.
Shipkiller: A Novel. Justin Scott. LC 78-18207. 10.00 (ISBN 0-8037-7949-6). Dial Press.
Shipmates. Morgan Robertson. LC 3-28137. 1901. D. Appleton and Company.

Shipmates. Mary Teresa Waggaman. LC 14-18465. 1914. Benziger Brothers.
Shipmates: A Tale of the Seafaring Women of New England. Isabel Hopestill Carter. LC 34-39886. W. R. Scott.
Shipment of Tarts. Edmund G Love. LC 67-22470. 1967. Doubleday.
Ships Across the Sea: Stories of the American Navy in the Great War. Ralph Delahaye Paine. LC 20-71393. 1920. 1.90. Houghton Mifflin Company.
Ships Aflame! A Mystery of the Sea. Jean Toussaint Samat & Abbott, Elizabeth, Tr. LC 35-7525. J. B. Lippincott Company.
Ships and Sailors: Tales of the Sea. Stanley Rogers. 1978. Repr. of 1929 ed. lib. bdg. 30.00 o.p. (ISBN 0-8495-4516-1). Arden Lib.
Ships by Day: A Novel. Edwin Allen Wyman. LC 9-1474. 1895. J. H. Earle.
Ship's Company. William Laurence Coleman. LC 55-7475. 1955. Little, Brown.
Ship's Company. Pauline Benedict Fischer. LC 37-270642. The Penn Publishing Company.
Ship's Company. William Wymark Jacobs. 1911. Hodder and Stoughton.
Ship's Company. William Wymark Jacobs. 1911. C. Scribner's Sons.
Ship's Doctor. Charles Stanley Strong. LC 41-16492. Phoenix Press.
Ships in the Bay! Dorothy Kathleen Broster. LC 31-21310. CowardMcCann, Inc.
Ships in the River. Gosta Larsson. LC 46-267340. 1946. Whittlesey House, McGraw-Hill Book Company, Inc.
Ship's Nurse. Dorothy Quentin. LC 47-11735. 1947. Arcadia House.
Ships of Youth: A Study of Marriage in Modern India. Katherine Helen Maud Marshall Diver. LC 51-15289. 1931. Houghton Mifflin Company.
Ship's Surgeon's Yarn, and Other Stories. Francis Brett Young. LC 72-134985. (Short story index reprint series). 1970. Books for Libraries Press.
Ship's Surgeon's Yarn: And Other Stories. Francis Brett Young. LC 40-11824. Reynal & Hitchcock.
Ships That Pass in the Night. Beatrice Harraden. (On cover: Seaside library. Pocket ed., no. 2071). 1894. G. Munro.
Ships That Pass in the Night. authorized american ed. Beatrice Harraden. 1894. G. P. Putnam's Sons.
Ships That Pass in the Night. new ed. Beatrice Harraden. LC 4-21550. 1900. Dodd, Mead and Company.
Ships That Pass in the Night. Beatrice Harraden. LC 12-24355. 1909. Dodd, Mead and Company.
Ships to the Stars. Fritz Leiber. 1976. 1.50. Ace.
Shipwreck in Europe. Joseph Bard. LC 28-7957. 1923. Harper.
Shipwreck: Or, The Desert Island. LC 49-41552. (Catholic presentation library). 1886. P. J. Kenedy.
Shipwrecked: A Novel. Graham Greene. 1953. Viking Press.
Shipwrecked: The Uniform Edition. Graham Greene. 1982. 16.95 (ISBN 0-670-64038-7). Viking Pr.
Shipyard. Juan Carlos Onetti. LC 68-12490. 1968. Scribner.
Shiralce. D'Arcy Niland. LC 55-102598. 1955. W. Sloane Associates.
Shirley. Charlotte Bronte. 1974. (ISBN 0-14-043095-4). Penguin Books.
Shirley. Charlotte Bronte. (Seaside library, v. 9, no. 162). 1877. G. Munro.
Shirley. Charlotte Bronte. (On cover: Lovell's library, v. 18, no. 897). 1887. J. W. Lovell Company.
Shirley. Charlotte Bronte. LC 99-5591. (Half-title: Life and works of the sisters Bronte... vol. II). 1899. Harper & Brothers.
Shirley. Charlotte Bronte. LC 12-19590. (Half-title:... Life and works of the sisters Bronte... vol. II). 1900. Harper & Brothers.
Shirley. Charlotte Bronte. LC 45-40835. (Half-title: The novels of Charlotte, Emily & Anne Bronte). 1922. J. M. Dent & Sons Ltd.
Shirley. Charlotte Bronte. Ed. by Margaret Smith. LC 78-40742. (Clarendon edition of the novels of the Brontes). 1979. 65.00 (ISBN 0-19-812565-8). Clarendon Press.
Shirley. A Tale. Charlotte Bronte. LC 31-19528. 1856. Derby & Jackson.
Shirley. A Tale. Charlotte Bronte. (On cover: Seaside library. Pocket ed., no. 57). 1883. G. Munro.
Shirley. A Tale. Charlotte Bronte. LC 6-17950. 1860. Derby & Jackson.
Shirley: An Entertainment. Howard Melvin Fast. LC 64-10774. 1964. Doubleday.
Shirley. 1st Ed. Pearl Eggers Jones. LC 59-123760. 1959. Greenwich Book Publishers.
Shirt Front. Charity Blackstock. 1977. 7.95 o.p. (ISBN 0-698-10831-0, Coward). Putnam Pub Group.
Shirt Front. Ursula Torday. LC 77-4823. 1977. 7.95 (ISBN 0-698-10831-0). Coward, McCann & Geoghegan.
Shirt of Flame... Ateshden Ceumlek. Halide Edib Adivar. LC 24-28227. 1924. Duffield & Company.
Shit on My Shoes. Duncan McNaughton. (Illus.). 1979. pap. 5.00 (ISBN 0-939180-12-X). Tombouctou.
Shiva Descending. Gregory Benford & Rotsler, William. 2.50 (ISBN 0-380-75168-2). Avon Books.
Shivering Bough. Dolores Birk Hitchens. LC 42-36296. 1942. E. P. Dutton & Company, Inc.
Shivering Bough. Dolores Birk Hitchens. LC 44-47728. (Bart house books, 7). 1944. Bartholomew House, Inc.
Shivering Mountain. Paul Somers. LC 59-13315. 1959. Harper.
Shivering Sands. Eleanor Hibbert. LC 69-10947. 1969. 5.95. Doubleday.
Shivering Sands. Victoria Holt, pseud. LC 69-10947. 1969. 6.95 (ISBN 0-385-06588-4). Doubleday.
Shivering Sands. Victoria Holt, pseud. 288p. 1981. pap. 2.75 (ISBN 0-449-23282-4, Crest). Fawcett.
Shkola Dlya Durakov. Sasha Sokolov. 1976. 10.00 (ISBN 0-88233-189-2); pap. 5.00 (ISBN 0-88233-188-4). Ardis Pubs.
Shmucks: A Novel. Seymour Blicker. LC 77-23084. 1977. 6.95 (ISBN 0-688-03244-3). Morrow.
Shoal Water. George Shepard Chappell. LC 33-305634. 1933. G. P. Putnam's Sons.
Shoal Water... Cecil William Mercer. LC 41-529. G. P. Putnam's Sons.
Shoals of Circumstances. William A Hatch. LC 38-32226. Dorrance and Company.
Shoals of Honour. Elisabeth Sanxay Holding. LC 26-6907. E. P. Dutton & Company.
Shock I: Thirteen Tales to Thrill and Terrify. Richard Matheson. (Berkley book). 1979. 1.95 (ISBN 0-425-04095-X). Berkley Pub. Corp.
Shock of Battle. Patrick Vaux. LC 6-27710. 1906. G. P. Putnam's Sons.
Shock Proof Sydney Skate. Marijane Meaker. 1973. 1.25. Curtis Books.
Shock Three. Richard Matheson. 1979. pap. 1.95 (ISBN 0-425-04209-X). Berkley Pub.
Shock to Society: A Novel. Florence Alice Price James. LC 7-7976. Lovell, Coryell & Company.
Shock Treatment. Winfred Van Atta. LC 61-12610. 1961. Published for the Crime Club by Doubleday.
Shock Troops. 1st Ed. Sherman, Malcolm Clarke. LC 62-1397. 1962. Vantage Pres.
Shock Value. Warren Murphy. (Destroyer Ser.: No. 51). 208p. 1983. pap. text ed. 2.25 (ISBN 0-523-41561-3). Pinnacle Bks.
Shock Value: A Tasteful Book About Bad Taste. John Waters. (Orig.). 1981. pap. 8.95 (ISBN 0-440-57871-X, Delta). Dell.
Shock Wave. Dorothy Salisbury Davis. LC 77-37200. 1972. 5.95 (ISBN 0-684-12748-2). Scribner.
Shock Wave. John Turner. (O.s.i.). (Orig.). pap. 0.60 o.s.i. (A220, Award). Univ Pub & Dist.
Shocking Bad Hat, a Victorian Novel. Dorothy Hewlett. LC 41-22357. The Bobbs-Merrill Company.
Shocking Example: And Other Sketches. Frances Courtenay Baylor Barnum. LC 6-865272. 1889. J. B. Lippincott Company.
Shocking Miss Anstey. Robert Neill. 1971. pap. 0.95 o.p. (09057). Curtis.
Shocking Miss Anstey: 1st Ed. in the U. S. A. Robert Neill. LC 65-14010. 4.95. Doubleday.
Shocking Pink Hat. Frances Kirkwood Crane. 1946. Random House.
Shocking Story. Wilkie Collins. LC 6-26935. (Atlas series. no. 6). A. S. Barnes & Company.
Shocking Tales. Robert Kendrick Brunner. LC 47-25. 1946. Current Books, Inc., A. A. Wyn.
Shocking Thing. Damon Knight. 1974. (pbk.) 0.95 (ISBN 0-671-77775-0). Pocket Books.
Shockproof Sydney Skate. Marijane Meaker. LC 70-175469. 1972. 5.95. Little, Brown.
Shocks. Algernon Blackwood. LC 36-20838. E. P. Dutton & Co., Inc.
Shockwave Rider. John Brunner. 1976. (pbk.) 1.50 (ISBN 0-345-24853-8). Ballantine.
Shockwave Rider. John Brunner. LC 74-23861. 1975. 8.95 (ISBN 0-06-010559-3). Harper & Row.
Shod with Flame. Helen Topping Miller. LC 46-7546. 1946. The Bobbs-Merrill Company.
Shoddy. Dan Brearley Brummitt. LC 28-7495. 1928. Willett, Clark & Colby.
Shoe-Bar Stratton. Joseph Bushnell Ames. LC 22-9194. 1922. The Century Co.
Shoe Binders of New York: Or, The Fields White to the Harvest. Julia MacNair Wright. LC 9-521. Presbyterian Publication Commitee.
Shoe the Wild Mare. Gene Fowler, pseud. LC 31-4812. H. Liveright.
Shoe the Wild Mare. Gene Fowler, pseud. LC 44-7526. 1944. New Avon Library.
Shoe the Wild Mare. Gene Fowler, pseud. LC 46-22513. 1946. The Sun Dial Press.
Shoelace Robin. William Norman Hall & Lawson, Robert, 1892- Illus. 1945. T. Y. Crowell.
Shoeless Joe. W. P Kinsella. LC 81-19196. 1982. 11.95 (ISBN 0-395-32047-X). Houghton Mifflin.
Shoepac Recollections: A Way-Side Glimpse of American Life. Orlando Bolivar Willcox. LC 8-36925. 1856. Bunce & Brother.
Shoes. J A Bentham. LC 23-18217. 1923. Frederick A. Stokes Company.
Shoes for Free People. David Runk. LC 75-25805. 1976. pap. 4.95 o.p. (ISBN 0-913300-44-6). Orenda-Unity.
Shoes for My Love. Jean Leslie. LC 48-9002. 1948. N. Y., Pub. for the Crime Club by Doubleday.
Shoes of Fortune. Neil Munro. 1901. Dodd, Mead and Company.
Shoes of Iron: A Tale of Witch Town. William McChesney Martin. LC 7-15543. 1907. Mayhew Publishing Co.
Shoes of the Fisherman. Morris L. West. 1974. (pbk.) 1.50 (ISBN 0-671-78685-7). Pocket Books.
Shoes of the Fisherman: A Novel. Morris L. West. LC 63-11743. 1963. Morrow.
Shoes That Had Walked Twice.. Jean Toussaint Samat & Abbott, Elisabeth, Tr. LC 33-17002. J. B. Lippincott Company.
Shoestring. Berton Braley. LC 31-14335. Sears Publishing Company.
Shoestring Symphony. David Broekman. LC 48-1318. 1948. Simon and Schuster.
Shoestrings. Maximilian Foster. LC 17-653316. 1917. 1.40. D. Appleton and Company.
Shogun. James Clavell. LC 74-77840. 1975. 19.95 (ISBN 0-689-10565-7). Atheneum.
Shogun. James Clavell. 1982. pap. 3.50 (ISBN 0-440-17800-2). Dell.
Shogun. James Clavell. 1983. 21.95 (ISBN 0-440-08721-X). Delacorte.
Shogun: A Novel of Japan. James Clavell. LC 74-77840. (Illus.). 1975. 12.50 (ISBN 0-689-10565-7). Atheneum.
Shogun: A Novel of Japan. James Clavell. 1976. 2.75. Dell.
Shogun's Daughter. Robert Ames Bennet. LC 10-321344. 1910. 1.35. A. C. McClurg & Co.
Shoot. Douglas Fairbairn. LC 72-89946. 168p. 1973. 5.95 o.p. (ISBN 0-385-08540-0). Doubleday.
Shoot! Luigi Pirandello. LC 76-52123. (Garland Classics of Film Literature; 24). 1978. 14.00 (ISBN 0-8240-2889-9). Garland Pub.
Shoot- Out at Sentinel Park. Richard Brister. (Ace double novel books, D-86). 1954. Ace Books.
Shoot: A Novel. Douglas Fairbairn. 1974. (pbk.) 1.50. Dell.
Shoot: A Novel. Douglas Fairbairn. LC 72-89946. 1973. 5.95 (ISBN 0-385-08540-0). Doubleday.
Shoot: A Novel. Elleston Trevor. LC 66-12823. 1966. Doubleday.
Shoot a Sitting Duck. David Alexander. LC 55-106301. 1955. Random House.
Shoot an Arrow to Stop the Wind. Clark Spurlock. LC 73-76968. 1970. 5.95. Dial Press.
Shoot an Arrow to Stop the Wind. Colin Stuart. (O.s.i.). 1969. 6.95 o.s.i. (ISBN 0-8037-7835-X). Dial.
Shoot at the Moon. William F Temple. (Bartell bk., 60239). 1967. Macfadden.
Shoot at the Moon. William F Temple. LC 66-16153. 1966. Simon and Schuster.
Shoot If You Must. Richard Pitts Powell. 1946. Simon and Schuster.
Shoot It. Paul Tynder. LC 68-11526. 1968. 5.75 o.p. (ISBN 0-316-86010-7, Pub. by Atlantic Monthly Pr). Little.
Shoot It Again. Ed Lacy. Orig. Title: Sex Castle. 1969. pap. 0.60 o.p. (63-134). Paperback Lib.
Shoot It Again, Sam. Michael Avallone. 1972. pap. 0.75 o.p. (07203). Curtis.
Shoot McAllister. Matt Chisholm, pseud. 1971. pap. 0.75 o.p. (94060). Beagle Bks.
Shoot Me Dacent. 1st Ed. Aaron Marc Stein. LC 51-10655. 1951. Published for the Crime Club by Doubleday.
Shoot Now or Never. (Bks. in Easy English Ser.: Stage 1). (Orig.). pap. 1.50 (ISBN 0-582-52707-4). Longman.
Shoot Out. Giles A Lutz. LC 77-14638. 1978. 6.95 (ISBN 0-385-13671-4). Doubleday.
Shoot Out. Giles A Lutz. 1979. 1.75 (ISBN 0-671-82821-5). Pocket Books.
Shoot-Out at Milk River. Lee Floren. (Belmont Tower Books). 1977. 1.50 (ISBN 0-505-51185-1). Tower Pubns.
Shoot Out at Sandcastle. Spencer Knight. 1978. pap. 1.25 (ISBN 0-532-12557-6). Woodhill.
Shoot-Out at Sioux Wells. Cliff Farrell. LC 73-75160. 1973. 4.95 (ISBN 0-385-04466-6). Doubleday.
Shoot-Out at Twin Buttes. Edwin Booth. (Berkley medallion book). 1974. (pbk.) 0.95 (ISBN 0-425-02612-4). Berkley Pub. Co.
Shoot! (Si Gira) The Notebooks of Serafino Gubbio, Cinematograph Operator. Luigi Pirandello. LC 74-12380. 1975. H. Fertig.
Shoot! Si Gira) the Notebooks of Serafino Gubbio, Cinematograph Operator. Luigi Pirandello & Scott-Moncrieff, Charles Kenneth, 1889-1930, Tr. LC 27-1243. E. P. Dutton & Company.
Shoot the Moon. Jake Page. LC 79-2031. 8.95 (ISBN 0-672-52608-5). Bobbs-Merrill.
Shoot the Movie Star. Frank Cutler. pap. 1.95 o.s.i. (TC-498, Travellers Comp). Olympia.
Shoot-the Movie Star. Frank Cutter. LC 74-28501. (Traveller's companion series, TC-498). 1971. 1.95. Traveller's Companion.
Shoot the Scene. Ellery Queen, pseud. LC 67-1933. (Dell mystery). 1966. Dell Pub. Co.
Shoot the Works. Richard Ellington. LC 48-5221. (A Morrow mystery). 1948. W. Morrow.
Shoot to Kill. Wade Miller, pseud. LC 51-14820. 1951. Farrar, Straus and Young.
Shoot to Kill: Michael Shayne's 49th Case. Davis Dresser. LC 64-16794. (Torquil book). 1964. Distributed by Dodd, Mead.
Shootin' Fools. Tex Holt, pseud. LC 42-20333. 1942. Gateway Books.
Shootin' Fools. Claude Rister. LC 42-20333. 1942. Gateway Books.
Shootin' Iron. Archie Joscelyn. LC 42-461241. 1942. Phoenix Press.
Shootin' Melody. Edward Beverly Mann. LC 52-9702. (Triple-A western classic). 1952. Jefferson House.
Shootin' Melody. Edward Beverly Mann. LC 38-18123. 1938. W. Morrow & Company.
Shootin' Melody see Trouble for Ben Melody.
Shootin' Sheriff. Nelson Coral Nye. LC 38-38331. Phoenix Press.
Shootin' Sheriff & The Bandit of Bloody Run. Nelson Nye. (Two-in One Western Ser.). 1979. pap. 1.95 (ISBN 0-89083-444-X). Zebra.
Shooting Gallery. Philip Basvic. LC 72-91939. 1973. 4.95 (ISBN 0-8059-1782-9). Dorrance.
Shooting Gallery. Hugh C Rae. LC 70-187153. 1972. 6.95 (ISBN 0-698-10454-4). Coward, McCann & Geoghegan.
Shooting of Dan McGregory: A Novel. Marvin Dana & Service, Robert William. LC 15-16445. Grosset & Dunlap.
Shooting of Dan McGrew. Michael Kenyon. LC 75-7905. (MW suspense). 1975. 5.95 (ISBN 0-679-50553-9). McKay.
Shooting of Dan McGrew. James J Tynan & Service, Robert William, 1876- LC 24-15192. Grosset & Dunlap.
Shooting of Storey James. 1st Ed. John Clifford. LC 62-808165. 1962. Doubleday.
Shooting of the Green. Joe Poyer, pseud. LC 73-9173. 1973. 5.95 (ISBN 0-385-04498-4). Doubleday.
Shooting Party. Anton Pavlovich Chekhov. Tr. by Chamot, Alfred Edward. LC 27-264419. (international library series). 1927. S. Paul & Co., Ltd.
Shooting Party. Isabel Colegate. LC 80-54194. 1981. 11.95 (ISBN 0-670-64064-6). Viking Press.
Shooting Script. Gavin Lyall. LC 66-18187. 4.95. Scribners.
Shooting Star. Lucien Waldo Emerson. LC 46-2396. 1946. Phoenix Press.
Shooting Star. Rodman Philbrick. LC 81-16710. 14.95 (ISBN 0-312-71757-1). St. Martin's Press.
Shooting Star. advance ed. Wallace Earle Stegner. LC 61-7037. 1961. Viking Press.
Shooting Stars: An Astrological Novel. Patricia Welles. LC 71-104946. 1970. 5.95. McCall Pub. Co.
Shooting Valley. Archie Joscelyn. LC 41-139381. Phoenix Press.
Shootist. Glendon Fred Swarthout. LC 74-17772. 1975. 6.95 (ISBN 0-385-06099-8). Doubleday.
Shootist. Glendon Fred Swarthout. LC 75-17915. 1975. 9.95 (ISBN 0-8161-6311-1). G. K. Hall.
Shootout. Jackson Flynn, pseud. (Gunsmoke Ser., No. 2). (O.s.i.). 160p. (Orig.). 1974. pap. 0.95 o.s.i. (AN1284, Award). Univ Pub & Dist.
Shootout at Clearwater. Merle M. Funk. (YA) 1979. 6.95 (Avalon). Bouregy.
Shootout at Las Cruces. Bret Sanders. (Hawk Ser.). (O.s.i.). (Orig.). 1976. pap. 1.25 o.s.i. (AQ1625, Award). Univ Pub & Dist.
Shootout at Shiprock. Lee O. Miller. (Orig.). 1981. pap. 1.75 (ISBN 0-505-51630-6). Tower Bks.
Shop Girl. Charles Norris Williamson & Alice Muriel Livingston Williamson. LC 16-162621. Grosset & Dunlap.
Shop of Dreams: A Tale of Love, Youth and Books. Charles Hanson Towne. LC 39-216574. 1939. D. Appleton-Century Company, Incorporated.
Shop on Main Street. Ladislav Grosman. LC 72-84389. (Illus.). 1970. 3.95. Doubleday.
Shop on Threnody Street. Mary Francis Shura, pseud. LC 71-184926. 1972. 5.95 (ISBN 0-448-02055-6). Grosset & Dunlap.
Shoplifter. Richard H. R Smithies. 1974. (pbk.) 1.25. Manor Books.

Shoplifter. Richard H. R Smithies. LC 68-23528. 1968. Horizon Press.
Shoplifter: Also, The Song of the Swan, and Aunt Ursula's Misfortune. Georges Ohnet. (On cover: The world library, no. 12). 1891. The Waverly Company.
Shoplifter: Also, The Song of the Swan, and Aunt Ursula's Misfortune. Georges Ohnet. (Liberty library, no. 1). 1891. Liberty Book Company.
Shoplifting Game. Tana Reiff. LC 78-75222. (LifeTimes Ser.). 1979. pap. 3.32 (ISBN 0-8224-4319-8). Pitman Learning.
Shops and Houses. Frank Arthur Swinnerton. LC 18-22825. George H. Doran Company.
Shore. St. John, David, pseud. LC 80-14018. 1980. 8.95 (ISBN 0-395-29473-8) (ISBN 0-395-29474-6). Houghton Mifflin.
Shore & the Wave. Aziz Ahmad. (Unesco Asian Fiction Ser). 167p. 1971. 8.75x o.p. (ISBN 0-8448-0026-0). Crane-Russak Co.
Shore Dimly Seen. Robert C Goldston. LC 63-7645. 1963. Random House.
Shore Excursion. Elizabeth Hall Yates. LC 36-30705. The Penn Publishing Company.
Shore Leave. Frederic Wakeman. LC 48-106007. 1948. Triangle Books.
Shore Leave. Frederic Wakeman. LC 44-271838. 1944. Farrar & Rinehart, Inc.
Shore of Two Worlds. Richard Marsh. (Illus.). 1978. pap. 2.75 o.s.i. (ISBN 0-915330-03-2). Mazgeen Pr.
Shorecliff. Marilyn Ross. 1970. pap. 0.60 o.p. (ISBN 0-446-63431-X, 63-431). Paperback Lib.
Shoreless Sea. Mollie Panter-Downes. LC 24-10302. 1924. G. P. Putnam's Sons.
Shoreline Nurse. Jeanne Bowman, pseud. 1971. pap. 0.75 o.p. (T2392). Pyramid Pubns.
Shoreline Nurse. Peggy O'More, pseud. LC 65-8164. 1965. Arcadia House.
Shorelines: A Novel. Roy MacGregor. LC 80-486992. 13.95 (ISBN 0-7710-5459-9). McClelland and Stewart.
Shores of Death. Michael Moorcock. LC 78-60740. 1978. pap. 1.95 o.s.i. (ISBN 0-89559-070-0). Dale Books Inc.
Shores of Greener Pastures: A Novel. 1st Ed. Jennie Ducoeur. LC 54-13411. 1955. Exposition Press.
Shores of Romance. George Fort Gibbs. LC 28-9056. 1928. D. Appleton and Company.
Shores of Space. Richard Matheson. LC 57-5194. (Bantam books, A 1571, 1). 1957. Bantam Books.
Shores of Space. Richard Matheson. 1979. 1.75 (ISBN 0-425-04024-0). Berkley Pub. Corp.
Shores of Tomorrow. Robert Silverberg. LC 76-28486. 1976. 6.95 (ISBN 0-8407-6526-6). T. Nelson.
Shores of Vespucci: Or, Romance Without Fiction. Marshall Shorewood Tufts. LC 8-6881. 1833. M. Tufts.
Shorn! Robert Grant. LC 28-102985. E. P. Dutton & Company.
Shorn Lamb. Hughie Florence Call. LC 69-19562. 1969. 4.95. Houghton Mifflin.
Shorn Lamb. Lucy Agnes Hancock. LC 41-19308. 1941. Macrae-Smith-Company.
Shorn Lamb. William John Locke. LC 30-27068. 1930. Dodd, Mead & Company.
Shorn Lamb. Emma Speed Sampson. LC 22-12019. The Reilly & Lee Co.
Short and Sweet. Harry Neville Gittins. LC 20-7428. 1919. John Lane.
Short As Any Dream. Elizabeth Shepley Sergeant. LC 29-24375. 1929. Harper & Brothers.
Short Bow's Big Medicine. James Willard Schultz. LC 40-5633. 1940. Houghton Mifflin Company.
Short Cases of Inspector Maigret. Georges Simenon. LC 59-9788. 1959. Published for the Crime Club by Doubleday.
Short Circuit. Noelle Loriot. LC 68-19331. 1968. World Pub. Co.
Short Circuit. Laurence Oriol. 1971. pap. 0.75 o.p. (B75-2110). Belmont-Tower.
Short Cruises. William Wymark Jacobs. LC 7-16484. 1907. C. Scribner's Sons.
Short Cut. George Elliot Flint. 1909. The Romance Press.
Short Cut. Herb Greer. LC 65-10806. 1965. bds., 4.95. Roy.
Short Cut. Jackson Gregory. LC 16-210598. 1916. Dodd, Mead and Company.
Short Cut. Translated from the Italian by Stuart Hood. Ennio Flaiano. LC 50-6659. 1950. Pellegrini & Cudahy.
Short Days Ago. Renee Brand. Tr. by Beigel, Margaret H. LC 41-1051. Farrar & Rinehart, Inc.
Short Dirty Life of a Mafia Killer. George Damico. (O.s.i.). (Orig.). 1975. pap. 1.25 o.s.i. (BT50836). Belmont-Tower.
Short End of the Stick. Gene L Coon. 1975. (pbk.) 1.50 (ISBN 0-523-00577-6). Pinnacle Books.
Short End of the Stick, and Other Stories. 1st Ed. Shulman, Irving. LC 59-10690. 1959. Doubleday.
Short Fiction: A Critical Collection. 2d ed. Ed. by James R. Frakes & Isadore Traschen. LC 69-11382. (Prentice-Hall English literature series). 1968. Prentice-Hall.
Short Fiction of Charles W. Chesnutt. Charles Waddell Chesnutt. Ed. by Sylvia Lyons Render. LC 73-88973. 1974. (ISBN 0-88258-012-4). Howard University Press.
Short Fiction of Charles W. Chesnutt. Ed. by Sylvia L. Render. LC 73-88973. 1981. pap. 7.95 (ISBN 0-88258-092-2). Howard U Pr.
Short Fiction of Charles W. Chesnutt. Ed. by Sylvia L. Render. LC 73-88973. 436p. 1974. 15.00 (ISBN 0-88258-012-4). Howard U Pr.
Short Fiction of Edgar Allan Poe. Edgar Allan Poe. Ed. by Stuart Levine & Susan Levine. LC 74-12377. (Library of literature, LL-40). (Illus.). 10.95, 6.95 (pbk.) (ISBN 0-672-51462-1) (ISBN 0-672-51462-1) (ISBN 0-672-61032-9). Bobbs-Merrill.
Short Fiction of Mary Wilkins Freeman & Sarah Orne Jewett. Ed. by Barbara Solomon. (Orig.). 1979. pap. 2.95 (ISBN 0-451-51192-1, CE1192, Sig Classics). NAL.
Short Fiction of Norman Mailer. Norman Mailer. LC 67-5099. 1967. Dell.
Short Fiction of Norman Mailer. Norman Mailer. LC 79-20189. 1980. 18.50. H. Fertig.
Short Fiction of Sarah Orne Jewett and Mary Wilkins Freeman: Including The Country of the Pointed Firs. Sarah Orne Jewett & Mary Eleanor Wilkins Freeman. LC 79-84605. (Signet classic). 2.95 (ISBN 0-451-51192-1). New American Library.
Short Fiction of the Masters. 2d ed. Ed. by Leo Hamalian & Frederick Robert Karl. LC 72-87641. 1973. 4.95 (ISBN 0-399-30023-6). Putnam.
Short Fiction of the Masters. Ed. by Leo Hamalian & Frederick Robert Karl. LC 63-11135. 1963. Putnam.
Short Fiction of the Seventeenth Century. Ed. by Charles C. Mish. (Seventeenth Century Ser). Orig. Title: Anchor Anthology of Short Fiction of the Seventeenth Century. 1968. pap. 2.95x (ISBN 0-393-00437-6, Norton Lib). Norton.
Short Fiction of the Seventeenth Century. Ed. by Charles C. Mish. LC 63-7685. (Stuart Editions). 458p. 1963. 15.00x o.p. (ISBN 0-8147-0313-5). NYU Pr.
Short Fiction: Shape and Substance. Ed. by William Harwood Peden. LC 76-129038. 1971. 4.95 (ISBN 0-395-10876-4). Houghton Mifflin.
Short Fictions. Richard Kostelanetz. LC 74-83297. 1974. Kulchur Foundation.
Short Friday. Isaac Bashevis Singer. 1978. pap. 2.50 (ISBN 0-449-24068-1, Crest). Fawcett.
Short Friday: And Other Stories. Isaac Bashevis Singer. LC 64-23122. 1964. Farrar, Straus and Giroux.
Short Grass. Thomas Wakefield Blackburn. LC 47-12024. (Essandess Western). 1947. Simon and Schuster.
Short Grass. Thomas Wakefield Blackburn. 1973. 0.75. Dell.
Short Grass. George Washington Ogden. LC 27-406106. 1927. Dodd, Mead and Company.
Short Hall. James B. Hall. 155p. 1981. 9.95 (ISBN 0-937050-06-7). Stonehenge.
Short History of Julia. Isa Glenn. LC 30-30572. 1930. A. A. Knopf.
Short-Horn Trail. Charles Stanley Strong. LC 46-3631. 1946. Phoenix Press.
Short Leash. Bertrand Leslie Shurtleff & Thorne, Diana, 1895- Illus. LC 45-34476. 1945. The Bobbs-Merrill Company.
Short Letter, Long Farewell. Peter Handke. LC 73-87695. 1974. 6.95 (ISBN 0-374-26318-3). Farrar, Straus and Giroux.
Short Life. Thomas Benton Allen. LC 77-11979. 8.95 (ISBN 0-399-11966-3). Putnam.
Short Life. Thomas Benton Allen. 1979. 2.25 (ISBN 0-425-03946-3). Berkley Pub. Corp.
Short Life: A Novel. Aharon Megged. LC 80-13001. 10.95 (ISBN 0-8008-7180-4). Taplinger.
Short Line War. Samuel Merwin & Henry Kitchell Webster. LC 99-2055. 1899. The Macmillan Company.
Short Line War: By Merwin-Webster. Samuel Merwin & Henry Kitchell Webster. LC 67-29273. (Americans in fic.). 1967. Gregg Pr.
Short March in Telengana. Michel Larneuil, pseud. LC 79-91601. 1969. 4.95. Morrow.
Short Methodist Stories. Robert Thomas Edwards. LC 9-100257. 1909. Cochrane Publishing Company.
Short Narratives. Ed. by Paul Milton Fulcher. LC 28-166240. The Century Co.
Short Night. Ronald Kirkbride. 1973. (pbk.) 0.95. New American Library.
Short Novel: An Anthology. Ed. by John Owen Beaty. Fitzhugh, Nannie M., Joint Ed. LC 40-952195. Farrar & Rinehart, Inc.
Short Novel Anthology. J. Golden Taylor. 1973. pap. text ed. price not set o.p. (3-55303). HM.
Short Novels. Sidonie Gabrielle Colette. Ed. by Glenway Westcott. 1951. 7.50 o.p. Dial.
Short Novels. Fedor Mikhailovich Dostoevskii. Ed. by T. Mann. 1945. 7.50 o.p. Dial.
Short Novels. Henry James. LC 61-15992. (Great illustrated classics: Titan editions). (Illus.). 1961. Dodd, Mead.
Short Novels. Thomas Wolfe. LC 61-7212. 1961. Scribner.
Short Novels and Other Writings. Theodor Fontane & Peter Demetz. LC 81-17505. (German Library; V. 46). 1982. 14.95 (ISBN 0-8264-0250-X) (ISBN 0-8264-0260-7). Continuum.
Short Novels of Balzac. Honore De Balzac. Tr. by Wormeley, Katharine Prescott. LC 48-5594. (Permanent library series). 1948. Dial Press.
Short Novels of Colette. Sidonie Gabrielle Colette. LC 76-7340. 1976. 14.95 (ISBN 0-8037-8120-2). Dial Press.
Short Novels of Dostoevsky. Fedor Mikhailovich Dostoevskii & Mann, Thomas, 1875- LC 46-555. 1945. Dial Press.
Short Novels of Jack Schaefer. Jack Warner Schaefer. LC 67-19133. 1967. Houghton Mifflin.
Short Novels of John Steinbeck. new ed. John Steinbeck. Bd. with Tortilla Flat; Of Mice & Men; Red Pony; Moon Is Down; Cannery Row; Pearl. 544p. 1963. 16.95 (ISBN 0-670-64138-3). Viking Pr.
Short Novels of the Masters. Ed. by Charles Neider. LC 48-8488. 1948. Rinehart.
Short Novels of Thomas Wolfe. Thomas Wolfe. LC 75-35061. 1962. lib. rep. ed. 17.50 (ISBN 0-684-14554-5, ScribT). Scribner.
Short Novels of Tolstoy. Lev Nikolaevich Tolstoi & Rahv, Philip, Ed. LC 46-7799. 1946. The Dial Press.
Short Novels; Stories of Love, Seduction, and Peasant Life. Lev Nikolaevich Tolstoi. Ed. by Ernest Joseph Simmons. LC 65-12448. (Modern library of the world's best books). Modern Library.
Short Novels: Stories of Love, Seduction, and Peasant Life; V.1. by Leo Tolstoy. Selected, Introd. by Ernest J. Simmons Tr. from Russian by Louise and Aylmer Maude, J. D. Duff. Lev Nikolaevich Tolstoi. Ed. by Ernest Joseph Simmons. LC 65-12448. (Mod. lib. of the world's best bks. 354). 2.45. Random.
Short Novels: Tortilla Flat, The Red Pony, Of Mice and Men, The Moon Is Down, Cannery Row, The Pearl. John Steinbeck. LC 53-9196. 1953. Viking Press.
Short Novels: With an Introd. by Glenway Wescott. Sidonie Gabrielle Colette. LC 51-13864. (Permanent library book). 1951. Dial Press.
Short of Murder. Thomas L Thienes. LC 48-2542. 1948. Phoenix Press.
Short Passages. Caleb Gattegno. 94p. 1968. pap. 2.20 (ISBN 0-87825-027-1). Ed Solutions.
Short Pleasures: A Novel. 1st Ed. Anne Bernays. LC 62-11365. 1962. Doubleday.
Short Rails. Cy Warman. LC 6727. 1900. S. Scribner's Sons.
Short Rations. Williston Fish. LC 99-550. 1899. Harper & Brothers.
Short Reign of Pippin IV: A Fabrication. John Steinbeck. LC 76-55799. 1977. (ISBN 0-14-004290-3). Penguin Books.
Short Reign of Pippin IV: A Fabrication. John Steinbeck. LC 57-7555. (Illus.). 1957. Viking Press.
Short Reign of Pippin IV: A Fabricator. John Steinbeck. 1977. pap. 2.50 o.p. (ISBN 0-14-004290-3). Penguin.
Short Sacred Right of Search & Destruction see Football.
Short Sentimental Journey & Other Stories. Italo Svevo. 1967. 21.50x o.p. (ISBN 0-520-01244-5). U of Cal Pr.
Short-Short Stories. Robert Oberfirst. LC 49-8606. 1949. B. Humphries.
Short Short Stories. Norvin Pallas. (Newbury Hse Readers Ser.: Stage 4 - Intermediate Level). (Illus.). (gr. 7-12). 1981. pap. cancelled o.p. (ISBN 0-88377-198-5). Newbury Hse.
Short Short Stories. Ed. by William Ransom Wood. LC 51-10636. 1951. Harcourt, Brace.
Short Shorts. Frances Dellingner. 2.00 o.p. Carlton.
Short Shorts: An Anthology of the Shortest Stories. Irving Howe & Iliana Wiener Howe. LC 81-85128. 1982. 12.95 (ISBN 0-87923-431-8). D.R. Godine.
Short Shorts for Shut-Ins: Simple Stories of Human Interest. Edna Harrison Baker. LC 41-66884. Brookhaven Press, Kellaway-Ide Company.
Short Shrift. Manning Long. LC 45-6212. 1945. Duell, Sloan and Pearce.
Short Sixes. Henry Cuyler Bunner. LC 68-55665. (American short story series, v. 5). (Illus.). 1968. Garrett Press.
Short Sixes.". Henry Cuyler Bunner. LC 72-8307. (American short story series, v. 5). 1972. (ISBN 0-8422-8014-6). MSS Information Corp.
Short Sixes" Stories to Be Read While the Candle Burns. Henry Cuyler Bunner. LC 4-15418. 1891. Keppler & Schwarzmann.
Short Skirts: A Story of Modern Youth. Rob Eden. LC 30-5171. Grosset & Dunlap.
Short Spanish Stories: Edited with Notes, Exercises, and Vocabulary. Ed. by Michael Angelo De Vitis. (Century modern language series, K. McKenzie, editor). D. Appleton-Century Company, Incorporated.
Short-Stop. Zane Grey. LC 9-18159. 1909. A. C. McClurg & Co.
Short Stories. Conrad Potter Aiken. LC 50-9750. 1950. Duell, Sloan, and Pearce.
Short Stories. Sherwood Anderson. LC 62-15213. (American century series, AC52). 1962. Hill and Wang.
Short Stories. Honore De Balzac. LC 21-9594. (Half-title: The modern library of the world's best books). Boni and Liveright, Inc.
Short Stories, 2 pts. Ed. by James A. Bellamy et al. (Contemporary Arabic Readers Ser.: Vol. IV). 1963. Set. 7.50 (ISBN 0-916798-14-3). Pt. 1, Texts; Xiii, 93p. Pt. 2, Notes & Glossaries; Iv, 274p. Dept NE Stud.
Short Stories. series 2 ed. Mary Josephine Brown. LC 3633. (The Catholic library, v. 40, 50, 60). 1900. C. Wildermann.
Short Stories. John Cullen Cameron. LC 77-361851. 1976. 1.25. Cameron.
Short Stories. Anton Pavlovich Chekhov. Tr. by Garnett, Constance (Black) Albright, Evelyn May. LC 28-218276. (modern readers' series). 1928. The Macmillan Company.
Short Stories. Rafaela Contreras de Dario. LC 65-21263. (Hispanic-American Studies Ser: No. 20). (Orig., Span.). 1965. pap. 2.00 (ISBN 0-87024-040-4). U of Miami Pr.
Short Stories. Alexandre Dumas. LC 72-5898. (Short story index reprint series). (Illus.). 1972. (ISBN 0-8369-4212-4). Books for Libraries Press.
Short Stories. Alexandre Dumas. LC 28-4071. Walter J. Black Co.
Short Stories. Ed. by Harold Thomas Eaton. LC 51-4138. 1951. American Book Co.
Short Stories. Ed. by Harold Thomas Eaton. LC 46-3083. 1945. American Book Company.
Short Stories. Maurice Francis Egan. LC 3663. (Catholic library, v. 35, 45, 55). C. Wildermann.
Short Stories. James Thomas Farrell. LC 51-2998. 1951. Vanguard Press.
Short Stories. James Thomas Farrell. 1962. Grosset & Dunlap.
Short Stories. Theophile Gautier. LC 73-122710. (Short story index reprint series). (Illus.). 1970. Books for Libraries Press.
Short Stories. Ed. by Constance Cary Harrison. LC 71-94731. (Short story index reprint series). 1969. Books for Libraries Press.
Short Stories. Ed. by Constance Cary Harrison. Stoddard, Elizabeth Drew (Barstow) 1823-1902 et al. LC 7-3039. (Half-title: The Distaff series). 1893. Harper & Brothers.
Short Stories. Nathaniel Hawthorne. Ed. by Newton Arvin (ISBN 0-394-75015-2, Vin). pap. 1.95 o.p. (ISBN 0-394-70015-5, V15). Random.
Short Stories. Henry James. 4.95 o.p. (G11); PLB 3.89 o.p. Modern Lib.
Short Stories. Rudyard Kipling. LC 72-181273. (Penguin modern classics). 1971. per vol. 0.35 (ISBN 0-14-003281-9) (ISBN 0-14-003282-7). Penguin.
Short Stories. A. M. Klein. Ed. by M. W. Steinberg. (Collected Works of A. M. Klein). 344p. 1983. 35.00x (ISBN 0-8020-5598-2); pap. 14.50 (ISBN 0-8020-6469-8). U of Toronto Pr.
Short Stories. Jack London. LC 68-12806. (Funk & Wagnalls paperbook, F30). Funk & Wagnalls.
Short Stories. Guy De Maupassant. Tr. by Marjorie Laurie. LC 37-31206. (Half-title: Everyman's library, ed. by Ernest Rhys. Fiction. no. 907). 1934. J. M. Dent & Sons, Ltd.
Short Stories. Guy De Maupassant. LC 37-16368. (Immortal masterpieces of literature. vol. xi). The Spencer Press.
Short Stories. Guy de Maupassant. Tr. by Marjorie Laurie. 1979. 8.95x (ISBN 0-460-00907-9, Evman); pap. 4.50x (ISBN 0-460-01907-4, Evman). Biblio Dist.
Short Stories. Guy de Maupassant. Tr. by Marjorie Laurie. 3.25x o.p. (E907, Evman). Dutton.
Short Stories. rev. facsimile ed. George Meredith. LC 73-144162. (Short Story Index Reprint Ser.). Repr. of 1898 ed. 18.00 (ISBN 0-8369-3777-5). Ayer Co.
Short Stories. Ursula Rose Moloney. LC 37-6577. 1935. Printed by Dunne Printing Co.
Short Stories. Ed. by Leonard Bowdoin Moulton. LC 15-12989. (Riverside literature series). Houghton Mifflin Company.
Short Stories. Elin Pelin. (International Studies & Translations Program Ser.). 6.50 o.p. (ISBN 0-8057-5033-9, Twayne). G K Hall.

Short Stories. Elin Pelin. (International Studies & Translations Ser.). lib. bdg. 6.50 o.p. (ISBN 0-8057-5033-9). Twayne.

Short Stories. Luigi Pirandello. Tr. by Frederick May. LC 65-2087. (Oxford library of Italian classics). 1965. Oxford University Press.

Short Stories. Edgar Allan Poe. Ed. by Glenn Munson. (Reading Shelf 1). (gr. 3-5). 1968. pap. 2.12 o.p. (ISBN 0-07-044047-6). McGraw.

Short Stories. L. W Reilly. LC 3750. (At head of special t.-p.: The Catholic library. v. 36, 46, 56). 1900. C. Wildermann.

Short Stories. Mary Anne Madden Sadlier. (Cathloic library, v. 32, 42, 52). 1900. C. Wildermann.

Short Stories. Saki. 1951. 3.95 o.p. (ISBN 0-394-60280-3, M280). Modern Lib.

Short Stories. Ed. by Harry Christian Schweikert. LC 25-6200. Harcourt, Brace and Company.

Short Stories. enl. ed. Ed. by Harry Christian Schweikert. LC 34-2345. 1934. Harcourt, Brace and Company.

Short Stories. Walter Scott. LC 34-27181. (Half-title: The world's classics, 414). 1934. H. Milford, Oxford University Press.

Short Stories. Irwin Shaw. LC 66-8416. 1966. Random House.

Short Stories. series ii. ed. Emma C Street. 1900. C. Wildermann.

Short Stories. James Howell Street. LC 45-5601. 1945. Dial Press.

Short Stories. Lev Nikolaevich Tolstoi. LC 60-10816. (Bantam Classic, NC75). 1960. Bantam Books.

Short Stories. Lev Nikolaevich Tolstoi. Ed. by Ernest Joseph Simmons. LC 64-11997. (Modern library of the world's best books ML346, 361). (Illus.). 1964-65. Random House.

Short Stories. Mark Van Doren. LC 51-12228. 1950. Abelard Press.

Short Stories. John O. Virtanen. Ed. by Barbara B. Ellis. 1978. write for info. o.p. Continent Pub.

Short Stories. T. Yovkov. 1965. 3.50x o.p. (B88). Vanous.

Short Stories. Yordan Yovkov. (International Studies & Translations Ser.). lib. bdg. 6.00 o.p. (ISBN 0-8057-5037-1). Twayne.

Short Stories, Vol. 1. Lev Nikolaevich Tolstoi. 2.95 o.p. (346, 361). Modern Lib.

Short Stories: A Collection for High School Students, Ed.by Henry I. Christ and Jerome Shostak. Ed. by Henry Irving Christ & Shostak, Jerome. 1948. Oxford Book Co.

Short Stories: A Collection of Types of the Short Story. Ed. by William Thomson Hastings. Clough, Benjamin Crocker, Joint Ed & Mason, Kenneth Oliver, Joint Ed. LC 29-67952. Houghton Mifflin Company.

Short Stories: A Collection of Types of the Short Story. rev. ed. Ed. by William Thomson Hastings. Clough, Benjamin Crocker, Joint Ed. LC 39-13546. Houghton Mifflin Company.

Short Stories: A Critical Anthology. Ensaf Thune & Ruth Prigozy. Ed. by D. Anthony English. 544p. 1973. pap. text ed. 12.95x (ISBN 0-02-420790-X). Macmillan.

Short Stories: a Critical Anthology. Ed. by Ensaf Thune. LC 72-80182. 1973. 4.95. Macmillan.

Short Stories: An Anthology for Secondary Schools. E. H. Sauer & H. M. Jones. (O.s.i.). (gr. 11-12). 1963. text ed. 4.68 o.s.i. (ISBN 0-03-003550-3, HoltC); tchrs' manual. 1.00 o.s.i. (ISBN 0-03-042310-4). HR&W.

Short Stories and Adventures. LC 41-20410. 1934. Jarman's Incorporated.

Short Stories and Reminiscences of the Last Fifty Years. Daniel Mallory. LC 5-3850. 1842. D. Mallory.

Short Stories and Selections: For Use in the Secondary Schools, Comp. and Annotated, with Questions for Study. Ed. by Emilie Kip Baker. LC 16-24322. (On verso of half-title: Macmillan's pocket American and English classics). 1916. The Macmillan Company.

Short Stories & Tall Tales. Walter Evans. 1980. 4.50 o.p. (ISBN 0-8062-1334-5). Carlton.

Short Stories As You Like Them. Ed. by William Ransom Wood. Husband, John Dillon, 1909- Joint Ed. LC 40-6328. Harcourt, Brace and Company.

Short Stories by Akutagawa. Ryunosuka Akutagawa. Tr. by Glenn W. Shaw. 1930. pap. 5.50 o.p. (ISBN 0-89346-040-0, Pub. by Hokuseido Pr). Heian Intl.

Short Stories: By Leo Tostoy; V.2. Selected, Introd. by Ernest J. Simmons. Lev Nikolaevich Tolstoi. (Mod. lib. of the world's best bks. ML 361). 2.45. Random.

Short Stories by Luigi Pirandello. Luigi Pirandello. (O.s.i.). 1960. pap. 1.95 o.s.i. (ISBN 0-671-65651-1, Touchstone Bks). S&S.

Short Stories by Modern Writers. R. W. Jepson. 1952. 10.00. Havertown Bks.

Short Stories by Present-Day Authors. Ed. by Raymond Woodbury Pence. LC 23-1839. 1922. The Macmillan Company.

Short Stories by Pushkin, Lermontov & Dostoevsky. Ed. by Helene Scriabine. (Orig., Rus.). pap. text ed. 4.00x o.p. (ISBN 0-06-045860-7, HarpC). Har-Row.

Short Stories by Sir Walter Scott. Walter Scott. LC 71-145286. 1971. Repr. of 1934 ed. 32.00 (ISBN 0-403-01200-7). Scholarly.

Short Stories by Tony Stokes. Tony Stokes. (Illus.). 1973. 1.50 o.p. (ISBN 0-87976-206-3). Amuru Pr.

Short Stories: Classic, Modern, Contemporary. Ed. by Marcus Klein. LC 67-17093. 1967. Little, Brown.

Short Stories: Edited and with an Introd. by Newton Arvin. Nathaniel Hawthorne. Ed. by Newton Arvin. LC 55-14436. (Vintage book, K-15). 1955. Vintage Books.

Short Stories: Edited and with an Introd. by Newton Arvin. 1st Borzoi Ed. Nathaniel Hawthorne. Ed. by Newton Arvin. LC 46-3911. 1946. Knopf.

Short Stories. Edited with an Introd. by Maxwell Geismar. Jack London. LC 60-141432. (American century series, AC33). 1960. Hill and Wang.

Short Stories: Five Decades. Irwin Shaw. 1983. pap. 6.95 (LE). Dell.

Short Stories for Class Reading. Ed. by Ralph Philip Boas. Hahn, Barbara M., Joint Ed. LC 25-20975. H. Holt and Company.

Short Stories for College Classes: Selected by Teachers of Narration in the Department of English, Hunter College of the City of New York. Ed. by Blanche Colton Williams. LC 29-93703. 1929. D. Appleton and Company.

Short Stories for English Classes. Ed. by Lewis Worthington Smith. LC 28-25026. J. B. Lippincott Company.

Short Stories for English Courses. rev. ed. Ed. by Rosa M. Mikels & Helen T. Munn. (gr. 10-12). 1963. text ed. 3.00 o.p. (ISBN 0-684-51536-9). Scribner.

Short Stories for English Courses: Edited with Introduction and Notes. Ed. by Rosa Mary Redding Mikels. LC 20-3193. C. Scribner's Sons.

Short Stories for English Courses... Edited with Introduction and Notes. Ed. by Rosa Mary Redding Mikels. LC 26-11037. C. Scribner's Sons.

Short Stories for English Courses: Edited with Introduction and Notes. Ed. by Rosa Mary Redding Mikels. LC 35-5463. C. Scribner's Sons.

Short Stories for High Schools: Ed., with Introduction and Biographies. Ed. by Nellie Octavia Plee. Miller, Edwin Lillie, 1868- Joint Ed. LC 16-23360. (On cover: Atlas series). Lyons & Carnahan.

Short Stories for High Schools: Edited with Introduction and Notes. Ed. by Rosa Mary Redding Mikels. LC 15-209139. C. Scribner's Sons.

Short Stories for Insigh. Ed. by Teresa Ferster. Glazier. LC 67-168237. 1967. pap., 3.25. Harcourt.

Short Stories for Spare Moments. Lippincott's Magazine. LC 8-25969. 1869-70. J. B. Lippincott and Co.

Short Stories for Study: An Anthology. Ed. by Raymond Wright Short. Sewall, Richard Benson, Joint Ed. LC 41-622986. H. Holt and Company.

Short Stories for Study: An Anthology. rev. ed. Ed. by Raymond Wright Short & Sewall, Richard Benson. LC 50-6799. 1950. Holt.

Short Stories for Study: An Anthology, by Raymond W. Short and Richard B. Sewall. 3d Ed. Ed. by Raymond Wright Short & Richard Benson Sewall. LC 56-6069. Holt.

Short Stories for Study and Enjoyment. Ed. by Harold Thomas Eaton. LC 29-134725. 1929. Doubleday, Doran & Company, Inc.

Short Stories for Study and Enjoyment. Ed. by Harold Thomas Eaton. LC 34-2902. Doubleday, Doran & Company, Inc.

Short Stories for Young & Old. G. Polizoides. (Greek.). 1977. pap. text ed. 2.00. Divry.

Short Stories from Around the World. Ed. by Lee A. Jacobus. LC 76-11728. (McKay English and humanities series). 2.95 (ISBN 0-679-30300-6). McKay.

Short Stories from Around the World: McKay English & Humanities Ser. Ed. by Lee A. Jacobus. LC 76-11728. 1976. pap. text ed. 2.95 o.p. (ISBN 0-679-30300-6, 2212250). McKay.

Short Stories from His Novels. James Fenimore Cooper. Ed. by Sidney Walter Finkelstein. LC 79-18760. (New World paperbacks, NW-S-11). 1970. 1.50. International Publishers.

Short Stories from Life: The 81 Prize Stories in "Life's" Shortest Story Contest. Life & Masson, Thomas Lansing. LC 16-17415. 1916. 1.25. Doubleday, Page & Company.

Short Stories from Southern Africa. Ed. by Alfred Gifford Hooper. LC 66-887. 1963. Oxford University Press.

Short Stories from Southern Africa. 5th imp. ed. Ed. by Alfred Gifford Hooper. LC 72-184073. 1970. 1.05. Oxford University Press.

Short Stories from the Balkans. Edna Worthley Underwood. LC 75-122590. 1970. AMS Press.

Short Stories from the Balkans: Tr. into English. Edna Worthley Underwood. LC 19-15082. 1919. Marshall Jones Company.

Short Stories from the Literary Magazines. Ed. by Jarvis A. Thurston. LC 79-99137. (Illus.). 1970. Scott, Foresman.

Short Stories from the New Yorker. The, New Yorker Magazine. (O.s.i.). 1940. pap. 5.00 o.s.i. (68927). S&S.

Short Stories from the New Yorker. The New Yorker. LC 40-27816. 1940. Simon and Schuster.

Short Stories from the Old North State. Ed. by Richard Gaither Walser. LC 59-9609. 1959. University of North Carolina Press.

Short Stories from Vanity Fair, 1926-1927: With a Foreword. Vanity Fair & Crowninshield, Frank, Ed. LC 28-299622. H. Liveright.

Short Stories in Context: Edited by Woodburn O. Ross and A. Dayle Wallace. Ed. by Woodburn O Ross & Alva Dayle Wallace. LC 53-845. 1953. American Book Co.

Short Stories in Parallel. Ed. by William F Bauer & Bowden, William Paul. LC 42-16497. 1942. D. C. Heath and Company.

Short Stories in Spanish. Cuentos Hispanicos. Ed. by Jean Franco. LC 67-81816. (Penguin parallel texts, 2500). 1966. Penguin.

Short Stories International. Ed. by Edward Warren Johnson. LC 75-2788. 1969. 2.95. Houghton Mifflin.

Short Stories. Introd. by Louis B. Salomon. Nathaniel Hawthorne. Ed. by Louis Bernard Salomen. LC 63-7411. (Great illustrated classics). 1962. Dodd, Mead.

Short Stories of America. Ed. by Robert Lee Ramsay. LC 22-1451. Houghton Mifflin Company.

Short Stories of Anton Chekhov. Anton Pavlovich Chekhov. LC 73-168277. (Illus.). 1973. Printed for the Members of the Limited Editions Club by the Cardavon Press.

Short Stories of Australia: The Moderns, Chosen with an Introd. by Beatrice Davis. Ed. by Beatrice Davis. LC 68-738721. 1967. 6.00. Angus & Robertson.

Short Stories of Charles Dickens. Charles Dickens. Limited Editions Club, Inc., New York. LC 75-28397. (Illus.). 1971. Printed for the Members of the Limited Editions Club.

Short Stories of Conrad Aiken. Conrad Potter Aiken. LC 72-178434. (Short story index reprint series). 1971. (ISBN 0-8369-4034-2). Books for Libraries Press.

Short Stories of De Maupassant. Guy de Maupassant. Repr. of 1941 ed. 35.00 (ISBN 0-89987-097-X). Darby Bks.

Short Stories of Dostoevsky. Fedor Mikhailovich Dostoevskii. Ed. by William Phillips. (O.s.i.). 614p. 1964. 7.50 o.s.i. (ISBN 0-8037-7857-0). Dial.

Short Stories of Dostoevsky. Fedor Mikhailovich Dostoevskii & Phillips, William, 1907- Ed. LC 46-8667. (Permanent library books). 1946. The Dial Press.

Short Stories of Edith Wharton, 1910-1937. Edith Newbold Jones Wharton. 1975. lib. rep. ed. 30.00x (ISBN 0-684-14420-4, ScribT). Scribner.

Short Stories of Ernest Hemingway. Ernest Hemingway. 1938. lib. rep. ed. 25.00x (ISBN 0-684-15155-3, ScribT); pap. 7.95 (ISBN 0-684-71806-5, SL141, ScribT). Scribner.

Short Stories of Ernest Hemingway: The First Forty-Nine Stories and the Play The Fifth Column. Ernest Hemingway. LC 42-36273. (Half-title: The Modern library of the world's best books). 1942. The Modern Library.

Short Stories of Five Decades. Irwin Shaw. (O.s.i.). 1978. 16.95 o.s.i. (ISBN 0-440-04147-3). Delacorte.

Short Stories of Frank Harris: A Selection. Frank Harris. LC 75-6883. 1975. (ISBN 0-8093-0721-9). Southern Illinois University Press.

Short Stories of Grace Livingston Hill. Grace Livingston Hill. LC 76-430. 1976. 6.95 (ISBN 0-89190-101-9). American Reprint Co.

Short Stories of Guy De Maupassant. Guy De Maupassant. Tr. by Michael Monahan. LC 39-17500. (Half-title: The modern library of the world's best books). The Modern Library.

Short Stories of Guy De Maupassant. Guy De Maupassant. Tr. by Michael Monahan. LC 32-17679. (Half-title: The modern library of the world's best books). 1932. The Modern Library.

Short Stories of H. G. Wells. Herbert George Wells. LC 30-13106. 1929. Doubleday, Doran & Company, Inc.

Short Stories of Henry James. Henry James & Fadiman, Clifton, 1904- Ed. LC 45-9328. 1945. Random House.

Short Stories of Henry James: Selected and Ed. Henry James & Fadiman, Clifton, 1904- Ed. LC 48-9351. (Modern library of the world's best books.Modern library giants.). 1948. Modern Library.

Short Stories of James T. Farrell. James Thomas Farrell. LC 37-37585. The Vanguard Press.

Short Stories of John Galsworthy. Jan Hendrik Smit. LC 68-877. 1966. Haskell House.

Short Stories of Katherine Mansfield. Katherine Mansfield. LC 82-21012. 1983. 9.95 (ISBN 0-88001-025-8). Ecco Press.

Short Stories of Katherine Mansfield. Ed. by John Middleton Murry. Murry, John Middleton, 1889- LC 37-21144. 1937. A. A. Knopf.

Short Stories of Latin America. Arturo Torres-Rioseco. (gr. 10 up). 1963. pap. 2.50 o.p. Las Americas.

Short Stories of Latin America. Ed. by Torres Rioseco, Arturo. LC 63-3493. 1963. Las Americas Pub. Co.

Short Stories of Love and Pathos. Evalyn Knickerbocker. LC 31-15688. The Chat Publishing Company, Inc.

Short Stories of Mark Twain. Samuel Langhorne Clemens. (Classics ser., CL171). 1968. Airmont.

Short Stories of Mark Twain. Samuel Langhorne Clemens. LC 67-282118. (Funk & Wagnalls paperbk. F18). 1967. pap., 1.50. Funk & Wagnalls.

Short Stories of Mark Twain. Samuel Langhorne Clemens. LC 67-28211. (Funk & Wagnalls paperbook F18). 1967. Funk & Wagnalls.

Short Stories of Mark Twain. Mark Twain. 1967. pap. 1.50 o.p. (ISBN 0-308-90018-9, F18, Paperbooks). Funk & W.

Short Stories of O. Henry. William Sydney Porter. LC 64-15725. 1966. Parents' Magazine Press.

Short Stories of Oscar Wilde. Oscar Wilde & Robert Gorham Davis. LC 77-6758. (Illus.). 1968. Printed at the Lane Press for the Members of the Limited Editions Club.

Short Stories of Padriac Pearse. Ed. by Desmond Malguire. 117p. (Dual language Irish & Eng.). 1968. pap. 4.75 (ISBN 0-85342-117-X). Irish Bk Ctr.

Short Stories of Robert Louis Stevenson. Robert Louis Stevenson. LC 23-15584. 1923. C. Scribner's Sons.

Short Stories of Russia Today. Translated by Tatiana Shebunina. 1st American Ed. Ed. by Yvonne Mayer Kapp. LC 58-9066. 1959. Houghton Mifflin.

Short Stories of Saki. Saki. 1930. 3.50 o.p. (ISBN 0-670-64204-5). Viking Pr.

Short Stories of Saki (H. H. Munro) Complete. Hector Hugh Munro & Munro, Ethel M. LC 30-27685. 1930. The Viking Press.

Short Stories of Tall Tales. Phil Di Pietro. 1979. 8.95 o.p. (ISBN 0-533-04164-3). Vantage.

Short Stories of the New America: Interpreting the America of This Age to High School Boys and Girls. Ed. by Mary Augusta Laselle. LC 19-5853. 1919. H. Holt and Company.

Short Stories of the Nineteenth Century. J. G. Fyfe. Repr. lib. bdg. 10.00 o.p. Folcroft.

Short Stories of the 'nineties: A Biographical Anthology. Ed. by Derek Stanford. LC 69-12324. (Illus.). 1969. 6.95. Roy Publishers.

Short Stories of the Sea. J. G. Fyfe. Repr. of 1935 ed. 10.00 o.p. Folcroft.

Short Stories of the Western World. Ed. by Current-Garcia, Eugene. LC 69-11519. (Key editions). 1969. Scott, Foresman.

Short Stories of the Western World. Walton R. Patrick & Eugene Current-Garcia. 1969. pap. 7.95x o.p. (ISBN 0-673-05678-3). Scott F.

Short Stories of Today. Ed. by Charles Lane Hanson. Gross, William J., Joint Ed. LC 28-6079. (Standard English classics). Ginn and Company.

Short Stories of Today. Ed. by Raymond Woodbury Pence. LC 34-2900. 1934. The Macmillan Company.

Short Stories of Today & Yesterday. Gerald Bullett. 1929. 10.00. Havertown Bks.

Short Stories of Various Types. Ed. by Laura F Freck. LC 20-231776. (Merrill's English texts). Charles E. Merrill Company.

Short Stories of Vietnam. Robert L. Henschel, Jr. LC 81-85593. 154p. (Orig.). 1982. pap. 3.95 (ISBN 0-941064-00-X). Guthrie Pub.

Short Stories of Wilkie Collins. Wilkie Collins. pap. 2.95 o.p. (ISBN 0-498-04015-1, Prpta). A S Barnes.

Short Stories of Yashpal: Author & Patriot. Tr. by Corinne Friend. LC 78-87939. 1970. 6.95 o.p. (ISBN 0-8122-7601-9). U of Pa Pr.

Short Stories of Yesterday. F. H. Pritchard. Repr. of 1929 ed. 8.50 (ISBN 0-8414-9274-3). Folcroft.

Short Stories of Youth. B. Kowiatek. 1978. 2.00 (ISBN 0-89502-022-X). FEB.

Short Stories: Old and New. Ed. by Charles Alphonso Smith. LC 16-24539. (Standard English classics). Ginn and Company.

Short Stories Out of Soviet Russia. Ed. by John Cournos. LC 29-23877. E. P. Dutton & Co., Inc.

Short Stories, Scraps and Shavings. George Bernard Shaw & Farleigh, John Illus. LC 34-12700. 1934. Dodd, Mead & Company.

Short Stories Selected: By J. I. Rodale With Wood Engravings by Fritz Eichenberg. Wilkie Collins. LC 50-11398. 1950. Story Classics.

Short Stories. Series 2. Bonaventure Hammer. (Catholic library, v. 31, 41, 51). 1900. C. Wildermann.

Short Stories: The Tale of Chloe--The House on the Beach--Farina--The Case of General Ople and Lady Camper. rev. ed. George Meredith. LC 1-19366. 1898. C. Scribner's Sons.

Short Stories: The Tale of Chloe; The House on the Beach; Farina; The Case of General Ople and Lady Camper. rev. ed. George Meredith. LC 73-144162. (Short story index reprint series). 1971. (ISBN 0-8369-3777-5). Books for Libraries Press.

Short Stories: Tr. by Marguerite Alexieva. Pelin Elin. LC 65-64887. 1965. bds., 3.75. Foreign Langs. Pr.

Short Stories. Tr. from Bulgarian by Marco Mincoff, Marguerite Alexieva. Ed.: Mercia MacDermott. Iordan Iovkov. LC 66-2259. 1965. bds., 2.50. Foreign Langs. Pr.

Short Stories. Tr. from French by Marjorie Laurie. Introd. by Gerald Gould. Guy De Maupassant. Tr. by Marjorie Laurie. (Everyman paperback, 1907). 1962. pap., 1.55. Dent.

Short Stories: Tradition and Direction. Ed. by William Merritt Sale. LC 49-48224. 1949. New Directions.

Short Stories. Translated from the Italian by Lily Duplaix. Introd. by Frances Keene. Luigi Pirandello. 1960. pap., 1.75. Simon and Schuster.

Short Stories. Translated from the Italian by Lily Duplaix. Introd. by Frances Keene. Luigi Pirandello. LC 58-137560. 1959. Simon and Schuster.

Short-Story. Ed. by William Patterson Atkinson. LC 16-20255. (On cover: Academy classics). Allyn and Bacon.

Short Story: A Thematic Anthology, Ed. by Dorothy Parker, Frederick B. Shroyer. Ed. by Dorothy Rothschild Parker & Frederick B. Shroyer. LC 65-14771. pap., 3.95. Scribners.

Short Story: an Inductive Approach. Gerald Henry Levin. LC 67-14187. 1967. Harcourt, Brace & World.

Short Story: An Introduction. Wilfred Healey Stone & Nancy Huddleston Packer. 1976. McGraw-Hill.

Short Story: An Introduction. 2nd ed. Wilfred Healey Stone & Nancy Huddleston Packer. LC 82-8925. (est.) 12.50 (ISBN 0-07-061693-0). McGraw-Hill.

Short Story: An Introductory Anthology. 2d ed. Ed. by Robert A. Rees. LC 74-15171. 1975. 6.95 (ISBN 0-316-73704-6). Little, Brown.

Short Story: An Introductory Anthology. Ed. by Robert A. Rees. LC 69-15951. 1969. Little, Brown.

Short Story and the Reader. Ed. by Robert Stanton. LC 60-7975. 1960. Holt.

Short Story: By James B. Hall and Joseph Langland. Ed. by James B Hall & Joseph Langland. LC 56-2729. 1956. Macmillan.

Short Story: By Willoughby Johnson, William C. Hamlin. Willoughby H Johnson & William C. Hamlin. LC 66-163808. pap., 3.40. Amer. Bk.

Short Story Case Book. Ed. by Edward Joseph Harrington O'Brien. LC 35-8977. Farrar & Rinehart, Incorporated.

Short Story: Classic & Contemporary, Ed. by R. W. Lid. Ed. by Richard Wald Lid. LC 66-19069. (Lippincott coll. Eng. ser.). 1966. 3.95. Lippincott.

Short Story Classics (American)... Ed. by William Patten. LC 6-35. P. F. Collier & Son.

Short Story Classics (Foreign)... Ed. by William Patten. LC 7-34777. P. F. Collier & Son.

Short Story: Fiction in Transition. 2nd ed. Ed. by J. Chesley Taylor. LC 69-14264. (Orig.). 1973. text ed. 8.95x o.p. (ISBN 0-684-13046-7, ScribC). Scribner.

Short Story: Fiction in Transition. 2d ed. Ed. by John Chesley Taylor. LC 72-2216. (Illus.). 1973. 4.95 (ISBN 0-684-13046-7). Scribner.

Short Story: Fiction in Transition. Ed. by John Chesley Taylor. LC 69-14264. 1969. Scribner.

Short Story: Fifty Masterpieces. Ed. by Ellen C. Wynn. LC 82-60462. 650p. 1983. pap. text ed. 7.95. St Martin.

Short Story Hits... An Intrepretative Anthology. Uzzell, Thomas H., Ed. LC 33-110769. Harcourt, Brace and Company.

Short Story: Ideas and Backgrounds. Ed. by Louis E Glorfeld. Broadus, Robert N., Joint Ed & Kakonis, Tom E., Joint Ed. LC 67-143766. 1967. C. E. Merrill Books.

Short-Story Masterpieces. Ed. by Joseph Berg Esenwein. LC 79-179299. (Short story index reprint series). (ISBN 0-8369-4038-5). Books for Libraries Press.

Short Story Masterpieces. Ed. by Robert P. Warren & Albert Erskine. pap. 3.50 (ISBN 0-440-37864-8, LE). Dell.

Short-Story Masterpieces:... Done into English and with Introductions. Ed. by Joseph Berg Esenwein. LC 13-663. The Home Correspondence School.

Short Story Masterpieces: Edited by Robert Penn Warren and Albert Erskine. Ed. by Robert Penn Warren & Albert Eskine. LC 54-7350. (Dell first edition, F16). 1954. Dell Books.

Short-Story Masterpieces: Vol. 3, Russian. facsimile ed. Compiled by Joseph B. Esenwein. Tr. by John Cournos from Rus. LC 79-179299. (Short Story Index Reprint Ser.). Repr. of 1913 ed. 12.50 (ISBN 0-8369-4038-5). Ayer Co.

Short Story Parade. Ed. by Mabel Holman. LC 40-6327. 1940. Harcourt, Brace and Company.

Short Story Reader. 3d ed. Ed. by Saundra Gould Berkley & Rodney A. Kimball. LC 72-12378. (Odyssey texts in types of literature). 1973. 4.40. Odyssey Press.

Short Story Reader. Ed. by Rodney A. Kimball. LC 46-2889. 1946. The Odyssey Press.

Short Story Three. Burton Raffel et al. (Orig.). pap. 2.45 o.p. Scribner.

Short Story: Twenty-Five Masterpieces. Ed. by Ellen C. Wynn. 448p. 1980. 10.95 (ISBN 0-312-72217-6). St Martin.

Short Story Writer's Handbook. Hallie Southgate Burnett. LC 82-48111. 9.95 (ISBN 0-06-015094-7). Harper & Row.

Short-Story Writing. Ed. by Grenville Kleiser. LC 29-12484. (Practical English series). Funk & Wagnallls Company.

Short Story. 1- LC 58-12310. Scribner.

Short Story, 25 Materpieces. Ed. by Ellen C. Wynn. LC 78-71722. 3.95 (ISBN 0-312-72218-4). St. Martin's Press.

Short Story's Mutations from Petronius to Paul Morand, by Frances Newman. Frances Newman. LC 25-2971. 1924. B. W. Heubsch, Inc.

Short Story's Mutations from Petronius to Paul Morand: By Frances Newman. Frances Newman. LC 25-6518. 1925. B. W. Huebsch, Inc.

Short Studies on Great Subjects. James Anthony Froude. 1964. Repr. of 1906 ed. 8.95x (ISBN 0-460-00013-6, Evman). Biblio Dist.

Short Studies on Great Subjects, 3 vols. James Anthony Froude. 1878. Set. 50.00 (ISBN 0-8274-3889-3). R West.

Short Takes. Michael Meltsner. LC 79-4778. 8.95 (ISBN 0-394-50606-5). Random House.

Short Takes: Readers' Choice of the Best Columns of America's Favorite Newspaperman, Damon Runyon. Damon Runyon. LC 46-3770. 1946. Whittlesey House, McGraw-Hill Book Company.

Short Talks to Young Toilers. Frederic Charles O'Neill. LC 6-3000. 1905. Christian Press Association Publishing Company.

Short Term. Arthur F Gliddings. LC 48-5710. 1948. Duell, Sloan and Pearce.

Short Term. 1st Ed. Jay Richard Kennedy. LC 59-11536. 1959. World Pub. Co.

Short Throat, the Tender Mouth. Doris Grumbach. LC 64-19304. 1964. Doubleday.

Short Time to Live. Mervyn Jones. LC 80-21891. 1981. 12.95 (ISBN 0-312-72221-4). St. Martin's Press.

Short-Timers. Gustav Hasford. LC 78-4742. 8.95 (ISBN 0-06-011782-6). Harper & Row.

Short Turns. Barry Benefield. LC 26-149224. 2.00. The Century Co.

Short Wait Between Trains: And Other Stories. Robert McLaughlin. LC 45-8406. 1945. A. A. Knopf.

Short Walk. Alice Childress. LC 79-14262. 9.95 (ISBN 0-698-10844-2). Coward, McCann & Geoghegan.

Short Walk. Alice Childress. (Bard book). 1981. 3.50 (ISBN 0-380-54239-0). Avon Books.

Short War, Short Lives. Zygmunt Frankel. LC 76-141560. 1971. (u.s.) 5.95 (ISBN 0-200-71777-4). Abelard-Schuman.

Short Weeks of Summer. Elisabeth Hargreave. 1981. 18.95x (Pub. by Remploy England). State Mutual Bk.

Short Year. Barbra Ward. LC 67-23137. 1967. Putnam.

Shortcut to Devil's Claw. William Oliver Turner. (Berkley Medallion Book). 1977. 1.25. Berkley Pub. Corp.

Shorter Finnegans Wake. James Augustine Aloysius Joyce. Ed. by John Anthony Burgess Wilson. LC 67-11267. 1967. Viking Press.

Shorter Finnegans Wake. Ed. by Anthony Burgess. James Augustine Aloysius Joyce. Ed. by John Anthony Burgess Wilson. LC 67-11267. (Compass bk., C224). 1968. pap., 1.65. Viking.

Shorter Imitations of Gulliver's Travels. Ed. by Jeanne K. Welcher. LC 74-7139. (Gulliveriana, 5). 1974. (ISBN 0-8201-1131-7). Scholars' Facsimiles & Reprints.

Shorter Novels of Herman Melville. Herman Melville. LC 78-19062. 1978. 4.95 (ISBN 0-87140-122-3). Liveright.

Shorter Novels of Herman Melville. Ed. by Raymond Weaver. 1977. pap. 2.50 (ISBN 0-449-30798-0, Prem). Fawcett.

Shorter Novels of Herman Melville: With an Introduction by Raymond Weaver. Herman Melville. Ed. by Weaver, Raymond Melbourne. LC 28-253508. (The black and gold library). H. Liveright.

Shorter Novels of Stendhal. Stendhal. Tr. by C. K. Scott-Moncrief. (Black & Gold Lib). 7.95 o.p. (ISBN 0-87140-832-5). Liveright.

Shorter Novels of Stendhal... Translated from the French by C. K. Scott-Moncrieff. Marie Henri Beyle & Charles Kenneth Scott-Moncrieff. LC 46-7901. 1946. Liveright Publishing Corporation.

Shorter Novels of the Seventeenth Century. Philip Henderson. 1972. pap. 1.50 o.p. (ISBN 0-460-01841-8, Evman). Dutton.

Shorter Tales. Joseph Conrad. LC 71-128727. (Short Story Index Reprint Ser). 1924. 22.00 (ISBN 0-8369-3618-3). Ayer Co.

Shorter Tales of Joseph Conrad. Joseph Conrad. LC 24-298307. 1924. Doubleday, Page & Company.

Shortest Gladdest Years. Scott Sullivan. LC 62-14284. 1962. Simon and Schuster.

Shortest Night. Gladys Bronwyn Stern. LC 31-18874. 1931. A. A. Knopf.

Shortest Street. Louise Platt Hauck. LC 37-7714. 1937. Macrae-Smith-Company.

Shortest Street. Jean Randall. LC 37-7714. 1937. Macrae Smith Company.

Shortgrass. Hal George Evarts. 1932. Little, Brown, and Company.

Shortstop: A Novel. Hamilton Maule. LC 62-10755. 1962. D. McKay Co.

Shortstop Shadow: Illustrated by Jay Hyde Barnum. Howard M Brier. LC 50-9580. 1950. Random House.

Shorty. Clifton Adams. LC 66-12238. (Double D western). 3.50. Doubleday.

Shorty. Clifton Adams. LC 66-12238. 1966. Doubleday.

Shorty. LC 64-19269. (Double D western). 1964. Doubleday.

Shorty & Patrick, U.S.S. Oklahoma. Stephen French Whitman. LC 11-313. P. F. Collier & Son.

Shorty in the Tank Corps. Edward W Keever. LC 29-17785. 1.75. The Century Co.

Shorty McCabe. Sewell Ford. LC 6-38890. M. Kennerley.

Shorty McCabe Gets the Hail. Sewell Ford. LC 7?-125211. (Short story index reprint series). 1970. Books for Libraries Press.

Shorty McCabe Gets the Hail. Sewell Ford. LC 1?-12721. E. J. Clode.

Shorty McCabe Looks 'em Over. Sewell Ford. LC 73-122702. (Short story index reprint series). (Illus.). 1970. Books for Libraries Press.

Shorty McCabe Looks 'em Over. Sewell Ford. LC 18-760419. 1918. E. J. Clode.

Shorty McCabe on the Job. Sewell Ford. LC 15-5294. 1.25. E. J. Clode.

Shosha. Isaac Bashevis Singer. LC 78-6921. 8.95 (ISBN 0-374-26336-1). Farrar, Straus and Giroux.

Shosha. Isaac Bashevis Singer. LC 79-10520. 1979. 15.95 (ISBN 0-8161-6710-9). G. K. Hall.

Shoshie, the Hindoo Zenana Teacher. Harriet G Brittan. T. Whittaker.

Shoshone Thunder. Bill Hotchkiss & Judith Shears. (American Indians Ser.: No. 12). (Orig.). 1983. pap. 2.95 (ISBN 0-440-07659-5). Dell.

Shoshonee Valley: A Romance... Timothy Fliut. LC 6-39999. 1830. E. H. Flint.

Shot. Sibyl Creed. LC 24-22675. George H. Doran Company.

Shot at Dawn. Cecil John Charles Street. LC 35-6052. 1935. Dodd, Mead & Company.

Shot from the Door. Charles Bryson. LC 35-438. E. P. Dutton & Co., Inc.

Shot in the Ass with Pesos: A Collection of Frontier Tales. Budge Ruffner, pseud. (Illus.). 112p. (Orig.). 1979. pap. 4.95 (ISBN 0-918080-11-8). Treasure Chest.

Shot in the Dark... Gerard Fairlie. LC 33-16670. Pub. for the Crime Club, Inc., by Doubleday, Doran & Company, Inc.

Shot in the Dark. Ed. by Judith Merril. LC 50-17825. (Bantam books, 751). 1950. Bantam Books.

Shot in the Dark. Richard Pitts Powell. LC 52-6703. (Inner sanctum mystery). 1952. Simon and Schuster.

Shot into Infinity. Otto Willi Gail. LC 75-410. (Garland Library of Science Fiction). 1975. 11.00 (ISBN 0-8240-1415-4). Garland Pub.

Shot of Murder. Jack Iams. LC 50-10231. 1950. Morrow.

Shot on Location. Helen Nielsen. LC 70-142404. 1971. 5.95. Morrow.

Shot on the Downs. Victor Lorenzo Whitechurch. LC 28-466387. 1928. Duffield & Company.

Shot Towers: A Novel. John Thomas McIntyre. LC 26-15577. 1926. Frederick A. Stokes Company.

Shot with Crimson. George Barr McCutcheon. LC 18-10583. 1918. Dodd, Mead and Company.

Shotgun. Ed McBain. 4.95 o.p. Doubleday.

Shotgun. William Wingate. LC 79-26873. 10.95 (ISBN 0-312-72228-1). St. Martin's Press.

Shotgun: An 87th Precinct Mystery. Evan Hunter. LC 69-15200. 1969. 4.95. Doubleday.

Shotgun Bottom. Bill Burchardt, pseud. LC 66-20980. (Doubel D western). 1966. Doubleday.

Shotgun Gap. William Frederick Bragg. 1981. pap. 1.75 (ISBN 0-8439-0895-5, Leisure Bks). Nordon Pubns.

Shotgun Gold. Wilbur C Tuttle. LC 40-111082. 1940. Houghton, Mifflin Company.

Shotgun Guard. Dwight Bennett Newton. LC 50-9564. 1950. Lippincott.

Shotgun House. Marie Moyers. 1978. 6.95 o.p. (ISBN 0-533-03506-6). Vantage.

Shotgun Law. Max Brand. 1976. 6.95 o.p. (ISBN 0-396-07371-9). Dodd.

Shotgun Law. Frederick Faust. LC 76-25506. (Silver star westerns). 1976. 6.95 (ISBN 0-396-07371-9). Dodd, Mead.

Shotgun Law. Frederick Faust. 1979. 1.75 (ISBN 0-671-81751-5). Pocket Books.

Shotgun Law. Nelson Nye. 1975. (pbk.) 0.95. Belmont Tower Books.

Shotgun Man. John Benteen. (Belmont Tower Book). 1977. 1.25 (ISBN 0-505-51155-X). Tower Pubns.

Shotgun Man. Frank O'Rourke. 1976. (pbk.) 1.25. Bantam Books.

Shotgun Marshal. Wade Everett. 1981. pap. 1.75 (ISBN 0-345-29434-3). Ballantine.

Shotgun Rider. Ray Hogan. (Shawn Starbuck). (Signet book). New American Library.

Shotgun Rider. Lauran Paine. LC 67-8721. 1967. Arcadia House.

Shotgunner. Ray Hogan. 1968. pap. 0.50 o.p. (50-434). Manor Bks.

Shotguns from Hell. Jake Logan. LC 79-90928. (Jake Logan Ser.). 208p. (Orig.). 1980. pap. 1.95 (ISBN 0-87216-866-2). Playboy Pbks.

Should Auld Acquaintance. Doris Miles Disney. 1967. pap. 0.60 o.p. (60-272). Manor Bks.

Should She Have Left Him? William Cadwalader Hudson. LC 7-5645. The Cassell Publishing Co.

Should She Tell? Margaret Wood. LC 33-19085. Grosset & Dunlap.

Should the Wind Be Fair. Garland Roark. 1970. pap. 0.95 o.p. (0502-09041). Curtis.

Should the Wind Be Fair. 1st Ed. Garland Roark. LC 60-8682. 1960. Doubleday.

Should Women Vote... Paul Morse. LC 7-32482. 1895. P. Morse.

Shoulder-Knot: Or, Sketches of the Three-Fold Life of Man. A Story of the Seventeenth Century. Benjamin Franklin Tefft. 1850. Harper & Brothers.

Shoulder-Straps. A Novel of New York and the Army, 1862. Henry Morford. T. B. Peterson & Brothers.

Shoulder-Straps and Sun-Bonnets. Edith Elmer Wood. LC 1-26200. 1901. H. Holt and Company.

Shoulder the Sky. James Gray. LC 35-38299. G. P. Putnam's Sons.

Shoulder the Sky. George Leonard. LC 59-12435. 1959. McDowell, Obolensky.

Shoulder the Sky. Dorothy Emily Stevenson. (D. E. Stevenson Romances). 1979. pap. 1.95 (ISBN 0-441-76180-1). Ace Bks.

Shoulder the Sky. Dorothy Emily Stevenson. 275p. 1976. lib. bdg. 17.95x (ISBN 0-89966-166-1). Buccaneer Bks.

Shoulder the Sky. Dorothy Emily Stevenson. 1972. 5.95 o.p. (ISBN 0-03-091355-1). HR&W.

Shoulder the Sky, a Story of Winter in the Hills. Dorothy Emily Stevenson. LC 51-12700. 1951. Rinehart.

Shoulder the Sky: A Story of Winter in the Hills. Dorothy Emily Stevenson. 1973. 0.95. Popular Library.

Shoulder the Sky: A Story of Winter in the Hills. new ed. Dorothy Emily Stevenson. LC 75-182764. (Illus.). 1972. 5.95 (ISBN 0-03-091355-1). Holt Rinehart and Winston.

Shoulder the Sky: A Story of Winter in the Hills. Dorothy Emily Stevenson. LC 51-12700. (Illus.). 1951. Rinehart.

Shoulders of Atlas. Mary Eleanor Wilkins Freeman. LC 76-51665. (Recovered Fiction by American Women). 1977. 22.00 (ISBN 0-405-10044-2). Arno Press.

Shoulders of Atlas: A Novel. Mary Eleanor Wilkins Freeman. LC 8-18373. 1908. Harper & Brothers.

Shout. Robert Graves. LC 77-1292. Repr. of 1929 ed. lib. bdg. 10.00 (ISBN 0-8414-4578-8). Folcroft.

Shout. Robert Graves. 1929. 4.00 o.s.i. Ridgeway Bks.

Shout! Philip Norman. (Illus.). 560p. 1982. pap. 3.95 (ISBN 0-446-30337-2). Warner Bks.
Shout & Other Stories. Robert Graves. 1979. pap. 2.95 o.p. (ISBN 0-14-004832-4). Penguin.
Shout at the Devil. Wilbur A Smith. LC 68-23364. 1968. Coward-McCann.
Show and Side Show. Joshua Rosett. LC 38-30606. Rodale Press.
Show & Tell Machine. Ross K. Goldsen. 1978. pap. 4.95 (ISBN 0-440-57666-0, Delta). Dell.
Show Boat. Edna Ferber. LC 26-16053. Doubleday, Page & Co.
Show Boat. Edna Ferber. LC 29-4760. 1928. Grosset & Dunlap.
Show Boat. Edna Ferber. LC 31-234. Grosset & Dunlap.
Show Boat. Edna Ferber. LC 44-51103. 1943. Pocket Books, Inc.
Show Boat. Edna Ferber. LC 25-31972. (Half title: The modern library of the world's best books). 1935. The Modern Library.
Show Boat: A Novel. Edna Ferber. 1926. Doubleday, Page & Company.
Show Boat: A Novel. Edna Ferber. LC 81-1937. 1981. 16.95 (ISBN 0-8161-3196-1). G.K. Hall.
Show Boat Girl. Peggy Gaddis, pseud. LC 40-35885. Gramercy Publishing Company.
Show Boy: A Novel. Marriott Coates Webster. LC 31-3681. The Macaulay Company.
Show Business. Thyra Samter Winslow. LC 26-6642. 1926. A. A. Knopf.
Show Business: A Mystery Novel. Bryant Ford. LC 39-20771. 1939. Dodd, Mead & Company.
Show Business is Murder. Carol-Lynn R. Waugh et al, pseud. 256p. (Orig.). 1983. pap. 2.75 (ISBN 0-380-81554-0). Avon.
Show Case. Charles Grayson. LC 36-125450. Green Circle Books.
Show Cases. Jacques Georges Clemenceau Le Clercq. LC 28-6088. 1928. Macv-Masius.
Show Down. Julia Houston Railey. LC 21-741020. 1921. 2.00. G. P. Putnam's Sons.
Show Girl. Max Pemberton. LC 9-16437. The J. C. Winston Company.
Show Gypsies. Leigh Brown. LC 75-23339. 352p. 1976. 8.95 o.p. (ISBN 0-88405-122-6). Mason Charter.
Show Gypsies: A Novel. Leigh Brown. LC 75-23339. 1975-1976. 8.95 (ISBN 0-88405-122-6). Mason/Charter.
Show Me. Janet Dailey. LC 77-355748. 1976. 0.30 (ISBN 0-263-72273-2). Mills and Boon.
Show Me: A Comedy of Amateur Theatricals. Harding Upton. LC 27-22049. 1927. G. H. Watt.
Show Me a Hero. Patrick Alexander. LC 79-20427. 1980. 9.95 (ISBN 0-670-64315-7). Viking Press.
Show Me a Hero: A Novel. Melvin B Voorhees. LC 54-8647. 1954. Simon and Schuster.
Show Me a Land. Clark McMeekin. LC 40-27164. 1940. D. Appleton-Century Company, Incorporated.
Show Me a Lawyer: Fiction. Lee Brahn. LC 79-65348. 2.25 (ISBN 0-89882-003-0). Distributed by Lane & Associates.
Show Me Death! W Redvers Dent. LC 30-9732. 1930. Harper & Brothers.
Show Me the Way. Leslie Waller. LC 47-235146. 1947. The Viking Press.
Show Me the Way. 1st Ed. Robert Portune. LC 60-7882. 1960. Doubleday.
Show Must Go on: A Novel. Elmer L. Rice. LC 49-11107. 1949. Viking Press.
Show of Force. Charles D Taylor. LC 79-23125. 10.95 (ISBN 0-312-72314-8). St. Martin's Press.
Show of Force. Stewart Thomson. LC 55-805094. 1955. Harper.
Show of Hands. Anna L. Etzel. 3.00 o.p. Carlton.
Show of Violence. Sara Woods, pseud. LC 75-10726. (MW suspense). 5.95 (ISBN 0-679-50542-3). D. McKay Co.
Show-off; a Novel. William Almon Wolff & Kelly, George Edward, 1887- LC 24-249491. 1924. Little, Brown, and Company.
Show on Ice: Part Two of Cesar Cascabel. Jules Verne. 3.95. Assoc Bk.
Show Piece. Booth Tarkington. LC 47-1180. 1947. Doubleday & Company, Inc.
Show Red for Danger; a Captain Heimrich Mystery, by Richard and Frances Lockridge. 1st Ed. Richard Lockridge & Frances Louise Davis Lockridge. LC 60-511095. (Main line mysteries). 1960. Lippincott.
Show Your Colors: Or, A Story of Boston Life. Justin Dewey Fulton. LC 29-25278. 1875. U. D. Ward.
Showbiz Priest. Robert Perella. 1973. 7.95 o.s.i. (ISBN 0-671-27112-1). Trident.
Showboat World. Jack Vance, pseud. (Science Fiction Ser.). 1981. pap. 2.25 (ISBN 0-87997-660-8, UE1660). DAW Bks.
Showboat World. Jack Vance, pseud. (Orig.). 1975. pap. 1.25 o.p. (ISBN 0-515-03698-6, V3698). Pyramid Pubns.
Showcase. Ed. by Roger Elwood. LC 72-9169. 1973. 5.95 (ISBN 0-06-011177-1). Harper & Row.
Showcase for Diane. Marjorie Mueller Freer. LC 51-2680. (Romance for young moderns). 1951. Messner.
Showdown. Max Brand. 1969. pap. 0.60 o.p. (63-170). Paperback Lib.
Showdown. Norman Daniels. 1972. pap. 0.75 o.s.i. (74-777). Lancer.
Showdown. Errol Leslie Flynn. LC 46-1162. 1946. Sheridan House.
Showdown at Bad Turn. Nathan Anton. (Illus.). 90p. 1975. 5.00 o.p. (ISBN 0-682-48345-1, Lochinvar). Exposition.
Showdown at Cibecue Creek. Dan Kirby. 288p. 1982. pap. 2.25 (ISBN 0-441-76179-8, Pub. by Charter Bks). Ace Bks.
Showdown at Emerald Canyon. Jack M Bickham. LC 74-15782. (Double D western). 1975. 4.95 (ISBN 0-385-01890-8). Doubleday.
Showdown at Emerald Canyon. jeff clinton. ed. Jack M Bickham. 1976. 1.25. Belmont Tower.
Showdown at Emerald Canyon. Jeff Clinton, pseud. (O.s.i.). 1976. pap. 1.25 o.s.i. (BT50995). Belmont-Tower.
Showdown at Fire Hill. Roe Richmond. (Orig.). 1979. pap. 1.95 (ISBN 0-89083-560-8). Zebra.
Showdown at Guyamas. Logan Winters. 1978. pap. 1.25 (ISBN 0-532-12558-4). Woodhill.
Showdown at Hell's Canyon. Robert E. Mills. (Kansan Ser.: No. 1). 1980. pap. 1.75 (ISBN 0-8439-0774-6). Nordon Pubns.
Showdown at Mesilla. Lewis B Patten. LC 77-150911. 1971. 4.95. Doubleday.
Showdown at Mesilla: The Trial of Judas Wiley. Lewis B. Patten. 1982. pap. 2.50 (ISBN 0-451-11631-3, AE1631, Sig). NAL.
Showdown at Mon Repos. Paul Rader. LC 76-111445. 1970. 5.95. Dial Press.
Showdown at Skeleton Flat. Orlando Rigoni. LC 67-5180. 1967. Arcadia House.
Showdown at Snakegrass Junction. Gary McCarthy. LC 77-92223. 1978. 6.95 (ISBN 0-385-13689-7). Doubleday.
Showdown at Snakegrass Junction. Gary McCarthy. 1979. 1.50 (ISBN 0-440-18278-6). Dell Publishing.
Showdown at Stony Crest: By Joseph Wayne Pseud. Wayne D Overholser. LC 57-826521. (Dell first edition, A138). 1957. Dell Pub. Co.
Showdown at the MB Ranch. James Wesley. 1976. 4.95. Avalon Books.
Showdown at the PTA Corral. William Johnston. LC 73-846. (Brady Bunch Ser, No. 2). (Orig.). 1969. pap. 0.60 o.p. Lancer.
Showdown at Yellow Butte. Louis L'Amour. 192p. 1982. pap. 2.25 (ISBN 0-449-14275-2, GM). Fawcett.
Showdown at Yellow Butte. Louis L'Amour. 1980. lib. bdg. 9.95 (ISBN 0-8398-2690-7, Gregg). G K Hall.
Showdown at Yellow Butte. Louis L'Amour. (Fawcett gold medal book). 1974. (pbk.) 0.95. Fawcett.
Showdown at Yellow Butte see Complete L'Amour.
Showdown Country. Charley Barstow. (Orig.). 1980. pap. 1.75 o.s.i. (ISBN 0-505-51491-5). Tower Bks.
Showdown Creek: A Western Novel. Lucas Todd. LC 55-14501. 1955. Macmillan.
Showdown Guns. Charles Stanley Strong. LC 46-604. 1946. Phoenix Press.
Showdown in Greenway Valley. James R. Haning. 1973. 4.95. Lenox Hill Pr.
Showdown in Sonora. Gordon D. Shirreffs. 160p. 1981. pap. 1.75 (ISBN 0-449-12710-9, GM). Fawcett.
Showdown in Sonora. Gordon D. Shirreffs. (Orig.). 1969. pap. 0.50 o.p. (D2070, GM). Fawcett World.
Showdown on Texas Flat. Ray Hogan. 1975. (pbk.) 0.95. Ace Books.
Showdown Trial. Leslie Scott. LC 60-283975. 1960. Arcadia House.
Shower of Summer Days. May Sarton. LC 52-9599. 1952. Rinehart.
Shower of Summer Days. May Sarton. LC 72-11247. 1970. 5.95. Norton.
Shower of Summer Days. May Sarton. LC 79-1140. (Norton paperback). 1979. 3.95 (ISBN 0-393-00925-4). Norton.
Showers of Sunlight. Donna K. Vitek. 192p. (Orig.). 1980. pap. 1.50 (ISBN 0-671-57047-1). S&S.
Shred of Lace. Franklyn Warner Lee. LC 7-12613. 1891. The Price-McGill Publishing Co.
Shreiber. Abraham Boyarsky. LC 81-4888. 1981. 13.95 (ISBN 0-8253-0060-6). Beaufort Books.
Shreiber's Choice. Dan Kirby. 128p. (Orig.). 1981. pap. 2.25 (ISBN 0-441-76198-4). Ace Bks.
Shrewsbury: A Romance. Stanley John Weyman. LC 8-34338. 1898. Longmans, Green and Co.
Shrewsbury Edition of the Works of Samuel Butler. Samuel Butler. Ed. by Jones, Henry Festing & Bartholomew, Augustus Theodore. LC 25-21802. 1923-26. J. Cape.
Shrewsdale Exit. John Buell. 1973. (pbk.) 1.50 (ISBN 0-671-78617-2). Pocket Books.
Shrewsdale Exit. John Buell. LC 72-81009. 1972. 6.95 (ISBN 0-374-26342-6). Farrar, Straus and Giroux.
Shriek: A Satirical Burlesque. Charles Somerville. LC 22-12632. W. J. Watt & Company.
Shriek with Pleasure. 1st Ed. Toni Howard. LC 50-3308. 1950. Prentice-Hall.
Shrieking Pit. Arthur John Rees. 1919. John Lane Company.
Shrimp Harris. Colin Davy. LC 47-303486. 1947. G. P. Putnam's Sons.
Shrimpers Woman. Patti Beckman. 192p. 1981. pap. 1.50 (ISBN 0-671-57054-4, Pub. by Silhouette Bks). S&S.
Shrimps for Tea. Josephine Blumenfeld. LC 30-23547. 1930. Doubleday, Doran & Company, Inc.
Shrine, and Other Stories. Mary Lavin. LC 77-24044. 1977. 6.95 (ISBN 0-395-25773-5). Houghton Mifflin.
Shrine of Fair Women. Ann Pinchot. LC 32-4111. 1932. R. Long & R. R. Smith, Inc.
Shrinking Man. Richard Matheson. (Berkley book). 1979. 1.95 (ISBN 0-425-04021-6). Berkley Pub. Corp.
Shrinking Man. Richard Matheson. LC 79-16582. (Gregg Press science fiction series). (Illus.). 1979. (ISBN 0-8398-2547-1). Gregg Press.
Shrinking Pond. Juanita Tyree Osborne. 192p. (YA) 1974. 6.95 (Avalon). Bouregy.
Shrinking: The Beginning of My Own Ending: a Novel. Alan Lelchuk. LC 77-28024. (Illus.). 12.95 (ISBN 0-316-52050-0). Little, Brown.
Shropshire Lad. Housman. 3.95 (ISBN 0-88088-306-5). Peter Pauper.
Shroud for a Nightingale. P. D James. LC 70-143933. 1971. 4.95 (ISBN 0-684-12372-X). Scribner.
Shroud for a Nightingale. P. D James. LC 81-20120. 1982. 14.95 (ISBN 0-8161-6791-5). G.K. Hall.
Shroud for Grandmama see Longstreet Legacy.
Shroud for Mr. Bundy. James M. Fox. (Raven House Mysteries Ser.). 224p. 1983. pap. cancelled (ISBN 0-373-63049-2, Pub. by Worldwide). Harlequin Bks.
Shroud for Mr. Bundy: By James M. Fox Pseud. 1st Ed. James M. W. Knipscheer. LC 52-9068. 1952. Little, Brown.
Shroud for Rowena. Virginia Rath. LC 47-352495. 1947. Ziff-Davis Publishing Company.
Shroud for Shylock. Frederick Clyde Davis. LC 39-31410. 1939. Published for the Crime Club, Inc., by Doubleday, Doran & Co., Inc.
Shroud for Shylock. Stephen Ransome. LC 39-314107. 1939. Pub. for the Crime Club, Inc., by Doubleday, Doran & Co., Inc.
Shroud of Darkness: By E. C. R. Lorac Pseud. 1st Ed. Edith Caroline Rivett. LC 54-10256. 1954. Published for the Crime Club by Doubleday.
Shroud of Fog. Willo Davis Roberts. (Ace Gothic). 1973. (pbk.) 0.95. Ace Books.
Shroud off Her Back: By Stephen Ransome Pseud. 1st Ed. Frederick Clyde Davis. LC 52-133691. 1953. Published for the Crime Club by Doubleday.
Shroud Society. Robert Crawford, pseud. LC 74-90513. (Red mask mystery). 1969. 4.50. Putnam.
Shrouded Planet. Robert Randall, pseud. LC 80-22472. (Starblaze editions). 4.95 (ISBN 0-915442-63-9). Donning.
Shrouded Planet. Robert Silverberg & Randall Garrett. LC 80-22472. 1980. pap. 5.95 (ISBN 0-89865-033-X). Donning Co.
Shrouded Planet. 1st Ed. Robert Randall, pseud. LC 57-14671. 1957. Gnome Press.
Shrouded Walls. Susan Howatch. LC 70-175942. 1971. 5.95 (ISBN 0-8128-1440-1). Stein and Day.
Shrouded Walls. Susan Howatch. (Fawcett crest book). 1974. (pbk.) 1.25. Fawcett.
Shrouded Walls of Boranga. Mike Sirota. (Ro-Lan Ser.: No. 2). 304p. (Orig.). 1980. pap. 1.95 (ISBN 0-89083-677-9). Zebra.
Shrovetide in Old New Orleans. Ishmael Reed. LC 76-42386. 1978. 8.95 o.p. (ISBN 0-385-05688-5). Doubleday.
Shtetl. Joachim Neugroschel. LC 82-5238. 1982. 10.95 (ISBN 0-399-50672-1). Perigee Books.
Shtetl and Other Yiddish Novellas. Ed. by Ruth R. Wisse. LC 73-10254. (Library of Jewish studies). 1973. 12.50 (ISBN 0-87441-201-3). Behrman House.
Shuddering Castle. Wilbur Finley Fauley. LC 36-21689. Green Circle Books.
Shuddering Fair One. Parley J Cooper. (Ravenswood gothic). 1974. (pbk.) 0.95 (ISBN 0-671-77729-7). Pocket Books.
Shudders. Lilian Edna Austin. LC 31-31342. 1931. Meador Publishing Company.
Shudders. Ed. by Ross Olney. (Griffon Ser). (Orig.). 1969. pap. 0.50 o.p. (Golden Pr). Western Pub.
Shudders, a Thatcher Colt Police Mystery. Fulton Oursler. LC 43-980. 1943. Farrar & Rinehart, Incorporated.
Shudders and Thrills: The Second Oppenheim Omnibus. Edward Phillips Oppenheim. LC 32-266615. 1932. Little, Brown, and Company.
Shudders Stories. Ed. by Cynthia Mary Evelyn Charteris Asquith. LC 29-24380. 1929. C. Scribner's Sons.
Shukar Balan: The White Lamb: the Story of Evaliz. Mela Meisner Lindsay. LC 75-39490. 6.95 (ISBN 0-914222-02-3). American Historical Society of Germans from Russia.
Shulamith. Meera Mahadevan. 208p. 1980. pap. 3.25 (ISBN 0-86578-061-7). Ind-US Inc.
Shulamith. Meera Mahadevan. (Indian Novel Ser.). 208p. 1976. 8.50 (ISBN 0-89253-047-2). Ind-US Inc.
Shule Agra: A Novel. Kathleen Coyle. LC 27-106480. E. P. Dutton & Company.
Shumway. Ronald K. Messer. 1975. 6.95 o.p. (ISBN 0-525-66419-X). Elsevier-Nelson.
Shut the Door Behind You. June Pat Wetherell. LC 44-5586. 1944. E. P. Dutton & Company, Inc.
Shut the Gate: An American Social Study, Washington Davis & Cole, Ashley W. 1889. The American News Company.
Shutter of Snow. Emily Holmes Coleman. LC 30-27771. 1930. The Viking Press.
Shuttered Doors: By Mrs. William Hicks Beach... Susan Emily Christian Hicks Beach. LC 20-7653. 1919. John Lane.
Shuttered Houses. pap. 1.95 o.p. (V1048T, Venus). Grove.
Shuttered Room. Charlotte A. Sherman. LC 75-21348. 192p. (Orig.). 1975. pap. 1.25 (ISBN 0-89041-033-X, 3033). Major Bks.
Shuttered Room: And Other Pieces by H. P. Lovecraft & Divers Hands. Compiled by August Derleth. Howard Phillips Lovecraft. LC 59-65100. 1959. Arkham House.
Shuttered Room, and Other Tales of Horror. Howard Philips Lovecraft & August William Derleth. LC 73-181015. (Panther horror). 1973. 0.35 (ISBN 0-586-03399-8). Panther.
Shutters. Olive Wadsley. LC 26-10926. 1926. Cassell and Company, Ltd.
Shutters. Olive Wadsley. LC 26-14628. 1926. Dodd, Mead and Company.
Shutters of Silence: The Romance of a Trappist. George Brown Burgin. 1903. The Smart Set Publishing Co.
Shuttle. Frances Hodgson Burnett. LC 7-29574. 1907. Frederick A. Stokes Company.
Shuttle. David C. Onley. (Orig.). 1982. pap. 3.25 (ISBN 0-89083-951-4). Zebra.
Shuttle Down. Lee Corey. 224p. (Orig.). 1981. pap. 2.25 (ISBN 0-345-29262-6, Del Rey). Ballantine.
Shy. William W. Thayer. 1978. pap. 1.25 (ISBN 0-532-12554-1). Woodhill.
Shy Cinderella. Wilson Collison. LC 32-289784. 1932. R. M. McBride & Company.
Shy Leopardess. Leslie Barringer. LC 77-154883. (His The Neustrian cycle; book 3). (Newcastle Forgotten Fantasy library; v. 13). 1977. 4.95. (ISBN 0-87877-112-3). Newcastle Pub. Co.
Shy Leopardess. Leslie Barringer. LC 80-19240. (His The Neustrian cycle; book 3). 1980. 11.95. Borgo Press.
Shy Leopardess: The Neustrian Cycle, Bk. 3. Leslie Barringer. Ed. by R. Reginald & Douglas Menville. LC 80-19240. (Newcastle Forgotten Fantasy Library Ser.: Vol. 13). 392p. 1980. Repr. of 1977 ed. lib. bdg. 12.95x (ISBN 0-89370-512-8). Borgo Pr.
Shy Leopardess: The Neustrian Cycle, Book Three. Leslie Barringer. (Forgotten Fantasy Library: Vol. 13). 1977. pap. 5.95 (ISBN 0-87877-112-3, F-112). Newcastle Pub.
Shy Nymphomaniac. Stanley Mitchell. (Orig.). 1969. pap. 1.75 o.p. (3053). Brandon.
Shy Photographer. Jock Carroll. LC 64-8503. (Olympia Press series). 1964. Stein and Day.
Shy Plutocrat. Edward Phillips Oppenheim. LC 41-8174. 1941. Little, Brown and Company.
Shy Yorkshireman: A Novel. William Richard Bird. LC 55-13556. 1955. Bouregy & Curl.
Shy Young Denbury. Audrey Blanshard. (Fawce tt Crest Book). 1978. 1.75 (ISBN 0-449-23666-8). Fawcett Publications.
Shylock's Daughter. A Novel. Margret Holmes Ernsperger Bates. LC 6-9073. 1894. C. H. Kerr & Company.
Shyster Lawyer. Leo Francis Schmitt. Leebodell Co., Inc.
Si Klegg: His Transformation from a Raw Recruit to a Veteran. 2d ed., rev. and enl. ed. John McElroy. The National Tribune Co.
Si Klegg: Si and Shorty Meet Mr. Rosenbaum, the Spry, Who Relates His Adventures. 2d ed., enl. and rev. ed. John McElroy. LC 10-17323. The National Tribune Co.
Si Klegg; Si and Shorty: With Their Boy Recruits, Enter on the Atlanta Campaign. 2d ed.--enl. and rev. ed. John McElroy. LC 16-1889. The National Tribune Company.
Si Klegg: Si, Shorty and the Boys, Are Captured at Kenesaw and Taken to Andersonville. 2d ed., enl. and rev. ed. John McElroy. LC 16-14721. The National Tribune Company.

Si Klegg: The Deacon's Adventures at Chattanooga in Caring for the Boys. John McElroy. LC 12-8141. The National Tribune Company.

Si Klegg Thru the Stone River Campaign and in Winter Quarters at Murfreesboro. By John McElroy. John McElroy. LC 10-92541. The National Tribune Co.

Si Nos Chemins se Croisent. Sonia Daquine. (Collection Colombine Ser.). 192p. 1983. pap. 1.95 (ISBN 0-373-48068-7). Harlequin Bks.

Siam Miami. Morris Renek. LC 78-75396. 1969. Macmillan.

Siamese Cat. Morse, Elizabeth. LC 30-4743. E. P. Dutton & Co., Inc.

Siamese Cat. Henry Milner Rideout. 1907. McClure, Phillips & Co.

Siamese Tales Old & New. Reginald S. Le May. LC 74-16311. 1974. Repr. of 1930 ed. lib. bdg. 25.00 (ISBN 0-8414-5747-6). Folcroft.

Siamese Twin Mystery. Ellery Queen. 360p. 1980. lib. bdg. 15.95x (ISBN 0-89966-145-9). Buccaneer Bks.

Siamese Twin Mystery. Emilie Baker Loring. 1976. Repr. of 1933 ed. lib. bdg. 6.95 o.p. (361). Amereon Ltd.

Siamese Twin Mystery. Ellery Queen, pseud. LC 40-13805. 1940. Triangle Books.

Siamese Twin Mystery. Ellery Queen, pseud. LC 43-3871. 1943. The Sun Dial Press.

Siamese Twin Mystery. Ellery Queen, pseud. LC 46-15769. 1946. Triangle Books, the Blakiston Company.

Siamese Twin Mystery: A Problem in Deduction. Ellery Queen, pseud. LC 33-32768. 1933. Frederick A. Stokes Company.

Siamese Twins. Michele Saraceno. LC 65-29032. 2.95. Harlo.

Siamese Twins. Michele Saraceno. LC 65-29032. 1965. Harlo Press.

Siballa the Sorceress: Or, The Flower Girl of London. A Tale of the Days of Richard Iii. William Henry Peck. LC 7-36473. (sea and shore series, no. 16). 1890. Street & Smith.

Siberian Encounter. Gaia Servadio. 241p. 1971. 7.95 o.p. (ISBN 0-374-26360-4). FS&G.

Siberian Exiles. A Novel. Thomas Wallace Knox. LC 7-22745. (ledger library, no. 77). 1893. R. Bonner's Sons.

Siberian Exiles' Children: Or, Thrown on the World. Edwin Hodder. LC 43-21548. Eaton & Mains.

Siberian Garrison. Rodion Markovits. Tr. by Halasz, George. LC 29-23490. 1929. H. Liveright.

Siberian Gold. Theodore Acland Harper & Harper, Winifred. LC 27-249552. 1927. Doubleday, Page & Company.

Siberian Gold. Theodore Acland Harper & Harper, Winifred. LC 37-21968. (Young moderns bookshelf). 1937. The Sundial Press, Inc.

Siberian Reservoir. Ian Bush. LC 82-11831. 1983. 16.95 (ISBN 0-395-32560-9). Houghton Mifflin.

Siberian Road. Henry Gibbs. LC 76-16316. 1976. 6.95. Walker.

Siberian Road. Henry Gibbs. LC 76-371426. (His The Asia in turmoil series). 1976. 3.60 (ISBN 0-09-125260-1). Hutchinson.

Siberian Road. Simon Harvester. 1976. 6.95 o.p. (ISBN 0-8027-5350-7). Walker & Co.

Sibert's Wold. A Tale. Matilda Anne MacKarness. 1856. J. Munroe and Company.

Sibil Cipher. Johannes Mario Simmel. 1979. pap. 2.25 (ISBN 0-445-04395-4). Popular Lib.

Sibling. Adam Hall, pseud. LC 79-83965. 304p. (Orig.). 1979. pap. 2.95 (ISBN 0-86721-058-3). Playboy Pbks.

Sibling. Elleston Trevor. LC 79-83965. 2.50 (ISBN 0-87216-522-1). Playboy Press.

Sibyl Huntington. A Novel. Julia Caroline Ripley Dorr. LC 6-33716. 1870. Carleton; Etc., Etc.

Sibyl Spencer. James Kent. LC 7-10962. 1878. G. P. Putnam's Sons.

Sibyl Sue Blue. Rosel George Brown. LC 66-17437. 3.95. Doubleday.

Sibyl Sue Blue. Rosel George Brown. LC 66-17437. 1966. Doubleday.

Sibyl. Translated by Naomi Walford. Par Fabian Lagerkvist. LC 57-10035. 1958. Random House.

Sibylla. Henry Stewart Cunningham. LC 22-10846. 1894. Macmillan and Co.

Sibylla. Adapted from the German. Agnes Vollmar & Nicholl, Mrs. Cornelia (Mather) Tr. LC 18-32693. 1888. Cranston & Stowe.

Sibyl's Dreams. Mary Helen. 1980. deluxe ed. 14.95 autographed (ISBN 0-912492-18-X). Pyquag.

Sibyl's Influence: Or, The Missing Link. Sarah Elizabeth Forbush G. S. Downs Downs. (select series. no. 16). 1888. Street & Smith.

Sic Vita Est. Such Is Life.) A Novel. Sue Froman Matthews. 1896. G. W. Dillingham Co.

Sicilian: A Novel. Georgette Brockman Hall. LC 74-31463. 1975. (ISBN 0-88289-060-3). Pelican Pub. Co.

Sicilian Affair. May Mackintosh. LC 73-18132. 1974. 6.95 (ISBN 0-440-03526-0). Delacorte Press.

Sicilian Carousel. Lawrence Durrell. 1978. pap. 3.95 (ISBN 0-14-004687-9). Penguin.

Sicilian Carousel. Lawrence Durrell. 1977. 13.95 (ISBN 0-670-64362-9). Viking Pr.

Sicilian Defense. John Nicholas Iannuzzi. LC 73-185910. 1973. (pbk) 1.25. New American Library.

Sicilian Heritage. Jack Higgins, pseud. Orig. Title: In the house Before Midnight. 1972. pap. 0.95 o.s.i. (75-396). Lancer.

Sicilian Marriage: By Douglas Sladen... Douglas Brooke Wheelton Sladen. LC 6-13421. 1906. J. Pott & Co.

Sicilian Romance. Ann Ward Radcliffe. LC 75-131338. (Gothic novels). 1972. (ISBN 0-405-00809-0). Arno Press.

Sicilian Romance. Ann Ward Radcliffe. LC 76-148596. (Belles lettres in English). 1971. Johnson Reprint Corp.

Sicilian Slaughter. Don Pendleton. (Executioner Ser. No. 16). pap. 1.95 (ISBN 0-523-41080-8). Pinnacle Bks.

Sicilian Specialist. Norman Lewis. LC 74-9057. 1974. 6.95 (ISBN 0-394-49008-8). Random House.

Sicilian Specialist. Norman Lewis. 1975. (pbk.) 1.95. Ballantine Books.

Sicilian Summer. Elizabeth Ashton. (Harlequin Romances Ser.). 192p. 1981. pap. 1.25 (ISBN 0-373-02401-0, Pub. by Harlequin). PB.

Sicily Ann: A Romance. Fannie Heaslip Lea. LC 14-17813. 1914. 1.00. Harper & Brothers.

Sicily Enough: A Novella. Claire Rabe. LC 76-28246. 1976. 10.00. (ISBN 0-88496-069-2) (ISBN 0-88496-070-6). Capra Press.

Sick-a-Bed Lady: And Also Hickory Dock, The Very Tired Girl, The Happy-Day, Something That Happened in October, The Amateur Lover, Heart of the City, The Pink Sash, Woman's Only Business. Eleanor Hallowell Abbott. LC 11-24125. 1911. The Century Co.

Sick-a-Bed Lady: And Also Hickory Dock, The Very Tired Girl, The Happy-Day, The Runaway Road, Something That Happened in October, The Amateur Lover, Heart of the City, The Pink Sash, Woman's Only Business. Eleanor Hallowell Abbott. LC 12-226591. 1912. The Century Co.

Sick and Full of Burning. Kelly Cherry. LC 73-14423. 1974. 8.95 (ISBN 0-670-64382-3). Viking Press.

Sick and Full of Burning. Kelly Cherry. 1975. (pbk.) 1.75. Ballantine Books.

Sick Fox. Paul Brodeur. LC 63-8955. 1963. Little, Brown.

Sick Friends: A Novel. Ivan Gold. LC 77-85923. 1969. 6.95. Dutton.

Sick to Death. Douglas Clark. LC 70-150944. 1971. 4.95 (ISBN 0-8128-1382-0). Stein and Day.

Sickness and Health: A Novel. Colin Douglas. LC 80-28316. 1982. 8.95 (ISBN 0-8008-7178-2). Taplinger Pub. Co.

Sickness and Health of the People of Bleaburn. 2d Ed. Harriet Mactineau. LC 7-17816. 1853. Crosby, Nichols, and Company.

Sicola, the Papal Bull: A Fantasy on the Escapades of an Itinerant Pope. John A Vitello. LC 78-71420. 11.95 (ISBN 0-87973-646-1). Our Sunday Visitor.

Side Effects. lst ed. Woody Allen, pseud. LC 79-5549. 8.95 (ISBN 0-394-51104-2). Random House.

Side Effects. Mel Silverstein & Karen Silverstein. LC 77-92231. 1978. 7.95. Doubleday.

Side Me at Sundown. L. P Holmes. 1974. (pbk.) 0.95. Ace Books.

Side of the Angels. Alexander Federoff. 1960. 10.00 (ISBN 0-8392-1103-1). Astor-Honor.

Side of the Angels. Robert McLaughlin. LC 47-1794. 1947. A. A. Knopf.

Side of the Angels. John Rowan Wilson. LC 68-24836. 1968. 5.95. Doubleday.

Side of the Angels. John Rowan Wilson. LC 74-481972. 1968. 0.85. Readers Book Club in Association with the Companion Book Club, London.

Side of the Angels: A Novel. Basil King. LC 42-26366. 1916. A. L. Burt Company.

Side of the Angels: A Novel. Basil King. LC 16-4427. 1916. Harper & Brothers.

Side of the Angels. Translated from the French by Humphrey Hare. Jean Louis Curtis. LC 56-102259. 1956. Putnam.

Side Show Studies. Francis Metcalfe. LC 6-11307. 1906. The Outing Publishing Company.

Side-Stepping with Shorty. Sewell Ford. LC 72-13046. (Short story index reprint series). 1973. (ISBN 0-8369-4242-6). Books for Libraries Press.

Side-Stepping with Shorty. Sewell Ford. LC 8-12803. M. Kennerley.

Side Street: A Powerful, Gripping Drama of New York's Racketeers. St. Clair, Mal & O'Hara, George, Joint Author. LC 30-15212. Jacobsen Publishing Company, Inc.

Side Street. 1st Ed. Nathaniel Benchley. LC 50-5875. 1950. Harcourt, Brace.

Sidehill Gouger or What's So Deadly About Caterpillars? Shane Dennison. LC 76-50761. 1977. 8.95 (ISBN 0-385-12515-1). Doubleday.

Sidelong Glances of a Pigeon Kicker. David Boyer. LC 68-16630. 1968. Viking Press.

Sideman: A Novel. Osborn Duke. LC 56-6209. 1956. Criterion Books.

Sidereality. Ellablanche K. Salmi. (Illus.). 240p. (Orig.). 1980. pap. 6.00 (ISBN 0-9601542-4-8). Ivy Hill.

Sideshow. Mike Resnick. (Tales of the Galactic Midway Ser.: No. 1). 160p. 1982. pap. 2.50 (AE1848, Sig). NAL.

Sideshows of a Big City: Tales of Yesterday and Today. Jack Tuthill. LC 33-2854. Kenfield-Leach Company.

Sidestreet. 1st Ed. Bowen, Robert O. LC 54-8755. 1954. Knopf.

Sidetripping. William Burroughs. 1975. pap. 6.95 o.p. Derbibooks.

Sidewalk Indian. Melvin Richard Ellis. LC 73-13980. 1974. (lib. bdg.) 5.95 (ISBN 0-03-012076-4). Holt, Rinehart and Winston.

Sidewalk Symphony. Janet Ford. LC 39-5405. Gramercy Publishing Company.

Sidewalks Are Free. Sam Ross. LC 50-5552. 1950. Farrar, Straus.

Sidewalks of New York. Nat Joseph Ferber. LC 28-56304. 1927. P. Covici.

Sidewinder. John Thomas Edson. 1979. pap. 1.75 (ISBN 0-425-04416-5). Berkley Pub.

Sidewinder. Jack Slade, pseud. (Lassiter Ser.). 1978. pap. 1.25 o.s.i. (ISBN 0-505-51307-2). Tower Bks.

Sidewinder Trail. George Brydges Rodney. LC 37-16220. Greenberg.

Sidewinder's Trail. Bill Haller. 1976. (pbk.) 1.25 (ISBN 0-523-00850-3). Pinnacle Books.

Sidewise in Time: And Other Scientific Adventures. William Fitzgerald Jenkins. LC 50-1899. 1950. Shasta Publishers.

Sidlatches Are Coming. M. T. Brown. (Illus.). 1980. pap. 9.95 o.p. (ISBN 0-930490-29-0). Future Shop.

Sidmouth Letters. Jane Gardam. LC 80-23940. 1980. 8.95 (ISBN 0-688-00134-3). Morrow.

Sidney. Margaret Wade Campbell Deland. LC 6-33379. 1890. Houghton, Mifflin and Company.

Sidney. 10th thousand ed. Margaret Wade Campbell Deland. LC 4-15445. Houghton, Mifflin and Company.

Sidney: A Love Story of the Old South. Modeste Hannis Jordan. LC 12-6225. 1912. 1.00. The Cosmopolitan Press.

Sidney Elliott: A Novel. Mary Dummett Nauman Robinson. LC 7-23112. 1869. Claxton, Remsen & Haffelfinger.

Sidney Forrester. Henry Leavitt Goodwin. LC 1-1604. 1895. H. W. Hagemann.

Sido. Sidonie Gabrielle Colette. Bd. with Vrilles De la Vigne. 1958. pap. 3.95 (373). French & Eur.

Sido see My Mother's House & Sido.

Sidonie. Fromont Jeune et Risler Aine). From the French of Alphonse Daudet. 8th thousand, american ed. from the 63d thousand, paris ed. Alphonse Daudet. Tr. by Sherwood, Mary Neal. LC 6-33041. (On cover: Lovell's library, v. 12, no. 604). J. W. Lovell Company.

Siege. Samuel Hopkins Adams. LC 24-4507. 1924. Boni and Liveright.

Siege. Victor B Miller. (Telly Savalas Kojak # 1). 1974. (pbk.) 1.25 (ISBN 0-671-78487-0). Pocket Books.

Siege. Jerrold Morgulas. LC 77-138882. 1972. 8.95 (ISBN 0-03-086003-2). Holt, Rinehart and Winston.

Siege. Peter Vansittart. LC 62-12749. 1962. Walker.

Siege: A Novel. Edwin Corley. LC 69-17948. 1969. 6.95. Stein and Day.

Siege: A Novel. Illes Kaczer. LC 53-572777. 1953. Dial Press.

Siege: A Novel of Love and War. John Silas Williams. LC 12-28701. 1912. The Cosmopolitan Press.

Siege at Forlorn River. Zane Grey. 1982. 18.00x (ISBN 0-86025-191-8, Pub. by Ian Henry Pubns England). State Mutual Bk.

Siege in the Sun. Dorothy Eden. 1979. pap. 2.25 (ISBN 0-449-23884-9, Crest). Fawcett.

Siege in the Sun: By Mary Paradise. Dorothy Eden. LC 67-21120. 1967. 4.95. Coward-McCann.

Siege of Battersea. Robert O Holles. LC 62-10639. 1962. Macmillan.

Siege of Calais. Claudine Alexandrine Guerin De Tencin & Pont De Veyle, Antoine De Ferriol. LC 74-16066. (Flowering of the Novel). 1974. (ISBN 0-8240-1101-5). Garland Pub.

Siege of Choczim: And Other Tales in Prose and Verse. Ed. by M Corbett. LC 42-26186. 1843.

Siege of Derry: Or, Sufferings of the Protestants: a Tale of the Revolution. Charlotte Elizabeth Browne Tonna. LC 1-11834. 1841. J. S. Taylor & Co.

Siege of Earth. John Faucette. (Peacemakers Ser). 1971. pap. 0.95 o.p. (B95-2194). Belmont-Tower.

Siege of Faltare. Arsen Darnay. 1978. 1.95 (ISBN 0-441-76341-3). Ace Books.

Siege of Hampton Mall. Brian Robertson. 1979. pap. 1.95 (ISBN 0-532-19252-4). Woodhill.

Siege of Harlem. Warren Miller. LC 64-22974. 1964. McGraw-Hill.

Siege of Innocence. Eugene MacCown. LC 49-49275. 1950. Doubleday.

Siege of Krishnapur. James Gordon Farrell. LC 74-1228. 1974. 7.95 (ISBN 0-15-182323-5). Harcourt Brace Jovanovich.

Siege of Krishnapur. James Gordon Farrell. 1976. (pbk.) 1.95. Warner Books.

Siege of Lady Resolute: A Novel. Harris Dickson. LC 2-6074. 1902. Harper & Brothers.

Siege of London see Lady Barbarina.

Siege of London, The Pension Beaurepas, and The Point of View. 2d ed. Henry James. LC 35-33415. 1883. J. R. Osgood and Company.

Siege of London, The Pension Beaurepas, and The Point of View. Henry James. LC 7-7434. 1883. J. R. Osgood and Company.

Siege of Orbitor. Richard L. Newman. 1980. pap. 2.25 (ISBN 0-8439-0814-9). Nordon Pubns.

Siege of Pleasure. Patrick Hamilton. LC 32-5660. 1932. Little, Brown and Company.

Siege of Quebec. John Knox. 1980. pap. 7.95. Pendragon Hse.

Siege of Spoleto: A Camp-Tale of Arlington Heights. Michael J. A McCaffery. LC 24-20800. 1864. P. O'Shea.

Siege of Superport. J. Bradford Olesker. LC 77-13812. Putnam.

Siege of the St. Lawrence. Herbert John Sugden. LC 48-2556. 1948. Christopher Pub. House.

Siege of the Seven Suitors. Meredith Nicholson. LC 10-249037. 1910. Houghton Mifflin Company.

Siege of the Villa Lipp. Eric Ambler. LC 76-53463. 8.95 (ISBN 0-394-49982-4). Random House.

Siege of Three Eighteen: Thirteen Mystical Stories. Davis Grubb. LC 78-61067. 180p. 1978. 9.00. Back Fork Bks.

Siege of Trencher's Farm. Gordon M. Williams. LC 78-80911. (Illus.). 1969. 5.95. Morrow.

Siege of Villa Lipp. Eric Ambler. LC 77-15578. 1978. 14.95 (ISBN 0-8161-6540-8). G. K. Hall.

Siege of Wonder. Mark S Geston. LC 75-36624. 1976. 5.95 (ISBN 0-385-11359-5). Doubleday.

Siege of Wonder. Mark S Geston. 1977. 1.50 (ISBN 0-87997-325-0). DAW Books.

Siege of Youth. Frances Asa Charles. LC 3-12963. 1903. Little, Brown, & Company.

Siege Perilous: And Other Stories. Katherine Helen Maud Marshall Diver. LC 78-122694. (Short story index reprint series). 1970. Books for Libraries Press.

Siege Perilous: And Other Stories. Katherine Helen Maud Marshall Diver. LC 24-30000. 1924. Houghton Mifflin Company.

Siege Perilous, & Other Stories. Katherine Helen Maud Marshall Diver. LC 78-122694. (Short Story Index Reprint Ser). 1924. 15.00 (ISBN 0-8369-3527-6). Ayer Co.

Siege. 1st Ed. Jay Williams. LC 55-6536. 1955. Little, Brown.

Siegfried the Mystic: A Novel. Ida Worden Wheeler. LC 8-36053. 1896. Arena Publishing Company.

Siegfried's Curse. Wayne Andrews. (Illus.). 1972. 10.95 o.p. (ISBN 0-689-10456-1). Atheneum.

Siegfried's Journey. Siegfried Sassoon. 224p. pap. 5.95 (ISBN 0-571-11917-4). Faber & Faber.

Sielanka: A Forest Picture, and Other Stories. Henryk Sienkiewicz. Tr. by Jeremiah Curtin. LC 98-796. 1898. Little, Brown, and Company.

Siempre Junto a Ti. Rafael Crespo. (Romance Real). 192p. (Span.). 1981. pap. 1.50 (ISBN 0-88025-004-6). Roca Pub.

Sierra Baron. Thomas Wakefield Blackburn. LC 55-5811. 1955. Random House.

Sierra Baron. Thomas Wakefield Blackburn. 1973. (pbk) 0.75. Dell.

Sierra Gold. Thomas Albert Curry. 1973. pap. 0.75 o.p. (07319). Curtis.

Sierra Massacre. Cliff Reno. (Fawcett gold medal book). 1974. (pbk.) 0.95. Fawcett.

Sierra Sierra, a Novel. John Joss. LC 77-82561. (Illus.). 1978. 8.95 (ISBN 0-688-03368-7). Morrow.

Sierra Silver. John W Hardin. (Fargo, # 16). 1974. (pbk.) 0.95. Belmont Tower Books.

Siesta. Fleming, Berry. LC 35-5115. Harcourt, Brace and Company.

Sieze the Day. Saul Bellow. 1977. 1.75 (ISBN 0-380-01649-4). Avon.

Sifted Wheat: Eleven Kernels. Roe Fulkerson. LC 23-12591. Gordon Bankers Publicity Corporation.

Sifting Matrimony. Cara Camera. LC 6-21858. T. B. Peterson & Brothers.

Sifting of Philip. Everett Titsworth Tomlinson. 1908. American Baptist Publication Society.

TITLE INDEX SILAS MARNER.

Siftings from Poverty Flat: Short Stories. Frances Asa Charles. 1893. The Californian Publishing Co.
Sig Byrd's Houston. Sigman Byrd. LC 55-6556. 1955. Viking Press.
Sigh for a Drumbeat. Patrick Doncaster. LC 48-2554. 1948. E. P. Dutton.
Sigh for a Strange Land. Monica Stirling. LC 59-5929. 1959. Little, Brown.
Sighard: The Tale of a Centvrion. William Schmidt & Schuette, Walter Erwin. LC 1-29810. 1900. Lvtheran Book Concern.
Sight of a Stranger. Sandra Field. (Harlequin Romances Ser.). 192p. 1982. pap. 1.50 (ISBN 0-373-02480-0). Harlequin Bks.
Sight of Death by Jeremy York Pseud. John Creasey. LC 57-187019. 1956. S. Paul.
Sight of Proteus. Charles Sheffield. (Ace Book). 1978. 1.75 (ISBN 0-441-76343-X). Grosset and Dunlap.
Sight to the Blind: A Story. Lucy Furman. LC 14-20368. 1914. 1.00. The Macmillan Company.
Sight Unseen. Raymond John Jeffreys. LC 52-6497. 1951. Capitol College Press.
Sight Unseen. Audrey Erskine Lindop. LC 68-21059. 1969. 5.95. Doubleday.
Sight Unseen, and The Confession. Mary Roberts Rinehart. LC 21-145441. George H. Doran Company.
Sighting. Luci Shaw. LC 81-9342. (Wheaton Literary Series). (Illus.). 3.95 (ISBN 0-87788-768-3). H. Shaw.
Sighting. John Wynne. (A Tree Line Story Book). (Orig.). 1978. pap. 2.00 o.s.i. (ISBN 0-931476-00-3); pap. 20.00 signed ed. o.s.i. Tree Line.
Sightless Horseman. Marque Trayde. Guild Publishers Inc.
Sights - Three Novellas. Anna Holmes. LC 63-22335. (Orig.). 1963. pap. 1.85 (ISBN 0-87376-001-8). Red Dust.
Sights a-Foot. Wilkie Collins. LC 13-1765. 1876. T. B. Peterson and Brothers.
Sights and Insights: Patience Strong's Story of Over the Way. Adeline Dutton Train Whitney. 1876. J. R. Osgood and Company.
Sightseer. Geoffrey Wolff. LC 73-13705. 1974. 6.95 (ISBN 0-394-48712-5). Random House.
Sigla of Finnegans Wake. LC 76-13577. 14.95 (ISBN 0-292-77528-8). University of Texas Press.
Sigma Phi: A Novel in Poetry and Prose. John Frederick Rachal. LC 74-30323. (Illus.). 1960. Vantage Press.
Sigmet Active: A Novel. Thomas Page. LC 78-53307. 8.95 (ISBN 0-8129-0774-4). Times Books.
Sign. Katharine Waldo Douglas Fedden. LC 12-15739. 1912. 1.25. Dodd, Mead and Company.
Sign. Robin Maugham. LC 74-189974. (Illus.). 1974. 2.25 (ISBN 0-491-01690-5). W. H. Allen.
Sign Above the Door. William Walker Canfield. LC 12-158136. 1912. 1.00. The Jewish Publication Society of America.
Sign at Six. Stewart Edward White. LC 12-19161. The Bobbs-Merrill Company.
Sign-Board, and Other Stories:...From the French by O. A. Bierstadt... Michel Masson et al. Tr. by Oscar Albert Bierstadt. LC 8-27037. (Rialto Ser.). (On cover: Rialto series, no. 37: No. 37). 1891. Rand, McNally & Company.
Sign for Cain. Grace Lumpkin. LC 35-19422. Lee Furman, Inc.
Sign in Sidney Brustein's Window see Raisin in the Sun.
Sign in the Dust. Lela P Tarbox. 3.50. Carlton Press Dist. Comet Press.
Sign of Arnim. Graham Seton Hutchison. LC 31-290697. 1931. Cosmopolitan Book Corporation.
Sign of Dawn. James Wylie. LC 80-52009. (Illus.). 1981. 13.95 (ISBN 0-670-64462-5). Viking Press.
Sign of Death. Barbara Merrell. (YA) 1981. pap. 2.50 (ISBN 0-89083-781-3). Zebra.
Sign of Evil. Robert McNair Wilson. LC 25-6618. 1925. J. B. Lippincott Company.
Sign of Fear: A Judge Peck Mystery. August William Derleth. LC 35-327700. Loring & Mussey.
Sign of Flame. Elisabeth Burstenbinder. LC 2-16199. (Manhattan library of new copyright fiction). 1902. A. L. Burt Co.
Sign of Four. Arthur Conan Doyle. LC 76-27104. (Illus.). 1977. 7.95 (ISBN 0-385-12285-3). Doubleday.
Sign of Four. Arthur Conan Doyle. LC 76-27104. 1977. 9.95 (ISBN 0-385-12285-3). Doubleday.
Sign of Four. Arthur Conan Doyle & Zangwill, Israel, 1864-1926. The Big Bow Mystery. LC 28-24488. (S. S. Van Dine detective library). 1928. C. Scribner's Sons.
Sign of Four: And A Study in Scarlet. Sir Arthur Conan Doyle. 1976. (pbk.) 1.25. Belmont Tower.
Sign of Freedom. Arthur Frederick Goodrich. LC 16-95433. 1916. D. Appleton and Company.
Sign of Jonah. Nancy Hale. LC 50-9783. 1950. Scribner.
Sign of Love. Barbara Cartland. LC 77-17353. 1977. 6.95 (ISBN 0-87272-032-2). Duron Books.
Sign of Taurus: A Novel. William Fifield. LC 60-8156. 1960. Holt, Rinehart and Winston.
Sign of the Blue Dragon. Jacquelyn Aeby. (Candlelight Historical Romance, 202). Dell.
Sign of the Burning Ship. Louis Arthur Cunningham. The Penn Publishing Company.
Sign of the Cobra. Nick Carter. (Nick Carter Ser.). 176p. 1981. pap. 2.25 (ISBN 0-441-76347-2, Pub. by Charter Bks). Ace Bks.
Sign of the Cobra. Nick Carter. (Nick Carter Ser.). (O.s.i.). 192p. (Orig.). 1974. pap. 0.95 o.s.i. (AN1270, Award). Univ Pub & Dist.
Sign of the Crescent Moon. Thomas J. Saunders. LC 76-56040. 1977. 7.00 o.p. (ISBN 0-682-48762-7). Exposition.
Sign of the Cross. Wilson Barrett. LC 6-8051. 1897. J. B. Lippincott Company.
Sign of the Cross. Wilson Barrett. LC 43-6571. 1943. The Sun Dial Press.
Sign of the Four. Arthur Conan Doyle. LC 5026. 1900. W. B. Conkey Co.
Sign of the Four. A Scandal in Bohemia, and Other Stories. Arthur Conan Doyle. LC 4-16519. (On cover: The home library). A. L. Burt Company.
Sign of the Four: Or the Problem of the Sholtos. Arthur Conan Doyle. 1975. (pbk.) 3.95 (ISBN 0-345-24715-9). Ballantine Books.
Sign of the Guardian. John A. Long. 256p. (Orig.). 1981. pap. 2.50 (ISBN 0-523-48005-9). Pinnacle Bks.
Sign of the Gun. Archie Joscelyn. LC 45-2941. 1945. Phoenix Press.
Sign of the Labrys. St. Clair, Margaret. LC 63-15233. 1963. Bantam Books.
Sign of the Morning. Irving Buckingham Holman. LC 12-22812. Jennings and Graham.
Sign of the Pagan. Roger Fuller, pseud. LC 54-10537. 1954. Dial Press.
Sign of the Prayer Shawl. Nick Carter. (Nick Carter Ser.). (O.s.i.). (Orig.). 1976. pap. 1.25 o.s.i. (AQ1590, Award). Univ Pub & Dist.
Sign of the Praying Tiger. Ben Lucien Burman. LC 66-17727. 1966. New American Library.
Sign of the Prophet: A Tale of Tecumseh and Tippecanoe. James Ball Naylor. LC 4-24839. 1901. The Saalfield Publishing Company.
Sign of the Ram. Margaret Ferguson. LC 45-2274. 1945. The Blakiston Company.
Sign of the Raven. Poul Anderson. (Last Viking Ser.: No. 3). (Orig.). 1981. pap. 2.50. Zebra.
Sign of the Raven. Poul Anderson. (Last Viking Ser.: No. 2). 352p. (Orig.). 1980. pap. 2.50 (ISBN 0-89083-625-6). Zebra.
Sign of the Scorpian. Bruce Abbott. pap. 1.95 o.p. (V1009T, Venus). Grove.
Sign of the Scorpion. LC 73-111002. 224p. 1981. pap. 2.95 o.p. (ISBN 0-394-17894-7, B-450, BC). Grove.
Sign of the Serpent. Sidney Floyd Gowing. LC 23-4138. 1923. G. P. Putnam's Sons.
Sign of the Snake. Derek Vane. LC 28-8134. Macrae Smith Company.
Sign of the Spider. Bertram Mitford. LC 3-1782. 1897. Dodd, Mead and Company.
Sign of the Thunderbird. Ron Montana. 1977. pap. 1.75 (ISBN 0-532-17167-5). Woodhill.
Sign of the Unicorn. Roger Zelazny. LC 74-12722. (Doubleday science fiction). 1975. 5.95 (ISBN 0-385-08515-X). Doubleday.
Sign of the Unicorn. roger zelazny. ed. Roger Zelazny. 1.50 (ISBN 0-380-00831-9). Avon Books.
Sign on for Tokyo. Alec Haig. LC 69-12469. (Red badge mystery). 1969. 3.95. Dodd, Mead.
Sign Upon My Hand. Marjorie Duhan Adler. LC 64-10023. 1964. Doubleday.
Signa. Louise De La Ramee. LC 6-33307. (On cover: Lovell's library. v. 18 no. 854). 1887. J. W. Lovell Company.
Signa. A Story. Louise De La Ramee. LC 6-33309. 1875. J. B. Lippincott & Co.
Signa. A Story. Louise De La Ramee. LC 6-33308. 1876. J. B. Lippincott & Co.
Signal, & Other Stories. facsimile ed. Wsewolod M. Garshin. Tr. by Rowland Smith from Rus. LC 77-163027. (Short Story Index Reprint Ser.). Repr. of 1915 ed. 19.00 (ISBN 0-8369-3941-7). Ayer Co.
Signal, Close Action! Alexander Kent. LC 74-16603. (Illus.). 1974. 7.95 (ISBN 0-399-11448-3). Putnam.
Signal-Close Action! Alexander Kent. (Berkley Medallion Book). 1976. (pbk.) 1.50 (ISBN 0-425-03035-0). G. P. Putnam.
Signal; Doc Smith, Town Promoter and Realtor: And His Interesting Family, Pioneers of West Texas. Ethel Jeanette Mauldin. LC 42-537. 1941. The Naylor Company.
Signal for Danger. Terry Harnan. LC 46-4358. 1946. Pub. for the Crime Club by Doubleday & Company, Inc.
Signal for Death. Cecil John Charles Street. LC 41-10973. 1941. Dodd, Mead & Company.
Signal Guns at Sunup. John Jo Carpenter. LC 50-7385. (Essandess western). 1950. Simon and Schuster.
Signal Guns at Sunup: By John Jo Carpenter Pseud. John Henry Reese. LC 50-7385. (Essandess western). 1950. Simon and Schuster.
Signal Lights: A Story of Life on the Prairies. Louise Martin Hopkins. LC 6-31387. 1906. The C. M. Clark Publishing Co.
Signal of Promise. Ella Booker Cook. LC 54-674872. 1954. Dorrance.
Signal Red. Harold Calin. pap. 0.75 o.p. Lancer.
Signal Red. Harold Calin. 1975. (pbk.) 1.25. Leisure Books.
Signal Thirty-Two: A Novel. MacKinlay Kantor. LC 50-9555. 1950. Random House.
Signal Victory. David Stacton. LC 60-13200. 1962. Pantheon Books.
Signals. Deborah Deutschman. LC 78-15266. 9.95 (ISBN 0-87223-513-0). Seaview Books: Trade Distribution by Simon and Schuster.
Signals. Deborah Deutschman. 1980. 2.50 (ISBN 0-87216-604-X). Playboy Press Paperbacks.
Signals from the Bay Tree. Henry Stanislaus Spalding. LC 21-18250. 1921. Benziger Brothers.
Signature. F. R. Scott. 56p. 1964. pap. 2.50 o.p. (ISBN 0-7735-9057-9). McGill-Queens U Pr.
Signature of Time. Walter Havighurst. LC 49-5790. 1949. Macmillan Co.
Signature of Venus. Desemea Wilson. LC 33-18478. E. P. Dutton & Co., Inc.
Signed in Yellow. Ethel H Loban. LC 30-102537. 1930. Pub. for The Crime Club, Inc., by Doubleday, Doran & Company, Inc.
Signed with Their Honour. James Aldridge. LC 42-17639. 1942. Little, Brown and Company.
Signet of King Solomon: Or, The Templar's Daughter. Augustus C. L Arnold. 1860. Macoy & Sickels.
Signet-Ring, and Other Gems. Jan De Liefde. LC 7-15842. Gould and Lincoln.
Signifcant Name in Terence. James C. Austin. pap. 7.00 (ISBN 0-384-02605-2). Johnson Repr.
Significant Contemporary Stories: Edtied by Edith Mirrielees... Edith Ronald Mirrielees. LC 29-5947. 1929. Doubleday, Doran & Company, Inc.
Significant Experience. Gwyn Griffin. LC 63-17964. 1963. Holt, Rinehart and Winston.
Signing off. John Thomas McIntyre. LC 38-17281. Farrar & Rinehart, Inc.
Signing the Contract, and What It Cost. Martha Finley. LC 6-412192. Dodd, Mead & Company.
Signor Monaldini's Niece. Mary Agnes Tincker. LC 34-37796. (No name series. 2d ser., v. 1). 1879. Roberts Brothers.
Signor Monaldini's Niece. Mary Agnes Tincker. LC 8-26772. (On cover: No name series). 1880. Roberts Brothers.
Signora. Gustav Kobbe. T. Y. Crowell & Co.
Signora, a Child of the Opera House. Gustav Kobbe. LC 2-26752. 1902. R. H. Russell.
Signorina. Henry Myers. LC 56-7187. 1956. Crown Publishers.
Signors of the Night. facs. ed. Max Pemberton. LC 74-132123. (Short Story Index Reprint Ser). 1899. 16.00 (ISBN 0-8369-3680-9). Ayer Co.
Signors of the Night: The Story of Fra Giovanni, the Soldier-Monk of Venice; and of Others in the "Silent City". Max Pemberton. LC 99-4970. 1899. Dodd, Mead and Company.
Signpost. Eileen Arbuthnot Robertson. LC 43-18120. 1944. The Macmillan Company.
Signpost to Love, No. 131. Barbara Cartland. 144p. (Orig.). 1981. pap. 1.75 (ISBN 0-553-14360-3). Bantam.
Signpost to Terror. 1969. pap. 0.60 o.p. (ISBN 0-448-05301-2, Tempo). G&D.
Signpost to Terror. Gretchen Sprague. LC 67-17648. 1967. Dodd, Mead.
Signs and Symptoms: Thomas Pynchon and the Contemporary World. Peter L Cooper. LC 82-6929. 19.95 (ISBN 0-520-04537-8). University of California Press.
Signs & Voices. M. Jurgensen. 1973. pap. 4.95x (ISBN 0-7022-0883-3). U of Queensland Pr.
Signs and Wonders. John Davys Beresford. LC 22-1458. 1921. G. P. Putnam's Sons.
Signs and Wonders. Leo Brady. LC 52-12335. 1953. Dutton.
Signs and Wonders. Ed. by Roger Elwood. LC 74-186535. 1972. 3.95 (ISBN 0-8007-0521-1). F. H. Revell Co.
Signs and Wonders: By Francoise Mallet-Joris. Tr. from French by Herma Briffault. Francoise Mallet-Joris. LC 67-13411. 1966-1967. 6.95. Farrar.
Signs Is Signs. Royal Dixon. LC 15-12885. 1915. 1.00. G. W. Jacobs & Company.
Signs of a Migrant Worker. Woolf, Douglas. LC 66-6077. 1965. Coyote's Journal.
Signs of a Migrant Worrier. Douglas Woolf. LC 75-317128. (Coyote book; no. 3). 1965. 1.75. Coyote's Journal.
Signs of Life. Sumner Locke Elliott. LC 80-21914. 288p. 1981. 11.95 (ISBN 0-89919-022-7). Ticknor & Fields.
Signs of Life. Francois Louvel & Louis J. Putz. 1970. pap. 0.95 o.p. (ISBN 0-8190-0363-8, Dome). Fides.
Signs of Life: A Novel. Sumner Locke Elliott. LC 80-21914. 1981. 11.95 (ISBN 0-89919-022-7). Ticknor & Fields.
Signs of Love & Glory. Hans Holzer. (Orig.). 1979. pap. 2.25 (ISBN 0-532-23103-1). Woodhill.
Signs of the Gods. Erich Von Daniken. 240p. 1981. pap. 2.75 (ISBN 0-425-05085-8). Berkley Pub.
Sigrid: An Icelandic Love Story. Jon Poroarsson Thoroddsen & Chrest, C., Tr. LC 8-19950. T. Y. Crowell & Co.
Sigrid and the Sergeant. Robert Buckner. LC 57-12518. 1957. Appleton-Century-Crofts.
Sigrid's Beautiful Frame. Gus Stevens. (Orig.). 1972. pap. 1.95 o.s.i. (TCP2338, Travellers Comp). Olympia.
Sigrid's Beautiful Frame. Gus Stevens. 1972. pap. 1.95 o.s.i. (TCP-2338). Olympia.
Sigurd Eckdal's Bride; a Romance of the Far North: By Richard Voss; Translated by Mary J. Safford; Illustrated by F. E. Schoonover. Richard Voss & Safford, Mary Joanna, D. 1916, Tr. LC 5177. 1900. Little, Brown, and Company.
Sigurd the Dragon Slayer. Kyaethi Sjurthar. Tr. by E. Smith-Dampier. 1934. 12.00 (ISBN 0-527-83200-6). Kraus Repr.
Silas Bradford's Boy. Joseph Crosby Lincoln. LC 42-470722. 1930. A. L. Burt Company.
Silas Bradford's Boy. Joseph Crosby Lincoln. LC 28-22461. 1928. D. Appleton & Company.
Silas Braunton. J Mills Whitham. LC 23-104509. 1923. The Macmillan Company; Etc., Etc.
Silas Brown, Pioneer: An Autobiographical Story. Alberto A Bennett. LC 77-95293. (Illus.). 1978. 5.95 (ISBN 0-912760-65-6). Valkyrie Press.
Silas Cobb: A Story of Supervision. Dan Voorhees Stephens. LC 1-12870. 1901. Hammond Bros. & Stephens.
Silas Crockett. Mary Ellen Chase. LC 35-253879. 1935. The Macmillan Company.
Silas Hood: A Novel. Henry Thornton. 1898. H. T. Jaynes & Company.
Silas Kirkendown's Sons. Margret Holmes Ernsperger Bates. LC 8-30933. 1908. The C. M. Clark Publishing Co.
Silas Marner. George Eliot. LC 66-1617. (Noble's comparative classics). (Illus.). 1965. Noble and Noble.
Silas Marner. George Eliot. (Lovell's library, v. 2, no. 71). 1883. J. W. Lovell Company.
Silas Marner. George Eliot & Barrie, Sir James Matthew, Bart., 1800-1937. The Little Minister. LC 43-34019. Globe Book Company.
Silas Marner. George Eliot & Colby, June Rose, 1856- Ed. LC 31-35208. (Half-title: Twentieth century text-books, ed. by A.F. Nightingale). D. Appleton and Company.
Silas Marner. George Eliot & Cross, Wilbur Lucius, 1862- Ed. LC 4-4977. (gateway series of English texts). American Book Company.
Silas Marner. George Eliot & Eaton, Mary P. Ed. LC 25-8545. (Winston companion classics). The John C. Winston Company.
Silas Marner. George Eliot & Fairley, Edwin, Ed. LC 13-26180. (Half-title: The Barnes English texts. General editor: E. Fairley). 1913. 0.35. The A.S. Barnes Company.
Silas Marner. George Eliot & Fairley, Edwin, Ed. LC 28-975. (Laidlaw English classics). Laidlaw Brothers, Incorporated.
Silas Marner. George Eliot & Gaston, Charles Robert, 1874- Ed. LC 23-86060. (Atlantic library of English classics). The Atlantic Monthly Press.
Silas Marner. George Eliot & Gulick, Edward Leeds, 1862- Ed. LC 90-2778. (On verso of half-title: Macmillan's pocket English classics). 1899. The Macmillan Company.
Silas Marner. George Eliot & Gulick, Edward Leeds, 1862- Ed. LC 29-20593. (Half-title: New pocket classics). The Macmillan Company.
Silas Marner. George Eliot & Hadsell, Sardis Roy, Ed. LC 26-15273. (Western series of English and American classics). 1926. Harlow Publishing Company.
Silas Marner. George Eliot & Hancock, Albert Elmer, Ed. LC 99-4192. (On cover: The Lake English classics). 1899. Scott, Foresman and Company.
Silas Marner. George Eliot & Hancock, Albert Elmer, 1870-1915, Ed. LC 19-17070. (Lake English classics). Scott, Foresman and Company.
Silas Marner. George Eliot & Jones, Richard, 1855- Ed. LC 1097. (On cover: Twentieth century text-books). 1900. D. Appleton and Company.

Silas Marner. George Eliot & Otto, Willaim Naill, Ed. LC 23-5362. (Half-title: Lippincott's classics, ed. by Edwin L. Miller). J.B. Lippincott Company.
Silas Marner. George Eliot & Scarson, James William, 1873- Ed. LC 24-21925. (Half-title: University classics for high schools--colleges--universities). 1924. The University Publishing Company.
Silas Marner. George Eliot & Shattuck, Marquis E., Ed. LC 28-255806. (Merrill's English texts). Charles E. Merrill Company.
Silas Marner. George Eliot & Stevenson, Robert Louis, 1850-1894. Kidnapped. LC 42-3903. (Prose and poetry individualized program. (The novel). 1942. The L.W. Singer Company.
Silas Marner. George Eliot & Wiggins, Evelina Oakley, 1878- Ed. LC 17-28606. (Lettered on cover: Graded classics series). B. F. Johnson Publishing Co.
Silas Marner see Three Nineteenth-Century Novels.
Silas Marner: Adapted by Lambert Greenawalt and Grace A. Benscoter. Eliot, George, Pseud., I. E. Marian Evans, Afterwards Cross & Lambert Greenawalt. LC 51-598. (Classics for enjoyment). Laidlaw Bros.
Silas Marner. Adapted by Lou P. Bunce; Illustrated by Seymour Fleishman. Eliot, George, Pseud., I. E. Marian Evans, Afterwards Cross. LC 51-7130. 1951. Scott, Foresman.
Silas Marner. Brother Jacob. George Eliot. LC 26-26995. (Half-title: The writings of George Eliot. Riverside ed. vol. vii). Houghton, Mifflin Company.
Silas Marner: By George Eliot. The Pearl, by John Steinbeck, Ed. by Jay E. Greene. George Eliot & John Steinbeck. LC 66-1617. (Noble's comparative classics). 1966. 3.16. Noble & Noble.
Silas Marner: By George Eliot. The Pearl, by John Steinbeck. Edited by Jay E. Greene. George Pseud. I. E. Marian Evans Afterwards Cross Eliot & John Steinbeck. LC 54-1069. (Noble's comparative classics). 1953. Noble and Noble.
Silas Marner. Magnatype Ed. George Eliot. LC 65-27229. 1966. 12.00. Stanwix House.
Silas Marner, The Lifted Veil and Brother Jacob. George Eliot. LC 41-33234. John W. Lovell Co.
Silas Marner: The Weaver of Raveloe. George Eliot. LC 68-2261. (Penguin English library, EL30). 1967. Penguin Books.
Silas Marner: The Weaver of Raveloe. George Eliot. LC 65-6722. (Perennial classic). 1965. Harper & Row.
Silas Marner, the Weaver of Raveloe. George Eliot. LC 11-25916.
Silas Marner, the Weaver of Raveloe. George Eliot. LC 6-40731. (Harper's Franklin square library. Duodecimo ed.). 1883. Harper & Brothers.
Silas Marner: The Weaver of Raveloe. George Eliot. (On cover: Seaside library. Pocket ed., no. 707). 1886. G. Munro.
Silas Marner, the Weaver of Raveloe. George Eliot. LC 6-40730. (On cover: Eclectic English classics). 1894. American Book Company.
Silas Marner, the Weaver of Raveloe. George Eliot. LC 6-40727. (On Cover: Riverside Literature Series, No. 83). 1895. Houghton, Mifflin and Company.
Silas Marner, the Weaver of Raveloe. George Eliot. (On Cover: Maynard's English Classic Series, No. 170-172). Maynard, Merrill, & Co.
Silas Marner, the Weaver of Raveloe. George Eliot. LC 6-40726. (On Cover: Riverside Literature Series, No. 83). Houghton, Mifflin and Company.
Silas Marner, the Weaver of Raveloe. George Eliot. (Half-title: Everymans's library, edited by Ernest Rhys. Fiction no. 121). 1907. J.M. Dent & Co.
Silas Marner, the Weaver of Raveloe. George Eliot & Atkinson, W. Patterson, Ed. LC 99-4390. (Academy Series of English Classics). Allyn And Bacon.
Silas Marner, the Weaver of Raveloe. George Eliot & Avent, John M., Ed. LC 28-5408. (Academy classics). Allyn and Bacon.
Silas Marner, the Weaver of Raveloe. George Eliot & Beare, Cornelia, Ed. LC 8-24868. (Merrill's English texts). C.E. Merrill Co.
Silas Marner, the Weaver of Raveloe. George Eliot & Carman, Bliss, 1861-1929. LC 99-3350. (On cover: Riverside literature series, no. 83). Houghton, Mifflin and Company.
Silas Marner, the Weaver of Raveloe. George Eliot & Church, Mrs. Virginia Woodson (Frame) 1880- Ed. LC 29-23134. (Lettered on cover: Stratford classics). Lyons & Carnshan.
Silas Marner, the Weaver of Raveloe. George Eliot & Hale, Edward Everett, 1863-1932, Ed. LC 2971. (On Cover: Standard Literature Series, No. 43). University Publishing Company.
Silas Marner, the Weaver of Raveloe. George Eliot & Witham, Rose Adelaide, 1873- Ed. LC 27-18973. Ginn and Company.
Silas Marner: The Weaver of Raveloe, Ed., Introd. by Q. D. Lewis. Eliot, George, Pseud, I.E. Marian Evans, Afterwards Cross. LC 68-2261. (Penguin English lib., EL30). 1967. pap., 1.25. Penguin.
Silas Marner, the Weaver of Raveloe: Ed., with Introduction and Notes by Franklin T. Baker... George Eliot & Baker, Franklin Thomas, 1864- Ed. LC 11-15194. (Half-title: The Scribner English classics, ed. by F.H. Sykes). 1911. 0.25. C. Scribner's Sons.
Silas Marner: The Weaver of Raveloe. Introd. by Charles Angoff. George Eliot. LC 57-3258. 1957. Fine Editions Press.
Silas Marner: The Weaver of Raveloe. Introd. by Michael Harrington. George Eliot. (Masterworks ser., d368). 1968. Fawcett.
Silas Marner: The Weaver of Raveloe, with Brother Jacob. George Eliot. LC 40-33699. (World juvenile library). 1937. The World Syndicate Publishing Company.
Silas Marner: With Illus. of Contemporary Scenes and a Foreword by Basil Davenport. George Eliot. LC 48-6156. (Great illustrated classics). 1948. Dodd, Mead.
Silas Snobden's Office Boy. Horatio Alger. LC 72-87500. (Illus.). 1973. 5.95 (ISBN 0-385-02551-3). Doubleday.
Silas Strong: Emperor of the Woods. Irving Bacheller. LC 6-9279. 1906. Harper & Brothers.
Silas Strong, Emperor of the Woods. Irving Bacheller. LC 42-48286. 1906. Grosset & Dunlap.
Silas Timberman. Howard Melvin Fast. LC 55-735. 1954. Blue Heron Press.
Silbermann. Jacques De Lacretelle. Tr. by Brian Lunn. LC 24-1307. 1923. Boni and Liveright.
Silbo Vulnerado see Rayo Que No Cesa.
Silcote of Silcotes. new ed. Henry Kingsley. LC 47-34984. 1895. Ward, Lock & Bowden, Limited.
Silence. Shusaku Endo. LC 76-365123. 1976. 4.25 (ISBN 0-7206-0354-4). P. Owen.
Silence. Shusaku Endo. LC 77-23391. 1977. 8.95 (ISBN 0-316-23860-0). Little, Brown.
Silence. Shusaku Endo. LC 78-27168. 1979. 9.95 (ISBN 0-8008-7183-9). Taplinger Pub. Co.
Silence. Alice Edna Gipson. LC 30-193631. 1930. The Caxton Printers, Ltd.
Silence: A Compound Problem Novel. Jean Louis De Esque. LC 8-24878. 1908. Connoisseur's Press.
Silence: A Novel. Iurii Vasilevich Bondarev. LC 66-11229. 1966. Houghton Mifflin.
Silence, and Other Stories. Mary Eleanor Wilkins Freeman. LC 74-101812. (Short story index reprint series). (Illus.). 1969. Books for Libraries Press.
Silence: And Other Stories. Mary Eleanor Wilkins Freeman. LC 6-40024. 1898. Harper & Brothers.
Silence & Other Stories. Krishna Balder Vaid. (Writers Workshop Greenbird Ser.). 94p. 1975. 14.00 (ISBN 0-88253-634-6); pap. text ed. 4.80 (ISBN 0-88253-633-8). Ind-US Inc.
Silence & Other Stories by Mary E. Wilkins. Mary Eleanor Wilkins Freeman. LC 74-101812. (Short Story Index Reprint Ser.). 1898. 16.00 (ISBN 0-8369-3200-5). Ayer Co.
Silence at Salerno: A Comedy of Intrigue. Francis Steegmuller. LC 77-17937. 8.95 (ISBN 0-03-041641-8). Holt, Rinehart and Winston.
Silence at Yorktown. William Ross McHale. Leisure Books.
Silence for His Worship. Bernard Ash. LC 54-5261. 1954. Knopf.
Silence for the Murderer. Freeman Wills Crofts. (Red badge detective). 1948. Dodd, Mead.
Silence in Bilbao. Margaret Cochran Shedd. LC 73-15365. 1974. 6.95 (ISBN 0-385-00586-5). Doubleday.
Silence in Court. Patricia Wentworth. LC 45-4021. 1945. J. B. Lippincott Company.
Silence in Crete. Elisabeth Ayrton. LC 64-10509. 1964. Morrow.
Silence in Eden. Jerry Allen Potter. LC 77-18639. 9.95 (ISBN 0-690-01742-1). Crowell.
Silence in Eden: Jerry Allen Potter. Jerry Allen Potter. 1979. 2.25 (ISBN 0-445-04430-6). Popular Library.
Silence Is Deadly. Lloyd Biggle, Jr. LC 76-56267. (Doubleday science fiction). (Illus.). 1977. 6.95 (ISBN 0-385-11033-2). Doubleday.
Silence Is Goldberg: By Julien Vedey Pseud. Julien Louis Robinson. LC 57-177508. 1956. Channel Island Publishers.
Silence Observed. Michael Innes. 1975. (pbk.) 1.25. Ballantine Books.
Silence Observed. John Innes Mackintosh Stewart. LC 61-12316. (Red badge detective). 1961. Dodd, Mead.
Silence of Colonel Bramble. Andre' Maurois. Tr. by Thurfrida Wake. Jackson, Wilfred, Tr. LC 20-4463. 1920. John Lane Company.
Silence of Colonel Bramble. Andre Maurois. Tr. by Thurfrida Wake. Jackson, Wilfrid Scarborough, 1871- Tr & Whitlock, Brand, 1869-1934. LC 30-21947. 1930. D. Appleton and Company.
Silence of Colonel Bramble. new ed. Andre Maurois. Tr. by Thurfrida Wake. Jackson, Wilfrid Scarborough, 1871- Tr. 1941. D. Appleton Century Company, Incorporated.
Silence of Dean Maitland. Mary Gleed Tuttiett. LC 1-2424. (The Antique library of standard and popular 12mos). 1901. Rand, McNally & Company.
Silence of Dean Maitland: A Novel, 3 vols. in 2. Maxwell Gray. LC 79-8209. Repr. of 1886 ed. Set. 84.50 (ISBN 0-404-62188-0). AMS Pr.
Silence of Dean Maitland: A Novel. Mary Gleed Tuttiett. LC 4-22822. 1903. D. Appleton and Company.
Silence of Desire. Kamala Purnaiya Taylor. LC 60-11299. 1960. John Day Co.
Silence of Gom. Kurt Mahr. (Perry Rhodan, #39). 1974. (pbk.) 0.75. Ace Books.
Silence of Herondale. Joan Aiken. LC 64-18703. 1964. Published for the Crime Club by Doubleday.
Silence of Herondale. Joan Aiken. 1973. 0.95 (ISBN 0-671-77625-8). Pocket Bks.
Silence of History. James Thomas Farrell. LC 61-12518. 1963. Doubleday.
Silence of History. James Thomas Farrell. LC 61-12518. 1974. (pbk.) 1.50. Manor Books.
Silence of Men. Henry Francis Prevost Battersby. LC 13-9722. 1913. John Lane.
Silence of Mrs. Harrold. Samuel Major Gardenhire. LC 5-3785. 1905. Harper & Brothers.
Silence of Sebastian. Anna Theresa Sadlier. LC 13-15268. The Ave Maria.
Silence of the Maharajah. Marie Corelli. LC 6-28741. (On cover: Merriam's series no. 3). The Merriam Company.
Silence of the North. Olive A. Fredrickson & Ben East. 208p. 1973. pap. 2.75 (ISBN 0-446-85559-6). Warner Bks.
Silence Over Sinai. Margery Awin. 1976. pap. 1.50 o.p. (ISBN 0-515-03958-6). BJ Pub Group.
Silence Over Sinai. Margery Awni. 1976. 1.50 (ISBN 0-515-03958-6). Pyramid Publications.
Silent. C. A. Fox. LC 23-193. C. A. Fox.
Silent and True; or, A Little Queen. A Novel. May Agnes Early Fleming. LC 6-39943. 1877. G. W. Carleton & Co.; Etc., Etc.
Silent Are the Dead. George Harmon Coxe. LC 41-282934. 1942. A. A. Knopf.
Silent Army. Kee Onn Chin. LC 53-8759. (Illus.). 1953. Longmans, Green.
Silent Barrier. Louis Tracy. LC 11-22024. E. J. Clode.
Silent Barrier. Louis Tracy. LC 21-86729. Grosset & Dunlap.
Silent Battle. George Fort Gibbs. LC 13-677137. 1913. 1.30. D. Appleton and Company.
Silent Bullet. Arthur Benjamin Reeve. 1981. 18.95x (Pub. by Remploy England). State Mutual Bk.
Silent Bullet: The Adventures of Craig Kennedy, Scientific Detective. Arthur Benjamin Reeve. LC 75-32795. (Literature of Mystery and Detection). (Illus.). 1976. (ISBN 0-405-07896-X). Arno Press.
Silent Bullet: The Adventures of Craig Kennedy, Scientific Detective. Arthur Benjamin Reeve. LC 12-245818. 1912. Dodd, Mead and Company.
Silent Bullet: The Adventures of Craig Kennedy, Scientific Detective. Arthur Benjamin Reeve. LC 21-13716. 1920. Grosset & Dunlap.
Silent Call. Edwin Milton Royle. LC 10-13217. 1910. 1.50. C. Scribner's Sons.
Silent Children: A Novel. Mai-Mai Sze. LC 48-5864. 1948. Harcourt, Brace.
Silent Cities: Mexico & the Maya. Norman F. Carver. (Illus., & Fr, Ger). 1965. 25.00x o.p. (ISBN 0-8150-0160-6). Wittenborn.
Silent Conflict: A Story of Industrial Warfare. Charles Carroll Swafford. LC 16-20434. Roxburgh Publishing Company, Inc.
Silent Cousin: 1st Amer. Ed. Elizabeth Fenwick. LC 66-12994. 1966. 3.95. Atheneum.
Silent Cry. Kenzaburo Oe. LC 75-322591. 1974-1975. 10.00 (ISBN 0-87011-232-5). Kodansha International.
Silent Cry. Kenzaburo Oe. LC 80-85382. 1981. 4.95 (ISBN 0-87011-466-2). Kodansha International.
Silent Don, 2 vols. Mikhail Aleksandrovich Sholokhov. Incl. And Quiet Flows the Don. Mikhail Sholokhov. 1959. 7.95 o.p. (ISBN 0-394-41520-5, 41520). 1959. 7.95 ea. o.p. (ISBN 0-394-44550-3); 14.95 o.p. (44550, Set). Knopf.
Silent Don: I. and Quiet Flows the Don. II. The Don Flows Home to the Sea. Mikhail Aleksandrovich Sholokhov & Garry, Stephen, Tr. 1942. A. A. Knopf.
Silent Door. Florence Wilkinson Evans. LC 7-10292. 1907. McClure, Phillips & Co.
Silent Dreams. Drusilla Campbell. (Hopewell Saga: No. 2). (Orig.). 1982. pap. 2.95 (ISBN 0-440-08450-4, Banbury). Dell.
Silent Drum. Grace Kellogg Griffith. LC 29-115863. Macrae Smith Company.
Silent Drum. Neil Harmon Swanson. LC 40-29472. Farrar & Rinehart, Inc.
Silent Duchess. Anne Green. LC 39-29722. 1939. Harper & Brothers.
Silent Dust. Bruno Fischer. LC 50-9277. (Red badge detective). 1950. Dodd, Mead.
Silent Enemy. John Benteen. (Leisure Books). 1977. 1.25 (ISBN 0-8439-0456-9). Nordon Pubns.
Silent Enemy. John Benteen. (Sundance Ser.: No. 21). 1981. pap. 1.75 (ISBN 0-8439-1052-6, Leisure Bks). Nordon Pubns.
Silent Enemy. Ernest T. Jahn. 1981. pap. 2.75 (ISBN 0-89083-763-5). Zebra.
Silent Five. Thomas Morris Longstreth. LC 24-19421. 1.75. The Century Co.
Silent Galaxy. William Tedford. 288p. (Orig.). 1981. pap. 2.50 (ISBN 0-8439-0997-8, Leisure Bks). Nordon Pubns.
Silent Guests. Alfred Edgar Forrest. LC 28-1591. 1927. P. Covici.
Silent Halls of Ashenden. Dorothy Daniels. 1973. 0.95. Warner Paperback Library.
Silent Hostage. Sarah Gainham. pap. 0.60 o.p. (73-712). Lancer.
Silent House. John Gordon Brandon. LC 28-10630. 1928. L. MacVeagh, The Dial Press.
Silent in the Saddle. Norman A Fox. 1945. Dodd, Mead & Company.
Silent Invaders. Robert Silverberg. 1977. 1.50. Ace Books.
Silent Joe. Stan Layne. LC 55-13620. 1955. Meador Pub. Co.
Silent Land. A Study. Minnie Willis Baines Miller. LC 11-10507. 1890. Cranston & Stowe.
Silent Legion. Annie Edith Foster Jameson. LC 18-9886. Hodder and Stoughton.
Silent Liars. John Michael Evelyn. LC 74-111186. 1970. 4.50. Published for the Crime Club by Doubleday.
Silent Liars. Michael Underwood. (Crime Club Ser). 1970. 4.50 o.p. Doubleday.
Silent Life and Silent Language: Or, The Inner Life of a Mute in an Institution for the Deaf and Dumb. Kate M Farlow. LC 6-38674. 1883. Christian Publishing House Print.
Silent Mill. Hermann Sudermann. LC 19-8991. Brentano's.
Silent Missions. Vernon A. Walters. LC 77-16853. 1978. 12.95 o.p. (ISBN 0-385-13500-9). Doubleday.
Silent Murder. Mildred Evelyn Flagg. 1977. 5.50 o.p. (ISBN 0-682-48758-9). Exposition.
Silent Murders. Archibald Gordon Macdonnell. LC 29-12619. 1929. Longmans, Green and Co.
Silent Murders. Archibald Gordon Macdonnell. LC 29-19785. 1930. Pub. for the Crime Club, Inc., by Doubleday, Doran & Company, Inc.
Silent One. Owen Cameron. LC 58-109552. (Random House mystery). 1958. Random House.
Silent Ones. Elisabeth Ogilvie. LC 81-3723. 11.95 (ISBN 0-07-047679-9). McGraw-Hill.
Silent Ones. Elisabeth Ogilvie. LC 81-20118. 1982. 16.95 (ISBN 0-8161-3343-3). G.K. Hall.
Silent Ones. E. Oglivie. 304p. 1981. 11.95 (ISBN 0-07-047679-9). McGraw.
Silent Partner. Leigh Brackett. LC 69-18167. 1969. 4.50. Putnam.
Silent Partner. Augustus Muir. LC 30-4297. The Bobbs-Merrill Company.
Silent Partner. Elizabeth Stuart Phelps Ward. LC 67-29276. (Americans in Fiction). 1967. Gregg Press.
Silent Partner. Elizabeth Stuart Phelps H. D. Ward Ward. LC 8-36034. 1871. J. R. Osgood and Company, Late Ticknor & Fields, and Fields, Osgood & Co.; Etc., Etc.
Silent Partner. Elizabeth Stuart Phelps H. D. Ward Ward. LC 99-1121. Houghton, Mifflin, and Company.
Silent Partner. 1st Ed. Kathleen Moore Knight. LC 50-11090. 1950. Published for the Crime Club by Doubleday.
Silent Partners. Albert Kovetz. 400p. (Orig.). 1980. pap. 2.50 (ISBN 0-89083-688-4). Zebra.
Silent People. Walter Macken. LC 62-19425. 1962. Macmillan.
Silent Pioneer. Lucy Cleaver McElroy. LC 2-7126. 1902. T. Y. Crowell & Co.
Silent Place. Rachel Cosgrove Payes. 1976. (pbk.) 1.25. Ace Books.
Silent Places. Stewart Edward White. LC 15-20278. 1909. Doubleday, Page & Company.
Silent Places. Stewart Edward White. LC 21-129725. Grosset & Dunlap.
Silent Places: A Story. Stewart Edward White. LC 4-963593. 1904. McClure, Philips & Co.
Silent Pool. Patricia Wentworth. LC 80-14579. 1980. 11.50 (ISBN 0-88411-740-5). Aeonian Press.
Silent Pool. 1st Ed. Patricia Wertworth. (Her A Miss Silver mystery). 1954. Lippincott.
Silent Prophet. Joseph Roth. LC 79-67676. 1980. 10.95 (ISBN 0-87951-110-9). Overlook Press.

Silent Pursuit. Denis J. Harrington. (Orig.). 1976. pap. 1.50 (ISBN 0-89041-108-5, 3108). Major Bks.

Silent Queen. W. Seymour Leslie. LC 27-20826. 1927. Boni & Liveright.

Silent Reach. Osmar White. LC 79-10508. 8.95 (ISBN 0-684-16155-9). Scribner.

Silent Reefs. Dorothy Wilkinson Cottrell. LC 52-141183. 1953. Morrow.

Silent Region. Annie Edith Foster Jameson. LC 18-106958. George H. Doran Company.

Silent River: By Wayne Roberts Pseud. Robert G Athearn. LC 56-13317. Avalon Books.

Silent Room. Francesca Chimenti. (O.s.i.). (Orig.). 1972. pap. 0.75 o.s.i. (T2688). Pyramid Pubns.

Silent Sage: A Very Ancient Tale. Ken Reed. LC 75-301809. (Illus.). 1974. (ISBN 0-914794-00-0). Wisdom Garden Institute.

Silent Salesman. Michael Z Lewin. LC 77-7936. 1978. 8.95 (ISBN 0-394-40433-5). Knopf.

Silent Salesman. Lewin, Michael Z. 1981. 2.25 (ISBN 0-425-04031-3). Berkley Publishing Corp.

Silent Sam, and Other Stories of Our Day. Harvey Jerrold O'Higgins. LC 73-2917. (Short story index reprint series). 1973. (ISBN 0-8369-4251-5). Books for Libraries Press.

Silent Sam: And Other Stories of Our Day. Harvey Jerrold O'Higgins. LC 14-4460. 1914. 1.25. The Century Co.

Silent Scream. Michael Collins, pseud. (Dan Fortune Detective Ser.). 192p. (Orig.). 1979. pap. 2.25 (ISBN 0-87216-930-8). Playboy Pbks.

Silent Scream. Jane Lake. LC 75-40778. 176p. 1976. pap. 1.25 (ISBN 0-89041-060-7, 3060). Major Bks.

Silent Scream. Dennis Lynds. LC 73-7486. (Red badge novel of suspense). 1973. 4.95 (ISBN 0-396-06844-8). Dodd, Mead.

Silent Scream: A Dan Fortune Mystery Novel. Michael Collins, pseud. LC 73-7486. 188p. 1973. 4.95 o.p. (ISBN 0-396-06844-8). Dodd.

Silent Sea. Harry Homewood. LC 80-27561. 12.95 (ISBN 0-07-029695-2). McGraw-Hill.

Silent Sea: A Novel. Catherine Edith Macaulay Mackay Martin. LC 7-16623. (On cover: Harper's Franklin square library, no. 728). 1892. Harper & Brothers.

Silent Search. Marjorie A Clark. LC 73-155688. 1971. 3.95. Moody Press.

Silent Shepherd: A Christmas Story. John Benjamin Magee. LC 31-2828. The Iron City Printing Co.

Silent Shore. A Romance. John Bloundelle-Burton. (On cover: Seaside library. Pocket ed., no. 913). 1887. G. Munro.

Silent Shore: Or, The Mystery of St. James' Park. John Edward Bloundelle-Burton. (On cover: Lovell's library, no. 1191). 1888. J. W. Lovell Company.

Silent Singer. Clara Morris. LC 99-3068. 1899. Brentano's.

Silent Sins. Sharon L. Ball. 1982. 8.95 (ISBN 0-533-05329-3). Vantage.

Silent Siren. Thomas L Sterling. LC 58-4465. (Inner sanctum mystery). 1958. Simon and Schuster.

Silent Siren. Thomas L. Sterling. LC 58-4465. (Inner sanctum mystery). 1958. Simon and Schuster.

Silent Six. Austin J Small. LC 27-13772. George H. Doran Company.

Silent Slain. Chad Pilgrim. LC 58-591586. 1958. Abelard-Schuman.

Silent Song: A Novel. Mary Vigliante Szydlowski. LC 79-92184. 8.95 (ISBN 0-89696-070-6). Everest House.

Silent South see Collected Works.

Silent Speaker. Rex Stout. LC 46-7679. 1946. The Viking Press.

Silent Spring. Rachael Carson. 304p. 1978. pap. 2.95 (ISBN 0-449-23871-7, Crest). Fawcett.

Silent Storms. Ernest Poole. LC 27-20759. 1927. The Macmillan Company.

Silent Tarn. Hannah Priebsch Closs. LC 63-7499. 1963. Vanguard Press.

Silent Terror. T. C. H Jacobs, pseud. LC 37-343. The Macaulay Company.

Silent Thunder. Robert Barnes. (Orig.). 1980. pap. text ed. 1.75 o.s.i. (ISBN 0-505-51551-2). Tower Bks.

Silent Thunder. Cleal Bradford & Terri B. Winder. LC 74-21667. (Illus.). 1974. (ISBN 0-88494-272-4). Bookcraft.

Silent Voice. Susan Claudia. Bd. with Madness at the Castle. 1978. pap. 1.95 (ISBN 0-451-08266-4, J8266, Sig). NAL.

Silent Voice. Berenice V Dell. LC 25-11321. The Four Seas Company.

Silent Voyage: A Novel. James Pattinson. LC 59-7115. 1959. McDowell, Obolensky.

Silent Walls. Mary Linn Roby. (Signet book). 1974. (pbk.) 0.95. New American Library.

Silent War. John Ames Mitchell. LC 68-57541. (American novels of muckraking, propaganda, and social protest). 1968. Gregg Press.

Silent War. John Ames Mitchell. LC 6-388934. 1906. Life Publishing Company.

Silent Watcher. Florence Stevenson. (Kitty Telefair Ser). (O.s.i.). 192p. (Orig.). 1975. pap. 1.25 o.s.i. (AQ1413, Award). Univ Pub & Dist.

Silent Watcher. Florence Stevenson. (Kitty Telefair gothic series,#6). 1975. (pbk.) 1.25. Award Books.

Silent Water, the Romance and Tragedy of the American Cliff Dwellers: A Saga of the Mesa Verde, Colorado, Cliff Dwellers. Arthur Worley Monroe. LC 51-843. 1950. Wetzel Pub. Co.

Silent Whisper. Frank Dorn. (Orig.). 1979. pap. 1.75. Woodhill.

Silent, White and Beautiful: And Other Stories. Clarence Aaron Robbins. LC 21-13860. Boni and Liveright.

Silent Witness. George Harmon Coxe. LC 72-8665. 1973. 5.95 (ISBN 0-394-48337-5). Knopf.

Silent Witness. George Harmon Coxe. 1974. (pbk.) 1.25. Manor Books.

Silent Witness. Richard Austin Freeman. LC 15-2001. 1.20. The John C. Winston Company.

Silent Witness. Richard Austin Freeman. 1929. Dodd, Mead & Company.

Silent Witness. Melville Davisson Post. LC 31-545. 1930. Farrar & Rinehart Incorporated.

Silent Witness. Ruth McCarthy Sear. (YA) 1973. 4.95 o.p. (Avalon). Bouregy.

Silent Witness. Jeannette Ritchie Hadermann Walworth. (On cover: Cassell's "rainbow" series, no. 25). Cassell & Company.

Silent Witness. Susan Yankowitz. LC 75-36807. 1976. 7.95 (ISBN 0-394-49943-3). Knopf: Distributed by Random House.

Silent Witness. Susan Yankowitz. 1977. 1.75 (ISBN 0-380-01684-2). Avon.

Silent Witness: A Novel of Computer Crime. Ed Yourdon. LC 82-90213. 12.95 (ISBN 0-917072-28-6). Yourdon Press.

Silent Witness: A Tale of a Kentucky Tragedy. Kate Slaughter McKinney. LC 6-46772. 1906. The Neale Publishing Company.

Silent Witness: A Thriller Novel. Margaret Yorke. LC 74-31914. 1975. 5.95 (ISBN 0-8027-5318-3). Walker and Co.

Silent Witnesses. Dorothy Stockbridge Tillet. LC 42-51184. 1942. The Sun Dial Press.

Silent Witnesses. Dorothy Stockbridge Tillet. LC 38-352993. 1938. Pub. for the Crime Club, Inc., by Doubleday, Doran & Co., Inc.

Silent Witnesses. Dorothy Stockbridge Tillet. LC 39-8131. The Sun Dial Press, Inc.

Silent Women. Margaret Page Hood. LC 53-11044. 1954. Coward-McCann.

Silent Wonder. Samantha Hughes. (Candlelight Ecstasy Ser.). (Orig.). 1983. pap. 1.95 (ISBN 0-440-18409-6). Dell.

Silent Workman: A Story. Clinton Ross. LC 8-67234. 1886. G. P. Putnam's Sons.

Silent World. A Novel. Florence Riddell. LC 34-130068. 1934. J. B. Lippincott Company.

Silent World of Nicholas Quinn. Colin Dexter. LC 76-56976. (Illus.). 1977. 7.95 (ISBN 0-312-72467-5). St. Martin's.

Silent Zero, in Search of Sound. Tr. by Eric Sackheim from Chinese. LC 68-18958. (Mushinsha Bks). 1968. pap. 3.95 o.p. (ISBN 0-670-64486-2, Grossman). Penguin.

Silhouette in Scarlet. Elizabeth Peters, pseud. LC 82-22174. 12.95 (ISBN 0-312-92773-8). Congdon & Weed: Distributed by St. Martin's Press.

Silhouette of Mary Ann: A Novel About George Eliot. Annie Edith Foster Jameson. LC 31-20071. 1931. Frederick A. Stokes Company.

Silhouettes of American Life. Rebecca Harding Davis. LC 68-55669. (American short story series, v. 9). 1968. Garrett Press.

Silhouettes of American Life. Rebecca Harding Davis. LC 11-105281. 1892. C. Scribner's Sons.

Silica Gel Pseudomorph and Other Stories. Edward Hart. LC 24-25639. 1924. The Chemical Publishing Co.; Etc., Etc.

Silicon Valley. Michael Rogers. 1982. 15.50 (ISBN 0-671-41030-X). S&S.

Silinski, Master Criminal. Edgar Wallace. LC 43-12318. (Murder of the month. No. 3). 1942. The Avon Book Company.

Silk: A Legend As Narrated in the Journals and Correspondence of Jan Po. Samuel Merwin. LC 23-15474. 1923. Houghton Mifflin Company.

Silk and Steel. Stephen Alter. LC 80-10215. 11.95 (ISBN 0-374-26411-2). Farrar Straus Giroux.

Silk and the Husk. 1st Ed. Albert George Haskell. LC 59-16043. 1959. Vantage Press.

Silk Coquette. Edith Bateman Morris. LC 26-11252. 1926. The Penn Publishing Company.

Silk-Cotton Tree. Esther Sietmann Warner, pseud. LC 58-6650. 1958. Doubleday.

Silk Ladder, & Other Stories. Belle Cross. 4.50 o.p. Vantage.

Silk Purse. Elisabeth Sanxay Holding. LC 28-19749. E. P. Dutton & Company.

Silk Road. Simon Harvester. pap. 0.60 o.p. (60-357). H-B Bks.

Silk Stockin' Row. Charles R Ward. LC 74-29019. (Illus.). 1975. 6.95 (ISBN 0-87012-206-1). McClain Print. Co.

Silk Stocking Murders: A Roger Sheringham Case. Anthony Berkeley Cox. LC 28-230442. 1928. Pub. for The Crime Club, Inc., by Doubleday, Doran & Company, Inc.

Silk Stocking Street. Rachel Paris. 1972. cloth over bds 6.95 o.p. (ISBN 0-87797-020-3). Cherokee.

Silken Bond. Flora Kidd. (Harlequin Presents Ser.). 192p. 1980. pap. 1.50 (ISBN 0-373-10379-4, Pub. by Harlequin). PB.

Silken Cage. Rebecca Stratton. (Harlequin Romances Ser.). 192p. 1981. pap. 1.50 (ISBN 0-373-02434-7). Harlequin Bks.

Silken Caresses. Samantha Carroll. (Second Chance at Love Ser.: No. 26). 192p. (Orig.). 1982. pap. 1.75 (ISBN 0-515-06108-5). Jove Pubns.

Silken Eyes. Francoise Quoirez. LC 77-21659. 6.95 (ISBN 0-440-08308-7). Delacorte Press/E. Friede.

Silken Eyes. Francoise Sagan, pseud. Tr. by Joanna Kilmartin from French. 1977. 6.95 o.p. (ISBN 0-440-08308-7, E Friede). Delacorte.

Silken Lines and Silver Hooks. T. E Apter. LC 76-365962. 1976. 3.50 (ISBN 0-434-02304-3). Heinemann.

Silken Net. Melvyn Bragg. LC 74-7719. 1974. 7.95 (ISBN 0-394-49307-9). Knopf: Distributed by Random House.

Silken Net. Rachelle Edwards. 1979. 1.75 (ISBN 0-449-24233-1). Fawcett Crest.

Silken Rapture. Cassie Edwards. 1983. pap. 3.50 (ISBN 0-8217-1172-5). Zebra.

Silken Scarf. L. C Hobart. LC 23-14482. E. P. Dutton & Company.

Silken Threads. A Detective Story. Harold Williams. LC 8-36915. 1885. Cupples, Upham, and Company.

Silken Threads. A Detective Story. Harold Williams. LC 8-36913. (On cover: The green paper series no. 2). 1889. Cupples and Hurd.

Silken Trap. Charlotte Lamb, pseud. (Harlequin Presents Ser.). 192p. 1980. pap. 1.50 (ISBN 0-373-10374-3). Harlequin Bks.

Silken Web. Miriam Lynch. pap. 0.75 o.s.i. (01-342). Lancer.

Silkie. Alfred Elton Van Vogt. 1982. pap. 2.25 (ISBN 0-87997-695-0, UE1695). Daw Bks.

Silkies: A Novel of the Shetlands. Charlotte Koplinka. LC 77-79123. (Illus.). 1979. 7.95 (ISBN 0-8397-7810-4). P. S. Eriksson.

Silky! A Detective Story. Leo Calvin Rosten. LC 78-20215. 10.00 (ISBN 0-06-013671-5). Harper & Row.

Silky! A Detective Story. Leo Calvin Rosten. 1980. 2.25 (ISBN 0-553-13547-3). Bantam Books.

Silky: An Incredible Tale. Elizabeth Jane Coatsworth. LC 52-10120. (Illus.). 1953. Pantheon Books.

Sillycomb. Hunce Voelcker. 1973. 4.95 (ISBN 0-915572-10-9). Panjandrum.

Silmarillion. John Ronald Reuel Tolkien. LC 77-8025. (Illus.). 1977. 10.95. Houghton Mifflin.

Silver Age: And Other Dramatic Memories. Temple Scott. LC 19-198513. 1919. Scott & Seltzer.

Silver and Gold: A Story of Luck and Love in a Western Mining Camp. Dane Coolidge. LC 19-13645. 1.75. E. P. Dutton & Company.

Silver and Pewter: A Tale of High Life and Low Life in New York. M. M Huet. H. Long & Brother.

Silver Answer. Marian Castle. LC 60-8108. 1960. Morrow.

Silver Answer... Rhoda Hoff. LC 45-183067. 1945. Dodd, Mead & Company.

Silver Arrow. Elizabeth Ashton. (Harlequin Romances Ser.). 192p. 1981. pap. 1.50 (ISBN 0-373-02425-8). Harlequin Bks.

Silver Arrow. Frank Laurence Donohue. (Dillingham's American authors library, no. 14). 1896. G. W. Dillingham.

Silver Bag. Thomas Cobb. LC 20-5233. 1919. John Lane.

Silver Bar Mystery. Wilbur C Tuttle. LC 33-27303. 1933. Houghton Mifflin Company.

Silver Baron: A Novel. Carlton Waite. LC 8-32828. 1896. Arena Publishing Company.

Silver Bear. Edna Adelaide Brown. LC 21-26985. 1921. Lothrop, Lee & Shepard Co.

Silver Bears. Paul Emil Erdman. LC 73-19261. 1974. (text ed.) 7.95 (ISBN 0-684-13842-5). Scribner.

Silver Blade: The True Chronicle of a Double Mystery. Charles Edmonds Walk. LC 8-9527. 1908. A. C. McClurg & Co.

Silver Brand: Or, The Secrets of Schwarzenberg. Charles T Manners. LC 7-20453. (select series. no. 69). 1890. Street & Smith.

Silver Bride. Ethel May Dell. LC 31-28683. 1932. G. P. Putnam's Sons.

Silver Bridge. Gray Barker. LC 79-119512. 1970. Saucerian Books.

Silver Bridge. Burton Wohl. LC 68-27159. 1968. Delacorte Press.

Silver Buckle: A Story of the Revolutionary Days, by M. Nataline Crumpton; Illustrations by Cornelia E. Bedford. M Nataline Crumpton. LC 1418. H. Altemus.

Silver Bullet Gang. Jack M Bickham. LC 73-10702. (Black bat mysery). 1974. (ISBN 0-672-51885-6). Bobbs-Merrill.

Silver Bullet Gang. John Miles, pseud. LC 73-10702. 176p. 1974. 5.95 o.p. (ISBN 0-672-51885-6). Bobbs.

Silver Bullet: Or The Young Relic Hunters of the Palmetto State. A Story of to-Day. A. S Rowell. LC 8-938. 1897. Shannon & Co.

Silver Butterfly. Nancy Mann Waddel Wilson Woodrow Woodrow. LC 8-30252. 1908. The Bobbs-Merrill Company.

Silver Canyon. Louis L'Amour. LC 56-13305. 1956. Avalon Books.

Silver Canyon. Logan Winters. (Spectros Ser.: No. 4). (Orig.). 1981. pap. 1.75 (ISBN 0-505-51638-1). Tower Bks.

Silver Casket. Patricia Lake. (Harlequin Presents Ser.). 192p. 1983. pap. 1.95 (ISBN 0-373-10578-9). Harlequin Bks.

Silver Castle. Erica Quest. LC 77-26527. 1978. 7.95 (ISBN 0-385-14172-6). Published for the Crime Club by Doubleday.

Silver Caves: A Mining Story. Ernest Ingersoll. LC 7-10522. Dodd, Mead & Company.

Silver Cayuse. Archie Joscelyn. LC 47-219435. 1947. Phoenix Press.

Silver Chalice. Thomas Bertram Costain. 1974. (pbk.) 1.50. Avon.

Silver Chalice: A Novel. 1st Ed. Thomas Bertram Costain. LC 52-3377. 1952. Doubleday.

Silver Christ: And A Lemon Tree. Louise De La Ramee. LC 6-33306. 1894. Macmillan and Company.

Silver Circus, Tales. Alfred Edgar Coppard. LC 29-5410. 1929. A. A. Knopf.

Silver City. Ion L. Idriess. 1967. Repr. pap. 1.60 o.s.i. Tri-Ocean.

Silver City. David Norman. (Frontier Rakers Ser.: No. 4). (Orig.). 1982. pap. 2.95 (ISBN 0-89083-921-2). Zebra.

Silver City. David Norman. (Frontier Rakers: No. 4). (Orig.). 1980. pap. 2.75 (ISBN 0-89083-681-7). Zebra.

Silver City: By Bradford Scott Pseud. Leslie Scott. LC 53-7226. 1953. Arcadia House.

Silver City Heyday. William Kehaly. LC 53-5508. 1953. Dorrance.

Silver City Rangers. Herbert Arthur, pseud. LC 44-5937. 1944. Phoenix Press.

Silver City Rangers. Herbert Shappiro. 1944. Phoenix Press.

Silver City Shootout. Jake Logan. 224p. (Orig.). 1983. pap. 2.25 (ISBN 0-425-06132-9). Berkley Pub.

Silver Cleek. John Campbell Haywood. LC 8-33905. M. Kennerley.

Silver Cobweb: A Ralph Lindsey Mystery. Ben Benson. LC 55-5967. 1955. M. S. Mill Co. and W. Morrow.

Silver Collar Boy. Constance Wright. LC 35-1979. E. P. Dutton & Co., Inc.

Silver Cord. Sallie Lee Bell. LC 58-330407. 1958. Zondervan Pub. House.

Silver Cord. George Agnew Chamberlain. LC 27-3371. 1927. G. P. Putnam's Sons.

Silver Cord. Eddie G. McNail. 1971. 2.95 o.p. (ISBN 0-8059-1543-5). Dorrance.

Silver Cord. A Novel. Shirley Brooks. LC 34-377599. 1861. Harper & Brothers.

Silver Cow. Frank Chester Robertson. LC 29-5412. Barse & Co.

Silver Cowboy. Gene Tuttle. 1981. pap. 6.95 (Avalon). Bouregy.

Silver Crescent. Edith Austin Holton. LC 44-2705. 1944. G. P. Putnam's Sons.

Silver Crescent. Frances M. Hoover. 1978. 7.95 (ISBN 0-533-03310-1). Vantage.

Silver Cross. Mary Johnston. LC 22-4980. 1922. 2.00. Little, Brown, and Company.

Silver Cross. Samuel Robert Keightley. LC 7-11432. 1898. Dodd, Mead and Company.

Silver Cross: A Story of the King's Daughters; and Miss Marigold's Tithes. Alice Eddy Curtiss. Congregational Sunday-School and Publishing Society.

Silver Cross: Or, The Carpenter of Nazareth; a Tale of Jerusalem. Eugene Sue & De Leon, Daniel, 1852-1914, Tr. LC 9-18158. 1909. New York Labor News Company.

Silver Crown of Glory. Horace Wilson Bennett. LC 36-8621. The John C. Winston Company.

Silver Darlings. Neil Miller Gunn. LC 45-351231. 1945. G. W. Stewart, Inc.

Silver Death. George Fort Gibbs. 1939. D. Appleton-Century Company, Incorporated.

Silver Desert. Ernest Haycox. LC 35-38587. 1935. Doubleday, Doran & Company, Inc.

Silver Dice. Emilie Benson Knipe & Knipe, Alden Arthur. LC 27-23605. 1928. Dodd, Mead and Company.

Silver Doll. Treynor, Blair. LC 52-11049. 1952. Holt.

Silver Dollar. Viola Helms. LC 60-16453. 1960. Dorrance.

Silver Dollar Rosebush. Gwendolen L. Hayden. 128p. 1971. 1.85 o.s.i. Review & Herald.

Silver Dolphin. Velda Johnston. LC 78-13011. 1979. 8.95 (ISBN 0-396-07626-2). Dodd, Mead.

Silver Dolphin. Velda Johnston. LC 79-28630. 1980. 12.95 (ISBN 0-8161-3068-X). G. K. Hall.

Silver Dove. Andrey Biely. Tr. by George Reavey from Rus. LC 73-21039. 1974. pap. 4.95 (ISBN 0-394-17859-9, E637, Ever). Grove.

Silver Dove. Boris Nikolaevich Bugaev. LC 73-21039. 1974. 8.95 (ISBN 0-8021-0046-5) (ISBN 0-394-17859-9). Grove Press; Distributed by Random House.

Silver Dove. Boris Nikolaevich Bugaev. LC 73-21040. 1974. 8.95 (ISBN 0-8021-0044-9). Grove Press: Distributed by Random House.

Silver Dress. Melesina Mary Blount. LC 12-258470. 1913. 1.25. Duffield & Company.

Silver Dunes. Ruby Lorraine Radford. LC 46-667097. 1946. Arcadia House, Inc.

Silver Eagle. William Riley Burnett. LC 31-31932. 1931. L. MacVeagh, The Dial Press.

Silver Elephant, & Other Stories. English Language Services. (Collier-Macmillan English Readers). pap. 1.40 (ISBN 0-02-971360-9). Macmillan.

Silver Falcon. Evelyn Anthony. LC 77-6663. 1977. 8.95 (ISBN 0-698-10755-1). Coward, McCann & Geoghegan.

Silver Falcon. Evelyn Anthony. (Signet Book). 1978. 2.25 (ISBN 0-451-08211-7). New American Library.

Silver Falcon. Yvonne Whittal. (Harlequin Presents Ser.). 192p. 1983. pap. 1.95 (ISBN 0-373-10598-3). Harlequin Bks.

Silver Fang. George Frank Worts. LC 30-8177. 1930. A. C. McClurg & Co.

Silver Flame. Leonard London Foreman. LC 66-20981. 1975. (pbk.) 0.95. Ace Books.

Silver Flame: By L. L. Foreman. 1st Ed. Leonard London Foreman. LC 66-20981. (Double D western). 1966. 3.50. Doubleday.

Silver Fleece: A Story of the Spanish in New Mexico. Florence Crannell Means & Carl Means. LC 50-7750. (Land of the Free series). 1950. Winston.

Silver Fleece: A Tale of the Swift Mines of Old Kentucky. J. H Kidwell. LC 27-23002. The Avondale Press, Incorporated.

Silver Flute. Liola Larrimore Thomas. LC 31-10984. 1931. Macrae Smith Company.

Silver for General Washington. Enid L. Meadowcroft. pap. 0.95 o.p. (2096, Starline). Schol Bk Serv.

Silver Forest. Ben Ames Williams. LC 26-118551. E. P. Dutton & Company.

Silver Fountain. Jane Ludlow Drake Abbott. 1932. J. B. Lippincott Company.

Silver Fountains. Dorothy Mackinder. LC 47-219517. 1947. The Declan X. McMullen Company.

Silver Fox. Bonnie Drake. (Candlelight Ecstacy Ser.: No. 132). (Orig.). 1983. pap. 1.95 (ISBN 0-440-18139-9). Dell.

Silver Fox. Rene Hansar. LC 38-34133. 1938. Wm. Morrow & Co.

Silver Fox. Violet Florence Martin & Somerville, Edith Anna CEnone, Joint Author. LC 4-8630. 1902. Longmans, Green, and Co.

Silver Fruit, a Novel. Patricia Campbell. LC 59-7971. 1959. Macmillan.

Silver Fruit Upon Silver Trees. Anne Mather. (Presents Ser.). 1975. pap. 1.25 (ISBN 0-373-70596-4, 70596, Pub. by Harlequin). PB.

Silver Ghost. Chuck Kinder. LC 78-22259. 8.95 (ISBN 0-15-124067-1). Harcourt Brace Jovanovich.

Silver Glade: A Novel. William Leo Murphy. LC 47-52463. 1947. Society of the Divine Savior (Salvatorian Seminary) Pub. Dept.

Silver Goblet. Raymond Foxall. LC 73-87405. 1974. 6.95. St. Martin's Press.

Silver Gulch. William L Hopson. LC 44-345235. 1944. Phoenix Press.

Silver Hat. Dane Coolidge. LC 34-20574. 1934. E. P. Dutton & Co., Inc.

Silver Hawk. William Byron Mowery. LC 29-9100. 1929. Doubleday, Doran and Company, Inc.

Silver Hook. Mortimer, John Clifford. LC 50-10202. 1950. Morrow.

Silver Horde. Rex Ellingwood Beach. LC 25-23761. 1911. A. L. Burt Company.

Silver Horde: A Novel. Rex Ellingwood Beach. 1909. Harper & Brothers.

Silver Huntress. Felicia Andrews. 2.95 (ISBN 0-441-76609-9). Ace Bks.

Silver Is the Fortune. Mildred Fielder. LC 78-66268. (Illus.). 1978. pap. 7.95 (ISBN 0-87970-145-5). North Plains.

Silver Jackass. Charles K Boston. LC 41-23059. Reynal & Hitchcock.

Silver Key... Edgar Wallace. LC 30-33612. 1930. Pub. for the Crime Club, Inc., by Doubleday, Doran & Company, Inc.

Silver Keys. Clifford Lindsey Alderman. LC 60-5261. 1960. Putnam.

Silver King. Alfred Wilson Barrett & Jones, Henry Arthur. LC 42-40106. 1.25. G. W. Dillingham Company.

Silver King Mystery. Ian Greig. LC 30-14664. H. Holt and Company.

Silver-Knife: Or, The Hunters of the Rocky Mountains. An Autobiography. John Hovey Robinson. LC 7-421665. 1854. W. V. Spencer.

Silver Ladies. Margaret Erskine. 1973. (pbk.) 0.95. Ace Books.

Silver Ladies. Wetherby Williams. LC 51-11593. 1951. Published for the Crime Club by Doubleday.

Silver Lady. Marguerite Collins. LC 43-14462. 1943. W. F. Lewis, Times-Mirror Press.

Silver Lady. James Facos. 1973. (pbk.) 1.25 (ISBN 0-671-78320-3). Pocket Books.

Silver Lady. James Facos. LC 74-184723. 1972. 5.95. Atheneum.

Silver Lake: Or, The Belle of Bayou Luie. A Tale of the South. by Theresa J. Freeman. Theresa J Freeman. LC 6-40026. P. M. Pinchard.

Silver-Leg. Emmuska Orczy. LC 18-1720. George H. Doran Company.

Silver Leopard. Zoe Cass. LC 76-14180. 7.95 (ISBN 0-394-40816-0). Random House.

Silver Leopard. Zoe Cass. 1978. 1.75 (ISBN 0-445-04323-7). Popular Library.

Silver Leopard. Helen Kieran Reilly. LC 46-7315. 1946. Random House.

Silver Leopard. 1st Ed. Francis Van Wyck Mason. LC 55-105145. 1955. Doubleday.

Silver Ley. Adrian Bell. LC 31-29969. 1931. Dodd, Mead & Company.

Silver Lining. Florence Eberhard. 1939. Gateway Books.

Silver Lining. Elizabeth Yates. LC 81-15392. 1981. 8.95 (ISBN 0-914016-81-4) (ISBN 0-914016-82-2). Phoenix Pub.

Silver Lining: Or, Fair-Hope Prospect. M J Guthrie. LC 6-46693. 1872.

Silver Linings. Joseph McCord. LC 32-6426. The Penn Publishing Company.

Silver Link. Elizabeth Ludlow Linscott. LC 42-51786. 1942. Gramercy Publishing Co.

Silver Lock: And Other Stories. Cassell's Magazine. (On cover: Cassell's "rainbow" series, no. 27). 1888. Cassell & Company, Limited.

Silver Lure. John Reid Turnbull. LC 46-21219. 1946. Wm. B. Eerdmans Publishing Company.

Silver Lust. Dallas Todd. 224p. (Orig.). 1982. pap. 2.50 (ISBN 0-8439-1090-9, Leisure Bks). Nordon Pubns.

Silver Magic. Elizabeth Carfrae, pseud. LC 32-343760. G. P. Putnam's Sons.

Silver Maple: A Story of Upper Canada. Mary Esther MacGregor. LC 6-34644. F. H. Revell Company.

Silver Matzoth. Gershon Kranzler, pseud. saddle-stitched 3.00 (ISBN 0-87559-131-0). Shalom.

Silver Mezzuzah. Gershon Kranzler, pseud. saddle-stitched 3.00 (ISBN 0-87559-133-7). Shalom.

Silver Mine Trail. Virgil Hart. (Orig.). 1981. pap. 1.95 (ISBN 0-505-51627-6). Tower Bks.

Silver Mine Trail. John Earl Lewis. (YA) 1979. 6.95 (Avalon). Bouregy.

Silver Miracles. Fayrene Preston. (Loveswept Ser.: No. 4). 1983. pap. 1.95. Bantam.

Silver Mistress. Chet Cunningham. (Pinkerton Agent Brad Spear Ser.: No. 2). 352p. (Orig.). 1981. pap. 2.25 (ISBN 0-440-07940-3, Banbury). Dell.

Silver Mistress. Peter O'Donnell. (Modesty Blaise Ser.). (Illus.). 256p. 1982. 10.95 (ISBN 0-915822-51-2). Archival Pr.

Silver Mistress. Peter O'Donnell. (Modesty Blaise Suspense Novel Ser.). 1977. 5.95 o.p. (ISBN 0-285-62112-2, Pub. by Souvenir Pr). Intl Schol Bk Serv.

Silver Moon. Eleanor Hallowell Abbott. LC 28-14567. E.P. Dutton & Company.

Silver Moon Cottage. Sara Ware Bassett. LC 45-572929. 1945. Doubleday, Doran and Company, Inc.

Silver Moth. Ann Sumner. LC 32-9239. A. L. Burt Company.

Silver Mountain. Dan Cushman. LC 57-12308. 1957. Appleton-Century-Crofts.

Silver Mountain: A Novel. 1st Ed. Rae Potter Roberts. LC 56-9455. 1956. PageantPress.

Silver Nightingale. Sylvia Thorpe. (Fawcett crest book). 1974. (pbk.) 0.95. Fawcett.

Silver Nutmeg. Norah Robinson Lofts. LC 47-31097. 1947. Doubleday.

Silver Oar. Howard Breslin. LC 54-9155. 1954. Crowell.

Silver Peaks: By Annie Duffield... Anne Duffield. LC 41-6367. 1941. Arcadia House, Inc.

Silver Peril. Marice Rutledge Hale. LC 31-19874. 1931. The Fiction League.

Silver Pilgrimage. M. Anantanarayanan. (Indian Novels Ser.). 160p. 1976. pap. 2.75 (ISBN 0-89253-022-7). Ind-US Inc.

Silver Pilgrimage. M. Anantanarayanan. 1961. 3.95 o.p. Criterion Bks.

Silver Pin. Alfred Wilson Barrett. LC 5-39866. The Saalfield Publishing Co.

Silver Platter. Laetitia McDonald Irwin. LC 34-901. 1934. Farrar & Rinehart.

Silver Platter. Laetitia McDonald. LC 34-901. Farrar & Rinehart, Incorporated.

Silver Plume. Arthur Meeker. LC 52-6406. 1952. Knopf.

Silver Pool. Eleanore Browne. LC 29-247373. Barse & Co.

Silver Poppy. Arthur John Arbuthnott Stringer. LC 24-20568. A. L. Burt Company.

Silver Rattle. Sylvia Thompson. LC 35-7025. 1935. Little, Brown, and Company.

Silver Ray. Abi S Jackman. LC 7-9476. 1885. R. R. Donnelley & Sons.

Silver Ribbons: A Novel. Christine Whiting Parmenter. LC 29-13374. 1929. Rae D. Henkle Co.

Silver River Ranch. Lawrence A Keating. LC 34-327585. E. J. Clode, Inc.

Silver Rock: By Luke Short Pseud. Frederick Dilley Glidden. LC 53-9247. 1953. Houghton Mifflin.

Silver Rose. Large Print ed. David Kaufelt. LC 82-16749. 394p. 1982. Repr. of 1982 ed. 10.95 (ISBN 0-89621-391-9). Thorndike Pr.

Silver Rose. Jennifer Stephens. 240p. 1982. pap. 2.75 (ISBN 0-505-51799-X). Tower Bks.

Silver Rose: A Novel. David A Kaufelt. LC 82-5135. 14.95 (ISBN 0-440-07945-4). Delacorte Press.

Silver Rose: A Novel. David A Kaufelt. LC 82-16749. 10.95 (ISBN 0-89621-391-9). Thorndike Press.

Silver Saber. Noel Bertram Gerson. LC 67-12890. 1967. Doubleday.

Silver Saddles. Austin Corcoran. LC 51-12223. (Dutton Diamond D western). 1951. Dutton.

Silver Sand. Samuel Rutherford Crockett. LC 14-9449. 1914. 0.60. Hodder and Stoughton.

Silver Sand: A Romance of Old Galloway. Samuel Rutherford Crockett. LC 14-15748. 1.25. Fleming H. Revell Company.

Silver Sandals. Clinton Holland Stagg. LC 16-13509. W. J. Watt & Company.

Silver Scale Mystery. Robert McNair Wilson. LC 31-220677. 1931. J. B. Lippincott Company.

Silver Shell. Chase, Mary Ellen. LC 30-21327. H. Holt and Company.

Silver Ship. Leon Lewis. (On cover: The sea and shore series, no. 2). 1888. Street & Smith.

Silver Ship of Mexico. A Tale of the Spanish Main. Joseph Holt Ingraham. 1846. H. L. William.

Silver Shoal Light. Edith Ballinger Price. LC 20-165021. 1920. 1.75. The Century Co.

Silver Shoals. Hamilton Cochran. 1945. The Bobbs-Merrill Company.

Silver Shores. Yvonne Kalman. LC 82-72069. 352p. 1982. 14.95 (ISBN 0-87795-432-1). Arbor Hse.

Silver Shot. Gary McCarthy. 176p. (Orig.). 1981. pap. 1.75 (ISBN 0-553-14477-4). Bantam.

Silver Shroud. Donna Creekmore. 1978. pap. 1.75 (ISBN 0-532-17198-5). Woodhill.

Silver Sixpence. Ruth Sawyer. LC 21-3913. Harper & Brothers.

Silver Skates. Ed. by William A. Kottmeyer. 1972. text ed. 5.76 o.p. (ISBN 0-07-034019-6, W). McGraw.

Silver Skull. Samuel Rutherford Crockett. LC 99-233. Frederick A. Stokes Company.

Silver Skull: A Novel of Sorcery. Les Daniels. LC 79-10057. 8.95 (ISBN 0-684-16141-9). Scribner.

Silver Skull: A Romance. Samuel Rutherford Crockett. LC 1-31276. F. A. Stokes Company.

Silver Slave, Dear Puritan & Rapture of the Desert, 3 Vols. Violet Winspear. (Harlequin Romances Series (3-in-1)). 576p. 1983. pap. 3.50 (ISBN 0-373-20069-2). Harlequin Bks.

Silver Slippers. Temple Bailey. LC 28-24956. The Penn Publishing Company.

Silver Song. Phyllis Yahnke. 1953. Arcadia House.

Silver Spade: Another Miss Julia Tyler Mystery. Louisa Revell. LC 50-6073. 1950. Macmillan.

Silver Spoon. John Galsworthy. LC 26-141071. 1926. C. Scribner's Sons.

Silver Spoon. Naka Kansuke. Tr. by Etsuko Terasaki from Japanese. LC 76-21917. 150p. 1977. 10.00 (ISBN 0-914090-14-3); pap. 4.95 (ISBN 0-914090-15-1). Chicago Review.

Silver Spoon. Clarence Budington Kelland. LC 41-519098. 1941. Harper & Brothers.

Silver Spoon: A Novel. Edwin Gilbert. LC 57-6831. 1957. Lippincott.

Silver Spoon: And Passers by. John Galsworthy. LC 75-8146. (His The Forsyte chronicles, v. 5). (Scribner library. Contemporary classics.). 1969. Scribner.

Silver Spooner. Darcy O'Brien. LC 80-22971. 13.95 (ISBN 0-671-25264-X). Simon and Schuster.

Silver Spoons. Nancie MacCullough Weir. LC 75-25722. 1975. 7.95 (ISBN 0-399-11548-X). Putnam.

Silver Spoons. Nancie MacCullough Weir. (Kangaroo Book). 1977. 1.75 (ISBN 0-671-80886-9). Pocket Books.

Silver Spurs: By Abel Shott Pseud. T. W. Ford. LC 50-7363. 1950. Phoenix Press.

Silver Stallion: A Comedy of Redemption. James Branch Cabell. 1926. R. M. McBride & Company.

Silver Star. Jackson Gregory. LC 31-247740. 1931. Dodd, Mead & Company.

Silver Star: By Will Ermine Pseud. 1st Ed. Harry Sinclair Drago. LC 51-11431. (Double D western). 1951. Doubleday.

Silver Star-Dust. Evelyn Everett Green. LC 25-19524. Greenberg, Inc.

Silver Strand. Gimone Hall. 1974. (pbk.) 0.95. Dell.

Silver Street. E. Richard Johnson. LC 68-17040. 1968. Harper & Row.

Silver Street Woman. 1st Ed. Les Savage. LC 54-5552. 1954. Hanover House.

Silver String. Cora Hardy Jarrett. LC 37-34672. Farrar & Rinehart, Inc.

Silver Sun. Nancy Springer. 1981. pap. 2.75 (ISBN 0-671-44244-9, Timescape). PB.

Silver Sundown. Marteen D. Grahm. (Orig.). 1982. pap. 3.50 (ISBN 0-440-17806-1). Dell.

Silver Swan. Bertrand Collins. LC 30-25627. 1930. Harper & Brothers.

Silver Thaw. Betty Neels. (Harlequin Romances Ser.). 192p. (Orig.). 1981. pap. 1.25 (ISBN 0-373-02386-3, Pub. by Harlequin). PB.

Silver Thorn: A Book of Stories. Hugh Walpole. LC 28-255513. 1928. Doubleday, Doran and Company, Inc.

Silver Threads to Love. Van Pelt, Ethel. 1976. 4.95. Avalon Books.

Silver Tiger. Reinhold Millers. 1977. pap. 2.00x o.p. (ISBN 0-912852-18-6). Echo Pubs.

Silver Toes of Fatima: And Other Stories. Edith Hecht. LC 42-2628. The Gillick Press.

Silver Tombstone... Frank Gruber. LC 45-8409. 1945. Farrar & Rinehart, Inc.

Silver Tombstones. J. D. Hardin. LC 81-80672. (J. D. Hardin Western Ser.). 224p. (Orig.). 1981. pap. 1.95 (ISBN 0-87216-839-5). Playboy Pbks.

Silver Trumpet: A Novel. James Wesley Ingles. LC 30-24517. (Green fund book, no. 27). The Union Press.

Silver Trumpets Calling. Lucille Papin Borden. LC 31-17130. 1931. The Macmillan Company.

Silver Unicorn. Catherine Christian. LC 48-20690. 1948. Didier.

Silver Urn. Foxhall Daingerfield. LC 27-18144. 1927. D. Appleton and Company.

Silver Veil. Margaret Way. (Harlequin Romances Ser.). 192p. 1983. pap. 1.75 (ISBN 0-373-02539-4). Harlequin Bks.

Silver Virgin. Ida Alexa Ross Wylie. LC 29-2965. 1929. Doubleday, Doran & Company, Inc.

Silver Visits the Attic. 1st. ed. Carol Hectus. (Illus.). 1974. 3.75 (ISBN 0-533-00776-3). Vantage Press.

Silver Warriors. Michael Moorcock. (Dell Book). 1977. 1.50 (ISBN 0-440-17994-7). Dell Pub. Co.

Silver Warriors. Michael Moorcock. 1973. (pbk.) 0.95. Dell.

Silver Web. Jean Nash. (Orig.). 1980. pap. 2.25 o.s.i. (ISBN 0-505-51473-7). Tower Bks.

Silver Wings. Grace Livingston Hill. Repr. lib. bdg. 15.70x (ISBN 0-89190-030-6). Am Repr-Rivercity Pr.

Silver Wings: A Novel. Eliza Marian Butler. LC 53-1252. 1953. Putnam.

Silver Wings: By Grace Livingston Hill. Grace Livingston Hill. LC 31-12124. 1931. J. B. Lippincott & Company.

Silver Wood. James Facos. 1977. pap. 1.50. Eldridge Pub.

Silver Wood. Deirdre Rowan. (Fawcett gold medal book). 1974. (pbk.) 0.95. Fawcett.

Silver Yoke. Sylvia Chatfield Bates. LC 51-7230. 1951. McGraw-Hill.

Silver Zone. King Hill, pseud. LC 36-10532. Greenberg.

Silverado. Logan Winters. (Spectros Ser.: No. 1). (Orig.). 1981. pap. 1.75 (ISBN 0-505-51612-8). Tower Bks.

Silverado Squatters. Robert Louis Stevenson. (On cover: Seaside library. Pocket ed. no. 1110). 1888. G. Munro.

Silverado Squatters. Robert Louis Stevenson. LC 44-274314. (With, as issued, his Strange case of Dr. Jekyll and Mr. Hyde. New York, 189-?). American Publishers Corporation.

Silverado: The Story of a Colorado Mining Town. Charles K Holmburg. LC 23-17993. 1923.

Silverfinger see Dedo De Plata.

Silverhill. Phyllis A. Whitney. 192p. 1978. pap. 2.50 (ISBN 0-449-24094-0, Crest). Fawcett.

Silverhill: By Phyllis A. Whitney. Phyllis A. Whitney. (T1135). 1968. Fawcett.

Silverhill: By Phyllis A. Whitney. 1st Ed. Phyllis A. Whitney. LC 67-153661. 1967. 4.95. Doubleday.

Silverleaf Syndrome. Eleanor Robinson. (Orig.). 1980. pap. text ed. 1.95 o.s.i. (ISBN 0-505-51556-3). Tower Bks.

Silverlock. John Myers Myers. LC 49-5070. 1949. E.P. Dutton.

Silvermead. Jean Middlemass. LC 9-3356. (On cover: Seaside library. Pocket ed., no. 539). 1885. G. Munro.

Silvern Secret; or, The Autobiography of a Silver Dollar... Lida Myra Keck. 1894. The Republican Publishing Co.

Silversmith. Joanne Stonebridge. (Orig.). 1969. pap. 1.75 o.s.i. (OPH148, Ophelia). Olympia.

Silverspurs. Charles Alden Seltzer. LC 74-21542. 1974. (ISBN 0-88411-109-1). Aeonian Press.

Silverspurs. Charles Alden Seltzer. 1935. Doubleday, Doran & Company, Inc.

Silvertip. Max Brand. LC 42-1100. 1942. Dodd, Mead & Company.

Silvertip. Frederick Faust. LC 76-20727. 1976. 7.95 (ISBN 0-89340-032-7). J. Curley & Associates.

Silvertip. Frederick Faust. 1973. (pbk) 0.75. Warner Paperback Library.

Silvertip Ranch. Archie Joscelyn. LC 49-49617. 1949. Phoenix Press.

Silvertip's Chase. Max Brand. 160p. 1973. pap. 1.50 (ISBN 0-446-98048-X). Warner Bks.

Silvertip's Chase. Frederick Faust. LC 44-1743. 1944. The Blakiston Company, Distributed by Dodd, Mead & Company, New York.

Silvertip's Chase. Frederick Faust. (Silvertip Adventure). 1973. (pbk.) 0.95. Warner Paperback Library.

Silvertip's Roundup. large print ed. Max Brand. 1981. cancelled 18.00x o.p. (ISBN 0-89340-120-X, Pub. by Curley Assoc England). State Mutual Bk.

Silvertip's Roundup. Max Brand. 144p. 1970. pap. 1.95 (ISBN 0-446-90318-3). Warner Bks.

Silvertip's Roundup. Frederick Faust. LC 43-3198. 1943. Dodd, Mead & Company.

Silvertip's Roundup. Frederick Faust. LC 77-14010. 1978. 7.95 (ISBN 0-89340-120-X). J. Curley.

Silvertip's Search. Max Brand. 1978. 1.50. Pocket Books.

Silvertip's Search. Frederick Faust. LC 45-1337. 1945. Dodd, Mead & Company.

Silvertip's Search. Frederick Faust. LC 80-10778. 1981. 11.50 (ISBN 0-89340-279-6). J. Curley & Associates.

Silvertip's Strike. Max Brand. 1973. pap. 1.50 (ISBN 0-446-98096-X). Warner Bks.

Silvertip's Strike. Frederick Faust. LC 42-23434. 1942. Dodd, Mead & Company.

Silvertip's Strike. Frederick Faust. (Silvertip adventure). 1973. (pbk.) 0.95. Warner Paperback Library.

Silvertip's Trap. Max Brand. LC 81-4844. 1981. 11.95 (ISBN 0-89340-324-5). J. Curley.

Silvertip's Trap. Frederick Faust. LC 43-11960. 1943. Dodd, Mead & Company.

Silverwool. Emily J Jenkinson. LC 11-124511. 1910. 1.50. The Baker and Taylor Company.

Silvia's in Town. Marion Strobel. LC 33-252015. Farrar & Rinehart, Incorporated.

Sim". Maude J Sullivan. LC 28-24794. Dorrance and Company.

Sim Greene: A Narrative of the Whisky Insurrection; Being a Setting Forth of the Memoirs of the Late David Freman, Esq. Richard Taylor Wiley. LC 6-27712. 1906. The J. C. Winston Company.

Simas. Jurgis Gliauda. 1971. 5.00 (ISBN 0-87141-042-7). Manyland.

Simba. Stewart Edward White. LC 18-550119. 1918. Doubleday, Page & Company.

Simeon Tetlow's Shadow. Jennette Barbour Perry Lee. LC 9-4193. 1909. The Century Co.

Simma & Other Stories. E. M. Black. 1978. 4.95 o.p. (ISBN 0-533-03215-6). Vantage.

Simms Revolutionary War Novels. William Gilmore Simms. LC 76-8879. 110.00(set). The Reprint Company.

Simon. Joseph Storer Clouston. LC 19-14472. 1.50. George H. Doran Company.

Simon and Schuster Present Show Girl. Joseph Patrick McEvoy. LC 28-18118. Simon and Schuster, Inc.

Simon and Schuster Present the Super-Colossal Wonder Picture Epoch of This or Any Other Century: Hollywood Girl. J P McEvoy. LC 29-20432. Simon and Schuster.

Simon Called Peter. Robert Keable. LC 21-19926. E. P. Dutton & Company.

Simon Dale. Anthony Hope Hawkins. LC 7-2187. F. A. Stokes Company.

Simon Dale. Anthony Hope Hawkins. LC 14-181921. F. A. Stokes Company.

Simon Dale. Anthony Hope Hawkins. LC 21-16860. 1901. International Association of Newspapers and Authors.

Simon Eichelkatz; The Patriarch; Two Stories of Jewish Life by Ulrich Frank Pseud. Tr. from the German. Ulla Wolff. LC 7-12639. 1907. The Jewish Publication Society of America.

Simon Girty: The Outlaw. Uriah James Jones. Ed. by Aurand, Ammon Monroe. LC 31-30266. 1931. The Aurand Press.

Simon Girty the Outlaw. Uriah James Jones. 1931. 15.00x. R S Barnes.

Simon Girty, the Outlaw. An Historical Romance. Uriah James Jones. LC 7-11690. 1846. G. B. Zeiber & Co.

Simon Hastings. Frederick Merrill Tibbott. LC 42-19354. 1942. The Bobbs-Merrill Company.

Simon Kenton: Or, the Scout's Revenge, an Historical Novel. James Weir. 1852. Lippincott, Grambo, and Co.

Simon Lash: Private Detective. Frank Gruber. LC 41-5876. Farrar & Rinehart, Inc.

Simon Lash: Private Detective. Frank Gruber. LC 44-46005. (Murder mystery monthly. No. 23). 1944. Avon Book Company.

Simon Lash, Private Detective. Frank Gruber. 1976. Repr. of 1941 ed. lib. bdg. 10.25 o.p. Buccaneer Bks.

Simon of Cyrene: Dimachaerus Splendens; or, The Story of a Man's (and a Nation's) Soul. Thomas Hall Shastid. LC 23-9539. 1923. G. Wahr; Etc., Etc.

Simon of Nazareth: A Story of the Foundations of Christianity. George Jackson Henry. LC 37-160019. Pub. by G. J. Henry in Association with Parker Printing Company.

Simon Peter and Simon Magus: A Legend of the Early Days of Christianity in Rome. Giovanni Giuseppe Franco. LC 6-43262. ("Messenger series," no. 2). 1871. P. F. Cunningham.

Simon Peter, Fisherman. Francis Bourne Upham. LC 4-62472. 1904. Eaton & Mains.

Simon Ryan the Peterite. Augustus Jessopp. LC 7-9929. A. D. F. Randolph and Company.

Simon Says: A Novel. Margaret Ritter. LC 66-20804. 1966. Little, Brown.

Simon Stone's Knight Missing. Howard Barrington. LC 45-2950. 1944. Pub. for the Crime Book Society by Hutchinson & Co., Ltd.

Simon Suggs Adventures and Travels. Comprising All the Scenes, Incidents and Adventures of His Travels, in a Series of Sketches of His Life; with Widow Rugby's Husband, and Twenty-Six Other Humorous Tales of Alabama. Being the Most Laughable and Side-Splitting Stories That Have Ever Appeared in Print. Johnson Jones Hosper. LC 13-33849. 1848. T. B. Peterson.

Simon Suggs' Adventures. Late of the Tallapossa Volunteers. Together with "Taking the Census," and Other Alabama Sketches. With a Portrait of Captain Simon Suggs. Johnson Jones Hooper. LC 9-2484. T. B. Peterson & Brothers.

Simon the Coldheart. Georgette Heyer. LC 25-10061. Small, Maynard & Company.

Simon the Coldheart. Georgette Heyer. LC 79-2609. 1979. 10.95 (ISBN 0-525-20459-8). Dutton.

Simon the Fox: Being an Account of the Activities of Simon Fraser, Lord of the Barony of Lovat During His Early Twenties. Patrick John Sinnott. (Nobel book). 1956. Comet Press Books.

Simon the Jester. William John Locke. LC 10-15396. 1910. 1.50. J. Lane.

Simon the Jester. William John Locke. LC 10-14369. 1910. John Lane Company.

Simon the Jester. William John Locke. LC 16-191648. 1911. John Lane.

Simon the Radical: Or, the Cap of Liberty. Charles Paul De Kock. 1847.

Simon Wheeler, Detective. Mark Twain. Ed. by Franklin R. Rogers. LC 63-18140. (Levy Pub. Ser.: No. 2). 1965. 15.00 (ISBN 0-87104-161-8). NY Pub Lib.

Simone. Roger Bequet. 160p. pap. 1.95 o.p. (MP-102). Montmartre.

Simone: A Novel. Lion Feuchtwanger & Hermann, G. A., Tr. LC 44-5840. 1944. The Viking Press.

Simonetta. Edwin Lefevre. LC 19-16356. George H. Doran Company.

Simonetta Perkins. Leslie Poles Hartley. LC 26-7350. 1925. G. P. Putnam's Sons, Ltd.

Simonetta Perkins. Leslie Poles Hartley. LC 26-894926. 1926. G. P. Putnam's Sons.

Simon's Night. Jon Hassler. LC 79-10900. 1979. 9.95 (ISBN 0-689-10981-4). Atheneum.

Simon's Soul. Stanley Shapiro. LC 77-6119. 7.95 (ISBN 0-399-11858-6). Putnam.

Simon's Waif. Mira Stables. 224p. 1981. pap. 1.95 (ISBN 0-449-50207-4, Coventry). Fawcett.

Simon's Wife: A Novel. Decla Dunning. LC 80-12493. 11.95 (ISBN 0-517-54211-0). Crown.

Simpkins Plot. James Owen Hannay. LC 12-35553. Hodder & Stoughton, George H. Doran Company.

Simpkinsville & Vicinity: The Arkansas Stories of Ruth McEnery Stuart. Ed. by Ethel C. Simpson. LC 82-16160. 208p. 1983. 19.00 (ISBN 0-938626-12-4); pap. 8.95 (ISBN 0-938626-16-7). U of Ark Pr.

Simpkinsville and Vicinity: The Arkansas Stories of Ruth McEnery Stuart. Ruth McEnery Stuart & Ethel C. Simpson. LC 82-16160. 1983. 19.00 (ISBN 0-938626-12-4). University of Arkansas Press.

Simple Act of Kindness: A Novel. Winston M. Estes. LC 72-3877. 1973. 6.50 (ISBN 0-397-00943-7). Lippincott.

Simple Act of Kindness: A Novel. Winston M. Estes. 1977. 1.75 (ISBN 0-380-01807-1). Avon Books.

Simple Adventures of a Memsahib. Sara Jeannette Duncan Cotes. LC 6-29019. 1893. D. Appleton and Company.

Simple Annals. Mary E. Sweetman Blundell. LC 6-35456. 1906. Longmans, Green, and Co.

Simple Art of Murder. Raymond Chandler. LC 68-3297. (Seagull library of mystery and suspense). 1968. Norton.

Simple Case of Ill-Will. Evelyn Berckman. LC 65-14967. 1965. bds., 3.50. Dodd.

Simple Case of Susan. Jacques Futrelle. 1908. D. Appleton and Company.

Simple Chinese Stories. George A. Kennedy. 2.25. Far Eastern Pubns.

Simple Country Tales of Bygone Days. Dean Haag. (Illus.). 1977. 5.95 o.p. (ISBN 0-8059-2348-9). Dorrance.

Simple Heart. Sarah Barnwell Elliott. LC 6-37574. 1887. J. Ireland.

Simple Honorable Man. 1st Ed. Conrad Richter. LC 62-11047. 1962. Knopf.

Simple Life Limited. Ford Madox Ford. LC 11-6001. 1911. John Lane.

Simple Peter Cradd. Edward Phillips Oppenheim. LC 31-18071. 1931. Little, Brown, and Company.

Simple Simon. Charles William Yerington. LC 5-38101. Broadway Publishing Company.

Simple Simon, His Adventures in the Thistle Patch. 3d ed. Albert Michael Neil Lyons. LC 14-4069. 1914. John Lane.

Simple Souls. John Hastings Turner. LC 18-26925. 1919. C. Scribner's Sons.

Simple Speaks His Mind. Langston Hughes. LC 50-7299. 1950. Simon and Schuster.

Simple Stories. Archibald Marshall. LC 27-20758. Harper & Brothers.

Simple Story. Elizabeth Simpson Inchbald. 299p. 1980. Repr. of 1908 ed. lib. bdg. 25.00 o.p. (ISBN 0-89984-296-8). Century Bookbindery.

Simple Story. Elizabeth Simpson Inchbald. 1908. Repr. 25.00 o.p. (ISBN 0-8274-3415-4). R West.

Simple Story. Elizabeth Simpson Inchbald. 299p. 1981. Repr. of 1908 ed. lib. bdg. 30.00 (ISBN 0-89760-377-X). Telegraph Bks.

Simple Story: By Charles-Louis Philippe; Translated from the French by Agnes Kendrick Gray... with Wood-Cuts by Franz Masereel. Charles Louis Philippe. Tr. by Gray, Agnes Kendrick. LC 24-4618. 1924. A. A. Knopf.

Simple Story: By Elizabeth Inchbald; Ed., Introd. by J. M. S. Tompkins. Elizabeth Simpson Inchbald. LC 67-88637. (Oxford English novels). 1967. 7.00. Oxford Univ. Pr.

Simple Takes a Wife. Langston Hughes. LC 53-155369. 1953. Simon and Schuster.

Simple Truth. Elizabeth Hardwick. LC 81-43389. 1982. 12.95 (ISBN 0-912946-98-9). Ecco Press.

Simple Truth. 1st Ed. Elizabeth Hardwick. LC 54-9718. Harcourt, Brace.

Simple Way of Poison. Zenith Jones Brown. LC 28-2668. Farrar & Rinehart, Inc.

Simple Way of Poison. Mona Naomi Anne Hocking Messer. LC 57-11041. (Chantecler mystery novel). 1957. Washburn.

Simples. Ian Irons. LC 24-27643. 1924. T. Seltzer.

Simples from the Master's Garden. Annie Trumbull Slosson. The Sunday-School Times Company.

Simple's Uncle Sam. Langston Hughes. 1965. pap. 7.25 (ISBN 0-8090-0087-3, AmCen). Hill & Wang.

Simpleton. Aleksei Feofilaktovich Pisemskii. LC 76-23893. (Classics of Russian literature). (Hyperion library of world literature). (Illus.). 1977. 10.50. (ISBN 0-88355-508-5) (ISBN 0-88355-507-7). Hyperion Press.

Simpleton: A Story of the Day. Charles Reade. LC 52-56514. (Harper's library of select novels, no. 400). 1873. Harper.

Simpleton, and The Wandering Heir. household ed. Charles Reade. LC 7-39656. 1873. J. R. Osgood and Company.

Simplicity: A Novel. A T G Price. LC 7-30107. Rand, McNally & Company.

Simplicius Simplicissimus. Hans Jacob Christoffel Von Grimmelshausen. LC 63-16934. (Library of liberal arts, 186). 1965. Bobbs-Merrill.

Simplicius Simplicissimus. Hans J. C. Von Grimmelshausen. 1982. pap. 11.95 (ISBN 0-7145-3910-4). Riverrun NY.

Simplicius Simplicissimus: By Johann Jakob Christoffel Von Grimmelshausen. Modern Tr. from German Introd., by George Schulz-Behrend. Hans Jacob Christoffel Von Grimmelshausen. (Lib. of liberal arts, 186) Bibl.). 5.00. Bobbs.

Simply a Love-Story. Francis C. Lowell. LC 11-7170. 1885. Cupples, Upham, and Company.

Simply Women: Selections from the Works of Marcel Prevost. Marcel Prevost. Tr. by Brandon-Vauvillez, R. I. LC 10-24711. 1910. 1.00. The Macaulay Company.

Simpson. Elinor Mordaunt, pseud. LC 13-20577. 1913. 1.35. Houghton Mifflin Company.

Simpson, a Life. Edward Sackville-West. LC 31-15288. 1931. A. A. Knopf.

Simultaneous Equations. Laurence Halley. LC 77-17637. 1978. 7.95 (ISBN 0-312-72595-7). St. Martin's Press.

Simultaneous Man: A Novel. Ralph Blum. LC 77-103953. 1970. 5.95. Little, Brown.

Sin. Robert Vaughan. (Orig.). 1979. pap. 2.50 (ISBN 0-89083-479-2). Zebra.

Sin: An Allegory of Truth. Francis Warrington Dawson. LC 24-1183. 1923. The Honest Truth Publishing Co.

Sin and Such, an Unconventional Novel. Josiah Pitts Woolfolk. LC 36-19983. 1936. Godwin.

Sin and Suffer. James Noble Gifford. LC 48-39141. 1948. Phoenix Press.

Sin-Child: Anonymous. Herman Alfred Kasen. LC 35-32570. 1933. G. H. Watt.

Sin Cinderella. Peggy Gaddis, pseud. LC 48-115231. 1948. Phoenix Press.

Sin Clinic. Sheila Matthew. pap. 1.95 o.p. (8022). Cameo.

Sin Eater. Alice T. Ellis. 1977. 5.95 o.p. (Pub. by Duckworth England). Biblio Dist.

Sin Eater, and Other Scientific Impossibilities. Elizabeth Walter. LC 68-16045. 1968. Stein and Day.

Sin-Eater, and Other Tales and Episodes. William Sharp. LC 74-167470. (Short story index reprint series). 1971. (ISBN 0-8369-3996-4). Books for Libraries Press.

Sin-Eater: And Other Tales and Episodes. William Sharp. LC 8-4799. (Carnation series). 1895. Stone & Kimball.

Sin Family Robinson. George Clayton. 192p. (Orig.). 1972. pap. 1.95 o.p. (ISBN 0-87682-266-9, 7266). Barclay Hse.

Sin Farm. James Malcolm. (Orig.). 1969. pap. 1.75 o.p. (3050). Brandon.

Sin File: By Stephen Ransome Pseud. Frederick Clyde Davis. LC 65-20907. (Red badge detective). bds., 3.50. Dodd.

Sin for Breakfast. Hamilton Drake. pap. 1.75 o.p. (3007). Brandon.

Sin for Breakfast. Hoffenberg. pap. 1.95 o.s.i. (TC-493, Travellers Comp). Olympia.

Sin for Breakfast. Mason Hoffenberg. 1968. pap. 1.25 o.s.i. (210, Travellers Comp). Olympia.

Sin Games with Daddy. Lester Blake. 192p. (Orig.). 1972. pap. 1.95 o.p. (ISBN 0-87682-282-0, 7282). Barclay Hse.

Sin in Haste. Gladys Sloan. LC 42-109425. 1942. Phoenix Press.

Sin in Haste. Leona Slottman. LC 42-10942. 1942. Phoenix Press.

Sin in Style. Gladys Sloan. LC 39-25555. Phoenix Press.

Sin in Style. Leona Slottman. LC 39-25555. 1939. Phoenix Press.

Sin Is Man's Twin: A Novel. Franklin P Jr Collier. LC 34-347493. W. Godwin, Inc.

Sin Mark. Margaret Page Hood. LC 63-10150. 1963. Coward-McCann.

Sin-O'-Man". Leah Weiss. LC 25-145170. 1924. Monfort & Company Press.

Sin of a Lifetime. Charlotte Mary Brame. LC 44-11144. (On cover: Lovell's library, v. 17, no. 809). John W. Lovell Company.

Sin of a Lifetime. Charlotte Mary Brame. LC 5339. (Bertha Clay library, no. 22). 1900. Street & Smith.

Sin of a Nation. Michael Kitsock. LC 50-12372. 1950. Dorrance.

Sin of Angels. Martha Gilbert Dickinson Bianchi. LC 12-180659. 1912. 1.30. Duffield & Company.

Sin of Eve. Helen Marion Edginton. LC 13-14817. 1913. Hodder and Stoughton.

Sin of Father Amara: A Novel. Jose Maria De Eca De Queiroz. LC 63-9413. 1963. St. Martin's Press.

Sin of Father Mouret. Emile Zola. LC 69-19595. (New library of French Classics). 1969. 9.95 (ISBN 0-13-810523-5). Prentice-Hall.

Sin of George Warrener. Marie Van Vorst. LC 6-20363. 1906. The Macmillan Company.

Sin of Her Youth. Rose Myles. LC 3524. 1900. A. D. Aldridge & Co.

Sin of Joost Avelingh. Jozua Marius Willem Van Der Poorten Schwartz. LC 8-2899. (On cover: Lovell's international series, no. 79). 1890. F. F. Lovell & Co.

Sin of Monseiur Pettipon: And Other Humorous Tales, by Richard Connell. Richard Edward Connell. LC 25-805126. 1925. Minton, Balch and Company.

Sin of Monsieur Pettipon and Other Humorous Tales. Richard Edward Connell. LC 77-106273. (Short story index reprint series). 1970. Books for Libraries Press.

Sin of Mousieur Pettipon, and Other Humorous Tales. Richard Edward Connell. LC 22-26482. 1922. George H. Doran Company.

Sin of Saint Desmond. Amy Cameron Fariss. 1905. R. G. Badger.

Sin of the Prophet. Truman John Nelson. LC 52-5007. 1952. Little, Brown.

Sin Pit. Paul Meskil. LC 54-37751. (Lion book, 198). 1954. Lion Books by Arrangement with Cornell Pub. Corp.
Sin Plan Family. Sterling Harkins. 192p. (Orig.). 1972. pap. 1.95 o.p. (ISBN 0-87682-222-7, 7222). Barclay Hse.
Sin Preacher. John Racine. 192p. (Orig.). 1973. pap. 1.95 o.p. (ISBN 0-87056-280-0, 6280). Brandon.
Sin Saber Quien Eras, y Repentino Despertar: Dos Novelas. Dalia D. St. Marie. 144p. 1975. 7.00 o.p. (ISBN 0-682-48248-X). Exposition.
Sin Shouter of Cabin Road. Cover Painting by Barye Phillips. John Faulkner, pseud. LC 55-258628. (Gold medal books, 455). 1955. Fawcett Publications.
Sin, Soul, and Circumstance: A Novel. Wilma M Prezzi. LC 54-6582. 1953. Padell Book Co.
Sin Street: A Novel. 1st Ed. Deadwiley, Paul N. LC 55-12324. Pageant Press.
Sin Students. David Bates. 192p. (Orig.). 1973. pap. 1.95 o.p. (ISBN 0-87682-288-X, 7288). Barclay Hse.
Sin Suits Me. Roy Booth. LC 35-8481. Godwin.
Sin-Teen Job. Jan Weaver. pap. 1.95 o.p. (8040). Cameo.
Sin That Was His. Frank Lucius Packard. LC 17-28602. George H. Doran Company.
Sin Time with Mother. John Racine. 192p. (Orig.). 1973. pap. 1.95 o.p. (ISBN 0-87682-310-X, 7310). Barclay Hse.
Sin to Symphony: A Novel. Charles Rollin Smith. LC 65-1632. 1964. Exposition Press.
Sin Underneath. Bentz Plagemann. Orig. Title: Into the Labyrinth. 1971. pap. 0.95 o.p. (N2509). Pyramid Pubns.
Sinai Tapestry: A Novel. Edward Whittemore. LC 76-28604. 8.95 (ISBN 0-03-018536-X). Holt, Rinehart and Winston.
Sinan, the Turkish Michelangelo: A Biographical Novel. Veronica De Osa. LC 80-50813. (Illus.). 10.95 (ISBN 0-533-04655-6). Vantage Press.
Sinbad; a Romance. Cyril Kay-Scott. LC 23-9240. 1923. T. Seltzer.
Sinbad Mines: A Tale of the Rockies. Edward Fayette Eldridge. The Reed Publishing Company.
Sinbad the Sailor. Boreslaw Lesmian. Tr. by Krystina Boron from Polish. (Illus.). 1980. 65.00; pap. 20.00. Pomegranate.
Sinbad the Soldier. Percival Christopher Wren. LC 35-1832. 1935. Houghton Mifflin Company.
Since We Love. Denise Robins. LC 41-6695. 1941. Arcadia House, Inc.
Since We Love. Denise Robins. 1975. (pbk.) 0.95 (ISBN 0-380-00339-2). Avon.
Since You Went Away... Letters to a Soldier from His Wife, Margaret Buell Wilder. Margaret Applegate Buell Wilder. LC 43-5937. 1943. Whittlesey House, McGraw-Hill Book Company, Inc.
Since You Went Away: Letters to a Soldier from His Wife, Margaret Buell Wilder. Margaret Applegate Buell Wilder. LC 44-7905. 1944. The Sun Dial Press.
Since You've Been Gone. Allison Kerry. (Orig.). 1982. pap. 2.95 (ISBN 0-515-05493-3). Jove Pubns.
Sincerely Peg. Peggy R. Dobler. (Illus.). 1976. pap. 4.95. New Expressions.
Sincerely, Ronald Reagan. Helene Von Damm. (Orig.). 1981. pap. 2.50 (ISBN 0-425-04855-1). Berkley Pub.
Sincerely: Willis Wayde. 1st Ed. John Phillips Marquand. LC 55-553485. Little, Brown.
Sincerely Yours. Josiah Pitts Woolfolk & John Burton Thompson. LC 51-10092. 1951. Arco Pub. Co.
Sincerite. Mortimer Henry Marion Durand. LC 24-229475. 1924. Longmans, Green and Co.
Sincerity: A Story of Our Time. John Erskine. LC 29-237928. The Bobbs-Merrill Company.
Sinclair Lewis: Our Own Diogenes. Vernon Louis Parrington. LC 27-22552. (Half-title: University of Washington chapter, no. 5). 1927. University of Washington Book Store.
Sinclairs of Old Fort Des Moines: A Historical Romance. Johnson Brigham. LC 28-5404. 1927. The Torch Press.
Sinews of Love. Alexander Cordell, pseud. LC 66-117615. 1966. 4.95. Doubleday.
Sinews of War: A Romance of London and the Sea. Eden Phillpotts & Arnold Bennett. LC 74-17139. (Collected works of Arnold Bennett). 1974. (ISBN 0-518-19155-9). Books for Libraries Press.
Sinfonia Pastoral. LC 33-32037. American Book Company.
Sinfonia Sexual. Hugo Escamilla. (Pimienta Collection Ser). (Span.). 1977. pap. 1.00 (ISBN 0-88473-259-2). Fiesta Pub.
Sinful. Bart Frame. Orig. Title: Scandals at the Country Club. pap. 0.60 o.p. (60-337). Manor Bks.
Sinful Bachelor and His Sinful Doings: A Novel. Nadage Doree. LC 18-17297. 1908. The News Company.
Sinful Cinderella. Henry Hale. LC 40-7289. Phoenix Press.
Sinful Daughter. Josiah Pitts Woolfolk. LC 51-13974. 1951. Arco Pub. Co.
Sinful Marriage. Watkins Eppes Wright. LC 39-33269. 1939. Phoenix Press.
Sinful Marriage: By Glen Watkins Pseud.... Wright Williams. Phoenix Press.
Sinful Ones. Fritz Leiber. LC 80-25744. (Gregg Press Science Fiction Series). 1980. 13.95 (ISBN 0-8398-2643-5). Gregg Press.
Sinful Pastor. Michel Starckenfeder & Henze, K., Tr. LC 44-25675. 1943. Serles Publishing Co.
Sinful Peck: A Novel. Morgan Robertson. LC 3-13930. 1903. Harper & Brothers.
Sinful Sadday: Son of a Cotton Mill; a Story of a Little Orphan Boy Who Lived to Triumph. Thornwell Jacobs. 1907. Smith & Lamar.
Sinful Sisters. Leona Slottman. LC 47-307839. 1947. Phoenix Press.
Sinful Stones. Peter Dickinson. LC 74-96805. 1970. 4.95. Harper & Row.
Sinful Town: A Novel. Leo P Walsh. LC 49-1761. 1948. Exposition Press.
Sinful Woman. James Mallahan Cain. LC 48-1363. (Avon monthly novel, 1). 1947. Avon Editions.
Sinful Woman. James Mallahan Cain. LC 49-176563. (New Avon library 174). 1948. Avon Pub. Co.
Sinfully Rich. Hulbert Footner. LC 40-38482. 1940. Harper & Brothers.
Sing a Song of Homicide. James R Langham. LC 40-33106. 1940. Simon and Schuster.
Sing a Song of Homicide. James Richard Langham. LC 40-33106. 1940. Simon and Schuster.
Sing a Song of Murder. Robert Portner Koehler. LC 41-5497. Phoenix Press.
Sing a Song of Murder. Jan Michaels. (Mystery Puzzler Ser.: No. 12). (Illus.). 1978. pap. 1.95 (ISBN 0-89083-424-5). Zebra.
Sing a Song of Sex. Sterling Harkins. 192p. pap. 1.95 o.p. (6142). Brandon.
Sing a Song of Six Guns. Burt Arthur, pseud. (O.s.i.). 1976. pap. 0.95 o.s.i. (BT50914). Belmont-Tower.
Sing a Song of Six-Guns. Burt Arthur. 1976. (pbk.) 0.95. Belmont Tower Books.
Sing All the Summer. Harriet Henry, pseud. LC 41-173229. 1941. Dodd, Mead & Company.
Sing Before Breakfast, Figures, Yacht and Island. Vincent McHugh. LC 33-6571. 1933. Simon and Schuster.
Sing, Brat, Sing. Translated from the German. Rene Fulop-Miller & Winston, Richard, Tr. LC 47-3088. 1947. H. Holt and Company.
Sing, Choirs of Angels. George Cuomo. LC 75-86897. 1969. 4.95. Doubleday.
Sing, Clubman, Sing! A Chico Brett Thriller, by Kevin O'Hara Pseud. Marten Cumberland. LC 52-2044. 1952. Hurst & Blackett.
Sing Cut the Glory. 1st Ed. Gladys Hasty Carroll. LC 57-11157. 1957. Little, Brown.
Sing Down the Moon. Scott O'Dell. 1976. pap. 1.75 (ISBN 0-440-97975-7, LFL). Dell.
Sing for a Penny. Clifford Dowdey. LC 41-2808. 1941. Little, Brown and Company.
Sing for Your Supper. Peggy Gaddis, pseud. LC 42-290511. 1941. Arcadia House, Inc.
Sing for Your Supper. Eleanor Bachman Lothrop. LC 52-8741. 1952. Rinehart.
Sing Me a Love Song. Jacob Benjamin. (Orig.). 1980. pap. 1.75 (ISBN 0-532-23173-2). Woodhill.
Sing Me a Murder. Helen Nielsen. LC 60-11076. 1960. Morrow.
Sing Me Back Home. Merle Haggard & Peggy Russell. 1983. pap. 2.95 (ISBN 0-671-45275-4). PB.
Sing, Morning Star. 1st American Ed. Jane Oliver, pseud. LC 56-6493. Putnam.
Sing No Sad Songs. Jean Carew. LC 40-102916. 1940. Arcadia House, Inc.
Sing No Sad Songs: A Novel. 1st Ed. John Hazard Wildman. LC 55-5725. 1955. Exposition Press.
Sing Once More. Helen Partridge. LC 37-3368. 1937. Arcadia House.
Sing One Song. Helen Topping Miller. LC 56-117798. 1956. Appleton-Century-Crofts.
Sing Sing Nights. Harry Stephen Keeler. LC 28-18755. E. P. Dutton & Company.
Sing to Me of Love. JoAnna Brandon. (Candlelight Ecstacy Ser.: No. 112). (Orig.). 1983. pap. 1.95 (ISBN 0-440-18119-4). Dell.
Sing to the Sun. Lucille Papin Borden. LC 33-305605. 1933. The Macmillan Company.
Sing Witch, Sing Death. Roberta Gellis. 1975. (pbk.) 0.95. Bantam Books.
Sing with the Wind. LC 68-56014. autographed gift ed. 4.95 (ISBN 0-918114-01-2). Inspiration Conn.
Singa at My Wake. Ruth Seid. LC 52-2952. (Permabooks, 169). 1952. Permabooks.
Singalee. John Henry Reese. LC 70-75702. 1969. 4.50. Doubleday.
Singapore Exile Murders. Francis Van Wyck Mason. LC 39-23192. 1939. Pub. for the Crime Club, Inc., by Doubleday, Doran & Company, Inc.
Singapore Grip. James Gordon Farrell. LC 78-10855. 1979. 10.95 (ISBN 0-394-50483-6). Knopf.
Singapore Grip. James Gordon Farrell. (Berkley book). 1980. 2.75. Berkley Pub. Corp.
Singapore Passage. Donald Barr Chidsey. LC 56-9449. (Dell first edition, 107). 1956. Dell Pub. Co.
Singapore Short Stories. Robert Yeo. LC 78-940680. (Writing in Asia series). 3.95. Heinemann Educational Books (Asia)
Singapore Wink. Ross Thomas. LC 69-13657. 1969. 5.95. W. Morrow.
Singer and the Summer Song. Beatrice Levin. (Berkley Highland book). 1974. (pbk) 0.75 (ISBN 0-425-02496-2). Berkley Pub. Co.
Singer at the Wedding. Bruce Arnold. LC 78-304890. 1978. 16.95 (ISBN 0-241-89825-0). Hamilton.
Singer from the Sea. Amelia Edith Huddleston Barr. LC 6-7972. Dodd, Mead & Company.
Singer Not the Song. Audrey Erskine Lindop. LC 52-14029. 1953. Appleton-Century-Crofts.
Singer of Seville: Novelized. Harry Sinclair Drago. LC 30-13183. A. L. Burt Company.
Singer of the Kootenay: A Tale of to-Day. Robert Edward Knowles. LC 11-26610. 1.25. Fleming H. Revell Company.
Singer of the Wilderness. William Byron Mowery. LC 31-28914. Doubleday, Doran & Company, Inc.
Singer Passes: An Indian Tapestry. Katherine Helen Maud Marshall Diver. LC 34-6196. 1934. Dodd Mead & Company.
Singermann. Myron Brinig. LC 74-27968. (Modern Jewish Experience). 1975. 27.00 (ISBN 0-405-06698-8). Arno Press.
Singermann. Myron Brinig. LC 29-368951. 1929. Farrar & Rinehart Incorporated.
Singers. Leonhard Frank. Tr. by Brooks, Cyrus Harry. LC 33-4730. H. Holt and Company.
Singer's Heart. Anna Farquhar Bergengren. LC 6-11335. 1897. Roberts Brothers.
Singer's Story. M. P. Hogan. (On cover: Seaside library. Pocket ed., no. 681). 1886. G. Munro.
Singing and the Gold. 1st Ed. A. B. Matthiessen. LC 55-5266. 1955. Doubleday.
Singing Arrow: A Navaho Indian Story of Love and Truth. Illustrated by Richard Holley. Nolie Mumey. LC 58-433168. 1958. Golden Bell Press.
Singing Beach: A Novel. Elizabeth Foster. LC 41-4624. Harper & Brothers.
Singing Birds Lie. Marjorie Vernon. 1973. (pbk) 0.75 (ISBN 0-671-75722-9). Pocket Books,
Singing Bone. Richard Austin Freeman. LC 65-9496. 1965. W. W. Norton.
Singing Bone. Richard Austin Freeman. LC 75-44972. (Fifty classics of crime fiction, 1900-1950; no. 18). 1976. 12.00 (ISBN 0-8240-2367-6). Garland Pub.
Singing Bone. Richard Austin Freeman. LC 22-25806. 1918. Hodder and Stoughton.
Singing Bone. Introd. by Vincent Starrett. Richard Austin Freeman. LC 65-949619. (Seagull lib. of mystery and suspense). 3.95. Norton.
Singing Captives. Emily Beatrix Coursolles Jones. LC 22-19475. Boni and Liveright.
Singing Clock. Virginia Perdue. LC 41-18052. 1941. Pub. for the Crime Club by Doubleday, Doran & Company.
Singing Corpse. Bernard Dougall. LC 43-605. 1943. Dodd, Mead & Company.
Singing Diamonds: And Other Stories. Helen McCloy. LC 65-277135. (Red badge detective). bds., 3.50. Dodd.
Singing Fiddles: A Story of the Jason Lee Missions in Early Oregon. Anne Tedlock Brooks. LC 50-9000. 1950. Arcadia House.
Singing Fool. Hubert Dail. LC 29-5227. Grosset & Dunlap.
Singing Frogs & Other Stories. Josephine Rioux. 2.50 o.p. Vantage.
Singing Glory! Georgiana L. Lahr. 3.95 (ISBN 0-533-01211-2). Vantage.
Singing Gold. Dorothy Cottrell. LC 29-800. 1929. Houghton Mifflin Company.
Singing Guns. Max Brand. LC 38-14381. 1938. Dodd, Mead & Company.
Singing Guns. Frederick Faust. LC 38-14881. 1938. Dodd, Mead & Company.
Singing Heart. Florence Jeannette Baier Ward. LC 19-188353. 1919. The James A. McCann Company.
Singing Hill. Bertha Muzzy Sinclair. LC 39-14803. 1939. Little, Brown and Company.
Singing Hills. Lillian K Craig. LC 51-6287. 1951. Crowell.
Singing Hills: A Novel About Welsh Settlers in Upstate New York. Howard Thomas. 1964. 4.50 o.p. (ISBN 0-913710-00-8). Prospect.
Singing in the Shrouds. Ngaio Marsh. LC 79-26218. 1980. 11.10 (ISBN 0-88411-494-5). Aeonian Press.
Singing in the Shrouds. 1st Ed. Ngaio Marsh. LC 58-5657. 1958. Little, Brown.
Singing in the Woods. Elizabeth Renier. 1981. pap. 1.95 (ISBN 0-441-76742-7). Ace Bks.
Singing Lariat. Harry Sinclair Drago. LC 48-826819. (Triple-A western classic). 1948. Jefferson House.
Singing Lariat. Harry Sinclair Drago. LC 39-32882. 1939. W. Morrow & Company.
Singing Lead. George C Henderson. LC 36-14928. Greenberg.
Singing Lizard. John Knowler. LC 67-11945. 1967. bds., 4.95. Farrar.
Singing Lizard. John Knowler. LC 67-11947. 1967. Farrar, Straus and Giroux.
Singing Mountains. Albert Benjamin Cunningham. LC 19-14344. 1.50. George H. Doran Company.
Singing Mouse Stories. Emerson Hough. LC 7-7143. 1895. Forest and Stream Pub. Co.
Singing Mouse Stories. Emerson Hough. The Bobbs-Merrill Company.
Singing River. Alice DeFord. LC 27-172273. 1927. Little, Brown, and Company.
Singing River. Wilbur C Tuttle. LC 39-27948. 1939. Houghton Mifflin Company.
Singing Sands. Elizabeth Mackintosh. (Kangaroo Book.). 1977. 1.75. Pocket Books.
Singing Sands. Josephine Tey. LC 81-47389. (Fifty Classics of Crime Fiction, 1950-1975). 1982. 14.95 (ISBN 0-8240-5000-2). Garland.
Singing Sands. Josephine Trey. Ed. by J. Barzun & W. H. Taylor. LC 81-47389. (Crime Fiction 1950-1975 Ser.). 192p. 1982. lib. bdg. 14.95 (ISBN 0-8240-5000-2). Garland Pub.
Singing Sands: By Josephine Tey Pseud. Elizabeth Mackintosh. LC 53-9282. 1953. Macmillan.
Singing Scorpion. William Colt MacDonald. LC 34-21153. Covici, Friede.
Singing Season: A Romance of Old Spain. Isabel Bowler Paterson. LC 24-15292. Boni and Liveright.
Singing Shadows. Jane Ludlow Drake Abbott. LC 33-16228. J. B. Lippincott Company.
Singing Soul. Arthur J Foxall. LC 32-17517. The Christopher Publishing House.
Singing Swans. Alexandra Manners, pseud. LC 75-18580. 1975. 7.95 (ISBN 0-399-11593-5). Putnam.
Singing Swans. Alexandra Manners, pseud. (Berkley Medallion Book). 1977. 1.50 (ISBN 0-425-03290-6). Berkley Pub. Corp.: Distributed by Putnam.
Singing to Sylvia: A Novel. Lucy Poate Stebbins. LC 34-16183. 1934. R. D. Henkle.
Singing Toads & Other Stories. Bea Bird. 1970. 2.95 o.p. Vantage.
Singing Waters. Elisabeth Stancy Payne. LC 25-9813. 1925. The Penn Publishing Company.
Singing Waters: A Novel. Mary Dolling Sanders O'Malley. LC 46-4610. 1946. The Macmillan Company.
Singing Wells. Roland Pertwee. LC 23-96881. 1923. A. A. Knopf.
Singing Widow. Veronica Parker Johns. LC 41-765247. Duell, Sloan and Pearce.
Singing Wind. Joy De Weese Wehen. LC 77-23984. 8.95 (ISBN 0-698-10857-4). Coward, McCann & Geoghegan.
Singing Winds: Stories of Gipsy Life. Konrad Bercovici. LC 26-19022. 1926. Doubleday, Page & Company.
Singing Winds: Stories of Gypsy Life. Konrad Bercovici. LC 79-133814. (BCL Ser. I). 1970. Repr. of 1926 ed. 22.00 (ISBN 0-404-00787-2). AMS Pr.
Singing Wire: And Other Stories. Hallie Erminie Rives. LC 7-41017. 1892. W. P. Titus, Printer.
Single: A Novel. Harriet Frank. LC 77-6481. 1977. 8.95 (ISBN 0-395-25778-6). Houghton Mifflin.
Single Bed. Leona Slottman. LC 45-9504. 1945. Phoenix Press.
Single-Code Girl: A Novel. Bell Elliott Palmer. LC 15-17980. 1915. Lothrop, Lee & Shepard Co.
Single File. Norman Fruchter. LC 74-106626. 1970. 5.95. Knopf.
Single Gentleman. Oliver Ellsworth. LC 8-29695. 1867. O. Ellsworth.
Single Girl. Mary Danby, pseud. 1974. (pbk.) 1.25. Dell.
Single Girl: A Novel. Mary Danby, pseud. LC 72-7736. 1973. 5.95. McGraw-Hill.
Single-Handed. Cecil Scott Forester. LC 20-14147. 1929. G. P. Putnam's Sons.
Single Heart. Robert Drake. LC 75-148010. 1971. 4.95 (ISBN 0-87695-142-6). Aurora Publishers.
Single Heart. Annie Edith Foster Jameson. LC 24-23492. 1924. Frederick A. Stokes Company.
Single Heart, and Double Face. Charles Reade. (Lovell's library v. 1, no. 28). 1882. J. W. Lovell Company.
Single Hound. May Sarton. LC 38-7060. 1938. Houghton Mifflin Company.

TITLE INDEX

SIOUX CITY.

Single in New York. Charles Oldfield. 1977. pap. 1.50 o.s.i. (ISBN 0-8439-0426-7, LB426DK, Leisure Bks). Nordon Pubns.
Single Jack. Max Brand. 1980. pap. 1.75 (ISBN 0-671-83417-7). PB.
Single Ladies. Vida Hurst. LC 41-231768. Gramercy Publishing Company.
Single Lady. John Saunders. LC 31-74053. 1931. Brewer & Warren Inc.
Single Lady. John Saunders. (Lost American Fiction Series). 1978. 1.95 (ISBN 0-445-04221-4). Popular Library.
Single Lady: A Novel. John Saunders. LC 75-37829. (Lost American Fiction Ser.). 411p. 1976. Repr. 8.95 (ISBN 0-8093-0761-8). S Ill U Pr.
Single Man. Christopher Isherwood. LC 64-17501. 1964. Simon and Schuster.
Single Pebble. John Richard Hersey. LC 56-7209. 1956. Knopf.
Single Pilgrim. Mary Christianna Milne Lewis. LC 46-1881. 1946. T. Y. Crowell Co.
Single Pilgrim: A Novel. Norman Lewis. LC 54-5888. 1954. Rinehart.
Single Reels. Albert Bigelow Paine. LC 23-840161. 1923. Harper & Brothers.
Single Secret: A Novel. Teo Savory. LC 61-657660. 1961. G. Braziller.
Single Session: And Other Stories About Schools. Charles William Bardeen. LC 17-28605. C. W. Bardeen.
Single Standard. St. John, Adela Rogers. LC 28-11054. 1928. Cosmopolitan Book Corporation.
Single Star. Francis Durham Grierson. LC 18-12231. 1918. 0.75. George H. Doran Company.
Single Star: A Novel of Cuba in the '90s. 1st ed. Walter Adolphe Roberts. LC 49-11126. 1949. Bobbs-Merrill Co.
Single Summer with Lord B. Derek Marlowe. LC 72-83235. (Illus.). 1970. 5.95. Viking Press.
Single Track. Isabel Egenton Ostrander. LC 20-128524. W. J. Watt & Company.
Single Voice: An Anthology of Contemporary Fiction. Ed. by Jerome Charyn. (Orig.). 1969. pap. 2.95 (ISBN 0-02-018900-1, Collier). Macmillan.
Singled Out. Steven Whitney. LC 78-4183. 1978. 8.95 (ISBN 0-688-03290-7). Morrow.
Singles. George Roland. (Orig.). 1971. pap. 0.75 o.p. (ISBN 0-446-64492-7, 64-492). Paperback Lib.
Singles City. John Brodman. 1972. pap. 0.95 o.p. (75-343). Lancer.
Singleton. Jack Cady. LC 81-8117. 1981. 13.95 (ISBN 0-914842-63-3). Madrona Publishers.
Singleton. Badger Clark, pseud. LC 78-2416. (Western Novels Ser.). 1978. 7.95 o.p. (ISBN 0-312-72599-X); large type 9.95 o.p. (ISBN 0-312-72600-7). St Martin.
Singleton. Lauran Paine. LC 78-2416. 1978. 7.95 (ISBN 0-312-72599-X) (ISBN 0-312-72600-7) (ISBN 0-312-72600-7) (ISBN 0-312-72600-7). St. Martin's Press.
Singleton Fontenoy, R. N. James Hannay. LC 7-132033. (On cover: Library of select novels, no. 151). 1851. Harper & Brothers.
Singoalla: A Romance Written in Swedish. autograph ed. Viktor Rydberg & Josephsson, Axel, 1868-1934, Tr. LC 3-32408. 1903. The Grafton Press.
Singreale Chronicles. Calvin Miller. LC 82-15850. 6.69 (ISBN 0-06-250573-4). Harper & Row.
Singular Adventures of Baron Munchausen. a definitive text edited, with an introd., by john carswell and illustrated by fritz kredel. ed. English Munchausen. Ed. by Carswell, John. LC 52-10595. 1952. Limited Editions Club.
Singular Case of the Multiple Dead. Mark McShane. LC 74-86259. (Red mask mystery). 1969. 4.50. Putnam.
Singular Conspiracy. Barry Perowne. LC 74-170899. 1974. 6.95 (ISBN 0-672-51892-9). Bobbs-Merrill.
Singular Fury. Howard Leoner Oleck. LC 68-13714. 1968. 4.95. World Pub. Co.
Singular Life. Elizabeth Stuart Phelps Ward. LC 4-15172. 1895. Houghton, Mifflin and Company.
Singular Man. James Patrick Donleavy. LC 63-21529. 1963. Little, Brown.
Singular Man. James Patrick Donleavy. 1973. (pbk.) 1.50. Dell.
Singular Miss Smith. Florence Morse Kingsley. LC 4-10543. 1904. The Macmillan Company.
Singular Sinner. Charles R Harker. LC 1-31628. The Abbey Press.
Singular Travels, Campaigns and Adventures of Baron Munchausen. By R. E. Raspe and Others. With an Introd. by John Carswell. With Illus. by Gustave Dore. Munchausen, English. (Dover T698). 1960. pap., 1.00. Dover Pubns.
Singular Travels, Campaigns and Adventures of Baron Munchausen: By R. E. Raspe, Others. Introd. by John Carswell. Illus. by Leslie Wood. Munchausen. English. (Dover bk. rebound). 1961. 3.01. Peter Smith.
Singularity Station. Brian N Ball. (Daw SF books, UQ1088). (Illus.). 1973. (pbk.) 0.95. Daw Books.
Singularly Deluded. Sarah Grand. LC 6-27663. (On cover: Seaside library. Pocket ed. no. 2088). G. Munro's Sons.
Sinister. Steve Dichter. LC 81-86420. 192p. 1983. 10.95 (ISBN 0-86666-043-7). GWP.
Sinister Abbey. Elsie Lee. 1973. (pbk.) 0.95. Dell.
Sinister Alibi. Carlton Wallace. LC 34-41051. 1934. Pub. for the Crime Club, Inc., by Doubleday, Doran & Company, Inc.
Sinister Cargo. Stanley Hart Page. LC 32-17260. 1932. A. A. Knopf.
Sinister Crag. Newton Gayle. LC 38-38828. 1939. C. Scribner's Sons.
Sinister Eden. Aylward Edward Dingle. LC 34-24635. J. B. Lippincott Company.
Sinister Errand. Peter Cheyney. LC 45-7538. 1945. Dodd, Mead & Company.
Sinister Errand. Peter Cheyney. LC 47-24309. (New Avon library. 114). 1947. Avon Book Co.
Sinister Gardens. Willo Davis Roberts. 1972. pap. 0.95 o.s.i. (75-405). Lancer.
Sinister History of Ambrose Hinkle. Thomas McMorrow. LC 29-5707. J. H. Sears & Company, Inc.
Sinister House. Caroline Farr. (Signet Book). 1978. 1.50. New American Library.
Sinister House. with illustrations by haydon jones. ed. Leland Hall. LC 19-232545. 1919. 1.50. Houghton Mifflin Company.
Sinister House: A Mystery Story of Southern California. Charles Gordon Booth. LC 26-16334. 1926. W. Morrow and Company, Inc.
Sinister Inn. Joseph Jefferson Farjeon. LC 34-251493. 1934. Dodd, Mead & Company.
Sinister Island. Charles Wadsworth Camp. LC 15-5384. 1915. 1.25. Dodd, Mead & Company.
Sinister Isle of Love. Ellen Morely. 1977. pap. 1.50 (ISBN 0-532-15269-7). Woodhill.
Sinister Light. Ethel L. White. Orig. Title: Put Out the Light. pap. 0.60 o.p. (53-374). Paperback Lib.
Sinister Madonna. Sax Rohmer, pseud. (Sumuru Ser). 1977. Repr. 6.50. Bookfinger.
Sinister Madonna. Arthur Sarsfield Ward. LC 56-1171. (Gold medal books, 555). 1956. Fawcett Publications.
Sinister Man. Edgar Wallace. LC 25-23587. Small, Maynard & Company.
Sinister Mark. Lee Thayer, pseud. LC 23-9854. 1923. Doubleday, Page & Company.
Sinister Quest. T. C. H Jacobs, pseud. LC 34-329455. The Macaulay Company.
Sinister Ranch. Bayne Hobart. LC 68-1543. 1968. Arcadia House.
Sinister Researches of C. P. Ransom. Homer Nearing, Jr. 1969. pap. 0.75 o.p. (0502-07051-075). Curtis.
Sinister Researches of C. P. Ransom. 1st Ed. Homer Nearing. LC 54-5168. 1954. Doubleday.
Sinister Revel. Lillian Barrett. LC 19-15018. 1919. A. A. Knopf.
Sinister Sequences. John Hawkes. LC 79-1707. 9.95 (ISBN 0-06-011808-3). Harper & Row.
Sinister Shadow: A Case for Inspector Silver, C.I.D., New Scotland Yard. Henry Holt. LC 34-5972. Pub. for The Crime Club, Inc., by Doubleday, Doran & Company, Inc.
Sinister Shelter. Mary Violet Heberden. LC 49-9321. 1949. Pub. for the Crime Club by Doubleday.
Sinister Stones. Arthur William Upfield. LC 54-9187. 1954. Published for the Crime Club by Doubleday.
Sinister Strangers. Clarence Budington Kelland. LC 61-12915. 1961. Dodd, Mead.
Sinister Street. Compton Mackenzie. LC 15-27374. 1914. D. Appleton and Company.
Sinister Street: A Quinny Hite Mystery. Richard Burke. LC 48-6425. (fingerprint mystery). 1948. Ziff-Davis Pub. Co.
Sinister Tapestry. Jane McCarthy. 192p. (YA) 1974. 4.95 o.p. (Avalon). Bouregy.
Sinister Tapestry. Jane McCarthy. (Avalon romances). 1974. 4.50. Avalon Books.
Sink the Grand Fleet. Fred Halliday. LC 78-74944. 1979. pap. 2.25 o.s.i. (ISBN 0-89516-068-4). Condor Pub Co.
Sinkiang Executive. Elleston Trevor. LC 77-82944. 1978. 7.95 (ISBN 0-385-12276-4). Doubleday.
Sinkiang Executive 1. Adam Hall, pseud. 1979. 2.50 (ISBN 0-440-17997-1). Dell Book.
Sinking of the Odradek Stadium and Other Novels. Harry Mathews. LC 74-15881. (Illus.). 12.50. (ISBN 0-06-012839-9) (ISBN 0-06-012841-0). Harper & Row.
Sinking of the Sarah Diamond. William D. Jennings. LC 73-83220. 416p. 1974. 5.95 (ISBN 0-8397-7814-7). Eriksson.
Sinking Ship. Eva Lathbury. LC 9-29256. 1909. 1.50. H. Holt and Company.
Sinking Spell. Edward Gorey. (Illus.). 1965. pap. 4.75 (ISBN 0-8392-1150-3). Astor-Honor.
Sinless Crime. John Russell Coryell. LC 6-39921. (On cover: Lovell's library, no. 1258). 1888. John W. Lovell Company.
Sinless Crime. John Russell Coryell. LC 1-30279. (On cover: Eagle series, no. 194). 1900. Street & Smith.
Sinless Crime. Geraldine Fleming. (On cover: Lovell's library. no. 1258). 1888. J. W. Lovell Company.
Sinless Crime. Geraldine Fleming. LC 1-30279. (On cover: Eagle series, no. 194). 1900. Street & Smith.
Sinless Secret. Eliza M. J. Humphreys. (On cover: Seaside library. Pocket ed., no. 252). 1884. G. Munro.
Sinless Secret... Eliza M. J. Humphreys & Wylde, Katharine. (On cover: Lovell's library, no. 1179). 1888. J. W. Lovell Company.
Sinless Sin. Kaye Holden. LC 33-976. Grosset & Dunlap.
Sinner. Stuart MacGregor. LC 72-95425. 1973. 6.95 (ISBN 0-87955-903-9). J. P. O'Hara.
Sinner and Saint. A Story of the Woman's Crusade. A Novel. Alphonso Alva Hopkins. LC 7-5250. D. Lothrop and Compnay.
Sinner Beloved: A Novel of the Life and Times of Hosea the Prophet. 1st Ed. Phillips Endecott Osgood. LC 56-7362. 1956. American Press.
Sinner from Toledo & Other Stories. Anton Pavlovich Chekhov. Tr. by Arnold Hinchliffe. LC 70-147269. 168p. 1972. 14.50 (ISBN 0-8386-7890-4). Fairleigh Dickinson.
Sinner in Gingham. Peggy Gaddis. LC 43-5568. 1943. Phoenix Press.
Sinner in Israel: A Romance of Modern Jewish Life. Pierre Costello. LC 11-4105. 1911. 1.50. John Lane Company.
Sinner in Orders. Edward Ansley Stokes. LC 8-16297. 1895. The Unionist Gazette Association.
Sinner of Saint Ambrose. Robert Raynolds. LC 52-5813. 1952. Bobbs-Merrill.
Sinner or Victim? Dora Delmar. (On cover: Library of American authors. no. 69). 1895. G. Munro's Sons.
Sinner Take All. William Arthur Neubauer. LC 48-254197. 1948. Phoenix Press.
Sinner Take All. Kerry Shaw. LC 36-31572. 1936. Godwin.
Sinner Within Their Home. Rosalind Bowen. LC 42-236389. 1942. Meador Publishing Company.
Sinner (Yoshe Kalb) Israel Joshua Singer & Samuel, Maurice, 1895- LC 33-7563. Liveright, Inc.
Sinners. Edward S. Aarons. 1970. pap. 0.75 o.p. (T2312, GM). Fawcett World.
Sinners: A Novelization of Owen Davis' Play. D. Torbett & Davis, Owen, 1874- LC 15-13559. E. J. Clode.
Sinners and Shrouds. Jonathan Latimer. LC 55-13534. (Inner sanctum mystery). 1955. Simon and Schuster.
Sinners Beware: Little, Brown, and Company. Edward Phillips Oppenheim. LC 32-26363.
Sinner's Castle. Samuel Andrew Wood. LC 42-79743. 1941. J. Swift.
Sinners' Castle... Samuel Andrew Wood. LC 45-1827. (Prize mystery novels). 1944.
Sinners, Come Away. Leon Wilson. LC 49-11648. 1949. Little, Brown.
Sinner's Comedy. Pearl Mary Teresa Richards Craigie. LC 12-24360. Cassell Publishing Company.
Sinners Game. Linton Baldwin. LC 55-22311. (Lion book, 227). 1954. Lion Books.
Sinners Go Secretly: Being Pages from the Diary of Dr. Eustace Hailey. Robert McNair Wilson. LC 27-18304. 1927. J. B. Lippincott Company.
Sinners in Heaven. Lily Clive Nutt. LC 23-13010. The Bobbs-Merril Company.
Sinners in Summertime. Sigurd Hoel & Sprigge, Elizabeth, 1900- LC 30-19282. 1930. Coward-McCann, Inc.
Sinners Never Die. A. E Martin. LC 44-721034. 1944. Simon and Schuster.
Sinners' Parish. Robert Temple. LC 62-9323. 1962. Doubleday.
Sinner's Sentence: A Novel. Alfred Larder. LC 7-13841. (On cover: Vanity fair series. no. 7). 1891. Chatto & Windus.
Sinners Twain: A Romance of the Great Lone Land. John Mackie. (On cover: Twentieth century series). F. A. Stokes Company.
Sinning Lens. Mark Tryon. LC 53-243024. 1953. Vixen Press.
Sinning with Annie. Paul Theroux. 1972. 9.95 (ISBN 0-395-25502-3). HM.
Sinning with Annie, and Other Stories. Paul Theroux. LC 72-2283. 1972. 5.95 (ISBN 0-395-13996-1). Houghton Mifflin.
Sinovariant. Allison Ind. LC 79-79505. 1969. 5.95. D. McKay Co.
Sins. Judith Gould. 1982. pap. 3.95 (ISBN 0-451-11859-6, AE1859, Sig). NAL.
Sin's Aftermath. William Benson Richter. LC 38-172. THe Christopher Publishing House.
**Sins of -- ** Jack George Thomas Grant. LC 24-6690. Dorrance & Company.
Sins of a Widow. Amelie L'Oiseau. LC 99-562. (Neely's booklet library, no. 2). 1899. F. T. Neely.
Sins of Bluenose Trogdon. Howell Raines. LC 74-26807. 1975. (ISBN 0-8128-1764-8). Stein and Day.
Sins of Commission: A Novel. Harold L Klawans. LC 81-71083. 13.95 (ISBN 0-8092-5761-0). Contemporary Books.
Sins of Herod. Frank Gill Slaughter. 370p. 1976. Repr. lib. bdg. 18.55x (ISBN 0-89190-284-8). Am Repr-Rivercity Pr.
Sins of Herod. Frank Gill Slaughter. LC 68-14208. (Pathways of Faith Ser). 1968. 5.95 o.p. Doubleday.
Sins of Herod: A Novel of Rome and the Early Church. Frank Gill Slaughter. 1.95 (ISBN 0-671-80828-1). Pocket Books.
Sins of Herod: A Novel of Rome and the Early Church. Frank Gill Slaughter. LC 68-14208. (Pathway of faith series). 1968. Doubleday.
Sins of Innocence: A Love Story. Claire Pomeroy. LC 31-33899. Chelsea House.
Sins of Leslie. Liz Genell. (Orig.). pap. 0.95 o.p. (1122). Brandon.
Sins of Maria. 1st Ed. Bruce Cameron. LC 58-104342. 1958. Duell, Sloan and Pearce.
Sins of Onan. John Hanforth. pap. 1.95 o.p. (6037). Brandon.
Sins of Philip Fleming: A Compelling Novel of a Man's Intimate Problem. Irving Wallace. LC 59-12485. 1959. F. Fell.
Sins of Philip Fleming: A Compelling Novel of a Man's Intimate Problem. new ed. Irving Wallace. LC 68-4881. 1968. F. Fell.
Sins of Rachel Ellis. Philip Caveney. LC 77-16763. 8.95 (ISBN 0-312-72603-1). St. Martin's Press.
Sins of Rachel Ellis. Philip Caveney. (Berkley Book). 1979. 2.25 (ISBN 0-425-04144-1). Berkley Pub. Corp.
Sins of Saint Anthony: Tales of the Theatre. Charles William Collins. LC 72-116948. (Short story index reprint series). 1970. Books for Libraries Press.
Sins of Saint Anthony: Tales of the Theatre. Charles William Collins. LC 25-12245. 1925. P. Covici.
Sins of Sally. Leslie Curtis. LC 37-5483. D. Ryerson.
Sins of Severac Bablon. Sax Rohmer, pseud. 1967. 8.50. Bookfinger.
Sins of Society: A Novel. Cecil Raleigh & Hamilton, Henry, 1853?-1918. The Sins of Society. LC 43-34444. G. W. Dillingham Company.
Sins of Sumuru. Sax Rohmer, pseud. 1977. Repr. 6.50. Bookfinger.
Sins of Surrender. Alison Hart. (Girls in Trouble). (Signet book: Vol. 5) (ISBN 0-451-07230-8). New American Library.
Sins of the Children: A Novel. Cosmo Hamilton. LC 16-21052. 1916. 1.40. Little, Brown, and Company.
Sins of the Children: A Study in Social Values. Horace W. C Newte. 1911. John Lane Company.
Sins of the Father: A Romance of the South. Thomas Dixon. LC 12-7620. 1912. D. Appleton and Company.
Sins of the Fathers. Lawrence Block. 192p. 1982. pap. 2.75 (ISBN 0-515-06729-6). Jove Pubns.
Sins of the Fathers. Lawrence Block. Dell.
Sins of the Fathers. Susan Howatch. LC 80-11290. 13.95 (ISBN 0-671-25463-4). Simon and Schuster.
Sins of the Fathers. Mary Ellen Burke Hyde. LC 14-22666. 1914. 1.35. Sherman, French & Company.
Sins of the Fathers. Stanley Schmidt. (Berkley Medallion Book). 1976. (pbk.) 1.25. Berkley Publishing Corp.
Sins of the Fathers: And Other Tales. George Robert Gissing. LC 24-30444. 1924. P. Covici.
Sins of the Fathers: Translated from Der Eid Des Stefan Huller, by Sarah J. I. Lawson. Felix Hollaender & Lawson, Sarah J. I., Tr. LC 27-20265. Payson & Clarke, Ltd.
Sins of the Lion. Annette Motley. LC 79-65115. 1979. 10.95 (ISBN 0-8128-2684-1). Stein and Day.
Sins of the Past. Helen S. Nuelle. 1977. pap. 1.50 (ISBN 0-532-15293-X). Woodhill.
Sinsation of a Sintury: A Novel by David O. Wilderness Pseud. 1st Ed. Peter S Brody. LC 56-8530. 1956. Pageant Press.
Sint and Sinner: Or, In Passions Thraldom. Fanny May Ramirez. (On cover: The sunnyside series, no. 84). J. S. Ogilvie Publishing Company.
Sioux: A Novel. Irene Handl. 5.95. New Amer. Lib.
Sioux Arrows. Donald Porter. (American Indians Ser.: No. 9). (Orig.). 1982. pap. 2.95 (ISBN 0-440-07914-4). Dell.
Sioux City: A Novel. John Hyatt Downing. LC 40-6909. 1940. G. P. Putnam's Sons.

Sioux Indian Wars: By John Conway Pseud. Joseph Chadwick. LC 62-5370. (Monarch books. Monarch American series, MA324). 1962. Monarch Books.
Sioux Spaceman. Alice Mary Norton. 1974. (pbk.) 1.25. Ace Books.
Sioux Spaceman. Andre Norton, pseud. LC 77-25468. (Norton, Andre. The Space Adventure Novels of Andre Norton). 1978. 7.95 (ISBN 0-8398-2420-3). Gregg Press.
Sioux Sunrise. Michael J. Stewart. 192p. (Orig.). 1981. pap. 1.95 (ISBN 0-505-51747-7). Tower Bks.
Sioux Uprising. George G. Gilman, pseud. (Edge Ser.: No. 11). 1974. pap. 1.75 (ISBN 0-523-41289-4). Pinnacle Bks.
Sioux Uprising. George G Gilman. (Edge,#11). 1974. (pbk.) 0.95 (ISBN 0-523-00360-9). Pinnacle Books.
Sioux Wildfire. E. J. Hunter. (White Squaw Ser.: No. 1). (Orig.). 1983. pap. 2.50 (ISBN 0-8217-1205-5). Zebra.
Sippi. John Oliver Killens. LC 67-16400. 1967. 5.95. Trident.
Sir. Mildred Cram. LC 73-77730. 1973. 4.95 (ISBN 0-913270-11-3). Sunstone Press.
Sir Adam Disappeared. Edward Phillips Oppenheim. LC 39-11402. 1939. Little, Brown and Company.
Sir Adam Disappeared. Edward Phillips Oppenheim. LC 43-390464. 1940. The Sun Dial Press.
Sir and Brother. Harry Lee. LC 48-8669. Appleton-Century-Crofts.
Sir Andrew Wylie of That Ilk. John Galt. LC 72-172056. (His Works, v. 3-4). (Illus.). 1968. AMS Press.
Sir Andrew Wylie, of That Ilk. John Galt. Ed. by Meldrum, David Storrar. LC 17-487. (Works of John Galt. Ed. by D. Storrar Meldrum). 1895. Roberts Brothers.
Sir Anthony's Secret: Or, A False Position. Adeline Sergeant. LC 3-19523. (On cover: Broadway series, no. 6). 1891. J. A. Taylor and Company.
Sir Bevill. Arthur Christopher Thynne. LC 34-37795. (Half-title: John Lane's Indian and colonial library). 1904. John Lane; Etc., Etc.
Sir Boss: A Tough Labor Story with Soft and Beautiful Women. Ralph Bushnell Potts. LC 76-375567. 1.75. Falcon Books.
Sir Boss. Limited 1st Ed. Ralph Bushnell Potts. LC 59-153896. 1959. N. P. Faversham House.
Sir Brook Fossbrooke. Charles James Lever. LC 24-11861. (On cover: Novels of Irish life). 1906. Little, Brown, and Company.
Sir Brook Fossbrooke. A Novel. Charles James Lever. LC 7-14398. 1866. Harper & Brothers.
Sir Christopher: A Romance of a Maryland Manor in 1644. LC 1-31536. 1901. Little, Brown, and Company.
Sir Christopher Leighton: Or, The Marquis De Vaudreuil's Story. Marie Longworth Storer. LC 15-19196. 1915. B. Herder.
Sir Cyril Black. Benjamin Grimm. (Orig.). 1969. pap. 1.75 o.s.i. (OPH139, Ophelia). Olympia.
Sir Edmund Orme see Altar of the Dead.
Sir Edward Graham: Or, Railway Speculators. Catherine Sinclair. LC 8-9006. 1850. Harper & Brothers.
Sir Edward Seaward's Narrative of His Shipwreck, and Consequent Discovery of Certain Islands in the Caribbean Sea: With a Detail of Many Extraordinary and Highly Interesting Events in His Life, from the Year 1733 to 1749, As Written in His Own Diary. Ed. by Jane Porter. LC 79-164393. (Black Heritage Library Collection). 1971. (ISBN 0-8369-8852-3). Books for Libraries Press.
Sir Edward Seaward's Narrative of His Shipwreck, and Consequent Discovery of Certain Islands in the Caribean Sea: With a Detail of Many Extraordinary and Highly Interesting Events in His Life, from the Year 1733 to 1749, As Written in His Own Diary. Ed. by Jane Porter. Porter, William Ogilvie. LC 7-37776. 1931. J. & J. Harper.
Sir Elyot of the Woods: A Novel. Emma Frances Brooke. 1907. Duffield & Company.
Sir Gawain & the Green Knight. Ed. by W. R. Barron. LC 74-21. (Manchester Medieval Classics Ser). 179p. 1976. pap. text ed. 9.50x (ISBN 0-06-490311-7). B&N Imports.
Sir Gawain & the Green Knight. Tr. by Marie Borroff. (Orig.). 1967. pap. 2.95x (ISBN 0-393-09754-4, NortonC). Norton.
Sir Gawain & the Green Knight. Tr. by Gwyn Jones. (Illus.). deluxe ed. 80.00 o.p. (ISBN 0-498-06121-3). Golden Cockerel.
Sir Gawain & the Green Knight. James R. Kreuzer. LC 59-6208. (Rinehart Editions). 1959. pap. text ed. 8.50 (ISBN 0-03-008880-1, HoltC). HR&W.
Sir Gawain & the Grene Gnome. Ed. by R. T. Jones. 1972. text ed. 3.75x o.p. (ISBN 0-435-14511-8). Heinemann Ed.
Sir Gawain & the Grene Gome. R. T. Jones. 1965. pap. 2.00 o.p. Verry.
Sir Gawayne & the Green Knight. Kenneth Hare. 1918. 20.00 (ISBN 0-8274-3421-9). R West.
Sir Gawayne and the Green Knight. Re-Edited from Cotton Ms. Nero, A. X., in the British Museum, by Richard Morris. Rev. in 1897, and Further in 1912, by I. Gollancz. Morris, Richard, 1833-1894- Ed & Gollancz, Sir Israel, 1864-1930, Ed. LC 22-19757. (On cover: Early English text society. Original series, 4). 1864-1921. Pub. for the Early English Text Society by H. Milford, Oxford University Press.
Sir George Tressady. Mary Augusta Arnold Humphry Ward Ward. LC 4-15341. 1896. The Macmillan Company; Etc., Etc.
Sir George's Objection. Lucy Lane Clifford. LC 10-186512. 1910. T. Nelson and Sons.
Sir George's Objection. Lucy Lane Clifford. LC 10-20180. 1910. Duffield and Company.
Sir Gibbie. George Macdonald. LC 52-16829. (Home library). --
Sir Gibbie. George Macdonald. LC 4-16562. D. McKay.
Sir Gibbie. George Macdonald. LC 12-183251. 1911. D. McKay.
Sir Gibbie. George Macdonald. LC 37-5601. (Half-title: Everyman's library, ed. by Ernest Rhys. Fiction. no. 678). 1929. J. M. Dent & Sons, Ltd.
Sir Gibbie. George Macdonald & Elizabeth Yates. LC 79-64123. 1979. 4.95 (ISBN 0-8052-0637-X) (ISBN 0-8052-3730-5). Schocken Books.
Sir Gibbie. A Novel. George Macdonald. (Seaside library, v. 25, no. 491). 1879. G. Munro.
Sir Gibbie. A Novel. George Macdonald. LC 7-15860. 1879. J. B. Lippincott & Co.
Sir Godfrey's Granddaughters: A Novel, by Rosa Nouchette Carey... Rosa Nouchette Carey. LC 6-22808. (On cover: Lippincott's series of select novels, no. 138). 1892. J. B. Lippincott Company.
Sir Guy and Lady Rannard: A Novel. H. N Dickinson. 1909. Duffield & Company.
Sir Harry: A Love Story. Archibald Marshall. LC 19-17478. 1919. 1.75. Dodd, Mead and Company.
Sir Harry Hotspur Humblethwaite. Anthony Trollope. LC 29-11583. (Half-title: The World's classics. cccxxxvi). 1928. H. Milford, Oxford University Press.
Sir Harry Hotspur of Humblethwaite. reprint ed. / introduction by john halperin. ed. Anthony Trollope. LC 80-1891. (Trollope, Anthony, 1815-1882. Selections. 1981). 1981. 35.00 (ISBN 0-405-14158-0). Arno Press.
Sir Henry. Robert Nathan. LC 79-12787. 1979. 10.95. (ISBN 0-89370-136-X) (ISBN 0-89370-236-6). Borgo Press.
Sir Henry Morgan, Buccaneer: A Romance of the Spanish Main, by Cyrus Townsend Brady... Cyrus Townsend Brady. LC 3-21013. 1903. G. W. Dillingham Company.
Sir Henry Morgan: The Buccaneer. Edward Howard. LC 7-7146. 1847. Burgess, Stringer & Co.
Sir Jaffray's Wife. Arthur Williams Marchmont. LC 12-368413. (On cover: Globe library, vol. ii. no. 279). Rand, McNally & Company.
Sir James Appleby, Bart. A Novel. Katharine Sarah Gadsden Macquoid. (Harper's Franklin square library, no. 550). 1886. Harper & Brothers.
Sir Jasper Carew, Knight: His Life and Experiences... Charles James Lever. (Seaside library, v. 31, no. 633). 1879. G. Munro.
Sir Jasper Carew, Knt. His Life and Experiences... Charles James Lever. LC 7-14399. 1854. Harper & Brothers.
Sir Jasper's Tenant. Mary Elizabeth Braddon Maxwell. (On cover: Lovell's library, no. 879). 1887. J. W. Lovell Company.
Sir Jasper's Tenant. A Novel. Mary Elizabeth Braddon Maxwell. (On cover: Seaside library. Pocket ed. no. 515). 1885. G. Munro.
Sir John and the American Girl. Lilian Lida Bell. LC 1-17620. (Lettered on cover: Harper's portrait collection of short stories. v. 2). 1901. Harper & Brothers.
Sir John Constantine. Arthur Thomas Quiller-Couch. (On verso of front.: Nelson's library). T. Nelson and Sons.
Sir John Constantine: Memoirs of His Adventures at Home and Abroad, and Particularly in the Island of Corsica; Beginning with the Year 1756. Arthur Thomas Quiller-Couch. LC 6-31381. 1906. C. Scribner's Sons.
Sir John Dering. Jeffery Farnol. LC 23-15820. 1923. Little, Brown, and Company.
Sir John Hawkwood: A Tale of the White Company in Italy. Marion Polk Angellotti. LC 11-215888. R. F. Fenno & Company.
Sir John Magill's Last Journey. Freeman Willis Crofts. 301p. 1977. Repr. lib. bdg. 13.95x (ISBN 0-89966-274-9). Buccaneer Bks.
Sir John Magill's Last Journey: An Inspector French Case. Freeman Wills Crofts. LC 30-30709. 1930. Harper & Brothers.
Sir Lancelot of the Lake: A French Prose Romance of the Thirteenth Century. Tr. by Lucy Allen Paton. LC 74-8340. (Series: Broadway Medieval Library.). (Illus.). 1974. 50.00. Folcroft Library Editions.
Sir Launcelot Greaves. Tobias George Smollett. Ed. by David Evans. (Oxford English Novels Ser.). 1973. 12.95x o.p. (ISBN 0-19-255364-X). Oxford U Pr.
Sir Mark: A Tale of the First Capital Philadelphia. Anna Robeson Brown Burr. 1896. D. Appleton and Company.
Sir Michael and Sir George: A Comedy of the New Elizabethans 1st Amer. Ed. John Boynton Priestley. LC 66-10621. 1966. bds., 4.95. Atlantic-Little.
Sir Michael and Sir George: A Tale of COMSA and DISCUS and the New Elizabethans. John Boynton Priestley. LC 65-2276. 1964. Heinemann.
Sir Mortimer. Mary Johnston. 1904. Repr. lib. bdg. 25.00 (ISBN 0-8414-5422-1). Folcroft.
Sir Mortimer: A Novel. Mary Johnston. LC 4-6876. 1904. Harper and Brothers.
Sir Nigel. Arthur Conan Doyle. bds., 2.50. Transatlantic Arts.
Sir Nigel. Arthur Conan Doyle. LC 75-31407. (Illus.). 8.95 (ISBN 0-8055-1171-7) (ISBN 0-8055-0252-1). Hart Pub. Co.
Sir Nigel. Arthur Conan Doyle. LC 6-34805. 1906. McClure, Phillips & Co.
Sir Nigel. Arthur Conan Doyle. 16.95 (ISBN 0-7195-3228-0). Transatlantic.
Sir Nigel: Boyhood of the Commander of the White Company. Arthur Conan Doyle. LC 31-11922. (windmill books). 1931. Doubleday, Doran and Company, Inc.
Sir Noel's Heir. A Novel. May Agnes Early Fleming. LC 6-39942. (On cover: The idle hour series. no. 3). 1892. The F. M. Lupton Publishing Company.
Sir or Madam: A Novel. Berta Ruck. LC 23-480739. 1923. Dodd, Mead and Company.
Sir Orfeo. Ed. by A. J. Bliss. (Illus.). 79p. 1981. Repr. of 1954 ed. lib. bdg. 35.00 (ISBN 0-8495-0486-4). Arden Lib.
Sir Pagan: A Novel of Love and Arms. Samuel Zimmerman. LC 47-11264. 1947. Creative Age Press.
Sir Patrick: The Puddock. Lucy Bethia Colquhoun Walford. LC 8-32807. 1899. Longmans, Green & Co.
Sir Percival; a Story of the Past and of the Present. Joseph Henry Shorthouse. LC 4-22077. 1886. Macmillan and Co.
Sir Percival, a Story of the Past and of the Present. Joseph Henry Shorthouse. (On cover: Lovell's library. v. 17. no. 832). 1886. J. W. Lovell Co.
Sir Percy Hits Back: An Adventure of the Scarlet Pimpernel. Emmuska Orczy. LC 27-199767. George H. Doran Company.
Sir Pompey and Madame Juno, and Other Tales. Martin Donisthorpe Armstrong. LC 75-163021. (Short story index reprint series). 1971. (ISBN 0-8369-3935-2). Books for Libraries Press.
Sir Pompey and Madame Juno and Other Tales. Martin Donisthorpe Armstrong. LC 27-276929. 1927. Houghton Mifflin Company.
Sir Pompey & Madame Juno: And Other Tales. facsimile ed. Martin Donisthorpe Armstrong. LC 75-163021. (Short Story Index Reprint Ser.). Repr. of 1927 ed. 15.00 (ISBN 0-8369-3935-2). Ayer Co.
Sir Quixote of the Moors: Being Some Account of an Episode in the Life of the Sieur De Rohaine. John Buchan. LC 6-19887. (On cover: Buckram series). 1895. H. Holt and Company.
Sir Raoul. James Meeker Ludlow. LC 5-33618. F. H. Revell Company.
Sir Richard Escombe: A Romance. Max Pemberton. LC 8-18372. 1908. Harper & Brothers.
Sir Robert's Fortune: A Novel. Margaret Oliphant Wilson Oliphant. LC 12-37532. 1894. Harper & Brothers.
Sir Rogue. Leslie Turner White. LC 54-6639. 1954. Crown Publishers.
Sir Rohan's Ghost. A Romance. Harriet Elizabeth Prescott Spofford. 1860. J. E. Tilton and Company.
Sir Roland Ashton. Catharine Walpole Long. LC 75-489. (Victorian Fiction: Novels of Faith and Doubt; V. 41). 1975. 35.00 (ISBN 0-8240-1565-7). Garland Pub.
Sir Roland Ashton: A Tale of the Times, 1841. Catherine Long. Ed. by Robert L. Wolff. Bd. with Mary Spencer: A Tale for the Times, 1844. Anne Howard. (Victorian Fiction Ser.). 1975. lib. bdg. 66.00 (ISBN 0-8240-1565-7). Garland Pub.
Sir!" She Said. Alec Waugh. LC 30-25820. Farrar & Rinehart, Inc.
Sir Superior: A Novel. Bettine Kavanaugh Phillips. LC 99-4975. 1899. J. A. Kavanaugh.
Sir Toby and the Regent. Paul Herring. LC 29-27797. 1929. J. B. Lippincott Company.
Sir Tom. Margaret Oliphant Wilson Oliphant. (Seaside library, v. 84, no. 1703). 1883. G. Munro.
Sir Tom. A Novel. Margaret Oliphant Wilson Oliphant. (Harper's Franklin square library, no. 327). 1883. Harper & Brothers.
Sir Tom. A Novel. Margaret Oliphant Wilson Oliphant. (On cover: Lovell's library. v. 4. no. 175). 1883. J. W. Lovell Company.
Sir Tommy: A Chronicle of Six Events in His Life. Frank Dunlap Frisbie. 1899. The Circuit Press.
Sir Tristrem: Ed. by George P. McNeill... Tristan & Anglo-Norman Poet Th Cent Thomas. (Half-title: Scottish text society. Pubns. 8). 13.00. Printed for the Society by W. Blackwood.
Sir Walter Scott's Ivanhoe. Walter Scott. Ed. by Bair, Frederick H. LC 30-14510. (Lippincott's classics, ed. by E. L. Miller). J. B. Lippincott Company.
Sir Walter Scott's Ivanhoe. Walter Scott & Williams, Herbert Pelham. LC 10-21023. 1910. 1.50. D. Appleton and Company.
Sir Walter Scott's Quentin Durward. Walter Scott. Ed. by Adams, Mary Elizabeth. LC 10-14671. (Half-title: Longmans' English classics...). 1910. Longmans, Green, and Co.
Sir Walter Scott's Quentin Durward. Walter Scott & Williams, Herbert Pelham. 1910. 1.50. D. Appleton and Company.
Sir Walter Scott's The Talisman. Walter Scott & Williams, Herbert Pelham. LC 10-21024. 1910. 1.50. D. Appleton and Company.
Sir Walter Scott's Woodstock. Walter Scott. Ed. by Perry, Bliss. LC 8-3035. (Longman's English classics, no. 3). 1895. Longmans, Green and Co.
Sir, You Bastard. G. F. Newman. 1973. pap. 1.25 o.s.i. (78-718). Lancer.
Sir, You Bastard. G. F. Newman. LC 70-139652. (Ism Ser). (O.S.I.). 1971. 5.95 o.s.i. (ISBN 0-671-20876-4). S&S.
Sirdar's Sabre: Being for the Most Part the Adventure of Sirdar Bahadur Mohammed Khan. Louis Tracy. LC 74-37568. (Short story index reprint series). 1972. (ISBN 0-8369-4127-6). Books for Libraries Press.
Sirdar's Sabre: Being for the Most Part the Adventures of Sirdar Bahadur Mohammed Khan. Louis Tracy. LC 20-16931. E. J. Clode.
Sire De Maletroit's Door. Robert Louis Stevenson. LC 2-25948. (The brocade series, xxiii). 1900. T. B. Mosher.
Siren. Linda C. Gray. LC 81-84144. 256p. (Orig.). 1982. pap. 2.50 (ISBN 0-86721-062-1). Playboy Pbks.
Siren. Thomas Adolphus Trollope. LC 75-32787. (Literature of Mystery and Detection). 1976. vols. in one) 49.00(three (ISBN 0-405-07902-8). Arno Press.
Siren. Thomas Adolphus Trollope. LC 44-32798. 1871. Harper & Brothers.
Siren City. William Romaine Paterson. LC 99-3830. 1899. Dodd, Mead and Company.
Siren in the Night. Zenith Jones Brown. LC 43-293945. 1943. C. Scribner's Sons.
Siren in the Night. Eddie Iroh. (African Writers Ser.). 207p. 1982. pap. 6.00x (ISBN 0-435-90255-5). Heinemann Ed.
Siren of Silver Valley, a New Western Novel. Paul Evan Lehman. LC 50-24476. (Handi-book western, 107). 1950. Handi-Book Editions.
Siren of the Snows. Stanley Shaw. LC 15-5743. 1915. Little, Brown and Company.
Siren Song. David Beaty. LC 64-22508. 1964. Morrow.
Siren Song. Robert Carse. LC 30-253012. Farrar & Rinehart Incorporated.
Siren Song. Roberta Gellis. LC 80-82657. 400p. (Orig.). 1981. pap. 2.75 (ISBN 0-87216-692-9). Playboy Pbks.
Siren Song. Roberta Gellis. LC 80-82657. 400p. 1982. pap. 2.95 (ISBN 0-86721-170-9). Playboy Pbks.
Siren Stars. Richard A. Carrigan, Jr. & Nancy J. Carrigan. 1971. pap. 0.75 o.p. (T2446). Pyramid Pubns.
Sirenas Insaciables. new ed. Manolo Andrade. (Pimienta Collection). 160p. (Span.). 1974. pap. 1.00 o.p. (ISBN 0-88473-210-X). Fiesta Pub.
Sirens. Eric Van Lustbader. 576p. 1982. pap. 3.95 (ISBN 0-449-24510-1). Fawcett.
Sirens. Eric Van Lustbader. LC 81-1482. 480p. 1981. 13.95 (ISBN 0-87131-346-4). M Evans.
Sirens: A Novel. Eric Van Lustbader. LC 81-1482. 13.95 (ISBN 0-87131-346-4). M. Evans.
Sirens & Others Stories. Azorin, pseud. Tr. by Warre B. Wells. 1978. Repr. of 1931 ed. lib. bdg. 30.00 (ISBN 0-8492-0062-8). R West.
Sirens Let Him Go. David Demarest Lloyd. LC 60-7146. 1960. Bobbs-Merrill.
Sirens of Titan. Kurt Vonnegut, Jr. 1971. 9.95 (ISBN 0-440-07948-9, Sey Lawr). Delacorte.
Sirens of Titan. Kurt Vonnegut, Jr. pap. 2.75 (ISBN 0-440-17948-3). Dell.
Sirens of Titan. Kurt Vonnegut, Jr. 1971. pap. 2.95 (ISBN 0-440-57948-1, Delta). Dell.

Siren's Son. Susie Lee Bacon. LC 6-5037. 1895. C. H. Kerr & Company.

Sirian Experiments. Doris May Lessing. LC 79-27710. 304p. 1981. 11.95 (ISBN 0-394-51231-6). Knopf.

Sirian Experiments. Doris May Lessing. LC 81-52259. 400p. 1982. Repr. of 1980 ed. 5.95 (ISBN 0-394-75195-7, Vin). Random.

Sirian Experiments: The Report by Ambien II, of the Five. Doris May Lessing. LC 79-27710. (Canopus in argos archives). 1980. 10.95 (ISBN 0-394-51231-6). Knopf.

Sirius: A Fantasy of Love and Discord. William Olaf Stapledon. LC 73-175519. 1972. (ISBN 0-14-001999-5). Penguin.

Sirius, a Volume of Fiction. Ellen Thorneycroft Fowler. LC 73-150543. (Short story index reprint series). 1971. (ISBN 0-8369-3840-2). Books for Libraries Press.

Sirius: A Volume of Fiction. Ellen Thorneycroft Fowler. LC 1-11778. 1901. D. Appleton and Company.

Sirius Mystery. Robert Temple. LC 74-83583. (Orig.). 1978. pap. 7.95 (ISBN 0-312-72731-3). St Martin.

Sirocco: A Novel. Kenneth H. Brown. LC 6-19771. M. Kennerley.

Sirocco: A Novel. Joseph Kessel & Woods, Katherine, 1886- 1947. Random House.

Sirocco and Other Stories. Ralph Bates. LC 30-27018. Random House.

Sironia, Texas. Decorations by William Barss. Madison A Cooper. LC 52-9585. 1952. Houghton Mifflin.

Sissie. John Alfred Williams. LC 63-8551. 1963. Farrar, Straus and Cudahy.

Sissie. John Alfred Williams. LC 79-9948. 1969. 1.45. Anchor Books.

Sister Act. Blossom Elfman. LC 78-15954. 1978. 7.95 (ISBN 0-395-26476-6). Houghton Mifflin.

Sister Act. Max F. Harris. 1981. pap. 1.95 (ISBN 0-8439-0907-2, Leisure Bks). Nordon Pubns.

Sister Aint Sulpice (La Hermana San Sulpicio) From the Spanish of Don Armando Palacio Valdes... Palacio Valdes, Armando. Tr. by Nathan Haskell Dole. LC 8-31900. T. Y. Crowell & Co.

Sister Bear. Herbert Burkholz. 1970. pap. 0.95 o.p. (M1412, Crest). Fawcett World.

Sister Bear: A Novel. Herbert Burkholz. LC 69-14278. 1969. 4.95. Simon and Schuster.

Sister Carrie. Louis Auchincloss. LC 69-13798. (gr. 9-12). 1969. text ed. 7.95x o.s.i.; pap. text ed. 3.50 (ISBN 0-675-09528-X). Merrill.

Sister Carrie. Theodore Dreiser. LC 65-6723. 1965. Harper & Row.

Sister Carrie. Theodore Dreiser. LC 69-13798. (Charles E. Merrill standard editions). (Charles E. Merrill program in American literature.). 1969. C. E. Merrill Pub. Co.

Sister Carrie. Theodore Dreiser. LC 69-16530. (Library of literature). 1970. 1.75. Bobbs-Merrill.

Sister Carrie. Theodore Dreiser. LC 78-183140. 1971. (ISBN 0-8376-0401-X). R. Bentley.

Sister Carrie. abridged ed. Theodore Dreiser. LC 49-53576. (Pocket books, 644). 1949. Pocket Books.

Sister Carrie. Theodore Dreiser. LC 1-29064. 1900. Doubleday, Page & Co.

Sister Carrie. Theodore Dreiser. LC 32-26342. (Half-title: The modern library of the world's best books). 1932. The Modern Library.

Sister Carrie. an abridged ed. by theodore dreiser and arthur henry. with a new introd. by jack salzman. ed. Theodore Dreiser & Arthur Henry. LC 68-54227. (Belles lettres in English). 1969. Johnson Reprint Corp.

Sister Carrie. Theodore Dreiser & James L. W West. LC 81-2082. (Penguin American library). (Illus.). 1981. 3.95 (ISBN 0-14-039002-2). Penguin Books.

Sister Carrie: A Novel. Theodore Dreiser. LC 12-24814. 1912. Harper & Brothers.

Sister Carrie: A Novel. Theodore Dreiser. 1917. Boni & Liveright, Inc.

Sister Carrie: A Novel. Theodore Dreiser. LC 23-3785. 1921. Boni & Liveright.

Sister Carrie: An Authoritative Text, Backgrounds, and Sources Criticism. Theodore Dreiser. LC 73-116120. (Norton critical edition). 1970. 6.00. Norton.

Sister Carrie. Introd. by James T. Farrell. Theodore Dreiser. LC 57-9756. (American century series, S-4). 1957. Sagamore Press.

Sister Carrie. Introd. by Kenneth S. Lynn. Theodore Dreiser. LC 56-13492. (Rinehart editions, 86). 1957. Rinehart.

Sister Carrie: The Pennsylvania Edition. Theodore Dreiser. Ed. by James L. West et al. 1981. 42.50x (ISBN 0-8122-7784-8); pap. 14.95x (ISBN 0-8122-1110-3). U of Pa Pr.

Sister Cat: A Novel. Felix Gould. LC 63-13722. 1963. L. Stuart.

Sister City & Other Tales. Norway Leif. (Illus.). 22p. (Orig.). 1971. pap. 2.50 (ISBN 0-932264-18-2). Trask Hse Bks.

Sister Clare. Marie Reynes-Monlaur & Arendrup, M. E., Tr. LC 19-9151. 1918. R. McBride & Company.

Sister Clare: A Novel. With Illus. by Pauline Baynes. Loretta Burrough. LC 60-5218. 1960. Houghton Mifflin.

Sister Clementia: A Novel. Frederick Houk Law. LC 10-26823. 1.50. R. F. Fenno & Company.

Sister Eleanor's Brood. Frances Irene Burge Smith Griswold. LC 40-17409. 1872. D. Lothrop & Co.

Sister Gin. June Arnold. LC 75-16510. (ISBN 0-913780-09-X). Daughters.

Sister Gratia: Satan's Simplicity. Chauncey Edgar Snow. LC 8-10205. 1895. C. H. Kerr and Company.

Sister-in-Chief: The L250 Prize Story for Girls. Dorothy A Beckett Terrell. LC 12-29135. 1912. Cassell and Company, Ltd.

Sister-in-Law: A Novel of Our Time. Gertrude Franklin Horn Atherton. LC 21-1279. Frederick A. Stokes Company.

Sister Innocent and the Wayward Miracle. Rosalie Lieberman. LC 65-25978. 1965. Newman Press.

Sister Jane: Her Friends and Acquaintances; a Narrative of Certain Events and Episodes Transcribed from the Papers of the Late William Wornum. Joel Chandler Harris. LC 7-2896. 1896. Houghton, Mifflin and Company.

Sister Jane: Her Friends and Acquaintances; a Narrative of Certain Events and Episodes Transcribed from the Papers of the Late William Wornum. Joel Chandler Harris. LC 41-31324. 1899. Houghton, Mifflin and Company.

Sister of a Saint: And Other Stories. Grace Ellery Channing Stetson. LC 8-12391. (Carnation series). 1895. Stone & Kimball.

Sister of Cain. Mary Garden Collins. LC 43-154709. 1943. C. Scribner's Sons.

Sister of the Angels. Elizabeth Goudge. LC 39-27982. Coward McCann, Inc.

Sister of the Bride. Natalie Shipman. LC 51-12723. 1951. Bouregy & Curl.

Sister of the Queen. Lorinda Hagen. (Belmont Tower Book). 1977. 1.95 (ISBN 0-505-51188-6). Tower Pubns.

Sister Philomene. Edmond De Goncourt & Jules De Goncourt. Tr. by L. Ensor. 292p. 1975. Repr. of 1890 ed. 21.00x (ISBN 0-86527-304-9). Fertig.

Sister Philomene. Edmond Louis Antoine Huot De Goncourt & Jules Alfred Huot De Goncourt. LC 75-11562. (Illus.). 1975. 12.50. H. Fertig.

Sister Philomene. Edmond Louis Antoine Huot De Goncourt & Goncourt, Jules Alfred Huot De. LC 6-43732. (On Cover: Primrose Series. No. 29). 1891. Street & Smith.

Sister Rosalee, the Gardening Nun. A. Holly Mrazik. 4.95 o.s.i. (ISBN 0-8181-0004-4). Pageant-Poseidon.

Sister Satan. George Dilnot. LC 34-24145. 1933. Houghton Mifflin Company.

Sister Sue. Eleanor Hodgman Porter. LC 21-26293. 1921. Houghton Mifflin Company.

Sister Sweethearts. Paul MacPherson. pap. 1.95 o.p. (8002). Cameo.

Sister Teresa. George Moore. LC 18-21374. 1918. Brentano's.

Sister Teresa: A Novel. George Moore. 1901. J. B. Lippincott Company.

Sister to Esau. Amelia Edith Huddleston Barr. LC 6-7971. Dodd, Mead & Company.

Sister to Esau. Amelia Edith Huddleston Barr. LC 42-437122. Hunt & Eaton.

Sister to Evangeline: Being the Story of Yvonne De Lamourie, and How She Went into Exile with the Villagers of Grand Pre. Charles George Douglas Roberts. LC 98-1651. 1898. Lamson, Wolffe and Company.

Sister to Evangeline: Being the Story of Yvonne De Lamourie, and How She Went into Exile with the Villagers of Grand Pre. new ed., with illustrations. ed. Charles George Douglas Roberts. LC 1-29112. Silver, Burdett and Company.

Sister Wolf. Ann Arensberg. 192p. 1981. pap. 3.50 (ISBN 0-671-43490-X). WSP.

Sister Wolf: A Novel. Ann Arensberg. LC 80-7659. 1980. 9.95 (ISBN 0-394-51021-6). Knopf: Distributed by Random House.

Sister X and the Victims of Foul Play... Carlene Hatcher Polite. LC 75-19343. 1975. 7.95 (ISBN 0-374-26521-6). Farrar, Straus and Giroux.

Sisterhood. Michael Palmer. 1982. pap. 3.50 (ISBN 0-553-22704-1). Bantam.

Sisters. Myron Brinig. LC 37-1526. Farrar & Rinehart, Inc.

Sisters. Joseph Conrad & Ford Madox Ford. LC 28-19009. 1928. C. Gaige.

Sisters. Mabel White Dearmer. LC 8-8089. 1908. The McClure Company.

Sisters. Georg Moritz Ebers. Tr. by Bell, Clara Courtenay (Poynter) (historical romances of Georg Ebers. vol. xii). 1915. D. Appleton and Company.

Sisters. Anne Lambton. LC 75-10467. 7.95 (ISBN 0-698-10683-0). Coward, McCann & Geoghegan.

Sisters. Anne Lambton. (Berkely medallion book). 1976. 1.95 (ISBN 0-425-03181-0). Berkley.

Sisters. Lucy Beatrice Malleson. LC 49-1192. 1949. Random House.

Sisters. Debby Mayer. LC 81-19888. 13.95 (ISBN 0-399-12700-3). Putnam.

Sisters. Cheryl Nash. 1975. (pbk.) 1.50. Dell.

Sisters. Andrew Neiderman. LC 77-160356. 1971. 6.95 (ISBN 0-8128-1404-5). Stein and Day.

Sisters. Kathleen Thompson Norris. LC 19-15019. 1919. Doubleday, Page & Company.

Sisters. Vikentii Vikentevich Smidovich. LC 74-10093. 1974. 16.50 (ISBN 0-88355-179-9). Hyperion Press.

Sisters. Vikenti V. Veresaev. Tr. by Juliet Soskice from Rus. LC 74-10093. (Soviet Literature in English Translation Ser). 288p. 1974. Repr. of 1934 ed. 19.50 (ISBN 0-88355-179-9). Hyperion Conn.

Sisters, a Domestic Tale. Barbara Wreaks Hoole Hofland. LC 7-6593. Porter & Coates.

Sisters. A Romance. Georg Moritz Ebers. Tr. by Clara Courtenay Bell. (On cover: Seaside library. Pocket ed., no. 1114). 1888. G. Munro.

Sisters: A Romance by George Ebers... authorized ed. Georg Moritz Ebers. Tr. by Clara Courtenay Bell. LC 42-30341. 1883. W. S. Gottsberger.

Sisters and Brothers: A Novel. Julian Moynahan. LC 60-121305. 1960. Random House.

Sisters and Brothers: A Novel. Janet Stevenson. LC 66-14248. 1966. Crown Publishers.

Sisters & Lovers. Nicola Thorne, pseud. LC 80-509. 1981. 14.95 (ISBN 0-385-15857-2). Doubleday.

Sisters and Strangers. Helen Van Slyke. LC 77-27720. 1978. 10.00 (ISBN 0-385-12776-6). Doubleday.

Sisters' Budget: A Collection of Original Tales in Prose and Verse. Ed. by M Corbett. LC 8-27035. 1832. W. & J. Neal.

Sisters in Love. Jacques Serguine. (Orig.). 1970. pap. 0.95 o.p. (N2337). Pyramid Pubns.

Sisters Liked Them Handsome. Stephen Longstreet. LC 46-5903. 1946. J. Messner.

Sisters Livingston... Natalie Anderson Scott. LC 46-4256. 1946. E. P. Dutton & Company, Inc.

Sisters Materassi: Translated by Angus Davidson. 1st Ed. Aldo Palazzeschi. LC 53-6938. 1953. Doubleday.

Sisters of Battle. Rebecca Drury. (Women at War Ser.: No. 8). (Orig.). 1982. pap. 2.95 (ISBN 0-440-08414-8, Banbury). Dell.

Sisters of Orleans. LC 8-9010. 1871. G. P. Putnam & Sons.

Sisters of Orleans: A Tale of Race and Social Conflict. LC 72-2025. (Black Heritage Library Collection). 1972. 14.00 (ISBN 0-8369-9063-3). Books for Libraries Press.

Sisters of Sorrow. Aola Vandergriff. 1974. (pbk.) 1.25. Warner Paperback Library.

Sisters of Torwood: A Novel. May Agnes Early Fleming. 1898. G. W. Dillingham Co.

Sisters Rondoli, and Other Stories. Guy De Maupassant. LC 79-157792. (Short story index reprint series). 1971. (ISBN 0-8369-3904-2). Books for Libraries Press.

Sisters Rondoli, & Other Stories: Collected Novels & Stories, Vol. 5. facsimile ed. Guy De Maupassant. Ed. by Ernest Boyd. LC 79-157792. (Short Story Index Reprint Ser.). Repr. of 1923 ed. 18.00 (ISBN 0-8369-3904-2). Ayer Co.

Sister's Sacrifice. John Russell Coryell. LC 6-39920. (On cover: Munro's library, v. 1, no. 315). 1885. N. L. Munro.

Sister's Sacrifice. Geraldine Fleming. LC 6-39920. (On cover: Munro's library. v. 1, no. 315). 1885. N. L. Munro.

Sister's Sin. A Novel. Emily Sharp H. Carmeron. LC 6-21848. (On cover: Lippincott's series of select novels, no. 139). 1893. J. B. Lippincott Company.

Sisters' Tragedy. Richard Arthur Hughes. Ed. by Edmund R. Brown. (International Pocket Library). pap. 3.00. Branden.

Sister's Vengeance. H. C. Hoffman. (On cover: Munro's library, popular novels. v. 1. no. 399). 1885. N. L. Munro.

Sister's Vocation: And Other Girls' Stories. Josephine Dodge Daskam Bacon. LC 1-29463. 1900. C. Scribner's Sons.

Sita: A Story of Child-Marriage Fetters. Olivia A Baldwin. LC 11-264173. 1.25. Fleming H. Revell Company.

Sitka. Louis L'Amour. LC 57-8126. 1957. Appleton-Century-Crofts.

Sitka. Louis L'Amour. LC 81-43100. (Illus.). 1981. 4.95 (ISBN 0-553-01351-3). Bantam Books.

Sitting Duck. George Bagby, pseud. LC 80-43251. 1981. 10.95 (ISBN 0-385-17802-6). Doubleday.

Sitting Ducks. Karl H. Meyer. 1978. pap. 1.50 (ISBN 0-532-15358-8). Woodhill.

Sitting Pretty. Al Young. (Signet Book). 1977. 1.75 (ISBN 0-451-07493-9). New American Library.

Sitting Pretty: A Novel. Al Young. LC 75-21461. 7.95 (ISBN 0-03-015266-6). Holt, Rinehart and Winston.

Sitting Target. Laurence Henderson. LC 70-184545. 1972. 5.95. St. Martin's Press.

Sitting up Dead. Aaron Marc Stein. LC 58-10041. 1958. Published for the Crime Club by Doubleday.

Situation Red, The UFO Siege. Leonard H. Stringfield. 1978. pap. 1.75 (ISBN 0-449-23654-4, Crest). Fawcett.

Situation Tragedy. Simon Brett. 1983. pap. 2.50 (ISBN 0-440-18792-3). Dell.

Situation Tragedy: A Charles Paris Mystery. Simon Brett. LC 81-9155. 9.95 (ISBN 0-684-17268-2). Scribner.

Sitzkrieg of Private Stefan. Translated from the German by Theodore H. Lustig. Erich Kuby. LC 62-18413. 1962. Farrar, Straus and Cudahy.

Six Against Scotland Yard, in Which Margery Allingham, Anthony Berkeley, Freeman Wills Crofts, Father Ronald Knox, Dorothy L. Sayers, Russell Thorndike Commit the Crime of Murder Which Ex-Superintendent Cornish, C.I.D., Is Called Upon to Solve. Allingham, Margery, 1904- et al. LC 33-3542. 1937. The Sun Dial Press, Inc.

Six Against the Rock. Clark Howard. 1978. pap. 2.25 (ISBN 0-515-04709-0). Jove Pubns.

Six a.m. Maxwell Bodenheim. LC 32-21669. 1932. Liveright, Inc.

Six Angels at My Back. John Bell Clayton. LC 52-2073. 1952. Macmillan.

Six Bells," A Volume of Naval Stories. 5th thousand. ed. Edward Horace Crebbin. 1942. Rich & Cowan.

Six Best Cellars. Harold Everett Porter & Kahler, Hugh. LC 19-14196. 1919. Dodd, Mead and Company.

Six Black Camels. Edwin Moultrie Lanham. 1961. bds. 3.50 o.p. (ISBN 0-15-182733-8). HarBraceJ.

Six Black Camels. 1st Ed. Edwin Moultrie Lanham. 1961. Harcourt, Brace.

Six Black Horses. Nolan Davis. LC 79-163408. 1971. 6.95. Putnam.

Six Bloody Summer Days. Nick Carter. (Nick Carter Ser.). 174p. 1981. pap. 2.25 (ISBN 0-441-76839-3, Pub. by Charter Bks). Ace Bks.

Six Bloody Summer Days. Nick Carter. (Killmaster spy chiller). 1975. (pbk.) 1.25. Award Books.

Six Came Flying. MacSwiney Of Mashanaglass. (Illus.). (YA) 1972. 6.95 o.s.i. (ISBN 0-394-47282-9). Knopf.

Six Cent Sam's. Julian Hawthorne. LC 70-101283. (Short story index reprint series). (Illus.). 1969. Books for Libraries Press.

Six Cent Sam's. Julian Hawthorne. LC 7-3889. The Price-McGill Company.

Six Contes. Guy De Maupassant. Ed. by Sloman, Harold Newman Penrose. (Cambridge modern French series. Senior group. General editor: A. Wilson-Green). 1930. The University Press.

Six Contes. Guy De Maupassant. Ed. by Slowman. (Fr). 1930. text ed. 1.25x o.p. Cambridge U Pr.

Six Cups of Chocolate: A Piece of Gossip in One Act; Freely Englished from a Kaffeeklatsch of E. Schmithof. E Schmithof. Tr. by Matthews, Edith Virginia Brander. LC 6308. 1897. Harper & Brothers.

Six Curtains for Natasha. Doris Caroline Abrahams & Simon Jasha Skidelsky. LC 46-586613. 1946. J. B. Lippincott Company.

Six-Cylinder Courtship. Edward Salisbury Field. LC 7-36410. 1907. The J. McBride Company.

Six Day Week. Alan Harold Gardner. LC 66-20150. 1966. Coward-McCann.

Six Days. Elinor Sutherland Glyn. LC 23-10586. 1923. J. B. Lippincott Company.

Six Days. Elinor Sutherland Glyn. LC 24-5945. 1924. J. B. Lippincott Company.

Six Days, Five Nites. Susana De Lyonne. 1.75 (ISBN 0-449-14028-8). Fawcett Gold Medal Books.

Six Days in Marapore. 1st Ed. Paul Scott. LC 53-9133. 1953. Doubleday.

Six Days of the Condor. James Grady. LC 73-22258. 1974. (ISBN 0-393-08692-5). Norton.

Six Days to Death. Peter Alding. 1975. 4.95 (ISBN 0-09-125390-X, Pub. by Hutchinson). Merrimack Pub Cir.

Six Days to Die. Gus Stevens. (Orig.). 1981. pap. 2.25 (ISBN 0-505-51696-9). Tower Bks.

Six Days to Suez. Harold Calin. Orig. Title: Desert War. 1970. pap. 0.95 o.p. (ISBN 0-447-75106-9). Lancer.

Six Days to Sunday: A Novel. Bernard Brunner. LC 75-4812. 1975. 7.95 (ISBN 0-07-008579-X). McGraw-Hill.

Six Dead Men. Stanislas Andre Steeman. Tr. by Benet, Rosemary. LC 32-16105. Farrar & Rinehart, Inc.

Six Deadly Dames. Frederick Nebel. LC 80-12129. (Gregg Press Mystery Fiction Series). 1980. 10.95 (ISBN 0-8398-2654-0). Gregg Press.

Six-Eleven. Albert Morgan. LC 63-8792. 1963. Morrow.

Six Exemplary Novels. Miguel de Cervantes de Saavedra. Ed. by Harriet De Onis. Incl. Dialogue of the Dogs; Gypsy Maid; Illustrious Kitchen Maid; Jealous Hidalgo; Master Glass; Rinconete & Cortadillo. LC 61-8942. (Illus.). (gr. 9 up). 1961. pap. text ed. 3.95 (ISBN 0-8120-0159-1). Barron.

Six Exemplary Novels. Introd. and Translation by Harriet De Onis. Miguel de Cervantes de Saavedra. LC 61-8942. 1961. Barron's Educational Series.

Six Feet Four. Jackson Gregory. 1918. Dodd, Mead and Company.

Six Feet of the Country: Fifteen Short Stories. Nadine Gordimer. LC 56-9927. 1956. Simon and Schuster.

Six Feet Under: A Luke Thanet Mystery. Dorothy Simpson. 192p. 1982. 10.95 (ISBN 0-684-17665-3, ScribT). Scribner.

Six Fingers of Time. Galaxy Magazine Editors. 1969. pap. 0.60 o.p. (60-428). Manor Bks.

Six for the Toff. John Creasey. LC 69-11777. 1969. 4.50. Walker.

Six Girls. Betty Evelyn Davies. LC 33-21279. 1933. L. MacVeagh, Dial Press, Inc.

Six Girls: A Home Story. Fannie Belle Irving. 1881. J. Q. Adams & Co.

Six Girls: A Home Story. Fannie Belle Irving. LC 7-9708. 1883. Estes and Lauriat.

Six Girls: A Home Story. Fannie Belle Irving. LC 3-17622. 1903. D. Estes & Company.

Six Golden Angels. Max Brand. LC 37-30401. 1937. Dodd, Mead & Company.

Six Golden Angels. Frederick Faust. LC 37-30401. 1937. Dodd, Mead & Company.

Six Golden Angels. Frederick Faust. 1973. 0.95. Warner.

Six Gothic Tales. Reader's Digest Editors. LC 77-83406. (Illus.). 640p. 1979. 16.50 (ISBN 0-89577-060-1, Pub. by RD Assn). Random.

Six Great Modern Short Novels. Dell Publishing Company, Inc., New York. LC 54-12209. (Dell first edition, F35). 1954. Dell Pub. Co.

Six Great Modern Short Novels. Incl. Dead. James Joyce; Billy Budd, Foretopman. Herman Melville; Noon Wine. Katherine A. Porter; Overcoat. Nikolai Gogol; Pilgrim Hawks. Glenway Wescott; Bear. William Faulkner. pap. 3.25 (ISBN 0-440-37996-2, LE). Dell.

Six Great Short Novels of Science Fiction: 1st Ed. Ed. by Groff Conklin. LC 53-13260. (Dell first edition, D9). 1954. Dell Pub. Co.

Six Greatest Novels of Anatole France... Anatole France, pseud. Tr. by Evans, Arthur William et al. LC 36-23270. The Literary Guild.

Six-Gun Boss: By Clay Randall Pseud. Clifton Adams. LC 52-5155. 1952. Random House.

Six-Gun Code. Clement Yore. LC 32-660. The Macaulay Company.

Six-Gun Country. Max Brand. LC 81-931. 1981. 11.95 (ISBN 0-8161-3226-7). G.K. Hall.

Six-Gun Country. Frederick Faust. LC 79-24209. (Silver star western). 1980. 7.95 (ISBN 0-396-07805-2). Dodd, Mead.

Six-Gun Cyclone. Amos Moore. LC 37-204346. I. Washburn, Inc.

Six-Gun Drive. Jon Sharpe. (Trailsman Ser.: No. 8). (Orig.). 1981. pap. 2.50 (AE2172, Sig). NAL.

Six-Gun Empire. Donald B. Hobart. 1969. pap. 0.60 o.p. (0502-06064-060). Curtis.

Six-Gun Gamble. Dwight Bennett Newton. LC 51-11196. 1951. Lippincott.

Six Gun Heritage. Samuel Anthony Peoples. LC 55-5340. (Dutton Diamond D western). 1955. Dutton.

Six-Gun Justice. Howard Roland Marsh. LC 39-25703. Dodge Publishing Company.

Six-Gun Kid. William MacLeod Raine. (Signet Brand Western, T5573). 1973. (pbk.) 0.75. New American Lib.

Six-Gun Melody. William Colt MacDonald. LC 33-144094. Covici, Friede.

Six-Gun Mission. John Earl Lewis. 1982. 6.95 (Avalon). Bouregy.

Six-Gun Outcast. Charles N Heckelmann. LC 46-19794. 1946. Arcadia House, Inc.

Six-Gun Planet. John Jakes. 1970. pap. 0.60 o.p. (63-313). Paperback Lib.

Six-Gun Poker, No. 11. Zeke Masters, pseud. (Orig.). 1981. pap. write for info. (ISBN 0-671-43810-7). PB.

Six Gun Samurai. Patrick Lee. (Six Gun Samurai Ser.: No. 1). 176p. (Orig.). 1981. pap. 1.95 (ISBN 0-523-41190-1). Pinnacle Bks.

Six-Gun Shadows. Glenn H Wichman. LC 57-4523. 1957. Arcadia House.

Six Gun Sheriff. Fred East. LC 49-7738. 1949. Macrae-Smith-Co.

Six-Gun Showdown. Fred East. LC 47-1269. 1947. E. P. Dutton & Co., Inc.

Six Gun Showdown. James Farnsworth, pseud. 1978. pap. 1.25 (ISBN 0-532-12582-7). Woodhill.

Six-Gun Song. Orlando Rigoni. LC 67-8798. 1967. Arcadia House.

Six Gun Sovereignty. Archie Joscelyn. LC 35-445. Phoenix Press.

Six-Gun Stampede. Jackson Cole, pseud. LC 37-34671. The Dodge Publishing Company.

Six-Gun Stampede. Oscar Schisgall. LC 37-34671. The Dodge Publishing Company.

Six-Gun Syndicate. Norman A Fox. LC 42-16051. 1942. Phoenix Press.

Six-Gun Vengeance. Buck Billings. LC 34-42180. 1933. G. H. Watt.

Six Gun Vengeance. Claude Rister. LC 34-42180. 1933. G. H. Watt.

Six-Gun Warrior, No. 7: Prairie Caesar. Patrick Lee. 208p. (Orig.). 1983. pap. 2.25. Pinnacle Bks.

Six-Guns for Hire. Charles Stanley Strong. LC 44-6550. 1944. Phoenix Press.

Six-Guns of Sandoval. Charles Horace Snow. LC 34-41289. 1935. Macrae Smith Company.

Six Guns South. Robert MacLeod, pseud. 1979. pap. 1.50 (ISBN 0-449-14235-3, GM). Fawcett.

Six-Horse Hitch. Janice Holt Giles. 408p. 1980. pap. 2.75 (ISBN 0-380-51532-6, 51532). Avon.

Six Horse Hitch. Janice Holt Giles. LC 69-15013. 1976. 18.00 o.p. (ISBN 0-910220-75-1). Larlin Corp.

Six-Horse Hitch. Janice Holt Giles. LC 69-15013. (Illus.). 1969. 6.95 o.p. (ISBN 0-395-07741-9). HM.

Six-Horse Hitch. Janice Holt Giles. 352p. 1972. pap. 0.95 o.p. (M1712, Crest). Fawcett World.

Six-Horse Hitch: A Novel. Janice Holt Giles. LC 69-15013. (Illus.). 1969. 6.95. Houghton Mifflin.

Six Horses. William Banning & Banning, George Hugh. LC 39-9516. The Century Co.

Six Hundred & Fforty-Six & the Troubleman. Charles Henry Oliver. LC 16-17648. 1916. 1.25. Rand McNally & Company.

Six Hundred & Sixty-Six. Jay Anson. LC 81-927. 12.95 (ISBN 0-671-25144-9). Simon and Schuster.

Six Hundred Sixty-Six Huntington Valley, Pa. Salem Kirban. LC 71-109942. (Illus.). 1970. 2.95.

Six Impossible Things. Elizabeth Cadell. 1961. 5.95 o.p. Morrow.

Six in All. Virginia Frances Townsend. LC 8-29815. Loring.

Six Iron Spiders. Phoebe Atwood Taylor. (Foul Play Press Bks.). 1979. pap. 4.95 (ISBN 0-914378-53-8). Countryman.

Six Iron Spiders. Phoebe Atwood Taylor. 1971. pap. 0.75 o.p. (T2599). Pyramid Pubns.

Six Iron Spiders: An Asey Mayo Mystery. Phoebe Atwood Taylor. 1942. W. W. Norton & Company, Inc.

Six Iron Spiders: An Asey Mayo Mystery. Phoebe Atwood Taylor. LC 43-13636. 1943. Triangle Books.

Six Iron Spiders: An Asey Mayo Mystery Reissue. Phoebe Atwood Taylor. LC 42-159801. 1966. bds., 3.95. Norton.

Six-Legged Watchdogs & Other Stories. Virginia Stead. 1970. 2.95 o.p. Vantage.

Six-Letter Word for Death. Patricia Moyes. LC 82-18738. 252p. 1983. 13.50 (ISBN 0-03-062978-0). HR&W.

Six-Letter Word for Death & Other Stories. Tommy Frierson. 1970. 3.95 o.p. Vantage.

Six Lost Women. Louis Sobol. LC 36-9465. C. Kendall, Inc.

Six Mad Men. Rix Faber. LC 7-16748. The Old Greek Press.

Six Maitres Contemporains. Ed. by Henri Peyre. (Fr.). 1969. pap. text ed. 5.50 o.p. (ISBN 0-15-581100-2, HC). HarBraceJ.

Six Middle English Romances. Ed. by Maldwyn Mills. (Rowman & Littlefield University Library). 224p. 1973. 9.25x o.p. (ISBN 0-87471-403-6); pap. 4.00x o.p. (ISBN 0-87471-396-X). Rowman.

Six Million Dollar Man: International Incidents. Mike Jahn. (Berkley Medallion Book). 1977. 1.25. Berkley Pub. Corp.

Six Modern Italian Novellas. Ed. by William Arrowsmith. LC 64-1716. (Permabook edition). 1964. Pocket Books.

Six Months with an Older Woman. David A Kaufelt. LC 73-75831. 1973. 6.95 (ISBN 0-399-11154-9). Putnam.

Six Moral Tales. Jules Laforgue & Frances Newman. LC 81-17609. 1982. 32.00 (ISBN 0-404-16327-0). AMS Press.

Six Moral Tales. Eric Rohmer. LC 79-23047. 1980. 10.00 (ISBN 0-670-64732-2). Viking Press.

Six Mrs. Greenes. Lorna Rea. LC 29-6663. 1929. Harper & Brothers.

Six Nights a Week. Evelyn Hawes. LC 78-160403. 1971. (ISBN 0-15-182740-0). Harcourt Brace Jovanovich.

Six Nights of Mystery: Tales of Suspense and Intrigue by William Irish Pseud. Hopley-Woolrich, Cornell George. LC 50-13516. (Popular library, 258). 1950. Popular Library.

Six Nights with the Washingtonians: And Other Temperance Tales. Timothy Shay Arthur. LC 6-3418. T. B. Peterson & Brothers.

Six Novels. Sidonie Gabrielle Colette. 2.95 o.p. (251). Modern Lib.

Six Novels of the Supernatural. Ed. by Edward Charles Wagenknecht. LC 44-8273. (Viking portable library). 1944. The Viking Press.

Six Nuns and a Shotgun. Colin Watson. LC 74-16621. (Red mask mystery). 1975. 5.95 (ISBN 0-399-11464-5). Putnam.

Six O'clock Casual. Henry W Clune. LC 60-13226. 1960. Macmillan.

Six O'clock Mass. Maurice Stephen Sheehy. LC 52-12284. 1952. Farrar, Straus and Young.

Six O'Clock Stud. Robert H. Sheldon. pap. 1.95 o.p. (8075). Cameo.

Six of One. Rita Mae Brown. LC 78-2057. 9.95 (ISBN 0-06-010524-0). Harper & Row.

Six of One by Half a Dozen of the Other. An Every Day Novel. Edward Everett Hale et al. LC 6-46196. 1872. Roberts Brothers.

Six of Swords. Carole N. Douglas. 1982. pap. 2.75 (Del Rey). Ballantine.

Six of Them. Alfred Neumann & Murad, Anatol, 1904- Illus. LC 45-6201. 1945. The Macmillan Company.

Six of Them: Translated from the German. Alfred Neumann & Murad, Anatol, 1904- Tr. 1945. Hutchinson International Authors Ltd.

Six Other Days. Andrew Meisels. (Orig.). 1973. pap. 0.95 o.p. (ISBN 0-515-02916-5, N2916). Pyramid Pubns.

Six People and Love: A Novel. Stella Zilliacus. LC 57-7414. 1957. J. Day Co.

Six-Pointed Cross in the Dust. John Rathbone Oliver. LC 17-494. Frederick A. Stokes Company.

Six Problems for Don Isidro Parodi. Jorge Luis Borges & Adolfo Bioy-Casares. LC 80-20107. 1981. 10.95 (ISBN 0-525-20480-6). Dutton.

Six Proud Walkers. Francis Beeding. LC 28-17206. 1928. Little, Brown, and Company.

Six Queer Things... Christopher St. John Sprigg. LC 37-149639. 1937. Pub. for the Crime Club, Inc., by Doubleday, Doran & Co., Inc.

Six Russian Short Novels: The Overcoat; Lady MacBeth of the Mtsensk District: A Lear of the Steppes; Master and Man; The Death of Ivan Llych; Ward No. 6. Ed. by Randall Jarrell. LC 63-11249. (Anchor books, A348). 1963. Doubleday.

Six Seconds a Year. Frederick Laing. LC 48-6362. 1948. T. Y. Crowell Co.

Six Seconds of Darkness. Octavus Roy Cohen. LC 21-755. 1921. Dodd, Mead and Company.

Six-Shooter Showdown. William Colt MacDonald. LC 41-4628. 1940. The Sun Dial Press.

Six-Shooter Showdown. A Double D Western. William Colt MacDonald. LC 39-29962. 1939. Doubleday, Doran and Company, Inc.

Six Short French Plays for the Use of Preparatory Schools. Alfred Spencer Johnson. LC 18-76. 1910. Longmans, Green, and Co.

Six Silver Handles. Daniel Mainwaring. LC 44-5324. 1944. W. Morrow and Company.

Six Six Six. Jay Anson. 286p. 1981. 12.95 o.s.i. (ISBN 0-671-25144-9). S&S.

Six Sixty-Six. Jay Anson. 1982. pap. 3.50 (ISBN 0-671-83126-7). PB.

Six Stars. Nelson McAllister Lloyd. LC 75-125229. (Short story index reprint series). (Illus.). 1970. Books for Libraries Press.

Six Stars: Stories. Nelson McAllister Lloyd. LC 6-116761. 1906. C. Scribner's Sons.

Six Stolen Souls. L. Ron Hubbard. 1979. 11.00 (ISBN 0-917972-05-8). Theta Bks.

Six Stories for Acting. Adapted by Geo. P. McCallum. 1976. pap. 3.75 (ISBN 0-89318-031-9); cassettes 29.50 (ISBN 0-89318-034-3). ELS Intl.

Six Stories Written in the First Person Singular. William Somerset Maugham. LC 75-26133. (Maugham, William Somerset, 1874-1965. Works. 1976). 1976. 15.00 (ISBN 0-405-07854-4). Arno Press.

Six Stories Written in the First Person Singular. William Somerset Maugham. LC 31-280687. 1931. Doubleday, Doran & Company, Inc.

Six Tales for All the Family: By Eva Rite Pseud. 1st Ed. Esther Victoria Anderson. LC 51-14983. 1951. Pageant Press.

Six Tales of the Jazz Age: And Other Stories. Francis Scott Key Fitzgerald. LC 60-6410. (Scribner lib., SL157). 1968. pap., 1.65. Scribners.

Six Tales of the Jazz Age, and Other Stories. Francis Scott Key Fitzgerald. LC 60-6410. 1960. Scribner.

Six Tennyson Essays. Charles Tennyson. 192p. 1972. Repr. of 1954 ed. 8.50x o.p. (ISBN 0-87471-072-3). Rowman.

Six Thousand Tons of Gold: By H. R. Chamberlain... Henry Richardson Chamberlain. LC 6-23346. 1894. Flood and Vincent.

Six Thousand Years Hence. Milton Worth Ramsey. LC 8-215. 1891. Press of A. Roper.

Six Times a Bride. Peggy Gaddis, pseud. LC 44-598468. 1944. Phoenix Press.

Six Times H. Robert Heinlein. 1972. 0.95 o.p. (ISBN 0-515-02822-3). Pyramid Pubns.

Six to Break Even. Mary Scott Adams. LC 67-20589. 1967. Rand McNally.

Six to Break Even. Priscilla D Willis. LC 67-20589. 1967. Rand McNally.

Six Trees. Mary Eleanor Wilkins Freeman. LC 74-94721. (Short Story Index Reprint Ser.). 1903. 16.00 (ISBN 0-8369-3100-9). Ayer Co.

Six Trees: Short Stories. Mary Eleanor Wilkins Freeman. LC 74-94721. (Short story index reprint series). (Illus.). 1969. Books for Libraries Press.

Six Trees: Short Stories. Mary Eleanor Wilkins Freeman. LC 3-4415. 1903. Harper & Brothers.

Six Vignettes. Robert L. Merriam. (Illus.). 38p. 1981. 9.50. R L Merriam.

Six-Way Swap. Kenneth Herbert. 192p. pap. 1.95 o.p. (6150). Brandon.

Six Ways of Dying. Lewis B. Patten. 144p. 1976. pap. 1.95 (ISBN 0-441-76843-1). Ace Bks.

Six Weeks. Lawrence Saunders. LC 32-22983. Covici, Friede.

Six Weeks. Fred M. Stewart. LC 76-8637. (F). 1976. 7.95 (ISBN 0-87795-136-5). Arbor Hse.

Six Weeks. Fred Mustard Stewart. 1982. pap. 2.95 (ISBN 0-553-22981-8). Bantam.

Six Weeks: A Novel. Fred Mustard Stewart. LC 76-8637. 7.95 (ISBN 0-87795-136-5). Arbor House.

Six Weeks in March. Constance Noyes Robertson. LC 52-7140. Random House.

Six Weeks in March. 1st Ed. Lane Kauffmann. LC 56-6562. 1956. Lippincott.

Six Were to Die... Kirk Wales. LC 44-53447. (Black cat detective series. No. 12). 1944.

Six Who Died Young. C. R Clumpner. 1978. 1.75 (ISBN 0-441-76846-6). Ace Books.

Six Who Ran. M. E. Chaber, pseud. (Milo March Mystery Ser). 1970. pap. 0.60 o.p. (ISBN 0-446-63380-1, 63-380). Paperback Lib.

Six Who Ran: A New Milo March Adventure. Kendell Foster Crossen. LC 64-21913. (Rinehart suspense novel). 1964. Holt, Rinehart and Winston.

Six Wives of Henry VIII. Gladys Malvern. LC 71-134678. (Illus.). 1972. 4.95 (ISBN 0-8149-0665-6). Vanguard Press.

Six Women Along the Way: From Bethlehem to Calvary. Margaret Elizabeth Sangster. LC 31-25229. 1931. Brewer, Warren & Putnam Inc.

Six Wounds. John A. Cuddon. 1965. 3.95 o.p. McKay.

Six Wounds: 1st Amer. Ed. John A Cuddon. LC 65-18889. 1965. bds., 3.95. McKay.

Six Years in Heaven: A True Story of Human Credulity and Unexampled Devotion, Embracing a Complete Expose of the Abominable Practices and Monstrous Professions of George Jacob Schweinfurth, the False Christ... Alexander McClenaghan. (On cover: Library of choice fiction, no. 71). 1894. Laird & Lee.

Six Years Later: Or, Taking the Bastile. Alexandre Dumas & Maquet, Auguste. (Seaside library, v. 14 no. 278). G. Munro.

Six Years Later: Or, Taking the Bastile. Alexandre Dumas & Maquet, Auguste. LC 6-42318. (American series no. 315). M. J. Ivers & Co.

Sixdays in the Metropolis: Or Phases of Life in Town. St. Clair, Frank. LC 8-3400. 1854. Redding & Company.

Sixes and Sevens. William Sydney Porter. LC 11-26407. 1911. Doubleday, Page & Company.

Sixes and Sevens. William Sydney Porter. LC 15-174113. 1915. Doubleday, Page & Company.

Sixes and Sevens. William Sydney Porter. LC 19-135203. 1919. Doubleday, Page & Company.

Sixes and Sevens. William Sydney Porter. LC 22-16023. 1919. Doubleday, Page & Company, for Review of Reviews Co.

Sixes and Sevens. William Sydney Porter. LC 25-237222. 1925. Doubleday, Page & Company.

Sixgun Mule-Skinner. Johanas L. Bouma. 176p. 1976. pap. 1.25 (ISBN 0-89041-081-X, 3081). Major Bks.

Sixgun Talk. Bradford Scott. (Orig.). 1969. pap. 0.60 o.p. (X2041). Pyramid Pubns.

Sixgun Town. Charles Morris Martin. LC 51-4815. 1951. Phoenix Press.

Sixpence in Her Shoe. Phyllis McGinley. 1964. 9.95 o.s.i. (ISBN 0-02-583360-X). Macmillan.

Sixpenny Dame. Eaton K Goldthwaite. LC 53-84021. (Red badge detective). 1953. Dodd, Mead.

Sixpenny Pieces. 2d ed. Albert Michael Neil Lyons. LC 11-410719. 1910. John Lane.

Sixshooters & Sagebrush: Cowboy Stories of the Southwest. Rowland W. Rider & Deirdre Paulsen. LC 79-15715. (Illus.). 1979. pap. 7.95x o.p. (ISBN 0-8425-1696-4). Brigham.

Sixteen Days. Jean Bekessy. Tr. by Basil Creighton. LC 40-27215. Harcourt, Brace and Company.

Sixteen Hands. Homer Croy. LC 33-5757. 1938. Harper & Brothers.

Sixteen Hundred Floogle Street. Don McGuire. LC 67-31125. 1967. Holloway House Pub. Co.

Sixteen Hundred One. Mark Twain. slipcase 6.50 o.p. (ISBN 0-8184-0081-1). Lyle Stuart.

TITLE INDEX SKILLED THROAT.

Sixteen Modern Marathi Short Stories. Tr. by Bal Gadgil from Marathi. 236p. 1974. 3.60 o.p. (ISBN 0-88253-460-2). InterCulture.
Sixteen Old Maids: And Other Stories. Henry D Taylor. LC 8-25664. 1888. The Phelps Publishing Co.
Sixteen People Who Live Downtown: Voices from an Inner City: a Novel. Tom Huey. LC 79-113659. 4.95. UNC-G: Purchase from Upstream Productions.
Sixteen Rue Cortambert: A Novel. Anne Green. 1937. E. P. Dutton & Co., Inc.
Sixteen Stories As They Happened. Michael Bullock. 116p. 1974. 12.95 o.p. (ISBN 0-913600-27-X). Kanchenjunga Pr.
Sixteen Stories by South African Writers. 3rd ed., 3rd. imp. ed. Ed. by Clive Millar. LC 77-358917. 1976. 2.95 (ISBN 0-623-00866-1). Maskew Miller.
Sixteen to Forty: A Woman's Story. Marina. LC 27-236403. 1927. D. Appleton and Company.
Sixteenth Pan Book of Horror Stories. Ed. by H. Van Thal. 1982. pap. 10.00x (ISBN 0-330-24544-9, Pub. by Pan Bks). State Mutual Bk.
Sixth Beatitude. Radclyffe Hall. LC 36-9230. Harcourt, Brace and Company.
Sixth Column. Peter Fleming. 1982. 15.00x (ISBN 0-86025-019-9, Pub. by Ian Henry Pubns England). State Mutual Bk.
Sixth Column. Peter Fleming. 1977. 5.20 o.p. State Mutual Bk.
Sixth Column: A Science Fiction Novel of a Strange Intrigue. Robert Anson Heinlein. LC 50-5003. 1949. Gnome Press.
Sixth Column: A Singular Tale of Our Times. Peter Fleming. LC 51-13667. 1951. Scribner.
Sixth Commandment. Lawrence Sanders. 1980. pap. 3.75 (ISBN 0-425-05943-X). Berkley Pub.
Sixth Commandment. Lawrence Sanders. LC 78-13158. 1979. 10.95 (ISBN 0-399-12305-9). Putnam Pub Group.
Sixth Commandment. Carolyn Wells. LC 27-12819. 1927. George H. Doran Company.
Sixth Commandment: A Novel. Lawrence Sanders. LC 78-13158. 10.95 (ISBN 0-399-12305-9). Putnam.
Sixth Directorate. 1st. ed. Joseph Hone. LC 75-1456. 1975. 7.95 (ISBN 0-525-20490-3). Dutton.
Sixth Directorate. Joseph Hone. 1976. 1.75 (ISBN 0-449-22938-6). Fawcett Crest.
Sixth Heaven. Leslie Poles Hartley. LC 47-4933. 1947. Doubleday.
Sixth Jar. first ed. Richard M Langsdale. 1973. 4.95 (ISBN 0-533-00617-1). Vantage Press.
Sixth Journey. Alice Grant Rosman. LC 31-270676. 1931. Minton, Balch & Company.
Sixth of June. Stanley Hopkins. LC 35-172322. 1935. Harper & Brothers.
Sixth of June. 1st Ed. Lionel S. B. Shapiro. LC 55-8410. 1955. Doubleday.
Sixth of October: A Novel. Robert Smythe SHichens. LC 36-19221. 1936. Doubleday, Doran and Company, Inc.
Sixth of the Cent Nouvelles Nouvelles. William Royall Tyler & Club of Odd Volumes, Boston. LC 72-176321. 1970. Club of Odd Volumes.
Sixth Seal. Mary Wesley. LC 77-163453. (Stein and Day mystery). 1971. 5.95 (ISBN 0-8128-1422-3). Stein and Day.
Sixth Sense. Stephen McKenna. LC 21-6903. George H. Doran Company.
Sixth Sense. Ramona Stewart. LC 78-12599. 8.95 (ISBN 0-440-08784-8). Delacorte Press.
Sixth Sense: And Other Stories. Margaret Sutton Briscoe Hopkins. LC 71-110199. (Short story index reprint series). (Illus.). 1970. Books for Libraries Press.
Sixth Sense: And Other Stories. Margaret Sutton Briscoe Hopkins. LC 99-3004. 1899. Harper & Brothers.
Sixth Sense & Other Stories. Margaret Sutton Briscoe Hopkins. LC 71-110199. (Short Story Index Reprint Ser.). 1899. 17.00 (ISBN 0-8369-3350-8). Ayer Co.
Sixth Sense: Or, Electricity. A Story for the Masses. Mary E Buell. LC 6-19649. 1891. Colby & Rich.
Sixth Speed. E. J Rath. LC 8-10277. 1908. Moffat, Yard & Company.
Sixth Wife. Eleanor Hibbert. LC 70-81642. 1969. 5.95. Putnam.
Sixth Winter. Douglas Orgill & John R. Gribbin. LC 79-19297. 10.95 (ISBN 0-671-25016-7). Simon and Schuster.
Sixty Days in Oriental Waters & Other Stories. Julian Brooks. LC 70-77440. 1969. 2.25 o.p. (ISBN 0-911782-13-3). New City.
Sixty-Eight. Peter Scaevola. LC 64-10572. 1964. Norton.
Sixty Fifth Tape. Frank Ross. LC 78-20367. 1979. 10.95 o.p. (ISBN 0-689-10965-2). Atheneum.
Sixty-Fifth Tape. Frank Ross. 304p. 1980. pap. 2.50 (ISBN 0-553-13747-6). Bantam.
Sixty-First Second. Owen McMahon Johnson. LC 13-35199. 1913. 1.30. Frederick A. Stokes Company.
Sixty-First Second. 3d ed. Owen McMahon Johnson. LC 16-936743. Frederick A. Stokes Company.
Sixty-Five on Time. Jean Katherine Baird. LC 9-26320. 1.25. The Saalfield Publishing Company.
Sixty-Five Short Stories. Ed. by Ognjen Lakicevic. LC 70-975813. 254p. 1970. pap. 6.50x (ISBN 0-8002-0133-7). Intl Pubns Serv.
Sixty-Four, Ninety-Four! Ralph Hale Mottram. LC 25-9298. 1925. L. Macveagh, The Dial Press.
Sixty Hours of Darkness. Arelo Sederberg. 254p. 1974. 6.95 o.s.i. Sherbourne.
Sixty Hours of Darkness: A Novel of Terror in Las Vegas. Arelo Sederberg. LC 75-306820. 6.95 (ISBN 0-8202-0166-9). Sherbourne Press.
Sixty Jane. John Luther Long. LC 76-103524. (Short Story Index Reprint Ser.). 1903. 15.00 (ISBN 0-8369-3266-8). Ayer Co.
Sixty Jane and The Strike on the Schlafeplatz Railroad. "Our Anchel", The Lady and Her Soul. The Beautiful Graveyard, Lucky Jim. The Outrageous Miss Dawn-Dream. The Little House in the Little Street Where the Sun Never Came. The Atonement. John Luther Long. LC 76-103524. (Short story index reprint series). (Illus.). 1969. Books for Libraries Press.
Sixty Jane and The Strike on the Schlafeplatz Railroad, "The Lady and Her Soul, The Beautiful Graveyard, Lucky Jim, The Outrageous Miss Dawn-Dream, The Little House in the Little Street Where the Sun Never Came, The Atonement. John Luther Long. LC 3-25875. 1903. The Century Co.
Sixty-Nine Diamonds. Jeremy Lord, pseud. LC 40-4888. 1940. Pub. for the Crime Club by Doubleday, Doran and Co., Inc.
Sixty-Nine Pleasures. Rod Gray. (Lady from L. U. S. T. Ser). 1970. pap. 0.95 o.p. (B95-2043). Belmont-Tower.
Sixty Nine Pleasures. Rod Gray. (The Lady from L.U.S.T. Ser.). (O.s.i.). 1973. pap. 0.95 o.s.i. (BT50559). Belmont-Tower.
Sixty-Nine Short Stories. O. Henry. 3.00 o.p. (ISBN 0-00-422550-3); lea. 5.00 o.p. (ISBN 0-00-423550-9). Collins-World.
Sixty-Nine South Walnut. O. R. Bassett. 224p. pap. 1.95 o.p. (6139). Brandon.
Sixty Seconds. Maxwell Bodenheim. LC 73-18549. 1975. 16.50 (ISBN 0-404-11364-8). AMS Press.
Sixty Seconds. Maxwell Bodenheim. LC 29-645116. H. Liveright.
Sixty Stories. Donald Barthelme. LC 81-8646. 18.95 (ISBN 0-399-12659-7) (ISBN 0-399-12675-9). Putnam.
Sixty Stories. Donald Barthelme. LC 82-72046. 8.95 (ISBN 0-525-48018-8). Dutton.
Sixty-Three; Dream Palace: A Novella. James Purdy. LC 56-11859. 1956. William-Frederick Press.
Sixty-Three: Dream Palace & Other Stories. James Purdy. 176p. 1981. pap. 4.95 (ISBN 0-14-005732-3). Penguin.
Sixty to Go. Ruth Landshoff Yorck. LC 44-3246. 1944. J. Messner, Inc.
Sixty-Two: A Model Kit. 1st. american ed. Julio Cortazar. LC 72-3406. 1972. 6.95 (ISBN 0-394-46822-8). Pantheon Books.
Sixty-Two: A Model Kit. Julio Cortazar. Tr. by Gregory Rabassa from Span. LC 72-3406. (O.s.i). 1972. 6.95 o.s.i. (ISBN 0-394-46822-8). Pantheon.
Sixty Years of the Life of Jeremy Levis... Laughton Osborn. LC 7-23695. 1831. G. & C. & H. Carvill.
Sizzling Platter. Peter Arno. (Illus.). 128p. 1977. 13.50 (ISBN 0-7156-1269-7, Pub. by Duckworth England). Biblio Dist.
Skarra. Henry V. M Richardson. LC 75-9739. 1975. 8.95 (ISBN 0-690-00909-7). Crowell.
Skarra. Henry V. M Richardson. 1976. 1.95 (ISBN 0-446-89126-6). Warner Books.
Skate. Jon Appleby. 224p. 1971. 6.95 o.p. (ISBN 0-374-26570-4). FS&G.
Skate: A Novel. Jon Appleby. LC 75-164534. 1971-1972. 6.95. Farrar, Straus and Giroux.
Skateboard: Novelization. Gail Kimberly. (Tempo Star Book). (Illus.). 1978. 1.95. Grosset & Dunlap.
Skater's Waltz. Philip Norman. 320p. 1980. 17.95 (ISBN 0-241-10255-3, Pub. by Hamish Hamilton England). David & Charles.
Skean. Robert McKay. LC 76-6904. 6.95 (ISBN 0-8407-6486-3). T. Nelson.
Skeeters Kirby: A Novel. Edgar Lee Masters. LC 23-4003. 1923. The Macmillan Company.
Skein of Life. William R. Mackay. LC 7-19416. 1897. J. B. Lippincott Company.
Skeleton. Kathleen Coyle. LC 33-246560. E. P. Dutton & Co., Inc.
Skeleton at the Feast: A Kenneth Carlisle Detective Story... Carolyn Wells. LC 31-163316. Pub. for the Crime Club, Inc., by Doubleday, Doran & Company, Inc.
Skeleton Coast Contract. Philip Atlee. (Contract Ser). 1970. pap. 0.60 o.p. (R2322, GM). Fawcett World.
Skeleton in Search of a Closet. E. X Ferrars, pseud. LC 82-45355. 1982. 11.95 (ISBN 0-385-18268-6). Published for the Crime Club by Doubleday.
Skeleton in the Clock. Carter Dickson, pseud. 1977. pap. 1.50 o.s.i. (ISBN 0-505-51194-0). Tower Bks.
Skeleton in the Clock: Another Adventure of Sir Henry Merrivale. John Dickson Carr. LC 48-8781. 1948. W. Morrow.
Skeleton in the Closet: A Novel. Emma Dorothy Eliza Nevitte Southworth. LC 8-14257. (Ledger library, no. 92). 1893. R. Bonner's Sons.
Skeleton in the Closet. 1st Ed. Albert Benjamin Cunningham. LC 51-9341. (Guilt edged mystery). 1951. Dutton.
Skeleton Key. Bernard Edward Joseph Capes. LC 20-7424. 1920. George H. Doran Company.
Skeleton Key. Lenore Glen Offord. LC 43-10069. 1943. Duell, Sloan and Pearce.
Skeleton Key to Finnegans Wake. Joseph Campbell & Henry Morton Robinson. LC 77-23061. 1977. 3.95 (ISBN 0-14-004663-1). Penguin Books.
Skeleton Key to Finnegans Wake. Joseph Campbell & Robinson, Henry Morton, 1806-Joint Author. LC 44-6502. 1944. Harcourt, Brace and Company.
Skeleton Key to Finnegans Wake: By Joseph Campbell, Henry Morton Robinson. Joseph Campbell & Henry Morton Robinson. (Compass bk. C74). 1961. pap., 1.65. Viking.
Skeleton of Chaucer's Canterbury Tales. Henry Bradshaw. LC 70-39518. Repr. of 1871 ed. 16.00 (ISBN 0-404-00929-8). AMS Pr.
Skeleton of Light. Thomas Vance. 1961. 3.95 o.p. (ISBN 0-8078-0819-9). U of NC Pr.
Skeleton Riders. Jackson Cole. 1975. (pbk.) 0.95. Popular Library.
Skeleton Staff. Morna Doris MacTaggart Brown. (Dell Book, 8061). 1973. 0.75. Dell.
Skeleton Staff. Morna Doris MacTaggart Brown. LC 78-86398. 1969. 4.50. Walker.
Skeleton Talks. Frederick George Eberhard. LC 33-10152. The Macaulay Company.
Skeletons. Glendon Fred Swarthout. LC 78-22370. 1979. 9.95 (ISBN 0-385-12824-X). Doubleday.
Skeletons. Glendon Fred Swarthouth. 1981. Pocket Books.
Skeletons: A Claim Agent's Stories. Guy Morrison Walker. LC 21-20191. 1921. The Stratford Co.
Skeletons and Cupboards. Ralph Arnold. LC 51-14459. 1951. Macmillan.
Skeletons in the Closet. Elizabeth Linington. LC 82-45075. (Crime Club Ser.). 192p. 1982. 10.95 (ISBN 0-385-18169-8). Doubleday.
Skeptic. Eliza Lee Cabot Follen. LC 9-944. (Added t.-p.: Scenes and characters illustrating Christian truth ed. by H. Ware no. ii). 1835. J. Munroe and Company.
Skerrett. Liam O'Flaherty. LC 32-31036. 1932. R. Long & R. R. Smith, Inc.
Sketch Book of a Cadet from Gascony. James Warner Bellah. LC 23-16464. 1923. A. A. Knopf.
Sketch Book of Geoffery Crayon Gentleman. Washington Irving. 5.00x o.p. (ISBN 0-460-00117-5, Evman). Dutton.
Sketch Book of Geoffrey Crayon, Gent. (Washington Irving) ed. de luxe... ed. Washington Irving. LC 7-94891. 1882. J. B. Lippincott & Co.
Sketch Books: The Paris Sketch Book of Mr. M. A. Titmarsh; The Irish Sketch Book; Notes of a Journey from Cornhill to Grand Cairo. William Makepeace Thackeray. LC 12-31088. (Half-title: The boigraphical edition. The works of... Thackeray... vol. V). 1898. Harper & Brothers.
Sketch in the Ideal, a Romance. Anna Reading Gazzam. LC 6-44257. 1891. J.B. Lippincott Company.
Sketch of a Sinner. Frank Arthur Swinnerton. LC 29-27450. 1929. Doubleday, Doran and Company, Inc.
Sketch of My Friend's Family: Intended to Suggest Some Practical Hints on Religion and Domestic Manners. 3d ed.... ed. Marshall. LC 11-3203. 1819. Pub. by Charles Ewer Sylvester T. Goss, Printer.
Sketch of My Friend's Family: Intended to Suggest Some Practical Hints on Religion and Domestic Manners. Marshall. 1821. J. Metcalf, Printer.
Sketches. Lydia Howard Huntley Sigourney. LC 8-8990. 1834. Key & Biddle.
Sketches and Travels in London. William Makepeace Thackeray. LC 8-28193. (On cover: Lovell's library, v. 6, no. 309). 1883. J. W. Lovell Company.
Sketches by Boz. Illustrative of Every-Day Life and Every-Day People... Charles Dickens. 1867. Hurd and Houghton.
Sketches by Boz: Illustrative of Every-Day Life & Every-Day People. Charles Dickens. LC 36-37122. (Half-title: Everyman's library, ed. by Ernest Rhys. Fiction. no. 237). 1929. J. M. Dent & Sons, Ltd.
Sketches from a Hunter's Album. Ivan Sergeevich Turgenev. Tr. by Richard Freeborn. LC 67-4223. (Penguin classics, L186). 1967. Penguin Books.
Sketches from a Hunter's Album. Ivan Sergeevich Turgenev. Tr. by Richard Freeborn. LC 67-93194. (Penguin classics, L186). 1967. Penguin.
Sketches from a Hunter's Album: By Ivan Turgenev. Ivan Sergeevich Turgenev & Richard Freeborn. LC 67-93194. (Penguin classics, L186). 1967. Penguin.
Sketches from the Bar. Grover Stephen McLeod. LC 67-6963. (Illus.). 1967. Manchester Press.
Sketches from Truth. Katharine Mary Cheever Meredith. 1892. Press of Nocton & Company.
Sketches from Truth. Katharine Mary Cheever Meredith. LC 42-30190. 1893. Press of Nocton Company.
Sketches in Black & White. Mariana Scott. (Illus.). 1967. 5.00 o.p. (ISBN 0-8283-1204-4). Branden.
Sketches in Ebony and Gold. Mary Cochran Thurman. LC 3-28562. Broadway Publishing Company.
Sketches in Lavender, Blue, and Green. Jerome Klapka Jerome. LC 72-37274. (Short story index reprint series). (Illus.). 1971. (ISBN 0-8369-4085-7). Books for Libraries Press.
Sketches in Lavender, Blue, and Green. Jerome Klapka Jerome. 1897. H. Holt and Company.
Sketches in Prose, and Occasional Verses. James Whitcomb Riley. LC 7-41649. 1891. The Bowen-Merrill Co.
Sketches of Aboriginal Life. V. V Vide. LC 75-7085. (Garland Library of Narratives of North American Indian Captivities; V. 62). (Series: American tableaux; no. 1.). 1975. (ISBN 0-8240-1686-6). Garland Pub.
Sketches of American Character. 6th stereotype ed. Sarah Josepha Hale. LC 7-3342. 1838. H. Perkins.
Sketches of American Character. Sarah Josepha Hale. LC 6-46210. 1843. Perkins & Purves.
Sketches of Character: And Tales Founded on Fact. Frederick William Thomas. LC 8-27047. 1849. Pub. at the Office of the Chronicle of Western Literature and Art.
Sketches of Domestic Life. LC 8-9020. 1831. Shirley, Hyde and Company.
Sketches of Gotham. Ike Swift. R. K. Fox.
Sketches of Irish Character. Anna Maria Fielding Hall. LC 24-27967. 1845. E. Ferrett and Company.
Sketches of Irish Character. Anna Maria Fielding Hall. LC 7-544. 1845. E. Ferrett and Company.
Sketches of Irish Character. Anna Maria Fielding Hall. LC 29-1650. 1858. J. Locken.
Sketches of the Irish Character. Anna Maria Fielding Hall. LC 79-15130. (Ireland from the Act of Union, 1800, to the Death of Parnell, 1891). 1979. 84.00 (ISBN 0-8240-3495-3). Garland Publishing.
Sketches of Life and Character. Timothy Shay Arthur. LC 45-47542. 1850. J. W. Bradley.
Sketches of Married Life. (3d bristol ed., rev. by the authoress) ed. Eliza Lee Cabot Follen. LC 6-41423. Philip and Evans, Printers.
Sketches of Young Couples. Charles Dickens. LC 6-33576. H. M. Caldwell Co.
Sketches Old and New. Walter Polk Phillips. LC 41-31251. J. H. Bunnell & Company.
Sketches. Three Tales: I. Walter Lorimer; II. The Emblems of Life; III. The Lost Inheritance. Elizabeth Missing Sewell. LC 42-28092. 1848. D. Appleton & Co.
Ski Bum. Romain Gary, pseud. LC 64-18076. 4.95. Harper.
Ski Lift to Love. Helen Murray. 1980. pap. 1.75 (ISBN 0-8439-8003-6, Tiara Bks). Nordon Pubns.
Ski Lodgers. William Hegner. (O.s.i.). 1976. pap. 1.75 o.s.i. WSP.
Ski Lodgers. William Hegner (ISBN 0-671-80792-7). Pocket Books.
Ski People. Burton Hersh. LC 68-24346. 1968. McGraw-Hill.
Ski Week. Edward Kuhn. (Berkley Medallion Book). 1977. 1.75 (ISBN 0-425-03317-1). Berkley Pub. Corp.
Ski Week: A Novel. Edward Kuhn. LC 72-89325. 1975. 8.95 (ISBN 0-385-02416-9). Doubleday.
Skid Puffer: A Tale of the Kankakee Swamp. French, Francis F. LC 10-9263. 1910. H. Holt and Company.
Skiddoo! George Vere Hobart. 1906. G. W. Dillingham Co.
Skies Are Falling. Winifred Peck. LC 36-17472. 1936. Frederick A. Stokes Company.
Skies of Europe. Frederic Prokosch. LC 41-14057. 1941. Harper & Brothers.
Skilled Throat. Barbara Devine. 192p. (Orig.). 1973. pap. 1.95 o.p. (ISBN 0-87682-334-7, 7334). Barclay Hse.

Skilled Workman. W. A Bodell. LC 6-141932. F. H. Revell Company.
Skin and Bones. Thorne Smith. LC 34-902. 1933. Doubleday, Doran & Company, Inc.
Skin and Bones. Thorne Smith. LC 35-12200. 1934. Doubleday, Doran & Company, Inc.
Skin Book. C. S Vanek. LC 77-9898. (Traveller's companion series). 1969. 1.95. Traveller's Companion, Inc.
Skin Dealer. Miles Tripp. LC 65-13415. 1965. bds., 4.95. Holt.
Skin Deep... Herman Irving Bloom. LC 34-200193. 1934. W. Godwin, Inc.
Skin Deep. Susan Hufford. 1978. 1.95 (ISBN 0-445-04258-3). Popular Library.
Skin Deep. Clarence Budington Kelland. LC 39-3294. 1939. Harper & Brothers.
Skin-Deep: Or, Portrait of Lucinda, with a Prologue and an Epilogue from the London Adventure of Arabell Holdenbrook. Naomi Gwladys Royde-Smith. LC 27-1996. 1927. A. A. Knopf.
Skin Flick. Joseph Hansen. LC 79-11077. (Rinehart suspense novel). 7.95 (ISBN 0-03-048931-8). Holt, Rinehart, and Winston.
Skin for Skin. Winifred Duke. LC 35-8103. 1935. Little, Brown, and Company.
Skin for Skin. James Douglas Rutherford McConnell. LC 68-27387. 1968. 3.95. Walker.
Skin Game Dame. Rod Gray. (Lady from L.U.S.T. Ser). (O.s.i.: No. 18). 1974. pap. 0.95 o.s.i. (BT50742). Belmont-Tower.
Skin Games. Jason F. Storm. 1973. pap. 1.95 o.s.i. (76-337). Lancer.
Skin O' My Tooth, His Memoirs: By His Confidential Clerk. Emmuska Orczy. LC 28-197518. 1928. Pub. for the Crime Club, Inc., by Doubleday, Doran & Company, Inc.
Skin of Dreams: A Novel. Raymond Queneau. Tr. by Kaplan, H. J. LC 48-9105. (Direction, 5). 1948. New Directions.
Skin of Dreams: A Novel. Raymond Queneau. LC 77-11668. 1978. 10.00. H. Fertig.
Skin of Dreams: A Novel. Raymond Queneau. LC 77-11668. 1979. 3.25 (ISBN 0-86527-305-7). H. Fertig.
Skin of Gods: Hycette. Sarah A Nassour. LC 40-31185. 1938. Suttonhouse.
Skin Summer. Ann Griffin. pap. 1.95 o.p. (8045). Cameo.
Skin. Tr. from Italian by David Moore. Curzio Malaparte. (N117). 1965. Avon.
Skin: Translated from the Italian by David Moore. Curzio Malaparte. LC 52-8275. 1952. Houghton Mifflin.
Skinman. Martin Tarmey. LC 73-126527. 1970. Harcourt Brace Jovanovich.
Skinner. Jay Gilbert. LC 60-11431. 1960. New Authors Guild.
Skinner. F. M Parker. LC 80-1863. (DD western). 1981. 9.95 (ISBN 0-385-17382-2). Doubleday.
Skinner: A Novel. Hugh C Rae. LC 65-19268. 1965. Viking Press.
Skinner Makes It Fashionable. Henry Irving Dodge. LC 20-6285. Harper & Brothers.
Skinner's Baby. Henry Irving Dodge. LC 17-25433. 1917. 1.25. Houghton Mifflin Company.
Skinner's Big Idea. Henry Irving Dodge. LC 18-5215. 1918. Harper & Brothers.
Skinner's Dress Suit. Henry Irving Dodge. LC 16-19955. 1916. Houghton Mifflin Company.
Skinner's Horse. Philip Mason. LC 79-1803. 1980. 9.95 (ISBN 0-06-013036-9). Harper & Row.
Skinny Angel. Thelma Jones. 6.95 (ISBN 0-87018-035-5). Ross.
Skinny Dynamite & Other Short Stories. Jack Micheline. Ed. by A. D. Winans. LC 79-63969. 96p. (Orig.). 1980. pap. 4.95 (ISBN 0-915016-27-3). Second Coming.
Skip to My Loo, My Darling. Elisabeth Offutt Allen. 1973. 4.50 o.p. (Avalon). Bouregy.
Skip to My Lou. William Martin Camp. LC 45-7981. 1945. Doubleday, Doran & Company, Inc.
Skipper. Barbara Corcoran. 1979. 7.95 (ISBN 0-689-30706-3). Atheneum.
Skipper & the Eagle. Gordon McGowan. 1960. pap. 5.95 (ISBN 0-442-25266-8). Van Nos Reinhold.
Skipper and the Skipped: Being the Shore Log of Cap'n Aaron Sproul. Holman Francis Day. LC 11-180033. 1911. 1.50. London, Harper & Brothers.
Skipper John of the Nimbus. Raymond McFarland. LC 18-18881. 1918. The Macmillan Company.
Skipper's Wooing: And The Brown Man's Servant. William Wymark Jacobs. LC 7-7425. F. A. Stokes Company.
Skippy. Percy Leo Crosby. LC 29-9372. 1929. G. P. Putnam's Sons.
Skippy Bedelle, His Sentimental Progress from the Urchin to the Complete Man of the World. Owen McMahon Johnson. LC 22-20277. 1922. Little, Brown, and Company.
Skippy Bedelle, His Sentimental Progress from the Urchin to the Complete Man of the World. Owen McMahon Johnson. LC 34-1837. 1931. Little, Brown, and Company.
Skippy Rambles. Percy Leo Crosby. LC 32-245442. 1932. G. P. Putnam's Sons.
Skippy Remembers: And Other Stories. Merle Merryday. LC 39-1832. The Crescent Press.
Skirmish. Bert Cloos. LC 57-12682. 1957. Avlon Books.
Skirmish. Clive Egleton. LC 74-16639. 1975. 7.95 (ISBN 0-698-10635-0). Coward, McCann & Geoghegan.
Skirmish. Clive Egleton. (Fawcett Crest Book). 1976. 1.50. Fawcett.
Skirmish at Fort Phil Kearny. Wayne C Lee. (Avalon Books). 4.95. Thomas Bouregy.
Skirmish: The Great Short Fiction of Clifford D. Simak. Clifford D Simak. (Berkley Book). 1978. 1.95 (ISBN 0-425-03821-1). Berkley Publishing Corporation.
Skirmishing. Henrietta Camilla Jackson Jenkin. 1863. Follett, Foster and Company.
Skirts of the Forest. Violet Quirk. LC 32-33995. 1931. The Macmillan Company.
Skitch: The Message of the Roses. Vincent G Perry. LC 75-20788. (ISBN 0-87714-032-4). Denlinger's.
Skittering Maching, the, Other Tales & Sketches. Edward J. Koch. 4.50 o.p. Vantage.
Skookum Chuck: A Novel. Stewart Edward White. LC 25-21915. 1925. Doubleday, Page & Company.
Skulamagee. Quoron Ostos. 1959. 3.75 o.p. (ISBN 0-8158-0159-9). Chris Mass.
Skulamagee: A Story of Early Vancouver. Quoron Ostos. LC 59-69265. 1959. Christopher Pub. House.
Skuldoggery. Fletcher Flora. (Orig.). pap. 0.50 o.p. (B50-738). Belmont-Tower.
Skulduggery: A Yellowthread Street Mystery. William Leonard Marshall. LC 79-1933. (Rinehart suspense novel). 1980. 8.95 (ISBN 0-03-047491-4). Holt, Rinehart, and Winston.
Skull Beneath the Skin. P. D James. LC 82-5981. 13.95 (ISBN 0-684-17773-0). Scribner.
Skull Beneath the Skin. P. D James. LC 83-205. 1983. 18.95 (ISBN 0-8161-3508-8). G.K. Hall.
Skull-Face. Robert A Howard. (Berkley Medallion Book). 1.95. Berkley Pub. Corp.
Skull-Face, and Others. Robert E. Howard. LC 46-7119. 1946. Arkham House.
Skull Gold. Ray Hogan. (Signet brand Western, T5497). 1973. (pbk.) 0.75. New American Lib.
Skull Mountain. Dean Hawkins. LC 41-13936. 1941. Pub. for the Crime Club by Doubleday, Doran & Company, Inc.
Skull of Adam. Stanley Moss. 1980. 7.95 (ISBN 0-8180-1578-0); pap. 3.95. Horizon.
Skull of the Waltzing Clown. Harry Stephen Keeler. LC 35-153184. E. P. Dutton & Co., Inc.
Skull Rack. Fred Truck & Bolon Dzacab. 250.00 o.p. Cookie Pr.
Skull Still Bone. John Wyllie. LC 74-12721. 1975. 4.95 (ISBN 0-385-07014-4). Published for the Crime Club by Doubleday.
Skullface Omnibus. Robert E. Howard. (O.s.i.). 8.95 o.s.i. Wehman.
Skutarevsky. Leonid Maksimovich Leonov. Tr. by Alec Brown. LC 76-135250. 1971. (ISBN 0-8371-5170-8). Greenwood Press.
Skutarevsky. Leonid Maksimovich Leonov & Brown, Alec, 1900- Tr. LC 36-19224. Harcourt, Brace and Company.
Sky: A Novel. Yvonne Yaw. LC 77-10025. 1977. 6.95 (ISBN 0-395-25693-3). Houghton Mifflin.
Sky Above Hell and Other Stories. Yuri Mamleyev. LC 79-66644. 1980. 7.95 (ISBN 0-8008-7236-3). Taplinger.
Sky Above Hell: And Other Stories. Yuri Mamleyev. Tr. by H. W. Tjalsma from Rus. LC 79-66644. 160p. 1980. 7.95 (ISBN 0-8008-7236-3). Taplinger.
Sky and the Forest. Cecil Scott Forester. LC 48-5977. 1948. Little, Brown.
Sky and Tomorrow. Thomas William Duncan. LC 72-92203. 1974. 8.95 (ISBN 0-385-02682-X). Doubleday.
Sky Attack. Canfield Cook. LC 42-17795. 1942. Grosset & Dunlap.
Sky Block. Steve Frazee. LC 53-9236. 1953. Rinehart.
Sky Blue, Grass Green. Ed. by Julian Ocean, pseud. LC 73-80966. (Illus.). 1974. 8.50 o.p. (ISBN 0-89002-017-5); pap. 4.45 o.p. (ISBN 0-89002-016-7). Northwoods Pr.
Sky Bride: A Romance of the Air. Bogart Rogers. LC 32-12758. Grosset & Dunlap.
Sky but Not the Heart: A Novel. Robert Luther Duffus. LC 36-17715. 1936. The Macmillan Company.
Sky Cage. Ann Prior. LC 67-90991. 1967. Chatto & Windus.
Sky Carnival: A Story of the Barnstorming Days. William F Hallstead. LC 69-13789. 1969. 3.95. D. McKay Co.
Sky Changes. Gilbert Sorrentino. LC 66-15895. 1966. Hill and Wang.
Sky Children. Donald Olson. 1975. (pbk.) 1.25 (ISBN 0-380-00427-5). Avon.
Sky Girl. Nellie Graf. LC 36-216873. Phoenix Press.
Sky Girls. Marilyn Lynch. (Modern career girl series). 1974. (pbk.) 1.25. Ace Books.
Sky Hawk: Novelized. Guy Fowler & Hughes, Llewellyn. LC 29-25350. Grosset & Dunlap.
Sky High. Michael Francis Gilbert. pap. 0.50 o.p. (72-751). Lancer.
Sky High. Tom Murphy. LC 76-45535. 8.95 (ISBN 0-399-11648-6). Putnam.
Sky in My Legs. Raymond Roseliep. (Haiku Ser.: No. 7). 1980. pap. 3.00. Juniper Pr WI.
Sky Is Falling. Clifford Comer Cawley. LC 72-148962. 1971. 5.00 (ISBN 0-87787-005-5). Mara Books.
Sky Is Falling. Oliver Jenkins. LC 31-31524. 1931. The St. Botolph Society.
Sky Is Falling. Esther Loewen Vogt. LC 68-20542. 1968. 3.50. Herald Press.
Sky Is My Tipi. Ed. by Mody Coggin Boatright. LC 49-1690. (Texas Folklore Society Publications: No. 22). (Illus.). 1966. Repr. of 1949 ed. 6.95 (ISBN 0-87074-010-5). SMU Press.
Sky Is Red. Giuseppe Berto. LC 76-138575. 1971. (ISBN 0-8371-5774-9). Greenwood Press.
Sky Is Red. Giuseppe Berto. Tr. by Davidson, Angus. LC 48-9030. 1948. New Directions.
Sky Kill. Daniel Da Cruz. (Jack Sargent). (Fawcett gold medal book: Vol. 3). 1974. (pbk.) 0.95. Fawcett.
Sky-Line Inn. Donal Hamilton Haines. LC 23-798607. 1923. Houghton Mifflin Company.
Sky Line of Spruce. Edison Marshall. LC 22-161482. 1922. 1.75. Little, Brown, and Company.
Sky-Liners. Louis L'Amour. 1972. pap. 2.25 (ISBN 0-553-20073-9). Bantam.
Sky Lines of Paradise. William Charles Smithson Pellowe. LC 41-12693. Fortuny's.
Sky-Man. Henry Kitchell Webster. 1910. The Century Co.
Sky Mates. Ilse Lefton Schlaitzer. LC 44-9355. 1944. W. H. Dietz, Inc.
Sky Phantom. Carolyn Keene, pseud. LC 75-17391. (Nancy Drew mystery stories; 53). (Illus.). 1976. 3.99 (ISBN 0-448-19553-4). Grosset & Dunlap,
Sky Phantom. 2.95 (ISBN 0-448-09553-X, G&D). Putnam Pub Group.
Sky Pilot: A Tale of the Foothills. Charles William Gordon. LC 73-104767. (Novel as American social history). 1970. University Press of Kentucky.
Sky Pilot: A Tale of the Foothills. Charles William Gordon. LC 6. 1899. F. H. Revell Company.
Sky Pilot: A Tale of the Foothills. Charles William Gordon. LC 40-37524. Grosset & Dunlap.
Sky Pilot: A Tale of the Foothills. Charles William Gordon. LC 4-15399. 1901. F. H. Revell Company.
Sky Pilot: A Tale of the Foothills. Charles William Gordon. LC 8-31160. F. H. Revell Company.
Sky Pilot: A Tale of the Foothills. Charles William Gordon. LC 40-9592. Grosset & Dunlap.
Sky-Pilot Cowboy. Walt Coburn. LC 37-10495. 1937. D. Appleton-Century Company, Incorporated.
Sky Pilot in No Man's Land. Charles William Gordon. LC 19-3537. 1.50. George H. Doran Company.
Sky Pirates of Callisto. Lin Carter. (Dell book). 1973. 0.95. Dell.
Sky Remembers. Dan Brennan. (Leisure Books). 1.50 (ISBN 0-8439-0484-4). Nordon Publications.
Sky-Sifter: The Great Chieftainess and "Medicine Woman" of the Mohawks. Remarkable Adventures and Experiences of Her White Foster Son As Related by Himself... William P Bennett. LC 7-34096. Pacific Press Publishing Co.
Sky Suspended. James E Bassett. LC 68-12197. 1968. Delacorte Press.
Sky Woman. Kenneth M. Cameron. 352p. 1982. pap. 3.50 (ISBN 0-445-04728-3). Popular Lib.
Skyaways for Doorian: 1st Ed. Zaara Van Tuyl. LC 67-17067. 1967. 3.95, 2.95 pap.,. C. Beaconsfield.
Skyblue the Badass. Dallas E Wiebe. LC 69-11989. 1969. 4.95. Doubleday.
Skycastle. Steve Krantz. LC 81-19283. 13.95. Macmillan.
Skychild. Suzanne Morris. LC 80-2752. 336p. 1981. 13.95 (ISBN 0-385-15305-8). Doubleday.
Skyclimber. Raymond Z. Gallun. (Orig.). 1981. pap. 2.25 (ISBN 0-505-51682-9). Tower Bks.
Skydive Girls. S. F. Mitchell. 192p. (Orig.). 1973. pap. 1.95 o.p. (ISBN 0-87056-294-0, 6294). Brandon.
Skye Cameron. Phyllis A Whitney. LC 57-903182. 1957. Appleton-Century-Crofts.
Skye O'Malley. Bertrice Small. LC 80-66549. 1980. 6.95 (ISBN 0-345-29256-1). Ballantine Books.
Skyfall. Harry Harrison. LC 77-367009. 1976. 3.50 (ISBN 0-571-10962-4). Faber.
Skyfall. Harry Harrison. 1978. 1.95 (ISBN 0-441-76942-X). Ace Books.
Skyfall. Harry Harrison. 1978. 1.95 (ISBN 0-441-76941-1). Ace Books.
Skyhigh Betrayers. Lionel Derrick. (Penetrator Ser.: No. 28). 1978. pap. 1.50 (ISBN 0-523-40268-6, Dist. by Independent News Co.). Pinnacle Bks.
Skylark. Samson Raphaelson. LC 39-20162. 1939. A. A. Knopf.
Skylark. Meredith Reed. LC 33-328531. Thomas Y. Crowell Company.
Skylark DuQuesne. Edward Elmer Smith. LC 75-432. (Garland Library of Science Fiction). 1975. 11.00 (ISBN 0-8240-1435-9). Garland Pub.
Skylark DuQuesne. Edward Elmer Smith. LC 75-237397. 1967. 0.60. Pyramid Books.
Skylark of Space. Edward Elmer Smith. LC 75-427. (Garland Library of Science Fiction). 1975. (ISBN 0-8240-1432-4). Garland Pub.
Skylark of Space. 2d ed. Edward Elmer Smith. LC 48-2219. 1947. Hadley Pub. Co.
Skylark of Space: The Tale of the First Inter-Stellar Cruise. Edward Elmer Smith & Garby, Lee (Hawkins) 1890- Joint Author. LC 46-16816. 1946. The Southgate Press, Inc.
Skylark of Valeron. Edward Elmer Smith. LC 75-430. (Garland Library of Science Fiction). 1975. 11.00 (ISBN 0-8240-1434-0). Garland Pub.
Skylark of Valeron. Edward Elmer Smith. LC 49-8714. 1949. Fantasy Press.
Skylark Three. Edward Elmer Smith. LC 75-429. (Garland Library of Science Fiction). 1975. 11.00 (ISBN 0-8240-1433-2). Garland Pub.
Skylark Three. Edward Elmer Smith. LC 48-9439. 1948. Fantasy Press.
Skylight. Robert Yates Kittredge. LC 57-5380. 1958. Random House.
Skylight. Carol Maske. LC 80-712. 1981. 5.95 (ISBN 0-385-17087-4). Doubleday.
Skyline. David Scott Milton. LC 82-5209. 15.95 (ISBN 0-399-12599-X). Putnam.
Skyline Riders. Francis W Hilton. LC 39-340174. 1939. H. C. Kinsey & Company, Inc.
Skyport. Curt Siodmak. LC 59-14017. 1959. Crown Publishers.
Skyprobe: A Commander Shaw Novel. Philip McCutchan. LC 67-24637. 1967. John Day Co.
Skyraiders. Alan Marks. 1979. pap. 1.95 o.s.i. (ISBN 0-505-51416-8). Tower Bks.
Skyrider. Bertha Muzzy Sinclair. LC 18-207764. 1918. Little, Brown, and Company.
Skyripper. David Drake. (Tor Bks.). 352p. (Orig.). 1983. pap. 3.50 (ISBN 0-523-48544-1). Pinnacle Bks.
Skyrocket. Adelaide Humphries. LC 36-7112. Greenberg.
Skyrocket: A New Novel. St. John, Adela Rogers. LC 25-7665. 1925. Cosmopolitan Book Corporation.
Skyrocket: A Novel About Glamour and Power. Eugenia Sheppard & Earl Blackwell. LC 79-8012. 1980. 12.95 (ISBN 0-385-15695-2). Doubleday.
Skyrocket Steele. Ron Goulart. Date not set. pap. 2.25 (ISBN 0-671-83410-X, Timescape). PB.
Sky's No Limit. W R Gwinn. LC 39-24927. 1939. Hillman-Curl, Inc.
Sky's the Limit. Wayne Dyer. 1981. pap. 3.50 (ISBN 0-671-43109-9). PB.
Sky's the Limit. A. D. Livingston. LC 66-11161. bds., 4.50. Lippincott.
Sky's the Limit. E. J. Rath. LC 29-7495. 1929. G. H. Watt.
Skyscraper. Faith Baldwin. 1976. Repr. of 1931 ed. lib. bdg. 16.60x (ISBN 0-88411-623-9). Amereon Ltd.
Skyscraper. Faith Baldwin Cuthrell. LC 76-40436. 1976. 6.95 (ISBN 0-88411-623-9). Aeonian Press.
Skyscraper. Faith Baldwin Cuthrell. LC 31-247801. 1931. Cosmopolitan Book Corporation.
Skyscraper Murder. Samuel Spewack. The Macaulay Company.
Skytip. Eliot Reed, pseud. LC 50-11192. 1950. Published for the Crime Club by Doubleday.
Skywinder Mystery. Alan Gregg. LC 42-20094. 1942. Doubleday, Doran & Company, Inc.
Skywinder Mystery. Gertrude Ethel Mallette. LC 42-20094. 1942. Doubleday, Doran.
Slab Happy. Richard S. Prather. (Shell Scott Ser). 1969. pap. 0.60 o.p. (R2118, GM). Fawcett World.
Sladd's Evil: A Novel. 1st Amer. Ed. Philip McCutchan. LC 67-14607. 1967. 4.50. John Day.
Slade. Warwick Deeping. LC 43-114633. 1943. Dial Press.
Slade of the Yard. Richard Harry Starr. LC 33-19708. 1933. R. M. McBride & Company.

Slade, Range Detective. Gene Tuttle. 1973. 4.50 o.p. Bouregy.
Slade Scores Again. Richard Harry Starr. LC 34-39249. 1933. R. M. McBride & Company.
Slade's Glacier. Robert F Jones. LC 80-28482. 10.95 (ISBN 0-671-25306-9). Simon and Schuster.
Slade's Marauder. Stephen Cade. 288p. (Orig.). 1981. pap. 2.75 (ISBN 0-553-20002-X). Bantam.
Slag. David Hare. 78p. 1971. pap. 4.95 (ISBN 0-571-09643-3). Faber & Faber.
Slag". John Thomas McIntyre. LC 27-213453. 1927. C. Scribner's Sons.
Slain by the Doones. Richard Doddridge Blackmore. LC 74-86137. (Short story index reprint series). 1969. Books for Libraries Press.
Slain by the Doones. Richard Doddridge Blackmore. LC 6-13139. 1895. Dodd, Mead and Company.
Slain by the Doones: And Other Stories. Richard Doddridge Blackmore. LC 6-13140. 1895. Dodd, Mead and Company.
Slam the Big Door. John Dann MacDonald. LC 60-2221. (Gold medal books, s961). 1960. Fawcett Publications.
Slambangaree: And Other Stories. Richard Kendall Munkittrick. 1897. R. H. Russell.
Slammer. Ben Greer. LC 74-20351. 1975. 8.95 (ISBN 0-689-10649-1). Atheneum.
Slammer. Ben Greer. 1977. 1.75 (ISBN 0-380-01845-4). Avon.
Slan. Alfred Elton Van Vogt. LC 51-14040. (Science fiction adventures). 1951. Simon and Schuster.
Slan. Alfred Elton Van Vogt. LC 75-439. (Garland Library of Science Fiction). 1975. 11.00 (ISBN 0-8240-1441-3). Garland Pub.
Slan. Alfred Elton Van Vogt. (Berkley medallion book). 1975. (pbk.) 0.95 (ISBN 0-425-02900-X). Berkley Pub. Co.
Slan. Alfred Elton Van Vogt. (A Berkley Medallion Book). 1977. 1.25. (ISBN 0-425-03352-X). Berkley Pub. Corp.
Slan. Alfred Elton Van Vogt. LC 47-924. (Arkham house novels of fantasy and terror. 3). 1946. Arkham House.
Slander. Arthur Somers Roche. LC 33-220473. Sears Publishing Company.
Slander of Witches. Richard Gehman. LC 54-10950. Rinehart.
Slandered. Vida Hurst. LC 36-17966. J. H. Hopkins & Son, Inc.
Slanderers. Warwick Deeping. LC 5-5441. 1905. Harper & Brothers.
Slane's Long Shots. Edward Phillips Oppenheim. LC 30-32844. 1930. Little, Brown, and Company.
Slang: A Story of Steel and Stocks. Donald McGibeny. LC 22-7757. The Bobbs-Merrill Company.
Slang Fables from Afar. Alfred Leon Kleberg. LC 3-13591. 1903. Phoenix Publishing Co.
Slant Eyed Angel. new ed. J. Van Der Hoeven. Tr. by Mike Zwart. 1978. pap. text ed. 5.00x (ISBN 0-901072-56-7). Humanities.
Slant of the Wild Wind. Garland Roark. LC 52-5127. 1952. Doubleday.
Slanting Earth: A Novel of Modern Science and Primitive Human Passions. 1st Ed. Blair A Haun. LC 60-14914. Greenwich Book Publishers.
Slanting Light. Gerda Charles. LC 63-18439. 1963. Knopf.
Slap Shot". Richard Woodley. (Berkley Medallion Book). (Illus.). 1.50 (ISBN 0-425-03339-2). Berkley Pub. Corp.
Slapstick. Kurt Vonnegut. 256p. 1982. pap. 2.95 (ISBN 0-440-18009-0). Dell.
Slapstick: Or Lonesome No More! Kurt Vonnegut. LC 77-357080. (Illus.). 1976. 3.50 (ISBN 0-224-01342-4). J. Cape.
Slapstick: Or, Lonesome No More! limited 1st ed. Kurt Vonnegut. LC 77-368812. (Illus.). 1976. Franklin Library.
Slapstick or Lonesome No More. Kurt Vonnegut. 1978. pap. 7.95 (ISBN 0-440-58009-9, Delta). Dell.
Slapstick: Or, Lonesome No More!: a Novel. Kurt Vonnegut. LC 76-15605. (Illus.). 7.95. Delacorte Press/S. Lawrence.
Slash G Hombre. Tom J Hopkins. LC 46-21124. 1946. Phoenix Press.
Slash-R Ranch. T. W. Ford. LC 49-11925. 1949. Phoenix Press.
Slash 44. Al P Nelson. LC 34-365627. Phoenix Press.
Slashed Portrait. Jeanne Hines. LC 73-14916. 1973. (pbk.) 0.75. Dell Pub. Co.
Slashed to Ribbons in Defense of Love & Other Stories. Felice Picano. 200p. (Orig.). 1983. pap. 6.95 (ISBN 0-9604724-2-8). Gay Pr NY.
Slasher. William Arden, pseud. LC 82-5176. 1982. 12.95 (ISBN 0-89340-398-9). J. Curley.
Slasher. Max Collins. (Berkley Medallion Book). 1977. 1.50 (ISBN 0-425-03499-2). Berkley Pub. Corp.
Slasher. Edson T. Hamill. 1976. (pbk.) 1.25. Leisure Books.
Slasher: A Novel of Suspense. Dennis Lynds. LC 79-27602. 7.95 (ISBN 0-396-07822-2). Dodd, Mead.
Slater's Book. James Wyckoff. LC 75-14847. 1976. 5.95 (ISBN 0-385-08662-8). Doubleday.
Slater's Book. James Wyckoff. LC 76-52377. 1977. 8.95 (ISBN 0-8161-6458-4). G. K. Hall.
Slater's Planet see Planeta Fantasma.
Slattery Stands Alone. Steven C Lawrence. 1976. (pbk.) 0.95. Leisure Books.
Slattery's Gun Says No. Steven C Lawrence. (Slattery#5). 1975. (pbk.) 0.95. Leisure Books.
Slattery's Hurricane. Herman Wouk. LC 56-6725. (Perma books, M-4050). 1956. Permabooks.
Slattery's Range. Richard Edward Wormser. LC 57-12162. 1957. Abelard -- Schuman.
Slaughter. Henry Clement. (Orig.). 1972. pap. 0.75 o.p. (07263). Curtis.
Slaughter at Crucifix Canyon. Johanas L. Bouma. LC 75-21648. 176p. (Orig.). 1975. pap. 1.75 (ISBN 0-89041-253-7, 3253). Major Bks.
Slaughter City. (Sergeant Ser.: No. 6). 208p. (Orig.). 1981. pap. text ed. 2.25 (ISBN 0-553-14712-9). Bantam.
Slaughter House. Stutely David Sikes. LC 31-10079. S. D. Sikes.
Slaughter Road. George G. Gilman, pseud. (Edge Ser.: No. 22). 160p. 1977. pap. 1.95 (ISBN 0-523-42029-3). Pinnacle Bks.
Slaughter Run. Axel Kilgore. (They Call Me the Mercenary Ser.). (Orig.). 1981. pap. 2.25 (ISBN 0-89083-719-8). Zebra.
Slaughter Summit. Mark Mandell. (Nazi Hunter Ser.: No. 2). 208p. (Orig.). 1982. pap. 2.25 (ISBN 0-523-41445-5). Pinnacle Bks.
Slaughterday. George G. Gilman, pseud. (Edge Ser: No. 24). 1977. pap. 1.75 (ISBN 0-523-41302-5). Pinnacle Bks.
Slaughtered Lovelies. Don Stanford, pseud. LC 51-26344. (Gold medal book, 116). 1950. Fawcett Publications.
Slaughterhouse-Five. Kurt Vonnegut, Jr. pap. 2.95 (ISBN 0-440-18029-5). Dell.
Slaughterhouse Five; or, the Children's Crusade. Kurt Vonnegut, Jr. 1974. pap. 3.95 (ISBN 0-440-58029-3, Delta). Dell.
Slaughterhouse Informer. Edward S Hyams. LC 55-35187. 1955. Longmans, Green.
Slaughterhouse Informer: A Novel. Edward S Hyams. LC 55-11319. 1955. Lippincott.
Slaughter's Big Rip-off. A. Kane. 1973. pap. 0.75 o.p. (07320). Curtis.
Slaughter's Way. John Thomas Edson. 1974. (pbk.) 0.75. Bantam Books.
Slav Soul, and Other Stories. Aleksandr Ivanovich Kuprin. Ed. by Stephen Graham. LC 78-150547. (Short story index reprint series). 1971. (ISBN 0-8369-3844-5). Books for Libraries Press.
Slav Soul: And Other Stories. Aleksandr Ivanovich Kuprin. Tr. by Graham, Stephen & Graham, Ross (Savary) (Half-title: Putnam's Russian library, under the editorship of Stephen Graham). 1916. G. P. Putnam's Sons.
Slave. Richard Hildreth. LC 72-8141. 1972. (ISBN 0-8422-8076-6). MSS Information Corp.
Slave. Richard Hildreth. LC 73-93626. 1970. (ISBN 0-512-00332-7). Garrett Press.
Slave. Isaac B. Singer. 1980. pap. 2.50 (ISBN 0-449-24188-2, Crest). Fawcett.
Slave. Isaac Bashevis Singer. Tr. by Cecil Hemley. 1962. 10.95 (ISBN 0-374-26580-1); pap. 4.95 (ISBN 0-374-50680-9). FS&G.
Slave. Isaac Bashevis Singer. 1979. pap. 4.95 o.p. (ISBN 0-374-50680-9). FS&G.
Slave: A Romance. Robert Smythe Hichens. LC 99-5078. 1899. H. S. Stone & Company.
Slave and Master: The Story of Spartacus. Jacques Perdue. 1960. Macaulay Co.
Slave Compulsion. X. 1972. pap. 1.75 o.s.i. (V1104K, Venus). Grove.
Slave Dreads Her Work. Nathan Whiting. 1980. pap. 3.00 (ISBN 0-914610-15-5). Hanging Loose.
Slave Empire. Norman Gant. (Orig.). 1969. pap. 0.95 o.p. (75070). Lancer.
Slave Girl. Buchi Emecheta. LC 77-77559. 1977. 7.95 (ISBN 0-8076-0872-6). G. Braziller.
Slave Girl: A Novel. 2d ed. Buchi Emecheta. LC 79-25651. 1980. 7.95 (ISBN 0-8076-0952-8). Braziller.
Slave Girl of Gor. John Norman. (Science Fiction Ser). 1977. pap. 2.95 (ISBN 0-87997-679-9, UE1679). DAW Bks.
Slave King. Robert Tralins. (Orig.). 1970. pap. 0.95 o.p. (65-470). Paperback Lib.
Slave King. From the Bug-Jargal of Victor Hugo Also Saint Domingo. Victor Marie Hugo. LC 7-660375. (Added t.-p.: The library of romance v. 6). 1833. Carey, Lea and Blanchard.
Slave Mistress. John Racine. 192p. 1973. pap. 1.95 o.p. (ISBN 0-87977-183-6, DBB183). Dansk Blue Bk.
Slave of Circumstances: A Story of New York. Ernest De Lancey Pierson. LC 7-35899. Belford, Clarke & Co.
Slave of Circumstances: A Story of New York. Ernest De Lancey Pierson. LC 5258. (On cover: Eagle series. no. 178). 1900. Street & Smith.
Slave of Ea: A Sumerian Legend. Eugene Frank Molnar. LC 35-562325. Dorrance & Company, Inc.
Slave of Frankenstein. Robert John Myers. LC 75-38877. 7.95 (ISBN 0-397-01126-1). Lippincott.
Slave of Passion. Katherine Tobias, pseud. (Orig.). 1978. pap. 2.25 (ISBN 0-89083-425-3). Zebra.
Slave of Passion: Or, The Fruits of Werter. A Novel... LC 11-17964. 1802. Printed by J. Hoff.
Slave of Sarma. Jeffrey Lord. (Blade Ser., No. 4). 192p. 1973. pap. 2.25 (ISBN 0-523-41721-7). Pinnacle Bks.
Slave of Sarma. Jeffrey Lord. (Richard Blade Ser). 1970. pap. 0.75 o.p. (75-305). Manor Bks.
Slave of Silence. Fred Merrick White. LC 6-24582. 1906. Little, Brown, and Company.
Slave of the Warmonger. Axel Kilgore. (They Call Me the Mercenary: No. 7). (Orig.). 1982. pap. 2.50 (ISBN 0-89083-917-4). Zebra.
Slave: Or, Memoirs of Archy Moore. Richard Hildreth. LC 68-57530. (Illus.). 1968. Gregg Press.
Slave: Or, Memoirs of Archy Moore Pseud.... 3d ed.... ed. Richard Hildreth. LC 16-7012. 1840. Massachusetts Anti-Slavery Society.
Slave Prince: A Story Founded on Fact. Archdeacon Chiswell. LC 70-99357. 1970. Repr. of 1890 ed. lib. bdg. 15.00 o.p. (ISBN 0-8411-0028-4). Afro Am.
Slave Rebellion. Norman Daniels. 1970. pap. 0.95 o.p. (65-378). Paperback Lib.
Slave Safari. Richard Sapir & Warren Murphy. LC 77-353532. (Destroyer: 13). 1976. 0.50 (ISBN 0-552-10082-X). Corgi.
Slave Ship. Harold Calin. 1977. pap. 1.75 o.s.i. (ISBN 0-8439-0478-X, Leisure Bks). Nordon Pubns.
Slave Ship. Eric Corder. LC 76-92067. 1969. 5.95. McKay.
Slave Ship. Mary Johnston. LC 24-27995. 1924. Little, Brown, and Company.
Slave Ship. Frederik Pohl. LC 56-13477. (Ballantine books, 192). 1957. Ballantine Books.
Slave Ship from Sergan. Gregory Kern. ("Cap Kennedy" Novel). 1973. (pbk.) 0.75. DAW Books.
Slave Ship. Translated by Eithne Wilkins and Ernst Kaiser. Bruno Erich Werner. LC 51-10869. 1951. Pantheon.
Slave Stealer. Boyd Upchurch. 1968. 6.95 o.p. Weybright.
Slave Stealer: A Novel. Boyd Upchurch. LC 68-12869. 1968. Weybright and Talley.
Slave to Duty: & Other Women. Alice French. LC 98-730. 1898. H. S. Stone & Company.
Slave Trade: A Novel. Herbert Gold. LC 78-73862. 8.95 (ISBN 0-87795-217-5). Arbor House.
Slave Who Was His Master. Elizabeth C. Isambard-Owen. 4.50 o.s.i. (ISBN 0-8181-0285-3). Pageant-Poseidon.
Slave Woman. Denise Robins. LC 35-4414. The Macaulay Company.
Slavers. Peter McCurtin. (Carmody Ser). (Orig.). 1971. pap. 0.75 o.p. (B75-2086). Belmont-Tower.
Slavers. Peter McCurtin. (Carmody Ser., No. 1). 1974. pap. 0.95 o.p. (LB127NK). Leisure Bks.
Slavers. C. C. Parx. 224p. (Orig.). 1980. pap. 2.25 (ISBN 0-441-76963-2, Pub. by Charter Bks). Ace Bks.
Slaver's Adventure on Land and Sea. William Henry Thomes. (On cover: The detective and adventure library, no. 11). 1889. A. T. Loyd & Co.
Slaver's Adventures on Land and Sea. William Henry Thomes. LC 13-12916. (Added t.-p.: The ocean life series). Lee and Shepard.
Slaver's Adventures on Land and Sea. William Henry Thomes. LC 12-16425. (Half-title: Ocean life series). 1884. A. T. Loyd & Company.
Slaver's Adventures on Sea and Land. William Henry Thomes. (On cover: The library of choice fiction, no. 21). 1891. Laird & Lee.
Slavery Unmasked. Philo Tower. Repr. of 1856 ed. 14.00 o.p. (ISBN 0-8398-1971-4). Gregg.
Slaves. Roderick Thorp. LC 77-179084. 1972. 6.95. M. Evans; Distributed by J. B. Lippincott, Philadelphia.
Slave's Blood. Robert R. Vaughan, Jr. (Orig.). 1969. pap. 0.95 o.p. (75-098). Lancer.
Slaves Cottage. George Locke Howe. LC 35-139041. Coward-McCann.
Slaves of Chance: A Novel. Ferrier Langworthy. 1900. L. C. Page & Company.
Slaves of Desire. Allan C Latson. LC 57-16372. 1956. Forum Pub. Co.
Slaves of Destiny. Pearl Doles Bell. LC 26-12980. W. J. Watt & Co.
Slaves of Folly: A Narrative. William Horace Brown. LC 6-17236. 1889. Rand, McNally & Company.
Slaves of Freedom. Coningsby William Dawson. LC 16-22979. 1916. 1.40. H. Holt and Company.
Slaves of Heaven. Edmund Cooper. LC 73-87180. 1974. 5.95 (ISBN 0-399-11284-7). Putnam.
Slaves of Paris... Emile Gaboriau. LC 6-44499. (On cover: Lovell's library. no. 1152). 1888. J. W. Lovell Company.
Slaves of Paris. From the French of Emile Gaboriau... Emile Gaboriau. LC 6-44500. Estes & Lauriat.
Slaves of Sabrehill. Raymond Giles. 1978. pap. 2.95 (ISBN 0-449-13970-0, GM). Fawcett.
Slaves of Sabrehill. Raymond Giles. (Fawcett gold medal book.). 1975. (pbk.) 1.75. Fawcett.
Slaves of Sleep. La Fayette Ronald Hubbard. LC 48-9282. 1948. Shasta Publishers.
Slaves of Society: A Comedy in Covers. Hlen Upward. LC 68395. 1900. Harper & Brothers.
Slaves of Success. Elliott Flower. LC 5-9060.
Slaves of Sumuru. Sax Rohmer, pseud. (Sumuru Ser.). 1979. 6.50. Bookfinger.
Slaves of the Eye. Charles Windburn. LC 78-68008. pap. 1.95 o.s.i. (ISBN 0-89516-050-1). Condor Pub Co.
Slaves of the Lamp. Pamela Frank. LC 64-105413. (Her Clothes of a king's son, a novel in three volumes; v.2). 5.95. Random.
Slaves of the Lamp: Being the Adventures of Yorke Norroy in This Quest of the Four Jade Plates; a Manhattan Nights' Entertainment. George Fitzalan Bronson Howard. LC 17-30730. W. J. Watt & Company.
Slaves of the Ring: Or, Before and After. Frederick William Robinson. LC 7-41988. 1863. T. O. H. P. Burnham.
Slaves of the Sawdust a Story. Amye Reade. J. W. Lovell Company.
Slave's Revenge. Robert Tralins. 1969. pap. 0.95 o.p. (75-094). Lancer.
Slaves Today: A Story of Liberia. George Samuel Schuyler. LC 70-76120. 1969. McGrath Pub. Co.
Slaves Today: A Story of Liberia. George Samuel Schuyler. LC 72-99887. 1969. AMS Press.
Slaves Today: A Story of Liberia. George Samuel Schuyler. LC 31-32949. 1931. Brewer, Warren & Putnam.
Slay Me a Sinner. Pierre Audemars. LC 79-92332. 1980. 9.95 (ISBN 0-8027-5417-1). Walker.
Slay Me Suddenly. Antony Brown. LC 69-15711. 1969. 4.50. Walker.
Slay Ride. Frank Kane. LC 50-5350. 1950. Washburn.
Slay Ride for a Lady. Harry Whittington. LC 50-11282. (Handi-book mystery, 120). 1950. Quinn Pub. Co.
Slay the Murderer: A Sheriff Macready Detective Story. Hugh Holman. LC 46-803. ("Mill Circle mysteries."). 1946. M. S. Mill Co., Inc.
Slay Time. Paul Muller. LC 68-8328. 1968. 3.95. Roy Publishers.
Slayboys. Philip Kirk. (Butler Ser.: No. 3). pap. 1.75 o.s.i. (ISBN 0-8439-0683-9, Leisure Bks). Nordon Pubns.
Slayer and the Slain. Helen McCloy. LC 57-10031. 1957. Random House.
Slayer of Souls. Robert William Chambers. 1.75. George H. Doran Company.
Slayer of Souls. Robert William Chambers. LC 77-84207. (Lost Race and Adult Fantasy Fiction). 1978. 20.00 (ISBN 0-405-10963-6). Arno Press.
Slayground. Richard Stark. 1971. 4.95 o.p. (ISBN 0-394-46430-3, 464303). Random.
Slayground. Donald E Westlake. LC 79-159379. 1971. 4.95 (ISBN 0-394-46430-3). Random House.
Slayride. Dick Francis. LC 73-14311. 1974. 5.95 (ISBN 0-06-011336-7). Harper & Row.
Sled Trails and White Waters. George Tracy Marsh. LC 29-23789. The Penn Publishing Company.
Sledge. Richard Voorhees Risley. (Half-title: The human tragedy v 1). R. G. Badger & Co.
Sledgehammer. Walter H Wager. LC 79-110986. 1970. 5.95. Macmillan.
Sleek for the Long Flight. William Matthews. 1972. pap. 1.95 o.p. (ISBN 0-394-70762-1). Random.
Sleep. John Creasey. 1971. pap. 0.75 o.p. (ISBN 0-447-74759-2). Lancer.
Sleep and His Brother. Peter Dickinson. LC 71-138800. 1971. 5.95 (ISBN 0-06-011039-2). Harper & Row.
Sleep & Learn. David Curtis. (Orig.). 1972. pap. 1.25 o.s.i. (33-009). Lancer.
Sleep Baters. John Lymington, pseud. 1971. pap. 0.75 o.p. (532-00456-075). Manor Bks.
Sleep Before Evening. Donald Olson. LC 79-16350. 8.95 (ISBN 0-312-72860-3). St. Martin's Press.
Sleep Eaters. John Lymington, pseud. 1978. pap. 1.50 (ISBN 0-532-15317-0). Woodhill.

Sleep Has His House. Anna Kavan. 1980. cloth 11.95 (ISBN 0-935576-00-2). Kesend Pub Ltd.
Sleep Has His House. Anna Kavan. 1980. 11.95 (ISBN 0-935576-01-0); pap. 6.95. Kesend Pub Ltd.
Sleep Has His House. Anna Kavan. LC 79-26730. 1980. Repr. 11.95 o.p. (ISBN 0-935576-00-2). Orenda-Unity.
Sleep in Peace. Phyllis Eleanor Bentley. LC 38-273133. 1938. The Macmillan Company.
Sleep in the Sun. Alan B Moody & Earle, Edwin, 1904- Illus. LC 45-3048. 1945. Houghton Mifflin Company.
Sleep in the Woods. Dorothy Eden. 256p. 1981. pap. 2.50 (ISBN 0-449-23706-0, Crest). Fawcett.
Sleep in Thunder. Ed Lacy. LC 63-15125. (Tempo books, T48). 1964. Grosset & Dunlap.
Sleep Is Deep. Hugh Lawrence Nelson. LC 52-9601. (Murray Hill mystery). 1952. Rinehart.
Sleep Is for the Rich. Donald MacKenie. 1972. Repr. lib. bdg. 8.95 o.p. (ISBN 0-8161-6030-9, Large Print Bks). G K Hall.
Sleep Is for the Rich. Donald MacKenzie. LC 78-152060. (Midnight novel of suspense). 1971. 5.95 (ISBN 0-395-12669-X). Houghton Mifflin.
Sleep Is for the Rich. Donald MacKenzie. LC 72-361. (Midnight novel of suspense). 1972. 8.95 (ISBN 0-8161-6030-9). G. K. Hall.
Sleep It off, Lady. Jean Rhys. 1978. 1.95 (ISBN 0-445-04208-7). Popular Library.
Sleep It off, Lady: Stories. Jean Rhys. LC 74-15889. 7.95 (ISBN 0-06-013572-7). Harper & Row.
Sleep Long, My Love. Hillary Waugh. LC 59-12657. 1959. Published for the Crime Club by Doubleday.
Sleep, My Love. Robert Lee Martin. LC 52-12950. (Red badge detective). 1953. Dodd, Mead.
Sleep My Love. Elizabeth Norman. 1980. pap. 2.50 (ISBN 0-380-48694-6, 48694). Avon.
Sleep No More. Margaret Erskine. (Ace gothic). 1974. (pbk.) 0.95. Ace Books.
Sleep No More. Sam S Taylor. LC 49-11488. (Gilt edged mystery). 1949. Dutton.
Sleep No More: Railway, Canal, and Other Stories of the Supernatural. Lionel Thomas Caswell Rolt. 1975. (ISBN 0-85527-022-5). Branchline.
Sleep No More: Twenty Masterpieces of Horror for the Connoisseur. Ed. by August William Derleth. LC 44-7662. 1944. Farrar & Rinehart, Inc.
Sleep No More. 1st Amer. Ed. George Sims. LC 66-22287. 1966. 3.95. Harcourt.
Sleep of Baby Filbertson, and Other Stories. Illustrated by Tom Keogh. 1st Ed. James Leo Herlihy. LC 59-5059. 1959. Dutton.
Sleep of Death. Anne Morice. LC 82-17023. 1983. 10.95 (ISBN 0-312-72863-8). St. Martin's Press.
Sleep of Life. Richard Gordon. (O.s.i.). 1975. 7.95 o.s.i. (ISBN 0-8037-6015-9). Dial.
Sleep of Life: A Novel. Gordon Ostlere. LC 75-1029. 1975. 7.95 (ISBN 0-8037-6015-9). Dial Press.
Sleep of Reason. Charles Percy Snow. LC 69-12600. (His Strangers and brothers, 10). 1969. 6.95. Scribner.
Sleep of Reason: A Novel. Warren Miller. LC 60-14149. 1960. Little, Brown.
Sleep of the Just: Novel. Mouloud Mammeri. LC 58-2141. 1958. Beacon Press.
Sleep off the Highway. Patricia J. Sherman. (Orig.). 1979. pap. 1.95. Woodhill.
Sleep-Rider: Or, The Old Boy in the Omnibus. Edward Sherman Gould. LC 6-27644. Winchester.
Sleep till Noon. Max Shulman. LC 50-6849. 1950. Doubleday.
Sleep, Two, Three, Four! John Neufeld. 1972. 0.75. Avon.
Sleep, Two, Three, Four! A Political Thriller. John Neufeld. LC 72-148422. 1971. 3.95 (ISBN 0-06-024378-3). Harper & Row.
Sleep-Walker. A Novel. Paul H Gerrard. (choice series, no. 103). (ledger library, no. 103). 1894. R. Bonner's Sons.
Sleep-Walkers. David Karp. LC 66-70228. 1966. Penguin.
Sleep with Strangers. 1st Ed. Dolores Birk Hitchens. LC 55-5297. 1955. Published for the Crime Club by Doubleday.
Sleep with the Devil. Day Keene. LC 54-41716. (Lion book, 204). 1954. Lion Books.
Sleep Without Dreams. Henry Kane. 1970. pap. 0.75 o.p. (ISBN 0-447-74694-4). Lancer.
Sleep Without Morning. Elinore Denniston. LC 71-180927. (Red badge novel of suspense). 1972. 4.95 (ISBN 0-396-06492-2). Dodd, Mead.
Sleep Without Morning. Elinore Denniston. 1973. 0.75. Dell.
Sleep Without Morning. Rae Foley. LC 71-180927. (Red Badge Suspense Novel Ser). 244p. 1972. 4.95 o.p. (ISBN 0-396-06492-2). Dodd.
Sleeper. Eric Clark. LC 79-5569. 1980. 11.95 (ISBN 0-689-11032-4). Atheneum.
Sleeper. Bruce Crowther. LC 76-57865. 1977. 6.95 (ISBN 0-8027-5372-8). Walker.
Sleeper. Holly Roth. LC 54-13496. (Inner sanctum mystery). 1955. Simon and Schuster.
Sleeper Agent. Ib Melchior. LC 74-15882. 1975. 7.95 (ISBN 0-06-012942-5). Harper & Row.
Sleeper Awakes. Herbert George Wells. 3.00 o.p. (ISBN 0-00-422691-7). Collins-World.
Sleeper of the Moonlit Ranges: A New Novel. Edison Marshall. LC 25-8267. 1925. Cosmopolitan Book Corporation.
Sleeper Wakes. George Fort Gibbs. LC 41-729822. 1941. D. Appleton-Century Company, Incorporated.
Sleepers Can Kill. Simon Jay, pseud. LC 68-17816. 1968. Published for the Crime Club by Doubleday.
Sleepers East. Frederick Nebel. LC 33-147930. 1933. Little, Brown, and Company.
Sleepers of Erin: A Lovejoy Novel of Suspense. Jonathan Gash, pseud. LC 82-14628. 13.95 (ISBN 0-525-24163-9). Dutton.
Sleepers of Roraima: A Carib Trilogy. Wilson Harris. (Illus.). 82p. 1970. 5.95 o.p. (ISBN 0-571-09272-1). Faber & Faber.
Sleeping & the Dead: Thirty Uncanny Tales. Ed. by August William Derleth. LC 47-11375. 1947. Pellegrini & Cudahy.
Sleeping and Waking. Bridget Chetwynd. LC 45-2043. 1944. Hutchinson & Co. Ltd.
Sleeping Around. Cheryl Nash. 1974. (pbk.) 1.50. Dell Book.
Sleeping Beauty. Faith Baldwin. 1976. Repr. of 1947 ed. lib. bdg. 14.40x (ISBN 0-88411-624-7). Amereon Ltd.
Sleeping Beauty. Faith Baldwin Cuthrell. LC 76-41704. 1976. 6.95 (ISBN 0-88411-624-7). Aeonian Press.
Sleeping Beauty. Faith Baldwin Cuthrell. LC 47-1630. 1947. Rinehart & Company, Inc.
Sleeping Beauty. Faith Baldwin Cuthrell. 1973. (pbk.) 0.95. Warner Paperback Lib.
Sleeping Beauty. L. L. Greene. (Orig.). 1982. pap. 2.50 (ISBN 0-451-11548-1, AE1548, Sig). NAL.
Sleeping Beauty. Kenneth Millar. LC 72-11037. 1973. 5.95 (ISBN 0-394-48474-6). Knopf.
Sleeping Beauty. Kenneth Millar. 1974. (pbk.) 1.50. Bantam Books.
Sleeping Beauty. Lillian O'Donnell. 1973. pap. 0.75 o.p. (94366-075). Beagle Bks.
Sleeping Beauty. Berta Ruck. LC 36-19987. 1936. Dodd, Mead & Company.
Sleeping Beauty. Elizabeth Taylor. LC 53-7288. 1953. Viking Press.
Sleeping Beauty Murders. Lillian O'Donnell. LC 66-24241. (Raven book). 1967. Abelard-Schuman.
Sleeping Bride. Dorothy Eden. 1976. (pbk.) 1.50. Ace Books.
Sleeping Car Murders. Sebastien Japrisot. (Crime Ser.). Orig. Title: Ten-Thirty from Marseille. 1978. pap. 1.95 o.p. (ISBN 0-14-004992-4). Penguin.
Sleeping-Car Murders. Jean Baptiste Rossi. LC 78-15185. 1978. 1.95 (ISBN 0-14-004992-4). Penguin Books.
Sleeping Cat. Isabel Egenton Ostrander. LC 26-7766. 1926. R. M. McBride & Company.
Sleeping Child. Alice Grant Rosman. LC 35-8754. Minton, Balch & Company.
Sleeping Death. George Douglas Howard Cole & Margaret Isabel Postgate Cole. LC 36-6998. 1936. Publ. for the Crime Club, Inc., by Doubleday, Doran & Company, Inc.
Sleeping Dogs. Frank Ross. LC 77-88911. 1978. 8.95 (ISBN 0-689-10850-8). Atheneum.
Sleeping Dogs. Carolyn Wells. LC 29-12916. 1929. Pub. for The Crime Club, Inc., by Doubleday, Doran & Company, Inc.
Sleeping Dogs: By E. X. Ferrars Pseud. 1st Ed. Morna Doris MacTaggart Brown. LC 60-15506. 1960. Published for the Crime Club by Doubleday.
Sleeping Dogs Lie. Julian Gloag. 1981. pap. 3.50 (ISBN 0-671-42494-7). PB.
Sleeping Dogs Lie: A Novel. Julian Gloag. LC 79-28204. 12.95. E. P. Dutton.
Sleeping Dogs Lying. Kenneth O'Hara. LC 62-9293. (Cock Robin mystery). 1962. Macmillan.
Sleeping Fires. George Robert Gissing. LC 6-43976. 1895. D. Appleton and Company.
Sleeping Fires. George Robert Gissing. 1896. D. Appleton and Company.
Sleeping Fires: A Novel. Gertrude Franklin Horn Atherton. LC 22-2602. Frederick A. Stokes Company.
Sleeping Fury. Martin Donisthorpe Armstrong. LC 29-21690. Harcourt, Brace and Company.
Sleeping Girls Don't Lie: A Mystery. Hansjorg Martin. LC 75-40797. 7.95. St. Martin's Press.
Sleeping Heiress. Phyllis Taylor Pianka. (Orig.). 1980. pap. 1.50 (ISBN 0-440-17551-8). Dell.
Sleeping House Party. Elisabeth Lambert, pseud. LC 51-14104. (Gargoyle mystery). 1951. Coward-McCann.
Sleeping Life. Ruth Rendell. LC 79-10521. 1980. 11.95 (ISBN 0-8161-6711-7). G. K. Hall.
Sleeping Memory. Edward Phillips Oppenheim. LC 2-25046. 1902. G. W. Dillingham Company.
Sleeping Memory. Edward Phillips Oppenheim. LC 10-6184. 1907. Little, Brown, and Company.
Sleeping Mines. 1st Ed. Gertrude E. Bridgeman Finney. LC 51-11672. 1951. Longmans, Green.
Sleeping Mountain. John Harris. LC 58-536721. 1958. W. Sloane Associates.
Sleeping Murder. Agatha Miller Christie. LC 76-21309. 7.95 (ISBN 0-396-07373-5). Dodd, Mead.
Sleeping Murder: Miss Marple's Last Case. Agatha Miller Christie. LC 77-355490. 1976. 3.50 (ISBN 0-00-231785-0). Collins for the Crime Club.
Sleeping on Fists. Alberto Rios. 36p. 1981. pap. 5.00 o.p. (ISBN 0-937160-02-4). Dooryard.
Sleeping Partner. Winston Graham. LC 56-9393. 1956. Doubleday.
Sleeping Planet. William R. Jr Burkett. LC 65-118067. 4.95. Doubleday.
Sleeping Salamander. Catherine Carfax, pseud. LC 73-79863. 228p. 1973. 6.95 o.p. (ISBN 0-8128-1603-X). Stein & Day.
Sleeping Salamander. Eleanor M Fairburn. LC 73-79863. 1973. 6.95 (ISBN 0-8128-1603-X). Stein and Day.
Sleeping Sphinx: A Doctor Fell Detective Story. John Dickson Carr. LC 47-173023. 1947. Harper & Brothers.
Sleeping Sword: A Biographical Novel (1798-1805. Pearl Frye. LC 52-6793. 1952. Little, Brown.
Sleeping Tiger. Dominic Devine. LC 68-17114. 1968. 3.95. Walker.
Sleeping Tiger. Marjorie McEvoy. LC 82-45362. (Starlight Romances). 1983. 7.95 (ISBN 0-385-18277-5). Doubleday.
Sleeping Tiger. Rosamunde Pilcher. LC 73-92054. 1974. 6.50. St. Martin's Press.
Sleeping Trees. Gilbert Maxwell. LC 49-11756. 1949. Little, Brown.
Sleeping Witness. 1st Ed. Mary Violet Heberden. LC 51-12101. 1951. Published for the Crime Club by Doubleday.
Sleepless Candle. Anne Frances Einselen. LC 41-4924. 1941. Macrae-Smith Company.
Sleepless Candle. Anne Paterson. LC 41-492427. 1941. Macrae-Smith-Company.
Sleepless Days. Jurek Becker. LC 79-1811. 7.95 (ISBN 0-15-182982-9). Harcourt Brace Jovanovich.
Sleepless Moon. 1st Ed. Herbert Ernest Bates. LC 56-5927. Little, Brown.
Sleepless Night of Eugene Delacroix. John Yau. LC 79-55713. (Illus.). 3.00 (ISBN 0-913722-20-0). Release Press.
Sleepless Nights. Elizabeth Hardwick. LC 78-21798. 8.95 (ISBN 0-394-50527-1). Random House.
Sleepless Nights. Elizabeth Hardwick. LC 79-23246. 1980. 2.50 (ISBN 0-394-74363-6). Vintage Books.
Sleepwalker: A Novel of Suspense. Helen McCloy. LC 73-15037. 1974. 4.95 (ISBN 0-396-06876-6). Dodd, Mead.
Sleepwalkers. Arthur Koestler. 1963. pap. 6.95 o.p. (ISBN 0-448-00159-4, G&D). Putnam Pub Group.
Sleepwalkers: A Trilogy. Hermann Broch & Muir, Mrs. Willa, Tr. LC 32-26961. 1932. Little, Brown, and Company.
Sleepwalker's World. Gordon R Dickson. LC 73-151488. 1971. 5.95. Lippincott.
Sleepwalking. Meg Wolitzer. LC 81-48290. 12.00 (ISBN 0-394-52155-2). Random House.
Sleepy Horse Range. William Colt MacDonald. LC 38-5360. Covici-Friede.
Sleepy Lagoon Mystery. S. Guy Endore. LC 72-85222. pap. 5.00 o.p. (ISBN 0-88247-187-2). R & E Res Assoc.
Sleeveless Errand: A Novel. Norah C James. LC 29-125307. 1929. W. Morrow & Company.
Sleigh Bell Trail. Mae Foster Jay. LC 37-280. W. A. Wilde Company.
Sleight of Crime. Ed. by Cedric E. Clute, Jr. & Nicholas Lewin. LC 76-6261. 10.00 (ISBN 0-8092-8081-7) (ISBN 0-8092-7978-9). H. Regnery Co.
Sleight of Crime: Sixteen Classic Tales of Murder, Mayhem & Magic. Ed. by Cedric E. Clute, Jr. & Nicholas Lewin. LC 76-6261. (Illus.). 1977. o. p. 10.00 o.p. (ISBN 0-8092-8081-7); pap. 4.95 o.p. (ISBN 0-8092-7978-9). Contemp Bks.
Slender Clue. Emma Murdoch Van Deventer. (library of choice fiction no. 35). 1891. Laird & Lee.
Slender Reed. Helen Huntington. LC 49-8097.
Slender Reed: A Biographical Novel of James Knox Polk, Eleventh President of the United States. Noel Bertram Gerson. LC 65-10643. 5.95. Doubleday.
Slender Thread. P. J. Merrill. LC 59-11767. 1959. Harcourt, Brace.
Slender Thread. Holly Roth. LC 59-11767. 1959. Harcourt, Brace.
Sleuth and the Liar. 1st Ed. John Sherwood. LC 61-9551. 1961. Published for the Crime Club by Doubleday.
Sleuth of St. James's Square. Melville Davisson Post. LC 20-18613. 1920. D. Appleton and Company.
Sleuth Patrol. Manly Wade Wellman. LC 47-30401. 1947. T. Nelson.
Sleuths and Consequences: An Anthology of Mystery Stories. Mystery Writers of America. Ed. by Thomas Blanchard Dewey. LC 66-26156. 1966. Simon and Schuster.
Sleuths of the Saddle. James Shaffer. LC 42-17838. 1942. Phoenix Press.
Sleuths: Twenty-Three Great Detectives of Fiction and Their Best Stories. Ed. by Kenneth Macgowan. LC 31-28030. Harcourt, Brace and Company.
Slice of Hell. John Roscoe. LC 54-6631. 1954. Crown Publishers.
Slice of Life. James Kisner. (Orig.). 1982. pap. text ed. 2.95 (ISBN 0-8217-1055-9). Zebra.
Slices from a Long Loaf. H. C Stiefel. LC 5-38105. Bissell Block Publishing Company.
Slices Of Ham. Peter M Bradley. 30p. (Orig.). 1982. pap. 4.00 (ISBN 0-9608222-0-8). Parsley Pr.
Slick. Charles T Hennigan. 1975. (pbk.) 1.50. Bantam Books.
Slick & the Dead. J. D. Hardin. LC 79-83968. (J.D. Hardin Western Ser.: No. 3). 208p. 1979. pap. 1.50 (ISBN 0-87216-555-8). Playboy Pbks.
Slick Revenge. Joseph Nazel. (Iceman). 1974. (pbk.) 1.50 (ISBN 0-87067-452-8). Holloway House.
Slide. Gerald A Browne. LC 75-40510. 8.95 (ISBN 0-87795-099-7). Arbor House.
Slide Area: Scenes of Hollywood Life. Gavin Lambert. LC 68-56618. 1968. 4.50. Dial Press.
Slides; a Novel. David Plante. LC 71-144341. 1971. 5.95 (ISBN 0-87645-043-5). Gambit.
Sliding: Short Stories. Leslie Norris. LC 76-20503. 6.95 (ISBN 0-684-14775-0). Scribner.
Slieve Bawn and the Croppy Scout: A Historical Tale of Seventeen Ninety-Eight in North Connaught. James Joseph Gibbons. LC 14-12893. 1.25. The Kistler Press.
Slight Indiscretion. Leroy Lindley Stineback. LC 9-22746. 1909. Cochrane Publishing Co.
Slight Misunderstanding. Prosper Merimee. Tr. by Douglas Parmee. 1980. pap. 2.95 (ISBN 0-7145-0529-3). Riverrun NY.
Slight Mourning. Catherine Aird, pseud. LC 75-21201. 1976. 5.95 (ISBN 0-385-11476-1). Published for the Crime Club by Doubleday.
Slight Romance. Edith Leverett Dalton. LC 6-33175. 1896. Damrell & Upham.
Slightest Distance. Henry Bromell. LC 74-9775. 1974. 6.95 (ISBN 0-395-19408-3). Houghton Mifflin.
Slightly Disjointed Affair. Irma Dunn. 3.75 o.p. Vantage.
Slightly Imperfect. Ann Chester. LC 56-124562. 1956. Arcadia House.
Slightly Perfect. George Malcolm-Smith. LC 41-126922. Random House C.
Slightly Scarlet. Percy Heath. LC 30-10095. World Wide Publishing Co., Inc.
Slightly Soiled Saint. Gordon F Morkel. 1960. Dorrance.
Slightly Used Woman. Peter Kortner. LC 73-174018. 1973. 2.50 (ISBN 0-491-00954-2). W. H. Allen.
Slightly Used Woman. Peter Kortner. 1974. (pbk.) 1.25 (ISBN 0-523-00296-3). Pinnacle Books.
Sligo. Brendan Wood. LC 47-11596. 1947. Ziff-Davis Pub. Co.
Slim. William Wister Haines. LC 34-227521. 1934. Little, Brown and Company.
Slimtonian Socker. Everett MacDonald. LC 22-9052. G. W. Jacobs & Company.
Sling and the Arrow. Stuart David Engstrand. LC 47-35330. 1947. Creative Age Press.
Slings and Arrows. Edwin Francis Edgett. LC 23-1007. 1922. B. J. Brimmer Company.
Slings and Arrows: And Miss River's Revenge. Frederick John Fargus. LC 6-38436. (On cover: Lovell's library. v. 12. no. 672). 1885. J. W. Lovell Company.
Slinky Jane. Catherine Cookson. 1976. 1.50. New American Library.
Slip-Carriage Mystery. Alister McAllister. LC 28-21975. 1928. Harper & Brothers.
Slip in the Fens, a Novel: With Illustrations by the Author. LC 8-9603. (Leisure hour series no.20). 1873. Holt & Williams.
Slip on a Fat Lady. Philip Norman. LC 79-123982. 1970. 5.95. Harper's Magazine Press.
Slip-up: Fleet Street, Scotland Yard & the Great Train Robbery. Anthony Delano. LC 75-8289. (Illus.). 256p. 1975. 8.95 o.p. (ISBN 0-8129-0576-8). Times Bks.
Sliphammer. Brian Wynne Garfield. 1979. pap. 1.75 (ISBN 0-449-24215-3, Crest). Fawcett.
Slipped Disc. J. Cyriax. 7.50x o.s.i. (ISBN 0-8277-0359-7). British Bk Ctr.
Slipperdown Chant. Jennifer Rigg. LC 76-44339. 6.95 (ISBN 0-679-50663-2). McKay.

Slipperdown Chant I.E. Chhant. Jennifer Rigg. LC 77-14070. 1978. 9.95 (ISBN 0-89340-127-7). J. Curley & Associates.

Slippery Hitch. Gerald Alfred Butler. LC 49-8915. 1949. Rinehart.

Slippery Step. Rae Foley. (Red Badge Novel of Suspence Ser.). 1977. 6.95 o.p. (ISBN 0-396-07404-9). Dodd.

Slippery Step: A Novel of Suspense. Elinore Denniston. LC 77-23321. (Red badge novel of suspense). 6.95 (ISBN 0-396-07404-9). Dodd, Mead.

Slipping-Down Life. Anne Tyler. 1977. 1.95 (ISBN 0-445-08596-7). Popular Library.

Slipping-Down Life. Anne Tyler. LC 76-98663. 1970. 4.95. Knopf.

Slippy McGee: Sometimes Known As the Butterfly Man. Marie Conway Oemler. LC 17-132196. 1917. The Century Co.

Slippy McGee: Sometimes Known As the Butterfly Man. Marie Conway Oemler. LC 20-22039. 1920. The Century Co.

Slippy McGee: Sometimes Known As the Butterfly Man. Marie Conway Oemler. LC 41-281841. 1921. Grosset & Dunlap.

Slippy McGee: Sometimes Known As the Butterfly Man. Marie Conway Oemler. LC 24-20462. 1922. The Century Co.

Slipstream. Roger McDonald. LC 82-84015. 15.50 (ISBN 0-316-55553-3). Little, Brown.

Slipway. Graham Billing. LC 73-4169. 1973. 6.95 (ISBN 0-670-65206-7). Viking Press.

Sliver Sphinx. Andrew Gail Combes. LC 21-12082. The Roxburgh Publishing Company, Inc.

Slocum & the Law. Jake Logan. 224p. (Orig.). 1983. pap. 2.25 (ISBN 0-425-06153-1). Berkley Pub.

Slocum & the Mad Major. Jake Logan. LC 81-85824. (Jake Logan Western Ser). 224p. (Orig.). 1982. pap. 1.95 (ISBN 0-86721-217-9). Playboy Pbks.

Slocum & the Widow Kate. Jake Logan. LC 75-21634. (Jake Logan Western Ser.: No. 3). 224p. 1975. pap. 1.95 (ISBN 0-86721-120-2). Playboy Pbks.

Slocum's Blood. Jake Logan. LC 78-59973. (Jake Logan Western Ser.). 192p. 1978. pap. 1.95 (ISBN 0-87216-880-8). Playboy Pbks.

Slocums Code. Jake Logan. LC 80-85107. (Jake Western Logan Ser.). 224p. (Orig.). 1981. pap. 1.95 (ISBN 0-87216-823-9). Playboy Pbks.

Slocum's Debt. Jake Logan. LC 81-84146. (Jake Logan Western Ser.). 224p. (Orig.). 1982. pap. 1.95 (ISBN 0-86721-071-0). Playboy Pbks.

Slocum's Drive. Jake Logan. 224p. (Orig.). 1983. pap. 2.25 (ISBN 0-425-05998-7). Berkley Pub.

Slocum's Fire. Jake Logan. LC 78-62020. (Jake Logan Western Ser.). 208p. 1979. pap. 1.95 (ISBN 0-87216-867-0). Playboy Pbks.

Slocum's Gamble. Jake Logan. LC 81-84139. (Jake Logan Western Ser.). 224p. (Orig.). 1982. pap. 1.95 (ISBN 0-86721-015-X). Playboy Pbks.

Slocum's Gold. Jake Logan. LC 75-40704. (Jake Logan Western Ser.: No. 6). 192p. 1976. pap. 1.95 (ISBN 0-86721-090-7). Playboy Pbks.

Slocum's Grave. Jake Logan. LC 79-89315. (Jake Logan Western Ser.). 224p. 1980. pap. 1.95. Playboy Pbks.

Slocum's Hell. Jake Logan. LC 79-83961. (Jake Logan Western Ser.). 208p. (Orig.). 1979. pap. 1.95 (ISBN 0-86721-023-0). Playboy Pbks.

Slocum's Rage. Jake Logan. LC 80-82659. (Jake Logan Western Ser.). 256p. (Orig.). 1981. pap. 1.95 (ISBN 0-87216-764-X). Playboy Pbks.

Slocum's Raid. Jake Logan. LC 81-80091. (Jake Logan Western Ser.). 224p. (Orig.). 1981. pap. 1.95 (ISBN 0-87216-863-8). Playboy Pbks.

Slocum's Revenge. Jake Logan. LC 78-59973. (Jake Logan Western Ser.). 208p. 1979. pap. 1.95 (ISBN 0-86721-087-7). Playboy Pbks.

Slocum's Run. Jake Logan. LC 81-82165. (Jake Logan Western Ser.). 224p. (Orig.). 1981. pap. 1.95 (ISBN 0-87216-927-8). Playboy Pbks.

Slocum's Slaughter. Jake Logan. LC 80-80996. (Jake Logan Western Ser.). 208p. (Orig.). 1980. pap. 1.95 (ISBN 0-87216-936-7). Playboy Pbks.

Slocum's Woman. Jake Logan. LC 76-9585. (Jake Logan Western Ser.: No. 9). 208p. 1977. pap. 1.95 (ISBN 0-86721-163-6). Playboy Pbks.

Slocum's Woman. Jake Logan. LC 76-9585. Playboy Press.

Slogum House. Mari Sandoz. LC 37-388709. 1937. Little, Brown and Company.

Slogum House. Mari Sandoz. LC 80-22077. 1981. 17.95 (ISBN 0-8032-4126-7) (ISBN 0-8032-9123-X). University of Nebraska Press.

Sloop of War. Alexander Kent. (Berkley medallion book). 1974. (pbk.) 1.25 (ISBN 0-425-02503-9). Putnam.

Sloop of War. Alexander Kent. LC 77-185055. 1972. 6.95 (ISBN 0-399-10975-7). Putnam.

Slot. John Clagett. LC 58-8320. 1958. Crown Publishers.

Sloth and Heathen Folly. Edward L Robinson. LC 76-167930. 1972. 7.95. Macmillan.

Slouching Towards Kalamazoo. Peter De Vries. LC 83-1026. 13.95 (ISBN 0-316-18172-2). Little, Brown.

Slouching Towards Kalamazoo. Peter De Vries. 228p. 1983. 13.95i (ISBN 0-316-18172-2). Little.

Slow Awakening. Catherine Cookson. LC 76-42259. 1977. 8.95 (ISBN 0-688-03136-6). Morrow.

Slow Awakening. Catherine Cookson. LC 76-363341. 1976. 3.60 (ISBN 0-434-45031-6). Heinemann.

Slow Awakening. Catherine Marchant, pseud. LC 76-42259. 1977. 8.95 o.p. (ISBN 0-688-03136-6). Morrow.

Slow Boat Across. 1st Ed. Harry B Antrotter. LC 52-10346. 1952. Psychological Library.

Slow Bow. Irving Ross Allen. 3.95 o.p. (ISBN 0-8062-1032-X). Carlton.

Slow Burner: By William Haggard Pseud. 1st American Ed. Richard Clayton. LC 58-7860. 1958. Little, Brown.

Slow Creek. Milton Harmon. 1969. 3.95 (ISBN 0-87012-034-4). McClain.

Slow Days, Fast Company: The World, the Flesh, & L.A. Eve Babitz. 1977. 7.95 o.s.i. (ISBN 0-394-40984-1). Knopf.

Slow Days, Fast Company: The World, Theflesh, and L.A.: Tales. Eve Babitz. (Kangaroo Book). 1978. 1.95 (ISBN 0-671-82001-X). Pocket Books.

Slow Days, Fast Company: The World, the Flesh, and L.A.: Tales. Eve Babitz. LC 76-47922. 1977. 7.95 (ISBN 0-394-40984-1). Knopf: Distributed by Random House.

Slow Death at Geneva. John Franklin Carter. LC 34-2424. 1934. Coward-McCann, Inc.

Slow Dies the Thunder. 1st Ed. Helen Topping Miller. LC 55-10900. 1955. Bobbs-Merrill.

Slow Down the World. Jeffrey Ashford, pseud. 186p. 1983. pap. 2.95 (ISBN 0-8027-3015-9). Walker & Co.

Slow Down the World. Roderic Jeffries. LC 76-24560. 6.95 (ISBN 0-8027-5354-X). Walker.

Slow Dying. William M. James, pseud. (Apache Ser.: No. 18). 160p. (Orig.). 1980. pap. 1.50 (ISBN 0-523-40695-9). Pinnacle Bks.

Slow Fall to Dawn. Stephen Leigh. 176p. (Orig.). 1981. pap. text ed. 1.95 (ISBN 0-553-14902-4). Bantam.

Slow Gallows: A Novel of Suspense. Whit Masterson, pseud. LC 78-31879. 7.95 (ISBN 0-396-07653-X). Dodd, Mead.

Slow Horses & Fast Women. Damon Runyon. Repr. lib. bdg. 12.95x (ISBN 0-89190-439-5). Am Repr-Rivercity Pr.

Slow Joe. Max Brand. 1933. Dodd, Mead & Company.

Slow Joe. Max Brand. LC 40-137291. 1940. Triangle Books.

Slow Joe. Frederick Faust. LC 33-1634. 1933. Dodd, Mead & Company.

Slow Natives. Thea Astley. LC 67-27295. 1967. M. Evans; Distributed in Association with Lippincott, Philadelphia.

Slow Sculpture. Theodore Sturgeon. (Orig.). 1982. pap. 2.95 (ISBN 0-671-44185-X, Timescape). PB.

Slow Smoke. Charles Malam. LC 31-10364. Farrar & Rinehart Incorporated.

Slow, Soft River: Seven Stories. Lawrence Dorr. LC 72-94606. 1973. 2.45 (ISBN 0-8028-1498-0). Eerdmans.

Slow Twitch. Richard Enders. 288p. (Orig.). 1982. pap. 2.95 (ISBN 0-671-43629-5). PB.

Slow Vision. Maxwell Bodenheim. LC 34-246339. The Macaulay Company.

Slow Wind in the West. George Garland. LC 72-92211. 192p. 1973. 4.95 o.p. (ISBN 0-385-01755-3). Doubleday.

Slow Wind in the West. Garland Roark. LC 72-92211. 1973. 4.95 (ISBN 0-385-01755-3). Doubleday.

Slow Wind in the West see Gunrunners.

Slowcoach. Edward Verrall Lucas. LC 10-26916. 1910. The Macmillan Company.

Slower Judas. Gladys Bronwyn Stern. LC 29-2131. 1929. A. A. Knopf.

Slowly by the Hand Unfurled. Romulus Linney. LC 65-19060. 1965. Harcourt, Brace & World.

Slowly the Poison. June Drummond. LC 76-24561. 1976. 6.95 (ISBN 0-8027-5357-4). Walker.

Slug It Slay. Edwin Moultrie Lanham. LC 46-7804. 1946. Harcourt, Brace and Company.

Slum Street, U. S. A. James Thomas Farrell. Orig. Title: Boarding House Blues. 1967. pap. 0.60 o.p. (53-588). Paperback Lib.

Slumgullion Trail. Tevis Miller. LC 35-13907. Phoenix Press.

Slump City. Andrew Friend & Andy Metcalf. pap. 7.95 (ISBN 0-86104-342-1). Pluto Pr.

Slums. Thomas Akare. LC 81-188793. (African Writers Series; 241). 1981. 6.50 (ISBN 0-435-90241-5). Heinemann.

Sly As a Serpent. John Creasey. LC 67-11567. (Cock Robin mystery). bds., 3.95. Macmillan.

Sly As a Serpent. Kyle Hunt, pseud. 1970. pap. 0.95 o.p. (95016). Beagle Bks.

Slyboots. Pat Flower. LC 77-21128. (A Jubilee mystery). 1977. 7.95 (ISBN 0-8128-2417-2). Stein and Day.

Slype. Arthur Russell Thorndike. LC 28-26856. 1928. L. MacVeagh, The Dial Press; Etc., Etc.

Smack Man. Nelson De Mille. (Keller Ser.: No. 1). 224p. (Orig.). 1975. pap. 1.25 o.p. (ISBN 0-532-12259-3). Woodhill.

Smack Man. Nelson De Mille. (Keller Ser.: No. 1). 224p. (Orig.). 1975. pap. 1.25 o.p. (ISBN 0-532-12259-3). Manor Bks.

Smacksmen: A Story of the Fishermen of Borough. George Goldsmith Carter. LC 48-7856. 1948. Houghton Mifflin Co.

Small Armageddon. Mordecai Roshwald. (Signet book). 1.50. New American Library.

Small Assassin. Ray Bradbury. LC 76-383964. 1976. 0.50 (ISBN 0-586-04228-8). Panther.

Small Bachelor. Pelham Grenville Wodehouse. LC 27-27697. George H. Doran Company.

Small Back Room. Nigel Balchin. LC 45-2273. 1945. Houghton Mifflin Company.

Small Beer. Ludwig Bemelmans. (Capricorn bk. CAP49). 1961. Putnam.

Small Beer. Ludwig Bemelmans. LC 39-24342. 1939. The Viking Press.

Small Bequest. Edmund G Love. LC 72-93398. 1973. 5.95 (ISBN 0-385-02726-5). Doubleday.

Small Ceremonies: A Novel. Carol Shields. LC 76-380985. 8.95 (ISBN 0-07-082340-5). McGraw-Hill Ryerson.

Small Change. Carnaby Brown. LC 58-12561. 1958. Roy Publishers.

Small Change. Charles Robert Mullong. LC 26-8066. Dorrance and Company.

Small Change: A Film Novel. Francois Truffaut. LC 76-44660. (Black cat book; B-399). (Illus.). 2.95 (ISBN 0-394-17921-8) (ISBN 0-394-17921-8). Grove Press: Distributed by Random House.

Small Changes. Hal Clement. LC 69-13647. (Science Fiction Ser). 1969. 4.95 o.p. (ISBN 0-385-09087-0). Doubleday.

Small Changes. Marge Piercy. LC 72-96253. 1973. 8.95 (ISBN 0-385-05666-4). Doubleday.

Small Changes. Marge Piercy. (Fawcett crest book). 1974. (pbk.) 1.75. Fawcett.

Small Changes. Harry C Stubbs. LC 69-13647. (Doubleday science fiction). 1969. 4.95. Doubleday.

Small Civil War. John Neufeld. 192p. 1982. pap. 1.95 (ISBN 0-449-70023-2, Juniper). Fawcett.

Small Corner. Roy Turner. LC 67-27030. 1967. Crown Publishers.

Small Dark Man: A Novel. Maurice Walsh. LC 29-21419. 1929. Frederick A. Stokes Company.

Small Farm in the Steppe. Valentin Petrovich Kataev. LC 74-10362. 1976. 16.25 (ISBN 0-8371-7674-3). Greenwood Press.

Small Fire. Gladys Schmitt. LC 56-121306. 1957. Dial Press.

Small General. Digby George Gerahty. LC 45-8892. 1945. The Macmillan Company.

Small Giant. Phyllis Woodruff Sapp. LC 58-20226. 1957. Zondervan Pub. House.

Small Gods & Mr. Barnum. Max Trell. LC 71-139544. 1971. 6.50 (ISBN 0-8415-0089-4). McCall Pub. Co.

Small Gust of Wind: A Novel of Action and Intrigue. Teodore Magnuson. LC 80-677. 1980. 10.00 (ISBN 0-672-52663-8). Bobbs-Merrill.

Small Hours of the Morning: A Thriller. Margaret Yorke. LC 75-24720. 1975. 6.95 (ISBN 0-8027-5331-0). Walker.

Small Hours of the Night. Timothy Angus Jones. LC 50-8608. 1950. Houghton Mifflin.

Small House at Allington. Anthony Trollope. (His The chronicles of Barsetshire, 5). 1962. Harcourt, Brace & World.

Small House at Allington. Anthony Trollope. LC 4-24967. (On cover: The chronicles of Barsetshire v). 1904. Dodd, Mead & Company.

Small House at Allington. Anthony Trollope. (Half-title: Everyman's library, ed. by Ernest Rhys. Fiction. no. 361). 1909. J. M. Dent & Co.

Small House at Allington. Anthony Trollope. LC 36-37172. (Half-title: EverymanS library, ed. by Ernest Rhys. Fiction. no. 361). 1934. J. M. Dent & Sons, Ltd.

Small House at Allington. Anthony Trollope. LC 39-277049. (Half-title: The world's classics. 472-473). 1939. H. Milford, Oxford University Press.

Small House at Allington. Anthony Trollope & Thorold, Algar Labouchere, Ed. LC 12-394511. (Half-title: The new pocket library). 1906. John Lane.

Small Locks. Lee Upton. 1979. pap. 2.00 o.p. (ISBN 0-931598-08-7). Fallen Angel.

Small Masterpiece. Tim Heald. LC 81-43394. (Crime Club Ser.). 192p. 1982. 10.95 (ISBN 0-385-17942-1). Doubleday.

Small Me: A Story of Shanghai Life. Stephen Piero Sergius Rudinger De Rodyenko. LC 22-2100. The James A. McCann Company.

Small Mine. Menna Gallie. LC 62-20122. Harper & Row.

Small Moments: Stories. Nancy Huddleston Packer. LC 76-7601. (Illinois short fiction). 6.95. (ISBN 0-252-00615-1) (ISBN 0-252-00616-X). University of Illinois Press.

Small Mosaics of Mr. and Mrs. Engel. Patricia Collinge. LC 59-13961. (Illus.). 1959. Doubleday.

Small Obligation & Other Stories of Hilo. Susan Nunes. LC 82-72555. (Orig.). 1982. pap. 5.00 (ISBN 0-910043-00-0). Bamboo Ridge Pr.

Small Person Far Away: A Novel. Judith Kerr. LC 78-13195. 1979. 7.95 (ISBN 0-698-20472-7). Coward, McCann & Geoghegan.

Small Pond. Ada Goepp. LC 56-9298. 1956. Westminster Press.

Small Potatoes. Emily Lansingh Muir. LC 40-11891. 1940. C. Scribner's Sons.

Small Rain. Nicholas Delbanco. LC 74-17481. 1975. 7.95 (ISBN 0-688-02885-3). Morrow.

Small Rain. Madeleine L'Engle. LC 45-2788. 1945. The Vanguard Press.

Small Rain. Diana Raymond. LC 55-6294. 1955. Lippincott.

Small Room. May Sarton. 256p. 1976. pap. 4.95 (ISBN 0-393-00832-0, Norton Lib). Norton.

Small Room: A Novel. May Sarton. LC 76-25230. (Norton library paperback series). 1976. 2.95 (ISBN 0-393-00832-0). Norton.

Small Room: A Novel. 1st Ed. May Sarton. LC 61-11317. 1961. Norton.

Small Rooms of Paris. Ezra De Richarnaud. pap. 1.75 o.p. (3016). Brandon.

Small Rooms of Paris. Ezra De Richarnaud. LC 68-1962. (Brandon House library edition). 1968. Brandon House.

Small Shadows Creep. Andre Norton. LC 74-5408. 1974. (ISBN 0-525-39505-9). Dutton.

Small Souls. Louis Marie Anne Couperus. Tr. by Teixeira De Mattos, Alexander Louis. 1914. Dodd, Mead and Company.

Small Stradivari. Deane Narayn. LC 61-6663. 1961. Abelard-Schuman.

Small Success. Albert Morgan. LC 60-6763. 1960. Rinehart.

Small Tawny Cat. easy eye ed. Virginia Coffman. (Orig.). 1968. pap. 0.75 o.p. (74-611). Lancer.

Small Texan. J. T Edson. 1974. (pbk.) 0.75. Bantam Books.

Small Things. Reese Rockwell. LC 7-397987. 1883. Philips & Hunt.

Small Town. Bradda Field. LC 32-223163. 1932. D. Appleton and Company.

Small Town. Sloan Wilson. LC 77-79535. (Illus.). 9.95 (ISBN 0-87795-172-1). Arbor House.

Small Town Corpse: By Clarence Hunt Pseud. Hugh Holman. LC 51-3128. 1951. Phoenix Press.

Small Town Family. Margaret H Francis. LC 45-6680. 1945. The Hobson Book Press.

Small Town Girl. Jeanne Judson. 1973. pap. 0.75 o.s.i. (01-392). Lancer.

Small Town Girl. William Arthur Neubauer. LC 45-29448. 1945. Gramercy Publishing Co.

Small-Town Girl. Lorena A. Olmsted. (YA) 1973. 4.50 o.p. (Avalon). Bouregy.

Small-Town Girl. Lorena Ann Olmsted. (Avalon romances). 1973. 4.50. Avalon Books.

Small Town Girl. Ben Ames Williams. LC 35-6880. E. P. Dutton & Co., Inc.

Small Town in Germany. John Le Carre. LC 67-15283. 1968. 6.95. Coward-McCann.

Small Town in Germany: By John le Carre. 1st Amer. Ed. David John Moore Cornwell. LC 67-152831. 1968. 6.95. Coward.

Small Town Is a World: The "Rabbi Stories" of David Kossoff. David Kossoff. LC 79-63191. (Illus.). 1979. 8.95 (ISBN 0-312-72985-5). St. Martin's Press.

Small Town Is Best for Waiting, and Other Stories. Warren C Miller. LC 80-105678. 2.00. Climate Books.

Small Town Kingdom. Ruth C Deitz. LC 41-10143. 1938. Pegasus Publishing Co.

Small Town Murder. Beatrice W Jefferson. LC 41-17323. 1941. E. P. Dutton & Co., Inc.

Small Town Nurse. Peggy O'More, pseud. LC 67-1213. Arcadia House.

Small Town Shoe. Dora Herbert Smith. LC 60-10368. 1960. Greenwich Book Publishers.

Small Town Summer. Carol Ellis. (Caprice Romance Ser.). 160p. 1982. pap. 1.95 (ISBN 0-448-17288-7, Pub. by Tempo). Ace Bks.

Small Town Tyrant. Heinrich Mann. LC 44-4457. 1944. Creative Age Press, Inc.

Small Unit Action in Vietnam: Summer 1966. Francis I. West. 133p. pap. 2.50 (ISBN 0-405-00018-9). Ayer Co.

Small Venom. William Mole. LC 81-47398. (Fifty Classics of Crime Fiction, 1950-1975). 1982. 14.95 (ISBN 0-8240-4966-7). Garland Pub.

Small Venom. William Antony Younger. LC 56-9694. (Red badge detective). 1956. Dodd, Mead.

Small Victory. Zelda Popkin. LC 47-11005. 1947. J. B. Lippincott Co.

Small War Made to Order. Norman Lewis. LC 66-12367. (Helen and Kurt Wolff bk.). 4.50. Harcourt.

Small Widow. Janet McNeill, pseud. LC 68-27443. 1968. Atheneum.
Small Wonder. Graham Porter. LC 57-6718. 1957. Macmillan.
Small World. Carol Deschere. LC 51-10850. 1951. Simon and Schuster.
Small World. Tabitha King. LC 80-25837. 10.95 (ISBN 0-02-563190-X). Macmillan.
Small World. Keith Wheeler. LC 58-11913. 1958. Dutton.
Small World, Long Gone. Avis D. Carlson. LC 75-25212. (Illus.). 1977. 7.95 (ISBN 0-914090-29-1). Chicago Review.
Small World of Murder. Morna Doris MacTaggart Brown. LC 73-83590. 1973. 4.95 (ISBN 0-385-06366-0). Published for the Crime Club by Doubleday.
Small World of Murder. E. X. Ferrars, pseud. LC 73-83590. (Crime Club Ser.). 192p. 1973. 4.95 o.p. (ISBN 0-385-06366-0). Doubleday.
Small World of Murder. Elizabeth Ferrars, pseud. (Crime Ser.). 160p. 1976. pap. 1.95 o.p. (ISBN 0-14-004067-6). Penguin.
Small World of Murder. Elizabeth Ferrars, pseud. (Crime Ser.). 160p. 1976. pap. 1.95 o.p. (ISBN 0-14-004067-6). Penguin.
Smallbone Deceased. Michael Francis Gilbert. LC 74-193359. (Illus.). 1974. 1.25 (ISBN 0-14-003810-8). Penguin Books.
Smallbone Deceased. Michael Francis Gilbert. LC 75-44976. (Fifty Classics of Crime Fiction, 1900-1950; 21). 1976. 12.00 (ISBN 0-8240-2370-6). Garland Pub.
Smallbone Deceased. Michael Francis Gilbert. LC 50-10225. (Illus.). 1950. Harper.
Smaller Penny. Charles Bryson. LC 28-14552. E. P. Dutton & Compamy.
Smaller Sky. John Barrington Wain. LC 70-480395. 1969. Penguin.
Smallest Orb. Ann Maturin. LC 74-80789. 8.95. Dorrance.
Smarre besattelser & Nya bersattelser see Rose of Jericho & Other Stories.
Smart As the Devil. Felice Picano. 1976. 1.75. Dell.
Smart As the Devil: A Novel. Felice Picano. LC 74-82235. 1975. 7.95 (ISBN 0-87795-097-0). Arbor House.
Smart Ass. Stark Simpson. LC 74-78810. 1974. 8.95 (ISBN 0-8059-2029-3). Dorrance.
Smart Bombs. Philip Kirk. (Butler Ser.: No. 2). 1979. pap. 1.75 o.s.i. (ISBN 0-8439-0676-6, Leisure Bks). Nordon Pubns.
Smart Setback. Wood Kahler. 1930. A. A. Knopf.
Smart Woman. Thelma Strabel. LC 33-22822. 1933. Dodd, Mead & Company.
Smartest Grave. 1st American Ed. Reginald James White. LC 61-12238. 1961. Harper.
Smartest Man in Ireland. Illus. by Charles Keeping. Mollie Hunter, pseud. LC 65-19342. 1965. 3.25. Funk & Wagnalls.
Smash. Hollis Alpert. LC 73-9553. 1973. 7.95. Dial Press.
Smash. Garson Kanin. 512p. 1982. pap. 3.25 (ISBN 0-425-05165-X). Berkley Pub.
Smash and Grab. Clifton Robbins. LC 34-21303. (Tired business man's library of adventure, detective, and mystery novels).
Smash Picture! Adventures of a News Camera Man. Robert Van Gelder. LC 38-34542. (Career books). 1938. Dodd, Mead & Company.
Smash the Wild Bunch. Giles A. Lutz. 192p. 1982. 10.95 (ISBN 0-8027-4000-6). Walker & Co.
Smash-up. Cover Painting by Jack Floherty, Jr. Theodore Pratt. LC 54-38451. (Gold medal books, 421). 1954. Fawcett Publications.
Smasher: A Suspense Novel. Talmage Powell. LC 58-136676. (Cock Robin mystery). 1959. Macmillan.
Smear Job. James Mitchell. LC 77-4917. 1977. 7.95 (ISBN 0-399-12024-6). Putnam.
Smear Job. James Mitchell. (Berkley Book). 1978. 1.95 (ISBN 0-425-03854-8). Berkley Pub. Corp.
Smedley Hoover, His Day. Barbara Ninde Byfield & Sara Krulwich. LC 76-2223. (Illus.). 1976. 2.95 (ISBN 0-385-11688-8). Doubleday.
Smedley on Swift see Swiftiana.
Smell of Burning: A Novel. Margaret Lane. LC 67-99. 1965. H. Hamilton.
Smell of Burning. 1st Amer. Ed. Margaret Lane. LC 66-123996. 1966. 4.95. Knopf.
Smell of Fraud. Gil Hogg. LC 74-14151. 8.95. St. Martin's Press.
Smell of Hay. Giorgio Bassani. LC 75-16222. 1975. 7.95 (ISBN 0-15-183146-7). Harcourt Brace Jovanovich.
Smell of It. Sonallah Ibrahim. Tr. by Denys Johnson-Davies from Arabic. 118p. (Orig.). 1971. 12.00 (ISBN 0-89410-194-3); pap. 6.00 (ISBN 0-89410-195-1). Three Continents.
Smell of Money. John Edwin Canaday. LC 43-1685. 1943. Simon and Schuster.
Smell of Onions. Peggy Appiah. 84p. (Orig.). 1979. pap. 4.00 o.p. (Dist. by Three Continents Pr). Longman.
Smetana & the Beetles. Albert Eugene Kahn & David Levine. (Illus.). 1967. 2.95 o.p. Random.
Smetana and the Beetles: A Funny Tale for Adults, by Albert E. Kahn. Illus. by David Levine. Albert Eugene Kahn. LC 67-31083. 1967. bds., 2.95. Random.
Smile. Harry Bernstein. LC 80-53806. (Illus.). 192p. (Orig.). 1980. pap. 5.00 (ISBN 0-931122-21-X). West End.
Smile a Minute,". Harry Charles Witwer. LC 19-10467. Small, Maynard & Company.
Smile and Be a Villain. Hamilton Jobson. LC 76-141674. (Raven books). 1971. (u.s.) 4.95 (ISBN 0-200-71784-7). Abelard-Schuman.
Smile at the Foot of the Ladder. Henry Miller. 1975. (pbk.) 1.95 (ISBN 0-8112-0556-8). New Directions.
Smile at the Foot of the Ladder. Henry Miller & Corle, Edwin, 1906- LC 48-9153. 1948. Duell, Sloan & Pearce.
Smile at the Foot of the Ladder: A Story. Henry Miller. LC 77-127742. (Illus.). 1971. 2.50 (ISBN 0-87529-173-2). Hallmark Editions.
Smile at the Storm. Mavis Areta Wynder, pseud. LC 67-4005. 1967. Moody Press.
Smile-Bringer, and Other Bits of Cheer. William Herschell. LC 19-19595. The Bobbs-Merrill Company.
Smile-Bringer, and Other Bits of Cheer. William Herschell. LC 26-18752. The Bobbs-Merrill Company.
Smile in a Mad Dog's I. 2nd ed. Richard Stine. 1977. 6.95 (ISBN 0-916860-02-7). Bean Pub.
Smile in His Lifetime. Joseph Hansen. LC 80-21420. 12.95 (ISBN 0-03-056064-0). Holt, Rinehart, and Winston.
Smile of Love. Jean Woodward. 1981. pap. 6.95 (Avalon). Bouregy.
Smile of the Sphinx. Marguerite Bouvet. LC 11-26255. 1911. A.C. McClurg & Co.
Smile of the Stranger. Joan Aiken. LC 77-25573. 1978. 8.95 (ISBN 0-385-13634-X). Doubleday.
Smile on the Face of the Lion: Tr. from Italian. P. M Pasinetti. LC 65-10457. 5.95. Random.
Smile on the Face of the Tiger. Douglas Hurd & Andrew Osmond. LC 77-90223. 1970. 5.95. Macmillan.
Smile on the Void. Stuart Gordon. 336p. 1982. pap. 2.75 (ISBN 0-425-05498-5). Berkley Pub.
Smile on the Void: The Mythhistory of Ralph M'Botu Kitaj. Stuart Gordon. LC 80-12808. 12.95 (ISBN 0-399-12503-5). Berkley Pub. Corp.: Distributed by Putnam.
Smile When You Say That. Paul Fairman. (Orig.). 1971. pap. 0.75 o.p. (ISBN 0-446-64771-3, 64-771). Paperback Lib.
Smile With Me. Karen Walden. LC 81-85806. pap. 3.95 (ISBN 0-86666-024-0). GWP.
Smiler Bunn, Gentleman-Adventurer. Bertram Atkey. LC 27-198941. 1926. L. MacVeagh, The Dial Press.
Smiler with the Knife. Nicholas Blake. 1978. pap. 1.95 o.p. (ISBN 0-06-080457-2, P 457, PL). Har-Row.
Smiler with the Knife. Cecil Day-Lewis. LC 39-30764. 1939. Harper & Brothers.
Smiles," a Rose of the Cumberlands. Eliot Harlow Robinson. LC 19-8989. 1919. The Page Company.
Smiles and Frowns. Sara A Wentz. LC 8-362352. 1857. D. Appleton and Company.
Smiley's Haven. Blanche Benjamin Crozier. LC 28-7753. 1928. Little, Brown, and Company.
Smiley's People. John Le Carre. LC 79-2299. 1980. 10.95 (ISBN 0-394-50843-2). Knopf.
Smiley's People. John Le Carre. LC 80-12138. 1980. 16.95 (ISBN 0-8161-3090-6). G. K. Hall.
Smiling Charlie. Max Brand. LC 31-181740. 1931. Dodd, Mead & Company.
Smiling Charlie. Frederick Faust. LC 31-1817. 1931. Dodd, Mead & Company.
Smiling Corpse. Ruth Lenore Marting. LC 41-180512. 1941. Doubleday, Doran and Company, Inc.
Smiling Corpse: Wherein G. K. Chesterton, S. S. Van Dine, Sax Rohmer and Dashiell Hammett Are Surprised to Find Themselves at a Murder. Ruth Lenore Marting. LC 35-3661. Farrar & Rinehart, Incorporated.
Smiling Death. Francis Durham Grierson. LC 28-673. E. J. Clode, Inc.
Smiling Desperado. Frederick Faust. (Warner paperback lib. western). 1974. (pbk) 0.95. Warner Paperback Lib.
Smiling Dogs. Kenneth Robeson. (Avenger). (Paperback Lib., 74-142: Vol. 10). 1973. 0.75. Warner Paperback Lib.
Smiling Harry. Stephen Adams. 3.50 o.p. Vantage.
Smiling House. Lee Belvedere, pseud. (YA) 1973. 4.95 o.p. (Avalon). Bouregy.
Smiling Kouros: A Novel of Ancient and Modern Greece. Mikhail Soloviev. LC 62-15778. 1962. D. McKay Co.
Smiling Medusa. Jean Muir. LC 75-91276. (Red badge mystery). 1969. 3.95. Dodd, Mead.
Smiling Moon. Marsha Manning. (Cameo romance). 1974. (pbk.) 0.75. Fawcett.
Smiling Pass: Being a Further Account of the Career of "Smiles": a Rose of the Cumberlands. Eliot Harlow Robinson. LC 21-178161. 1921. The Page Company.
Smiling Rebel. Harnett Thomas Kane. 1972. pap. 0.95 o.p. (09131). Curtis.
Smiling Rebel: A Novel Based on the Life of Belle Boyd. Harnett Thomas Kane. LC 55-9985. 1955. Doubleday.
Smiling Road. Hanna Rion Ver Beck. LC 10-27190. E. J. Clode.
Smiling, the Boy Fell Dead. Michael Delving, pseud. LC 67-11395. 1967. Scribner.
Smiling, the Boy Fell Dead. Jay Williams. LC 67-11395. 1967. Scribner.
Smiling Tiger. Lenore Glen Offord. LC 49-11204. 1949. Duell, Sloan and Pearce.
Smire: An Acceptance in Third Person. James Branch Cabell. LC 37-6125. 1937. Doubleday, Doran & Company, Inc.
Smirt: An Urbane Nightmare. James Branch Cabell. 1934. R. M. McBride & Company.
Smith. Warwick Deeping. LC 32-25316. 1932. A. A. Knopf.
Smith: A Novel. David Gray & Maugham, William Somerset. LC 11-25440. 1911. 1.20. Duffield & Company.
Smith: A Sylvan Interlude. James Branch Cabell. LC 35-223907. 1935. R. M. McBride & Company.
Smith and Jones. Nicholas Monsarrat. LC 63-13219. (His Signs of the times, 2). 1963. W. Sloane Associates.
Smith and the Pharaohs and Other Tales. Henry Rider Haggard. LC 21-14289. 1921. Longmans, Green & Co.
Smith Brunt: A Story of the Old Navy. Waldron Kintzing Post. LC 99-5533. 1899. G. P. Putnam's Sons.
Smith College Stories. facsimile ed. Josephine Dodge Daskam Bacon. LC 70-94701. (Short Story Index Reprint Ser.). 1900. 17.00 (ISBN 0-8369-3079-7). Ayer Co.
Smith College Stories: Ten Stories. Josephine Dodge Daskam Bacon. LC 70-94701. (Short story index reprint series). (Illus.). 1969. Books for Libraries Press.
Smith College Stories. Ten Stories. Josephine Dodge Daskam Bacon. LC 1793. 1900. C. Scribner's Sons.
Smith Everlasting. Dillwyn Parrish. LC 26-17280. 1926. Harper & Brothers.
Smith of Wootton Major. John Ronald Reuel Tolkien. LC 67-30683. (Illus.). 1967. Houghton Mifflin.
Smiths. Janet Ayer Fairbank. LC 25-10884. The Bobbs-Merrill Company.
Smiths: A Comedy Without a Plot. John Keble Bell. LC 7-16483. 1907. McClure, Phillips & Co.
Smith's Dream. C. K. Stead. 142p. 1974. pap. 5.00x (ISBN 0-582-71723-X). Intl Pubns Serv.
Smith's Dream. C. K Stead. 1973. (ISBN 0-582-71723-X). Longman Paul.
Smith's Gazelle. Lionel Davidson. LC 77-136321. 1971. 5.95 (ISBN 0-394-46862-7). Knopf.
Smith's Gazelle. Lionel Davidson. 1974. (pbk.) 1.50. Bantam.
Smiths in War Time. John Keble Bell. LC 17-302821. 1917. John Lane.
Smithsburg. Michael Brondoli. (Treacle Story Ser.: No. 2). (Illus.). 48p. 1976. signed ed. 8.00 (ISBN 0-914232-09-6); pap. 2.50 (ISBN 0-914232-08-8). McPherson & Co.
Smithy of Burgwald. Gershon Kranzler, pseud. saddle-stitched 3.00 (ISBN 0-87559-135-3). Shalom.
Smiting of the Rock: A Tale of Oregon. George Palmer Putnam. LC 18-16017. 1918. 1.50. G. P. Putnam's Sons.
Smiting of the Rock: A Tale of Oregon. George Palmer Putnam. LC 33-780601. 1921. Grosset & Dunlap.
Smog. John Creasey. 160p. 1980. pap. 1.95 o.p. (ISBN 0-441-77180-7). Charter Bks.
Smog. John Creasey. 1971. 4.95 o.p. (ISBN 0-8027-5226-8). Walker & Co.
Smog. John Creasey. 160p. 1980. pap. 1.95 o.p. (ISBN 0-441-77180-7). Charter Bks.
Smog. John Creasey. (Dr. Palfrey Ser.). (O.s.i.). 192p. 1972. pap. 0.95 o.s.i. (AN1028, Award). Univ Pub & Dist.
Smog: A Story of Dr. Palfrey. John Creasey. LC 79-142846. 1971. 4.95 (ISBN 0-8027-5226-8). Walker.
Smoke. Ivan Sergeevich Turgenev. (Half-title: The modern library of the world's best books). The Modern Library.
Smoke: A Novel. Ivan Sergeevich Turgenev. LC 75-10319. (His Novels, v. 5). 1970. AMS Press.
Smoke: A Russian Novel. Ivan Sergieevich Turgenev & West, William F., Tr. LC 8-32673. (On cover: Leisure hour series. no. 2). 1872. Holt & Williams.
Smoke Against the Sky. Archie Joscelyn. 1965. Arcadia House.
Smoke and Ashes. Rafael Escandon. LC 72-97809. 1973. 4.95 (ISBN 0-8059-1832-9). Dorrance.
Smoke and Ashes. Fedor Kuzmich Teternikov. LC 78-74210. (His The created legend; pt. 3). v. 3 13.00 (ISBN 0-88233-144-2). Ardis.
Smoke, and Other Early Stories. Djuna Barnes & Douglas Messerli. LC 82-10627. (Illus.). 1982. 12.95 (ISBN 0-940650-17-7) (ISBN 0-940650-12-6). Sun & Moon Press.
Smoke: Another Jimmy Carter Adventure. Alexander Cockburn & James Ridgeway. LC 78-58159. (Illus.). 7.50 (ISBN 0-8129-0784-1). Times Books.
Smoke Away! May Wilson. 1981. pap. 1.15 (ISBN 0-85363-138-7). OMF Bks.
Smoke Bellew. Jack London. LC 12-223133. 1912. The Century Co.
Smoke Bellew. Rev. Ed. Jack London. LC 52-13236. 1953. World Pub. Co.
Smoke Beyond the Rim. Ney N Geer. LC 39-7584. L. Furman, Inc.
Smoke-Eater. Carl Henry Rathjen. LC 54-10280. 1954. Dodd, Mead.
Smoke-Eaters: The Story of a Fire Crew. Harvey Jerrold O'Higgins. LC 73-271. (Short story index reprint series). 1973. 13.50 (ISBN 0-8369-4249-3). Books for Libraries Press.
Smoke-Eaters: The Story of a Fire Crew. Harvey Jerrold O'Higgins. LC 5-5065. 1905. The Century Co.
Smoke-Filled Boudoir. Lawrence Williams. LC 65-185629. 4.95. S. & S.
Smoke in Her Eyes. Allene Soule Corliss. LC 36-748130. Farrar & Rinehart, Inc.
Smoke Island: A Novel. Antony Trew. LC 64-20019. (Illus.). 1964. Random House.
Smoke of Battle. Robert William Chambers. LC 38-4652. 1938. D. Appleton-Century Company, Incorporated.
Smoke of the .45. Harry Sinclair Drago. LC 23-13890. The Macaulay Company.
Smoke on the Ground. Miguel Delibes, pseud. LC 79-186031. 1972. 5.00. Doubleday.
Smoke on the Mountain. Ellen Crain. LC 67-13366. 1967. Dodd, Mead.
Smoke on the Range. King Phillips. LC 41-950042. Dodge Publishing Company.
Smoke on the River. Anne Tedlock Brooks. LC 49-867917. 1949. Acadia House.
Smoke Rings. Gladys Bronwyn Stern. LC 72-10810. (Short story index reprint series). 1973. (ISBN 0-8369-4229-9). Books for Libraries Press.
Smoke Rings. Gladys Bronwyn Stern. 1924. A. A. Knopf.
Smoke Screen. Lawrence Saunders. LC 30-14885. Sears Publishing Company, Inc.
Smoke Screen. Frances Moyer Ross Stevens. LC 35-23324. Harcourt, Brace and Company.
Smoke Talk: By Clem Colt Pseud. Nelson Coral Nye. LC 54-6491. (Silver star westerns). 1954. Dodd, Mead.
Smoke Tree Range. Arthur Henry Gooden. LC 36-19261. 1936. H. C. Kinsey & Company, Inc.
Smoke-Wagon Kid. Nelson Coral Nye. LC 43-16528. 1943. Phoenix Press.
Smoked Glass. Robert Henry Newell. LC 70-171060. Repr. of 1868 ed. 16.45 (ISBN 0-404-03663-5). AMS Pr.
Smoked Out. (Digger Ser.: No. 1). (Orig.). 1982. pap. 2.25 (ISBN 0-671-42610-9). PB.
Smokefires in Schoharie. Donald Cameron Shafer. LC 38-32614. 1938. Longmans, Green and Co.
Smokejumper: A Summer in the American Wilderness. Dale L. Schmaljohn. (Illus.). 163p. (gr. 6-12). 1982. 9.95 (ISBN 0-9608454-0-2); pap. 6.95 (ISBN 0-9608454-1-0). Hyde Park Pr.
Smokeless Burning. Constance I Smith. LC 23-56245. 1922. A. Melrose, Ltd.
Smokescreen. Dick Francis. LC 73-6763. 1973. 8.95 (ISBN 0-8161-6112-7). G. K. Hall.
Smokescreen. Dick Francis. (Edgar Allan Poe Mystery Award winner). 1973. (pbk) 0.95. Bantam Books.
Smokescreen. Anne Mather. (Harlequin Presents Ser.). 192p. 1982. pap. 1.75 (ISBN 0-373-10509-6). Harlequin Bks.
Smokestack Lightning: A Novel. John Eskow. LC 80-15505. 8.95. Delacorte Press.
Smokey & the Bandit. Delmas Hanks. 192p. (Orig.). 1981. pap. text ed. 2.50 (ISBN 0-553-20317-7). Bantam.
Smokey River. Lee Floren. LC 79-28243. 1980. 10.95 (ISBN 0-8161-3027-2). G. K. Hall.
Smoking Alters. St. John-Loe, Gladys. LC 37-1674. 1936. C. Kendall, Inc.
Smoking Flax. Patrick Joseph Carroll. LC 39-239855. The Ave Maria Press.
Smoking Flax. Hallie Erminie Rives. LC 72-2026. (Black Heritage Library Collection). 1972. 11.75 (ISBN 0-8369-9057-9). Books for Libraries Press.
Smoking Flax. Robert James Campbell Stead. LC 24-24806. George H. Doran Company.
Smoking Flax: A Story. Hallie Erminie Rives. LC 7-41018. (Neely's prismatic library). F. T. Neely.

Smoking Iron: "a Powder Valley Western,". Peter Field. LC 43-18853. 1944. Books Inc., Distributed by W. Morrow & Company.

Smoking Land: A Novel of Super-Science & Amazing Adventure. Max Brand. (Max Brand Popular Classics Ser.). 112p. 1980. pap. 5.95 (ISBN 0-88496-155-9). Capra Pr.

Smoking Land: A Novel of Super-Science and Amazing Adventure. Frederick Faust. LC 80-17333. (Series: Max Brand Popular Classic.). 1980. 5.95 (ISBN 0-88496-155-9). Capra Press.

Smoking Leg: And Other Stories. John Metcalfe. LC 74-152950. (Short story index reprint series). 1971. (ISBN 0-8369-3828-3). Books for Libraries Press.

Smoking Leg: And Other Stories. John Metcalfe. LC 26-975028. 1926. Doubleday, Page & Company.

Smoking Leg, & Other Stories. facsimile ed. John Metcalfe. LC 74-152950. (Short Story Index Reprint Ser.). Repr. of 1926 ed. 16.00 (ISBN 0-8369-3828-3). Ayer Co.

Smoking Mirror. Helen McCloy. (Red Badge Novel of Suspense Ser.). (O.s.i.). 1979. 7.95 o.s.i. (ISBN 0-396-07596-7). Dodd.

Smoking Mountain: Stories of Post War Germany. Kay Boyle. LC 51-10197. 1951. McGraw-Hill.

Smoking Rector: An Illuminating Composition, True to Fact and Experience in Real Life and of Vital Import in Its Striking Contrasts in Relation to the Spiritual and Non-Spiritual Influence in Individual Life As Affecting Humanity As a Whole. Charles Giffin Pease. LC 36-10498. 1936. The Restoration Publishing Company.

Smoky Canvas. Desemea Wilson. LC 35-239182. E. P. Dutton & Co., Inc.

Smoky City: A Tale of Crime. Samuel Young. LC 9-1197. 1845. Printed by A. A. Anderson.

Smoky God: Or, A Voyage to the Inner World. Willis George Emerson. LC 8-22549. 1908. Forbes & Company.

Smoky God: Or, A Voyage to the Inner World. With Illus. by John A. Williams. new ed. Willis George Emerson. LC 66-3179. Fieldcrest Pub. Co.

Smoky Joe. William Frederick Bragg. LC 49-48505. 1949. Phoeni Press.

Smoky Pass. Aubrey Boyd. LC 32-5859. 1932. E. P. Dutton & Co., Inc.

Smoky Range. 1st Ed. Eugene E Halleran. LC 51-10024. 1951. Lippincott.

Smoky Read. Frank Gruber. 1977. 1.25 (ISBN 0-380-00877-7). Avon Books.

Smoky River. Lee Floren. 1980. lib. bdg. 10.95 o.p. (ISBN 0-8161-3027-2, Large Print Bks). G K Hall.

Smoky River. Lee Floren. 1970. pap. 0.60 o.p. (ISBN 0-447-73895-X). Lancer.

Smoky River. Tom Roan. LC 35-15164. Godwin.

Smoky River: By Lew Smith Pseud. Lee Floren. LC 53-130626. 1953. Arcadia House.

Smoky Road. Frank Gruber. LC 49-93039. 1949. Rinehart.

Smoky: The Cow Horse. Will James. 324p. 1981. pap. 2.45 (ISBN 0-684-71819-7, ScribT). Scribner.

Smoky Trail: By Matt Stuart Pseud. 1st Ed. Llewellyn Perry Holmes. LC 51-11207. 1951. Lippincott.

Smoky Valley. Donald Hamilton. LC 54-8054. (First edition, 18). 1954. Dell Pub. Co.

Smoky Valley. Donald Hamilton. (Gold Medal book). 1976. 1.50 (ISBN 0-449-13677-9). Fawcett.

Smoky Waters. Raymond A Berry. LC 35-21568. 1935. Macrae Smith Company.

Smoky Years. Alan Le May. LC 35-9295. Farrar & Rinehart, Incorporated.

Smoldering Embers, No. 65. Marie Charles. 1982. pap. 1.75 (ISBN 0-515-06676-1). Jove Pubns.

Smoldering Fire. Harry Harrison Kroll. LC 55-42205. (Ace books, S-111). 1955. Ace Books.

Smoldering Flames: Adventures and Emotions of a Flapper. Clara Palmer Goetzinger. LC 28-20130. The Zuriel Publishing Co.

Smoldering Sea. Uell Stanley Andersen. LC 53-5892. 1953. A. A. Wynn.

Smooth. James Noble Gifford. LC 38-209882. Phoenix Press.

Smooth in the Saddle. Miles Merkel. LC 74-156825. 1973. 4.95 (ISBN 0-517-51415-X). Lenox Hill Press.

Smooth Justice. Michael Underwood. LC 78-21419. 1979. 7.95 (ISBN 0-312-73033-0). St. Martin's Press.

Smooth Runs the Water. James C Bryant. LC 73-78214. 1973. (ISBN 0-8054-7308-4). Broadman Press.

Smooth with Women. James Mandeville Neville. LC 32-21192. Coward-McCann, Inc.

Smothered Fires. Harriet Theresa Smith Comstock. LC 24-25414. 1924. Doubleday, Page & Company.

Smouldering Ashes & Other Stories. Marlene Johnson. 2.00 o.p. Carlton.

Smouldering: By Jack Woodford Pseud. & Gordon Greene. Josiah Pitts Woolfolk & Gordon Greene. LC 53-247953. 1953. Signature Press.

Smouldering Fire. new ed. Dorothy Emily Stevenson. LC 72-78109. 1972. 6.95 (ISBN 0-03-001311-9). Holt, Rinehart and Winston.

Smouldering Fire: A Romance. Dorothy Emily Stevenson. LC 38-19255. Farrar & Rinehart, Inc.

Smouldering Fires. Anya Seton. (Signet Book). 1977. 1.95. New American Library.

Smouldering Flame. Anne Mather. (Alpha Books). (Orig.). 1979. pap. text ed. 2.95x (ISBN 0-19-424164-5). Oxford U Pr.

Smudge. Nicholas Armfelt. 1975. 3.95 (ISBN 0-09-123060-8, Pub. by Hutchinson). Merrimack Pub Cir.

Smuggled Atom Bomb. Philip Wylie. 1968. pap. 0.60 o.p. (73-692). Lancer.

Smuggled Heart. Barbara Cartland. 1982. pap. 1.95 (ISBN 0-515-06213-8). Jove Pubns.

Smuggler. George Payne Rainsford James. (Seaside library, v. 37, no. 755). 1880. G. Munro.

Smuggler. Ella Middleton Tybout. LC 7-31227. 1907. J. B. Lippincott Company.

Smuggler Hero. A Story. rev. and ed. by percy b. st. john. ed. Gustave Aimard & St. John, Percy Bolingbroke, 1821-1889, Ed. (On cover: Lovell's library, no. 1118). 1888. J. W. Lovell Company.

Smuggler of King's Cove: Or, The Old Chapel Mystery. Sylvanus Cobb. LC 6-207157. Cassell & Company.

Smuggler of King's Cove: Or, The Old Chapel Mystery. Sylvanus Cobb. (On cover: Cassell's sunshine series, no. 29). The Cassell Publishing Co.

Smuggler of St. Malo. A Tale of Sea and Shore. Sylvanus Cobb. (New York boys' library, v. 2, no. 35). N. L. Munro.

Smugglers. Paul Petersen. (Smugglers#1). 1974. (pbk.) 0.95. Pocket Books.

Smugglers: A Novel. Noel Bertram Gerson. LC 77-8162. 6.95 (ISBN 0-690-01468-6). Crowell.

Smuggler's Bible. Joseph McElroy. (Bard Book). 1977. 2.50 (ISBN 0-380-01687-7). Avon Books.

Smuggler's Bride. Rosalind Laker. LC 74-27638. 1975. 5.95 (ISBN 0-385-08997-X). Doubleday.

Smuggler's Bride. Rosalind Laker. (Signet book). 1976. 1.50. New American Library.

Smugglers' Cave. J. M. Simpson. LC 27-2146. The Bobbs-Merrill Company.

Smuggler's Luck: Being the Adventures of Timothy Pinkham of Nantucket Island During the War of the Revolution. educational ed. Edouard A. Stackpole. LC 38-12770. Published by Doubleday, Doran & Company, Inc. by Arrangement with W. Morrow & Company.

Smuggler's Luck: Being the Adventures of Timothy Pinkham of Nantucket Island During the War of the Revolution. Edouard A. Stackpole. LC 31-181741. 1931. W. Morrow & Company.

Smugglers' Moon: A Novel of Suspense by Charlotte and BobSpringer. 1st Ed. Charlotte Springer & Bob Springer. LC 54-7050. 1954. Exposition Press.

Smugglers of Chestnut. Clarence Blendon Burleigh. LC 6-18653. (Raymond Benson series v. 1). 1891. E. E. Knowles and Company.

Smugglers of the Swedish Coast: Or, The Rose of Thistle Island. A Romance. Emilia Smith Flygare Carlen. Tr. by Hebbe, Gustaf Clemens & Deming, Henry Champion. LC 6-20142. J. Winchester.

Smugglers' Ranch. Charles Horace Snow. LC 34-12972. Macrae Smith Company.

Smuggler's Secret. A Novel. Frank Barrett. LC 6-8661. (On cover: Lovell's international series, no. 74). J. W. Lovell Company.

Smugglers' Trail. Max Brand. 1969. pap. 0.60 o.p. (63-117). Paperback Lib.

Smuggler's Trail. Evan Evans, pseud. 241p. 1976. Repr. of 1950 ed. lib. bdg. 12.05x (ISBN 0-89190-209-0). Am Repr-Rivercity Pr.

Smuggler's Trail. Frederick Faust. LC 75-32516. 1975-1976. 5.95 (ISBN 0-89190-209-0). American Reprint Co.

Smuggler's Wench. Monica Mugan. (Signet Book). 1975. (pbk.) 1.25. New American Library.

Smugtown, U. S. A. Curt Gerling. 203p. 1957. 5.95 o.p. Plaza Pubs.

Smut King. George Bishop. 1974. (pbk.) 1.50. Dell.

Snail-Watcher, and Other Stories. Patricia Highsmith. LC 78-103755. 1970. 4.95. Doubleday.

Snake. John Godey. LC 78-1305. 8.95 (ISBN 0-399-12184-6). Putnam.

Snake. James McClure. LC 75-30353. (Harper Novel of suspense). 7.95 (ISBN 0-06-012884-4). Harper & Row.

Snake. F. Inglis Powell. LC 12-11859. 1912. John Lane.

Snake. Frank Morrison Spillane. LC 63-8603. 1964. Dutton.

Snake & the Womb. K. C. Carmichael. pap. 1.25 o.p. (2050). Brandon.

Snake Bit Jones. Dane Coolidge. LC 36-14274. E. P. Dutton & Co., Inc.

Snake-Bite, and Other Stories. Robert Smythe Hichens. LC 19-113645. 1919. Cassell and Company, Ltd.

Snake-Bite, and Other Stories. Robert Smythe Hichens. LC 19-11943. George H. Doran Company.

Snake Breed. Burt Kroll. 3.95 o.p. Lenox Hill.

Snake Breed. Burt Kroll. 1970. Repr. of 1968 ed. 3.95 o.p. B Franklin.

Snake Doctor, and Other Stories. Irvin Shrewsbury Cobb. LC 23-109047. George H. Doran Company.

Snake Eyes. Edwin Silberstang. LC 77-23856. 8.95. Dutton.

Snake Eyes. Edwin Silberstang. 1979. 2.25. Pocket Books.

Snake Flag Conspiracy. Nick Carter. (Nick Carter Ser.). 176p. 1981. pap. 2.25 (ISBN 0-441-77193-9, Pub. by Charter Bks). Ace Bks.

Snake Flag Conspiracy. Nick Carter. (Nick Carter Ser). (O.s.i.). 176p. (Orig.). 1976. pap. 1.25 o.s.i. (AQ1576, Award). Univ Pub & Dist.

Snake Gold: A Tale of Indian Treasure; of an Ancient Emblem and Its Power Over Men to-Day; and of the Hazard of Casa Blanca. Hervey White. LC 26-14157. 1926. The Macmillan Company.

Snake Harvest. Francis John Thornton. LC 77-20651. 8.95 (ISBN 0-698-10904-X). Coward, McCann & Geoghegan.

Snake in the Glass: A Novel. Hal Kanter. LC 72-140948. 1971. 6.95. Delacorte Press.

Snake in the Grass. Hal Kantor. 1971. 6.95 o.p. (9829-6). Delacorte.

Snake in the Grass. James Howard Wellard. LC 42-21303. 1942. Dodd, Mead & Company.

Snake Lady: And Other Stories by Vernon Lee Pseud. Edited and with an Introd. by Horace Gregory. Violet Paget. LC 53-13497. Grove Press.

Snake of Luvercy. Maurice Renard & Crewe-Jones, Florence, Tr. LC 30-30570. E. P. Dutton & Co., Inc.

Snake on the Grave. George Beare. LC 73-19795. (Midnight novel of suspense). 1974. 5.95 (ISBN 0-395-18468-1). Houghton, Mifflin.

Snake Pit. Sigrid Undset & Chater, Arthur G., Tr. LC 29-1082. 1929. A. A. Knopf.

Snake Pit. Mary Jane Ward. LC 46-26431. 1946. Random House.

Snake Pit. Mary Jane Ward. (Signet Book). 1973. (pbk) 1.25. New American Library.

Snake River Rescue. J. D. Hardin. LC 81-86256. (J. D. Hardin Western Ser.). 224p. (Orig.). 1982. pap. 1.95 (ISBN 0-86721-133-4). Playboy Pbks.

Snake River to Hell. Frank Chester Robertson. LC 41-109716. 1941. E. P. Dutton & Co., Inc.

Snake Stomper. Wayne D Overholser. LC 51-11049. (Dutton Diamond D western). 1951. Dutton.

Snake Venom. Sekender A. Kahn. 2.00 o.p. Carlton.

Snake Water. Alan Williams. LC 65-26106. 1965. Harper & Row.

Snakegod. Ron Goulart. (Vampirella #6). 1976. 1.25. Warner Books.

Snakehunter. Chuck Kinder. LC 73-7274. 1973. 5.95 (ISBN 0-394-48510-6). Knopf; Distributed by Random House.

Snakes. Al Young. LC 77-105434. 1981 (ISBN 0-916870-34-0). Creative Arts Book Company.

Snakes: A Novel. Al Young. LC 77-105434. 1970. 4.95 (ISBN 0-03-084535-1). Holt, Rinehart and Winston.

Snake's Nest, or, A Tale Badly Told: A Novel. Ledo. Ivo. LC 81-3956. 1981. 12.95 (ISBN 0-8112-0806-0) (ISBN 0-8112-0807-9). New Directions Pub. Corp.

Snakes of St. Cyr. William O'Farrell. LC 51-10421. 1951. Duell, Sloan and Pearce.

Snake's Pass, a Novel. Bram Stoker. LC 8-16296. (On cover: Harper's Franklin square library, no. 685). 1890. Harper & Brothers.

Snaketrack. Frank Bonham. LC 52-10349. (Essandess western). 1952. Simon and Schuster.

Snap. 1st. u.s. ed. A. J Quinnell. LC 82-20802. (Illus.). 1983. 14.95 (ISBN 0-688-01898-X). Morrow.

Snap. Jacqueline Wilson. 1982. 15.00x (ISBN 0-333-16638-8, Pub. by Macmillan England). State Mutual Bk.

Snap: A Novel. Melville Philips. LC 7-36063. 1881. Harper & Brothers.

Snap Box. Paul Gogarty. 1972. 6.00 (Pub. by Trigram Pr); signed ed. 12.00; pap. 3.50. SBD.

Snap Shots. A Volume of Short Stories. Helen Margaret Graham.

Snap. The Ox-Train Era. Early Troubles of Border Trade. T. Buchanan Price. 1881. W. B. Smith & Co.

Snapdragon. Horace Hazeltine. LC 13-5066. D. FitzGerlad, Inc.

Snapdragon. Charles Stokes Wayne. LC 13-5066. 1913. D. FitzGerald.

Snappy Western Stories. Elois Felicia Elden. LC 26-16144. 1926. The Stratford Company.

Snapshots. Del Cogswell Brebner. LC 78-2486. 7.95 (ISBN 0-397-01273-X). Lippincott.

Snapshots. Alain Robbe-Grillet. LC 67-27889. (Evergreen original, E-435). 1968. 1.45. Grove Press.

Snapshots by the Way. Gilbert Guest. LC 20-22796. 1920. Burkley Printing Company.

Snare. Sallie Lee Bell. 1959. Zondervan Pub. House.

Snare. Rafael Sabatini. LC 17-29537. 1917. M. Secker.

Snare. Rafael Sabatini. LC 23-4987. 1922. Houghton Mifflin Company.

Snare. Rafael Sabatini. LC 26-7510. 1925. Grosset & Dunlap.

Snare. Elizabeth Spencer. LC 72-3846. 384p. 1972. 8.95 o.p. (ISBN 0-07-060178-X, GB). McGraw.

Snare. George Vane. LC 15-8433. 1915. John Lane.

Snare: A Novel. Elizabeth Spencer. LC 72-3846. 1972. 7.95 (ISBN 0-07-060178-X). McGraw-Hill.

Snare Andalucian. Aaron Marc Stein. LC 68-10678. 1968. Doubleday.

Snare for Sinners. Ruth Fenisong. LC 49-9743. 1949. Pub. for the Crime Club by Doubleday.

Snare for Witches. Elinor Chamberlain. LC 48-8216. 1948. Dodd, Mead.

Snare in the Dark. Frank Parrish. LC 81-9769. (Dan Mallett Novel of Suspense Ser.). 224p. 1981. 8.95 (ISBN 0-396-08025-1). Dodd.

Snare in the Dark. Frank Parrish. LC 82-48814. 224p. 1983. pap. 2.84i (ISBN 0-06-080650-8, P 650, PL). Har-Row.

Snare in the Dark: A Dan Mallett Novel of Suspense. Frank Parrish. LC 81-9769. 8.95 (ISBN 0-396-08025-1). Dodd, Mead.

Snare of Circumstance. Edith E Buckley. LC 10-35334. 1910. 1.50. Little, Brown, and Company.

Snare of Strength. Randolph Bedford. LC 6-13688. 1906. H.B. Turner & Co.

Snare of the Fowler. Gerald William Bullett. LC 36-23525. 1936. A. A. Knopf.

Snare of the Fowler. Annie French Hector. Cassell Publishing Company.

Snare of the Fowler. Tom Taylor. LC 77-22322. 1.50 (ISBN 0-8024-8104-3). Moody Press.

Snare of the Hunter. Helen MacInnes. LC 73-17478. (Illus.). 1974. 7.50 (ISBN 0-15-183180-7). Harcourt Brace Jovanovich.

Snare of the Hunter. Helen MacInnes. LC 74-18305. (Illus.). 1975. 7.50 (ISBN 0-8161-6246-8). G. K. Hall.

Snared Nightingale. Geoffrey Trease. LC 58-8070. 1958. Vanguard Press.

Snark Was a Boojum... Dora Richards Shattuck. LC 41-6048. 1941. Morrow.

Snark Was a Boojum... Richard Shattuck. LC 41-6048. 1941. W. Morrow and Company.

Snarl of the Beast. Carroll John Daly. LC 27-20083. E. J. Clode, Inc.

Snarl of the Beast. Carroll John Daly. LC 81-4771. (Gregg Press Mystery Fiction Series). 1981. 13.95 (ISBN 0-8398-2658-3). Gregg Press.

Snarleyyow: Or, The Dog Fiend. Frederick Marryat. 1880. D. Appleton and Company.

Snarleyyow: Or, The Dog Fiend. An Historical Novel. Frederick Marryat. LC 7-17566. 1837. Carey and A. Hart.

Snatch. Rennie Airth. LC 69-14276. 1969. 4.95. Simon and Schuster.

Snatch. Raymond Leslie Goldman. LC 40-9008. Coward-McCann, Inc.

Snatch. Bill Pronzini. LC 70-159366. 1973. (pbk.) 0.95 (ISBN 0-671-77663-0). Pocket Books.

Snatch! Roger Taylor. 304p. (Orig.). 1981. pap. text ed. 2.95 (ISBN 0-553-20091-7). Bantam.

Snatch a Dream. Joan Garrison, pseud. pap. 0.50 o.p. (B50-654). Belmont-Tower.

Snatch a Dream. William Arthur Neubauer. LC 64-9299. 1964. Arcadia House.

Snatch an Eye. Henry Kane. 1971. pap. 0.75 o.p. (ISBN 0-447-74562-X). Lancer.

Snatch of Music. Ludovic Peters. LC 62-795992. (Raven book). 1962. Abelard-Schuman.

Sneakers in the Dryer. Mary Ann Bohrs. LC 75-10085. 1975. 3.50 (ISBN 0-87680-983-2). Word Books.

Sneaks. Edith Pinero Green. LC 79-1300. 9.95 (ISBN 0-525-20632-9). Dutton.

Sneaks. Edith Pinero Green. LC 80-12707. 13.50 (ISBN 0-89340-287-7). J. Curley & Associates.

Sneaky People. Thomas Berger. 1.95. Dell.

Sneaky People: A Novel. Thomas Berger. LC 74-22320. 1975. 7.95 (ISBN 0-671-21897-2). Simon and Schuster.

Sneeze & Be Slain. Hunter. 127p. 8.95 (ISBN 0-370-30313-X, Pub. by Chatto-Bodley-Jonathan). Merrimack Pub Cir.

Snibs. Irena Dell Harkness. LC 45-5488. 1945. Dorrance & Company.

Snickerty Nick. Julia Ellsworth Shaw Ford & Bynner, Witter, 1881- LC 19-19589. 1919. Moffat, Yard & Co.

Snider's Wickedness: And Other Stories. Seneca E Truesdell. LC 8-28482. 1892. Pioneer Press Company.

Snipe Hunt. Amber Dean. LC 49-114697. 1949. Published for the Crime Club by Doubleday.

Sniper. Anthony V La Penta. LC 75-16563. 6.95 (ISBN 0-87949-042-X). Ashley Books.

Sniper. Judson Penetcost Philips. LC 65-14519. (Red badge detective). Dodd, Mead.

Sniper. Michael Stratford. (Adam-12 Ser.). (O.s.i.). 192p. (Orig.). 1974. pap. 0.95 o.s.i. (AN1266, Award). Univ Pub & Dist.

Snob Papers: A Humorous Novel. Adair Welcker. LC 8-367334. T. B. Peterson & Brothers.

Snob: The Story of a Marriage. Helen Reimensnyder Martin. LC 24-164534. 1924. 2.00. Dodd, Mead and Company.

Snobs. Marian Edna Sharrock. LC 31-96259. 1931. D. Appleton and Company.

Snookie Gets Around. Ida Elson. LC 48-62765. 1948. Christopher Pub. House.

Snoopy Festival. Charles M. Schulz. LC 74-4809. (Peanuts Ser.). 224p. 1980. pap. 7.95 (ISBN 0-03-057503-6). HR&W.

Snooty Baronet. Wyndham Lewis. LC 77-176492. 1971. (ISBN 0-8383-1359-0). Haskel House Publishers.

Snopes: A Trilogy, 3 vols. William Faulkner. Incl. Vol. 1. Hamlet; Vol. 2. Town; Vol. 3. Mansion. 1964. Set. boxed 20.00 o.p. (ISBN 0-394-44592-9). Random.

Snoqualmi Falls Apocalypse. Nelson Bentley. 1981. pap. 3.50 (ISBN 0-917652-25-8). Confluence Pr.

Snow. Tomaz Salamun. 1974. pap. 1.50 o.p. (ISBN 0-915124-02-5). Toothpaste.

Snow: A Love-Story. Ruth Pine Furniss. LC 29-18542. Harcourt.

Snow Above Town. Donald Hough. LC 43-2820. 1943. W. W. Norton & Company Inc.

Snow Against the Sky: A Novel. Mary Dunstan. LC 35-35683. 1936. Frederick A. Stokes Company.

Snow Along the Border. Raymond H. Sawkins. LC 68-20072. 1968. Harcourt, Brace & World.

Snow and Other Stories. Philip Freund. LC 35-6883. 1935. Pilgrim House.

Snow and Roses". Worthington Newton. LC 33-477. Brown-Morrison Co., Inc.

Snow and Roses: A Novel. Lettice Ulpha Cooper. LC 76-368156. 1976. 3.95 (ISBN 0-575-02098-9). Gollancz.

Snow and Steel. Sommi-Picenardi, Girolamo. LC 77-130072. (Short story index reprint series). 1970. Books for Libraries Press.

Snow and Steel. Girolamo Sommi-Picenardi & Altrocchi, Rudolph, 1882- Tr. LC 26-15371. 1926. D. Appleton and Company.

Snow Ball. Brigid Brophy. 144p. 1980. 12.95 (Pub. by Allison & Busby England); pap. 4.95 (ISBN 0-8052-8006-5, Pub. by Allison & Busby England). Schocken.

Snow Ball. The Finishing Touch. Brigid Brophy. LC 64-12066. 1964. World Pub. Co.

Snow Birch. 1st Ed. John Mantley. 1958. Dutton.

Snow-Blind. Katharine Newlin Burt. LC 21-15108. 1921. 1.50. Houghton Mifflin Company.

Snow-Blind. Katharine Newlin Burt. (Signet rainbow romance, T5297). 1972. New American Lib.

Snow-Blind. Albert M Treynor. LC 29-54149. 1929. Dodd, Mead & Company.

Snow-Bound at Eagle's. Bret Harte. LC 7-3650. 1886. Houghton, Mifflin and Company.

Snow Bride. Shannon Clare. (Superromances Ser.). 384p. 1983. pap. 2.95 (ISBN 0-373-70078-4). PB.

Snow-Burner. Henry Oyen. LC 16-22899. George H. Doran Company.

Snow Country. Yasunari Kawabata. LC 80-39979. 1981. 4.95 (ISBN 0-399-50525-3). Perigee Books.

Snow Country: And Thousand Cranes. Yasunari Kawabata. LC 69-17239. (Illus.). 1969. 5.95. Knopf.

Snow Country. Translated, with an Introd. by Edward G. Seidensticker. 1st American Ed. Yasunari Kawabata. (UNESCO series of contemporary works: Japanese series). 1956. Knopf.

Snow Falcon. Craig Thomas. LC 79-3435. 1980. 10.95 (ISBN 0-03-045496-4). Holt, Rinehart and Winston.

Snow-Fire: A Story of the Russian Court. Marguerite De Godart Cunliffe-Owen. LC 40-926738. 1910. 1.50. Harper & Brothers.

Snow Flame. Susanna Howe. 304p. (Orig.). 1981. pap. 2.95 (ISBN 0-515-05391-0). Jove Pubns.

Snow Fury. Richard Holden. LC 55-6933. 1955. Dodd, Mead.

Snow Ghost. Paul Kropp. LC 82-12930. (Encounters Ser.). (Illus.). 96p. 1982. pap. text ed. 3.95 (ISBN 0-88436-964-1); wkbk. 1.20 (ISBN 0-88436-968-4). EMC.

Snow Gods. Frederic Morton. 1969. 5.95 o.p. (HO267, NAL). Norton.

Snow Gods: A Novel. Frederic Morton. LC 68-28114. (Nal book). 1968. 5.95. World Pub. Co.

Snow Goose. Paul Gallico. LC 41-4260. 1941. A. A. Knopf.

Snow Image. Nathaniel Hawthorne. LC 30-31804. (On cover: The little library). 1930. The Macmillan Company.

Snow-Image: A Childish Miracle. Nathaniel Hawthorne. LC 7-1614. 1868. Hurd and Houghton.

Snow Image and Other Twice-Told Tales. Nathaniel Hawthorne. LC 75-116954. (Short story index reprint series). (Illus.). 1970. Books for Libraries Press.

Snow-Image: And Other Twice-Told Tales. Nathaniel Hawthorne. LC 7-3773. (On cover: Standard literature series, no. 20). University Publishing Company.

Snow Image: And Other Twice-Told Tales. Nathaniel Hawthorne. LC 99-3359. T. Y. Crowell & Company.

Snow-Image and Uncollected Tales. Nathaniel Hawthorne. LC 73-5365. (centenary edition of the works of Nathaniel Hawthorne; v. 11). 1974. 17.00 (ISBN 0-8142-0204-7). Ohio State University Press.

Snow-Image: The Great Stone-Face, Little Daffydowndilly. Nathaniel Hawthorne. LC 7-3772. (On cover: Maynard's English classic series, no. 208). 1898. Maynard, Merrill & Co.

Snow in April. Rosamunde Pilcher. LC 74-33911. 1975. 6.95. St. Martin's Press.

Snow in Eden. Ione Samuel Williams. LC 38-696100. 1938. C. Scribner's Sons.

Snow in Paradise. Raymond H. Sawkins. LC 67-20304. 1967. Harcourt, Brace & World.

Snow in the River: A Novel, by Carol Brink. Carol Ryrie Brink. LC 64-17377. 1964. Macmillan.

Snow Job. Alfred Baker. LC 52-14890. 1952. Arco.

Snow Leopard. Paul West. 1965. 2.95 o.p. HarBraceJ.

Snow Man... George Sand. LC 4-17507. 1898. Little, Brown, and Company.

Snow Man: A Novel. George Sand & Vaughan, Virginia, Tr. LC 13-2061. (Half-title: George Sands' novels. The snow man). 1871. Roberts Brothers.

Snow Mountain. Catherine Irvine Gavin. LC 73-19752. (Illus.). 1974. 8.95 (ISBN 0-394-49179-3). Pantheon Books.

Snow Mountain. Catherine Irvine Gavin. 1977. 1.95 (ISBN 0-671-81189-4). Pocket Books.

Snow on High Ground. Raymond H. Sawkins. LC 67-10769. 1967. Harcourt, Brace & World.

Snow on the Headlight: A Story of the Great Burlington Strike. Cy Warman. LC 99-3430. 1899. D. Appleton and Company.

Snow on the Mountain. John Tedman & Alison Tedman. (New Oxford Supplementary Readers Ser). (Illus.). 96p. 1961. pap. text ed. 0.75x o.p. (ISBN 0-19-422433-3). Oxford U Pr.

Snow-on-the-Mountain: And Other Stories. David Cornel De Jong. LC 46-7690. 1946. Reynal & Hitchcock.

Snow Over Elden: A Story of Today. Thomas Moult. LC 21-49127. 1920. George H. Doran Company.

Snow Patrol. Harry Sinclair Drago. LC 25-16971. The Macaulay Company.

Snow Queen. Joan D Vinge. LC 79-20555. (Quantum novel). 10.95 (ISBN 0-8037-7739-6). Dial Press.

Snow Rattlers. Shepard Rifkin. LC 76-23311. 7.95. Putnam.

Snow Rubies. Martin Louis Alan Gompertz. LC 25-19429. 1925. Houghton Mifflin Company.

Snow Salmon Reached the Andes Lake. Willis Barnstone. LC 80-65064. 1980. 6.95 (ISBN 0-931604-02-8); pap. 3.95 (ISBN 0-931604-03-6). Curbstone Pub NY TX.

Snow Shadow. Andre Norton, pseud. 1979. 1.95 (ISBN 0-449-23963-2). Fawcett Crest Books.

Snow, Stars & Wild Honey. George P. Morrill. 1975. 8.95 o.p. (ISBN 0-397-01029-X). Lippincott.

Snow Storm & Other Stories. Lev Nikolaevich Tolstoi. (World's Classics). 5.95 o.p. (ISBN 0-19-250420-7). Oxford U Pr.

Snow Tiger. Desmond Bagley. LC 74-12674. 1975. 7.95 (ISBN 0-385-04841-6). Doubleday.

Snow Tiger. Desmond Bagley. (Fawcett Crest Book). 1977. 1.75 (ISBN 0-449-23107-0). Fawcett Pubns.

Snow Trenches. Dan Steele. LC 31-29960. 1931. A. C. McClurg & Co.

Snow Upon the Desert. Sarah Broom Macnaughton. LC 13-21363. Hodder and Stoughton.

Snow Upon the Desert. Sarah Broom Macnaughton. LC 13-228173. E. P. Dutton & Company.

Snow Walker. Farley Mowat. LC 75-35956. 8.95 (ISBN 0-316-58693-5). Little, Brown.

Snow Water. Dorothy Gardiner. LC 39-4901. 1939. Doubleday, Doran & Company, Inc.

Snow Water. Jean Slattery. LC 30-33. Dorrance and Company.

Snow White. Donald Barthelme. (N3802). 1968. Bantam.

Snow-White Soliloquies. Sheila MacLeod. LC 74-104132. 1970. 4.95. Viking Press.

Snow White. 1st Ed. Donald Barthelme. LC 67-14324. 1967. 4.50. Atheneum.

Snow World. Kevin Urick. LC 82-51026. 477p. 1983. 16.95 (ISBN 0-917976-16-9). White Ewe.

Snowball. Ted Allbeury. LC 73-19974. 1974. 6.95 (ISBN 0-397-01020-6). Lippincott.

Snowball. Stanley John Weyman. (On cover: Merriam's violet series, no. 6). The Merriam Company.

Snowball. Hants A White. LC 74-108568. 1970. 3.50. Dorrance.

Snowball Berry Red & Other Stories. Vasilii Makarovich Shukshin. LC 79-103566. (Illus.). 13.95 (ISBN 0-88233-283-X). Ardis.

Snowballing. Frank Covino. (Orig.). 1975. pap. 1.50 o.p. (LB290DK, Leisure Bks). Nordon Pubns.

Snowbound. Bill Pronzini. LC 73-87200. 1974. 6.95 (ISBN 0-399-11264-2). Putnam.

Snowbound. John Greenleaf Whittier. 1967. 1.95 o.p. (ISBN 0-442-82459-9). Peter Pauper.

Snowbound Heart. Maxine Patrick. (Signet Book). 1.75 (ISBN 0-451-08935-9). New American Library.

Snowbound Six. Richard Martin Stern. LC 77-77551. 1977. 7.95 (ISBN 0-385-12320-5). Doubleday.

Snowbound Weekend. Amii Loren. (Candlelight Ecstasy Ser.: No. 50). (Orig.). 1982. pap. 1.75 (ISBN 0-440-18027-9). Dell.

Snowboys. Forrest Webb. LC 73-79728. 1973. 5.95 (ISBN 0-385-05442-4). Doubleday.

Snowboys. Forrest Webb. 1976. (pbk.) 1.50. Bantam Books.

Snowcastles. Duncan McGeary. (Orig.). 1981. pap. text ed. 1.75 o.s.i. (ISBN 0-505-51625-X). Tower Bks.

Snowdrift: A Story of the Land of the Strong Cold. James Beardsley Hendryx. LC 22-3497. 1922. G. P. Putnam's Sons.

Snowed up. Rosalie K. Fry. pap. 0.75 o.p. (ISBN 0-671-29547-0). Archway.

Snowfall, and Other Chilling Events. Elizabeth Walter. LC 66-17151. 1966. Stein and Day.

Snowfire. Phyllis A. Whitney. LC 72-84953. 1973. 6.95 (ISBN 0-385-02264-6). Doubleday.

Snowfire. Phyllis A. Whitney. LC 73-4678. 1973. 10.95 (ISBN 0-8161-6105-4). G. K. Hall.

Snowfire. Phyllis A. Whitney. (Crest Book, P2041). 1974. (pbk.) 1.25. Fawcett Pubns.

Snowflake. Paul Gallico. (Illus.). 1957. 3.50 o.p. Doubleday.

Snowflake. Decorations by David Knight and Reisie Lonette. 1st American Ed. Paul Gallico. LC 53-9137. 1953. Doubleday.

Snowflakes in the Sun. Audrey Brent. 192p. 1981. pap. 1.50 (ISBN 0-671-57063-3). S&S.

Snowing in Paradise. J. R. Williams, pseud. (Orig.). 1980. pap. 2.25 (ISBN 0-532-23147-3). Woodhill.

Snowkill. Ron Faust. 208p. 1981. pap. 2.25 (Leisure Bks). Nordon Pubns.

Snowline. Berkely Mather. LC 72-11130. 1973. 6.95 (ISBN 0-684-13282-6). Scribner.

Snowline. Berkely Mather. 1978. 1.95 (ISBN 0-671-81978-X). Pocket Books.

Snowman. Norman Bogner. 1978. pap. 1.95 (ISBN 0-440-18152-6). Dell.

Snowman. Charles Haldeman. LC 65-24676. bds., 4.50. S. & S.

Snowman. Arthur Maling. LC 72-9172. 1973. 5.95 (ISBN 0-06-012778-3). Harper & Row.

Snowman: A Novel. Thomas Lee York. LC 76-18378. (Illus.). 1976. 8.95 (ISBN 0-385-12278-0). Doubleday.

Snowman. Snowman, Fables and Fantasies. Janet Frame, pseud. LC 63-15826. 1963. G. Braziller.

Snowmobile Kidnapping. Judy Hughes. (Orig.). 1980. pap. text ed. 1.75 o.s.i. (ISBN 0-505-51566-0). Tower Bks.

Snows of December. Translated from the French by Frances Frenaye. 1st Ed. Daria Olivier. LC 58-14358. 1959. McGraw-Hill.

Snows of Helicon. Henry Major Tomlinson. LC 33-20518. 1933. Harper & Brothers.

Snows of Kilimanjaro, and Other Stories. Ernest Hemingway. LC 61-1437. (Scribner library, SL32). 1961. Scribner.

Snows of Yester-Year: A Novel. Wilbertime-Teters Worden. 1895. Arena Publishing Company.

Snows of Yesterday. Betty De Forrest. (Ace gothic read easy large type). 1973. (pbk.) 0.95. Ace.

Snowshoe Al's Bed Time Stories: And Uther Times. Albert J Bromley. LC 26-8382. 1926. The Contributors' Guild.

Snowshoe Thompson. Adrien Stoutenburg & Baker, Laura Nelson. LC 57-8491. 1957. Scribner.

Snowshoe Trail. Edison Marshall. LC 21-16002. 1921. 1.90. Little, Brown, and Company.

Snowslide. 1st Ed. Carl Jonas. LC 50-7740. 1950. Little, Brown.

Snowy Hills of Innocence. Ann Boyle. (Avalon Books). 1977. 4.95. Thomas Bouregy.

Snuffs and Butters... Ellen Newbold La Motte. 1.75. The Century Co.

Snuffs and Butters: And Also The Malay Girl, The Golden Stars, The Middle-Class Mind, Proof, Widows and Orphans, The Cardiff Giant, The Onlookers and In Mashonaland. Ellen Newbold La Motte. LC 74-125226. (Short story index reprint series). 1970. Books for Libraries Press.

Snug Harbour. William Wymark Jacobs. LC 31-28022. 1931. C. Scribner's Sons.

So. Adam Pilgrim. LC 72-185653. 1970. 3.95 (ISBN 0-909893-00-4). Owen Webster.

So a Leader Came. Frederick Palmer. LC 32-24283. 1932. R. Long & R. R. Smith, Inc.

So As by Fire. Jean Connor. LC 10-1142. 1909. Benziger Brothers.

So-Big. Edna Ferber. LC 24-26188. 1924. Doubleday, Page & Company.

So Big: A Novel. Edna Ferber. LC 81-1845. 1981. 15.95 (ISBN 0-8161-3193-7). G.K. Hall.

So Big: But Not Too Big. Anthony Basile, Sr. 1980. 4.95 (ISBN 0-533-04658-0). Vantage.

So Blue Marble. Dorothy Belle Flanagan Hughes. LC 40-7242. Duell, Sloan & Pearce.

So Blue Marble. Dorothy Belle Flanagan Hughes. LC 80-12749. 1981. 13.50 (ISBN 0-89340-269-9). J. Curley & Associates.

So Brief a Spring: A Magnificent Story of the Hundred Days. Translated by Humphrey Hare. Claude Manceron. LC 57-12214. 1958. Putnam.

So Brief the Spring. Walter Greenwood. LC 52-1225. 1952. Hutchinson.

So Brief the Years. Natalie Anderson Scott. LC 35-3050. 1935. Dodd, Mead & Company.

So Brief the Years. Natalie B Sokoloff. LC 35-3050. 1935. Dodd, Mead & Company.

So Bright the Vision. Clifford D Simak. 1976. 1.50. Ace.

So Build We. Mary Sewall Gardner. LC 42-224218. 1942. The Macmillan Company.

So Cold, My Bed. 1st Ed. Sam S Taylor. LC 53-103346. (Guilt edged mystery). 1953. Dutton.

So Cold the Night. Ruth Landshoff Yorck. LC 48-834171. 1948. Harper.

So Dark a Shadow. Freda Hurt. (Gothic Ser). 1969. pap. 0.60 o.p. (63-136). Paperback Lib.

So Dead My Lovely. Day Keene. 0.60 o.p. (60-354). Manor Bks.

So Dead the Rose. M. E. Chaber, pseud. (Milo March). 1970. pap. 0.60 o.p. (ISBN 0-446-63396-8, 63-396). Paperback Lib.

So Deadly My Love: By Stephen Ransome Pseud. 1st Ed. Frederick Clyde Davis. 1957. Published for the Crime Club by Doubleday.

So Dear, So Deadly. Linda DuBreuil. 1979. pap. 1.75 o.s.i. (ISBN 0-8439-0657-X, Leisure Bks). Nordon Pubns.

So Dear to My Heart. Sterling North. LC 68-15398. (Illus.). 1968. Doubleday.

So Dear to My Heart. Sterling North. LC 47-31241. 1947. Doubleday.

So Dear to My Heart: A Novel of Lamplight Days on a Farm. Sterling North. LC 49-5619. (Dell book, 291). Dell Pub. Co.

So Deep My Love. Vivien Grey. LC 44-5323. 1944. Arcadia House, Inc.

So Dies the Dreamer. Ursula Reilly Curtiss. (Kangaroo Book). 1977. 1.50 (ISBN 0-671-81058-8). Pocket Books.

So Dream All Night. Kenneth Payson Kempton. LC 41-522103. G. P. Putnam's Sons.

So Evil My Love. Joseph Shearing. LC 47-31024. 1947. Harper.

So Fair a House. Welbourn Kelley. LC 36-12118. 1936. W. Morrow & Company.

So Fair a House. Robert Neill. 1970. pap. 0.95 o.p. (0502-09040). Curtis.

So Fair a House. 1st Ed. Robert Neill. LC 61-63288. 1961. Doubleday.

So Fair, So Evil: By Paul Connelly I. E. Connoly, Pseud. Tom Wicker. LC 55-56515. (Gold medal books, 500). 1955. Fawcett Publications.

So Far. Debby Boone & Dennis Baker. 224p. 1982. pap. 2.95 (ISBN 0-515-06323-1). Jove Pubns.

So Far Away. Harriet Rochlin. 352p. (Orig.). 1981. pap. 2.95 (ISBN 0-515-06125-5). Jove Pubns.

So Far from Heaven. Richard Bradford. LC 73-7885. 1973. 6.95 (ISBN 0-397-00853-8). Lippincott.

So Far from Heaven. Richard Bradford. 1974. (pbk.) 1.50 (ISBN 0-671-78679-2). Pocket Books.

So Far from Spring, a Novel. Peggy Simson Curry. LC 56-5071. 1956. Viking Press.

So Far No Further. Judah Waten. 230p. 1973. 3.50 (ISBN 0-85885-000-1). David & Charles.

So Free We Seem. Jamie Brown. LC 76-378942. 8.95 (ISBN 0-7720-1052-8). Clarke, Irwin.

So Free We Seem: A Novel. Helen Todd. LC 36-285622. Reynal & Hitchcock.

So Gentle, So Fierce. Beverly Friedlander. 1978. pap. 1.95 (ISBN 0-89041-226-X, 3226). Major Bks.

So Great a Cloud of Witnesses. David O. Rankin. LC 78-2584. (Illus., Orig.). 1978. pap. 6.95 (ISBN 0-89407-014-2). Strawberry Hill.
So Great a Man. David Pilgrim, pseud. LC 37-28471. 1937. Harper & Brothers.
So Great a Queen: The Story of Esther, Queen of Persia. Paul Frischauer. LC 50-9696. 1950. Scribner.
So Green the Spring Pastures. 1st Ed. Leonora Barrett. LC 55-10009. 1955. Greenwich Book Publishers.
So Help Me God! Herbert Tarr. LC 79-10905. 8.95 (ISBN 0-8129-0827-9). Times Books.
So Help Me God: A Novel. Felix Jackson. LC 55-9026. 1955. Viking Press.
So I Killed Her. Leonard Oswald Mosley. LC 37-1605. 1937. Doubleday, Doran and Company, Inc.
So It Doens't Whistle. Robert Paul Smith. LC 41-18116. Harcourt, Brace and Company.
So It Goes. Giuseppe Cassieri. LC 62-14266. 1963. Pantheon Books.
So It Was. Zelon B. Jones. 120p. 1975. 5.00 o.p. (ISBN 0-8059-2205-9). Dorrance.
So It Was Just a Simple Wedding. Sara Kasdan. LC 61-13280. 1961. Vanguard Press.
So Joined: A Novel. Harlow Wilson Estes. LC 47-23974. 1947. Rinehart.
So Life Goes on. Mary Lee Russell. LC 45-8457. 1945. House of Field-Doubleday, Inc.
So Little Cause for Caroline. Eric Bercovici. LC 81-65999. 1981. 9.95 (ISBN 0-689-11176-2). Atheneum.
So Little Cause for Caroline. large print ed. Eric Bercovici. LC 82-13982. 1983. 10.95 (ISBN 0-89340-537-X). J. Curley.
So Little Time. Sharon Combes. 1982. pap. 2.50 (ISBN 0-89083-974-3). Zebra.
So Little Time. Sharon Combes. (Orig.). 1980. pap. 2.50 (ISBN 0-89083-585-3). Zebra.
So Little Time. John Phillips Marquand. LC 43-12144. 1943. Little, Brown and Company.
So Long As Love Remembers. Russell Janney. LC 53-10613. 1953. Hermitage House.
So Long As We Love... Peter Goulding. LC 43-177530. 1943. W. A. Wilde Company.
So Long As You Both Shall Live. Ed McBain. (87th precinct mystery). (Signet Book). 1977. 1.50 (ISBN 0-451-07749-0). New American Library.
So Long As You Both Shall Live. Lois Redmon. LC 44-5026. 1944. Dorrance & Company.
So Long As You Both Shall Live: An 87th Precinct Mystery. Evan Hunter. LC 75-37345. 6.95 (ISBN 0-394-48583-1). Random House.
So Long As You're Healthy. Harry Golden. 1971. pap. 0.95 o.p. (N2590). Pyramid Pubns.
So Long at the Fair. Bonner McMillion. LC 64-19305. 1964. Doubleday.
So Long at the Fair. Janet Gregory Vermandel. LC 68-12813. (Red badge mystery). 1967. Dodd, Mead.
So Long at the Fair: A Novel. Anthony Thorne. LC 47-2787. 1947. Random House.
So Long, Daddy. H. B Gilmour. LC 82-22417. 14.95 (ISBN 0-937858-13-7). Newmarket Press.
So Long, See You Tomorrow. William Maxwell. LC 79-2247. 1980. 7.95 (ISBN 0-394-50835-1). Knopf.
So Long, See You Tomorrow. William Maxwell. LC 80-14393. 1980. 10.95 (ISBN 0-8161-3093-0). G. K. Hall.
So Long, Snowman. Tana Reiff. LC 78-75224. (LifeTimes Ser.). 1979. pap. 3.32 (ISBN 0-8224-4321-X). Pitman Learning.
So Long, Sucker. Charles Alden Seltzer. LC 41-254276. 1941. Doubleday, Doran and Company, Inc.
So Long to Learn. Doreen Eileen Agnew Wallace, pseud. LC 36-123105. 1936. The Macmillan Company.
So Love Returns. Robert Nathan. pap. 0.50 o.p. (R772). Pyramid Pubns.
So Many Doors. Oakley M Hall. LC 50-8503. 1950. Random House.
So Many Doors. Laurence Walter Meynell. LC 33-153883. J. B. Lippincott Company.
So Many Doors. Punshon, Ernest Robertson. LC 50-5668. 1950. Macmillan.
So Many Hours. Desemea Wilson. LC 39-11745. 1939. E. P. Dutton & Co., Inc.
So Many Miles. Ruby Mildred Ayres. LC 32-300204. 1932. Doubleday, Doran & Company, Inc.
So Many Partings: A Novel. Cathy Cash Spellman. LC 83-835. 16.95 (ISBN 0-440-07812-1). Delacorte Press.
So Many Steps to Death. Agatha Miller Christie. LC 55-6199. (Red badge detective). 1955. Dodd, Mead.
So Many Steps to Death. Agatha Miller Christie. 1973. (pbk.) 0.95. Pocket Books.
So Many Voices. Gertrude Schweitzer. LC 64-20290. 1964. Prentice-Hall.
So Many Worlds. Anita Blackmon Smith. LC 35-126773. Arcadia House.
So Merciful a Queen, So Cruel a Woman. Alice Harwood. LC 58-9152. 1958. Bobbs-Merrill.
So Moses Was Born. Joan Marshall Grant. LC 78-20230. (Grant, Joan Marshall, 1907-. Works). (Works.). (Illus.). 1980. 18.00 (ISBN 0-405-11791-4). Arno Press.
So Move the Body. Carter Brown, pseud. (Signet Book). 1973. (pbk.) 0.75. New American Library.
So Much As Beauty Does. Muriel Elwood. LC 41-77979. Liveright Publishing Corporation.
So Much Blood. Simon Brett. LC 76-42083. 6.95 (ISBN 0-684-14804-8). Scribner.
So Much Blood... Bruno Fischer. LC 47-21435. (On cover: A Golden willow mystery, no. 52). 1946.
So Much Blood: A Mystery Novel. Zelda Popkin. LC 44-485494. 1944. J. B. Lippincott Company.
So Much for Love. Cella Vaughan. LC 36-6966. Godwin.
So Much Good: A Novel in a New Manner. Gilbert Frankau. LC 28-2380. 1928. Harper & Brothers.
So Much Love. Lucy Walker, pseud. LC 77-6140. 1977. 1.50 (ISBN 0-345-25858-4). Ballantine Books.
So Much of the Diary of Lady Willoughby: As Relates to Her Domestic History, and to the Eventful Period of the Reign of Charles the First. Hannah Mary Reynolds Rathbone. LC 38-35033. (Half-title: Wiley and Putnam's library of choice reading. Diary of Lady Willoughby). 1845. Wiley and Putnam.
So Much to Say. Edmund B. Bolles. (Illus.). 288p. 1982. 16.95 (ISBN 0-312-73120-5); pap. 9.95 (ISBN 0-312-73121-3). St Martin.
So Narrow the Bridge & Deep the Water. Lisa Thomas. LC 80-52865. 156p. 1980. pap. 4.95 (ISBN 0-931188-08-3). Seal Pr WA.
So Near & Yet.; see Castle in Spain.
So Now You're Alone. Jo Kimmel. 1976. pap. 1.25x o.p. (ISBN 0-8358-0340-6). Upper Room.
So Perilous, My Love. Clarissa Ross, pseud. 1979. pap. 2.25 o.s.i. (ISBN 0-8439-0606-5, Leisure Bks). Nordon Pubns.
So Perish the Roses. Stephen Southwold. LC 40-31636. 1940. The Macmillan Company.
So Red the Rose. Stark Young. LC 34-218320. 1934. C. Scribner's Sons.
So Red the Rose. Stark Young. LC 78-10963. 1978. 15.00 (ISBN 0-89783-006-7). Larlin Corp.
So Red the Rose. With an Introd. by Donald Davidson. Stark Young. LC 53-11471. (Modern standard authors). 1953. Scribner.
So Restless, So Lonely. Bernard Alvin Palmer. (Dimension Books). 1973. (pbk.) 0.95. Bethany Fellowship.
So Rich, So Lovely, & So Dead. Harold Q. Masur. 1971. pap. 0.75 o.p. (T2391). Pyramid Pubns.
So Rich, So Lovely, and So Dead: A Scott Jordan Story. Harold Q. Masur. LC 52-14149. (Inner sanctum mystery). 1952. Simon and Schuster.
So Runs the World Away. A Novel. Edith May Dickinson & Stokes, Edward Ansley. LC 6-36828. 1891. G. W. Dillingham.
So Shadows Pass. Dorothy Quentin. LC 43-14569. 1943. Arcadia House, Inc.
So Shall They Reap. John Henry Van Sweringen Bennett. LC 44-786. 1944. Doubleday, Doran and Company, Inc.
So Simply Means the Rain. Ronald Moran. 1965. 3.00; pap. 2.00. Claitors.
So Slow the Dawning. Inge Trachtenberg. LC 72-8970. 1973. (ISBN 0-393-08538-4). Norton.
So Soon to Die: By Jeremy York Pseud. John Creasey. LC 56-239735. 1955. S. Paul.
So Soon to Die by Jeremy York Pseud. John Creasey. LC 57-586073. 1957. Scribner.
So Speaks My Heart. Rose Michaels. (Orig.). 1979. pap. 1.75 (ISBN 0-532-23172-4). Woodhill.
So Speaks the Heart. Johanna Lindsey. 368p. 1983. pap. 3.95 (ISBN 0-380-81471-4). Avon.
So Stands the Rock. Anne Miller Downes. LC 39-20249. 1939. Frederick A. Stokes Company.
So Stood I... Jane Culver. LC 34-5822. 1934. Houghton Mifflin Company.
So That's That. Inez Specking. LC 29-15661. 1929. B. Herder Book Co.
So the Lights Will Keep Burning. Henry P. Wheeler, Jr. 3.50 o.p. Carlton.
So the Loud Torrent. Richard C House. LC 78-104915. (Illus.). 6.95 (ISBN 0-87839-028-6) (ISBN 0-87839-027-8). North Star Press.
So the Wind Won't Blow It All Away. Richard Brautigan. LC 82-2504. 13.95 (ISBN 0-440-08195-5). Delacorte Press/Seymour Lawrence.
So the World Goes. James William Sullivan. LC 8-17667. 1898. C. H. Kerr & Company.
So They Were Married." A Novel. Walter Besant & Rice, James. (Harper's Franklin square library, no 261). 1882. Harper & Brothers.
So Thick the Fog. Catherine Pomeroy Stewart. LC 44-7100. 1944. C. Scribner's Sons.
So Thin Is the Veil: A Novel. Delmar Eil Bordeaux. LC 48-7332. 1948. Bellevue Books.
So This Is What Happened to Charlie Moe. Douglass Wallop. LC 65-18777. 4.50. Norton.
So Tiberius... Decorated by A. H. Eisner. 1st American Ed. Ethel Edith Mannin. LC 55-10109. 1955. Putnam.
So True a Love. A Novel. Maria M Grant. LC 6-44840. 1884. G. W. Carleton & Co.; Etc., Etc.
So Unlike the English. Noel Langley. LC 37-3366. 1937. W. Morrow & Co.
So We'll Live. Priscilla Hovey Wright. LC 37-29167. 1937. Houghton Mifflin Company.
So Well Remembered... James Hilton. LC 46-553. 1945. Little, Brown and Company.
So What Killed the Vampire? Alan Geoffrey Yates. LC 66-5647. (His the Carter Brown mystery series). New American Library.
So White Your Hands: A Novel. Erwin L Gienke. LC 51-9005. 1950. Exposition Press.
So Wicked My Desire. Stephanie Blake. LC 78-70092. (Orig.). 1979. pap. 2.95 (ISBN 0-87216-892-1). Playboy Pbks.
So Wicked the Heart. Barbara Riefe. LC 79-92154. 368p. (Orig.). 1980. pap. 2.75 (ISBN 0-87216-658-9). Playboy Pbks.
So Wild a Heart. Veronica Jason. (Orig.). 1981. pap. 2.95 (ISBN 0-451-11067-6, AE1067, Sig). NAL.
So Wild a Love. Barbara Bennett. (Dell Book). 1977. 1.50 (ISBN 0-440-18470-3). Dell Pub. Co.
So Wild a Rapture. Andrea Layton, pseud. LC 78-59974. 368p. (Orig.). 1978. pap. 1.95 (ISBN 0-87216-489-6). Playboy Pbks.
So Wild, So Wonderful. Justine Sommers. 1978. 1.25 (ISBN 0-441-78730-4). Ace Books.
So Wild the Heart. Geoffrey Trease. LC 59-12394. 1959. Vanguard Press.
So Wild the Wind. Translated from the French by Peter Wiles. Maurice Guy. LC 59-110143. 3.95. Putnam.
So Winds the River. Yale Samuel Nathanson. LC 70-140241. 7.50. Impress House.
So Wise, So Young. Agnes Burke Hale. LC 35-12674. Minton, Balch & Company.
So Wise We Grow. Christine Whiting Paramenter. LC 30-314863. Hale, Cushman & Flint.
So Wondrous Free. Maryhelen Clague. LC 77-8771. (Illus.). 1978. 8.95 (ISBN 0-8128-2355-9). Stein and Day.
So You Think Sex Is Dirty? Odette Newman. LC 71-9970. (Traveller's companion series, TC-442). 1969. 1.75. Olympia Press.
So Young a Body. Frank Bunce. LC 50-5272. (Inner sanctum mystery). 1950. Simon and Schuster.
So Young, So Fair. Elizabeth Seifert. LC 73-79150. 1973. 6.95. Aeonian Press.
So Young, So Fair. Elizabeth Seifert. LC 47-2362. 1947. Dodd, Mead & Company.
So Young the Warriors. Thomas S. Byrd. 5.00 o.p. Vantage.
So Young to Burn. John Creasey. LC 68-12492. 1968. Scribner.
So Young to Die. Gregory Tree, pseud. LC 53-10754. 1953. Scribner.
Soakum: A Story. Harry Edmund Danford. LC 13-37915. 1912. 1.35. The Author.
Soames and the Flag. John Galsworthy. LC 30-15143. 1930. C. Scribner's Sons.
Soames Green. Margaret Rivers Larminie Tragett. LC 25-16607. 1925. Houghton Mifflin Company.
Soap. Francis Ponge. Tr. by Lane Dunlop. (Cape Editions Ser). 1969. pap. 1.50 o.p. (ISBN 0-670-65418-3, Grossman). Penguin.
Soap Man & the Railroad of Death. Dick Scroggs. 1975. 4.95 o.p. (ISBN 0-8059-2166-4). Dorrance.
Soap Opera Slaughter. Marvin Kaye. LC 82-45530. (Crime Club Ser.). 1982. 11.95 (ISBN 0-385-18361-5). Doubleday.
Soapy Smith. Frank C. Robertson & Beth K. Harris. 1961. 8.50 (ISBN 0-8038-6661-5). Hastings.
Soaring "...an Odyssey of the Soul". Roger Elwood. LC 78-55676. (Illus.). 1978. pap. 1.95 o.p. (ISBN 0-87239-225-2, 3163). Standard Pub.
Sob Sister. Florenz Branch. LC 40-8382. Phoenix Press.
Sob Sister. Mildred Evans Gilman. LC 31-521694. J. Cape & H. Smith.
Sob Sister. Florence Stonebraker. LC 40-8382. 1940. Phoenix Press.
Sob-Squad: A Novel. Winfield H Caslow. LC 28-29083. The Grand Rapids Calendar Co., Co-Operating with J. Thomas Co.
Sobbing Sounds. Omunjakko Nakibimbiri. LC 75-333033. (African creative writing series). 1975. 2.25 (ISBN 0-582-64157-8). Longman.
Sober As a Judge. Henry Cecil. LC 58-12468. 1958. Harper.
Sober Feast. Barbara Blackburn. LC 29-161623. 1929. Little, Brown, and Company.
Sobranie Sochinenii V 4 Tomakh, Vol. 1. Evgeny Ivanovich Zamyatin. Ed. by Alexi Tsvetkov. 300p. (Rus.). 1982. 25.00 (ISBN 0-88233-767-X). Ardis Pubs.
Sobranie Sochinenii V 5-i Tomakh, Vol 1. Vladislav Khodasevich. Ed. by Robert Hughes & John Malmstad. 330p. (Rus.). 1983. 25.00 (ISBN 0-88233-686-X). Ardis Pubs.
Sobranie Sochinenii: Vol. 1. Mikhail Bulgakov. Tr. by Tom I. Ranniaia. 421p. (Rus.). 1982. 25.00 (ISBN 0-88233-506-5). Ardis Pubs.
Sociable Ghost. Being the Adventures of a Reporter... HelenBurnell D'Apery. LC 3-19178. J. S. Ogilvie Publishing Company.
Social Bucaneer. Frederic Stewart Isham. LC 10-23396. The Bobbs-Merrill Company.
Social Cancer: A Complete Version of Noli Me Tangere from the Spanish of Jose Rizal. Jose Rizal Y Alonso. Tr. by Derbyshire, Charles. LC 13-138201. 1912. Philippine Education Company.
Social Club. Albert Quandt. LC 54-31853. (Carnival books, no. 980). 1954. Hanro Corp.
Social Comedy see Insight: English Literature.
Social Conspiracy: Or, Under the Ban. A Novel. Ione G Daniels. LC 6-34207. 1888. G. C. Pound.
Social Crime. Minnie L Armstrong & Sceets, George N., Joint Author. W. L. Allison Company.
Social Departure. Sara Jeannette Duncan Cotes. LC 5-2455. (On cover: Seaside library. Pocket ed., no. 2137). 1895. G. Munro's Sons.
Social Departure: How Orthodocia and I Went Round the World by Ourselves. Sara Jeannette Duncan Cotes. LC 42-26000. 1893. D. Appleton and Company.
Social Departure. How Orthodocia and I Went Round the World by Ourselves. Sara Jeannette Duncan Cotes. LC 5-27600. 1891. D. Appleton and Company.
Social Diplomat. Flora Adams Darling. LC 6-33069. (On cover: American novelists' series, no. 1). 1889. F. F. Lovell & Company.
Social Distinction: Or, Hearts and Home. Sarah Stickney Ellis. LC 6-37842. 1848-49. J. & F. Tallis.
Social Evil: Or, The Woman Lalarge. Pauline Grayson. (peerless series, no. 67). 1893. J. S. Ogilvie.
Social Experiment. Annie E P Searing. LC 8-3379. 1885. G. P. Putnam's Sons.
Social Fetters: Or, Within a Shadow. Henry Thompson Stanton. LC 8-13452. 1889. W. H. Morrison.
Social Firebreak: World War III, June 12, 1986. Robert Sotrell. LC 81-84587. 260p. 1982. pap. 2.95 (ISBN 0-9606458-0-2). Select Pub.
Social Gangster: Adventures of Craig Kennedy, Scientific Detective. Arthur Benjamin Reeve. LC 16-16715. 1916. Hearst's International Library Co.
Social Highwayman. Elizabeth Phipps Train. LC 8-29725. (On cover: The lotus library). 1896. J. B. Lippincott Company.
Social Insight Through Short Stories: An Anthology. Ed. by Josephine Strode. LC 46-6884. 1946. Harper & Brothers.
Social Lion. Margaret Horton Potter. LC 2-2770. 1901. The Lion Publishing Co.
Social Meteor. Clement R Marley. LC 7-24689. (primrose series. no. 17). Street & Smith.
Social Problems Through Science Fiction. Martin Harry Greenberg. LC 74-24713. 1975. 4.95. St. Martin's Press.
Social Psychology Through Literature. Ed. by Ronald Fernandez. LC 70-161134. 1971. (ISBN 0-471-25760-5). Wiley.
Social Revolution. A Novel. Henry Martel. 1891. G. W. Dillingham.
Social Secretary. Shirley Brander. LC 33-863179. E. J. Clode, Inc.
Social Secretary. David Graham Phillips. LC 72-84627. (Illus.). 1974. 8.95 (ISBN 0-403-03051-X). Scholarly Press.
Social Secretary. David Graham Phillips. LC 74-104542. (Illus.). 1970. Literature House.
Social Secretary. David Graham Phillips. LC 5-28184. 1905. The Bobbs-Merrill Company.
Social Silhouettes. Edgar Fawcett. LC 75-1846. (Leisure Class in America). 1975. 22.00 (ISBN 0-405-06913-8). Arno Press.
Social Silhouettes (Being the Impressions of Mr. Mark Manhattan) Edgar Fawcett. LC 6-38780. 1885. Ticknor and Company.
Social Sinners. Emile Palier. The Abbey Press.
Social Strugglers: A Novel. Hjalmar Hjorth Boyesen. 1893. C. Scribner's Sons.
Social Tragedies. S. T Satterthwaite. LC 8-1827. W. B. Conkey Company.
Social Vicissitudes. Francis Charles Philips. (On cover: Seaside library. Pocket ed. no. 1041). 1887. G. Munro.
Social Worker. Barry N. Malzberg. Orig. Title: Horizontal Woman. 1977. pap. 1.50 o.s.i. (ISBN 0-8439-0511-5, Leisure Bks). Nordon Pubns.
Socialist. Cyril Arthur Edward Ranger Gull. LC 9-31022. 1909. G. P. Putnam's Sons.
Socialist and the Prince. Cora Miranda Baggerly Older. LC 3-5534. 1903. Funk & Wagnalls Company.

Socialist Countess: A Story of to-Day. Horace W. C Newte. LC 11-17103. 1911. John Lane Company.
Society and Souls. Elizabeth Ransom Inglis. LC 35-527. The Christopher Publishing House.
Society As It Found Me Out. Alfred Thompson. LC 8-19977. 1890. Carlton-Regand.
Society Be Damned. Bonnie Melbourne Busch. LC 52-130871. 1953. Dorrance.
Society Detective. Oscar Maitland. (secret service series, no. 22). 1889. Street & Smith.
Society Editor. Helen Welshimer. LC 39-152755. Gramercy Publishing Co.
Society Editor: A Newspaper Mystery Story. Henry Charlton Beck. LC 32-317233. E. P. Dutton and Company, Inc.
Society Girl: A Love Story. Vivien Grey. LC 38-13407. Chelsea House.
Society in Search of Truth: Or, Stock Gambling in San Francisco. A Novel. J. F. Clark. 1878. Pub. by the Author.
Society Is Nuts. J. Janu. (Geneva Books). 1968. 2.75 o.p. Carlton.
Society Nurse. Ruth McCarthy Sears. 1975. 4.95. Avalon Books.
Society of Friends: A Domestic Narrative, Illustrating the Peculiar Doctrines Held by the Disciples of George Fox. Sarah D Greer. LC 6-45443. 1853. M. W. Dodd.
Society of the Dispossessed. Raymond Foxall. (Highwayman). (Signet book: Vol. 1) (ISBN 0-451-07216-2). New American Library.
Society Play-Girl. Carlotta Baker. LC 39-158028. Phoenix Press.
Society Play-Girl. Leona Slottman. LC 39-15802. 1939. Phoenix Press.
Society Rapids. High Life in Washington, Saratoga and Bar Harbor. Cara Camera. LC 7-3311. T. B. Peterson & Brothers.
Society Silhouettes: Collection of Short Stories. Laura Cooke Barker. 1898. The Helman-Taylor Company.
Society Wolf. John Russell. LC 10-7824. 1.50. Cupples & Leon Company.
Society's Prodigal: A Novel. Patrick T Crowe. J. S. Ogilvie Publishing Company.
Society's Protegee. A Novel. Also, A Modern Sinner. Maude James Chilton. LC 6-20975. (On cover: Union square series, no. 3). Cleveland Publishing Company.
Society's Verdict. A Novel. LC 8-10208. (On cover: Seaside library. Pocket ed. no, 778). G. Munro.
Sociology Through Science Fiction. Ed. by Martin Harry Greenberg et al. 350p. (Orig.). 1974. 14.95 o.p. (ISBN 0-312-74130-8); pap. text ed. 10.95 (ISBN 0-312-74165-0). St Martin.
Sock It to Me. Rod Gray. (The Lady from L.U.S.T. Ser.). (O.s.i.). Orig. Title: Poison Pussy. 1973. pap. 0.95 o.s.i. (BT50604). Belmont-Tower.
Sock It to Me, Zombie. F. W. Paul. pap. 0.60 o.p. (73-759). Lancer.
Socks on a Rooster. Richard McCaughan. 1967. 6.00. Claitors.
Sod House. Elizabeth Jane Coatsworth. 1967. 8.95 (ISBN 0-02-721690-X). Macmillan.
Sodbuster Law. Ford Bowne, pseud. 192p. (OSI). 1972. 3.95 o.s.i. Lenox Hill.
Soddy. Sarah Comstock. LC 12-22314. 1912. 1.30. Doubleday, Page & Company.
Sodom and Gomorrah Business. Barry N Malzberg. 1974. (pbk.) 0.95 (ISBN 0-671-77789-0). Pocket Books.
Sodom Thy Sister. S. P. Johnson. 192p. 1974. text ed. 5.95x o.s.i. (ISBN 0-8277-2903-0). British Bk Ctr.
Soeur Angele and the Bell Ringer's Niece: By Henri Catalan Pseud. Henry Dupuy-Mazuel. LC 57-10175. 1957. Sheed and Ward.
Soeur Angele and the Embarrassed Ladies: By Henry Catalan Pseud. Henry Dupuy-Mazuel. LC 55-944613. 1955. Sheed & Ward.
Soeur Angele & the Embarrassed Ladies. Henri Catalan. 2.50 o.p. (ISBN 0-8362-0265-1, Pub. by Sheed). Guild Bks.
Soeur Angele and the Ghosts of Chambord. By Henri Catalan Pseud. Henry Dupuy-Mazuel. LC 56-6124. 1956. Sheed and Ward.
Soeur Louise. Tr. by Vairin, Minnie. LC 8-10209. (On cover: Lovell's library, no. 1019). 1887. J. W. Lovell Co.
Sofa. Claude P. De Crehillon, Jr. (Orig.). 1968. pap. 0.95 o.p. (B95-108). Belmont-Tower.
Soft & Savage. Hector Casale. 160p. pap. 1.95 o.p. Montmartre.
Soft Answer. Patricia Frane. LC 37-1121. Arcadia House.
Soft Answers. Richard Aldington. LC 67-13046. (Crosscurrents: modern fiction). 1967. Southern Illinois University Press.
Soft Answers. Richard Aldington. LC 32-125176. 1932. Doubleday, Doran & Company, Inc.
Soft As Silk. Louise Platt Hauck. LC 42-11121. 1942. Macrae-Smith-Company.
Soft As Silk. Jean Randall. LC 42-11121. 1942. Macrae-Smith-Company.
Soft As Steel. Henry Ralph Pruett. LC 51-13. 1950. Christopher.
Soft Clay, Anonymous. Josiah Pitts Woolfolk. LC 34-20215. Authors Publications, Inc.
Soft in the Middle. Michael Storey. LC 74-171132. 1972. 6.95 (ISBN 0-394-47476-7). Knopf.
Soft Machine. William S. Burroughs. 1966. pap. 2.45 o.p. (ISBN 0-394-17115-2, B131, BC). Grove.
Soft Machine: Nova Express; The Wild Boys: Three Novels. William S. Burroughs. LC 80-8062. 1980. 4.95 (ISBN 0-394-17749-5). Grove Press: Distributed by Random House.
Soft Money. Henry Barnard Safford. The Penn Publishing Company.
Soft Night. Liz Vibert. LC 77-82784. 1977. pap. 1.95 o.p. (ISBN 0-87216-421-7, E16421, Dist. by PB). Playboy.
Soft, Savage Cat. Peter Keyes. (Orig.). pap. 0.95 o.p. (1106). Brandon.
Soft Shoulders. Ashford Grainge. LC 32-14018. Sears Publishing Company.
Soft Shoulders. Peter Shelley, pseud. LC 35-229603. Godwin.
Soft Side. Henry James. LC 77-140330. (Short story index reprint series). 1970. Books for Libraries Press.
Soft Side. Henry James. LC 5075. 1900. The Macmillan Company.
Soft Soap see Three Novels: Bibliotheca Neerlandica Ser.
Soft Spot. Arthur Stuart-Menteth Hutchinson. LC 33-272628. 1933. Little, Brown, and Company.
Soft Targets. Dean Ing. LC 80-113242. 4.95 (ISBN 0-441-77405-9). Ace Books.
Soft Thighs. Aremus Maginot. 160p. pap. 1.95 o.p. (MP-110). Montmartre.
Soft Touch. Robert Brooks. pap. 1.95 o.s.i. (Venus). Grove.
Soft Touch. John Dann MacDonald. 1978. pap. 1.95 (ISBN 0-449-13957-3, GM). Fawcett.
Soft Touch of Love. Cornell Wiley. 4.50 o.p. Carlton.
Soft Voice of the Serpent: And Other Stories. Nadine Gordimer. LC 52-9515. 1952. Simon and Schuster.
Softie. Howard Warren. LC 39-15796. Phoenix Press.
Softly in the Night. M. E. Chaber, pseud. (Milo March Mystery Ser). 1970. pap. 0.60 o.p. (63-288). Paperback Lib.
Softly in the Night: A New Milo March Adventure. Kendell Foster Crossen. LC 63-7269. (Rinehart suspense novel). 1963. Holt, Rinehart and Winston.
Softly Roars the Lion. Melvin Richard Ellis. LC 68-23573. 1968. 3.95. Holt, Rinehart and Winston.
Softness on the Other Side of the Hole. Kenneth Davids. LC 67-27883. (Black circle bk.). 1968. 3.50. Grove.
Softness on the Other Side of the Hole. Kenneth Davids. LC 67-27883. (Black circle book). 1968. Grove Press.
Software. Rudy Rucker. 176p. (Orig.). 1982. pap. 2.25 (ISBN 0-441-77408-3). Ace Bks.
Soganannten Sententiae Vorronis. Peter Germann. pap. 6.00 (ISBN 0-384-18030-2). Johnson Repr.
Sogliadatai. Vladimir Nabokov. (Sobranie Rasskazov I Povestei: Vol. 2). (Rus.). 1978. 15.00 (ISBN 0-88233-287-2); pap. 7.00 (ISBN 0-88233-288-0). Ardis Pubs.
Soho. C. L Byrd. LC 80-2856. 1981. 16.95 (ISBN 0-385-17185-4). Doubleday.
Soho Square. Claire Rayner. LC 77-361841. (Her The performers; book 4). (Illus.). 1976. 4.25 (ISBN 0-304-29736-4). Cassell.
Soho Square. Claire Rayner. (Signet Book). 1977. 1.95 (ISBN 0-451-07783-0). New American Library.
Soho Square: A Novel. Claire Rayner. LC 76-42180. 8.95 (ISBN 0-399-11879-9). Putnam.
Soho Summer of Mr. Green. Cyril Kersh. LC 74-192899. 1974. 2.50 (ISBN 0-491-01523-2). W. H. Allen.
Soil Runs Red. Matthew Semple Evans. LC 48-1369. 1948. Van Kampen Press.
Soil, the Master. Rosena A Giles. LC 24-298242. The Cornhill Publishing Company.
Sojourn: A Diary of Deliberate Death. Paul Morgan. LC 75-123354. (Genesis Press book). (Illus.). 1970. 4.95. Hallux.
Sojourn Among Shadows. Murrell Edmunds. LC 36-1742. 1936. The Caxton Printers, Ltd.
Sojourn in Mosaic. Robert A Elfers. LC 79-10244. 2.95 (ISBN 0-377-00089-2). Friendship Press.
Sojourn in Persepolis: Xerxes After Salamis. Elbert L Harris. LC 76-362674. 2.25. Adams Press.
Sojourn of a Stranger. Walter Sullivan. LC 57-10426. 1957. Holt.
Sojourner. Robert Dull Elder. LC 13-7081. 1913. 1.30. Harper & Brothers.
Sojourner. Marjorie Kinnan Rawlings. LC 52-14613. 1953. Scribner.
Sol. Mario Satz. LC 78-66998. 1979. 12.95 (ISBN 0-385-11579-2). Doubleday.
Sol Myers. Judah Stampfer. LC 62-12420. 1962. Macmillan.
Solal. Albert Cohen & Benson, Wilfrid, 1899- Tr. LC 33-8148. 1933. E. P. Dutton & Co., Inc.
Solan. Ernest Gordon. LC 73-76256. 1973. 5.95. Word Books.
Solange Stories. Fryniwyd Tennyson Jesse. LC 31-119123. 1931. The Macmillan Company.
Solar Assassins. Kurt Mahr. (Perry Rhodan, #49). 1974. (pbk.) 0.95. Ace Books.
Solar Barque. Illus. by Peter Loomer. 1st Ed. Anais Nin. LC 58-46358. 1958.
Solar Lottery. Philip K Dick. LC 55-33828. (Ace double novel books, D-103). 1955. Ace Books.
Solar Lottery. frontispiece ill. by richard powers. ed. Philip K Dick. LC 76-10716. (Gregg Press science fiction series). 1976. 9.50 (ISBN 0-8398-2330-4). Gregg Press.
Solar Menace. Nick Carter. (Nick Carter Ser.). 224p. (Orig.). 1981. pap. 2.50 (ISBN 0-441-77413-X). Ace Bks.
Solar Pons Omnibus. August William Derleth & Basil Copper. LC 76-17995. (Illus.). 39.95 (ISBN 0-87054-009-2) (ISBN 0-87054-010-6) (ISBN 0-87054-006-8). Arkham House.
Solarians. Norman Spinrad. (Orig.). 1969. pap. 0.60 o.p. (63-044). Paperback Lib.
Solarians. Norman Spinrad. 1976. (pbk.) 1.25. Leisure Books.
Solaris. Stanislaw Lem. LC 75-123267. 1970. 4.95 (ISBN 0-8027-5526-7). Walker.
Solaris Farm: A Story of the Twentieth Century. Milan C. Edson. LC 78-154440. (Utopian Literature Ser). (Illus.). 1971. Repr. of 1900 ed. 23.00 (ISBN 0-405-03523-3). Ayer Co.
Solarman: The Beginning. David Oliphant & Alison Bellack. (Pendulum Illustrated Originals Ser.). (Illus.). (gr. 4-12). 1979. pap. text ed. 2.45 (ISBN 0-88301-425-4); wkbk. 1.25 (ISBN 0-88301-435-1). Pendulum Pr.
Sold! Nan Lyons & Ivan Lyons. LC 81-19576. 12.95 (ISBN 0-698-11148-6). Coward, McCann & Geoghegan.
Sold: A Novel. William G Hosie. LC 32-25593. The Macaulay Company.
Sold for a Song. Elizabeth Hamilton Herbert. Farrar & Rinehart, Incorporated.
Sold for Gold. Emma Augusta Sharkey. (On cover: Library of American authors, no. 31). 1891. G. Munro.
Sold South. William Almon Wolff. LC 21-184734. 1921. G. P. Putnam's Sons.
Soldato. Al Conroy. (Orig.). 1972. pap. 0.95 o.p. (75-315). Lancer.
Soldato No. 3: Strange Hold. Al Conroy. (Orig.). 1973. pap. 0.95 o.s.i. (75-433). Lancer.
Soldato Number Four: Murder Mission! Al Conroy. 1973. pap. 0.95 o.s.i. (75-459). Lancer.
Soldier. John Alexander Lee. LC 77-361855. 1976. (ISBN 0-589-00986-9). A. H. & A. W. Reed.
Soldier. Richard Pitts Powell. LC 60-12606. 1960. Scribner.
Soldier and a Gentleman. James Maclaren Cobban. LC 6-26760. Lovell, Coryell & Company.
Soldier and a Gentleman. James MacLaren Cobban. Street & Smith.
Soldier and the Gentlewoman. Hilda Vaughan. LC 32-216861. 1932. C. Scribner's Sons.
Soldier & the Lady. Barriss Mills. 1975. 16.00 (Pub. by Elizabeth Pr); pap. 8.00. SBD.
Soldier and the Rose. Translated by Monroe Stearns. Marcel Haedrich. LC 62-10967. 1962. Putnam.
Soldier and the Sage. A Novel About Akiba. Richard Gibson Hubler. LC 66-15108. 4.95. Crown.
Soldier and the Sage: A Novel About Akiba. Richard Gibson Hubler. LC 66-15108. 1966. Crown Publishers.
Soldier and the Sorceress: Or, The Adventures of Jane Seton. James Grant. LC 41-31318. 1890. The Keystone Publishing Co.
Soldier, Ask Not. Gordon R. Dickson. 320p. 1982. pap. 2.25. Ace Bks.
Soldier, Ask Not. Gordon R. Dickson. 1980. pap. 2.25 (ISBN 0-441-77418-0). Ace Bks.
Soldier, Ask Not. Gordon R Dickson. (Dorsai Novels). (DAW Science Fiction Books, no. 172: Vol. 2). (Illus.). 1975. (pbk.) 1.50. Daw Books.
Soldier Boy: A Collection of Short Stories. Michael Shaara. 191p. (Orig.). 1982. pap. 2.50 (ISBN 0-671-83342-1, Timescape). PB.
Soldier Erect. Brian Wilson Aldiss. LC 70-161539. 1971. 6.95. Coward, McCann & Geoghegan.
Soldier for Hire. Red Cushing. 1962. 4.00 o.p. Fernhill.
Soldier for Hire, No. 1: Commando Squad. Mark K. Roberts. 1982. pap. 2.50 (ISBN 0-8217-1094-X). Zebra.
Soldier for Hire, No. 1: Zulu Blood. Robert Skimin. 1981. pap. 2.50 (ISBN 0-89083-777-5). Zebra.
Soldier for Hire, No. 2: Trojan in Iran. Robert Skimin. (Orig.). 1981. pap. 2.50 (ISBN 0-89083-793-7). Zebra.
Soldier for Hire, No. 3: U. N. Sabotage. Robert Skimin. (Orig.). 1981. pap. 2.50 (ISBN 0-89083-894-1). Zebra.
Soldier for Hire, No. 4: Bloodletting! Robert Skimin. (Orig.). 1982. pap. 2.50 (ISBN 0-89083-939-5). Zebra.
Soldier for Hire, No. 5: Libyan Warlord. Robert Skimin. 1982. pap. 2.50 (ISBN 0-89083-988-3). Zebra.
Soldier for Hire, No. 7: Pathet Vengeance. Mark K. Roberts. 1983. pap. 2.50 (ISBN 0-8217-1140-7). Zebra.
Soldier from Virginia. Marjorie Bowen. LC 12-22518. 1912. 1.30. D. Appleton and Company.
Soldier: His Daily Life Through the Ages. Philip Warner. LC 75-10062. (Illus.). 1976. 8.95 (ISBN 0-8008-7248-7). Taplinger Pub. Co.
Soldier in Paradise. Burton Wohl. LC 77-8852. (Illus.). 8.95 (ISBN 0-399-11928-0). Putnam.
Soldier Lover. A Romance of Grant's Seige ! of Petersburg. Edward S Brooks. (On cover: Flag series, no. 2). Street & Smith.
Soldier Men. Yeo. LC 18-588321. 1917. John Lane.
Soldier No More. Anthony Price. LC 81-43619. 1982. 13.95 (ISBN 0-385-18048-9). Published for the Crime Club by Doubleday.
Soldier of Fortune. Ernest Kellogg Gann. (Kangaroo Book). 1977. 1.95 (ISBN 0-671-81198-3). Pocket Books.
Soldier of Fortune. Ernest Kellogg Gann. LC 54-9184. 1954. W. Sloane Associates.
Soldier of Fortune. Elizabeth Thomasina Meade Smith. LC 8-8653. R. F. Fenno & Company.
Soldier of Fortune, Spoils of War. Peter McCurtin. (O.s.i.). 1976. pap. 1.25 o.s.i. (BT50967). Belmont-Tower.
Soldier of Fortune: The Guns of Palembang. Peter McCurtin. (Belmont Tower Book). 1.25. Tower Publications.
Soldier of Fortune: The True Story of a Prodigal Who Learned That the Way of the Transgressor Is Hard, and That God Used His Angels to Guide Him Through Many Dangers and Bring Him Safely Back to 'the Shadow of the Almighty.' Illustrated by Stanley Fleming. William L Barclay. LC 59-25927. 1958. Southern Pub. Association.
Soldier of God. James S Diemer. 1973. 4.50 (ISBN 0-533-00312-1). Vantage.
Soldier of Good Fortune: An Historical Novel. Ruth Cross. LC 37-658. B. Upshaw and Company.
Soldier of India. Tom Gibson. LC 81-52952. 1982. 11.95 (ISBN 0-312-74245-2). St. Martin's Press.
Soldier of Life. Hugh De Selincourt. LC 17-2025. 1917. 1.50. The Macmillan Company.
Soldier of Lyons: A Tale of the Tuileries. Catherine Grace Frances Moody Gore. LC 71-162906. (Bentley's Standard Novels: No. 82). Repr. of 1841 ed. 18.50 (ISBN 0-404-54482-7). AMS Pr.
Soldier of Manhattan, and His Adventures at Ticonderoga and Quebec. Joseph Alexander Altsheler. LC 6-508. (Half-title6 Appletons' town and country library, no. 225). 1897. D. Appleton and Company.
Soldier of Orange. Erik H. Roelfzema. 1980. pap. 2.50 (ISBN 0-345-28849-1). Ballantine.
Soldier of the Confederacy. Andrew Magnus Fleming. LC 34-42867. 1934. Meador Publishing Company.
Soldier of the Future. William James Dawson. LC 8-24464. F. H. Revell Company.
Soldier of the Legion. Charles Norris Williamson & Alice Muriel Livingston Williamson. LC 14-18424. 1914. Doubleday, Page & Co.
Soldier of the Queen. John Harris. LC 80-65993. 1980. 9.95 (ISBN 0-689-11074-X). Atheneum.
Soldier of the Revolution. Ward S Just. LC 76-112990. 1970. 5.95. Knopf.
Soldier of the Sea. Robert Welter Daly. LC 42-19443. 1942. W. Morrow and Company.
Soldier of the Valley. Nelson McAllister Lloyd. LC 4-25389. 1904. C. Scribner's Sons.
Soldier of Valley Forge: A Romance of the American Revolution. Robert Neilson Stephens & Goodridge Roberts, Theodore. LC 11-7746. 1911. 1.50. L. C. Page & Company.
Soldier of Virginia: Tale of Colonel Washington & Braddock's Defeat. Burton Egbert Stevenson. 1901. lib. bdg. 14.50 o.s.i. (ISBN 0-512-00874-4). Garrett Pr.
Soldier Rigdale: How He Sailed in the "Mayflower" and How He Served Miles Standish. Beulah Marie Dix. LC 99-55033. 1899. The Macmillan Company.
Soldier Room: 1st Ed. Anne Chamberlain. LC 56-760929. 1956. Bobbs-Merrill.
Soldier Stories. Rudyard Kipling. LC 70-110205. (Short story index reprint series). (Illus.). 1970. Books for Libraries Press.
Soldier Stories. Rudyard Kipling. LC 4-153191. 1896. The Macmillan Company.
Soldier Stories. Rudyard Kipling. 1897. The Macmillan Company.
Soldier Stories. Rudyard Kipling. LC 4-165429. 1899. Doubleday & McClure Co.

Soldier Stories. Rudyard Kipling. LC 18-21829. 1914. Doubleday, Page & Company, for Review of Reviews Co.

Soldier Tales. Rudyard Kipling. LC 50-41960. 1896. Macmillan.

Soldier's Art. 1st Amer. Ed. Anthony Dymoke Powell. LC 67-11219. (His The music of time). bds., 4.95. Little.

Soldiers Both: A Novel. Gustave Guiches. Tr. by Cooper, Frederic Taber. LC 18-9497. Frederick A. Stokes Company.

Soldier's Bride. James Noble Gifford. LC 43-5573. 1943. Gramercy Publishing Co.

Soldier's Bride, and Other Tales. James Noble Gifford. LC 43-30001. 1829. J. P. Ayres and Co.

Soldier's Bride: And Other Tales. James Hall. LC 7-315. 1833. Key and Biddle.

Soldier's Christmas Eve. Villy Soerensen et al. Tr. by Nadia Christensen & Alexander Taylor. 1973. pap. 3.00 o.p. (ISBN 0-915306-00-X). Curbstone.

Soldier's Daughter. Gerhard Lewis Wind. LC 47-15249. 1946. Concordia Publishing House.

Soldier's Daughters Never Cry: A Novel. Audrey Lindop. LC 48-3949. 1948. Simon and Schuster.

Soldier's Embrace: Stories. Nadine Gordimer. LC 81-11975. 1982. 3.95 (ISBN 0-14-005925-3). Penguin Books.

Soldiers March! Theodore Fredenburgh. LC 30-24850. Harcourt, Brace and Company.

Soldiers of Fortune. Peter Bourne, pseud. 1981. 18.95x (Pub. by Remploy England). State Mutual Bk.

Soldiers of Fortune. Richard Harding Davis. LC 73-129186. (Illus.). 1970. Scholarly Press.

Soldiers of Fortune. Richard Harding Davis. LC 74-96880. (Illus.). 1969. Literature House.

Soldiers of Fortune. Richard Harding Davis. LC 6-322633. 1897. C. Scribner's Sons.

Soldiers of Fortune. Richard Harding Davis. LC 99-5385. 1899. C. Scribner's Sons.

Soldiers of Fortune. Richard Harding Davis. LC 2-10343. 1902. C. Scribner's Sons.

Soldiers of Fortune. Richard Harding Davis. 1940. C. Scribner's Sons.

Soldiers of Fortune. Richard Harding Davis. LC 16-63178. 1913. C. Scribner's Sons.

Soldiers of Fortune. Richard Harding Davis. LC 20-15630. 1920. C. Scribner's Sons.

Soldiers of Fortune. Graham Montague Jeffries. LC 63-9653. 1963. Putnam.

Soldiers of Fortune. Lee D. Willoughby. (Making of America Ser.: No. 32). (Orig.). 1982. pap. 3.25 (ISBN 0-440-08199-8, Bryans). Dell.

Soldiers of Misfortune: The Story of Otho Belleme... Percival Christopher Wren. LC 29-155693. 1929. Frederick A. Stokes Company.

Soldiers of Sodom. Jonathan Martin. 192p. pap. 1.95 o.p. (6108). Brandon.

Soldiers of '44. William P McGivern. LC 78-72919. 10.95 (ISBN 0-87795-208-6). Arbor House.

Soldier's Orphans. Ann Sophia Winterbotham Stephens. LC 8-12406. T. B. Peterson and Brothers.

Soldiers' Pay. William Faulkner. LC 79-114374. 1970. 2.47. Liveright.

Soldiers' Pay. William Faulkner. LC 26-6911. 1926. Boni & Liveright.

Soldiers' Pay. William Faulkner. LC 37-11251. 1937. The Sun Dial Press, Inc.

Soldier's Pay. Afterword by Robie Macauley. William Faulkner. (Signet modern classic, CQ411). 1968. New Amer. Lib.

Soldiers' Peaches: And Other African Stories. Stuart Cloete. LC 59-8855. 1959. Houghton Mifflin.

Soldier's Revenge: Or, Roland and Wilfred. Florence Nightingale Craddock. LC 1-30040. The Abbey Press.

Soldiers' Revolt. Hans Hellmut Kirst. LC 66-10645. 1966. Harper & Row.

Soldiers' Revolt. Tr. from German by J. Maxwell Brownjohn. Hans Hellmut Kirst. (N3451). 1967. Bantam.

Soldiers, Sailors, and Dogs. Peter Bernard Kyne. LC 36-19257. 1936. H. C. Kinsey & Company, Inc.

Soldier's Son. Maude Mary Butler. LC 13-23419. 1.00. Davis & Bond.

Soldier's Sweetheart. James Noble Gifford. 1942. Gramercy Pub. Co.

Soldier's Sweetheart. Carol Holliston. LC 42-1189. Gramercy Publishing Company.

Soldier's Sweetheart: And Other Stories. Thomas H Wilson. LC 8-37047. 1894. J. L. Gideon & Co.

Soldier's Tale. Michael J. Joseph. 152p. 1976. 12.50x (ISBN 0-8002-1989-9). Intl Pubns Serv.

Soldiers Three. Rudyard Kipling. LC 4875. H. M. Caldwell Company.

Soldiers Three: A Collection of Stories Setting Forth Certain Passages in the Lives and Adventures of Privates Terence Mulvaney, Stanley Ortheris, and John Learoyd. Rudyard Kipling. LC 9-3023. F. F. Lovell Company.

Soldiers Three: A Collection of Stories Setting Forth Certain Passages in the Lives and Adventures of Private Terence Mulvaney, Stanley Ortheris and John Learoyd. authorized ed. Rudyard Kipling. LC 7-12346. (On cover: Lovell's international series, no. 98). 1890. J. W. Lovell Company.

Soldiers Three: A Collection of Stories Setting Forth Certain Passages in the Lives and Adventures of Privates Terence Mulvaney, Stanley Ortheris, and John Learoyd. Rudyard Kipling. LC 19-723. A. L. Burt Company.

Soldiers Three: The Story of the Gadsbys, In Black and White. new ed., rev. with additions. ed. Rudyard Kipling. LC 7-12347. 1895. Macmillan and Co.

Soldiers Three: The Story of the Gadsbys, In Black and White. copyright ed. Rudyard Kipling. LC 99-3032. 1899. Doubleday & McClure Co.

Soldiers Three: The Story of the Gadsbys, In Black and White. Rudyard Kipling. 1922. Doubleday, Page & Company.

Soldiers Three. The Works of Rudyard Kipling. Rudyard Kipling. LC 9-16423. 1909. The Nottingham Society.

Soldier's Trial: An Episode of the Canteen Crusade. Charles King. LC 6-744. 1905. The Hobart Company.

Soldier's Ward: Or, Saved for Martyrdom. A Sequel to Walter Harmsen. Eduard Gerdes. Tr. by Van Pelt, Daniel. LC 6-44239. Presbyterian Board of Publication and Sabbath-School Work.

Soldiers' Women. Otto Bernhard Wendler & Morrow, Ian Fitzherbert Despard, 1806- Tr. LC 30-25154. 1930. Harper & Brothers.

Sole Agent. Kenneth Benton. LC 73-90462. 1974. 5.95 (ISBN 0-8027-5286-1). Walker.

Sole Survivor. Louis Falstein. LC 54-8049. (Dell first edition, 29). 1954. Dell Pub. Co.

Sole Survivor; and, The Kynsard Affair. Roy Vickers. LC 82-17733. 1983. 3.95 (ISBN 0-486-24433-4). Dover Publications.

Soleil Cou Coupe see Cadastre.

Solemn Boy. Hector Bolitho. LC 27-16473. George H. Doran Company.

Solemn High Murder. Barbara Ninde Byfield & Frank L. Tedeschi. LC 74-9477. 1975. 4.95. Doubleday.

Solemn Hour. William P. McKenzie. 3.50 o.p. Carlton.

Solemn Johnson Plus. Earl Wayland Bowman. LC 28-5561. Grosset & Dunlap.

Solid for Mulhooly. Rufus Edmonds Shapley. LC 76-96894. 1969. (ISBN 0-8398-1855-6). Literature House.

Solid for Mulhooly - I'm Fur'Im. Rufus Shavley. LC 76-96894. 1969. Repr. of 1881 ed. lib. bdg. 9.00x o.p. (ISBN 0-8398-1855-6). Gregg.

Solid Gold Circle. Sheila Schwartz. LC 80-12486. 1980. 9.95 (ISBN 0-517-54163-7). Crown.

Solid Gold Kidnapping. Evan Richards. (Six million dollar man#2). 1975. (pbk.) 1.25 (ISBN 0-446-76834-0). Warner Paperback Library.

Solid Gold Screw. F. W. Paul. pap. 0.60 o.p. Lancer.

Solid Mandala. Patrick White. LC 66-10984. 1975. (pbk.) 1.95 (ISBN 0-380-00375-9). Avon.

Solid Mandala: A Novel. Patrick White. LC 66-10984. 1966. Viking Press.

Solid Rock: A Story. Gladys Mae Walter. LC 41-25428. 1941. Herald Publishing House.

Solidaritat Auf der Drehscheibe: Eine Kindergeschichte und Fur Erwachsene. Ute Tempel. LC 76-450222. 1975. (ISBN 3-921433-05-3). Verlag PE. CH.

Solider Monk. Upton Beall Sinclair. LC 99-3262. (On cover: Columbia library. War stories of to-day. vol. 1, no. 17). 1899. Street & Smith.

Solider's Embrace: Stories. Nadine Gordimer. LC 79-56266. 1980. 8.95 (ISBN 0-670-65638-0). Viking Press.

Soliloquy. Stephen McKenna. LC 23-5619. George H. Doran Company.

Solitaire. Edwin Corle. LC 40-518559. 1940. E. P. Dutton & Co., Inc.

Solitaire. Sara Craven. (Harlequin Presents Ser.). (Orig.). 1979. pap. 1.50 (ISBN 0-373-70825-4, Pub. by Harlequin). PB.

Solitaire. Mojmir Drvota. LC 74-9557. 1974. 6.00 (ISBN 0-8142-0212-8). Ohio State University Press.

Solitaire. Pierre Henri Larthomas. LC 51-12687. 1951. Houghton Mifflin.

Solitaire. Graham Masterton. LC 82-14197. 576p. 1982. 15.95 (ISBN 0-688-01555-7). Morrow.

Solitaire, a Novel. Mojmir Drvota. LC 74-9557. 1974. 6.00 (ISBN 0-8142-0212-8). Ohio St U Pr.

Solitana. Unamuno y Jugo, Miguel De. LC 78-102372. (Illus.). 1970. Washington Irving Pub. Co.

Solitaria. Vasilii Vasilevich Rozanov & Erikh Fedorovich Gollerbakh. LC 79-13120. (Illus.). 1979. 16.75 (ISBN 0-313-22004-2). Greenwood Press.

Solitaries. A Tale. Paul Johann Von Heyse. LC 7-6608. 1870. Claxton, Remsen, and Haffelfinger.

Solitary Blackbird. E. Clephan Palmer. 2.00 o.p. (ISBN 0-8149-0582-X). Vanguard.

Solitary Dance. Robert G. Lane. LC 82-81020. (Illus.). 240p. (Orig.). 1983. 11.95 (ISBN 0-943104-82-3); pap. 6.95 (ISBN 0-943104-83-1). Serrell-Simons.

Solitary Eden. Dirk Vanden. 1970. 3.95 o.s.i. Guild Pr Ltd.

Solitary Farm. Fergus Hume. LC 9-7827. G. W. Dillingham Company.

Solitary Heart. Ruth McCarthy Sears. 1976. 4.95. Avalon Books.

Solitary Horseman. Emilie Baker Loring. LC 27-681022. 1927. The Penn Publishing Company.

Solitary House. Ernest Robertson Punshon. LC 18-23508. (On verso of half-title: The Borzol mystery stories. ii). 1918. A. A. Knopf.

Solitary Island: A Story of the St. Lawrence. 3d ed. John Talbot Smith. LC 8-8174. 1897. W. H. Young & Company.

Solitary Man. Jack Winchester. LC 80-14126. 1980. 10.95 (ISBN 0-698-11034-X). Coward, McCann & Geoghegan.

Solitary of Juan Fernandez: Or, The Real Robinson Crusoe. Joseph Xavier Boniface Saintine & Wood, Mrs., Anne Toppan (Wilbur) 1817-1864, Tr. LC 8-3731. 1851. Ticknor, Reed, and Fields.

Solitary: Or, The Mysterious Man of the Mountain. Charles Victor Prevot Arlincourt. LC 6-2046. 1822. H. Durell.

Solitary Summer. Elizabeth. 1973. pap. 0.95 o.p. (09252). Curtis.

Solitary Summer. Mary Annette Beaucham Russell Russell. LC 13-338668. The York.

Solitary Summer. Mary Annette Beauchamp Russell Russell. LC 6573. 1900. The Macmillan Company.

Solitary Summer. Mary Annette Beauchamp Russell Russell. LC 2-17486. 1901. The Macmillan Company.

Solitude de la Pitie. Jean Giono. pap. 1.25 o.p. (2759). French & Eur.

Solitude de la Pitie see Oeuvres Romanesques.

Solitudes: A Novel. R. G. Vliet. LC 76-54310. 8.95 (ISBN 0-15-183669-8). Harcourt Brace Jovanovich.

Solo. Frank Cyril Davison. LC 24-25415. 1924. G. P. Putnam's Sons.

Solo. Leo Hamalian & Linda Hamalian. 1977. 10.00 o.p. (ISBN 0-440-08068-1). Delacorte.

Solo. Jack Higgins, pseud. LC 79-3890. 1980. 11.95 (ISBN 0-8128-2713-9). Stein and Day.

Solo. Jack Higgins, pseud. LC 80-19284. 1980. 13.95 (ISBN 0-8161-3120-1). G. K. Hall.

Solo Blues. Paula Gosling. LC 81-5403. 11.95 (ISBN 0-698-11107-9). Coward, McCann & Geoghegan.

Solo Faces. James Salter. LC 78-27840. (ISBN 0-316-76965-7). Little, Brown.

Solo Faces. James Salter. LC 79-27436. 1980. 2.95 (ISBN 0-14-005564-9). Penguin Books.

Solo for No Voices. Wreford Paddon. LC 55-44859. (British bloodhound no. 102). 1955. T. V. Boardman.

Solo for Several Players. Barbara Jerfferis. LC 61-112157. 1961. W. Sloane Associates.

Solo in Black. Freddie Robinson. 1974. pap. 1.50 o.p. (ISBN 0-913358-06-1). El-Shabazz Pr.

Solo in Black. Freddie Robinson. 1974. pap. 1.50 o.p. (ISBN 0-913358-06-1). El-Shabazz Pr.

Solo Kid. T. W. Ford. 1948. Phoenix Press.

Solo Kill. William E Cochrane. (Berkley Medallion Book). 1977. 1.50 (ISBN 0-425-03560-3). Berkley Pub. Corp.

Solo Run. Hans Herlin. Tr. by J. Maxwell Brownjohn. LC 82-45145. 288p. 1983. 15.95 (ISBN 0-385-17621-X). Doubleday.

Solo Saddles. T. W. Ford. 1949. Phoenix Press.

Solo: Women on Woman Alone. Linda Hamalian & Leo Hamalian. LC 77-11861. 10.00. Delacorte Press.

Solo. 1st Ed. Stanford Whitmore. LC 55-101519. 1955. Harcourt, Brace.

Solomon & Sheba. Faye Levine. LC 79-24671. 10.95 (ISBN 0-399-90069-1). R. Marek.

Solomon and Shebs. Jay Williams. LC 59-5706. 1959. Random House.

Solomon and the Queen of Sheba. Czenzi Ormonde. LC 54-7306. 1954. Farrar, Straus and Young.

Solomon Crow's Christmas Pockets: And Other Tales. Ruth McEnery Stuart. LC 70-94744. (Short story index reprint series). (Illus.). 1969. Books for Libraries Press.

Solomon Crow's Christmas Pockets: And Other Tales. Ruth McEnery Stuart. LC 8-16869. 1897. Harper & Brothers.

Solomon Kane. Robert E. Howard. (Time-Lost Ser). Orig. Title: Red Shadows. (Illus.). 1971. pap. 1.50 o.p. (ISBN 0-87818-005-2). Centaur.

Solomon Levi. Claudius Gregory. LC 35-39243. 1935. Kyle & Hovendon.

Solomon, My Son! John Erskine. LC 35-9327. The Bobbs-Merrill Company.

Solomon Shilling, Come to Court. Frances Dietz Parsons. LC 44-3242. 1944. Dorrance & Company.

Solomon's Daughter. C. E. Poverman. (Contemporary American Fiction Ser.). 1983. pap. 5.95 (ISBN 0-14-006280-7). Penguin.

Solomon's Folly. Leslie Croxford. LC 75-1458. 1978. 8.95 (ISBN 0-8149-0763-6). Vanguard.

Solomon's Palace. Sam Ross. LC 72-10575. 1973. 7.95. Delacorte Press.

Solomon's Place. Sam Ross. 1974. (pbk.) 1.50. Dell.

Solomons Seal. Hammond Innes. LC 80-7632. 1980. 11.95 (ISBN 0-394-51326-6). Knopf.

Solomon's Stone. Lyon Sprague De Camp. LC 57-12678. 1957. Avalon Books.

Solomon's Story. A Novel. W J Shaw. LC 12-143512. 1880. P. G. Thomson.

Solomon's Temple. Stanley Hoffman. LC 73-2335. 1974. 7.95 (ISBN 0-670-65640-2). Viking Press.

Solomon's Wisdom: A Collection of Short Stories. Roberta Kalechofsky. LC 78-62032. 190p. 1978. pap. 5.00x (ISBN 0-916288-05-6). Micah Pubns.

Solstad, the Old and the New: A Story. James A Peterson. LC 23-173443. Augsburg Publishing House.

Solstice Cipher. Bruce Hatton Boyer. LC 79-740. 8.95 (ISBN 0-397-01346-9). Lippincott.

Solstice II. Paul J. Payack. Ed. by Merritt Clifton. (Illus.). 1976. pap. 1.00. Chthon Pr.

Solstice Man. Derry Quinn. LC 77-16762. 1978. 7.95 (ISBN 0-312-74296-7). St. Martin's Press.

Soltaire: A Romance of the Willey Slide and the White Mountains. George Franklyn Willey. LC 2-30147. 1902. New Hampshire Publishing Corporation.

Solution: A Story of the New Medication. Carolyn Scofield Smith. LC 22-199126. R. G. Badger.

Solution of a Mystery: Documents Relative to the Murder of Roger Maidment at Ullathwaite in the County of Yorkshire in October, 1899; Collected by Philip Wynyard Wrenne, M.A., J. P., D. L., and Edited. Joseph Smith Fletcher. LC 32-1645. Pub. for the Crime Club, Inc., by Doubleday, Doran & Company, Inc.

Solution, T-25. Theodora McCormick Du Bois. 1970. pap. 0.75 o.p. (0502-07076). Curtis.

Solution T-25: 1st Ed. Theodora McCormick Du Bois. LC 51-1623. 1951. Doubleday.

Solution Three. Naomi Mitchison. 1975. (pbk.) 1.25. Warner Books.

Solyman and Almena. An Oriental Tale. John Langhorne. LC 7-14080. 1799. Printed.

Solzhenitsyn: A Documentary Record, with the Nobel Prize Lecture. enl. ed. Ed. by Leopold Labedz. LC 72-94815. (Midland Bks.: No. 164). 1973. pap. 3.50x o.p. (ISBN 0-253-20164-0). Ind U Pr.

Som Havets Navka Vind see Naked As the Wind from the Sea.

Somber Memory. Hilda Van Siller. LC 45-886984. 1945. Pub. for the Crime Club, by Doubleday, Doran & Co., Inc.

Sombre Flame. Samuel Rogers. LC 27-8774. Payson & Clarke, Ltd.

Sombrero de tres picos. Pedro Antonio de Alarcon. Ed. by J. P. Crawford. 1930. pap. 1.95 o.p. (ISBN 0-02-301260-9). Macmillan.

Sombrero Fallout. Richard Brautigan. 1978. pap. 4.95 (ISBN 0-671-23025-5, Touchstone Bks). S&S.

Sombrero Fallout: A Japanese Novel. Richard Brautigan. LC 76-16137. 6.95 (ISBN 0-671-22331-3). Simon and Schuster.

Sombrero for Miss Brown. Charlotte Baker. LC 41-12289. 1941. E. P. Dutton & Co., Inc.

Some Account of Mr. Mark Beatty and His Family. Samuel Rodgers. LC 7-39806. 1890. Publishing House of the M. E. Church, South.

Some Achieve Greatness. Frank Arthur Swinnerton. LC 75-44527. 1976. 7.95 (ISBN 0-385-12082-6). Doubleday.

Some Achieve Greatness. Frank Arthur Swinnerton. LC 76-372798. 1976. 3.75 (ISBN 0-241-89415-8). H. Hamilton.

Some Achieve Greatness. Frank Arthur Swinnerton. LC 76-51431. 1977. 11.95 (ISBN 0-8161-6452-5). G. K. Hall.

Some Adventures of Capt. Simon Suggs. Johnson Jones Hooper. LC 73-104487. (Illus.). 1970. (ISBN 0-8398-0789-9). Literature House.

Some Adventures of Samson Cogg. R. H. Clark. 1976. text ed. 10.50x o.s.i. (ISBN 0-8277-4603-2). British Bk Ctr.

Some Angry Angel: A Mid-Century Faerie Tale. Richard Condon. LC 60-8826. 1960. McGraw-Hill.

Some Are Friends: A Novel. Lewis T Apple. LC 51-10892. 1951. Crown Publishers.

Some Avenger, Rise! By Lesley Egan. Pseud. Elizabeth Linington. LC 66-20755. bds., 4.50. Harper.

Some Beast No More. Kenneth Giles. LC 68-27389. 1968. 3.95. Walker.

Some Beckoning Wraith. easy eye ed. Paulette Warren. pap. 066 o.p. Lancer.
Some Brief Folly. Patricia Veryan. LC 80-28024. 1981. 11.95 (ISBN 0-312-74301-7). St. Martin's Press.
Some Brief Folly. Patricia Veryan. LC 81-23527. 1982. 15.95 (ISBN 0-8161-3352-2). G.K. Hall.
Some Brighter Dream. Nina Kaye. LC 37-38600. Phoenix Press.
Some Buried Caesar. Rex Stout. LC 82-920. 1982. 13.95 (ISBN 0-8161-3286-0). G.K. Hall.
Some Buried Caesar: A Nero Wolfe Mystery. Rex Stout. LC 39-27151. Farrar & Rinehart, Incorporated.
Some Call It Love. Bennie Caroline Hall. LC 46-223544. 1946. Phoenix Press.
Some Call It Love. Rian James. LC 33-18426. 1933. A. H. King.
Some Call It Perjury. Linda DuBreuil. (Leisure Book). 1.75 (ISBN 0-8439-0633-2). Nordon Publications.
Some Call It Perjury. Linda DuBreuil. 1979. pap. 1.75 o.s.i. (ISBN 0-8439-0633-2, Leisure Bks). Nordon Pubns.
Some Came Running. James Jones. LC 57-8932. 1957. Scribner.
Some Came Running. special abridged ed. James Jones. (Signet novel, E5337). 1973. 1.75. New American Lib.
Some Came Running. newly abridged ed. James Jones. 1979. 2.75 (ISBN 0-440-18261-1). Dell Pub. Co.
Some Children of Adam. R. M Manley. LC 7-20460. (On cover: The rose library. no. 12). 1892. Worthington Company.
Some Chinese Ghosts. Ed. by Lafcadio Hearn. LC 68-55681. (American short story series, v. 22). 1969. Garrett Press.
Some Corner of an English Field: A Novel. Dannie Abse. 1956. Criterion Books.
Some Darling Folly, a Novel. Monica Stirling. LC 56-11523. 1956. Coward-McCann.
Some Darling Sin. Ronald De Levington Kirkbride. LC 73-174754. 1973. 2.00 (ISBN 0-491-00934-8). W. H. Allen.
Some Day... Ruby Mildred Ayres. LC 35-156198. 1935. Doubleday, Doran & Company, Inc.
Some Day... Ruby Mildred Ayres. LC 37-10654. 1937. The Sun Dial Press, Inc.
Some Day I'll Be a Millionaire," 34 More Great Stories. William Saroyan. LC 45-7298. (On cover: Avon modern short story monthly. No. 12).
Some Day I'll Find Her. Allen Eppes. LC 39-17110. Gramercy Publishing Co.
Some Day I'll Find Her. Watkins Eppes Wright. LC 39-17110. 1939. Gramercy Pub. Co.
Some Day I'll Kill You. Albert Leffingwell. LC 39-6481. 1939. The Dial Press.
Some Die Eloquent. Catherine Aird, pseud. LC 79-8046. 1980. 8.95 (ISBN 0-385-15747-9). Published for the Crime Club by Doubleday.
Some Die Hard. Stephen Brett. (Orig.). 1979. pap. 1.75 (ISBN 0-532-17221-3). Woodhill.
Some Distant Shore. Margaret Pemberton. 1981. Pocket Books.
Some Distinguished Americans: Imaginary Portraits. Harvey Jerrold O'Higgins. LC 78-144166. (Short story index reprint series). 1971. (ISBN 0-8369-3781-3). Books for Libraries Press.
Some Do Not... Ford Madox Ford. LC 24-23089. 1924. T. Seltzer.
Some Doves and Pythons. 1st Ed. Sumner Locke-Elliott, pseud. LC 66-11475. 1966. Harper & Row.
Some Dreams Are Nightmares. James E. Gunn. LC 73-19263. (Illus.). 1974. 6.95 (ISBN 0-684-13779-8). Scribner.
Some Emotions and a Moral. Pearl Mary Teresa Richards Craigie. ("unknown" library, v. 8). Cassell Publishing Company.
Some Experiences of an Irish R.M. Edith Anna CEnone Somerville & Violet Florence Martin. LC 8-10210. 1899. Longmans, Green and Co.
Some Experiences of an Irish R.M. Edith Anna CEnone Somerville & Violet Florence Martin. LC 26-3651. 1903. Longmans, Green and Co.
Some Experiences of an Irish R.M. Edith Anna CEnone Somerville & Violet Florence Martin. LC 14-10512. 1910. Longmans, Green and Co.
Some Experiences of an Irish R.M. Edith Anna CEnone Somerville & Violet Florence Martin. LC 37-17355. (The Longman stories of laughter. no. 3). 1934. Longmans, Green and Co.
Some Faces in the Crowd: Short Stories. Budd Schulberg. LC 53-5011. 1953. Random House.
Some Fell Among Thorns: A Novel. Mary Frances Doner. LC 39-13361. The Penn Publishing Company.
Some Final Words of Advice. Saikaku Ihara & Peter Nosco. LC 78-66086. (Illus.). 1980. 12.00 (ISBN 0-8048-1249-7). C. E. Tuttle Co.
Some Find a New Dawn. Maide O'Heeron Moyer. LC 37-2247. 1937. Burney Brothers Publishing Co.
Some Folks. By John Habberton... John Habberton. LC 6-40672. 1877. Derby Brothers.
Some for the Glory. Louis Zara. LC 37-37590. 1937. The Bobbs-Merrill Company.
Some Found Adventure. Robert E McClure. LC 26-23130. 1926. Doubleday, Page & Company.
Some Friends. Henry Miller. 1978. 14.50. Porter.
Some Get the Orchids. Virginia Hudson Brightman. LC 33-16996. The Macaulay Company.
Some Ghost Stories. Alfred McLelland Burrage. 1981. 8.50. Bookfinger.
Some Girls Don't". Besse Sprague. LC 22-255947. A. L. Burt Company.
Some Go up... Samuel Tupper. LC 31-31845. 1931. R. M. McBride & Company.
Some Good Intentions and a Blunder. Pearl Mary Teresa Richards Craigie. LC 6-31093. (On cover: Merriam's violet series, no. 4). The Merriam Company.
Some Gorgeous Accident. James Kennaway. LC 67-25470. 1967. Atheneum.
Some Happenings. Horace Annesley Vachell. George H. Doran Company.
Some Have Too Much. Marcus Van Heller, pseud. (Orig.). 1968. pap. 1.75 o.s.i. (117, Ophelia). Olympia.
Some Honeymoon! Charles Everett Hall. LC 18-68005. G. Sully & Company.
Some Inner Fury: By Kamala Markandaya Pseud. 1st American Ed. Kamala Purnaiya Taylor. LC 56-5983. 1956. J. Day Co.
Some Instructions. Stanley G. Crawford. LC 77-14298. 1978. 7.95 (ISBN 0-394-42835-8). Knopf: Distributed by Random House.
Some Irish Loving. Edna O'Brien. (Penguin Fiction Ser.). 256p. 1980. pap. 4.25 (ISBN 0-14-004982-7, Pub. by Penguin England). Irish Bk Ctr.
Some Just Like You. Sol Yurick. LC 75-156569. 1974. (pbk.) 1.50. Manor Books.
Some Kind of Hero. James Kirkwood. (Signet book). 1976. 1.95. New American Library.
Some Kind of Hero: A Novel. James Kirkwood. LC 75-5725. 1975. 8.95 (ISBN 0-690-00757-4). Crowell.
Some Kind of Innocence: A Novella. Jane Lazarre. LC 79-24191. 7.95 (ISBN 0-8037-8192-X). Dial Press.
Some Ladies Demand Marriage. Barry Caldwell. LC 36-6965. Godwin.
Some Ladies in Haste. Robert William Chambers. 1908. D. Appleton and Company.
Some Ladies in My Life. John Sinor. LC 79-87472. 1979. 9.95 (ISBN 0-89325-015-5). Joyce Press.
Some Laughter, Some Tears. Sholom Aleichem. LC 79-13849. 1979. pap. 4.95 (ISBN 0-399-50395-1, Perige). Putnam Pub Group.
Some Laughter, Some Tears: Tales from the Old World and the New. Shalom Rabinowitz. Ed. by Curt Leviant. LC 68-25445. 1968. Putnam.
Some Laughter, Some Tears: Tales from the Old World and the New. Shalom Rabinowitz & Sholom Aleichem. Ed. by Curt Leviant. 1968. Putnam.
Some Laughter, Some Tears: Tales from the Old World an:l the New. Shalom Rabinowitz & Curt Leviant. LC 79-13849. 1979. 4.95 (ISBN 0-399-50395-1). Putnam.
Some Lie and Some Die. Ruth Rendell. LC 73-83604. (Illus.). 1973. 4.95 (ISBN 0-385-07428-X). Doubleday.
Some Lie and Some Die. Ruth Rendell. 1975. (pbk.) 0.95. Bantam Books.
Some Like 'em Shot. Fred Malina. LC 49-80649. 1949. M. S. Mill Co.
Some Like It Dark. Kipp Washington. (Orig.). 1977. pap. 1.75 (ISBN 0-87067-527-3, BH527). Holloway.
Some Like It Hot. Dorothy Herzog. LC 30-7296. The Macaulay Company.
Some Like It Hot. Sidney Marshall. LC 41-16061. 1941. W. Morrow and Company.
Some Little of the Angel Still Left: A Novel. Josephine Russell Clay. LC 6-21366. 1893. R. Clarke & Co.
Some Lose Their Way. Eloise S Liddon. LC 41-17613. 1941. E. P. Dutton & Co., Inc.
Some Love: Some Hunger. Millen Brand. LC 55-7225. 1955. Crown Publishers.
Some Marked Passages: And Other Stories. Jeanne Gillespie Pennington. 1898. Fords, Howard, and Hulbert.
Some Men and Women. Marie Adelaide Belloc Lowndes. LC 75-150549. (Short story index reprint series). 1971. (ISBN 0-8369-3846-1). Books for Libraries Press.
Some Men and Women. Marie Adelaide Belloc Lowndes. LC 29-66794. 1928. Doubleday, Doran & Company.
Some Men in Their Time. George Pattullo. LC 59-148194. 1959. Naylor Co.
Some Modern Heretics: A Novel. Cora Maynard. LC 7-25871. 1896. Roberts Bros.
Some More Horse Tradin' Ben K. Green. (Illus.). (YA) 1972. 11.95 (ISBN 0-394-46123-1). Knopf.
Some Must Die. Cover Painting by Ray Johnson. Gil Brewer. LC 54-33170. (Gold medal books, 409). 1954. Fawcett Publications.
Some Must Watch. Edwin Daly. LC 57-585713. Scribner.
Some Must Watch: A Novel. Ethel Lina White. LC 41-5984. 1941. Harper & Brothers.
Some Nephew! A Laugh Movie in Six Reels. Carleton Stevens Montanye. LC 20-7645. 1920. Moffat, Yard and Company.
Some Notes to Gary Snyder's Myths & Texts. Howard McCord. 1971. pap. 1.00 o.p. Sand Dollar.
Some of My Best Friends. Donald Warman. pap. 1.95 o.s.i. (OPH-223, Ophelia). Olympia.
Some of My Best Friends Are Soldiers, a Kind of Novel. Margaret Halsey. LC 44-7915. 1944. Simon and Schuster.
Some of New York's "400.". Adella Octavia Clouston & A. O. C. LC 67-124609. 1898. American Humane Education Society.
Some of Our Girls. A Novel. Elizabeth C. J. Eiloart Eiloart. (On cover: Seaside library. Packet ed., no. 114). 1883. G. Munro.
Some of Our People. Lynn Roby Meekins. LC 7-25858. 1898. Williams & Wilkins Company.
Some of Snooksie's Sayings, Stories & Pictures: Words of Wisdom. Edwin Mumford. (Illus.). 101p. 1980. pap. 7.50 (ISBN 0-682-49639-1). Exposition.
Some of Us Are Married. Mary Stewart Doubleday Cutting. LC 20-6842. 1920. Etc. Doubleday, Page & Company.
Some Old Love Stories. Thomas Power O'Connor. 1979. Repr. of 1895 ed. lib. bdg. 35.00 (ISBN 0-8495-4208-1). Arden Lib.
Some One Else. A Novel. Bithia Mary Sheppard Croker. LC 6-32160. (Harper's Franklin square library. no. 455). 1885. Harper & Brothers.
Some One Shall Love Me. Ethel Owen. LC 39-31791. L. Furman, Inc.
Some One Sweet Angel Chile. Sherley A. Williams. LC 81-18752. 1982. 11.50 (ISBN 0-688-01012-1); pap. 7.50 (ISBN 0-688-01177-2). Morrow.
Some Other Beauty. Ida Alexa Ross Wylie. LC 30-14196. 1930. Doubleday, Doran & Company, Inc.
Some Other Folks. Sarah Pratt McLean Greene. LC 74-98570. (Short story index reprint series). 1969. Books for Libraries Press.
Some Other Folks. Sarah Pratt McLean Greene. LC 6-45564. 1884. Cupples, Upham and Company.
Some Other Place: The Right Place. Donald Harington. 1974. pap. 1.75 o.p. (M3309). BJ Pub Group.
Some Other Place. The Right Place; a Novel. Donald Harington. LC 72-5106. 1972. 8.95 (ISBN 0-316-34640-3). Little, Brown.
Some Other Time. 1st Ed. Hollis Alpert. LC 60-11425. 1960. Knopf.
Some Others and Myself: Seven Stories and a Memoir. Ruth Suckow. LC 51-14899. 1952. Rinehart.
Some Others and Myself: Seven Stories and a Memoir. Ruth Suckow. LC 79-143311. 1972. (ISBN 0-8371-5967-9). Greenwood Press.
Some Parts in the Single Life. Jimmy Miller. LC 76-111236. 1970. 5.95. Knopf.
Some Passages in the Life of Mr. Adam Blair, Minister of the Gospel at Cross-Meikle. With an Introd. by David Craig. John Gibson Lockhart. LC 64-843. (Scottish Reprints, No. 1). 1963. Edinburgh University Press; U.S.A. Agent: Aldine Ub. Co., Chicago.
Some Passages in the Life of Sir Frizzle Pumpkin: The Picnic, and Other Tales. James White. LC 8-27033. 1834. E. L. Carey & A. Hart.
Some Passages in the Practice of Dr. Martha Scarborough. Helen Stuart Campbell. LC 6-21486. 1893. Roberts Brothers.
Some People. William Neville Scott. LC 70-405982. 1968. 3.50. Jacaranda.
Some People, Places, and Things That Will Not Appear in My Next Novel. John Cheever. LC 79-116947. (Short story index reprint series). 1970. Books for Libraries Press.
Some Persons Unknown. Ernest William Hornung. LC 96-1554. 1898. C. Scribner's Sons.
Some Plant Olive Trees. Emma Gelders Sterne. LC 37-30406. 1937. Dodd, Mead & Company.
Some Pleasure There to Find. Elizabeth Rossiter. LC 75-34383. 7.95 (ISBN 0-399-11728-8). Putnam.
Some Pleasure There to Find. Elizabeth Rossiter. 1977. 1.50 (ISBN 0-380-01640-0). Avon.
Some Poisoned by Their Wives. Stanton Forbes, pseud. LC 73-83631. 1974. 4.95 (ISBN 0-385-07057-8). Published for the Crime Club by Doubleday.
Some Prefer Nettles. Junichiro Tanizaki. LC 55-5616. (Illus.). 1955. Knopf.
Some Prefer Nettles. Junichiro Tanizaki. LC 80-39932. 1981. 4.95 (ISBN 0-399-50521-0). Perigee Books.
Some Rain Must Fall. William A Adler. LC 49-4870. 1949. Exposition Press.
Some Run Crooked. John Buxton Hilton. LC 77-10182. 1978. 7.95 (ISBN 0-312-74355-6). St. Martin's Press.
Some Short Stories ... Impressionist Publishing Co.
Some Short Stories About Nasty People I Don't Like. John Mitzel. 100p. 1976. pap. 3.00 o.p. (ISBN 0-914852-03-5). Manifest Destiny.
Some Short Stories About Nasty People I Don't Like. John Mitzel. 100p. 1976. pap. 3.00 o.p. (ISBN 0-914852-03-5). Manifest Destiny.
Some Silent Shore. Sigrid Johannesson. LC 80-53307. (Illus.). (10.95, 11.95 can) (ISBN 0-86629-020-6). Sunrise Pub. Co.
Some Slips Don't Show: By A.A.Fair (Erle Stanley Gardner. Erle Stanley Gardner. LC 57-104061. 1957. W. Morrow.
Some State of Affairs. Eugene Vale. LC 73-158889. 1972. 2.50 (ISBN 0-491-00429-X). W. H. Allen.
Some Stories. Walter De La Mare. (Orig.). 1962. pap. 4.95 o.p. (ISBN 0-571-04581-2, Pub. by Faber & Faber). Merrimack Pub Cir.
Some Successful Marriages. Abby Meguire Roach. LC 76-152956. (Short story index reprint series). (Illus.). 1971. (ISBN 0-8369-3871-2). Books for Libraries Press.
Some Successful Marriages. Abby Meguire Roach. LC 6-37923. 1906. Harper & Brothers.
Some Summer Lands. Jane Gaskell. LC 77-9179. (Gaskell, Jane, 1941-. The Atlan Ser.: Vol. 5). 1979. 8.95 (ISBN 0-312-74362-9). St. Martin's Press.
Some Sweet Day. Bryan Woolley. LC 73-13701. 1974. 5.95 (ISBN 0-394-48714-1). Random House.
Some Take a Lover. Ann Du Pre. LC 33-781. The Macanlay Company.
Some Tame Gazelle. Barbara Pym. 252p. 1983. 12.95 (ISBN 0-525-24178-7, 01258-370). Dutton.
Some Things Dark and Dangerous. Joan Kahn. LC 78-121804. 1974. (pbk.) 0.95. Avon.
Some Things Dark and Dangerous. Joan Kahn. LC 78-121804. 1970. 4.95. Harper and Row.
Some Things Fierce and Fatal. Joan Kahn. LC 73-157903. 1971. 4.95 (ISBN 0-06-023084-3). Harper & Row.
Some Things Fierce and Fatal. Joan Kahn. LC 82-45467. (Avon/Flare book). (Flare mystery). 1982. 2.25 (ISBN 0-380-00388-0). Avon Books.
Some Things Strange and Sinister. Joan Kahn. LC 72-9871. 1973. 4.95 (ISBN 0-06-023086-X) (ISBN 0-06-023086-X). Harper & Row.
Some Things Strange and Sinister. Joan Kahn. LC 82-6780. (Avon/Flare book). (Flare mystery). 1982. 2.25 (ISBN 0-380-00084-9). Avon Books.
Some Things Weird and Wicked: Twelve Stories to Chill Your Bones. Joan Kahn. LC 75-35855. 5.95 (ISBN 0-394-83244-2). Pantheon Books.
Some Thoughts for My Friends. rev. ed. Mari Stein. (Illus.). 1977. pap. 4.95 (ISBN 0-918546-02-8). Quarterdeck.
Some Time in the Sun. Tom Dardis. 1981. pap. 5.95 (ISBN 0-14-005831-1). Penguin.
Some Time Never: A Fable for Supermen. Roald Dahl. LC 48-137497. 1948. C. Scribner's Sons.
Some Trails Never End. Darragh Aldrich. LC 42-100142. 1941. H. C. Kinsey & Company, Inc.
Some Trust in Chariots. Jack Jones. LC 49-7932. 1948. W. Sloane Associates.
Some Trust in Chariots. Fiswoode Tarleton. LC 30-243472. 1930. L. MacVeagh, The Dial Press.
Some Trust in Chariots. Jack Weeks. (Signet bk., Q2559). 1965. New Amer. Lib.
Some Trust in Chariots. Jack Weeks. LC 63-20726. 1964. McGraw-Hill.
Some Try Murder. Robert Portner Koehler. LC 43-150644. 1943. Phoenix Press.
Some Unconventional People. John Beveridge Gladwyn Jebb. LC 7-10188. 1895. Roberts Brothers.
Some Unease & Angels. Elaine Feinstein. LC 77-11250. pap. 5.00 (ISBN 0-940580-05-5). Green River.
Some Unknown Person. Sandra Scoppettone. LC 77-2910. 8.95 (ISBN 0-399-11928-0). Putnam.
Some Unrenowned Folks. Maria Hadwin. LC 35-8923. 1935. Meador Publishing Company.
Some Valiant Ones. Robert Barrington. LC 36-18234. 1937. Falmouth Book House.
Some Ways of Life. Helen Wales. LC 72-11744. 1969. 3.95. Prairie Press Books.
Some We Loved. Edward Harris Heth. LC 35-190014. 1935. Houghton Mifflin Company.
Some Whims of Fate. Menie Muriel Dowie. LC 7-33307. 1896. J. Lane.
Some Will Not Die. Algis Budrys & Polly Freas. LC 78-2193. (Illus.). 1978. 4.95 (ISBN 0-915442-52-3). Starblaze Editions.
Some with Steel. Robert T Crowley. LC 65-17260. Doubleday.
Some with Steel. Robert T Crowley. LC 65-17260. 1965. Doubleday.

Some Women and a Man: A Comedy of Contrasts. William John Locke. LC 7-15171. (Publisher's lettering: Neely's library of choice literature. no. 59). 1896. F. T. Neely.
Some Women I Have Known. Jozua Marius Willen Van Der Poorten Schwartz. 1899. D. Appleton and Company.
Some Women I Have Known. Jozua Marius Willen Van Der Poorten Schwartz. LC 1-24551. 1901. D. Appleton and Company.
Some Women of to-Day: A Novel. W. H. White. LC 8-36562. 1880. G. W. Carleton & Co.; Etc., Etc.
Some Women Won't Wait: By A.A. Fair Pseud. Erle Stanley Gardner. LC 53-9229. (Morrow mystery). 1953. Morrow.
Some Women's Hearts. Louise Chandler Moulton. LC 7-32314. 1874. Roberts Brothers.
Some Women's Ways. Mary Angela Dickens. LC 6-36834. R. F. Fenno & Company; Etc., Etc.
Some Worlds. Anselm Hollo. 1974. pap. 6.00 o.p. (Pub. by Elizabeth Pr). SBD.
Some Writings of Richard DeVeaux: Pseud. Gwendolen Foulke Andrews. LC 39-106651. 1938. Edwards Brothers, Inc.
Somebody at the Door. Raymond William Postgate. LC 76-382854. 1976. 2.65 (ISBN 0-86025-026-1). Ian Henry Publications Ltd.
Somebody at the Door. Raymond William Postgate. LC 43-7755. 1943. A. A. Knopf.
Somebody Else. Ruby Mildred Ayres. LC 36-343966. 1936. Doubleday, Doran & Company, Inc.
Somebody Else. George Parsons Lathrop. LC 7-13853. 1878. Roberts Brothers.
Somebody Else's Wife: A Novel. Adam Kennedy. LC 74-1135. 1974. 7.95 (ISBN 0-671-21739-9). Simon and Schuster.
Somebody in Boots. Nelson Algren. LC 71-581. (Berkley medallion book, S1125). 1965. 0.75. Berkley Pub. Corp.
Somebody Just Grabbed Annie! Charles Dennis. LC 75-9477. 1975. 7.95. St. Martin's Press.
Somebody Killed Reddy Fox. Susan K. Sibley, pseud. Ed. by Ronald H. Bayes. 64p. (Orig.). 1980. pap. 5.00 (ISBN 0-932662-33-1). St Andrews NC.
Somebody Knew. Mary Montgomery. pap. 0.75 o.s.i. (01-349). Lancer.
Somebody Loves Me. Cover Painting by Saul Tepper. Nancy Morgan. LC 55-157377. (Gold medal giant, S 433). 1954. Fawcett Publications.
Somebody Must. Alice Grant Rosman. LC 34-271775. Minton, Balch and Company.
Somebody on the Phone: By William Irish Pseud. 1st Ed. Cornell George Hopley-Woolrich. LC 50-8511. (Main line mysteries). 1950. Lippincott.
Somebody Owes Me Money. Donald E Westlake. LC 69-16473. 1969. 4.50. Random House.
Somebody to Kill. Richard Reinsmith. (Bodyguard Ser.: No. 4). 224p. (Orig.). Date not set. pap. cancelled o.p. (ISBN 0-505-51798-1). Tower Bks.
Somebody to Kill. Richard Reinsmith. (Bodyguard Ser.: No. 4). 224p. (Orig.). 1982. pap. 2.50 o.s.i. (ISBN 0-8439-1177-8, Leisure Bks). Nordon Pubns.
Somebody's Darling. Larry McMurtry. LC 78-16781. 9.95 (ISBN 0-671-24394-2). Simon and Schuster.
Somebody's Darling: A Novel. Larry McMurtry. 1979. 2.50 (ISBN 0-445-04498-5). Popular Library.
Somebody's Daughter, Somebody's Wife. Lorinda Hagen. (Orig.). 1980. pap. 2.50 (ISBN 0-8439-8000-1, Tiara Bks). Nordon Pubns.
Somebody's Got to Want Me... Edwina Levin MacDonald. LC 38-5406. 1938. Godwin.
Somebody's Hanging in Unruh Street: A Tragicomic Novel. Marvin Rose. LC 66-28151. 1967. 4.75. William-Frederick.
Somebody's Hanging in Unruh Street: An Experimental Novel. Marvin Rose. 1973. 4.75 (ISBN 0-87164-066-X). William-F.
Somebody's Luggage. Frederick John Randall. LC 14-10524. 1914. John Lane.
Somebody's Ned. A M Freeman. LC 7-299. 1879. S. C. Griggs and Company.
Somebody's Neighbors. Rose Terry Cooke. LC 69-11883. (American short story series, v. 41). 1969. Garrett Press.
Somebody's Neighbors. Rose Terry Cooke. LC 72-8165. (American short story series, v. 41). 1972. (ISBN 0-8422-8028-6). MSS Information Corp.
Somebody's Neighbors. Rose Terry Cooke. LC 4-23599. 1881. J. R. Osgood and Company.
Somebody's Neighbors. Rose Terry Cooke. LC 4-15084. Houghton, Mifflin and Company.
Somebody's Sister. Derek Marlowe. LC 74-3681. 1974. 6.95 (ISBN 0-670-65652-6). Viking Press.
Somebody's Sister. Derek Marlowe. LC 75-8832. 1975. 8.95 (ISBN 0-8161-6286-7). G. K. Hall.
Somebody's Sweetheart. William Arthur Neubauer. LC 64-57220. 1964. Arcadia House.
Someday, Boy. Sam Ross. LC 48-21701. 1948. Farrar, Straus.
Someday I'll Be Somebody. Mickey Jordan. 1975. 5.95 o.p. (ISBN 0-88270-134-7); pap. 2.95 o.p. (ISBN 0-88270-135-5). Logos.
Someday I'll Find You. Margaret Widdemer. LC 40-11110. Farrar & Rinehart, Inc.
Someday the Dream. Magdalena Mondragon Aguirre & Putnam, Samuel, 1892- Tr. LC 47-23663. 1947. The Dial Press.
Someday You Can. June Knight. 1975. 7.95 o.p. (ISBN 0-8283-1604-X). Branden.
Somehow Good. William Frend De Morgan. LC 8-4365. 1908. H. Holt and Company.
Somehow I Had to Find a Brass Band: A Novel. Angela Huth. LC 74-121330. 1970. 5.95. Coward-McCann.
Someone and Somebody. Porter Emerson Browne. LC 17-14136. 1.35. The Bobbs-Merrill Company.
Someone Called Maggie Lane. Frances Shelley Wees. LC 47-31005. 1947. Macrae-Smith Co.
Someone Else. Gillian Tindall. LC 75-86401. 1969. 5.95. Walker.
Someone Else's Dreams. John Yamrus. LC 80-70611. (Illus.). 60p. (Orig.). 1981. pap. 4.95 (ISBN 0-930090-13-6); pap. 10.00 special ltd. ed. Applezaba.
Someone Else's War. Jon Burmeister. LC 73-93694. 1974. 6.95. St. Martin's Press.
Someone from the Past. 1st Ed. Margot Bennett. 1958. Dutton.
Someone Great. Robert Grossbach. 1970. price not set o.p. Harper Mag Pr.
Someone Great: A Novel. Robert Grossbach. LC 75-160657. 1971. 6.00 (ISBN 0-06-122607-6). Harper's Magazine Press Book.
Someone in the Dark. August William Derleth. 1941. Arkham House.
Someone in the House. Barbara Michaels. LC 81-5572. 10.95 (ISBN 0-396-08022-7). Dodd, Mead & Co.
Someone in the House. Barbara Michaels. LC 81-20089. 1982. 13.95 (ISBN 0-8161-3306-9). G.K Hall.
Someone in the Room. Alfred McLelland Burrage. LC 75-46259. (Supernatural and Occult Fiction). 1976. 16.00 (ISBN 0-405-08118-9). Arno Press.
Someone Is Killing the Great Chefs of Europe. Nan Lyons & Ivan Lyons. LC 75-45140. 7.95 (ISBN 0-15-183760-0). Harcourt Brace Jovanovich.
Someone Is Watching. Penelope Field, pseud. (Spring Adult Ser.). 1977. lib. bdg. 10.95 o.p. (ISBN 0-8161-6453-3, Large Print Bks). G K Hall.
Someone Is Watching. Penelope Field, pseud. 1977. pap. 1.50 o.p. (ISBN 0-515-04387-7). BJ Pub Group.
Someone Is Watching. Dorothy Giberson. LC 76-30766. 1977. 10.95 (ISBN 0-8161-6453-3). G. K. Hall.
Someone Is Watching: A Novel. Dorothy Giberson. LC 76-13587. 7.95 (ISBN 0-316-28166-2). Little, Brown.
Someone Just Like You. Sol Yurick. LC 75-156569. 1972. 6.95 (ISBN 0-06-014783-0). Harper & Row.
Someone Like You. Roald Dahl. LC 53-6841. 1953. Knopf.
Someone There. Shelagh Brown. 96p. (Orig.). 1982. pap. 1.70 (ISBN 0-88028-019-0). Forward Movement.
Someone to Love. Vernie E Connelly. LC 35-61990. 1933. A.L. Burt Company.
Someone to Love. Peggy Gaddis, pseud. LC 47-20370. 1947. Arcadia House.
Someone to Love. Iris Weigh. Ed. by Gene DeRoin. (Aston Hall Presents Ser.). (Orig.). 1979. pap. 1.50 (ISBN 0-89936-014-9). Aston Hall.
Someone to Remember: A Novel. Jean Potts. LC 43-57992. 1943. The Westminster Press.
Someone Watching. J. W Donohue. LC 74-81609. 1974. 6.95 (ISBN 0-8059-2052-8). Dorrance.
Someone Will Conquer Them. Elizabeth Kata. LC 62-187244. 1962. St Martin's Press.
Someone's Death. Charles Larson. LC 73-443. 1973. 5.95 (ISBN 0-397-00977-1). Lippincott.
Somerset Dreams and Other Fictions. Kate Wilhelm. LC 77-11776. 9.95 (ISBN 0-06-014649-4). Harper & Row.
Somerset Dreams and Other Fictions. Kate Wilhelm. 1979. 1.95 (ISBN 0-06-080476-9). Harper & Row.
Somerset Murder Case. Brian Flynn. LC 38-31440. 1937. M.S. Mill Co., Inc.
Something About a Sailor. Peggy O'More, pseud. LC 44-8149. 1944. Grammercy Publishing Co.
Something About a Soldier. Mark Harris. LC 57-11227. 1957. Macmillan.
Something About a Soldier. Mark Harris. 1976. (pbk.) 1.50. Ballantine Books.
Something About Arthur. Charlotte Bronte. Ed. by Christine Alexander. 1981. 12.95 (ISBN 0-87959-095-5). U of Tex Hum Res.
Something About Cats, and Other Pieces. Howard Phillips Lovecraft. Ed. by August William Derleth. LC 79-156681. (Essay index reprint series). 1971. (ISBN 0-8369-2410-X). Books for Libraries Press.
Something About Eve: A Comedy of Fig-Leaves. James Branch Cabell. LC 70-22275. (Illus.). 1971. 0.95 (ISBN 0-345-02067-7). Ballantine Books.
Something About Eve: A Comedy of Fig-Leaves. James Branch Cabell. LC 29-23486. 1929. R. M. McBride & Company.
Something About Midnight: By D. B. Olsen Pseud. 1st Ed. Dolores Birk Hitchens. LC 50-5164. 1950. Published for the Crime Club by Doubleday.
Something About My Father: And Other People. Charles Angoff. LC 55-120654. 1956. T. Yoseloff.
Something About Singlefoot: Chapters in the Life of an Oshkosh Man. John Hicks. LC 10-7023. 1910. Cochrane Publishing Company.
Something Beautiful. Garnett A. Schultz. 1966. 3.75 o.p. (ISBN 0-8059-0255-4). Dorrance.
Something Better. LC 8-10212. 1878. Lee and Shepard.
Something Between. Marian Cockrell. LC 46-4172. 1946. Harper & Brothers.
Something Big. Grant Freeling. (Orig.). 1971. pap. 0.75 o.p. (A904S, Award). Univ Pub & Dist.
Something Blue. Charlotte Armstrong. 1975. (pbk.) 1.25. Ace Books.
Something Doing. Frederic Van Rensselaer Dey. LC 19-14696. 1.50. The Macaulay Company.
Something Else: A Novel. John Breckenridge Ellis. 1911. 1.35. A. C. McClurg & Co.
Something Evil. Dorothy Quick. LC 64-9197. 1958. Arcadia House.
Something Foolish, Something Gay. Glen Sire & Jane Sire. LC 58-10355. (Illus.). 1958. Simon and Schuster.
Something for Every Body: Gleaned in the Old Purchases, from Fields Often Reaped. Baynard Rush Hall. (On cover: Appleton's literary miscellany. no. 16). 1846. D. Appleton & Company.
Something for Everybody. Martin A. Labb. LC 72-854420. 54p. 1973. 2.95 o.p. (ISBN 0-8059-1733-0). Dorrance.
Something for Everybody Is Not Enough. William Birenbaum. 1972. 7.95 o.p. (ISBN 0-394-46037-5). Random.
Something for Joey. Richard E. Peck. (gr. 8-10). 1978. pap. 2.25 (ISBN 0-553-11640-1, 13352-7, B14225-9). Bantam.
Something for Nothing. Kathryn Kilgore. LC 81-52068. 12.98 (ISBN 0-87223-740-0). Seaview Books.
Something for Nothing. E. J. Rath. LC 28-13497. 1928. G. H. Watt.
Something for Nothing. 1st Ed. Harry Vernor Dixon. LC 50-5657. 1950. Harper.
Something Gleamed. Theda Kenyon. LC 48-873755. 1948. J. Messner.
Something Going. Robert Lipsyte & Steve Cady. LC 72-94681. 1973. 6.95 (ISBN 0-525-20678-7). Dutton.
Something Happened. Joseph Heller. LC 74-8550. 1974. 10.00 (ISBN 0-394-46568-7). Knopf; Distributed by Random House.
Something Human. Shirley Darbyshire. LC 34-4672. G. P. Putnam's Sons.
Something in Common, and Other Stories. Langston Hughes. LC 63-8189. (American century series). 1963. Hill and Wang.
Something in Disguise. Elizabeth Jane Howard. 1974. (pbk.) 1.50. Dell.
Something in Disguise. Elizabeth Jane Howard. LC 75-94846. 1970. 5.95. Viking Press.
Something in the Air. John Alexander Graham. LC 70-103951. 1970. 5.95. Little, Brown.
Something in the Blood: A Novel. Stephen Lewis. (Fawcett Gold Medal Book). 1.75 (ISBN 0-449-13770-8). Fawcett Publications.
Something in the Blood: Short Stories. Trevor Shearston. LC 80-460943. 1979. 18.00 (ISBN 0-7022-1335-7). University of Queensland Press.
Something in the Shadows. Vin Packer. (O.s.i.). 1971. pap. 0.75 o.s.i. (532-75420-025). Manor Bks.
Something in the Wind. Lee Smith. LC 73-123986. 1971. 6.95 o.p. (ISBN 0-06-013941-2, HarpT). Har-Row.
Something is Happening Here. Ramon Hernandez. LC 82-61182. 300p. (Orig.). 1983. pap. 15.00 (ISBN 0-89295-025-0). Society Sp & Sp-Am.
Something I've Been Meaning to Tell You. Alice Munro. LC 73-4443. 224p. 1974. 7.95 o.p. (ISBN 0-07-077760-8, GB). McGraw.
Something I've Been Meaning to Tell You... Thirteen Stories. Alice Munro. LC 74-187. 1974. 6.95 (ISBN 0-07-077760-8). McGraw-Hill Ryerson.
Something Left to Lose. Robin F. Brancato. 1979. pap. 1.75 (ISBN 0-553-12171-5). Bantam.
Something Less Than Love. Daphne Clair. (Presents Ser.). 192p. (Orig.). 1980. pap. text ed. 1.50 (ISBN 0-373-10367-0, Pub. by Harlequin). PB.
Something Lighter. John Otway Percy Bland. LC 25-98793. 1924. Houghton Mifflin Company.
Something Like Passion. James Noble Gifford. LC 49-2096. 1949. Phoenix Press.
Something Marvelous Is About to Happen. James Stevenson. LC 71-138764. (Illus.). 1971. 7.50 (ISBN 0-06-014118-2). Harper & Row.
Something More Than Earth. Helen Norris. LC 40-31343. 1940. Little, Brown and Company.
Something Nasty in the Woodshed. Kyril Bonfiglioli. LC 77-356301. 1976. 2.95 (ISBN 0-333-19443-8). Macmillan.
Something Near. August William Derleth. LC 45-5188. 1945. Arkham House.
Something New. Pelham Grenville Wodehouse. LC 15-18283. 1915. D. Appleton and Company.
Something New. Pelham Grenville Wodehouse. LC 30-18870. 1930. Dodd, Mead & Company.
Something New Under the Sun. Susanne Chambers Wheat. 62p. 1972. 3.50 o.p. (ISBN 0-682-47615-3). Exposition.
Something Occured. Benjamin Leopold Farjeon. LC 6-38765. G. Routledge and Sons, Limited.
Something of a Hero... Israel James Kapstein. LC 41-5377. 1941. A. A. Knopf.
Something of an Achievement. Gwyn Griffin. LC 60-6954. 1960. Holt.
Something of the Night. Mary McMullen. LC 80-1035. 1980. 8.95 (ISBN 0-385-17182-X). Published for the Crime Club by Doubleday.
Something of the Night. large print ed. Mary McMullen. LC 81-6215. 1981. 12.95 (ISBN 0-8161-3244-5). G.K. Hall.
Something of Value. Robert Chester Ruark. LC 55-7158. (Illus.). 1955. Doubleday.
Something Old, Something New. Lillian Africano. 384p. 3.50 (ISBN 0-515-05865-3). Jove Pubns.
Something on the Wind. Barbara Moore. LC 77-80483. 1978. 6.95 (ISBN 0-385-13171-2). Doubleday.
Something Singing. Margaret Perry. LC 16-23045. 1916. 1.00. Sherman, French & Company.
Something Soft. Roland Starke. 1971. pap. 0.75 o.p. (07118). Curtis.
Something Soft, and Other Stories. Roland Starke. LC 69-10965. 1969. 4.95. Doubleday.
Something Special". Faith Baldwin Cuthrell. LC 40-90063. Farrar & Rinehart, Inc.
Something Special,". Faith Baldwin Cuthrell. LC 47-19999. 1946. Triangle Books, the Blakiston Company.
Something Strange. Marjorie B. Smiley et al. (Macmillan Gateway English Ser: Level 3). (gr. 7-12). 1969. pap. 2.20, s.p. 1.65 o.p. (27575). Macmillan.
Something Terrible, Something Lovely. William Sansom. LC 54-9721. 1954. Harcourt, Brace.
Something That Begins with "T".C. Kay Cleaver Strahan. C.
Something to Answer for: A Novel. Percy Howard Newby. LC 69-14494. 1969. 5.95. Lippincott.
Something to Do. A Novel. Cecilia Viets Dakin Jamison. LC 8-10803. 1871. J. R. Osgood and Company.
Something to Hide. Philip MacDonald. LC 52-12388. 1952. Published for the Crime Club by Doubleday.
Something to Hide. Nicholas Monsarrat. LC 66-112381. (His Signs of the times, 4). 1966. 3.50. Sloane, Dist. Morrow.
Something to Live for. Mona L. Caldwell. 160p. 1972. 6.00 o.p. (ISBN 0-682-47570-X). Exposition.
Something to Live for. Joseph Romani. LC 54-11895. 1955. Vantage Press.
Something to Make Us Happy. Linda Crawford. LC 78-16495. 1978. 12.95 (ISBN 0-8161-6599-8). G. K. Hall.
Something to Make Us Happy: A Novel. Linda Crawford. LC 77-12562. 8.95 (ISBN 0-671-22817-X). Simon and Schuster.
Something to Read. Leonard Wibberley. 1967. 3.75 o.p. Washburn.
Something to Remember. Elisabeth Stancy Payne. LC 36-25283. 1936. Dodd, Mead & Company.
Something up a Sleeve. Richard Lockridge. LC 71-37929. 1972. (ISBN 0-397-00867-8). Lippincott.
Something Wicked. Stuart Hamill. LC 43-4375. 1943. J. Swift, Inc.
Something Wicked This Way Comes. Ray Bradbury. LC 82-48732. 1983. 13.95 (ISBN 0-394-53041-1). Knopf.
Something Wicked This Way Comes: A Novel. Ray Bradbury. LC 62-9604. 1962. Simon and Schuster.
Something Wonderful Right Away. Jeffrey Sweet. 432p. 1982. pap. 3.95 (ISBN 0-380-01884-5, 79707-0, Discus). Avon.
Something Wrong. Elizabeth Linington. LC 67-22519. 1967. Harper & Row.
Something You Do in the Dark. Daniel Curzon. LC 71-150268. 1971. 6.95. Putnam.

Something's Got to Give: A Novel. Marion Hargrove. LC 48-6673. 1948. W. Sloane Associates.
Something's Happened to Kate: By Genevieve Holden Pseud. 1st Ed. Genevieve Long Pou. LC 58-5580. 1958. Published for the Crime Club by Doubleday.
Somethings Strange and Sinister. Joan Kahn. 1974. (pbk.) 0.95 (ISBN 0-380-00084-9). Avon.
Something's Waiting for You, Baker D. A Story of Suspense. Patricia Windsor. LC 74-3588. 1974. 5.11. Harper & Row.
Sometime. Robert Herrick. LC 33-16579. Farrar & Rinehart, Incorporated.
Sometime see Collected Works.
Sometime After the Equinox. Jorj Bent. (Orig.). 1981. pap. 2.25 (ISBN 0-505-51695-0). Tower Bks.
Sometime, Never: Three Tales of Imagination, by William Golding, John Wyndham and Mervyn Peake. William Gerald Golding. LC 57-11580. (Ballantine books, 215). 1957. Ballantine Books.
Sometime: Somewhere. Martin Ruben Aceves Gonzalez. LC 35-22664. Alliance Press.
Sometimes. Olive Wadsley. LC 23-15035. 1923. Cassell and Company, Ltd.
Sometimes. Olive Wadsley. LC 23-16661. 1923. Dodd, Mead and Company.
Sometimes a Great Notion. Ken Kesey. (N2998). 1965. Bantam.
Sometimes a Great Notion: A Novel. Ken Kesey. LC 77-4998. 1977. 4.95 (ISBN 0-14-004529-5). Penguin Books.
Sometimes a Hero. Leslie H. Whitten. LC 78-19717. 1979. 12.50 (ISBN 0-385-14301-X). Doubleday.
Sometimes, but Not Always. James Stevenson. LC 67-18107. 1967. Little, Brown.
Sometimes They Bite. Lawrence Block. 304p. 1983. 14.50 (ISBN 0-87795-485-2). Arbor Hse.
Sometimes We Laugh, Sometimes We Cry. Rupert L. McCanon. 3.95 o.p. Vantage.
Sometimes Wife: The Savage Sisters. Carter Brown, pseud. 288p. 1983. pap. 2.95 (ISBN 0-451-12014-0, Sig). NAL.
Somewhat Angels. David Cornel De Jong. LC 45-9495. 1945. Reynal & Hitchcock.
Somewhat of a Liar Myself: A Story. James William De Vore. LC 2-3571. 1901. F. T. Neely Co.
Somewhere a Master: Further Tales of the Hasidic Masters. Elie Wiesel. 336p. 1982. 15.50 (ISBN 0-671-44170-1). Summit Bks.
Somewhere a Voice Is Calling: A Novel. John Lodwick. LC 53-9777. 1953. Roy Publisher.
Somewhere an Empire. Fleming Healy. LC 85-85883. 1935. R. Speller, Inc.
Somewhere at Sea, and Other Tales. John Fleming Wilson. LC 24-1639. E. P. Dutton & Company.
Somewhere Between the Two. Jay Little. pap. 0.75 o.p. (54-831). Paperback Lib.
Somewhere Between the Two: A New Novel by Jay Little Pseud. 1st Ed. Clarence L Miller. LC 56-106135. 1956. Pageant Press.
Somewhere Beyond the Clouds: A Novel. Robert Richard Rice. LC 52-8640. 1952. Exposition Press.
Somewhere Beyound Reproach. Tim Jeal. LC 68-58210. 1969. McGraw-Hill.
Somewhere Child. Bonnie L. Black. 1983. pap. 3.50 (ISBN 0-553-22923-0). Bantam.
Somewhere Else. Robert Kotlowitz. LC 72-84211. 1972. 7.95. Charterhouse.
Somewhere I'll Find You. Charles Hoffman. LC 41-6655. 1941. A. A. Knopf.
Somewhere in England. Reg Gadney. LC 76-174645. 1971. 5.95. St. Martin's Press.
Somewhere in France. Richard Harding Davis. LC 15-26506. 1915. C. Scribner's Sons.
Somewhere in Red Gap. Harry Leon Wilson. LC 16-19217. 1916. Doubleday, Page & Company.
Somewhere in the House... Elizabeth Daly. 1946. Rinehart & Company, Inc.
Somewhere in the Whirlwind. Amanda York, pseud. 1980. pap. 2.50 (ISBN 0-671-82606-9). PB.
Somewhere in This City. 1st American Ed. Maurice Procter. LC 54-121951. Harper.
Somewhere in This House. Rufus King. LC 30-7559. 1930. Pub. for The Crime Club, Inc., by Doubleday, Doran & Company, Inc.
Somewhere South in Sonora: A Novel. Will Levington Comfort. LC 25-171150. 1925. Houghton Mifflin Company.
Somewhere the Tempest Fell. Josephine Herbert. LC 47-115761. 1947. C. Scribner's Sons.
Somewhere There's Music. David Rogers. LC 76-50917. 8.95. St. Martin's Press.
Somewhere There's Music. 1st Ed. George Lea. LC 57-11951. 1958. Lippincott.
Somewhere They Die. Llewellyn Perry Holmes. LC 55-9838. 1955. Little, Brown.
Somewhere to the Sea. Kenneth Sheils Reddin. LC 36-18259. 1936. Houghton Mifflin Company.
Somewhere to the Sea. Kenneth Sheils Reddin. LC 36-17317. 1936. T. Nelson & Sons Ltd.
Somewhere Within This House. Jean Francis Webb. LC 73-79949. (Illus.). 1973. 6.95. McKay.
Somos Como Somos. Andres Rivero. LC 81-70535. (Short Stories in Spanish). 52p. (Orig.). 1982. pap. 3.00x (ISBN 0-933648-04-9). Cruzada Span Pubns.
Son. Hildur Dixelius. Tr. by Settergren, Anna Ch. LC 28-5565. 1928. E. P. Dutton & Company.
Son". Ethel Kissam Train. LC 11-23842. 1911. C. Scribner's Sons.
Son and Daughter. Helen Reimensnyder Martin. LC 38-513924. 1938. D. Appleton-Century Company, Incorporated.
Son and Heir. 1st Ed. Edith P Begner. LC 60-13109. 1960. Holt, Rinehart and Winston.
Son" and Other Stories of Childhood and Age. Ethel Kissam Train. LC 23-18067. 1923. C. Scribner's Sons.
Son and Stranger. David Demarest Lloyd. LC 50-7520. 1950. Houghton Mifflin.
Son and Stranger: A Novel. Charlotte Underwood. LC 45-2913. 1945. Harper & Brothers.
Son (Andre Cornelis) Paul Charles Joseph Bourget. LC 6-14923. (On cover: World library, no. 21)). 1893. The Waverly Company.
Son at the Front. Edith Newbold Jones Wharton. LC 23-12336. 1923. C. Scribner's Sons.
Son Avenger. Sigrid Undset & Chater, Arthur G., Tr. LC 30-23438. 1930. A. A. Knopf.
Son Decides: The Story of a Young German-American. Arthur Stanwood Pier. LC 18-9494. 1918. Houghton Mifflin Company.
Son Long, Sucker. Charles Alden Seltzer. LC 43-7708. 1943. The Sun Dial Press.
Son of a Cowthief. Paul Evan Lehman. LC 35-9121. The Macaulay Company.
Son of a Fiddler. Jennette Barbour Perry Lee. LC 2-9344. 1902. Houghton, Mifflin and Co.
Son of a Gunman. Wayne C Lee. (Ace double Westerns). 1973. (pbk.) 0.95. Ace.
Son of a Hundred Kings. Thomas Bertram Costain. 1974. (pbk.) 1.75. Avon.
Son of a Hundred Kings: A Novel of the Nineties. 1st Ed. Thomas Bertram Costain. LC 50-9942. 1950. Doubleday.
Son of a Klansman. Albert Sydney Gaffney. LC 26-19348. F. Hudson.
Son of a Prophet. George Anson Jackson. LC 7-9475. 1893. Houghton, Mifflin and Company.
Son of a Servant. August Strindberg & Field, Claud Herbert Alwyn, 1863- Tr. LC 13-11633. 1913. G. P. Putnam's Sons.
Son of a Servant: The Story of the Evolution of a Human Being. Newly Tr. with Introd., Notes, by Evert Sprinchorn. August Strindberg. (Anchor bk., A492). pap., 1.25. Doubleday.
Son of a Servant: The Story of the Evolution of a Human Being. August Strindberg. LC 66-11748. 1966. Anchor Books.
Son of a Smaller Hero. Mordecai Richler. 1968. pap. 0.95 o.p. (ISBN 0-446-55783-8, 55-783). Paperback Lib.
Son of a Star. Andrew Meisels. LC 69-18189. 1969. 6.95. Putnam.
Son of a Star: A Romance of the Second Century. Benjamin Ward Richardson. LC 44-240189. 1888. Longmans, Green, and Co.
Son of a Tinker. Maurice Walsh. LC 52-5048. 1952. Lippincott.
Son of a Troy: A Narrative of the Experiences of Wilton Aubrey in the Mohawk Valley and Elsewhere During the Summer of 1777, Now for the First Time. Clinton Scollard. 1901. R. G. Badger & Company (Incorporated.
Son of a Witch. Troy Conway, pseud. (Coxeman Ser). 1971. pap. 0.75 o.p. (ISBN 0-446-64548-6, 64-548). Paperback Lib.
Son of an Undying Race. Hagop Keverian. LC 34-23277. 1934. Efficient Printing Company.
Son of Apple. Maurice Walsh & MacLeod, Catriona. LC 40-7356. 1940. Frederick A. Stokes Company.
Son of Arizona. Charles Alden Seltzer. LC 31-18587. Doubleday, Doran & Company, Inc.
Son of Carolina. Eugenia Orchard Stovall. LC 9-29765. 1909. The Neale Publishing Company.
Son of Columbus. Molly Elliot Seawell. LC 12-212766. 1912. Harper & Brothers.
Son of Courage. Archie P. McKishnie. LC 20-17187. The Reilly & Lee Co.
Son of Destiny: The Story of Andrew Jackson. Mary Cornelia Francis. LC 2-30269. 1902. The Federal Book Company.
Son of Dr. Tradusac. Elizabeth Huntington. LC 29-8393. 1929. Duffield & Company.
Son of Dust. Hilda Frances Margaret Prescott. LC 56-133387. 1956. Macmillan.
Son of Earth. Howard Erickson. LC 33-9096. 1933. L. MacVeagh, Dial Press, Inc.
Son of Emma. James Girard Blower. LC 52-8347. 1952. Dorrance.
Son of Esau. Minnie L Gilmore. LC 6-43992. Lovell, Coryell & Company.
Son of Fanny Hill. 192p. pap. 1.95 o.p. (6121). Brandon.
Son of Hagar. Hall Caine. LC 6-21868. R. F. Fenno and Company.
Son of Hagar: She's All the World to Me. by hall caine... ed. Hall Caine. LC 16-19157. (Hall Caine's best books in three volumes. vol. iii). P. F. Collier & Son.
Son of Haman. Louis Cochran. LC 37-799895. 1937. The Caxton Printers, Ltd.
Son of Han. Richard Tracy LaPiere. LC 37-4390. 1937. Harper & Brothers.
Son of His Country: An Imaginative Novel Dealing with George Washington's Youth. Walter Bloem & Martens, Frederick Herman, 1874- Tr. LC 28-25553. 1928. Harper & Brothers.
Son of His Father. Ridgwell Cullum. LC 15-257008. 1915. 1.35. G. W. Jacobs & Company.
Son of His Father. Margaret Oliphant Wilson Oliphant. (On cover: Lovell's library, v. 17, no. 831). 1886. J. W. Lovell Company.
Son of His Father. Margaret Oliphant Wilson Oliphant. (On cover: Seaside library. Pocket ed., no. 880). 1886. G. Munro.
Son of His Father. Harold Bell Wright. LC 25-13865. 1925. D. Appleton and Company.
Son of His Father. Harold Bell Wright. LC 33-28371. 1925. A. L. Burt Company.
Son of His Father. A Novel. Margaret Oliphant Wilson Oliphant. (Harper's Franklin square library, no. 554). 1886. Harper & Brothers.
Son of His Mother. Clara Viebig Cohn & Raahauge, H., Tr. LC 13-7851. 1913. 1.25. John Lane.
Son of Ingar. Katharine Pearson Woods. LC 8-37249. 1897. Dodd, Mead and Company.
Son of Ishmael: A Novel. Elizabeth Thomasina Meade Smith. LC 8-8654. (On cover: Netherland library, no. 7). New Amsterdam Book Company; Etc., Etc.
Son of Israel: An Original Story. Caroline McCoy Willard. LC 8-37014. 1898. J. B. Lippincott Company.
Son of John Winteringham. Warrene Piper. LC 30-6153. 1930. Houghton Mifflin Company.
Son of Judah. Dan Levin. LC 61-15820. 1961. Appleton-Century-Crofts.
Son of Justin. Richard Vaughan. LC 55-5466. 1955. Dutton.
Son of Man. Robert Silverberg. 224p. 1980. pap. 2.25 (ISBN 0-345-28884-X). Ballantine.
Son of Marietta. Johan Wigmore Fabricius. Tr. by Clephane, Irene. LC 36-711. 1936. Little, Brown, and Company.
Son of Mars. St. George Rathborne. LC 8-590. (On cover: Neely's library of choice literature, no. 74). F. T. Neely.
Son of Mars: A Novel. St. George Rathborne. (On cover: Eagle library, no. 108). Street & Smith.
Son of Mary Bethel. Elsa Barker. LC 9-24253. 1909. Duffield & Company.
Son of Minos: A Novel. David MacGregor Cheney. LC 64-25838. 1964. 3.50. Biblo & Tannen.
Son of Minos: A Novel. David MacGregor Cheney. LC 30-29557. 1930. R. M. McBride & Company.
Son of Minos: A Novel. David MacGregor Cheney. LC 41-5871. Bruce Humphries, Inc.
Son of Monte-Cristo. A Continuation of Monte-Cristo and the Countess, and Sequel to the Count of Monte-Cristo. authorized ed. tr. from the french by j. abarbanell... ed. Jules Hippolyte Lermina & Abarbanell, Jacob Ralph, 1852- Tr. LC 8-12386. (On cover; Munro's library, v. 1, no. 218). N. L. Munro.
Son of Monte Cristo... A Sequel to The Count of Monte Cristo. Jules Hippolyte Lermina & Dumas, Alexandre, 1802-1870. LC 8-12387. (On cover: Lovell's library, no. 884). 1887. J. W. Lovell Company.
Son of Monte-Cristo. Sequel to The Wife of Monte-Cristo, and End of the Continuation to Alexander Dumas' Celebrated Novel of "The Count of Monte-Cirsto"... Jules Hippolyte Lermina. LC 8-12388. T. B. Peterson & Brothers.
Son of Normandy: A Novel of Modern France. B. M Sawdon. LC 45-7204. 1945. S. Curl, Inc.
Son of Old Harry: A Novel. Albion Winegar Tourgee. LC 8-29839. (Ledger library, no. 68). 1892. R. Bonner's Sons.
Son of Perdition. James Gould Cozzens. LC 29-17388. 1929. W. Morrow & Company.
Son of Perdition. William Alexander Hammond. LC 98-1390. 1898. H. S. Stone & Co.
Son of Pio. Carl Laurence Carlsen. LC 19-4850. 1.75. E. P. Dutton & Company.
Son of Porthos: Or, The Death of Aramia. Alexandre Dumas. Tr. by William, Henry Liewellyn, Jr. LC 6-42317. (American series. no. 303). M. J. Ivers & Co.
Son of Porthos: Or, The Death of Aramis. Alexandre Dumas. Tr. by Williams, Henry Llewellyn, Jr. LC 6-42316. (On cover: The souvenir series, no. 61). F. M. Lupton Publishing Company.
Son of Power. Will Levington Comfort & Armstrong, Willimina Leonora. LC 20-211821. 1920. Doubleday, Page & Company.
Son of Rhubarb: By H. Allen Smith. Illus. by Leo Hershfield. Harry Allen Smith. LC 67-16405. 1967. 4.95. Trident.
Son of Richard Carden. Stephen Southwold. LC 35-4300. 1935. Little, Brown, and Company.
Son of Royal Langbirth: A Novel. William Dean Howells. LC 4-27128. 1904. Harper & Brothers.
Son of Royal Langbrith. William Dean Howells & David J Burrows. LC 75-79476. (His A Selected edition of W. D. Howells, v. 26). (Illus.). 1969. 10.50. Indiana University Press.
Son of Sato. William Lewis. 1978. 25.00x (ISBN 0-918824-10-9); pap. 3.00 (ISBN 0-918824-09-5). Turkey Pr.
Son of Siam. Frank Harrison Beckmann. LC 39-31790. The Stratford Company.
Son of Siro: A Story of Lazarus. John Edwin Copus. LC 9-561. 1909. 1.35. Benziger Brothers.
Son of Song. Alfred Eichler. LC 41-3421. R. Speller.
Son of Tarzan. Edgar Rice Burroughs. LC 17-7816. 1917. A. C. McClurg & Co.
Son of Tarzan. Edgar Rice Burroughs. LC 21-136944. 1918. A.L. Burt Co.
Son of Tarzan, No. 4. Edgar Rice Burroughs. 224p. 1975. pap. 1.95 (ISBN 0-345-29415-7). Ballantine.
Son of Tears: A Novel on the Life of Saint Augustine. Henry W Coray. 1966. pap., 1.95. Eerdmans.
Son of Tears: A Novel on the Life of Saint Augustine. Henry W Coray. LC 57-6722. 1957. Putnam.
Son of Tears: A Novel on the Life of St. Augustine. Henry W. Coray. 1957. pap. 1.95 o.p. (6005). Eerdmans.
Son of the Ages: The Reincarnations and Adventures of Scar, the Link; a Story of Man from the Beginning. Stanley Waterloo. LC 14-5427. 1914. Doubleday, Page & Company.
Son of the Bayou. John Murray. LC 40-32365. The Ave Maria Press.
Son of the Bondwoman. Pardo Bazan, Emilia. LC 75-23344. 1976. 13.50. H. Fertig.
Son of the Carolinas: A Story of the Hurricane Upon the Sea Islands. Elisabeth Carpenter Satterthwait. LC 72-2064. (Black Heritage Library Collection). 1972. 12.50 (ISBN 0-8369-9062-5). Books for Libraries Press.
Son of the Carolinas: A Story of the Hurricane Upon the Sea Islands. Elisabeth Carpenter Satterthwait. LC 98-528. 1898. H. Altemus.
Son of the Cincinnati. Montague Brisard. LC 25-11040. Small, Maynard & Company.
Son of the Czar. An Historical Romance. James M Graham. LC 6-27658. F. A. Stokes Comany.
Son of the Gamblin' Man: The Youth of an Artist: a Novel. Mari Sandoz. LC 76-17066. 1976. 14.95 (ISBN 0-8032-0895-2) (ISBN 0-8032-5833-X). University of Nebraska Press.
Son of the Gamblin Man: The Youth of an Artist, a Novel. 1st Ed. Mari Sandoz. LC 60-7340. 1960. C. N. Potter.
Son of the Giant. Stuart David Engstrand. LC 50-5867. 1950. Creative Age Press.
Son of the Gods. Rex Ellingwood Beach. 1929. Harper & Brothers.
Son of the Gods and A Horseman in the Sky. Ambrose Gwinnett Bierce. LC 7-38028. (Half-title: Western classics, no. 4). P. Elder and Company.
Son of the Grand Eunuch. Charles Pettit. LC 49-179141. (New Avon library 197). 1949. Avon Pub. Co.
Son of the Grand Eunuch. Charles Pettit. LC 27-14209. 1927. Boni & Liveright.
Son of the Great American Novel. James Fritzhand. LC 75-143396. 1971. 5.75 (ISBN 0-8076-0579-4). G. Braziller.
Son of the Great American Novel. James Fritzhand. 1978. 1.95 (ISBN 0-380-01962-0). Avon.
Son of the Hawk. Thomas Head Raddall. LC 50-6022. 1950. Winston.
Son of the Hidalgos. Ricardo Leon & MacManus, Mrs. Catalina Violante (Paez) Tr. LC 21-26551. 1921. Doubleday, Page & Company.
Son of the Hills. Harriet Theresa Smith Comstock. LC 13-23215. 1913. Doubleday, Page & Company.
Son of the House. Agnes Russell Weekes. LC 26-6257. 1926. Dodd, Mead and Company.
Son of the Immortals. Louis Tracy. LC 9-29369. E. J. Clode.
Son of the Lost Son. Soma Morgenstern & Leftwich, Joseph, 1892- Tr. LC 46-25123. 1946. Rinehart & Company, Inc.
Son of the Lost Son. Soma Morgenstern & Leftwich, Joseph, 1892- Tr. LC 46-143947. 1706. The Jewish Publication Society of America.
Son of the Middle Border see Collected Works.
Son of the Moon: A Novel. Joseph George Hitrec. LC 48-5764. 1948. Harper.

Son of the Morning. Joyce Carol Oates. 1979. pap. 2.75 (ISBN 0-449-24073-8, Crest). Fawcett.

Son of the Morning. Joyce Carol Oates. LC 78-56428. 1978. 12.95 (ISBN 0-8149-0800-4). Vanguard.

Son of the Morning: A Novel. Joyce Carol Oates. LC 78-56428. 10.00 (ISBN 0-8149-0793-8). Vanguard Press.

Son of the Morning: A Novel. Joyce Carol Oates. 1979. 2.75 (ISBN 0-449-24073-8). Fawcett Crest.

Son of the Mountain. Harlin Rex Cokeley. LC 36-7621. Chapman & Grimes.

Son of the Nile. Simon Robert Hoover. 1927. The Stratford Company.

Son of the North. Osseannah Roberts. LC 9-8. 1908. The C. M. Clark Publishing Co.

Son of the Organ-Grinder. Marie Sofle Birath Schwartz. Tr. by Borg, Selma & Shipley, Marie Adelaide (Brown) Porter & Coates.

Son of the Otter. George Gray Van Schaick. LC 15-25697. 1915. Small, Maynard & Company.

Son of the People: A Romance of the Hungarian Plains. Emmuska Orczy. LC 6-20452. 1906. G. P. Putnam's Sons.

Son of the Plains. Arthur Henry Paterson. LC 7-34082. 1895. Macmillan and Co.

Son of the Prefect: A Story of the Reign of Tiberius. Edmund Hamilton Sears. LC 14-18802. 1.25. R. G. Badger; Etc., Etc.

Son of the Saddle. Al Cody, pseud. 1971. pap. 0.60 o.p. (60-492). Manor Bks.

Son of the Saddle. Archie Joscelyn. LC 39-171083. Phoenix Press.

Son of the Sahara. Louise Gerard. LC 22-10391. The Macaulay Company.

Son of the Sea. Sara Ware Bassett. LC 39-27552. 1939. Doubleday, Doran & Company, Inc.

Son of the Sioux. Gerald Drayson Adams. (Orig.). 1981. pap. 1.95 (ISBN 0-505-51703-5). Tower Bks.

Son of the Soil. Leon Lester. LC 13-20576. 1913. The Minleon Shop.

Son of the Soil. 2d ed. Leon Lester. LC 16-4428. 1915. The Minleon Shop.

Son of the Soil. A Novel. Margaret Oliphant Wilson Oliphant. LC 7-32630. 1865. Harper & Brothers.

Son of the Star: A Novel. Carl Krueger. LC 64-15964. 1964. Citadel Press.

Son of the Stars. Jacket Illus. by Alex Schomburg. 1st Ed. Raymond F Jones. LC 52-5494. (Science fiction novel). 1952. Winston.

Son of the State. William Pett Ridge. LC 99-5458. 1899. Dodd, Mead and Company.

Son of the Sun. Orfeo M Angelucci. LC 59-48655. 1959. De Vorse.

Son of the Sun. Jack London. LC 12-121365. 1912. Doubleday, Page & Company.

Son of the Three Musketeers. Henri Cami & Gorman, Jean Wright, Tr. LC 30-23900. Farrar & Rinehart Incorporated.

Son of the Turk. Vere Lockwood. (Orig.). 1980. pap. 1.50 (ISBN 0-553-13931-2). Bantam.

Son of the Typhoon: A Novel. James W Bennett. LC 28-284828. 1928. Duffield & Company.

Son of the White Wolf. Robert E. Howard. LC 77-73604. (Illus.). 1977. 12.95 (ISBN 0-913960-09-8). FAX.

Son of the White Wolf. Robert E. Howard. (Berkley Book). 1978. 1.95 (ISBN 0-425-03709-6). Berkley Pub. Corp.

Son of the Wilderness. Maurice B Gardner. LC 39-2940. 1939. Meador Publishing Company.

Son of the Wind. Lucia Chamberlain. LC 10-25792. 1.50. The Bobbs-Merrill Company.

Son of the Wolf. Jack London. LC 68-55683. (American short story series, v. 24). (Illus.). 1969. Garrett Press.

Son of the Wolf: Tales of the Far North. Jack London. LC 2266. 1900. Houghton, Mifflin and Company.

Son of the Wolf: Tales of the Far North. Jack London. LC 31-26194. (Riverside library). 1930. Houghton Mifflin Company.

Son of the Wolf: Tales of the Far North. Jack London. LC 78-104496. 1978. 11.00. Scholarly Press.

Son of Three Fathers. Gaston Leroux & Bennett, Hannaford, Tr. LC 28-9841. The Macaulay Company.

Son of Ti-Coyo. Translated from the French by Gerard Hopkins. 1st American Ed. Clement Richer. LC 54-7200. 1954. Knopf.

Son of Tomorrow. Earl Reed Silvers. LC 47-11243. 1947. Westminister Press.

Son of Wallingford. George Randolph Chester & Chester, Mrs. Lilian Eleanor (Hauser) 1888-Joint Author. LC 21-14133. Small, Maynard & Company.

Son of Zelman. Oscar Pinkus. LC 81-21397. 1982. 14.95 (ISBN 0-87073-548-9) (ISBN 0-87073-549-7). Schenkman Pub. Co.

Son Who Was Older Than His Father. 2nd ed. Joseph H. Hughes, Jr. LC 77-926281. 1977. 10.00; pap. 3.25, signed 3.50. Aaron-Jenkins.

Son Who Was Older Than His Father. Joseph H. Hughes, Jr. 100p. (Orig.). 6.95 o.p. (ISBN 0-89185-035-X); pap. 2.25 o.p. (ISBN 0-89185-034-1). Anthelion Pr.

Sonador Para un Pueblo see Historia de una Escalera.

Sonata De Primavera. Ramon Del Valle-Inclan & Salas, Manuel, Ed. LC 41-23550. (Half-title: The Drydon press. Modern language publications; general editor, Frederic Ernst). The Dryden Press, Inc.

Sonata of Icarus: By Jurgis Gliauda. Tr. from Lithuanian by Ralphael Sealey. Introd. by Charles Angoff. Illus. by Mikalorus K. Ciurlionis. Jurgis Gliauda. LC 67-31646. 1968. 5.00. Manyland Bks.

Sondra O'Moore. Florance Barrett Willoughby. LC 39-22732. 1939. Little, Brown and Company.

Sondra Pass. abr ed. Jay Hayden, pseud. Ed. by Alice Sachs. 1970. Repr. of 1967 ed. 3.95 o.p. Lenox Hill.

Song Across the Wave: A Novel. Catherine Stadtler. LC 42-106875. 1942. Zondervan Publishing House.

Song After Midnight. Helen Topping Miller. LC 39-328219. 1939. D. Appleton-Century Company, Incorporated.

Song and a Sigh. Rose Porter. LC 7-374263. A. D. F. Randolph & Company.

Song and You. Vivien Grey. LC 42-14394. 1942. Arcadia House, Inc.

Song at the Scaffold. Gertrud Von Le Fort. LC 33-117870. (Half-title: The Malta books). H. Holt and Company.

Song at the Scaffold. Tr. from German by Olga Marx. Gertrud Von Le Fort. (Image bk., D126). Doubleday.

Song Before Sunrise. Jonreed Lauritzen. LC 48-8578. 1948. Doubleday.

Song Beneath the Keys. Emma Beaver Byrne. LC 16-17411. 1.50. The Roxburgh Publishing Company Inc.

Song Bird. Sophia Cleugh. LC 30-878825. 1930. Houghton Mifflin Company.

Song Comes Native. Hobie Mills. LC 81-9864. 11.95 (ISBN 0-914378-84-8). Countryman Press.

Song Everlasting. Paul Dayton Bailey. LC 46-1841. 1946. Westernlore Press.

Song for Christina. Blakely St. James. LC 76-22218. (Christina Van Bell Ser.). 256p. (Orig.). 1976. pap. 2.95 (ISBN 0-86721-081-8). Playboy Pbks.

Song for Christina. Blakely St. James. LC 76-22218. Playboy Press.

Song for Jenny. Susan D Winkler. LC 55-148334. 1955. Avalon Books.

Song for Lya: And Other Stories. George R. R Martin. LC 76-620. 1976. (pbk.) 1.25 (ISBN 0-380-00521-2). Avon Books.

Song for Mumu: A Novel. Lindsay Barrett. LC 73-99065. (Illus.). 1974. 6.95 (ISBN 0-88258-006-X). Howard University Press.

Song for My Father. Schavi M. Diara. LC 75-11025. 1976. 2.50 (ISBN 0-913358-08-8). Agascha Productions.

Song for My Time. Meridel Le Sueur. LC 77-14827. (Illus.). 1977. pap. 2.50 o.p. (ISBN 0-931122-04-X). West End.

Song for My Time: Stories of the Period of Repression. Meridel Le Sueur. LC 77-156060. (Illus.). 1977. 2.50 (ISBN 0-931122-04-X). West End Press.

Song for Pamela. 1st Ed. Rose A Livant. LC 63-15333. 1963. Chilton Books.

Song for the River. James Hale Carlisle. LC 57-59554. (Milestone book). 1957. Comet Press Books.

Song for Two Voices. Barbara Corcoran. 128p. 1981. pap. 1.95 (ISBN 0-345-29012-7). Ballantine.

Song Forever. Paul Hutchens. LC 36-762637. 1936. W. B. Eerdmans Publishing Co.

Song Goes on. Barbara Hedworth. LC 47-56343. 1947. Hurst & Blackett.

Song in Her Heart. Peggy Gaddis. LC 38-4647. Arcadia House.

Song in My Heart. Janet Doran. LC 38-152262. Gramercy Publishing Co.

Song in the Green Thorn Tree: A Novel of the Life and Loves of Robert Burns. James Barke. LC 48-2552. 1948. Macmillan Co.

Song in the Night. LeRoy Brown. (Orig.). 1971. pap. 1.50 o.p. Nazarene.

Song in the Night. Josephine Lawrence. LC 52-7498. 1952. Morrow.

Song of a Heart: Christmas Milestones. Helen Mason Boynton. LC 1-29498. 1901. The Robert Clarke Co.

Song of a Single Note: A Love Story. Amelia Edith Huddleston Barr. LC 2-24726. 1902. Dodd & Company.

Song of Abraham. Ellen Gunderson Traylor. 1975. pap. 2.45 (ISBN 0-8423-6070-0). Tyndale.

Song of Africa. Leland Tracy. pap. 0.95 o.p. Lancer.

Song of Aino: A Tale of Finland in America. Olav K Lundeberg. LC 42-571925. Augsburg Publishing House.

Song of Bernadette. Franz Werfel. 1975. (pbk.) 1.95 (ISBN 0-380-00502-6). Avon.

Song of Bernadette. Franz V Werfel. Tr. by Lewisohn, Ludwig. LC 48-41804. 1943. Viking Press.

Song of Bernadette. Franz V. Werfel. Tr. by Ludwig Lewisohn. LC 42-104304. 1942. The Viking Press.

Song of Bernadette. Franz V. Werfel. Tr. by Ludwig Lewisohn. LC 46-438868. 1943. The Viking Press.

Song of Bernadette. Franz V. Werfel. Tr. by Ludwig Lewisohn. LC 44-772643. 1944. The Sun Dial Press.

Song of Corpus Juris. Joe L. Hensley. LC 74-3694. 1974. 4.95 (ISBN 0-385-09555-4). Published for the Crime Club by Doubleday.

Song of Cyrana: A Story. Hales-Tooke, John. LC 74-168887. (Illus.). 1973. 0.30 (ISBN 0-903955-00-8). Causeway Press.

Song of David Freed: A Novel. Abraham Rothberg. LC 68-12110. 1968. Putnam.

Song of Deborah: A Novel. Bette M Ross. LC 80-28351. 9.95 (ISBN 0-8007-1263-3). F. H. Revell Co.

Song of Desire. Rosalind Carson. (Superromances Ser.). 384p. 1982. pap. 2.50 (ISBN 0-373-70040-7, Pub. by Worldwide). Harlequin Bks.

Song of Everything, and Other Stories. Tracy Leddy. LC 75-9243. (Illus.). 1975. 2.95 (ISBN 0-89142-020-7). Sant Bani Press.

Song of Friendship: A Novel. Bernhard Kellermann. Tr. by Gribble, George Dunning. LC 37-1362. The Bobbs-Merrill Company.

Song of Heyoehkah. Hyemeyohsts Storm. LC 80-8359. (Illus.). 17.95 (ISBN 0-06-452000-5). Harper & Row.

Song of Hyeyoehkah: A Novel. Hyemeyohsts Storm. LC 80-8359. (Native American Publishing Program). (Illus.). 224p. 1981. 4.00i (ISBN 0-06-452000-5, HarpR). Har-Row.

Song of India. Mozelle Richardson. LC 74-17136. 1975. 5.95 (ISBN 0-688-00336-2). Morrow.

Song of India. Mozelle Richardson. LC 75-8660. 1975. 10.95 (ISBN 0-8161-6290-5). G. K. Hall.

Song of Lawino. Okot Bitek. 1966. pap. 2.00 o.p. (Pub. by East African Publ Hse). Northwestern U Pr.

Song of Life. Fannie Hurst. LC 27-4634. 1927. A. A. Knopf.

Song of Love. Barbara Cartland. 208p. 1980. pap. 1.75 (ISBN 0-515-05444-5). Jove Pubns.

Song of Love. Irwin R Franklyn. LC 30-552. Grosset & Dunlap.

Song of Man: A Novel Based Upon the Life of Eugene V. Debs. Nissenson, Aaron. LC 64-13961. 1964. Whittier Books.

Song of Metamoris: A Story That Remains of a People Who Passed This Way. Milford E Anness. LC 63-11312. 1964. Caxton Printers.

Song of Miriam: And Other Stories. Marie Corelli. LC 71-37263. (Short story index reprint series). 1971. (ISBN 0-8369-4074-1). Books for Libraries Press.

Song of Miriam: And Other Stories. Marie Corelli. (On cover: Seaside library, Pocket ed., no. 2186). 1898. G. Munro's Sons.

Song of Renny. Maurice Henry Hewlett. LC 11-25013. 1911. C. Scribner's Sons.

Song of Rhiannon: The Third Branch of the Mabinogion. Evangeline Walton. LC 72-197185. (Adult fantasy). 1972. 1.25 (ISBN 0-345-02773-6). Ballantine Books.

Song of Roland. F. B. Luquiens. 1960. pap. 2.95 o.s.i. (ISBN 0-02-069850-X). Macmillan.

Song of Roland. Tr. by Scott-Moncrieff, Charles Kenneth. LC 59-16354. (Ann Arbor paperbacks, AA32). 1959. University of Michigan Press.

Song of Ruth. Frank Gill Slaughter. (Kangaroo Book). 1977. 1.95 (ISBN 0-671-80965-2). Pocket Books.

Song of Ruth: A Love Story from the Old Testament. Frank Gill Slaughter. LC 54-6247. 1954. Doubleday.

Song of Saturn. Connie Menger. (Illus.). 1968. pap. 3.95 o.p. Saucerian.

Song of Sixpence. Archibald Joseph Cronin. LC 64-15052. 1964. Little, Brown.

Song of Sixpence. Frederic Arnold Kummer. LC 13-2839. 1.25. W. J. Watt & Company.

Song of Sixpence. William Almon Wolff. LC 31-80597. 1931. Minton, Balch & Company.

Song of Solomon. Toni Morrison. LC 77-874. 1977. 8.95 (ISBN 0-394-49784-8). Knopf.

Song of Songs. 1.95 o.p. (ISBN 0-442-82424-6). Peter Pauper.

Song of Songs. Hermann Sudermann. LC 31-30708. (Half-title: The modern library of the world's best books). The Modern Library.

Song of Songs: Das Hohe Lied. Hermann Sudermann & Seltzer, Thomas, Tr. LC 10-743. 1909. B. W. Huebsch.

Song of Songs: Das Hohe Lied. Hermann Sudermann & Seltzer, Thomas, Tr. LC 20-18820. 1919. B. W. Huebsch.

Song of Songs: Das Hohe Lied. Hermann Sudermann & Seltzer, Thomas, Tr. 1923. B. W. Huebsch, Inc.

Song of the Axe. N. C. McDonald. LC 57-146801. 1957. Ballantine Books.

Song of the Black Witch. Elisabeth Barr. LC 81-80775. 304p. (Orig.). 1981. pap. 2.95 (ISBN 0-87216-923-5). Playboy Pbks.

Song of the Blood-Red Flower. Vihtori Pelton. Tr. by Worster, W. W. LC 21-16802. 1921. Moffat, Yard & Company.

Song of the Cardinal. Gene Stratton Porter. LC 53-386519. 1953. Grosset & Dunlap.

Song of the Cardinal. Gene Stratton Porter. LC 12-18615. The Bobbs-Merrill Company.

Song of the Cardinal. new and rev. ed. Gene Stratton Porter. LC 15-165343. 1915. Doubleday, Page & Company.

Song of the Cardinal. Gene Stratton-Porter. 1977. Repr. of 1903 ed. lib. bdg. 25.00 (ISBN 0-8414-7939-9). Folcroft.

Song of the Cave: A Tale of Ruth and Noemi. Edward Francis Murphy. LC 50-9050. 1950. Bruce.

Song of the Deep: A Narrative in Three Parts. Gustav Olson. LC 49-167292. 1948. House of Edinboro.

Song of the Dnieper. Zalman Shneur. Tr. by Joseph Leftwich. LC 45-8808. 1945. Roy Publishers.

Song of the Dragon. John Taintor Foote. LC 23-28843. 1923. D. Appleton and Company.

Song of the Dusty Stars. William S Murray. LC 72-142524.

Song of the Earth: A Novel. Alexander Cordell, pseud. LC 70-101870. 1970. 6.50. Simon and Schuster.

Song of the Evening. Nandini Satpathi. Tr. by J. B. Mohanty from Oriya. 110p. (Orig.). 1975. pap. 1.50 (ISBN 0-88253-770-9). Ind-US Inc.

Song of the Flea. Gerald Kersh. LC 48-660734. 1948. Doubleday.

Song of the Flesh. Ruth Cummings. LC 34-325689. The Macaulay Company.

Song of the Frog. Taylor, Raymond H. LC 50-7915. 1950. Bobbs-Merrill.

Song of the Kingdom. Andy Stone. LC 78-22424. (Illus.). 1979. 8.95 (ISBN 0-385-15035-0). Doubleday.

Song of the Lark. Willa Sibert Cather. LC 15-19408. 1915. Houghton Mifflin Company.

Song of the Lark. Willa Sibert Cather. LC 15-19406. 1915. Houghton Mifflin Company.

Song of the Lark... Willa Sibert Cather. LC 38-885. (Half-title: The novels and stories of Willa Cather, no. 2, autograph edition). 1937. Houghton Mifflin Company.

Song of the Lark. Willa Sibert Cather. LC 77-15596. 1978. 4.95 (ISBN 0-8032-6300-7). University of Nebraska Press.

Song of the Ocean. Helene Chambers Schellenberg. C.

Song of the Oxen. 1st Ed. Hallie Ray Dolin. LC 53-20943. 1952. Pageant Press.

Song of the Pedernales: A Novel of Reconstruction Texas. John L Mortimer. LC 76-40637. 8.95 (ISBN 0-89052-021-6). Madrona Press.

Song of the Pines. Robert Valentine Mathews. LC 6-27703. 1906. E. C. Hill Company.

Song of the Pines. Ethelbert Sheb Ray. 1909. 1.50. The C. M. Clark Publishing Company.

Song of the Plains. Fred N Kimmel. LC 63-18126. Macmillan.

Song of the Red Ruby. Translated by Maurice Michael. 1st American Ed. Agnar Mykle. LC 61-6002. 1961. Dutton.

Song of the River. Drawings by Ezra Jack Keats. Billy C Clark. LC 57-9241. 1957. Crowell.

Song of the Scorpions. Paul Tabori. (O.s.i.). 1976. pap. 1.25 o.s.i. (BT50905). Belmont-Tower.

Song of the Scorpions. Paul Tabori. 1976. (pbk.) 1.25. Belmont Tower.

Song of the Siren. Philippa Carr, pseud. pap. 2.75 (ISBN 0-449-24371-0, Crest). Fawcett.

Song of the Siren. Philippa Carr, pseud. LC 79-10124. 1980. 10.95 (ISBN 0-399-12426-8). Putnam Pub Group.

Song of the Siren. Eleanor Hibbert. LC 79-10124. 10.00. Putnam.

Song of the Sirens. Ernest Kellogg Gann. 256p. 1981. pap. 2.50 (ISBN 0-515-05482-8). Jove Pubns.

Song of the Stars. Anne Stewart. LC 40-294703. Phoenix Press.

Song of the Susquehanna. Herbert E Stover. LC 49-2533. 1949. Dodd, Mead.

Song of the Trail. Mabel E. Cason. LC 53-10772. (Destiny Ser.). 1979. pap. 4.95 o.p. (ISBN 0-8163-0245-6). Pacific Pr Pub Assn.

Song of the Trumpet. Mamie Peters Call. LC 54-9129. 1954. Vantage Press.

Song of the Undersea. Ronald De Levington Kirbride. LC 67-31111. 1967. Astor-Honor.

Song of the Valley. Shalom Asch & Krauch, Elsa, Tr. LC 39-27222. G. P. Putnam's Sons.

Song of the Wheatfields. Ferenc Mora. Tr. by Halasz, George. LC 30-30230. 1930. Brewer & Warren, Inc.

Song of the Whip. Max Brand. 1969. pap. 0.60 o.p. (63-151). Paperback Lib.
Song of the Whip. Evan Evans, pseud. LC 36-15161. 1936. Harper & Brothers.
Song of the Whip. Frederick Faust. LC 75-42201. 1975. 5.95 (ISBN 0-89190-210-4). American Reprint Co.
Song of the Wild. Allan W Eckert. LC 80-15633. 10.95 (ISBN 0-316-20877-9). Little, Brown.
Song of the Wolf. Frank Mayer. LC 10-11139. 1910. Moffat, Yard and Company.
Song of the World. Jean Giono. LC 74-23512. 1975. 13.50. H. Fertig.
Song of the World. Jean Giono. Tr. by Fluchere, Henri. LC 37-28508. 1937. The Viking Press.
Song of the World. Jean Giono. LC 80-28523. 1981. 8.50 (ISBN 0-86547-038-3). North Point Press.
Song of the Young Sentry. David Westheimer. LC 68-24237. 1968. 6.95. Little, Brown.
Song of Tomorrow. Charlie May Hogue Simon. LC 43-151673. 1943. E. P. Dutton and Company, Inc.
Song of Triumphant Love. Ivan Sergieevich Turgenev & Ford, Marian, Tr. 1882. G. Munro.
Song of Years. Bess Streeter Aldrich. LC 75-29208. 1975. 6.95. Aeonian Press.
Song of Years. Bess Streeter Aldrich. LC 45-132879. 1944. The Sun Dial Press.
Song of Zion. Clara Bernhardt. LC 44-8147. 1944. Wm. B. Eerdmans Publishing Company.
Song on Your Bugles. Eric Mowbray Knight. LC 37-17035. 1937. Harper & Brothers.
Song-Sister, Sing. Vicki Baum. Tr. by Creighton, Basil. LC 37-349. 1936. Doubleday, Doran & Company, Inc.
Song-Story of Aucassin and Nicolete. Tr. by Lang, Andrew. Elston Press. LC 2-30150. 1908. The Elston Press.
Song-Story of Aucassin & Nicolette. The Andrew Lang Translation. Aucassin Et Nicolette. Tr. by Andrew Lang. Fritz Kredel. LC 58-964. 1957. Gravesend Press.
Song-Story of Aucassin and Nicolette. The Andrew Lang Translation. Andrew Lang. LC 58-964. (Illus.). 1957. Gravesend Press.
Song Without Sermon. James Woolf. LC 50-5713. 1950. Creative Age Press.
Songbird. Ralph Benner. 192p. 1975. pap. 1.25 (ISBN 0-532-12294-1). Woodhill.
Songbird. Ralph Benner. (Orig.). 1970. pap. 0.95 o.p. (95-139). Manor Bks.
Songbird of the Sierras. Basil William Miller. LC 43-209. 1942. Zondervan Publishing House.
Songes Merveilleux Du Dormeur Eveille: Le Chant Du Dvgne: Contes Parles D'Oscar Wilde. Guillot De Saix. LC 76-25932. (Decadent Consciousness Ser.). lib. bdg. 38.00 (ISBN 0-8240-2785-X). Garland Pub.
Songmaster. Orson Scott Card. LC 80-10380. (Quantum novel). 10.95 (ISBN 0-8037-7711-6). Dial Press.
Songs and Stories from Tennessee. John Trotwood Moore. LC 70-94739. (Short story index reprint series). (Illus.). 1969. Books for Libraries Press.
Songs, Ballads, & Stories. William Allingham. LC 75-148743. Repr. of 1877 ed. 24.00 (ISBN 0-404-00347-8). AMS Pr.
Songs for the Little Ones at Home. Mary O. Ward. LC 41-267198. American Tract Society.
Songs for the Master. Ruth Plummer. LC 28-18820. Powell & White.
Songs from the Night Before. Anthony Tuttle. 1974. (pbk.) 1.50. Dell.
Songs from the Night Before. Anthony Tuttle. LC 73-157631. 1972. 6.95. Doubleday.
Songs from the Stars. Norman Spinard. 1981. pap. 2.50 (ISBN 0-671-82826-6, Timescape). PB.
Songs from the Stars. Norman Spinrad. LC 79-23299. 10.95 (ISBN 0-671-25326-3). Simon and Schuster.
Songs My Mother Taught Me. Audrey Callahan Thomas. LC 73-1737. 1973. 6.95 (ISBN 0-672-51792-2). Bobbs-Merrill.
Songs My Mother Taught Me. Audrey Callahan Thomas. 1974. (pbk.) 1.25. Ballantine Books.
Songs of Light. Georgiana L. Lahr. 1977. 5.95 (ISBN 0-533-02845-0). Vantage.
Songs of Love. Gwen Shaw. 1975. pap. 2.95 o.p. (ISBN 0-89221-003-6). New Leaf.
Songs of Sentimentality. Susan Lizotte. 2.50 o.p. Vantage.
Songs of Stars & Shadows. George R. R Martin. (Kangaroo Book). 1977. 1.75 (ISBN 0-671-81277-7). Pocket Books.
Songs of the Wild Land. 1st Ed. Michael Grinnell. LC 53-8092. Pageant Press.
Songs of Years. Bess Streeter Aldrich. LC 38-20081. 1939. D. Appleton-Century Company, Incorporated.
Songs, Set Two: A Short Count. Edward Dorn. 28p. (Orig.). 1970. pap. 1.00. Frontier Press Calif.
Songs Under Open Skies. M. Jay Flannery. LC 12-25603. 1912. Steward & Kidd Company.
Sonia. Vida Hurst. LC 27-137647. Grosset & Dunlap.
Sonia. A Russian Story. Alice Marie Celeste Durand. Tr. by Sherwood, Mary (Neal) LC 6-35683. T. B. Peterson & Brothers.
Sonia: Between Two Worlds. Stephen McKenna. LC 17-20668. George H. Doran Company.
Sonia by Night. Pierre Berg. Tr. by Andrea Gilbert. 1968. pap. 1.75 o.p. Brandon.
Sonia Married. Stephen McKenna. LC 19-275798. George H. Doran Company.
Sonia: Novela. Rafael Echeverri. LC 67-50731. 1962. Colombia.
Sonic Slave. Paul Kenyon. 1974. (pbk.) 0.95 (ISBN 0-671-77949-4). Pocket Books.
Sonnica. Vicente Blasco Ibanez & Douglas, Frances, 1870- Tr. LC 12-25824. 1912. Duffield & Company.
Sonnie-Boy's People. James Brendan Connolly. LC 13-205753. 1913. C. Scribner's Sons.
Sonntag. Michael Sinclair. LC 72-151217. 1971. 5.95. Putnam.
Sonny. Virginia Brightman. LC 24-4262. W. J. Watt & Co.
Sonny: A Christmas Guest. Ruth McEnery Stuart. LC 4-31821. 1904. The Century Co.
Sonny: A Christmas Guest. Ruth McEnery Stuart. LC 22-14549. 1914. The Century Co.
Sonny: A Story. Ruth McEnery Stuart. 1896. The Century Co.
Sonny's Father: In Which the Father, Now Become Grandfather, a Kindly Observer of Life and a Genial Philosopher, in His Desultory Talks with the Family Doctor, Carries Along the Story of Sonny. Ruth McEnery Stuart. 1910. The Century Co.
Sonoma. Leonard Sanders. LC 80-22902. 12.95 (ISBN 0-440-08111-4). Delacorte Press.
Sonora Guns. Robert Poole. (Orig.). 1979. pap. 1.50 (ISBN 0-532-15395-2). Woodhill.
Sonora Mutation. Albert J Elias. LC 78-55631. 1978. 1.95 (ISBN 0-380-01963-9). Avon.
Sonora Slaughter. William M James. (Apache series#6). 1976. (pbk.) 1.25 (ISBN 0-523-00827-9). Pinnacle Books.
Sonora Stage. Lee Floren. LC 53-856466. 1953. Arcadia House.
Sonora Stage. Lee Floren. 1976. (pbk.) 0.95. Belmont Tower.
Sonotaw. William Sayres. LC 59-11201. 1959. Simon and Schuster.
Sons. Pearl Sydenstricker Buck. 1975. (pbk.) 1.50 (ISBN 0-671-78796-9). Pocket Books.
Sons. Pearl Sydenstricker Buck. LC 32-27061. 1932. The John Day Company.
Sons. Evan Hunter. LC 78-79415. 1969. 6.95. Doubleday.
Sons. Viktor A Smirnov. Tr. by Yohel, Naomi Y. LC 47-30162. 1947. Doubleday.
Sons and Comrades: A Novel of Modern Poland Translated from the Polish by D.J. Welsh. Kazimierz Brandys. LC 61-10905. (Evergreen original E-302). 1961. Grove Press.
Sons and Daughters. William Johnston. 1974. (pbk.) 1.25. Ballantine.
Sons and Daughters. Ellen Warner Olney Kirk. LC 7-12364. 1887. Ticknor and Company.
Sons and Fathers. Harry Stillwell Edwards. LC 6-36576. 1896. Rand, McNally & Company.
Sons and Fathers. Harry Stillwell Edwards. LC 38-41004. Brown Publishing Company.
Sons and Fathers. Maurice Gerschon Hindus. LC 40-271503. 1940. Doubleday, Doran & Co., Inc.
Sons and Lovers. David Herbert Lawrence. LC 63-1407. (Modern library of the world's best books, 833). Modern Library.
Sons and Lovers. David Herbert Lawrence. 1976. 2.25 (ISBN 0-14-004217-2). Penguin.
Sons and Lovers. David Herbert Lawrence. Ed. by Julian Moynahan. LC 68-6512. (Viking critical library). (Illus.). 1968. 4.75. Viking Press.
Sons and Lovers. David Herbert Lawrence. LC 68-28024. 1968. 4.50. Viking Press.
Sons and Lovers. David Herbert Lawrence. LC 76-359185. (Illus.). 1975. Printed for the Limited Editions Club.
Sons and Lovers. David Herbert Lawrence. LC 13-21105. 1913. M. Kennerley.
Sons and Lovers. David Herbert Lawrence. LC 23-18621. (Half-title: The modern library of the world's best books). 1922. Boni and Liveright.
Sons and Lovers. David Herbert Lawrence. LC 26-23543. 1922. M. Kennerley.
Sons and Lovers. David Herbert Lawrence. Ed. by Macy, John Albert. LC 31-251. (Half-title: The modern library of the world's best books). 1923. The Modern Library.
Sons and Lovers: Text, Background, and Criticism. David Herbert Lawrence & Julian Moynahan. LC 76-51771. 1977. 4.95 (ISBN 0-14-015504-X). Penguin Books.
Sons and Lovers: With an Introd. by Mark Schorer. David Herbert Lawrence. LC 51-6232. (Harper's modern classics). 1951. Harper.
Sons & Sinners. J. D. Hardin. LC 81-83490. (J. D. Hardin Western Ser.). 224p. (Orig.). 1982. pap. 1.95 (ISBN 0-86721-039-7). Playboy Pbks.
Sons for King Yah. Linda Howard. LC 75-7480. (Illus.). 2.25. Logos International.
Sons for the Return Home. Albert Wendt. LC 74-191754. 1973-1974. 7.90 (ISBN 0-582-71718-3). Longman Paul.
Sons O' Cormac: An' Tales of Other Men's Sons. Effie Barnhurst Kaemmerling. LC 20-22231. 1921. E. P. Dutton & Company.
Sons O' Cormac: An' Tales of Other Men's Sons. Effie Barnhurst Kaemmerling. LC 29-56905. E. P. Dutton & Co., Inc.
Sons of Adam: A Novel. Frederick Feikema Manfred. LC 80-12648. 12.95 (ISBN 0-517-54186-6). Crown Publishers.
Sons of Adam: Stories of Somalia. Omar Eby. LC 73-113819. (Illus.). 1970. 3.95. Herald Press.
Sons of Adversity: A Romance of Queen Elizabeth's Time. Leslie Cope Cornford. 1898. L. C. Page and Company.
Sons of Avfom. Translated by Leonard M. Friedman and Maxwell Singer. Roger Ikor. LC 57-6728. 1958. Putnam.
Sons of Belial. William Westall. LC 8-36227. The Cassell Publishing Co.
Sons of Cain. James Warner Bellah. LC 28-230432. 1928. D. Appleton & Company.
Sons of Darkness, Sons of Light. John A. Williams. LC 69-16977. (An explosive new novel). 1969. 6.95 o.p. (ISBN 0-316-94348-7). Little.
Sons of Darkness, Sons of Light: A Novel of Some Probability. John Alfred Williams. LC 69-16977. 1969. 5.95. Little, Brown.
Sons of Earth. Richard Rhodes. 240p. 1982. pap. 2.75 (ISBN 0-441-77515-2, Pub. by Charter Bks). Ace Bks.
Sons of Earth: A Novel. Richard Rhodes. LC 80-25178. 12.95 (ISBN 0-698-11055-2). Coward, McCann & Geoghegan.
Sons of Eli. Ralph Delahaye Paine. LC 17-24274. 1917. C. Scribner's Sons.
Sons of Elohim. Harry Lascelles Burnette. LC 22-239174. 2.00. Randolph, Sterling & Van Ess.
Sons of Fortune. Malcolm MacDonald. LC 77-11637. (Illus.). 1978. 10.00 (ISBN 0-394-41814-X). Knopf.
Sons of Fortune. Malcolm Macdonald. 1979. 2.75 (ISBN 0-451-08595-7). New American Library.
Sons of Ham. A Tale of the New South. Louis Beauregard Pendleton. 1895. Roberts Brothers.
Sons of Israel. Joseph Mendel Kesslinger. LC 27-21341. Dorrance and Company.
Sons of Kings: Les Pleiades) Tr. from French Introd. by Douglas Parmee. Joseph Arthur Gobineau. LC 66-1708. (Oxford lib. of French classics). 5.60. Oxford.
Sons of Light. David Rudkin. 1982. pap. 7.50 (ISBN 0-413-49120-X, NO. 3644). Methuen Inc.
Sons of Martha, & Other Stories. Richard McKenna. 1967. 4.95 o.p. (ISBN 0-06-012913-1). Har-Row.
Sons of Martha: And Other Stories. Ed., Introd. by M. S. Wyeth, Jr. 1st Ed. Richard McKenna. LC 67-11335. 1967. 4.95. Harper.
Sons of Men. Herschel Steinhardt. 1959. 3.00 o.p. Twayne.
Sons of Mrs. Aab. Sarah Gertrude Liebson Millin. LC 31-28032. H. Liveright, Inc.
Sons of My Skin. Peter Redgrove. 1975. 14.95 (ISBN 0-7100-8073-5). Routledge & Kegan.
Sons of Noah. Negley Farson. LC 49-8553. 1949. Harcourt, Brace.
Sons of Saintly Women. Bernard Packer. LC 81-3571. 1981. 12.95 (ISBN 0-689-11177-0). Atheneum.
Sons of Sheba. Stuart Bergsma. LC 34-12976. 1933. W. B. Eerdmans Publishing Co.
Sons of Sinbad. Alan Villiers. (Emblem Edition Ser). (Illus.). 1970. pap. 3.50 o.p. (ISBN 0-684-71919-3, 237, SL). Scribner.
Sons of Strength: A Romance of the Kansas Border Wars. William Rheem Lighton. LC 99-5098. 1899. Doubleday & McClure Co.
Sons of the Border. Sketches of the Life and People of the Far Frontier. James William Steele. 1873. Commonwealth Printing Company.
Sons of the Covenant: A Tale of London Jewry. Samuel Gordon. 1900. The Jewish Publication Society of America.
Sons of the Fathers. Beatrice Ann Wright. LC 59-9304. 1959. Macmillan.
Sons of the Fathers: By Albert Halper. Albert Halper. LC 40-333633. Harper & Brothers.
Sons of the Mammoth. Vladimir Germanovich Bogoraz & Graham, Stephen, 1884- Tr. LC 29-19241. 1929. Cosmopolitan Book Corporation.
Sons of the Martian. Donald Culross Peattie. LC 32-30526. 1932. Longmans, Green and Co.
Sons of the Morning. Eden Phillpotts. LC 4612. 1900. G. P. Putnam's Sons.
Sons of the Morning, Otto Schroq. LC 95-10358. 1945. Doubleday, Doran and Company, Inc.
Sons of the Others, a Novel. Philip Hamilton Gibbs. 1941. Doubleday, Doran and Company, Inc.
Sons of the Pioneers. John Givens. LC 77-73052. 10.00. (ISBN 0-15-183775-9) (ISBN 0-15-683815-X). Harcourt Brace Jovanovich.
Sons of the Puritans: With a Preface by Christopher Morley. Don Marquis & Morley, Christopher Darlington. LC 39-27146. 1939. Doran & Co., Inc.
Sons of the Red Rose: A Story of the Rail in the Early '80's. Matthias Bodine De Courcy. LC 6-456927. J. W. Cannon.
Sons of the Rhine (Die Wiskottens) Rudolf Herzog. Tr. by Lazell, Louise T. LC 14-201138. 1.25. Desmond Fitzgerald, Inc.
Sons of the Saddle. William MacLeod Raine. LC 38-27834. 1938. Houghton Mifflin Company.
Sons of the Saddle. William MacLeod Raine. (Signet Brand Western, T5572). 1973. (pbk.) 0.75. New American Lib.
Sons of the Sea. Raymond McFarland. LC 21-3810. 1921. G. P. Putnam's Sons.
Sons of the Seigneur. Helen Wallace. LC 7-207110. 1907. The Outing Publishing Company.
Sons of the Sheik. Edith Maude Hull. LC 25-145104. Small, Maynard and Company.
Sons of the Soil. Balzac, Honore De. Tr. by Katharine Prescott Wormeley. LC 3-23180. (Half-title: The comedy of human life... Scenes from country life). 1890. Roberts Brothers.
Sons of the Sword: A Romance of the Peninsular War. Margaret Louisa Bradley Woods. LC 1-27053. 1901. McClure, Phillips & Co.
Sons of the Sword Maker. Maurice Walsh. LC 38-29078. 1939. Frederick A. Stokes Company.
Sons of the Western Frontier. Henry Allen. LC 66-15713. 1966. Chilton Books.
Sons of the Western Frontier: By Will Henry. Henry Allen. LC 66-15713. 3.95. Chilton.
Sons of the Wolf. Barbara Mertz. LC 67-24433. 1967. Meredith Press.
Sons of Vengeance: A Tale of the Cumberland Highlanders. Joseph S Malone. F. H. Revell Company.
Sons to Fortune. Vingie Eve Roe. LC 34-30881. 1934. Doubleday, Doran & Company, Inc.
Son's Victory: A Story of the Land of the Honey-Bee. Fannie E Newberry. LC 1-25798. The Pilgrim Press.
Sons Without Anger. Stanley Young. LC 39-19491. Farrar & Rinehart, Incorporated.
Sonya Babushka: A Novel of the Russians. Maurice Chideckel. LC 28-6087. The Four Seas Company.
Soo Canal! William Ratigan. LC 54-623875. 1954. W. B. Eerdmans Pub. Co.
Soo Thah: A Tale of the Making of the Karen Nation. Alonzo Bunker. LC 2-21579. 1902. F.H. Revell Company.
Sookey. Angelo D'Arcangelo. LC 70-15997. (Traveller's companion series TC-465). 1969. 1.95. Olympia Press.
Sookey. Wilfrid Douglas Newton. LC 26-720924. 1925. Cassell and Company, Ltd.
Sookey. Wilfrid Douglas Newton. LC 26-5444. 1926. Dodd, Mead and Company.
Soon to Be Immortal. Ellen Alexander Conley. LC 81-23188. 1982. 13.95 (ISBN 0-312-74504-4). St. Martin's Press.
Sooner Land. George Washington Ogden. LC 29-421263. 1929. Dodd, Mead & Company.
Sooner or Later. Millie R. Hynes. (Illus.). 106p. (Orig.). 1982. pap. 4.95 (ISBN 0-939688-07-7). Directed Media.
Sooner to Sleep. Van De Water, Frederic Franklyn. LC 46-2157. 1946. Duell, Sloan and Pearce.
Sooners: A Romance of Early Oklahoma. Roderic Horton. LC 27-4646. Gem Publishing Company.
Soothsayer: A Novel. Laurene Chambers Chinn. LC 72-104. (Illus.). 1972. (ISBN 0-688-00022-3). Morrow.
Sophia. St. John Greer Ervine. LC 41-19303. 1941. The Macmillan Company.
Sophia. Charlotte Ramsay Lennox. LC 74-17442. (Flowering of the Novel). 1974. (ISBN 0-8240-1160-0). Garland Pub.
Sophia: A Romance. Stanley John Weyman. LC 21713. 1900. Longmans, Green, and Co.
Sophia-Adelaide: A Chapter in Contemporaneous History. Charlotte Louise Kent. LC 5-30544. 1887. Belford. Clarke & Company.
Sophia and Augusta. Norma Lee Clark. 1.75 (ISBN 0-449-23916-0). Fawcett Crest.
Sophia Sparkhall: Or, How She Attended Her Own Funeral... T. Aldiffe Teske. 1885. Clark & Smith, Book and Job Printers.
Sophie. Frances Roberta Sterrett. LC 30-21335. The Penn Publishing Company.
Sophie. Geoffrey Atheling Wagner. 320p. 1982. pap. 2.95 (ISBN 0-505-51795-7). Tower Bks.
Sophie: A Novel. Geoffrey Atheling Wagner. LC 58-12131. 1958. J. Day Co.
Sophie Halenczik: American. Rose Caroline Feld & Alajalov, Constantin, 1900- Illus. LC 43-6809. 1943. Little, Brown and Company.
Sophie's Choice. William Styron. LC 78-21835. 12.95 (ISBN 0-394-46109-6). Random House.

Sophisticates. Gertrude Franklin Horn Atherton. LC 31-96560. H. Liveright.

Sophomore. Barry Spacks. LC 68-11274. 1968. Prentice-Hall.

Sophomore Jinx. Allen Trask. 1970. 3.00 o.p. Carlton.

Sophomores. Betty Berra. LC 76-58612. 1977. pap. 5.95 o.p. (ISBN 0-8283-1694-5). Branden.

Sophomores Abroad. Charles Macomb Flandrau. LC 35-13818. 1935. D. Appleton-Century Company, Incorporated.

Sophronia. LC 74-16158. (Flowering of the Novel). 1974. (ISBN 0-8240-1158-9). Garland Pub.

Sophy Carmine. Henrietta Eliza Vaughan Stannard. (On cover: Lovell's international series, no. 25). 1889. F. F. Lovell & Company.

Sophy Carmine. Henrietta Eliza Vaughan Stannard. (On cover: Seaside library. Pocket ed. no. 1171 A). 1889. G. Munro.

Sophy Cassmajor. Margery Sharp. LC 36-4880. 1934. G. P. Putnam's Sons.

Sophy of Kravonia: A Novel. Anthony Hope Hawkins. 1906. Harper & Brothers.

Sopping Thursday. Edward Gorey. (Illus.). 66p. (Orig.). 1971. pap. 4.95 (ISBN 0-912264-21-7). Capra Pr.

Soprano: A Musical Story. Charles Barnard. LC 6-7194. Loring.

Sorcerer. Anne Eliot Crompton. LC 82-61042. 176p. 1982. Repr. of 1971 ed. 16.95 (ISBN 0-933256-36-1). Second Chance.

Sorcerer. Anne Eliot Crompton. LC 82-61042. (Illus.). 176p. pap. 8.95 (ISBN 0-933256-37-X). Second Chance.

Sorcerer. Eric Ericson. LC 78-19530. 8.95 (ISBN 0-312-74506-0). St. Martin's Press.

Sorcerer of the Castle. Florence Stevenson. (Kitty Telefair Ser). (O.s.i.). 160p. (Orig.). 1974. pap. 0.95 o.s.i. (AN1219, Award). Univ Pub & Dist.

Sorcerers. Howard Hunt. LC 74-95055. 1969. 5.00. Weybright and Talley.

Sorcerers. David St. John, pseud. 1969. 5.50 o.p. Weybright.

Sorcerers. David St. John, pseud. 1971. pap. 0.75 o.p. (T1566, Crest). Fawcett World.

Sorcerers: A Laotian Tale. Knute Skinner. (Illus.). 1973. pap. 1.50. Goliards Pr.

Sorcerer's Amulet. Michael Moorcock. (Orig.). 1968. pap. 0.60 o.p. (73-707). Lancer.

Sorcerer's Apprentice: Translated from the German of Hanns Heinz Ewers. Hanns Heinz Ewers. Tr. by Lewisohn, Ludwig. LC 27-7925. 1927. The John Day Company.

Sorcerer's Apprentice: Translated from the German of Hanns Heinz Ewers. Hanns Heinz Ewers. Tr. by Lewisohn, Ludwig. LC 31-764523. 1927. The John Day Company.

Sorcerer's Blood. Ross A. Coe. (Warrior of Vengeance Ser.: No. 1). 224p. (Orig.). 1982. pap. 2.25 (ISBN 0-523-41709-8). Pinnacle Bks.

Sorcerer's Legacy. Janny Wurts. 256p. 1982. pap. 2.50 (ISBN 0-441-77540-3, Pub. by Ace Science Fiction). Ace Bks.

Sorcerer's Shadow. David C. Smith. 1978. pap. 1.95 (ISBN 0-89083-387-7). Zebra.

Sorcerer's Shadow. David C. Smith. 1982. pap. 2.50. Zebra.

Sorcerer's Skull. David Mason. 1973. pap. 0.75 o.p. (74-628). Lancer.

Sorcerer's Skull. Robert Vardeman. pap. 2.75 (ISBN 0-441-77541-1, Ace Science Fiction). Ace Bks.

Sorcerer's Son. Phyllis Eisenstein. 1979. pap. 2.50 (ISBN 0-345-29766-0, Del Rey Bks). Ballantine.

Sorcerer's Son: And Other Stories. Josephine Winslow Johnson. LC 65-11164. bds., 4.50. S. & S.

Sorcerer's Stone. Beatrice Ethel Grimshaw. LC 14-16237. 1.20. The John C. Winston Company.

Sorceress. Anthony DeStefano. 1977. pap. 1.50 (ISBN 0-532-15285-9). Woodhill.

Sorceress. John Jakes. (Brak Ser.: No. 3). 1981. pap. 2.25 (ISBN 0-505-51709-4). Tower Bks.

Sorceress. Margaret Oliphant Wilson Oliphant. LC 7-32632. (On cover: Broadway series, no. 22). 1893. J. A. Taylor and Company.

Sorceress. Nathaniel Norsen Weinreb. LC 54-9836. (Illus.). 1954. Doubleday.

Sorceress of Qar. Ted White. LC 82-23471. (Quest of the wolf; 2). ((Series: White, Ted.). (Quest of the wolf; 2.). 5.95 (ISBN 0-89865-288-X). Donning.

Sorceress of Qar. Ted White. (Orig.). 1968. pap. 0.60 o.p. (73-528). Lancer.

Sorceress of Qar. Ted White. LC 74-592. 1969. pap. 0.75 o.p. Lancer.

Sorceress of Rome. Nathan Gallizier. 1907. L. C. Page & Company.

Sorceress of Rome. Nathan Gallizier. LC 41-42335. Grosset & Dunlap.

Sorceress of the Witch World. Andre Norton, pseud. LC 77-23226. (Norton, Andre. The Witch Would Novels of Andre Norton). 1977. 7.95. Gregg Press.

Sorcery. Francis Charles MacDonald. LC 19-143554. 1919. The Century Co.

Sorcery Club. Elliot O'Donnell. LC 75-46295. (Supernatural and Occult Fiction). 1976. 20.00 (ISBN 0-405-08156-1). Arno Press.

Sordello's Story, Retold in Prose. Annie Russell Wall & Robert Browning. LC 76-47474. 1976. 17.50 (ISBN 0-8414-9607-2). Folcroft Library Editions.

Sore Foots. Donald J Cotton. LC 72-78027. 1972. 6.95. Librattërian Books.

Soren Qvist. Katie Lou Negy. LC 52-42169. 1952. Story Book Press.

Sorority of Submissive Girls. Carl Buono. pap. 1.95 o.s.i. (Venus). Grove.

Sorpresivamente. Andres Rivero. LC 1-67366. (Short Stories in Spanish Ser.). 80p. 1981. pap. 4.00 (ISBN 0-933648-03-0). Cruzada Span Pubns.

Sorrell and Son. Warwick Deeping. 1966. bds., 3.75. Cassell.

Sorrell and Son. Warwick Deeping. LC 25-238182. 1925. Casell and Company, Ltd.

Sorrell and Son. Warwick Deeping. LC 26-26480. 1926. A. A. Knopf.

Sorrell and Son. Warwick Deeping. LC 29-237967. 1926. Grossett & Dunlap.

Sorrell and Son. Warwick Deeping. LC 28-17917. 1927. Grosset & Dunlap.

Sorrell and Son. Warwick Deeping. LC 28-4668. 1927. A. A. Knopf.

Sorrow by Day. Marjorie Coryn. LC 50-6672. 1950. Appleton-Century-Crofts.

Sorrow for Angels. Helen Arvonen. 1973. (pbk) 0.95. Ace Books.

Sorrow of a Secret: A Story. Mary Cecil Hay. LC 7-375467. (On cover: Harper's half-hour series no. 88). 1879. Harper & Brothers.

Sorrows of a Show Girl: A Story of the Great "White Way,". Kenneth McGaffey. 1908. J. I. Austen Company.

Sorrows of Elsie. Andre Savignon & Dingle, Reginald J., Tr. LC 27-3821. Payson & Clarke, Ltd.

Sorrows of Noma. Abraham Mapu. Tr. by Marymont, Joseph. LC 20-4891. National Book Publishers.

Sorrows of Sap'ed: A Problem Story of the East. James Jeffrey Roche. LC 4-27990. 1904. Harper & Brothers.

Sorrows of Satan. Marie Corelli. 1965. 4.50 o.p. (Pub. by Methuen). Wehman.

Sorrows of Satan: Or, The Strange Experience of One Geoffrey Tempest, Millionaire. A Romance. Marie Corelli. LC 6-28740. 1896. J. B. Lippincott Company.

Sorrows of Travel: A Novel. John Breon. LC 55-10090. 1955. Putnam.

Sorrows of Young Werther. Johann Wolfgang Von Goethe. Tr. by Elizabeth Mayer et al. Bd. with Novella. 1973. pap. 3.95 (ISBN 0-394-71958-1, Vin). Random.

Sorrows of Young Werther and Novella. Johann Wolfgang Von Goethe. Tr. by Elizabeth Mayer & Louise Bogan. LC 73-4285. 1973. 1.95 (ISBN 0-394-71958-1). Vintage Books.

Sorrows of Young Werther, and Novella. Johann Wolfgang Von Goethe. Tr. by Elizabeth Mayer & Louise Bogan. LC 77-141780. 1971. 7.95 (ISBN 0-394-47024-9). Random House.

Sorrows of Young Werther, the New Melusina, Novelle. Johann Wolfgang Von Goethe. (Rinehart Editions). 1949. pap. text ed. 5.95 (ISBN 0-03-008900-X, HoltC). HR&W.

Sorrowstones. William Robinson Calvert. LC 30-302365. 1930. Putnam.

Sorry, Chief... William Johnston. LC 66-4013. (Tempo books, T-119). 1966. Grosset & Dunlap.

Sorry Her Lot Who Loves Too Well. A Novel. Maria M Grant. LC 6-44839. 1879. G. W. Carleton & Co.

Sorry Seasons. Loyta Wooding. LC 73-100969. 1970. 5.95. Dorrance.

Sorry State. Michael Kenyon. LC 74-77480. (MW suspense). 1974. 4.95 (ISBN 0-679-50463-X). D. McKay Co.

Sorry Tale: A Story of the Time of Christ. Patience Worth. Curran, Mrs. Pearl Lenore (Pollard) 1868- & Yost, Casper Selethiel, 1864- Ed. LC 17-19505. 1917. H. Holt and Company.

Sorry to Be So Cheerful. Stories With Illus. by Paul Galdone. Hildegarde Dolson. LC 55-8144. 1955. Random House.

Sort of Life, Vol. 1. Graham Greene. 1982. pap. 2.95 (ISBN 0-671-45198-7). WSP.

Sort of Madness: By E. B. Ronald Pseud. Ronald Ernest Barker. LC 59-11836. 1959. Abelard-Schuman.

Sort of Samurai. James Melville. LC 81-16750. 9.95 (ISBN 0-312-74558-3). St. Martin's Press.

S.O.S. A Story of the World War at Sea. John Downes Whiting. LC 28-209253. The Bobbs-Merrill Company.

SOS: Spaceship Titan! Kurt Brand. (Perry Rhodan #34). 1973. (pbk.) 0.75. Ace Books.

SOS the Rope. Piers Anthony, pseud. 1968. pap. 0.60 o.p. (X1890). Pyramid Pubns.

Sostoianie Sna. Alexei Tsvetkov. 115p. (Rus.). 1981. 11.50 (ISBN 0-88233-710-6); pap. 4.00 (ISBN 0-88233-711-4). Ardis Pubs.

Sot. Leonid Maksimovich Leonov. Tr. by Ivor Goldsmid Samuel Montagu. Nolbandov, Sergei, Joint Tr. LC 32-671. 1931. Putnam.

Sot-Weed Factor. John Barth. (Universal lib. bk., UL153 rebound). 1965. 5.00. P. Smith.

Sot-Weed Factor. John Barth. (1096). 1966. pap., 1.50. Grosset.

Sot-Weed Factor. rev. ed. John Barth. LC 67-10411. 1967. Doubleday.

Sot-Weed Factor. 1st Ed. John Barth. LC 60-9467. 1960. Doubleday.

Sotileza: A Novel. Jose Maria De Pereda. LC 76-50003. 1976. 14.00. H. Fertig.

Sotileza, a Novel. Translated by Glenn Barr. 1st Ed. Jose Maria De Pereda. LC 59-651412. (Exposition-banner book). 1959. Exposition Press.

Souci. A Novel. Julia Helen Watts Twells. LC 8-32304. 1878. J. B. Lippincott & Co.

Sought and Found. Tr. from the German of Golo Raimund Pseud. Bertha Heyn Frederich. Tr. by Burkley, Adelade S. LC 6-42852. 1888. Funk & Wagnalls.

Soul and the Hammer: A Tale of Paris. Lina Bartlett Ditson. LC 2515. 1900. G. A. S. Wieners.

Soul Appears. Charles Stewart McMillan. LC 73-81017. (Illus.). 1973. (pbk.) 3.95. Franklin Pub. Co.

Soul Catcher. Frank Herbert. 1973. (pbk.) 1.25. Bantam Books.

Soul Clap Hands and Sing. Paule Marshall. LC 78-170921. 1971. (ISBN 0-911860-06-1). Chatham Bookseller.

Soul Clap Hands and Sing. 1st Ed. Paule Marshall. LC 61-16515. 1961. Atheneum.

Soul Eater. Mike Resnick. (Orig.). 1981. pap. 2.25 (ISBN 0-451-11092-7, AE1092, Sig). NAL.

Soul Hit. Charlie Haas & Tim Hunter. LC 76-26269. 7.95 (ISBN 0-06-011708-7). Harper & Row.

Soul in Chains. Elizabeth Helene Freston. LC 41-4919. House of Field, Inc.

Soul Job. Robert H. Sheldon. pap. 1.95 o.p. (8052). Cameo.

Soul Merchants. Joan Bagnel. (Kangaroo Book). 1977. 1.95 (ISBN 0-671-80893-1). Pocket Books.

Soul Nurse. Rose Dana, pseud. 1970. pap. 0.60 o.p. (ISBN 0-447-73894-1). Lancer.

Soul of a Bishop. Herbert George Wells. LC 17-24100. 1917. The Macmillan Company.

Soul of a Child. Edwin August Bjorkman. LC 79-144883. 1971. (ISBN 0-403-00869-7). Scholarly Press.

Soul of a Child. Edwin August Bjorkman. LC 22-660646. 1922. A. A. Knopf.

Soul of a Mummy: And Other Stories. Blanche Bloor Schleppey. 1908.

Soul of a Priest. Pompeo Litta-Visconti-Arese. LC 8-33161. 1908. Doubleday, Page & Company Edinburgh Printed.

Soul of a Serf: A Romance of Love and Valor Among the Angles and Saxons. John Breckenridge Ellis. LC 10-14853. 1.50. Laird & Lee.

Soul of a Tenor: A Romance. William James Henderson. LC 12-24057. 1912. H. Holt and Company.

Soul of a Young Girl. Alma Lillian Wormington. LC 22-3015. 1921. Franklin Hudson Publishing Co.

Soul of Abe Lincoln. Bernie Smade Babcock. LC 23-11081. 1932. J. B. Lippincott Company.

Soul of an Artist. Anna Zuccari Radius. Tr. by Murison, Elizabeth Livingstone. LC 6-3001. P. Elder and Company.

Soul of an Organ. Louise Vescelius Sheldon. LC 26-2447. The Goodyear Book Shop.

Soul of Ann Rutledge: Abraham Lincoln's Romance. Bernie Smade Babcock. 1919. J. B. Lippincott Company.

Soul of Ann Rutledge: The True Story of Abraham Lincoln's First Love 4th Ed., Rev. and Enl. Bernie Smade Babcock. LC 54-11682. (Banner book). 1954. Exposition Press.

Soul of Anna Klane. Terrel Miedaner. LC 76-58447. 8.95 (ISBN 0-698-10826-4). Coward, McCann & Geoghegan.

Soul of China, Glimpsed in Tales of Today and Yesterday. Louise Jordan Miln. LC 25-1250. 1925. Frederick A. Stokes Company.

Soul of Countess Adrian. authorized ed. Rosa Caroline Murray-Prior Praed. LC 7-30295. (Lovell's international series, no. 160). United States Book Company, Successors to J. W. Lovell Company.

Soul of Croesus. Gerald Villiers Stuart. LC 8-17792. Cupples & Leon Company.

Soul of Henry Harrington: And Other Stories. Frank Emory Bunts. LC 17-4617. 1916. 3.00. The Gardner Printing Co.

Soul of Kindness. Elizabeth Taylor. LC 83-2053. (Virago Modern Classic). 1983. 6.95 (ISBN 0-385-27922-1). Dial Press.

Soul of Kindness: A Novel. Elizabeth Taylor. LC 64-15058. 1964. Viking Press.

Soul of Kol Nikon. Eleanor Farjeon. LC 23-13122. 1923. Frederick A. Stokes Company.

Soul of Lady Agnes. Marie Virginia Harding. LC 7-1925. 1889. G. W. Dillingham.

Soul of Life: Or, What Is Love? David Lisle. LC 13-23491. 1913. 1.25. Frederick A. Stokes Company.

Soul of Lilith. Marie Corelli. LC 6-28739. J. W. Lovell Company.

Soul of Lilith. Marie Corelli. LC 16-19158. Grosset & Dunlap.

Soul of Lilith. Marie Corelli. J. W. Lovell Company.

Soul of Love. Elizabeth Toldridge. LC 10-31004. Broadway Publishing Co.

Soul of Malaya. Henri Fauconnier. LC 66-77163. 1965. Oxford U.P.

Soul of Melicent. James Branch Cabell. LC 13-199372. 1.50. Frederick A. Stokes Company.

Soul of Pierre. Georges Ohnet. Tr. by Serrano, Mary Jane (Christie) LC 7-325112. Cassell Publishing Company.

Soul of Susan Yellam. Horace Annesley Vachell. LC 18-15779. George H. Doran Company.

Soul of Tad Winslow. Lowell Morrell. LC 29-6454. 1928. Threlkeld-Morrell Book Co.

Soul of the Bishop. Henrietta Eliza Vaughan Stannard. LC 8-27040. J. S. Tait & Sons.

Soul of the Robot. Barrington J Bayley. LC 73-15325. 1974. 5.95. Doubleday.

Soul of the Robot. Barrington J Bayley. LC 77-353894. 1976. 3.50 (ISBN 0-85031-145-4). Allison and Busby.

Soul of the Sea. Leonid Sergeevich Sobolev & Orloff, Nicholas, Tr. LC 46-29173. 1946. J. B. Lippincott Company.

Soul of the Street: Correlated Stories of the New York Syrian Quarter. Norman Duncan. LC 1-29296. 1905. McClure, Phillips & Company.

Soul of the World. Estella Bachman Brokaw. LC 9-11535. 1909. Equitist Publishing House.

Soul of Wood, & Other Stories. Tr. from German by Ralph Manheim. Jakov Lind. LC 64-13782. 1965. 3.95. Grove.

Soul on Fire. Clarence Farmer. LC 95-1057. (Orig.). 1969. pap. 0.95 o.p. (B95-1057). Belmont-Tower.

Soul on Fire. Frances Fenwick Williams. LC 15-201422. 1915. John Lane Company.

Soul Retrievers. George Bullock. 4.95 o.p. Carlton.

Soul Scar: A Craig Kennedy Scientific Mystery Novel. Arthur Benjamin Reeve. LC 19-15545. Harper & Brothers.

Soul Sisters. Joan Blair. (Orig.). 1970. pap. 0.95 o.p. (A666, Award). Univ Pub & Dist.

Soul Stealers. Charles Huntington. (Space Probe 6). 1972. 0.75. Award Books.

Soul Sucker. Cherry Hawkins. pap. 1.95 o.p. (8079). Cameo.

Soul Toys. Alvin David Hersch. LC 24-353351. R. G. Badger.

Soul Wounds: A Novel of the World War. Al Schak. LC 35-4338. The Missoulian Publishing Co.

Soulcatcher: A Novel. Barbara Leslie Austin. LC 72-91575. 1975. (ISBN 0-03-007566-1). Holt, Rinehart and Winston.

Soulless Saints: A Strange Revelation. Bailey Kay Leach. LC 7-13235. American Publishing Company.

Soulless Singer. Mary Catherine Jenkins Lee. LC 7-125945. 1895. Houghton, Mifflin and Company.

Soulmate. Charles W Runyon. 1974. (pbk.) 0.95. Avon.

Souls Aflame. Patricia Hagan. LC 80-65145. 1980. 2.75 (ISBN 0-380-75507-6). Avon Books.

Souls and Bodies. David Lodge. LC 81-14026. 1982. 12.50 (ISBN 0-688-00933-6). Morrow.

Soul's End. Joy Carroll. (Dell book). 1974. (pbk.) 1.25. Dell.

Soul's Fire. Jeremiah Stokes. LC 41-307475. 1936. Suttonhouse Ltd.

Souls for Sale. Rupert Hughes. LC 22-11083. Harper & Brothers.

Souls for Sale. Rupert Hughes. LC 76-52109. (Garland Classics of Film Literature). 1978. 15.00 (ISBN 0-8240-2880-5). Garland Pub.

Soul's Gymnasium. Harold Acton. 165p. 1982. 16.95 (ISBN 0-241-10740-7, Pub. by Hamish Hamilton England). David & Charles.

Souls in Hell: A Mystery of the Unseen. John O'Neill. LC 24-129. 1924. N. L. Brown.

Souls in Metal: An Anthology of Robot Futures. Michael Ashley. LC 76-20430. 1977. 6.95. St. Martin's Press.

Souls in Pawn: A Story of New York Life. Margaret Blake Robinson. F. H. Revell Company.

Soul's Island. Marjorie Bevier Jackson. LC 39-32048. 1939. Meador Publishing Company.

Souls of Lambs: A Fable. Donald Earl Mitchell & Georgann Schroeder. LC 78-25835. (Illus.). 1979. 7.95. (ISBN 0-395-27572-5) (ISBN 0-395-27571-7). Houghton Mifflin.

Souls of Men. Martha Melean Burgess Stanley. LC 13-4990. G. W. Dillingham Company.
Souls of Passage... Amelia Edith Huddleston Barr. LC 1-31255. 1901. Dodd, Mead & Co.
Souls on Fire. Elie Wiesel. 320p. (Orig.). 1982. 17.50 (ISBN 0-671-45210-X); pap. 7.95 (ISBN 0-671-44171-X). Summit Bks.
Souls on Fire. Elie Wiesel. Date not set. price not set. S&S.
Souls Resurgent. Marion Hamilton Carter. LC 16-18914. 1916. 1.35. C. Scribner's Sons.
Sound an Alarm: By Genevieve Holden Pseud. 1st Ed. Genevieve Long Pou. LC 54-5353. 1954. Published for the Crime Club by Doubleday.
Sound and Fury. James Henle. LC 24-21358. 1924. A. A. Knopf.
Sound and the Fury. a limited ed. William Faulkner. LC 77-357221. (Illus.). 1976. Franklin Library.
Sound and the Fury. William Faulkner. LC 72-7461. 1973. (ISBN 0-394-70005-8). Vintage Books.
Sound and the Fury. William Faulkner. LC 29-20977. J. Cape and H. Smith.
Sound and the Fury & As I Lay Dying. William Faulkner. LC 47-1273. (Half-title: The Modern library of the world's best books 187). 1946. The Modern Library.
Sound and the Fury. By William Faulkner. Appendix by the Author. William Faulkner. (Modern lib. coll. ds., T94). 1967. pap., 1.45. Modern Lib.
Sound of a City. James Thomas Farrell. LC 63-790. 1962. Paperback Library.
Sound of a Distant Horn. Sven Stolpe. LC 57-7633. 1957. Sheed & Ward.
Sound of a Harp. E MacRan. 1976. 7.95 (ISBN 0-8059-2284-9). Dorrance.
Sound of Always. Lee Priestley. 1975. 4.95. Avalon Books.
Sound of an American: A Novel. Stephen Longstreet. LC 42-19131. 1942. E. P. Dutton & Co., Inc.
Sound of Bow Bells. Jerome Weidman. LC 62-12732. 1962. Random House.
Sound of Chariots: A Novel of John Sevier and the State of Franklin. Helen Topping Miller. LC 47-30850. 1947. Bobbs-Merrill Co.
Sound of Coaches. Leon Garfield. 1976. 1.75 (ISBN 0-670-65834-0). Popular Library.
Sound of Dreams. Hermann Weiss. LC 80-68429. 2.50 (ISBN 0-380-76976-X). Avon Books.
Sound of Drums and Cymbals. Robert Wilder. LC 72-87632. 1973. 7.95 (ISBN 0-399-11067-4). Putnam.
Sound of Drums and Cymbals. Robert Wilder. 1974. (pbk.) 1.75. Bantam Books.
Sound of Footsteps... Zenith Brown. LC 31-30510. Pub. for the Crime Club, Inc., by Doubleday, Doran & Company, Inc.
Sound of Gunfire. Frank Bonham. 192p. 1981. pap. 1.95 (ISBN 0-425-05090-4). Berkley Pub.
Sound of Gunfire. Frank Bonham. 1979. pap. 1.75 (ISBN 0-425-04097-6). Berkley Pub.
Sound of Insects. Mildred B Davis. LC 66-12239. 1966. Published for the Crime Club by Doubleday.
Sound of Lightning. Jon Cleary. LC 76-1859. 1976. 7.95 (ISBN 0-688-03030-0). Morrow.
Sound of Midnight. Charles L Grant. LC 77-15157. 1978. 7.95 (ISBN 0-385-13695-1). Doubleday.
Sound of Mountain Water. Wallace Earle Stegner. 1972. pap. 1.25 o.p. (ISBN 0-345-02651-9). Comstock.
Sound of Murder. John Bonett & Emery Bonett. LC 82-48809. 224p. 1983. pap. 2.84i (ISBN 0-06-080642-7, P 642, PL). Har-Row.
Sound of Murder. John Bonnet & Emory Bonnet. 4.95 o.p. (ISBN 0-8027-5213-6). Walker & Co.
Sound of Murder. John Coulson & Felicity Winifred Carter. LC 78-120405. 1971. 4.95. Walker.
Sound of Murder. Rex Stout. Orig. Title: Alphabet Hicks. 1973. pap. 1.25 o.p. (ISBN 0-515-03083-X, N3083). BJ Pub Group.
Sound of One Hand. 1st Ed. Laurence D Savadove. LC 60-5456. 1960. Duell, Sloan and Pearce.
Sound of Revelry. Octavus Roy Cohen. 1943. The Macmillan Company.
Sound of Rowlocks. Wilbur Daniel Steele. LC 38-7319. 1938. Harper & Brothers.
Sound of Running Feet. Josephine Lawrence. LC 37-559. 1937. Frederick A Stokes Company.
Sound of Shadows. Wilkins-Foster. 2.00 o.p. Swallow.
Sound of Silence. Mary Rickwood. LC 56-131901. 1956. Dutton.
Sound of Silence. Mary Rickwood. LC 56-13190. 1956. Dutton.
Sound of Silence. Bill Riley. LC 68-31576. 1968. 4.00. Dorrance.
Sound of Small Hammers; a Novel of Divided Germany. Bynum Shaw. LC 62-11352. Morrow,
Sound of Spanish Voices: By Lonnie Coleman. 1st Ed. William Laurence Coleman. LC 51-12492. 1951. Dutton.
Sound of Summer Voices. Helen Tucker. LC 72-87959. 1969. 5.95. Stein and Day.
Sound of the Mountain. Yasunari Kawabata. LC 75-305158. 1974. 0.35 (ISBN 0-14-003735-7). Penguin.
Sound of the Mountain. Yasunari Kawabata. LC 77-98666. 1970. 6.95. Knopf.
Sound of the Mountain. Yasunari Kawabata. LC 80-39980. 1981. 5.95 (ISBN 0-399-50527-X). Perigee Books.
Sound of the Sea. Adel Pryor, pseud. LC 68-12950. 1968. Zondervan Pub. House.
Sound of the Snore: A Collection of Short Stories. M. Varadarajan. LC 76-902783. 1976. 15.00. Makkal Nalvaalvu Manram.
Sound of the Stars. Frances M. Parsons. 5.95 o.p. Vantage.
Sound of the Sun. 1st Ed. Margaret Cobb Shipley. LC 58-10040. 1958. Doubleday.
Sound of the Trumpet. Grace Livingston Hill. LC 43-9933. 1943. J. B. Lippincott Company.
Sound of the Trumpet. 1st Ed. Leicester Hemingway. LC 53-9587. 1953. Holt.
Sound of the Weir: A Novel of Suspense. Mary Ingate. LC 73-19080. 1974. 5.95 (ISBN 0-396-06921-5). Dodd, Mead.
Sound of Thunder. Taylor Caldwell. LC 57-10450. 1957. Doubleday.
Sound of Thunder. 1st Ed. Taylor Caldwell. LC 57-10450. 1957. Doubleday.
Sound of Trumpets. James Howard Wellard. LC 61-14548. Little, Brown.
Sound of Voices Dying. Glenn Scott. LC 54-5042. 1954. Dutton.
Sound of Water. Margarita Spalding Gerry. LC 14-17620. 1914. 1.00. Harper & Brothers.
Sound of Waves. Kimitake Hiraoka. LC 56-8911. (Illus.). 1956. A. A. Knopf.
Sound of Waves. Yukio Mishima, pseud. LC 80-14994. 1980. 3.95 (ISBN 0-399-50487-7). Putnam.
Sound of Waves. Translated by Meredith Weatherby, Drawings by Yoshinori Kinoshita. 1st Ed. Yukio Mishima, pseud. LC 56-8911. 1956. Knopf.
Sound of White Water. Hugh Fosburgh. LC 55-9670. 1955. Scribner.
Sound of Wings. Arthur Frederick Goodrich. LC 41-12689. 1941. D. Appelton-Century, Incorporated.
Sound of Winter. Arthur Byron. (Orig.). 1976. pap. 1.25 o.p. (ISBN 0-515-04017-7). BJ Pub Group.
Sound of Years. Merriam Modell. LC 46-36332. 1946. Simon and Schuster.
Sound off, Tumbleweeds! Tom K. Ryan. 128p. 1983. pap. 1.95 (ISBN 0-449-12386-3, GM). Fawcett.
Sound Retreat for the Conquistadores. John E. Baca. 4.50 o.p. Carlton.
Sound Sense for Successful Living. D. Stuart Briscoe. Ed. by James A. Kuse. (Illus.). 1979. pap. 5.95 (ISBN 0-89542-074-0). Ideals.
Sound the Great Trumpet: The Story of Israel Through the Eyes of Those Who Built It. Ed. by Moses Zebi Frank. LC 55-14860. 1955. Whittier Books.
Sound the Retreat. Simon Raven. LC 72-183746. (Alms for Oblivion Ser.: No. 7). 1973. Repr. of 1971 ed. 12.50x (ISBN 0-85634-998-4). Intl Pubns Serv.
Sound Wagon. Thomas Sigismund Stribling. LC 36-211. 1935. Doubleday, Doran & Company, Inc.
Sound Wagon. Thomas Sigismund Stribling. LC 36-33145. 1936. The Literary Guild.
Sound. 1st Ed. Ross Russell. LC 61-11014. 1961. Dutton.
Sounder. William H. Armstrong. 1972. pap. 1.25 o.p. (ISBN 0-06-087032-X, HW). Har-Row.
Sounder of Swine: A Novel of Suspense. Patrick Buchanan, pseud. LC 74-12531. 1974. 5.95 (ISBN 0-396-06999-1). Dodd, Mead.
Sounding. Hank Searls. LC 81-48297. 1982. 13.50 (ISBN 0-394-52471-3). Ballantine Books.
Sounding Brass. Edythe Latham. LC 53-7297. 1953. Little, Brown.
Sounding Brass. Ethel Edith Mannin. LC 26-12830. 1926. Duffield & Company.
Sounding Brass: A Christian Novel. Capwell Wyckoff. LC 43-853780. 1943. Wm. B. Eerdmans Publishing Company.
Sounding Brass. A Novel. Carrie A. Morgan. LC 7-260019. The American News Company.
Sounding Brass. 1st Ed. Beryhl Howard Wier. LC 56-5508. 1956. Vantage Press.
Sounding Harbors. Eleanor Mercein Kelly. LC 35-520. 1935. Harper & Brothers.
Sounding the Territory. Laurel Goldman. LC 81-12409. 1982. 13.50 (ISBN 0-394-51935-3). Distributed by Random House.
Soundings. Arthur Hamilton Gibbs. LC 25-616217. 1925. Little, Brown, and Company.
Soundings of Hell. Sidney C Kendall. LC 3-25208. 1903.
Soundless Scream. Michael Butterworth. LC 67-22471. 1967. Published for the Crime Club by Doubleday.
Sounds in the Jungle. H. Douglass Harriman. LC 52-13887. Vantage Press.
Sounds of a Drunken Summer. Ursule Molinaro. LC 69-15282. 1969. 4.95. Harper & Row.
Sounds of Home. Ilka Chase. LC 76-150880. 1971. 5.95. Doubleday.
Sounds of Rescue, the Signs of Hope. Robert Flynn. LC 73-111246. 1970. 5.95. Knopf.
Sounds of Silence. Judith Richards. LC 76-56396. 7.95. Putnam.
Sounds of Silence. Judith Richards. (Kangaroo book). 1979. 2.25. Pocket Books.
Sour Apple Tree. John Blackburn. LC 59-7400. 1959. M. S. Mill Co., and W. Morrow.
Sour Cream with Everything. Joyce Porter. LC 66-22526. 1966. 3.95. Scribners.
Sour Saints and Sweet Sinners. Carlos Martyn. LC 98-1855. F. T. Neely.
Source. James A. Michener. (Illus.). 1978. pap. 3.95 (ISBN 0-449-23859-8, Crest). Fawcett.
Source: A Novel. Clarence Budington Kelland. LC 18-5745. 1918. Harper & Brothers.
Source: A Novel. James Albert Michener. LC 65-11255. (Illus.). 1965. Random House.
Source of Evil. Mary Vigliante, pseud. (Orig.). 1979. pap. 1.95 (ISBN 0-532-23104-X). Woodhill.
Source of Light. Reynolds Price. LC 80-69650. 1981. 12.95 (ISBN 0-689-11136-3). Atheneum.
Source of Magic. Piers Anthony, pseud. 1979. pap. 2.25 (ISBN 0-345-28765-7, Del Rey Bks). Ballantine.
Source of Magic Piers Anthony. Piers Anthony, pseud. LC 78-61817. (Dell Rey book). 1979. 1.95 (ISBN 0-345-27284-6). Ballantine Books.
Source of the Thunder. Roger A. Caras. LC 70-121419. 1970. 5.95 o.p. (ISBN 0-316-12838-4). Little.
Sources of Jane Eyre. Florence Swinton Dry. LC 76-4104. 1976. 10.00 (ISBN 0-88305-484-1). Norwood Editions.
Sources of "Wuthering Heights.". Florence Swinton Dry. LC 73-22134. (Dry, Florence Swinton. Bronte Sources: 1). 1973. (lib. bdg.). 5.50. Folcroft Library Editions.
Sourdough Gold. James Beardsley Hendryx. LC 52-8059. (Double D western). 1952. Doubleday.
Sourwood Tales: Stories. Billy C Clark. LC 68-15044. (Illus.). 1968. Putnam.
Sous la Lune des Tropiques. Robyn Donald. (Collection Harlequin). 192p. 1983. pap. 1.95 (ISBN 0-373-49323-1). Harlequin Bks.
Souter's Lamp. Hector MacGregor. 1903. F. H. Revell Company.
South. Frederick Stallknecht Wight. LC 35-15314. Farrar & Rinehart, Inc.
South African Short Stories. E. R. Seary. Repr. of 1947 ed. 20.00 (ISBN 0-8414-8141-5). Folcroft.
South American Romances. William Henry Hudson. 1966. 18.95 o.p. (ISBN 0-7156-0348-5). Dufour.
South American Romances: The Purple Lane; Green Mansions; el Ombu. William Henry Hudson. 823p. 1981. Repr. of 1930 ed. lib. bdg. 40.00 (ISBN 0-89987-368-5). Darby Bks.
South American Variant. Sergei Pavlovich Zalygin. LC 79-322489. 1979. 15.75 (ISBN 0-7022-1327-6). University of Queensland Press.
South: Aspects and Images from Corsica, Italy, and Southern France. William Sansom. LC 50-9477. 1950. Harcourt, Brace.
South by Java Head. Alistair MacLean. LC 75-31797. 1975. 9.95. American Reprint Co.
South by Java Head. 1st Ed. Alistair MacLean. LC 58-5576. 1958. Doubleday.
South by Southwest. Rudolph Mellard. LC 60-9928. 1960. Sage Books.
South Carolina Folktales. Federal Writers' Project, South Carolina. LC 73-3651. (American Guide Ser). Repr. of 1941 ed. 10.00 (ISBN 0-404-57951-5). AMS Pr.
South Carolina Ghost Tales. Nell S. Graydon. 10.95 (ISBN 0-910206-06-6). Beaufort Bk Co.
South-County Neighbors. Esther Bernon Carpenter. LC 6-24228. 1887. Roberts Brothers.
South Cove Summer. 1st Ed. Sara Ware Bassett. LC 56-765219. 1956. Doubleday.
South Florida Book of the Dead. Robert Merkin. LC 81-22598. 1982. 15.00 (ISBN 0-688-00988-3). Morrow.
South Foreland Murder. Joseph Smith Fletcher. LC 30-24622. 1930. A. A. Knopf.
South from Yesterday. Willard Robertson. LC 43-4859. 1943. J. B. Lippincott Company.
South Maintain Sketches: Folk Tales and Legends Collected in the Mountains of Southern Pennsylvania. Henry Wharton Shoemaker. LC 20-18663. 1920. Times Tribune Company.
South Meadows. A Tale of Long Ago. Ella Taylor Disosway. Porter and Coates.
South Moon Under. Marjorie Kinnan Rawlings. LC 33-548586. 1933. C. Scribner's Sons.
South-Mountain Magic. Madeleine Vinton Dahlgren. 1882. Repr. of 1975 ed. 8.00 (ISBN 0-87012-202-9). McClain.
South of Capricorn. Anne Hampson. (Harlequin Presents Ser.). 192p. 1982. pap. 1.75 (ISBN 0-373-10507-X). Harlequin Bks.
South of Heaven. Lettie Hamlett Rogers. LC 46-7331. 1946. Random House.
South of No North. Charles Bukowski. 189p. (Orig.). 1981. 14.00 (ISBN 0-87685-190-1); pap. 6.00 (ISBN 0-87685-189-8). Black Sparrow.
South of No North: Stories of the Buried Life. Charles Bukowski. LC 73-19672. (Illus.). 1973. (ISBN 0-87685-190-1) (ISBN 0-87685-190-1). Black Sparrow Press.
South of Nogales. Steve Mensing. (Orig.). 1980. pap. 1.75 (ISBN 0-505-51599-7). Tower Bks.
South of Nowhere. Antonio L. Antunes. Tr. by Elizabeth Lowe. 1983. 11.95 (ISBN 0-394-52574-4). Random.
South of Rio Grande. Max Brand. LC 36-252827. 1936. Dood, Mead & Company.
South of Rio Grande. Frederick Faust. LC 74-5014. 1974. (lib. bdg.) 10.95 (ISBN 0-8161-6209-3). G. K. Hall.
South of Rio Grande. Frederick Faust. LC 36-25282. 1936. Dodd, Mead & Company.
South of Rio Grando. Max Brand. 1981. pap. 2.25 (ISBN 0-671-83368-5). PB.
South of the Angels. Jessamyn West. LC 60-6714. 1960. Harcourt, Brace.
South of the Bordello. Rod Gray. (The Lady from L.U.S.T. Ser.). (O.s.i.). 1973. pap. 0.95 o.s.i. (BT50582). Belmont-Tower.
South of the Border. Arthemise Goertz. LC 40-33582. 1940. The Macmillan Company.
South of the Heart: A Novel of Modern Arabia. Hans Ruesch. LC 57-10717. 1957. Coward-McCann.
South of the Line. Ralph Stock. LC 22-21183. 1922. Doubleday, Page & Company.
South of the Main Offensive. Grigorii Iakovlevich Baklanov. LC 64-25464. 1963. 9.95 (ISBN 0-8023-1006-0). Dufour.
South of the Main Offensive. Tr. from Russian. Grigorii IAkovlevich Baklanov. LC 64-25464. 1965. bds., 4.50. Dufour.
South of the Matterhorn: A World War Romance in Italy. Daniel Maurice Robins. LC 40-35997. (Turnercrest series). Fleming H. Revell Company.
South of the Moon. Anne Hampson. (Harlequin Romances Ser.). 1979. pap. 1.25 (ISBN 0-373-02266-2). Harlequin Bks.
South of the Pass. Johnston McCulley. 1944. Arcadia House, Inc.
South of the Rio Grande. Laurence Clarke. LC 24-5102. 1924. The Macaulay Company.
South of the Sun. (Gold medal books, 331). 1953. Fawcett Publications.
South of the Sunset: An Interpretation of Sacajawea, the Indian Girl That Accompanied Lewis and Clark. Claire Warner Churchill. LC 37-22647. 1936. R. R. Wilson, Inc.
South Pacific Affair. Ed Lacy. LC 61-255434. 1961. Belmont Books.
South Pole Terror. Kenneth Robeson. (amazing adventures of Doc Savage, 77). 1974. (pbk.) 0.75. Bantam Books.
South Riding. Winifred Holtby. 1972. pap. 1.50 o.p. (02001). Curtis.
South Riding: A Novel by Winifred Holtby. Holtby, Winifred & Holtby, Winifred. LC 36-7597. 1936. The Macmillan Company.
South-Sea Idyls. Charles Warren Stoddard. LC 22-14547. 1873. J. R. Osgood and Company.
South-Sea Idyls. Charles Warren Stoddard. LC 4-16770. 1892. C. Scribner's Sons.
South Sea Supercargo. Edited with an Introd. by A. Grove Day. Louis Becke. LC 68-18937. 1967. University of Hawaii Press.
South Sea Tales. Jack London. 1961. Macmillan.
South Sea Tales. Jack London. LC 11-25011. 1911. The Macmillan Company.
South Street. David Bradley. LC 75-14343. 1975. 8.95 (ISBN 0-670-65935-5). Grossman Publishers.
South Street. William Gardner Smith. LC 54-5687. 1954. Farrar, Straus and Young.
South Swell. Leonard Patrick O'Connor Wibberley. LC 67-15043. 1967. Washburn.
South to Destiny. Dobrica Cosic. LC 80-8764. 1981. 19.95 (ISBN 0-15-184486-0). Harcourt Brace Jovanovich.
South to Heaven. Christine Chester. LC 46-177672. 1946. Arcadia House, Inc.
South to Panama. 1st Ed. Amy Vincent McCormack. LC 60-1377. 1960. Vantage Press.
South to Sonora. W. Ryerson Johnson. LC 46-6773. 1946. S. Curl, Inc.
South Town. Lorenz B Graham. LC 58-13128. 1958. Follett Pub. Co.
South Ward. Katharine Dooris Sharp. 1891. Cranston & Stowe.
South Wind. Norman Douglas. (Penguin modern classics, 11). pap., 1.25. Penguin.
South Wind. Norman Douglas. LC 73-144982. (Bonibooks). 1971. Scholarly Press.
South Wind. Norman Douglas. LC 48-41805. (Modern Library of the World's Best Books). Modern Library.
South Wind. 12th impression. ed. Norman Douglas. LC 24-26888. 1924. Dodd, Mead & Company.

South Wind. Norman Douglas. LC 25-26572. (Half-title: The modern library of the world's best books). Boni and Liveright.

South Wind. Norman Douglas. LC 28-219655. 1928. Dodd, Mead & Company.

South Wind. Norman Douglas. LC 29-17531. (modern readers' series). 1929. The Macmillan Company.

South Wind. Norman Douglas. LC 38-32638. 1938. The Sun Dial Press, Inc.

South Wind. Norman Douglas. LC 82-4555. 1982. 6.00 (ISBN 0-486-24361-3) (ISBN 0-486-24362-1). Dover Publications.

South Wind. Norman Douglas & Austen, John, Illus. LC 30-5336. 1929. Argus Books.

South Wind. Norman Douglas & Petrina, Mrs. Carlotta, 1901- Illus. LC 39-12842. 1939. Printed for the Members of the Heritage Club.

South Wind. Norman Douglas & Van Doren, Carl Clinton, 1885- LC 32-32403. Limited Editions Club.

South Wind. Esther J. Neely. 320p. 1983. pap. 3.25 (ISBN 0-8439-2019-X, Leisure Bks). Dorchester Pub Co.

South Wind. Thomas O'Reilly. LC 82-109850. 1981. 5.95 (ISBN 0-7986-0869-2). HAUM.

South Wind Blew Softly. James L. Dial. 5.95 o.p. Vantage.

South Wind Blew Softly. Ruth Livingston Hill Munce. LC 75-35722. 1975. 9.95 (ISBN 0-89190-253-8). American Reprint Co.

South Wind Blew Softly. 1st Ed. Ruth Livingston Hill Munce. LC 59-13074. 1959. Lippincott.

South Wind Blow Softly. Ruth L. Hill, pseud. 255p. 1975. Repr. of 1959 ed. lib. bdg. 14.40x (ISBN 0-89190-253-8). Am Repr-Rivercity Pr.

South Wind Blows. Clark Porteous. LC 48-2894. 1948. Current Books.

South Wind of Love. Compton Mackenzie. LC 37-23348. 1937. Dodd, Mead & Company.

Southbooke. Sutton Selwyn Scott. LC 8-2906. 1880. T. Gilbert, Printer.

Southbound. Barbara Tunnell Anderson. LC 49-7988. 1949. Farrar, Straus.

Southennan: A Novel. John Galt. 1830. Printed by J. & J. Harper.

Southern Album: Edited, with a Preface. Sara Haardt & Mencken, Henry Louis, 1880- Ed. LC 36-70021. 1936. Doubleday, Doran & Co., Inc.

Southern Atmosphere & Other Stories. Blanche Cronheim. 3.50 o.p. Vantage.

Southern Belle. Watkins Eppes Wright. LC 49-9540. 1949. Gramercy Pub. Co.

Southern Blood. Justin Channing. 400p. 1980. pap. 2.50 (ISBN 0-553-13132-X). Bantam.

Southern Buds and Sons of War... William Henry Winslow. LC 7-40001. 1907. The C. M. Clark Publishing Co.

Southern Character Sketches. Idora McClellan Moore. LC 38-156897. 1937. The Dietz Press.

Southern Charm. Isa Glenn. LC 28-674. 1928. A. A. Knopf.

Southern Comfort. Michael Largo. 1977. pap. 3.95x (ISBN 0-918258-02-2). New Earth.

Southern Comfort. Gerrold Wilkins. (Orig.). 1969. pap. 1.95 o.s.i. (TC460, Travellers Comp). Olympia.

Southern Cousin. Bennie Caroline Hall. LC 52-3394. 1952. Arcadia House.

Southern Cross. Leland Wellington Brignall. LC 28-22328. The Christopher Publishing House.

Southern Cross. Terry Coleman. LC 78-26876. 1979. 10.95 (ISBN 0-670-65937-1). Viking Press.

Southern Cross: A Novel of the South Seas Told in Wood Engravings. Laurence Hyde. (Illus.). 1951. 5.00 o.p. (ISBN 0-378-09901-9). Ritchie.

Southern Cross, a Novel. 1st Ed. Brigid Knight. LC 49-7140. 1949. Doubleday.

Southern Cross: Poems. Charles Wright. 1981. 10.50 (ISBN 0-394-52148-X); pap. 5.95 (ISBN 0-394-74888-3). Random.

Southern Discomfort. Rita Mae Brown. LC 81-47683. 12.98 (ISBN 0-06-014928-0). Harper & Row.

Southern Echoes. Louise Pike. LC 72-1519. (Black Heritage Library Collection). 1972. 9.00 (ISBN 0-8369-9046-3). Books for Libraries Press.

Southern Echoes. Louise Pike. LC 1-29366. 1900. Eastern Publishing Company.

Southern Field & Fireside Novelette No. 1. Incl. Myra Bruce; or, True Love Running Roughly. (Illus.); Riverlands; Five Chapters of a History, A Georgia Court, Forty Years Ago. LC 70-162229. (Confederate Imprints Collection Ser.). 95p. 1973. Repr. of 1863 ed. 7.00 o.p. (ISBN 0-405-04335-X). Arno.

Southern Fried Plus Six. William Price Fox. 1980. pap. 2.25 (ISBN 0-89176-030-X, 6030). Mockingbird Bks.

Southern Fried Plus Six: Short Stories of Fiction. William Price Fox. LC 68-17498. 1968. Lippincott.

Southern Glamour. Juanita Savage. LC 36-10012. The Macaulay Company.

Southern Harvest: Short Stories by Southern Writers. Ed. by Robert Penn Warren. LC 72-171033. 1972. 10.00 (ISBN 0-910220-35-2). N. S. Berg.

Southern Harvest: Short Stories by Southern Writers. Ed. by Robert Penn Warren. LC 37-351877. 1937. Houghton Mifflin Company.

Southern Hearts. Florence Hull Winterburn. LC 4-32747. 1900. The F. M. Lupton Publishing Company.

Southern Heritage: A Novel. William Horace Brown. LC 6-17235. (On cover: Vanity fair series, no. 6). 1891. E. Brandus & Co.

Southern Hill and the Land Beyond. Pauline Davies. LC 75-4816. 1975. 2.45 (ISBN 0-8028-1601-0). Eerdmans.

Southern Indian Boy. Caroline Dormon. (Illus.). 1967. 3.50. Claitors.

Southern Life in Fiction. Jay Broadus Hubbell. LC 60-9898. (Eugenia Dorothy Blount Lamar Memorial Lectures, 1959). 2.50. University of Georgia Press.

Southern Lights and Shadows... Ed. by William Dean Howells. LC 7-9555. (Harper's novelettes). 1907. Harper & Brothers.

Southern Literary Messenger, 36 Vols. 1834-64. Set. lib. bdg. 975.00 o.p.; lib. bdg. 27.50 ea. o.p.; Set. pap. 900.00 o.p.; pap. 25.00 ea. o.p. Ams Pr.

Southern Mail. Antoine De Saint Exupery. Tr. by Curtis Cate. LC 79-182749. (Harbrace paperbound library). 1972. (ISBN 0-15-683901-6). Harcourt Brace Jovanovich.

Southern Mail. Antoine De Saint Exupery & Gilbert, Stuart, Tr. LC 33-31418. 1933. H. Smith and R. Haas.

Southern Medical Student's Portfolio. George M Wharton. LC 8-36060. 1872. Claxton, Remsen & Haffelfinger.

Southern Moon. Narena Easterling. LC 38-221301. Gramercy Publishing Co.

Southern Nights. Janet Dailey. (Harlequin Presents Ser.). 192p. (Orig.). 1980. pap. text ed. 1.50 (ISBN 0-373-10369-7). Harlequin Bks.

Southern Plantation Stories and Sketches. George E Wiley. LC 78-161277. (Black Heritage Library Collection). (Illus.). 1971. (ISBN 0-8369-8836-1). Books for Libraries Press.

Southern Plantation Stories and Sketches. George E Wiley. LC 6-3548. 1905. Press of J. J. Little & Co.

Southern Pride. William R. Sinclair. 1977. 6.98. CLCB Pr.

Southern Reporter and Other Stories. John William Corrington. LC 80-26204. 1981. 9.95 (ISBN 0-8071-0869-3). Louisiana State University Press.

Southern Rose. Paula Fairman. 384p. (Orig.). 1980. pap. 2.95 (ISBN 0-523-41800-0). Pinnacle Bks.

Southern Scenes and Scenery: I. Father Cyril, in Georgia. II. The Last Vacation. III. The Old Planter. A Southern Lady, Pseud. LC 8-10219. 1856. Southern Baptist Publication Society.

Southern Soldier Stories. George Cary Eggleston. LC 4-15099. 1898. The Macmillan Company.

Southern Songs, Rhymes and Jingles: By Elizabeth M. Montague... Elizabeth May Montague. LC 16-23429. 1916. 1.25. The Cameo Press.

Southern Star: By Mary Douglas Warren Pseud. Maysie Greig. LC 50-13684. 1950. Arcadia House.

Southern Star Mystery. Jules Verne. 3.95. Assoc Bk.

Southern Stories. Jessie Watson Spinks. The Christopher Publishing House.

Southern Stories. Ed. by Arlin Turner. LC 60-7870. (Rinehart editions, 106). 1960. Rinehart.

Southern Strategy. Bob Lancaster. LC 80-54522. (ISBN 0-87223-695-1). Seaview Books.

Southern Territory: A Novel. Tallant, Robert. LC 51-11537. 1951. Doubleday.

Southern Wild. Ruth Chatterton. LC 58-7352. 1958. Doubleday.

Southern Wind. Gene Lancour. (Carlisles Ser.: No. 3). (Orig.). 1982. pap. 2.75 (ISBN 0-440-08039-8, Standish). Dell.

Southerner. Douglas Kiker. LC 57-10619. 1957. Rinehart.

Southerner, a Novel: Being the Autobiography of Nicholas Worth Pseud. Walter Hines Page. LC 9-26438. 1909. Doubleday, Page & Company.

Southerner: A Romance of the Real Lincoln. Thomas Dixon. LC 13-12599. 1913. D. A. Appleton and Company.

Southerner: A Romance of the Real Lincoln. Thomas Dixon. LC 23-17908. 1925. D. Appleton and Company.

Southerners. Edna L. Mooney Lee. LC 54-50760. 1953. Appleton-Century-Crofts.

Southerners: A Story of the Civil War. Cyrus Townsend Brady. LC 3-6871. 1903. C. Scribner's Sons.

Southernwood. Erica Isobel Oxenham. LC 29-1971. 1928. Longmans, Green and Co.

Southland. Amanda Carlisle. 448p. (Orig.). 1982. pap. 3.50 (ISBN 0-523-41686-5). Pinnacle Bks.

Southland Stories. James B Hodgkin. LC 42-290153. 1903. The Journal Press.

Southpaw. Mark Harris. 1982. lib. bdg. 16.95x (ISBN 0-89966-394-X). Buccaneer Bks.

Southpaw: By Henry W. Wiggen; Punctuation Freely Inserted and Spelling Greatly Improved by Mark Harris. 1st Ed. Mark Harris. LC 53-5845. 1953. Bobbs-Merrill.

Southpaw Fly Hawk. Adolph Casper Regli. LC 52-5641. 1952. Longmans, Green.

Southward Ho! A Spell of Sunshine. William Gilmore Simms. LC 75-116012. 1970. AMS Press.

Southward Ho! A Spell of Sunshine. William Gilmore Simms. LC 8-11014. (With his The Yemassee. New York, 1882). 1882. A. C. Armstrong & Son.

Southward Ho! a Spell of Sunshine. William Gilmore Simms. (On cover: Lovell's library, v. 12, no. 662). 1885. J. W. Lovell Company.

Southways. Erskine Caldwell. LC 38-14891. 1938. The Viking Press.

Southwest. John Houghton Allen. LC 76-57532. (Zia book). 1977. 3.45 (ISBN 0-8263-0446-X). University of New Mexico Press.

Southwest. Laura Adams Armer. LC 35-353677. 1935. Longmans, Green and Co.

Southwest Corner. Mildred Walker, pseud. LC 51-2761. 1951. Harcourt, Brace.

Southwest Drifter. Gordon D. Shirreffs. 1971. pap. 0.60 o.p. (R2423, GM). Fawcett World.

Southwest Fiction Anthology. Ed. by Max Apple. 368p. (Orig.). 1981. pap. 2.95 (ISBN 0-553-14256-9). Bantam.

Southwest of the Law. Hamilton Craigie. LC 32-8308. E. J. Clode, Inc.

Southwind. Esther J. Neely. 1979. pap. 2.25 o.s.i. (ISBN 0-8439-0666-9, Leisure Bks). Nordon Pubns.

Southwind Calling. Janet Gregory Vermandel. (Orig.). 1979. pap. 1.75 (ISBN 0-532-23106-6). Woodhill.

Souvenir. Benedict Joseph Murdoch. LC 26-6264. 1926. Wickersham Press.

Souvenir: A Novel by Floyd Dell. Floyd Dell. 1929. Doubleday, Doran and Company, Inc.

Souvenir from Qam. Marcus Cook Connelly. LC 65-10126. 4.50. Holt.

Sovereign. R. M. Meluch. 1979. pap. 2.25 (ISBN 0-451-09883-8, E9883, Sig). NAL.

Sovereign Good. Helen Manchester Gates Granville-Barker. LC 8-28983. 1908. G. P. Putnam's Sons.

Sovereign Guide; a Tale of Eden. William Amos Miller. LC 99-399. 1898. G. Rice & Sons.

Sovereign Power. Mark Lee Luther. LC 11-11282. 1911. The Macmillan Company.

Sovereign Remedy. Flora Annie Webster Steel. LC 6-26482. 1906. The Trow Press.

Sovereign Solution. Michael M. McNamara. LC 78-27373. 8.95 (ISBN 0-517-53690-0). Crown Publishers.

Soviet Eight: Contemporary Russian Short Stories, Translated from the Russian. U. N. Owen. LC 63-20330. 1963. Pageant Press.

Soviet Literature. Ed. by George Reavey & Marc Slonim. Tr. by George Reavey & Marc Slonim. LC 77-138176. 426p. 1972. Repr. of 1934 ed. lib. bdg. 18.00x (ISBN 0-8371-5633-5, REAA). Greenwood.

Soviet River. Leonid Maksimovich Leonov. LC 72-90298. 1973. (ISBN 0-88355-009-1). Hyperion Press.

Soviet River. Leonid Maksimovich Leonov. Tr. by Ivor Goldsmid Samuel Montagu. Nolbandov, Sergie, Joint Tr. LC 32-937782. 1932. L. MacVeagh, Dial Press, Inc.

Soviet Russian Stories of the 1960's & 1970's. Y. Bochkarev. 419p. 1977. 7.45 (ISBN 0-8285-0949-2, Pub. by Progress Pubs USSR). Imported Pubns.

Soviet Science Fiction. Ed. by Isaac Asimov. (Orig.). 1962. pap. 1.75 o.p. (ISBN 0-02-016550-1, Collier). Macmillan.

Soviet Short Stories. Ed. by Avrahm Yarmolinsky. LC 60-13565. (Anchor books, A218). 1960. Anchor Books.

Soviet Short Stories. Ed. by Avrahm Yarmolinsky. LC 75-17467. 1975. 16.00 (ISBN 0-8371-8310-3). Greenwood Press.

Soviet Short Stories, Vol. 2. Ed. by Peter Reddaway. (Orig., Rus. & Eng.). (YA) (gr. 9 up). 1968. pap. 1.25 o.p. (ISBN 0-14-002555-3). Penguin.

Soviet Short Stories: Nineteen Twenty-Nine to Sixty-One. Ed. by Richard Newnham. (Orig., Rus. & Eng.). (YA) (gr. 9 up). pap. 0.95 o.p. (ISBN 0-14-001793-3). Penguin.

Soviet Stories of the Last Decade. Elisaveta Fen. Repr. of 1945 ed. 10.00 o.p. (ISBN 0-89987-101-1). Darby Bks.

Soviet War Stories. Sholokhow, Mikhall Aleksandrovich, 1905- et al. LC 44-4181. Hutchinson & Co. Ltd.

Sow Death, Reap Death. Hugh Pentecost. LC 81-9712. (Red badge novel of suspense). 8.95 (ISBN 0-396-08006-5). Dodd, Mead.

Sow Not in Anger: A Novel. 1st Ed. Jack Hoffenberg. LC 61-6011. 1961. Dutton.

Sow Not in Anger: A Novel. 1st Ed. John Hoffenberg. LC 61-6011. 1961. Dutton.

Sow the Seeds of Hemp. Gary Jennings. LC 75-42202. 7.95 (ISBN 0-393-08733-6). Norton.

Sow the Wild Wind: By John Vail Pseud. Cover Painting by Clark Hulings. Robert Carse. LC 55-20536. (Gold medal books, 441). 1954. Fawcett Publications.

Sow the Wind. Theodore Fredenburgh. LC 36-218261. Green Circle Books.

Sow the Wind. La Selle Gilman. LC 55-6210. 1955. W. Sloane Associates.

Sower of the Wind. Clotilde Inez Mary Graves. LC 27-16668. 1927. Little, Brown, and Company.

Sowers. Hugh Stowell Scott. LC 68-12383. (Doughty library, no. 7). 1968. Stein and Day.

Sowers. Hugh Stowell Scott. LC 99-4308. 1899. Harper & Brothers.

Sowers: A Novel. Hugh Stowell Scott. LC 8-2913. 1895. Harper & Brothers.

Sowers Not Reapers: Or, Chatham and Mary Kay. Harriet Martineau. (On cover: Lovell's library, v. 7, no. 395). 1884. J. W. Lovell Company.

Sowers of the Thunder. With Illus. and Decorations by Roy G. Krenkel. Robert E. Howard. LC 73-172140. (Illus.). 1973. 12.00. D. M. Grant.

Sowing and Reaping. William Burns McGregor. LC 22-20997. P. G. Boyle.

Sowing Glory: The Memoirs of "Mary Ambree", the English Woman-Legionary. Percival Christopher Wren. LC 31-22438. 1931. Frederick A. Stokes Company.

Sowing of Alderson Cree. Margaret Prescott Montague. LC 7-12272. 1907. The Baker & Taylor Company.

Sowing of Swords: Or, The Soul of the 'sixties, by Hannah Parting of New England. Elizabeth Avery Meriwether. LC 10-22984. 1910. 1.50. The Neale Publishing Company.

Sowing of the Seed. Ezio Taddei & Putnam, Samuel, 1892- Tr. LC 46-85296. 1946. The Dial Press.

Sowing Seeds in Danny. Nellie Letitia Mooney McClung. LC 8-9810. 1908. Doubleday, Page & Company.

Sowing the Wind. Martha Dodd. LC 45-78457. 1945. Harcourt, Brace and Company.

Sowing the Wind and Other Stories. Timothy Shay Arthur. LC 70-137721. (His Arthur's home stories). (American fiction reprint series.). 1970. Books for Libraries Press.

Sowing Wind. M. Herbert Wolf. LC 32-24138. 1932. Gage & Moran.

Sown Among Thorns. Ethel May Dell. LC 39-247273. 1939. Doubleday, Doran & Company, Inc.

Sown in the Darkness, A.D. 2,000. William Richard Twiford. LC 41-13947. 1941. Orlin Tremaine Company.

Sow's Ear. Irving J Bissell. LC 37-21964. J. Messner, Inc.

Sow's Ear. 1st Ed. Georgia Archer. LC 53-127595. 1953. Pageant Press.

Space. James A Michener. LC 82-40127. (Illus.). 17.95 (ISBN 0-394-50555-7) (ISBN 0-394-52764-X). Random House.

Space Adventure Novels. Andre Norton, pseud. 1978. 50.00 (Gregg). G K Hall.

Space-Age Bible Stories. Margaret Ehlenbeck. 3.00 o.p. Carlton.

Space Apart. Meredith Sue Willis. LC 78-20998. 8.95 (ISBN 0-684-16071-4). Scribner.

Space Apart. Meredith Sue Willis. LC 82-5164. 1982. 12.95 (ISBN 0-89340-516-7). John Curley & Associates.

Space Apprentice. Arkadii Natanovich Strugatskii & Boris Natanovich Strugatskii. LC 81-171. (MacMillan's Best of Soviet Science Fiction). 10.95 (ISBN 0-02-615220-7). Macmillan.

Space Apprentice. Arkady Strugatsky & Arkadii Natanovich Strugatskii. (Best of Soviet Science Fiction Ser.). 141p. 1981. 11.95 o.p. (ISBN 0-02-615220-7). Macmillan.

Space Ark. Thomas Hubschman. (Orig.). 1981. pap. 1.95 (ISBN 0-505-51635-7). Tower Bks.

Space Behind the Clock. Ed. by Van K. Brock. pap. 3.00 o.s.i. Anhinga Pr.

Space Between. Sharon Spencer. LC 72-9178. 256p. 1973. 7.95 o.p. (ISBN 0-06-013961-7, HarpT). Har-Row.

Space Between. Ruth Wolff. (YA) 1970. 6.95 o.p. (ISBN 0-381-98202-5, A73450). John Day.

Space Between: A Novel. Sharon Spencer. LC 72-9178. (Illus.). 1973. 7.95 (ISBN 0-06-013961-7). Harper & Row.

Space Between: A Novel. Ruth Wolff. LC 78-89314. 1970. 5.95. J. Day.

Space Beyond. John Wood Campbell. 1976. pap. 1.75 o.p. (ISBN 0-515-03742-7). BJ Pub Group.

Space Child's Mother Goose. rev. ed. Frederick Winsor. 1972. pap. 2.95 (ISBN 0-671-21316-4, Fireside). S&S.

Space Circus. Alex Raymond. (Flash Gordon adventures). 1974. (pbk.) 0.95 (ISBN 0-380-00064-4). Avon.
Space Doctor. Lee Corey. 256p. (Orig.). 1981. pap. 2.50 (ISBN 0-345-29263-4, Del Rey). Ballantine.
Space Dreamers. Arthur C. Clarke. Orig. Title: Prelude to Space. 1969. pap. 0.75 o.p. (74-524). Lancer.
Space Egg. Russell Robert Winterbotham. LC 58-12507. 1958. Avalon Books.
Space Enterprise. G. Harry Stine. 256p. 1982. pap. 2.95 (ISBN 0-441-77756-2). Ace Bks.
Space Four. Ed. by Richard Davis. 1978. 10.75 o.p. (ISBN 0-200-72512-2). Transatlantic.
Space Frontiers. Roger Lee Vernon. LC 55-104477. (Signet book, 1224). 1955. New American Library.
Space-Gods Revealed: A Close Look at the Theories of Enrich Von Daniken. Ronald Story. pap. 3.95 (ISBN 0-06-464040-X, BN). B&N NY.
Space Guardian. Max Daniels. (Kangaroo Book). 1.75 (ISBN 0-671-81888-0). Pocket Books.
Space Guardians. Brian Ball. (Space: 1999 no. 3). (Illus.). 1975. (pbk.) 1.50 (ISBN 0-671-80198-8). Pocket Books.
Space Guardians. Brian N. Ball. (Space - 1999). 142p. 1975. lib. bdg. 5.95 (ISBN 0-88411-673-5). Amereon Ltd.
Space Hawk, the Greatest of Interplanetary Adventurers. Harry Bates. LC 52-6108. 1952. Greenberg.
Space Lawyer. Nathan Schachner. LC 53-12603. 1953. Gnome Press.
Space Lords. Cordwainer Smith, pseud. 1979. pap. 1.75 (ISBN 0-515-05122-5). Jove Pubns.
Space Lords. Cordwainer Smith, pseud. 1968. pap. 0.60 o.p. (X1911). Pyramid Pubns.
Space Machine: A Scientific Romance. Christopher Priest. LC 75-25095. 8.95 (ISBN 0-06-013429-1). Harper & Row.
Space Machine: A Scientific Romance. Christopher Priest. LC 76-365138. 1976. 3.50 (ISBN 0-571-10931-4). Faber.
Space Magicians. Ed. by Samuel Moskowitz & Alden Norton. 1971. pap. 0.75 o.p. (T2393). Pyramid Pubns.
Space Mail. Ed. by Isaac Asimov. 416p. (Orig.). 1980. pap. 2.50 (ISBN 0-449-24312-5, Crest). Fawcett.
Space Merchants. Frederik Pohl. LC 69-13672. 1969. 4.50. Walker.
Space Merchants: By Frederik Pohl and C. M. Kornbluth. Frederik Pohl & Cyril M. Kornbluth. LC 53-6886. 1953. Ballantine Books.
Space No Barrier see Man of Metal.
Space Novels: To the Sun! Off on a Comet! Jules Verne. LC 60-50100. 1960. Dover Publications.
Space Odysseys: A New Look at Yesterday's Futures. Brian Wilson Aldiss. LC 75-36576. 1976. 7.95 (ISBN 0-385-07851-X). Doubleday.
Space Odysseys: A New Look at Yesterday's Futures. Brian Wilson Aldiss. (Berkley Book). 1978. 1.95 (ISBN 0-425-03681-2). Berkley Pub. Corp.
Space of the Heart. Patricia Wright. LC 75-17896. (Illus.). 1976. 7.95 (ISBN 0-385-03648-5). Doubleday.
Space of the Heart. Patricia Wright. 1.95 (ISBN 0-446-89241-6). Warner.
Space on My Hands. Fredric Brown. LC 51-5685. 1951. Shasta Publishers.
Space Opera. Jack Vance, pseud. 1979. 1.75 (ISBN 0-87997-457-5). DAW Books.
Space Opera: An Anthology of Way-Back-When Futures. Ed. by Brian Wilson Aldiss. LC 74-9473. (Doubleday science fiction). 1975. 7.95 (ISBN 0-385-07873-0). Doubleday.
Space Opera: An Anthology of Way-Back-When Futures. Ed. by Brian Wilson Aldiss. (Berkeley Medallion Book). 1977. 1.50 (ISBN 0-425-03344-9). Berkley Pub. Corp.
Space Outside. Guy Russell. LC 75-35693. 1975. pap. 15.00 (ISBN 0-916348-07-5). Sigga Pr.
Space Patrol. Steven Caldwell. LC 79-52774. 3.98 (ISBN 0-517-29228-9). Crescent Books.
Space Pioneers: Stories by Eric Frank Russell and Others Edited with an Introd. and Notes by Andre Norton Pseud. 1st Ed. Ed. by Alice Mary Norton. LC 54-5338. 1954. World Pub. Co.
Space Pirates. E. E. Smith & Gordon Eklund. 1979. pap. 4.95 (ISBN 0-89437-056-1). Baronet.
Space Police: Stories Edited with an Introd. and Notes by Andre Norton Pseud. 1st Ed. Ed. by Alice Mary Norton. LC 56-5309. World Pub. Co.
Space Power. G. Harry Stine. 256p. (Orig.). 1981. pap. 2.50 (ISBN 0-441-77744-9). Ace Bks.
Space Relations: A Slightly Gothic Interplanetary Tale. Donald Barr. LC 73-79958. 1973. 6.95. Charterhouse.
Space Scavengers. Cleve Cartmill. LC 75-13499. (O.s.i.). 192p. (Orig.). 1975. pap. 1.25 o.s.i. (ISBN 0-89041-013-5, 3013). Major Bks.
Space Service: Stories by Theodore R. Cogswell and Others Edited, with an Introd. and Notes, by Andre Norton Pseud. Ed. by Alice Mary Norton. LC 52-13235. 1953. World Pub. Co.
Space Skimmer. David Gerrold. 1976. Repr. of 1972 ed. lib. bdg. 14.40x (ISBN 0-88411-192-X). Amereon Ltd.
Space Skimmer. David Gerrold. 1981. pap. 2.50 (ISBN 0-345-29851-9, Del Rey). Ballantine.
Space, Space, Space: Stories About the Time When Men Will Be Adventuring to the Stars. Ed. by William Milligan Sloane. LC 53-9924. (Terrific triple title series). 1953. F. Watts.
Space Station Eight. Carlton C. Allen. 1978. 7.95 o.p. (ISBN 0-533-03076-5). Vantage.
Space Three. Ed. by Richard Davis. (Illus.). 1977. 7.75 o.p. (ISBN 0-200-72447-9). Transatlantic.
Space Three: A Collection of Science Fiction Stories. Ed. by Richard Davis. 1977. 10.00 o.s.i. (ISBN 0-8277-5421-3). British Bk Ctr.
Space Trilogy. Clive Staples Lewis. Incl. Out of the Silent Planet; Perelandra; That Hideous Strength. 768p. 1975. pap. 8.95 boxed set (ISBN 0-02-022350-1). Macmillan.
Space Tug. 2nd ed. Murray Leinster, pseud. (Orig.). 1968. pap. 0.50 o.p. (B50-846). Belmont-Tower.
Space Two: A New Collection of Science Fiction Stories. Richard Davis. 140p. 1975. 8.95 o.p. (ISBN 0-200-72275-1). Transatlantic.
Space Vampires. Colin Wilson. LC 75-31605. 7.95 (ISBN 0-394-40093-3). Random House.
Space Vampires. Colin Wilson. (Kangaroo Book)). 1977. 1.75 (ISBN 0-671-80916-4). Pocket Books.
Space Vampires. Colin Wilson. LC 77-366416. 1976. 3.50 (ISBN 0-246-10913-0). Hart-Davis, MacGibbon.
Space Viking. H. Beam Piper. LC 75-422. (Garland Library of Science Fiction). 1975. 11.00 (ISBN 0-8240-1427-8). Garland Pub.
Space Viking. H. Beam Piper. 1977. 1.50. Ace.
Space Visitor. Mack Reynolds. 1977. 1.50 (ISBN 0-441-77782-1). Ace Books.
Space War Blues. Richard A. Lupoff. LC 79-9214. (Gregg Press science fiction series). (Illus.). 1980. 15.00 (ISBN 0-8398-2596-X). Gregg Press.
Space War. John W Macvey. LC 78-24147. 1979. 9.95 (ISBN 0-8128-2579-9). Stein and Day.
Space Weapons-Space Wars. John W. Macvey. LC 78-24147. (Illus.). 264p. 1982. pap. 7.95 (ISBN 0-8128-6111-6). Stein & Day.
Space Within the Heart. Aubrey Menen. LC 78-124140. 1970. McGraw-Hill.
Space 1: A Collection of Science Fiction Stories. Ed. by Richard Davis. 1973. (ISBN 0-200-71967-X). Abelard-Schuman.
Space 3: A Collection of Science Fiction Stories. Richard Davis. LC 77-360699. 1976. Abelard.
Spacedust One. C. C. Coffman. LC 78-63089. (Illus.). 1979. 6.50 o.p. (ISBN 0-533-03958-4). Vantage.
Spaceflight Venus. Philip Wilding. LC 56-2316. 1955. Philosophical Library.
Spacehawk, Inc. Ron Goulart. 1974. (pbk.) 0.95. DAW Books.
Spacehounds of IPC: A Tale of the Inter-Planetary Corporation. Edward Elmer Smith. LC 47-17967. 1947. Fantasy Press.
Spacejacks. Robert Wells. (Berkley medallion book). 1975. (pbk.) 0.95 (ISBN 0-425-02847-X). Berkley Pub. Co.
Spaceling. Doris Piserchia. 1979. 1.75 (ISBN 0-87997-460-5). DAW.
Spacepaw. Gordon R. Dickson. 1983. pap. 2.50 (ISBN 0-441-77759-7, Pub. by Ace Science Fiction). Ace Bks.
Spaceship for the King. Jerry Pournelle. (Science Fiction Ser.). (Orig.). 1973. pap. 0.95 o.p. (UQ1042). DAW Bks.
Spaceship to Saturn. Hugh Walters, pseud. LC 67-11915. 1967. Criterion Books.
Spaceships of Ancestors. Clark Darlton. (Perry Rhodan#73). (Illus.). 1975. (pbk.) 1.25. Ace Books.
Spacetime Donuts. Rudy Rucker. 224p. (Orig.). 1981. pap. 2.50 (ISBN 0-441-77775-9). Ace Bks.
Spacewater Blues. Homer Weiner. LC 80-53163. 12.95 (ISBN 0-937110-00-0). Sonica Press.
Spaceways: Corundum's Woman. John Cleve, pseud. LC 81-83489. (Spaceways Ser.: No. 2). 224p. (Orig.). 1982. pap. 2.50 (ISBN 0-86721-037-0). Playboy Pbks.
Spaceways, No. 10: The Yoke of Shen. John Cleve, pseud. (Orig.). 1983. pap. 2.50 (ISBN 0-425-06063-2). Berkley Pub.
Spaceways, No. 11: The Iceworld Connection. John Cleve, pseud. 224p. (Orig.). 1983. pap. 2.50 (ISBN 0-425-06067-5). Berkley Pub.
Spaceways Number Eight: Under Twin Suns. John Cleve, pseud. LC 82-81997. (Spaceways Ser.). 224p. 1982. pap. 2.75 (ISBN 0-86721-204-7). Playboy Pbks.
Spaceways Number Seven: The Manhuntress. LC 82-81380. (Spaceways Ser.: No. 7). 224p. (Orig.). 1982. pap. 2.50 (ISBN 0-86721-175-X). Playboy Pbks.
Spaceways Number Six: Purrfect Plunder. John Cleve, pseud. LC 82-80838. (Spaceways Ser.: No. 6). 224p. (Orig.). 1982. pap. 2.50 (ISBN 0-86721-148-2). Playboy Pbks.
Spaceways: Of Alien Bondage. John Cleve, pseud. LC 81-83488. (Spaceways Ser.: No. 1). 240p. (Orig.). 1982. pap. 2.50 (ISBN 0-86721-036-2). Playboy Pbks.
Spaceways Satellite: By Charles Eric Maine Pseud. David McIlwain. LC 58-7591. 1958. Avalon Books.
Spade in the Sensorium. David Wulf Anderson. 1974. saddlestitched in wrappers 1.50 (Pub. by Big Sky Bks). SBD.
Spadeful of Spacetime. Ed. by Fred Saberhagen. 224p. (Orig.). 1981. pap. 2.25 (ISBN 0-441-77766-X). Ace Bks.
Spaewife: Or, The Queen's Secret. A Story of the Reign of Elizabeth. John Boyce. LC 6-16077. 1853. J. Murphy & Co.; Etc., Etc.
Spaghetti on the Wall. Mary Crisafulli. 3.50 o.p. Carlton.
Spagyric Quest of Beroaldus Cosmopolita. Arthur Machen. (Illus.). 24p. 1976. Repr. of 1888 ed. pap. 2.00 (ISBN 0-9603300-1-1). Purple Mouth.
Span O' Life: A Tale of Louisbourg & Quebec. William McLennan & McIlwraith, Jean Newton, Joint Author. LC 99-1579. 1899. Harper & Brothers.
Span of the Year. Vera Fedorovna Panova. LC 75-39007. (Early Soviet Literature). 1977. 18.75 (ISBN 0-88355-410-0). Hyperion Press.
Spandau: The Secret Diaries. Albert Speer. 1981. pap. 3.95 (ISBN 0-671-42447-5). PB.
Spandau Warrant. Allan Morgan. (Blood Ser.). (O.s.i.: No. 2). 208p. (Orig.). 1974. pap. 1.25 o.s.i. (AQ1296, Award). Univ Pub & Dist.
Spanglers. Henry Castor. LC 48-8526. 1948. Doubleday.
Spanglers and Tingles: Or, The Rival Belles. A Tale, Unveiling Some of the Mysteries of Society and Politics As They Exist at the Present Time in the United States. John Beauchamp Jones. LC 7-11917. (On cover: Library of humours American works). 1852. A. Hart.
Spangles. Joseph J Quinn. LC 30-30. The Stratford Company.
Spangles". Nellie Revell. LC 26-236869. Grosset & Dunlap.
Spaniard. Bernard Clavel. LC 70-143849. 1971. 6.95 o.p. (ISBN 0-8092-9615-2). Regnery.
Spaniard. Juanita Savage. LC 29-25279. 1924. A. L. Burt Company.
Spaniard. 1st American Ed. Paul Pettit. LC 54-6289. 1954. Harper.
Spaniard's Gift. Elisabeth Welles. (Kangaroo Book). 1.50 (ISBN 0-671-80901-6). Pocket Books.
Spanish Acres. Hal George Evarts. LC 25-158502. 1925. Little, Brown, and Company.
Spanish American Short Stories. Sherman H. Eoff & Paul C. King. (Orig., Span.). 1953. pap. text ed. 2.95x o.p. (ISBN 0-02-333830-X). Macmillan.
Spanish Bayonet. Stephen Vincent Benet. LC 77-131621. 1971. Scholarly Press.
Spanish Bayonet. Stephen Vincent Benet. LC 26-4705. George H. Doran Company.
Spanish Blood: A Collection of Short Stories. Raymond Chandler. LC 46-6327. 1946. The World Publishing Company.
Spanish Bride. Georgette Heyer. LC 65-11840. 1965. 4.95. Dutton.
Spanish Bride. Georgette Heyer. LC 40-30108. 1940. Doubleday, Doran and Company, Inc.
Spanish Bride. Walter O'Meara. LC 54-11402. 1954. Putnam.
Spanish Bridegroom. Eleanor Hibbert. LC 75-151215. 1971. 6.95. Putnam.
Spanish Bridegroom. Jean Plaidy. 1971. 6.95 o.p. (ISBN 0-399-10761-4). Putnam Pub Group.
Spanish Bridegroom: By Jean Plaidy Pseud. Eleanor Hibbert. LC 56-11978. 1956. Macrae Smith Co.
Spanish Brothers: A Tale of the Sixteenth Century. Deborah Alcock. LC 67-1695. 1966. Bethany Fellowship.
Spanish Cape Mystery. Ellery Queen. 354p. 1976. lib. bdg. 16.95x (ISBN 0-89966-146-7). Buccaneer Bks.
Spanish Cape Mystery. large print ed. Ellery Queen, pseud. LC 82-7356. 1982. 13.95 (ISBN 0-89340-523-X). J. Curley & Associates.
Spanish Cape Mystery: A Problem in Deduction. Ellery Queen, pseud. LC 35-5190. 1935. Frederick A. Stokes Company.
Spanish Cape Mystery: A Problem in Deduction. Ellery Queen, pseud. LC 43-13937. 1943. Triangle Books.
Spanish Cape Mystery: A Problem in Deduction. Ellery Queen, pseud. LC 46-205543. 1946. Triangle Books, the Blakiston Company.
Spanish Castles by the Rhine: A Triptychal Yarn. David Skaats Foster. (Buckram series). 1897. H. Holt and Company.
Spanish Cavaliers: A Tale of the Moorish Wars in Spain. Tr. from the French. Sadlier, Mary Anne (Madden) "Mrs. James Sadlier," 1820-1903, Tr. LC 8-25955. (On cover: Parlor & cottage library). 1866. D. & J. Sadlier & Co.
Spanish Chapel. Dorothy Daniels. (Inflation Fighters Ser.). 192p. 1982. pap. 1.50 (ISBN 0-8439-1066-6, Leisure Bks). Nordon Pubns.
Spanish Chapel. Dorothy Daniels. 1977. pap. text ed. 1.25 o.s.i. (ISBN 0-505-51165-7, BT51165). Tower Bks.
Spanish Connection. Nick Carter. (Nick Carter Ser.). (O.s.i.). (Orig.). 1977. pap. 1.50 o.s.i. (AD 1656, Award). Univ Pub & Dist.
Spanish Daughter. By the Rev. George Butt... Rev. and Cor. by His Daughter, Mrs. Sherwood... George Butt & Sherwood, Mary Martha (Butt) 1824. S. T. Armstrong Etc.
Spanish Doll. Elizabeth Renier. 192p. 1981. pap. 1.75 (ISBN 0-441-77757-0). Ace Bks.
Spanish Doubloons. Camilla Kenyon. LC 19-155534. 1.50. The Bobbs-Merrill Company.
Spanish Duet. Francis Clifford. (YA) 1966. 4.95 o.p. Coward.
Spanish Duet: Two Novels of Suspense. Arthur Leonard Bell Thompson. LC 66-26530. 1966. Coward-McCann.
Spanish Eyes That Smile. Hattie Horner Louthan. LC 38-24741. Library Service Guild.
Spanish Faith: A Romance of Old Mexico and the Caribbean. Francis Rufus Bellamy. LC 26-9263. 1926. Harper & Brothers.
Spanish Farm. Ralph Hale Mottram. LC 24-21587. 1924. L. MacVeagh, The Dial Press.
Spanish Farm. Ralph Hale Mottram. LC 41-6370. (On cover: Penguin books. 52). 1938. Penguin Books Limited.
Spanish Farm Trilogy, 1914-1918. Ralph Hale Mottram. LC 27-6203. 1927. L. MacVeagh, The Dial Press.
Spanish Gardener. Archibald Joseph Cronin. 1968. pap. 0.75 o.p. (T1769). Pyramid Pubns.
Spanish Gardener. Archibald Joseph Cronin. 1973. pap. 1.25 o.p. (ISBN 0-515-03191-7, V3191). BJ Pub Group.
Spanish Gardener. 1st Ed. Archibald Joseph Cronin. LC 50-13122. 1950. Little, Brown.
Spanish Gold. Peter Germano. LC 64-9175. Arcadia House.
Spanish Gold. James Owen Hannay. LC 12-35374. 1912. Hodder and Stoughton Etc.
Spanish Gold. James Owen Hannay. LC 14-10503. G. H. Doran Company.
Spanish Gold. James Owen Hannay. LC 21-412203. 1919. Grosset & Dunlap.
Spanish Gold. James Owen Hannay. LC 33-283488. (The pocket books). George H. Doran Company.
Spanish Grant. Leonard London Foreman. 1975. (pbk.) 0.95. Ace Books.
Spanish Hate. Juanita Savage. LC 31-8220. 1931. L. MacVeagh, The Dial Press.
Spanish Heroine: A Tale of Cuban Patriotism... William C. Falkner. LC 22-5172. 1856. H. B. Pearson.
Spanish Heroine: A Tale of War and Love. William C Falkner. LC 6-3842. 1851. I. Hart & Co.
Spanish Holiday. Eleanor Mercein Kelly. LC 30-10715. 1930. Harper & Brothers.
Spanish House. Eleanor Furneaux Smith. LC 38-27669. 1938. Doubleday, Doran & Company, Inc.
Spanish Inn. Jean Louis Bergonzo. LC 68-22004. 1968. 3.95. Grove Press.
Spanish Jade. Maurice Henry Hewlett. 1908. Doubleday, Page & Company.
Spanish John: Being a Memoir, Now First Published in Complete Form, of the Early Life and Adventures of Colonel John McDonell, Known As "Spanish John," When a Lieutenant in the Company of St. James of the Regiment Irlandia, in the Service of the King of Spain Operating in Italy. William McLennan. 1898. Harper & Brothers.
Spanish Ladie & Two Other Stories from Cervantes. Miguel de Cervantes Saavedra. Tr. by James Mabble. (Illus.). 197p. 1981. Repr. of 1928 ed. lib. bdg. 45.00 (ISBN 0-89987-770-2). Darby Bks.
Spanish Lady. Frederic Arnold Kummer. LC 33-16587. Sears Publishing Company.
Spanish Lady. Maurice Walsh. LC 43-11747. 1943. J. B. Lippincott Company.
Spanish Lover. Frank Hamilton Spearman. 1930. C. Scribner's Sons.
Spanish Musketeer. A Tale of Military Life. Maturin Murray Ballou. LC 9-1818. 1847. Gleason's Publishing Hall.
Spanish Necklace. Bithia Mary Sheppard Croker. LC 9-102. Cupples & Leon Company.
Spanish Nun. Thomas De Quincey. (Lovell's library, no. 20). 1882. J. W. Lovell Company.
Spanish Peggy: A Story of Young Illinois. Mary Hartwell Catherwood. LC 99-5806.
Spanish Pesos: A Western Story. William Colt MacDonald. LC 37-374436. Covici, Friede.
Spanish Plot. Frederick Alanson Randle. LC 8-225. (On cover: Neely's continental library, no. 5). F. T. Neely.

Spanish Pole-Cat: The Adventures of Seniora Rufina. Alonso De Castillo Solorzano. Ed. by Roger L'Estrange & John Ozell. LC 80-2472. Repr. of 1717 ed. 62.50 (ISBN 0-404-19104-5). AMS Pr.
Spanish Prisoner. Frank Gruber. LC 73-87182. 1969. 4.95. Dutton.
Spanish Prisoner. Freeman Tilden. LC 28-11057. 1928. Doubleday, Doran & Company, Inc.
Spanish Range. Lee E Wells. LC 51-13164. 1951. Rinehart.
Spanish Rapture. Juanita Savage. LC 34-32755. The Macaulay Company.
Spanish Ridge. Eugene E Halleran. LC 57-12240. (Ballantine books, 219). 1957. Ballantine Books.
Spanish Scene. Chandler Brossard. LC 68-16634. 1968. Viking Press.
Spanish Season. Bernard Stanley Oldsey. LC 74-95875. 1970. 6.95. Harcourt, Brace & World.
Spanish Short Stories, Vol. 2. Ed. by Gudie Lawaetz. 1972. pap. 1.95 o.p. (ISBN 0-14-003378-5, 3378). Penguin.
Spanish Short Stories of the Sixteenth Century in Contemporary Translations: Revised, with an Introduction. Ed. by John Brande Trend. LC 29-5417. (Half-title: The world's classics. CCCXXVI). 1928. H. Milford, Oxford University Press.
Spanish Soldier. Herburt Burkholz. LC 72-84219. 352p. 1973. 7.95 o.p. (ISBN 0-88327-006-4). Charterhouse.
Spanish Soldier: A Novel. Herbert Burkholz. LC 72-84219. 1972. 7.95. Charterhouse.
Spanish Stirrup, and Other Stories. John Prebble. LC 72-78537. 1973. 6.95 (ISBN 0-03-001461-1). Holt, Rinehart and Winston.
Spanish Stirrups: Illustrated by Gil Walker. 1st American Ed. John Prebble. LC 58-108900. 1958. Harcourt, Brace.
Spanish Stories. Ed. by Angel Flores. (Eng. & Span.). (gr. 10-12). pap. 2.50 (ISBN 0-553-20018-6, 12936-8). Bantam.
Spanish Stories & Tales. Harriet De Onis. Repr. of 1954 ed. 20.00 o.p. (ISBN 0-89987-103-8). Darby Bks.
Spanish Stories & Tales. Ed. by Harriet De Onis. (Fr). 1968. pap. 0.60 o.p. (W0536). WSP.
Spanish Stories and Tales. 1st Ed. Ed. by Harriet De Onis. LC 53-9479. (Borzoi series of stories and tales). 1954. Knopf.
Spanish Sunlight. Agnes Russell Weekes. LC 25-5461. 1925. Dodd, Mead and Company.
Spanish Tales. H. L. Prosser. 16p. 1977. pap. 2.00x o.p. (ISBN 0-918534-02-X). Mafdet.
Spanish Trails to California. Trevino De La Rhue. LC 37-27300. 1937. The Caxton Printers, Ltd.
Spanish Treasure: A Novel. Elizabeth Campbell Winter. LC 8-37112. (choice series. no. 78). 1893. R. Bonner's Sons.
Spanish Urne: A Novel. Frank James Mathew. 1897. J. Lane.
Spanish Village. Marvin H Tuma. LC 56-11351. 1956. Pageant Press.
Spanish World in English Fiction. Cony Sturgis. 1927. 2.00 o.p. (ISBN 0-87305-034-7). Faxon.
Spanking Game. Norman Smith. pap. 2.25 o.s.i. (Venus). Grove.
Spanking Girls. Carter Brown, pseud. 1979. pap. 1.50 (ISBN 0-505-51383-8). Tower Bks.
Spanking Room. M. Le Compte Du Bouleau. 1972. pap. 1.75 o.s.i. (V1109K, Venus). Grove.
Spanking the Maid: A Novel. Robert Coover. LC 81-48546. 1982. 10.95 (ISBN 0-394-52561-2) (ISBN 0-394-17971-4). Grove Press.
Spare Not for Their Crying. John Skinner. LC 59-6921. 1959. Christopher Pub. House.
Spare Parts. Charles Henri Ford. 30.00 o.p. Horizon.
Spare Parts. David A Kaufelt. 1978. 2.50 (ISBN 0-446-81889-5). Warner Books.
Spare Room: A Novel. Nelia Gardner White. LC 54-5764. 1954. Viking Press.
Spare the Rod. Michael Croft. LC 54-4652. 1954. Longmans, Green.
Spargo. Jack D. Scott. 1975. pap. 1.75 o.p. (ISBN 0-515-03873-3, M3873). Pyramid Pubns.
Spargo: A Novel of Espionage. Jack Denton Scott. LC 70-158532. 1971. 7.95. World Pub. Co.
Sparhawk. Lionel Webb. (Orig.). 1968. pap. 0.95 o.p. (75-052). Lancer.
Sparhawk. Lionel Webb. (O.s.i.). 1976. pap. 1.50 o.s.i. (AD1639, Award). Univ Pub & Dist.
Sparing to Spend: Or, The Loftons and Pinkertons. Timothy Shay Arthur. LC 6-3419. 1853. C. Scribner.
Spark see Old New York.
Spark and the Exodus. Benedict Freedman & Nancy Mars Freedman. LC 54-6627. 1954. Crown Publications.
Spark of Fire in the Night. Elise Randolph. (Candlelight Ecstasy Ser.: No. 73). (Orig.). 1982. pap. 1.95 (ISBN 0-440-18805-9). Dell.
Spark of Godness. Charles Brady. LC 82-11949. 1982. 14.95 (ISBN 0-395-31257-4). Houghton Mifflin.
Spark of Life. Erich Maria Remarque. LC 52-6136. 1952. Appleton-Century-Crofts.
Spark Plug at Short. Jackson Volney Scholz. LC 66-15133. 1966. W. Morrow.
Spark Plug Thief: Stories. Marc Plourde. LC 77-373064. New Delta.
Spark: The 'sixties. Edith Newbold Jones Wharton. LC 24-114724. (Her Old New York. v. 3). 1924. D. Appleton and Company.
Sparkenbroke. Charles Morgan. LC 36-801411. 1936. The Macmillan Company.
Sparkle. Richard Perry. 1976. (pbk.) 1.50. Warner Books.
Sparkle from the Coal: 1st Amer. Ed. Prudence Andrew. LC 65-13970. 1965. 4.95. Putnam.
Sparkles in the Water. William Arthur Neubauer. LC 65-8088. 1965. Arcadia House.
Sparkling Windows. William Arthur Neubauer. LC 48-2944. 1948. Arcadia House.
Sparks. Elizabeth Fritch. (Richmond Ser.: Vol. 4). (Orig.). 1982. pap. 3.50 (ISBN 0-89083-962-X). Zebra.
Sparks. Maureen Strange. LC 81-50326. 12.95 (ISBN 0-87223-703-6). Seaview Books.
Sparks Fly Upward. James Ronald. LC 53-92984. 1953. J. Messner.
Sparks Fly Upward: A Novel. Oliver La Farge. LC 31-30506. 1931. Houghton Mifflin Company.
Sparks from the Anvil of Thought and Industry. William Yancey Erwin. LC 31-1745. Pub. for the Author by Standard Printing & Publishing Company.
Sparks on the Wind. Morton D. Prouty, Jr. 1961. 2.00 o.p. (ISBN 0-8042-2544-3). John Knox.
Sparrow Falls. Wilbur A Smith. LC 78-218. 1978. 10.95 (ISBN 0-385-13603-X). Doubleday.
Sparrow Farm. Rudolf Ditzen, pseud. LC 38-6969. 1938. G. P. Putnam's Sons.
Sparrowgrass Papers. Frederick Swartwout Cozzens. LC 72-76922. (American fiction reprint series). (Illus.). 1969. Books for Libraries Press.
Sparrowgrass Papers: Or, Living in the Country. Frederick Swartwout Cozzens. 1856. Derby & Jackson.
Sparrowgrass Papers: Or. Living in the Country. Frederick Swartwout Cozzens. 1869. J. B. Lippincott & Co.
Sparrows. Marie Coolidge-Rask & Dunn, Winifred. LC 26-20888. Grosset & Dunlap.
Sparrow's Fall. Fred Bodsworth. (Signet bk. T3590). 1968. New Amer. Lib.
Sparrow's Fall. Fred Bodsworth. LC 67-10412. 1967. Doubleday.
Sparrows of Paris. Mario Andrew Pei. LC 58-4324. 1958. Philosophical Library.
Spartacus. Howard Melvin Fast. LC 52-1048. 1951.
Spartan. Donald Harrison. (Illus.). 180p. 1982. pap. 5.95 (ISBN 0-932870-20-1). Alyson Pubns.
Spartan. Caroline Dale Parke Snedeker. LC 13-382. 1949. Doubleday, Page & Company.
Spartan. Caroline Dale Parke Snedeker. LC 36-13886. 1936. Doubleday, Doran & Company, Inc.
Spartan Education. Albert D Werder. LC 78-7134. 1979. 9.95 (ISBN 0-8464-0040-5). Beekman Publishers.
Sparterville Surgeon. James L Mercadante. LC 77-82608. (Illus.). 1978. 8.00. Mercadante.
Spawn. Robert O Holles. LC 78-218. 1978. 7.95 (ISBN 0-385-13635-8). Doubleday.
Spawn. Robert O Holles. (Berkley book). 2.50 (ISBN 0-425-04570-6)., C.
Spawn. L. J. Key. 384p. (Orig.). 1983. pap. 3.50 (ISBN 0-440-19043-6). Dell.
Spawn: A Novel of Degeneration. Nat Joseph Ferber. LC 30-30577. Farrar & Rinehart, Incorporated.
Spawn of Laban. Gregory Kern. (Cap Kennedy,#11). 1974. (pbk.) 0.95. DAW Books.
Spawn of the Death Machine. Ted White. (Science Fiction Ser). (Orig.). 1968. pap. 0.60 o.p. (53-680). Paperback Lib.
Spawn of the North. Florance Barrett Willoughby. LC 32-10750. 1932. Houghton Mifflin Company.
Spawn of the Vortex. Harold Gayle. LC 57-10651. (Milestone book). 1957. Comet Press Books.
Spawning. Fritzen Ravenswood. (Orig.). 1981. pap. 2.95 (ISBN 0-89083-866-6). Zebra.
Speak Easily. Clarence Budington Kelland. LC 32-9369. 1932. Harper & Brothers.
Speak for the Dead. Rex Burns. LC 77-11792. 8.95 (ISBN 0-06-010526-7). Harper & Row.
Speak for Yourself, Michael. Janet Doran. LC 37-36098. 1937. Hillman-Curl, Inc.
Speak Ill of the Dead. Peter Chambers, pseud. LC 69-12988. 1969. 3.95 o.p. Roy.
Speak Ill of the Dead. Dennis John Andrew Phillips. LC 69-12998. 1969. 3.95. Roy Publishers.
Speak Justly of the Dead. Edith Caroline Rivett. LC 52-13682. 1953. Published for the Crime Club by Doubleday.
Speak No Evil. Mignon Good Eberhart. LC 41-515813. Random House.
Speak No Evil. Mignon Good Eberhart. 1973. 0.75. Popular Lib.
Speak No Evil. Joyce Morton. (YA) 1979. 6.95 (Avalon). Bouregy.
Speak Not Evil. Edwin Moultrie Lanham. (N3031). 1965. Bantam.
Speak Now. Frank Yerby. 1975. (pbk.) 1.50. Dell.
Speak Now: A Modern Novel. Frank Yerby. LC 74-91119. 1969. 5.95. Dial Press.
Speak of the Devil. Alfred Hitchcock. 1980. pap. 2.25 (ISBN 0-440-17654-9). Dell.
Speak of the Devil: By Elisabeth Sanxay Holding. Elisabeth Sanxay Holding. LC 41-5576. Duell, Sloan and Pearce.
Speak Out My Heart. Robin Jordan. 1976. 4.00. The Naiad Press: Distributed by The Ladder.
Speak Softly To My Soul. Dorothy A. Bernard. (Candlelight Ecstasy Ser.: No. 104). (Orig.). 1982. pap. 1.95 (ISBN 0-440-18827-X). Dell.
Speak the Sin Softly: A Novel. Cyril Cassidy Caldwell. LC 46-18715. 1946. J. Messner, Inc.
Speak to Me, Brother. Anne Miller Downes. LC 54-9418. 1954. Lippincott.
Speak to Me of Love. Dorothy Eden. (Crest Book, P2014). 1973. (pbk.) 1.25. Fawcett Pubns.
Speak to Me of Love. Dorothy Eden. LC 72-76679. 1972. 7.95 (ISBN 0-698-10462-5). Coward, McCann & Geoghegan.
Speak to the Earth. Sarah Comstock. 1927. Doubleday, Page & Company.
Speak to the Winds. Ruth Moore. LC 56-9811. 1956. W. Morrow.
Speakeasy: A Novel. Nathaniel Benchley. LC 81-43406. 1982. 15.95 (ISBN 0-385-17385-7). Doubleday.
Speakeasy Girl. Bobbie Meredith. LC 31-20648. 1931. Covici Friede.
Speaker of the House: A Novel. Angeline Teal. LC 8-26033. (On cover: Pastime series, no. 129). 1894. Laird & Lee.
Speaking Dust: Thomas and Jane Carlyle, a Biographical Novel. Elsie Prentys Thornton-Cook. LC 38-11326. 1938. C. Scribner's Sons.
Speaking Likeness. Shelia Bishop. (Fawcett Crest Book). 1976. (pbk.) 1.25. Fawcett.
Speaking Oak: And 300 Other Tales of Life, Love and Achievement. Ferdinand Cowle Iglehart. LC 2-28500. 1902. The Christian Herald.
Speaking of Ellen. Linn Boyd Porter. LC 7-37765. (On cover: The albatross novels). 1890. G. W. Dillingham.
Speaking of Maine: A Selection from the Writings of Virginia Chase. Virginia Chase. Ed. by Margaret Shea. (Illus.). 128p. (Orig.). 1983. pap. price not set (ISBN 0-89272-164-2). Down East.
Speaking of Murder. Virginia Van Urk. LC 51-13773. 1931. Phoenix Press.
Speaking of Women. Louis Joseph Vance. LC 30-34414. 1930. J. B. Lippincott Company.
Speaking Stones. Sara Cardiff. LC 75-28035. 7.95 (ISBN 0-698-10701-2). Coward, McCann & Geoghegan.
Spear. James Herbert. (Orig.). 1980. pap. 2.50 (ISBN 0-451-09060-8, E9060, Sig). NAL.
Spear in the Sand: A Novel. Raoul Cohen Faure. LC 46-7211. 1946. Harper & Brothers.
Spear Penny: A Novel. Dorothy Davis Willette. LC 49-1789. 1949. Coward-McCann.
Spear. 1st Ed. Louis De Wohl. LC 55-6296. 1955. Lippincott.
Spearfield's Daughter. Jon Cleary. LC 82-14542. 567p. 1983. Repr. 15.95 (ISBN 0-688-01736-3). Morrow.
Spearhead: A Novel. John Brophy. LC 43-8696. 1943. Harper & Brothers.
Spearmen of Arn. Del DowDell. 1978. pap. 1.75 o.s.i. (ISBN 0-505-51326-9). Tower Bks.
Spears Against Us. Cecil Roberts. LC 32-182488. 1932. D. Appleton and Company.
Spears in the Sun. James Edwin Baum. LC 28-21062. The Reilly & Lee Co.
Spears of Destiny: A Story of the First Capture of Constantinople. Arthur Douglas Howden Smith. LC 19-6410. George H. Doran Company.
Special Agent. Noel Bertram Gerson. LC 76-14776. 7.95 (ISBN 0-8415-0451-2). Dutton.
Special Agent, an FBI Mystery. James Remington McCarthy. LC 38-5599. The Bobbs-Merrill Company.
Special Boys. Peter Fisher & Marc Rubin. LC 78-19417. 10.00. (ISBN 0-312-75151-6) (ISBN 0-312-75152-4). St. Martin's Press.
Special Circumstances. Brian Lysaght. LC 83-2938. 1983. 13.95 (ISBN 0-312-75116-8). St. Martin's.
Special Correspondent: Or, The Adventures of Claudius Bombarnac by Jules Verne... Jules Verne. LC 1-9794. Lovell, Coryell & Company.
Special Deliverance. Clifford D. Simak. LC 81-12893. 1982. 12.50 (ISBN 0-345-29897-7). Ballantine Books.
Special Delivery. Gordon R. Dickson. pap. 1.95 (Pub. by Ace Science Fiction). Ace Bks.
Special Detail. Howard Blakemore. LC 44-8657. 1944. Dorrance & Company.
Special Duty Nurse. Ann Rush. LC 58-913566. 1958. Avalon Books.
Special Effects. Harriet Frank. LC 78-11679. 1979. 8.95 (ISBN 0-395-27219-X). Houghton Mifflin.
Special Feature. Charles V DeVet. 1975. (pbk.) 0.95 (ISBN 0-380-00362-7). Avon.
Special Friendships. Roger Peyrefitte. 1950. Vanguard Press.
Special Gift: The Story of Jan. T. De Vries-Kruyt. LC 74-76906. 1974. 4.95 o.p. (ISBN 0-88326-072-7, Wyden). McKay.
Special Hunger. George O'Neil. LC 31-30611. H. Liveright, Inc.
Special Kind of Crime. Lawrence Treat. LC 81-43452. 1982. 10.95 (ISBN 0-385-17993-6). Published for the Crime Club by Doubleday.
Special Kind of Love. Kirstin Michaels. Bd. with Enchanted Journey. 1981. pap. 1.95 (ISBN 0-451-09619-3, J9619, Sig). NAL.
Special Kind of Love. Kristin Michaels. (Signet Book). 1976. New American Library.
Special Messenger. Robert William Chambers. 1909. 1.50. D. Appleton and Company.
Special Nurse. Lucy Agnes Hancock. LC 48-208549. 1948. Macrae-Smith-Co.
Special Nurse: By Margaret Howe Pseud. Margaretta Brucker. LC 55-149436. 1955. Avalon Books.
Special Offer. Jerry Bumpus. LC 80-20671. 1981. pap. 5.95x (ISBN 0-914140-08-6). Carpenter Pr.
Special Olympics. John Sacret Young. 1978. 1.95 (ISBN 0-446-89718-3). Warner Books.
Special Passion. Ruth Ray. LC 43-15764. 1943. Phoenix Press.
Special Patient. Carlotta Baker. LC 41-11802. Phoenix Press.
Special Patient. Leona Slottman. LC 41-11802. 1941. Phoenix Press.
Special People. Translated from the French by Richard Howard. Jacques Serguine. LC 61-8403. 1961. Farrar, Straus and Cudahy.
Special Providence. Richard Yates. LC 74-88750. 1969. 5.95. Knopf.
Special Relationship. William Clark. LC 69-15007. 1969. 4.95. Houghton Mifflin.
Special Sparrow. Jo Calloway. 1978. pap. 1.50 (ISBN 0-532-15350-2). Woodhill.
Special Wonder, Vol. 1. Ed. by J. Francis McComas. 1971. pap. 0.95 o.p. (95044-095). Beagle Bks.
Special Wonder, Vol. 2. Howard Schoenfeld et al. Ed. by J. Francis McComas. 1971. pap. 0.95 o.p. (95057). Beagle Bks.
Special Wonder: The Anthony Boucher Memorial Anthology of Fantasy and Science Fiction. Ed. by J. Francis McComas. William Anthony Parker White. LC 76-102342. 1970. 7.95. Random House.
Specialist: A Novel. Amy Mary Irvine. LC 4-32326. 1904. J. Lane.
Specialty of the House. Jack Warren. pap. 1.95 o.s.i. (Venus). Grove.
Specialty of the House & Other Stories: The Complete Mystery Tales, 1948-1978. Stanley Ellin. LC 79-67149. 557p. 1979. limited ed. 35.00 (ISBN 0-89296-050-7); 15.00 (ISBN 0-89296-049-3). Mysterious Pr.
Specimen Case. Ernest Bramah Smith. LC 25-7086. George H. Doran Company.
Specimens. Fred Saberhagen. 224p. 1981. pap. 2.25 (ISBN 0-441-77791-0). Ace Bks.
Specimens of the Short Story. George Henry Nettleton. LC 75-94740. (Short story index reprint series). 1969. (ISBN 0-8369-3120-3). Books for Libraries Press.
Speckled Bird. Robert Cutler. LC 23-3438. 1923. The Macmillan Company.
Speckled Bird. Augusta Jane Evans Wilson. LC 2-18338. 1902. G. W. Dillingham Company.
Speckled Bird. William Butler Yeats & William H. O'Donnell. LC 76-359241. 1973. Cuala Press.
Speckled Bird. William Butler Yeats & William H. O'Donnell. LC 78-305913. (Yeats Studies Series). (Illus.). 1977. 25.00 (ISBN 0-7710-9066-8). McClelland and Stewart.
Spectacle. Rayne Kruger. LC 53-2634. 1953. Longmans, Green.
Spectacle. Rayne Kruger. 1954. Macmillan.
Spectacle of a Man. Alvan Leroy Barach. LC 37-20751. 1937. Jefferson House.
Spectacle of a Man. Alvan Leroy Barach. LC 41-12242. 1941. Duell, Sloan and Pearce.
Spectacle of a Man. John Coignard. LC 37-20751. 1937. Jefferson House.
Spectacle of a Man. John Coignard. LC 41-12242. Duell, Sloan and Pearce.
Spectacles of Mr. Cagliostro. Harry Stephen Keeler. LC 29-1190. E. P. Dutton & Company, Inc.
Spectacular Romances. William Hosea Ballou. LC 6-6088. (On cover: Farm and fireside library, no. 112). 1894. Mast, Crowell & Kirkpatrick.
Spectacular Romances: Including "The Jewess". William Hosea Ballou. LC 6-6089. (On cover: Leisure-time series, no. 15). 1892. W. D. Rowland.

Spectator Bird. Wallace Earle Stegner. LC 75-38171. 1976. 7.95 (ISBN 0-385-07890-0). Doubleday.

Spectator Bird. Wallace Earle Stegner. LC 76-51369. 1977. 10.95 (ISBN 0-8161-6443-6). G. K. Hall.

Spectator Bird. Wallace Earle Stegner. LC 77-364849. (Illus.). 1976. Franklin Library.

Spectator Bird. Wallace Earle Stegner. LC 78-26789. 1979. 3.50 (ISBN 0-8032-9107-8). University of Nebraska Press.

Spectator Sport. James Alexander Thom. LC 78-52909. 1978. 1.95 (ISBN 0-380-01925-6). Avon Books.

Specter. Maksim Gorkii. LC 38-27446. 1938. D. Appleton-Century Company, Incorporated.

Specter! A Chrestomathy of "Spookery". Bill Pronzini. LC 81-71682. 1982. 13.95 (ISBN 0-87795-391-0); pap. 6.95 (ISBN 0-87795-403-8). Arbor Hse.

Specter Is Haunting Texas. Fritz Leiber. LC 69-13140. 1969. 4.95. Walker.

Specter Is Haunting Texas. Fritz Leiber. 1978. 1.95 (ISBN 0-87997-359-5). DAW Books.

Specter of Dolphin Cove. Katheryn Kimbrough. (Queen-size gothic). 1973. (pbk.) 0.95. Popular Library.

Specter of the Dunes. Kate Ostrander. (Queen-size gothic). 1974. (pbk.) 0.95. Popular Library.

Spector. Marc David. 1970. 5.95 o.p. (ISBN 0-684-10105-X). Scribner.

Spector: A Novel. Marc Davis. LC 74-106539. 1970. 5.95. Scribner.

Spectral Bride. Margaret Campbell. (Signet book). 1975. (pbk.) 1.25. New American Library.

Spectral Bride. Joseph Shearing & Roughead, William, 1870- The Ambiguities of Miss Smith. LC 42-19355. 1942. Smith & Durrell, Inc.

Spectral Mist. Clarissa Ross, pseud. 1972. pap. 0.95 o.p. (75-348). Lancer.

Spectral Santa Claus: And Other Christmas Stories, by Harold T. Davis and Agnes M. Davis. Illus. by Vera Fisher and Helen Dagmar Davis. Harold Thayer Davis & Agnes M. Davis. LC 67-30473. 1967. Naylor Co.

Spectral Santa Claus, and Other Christmas Stories. Harold Thayer Davis & Agnes M. Davis. LC 67-30473. (Illus.). 1967. Naylor Co.

Spectre Bridegroom and Other Horrors. R. Reginald & Douglas Alver Menville. LC 75-46305. (Supernatural and Occult Fiction). (Illus.). 1976. 17.00 (ISBN 0-405-08165-0). Arno Press.

Spectre Lover. Emma Dorothy Eliza Nevitte Southworth & Frances Henshaw Baden. LC 8-10836. 1875. T. B. Peterson & Brothers.

Spectre of Masuria. Charles Stanley Strong. LC 32-251694. 1932. The Caxton Printers, Ltd.

Spectre of Power. Mary Noailles Murfree. LC 3-129663. 1903. Houghton, Mifflin and Company.

Spectre of the Forest: Or, Annals of the Housatonic, a New-England Romance. James Mohenry. LC 1-17015. 1823. E. Bliss and E. White.

Spectre Spread. Fred East. LC 48-774938. 1948. E. P. Dutton.

Spectre Steamer, and Other Tales. Joseph Holt Ingraham. LC 7-9718. 1846. United States Publishing Company.

Spectre Two: A Collection of Stories of the Supernatural. Ed. by Richard Davis. 1977. 8.95 o.s.i. (ISBN 0-8277-5422-1). British Bk Ctr.

Spectre's Secret. A Novel. Sylvanus Cobb. (On cover: The popular series, no. 20). 1892. R. Bonner's Sons.

Spectre's Secret: A Novel. Sylvanus Cobb. LC 99-1413. (On cover: Ledger library, no. 140). 1899. R. Bonner's Sons.

Spectres, Spooks and Shuddery Shades. Helen Hoke & Charles Keeping. LC 78-310518. (Illus.). 1977. 3.50 (ISBN 0-85166-620-5). F. Watts.

Spectrum. David Wise. LC 80-17418. 1981. 12.95 (ISBN 0-670-66219-4). Viking Press.

Spectrum: A Science Fiction Anthology. 1- Ed. by Amis, Kingsley & Conquest, Robert. LC 63-13497. Harcourt, Brace & World.

Spectrum; a Science Fiction Anthology. 1- Ed. by Kingsley Amis & Robert Conquest. LC 63-13497. Harcourt, Brace & World.

Spectrum of a Forgotten Sun. E. C. Tubb. (Science Fiction Ser.: Dumarest No. 15). 1976. pap. 1.25 o.p. (ISBN 0-87997-265-3, UY1265). DAW Bks.

Spectrum of a Forgotten Sun. E C Tubb (ISBN 0-87997-265-3). Daw Books.

Spectrum of Worlds. Ed. by Thomas D. Clareson. LC 72-76139. (Doubleday science fiction). 1972. 5.95. Doubleday.

Speculation. A Novel. Julia Pardoe. LC 7-35602. 1834. Harper & Brothers.

Speculations. Isaac Asimov & Alice Laurance. LC 81-13369. 1982. 12.95 (ISBN 0-395-32065-8). Houghton Mifflin.

Speculations About Jakob. Uwe Johnson. LC 62-17528. 1963. Grove Press.

Speculations: Fantasy - Science Fiction. Thomas E. Sanders. LC 72-86794. 608p. 1973. pap. text ed. 8.95x (ISBN 0-02-477630-0). Macmillan.

Speculations of John Steele. Robert Barr. LC 5-32732. 1905. F. A. Stokes Company.

Speculator: A Story. Clinton Ross. LC 8-673. 1891. G. P. Putnam's Sons.

Speculator in Petticoats. Hector Henri Malot & Sherwood, Mrs. Mary (Neal) Tr. LC 7-24359. T. B. Peterson & Brothers.

Speculators. John Gerstine. LC 63-12063. 1963. Crown Publishers.

Sped Arrow. Valerie Watkinson, pseud. LC 64-11011. 1964. Scribner.

Speech for Life. Illus. by Alison Taylor. Christabel Burniston. LC 66-16687. (Commonwealth & intl. lib., C.S.E. div.). bds., 4.95. Pergamon.

Speeches of Prime Minister Shastri, June 1964-May 1965. L. B. Shastri. 1965. 5.00x (ISBN 0-8426-1499-0). Verry.

Speed. William Burroughs, Jr. pap. 1.25 o.s.i. (OPS-2). Olympia.

Speed Boat. Renata Adler. 1978. 1.95 (ISBN 0-445-04192-7). Popular Library.

Speed Bunnies. Barney Stewart. 1973. (pbk.) 1.95. Brandon Books.

Speed of Light. Gwyneth Cravens. LC 79-17778. 9.95 (ISBN 0-671-25127-9). Simon and Schuster.

Speedboat. Renata Adler. LC 76-14919. (ISBN 0-394-48876-8). Random House.

Speedwell Sketches. 2d Ed. Lawrence Edwards. LC 52-8907. B. Humphries.

Speedy. Max Brand. LC 55-6200. 1974. (pbk.) 0.95. Warner Paperback Library.

Speedy. Frederick Faust. 1974. (pbk.) 0.95. Warner Paperback Library.

Speedy. Russell Holman. LC 28-11052. Grosset & Dunlap.

Speedy Death. Gladys Mitchell. LC 29-19243. L. MacVeagh, The Dial Press.

Speedy Finds Happiness. Naomi Derrick. 1980. 4.95 (ISBN 0-533-04525-8). Vantage.

Spell. William Dana Orcutt. LC 9-2773. 1909. 1.20. Harper & Brothers.

Spell: A Novel. Gustav Breuer. LC 50-11620. 1951. Houghton Mifflin.

Spell, an Extravaganza. Charlotte Bronte. Ed. by George Edwin MacLean. LC 72-191958. 1972. Folcroft Library Editions.

Spell: An Extravaganza. Charlotte Bronte. LC 32-4222. 1931. H. Milford, Oxford University Press.

Spell: An Extravaganza: an Unpublished Novel. Charlotte Bronte. LC 75-28396. 1975. 20.00 (ISBN 0-88305-865-0). Norwood Editions.

Spell: An Extraveganza. Charlotte Bronte. 1979. Repr. of 1931 ed. lib. bdg. 20.00 (ISBN 0-8495-0511-9). Arden Lib.

Spell for Chameleon. Piers Anthony, pseud. LC 77-1666. 1977. 1.95 (ISBN 0-345-25855-X). Ballantine Books.

Spell for Old Bones. Eric Robert Russell Linklater. LC 77-84250. (Lost Race and Adult Fantasy Fiction). 1978. 15.00 (ISBN 0-405-10996-2). Arno Press.

Spell Is Cast. Eleanor Cameron. (gr. 5-7). 1974. pap. 1.25 o.s.i. (ISBN 0-671-29586-1). Archway.

Spell Is Cast. Eleanor Cameron. (gr. 5-7). 1974. pap. 1.25 o.s.i. (ISBN 0-671-29586-1). Archway.

Spell Land: The Story of a Sussex Farm. Sheila Kaye-Smith. LC 27-2566. 1926. E. P. Dutton & Company.

Spell of Ashtaroth. Duffield Osborne. LC 7-23177. 1888. C. Scribner's Sons.

Spell of Egypt: A Novel. Victoria Wolf & Demuth, Dora H., Tr. LC 43-3877. 1943. L. B. Fischer.

Spell of Mary Stewart: Three Complete Books. Mary Stewart. LC 68-1348. (Illus.). 1968. N. Doubleday.

Spell of Sarnia. Gertrude M. Robins Reynolds. LC 25-19165. George H. Doran Company.

Spell of Seven. Lyon Sprague De Camp. 1969. pap. 0.75 o.p. (T2133). Pyramid Pubns.

Spell of Siris. Muriel Hine Coxon. LC 23-17384. 1923. 2.00. Dodd, Mead and Company.

Spell of the Desert. Samuel Anthony Peeples. LC 51-6943. (Dutton Diamond D western). 1951. Dutton.

Spell of the Witch World. Andre Norton, pseud. LC 77-23206. (Norton, Andre. The Witch Would Novels of Andre Norton). 1977. 7.95 (ISBN 0-8398-2354-1). Gregg Press.

Spell of Time: A Tale of Love in Jerusalem. Meyer Levin. LC 74-8050. (Illus.). 1974. 5.95. Praeger.

Spell of Ursula. Effie Adelaide Maria Albanesi. LC 7-12331. (On cover: Lippincott's select novels, no. 164). 1894. J. B. Lippincott Company.

Spell Sword. Marion Zimmer Bradley. LC 78-21231. (Gregg Press Science fiction series). (Illus.). 1979. 8.00 (ISBN 0-8398-2503-X). Gregg Press.

Spell Sword: A Darkover Novel. Marion Zimmer Bradley. (Science Fiction Ser). pap. 1.95 (ISBN 0-87997-675-6, UJ1675). DAW Bks.

Spell Sword: A Darkover Novel. Marion Zimmer Bradley. (Science Fiction Ser.). 160p. (Orig.). 1974. pap. 0.95 o.p. (UQ1131). DAW Bks.

Spell Sword: A Darkover Novel. Marion Zimmer Bradley. 1974. (pbk.) 0.95. DAW Books.

Spella Ho. Herbert Ernest Bates. LC 38-32625. 1938. Little, Brown and Company.

Spellbinder. Seth Kohlhaas. 240p. (Orig.). 1982. pap. 2.75 (ISBN 0-8439-1024-0, Leisure Bks). Nordon Pubns.

Spellbinder. Harold Robbins. LC 82-10291. 14.50 (ISBN 0-671-41634-0). Simon and Schuster.

Spellbinder. Leonard Rossiter. LC 28-7750. E. P. Dutton & Company.

Spellbinder. Collin Wilcox. 256p. 1981. pap. 2.50 (ISBN 0-449-14436-4). Fawcett.

Spellbinders. Margaret Culkin Banning. LC 22-188582. George H. Doran Company.

Spellbound. Jayne Castle. (Candlelight Ecstasy Ser.: No. 91). (Orig.). 1982. pap. 1.95 (ISBN 0-440-18034-1). Dell.

Spellbound. Margaret Way. (Harlequin Romances Ser.). 192p. 1983. pap. 1.75 (ISBN 0-373-02537-8). Harlequin Bks.

Spellbound Fiddler: A Norse Romance. Kristofer Nagel Janson. Tr. by Moore, Annie Aubertine (Woodward) Anderson, Rasmus Bjorn. LC 10-22198. 1884. S. C. Griggs and Company.

Spellbound Village: A Novel. Julia Truitt Yenni. LC 51-11574. 1951. Harcourt, Brace.

Spellcoats. Diana W. Jones. 1980. pap. 2.25 (ISBN 0-671-83599-8, Timescape). PB.

Spells of Evil. Pierre Boileau & Thomas Narcejac. 1961. 3.50x o.p. Verry.

Spells of Evil: By Boileau-Narcejac. Tr. from French by Daphne Woodward. Pierre Boileau & Thomas Narcejac. LC 66-2804. 1966. bds., 2.50. H. Hamilton.

Spells of Lamazee. James S. White. LC 82-14578. 1982. limited signed 60.00 (ISBN 0-932576-13-3); pap. 8.95 (ISBN 0-932576-12-5). Breitenbush Pubns.

Spellsinger. Alan Dean Foster. 288p. 1983. pap. 2.95 (ISBN 0-446-90352-3). Warner Bks.

Spellstone of Shaltus. Linda E. Bushyager. (Orig.). 1980. pap. 1.95 (ISBN 0-440-18274-3). Dell.

Spence and the Holiday Murders. Michael Derek Allen. LC 78-51976. 1978. 7.95 (ISBN 0-8027-5390-6). Walker.

Spence at the Blue Bazaar. Michael Derek Allen. LC 79-64148. 1979. 7.95 (ISBN 0-8027-5408-2). Walker.

Spencer Brade, M.D. Frank Gill Slaughter. 375p. 1975. Repr. of 1942 ed. lib. bdg. 18.55x (ISBN 0-89190-287-2). Am Repr-Rivercity Pr.

Spencer Brade, M.D. A Novel. Frank Gill Slaughter. LC 75-31975. 1975-1976. 9.95 (ISBN 0-89190-287-2). American Reprint Co.

Spencer Brade: M.D., a Novel. Frank Gill Slaughter. LC 42-7503. 1942. Doubleday, Doran and Company, Inc.

Spencer Holst Stories. Spencer Holst. LC 75-37062. (Illus.). 6.95 (ISBN 0-8180-0622-6). Horizon Press.

Spencer Problem. E. W. Nash. 1969. pap. 0.75 o.p. (0502-07047-075). Curtis.

Spencer Problem: A Novel. Edmund W Nash. LC 66-111756. 4.95. Doubleday.

Spencers: a Story of Home Influence. Paul Tynder. LC 30-12311. American Tract Society.

Spencer's Bag. William M. Green. LC 78-139622. (Inner sanctum mystery). 1971. 4.95 (ISBN 0-671-20835-7). Simon and Schuster.

Spencer's Mountain. Earl Hammur. 1973. (pbk) 0.95. Dell.

Spencer's Mountain. Earl Hamner. LC 61-15508. 1961. Dial Press.

Spend Game. Jonathan Gash, pseud. LC 80-26266. 1981. 8.95 (ISBN 0-89919-030-8). Ticknor & Fields.

Spend Game. Jonathan Gash, pseud. LC 81-19271. 1982. 2.95 (ISBN 0-14-006190-8). Penguin Books.

Spend It Foolishly. Mary Gallagher. LC 77-23661. 1978. 10.95 (ISBN 0-689-10859-1). Atheneum.

Spend It Foolishly. Mary Gallagher. 1979. 2.25 (ISBN 0-380-46011-4). Avon Books.

Spend the Night. Stephen Gould Fisher. LC 35-8474. Phoenix Press.

Spend the Night. Stephen Gould Fisher & Stephen Gould Fisher. LC 35-15042. Phoenix Press.

Spend Your Heart. Alice Margaret Huggins & Robinson, Hugh Laughlin. LC 65-10771. 1965. Westminster Press.

Spenders: A Tale of the Third Generation. Harry Leon Wilson. LC 2-16003. 1902. Lothrop Publishing Company.

Spendthrift: By Porter Emerson Browne; a Story of American Life, Novelized from the Play. Edward Marshall. LC 10-25791. 1.50. G. W. Dillingham Company.

Spendthrift Town: A Novel. Henry Hudson. LC 20-22444. 1920. Houghton Mifflin Company.

Spendthrifts. Perez Galdos, Benito. LC 52-905837. (illustrated novel library). (Illus.). 1952. Farrar, Straus & Young.

Spendthrifts. Benito Perez Galdos. 1978. Repr. of 1952 ed. lib. bdg. 30.00 (ISBN 0-8495-1919-5). Arden Lib.

Spenlove in Arcady. William McFee. LC 41-51993. Random House.

Spenser's Art: A Companion to Book One of the Faerie Queene. Mark Rose. LC 74-21229. 160p. 1975. text ed. 8.95x (ISBN 0-674-83193-4). Harvard U Pr.

Spenser's "Faerie Queene" & the Cult of Elizabeth. Robin H. Wells. LC 82-11568. 192p. 1982. text ed. 27.50x (ISBN 0-389-20324-6). B&N Imports.

Spent, a Novel. Russell Murphy. LC 81-68148. (Illus.). 1981. 9.95 (ISBN 0-935304-27-4) (ISBN 0-935304-28-2). August House.

Sperry Stories. Arthur Sperry. LC 8-14067. (Potomac series, no. 2). 1894. H. B. Sperry.

Sphereland. Dionys Burger. Tr. by Cornelie J. Rheinboldt from Fr. (Illus.). 224p. 1983. pap. 4.76i (ISBN 0-06-463574-0, EH 574). B&N NY.

Sphinx. Florence Converse. LC 31-1200. E. P. Dutton & Co., Inc.

Sphinx. Robin Cook. LC 79-1071. 10.95 (ISBN 0-399-12328-8). Putnam.

Sphinx. Robin Cook. LC 79-23076. 1979. 13.95 (ISBN 0-8161-3014-0). G. K. Hall.

Sphinx. Robin Cook. (Signet Book.). 1980. 2.95 (ISBN 0-451-09194-9). New American Library.

Sphinx. Graham Masterton. 1978. pap. 2.95 (ISBN 0-523-48067-9). Pinnacle Bks.

Sphinx Has Spoken. Maurice DeKobra, pseud. Tr. by Wood, Metcalfe. LC 30-321409. Brewer and Warren, Inc.

Sphinx in Aubrey Parish: A Novel. Nathan Henry Chamberlain. LC 6-23544. (Half-title: The Algonquin press library... v. 2). 1889. Cupples and Hurd.

Sphinx in the Labyrinth. Maude Annesley. LC 13-12598. 1913. Duffield & Company.

Sphinx of Eaglehawk: A Tale of Old Bendigo. Thomas Alexander Browne. LC 6-172243. 1895. Macmillan and Co.

Sphinx: Or, Striving with Destiny. A Novel, Tr. from the German of Robert Byr Pseud. by Auber Forestier Pseud. Robert Von Bayer & Moore, Mrs. Annie Aubertine (Woodward) 1841- Tr. LC 6-10359. 1871. G. Maclean.

Sphinx Smiles Twice. Antigone Maroudis. 1976. 8.00x; pap. 6.75x. Intl Learn Syst.

Sphinx Wore an Orchid. Marian Cox. 3.95 o.p. Vantage.

Sphinx's Children and Other People. Rose Terry Cooke. LC 69-11884. (American short story series, v. 42). 1969. Garrett Press.

Sphinx's Children and Other People's. Rose Terry Cooke. LC 4-23600. 1886. Ticknor and Company.

Sphinx's Children: And Other People's. Rose Terry Cooke. LC 4-15085. Houghton Mifflin and Company.

Sphinx's Lawyer. Julia Davis Frankau. LC 6-21385. 1906. F. A. Stokes Company.

Spice Box. Grace Livingston Hill. LC 43-2713. 1943. J. B. Lippincott Company.

Spice Box. Grace Livingston Hill. 1974. (pbk.) 0.95. Bantam Books.

Spice-Box Earth. Leonard Cohen. 1965. 3.75 o.p. (ISBN 0-670-66261-5). Viking Pr.

Spice of Life. Gilbert Keith Chesterton. 1966. 4.50 o.p. Dufour.

Spice of Life. Berta Ruck. LC 52-10156. 1952. Dodd, Mead.

Spicy. A Novel. Martha Joanna Read Nash Lamb. LC 7-14112. 1873. D. Appleton and Company.

Spicy: Breezes from Minnesota Prairies. Boston W Smith. American Baptist Publication Society.

Spicy Lady. Joseph A Daley. LC 73-77762. 1973. 6.95. St. Martin's Press.

Spider. Grace Perkins Oursler & Oursler, Fulton. LC 29-7394. Grosset & Dunlap.

Spider. Marguerite Steen. LC 33-313841. 1933. Little, Brown, and Company.

Spider: And Other Tales. Carl Ewald. Tr. by Teixeira De Mattos, Alexander Louis. LC 7-15116. 1907. C. Scribner's Sons.

Spider & Other Tales. Carl Ewald. Repr. of 1907 ed. 7.50 o.p. (ISBN 0-89987-104-6). Darby Bks.

Spider and the Fly. Graham Lord. LC 74-6849. 1975. 7.95 (ISBN 0-670-66269-0). Viking Press.

Spider and the Fly. Lily Clive Nutt. LC 28-29729. The Bobbs-Merrill Company.

Spider and the Fly. Robert Alfred John Walling. LC 40-127399. 1940. W. Morrow & Company.

Spider and the Fly: Cinq Mars) Alfred Victor Vigny. LC 76-48463. (Classics of European Literature). (Hyperion library of world literature). 1977. 13.95. (ISBN 0-88355-620-0) (ISBN 0-88355-621-9). Hyperion Press.
Spider Boy: A Scenario for a Moving Picture. Carl Van Vechten. LC 28-19963. 1928. A. A. Knopf.
Spider Girl. Peter Lear. 300p. 1980. 10.95 o.p. (ISBN 0-670-66274-7). Viking Pr.
Spider Girl. Peter Lovesey. LC 80-14713. 1980. 10.95 (ISBN 0-670-66274-7). Viking Press.
Spider House. Francis Van Wyck Mason. LC 33-21385. 1932. The Mystery League, Inc.
Spider in the Cup. Joseph Shearing. LC 34-5282. 1934. H. Smith and R. Haas.
Spider in the Morning. Duff Hart-Davis. LC 70-171296. 1972. 5.95 o.p. (ISBN 0-385-00580-6). Doubleday.
Spider in the Morning: A Suspense Novel. Hart-Davis, Duff. LC 70-171296. 1972. 5.95. Doubleday.
Spider King: A Biographical Novel of Louis XI of France. Lawrence L Schoonover. LC 54-693. 1954. Macmillan.
Spider King: A Biographical Novel of Louis Xi of France. Lawrence L Schoonover. LC 65-87309. 1954. Macmillan.
Spider Lily... Bruno Fischer. LC 46-6086. 1946. David McKay Company.
Spider Love: A Novel. 1st Ed. Samuel Hilburn. LC 62-531124. 1962. Exposition Press.
Spider-Men: A Science-Fantasy Short Novel. Ralph Annan. 1979. 5.95 o.p. (ISBN 0-533-03684-4). Vantage.
Spider of Brooklyn Heights. Nancy Veglahn. LC 67-15493. (Illus.). 1967. Scribner.
Spider of the Mind: A Novel. Cole Atwood. LC 54-11791. 1955. Chapman & Grimes.
Spider of Truxillo. The Passing Show); Exciting Adventures on Land and Sea. Richard Henry Savage. (On cover: Neely's popular library, no. 53). 1895. F. T. Neely.
Spider-Orchid. Celia Fremlin, pseud. LC 77-92212. 1978. 6.95 (ISBN 0-385-14052-5). Published for the Crime Club by Doubleday.
Spider Stone. Eleanor Elford Cameron, pseud. 1973. (pbk.) 0.95. Dell.
Spider Strikes: A Detective Story. John Innes Mackintosh Stewart. LC 39-31413. 1939. Dodd, Mead & Company.
Spider Web. 2nd ed. T. D. Hallam. LC 80-25024. (Great War Stories Ser.). (Illus.). 278p. Repr. of 1919 ed. 15.95 (ISBN 0-933852-19-3). Nautical & Aviation.
Spider Web. Marjorie Muir Worthington. LC 30-3235. J. Cape and H. Smith.
Spider Woman Stories. G. M. Mullett. LC 78-11556. 1979. 11.95 o.p. (ISBN 0-8165-0669-8); pap. 7.50 (ISBN 0-8165-0621-3). U of Ariz Pr.
Spiders. Richard Lewis. (YA) 1980. pap. 1.75 (ISBN 0-451-09250-3, E9250, Sig). NAL.
Spiders and Rice Pudding. Sarah G Barbour. LC 6-7214. (On cover: Satchel series no. 18). The Authors' Publishing Company.
Spider's House. Paul Frederic Bowles. LC 55-816920. 1955. Random House.
Spider's Parlour. Patrick Wynnton. LC 33-11088. 1933. Longmans, Green and Co.
Spider's Touch: A Clubfoot Story. Valentine Williams. LC 36-19838. 1936. Houghton Mifflin Company.
Spiders' War: A Fantasy Novel. Sydney Fowler Wright. LC 54-5233. 1954. Abelard Press.
Spider's Web. Reginald Wright Kauffman. LC 13-237351. 1913. 1.35. Moffat, Yard and Company.
Spider's Web. Joseph Nazel. (Orig.). 1978. pap. 1.75 (ISBN 0-87067-541-9, BH541). Holloway.
Spider's Web. St. George Rathborne. (On cover: The Eagle library, no. 71). Street & Smith.
Spider's Web. Mansfield Scott. LC 29-177312. E. J. Clode, Inc.
Spiderweb. Robert Bloch. LC 54-31249. (Ace double novel books, D-59). 1954. Ace Books.
Spiderweb. Alice Ormond Campbell. LC 41-6690. (On cover: Penguin books. 142). 1940. Penguin Books Limited.
Spiderweb. Joseph E Persico. LC 79-14102. 10.00 (ISBN 0-517-53925-X). Crown Publishers.
Spiderweb Clues. Paul Thorne. LC 28-40709. 1928. The Penn Publishing Company.
Spiderweb Ridge. Walt Coburn. 1978. pap. 1.25 o.s.i. (ISBN 0-8439-0539-5, Leisure Bks). Nordon Pubns.
Spiderweb Trail: A Texas Ranger Novel. Eugene Cunningham. LC 40-31871. 1940. Houghton Mifflin Company.
Spiegel der Zeit. Paulene H. Roth & M. L. Nielsen. (Ger). 1960. pap. 3.50x o.p. (3-48840). HM.
Spiegel the Cat. David Lozell Martin. (Illus.). 1971. 3.95 o.p. Potter.
Spieler for the Holy Spirit: A Novel. David Chagall. LC 72-78505. (Illus.). 1972. 7.95 (ISBN 0-87949-003-9). Ashley Books.
Spies. Thea Von Harbou & Stiegler, Helen J., Tr. LC 29-1962. 1929. G. P. Putnam's Sons.
Spies. Scott C. S Stone. LC 79-27137. 10.00 (ISBN 0-312-75230-X). St. Martin's Press.
Spies Among Us. Agatha Miller Christie. LC 68-24023. 1968. Dodd, Mead.
Spies and Intrigues: The Oppenheim Secret Service Omnibus. Edward Phillips Oppenheim. 1936. Little, Brown, and Company.
Spies and More Spies. Ed. by Robert Arthur. LC 67-20604. (Illus.). 1967. Random House.
Spies, Inc. Jack D Hunter. LC 69-13337. 1969. 5.50. Dutton.
Spies of Good Intent. Gabriel Veraldi. LC 68-12548. 1969. 5.95. Atheneum.
Spike. Charles Badger Clark. LC 25-8375. R. G. Badger.
Spike. Arnaud De Borchgrave & Robert Moss. LC 79-25705. 12.95 (ISBN 0-517-53624-2). Crown Publishers.
Spikebit. Sam Victor. (Berkley medallion book). 1974. (pbk.) 0.95 (ISBN 0-425-02683-3). Berkley Pub. Co.
Spiked Heel: By Richard Marsten Pseud. 1st Ed. Evan Hunter. LC 56-10516. 1956. Holt.
Spiked Lion: An Anthony Bathurst Story. Brian Flynn. LC 34-142318. 1934. Macrae Smith Company.
Spikes Gang. Giles Tippette. LC 70-117966. 1974. (pbk.) 1.25 (ISBN 0-671-78431-5). Pocket Books.
Spiks. Pedro Juan Soto. Tr. & intro. by Victoria Ortiz. LC 73-8057. 96p. 1974. pap. 4.50 (ISBN 0-85345-331-4, PB3314). Monthly Rev.
Spiks: Stories. Pedro Juan Soto. LC 73-8057. 1973. 6.50 (ISBN 0-85345-299-7). Monthly Review Press.
Spill the Jackpot! A. A. Fair, pseud. LC 41-520645. 1941. W. Morrow & Company.
Spill the Jackpot! Erle Stanley Gardner. LC 41-5296. 1941. W. Morrow.
Spilled Wine. St. John-Loe, Gladys. LC 23-43593. 1923. T. Seltzer.
Spillway. Djuna Barnes. LC 73-152892. (Harper colophon Books, CN 282). 1972. 2.25 (ISBN 0-06-090282-5). Harper & Row.
Spilt Milk. John Daniel. 1977. pap. 1.00 o.p. (ISBN 0-931832-09-8). No Dead Lines.
Spin a Dream. Cynthia Millburn, pseud. (Contemporary Teens Ser.). 224p. (Orig.). 1981. pap. 2.25 (ISBN 0-89531-142-9, 0146-96). Sharon Pubns.
Spin a Yarn, Sailor. Aylward Edward Dingle. LC 35-12197. 1935. J. B. Lippincott Company.
Spin the Glass Web. Max Simon Ehrlich. LC 51-11906. 1952. Harper.
Spin Your Web, Lady! A Captain Heimrich Myster. Richard Lockridge & Frances Louise Davis Lockridge. LC 49-746814. (Main line mysteries). 1949. J. B. Lippincott Co.
Spinach and Reconcilation. Edward Frederic Benson. LC 24-222763. George H. Doran Company.
Spindle & Plough. Alice Dudeney. LC 1-24574. 1901. Dodd, Mead & Co.
Spindle and Plough. Alice Dudeney. LC 2-8860. 1902. Dodd, Mead & Company.
Spindrift. Jesse Lenard Lasky. LC 48-154379. 1948. Prentice-Hall.
Spindrift. Phyllis A. Whitney. LC 74-14384. 1975. 7.95. (ISBN 0-385-08454-4). Doubleday.
Spindrift. Phyllis A. Whitney. LC 75-17872. 1975. 13.95 (ISBN 0-8161-6312-X). G. K. Hall.
Spindrift. Phyllis A. Whitney. 1976. (pbk.) 1.95. Fawcett.
Spindrift: A Novel of the Great Lakes. by harold titus. ed. Harold Titus. LC 25-982414. 1925. Doubleday, Page & Company.
Spinnaker: A Novel. Ralph M McInerny. LC 77-81436. 8.95 (ISBN 0-89526-696-2). Gateway Editions.
Spinner. Doris Piserchia. (Science Fiction Ser.). 1980. pap. 1.95 (ISBN 0-87997-548-2, UJ1548). DAW Bks.
Spinner in the Sun. Myrtle Reed. LC 6-33577. 1906. G. P. Putnam's Sons.
Spinner in the Sun. Myrtle Reed. LC 9-32290. 1907. G. P. Putnam's Sons.
Spinner in the Sun. Myrtle Reed. LC 10-15483. 1909. G. P. Putnam's Sons.
Spinner of the Dream. 1st Ed. John H Secondari. LC 55-107623. 1955. Little, Brown.
Spinner of the Years. Phyllis Eleanor Bentley. LC 34-27171. 1934. The Macmillan Company.
Spinner of the Years. Phyllis Eleanor Bentley. LC 29-4995. Rae D. Henkle Co., Inc.
Spinner of Webs. Catharine Morris Plumer Bement. LC 19-183004. 1919. The Four Seas Company.
Spinners. Eden Phillpotts. LC 18-19511. 1918. The Macmillan Company.
Spinners' Book of Fiction. Gertrude Atherton et al. 1979. lib. bdg. 9.95 (ISBN 0-8398-2582-X, Gregg). G K Hall.
Spinners' Book of Fiction. Spinners' Club & Gertrude Franklin Horn Atherton. LC 79-16762. (Series: Gregg Press Western Fiction Series.). (Illus.). 1979. 9.95 (ISBN 0-8398-2582-X). Gregg Press.
Spinners' Book of Fiction. Spinners' Club & Atherton, Mrs. Gertrude Franklin (Horn) 1857- LC 7-32566. P. Elder and Company.
Spinners of Life. Vance Thompson. LC 3-6863. 1903. J. B. Lippincott Company.
Spinning Dust. Brainerd Beckwith. LC 29-551. 1928. W. Hebberd.
Spinning Target. Joseph Nazel. 1974. (pbk.) 1.50 (ISBN 0-87067-457-9). Holloway House Pub Co.
Spinoza. by berthold auerbach... from the german by e. nicholson... ed. Berthold Auerbach. Tr. by Nicholson, E. LC 6-4498. (Leisure hour series, no. 135). 1882. H. Holt and Company.
Spinoza of Market Street. Isaac Bashevis Singer. LC 61-13676. 1961. Farrar, Straus & Cudahy.
Spinoza of Market Street & Other Stories. Isaac Bashevis Singer. Tr. by Elaine Gottleib et al. 1961. 8.95 (ISBN 0-374-26776-6); pap. 4.95 (ISBN 0-374-50256-0). FS&G.
Spinster. Sylvia Ashton-Warner. (O.s.i.). 1971. pap. 2.95 o.s.i. (ISBN 0-671-20916-7, Touchstone Bks). S&S.
Spinster. Hubert Wales. LC 12-16852. 1912. W. Rickey & Co.
Spinster: A Novel. Sylvia Ashton-Warner. 1959. Simon and Schuster.
Spinster: A Novel Wherein a Nineteenth Century Girl Finds Her Place in the Twentieth. Sarah Norcliffe Cleghorn. LC 16-90699. 1916. 1.35. H. Holt and Company.
Spinster & the Boys Next Door. Eric Anderson. 192p. (Orig.). 1973. pap. 1.95 o.p. (ISBN 0-87682-298-7, 7298). Barclay Hse.
Spinster & the Rake. Anne Stuart. (Candlelight Regency Ser.: No. 711). (Orig.). 1982. pap. 2.25 (ISBN 0-440-18597-1). Dell.
Spinster Farm. Helen Maria Winslow. 1908. L. C. Page & Company.
Spinster of This Parish. William Babington Maxwell. LC 22-16759. 1922. Dodd, Mead and Company.
Spinster of This Parish. William Babington Maxwell. LC 33-27402. 1933. Dodd, Mead & Company.
Spinsters in Jeopardy. Ngaio Marsh. LC 53-7306. 1953. Little, Brown.
Spinsters in Jeopardy. Ngaio Marsh. 1978. 1.75 (ISBN 0-425-03998-6). Berkley Publishing Corp.
Spinster's Leaflets. Wherein Is Written the History of Her "Doorstep Baby", a Fancy Which in Time Became a Fact and Changed a Life. Eugenia Laura Morris. 1894. Lee and Shepard.
Spinster's Progress: A New Novel. Berta Ruck. LC 42-4614. 1942. Dodd, Mead & Company.
Spinster's Story. Mary Ann Fisher. LC 6-41212. 1866. Carleton.
Spira, a Novel: Written to Encourage and Inspire, in the Hope That Some Good Will Result from It. Monroe E Miller. LC 41-28266. Press of H. L. & J. B. McQueen, Inc.
Spiral of Mist. Michele Prisco. LC 69-10299. 1969. 5.95. Dutton.
Spiral Road. Jan De Hartog. 465p. 1976. Repr. of 1957 ed. lib. bdg. 17.95x (ISBN 0-89244-092-9). Queens Hse.
Spiral Road. 1st Ed. Jan De Harteg. LC 56-12237. 1957. Harper.
Spiral: the World of Alan Brett. Robert Garrett. LC 72-78286. 1972. 4.95 (ISBN 0-689-10513-4). Atheneum.
Spirals. Aaron Marc Stein. LC 30-3228. 1930. Covici, Friede.
Spire. Gerald Warner Brace. 380p. 1976. Repr. of 1952 ed. lib. bdg. 11.95x o.p. Queens Hse.
Spire. William Gerald Golding. LC 63-15314. 1964. Harcourt, Brace & World.
Spire: A Novel. Gerald Warner Brace. LC 52-11303. 1952. Norton.
Spirit. Thomas Page. LC 77-77000. 1977. 8.95 (ISBN 0-89256-032-0). Rawson Associates.
Spirit and the Bride. 1st Ed. Harold J Kaplan. LC 51-6204. 1951. Harper.
Spirit and the Clay. 1st Ed. Shevawn Lynam. LC 54-6862. 1954. Little, Brown.
Spirit & the Flesh. J. D. Hardin. LC 80-80990. (J.D. Hardin Ser.: No. 7). 208p. (Orig.). 1980. pap. 1.95 (ISBN 0-87216-869-7). Playboy Pbks.
Spirit and the Flesh: A Novel Inspired by the Life of Isadora Duncan. David Weiss. LC 59-13659. 1959. Doubleday.
Spirit Hand. Robert Stern. LC 78-11247. 1978. cloth 15.50 (ISBN 0-916906-14-0); signed ed 30.00 (ISBN 0-916906-15-9); pap. 10.00 (ISBN 0-916906-13-2). Konglomerati.
Spirit Hedi. Maria Akiya. 200p. (Orig.). 1975. pap. 3.95 o.p. (ISBN 0-917200-11-X). ESPress.
Spirit Horses. Lou Cameron. LC 76-7059. 1976. 1.25 (ISBN 0-345-24915-1). Ballantine Books.
Spirit in Prison. Robert Smythe Hichens. LC 8-25367. 1908. Harper & Brothers.
Spirit Lake. Arthur Henry Howard Heming. LC 7-21229. 1907. The Macmillan Company.
Spirit Lake. 1st Ed. MacKinlay Kantor. LC 61-8164. 1961. World Pub. Co.
Spirit of an Illinois Town: And The Little Rensault; Two Stories of Illinois at Different Periods. Mary Hartwell Catherwood. LC 6-201723. 1897. Houghton, Mifflin and Company.
Spirit of Atlantis. Anne Mather. (Harlequin Presents). (Orig.). 1980. pap. 1.50 (ISBN 0-373-10351-4, Pub. by Harlequin). PB.
Spirit of Bambatse: A Romance. Henry Rider Haggard. LC 6-27709. 1906. Longmans, Green, and Co.
Spirit of Bambatse: A Romance. Henry Rider Haggard. LC 79-15278. (Newcastle Forgotten Fantasy library; 22). 1979. 10.95. (ISBN 0-87877-521-8) (ISBN 0-87877-121-2). Newcastle Pub. Co.
Spirit of Bambatse: A Romance. Henry Rider Haggard. LC 80-19674. (Newcastle Forgotten Fantasy library; v. 22). 1980. 11.95. Borgo Press.
Spirit of Brynmaster Oaks. Anne J Griffin. (Avon gothic original). 1974. (pbk.) 0.95 (ISBN 0-380-00037-7). Avon.
Spirit of Cove Island. Ruth McCarthy Sear. (YA) 1972. 4.50 o.p. (Avalon). Bouregy.
Spirit of Cove Island. Ruth McCarthy Sear. 1975. pap. 0.95 o.s.i. (LB263NK, Leisure Bks). Nordon Pubns.
Spirit of Dorsai. Gordon R Dickson. LC 79-124167. (Illus.). 1979. 5.95 (ISBN 0-441-77802-X). Ace Books.
Spirit of Fog Island. Margaret Sutton. (Judy Bolton Mysteries). 1976. Repr. of 1951 ed. lib. bdg. 12.95x (ISBN 0-88411-713-8). Amereon Ltd.
Spirit-of-Iron (Manitou-Pewabic) An Authentic Novel of the North-West Mounted Police. Harwood Elmes Robert Steele. LC 23-13312. 2.00. George H. Doran Company.
Spirit of Melissa Norgate. Elizabeth E. Mande. pap. 0.75 o.p. (T2617). Pyramid Pubns.
Spirit of Mirth. Peggy Webling. LC 11-225494. 1911. E. P. Dutton and Company.
Spirit of Penn." A Tale Founded Upon the Faith of the Quakers... Charles Edward Hewitt. LC 9-17585. J. S. Ogilvie Publishing Company.
Spirit of Poor Fork. Lee Pennington. 1976. pap. 1.00 (ISBN 0-915216-07-8). Love Street.
Spirit of Revolt. Philip Hamilton Gibbs. LC 26-13014. 1926. Methuen & Co.
Spirit of Service and Other Stories. Ross Ellis. LC 15-4584. 1914. The Inland Trade Press Company.
Spirit of Seventeen Seventy-Six. Ed. by Peter Seymour. LC 77-157754. (Illus.). 64p. 1972. 2.50 o.p. (ISBN 0-87529-212-7). Hallmark.
Spirit of Sunrise. Bill Bahan et al. 192p. 1980. 16.00x (ISBN 0-7051-0270-X, Pub. by Skilton & Shaw England); pap. 6.00x (ISBN 0-7051-0271-8). State Mutual Bk.
Spirit of Sunrise. Michael Cecil et al. 1979. 7.00 (ISBN 0-7051-0270-X); pap. 2.95 (ISBN 0-7051-0271-8). Cole-Outreach.
Spirit of Sweetwater. Hamlin Garland. LC 7-3333. (Ladies' home journal library of fiction). Curtis Publishing Company.
Spirit of the Age. Channing, William Henry, 1810-1864, Ed. LC 1-19197. 1850. Fowlers & Wells.
Spirit of the Andes. Jose S. Chocano. Tr. by E. W. Underwood. 1977. lib. bdg. 59.95 (ISBN 0-8490-2660-1). Gordon Pr.
Spirit of the Border. Grey, Zane. LC 64-9041. (His Great western edition, 34). Grosset & Dunlap.
Spirit of the Border. Zane Grey. LC 82-17951. 1983. 13.95 (ISBN 0-89340-546-9). J. Curley.
Spirit of the Border: A Popular Condensation of a Story of Early Settlers in the Ohio Valley. Zane Grey. LC 50-33958. (Falcon books, A-51). 1950. World Pub. Co.
Spirit of the Border: A Romance of the Early Settlers in the Ohio Valley. Zane Grey. LC 6-20980. A. L. Burt Company.
Spirit of the Border: A Romance of the Early Settlers in the Ohio Valley. Zane Grey. LC 22-247482. 1916. A. L. Burt Company.
Spirit of the Border: An Abridged Edition of the Novel. Zane Grey. LC 40-10442. The Saalfield Publishing Company.
Spirit of the Border, Retold for Young Readers. Illustrated by Earl Sherwan. Zane Grey. LC 50-12231. 1950. Whitman Pub. Co.
Spirit of the Border: Retold for Young Readers; Illustrated by Earl Sherwan. Authorized Ed. Zane Grey. LC 54-370503. 1954. Whitman Pub. Co.
Spirit of the Chase. Illus. by Miross. Vasiliu. Robert Bright. LC 56-9470. 1956. Scribner.
Spirit of the Eagle. Merritt Parmelee Allen. LC 47-4699. 1947. Longmans, Green.
Spirit of the House. Anna Vernon Dorsey Williams. LC 24-11020. 1924. D. Appleton and Company.
Spirit of the Island. Joseph Hornor Coates. LC 11-112799. 1911. 1.25. Little, Brown, and Company.
Spirit of the Land. (Illus.). 64p. 1.00 o.p. Peoples Pr.

Spirit of the Pines. Margaret Fessenden Morse. LC 6-5134. 1906. Houghton, Mifflin & Company.
Spirit of the Rails: By Burton N. Brin and Richard S. Prosser. With Scratchboard Illus. by Marshall Thomas. Burton N Brin & Richard S. Prosser. LC 60-53652. 1960. West Colton Press.
Spirit of the Range. Bertha Muzzy Sinclair. LC 40-122687. 1940. Little, Brown and Company.
Spirit of the South. William Wallace Harney. LC 9-16472. 1909. R. G. Badger.
Spirit of the Time: A Novel of Today. Robert Smythe Hichens. LC 21-26414. George H. Doran Company.
Spirit of the Town: A Novel Presentation in Fiction Form of the Impulse and Desire Which Mould the Lives of Men. Clarence Aaron Robbins. LC 12-294742. J. S. Ogilvie Publishing Company.
Spirit of the Wild Rosebush: A Novel of the Pioneer Period of the Inland Empire. Albert J Laughon. LC 38-38715. 1938.
Spirit of the Winding Water: A Novel of the Epic 1877 Wilderness Plight of the Nez Perce Indians. Judy B. Hanson. 1979. 7.50 o.p. (ISBN 0-682-49345-7, Lochinvar). Exposition.
Spirit of '76: A Political Novel of the Near Future. Holmes Moss Alexander. LC 66-25069. 1966. Arlington House.
Spirit Returneth... A Novel. Selma Stern & Lewisohn, Ludwig, 1882- Tr. LC 46-7933. The Jewish Publication Society of America.
Spirit Rises: Stories. Sylvia Townsend Warner. LC 62-11675. 1962. Viking Press.
Spirit Run. Houston A. Baker, Jr. LC 81-82664. 38p. 1982. pap. 3.00 (ISBN 0-916418-35-9). Lotus.
Spirit Trail. Kate Boyles Bingham & Boyles, Virgil Dillin. LC 10-24900. 1910. 1.50. A. C. McClurg & Co.
Spirit Was Willing. Milton Luban. LC 51-11544. 1951. Greenberg.
Spirit Wrestler. James A. Houston. LC 79-1829. (Illus.). 12.50 (ISBN 0-15-184755-X). Harcourt Brace Jovanovich.
Spirit Wrestler. James A. Houston. 1981. 2.75 (ISBN 0-380-56911-6). Avon Books.
Spirite. Theophile Gautier. LC 76-1433. (Supernatural and Occult Fiction). (Series: Rialto series; no. 27-28.). 1976. 18.00 (ISBN 0-405-08419-6). Arno Press.
Spirite. Theophile Gautier. Tr. by Arthur D. Hall. 1890. Rand, McNally & Company.
Spirite: A Fantasy, from the French of Theophile Gautier. Theophile Gautier. LC 6-44267. (Half-title: Collection of foreign authors, no. 3). 1877. D. Appleton and Company.
Spiritmist. Herman Arthur Haubold. LC 9-12619. D. W. Newton.
Spirits Unchained: Paeans. Keorapetse Kgositsile. LC 71-78644. 1969. 1.00. Broadside Press.
Spiritual Adventures. Arthur Symons. LC 76-19996. (Decadent Consciousness). 1977-1978. 26.00 (ISBN 0-8240-2773-6). Garland Pub.
Spiritual Curiosities. Marian Metcalf Cox. LC 12-12138. 1911. 1.30. M. Kennerley.
Spiritual Divorce and Other Stories. Heather Ross Miller. LC 74-16654. 1974. 6.95 (ISBN 0-910244-82-0). J. F. Blair.
Spiritual Journey of Joel S. Goldsmith. Lorraine Sinkler. 1977. pap. 5.95i (RD 243, HarpR). Har-Row.
Spiritual Quixote. Richard Graves. LC 74-20651. (Flowering of the Novel). 1974. 25.00 (ISBN 0-8240-1201-1). Garland Pub.
Spiritual Quixote, or The Summer's Ramble of Mr. Geoffrey Wildgoose: A Comic Romance. Richard Graves. Ed. by Clarence Rupert Tracy. LC 67-93705. (Oxford English novels). (Illus.). 1967. Oxford U.P.
Spiritual Quixote: Or, The Summer's Ramble of Mr. Geoffry Wildgoose. A Comic Romance. To Which Is Prefixed the Life of the Author... Richard Graves. LC 6-45534. 1816. Robinson & Howland Etc.
Spit and the Stars. Robert Mende. LC 49-8053. 1949. Rinehart.
Spite of Heaven. Oliver Onions. LC 26-7448. George H. Doran Company.
Spite Wife. Ann Forester. LC 33-7379. 1933. L. MacVeagh, Dial Press, Inc.
Spitfire. Lindsay Armstrong. (Harlequin Romances Ser.). 192p. 1981. pap. 1.50 (ISBN 0-373-02443-6). Harlequin Bks.
Spitfire. Frederick Chamier. LC 6-20165. 1840. Carey and Hart.
Spitfire. Edward Henry Peple. 1908. Moffat, Yard and Company.
Spitfire. Barbara Phillips. (Orig.). 1981. pap. 1.95 (ISBN 0-8439-8044-3, Tiara Bks). Nordon Pubns.
Spitfire Pilot. Canfield Cook. LC 42-176397. Groseet & Dunlap.
Spitting Image. Michael Avallone. 1973. pap. 0.75 o.p. (07318). Curtis.
Spitting Image: A Novel of Suspense. 1st Ed. Michael Avallone. LC 53-8974. 1953. Holt.
Spitz: The Wandering Dog. Marianne Richter. LC 66-728285. 1966. 1.95, 2.50 lib. ed.,. Childrens.
Splash of Red. Antonia Fraser. LC 81-9543. 12.95 (ISBN 0-393-01511-4). W.W. Norton.
Splashing into Society. Iris Barry. LC 23-13654. E. P. Dutton & Company.
Spleen & Other Stories. Pierre-Victor Besenval. 10.00 o.p. Blom.
Splendid Californians. Sidney Herschel Small. LC 26-10829. The Bobbs-Merrill Company.
Splendid Chance. Mary Hastings Bradley. LC 15-11869. 1915. 1.30. D. Appleton and Company.
Splendid Cousin. Cecily Sidgwick. LC 8-6888. ("Unknown" library. 18). Cassell Publishing Co.
Splendid Earth. Victor J. Banis. 1979. 2.25 (ISBN 0-449-23835-0). Fawcett Crest.
Splendid Egotist: A Novel. Jeannette Ritchie Hadermann Walworth. LC 8-33129. Belford, Clarke & Company.
Splendid Egotist: A Novel. Jeannette Ritchie Hadermann Walworth. LC 3391. (On cover: Eagle library. no. 168). 1900. Street & Smith.
Splendid Fairing (Femina-Vie Heureuse Prize) Constance Holme. LC 38-272735. (On cover: The Oxford bookshelf). 1937. Oxford University Press.
Splendid Folly. Margaret Bass Pedler. LC 21-2757. George H. Doran Company.
Splendid Folly. Margaret Bass Pedler. LC 33-17479. 1923. Grosset & Dunlap.
Splendid Hazard. Harold MacGrath. LC 10-13393. 1.50. The Bobbs-Merrill Company.
Splendid Idle Forties. Gertrude Franklin Horn Atherton. 1901. lib. bdg. 20.00 (ISBN 0-8414-3095-0). Folcroft.
Splendid Idle Forties: Six Stories of Spanish California. Gertrude Franklin Horn Atherton. LC 74-28962. (Illus.). 1960. 100.00. Allen Press.
Splendid Idle Forties: Stories of Old California. Gertrude Franklin Horn Atherton. LC 68-20004. (Americans in Fiction). (Illus.). 1968. Gregg Press.
Splendid Idle Forties: Stories of Old California. Gertrude Franklin Horn Atherton. LC 2-24243. 1902. The Macmillan Company.
Splendid Idle Forties: Stories of Old California. Gertrude Franklin Horn Atherton. LC 22-14565. 1908. The Macmillan Company.
Splendid in Ashes: A Novel. Josephine Pinckney. LC 58-70689. 1958. Viking Press.
Splendid Joy. Marguerite Williams. LC 27-6912. 1927. The Penn Publishing Company.
Splendid Lives: Stories. Penelope Gilliatt. LC 77-10865. 1978. 7.95 (ISBN 0-698-10878-7). Coward, McCann & Geoghegan.
Splendid Murder. Reynolds H. Hayden. 1977. 11.50 o.p. (ISBN 0-682-48675-2). Exposition.
Splendid Outcast. George Fort Gibbs. LC 20-225859. 1920. D. Appleton and Company.
Splendid Outcast. Ethel Winifred Savi. LC 30-3355. The Curtiss Press.
Splendid Passion. Marianne Evans. (Orig.). 1980. pap. 2.50 (ISBN 0-446-81945-X). Warner Bks.
Splendid Quest. Edison Marshall. LC 34-29903. 1934. H. C. Kinsey & Company, Inc.
Splendid Rascal. George Challis. LC 26-11039. The Bobbs-Merrill Company.
Splendid Renegade. John Herries McCulloch. LC 28-19964. 1928. Coward-McCann, Inc.
Splendid Road. Vingie Eve Roe. LC 25-6946. 1925. Duffield and Company.
Splendid Savage. Zandra Colt. (Second Chance at Love Ser.: No. 92). 1982. pap. 1.75. Jove Pubns.
Splendid Shilling. Idwal Jones. LC 26-9671. 1926. Doubleday, Page & Company.
Splendid Silence. Alan Sullivan. E. P. Dutton & Co., Inc.
Splendid Sin. Grant Allen. LC 99-4137. 1899. F. M. Buckles & Company; Etc., Etc.
Splendid Sisters. Alan Mitchell. 14.50 (ISBN 0-392-04716-0, SpS). Sportshelf.
Splendid Spur: Being Memoirs of the Adventures of Mr. John Marvel, a Servant of His Late Majesty King Charles I., in the Years 1642-3. Arthur Thomas Quiller-Couch. (On cover: Cassell's sunshine series of choice fiction, v. 1, no. 40). 1890. Cassell & Company, Limited.
Splendid Spur: Being Memoirs of the Adventures of Mr. John Marvel, a Servant of His Late Majesty King Charles I, in the Years 1642-3. Arthur Thomas Quiller-Couch. LC 6-29004. (On cover: Harper's Franklin square library, no. 667). 1890. Harper & Brothers.
Splendid Spur: Being Memoirs of the Adventures of Mr. John Marvel, a Servant of His Late Majesty King Charles I., in the Years 1642-3. Arthur Thomas Quiller-Couch. LC 6-29005. R. F. Fenno & Company.
Splendid Spur: Being Memoirs of the Adventures of Mr. John Marvel, a Servant of His Late Majesty King Charles I, in the Years 1642-43. Arthur Thomas Quiller-Couch. LC 4-16297. 1898. C. Scribner's Sons.
Splendid Spur: Being Memoirs of the Adventure of Mr. John Marvel, a Servant of His Late Majesty King Charles I., in the Years 1642-43. Arthur Thomas Quiller-Couch. LC 1-29678. (On cover: Arrow library. no. 151). 1900. Street & Smith.
Splendid Spur: Being Memoirs of the Adventures of Mr. John Marvel, a Servant of His Late Majesty King Charles I., in the Years 1642-3. Arthur Thomas Quiller-Couch. LC 27-19645. George H. Doran Company.
Splendid Spur: Being Memoris of the Adventures of Mr. John Marvel, a Servant of His Late Majesty King Charles I., in the Years 1642-3. Arthur Thomas Quiller-Couch. LC 37-30936. 1937. Garden City Publishing Co., Inc.
Splendid Summits. Charles Alexander, pseud. LC 25-23366. 1925. Dodd, Mead and Company.
Splendid Torment. Natasha Peters. 476p. 1981. pap. 3.25 (ISBN 0-441-77798-8). Ace Bks.
Splendid Torments: A Novel. Margaret Culkin Banning. LC 76-5107. (Cass Canfield book). 8.95 (ISBN 0-06-010207-1). Harper & Row.
Splendid Victory. Rebecca Drury. (Woman at War Ser.: No. 10). 352p. (Orig.). 1983. pap. 3.25 (ISBN 0-440-08016-9, Emerald). Dell.
Splendor & Misery: A Novel of Harvard. Faye Levine. 288p. 1983. 13.95 (ISBN 0-312-75269-5, Pub. by Mareu). St Martin.
Splendor by the Sea. Darla Benton. (Candlelight Romance Ser.: No. 684). 192p. (Orig.). 1981. pap. 1.75 (ISBN 0-440-17257-8). Dell.
Splendor of Eagles. Helen Topping Miller. LC 35-4527. The Penn Publishing Company.
Splendor of God. Honore McCue Willsie Morrow. LC 29-16395. 1929. W. Morrow & Company.
Splendor of Love. Winifred Mary Watson Scott. LC 41-5982. 1941. H. C. Kinsey & Company, Inc.
Splendor of Torches. Cosmo Hamilton. LC 34-8580. 1934. R. M. McBride & Company.
Splendor Stays: An Historic Novel Based on the Lives of the Seven Hart Sisters of Saybrook, Connecticut. Marguerite Allis. LC 42-24491. 1942. G. P. Putnam's Sons.
Splendora. Edward Swift. 264p. 1981. pap. 3.95 (ISBN 0-14-005756-0). Penguin.
Splendora: A Novel. Edward Swift. LC 77-28453. 1978. 8.95 (ISBN 0-670-66410-3). Viking Press.
Splendors of Passion. Daniel Robert. Tr. by L. E. LaBan. pap. 1.75 o.p. (3033). Brandon.
Splendors of the Heart. Candice Arkham. 1979. 1.25 (ISBN 0-440-11890-5). Dell Pub. Co.
Splendour Falls. Norah Burke. LC 53-82973. 1953. Morrow.
Splendour of the Dawn. John Oxenham, pseud. LC 30-25626. 1930. Longmans, Green and Co.
Splint Road: A Novel. May Mellinger. LC 52-5269. 1952. Putnam.
Splinter of Glass. John Creasey. 1976. (pbk.) 1.25. Award Books.
Splinter of Glass. John Creasey. LC 72-37625. 1972. 4.95 (ISBN 0-684-12840-3). Scribner.
Splinter of the Mind's Eye. Alan Dean Foster. (Del Rey Book). 1978. 1.95 (ISBN 0-345-26062-7). Ballantine Books.
Splinter of the Mind's Eye: From the Adventures of Luke Skywalker. Alan Dean Foster. LC 77-28428. 1978. 1.95 (ISBN 0-345-27566-7). Ballantine Books.
Splintered Man. M. E. Chaber, pseud. 1970. pap. 0.60 o.p. (63-308). Paperback Lib.
Splintered Man: By M. E. Chaber Pseud. Kendell Foster Crossen. LC 55-108798. 1955. Rinehart.
Splinters. Richard Brooks. LC 42-9574. Suttonhouse.
Splinters: A New Anthology of Modern Macabre Fiction. Alex Hamilton. LC 79-86402. 1969. 5.95. Walker.
Split Atom, Last Human Pair on Earth: The Whirling of Ideas. Benjamin Belove. LC 46-8411. 1946. B. Ackerman.
Split Bamboo: By Leon Phillips. Noel Bertram Gerson. LC 66-174463. price unreported lib. ed., 3.25,. Doubleday.
Split End. George Blaire. 1971. pap. 1.50 o.s.i. (71-347). Lancer.
Split Ends. Pamela Herbert Chais. LC 76-50136. 7.95 (ISBN 0-397-01197-0). Lippincott.
Split Images. Elmore Leonard. LC 81-67524. 288p. 1981. 12.50 (ISBN 0-87795-354-6). Arbor Hse.
Split Images. Elmore Leonard. 288p. pap. 2.95 (ISBN 0-380-63107-5). Avon.
Split Infinity. Piers Anthony, pseud. LC 79-20282. (Illus.). 9.95 (ISBN 0-345-28645-6). Ballantine Books.
Splitsville. Frank Baginski & Reynolds Dodson. (Illus.). 96p. 1980. pap. 4.95 o.p. (ISBN 0-8015-7042-5, Hawthorn). Dutton.
Splitting Firewood. David Tresemer. (Illus.). 160p. (Orig.). 1981. pap. 6.95 (ISBN 0-938670-01-8). By Hand & Foot.
Spock, Messiah! Theodore R Cogswell & Charles A. Spano (ISBN 0-553-10159-5). Bantam.
Spoil. Ernest G. Perrault. LC 74-2722. 264p. 1975. 6.95 o.p. (ISBN 0-385-05143-3). Doubleday.
Spoil of Office. Hamlin Garland. LC 77-79656. (Series in American Studies). 1969. Johnson Reprint Corp.
Spoil of Office. A Story of the Modern West. Hamlin Garland. LC 3-148062. 1892. Arena Publishing Company.
Spoil of Office: A Story of the Modern West. new and rev. ed. Hamlin Garland. LC 3-14807. 1897. D. Appleton and Company.
Spoil of the Flowers. 1st Ed. Doris Grumbach. LC 62-15931. 1962. Doubday.
Spoiled Children. Philippe Heriat. LC 55-5666. 1956. Putnam.
Spoiled Priest, and Other Stories: An Anthology of Short Stories and Sketches from the Thinker's Digest. The Thinker's Digest. Ed. by Miriam, Sister. LC 51-9. 1950. P. J. Kenedy.
Spoilers. Desmond Bagley. LC 78-83310. 1970. 5.95. Doubleday.
Spoilers. Rex Ellingwood Beach. LC 76-144869. (Illus.). 1972. (ISBN 0-403-00856-5). Scholarly Press.
Spoilers. Rex Ellingwood Beach. LC 71-96874. 1969. (ISBN 0-8398-0157-2). Literature House.
Spoilers. Rex Ellingwood Beach. 1906. A. L. Burt Company.
Spoilers. Rex Ellingwood Beach. LC 7-32033. 1907. Harper & Brothers.
Spoilers. Rex Ellingwood Beach. LC 13-23587. Harper & Brothers.
Spoilers. Rex Ellingwood Beach. LC 24-28538. 1922. A. L. Burt Company.
Spoilers. Rex Ellingwood Beach. LC 6-11542. 1906. Harper & Brothers.
Spoilers. Matthew Braun. 224p. (Orig.). 1981. pap. 1.95 (ISBN 0-671-82034-6). PB.
Spoilers of the Valley. Robert Watson. LC 21-155062. George H. Doran Company.
Spoils of Ararat: A Novel. Robert Katz. LC 78-1966. 1978. 7.95 (ISBN 0-395-25702-6). Houghton Mifflin.
Spoils of Eden. Cary Morgan. (Orig.). 1981. pap. 2.95 (ISBN 0-451-09967-2, E9967, Sig). NAL.
Spoils of Empire: A Romance of the Old World and the New. Francis Newton Thorpe. LC 3-11160. 1903. Little, Brown, and Company.
Spoils of Marriage. Edward Linder & Goldberg, Nathan. Publix Publishing Co.
Spoils of Poynton. Henry James. LC 43-51343. (New classics series). 1943. New Directions.
Spoils of Poynton. Henry James & Bernard Arthur Richards. LC 82-6506. (World's classics). 1982. 4.95 (ISBN 0-19-281605-5). Oxford University Press.
Spoils of Poynton see Bodley Head Henry James.
Spoils of Poynton, and Other Stories. Henry James. LC 76-160885. 1971. 6.95. Doubleday.
Spoils of the Strong. Eleanor Talbot Kinkead. LC 20-164963. 1920. The James A. McCann Company.
Spoils of the Victors. Paul Edmondson. LC 64-12482. 1964. Simon and Schuster.
Spoils of War. Peter McCurtin. (Soldier of Fortune Ser.: No. 3). 192p. 1982. pap. 2.25 (ISBN 0-505-51779-5). Tower Bks.
Spoils of War. Peter McCurtin. Belmont Tower.
Spoils of War. Warren Murphy. (Destroyer Ser.: No. 45). 192p. (Orig.). 1981. pap. 1.95 (ISBN 0-523-40719-X). Pinnacle Bks.
Spoils of War. Douglas Scott. LC 77-14032. 1978. 8.95 (ISBN 0-698-10868-X). Coward, McCann & Geoghegan.
Spoilsmen. Elliott Flower. LC 3-686264. 1903. L.C. Page & Company.
Spoilt City. 1st American Ed. Olivia Manning. LC 62-15920. 1962.
Spoilt Girl. Florence Alice Price James. LC 7-797532. (On cover: Lippincott's series of select novels no. 173). 1895. J. B. Lippincott Company.
Spoilt Kill. Mary Kelly. LC 62-160190. 1961. M. Joseph.
Spoilt Kill. Mary Kelly. LC 68-13440. 1968. Walker.
Spoilt Music. Ruby Mildred Ayres. LC 26-12593. George H. Doran Company.
Spokane Saga: A Novel of the Rebuilding of a City Destroyed. 1st Ed. Zola Helen Ross. LC 57-128577. 1957. Bobbs-Merrill.
Spokes for the Wheel. Robert Deal Broadus. LC 61-59588. 1961. Kingsman Press.
Sponsors Are Always Right. David Halpern & Halpern, Ann, Joint Author. LC 40-5157. 1940. Discovery House.
Spook Stories. Edward Frederic Benson. LC 75-46252. (Supernatural and Occult Fiction). 1976. 16.00. Arno Press.
Spook Who Sat by the Door: A Novel. Sam Greenlee. LC 77-90885. 1969. 4.95. R. W. Baron.
Spooky Hollow: A Fleming Stone Story. Carolyn Wells. LC 23-15162. 1923. J. B. Lippincott Company.
Spoon. John Christgau. LC 77-22081. (Illus.). 1978. 8.95 (ISBN 0-670-66455-3). Viking Press.

Spoon-River Dan. Laura Everingham Scammon. LC 8-2021. 1894. Hudson-Kimberly Publishing Co.
Spoonhandle: A Novel... Ruth Moore. LC 46-3808. 1946. W. Morrow and Company.
Spore Seven. Clancy Carlile. LC 78-23851. 1979. 9.95 o.p. (ISBN 0-688-03423-3). Morrow.
Spore 7. Clancy Carlile. LC 78-23851. 1979. 9.95 (ISBN 0-688-03423-3). Morrow.
Spore 7. Clancy Carlile. 1980. 2.25 (ISBN 0-380-49031-5). Avon Books.
Sport and a Pastime. James Salter. (N3740). 1968. Bantam.
Sport and a Pastime. James Salter. LC 67-10413. 1967. Doubleday.
Sport and a Pastime. James Salter. LC 80-11577. 1980. 2.95 (ISBN 0-14-005638-6). Penguin Books.
Sport for the Baron. John Creasey. LC 72-86403. 1969. 4.50. Walker.
Sport for the Baron. Anthony Marton. LC 72-86403. (Mystery Ser). 1969. 4.50 o.p. (ISBN 0-8027-5166-0, 21060). Walker & Co.
Sport of Kings. Arthur Somers Roche. LC 17-18594. The Bobbs-Merrill Company.
Sport of Kings: Racing Stories. Josephine Russell Clay. LC 12-12489. 1.00. Broadway Publishing Co.
Sport of My Mad Mother. Ann Jellicoe. 1964. pap. 4.95 (ISBN 0-571-05935-X). Faber & Faber.
Sport of Queens. Dick Francis. LC 69-14574. (Illus.). 1969. 10.95 o.p. (ISBN 0-06-011329-4, HarpT). Har-Row.
Sport of the Gods. Paul Laurence Dunbar. LC 69-18588. (American Negro, His History and Literature). (Afro-American culture series.). 1969. 8.00. Arno Press.
Sport of the Gods. Paul Laurence Dunbar. LC 74-81114. 1969. Mnemosyne Pub. Inc.
Sport of the Gods. Paul Laurence Dunbar. LC 75-127215. 1970. Collier Books.
Sport of the Gods. Paul Laurence Dunbar. LC 2-11733. 1902. Dodd, Mead and Co.
Sport of the Gods. Paul Laurence Dunbar. LC 81-1283. (Dodd, Mead quality paperback). 5.95 (ISBN 0-396-07945-8). Dodd, Mead.
Sport of the Gods: A Novel. Grove Wilson. LC 26-122407. 1926. Frank-Maurice, Inc.
Sport Royal. Anthony Hope Hawkins. LC 7-34772. 1907. Harper & Brothers.
Sport Royal and Other Stories. Anthony Hope Hawkins. (On cover: Seaside library. Pocket ed., no. 2140). 1895. G. Munro's Sons.
Sport Royal: By Anthony Hope Pseud. Illustrated by Arno E. Schuele. Anthony Hope Hawkins. LC 52-3696. 1952. Story Classics.
Sport Stories: Selected and with an Introd. by "Red" Smith. The Saturday Evening Post. Ed. by Smith, Walter Wellesley. LC 50-5428. 1950. Pocket Books.
Sporting Blood: The Great Sports Detective Stories. Ed. by Ellery Queen, pseud. LC 42-25351. 1942. Little, Brown and Company.
Sporting Chance. James Edward Amesbury. LC 80-16251. 9.95 (ISBN 0-8037-7865-1). Dial Press.
Sporting Chance. Margaret H. C. Cameron. LC 26-7763. 1926. Harper & Brothers.
Sporting Chance. Donal Hamilton Haines. LC 35-16202. Farrar & Rinehart, Inc.
Sporting Club. Thomas McGuane. LC 75-305065. (Noonday; 488). 1974. 3.95 (ISBN 0-374-51205-1). Farrar, Straus, and Giroux.
Sporting Club. Thomas McGuane. LC 79-20433. 1979. 2.95 (ISBN 0-14-005275-5). Penguin Books.
Sporting Club: A Novel. Thomas McGuane. LC 69-12091. 1969. 4.95. Simon and Schuster.
Sporting Days. John Taintor Foote. LC 72-121544. (Short story index reprint series). (Illus.). 1970. Books for Libraries Press.
Sporting Days. John Taintor Foote. LC 37-34925. D. Appleton-Century Company, Incorporated.
Sporting Gesture: Stories of Some Who Played the Game. Ed. by Thomas Louis Stix. LC 34-7609. 1934. D. Appleton-Century Company, Incorporated.
Sporting Gesture: Stories of Some Who Played the Game. student's ed., edited by frank a. smerling... ed. Ed. by Thomas Louis Stix. Smerling, Frank A., Ed. LC 40-4196. D. Appleton-Century Company, Incorporated.
Sporting Lady. Gene Gauntier. LC 33-287261. 1933. A.H. King.
Sporting Life. William Fain. LC 61-17474. 1961. Crown Publishers.
Sporting Print. Gus March-Phillipps. LC 38-29716. E. P. Dutton & Co., Inc.
Sporting Proposition. James Aldridge. LC 73-7845. 1973. 5.95 (ISBN 0-316-03119-4). Little, Brown.
Sporting Proposition. James Aldridge. (Laurel leaf library). 1975. (pbk.) 1.25. Dell.
Sporting Spinster. Harold MacGrath. LC 26-6736. 1926. Doubleday, Page & Co.
Sporting Spirit: An Anthology. Ed. by Charles Wright Gray. 1925. Holt and Company.
Sporting Youth. McKinley Bryant. LC 31-6271. A. H. King.
Sports Action; Eight Short Stories. Ed. by Robert Vitarelli. LC 72-83374. (Pal paperback, R6). (Illus.). 1972. (pbk.) 0.75. Xerox Education Publications.
Sports Car Menopause: A Novel. Page Stegner. LC 77-5505. 8.95 (ISBN 0-316-81224-2). Little, Brown.
Sports Freak. Shannon O'Cork. LC 79-22850. 10.00 (ISBN 0-312-75331-4). St. Martin's Press.
Sports Stories. The Saturday Evening Post. Ed. by Smith, Walter Wellesley. LC 49-840334. 1949. A. S. Barnes.
Sportsman-Detective. Mansfield Scott. LC 30-33142. E. J. Clode, Inc.
Sportsman "Joe,". Edwyn Sandys. LC 4-24568. 1904. The Macmillan Company.
Sportsman on the Sofa. Frank Durfey. LC 32-14945. 1932. Covici, Friede.
Sportsman on Wheels. Erwin Bauer. (Outdoor Life Bks). (Illus.). 1969. 4.50 o.p. (ISBN 0-87468-055-7, Dist. by Dutton). Times Mirror Mag.
Sportsman's Anthology. Ed. by Robert Fulton Kelley. LC 44-75211. 1944. Howell, Soskin.
Sportsman's Notebook. Ivan Sergeevich Turgenev. LC 50-8497. (Cresset library). 1950. Chanticleer Press.
Sportsman's Sketches. Ivan Sergeevich Turgenev. LC 73-10269. (His Novels, v. 8-9). 1970. AMS Press.
Sportsman's Sketches. Ivan Sergieevich Turgenev & Garnett, Mrs. Constance (Black) 1862- Tr. LC 32-26963. (Half-title: Open-air library, edited by E. F. Daglish). 1932. E. P. Dutton & Co., Inc.
Spot of Evil. R. Matson. 3.75 o.p. Carlton.
Spot of Purple is Deaf. Ed. by Van K. Brock & Francis Poole. pap. 3.50. Anhinga Pr.
Spotless Reputation. Dorothea Gerard Longard De Longgarde. LC 3-3611. (Half-title: Appletons' town and country library. no. 213). 1897. D. Appleton and Company.
Spotlight. Harriet Works Corley. Grosset & Dunlap.
Spotlight. Clarence Budington Kelland. LC 37-1017. 1937. Harper & Brothers.
Spotlight. Judith Korotkin. 1974. (pbk.) 0.95. Popular Library.
Spotlight. Helen Topping Miller. 1946. D. Appleton Century Company, Inc.
Spotlight for Megan. Marcia Miller. LC 64-9018. (Avalon careers). 1964. Avalon Books.
Spotlight Madness: A Novel. Charles Grayson. LC 31-4965. H. Liveright.
Spotlight on Romance. Marcia Miller. 1975. 4.95. Avalon Books.
Spotlight on Romance-Broken Dream. Marcia Miller. 1982. pap. 2.50 (ISBN 0-451-11870-7, AE1778, Sig). NAL.
Spots of Time. Marcel Weinberg. LC 74-173693. 1972. 6.95. Macmillan.
Spotted Hawk. Olive Tilford Dargan. LC 58-59765. 1958. 3.00 o.p. (ISBN 0-910244-13-8). Blair.
Spotted Horse: By Jack Dillon. John Dillon. LC 57-7710. (Ballantine books, 194). Ballantine Books.
Spotted Lamb. Anican Soholt. LC 27-1841. Gem Publishing Company.
Spotted Panther. James Francis Dwyer. LC 13-201271. 1913. Doubleday, Page & Company.
Spotter, a Romance of the Oil Region. William Walker Canfield. 1907. R. F. Fenno & Company.
SPQR: A Romance. Paul Hyde Bonner. LC 52-8112. 1952. Scribner.
Spragge's Canyon: A Character Study. Horace Annesley Vachell. George H. Doran Company.
Spray on the Windows. Annie Edith Foster Jameson. 1.25. George H. Doran Company.
Spread. Barry N. Malzberg. 1977. pap. 1.50 o.s.i. (ISBN 0-505-51180-0). Tower Bks.
Spread. Barry N. Malzberg. (Orig.). 1971. pap. 0.75 o.p. (B75-2167). Belmont-Tower.
Spread Circles. Florence Jeannette Baier Ward. LC 27-854918. Macrae Smith Company.
Spread Eagle: And Other Stories. Gouverneur Morris. LC 10-228620. 1910. C. Scribner's Sons.
Spreadeagle. Marcus Van Heller, pseud. (Orig.). 1969. pap. 1.95 o.s.i. (OPH163, Ophelia). Olympia.
Spreading Dawn: Stories of the Great Transition. Basil King. LC 27-17786. 1927. Harper & Brothers.
Spreading Fires. John Knowles. LC 73-5038. 1974. 5.95 (ISBN 0-394-46915-1). Random House.
Spreewald Collection. Donald MacKenzie. LC 74-20706. (Midnight novel of suspense). 1975. 6.95 (ISBN 0-395-20286-8). Houghton Mifflin.
Sprig Muslin. Georgette Heyer. 256p. 1981. pap. 2.50 (ISBN 0-515-06020-8). Jove Pubns.
Sprig Muslin. Georgette Heyer. 256p. 1983. pap. 2.75 (ISBN 0-515-07148-X). Jove Pubns.
Sprig Muslin. Georgette Heyer. (YA) 1972. 7.95 o.p. (ISBN 0-399-11093-3). Putnam.
Sprig of Hemlock: A Novel About Shays' Rebellion. Robert Muir. LC 57-5849. 1957. Longmans, Green.
Sprig of Plantagenet: Or, The National Debt of England... by J. H. Mortimer... James Howard Mortimer. LC 9-6844. The Independent Publishing Co.
Sprig of Sea Lavender. J. R. Anderson. LC 78-19419. 1979. 7.95 o.p. (ISBN 0-312-75377-2). St Martin.
Sprig of Sea Lavender: A Novel. John Richard Lane Anderson. LC 78-19419. 1979. 7.95 (ISBN 0-312-75377-2). St. Martin's Press.
Spriggles: A Tale of Youth. frontispiece by george gibbs. ed. Edward Laurence Dudley. LC 19-13367. 1919. 1.60. D. Appleton and Company.
Sprightly Romance of Marsac. Molly Elliot Seawell. LC 8-6430.
Sprigs. Benedict Joseph Murdoch. LC 27-24662. The Torch Press.
Sprigs O' Mint. James Tandy Ellis. LC 6-15403. 1906. The Neale Publishing Company.
Spriit Gold. Louise Kiisel. LC 20-15070. 1920. The Stratford Co.
Spring. Sophia Cleugh. LC 29-126586. 1929. The Macmillan Company.
Spring Always Comes. Barbara K. Hodges. LC 38-19065. 1938. G. P. Putnam's Sons.
Spring Always Comes. Emilie Baker Loring. LC 79-10584. 1979. 12.50 (ISBN 0-8161-6730-3). G. K. Hall.
Spring Always Comes: By Emilie Loring. Emilie Baker Loring. LC 66-16685. 1966. Little, Brown.
Spring & Asura. Kenji Miyazawa. Tr. by Hiroaki Sato. LC 73-85173. 104p. 1975. 6.00 (ISBN 0-914090-00-3); pap. 3.50 (ISBN 0-914090-01-1). Chicago Review.
Spring Begins. Katherine Dunning. LC 34-24356. E. P. Dutton & Co., Inc.
Spring Begins: A Novel. Helen Rich. LC 47-3827. 1947. Simon and Schuster.
Spring Blossoms: An Easter Story. Mary Lowe Dickinson. LC 6-37028. C. H. Banes.
Spring by the River. Peggy O'More, pseud. LC 38-6338. Gramercy Publishing Co.
Spring Came on Forever. Bess Streeter Aldrich. LC 62-5010. Grosset & Dunlap.
Spring Came on Forever. Bess Streeter Aldrich. LC 35-18847. 1935. D. Appleton-Century Company, Incorporated.
Spring Came on Forever. Bess Streeter Aldrich. LC 44-8411. 1944. The Sun Dial Press.
Spring Came Too Late. Kathleen Rollins. LC 36-31242. 1936. Arcadia House.
Spring Comedies. Mary Anne Stewart Barker Broome. LC 22-10811. 1871. Macmillan.
Spring Comes. Berta Ruck. LC 36-6128. 1936. Dodd, Mead & Company.
Spring Dance: A Novel. Paul Tembler. LC 59-6030. 1959. Viking Press.
Spring Day in Autumn. Geoffrey Lehmann. LC 75-320798. 1974. 5.95 (ISBN 0-17-005010-6). Thomas Nelson (Australia)
Spring Dream. James Noble Gifford. 1948. Arcadia House.
Spring Dream. Rosamund Hunt. LC 63-6795. 1963. Avalon Books.
Spring Dust. Olive Wadsley. LC 30-16605. 1930. Dodd, Mead & Company.
Spring Fever. Kerry Allyne. (Harlequin Romances Ser.). 192p. 1983. pap. 1.50 (ISBN 0-373-02527-0). Harlequin Bks.
Spring Fever. Simone Hadary. (Second Chance at Love Ser.: No. 108). pap. 1.75 (ISBN 0-515-06872-1). Jove Pubns.
Spring Fever. Marcus Van Heller, pseud. LC 75-7583. 1969. 1.75. Ophelia Press.
Spring Fever. Pelham Grenville Wodehouse. LC 77-371554. 1976. 3.95 (ISBN 0-257-66290-1). Barrie and Jenkins.
Spring Fever. Pelham Grenville Wodehouse. LC 48-6922. 1948. Doubleday.
Spring Fire. Vin Packer. 1971. pap. 0.95 o.p. (95-149). Manor Bks.
Spring Fires. Cynthia Wright. 432p. (Orig.). 1983. pap. 3.50 (ISBN 0-345-27514-4). Ballantine.
Spring Flight. William Maier. LC 43-51052. 1943. Duell, Sloan and Pearce.
Spring Flight: A Novel. Lee J Smits. LC 25-8373. 1925. A. A. Knopf.
Spring Gambit. Claudette Williams (ISBN 0-449-23025-2). Fawcett Crest.
Spring Harrowing. Phoebe Atwood Taylor. 1971. pap. 0.75 o.p. (T2581). Pyramid Pubns.
Spring Harvest. Gladys Bagg Taber. LC 59-7846. 1959. Putnam.
Spring Harvest: A Collection of Stories from Alabama, Selected with an Introduction. Ed. by Hudson Strode. LC 44-4716. 1944. A. A. Knopf.
Spring Harvest: A Romance. Peggy Gaddis. LC 41-7328. 1941. Arcadia House, Inc.
Spring Horizon: A Novel. Thomas C Murray. LC 38-36746. 1937. T. Nelson and Sons, Limited.
Spring in Morocco. Anne Betteridge, pseud. 1973. pap. 0.75 o.p. (ISBN 0-345-20728-9). Beagle Bks.
Spring in the Bishop's Palace: A Novella. Alice Bliss. LC 70-259780. 1969. 2.50. Bozart Press.
Spring in the Desert. Cecil John Eustace. LC 69-12235. 1969. 5.95. Doubleday.
Spring Is a Woman. Natalie Shipman. LC 38-14450. The Greystone Press.
Spring Is Not Gentle. Ronald De Levington Kirkbride. LC 49-7512. 1949. Doubleday.
Spring Journey. Geneva Stephenson. LC 39-27158. 1939. The Macmillan Company.
Spring Lady. Mary Brecht Pulver. LC 14-15561. 1.25. The Bobbs-Merrill Company.
Spring List. Ralph Arnold. LC 57-5544. 1957. Macmillan.
Spring Magic. Dorothy Emily Stevenson. LC 41-52074. Farrar & Rinehart, Inc.
Spring Magic. Dorothy Emily Stevenson. 1978. 1.95 (ISBN 0-441-77841-0). Ace Books.
Spring May Be Late: By G. A. Clevenger. G. A Clevenger. LC 36-28261. Phoenix Press.
Spring Moon. Bette B. Lord. 1982. pap. 3.95 (ISBN 0-380-59923-6, 59923). Avon.
Spring Moon: A Novel of China. Bette B. Lord. LC 78-20210. 13.95 (ISBN 0-06-014893-4). Harper & Row.
Spring Moon: A Novel of China. Bette B. Lord. LC 82-6046. 1982. 18.95 (ISBN 0-8161-3385-9). G.K. Hall.
Spring Muslin. Georgette Heyer. LC 56-10231. 1956. Putnam.
Spring Must Come: A European Love Story. Frederique Hebrard. LC 79-28570. 1980. 8.95 (ISBN 0-312-75384-5). St. Martin's Press.
Spring of Fifty-Second Street. Dorothy Speare. LC 47-30397. 1947. Rinehart.
Spring of Love. Celia Dale. LC 67-13225. 1967. Walker.
Spring of Malice. John Harris. LC 62-18518. 1962. W. Sloane Associates.
Spring of Prosperity. Torkom Saraydarian. 1982. o. s. i. 7.00 (ISBN 0-911794-12-3); pap. 5.00 (ISBN 0-911794-13-1). Aqua Educ.
Spring of the Thief. John Logan. 1963. 4.50 o.p. Knopf.
Spring of the Tiger. Eleanor Hibbert. LC 78-22814. 1979. 10.00 (ISBN 0-385-15261-2). Doubleday.
Spring of the Tiger. Eleanor Hibbert. LC 79-20188. 1979. 15.95 (ISBN 0-8161-6782-6). G. K. Hall.
Spring of the Tiger. Victoria Holt, pseud. LC 78-22814. 1979. 13.95 (ISBN 0-385-15261-2). Doubleday.
Spring of the Tiger. Victoria Holt, pseud. 384p. 1980. pap. 2.75 (ISBN 0-449-24297-8, Crest). Fawcett.
Spring of the Tiger. Virginia Holt. (General Ser.). 1979. lib. bdg. 15.95 (ISBN 0-8161-6782-6, Large Print Bks). G K Hall.
Spring of Violence. Elizabeth Linington. LC 73-9723. 1973. 5.95 (ISBN 0-688-00209-9). Morrow.
Spring Offensive. Herbert Clyde Lewis. LC 40-7421. 1940. The Viking Press.
Spring Prairie. Ernie Roberts. 255p. 1981. pap. 5.95 o.p. (ISBN 0-89260-199-X). Hwong Pub.
Spring Returns. William Arthur Neubauer. LC 50-13852. 1950. Arcadia House.
Spring Returns. Pref. by Anne Morrow Lindbergh. Haniel Long. LC 58-7203. 1958. Pantheon.
Spring Riot, a Novel. Jay Presson. LC 48-8617. 1948. Rinehart.
Spring Running. Francis Woolsey Bronson. LC 26-681489. George H. Doran Company.
Spring Shall Plant. Beatrice Harraden. LC 21-6502. 1920. Hodder and Stoughton, Limited.
Spring Shall Plant. Beatrice Harraden. LC 21-5082. 2.00. George H. Doran Company.
Spring Silkworms & Other Stories. 2nd ed. Mao Dun. 1980. 6.95 (ISBN 0-8351-0615-2). China Bks.
Spring Silkworms, and Other Stories. Yen-Ping Shen. LC 72-5086. (Illus.). 1970. Center for Chinese Research Materials, Association of Research Libraries.
Spring Silkworms, and Other Stories. Yen-Ping Shen. LC 75-36238. (Illus.). 1979. 24.50 (ISBN 0-404-14486-1). AMS Press.
Spring Snow. Yukio Mishima, pseud. (Unesco Collection of Representative Works: Japanese Ser.). 1973. (pbk.) 1.50 (ISBN 0-394-44239-3). Pocket Books.
Spring Snow. Yukio Mishima, pseud. LC 79-154940. (UNESCO Collection of Representative Works: Japanese Series). (His The Sea of fertility 1). 1972. 7.95 (ISBN 0-394-44239-3). Knopf.
Spring Snow and Algy. Peter De Polnay. LC 74-81464. 1975. 6.50. St. Martin's Press.
Spring Snow & Algy. Peter De Polnay. 192p. 1975. 6.50 o.p. (ISBN 0-312-75390-X). St Martin.
Spring Song. Forrest Reid, pseud. LC 17-8741. 1917. Houghton Mifflin Company.

Spring Song, and Other Stories. Joyce Cary. LC 75-116946. (Short story index reprint series). 1970. Books for Libraries Press.
Spring Sorrel. Douglas Pulleyne. LC 26-15399. George H. Doran Company.
Spring Sowing. Liam O'Flaherty. LC 72-10748. (Short story index reprint series). 1973. (ISBN 0-8369-4221-3). Books for Libraries Press.
Spring Storm. Alvin Saunders Johnson. LC 36-8945. 1936. A. A. Knopf.
Spring Street: A Story of Los Angeles. James H Richardson. LC 23-802. 1922. Times-Mirror Press.
Spring Symphony: A Novel. Eleanor Painter. LC 41-51538. Harper & Brothers.
Spring Term. Joseph Carrigan Higgins. LC 40-34069. Cullom & Ghertner.
Spring Tide. Octavus Roy Cohen. LC 28-10865. 1928. D. Appleton and Company.
Spring Tides: A Novel. Robert Eugene Pinkerton. LC 27-12820. The Reilly & Lee Co.
Spring Torrents. Ivan Sergeevich Turgenev. Tr. by Leonard Shapiro from Rus. (Classics Ser.). 1980. pap. 3.95 (ISBN 0-14-044369-X). Penguin.
Spring Vacation: By Warren Howard Pseud. James Noble Gifford. LC 56-129345. 1956. Arcadia House.
Spring Will Come Again. Florence Glass Palmer. LC 40-5228. The Bobbs-Merrill Company.
Spring Will Come Again. June Slyvia Thimblethrone. (Fawcett Crest Book). 1977. 1.50 (ISBN 0-449-23346-4). Fawcett Books.
Spring Will Come Again. Sylvia Thorpe. LC 78-3758. 1978. 8.95 (ISBN 0-89340-149-8). J. Curley.
Spring Will Come Again. Dorothy Worley. LC 53-7479. 1953. Bouregy & Curl.
Spring 1940. Stuart David Engstrand. LC 39-27860. 1941. Doubleday, Doran and Co., Inc.
Springboard. Robert Wolf. LC 27-7725. 1927. A. & C. Boni.
Springer's Progress. David Markson. LC 76-43496. 8.95 (ISBN 0-03-020341-4). Holt, Rinehart and Winston.
Springfield Forty-Five Seventy. John Henry Reese. 192p. 1982. pap. 1.95 (ISBN 0-505-51789-2). Tower Bks.
Springfield .45-70. John Henry Reese. LC 72-79421. (Doubleday western). 1972. 4.95 (ISBN 0-385-08928-7). Doubleday.
Springhaven. Richard Doddridge Blackmore. (On cover: Seaside library. Pocket ed. no. 926). G. Munro.
Springhaven. Richard Doddridge Blackmore. LC 6-131383. (On cover: Lovell's library, no. 961). J. W. Lovell Company.
Springhaven. A Novel. Richard Doddridge Blackmore. (Harper's Franklin square library, no. 568). Harper & Brothers.
Springhaven: A Tale of the Great War. Richard Doddridge Blackmore. (Half-title: Everyman's library, ed. by Ernest Rhys. Fiction). 1909. J. M. Dent & Co.
Springhaven: A Tale of the Great War. Richard Doddridge Blackmore. LC 36-37162. (Half-title: Everyman's library, ed. by Ernest Rhys. Fiction. no. 350). 1925. J. M. Dent & Sons, Ltd.
Springhaven: A Tale of the Great War. Richard Doddridge Blackmore & Parsons, Alfred, 1847-1920, Illus. LC 43-43116. 1887. Harper & Brothers.
Springs. Anne Goodwin Winslow. LC 49-74162. 1949. A. A. Knopf.
Spring's Banjo: A Portmanteau Historical Novel and Hymn to Youth, with a Musical Accompaniment and Fashion Notes of the Period. Horatio Gates Winslow. LC 27-7733. 1927. Frank-Maurice, Inc.
Spring's Green Shadow. Cecily Mackworth. LC 53-11165. 1953. Dutton.
Springs of the Waters: A Story of a Love That Transcends All Human Barriers. 1st Ed. Austin Ballard. LC 58-122445. 1959. Greenwich Book Publishers.
Springs of Violence: By Edward Lindall Pseud. Edward Ernest Smith. LC 63-17680. 1963. Morrow.
Springtime & Harvest. Upton Beall Sinclair. 1901. Repr. 23.00 (ISBN 0-403-00292-3). Scholarly.
Springtime Fancy. Frank O'Rourke. LC 61-8074. 1961. Morrow.
Springtime for a Goddess: A Novel. Thomas J Limoli. LC 52-5703. 1952. Exposition Press.
Springtime of Life. Jean Dutourd. LC 73-15351. 1974. 6.95 (ISBN 0-385-06749-6). Doubleday.
Spuddy: A Novel. rev. american ed. Lillian Beckwith. LC 75-17599. 1976. 6.95 (ISBN 0-440-07681-1). Delacorte Press.
Spun by an Angel. Martha Louise Cheavens. LC 48-7642. 1948. Broadman Press.
Spun Gold. Ruth Hammitt Kauffman. LC 36-1430. The Penn Publishing Company.
Spun Sugar Hole. Jerry Sohl. (Signet bk., Y5314). 1973. 1.25. New American Lib.
Spun Sugar Hole. Jerry Sohl. LC 73-139661. 1971. 6.95 (ISBN 0-671-20874-8). Simon and Schuster.
Spun-Yarn. Morgan Robertson. LC 76-98592. (Short Story Index Reprint Ser.). 1898. 15.00 (ISBN 0-8369-3166-1). Ayer Co.
Spun-Yarn Sea Stories. Morgan Robertson. LC 76-98592. (Short story index reprint series). 1969. Books for Libraries Press.
Spur. Ardyth Kennelly. LC 51-2015. 1951. J. Messner.
Spur of Danger. Chauncey Crafts Hotchkiss. LC 15-19973. W. J. Watt & Company.
Spur of Monmouth: Or, Washington in Arms. A Historical and Centennial Romance of the Revolution, from Personal Relations and Documents Never Before Made Public. Henry Morford. LC 7-17263. 1876. Claxton, Remsen & Haffelfinger.
Spur of Pride. Percival Christopher Wren. LC 37-674. 1937. Houghton Mifflin Company.
Spur: Or, The Bondage of Kin Severne. Edith J. Lyttleton. LC 6-11312. 1906. Doubleday.Page & Company.
Spur to the Smoke. Steve Frazee. LC 55-21025. (Perma books, M-3008 3). 1955. Perma Books.
Spurs from San Isidro: A Novel of the Southwest. Birdsall Briscoe. LC 51-9029. 1951. Dutton.
Spurs West. Western Writers of America. LC 70-113692. (Short story index reprint series). 1970. Books for Libraries Press.
Spurs West: By Members of the Western Writers of America. Western Writers of America. LC 60-15196. 1960. Doubleday.
Sputnik Rapist: A Novel. Carl Jonas. LC 72-8302. 1973. 6.95 (ISBN 0-393-08527-9). Norton.
Spuytenduyvel Chronicle. LC 8-14039. 1856. Livermore & Rudd.
Spy. James Fenimore Cooper. LC 72-367009. (Classic American texts). 1968 (ISBN 0-19-812309-4). Oxford U.P.
Spy. James Fenimore Cooper. LC 6-32153. (Standard literature ser. no. 1). 1895. University Publishing Co.
Spy. James Fenimore Cooper. LC 24-23805. 1924. Minton, Balch & Co.
Spy. James Fenimore Cooper. Ed. by Boynton, Percy Holmes. LC 28-8701. (modern readers' series). 1928. The Macmillan Company.
Spy. James Fenimore Cooper. LC 36-13305. The Saalfield Publishing Company.
Spy. James Fenimore Cooper. (Great Illustrated Classics). 1949. Dodd, Mead.
Spy. James Fenimore Cooper & Baldridge, Cyrus LeRoy, 1889- Illus. LC 42-51780. 1942. Garden City Publishing Co., Inc.
Spy. James Fenimore Cooper & Campbell, Katherine L. LC 25-11316. (Instructor literature series). F. A. Owen Publishing Company.
Spy. Norman Garbo. LC 80-216. 10.95 (ISBN 0-393-01321-9). Norton.
Spy: A Tale of the Neutral Ground... James Fenimore Cooper. LC 31-35213. 1829. Carey, Lea, & Carey.
Spy: A Tale of the Neutral Ground... 6th ed. James Fenimore Cooper. LC 6-29676. 1834. Carey & Lea.
Spy: A Tale of the Neutral Ground... new ed. James Fenimore Cooper. 1836. Carey, Lea, & Blanchard.
Spy. A Tale of the Neutral Ground... new ed. James Fenimore Cooper. LC 6-32150. 1845. Burgess, Stringer & Co.
Spy: A Tale of the Neutral Ground. James Fenimore Cooper. LC 9-300286. 1893. D. Appleton and Company.
Spy: A Tale of the Neutral Ground. James Fenimore Cooper. LC 4-19556. 1896. D. Appleton and Company.
Spy: A Tale of the Neutral Ground. James Fenimore Cooper. LC 4-15436. (In his Works. Mohawk ed.). 1896. G. P. Putnam's Sons.
Spy: A Tale of the Neutral Ground. James Fenimore Cooper. LC 26-23544. H. T. Coates & Co.
Spy: A Tale of the Neutral Ground. James Fenimore Cooper. Ed. by Thurber, Samuel. (Macmillan's pocket American and English classics). 1909. The Macmillan Company.
Spy: A Tale of the Neutral Ground. James Fenimore Cooper. Ed. by Thomas, Charles Swain. LC 11-23509. (Riverside literature series). Houghton Mifflin Company.
Spy: A Tale of the Neutral Ground. James Fenimore Cooper. Ed. by Revell, Ellen Isabel. Educational Publishing Company.
Spy: A Tale of the Neutral Ground. James Fenimore Cooper. Ed. by Damon, Lindsay Todd. LC 14-1910. (Half-title: The Lake English classics, ed. by L. T. Damon). 0.40. Scott, Foresman and Company.
Spy: A Tale of the Neutral Ground. James Fenimore Cooper. Ed. by Barnes, Nathaniel Waring. LC 15-7280. (Eclectic English classics). American Book Company.
Spy: A Tale of the Neutral Ground. James Fenimore Cooper. Ed. by Damon, Lindsay Todd. LC 20-8236. (Half-title: The Lake English classics, general editor: L. T. Damon). Scott, Foresman and Company.
Spy: A Tale of the Neutral Ground. James Fenimore Cooper. LC 24-23176. (Riverside book-shelf). 1924. Houghton Mifflin Company.
Spy: A Tale of the Neutral Ground. James Fenimore Cooper & Canby, Henry Seidel. LC 29-250391. 1929. Bowling Green Press.
Spy: A Tale of the Neutral Ground. James Fenimore Cooper & Griffin, Beatrice Adams. LC 18-7646. Ginn and Company.
Spy: A Tale of the Neutral Ground. James Fenimore Cooper & McDowell, Tremaine. LC 31-32070. (Half-title: The modern student's library). C. Scribner's Sons.
Spy at Angkor Wat. William Sanborn Ballinger. LC 66-9097. (Signet book, D2899). 1966. New American Library.
Spy at Evening. Donald James. 256p. 1981. pap. 2.50 (ISBN 0-445-04686-4). Popular Lib.
Spy at the Villa Miranda. Elsie Lee. pap. 0.60 o.p. Lancer.
Spy at the Villa Miranda. Elsie Lee. 1973. (pbk.) 0.95. Dell.
Spy Castle. Nick Carter. (Nick Carter Killmaster Ser.). 160p. 1968. pap. 0.60 o.p. (A289X, Award). Univ Pub & Dist.
Spy Company: A Story of the Mexican War. Archibald Clavering Gunter. LC 7-132. 1902. The Home Publishing Company.
Spy Concerto. Christina Merlin. LC 79-5353. 1980. 9.95 (ISBN 0-312-75416-7). St. Martin's Press.
Spy for a Spy. Berkely Mather. LC 68-27792. 1968. 4.95. Scribner.
Spy for Mr. Crook. Lucy Beatrice Malleson. LC 44-1707. 1944. A. S. Barnes and Company.
Spy for Sale. Laurence Payne. LC 70-116244. 1970. 4.50. Doubleday.
Spy for the General: A Story of the Philippine Insurrection. Perry Coler. LC 48-35061. 1932-1948. News.
Spy Game. Marc Lovell, pseud. LC 80-499. 1980. 8.95 (ISBN 0-385-17073-4). Published for the Crime Club by Doubleday.
Spy Game. John McNeil. LC 80-13189. 11.95 (ISBN 0-698-11046-3). Coward, McCann & Geoghegan.
Spy in Black. Joseph Storer Clouston. LC 18-94912. 1.35. George H. Doran Company.
Spy in Chancery. Kenneth Benton. LC 72-95772. 1973. 4.95 (ISBN 0-8027-5273-X). Walker.
Spy in the Family: An Erotic Comedy. Alec Waugh. LC 70-97616. 1970. 5.95. Farrar, Straus and Giroux.
Spy in the House of Love. Anais Nin. 1974. (pbk.) 1.65. Bantam Books.
Spy in the House of Love. Anais Nin. LC 73-168463. 1973. 0.25 (ISBN 0-14-003600-8). Penguin.
Spy in the House of Love. Anais Nin. LC 66-6833. (Illus.). 1959. Swallow Press.
Spy in the House of Love. 1st American Ed. Anais Nin. LC 54-3920. (New-story book). 1954. British Book Centre.
Spy in the Ointment. Donald E Westlake. LC 66-21503. 1966. Random House.
Spy in the Room. Denison Halley Clift. LC 44-7577. 1944. Mystery House.
Spy Is Forever. Richard P French. LC 73-109408. 1970. 3.95. C. E. Tuttle Co.
Spy Island Mystery: Mrs. Matthews' Emeralds. Alfred Augustus Gardner. LC 30-446. The Evening Post Job Printing Office, Inc.
Spy Meets Spy: A Thrilling Story of International Intrigue Featuring Anthony Hamilton, America's Secret Agent Number One. Frederick Frost. LC 37-2250. 1937. Macrae Smith Company.
Spy Net. Ared White. 1931. Houghton Mifflin Company.
Spy Next Door. Lawrence Kessner. 250p. 1981. 12.95 (ISBN 0-517-54818-6, Arlington Hse). Crown.
Spy Next Door: A Novel. Lawrence Kessner. LC 81-12871. 1981. 12.95 (ISBN 0-87000-521-9). Arlington House.
Spy of Napoleon. Emmuska Orczy. LC 34-227580. G. P. Putnam's Sons.
Spy of Osawatomie: Or, The Mysterious Companions of Old John Brown. Mary E Jackson. LC 7-9467. 1881. W. S. Bryan.
Spy on Riverside Drive. Constance Rauch. 1977. 1.75 (ISBN 0-445-04135-8). Popular Library.
Spy on the Run. Marc Lovell, pseud. LC 81-43778. 1982. 10.95 (ISBN 0-385-18095-0). Published for the Crime Club by Doubleday.
Spy Paramount. Edward Phillips Oppenheim. LC 35-448. 1935. Little, Brown, and Company.
Spy Story. Len Deighton. LC 74-3124. 1974. 6.95 (ISBN 0-15-184838-6). Harcourt Brace Jovanovich.
Spy Story. Len Deighton. LC 74-3124. 1975. (pbk.) 1.95 (ISBN 0-671-80058-2). Pocket Books.
Spy, the Lady, the Captain & the Colonel. Richard Stiller. (Firebird Library). (Illus.). (gr. 4-8). 1970. 3.95 o.p. Schol Bk Serv.
Spy: The Story of a Superfluous Man. Maksim Gorkii & Seltzer, Thomas, Tr. LC 8-33904. 1908. B. W. Huebsch.
Spy Trap. Burton Graham. LC 72-90174. 1972. 4.95. Weybright and Talley.
Spy Who Came, and Came, and Came, and Came. Ray Kainen. LC 79-9885. (Traveller's companion series). 1969. 1.75. Traveler's Companion, Inc.
Spy Who Came in from the Cold. John Le Carre. LC 64-10430. 1964. Coward-McCann.
Spy Who Came in from the Cold. John Le Carre. LC 78-1799. 1978. 9.95 (ISBN 0-698-10916-3). Coward, McCann & Geoghegan.
Spy Who Came in from the Cold: By John Le Carre Pseud. David John Moore Cornwell. (8221). 1965. Dell.
Spy Who Came in from the Cold: By John le Carre Pseud. Large Type Ed. David John Moore Cornwell. (Keith Jennison bk.). 1966. 6.95. Watts.
Spy Who Died of Boredom. George Mikes. LC 73-17634. 240p. 1974. 6.95 o.p. (ISBN 0-06-012931-X, HarpT). Har-Row.
Spy Who Died of Boredom: A Novel. George Mikes. LC 73-17634. 1974. 6.95 (ISBN 0-06-012931-X). Harper & Row.
Spy Who Died Twice. Michael Bar-Zohar. LC 74-26598. 1975. 6.95 (ISBN 0-395-19417-2). Houghton Mifflin.
Spy Who Died Twice. Michael Bar-Zohar. LC 74-26598. 1975. 6.95 o.p. (ISBN 0-395-20444-5). HM.
Spy Who Fell into the Borscht. Ed. by Jack Heller. (O.s.i.). (Orig.). pap. 0.50 o.s.i. (A167F, Award). Univ Pub & Dist.
Spy Who Loved Me. Ian Fleming. pap. 4.50 fr. ed. French & Eur.
Spy Who Loved Me. Ian Fleming. 192p. 1982. pap. 2.75 (ISBN 0-425-05372-5). Berkley Pub.
Spy Who Loved Me" A Novel. Christopher Wood. 1977. 1.75 (ISBN 0-446-84544-2). Warner Books.
Spy Who Never Was. Sheila Martin. 192p. (Orig.). 1982. pap. 2.25 (ISBN 0-8439-1036-4, Leisure Bks). Nordon Pubns.
Spy Who Sat and Waited. R. Wright Campbell. 1979. 2.50 (ISBN 0-671-82111-3). Pocket Books.
Spy Who Sat and Waited: A Novel. R. Wright Campbell. LC 74-16580. 1975. 7.95 (ISBN 0-399-11424-6). Putnam.
Spy Who Spoke Porpoise. Philip Wylie. LC 74-79970. (Illus.). 1969. 5.95. Doubleday.
Spy Who Wasn't Exchanged. Alfred Tack. LC 69-15201. 1969. 4.50. Published for the Crime Club by Doubleday.
Spy with His Head in the Clouds. Marc Lovell, pseud. LC 81-43281. 1982. 10.95 (ISBN 0-385-17859-X). Published for the Crime Club by Doubleday.
Spy with Two Hats. Rosamond McPherson Young. LC 67-1105. 1966. D. McKay.
Spy Without a Country. H. H. Ronblum. (YA) 1965. 4.50 o.p. Coward.
Spybot! Clark Darlton. (Perry Rhodan#53). (Illus.). 1974. (pbk.) 0.95. Ace Books.
Spyglass Range. George M Johnson. LC 33-109722. E. J. Clode, Inc.
Spykill. L. W. Blanco. pap. 0.50 o.p. Lancer.
Spylight. James Leasor. LC 66-14696. (Heinemann) has title: Passport to peril.). 1966. Lippincott.
Spymaster. rev. ed. Donald Freed. 448p. 1981. pap. 2.95 (ISBN 0-553-14719-6). Bantam.
Spymaster. Edward Phillips Oppenheim. LC 38-33401. 1938. Little, Brown and Company.
Spymaster. Edward Phillips Oppenheim. LC 40-7423. 1940. The Sun Dial Press.
Spymaster, a Novel of America. Donald Freed. LC 78-72922. 12.95 (ISBN 0-87795-211-6). Arbor House.
Spymaster: 1st Amer. Ed. Philip Freund. LC 66-142352. 1966. bds., 3.95. Washburn.
S.P.Y.S. T. Robert Joyce. 1974. (pbk.) 0.95 (ISBN 0-671-77939-7). Pocket Books.
Spy's Wife. Reginald Hill. LC 80-7929. 8.95 (ISBN 0-394-51402-5). Pantheon Books.
Spyship. Tom Keene & Brian Haynes. LC 79-20241. 11.95 (ISBN 0-399-90068-3). R. Marek Publishers.
Spytrap. William Crisp. 200p. 1983. 12.95 (ISBN 0-394-52971-5). Pantheon.
Squad. Harry Tedesco. 6.95 o.p. (ISBN 0-8062-0675-6). Carlton.
Squad. James B Wharton. LC 28-21978. 1928. Coward-McCann, Inc.
Squad. James B Wharton. LC 30-123407. 1929. Grosset & Dunlap.
Squad Goes Out: A Novel. Robert Greenwood. LC 43-6645. 1943. The Bobbs-Merrill Company.
Squadron Airborne. Elleston Trevor. LC 56-7338. 1956. Macmillan.
Squadron Alert! A Civil Air Patrol Adventure Story. John Berchman Stanley. LC 54-11135. 1954. Dodo, Mead.
Squadron Forty-Four: By Arch Whitehouse. Arthur George Joseph Whitehouse. LC 65-118020. 4.95. Doubleday.
Squadron Shilling. Arthur George Joseph Whitehouse. LC 68-22630. 1968. 5.95. Doubleday.

TITLE INDEX STAIRS OF SAND.

Squandering. Dorothy Monet. LC 70-117268. 1971. 5.95 (ISBN 0-03-085072-X). Holt, Rinehart and Winston.
Squarcio the Fisherman. Translated from the Italian by Frances Frenaye. 1st Ed. Franco Solinas. LC 58-7819. 1958. Dutton.
Square. Marguerite Duras. 1955. pap. 2.50 o.p. French & Eur.
Square. Maud Lalita Johnson. LC 34-5284. 1934. The Order of Loving Service.
Square. Haidee Terrill. LC 49-11215. 1949. Macmillan Co.
Square see Four Novels.
Square Called Silence. Desmond Meiring, pseud. LC 66-11591. 1966. Houghton Mifflin.
Square Circle. Denis George Mackail. LC 41-31117. 1931. Houghton Mifflin Company.
Square Crib. Graham Jackson. LC 82-133305. 14.95 (ISBN 0-7022-1640-2). University of Queensland Press.
Square Dance. John William Wainwright. LC 74-24701. 1975. 6.95. St Martin's Press.
Square Deal Sanderson. Charles Alden Seltzer. LC 22-7206. 1922. A. C. McClurg & Co.
Square Egg. Ronald Searle. (Illus.). 96p. (Orig.). 1981. pap. 2.95 (ISBN 0-14-005467-7). Penguin.
Square Emerald. Gilbert Vivian Seldes. LC 28-7330. 1928. The John Day Company.
Square Game. Theophile Gautier & Miller, Hettie E., Tr. (On cover: The optimus series, no. 15). 1892. Donohue, Henneberry & Co.
Square in the Middle. William Campbell Gault. LC 56-5209. Random House.
Square Jungle. J. Jason Grant. 1979. 1.95 (ISBN 0-87067-632-6). Holloway House.
Square Mark. Grace M White & Deakin, H. L., Joint Author. LC 30-21637. E. P. Dutton & Co., Inc.
Square of Acceptance. John Forte. LC 73-87875. 1973. 2.95 (ISBN 0-8059-1947-3). Dorrance.
Square Peg. Walter Ernest Allen. LC 51-9333. 1951. Morrow.
Square Peg. Sylvia L. Klein. 1969. 3.95 o.p. (ISBN 0-8059-1402-1). Dorrance.
Square Peg. Philip Macer-Wright. LC 25-14523. 1925. Longmans, Green, and Co.
Square Peg. George Malcolm-Smith. LC 52-6308. 1952. Doubleday.
Square Peg: Or, The Gun Fella. John Masefield. LC 37-36661. 1937. The Macmillan Company.
Square Peggy. Josephine Dodge Daskam Bacon. LC 19-149083. 1.60. D. Appleton and Company.
Square Pegs. Adeline Dutton Train Whitney. 1899. Houghton, Mifflin and Company.
Square Root of Man. William Tenn. 224p. (Orig.). 1981. pap. 2.25 (ISBN 0-345-29230-8, Del Rey). Ballantine.
Square Root of Valentine. Berry Fleming. LC 32-6311. W. W. Norton & Company, Inc.
Square Shooter. Tony Adams. LC 35-182898. Phoenix Press.
Square Shooter. Walt Coburn. 1978. pap. 1.25 o.s.i. (ISBN 0-505-51228-9). Tower Bks.
Square Shooter. Walt Coburn. 1970. pap. 0.60 o.p. (60-453). Manor Bks.
Square-Shooter. William MacLeod Raine. LC 35-519. 1935. Houghton Mifflin Company.
Square-Shooter. William MacLeod Raine. LC 44-7840. 1944. Triangle Books.
Square-Shooter. William Macleod Raine. 1974. (pbk.) 0.75. Popular Library.
Square Trap. Irving Shulman. LC 76-1585. (Chicano Heritage). 1976. 21.00 (ISBN 0-405-09525-2). Arno Press.
Square Trap. Irving Shulman. LC 53-5260. 1953. Little, Brown.
Squareheads: The Story of a Socialized State, a Futuristic Novel. William Salisbury. LC 29-21544. 1929. The Independent Publishing Company.
Squares of the City. John Brunner. LC 65-29848. (Ballantine science fiction original). 1965. Ballantine Books.
Square's Progress. Wilfrid Sheed. 309p. 1965. 5.95 (ISBN 0-374-26832-0). FS&G.
Square's Progress: A Novel. Wilfrid Sheed. LC 65-17023. 4.95. Farrar.
Squaretail. Charles M. Kroll. 5.95 o.p. Vantage.
Squaring the Circle. Niel Hancock. (Circle of Light Ser: No. 4). 1982. pap. 2.95 (ISBN 0-445-04089-0). Popular Lib.
Squatter and the Don. A Novel Descriptive of Contemporary Occurrences in California. Maria Amparo Ruiz Burton. LC 6-22255. 1885. S. Carson & Co.
Squatter Sovereign, or Kansas in the '50's. A Life Picture of the Early Settlement of the Debatable Ground. A Story, Founded Upon Memorable, and Historical Events... Mary A. Vance Humphrey. LC 5-40608. 1883. Coburn & Newman Publishing Co.
Squatter's Dream: A Story of Australian Life. new ed. Thomas Alexander Browne. LC 41-34781. 1890. Macmillan and Co.
Squaw Book. The Squaws of the Onondagas Made This Book That the Great Chiefs Might Give Them Wampum for It, So That the Squaws, Having Wampum, Might Bribe Medicine Men to Cure with Weird Charms Those Who Have Been Wounded in the Long Battle and Cannot Fight for Themselves... Syracuse, N.Y. Free Dispensary. LC 10-114031. Pub. for the Benefit of the Free Dispensary.
Squaw Elouise. Marah Ellis Martin Ryan. LC 8-13586. (On cover: Rialto series, no. 47). 1892. Rand, McNally & Company.
Squaw Man. Julie Opp Faversham & Edwin Milton Royle. LC 77-104559. (Illus.). 1972. (ISBN 0-8398-1769-X). Literature House.
Squaw Man: A Novel. Julie Opp Faversham & Boyle, Edwin Milton, 1862- LC 6-45695. 1906. Harper & Brothers.
Squaw Point. Ruth H Shimer. LC 73-175155. 1972. 5.95 (ISBN 0-06-013848-3). Harper & Row.
Squaw Valley War. James D. Sayers. 1971. pap. 0.60 o.p. (ISBN 0-447-73210-2). Lancer.
Squaw Winter: A Love Story Based on the Indian Folklore of Highland County. Limited 1st Ed. Violet Morgan. LC 56-20438. 1955. Greenfield Print. & Pub. Co.
Squealer. Edgar Wallace. LC 28-3438. 1928. Doubleday, Doran & Company, Inc.
Squealer... Edgar Wallace. LC 47-21039. (On cover: New Avon library. 112). 1946.
Squeegee: A Novel. Jack Siegel, pseud. LC 65-16926. 4.95. Horizon.
Squeeze. David Craig. LC 73-92192. 1974. 25.00x o.s.i. (ISBN 0-8128-1697-8). Stein & Day.
Squeeze. Allan James Tucker. LC 73-92192. 1974. 5.95 (ISBN 0-8128-1697-8). Stein and Day.
Squeeze Play. Paul Benjamin. 1982. 10.95 o.p.; pap. 5.95 o.p. Caroline Hse.
Squeeze Play. Paul Benjamin. 200p. (Orig.). 1982. 10.95 (ISBN 0-938764-03-9); pap. 5.95 (ISBN 0-938764-04-7). Alpha-Omega Bks.
Squid Soup. Michael Mooney. LC 80-13000. (Illus.). 160p. 1980. 10.50 (ISBN 0-931704-05-7); pap. 3.95 (ISBN 0-931704-04-9). Story Pr.
Squire. Louisa Taylor Parr. LC 7-34715. Cassell Publishing Company.
Squire Arden. Margaret Oliphant Wilson Oliphant. (Seaside library, v. 25, no. 511). 1879. G. Munro.
Squire Arden. A Novel. Margaret Oliphant Wilson Oliphant. LC 9-3855. 1875. Harper & Brothers.
Squire John: A Tale of the Cuban War. St. George Rathbonne. LC 8-591. (On cover: Neely's continental library, no. 4). 1897. F. T. Neely.
Squire of Ash. Frank Dilnot. LC 29-13071. 1929. Brentano's Ltd.
Squire of Bor Shachor. Chaim I. Bermant. 1977. 7.95 o.p. (ISBN 0-312-75442-6). St. Martin.
Squire of Bor Shachor: A Novel. Chaim I Bermant. LC 76-62752. 8.95 (ISBN 0-312-75442-6). St. Martin's Press.
Squire of Death. Richard Lockridge. LC 65-14896. (Main line mysteries). 1965. Lippincott.
Squire of Low Degree. Lily Augusta Long. LC 7-15151. (On cover: Appleton's town and country library. no. 68). 1890. D. Appleton and Company.
Squire of Sandal-Side: A Pastoral Romance. Amelia Edith Huddleston Barr. Dodd, Mead and Company.
Squire Phin: A Novel. Holman Francis Day. LC 5-32389. 1905. A. S. Barnes & Company.
Squire Phin: A Novel. Holman Francis Day. LC 13-194191. 1913. Harper & Brothers.
Squire Trevlyn's Heir: Or, Trevlyn Hold. Ellen Price Henry Wood Wood. (Seaside library, v. 7, no. 124). 1877. G. Munro.
Squireen. Shan F Bullock. 1906. McClure, Phillips and Company.
Squire's Darling. Charlotte Mary Brame. LC 44-111385. (On cover: Lovell's library, no. 1012). John W. Lovell Company.
Squire's Daughter. Archibald Marshall. 1912. Dodd Mead and Company.
Squire's Daughter. Archibald Marshall. LC 21-168707. 1920. Dodd, Mead and Company.
Squire's Daughter. Flora Macdonald Mayor. LC 44-14018. 1931. Coward, McCann, Inc.
Squire's Legacy. Mary Cecil Hay. (Seaside library, v. 2, no. 23). 1877. G. Munro.
Squire's Legacy. Mary Cecil Hay. (On cover: Lovell's library, v. 20, no. 972). 1887. J. W. Lovell Company.
Squirm. Richard Curtis. Ace.
Squirrel-Cage. with illustrations by john alonzo williams. ed. Dorothea Frances Canfield Fisher. LC 12-7966. 1912. 1.35. H. Holt and Company.
Squirrel Cage. Edwin Gilbert. LC 47-31284. 1947. Doubleday.
Squirrel Forever. Douglas Fairbairn. (O.s.i.). 1973. 6.95 o.s.i. (ISBN 0-671-21587-6). S&S.
Squirrel Inn. Frank Richard Stockton. LC 8-15537. 1891. The Century Co.
Srengenge. Shahnon Ahmad. Tr. by Harry Aveling. (Writing in Asia Ser.). 1979. pap. text ed. 5.50x (00240). Heinemann Ed.
Sri Sumarah & Other Stories. Umar Kayam. Tr. by Harry Aveling. (Writing in Asia Ser.). 1981. pap. text ed. 6.50x (00211). Heinemann Ed.
Srikanta. Saratchandra Chatterji. Tr. by Sen, K. C. Thompson Edward Joseph. LC 23-104743. (Half-title: An Eastern library. no. ii). H. Milford, Oxford University Press.
S.R.O. Robert Deane Pharr. LC 74-144287. 1971. 7.95. Doubleday.
SS-GB. Len Deighton. 1982. pap. 3.50 (ISBN 0-345-30454-3). Ballantine.
SS-GB. Len Deighton. 1980. pap. 2.95 (ISBN 0-345-29317-7). Ballantine.
SS-GB: Nazi-Occupied Britain, 1941. Len Deighton. LC 79-16424. 1979. 18.95 (ISBN 0-8161-6748-6). G. K. Hall.
SS-GB: Nazi-Occupied Britain, 1941: a Novel. Len Deighton. LC 78-14563. 1979. 10.00 (ISBN 0-394-50409-7). Knopf.
S.S. General. Sven Hassel. LC 72-8836. 1972. 0.95. Bantam Books.
Stab. Robert Alley. 224p. 1982. pap. 2.50 (ISBN 0-345-30689-9). Ballantine.
Stab in the Back. Charles Drummond. 4.95 o.p. (ISBN 0-8027-5211-X). Walker & Co.
Stab in the Back. Kenneth Giles. LC 70-120403. 1970. 4.95 (ISBN 0-8027-5211-X). Walker.
Stab in the Dark. Lawrence Block. LC 81-66971. 192p. 1981. 10.95 (ISBN 0-87795-340-6). Arbor Hse.
Stab in the Dark. Lawrence Block. 192p. 1982. pap. 2.75 (ISBN 0-515-06717-2). Jove Pubns.
Stab in the Dark: By Joe Rayter Pseud. Mary F McChesney. LC 55-10233. (A Mill mystery). 1955. M.S. Mill Co., and W. Morrow.
Stabbed in the Dark. Elizabeth Lynn Linton. (On cover: Seaside library. Pocket ed. no 817). 1886. Gr. Munro.
Stable Boy: By Adam Rebel Pseud. Tom Roan. LC 55-32122. (Beacon book original, no. 107). 1954. Beacon PublicationsCorp.
Stable for Nightmares: Or, Weird Tales : an Anonymous Anthology. LC 75-46286. (Supernatural and Occult Fiction). 1976. 15.00 (ISBN 0-405-08147-2). Arno Press.
Stacey. Alexander Black. LC 25-890. The Bobbs-Merrill Company.
Stacey. William Sherman. LC 76-51624. (Orig.). 1977. pap. 1.50 o.p. (ISBN 0-87216-393-8, C16393). Playboy.
Stacy. Kim Townsend. (Leisure Books). 1977. 1.95 (ISBN 0-8439-0507-7). Nordon Pubns.
Stacy Tower: A Novel. Robert H K Walter. LC 63-11813. 1963. Macmillan.
Stadium. Francis Wallace. LC 31-25216. Farrar & Rinehart Incorporated.
Stadium Beyond the Stars. 1st Ed. Milton Lesser. LC 60-5840. 1960. Winston.
Staff Nurse. Lucy Agnes Hancock. LC 42-21091. 1942. Macrae-Smith-Company.
Staff Nurse. Lucy Agnes Hancock. LC 44-21218. 1944. Triangle Books.
Staff Officer: Or, The Soldier of Fortune. A Tale of Real Life. Oliver Moore. LC 7-19166. 1833. E. L. Carey & A. Hart.
Stafford's Island. Florence Olmstead. 1920. C. Scribner's Sons.
Stag at Eve. Henry C Wilkinson. LC 78-116751. 1970. 5.00. Dorrance.
Stag at Large: Confessions of a Bachelor Abroad. Roger St. Martin O'Toole. LC 68-19824. 1968. Macmillan.
Stag Film Nymph. Dan Turk. pap. 1.95 o.p. (8041). Cameo.
Stag Girls. Jack Michaels. 192p. pap. 1.95 o.p. (6132). Brandon.
Stag Line. Graeme Lorimer & Lorimer, Sarah. LC 34-9620. 1934. Little, Brown and Company.
Stag Night. Albert Edward Idell. LC 46-4512. 1946. Prentice-Hall, Inc.
Stag Night. Philips Rogers. 2.95 o.p. Wehman.
Stag Party. 1st Ed. William Krasner. LC 56-111034. 1957. Harper.
Stage Baby: The Romance of a Trouper. Alexander McKenzie. LC 15-16010. 1915. 0.50. The Franklin Company.
Stage-Coach. Founded on Fact. 4th ed. Lucius Manlius Sargent. LC 7-1623. 1838. Whipple & Damrell.
Stage Daughter. Darrell Husted. LC 81-43414. (Starlight Romances). 1982. 10.95 (ISBN 0-385-17629-5). Doubleday.
Stage Door. Charles Belmont Davis. LC 74-122693. (Short story index reprint series). (Illus.). 1970. Books for Libraries Press.
Stage Door. Charles Belmont Davis. 1908. C. Scribner's Sons.
Stage Door Canteen: "a Story of Lovetime in Wartime,". Delmer Lawrence Daves. LC 44-871487. New Avon Library.
Stage for Fools. Michael Norday. LC 55-448385. 1955. Vixen Press.
Stage Mother. Marcia Miller. 1974. 4.50. Avalon Books.
Stage Mother. Bradford Ropes. LC 33-11631. 1933. A. H. King.
Stage of Fools. 1st Ed. Charles Andrew Brady. LC 52-129471. 1953. Dutton.
Stage of Love. Cecily Shelbourne. LC 77-9005. 8.95. Putnam.
Stage of Love. Cecily Shelbourne. (Berkley Medallion Books). 1978. 1.95 (ISBN 0-425-03879-3). Berkley Pub. Corp.
Stage Rider: By Chuck Stanleypseud. Charles Stanley Strong. LC 53-129227. 1953. Arcadia House.
Stage Road to Denver. Allan Vaughan Elston. LC 53-8938. 1953. Lippincott.
Stage Stop. James B Kelly. 1974. 4.95. Lenox Hill Press.
Stage Struck. Jean Carew. (Contemporary Teens Ser.). 224p. (Orig.). 1981. pap. 2.25 (ISBN 0-89531-137-2, 0146-96). Sharon Pubns.
Stage Struck. Simon Gray. LC 80-25312. 64p. 1981. 9.95 (ISBN 0-394-51804-7); pap. 4.95 (ISBN 0-394-17882-3). Seaver Bks.
Stage-Struck: Or, She Would Be an Opera-Singer. Blanche Roosevelt Macchetta. LC 7-15179. 1884. Fords, Howard, & Hulbert.
Stage to Link City. Dan Roberts. LC 66-5429. 1966. Arcadia House.
Stage to Link City. William Edward Daniel Ross. LC 66-5429. 1966. Arcadia House.
Stage to Rawhide. Floyd Day. LC 56-10909. 1956. Arcadia House.
Stage to Seven Springs. James Powell. 1979. pap. 1.75 (ISBN 0-441-77918-2). Ace Bks.
Stagecoach & Other Stories. Ernest Haycox. (Westerns Ser.). 1981. lib. bdg. cancelled o.s.i. (ISBN 0-8398-2677-X, Gregg). G K Hall.
Stagecoach Kingdom. Harry Sinclair Drago. LC 43-163449. 1943. Doubleday, Doran & Company, Inc.
Stagecoach to Hell. Giles A Lutz. LC 74-12700. 1975. 4.95 (ISBN 0-385-09951-7). Doubleday.
Stagecoach to Nowhere. Roger Margason. LC 75-36903. 176p. (Orig.). 1976. pap. 0.95 (ISBN 0-89041-056-9, 3056). Major Bks.
Stagecoach to the Brazos. Ford Bowne, pseud. Ed. by Alice Sachs. 1971. 3.95 o.p. Lenox Hill.
Staged for Death. Patricia Bird. 1976. 4.95. Avalon Books.
Stages of Love. Beverly Sommers. (Candlelight Ecstasy Ser.: No. 28). 192p. (Orig.). 1981. pap. 1.75 (ISBN 0-440-18363-4). Dell.
Stagger Lee. John Dee. LC 73-83800. 1973. IMAC, Inc.
Staggerford. Jon Hassler. LC 76-57757. 1977. 8.95 (ISBN 0-689-10793-5). Atheneum.
Stagline Feud. Jonathan H. Glidden. LC 41-16057. 1941. Dodd, Mead & Company.
Stain. Forrest Halsey. LC 13-4149. 1913. F. G. Browne & Co.
Stain: A Novel. Elfrieda Hochbaum. LC 55-15236. 1954. Big Mountain Press.
Stain of Suspicion. Charles Williams. 1973. (pbk.) 0.95 (ISBN 0-671-77669-X). Pocket Books.
Stain on the Snow. Georges Simenon. pap. 0.95 o.p. (ISBN 0-14-002178-7). Penguin.
Stained Glass. William Frank Buckley. LC 77-91557. 1978. 7.95 (ISBN 0-385-12542-9). Doubleday.
Stained Glass. William Frank Buckley. 1979. 2.25 (ISBN 0-446-82323-6). Warner Books.
Stained Glass Jungle. Gregory Wilson, pseud. LC 61-12605. 1962. Doubleday.
Stained Glass Lady: An Idyl. Blanche Elizabeth Wade. LC 6-36881. 1906. A. C. McClurg & Co.
Stained Glass Reflections. Carole Cullenbine. LC 76-8072. (Illus., Orig.). 1977. pap. 3.95 o.p. (ISBN 0-8256-3815-1, Hidden Hse). Music Sales.
Stained Sails: A Novel. John Thomas McIntyre. LC 28-5166. 1928. Frederick A. Stokes Company.
Stainless Steel Kimono. Elliott Chaze. LC 47-12461. 1947. Simon and Schuster.
Stainless Steel Rat. Harry Harrison. LC 74-103005. 1970. 4.95. Walker.
Stainless Steel Rat for President. Harry Harrison. 192p. 1982. pap. 2.50. Bantam.
Stainless Steel Rat Saves the World. Harry Harrison. LC 72-83853. 1972. 5.95 (ISBN 0-399-11047-X). Putnam.
Stainless Steel Rat Wants You! Harry Harrison. 1979. pap. 1.95 (ISBN 0-553-12625-3). Bantam.
Stainless Steel Rat's Revenge. Harry Harrison. LC 79-123268. 1970. 4.95. Walker.
Staircase. Charles Dyer. LC 79-86898. 1969. 5.95. Doubleday.
Staircase of Surprise. Frances Aymar Mathews. 1905. D. Appleton and Company.
Staircase 4. Helen Kieran Reilly. LC 49-7740. 1949. Random House.
Stairs of Sand. Nancy Huston Banks. (On cover: Globe library, v. 1, no. 132). 1890. Rand McNally & Company.
Stairs of Sand. Zane Grey. LC 43-100646. 1943. Harper & Brothers.

Stairs That Kept Going Down. Sir Compton Mackenzie. (Illus.). 1973. 3.95 (ISBN 0-385-05376-2). Doubleday.
Stairs to Nowhere. Gabriella Z. Psenitznik. 3.50 o.p. Vantage.
Stairs to Nowhere. first ed. Gabriella Z. Psenitznik. Tr. by Sylvia Zaoral. 1972. 3.50. Vantage.
Stairway. Alice Amelia Chown. LC 21-8168. The Cornhill Company.
Stairway. Ursula Reilly Curtiss. (Red badge detective). 1957. Dodd, Mead.
Stairway of the Sun. Robert Welles Ritchie. LC 24-35355. 1924. 2.00. Dodd, Mead and Company.
Stairway on the Wall. Augusta Prescott. LC 11-7303. 1911. 1.35. The Alice Harriman Company.
Stairway to an Empty Room. 1st. Ed. Dolores Birk Hitchens. LC 51-11334. 1951. Published for the Crime Club by Doubleday.
Stairway to Heaven. Zecharia Sitchin. 336p. 1983. pap. 3.50 (ISBN 0-380-63339-6). Avon.
Stairway to the Stars: A Novel. Treve Collins. LC 36-19254. 1936. Godwin.
Stake: A Story of the New England Coast. Jay Cady. LC 12-6557. 1912. 1.25. G. W. Jacobs & Company.
Stake in the Game. Evelyn Berckman. LC 72-84889. 1973. 5.95 (ISBN 0-385-05285-5). Doubleday.
Stake in the Game. Evelyn Berckman. (Dell Book). 1977. 1.50 (ISBN 0-440-15723-4). Dell Pub. Co.
Staked Plain. Frank X Tolbert. LC 56-11105. 1958. Harper.
Staked Plains Rendezvous. Roe Richmond. (Lashtrow Ser.: No. 7). 208p. (Orig.). 1981. pap. 1.95 (ISBN 0-8439-1019-4, Leisure Bks). Nordon Pubns.
Stakes Are High. 1st Ed. Ed. by Brent Ashabranner. LC 54-43099. (Pennant books, p64: 4). 1954. Bantam Books.
Staking Claims. Page Edwards, Jr. LC 79-66572. 160p. 1980. 11.95 (ISBN 0-7145-2689-4, Pub. by M Boyars). Merrimack Pub Cir.
Staking Claims: Stories. Page Edwards. LC 79-66572. 1980. 11.95 (ISBN 0-7145-2689-4). M. Boyars.
Stalemate. Evelyn Berckman. LC 66-17394. 1966. Published for the Crime Club by Doubleday.
Stalemate. Icchokas Meras. LC 79-26347. 10.00 (ISBN 0-8184-0296-2). Lyle Stuart.
Stalemate at Panmunjon: A Novel. Wilbert L Walker. LC 79-90648. 9.00 (ISBN 0-935428-00-3). Heritage Press.
Stalin, Tommy Tucker, and God. Stewart H. Quinn. LC 68-26050. 1969. 6.95. Dorrance.
Stalin's Tanks. 1980. pap. text ed. write for info. (ISBN 0-88074-162-7). Metagam.
Stalk the Hunter. Mitchell A Wilson. LC 43-12647. 1943. Simon and Schuster.
Stalked. Frances Rickett. 240p. 1983. pap. 2.95 (ISBN 0-380-81463-3). Avon.
Stalker. Bill Pronzini. 1973. Pocket Bks.
Stalker. Bill Pronzini. LC 73-140723. 1971. 5.95 (ISBN 0-394-46291-2). Random House.
Stalker Lord. Brenda G. Spielman. (Orig.). 1979. pap. 2.25 (ISBN 0-532-22174-5). Woodhill.
Stalkers. Luke Short. LC 73-4763. 1973. (pbk.) 0.75. Bantam Books.
Stalkers of the Sea. Ken Stanton. (Aquanauts Ser.). 1972. pap. 0.95 o.p. (95-173). Manor Bks.
Stalking. Tom Seligson. LC 78-65528. 8.95 (ISBN 0-89696-037-4). Everest House.
Stalking Blind. Steven Ashley. LC 76-21074. 1976. 6.95 (ISBN 0-8037-7909-7). Dial Press.
Stalking-Horse. Val Henry Gielgud. LC 49-50386. 1950. Morrow.
Stalking Horse. Abraham Rothberg. LC 72-80672. 1972. 5.95 (ISBN 0-8415-0209-9). Saturday Review Press.
Stalking Horse. Rafael Sabatini. LC 33-126473. 1933. Houghton Mifflin Company.
Stalking Horse. 1972. 5.95 o.p. (ISBN 0-8415-0209-9). Sat Rev Pr.
Stalking Horse: A Mystery. Collin Wilcox. 1982. 10.50 (ISBN 0-394-51173-5). Random.
Stalking Man. William Jeremiah Coughlin. (O.s.i.). 1979. 8.95 o.s.i. (ISBN 0-440-08334-6). Delacorte.
Stalking Man: A Novel. William Jeremiah Coughlin. LC 78-13359. 8.95. Delacorte Press.
Stalking Moon. Theodore V Olsen. LC 65-23799. 3.50. Doubleday.
Stalking of Adrian Lawford. Roderick Grant. 1975. pap. 1.25 o.p. (ISBN 0-515-03610-2, V3610). Pyramid Pubns.
Stalking Point. Duncan Kyle. LC 81-16729. 10.95 (ISBN 0-312-75540-6). St. Martin's Press.
Stalking Terror. (Signet Book). 1977. 1.50 (ISBN 0-451-07367-3). New American Library.
Stalking Terror. (Signet Book). 1977. 1.50 (ISBN 0-451-07367-3). New American Library.
Stalking the Far Away Places. Euell Gibbons. 1973. 7.95 o.p. (ISBN 0-679-50394-3). McKay.
Stalking the Golden Lion: A Historic-Fiction Novel. Robert L Peters. LC 52-11104. 1952. Meador Pub. Co.
Stalking the Nightmare. Harlan Ellison. LC 82-235745. 1982. 16.00 (ISBN 0-932096-16-6) (ISBN 0-932096-17-4). Phantasia Press.
Stalky & Co. Rudyard Kipling. LC 99-4556. 1899. Doubleday & McClure Co.
Stalky & Co. Rudyard Kipling. LC 18-21830. 1914. Doubleday, Page & Company, for Review of Reviews Co.
Stalky & Co. Rudyard Kipling. LC 28-1676. 1922. Doubleday, Page & Company.
Stalky & Co. With a New Introd. by Steven Marcus. Rudyard Kipling. LC 62-189946. (Collier books, AS383V. Classic). 1962. Collier Books.
Stalky & Company. Rudyard Kipling. (Orig.). 1962. pap. 0.95 o.p. (04419, Collier). Macmillan.
Stallion. William Chaffey. pap. 1.95 o.p. (8074). Cameo.
Stallion. Marguerite Steen. LC 33-7951. 1971. 6.50x (ISBN 0-7182-0699-1). Intl Pubns Serv.
Stallion: A Novel. Marguerite Steen. 1933. Little, Brown, and Company.
Stallion from the North. Daniel Joseph Clinton. LC 32-22990. 1932. Farrar & Rinehart, Incorporated.
Stallion Man. Judith Glover. LC 82-17049. 1983. 11.95 (ISBN 0-312-75542-2). St. Martin's Press.
Stallion of a Dream. Robert Vavra. LC 80-82431. (Illus.). 56p. 1980. 14.95 (ISBN 0-688-03746-1). Morrow.
Stallion Road: A Novel. Stephen Longstreet. LC 45-4613. 1945. J. Messner, Inc.
Stalwarts: How Oxford Students Stood for Protestantism. Frank Ernest Channon. LC 12-22124. 0.50. American Tract Society.
Stalwarts: Or, Who Were to Blame? A Novel, Portraying Fifty Years of American History. Showing Those Political Complications Which Have, in the United States Culminated in Civil War, and Even in the Assassination of Two Good Presidents. Francers Marie Norton. LC 7-33280. 1888. Frances M. Norton.
Stamboul Intrigue. Robert Charles, pseud. 1968. 3.50 o.p. Roy.
Stamboul Intrigue. Robert Charles Smith. LC 68-15898. 1968. Roy Publishers.
Stamboul Love. Anne Duffield. LC 34-103761. 1934. A. A. Knopf.
Stamboul Nights. Harrison Griswold Dwight. LC 16-6762. 1916. Doubleday, Page and Company.
Stamboul Nights. Harrison Griswold Dwight. LC 22-12088. 1922. Etc. Doubleday, Page & Company.
Stamp of Possession. Sheila Strutt. (Harlequin Romances Ser.). 192p. 1982. pap. 1.50. Harlequin Bks.
Stamped for Murder: A Wade Paris Mystery. Ben Benson. LC 52-5059. 1952. M. S. Mill Co., and W. Morrow.
Stampede. Will C Knott. (Berkley Medallion Book). 1978. 1.25 (ISBN 0-425-03665-0). Berkley Pub. Corp.
Stampede. Edward Beverly Mann. LC 34-2224. 1934. W. Morrow & Co.
Stampede! Lancelot De Giberne Sieveking. LC 28-30705. 1928. Brentano's.
Stampede. Stewart Edward White. LC 42-216. 1942. Doubleday, Doran and Company, Inc.
Stampede at Blue Springs. Gene Olson. LC 56-111819. (Dodd, Mead silver star westerns). 1956. Dodd, Mead.
Stampede Canyon. Robert J Hogan. LC 52-8984. (Silver star westerns). 1952. Dodd, Mead.
Stampede Jones. William Frederick Bragg. LC 54-11467. 1954. Arcadia House.
Stampede Kid. Norman A Fox. LC 43-206. 1942. Phoenix Press.
Stampeders. James Beardsley Hendryx. LC 51-9260. (Double D western). 1951. Doubleday.
Stamping Ground. Loren D Estleman. LC 79-7673. 1980. 8.95 (ISBN 0-385-15563-8). Doubleday.
Stan Ball of the Rangers. Rutherford George Montgomery. LC 41-13061. David McKay Company.
Stanbroke Girls: A Novel of Regency England. Fiona Hill. LC 80-21474. 10.95 (ISBN 0-312-75570-8). St. Martin's Press.
Stanbroke Girls: A Novel of Regency England. large print ed. Fiona Hill. LC 81-6244. 1981. 13.95 (ISBN 0-8161-3252-6). G.K. Hall.
Stand. Stephen King. LC 77-16928. 1978. 12.50 (ISBN 0-385-12168-7). Doubleday.
Stand and Give Challenge. Francis MacManus. LC 36-4468. 1935. Loring & Mussey.
Stand Before Kings. Gertrude Schweitzer. LC 81-15723. 14.95 (ISBN 0-399-12702-X). Putnam.
Stand by. Carolyn Cox. LC 25-15758. 1925. Harper & Brothers.
Stand-by: A Novel. Edmund Pearson Dole. LC 6-33851. 1897. The Century Co.
Stand by for Romance. Portia Maxwell. LC 41-165991. Gramercy Publishing Company.
Stand by for Romance (Stand by for Love) By Kathleen Harris Pseud. Adelaide Humphries. LC 52-11396. 1952. Arcadia House.
Stand by-y-y to Start Engines. Daniel V Gallery. LC 66-11645. 1966. W. W. Norton.
Stand Clear of Thunder. Hagar Wilde. LC 33-347841. 1933. Little, Brown, and Company.
Stand Fast Craig-Royston! A Novel. William Black. LC 6-12916. (Harper's Franklin square library, no. 68). 1890. Harper & Brothers.
Stand Fast, Craig-Royston! A Novel. William Black. LC 41-32188. 1891. Harper & Brothers.
Stand-in. Merriam Modell. LC 70-106606. 1970. 4.95. McKay.
Stand-In. Evelyn Piper. LC 70-106606. 1970. 4.95 o.p. McKay.
Stand-in Bride. Carole Halston. 192p. 1981. pap. 1.50 (ISBN 0-671-57062-5). S&S.
Stand-in for Death. Margaret Echard. LC 40-5219. 1940. Pub. for the Crime Club by Doubleday, Doran & Co., Inc.
Stand-in for Murder. Leonard Reginald Gribble. Roy Publishers.
Stand-in for Passion. William Arthur Neubauer. LC 50-13801. 1950. Phoenix Press.
Stand-in for Romance. Marcia Miller. (YA) 1973. 4.50 o.p. (Avalon). Bouregy.
Stand-in for Romance. Marcia Miller. (Fawcett Gold Medal Book). 1976. (pbk.) 0.95. Fawcett.
Stand in the Rain. Jean Watson. 1968. 3.50 o.s.i. Tri-Ocean.
Stand in the Rain: A Novel. Jean Watson. LC 66-24942. 1966. 3.95. Bobbs.
Stand in the Sun. Max Von Kreisler. LC 77-11755. (A Double D. western). 1978. 6.95 (ISBN 0-385-13670-6). Doubleday.
Stand into Danger. Alexander Kent. LC 80-23766. 1981. 10.95 (ISBN 0-399-12539-6). Putnam.
Stand Like Men: A Novel. James Sherburne. LC 72-12399. 1973. 6.95 (ISBN 0-395-17117-2). Houghton Mifflin.
Stand on It. Stroker Ace. LC 73-10414. 1973. 6.95 (ISBN 0-316-66870-2). Little, Brown.
Stand on It. Stroker Ace. 1974. (pbk.) 1.50 (ISBN 0-345-24226-2). Ballantine Books.
Stand on Zanzibar. John Brunner. LC 68-22631. (Doubleday science fiction). 1968. 6.95. Doubleday.
Stand on Zanzibar. John Brunner. LC 79-19062. 1979. 15.00 (ISBN 0-8376-0438-9). R. Bentley.
Stand Pat: Or, Poker Stories from the Mississippi. David A Curtis. LC 6-16996. 1906. L. C. Page & Company.
Stand Still Like the Hummingbird. Henry Miller. LC 62-10408. (Cloth ed. 6.50 o.p.). 1967. pap. 4.95 (ISBN 0-8112-0322-0, NDP236). New Directions.
Stand up and Die: A Captain Heimrich Mystery. Richard Lockridge & Frances Louise Davis Lockridge. LC 53-8928. (Mainline mysteries). 1953. Lippincott.
Stand We at Last. Zoe Fairbairns. LC 82-15624. 1983. 15.95 (ISBN 0-395-32863-2). Houghton Mifflin.
Standard Bearer. Samuel Rutherford Crockett. LC 6-31591. 1898. D. Appleton and Company.
Standard Bearer. Efraim Sevela. LC 82-12060. 1982. 14.95 (ISBN 0-89651-701-2) (ISBN 0-89651-703-9). Icarus Press.
Standard Dreaming. Hortense Calisher. LC 72-82176. 1972. 5.95 (ISBN 0-87795-043-1). Arbor House.
Standard Dreaming. Hortense Calisher. 1974. (pbk.) 1.50. Dell.
Standard in the Sulu Sea. 1st Ed. Floyd Clinton Turner. LC 56-12760. Pageant Press.
Standby Nurse. Mary Collins Dunne. 192p. (YA) 1974. 4.95 o.p. (Avalon). Bouregy.
Standin' Short. Charles Edgar & Mary Edgar. 6.95 o.p. Vantage.
Standing Fast. Harvey Swados. LC 73-121957. 1970. 8.95. Doubleday.
Standing in Others' Way. G. S Hoyt. LC 7-5666. 1882. H. Gannett.
Standing on a Drum. Irwin R Blacker. LC 68-12097. 1968. Putnam.
Standing Room Only: Or, A Laugh in Every Line. Walter Greenwood. LC 36-32135. 1936. Doubleday, Doran & Company, Inc.
Standish Gaunt Case. Innis Patterson. LC 31-24658. Farrar & Rinehart, Incorporated.
Standish of Standish: A Story of the Pilgrims. Jane Goodwin Austin. LC 41-82187. 1890. Houghton, Mifflin and Company.
Standish of Standish. A Story of the Pilgrims. Jane Goodwin Austin. LC 6-5042. 1895. Houghton, Mifflin and Company.
Standish of Standish: A Story of the Pilgrims. 28th impression. ed. Jane Goodwin Austin. LC 4-16451. Houghton, Mifflin and Company.
Standish the Puritan. A Tale of the American Revolution. Robert Hare. LC 7-2861. 1850. Harper & Brothers.
Stands a Calder Man. Janet Dailey. (Orig.). 1983. pap. price not set (ISBN 0-671-83609-9). PB.
Stanfield Harvest. Richard Martin Stern. (Crest Book, P2015). 1973. (pbk.) 1.25. Fawcett.
Stanfield Harvest. Richard Martin Stern. LC 74-178815. 1972. 7.95 (ISBN 0-529-04518-4). World Pub.
Stanford Short Stories. Ed. by Wallace Earle Stegner & Richard Scowcroft. Incl. 1962. 7.50x (ISBN 0-8047-0392-2); 1964. 168p. 7.50x (ISBN 0-8047-0393-0); 1968. 170p. 7.50x (ISBN 0-8047-0396-5). Stanford U Pr.
Stanford Short Stories: Ed. by Wallace Stegner, Richard Scowcroft, Nancy Packer.
Stanford Short Stories, 1946- Stanford University. LC 47-5367. Stanford University Press; Etc., Etc.
Stanford Short Stories: 1962. Stanford University. LC 47-5367. 3.50. Stanford Univ. Pr.
Stanford Stories: Tales of a Young University. 2d ed. Charles Kellogg Field & William Henry Irwin. LC 71-121541. (Short story index reprint series). (Illus.). 1970. (ISBN 0-8369-3497-0). Books for Libraries Press.
Stanford Stories: Tales of a Young University. Charles Kellogg Field & Leland, Stanford Junior University--Fiction. LC 2976. 1900. Doubleday, Page & Company.
Stanford Stories: Tales of a Young University. Charles Kellogg Field & Leland Stanford Junior Univeristy--Fiction. LC 14-14265. 1913. A. M. Robertson.
Stanhope Burleigh. The Jesuits in Our Homes. Charles Edwards Lester. LC 2-3523. 1855. Stringer & Townsend.
Stanhope Burleigh. The Jesuits in Our Homes. A Novel. Helen Black. LC 2-3523. 1855. Stringer & Townsend.
Stanhope of Chester. Percy Andreae. LC 6-2454. (On cover: Globe library, v. 1, no. 233). 1896. Rand, McNally & Company.
Stanley Buxton: Or, The Schoolfellows... John Galt. LC 6-45963. 1833. E. L. Carey & A. Hart.
Stanley Buxton: Or, The Schoolfellows... John Galt. LC 6-45962. 1833. E. L. Carey & A. Hart.
Stanley Elkin's Greatest Hits. Stanley Elkin. LC 80-15891. 9.95 (ISBN 0-525-20940-9). Dutton.
Stanley Elkin's Greatest Hits. Stanley Elkin. LC 81-2826. 7.95 (ISBN 0-446-97674-1). Warner Books.
Stanley Huntingdon. A Novel. Sydney J Wilson. LC 8-370482. 1886. Press of J. B. Lippincott Company.
Stanley John's Wife. Katharine Haviland Taylor. LC 26-478119. George H. Doran Company.
Stanley: Or, The Recollections of a Man of the World... Horace Binney Wallace. LC 8-33281. 1838. Lea & Blanchard.
Stanley: The Don Juan of Second Avenue. Rick Allmen. LC 73-14303. 1974. 7.95 (ISBN 0-06-010094-X). Harper & Row.
Stanley: The Don Juan of 2nd Avenue. Rick Allmen. LC 73-14303. 352p. 1974. 7.95 o.p. (ISBN 0-06-010094-X, HarpT). Har-Row.
Stanmore Hall and Its Inmates. Herbert Spring. LC 13-3302. 1913. B. Herder.
Stanton Bishop, M. D. easy eye ed. Norman Daniels. (Orig.). 1969. pap. 0.60 o.p. (73825). Lancer.
Stanton Wins. Eleanor Marie Ingram. LC 11-112817. 1.00. The Bobbs-Merrill Company.
Stapleton. Grif Alexander. LC 56-11544. 1956. Dorrance.
Star. Charlemagne Ischir Defontenay. (Science Fiction Ser). 1975. pap. 1.25 o.p. (UY1200). DAW Bks.
Star. James Noble Gifford. LC 44-2704. 1944. Arcadia House.
Star. Warren Howard. LC 44-270429. 1944. Arcadia House, Inc.
Star. Michael McClure. 1970. 4.75 o.p. (GP612). Grove.
Star. David Meltzer. 192p. pap. 1.95 o.p. (6135). Brandon.
Star. Allan Nixon. pap. 0.75 o.p. (54-717-X). Paperback Lib.
Star-Anchored, Star-Angered. Suzette Haden Elgin. LC 78-14699. (Doubleday science fiction). 1979. 7.95 (ISBN 0-385-13564-5). Doubleday.
Star and a Heart. Florence Marryat Church Lean. LC 7-13225. (On cover: Lovell's library. v. 19. no. 944). 1887. J. W. Lovell Company.
Star & Gate Diary of Discovery: A Record of Personal Insights. Richard Geer. 80p. (Orig.). 1980. pap. 6.00 (ISBN 0-911167-00-5). Cloud Ent.
Star Anise. Theodore Enslin. (Illus.). 1980. pap. 5.00 (ISBN 0-915316-82-X). Pentagram.
Star-Apple Kingdom. Derek Walcott. LC 78-11323. 8.95 (ISBN 0-374-26974-2). Farrar, Straus, and Giroux.
Star at Noon. Louis Redfield Peattie. LC 39-9058. 1939. Doubleday, Doran & Co., Inc.
Star Axe. Duncan McGreary. (Orig.). 1980. pap. text ed. 2.25 o.s.i. (ISBN 0-505-51579-2). Tower Bks.
Star Babies. Raymond Strait. 224p. 1981. pap. 2.75 (ISBN 0-425-04930-2). Berkley Pub.

TITLE INDEX STAR-SPANGLED HUSTLE.

Star Begotten. Herbert George Wells. 1977. Repr. pap. 1.25 (ISBN 0-532-12512-6). Woodhill.
Star-Begotten. Herbert George Wells. 176p. 1975. pap. 0.95 o.p. (532-95394-095). Manor Bks.
Star-Begotten. Herbert George Wells. 1975. (pbk.) 0.95. Manor Books.
Star-Begotten: A Biological Fantasia. Herbert George Wells. LC 37-27374. 1937. The Viking Press.
Star Born. Andre Norton, pseud. 1980. pap. 2.25 (ISBN 0-441-78016-4). Ace Bks.
Star Bridge: By Jack Williamson and James E. Gunn. 1st Ed. Jack Williamson & James Edward Gunn. LC 55-5463. 1955. Gnome Press.
Star Bright. Martin Caidin. (Orig.). 1979. pap. 2.25 (ISBN 0-553-12621-0). Bantam.
Star-Chamber: An Historical Romance. William Harrison Ainsworth & Browne, Hablot Knight, 1815-1882, Illus. LC 6-8356. 1873. G. Routledge and Sons.
Star Chase. Brian James Royal. LC 79-18749. 7.95 (ISBN 0-525-66671-0). Elsevier/Nelson Books.
Star Chase: A Science Fiction Novel. Brian James Royal. LC 79-18749. 1979. 8.95 (ISBN 0-525-66671-0). Lodestar Bks.
Star Child. Fred M. Stewart. LC 74-80712. 1974. 6.95 (ISBN 0-87795-093-8). Arbor Hse.
Star Child: A Novel. Fred Mustard Stewart. LC 74-80712. 1974. 6.95 (ISBN 0-87795-093-8). Arbor House.
Star Child: A Novel. Fred Mustard Stewart. 1975. (pbk.) 1.75. Bantam.
Star Child Trilogy. Frederik Pohl & Jack Williamson. 1977. pap. 2.50 (ISBN 0-671-82284-5). PB.
Star Colony. Keith Laumer. LC 81-5731. 1981. 14.95 (ISBN 0-312-15087-3). St Martin's Press.
Star Courier. A. Bertram Chandler. (Science Fiction Ser.). 1977. pap. 1.25 o.p. (ISBN 0-87997-292-0, UY1292). DAW Bks.
Star Courier. Chandler, A. Bertrum. 1977. 1.25 (ISBN 0-87997-292-0). DAW Books.
Star-Crossed. Charlotte Lamb, pseud. (Alpha Books). (Orig.). 1979. pap. text ed. 2.95x (ISBN 0-19-424160-2). Oxford U Pr.
Star-Crossed Lover. Carter Brown, pseud. 1974. (pbk.) 0.95. New American Library.
Star-Crossed: The Life and Love of an Actress. Lillian Spencer. LC 8-15506. 1888. The Judge Publishing Company.
Star-Crossed Woman. Maribelle Cormack. LC 62-20043. 1962. Crown Publishers.
Star-Crowned Kings. Robert Chilson. (Science Fiction Ser.). pap. 1.95 (ISBN 0-87997-606-3, UJ 1606). DAW Bks.
Star-Crowned Kings. Robert Chilson. (Science Fiction Ser). 1975. pap. 1.25 o.p. (ISBN 0-87997-190-8, UY1190). DAW Bks.
Star-Crowned Kings. Robert Chilson. 1975. (pbk.) 1.25. DAW Books.
Star Diaries. Stanislaw Lem. LC 75-44428. (Continuum book). (Illus.). 8.95 (ISBN 0-8164-9283-2). Seabury Press.
Star Diaries. Stanislaw Lem. LC 77-360458. (Illus.). 1976. 3.90 (ISBN 0-436-24421-7). Secker and Warburg.
Star Diaries. Stanislaw Lem. (Illus.). 1977. 1.75 (ISBN 0-380-01812-8). Avon Books.
Star-Dreams. Frederic Perkins. LC 29-20551. 1928. Private Print at The Riverside Press.
Star Driver. Lee Correy, pseud. 1980. pap. 1.95 (ISBN 0-345-28994-3). Ballantine.
Star-Dust: The Story of an American Girl. Fannie Hurst. LC 21-4908. Harper & Brothers.
Star Dwellers. James Blish. 112p. 1982. pap. 1.95 (ISBN 0-380-57976-6, 57976). Avon.
Star Eternal. Ka-Tzetnik. LC 75-141639. 1971. 4.95 (ISBN 0-87795-009-1). Arbor Hse.
Star Eternal. Ka-Tzetnik 135633. LC 75-141639. 1971. 4.95. Arbor House.
Star Eyes. Ann Ashton. LC 82-45282. 1983. 11.95 (ISBN 0-385-18130-2). Doubleday.
Star Fell. Sylvia Leonore Brett Brooke. LC 40-8816. Harrison-Hilton Books, Inc.
Star Fighter. Robert E. Mills. (Star Quest Ser.: No. 2). 1978. pap. 1.75 o.s.i. (ISBN 0-505-51283-1). Tower Bks.
Star Fighters. Robert E Mills. (Belmont Tower Book.). 1978. 1.75 (ISBN 0-505-51283-1). Tower Pubns.
Star-Fire Prophecy. Jane Toombs. (Berkley Medallion) (ISBN 0-425-03257-4). Berkley.
S.T.A.R. Flight. E. C. Tubb. (Orig.). 1969. pap. 0.50 o.p. (62-009). Paperback Lib.
Star Flower. Jim Kelly. (Small Star Stories). (Illus.). 1975. 5.95 o.p. (ISBN 0-02-645710-5, 64571); cassette 6.95 o.p. (ISBN 0-02-645720-2, 64572). Glencoe.
Star for a Night: A Story of Stage Life. Elsie Janis. LC 11-26176. 1911. 1.00. W. Rickey & Company.
Star for Christina. Blakely St. James. LC 81-82362. (Christina Van Bell Ser.). 256p. (Orig.). 1982. pap. 2.95 (ISBN 0-87216-985-5). Playboy Pbks.
Star for Susan. Frances Shelley Wees. LC 43-2623. 1942. The Sun Dial Press.
Star for Susan. Frances Shelley Wees. LC 40-321393. 1940. Macrae-Smith Company.
Star Force. Robert E. Mills. (Star Quest Ser.: No. 3). 1978. pap. 1.75 o.s.i. (ISBN 0-505-51312-9). Tower Bks.
Star Fox. Poul Anderson. LC 65-17261. 1965. Doubleday.
Star Gate. Alice Mary Norton. 1.50. Ace Books.
Star Gate: By Andre Norton Pseud. 1st Ed. Alice Mary Norton. LC 58-862619. 1958. Harcourt, Brace.
Star-Gazer. Zsolt Harsanyi. Tr. by Tabor, Paul. LC 39-15266. 1939. G. P. Putnam's Sons.
Star-Gazers. Abbe Carter Goodloe. LC 10-21635. 1910. 1.00. C. Scribner's Sons.
Star Ghosts. Hans Holzer. 1979. pap. 1.75 o.s.i. (ISBN 0-8439-0686-3, Leisure Bks). Nordon Pubns.
Star Giant. Dorothy Shinkle. (Belmont Tower book). 1978. 1.50 (ISBN 0-505-51267-X). Tower Pubns.
Star Giant. Dorothy Skinkle. 1978. pap. 1.50 o.s.i. (ISBN 0-505-51267-X). Tower Bks.
Star God. Allen Wold. LC 79-23373. 8.95 (ISBN 0-312-75578-3). St. Martin's Press.
Star Gods. Jack Lovejoy. 1979. pap. 1.75 (ISBN 0-89041-230-8, 3230). Major Bks.
Star Guard. Andre Norton, pseud. 1978. pap. 2.25 (ISBN 0-449-23646-3, Crest). Fawcett.
Star Guard: By Andre Norton Pseud. 1st Ed. Alice Mary Norton. LC 55-7612. 1955. Harcourt, Brace.
Star Hawks Empire Ninety-Nine. Ron Goulart & Gil Kane. LC 79-90921. (Illus.). 192p. 1980. pap. 1.95 (ISBN 0-87216-637-6). Playboy Pbks.
Star Hawks: The Cyborg King. Ron Goulart & Gil Kane. LC 81-81985. 192p. (Orig.). 1981. pap. 2.25 (ISBN 0-87216-910-3). Playboy Pbks.
Star Heights, and Other Stories, Pastels and Poems. Leonora Beck. LC 6-9780. 1895. The Foote & Davies Co.
Star House. Rosemary Newell. (Queen-size Gothic). 1973. (pbk) 0.95. Popular Library.
Star Hunter. Andre Norton, pseud. Bd. with Voodoo Planet. 1980. pap. 1.95 (ISBN 0-441-78194-2). Ace Bks.
Star Hunters. Jo Clayton. (Science Fiction Ser.). 1980. pap. 1.75 (ISBN 0-87997-550-4, UE1550). DAW Bks.
Star in a Mist: A Novel. Arthur John Arbuthnott Stringer. LC 43-12692. 1943. The Bobbs-Merrill Company.
Star in a Prison: A Tale of Canada. Anna May Wilson. LC 8-37108. (On cover: New Sabbath library. v. l., no. 8). D. C. Cook Publishing Company.
Star in Love. Berta Ruck. LC 35-353536. 1935. Dodd, Mead & Company.
Star in the Desert: By the Author of A Trap to Catch a Sunbeam, Old Jolliffe... Matilda Anne Mackarness. LC 7-16433. 1853. J. Munroe and Company.
Star in the East. Hans Holzer. 1973. pap. 1.25 o.p. (ISBN 0-515-02878-9, V3260). Pyramid Pubns.
Star in the Family. Irvin Faust. LC 74-9445. 1975. 7.95 (ISBN 0-385-01023-0). Doubleday.
Star in the Family. Irvin Faust. 1976. (pbk.) 1.95. Ballantine.
Star in the Rigging. Garland Roark. 1969. pap. 0.75 o.p. (0502-07034-075). Curtis.
Star in the Rigging: A Novel of the Texas Navy. 1st Ed. Garland Roark. LC 54-73166. 1954. Doubleday.
Star in the Well: A Christmas Story. Temple Bailey. LC 29-3498. The P. F. Volland Company.
Star in the West. Richard Emery Roberts. LC 51-12136. 1951. Random House.
Star in the Wind. Robert Nathan. 1962. 5.95 o.p. (ISBN 0-394-44689-5). Knopf.
Star in the Window: A Novel. Olive Higgins Prouty. LC 18-17608. Frederick A. Stokes Company.
Star Inn. Sue Mildred Lee Johnston. LC 53-5945. 1953. Ave Maria Press.
Star Is Made. Marcus Van Heller, pseud. pap. 1.95 o.s.i. (OPH-241, Ophelia). Olympia.
Star Killers. James R Singleton. LC 77-80980. 2.95 (ISBN 0-89343-025-0). Ermine Publishers.
Star King. Jack Vance, pseud. 1978. 1.75 (ISBN 0-87997-402-8). DAW Books.
Star Kings. Edmond Hamilton. LC 49-118021. (Fell's science-fiction library). 1949. F. Fell.
Star Light, Star Bright. Alfred Bester. LC 77-15050. (great short fiction of Alfred Bester; v. 2). 7.95 (ISBN 0-399-11816-0). Berkley Pub. Corp.: Distributed by Putnam.
Star Light, Star Bright. Stanley Ellin. LC 78-11519. 8.95 (ISBN 0-394-42217-1). Random House.
Star Light, Star Bright. Amy Williamson. 192p. (Orig.). 1982. pap. 1.95 (ISBN 0-449-70031-3, Juniper). Fawcett.
Star Listeners. Donald O Johnson. LC 67-22548. 1967. Academe Press.
Star Loot. A. Bertram Chandler. (Science Fiction Ser.). 1980. pap. 1.75 (ISBN 0-87997-564-4, UE1564). Daw Bks.
Star Lust. Jack Hanley. LC 34-37836. W. Godwin, Inc.
Star Magic. Channing Pollock. LC 33-22469. Farrar & Rinehart, Incorporated.
Star Maker. William Olaf Stapledon. LC 73-157939. 1972. (u.s.) 1.25 (ISBN 0-14-003541-9). Penguin Books.
Star Maker see Last & First Men.
Star Man's Son. Andre Norton, pseud. 1978. pap. 1.95 (ISBN 0-449-23614-5, Crest). Fawcett.
Star Money. Kathleen Winsor. LC 50-6054. 1950. Appleton-Century-Crofts.
Star Money. Kathleen Winsor. LC 51-26342. (Signet book, 868 AB). 1951. New American Library.
Star Mother. Sydney J Van Scyoc. LC 75-26766. (Berkley Medallion Book). 1977. 1.50 (ISBN 0-425-03345-7). Berkley Pub. Corp.
Star of Bethlehem. Ed. by John C. Rhodes & Joseph G. Beery. (O.s.i.). 1969. Repr. of 1889 ed. 3.75x o.s.i. (ISBN 0-87813-101-9). Park View.
Star of Danger. Marion Zimmer Bradley. LC 79-17575. (Gregg Press science fiction series). (Illus.). 1979. 8.00 (ISBN 0-8398-2512-9). Gregg Press.
Star of Danger. Marion Zimmer Bradley. 1975. (pbk.) 1.25. Ace Books.
Star of David. Jerry Hoffmann. LC 75-2173. 1975. 4.95 (ISBN 0-517-52169-5). Lenox Hill Press.
Star of Earth. Octavus Roy Cohen. LC 32-5295. 1932. D. Appleton and Company.
Star of Earth. Morris Dallett. LC 23-2885. 1923. A. A. Knopf.
Star of Empire: A Novel. Grant Lewi. LC 35-2725. The Vanguard Press.
Star of Gettysburg. Joseph Alexander Altsheler. 1976. Repr. of 1915 ed. lib. bdg. 18.55x (ISBN 0-88411-945-9). Amereon Ltd.
Star of Gettysburg: A Story of Southern High Tide. Joseph Alexander Altsheler. LC 15-4796. 1915. D. Appleton and Company.
Star of Glass. Ann Birstein. LC 50-9577. (Intercollegiate literary fellowship prise novel). 1950. Dodd, Mead.
Star of Hollywood. Edward Stilgebauer & Wilson, E. E. Tr. LC 30-12381. International Library.
Star of Hope. Lillian Taft Maize. LC 39-19895. The Penn Publishing Company.
Star of Lancaster. Jean Plaidy. (Plantagenet Saga Ser.). 320p. 1982. 12.95 (ISBN 0-399-12758-5). Putnam Pub Group.
Star of Life. Edmond Hamilton. LC 59-663872. (Torquil book). 1959. Distributed by Dodd, Mead.
Star of Light. J. St. John. pap. 1.50 o.p. Believers Bkshelf.
Star of Macedon: A Novel. Karl V Eiker. LC 57-6724. 1957. Putnam.
Star of Midnight. Arthur Somers Roche. LC 36-1122. 1936. Dodd, Mead & Company.
Star of Satan. Georges Bernanos. LC 75-20060. 1975. 14.00. H. Fertig.
Star of Stars. 1st Ed. Ed. by Frederik Pohl. LC 60-13554. (Doubleday science fiction). 1960. Doubleday.
Star of the Alamo. Willis Vernon Cole. LC 26-1390. 1926. The Writers Guild.
Star of the Hills. Wilder Anthony. The Macaulay Company.
Star of the North. Francis William Sullivan. LC 16-12401. 1916. G. P. Putnam's Sons.
Star of the Orsini. Ludwig Huna & Pemberton, Madge, Tr. LC 31-604. 1930. Brewer and Warren Inc.
Star of the Sea. Linda Haldeman. LC 77-82759. 1978. 6.95 (ISBN 0-385-13363-4). Doubleday.
Star of the Sea. Linda Haldeman. LC 78-23928. 1980. 11.50 (ISBN 0-8161-6654-4). G. K. Hall.
Star of the Sea. Linda Haldeman. 1981. 2.25 (ISBN 0-380-54114-9). Avon Books.
Star of the Unborn. Franz Werfel. 1976. (pbk.) 1.95. Bantam Books.
Star of the Unborn. Franz V. Werfel. Tr. by Gustave Otto Arlt. LC 46-1349. 1946. The Viking Press.
Star of the West: The Romance of the Lewis and Clark Expedition. Ethel Powelson Hueston. LC 35-6161. The Bobbs-Merrill Company.
Star of the Wilderness: A Novel. Karle Wilson Baker. LC 42-12646. Coward-McCann, Inc.
Star of Valhalla: A Romance of Early Christianity in Norway. Myra Geraldine Gross. LC 7-17387. 1907. F. A. Stokes Company.
Star on the Mountain. Renee Shann. LC 52-31005. 1952. Arcadia House.
Star Over Adobe. Dorothy L. Pillsbury. LC 63-21376. (Illus.). 1977. pap. 4.95 o.p. (ISBN 0-8263-0179-7). U of NM Pr.
Star Over Flushing. Stella Eugenie Asling Riis. LC 40-633. B. Humphries, Inc.
Star-Packers. Nelson Coral Nye. LC 37-173502. Greenberg.
Star People. Brad Steiger & Francie Steiger. (Orig.). 1981. pap. 2.50 (ISBN 0-425-04823-3). Berkley Pub.
Star Pointed North. Edmund Fuller. LC 46-11801. 1946. Harper & Brothers.
Star Probe. Joseph Green. LC 77-360343. 3.00 (ISBN 0-86000-057-5). Millington Books.
Star (Psi Cassiopeia) C. I Defontenay. (Illus.). 1975. (pbk.) 1.25. DAW Books.
Star: Psi Cassiopeia) Charlemagne Ischir Defontenay. LC 75-330091. (Illus.). 1975. 1.25. Daw Books.
Star: Psi Cassiopeia) Charlemagne Ischir Defontenay. LC 76-10806. (Gregg Press science fiction series). 1976. 9.50 (ISBN 0-8398-2324-X). Gregg Press.
Star (Psi Cassiopeia) Charlemagne Ischir Defontenay. (Science Fiction Ser.). 208p. 1976. Repr. of 1854 ed. lib. bdg. 10.95 o.p. (ISBN 0-8398-2324-X, Gregg). G K Hall.
Star Quality: Six Stories. Noel Pierce Coward. LC 75-109288. 1970. Greenwood Press.
Star Quality; Six Stories. Noel Pierce Coward. LC 51-1321. 1951. Doubleday.
Star Quality: Six Stories. 1st Ed. Noel Pierce Coward. LC 51-1321. 1951. Doubleday.
Star Quest. Robert E Mills. (Belmont Tower Book.). 1978. 1.75 (ISBN 0-505-51259-9). Tower Pubns.
Star Quest: An Incredible Voyage into the Unknown. Steven Caldwell. LC 79-52717. (Illus.). 3.98 (ISBN 0-517-29224-6). Crescent.
Star-Raker. Donald Gordon Payne. LC 62-8856. 1962. Morrow.
Star Rangers. Andre Norton, pseud. 1979. pap. 1.95 (ISBN 0-449-24076-2, Crest). Fawcett.
Star Rangers: By Andre Norton Pseud. 1st Ed. Alice Mary Norton. 1953. Harcourt, Brace.
Star Rider. Doris Piserchia. (Bantam science fiction). 1974. (pbk.) 1.25. Bantam Books.
Star Riders of Ren. Calvin Miller. LC 82-48408. (Singreale Chronicles Ser.: Vol. 2). (Illus.). 224p. 1983. pap. 7.95 (ISBN 0-06-250576-9, HarpT). Har-Row.
Star Rising. Jess Carr. (Orig.). 1980. pap. 3.50 o.s.i. (ISBN 0-505-51575-X). Tower Bks.
Star Rising. Clarence Budington Kelland. LC 38-343117. 1938. Harper & Brothers.
Star Road. Gordon R Dickson. LC 72-89304. (Doubleday science fiction). 1973. 5.95 (ISBN 0-385-06811-5). Doubleday.
Star Road. Gordon R Dickson. 1974. (pbk.) 1.25. DAW Books.
Star Rogue. Lin Carter. (Orig.). 1970. pap. 0.75 o.p. (ISBN 0-447-74649-9). Lancer.
Star Rover. Jack London. LC 15-19808. 1915. The Macmillan Company.
Star Rover. Jack London. LC 33-28354. 1929. The Macmillan Company.
Star Rover. Autobiographical Introd. Jack London. LC 62-21212. 1963. Macmillan.
Star Rovers. H. U. Bevis. Ed. by Alice Sachs. 1970. 3.95 o.p. Lenox Hill.
Star Sailors. Gary L Bennett. LC 79-27175. 12.95 (ISBN 0-312-75582-1). St. Martin's Press.
Star Sapphire. Rebecca Danton, pseud. 1979. pap. 1.75 (ISBN 0-449-50058-6, Coventry). Fawcett.
Star Sapphire: A Novel. Mabel Collins Cook. LC 6-28077. 1896. Roberts Brothers.
Star Science Fiction Stories. No. 1- Frederik Pohl. LC 53-5671. Ballantine Books.
Star Seed. David Andreissen & Hank Stine. LC 81-5402. (Starblaze Editions). (Illus.). 1982. 4.95 (ISBN 0-89865-021-6). Donning.
Star Seekers. Jacket Design by Paul Calle; Endpaper Design by Alex Schomburg. 1st Ed. Milton Lesser. LC 53-7338. (Science fiction novel). 1953. Winston.
Star Ship Invincible: Science Fiction Stories of the 30s. Frank K. Kelly. LC 79-9076. 1979. 4.95 (ISBN 0-88496-139-7). Capra Press.
Star Short Novels. Ed. by Frederik Pohl. LC 54-11986. 1954. Ballantine Books.
Star Smashers of the Galaxy Rangers. Harry Harrison. LC 73-78643. 1973. 5.95 (ISBN 0-399-11186-7). Putnam.
Star Smashers of the Galaxy Rangers. Harry Harrison. (Berkley medallion book). 1974. (pbk.) 0.95. Berkley Pub. Co.
Star Songs & Unicorns. Eric Norden. 1978. pap. 1.75 (ISBN 0-532-17189-6). Woodhill.
Star Songs of an Old Primate. James Tiptree. LC 77-6129. 1978. 1.75 (ISBN 0-345-25417-1). Ballantine Books.
Star Spangled Contract. Jim Garrison. LC 75-46575. 8.95 (ISBN 0-07-022890-6). McGraw-Hill.
Star Spangled Contract. Jim Garrison. 1977. 1.95 (ISBN 0-446-89259-9). Warner Books.
Star Spangled Crunch. Richard Condon. 1974. (pbk.) 1.50. Bantam.
Star-Spangled Hustle. Arthur I. Blaustein & Geoffrey Faux. LC 72-79376. 312p. 1973. pap. 2.95 o.p. (ISBN 0-385-06272-9, Anch). Doubleday.

Star Spangled Virgin. Du Bose Heyward. LC 39-27656. Farrar & Rinehart, Inc.
Star Spring. David F. Bischoff. 1982. pap. 2.25 (ISBN 0-425-05440-3). Berkley Pub.
Star Stalker. Robert Bloch. 1968. pap. 0.75 o.p. (T1869). Pyramid Pubns.
Star Surgeon. James White. 160p. (Orig.). 1981. pap. 1.95 (ISBN 0-345-29169-7, Del Rey). Ballantine.
Star to Hold. William Arthur Neubauer. LC 44-8032. 1944. Gramercy Publishing Company.
Star to Steer by: A Novel. Gladys Bagg Taber. LC 38-32618. 1938. Macrae Smith Company.
Star to the North. Barbara Corcoran & Bradford Angier. LC 79-119362. 1970. T. Nelson.
Star Trail. Irving A. Greenfield. 1977. pap. 1.50 (ISBN 0-532-15276-X). Woodhill.
Star Trap. Simon Brett. 1981. pap. 2.25 (ISBN 0-425-04936-1). Berkley Pub.
Star Trap. Robert Colby. 176p. 1974. pap. 1.25 o.p. (ISBN 0-532-12247-X). Woodhill.
Star Trap. Robert Colby. 176p. 1974. pap. 1.25 o.p. (ISBN 0-532-12247-X). Manor Bks.
Star Trap. Robert Colby. 1974. (pbk.) 0.95. Manor Books.
Star Trap: A Crime Novel. Simon Brett. LC 77-78114. 7.95 (ISBN 0-684-15190-1). Scribner.
Star Trap: A Crime Novel. Simon Brett. 1980. 1.95 (ISBN 0-425-04219-7). Berkley Publishing Corp.
Star Treasure: A Science Fiction Novel. Keith Laumer. LC 79-147057. 1971. 4.95. Putnam.
Star Trek, No. 1. James Blish. (gr. 6-12). 1970. pap. 1.95 (ISBN 0-553-13869-3, Y13869-3). Bantam.
Star Trek, No. 2. James Blish. 128p. (Orig.). (gr. 6-12). 1975. pap. 1.95 (ISBN 0-553-13877-4, Y13877-4). Bantam.
Star Trek, No. 5. James Blish. (Orig.). (gr. 6-12). 1972. pap. 1.95 (ISBN 0-553-12325-4, Y14383-2). Bantam.
Star Trek, No. 6. James Blish. 128p. (Orig.). (gr. 6-12). 1972. pap. 1.95 (ISBN 0-553-13874-X, Y13874-X). Bantam.
Star Trek, No. 7. James Blish. 160p. (gr. 6-12). 1976. pap. 1.95 (ISBN 0-553-13873-1, Y13873-1). Bantam.
Star Trek, No. 9. James Blish. (Pathfinder Ser.). 192p. (Orig.). (gr. 6-12). 1973. pap. 1.75 (ISBN 0-553-12111-1, 12111-1). Bantam.
Star Trek, No. 10. James Blish. 176p. (Orig.). (gr. 6-12). 1976. pap. 1.95 (ISBN 0-553-13866-9, Y13866-9). Bantam.
Star Trek, No. 12. James Blish & J A Lawrence. (gr. 6-12). 1977. pap. 1.75 (ISBN 0-553-11382-8). Bantam.
Star Trek II: The Wrath of Kahn. Vonda N. McIntyre. 1982. pap. 2.50. Bantam.
Star Trek II: The Wrath of Khan. Vonda N. McIntyre. 1982. pap. 2.50 (ISBN 0-671-45610-5). PB.
Star Trek Log. Alan Dean Foster. LC 74-8477. 0.95 (ISBN 0-345-24014-6). Ballantine Books.
Star Trek Log: Based on the Popular Series Created by Gene Roddenberry. Alan Dean Foster. LC 75-15492. 1975. per vol. 7.95 (ISBN 0-88411-081-8). Aeonian Press.
Star Trek Log Five. Alen Dean Foster. 1975. Repr. of 1974 ed. lib. bdg. 12.70x (ISBN 0-88411-085-0). Amereon Ltd.
Star Trek Log Four. Alan Dean Foster. 1975. Repr. of 1974 ed. lib. bdg. 13.25x (ISBN 0-88411-084-2). Amereon Ltd.
Star Trek Log Nine. Alan Dean Foster. LC 74-8477. 1977. 1.50 (ISBN 0-345-25557-7). Ballantine Books.
Star Trek Log One. Alan Dean Foster. 1975. Repr. of 1974 ed. lib. bdg. 12.05x (ISBN 0-88411-081-8). Amereon Ltd.
Star Trek; Log One. Alan Dean Foster. 1974. (pbk.) 0.95 (ISBN 0-345-24014-6). Ballantine Books.
Star Trek Log Seven. Alan Dean Foster. 1976. 1.50. Ballantine Books.
Star Trek Log Six. Alan Dean Foster. 1976. (pbk.) 1.50. Ballantine Books.
Star Trek Log Ten. Alan Dean Foster. 215p. Repr. of 1977 ed. lib. bdg. 12.95x (ISBN 0-88411-090-7). Amereon Ltd.
Star Trek Log Three. Alan Dean Foster. 1975. Repr. of 1974 ed. lib. bdg. 13.25x (ISBN 0-88411-083-4). Amereon Ltd.
Star Trek Log Two. Alan Dean Foster. 1975. Repr. of 1974 ed. lib. bdg. 11.75x (ISBN 0-88411-082-6). Amereon Ltd.
Star Trek Maps. New Eye Photography. 1980. pap. 8.95 (ISBN 0-553-01202-9). Bantam.
Star Trek Reader. James Blish. LC 76-200260. 1976. 8.95 (ISBN 0-8415-0467-9). E.P. Dutton.
Star Trek Reader. James Blish & Gene Roddenberry. LC 76-20260. 1976. 8.95 (ISBN 0-8415-0467-9). Dutton.
Star Trek Reader II. James Blish & Gene Roddenberry. LC 77-150066. 1977. 8.95 (ISBN 0-525-20960-3). Dutton.
Star Trek Reader III. James Blish & Gene Roddenberry. LC 77-152626. 1977. 8.95 (ISBN 0-525-20961-1). Dutton.
Star Trek Reader IV. James Blish & Gene Roddenberry. LC 78-102307. 1978. 9.95 (ISBN 0-525-20962-X). E. P. Dutton.
Star Trek, the Motion Picture. Gene Roddenbury. (Orig.). 1979. pap. 2.50 (ISBN 0-671-83088-0, Timescape). PB.
Star Trek-the Motion Picture: A Novel. Gene Roddenberry & Harold Livingston. LC 79-25970. 9.95 (ISBN 0-671-25324-7). Simon & Schuster.
Star Trek, the Motion Picture: A Photonovel. Gene Roddenbury. (Orig.). 1980. pap. 2.95 (ISBN 0-671-83089-9, Timescape). PB.
Star Trek: The New Voyages. Myrna Culbreath & Sondra Marshak. 256p. (gr. 6-12). 1976. pap. 2.25 (ISBN 0-553-14323-9, 12753-5). Bantam.
Star Trek: The New Voyages. Ed. by Sondra Marshak. 1976. (pbk.) 1.75. Bantam.
Star-Wagon. Peggy Wood. LC 36-838417. Farrar & Rinehart, Incorporated.
Star Wars Book. Carol W. Titelman. (Illus.). 1979. 17.95 (ISBN 0-345-28273-6); pap. 8.95 (ISBN 0-345-27666-3). Ballantine.
Star Wars: From the Adventures of Luke Skywalker. George Lucas. LC 77-88169. 1976. pap. 1.95 (ISBN 0-345-26079-1). Ballantine.
Star Wars: From the Adventures of Luke Skywalker: a Novel. George Lucas. LC 78-103103. (Illus.). 1976. 1.95. Ballantine Books.
Star Ways. Poul Anderson. LC 56-13319. Avalon Books.
Star Web. Joan Cox. 336p. 1980. pap. 2.50 (ISBN 0-380-75697-8, 75697). Avon.
Star Winds. Barrington J Bayley. 1978. 1.75 (ISBN 0-87997-384-6). DAW Books.
Star Witches. John Lymington, pseud. 1978. pap. 1.50 (ISBN 0-532-15313-8). Woodhill.
Star Witches. John Lymington, pseud. 1970. pap. 0.60 o.p. (60-445). Manor Bks.
Star Within. Donald Robinson. LC 65-16476. 1965. Christopher Pub. House.
Star Witness. Richard Kluger. LC 78-7760. 1979. 10.95 (ISBN 0-385-13505-X). Doubleday.
Star Woman. Henry Bedford-Jones. 1924. Dodd, Mead and Company.
Starblood. Dean R. Koontz. (Orig.). 1972. pap. 0.95 o.p. (75-306). Lancer.
Starborn: A Mystical Tale. John Nelson. LC 78-22108. (Unilaw library book). 4.95 (ISBN 0-915442-68-X). Donning.
Starbow. Frederik Pohl. 1982. write for info. (ISBN 0-345-30195-1). Ballantine.
Starbrace. Sheila Kaye-Smith. LC 26-311720. 1926. E. P. Dutton & Company.
Starbrat. John Morressy. LC 78-188478. 1972. 5.95 (ISBN 0-8027-5549-6). Walker.
Starbrat. John Morressy. 1973. 0.75. Curtis Books.
Starbridge. Jack Williamson & James E Gunn. (Berkley Medallion Book). 1.50 (ISBN 0-425-03294-9). Berkley Pub. Corp.,C.
Starbright, Starlight: A Novel. Joseph C Spangler. LC 45-977543. 1945. Osborne House.
Starbuck. John Selby. LC 43-755244. 1943. Farrar & Rinehart, Inc.
Starbucks: A New Novel. Opie Percival Read. LC 2-19292. 1902. Laird & Lee.
Starbuck's Brand. Theodore V Olsen. LC 73-76957. (Double D Western). 1973. 4.95 (ISBN 0-385-07012-8). Doubleday.
Starburn, the Story of Jenni Love. Rosalyn Drexler. (O.s.i.). 1979. 9.95 o.s.i. (ISBN 0-671-22493-X). S&S.
Starburst. Tess Ewing. (Second Chance at Love Ser.: No. 48). (Orig.). 1982. pap. 1.75 (ISBN 0-515-06541-2). Jove Pubns.
Starburst. Frederik Pohl. LC 81-17624. 1982. 12.50 (ISBN 0-345-30195-1). Ballantine Books.
Starcrossed. Benjamin Bova. LC 75-23092. 1975. 6.95 (ISBN 0-8019-6072-X). Chilton Book Co.
Stardance. Spider Robinson & Jeanne Robinson. LC 78-11231. (Quantum Science Fiction). 8.95. Dial Press/James Wade.
Stardreamer. Cordwainer Smith, pseud. (Boxer Ser). (Orig.). 1971. pap. 0.95 o.p. (95127). Beagle Bks.
Stardrifter. Dale Aycock. 1981. pap. 1.95 (ISBN 0-8439-0855-6, Leisure Bks). Nordon Pubns.
Stardroppers. John Brunner. (Orig.). 1972. pap. 0.95 o.p. (UQ1023). Daw Bks.
Stardust. William Bayer. 1974. (pbk.) 1.25. Dell.
Stardust. Parris Afton Bonds. 256p. (Orig.). 1983. pap. 2.95 (ISBN 0-449-12539-4, GM). Fawcett.
Stardust. David Leslie Murray. LC 31-21886. 1931. Little, Brown, and Company.
Stardust in Her Eyes. Lee Olsen. LC 46-6097. 1946. Arcadia House, Inc.
Stardust Kid. Pat Richoux. LC 73-78622. 1973. 6.95 (ISBN 0-399-11156-5). Putnam.
Starduster. D B Mills. 1965. Arcadia House.
Starett. Arthur V Deutcsh. LC 78-57329. 8.95 (ISBN 0-87795-199-3). Arbor House.
Starfall. John M. Cunningham. 1972. pap. 0.95 o.p. (09138). Curtis.
Starfinder: Robert F. Young. Robert F. Young. (Illus.). 1980. 2.50 (ISBN 0-671-83282-4). Pocket Books.
Starfire. Gordon T. Allred. LC 81-67182. 190p. 1981. 6.95 (ISBN 0-87747-871-6). Deseret Bk.
Starfire. Arlene Morgan, pseud. Ed. by Gene DeRoin. (Aston Hall Presents Ser.). (Orig.). 1979. pap. 1.50 (ISBN 0-89936-004-1). Aston Hall.
Starfire. Lauran Paine. LC 81-363. 9.95 (ISBN 0-89621-271-8). Thorndike Press.
Starfishers. Glen Cook. 384p. (Orig.). 1982. pap. 2.95 (ISBN 0-446-30155-8). Warner Bks.
Starflight to Faroul. Patrick Dearen. (Orig.). 1980. pap. 1.95 (ISBN 0-505-51600-4). Tower Bks.
Starforth. Lucille Papin Borden. LC 37-36660. 1937. The Macmillan Company.
Stargate. Pauline Gedge. LC 81-19473. 1982. 14.95 (ISBN 0-385-27420-3). Dial Press.
Stargate. Stephen Robinett. LC 75-26195. 7.95. St. Martin's Press.
Stargate. Stephen Robinett. (Signet Book). 1977. 1.50 (ISBN 0-451-07757-1). New American Library.
Starhaven. Ivar Jorgenson. LC 58-9140. 1958. Avalon Books.
Starhiker. Jack Dann. LC 76-47256. 1977. 7.95 o.p. (ISBN 0-06-010958-0, HarpT). Har-Row.
Starhiker. Jack Dann. LC 76-15140. 1976. 7.95 o.p. (ISBN 0-672-52069-9). Bobbs.
Starhiker: A Novel. Jack Dann. LC 76-15140. 7.95 (ISBN 0-672-52069-9). Harper & Row.
Stark Island. Lynna Cooper. (Avon gothic). 1974. (pbk.) 0.95 (ISBN 0-380-00041-5). Avon.
Stark Munro Letters: Being a Series of Twelve Letters Written by J. Stark Munro, M.D., to His Friend and Former Fellow-Student, Herbert Swanborough... During the Years 1881-1884. ed. and arranged by a. conan doyle... ed. Arthur Conan Doyle. LC 6-34235. 1895. D. Appleton and Company.
Stark Murder. Lee Thayer, pseud. LC 39-21179. 1939. Dodd, Mead & Company.
Stark Mysteries, 6 bks. Richard Stark. 1981. Set. lib. bdg. 60.00 (ISBN 0-8398-2732-6, Gregg). G K Hall.
Stark Naked. Norton Juster. 1969. 2.95 o.p. (ISBN 0-394-44695-X). Random.
Stark Summer: A Novel of Correlated Incidents. James Robert Peery. LC 39-22579. 1939. Harper & Brothers.
Starkahn of Rhada. Alfred Coppel. LC 70-102441. 1970. Harcourt, Brace & World.
Starkenden Quest. Gilbert Collins. LC 25-18705. 1925. R. M. McBride & Company.
Starless Crown. A Story. Jane Roseboom. 1889. L. Thompson, Printer.
Starless Realm. Clark Darlton. (Perry Rhodan#87). 1976. (pbk.) 1.25. Ace Books.
Starlight. Anne Stanton Drew. LC 34-4190. Loring & Mussey.
Starlight. Terence Kennedy. LC 54-5637. 1954. Roy Publishers.
Starlight. Thomas E. Kipp. (Illus.). 75p. 1983. 5.50 (ISBN 0-682-49946-3). Exposition.
Starlight Basin. Gifford Paul Cheshire. LC 54-7455. 1954. Random House.
Starlight Furnace: An Historical Novel. Clifford T. Stafford. 1979. 10.00 (ISBN 0-682-49289-2). Exposition.
Starlight of the Hills: A Romance of the Kentucky Mountains. Jason Rolfe Strong. LC 23-10972. 1923. F. Pustet Co. (Inc.); Etc., Etc.
Starlight on the Bayou. Ethel Lockwood. 1973. 4.95. Lenox Hill Press.
Starlight Pass. Tom Gill. LC 35-701649. Farrar & Rinehart, Incorporated.
Starlight Ranch: And Other Stories of Army Life on the Frontier. Charles King. LC 73-94737. (Short story index reprint series). 1969. Books for Libraries Press.
Starlight Ranch: And Other Stories of Army Life on the Frontier. Charles King. LC 7-12217. 1890. J. B. Lippincott Company.
Starlight Ranch: And Other Stories of Army Life on the Frontier. Charles King. LC 42-29440. 1896. J. B. Lippincott Company.
Starlight Ranch: And Other Stories of Army Life on the Frontier. Charles King. LC 16-131167. 1905. J. B. Lippincott Company.
Starlight Ranch & Other Stories of Army Life on the Frontier. Charles King. LC 73-94737. (Short Story Index Reprint Ser.). 1890. 15.00 (ISBN 0-8369-3117-3). Ayer Co.
Starlight Rider. Ernest Haycox. 1933. Doubleday, Doran & Company, Inc.
Starlight Seduction. Anne Reed. (Second Chance at Love: No. 29). 192p. (Orig.). 1982. pap. 1.75 (ISBN 0-515-06281-2). Jove Pubns.
Starlight: The Great Short Fiction of Alfred Bester. Alfred Bester. (Berkley Medallion Book). 1977. 1.95 (ISBN 0-425-03451-8). Berkley Pub. Corp.
Starling. Doris Oppenheim Leslie. LC 27-13126. The Century Co.
Starling. Juliet Wilbor Tompkins. LC 19-111503. The Bobbs-Merrill Company.
Starling: A Scotch Story. Norman Macleod. LC 3-14791. (On cover: Round table library). 1896. J. Knight Company.
Starling: A Story of Husbands and Wives. Christopher Ward. LC 27-5946. 1927. Harper & Brothers.
Starling Street. Dinah Palmtag. 1973. (pbk.) 0.95. Dell.
Starlit Corridor: Modern Science Fiction, Short Stories, and Poems. trade ed. 1st ed. Ed. by Roger Mansfield. LC 67-26690. (Commonwealth and international library). (Pergamon Oxford English series.). 1967-1968. (ISBN 0-08-203381-1). Pergamon Press.
Starlit Seduction, No. 83. Anne Reed. 1982. pap. 1.75 (ISBN 0-515-06694-X). Jove Pubns.
Starmaker. Henry Denker. LC 76-55323. 9.95 (ISBN 0-671-22431-X). Simon and Schuster.
Starmaker. Henry Denker. (Kangaroo Book). 1978. 2.50 (ISBN 0-671-81644-6). Pocket Books.
Starmaker. Wilfred McCormick. 1963. 3.00 (ISBN 0-8315-0109-X). Speller.
Starman Jones. Robert Anson Heinlein. Ed. by Judy L. Del Rey. 256p. 1975. pap. 1.50 (ISBN 0-345-24354-4). Ballantine.
Starman's Quest. Robert Silverberg. 1969. 4.95 o.p. (ISBN 0-8015-7104-9). Hawthorn.
Starmasters' Gambit. Gerard Klein. (Daw sf, no. 58). (Illus.). 1973. (pbk.) 0.95. Daw Books.
Starmen of Llyrdis. Leigh Brackett. 176p. 1976. pap. 1.95 (ISBN 0-345-24668-3). Ballantine.
Starmen. 1st Ed. Leigh Brackett. LC 52-13840. 1952. Gnome Press.
Starmother. Sydney J Van Scyoc. LC 75-26766. 6.95 (ISBN 0-399-11674-5). Berkley Pub. Co.: Distributed by Putnam.
Starr, of the Desert. Bertha Muzzy Sinclair. LC 17-130756. 1917. 1.35. Little, Brown, and Company.
Starr of Wyoming. William Frederick Bragg. 1981. pap. 2.25 (ISBN 0-8439-0860-2, Leisure Bks). Nordon Pubns.
Starrbelow. Mary Christianna Milne Lewis. LC 76-52384. 1977. 7.95 (ISBN 0-912588-16-0). Brooke House.
Starrbelow. China Thompson, pseud. LC 58-10861. 1958. Scribner.
Starring. James Fritzhand. LC 77-79340. 1977. 1.95 (ISBN 0-380-01653-2). Avon Books.
Starring Dulcy Jayne. Virginia Tracy. LC 28-28321. 1927. George H. Doran Company.
Starring Miss Marple. Agatha Miller Christie. LC 76-54722. 10.95 (ISBN 0-396-07451-0). Dodd, Mead.
Starrs of Texas: A Novel. Warren Leslie. LC 78-7902. 10.95 (ISBN 0-671-24011-0). Simon and Schuster.
Starrs of Texas: A Novel. Warren Leslie. 1979. 2.50 (ISBN 0-671-81773-6). Pocket Books.
Starry Adventure. Mary Hunter Austin. LC 31-27003. 1931. Houghton Mifflin Company.
Starry Messenger: The Best of Galileo. Chales C Ryan. LC 79-16604. 1979. 8.95 (ISBN 0-312-75599-6). St. Martin's Press.
Starry Night. Bertha Muzzy Sinclair. LC 39-2541. 1939. Little, Brown and Company.
Stars: A Slumber Story. Eugene Field. LC 6-34078. 1906. C. Scribner's Sons.
Stars Abide. Ramona Stewart. LC 61-11826. 1961. Morrow.
Stars: An Astrological Romance. Harriet Doan Prentiss. LC 37-33116. B. Humphries, Inc.
Stars and Bars; or, The Reign of Terror in Missouri. Isaac Kelso. LC 7-10977. 1864. A. Williams & Co.
Stars & Other Korean Short Stories. Hwang Sun-won. Tr. by Edward W. Poitrass. (Writing in Asia Ser.). 227p. (Orig., Korean.). 1980. pap. text ed. 8.95x. Heinemann Ed.
Stars and Stripes Forever. Elliot Harold Paul. LC 39-273322. Random House.
Stars & Swipes Forever. David King. 1969. pap. 0.60 o.p. (63-052). Paperback Lib.
Stars Are Dark. Peter Cheyney. LC 43-15060. 1943. Dodd, Mead & Company.
Stars Are Ours. Andre Norton, pseud. 192p. 1981. pap. 1.95 (ISBN 0-441-78434-8). Ace Bks.
Stars Are the Styx. Theodore Sturgeon. 1981. pap. 2.75 (ISBN 0-440-18006-6). Dell.
Stars Are Too High. Agnew H Bahnson. LC 59-5720. 1959. Random House.
Stars Came Down. Joseph Lawrence Morrissey. LC 67-5895. 1967. Arcadia House.
Stars Cast No Shadows. William Hegner. 1974. (pbk.). 1.50 (ISBN 0-671-78692-X). Pocket Books.
Stars Come Close. Margaret Elizabeth Sangster. LC 36-9937. Greenberg.
Stars' End. Glen Cook. 352p. (Orig.). 1982. pap. 2.95 (ISBN 0-446-30156-6). Warner Bks.
Stars for Sale. Ruth Hammitt Kauffman. LC 30-7298. The Penn Publishing Company.
Stars for the Toff. John Creasey. LC 68-16679. 1968. Walker.
Stars Give Warning. Brenda Conrad. LC 41-154881. 1941. C. Scribner's Sons.
Stars Grow Pale. Karl Bjarnhof. LC 58-7559. 1958. Knopf.

Stars in My Crown. Joe David Brown. 1974. (pbk.) 1.25. New American Library.
Stars in My Heart. Barbara Cartland. (Barbara Carrtland Ser.: No. 12). 1981. pap. 1.75 (ISBN 0-515-05570-0). Jove Pubns.
Stars in My Heart. Barbara Cartland. 1971. pap. 1.25 o.p. (V2429). Pyramid Pubns.
Stars in My Heart. Barbara Cartland. 1976. pap. 1.25 o.p. (ISBN 0-515-04161-0). BJ Pub Group.
Stars in My Heaven: A Novel. Grace Wallace Doonan. LC 41-2087. Catholic Literary Guild.
Stars in Shroud. Gregory Benford. LC 78-242. 8.95. Berkley Pub. Corp.: Distributed by Putnam.
Stars in the Water. John Appleby. LC 52-11715. 1953. Coward-McCann.
Stars in Their Courses. Isaac Asimov. LC 71-131065. (Illus.). 1971. 5.95 o.p. (ISBN 0-385-01049-4). Doubleday.
Stars in Their Courses. Hilda Mary Sharp. LC 17-7812. 1917. G. P. Putnam's Sons.
Stars in Their Courses. 1st Ed. Harry Peter M'Nab Brown. LC 60-7491. 1960. Knopf.
Stars in Your Eyes. Emilie Baker Loring. LC 76-41719. 1976. 6.95 (ISBN 0-88411-362-0). Aeonian Press.
Stars in Your Eyes. Emilie Baker Loring. LC 41-21543. 1941. Little, Brown and Company.
Stars Incline. Clyde Brion Davis. LC 45-10692. 1946. Farrar & Rinehart, Inc.
Stars Incline. Jeanne Judson. LC 20-2647. 1920. 1.75. Dodd, Mead and Company.
Stars Is God's Lanterns. Charles M. Wilson. 1973. pap. 1.25 o.p. (23739-0-125). Mockingbird Bks.
Stars Is God's Lanterns: An Offering of Ozark Tellin' Stories. Charles M. Wilson. LC 75-88142. 1970. 6.95 o.p. (ISBN 0-8061-0882-7). U of Okla Pr.
Stars, Like Dust. Isaac Asimov. 1978. pap. 2.25 (ISBN 0-449-23595-5, Crest). Fawcett.
Stars Like Dust. Isaac Asimov. pap. 0.60 o.p. (73-704). Lancer.
Stars: Like Dust. 1st Ed. Isaac Asimov. LC 51-1170. 1951. Doubleda.
Stars Look Down. Archibald Joseph Cronin. LC 35-27304. 1935. Little, Brown, and Company.
Stars Look Down. Archibald Joseph Cronin. 1935. 14.95 (ISBN 0-575-00276-X, Pub. by Gollancz England). David & Charles.
Stars Look Down. Archibald Joseph Cronin. 1935. 6.95 o.p. (ISBN 0-316-16171-3). Little.
Stars My Destination. Alfred Bester. LC 57-803155. (Signet book, S1389). 1957. New American Library.
Stars My Destination. Alfred Bester. LC 75-5632. (Gregg Press science fiction series). 1975. 10.00 (ISBN 0-8398-2301-0). Gregg Press.
Stars My Destination. Alfred Bester. LC 57-8031. (Berkley medallion book). 1975. (pbk.) 1.25 (ISBN 0-425-02780-5). Berkley Pub. Co.
Stars of Albion. Ed. by R. Holdstock & C. Priest. 1982. pap. 10.00x (ISBN 0-330-25872-9, Pub. by Pan Bks). State Mutual Bk.
Stars of Love: By Norma Newcomb Pseud. William Arthur Neubauer. LC 53-113023. 1953. Arcadia House.
Stars on the Sea. Francis Van Wyck Mason. J. B. Lippincott Company.
Stars on the Sea. F. Van Wyck Mason. (Mason Bicentennial Ser: No. 2). 1975. pap. 1.95 (ISBN 0-425-02975-1, Medallion). Berkley Pub.
Stars Over Sarawak. Anne Hampson. (Presents Ser.). 1974. pap. 1.25 (ISBN 0-373-70563-8, 70563, Pub. by Harlequin). PB.
Star's Progress. 1st Ed. Katherine Everard. LC 50-5359. 1950. Dutton.
Star's Road: A Novel. Lloyd Stern. LC 32-29900. The Vanguard Press.
Stars Scream Murder: A Craig Kennedy Novel. Arthur Benjamin Reeve. LC 36-5511. (Tired business man's library of adventure, detective, and mystery novels). 1936. D. Appleton-Century Company Incorporated.
Stars Shine Tomorrow. Richard Williams. 3.00 o.p. Carlton.
Stars Spell Death. Jonathan Stagge, pseud. LC 39-29431. 1939. Pub. for the Crime Club by Doubleday, Doran & Company, Inc.
Stars Still Shine. Rembert Gilman Smith. LC 44-40366. 1944. Columbia Publishing Company.
Stars Still Shine. Lida Larrimore Thomas. LC 40-959698. 1940. Macrae-Smith Company.
Stars Through the Mist, Winter of Change & Three for a Wedding. Betty Neels. (Harlequin Romances Ser.: 3 Vols. in 1). 576p. 1983. pap. 3.95 (ISBN 0-373-20073-0). Harlequin Bks.
Stars Were Born. Barbara Lucas, pseud. 1935. Harper & Brothers.
Stars Will Judge. Irving A Greenfield. (Dell book). 1974. (pbk.) 0.95. Dell.
Starset and Sunrise. Nicholas Sandys. LC 51-12360. 1951. Sheed and Ward.
Starshadows. Pamela Cargent. (Ace Book). 1977. 1.75 (ISBN 0-441-78318-X). Ace Books.
Starshine. Theodore Sturgeon. 1972. pap. 0.75 o.p. (T2658). Pyramid Pubns.
Starship. Brian Wilson Aldiss. LC 59-6560. 1959. Criterion Books.
Starship. Poul Anderson. (Psychotechnic League Ser.: Vol. III). 288p. (Orig.). 1982. pap. 2.75 (ISBN 0-523-48533-6). Pinnacle Bks.
Starship & Haiku. Somtow Sucharitkul. (Orig.). 1981. pap. 2.50 (ISBN 0-671-83601-3, Timescape). PB.
Starship & the Canoe. Kenneth Brower. 1979. pap. 2.95 (ISBN 0-553-12451-X). Bantam.
Starship Death. Randall Garrett. 240p. 1982. pap. 2.50 (ISBN 0-8439-1074-7, Leisure Bks). Nordon Pubns.
Starship Orpheus: Cosmic Carnage, No. 2. Symon Jade. 208p. (Orig.). 1982. pap. 2.25 (ISBN 0-523-41647-4). Pinnacle Bks.
Starship Orpheus: Return from the Dead, No. 1. 161p. 1982. pap. 2.25 (ISBN 0-523-41646-6). Pinnacle Bks.
Starships: Stories Beyond the Boundaries of the Universe. Ed. by Isaac Asimov et al. 352p. (Orig.). 1983. pap. 3.50 (ISBN 0-449-20126-0, Crest). Fawcett.
Starsky and Hutch. Richard Deming & William Blinn. LC 75-38993. 1976. 1.50. Ballantine Books.
Starsky & Hutch. Max Franklin, pseud. (Orig.). 1976. pap. 1.50 (ISBN 0-345-24996-8). Ballantine.
Starsky & Hutch, No. 2. Max Franklin, pseud. (Orig.). 1976. pap. 1.50 (ISBN 0-345-25124-5). Ballantine.
Starsky & Hutch Number Five: Terror on the Docks. Richard Deming. LC 76-56756. 1977. 1.50 (ISBN 0-345-25709-X). Ballantine Books.
Starsky & Hutch, Number Seven: The Setup. Richard Deming. LC 77-25146. 1978. 1.75 (ISBN 0-345-27340-0). Ballantine Books.
Starsky & Hutch, Number Six: The Psychic. Richard Deming. LC 76-56757. 1977. 1.50 (ISBN 0-345-27340-0). Ballatine Books.
Starsky & Hutch Number Two; Kill Huggy Bear. Richard Deming & William Blinn. LC 76-10729. 1976. 1.50 (ISBN 0-345-25124-5). Ballantine Books.
Starspinner. Dale Aycock. 240p. 1981. pap. 2.25 (ISBN 0-8439-0973-0, Leisure Bks). Nordon Pubns.
Starstruck. Linda Palmer. LC 81-11878. 13.95 (ISBN 0-399-12512-4). Putnam.
Starswarm. Brian Wilson Aldiss. LC 78-2194. (Gregg Press science fiction series). (Illus.). 1978. 9.00 (ISBN 0-8398-2408-4). Gregg Press.
Start in Life. Alan Sillitoe. LC 77-162736. 1971. 6.95 o.p. (ISBN 0-684-12537-4). Scribner.
Start in Life: And Other Stories. Honore De Balzac. Tr. by Katharine Prescott Wormeley. LC 3-23193. (Half-title: The comedy of human life... Scenes from private life). 1895. Roberts Brothers.
Start of the Road: A Novel. John Erskine. LC 38-32860. 1938. Frederick A. Stokes Company.
Start Point: Six Studies in Violence. Otis Dunbar Richardson. 1973. 8.00 o.p. (ISBN 0-682-47672-2). Exposition.
Starting from Tomorrow. Tony Gray. LC 65-18955. 1965. Little, Brown.
Starting Gun. Aaron Marc Stein. LC 48-2625. 1948. Pub. for the Crime Club by Doubleday.
Starting Out in the Thirties. Alfred Kazin. LC 79-22491. 1980. pap. 2.95 (ISBN 0-394-74336-9, Vin). Random.
Starting Over. Dan Wakefield. LC 73-1930. 1973. 7.95. Delacorte Press/Seymour Lawrence.
Starting Over. Dan Wakefield. 1974. (pbk.) 1.75. Dell.
Starting Over Again. Jane F. Thornton. (O.s.i.). 1977. pap. 1.50 o.s.i. (BT51110). Belmont-Tower.
Starting Over Again. Jane Foster Thornton. (Belmont Tower Book). 1.50. Tower Publications.
Starting Point. Cecil Day-Lewis. LC 38-5131. 1938. Harper & Brothers.
Starting Point. Hiram Wallace Hayes. LC 22-189. The Harmony Shop.
Startling Exploits of Dr. J. B. Quies: From the French of Paul Celiere ! Paul Celieres. Tr. by Hoey, Frances Sarah (Johnston) & Lillie, John. LC 6-22273. 1887. Harper & Brothers.
Startling Stories About Pennsylvania. Patrick M. Reynolds. (Pennsylvania Profiles Ser.: Vol. IV). (Illus.). 56p. (Orig.). 1980. pap. 3.65 (ISBN 0-932514-04-9). Red Rose Studio.
Starvecrow Farm. Stanley John Weyman. LC 5-17594. 1905. Longmans, Green, and Co.
Starvecrow Farm. Stanley John Weyman. LC 5-32695. 1905. Longmans, Green, and Co.
Starved: By Jack Woodford Pseud. & Conrad Carter. Josiah Pitts Woolfolk & Conrad Carter. LC 53-329134. 1953. Signature Press.
Starved Fields. Elizabeth Inglis-Jones. LC 30-4495. Minton, Balch & Company.
Starvel Hollow Tragedy: An Inspector French Case. Freeman Wills Crofts. LC 27-18770. 1927. Harper & Brothers.
Starvel Hollow Tragedy: An Inspector French Case. Freeman Wills Crofts. LC 38-27268. 1938. Dodd, Mead & Company.
Starveling: A Christmas Story. Nina Warner Hooke. (Illus.). 1968. 4.50 o.p. John Day.
Starwolf. Edmond Hamilton. 1982. pap. 3.50 (ISBN 0-441-78422-4, Pub. by Ace Science Fiction). Ace Bks.
Starworld. Harry Harrison. 208p. (Orig.). 1981. pap. 2.25 (ISBN 0-553-14647-5). Bantam.
Stash Spots a Murder. Ron Peters. 1973. (pbk) 0.75. Curtis Books.
State Department Murders. Edward Sidney Aarons. 1970. pap. 0.60 o.p. (R2260, GM). Fawcett World.
State Department Murders. Edward Sidney Aarons. 160p. 1973. pap. 0.75 o.p. (T2799, GM). Fawcett World.
State Department Murders: By Edward Ronns Pseud. Edward Sidney Aarons. LC 51-24858. (Gold medal book, 117). 1950. Fawcett Publications.
State Fair. Philip Duffield Stong. LC 32-262. The Century.
State in Mimosa: A Novel. Tallant, Robert. LC 50-10583. 1950. Doubleday.
State of Almost Happiness. Bryn Beorse. LC 72-77854. 1972. 4.95 (ISBN 0-87141-044-3). Manyland Books.
State of Change. Penelope Gilliatt. LC 68-14501. 1968. Random House.
State of Emergency. Basil Jackson. LC 82-6409. 13.95 (ISBN 0-393-01605-6). Norton.
State of Emergency: A Novel of Alternatives. Dennis Guerrier & Joan Richards. LC 70-96067. (Illus.). 1970. 5.95. Houghton Mifflin.
State of Emergency: A Programmed Entertainment. Dennis Guerrier & Joan Richards. LC 71-488092. (Illus.). 1969 (ISBN 0-14-003021-2). Penguin.
State of Grace. Robert Tine. LC 80-14538. 1980. 10.95 (ISBN 0-670-66851-6). Viking Press.
State of Grace. Joy Williams. LC 72-89954. 1973. 6.95. Doubleday.
State of Ireland: A Novella & Seventeen Short Stories. Benedict Kiely. LC 79-92210. 352p. 1980. 16.95 (ISBN 0-87923-320-6). Godine.
State of Ireland: A Novella and Seventeen Stories. Benedict Kiely. LC 81-15886. (Illus.). 1982. 6.95 (ISBN 0-14-006083-9). Penguin Books.
State of Justice. Tom Paulin. 48p. 1977. pap. 4.95 (ISBN 0-571-10982-9). Faber & Faber.
State of Mind. Mark Schorer. LC 47-235039. 1947. Houghton Mifflin Company.
State of Mind: Thirty-Two Stories. Mark Schorer. LC 73-156208. 1972. (ISBN 0-8371-6158-4). Greenwood Press.
State of Nature. Paul Goodman. LC 46-5254. 1946. The Vanguard Press.
State of Peace. Janice Elliott. 1971. 6.95 o.p. (ISBN 0-394-46919-4). Knopf.
State of Siege. Janet Frame, pseud. LC 66-20188. 5.00. Braziller.
State of Siege. Franco Solinas. 1973. 1.50. Ballantine.
State of Siege. 1st American Ed. Eric Ambler. 1956. Knopf.
State Preferences. Marshall Ford. 1974. (pbk.) 1.25. Dell.
State Secret: And Other Stories. Bithia Mary Sheppard Croker. 1901. F. M. Buckles & Company; Etc., Etc.
State Trooper. Noel Bertram Gerson. LC 72-88706. 1973. 6.95 (ISBN 0-385-03894-1). Doubleday.
State Trooper. Noel Bertram Gerson. 1973-1974. (pbk.) 1.75. Popular Library.
State Versus Elinor Norton. Mary Roberts Rinehart. Farrar & Rinehart, Incorporated.
State Versus Elna Jepson. Nancy Barr Mavity. LC 37-127211. 1937. Doubleday, Doran & Company, Inc.
State Vs. Elinor Norton. Mary Roberts Rinehart. LC 80-29644. 1981. 13.50 (ISBN 0-8161-3235-6). G. K. Hall.
Stateline. John Van Der Zee. LC 75-33627. 7.95 (ISBN 0-15-184905-6). Harcourt Brace Jovanovich.
Stately Home Murder. Catherine Aird, pseud. LC 79-89140. (Illus.). 1970. 4.50. Published for the Crime Club by Doubleday.
Stately Timber. Rupert Hughes. LC 39-27132. 1939. C. Scribner's Sons.
Statement of Stella Maberly. Thomas Anstey Guthrie. LC 8-20116. 1896. D. Appleton and Company.
Statements: New Fiction from the Fiction Collective. Jonathan Baumbach. LC 74-25083. (Venture book). 1975. 8.95. (ISBN 0-8076-0777-0) (ISBN 0-8076-0778-9). G. Braziller.
Statements Two. Ed. by Jonathan Baumbach & Peter Spielberg. LC 76-56053. 1977. 8.95 (ISBN 0-914590-36-7); pap. 2.95 (ISBN 0-914590-37-5). Fiction Coll.
Stateroom for Two. Glenna Finley, pseud. (Orig.). 1980. pap. 1.95 (ISBN 0-451-11497-3, AJ1497, Sig). NAL.
Stateroom Opposite. Arthur Henry Veysey. (Dillingham's American authors library, no. 61). 1900. G. W. Dillingham Co.
States General (from "The Story of a Peasant") Emile Erckmann & Chatrian, Alexandre, 1826-1890, Joint Author. LC 4-17213. (On cover: Chautauqua home reading series). 1904. The Chatauqua Press.
States of Grace: A Novel by Francis Steegmuller. Francis Steegmuller. LC 46-32943. 1946. Reynal & Hitchcock, Inc.
State's Scandal. Carl Franklin Hutcheson. LC 17-10161. 1917.
Stateside Soldier. Wayne E Kampmeier. LC 55-7684. 1955. Bellevue Books Pub. Co.
Statesman's Game. James Aldridge. LC 66-234102. 4.95. Doubleday.
Statesmen Snowbound: By Robert Fitzgerald; Illustrated by Wad-el-Ward. Robert Fitzgerald. LC 9-18157. 1909. The Neale Publishing Company.
Stat'i. Aleksandr Konstantinovich Voronskii. (Rus.). 1981. 15.00 (ISBN 0-88233-512-X); pap. 6.00 (ISBN 0-88233-513-8). Ardis Pubs.
Stat'i O Literature. Vladislav Khodasevich. 124p. (Rus.). 1982. 18.00 (ISBN 0-88233-408-5); pap. 9.00 (ISBN 0-88233-409-3). Ardis Pubs.
Static. Rupert Hughes. LC 32-9370. 1932. Harper & Brothers.
Station in Space. James Edward Gunn. LC 58-9789. (Bantam books, A1825-5). 1958. Bantam Books.
Station in the Delta. John Cassidy. 320p. 1981. pap. 2.50 (ISBN 0-345-28846-7). Ballantine.
Station in the Delta: A Novel. John Cassidy. LC 79-9819. 9.95 (ISBN 0-684-16156-7). Scribner.
Station Wagon in Spain. Frances Parkinson Wheeler Keyes. 256p. 1977. pap. 1.50 (ISBN 0-449-23193-3, Crest). Fawcett.
Station Wagon in Spain: A Novel. Frances Parkinson Wheeler Keyes. LC 59-10000. 1959. Farrar, Straus and Cudahy.
Station Wagon Murder. Milton Morris Propper. LC 40-31634. Harper & Brothers.
Station Wagon Murder. Milton Morris Propper. LC 44-3608. (Prize mystery novels). 1944. Crestwood Publishing Co., Inc.
Station Wagon Set. Faith Baldwin. 1976. Repr. of 1939 ed. lib. bdg. 19.10x (ISBN 0-88411-604-2). Amereon Ltd.
Station Wagon Set. Faith Baldwin Cuthrell. LC 73-86739. 1973. 5.95. Aeonian Press.
Station Wagon Set. Faith Baldwin Cuthrell. LC 39-33520. Farrar & Rinehart, Inc.
Station Wagon Set. Faith Baldwin Cuthrell. 1974. (pbk.) 1.25. Warner Paperback Library.
Station West. Frederick Dilley Gidden. LC 47-12192. 1947. Houghton Mifflin Co.
Station X. George McLeod Winsor. LC 75-9591. (Gregg Press science fiction series). 1975. 13.50 (ISBN 0-8398-2319-3). Gregg Press.
Station Zero-Zero. Mike Sullivan. 1978. pap. 1.75 (ISBN 0-89041-221-9, 3221). Major Bks.
Stations. Burt Blechman. LC 64-20023. 1964. Random House.
Stations of the Nightmare. Philip Jose Farmer. 288p. (Orig.). 1982. pap. 2.75 (ISBN 0-523-48522-0). Pinnacle Bks.
Statue. Eden Phillpotts & Arnold Bennett. LC 74-17141. (Collected works of Arnold Bennett). 1974. (ISBN 0-518-19156-7). Books for Libraries Press.
Statue: A Story of International Intrigue and Mystery. Eden Phillpotts & Bennett, Arnold. LC 8-22564. 1908. Moffat, Yard and Company.
Statue in the Air. Caroline Eaton Le Conte. LC 7-12782. 1897. The Macmillan Company.
Statue in the Wood. Richard Pryce. LC 18-9079. 1918. 1.50. Houghton Mifflin Company.
Statues in a Garden. Isabel Colegate. 1964. pap. 2.95. Avon.
Statues in a Garden: 1st Amer. Ed. Isabel Colegate. LC 66-10528. 1966. bds., 3.95. Knopf.
Statuette. Jane Wald & Kathleen Wakefield. LC 77-80311. 1977. pap. 1.95 o.s.i. (ISBN 0-89516-006-4). Condor Pub Co.
Stature of Thomas Mann: A Critical Anthology. Ed. by Charles Neider. LC 48-5734. 1947. New Directions.
Status Civilization. Robert Sheckley. LC 77-356746. 1976. 3.50 (ISBN 0-575-02108-X). Gollancz.
Status 1SQ. Roger E. Herst. LC 77-27707. (Illus.). 1979. 8.95 (ISBN 0-385-14242-0). Doubleday.
Staves for Louisville. William Carigan. LC 81-81067. (Illus.). 10.95 (ISBN 0-9605986-0-X). Juniper Publishers.
Stavrogin's Confession, and the Plan of The Life of a Great Sinner. With Introductory and Explanatory Notes. Fedor Mikhailovich Dostoevskii. LC 72-2556. 1972. 8.95 (ISBN 0-8383-1494-5). Haskell House Publishers.
Stavrogin's Confession & the Plan of the Life of a Great Sinner. Fedor Mikhailovich Dostoevskii. LC 72-2556. (Studies in Fiction, No. 34). 1972. Repr. of 1922 ed. lib. bdg. 48.95x (ISBN 0-8383-1494-5). Haskell.

Stay-at-Home. Lawrence Nelson. LC 35-15160. Arcadia House.

Stay Away, Joe: A Novel. Dan Cushman. LC 52-12887. 1953. Viking Press.

Stay but till Tomorrow. Iris Bromige. (Beagle romance#35). 1975. (pbk.) 0.95. Ballantine Books.

Stay for Breakfast. Nelson Robins. LC 36-7486. Phoenix Press.

Stay Hungry. Charles Gaines. 1974. (pbk.) 1.50. Bantam.

Stay Hungry. Charles Gaines. LC 79-186023. 1972. 5.95. Doubleday.

Stay Loose: By Bud Nye. 1st Ed. Harry Nye. LC 59-11605. 1959. Doubleday.

Stay Out of My Life. Sophie Kerr. LC 34-4063. Farrar & Rinehart, Incorporated.

Stay Out of My Life. Sophie Kerr. LC 42-25555. 1942. The Sun Dial Press.

Stay Out of My Parlor. Frances Nichols Hanna. LC 38-13180. 1938. Arcadia House.

Stay That Swift Courier, a Novel. 1st Ed. Charles E Harris. LC 53-563021. 1953. Exposition Press.

Stay with It Snoopy: Selected Cartoons from, Summers Fly, Winters Walk, Vol. III. Charles M. Schulz. 128p. 1980. pap. 1.50 (ISBN 0-449-24310-9, Crest). Fawcett.

Staying on. Paul Scott. LC 78-2352. 1978. 9.95 (ISBN 0-89340-157-9). J. Curley.

Staying on. Paul Scott. 1979. 2.25 (ISBN 0-380-46045-9). Avon Books.

Staying on: A Novel. Paul Scott. LC 77-1491. 1977. 8.95 (ISBN 0-688-03205-2). Morrow.

Staying Power, 2 Stories. Educational Challenges, Inc. Incl. Match for Sara; Ward Two. (Turning Point I Ser.). (gr. 7-12). pap. text ed. 3.40 (ISBN 0-8009-1892-4). McCormick-Mathers.

Staying with Relations. Rose Macaulay. LC 30-27116. H. Liveright.

Stead. Cid Corman, pseud. 1966. pap. 6.00 (Pub. by Elizabeth Pr). SBD.

Steadfast Heart. Nora Hampton. 1.75 (ISBN 0-449-23772-9). Fawcett Crest.

Steadfast Heart. Clarence Budington Kelland. LC 24-207517. Harper & Brothers.

Steadfast Light. Elisabeth Stancy Payne. LC 39-24443. 1939. Dodd, Mead & Company.

Steadfast Love. Woodrum, Lon Riley. LC 63-15738. 1963. Zondervan Pub. House.

Steadfast: The Story of a Saint and a Sinner. Rose Terry Cooke. LC 4-15086. 1889. Ticknor and Company.

Steady Flame. Beth Meyers. (YA) 1972. 6.95 (Avalon). Bouregy.

Steady Flame. Beth McHenry Myers. LC 52-14353. 1952. Bouregy & Curl.

Steady Flame. Beth McHenry Myers. (Candlelight Romance#189). (Illus.). 1976. (pbk.) 0.75. Dell.

Steagle. Irvin Faust. LC 66-18324. bds., 4.95. Random.

Steagle. Irvin Faust. LC 66-18324. 1966. Random House.

Steal Big. Patrick Mann, pseud. 208p. 1981. 9.95 (ISBN 0-312-76139-2). St Martin.

Steal Big. LC 60-37413. (Gold medal books, 998). 1960. Fawcett Publications.

Steal Big. Leslie Waller. LC 80-53082. 1981. 9.95 (ISBN 0-312-76139-2). St. Martin's Press.

Steal the Sun. A. E Maxwell. LC 81-11760. 12.95 (ISBN 0-399-90129-9). R. Marek Publishers.

Stealer of Souls. Michael Moorcock. (Orig.). 1968. pap. 0.60 o.p. (73-545). Lancer.

Stealing Heaven. Marrion Meade. 448p. 1980. pap. 2.95 (ISBN 0-380-50674-2, 50674). Avon.

Stealing Heaven: The Love Story of Heloise and Abelard. Marion Meade. LC 79-1182. 1979. 9.95 (ISBN 0-688-03477-2). W. Morrow.

Stealing Home. Philip F. O'Connor. 288p. 1981. pap. 2.75 (ISBN 0-345-28478-X). Ballantine.

Stealing Home: A Novel. Philip F O'Connor. LC 78-13791. 1979. (ISBN 0-394-50186-1). Knopf.

Stealing Lillian. Tony Kenrick. LC 75-17984. 1975. 6.95 (ISBN 0-679-50544-X). McKay.

Stealing Lillian. Tony Kenrick. 1976. 1.75. Warner Books.

Stealthy Terror. John Alexander Ferguson. LC 18-7924. 1918. John Lane Company.

Steam Against Steam: Tales of the Classic Connecticut River Battle of Steamboats Vs. Railroads. Carl Daniel Lane. LC 75-183875. 1973. 3.95 (ISBN 0-87106-109-0). Pequot Press.

Steam-Boat. John Galt. LC 20-13631. 1823. S. Campbell and Son Etc.

Steam House. Jules Verne. LC 60-140. (Fitzroy edition of Jules Verne). 1960. Associated Booksellers.

Steam House, Part One: The Demon of Cawnpore. Jules Verne. (Illus.). 1976. Repr. of 1886 ed. lib. bdg. 10.60x (ISBN 0-88411-908-4). Amereon Ltd.

Steam House, Part Two: Tigers & Traitors. Jules Verne. (Illus.). 1976. Repr. of 1886 ed. lib. bdg. 14.85x (ISBN 0-88411-909-2). Amereon Ltd.

Steam Peg. James McClure. 1974. (pbk.) 1.25. Avon.

Steam Pig. James McClure. LC 72-410. 1972. 5.95 (ISBN 0-06-012896-8). Harper & Row.

Steam Pig. James McClure. LC 81-48254. (Pantheon International Crime). 1982. 2.95 (ISBN 0-394-71021-5). Pantheon Books.

Steam-Shovel Man. Ralph Delahaye Paine. LC 13-18714. 1913. 1.00. C. Scribner's Sons.

Steamboat Gold. George Washington Ogden. LC 31-2904. 1931. Dodd, Mead & Company.

Steamboat Gothic. A Novel. Frances Parkinson Wheeler Keyes. LC 52-13868. 1952. Messner.

Steamboat on the River: A Novel. Darwin Le Ora Teilhet. LC 52-12479. (Illus.). 1952. Sloane.

Steamboat Round the Bend. Ben Lucien Burman. LC 33-309931. Farrar & Rinehart, Incorporated.

Steamboat Round the Bend. Ben Lucien Burman. LC 41-264189. Grosset & Dunlap.

Steamboat Round the Bend. mississippi river ed. Ben Lucien Burman. LC 35-32207. 1935. Little, Brown, and Company.

Steamboat Round the Bend. Ben Lucien Burman. LC 46-4173. 1946. E. P. Dutton & Co., Inc.

Steamboat Round the Bend. Sketches by Alice Caddy. With an Introd. by Harry Hansen and a New Pref. by the Author. Ben Lucien Burman. (Collier books, AS49X). 1962. Collier Books.

Steaming to Bamboola. Christopher Buckley. 320p. 1982. 14.95 (ISBN 0-312-92792-4). St Martin.

Steel. Forest Hill. (Orig.). 1983. pap. cancelled (ISBN 0-523-40637-1). Pinnacle Bks.

Steel and Iron: A Novel. Israel Joshua Singer. LC 69-19656. 1969. 6.95. Funk & Wagnalls.

Steel and Jade. Achmed Abdullah. LC 27-18773. George H. Doran Company.

Steel Bird, and Other Stories. Vasilii Pavlovich Aksenov. LC 79-103556. 12.95 (ISBN 0-88233-295-3). Ardis.

Steel Chips. Idwal Jones. LC 29-14378. 1929. A. A. Knopf.

Steel Cocoon, a Novel. Bentz Plagemann. 1958. Viking Press.

Steel Crocodile. David Guy Compton. LC 76-10754. (Gregg Press science fiction series). 1976. 11.50 (ISBN 0-8398-2327-4). Gregg Press.

Steel Crown. Fergus Hume. LC 11-25747. G. W. Dillingham Company.

Steel Decks. James Brendan Connolly. LC 25-21216. 1925. C. Scribner's Sons.

Steel Flea: Adapted from the Russian of Nicholas Leskov. Nikolai Semenovich Leskov & Deutsch, Babette, 1895- LC 43-17239. 1943. Harper & Brothers.

Steel Horizon. Edward Churchill. LC 50-6720. 1950. Avalon Books.

Steel Killer. Robert Charles, pseud. 304p. (Orig.). 1981. pap. 2.75 (ISBN 0-515-05543-3). Jove Pubns.

Steel Mirror. Donald Hamilton. LC 48-9185. 1948. Rinehart.

Steel Necklace. Fortune Du Boisgobey. LC 6-34410. (Secret service series, no. 47). Street & Smith.

Steel of Raithskar. Randall Garrett & Vicki A. Heydron. 192p. (Orig.). 1981. pap. 2.25 (ISBN 0-553-14607-6). Bantam.

Steel Palace. Hugh Pentecost. (Julian Quist Mystery Novel & Red Badge Novel of Suspense Ser.). 1977. 6.95 o.p. (ISBN 0-396-07491-X). Dodd.

Steel Preferred. Herschel Salmon Hall. LC 20-12451. E.P. Dutton & Company.

Steel Safe: Or, The Stains and Splendors of New York Life. A Story of Our Day and Night. Henry Llewellyn Williams. (On cover: De Witt's series of choice novels, no. 10). 1868. R. M. De Witt.

Steel Saraband. Roger Dataller. LC 39-23305. 1938. T. Nelson and Sons, Ltd.

Steel Saraband. Archibald Arthur Eaglestone. LC 39-23305. 1938. Nelson.

Steel Shark. Bruno Krauss. (Sea Wolf Ser.: No. 1). 1981. pap. 2.25 (ISBN 0-89083-755-4). Zebra.

Steel Spring. Per Wahloo. LC 74-120849. 1970. Delacorte Press.

Steel Tiger. Sterling Silliphant. 320p. (Orig.). 1983. pap. 3.50 (ISBN 0-345-30428-4). Ballantine.

Steel to the South. Wayne D Overholser. LC 51-9373. 1951. Macmillan.

Steel to the Sunset. Alamo Boyd, pseud. LC 41-654520. 1941. Arcadia House, Inc.

Steel Tsar. Michael Moorcock. 160p. 1982. pap. 2.50. DAW Bks.

Steel Under Velvet. Julia Christina Lieb. LC 39-24573. 1939. Margent Press.

Steel Web. 1st Ed. Thomas Thompson. LC 53-9126. (Double D western). 1953. Doubleday.

Steele Heart. Jocelyn Day. LC 82-19865. 1983. 11.95 (ISBN 0-89340-542-6). J. Curley.

Steele: The Big Game, No. 22. George G. Gilman, pseud. 192p. (Orig.). 1982. pap. 1.95 (ISBN 0-523-41455-2). Pinnacle Bks.

Steele: The Tarnished Star, No. 19. George G. Gilman, pseud. 160p. 1981. pap. 1.75 (ISBN 0-523-41452-8). Pinnacle Bks.

Steelwork. Gilbert Sorrentino. LC 79-119484. 1970. 5.95. Pantheon Books.

Steelyard Blues. Timothy Harris & David S Ward. LC 72-6562. 1972. 0.95. Bantam Books.

Steep Ascent. Anne Morrow Lindbergh. LC 44-40062. 1944. Harcourt, Brace and Company.

Steep Ascent: The Story of a Surgeon. Dorothy Dennison. (YA) 1967. pap. 1.35 o.p. (38-16). Moody.

Steep Ascent: The Story of a Surgeon, by Dorothy Dennison. Dorothy Dennison. LC 53-13446. Moody Press.

Steep Hill: By Carol Holliston Pseud. James Noble Gifford. LC 53-130645. 1953. Arcadia House.

Steep Valley. Ada Horner & Thelma Bailey. 1978. 6.95 o.p. (ISBN 0-533-03558-9). Vantage.

Steeper Cliff: A Novel. David Albert Davidson. LC 47-5079. 1947. Random House.

Steering Wheel. Robert Alexander Wason. LC 10-22536. The Bobbs-Merrill Company.

Steffi: A Novel. Eunice Gray. LC 51-1931. 1951. Exposition Press.

Steinbeck. John Steinbeck & Covici, Pascal, Comp. LC 43-11292. (Viking portable library). 1943. The Viking Press.

Steinway Quintet: Plus Four. Leslie Epstein. LC 76-15615. 8.95 (ISBN 0-316-24569-0). Little, Brown.

Stella. Fanny Lewald-Stahr & Marshall, Beatrice. (On cover: The seaside library. Pocket ed. no. 436). 1885. G. Munro.

Stella and an Unfinished Communication: Studies of the Unseen... Charles Howard Hinton. LC 1-16437. 1895. S. Sonnenschein & Co.

Stella Dallas. Olive Higgins Prouty. pap. 0.60 o.p. (53-535). Paperback Lib.

Stella Dallas, a Novel. Olive Higgins Prouty. LC 24-3792. Houghton Mifflin Company.

Stella Dallas: A Novel. Olive Higgins Prouty. LC 42-50419. 1942. Triangle Books.

Stella Dallas, Novel. Olive Higgins Prouty. 1923. Houghton Mifflin Company.

Stella, Daphne see Oeuvres Completes.

Stella Defiant. Clare Consuelo Frewen Sheridan. LC 25-8544. 1925. Greenberg, Inc.

Stella Fregelius: A Tale of Three Destinies. Henry Rider Haggard. 1903. Longmans, Green, and Co.

Stella Hope. Emily Woodson Barksdale. 1907. The Neale Publishing Company.

Stella Maris. William John Locke. LC 13-35200. 1913. John Lane Company.

Stella Marvin. Marie Tello Phillips. LC 27-249497. 1927. H. Vinal, Ltd.

Stella Nash. Martin Louis Alan Gompertz. LC 24-233768. 1924. Houghton Mifflin Company.

Stella Rosevelt. A Novel. Sarah Elizabeth Forbush G. S. Downs Downs. LC 6-45952. (primrose series. no. 10). 1890. Street & Smith.

Stella Russell. Katherine Virginia Bell. LC 7-23534. 1907. The Neale Publishing Company.

Stella the Star: Or, A Drama of the Stage. Florence Blackburn White Schoeffel. LC 2643. (On cover: Eagle library, no. 158). 1900. Street & Smith.

Stella the Star: Or, A Drama off the Stage. The Romance of an Actress' Private Life. Florence Blackburn White Schoeffel. (On cover: Munro's library v. 50 no. 794). 1887. N. L. Munro.

Stellar Conquest. 1974. pap. write for info. (ISBN 0-88074-600-9). Metagam.

Stellar Missiles. Edward Earl Repp. LC 50-5641. 1949. Fantasy Pub. Co.

Stellar Science Fiction, No. 2. Judy-Lynn Del Rey. LC 75-34193. 1976. 1.50 (ISBN 0-345-24584-9). Ballantine Books.

Stellar Science Fiction, No. 3. Judy-Lynn Del Rey. LC 77-4376. (Del Rey book). 1.95 (ISBN 0-345-25152-0). Ballantine Books.

Stellar Science Fiction, No. 6. Judy-Lynn Del Rey. LC 80-68216. 1981. 2.25 (ISBN 0-345-28969-2). Ballantine Books.

Stellar Science Fiction, No. 7. Judy-Lynn Del Rey. LC 81-66549. 1981. 2.50 (ISBN 0-345-29473-4). Ballantine Books.

Stellar Science-Fiction Stories. Ed. by Judy-Lynn Del Rey. (Del Rey book). 1978. 1.95 (ISBN 0-345-27302-8). Ballantine Books.

Stellar Short Novels. LC 76-18081. 1976. 1.50 (ISBN 0-345-25501-1). Ballantine Books.

Stella's Roomers: The Astonishing Story of a New York Rooming-House. Elizabeth Bang. LC 11-255542. Brandu's.

Stelmark: A Family Recollection. Harry Mark Petrakis. LC 76-124685. 1970. 4.95. McKay.

Stem of the Crimson Dahlia. James Locke. 1908. Moffat, Yard & Company.

Stem to Stern: Or, Building the Boat. William Taylor Adams. LC 12-37487. (Added t.-p.: Oliver Optic's boat-builder series. v. 4). 1886. Lee and Shepard.

Sten. Allan Cole & Chris Bunch. 288p. 1982. pap. 2.50 (ISBN 0-345-28503-4, Del Rey). Ballantine.

Stench of Poppies. Ivor Drummond. LC 77-91888. 7.95 (ISBN 0-312-76147-3). St. Martin's Press.

Stendahl: Notes on a Novelist. Robert Martin Adams. LC 73-796. 1969. 5.95. Funk & Wagnalls.

Stendhal. John Atherton. LC 64-16140. (Studies in mod. European lit. and thought) Bibl.). 1965. bds., 2.50. Hillary.

Stendhal. Wallace Fowlie. LC 70-75903. (Masters of world literature series). 1969. Macmillan.

Stendhal. Michael Wood. LC 73-164669. 1971. 7.50 (ISBN 0-8014-0680-3). Cornell University Press.

Stendhal: A Collection of Critical Essays. Ed. by Victor H. Brombert. LC 62-9306. (Twentieth century views). (Spectrum book, S-TC-7.). 1962. Prentice-Hall.

Stendhal: Notes on a Novelist. Robert Martin Adams. LC 59-9455. 1959. Noonday Press.

Stendhal's The Red and the Black. Marie Henri Beyle. Ed. by Maugham, William Somerset. LC 49-10799. (Ten Greatest H Novels of the World). 1949. J. C. Winston Co.

Step- Daughter of Jerusalem: The Virgin of No-Man's Land) A Novel. Translated from the Hebrew by the Author with the Kind Assistance of B. Preiskel and R. C. Burbank. David Satty Kinarthy. LC 58-42604. 1958. Oxford Press.

Step--Mother. Annie French Hector. LC 99-4075. 1900. J. B. Lippincott Company.

Step Aside. Charlotte Dunning Wood. LC 9-5118. 1886. Houghton, Mifflin and Company.

Step Backwards. Patricia Lake. (Harlequin Presents Ser.). 192p. 1983. pap. 1.75 (ISBN 0-373-10570-3). Harlequin Bks.

Step Beyond Innocence. 1st Ed. Nora Johnson. LC 61-5750. 1961. Little, Brown.

Step by Step: A Story of High Ideals. Sarah Elizabeth Forbush G. S. Downs Downs. 1906. G. W. Dillingham Company.

Step by Step: Or, Delia Arlington. A Fireside Story. Frances West Pike. LC 26-365795. 1857. J. Munroe and Company.

Step by Step: Or, The Lord's Leading. Alice T Pickford. LC 7-35914. 1891. American Baptist Publication Society.

Step-Child. Rob Eden. LC 30-32906. Grosset & Dunlap.

Step Children of the World. Jacob Manuel Mayer. LC 34-5278. 1934. Bloch Publishing Company.

Step Down, Elder Brother: A Novel. Josephina Niggli. LC 47-11652. 1947. Rinehart.

Step in the Dark. Elizabeth Lemarchand. LC 76-24554. (Illus.). 1977. 6.95 (ISBN 0-8027-5360-4). Walker.

Step in the Dark. Ethel L. White. pap. 0.50 o.p. (52-988). Paperback Lib.

Step in the Dark: A Novel. Ethel Lina White. LC 39-110498. 1939. Harper & Brothers.

Step in the River: A Novel. Francis Irby Gwaltney. LC 60-159798. 1960. Random House.

Step into Terror. Marilyn Ross. 1973. 0.95. Warner.

Step Lively. Elva Williams. LC 31-603. Sears Publishing Company, Inc.

Step on the Stair. Alice French. LC 13-6077. 0.50. The Bobbs-Merrill Company.

Step on the Stair. Anna Katharine Green Rohlfs. LC 23-1441. 1923. Dodd, Mead and Company.

Step-Sister: A Novelette. LC 74-162230. (Confederate Imprints Collection Ser.). 260p. 1973. Repr. of 1863 ed. 11.00 o.p. (ISBN 0-405-04336-8). Arno.

Step Softly on My Grave. Margaret Ann Hubbard. LC 66-297124. 1966. 4.95. Bruce.

Step Softly on the Beaver. Frank Harrison. LC 77-161101. 1971. 6.95 (ISBN 0-8027-0354-2). Walker.

Step Softly on the Beaver see Wild Call of Love.

Step-Sons of France. Percival Christopher Wren. LC 28-25638. Grosset & Dunlap.

Step to Destiny and Other Short Stories: An Anthology. Gabriel. LC 76-4650. 1976. 3.25 (ISBN 0-89144-017-8). Crescent Publications.

Step to the Music. Phyllis A Whitney. LC 53-8425. (Signet book). 1974. (pbk.) 1.25. New American Library.

Stepan Razin. Aleksei Pavlovich Chapygin. Tr. by Cedar Paul from Rus. LC 72-14051. (Soviet Literature in English Translation Ser). (o.s.i.). 480p. 1973. Repr. of 1946 ed. 27.50 (ISBN 0-88355-002-4). Hyperion Conn.

Stepchild. Joanne Fluke. (Orig.). 1980. pap. 2.25 (ISBN 0-440-18408-8). Dell.

Stepchild of the Moon. Fulton Oursler. LC 26-16084. 1926. Harper & Brothers.

Stepdaughter. Caroline Blackwood. LC 77-3500. 5.95 (ISBN 0-684-14934-6). Scribner.

Stepdaughter. Caroline Blackwood. (Quokka Book). 1978. 1.95 (ISBN 0-671-82040-0). Pocket Books.

Stepdaughter. Iris Bromige. 1972. pap. 0.75 o.p. (94240). Beagle Bks.
Stepdaughters of War. Helen Zenna Smith. LC 30-10064. E. P. Dutton & Co., Inc.
Stepfather: By Charlotte Jay Pseud. 1st American Ed. Geraldine Jay. LC 59-10621. Harper.
Stepford Wives. Ira Levin. LC 72-13475. 1973. 6.95. G. K. Hall.
Stepford Wives. Ira Levin. 1979. 2.25 (ISBN 0-440-18294-8). Dell Publishing Co.
Stepford Wives: A Novel. Ira Levin. (Crest Book, P1876). 1973. (pbk.) 1.25. Fawcett.
Stepford Wives: A Novel. Ira Levin. LC 72-2481. 1972. 4.95 (ISBN 0-394-48199-2). Random House.
Stephan Crane's Red Badge of Courage & Related Readings. Ed. by J. Green & L. Bertrand. 1965. pap. text ed. 4.72 o.p. (ISBN 0-13-846519-3). P-H.
Stephania. Ilona Karmel. LC 52-10908. 1953. Houghton Mifflin.
Stephanie: The Emperor's Agent. Marceline Gobineau. LC 77-89187. 1977. 1.75. Avon Books.
Stephanie: The Passions of Spring. Marcel Gobineau. 1976. 1.50 (ISBN 0-380-00602-2). Avon.
Stephanie: The Snows of Sebastopol. Marceline Gobineau. 1.50 (ISBN 0-380-00833-5). Avon.
Stephanie: The Story of a Christian Maiden's Love. Louis Francois Veuillot. LC 16-7009. 1883. J. B. Piet & Co.
Stephanie's Son: A Novel. Philip Freund. LC 47-11159. 1947. Beechhurst Press.
Stephen, a Soldier of the Cross. Florence Morse Kingsley. LC 7-128144. 1896. H. Altemus.
Stephen & the Sleeping Saints. Pamela Bennatts. LC 76-28071. (O.s.i.). 1977. 7.95 o.s.i. (ISBN 0-312-76160-0). St Martin.
Stephen and the Sleeping Saints. Pamela Bennetts. LC 76-28071. 1977. 7.95. St. Martin's Press.
Stephen Archer, and Other Tales. George Macdonald. LC 79-152946. (Short story index reprint series). (Illus.). 1971. (ISBN 0-8369-3805-4). Books for Libraries Press.
Stephen Archer: And Other Tales. George Macdonald. LC 12-18321. 1911. D. McKay.
Stephen Ayers. James McConnaughey. LC 39-20726. Farrar & Rinehart, Inc.
Stephen Crane: Sullivan County Tales & Sketches. facsimile ed. R. W. Stallman. (Illus.). 1968. pap. 8.90x (ISBN 0-8138-2310-2). Iowa St U Pr.
Stephen Crane's Red Badge of Courage. Edit. Bd. of Consultants: Stanley Cooperman, Charles Leavitt, Unicio J. Violi. Joseph E Grennen. LC 65-8278. (Monarch notes and study guides, 660-1). pap., 1.00. Dist. by Monarch Pr.
Stephen Crane's The Red Badge of Courage. David Reuben Turner. LC 76-82586. (Arco notes). 1969. 0.95. Arco.
Stephen Dane. Amanda Minnie Douglas. LC 6-33466. 1867. Lee and Shepard.
Stephen Dane. Amanda Minnie Douglas. LC 6-33464. Lee and Shepard.
Stephen Ellicott's Daughter. A Novel. Mary Anna Lupton Needell. LC 9-15523. 1902. F. Warne and Co.
Stephen Escott. Ludwig Lewisohn. LC 30-7110. 1930. Harper & Brothers.
Stephen Hayne. Albert Edward Idell. LC 51-7951. 1951. Sloane.
Stephen Hero. James Augustine Aloysius Joyce. LC 63-14454. (A New Directions paperbook, 133). (Illus.). 1963. New Directions.
Stephen Hero: A Part of the First Draft of A Portrait of the Artist As a Young Man. James Joyce & Spencer, Theodore, 1902- Ed. LC 45-265435. New Directions.
Stephen Hero, Edited from the Ms. in the Harvard College Library by Theodore Spencer. A New Ed., Incorporating the Additional Ms. Pages in the Yale University Library, Edited by John J. Slocum and Herbert Cahoon. James Joyce. LC 55-12451. (New Directions book).
Stephen Holton: A Story of Life As It Is in Town and Country. Charles Felton Pidgin. LC 2-12946. 1902. L. C. Page & Company.
Stephen Kent. Hallie Ferron Dickerman. LC 35-15471. 1935. The Hartney Press.
Stephen King's Danse Macabre. Stephen King. 1981. 13.95 (ISBN 0-89696-076-5, An Everest House Book). Dodd.
Stephen Lescombe, Bachelor of Arts: A Novel. Julius H Hurst. 1897. G. P. Putnam's Sons.
Stephen March's Way. Henry Herbert Knibbs. LC 13-4613. 1913. 1.25. Houghton Mifflin Company.
Stephen Moreland. A Novel ... 1834. Key & Biddle.
Stephen Morris. Nevil Shute. pap. 0.60 o.p. (73-435). Lancer.
Stephen Morris: By Nevil Shute Pseud. Nevil Shute Norway. 1961. Morrow.
Stephen Mulhew: The Making of a Gentle Man. Howard Buckwalter Seitz. LC 12-213946. 1912. The Cosmopolitan Press.
Stephen Remarx. James Granville Adderley. LC 75-485. (Victorian Fiction: Novels of Faith and Doubt; 38). 1975. 35.00 (ISBN 0-8240-1562-2). Garland Pub.
Stephen the Black. Caroline H Pemberton. LC 72-1520. (Black Heritage Library Collection). 1972. 12.50 (ISBN 0-8369-9044-7). Books for Libraries Press.
Stephen the Black. Caroline H Pemberton. LC 1-29361. G. W. Jacobs & Co.
Stephen the Well-Beloved. Harold E Scarborough. LC 25-15513. 1924. D. Appleton and Company.
Stephen's Bridge: By Laurence Lafore. 1st Ed. Laurence Davis Lafore. LC 67-191206. 1968. Doubleday.
Stephen's Passion. Roberta Kalechofsky. LC 75-30158. (Illus.). 3.33. Micah Publications.
Stepmother: A Novel. Ray Coryton Hutchinson. LC 55-7895. 1955. Rinehart.
Stepmother in Bondage. O. R. Bassett. 192p. (Orig.). 1973. pap. 1.95 o.p. (ISBN 0-87977-181-X, DBB181). Dansk Blue Bk.
Stepmother's House. (Orig.). 1972. pap. 0.75 o.p. (94263). Beagle Bks.
Steppe & Other Stories. Anton Pavlovich Chekhov. LC 70-106263. (Short story index reprint series). 1970. Books for Libraries Press.
Steppe: And Other Stories. Anton Pavlovich Chekhov. Tr. by Kaye, Adeline Lister. LC 16-10126. 1915. Frederick A. Stokes Company.
Steppenwolf. Hermann Hesse. LC 63-12171. (Modern library of the world's best books). 1963. Modern Library.
Steppenwolf. Hermann Hesse. Tr. by Creighton, Basil. LC 29-18164. H. Holt and Company.
Steppenwolf. Translated from the German by Basil Creighton. Hermann Hesse. (Atlantic paperbacks 2101). 1960. pap., 1.75. F. Ungar.
Stepping. Nancy Thayer. LC 79-7214. 1980. 10.95 (ISBN 0-385-15203-5). Doubleday.
Stepping from the Shadows. Patricia A McKillip. LC 81-69151. 1982. 12.95 (ISBN 0-689-11211-4). Atheneum.
Stepping Heavenward. Elizabeth Payson Prentiss. LC 31-19503. 1869. A. D. F. Randolph & Co.
Stepping Heavenward. Elizabeth Payson Prentiss. LC 7-30126. 1870. A. D. F. Randolph & Co.
Stepping Heavenward. new stereotype ed., with a sketch of the author. ed. Elizabeth Payson Prentiss. LC 7-30125. 1880. A. D. F. Randolph & Company.
Stepping Heavenward. illustrated ed. Elizabeth Payson Prentiss. LC 7-30124. 1889. A. D. F. Randolph and Company.
Stepping Heavenward. new ed. with a sketch of the author. ed. Elizabeth Payson Prentiss. LC 7-30123. A. D. F. Randolph Company.
Stepping Heavenward. new and rev. ed. Elizabeth Payson Prentiss. LC 29-8259. 1901. D. C. Cook Publishing Company.
Stepping High. Gene Markey. LC 29-8723. 1929. Doubleday, Doran & Company, Inc.
Stepping Out. Deborah Beckerman. 1975. 3.95 o.s.i. (ISBN 0-913390-13-5). Pathmark Bks.
Stepping Out: A Love Story. Rolaine A Hochstein. LC 77-24702. 7.95 (ISBN 0-393-08787-5). Norton.
Stepping Stones. James McShan. LC 76-527. 1976. 7.95 o.p. (ISBN 0-89002-067-1); pap. 2.95 o.p. (ISBN 0-89002-066-3). Northwoods Pr.
Stepping-Stones. Mary Virginia Terhune & Townsend, Virginia Frances, 1836- (select series, no. 57). Street & Smith.
Stepping Under Ladders. Maysie Greig. LC 39-229329. 1939. Doubleday, Doran & Co., Inc.
Stepping Westward. Malcolm Bradbury. 1966. 4.95 o.p. HM.
Stepping Westward: A Novel 1st Amer. Ed. Malcolm Bradbury. LC 66-11228. 1966. 4.95. Houghton.
Steps. Jerzy N. Kosinski. LC 68-28544. 1968. 4.95. Random House.
Steps Going Down. John Thomas McIntyre. LC 36-18911. Farrar & Rinehart, Incorporated.
Steps in Darkness. Krishna Baldev Vaid. LC 62-10330. 1962. Orion Press.
Steps in the Dark. Marten Cumberland. 1945. Pub. for the Crime Club, by Doubleday, Doran & Co., Inc.
Steps in the Dark. Marten Cumberland. 1945. Pub. for the Crime Book Society by Hurst & Blackett Ltd.
Steps of Honor. Basil King. LC 4-9500. 1904. Harper & Brothers.
Steps of the Quarry. Robert Terrall. LC 51-3930. 1951. Crown Publishers.
Steps of the Sun. Olivia Davis. LC 78-170160. 1972. 6.95 (ISBN 0-395-13518-4). Houghton Mifflin.
Steps of the Sun. Emily Hahn. LC 40-32133. 1940. The Dial Press.
Steps of the Sun. Walter S Tevis. LC 81-43899. 1982. 15.95 (ISBN 0-385-17037-8). Doubleday.
Steps to Destiny & Other Short Stories: An Anthology. Gabriel. Ed. by Joseph Lawrence. LC 76-4650. 112p. 1976. pap. text ed. 3.25 o.p. (ISBN 0-89144-017-8). Crescent Pubns.
Steps to Murder. Robert Portner Koehler. LC 43-556744. 1943. Phoenix Press.
Steps to Nowhere: A Novel of Suspense. Constance Leonard. LC 74-103. 1974. 4.95 (ISBN 0-396-06941-X). Dodd, Mead.
Steps to the Empty Throne: The First of a Triology of Novels About Robert the Bruce. Nigel G Tranter. 1973. 1.25. Ballantine Books.
Steps to the Grotto. Cassandra Nye. (Berkley medallion book). 1974. (pbk) 0.95 (ISBN 0-425-02498-9). Berkley Pub. Co.
Steps to the Moon. Adelaide Humphries. LC 37-235342. 1937. Hillman-Curl, Inc.
Steps Toward Heaven. Ida Viola Best Houck. LC 12-12012. I. B. Houck.
Steps Unto Heaven. Edward S Mullins. LC 41-27320. 1941. Meador Publishing Company.
Stepsons of France. new and enl. ed. Percival Christopher Wren. LC 74-169570. (Short story index reprint series). 1971. (ISBN 0-8369-4033-4). Books for Libraries Press.
Stepsons of France. new and enl. ed. Percival Christopher Wren. LC 49-34597. 1926. F. A. Stokes Co.
Stepsons of Light. new ed. Eugene Manlove Rhodes. LC 69-16714. (Western frontier library). (Illus.). 1969. University of Oklahoma Press.
Stepsons of Light. Eugene Manlove Rhodes. LC 21-9518. 1921. Houghton Mifflin Company.
Stepsons of Terra. Robert Silverberg. 1977. 1.50. Ace Books.
Stereopticon. Susan Ries Lukas. LC 74-26888. 220p. 1975. 7.95 o.p. (ISBN 0-8128-1774-5); pap. 1.95 (ISBN 0-8128-7015-8). Stein & Day.
Stereopticon: A Novel. Susan Ries Lukas. LC 74-26888. 1975. 7.95 (ISBN 0-8128-1774-5). Stein and Day.
Sterile Cuckoo. John Treadwell Nichols. LC 64-23047. (Illus.). 1965. D. McKay Co.
Sterile Cuckoo. John Treadwell Nichols. 1979. 2.50 (ISBN 0-671-82321-3). Pocket Books.
Sterile Sun. Caroline Beach Slade. LC 36-10628. The Vanguard Press.
Stern. Bruce Jay Friedman. Bd. with Mother's Kisses. 1966. pap. 2.25 o.p. (ISBN 0-671-68830-8, Touchstone Bks). S&S.
Stern. Bruce Jay Friedman. (O.S.I.). 1962. 3.95 o.s.i. (ISBN 0-671-68820-0). S&S.
Stern, and A Mother's Kisses: Two Novels. Bruce Jay Friedman. LC 66-21929. 1966. Simon and Schuster.
Stern Chase. A Story in Three Parts. Frances Sarah Johnston Cashel Hoey Hoey. (On cover: Seaside library. Pocket ed. no. 802). 1886. G. Munro.
Stern Necessity. Frederick William Robinson. (seaside library, v. 65, no. 1312). 1882. G. Munro.
Sterns. Brooke Miller. (American Dynasty Ser.: Vol. III). 1982. pap. 3.75 (ISBN 0-440-07639-0, Emerald). Dell.
Sterope: The Veiled Pleiad. William Hayes Acklan. LC 78-38637. (Black Heritage Library Collection). 1972. (ISBN 0-8369-8963-5). Books for Libraries Press.
Stettin Secret. James Stewart Thayer. 1980. pap. 2.50 (ISBN 0-445-04556-6). Popular Lib.
Stettin Secret: A Novel. James Stewart Thayer. LC 78-27527. 19.50 (ISBN 0-691-09238-9). Putnam.
Steve Douglas of Sleepycat Ranch. E. H. Manring. (Orig.). 1971. pap. 0.75 o.p. (B75-2105). Belmont-Tower.
Steve of the Bar Gee Ranch: A Thrilling Story of Life on the Plains of Colorado. Marion Reid-Girardot. LC 14-11804. Broadway Publishing Company.
Steve Train's Ordeal. Max Brand. LC 82-859. 1982. 10.95. Thorndike Press.
Steve Train's Ordeal: By Max Brand. Frederick Faust. LC 67-127133. (Silver star western). 1967. bds., 3.50. Dodd.
Steve Yeager. William MacLeod Raine. LC 15-22997. 1915. Houghton Mifflin Company.
Stevedore Mystery: Or, A Romance of Love and Crime. William Cadwalader Hudson. LC 4863. (On cover: Magnet detective library, no. 146). 1900. Street & Smith.
Steven Lawrence. Annie Edwards. (On cover: Seaside library. Pocket ed. no. 846). 1886. G. Munro.
Stevenson Companion. Robert Louis Stevenson. Ed. by John Hampden. LC 50-326414. 1950. McBride.
Stevenson's Stories for Boys. Robert Louis Stevenson. LC 38-31289. Cupples & Leon Company.
Stevenson's Treasure Island. Robert Louis Stevenson. Ed. by Hersey, Frank Wilson Cheney. LC 11-16561. (Standard English classics). 0.45. Ginn and Company.
Stevenson's Treasure Island. Robert Louis Stevenson. Ed. by Sherman, Stuart Pratt. LC 11-147548. (Half-title: English readings for schools). 1911. 0.40. H. Holt and Company.
Stevenson's Treasure Island. Robert Louis Stevenson. Ed. by Hersey, Frank Wilson Cheney. LC 26-5478. Ginn and Company.
Stevenson's Treasure Island. Robert Louis Stevenson. Ed. by Hersey, Frank Wilson Cheney. LC 28-20570. (Standard English classics). Ginn and Company.
Stevenson's Treasure Island. Robert Louis Stevenson. Ed. by Rutland, James Richard. (Lippincott's classics, ed. by Edwin L. Miller). J. B. Lippincott Company.
Stevenson's Treasure Island: A Story of the Spanish Main. Robert Louis Stevenson. Ed. by Law, Frederick Houk. LC 16-155931. (Twentieth century text-books). 0.25. D. Appleton and Company.
Steve's Woman. Edith Mary Oldham Lees Ellis. LC 9-28072. 1909. The J. McBride Co.
Stevie. Benedict Thielen. LC 41-4629. 1941. The Dial Press.
Stewardess. Robert J Serling. LC 81-21487. 13.95 (ISBN 0-312-76193-7). St. Martin's/Marek.
Stewart Edward White. Judy Alter, pseud. LC 75-7011. (Western Writers Ser.: No. 18). (Illus., Orig.). 1975. pap. 2.00x (ISBN 0-88430-017-X). Boise St Univ.
Stick. Elmore Leonard. LC 82-72073. 1983. 14.50 (ISBN 0-87795-436-4). Arbor Hse.
Stick Your Neck Out. Mordecai Richler. 1963. 3.95 o.p. (68906). S&S.
Sticking Place. Jessica Mann. LC 74-83694. 1974. 5.95 (ISBN 0-679-50481-8). David McKay.
Sticking Point! Ken Jackson. LC 79-139633. (Inner sanctum mystery). 1971. 4.95 (ISBN 0-671-20884-5). Simon and Schuster.
Stickit Minister: And Some Common Men. 2d ed. Samuel Rutherford Crockett. LC 72-163023. (Short story index reprint series). 1971. (ISBN 0-8369-3937-9). Books for Libraries Press.
Stickit Minister: And Some Common Men. Samuel Rutherford Crockett. LC 26-36407. 1894. R. F. Fenno & Co.
Stickit Minister and Some Common Men. Samuel Rutherford Crockett. LC 4-16514. 1902. The Macmillan Company.
Stickit Minister and Some Common Men. Samuel Rutherford Crockett. LC 4559. W. B. Conkey Company.
Stickit Minister's Wooing. Samuel Rutherford Crockett. LC 6608. 1900. Doubleday & McClure Co.
Sticks & Stones. Mary L. Dodge. (Orig.). 1979. pap. 1.75 (ISBN 0-532-23279-8). Woodhill.
Sticks & Stones. Lynn Hall. 192p. 1972. pap. 1.50 (ISBN 0-440-98266-9, LFL). Dell.
Sticks & Stones. 1978. pap. text ed. write for info. (ISBN 0-88074-011-6). Metagam.
Sticky Fingers. Eleanor Bartlett. pap. 1.50 o.p. (Z1052D, Zebra). Grove.
Stiff As a Broad. G. G. Fickling, pseud. (Honey West Ser., No. 11). (Orig.). 1971. pap. 0.75 o.p. (T2494). Pyramid Pubns.
Stiff Proposition. Troy Conway, pseud. (Coxeman Ser., No. 28). (Orig.). 1971. pap. 0.75 o.p. (ISBN 0-446-64661-X, 64-661). Paperback Lib.
Stiff Upper Lip. Peter Israel. 1980. 1.95 (ISBN 0-380-46086-6). Avon Books.
Stiff Upper Lip see Esprit De Corps.
Stiff Upper Lip: A Novel. Peter Israel. LC 78-3325. 9.95 (ISBN 0-690-01412-0). Crowell.
Stiff Upper Lip, Jeeves. Wodehouse, Pelham Grenville. LC 63-7423. 1963. Simon and Schuster.
Stiffs. Melbourne Garahan. LC 24-4502. 1924. T. Seltzer.
Stigma. Hugo Ballin. LC 28-14554. The Macaulay Company.
Stigma. Williams Forrest. LC 57-12819. 1957. Crown Publishers.
Stigma: A Novel. Emily Selkirk. LC 6-11308. 1906. H. B. Turner & Co.
Stigmata of Dr. Constantine. Thomas J Dulack. 1976. 1.75 (ISBN 0-553-02195-8). Bantam.
Stigmata of Dr. Constantine. Thomas J. Dulack. LC 73-18662. 1974. 8.95 (ISBN 0-06-122100-7). Harper's Magazine Press.
Stigmata of Palmer Eldritch Three. Philip K. Dick. 1971. pap. 0.75 o.p. (75-399). Manor Bks.
Stiletto. Ernest Goodwin. LC 24-172493. The Bobbs-Merrill Company.
Stiletto. Harold Robbins. 1982. pap. 3.25 (ISBN 0-440-18284-0). Dell.
Stiletto Signature- Jon Messmann. (Revenger). (Signet book: Vol. 4). 1974. (pbk.) 0.95. New American Library.
Still and Woven Blue. Richard Stookey. LC 73-21637. 1974. 6.95 (ISBN 0-395-18493-2). Houghton Mifflin.
Still As the Grave. Mary Linn Roby. LC 64-17562. (Red badge detective). 1964. Dodd, Mead.
Still Circling Moose Jaw. Richard Pike Bissell. LC 65-16866. bds., 5.00. McGraw.
Still Circling Moose Jaw. Richard Pike Bissell. LC 65-16866. 1965. McGraw-Hill.

Still Dead. Ronald Arbuthnott Knox. LC 34-32402. E. P. Dutton & Co., Inc.
Still Falls the Rain. Chloe Gartner. (Orig.). 1983. pap. 3.95 (ISBN 0-440-18329-4). Dell.
Still Forms on Foxfield. Joan Slonczewski. 1980. pap. 1.95 (ISBN 0-345-28762-2). Ballantine.
Still Full of Sap, Still Green. Alfred Henry Deutsch. LC 79-21558. (Illus.). 5.95 (ISBN 0-8146-1051-X). Liturgical Press.
Still Glides the Stream. Dorothy Emily Stevenson. LC 59-13403. 1959. Rinehart.
Still Glides the Stream. 2d ed. Dorothy Emily Stevenson. LC 79-1918. 1979. 8.95 (ISBN 0-03-052086-X). Holt, Rinehart and Winston.
Still Glides the Stream. Flora Thompson. LC 80-49680. (Illus.). 1981. 13.95 (ISBN 0-19-217414-2). Oxford University Press.
Still Is the Summer Night. August William Derleth. LC 37-27184. 1937. C. Scribner's Sons.
Still Jim. Honore McCue Willsie Morrow. LC 15-842526. 1915. Frederick A. Stokes Company.
Still Life. Sanford Friedman. 320p. 1975. 8.95 o.p. (ISBN 0-8415-0368-0). Dutton.
Still Life. Peter Nadin. 96p. (Orig.). 1983. 12.95 (ISBN 0-934378-35-5); pap. 5.95 (ISBN 0-934378-36-3). Tanam Pr.
Still Life: Two Short Novels. Sanford Friedman. LC 74-28060. 1975. 8.95 (ISBN 0-8415-0368-0). Saturday Review Press.
Still Life with Woodpecker. Tom Robbins. LC 81-103498. 1980. 12.95 (ISBN 0-553-01260-6). Bantam Books.
Still Lives. Rob Swigart. 1976. pap. 3.00 o.p. (ISBN 0-931832-03-9). No Dead Lines.
Still Missing. Beth Richardson Gutcheon. LC 80-25621. 11.95 (ISBN 0-399-12578-7). Putnam.
Still Missing. Beth Richardson Gutcheon. LC 81-13209. 1981. 14.95 (ISBN 0-8161-3327-1). G.K. Hall.
Still No Answer. Emma Redington Lee Thayer. LC 58-5981. (Red badge detective). 1958. Dodd, Mead.
Still of the Night. Robert Alley. 224p. (Orig.). 1982. pap. 2.50. Ballantine.
Still, Small Voice of Trumpets. Lloyd Biggle, Jr. 1975. (pbk.) 1.25. Leisure Books.
Still, Small Voice of Trumpets. Lloyd Biggle, Jr. LC 68-14209. (Doubleday science fiction). 1968. Doubleday.
Still the Heart Sings. Ronald De Levington Kirkbride. LC 50-7671. 1950. Fell.
Still the Mighty Waters. Janice Y. Brooks. (Orig.). 1983. pap. 3.95 (ISBN 0-440-17630-1). Dell.
Still the Night Winds. James E. Rady. 3.75 o.p. Vantage.
Still to the West. Nard Jones. LC 46-188510. 1946. Dodd, Mead & Company.
Still und Bewegt: Contemporary German Stories. Ed. by William Diamond & Rosenfeld, Selma. LC 32-715528. H. Holt and Company.
Still Water. Katharine Newlin Burt. LC 48-51087. 1948. Macrae-Smith-Co.
Still Waters. Ruby Mildred Ayres. LC 41-525. 1941. Doubleday, Doran and Company, Inc.
Still Waters. Ruby Mildred Ayres. LC 42-17831. 1942. The Sun Dial Press.
Still Waters. Dorothy Fletcher. (Orig.). 1969. pap. 0.60 o.p. (63-215). Paperback Lib.
Still Waters. Stanley Middleton. LC 77-350534. 1976. 8.95 (ISBN 0-09-127260-2). Hutchinson.
Still Waters. Frederic Franklyn Van De Water. LC 30-555286. 1929. Pub. for The Crime Club, Inc., by Doubleday, Doran & Company, Inc.
Stillborn. Lillian Eichler Watson. LC 29-4538. 1929. D. Appleton & Company.
Stille Wasser: Erzahlungen, Von Anna Von Krane, Hans Hoffmann und Ernst Von Wildenbruch. Ed. by Wilhelm Bernhardt. Krane, Anna, Frelin Von & Hoffman, Hans. LC 99-2201. (Health's modern language series). 1899. D. C. Health & Co.
Stillman Gott, Farmer and Fisherman. Edwin Day Sibley. LC 2-20469. 1902. J. S. Brooks & Company.
Stillmeadow Seasons. Gene Stratton Porter. Repr. lib. bdg. 14.65x (ISBN 0-89190-594-4). Am Repr-Rivercity Pr.
Stillness. Nicholas Delbanco. LC 80-14395. 1980. 8.95 (ISBN 0-688-03708-9). Morrow.
Stillness. Nicholas Delbanco. LC 81-21020. 1982. 6.95 (ISBN 0-688-00978-6). Quill.
Stillness at Sea. Ashley Aasheim. 368p. (Orig.). 1983. pap. 3.50 (ISBN 0-440-08250-1, Emerald). Dell.
Stillwater Tragedy. Thomas Bailey Aldrich. LC 68-20001. (Americans in Fic.). 1968. 10.00. Gregg Pr.
Stillwater Tragedy. Thomas Bailey Aldrich. LC 4-15060. 1880. Houghton, Mifflin and Company.
Stillwater Tragedy. Thomas Bailey Aldrich. LC 8-22611. Houghton, Mifflin Company.
Stillwater Tragedy. 18th ed. Thomas Bailey Aldrich. LC 44-23383. 1888. Houghton, Mifflin and Company.
Sting. Robert Heverka. (Bantam book, N8272). 1974. (pbk.) 0.95. Bantam Books.
Sting. William Le Queux. LC 28-23665. The Macaulay Company.
Sting Man. Robert W. Greene. 1982. pap. 2.95 (ISBN 0-345-30324-5). Ballantine.
Sting of Death. Jessica Mann. LC 82-45868. (Crime Club Ser.). 192p. 1983. 11.95 (ISBN 0-385-18701-7). Doubleday.
Sting of Death. Perry D Westbrook. LC 55-124902. 1955. Arcadia House.
Sting of Glory. Ann Willets. LC 54-7456. 1954. Random House.
Sting of the Bee. Judith Worrell. 240p. (Orig.). 1982. pap. 2.50 (ISBN 0-505-51809-0). Tower Bks.
Sting of the Honeybee. Frank Parrish. LC 82-48816. 192p. 1983. pap. 2.84i (ISBN 0-06-080652-4, P 652, PL). Har-Row.
Sting of the Honeybee: A Novel of Suspense. Frank Parrish. LC 79-10518. 1979. 7.95 (ISBN 0-396-07702-1). Dodd, Mead.
Sting of the Scorpion. Joseph Coddington. (Orig.). 1981. pap. 1.95 (ISBN 0-505-51699-3). Tower Bks.
Stingaree. Max Brand. LC 81-38512. 1981. 12.50 (ISBN 0-8376-0461-3). R. Bentley.
Stingaree. Frederick Faust. LC 68-23092. 1968. 3.95. Dodd, Mead.
Stingaree. Ernest William Hornung. LC 71-110200. (Short story index reprint series). (Illus.). 1970. Books for Libraries Press.
Stingaree. Ernest William Hornung. LC 5-12707. 1905. C. Scribner's Sons.
Stingaree Murders. W. Shepard Pleasants. LC 33-4987. 1932. The Mystery League.
Stinging Nettles. Marjorie Bowen. LC 23-13314. Small, Maynard & Company.
Stingy Receiver. Eleanor Hallowell Abbott. LC 17-7926. 1917. 1.00. The Century Co.
Stinsons. Frances Casey Kerns. 384p. (Orig.). 1982. pap. 2.95 (ISBN 0-446-90649-2). Warner Bks.
Stinsons. Frances Casey Kerns. 1972. pap. 1.25 o.p. (01033). Curtis.
Stinsons. Frances Casey Kerns. 1.75 (ISBN 0-380-00803-3). Avon.
Stir of Echoes. Richard Matheson. (Berkley book). 1979. 1.95 (ISBN 0-425-04107-7). Berkley Pub. Corp.
Stir of Echoes. 1st Ed. Richard Matheson. LC 58-5846. 1958. Lippincott.
Stirred, Not Shaken: The Dry Martini. John Doxat. 1976. pap. 2.95 (ISBN 0-09-127661-6, Pub. by Hutchinson). Merrimack Pub Cir.
Stirrup Boss. Jonathan H Glidden. LC 49-10970. (Silver star westerns). 1949. Dodd, Mead.
Stirrup Brother. Cherry Wilson. LC 35-1208. A. H. King.
Stirrup Latch. Mary Fenollosa. LC 15-22541. 1905. 1.35. Little, Brown, and Company.
Stirrups in the Dust: By Burt Arthur. 1st Ed. Herbert Arthur, pseud. LC 50-9678. (Double D western). 1950. Doubleday.
Stitch. Richard G Stern. LC 65-20989. 1965. Harper & Row.
Stitch in Time. Emma Lathen, pseud. LC 68-17201. 1968. Macmillan.
Stitch in Time. Emma Lathen, pseud. LC 68-17201. 1975. (pbk.) 1.25 (ISBN 0-671-80046-9). Pocket Books.
Stjorn. Ed. by C R Unger. LC 80-1947. Repr. of 1862 ed. 72.00 (ISBN 0-404-18717-X). AMS Pr.
Stochastic Man. Robert Silverberg. LC 75-6378. 1975. 7.95 (ISBN 0-06-013868-8). Harper & Row.
Stochastic Man. Robert Silverberg. 1976. 1.50 (ISBN 0-449-13570-5). Fawcett Publications.
Stock Car Racer. William E. Butterworth. 4.25 o.p. (21200); PLB 3.93 o.p. G&D.
Stockade. Kenneth Church Lamott. LC 52-5868. 1952. Little, Brown.
Stockade. Jack Pearl, pseud. LC 64-242812. 1965. 4.95. Trident.
Stockbroker, the Bitter Young Man & the Girl. Alfred Hayes. 1971. price not set o.p. Atheneum.
Stockholders in Death. Kenneth Robeson. (Avenger, #7). 1972. Warner Paperback Lib.
Stockholm Syndicate. Colin Forbes, pseud. LC 81-17525. 12.75 (ISBN 0-525-24102-7). Dutton.
Stocking Our Selection. Arthur Hoey Davis. LC 78-497119. (Illus.). 1970. 3.95. University of Queensland Press.
Stockman Stories. National Stockman and Farmer. LC 13-25610. 0.50. The Stockmanfarmer Publishing Co.
Stockton's Stories... By Frank R. Stockton...1st-2d Ser. Frank Richard Stockton. LC 8-15536. 1886. C. Scribner's Sons.
Stockton's Stories, First Series. Frank Richard Stockton. LC 74-98597. (Short Story Index Reprint Ser.). 1886. 15.00 (ISBN 0-8369-3271-4). Ayer Co.
Stockton's Stories, Second Series. Frank Richard Stockton. LC 74-98597. (Short Story Index Reprint Ser.). 1886. 16.00 (ISBN 0-8369-3172-6). Ayer Co.
Stockton's Stories: Second Series: The Christmas Wreck, and Other Stories. Frank Richard Stockton. LC 74-98597. (Short story index reprint series). 1969. Books for Libraries Press.
Stockyards Cowboy. George Washington Ogden. LC 39-7780. Triangle Books.
Stockyards Cowboy. George Washington Ogden. LC 37-19883. 1937. Dodd, Mead & Company.
Stockyards Cowboy. George Washington Ogden. 1938. Triangle Books.
Stoenberg Affair. Ralph A Goodwin. LC 13-9473. 1913. 1.25. Sully and Kleinteich.
Stoic. Theodore Dreiser. LC 52-9798. 1952. World Pub. Co.
Stoic. Theodore Dreiser. LC 47-11518. 1947. Doubleday.
Stoke of Brier Hill. Zenobia Bird. LC 36-21198. 1936. Fleming H. Revell Company.
Stoke of Brier Hill. Zenobia Bird. LC 36-21198. Fleming H. Revell Company.
Stoke Silver Case. Alister McAllister. LC 29-10217. 1929. Harper & Brothers.
Stoker Bush. James Hanley. LC 36-484. 1936. The Macmillan Company.
Stolen America: A Novel. Isobel Henderson Reid Floyd. LC 6-41428. Cassell Publishing Comapny.
Stolen Child. A Tale of the Town, Founded on a Certain Interesting Fact. John Galt. LC 7-158413. (Added t.-p.: The library of romance v. 4). 1833. Carey, Lea and Blanchard.
Stolen Child. And, The Sorcerer. Hendrik Conscience. LC 6-28058. 1892. J. Murphy & Co.
Stolen Credentials: A Tale of French Chivalry. Max Everhart Smith. LC 18-23505. R. J. Shores.
Stolen Empire. Lee E. Wells. 1973. pap. 0.60 o.p. (06188). Curtis.
Stolen Expedition. Lionel Edwin Oswald Charlton. LC 35-15167. 1934. T. Nelson and Sons Ltd.
Stolen Faces. Michael Bishop. LC 76-26262. 7.95 (ISBN 0-06-010362-0). Harper & Row.
Stolen God. Edison Marshall. LC 36-18151. 1936. H. C. Kinsey & Company, Inc.
Stolen Goddess. Richard L. Purtill. 1980. 1.75 (ISBN 0-87997-584-9). DAW Books.
Stolen Goods. 1st Ed. Clarence Budington Kelland. LC 50-8725. 1950. Harper.
Stolen Halo. Barbara Cartland. 1973. pap. 1.25 o.p. (ISBN 0-515-02887-8, V2887). BJ Pub Group.
Stolen Halo. Barbara Cartland. 1973. 0.95. Pyramid.
Stolen Holiday. Marjorie Eatock. (Candlelight Ecstasy Ser.: No. 34). (Orig.). 1982. pap. 1.75 (ISBN 0-440-17742-1). Dell.
Stolen Holiday. Arthur Gainess. LC 31-3684. H. Liveright.
Stolen Honey. Rachel Swete Macnamara. 1924. Small, Maynard & Company.
Stolen Honeymoon. Helen Marion Edginton. LC 43-5942. 1943. Macrae-Smith-Company.
Stolen House. Jack Remick. LC 79-91912. 4.00 (ISBN 0-917530-13-6). Pig Iron Press.
Stolen Husband: A Chicago Novel. Robert Douglas Andrews, pseud. LC 31-3686. Grosset & Dunlap.
Stolen Idols. Edward Phillips Oppenheim. LC 25-9634. 1925. 2.00. Little, Brown, and Company.
Stolen Images. Ulli Beier. (Illus.). 1976. 1.50. Cambridge University Press.
Stolen Jew. Jay Neugeboren. LC 80-19019. 14.95 (ISBN 0-03-056223-6). Holt, Rinehart, and Winston.
Stolen Laces: An Episode in the History of Chicago Crime. From the Diary of Ex-Chief Denis Simmons of the Chicago Police. John W Postgate. (Pinkerton detective series, v. 28). 1889. Laird & Lee.
Stolen Land. Ian Downs. LC 75-873501. 1970. 4.95 (ISBN 0-7016-8124-1). Jacaranda Press.
Stolen Letter: Or, Frank Sharp, the Washington Detective. Charles Morris. (Globe detective series, no. 1). 1887. Rand, McNally & Company.
Stolen Love. Hazel Livingston. LC 29-2735. Grosset & Dunlap.
Stolen March. Cecil William Mercer. LC 33-22163. 1933. Minton, Balch & Company.
Stolen Millionaire. Seldon Truss, pseud. LC 29-15480. 1929. Coward-McCann, Inc.
Stolen Passions. Drusilla Campbell. 384p. 1982. pap. 2.95 (ISBN 0-440-08130-0, Banbury). Dell.
Stolen Past. John Knowles. LC 82-15472. 211p. 1983. 14.95 (ISBN 0-03-062209-3). HR&W.
Stolen Pay Train. Nick Carter. LC 74-15733. (Popular Culture in America Ser.). 128p. 1975. Repr. 9.00x (ISBN 0-405-06368-7). Ayer Co.
Stolen Pay Train. John Russell Coryell. LC 74-15733. (Popular Culture in America). 1974. 7.00 (ISBN 0-405-06368-7). Arno Press.
Stolen Pay Train: The Case of the Burned Car; The Passenger in Stateroom Thirty-Three; Three Complete Stories the Exploits of Nicholas Carter Pseud.... John Russell Coryell. LC 99-4893. (On cover: Magnet detective library, no. 101). 1899. Street & Smith.
Stolen Plans Mystery. Norvin Pallas. LC 59-9052. 1959. Washburn.
Stolen Promises. Barbara Andrews. (Candlelight Ecstacy Ser.: No. 111). (Orig.). 1983. pap. 1.95 (ISBN 0-440-17522-4). Dell.
Stolen Race-Horse. The Five Kernels of Corn. Nick Carter's One Cent Fee; Three Complete Stories of the Exploits of Nicholas Carter Pseud.... John Russell Coryell. LC 1090. (On cover: Magnet detective library. no. 111). 1899. Street & Smith.
Stolen Rapture. Lydia Lancaster. 1978. 2.50 (ISBN 0-446-81777-5). Warner Books.
Stolen Secrets. Marilyn Austin. (Orig.). 1981. pap. 1.95 (ISBN 0-8439-8045-1, Tiara Bks). Nordon Pubns.
Stolen Signet. Frederick Miller Smith. 1909. Duffield & Company.
Stolen Singer. Martha Bellinger. LC 11-11896. 1.25. The Bobbs-Merrill Company.
Stolen Sins. Davis Dresser. LC 36-101198. Godwin.
Stolen Souls. William Le Queux. LC 7-13135. (Half-title: West end series). F. A. Stokes Company.
Stolen Souls. William Le Queux. LC 7-13136. F. A. Stokes Company.
Stolen Spring. Hans Scherfig. Tr. by Jack Brondum from Danish. Orig. Title: Det Forsoemte Foraar. 192p. (Orig.). 1983. pap. 6.95 (ISBN 0-940242-00-1). Fjord Pr.
Stolen Squadron. Mary Violet Heberden. LC 42-51967. 1942. Pub. for the Crime Club by Doubleday, Doran and Company, Inc.
Stolen Stallion. Max Brand. 1979. pap. 1.75 (ISBN 0-671-83023-6). PB.
Stolen Statesman. Leonard Reginald Gribble. LC 32-157699. 1932. Dodd, Mead & Company.
Stolen Steers: A Tale of the Big Thicket. Bill Brett. LC 76-51651. (Illus.). 6.75 (ISBN 0-89096-026-7). Texas A & M University Press.
Stolen Steps: A Story. Squier L Pierce. LC 7-35906. 1892. J. B. Lippincott Company.
Stolen Story: And Other Newspaper Stories. Jesse Lynch Williams. LC 76-98604. (Short story index reprint series). 1969. Books for Libraries Press.
Stolen Story: And Other Newspaper Stories. Jesse Lynch Williams. LC 99-1784. 1899. C. Scribner's Sons.
Stolen Story & Other Newspaper Stories. Jesse Lynch Williams. LC 76-98604. (Short Story Index Reprint Ser.). 1899. 16.00 (ISBN 0-8369-3178-5). Ayer Co.
Stolen Sun. Emil Petaja. (Daw Science Fiction Ser.). 1979. pap. 1.95 o.p. (ISBN 0-87997-490-7, UJ1490). Daw Bks.
Stolen Throne. Herbert Kaufman & Fisk, May Isabel. LC 7-14250. 1907. Moffat, Yard & Company.
Stolen Treasure. Howard Pyle. LC 7-18095. 1907. Harper & Brothers.
Stolen Vail. Elisabeth Burstenbinder & Holtz, E. Von. Tr. by Safford, Mary Joanna. (popular series, no. 23). 1892. R. Bonner's Sons.
Stolen Waters Are Sweet: A Novel of a Woman's Faith in a Man's Weakness. Theresa Abeles Rosenberg. LC 47-220. 1946. The William-Frederick Press.
Stolen White Elephant, Etc. Samuel Langhorne Clemens. LC 70-121530. (Short story index reprint series). 1970. Books for Libraries Press.
Stolen White Elephant, Etc. Samuel Langhorne Clemens. LC 31-246. 1888. C. L. Webster & Co.
Stolen Woman. Wade Miller, pseud. LC 51-17382. (Gold medal book, 139). 1950. Fawcett Publications.
Stolen Years. Sara Zyskind. 240p. 1983. pap. 3.50 (ISBN 0-451-12011-6, Sig). NAL.
Stomping Ground. Denis Hamill. LC 79-28428. 9.95 (ISBN 0-440-07741-9). Delacorte Press.
Stomping Ground. 1981. pap. 2.95 (ISBN 0-440-17615-8). Dell.
Stomping the Goyim. Michael Disend. LC 73-77370. 1969. 5.00. Croton Press.
Stone. Anthea Fraser. LC 79-26746. 1980. 8.95 (ISBN 0-312-76205-4). St. Martin's Press.
Stone. James Tucker. (Orig.). 1981. pap. 2.95 (ISBN 0-89083-760-0). Zebra.
Stone: A Novel. Nigel G Tranter. LC 59-5675. 1959. Putnam.
Stone: A Novel. Douglass Wallop. LC 70-160484. 1971. 5.95 (ISBN 0-393-08653-4). Norton.
Stone Amulet. Louise Boggan. 1975. 4.95 o.p. (ISBN 0-88289-016-6). Pelican.
Stone & the Violets. Milovan Djilas. LC 76-174507. 1972. 6.95 (ISBN 0-15-185100-X). HarBraceJ.
Stone Angel. Margaret Laurence. LC 64-13448. 1964. Knopf.

Stone Arbor: And Other Stories. Roger Angell. LC 79-121519. (Short story index reprint series). 1970. Books for Libraries Press.
Stone Arrow. Richard Herley. LC 78-19531. 1979. 8.95 (ISBN 0-312-76207-0). St. Martin's Press.
Stone Baby. Ben Healey. LC 73-22422. 1974. 7.95 (ISBN 0-8161-6191-7). G. K. Hall.
Stone Baby. Ben Healey. LC 73-667. 1973. 5.95 (ISBN 0-397-00957-7). Lippincott.
Stone Blunts Scissors. Gerard Fairlie. LC 29-499209. 1929. Little, Brown, and Company.
Stone Bull. Phyllis A. Whitney. LC 76-50802. 1977. 7.95 (ISBN 0-385-12891-6). Doubleday.
Stone Bull. Phyllis A. Whitney. LC 77-15574. 1977. 13.95 (ISBN 0-8161-6535-1). G. K. Hall.
Stone Bull: Phyllis A. Whitney. Phyllis A Whitney. 1978. 2.25 (ISBN 0-449-23638-2). Fawcett Crest.
Stone Came Rolling: A Novel. Olive Tilford Dargan. LC 35-27437. 1935. Longmans, Green and Co.
Stone Carnation. Naomi A Hintze. LC 79-140711. 1971. 5.95 (ISBN 0-394-46244-0). Random House.
Stone Cold Blonde: By Adam Knight Pseud. Lawrence Lariar. LC 51-1295. 1951. Crown Publishers.
Stone Cold Dead. Richard Ellington. LC 50-7065. 1950. Morrow.
Stone Cold Dead in the Market. Christopher Landon. LC 81-47404. (Fifty Classics of Crime Fiction, 1950-1975). 1982. 14.95 (ISBN 0-8240-4973-X). Garland Pub.
Stone Country. Alex La Guma. LC 75-316237. (African writers series; 152). 1974-1975. 2.00 (ISBN 0-435-90152-4). Heinemann Educational.
Stone Creek Wreck: A Modern Will-O-the-Wisp. W. F. Combs. LC 98-2243. F. T. Neely.
Stone-Cutter of Memphis. William Patrick Kelly. LC 25-3169. 1907. G. Routledge & Sons, Limited.
Stone Daugherty. John Porter Fort. 1929. Dodd, Mead & Company.
Stone Dawn: An Antediluvian Tale. Will Baker. LC 75-31661. (Capra chapbook series; no. 36.). (Illus.). 1975. 10.00. (ISBN 0-88496-045-5) (ISBN 0-88496-046-3). Capra Press.
Stone Dead. Amelia Reynolds Long. LC 45-6562. 1945. Phoenix Press.
Stone Dead. San Antonio. Tr. by Cyril Buhler. (San Antonio Ser). 1970. pap. 0.60 o.p. (63-283). Paperback Lib.
Stone Desert. Gustavo Adolfo Martinez Zuviria. Tr. by Louis Imbert. Le Clercq, Jacques Georges Clemenceau, 1898- Joint Tr. LC 28-254649. 1928. Longmans, Green and Co.
Stone Desert see Novels by Hugo Wast.
Stone Door. Leonora Carrington. LC 77-76629. 7.95 (ISBN 0-312-76210-0). St. Martin's Press.
Stone Face. William Gardner Smith. 213p. 1975. Repr. of 1963 ed. 7.95x (ISBN 0-911860-48-7). Chatham Bkseller.
Stone Face: A Novel. William Gardner Smith. LC 63-11184. 1963. Farrar, Straus.
Stone Field. Martha Ostenso. LC 37-344618. 1937. Dodd, Mead & Company.
Stone Flower. Alan Scholefield. LC 81-22397. 1982. 15.00 (ISBN 0-688-00981-6). W. Morrow.
Stone for Danny Fisher. Harold Robbins. 1979. pap. 3.95 (ISBN 0-671-41716-9). PB.
Stone for Danny Fisher. Harold Rubins. LC 51-13212. 1952. Knoft.
Stone for Danny Fisher: By Harold Robbins Pseud. 1st Ed. Harold Rubin. LC 51-13212. 1952. Knopf.
Stone from Mnar: A Fragment from the 'Necronomicon' Lin Carter. 128p. (Orig.). 1974. pap. 4.00 o.p. (ISBN 0-88358-018-7). Mirage Pr.
Stone from the Brook. Robert Greenwood. LC 60-11111. 1960. Appleton-Century Crofts.
Stone Giant. A Story of the Mammoth Cave. C. C Dail. LC 11-10529. (On cover: Neely's Continental library, no. 7). F. T. Neely.
Stone God Awakens. Philip Jose Farmer. 192p. 1975. pap. 2.25 (ISBN 0-441-78654-5). Ace Bks.
Stone God Awakens. Philip Jose Farmer. 1973. (pbk) 0.95. Ace.
Stone House. Dorothy Daniels. 1973. 0.95. Warner.
Stone Humpers. Donald Marsh. 1970. 5.95 o.p. (8209-6). Delacorte.
Stone in Heaven. Poul Anderson. LC 79-124196. (Illus.). 5.95 (ISBN 0-441-78656-1). Ace Books.
Stone in the Hourglass. Donald Windham. 1981. wrappers, ltd. ed. 15.00x (ISBN 0-917366-05-0). S Campbell.
Stone in the Path. Maud Louise Hudnut Chapin. LC 22-18400. 1922. 1.75. Duffield and Company.
Stone in the Rain. Laurette MacDuffie. LC 46-1387. 1946. Doubleday & Co., Inc.
Stone Island. Peter Boynton. LC 73-4379. 1973. 7.95 o.p. (ISBN 0-15-185140-9). HarBraceJ.
Stone Killer. John Gardner. 1975. (pbk.) 1.25. Award Books.
Stone Killer. Frank Scarpetta. (marksman,#8). 1974. (pbk.) 0.95. Belmont Tower Books.
Stone Knife: A Novel. Jose Revueltas & Hays, H. R., Tr. LC 47-4724. 1947. Reynal & Hitchcock.
Stone Lands. (Stone Ser.: No. 12). 1979. pap. 2.00. Stone Pr Calif.
Stone Leopard. Colin Forbes, pseud. 1976. 7.95 o.p. (ISBN 0-525-21002-4). Dutton.
Stone Leopard. Raymond H. Sawkins. LC 75-32661. 1976. 7.95 (ISBN 0-525-21002-4). Dutton.
Stone Leopard. Raymond H Sawkins. (Fawcett Crest Book). 1977. 1.95 (ISBN 0-449-23129-1). Fawcett Pubns.
Stone Maiden. H Clark Brown. LC 40-2309. 1939. The Seton Village Press.
Stone Maiden. Velda Johnston. LC 80-16109. 8.95 (ISBN 0-396-07882-6). Dodd, Mead.
Stone Maiden. large print. ed. Velda Johnston. LC 81-7267. 1981. 13.95 (ISBN 0-8161-3310-7). G.K. Hall & Co.
Stone Maiden. Alexandra Manners, pseud. LC 72-97302. 1973. 6.95 (ISBN 0-399-11123-9). Putnam.
Stone Maiden. Alexandra Manners, pseud. (Berkley medallion book). 1974. (pbk.) 1.25 (ISBN 0-425-02524-1). Putnam.
Stone Man. Kenneth Robeson. (Doc Savage Series#81). 1976. (pbk.) 1.25. Bantam Books.
Stone Man, Yes: A Novel. Daniel Curley. LC 64-17545. 1964. Viking Press.
Stone-Mason of Saint Point. A Village Tale. Alphonse Marie Louis De Lamartine. LC 7-3527. 1851. Harper & Brothers.
Stone, No. 13: Featured Writers. 1981. pap. 3.50. Stone Pr Calif.
Stone of Blood. Juanita Coulson. (Birthstone gothic#3). 1975. (pbk.) 0.95 (ISBN 0-345-26694-3). Ballantine Books.
Stone of Chastity. Margery Sharp. LC 75-41248. 1976. 14.50. AMS Press.
Stone of Chastity. Margery Sharp. LC 48-10517. (New Avon Library, 165). 1948. Avon Pub. Co.
Stone of Chastity. Margery Sharp. LC 40-31530. 1940. Little, Brown and Company.
Stone of Destiny. Katherine Mackay. LC 4-3939. 1904. Harper & Brothers.
Stone of Jacob. 1st Ed. Edith E Clements. LC 56-11209. 1957. Vantage Press.
Stone of Kannon. Oswald A Bushnell. LC 79-2563. 10.95 (ISBN 0-8248-0663-8). Published for the Friends of the Library of Hawaii by the University Press of Hawaii.
Stone Offering: A Septimus Mystery. Stephen Chance. LC 77-1485. 6.95 (ISBN 0-8407-6547-9). T. Nelson.
Stone Roses. Sarah Gainham. LC 76-376472. 1976. 3.15 (ISBN 0-7278-0109-0). Severn House: Distributed by Hutchinson.
Stone That Never Came Down. John Brunner. LC 73-79652. (Doubleday science fiction). 1973. 5.95 (ISBN 0-385-03716-3). Doubleday.
Stone That Stopped: A Story of Holmes, M.D. Kenneth Rose McAlpin. LC 38-19936. Fleming H. Revell Company.
Stone Upon His Shoulder: A Novel. Helen Butler. LC 53-9209. 1953. Westminster Press.
Stonecliff. Robert Nathan. LC 67-11140. 1967. Knopf.
Stonecloud Seven. Ed. by Dan Ilves et al. (Illus.). 1978. pap. 3.50 o.s.i. (ISBN 0-914664-04-2). Pacific Perceptions.
Stonecloud Six. Ed. by Daniel Ilves et al. (Illus.). 1976. pap. 2.95 o.s.i. (ISBN 0-914664-02-6). Pacific Perceptions.
Stonecrop: A Novel. Cecile Tormay. LC 23-26471. 1923. R. M. McBride & Company.
Stonecrop: The Country I Remember. Teo Savory. LC 75-43072. (Illus.). 10.00 (ISBN 0-87775-105-6). Unicorn Press.
Stoned. W. Kaerf. 2.95 o.p. Vantage.
Stoned Apocalypse. Marco Vassi. LC 79-169251. 1973. pap. 1.25. (ISBN 0-671-78286-X). Pocket Books.
Stoned Apocalypse. Marco Vassi. LC 79-169251. 1972. 6.95 (ISBN 0-671-27085-0). Trident Press.
Stonedancer. Mike Doyle. 1976. pap. 5.95x o.p. (ISBN 0-19-647945-2). Oxford U Pr.
Stonefield Silhouettes: Stories from a Quainter Day. Cornelia Minor Arnold. LC 11-31855. Broadway Publishing Co.
Stonefish. John McIntosh. LC 70-95863. 1970. Harcourt, Brace & World.
Stonehaven. Kay Richardson. (Avalon romances). 1973. 4.50. Avalon Books.
Stonehaven. Elizabeth St. Clair. 1974. (pbk.) 0.95. New American Library.
Stoneheart. A Romance. rev. and ed. by percy b. st. john. ed. Gustave Aimard & St. John, Percy Bolingbroke, 1821-1889, Ed. LC 5-42193. (On cover: Lovell's library, no 1107). 1887. J. W. Lovell Company.
Stonehenge. Harry Harrison & Leon E. Stover. LC 71-38279. 1972. 5.95 (ISBN 0-684-12831-4). Scribner.
Stoneholt. Sally Bullock Cave. LC 54-42472. 1954. Christopher Pub. House.
Stoneman's Gap: A Novel. Robert J McCaig. LC 75-35972. 1976. 0.95 (ISBN 0-345-24883-X). Ballantine Books.
Stonepastures. Eleanor Stuart Childs. LC 8-16875. 1895. D. Appleton and Company.
Stoner. John Edward Williams. LC 65-15219. 1965. Viking Press.
Stoner, No. 2: The Satan Stone. Ralph Hayes. (Orig.). 1976. pap. 1.25 o.p. (ISBN 0-532-12384-0). Woodhill.
Stoner, No. 2: The Satan Stone. Ralph Hayes. (Orig.). 1976. pap. 1.25 o.p. (ISBN 0-532-12384-0). Manor Bks.
Stones. Erica Pedretti. (Swiss Library). 220p. 1982. 14.95 (ISBN 0-7145-3929-5); pap. 7.95 (ISBN 0-7145-3942-2). Riverrun NY.
Stones Awake: A Novel of Mexico. Carleton Beals. J. B. Lippincott Company.
Stones Begin to Dance. Aben Kandel. LC 42-21072. 1942. Duell, Sloan and Pearce.
Stones Cry Out: A Novel of Camilo Torres. Wim Hornman. LC 72-163224. 1971. 7.50. Lippincott.
Stones for Bread. Edwin Carlile Litsey. LC 40-170277. 1940. The Caxton Printers, Ltd.
Stones of Fire. 1st Ed. Arthur Trevenning Harris. LC 56-12712. 1956. Pageant Press.
Stones of Jehoshaphat. Jerome Irving Rodale. LC 54-12538. (His 64 series). 1954. Rodale Books.
Stones of Silence. George B. Shaller. 320p. 1982. 3.95 (ISBN 0-553-14908-3). Bantam.
Stones of Strendleigh. Geraldine Killoran. (Ace Gothic). 1974. (pbk.) 0.95. Ace Books.
Stones of Summer. Dow Mossman. LC 79-142479. 1972. 9.95 o.p. (ISBN 0-672-51302-1). Bobbs.
Stones of Summer: A Yeoman's Notes, 1942-1969. Dow Mossman. 1973. 1.50. Popular Lib.
Stones of Summer: A Yeoman's Notes, 1942-1969. Dow Mossman. LC 79-142479. 1972. 9.95. Bobbs-Merrill.
Stones of the Abbey. Fernand Pouillon. LC 70-95858. (Illus.). 1970. Harcourt, Brace & World.
Stones of the House. Theodore Morrison. LC 53-5319. 1953. Viking Press.
Stones of Venice. John Ruskin. (Illus.). 5.00 o.p. (ISBN 0-8090-8850-9). Hill & Wang.
Stonewall Brigade. Frank Gill Slaughter. LC 74-2524. (Illus.). 1975. 8.95 (ISBN 0-385-01679-4). Doubleday.
Stonewall Brigade. Frank Gill Slaughter. 1976. (pbk.) 1.95 (ISBN 0-671-80300-X). Pocket Books.
Stonewall Ladies. Elizabeth O. Verner. 1963. 10.00 (ISBN 0-937684-07-4). Tradd St Pr.
Stoneware Monkey. Richard Austin Freeman. LC 39-5404. 1939. Dodd, Mead & Company.
Stoneware Monkey & the Penrose Mystery: Two Dr. Thorndyke Novels. R. Austin Freeman. 8.50 (ISBN 0-8446-5108-7). Peter Smith.
Stoneware Monkey: & The Penrose Mystery; Two Dr. Thorndyke Novels. Richard Austin Freeman. LC 72-82073. 1973. (pbk.) 3.50 (ISBN 0-486-22963-7). Dover Publications.
Stonewulf. Elizabeth Dugan Whitehead. LC 62-10629. 1962. Dorrance.
Stoney Batter: A Novel of the Nineteenth-Century Pennsylvania Dutch and the Discovery of Oil. Zoda Elizabeth Anderson. LC 51-8853. 1951. W. B. Eerdmans Pub. Co.
Stonor Eagles. William Horwood. LC 82-50710. (Illus.). 1982. 13.95 (ISBN 0-531-09873-7). F. Watts.
Stony Cliff People. Effie Woodward. LC 30-10081. 1930. The Midwest Company.
Stony Gulch. 1st Ed. Mabel E Stanton. LC 55-10846. Vantage Press.
Stony Lonesome. Scott Hart. LC 54-10147. 1954. Coward-McCann.
Stooping Lady. Maurice Henry Hewlett. LC 7-30839. 1907. Dodd, Mead and Company.
Stooping Venus: A Novel. Bruce Marshall. LC 26-14491. E. P. Dutton & Company.
Stop Angel. Frederick H Christian. (Angel series#9). 1976. (pbk.) 0.95 (ISBN 0-523-00859-7). Pinnacle Books.
Stop at a Winner. Ronald Frederick Delderfield. LC 78-6931. 1978. 8.95 (ISBN 0-671-24229-6). Simon and Schuster.
Stop Here, My Friend: Stories. Merrill Joan Gerber. LC 64-24645. 1965. 4.50. Houghton.
Stop It I Love It. Laurence Schwab & Karen Markham. LC 75-97123. 1972. limited ed. 7.00 o.s.i. Great Ideas.
Stop, Look, and Laugh. Drawings by Alan Moyler. Ed. by William B. Coates. LC 60-11474. 1960. Nelson.
Stop on the Green Light! Denis William Brogan. LC 42-14049. 1942. Harper & Brothers.
Stop Press--Murder! David Stern. LC 47-17965. 1947. Phoenix Press.
Stop the Clocks. David Watson. LC 68-55522. 1969. 4.00. Dorrance.
Stop the Presses, I Want to Get off: Tales of the News Business from the Pages of MORE Magazine. Ed. by Richard Pollak. 1975. 8.95 o.p. (ISBN 0-394-49742-2). Random.
Stop Thief! George C Jenks & Moore, Carlyle. LC 13-218231. 1.25. The H. K. Fly Company.
Stop This Man! Cover Painting by Lu Kimmal. Peter Rabe. LC 55-43679. (Gold medal books, 606). 1955. Fawcett Publications.
Stop-Time. Frank Conroy. (O.s.i.). 5.95 o.s.i. (ISBN 0-670-67190-8). Viking Pr.
Stopgap. T. A. Schock. (Daniel Keel Mystery: No. 3). 240p. 1981. pap. 2.25 (ISBN 0-8439-0972-2, Leisure Bks). Nordon Pubns.
Stopover. Carol Ryrie Brink. LC 51-10008. 1951. Macmillan.
Stopover for Murder: A Mystery Novel. Floyd Mahannah. LC 53-10084. 1953. Macrae Smith.
Stopover in Paradise. Maysie Greig. LC 38-6758. 1938. Doubleday, Doran and Co., Inc.
Stopover: Tokyo. 1st Ed. John Phillips Marquand. LC 57-5508. Little, Brown.
Stopover: Tokyo. 1st Ed. John Phillips Marquand. LC 57-5508. Little, Brown.
Stopped Clock. Joel Townsley Rogers. LC 58-147380. (Inner sanctum mystery). 1958. Simon and Schuster.
Stopping Place. A. G. Mojtabai. LC 79-18796. (ISBN 0-671-23083-2). Simon and Schuster.
Store. Knight Isaacson. LC 73-93297. 1974. 6.95 (ISBN 0-8027-0454-9). Walker.
Store. Knight Isaacson. 1975. (pbk.) 1.50. Dell.
Store. Michael Pearson. LC 80-18266. 13.95 (ISBN 0-671-25114-7). Simon and Schuster.
Store. Thomas Sigismund Stribling. LC 68-1966. 1968. N. S. Berg.
Store. Thomas Sigismund Stribling. LC 32-266716. 1932. Doubleday, Doran & Company, Inc.
Store. Thomas Sigismund Stribling. LC 33-175109. 1933. Doubleday, Doran & Company, Inc.
Store. Thomas Sigismund Stribling. LC 38-233647. 1938. The Sun Dial Press, Inc.
Store of Ladies. Louis Golding. 1927. A. A. Knopf.
Store of Wrath. Seldon Truss, pseud. LC 56-7661. 1956. Published for the Crime Club by Doubleday.
Store up the Anger. Wessel Ebersohn. LC 80-2076. 1981. 11.95 (ISBN 0-385-17406-3). Doubleday.
Storehouses of the Snow. Woodard & Bischoff. 1980. pap. 1.95 (ISBN 0-8439-0746-0). Nordon Pubns.
Stories. John Cheever et al. 1966. 4.95 o.p. FS&G.
Stories. Fedor Mikhailovich Dostoevskii. 334p. 1971. 5.95 (ISBN 0-8285-0959-X, Pub. by Progress Pubs USSR). Imported Pubns.
Stories. Fedor Mikhailovich Dostoevskii. 374p. 1981. pap. 4.00 (ISBN 0-8285-2190-5, Pub. by Progress Pubs USSR). Imported Pubns.
Stories. Gottfried Keller & Frank Glessner Ryder. LC 81-22067. (German Library; V. 44). 1982. 17.50 (ISBN 0-8264-0256-9) (ISBN 0-8264-0266-6). Continuum.
Stories. Ram Kumar. 1976. lib. bdg. 9.00 (ISBN 0-89253-085-5); flexible bdg. 6.00 (ISBN 0-89253-267-X). Ind-US Inc.
Stories. Doris May Lessing. LC 77-20797. 1978. 15.00 (ISBN 0-394-50009-1). Knopf: Distributed by Random House.
Stories. Doris May Lessing. LC 79-22320. 1980. 4.95 (ISBN 0-394-74249-4). Vintage Books.
Stories. Katherine Mansfield. LC 56-46420. (Vintage book, K36). 1956. Vintage Books.
Stories. Ed. by John Middleton Murry. Murry, John Middleton, 1889- Ed. LC 30-307151. 1930. A. A. Knopf.
Stories. Ed. by John Middleton Murry. Murry, John Middleton, 1880- Ed. LC 46-8608. (Half-title: The Living library). 1946. The World Publishing Company.
Stories. Frank O'Conner. (O.s.i.). 1956. pap. 2.95 o.s.i. (ISBN 0-394-70029-5, Vin). Random.
Stories. William R Rose. LC 27-24951. 1927. The Stratford Press Co.
Stories. William Sansom. LC 63-8321. 1963. Little, Brown.
Stories. Mikhail Aleksandrovich Sholokhov. 166p. 1975. pap. 2.95 (ISBN 0-8285-1043-1, Pub. by Progress Pubs USSR). Imported Pubns.
Stories. Stafford, Jean, 1915- LC 66-6287. 1966. Farrar, Straus and Giroux.
Stories. LC 4-15337. 1884. C. Scribner's Sons.
Stories. LC 8-30407. 1891-98. C. Scribner's Sons.
Stories. LC 4-15338. 1896. C. Scribner's Sons.
Stories. LC 6-1269. 1898. C. Scribner's Sons.
Stories. Ed. by Willis Thomson. Souba, Jane, Joint Ed. LC 39-10862. C.
Stories. Oscar Wilde. 3.00 o.p. (ISBN 0-00-422701-8); lea. 5.00 o.p. (ISBN 0-00-423701-3). Collins-World.
Stories. Thomas Wolfe & Wolfe, Thomas, 1900-1938. The Hills Beyond. LC 44-47299. (On cover: Avon modern short story monthly. No. 17). 1944. Avon Book Company.

Stories About Children Every Child Should Know: A Delightful Child-Study Containing the Beautiful Life Stories of Young Heroes and Heroines of... Charles Dickens & Dickens, Mary Angela. LC 7-33908.

Stories About Ghosts. Chin Hao. Ed. by Lin Lan. (Tales from the Orient Ser.: No. 14). (Chinese.). 12.00x (ISBN 0-89986-238-1, Pub. by E Langstaff). Oriental Bk Store.

Stories About Workers. Benjamin Piltch. (Illus.). 1975. pap. 2.75x (ISBN 0-88323-120-4, 208). Richards Pub.

Stories. Adapted with Notes and Exercises by Kenneth Croft and Edith Fries Croft. 3000 Word Level. Edith Newbold Jones Wharton & Kenneth Croft. LC 62-19682. (Graded readers for students of English as a second language). 1962. Prentice-Hall International.

Stories & Fables of Ambrose Bierce. Ambrose Gwinnett Bierce. Ed. by Edward Wagenknecht. LC 77-20146. (Illus.). 1977. 14.95 (ISBN 0-916144-19-4); pap. 7.95 (ISBN 0-916144-20-8). Stemmer Hse.

Stories & Fables: The Reservoir (With Snowman Snowman) Janet Frame. (O.s.i.). 2 vols. boxed 7.00 o.s.i. (ISBN 0-8076-0233-7). Braziller.

Stories & Fantasies. Emil Bernhard Cohn. 1951. 4.00 o.p. Jewish Pubn.

Stories & Fantasies from the Jewish Past. Emil Bernhard Cohn. Tr. by Charles Reznikoff. 1951. 4.00 o.p. Jewish Pubn.

Stories and Fantasies from the Jewish Past: Translated from the German Manuscript by Charles Reznikoff. Emil Bernhard Cohn. LC 52-1224. 1951. Jewish Publication Society of America.

Stories and Interludes. Barry Eric Odell Pain. LC 7-35789. 1892. Harper & Brothers.

Stories and Novels. Fanny Lewald-Stahr. LC 8-28107. (Overland library, no. 2). L. Schick.

Stories and Novels: From the German of Rudolf Lindau... Rudolf Lindau. LC 7-19015. (Overland library. no. 1). 1885. L. Schick.

Stories and Pictures. Isaac Loeb Peretz. LC 75-44361. 1976. 44.95 (ISBN 0-87968-376-7). Gordon Press.

Stories and Pictures. Isaac Loeb Peretz. LC 75-152953. (Short story index reprint series). 1971. (ISBN 0-8369-3868-2). Books for Libraries Press.

Stories and Pictures. Isaac Loeb Peretz. Tr. by Frank, Helena. LC 6-26193. 1906. The Jewish Publication Society of America.

Stories and Pictures. Isaac Loeb Peretz & Frank, Helena, Tr. LC 6-26193. 1906. The Jewish Publication Society of America.

Stories & Poems. Bret Harte. 1915. Repr. lib. bdg. 20.00 (ISBN 0-8414-5013-7). Folcroft.

Stories and Poems. Edgar Allan Poe. Ed. by Ollie Depew. LC 51-2534. 1951. Globe Book Co.

Stories and Poems of Bret Harte. Bret Harte. LC 42-6433. (The Companion classics). 1932. W. J. Black, Inc.

Stories and Prose Poems. Aleksandr Isaevich Solzhenitsyn. LC 74-148708. 1971. 7.95 (ISBN 0-374-27033-3). Farrar, Straus and Giroux.

Stories and Romances. Horace Elisha Scudder. LC 8-3392. 1880. Houghton, Mifflin and Company.

Stories & Satires. Sholom Aleichem. Tr. by Curt Leviant. (Illus.). 2.95 o.p. (ISBN 0-498-07276-2, Encore). A S Barnes.

Stories & Satires. Sholom Aleichem. Tr. by Curt Leviant. (O.s.i). (Illus.). 1970. pap. 1.95 o.s.i. (01614, Collier). Macmillan.

Stories & Sketches. Saros Cowasjee. (Writers Workshop Greenbird Ser.). 85p. 1975. 11.00 (ISBN 0-88253-646-X); pap. text ed. 6.00 (ISBN 0-88253-645-1). Ind-US Inc.

Stories and Sketches. Mary Putnam Jacobi. LC 8-11830. 1907. G. P. Putnam's Sons.

Stories and Sketches. Sara Jane Clarke Lippincott. LC 7-19005. Tait, Sons & Company.

Stories and Sketches. LC 8-16110. 1867. Lee and Shepard.

Stories and Story-Telling. Angela Mary Keyes. LC 11-14714. 1911. D. Appleton and Company.

Stories and Storytellers. Ed. by David Aloian. LC 68-1107. (Illus.). 1968. Addison-Wesley Pub. Co.

Stories & Tales. William Gilmore Simms. LC 68-9190. (Centennial Edition of the Writings of William Gilmore Simms: Vol. 5). xxiv, 880p. 1974. 34.95x (ISBN 0-87249-144-7). U of SC Pr.

Stories and Tales. Edited by Robert Wooster Stallman. Stephen Crane. LC 55-159. (Vintage book, K-10). 1955. Vintage Books.

Stories and Tales of Joseph Conrad. Joseph Conrad. LC 68-12807. (Funk & Wagnalls paperbook, F29). 1968. 2.50. Funk & Wagnalls.

Stories & Texts for Nothing. Samuel Beckett. LC 67-20341. (Illus.). 1967. Grove Press.

Stories: British & American. J. B. Ludwig & W. R. Poirier. 1953. 7.50 o.p. (3-33905). HM.

Stories: British and American. Editors: Jack Barry Ludwig and W. Richard Poirier. Ed. by Jack Barry Ludwig & W. Richard Poirier. LC 53-7968. 1953. Houghton Mifflin.

Stories by American Authors, 10 vols in 5. Ed. by Charles Scribner's Sons Editorial Staff. 1972. Repr. of 1884 ed. lib. bdg. 100.00 set; Vols. 1-2. (ISBN 0-8422-8142-8); Vols. 3-4. (ISBN 0-8422-8143-6); Vols 5-6. (ISBN 0-8422-8144-4); Vols 7-8. Vols. 9-10. (ISBN 0-8422-8146-0); lib. bdg. 25.00 ea., 5 individual vols. Irvington.

Stories by American Authors, 10 Vols. Bound as 5. Ed. by Scribners Editorial Staff. LC 4-15337. (Important Literary Anthologies Ser). 1969. Repr. of 1884 ed. lib. bdg. 65.00 o.s.i. (ISBN 0-512-00672-5). Garrett Pr.

Stories by Anton Chekhov. 2nd rev. ed. Anton Pavlovich Chekhov. Ed. by Oleg A. Maslenikov. (Advanced Russian Readers). (£0.85: No. 1). (Rus). 1961. pap. 3.75x o.p. (ISBN 0-520-00226-1). U of Cal Pr.

Stories by Contemporary Japanese Women Writers. Noriko Mizuta Lippit & Kyoko Selden. LC 82-10270. 1982. 25.00 (ISBN 0-87332-193-6) (ISBN 0-87332-223-1). M.E. Sharpe.

Stories by English Authors. Charles Reade. Repr. 10.00 (ISBN 0-8414-7415-X). Folcroft.

Stories by English Authors, 10 Vols. Ed. by Scribners Editorial Staff. LC 4-15338. (Important Literary Anthologies Ser). 1969. Repr. of 1896 ed. lib. bdg. 65.00 o.s.i. (ISBN 0-512-00673-3). Garrett Pr.

Stories by Erskine Caldwell: Twenty-Four Representative Stories. Erskine Caldwell & Canby, Henry Seidel, 1878- LC 44-40335. 1944. Duell, Sloan and Pearce.

Stories by Foreign Authors, 10 vols in 5. Ed. by Charles Scribner's Sons Editorial Staff. 1972. Repr. of 1896 ed. lib. bdg. 125.00 set; Vols 1-2. Fr. (ISBN 0-8422-8152-5); Vols 3-4. Fr. - Ger. (ISBN 0-8422-8153-3); Vols 5-6. Ger. - It. (ISBN 0-8422-8154-1); Vols. 7-8. Rus.-Scand. (ISBN 0-8422-8155-X); Vols. 9-10. Span. & Polish (ISBN 0-8422-8156-8); lib. bdg. 30.00 ea., 5 individual vols. Irvington.

Stories by Foreign Authors, 10 Vols. Bound as 5. Ed. by Scribners Editorial Staff. (Important Literary Anthologies Ser). 1969. Repr. of 1896 ed. lib. bdg. 65.00 o.s.i. (ISBN 0-512-00674-1). Garrett Pr.

Stories by Foreign Authors. LC 72-110211. (Short story index reprint series). (Illus.). 1970. Books for Libraries Press.

Stories by Foreign Authors: German, 2 Vols. facsimile ed. LC 72-110211. (Short Story Index Reprint Ser.). 1898. 21.50 (ISBN 0-8369-3363-X). Ayer Co.

Stories by Foreign Authors: Italian. facsimile ed. LC 72-110211. (Short Story Index Reprint Ser.). 1898. 10.00 (ISBN 0-8369-3364-8). Ayer Co.

Stories by Foreign Authors: Polish Greek Belgian Hungarian. facsimile ed. LC 72-110211. (Short Story Index Reprint Ser.). 1898. 10.50 (ISBN 0-8369-3365-6). Ayer Co.

Stories by Foreign Authors: Russian. facsimile ed. LC 72-110211. (Short Story Index Ser.). 1898. 10.25 (ISBN 0-8369-3366-4). Ayer Co.

Stories by Foreign Authors: Scandinavian. facsimile ed. LC 72-110211. (Short Story Index Reprint Ser.). 1898. 10.25 (ISBN 0-8369-3367-2). Ayer Co.

Stories by Foreign Authors: Spanish. facsimile ed. LC 72-110211. (Short Story Index Reprint Ser.). 1898. 12.50 (ISBN 0-8369-3368-0). Ayer Co.

Stories by Frank O'Connor: Pseud. Michael O'Donovan. LC 56-136914. (Vintage book, K-29). 1956. Vintage Books.

Stories: By Jean Stafford and Others. Jean Stafford. LC 56-11963. 1956. Farrar, Straus, and Cudahy.

Stories: By O. Henry Pseud. Adapted with Notes and Exercises by Mildred H. Larson. William Sydney Porter. (Graded readers for students of English as a second language). 1962. Prentice-Hall International.

Stories by the Man Nobody Knows: Nine Tales. B Traven. LC 61-66312. 1961. Regency Books.

Stories Come Home from India & Pakistan. Helen C. Rockey. 1970. 2.00 o.p. Carlton.

Stories Created by Life. Nonna Osipova. (Illus.). 60p. (Rus.). pap. cancelled (ISBN 0-935500-26-X, TX 198-101). Am Samizdat.

Stories, Dreams and Allegories. Olive Schreiner. LC 23-6694. 1923. Frederick A. Stokes Company.

Stories East and West. Ed. by James Gettier Kennedy. LC 70-140505. 1971. Scott, Foresman.

Stories: Edited by Frank G. Jennings and Charles J. Calitri. Ed. by Frank G Jennings & Charles J. Calitri. LC 58-247. 1957. Harcourt, Brace.

Stories: Edited by Frank G. Jennings and Charles J. Calitri. Teacher's Ed. Ed. by Frank G Jennings & Charles J. Calitri. LC 57-1874. 1957. Harcourt, Brace.

Stories, Fables & Other Diversions. Howard Nemerov. LC 75-143388. 1971. Godine.

Stories for Boys. Richard Harding Davis. LC 4-16128. 1891. C. Scribner's Sons.

Stories for Christmas. Ed. by Mary Virginia Robinson. LC 67-11202. (Illus.). 1967. John Knox Press.

Stories for Every Holiday. Carolyn Sherwin Bailey. LC 73-20149. 277p. 1974. Repr. of 1918 ed. 44.00x (ISBN 0-8103-3957-9). Gale.

Stories for Here and Now: Edited by Joseph Greene and Elizabeth Abell. 1st Ed. Ed. by Joseph Ingham Greene. LC 51-34007. (Bantam giant, A914). 1951. Bantam Books.

Stories for Home-Folks: Young and Old. Sara Jane Clarke Lippincott. 1884. J. B. Alden.

Stories for Junior High Schools. Ed. by William Louis Rabenort. LC 26-10842. C. Scribner's Sons.

Stories for Late at Night. Ed. by Alfred Hitchcock. (YA) 1961. 8.95 (ISBN 0-394-41346-6, BYR). Random.

Stories for Men: An Anthology. Ed. by Charles Grayson. LC 36-17728. 1936. Little, Brown, and Company.

Stories for Men: An Anthology. de luxe ed. Ed. by Charles Grayson. 1938. Garden City Publishing Co., Inc.

Stories for Parents. Timothy Shay Arthur. LC 6-3420. (On cover: Lovell's library, v. 11, no. 554). 1885. J. W. Lovell Co.

Stories for Paulette. Jack Costello. 93p. 1975. 5.00 o.p. (ISBN 0-682-48271-4). Exposition.

Stories for Ramu. Deepak Dubey. LC 75-907478. 1976. 10.00 (ISBN 0-89253-794-9) (ISBN 0-89253-795-7). Writers Workshop.

Stories for Talks with Boys & Girls. J. A. Cheley. 1958. 4.95 o.p. Assn Pr.

Stories for the Dead of Night. Ed. by Don Congdon. LC 57-6999. (Dell first edition, B107). 1957. Dell Pub. Co.

Stories for the Sixties. Ed. by Richard Yates. LC 63-8943. (Bantam seventy-five). 1963. Bantam Books.

Stories for the Sophisticated. Lionel A. Canaan. 1981. 7.95 (ISBN 0-533-04871-0). Vantage.

Stories for the Thirties, Bk. 1. Ye Shengtao. Tr. by Gladys Yang from Chinese. 456p. (Orig.). 1982. pap. 5.95 (ISBN 0-8351-1019-2). China Bks.

Stories for Tomorrow: An Anthology of Modern Science Fiction by Bradbury and Others. Ed. by William Milligan Sloane. LC 53-10794. 1954. Funk & Wagnalls.

Stories for Young Housekeepers. Timothy Shay Arthur. LC 7-3329. 1851. Lippincott, Grambo & Co.

Stories for Young Housekeepers. Timothy Shay Arthur. LC 6-3421. (On cover: Lovell's library, v. 11, no. 574). J. W. Lovell Company.

Stories for Youth. Ed. by A. H. Lass & Arnold Horowitz. (gr. 9-12). 1950. text ed. 5.32, s.p. 3.99 o.p. McGraw.

Stories for Youth. Abraham H. Lass & A. Horowitz. 1950. 5.32 o.p. (ISBN 0-07-036515-6). McGraw.

Stories for Youth: Edited by A. H. Lass and Arnold Horowitz. Ed. by Abraham Harold Lass & Arnold Horowits. LC 50-5634. 1950. Harper.

Stories from a Ming Collection. Tr. by Cyril Birch. 1968. pap. 5.95 (ISBN 0-394-17308-2, E473, Ever). Grove.

Stories from a Ming Collection. Tr. by Cyril Birch. (Illus.). 1958. 5.00 o.p. (ISBN 0-253-18430-4). Ind U Pr.

Stories from a Ming Collection. Ed. by Meng-Lung Feng. Tr. by Cyril Birch. LC 68-44187. (UNESCO Collection of Representative Works: Chinese Series). (Evergreen book, E-473.). (Illus.). Grove Press.

Stories from a Ming Collection: Translations of Chinese Short Stories Published in the 17th Century. Feng Meng-Lung. Tr. by Cyril Birch. LC 77-26340. (UNESCO Collection of Representative Works: Chinese Ser.). (Illus.). 1978. Repr. of 1959 ed. lib. bdg. 19.25x (ISBN 0-313-20067-X, FESM). Greenwood.

Stories from Balzac: Ed. with Notes and Vocabulary by Douglas Labaree Buffum... Honore De Balzac. Ed. by Douglas Labaree Buffum. LC 17-28106. H. Holt and Company.

Stories from Beyond the Borderland. Hudson Tuttle & Tuttle, Mrs. Emma (Rood) Joint Author. LC 10-2658. 1910. The Tuttle Publishing Company.

Stories from Beyond the Double Rainbow. Elaine Hardt. LC 81-85199. 1982. pap. 8.95 (ISBN 0-932960-03-0). Horizons.

Stories from "Blackwood". Blackwood's Edinburgh Magazine. LC 26-7522. (Half-title: Appleton's popular library of the best authors). 1852. D. Appleton & Company.

Stories from Carleton. William Carleton. LC 72-87971. (Series: The Camelot Series.). 1973. 15.00 (ISBN 0-87696-040-9). Lemma Pub. Corp.

Stories from Dickens. Charles Dickens. Ed. by McSpadden, Joseph Walker. LC 24-13706. Thomas Y. Crowell Company.

Stories from Dickens. Charles Dickens & McSpadden, Joseph Walker. LC 6-29037. T. Y. Crowell & Company.

Stories from Dickens. Charles Dickens & McSpadden, Joseph Walker. LC 6-33590. T. Y. Crowell & Co.

Stories from Dickens. Charles Dickens & McSpadden, Joseph Walker, 1874- Ed. LC 49-10828. 1949. T. Y. Crowell Co.

Stories from Dickens: Arranged and Annotated for Use in Schools, with a Biographical Notice of the Author. Charles Dickens. 1899. Educational Publishing Company.

Stories from Don Quixote. Miguel de Cervantes de Saavedra & Havell, Herbert Lorde. LC 8-24872. T. Y. Crowell & Company.

Stories from Epoch: The First Fifty Issues, 1947-1964. Ed. by Baxter Hathaway. 1966. 14.50x o.p. (ISBN 0-8014-0178-X). Cornell U Pr.

Stories from Epoch: The First Fifty Issues, 1947-1964. Ed. by Baxter Hathaway. Epoch. Ed. by Baxter Hathaway. LC 66-23557. 1966. 7.50. Cornell Univ. Pr.

Stories from Far and Near. Lion Feuchtwanger. LC 45-9985. 1945. The Viking Press.

Stories from Four Languages. Tr. by Walter Brooks. LC 6-126341. I. Kimball.

Stories from Four Languages Retold in English. Walter Brooks. Repr. of 1905 ed. lib. bdg. 10.00 o.p. Folcroft.

Stories from India. Ed. by Khyswant Singhi & Quarratulain Hyder. 1975. (ISBN 0-88253-776-8). A Sterling Pubs.

Stories from Italy. Georgiana Sarah Godkin. 1897. A. C. McClurg and Company.

Stories from Life. Sarah Knowles Bolton & C. E. Bolton. LC 6-14179. T. Y. Crowell & Co.

Stories from Literature for Our Time: Editedby Harlow O. Waite and Benjamin P. Atkinson. revised edition ed. Ed. by Harlow O Waite & Benjamin P. Atkinson. LC 56-6070. 1956. Holt.

Stories from Literature for Our Time,3d Ed. Ed. by Harlow O Waite & Atkinson, Benjamin P. LC 59-14160. 1959. Holt.

Stories from Many Lands. Ed. by Morris Rosenblum. LC 55-4859. (Students pocket library). 1955. Oxford Book Co.

Stories from Modern Russia. Ed. by Charles Percy Snow & P. H. Johnson. (Winter's Tables, Vol. 7). 1962. 4.95 o.p. St Martin.

Stories from Morris. William Morris & Edgar, Madalen. T. Y. Crowell & Company.

Stories from New England Life: Or, Leaves from the Tree Igdrasyl. Martha Russell. LC 8-1342. 1856. J. P. Jewett and Company.

Stories from Old English Poetry. Abby Sage Richardson. LC 14-19347. 1871. Hurd and Houghton.

Stories from Quebec. Ed. by Philip Stratford. LC 72-11215. (Illus.). 1974. 7.95. (ISBN 0-442-27910-8). Van Nostrand Reinhold.

Stories from Quebec. Ed. by Philip Stratford. LC 72-11215. (Illus.). 1974. 7.95. (ISBN 0-442-27910-8) (ISBN 0-442-29910-9). Van Nostrand Reinhold.

Stories from Shakespeare. Marchette Gaylord Chute. LC 78-31326. 1979. 9.95 (ISBN 0-529-05533-3). Collins.

Stories from Six Authors. Arnold Sklare & William E. Buckler. 1966. text ed. 10.95 o.p. (ISBN 0-07-057907-5); pap. text ed. 7.95 o.p. (ISBN 0-07-057906-7). McGraw.

Stories from Six Authors: Edited by William E. Buckler and Arnold B. Sklare. Ed. by William Earl Buckler & Arnold B. Sklare. LC 59-13194. 1960. McGraw-Hill.

Stories from Six Authors: Second Ser., Ed. by Arnold B. Sklare, William E. Buckler. Ed. by Arnold B. Sklare & William Earl Buckler. LC 66-19305. 5.95. McGraw.

Stories from Six Authors, Second Series. Ed. by Arnold B Sklare & Buckler, William Earl. LC 66-19305. 1966. McGraw-Hill.

Stories from Six Authors: 2d Ser. by William E.Buckler. Arnold B. Sklare. Ed. by William Earl Buckler & Arnold B. Sklare. LC 59-13194. pap., 3.95. McGraw.

Stories from Sri Lanka. Ed. by Yasmite Gooneratne. (Writing in Asia Ser.). 1979. pap. text ed. 5.50x (00218). Heinemann Ed.

Stories from Tennessee. Linda Burton. LC 82-16016. 27.95 (ISBN 0-87049-376-0) (ISBN 0-87049-377-9). University of Tennessee Press.

Stories from the Adirondacks. Albert A Young. LC 99-3881. F. T. Neely.

Stories from the Arabian Nights. 1968. pap. 0.35 o.p. (LP29). Pyramid Pubns.

Stories from the Arusi Hills. Daniel F. Close. 3.95 o.p. Vantage.

TITLE INDEX STORIES OF SCHOOL AND

Stories from the Caribbean: A Collection of West Indian Stories. Ed. by Andrew Salkey. 1968. Repr. of 1965 ed. 8.95 o.p. (ISBN 0-236-17797-4). Dufour.
Stories from the Chap-Book: Being a Miscellany of Curious and Interesting Tales, Histories, &C. The, Chap-Book et al. 1896. Printed for H. S. Stone & Company.
Stories from the Chap-Book: Being a Miscellany of Curious and Interesting Tales, Histories, &C; Newly Composed by Many Celebrated Writers and Very Delightful to Read. The Chap-Book. LC 45-29159. 1896. H. S. Stone & Company.
Stories from the Dial. The Dial. LC 24-21360. 1924. L. MacVeagh, The Dial Press.
Stories from the Diary of a Doctor. L. T. Meade. LC 75-32767. (Literature of Mystery & Detection). (Illus.). 1976. Repr. of 1895 ed. 21.00x (ISBN 0-405-07886-2). Ayer Co.
Stories from the Diary of a Doctor. Elizabeth Thomasina Meade Smith & Clifford Halifax. LC 75-32767. (Literature of Mystery and Detection). (Illus.). 1976. 21.00 (ISBN 0-405-07886-2). Arno Press.
Stories from the French... Tr. by William Henry Scudder. LC 8-16109. (On cover: Idylwild series, v. 1, no. 14). 1892. Morrill, Higgins & Co.
Stories from the Harvard Advocate. Being a Collection of Stories Selected from the Advocate from Its Founding, Eighteen Hundred and Sixty-Six, to the Present Day. The Harvard Advocate. LC 17-230035. 1896. Harvard University.
Stories from the Hugo Winners, Vol. II. Ed. by Isaac Asimov. 1978. pap. 1.95 (ISBN 0-449-23791-5, Crest). Fawcett.
Stories from the Husk. The Husk. Ed. by Tull, Clyde & Plummer, Anya. Cornell College, Mount Vernon, Ia. LC 41-729. 1940. The English Club of Cornell College.
Stories from the Indian Classics: Selected and Retold by V. S. Naravane. Vishwanath S Naravane. LC 62-51476. 1962. Asia Pub. House.
Stories from the Italian Poets: Being a Summary in Prose of the Poems of Dante, Pulci, Boiardo, Ariosto and Tasso; with Comments Throughtout Occasional Passages Versified, and Critical Notices of the Lives and Genius of the Authors. Leigh Hunt et al. LC 7-9046. (Wiley & Putnam's Library of Choice Reading). (On cover: Wiley and Putnam's library of choice reading, 52-54: 52-54). 1846. Wiley and Putnam.
Stories from the Literary Review. Ed. by Charles Angoff. LC 68-21271. 1969. 8.00. Fairleigh Dickinson University Press.
Stories from the London Magazine. London Magazine. Ed. by Alan Ross. 1964. 5.00 o.p. Dufour.
Stories from the London Magazine: Ed. by Alan Ross. London Magazine (The) Ed. by Alan Ross. LC 65-770527. 1964. 5.00. Eyre & Spottiswoode.
Stories from the Midland. The Midland & Frederick, John Towner, 1893- Ed. LC 24-5502. 1924. A. A. Knopf.
Stories from the Moorland; or, Tales of the Convenanters. Lizzie Bates. LC 29-30779. (Lettered on cover: Little Ben Hadden series). 1869. American Tract Society.
Stories from the New Yorker, 1950-1960. LC 60-12590. 1960. Simon and Schuster.
Stories from the New Yorker 1950-1960. The, New Yorker Magazine. (O.s.i.). pap. 2.95 o.s.i. (68929). S&S.
Stories from the Note-Book of a Detective. Joyce Emmerson Preston Muddock. LC 1-2116. (With Taylor, Judson R. Phil Scott, the detective. New York 531909). 1900. Street & Smith.
Stories from The Quarto. Ed. by Leonard Stanley Brown. LC 68-14624. 1968. Scribner.
Stories from the Rabbis. Abram Samuel Isaacs. LC 7-9480. 1893. C. L. Webster & Company.
Stories from the Rabbis. 2d and enl. ed. Abram Samuel Isaacs. 1911. Bloch Publishing Company.
Stories from the Rest of the Robots. Isaac Asimov. 1974. pap. 1.25 o.p. (ISBN 0-515-03296-4, V3296). BJ Pub Group.
Stories from the Sixties. Ed. by Stanley Elkin. LC 71-144262. 1971. 6.95. Doubleday.
Stories from the Transatlantic Review. Ed. by Joseph F. McCrindle. LC 75-103548. 1970. 8.95 (ISBN 0-03-084524-6). Holt, Rinehart and Winston.
Stories from the Ukraine. Cyvi Khvyl. pap. 1.65 (76, WL). Citadel Pr.
Stories from the Ukraine. Translated with an Introd. by George S. N. Luckyj. Mykola Khvyl Cvyi. LC 60-13648. 1960. Philosophical Library.
Stories from Three Worlds. Ed. by A. McKenzie & J. McKenzie. 1978. pap. text ed. 6.95x o.p. (ISBN 0-85859-184-7, 00535). Heinemann Ed.
Stories from Virgil. Publius Vergilius Maro & Church, Alfred John, 1829-1912. LC 4-14047. Dodd, Mead & Company.
Stories from Wales. C. M. Duncan-Jones. Repr. lib. bdg. 10.00 (ISBN 0-8414-3871-4). Folcroft.
Stories in Black and White. Ed. by Eva H. Kissin. LC 77-101896. 1970. 4.95. Lippincott.
Stories in Fantasia. Damon Lahman. 1967. 4.00 o.p. (ISBN 0-682-45763-9). Exposition.
Stories in Light and Shadow. Bret Harte. LC 78-116952. (Short story index reprint series). (Illus.). 1970. Books for Libraries Press.
Stories in Light and Shadow. Bret Harte. LC 98-1391. 1898. Houghton, Mifflin and Company.
Stories in Light and Shadow. Bret Harte. LC 42-534139. Houghton Mifflin Company.
Stories in the Modern Manner: A Collection of Stories from the Partisan Review. Partisan Review. LC 53-3942. (Avon, AT-61). 1953. Avon Publications.
Stories into Film. William Kittredge & Steven M Krauzer. LC 78-73542. (Harper colophon books). 4.95 (ISBN 0-06-090638-3). Harper and Row.
Stories Near and Far. William John Locke. LC 27-4322. 1927. Dodd, Mead & Company.
Stories New and Old: Typical American and English Tales, Selected with Introductions. Ed. by Hamilton Wright Mabie. LC 8-18574. 1908. The Macmillan Company.
Stories Not to Be Missed. Ellery Queen, pseud. LC 78-104105. (Masterpieces of mystery). (Illus.). Davis Publications.
Stories of a Salesman. Murli D. Melwani. 1976. lib. bdg. 8.00 (ISBN 0-89253-084-7); flexible bdg. 6.75 (ISBN 0-89253-268-8). Ind-US Inc.
Stories of a Sanctified Town. Lucy S Furman. LC 6-44569. 1896. The Century Co.
Stories of a Western Town. Alice French. LC 69-11898. (American short story series, v. 56). (Illus.). 1969. Garrett Press.
Stories of a Western Town. Alice French. LC 72-8083. (American short story series, v. 56). 1972. (ISBN 0-8422-8055-3). MSS Information Corp.
Stories of a Western Town. Alice French. LC 4-151129. 1893. C. Scribner's Sons.
Stories of Adventure, Selected and Edited. Ed. by Max John Herzberg. LC 27-4636. (Academy classics for junior high schools). Allyn and Bacon.
Stories of American Life. Ed. by Mary Russell Mitford. LC 78-93646. 1969. Garrett Press.
Stories of American Life, 3 vols. LC 72-78787. 1830. Repr. 25.00 ea o.p.; 72.00 o.p. (ISBN 0-403-08941-7). Somerset Pub.
Stories of Anton Tchekov. Anton Pavlovich Chekhov. Ed. by Linscott, Robert Newton. LC 32-6306. (Half-title: The modern library of the world's best books). The Modern Library.
Stories of Breece D'J Pancake. Breece D'J Pancake. LC 82-17226. 13.50 (ISBN 0-316-69012-0). Little, Brown.
Stories of Buddha's Births: A Jataka Reader. C. S. Jossan. LC 76-30762. (Foreign & Comparative Studies-South Asian Special Publications Ser.: No. 1). 130p. 1976. pap. text ed. 5.00x (ISBN 0-915984-77-6). Syracuse U Foreign Comp.
Stories of C. F. Meyer. William David Williams. LC 63-106. 5.60. Clarendon Pr. Dist. New York, Oxford.
Stories of Champions: And the National Arabian Shows, Vol. 1. Dixie Ryan. (Illus.). 1975. 13.95 (ISBN 0-912830-25-5). Printed Horse.
Stories of China at War. Ed. by Wang Chi-Chen. LC 75-26630. 1975. 11.75 (ISBN 0-8371-8369-3). Greenwood Press.
Stories of Chinatown. Sketches from Life in the Chinese Colony of Mott, Pell and Doyers Streets. William Norr. LC 7-33306. 1892. W. Norr.
Stories of Classical Fables: A Wonder Book for Boys and Girls. Nathaniel Hawthorne. LC 8-191537. McLoughlin Brothers.
Stories of Courage and Devotion. Christine Whiting Parmenter. LC 39-303243. J. Messner. Inc.
Stories of Crime & Detection. Ed. by Joan D. Berbrich. LC 73-8832. (Patterns in Literary Art Ser). (Illus.). 312p. (gr. 9-12). 1972. pap. text ed. 9.16 (ISBN 0-07-004826-6, W). McGraw.
Stories of Darkness and Dread. Joseph Payne Brennan. LC 73-81267. 1973. 6.00. Arkham House.
Stories of Detection: By Modern Writers. R. W. Jepson. 10.00. Havertown Bks.
Stories of Doctors, for Doctors, by a Doctor. William T Bertrand. 1.00. The Roxburgh Publishing Company, Inc.
Stories of Don Quixote: Written Anew for Young People. James A. Baldwin. LC 11-1522. (On cover: Ecletic readings). American Book Company.
Stories of Eliyah Hanavi, 4 vols. 1982. Set. 32.00. Feldheim.
Stories of Elizabeth Spencer. Elizabeth Spencer. LC 79-6601. 1981. 14.95 (ISBN 0-385-15697-9). Doubleday.
Stories of Eric Linklater. Eric Robert Russell Linklater. LC 76-85336. 1969. 6.50. Horizon Press.
Stories of Ernest Dowson. Ernest Christopher Dowson & Longaker, John Mark, 1900- Ed. LC 47-31063. 1947. Univ. of Pennsylvania Press.
Stories of F. Scott Fitzgerald. Francis Scott Key Fitzgerald. 1951. pap. 5.95 o.p. (ISBN 0-684-71737-9, SL135, ScribT); lib. rep. ed. 17.50x o.p. (ISBN 0-684-15366-1). Scribner.
Stories of F. Scott Fitzgerald: A Selection of 28 Stories. Francis Scott Key Fitzgerald. LC 51-9861. 1951. Scribner.
Stories of F. Scott Fitzgerald: A Selection of 28 Stories. Introd. Notes by Malcolm Cowley. Francis Scott Key Fitzgerald. (Scribner lib. Omnibus volume, SL 135). 1966. pap., 2.95. Scribners.
Stories of Five Decades. Hermann Hesse. LC 72-81010. 1972. 8.95 (ISBN 0-374-27050-3). Farrar, Straus and Giroux.
Stories of Five Decades. 1974. (pbk.) 1.95. Bantam Books.
Stories of Frank O'Connor. Frank O'Connor, pseud. (YA) 1952. 10.00 o.p. (ISBN 0-394-44732-8). Knopf.
Stories of Frank O'Connor Pseud. Michael O'Donovan. LC 52-10153. 1952. Knopf.
Stories of Frank Sargeson. Frank Sargeson. 351p. 1974. 13.00x (ISBN 0-582-71721-3). Intl Pubns Serv.
Stories of Georgia. Joel Chandler Harris. (Illus.). 315p. 1971. Repr. of 1896 ed. bds. 6.50 (ISBN 0-87797-018-1). Cherokee.
Stories of God. Rainer Maria Rilke. LC 63-11685. 1963. Norton.
Stories of God. Rainer Maria Rilke. Tr. by Herter Norton, Mary Dows. LC 32-32272. W. W. Norton & Company, Inc.
Stories of H. C. Bunner. Henry Cuyler Bunner. LC 72-5900. (Short story index reprint series). (Illus.). 1972. (ISBN 0-8369-4194-2). Books for Libraries Press.
Stories of Hawaii. Jack London. Ed. by Arthur Grove Day. LC 65-11682. 1965. Appleton-Century.
Stories of H.C. Bunner. Henry Cuyler Bunner. LC 16-11385. 1916. C. Scribner's Sons.
Stories of H.C. Bunner. second series. ed. Henry Cuyler Bunner. LC 16-265449. 1916. C. Scribner's Sons.
Stories of H.C. Bunner. More "Short Sixes"; The Runaway Browns, a Story of Small Stories. Henry Cuyler Bunner. 1917. C. Scribner's Sons.
Stories of H.C. Bunner: "Short Sixes", Stories to Be Read While the Candle Burns; The Suburban Sage, Stray Notes and Comments on His Simple Life. Henry Cuyler Bunner. LC 17-13500. 1917. C. Scribner's Sons.
Stories of Henry Lawson, 3 Vols. Cecil Mann. Vol. 1. 7.00 o.s.i. (Pub. by Cowman); Vol. 2. 9.00 o.s.i.; Vol. 3. 6.75 o.s.i. Tri-Ocean.
Stories of Hoaxes. Irving Adler. (O.s.i.). 1962. pap. 0.95 o.s.i. (ISBN 0-02-016070-4, Collier). Macmillan.
Stories of Home Folks: Actual Incidents from Real Life. Mabel Hale. LC 28-13794. Gospel Trumpet Company.
Stories of India: Moral, Mystical, Spiritual and Romantic. Rose Reinhardt Anthon. 1906. Times-Mirror Printing & Binding House.
Stories of Ireland: Castle Rackrent. The Absentee. 2d ed. Maria Edgeworth. LC 45-53917. (Half-title: Morley's universal library. 36). 1886. G. Routledge and Sons.
Stories of Italy. LC 4-18268. (Stories from Scribner). 1894. C. Scribner's Sons.
Stories of James Stern. James Stern. LC 69-12049. 1969. 4.95 o.p. (ISBN 0-15-185200-6). HarBraceJ.
Stories of Jewish Home Life. Salomon Hermann Mosenthal. LC 75-160945. (Short story index reprint series). 1971. (ISBN 0-8369-3924-7). Books for Libraries Press.
Stories of Jewish Home Life. Salomon Hermann Ritter Von Mosenthal. LC 7-407965. 1907. The Jewish Publication Society of America.
Stories of John Cheever. John Cheever. LC 78-160. 1978. 15.95 (ISBN 0-394-50087-3). Knopf.
Stories of John Cheever. John Cheever. LC 81-40192. 1981. 7.95 (ISBN 0-394-74799-2). Vintage Books.
Stories of King Arthur & His Knights. Barbara Leonie Picard. (Illus.). 300p. 1955. 12.95 o.p. (ISBN 0-19-274510-7). Oxford U Pr.
Stories of Liam O'Flaherty. Introd. by Vivian Mercier. Liam O'Flaherty. LC 56-8128. 1956. Devin-Adair Co.
Stories of Life and Love. Amelia Edith Huddleston Barr. (On cover: The Christian herald library). The Christian Herald.
Stories of Life, North & South: Selections from the Best Short Stories of Erskine Caldwell. Erskine Caldwell & Edward Connery Lathem. LC 82-19922. 14.95 (ISBN 0-396-08133-9). Dodd, Mead.
Stories of Light. Edmund Wilson. 1952. 9.95 o.p. (ISBN 0-374-51045-8). FS&G.
Stories of Love & Devotion. Hannah Shenton. 3.00 o.p. Carlton.
Stories of Love and Intrigue from The Mixture As Before. William Somerset Maugham. LC 48-1425. (Avon modern short story monthly, 38). 1947. Avon Book Co.
Stories of Love and Life, of Fact and Fancy Woven. William Josephus Robinson. LC 13-7850. 1913. The Critic and Guide Company.
Stories of Love and Passion. Honore De Balzac. Tr. by Kent, Philip. LC 48-40911. (Arundel series). Arundel Print.
Stories of Love, Courage and Compassion. Warwick Deeping. LC 30-27115. 1930. A. A. Knopf.
Stories of Love, Courage and Compassion. Warwick Deeping. LC 32-6531. 1930. A. A. Knopf.
Stories of Love: Intrigue and Battle. Rafael Sabatini. 1931. Houghton Mifflin Company.
Stories of Many Nations. Ed. by Irwin H Braun & Safarjian, David Edward. LC 42-3941. D. C. Heath and Company.
Stories of Michael Robartes & His Friends. William Butler Yeats. 58p. 1970. Repr. of 1931 ed. 13.00x (ISBN 0-7165-1373-0, Pub. by Cuala Press Ireland). Biblio Dist.
Stories of Modern Italy: From Verga, Svevc and Pirandello to the Present. Edited, with an Introd., by Ben Johnson. Ed. by Ben Johnson. LC 60-10264. (Modern library, 118). 1960. Modern Library.
Stories of Naples and the Camorra. Charles Grant & Capper, J. B. LC 4-15311. 1896. Macmillan and Co., Ltd.
Stories of New Jersey. Frank Richard Stockton. (Illus.). 1961. pap. 6.95 (ISBN 0-8135-0369-8). Rutgers U Pr.
Stories of New York. LC 4-18269. (Stories from Scribner). 1894. C. Scribner's Sons.
Stories of O. Henry: New Ed. Chosen, Introd. by Harry Hansen. Illus. by John Groth. William Sydney Porter. Ed. by Harry Hansen. John Groth. LC 66-815. 1966. bds., 7.50. Heritage Pr. Dist: Dial.
Stories of Old New Spain. Thomas Allibone Janvier. LC 69-11905. (American short story series, v. 64). (Illus.). 1969. Garrett Press.
Stories of Old New Spain. Thomas Allibone Janvier. LC 72-8162. (American short story series, v. 64). 1972. (ISBN 0-8422-8081-2). MSS Information Corp.
Stories of Old New Spain. Thomas Allibone Janvier. LC 7-10334. (On cover: Appletons' town and country library, no. 71). 1891. D. Appleton and Company.
Stories of Old Oregon. George Andrew Waggoner. LC 5-8674. 1905. Statesman Publishing Co.
Stories of Old Samoa. Fanaafi Ma'Ia'I. 1960. pap. 1.25 o.s.i. Tri-Ocean.
Stories of Our Century by Catholic Authors. Ed. by John Gilland Brunini & Connolly, Francis Xavier. LC 49-6993. 1948. J. B. Lippincott Co.
Stories of Peace and War. Frederic Remington. LC 75-125237. (Short story index reprint series). (Illus.). 1970. Books for Libraries Press.
Stories of Peace and War. Frederic Remington. (Little books by famour writers). 1899. Harper & Brothers.
Stories of Pennsylvania... Elsie Singmaster. LC 37-2381. The Pennsylvania Book Service.
Stories of Provence. From the French of Alphonse Daudet (Lettres De Mon Moulin). Alphonse Daudet. Ed. by Lee, S. L. (Harper's handy series, no. 51). 1886. Harper & Brothers.
Stories of Rainbow and Lucky. Jacob Abbott. LC 4-16448. 1887-88. Harper & Brothers.
Stories of Ray Bradbury. Ray Bradbury. LC 80-7655. 1980. 15.00 (ISBN 0-394-51335-5). Knopf: Distributed by Random House.
Stories of Red Hanrahan. William Butler Yeats. 72p. 1971. Repr. of 1904 ed. 13.00x (ISBN 0-7165-1330-7, Pub. by Cuala Press Ireland). Biblio Dist.
Stories of Red Hanrahan. The Secret Rose, Rosa Alchemica. William Butler Yeats. LC 14-615415. 1914. The Macmillan Company.
Stories of Russian Life. Anton Pavlovich Chekhov. Tr. by Fell, Marian. LC 14-10072. 1914. C. Scribner's Sons.
Stories of Sahabah. M. Zakariya. 1970. 3.00 o.p. (ISBN 0-87902-194-2). Orientalia.
Stories of School and College Days. LC 2-12954. (Added t.-p.: The young folks' library. vol. VII). 1901. Hall & Locke Company.

Stories of School and College Days: Edited by Kirk Munroe and Mary Hartwell Catherwood. Kirk Munroe. Ed. by Mary Hartwell Catherwood. LC 54-2438. (Young Folks Library 7). Auxiliary Educational League.
Stories of School and College Life: September to June. Ed. by Robert J Cadigan. LC 42-3942. D. Appleton-Century Company, Incorporated.
Stories of Scientific Imagination. Ed. by Joseph Gallant. LC 54-10170. (Students pocket library). 1954. Oxford Book Co.
Stories of Sean O'Faolain. Sean O'Faolain. LC 72-176410. 1970. 0.40 (ISBN 0-14-003195-2). Penguin.
Stories of Sherlock Holmes... Arthur Conan Doyle. LC 4-2990. 1904. Harper & Brothers.
Stories of Sicily. Alfred Alexander. LC 75-9843. 1975. 8.95 (ISBN 0-8052-3592-2). Schocken Books.
Stories of Strange Places. Cyril E Goode. LC 73-170036. 1973. 5.95 (ISBN 0-7256-0095-0). Hawthorn Press.
Stories of Sudden Truth. Ed. by Joseph Ingham Greene & Elizabeth Abell. Repr. of 1953 ed. 7.50 o.p. (ISBN 0-89987-108-9). Darby Bks.
Stories of Sudden Truth: Edited by Joseph Green and Elizabeth Abell. Ed. by Joseph Ingham Greene & Elizabeth Abell. LC 53-6125. 1953. Ballantine Books.
Stories of the American Experience. Ed. by Leonard Kriegel. LC 73-75330. (Mentor book). 1973. (pbk.) 1.95. New American Library.
Stories of the Ants. Robert L. Merriam. (Illus.). 19p. (Orig.). 1981. pap. 6.50. R L Merriam.
Stories of the Army. Brander Matthews. LC 76-113683. (Short story index reprint series). (Illus.). 1970. Books for Libraries Press.
Stories of the Army. Brander Matthews & Heard, John, Jr. (Stories from Scribner). 1894. C. Scribner's Sons.
Stories of the Benin Empire. Joseph E. Sidahome. 1964. 3.25x o.p. (ISBN 0-19-428212-0). Oxford U Pr.
Stories of the Cherokee Hills. Maurice Thompson. LC 77-113686. (Short story index reprint series). (Illus.). 1970. Books for Libraries Press.
Stories of the Cherokee Hills. Maurice Thompson. LC 98-955. 1898. Houghton, Mifflin and Company.
Stories of the City. Ed. by Henry Goodman & Carpenter, Bruce. LC 31-11376. (Modern America Series of English Texts, H. A. Watt, Ed.). The Ronald Press Company.
Stories of the Colleges: Being Tales of Life at the Great American Universities Told by Noted Graduates. LC 1-27045. 1901. J. B. Lippincott Company.
Stories of the Double. Ed. by Albert J. Guerard. Incl. Double. Fedor Dostoyevsky; Doctor Jekyll & Mister Hyde. Robert L. Stevenson; Secret Sharer. Joseph Conrad. (Contrasts in Literature Ser.). (Orig.). 1967. Lippincott.
Stories of the Early West: The Luck of Roaring Camp, and 16 Other Exciting Tales of Mining and Frontier Days. Each Story Complete. Forward by Walter Van Tilburg Clark. Bret Harte. LC 64-15905. (Platt & Munk great writers collection). 1964. Platt & Munk.
Stories of the Foot-Hills. Margaret Collier Graham. LC 76-94727. (Short story index reprint series). 1969. Books for Libraries Press.
Stories of the Foot-Hills. Margaret Collier Graham. LC 6-27654. 1895. Houghton, Mifflin and Company.
Stories of the Foreign Legion: Selected from the Book Appearing in England Under the Same Title. Percival Christopher Wren. LC 48-706685. 1948. Macrae, Smith Co.
Stories of the Great Lakes. St. Nicholas. 185p. 1972. Repr. of 1907 ed. 9.00 o.p. Gale.
Stories of the Great Lakes see Early Stories of the Great Lakes.
Stories of the Irish Peasantry. Anna Maria Fielding Hall. LC 79-12010. (Ireland, from the Act of Union, 1800, to the Death of Parnell, 1891; 49). 1979. 32.00 (ISBN 0-8240-3498-8). Garland Pub.
Stories of the Land of Evangeline. Grace Dean McLeod. LC 7-20433. D. Lothrop Company.
Stories of the Modern South. Ben Forkner & Patrick H Samway. LC 81-426. 1981. 4.95 (ISBN 0-14-005848-6). Penguin Books.
Stories of the Occult. Daniel Ahrens Stitzer. LC 17-12958. 1917. R. G. Badger; Etc., Etc.
Stories of the Old Duck Hunters. Gordon F. MacQuarrie. 1979. pap. 7.95 (ISBN 0-932558-10-0). Willow Creek.
Stories of the Old Duck Hunters: & Other Drivel. Gordon F MacQuarrie. Ed. by Zack Taylor. LC 67-12929. (Stackpole easy-chair book). 1967. Stackpole Co.
Stories of the Old Missions of California. Charles Franklin Carter. LC 71-116945. (Short story index reprint series). (Illus.). 1970. Books for Libraries Press.
Stories of the Old Missions of California. Charles Franklin Carter. LC 17-31618. 1917. P. Elder & Company.
Stories of the Old Santa Fe Trail. Henry Inman. LC 7-9717. 1881. Ramsey, Millett & Hudson.
Stories of the Prairie, and Other Adventures of the Border. James Fenimore Cooper. LC 6-29675. 1868. Hurd and Houghton.
Stories of the Railroad. John Alexander Hill. LC 99-4656. 1899. Doubleday & McClure Co.
Stories of the Railway. George Abiah Hibbard. LC 70-113684. (Short story index reprint series). (Illus.). 1970. Books for Libraries Press.
Stories of the Railway. George Abiah Hibbard & Davison, Charles Stewart, 1855- LC 4-182715. (Stories from Scribner). 1893. C. Scribner's Sons.
Stories of the Railway. Victor Lawrence Whitechurch. LC 78-318924. (Illus.). 1978. 8.25 (ISBN 0-7100-8635-0). Routledge & Kegan Paul.
Stories of the Riverina. Selected, Introd. by Clement Semmler. E. O Schlunke. LC 66-811426. 1965. 4.50. Angus & Robertson.
Stories of the Sea. John Randolph Spears. LC 73-113685. (Short story index reprint series). (Illus.). 1970. Books for Libraries Press.
Stories of the Sea. John Randolph Spears & Blunt, Maria. LC 4-18272. (Stories from Scribner). 1893. C. Scribner's Son.
Stories of the Sea: Being Narratives of Adventures, Selected from the "Sea Tales,". James Fenimore Cooper. LC 6-29674. 1863. J. G. Gregory.
Stories of the Seen and the Unseen. Margaret Oliphant Wilson Oliphant. LC 72-113682. (Short story index reprint series). 1970. Books for Libraries Press.
Stories of the Seen and the Unseen. Margaret Oliphant Wilson Oliphant. LC 41-311311. 1889. Roberts Brothers.
Stories of the Seen and the Unseen. Margaret Oliphant Wilson Oliphant. LC 4-165702. 1900. Little, Brown, and Company.
Stories of the South. Thomas Nelson Page. LC 74-110217. (Short story index reprint series). (Illus.). 1970. Books for Libraries Press.
Stories of the South. Thomas Nelson Page & Robertson, Harrison, 1856-1939. (Stories from Scribner). 1894. C. Scribner's Sons.
Stories of the South, Old & New. Ed. by Clarence Addison Hibbard. 1978. Repr. of 1931 ed. 35.00 (ISBN 0-8492-5311-X). R West.
Stories of the South, Old and New, Edited: By Addison Hibbard, with an Introduction, Biographical Notes, and Bibliography by the Editor. Ed. by Clarence Addison Hibbard. LC 31-86832. The University of North Carolina Press.
Stories of the South Seas. E. C. Parnwell. Repr. of 1928 ed. 10.00 o.p. Folcroft.
Stories of the Spanish Southwest. Cuentos De los Ninos Chicanos. Thomas Matthews Pearce. LC 73-211053. (Illus.). 1973.
Stories of the Spanish-Speaking World: Selected and Edited with Introductory Comment, Footnotes, Exercises, and Vocabulary, by James R. Browne. Ed. by James Roll Browne. LC 51-1480. 1950. Ginn.
Stories of the Steppe. Maksim Gorkii. Tr. by Henry Thomas. LC 72-121552. (Short story index reprint series). 1970. Books for Libraries Press.
Stories of the Steppe. Maksim Gorkii. LC 72-121552. (Short Story Index Reprint Ser). 1918. 10.00 (ISBN 0-8369-3508-X). Ayer Co.
Stories of the Steppe. Maksim Gorkii & Schnittkind, Henry Thomas, 1888- Tr. LC 18-14420. (Stratford universal library). 1918. The Stratford Company.
Stories of the Struggle. Morris Winchevsky. LC 8-17790. 1908. C. H. Kerr & Company.
Stories of the Supernatural. Henry James. Ed. by Leon Edel. LC 78-125479. 1970. 7.95. Taplinger Pub. Co.
Stories of the Supernatural. Dorothy Leigh Sayers. 1963. pap. 0.50 o.p. (50-300). Manor Bks.
Stories of the Supernatural. 3rd ed. Dorothy Leigh Sayers. 176p. 1974. pap. 0.95 o.p. (532-95313-095). Manor Bks.
Stories of the Three Burglars. Frank Richard Stockton. LC 8-15535. Dodd, Mead & Company.
Stories of the Tragedy & Comedy of Life: With an Introduction. Guy De Maupassant. LC 4-150069. (Dunne imprints). 1904. M. W. Dunne.
Stories of the Unforseen. Rondall Isaac. 1979. 6.95 o.p. (ISBN 0-533-04170-8). Vantage.
Stories of the World's Holidays. Grace Humphrey. Repr. of 1924 ed. lib. bdg. 10.00 o.p. Folcroft.
Stories of Thornton Wilder: The Bridge of San Luis Rey, The Cabala, The Woman of Andros. Thornton Niven Wilder. LC 35-787146. 1934. Longmans, Green and Co.
Stories of Three Decades. Thomas Mann. Tr. by Helen Tracy Porter Lowe. LC 46-43883. (Borzoi book). 1966. A. A. Knopf.
Stories of Three Decades. Thomas Mann. Tr. by Helen Tracy Lowe. LC 36-119569. 1936. A. A. Knopf.
Stories of Three Decades. Thomas Mann. Tr. by Helen Tracy Lowe. LC 46-43883. 1936. A. A. Knopf.
Stories of to-Day and Yesterday: Thirty Selected Short Stories, Nine Imitative Stories by Students, Questions for Class Discussion, Directions for Creative Narration. Ed. by Frederick Houk Law. LC 30-8266. 1.10. The Century Co.
Stories of William Sansom. William Sansom. LC 77-144171. (Short story index reprint series). 1971. (ISBN 0-8369-3786-4). Books for Libraries Press.
Stories of York State. Harold Frederic. Ed. by Thomas Francis O'Donnell. LC 66-17031. 1966. Syracuse University Press.
Stories of York State. Ed. by Thomas F. O'Donnell,Introd. by Edmund Wilson. Harold Frederic. Ed. by Thomas Francis O'Donnell. LC 66-170317. 6.50. Syracuse Univ. Pr.
Stories Plus: Canadian Stories with Authors' Commentaries. John Metcalf. LC 81-104232. (Illus.). 1979. 6.29 (ISBN 0-07-082983-7). McGraw-Hill Ryerson.
Stories Revived; First Series. Henry James. LC 72-12605. (Short Story Index Reprint Ser.). 1973. Repr. of 1885 ed. 25.00 (ISBN 0-8369-4237-X). Ayer Co.
Stories Revived. 1st Ser. Henry James. LC 72-12605. (Short story index reprint series). 1973. (ISBN 0-8369-4237-X). Books for Libraries Press.
Stories: Second Stories, Vol. 1. Henry Cuyer Bunner. LC 72-5900. (Short Story Index Reprint Ser). Repr. of 1916 ed. 21.00 (ISBN 0-8369-4194-2). Ayer Co.
Stories. Selected, Introd. by William R. Roff. Hugh Charles Clifford. Ed. by William R. Roff. (Oxford in Asia hist. reprints). 1966. 5.50. Oxford Univ. Pr.
Stories That Count. Ed. by William A. Roecker. LC 78-126799. 1971. (ISBN 0-03-084146-1). Holt, Rinehart and Winston.
Stories That End Well. Alice French. LC 11-225465. The Bobbs-Merrill Company.
Stories That Live. Ralph Cutlip. (gr. 7-12). 1973. 5.42 (ISBN 0-87720-352-0). AMSCO Sch.
Stories That Live. Lucy G. Thomson. 1.25 o.p. (ISBN 0-87747-246-7). Deseret Bk.
Stories They Wouldn't Let Me Do on Tv. Ed. by Alfred Hitchcock. 1957. 4.50 o.p. S&S.
Stories to Brighten up Your Mondays. Dick Bothwell. (Illus.). 1979. pap. 3.95 o.p. (ISBN 0-8200-9905-8). Great Outdoors.
Stories to Enjoy. Ed. by Hoopes. (Macmillan Lit. Heritage Ser. Gr. 7: Literature to Enjoy). pap. text ed. 1.48, s.p. 1.11 o.p. Macmillan.
Stories to Make You Feel Better. Bennett Alfred Cerf. (General Ser.). 1973. lib. bdg. 6.95 (ISBN 0-8161-6081-3, Large Print Bks). G K Hall.
Stories to Make You Feel Better. Bennett Alfred Cerf. 1972. 8.95 (ISBN 0-394-47553-4, BYR). Random.
Stories to Read at Christmas. Elsie Singmaster. LC 40-32568. 1940. Houghton Mifflin Company.
Stories to Remember. Ed. by Thomas Bertram Costain & John Beecroft. LC 56-11620. (Illus.). 1956. Doubleday.
Stories to Remember. Ed. by Schlakman. (Macmillan Lit. Heritage Ser. Gr. 8: Literature to Remember). pap. text ed. 1.52, s.p. 1.14 o.p. Macmillan.
Stories to Remember: V.1&2, Selected by Thomas B. Costain, John Beecroft. Ed. by Thomas Bertram Costain & John Beecroft. (W1172, W1173). 1965. Popular Lib.
Stories to Surprise You. English Language Services. (Collier-Macmillan English Readers). pap. 1.40 (ISBN 0-02-971300-5). Macmillan.
Stories Told for Revenue Only. St. Paul Press Club St. Paul, Minn & Conway, John Joseph, Ed. LC 6-3659. 1893.
Stories Told in the Kitchen. Kendall Morse. LC 81-8775. 3.95 (ISBN 0-89621-064-2). Thorndike Press.
Stories Toto Told Me. Frederick B. Corvo. LC 72-145439. 254p. 1971. 5.95x o.p. (S62500). St Martin.
Stories Toto Told Me. Frederick William Rolfe. LC 72-145439. 1971. 5.95. St. Martin's Press.
Stories up to a Point. Bette Pesetsky. LC 81-47519. 1981. 9.50 (ISBN 0-394-52079-3). Knopf.
Stories We Love. John F. Bradosky & Jon L. Joyce. (Orig.). 1981. pap. 9.95 (ISBN 0-937172-21-9). JLJ Pubs.
Stories with a Moral, Humourous and Descriptive of Southern Life a Century Ago. Augustus Baldwin Longstreet. Ed. by Longstreet, Fitz Randolph. LC 12-14112. 1912. The John C. Winston Company.
Stories Without Morals. Raymond Stephen McAtee. LC 49-2382. 1949. M. L. Ramsey Co.
Stories Without Women and a Few with Women. Donn Byrne. LC 74-103502. (Short story index reprint series). 1970. Books for Libraries Press.
Stories Without Women: And a Few with Women. Donn Byrne. LC 15-246. 1915. Hearst's International Library Co.
Stories Without Women and a Few with Women. Donn Byrne. LC 31-26377. 1931. The Century Co.
Stories Without Words, 16 vols. (Adventures in Living Ser.). Set. 10.67 o.p. (ISBN 0-672-75038-4). Bobbs.
Stories You Can Sell. author's ed. Laurence R D'Orsay. LC 33-2320. 1932. Parker, Stone & Baird Co.
Stories You Can Sell. 3d ed., march, 1935. ed. Laurence R D'Orsay. LC 35-9871. Parker, Stone & Baird Co.
Stories You Won't Forget. Robert O'Neal. LC 32-255901. Dorrance & Company, Inc.
Stories. 3v. Ed. by Cecil Mann. Henry Archibald Hertzberg Lawson. Ed. by Cecil Mann. LC 64-256978. 1965. Angus and Robertson.
Storington Papers. Dorothy Eden. 1980. 2.50 (ISBN 0-449-24239-0). Fawcett Crest Books.
Stork. Denison Hatch. LC 76-46420. 1977. 8.95 (ISBN 0-688-03160-9). Morrow.
Stork. Denison Hatch. (Jove/HBJ Bok). 1978. 1.95 (ISBN 0-515-04747-3). Jove Publications.
Stork and the Jewels: A Parable Translated from the French by Gerold Lauck. Illustrated by Peter Lauck. Raymond Leopold Bruckberger. LC 51-13664. 1951. Harper.
Stork Factor. Zachary Hughes. (Berkley medallion book). 1975. (pbk.) 0.95 (ISBN 0-425-02781-3). Berkley Pub. Co.
Stork's Nest. John Breckenridge Ellis. LC 5-33023. 1905. Moffat, Yard & Company.
Stork's Nest: Or Pleasant Reading from the North. Ed. by John Fulford Vicary. LC 41-32447. F. Warne and Co.
Storm. Jacquelyn Aeby. (Candlelight Romance, 199). Dell.
Storm. Ilya Grigorevich Ehrenburg. LC 49-49307. 1949. Gaer Associates.
Storm. Elsie Frances Wilson Mack. LC 51-14978. 1951. Bouregy & Curl.
Storm. Frances S. Moore. 256p. (YA) 1973. 6.95 (Avalon). Bouregy.
Storm. Wilbur Daniel Steele. LC 14-5167. 1914. 1.35. Harper & Brothers.
Storm. George Rippey Stewart. LC 41-51984. Random House.
Storm: A Novel. George Rippey Stewart. LC 82-16098. 1983. 8.95 (ISBN 0-8032-9135-3). University of Nebraska Press.
Storm. A Novel. LC 7-4433. 1801. Printed by David Sower.
Storm: A Novel; with a New Introd. George Rippey Stewart. LC 48-243. (modern library of the world's best books). 1947. Modern Library.
Storm Against the Wall. Fannie Cook. LC 48-583910. 1948. Doubleday.
Storm Against the Wall. Laurence Walter Meynell. LC 31-160035. 1931. J. B. Lippincott Company.
Storm Against the Wind. Helen Hull Jacobs. LC 44-3826. 1944. Dodd, Mead & Company.
Storm Along the Rattlesnake. Archie Joscelyn. LC 64-57497. 1964. Arcadia House.
Storm: An Epic Novel of the Sea. Charles Rodda. LC 33-19403. 1933. Roland Swain Company.
Storm and Echo. Frederic Prokosch. LC 48-8302. 1948. Doubleday.
Storm & Other Stories. Kate O'Flaherty Chopin. Ed. by Per Seyersted. 384p. 1975. pap. 5.00 o.p. (ISBN 0-912670-37-1). Feminist Pr.
Storm & Other Stories. Sharat Kumar. 1976. 9.00 (ISBN 0-89253-815-5); flexible cloth 6.75 (ISBN 0-89253-816-3). Ind-US Inc.
Storm, and Other Stories: With The Awakening. Kate O'Flaherty Chopin. LC 75-9718. (Illus.). 1974. 5.00. Feminist Press.
Storm and the Silence. David Harry Walker. LC 49-11592. 1949. Houghton Mifflin Co.
Storm & the Splendor. Jennifer Blake. (Orig.). 1979. pap. 2.95 (ISBN 0-449-14282-5, GM). Fawcett.
Storm Ashore. James H. Connelly. LC 6-30685. (On cover: The household library, v. 4, no. 24). 1888. Belford, Clarke and Company; Etc., Etc.
Storm at Dusk. Katherine Ursula Parrott. LC 43-270949. 1943. Dodd, Mead & Company.
Storm at Sable Island. Edmund Gilligan. LC 48-8559. 1948. Little, Brown.
Storm at the Crossroads and Other Stories. Tristram Tupper. LC 31-146292. 1930. J. B. Lippincott Company.
Storm Beach. Virginia Davis Hersch. LC 33-10971. 1933. Houghton Mifflin Company.
Storm Before Dawn. Fred J Cook. LC 78-52969. 2.25 (ISBN 0-89516-027-7). Condor.

Storm Before Daybreak. Marian McCamy Sims. LC 46-827025. 1946. J. B. Lippincott Company.
Storm Bird. Mollie Panter-Downes. LC 30-5170. 1930. G. P. Putnam's Sons.
Storm Birds. Schroeder Davis. LC 10-127837. 1910. 1.50. Moffat, Yard and Company.
Storm Blows Over. Judith Ravel & Brentano, Lowell. LC 34-157396. Covici, Friede.
Storm-Bound: A Romance of Shell Beach. Eleanor Cecilia Donnelly. LC 6-33727. H L. Kilner & Co.
Storm Canvas. Armstrong Sperry. LC 44-5270. 1944. The John C. Winston Company.
Storm Center: A Novel About Andy Johnson. Joseph Walker McSpadden. LC 47-1775. 1947. Dodd, Mead & Company.
Storm-Center: A Romance. Burton Egbert Stevenson. LC 24-1644. 1924. 2.00. Dodd, Mead and Company.
Storm Centre. Charlotte Lamb, pseud. (Presents Ser.). 192p. (Orig.). 1980. pap. text ed. 1.50 (ISBN 0-373-10371-9, Pub. by Harlequin). PB.
Storm Centre: A Novel. Mary Noailles Murfree. LC 5-19420. 1902. The Macmillan Company.
Storm Centre: By Robert Standish Pseud. Digby George Gerahty. LC 51-13134. 1951. Macmillan.
Storm Child. Ruth Carmen. LC 37-37802. John C. Publishing Co.
Storm Cloud. Lettie Hamlett Rogers. LC 51-359. 1951. Random House.
Storm Country Polly. Grace Miller White. LC 20-8242. 1920. Little, Brown, and Company.
Storm Cycle. Margaret Way. (Harlequin Presents Ser.). 192p. 1982. pap. 1.75 (ISBN 0-373-10548-7). Harlequin Bks.
Storm Drift. Ethel May Dell. LC 31-368572. 1931. G. P. Putnam's Sons.
Storm Dust. Constance I Smith. LC 26-7210. 1925. A. Melrose, Ltd.
Storm Dust. Constance I Smith. LC 26-647610. H. Holt and Company.
Storm Fear: A Novel. 1st Ed. Clinton Seeley. LC 54-11864. 1954. Holt.
Storm Front. Phillip Finch. LC 77-12077. 7.95 (ISBN 0-698-10830-2). Coward, McCann & Geoghegan.
Storm Girl. Joseph Crosby Lincoln. LC 37-17511. 1937. D Appleton-Century Company, Incorporated.
Storm Haven. Frank Gill Slaughter. LC 75-33035. 1975-1976. 9.95 (ISBN 0-89190-285-6). American Reprint Co.
Storm Haven. 1st Ed. Frank Gill Slaughter. LC 53-99972. 1953. Doubleday.
Storm House. Florence Hard. (Manor Books gothic). 1973. (pbk.) 0.95. Manor Books.
Storm House. new ed. Florence Hurd. 192p. 1975. pap. 1.25 o.p. (ISBN 0-532-12397-2). Woodhill.
Storm House. Florence Hurd. 1973. pap. 0.95 o.p. (532-95258-095). Manor Bks.
Storm House. new ed. Florence Hurd. 192p. 1975. pap. 1.25 o.p. (ISBN 0-532-12397-2). Manor Bks.
Storm House. Kathleen Thompson Norris. LC 29-9219. 1929. Doubleday, Doran & Company Incorporated.
Storm House. Kathleen Thompson Norris. LC 31-19524. 1930. A. L. Burt Company.
Storm in a Teacup. Gus March-Phillipps. LC 37-2171. 1937. E. P. Dutton & Co., Inc.
Storm in a Teacup. Eden Phillpotts. LC 19-13364. 1919. 1.60. The Macmillan Company.
Storm in Chandigarh. Nayantara Pandit Sahgal. LC 68-56268. 1969. 4.95. Norton.
Storm in Her Heart. Gloria Young. LC 38-118898. 1933. Wm. B. Eerdmans Publishing Company.
Storm in the Backwoods. Anne Osborne. 300p. (Orig.). 1981. pap. 5.95 (ISBN 0-9606508-0-6). Holly Hill.
Storm in the South. Jonathan Scofield, pseud. (Freedom Fighters Ser.: No. 6). 1981. pap. 2.75 (ISBN 0-440-07685-4, Bryans). Dell.
Storm in the Valley. Carolyn MacDonald. 1973. (pbk) 0.95 (ISBN 0-671-77658-4). Pocket Books.
Storm in the Village. Miss Read. (Illus.). 1959. 3.50 o.p. HM.
Storm in the Village: By Miss Read Pseud. Illustrated by J. S. Goodall. 1st American Ed. Dora Jessie Saint. LC 59-5848. 1959. Houghton Mifflin.
Storm in the West. rev. ed. Sinclair Lewis & Dore Schary. LC 63-13228. (Illus.). 200p. 1981. pap. 5.95 (ISBN 0-8128-6079-9). Stein & Day.
Storm Is Rising. George Dyer. 1934. Houghton Mifflin Company.
Storm Island. Theodore J Waldeck. LC 35-8859. Alliance Press.
Storm King. A Story of Want and Wealth. Mansfield Lovell Hillhouse. (Dillingham's American authors library, no. 5). 1895. G. W. Dillingham.
Storm King Riders. Galen C Colin. E. J. Clode, Inc.
Storm Lord. Tanith Lee. (Science Fiction Ser.). 1978. pap. 1.95 (ISBN 0-87997-361-7, US1361). DAW Bks.
Storm-Lord. Tanith Lee. (Science Fiction Ser.). 1976. pap. 1.75 o.p. (UE1233). DAW Bks.
Storm Lord. Tanith Lee. (Daw Science Fiction#193). 1976. (pbk.) 1.75. Daw Books.
Storm Music. Cecil William Mercer. LC 34-14908. 1934. Minton, Balch & Company.
Storm of Desire. Paula Fairman. 1979. pap. 2.95 (ISBN 0-523-41797-7). Pinnacle Bks.
Storm of Desire. Glenna Finley, pseud. (Signet Book). 1977. 1.25 (ISBN 0-451-07356-8). New American Library.
Storm of Destiny. Hymen Willem Johannes Picard. LC 77-351600. 1976. Hollandsch Afrikaansche Uitgevers Maatschappij.
Storm of Destiny. Vicki Richey. LC 59-12687. 1959. Pageant Press.
Storm of Fortune: A Novel. Austin Chesterfield Clarke. LC 72-12805. 1973. 7.95 (ISBN 0-316-14700-1). Little, Brown.
Storm of Spears. Alfred Coppel. LC 75-153689. 1971. 5.95 (ISBN 0-15-185214-6). Harcourt Brace Jovanovich.
Storm of Spears. A. C. Marin. LC 75-153689. 192p. 1971. 5.95 o.p. (ISBN 0-15-185214-6). HarBraceJ.
Storm of Steel. Ernst Junger. Tr. by B. Creighton from Ger. LC 75-22372. xiii, 319p. 1975. Repr. of 1929 ed. 15.00x (ISBN 0-86527-310-3). Fertig.
Storm of the Old Frontier. Marshall R Hall. LC 27-508113. Henry Altemus Company.
Storm of Time. Eleanor O'Reilly Dark. LC 50-5357. 1950. Whittlessy House.
Storm of Wings. M. John Harrison. LC 79-7198. (Double D Science Fiction Ser.). 1980. 10.95 o.p. (ISBN 0-385-14765-1). Doubleday.
Storm of Wings. M. John Harrison. 1982. pap. 2.50 (ISBN 0-671-83585-8, Timescape). PB.
Storm of Wings: Being the Second Volume of the "Viriconium" Sequence, in Which Benedict Paucemanly Returns from His Long Frozen Dream in the Far Side of the Moon, and the Earth Submits Briefly to the Charisma of the Locust. Mike John Harrison. LC 79-7198. (Doubleday science fiction). 1980. 8.95 (ISBN 0-385-14765-1). Doubleday.
Storm of Wrath. Dwyer-Joyce, Alice. LC 77-6153. 1978. 7.95 (ISBN 0-312-76248-8). St. Martin's Press.
Storm on the Range. Max Brand. LC 83-200. 1983. 13.95. G.K. Hall.
Storm on the Range. Max Brand. 1978. 6.95 o.p. (ISBN 0-396-07599-1). Dodd.
Storm on the Range. Frederick Faust. LC 78-16728. (Silver star western). 6.95 (ISBN 0-396-07599-1). Dodd, Mead.
Storm Out of Cornwall: A Tale of the Prayer Book Rebellion, by S. M. C. Mary Catherine. LC 59-8441. 1959. P. J. Kenedy.
Storm Over Bitterhill. Paulette Warren. 256p. 1976. pap. 1.25 (ISBN 0-532-12405-7). Woodhill.
Storm Over Bitterhill. easy eye ed. Paulette Warren. pap. 0.60 o.p. Lancer.
Storm Over Eden. Helen Topping Miller. LC 37-172359. 1937. D. Appleton-Century Company, Incorporated.
Storm Over Fox Hill. Gwen Addison. (Ravenswood Gothic). 1974. (pbk.) 0.95 (ISBN 0-671-77716-5). Pocket Books.
Storm Over Paris: A Novel. Blanche Lempel. LC 54-2240. 1954. Philosophical Library.
Storm Over Paris: A Novel. Sterling Noel. LC 55-11164. 1955. Farrar, Straus and Cudahy.
Storm Over Rockall. W. Howard Baker. 1966. pap. 0.50 o.p. (50-284). Manor Bks.
Storm Over Sabrehill. Raymond Giles. 1978. 1.95 (ISBN 0-449-14018-0). Fawcett Gold Medal Books.
Storm Over the Caucasus. Barbara Bartos-Hoppner. LC 68-11226. 1968. H. Z. Walck.
Storm Over Warlock. Andre Norton, pseud. 1980. lib. bdg. 9.95 (ISBN 0-8398-2635-4, Gregg). G K Hall.
Storm Over Warlock. Andre Norton, pseud. 208p. 1982. pap. 2.25 (ISBN 0-441-78745-2, Pub. by Ace Science Fiction). Ace Bks.
Storm Over Windhaven. Marie De Jourlet. 1977. pap. 3.50 (ISBN 0-523-41967-8). Pinnacle Bks.
Storm Over Windmere. Cynthia Alcott. (Ace gothic read easy large type). 1973. (pbk.) 0.95. Ace.
Storm Over Yellowstone. C. William Harrison. (Orig.). 1972. pap. 0.60 o.p. (06181). Curtis.
Storm Point: A Novel. Ruth Eleanor McKee. LC 42-24443. 1942. Doubleday, Doran and Company, Inc.
Storm Season. Robert L. Asprin. 1982. pap. 2.95 (ISBN 0-441-78710-X, Pub. by Ace Science Fiction). Ace Bks.
Storm Signal. Gustave Frederick Mertins. 1905. The Bobbs-Merrill Company.
Storm Signals. Joseph Crosby Lincoln. LC 35-10852. 1935. D. Appleton-Century Company, Incorporated.
Storm Signals: The Anarchist) A Story of to-Day. Richard Henry Savage. LC 12-38254. (On cover: Oriental library, vol. I, no. 5). Rand, McNally & Company.
Storm-Swept: Or, Saved to Serve. Estella J Mills. 1897. J. H. Earle.
Storm the Last Rampart. David Taylor. LC 60-6392. 1960. Lippincott.
Storm Tide. Allan R Bosworth. LC 65-20981. Harper & Row.
Storm Tide. Elisabeth Ogilvie. LC 76-2371. 1976. 8.95 (ISBN 0-88411-184-9). Aeonian Press.
Storm Tide. Elisabeth Ogilvie. LC 45-8184. 1945. Thomas Y. Crowell Company.
Storm Tide. Elisabeth Ogilvie. 1975. (pbk.) 1.75 (ISBN 0-380-00551-4). Avon.
Storm to the South. Thelma Strabel. LC 44-57104. 1944. Doubleday, Doran and Co., Inc.
Storm to the South. Thelma Strabel. LC 45-9219. 1945. The Blakiston Company.
Storm-Tossed: If Communists Had the Truth... or Catholics Had the Zeal... Daniel Aloysius Lord. LC 36-7825. The Queen's Work.
Storm Trail. Arthur Moore. 1973. (pbk) 0.95. Popular Lib.
Storm Upon Ulster. Kenneth C. Flint. 320p. (Orig.). 1981. pap. 2.50 (ISBN 0-553-14622-X). Bantam.
Storm Warning. Jack Higgins, pseud. 1977. pap. 2.75 (ISBN 0-553-14054-X). Bantam.
Storm Warning. Jack Higgins, pseud. 1977. lib. bdg. 11.95 o.p. (ISBN 0-8161-6439-8, Large Print Bks). G K Hall.
Storm Warning. Jack Higgins, pseud. LC 76-3974. 1976. 8.95 (ISBN 0-03-017761-8). HR&W.
Storm Warning. Henry Patterson. LC 76-382504. (Illus.). 1976. 3.95 (ISBN 0-00-222460-7). Collins.
Storm Watch. Stephen Longstreet. 1981. pap. 2.50 (ISBN 0-8439-0882-3, Leisure Bks). Nordon Pubns.
Storm Watch: A Novel. Stephen Longstreet. LC 79-1293. 10.95 (ISBN 0-399-12330-X). Putnam.
Storm Wind Rising. Jean Rouverol. (Fawcett gold medal). 1974. (pbk.) 0.95. Fawcett.
Storm Winds. Bernard Alvin Palmer. LC 43-600. 1942. Wm. B. Eerdmans Publishing Co.
Storm Witch. Elisabeth Barr. LC 76-1638. 1976. 5.95 (ISBN 0-385-12035-4). Doubleday.
Storm Wrack. Charles Root. LC 73-139783. 1971. 5.00 (ISBN 0-8059-1523-0). Dorrance.
Stormalong. Kenneth Cook. LC 73-167445. 1972. 1.65 (ISBN 0-7260-0065-5). Gold Star Publications.
Stormalong Gert. Martha Banning Thomas. LC 36-21688. Green Circle Books.
Stormbringer. Michael Moorcock. 1977. 1.50 (ISBN 0-87997-335-8). DAW Books.
Stormbringer: Elric No. 6. Michael Moorcock. (Science Fiction Ser.). 1977. pap. 2.25 (ISBN 0-87997-335-8, UE1629). DAW Bks.
Stormbury. Eden Phillpotts. LC 32-3900. 1932. The Macmillan Company.
Stormcliff. A Tale of the Highlands. Mansfield Tracy Walworth. LC 42-26370. 1866. Carleton.
Stormcliff. A Tale of the Highlands. Mansfield Tracy Walworth. 1889. G. W. Dillingham.
Stormhaven. Jennifer Hale. pap. 0.95 o.s.i. (75-492). Lancer.
Storming Heaven. Ralph Winston Fox. LC 28-207272. Harcourt, Brace & Company.
Storming Heaven. Ralph Winston Fox. LC 28-20727. Harcourt, Brace & Company.
Storming Heaven. Richard O'Brien. (Jazz Age Ser.: No. 6). 352p. (Orig.). 1983. pap. 3.25 (ISBN 0-440-08381-8, Emerald). Dell.
Stormqueen! Marion Zimmer Bradley. LC 79-9386. (Gregg Press science fiction series). (Illus.). 1979. 9.95 (ISBN 0-8398-2504-8). Gregg Press.
Stormqueen! A Darkover Novel. Marion Zimmer Bradley. 1978. 1.95 (ISBN 0-87997-381-1). DAW Books, Inc.
Storms Blow Over. Vera Murdock Stuart Jervis. LC 43-251372. 1942. Arcadia House, Inc.
Storm's End. Rebecca Salsbury James. LC 73-20516. 1974. 6.95 (ISBN 0-385-02633-1). Doubleday.
Storm's End. Sondra Stanford. 192p. (Orig.). 1980. pap. 1.50 (ISBN 0-671-57035-8, Pub. by Silhouette Bks). S&S.
Storm's Landing. Zelda Norman Thorne. LC 73-76446. 1973. 5.95 (ISBN 0-8059-1849-3). Dorrance.
Storms of Fate. Patricia Wright. LC 80-1695. 1981. 13.95 (ISBN 0-385-17117-X). Doubleday.
Storms of Lookout Pass. E. Ellery. 5.75 o.p. Carlton.
Storms of Our Journey: And Other Stories. David Harry Walker. LC 62-13697. 1962. Houghton Mifflin.
Storms of Spring. Sandra Field. (Harlequin Romances Ser.). 192p. 1982. pap. 1.50 (ISBN 0-373-02457-6). Harlequin Bks.
Storms of Youth. Viola Roseboro' LC 20-8273. 1920. C. Scribner's Sons.
Stormspell. Anne Mather. 1982. pap. 2.95 (ISBN 0-373-89010-9). Harlequin Bks.
Stormtide. Bill Knox. LC 72-84924. 1973. 4.95 (ISBN 0-385-08539-7). Published for the Crime Club by Doubleday.
Stormtrack. James Sutherland. LC 73-21121. (Harlan Ellison discovery series:#1). 1974. (pbk.) 0.95 (ISBN 0-515-03297-2). Pyramid Books.
Stormy & the Treehouse Gang. Gerry Turner. 1966. 3.75 o.p. Concordia.
Stormy Crossing. White, Roy. LC 63-4970. 1963. Brethren Press.
Stormy Fires. Florence Jeannette Baier Ward. LC 31-1922. Macrae, Smith Company.
Stormy Hearts. Dorothy Clewes. LC 44-3341. 1944. Arcadia House, Inc.
Stormy in the West. Norman A Fox. LC 50-6974. (Silver star westerns). 1950. Dodd, Mead.
Stormy Masquerade. Anne Hampson. 192p. (Orig.). 1980. pap. 1.50 (ISBN 0-671-57004-8, Pub. by Silhouette Bks). S&S.
Stormy Night... Frances Moyer Ross Stevens. LC 37-170613. 1937. Pub. for the Crime Club, Inc., by Doubleday, Doran and Company, Inc.
Stormy Night with The Turn of the Screw. Ed. by Muriel West. LC 64-22898. 1964. Frye & Smith.
Stormy Paradise. Joy Howard. (Super Romances Ser.). 384p. 1983. pap. 2.95 (ISBN 0-373-70060-1, Pub. by Worldwide). Harlequin Bks.
Stormy Passage. Vera Murdock Stuart Jervis. 1947. Hurst & Blackett, Ltd.
Stormy Passage, No. 66. Laurel Blake. 1982. pap. 1.75 (ISBN 0-515-06677-X). Jove Pubns.
Stormy Petrel. Eleanor Elliott Carroll. LC 37-124296. The Penn Publishing Company.
Stormy Petrel. Oswald Kendall. LC 25-17934. 1925. Houghton Mifflin Company.
Stormy Petrel: An Historical Romance. John Bowles. LC 6-18281. A. Lovell & Co.; Etc., Etc.
Stormy Petrel: An Historical Romance of the Civil War. illustrated ed. John Bowles. LC 6-18280. (On cover: Modern novelists' series. no. 10). Home Book Company.
Stormy Present. Hope Field. LC 42-17989. 1942. E. P. Dutton & Co., Inc.
Stormy Range. easy eye ed. Dwight Bennett. 1968. pap. 0.60 o.p. (75-334). Lancer.
Stormy Range. Dwight Bennett Newton. LC 51-1169. (Double D western). 1951. Doubleday.
Stormy Range. Frank Chester Robertson. LC 36-6959. Godwin.
Stormy Reunion, No. 80. Jasmine Craig. 1982. pap. 1.75 (ISBN 0-515-06691-5). Jove Pubns.
Stormy Road. Thomas Rowan. LC 34-29907. 1934. I. Washburn, Inc.
Stormy Road to Freedom: A Novel. Nicholas F. Prychodko. LC 68-1925. 1968. Vantage Press.
Stormy Sea of Love. Arlene Hale. LC 80-20855. (Arlene Hale romance). 1981. 13.50 (ISBN 0-89340-292-3). J. Curley.
Stormy Sea of Love. Arlene Hale. (Signet Book). 1976. (pbk.) 0.95. New American Library.
Stormy Spring. Alice Acland. LC 55-10074. 1955. Coward-McCann.
Stormy Surrender. Janette Radcliffe, pseud. 1978. pap. 2.25 (ISBN 0-440-16941-0). Dell.
Stormy Surrender. Janette Radcliffe. (Dell Book.). 1978. 2.25 (ISBN 0-440-16941-0). Dell.
Stormy Tide. Cleo M. Stephens. (YA) 1974. 4.95 o.p. (Avalon). Bouregy.
Stormy Vigil. Elizabeth Graham, pseud. (Harlequin Romances Ser.). 192p. 1982. pap. 1.75 (ISBN 0-373-10543-6). Harlequin Bks.
Stormy Voyage. Virginia E Beck. LC 55-8984. 1955. Arcadia House.
Stormy Voyage. Joye Hoekzema. 1947. Zondervan Pub. House.
Stormy Waters. A Story of to-Day. Robert Williams Buchanan. (On cover: Seaside library. Pocket ed., no. 1074). 1888. G. Munro.
Stormy Weather. Edith Austin Holton. LC 36-13046. The Penn Publishing Company.
Stormy Wedding. Mary Edwards Bryan. (On cover: Street & Smith's select series, no. 6). 1888. Street & Smith.
Stormy Wind Fulfilling. Stephen Edward Rose. LC 47-38234. 1947. Dorrance & Company.
Storrington Papers. Dorothy Eden. LC 78-11782. 1978. 9.95 (ISBN 0-698-10962-7). Coward, McCann & Geoghegan.
Storrington Papers. Dorothy Eden. LC 79-10583. 1979. 12.95 (ISBN 0-8161-6714-1). G. K. Hall.
Story: A Critical Anthology. Ed. by Mark Schorer. LC 50-4884. (Prentice-Hall composition and introduction to literature series). 1950. Prentice-Hall.
Story: A Critical Anthology. 2d ed. Ed. by Mark Schorer. LC 67-10315. (Prentice-Hall English literature series). 1967. Prentice-Hall.
Story About a Real Man. Boris Nikolaevich Polevoi. LC 79-98870. (Library of selected Soviet literature). (Illus.). 1970. (ISBN 0-8371-3993-7). Greenwood Press.

Story and Critic. Ed. by Myron Matlaw & Leonard Lief. LC 62-16884. 1963. Harper & Row.

Story and Song. Frances Stoughton Bailey. LC 6-5027. Snow & Farnham.

Story and Structure. Laurence Perrine. LC 59-7738. 1959. Harcourt, Brace.

Story and Structure. 4th ed. Laurence Perrine. LC 73-15238. 1974. (pbk.) 5.50 (ISBN 0-15-583784-2). Harcourt Brace Jovanovich.

Story and Structure. 2d ed. Laurence Perrine. LC 66-10759. 1966. Harcourt, Brace & World.

Story and Structure. 3d ed. Laurence Perrine. LC 73-111325. 1970. Harcourt, Brace & World.

Story and Structure. 5th ed. Laurence Perrine. LC 78-104946. 6.95 (ISBN 0-15-583786-9). Harcourt Brace Jovanovich.

Story Anthology, 1931-1933: Thirty-Three Selections from the European Years of "Story", the Only Magazine Devoted Solely to the Short Story. Story. Ed. by Whit Burnett. Foley, Martha, Joint Ed. LC 33-31314. 1933. The Vanguard Press.

Story Anthology, 1931-1933: Thirty-Three Selections from the European Years of "Story," the Only Magazine Devoted Solely to the Short Story. Story (New York, 1931-) & Burnett, Whit, 1899- Ed. LC 33-31314. 1933. Vanguard Press.

Story at Canona. Based on Fact. Harold Elvin. LC 52-6240. 1950. Roy Publishers.

Story at Work: An Anthology. Ed. by Jessie C Rehder. LC 63-12620. 1963. Odyssey Press.

Story Behind the Verdict. Julia Davis Frankau. LC 15-19082. 1915. Cassell and Company, Ltd.

Story Behind the Verdict. Julia Davis Frankau. LC 15-19627. 1915. 1.35. Dodd, Mead and Company.

Story for Icarus: Projects, Incidents, and Conclusions from the Life of D., Engineer. Translated from the German by J. J. Dunbar. 1st American Ed. Ernst Schnabel. LC 60-109178. Harcourt, Brace.

Story for Teddy: And Others. Harvey Swados. LC 65-171045. 5.00. S. &S.

Story from Life. Kathleen Shepard. LC 39-34155. J. Messner.

Story Girl. Lucy Maud Montgomery. LC 11-115641. 1911. 1.50. L. C. Page & Company.

Story I Love to Tell. Victor A. Myers. (Orig.). 1980. pap. 4.25 (ISBN 0-937172-02-2). JLJ Pubs.

Story in America, 1933-1934: Thirty-Four Selections from the American Issues of "Story," the Magazine Devoted Solely to the Short Story. Story & Burnett, Whit, Ed. LC 34-36784. 1934. The Vanguard Press.

Story in America, 1933-1934: Thirty-Four Selections from the American Issues of "Story," the Magazine Devoted Solely to the Short Story. Story (New York, 1931-) & Burnett, Whit, 1890- Ed. LC 34-36784. 1934. Vanguard Press.

Story Jubilee. Story (New York, 1931-) & Burnett, Whit, 1899- Ed. LC 64-19312. 1965. Doubleday.

Story Like the Wind. Laurens Van Der Post. LC 76-182968. 1972. 7.95. Morrow.

Story Like the Wind. Laurens Van Der Post. LC 78-5688. (Harvest/HBJ book). 1978. 3.95 (ISBN 0-15-685261-6). Harcourt Brace Jovanovich.

Story: New York, 1931-) Story Jubilee. Ed. by Whit and Hallie Burnett. Ed. by Whit Burnett & Hallie Southgate Burnett. LC 64-19312. 5.95. Doubleday.

Story of a Boy. Richard Jefferies. (Puffin book). 1974. (ISBN 0-14-030677-3). Penguin.

Story of a Canon,". Beveridge Hill. 1895. Arena Publishing Company.

Story of a Cat. Emile Gigault De La Bedolliere. Tr. by Aldrich, Thomas Bailey. LC 12-360491. 1879. Houghton, Osgood and Company.

Story of a Child: Translated from the French of Pierre Loti Pseud. Julien Viaud & Smith, Caroline F., Tr. LC 1-17624. 1901. C. C. Birchard & Co.

Story of a Clergyman's Daughter: Or, Reminiscences from the Life of My Old Friend. Bertha Behrens & Wylie, Jean W., Tr. (On cover: Seaside library. Pocket ed. no. 1216). G. Munro.

Story of a Country Boy. Dawn Powell. LC 34-58987. Farrar & Rinehart, Incorporated.

Story of a Country Place. Russell Neale. LC 31-31123. 1931. Harper & Brothers.

Story of a Country Town. Edgar Watson Howe. LC 64-8889. (Rinehart editions). Holt, Rinehart and Winston.

Story of a Country Town. Edgar Watson Howe. LC 65-3274. (Signet classic, CT275). 1964. New American Library.

Story of a Country Town. Edgar Watson Howe. LC 72-84671. 1974. (ISBN 0-403-03053-6). Scholarly Press.

Story of a Country Town. Edgar Watson Howe. LC 11-17971. Houghton, Mifflin and Company.

Story of a Country Town. Edgar Watson Howe. LC 7-7123. 1884. J. R. Osgood and Company.

Story of a Country Town. Edgar Watson Howe. LC 1-274613. 1889. Houghton, Mifflin and Company.

Story of a Country Town. Edgar Watson Howe. LC 26-26999. (The American library). 1926. A. & C. Boni.

Story of a Country Town. Edgar Watson Howe. LC 28-2241. 1927. Dodd, Mead & Company.

Story of a Country Town. Edgar Watson Howe. LC 45-45006. 1883. Howe & Co.

Story of a Country Town see Collected Works.

Story of a Country Town. Ed. by Brom Weber. Edgar Watson Howe. LC 64-8889. (Rinehart eds. 127). pap., 1.45. Holt.

Story of a Country Town. Edited by Claude M. Simpson. Edgar Watson Howe. LC 61-13736. (John Harvard library). 1961. Belknap Press of Harvard University Press.

Story of a Country Town. Edited by Sylvia E. Bowman. Edgar Watson Howe. LC 61-16903. (Twayne's United States classics series). 1962. Twayne Publishers.

Story of a County Pastor. J. M. Johnson. 5.00 o.p. Vantage.

Story of a Cowhorse, Gotch. Luke Decatur Sweetman. LC 78-116053. (Illus.). 1970. 1.95. University of Nebraska Press.

Story of a Cowhorse, Gotch. Luke Decatur Sweetman. LC 36-149211. 1936. The Caxton Printers, Ltd.

Story of a Day in London. Samuel Serene. LC 8-6452. 1888. G. W. Dillingham.

Story of a Dream. Ethel Maude Colson Brazelton. LC 8-28105. 1896. C. H. Kerr & Company.

Story of a Flower: And Other Fragments Twice Gathered. Rose Porter. LC 7-374257. A. D. F. Randolph & Company.

Story of a Governess. Margaret Oliphant Wilson Oliphant. LC 7-32499. R. F. Fenno & Company.

Story of a Humble Christian. Ignazio Silone. Tr. by William Weaver from It. LC 79-95982. 1971. 5.95 o.p. (ISBN 0-06-013873-4, HarpT). Har-Row.

Story of a Lake. Negley Farson. LC 39-4168. Harcourt, Brace and Company.

Story of a Lie: And Other Tales. Stevenson, Robert Louis. LC 47-392828. 1907. Small, Maynard & Co.

Story of a Life. James B Goode. (On cover: Goode's monthly stories. no. 1). 1894. The Kansas City Novel Publishing Co.

Story of a Love. Ivan Sergieevich Shmelev & Taytovitch, Natalie, Tr. LC 31-31850. E. P. Dutton & Company, Inc.

Story of a Millionnaire. Klara Muller Mundt. Tr. by Greene, Nathaniel. LC 7-31820. 1872. D. Appleton and Company.

Story of a Mine. Bret Harte. LC 34-25490. 1878. J. R. Osgood & Company.

Story of a Mine. Bret Harte. LC 5-26225. Houghton, Mifflin and Company.

Story of a Modern Woman. Ella Hepworth Dixon. LC 6-83367. The Cassel Publishing Co.

Story of a New York House. Henry Cuyler Bunner. LC 4-15071. 1887. C. Scribner's Sons.

Story of a New Zealand River. Jane Mander. LC 20-4462. 1920. John Lane Company.

Story of a Novel: And Other Stories. Maksim Gorkii & Zakrevskain, Tr. LC 25-21418. 1925. L. MacVeagh, The Dial Press.

Story of a Pathfinder. Philander Deming. LC 77-128731. (Short story index reprint series). (Illus.). 1970. Books for Libraries Press.

Story of a Pathfinder. Philander Deming. 1907. Houghton, Mifflin and Company.

Story of a Penitent Soul. Adeline Sergeant. LC 8-6860. J. W. Lovell Company.

Story of a Play: A Novel. William Dean Howells. LC 7-57633. 1898. Harper & Brothers.

Story of a Ploughboy. James Bryce. LC 12-155655. 1912. John Lane Company.

Story of a Ploughboy. James Bryce & Markham, Edwin I. E. Charles Edwin. LC 12-10757. 1912. 1.25. John Lane Company.

Story of a Pocket Bible. A Book for All Classes of Readers. Ten Illustrations. George Etell Sargent. LC 34-38291. Carlton & Porter.

Story of a Pocket Bible. New Ed., with Corrections and Additions... George Etell Sargent. 1857. Wiley & Halsted.

Story of a Ranch. Alice Wellington Rollins. LC 7-40755. Cassell & Company, Limited.

Story of a Round Loaf. 1979. 5.95 o.p. (ISBN 0-13-850834-8). P-H.

Story of a Sculptor: And Other Stories. Frederick John Fargus. LC 6-38434. (On cover: Lovell's library. v. 12. no. 667). 1885. J. W. Lovell Company.

Story of a Shot Life. Juliana Horatia Gatty Ewing. Little, Brown, and Company.

Story of a Sin. Helen Buckingham Mathers Reeves. LC 7-30674. (On cover: Lovell's library. no. 1048). 1887. J. W. Lovell Company.

Story of a Slave: A Realistic Revelation of a Social Relation of Slave Times--Hitherto Unwritten--from the Pen of One Who Has Felt Both the Lash and the Caress of a Mistress. LC 8-16286. (On cover: The web series, no. 1). 1894. Wesley, Elmore & Benson.

Story of a Small Life. Beatrice Joy Chute. LC 70-165597. 1971. 6.95. Dutton.

Story of a Star. Fanny Du Tertre. (On cover: Once a week library, v. 10, no. 3). 1892. P. F. Collier.

Story of a Story. Margaret Lee. LC 7-12778. 1884. Ward & Drummond.

Story of a Story: And Other Stories. Brander Matthews. LC 70-98585. (Short story index reprint series). (Illus.). 1969. Books for Libraries Press.

Story of a Story: And Other Stories. Brander Matthews. LC 1-25399. 1893. Harper & Brothers.

Story of a Story & Other Stories. Brander Matthews. LC 70-98585. (Short Story Index Reprint Ser.). 1893. 16.00 (ISBN 0-8369-3159-9). Ayer Co.

Story of a Telegraph Operator. M J Herrington. (sunnyside series, no. 73). 1893. J. S. Ogilvie.

Story of a Train of Cars. A Tale of Travel... Wallace Peck. Authors Publishing Association.

Story of a Vocation. How It Came, and What Came of It. Tr. from the French. LC 8-16285. 1876. The Catholic Publication Society.

Story of a Watch and Other Sketches. B Marshall. LC 7-24669. (Silver lining series, no. 2). 1894. W. Doxey.

Story of a Welsh Girl. H. Pomeroy Brewster. LC 6-16103. 1888.

Story of a Western Claim: A Tale of How Two Boys Solved the Indian Question. Samuel C Gilman. LC 6-44034. 1893. Printed by J. B. Lippincott Company.

Story of a Whim. Grace Livingston Hill. LC 76-41322. 1975. 8.95 (ISBN 0-89190-023-3). American Reprint Co.

Story of a Whim. Grace Livingston Hill. LC 24-21145. 1924. J. B. Lippincott Company.

Story of a Whim. Grace Livingston Hill. LC 81-19939. 5.95 (ISBN 0-8007-1298-6). Revell.

Story of a Whim: By Grace Livingston Hill; Illustrations by Etheldred B. Barry. Grace Livingston Hill. LC 3-11162. The Golden Rule Co.

Story of Aaron (So Named) the Son of Ben Ali: Told by His Friends and Acqaintances. Joel Chandler Harris. LC 4-23573. 1896. Houghton, Mifflin and Company.

Story of Ab: A Tale of the Time of the Cave Man. Stanley Waterloo. LC 74-16524. (Science Fiction). (Illus.). 1975. 20.00 (ISBN 0-405-06316-4). Arno Press.

Story of Ab: A Tale of the Time of the Cave Man. 3d ed. Stanley Waterloo. LC 4-15176. 1897. Way & Williams.

Story of Ab: A Tale of the Time of the Cave Man. Stanley Waterloo. LC 35-32780. 1934. Doubleday, Doran & Company, Inc.

Story of Acadia. Grace Kinnicutt. LC 3-22104. A. Flanagan Company.

Story of Achilles: A Translation of Homer's "Iliad" into Plain English. Tr. by Rouse, William Henry Denham. LC 38-37554. 1938. T. Nelson and Sons, Ltd.

Story of Adamsville. Agnes Czerwinski Riedmann. LC 79-25624. (Illus.). 3.50 (ISBN 0-534-00823-2). Wadsworth Pub. Co.

Story of Adele H. Francois Truffaut. LC 75-42798. (Illus.). 1975. pap. 2.45 (ISBN 0-394-17908-0, B395, BC). Grove.

Story of Agatha Ann. Georgie Tillman Snead. LC 13-243196. 1913. 1.00. The John C. Winston Co.

Story of an Abduction in the Seventeenth Century. Jacob Van Lennep. LC 8-348655. 1891. W.S. Gottsberger & Co.

Story of an African Farm. Olive Schreiner. LC 76-9143. 1976. 4.95 (ISBN 0-8052-0547-0). Schocken Books.

Story of an African Farm. Olive Schreiner. LC 75-1530. (Victorian Fiction: Novels of Faith and Doubt; V. 78). 1975. (ISBN 0-8240-1602-5). Garland Pub.

Story of an African Farm. Olive Schreiner. LC 79-26665. (Penguin modern classics, 197). 1971. (u.s.) 1.45 (ISBN 0-14-000197-2). Penguin Books.

Story of an African Farm. Olive Schreiner. LC 24-16886. Little, Brown, and Company.

Story of an African Farm. Olive Schreiner & Young, Francis Brett. LC 27-26628. (Half-title: The modern library of the world's best books). 1927. The Modern Library.

Story of an African Farm. A Novel. Olive Schreiner. LC 8-30411. 1888. Roberts Brothers.

Story of an African Farm: A Novel. Olive Schreiner. (On cover: Lovell's library, no. 1203). 1888. J. W. Lovell Company.

Story of an African Farm. A Novel. Olive Schreiner. (On cover: Seaside library. Pocket ed. no. 1120). 1888. G. Munroe.

Story of an African Farm. A Novel. Olive Schreiner. LC 24-28520. (On cover: The home library). A. L. Burt.

Story of an African Farm. A Novel. Olive Schreiner. LC 4-17549. 1900. Little, Brown, and Company.

Story of an African Farm. A Novel. Olive Schreiner. LC 19-18458. 1918. Little, Brown, and Company.

Story of an African Farm. A Novel. Olive Schreiner. LC 20-23163. 1920. Little, Brown, and Company.

Story of an African Farm. A Novel. Olive Schreiner. LC 46-43885. Little, Brown, and Company.

Story of an African Farm: By Olive Schreiner. Afterword by Doris Lessing. Olive Schreiner & Francis Brett Young. (Master work ser., R374). 1968. Fawcett.

Story of an American Farm: A Novel. Olive Schreiner. 1978. Repr. of 1883 ed. lib. bdg. 15.00 (ISBN 0-8495-4832-2). Arden Lib.

Story of an East-Side Family. Lillian Williams Betts. 1903. Dodd, Mead and Company.

Story of an Enthusiast. Told by Himself. Cecilia Viets Dakin Jamison. LC 7-10328. 1888. Ticknor and Company.

Story of an Heiress. Mabel Collins Cook. LC 11-10565. United States Book Company.

Story of an Honest Man. Edmond Francois Valentin About. LC 1-1608. 1880. D. Appleton and Company.

Story of an Old House: The Strategy of Grandma Terrence. Aurelia Rice. LC 22-4676. T. Todd.

Story of an Unfamed Hero. N Eleanor Dement. LC 26-10841. 1926. Morehouse Publishing Company.

Story of an Untold Love. Paul Leicester Ford. LC 6-41392. 1897. Houghton, Mifflin and Company.

Story of an Untold Love. 18th thousand ed. Paul Leicester Ford. LC 9-1823. 1897. Houghton, Mifflin and Company.

Story of an Untold Love. 73d thousand ed. Paul Leicester Ford. LC 16-25050. Houghton, Mifflin and Company.

Story of an Untold Love. 30th thousand ed. Paul Leicester Ford. LC 6-413910. 1898. Houghton, Mifflin and Company.

Story of Andrea Fields. Elizabeth Seifert. 1974. (pbk.) 0.95. New American Library.

Story of Andrea Fields: A New Novel. Elizabeth Seifert. LC 50-10178. 1950. Dodd, Mead.

Story of Andrea Fields: A New Novel. Elizabeth Seifert. LC 73-79156. 1973. 6.95. Aeonian Press.

Story of Antony Grace. George Manville Fenn. LC 42-26803. 1888. D. Appleton and Company.

Story of Antony Grace. George Manville Fenn. LC 6-39255. (On cover: Lovell's library, no. 1129). 1888. J. W. Lovell Company.

Story of Aranka Ickovic Lowy: The Ugly Duckling (Non-Fiction Autobiography with Reference to WW II in Europe) Aranka I. Lowy. LC 81-90799. (Illus.). 52p. (Orig.). 1982. pap. 3.00x (ISBN 0-9602940-1-5). Lowy Pub.

Story of Atlantis & the Lost Lemuria. W. Scott-Elliott. 4.00 o.p. (ISBN 0-7229-0030-9). Theos Pub Hse.

Story of Aunt Shlomzion the Great. Yoram Kaniuk. LC 78-2066. 10.00 (ISBN 0-06-012259-5). Harper & Row.

Story of Avis. Elizabeth Stuart Phelps Ward. LC 76-51681. (Recovered Fiction by American Women). 1977. 22.00 (ISBN 0-405-10058-2). Arno Press.

Story of Avis. Elizabeth Stuart Phelps Ward. LC 3-24492. 1877. J. R. Osgood and Company.

Story of Avis. Elizabeth Stuart Phelps Ward. LC 5-33980. Houghton, Mifflin and Company.

Story of Babette: A Little Creole Girl. Ruth McEnery Stuart. LC 4-16160. 1894. Harper & Brothers.

Story of Baloney with Beans & Macaroni. Eduardo L. DiGirolamo. 64p. 1976. 4.00 o.p. (ISBN 0-682-48589-6). Exposition.

Story of Bawn. Katharine Tynan Hinkson, pseud. 1907. A. C. McClurg & Co.

Story of Beryl. Charles Woodward Hutson. LC 7-9025. 1888. J. B. Alden.

Story of Bessie Costrell. Mary Augusta Arnold Humphry Ward Ward. LC 8-34856. 1895. Macmillan and Co.

Story of Billy Owen: An Historical Novel of the Great Oil Industry. John Garretson. LC 18-21533. 1918. 1.25. The Neale Publishing Company.

Story of Borge. Hans Christian Branner. Tr. by Kristi Planck from Danish. LC 73-1593. (Library of Scandinavian Literature). 1973. lib. bdg. 18.50x (ISBN 0-8057-3359-0). Irvington.

Story of Burnt Njal. George W. Dasent. 1971. 9.95x (ISBN 0-460-00558-8, Evman); pap. 3.50x (ISBN 0-460-01558-3, Evman). Biblio Dist.

Story of California. Stewart Edward White. LC 75-126679. 1975. 48.50 (ISBN 0-404-06936-3). AMS Press.

Story of California... Stewart Edward White. LC 32-35814. 1932. Doubleday, Doran & Company, Inc.

Story of California... Stewart Edward White. LC 37-112522. 1937. The Sun Dial Press, Inc.

Story of California... Stewart Edward White. LC 40-12664. 1940. Halcyon House.

Story of Carnival. Mary A. M. Hoppus Marks. LC 7-24675. (Seaside library, v. 80, no. 1612). 1883. G. Munro.

Story of Cecilia. Katharine Tynan Hinkson, pseud. LC 11-28366. 1911. 1.25. Benzinger Brothers.

Story of Champ D'Asile. Ed. by Fannie E. Ratchford. Tr. by Donald Joseph. 1969. Repr. of 1937 ed. 7.95 o.p. (ISBN 0-8114-7696-0). Steck-V.

Story of Chester Lawrence: Being the Completed Account of One Who Played an Important Part in "Piney Ridge Cottage,". Nephi Anderson. LC 14-502. 1913. 0.75. The Deseret News.

Story of Ch'ing. John LaCrosse. 1979. pap. 3.00 (ISBN 0-932282-46-6). Caledonia Pr.

Story of Christina. Mary Harriott Norris. LC 7-21537. 1907. The Neale Publishing Company.

Story of Christine Rochefort. Helen Choate Pratt Prince. 1895. Houghton, Mifflin and Company.

Story of Colette: From the French, "La Neuvaine De Colette" in the "Revue Des Deux Mondes.". Jeanne Shultz. LC 3-28193. D. Appleton and Company,

Story of Colette: From the French of La Neuvaine De Colette; with Six Full-Page Illustrations and Thirty Vignettes. Jeanne Schultz. LC 8-2051. 1891. D. Appleton and Company.

Story of Cyrano De Bergerac. Founded Upon and Written from the Play of That Name Which Was Written. Anne O'Hagan & Rostand, Edmond. LC 98-1347. (peerisess series, no. 110). 1898. J. S. Ogilvie Publishing Company.

Story of Daisy. A True Record of the Life of a Little Child. Mary J Cravens. LC 99-22. 1898. The B. F. Wade Co., Printers.

Story of Damon and Pythias. Albert Payson Terhune. LC 15-2390. Grosset and Dunlap.

Story of Dan. Mary E. Sweetman Blundell. LC 6-14200. 1804. Houghton Mifflin and Company.

Story of Daphnis and Chloe: A Greek Pastoral. Longus & William Douglas Lowe. LC 78-18586. (Greek Texts and Commentaries). 1979. 15.00 (ISBN 0-405-11428-1). Arno Press.

Story of Doctor King. Grace Doonan & Franciscans. Commissariat of the Holy Land. LC 44-9353. 1944. The Commissariat of the Holy Land.

Story of Dr. Wassell... James Hilton. LC 43-511186. 1943. Little, Brown and Company.

Story of Don Miff: As Told by His Friend John Bouche Whacker. A Symphony of Life. 2d ed. Virginius Dabney. LC 24-149479. 1886. J. B. Lippincott Company.

Story of Doris Summerday. Findlay Sackett. LC 27-12294. E. R. Starr Co.

Story of Dorothy Grape, and Other Tales. Ellen Price Henry Wood Wood. (On cover: Seaside library. Pocket ed. no. 610). 1885. G. Munro.

Story of Dorothy Stanfield: Based on a Great Insurance Swindle, and a Woman! Oscar Micheaux. LC 46-250742. 1946. Book Supply Company.

Story of Duciehurst: A Tale of the Mississippi. Mary Noailles Murfree. LC 14-122853. 1914. The Macmillan Company.

Story of Edah. Mary Ruth Evans. LC 15-401. 1914. 1.50. Broadway Publishing Co.

Story of Eddystone. (Illus.). 1974. Repr. of 1928 ed. 8.95 o.s.i. (ISBN 0-911760-16-4). Glenwood.

Story of Eden. Dolf Wyllarde. 1902. J. Lane.

Story of Elizabeth. A Novel. Anne Isabella Thackeray Ritchie. LC 8-28088. T. B. Peterson & Brothers.

Story of Esther Costello. Nicholas Monsarrat. LC 53-6845. 1953. Knopf.

Story of Food: A History of Man's Search for Things to Eat. Anne Jolliffe. LC 75-9056. (Illus.). 1967. Hawthorn Books.

Story of Fort Frayne. Charles King. LC 7-1495. F. T. Neely.

Story of Fort Hill. Giving an Account of Many Interesting Adventures Between the Whites and Indians, Previous to the Settlement of Auburn, and When Fort Hill Was an Indian Battle Ground. Frederic Prince. LC 7-30095. 1859. P. J. Becker.

Story of Francis Cludde. Stanley John Weyman. LC 13-9695. Cassell Publishing Company.

Story of Francis Cludde. Stanley John Weyman. 1898. Longmans, Green, and Co.

Story of Gosta Berling. Selma Ottiliana Lovisa Lagerlof. LC 76-48430. (Classics of European Literature). (Hyperion library of world literature). 1977. 14.95. (ISBN 0-88355-556-5) (ISBN 0-88355-557-3). Hyperion Press.

Story of Gosta Berling. Selma Ottiliana Lovisa Lagerlof. Tr. by Flach, Pauline Bancroft. 1910. Little, Brown, and Company.

Story of Gosta Berling. Selma Ottiliana Lovisa Lagerlof. Tr. by Flach, Pauline Bancroft. LC 26-26898. 1926. Doubleday, Page & Company.

Story of Gosta Berling. Selma Ottiliana Lovisa Lagerlof. Tr. by Flach, Pauline Bancroft. 1898. Little, Brown and Company.

Story of Gotton Connixloo: Followed by Forgotten. Camille Mayran. Tr. by Van Wyck Brooks. LC 20-110728. (Half-title: The library of French fiction, ed. by B. J. Beyer). E. P. Dutton & Company.

Story of Grettir the Strong. Eirikr Magnusson & William Morris. LC 79-41587. (Illus.). 1980. 17.50 (ISBN 0-8154-0517-0). G. Prior Publishers.

Story of Hannah. Jennie Maria Drinkwater Conklin. R. Carter & Brothers.

Story of Happinolande: And Other Legends. Oliver Bell Bunce. LC 6-18677. (On cover: The Gainsborough series). 1889. D. Appleton and Company.

Story of Harold. Terry Andrews. (Equinox Book). 1975. (pbk.) 4.95 (ISBN 0-380-00403-8). Avon.

Story of Harold: A Novel. Terry Andrews. LC 73-9313. 1974. 7.95 (ISBN 0-03-011791-7). Holt, Rinehart and Winston.

Story of Hassan (Hassan Ali Shah) A Novel of India. John Anthony. LC 29-20443. E.P. Dutton & Co. Inc.

Story of Helen Troy. Constance Cary Harrison. LC 7-2887. 1881. Harper & Brothers.

Story of Helen Troy. Constance Clay Harrison. LC 9-100398. Harper & Brothers.

Story of Helga. Rudolf Herzog. Tr. by Lewisohn, Adele (Guggenheimer) LC 13-254002. 1.35. E. P. Dutton & Company.

Story of Induraja. A Novel. Hilda Wernher. LC 48-858675. 1948. Doubleday.

Story of Inyo. W. A. Chalfant. 1980. 18.95 (ISBN 0-912494-34-4); pap. 12.50 (ISBN 0-912494-35-2). Chalfant Pr.

Story of Ivy. Marie Adelaide Belloc Lowndes. LC 26-102973. 1928. N. Y., Doubleday, Doran & Company, Inc.

Story of Ivy: By Emily Noble Pseud. James Noble Gifford. LC 54-131191. 1954. Arcadia House.

Story of Janet Court. Glenn Eldridge Sheley. LC 48-9055. 1948. Murray & Gee.

Story of Jean Valjean: From Victor Hugo's Les Miserables. Victor Marie Hugo & Wiltse, Sara Elize, 1849- Ed. (On cover: Classics for children). 1897. Ginn & Company.

Story of Joanna. Gerard Damiano & Justin Collin. LC 76-1821. 1976. pap. 1.95 o.p. (ISBN 0-8021-4023-8, GP4023). Grove.

Story of Joanna: A Film by Gerard Damiano. Justin Collin & Gerard Damiano. LC 76-1821. 1.95 (ISBN 0-8021-4023-8). Strawberry Hill Pub. Co.: Distributed by Whirlwind Book Co.

Story of John Trevennick. Walter C Rhoades. LC 7-30590. 1893. Macmillan and Co.

Story of Joseph. Ellen Thompson. LC 12-7204. The C. M. Clark Publishing Co.

Story of Julia Page. Kathleen Thompson Norris. LC 15-18568. 1915. Doubleday, Page & Company.

Story of Julia Page. Kathleen Thompson Norris. LC 17-835168. 1916. Doubleday, Page & Company.

Story of Julia Page. Kathleen Thompson Norris. LC 21-867368. 1920. Doubleday, Page & Company.

Story of Julian. Susan Ertz. LC 31-22244. 1931. D. Appleton and Company.

Story of Kastan: A Novel. 1st Ed. C Whitworth Ekberg. LC 54-5554. 1954. Exposition Press.

Story of Keedon Bluffs. Mary Noailles Murfree. LC 22-108422. 1899. Houghton, Mifflin, and Company.

Story of Kennett. cedarcroft ed. Bayard Taylor. LC 3-19668. 1903. G. P. Putnam's Sons.

Story of Kennett. household ed. Bayard Taylor. LC 8-25657. (Publisher's lettering on book: Bayard Taylor's works). 1894. G. P. Putnam's Sons.

Story of King Sylvain and Queen Aimee. Margaret Pollock Sherwood. LC 4-7533. 1904. The Macmillan Company.

Story of Lawrence Garthe. Ellen Warner Olney Kirk. LC 7-12507. 1894. Houghton, Mifflin and Company.

Story of Layla and Majnun. Nizami Ganjavi & Rudolf Gelpke. LC 78-58219. 1978. 5.95 (ISBN 0-87773-133-0). Shambhala.

Story of Leatherstocking. James Fenimore Cooper. Ed. by Marble, Mrs. Annie (Russell) LC 26-17968. 1926. D. Appleton and Company.

Story of Leland Gay. Weekes, Agnes Russell, pseud. LC 32-574827. 1932. Dodd, Mead & Company.

Story of Little Black Sambo. Helen Bannerman. LC 31-9804. Henry Altemus Company.

Story of Little Black Sambo: With "Pop-up" Picture by C. Carey Cloud. (On cover: The midget pop-up books). Blue Ribbon Press.

Story of Little Black Sambo: With Twenty-Seven Full-Page Illustrations in Color by Kurt Wiese; Animations by A. V. Warren. LC 33-36721. Garden City Publishing Co., Inc.

Story of Little David. Charles Dickens. LC 3-20058. (Famous children of literature series...). 1903. D. Estes & Company.

Story of Little Nell. Charles Dickens. Ed. by Gordon, Jane. LC 1-31852. (Eclectic school readings). 1901. American Book Company.

Story of Little Nell: From Old Curiosity Shop. Charles Dickens. (Standard literature series. no. 22). University Publishing Company.

Story of Little Nell: From The Old Curiosity Shop of Charles Dickens; Illustrated by Etheldred B. Barry. Charles Dickens. LC 2-18034. (Famous children of literature series...). 1902. D. Estes & Company.

Story of Little Paul: From the Dombey and Son. Charles Dickens. LC 4-22838. (Famous children of literature series). 1904. D. Estes & Company.

Story of Little Tom and Maggie from The Mill on the Floss of George Eliot; Illustrated by Frank T. Merrill and Others. George Eliot. LC 3-20449. (Famous children of literature series). 1903. D. Estes & Company.

Story of Lola Gregg. Howard Melvin Fast. LC 56-319973. 1956. Blue Heron Press.

Story of Manon Lescaut and of the Chevalier Des Grieux. Antoine Francois Prevost. Tr. by Gundry, Arthur W. LC 22-4766. Belford Company.

Story of Manon Lescaut and of the Chevalier Des Grieux. Antoine Francois Prevost. Tr. by Gundry, Arthur W. LC 7-30054. 1887. F. T. Jones & Co.

Story of Manon Lescaut and the Chevalier Des Grieux. Antoine Francois Prevost. Tr. by Waddell, Heleh Jame. LC 36-70. 1935. The Heritage Press.

Story of Many Colors: Or, Romance in a Lodging-House. William J. B Stabb. LC 4-1650. 1903. Dickerman Publishing Co.

Story of Marcel, the Little Mettray Colonist: And Other Tales, Original, Translated, and Selected. LC 8-16108. 1876. The Catholic Publication Society.

Story of Marco. Eleanor Hodgman Porter. LC 11-28359. Jennings and Graham.

Story of Margaret Kent: A Novel. Ellen Warner Olney Kirk. 1886. Ticknor and Company.

Story of Margaret Kent: A Novel. 2d ed. Ellen Warner Olney Kirk. 1886. Ticknor and Company.

Story of Margredel: Being a Fireside History of a Fifeshire Family. copyright american ed. David Storrar Meldrum. LC 7-25854. 1894. G. P. Putnam's Sons.

Story of Marie De Rozel: Huguenot. Alicia Stuart Aspinwall. LC 6-31383. 1906. E. P. Dutton and Company.

Story of Martin Coe. Ralph Delahaye Paine. 1906. The Outing Publishing Co.

Story of Mary. William Loring Spencer. LC 8-14076. 1885. G. W. Carleton & Co.; Etc., Etc.

Story of Mary. William Loring Nunez Spencer. LC 72-2124. (Black Heritage Library Collection). 1972. 14.75 (ISBN 0-8369-9064-1). Books for Libraries Press.

Story of Mary MacLane. Mary MacLane. 1902. H. S. Stone and Company.

Story of Mary MacLane. new ed., with a chapter on the present (1911) ed. Mary MacLane. LC 11-18977. 1911. Duffield & Company.

Story of Matka: A Tale of the Mist-Islands. David Starr Jordan & Clark, George Archibald. LC 10-739. 1910. Whitaker & Ray-Wiggin Co.

Story of Matka: A Tale of the Mist Islands. David Starr Jordan & Clark, George Archibald. LC 21-10020. (Animal life series). 1921. World Book Company.

Story of Mia. Judith Piccone. 1969. pap. 0.75 o.p. (75-254). Manor Bks.

Story of Misjean: A Work of Misjean & Her Uncle. George Hetherington Smith. 1942. G. H. Smith.

Story of Moby Dick: The White Whale. Herman Melville. Retold by Frank Lee Beals. LC 49-48155. (Famous Story Series). 1949. B. H. Sanborn.

Story of Mollie. Marian Bower. LC 6-16085. 1897. Roberts Brothers.

Story of Mona Sheehy. Edward John Moreton Drax Plunkett Dunsany. LC 40-4884. 1940. Harper & Brothers.

Story of Monica & Her Son Augustine. Leon Cristiani. 1977. 3.95 o.s.i. (ISBN 0-8198-0461-4); pap. 2.95 o.s.i. (ISBN 0-8198-0462-2). Dghtrs St Paul.

Story of Mrs. Murphy... Natalie Anderson Scott. LC 47-303629. 1947. E. P. Dutton & Company, Inc.

Story of Muhammad Hanafiyyah: A Medieval Muslim Romance. Tr. by L. F. Brakel. (Bibliotheca Indonesica: No. 16). 1977. pap. 22.00 (ISBN 90-247-2010-9, Pub. by Martinus Nijhoff Netherlands). Kluwer Boston.

Story of My Desire: A Novel. Philip Callow. LC 76-382649. 1976. 3.50 (ISBN 0-370-10557-5). Bodley Head.

Story of My Life. new ed. Helen Keller. Ed. by C. N. Douglas. (Illus.). 64p. (gr. 5-10). 1974. 5.00 (ISBN 0-88301-216-2); pap. text ed. 1.95 (ISBN 0-88301-140-9). Pendulum Pr.

Story of My Misfortunes. Peter Abelard. Tr. by Henry A. Bellows. (o.s.i.). 128p. 1972. pap. 1.95 o.s.i. (ISBN 0-02-083020-3). Macmillan.

Story of My Village. Henry De Vere Stacpoole. LC 47-210404. Hutchinson & Co., Ltd.

Story of Nancy Meadows. Louise Platt Hauck. LC 33-2525. The Penn Publishing Company.

Story of Niagara. To Which Are Appended Reminiscences of a Custom House Officer. Charles R Edwards. LC 6-36571. 1870. Breed, Lent & Co.

Story of O. Pauline Reage. 1973. pap. 2.50 (ISBN 0-345-28913-7). Ballantine.

Story of O. Pauline Reage. LC 77-93975. (Illus.). 1978. 25.00 o.p. (ISBN 0-8021-0159-3, GP0159). Grove.

Story of O. Pauline Reage. Tr. by Sabine D'Estree from Fr. (Illus.). 1966. pap. 1.95 o.p. (ISBN 0-394-17909-9, B396, BC). Grove.

Story of O. Pauline Reage. Tr. by Sabine D'Estree from Fr. LC 66-13262. (Illus.). 1976. pap. 1.95 o.p. (ISBN 0-8021-4002-5, GP4002, Dist. by Whirlwind Bk. Co.). Grove.

Story of O. Pauline Reage. Tr. by Sabine D'Estree from Fr. (Illus.). 1966. pap. 1.95 o.p. (ISBN 0-394-17909-9, B396, BC). Grove.

Story of O: Part Two, Return to the Chateau. Pauline Reage. Tr. by Sabine D'Estree from Fr. LC 77-155130. Orig. Title: Retour a Roissy. 158p. 1980. pap. 2.95 (ISBN 0-394-17658-8, B364, BC). Grove.

Story of Old Bill Marshall: A Sage of the Schoharie Valley. Horatio Milo Pollock. LC 48-28261. 1948. Printed by the Middleburgh Pub. Co.

Story of Old Fort London. Mary Noailles Murfree. The Macmillan Company; London.

Story of Old Fort Loudon. Mary Noailles Murfree. LC 73-104531. (Illus.). 1970. Literature House.

Story of Oliver Twist. Charles Dickens. Ed. by Kirk, Ella Boyce. LC 6-26418. (Half-title: Appletons' home reading books... Division iii, biography, etc.). 1897. D. Appleton and Company.

Story of Oliver Twist. Charles Dickens. LC 35-14890. Whitman Publishing Company.

Story of Paul Jones: An Historical Romance. Alfred Henry Lewis. LC 6-16735. 1906. G. W. Dillingham Company.

Story of Peace and Other War Stories. Harry Fornari. LC 76-54818. 1977. 5.95. Aurora Publishers.

Story of Phaedrus: How We Got the Greatest Book in the World. Newell Dwight Hillis. LC 14-7074. 1914. The Macmillan Company.

Story of Philip Methuen. authorized ed. Mary Anna Lupton Needell. LC 7-23097. 1895. D. Appleton and Company.

Story of Queen Esther. E Leuty Collins. (On cover: Alliance library, no. 7). Street & Smith.

Story of Realmah. Arthur Helps. LC 7-13287. 1888. Roberts Brothers.

Story of Richard Trent. Mary Hornibrook Cummins. LC 15-20987. 1915. 1.00. Davis & Bond.

Story of Rob Roy. Walter Scott & Harris, Edith D. (Appletons' home reading books). 1898. D. Appleton & Co.

Story of Rodman Heath: Or, Mugwumps. Robert Thaxter Edes. 1894. Arena Publishing Company.

Story of Rolf and the Viking's Bow. Allen French. LC 4-24565. 1904. Little, Brown, and Company.

Story of Ronald Kestrel. Alec John Dawson. LC 118. (Half-title: Appletons' town and county library, no. 277). 1899. D. Appleton and Company.

Story of Rosabelle Shaw. Dorothy Emily Stevenson. LC 39-1744. Farrar & Rinehart, Incorporated.

Story of Roy Bean: Law West of the Pecos. C. L. Sonnichsen. (Illus.). 1972. pap. 0.95 o.p. (M2547, GM). Fawcett World.

Story of Sam Tag, Age from Ten to Fifteen: From 1860 to 1865. Samuel Jackson Kennerly. LC 12-61967. 1911. 1.00. The Cosmopolitan Press.

Story of Sarah. Mary Louise Foster. LC 1-30982. 1901. Brentano's.

Story of Seven Maidens. 1972. pap. 1.95 o.s.i. (V1065T, Venus). Grove.

Story of Shep. Bertha E Jaques. LC 12-25537. 1912. 1.00. T. Rubovits, Printer.

Story of Sibylle. Octave Feuillet & T. M. H., Tr. LC 6-39538. (On cover: Osgood's library of novels, no. 28). 1872. J. R. Osgood and Company.
Story of Siegfried. James A. Baldwin. 1898. Repr. 30.00 (ISBN 0-8274-3520-7). R West.
Story of Silas Woodward. Elisabeth Wilkins Thomas. LC 32-280950. Brewer, Warren and Putnam.
Story of Sir Charles Vorcker: A Tale of Romance and Adventure. Jessie A Gaugham. LC 27-25428. 1927. P.J. Kenedy & Sons.
Story of Six Loves. Richard Carroll Johnson. LC 55-12517. 1955. Pageant Press.
Story of Skippy. Percy Leo Crosby. LC 34-12695. (On cover: The big little books). Whitman Publishing Company.
Story of Sodom, a Biblical Episode. W. C Kitchin. LC 7-14758. 1891. Hunt & Eaton.
Story of Stephen Compton: A Novel. John Edward Patterson. LC 13-122. 1.25. Hodder & Stoughton, George H. Doran Company.
Story of Susan. Alice Dudeney. LC 4-3935. 1904. Dodd, Mead & Company.
Story of Swan-Like. Antoinette Elizabeth Gazzam Galvin. LC 12-212821. R. G. Badger.
Story of Terry: A Romantic Novel... Harriet Theresa Smith Comstock. LC 45-21688. (On cover: A Bart house novel, 18). 1945.
Story of the Bed. Walter Dusenbery. 1970. pap. 2.00. White Rabbit.
Story of the Carol. Edmondstoune Duncan. LC 69-16805. 1968. Repr. of 1911 ed. 31.00 o.p. (ISBN 0-8103-3547-6). Gale.
Story of the Champions of the Round Table. Howard Pyle. (Illus.). 9.50 (ISBN 0-8446-0229-9). Peter Smith.
Story of the Days to Come. Herbert George Wells. LC 77-360463. (Corgi book). 1976. 0.45 (ISBN 0-552-10185-0). Corgi.
Story of the Days to Come see Three Prophetic Novels.
Story of the Edinburgh Burns Relics with Fresh Facts About Burns & His Family. Robert Duncan. LC 75-42242. 1976. Repr. of 1910 ed. lib. bdg. 20.00 (ISBN 0-8414-3722-X). Folcroft.
Story of the Eye. Georges Bataille. LC 77-11983. 5.95 (ISBN 0-916354-90-3). Urizen Books.
Story of the Fast Mail: Lincoln J. Carter's Great Play. A Novel. Charles Thornton. (patrol detective series, no. 3). 1891. The Continental Publishing Co.
Story of the Foss River Ranch: A Tale of the Northwest. Ridgwell Cullum. 1903. L. C. Page & Company.
Story of the Gadsbys. Rudyard Kipling. LC 9-3024. F. F. Lovell Company.
Story of the Gadsbys. Rudyard Kipling. LC 42-274851. (With, as issued, his In black and white. New York, 1899). 1899. R. F. Fenno & Company.
Story of the Gadsbys: A Tale Without a Plot. authorized ed. Rudyard Kipling. LC 7-12348. (On cover: Lovell's Westminster series, no. 4). 1890. J. W. Lovell Company.
Story of the Gadsbys. In Black and White. Rudyard Kipling & Bridgman, Lewis Jesse, 1857- Illus. LC 4876. H. M. Caldwell Company.
Story of the Gadsbys. In Black and White. The Works of Rudyard Kipling. Rudyard Kipling. LC 9-16422. 1909. The Nottingham Society.
Story of the Glittering Plain see Glittering Plain.
Story of the Glittering Plain: Which Has Also Been Called the Land of Living Men or the Acre of the Undying. new ed. William Morris. LC 4-16844. 1898. Longmans, Green, and Co.
Story of the Glittering Plain: Which Has Been Also Called the Land of Living Men or the Acre of the Undying. William Morris. (Newcastle forgotten fantasy library). (Illus.). 1973. (pbk.) 2.45 (ISBN 0-87877-100-X). Newcastle Pub. Co.
Story of the Glittering Plain: Which Has Been Also Called the Land of Living Men or the Acre of the Undying. pocket ed.; new impression. ed. William Morris. LC 36-138907. (Longmans' pocket library). 1924. Longmans, Green and Co.
Story of the Glittering Plain Which Has Been Also Called the Land of Living Men or the Acre of the Undying. William Morris. LC 80-19460. (Newcastle Forgotten Fantasy library; v. 1). 1980. 9.95 (ISBN 0-87877-500-5). Borgo Press.
Story of the Grateful Crane: A Japanese Folktale. Jennifer Bartoli & Kozo Shimizu. LC 77-3969. (Illus.). 1977. 6.25 (ISBN 0-8075-7630-1). A. Whitman.
Story of the Heavenly Camp-Fires: By One with a New Name. Edward Payson Tenney & One with a New Name, Pseud. LC 8-26045. 1896. Harper & Brothers.
Story of the House of Israel: Or, The Hebrew's Pilgrimage to the. Holy City: Comprising a Picture of Judaism in the Century Which Proceded. the Birth of Our Saviour. Gerhard Friedrich Abraham Strauss & Kenrick, John, 1788-1877, Tr. LC 8-16893. 1839. J. B. Lippincott & Co.
Story of the Huguenots: A Sixteenth Century Narrative Wherein the French Spaniards, and Indians Were the Actors. Florian Alexander Mann. LC 99-1320. (Florida historical tales). 1898. Mann & Mann.
Story of the Iliad. Eric Trevor Owen. LC 47-30648. (Ann Arbor paperbacks, AA117). 1966. University of Michigan Press.
Story of the Little Angels. Laura Spencer Portor. LC 17-24282. 1917. 0.50. Harper & Brothers.
Story of the Other Wise Man. Henry Van Dyke. LC 59-11521. (Revell Inspirational Classic). 1959. Revell.
Story of the Other Wise Man. Henry Van Dyke. LC 73-180912. (Inspiration Three V. 5). (Pivot family reader). 1973. (pbk.). 1.25. Keats Pub.
Story of the Other Wise Man. Henry Van Dyke. LC 8-30224. 1896. Harper & Brothers.
Story of the Other Wise Man. Henry Van Dyke. LC 7-74396. 1898. Harper & Brothers.
Story of the Other Wise Man. Henry Van Dyke. LC 99-5766. (Little books by famous writers). 1899. Harper & Brothers.
Story of the Other Wise Man. Henry Van Dyke. LC 41-12282. 1940. Harper & Brothers.
Story of the Other Wise Man. Henry Van Dyke. LC 43-27343. 1900. Harper & Brothers.
Story of the Other Wise Man. Henry Van Dyke & Flanagan, J. R., Illus. LC 20-20004. Harper & Brothers.
Story of the Peasant-Boy Philosopher: Or, "The Child Gathering Pebbles on the Sea-Shore." (Founded on the Early Life of Ferguson, the Shepherd-Boy Astronomer, and Intended to Show How a Poor Lad Became Acquainted with the Principles of Natural Science. Henry Mayhew. LC 4-31675. 1856. Harper & Brothers.
Story of the Seas. A Romance in Reality of a Sailor's Life. Fred D Baars. LC 6-5041. Baars and Neeley.
Story of the Seven Princesses. Nizami. Ed. & tr. by R. Gelpke. 1976. pap. text ed. 12.75x (ISBN 0-85181-042-X). Verry.
Story of the Stone: A Chinese Novel in Five Volumes. Chan Ts'Ao. Tr. by David Hawkes. LC 74-165360. (Penguin classics). (Illus.). (v. 1) 0.75 (ISBN 0-14-044293-6). Penguin.
Story of the Stone: A Chinese Novel in Five Volumes. Chan Ts'Ao & David Hawkes. LC 78-20279. (Chinese Literature in Translation). 25.00 (ISBN 0-253-19266-8). Indiana University Press.
Story of the Stone (The Dream of the Red Chamber), Vol. 1: The Golden Days. Xuequin Cao. Tr. by David Hawkes from Chinese. LC 78-20279. (Chinese Literature in Translation Ser.). 544p. 1979. 25.00x (ISBN 0-253-19261-7). Ind U Pr.
Story of the Stone (The Dream of the Red Chamber), Vol. 2: The Crab-Flower Club. Xuequin Cao. Tr. by David Hawkes from Chinese. LC 78-20279. (Chinese Literature in Translation Ser.). 608p. 1979. 25.00x (ISBN 0-253-19262-5). Ind U Pr.
Story of the Stone: The Dream of the Red Chamber, 2 vols. Xuequin Cao. Tr. by David Hawkes from Chinese. LC 78-20279. (Chinese Literature in Translation Ser.). 1979. 25.00x ea. Ind U Pr.
Story of the Stone, Vol. 1: The Golden Days. Xuequin Cao. Tr. by David Hawkes. (Classics Ser.). 1974. pap. 6.95 (ISBN 0-14-044293-6). Penguin.
Story of the Stone, Vol. 2: The Crab-Flower Club. Xuequin Cao. Tr. by David Hawks. (Classics Ser.). 1977. pap. 8.95 (ISBN 0-14-044326-6). Penguin.
Story of the Stone, Vol. 3: The Warning Voice. Xuequin Cao. Tr. by David Hawkes. 1981. pap. 8.95 (ISBN 0-14-044370-3). Penguin.
Story of The Three Musketeers. Frank Lee Beals & Bailey, Bernadine (Freeman) (Famous Story Series). 1948. B. H. Sanborn.
Story of the Tomb of Gold. Thomas Alva Stubbins. LC 33-775. 1932. Meador Publishing Company.
Story of the Volsungs & Niblungs: With Certain Songs from the Elder Edda. Eirikr Magnusson & William Morris. LC 79-41588. 1980. 17.50 (ISBN 0-86043-403-6). G. Prior Publishers.
Story of the Weasel. Carolyn Slaughter. LC 76-367238. 1976. 3.25 (ISBN 0-246-10887-8). Hart-Davis MacGibbon.
Story of Three Girls (Women Must Weep) A Novel. Edgar Fawcett. LC 6-38779. (On cover: The library of choice fiction. no. 38). Laird & Lee.
Story of Three Sisters. Cecil Maxwell. LC 7-17921. (Leisure hour series. no. 64). 1876. H. Holt and Company.
Story of Thyrza. Alice Brown. LC 9-5521. 1909. Houghton Mifflin Company.
Story of Tonty. Mary Hartwell Catherwood. LC 6-20171. 1890. A. C. McClurg and Company.
Story of Tonty. 6th ed., with new introduction by the author. ed. Mary Hartwell Catherwood. LC 2-1062. 1901. A. C. McClurg & Co.
Story of Troilus. Ed. by R. K. Gordon. (Mediaeval Academy Reprints for Teaching Ser.). 1979. pap. 6.50 (ISBN 0-8020-6368-3). U of Toronto Pr.
Story of Two Lives. Gertrude Bloede. LC 6-14213. Cassell Publishing Company.
Story of Ulla. Edwin Lester Linden Arnold. LC 1-21252. 1895. Longmans, Green, and Co.
Story of Valentine and His Brother. Margaret Oliphant Wilson Oliphant. (Seaside library, v. 26, no. 542). 1879. G. Munro.
Story of Valentine and His Brother. A Novel. Margaret Oliphant Wilson Oliphant. LC 24-14946. 1875. Harper & Brothers.
Story of Venus and Tannhauser.... a Romantic Novel, by Aubrey Beardslly. Aubrey Vincent Beardsley. (A235N K). Tandem Bks.
Story of Waitstill Baxter. Kate Douglas Smith Wiggin. LC 13-21262. 1913. Houghton Mifflin Company.
Story of Waldemar Krone's Youth. Herman Frederik Ewald. LC 6-38134. 1868. J. B. Lippincott & Co.
Story of Wan and the Remarkable Shrub: And The Story of Ching-Kwei and the Destinies. Ernest Bramah Smith. LC 28-10389. Doubleday, Doran & Company, Inc.
Story of Welthy Ann. Norma Smith Tweedie, Illustrator. Gladys Sylvester Tweedie. LC 54-255733. 1953. Prestile Pub. Co.
Story of Wool. Sara Ware Bassett. LC 13-241132. 1913. The Penn Publishing Company.
Story of Wunnee-Neetunah: Or, The Life of an Indian Princess of Connecticut; a Tale of Truth. Mathias Spiess. LC 34-22744. 1934. Meador Publishing Company.
Story or Two from an Old Dutch Town. Robert Traill Spence Lowell. 1878. Roberts Brothers.
Story Pocket Book. Story. Ed. by Whit Burnett. LC 45-2042. 1944.
Story Pocket Book. Story (New York, 1931-) & Burnett, Whit, 1899- Ed. LC 45-2042. 1944. Pocket Books.
Story Reader's Garland: A Cluster of Tales. Rufus Charles Maclellan. LC 21-8709. 1849. Printed by J. D. Toy.
Story So Far. George Bowering. LC 72-183860. (Illus.). 1971. 3.00. Coach House Press.
Story Survey. Ed. by Harold William Blodgett. LC 39-15270. J. B. Lippincott Company.
Story Survey. Rev. Ed. Ed. by Harold William Blodgett. LC 53-543. 1953. Lippincott.
Story-Tell Lib. Annie Trumbull Slosson. LC 5144. 1900. C. Scribner's Sons.
Story-Tell Lib. Annie Trumbull Slosson. LC 13-33857. 1903. C. Scribner's Sons.
Story-Teller. Highsmith, Patricia. LC 65-22584. 1965. Published for the Crime Club by Doubleday.
Story Teller. MacKinlay Kantor. LC 67-10415. 1967. Doubleday.
Story Teller. Norton, Charles Eliot, 1827-1908, Ed. LC 10-10551. (Young folks' library... T. B. Aldrich, editor-in-chief. v. 1). Hall and Locke Company.
Story-Teller's Holiday. George Moore. LC 29-12465. 1928. Issued for Subscribers Only by H. Liveright.
Story-Teller's Pack. Frank Richard Stockton. LC 72-3287. (Short story index reprint series). 1972. (ISBN 0-8369-4162-4). Books for Libraries Press.
Story-Teller's Pack. Frank Richard Stockton. LC 4-15162. 1897. C. Scribner's Sons.
Story Teller's Story. Sherwood Anderson. Ed. by Ray L. White. (Major Fiction of Sherwood Anderson Ser.). 1968. 8.95 o.p. (ISBN 0-8295-0129-0). Pr of Case WR.
Story That Ends with a Scream, and Eight Others. James Leo Herlihy. LC 67-20795. 1967. Simon and Schuster.
Story That the Keg Told Me: And The Story of the Man Who Didn't Know Much. William Henry Harrison Murray. LC 7-32492. (Half-title: The Adirondack tales, v. 1). Cupples and Hurd.
Story, the Fiction of the Forties. Story. Ed. by Burnett, Whit & Burnett, Hallie Southgate. LC 49-49094. 1949. Dutton.
Story, the Yearbook of Discovery.
Story: The Yearbook of Discovery, Third Series. Ed. by Whit Burnett & Hallie Southgate Burnett. LC 70-105337. 1970. pap. 3.65 o.p. (1619, Four Winds). Schol Bk Serv.
Story to Tell: And Other Tales. Peter Fleming. LC 42-10018. 1942. C. Scribner's Sons.
Story Without a Name. Jules Amedee Barbey D'Aurevilly. Tr. by Edgar Evertson Saltus. LC 7-2160. (On cover: The Bel-espirit series. v. 1. no. 1). Belford and Company.
Story Without a Name. Barbey D'Aurevilly, Jules Amedee & Saltus, Edgar Evertson, 1858- Tr. LC 19-7719. 1919. Brentano's.
Story Without a Name. Arthur John Arbuthnott Stringer & Holman, Russell, Joint Author. LC 24-29639. Grosset & Dunlap.
Story Without Ending (Hekeyah bela Bidayah) Najib Mahfuz. (Arabic.). 5.50x (ISBN 0-86685-155-0). Intl Bk Ctr.
Story Workshop. Wilbur Lang Schramm. LC 38-22496. 1938. Little, Brown and Company.
Story: Yearbook of Discovery, Fourth Series. Whit Burnett & Hallie Burnett. 1971. pap. 3.85 o.p. (1869, Four Winds). Schol Bk Serv.
Storyteller. Leslie Marmon Silko. LC 80-20251. (Illus.). 9.95 (ISBN 0-86579-004-3). Seaver Books.
Storyteller. Alan Sillitoe. LC 80-17998. 1980. 11.95 (ISBN 0-671-41263-9). Simon and Schuster.
Storytelling, It's Easy. Ethel Barrett. pap. 5.95 (ISBN 0-310-20561-1, Pub. by Cowman). Zondervan.
Storytime. (Illus.). 1973. William Collins Sons.
Storytime Blue. Charles J. Quarto. 1982. write for info. (ISBN 0-9609344-0-5); pap. 9.95 (ISBN 0-9609344-1-3). G D Kieffer.
Stove. Jakov Lind. 110p. 1983. 13.95 (ISBN 0-935296-26-3); pap. 7.95 (ISBN 0-935296-27-1). Sheep Meadow.
Stover at Yale. Owen McMahon Johnson. LC 68-22128. 1968. 1.50. Collier Books.
Stover at Yale. Owen McMahon Johnson. LC 12-814220. 1912. 1.35. Frederick A. Stokes Company.
Stover at Yale. 7th ed. Owen McMahon Johnson. LC 21-8679. Frederick A. Stokes Company.
Stover at Yale. Owen McMahon Johnson. LC 26-7519. 1925. Little, Brown, and Company.
Stowaway. Francisco Coloane. 3.00 o.p. Twayne.
Stowaway. Charles Munoz. LC 57-5375. 1957. Random House.
Stowaway. Louis Tracy. LC 9-28271. E. J. Clode.
Stowaway: A Novel. 1st Ed. Lawrence Sargent Hall. LC 61-5314. 1961. Little, Brown.
Stowaway from St. Tropez. 1st Ed. Charles Terrot. LC 60-12097. 1960. Dutton.
Stowaway Girl. Louis Tracy. LC 12-337593. 1912. E. J. Clode.
Stowaway to Mars. John Beynon Harris. (Gold medal bk., T2646). 1972. Fawcett.
Stowaway to Mars. John Wyndham, pseud. (Orig.). 1972. pap. 0.75 o.p. (T2646, GM). Fawcett World.
Stowaway to the Moon: The Camelot Odyssey. William Roy Shelton. LC 73-79709. 1973. 5.95 (ISBN 0-385-08447-1) (ISBN 0-385-08447-1). Doubleday.
Stowaway. 1st Amer. Ed. Ronald Johnston. LC 66-222787. 1966. 4.50. Harcourt.
Stowaway's Inheritance. Margaret Carter. LC 13-1642. 1912. 1.25. The Bookery.
Stowmarket Mystery: Or, A Legacy of Hate. Louis Tracy. LC 4-10076. 1904. R. F. Fenno & Company.
Strack Selections from Booth Tarkington's Stories. Booth Tarkington & Strack, Lilian Holmes. LC 26-17112. 1926. Walter H. Baker Company.
Stradella. Francis Marion Crawford. LC 9-249437. 1909. The Macmillan Company.
Stradella. rev. ed. James Sherwood. LC 67-24104. 1967. Grove Press.
Stradella. Rev.Ed. James Sherwood. (Zebra bks., Z1020). 1968. pap., 1.25. Grove.
Straggler. A. Holk. 3.95 o.p. Wehman.
Straight. Steve Knickmeyer. LC 75-40017. 6.95 (ISBN 0-394-40190-5). Random House.
Straight. Steve Knickmeyer. (Kangaroo Book). 1977. 1.75 (ISBN 0-671-80946-6). Pocket Books.
Straight and Narrow Path. Honor Lilbush Wingfield Tracy. LC 56-8791. 1956. Random House.
Straight and Narrow Path. Honor Lilbush Wingfield Tracy. LC 58-3470. (Modern library paperbacks, P43). 1958. Random House.
Straight Cut Ditch. Richard Andersen. LC 79-101026. 1979. 8.95 (ISBN 0-87949-139-6). Ashley Books.
Straight Down a Crooked Lane. Francena Harriet Arnold. LC 59-4911. 1959. Moody Press.
Straight Down: Memoirs by the King of the Beach. Ron Bernstein. 218p. 1977. pap. 4.95 (ISBN 0-915520-08-7). Ross-Erikson.
Straight Down the Crooked Lane. Bertha Runkle. LC 15-190731. 1915. 1.35. The Century Co.
Straight from Boothill. William L Hopson. LC 47-4517. 1947. Phoenix Press.
Straight from the Heart. Clara B. Brooks. 1977. 5.00 o.p. (ISBN 0-533-02827-2). Vantage.
Straight Man. Kent Nelson. LC 77-88656. (Black lizard book). 3.50 (ISBN 0-916870-11-1). Creative Arts Book Co.
Straight Road. Grace MacGowan Cooke & MacGowan, Alice. LC 17-13077. 1917. George H. Doran Company.
Straight Sapling. Rachel Swete Macnamara. LC 26-17281. Small, Maynard & Company.
Straight Shooting. Wilbur Tuttle. LC 26-22318. 1926. Garden City Publishing Co., Inc.
Strain of White. Ada Woodruff Anderson. LC 9-10650. 1909. Little, Brown, and Company.

Strait and Narrow: A Novel. 1st American Ed. Geoffrey Cotterell. LC 51-9340. 1951. Lippincott.

Strait Gate. Ruth Comfort Mitchell. LC 35-164773. 1935. D. Appleton-Century Company, Incorporated.

Strait Is the Gate: A Novel. Albert Benjamin Cunningham. LC 46-785. 1946. E. P. Dutton & Company, Inc.

Strait Is the Gate: La Porte Etroite. Andre Paul Guillaume Gide. LC 79-23999. 1980. 10.00 (ISBN 0-8376-0453-2). R. Bentley.

Strait Is the Gate (La Porte Etroite) Translated from the French of Andre Gide. Andre Paul Guillaume Gide. Tr. by Bussy, Dorothy (Strachey) LC 24-461918. 1924. A. A. Knopf.

Straitjacket. Edita Morris. 1978. 7.95 o.p. (ISBN 0-517-53257-3). Crown.

Strand. Vi Englund. LC 77-76176. 6.95 (ISBN 0-9601258-0-9). Golden Owl Publishers.

Strand. Claire Rayner. LC 80-39954. (Her The Performers; book 8). 1981. 11.95 (ISBN 0-399-12537-X). Putnam.

Strand see Trafalgar Square.

Stranded, a Story of New York in 1875. Peter Burchard. LC 67-24211. (Illus.). 1967. Coward-McCann.

Stranded: A Story of the Garden City. Edgar Rice Beach. LC 6-10284. (On cover: The sterling series, no. 1). 1890. Donohue, Henneberry & Co.

Stranded in Arcady. Francis Lynde. LC 17-14177. 1917. C. Scribner's Sons.

Stranded in the Sulu Sea. Floyd Clinton Turner. LC 56-12760. Pageant Press.

Strange Adventures of a House Boat. William Black. LC 6-12913. (Lovell's library. no. 1182). 1888. J. W. Lovell Company.

Strange Adventures of a House-Boat. A Novel. William Black. LC 42-27062. Harper & Brothers.

Strange Adventures of a House-Boat. A Novel. William Black. (Harper's Franklin square library, no. 622). 1888. Harper & Brothers.

Strange Adventures of a House-Boat. A Novel. William Black. LC 13-17738. (Seaside library. Pocket ed., no. 1096). 1887. G. Munro's Sons.

Strange Adventures of a Phaeton. William Black. (Lovell's library, v. 4, no. 143). J. W. Lovell Company.

Strange Adventures of a Phaeton. William Black. (Seaside library. Pocket ed., no. 50). G. Munro.

Strange Adventures of a Phaeton: Novel. library ed. William Black. LC 4-16500. Harper & Brothers.

Strange Adventures of Bromley Barnes. George Barton. LC 18-19575. 1918. The Page Company.

Strange Adventures of Captain Dangerous. A Narrative in Plain English, Attempted. George Augustus Henry Sala. LC 8-5792. 1863. T. O. H. P. Burnham.

Strange Adventures of Captain Dangerous: Who Was a Soldier, a Pirate, a Merchant, a Spy, a Slave Among the Moors, a Bashaw in the Serive of the Great Turk, and Died at Last in His Own House in Hanover Square. A Narrative in Plain English Attempted. George Augustus Henry Sala. (Harper's Franklin square library, no. 517). 1886. Harper & Brothers.

Strange Adventures of Captain Runnelstoke. Alfred James Fritchey. LC 12-6822. 1912. 1.00. The Cosmopolitan Press.

Strange Adventures of James Shervinton: And Other Stories. Louis Becke. LC 26-27689. 1926. J. B. Lippincott Company.

Strange Adventures of Jonathan Drew, a Rolling Stone: During His Travels Through Massachusetts, Connecticut, Rhode Island, New York, Pennsylvania, Virginia, Ohio, Indiana, Illinois, Missouri & Kentucky in the Years 1821-24; Together with Some Account of the People He Met, the Things They Did and Said, the Songs They Sang and the Roads They Travelled, As Taken Down. Christopher Ward. LC 32-6890. 1932. Simon and Schuster, Inc.

Strange Adventures of Lucy Smith. Francis Charles Philips. (On cover: Lovell's library, no. 1082). 1887. J. W. Lovell Company.

Strange Adventures of Lucy Smith. Francis Charles Philips. (On cover: Seaside library. Pocket ed. no. 1038). 1887. G. Munro.

Strange Adventures of Mr. Collin. Gunnar Serner & Lee, Robert Emmons, Tr. LC 26-326724. Thomas Y. Crowell Company.

Strange Adventures of Mr. Middleton. Wardon Allan Curtis. LC 3-25883. 1903. H. S. Stone & Company.

Strange Adventures on Other Worlds. Leigh Brackett. (best of planet stories, 1). 1975. (pbk.) 1.25 (ISBN 0-345-24334-X). Ballantine Books.

Strange Adventures Under the Sea. S. H. Skaife. 1964. 1.65 o.s.i. Tri-Ocean.

Strange Alphabet: A Novel. Alexis Lykiard. LC 78-104649. 1970. 5.95 (ISBN 0-8128-1281-6). Stein and Day.

Strange and Fantastic Stories: Fifty Tales of Terror, Horror and Fantasy. Ed. by Joseph A. Margolies. LC 46-7566. Whittlesey House, McGraw-Hill Book Company, Inc.

Strange and Gracious Gift. Letty M Shaw. LC 55-21254. Story Book Press.

Strange and Ill-Starred Marriage. Helen Tucker. (Fawcett Crest Book). 1978. 1.50 (ISBN 0-449-23535-1). Fawcett Pub.

Strange & the Unknown. Ed. by Fate Magazine Editors. (Fate Mysteries Ser., No. 2). 1971. pap. 0.75 o.p. (64-559). Paperback Lib.

Strange Attraction. Jane Mander. LC 22-199102. 1922. Dodd, Mead and Company.

Strange Avenue. Ethel May Kelley. LC 32-4751. Farrar & Rinehart, Incorporated.

Strange Awakening. Jacques Perdue. LC 55-35049. 1955. Castle Books.

Strange Awakening. Dorothy Quick. LC 39-17503. House of Field, Inc.

Strange Barriers see Black & the White.

Strange Beasts and Unnatural Monsters. Philip Van Doren Stern. LC 68-29492. (Fawcett crest book). 1968. 0.60. Fawcett Publications.

Strange Beauty. Maysie Greig. LC 38-38329. 1938. Doubleday, Doran and Company, Inc.

Strange Beauty. Maysie Greig. LC 40-33289. 1939. The Sun Dial Press, Inc.

Strange Bed. Brownie Cole. LC 46-4276. 1946. Phoenix Press.

Strange Bedfellow. Evelyn Berckman. LC 56-57408. (Read badge detective). 1956. Dodd, Mead.

Strange Bedfellow. Evelyn Berckman. LC 56-5740. (Signet book). 1975. (pbk.) 1.25. New American Library.

Strange Bedfellows. Evelyn Berckman. 1977. Repr. of 1956 ed. lib. bdg. 7.95 o.p. (ISBN 0-89244-032-5). Queens Hse.

Strange Bedfellows. Maggie MacKeever. (Coventry Romance Ser.: No. 189). 192p. 1982. pap. 1.50 (ISBN 0-449-50292-9, Coventry). Fawcett.

Strange Bedfellows. Ed. by Thomas N. Scortia. LC 72-2749. 1973. 5.95 o.p. (ISBN 0-394-48155-0). Random.

Strange Bedfellows of Montague Hmes. Norton S Parker. LC 53-9726. 1953. Hermitage House.

Strange Bedfellows: Sex and Science Fiction. Ed. by Thomas N. Scortia. LC 72-5611. 1972. 5.95 (ISBN 0-394-48155-0). Random House.

Strange Bedfellows: Sex and Science Fiction. Ed. by Thomas N. Scortia. 1974. (pbk.) 0.95 (ISBN 0-671-77794-7). Pocket Books.

Strange Bedmates. Elliot Storm. LC 35-2183. W. Godwin, Inc.

Strange Betrothal. Mary Grace Halpine. (On cover: Munro's library. v. 1. no. 404). 1885. N. L. Munro.

Strange Blooming. Francis Rufus Bellamy. LC 48-1511. 1948. E. P. Dutton.

Strange Blue Yawl. Lucille Fletcher, pseud. LC 64-11994. 1964. Random House.

Strange Boarders of Palace Crescent. Edward Phillips Oppenheim. LC 34-29558. 1934. Little, Brown, and Company.

Strange Brigade: A Story of the Red River and the Opening of the Canadian West. John Edward Jennings. LC 52-5517. 1952. Little, Brown.

Strange Brother. Blair Niles. LC 75-12341. (Homosexuality). 1975. 12.00 (ISBN 0-405-07390-9). Arno Press.

Strange Brother. Blair Niles. LC 31-214313. H. Liveright, Inc.

Strange Capers. Arthur Meeker. LC 21-119087. 1931. Covici, Friede.

Strange Career of Bishop Sterling: A Novel. Stephen Endicott. LC 32-12601. The Meteor Press.

Strange Career of Bishop Sterling: A Novel. Walter Adolphe Roberts. LC 73-18603. 1974. (ISBN 0-404-11413-X). AMS Press.

Strange Case of Big Harry. Frosty Johnson, pseud. 1972. 6.00 o.p. (ISBN 0-682-47556-4). Exposition.

Strange Case of Billy Biswas. Arun Joshi. 1971. 6.00x o.p. (ISBN 0-210-22385-5). Asia.

Strange Case of Billy Biswas. Arun Joshi. 1974. pap. 3.50 (ISBN 0-88253-387-8). Ind-US Inc.

Strange Case of Cavendish. Randall Parrish. LC 19-26545. George H. Doran Company.

Strange Case of Deacon Brodie. Forbes Bramble. LC 75-31754. 1976. 8.95 (ISBN 0-698-10723-3). Coward, McCann & Geoghegan.

Strange Case of Dr. Bruno. Ferdinand Eugene Daniel. LC 6-437873. Guarantee Publishing Co.

Strange Case of Dr. Earle. Freeman Wills Crofts. LC 33-768826. 1933. Dodd, Mead & Company.

Strange Case of Dr. Jekyll and Mr. Hyde, and Other Stories. Robert Louis Stevenson & Jenni Calder. LC 81-133520. (Penguin English library). 1979. 2.95 (ISBN 0-14-043117-9). Penguin Books.

Strange Case of Dr. Jekyll and Mr. Hyde: And Their Famous Tales. Robert Louis Stevenson. LC 61-8312. (Great illustrated classics). 1961. Dodd, Mead.

Strange Case of Dr. Jekyll and Mr. Hyde. The Merry Men and Other Tales and Fables. medallion ed. Robert Louis Stevenson. LC 14-13024. 1909. Current Literature Publishing Co.

Strange Case of Dr. Jekyll & Mr. Hyde, the Merry Men, & Other Tales. Robert Louis Stevenson. 1977. 9.95x (ISBN 0-460-00767-X, Evman); pap. 2.95x (ISBN 0-460-01767-5, Evman). Biblio Dist.

Strange Case of Dr. Jekyll and Mr. Hyde. Robert Louis Stevenson. 1952. Limited Editions Club.

Strange Case of Dr. Jekyll and Mr. Hyde. Robert Louis Stevenson. LC 67-10994. (Illus.). 1967. F. Watts.

Strange Case of Dr. Jekyll and Mr. Hyde. Robert Louis Stevenson. (On cover: Seaside library. Pocket ed. no. 686). 1886. G. Munro.

Strange Case of Dr. Jekyll and Mr. Hyde. authorized ed. Robert Louis Stevenson. LC 24-28519. 1888. C. Scribner's Sons.

Strange Case of Dr. Jekyll and Mr. Hyde. Robert Louis Stevenson. 1904. Scott-Thaw Company.

Strange Case of Dr. Jekyll and Mr. Hyde. Robert Louis Stevenson. Ed. by Burton, Richard. LC 20-823312. (Living literature series, R. Burton, PH. D., editor-in-chief). The Gregg Publishing Company.

Strange Case of Dr. Jekyll and Mr. Hyde. Robert Louis Stevenson. LC 44-27430. American Publishers Corporation.

Strange Case of Eleanor Cuyler. Kingsland Crosby. LC 10-234038. 1910. 1.20. Dodd, Mead and Company.

Strange Case of Eric Marotte: A Modern-Historical Problem-Romance of Chicago. John Irving Pearce. LC 13-25611. 1913. 1.50. Press of P. F. Pettibone & Company.

Strange Case of Gunner Rawley. Walter Frederick Morris. LC 30-27752. 1930. Dodd, Mead & Company.

Strange Case of John R. Graham. Victor Kutchin. LC 29-9366. 1929. Dean & Company.

Strange Case of Mary Page. Frederick Lewis Collins. LC 16-7235. 1916. E. J. Clode.

Strange Case of Mary Page. Frederick Lewis. LC 16-723564. E. J. Clode.

Strange Case of Miss Annie Spragg. Louis Bromfield. LC 28-21419. 1928. Frederick A. Stokes Company.

Strange Case of Miss Annie Spragg. Louis Bromfield. LC 34-38269. 1930. Grosset & Dunlap.

Strange Case of Mr. Henry Marchmont. Joseph Smith Fletcher. LC 27-22484. 1927. A. A. Knopf.

Strange Case of Mr. Pelham. Anthony Armstrong. 1981. 18.95x (Pub. by Remploy England). State Mutual Bk.

Strange Case of Mr. Pelham. Anthony Armstrong Willis. LC 57-5779. 1957. Published for the Crime Club by Doubleday.

Strange Case of Mortimer Fenley. Louis Tracy. LC 20-2642. E. J. Clode.

Strange Case of Pauline Wilton. James Gardner. LC 17-13189. Broadway Publishing Company.

Strange Case of Peter the Lett. Georges Simenon. LC 33-18218. Covici, Friede.

Strange Case of "William" Cook. Clifford James Wheeler Hosken. LC 29-7209. 1928. Harper & Brothers.

Strange Case: Or, The Convict's Plot. Dennis O'Sullivan. (On cover: Munro's library, popular novels, v. 1, no. 416). N. L. Munro.

Strange Cases of Dr. Stanchon. Josephine Dodge Daskam Bacon. LC 13-8320. 1913. 1.30. D. Appleton and Company.

Strange Cases of Magistrate Pao. Leon Comber. (Writing in Asia Ser.). 1972. pap. text ed. 5.50x (00200). Heinemann Ed.

Strange Cases of Magistrate Pao: Chinese Tales of Crime and Detection. Translated from the Chinese and Retold by Leon Comber. Illus. by Lo Koon-Chiu. Tr. by Comber, Leon. LC 64-19359. 1964. C. E. Tuttle Co.

Strange Cases of Mason Brant. Nevil Monroe Hopkins. LC 16-11041. 1916. J. B. Lippincott Company.

Strange Chief: The Story of a Glorious Heritage. Grace Isabel Lane Berkeley. LC 29-6444. The Judson Press.

Strange Children. Caroline Gordon. LC 51-12447. 1951. Scribner.

Strange Children. Caroline Gordon. LC 71-164525. 1971. (ISBN 0-8154-0394-1). Cooper Square Publishers.

Strange Code of Justice. Reymoure Keith Isely. LC 73-22659. (Black bat mystery). 1974. 6.50 (ISBN 0-672-51935-6). Bobbs-Merrill.

Strange Code of Justice. Reymoure K. Isley. LC 73-22659. (Black Bat Mystery Ser). 208p. 1974. 6.50 o.p. (ISBN 0-672-51935-6). Bobbs.

Strange Combat. Coralie Hobson. LC 31-75643. 1931. Brewer & Warren Inc.

Strange Companion: A Story of Survival. Dayton O. Hyde. LC 74-22309. (Illus.). 1975. 7.95 (ISBN 0-87690-156-9). Dutton.

Strange Companion: A Story of Survival. Dayton O. Hyde. (Fawcett Crest Book). (Illus.). 1977. 1.50 (ISBN 0-449-23298-0). Fawcett Pubns.

Strange Companions. John Cranstoun Nevill. LC 29-3181. 1929. Little, Brown, and Company.

Strange Conditions. Fannie E Newberry. A. I. Bradley & Company.

Strange Conflict. Dennis Yates Wheatley. 1978. 9.50 (ISBN 0-09-043531-1, Pub. by Hutchinson). Merrimack Pub Cir.

Strange Conflict. Translated by James A. Galston. 1st Ed. Olga Woller. LC 55-837794. 1955. Pageant Press.

Strange Conquest: Translaied by Ransom T. Taylor. Alfred Neumann. LC 54-9672. (Ballantine books, 88).

Strange Corner. Mildred B Davis. LC 67-11193. 1967. Published for the Crime Club by Doubleday.

Strange Countess. Edgar Wallace. LC 26-6477. Small, Maynard & Company.

Strange Courage. Evan Evans, pseud. 213p. 1975. Repr. of 1952 ed. lib. bdg. 12.95x (ISBN 0-89190-211-2). Am Repr-Rivercity Pr.

Strange Courage. Frederick Faust. LC 76-41739. 1976. 7.95 (ISBN 0-89190-211-2). American Reprint Co.

Strange Crime in Bermuda. Elisabeth Sanxay Holding. LC 37-19753. 1937. Dodd, Mead & Company.

Strange Crimes. William Westall. LC 8-36226. (On cover: Lovell's international series, no. 94). J. W. Lovell Company.

Strange Crimes of Passion. Leonard Gribble. 1970. 8.00 o.p. (ISBN 0-09-100350-4, LTB). Soccer.

Strange Daughter. Louella Annette Pitts Woolfolk. LC 42-9587. 1942. J. Swift.

Strange Death of a Doctor. Louise Platt Hauck. LC 33-7569. The Penn Publishing Company.

Strange Death of Manny Square. Albert Benjamin Cunningham. LC 41-172461. 1941. E. P. Dutton & Co., Inc.

Strange Death of Martin Green... Zenith Jones Brown. LC 31-2439. 1931. Pub. for the Crime Club, Inc., by Doubleday, Doran & Company, Inc.

Strange Desires. Originally Titled What D'ya Know for Sure. Len Zinberg. LC 48-10521. (Avon monthly novel, 6). 1948. Avon Novels.

Strange Desires. Twelve Stories. Ed. by J Vernon Shea. LC 54-30495. (Lion book, 191). 1954. Lion Books by Arrangement with Classic Syndicate.

Strange Disappearance. Anna Katharine Green Rohlfs. LC 11-7140. (On cover: Knickerbocker novels). 1880. G. P. Putnam's Sons.

Strange Disappearance of Eugene Comstocks. Mary R. Platt Hatch. LC 7-2838. 1895. G. W. Dillingham.

Strange Disappearance of Mary Young. Milton Morris Propper. LC 29-854634. 1929. Harper & Brothers.

Strange Disapperance. Mary Grace Halpine. LC 7-12023. (On cover: Munro's library. v. 1. no. 409). N. L. Munro.

Strange Disclosure: A Tale of New England Life... Lydia Louisa Anna Very. J. H. Earle.

Strange Discovery. Charles Romyn Dake. LC 75-17518. (Gregg Press science fiction series). 1975. 14.00 (ISBN 0-8398-2302-9). Gregg Press.

Strange Discovery. Charles Romyn Dake. 1899. H. I. Kimball.

Strange Doings. R. A Lafferty. (Illus.). 1973. 0.95. Daw Books.

Strange Doings. R. A Lafferty. LC 72-162759. 1972. (ISBN 0-684-12530-7). Scribner.

Strange Doings on Halfaday Creek. James Beardsley Hendryx. LC 43-510094. 1943. Doubleday, Doran and Company, Inc.

Strange Doings on Halfaday Creek. James Beardsley Hendryx. LC 45-20695. The Sun Dial Press.

Strange Duel: Or, Helene Buderoff. Martha Morton. LC 7-32481. (On cover: Series of American novels, no. 28). Lovell, Coryell & Company.

Strange Elation. Prudence Martin. (Candlelight Ecstasy Ser.: No. 93). (Orig.). 1982. pap. 1.95 (ISBN 0-440-17505-4). Dell.

Strange Elopment. William Clark Russell. LC 13-7656. 1892. Macmillan and Co.

Strange Enchantment. Hermina Black. 1972. pap. 0.75 o.p. (94206). Beagle Bks.

Strange Enchantment. Geoffrey Cotterell. LC 57-6236. 1957. Lippincott.

Strange Eons. Robert Bloch. LC 78-66962. (Illus.). 1979. 12.00 (ISBN 0-918372-30-5); signed-slipcased ed 25.00x (ISBN 0-918372-29-1). Whispers.

Strange Exile. Laura Saunders. LC 52-7002. 1952. Bouregy.

Strange Exile. Laura Saunders. 1974. (pbk.) 0.75. Dell.

Strange Fancies: A Novel. Fred S Brown. LC 6-18945. 1888. F.S. Brown.

Strange Fate No. 1. Ed. by Fate Magazine Editors. 1971. pap. 0.75 o.p. (64-516). Paperback Lib.

Strange Fires. Clement Wood. LC 51-5877. 1951. Woodford Press.
Strange Flaw. Henry S. Wilcox. LC 6-28450. 1906. Thompson & Thomas.
Strange Fraternity: By M. Coates Webster... Marriott Coates Webster. LC 34-8138. The Macaulay Company.
Strange Friend of Tito Gil. Pedro Antonio De Alarcon & Darr, Lizzie (Townsend) "Mrs. Francis J. A. Darr.". LC 6-33059. A. Lovell & Co.
Strange Fruit. Phyllis Bottome. LC 28-249480. 1928. Houghton Mifflin Company.
Strange Fruit. Lillian Eugenia Smith. LC 44-4605. 1944. Reynal & Hitchcock.
Strange Fugitive. Morley Callaghan. LC 28-204203. 1928. C. Scribner's Sons.
Strange Games. new ed. Heller Toren. (Osi). 1973. 5.95 o.s.i. (ISBN 0-671-27099-0). Trident.
Strange Games: A Novel. Heller Toren. LC 72-93486. 1973. 5.95 (ISBN 0-671-27099-0). Trident Press.
Strange Gateways. E. Hoffmann Price. LC 68-549. 1967. Arkham House.
Strange Gift. Adelyn Bushnell. LC 51-10939. 1951. Coward-McCann.
Strange Gifts: Eight Stories of Science Fiction. Robert Silverberg. LC 75-14036. 1975. 6.95 (ISBN 0-8407-6460-X) (ISBN 0-8407-6460-X). T. Nelson.
Strange Glory. Paul C. Brown. (Geneva Books). 1968. 3.00 o.p. Carlton.
Strange Glory. Gerry Goldberg. LC 77-76635. (Illus.). 1977. 10.95 o.p. (ISBN 0-312-76387-5); pap. 5.95 o.p. (ISBN 0-312-76388-3). St Martin.
Strange Glory. Leopold Hamilton Myers. LC 36-9229. Harcourt, Brace and Company.
Strange God. Thomas Savage. LC 74-1230. 1974. 7.95 (ISBN 0-316-77143-0). Little, Brown.
Strange Gods. Ed. by Roger Elwood. 1974. (pbk.) 0.95 (ISBN 0-671-77754-8). Pocket Books.
Strange Gods: A Novel. Constance Woodbury Dodge. LC 39-23865. The Penn Publishing Company.
Strange Happenings: Tales of the Caribbean. Lionel Belasco. LC 74-132375. 90p. 1973. pap. 1.95 (ISBN 0-88238-076-1). Law-Arts.
Strange Harvest. Mildred Burcham Hart. LC 36-10239. 1936. The Caxton Printers, Ltd.
Strange Harvest. Inez Haynes Irwin. LC 34-6195. The Bobbs-Merrill Company.
Strange Harvest. Donald Wandrei. LC 65-29534. 1965. 4.00. Arkham.
Strange Holiness. Robert P. Coffin. LC 78-8151. 1978. lib. bdg. 8.50 o.p. (ISBN 0-89621-003-0); pap. 3.95 (ISBN 0-89621-002-2). Thorndike Pr.
Strange Honeymoon. Lucinda M. Bersch. 1974. 4.95 o.s.i. (ISBN 0-8181-0327-2). Pageant-Poseidon.
Strange Honeymoon. Octavus Roy Cohen. LC 39-17095. 1939. D. Appleton Century Company, Incorporated.
Strange Houses: A Tale, by Cora Jarrett. Cora Hardy Jarrett. LC 36-130499. Farrar & Rinehart, Incorporated.
Strange Husband. Peggy O'More, pseud. LC 45-10122. 1945. Grammercy Publishing Co.
Strange Infatuation. Lewis H. Watson. LC 8-367573. (On cover: The Rialto series, v. 1, no. 22). 1890. Rand, McNally & Company.
Strange Invasion of Catfish Bend. Ben Lucien Burman. LC 79-67487. (Catfish Bend Stories). (Illus.). 160p. 1980. 8.95 (ISBN 0-8149-0828-4). Vanguard.
Strange Journey. Kathleen Hasting Curzon-Herrick. LC 35-27266. W. W. Norton & Company, Inc.
Strange Journey. abr. ed. Marjorie Harte. Ed. by Alice Sachs. 1971. Repr. of 1968 ed. 3.95 o.p. Lenox Hill.
Strange Journey. Rick Lucas. LC 54-114879. 1954. Vixen Press.
Strange Journey: Or, Pictures from Egypt and the Soudan. Christina Georgina Rossetti. (Harper's Franklin square library, no. 270). 1882. Harper & Brothers.
Strange Journeys. Denys Val Baker. (Orig.). 1969. pap. 0.75 o.p. (T2000). Pyramid Pubns.
Strange Journeys of Colonel Polders. Dunsany, Edward John Moreton Drax Plunkett. LC 51-26340. 1950. Jarrolds.
Strange Lady. Robert Smythe Hichens. LC 50-10261. 1950. Macrae Smith.
Strange Land. Ned Calmer. LC 50-518221. 1950. Scribner.
Strange Landscape. Tony Duvert. LC 75-13553. 1975. 7.50. (ISBN 0-8021-0100-3) (ISBN 0-394-49932-8). Grove Press: Distributed by Random House.
Strange Laughter: Translated by Eithne Wilkins. Pierre Molaine. Roy Publishers.
Strange Legacy of Aunt Betina. Lou Crail. 1978. pap. 1.50 (ISBN 0-532-15374-X). Woodhill.
Strange Life of Ivan Osokin: A Novel. Petr Dem'Ianovich Uspenskii. LC 47-288179. 1947. Holme Press.
Strange Life of Ivan Osokin: A Novel. Petr Den'Ianovich Uspenskii. LC 55-14166. 1955. Hermitage House.
Strange Love. Georges Eekhoud. 1965. 6.00 o.s.i. Guild Pr Ltd.
Strange Lovers. John Trinian. Orig. Title: North Beach Girl. 1967. pap. 0.60 o.p. (60-301). Manor Bks.
Strange Lovers: Translated from the Italian by Elizabeth Abbott. 1st Ed. Armando Meoni. LC 52-10422. 1953. Dutton.
Strange Loves of Lady S. Max Nortik. (Orig.). pap. 1.75 o.p. (3035). Brandon.
Strange Loyalty of Dr. Carlisle. Elizabeth Seifert. LC 73-79160. 1973. 6.95. Aeonian Press.
Strange Man. Solomon Alexander Amu Djoleto. LC 67-110096. 1968. 4.00. Heinemann.
Strange Man on the Creek. Rufus Henderson Click. LC 55-15732. 1954. Christopher Pub. House.
Strange Manuscript Found in a Copper Cylinder. James De Mille. LC 74-15964. (Science Fiction). (Illus.). 1975. 16.00 (ISBN 0-405-06285-0). Arno Press.
Strange Manuscript Found in a Copper Cylinder. James De Mille. LC 13-177273. 1888. Harper & Brothers.
Strange Manuscript Found in a Copper Cylinder. James De Mille. LC 8-25957. (On cover: Harper's Franklin square library, no. 639). 1889. Harper & Brothers.
Strange Marriage. James Colton, pseud. LC 65-23705. Argyle Books.
Strange Marriage. Gerald Foster. LC 34-9919. 1934. W. Godwin, Inc.
Strange Marriage. Netta Syrett. LC 31-8411. 1931. Dodd, Mead & Company.
Strange Meeting. Susan Hill. LC 74-182473. 1972. 5.95 (ISBN 0-8415-0147-5). Saturday Review Press.
Strange Meeting. Denise Robins. 1974. pap. 0.75 o.p. (26586-6-075). Beagle Bks.
Strange Melody: A Novel. Stephen Southwold. LC 36-164996. 1936. Doubleday, Doran & Company, Inc.
Strange Memories. Death-Bed Scenes; Extraordinary Conversions; Incidents of Travel, Etc. Augustine J O'Reilly. 1880. D. & Saflier & Co.; Etc., Etc.
Strange Message: By Dora Russell... Dora Russell. (On cover: Lovell's library, no. 1211). 1888. J. W. Lovell Company.
Strange Moon. Thomas Sigismund Stribling. LC 29-11670. 1929. Doubleday, Doran and Company, Inc.
Strange Ms. Alexander Pitts Bettersworth. LC 6-13112. 1883. H. W. Rokker, Printer.
Strange Murder of Hatton, K. C. Herbert Adams. LC 33-256927. J. B. Lippincott Company.
Strange Murders at Greystones. Elsie Wright. LC 31-1818. 1931. International Fiction Library.
Strange Mysteries of the Sea. Len Ortzen. LC 76-24980. 1977. 7.95 o.p. (ISBN 0-312-76405-7). St Martin.
Strange Negro Stories of the Old Deep South. Harry D Howell. LC 78-122722. (Short story index reprint series). (Illus.). 1970. Books for Libraries Press.
Strange Negro Stories of the Old Deep South. Harry D Howell. LC 37-1006. Wetzel Publishing Co., Inc.
Strange News from Another Star. Hermann Hesse. Tr. by Denver Lindley from Ger. 160p. 1972. pap. 4.95 (ISBN 0-374-51018-0, N432). FS&G.
Strange News from Another Star and Other Tales. Hermann Hesse. LC 73-14597. 1973. 6.95 (ISBN 0-8161-6154-2). G. K. Hall.
Strange News from Another Star: And Other Tales. Hermann Hesse. LC 70-179791. 1972. 5.95 (ISBN 0-374-27088-0). Farrar, Straus and Giroux.
Strange News from Heaven. Alan Griffiths. LC 35-12783. 1935. Doubleday, Doran & Company, Inc.
Strange Nigerian Tales of Doctor Morgu. B. E. Ikezuagu. 6.25 o.p. (ISBN 0-8062-0660-8). Carlton.
Strange Notes of Samuel Butler. Samuel Butler. Ed. by Gunn, John W. (Pocket series, no. 472, ed. by E. Haldeman-Julius). Haldeman-Julius Company.
Strange Obsession. George Alexander. LC 61-26340. 1959. Macaulay.
Strange Occurrences. Leopold Davis. 1877. Published for the Author.
Strange of Dr. Jekyll and Mr. Hyde. authorized ed. Robert Louis Stevenson. LC 9-3860. 1893. C. Scribner's Sons.
Strange One. Fred Bodsworth. LC 59-11735. 1960. Dodd, Mead.
Strange Orbits: An Anthology of Science Fiction. Williams-Ellis, Amabel & Michael Pearson. LC 76-382972. 1976. Blackie.
Strange Papers of Dr Blayre. Heron-Allen, Edward. LC 76-1432. (Supernatural and Occult Fiction). 1976. 15.00 (ISBN 0-405-08418-8). Arno Press.
Strange Paradise. Dorothy Daniels. (Orig.). 1969. pap. 0.60 o.p. (63-259). Paperback Lib.
Strange Paradise No. 2: Island of Evil. Dorothy Daniels. (Strange Paradise Ser). (Orig.). 1970. pap. 0.60 o.p. (63-321). Paperback Lib.
Strange Passage. Theodore D Irwin. LC 35-32776. H. Smith and R. Haas.
Strange Pastures. Sandra Sobel. LC 51-4169. 1951. De Vorsa.
Strange Paths. Louise Gerard. LC 34-1301. The Macaulay Company.
Strange Peaches: A Novel. Edwin Shrake. LC 79-181662. 1972. 7.95 (ISBN 0-06-127773-8). Harper's Magazine Press.
Strange People. John M Batchelor. LC 6-90903. (On cover: Fireside series, no. 60). 1888. J. S. Orilvie.
Strange Pilgrimage. A Novel. Jeannette Ritchie Hadermann Walworth. (On cover: The Manhattan series, no. 7). A. L. Burt.
Strange Pilgrimage. A Novel. Jeannette Ritchie Hadermann Walworth. (select series, no. 62). 1890. Street & Smith.
Strange Place for Murder. Clare Barroll. LC 79-222. 8.95 (ISBN 0-684-16149-4). Scribner.
Strange Ports of Call. Ed. by August William Derleth. LC 48-6688. 1948. Pellegrini & Cudahy.
Strange Possession. Johanna Phillips. (Second Chance at Love Ser.: No. 43). (Orig.). 1982. pap. 1.75 (ISBN 0-515-06521-8). Jove Pubns.
Strange Proposal. Grace Livingston Hill. LC 35-170947. J. B. Lippincott Company.
Strange Pursuit. Patrick Wynnton. LC 30-23087. 1930. J. B. Lippincott Company.
Strange Rapture. Denise Robins. 1973. pap. 0.75 o.p. (94355-075). Beagle Bks.
Strange Recluse: Or, Ye Did It Unto Me... Lydia Louisa Anna Very. 1899. The Salem Press Co.
Strange Record. Mary Gill. LC 8-18002. 1908. The Neale Publishing Company.
Strange Record. Mount Houmas. LC 8-18002. 1908. The Neale Publishing Company.
Strange Relations. Jerome Barry. LC 62-11425. 1962. Published for the Crime Club by Doubleday.
Strange Report. John Burke. 1971. pap. 0.60 o.p. (ISBN 0-447-73219-6). Lancer.
Strange Return. Albert Benjamin Cunningham. LC 52-5299. (Guilt edged mystery). 1952. Dutton.
Strange River. Julien Green. Tr. by Holland, Vyvyan. LC 32-216826. 1932. Harper & Brothers.
Strange, Sad Comedy. Molly Elliot Seawell. LC 8-6431. 1896. The Century Co.
Strange Schemes of Randolph Mason. Melville Davisson Post. LC 75-32776. (Literature of Mystery and Detection). (Series: Hudson library; no. 16.). 1976. 16.00 (ISBN 0-405-07895-1). Arno Press.
Strange Schemes of Randolph Mason. new ed. Melville Davisson Post. LC 73-169411. (Series: Hudson Library, No. 16.). 1973. 6.00. O. Train.
Strange Schemes of Randolph Mason. Melville Davisson Post. (Added t.-p.: The Hudson library, no. 16). 1896. G. P. Putnam's Sons.
Strange Schemes of Randolph Mason. Melville Davisson Post. LC 14-1825. G. P. Putnam's Sons.
Strange Schemes of Randolph Mason: Stories of Mystery and Crime. Melville Davisson Post. LC 74-10490. (Series: Hudson Library; 16.). 1975. 10.00 (ISBN 0-88355-204-3). Hyperion Press.
Strange Sea Stories & Legends. Bill Wisner. (Orig.). 1981. pap. 3.50 (ISBN 0-451-12358-1, AE2358, Sig). NAL.
Strange Seas and Shores: A Collection of Short Stories. Avram Davidson. LC 79-140064. 1971. 4.95. Doubleday.
Strange Secret. A Story of the American Revolution. Sylvanus Cobb. (On cover: The fireside series, no. 85). J. S. Ogilvie.
Strange Secrets. Virginia Coffman. (Signet Book). 1976. (pbk.) 1.25. New American Library.
Strange Secrets. Arthur Conan Doyle. LC 10-419189. R. F. Fenno & Company.
Strange Seed. T. M Wright. 1980. 2.25 (ISBN 0-87216-673-2). Playboy Press.
Strange Seed: A Contemporary Novel of Unutterable Terror. T. M. Wright. LC 78-57400. 1978. 7.95 o.p. (ISBN 0-89696-021-8, An Everest House Book). Dodd.
Strange Seed: A Novel. T. M. Wright. LC 78-57400. 8.95 (ISBN 0-89696-021-8). Everest House.
Strange Sensations. Andrew Miller. pap. 1.95 o.s.i. (Venus). Grove.
Strange Signposts: An Anthology of the Fantastic. Ed. by Samuel Moskowitz & Elwood, Roger. LC 66-13106. 1966. Holt, Rinehart and Winston.
Strange Signposts: An Anthology of the Fantastic, Ed. by Sam Moskowitz, Roger Elwood. Ed. by Samuel Moskowitz & Roger Elwood. LC 66-13106. bds., 5.50. Holt.
Strange Signposts: Anthology of the Fantastic. Ed. by R. Elwood & S. Moskowitz. 1966. 5.50 o.p. (ISBN 0-03-057495-1). HR&W.
Strange Sinner. Florence Stonebraker. pap. 0.60 o.p. (60-383). Manor Bks.
Strange Sinner. 1st Ed. Elsie Jordan. LC 54-7603. 1954. Pageant Press.
Strange Sisters. Fletcher Flora. LC 54-424803. (Lion book, 215). Lion Books.
Strange Solitude. Philippe Sollers. LC 59-12221. 1959. Grove Press.
Strange Stories. Algernon Blackwood. LC 75-46255. (Supernatural and Occult Fiction). 1976. 42.00 (ISBN 0-405-08114-6). Arno Press.
Strange Stories. Contes Fantastiques. Emile Erckmann & Chatrian, Alexandre, 1826-1890, Joint Author. LC 6-38165. (Appletons' new handy-volume ser. V. 58). 1880. D. Appleton and Company.
Strange Stories from a Chinese Studio. Herbert A. Giles. 1970. pap. 3.50 o.p. (ISBN 0-486-22395-7). Dover.
Strange Stories from a Chinese Studio. Sung-Ling Pu. Tr. by Herbert Allen Giles. LC 73-94319. 1969. 3.50 (ISBN 0-486-22395-7). Dover Publications.
Strange Story... Hilda Winifred Lewis. LC 47-17006. 1945. Jarrold's, Limited.
Strange Story. Hilda Winifred Lewis. LC 47-4016. 1947. Random House.
Strange Story. Edward George Earle Lytton Bulwer-Lytton Lytton. LC 9-3830. 1863. S. H. Goetzel & Co.
Strange Story. A Novel. Edward George Earle Lytton Bulwer-Lytton Lytton. LC 7-8091. (On cover: Seaside library. Pocket ed. no. 83). 1883. G. Munro.
Strange Story. A Novel. Edward George Earle Lytton Bulwer-Lytton Lytton. LC 21-15378. (Seaside library, v. 75, no. 1529). 1883. G. Munro.
Strange Story: An Alchemical Novel. Edward George Earle Lytton Bulwer-Lytton Lytton. LC 73-163896. 1973. 3.95. Shambala.
Strange Story and The Haunted and the Haunters. Edward George Earle Lytton Bulwer-Lytton Lytton. LC 49-32960. 1879. J.B. Lippincott.
Strange Story and The Haunted & the Haunters. Edward George Earle Lytton Bulwer-Lytton Lytton. LC 8-11031. G. Routledge and Sons.
Strange Story of Hester Wynne, Told by Herself; with a Prologue by G. Colmore Pseud.... Mrs. Gertrude Weaver. (Half-title: Appletons' town and country library, no. 270). 1899. D. Appleton and Company.
Strange Story of My Life: The Colonel's Daughter. Henrietta Eliza Vaughan Stannard. LC 8-27069. Rand, McNally & Company.
Strange Story of the Great Whale Also Known As Big Mac. Erih Kos. Tr. by Lovett F. Edwards. LC 62-16725. 1962. 3.50 o.p. (ISBN 0-15-185480-7). HarBraceJ.
Strange Story of William Hyde. Patrick Casey & Casey, Terence. LC 16-6817. 1916. 1.25. Hearst's International Library Co.
Strange Story. To Which Is Added The Haunted and the Haunters. Edward George Earle Lytton Bulwer-Lytton Lytton. LC 4-23579. (Half-title: Novels of Sir Edward Bulwer Lytton. Library ed. Romances, vol. IV-V). 1893. Little, Brown, and Company.
Strange Story. To Which Is Added, The Haunted and the Haunters. Edward George Earle Lytton Bulwer-Lytton Lytton. LC 4-16553. (Half-title: Novels of Sir Edward Bulwer Lytton. Library edition. Romances, vol. IV-V). 1896. Little, Brown, and Company.
Strange Story, Zanoni. Edward George Earle Lytton Bulwer-Lytton Lytton. LC 31-322935. (The novels and romances of Edward Bulwer Lytton. v. 14). Aldine Book Publishing Co.
Strange, Stranger, Strangest. Ed. by Borderline Magazine. (O.S.I.). 1971. pap. 0.75 o.s.i. (ISBN 0-446-64620-2, 64-620). Paperback Lib.
Strange Tale from Overseas. Kaigai L. Hatsvtaro. Tr. by Richard Zumwinkle. 12.50 o.p. (ISBN 0-87093-220-9). Dawsons.
Strange Tales. Retold by B. Mendelssohn. (Tales Retold for Easy Reading Ser). 116p. 1939. pap. text ed. 1.25x o.p. (ISBN 0-19-422236-5). Oxford U Pr.
Strange Tales. 3rd ed. Ed. by Basil Rathbone. 1968. pap. 0.50 o.p. (B50-839). Belmont-Tower.
Strange Tales from the CBS Radio Mystery Theater. Ed. by Himan Brown (ISBN 0-445-00422-3). Popular Library.
Strange Tales of a Nihilist. William Le Queux. LC 7-13134. (On cover: Cassell's sunshine series. no. 130). Cassell Publishing Company.
Strange Things Happen. Chowan College Creative Writing Group & North Carolina Writers Conference. Ed. by Bernice K. Harris. 1971. 7.50 (ISBN 0-930230-24-8). Johnson NC.
Strange Things Happen Here: Twenty-Six Short Stories and a Novel. Luisa Valenzuela. LC 78-22274. 9.95 (ISBN 0-15-185782-2). Harcourt Brace Jovanovich.
Strange Thoroughfare. Sonia Ruthele Novak. LC 31-26870. 1931. The Macmillan Company.

Strange Threads. J Douglas. LC 42-35081. 1888. J. B. Alden.
Strange to Tell: Stories of the Marvelous and Mysterious. Ed. by Marjorie Fischer. Humphries, Rolfe, Joint Ed. LC 47-296279. 1946. J. Messner, Inc.
Strange Tomorrows. Ed. by Robert Hoskins. 1972. pap. 1.25 o.s.i. (78-713). Lancer.
Strange Triangle of G. B. S. Biographical Novel. Tullah Innes Hanley. LC 56-7360. 1957. Bruce Humphries.
Strange True Stories of Louisiana. George Washington Cable. LC 72-84530. 1974. (lib. ed.) 14.50 (ISBN 0-403-02952-X). Scholarly Press.
Strange True Stories of Louisiana. George Washington Cable. LC 78-116944. (Short story index reprint series). (Illus.). 1970. (ISBN 0-8369-3446-6). Books for Libraries Press.
Strange True Stories of Louisiana. George Washington Cable. LC 6-22249. 1889. C. Scribner's Sons.
Strange True Stories of Louisiana see Collected Works.
Strange Understanding. Harriet Theresa Smith Comstock. LC 33-15238. 1933. Doubleday, Doran & Company, Inc.
Strange Victory. Franken Meloney. LC 39-16850. Farrar & Rinehart, Inc.
Strange Victory: A Novel. Edward Dudowicz. LC 45-59188. House of Field-Doubleday, Inc.
Strange Visitation of Josiah McNason: A Christmas Ghost Story. Marie Corelli. LC 75-46262. (Supernatural and Occult Fiction). 1976. 10.00 (ISBN 0-405-08120-0). Arno Press.
Strange Visitation of Josiah McNason: A Christmas Ghost Story. Mary MacKay. Ed. by R. Reginald & Douglas Menville. LC 75-46262. 1976. Repr. of 1904 ed. lib. bdg. 10.00x (ISBN 0-405-08120-0). Ayer Co.
Strange Visitor. Dorothy Phoebe Ansle. LC 74-25030. 1975. 6.95 (ISBN 0-8415-0364-8). Saturday Review Press.
Strange Visitor. Laura Conway. LC 74-25030. 160p. 1975. 6.95 o.p. (ISBN 0-8415-0364-8). Dutton.
Strange Voyage. William Clark Russell. (On cover: Seaside library. Pocket ed., no. 592). 1885. G. Munro.
Strange Voyage. A Novel. William Clark Russell. (Harper's Franklin square library, no. 492). 1885. Harper & Brothers.
Strange Voyage. A Revision of The Key of Industrial Co-Operative Government. An Interesting and Instructive Description of Life on Planet Venus. Harry Francis Allen. LC 6-486. 1891. The Monitor Publishing Company.
Strange Way Home. Nancy W Faber. LC 63-18318. 1963. H. Regnery Co.
Strange Way Home: By Renee Easterling. Easterling, Narena. LC 52-14508. 1952. Pageant Press.
Strange Ways of Love. Clayton Matthews. 1969. pap. 0.75 o.p. (75-285). Manor Bks.
Strange Week-End: A Novel. Mary Borden. 1938. Harper & Borhters.
Strange Welcome. Frank Albert Chittenden. LC 50-4881. 1949. T. V. Boardman.
Strange Welcome. Frank Albert Chittenden. LC 51-9322. (Gargoyle mystery). Coward-McCann.
Strange Wine. Harlan Ellison. 1979. pap. 2.50 (ISBN 0-446-91946-2). Warner Bks.
Strange Wine: Fifteen New Stories from the Nightside of the World. Harlan Ellison. LC 77-89060. 9.95 (ISBN 0-06-011113-5). Harper & Row.
Strange Wine: Fifteen New Stories from the Nightside of the World. Harlan Ellison. 1979. 1.95 (ISBN 0-446-89489-3). Warner Booksnc.
Strange Witness. Day Keene. 1970. pap. 0.75 o.p. (75-369). Manor Bks.
Strange Wives. Shirley Barker. LC 63-12062. 1963. Crown Publishers.
Strange Woman. Elmer Holmes Davis. LC 27-20760. 1927. R. M. McBride & Company.
Strange Woman. Mary Fenollosa & Hurlbut, William. J. LC 14-20501. 1914. 1.30. Dodd, Mead and Company.
Strange Woman. Ernest Aime Feydeau. (On cover: The crescent library, no. 7). 1893. The Price-McGill Company.
Strange Woman. Ben Ames Williams. LC 41-18119. 1941. Houghton Mifflin Company.
Strange Woman: By Sarah-Elizabeth Rodger. Sarah Elizabeth Rodger. LC 38-529628. J. B. Lippincott Company.
Strange Women. LC 32-20309. The Mohawk Press.
Strange World. Mary Elizabeth Braddon Maxwell. (On cover: Lovell's library, no. 887). 1887. J. W. Lovell Company.
Strange World. A Novel. Mary Elizabeth Braddon Maxwell. (On cover: Seaside library. Pocket ed. no. 511). 1885. G. Munro.
Strange World of Arthur Machen. Arthur Machen. LC 60-183196. (Classics of mystery, v. 6). 1960. Juniper Press.
Strange Yesterday. Howard Melvin Fast. LC 34-300396. 1934. Dodd, Mead & Company.
Strange Young Man. Louise Gerard. LC 31-6489. The Macaulay Company.
Strangeling, a Victorian Novel. 1st Ed. Alice Harwood. LC 53-10554. 1954. Bobbs-Merrill.
Strangeness. Thomas M Disch & Charles Naylor. 1978. 2.50 (ISBN 0-380-41434-1). Avon.
Strangeness: A Collection of Curious Tales. Thomas M Disch & Charles Naylor. LC 77-23239. 8.95 (ISBN 0-684-14899-4). Scribner.
Strangeness of Noel Carton. William Caine. LC 20-114972. 1920. 1.75. G. P. Putnam's Sons.
Stranger. Max Brand. 208p. 1976. pap. 1.75 (ISBN 0-446-94508-0). Warner Bks.
Stranger. Arthur Bullard. LC 20-792039. 1920. The Macmillan Company.
Stranger. James Fitz James Caldwell. LC 7-9557. 1907. The Neale Publishing Company.
Stranger. Albert Camus. Tr. by Stuart Gilbert. LC 72-8033. 1973. (ISBN 0-394-70002-3). Vintage Books.
Stranger. Albert Camus & Kate Griffith. LC 81-19846. 17.95 (ISBN 0-8191-2141-X) (ISBN 0-8191-2142-8). University Press of America.
Stranger. Claire Dumas, pseud. LC 76-56405. 1977. 1.50 (ISBN 0-345-25402-3). Ballantine Books.
Stranger. Bryan Forbes. LC 79-7811. 1980. 10.95 (ISBN 0-385-15527-1). Doubleday.
Stranger. Giles A Lutz. 1976. (pbk.) 1.25. Ace Books.
Stranger. Fred J. Payne. 6.75 o.p. (ISBN 0-8062-0594-6). Carlton.
Stranger. Rose Albert Porter. LC 40-7016. 1940. The Dial Press.
Stranger: A Novel. Malachy Gerard Carroll. LC 52-8686. 1952. Bruce.
Stranger: A Novel. Maria Szczepanska Kuncewiczowa. LC 45-7648. 1945. L. B. Fischer.
Stranger: A Novel of the Big Sur. Lillian Bos Ross. LC 42-21690. 1942. W. Morrow and Company.
Stranger and Afraid. Morna Doris MacTaggart Brown. LC 72-142839. 1971. 4.95 (ISBN 0-8027-5219-5). Walker.
Stranger & Afraid. E. X. Ferrars, pseud. 1971. 4.95 o.p. Walker & Co.
Stranger and Afraid. Michael Hardt. LC 43-7712. 1943. The Bobbs-Merrill Company.
Stranger and Afraid. Marika Robert. LC 64-13861. 1964. Doubleday.
Stranger and Afraid. Marika Robert. LC 64-4627. 1964. McClelland and Stewart.
Stranger and Alone: A Novel. Jay Saunders Redding. LC 50-5405. 1950. Harcourt, Brace.
Stranger-Artist: Or, Through Shadowland. Edith C Kenyon. LC 7-10966. (Once a week library, v. 10, no. 25). 1893. P. F. Collier.
Stranger at Home. George Sanders. LC 55-19315. (Ace double novel books, D-77). Ace Books.
Stranger at Home. George Sanders. LC 46-610433. 1946. Simon and Schuster.
Stranger at Killknock. Leonard Patrick O'Connor Wibberley. LC 61-8352. 1961. Putnam.
Stranger at My Door. Mary Kistler. LC 78-14704. 1979. 7.95 (ISBN 0-385-13510-6). Doubleday.
Stranger at Pembroke. Lois Dwight Cole. LC 74-150144. 1971. 5.95. Hawthorn Books.
Stranger at Pembroke. Anne Eliot, pseud. 1971. 5.95 o.p. Hawthorn.
Stranger at Plantation Inn. Patricia Maxwell. 160p. 1973. pap. 0.75 o.p. (T2687, GM). Fawcett World.
Stranger at Storm Ranch. James Denson Sayers. LC 36-20254. 1936. Godwin.
Stranger at the Crossroads. Annette Hard. 1976. (pbk.) 1.50. Warner Books.
Stranger at the Door. Gil Meynier. LC 48-5172. 1948. C. Scribner's Sons.
Stranger at the Feast. George Agnew Chamberlain. LC 28-84083. 1928. G. P. Putnam's Sons.
Stranger at the Gate. Josephine Edgar. (Ravenswood gothic). 1975. (pbk.) 0.95 (ISBN 0-671-77990-7). Pocket Books.
Stranger at the Gate. Lynn Williams. (Candlelight romance). 1975. (pbk.) 0.75. Dell.
Stranger at the Gate: A Story of Christmas. Mabel Osgood Wright. LC 13-24118. 1913. The Macmillan Company.
Stranger at the Gates. Evelyn Anthony. LC 73-78736. 1978. 9.95 o.p. (ISBN 0-698-10946-5, Coward). Putnam Pub Group.
Stranger at the Gates. Evelyn Anthony. 304p. 1974. pap. 1.50 (ISBN 0-451-06019-9, W6019, Sig). NAL.
Stranger at the Gates. Evelyn Anthony. 320p. (YA) 1973. 7.95 o.p. (ISBN 0-698-10541-9). Coward.
Stranger at the Gates. Eve Stephens, pseud. LC 73-78736. 1973. 7.95 (ISBN 0-698-10541-9). Coward, McCann & Geoghegan.
Stranger at the Gates. Eve Stephens, pseud. 1974. (pbk.) 1.50. New American Library.
Stranger at the Hearth. Katharine Metcalf Roof. LC 16-228942. 1.35. Small, Maynard & Company.
Stranger at the Inlet: A Roger Baxter Mystery. Samuel Epstein & Wonsetler, John Charles, 1900- Illus. LC 46-25170. 1946. J. Messner, Inc.
Stranger at the Wedding. Frances Lynch. LC 76-28044. 8.95 (ISBN 0-312-76422-7). St. Martin's Press.
Stranger at the Wedding. Frances Lynch. LC 78-2357. 1978. 9.95 (ISBN 0-89340-132-3). J. Curley.
Stranger at Wildings. Madeleine Brent. LC 75-6152. 1976. 7.95 (ISBN 0-385-11101-0). Doubleday.
Stranger Beside Me. Ann Rule. (Illus.). 1981. pap. 3.95 (ISBN 0-451-12169-4, AE2169, Sig). NAL.
Stranger Beside Me. Mabel Seeley. LC 51-12483. 1951. Doubleday.
Stranger: By Burt and Budd Arthur. 1st Ed. Herbert Arthur & Budd Arthur. LC 59-12612. (Double D western). 1959. Doubleday.
Stranger Came Ashore. Mollie Hunter. LC 75-10814. 1975. 5.95. Harper & Row.
Stranger Came to Port: A Novel. Max Miller. LC 38-289064. Reynal & Hitchcock.
Stranger Came to the Farm. Mika Toimi Waltari. LC 52-9848. 1952. Putnam.
Stranger Came to the Lucias. Beatrice Vivian Casey. 1973. 7.95 (ISBN 0-533-00217-6). Vantage.
Stranger City Caper. Ross H Spencer. LC 79-55394. 1980. 1.95 (ISBN 0-380-75036-8). Avon.
Stranger, Come Home. William Lawrence Shirer. LC 54-6891. 1954. Little, Brown.
Stranger Fidelities. Mathilde Eiker. LC 29-18937. 1929. Doubleday, Doran & Company Inc.
Stranger from Arizona. Norman A Fox. LC 56-9755. (Dodd, Mead silver star westerns). 1956. Dodo, Mead.
Stranger from Cheyenne. Joseph Bushnell Ames. LC 27-3406. The Century Co.
Stranger from Home. Leonie Simpson. LC 78-59770. (Illus., Orig.). 1979. pap. 4.00 (ISBN 0-912292-51-2). The Smith.
Stranger from Texas. Allan K. Echols. 1970. Repr. pap. 0.60 o.p. (60-457). Manor Bks.
Stranger from the North. Lucy Walker, pseud. 1976. pap. 1.25 (ISBN 0-345-25233-0). Ballantine.
Stranger from the Past. Lorimer DeKalb, pseud. LC 74-34348. (Spire books). 1975. 1.75 (ISBN 0-8007-8181-3). F. H. Revell Co.
Stranger from the Sea: A Novel of Cornwall, 1810-1811. Winston Graham. LC 81-43400. 1982. 16.95 (ISBN 0-385-17967-7). Doubleday.
Stranger from the Sky. Nicholas Farkas. LC 42-50212. 1942. Citizen Union Press.
Stranger from the Tonto. Zane Grey. LC 78-2659. 1978. 9.95 (ISBN 0-89340-133-1). J. Curley.
Stranger from the Tonto. 1st Ed. Zane Grey. LC 56-8781. 1956. Harper.
Stranger from up-Along. Roberts Theodore Goodridge. LC 24-24140. 1924. Doubleday, Page & Company.
Stranger Here: A Novel. Robert David Quixano Henriques. LC 53-5200. 1953. Viking Press.
Stranger Here, Myself. Thelma Campbell Nason. Ed. by Constance Hunting. 1980. pap. 3.50 (ISBN 0-913006-11-4). Puckerbrush.
Stranger Here, Myself: Short Stories. Thelma Campbell Nason. LC 77-151587. 3.50. Puckerbrush Press.
Stranger-Husband. Peggy Gaddis, pseud. LC 44-403684. 1944. Arcadia House, Inc.
Stranger in a Dark Land. easy eye ed. Julie Wellsley. pap. 0.75 o.p. (75-369). Lancer.
Stranger in a Dark Land. Julie Wellsley. (Orig.). 1972. pap. 0.95 o.s.i. (75-369). Lancer.
Stranger in a Strange Land. Robert Anson Heinlein. LC 61-11702. 1961. Putnam.
Stranger in Angel Town. Nancy Lester. LC 52-10160. (Illus.). 1952. Dodd, Mead.
Stranger in Black Butte. Hoffman Birney. LC 36-14284. The Penn Publishing Company.
Stranger in Boots. Bradford Scott. 1971. pap. 0.60 o.p. (X2545). Pyramid Pubns.
Stranger in Canebrake. Will Houston, pseud. LC 67-1218. Arcadia House.
Stranger in Dodge. Robert V. Bell. 192p. (Orig.). 1983. pap. 2.25 (ISBN 0-345-30875-1). Ballantine.
Stranger in Galah. Michael Barrett. LC 59-1976. 1958. Longmans, Green.
Stranger in Heaven. Harold Vinal. 5.00 o.p. (ISBN 0-8283-1236-2). Branden.
Stranger in Her House. Helen Arvonen. 1970. pap. 0.60 o.p. (ISBN 0-446-63093-4, 63-093). Paperback Lib.
Stranger in My Grave. Margaret Millar. LC 60-55468. 1960. Random House.
Stranger in Our Darkness. Joyce Crawford. LC 68-57163. 1968. 8.95 (ISBN 0-87716-000-7, Pub. by Moore Pub Co). F Apple.
Stranger in Our Midst. Robert Carson. LC 47-23975. 1947. G. P. Putnam's Sons.
Stranger in Texas. Clarence O Lawson. LC 60-284016. 1960. Arcadia House.
Stranger in the Dark. Helen Nielsen. LC 55-430225. 1955. I. Washburn.
Stranger in the Earth. Thomas Sugrue. 1971. pap. 0.95 o.p. (ISBN 0-446-65456-6, 65-456). Paperback Lib.
Stranger in the Family. Claire Burch. LC 76-173211. 1972. 6.95 o.p. (ISBN 0-672-51566-0). Bobbs.
Stranger in the House. Patricia J. MacDonald. (Orig.). 1983. pap. 3.50 (ISBN 0-440-18455-X). Dell.
Stranger in the House. Georges Simenon. LC 67-110685. (B 67-11237). 1967. Penguin.
Stranger in the Land. Ward Thomas. LC 49-9471. 1949. Houghton Mifflin Co.
Stranger in the Land. Colby Wolford. LC 58-5989. 1958. Dodd, Mead.
Stranger in the Mirror. Sidney Sheldon. LC 75-34328. 1976. 8.95 (ISBN 0-688-03002-5). Morrow.
Stranger in the Mirror. Sidney Sheldon. 1977. 1.95 (ISBN 0-446-89204-1). Warner Books.
Stranger in the Night. Charlotte Lamb, pseud. (Harlequin Presents Ser.). 192p. 1981. pap. 1.50 (ISBN 0-373-10417-0, Pub. by Harlequin). PB.
Stranger in the Snow. Lester Goran. 4.95. New Amer. Lib.
Stranger in Town. Howard Hunt. LC 47-1651. 1947. Random House.
Stranger in Town: By Brett Halliday Pseud. Davis Dresser. LC 55-149333. (Torquil book). 1955. Distributed by Dodd, Mead.
Stranger in Town: By Robert Bloomfield Pseud. 1st Ed. Leslie Edgley. LC 53-6629. 1953. Published for the Crime Club by Doubleday.
Stranger in Town. 1st Ed. Clifton Adams. LC 60-9466. (Double-D western). 1960. Doubleday.
Stranger in Two Worlds. Hugh Clevely. LC 59-13773. 1959. Appleton-Century-Crofts.
Stranger Is Watching. Mary Higgins Clark. LC 77-20505. 1978. 8.95 (ISBN 0-671-23071-9). Simon and Schuster.
Stranger Is Watching. Mary Higgins Clark. LC 78-16210. 1978. 11.95 (ISBN 0-8161-6597-1). G. K. Hall.
Stranger Is Watching. Mary Higgins Clark. (Dell Book). 1979. 2.50 (ISBN 0-440-18125-9). Dell Publishing Co.
Stranger Knocked. E M Nightingale. LC 53-5489. 1953. Dorrance.
Stranger Notes. Gary Carey. (Orig.). 1979. pap. 2.25 (ISBN 0-8220-1229-4). Cliffs.
Stranger on the Beach. Arlene Hale. (Candlelight Romance.). 1977. 0.95 (ISBN 0-440-18176-3). Dell Pub. Co.
Stranger on the Beach. Lilian Peake. (Harlequin Romance Ser.). 1979. pap. 1.25 (ISBN 0-373-02279-4, Pub. by Harlequin). PB.
Stranger on the Highway. Hoffman Reynolds Hays. LC 43-6285. 1943. Little, Brown and Company.
Stranger on the Island. Brand Whitlock. LC 33-4812. 1933. D. Appleton and Company.
Stranger on the Stair. Mortimer, Chapman. LC 50-14492. 1950. McGraw-Hill.
Stranger Prince: The Story of Rupert of the Rhine. Margaret Emma Faith Irwin. LC 37-271638. Harcourt, Brace and Company.
Stranger Than Fiction. A Novel. Kenneth Lee. (On cover: Echo series. no. 87). Pollard & Moss.
Stranger Than Fiction: A Series of Short Stories. souvenir ed. John Joseph Bent. LC 16-24538. 1.00. Matthew F. Sheehan Co.
Stranger Than Truth: A Novel. Vera Caspary. LC 46-11808. 1946. Random House.
Stranger Things. Mildred Cram. LC 78-121532. (Short story index reprint series). 1970. Books for Libraries Press.
Stranger Things. Mildred Cram. LC 23-15251. 1923. 2.00. Dodd, Mead and Company.
Stranger to Himself. Joseph Hansen. 1977. pap. 1.75 (ISBN 0-89041-171-9, 3171). Major Bks.
Stranger to the Shore. 1st Ed. Kenneth Dodson. LC 56-6770. 1956. Little, Brown.
Stranger to Town. Leslie Purnell Davies. LC 69-12236. 1969. 3.95. Published for the Crime Club by Doubleday.
Stranger, Tread Light. Jean Muir. LC 70-165668. (Red badge novel of suspense). 1971. 4.95 (ISBN 0-396-06416-7). Dodd, Mead.
Stranger, Tread Light. Jean Muir. LC 79-37947. (Red badge novel of suspense). 1971. 7.95 (ISBN 0-8161-6002-3). G. K. Hall.
Stranger, Tread Light. Jean Muir. 1974. (pbk.) 0.75. Dell.
Stranger with a Gun. Harry Sinclair Drago. LC 57-11390. (Silver star westerns). 1957. Dodd, Mead.
Stranger with a Watch. Knute Skinner. 1965. 3.00 o.p. (ISBN 0-8233-0099-4). Golden Quill.
Stranger with My Face. Patricia McGerr. LC 68-31496. 1968. 5.95. R. B. Luce.
Stranger Within. Matthew Trill. LC 35-16059. 1935. Frederick A. Stokes Company.

Stranger Within the Gates. Constance Antonina Boyle. LC 26-701323. 1926. T. Seltzer.

Stranger Within the Gates. Grace Livingston Hill. LC 30-23416. J. B. Lippincott Company.

Stranger Woman... Henrietta Eliza Vaughan Stannard. LC 8-27038. (Half-title: Pseudonym library v. 7). 1894. J. S. Tait & Sons.

Strangers. Gardner Dozois. LC 77-10108. 7.95. Berkley Pub. Corp.: Distributed by Putnam.

Strangers. Gardner Dozois. (Berkley Book). 1978. 1.75 (ISBN 0-425-03924-2). Berkley Pub. Corp.

Strangers. Barbara Ewing. LC 77-15348. 1978. 6.95 (ISBN 0-689-10855-9). Atheneum.

Strangers. Claude Houghton Oldfield. LC 38-6347. 1938. The Macmillan Company.

Strangers. Dorothy Graffe Van Doren. LC 26-16534. George H. Doran Company.

Strangers. Antonia White. LC 82-12852. (Virago Modern Classic Ser.). 192p. 1983. pap. 6.95 (ISBN 0-385-27786-5). Dial.

Strangers Among Us. Ruth Montgomery. 256p. 1982. pap. 2.95 (ISBN 0-449-24487-3, Crest). Fawcett.

Strangers and Afraid: A Novel. Thomas L Sterling. LC 52-11162. 1952. Simon and Schuster.

Strangers and Brothers. Charles Percy Snow. LC 60-12605. (His Strangers and brothers 1). 1960. Scribner.

Strangers and Brothers. omnibus ed. Charles Percy Snow. LC 74-37229. 1972. per vol. 15.00. Scribner.

Strangers and Comrades. Alfred Slote. (55-903). 1965. Paperback Lib.

Strangers and Comrades. Alfred Slote. LC 64-13345. 1964. Simon and Schuster.

Strangers and Graves: Four Short Novels by Peter S.Feibleman. 1st Ed. Peter S Feibleman. LC 66-235697. 1966. 5.95. Atheneum.

Strangers & Journeys. Maurice Shadbolt. LC 72-94597. 1973. 10.00 o.p. St Martin.

Strangers and Lovers. Edwin Granberry. LC 51-26341. (Signet book, 864). 1951. New American Library.

Strangers and Lovers. Edwin Granberry. The Macaulay Company.

Strangers and Pilgrims. Mary Elizabeth Braddon Maxwell. (On cover: Seaside library. Pocket ed. no. 524). 1885. G. Munro.

Strangers and Pilgrims. Mary Elizabeth Braddon Maxwell. (On cover: Lovell's library, no. 886). 1887. J. W. Lovell Company.

Strangers and Wayfarers. Sarah Orne Jewett. LC 69-11906. (American short story series, v. 65). 1969. Garrett Press.

Strangers and Wayfarers. Sarah Orne Jewett. LC 7-9729. 1890. Houghton, Mifflin and Company.

Strangers and Wayfarers. Sarah Orne Jewett. LC 79-10824. 1979. 20.00 (ISBN 0-403-03184-2). Scholarly Press.

Strangers & Wayfarers see Collected Works.

Strangers Are Coming. Ida Alexa Ross Wylie. LC 41-24081. Random House.

Strangers at Collins House. Marilyn Ross. (Orig.). 1967. pap. 0.50 o.p. (52-543). Paperback Lib.

Strangers at Lisconnel. A Second Series of Irish Idylls. Jane Barlow. LC 73-150535. (Short story index reprint series). 1971. (ISBN 0-8369-3832-1). Books for Libraries Press.

Strangers at Lisconnel. A Second Series of Irish Idylls. Jane Barlow. LC 6-7222. 1895. Dodd, Mead and Company.

Strangers at Sea. Alice Mary Ross Colver. 1936. Dodd, Mead & Company.

Strangers at the Gate: Tales of Russian Jewry. Samuel Gordon. 1902. The Jewish Publication Society of America.

Strangers' Banquet. Donn Byrne. LC 19-19596. Harper & Brothers.

Strangers Come Home. Ronald MacDonald Douglas. LC 35-9402. 1935. The Macmillan Company.

Stranger's Eyes. Bettie Wysor. 352p. (Orig.). 1981. pap. 2.75 (ISBN 0-515-05564-6). Jove Pubns.

Strangers' Forest. Pamela Hill. LC 77-9183. 8.95 (ISBN 0-312-76426-X). St. Martin's Press.

Strangers' Forest: A Novel. Pamela Hill. 1978. 1.95 (ISBN 0-449-23907-1). Fawcett Crest.

Strangers from Earth: Eight Tales of Vaulting Imagination. Poul Anderson. LC 61-301234. 1961. Ballantine Books.

Strangers from the Skies. Brad Steiger. (O.s.i.). (Orig.). pap. 0.60 o.s.i. (A171X, Award). Univ Pub & Dist.

Strangers' Gate. Edward Phillips Oppenheim. LC 39-310505. 1939. Little, Brown and Company.

Stranger's Grave. A Tale of the Seventeenth Century. Founded on Facts. Henry Grattan Plunkett. LC 7-38191. (On cover: Bunce's ten cent novels. no. 1)). 1860. W. J. Bunce.

Strangers, Healers. Benjamin Siegel. 352p. (Orig.). 1981. pap. 2.75 (ISBN 0-345-29439-4). Ballantine.

Strangers in Company. Jane Aiken Hodge. LC 72-87582. 1973. 6.95 (ISBN 0-698-10499-4). Coward, McCann & Geoghegan.

Strangers in Love. Josiah Pitts Woolfolk. LC 34-34197. W. Godwin, Inc.

Strangers in Love: A Romance. Mary Howard, pseud. LC 41-118049. 1941. Doubleday, Doran and Company, Inc.

Strangers in My House. Clifford F Thomallo. LC 59-8904. 1959. Pageant Press.

Strangers in Paradise. Christopher Anvil. 1970. pap. 0.75 o.p. (T075-4). Tower.

Strangers in the Dark see Easy Score.

Strangers in the Forest. Carol Ryrie Brink. LC 59-10100. 1959. Macmillan.

Strangers in the House. Jane Ludlow Drake Abbott. LC 35-7812. J. B. Lippincott Company.

Strangers in the House. Les Inconnus Dans la Maison. Georges Simenon. LC 54-7315. 1954. Doubleday.

Strangers in the Land. E. B Ashton. LC 40-9243. 1939. C. Scribner's Sons.

Strangers in the Land. LC 40-9243. 1939. C. Scribner's Sons.

Strangers in the Sun. Mary Sheppard. 1972. 4.95. Lenox Hill Pr.

Strangers in the Universe: Schience-Fiction Stories. Clifford D Simak. LC 56-111892. 1956. Simon and Schuster.

Strangers in The Vly. Edmund Gilligan. LC 41-19190. 1941. C. Scribner's Sons.

Strangers in the Wilderness. L. S. Rickard. (Illus.). 14.50x (ISBN 0-392-04800-0, ABC). Sportshelf.

Strangers in the Wilderness: By L. S. Rickard. L. S Rickard. LC 68-93058. 1967. bds., 7.50. Minerva.

Strangers in 7-A: A Novel of Suspense. Fielden Farrington. LC 73-179347. 1972. 5.95. D. McKay Co.

Strangers into Lovers. Lilian Peake. (Harlequin Presents Ser.). 192p. 1981. pap. 1.75 (ISBN 0-373-10454-5). Harlequin Bks.

Stranger's Kiss. Sondra Stanford. (Romances Ser.). 1978. pap. 0.95 (ISBN 0-373-02208-5, Pub. by Harlequin). PB.

Strangers Married. Vida Hurst. M. S. Mill Co., Inc.

Strangers May Kiss. Katherine Ursula Parrott. LC 30-20356. J. Cape & H. Smith.

Strangers May Love. Georgia Craig. LC 38-5285. The Dodge Publishing Company.

Strangers May Love. Peggy Gaddis, pseud. LC 38-5285. 1938. Dodge Pub. C.

Strangers No Longer. Annie Barclay Kerr. LC 43-5433. 1943. Friendship Press.

Strangers of Rome: A Novel. Isabel Constance Clarke. LC 28-251777. 1928. Longmans, Green and Co.

Strangers on a Train. Patricia Highsmith. 1974. (pbk.) 1.50. Penguin.

Strangers on a Train: 1st Ed. Patricia Highsmith. LC 50-6429. 1950. Harper.

Strangers on Earth. Sara Hancock Black & Irene Black. LC 66-29997. 1966. Deseret Book Co.

Strangers on Earth. Translated from the French by Anthony Hinton. Henri Troyat. LC 58-100861. Crowell.

Strangers on Friday. Harry Whittington. LC 59-8932. 1959. Abelard-Schuman.

Strangers on My Roof. Eileen Arbuthnot Robertson. LC 64-14030. 1964. Macmillan.

Strangers on the Moor. Sylvia Thorpe. 1974. pap. 0.95 o.p. (ISBN 0-515-03298-0, N3298). Pyramid Pubns.

Stranger's Return. Philip Duffield Stong. LC 33-17944. Harcourt, Brace and Company.

Strangers South. Richard Poole. LC 72-79416. 192p. 1972. 4.95 o.p. (ISBN 0-385-06679-1). Doubleday.

Strangers South. Lee E Wells. LC 72-79416. 1972. 4.95 (ISBN 0-385-06679-1). Doubleday.

Strangers: The Story of a Mother and Daughter. Michael De Guzman. (Dell book). 1979. 2.25 (ISBN 0-440-17952-1). Dell Pub. Co.

Strangers. Translated from the French by Brian Rhys. Albert Memmi. LC 60-136143. 3.50. Orion Press.

Stranger's View. David Pryce-Jones. LC 68-12214. 1968. Holt, Rinehart and Winston.

Stranger's Visit. Franklin Pope. LC 8-37188. Zuriel Publishing Company.

Strangers' Wedding: The Comedy of a Romantic. Walter Lionel George. LC 16-1396. 1916. Little, Brown and Company.

Strangers Were There: Selected Stories. John Bell Clayton. LC 57-7908. 1957. Macmillan.

Strangers When We Meet. Evan Hunter. LC 58-7513. 1958. Simon and Schuster.

Strangers When We Meet. Evan Hunter. LC 77-71171. 1977. 1.75 (ISBN 0-380-00617-0). Avon Books.

Strangers Within Our Gates. James S. Woodsworth. LC 76-163836. (Social History of Canada Ser.). 1972. pap. 8.50 (ISBN 0-8020-6149-4). U of Toronto Pr.

Strangest Game. Stark Cole. (Orig.). 1968. pap. 1.25 o.p. (2080). Brandon.

Strangest Grand National. Frank Johnston. LC 48-1060. 1947. J. Long.

Strangle Hold! Al Conroy. (Soldate #3). 1973. (pbk) 0.95. Lancer.

Strangle Hold. Mary McMullen. LC 51-11693. 1951. Harper.

Strangled Queen. Translated from the French by Humphrey Hare. Maurice Druon. LC 57-6063. (His The accursed kings, 2). 1957. Scribner.

Strangled Witness. Zenith Jones Brown. LC 34-18832. Farrar & Rinehart, Incorporated.

Stranglehold. M. G. Bagby. 1976. pap. 1.50 (ISBN 0-89041-125-5, 3125). Major Bks.

Stranglehold. Gregory Cromwell Knapp. LC 73-6590. 1973. 6.95 (ISBN 0-316-49921-8). Little, Brown.

Stranglehold. Gregory Cromwell Knapp. 1974. (pbk.) 1.50 (ISBN 0-446-78525-3). Warner Paperback Library.

Stranglehold. Coleman Posard. 384p. (Orig.). 1981. pap. 2.95 (ISBN 0-523-41214-2). Pinnacle Bks.

Stranglehold... Gertrude M. Robins Reynolds. LC 30-17704. 1930. Pub. for The Crime Club, Inc., by Doublday, Doran & Company, Inc.

Strangler. San Antonio. (San Antonio Mystery Ser.). 1970. pap. 0.60 o.p. (ISBN 0-446-63326-7, 63-326). Paperback Lib.

Strangler. David Black. 224p. 1974. pap. 1.25 o.p. (ISBN 0-532-12211-9). Woodhill.

Strangler. David Black. 1974. (pbk.) 1.25. Manor Books.

Strangler. Molly Thynne. LC 29-18557. 1929. Minton, Balch & Company.

Strangler Fig... Dorothy Stockbridge Tillet. LC 30-234391. 1930. Pub. for the Crime Club, Inc., by Doubleday, Doran & Company, Inc.

Strangler Who Couldn T Let Go: By Hampton Stone Pseud. Aaron Marc Stein. LC 56-13715. (Inner sanctum mystery). 1956. Simon and Schuster.

Strangler Who Couldn't Let Go. Hampton Stone, pseud. (Hampton Stone Mystery Ser.). 1971. pap. 0.75 o.p. (ISBN 0-446-64547-8, 64-547). Paperback Lib.

Stranglers. Adolphe Belot & De Cordova, Robert J. (Seaside library, v. 41, no. 845). G. Munro.

Strangler's Holiday. Rudolf Kagey. LC 43-12459. (On cover: A Crime novel selection. No.1). 1942. Select Publications, Inc.

Strangler's Moon. E. E. Smith & Stephen Goldin. (D'Alembert Ser.: No. 2). 160p. 1982. pap. 2.25 (ISBN 0-425-05630-9). Berkley Pub.

Stranglers of Paris. "Lee Etrangleurs.". Adolphe Belot. Tr. by Cox, George D. LC 6-11351. T. B. Peterson & Brothers.

Strangler's Serenade: By William Irish Pseud. Hopley-Woolrich, Cornell George. LC 51-9552. (Murray Hill mystery). 1951. Rinehart.

Strasbourg Legacy. William Craig. LC 75-12795. 1975. 5.95 (ISBN 0-88349-062-5). Reader's Digest Press: Distributed by Crowell.

Strata. Terry Pratchett. LC 81-51199. 1981. 10.95 (ISBN 0-312-76429-4). St. Martin's Press.

Stratagem, and Other Stories. Aleister Crowley, pseud. LC 74-167446. (Short story index reprint series). 1971. (ISBN 0-8369-3972-7). Books for Libraries Press.

Stratagem: And Other Stories. facsimile ed. Aleister Crowley, pseud. LC 74-167446. (Short Story Index Reprint Ser.). Repr. of 1929 ed. 11.00 (ISBN 0-8369-3972-7). Ayer Co.

Stratagem Rex. Stephen Dolinar. LC 75-13343. 8.95 (ISBN 0-8283-1625-2). Branden Press.

Stratagems and Spoils: Stories of Love and Politics. William Allen White. LC 70-79665. (Series in American Studies). (Illus.). 1969. Johnson Reprint Corp.

Stratagems and Spoils: Stories of Love and Politics. William Allen White. LC 1-24648. 1901. C. Scribner's Sons.

Strategem Rex. Stephen Dolinar. LC 73-13343. 210p. 1976. 8.95 o.p. (ISBN 0-8283-1625-2). Branden.

Strategems and Spoils: Stories of Love and Politics. William Allen White. LC 68-55689. (American short story series, v. 29). 1969. Garrett Press.

Strategie Pour Deux Jambons see Death Sty: A Pig's Tale.

Stratford-by-the-Sea: A Novel. Alice Brown. LC 8-17652. (On cover: American novel series no. 4)). 1884. H. Holt and Company.

Stratford-by-the-Sea: A Novel. Alice Brown. LC 8-17652. (American novel series. No. 4). 1884. H. Holt and Company.

Strathcairn: A Novel, 2 vols. in 1. Charles A. Collins. LC 79-8257. Repr. of 1864 ed. 44.50 (ISBN 0-404-61832-4). AMS Pr.

Strathgallant. Laura Black. LC 81-8850. 1981. 11.95 (ISBN 0-312-76481-2). St Martin's Press.

Strathgallant. Laura Black. LC 81-20334. 1982. 15.95 (ISBN 0-8161-3361-1). G.K. Hall.

Strathmore: A Novel. Jessica Stirling. LC 74-28322. 1975. (ISBN 0-440-05971-2). Delacorte Press.

Strathmore: Or, Wrought by His Own Hand. A Life Romance. Louise De La Ramee. LC 12-313922. 1866. J. B. Lippincott & Co.

Strathmore: Or, Wrought by His Own Hand. A Life Romance. Louise De La Ramee. LC 3-28192. (On cover: Lippincott's popular fiction). 1896. J. B. Lippincott Company.

Straus. Anders Bodelsen. LC 73-4140. 1974. 6.95 (ISBN 0-06-010402-3). Harper & Row.

Straw. Rina Ramsay. LC 9-5527. 1909. The Macmillan Company.

Straw Boss. Stephen Longstreet. 1981. pap. 2.95 (ISBN 0-8439-0980-3, LB980, Leisure Bks). Nordon Pubns.

Straw Boss. Stephen Longstreet. LC 78-5258. 1978. 10.95 o.p. (ISBN 0-399-12196-X). Putnam Pub Group.

Straw Boss: A Novel. Stephen Longstreet. LC 78-5258. 8.95 (ISBN 0-399-12196-X). Putnam.

Straw Boss. 1st Ed. Eugene E Halleran. LC 52-5085. 1952. Lippincott.

Straw Donkey Case. Albert Sidney Fleischman. LC 48-28173. 1948. Phoenix Press.

Straw Fire: A Novel. Kathleen Crawford. LC 47-30873. 1947. W. Morrow.

Straw for the Fire. Ed. by David Wagoner. 264p. 1974. pap. 3.95 o.p. (ISBN 0-385-06675-9, Anch). Doubleday.

Straw for the Fire: From the Notebooks of Theodore Roethke, 1943-63. Theodore Roethke. Ed. by David Wagoner. LC 80-13970. 262p. 1980. pap. 8.95 (ISBN 0-295-95753-0). U of Wash Pr.

Straw Hammocks. Victoria Ferguson. LC 40-37523. B. Humphries, Inc.

Straw Hat: A Novel. Joseph Vogel. LC 40-347508. Modern Age Books.

Straw in the Sun. Charlie May Hogue Simon. LC 45-25411. 1945. E. P. Dutton & Company, Inc.

Straw in the Wind. Ruth Lininger Dobson. LC 37-1266. 1937. Dodd, Mead & Company.

Straw Man. Jean Giono. Tr. by Phyllis Johnson. LC 82-73715. 472p. 1982. pap. 14.00 (ISBN 0-86547-071-5). N Point Pr.

Straw Man. Barbara Goldsmith. LC 74-34398. 1975. 8.95 (ISBN 0-374-27090-2). Farrar, Straus, Giroux.

Straw Man. Barbara Goldsmith. 1976. (pbk.) 1.75. Ballantine.

Straw Man. 1st Ed. Doris Miles Disney. LC 51-13068. 1951. Published for the Crime Club by Doubleday.

Straw Obelisk. Adolph Caso. 1972. 6.95 (ISBN 0-8283-1293-1). Branden.

Straw Sandals: Chinese Stories of Social Realism. Ed. by Harold Robert Isaacs. 432p. 1974. 17.50x (ISBN 0-262-09014-7); pap. 5.95 (ISBN 0-262-59006-9). MIT Pr.

Straw to Make Brick. Alan Marcus. LC 48-518643. 1948. Little, Brown.

Straw Wife: A Novel. William John Kehoe. LC 46-7277. 1946. E. P. Dutton & Company, Inc.

Strawberries in the Sea. Elisabeth Ogilvie. LC 73-3474. 1973. 7.95 (ISBN 0-07-047621-7). McGraw-Hill.

Strawberries in the Sea. Elisabeth Ogilvie. 1977 (ISBN 0-380-00732-0). Avon Books.

Strawberry Acres. Grace Louise Smith Richmond. LC 11-264062. 1911. Doubleday, Page & Company.

Strawberry-Blonde Jungle. Carter Brown, pseud. 1979. pap. 1.50 (ISBN 0-505-51405-2). Tower Bks.

Strawberry Boy. Jennifer Dawson. LC 76-381248. 1976. 3.95 (ISBN 0-7043-2067-3). Quartet Books.

Strawberry Fields of Heaven. Blossom Elfman. 1982. 14.95 (ISBN 0-517-54830-5). Crown.

Strawberry Handkerchief: A Romance of the Stamp Act. Amelia Edith Huddleston Barr. LC 8-24302. 1908. Dodd, Mead & Company.

Strawberry Moon. Jean Carew. LC 38-779240. Arcadia House.

Strawberry Roan. Nelson Nye. 1975. (pbk.) 0.95. Belmont Tower Books.

Strawberry Roan. large print ed.. ed. Nelson Coral Nye. LC 81-12649. 1982. 11.95 (ISBN 0-89340-368-7). J. Curley & Associates.

Strawberry Roan. Arthur George Street. LC 33-7852. Harcourt, Brace and Company.

Strawberry Roan: By Clem Colt Pseud. Nelson Coral Nye. LC 52-141956. (Silver star westerns). 1953. Dodd, Mead.

Strawberry Sunday: A Novel. Jessie Allen Siple. LC 51-32211. 1951. Erle Press.

Straws in Amber. Naomi Ellington Jacob. LC 39-448685. 1939. The Macmillan Company.

Straws in the Wind. Wilbur C. Tuttle. LC 48-1373. 1948. Houghton Mifflin Co.

Strawstack. Dorothy Cameron Disney. LC 39-8477. Random House.

Stray in the South Wind. Donald Joseph. LC 46-2670. 1946. The Macmillan Company.

Stray Lamb. Thorne Smith. LC 29-19245. 1929. Cosmopolitan Book Corporation.

Stray Lamb. Thorne Smith. LC 38-35055. 1935. Grosset & Dunlap.

Stray Leaves from Newport. Esther Gracie Lawrence Wheeler. LC 8-6421. 1888. Cupples and Hurd.

Stray Leaves from Newport: A Book of Fancies. 4th ed. illustrated. ed. Esther Gracie Lawrence Wheeler. LC 8-6422. 1890. J. G. Cupples Company.

Stray Leaves from Strange Literature: Stories Reconstructed from the Anvari-Soheili, Baital Pachisi, Mahabharata, Pantchatantra, Gulistan, Talmud, Kalewala, Etc. Lafcadio Hearn. LC 74-3418. 1974. (ISBN 0-8414-4811-6). Folcroft Library Editions.

Stray Pearls. Memoirs of Margaret De Ribaumont, Viscountess of Bellaise. Charlotte Mary Yonge. (Harper's Franklin square library, no. 305). 1883. Harper & Brothers.

Stray Pussycat. Tony Trelos, pseud. (Orig.). pap. 0.95 o.p. (1100). Brandon.

Stray Steps,". Addison Beecher Colvin. LC 21-1359. The Glens Falls Publishing Company.

Stray Subjects, Arrested and Bound Over. Being the Fugitive Offspring of the "Old 'un" and the "Young 'un." That Have Been "Lying Round Loose," and Are Now "Tied up" for Fast Keeping. Illustrated by Darley. Francis Alexander Durivage & Burnham, George P. LC 6-36402. 1848. Carey and Hart.

Stray Yankee in Texas. Samuel Adams Hammett. LC 7-933. 1853. Redfield.

Strayed Angel. Dolf Wyllarde. LC 33-35483. The Macaulay Company.

Strayed Revellers: A Novel of Modernistic Truth and Intruding War. Allan Eugene Updegraff. LC 18-168921. 1918. H. Holt and Company.

Strayed Sheep of Charun. John Maddox Roberts. LC 77-74309. 1977. 6.95 (ISBN 0-385-13066-X). Doubleday.

Strayers from Sheol. Herbert Russell Wakefield. LC 61-2701. 1961. Arkham House.

Strayhorn. William Herrick. LC 68-13108. 1968. McGraw-Hill.

Streak. Paul Darcy Boles. LC 53-11143. (Illus.). 1953. Macmillan.

Streak. Max Brand. LC 37-12762. 1937. Dodd, Mead & Company.

Streak. Max Brand. LC 39-168588. 1939. The Sun Dial Press, Inc.

Streak. Frederick Faust. LC 37-12762. 1937. Dodd, Mead & Company.

Streak. Frederick Faust. LC 39-16858. 1939. The Sun Dial Press, Inc.

Streak. David Potter. LC 13-21029. 1913. 1.25. J. B. Lippincott Company.

Streak of Light. Richard Lockridge. LC 76-23291. 7.95 (ISBN 0-397-01177-6). Lippincott.

Streaked with Crimson. Charles Judson Dutton. LC 29-865223. 1929. Dodd, Mead & Company.

Streaker Murders. Philip Dorian. 1976. pap. 5.95 o.p. (ISBN 0-8059-2298-9). Dorrance.

Streaks of Squatter Life, and Far-West Scenes. A Series of Humorous Sketches Descriptive of Incidents and Character in the Wild West. To Which Are Added Other Miscellaneous Pieces. John S Robb. LC 7-41019. (On cover: Carey & Hart's library of humorous American works). 1847. Carey and Hart.

Streaks of Squatter Life, and Far-West Scenes. A Series of Humorous Sketches Descriptive of Incidents and Character in the Wild West. To Which Are Added Other Miscellaneous Pieces. John S Robb. LC 29-25276. (In Lewis, H. C. The swamp doctors adventures in the South-west. Philadelphia 1858). 1858. T. B. Peterson and Brothers.

Stream. Robert William Murphy. LC 76-139339. (Illus.). 1971. 6.95. Farrar, Straus and Giroux.

Stream of Consciousness and Beyond in Ulysses. Erwin Ray Steinberg. LC 72-78932. 1973. 9.95 (ISBN 0-8229-3245-8). University of Pittsburgh Press.

Stream of Life. 1st. ed. James H Smith. 1974. 5.00 (ISBN 0-682-48063-0). Exposition.

Stream Sinister. Kathleen Moore Knight. LC 45-2937. 1945. Pub. for the Crime Club, by Doubleday, Doran and Company, Inc.

Streamline Marriage. Thelma Strabel. LC 37-6309. J. B. Lippincott Company.

Streamlined Murder. Sue MacVeigh. LC 40-9311. 1940. Houghton Mifflin Company.

Streamlined Murder. Elizabeth Nearing. LC 40-9311. 1940. Houghton Mifflin Company.

Streams in the Wilderness. Chayym Zeldis. LC 62-10190. 1962. T. Yoseloff.

Streams of Ocean. Aubrey De Selincourt. 1923. Repr. 15.00 (ISBN 0-8274-3527-4). R West.

Street. Donald Lindquist. 1979. 12.95 o.p. (ISBN 0-525-21109-8, Thomas Congdon Book). Dutton.

Street. Sydney Marsh. LC 61-13246. 1961. Dorrance.

Street. Ann Lane Petry. LC 46-1079. 1946. Houghton Mifflin Company.

Street: An Autobiographical Novel. Aram Saroyan. LC 74-82227. 2.95. Bookstore Press.

Street & Smith's Love Story Anthology. LC 50-15996. Street & Smith.

Street & Smith's Love Story Anthology. LC 50-15996. Street & Smith Publications.

Street Beat. Stewart Benedict. 288p. (Orig.). 1982. pap. 2.75 (ISBN 0-523-41188-X). Pinnacle Bks.

Street Beyond Darkness: A Novel. Robert Rogers Hubach. LC 68-20957. 1968. 3.50. Dorrance.

Street Called Straight: A Novel. Basil King. LC 41-35138. 1912. Grosset & Dunlap.

Street Called Straight: A Novel. Basil King. LC 12-124812. 1912. Harper & Brothers.

Street Cops. William Klasne. LC 79-26745. 10.95 (ISBN 0-13-851568-9). Prentice-Hall.

Street Games. Rosellen Brown. LC 73-18774. 1974. 6.95 (ISBN 0-385-09897-9). Doubleday.

Street Games. Alan Lechner. LC 81-85823. 192p. 1982. pap. 2.95 (ISBN 0-86721-112-1). Playboy Pbks.

Street Games. Eddie Stone. 1977. 1.75 (ISBN 0-87067-518-4). Holloway House.

Street Girl. James Noble Gifford. LC 41-8356. Phoenix Press.

Street Has Changed. Elizabeth Daly. LC 41-200467. Farrar & Rinehart, Inc.

Street Hustler. Norman Rubington. 1975. pap. 1.50 o.p. (LB301DK, Leisure Bks). Nordon Pubns.

Street in Moscow. Ilya Grigorevich Ehrenburg & Volochova, Sonia, Tr. LC 32-26440. Covici, Friede.

Street in Suburbia. Edwin William Pugh. LC 7-42192. 1895. D. Appleton and Company.

Street Music. Theodora Keogh. LC 51-6886. 1951. Farrar, Straus, and Young.

Street of a Thousand Delights. Jay Gelzer. LC 75-167449. (Short story index reprint series). 1971. (ISBN 0-8369-3975-1). Books for Libraries Press.

Street of a Thousand Delights. Jay Gelzer. LC 21-12706. 1921. R. M. McBride & Company.

Street of Adventure. Philip Hamilton Gibbs. 1920. E. P. Dutton & Company.

Street of Chains. Lilian Laufferty. LC 29-18267. 1929. Harper & Brothers.

Street of Crocodiles. Bruno Schulz. LC 76-48335. (Writers from the Other Europe). 1977. 2.95 (ISBN 0-14-004227-X). Penguin Books.

Street of Grass. Pierre Audemars. LC 63-20608. 1963. Harper & Row.

Street of Ho's. Leo Guild. (Orig.). 1976. pap. 1.50 (ISBN 0-87067-495-1, BH025). Holloway.

Street of Kings. Charles Dexter. LC 57-7354. 1957. Holt.

Street of Knives. Cyril Harris. LC 50-9023. 1950. Little, Brown.

Street of Many Arches. Joan Conquest & Lally, Gwen, Joint Author. LC 23-176504. 1923. Cassell and Company, Ltd.

Street of Many Arches. Joan Conquest & Lally, Gwen, Joint Author. LC 24-510576. The Macaulay Company.

Street of No Return. Cover Painting by Barye Phillips. David Goodis. LC 54-42479. (Gold medal books, 428). 1954. Fawcett Publications.

Street of Painted Lips. Maurice DeKobra, pseud. Tr. by Wainwright, Neal. LC 34-2642. The Macaulay Company.

Street of Queer Houses & Other Tales. David Henry Keller. Ed. by R. Reginald & Douglas Menville. LC 75-46285. (Supernatural & Occult Fiction Ser.). 1976. Repr. of 1925 ed. lib. bdg. 13.00x (ISBN 0-405-08146-4). Ayer Co.

Street of Queer Houses and Other Tales. Vernon Knowles. LC 75-46285. (Supernatural and Occult Fiction). 1976. 13.00 (ISBN 0-405-08146-4). Arno Press.

Street of Riches. Garbrielle Carbotte Roy. LC 67-106643. (New Canadian library, no. 56) $1.50 Can.). McClelland and Stewart.

Street of Riches: Translated by Harry Binsse. 1st Ed. Gabrielle Carbotte Roy. LC 57-100653. 1957. Harcourt, Brace.

Street of Seven Monks. William Howard Woods. LC 48-903. 1948. Little, Brown.

Street of Seven Stars. Mary Roberts Rinehart. LC 14-20856. 1914. 1.25. Houghton Mifflin Company.

Street of Stairs. Ronald Tavel. LC 79-3029. 1969. 3.95. Olympia Press.

Street of Strange Faces. Louis Joseph Vance. LC 34-2150. J. B. Lippincott Company.

Street of the Barefoot Lovers. 1st Ed. Joseph O'Kane Foster. LC 53-9326. 1953. Deull, Sloan and Pearce.

Street of the Blank Wall: And Other Stories. Jerome Klapka Jerome. LC 16-23590. 1916. 1.35. Dodd, Mead and Company.

Street of the Blank Wall: And Other Stories. Jerome Klapka Jerome. LC 18-11271. 1917. Dodd, Mead and Company.

Street of the Blues. Kate Nickerson. 1969. pap. 0.75 o.p. (75-287). Manor Bks.

Street of the City. Grace Livingston Hill. LC 42-232263. 1942. J. B. Lippincott Company.

Street of the Crying Woman. Daniel Mainwaring. LC 42-168383. 1942. W. Morrow and Company.

Street of the Eye, and Nine Other Tales. Gerald William Bullett. LC 77-167444. (Short story index reprint series). 1971. (ISBN 0-8369-3970-0). Books for Libraries Press.

Street of the Fishing Cat. Jolan Foldes & Jacobi, Elizabeth Pongracz, Tr. LC 37-4744. Farrar & Rinehart, Incorporated.

Street of the Five Moons. Elizabeth Peters, pseud. LC 78-4278. 7.95 (ISBN 0-396-07528-2). Dodd, Meade.

Street of the Flute-Player: A Romance. Henry De Vere Stacpoole. LC 12-24621. 1912. 1.25. Duffield & Company.

Street of the Islands. Stark Young & Bischoff, Ilse, 1901- Illus. LC 30-25745. 1930. C. Scribner's Sons.

Street of the Laughing Camel. Ben Lucien Burman. 4.95. Taplinger.

Street of the Laughing Camel. Drawings by Alice Caddy. 1st Ed. Ben Lucien Burman. LC 59-11925. 1959. McGraw-Hill.

Street of the Madwoman. Phyllis G Leonard. LC 78-592. 9.95 (ISBN 0-698-10911-2). Coward, McCann & Geoghegan.

Street of the Malcontents: And Other Stories. Cyril Hume. LC 27-11492. George H. Doran Company.

Street of the Sandalmakers: A Tale of Rome in the Time of Marcus Aurelius. Nis Petersen. Tr. by Sprigge, Elizabeth. LC 33-796801. 1933. The Macmillan Company.

Street of the Serpents. Francis Beeding. LC 34-188360. 1934. Harper & Brothers.

Street of the Seven Little Sisters: A Tale of Old Cario and the Great Desert. Gladys Parvin. LC 25-159877. R. F. Seymour.

Street of the Small Steps. Ruth Willock. LC 73-179111. 1972. 5.95. Hawthorn Books.

Street of the Small Steps. Ruth Willock. 1975. (pbk.) 1.25. Dell.

Street of the Sun. Lance Horner. Abelard-Schuman.

Street of the Three Friends. Myron Brinig. LC 52-13576. 1953. Rinehart.

Street of the Two Friends. Frank Berkeley Smith. LC 12-249197. 1912. Doubleday, Page & Company.

Street of to-Day. John Masefield. LC 11-29730. 1911. J. M. Dent & Sons, Ltd.

Street of Women. Polan Banks. LC 31-23589. J. Cape & H. Smith.

Street Players. Donald Goines. 192p. (Orig.). 1973. pap. 1.95 (ISBN 0-87067-644-X, BH024). Holloway.

Street Players. Donald Goines. 1973. 1.50 (ISBN 0-87067-430-7). Holloway House.

Street Singer. Sallie Lee Bell. LC 51-2266. 1951. Zondervan.

Street Smarts. Bruce Reeves. (Illus.). 224p. 1982. pap. 2.25 (ISBN 0-448-16930-4, Pub. by Tempo). Ace Bks.

Street Sparrows. Rose Ayers. LC 78-9354. 10.95 (ISBN 0-698-10935-X). Coward, McCann & Geoghegan.

Street Where I Live. Maara Haas. (Illus.). 224p. 1976. 7.95 o.p. (ISBN 0-07-092771-5). McGraw.

Street Where I Live: A Novel. Maara Haas. LC 76-379935. (Illus.). 8.95 (ISBN 0-07-092771-5). McGraw-Hill Ryerson.

Street Where the Heart Lies. Ludwig Bemelmans. LC 62-17156. 1963. World Pub. Co.

Street 8: A Novel. Douglas Fairbairn. LC 76-28245. 7.95 (ISBN 0-440-06167-9). Delacorte Press/Seymour Lawrence.

Streetbird. Janwillem Van De Wetering. 288p. 1983. 13.95 (ISBN 0-399-12808-5). Putnam Pub Group.

Streetful of People. Winston M. Estes. LC 71-38307. 1972. 5.95 (ISBN 0-397-00768-X). Lippincott.

Streetful of People. Winston M. Estes. 1978. 1.75 (ISBN 0-380-01917-5). Avon.

Streets. Joseph Trigoboff. LC 73-138846. 1970. 4.00 (ISBN 0-911838-07-4). Windy Row.

Streets Are Not Paved with Gold. Terez D Stibran. LC 61-10299. 1961.

Streets of Ascalon: Episodes in the Unfinished Carreer of Richard Quarren. Esq. Robert William Chambers. LC 12-21917. 1912. D. Appleton and Company.

Streets of Askelon. Tony Aspler. LC 72-83731. 1972. 5.95. M. Evans; Distributed in Association with Lippincott, Philadelphia.

Streets of Askelon. Don Tracy. LC 51-10287. 1951. Dial Press.

Streets of Blood. Philip Rawls. (Bronson Ser: No. 2). 192p. (Orig.). 1975. pap. 1.25 o.p. (ISBN 0-532-12292-5). Woodhill.

Streets of Blood. Philip Rawls. (Bronson Ser: No. 2). 192p. (Orig.). 1975. pap. 1.25 o.p. (ISBN 0-532-12292-5). Manor Bks.

Streets of Death. Elizabeth Linington. LC 76-14423. 1976. 6.95 (ISBN 0-688-03122-6). Morrow.

Streets of Death. Dell Shannon. 192p. 1980. pap. 1.95 (ISBN 0-553-13952-5). Bantam.

Streets of Death. Dell Shannon. LC 76-14423. 1976. 7.95 (ISBN 0-688-03122-6). Morrow.

Streets of Death. Dell Shannon. LC 80-24140. 315p. 1980. Repr. of 1976 ed. large print ed. 9.95x (ISBN 0-89621-250-5). Thorndike Pr.

Streets of Death. Guy Carlton Williams. LC 39-7437. 1939. Orion Publishers.

Streets of Death: A Luis Mendoza Mystery. Elizabeth Linington. LC 80-24140. 1980. 9.95 (ISBN 0-89621-250-5). Thorndike Press.

Streets of Gold. Evan Hunter. LC 74-6980. 1974. 8.95 (ISBN 0-06-012012-6). Harper & Row.

Streets of Night. John Dos Passos. LC 23-17922. George H. Doran Company.

Streets of Shadow. Leslie McFarlane. LC 30-102550. E. P. Dutton & Co., Inc.

Strega - Other Stories. Louise De La Ramee. LC 72-101797. (Short Story Index Reprintser.). 1899. 16.00 (ISBN 0-8369-3185-8). Ayer Co.

Strega, & Other Stories. Louise De La Ramee. LC 6-33877. 1899. D. Biddle.

Strengleikar. Rudolf Meissner. LC 80-1954. Repr. of 1902 ed. 42.00 (ISBN 0-404-18711-0). AMS Pr.

Strengleikar Etha Ljothabok. Ed. by C R Unger & R. Keyser. LC 80-1945. Repr. of 1850 ed. 28.00 (ISBN 0-404-18719-6). AMS Pr.

Strength of Gideon: And Other Stories. Paul Laurence Dunbar. LC 69-18589. (Afro-American Culture Series.). (American Negro, his history and literature). (Illus.). 1969. Arno Press.

Strength of Gideon: And Other Stories. Paul Laurence Dunbar. LC 78-81115. (Illus.). 1969. Mnemosyne Pub. Inc.

Strength of Gideon: And Other Stories. Paul Laurence Dunbar. LC 2516. 1900. Dodd, Mead & Company.

Strength of Gideon & Other Stories. Paul Laurence Dunbar. LC 69-18589. (American Negro: His History & Literature Ser., No. 2). 1969. Repr. of 1899 ed. 15.00 (ISBN 0-405-01860-6). Ayer Co.

Strength of Gideon, & Other Stories. facs. ed. Paul Laurence Dunbar. LC 78-81115. (Black Heritage Library Collection Ser). (Illus.). 1900. 14.50 (ISBN 0-8369-8566-4). Ayer Co.

Strength of Gideon & Other Stories. Paul Laurence Dunbar. 3.45 o.p. (0606). G&D.

Strength of Love. Julienne Bonin. LC 56-13098. (Pan Press inspirational book). Pan Press.

Strength of Lovers. Gustavo Adolfo Martinez Zuviria & Imbert, Louis, Tr. LC 30-4857. 1930. Longmans, Green and Co.

Strength of Lovers see Novels by Hugo Wast.

Strength of Stones, Flesh of Brass. Gregory Bear. 256p. (Orig.). 1981. pap. 2.50 (ISBN 0-441-79069-0). Ace Bks.

Strength of the Hills. William Aden French. LC 44-7846. 1944. The Current Wave Press.

Strength of the Hills. Bertha B. Moore McCurry. LC 52-4351. 1952. Moody Press.

Strength of the Hills: A Novel. Florence Wilkinson Evans. LC 1-24836. 1901. Harper & Brothers.

Strength of the Hills: A Story of Andrew Jackson, and of the Pioneers of Tennessee. Ellery Harding Clark. LC 29-18073. Thomas Y. Crowell Company.

Strength of the Pines. Edison Marshall. LC 21-2387. 1921. Little, Brown, and Company.

Strength of the Spirit. Margaret Leonora Pitcairn Eyles. 1930. R. R. Smith. Inc.

Strength of the Weak. May Dixon Thacker. 1910. Broadway Publishing Co.

Strength of the Weak: A Romance. Chauncey Crafts Hotchkiss. LC 2-2773. 1902. D. Appleton and Company.

Strength of Tradition: Stories of the Immigrant Presence in Australia. Ed. by R. F. Holt. LC 82-10874. 288p. 1983. 16.50 (ISBN 0-7022-1691-7); pap. 8.95 (ISBN 0-7022-1701-8). U of Queensland Pr.

Strength to Yield: The Psychology of a Great Temptation. Virgilia Bogue. LC 9-23808. 1909. Cunningham, Curtiss & Welch.

Strenth of the Strong. Jack London. LC 14-9528. 1914. 1.25. The Macmillan Company.

Stress Patterns. Neal Jr. Barrett. 1974. (pbk.) 0.95. DAW Books.

Stretch-Berry Smile. Dorothy Scarborough. LC 32-4557. The Bobbs-Merrill Company.

Stretch Dawson. William Riley Burnett. LC 50-8355. (Gold medal book, 106). 1950. Fawcett Publications.

Stretch on the River. 1st Ed. Richard Pike Bissell. LC 50-8516. 1950. Little, Brown.

Stretelli Case and Other Mystery Stories. Edgar Wallace. LC 30-22435. International Fiction Library.

Strettam: A Novel. Elva Arline McAllaster. LC 75-189580. 1972. 4.95. Zondervan Pub. House.

Stretton Street Affair. William Le Queux. LC 22-4826. The Macaulay Company.

Stribling: A Novel. Lucas Webb. LC 72-92250. 1973. 6.95 (ISBN 0-385-00257-2). Doubleday.

Stricken Field. Martha Gellhorn. LC 40-27213. Duell, Sloan and Pearce.

Stricklands. Edwin Moultrie Lanham. LC 39-500801. 1939. Little, Brown and Company.

Strictly a Loser. Edna Sherry. LC 65-14522. (Red badge detective). 1965. Dodd, Mead.
Strictly a Wolf. William Arthur Neubauer. LC 44-5098. 1944. Phoenix Press.
Strictly Amateur. Tom McCormack. 288p. (Orig.). 1982. pap. 2.75 (ISBN 0-523-41486-2). Pinnacle Bks.
Strictly Business". F. Morton Howard. LC 23-8242. E. P. Dutton & Company.
Strictly Business. Gloria Renwick. (Candlelight Ecstasy Ser.: No. 69). (Orig.). 1982. pap. 1.95 (ISBN 0-440-17727-8). Dell.
Strictly Business: More Stories of the Four Million. William Sydney Porter. LC 10-5307. 1910. Doubleday, Page & Company.
Strictly Business: More Stories of the Four Million. William Sydney Porter. LC 15-17410. 1911. Doubleday, Page & Company.
Strictly Business: More Stories of the Four Million. William Sydney Porter. LC 19-135255. 1918. Doubleday, Page & Company.
Strictly Business: More Stories of the Four Million. William Sydney Porter. LC 21-8695. 1920. Doubleday, Page & Company.
Strictly Dishonorable. Joseph Weil & Sturges, Preston. Strictly Dishonorable. LC 31-25224. Grosset & Dunlap.
Strictly Feminine. Allen Eppes. LC 38-152231. Gramercy Publishing Co.
Strictly Feminine. Watkins Eppes Wright. LC 38-15223. 1938. Gramercy Pub. Co.
Strictly for Cash. Rene Raymond. 1973. (pbk) 0.75. Pocket Books.
Strictly for Laughs. Joey Adams. 4.95 o.p. Wehman.
Strictly from Brooklyn. William Heuman. LC 56-5675. 1956. Morrow.
Strictly Legal: A Novelette. Kenneth C Davis. LC 34-410616. 1934.
Strictly Personal. Julie Closson Kenly. LC 29-14912. 1929. D. Appleton and Company.
Strictly Private. Therese Benson. LC 31-119982. 1931. Dodd, Mead & Company.
Stride of Man. Thames Ross Williamson. LC 28-27809. 1928. Coward-McCann, Inc.
Strife. A Romance of Germany and Italy. 2d ed. E. D. Wallace. LC 8-332835. 1872. Claxton, Remsen & Haffelfinger.
Strife and Peace: Or, Scenes in Norway. Fredrika Bremer. LC 6-17396. 1843. J. Munroe and Company.
Strife Before Dawn. Mary Schumann. LC 39-31681. 1939. The Dial Press.
Strife of the Sea. Thornton Jenkins Hains. LC 72-103515. (Short story index reprint series). (Illus.). 1969. Books for Libraries Press.
Strike. Isabel Alvarez. Tr. by William Rose from Span. LC 76-111027. 1971. 6.95 o.p. (ISBN 0-394-47566-6, GP592). Grove.
Strike. Alvarez De Toledo, Luisa Isabel. LC 76-111027. 1971. 6.95. Grove Press.
Strike! Mary Marvin Heaton Vorse. LC 30-279295. H. Liveright.
Strike. William Wilfrid Whalen. LC 27-2652. Dorrance and Company.
Strike: A Novel. Yvonne Burgess. LC 79-23680. 1980. 8.95 (ISBN 0-8008-7471-4). Taplinger Pub. Co.
Strike at Cripple Creek. Bob Haning. 1975. (pbk.) 0.95. Belmont Tower Books.
Strike at Cripple Creek. James R. Haning. 1973. 4.95 (ISBN 0-517-51498-2). Lenox Hill Press.
Strike at Shane's... Sequel to "Black Beauty." A Prize Story of Indiana... James S. Shelton. LC 8-5110. (Gold mine series, no. 2). American Humane Education Society.
Strike Deep. Anthony North. LC 74-4145. 1974. 6.95 (ISBN 0-8037-8338-8). Dial Press.
Strike for the Heart. Kay Beliveau. LC 47-31154. 1947. Doubleday.
Strike for Tomahawk: A Powder Valley Western. Peter Field. LC 56-9701. 1956. Jefferson House.
Strike Force see Killer Tank.
Strike Force Terror. Nick Carter. (Nick Carter Ser.). (O.s.i.). 192p. (Orig.). 1974. pap. 1.25 o.s.i. (AQ1298, Award). Univ Pub & Dist.
Strike Force 7. Ian MacAlister. (Fawcett gold medal book). 1974. (pbk.) 0.95. Fawcett.
Strike from the Sea. Douglas Reeman. LC 78-58389. 1978. 8.95 (ISBN 0-688-03319-9). Morrow.
Strike from the Sea. Douglas Reeman. (Berkley Book). 1979. 2.25 (ISBN 0-425-04189-1). Berkley Pub Corp.
Strike Heaven on the Face, a Novel. Charles J Calitri. LC 58-128803. 1958. Crown Publishers.
Strike North. easy eye ed. W. Howard Baker. (Super Hero Collection). 1968. pap. 0.60 o.p. (73-698). Lancer.
Strike of a Sex and Zugassent's Discovery: Or, After the Sex Struck. George Noyes Miller. LC 73-20636. (Sex, Marriage, and Society). 1974. 7.00 (ISBN 0-405-05812-8). Arno Press.
Strike of a Sex.A Novel. By? George Noyes Miller. 1890. G. W. Dillingham.
Strike Out Where Not Applicable. Nicolas Freeling. LC 68-15981. 1968. 4.95 o.p. (ISBN 0-06-011357-X, HarpT). Har-Row.
Strike Out Where Not Applicable. 1st U.S. Ed. Nicolas Freeling. LC 68-15981. 4.95. Harper.
Strike Terror. Hy Steirman. (Orig.). 1968. pap. 0.75 o.p. (54-722). Paperback Lib.
Strike the Bell Boldly: A Novel. Stephen Longstreet. LC 76-51426. 8.95. Putnam.
Strike the Bell Boldly: A Novel. Stephen Longstreet. (Berkley Medallion Book). 1978. 1.95 (ISBN 0-425-03765-7). Berkley Pub. Corp.
Strike the Father Dead: A Novel. John Barrington Wain. LC 62-18721. 1962. St. Martin's Press.
Strike the Lutin Bell. 1st Ed. Victor Hugo Johnson. LC 58-12264. 1958. Duell, Sloan and Pearce.
Strike Zone. Richard Curtis. (Pro#3). 1975. (pbk.) 1.25 (ISBN 0-446-76837-5). Warner Paperback Library.
Striker Schneiderman. Jack Gray. LC 72-954459. (Canadian Play Ser.). 1973. pap. 3.00 (ISBN 0-8020-6172-9). U of Toronto Pr.
Strikers: A Novel. Goetze Jeter. LC 37-122329. 1937. Frederick A. Stokes Company.
Strikes Portfolio. Adam Hall, pseud. LC 69-12088. (O.S.I.). 1969. 4.95 o.s.i. (ISBN 0-671-20175-1, 20175). S&S.
Striking Hours. Eden Phillpotts. LC 1-22004. Frederick A. Stokes Company.
Striking Resemblance. Joseph Real Brown. LC 32-17154. 1932. Meador Publishing Company.
String Bean. Edmond Sechan. LC 81-43242. (Illus.). 12.95 (ISBN 0-385-17135-8). Doubleday.
String Horses. Ursula Holden. LC 76-376183. (London Magazine editions). 1976. 3.75 (ISBN 0-904388-11-5). London Magazine Editions.
String of Blue Beads. Illustrated by Reisie Lonette. 1st Ed. Fulton Oursler. LC 56-113072. 1956. Doubleday.
String of Chinese Pearls: Ten Tales of Chinese Girls Ancient & Modern. W. Fisher. lib. bdg. 59.95 (ISBN 0-87968-518-2). Krishna Pr.
String of Pearls. Hedwig Mahler Courths. 1929. J. B. Lippincott Company.
String of Pearls. Elizabeth H. Mace. LC 99-4750. (Neely's universal library, no. 86). 1899. F. T. Neeley.
String That Went up. Otis Kidwell Burger. LC 63-9425. 1963. St Martin's Press.
Stringer. Ward S Just. LC 73-13682. 1974. 5.95 (ISBN 0-316-47721-4). Little, Brown.
Strings of Steel: Novelized by Paul Gulick, from the University Picture of the Same Name of Philip Hurn and Oscar Lund, Illustrated with Scenes from the Photoplay. Paul Gulick & Hurn, Philip. LC 26-15064. Grosset & Dunlap.
Strings to Love. Anne Maguire, pseud. (YA) 1981. 6.95 (Avalon). Bouregy.
Stringtown on the Pike: A Folk-Lore Tale of Northernmost Kentucky. John Uri Lloyd. LC 34-406782. 1934. The Ruter Press.
Stringtown on the Pike: A Tale of Northernmost Kentucky. John Uri Lloyd. 1900. Dodd, Mead and Company.
Strip Death Naked. Norman Longmate. LC 81-47351. (Fifty Classics of Crime Fiction, 1950-1975). 1982. 14.95 (ISBN 0-8240-4972-1). Garland Pub.
Strip for Murder. Richard S Prather. LC 55-43681. (Gold medal books, 508). 1955. Fawcett Publications.
Strip Jack Naked. Alexander Baron. LC 66-24654. 1967. 4.50. Yoseloff.
Strip Jack Naked. William Garner. LC 75-142478. 1971. 5.95. Bobbs-Merrill.
Striped Suitcase. 1st. american ed. Edith Caroline Rivett. LC 47-586030. 1947. Pub. for the Crime Club by Doubleday.
Stripling. Youel Benjamin Mirza. LC 40-32085. W. Funk, Inc.
Striplings. Nina Warner Hooke. LC 34-3285. E. P. Dutton & Co., Inc.
Stripped to the Hide. Herman Edwin Mootz. LC 27-21131. The Roxburgh Publishing Company, Inc.
Stripper. Emarcus Lee Adams. LC 54-415701. 1954.
Stripper. Carter Brown, pseud. LC 62-2012. (Signet books, S1961). 1961. New American Library of World Literature.
Stripper. Wright Williams. LC 41-11977. Phoenix Press.
Stripper. Watkins Eppes Wright. LC 41-11977. 1941. Phoenix Press.
Stripper. Alan Geoffrey Yates. LC 62-2012. (Signet books, S1981). 1961. New American Library of World Literature.
Stripper: The Life and Times of Jennifer Diamond. Charlene Keel. 1975. (pbk.) 1.50. Belmont Tower Books.
Striptease; Tango; Vatzlav: Three Plays. Sawomir. Mrozek. LC 81-47635. 8.95 (ISBN 0-394-17933-1). Grove Press.
Stripwell & Claw. Howard Barker. 1980. pap. 4.95 (ISBN 0-7145-3572-9). Riverrun NY.
Strode Venturer. Hammond Innes. LC 65-18759. 1965. Knopf.
Stroka Prospekt. Richard A. Lupoff. LC 82-19269. (Singularities; 2nd). 1982. 35.00 (ISBN 0-915124-72-6) (ISBN 0-915124-73-4). Toothpaste Press.
Stroke Oar. Ralph Delahaye Paine. 1908. The Outing Publishing Company.
Stroke of Death. Josephine Bell. LC 77-79963. 1977. 6.95 (ISBN 0-8027-5378-7). Walker.
Stroke of Diplomacy. From the French of Victor Cherbuliez... Victor Cherbuliez. LC 6-26964. (Appletons' new handy volume series v. 49). 1880. D. Appleton and Company.
Stroke of Genius. Ted Mark, pseud. (Orig.). 1982. pap. 2.50 (ISBN 0-89083-976-X). Zebra.
Stroke of Light. George Brandon Saul. 1974. 5.00 (ISBN 0-8233-0201-6). Golden Quill.
Stroke of Lightning. Ted Mark, pseud. (Stroke Ser.). 1982. pap. cancelled (ISBN 0-8217-1078-8). Zebra.
Stroke of Luck and Dream of Destiny. Arnold Bennett. LC 32-143337. 1932. Doubleday, Doran & Company, Inc.
Stroke of Luck and Dream of Destiny: An Unfinished Novel. Arnold Bennett. LC 74-17075. (Collected works of Arnold Bennett). 1974. (ISBN 0-518-19157-5). Books for Libraries Press.
Stroke of One. Robert Alfred John Walling. LC 31-5251. 1931. W. Morrow & Co.
Stroke of Seven: By Robert Wade. Bob Wade, pseud. LC 65-18519. bds., 4.95. Morrow.
Stroke: The Condition & the Patient. John Sarno & Martha Sarno. 1969. 9.95 o.p. (ISBN 0-07-054739-4, GB). McGraw.
Strollers. Frederic Stewart Isham. LC 2-9136. 1902. The Bowen-Merrill Co.
Strolling Piper of Brittany. John William Harding. LC 13-177269. (On cover: Neely's continental library, no. 3). 1897. F. T. Neely.
Strolling Players. Dwyer-Joyce, Alice. LC 74-18735. 1975. 6.95 (ISBN 0-7091-4351-6). St. Martin's Press.
Strolling Saint: Being the Confessions of the High and Mighty Agostino D'Anguissola, Tyrant of Mondolfo and Lord of Carmina, in the State of Piacenza. Rafael Sabatini. LC 25-26900. 1925. Houghton Mifflin Company.
Strong & Steady: Or Paddle Your Own Canoe. Horatio Alger. 172p. 1975. pap. 1.25 (ISBN 0-89041-004-6, 3004). Major Bks.
Strong & Tender Thread. Jackie Weger. (American Romance Ser.). 192p. 1983. pap. 2.25 (ISBN 0-373-16005-4). Harlequin Bks.
Strong Arm. Robert Barr. LC 99-2871. 1899. Frederick A. Stokes Company.
Strong As Death: A Novel. Guy De Maupassant. Tr. by Teofilo Ernesto Combs. LC 99-4567. 1899. D. Biddle.
Strong Citadel. Katharine Newlin Burt. LC 49-788. 1949. C. Scribner's Son.
Strong City. Taylor Caldwell. LC 75-702. 1975. 11.95 (ISBN 0-88411-158-X). Aeonian Press.
Strong City. Taylor Caldwell. LC 42-10015. 1942. C. Scribner's Sons.
Strong Enchantments: A Novel. Mary Schumann. LC 33-10151. 1933. Macrae Smith Company.
Strong Hand. Warwick Deeping. LC 12-23515. 1912. 1.35. Cassell & Company, Limited.
Strong Hand. 1st Ed. Michael Blankfort. LC 56-5620. 1956. Little, Brown.
Strong Heart: Being the Story of a Lady. Arthur Rhys Goring-Thomas. LC 14-4464. 1914. 1.25. John Lane.
Strong Hearts. George Washington Cable. LC 72-84533. 1974. (lib. ed.) 8.50 (ISBN 0-403-02990-2). Scholarly Press.
Strong Hearts. George Washington Cable. LC 77-96495. (Illus.). 1970. Garrett Press.
Strong Hearts. George Washington Cable. LC 99-1236. 1899. C. Scribner's Sons.
Strong Hearts see Collected Works.
Strong Hours. Katherine Helen Maud Marshall Diver. LC 19-17180. 1919. Houghton Mifflin Company.
Strong Mac. Samuel Rutherford Crockett. LC 4-7709. 1904. Dodd, Mead and Company.
Strong Man Needed. Maurice Richardson. LC 32-3745. H. Liveright, Inc.
Strong Man of Nevada. Neve Conklin. LC 75-326916. 6.95 (ISBN 0-8059-2144-3). Dorrance.
Strong Man's House. Francis Neilson. LC 16-189098. The Bobbs-Merrill Company.
Strong Man's House. Francis Neilson. LC 24-20612. 1924. B. W. Huebsch, Inc.
Strong-Minded Woman: Or, Two Years After. William Alexander Hammond. LC 7-556. 1885. D. Appleton and Company.
Strong Opinions. Vladimir Nabokov. LC 73-6604. 352p. 1973. 8.95 (ISBN 0-07-045737-9, GB). McGraw.
Strong Poison. Dorothy Leigh Sayers. (Lord Peter Wimsey novel. Keith Jennison bk.; large type ed.). 1965. 6.95. Watts.
Strong Poison. Dorothy Leigh Sayers. LC 58-8893. 1958. Harper.
Strong Poison. Dorothy Leigh Sayers. LC 75-44999. (Fifty Classics of Crime Fiction, 1900-1950; 43). 1976. 12.00 (ISBN 0-8240-2392-7). Garland Pub.
Strong Poison. Dorothy Leigh Sayers. LC 30-25305. Brewer & Warren Inc.
Strong Poison. Dorothy Leigh Sayers. LC 80-20970. 1980. 15.95 (ISBN 0-8161-3042-6). G. K. Hall.
Strong Poison see Wimsey Set II.
Strong Poison and Have His Carcase. Dorothy Leigh Sayers. LC 37-270251. 1936. Harcourt, Brace and Company.
Strong Shall Hold. Theodore Wayland Douglas. 1943. Macrae-Smith-Company.
Strong Tea. John B. Keane. 1966. pap. 4.50 (ISBN 0-85342-255-9). Irish Bk Ctr.
Strong Tower. Martha Wall. LC 76-109938. 1970. 4.95. Herald Press.
Strong Wind. Miguel Angel Asturias. (Laurel edition). 1975. (pbk.) 1.25. Dell.
Strong Wind. Miguel Angel Asturias. LC 68-30987. 1968. 6.95. Delacorte Press.
Strong Wine, Red As Blood: A Novel. Robert Daley. LC 74-27300. 1975. 10.00 (ISBN 0-06-121875-8). Harper's Magazine Press.
Strongbox. Howard Swiggett. LC 55-6552. 1955. Houghton Mifflin.
Stronger Claim. Alice Robinson Perrin. LC 10-8338. 1910. Duffield & Company.
Stronger Climate: 9 Stories. Ruth Prawer Jhabvala. LC 68-13486. 1968. 4.95. Norton.
Stronger God. Eric Waring. LC 27-2301. 1927. Brentano's.
Stronger Heart. Pauline Vance. LC 47-19189. 1947. Arcadia House.
Stronger Light. Mary Gertrude Balch. LC 22-11790. The Cornhill Publishing Company.
Stronger Than Death: Adapted from the French of Emile Richebourg. Emile I. E. Jules Emile Richebourg & Loranger, Alexina, Tr. LC 7-41228. (On cover: Idylwild series. v. 1, no. 11). 1892. Morrill, Higgins & Co.
Stronger Than Death: Or, Spirite. Theophile Gautier. Tr. by Arthur D. Hall. LC 98-1515. (On cover: Globe library, vol. I, no. 14). 1898. Rand, McNally & Company.
Stronger Than Fear. Richard William Tregaskis. LC 45-5191. 1945. Random House.
Stronger Than His Sea. Robert Watson. LC 20-18387. George H. Doran Company.
Stronger Than Love. Annie French Hector. 1902. Brentano's.
Stronger Than We Think. Elizabeth G. Conley. 1962. 4.00 o.p. (ISBN 0-682-40034-3). Exposition.
Stronger Will. Evelyn Everett Green. LC 6-455502. Bradley & Woodruff.
Strongest (Les Plus Fort) Georges Eugene Benjamin Clemenceau. LC 19-155429. 1919. Doubleday, Page & Company.
Strongest Man in the World. Barry Collins. 96p. (Orig.). 1980. pap. 9.95 (ISBN 0-571-11111-4). Faber & Faber.
Strongest Master. Helen Choate Pratt Prince. LC 2-21981. 1902. Houghton, Mifflin and Company.
Strongest Son. Barbara B Stevens. LC 38-757036. 1938. Houghton Mifflin Company.
Stronghand. A Tale of the Disinherited. rev. and ed. by percy b. st. john. ed. Gustave Aimard & St. John, Percy Bolingbroke, 1821-1889, Ed. LC 5-42186. (On cover: Lovell's library, no. 1101). 1887. J. W. Lovell Company.
Strongheart: A Novel. Frederick Russell Burton & De Mille, William C. LC 8-24461. G. W. Dillingham Company.
Stronghold. Gifford Paul Cheshire. LC 63-17128. (Double D western). 1963. Doubleday.
Stronghold. Donald Barr Chidsey. LC 48-562048. 1948. Doubleday.
Stronghold. Stanley Ellin. LC 74-9064. 1974. 5.95 (ISBN 0-394-48558-0). Random House.
Stronghold: A Novel. Meyer Levin. LC 65-22264. 1965. 5.95. S. & S.
Strongholds. Lucy Maria Boston. LC 68-24383. 1969. Harcourt, Brace & World.
Strongmen. John Brick. LC 59-12617. 1959. Doubleday.
Strontium Code. Nick Carter. (Nick Carter Ser.). 208p. (Orig.). 1981. pap. 2.50 (ISBN 0-441-79073-9). Ace Bks.
Struan. Julia Magruder. 1899. R. G. Badger & Co.
Struck a Lead. An Historical Tale of the Upper Lead Region. James M Goodhue. 1883. J. Cover, Jr.
Struck by Lightning: The Comedy of Being a Man. Burton Kline. LC 16-8807. 1916. 1.30. John Lane Company.
Struck Down. A Novel. Hawley Smart. (On cover: Seaside library. Pocket ed. no. 550). 1885. G. Munro.
Structure and Motif in Finnegans Wake. Clive Hart. LC 62-14296. (Illus.). 1962. Northwestern University Press.
Struggle. Sidney C. Tapp. LC 6-3126. 1906. A. Wessels Company.
Struggle. A Story in Four Parts. Barnet Phillips. (Appletons' new handy-volume series no. 2). 1878. D. Appleton and Company.
Struggle: By Harmon Bellamy (Pseud. Herman Irving Bloom. LC 35-18232. Godwin.

TITLE INDEX STUMBLING STONE.

Struggle for a Heart: Or Crystabel's Fatal Love. Laura Jean Libbey. (On cover: The library of American authors, no. 15). 1889. G. Munro.
Struggle for a Ring. A Novel. Charlotte Mary Brame. 1883. G. W. Carleton & Co.
Struggle for a Ring: A Novel. Charlotte Mary Brame. LC 6174. (Bertha Clay library, no. 26). 1900. Street & Smith.
Struggle for a Ring. A Novel. Charlotte Mary Brame & Clark, Charlotte (Moon) 1829-1895, Supposed Author. LC 44-11964. 1883. G. W. Carleton & Co.
Struggle for Existence: Or, As 'tis in Life. (Comme Dans la Vie. Albert Delpit. Tr. by Bramwell, Remington. (On cover: World library. no. 4). The Waverly Company.
Struggle for Fame. A Novel. Charlotte Eliza Lawson Cowan Riddell. (Harper's Franklin square library, no. 337). 1883. Harper & Brothers.
Struggle for Fame. A Novel. Charlotte Eliza Lawson Cowan Riddell. (On cover: Seaside library. Pocket ed., no. 71). 1883. G. Munro.
Struggle: For Fame, Love, Honor and Treasure. Robert Elmer Callahan. LC 26-4417. 1926.
Struggle for Honor: Or, The World Against Her. Edna Winfield, pseud. LC 2176. (On cover: Holly libarary. no. 157)). 1900. The Mershon Co.
Struggle for Justice. Pierce Egan. LC 13-3074. 1913. Tribune Company, Printers.
Struggle for Life. Albert Delpit. Tr. by Robins, E. P. (On cover: elite ser. no. 13). The F. M. Lupton Publishing Company.
Struggle for Life. Lucretia Peabody Hale. 1861. Walker, Wise, & Co.
Struggle for Life: Or, Board Court and Langdale. A Story of Home. 4th ed. Lucretia Peabody Hale. LC 6-46205. 1868. A. Williams and Company.
Struggle for Maverick. A Dramatic Story, in Three Parts. James Franklin Fitts. (On cover: Sea and shore series, no. 22). 1890. Street & Smith.
Struggle for Millions: Or, The Baffled Detectives. Arthur Arnould. LC 7-22758. (On cover: The Pinkerton detective series. no. 52). 1892. Laird & Lee.
Struggle for the Right: Or, Tracking the Truth. (On cover: Seaside library. Pocket ed., no. 964). 1887. G. Munro.
Struggle in the Kremlin: A Novel. Nikodems Elijs Bojars. LC 78-105510. 8.95 (ISBN 0-533-03071-4). Vantage Press.
Struggle of the Naga Tribe: A Play. W. S Rendra. LC 79-16537. 16.95 (ISBN 0-312-76876-1). St. Martin's Press.
Struggle Outside: A Funny Serious Novel. Raymond Joseph Fraser. LC 75-314918. 1975. 6.95. McGraw-Hill Ryerson.
Struggle to Win: Or, A Gypsy Boy's Secret. Harlan Page Halsey. LC 7-117705. (Old Sleuth's own, no. 117). 1898. The Parlor Car Publishing Co.
Struggle with Destiny: Or, Nick Carter's Gentle Persuader. Nick Carter & Dey, Frederic Van Rensselaer. LC 34-382763. (On cover: New magnet library. no. 871). Street & Smith.
Strugglers: A Story. Uno Upton. LC 11-19660. Dearborn Publishing Co.
Struggles & Triumphs. Phineas Taylor Barnum. Ed. by Carl Bode. (Penguin American Library). 1981. pap. 4.95 (ISBN 0-14-039004-9). Penguin.
Struggles and Triumphs: Or, Forty Years' Recollections of P. T. Barnum. Phineas Taylor Barnum. LC 21-16881. (Seaside library, v. 32, no. 662). 1879. G. Munro.
Struggles for Life: Or, The Autobiography of a Dissenting Minister... William Leask. LC 8-28908. 1854. Lindsay & Blakiston.
Struggles of Albert Woods. Harry Summerfield Hoff. LC 53-5285. 1953. Doubleday.
Struggles of Brown, Jones, and Robinson. reprint ed. / introduction by n. john hall. ed. Anthony Trollope. LC 80-1889. (Trollope, Anthony, 1815-1882. Selections. 1981). 1981. 29.00 (ISBN 0-405-14156-4). Arno Press.
Struggles of Capt. Thomas Keith in America. LC 75-7048. (Garland Library of Narratives of North American Indian Captivities ; V. 26). (Illus.). 1977. 25.00 (ISBN 0-8240-1650-5). Garland Pub.
Struggling Upward: Or Luke Larkins Luck. Horatio Alger. 1974. (pbk.) 1.25 (ISBN 0-89014-109-6). Canyon Books.
Strumpet City: A Novel. James Plunkett. LC 73-84909. 1969. 6.95. Delacorte Press.
Strumpet Sea. Ben Ames Williams. LC 38-5860. 1938. Houghton Mifflin Company.
Strumpet Wind. Gertrude Bosworth Crum. LC 38-7061. Covici, Friede.
Strumpet Wind. Gordon Merrick. LC 47-300845. 1947. W. Morrow & Company.
Struthers: And The Comedy of the Masked Musicians. Anna Bowman Blake Dodd. LC 6-33862. Lovell, Coryell & Company.
Stryker: A Novel. Chuck Scarborough. LC 78-17284. 9.95 (ISBN 0-02-606920-2). Macmillan.
Stuart and Bamboo: A Novel. Sarah Pratt McLean Greene. 1897. Harper & Brothers.
Stuart Legacy. Robert Kerr. LC 73-81732. 1973. 7.95 (ISBN 0-8128-1631-5). Stein and Day.
Stuart Legacy. Robert Kerr. (Fawcett crest book). 1974. (pbk.) 1.25. Fawcett.
Stuart Stain. Willo Davis Roberts. (Black Pearl Ser: No. 3). 1978. pap. 1.75 (ISBN 0-445-04306-7). Popular Lib.
Stuart Women. Matthew Braun. LC 79-17245. 11.95 (ISBN 0-399-12050-5). Putnam.
Stuart's Hill. Eleanor Saltzman. LC 45-3912. 1945. B. Ackerman, Incorporated.
Stubble. George Looms. LC 22-18472. 1922. Doubleday, Page & Company.
Stubble or Wheat? A Story of More Lives Than One. Samuel Bayard Dod. LC 6-33864. A. D. F. Randolph & Company.
Stubborn Breed. Giles A Lutz. LC 75-12225. 1975. 5.95. (ISBN 0-385-11239-4). Doubeday.
Stubborn Breed. Giles A Lutz. (Kangaroo Book). 1978. 1.50 (ISBN 0-671-81929-1). Pocket Books.
Stubborn Case: A Novel. Charles Frankel. LC 72-3426. 1972. (ISBN 0-393-08472-8). Norton.
Stubborn Fate. Obi Okonkwo. 1979. pap. 2.95 o.p. (ISBN 0-89260-146-9). Hwong Pub.
Stubborn Heart. Frank Gill Slaughter. LC 50-8218. 1950. Doubleday.
Stubborn Heart. reprint ed. Frank Gill Slaughter. LC 51-6295. 1951. Garden City Books.
Stubborn Roots. Elma Godchaux. LC 36-7830. 1936. The Macmillan Company.
Stubborn Way: A Novel. Baxter Hathaway. LC 37-24109. 1937. The Macmillan Company.
Stubborn Wood. Emily Pseud Harvin. LC 47-7151. 1947. Ziff-Davis Pub. Co.
Stubb's Run. Peter L. Sandberg. LC 79-9203. 1979. 8.95 (ISBN 0-395-28423-6). Houghton Mifflin.
Stucco House. Gilbert Cannan. LC 18-316911. 1918. George H. Doran Company.
Stud. Phil Andros. 1965. 5.00 o.s.i. Guild Pr Ltd.
Stud. Jackie Collins. LC 75-120127. 1970. 5.95. World Pub. Co.
Stud. Devon Shire. (Illus., Orig.). 1969. pap. 1.75 o.p. (3075). Brandon.
Stud Pack for the Housewife. Mark S. Wolin. 192p. (Orig.). 1972. pap. 1.95 o.p. (ISBN 0-87977-175-5, DBB-175). Dansk Blue Bk.
Stud Prof. Ira Henning. pap. 1.95 o.p. (8029). Cameo.
Stud Up. Elton Gannaway. pap. 1.95 o.p. (8001). Cameo.
Student Body. M. R Hodgkin. LC 49-9573. 1949. C. Scribner's Sons.
Student Body. Marion Rous Hodgkin. LC 49-9573. 1949. Scribner.
Student Cavaliers. Joshua Rhodes Forrest. R. F. Fenno & Company.
Student Fraternity Murder. Milton Morris Propper. LC 32-24976. The Bobbs-Merrill Company.
Student Life at Harvard... George Henry Tripp. LC 8-29714. 1876. Lockwood, Brooks, & Company.
Student Nurse. Peggy Gaddis, pseud. Orig. Title: Grass Roots Nurse. 1972. pap. 0.60 o.p. (532-00497-060). Manor Bks.
Student Nurse. Lucy Agnes Hancock. LC 44-3412. 1944. Macrae-Smith-Company.
Student Nurse. Patricia Rae. (Nurse Ser.). 1983. pap. 2.95 (ISBN 0-8217-1123-7). Zebra.
Student Nurse. Renee Shann. LC 41-1833. Carlton House.
Student of Blenheim Forest. Anna Hanson McKenney Dorsey. LC 41-34708. 1888. J. Murphy & Co.
Student of Blenheim Forest. 2d thousand. ed. Anna Hanson McKenney Dorsey. LC 6-33708. J. Murphy & Co.
Student of Blenheim Forest: Or, The Trials of a Convert. 2d rev. ed. Anna Hanson McKenney Dorsey. LC 6-33709. 1867. J. Murphy & Co.
Students Choice. Richard Kraus & William Wiegand. LC 75-112876. 1970. pap. text ed. 3.95x o.s.i. (ISBN 0-675-09342-2). Merrill.
Students of Spalato: A Novel. Istvan Tamas & Dohanos, Katherine Kovach, Tr. LC 44-269843. 1944. The Blakiston Co., Distributed by E. P. Dutton & Co., Inc., New York.
Student's Romance. Richard Burleigh Kimball. LC 7-12232. 1893. G. W. Dillingham.
Studhorse Man: A Novel. Robert Kroetsch. LC 78-101880. 1970. 4.95. Simon and Schuster.
Studien Zum Altenglischen Computus. Heinrich Henel. 1934. pap. 6.00 (ISBN 0-384-22300-1). Johnson Repr.
Studies for Stories. Jean Ingelow. LC 25-15518. 1865. Roberts Brothers.
Studies in Black and White: A Novel... Jerome Bruce. LC 72-6487. (Black Heritage Library Collection). 1972. (ISBN 0-8369-9160-5). Books for Libraries Press.
Studies in Black and White: A Novel in Which Are Exemplified the Lights and Shades in the Friendship and Trust Between Black and White--Master and Slave--in Their Intercourse with Each Other in Antebellum Days. Jerome Bruce. LC 6-43783. 1906. The Neale Publishing Company.
Studies in Brown Humanity, Being Scrawls and Smudges in Sepia, White, and Yellow. Hugh Charles Clifford. LC 72-13855. (Black Heritage Library Collection). 1973. (ISBN 0-8369-9240-7). Books for Libraries Press.
Studies in Change: A Book of the Short Story. Ed. by Hugh Kenner. LC 65-10148. (Prentice-Hall introduction to literature series). 1965. Prentice-Hall.
Studies in Fiction: By Blaze O. Bonazza, Emil Roy. Ed. by Blaze O. Bonazza & Emil Roy. LC 65-104248. 1964. pap., 3.95. Harper.
Studies in Hearts. Julia MacNair Wright. LC 2-20386. 1902. American Tract Society.
Studies in Love and in Terror. Marie Adelaide Belloc Lowndes. LC 74-167462. (Short story index reprint series). 1971. (ISBN 0-8369-3988-3). Books for Libraries Press.
Studies in Love and in Terror. Marie Adelaide Belloc Lowndes. LC 14-6991. 1913. C. Scribner's Sons.
Studies in Short Fiction: Five Short Novels and Twenty-Five Stories. Ed. by Douglas A. Hughes. LC 70-131287. 1971. (ISBN 0-03-084188-7). Holt, Rinehart and Winston.
Studies in Short Fiction: Five Short Novels & Thirty Stories. 2d ed. Ed. by Douglas A. Hughes. LC 74-14924. 1975. 6.95 (ISBN 0-03-089217-1). Holt, Rinehart and Winston.
Studies in the Short Stories of William Carleton. Margaret Chesnutt. LC 77-467827. (Gothenburg Studies in English; 34). 1976. 13.50 (ISBN 9-17-346027-3). Acta Universitatis Gothoburgensis.
Studies in the Short Story. 3d ed. by virgil scott. ed. Ed. by Adrian H. Jaffe. Virgil Scott. LC 68-10540. 1968. Holt, Rinehart and Winston.
Studies in the Short Story. 4th ed. Ed. by Virgil Scott. Ed. by Adrian H. Jaffe. LC 75-25515. (ISBN 0-03-089835-8). Holt, Rinehart and Winston.
Studies in the Short Story. 5th ed. / edited by by david madden. ed. Ed. by Virgil Scott. LC 79-19576. 8.95 (ISBN 0-03-043131-X). Holt, Rinehart and Winston.
Studies in the Short Story. alternate ed. Ed. by Virgil Scott & Adrian H. Jaffe. LC 77-139000. 1971. (ISBN 0-03-081159-7). Holt, Rinehart and Winston.
Studies in the Short Story: Edited by Adrian H. Jaffe and Virgil Scott. Rev. Ed. by Viroil Scott. Ed. by Adrian H. Jaffe. Virgil Scott. LC 60-14981. 1960. Holt, Rinehart and Winston.
Studies in Victor Hugo's Dramatic Characters. James Dowden Bruner. LC 73-5975. 1973. (ISBN 0-8414-3112-4). Folcroft Library Editions.
Studies in Wives. Marie Adelaide Belloc Lowndes. LC 10-952133. 1910. 1.50. M. Kennerley.
Studio. Leo Guild. (Orig.). 1969. pap. 1.75 (ISBN 0-87067-168-5, BH168). Holloway.
Studio. Thomas Maremaa. 1980. 2.25 (ISBN 0-87216-528-0). Playboy Press.
Studio: A Novel. Thomas Maremaa. LC 77-27095. 1978. 9.95 (ISBN 0-688-03300-8). Morrow.
Studio Affair. Dorothy Brenner Francis. (YA) 1972. 4.50 o.p. (Avalon). Bouregy.
Studio Apartment. Leona Slottman. LC 46-21123. 1946. Phoenix Press.
Studio Apartment. Leona Slottman. LC 46-21123. 1946. Phoenix Press.
Studio Apartment. Leona Slottman. LC 46-211233. 1946. Phoenix Press.
Studio Baby: And Some Other Children. Modeste Hannis Jordan. LC 12-6554. 1912. 1.25. The Cosmopolitan Press.
Studio Murder Mystery. Arlo C Edington & Edington, Mrs. Carmen Ballen,1894- Joint Author. LC 29-112840. The Reilly & Lee Co.
Studs Lonigan: A Trilogy. James Thomas Farrell. LC 36-214. The Vanguard Press.
Studs Lonigan: A Trilogy Containing Young Lonigan, The Young Manhood of Studs Lonigan, Judgment Day. James Thomas Farrell. LC 78-56426. 1978. 17.50 (ISBN 0-8149-0791-1). Vanguard Press.
Studs Lonigan: A Triology Containing Young Lonigan, The Young Manhood of Studs Lonigan, Judgment Day. James Thomas Farrell. LC 36-31286. (modern library of the world's best books). 1938. The Modern Library.
Stud's Vengeance. Ward C. Baxter. 192p. 1972. pap. 1.95 o.p. (ISBN 0-87977-151-8, DBB151). Dansk Blue Bk.
Study Book of Canals. Drawings by Heather Copley. Geoffrey Middleton & Heather Illus Copiey. (Study bks.). 1961. bds., 2.95. Bodley Head.
Study Book of Ships. Drawings by Heather Copley and Christopher Chamberlain. Eric Baxter & Heather Illus Copley. (Study bks.). 1966. bds., 2.95. Bodley Head.
Study in Bronze. Esther Hyman. LC 28-22140. H. Holt and Company.
Study in Ebony. Dotia Trigg Cooney. LC 11-188398. 1911. 1.50. The Neale Publishing Company.
Study in Life Tints. Clara Viola Fleharty. LC 7-39195. 1907. M. A. Long Book and Publishing House.
Study in Prejudices. Emily Morse Symonds. LC 8-25587. 1895. D. Appleton and Company.
Study in Scarlet. Arthur Conan Doyle. LC 75-43272. (Illus.). 6.95. (ISBN 0-8055-1179-2) (ISBN 0-8055-0264-5). Hart Pub. Co.
Study in Scarlet. Arthur Conan Doyle. LC 76-27105. (Illus.). 1977. 7.95 (ISBN 0-385-12283-7). Doubleday.
Study in Scarlet. Arthur Conan Doyle. LC 22-24754. American Publishers Corporation.
Study in Scarlet. Arthur Conan Doyle. 192p. 1981. pap. 2.25 (ISBN 0-441-79076-3, Pub. by Charter Bks). Ace Bks.
Study in Scarlet: A Novel. Arthur Conan Doyle. LC 4-16520. (On cover: The home library). A. L. Burt.
Study in Scarlet and the Sign of Four. Sir Arthur Conan Doyle. (Berkley medallion book). 1975. (pbk.) 1.25. Berkley Pub. Co.
Study in Scarlet: And The Sign of the Four. Arthur Conan Doyle. LC 12-18724. 1904. Harper & Brothers.
Study in Scarlet: Based on the Story by Sir Arthur Conan Doyle. Ed. by Simon Goodenough. (Illus.). 120p. (Orig.). 1983. pap. 17.95 incl. facsimile documents & clues (ISBN 0-688-01951-X). Quill NY.
Study in Temptations. Pearl Mary Teresa Richards Craigie. LC 6-31092. ("unknown" library, v. 23). Cassell Publishing Company.
Study in Terror. Ellery Queen, pseud. (Orig.). 1969. pap. 0.60 o.p. (73-814). Lancer.
Study of Browning's The Ring and the Book. Edith Mary Steane Story & Robert Browning. LC 74-117581. 1971. (ISBN 0-8383-1014-1). Haskell House Publishers.
Study of HadithIsa Ibn Hisham, Muhammad Al-Muwaylihi's View of Egyptian Society During the British Occupation: With an English Translation of the Third Edition. Muhammad Al-Muwaylihi & Roger M. A Allen. LC 74-3054. 1974. (ISBN 0-87395-088-7). State University of New York Press.
Study War No More: A Selection of Alternatives. Joe W Haldeman. LC 77-9517. 1977. 7.95 (ISBN 0-312-77315-3). St. Martin's Press.
Stuff of a Man. Katharine Evans Blake. LC 8-83011. 1908. The Bobbs-Merrill Company.
Stuff of Dreams. Edith Sessions Tupper. LC 8-32647. 1908. B. W. Dodge & Company.
Stuffed Dog. Peter De Polnay. LC 77-76632. 7.95 (ISBN 0-312-77325-0). St. Martin's Press.
Stuffed Dog. Peter De Polnay. LC 76-383455. 1976. 3.75 (ISBN 0-491-01568-2). W. H. Allen.
Stuffed Men. Anthony M Rud. LC 35-18569. The Macaulay Company.
Stuffed Owl. Ed. by D. B. Lewis & Charles Lee. 1978. 9.95x (ISBN 0-460-00186-8, Evman). Biblio Dist.
Stuffed Peacocks. Emily Tapscott Clark Balch. LC 75-110181. (Short story index reprint series). (Illus.). 1970. Books for Libraries Press.
Stuffed Peacocks. Emily Clark. LC 27-19778. 1927. A.A. Knopf.
Stuffed Shirts. Clare Boothe. LC 31-38680. H. Liveright, Inc.
Stuffed Shirts. Clare Boothe Luce. LC 77-163043. (Short story index reprint series). (Illus.). 1971. Books for Libraries Press.
Stumble on the Threshold. James Payn. LC 7-33769. (On cover: Appletons' town and country library, no. 106). 1892. D. Appleton and Company.
Stumble Upon the Dark Mountains. Lon Riley Woodrum. LC 56-13795. 1956. Broadman Press.
Stumbler in Wide Shoes: A Novel. E. Sutcliffe March. LC 8-29692. (Protean series, no. 6). 1896. H. Holt and Company.
Stumbling. Dave E Smalley. LC 29-7724. Barse & Co.
Stumbling Block. Justus Miles Forman. LC 7-24156. 1907. Harper & Brothers.
Stumbling-Block. Edwin William Pugh. LC 3-7163. 1903. A. S. Barnes and Company.
Stumbling Block: A Novel. Henry Howard Harper. LC 13-816. 1912. 5.00.
Stumbling-Blocks and Stepping-Stones. Nell R Latimer. 1973. 3.95 (ISBN 0-533-00423-3). Vantage.
Stumbling Herd. John Antonio Moroso. LC 23-6142. The Macaulay Company.
Stumbling Stone. Aubrey Menen. LC 49-9745. 1949. C. Scribner's Sons.

Stump. Alexis Lykiard. LC 73-179102. 1973. 1.75 (ISBN 0-246-10610-7). Hart-Davis, MacGibbon Ltd.
Stunset Touch. Moira Pearce. LC 60-12595. 1960. Scribner.
Stunt Girl. Rose Gordon & Reed, Ione. G. P. Putnam, Inc.
Stunt Man. Paul Brodeur. 1973. 1.25 (ISBN 0-345-03153-9). Ballantine Books.
Stunt Man. Paul Brodeur. LC 73-105677. 1970. 5.95. Atheneum.
Stunt Man. John Weld. LC 32-21441. 1932. R. M. McBride & Company.
Stunt Man's Holiday. John Whitlatch. 1973. 0.95. Pocket Books.
Stuore. Michael Earls. LC 11-26026. 1911. Benziger Brothers.
Sturbridge Dynasty. Joan Bagnel. 704p. (Orig.). 1982. pap. 3.50 (ISBN 0-446-80297-2). Warner Bks.
Sturdy Beggar: A Novel. Charles Charrington. LC 6-23442. 1896. Stone & Kimball.
Sturdy Oak: A Composite Novel of American Politics by Fourteen American Authors. Jordan, Elizabeth Oliver, 1867- Ed & Austin, Mrs. Mary (Hunter) 1868- LC 17-31033. 1917. H. Holt and Company.
Sturgeon Is Alive and Well. Edward Hamilton Waldo, pseud. LC 70-136811. 1971. 4.95. Putnam.
Sturgeon's West. Theodore Sturgeon & Don Ward. LC 73-135717. 1973. 5.95 o.p. (ISBN 0-385-05393-2). Doubleday.
Sturgeon's West. Edward Hamilton Waldo & Don Ward. LC 73-135717. 1973. 5.95 (ISBN 0-385-05393-2). Doubleday.
Sturgis Wager: A Detective Story. Edgar Morette. LC 99-1167. Frederick A. Stokes Company.
Sturlunga Saga, 2 vols. Ed. by Gudbrand Vigfusson. LC 80-1944. (Illus.). Repr. of 1878 ed. 135.00 (ISBN 0-404-18720-X). AMS Pr.
Sturmer: A Tale of Mesmerism. To Which Are Added, Other Sketches from Life. Isabella Frances Romer. LC 7-40761. 1842. Lea & Blanchard.
Sturmsee, Man and Man. Henry Holt. LC 5-161219. 1905. The Macmillan Company.
Stuttering Six-Guns. Merle M Funk. 1973. 4.95 (ISBN 0-517-51496-6). Lenox Hill Press.
Styles by Suzy. Karla H Wiley. LC 65-14129. 1965. D. McKay Co.
Stylish Marriage. Alec Rackowe. LC 48-7069. 1948. Farrar, Straus.
Styrbiorn the Strong. Eric Rucker Eddison. LC 26-15960. A. & C. Boni,
Styrbiorn the Strong. Eric Rucker Eddison. LC 77-84222. (Lost Race and Adult Fantasy Fiction). 1978. 18.00 (ISBN 0-405-10975-X). Arno Press.
Styx. Christopher Hyde. 272p. (Orig.). 1982. pap. 2.95 (ISBN 0-86721-173-3). Playboy Pbks.
Styx Complex. Russell L Rhodes. LC 77-654. 9.95 (ISBN 0-396-07435-9). Dodd, Mead.
Sub: Being the Autobiography of David Munro, Sub-Lieutenant, Royal Navy. Henry Taprell Dorling, pseud. LC 18-12229. George H. Doran Company.
Sub Rosa. A Novel. Charles Theodore Murray. LC 10-419297. 1880. G. W. Carleton & Co.; Etc., Etc.
Sub Wars, No. 1: Target Delta V. James Good. (Orig.). 1982. pap. 2.50 (ISBN 0-8217-1046-X). Zebra.
Sub Wars, No. 2: Target Sosus. James Good. 1982. pap. 2.50 (ISBN 0-8217-1092-3). Zebra.
Sub-Zero! Robert W Walker. (Belmont Tower books). 1.75 (ISBN 0-505-51395-1). Tower Pubns.
Subaltern. Duncan MacNeil. (Belmont Tower Books). 1977. 1.50 (ISBN 0-505-51148-7). Tower Pubns.
Subaltern's Choice. Duncan MacNeil. LC 74-78694. 224p. 1974. 6.95 o.p. St Martin.
Subaltern's Choice: An 'Ogilvie' Novel. Philip McCutchan. LC 74-78694. 1974. 6.95. St. Martin's Press.
Subb. C. C. MacApp. (Orig.). 1971. pap. 0.75 o.p. (ISBN 0-446-64532-X, 64-532). Paperback Lib.
Subconscious Courtship: A Novel. Berta Ruck. LC 22-19908. 1922. Dodd, Mead and Company.
Subdued Southern Nobility: A Southern Ideal. LC 72-2035. (Black Heritage Library Collection). 1972. 16.50 (ISBN 0-8369-9070-6). Books for Libraries Press.
Subdued Southern Nobility: A Southern Ideal. LC 8-16856. Sharps Publishing Company.
Sube Tu Apuesta. new ed. Glen Chase, pseud. Tr. by Jacinto De Torres from Eng. (Pimienta Collection, Cereza Delicias: No. 4). 160p. (Span.). 1974. pap. 1.00 (ISBN 0-88473-220-7). Fiesta Pub.
Subi, the Volcano. Burt Cole. LC 57-9365. 1957. Macmillan.
Subject of Harry Egypt. Daniel Broun. LC 63-7270. (Rinehart suspense novel). 1963. Holt, Rinehart and Winston.
Subject to Authority. Isabel Constance Clarke. LC 46-3592. 1946. Longmans, Green and Co.
Subjugation of Rose Bolton. Pierre Lavalle. pap. 1.95 o.s.i. (Venus). Grove.
Sublime Fire. Frieda Meitzen-Williams. LC 41-7799. Fortuny's Publishers, Inc.
Sublime Jester... Ezra Selig Brudno. LC 25-91433. 1924. N. L. Brown.
Sublunary: A Novel. L. E Martin. LC 33-33457. E. P. Dutton & Co., Inc.
Submarine. John Wingate. LC 81-23198. 1982. 10.95 (ISBN 0-312-77476-1). St. Martin's Press.
Submarine Signaled... Murder! Allan R Bosworth. LC 43-123163. (On cover: A Crime novel selection. No. 3). Select Publications, Inc.
Submarine Z-1, a Novel. Translated from the Yiddish by Max Rosenfield. Leon Chanukoff. LC 60-139323. 1960. Citadel Press.
Submariner. Edward Carl Stephens. LC 73-79715. 1973. 6.95 (ISBN 0-385-08884-1). Doubleday.
Submission of Lilly. J. J. Montague. 192p. 1972. pap. 1.95 o.p. (ISBN 0-87977-149-6, DBB149). Dansk Blue Bk.
Subpoena. Irwin Stark. LC 66-188144. 5.95. Amer. Lib.
Subscription to Murder. Mary Violet Heberden. LC 40-5630. 1940. Pub. for the Crime Club by Doubleday, Doran & Company, Inc.
Subsoil: From the Chronicle of a Village. George Frederick Hummel. Boni and Liveright.
Subspace Explorers. Edward Elmer Smith. LC 64-25828. (Illus.). 1965. Canaveral Press.
Substance of a Dream: By Garth Hale Pseud. 1st Ed. Albert Benjamin Cunningham. LC 51-9487. 1951. Dutton.
Substance of a Dream: Tr. from the Original Manuscript. Francis William Bain. LC 19-195980. 1919. 1.50. G. P. Putnam's Sons.
Substance of His House. Ruth Holt Boucicault. LC 14-3177. 1914. 1.30. Little, Brown, and Company.
Substance X. David Houston. (Tales of Tomorrow Ser.: No. 3). 208p. (Orig.). 1982. pap. 2.25 (ISBN 0-8439-0961-7, Leisure Bks). Nordon Pubns.
Substitute. William Nathaniel Harben. LC 3-71685. 1903. Harper & Brothers.
Substitute Angel. Georgia Craig. LC 44-598567. 1944. Arcadia House, Inc.
Substitute Angel. Peggy Gaddis, pseud. LC 44-5985. 1944. Arcadia House.
Substitute Bride. Lynna Cooper, pseud. Bd. with My Treasure, My Love. 1981. pap. 2.25 (ISBN 0-451-09739-4, E9739, Sig). NAL.
Substitute Bride. Lynna Cooper. (Signet Book). 1977. 1.25 (ISBN 0-451-07296-0). New American Library.
Substitute Bride. Dorothy Mack. (Candlelight Regency special; 225). 1977. 1.25 (ISBN 0-440-18375-8). Dell Pub. Co.
Substitute Bride. Margaret Pargeter. (Harlequin Presents Ser.). 192p. 1983. pap. 1.95 (ISBN 0-373-10580-0). Harlequin Bks.
Substitute Bride. Clare Consuelo Frewen Sheridan. LC 31-20844. 1931. Longmans, Green and Co.
Substitute Doctor. Elizabeth Seifert. LC 57-642278. 1957. Dodd, Mead.
Substitute Doctor. Elizabeth Seifert. 6.95. Aeonian Press.
Substitute Guest. Grace Livingston Hill. LC 36-29009. J. B. Lippincott Company.
Substitute Lover. Alice Mary Ross Colver. LC 36-218201. 1936. Dodd, Mead & Company.
Substitute Millionaire. Hulbert Footner. LC 19-152243. George H. Doran Company.
Substitute Nurse. Adelaide Humphries. LC 44-9551. 1944. Arcadia House, Inc.
Substitute Prisoner. Max Marcin. LC 11-292322. 1911. 1.25. Moffat, Yard and Company.
Substitute Sweetheart. Besse Sprague. LC 36-101205. J. H. Hopkins & Son, Inc.
Subterranean World. Timothy G. Beckley. 1971. pap. 6.95 o.p. Saucerian.
Subterraneans. John Kerouac. LC 58-6703. (Evergreen books, E-99). 1958. Grove Press.
Subterraneans. John Kerouac. LC 81-47644. 1981. 3.50 (ISBN 0-394-17952-8). Grove Press.
Subtle Adversary: A Tale of Callitso County. Charles Josiah Scofield. LC 8-2059. 1891. The Author.
Subtle Trail: Another Goldfish Story. Joseph Gollomb. LC 29-226928. 1929. The Macmillan Company.
Suburban Doctor. Charles Stanley Strong. LC 41-270832. Phoenix Press.
Suburban Pastoral: And Other Tales. Henry Augustin Beers. LC 6-9760. (On cover: Buckram series). 1894. H. Holt and Company.
Suburban Sage. facs. ed. Henry Cuyer Bunner. LC 76-90578. (Short Story Index Reprint Ser). 1896. 12.00 (ISBN 0-8369-3061-4). Ayer Co.
Suburban Sage: Stray Notes and Comments on His Life. Henry Cuyler Bunner. LC 76-90578. (Short story index reprint series). (Illus.). 1969. Books for Libraries Press.
Suburban Saraband. Richard Harrison. LC 52-1453. 1952. Jarrolds.
Suburban Sketches. William Dean Howells. LC 78-86146. (Short story index reprint series). (Illus.). 1969. Books for Libraries Press.
Suburban Souls. 1969. pap. 1.75 o.p. (Z1032K, Zebra). Grove.
Suburban Souls: The Erotic Psychology of a Man and a Maid. Jacky S- LC 68-29442. 1968. 10.00. Grove Press.
Suburban Souls: The Erotic Psychology of a Man and a Maid : Also Contains the Complete Text of Another Novel, The Yellow Room by M. Le Compte Du Bouleau. LC 79-2348. 1979. 12.50 (ISBN 0-394-50518-2). Grove Press : Distributed by Random House.
Suburban Whirl: And Other Stories of Married Life. Mary Stewart Doubleday Cutting. LC 7-332069. 1907. The McClure Company.
Suburbs. Robert H. Baker. Ed. by Sylvia Ashton. LC 77-82652. 1979. 12.95 (ISBN 0-87949-102-7). Ashley Bks.
Suburbs of Pleasure. John Frederick Burke. LC 67-18372. 1967. Delacorte Press.
Subway Murder. Madeleine Sharpe Buchanan. LC 30-24948. 1930. A. C. McClurg & Co.
Subway to Samarkand. John R. Humphreys. LC 75-36595. 1977. 8.95 (ISBN 0-385-11079-0). Doubleday.
Subway to Samarkand. John R. Humphreys. LC 78-7409. 1978. 12.95 (ISBN 0-8161-6588-2). G. K. Hall.
Subway to Semarkand. John R. Humphreys. 2.25. Berkley Pub. Corp., C.
Success. Constance Leonie Caroline Borgstrom Aminoff. LC 24-11880. (Her Torchlight series of Napoleonic romances. iv). E. P. Dutton & Company C.
Success. Robert B. Graham. LC 71-103512. (Short Story Index Reprint Ser.). 1902. 15.00 (ISBN 0-8369-3254-4). Ayer Co.
Success. Walter Winward. LC 67-24930. bds., 5.95. Delacorte.
Success: A Novel. Samuel Hopkins Adams. LC 21-18946. 1921. Houghton Mifflin Company.
Success: A Novel. Lion Feuchtwanger & Muir, Willa, Tr. LC 30-30575. 1930. The Viking Press.
Success: A Novel. Helen Huntington Howe. LC 56-9919. 1956. Simon and Schuster.
Success and Other Sketches. Robert Bontine Cunninghame Graham. LC 71-103512. (Short story index reprint series). 1969. Books for Libraries Press.
Success and Plenty. James Lawrence Campbell. LC 32-25728. E. P. Dutton & Co., Inc.
Success Easier Than Failure see Collected Works.
Success of Failure. Lillian Smith Tapman. LC 13-244002. Tapman Publishing Company.
Success of Mark Wyngate. Una Lucy Silberrad. LC 3-2224. 1902. Doubleday, Page & Company.
Success of Patrick Desmond. Maurice Francis Egan. LC 6-37569. 1893. Office of the "Ave Maria".
Success-the Bloom or Blight. Emily C Marquardt. 1973. 6.95 (ISBN 0-533-00714-3). Vantage Press.
Successful Failure. Robert P. Dews. 1970. 5.00 o.p. Carlton.
Successful Failure. An Outline... Cary Glasgow. LC 6-43964. 1883. West, Johnston & Co.
Successful Love: And Other Stories. Delmore Schwartz. LC 61-14981. 1961. Corinth Books.
Successful Man. Julie Grinnell Storrow Cruger. LC 11-10569. 1891. J. B. Lippincott Company.
Successful Mr. Bagley. John Francis. LC 26-8007. L. C. Page & Company.
Successful Wife: A Story. Gerald Dorset. LC 10-19389. 1910. Harper & Brothers.
Succession; a Comedy of the Generations. Ethel Sidgwick. LC 13-12595. Small, Maynard and Company.
Succession: A Story. Joseph Hyman. LC 80-65255. 6.00 (ISBN 0-9604040-0-7). Court House Books.
Successor: A Novel. Richard Pryce. 1907. Duffield & Company.
Successors. William Hegner. 1976. 1.75 (ISBN 0-671-80534-7). Pocket Books.
Successors of Mary the First. Elizabeth Stuart Phelps H. D. Ward Ward. LC 1-31800. 1901. Houghton, Mifflin and Company.
Successors to the Title. Lucy Bethia Colquhoun Walford. LC 8-32806. (Half-title: Appletons' town and country library, no. 184). 1896. D. Appleton and Company.
Succubus. Kenneth R. Johnson. (Orig.). 1980. pap. 2.50 (ISBN 0-440-17716-2). Dell.
Succubus. Campo Verdi. 1977. pap. 1.50 (ISBN 0-532-15257-3). Woodhill.
Such a Folly. Jettie Irving Felps. LC 57-16787. 1956. Meador Pub. Co.
Such a Gorgeous Kid Like Me. Henry Farrell. (8385). 1968. Dell.
Such a Gorgeous Kid Like Me. Henry Farrell. LC 67-13468. 1967. Delacorte Press.
Such a Woman. Owen Frawley Kildare & Kildare, Mrs. Leita, Joint Author. LC 11-20824. G. W. Dillingham Company.
Such an Enmity. Roland Pertwee. LC 36-80577. 1936. Little, Brown, and Company.
Such Are the Valiant. John C. Andrews. (Inflation Fighter Ser.). 160p. 1982. pap. cancelled o.s.i. (ISBN 0-8439-1122-0, Leisure Bks). Nordon Pubns.
Such Are the Valiant. John C. Andrews. 1978. pap. 1.50 o.s.i. (ISBN 0-505-51314-5). Tower Bks.
Such As We. Pierre Sichel. LC 48-6312. 1948. Reynal & Hitchcock.
Such Darling Dodos, and Other Stories. Angus Wilson. LC 51-319. 1951. Morrow.
Such Friends Are Dangerous. Walter Tyrer. LC 81-47390. (Fifty Classics of Crime Fiction, 1950-1975). 1982. 14.95 (ISBN 0-8240-4974-8). Garland Pub.
Such Good Friends. Lois Gould. LC 77-102353. 1970. 6.95. Random House.
Such Happy People. James Noble Gifford. LC 49-4831. 1949. Arcadia House.
Such Harmony: A Novel. Margaret Matthews. 1939. C. Scribner's Sons.
Such Interesting People. Margaret Culkin Banning. LC 78-20199. 8.95. Harper & Row.
Such Interesting People. Margaret Culkin Banning. LC 80-11526. 1980. 15.95 (ISBN 0-8161-3080-9). Hall.
Such Is Life see Australian Classics.
Such Is Life: Being Certain Extracts from the Diary of Tom Collins Pseud. Joseph Furphy. LC 48-440489. 1948. Univ. of Chicago Press.
Such Is Life (Comme Dans la Vie) Albert Delpit. Tr. by Donovan, Alexina (Loranger) LC 11-10535. (library of choice fiction no. 16). 1891. Laird & Lee.
Such Is My Beloved. Morley Callaghan. LC 34-590436. 1934. C. Scribner's Sons.
Such Is the Kingdom. Thomas Sugrue. LC 40-14502. H. Holt and Company.
Such Men Are Dangerous. Elinor Sutherland Glyn. LC 33-38985. The Macaulay Company.
Such Men Are Dangerous: A Novel of Violence. Paul Kavanagh. LC 69-20406. 1969. Macmillan.
Such Men Are Rare: From the Diaries of Samuel Pepys. Arthur Richard Rawlinson. LC 78-437990. 1969. A. Wingate; H. Baker.
Such Nice People. Sandra Scoppettone. LC 79-22855. 12.95 (ISBN 0-399-12353-9). Putnam.
Such Power Is Dangerous. Dennis Yates Wheatley. 1979. 9.95 (ISBN 0-09-043791-8, Pub. by Hutchinson). Merrimack Pub Cir.
Such Sad Tidings. Elisabeth Plessen. LC 78-12211. 1979. 8.95 (ISBN 0-670-68106-7). Viking Press.
Such Things from the Valley. Arthenia Bates Millican. LC 77-362603. Millican.
Such Waltzing Was Not Easy: Stories. Gordon Weaver. LC 75-2288. (Illinois short fiction). 1975. 6.95. (ISBN 0-252-00476-0) (ISBN 0-252-00533-3). University of Illinois Press.
Such Waltzing Was Not Easy Stories. Gordon Weaver. LC 75-2288. (Short Fiction Ser). 140p. 1974. pap. 4.95 (ISBN 0-252-00533-3). U of Ill Pr.
Such Ways Are Dangerous. Constance Grenelle Wilcox. LC 39-23189. R. M. McBride & Company.
Such Women Are Deadly. Leonard Gribble. 1965. lib. bdg. 4.95 o.p. (ISBN 0-668-01852-6). Arco.
Sucker Bet. Zeke Masters, pseud. (Faro Blake Ser.: No. 17). 176p. (Orig.). Date not set. pap. 1.95 (ISBN 0-671-43816-6). PB.
Sucker Trap. Mark Kane. LC 68-26891. 1968. 3.95. Roy Publishers.
Sucker's Teeth. Joe Back. LC 65-25805. 2.95. Sage Bks. Dist. Swallow.
Sudden Bill Dorn. Jackson Gregory. LC 37-21728. 1937. Dodd, Mead & Company.
Sudden Country. Nelson Nye. 1976. (pbk.) 1.25. Ace Books.
Sudden Death. Peter Brennan. LC 77-92076. 9.95 (ISBN 0-89256-053-3). Rawson Associates.
Sudden Death. Rita Mae Brown. 288p. 1983. 14.95 (ISBN 0-553-05037-0). Bantam.
Sudden Death. Freeman Wills Crofts. LC 32-223007. 1932. Harper & Brothers.
Sudden Death. David Delman. LC 72-76149. 1972. 4.95 (ISBN 0-385-08159-6). Published for the Crime Club by Doubleday.
Sudden Death. Lee Thayer, pseud. LC 35-13556. 1935. Dodd, Mead & Company.
Sudden Endings. Vin Packer. (Orig.). 1970. pap. 0.75 o.p. (T2248, GM). Fawcett World.
Sudden Fear. Edna Sherry. LC 48-5590. 1948. Dodd, Mead.
Sudden Glory: A Novel. Cid Ricketts Sumner. LC 51-11048. 1951. Bobbs-Merrill.
Sudden Guest... Christopher La Farge. LC 46-6673. 1946. Coward-MCann, Inc.
Sudden Guns. 1st Ed. Gifford Paul Cheshire. LC 59-9134. (Double D western). 1959. Doubleday.
Sudden Insurrection. Philip L. Sawyer. pap. 2.75 o.p. William F.

Sudden Insurrection: Twelve Short Stories. Philip L Sawyer. LC 75-126427. 1970. 2.75. William-Frederick Press.

Sudden Jim: A Novel. Clarence Budington Kelland. LC 17-6325. 1917. 1.35. Harper & Brothers.

Sudden Lady. 1st American Ed. Marjorie G Lowe. LC 61-15078. 1961. Putnam.

Sudden Land. Dale Oldham. (Orig.). 1980. pap. 1.75 o.s.i. (ISBN 0-505-51480-X). Tower Bks.

Sudden Madness. Ralph Hayes. (Orig.). 1981. pap. 2.25 (ISBN 0-505-51693-4). Tower Bks.

Sudden Rides Again. Oliver Strange. LC 39-271672. 1939. Doubleday, Doran & Company, Inc.

Sudden Rides Again. Oliver Strange. LC 40-5533. 1940. The Sun Dial Press.

Sudden Silence. John Minahan. LC 63-7486. 1963. Morrow.

Sudden Silence: The Case of the Murdered Band-Leader. Cortland Fitzsimmons. LC 38-1968. 1938. Frederick A. Stokes Company.

Sudden Sky: A Novel. B Michelaard. LC 73-84083. 1974. 9.95 (ISBN 0-88327-030-7). Charterhouse.

Sudden Squall: A Lace White Mystery. Jeannette Covert Nolan. LC 55-14378. 1955. L. Washburn.

Sudden Star. Pamela Sargent. 1.95 (ISBN 0-449-14114-4). Fawcett Gold Medal.

Sudden Strangers. William Edmund Barrett. LC 56-5581. 1956. Doubleday.

Sudden Sun: A Novel. Translated by Elsa Kruuse. Olov Hartman. LC 64-10649. 1964. Fortress Press.

Sudden Sweetheart. Berta Ruck. LC 33-222646. 1933. Dodd, Mead & Company.

Sudden Takes Charge. Oliver Strange. LC 40-31458. 1940. Doubleday, Doran and Company, Inc.

Sudden Thunder. Pat Brooks. LC 78-70386. 1.95 (ISBN 0-932050-02-6). New Puritan Library.

Sudden Thunder. Warren T. Longtree. (Ruff Justice Ser.: No. 1). (Orig.). 1981. pap. 2.50 (ISBN 0-451-11028-5, AE1028, Sig). NAL.

Sudden Vengeance. Robert Bruce Montgomery. LC 50-6529. (Red badge mystery). 1950. Dodd, Mead.

Sudden Wealth. Henry James Forman. LC 24-23733. 1924. Boni and Liveright.

Sudden Woman. Martha Albrand. LC 64-1017. 1964. Atheneum.

Sudden Woman. Christine Lambert, pseud. 1964. 5.00 o.p. Atheneum.

Suddenly a Corpse: A Scott Jordan Story. Harold Q Masur. LC 49-9609. (Inner sanctum mystery). 1949. Simon and Schuster.

Suddenly a Widow. 1st Ed. George Harmon Coxe. LC 55-110598. 1956. Knopf.

Suddenly He Knew: A Modern Crime Story. Walger Vinn. LC 57-14512. 1957-1958. Greenwich Book Publishers.

Suddenly, in Paris. Alexandra Roudybush. LC 74-33687. 1975. 5.95 (ISBN 0-385-06065-3). Published for the Crime Club by Doubleday.

Suddenly, in the Air. Karen Campbell, pseud. LC 70-87961. 1969. 4.95. Stein and Day.

Suddenly It's Love. Joseph Bonuccelli. 1978. 6.50 o.p. (ISBN 0-533-03530-9). Vantage.

Suddenly It's Love. Peggy Gaddis, pseud. LC 49-6143. 1949. Arcadia House.

Suddenly It's Tomorrow: A Novel. 1st Ed. Shirley Hymson. LC 59-14967. 1959. Greenwich Book Publishers.

Suddenly of Age. Wal Watkins. LC 73-163292. 1972. 1.65 (ISBN 0-7260-0010-8). Gold Star Publications.

Suddenly One Night. Kelley Roos. LC 77-129956. (Red badge novel of suspense). 1970. 4.50 (ISBN 0-396-06247-4). Dodd, Mead.

Suddenly Tomorrow. P. M. Pasinetti. 1973. 5.95 o.p. (ISBN 0-394-47552-6). Random.

Suddenly Tomorrow: A Novel. P. M Pasinetti. LC 72-8389. 1973. 5.95 (ISBN 0-394-47552-6). Random House.

Suddenly While Gardening. Elizabeth Lemarchand. LC 78-67180. (Illus.). 1978. 7.95 (ISBN 0-8027-5395-7). Walker.

Suddenly, Wonderfully Gay. Peter Kanto. (Orig.). pap. 1.25 o.p. (2046). Brandon.

Sudina. Jessie Schell. LC 77-82086. 1977. 1.50 (ISBN 0-380-01763-6). Avon.

Sudina. 1st Ed. Jessie Rosenberg. LC 67-20532. 1967. bds., 4.95. Dutton.

Suds in Your Eye. Mary Lasswell. LC 42-258128. 1942. Houghton Mifflin Company.

Suds in Your Eye. Mary Lasswell. LC 43-109164. Houghton Mifflin Company.

Suds in Your Eye. With Illus. by George Price. Mary Lasswell. LC 60-51026. 1959. Houghton Mifflin.

Sudsy. Madge I. Enos. 3.00 o.p. Carlton.

Sue Ann, the Million Dollar Tramp. Warren Ashley & Kelly James. 1978. 6.95 o.p. (ISBN 0-533-03402-7). Vantage.

Sue Barton, Neighborhood Nurse. Helen Dore Boylston. LC 49-11907. 1949. Little, Brown.

Sue Barton, Senior Nurse. Helen Dore Boylston. 1973. 0.75. Popular Lib.

Sue Barton, Student Nurse. Helen Dore Boylston. 1973. 0.75. Popular Lib.

Sue Barton, Superintendent of Nurses. Helen Dore Boylston. 1973. (pbk) 0.75. Popular Library.

Sue Barton, Visiting Nurse. Helen Dore Boylston. 1973. (pbk) 0.75. Popular Library.

Sue Comes Home. Peggy O'More, pseud. LC 45-2148. 1945. Grammercy Publishing Company.

Sue Downer: What Selfishness Did for Her. Sarah Stuart Robbins. LC 12-38125. (Half-title: Rock Cove series, v). 1890. Leonard Publishing Company.

Sue Ella: A Historical Romance Founded on Incidents of the War Between the States. Robert H Jetton. LC 16-13102.

Sue Ella: A Historical Romance, Founded on Incidents of the War Between the States. Robert H Jetton. LC 15-21141. 1.00. Printed by the Author.

Sue Ellen. Margaretta Brucker. LC 41-11796. Gramercy Publishing Co.

Sue McFarland, Schoolmarm. Edith K Cocayne. LC 19-1339. 1918. Saulsbury Publishing Company.

Sue Suckit. Justine. pap. 1.25 o.p. (V1042Z, Venus). Grove.

Sue Warren: Decorator by Frances Dean Hancock Pseud. Jeanne Judson. LC 58-7587. 1958. Avalon Books.

Sue. 1st Ed. Hayward Rice. LC 56-8082. 1956. Vantage Press.

Suede Butterfly. Charles Miron. 1973. (pbk). 0.95. Manor Books.

Suede Holloway. William Baldwin. 1978. pap. 3.95 (ISBN 0-9602170-0-2). Ars Eterna.

Suevian. Edgar W Kiefer. LC 57-34240.

Suffer a Sea Change. Celeste De Blasis. 1979. pap. 1.95 (ISBN 0-449-23954-3, Crest). Fawcett.

Suffer a Sea Change. Celeste De Blasis. LC 75-26957. 7.95 (ISBN 0-698-10708-X). Coward, McCann & Geoghegan.

Suffer a Witch. Nigel Fitzgerald. LC 81-47411. 1983. 14.95 (ISBN 0-8240-5001-0). Garland.

Suffer a Witch. Nigel Fitzgerald. Ed. by J. Barzun & W. H. Taylor. LC 81-47411. (Crime Fiction 1950-1975 Ser.). 256p. 1982. lib. bdg. 14.95 (ISBN 0-8240-5001-0). Garland Pub.

Suffer a Witch. easy eye ed. Rae Foley. Orig. Title: Gilt Edge. 1968. pap. 0.95 o.s.i. (75-257). Lancer.

Suffer a Witch: By Rae Foley Pseud. Elinore Denniston. LC 65-10716. (Red badge detective). bds., 3.50. Dodd.

Suffer All Children. Jennie Dethloffs Klein. LC 44-498914. 1944. Dorrance and Company.

Suffer! Little Children: A Novel. Peter Van Greenaway. LC 77-351576. 1976. 3.95 (ISBN 0-575-02125-X). Gollancz.

Suffer the Children. John Saul. 1979. pap. 3.50 (ISBN 0-440-18293-X). Dell.

Suffer the Little Ones. James H Ryan. LC 76-187956. 1972. 5.95 (ISBN 0-87695-145-0). Aurora.

Suffering Husbands. Wallace Irwin. LC 20-10767. George H. Doran Company.

Suffering Millions: A Novel. Rosetta Otwell Cross. LC 6-319514. 1890. The Courier Office, Printers.

Sufferings of Young Werther. Johann Wolfgang Von Goethe. Tr. by Harry Steinhauer. LC 70-95519. 1970. 6.00. Norton.

Sufferings of Young Werther. Johann Wolfgang Von Goethe. Tr. by J. Q. Morgan. 1980. pap. 4.50 (ISBN 0-7145-0542-0). Riverrun NY.

Suffrage of Elvira. Vidiadhar Surajprasad Naipaul. LC 73-173538. 1969. 0.25. Penguin.

Sugar and Mr. Duck. Martha Manker Moran. (Illus.). 1973. 4.00 (ISBN 0-682-47763-X). Exposition Pr.

Sugar Bush Nurse. Virginia K. Smiley. (YA) 1981. 6.95 (Avalon). Bouregy.

Sugar Creek Gang Flies to Cuba. Paul Hutchens. 1944. Wm. B. Eerdmans Publishing Company.

Sugar Dragon. Victoria Gordon. (Harlequin Romances Ser.). 192p. 1981. pap. 1.50 (ISBN 0-373-02427-4). Harlequin Bks.

Sugar Hill. Amanda Hart Douglass. 1979. pap. 2.25 o.s.i. (ISBN 0-505-51412-5). Tower Bks.

Sugar in the Air: A Romance. Ernest Charles Large. LC 37-16649. 1937. C. Scribner's Sons.

Sugar in the Gourd. Evelyn Hanna. LC 41-26741. 1942. E. P. Dutton & Company, Inc.

Sugar Loaf. Patricia C. Summers. 5.00 o.p. Vantage.

Sugar Loaf. Patricia Celley Summers. 1974. 5.00 (ISBN 0-533-00761-5). Vantage Press.

Sugar Mouse. Mary Ann Gibbs. 1974. pap. 0.95 o.p. (26556-4-095). Beagle Bks.

Sugar on the Slate. Don Fontaine. LC 51-12796. 1951. Farrar, Straus and Young.

Sugar-Pine Murmurings. Elizabeth Sargent Wilson & Sargent, Jacob Livermore, 1865- LC 3-281890. 1899. For the Authors by the Whitaker & Ray Company, Incorporated.

Sugar Princess. Linn Boyd Porter. LC 4392. (On cover: Dillingham's American author's library, no. 65). 1900. G. W. Dillingham Co.

Sugarbird. Kate Thompson. 1971. pap. 0.95 o.p. (95087). Beagle Bks.

Sugarfields. Barbara Mahone. 1970. pap. 1.00 o.p. Broadside.

Sugarfoot. Clarence Budington Kelland. LC 42-24977. 1942. Harper & Brothers.

Sugarland: A Novel. Paul Foreman. LC 77-25171. 1978. 8.50 (ISBN 0-914476-76-9). Thorp Springs Press.

Sugarland: A Novel of Texas & Prison. Paul Foreman. LC 77-25171. 1978. 7.50 (ISBN 0-914476-76-9). Thorp Springs.

Sugarland Express. Henry Clement. 1974. (pbk.) 1.25. Popular Library.

Sugarplum Staircase. Richard English. LC 47-11922. (inner sanctum mystery). 1947. Simon and Schuster.

Suggestion. Mabel Collins Cook. LC 6-28076. Lovell, Gestefeld & Company.

Suicide. Nicolai Erdman. 52p. (Orig.). 1981. pap. 4.95 (ISBN 0-86104-203-4). Pluto Pr.

Suicide Academy. Daniel Stern. LC 68-22769. 1968. McGraw-Hill.

Suicide Club and Other Stories. Robert Louis Stevenson. LC 79-120692. (Pergamon English Library). (Athena books.). 1970. (ISBN 0-08-006703-4). Pergamon Press.

Suicide Command. M. M. Michaeles. 1971. pap. 0.75 o.p. (ISBN 0-447-74732-0). Lancer.

Suicide Excepted. Alfred Alexander Gordon Clark. LC 54-12836. (Murder revisited mystery novel, no. 7). 1954. Macmillan.

Suicide Excepted. Cyril Hare. LC 81-17346. 1982. 3.75 (ISBN 0-486-24245-5). Dover Publications.

Suicide Excepted. Cyril Hare. LC 82-48244. (636). 1983. 2.95 (ISBN 0-06-080636-2). Harper & Row.

Suicide Most Foul. J. G Jeffreys, pseud. LC 80-52078. 1981. 9.95 (ISBN 0-8027-5430-9). Walker.

Suicide Note. Christopher Davis. LC 77-3787. 1977. 7.95 o.p. (ISBN 0-06-010988-2, HarpT). Har-Row.

Suicide Note: A Novel. Christopher Davis. LC 77-3787. 7.95 (ISBN 0-06-010988-2). Harper & Row.

Suicide of the Empires. Alan Clark. (Twentieth Century Library - B. P. C. Ser). (Illus.). 1972. pap. 2.95 o.p. (ISBN 0-07-011126-X). McGraw.

Suicide Plague. Ed Naha. 1982. pap. 2.75 (ISBN 0-553-22588-X). Bantam.

Suicide Ranch. Edward Earl Repp. LC 36-19263. 1936. Godwin.

Suicide Seat. Nick Carter. 192p. (Orig.). 1980. pap. 2.25 (ISBN 0-441-79077-1, Pub. by Charter Bks). Ace Bks.

Suicide Squadron. Dan Brennan. 1978. pap. 1.75 o.p. (ISBN 0-505-51282-3). Tower Bks.

Suicide Submarine. Yutaka Yokota & Joseph D. Harrington. 1980. pap. 1.75 o.s.i. (ISBN 0-8439-0723-1, Leisure Bks). Nordon Pubns.

Suicide Trail. Wayne C. Lee. 1972. 3.95 o.p. Crown.

Suicide's Wife. David Madden. LC 78-55644. 1978. 8.95 o.p. (ISBN 0-672-52492-9). Bobbs.

Suitable Child. Norman Duncan. LC 9-28038. 1.00. F. H. Revell Company.

Suitable for Framing. Marion Holbrook. LC 41-19644. 1941. Dodd, Mead & Company.

Suitable for Framing. James Atlee Phillips. LC 49-987812. 1949. Macmillan Co.

Suitable Marriage. Marlaine Kyle, pseud. (Candlelight Regency Special Ser.: No. 692). (Orig.). 1981. pap. 1.75 (ISBN 0-440-18406-1). Dell.

Suitable Match. Joy Freeman. 336p. 1980. 11.95 (ISBN 0-312-77537-7). St Martin.

Suitable Match. Joy Freemen. LC 80-14195. 1980. 11.95 (ISBN 0-312-77537-7). St. Martin's Press.

Suitcase Full of Money. W. Crawford Thompson. 1973. pap. 0.75 o.p. (07282). Curtis.

Suitcase Full of Money. W. Crawford Thompson. 1973. 0.75. Curtis Books.

Suitor Too Many. Mildred Barbour. LC 28-14240. Grosset & Dunlap.

Suitors of Yvonne: Being a Portion of the Memoirs of the Sieur Gaston De Luynes. Rafael Sabatini. LC 2-15211. 1902. G. P. Putnam's Sons.

Suivez la Piste. Emile De Harven. LC 77-10091. 1972. pap. 4.75 (ISBN 0-912022-30-2). EMC.

Sula. Toni Morrison. LC 73-7278. 1974. 5.95 (ISBN 0-394-48044-9). Knopf; Distributed by Random House.

Sula. Toni Morrison. 1975. (pbk.) 1.50. Bantam.

Sullivan. Clyde Brion Davis. LC 40-30098. Farrar & Rinehart, Inc.

Sullivan. Walter Macken. LC 57-9116. 1957. Macmillan.

Sullivan County Sketches of Stephen Crane. Stephen Crane. Ed. by Schoberlin, Melvin. LC 49-929383. 1949. Syracuse Univ. Press.

Sullivan's Law. George G. Gilman, pseud. (Edge Ser.: No. 20). 1976. pap. 1.95 (ISBN 0-523-41774-8). Pinnacle Bks.

Sulphur Fumes: Or, In the Garden of Hell. George Wesley Davis. LC 23-13490. 1923. The Times-Mirror Press.

Sultan and the Lady: A Story of His Highness Zafrullah Bin Ismail Bin Said, Sultan of Namua, Lord of the Island Sea Who Retained Also His Grandfather's Title of Honour: Faithful Ally of Queen Victoria. 1st American Ed. Eric Robert Russell Linklater. LC 55-531718. Harcourt, Brace.

Sultana. Michel. LC 82-48685. 16.95 (ISBN 0-06-015166-8). Harper & Row.

Sultana. Henry Cottrell Rowland. LC 14-7875. 1914. 1.25. Dodd, Mead and Company.

Sultans. Noel Barber. (O.s.i.). 1973. 10.95 o.s.i. (ISBN 0-671-21624-4). S&S.

Sultan's Jewels: A Novel by Moritz Wm. Boehm. Moritz William Boehm. LC 40-13624. Dorrance and Company.

Sultan's Rival: A Story for Boys. Bradley Gilman. LC 11-25677. 1.20. Small, Maynard and Company.

Sultan's Warrior: By Bates Baldwin Pseud. John Edward Jennings. LC 51-11271. 1951. Holt.

Sultan's Warrior. 1st Ed. Bates Baldwin, pseud. LC 51-11271. 1951. Holt.

Sultry Nights, No. 74. Ariel Tierney. 1982. pap. 1.75 (ISBN 0-515-06685-0). Jove Pubns.

Sulu Sea Murders: A Case for Captain North, D.C.I.... Francis Van Wyck Mason. LC 33-35698. 1933. Pub. for the Crime Club, Inc., by Doubleday, Doran & Company, Inc.

Sum and Total of Now: A Novel. Don Robertson. LC 66-155912. 4.95. Putnam.

Sum of Things. Olivia Manning. LC 80-7924. 1981. 10.95 (ISBN 0-689-11096-0). Atheneum.

Sum VII: A Novel. T. W Hard. LC 78-2062. (Illus.). 8.95 (ISBN 0-06-011702-8). Harper & Row.

Sumatra. Donald Moore. LC 59-10680. 1959. Doubleday.

Sumatra Seven Zero. Oswald Wynd. LC 68-12608. 1968. Harcourt, Brace & World.

Summer. Jack Ansell. LC 73-82179. 1973. 7.95 (ISBN 0-87795-063-6). Arbor House.

Summer... Romain Rolland & Stimson, Eleanor, Tr. LC 25-180605. (His The soul enchanted. II). 1925. H. Holt and Company.

Summer. Edith Newbold Jones Wharton. (Scribners lib. 116). 1965. pap., 1.45. Scribners.

Summer. Edith Newbold Jones Wharton. 1981. 2.75 (ISBN 0-425-04610-9). Berkley Publishing Corp.

Summer: A Novel. Edith Newbold Jones Wharton. LC 73-115288. 1970. Scholarly Press.

Summer: A Novel. Edith Newbold Jones Wharton. LC 17-175164. 1917. D. Appleton and Company.

Summer After Summer. Richard Sullivan. LC 42-22860. 1942. Doubleday, Doran & Company, Inc.

Summer After Summer. Richard Sullivan. LC 77-11315. (American Catholic Tradition). 1978. 19.00 (ISBN 0-405-10860-5). Arno Press.

Summer After the War. James Whitfield Ellison. LC 72-3723. 1972. 6.95 (ISBN 0-396-06646-1). Dodd, Mead.

Summer Assembly Days: Or, What Was Seen, Heard and Felt at the Nebraska Chautauqua. Anna E Hahn. LC 6-46156. Congregational Sunday-School and Publishing Society.

Summer at Awakopu. Robyn Donald. (Harlequin Presents Ser). (Orig.). 1979. pap. 1.25 (ISBN 0-373-70785-1). Harlequin Bks.

Summer at Chateau Oirad. Paul Lester. 1972. pap. 1.95 o.s.i. (OPH-4059, Ophelia). Olympia.

Summer at Dorne. Mira Stables. (Coventry Romance Ser.: No. 181). 224p. 1982. pap. 1.50 (ISBN 0-449-50282-1, Coventry). Fawcett.

Summer at Hope House. Marjorie Warby. Ed. by Gene DeRoin. (Aston Hall Presents Ser.). (Orig.). 1979. pap. 1.50 (ISBN 0-89936-011-4). Aston Hall.

Summer at Raven's Roost. Elissa Grandower, pseud. LC 76-5342. 1976. 7.95 o.p. (ISBN 0-385-11627-6). Doubleday.

Summer at Raven's Roost. Hillary Waugh. LC 76-5342. 1976. 7.95 (ISBN 0-385-11627-6). Doubleday.

Summer at the Castle. James Howard Wellard. LC 53-12513. 1953. St. Martin's Press.

Summer Bachelors. Warner Fabian. LC 26-15271. 1926. Boni and Liveright.

Summer Before Dark. Doris May Lessing. 1974. (pbk.) 1.75. Bantam Books.

Summer Before the Dark. 1st. american ed. Doris May Lessing. LC 72-11044. 1973. 6.95 (ISBN 0-394-48428-2). Knopf; Distributed by Random House.

Summer Begins. Sandy Asher. 176p. 1982. 1.95 (ISBN 0-553-22512-X). Bantam.

Summer Bird-Cage. Margaret Drabble. LC 68-89890. (B67-24882). 1967. Penguin.

Summer Bird-Cage. Margaret Drabble. 1977. 1.95 (ISBN 0-445-08584-3). Popular Library.

Summer Boarders. Adele M Garrigues. LC 6-40712. 1880. The Authors' Publishing Company.

Summer Book. Tove Jansson. LC 74-22195. 1975. 6.95 (ISBN 0-394-49249-8). Pantheon Books.

Summer Book. Tove Jansson. LC 77-1836. 1977. 9.95 (ISBN 0-8161-6471-1). G. K. Hall.

Summer Brings Gifts. 1st Ed. Ann Katherine Gilliland Ritner. LC 56-108063. 1956. Lippincott.

Summer Burning. Harry J Boyle. LC 64-13863. 1964. Doubleday.

Summer Camp. Richard Woodley. 1.95 (ISBN 0-440-18331-6). Dell Publishing Co.

Summer Camp Arts & Crafts - & Sex. Garth Brandtson. 192p. (Orig.). 1973. pap. 1.95 o.p. (ISBN 0-87682-315-0, 7315). Barclay Hse.

Summer Camp Mystery. Cecil Day-Lewis. LC 40-80756. Harper & Brothers.

Summer Clouds and Other Stories. Eden Phillpotts. LC 7-36053. (breezy library, no. 2). R. Tuck & Sons.

Summer Companions. Olivia Manning. (Inflation Fighter Ser.). 192p. 1982. pap. cancelled o.s.i. (ISBN 0-8439-1120-4, Leisure Bks). Nordon Pubns.

Summer Crossing. Steve Tesich. LC 82-40125. 374p. 1982. 14.95 (ISBN 0-394-52759-3). Random.

Summer Crossing: A Novel. Steve Tesich. LC 82-40125. 14.95 (ISBN 0-394-52759-3). Random House.

Summer Dancers. Clyde Miller. LC 61-15161. 1961. Macmillan.

Summer Day at Ajaccio. E. G. Bartlett. 168p. 1980. 15.00x (ISBN 0-7050-0075-3, Pub. by Skilton & Shaw England). State Mutual Bk.

Summer Day Is Done. R. T Stevens. LC 76-2822. 1976. 7.95 (ISBN 0-385-12041-9). Doubleday.

Summer Dreams. Cynthia Applewhite. LC 80-52408. 288p. 1982. 12.50 (ISBN 0-87223-714-1, Seaview Bks). Putnam Pub Group.

Summer Dreams and the Kleig Light Gas Company. Cynthia Applewhite. LC 80-52408. 12.50. Seaview Books.

Summer Drift-Wood for the Winter Fire. Rose Porter. 1870. A. D. F. Randolph & Co.

Summer Ends Now: Stories. John Emery. LC 80-486107. 1980. 10.95 (ISBN 0-7022-1467-1) (ISBN 0-7022-1468-X). University of Queensland Press.

Summer Fire. Sally Wentworth. (Harlequin Presents Ser.). 192p. 1981. pap. 1.75 (ISBN 0-373-10456-1). Harlequin Bks.

Summer Fires: A Novel. Bob Reiss. LC 79-17642. 9.95 (ISBN 0-671-24655-0). Simon and Schuster.

Summer Fires and Winter Country. Maurice Shadbolt. LC 66-16353. 1966. Atheneum.

Summer Flood. Goronwy Rees. LC 33-249223. 1933. The John Day Company.

Summer Friends. Peter McCurtin. 384p. (Orig.). 1983. pap. 3.50 (ISBN 0-8439-1167-0, Leisure Bks). Dorchester Pub Co.

Summer Fruit. Cecil William Mercer. LC 29-79608. 1929. Minton, Balch & Company.

Summer Game. Roger Angell. LC 76-183512. (O.s.i.). 320p. 1972. 7.50 o.s.i. (ISBN 0-670-68164-4). Viking Pr.

Summer Games. Babs H Deal. LC 72-157584. 1972. 6.95. Doubleday.

Summer Girl. Caroline Crane. LC 79-15811. 1979. 8.95 o.p. (ISBN 0-396-07735-8). Dodd.

Summer Girl: A Novel of Suspense. Caroline Crane. LC 79-15811. 8.95 (ISBN 0-396-07735-8). Dodd, Mead.

Summer Hail. Valerie Dade Savage. LC 36-109437. 1936. Doubleday, Doran and Company, Inc.

Summer Half. Angela Mackail Thirkell. LC 38-27472. 1938. A. A. Knopf.

Summer Heart: A Novel. Margaret Granville. (Dillingham's American authors library, no. 7). 1895. G. W. Dillingham.

Summer Holiday. Alice Duer Miller. LC 41-164902. 1941. Dodd, Mead & Company.

Summer Hostess. Lucy Poate Stebbins. LC 38-3532. The Penn Publishing Company.

Summer Hotel. P. J Wolfson. LC 32-10832. The Vanguard Press.

Summer House. Dorothy Daniels. 1976. (pbk.) 1.25. Warner Books.

Summer Houses. James Stevenson. LC 63-12515. 1963. Macmillan.

Summer Hymnal: A Romance of Tennessee. John Trotwood Moore. LC 1-11787. 1901. H. T. Coates & Company.

Summer Idyl. Frances Christine Tiernan. LC 8-19800. (On cover: Appletons' new handy-volume series, no. 12). 1878. D. Appleton and Company.

Summer in April: A Novel. Donald Macardle. LC 46-5571. 1946. J. B. Lippincott Company.

Summer in Arcady. James Lane Allen. Repr. of 1899 ed. lib. bdg. 15.00 (ISBN 0-8414-3071-3). Folcroft.

Summer in Arcady: A Tale of Nature. James Lane Allen. LC 7-4432. 1896. The Macmillan Company.

Summer in Arcady: A Tale of Nature. James Lane Allen. LC 2-17485. 1902. The Macmillan Company.

Summer in New York: A Love Story Told in Letters. Edward Waterman Townsend. LC 3-6565. 1908. H. Holt and Company.

Summer in Oldport Harbor. A Novel. W H Metcalf. LC 7-25875. 1887. J. B. Lippincott Company.

Summer in Prague. Zdena Salivarova, pseud. Tr. by Marie Winn from Czech. LC 75-181661. 288p. (YA) 1973. 8.95 o.p. (ISBN 0-06-013746-0, HarpT). Har-Row.

Summer in Salandar. 1st Ed. Herbert Ernest Bates. LC 57-11155. 1957. Little, Brown.

Summer in Sodom. Edwin Fey. LC 65-4505. Argyle Books.

Summer in Sodom with Kitchen Privileges. Florence Holland. 1977. 6.50 o.p. (ISBN 0-682-48968-9). Exposition.

Summer in Spoleto. Natalja Wendel. LC 67-20436. 1967. F. Fell.

Summer in the Gravel Pit. Maurice Duggan. 176p. 1965. pap. 3.90x (ISBN 0-582-71014-6). Intl Pubns Serv.

Summer in the Gravel Pit. Maurice Duggan. 176p. 1965. pap. 3.90x o.p. (ISBN 0-582-71014-6). Intl Pubns Serv.

Summer in the Greenhouse. Elizabeth Mavor. LC 60-8106. 1960. Morrow.

Summer in the Twenties. Peter Dickinson. LC 80-8652. 10.95 (ISBN 0-394-51330-4). Pantheon Books.

Summer in Vermont: By Rebecca Marsh Pseud. William Arthur Neubauer. LC 55-102035. 1955. Arcadia House.

Summer in Williamsburg: A Novel. Daniel Fuchs. LC 34-362236. The Vanguard Press.

Summer Interlude: By Emily Noble Pseud. James Noble Gifford. LC 52-6493. 1952. Arcadia House.

Summer Is Ended. John Herrmann. LC 32-24548. Covici, Friede.

Summer Job. Charlotte Montgomery. LC 42-172229. 1942. Arcadia House, Inc.

Summer Journey South. Walter H. Carnaham. LC 68-1972. 1968. Adams Press.

Summer Lace. Jenny Nolan. (Second Chance at Love: No. 33). 192p. (Orig.). 1982. pap. 1.75 (ISBN 0-515-06249-9). Jove Pubns.

Summer Land. Burke Davis. LC 65-11269. (Illus.). 1965. Random House.

Summer-Land: A Southern Story. A Child of the Sun. LC 8-17660. 1855. D. Appleton and Company.

Summer Landmark. Richard Riggs Day. LC 47-31038. 1947. Macmillan Co.

Summer Leaves. Denis George Mackail. LC 34-40673. 1934. Doubleday, Doran & Company, Inc.

Summer Legends. Rudolf Baumbach & Dole, Mrs. Helen James (Bennett) Tr. LC 6-10285. T. Y. Crowell & Co.

Summer Light. Herbert Mason. LC 79-25803. 9.95 (ISBN 0-374-27176-3). Farrar, Straus, Giroux.

Summer Lightning. Allene Soule Corliss. LC 36-24945. Toronto, Farrar & Rinehart, Incorporated.

Summer Lightning. George Frederick Hummel. LC 29-740019. 1929. H. Liveright.

Summer Lightning. Judith Richards. LC 77-16761. 1978. 8.95 (ISBN 0-312-77544-X). St. Martin's Press.

Summer Lightning. Judith Richards. 1979. 2.50 (ISBN 0-380-42960-8). Avon Books.

Summer Lightning. Judith Richards. LC 78-23881. 1980. 13.50 (ISBN 0-8161-6647-1). G. K. Hall.

Summer Lightning. P. G. Wodehouse. 1964. 11.95 o.s.i. (ISBN 0-8277-0230-2). British Bk Ctr.

Summer Lovers. 1st Ed. Hollis Alpert. LC 58-10963. 1958. Knopf.

Summer Magic. F. C. Martanga. 1979. pap. 1.25 (ISBN 0-440-17962-9). Dell.

Summer Masquerade. Donna Ball. LC 81-43285. 1982. 10.95 (ISBN 0-385-17828-X). Doubleday.

Summer Masquerade. Blanche Chenier. 1978. 1.75 (ISBN 0-449-23820-2). Fawcett Crest Books.

Summer Meadows. Robert Nathan. LC 73-5829. 1973. 5.95. Delacorte Press.

Summer Moonshine. Pelham Grenville Wodehouse. LC 73-164025. 1972. 0.35 (ISBN 0-14-002547-2). Penguin.

Summer Moonshine. Pelham Grenville Wodehouse. LC 37-28699. 1937. Doubleday, Doran and Company, Inc.

Summer Moonshine. Pelham Grenville Wodehouse. LC 39-25330. 1938. Doubleday, Doran and Company, Inc.

Summer Never Ends: A Modern Love Story. Waldo David Frank. LC 41-14049. Duell, Sloan and Pearce.

Summer Night. Alan Moorehead. LC 55-788. Harper.

Summer Obsession. Myra M Lorenz. LC 53-10298. Vantage Press.

Summer of a Dormouse. Monica Stirling. LC 67-20322. 1967. Harcourt, Brace & World.

Summer of Change. Russ Cornell. LC 76-381141. 1976. Simon & Schuster of Canada.

Summer of Decision. Ruby C Tolliver. LC 78-74499. 3.95 (ISBN 0-8054-7310-6). Broadman Press.

Summer of Discovery. Isabel Cabot. (YA) 1980. 6.95 (Avalon). Bouregy.

Summer of Enchantment. Kathleen Harris. LC 40-51876. 1940. Arcadia House.

Summer of Enchantment. Kathleen Harris, pseud. LC 40-31876. 1940. Arcadia House, Inc.

Summer of Fear. Lois Duncan. (YA) 1977. pap. 2.25 (ISBN 0-440-98324-X, LFL). Dell.

Summer of Forty Two. Herman Raucher. 1978. pap. 1.95 (ISBN 0-440-18348-0). Dell.

Summer of Good Hope. Georgiana Cushman Philips. LC 39-4386. 1939. G. P.Putnam's Sons.

Summer of Katya. Trevanian. LC 83-1790. 13.95 (ISBN 0-517-54829-1). Crown.

Summer of Katya. Trevanian. 256p. 1983. 12.95 (ISBN 0-517-54829-1). Crown.

Summer of Life. Beatrice Kean Stapleton Seymour. LC 36-24396. 1936. Little, Brown, and Company.

Summer of Love. Daisy H. Thomson. 1976. pap. 1.25 o.p. (ISBN 0-515-03869-5). BJ Pub Group.

Summer of My First Love. Isabelle Holland. 256p. (Orig.). 1981. pap. 2.25 (ISBN 0-449-70007-0, Juniper). Fawcett.

Summer of Sir Lancelot. Gordon Ostlere. LC 65-17965. 1965. Doubleday.

Summer of Stones: A Novel. Raoul Cohen Faure. LC 63-21123. Crown Publishers.

Summer of the Dragon. Elizabeth Peters, pseud. LC 79-9782. 8.95 (ISBN 0-396-07689-0). Dodd, Mead.

Summer of the Dragon. Elizabeth Peters, pseud. 1980. 1.95. Ballantine Books.

Summer of the Dragon. Elizabeth Peters, pseud. 1980. 2.25 (ISBN 0-449-24291-9). Fawcett Crest Books.

Summer of the Drums. Theodore V. Olsen. LC 72-79413. 160p. 1972. 4.95 o.p. (ISBN 0-385-05694-X). Doubleday.

Summer of the Drums. Theodore V. Olsen. 160p. 1974. pap. 0.95 o.p. (532-95361-095). Manor Bks.

Summer of the Drums. Theodore A. Olson. 1978. pap. 1.25 (ISBN 0-532-12545-2). Woodhill.

Summer of the Flea. Patricia Bailey. LC 81-80163. 160p. 1983. 10.95 (ISBN 0-86666-013-5). GWP.

Summer of the Gun. Henry Wilson Allen. LC 78-15282. 8.95 (ISBN 0-397-01309-4). Lippincott.

Summer of the Gun. Will Henry, pseud. 1978. 11.49i (ISBN 0-397-01309-4). Har-Row.

Summer of the Monkeys. Wilson Rawls. LC 75-32295. 1976. 7.95 (ISBN 0-385-11450-8). Doubleday.

Summer of the Raven. Sara Craven. (Harlequin Presents Ser.). 192p. 1981. pap. 1.50 (ISBN 0-373-10440-5). Harlequin Bks.

Summer of the Red Wolf. Morris L. West. 1972. Repr. lib. bdg. 9.95 o.p. (ISBN 0-8161-6029-5, Large Print Bks). G K Hall.

Summer of the Red Wolf: A Novel. Morris L. West. LC 70-155497. 1971. 6.95. Morrow.

Summer of the Red Wolf: A Novel. Morris L. West. LC 72-1971. 1972. (ISBN 0-8161-6029-5). G. K. Hall.

Summer of the Shaman. Clarissa Ross, pseud. 240p. (Orig.). 1982. pap. 1.95 (ISBN 0-446-90796-0). Warner Bks.

Summer of the Sioux. Tim Champlin. 224p. 1982. pap. 1.95 (ISBN 0-345-29268-5). Ballantine.

Summer of the Spanish Woman. Catherine Gaskin. LC 76-56292. 1977. 10.00 (ISBN 0-385-07414-X). Doubleday.

Summer of the Spanish Woman. Catherine Gaskin. 1979. 2.50 (ISBN 0-449-23809-1). Fawcett Crest.

Summer of the Weeping Rain. Yvonne Whittal. (Harlequin Romances Ser.). 192p. 1981. pap. 1.25 (ISBN 0-373-02412-6, Pub. by Harlequin). PB.

Summer of Thirty-Two. Lorinda Hagen. 1979. pap. 1.75 o.s.i. (ISBN 0-8439-0656-1, Leisure Bks). Nordon Pubns.

Summer of Uncle Jean-Marie. Jacot De Boinod, Bernard Louis. LC 64-12297. 1964. Knopf.

Summer of '42. Herman Raucher. LC 76-146106. 1971. 5.95. Putnam.

Summer on a Mountain of Spices. Harvey Jacobs. LC 74-1887. 1975. 9.95 (ISBN 0-06-012156-4). Harper & Row.

Summer on the Shore. William Arthur Neubauer. LC 67-8606. 1967. Arcadia House.

Summer on the Water: A Novel. David Westheimer. LC 48-6911. 1948. Macmillan Co.

Summer People. Janice Elliott. LC 81-108270. 1980. 25.00 (ISBN 0-340-25172-7). Hodder and Stoughton.

Summer People. Fannie Heaslip Lea. LC 33-253740. 1933. Dodd, Mead and Company.

Summer Place: A Novel. Sloan Wilson. LC 58-7506. 1958. Simon and Schuster.

Summer Queen. Alice Walworth Graham. LC 72-84916. 1973. 6.95 (ISBN 0-385-05111-5). Doubleday.

Summer Queen. Alice Walworth Graham. 1973. (pbk.) 1.25. Popular Library.

Summer Rain. Yvonne Kalman. (Orig.). pap. 2.50 (ISBN 0-515-05702-9). Jove Pubns.

Summer Range. Llewellyn Perry Holmes. LC 51-4993. (Double D western). 1951. Doubleday.

Summer Romance. Joanne Gille Aldrich. 192p. (YA) 1974. 4.95 o.p. (Avalon). Bouregy.

Summer Season. Jane Rossiter, pseud. 1969. pap. 0.60 o.p. (83-854). Lancer.

Summer Share. Jessica Hyatt. (Belmont Tower). 2.25 (ISBN 0-505-51404-4). Tower Publications.

Summer Shock. Thorne Lee. LC 56-5914. 1956. Abelard-Schuman.

Summer Showers: By Harry Arthur Pseud. 1st Ed. Harry Arthur Bates. LC 53-20517. 1952. Pageant Press.

Summer Sin. Gladys Sloan. LC 41-19651. Phoenix Press.

Summer Sin. Leona Slottman. LC 41-19651. 1941. Phoenix Press.

Summer Situations. Ann Birstein. LC 70-175276. 1972. 5.95. Coward, McCann & Geoghegan.

Summer Soldier. Nicholas Guild. LC 77-27125. 8.95 (ISBN 0-87223-499-1). Seaview Books: Trade Distribution by Simon and Schuster.

Summer Soldier. Leane Zugsmiht. LC 38-20482. Random House.

Summer Soldiers. 1st Ed. David Mark. 1957. Doubleday.

Summer Solstice. Michael T Hinkemeyer. (Berkley Medallion Book). 1977. 1.50 (ISBN 0-425-03329-5). Berkley Pub. Corp.

Summer Solstice. Elizabeth North. 1973. 0.75. Popular Lib.

Summer Solstice. Elizabeth North. LC 79-171144. 1972. 5.95 (ISBN 0-394-47304-3). Knopf.

Summer Solstice: A Novel. Michael T Hinkemeyer. LC 75-33348. (ISBN 0-399-11645-1). Berkeley Pub. Co.: Distributed by Putnam.

Summer Song. Marsha Manning. (Cameo Romance). (Fawcett gold medal book: Vol. 22). 1975. (pbk.) 0.95. Fawcett.

Summer Star. William Edward Daniel Ross. pap. 0.50 o.p. (52-890). Paperback Lib.

Summer Star. Jane Rossiter, pseud. LC 64-7422. 1964. Avalon Books.

Summer Station. Maud Lang, pseud. LC 75-38763. 1976. 7.95 (ISBN 0-698-10732-2). Coward, McCann & Geoghegan.

Summer Station. Maud Lang, pseud. (Signet Book). 1977. 1.75 (ISBN 0-451-07489-0). New American Library.

Summer Storm. Charles Angoff. LC 63-18234. 1963. T. Yoseloff.

Summer Storm. Letitia Healey. 192p. (Orig.). 1980. pap. 1.50 (ISBN 0-671-57024-2). S&S.

Summer Storm. Jane Lane. LC 76-379545. 1976. 3.50 (ISBN 0-432-08577-7). P. Davies.

Summer Storm. Louis Paul. LC 49-9182. 1949. Crown Publishers.

Summer Storm. Cesare Pavese. Tr. by A. E. Murch. 204p. 1982. 13.95 (ISBN 0-7206-8650-4, Pub. by Peter Owen). Merrimack Pub Cir.

Summer Storm. Frank Arthur Swinnerton. LC 26-17244. George H. Doran Company.

Summer Storms. Stephanie St. Clair. (Candlelight Ecstasy Ser.: No. 38). (Orig.). 1982. pap. 1.75 (ISBN 0-440-18444-4). Dell.

Summer Story: A Novel. Robert Houston. 1.75 (ISBN 0-449-14019-9). Fawcett Gold Medal Books.

Summer Stranger. Louise Field Cooper. LC 47-18675. 1947. Harper & Brothers.

Summer Street. Hal Ellson. LC 53-8522. 1953. Balla Tine Books.

Summer Sunday at Sundown. Sara S. Sims. 3.50 o.p. Vantage.

Summer Tempest. Doris M Hume. LC 41-6796. 1941. Arcadia House, Inc.

Summer That Bled. Anthony Masters. 1974. pap. 1.65 o.p. (48652-7). WSP.

Summer Time Ends. John Hargrave. LC 35-17681. The Bobbs-Merrill Company.

Summer to Decide. Carol Gaye. pap. 0.50 o.p. (52-347). Paperback Lib.

Summer to Decide. Pamela Hansford Johnson. LC 74-25239. 1975. 10.00 (ISBN 0-684-14191-4). Scribner.

Summer to Decide. Renee Shann. 1972. pap. 0.75 o.p. (94271). Beagle Bks.

Summer to Remember. Vera Fedorovna Panova. LC 62-3165. 1962. T. Yoseloff.

Summer Vacation Swap. J. K. Marshall. pap. 1.95 o.p. (8095). Cameo.

Summer Visits. Margery Sharp. LC 77-15364. 8.95 (ISBN 0-316-78312-9). Little, Brown.

Summer Will Come Again. Maud McCurdy Welch. LC 46-18348. 1946. Arcadia House, Inc.

Summer Will Show. Sylvia Townsend Warner. LC 36-13045. 1936. The Viking Press.

Summer with Danica. H. G. Gunther. (Gunther Ser.: No. 3). 224p. (Orig.). 1981. pap. 1.95 (ISBN 0-515-05674-X). Jove Pubns.
Summer 1914. Roger Martin Du Gard. Tr. by Stuart Gilber. LC 41-51575. 1941. The Viking Press.
Summerblood. Anne Rudeen. 1978. 2.25 (ISBN 0-446-82535-2). Warner Books.
Summerfair. Ansen Dibell, pseud. 272p. 1982. pap. 2.75 (ISBN 0-87997-759-0). DAW Bks.
Summerfield; or, Life on a Farm. Day Kellogg Lee. LC 7-12608. 1852. Derby and Miller.
Summergreen. Janet Cox. LC 81-66051. 1981. 6.95 (ISBN 0-87747-864-3). Deseret Book Co.
Summerhaven. Linda Masterson. (Illus.). 1979. pap. 1.95 (ISBN 0-89083-471-7). Zebra.
Summerhills. Dorothy Emily Stevenson. LC 56-101806. 1956. Rinehart.
Summerhouse. Patricia Wentworth. 1972. pap. 0.95 o.p. (ISBN 0-515-02772-3, N2772). Pyramid Pubns.
Summering. Joanne Greenberg. (Bard book). 1974. (pbk.) 1.65. Avon.
Summering. Joanne Greenberg. 1974. (pbk.) 1.65. Bard Books/Published by Avon.
Summering: A Book of Short Stories. Joanne Greenberg. LC 66-13100. 1966. Holt, Rhinehart and Winston.
Summer's End. William Edward Daniel Ross. (Avalon romances). 1973. 4.50. Avalon Books.
Summer's End. William Edward Daniel Ross. (Gold Medal Book). 1976. 1.25 (ISBN 0-449-13613-2). Fawcett.
Summer's End. Danielle Steel. 1981. pap. 3.75 (ISBN 0-440-18405-3). Dell.
Summer's End. Mary Dallas Street. LC 36-4915. 1936. W. Morrow & Company.
Summer's Lease. Susan Ertz. LC 79-181654. 1972. 6.95 (ISBN 0-06-011182-8). Harper & Row.
Summer's Lease. Celia Larner. LC 74-81469. 7.50. St. Martin's.
Summer's Lease. Constance Pendergast. LC 59-71164. 1959. McDowell, Obolensky.
Summer's Lease. Eileen Arbuthnot Robertson. LC 40-6441. 1940. Houghton Mifflin Company.
Summer's Lie: A Novel. Alan Boatman. LC 76-95992. 1970. 6.95. Harper & Row.
Summer's Love. Isabel Cabot. 1972. pap. 0.75 o.s.i. (01-352). Lancer.
Summers Night. Sylvia Thompson. LC 31-28627. 1932. Little, Brown, and Company.
Summer's Play: A Novel. Charlotte Underwood. LC 78-69512. 9.95 (ISBN 0-06-014471-8). Harper & Row.
Summer's Play: An Exaggeration... Gladys Bronwyn Stern. LC 34-4061. 1934. A. A. Knopf.
Summer's Romance. Marie Healy Bigot. 1872. Roberts Brothers.
Summer's Tale, a Novel. Gerald Warner Brace. LC 49-9215. 1949. W. W. Norton.
Summer's Tales, 3 vols. Kylie Tennant & J. Iggulden. 1964-66. 4.95 ea o.p. St Martin.
Summer's Tales. 2. Ed. by Kylie Tennant. Ed. by Kylie Tennant. LC 65-13195. 1966. bds., 4.95. Macmillan.
Summer's Tales. 3 Melbourne, Macmillan. LC 65-131955. 4.95. St. Martin's.
Summersea. Eileen Lottman. LC 75-10468. 7.95 (ISBN 0-698-10684-9). Coward, McCann & Geoghegan.
Summertime. Denis George Mackail. LC 24-263181. 1924. Houghton Mifflin Company.
Summertime Island. Erskine Caldwell. LC 68-28111. 1968. World Pub. Co.
Summertime Love. Kay Kirby. (Adventures in Love Ser.: No. 25). 1982. pap. 1.75 (ISBN 0-451-11567-8, AE1567, Sig). NAL.
Summerwild. Annette Lucile Noble. LC 42-27128. 1893. The National Temperance Society and Publication House.
Summit. Stephen Marlowe. LC 75-97592. 1970. 5.95 o.p. (75-97592). Geis.
Summit, a Novel. Stephen Marlowe. LC 75-97592. 1970. 5.95. Bernard Geis Associates.
Summit Kill. Clark Howard. 1975. (pbk.) 1.25 (ISBN 0-523-00470-2). Pinnacle Books.
Summits Move with the Tide. Mei Berssenbrugge. (O.s.i.). staple bdg 1.95 o.s.i. (ISBN 0-912678-15-1). Greenfld Rev Pr.
Summitt: A Novel. William P McGivern. LC 79-57078. 14.95 (ISBN 0-87795-251-5). Arbor House.
Summon the Bright Water. Geoffrey Household. LC 81-8171. (Illus.). 11.95 (ISBN 0-316-37439-3). Little, Brown.
Summoned to Darkness. Anne-Marie Sheridan. LC 78-3843. 8.95 (ISBN 0-671-24007-2). Simon and Schuster.
Summoning. John Pintoro. LC 79-88559 (ISBN 0-380-47639-8). Avon Books.
Summoning. Robert Towers. LC 82-48686. 288p. 1983. 13.41i (ISBN 0-06-015168-4, HarpT). Har-Row.
Summons. Alfred Edward Woodley Mason. LC 20-186563. George H. Doran Company.
Summons from Baghdad. 1st Ed. Allan MacKinnon. LC 58-6646. 1958. Published for the Crime Club by Doubleday.
Summons to Love. Daisy H. Thomson. 1974. pap. 1.25 o.p. (ISBN 0-515-03452-5, N3452). BJ Pub Group.
Sumner Intrigue. 1st Ed. Frank Arthur Swinnerton. LC 55-11603. 1955. Doubleday.
Sumner Street. Rod Townley. 1976. 1.00 o.p. The Smith.
Sumuru. Arthur Sarsfield Ward. LC 52-18391. (Gold medal books, 199). 1951. Fawcett Publications.
Sun a Honeydew, Moon a Cantaloupe. Jack Libert. (Illus., Orig.). 1970. pap. 2.00 (ISBN 0-911732-53-5). Irego.
Sun Across the Sky. Eleanor O'Reilly Dark. LC 37-29651. 1937. The Macmillan Company.
Sun Also Rises. Ernest Hemingway. LC 57-4130. 1956. Scribner.
Sun Also Rises. Ernest Hemingway. LC 26-191067. 1926. C. Scribner's Sons.
Sun Also Rises. Ernest Hemingway. LC 28-763126. 1927. C. Scribner's Sons.
Sun Also Rises. Ernest Hemingway. LC 29-668036. 1928. C. Scribner's Sons.
Sun Also Rises. Ernest Hemingway. LC 35-285616. 1930. Grosset & Dunlap.
Sun Also Rises. Ernest Hemingway. LC 30-263873. (Half-title: The modern library of the world's best books). 1930. The Modern Library.
Sun Also Rises. Ernest Hemingway. LC 33-7792. (Half title: The modern library of the world's best books)). The Modern Library.
Sun & Catriona. Rosemary Pollock. (Harlequin Romance Ser.). 192p. 1982. pap. 1.50 (ISBN 0-373-02486-X). Harlequin Bks.
Sun and Grey Shadow. Patrick Hall. LC 75-316317. 1974. 2.50 (ISBN 0-491-01750-2). W. H. Allen.
Sun and Moon. Vincent Herbert Gowen. LC 27-12368. 1927. Little, Brown, and Company.
Sun and Storm: By Unto Seppanen. Unto Seppanen & Kaufman, Kenneth Carlyle, 1887- Tr. LC 39-25958. The Bobbs-Merrill Company.
Sun and the Barrow. Edward Verdier. LC 48-5244. 1948. Ziff-Davis Pub. Co.
Sun and the Moon. Niccolo Tucci. LC 76-39918. 1977. 10.95 (ISBN 0-394-46640-3). Knopf: Distributed by Random House.
Sun & the Moon & Other Fictions. P. K. Page. (Found Books: No. 1). 204p. 1973. 11.95 (ISBN 0-88784-429-4, Pub. by Hse Anansi Pr Canada); pap. 6.95 (ISBN 0-88784-327-1). U of Toronto Pr.
Sun and the Rain. Patrick Cassidy. LC 34-305491. R. Hill.
Sun and the Sea. Ruby Mildred Ayres. LC 35-59703. 1935. Doubleday, Doran & Company, Inc.
Sun and the Snow. Translated by Anthony Karrigan. Rodrigo Royo. LC 56-8243. 1956. H. Regnery Co.
Sun at Noon. Charles Angoff. LC 54-10689. 1955. Beechhurst Press.
Sun Beats Down: A Novella of the Cuban Revolution. Translated from the Spanish by Joseph M. Bernstein. Humberto Arenal. LC 59-14144. 1959. Hill and Wang.
Sun Bird. Alice Alberthe Robertson. LC 27-25415. 1927. H. Vinal, Ltd.
Sun-Blazoned. Judy Hogan. 90p. 1982. pap. 5.00. Carolina Wren.
Sun Blight: A Novel. Robert Holles. LC 82-144839. 1982. 16.95 (ISBN 0-241-10733-4). H. Hamilton.
Sun Boy. Robert J. Steelman. LC 75-2855. 1975. 5.95 (ISBN 0-385-08911-2). Doubleday.
Sun Chemist. Lionel Davidson. LC 77-371283. 1976. 7.95 (ISBN 0-394-40693-1). Knopf.
Sun Chemist. Lionel Davidson. 1978. 1.95 (ISBN 0-14-004479-5). Penguin Books.
Sun City. Tove Jansson. LC 75-28321. 7.95 (ISBN 0-394-49907-7). Pantheon Books.
Sun City. Tove Jansson. (Bard Book). 1977. 1.95 (ISBN 0-380-00955-2). Avon Books.
Sun Climbs Slow. Julia Davis. LC 42-5122. 1942. E. P. Dutton & Co., Inc.
Sun Cure. Alfred Noyes. LC 29-16435. 1929. Cosmopolitan Book Concern.
Sun Dance. Fred Grove. LC 58-815207. (Ballantine books, 251). 1958. Ballantine Books.
Sun Dance Murders. Peter McCurtin. (Orig.). 1970. pap. 0.75 o.p. (B75-2065). Belmont-Tower.
Sun Dancers. Barbara Faith. (Richard Gallen Book). 1981. Pocket Books.
Sun Dial: By Richard Austin Smith. Richard Austin Smith. LC 42-12641. 1942. A. A. Knopf.
Sun Dial Time. Don Marquis. LC 79-132119. (Short story index reprint series). 1970. Books for Libraries Press.
Sun Dial Time. Don Marquis. LC 36-33982. 1936. Doubleday, Doran & Company, Inc.
Sun Doctor: A Novel, 1st American Ed. Robert Shaw. LC 61-13351. 1961. Harcourt, Brace & World.
Sun-Dog Trail, and Other Stories. Jack London. LC 51-11745. 1951. World Pub. Co.
Sun Dogs. Robert Olen Butler. LC 82-48104. 12.95 (ISBN 0-8180-0636-6). Horizon Press.
Sun Field. Heywood Campbell Broun. LC 23-144799. 1923. G. P. Putnam's Sons.
Sun-Gazers. James Howard Wellard. LC 73-455601. 1969. 3.80. Hutchinson of Australia.
Sun Gold. Irene Lindsay. 2.50 o.p. Vantage.
Sun Grows Cold. Howard Berk. LC 72-124720. 1971. 6.95. Delacorte Press.
Sun Harvest. Susan Zinkhan. 3.75 o.p. Carlton.
Sun Hawk. Robert William Chambers. LC 28-9649. 1928. D. Appleton and Company.
Sun, He Dies. Jamake Highwater. (Illus.). 256p. 1980. 11.95i (ISBN 0-690-01695-6). Har-Row.
Sun, He Dies. Jamake Highwater. 1981. pap. 2.95 (ISBN 0-451-11110-9, AE1110, Sig). NAL.
Sun, He Dies: A Novel About the End of the Aztec World. Jamake Highwater. LC 79-25859. (Illus.). 9.95 (ISBN 0-690-01695-6). Lippincott & Crowell.
Sun in Capricorn. Hamilton Basso. LC 42-209921. 1942. C. Scribner's Sons.
Sun in Eclipse: Part One of the Fur Country. Jules Verne. 3.95. Assoc Bk.
Sun in His Own House. Warrene Piper. LC 31-268933. 1931. Houghton Mifflin Company.
Sun in Mid-Career. Christopher Davis. LC 73-14309. 1975. 10.00 (ISBN 0-06-010989-0). Harper & Row.
Sun in My Hands. Ellen Dymphna. Cusack. LC 52-5058. 1952. Morrow.
Sun in Scorpio. 1st Amer. Ed. Margery Sharp. LC 65-21353. 1965. 4.95. Little.
Sun in Splendour. Thomas Burke. LC 26-17796. George H. Doran Company.
Sun in the Hunter's Eyes. Harry Wilcox. LC 58-5401. 1958. Viking Press.
Sun in the Street... John Leonard Lovdahl. LC 47-19014. 1947. Moody Press.
Sun in Their Eyes: A Novel of Texas in 1812. Monte Barrett. 1944. The Bobbs-Merrill Company.
Sun Is a Witness. Aaron Marc Stein. LC 40-33710. 1940. Pub. for the Crime Club by Doubleday, Doran and Co., Inc.
Sun Is God. Michael Noonan. LC 73-20145. 1974. 6.95 (ISBN 0-440-08496-2). Delacorte Press.
Sun Is My Shadow. Robert Wilder. LC 60-8484. 1960. Putnam.
Sun Is My Undoing: A Novel. Marguerite Steen. LC 41-220756. 1941. The Viking Press.
Sun Is Near: A Novel. Dorothy Black. 1943. Macrae-Smith-Company.
Sun Is Silent. Saul Levitt. LC 51-10293. 1951. Harper.
Sun Lovers. Charles Rigdon. (Kangaroo Book.). 1978. 1.95 (ISBN 0-671-81818-X). Pocket Books.
Sun-Maid. A Romance. Maria M Grant. LC 6-44838. (Seaside library, v. 20, no. 383). G. Munro.
Sun-Maid. A Romance. Maria M Grant. LC 6-448378. (On cover: Seaside library. Pocket edition. no. 222). G. Munro.
Sun Mountain Slaughter. Clint Reno. (Vigilante series,#1). 1974. (pbk.) 0.95. Fawcett.
Sun Mountain Slaughter. Clint Reo. 176p. 1981. pap. 1.75 (ISBN 0-449-12976-4, GM). Fawcett.
Sun Never Sets. Constantine J Skouras. LC 44-5093. 1944.
Sun Never Shines. Steve Pantano. LC 76-4072. 1.50 (ISBN 0-914042-12-2). Neptune Books.
Sun of Saratoga: A Romance of Burgoyne's Surrender. Joseph Alexander Altsheler. LC 6-510. (Half-title: Appletons' town and country library, no. 216). 1897. D. Appleton and Company.
Sun of the Dead. Ivan Sergeevich Shmelev & Hogarth, C. J., Tr. LC 28-13797. 1927. J. M. Dent and Sons, Ltd.
Sun of the Dead. Ivan Sergieevich Shmelew & Hogarth, C. J., Tr. LC 28-13797. 1927. J. M. Dent and Sons Ltd.
Sun on the Hills. Margaret Lucas Trist. LC 46-2713. 1946. Harper & Brothers.
Sun on the Wall. Wayne D. Overholser. 1981. pap. 1.75 (ISBN 0-345-29493-9). Ballantine.
Sun on Their Shoulders. Elizabeth Eastman. LC 34-20568. 1934. W. Morrow and Company.
Sun Over Costa Rica: A Novel. Jaromir Sladek. LC 57-9940. 1957. Pageant Press.
Sun Place. Ray Connolly. 368p. 1981. pap. 2.95 (ISBN 0-380-78816-0, 78816). Avon.
Sun Queen: A Novel About Nefertiti. Emma Lillie Patterson. LC 67-28223. 1967. D. McKay Co.
Sun Rises into the Sky. Fielding Dawson. (Ltd. signed ed. 15.00 o.p.). 130p. (Orig.). 1974. pap. 4.00 o.p. (ISBN 0-87685-114-6). Black Sparrow.
Sun Rises into the Sky, and Other Stories, 1952-1966. Fielding Dawson. LC 73-15891. (Illus.). 1974. (ISBN 0-87685-115-4) (ISBN 0-87685-114-6). Black Sparrow Press.
Sun Sets in the West. Myron Brinig. LC 35-16054. Farrar & Rinehart, Incorporated.
Sun Sets Red. Stanley Hart Cauffman. LC 30-28180. The Penn Publishing Company.
Sun Shall Greet Them. Arthur Durham Divine. LC 41-16059. 1941. The Macmillan Company.
Sun Shines Bright. Norma Patterson. LC 32-28831. Farrar & Rinehart, Incorporated.
Sun Shines West. Nathan Schachner. LC 43-145608. 1943. D. Appleton-Century Company, Incorporated.
Sun Song. Sebastian Clarke. (Heritage Ser). 1973. pap. 2.50x. Broadside.
Sun Stood Still and Other Dud Dean Stories. Arthur Raymond Macdougall. LC 39-17106. 1939. A. R. Macdougall, Jr.
Sun Virgin. Thomas Dixon. LC 29-720246. 1929. H. Liveright.
Sun-Way. Margaret Sperry. LC 30-33141. (Paper books). 1930. C. Boni.
Sun Will Shine. Helen Marion Edginton. LC 35-3122. 1934. The Macaulay Company.
Sun Woman: A Novel. James Willard Schultz. LC 26-13913. 1926. Houghton Mifflin Company.
Sunbeam Stories. By the Author of "A Trap to Catch a Sunbeam"... Matilda Anne Mackarness. LC 7-16432. 1856. J. Munroe and Company.
Sunbeams and Shadows: A Novel. Edgar C Blum. LC 6-142066. (On Cover: The Pastime Series, No. 138). 1895. Laird & Lee.
Sunbeams and Shadows: And Buds and Blossoms; or, Leaves from Aunt Minnie's Portfolio. Georgiana A Hulse. LC 7-5853. 1851. D. Appleton & Co.
Sunbeams, Inc. Julian Leonard Street. LC 20-16499. 1920. Doubleday, Page & Company.
Sunbeams: Sequel to "Shadows". Herman August Schroeder. LC 29-21550. 1929. Concordia Publishing House.
Sunbelt. James Wakefield Burke. 1.95 (ISBN 0-449-14029-6). Fawcett Gold Medal Books.
Sunbird. Wilbur A Smith. LC 72-94173. 1973. 7.95 (ISBN 0-385-00710-8). Doubleday.
Sunblade. Lewis B Patten. LC 58-679316. 1958. Abelard-Schuman.
Sunblind Range. John Henry Reese. LC 68-24840. (Double D western). 1968. 3.95. Doubleday.
Sunbonnet: Filly of the Year. Barbara Van Tuyl. (Signet Book, Q5658). 1973. (pbk.) 0.95. New American Library.
Sunburn. John Lescroart. 224p. (Orig.). 1981. pap. 2.25 (ISBN 0-523-41187-1). Pinnacle Bks.
Sunburned Corpse: By Adam Knight Pseud. Lawrence Lariar. LC 52-10773. 1952. Crown Publishers.
Sunburst. Desmond Cory, pseud. 1971. 4.95 o.p. (ISBN 0-8027-5227-6). Walker & Co.
Sunburst. Phyllis Bloom Gotlieb. ("A Berkley Medallion book"). 1978. 1.50 (ISBN 0-425-03622-7). Berkley Pub. Corp.
Sunburst. Phyllis Bloom Gotlieb. LC 78-21597. (Gregg Press Science Fiction Series). 1978. 12.00 (ISBN 0-8398-2500-5). Gregg Press.
Sunburst. Shaun McCarthy. LC 72-142847. 1971. 4.95 (ISBN 0-8027-5227-6). Walker.
Sunburst. Mauricio Magdaleno & Brenner, Anita, 1905- Tr. LC 43-17979. 1944. The Viking Press.
Sunburst. Berta Ruck. LC 34-20798. 1934. Dodd, Mead & Company.
Sunclouds. Octavus Roy Cohen. LC 24-21921. 1924. 2.00. Dodd, Mead and Company.
Sundance: The Marauders. Peter McCurtin. (Orig.). 1980. pap. 1.75 o.s.i. (ISBN 0-8439-0740-1, Leisure Bks). Nordon Pubns.
Sundancer. Edward Hays. LC 82-83135. (Illus.). 64p. (Orig.). 1982. pap. 5.95 (ISBN 0-939516-04-7). Forest Peace.
Sunday. Georges Simenon. LC 75-29341. (Harbrace paperbound library; HPL 68). 1976. 2.25 (ISBN 0-15-686301-4). Harcourt Brace Jovanovich.
Sunday After the War. Henry Miller. LC 44-8815. 1961. 6.50 o.p. (ISBN 0-8112-0323-9). New Directions.
Sunday Alibi. Ray Lilly, pseud. 1977. pap. 1.50 (ISBN 0-532-15254-9). Woodhill.
Sunday at Six. Elizabeth Frances Corbett. 1971. 5.95 o.p. Hawthorn.
Sunday at Six. Elizabeth Frances Corbett. 1973. pap. 0.95 o.p. (95332). Beagle Bks.
Sunday at Six: A Novel. Elizabeth Frances Corbett. LC 74-158012. 1971. 5.95. Hawthorn Books.
Sunday Best: A Novel. Bernice Rubens. LC 79-27131. 9.95 (ISBN 0-671-40081-9). Summit Books.
Sunday Evening. Gladys Starkey Battye. LC 72-131092. 1971. 4.50. Published for the Crime Club by Doubleday.
Sunday Evening. Margaret Lynn. LC 72-131092. 1971. 1.95 o.p. (ISBN 0-385-00224-6). Doubleday.

Sunday Father. John Neufeld. (Signet Book). 1977. 1.50 (ISBN 0-451-07292-8). New American Library.

Sunday Gentleman. Irving Wallace. (O.s.i.). 1965. 5.95 o.s.i. (ISBN 0-671-69912-1). S&S.

Sunday Girl. Lee Langley. LC 73-78734. 1973. 5.95 (ISBN 0-698-10549-4). Coward, McCann & Geoghegan.

Sunday Hangman. James McClure. LC 77-6890. 8.95 (ISBN 0-06-012859-3). Harper & Row.

Sunday Hangman. James McClure. 1979. 2.50 (ISBN 0-380-43570-5). Avon.

Sunday Heroes. Noel Bertram Gerson. 1973. (pbk.) 1.50 (ISBN 0-515-03136-4). Pyramid.

Sunday Heroes. Noel Bertram Gerson. LC 75-170241. 1972. 6.95. W. Morrow.

Sunday in the Making. Charles H. Huestis. 1929. Repr. 13.00 o.s.i. Finch Pr.

Sunday Is the Day You Rest. John Upton Terrell. LC 39-4659. Coward-McCann, Inc.

Sunday Kind of Love. Mullin Garr. (Orig.). 1969. pap. 1.75 o.s.i. (OPH130, Ophelia). Olympia.

Sunday Love. Ursula Bloom. 1978. pap. 1.95 (ISBN 0-89041-183-2, 3183). Major Bks.

Sunday, Monday, and Always. Dawn Powell. LC 52-5257. 1952. Houghton Mifflin.

Sunday of Life. Raymond Queneau. LC 76-381805. 1976. 5.95 (ISBN 0-7145-3521-4). J. Calder.

Sunday of Life: A Novel. Raymond Queneau. LC 76-49628. 1977. 12.00 (ISBN 0-8112-0645-9) (ISBN 0-8112-0646-7). New Directions.

Sunday Paper: "Trifling" Stories Behind the News. Frieda W. Van Emden. LC 39-9821. 1939. The Naylor Company.

Sunday Pigeon Murders. Craig Rice. LC 42-24669. 1942. Simon and Schuster.

Sunday Punch. Edwin Newman. LC 79-1289. 1979. 9.95 (ISBN 0-395-28050-8). Houghton Mifflin.

Sunday Punch: Edwin Newman. Edwin Newman. 1980. 2.50 (ISBN 0-425-04671-0). Berkley Books.

Sunday Seducer. Linda DuBreuil. 1975. pap. 1.50 o.p. (LB246DK, Leisure Bks). Nordon Pubns.

Sunday Seducer. Linda DuBreuil. 1975. (pbk.) 1.50. Leisure Books.

Sunday Shoes. 1st Ed. Margaret Crowder Belcher. LC 55-120371. Pageant Press.

Sunday. The Little Man from Archangel. Tr. from French by Nigel Ryan. 1st Amer. Ed. Georges Simenon. LC 66-23802. 1966. 4.95. Harcourt.

Sunday the Rabbi Stayed Home. Harry Kemelman. LC 77-21552. 1977. 11.95 (ISBN 0-8161-6499-1). G. K. Hall.

Sunday the Rabbi Stayed Home. Harry Kemelman. LC 68-25443. 1969. 5.95. Putnam.

Sunday Woman. Carlo Fruttero & Franco Lucentini. LC 73-6981. 1973. 7.50 (ISBN 0-15-186720-8). Harcourt Brace Jovanovich.

Sunday Woman. Carlo Fruttero & Franco Lucentini. 1.75 (ISBN 0-380-00865-3). Avon.

Sunday World. Camilla R Bittle. LC 66-13113. 4.50. Coward.

Sundays. Cynthia Applewhite. LC 78-67250. 1979. 1.95 (ISBN 0-380-42358-8). Avon Books.

Sunday's Child. Claudette Williams. (Fawcett Crest Book). 1977. 1.50 (ISBN 0-449-23230-1). Fawcett Pubns.

Sunday's Children. Decorations by David Hendrickson. James Knox. 1955. Houghton Mifflin.

Sundays from Two to Six. Virginia Abaunza. LC 56-13045. 1956. Bobbs-Merrill.

Sundered Hearts: Also, Jack Mainwaring's Love Story. Odah M. Howard. (On cover: Munro's library. v. 1. no. 90). N. L. Munro.

Sundered Realm. Robert E. Vardeman & Victor Milan. LC 80-81634. 224p. 1980. pap. 2.25 (ISBN 0-87216-732-1). Playboy Pbks.

Sundered Worlds. Michael Moorcock. pap. 0.50 o.p. (52-368). Paperback Lib.

Sundering Flood. William Morris. LC 4-15326. 1898. Longmans, Green, and Co.

Sundial. Shirley Jackson. LC 58-64570. 1958. Farrar, Straus and Cudahy.

Sundial. Fred Merrick White. LC 8-31687. 1908. B. W. Dodge & Company.

Sundiver. David Brin. 1980. pap. 1.95 (ISBN 0-553-13312-8). Bantam.

Sundown. Archie Joscelyn. LC 50-8283. (Silver star westerns). 1950. Dodd, Mead.

Sundown. Barre Lyndon. LC 41-8543. Frederick A. Stokes Company.

Sundown. John Joseph Mathews. LC 34-41056. 1934. Longmans, Green and Co.

Sundown. John Joseph Mathews. LC 79-9365. (Series: Gregg Press Western Fiction Series.). 1979. 11.95 (ISBN 0-8398-2588-9). Gregg Press.

Sundown: An Epic Drama of to-Day. Walter F Eberhardt & Hudson, Earl J. LC 24-16568. Grosset & Dunlap.

Sundown Gun. easy eye ed. Wade B. Cantrell. (Orig.). 1968. pap. 0.60 o.p. (73-773). Lancer.

Sundown Gun. Dean Owen. 192p. 1974. pap. 0.95 o.p. (ISBN 0-532-95362-2). Woodhill.

Sundown Gun. Dean Owen. 192p. 1974. pap. 0.95 o.p. (ISBN 0-532-95362-2). Manor Bks.

Sundown Jim. Ernest Haycox. LC 38-3231. 1938. Little, Brown and Company.

Sundown Jim. Ernest Haycox. LC 40-11549. 1940. Triangle Books.

Sundown Jim. Ernest Haycox. LC 82-15777. 1982. 13.95 (ISBN 0-8161-3357-3). G.K. Hall.

Sundown Kid. Hal George Evarts. (Orig.). 1969. pap. 0.60 o.p. (R2047, GM). Fawcett World.

Sundown Leflare. Frederic Remington. LC 99-313. 1899. Harper & Brothers.

Sundown Man-Sunday in Choctaw Country. Shad Denver & Brett McKinley. 1980. pap. 2.25 o.s.i. (ISBN 0-8439-0732-0, Leisure Bks). Nordon Pubns.

Sundown on the Pacific Shore: Historical Novel About Southern California. Renan Prevost. LC 57-48995. 1957.

Sundown Riders. Thomas Thompson. LC 50-9381. (Double D western). 1950. Doubleday.

Sundown Searchers. Jon Sharpe. (Trailsman Ser.: No. 4). (Orig.). 1980. pap. 2.50 (ISBN 0-451-12200-3, AE2200, Sig). NAL.

Sundown Slim. Henry Herbert Knibbs. LC 15-11001. 1915. Houghton Mifflin Company.

Sundowners. Jon Cleary. LC 52-7811. 1952. Scribner.

Sundowners. Jon Cleary. LC 65-8252. 1965. Scribner.

Sundowners. school ed. Jon Cleary. LC 67-14015. 1967. Scribner.

Sundowners. Jon Cleary. LC 70-4920. (Scribner school paperbacks, 24). (Illus.). 1969. Scribner.

Sundowners. Ward Allison Dorrance. LC 42-18491. 1942. C. Scribner's Sons.

Sundowners. Archie Joscelyn. LC 56-3371. 1956. Avalon Books.

Sundry Accounts. Irvin Shrewsbury Cobb. LC 22-8944. George H. Doran Company.

Sundry Creditors. Nigel Balchin. 1979. 15.00 (Pub. by Ian Henry Pubns England). State Mutual Bk.

Sundry Fell Designs. Vivian Collin Brooks. LC 68-9681. 1968. 3.95. Roy Publishers.

Sundry Fell Designs. Osmington Mills. LC 68-9681. 1969. 3.95 o.p. Roy.

Sunfall. C. J. Cherryh. (Science Fiction Ser.). 1981. pap. 2.25 (ISBN 0-87997-618-7, UE1618). DAW Bks.

Sunflower. Marilyn Sharp. LC 78-24428. 9.95 (ISBN 0-399-90035-7). R. Marek.

Sunflower Gold: A Novel of Western Kansas. 1st Ed. Effie Lawrence Marshall. LC 53-8511. 1953. Exposition Press.

Sunflower: With a Symposium. Simon Wiesenthal. LC 75-35446. 1977. 7.50 (ISBN 0-8052-3612-0); pap. 5.95 (ISBN 0-8052-0578-0). Schocken.

Sunflowers. rev. 6th ed. Ric Masten. 1979. pap. 3.95 o.p. (ISBN 0-931104-00-9). Sunflower Ink.

Sungazers. Henry Herbert Knibbs. LC 26-5144. 1926. Houghton Mifflin Company.

Sunia: a Himalayan Idyll: And Other Stories. Katherine Helen Maud Marshall Diver. LC 13-12281. 1913. 1.25. G. P. Putnam's Sons.

Sunk Island. 1st American Ed. Hubert Nicholson. LC 57-6281. 1957. Coward-McCann.

Sunk Without Trace. Dominic Devine. LC 79-5107. 1979. 8.95 (ISBN 0-312-77568-7). St. Martin's Press.

Sunken Fleet. Helmut Lorenz. Tr. by Cross, Samuel Hazzard. LC 30-6482. 1930. Little, Brown, and Company.

Sunken Garden. Nathalia Clara Ruth Crane. LC 26-10311. 1926. T. Seltzer.

Sunken Garden. 1st Ed. Douglass Wallop. LC 55-13924. 1956. Norton.

Sunken Gold. Andre Savignon & Jepson, Edgar, 1864- Tr. LC 25-11074. 1925. D. Appleton and Company.

Sunken Rock. A Tale of the Mediterranean. George Cupples. LC 6-34002. (On cover: Harper's half-hour ser. v. 128). 1879. Harper & Brothers.

Sunken Submarine. Emile Augustin Cyprien Driant & Lawton, Frederick, Tr. LC 11-31638. 1912. Little, Brown, and Company.

Sunken Valley Pass. Buck Billings. LC 38-7725. The Dodge Publishing Company.

Sunken Valley Pass. Claude Rister. LC 38-7725. 1938. The Dodge Publishing Company.

Sunken World. Stanton Arthur Coblentz. LC 48-8318. 1948. Fantasy Pub. Co.

Sunless Day. Sarah Nichols. (Queen-size gothic). 1975. (pbk.) 1.25. Popular Library.

Sunless Sea: A Novel. Stanley Burnshaw. LC 49-7944. 1949. Dial Press.

Sunlight and Gloom: Or, From the Workhouse to the Peerage. John Russell Coryell. LC 1-680. (On cover: Munro's library, v. 1, no. 302). 1885. N. L. Munro.

Sunlight and Gloom: Or, From the Workhouse to the Peerage. Geraldine Fleming. LC 1-680. (On cover: Munro's library, v. 1, no. 302). 1885. N. L. Munro.

Sunlight Dialogues. John Champlin Gardner. (Illus.). 1973. (pbk.) 1.95. Ballantine Books.

Sunlight Dialogues. John Champlin Gardner. LC 72-2226. (Illus.). 1972. 8.95 (ISBN 0-394-47144-X). Knopf; Distributed by Random House.

Sunlight on the Hills. Elizabeth Carfrae, pseud. LC 34-353066. G. P. Putnam's Sons.

Sunlight on the Lawn. Beverley Nichols. (Illus.). 1957. 4.50 o.p. (ISBN 0-525-21236-1). Dutton.

Sunlight on the Lawn. With Drawings by William McLaren. 1st American Ed. Beverley Nichols. LC 57-5350. Dutton.

Sunlight Patch. Credo Fitch Harris. LC 15-25939. 1915. 1.35. Small, Maynard & Company.

Sunlit Ambush. Mark Derby. LC 55-8925. 1955. Viking Press.

Sunlit Ambush: By Mark Derby Pseud. Harry Wilcox. LC 55-8925. 1955. Viking Press.

Sunlit Field: A Novel. Lucy Kennedy. LC 50-8067. 1950. Crown Publishers.

Sunne in Splendour. Sharon Kay Penman. LC 81-20149. (Illus.). 19.95 (ISBN 0-03-061368-X). Holt, Rinehart, and Winston.

Sunnier Side: Twelve Arcadian Tales. Charles Reginald Jackson. LC 50-6626. 1950. Farrar, Straus.

Sunnier Side: Twelve Arcadian Tales. Charles Reginald Jackson. LC 70-157779. (Short story index reprint series). 1971. (ISBN 0-8369-3891-7). Books for Libraries Press.

Sunningwell. Francis Warre Cornish. LC 9-4966. 1900. A. Constable and Co.

Sunny. Margaret Ann Frost. LC 7-13949. 1907. Griffith and Rowland Press.

Sunny Ducrow. Henry St. John Cooper. LC 20-663517. 1920. 1.90. G. P. Putnam's Sons.

Sunny Hill: A Norwegian Idyll. Bjornstjerne Bjornson. LC 32-30644. (The Green and blue library). 1932. The Macmillan Company.

Sunny Island: By Mary Douglas Warren Pseud. Maysie Greig. LC 52-12758. 1952. Arcadia House.

Sunny Life. Robert Broomfield. LC 6-19374. (On cover: American Sunday library). W. B. Smith & Co.

Sunny Mateel. Henry Herbert Knibbs. LC 27-381344. 1927. Houghton Mifflin Company.

Sunny Night. Nodar Vladimirovich Dumbadze. LC 68-18513. (Russian library). 1968. Washington Square Press.

Sunny-Sab. Winnifred Eaton Babcock. LC 22-9055. 1922. 2.00. George H. Doran Company.

Sunny Side of the Cumberland. A Story of the Mountains. William Allen Dromgoole. 1886. J. B. Lippincott Company.

Sunny Side of the Hill. Rosa Nouchette Carey. LC 8-26685. 1908. J. B. Lippincott Company.

Sunny Side: Or, The Country Minister's Wife. Elizabeth Steward Phelps. LC 8-28113. 1851. American Sunday-School Union.

Sunny Slopes. Ethel Powelson Hueston. LC 17-22006. The Bobbs-Merrill Company.

Sunny Southerner. Julia Magruder. LC 1-8310. 1901. L. C. Page & Company.

Sunny Stories and Some Shady Ones. authorized ed. James Payn. LC 7-33768. (Lovell's international series, no. 162). J. W. Lovell Company.

Sunnybank. Mary Virginia Terhune. LC 8-26063. 1866. Sheldon and Company.

Sunnybank. Mary Virginia Terhune. (American Historical Novel Ser). 1866. 11.50 o.s.i. (ISBN 0-512-00878-7). Garrett Pr.

Sunnybank. A Novel. Mary Virginia Terhune. LC 8-26064. 1889. G. W. Dillingham.

Sunnyridge: A Story of the Missouri Hills. Clark Duncan. LC 45-7352. 1945. Wm. B. Eerdmans Publishing Co.

Sunnyside Tad. Philip Verrill Mighels. 1907. Harper & Brothers.

Sunrise. William Black. LC 6-12417. (On cover: Lovell's library, v. 4, no. 153). J. W. Lovell Company.

Sunrise. Charles R Cottle. LC 77-79098. 3.25 (ISBN 0-916818-02-0). Visage Press.

Sunrise. Charles R Cottle. LC 77-8540. 1977. 6.95 (ISBN 0-916818-03-9) (ISBN 0-916818-02-0). Visage Press.

Sunrise. Anne Duffield. 1944. Arcadia House, Inc.

Sunrise. Grace Livingston Hill. LC 37-16665. J. B. Lippincott Company.

Sunrise. Marie Van Vorst. LC 24-205523. 1924. Dodd, Mead and Company.

Sunrise. G. C. Wilson. (Caprice Romance Ser.). (Illus.). 1982. pap. 1.95 (ISBN 0-448-16981-9, Pub. by Tempo). Ace Bks.

Sunrise. A Novel. William Black. (Franklin square library. no. 162). 1881. Harper & Brothers.

Sunrise: A Story of These Times. William Black. LC 6-12418. 1881. Harper & Brothers.

Sunrise: A Story of These Times. William Black. (Seaside library, v. 46. no. 950). G. Munro.

Sunrise and Sunset: A True Tale. Helen Eliza Fitch Parker. 1854. Derby and Miller.

Sunrise by Request. Ethel Owen. LC 38-29546. Lee Furman, Inc.

Sunrise Calling. Henry Gardner Hunting. LC 29-4418. 1929. D. Appleton and Company.

Sunrise from the Hill-Top. Beatrice Barmby. LC 19-166642. George H. Doran Company.

Sunrise in the West. David Carb. LC 31-19276. 1931. Brewer, Warren & Putnam.

Sunrise in the West: An Absurdity. Carl Eric Bechhofer Roberts. LC 46-16348. 1945. Jarrolds Limited.

Sunrise: No. 25. Grace Livingston Hill. 208p. 1980. pap. 1.95 (ISBN 0-553-14169-4). Bantam.

Sunrise of the Menominees: A Story of Wisconsin Indians. Phebe Jewell Nichols. LC 30-33973. The Stratford Company.

Sunrise on Guam. James Jean Steward. LC 50-34661. 1950. White Wing Pub. House & Press.

Sunrise: Story of Eternal Love & Live. Enrica In Tala & Antita In Tala. 4.50 o.p. Vantage.

Sunrise to Sunset. Samuel Hopkins Adams. LC 50-7919. 1950. Random House.

Sunrise Valley. Marion Hill. LC 14-6195. Small, Maynard and Company.

Sunrise West. William K Carlson. LC 79-7043. 1981. 9.95 (ISBN 0-385-14498-9). Doubleday.

Sun's Attendant. Charles Haldeman. (O.S.I.). 1964. 4.95 o.s.i. (69917). S&S.

Sun's Gold. Smith Kirkpatrick. LC 73-19611. 1974. 5.95 (ISBN 0-395-18467-3). Houghton Mifflin.

Sun's Net. George Mackay Brown. 268p. 1979. 8.95 o.p. (ISBN 0-7012-0419-2, Pub. by Chatto Bodley Jonathan). Merrimack Pub Cir.

Suns of Badarane. Pierre Lauer. LC 75-151913. 1972. 6.95. Morrow.

Suns of Independence. Tr. by Adrian Adams from Fr. LC 80-8891. 160p. 1982. text ed. 14.50 (ISBN 0-8419-0626-2, Africana); pap. text ed. 8.50 (ISBN 0-8419-0688-2, Africana). Holmes & Meier.

Suns of Independence. Ahmadou Kourouma. LC 80-8891. 1981. 24.50 (ISBN 0-8419-0626-2). Africana Pub. Co.

Suns of Scorpio. Alan Burt Akers. (Science Fiction Ser). 1975. pap. 1.25 o.p. (ISBN 0-87997-191-6, UY1191). DAW Bks.

Suns of Scorpio. Alan Burt Akers. (Science Fiction Ser.). 192p. (Orig.). 1973. pap. 0.95 o.p. (UQ1049). DAW Bks.

Sunser Pass: Or, Running the Gauntlet Through Apache Land. Charles King. LC 7-12218. (American authors' series, no. 11). J. W. Lovell Company.

Sunset. Christopher Nicole. LC 77-16750. (Illus.). 10.00 (ISBN 0-312-77575-X). St. Martin's Press.

Sunset. Albert Henry Ross. LC 32-20229. The Century Co.

Sunset. Beatrice Whitby. LC 8-36041. 1897. D. Appleton and Company.

Sunset. Beatrice Whitby. (Half-title: Appletons' town and country library, no. 232). 1898. D. Appleton and Company.

Sunset at Blandings. Pelham Grenville Wodehouse & Richard Usborne. LC 78-2188. (Illus.). 8.95 (ISBN 0-671-24293-8). Simon and Schuster.

Sunset at Noon. Seymour Peyton. 3.95 o.p. Vantage.

Sunset at Noon: The Story of a Career. Ruth Feiner & Alexander, Norman, Tr. LC 37-170229. J. B. Lippincott Company.

Sunset at Sheba. John Harris. LC 60-5462. 1960. W. Sloane Associates.

Sunset Cloud. Anne Hampson. (Alpha Books). (Orig.). 1979. pap. text ed. 2.95x (ISBN 0-19-424161-0). Oxford U Pr.

Sunset Gang. Warren Adler. LC 77-9085. 1977. 7.95 (ISBN 0-670-68437-6). Viking Press.

Sunset Graze. Frederick Dilley Glidden. LC 42-15040. 1942. Doubleday, Doran & Company, Inc.

Sunset Graze. Frederick Dilley Glidden. LC 44-992. The Sun Dial Press.

Sunset Graze. Luke Short. LC 42-150405. 1942. Doubleday, Doran & Company, Inc.

Sunset Gun. George Bartram. 384p. (Orig.). 1983. pap. 3.50 (ISBN 0-523-41867-1). Pinnacle Bks.

Sunset Harbor: A Modern Idyll. Charles Wharton Stork. LC 33-18227. 1933. Roland Swain Company.

Sunset Hill. Kathleen Mary Abbott. LC 26-20526. Dorrance and Company.

Sunset in Cremona: A Fanciful Tale; Being the Romance of Joseph Guarnerius. Albert Wingate Green. LC 54-43757. 1954.

Sunset Law. John Buxton Hilton. LC 82-5645. 1982. 9.95 (ISBN 0-312-77576-8). St. Martin's Press.

Sunset Marshal. Lauran Paine. LC 67-8896. 1967. Arcadia House.

Sunset on the Window-Panes. Walter Macken. LC 55-769017. 1955. St. Martin's Press.

Sunset Over Sotto. Gladys Mitchell. 1981. 18.95x (Pub. by Remploy England). State Mutual Bk.

Sunset Pass. Zane Grey. LC 31-521. 1931. Harper & Brothers.

Sunset Pass. Zane Grey. 1975. (pbk.) 0.95 (ISBN 0-671-77976-1). Pocket Books.

Sunset Pass: Or, Running the Gauntlet Through Apache Land. Charles King. LC 1613. (On cover: Eagle library, no. 150). Street & Smith.

Sunset Patriots. Charles D. Taylor. 464p. (Orig.). 1982. pap. 3.50 (ISBN 0-441-79108-5, Pub. by Charter Bks). Ace Bks.
Sunset Ranch. William L Hopson. LC 43-455. 1943. Phoenix Press.
Sunset Range. Lawrence A Keating. LC 33-362286. E. J. Clode, Inc.
Sunset Rider: By Matt Stuart Pseud. 1st Ed. Llewellyn Perry Holmes. LC 52-5099. 1952. Lippincott.
Sunset Rim. Curtis Kent Bishop. LC 46-376297. 1946. The Macmillan Company.
Sunset Song. J. Leslie Mitchell. LC 33-4884. The Century Co.
Sunset Song. James Leslie Mitchell. LC 81-9114. 1981. 5.95 (ISBN 0-8052-0688-4). Schocken Books.
Sunset Touch. 1st Ed. Howard Spring. LC 53-7744. 1953. Harper.
Sunset Trail. Alfred Henry Lewis. LC 5-12392. 1905. A. S. Barnes & Co.
Sunset Trail. Alfred Henry Lewis. LC 14-10517. A. L. Burt Company.
Sunset Valley: A Romance of the Oregon Country. Cloy Alvin Sloat. LC 58-69. (Milestone book). 1957. Comet Press Books.
Sunset Village. Frank Sargeson. LC 77-357867. 1976. 3.00 (ISBN 0-85616-380-5). Martin Brian and O'Keeffe.
Sunset Warrior. Eric Van Lustbader. LC 76-58101. 1977. 6.95 (ISBN 0-385-12967-X). Doubleday.
Sunshine. Clifford Hagen. LC 78-95998. 1971. 5.00. Harper & Row.
Sunshine. Norma Klein. LC 75-10787. 224p. 1975. 7.95 (ISBN 0-03-015196-1). HR&W.
Sunshine. Norma Klein. 224p. 1982. pap. 2.25 (ISBN 0-380-00049-0, 80341-0, Flare). Avon.
Sunshine: A Novel. Norma Klein. LC 75-10787. 1975. 6.95 (ISBN 0-03-014021-8). Holt, Rinehart and Winston.
Sunshine: A Novel. Norma Klein. LC 82-1751. (Avon/Flare book). 1982. 2.25 (ISBN 0-380-00049-0). Avon Books.
Sunshine: A Novel. Norma Klein. 1974. (pbk.) 1.50 (ISBN 0-380-00049-0). Avon.
Sunshine Acres. Alice Marie Dodge. LC 36-104369. Arcadia House.
Sunshine After Rain. Winifred Mary Scott. LC 38-12692. 1938. Doubleday, Doran & Company.
Sunshine After Storm: By Norman E. King Pseud. Kenneth Anderson. LC 50-11747. 1950. Zondervan.
Sunshine Ahead. Vivian Radcliffe. LC 37-201982. Gramercy Publishing Co.
Sunshine Among the Clouds: Or, The Macdonalds. A Story of Trust on Trial. William D Hedden. U. D. Ward.
Sunshine and Roses. Charlotte Mary Brame. LC 44-38284. (On cover: Lovell's library, v. 9, no. 458). 1884. John W. Lovell Company.
Sunshine and Roses. Charlotte Mary Brame. LC 44-378223. (On cover: Seaside library. Pocket ed. No. 250). G. Munro.
Sunshine and Salt. Sylvia Rothchild. LC 64-17281. 1964. Simon and Schuster.
Sunshine and Shadow. Antonia Van-Loon. LC 81-8848. 1981. 12.95 (ISBN 0-312-77577-6). St. Martin's Press.
Sunshine and Shadow. large print ed. Antonia Van-Loon. LC 82-3278. 1982. 12.95 (ISBN 0-89621-359-5). Thorndike Press.
Sunshine & Shadow. large print ed. Antonia Van Loon. LC 82-3278. 568p. 1982. Repr. of 1981 ed. 12.95 (ISBN 0-89621-359-5). Thorndike Pr.
Sunshine and Shadow: By Beth McBryde Pseud. Elizabeth C Jaros. LC 50-1186. 1950. New Voices Pub. Co.
Sunshine and Shadow; or, Paul Burton's Surprise. A Romance of the American Revolution. Julia A Davis Moore. LC 15-20395. 1915.
Sunshine and Shadows. Anna Margaret Denbo. LC 35-328. Dorrance & Company, Inc.
Sunshine & Shadows. Jacy Showers. LC 78-67733. (Illus.). 1979. pap. 4.95 (ISBN 0-89087-236-8). Celestial Arts.
Sunshine at Home, and Other Stories. Timothy Shay Arthur. LC 74-137722. (His Arthur's home stories, 3). (American fiction reprint series.). 1970. Books for Libraries Press.
Sunshine Beggars. Mary Fenollosa. LC 18-4256. 1918. 1.50. Little, Brown, and Company.
Sunshine in the Palace and Cottage: Or, Bright Extremes in Human Life. Levina Buoncuore Urbino. 1854. Heath and Graves.
Sunshine in Underwood. Jessie Champion. LC 20-743018. 1919. John Lane.
Sunshine Killers. Giles Tippette. 1980. pap. 1.95 (ISBN 0-440-15895-8). Dell.
Sunshine Lost. Patricia Bird. (YA) 1979. 6.95 (Avalon). Bouregy.
Sunshine Love. T. Germon. 4.00 o.p. (ISBN 0-8062-0995-X). Carlton.
Sunshine Man: A Novel. Delwin Mark Clark. LC 77-72370. 1977. 8.95. St. Martin's Press.
Sunshine Man: A Novel. Delwin Mark Clark. LC 77-362360. 10.00 (ISBN 0-7710-2148-8). McClelland and Stewart.
Sunshine Patriot: A Novel of Benedict Arnold. Norman Partington. LC 74-21099. 1975. 8.95. St. Martin's Press.
Sunshine Soldiers. Peter Tauber. LC 70-139663. (O.s.i.). 1971. 6.95 o.s.i. (ISBN 0-671-20844-6). S&S.
Sunshine Sonniksen: An Idyl of the Shetland Islands. Thomas Harold Grimshaw. LC 54-7979. 1954. Vantage Press.
Sunshine Stampede. Dote Fulton. LC 34-182524. The Macaulay Company.
Sunshine Stealer. Berta Ruck. LC 35-16319. 1935. Dodd, Mead and Company.
Sunshine Years. Norma Klein. 1975. (pbk.) 1.50. Dell.
Sunspot. Desmond Lowden. LC 80-24994. (Suspense Novel Ser.). 224p. 1982. 12.95 (ISBN 0-03-047616-X, Owl Bks). HR&W.
Sunstop 8. Lou Fisher. (Dell Book). 1978. 1.50 (ISBN 0-440-12662-2). Dell Pub. Co.
Sunstop 8. Lou Fisher. (Dell Book). (Illus.). 1.50 (ISBN 0-440-12662-2). Dell Pub. Co.
Sunwatch. Frank Dorn. (Orig.). 1980. pap. 1.95 (ISBN 0-532-23239-9). Woodhill.
SunWoman. Bette M. Ross. 1977. pap. 1.95 (ISBN 0-916608-09-3). Quill Pubns.
Sunworld. Leo P. Kelley. LC 79-51080. (Space Police Bks.). 1979. pap. 4.24 (ISBN 0-8224-6381-4). Pitman Learning.
Suomiria: A Fantasy. James Carnegie. Ed. by R. Reginald & Douglas Menville. LC 75-46307. (Supernatural & Occult Fiction Ser.). 1976. Repr. of 1899 ed. lib. bdg. 18.00x (ISBN 0-405-08170-7). Ayer Co.
Suomiria: A Fantasy. James Carnegie Southesk. LC 75-46307. (Supernatural and Occult Fiction). 1976. 18.00 (ISBN 0-405-08170-7). Arno Press.
Sup with the Devil. Sara Craven. (Harlequin Presents Ser.). 192p. 1983. pap. 1.95 (ISBN 0-373-10599-1). Harlequin Bks.
Super. John Cornwell. 1972. pap. 2.25 o.s.i. (ISBN 0-8439-0682-0, Leisure Bks). Nordon Pubns.
Super. C. D. Wilde. (Orig., Osi). 1970. pap. 0.95 o.s.i. (B95-2060). Belmont-Tower.
Super. C. D. Wilde. (O.s.i.). 1972. pap. 0.95 o.s.i. (BT50291). Belmont-Tower.
Super-Barbarians. William Carlton Lanyon Dawe. 1916. 1.25. John Lane.
Super-City. Harry Hershfield. LC 30-28394. 1930. The Elf.
Super-Dude: A Novel. John Craig. 1974. (pbk.) 1.25. Warner Paperback Library.
Super-Gangster. Frederick George Eberhard. LC 32-654. The Macaulay Company.
Super Girls. William Dare. (O.s.i.). 160p. 1976. pap. 1.25 o.s.i. (AQ1548, Award). Univ Pub & Dist.
Super Mad. (Mad Ser.: No. 51). (Illus., Orig.). 1979. pap. 1.95 (ISBN 0-446-90442-2). Warner Bks.
Super ManChu. Sean Mei Sullivan. (Illus.). 1974. (pbk.) 1.25 (ISBN 0-345-23894-X). Ballantine Books.
Super Sam and the Salad Garden. Patty Wolcott. 1975. (lib. bdg.) 3.95. Addison-Wesley.
Super Seduction. Hans Holzer. 1979. pap. 1.95 (ISBN 0-532-19223-0). Woodhill.
Super Sex. Max Brodnick. (O.s.i.). 1977. pap. 1.25 o.s.i. (BT 51116). Belmont-Tower.
Super Star. Paul J Gillette. (Dell book). 1974. (pbk.) 1.50. Dell.
Super Stud. William Rotsler. 1975. pap. 1.50 (ISBN 0-87067-479-X, BH479, Melrose Sq). Holloway.
Super Summer of Jamie MacBride. Jack Shepherd & Christopher Wren. LC 70-133100. 1971. 5.95 o.p. (ISBN 0-671-20799-7). S&S.
Super Summer of Jamie McBride. Christopher S. Wren & Jack Shepherd. LC 70-133100. 1971. 5.95 (ISBN 0-671-20799-7). Simon and Schuster.
Super Tour. Marilyn Allen. LC 73-11695. 1974. 6.95 (ISBN 0-385-02437-1). Doubleday.
Super Tour. Marilyn Allen. 1976. 1.50 (ISBN 0-515-03914-4). Pyramid Publications.
Superbaby. Felix Mendelsohn. LC 73-95375. 1969. 4.95. Nash Pub.
Superball. Nicole Warfield. 1974. (pbk.) 1.25. Bantam Books.
Supercargo. Earl Whitehorne. LC 39-271633. 1939. Funk & Wagnalls Company.
Supercock. Chuck Kelly. (Orig.). 1975. pap. 1.50 (ISBN 0-87067-482-X, BH482). Holloway.
Supercock. Chuck Kelly. (Illus.). 1975. (pbk.) 1.50 (ISBN 0-87067-482-X). Holloway House.
Supercrip. William Jacks, Jr. 180p. (Orig.). 1981. pap. 5.00 (ISBN 0-930012-30-5). Bandanna Bks.
Superdoll. Leo August. (Orig.). 1969. pap. 0.60 o.p. (A427, Award). Univ Pub & Dist.
Superfan. Nick Meglin. (Signet, T5136). (Illus.). 1973. (pbk.) 0.75. New American Lib.
Superfiction: Or, The American Story Transformed: an Anthology. Joe David Bellamy. LC 75-13368. (Illus.). 1975. 3.95 (ISBN 0-394-71523-3). Vintage Books.
Superfluous Woman. Emma Frances Brooke. The Cassell Publishing Co.
Superfolks: A Novel. Robert Mayer. LC 76-53033. 1977. 8.95 (ISBN 0-8037-8211-X). Dial Press.
Superforce. Rorke Garfield. 1976. pap. 4.50 o.p. (ISBN 0-87728-353-2). Weiser.
Superhorror. J. Ramsey Campbell. LC 77-360977. 1976. W. H. Allen.
Superhorror. J. Ramsey Campbell. LC 76-40517. 1977. 7.95. St. Martin's Press.
Superintendent Wilson's Holiday. George Douglas Howard Cole & Margaret Isabel Postgate Cole. LC 29-5408. 1929. Payson & Clarke Ltd.
Superintendent's Room. Jeffrey Ashford, pseud. LC 65-14666. 1965. 3.95. Harper.
Superintendent's Room. Roderic Jeffries. LC 65-14666. 1965. Harper & Row.
Superior to Circumstances. Emily Lucas Blackall. LC 6-13134. D. Lothrop Company.
Superior Woman. Jane Woolsey Yardley. LC 9-1470. (No name series, 3d series). 1885. Roberts Brothers.
Supermale. Alfred Jarry. Tr. by Ralph Gladstone & Barbara Wright. LC 76-45646. 1977. 7.50 (ISBN 0-8112-0632-7); pap. 2.45 (ISBN 0-8112-0633-5, NDP426). New Directions.
Superman. Frank Willoughby. LC 23-650120. 1922. Authors & Publishers Corporation.
Superman & Spiderman. Jim Shooter et al. (Illus.). 160p. (Orig.). 1981. pap. 2.50 (ISBN 0-446-91757-5). Warner Bks.
Superman: From the Thirties to the Seventies. Intro. by Nelson Bridwell. 1971. 12.95 (0-517-L07162). Crown.
Superman III. William Kotzwinkle. 240p. 1983. pap. 2.95 (ISBN 0-446-30699-1). Warner Bks.
Supermind. Alfred Elton Van Vogt. (Science Fiction Ser.). 1977. pap. 1.75 o.p. (ISBN 0-87997-445-1, UE1445). DAW Bks.
Supermind. Alfred Elton Van Vogt (ISBN 0-87997-275-0). Daw.
Supermouth. William Rotsler. 1975. pap. 1.50 (ISBN 0-87067-484-6, BH484, Melrose Sq). Holloway.
Supernatural. Ed. by Phil Hirsch. (Orig.). 1968. pap. 0.60 o.p. (X1833). Pyramid Pubns.
Supernatural Cats: An Anthology. Ed. by Claire Necker. LC 72-79412. (Doubleday science fiction). 1972. 6.95 (ISBN 0-385-07561-8). Doubleday.
Supernatural Cats: An Anthology. Ed. by Claire Necker. 1974. (pbk.) 1.75. Warner Paperback Library.
Supernatural Omnibus. Ed. by Montague Summers. 1962. 5.00 o.p. Verry.
Supernatural Omnibus. Ed. by Montague Summers. 624p. 1975. 12.50 o.p. (ISBN 0-88356-037-2). Causeway.
Supernatural Omnibus: Being a Collection of Stories of Apparitions, Witchcraft, Werewolves, Diabolism, Necromancy, Satanism, Divination, Sorcery, Goetry, Voodoo, Possession, Occult, Doom and Destiny. Ed. by Montague Summers. LC 74-43210. 12.50 (ISBN 0-88356-037-2). Causeway Books.
Supernatural Omnibus: Being a Collection of Stories of Apparitions, Witchcraft, Werewolves, Diabolism, Necromancy, Satanism, Divination, Sorcery, Gosty, and Voodoo. Ed. by Montague Summers. LC 32-26476. 1932. Doubleday, Doran & Company, Inc.
Supernatural Reader. Ed. by Groff Conklin. (O.s.i.). 1962. pap. 1.50 o.s.i. (ISBN 0-02-019110-3, Collier). Macmillan.
Supernatural Reader: Edited by Groff and Lucy Conklin. 1st Ed. Ed. by Groff Conklin & Lucy Conklin. LC 53-5415. 1953. Lippincott.
Supernatural Short Stories of Charles Dickens. Charles Dickens & Michael Hayes. LC 78-316959. 1978. 8.95 (ISBN 0-7145-3678-4). J. Calder.
Supernatural Short Stories of Charles Dickens. Ed. by Michael Hayes. 1979. 9.95 (ISBN 0-7145-3678-4). Riverrun NY.
Supernatural Short Stories of R. L. Stevenson. Robert Louis Stevenson. Ed. by Michael Hayes. 1982. 11.95 (ISBN 0-7145-3550-8). Riverrun NY.
Supernatural Short Stories of Robert Louis Stevenson. Ed. by Michael Hayes. (Scottish Library). 1976. text ed. 13.00x (ISBN 0-7145-3550-8). Humanities.
Supernatural Short Stories of Robert Louis Stevenson. Robert Louis Stevenson. LC 76-371972. (Scottish library). 1976. 4.95 (ISBN 0-7145-3550-8). John Calder (Publishers) Ltd.
Supernatural Short Stories of Sir Walter Scott. Ed. by Michael Hayes. (Scottish Library). 1977. text ed. 13.75x (ISBN 0-7145-3616-4). Humanities.
Supernatural Solution: Chilling Stories of Spooks and Sleuths. Michel Parry. LC 75-27979. 1976. 8.95 (ISBN 0-8008-7497-8). Taplinger Pub. Co.
Supernatural Stories. E. Webster. 4.50 o.p. (ISBN 0-8062-0556-3). Carlton.
Supernatural Stories of Sir Walter Scott. Walter Scott. Ed. by Michael Hayes. 1982. 11.95 (ISBN 0-7145-3616-4). Riverrun NY.
Superseded. May Sinclair. 1906. H. Holt and Company.
Supersonic. Basil Jackson. LC 74-28005. 1975. 6.95 (ISBN 0-393-08701-8). Norton.
Supersonic. Basil Jackson. (Berkley Medallion Book). 1976. (pbk.) 1.50 (ISBN 0-425-03109-8). Berkley Publishing Corp.
Superspade, No. 4# Mother Of The Year. B. B. Johnson. (Orig.). 1970. pap. 0.75 o.p. (64-343). Paperback Lib.
Superspade No. 2: Black Is Beautiful. B. B. Johnson. (Superspade Ser). (Orig.). 1970. pap. 0.75 o.p. (64-305). Paperback Lib.
Superspade Number Five - Bad Day for a Black Brother. B. B. Johnson. (Superspade Ser). (Orig.). 1970. pap. 0.75 o.p. (64-482). Paperback Lib.
Superspade 3, That's Where the Cat's At, Baby. B. B. Johnson. (Superspade 3). (Orig.). 1970. pap. 0.75 o.p. (64-388). Paperback Lib.
Superspill: An Account of the 1978 Grounding at Bird Rocks. Mary Kay Becker & Patricia Coburn. LC 74-76954. (Illus.). 1974. 3.95. Madrona Press.
Superstar. Barry Mazer. (Belmont Tower Book). 1.50 (ISBN 0-505-51200-9). Tower Pubns.
Superstar... A Novel. Viva. LC 78-129959. 1970. 6.95. Putnam.
Superstar Murder?: a Prose Flick. john paul hudson, warren wexler. ed. John Paul Hudson & Warren Wexler. LC 75-45845. (Strawberry Hill book.). 9.50. Insider Press: Distributed by Lieber-Atherton.
Superstar Promoters. John Racine. 192p. (Orig.). 1973. pap. 1.95 o.p. (ISBN 0-87056-316-5). Brandon.
Superstition. Howard Lee. (Kung Fu #3.). 1973. (pbk.) 1.25. Warner Paperback Lib.
Superstition Corner. Sheila Kaye-Smith. LC 34-516651. 1934. Harper & Brothers.
Superstition Corner. Pref. by G. B. Stern. Sheila Kaye-Smith. LC 55-14013. (Thomas More book to live). 1955. H. Regnery Co.
SuperStock: A Novel. Stuart M Speiser. LC 81-19631. 14.95 (ISBN 0-89696-165-6). Everest House.
Superstoe. William Borden. LC 68-15973. 1968. Harper & Row.
Superswine. Illus. by Tom Ballenger. Richard Carter, pseud. LC 66-24827. 1966. bds., 3.95. Trident.
Superthreats. John Striker. 1981. pap. 2.95 (ISBN 0-440-17828-2). Dell.
Supertongue & Other Turn Ons. William Rotsler. 1975. pap. 1.50 (ISBN 0-87067-478-1, BH478, Melrose Sq). Holloway.
Superurimpus. J. Emmerichs. 1978. pap. 6.00 (ISBN 0-07-019342-8). McGraw.
Superworm. George Deaux. LC 68-12166. 1968. Simon and Schuster.
Supper at the Maxwell House: A Novel of Recaptured Nashville. Alfred Leland Crabb. 1943. The Bobbs-Merrill Company.
Supper with the Borgias. Richard Jones. (A novel). 1969. 5.95 o.p. (ISBN 0-316-47264-6, Pub. by Atlantic Monthly Pr). Little.
Supper with the Borgias: A Novel. Richard Jones. LC 69-12635. 1969. 5.95. Little, Brown.
Supplanter. Grace Duffle Boylan. LC 13-17414. 1913. 1.25. Lothrop, Lee & Shepard Co.
Supply Train: By Chuck Stanley. pseud. ed. Charles Stanley Strong. LC 59-65477. 1959. Arcadia House.
Support. Margaret Eliza Ashmun. LC 22-20172. 1922. The Macmillan Company.
Suppressed Desires: A Novel. Karl Ashton. LC 34-30894. W. Godwin, Inc.
Supreme Court: A Novel. Andrew Tully. LC 63-9276. 1963. Simon and Schuster.
Supreme Gift. Grace Denio Litchfield. LC 8-9529. 1908. Little, Brown, and Company.
Supreme Sacrifice: Or, Gillette's Marriage. Mamie Bowles. LC 1-249654. 1901. G. W. Dillingham Company.
Supreme Struggle: A Novel. Wright, James Richmond. LC 35-2186. 1934. Western Baptist Publishing Company.
Supreme Test. Gertrude M. Robins Reynolds. LC 8-31471. 1908. Brentano's.
Supremo. Edward White. 1967. 10.00 o.p. (ISBN 0-525-09744-9). Dutton.
Supremo. 2nd ed. Edward Lucas White. 1967. 10.00 o.p. (ISBN 0-525-09744-9). Dutton.
Sur L'eau, The Magic Couch, and Other Stories. Guy De Maupassant. Tr. by Albert M. C. McMaster. Henderson, A. E., Tr & Quesada, Mme. Louise Charlotte Garstin, 1864?- Tr. LC 23-10448. (Guy de Maupassant stories. vol. ix). 1923. Thompson-Barlow Company, Inc.
Surakarta. William MacHarg. LC 13-199411. 1.25. Small, Maynard & Company.

Sure-Dart: A Story of Strange Hunters and Stranger Game in the Days of Monsters. Frederick Hankerson Costello. LC 9-25176. 1909. 1.25. A. C. McClurg & Co.
Sure-Fire Kid. Nelson Coral Nye. LC 42-5120. 1942. Phoenix Press.
Sure Hand of God. Erskine Caldwell. 1961. Grosset & Dunlap.
Sure Hand of God: A Novel. Erskine Caldwell. LC 47-11204. 1947. Duell, Sloan and Pearce.
Sure;" Now "Chimmie Fadden" Stories. Edward Waterman Townsend. LC 4-6735. 1904. Dodd, Mead & Company.
Sure Salvation. John Hearne. 224p. 1982. 10.95 (ISBN 0-312-77685-3). St Martin.
Sure Shot Shapiro. John Henry Reese. LC 68-12041. (Double D western). 1968. Doubleday.
Sure Thing. Merle Miller. LC 49-102222. 1949. W. Sloane Associates.
Sure Thing. Richard S Prather. 1975. (pbk.) 1.25 (ISBN 0-671-78949-X). Pocket Books.
Surely the Night. Claire Augusta Wilcox Noall. LC 72-84791. (Bonneville Bks). 288p. (Orig.). 1972. pap. 4.00 o.p. (ISBN 0-87480-039-0). U of Utah Pr.
Surely the Night: A Novel. Claire Augusta Wilcox Noall. LC 72-84791. 1972. 6.00 (ISBN 0-87480-039-0). Bonneville Books.
Surety for a Stranger. Mary Raymond. (Orig.). 1974. pap. 0.75 o.p. (26608-0-075). Beagle Bks.
Surf: A Summer Pilgrimage. F. T. Wilson. LC 8-37101. Fords, Howard, & Hulbert.
Surf Skiff: Or, The Heroine of the Kennebec. Joseph Holt Ingraham. 1847. Williams Brothers.
Surface of Earth. Reynolds Price. LC 74-32615. 1975. 10.95 (ISBN 0-689-10662-9). Atheneum.
Surface of Earth. reynolds price. ed. Reynolds Price. 1.95 (ISBN 0-380-00664-2). Avon Books.
Surface of the Earth: A Novel. Reynolds Price. LC 74-32615. 1981. 9.95 (ISBN 0-689-11170-3). Atheneum.
Surface of Things. Charles Walston. LC 99-5558. 1899. Small, Maynard & Company.
Surface with Daring. Douglas Reeman. LC 76-39920. 1977. 8.95 (ISBN 0-399-11891-8). Putnam.
Surface with Daring. Douglas Reeman. (Berkley Medallion Book.). 1978. 1.95 (ISBN 0-425-04006-2). Berkley Publishing Corp.
Surface with Daring: Douglas Reeman. (Berkley book). 1978. 1.95 (ISBN 0-425-04006-2). Berkley Pub. Corp.
Surfaces of a Diamond. Louis Decimus Rubin. LC 81-6034. 1981. 12.95 (ISBN 0-8071-0897-9). Louisiana State University Press.
Surfaces of a Diamond: A Novel by Louis D. Rubin Jr. Louis D. Rubin, Jr. 232p. 1981. 12.95 (ISBN 0-8071-0897-9). La State U Pr.
Surfacing. Margaret Eleanor Atwood. LC 72-86983. 1973. 6.95 (ISBN 0-671-21450-0). Simon and Schuster.
Surfacing. Margaret Eleanor Atwood. 1974. (pbk.) 1.50. Popular Library.
Surfeit of Alibis. Philip Lauben. LC 83-2892. 1983. 10.95 (ISBN 0-312-77688-8). St. Martin's Press.
Surfeit of Sun: A Novel 1st Ed. in the U. S. A. Sean Graham. LC 66-117620. 1966. 4.50. Doubleday.
Surge and Thunder: Critical Readings in Homer's Odyssey. Homerus. Ed. by David Martin Gaunt. LC 70-28543. 1971. 0.75 (ISBN 0-19-912015-3). Oxford University Press.
Surgeon. Doctor Bowman. 1971. pap. 0.95 o.p. (N2530). Pyramid Pubns.
Surgeon. Heinz, Wilfred Charles. LC 63-7727. 1963. Doubleday.
Surgeon in Black. Owen M Andrews. LC 56-12155. 1956. Comet Press Books.
Surgeon in Charge. Elizabeth Seifert. LC 73-79140. 1973. 5.95. Aeonian Press.
Surgeon in Charge. Elizabeth Seifert. LC 42-21080. 1942. Dodd, Mead & Company.
Surgeon in Uniform. Peggy O'More, pseud. LC 44-3448. 1944. Grammercy Publishing Co.
Surgeon of Gaster Fell. Arthur Conan Doyle. (American ser. no. 362). 1895. M. J. Ivers & Co.
Surgeon of St. Christopher's. Edward Somerville Stevens. LC 39-30178. Essex Publishing Concern.
Surgeon to the Sioux. Robert J Steelman. LC 78-22799. 1979. 7.95 (ISBN 0-385-14430-X). Doubleday.
Surgeon, U. S. A. Frank Gill Slaughter. 1973. (pbk.) 0.95 (ISBN 0-671-77603-7). Pocket Books.
Surgeon, U.S.A. Frank Gill Slaughter. LC 66-16328. 1966. Doubleday.
Surgeons. Shirley Hartman & Walter P. Ellerbeck. LC 74-83692. 1974. 8.95 (ISBN 0-679-50473-7). D. McKay Co.
Surgeons Blue Coal: A Novel. Fred Winner. LC 68-2799. 1968. Murphy Pub.
Surgeon's Call. Elizabeth Harrison. 1974. (pbk.) 0.95 (ISBN 0-671-77931-1). Pocket Books.
Surgeon's Choice. Frank Gill Slaughter. (Kangaroo Book). 1977. 1.95 (ISBN 0-671-81194-0). Pocket Books.
Surgeon's Choice: A Novel of Medicine Tomorrow. Frank Gill Slaughter. LC 69-20072. 1969. 5.95. Doubleday.
Surgeon's Crisis. Bruce Cassiday. (General Hospital Ser.). (O.s.i.). (Orig.). pap. 0.75 o.s.i. (AS1024, Award). Univ Pub & Dist.
Surgeon's Daughter. Margaret Hertzler Brown. LC 40-636. Wetzel Publishing Co., Inc.
Surgeon's Daughter. Walter Scott. (On cover: Seaside library. Pocket ed. no. 363). 1885. G. Munro.
Surgeon's Daughters. Ellen Price Henry Wood Wood. (On cover: Seaside library. Pocket ed. no. 277). 1884. G. Munro.
Surgeon's Don't Cry. Albert R. Greenfeld. 1974. pap. 0.95 o.p. (LB0010). Leisure Bks.
Surgeon's Knot. Arthur Young. LC 82-17061. 1982. 14.95 (ISBN 0-312-77693-4). St. Martin's Press.
Surgeon's Log. Andrew V Mason. LC 79-56916. (Illus.). 9.75 (ISBN 0-8158-0394-X). Christopher Pub. House.
Surgeon's Oath. William Johnston. 1973. pap. 0.95 o.s.i. (75-463). Lancer.
Surgeon's Ordeal. Edith P. Begner. 1972. pap. 0.95 o.s.i. (75-360). Lancer.
Surgical Call. Margaret Elizabeth Sangster. LC 37-22646. 1937. Greenberg.
Surgical Nurse. Ruth Dorset, pseud. Ed. by Alice Sachs. 1970. 3.95 o.p. Lenox Hill.
Surly Sullen Bell. Russell Kirk. (Illus.). 4.50 o.p. (ISBN 0-8303-0014-7). Fleet.
Surly Sullen Bell: Ten Stories and Sketches, Uncanny or Uncomfortable. With a Note on the Ghostly Tale. Russell Kirk. LC 62-17193. 1962. Fleet Pub. Corp.
Surly Tim: And Other Stories. Frances Hodgson Burnett. LC 77-103500. (Short story index reprint series). (Illus.). 1969. Books for Libraries Press.
Surly Tim, and Other Stories. Frances Hodgson Burnett. LC 6-17370. 1877. Scribner, Armstrong & Co.
Surly Tim: And Other Stories. by frances hodgson burnett. ed. Frances Hodgson Burnett. LC 5-24198. 1905. C. Scribner's Sons.
Surplus. Sylvia Stevenson. LC 24-9437. 1924. D. Appleton and Company.
Surplus of Riches. Robert B. Spindle. LC 68-16249. 1968. 3.00 o.p. (ISBN 0-8059-0272-4). Dorrance.
Surprise. Brian Burland. LC 74-1878. 1974. 6.95 (ISBN 0-06-010592-5). Harper & Row.
Surprise Ending, No. 68. Elinor Stanton. 1982. pap. 1.75 (ISBN 0-515-06679-6). Jove Pubns.
Surprise Endings by Hercule Poirot: Including The A. B. C. Murders, Murder in Three Acts, and Cards on the Table. Agatha Miller Christie. LC 56-6290. 1956. Dodd, Mead.
Surprise Engagement. Berta Ruck. LC 46-7900. 1946. Dodd, Mead & Company.
Surprise Party Complex. Ramona Stewart. LC 63-7382. 1963. Morrow.
Surprise Party Murder. Eugene Valentine Brewster. LC 36-14926. Greenberg.
Surprise Surprise. Agatha Miller Christie. 1979. pap. 2.50 (ISBN 0-440-18389-8). Dell.
Surprises of Life. Georges Eugene Benjamin Clemenceau. Tr. by Grace Hall. LC 77-132113. (Short story index reprint series). 1970. Books for Libraries Press.
Surprises of Life. Georges Eugene Benjamin Clemenceau. LC 20-164973. 1920. Doubleday, Page & Company.
Surrender. Helen Mittermeyer. (Loveswept Ser.: No. 2). 1983. pap. 1.95. Bantam.
Surrender. John Collis Snaith. LC 28-19626. 1928. D. Appleton and Company.
Surrender. Irma Walker. (Love & Life Romance Ser.). 176p. (Orig.). 1983. pap. 1.75 (ISBN 0-345-30450-0). Ballantine.
Surrender: By Jack Woodford Pseud. & Todd Marshall. Josiah Pitts Woolfolk & Todd Marshall. LC 53-329129. 1953. Signature Press.
Surrender by Moonlight. Bonnie Drake. (Orig.). 1981. pap. 1.75 (ISBN 0-440-18426-6). Dell.
Surrender in Paradise. Sandra Robb. 192p. (Orig.). 1980. pap. 1.50. S&S.
Surrender My Love. Glenna Finley, pseud. 1974. pap. 1.50 (ISBN 0-451-07916-7, W7916, Sig). NAL.
Surrender of a Young Secretary. Wayne Towne. 192p. pap. 1.95 o.p. Dansk Blue Bk.
Surrender of Helen. Samuel Hugh McGrady. LC 34-42575. 1934. C. Kendall.
Surrender of Margaret Bellarmine. ed. by adeline sergeant... ed. Adeline Sergeant. LC 8-6861. (On cover: The authors' library, no. 4). 1894. The Interantional News Company.
Surrender the Dream. J. M Boullon. 4.95 (ISBN 0-8059-2315-2). Dorrance.
Surrender the Heart. Elizabeth Grey Stewart. LC 47-2102. 1947. The Bobbs-Merrill Company.
Surrender! The Romance of a Woman's Soul. LC 25-11435. The Macaulay Company.
Surrender the Seasons. Catherine Turney. (Orig.). 1981. pap. 2.75 (ISBN 0-671-83380-4). PB.
Surrender to Love. Rosemary Rogers. 624p. 1982. pap. 3.95 (ISBN 0-380-80630-4, 80630). Avon.
Surrender to Mistress: A Novel. Richard A Meincke. 1973. 4.50 (ISBN 0-682-47681-1). Exposition Pr.
Surrender to the Night. Shirley Hart. (Candlelight Ecstasy Ser.: No. 144). (Orig.). 1983. pap. 1.95 (ISBN 0-440-18473-8). Dell.
Surrender Value. John Buxton Hilton. LC 81-8820. 1981. 9.95 (ISBN 0-312-77710-8). St. Martin's Press.
Surrey: Henry the Eighth, Pt. 6. Mark Dunster. 1980. pap. 4.00 (ISBN 0-89642-061-2). Linden Pubs.
Surrogate. David Combs. 208p. 1982. pap. 2.50 (ISBN 0-380-81133-2, 81133). Avon.
Surrogate. Elizabeth Hanley, pseud. 1977. pap. 1.50 o.s.i. (ISBN 0-8439-0443-7, Leisure Bks). Nordon Pubns.
Surrogate. Robert B. Parker. 40p. 1982. limited signed ed. 38.00 (ISBN 0-935716-12-2). Lord John.
Surrogate Womb. Bruce Cassiday. (Bold Ones Ser.: No. 1). (Orig.). 1973. pap. 0.95 o.p. (532-95260-095). Manor Bks.
Surrounded. Brian Coffey. LC 73-11797. 1974. 5.95 o.p. (ISBN 0-672-51859-7). Bobbs.
Surrounded. Dean Koontz. LC 73-11797. (Black bat mystery). 1974. 5.95 (ISBN 0-672-51859-7). Bobbs-Merrill.
Surrounded. D'Arcy McNickle. LC 36-4310. 1936. Dodd, Mead & Company.
Surrounded. D'Arcy McNickle. LC 77-91886. (Zia book). 1978. 3.95 (ISBN 0-8263-0469-9). University of New Mexico Press.
Surrounded on Three Sides. John Keasler. 224p. 1974. pap. 1.50 o.p. (6274). Mockingbird Bks.
Surrounded on Three Sides: A Novel. 1st Ed. John Keasler. LC 58-11129. 1958. Lippincott.
Surry Family. Helen Rose Hull. LC 25-227565. 1925. The Macmillan Company.
Surry of Eagle-Nest: Or, The Memoirs of a Staff-Officer Serving in Virginia. John Esten Cooke. LC 38-1585. M. A. Donohue & Company.
Surry of Eagle's Nest. John Esten Cooke. LC 68-23718. (Americans in Fiction Ser.). Repr. of 1866 ed. lib. bdg. 14.00 (ISBN 0-8398-0273-0). Irvington.
Surry of Eagle's Nest. John Esten Cooke. LC 68-23718. (Americans in Fiction Ser). 1968. Repr. of 1866 ed. lib. bdg. 11.50x o.p. (ISBN 0-8398-0273-0). Gregg.
Surry of Eagle's-Nest: Or, The Memoirs of a Staff-Officer Serving in Virgina. Ed., from the MSS of Colonel Surry, by John Esten Cooke. John Esten Cooke. LC 68-23718. 1968. 10.00. Gregg Pr.
Surry of Eagle's-Nest: Or, The Memoirs of a Staff-Officer Serving in Virginia. John Esten Cooke. LC 68-23718. (Illus.). 1968. Gregg Press.
Surry of Eagle's-Nest: Or, The Memoirs of a Staff-Officer Serving in Virginia. John Esten Cooke. LC 34-4938. 1866. Bunce and Huntington.
Surry of Eagle's-Nest: Or. The Memoirs of a Staff-Officer Serving in Virginia. John Esten Cooke. LC 16-7550. G. W. Dillingham Co.
Surry of Eagle's Nest: Or, The Memoirs of a Staff Officer Serving in Virginia. John Esten Cooke. (On cover: The novels of John Estem Cooke). 1894. G. W. Dillingham.
Surry of Eagle's Nest: Or, The Memoirs of a Staff-Officer Serving in Virginia. John Esten Cooke. LC 38-35062. G. W. Dillingham Co.
Survey Ship. Marion Zimmer Bradley. LC 81-112639. (Ace science fiction). (Illus.). 6.95 (ISBN 0-441-79110-7). Ace Books.
Surveyor. Truman John Nelson. LC 60-8876. (Illus.). 1960. Doubleday.
Survival. Phyllis Bottome. LC 43-51227. 1943. Little, Brown and Company.
Survival. Evelyn Campbell. LC 28-25025. 1928. L. MacVeagh, The Dial Press.
Survival. Vernon L. Doss. (Orig.). 1981. pap. 2.50 (ISBN 0-505-51727-2). Tower Bks.
Survival... Zero! Frank Morrison Spillane. LC 77-122789. 1970. 4.95. Dutton.
Survival: Adapted from the Mark IV Picture "Survival". Bob Friedman. LC 75-1668. (Orig.). 1975. pap. 2.50 o.p. (ISBN 0-8307-0364-0, 54-024-09). Regal.
Survival Game. Colin Kapp. LC 76-11820. 1976. 1.50 (ISBN 0-345-25192-X). Ballantine Books.
Survival of the Fittest. Sherry, Edna. LC 60-11926. 1960. Dodd, Mead.
Survival of the Fittest: A Novel. Pamela Hansford Johnson. LC 68-17332. 1968. Scribner.
Survival of the Fittest: A Novel. Louis Bond Mason & Elliot, Norman, Joint Author. LC 7-25572. (On cover: Nile series, v. 2, no. 3). 1892. The Nile Publishing Company.
Survival Planet: A Novel of the Future. Arthur Tofte. LC 76-43602. 1977. 7.95 (ISBN 0-672-52204-7). Bobbs-Merrill.
Survival Printout. Leonard Allison & Leonard Jenkin. LC 72-3237. 1973. (pbk) 1.95 (ISBN 0-394-71857-7). Vintage Books.
Survival Printout: Science Fact, Science Fiction. Ed. by Total Effect. 352p. 1973. pap. 1.95 o.p. (ISBN 0-394-71857-7, Vin). Random.
Survival Prose: An Anthology of New Writings. Ed. by John Bart Gerald. LC 78-142468. 1971. 5.95. Bobbs-Merrill.
Survival with Style. Bradford Angier. 1974. pap. 4.95 (ISBN 0-394-71982-4, V-982, Vin). Random.
Survival World. Frank Belnap Long. 1971. pap. 0.75 o.p. (ISBN 0-447-74750-9). Lancer.
Survival: Zero. Mickey Spillane, pseud. 1970. 4.95 o.p. (ISBN 0-525-21304-X). Dutton.
Survivalist. Giles Tippette. LC 74-22042. 1975. 7.95 (ISBN 0-02-619020-6). Macmillan.
Survivalist, No. 1: Total War. Jerry Ahern. (Orig.). 1981. pap. 2.25 (ISBN 0-89083-768-6). Zebra.
Survivalist, No. 2: The Nightmare Begins. Jerry Ahern. (Orig.). 1981. pap. 2.50 (ISBN 0-89083-810-0). Zebra.
Survivalist, No. 3: The Quest. Jerry Ahern. (Illus.). 1981. pap. 2.50 (ISBN 0-89083-851-8). Zebra.
Survivalist, No. 4: The Doomsayer. Jerry Ahern. (Orig.). 1981. pap. 2.50 (ISBN 0-89083-893-3). Zebra.
Survivalist, No. 5: The Web. Jerry Ahern. 1983. pap. 2.50 (ISBN 0-8217-1145-8). Zebra.
Survivalists. Patrick Rivers. LC 75-33484. 224p. 1976. 8.50x o.p. (ISBN 0-87663-272-X); pap. 4.95 (ISBN 0-87663-931-7). Universe.
Survive. Evan L. Heyman. 1971. pap. 0.75 o.p. (ISBN 0-447-74743-6). Lancer.
Survive the Savage Sea. Dougal Robertson. (Adult Ser.). 420p. 1974. Repr. lib. bdg. 10.95 o.p. (ISBN 0-8161-6235-2, Large Print Bks.). G K Hall.
Survivers. Hammond Innes. pap. 0.95 o.p. (02151, Collier). Macmillan.
Surviving Adverse Seasons: Stories. Barry Targan. LC 79-20191. (Illinois short fiction). 10.00 (ISBN 0-252-00786-7) (ISBN 0-252-00787-5). University of Illinois Press.
Surviving Sisters. Gail Pass. LC 80-69373. 1981. 10.95 (ISBN 0-689-11134-7). Atheneum.
Surviving the Flood. Stephen Minot. LC 81-66006. (Illus.). 1981. 12.95 (ISBN 0-689-11180-0). Atheneum.
Survivor. Marc Brandel. LC 75-23090. 1975. 7.95 (ISBN 0-671-22158-2). Simon and Schuster.
Survivor. Marc Brandel. 1977. 1.50 (ISBN 0-380-00953-6). Avon Books.
Survivor. Marc Brandel. LC 77-352556. 1976. 3.50 (ISBN 0-241-89373-9). Hamilton.
Survivor. Octavia E Butler. LC 77-81548. (Doubleday science fiction). 1978. 6.95 (ISBN 0-385-13385-5). Doubleday.
Survivor. James Herbert. 1977. pap. 2.50 (ISBN 0-451-11395-0, AE1395, Sig). NAL.
Survivor. James Herbert. (Signet Book)). 1977. 1.75 (ISBN 0-451-07393-2). New American Library.
Survivor. Laurence M Janifer. 1.50 (ISBN 0-441-79111-5). Ace Books.
Survivor. Mervyn Jones. LC 68-16865. 1968. Atheneum.
Survivor. Thomas Keneally. LC 77-104130. 1970. 5.95. Viking Press.
Survivor. Siegfried Lenz. LC 65-12947. 1965. Hill and Wang.
Survivor. George MacBeth. LC 77-379697. 1977. 4.95 (ISBN 0-7043-2125-4). Quartet Books.
Survivor. George MacBeth. LC 78-53902. 1978. 7.95 (ISBN 0-15-187046-2) (ISBN 0-15-187046-2). Harcourt, Brace, Jovanovich.
Survivor. Edward Phillips Oppenheim. LC 12-6834. 1904. Ward, Lock & Co., Limited.
Survivor... Dennis Parry. LC 42-2016. 1941. H. Holt and Company.
Survivor. Sydney Smith. LC 78-19422. 8.95 (ISBN 0-312-77953-4). St. Martin's Press.
Survivor. Robb White. LC 64-16238. 1964. Doubleday.
Survivor, a Novel. 1st Ed. Carl Marzani. LC 59-3850. 1958. Cameron Associates.
Survivor: A Selection of Stories. Arun Joshi. LC 75-902683. 1975. 2.50 (ISBN 0-88253-777-6). Sterling Publishers.
Survivor and Others: By H. P. Lovecraft and August Derleth. Howard Phillips Lovecraft & August William Derleth. LC 57-28108. 1957. Arkham House.
Survivor of Babi Yar. Othniel J Seiden. LC 80-51028. 1980. 12.95 (ISBN 0-937050-02-4). Stonehenge Books.
Survivor of Darkness. Virginia Coffman. 1973. pap. 0.95 o.s.i. (75-230). Lancer.
Survivor of Darkness. Dorothy Daniels. 1969. pap. 0.95 o.p. (75-230). Lancer.
Survivor. Tr. from German by Michael Bullock 1st Amer. Ed. Siegfried Lenz. LC 65-12947. 4.50. Hill & Wang.
Survivors. Marion Zimmer Bradley & Zimmer, Paul Edwin. 1979. 1.95 (ISBN 0-87997-435-4). DAW Books.

TITLE INDEX SWAN AND THE LAKE.

Survivors. Mary Canon. (O'Hara Dynasty Ser.). 1982. pap. 2.95 (ISBN 0-373-89002-8). Harlequin Bks.
Survivors. Anne Edwards. LC 68-11825. 1968. Holt, Rinehart and Winston.
Survivors. Mary St. Leger Kingsley Harrison. LC 23-7725. 1923. 2.00. Dodd, Mead and Company.
Survivors. Kristin Hunter. LC 75-612. 1975. 7.95 (ISBN 0-684-14201-5). Scribner.
Survivors. John Nahmlos. (Orig.). 1982. pap. 3.25 (ISBN 0-8217-1071-0). Zebra.
Survivors. Terry Nation. LC 74-30612. 1976. 8.95 (ISBN 0-698-10664-4). Coward, McCann & Geoghegan.
Survivors. Simon Raven. LC 76-375700. 1976. 3.95 (ISBN 0-85634-034-0). Blond and Briggs.
Survivors. Francis H Sibson. LC 32-10834. 1932. Doubleday, Doran & Company, Inc.
Survivors: By Hammond Innes Pseud. 1st American Ed. Hammond-Innes, Ralph. LC 50-7448. 1950. Harper.
Survivors. 1st American Ed. Hammond Innes. LC 50-7448. 1950. Harper.
Susan. Ernest James Oldmeadow. LC 7-22115. 1907. J. W. Luce and Company, Inc.
Susan. C. E. Poverman. LC 76-49931. 1977. 8.95 (ISBN 0-670-68521-6). Viking Press.
Susan Aked. pap. 1.75 o.p. (V1049K, Venus). Grove.
Susan and Joanna. Barbara K. Hodges. LC 35-6157. G. P. Putnam's Sons.
Susan Clegg and a Man in the House. Anne Warner French. LC 7-31418. 1907. Little, Brown, and Company.
Susan Clegg and Her Friend Mrs. Lathrop. Anne Warner French. LC 71-94723. (Short story index reprint series). 1969. (ISBN 0-8369-3102-5). Books for Libraries Press.
Susan Clegg and Her Friend Mrs. Lathrop. Anne Warner French. LC 4-24560. 1904. Little, Brown, and Company.
Susan Clegg and Her Love Affairs. Anne Warner French. LC 16-10880. 1916. Little, Brown, and Company.
Susan Clegg and Her Neighbors' Affairs. Anne Warner French. LC 70-150474. (Short story index reprint series). 1971. (ISBN 0-8369-3814-3). Books for Libraries Press.
Susan Clegg and Her Neighbors' Affairs. Anne Warner French. LC 6-19936. 1906. Little, Brown, and Company.
Susan Clegg, Her Friend and Her Neighbors. Anne Warner French. LC 10-22531. 1910. 1.50. Little, Brown, and Company.
Susan Drummond. A Novel. Charlotte Eliza Lawson Cowan Riddell. LC 26-364931. (Munro's library, no. 138). N L. Munro.
Susan Drummond: A Novel. Charlotte Eliza Lawson Cowan Riddell. (Harper's Franklin square library. no. 361). 1884. Harper & Brothers.
Susan Errant. Nancy Hoyt. LC 34-309085. The Bobbs-Merrill Company.
Susan Fielding. A Love Story. Annie Edwards. (On cover: Seaside library. Pocket ed. no. 344). 1886. G. Munro.
Susan Fielding. A Novel. Annie Edwards. 1870. Sheldon and Company.
Susan Grows up. Mary Finley Leonard. LC 14-18302. Thomas Y. Crowell Company.
Susan Howatch Treasury. Susan Howatch. LC 78-58879. 1978. per vol. 10.95 (ISBN 0-8128-2538-1). Stein and Day.
Susan Latimer, Clinic Nurse. Maud McCurdy Welch. LC 57-8721. 1957. Avalon Books.
Susan Latimer: Clinic Nurse. Maud McCurdy Welkh. LC 57-8721. 1957. Avalon Books.
Susan Lenox. David Graham Phillips. 1978. 2.50 (ISBN 0-445-04155-2). Popular Library.
Susan Lenox: Her Fall and Rise. David Graham Phillips. LC 76-21767. (Lost American fiction). 12.95 (ISBN 0-8093-0773-1). Southern Illinois University Press.
Susan Lenox: Her Fall and Rise. David Graham Phillips. LC 68-57548. (American novels of muckraking, propaganda, and social protest). (Illus.). 1968. Gregg Press.
Susan Lenox: Her Fall and Rise. David Graham Phillips. LC 70-121842. (Illus.). 1970. (ISBN 0-404-05029-8). AMS Press.
Susan Lenox: Her Fall and Rise. David Graham Phillips. LC 72-84643. 1974. (ISBN 0-403-02288-6). Scholarly Press.
Susan Lenox, Her Fall and Rise... With a Portrait of the Author. David Graham Phillips. LC 17-6327. 1917. D. Appleton and Company.
Susan Merton, Civilian. Louise Logan. LC 46-197925. 1946. Arcadia House, Inc.
Susan Merton, First Lieutenant. Louise Logan. LC 42-203201. 1942. Arcadia House, Inc.
Susan Merton: Nurse. Louise Logan. LC 41-154464. 1941. Arcadia House, Inc.
Susan Merton on the Home Front. Louise Logan. LC 44-4510. 1944. Arcadia House, Inc.
Susan Merton's Daughter. Louise Logan. LC 47-17701. 1947. Arcadia House, Inc.
Susan of the Storm. Grace Miller White. LC 27-139732. The Macaulay Company.
Susan Shane: A Story of Success. Roger Burlingame. LC 27-446. 1926. C. Scribner's Sons.
Susan Sins. Marian Eddy Standish. LC 41-17254. Fortuny's Publishers, Inc.
Susan Spray. Sheila Kaye-Smith. LC 31-224008. 1931. Harper & Brothers.
Susan to You. Gertrude Carrick. LC 43-106813. 1943. J. B. Lippincott Company.
Susanna. Suzanne Borrelli. (Orig.). 1979. pap. 2.25 (ISBN 0-532-22154-0). Woodhill.
Susanna. Joan Dial. (Fawcett Gold Medal Book.). 1978. 1.75 (ISBN 0-449-13961-1). Fawcett Books.
Susanna and Sue. with illustrations by alice barber stephens and n. c. wyeth. ed. Kate Douglas Smith Wiggin. LC 9-27270. 1909. Houghton Mifflin Company.
Susanna, Don't You Cry! Mary Plum. LC 46-2492. 1946. Pub. for the Crime Club by Doubleday & Company, Inc.
Susannah, Beware. T. E Huff. 1976. 1.25. Dell.
Susannah Screaming. Carolyn Weston. LC 75-6767. 1975. 6.95 (ISBN 0-394-49417-2). Random House.
Susannah, the Righteous. Katheryn Kimbrough, pseud. (Saga of the Phenwick Women: Bk. 6). 1975. pap. 1.25 (ISBN 0-445-00312-X). Popular Lib.
Susanne. Johannes Buchholtz. Tr. by Bjorkman, Edwin August. LC 33-449993. Liveright, Inc.
Susan's Escort: And Others. Edward Everett Hale. LC 6-46198. 1897. Harper & Brothers.
Susan's Sheaves: And Other Stories. C M Livingston. LC 7-194017. 1887. The National Temperance Society and Publication House.
Susette: A Romance of Two Young People. Dion Clayton Calthrop. LC 13-190812. 1.25. Frederick A. Stokes Company.
Sushila, a Novel. Graham McInnes. LC 57-6733. 1957. Putnam.
Susie's Dream. Katherin Longenecker. 3.95 o.p. Vantage.
Susie's Girls. Susanna Sheldon. 1975. pap. 1.50 o.p. (LB314DK, Leisure Bks). Nordon Pubns.
Susie's Girls. Susanna Sheldon. 1979. pap. 1.75 o.s.i. (ISBN 0-505-51362-5). Tower Bks.
Susie's Wish. Sharon Camotta. 35p. (Orig.). 1982. pap. 4.95 (ISBN 0-931494-31-1). Brunswick Pub.
Suspect... Gerard Fairlie. LC 30-311862. 1930. Pub. for the Crime Club, Inc., by Doubleday, Doran & Company, Inc.
Suspect. B. M Gill. LC 81-9000. 8.95 (ISBN 0-684-16885-5). Scribner's.
Suspect. large print ed. B. M Gill. LC 82-7362. 1982. 12.95 (ISBN 0-89340-526-4). J. Curley & Associates.
Suspect. Hugh Lawrence Nelson. LC 54-624353. (Murray Hill mystery). 1954. Rinehart.
Suspect. Gertrude Walker. 1979. pap. 1.95 (ISBN 0-89041-244-8, 3244). Major Bks.
Suspected. George Dilnot. LC 20-8448. E. J. Clode.
Suspended Man. Translated from the German by Robert Molloy. Denis F Bernard. LC 60-13188. 1960. Putnam.
Suspense. Isabel Egenton Ostrander. LC 18-9776. 1918. R. M. McBride & Co.
Suspense. Hugh Stowell Scott. LC 529. 1899. Dodd, Mead and Company.
Suspense: A Napoleonic Novel. Joseph Conrad. LC 25-12983. 1925. Doubleday, Page & Company.
Suspense: Four Short Novels. Richard Martin Stern. LC 61-6902. (Ballantine suspense book, 331K). 1959. Ballantine Books.
Suspense Stories. Ed. by Alfred Hitchcock. LC 46-618305. (On cover: A Dell book. 92). 1945. Dell Publishing Company.
Suspension of Mercy. Patricia Highsmith. 1982. pap. 3.50 (ISBN 0-14-003470-6). Penguin.
Suspicion. Dominique Dunois. LC 33-24347. The Macaulay Company.
Suspicion. Florence Riddell. LC 31-8414. 1931. J. B. Lippincott Company.
Suspicion. Lee Roberts, pseud. 1971. pap. 0.75 o.p. (07161). Curtis.
Suspicion. Jo Sullivan. (Harlequin Romances Ser.). 192p. 1983. pap. 1.75 (ISBN 0-373-02544-0). Harlequin Bks.
Suspicions. Barbara Betcherman. LC 79-16927. 10.95 (ISBN 0-399-12439-X). Putnam.
Suspicions. Barbara Betcherman. 1981. 2.75 (ISBN 0-425-04839-X). Berkley Books.
Suspicions of Mrs. Allonby. Mary Gleed Tuttiett. LC 8-23105. 1908. D. Appleton and Company.
Suspicious Characters: A Lord Peter Wimsey Mystery. Dorothy Leigh Sayers. LC 44-5853. 1943. New Avon Library.
Suspicious Characters: The New Lord Peter Mystery. Dorothy Leigh Sayers. LC 31-28160. 1931. Brewer, Warren & Putnam.
Suspicious Circumstances. Patrick Quentin. LC 58-200. (Inner sanctum mystery). 1957. Simon and Schuster.
Suspicious Heart. Amber Fitzgerald. LC 81-43009. 1981. 10.95 (ISBN 0-385-17459-4). Doubleday.
Susquehanna Legends: Collected in Central Pennsylvania. Henry Wharton Shoemaker. LC 13-16336. 1913. The Bright Printing Company.
Sussex Gorse, the Story of a Fight. Sheila Kaye-Smith. LC 17-8740. 1916. A. A. Knopf.
Sustained Honor: A Story of the War of 1812. John Roy Musick. LC 7-33325. (On cover: Columbian historical novels. v. 10). 1893. Funk & Wagnalls Company.
Susurrations. Michael R. Conroy. 1976. 1.00 (ISBN 0-915626-05-5). Yellow Jacket.
Susy: A Story of the Plains. Bret Harte. LC 11-7154. 1893. Houghton, Mifflin and Company.
Susy Smith's Supernatural World. Susy Smith. (O.s.i.). 1971. pap. 0.95 o.s.i. (532-95153-095). Manor Bks.
Sutherlands. 11th ed. Miriam Coles Harris. LC 7-29163. 1871. C. Scribner & Company.
Sutherlands. Miriam Coles Harris. LC 7-2917. 1889. Houghton, Mifflin and Company.
Suttee of Safa: A Hindoo Romance. Dulcie Deamer. LC 13-11540. 1.25. G. W. Dillingham Company.
Sutter House. Ellen Orford. (Queen-size gothic). 1975. (pbk.) 1.25. Popular Library.
Sutter's Sands. Marilyn Donahue. (Orig.). 1971. pap. 0.75 o.p. (B75-2123). Belmont-Tower.
Sutton Papers. Selwyn Jepson. LC 24-215902. 1924. L. MacVeagh, The Dial Press.
Sutton Place Murders... Robert George Dean. LC 36-5103. 1936. Pub. for the Crime Club, Inc., by Doubleday, Doran & Co., Inc.
Suttree. Cormac McCarthy. LC 78-57101. (ISBN 0-394-48213-1). Random House.
Suvarov Adventure. Duncan Kyle. LC 73-88173. 1974. 6.95. Saint Martin's Press.
Suvarov Adventure. Duncan Kyle. 1974. (pbk.) 1.25. Bantam Books.
Suwanee River Tales. facsimile ed. Sherwood Bonner. LC 73-38641. (Black Heritage Library Collection). Repr. of 1884 ed. 18.25 (ISBN 0-8369-8999-6). Ayer Co.
Suwannee Valley. Bernard Fendig Borchardt & Sears, Eugene, Joint Author. LC 41-311131. Harbinger House.
Suzanna: A Romance of Early California. Harry Sinclair Drago. LC 22-25008. The Macaulay Company.
Suzanna Stirs the Fire. Emily Calvin Blake. LC 15-191872. 1915. A.C. McClurg & Co.
Suzanne... Sophy Beckett. LC 6-9769. (On cover: Seaside library. Pocket edition, no. 1187). 1889. G. Munro.
Suzanne and the Pacific. Jean Giraudoux. LC 75-5831. 1975. 12.50. H. Fertig.
Suzanne and the Pacific. Jean Giraudoux. Tr. by Redman, Ben Ray. LC 23-4142. 1923. 2.00. G. P. Putnam's Sons.
Suzanne De L'Orme: A Story of Huguenot Times. G., H. LC 8-25648. 1871. Hitchcock and Walden.
Suzanne. Novel. 1st Ed. Jonreed Lauritzen. LC 55-5594. Hanover House.
Suzette; a Novel. Mary Spear Nicholas Tiernan. LC 8-19797. 1885. H. Holt and Company.
Suzie. John Benton. LC 78-27010. (Spire books). (Illus.). 1.95 (ISBN 0-8007-8358-1). Revell.
Suzuki Beane. Drawings by Louise Fitzhugh. 1st Ed. Sandra Scoppettone. LC 61-7513. 1961. Doubleday.
Suzuki Concept. Elizabeth Mills & Therese C. Murphy. 1974. pap. 4.95 lyceum ed. o.p. (ISBN 0-87297-003-5, SL521). Scribner.
Suzy. Herbert Sherman Gorman. LC 34-39745. Farrar & Rinehart, Incorporated.
Suzy Falls off. Jack Kahane. LC 29-22148. 1929. A. and C. Boni.
Svalbard Passage. Thomas Kirkwood & Geir Finne. (Illus.). 307p. 1981. 13.95 o.p. (ISBN 0-02-563560-3). Macmillan.
Swag. Charles Francis Coe. LC 28-24957. 1928. G. P. Putnam's Sons.
Swag. Elmore Leonard. LC 75-29140. 8.95. Delacorte Press.
Swallow. Henry Rider Haggard. 1898. Longmans, Green and Co.
Swallow: A Novel Based Upon the Actual Experiences of One of the Survivors of the Famous Lafayette Escadrille. Ruth Dunbar. LC 19-8806. 1919. Boni and Liveright.
Swallow: A Tale of the Great Trek. Henry Rider Haggard. LC 12-23271. 1899. Longmans, Green, and Co.
Swallow and the Tom Cat: A Grown-up Love Story. Jorge Amado. LC 82-10038. 9.95 (ISBN 0-440-08325-7). Delacorte.
Swallow & the Tom Cat: A Love Story. Jorge Amado. Tr. by Barbara S. Merello from Port. (Illus.). 96p. 1982. 10.95 (ISBN 0-440-08325-7, E Friede). Delacorte.
Swallow Barn, 2 Vols. John Pendleton Kennedy. Ed. by Joseph V. Ridgely. LC 76-93632. (American Fiction Ser). 1970. lib. bdg. 27.50 o.s.i. (ISBN 0-512-00440-4). Garrett Pr.
Swallow Barn, or A Sojourn in the Old Dominion... John Pendleton Kennedy. LC 7-3061. 1832. Carey & Lea.
Swallow Barn, or A Sojourn in the Old Dominion. rev. ed. with twenty illustrations by strother. ed. John Pendleton Kennedy. LC 3-28156. 1851. G. P. Putnam.
Swallow Barn, or A Sojourn in the Old Dominion. rev. ed. with twenty illustrations by strother. ed. John Pendleton Kennedy. LC 3-28157. 1856. G. P. Putnam & Company.
Swallow Barn; or, A Sojourn in the Old Dominion. John Pendleton Kennedy. Ed. by Hubbell, Jay Broadus. LC 29-9094. (American authors series, general editor, S. T. Williams). Harcourt, Brace and Company.
Swallow Barn: Or, A Sojourn in the Old Dominion. rev. ed. John Pendleton Kennedy. LC 72-78763. (Illus.). 1978. 39.00 (ISBN 0-403-08617-5). Scholarly Press.
Swallow Dive. Sylvia Dryhurst Lynd. LC 21-8373. 1921. Cassell and Company, Ltd.
Swallowed up. Nancy Mann Waddel Wilson Woodrow Woodrow. LC 22-21568. Brentano's.
Swallowfork Bulls. Bertha Muzzy Sinclair. LC 29-550. 1929. Little, Brown and Company.
Swallowing the Anchor. William McFee. LC 70-128275. (Essay Index Reprint Ser). 1925. 19.00 (ISBN 0-8369-1986-6). Ayer Co.
Swallows & Amazons. Arthur Ransome. (Illus.). 343p. 1980. Repr. of 1931 ed. lib. bdg. 25.00 (ISBN 0-89987-021-X). Darby Bks.
Swallow's Wing: A Tale of Pekin. Charles Hannan. (On cover: Cassell's sunshine series, v. 1, no. 32). Cassell & Company, Limited.
Swami and Friends. R. K. Narayan. LC 80-16119. 1980. 3.95 (ISBN 0-226-56831-8) (ISBN 0-226-56829-6). University of Chicago Press.
Swami and Friends: A Novel of Malgudi. R. K. Narayan. LC 54-8878. 1954. Michigan State College Press.
Swami & Friends & the Bachelor of Arts: Two Novels of Malgudi. R. K. Narayan. 1954. 3.95 o.p. (ISBN 0-87013-008-0). Mich St U Pr.
Swami & the Comrade. K. K. Roy. 1975. 12.00 o.p. (ISBN 0-8283-1633-3). Branden.
Swami & the Comrade. K. K. Roy. 1975. 12.00 o.p. (ISBN 0-8283-1633-3). Branden.
Swamp. Bill Thomas. (Illus.). 1976. 29.95 (ISBN 0-393-08747-6). Norton.
Swamp Angel. George W Hodges. LC 58-2418. 1958. New Voices Pub. Co.
Swamp Angel. Dorothy Langley. LC 82-18421. 1982. 14.95 (ISBN 0-89733-060-9) (ISBN 0-89733-061-7). Academy Chicago.
Swamp Angel: A Novel. James Bruce Eure. 1974. 6.00 (ISBN 0-682-47878-4). Exposition Press.
Swamp Angel: A Realistic Portrayal of Life in the Missouri 'Boot' in the Early 1900's. Illus. by Robert W. Murray. Delia Cash Jenkins. LC 53-3885. 1953. Naylor Co.
Swamp Angel. 1st Ed. Ethel Davis Wilson. LC 54-9003. 1954. Harper.
Swamp Breath. Robert Simpson. LC 21-927. 1921. The James A. McCann Company.
Swamp Doctor's Adventures in the Southwest. Containing the Whole of the Louisiana Swamp Doctor; Streaks of Squatter Life; and Far Western Scenes; in a Series of Forty Two Humorous Southern and Western Sketches... Henry Clay Lewis & Robb, John S. LC 8-30879. (On cover: Peterson's illustrated uniform edition of humorous American works). T. B. Peterson and Brothers.
Swamp Fox, Francis Marion. Noel Bertram Gerson. LC 67-10376. 1967. Doubleday.
Swamp Foxes. Jake Logan. LC 82-80844. (Jake Logan Ser.). 224p. (Orig.). 1982. pap. 1.95 (ISBN 0-86721-179-2). Playboy Pbks.
Swamp Girl: By Perry Lindsay Pseud. Peggy Gaddis, pseud. LC 50-12679. 1950. Phoenix Press.
Swamp Man. Donald Goines. (Orig.). 1974. pap. 1.95 (ISBN 0-87067-624-5, BH026). Holloway.
Swamp Man. Donald Goines. 1974. (pbk.) 1.50 (ISBN 0-87067-446-3). Holloway House.
Swamp Rats. Lee Falk. (Adventures of the Phantom). 1974. (pbk.) 0.95. Avon.
Swamp Shadow. Katherine Hamill. LC 36-10718. A. A. Knopf.
Swamp Thing. Len Wein. 224p. (Orig.). 1982. pap. 2.50 (ISBN 0-523-48039-3). Pinnacle Bks.
Swamp Water. Vereen Bell. LC 41-1942. 1941. Little, Brown and Company.
Swamp Willow. Edwina Elroy. LC 47-30747. 1947. G. P. Putnam's Sons.
Swamps: A Record of Pioneer Days in the Middle West. Sigel Roush. LC 30-846. 1929. Printed by Shenandoah Publishing House, Inc.
Swan. Margaret Kennedy. LC 57-5682. 1957. Rinehart.
Swan: A Novel with Illus. by Walter Goetz. Marguerite Steen. LC 52-13390. 1953. Houghton Mifflin.
Swan & the Eagle. C. D. Narasimhaiah. 1969. 5.50 o.p. Intl Pubns Serv.
Swan and the Lake. James Copray De Wilde. LC 50-9074. 1950. Dorrance.

Swan and the Mule: A Novel. Della Campbell MacLeod. LC 22-18852. 1922. Houghton Mifflin Company.

Swan and the Rose. Francis W Leary. LC 53-5898. 1953. A. A. Wyn.

Swan Dive. Keith Korman. LC 79-5523. 10.00 (ISBN 0-394-50849-1). Random House.

Swan Island Murders. Victoria Lincoln. LC 30-23889. Farrar & Rinehart Incorporated.

Swan of Usk: A Historical Novel. Helen Ashton. LC 40-6293. 1940. The Macmillan Company.

Swan of Vilamorta. Pardo Bazan, Emilia. Tr. by Serrano, Mary Jane (Christie) LC 7-35609. Cassell Publishing Company.

Swan Sang Once. Marjorie Chalmers Carleton. LC 47-601. 1947. W. Morrow & Company.

Swan Song. Edmund Crispin, pseud. 192p. Repr. of 1947 ed. lib. bdg. 12.05c (ISBN 0-89190-692-4). Am Repr-Rivercity Pr.

Swan Song. Edmund Crispin, pseud. 192p. 1981. pap. 2.50 (ISBN 0-380-55145-4, 59733). Avon.

Swan Song. Helen Jean Mary Edmiston. LC 60-6872. 1960. Published for the Crime Club by Doubleday.

Swan Song. John Galsworthy. LC 74-8100. (His The Forsyte chronicles, v. 6). (Scribner library. Contemporary classics.). 1969. 1.95. Scribner.

Swan Song. John Galsworthy. LC 28-17388. 1928. C. Scribner's Sons.

Swan Song. Robert Bruce Montgomery. LC 80-80453. 1980. 9.95 (ISBN 0-8027-5420-1). Walker.

Swan Song. Helen Robertson. LC 81-47394. (Fifty Classics of Crime Fiction, 1950-1975). 1982. 14.95 (ISBN 0-8240-4957-8). Garland Pub.

Swan Song. Brian M Stableford. 1975. (pbk.) 1.25. DAW Books.

Swan Swanson: The American Citizen; Showing How He Joined and Why He Abandoned the A. P. A. Michael J Doyle. LC 6-34233. 1895. J. S. Hyland & Company.

Swan Villa. Martin Walser. Tr. by Leila Vennewitz. 1982. 15.50 (ISBN 0-03-059372-7). HR&W.

Swann. Dan Sherman. LC 78-57325. 8.95 (ISBN 0-87795-195-0). Arbor House.

Swann's Way. Marcel Proust. Tr. by Scott-Moncrieff, Charles Kenneth. LC 71-9169. (Modern library books, 59). 1956. 2.45. Modern Library.

Swann's Way. Marcel Proust. LC 72-26737. (His Remembrance of things past). 1970. 1.95 (ISBN 0-394-70594-7). Vintage Books.

Swann's Way. Marcel Proust. Tr. by Scott-Moncrieff, Charles Kenneth. LC 23-26026. (His Remembrance of things past. i). 1922. H. Holt and Company.

Swann's Way. Marcel Proust. Tr. by Scott-Moncrieff, Charles Kenneth. Galantiere, Lewis. LC 29-3969. (Half-title: The Modern library of the world's best books). The Modern Library.

Swann's Way. Marcel Proust. Tr. by Scott-Moncrieff, Charles Kenneth. Krutch, Joseph Wood. LC 34-34439. (His Remembrance of things past. i-ii). 1934. Random House.

Swan's Harbor. Eleanor R Mayo. LC 52-131285. 1953. Crowell.

Swans of Brhyadr. Vivienne Couldrey. LC 78-11777. 8.95 (ISBN 0-698-10945-7). Coward, McCann & Geoghegan.

Swans on an Autumn River: Stories. Sylvia Townsend Warner. LC 66-11352. 1966. Viking Press.

Swansea Dan. Arthur Mason. LC 29-595023. 1929. Cosmopolitan Book Corporation.

Swanson: A Novel. Timothy Pember. LC 51-5288. 1951. Harcourt, Brace.

Swansong for a Rare Bird. Alfred Draper. LC 71-113533. 1970. 4.95. Coward-McCann.

Swap. Walter H Wager. LC 72-81657. 1973. (pbk.) 1.25 (ISBN 0-671-78335-1). Pocket Books.

Swap Beach Weekend. Jake Danjo. pap. 1.95 o.p. (8065). Cameo.

Swap Carnival. Sandy Taylor. pap. 1.95 o.p. (8072). Cameo.

Swap Circle. James L. Brown. pap. 1.95 o.p. (8062). Cameo.

Swap City. Geoffrey Kyle. 224p. pap. 1.95 o.p. (6138). Brandon.

Swap City Hustler. Marsha Alexander. 1973. (pbk.) 1.95 (ISBN 0-87682-361-4). Barclay House.

Swap-Club Stud. Kevin Charters. 192p. (Orig.). 1973. pap. 1.95 o.p. (ISBN 0-87682-294-4, 7294). Barclay Hse.

Swap Factory. Walter Defowe. 192p. pap. 1.95 o.p. (6158). Brandon.

Swap Island. Frank Anvic, pseud. 192p. pap. 1.95 o.p. (ISBN 0-87056-163-4, 6163). Brandon.

Swap Mates. Pat Elwood. pap. 1.95 o.p. (8085). Cameo.

Swap Neighbors. Thomas H. Hilton. 192p. (Orig.). 1973. pap. 1.95 o.p. (ISBN 0-87682-308-8, 7308). Barclay Hse.

Swap Season. Sterling Harkins. 192p. pap. 1.95 o.p. (6142). Brandon.

Swap Street. Robert H. Sheldon. pap. 1.95 o.p. (8020). Cameo.

Swap Street Revisited. Robert H. Sheldon. pap. 1.95 o.p. (8047). Cameo.

Swap Time. Jack Milton, pseud. 224p. pap. 1.95 o.p. (6146). Brandon.

Swappers in Building A. Gene North. 192p. pap. 1.95 o.p. (6155). Brandon.

Swappers Wild. Rina Black. pap. 1.95 o.s.i. (Venus). Grove.

Swapping Experiment. Rick West. pap. 1.95 o.p. (8083). Cameo.

Swapping: Thrills and Sensuality. Matt Galant & Kathleen Galant. LC 72-186003. (API, 105). 1967. 1.95. Nu-Triumph, Introd.

Swarm. Arthur Herzog. LC 74-164327. (Illus.). 1974. 6.95 (ISBN 0-671-21709-7). Simon and Schuster.

Swastika. Robert Kail. (Belmont Tower Book). 2.25 (ISBN 0-505-51422-2). Tower Publications.

Swastika. Oscar Schisgall. LC 39-11747. 1939. A. A. Knopf.

Swastika Hunt. Desmond Cory, pseud. (Johnny Fedora Ser., No. 7). Orig. Title: Johnny Goes North. 1969. pap. 0.60 o.p. (A475X, Award). Univ Pub & Dist.

Sway of the Black... Augustin Fleming. LC 6-39930. 1890. The Lakeside Press.

Swaying Corpse. Robert Platt. LC 41-54401. Phoenix Press.

Swaying Elms: And Other Stories. Ernest Richard Blackburn. LC 50-9022. (Provident books). 1950. Moody Press.

Swaying Pillars. Morna Doris MacTaggart Brown. LC 69-15721. 1969. 4.50. Walker.

Swaying Pillars. E. X. Ferrars, pseud. 1969. 4.50 o.p. Walker & Co.

Swaying Pillars. Elizabeth Ferrars. 1973. 0.75. Dell.

Swaying Rock. Arthur John Rees. LC 31-12126. 1931. Dodd, Mead & Company.

Swear by Apollo. Shirley Barker. LC 58-5282. 1958. Random House.

Sweat of Fear. Robert C Dennis. LC 72-89692. (Black bat mystery). 1973. 5.95. Bobbs-Merrill.

Sweathog Trail. William Johnston. (Welcome Back, Kotter#1). 1976. (pbk.) 1.25 (ISBN 0-448-12406-8). Tempo Books.

Sweden's Best Stories. Hanna A. Larsen. Repr. of 1928 ed. lib. bdg. 20.00 (ISBN 0-8414-5779-4). Folcroft.

Sweden's Best Stories: An Introduction to Swedish Fiction. Ed. by Hanna Astrup Larsen. LC 70-37276. (Short story index reprint series). (Illus.). 1971. (ISBN 0-8369-4087-3). Books for Libraries Press.

Sweden's Best Stories: An Introduction to Swedish Fiction. Ed. by Hanna Astrup Larsen. Tr. by Stork, Charles Wharton. (Half-title: Scandinasvian classics, vol. xxx). The American-Scandinavian Foundation; W. W. Norton & Company, Inc.

Swedey. Ethel Powelson Hueston. LC 25-19829. The Bobbs-Merrill Company.

Swedish Passions. P. LC 72-163555. (Venus library). 1971. 1.25. Grove Press.

Swedo-Finnish Short Stories. Ed. by George C. Schoolfield. LC 74-8724. (Library of Scandinavian Literature, V. 27). 1975. (ISBN 0-8057-3367-1). Twayne Publishers.

Sweeney: A Novel. 1st Ed. William Bolger. LC 56-12278. 1956. Exposition Press.

Sweeney Squadron: A Novel. 1st Ed. Donald J Plantz. LC 61-9542. 1961. Doubleday.

Sweeney Todd: Or, The Ruffian Barber. A Tale of the Terrors of the Seas and the Mysteries of the City. Merry. H. Long & Brother.

Sweeney's Honor. Brian Wynne Garfield. 192p. 1980. pap. 1.95 (ISBN 0-449-24330-3, Crest). Fawcett.

Sweeney's Island. John Christopher. LC 64-13347. 1964. Simon and Schuster.

Sweep of Dusk. William John Kehoe. LC 45-430126. 1945. E. P. Dutton & Company, Inc.

Sweeper. Gary Paulsen. (Raven House Mysteries Ser.). 224p. 1981. pap. 2.25 (ISBN 0-373-63011-5, Pub. by Worldwide). Harlequin Bks.

Sweeper to Saint. Hari Dass. LC 80-52021. (Illus.). 1980. 6.95 (ISBN 0-918100-03-8). Sri Rama Pub.

Sweepers of the Sea: The Story of a Strange Navy. Claude Hazeltine Wetmore. LC 2666. The Bowen-Merrill Company.

Sweepings. Lester Cohen. LC 26-18162. 1926. Boni & Liveright.

Sweeps. Bill Granger. 1980. pap. 2.50 (ISBN 0-449-14351-1, GM). Fawcett.

Sweepstake Murders. Alfred Walter Stewart. LC 32-6588. 1932. Little, Brown, and Company.

Sweepstakes. Emily Greenaway. LC 41-2314. 1941. Houghton Mifflin Company.

Sweet Abandon. Diana Mars. (Second Chance at Love Ser.: No. 122). 1983. pap. 1.75 (ISBN 0-515-07210-9). Jove Pubns.

Sweet Adelaide. Julian Symons. LC 80-7610. 10.00 (ISBN 0-06-014207-3). Harper & Row.

Sweet Adelaide. Julian Symons. LC 81-1714. 1981. 3.50 (ISBN 0-14-005792-7). Penguin.

Sweet Adin. George A Kirkland. LC 7-12513. 1891. Laird & Lee.

Sweet Adventure. Barbara Cartland. (Historical Romance Ser., No. 17). 1972. pap. 1.25 o.p. (V2689). Pyramid Pubns.

Sweet Adventure. Barbara Cartland. 1976. pap. 1.25 o.p. (ISBN 0-515-04110-6). BJ Pub Group.

Sweet Adversity. Donald Newlove. 1978. pap. 2.95 (ISBN 0-380-38364-0, 38364, Bard). Avon.

Sweet Alice. William Arthur Neubauer. LC 49-49118. 1949. Arcadia House.

Sweet Anarchy. Nathaniel Benchley. LC 79-7039. 1979. 10.00 (ISBN 0-385-14867-4). Doubleday.

Sweet Anarchy. Nathaniel Benchley. LC 80-23869. 1980. 15.50 (ISBN 0-8161-3134-1). G. K. Hall.

Sweet and Bitter Land. Wayne D Overholser. LC 50-8993. (Dutton Diamond D western). 1950. Dutton.

Sweet and Deadly. Charlaine Harris. LC 80-25712. 1981. 8.95 (ISBN 0-395-30532-2). Houghton Mifflin.

Sweet & Faraway. Lucy Walker, pseud. 192p. 1976. pap. 1.75 (ISBN 0-345-29274-X). Ballantine.

Sweet and Hot. Ann Lawrence. 1934. W. Godwin, Inc.

Sweet and Lovely. Herman Irving Bloom. LC 38-148851. Gramercy Publishing Co.

Sweet and Low. Emma Lathen, pseud. LC 74-2344. (Simon and Schuster novel of suspense). 1974. 5.95 (ISBN 0-671-21785-2). Simon and Schuster.

Sweet and Low. Emma Lathen, pseud. LC 74-30191. 1975. 10.95 (ISBN 0-8161-6261-1). G. K. Hall.

Sweet and Low. Emma Lather. LC 74-2344. 1975. (pbk.) 1.25. Pocket Books.

Sweet and Low-Down. Carlotta Baker. LC 42-17832. 1942. The Phoenix Press.

Sweet and Sour. John O'Hara. LC 54-9511. 1974. (pbk.) 1.25. Popular Library.

Sweet and Sour. Olive Page. 1966. bds., 3.85. Rigby.

Sweet and Sour. Olive Page. LC 65-25108. 1966. Rigby; San Francisco, Tri-Ocean Books.

Sweet & Sour Milk. Nuruddin Farah. (African Writers Ser.: No. 226). 237p. (Orig.). 1980. pap. text ed. 5.00x (ISBN 0-435-90226-1). Heinemann Ed.

Sweet and the Wretched. Allen A Baldwin. LC 62-18186. Greenwich Book Publishers.

Sweet and Twenty. Don Morrc. LC 55-4482. 1955. Vixen Press.

Sweet and Twenty. Mary Farley Sanborn Sanborn. LC 8-3756. (On cover: Good company series. no. 10). 1891. Lee and Shepard.

Sweet and Twenty. Joan Smith. LC 79-10050. (Series: Regency Romance.). 1981. 6.95 (ISBN 0-89340-207-9). J. Curley & Associates.

Sweet Bait of Money. Clayton Fox. 1977. pap. 1.50 (ISBN 0-532-15284-0). Woodhill.

Sweet Bells Jangled: A Dramatic Love Tale. Cara Oakey Hall. LC 7-321. (Library of select novels). 1876. American News Company.

Sweet Bells Jangled Out of Tune. Robin F. Brancato. LC 81-14283. 224p. 1982. PLB 9.99 (ISBN 0-394-94809-2); 9.95 (ISBN 0-394-84809-8). Knopf.

Sweet Bells Out of Tune. Constance Cary Harrison. LC 7-2888. 1893. The Century Co.

Sweet Beulah Land. Roderick Finlayson. LC 43-12314. 1942. The Griffin Press.

Sweet Beulah Land. Bernice Kelly Harris. LC 43-384892. 1943. Doubleday, Doran & Co., Inc.

Sweet Birds of Gorham. Ann Birstein. LC 66-147996. bds., 3.95. McKay.

Sweet Birds of Gorham. Ann Birstein. 1972. Ballantine.

Sweet Blossoms 'neath Frosted Leaves. Jennie M Wunderlich. LC 99-5366. 1899. P. Anstadt & Sons.

Sweet Bobby: A Novel. Joel Kurtzman. LC 73-13702. 1974. 5.95 (ISBN 0-07-035671-8). McGraw-Hill.

Sweet Bravado. Alicia Meadows. 1979. 1.95 (ISBN 0-446-89936-4). Warner Books.

Sweet-Brier. Mary Elizabeth Wilson Sherwood. LC 8-7347. 1889. D. Lothrop Company.

Sweet Cane. Bruce McGinnis. LC 81-16126. 11.95 (ISBN 0-8149-0857-8). Vanguard Press.

Sweet Caroline. Con Sellers. 1979. 2.50 (ISBN 0-671-81750-7). Pocket Books.

Sweet Chariot: A Novel. Frank Baker. LC 43-47321. 1943. Coward-McCann, Inc.

Sweet Cheat. Herbert Crooker. LC 32-16256. The Macaulay Company.

Sweet Cheat Gone. Marcel Proust. LC 70-22050. (His Remembrance of things past). 1970. 1.95 (ISBN 0-394-70599-8). Vintage Books.

Sweet Cheat Gone. Marcel Proust. Tr. by Scott-Moncrieff, Charles Kenneth. LC 30-9311. (His Remembrance of things past, vii). 1930. A. & C. Boni.

Sweet Cicely; or, Josiah Allen As a Politician. Marietta Holley. LC 7-6040. 1885. Funk & Wagnalls.

Sweet Clover: A Romance of the White City. Clara Louise Root Burnham. LC 6-19672. 1894. Houghton, Mifflin and Company.

Sweet Country. Caroline Richards. LC 78-14078. 9.95. Harcourt Brace Jovanovich.

Sweet Cymbeline. Charlotte Mary Brame. (On cover: Lovell's library. v. 20 no. 989). J. W. Lovell Company.

Sweet Cymbeline. Charlotte Mary Brame. (On cover: Seaside library. Pocket ed. no. 927). G. Munro.

Sweet Cymbeline. Charlotte Mary Brame. LC 44-116591. (On cover: Seaside library. Pocket ed. No. 927). G. Munro.

Sweet Cymbeline. Bertha M. Clay. LC 44-11676. (On cover: Lovell's library, v. 20, no. 989). J. W. Lovell Company.

Sweet Danger. Margery Allingham. 1950. pap. 1.95 o.p. (ISBN 0-14-000769-5). Penguin.

Sweet Danger. Maysie Greig. 1935. Doubleday, Doran & Company, Inc.

Sweet Danger. Ella Wheeler Wilcox. LC 12-40381. M. A. Donohue & Co.

Sweet Dawn of Desire. Meg Hudson. (Superromances Ser.). 384p. 1981. pap. 2.50 (ISBN 0-373-70009-1, Pub. by Worldwide). Harlequin Bks.

Sweet Deadly Passión. Violet Hawthorne. LC 76-7424. 1976. 1.25 (ISBN 0-345-25071-0). Ballantine Books.

Sweet Death of Candor. Elizabeth Head Fetter. LC 69-14836. 1969. Harcourt, Brace & World.

Sweet Death of Candor. Hannah Lees, pseud. 1969. 5.95 o.p. (ISBN 0-15-187334-8). HarBraceJ.

Sweet Desperations. Will Jackson. 1973. 4.00 o.p. (ISBN 0-682-47766-4). Exposition.

Sweet Desperations. 1st. Ed. Will Jackson. 1974. 4.00 (ISBN 0-682-47766-4). Exposition Press.

Sweet Disorder. Claudette Williams. 224p. 1981. pap. 1.95 (ISBN 0-449-50206-6, Coventry). Fawcett.

Sweet Dove Died. american ed. Barbara Pym. LC 78-74024. 1979. 8.95 (ISBN 0-525-21318-X). Dutton.

Sweet Dream. James Wakefield Burke. LC 64-18661. 1964. Fountainhead Publishers.

Sweet Dreams. Michael Frayn. LC 73-3504. 1974. 5.95 (ISBN 0-670-68637-9). Viking Press.

Sweet Dreams. Warren Murphy. (Destroyer Ser.: No. 25). 1976. pap. 1.75 (ISBN 0-523-40901-X). Pinnacle Bks.

Sweet Elixir. P. F Catcher. LC 70-28500. (Traveller's companion series, TC-499). 1971. 1.95. Traveller's Companion.

Sweet Ember. Bonnie Drake. (Candlelight Ecstacy Ser.: No. 18). (Orig.). 1981. pap. 1.75 (ISBN 0-440-18459-2). Dell.

Sweet Enchantress. Barbara Cartland. 1979. pap. 1.50 (ISBN 0-515-05100-4). Jove Pubns.

Sweet Enchantress. Barbara Cartland. 1973. pap. 1.25 o.p. (ISBN 0-515-03189-5, V3189). Pyramid Pubns.

Sweet Enchantress. Barbara Cartland. 1976. pap. 1.25 o.p. (ISBN 0-515-04153-X). BJ Pub Group.

Sweet Enchantress, No. 48. Barbara Cartland. (Orig.). 1982. pap. 1.95 (ISBN 0-515-06214-6). Jove Pubns.

Sweet Epitaph. Gladys Starkey Battye. LC 72-76187. 1972. 4.95. Published for The Crime Club by Doubleday.

Sweet Epitaph. Margaret Lynn. LC 72-76187. 216p. 1972. 4.95 o.p. (ISBN 0-385-00439-7). Doubleday.

Sweet Evil. Charles Platt. (Berkley Medallion Book). 1977. 1.25 (ISBN 0-425-03298-1). Berkley Pub. Corp.

Sweet Familiarity: A Novel. Daoma Winston. LC 81-66963. 11.95 (ISBN 0-87795-331-7). Arbor House.

Sweet Fantasy. Pfirman. 3.50 o.p. (ISBN 0-8062-0388-9). Carlton.

Sweet Fire. Kate Fairfax. 272p. pap. 2.95 (ISBN 0-441-79119-0). Ace Bks.

Sweet for a Season. Joseph McCord. 1939. Macrae Smith Company.

Sweet Friday. Marsha Manning. (Cameo Romance). (Fawcett gold medal book). (Cameo romance). 1974. (pbk.) 0.75. Fawcett.

Sweet Genevieve. August William Derleth. LC 42-12601. 1942. C. Scribner's Sons.

Sweet Gogarty. Matthew Hochberg. LC 80-28358. 10.95 (ISBN 0-8253-0048-7). Beaufort Books.

Sweet Golden Son. Parris Afton Bonds. 1978. 1.95 (ISBN 0-445-04226-5). Popular Library.

Sweet Grass. Bertha Muzzy Sinclair. LC 40-211554. 1940. Little, Brown and Company.

Sweet Harvest. Kerry Allyne. (Romances Ser.). 192p. (Orig.). 1980. pap. text ed. 1.25 (ISBN 0-373-02341-3, Pub. by Harlequin). PB.

Sweet Healing Passion. (Candlelight Ecstasy Ser.: No. 64). (Orig.). 1982. pap. 1.95 (ISBN 0-440-18033-3). Dell.

Sweet Humiliation. Christel. Bd. with Dusky Flesh. Francoise Noule. 160p. pap. 1.95 o.p. Montmartre.

Sweet Illusions: By S. L. Regberg. Illustrations by S. Rick Regberg. Scott L Regberg. (Illus.). 1972-1974. 4.95. Maiter.

Sweet Imposter. Rosemary Carter. (Harlequin Presents Ser). 1979. pap. 1.25 (ISBN 0-373-70783-5, Pub. by Harlequin). PB.

Sweet Is Revenge. Joseph Fitzgerald Molloy. LC 7-25311. (On cover: Broadway series. no. 1). J. A. Taylor & Co.

Sweet Is the Rose. Helen Douglas-Irvine. LC 44-747856. 1944. Longmans, Green and Co.

Sweet Is True Love: And Other Tales. Margaret Wolfe Hungerford. (On cover: The seaside library. Pocket ed., no. 123). 1884. G. Munro.

Sweet Jesse, Sweet Jesus. Steve Winsten. (Orig.). 1973. pap. 0.75 o.p. (09210). Curtis.

Sweet Kate, A Time Remembered: Dangerous Stranger. Lucy Gillen. (Harlequin Romances Ser.). 576p. 1982. pap. 3.50 (ISBN 0-373-20060-9). Harlequin Bks.

Sweet Land of Liberty. Edwin Silberstang. 320p. 1972. 6.95 o.p. (ISBN 0-399-10941-2). Putnam.

Sweet Land of Liberty: A Novel. Edwin Silberstang. LC 71-188724. 1972. 6.95. Putnam.

Sweet Land of Michigan. August William Derleth. 1962. 2.95 o.p. (ISBN 0-696-82183-4). Hawthorn.

Sweet Land of Michigan. August William Derleth. 4.95 o.p. (ISBN 0-88361-068-X). Stanton & Lee.

Sweet Lavender. Founded Under Special Permission, on the Celebrated Play. Williams, Henry Llewellyn. (On cover: The Cosmopolitan series, no. 36). Hurst & Co.

Sweet Liberty: A Novel. Clarabelle Eberle Rundel. LC 44-3944. 1944. Cartwright, Mueller, Benjamin & Robison.

Sweet Lies. Diana Hammond. 304p. 1981. pap. 2.95 (ISBN 0-446-80986-1). Warner Bks.

Sweet Lies: A Novel. Diana Hammond. LC 78-12601. 9.95 (ISBN 0-07-025890-2). McGraw-Hill.

Sweet Life of Jimmy Riley: A Novel. James Reardon. LC 80-24579. 14.95 (ISBN 0-671-61014-7). Wyndam Books.

Sweet Love, Bitter Love. Anna James. 1978. pap. 2.25 (ISBN 0-515-04697-3, 04697-3). Jove Pubns.

Sweet Love Remembered. Helen Cortez Stafford. LC 47-107046. 1946. Deseret Book Company.

Sweet Lucy. Players Magazine. (Orig.). 1976. pap. 1.50 (ISBN 0-87067-813-2, BH813). Holloway.

Sweet Lucy. (ISBN 0-87067-813-2). Holloway House.

Sweet Mace: a Sussex Legend of the Iron Times. George Manville Fenn. LC 44-14003. 1885. Cassell & Company, Limited.

Sweet Madness. Robert Lalonde. LC 82-4372. 144p. 1982. 12.95 (ISBN 0-8253-0096-7). Beaufort Bks NY.

Sweet Man. Gilmore Millen. LC 30-16614. 1930. The Viking Press.

Sweet Marie-Antoinette. Lozania Prole. 1973. (pbk) 0.95. Pocket Books.

Sweet Marpessa. George Revelli. LC 73-3091. 1973. (pbk.) 1.25. Bantam Books.

Sweet Medicine's Propehcy: Sun Dancer's Passion. Karen A. Bale. 1981. pap. 2.95 (ISBN 0-89083-776-7). Zebra.

Sweet Medicine's Prophecy, No. 3: Winter's Love Song. Karen A. Bale. 1983. pap. 3.50 (ISBN 0-8217-1154-7). Zebra.

Sweet Money Girl. Cover Painting by Barye Phillips. Benjamin Appel. LC 54-24967. (Gold medal books, 885). 1954. Fawcett Publications.

Sweet Moon. Margaretta Brucker. LC 40-337821. Gramercy Publishing Company.

Sweet Morn of Judas' Day. 1st Ed. Llewellyn, Richard. LC 64-17731. 1964. Doubleday.

Sweet Murder. Milton Scott Michel. LC 43-10914. 1943. Coward-McCann, Inc.

Sweet Nineteen. Frederick William Robinson. (seaside library. v. 38, no. 777). 1880. G. Munro.

Sweet Nothing. Roland Pease. LC 57-8800. 1957. Doubleday.

Sweet Nothings. Laura Cunningham. LC 76-48602. 1977. 8.95 (ISBN 0-385-12751-0). Doubleday.

Sweet Nothings. Laura Cunningham. 1978. 1.95 (ISBN 0-380-38562-7). Avon Books.

Sweet One. Rob Eden. LC 48-142889. 1947. Gramercy Pub. Co.

Sweet Peggy. Linnie Sarah Harris. LC 4-24577. 1904. Little, Brown, and Company.

Sweet Pepper. Geoffrey McNeill-Moss. LC 23-8481. E. P. Dutton & Company.

Sweet Persuasion. Ginger Chambers. (Candlelight Ecstasy Ser.: No. 102). (Orig.). 1982. pap. 1.95 (ISBN 0-440-17524-0). Dell.

Sweet Peter Deeder. Odie Hawkins. (Orig.). 1979. pap. 1.95 (ISBN 0-87067-633-4, BH633). Holloway.

Sweet Pilgrimage. Hermina Black. 1972. pap. 0.75 o.p. (94205). Beagle Bks.

Sweet Piracy. Patricia Maxwell. (Fawcett Gold Medl Book.). 1978. 1.95 (ISBN 0-449-13990-5). Fawcett Gold Medal Books.

Sweet Promise. Janet Dailey. (Harlequin Presents Ser.). 1979. pap. 1.50 (ISBN 0-373-70808-4, Pub. by Harlequin). PB.

Sweet Punishment. Barbara Cartland. 1973. pap. 1.25 o.p. (ISBN 0-515-02920-3, V2920). BJ Pub Group.

Sweet Punishment. Barbara Cartland. 1973. (pbk) 0.95 (ISBN 0-515-02920-3). Pyramid.

Sweet Reason. Robert Littell. 1976. 1.75. Popular Library.

Sweet Reason. Robert Littell. LC 73-12079. 1974. 5.95 (ISBN 0-395-18280-8). Houghton Mifflin.

Sweet Revenge. Dick Beaird. (Orig.). 1982. pap. 2.95 (ISBN 0-89083-911-5). Zebra.

Sweet Revenge. Thom Racina. 1977. pap. 1.50 (ISBN 0-425-03559-X, Medallion). Berkley Pub.

Sweet Revenge: A Romance of the Civil War. Frederick Augustus Mitchel. 1897. Harper & Brothers.

Sweet Ride. William Murray. LC 67-11791. 1967. New American Library.

Sweet River in the Morning. Winston David Armstrong Clewes. LC 73-153990. 1972. 5.95 (ISBN 0-85617-841-1). White Lion Publishers.

Sweet River in the Morning: A Novel. Winston David Armstrong Clewes. LC 46-6431. 1946. D. Appleton-Century Co.

Sweet River in the Morning: A Novel. Winston David Armstrong Clewes. LC 46-643148. 1946. D. Appleton-Century Company, Inc.

Sweet Rocket. Mary Johnston. LC 20-185092. Harper & Brothers.

Sweet Rome: A Novel. Audrey Stainton. LC 81-7026. 14.95. Holt, Rinehart, and Winston.

Sweet Salt. Felix E. Goodson. LC 75-40585. 8.95 (ISBN 0-8048-1173-3). C. E. Tuttle Co.

Sweet Sam. David Morgan. 1973. (pbk.) 1.25. Dell.

Sweet Savage Love. Rosemary Rogers. 640p. 1979. pap. 3.95 (ISBN 0-380-00815-7, 81877-9). Avon.

Sweet-Scented Name & Other Fairy Tales & Stories. Fyodor Sologub. Ed. by S. Graham. LC 76-23900. (Classics of Russian Literature). 1977. 11.95 (ISBN 0-88355-519-0); pap. 3.95 (ISBN 0-88355-520-4). Hyperion Conn.

Sweet-Scented Name, and Other Fairy Tales, Fables, and Stories. Fedor Kuzmich Teternikov. LC 73-37565. (Short story index reprint series). 1972. (ISBN 0-8369-4124-1). Books for Libraries Press.

Sweet-Scented Name: And Other Fairy Tales, Fables and Stories. Fedor Kuznich Teternikov & Graham, Stephen, 1884- Ed. LC 15-20397. 1915. G. P. Putnam's Sons.

Sweet Second Summer of Kitty Malone. Matthew Cohen. LC 79-313581. 1979. 12.95 (ISBN 0-7710-2221-2). McClelland and Stewart.

Sweet Seduction. Travis Forsyth. (Orig.). 1982. pap. 2.95 (ISBN 0-440-18017-1). Dell.

Sweet Seduction. Maura MacKenzie. 1981. pap. 2.50 (ISBN 0-373-70006-7). Harlequin Bks.

Sweet Seventeen. Bennie Caroline Hall. 1946. Gramercy Publishing Co.

Sweet Short Grass. Peter Inchbald. LC 82-45359. 1982. 11.95 (ISBN 0-385-18255-4). Published for the Crime Club by Doubleday.

Sweet Sinner. Lorinda Hagen. 1979. pap. 1.95 o.s.i. (ISBN 0-505-51330-7). Tower Bks.

Sweet Sinner. June Jennifer. LC 36-202411. 1936. Godwin.

Sweet Sister. James Noble Gifford. LC 45-371. 1944. Gramercy Publishing Company.

Sweet Sisters of Inchvarra: Or, The Vampire of the Guillamores. J. M. Simpson. (On cover: The select series, no. 71). 1890. Street & Smith.

Sweet Smell of Mangoes: A Journey Through the Congo. Sigfrid Sodergren. LC 67-20546. (Illus.). 1968. 5.95 o.p. Dutton.

Sweet Smell of Success: And Other Stories. Ernest Lehman. LC 57-11134. (Signet book, S1413). 1957. New American Library.

Sweet Sorrow. Denise Robins. 1974. (pbk.) 0.95 (ISBN 0-380-00178-0). Avon.

Sweet Spot in Time. John Jerome. 352p. 1982. pap. 5.95 (ISBN 0-380-57026-2, 57026). Avon.

Sweet Spring of April. Ursula Bloom. 1979. pap. 2.25 (ISBN 0-89041-260-X). Major Bks.

Sweet Stranger. Berta Ruck. LC 21-5541. 1921. 2.00. Dodd, Mead and Company.

Sweet Street Blues. Laurence Blaine. 1978. 1.75 (ISBN 0-87067-531-1). Holloway House Pub. Co.

Sweet Summer Love. William Arthur Neubauer. LC 54-114703. 1954. Arcadia House.

Sweet Surrender. Diana Mars. (Second Chance at Love Ser.: No. 95). 192p. 1983. pap. 1.75 (ISBN 0-515-06859-4). Jove Pubns.

Sweet Sweet Summer. Jane Gaskell. 223p. 1973. 6.95 o.p. St Martin.

Sweet Talk. Beatrice Burton Morgan. LC 34-36037. Farrar & Rinehart, Incorporated.

Sweet Taste of Burning. Paul Andreota. LC 73-81394. 1973. 5.95. D. McKay.

Sweet Taste of Burning. Paul Andreota. 1974. (pbk.) 1.25. Warner Paperback Library.

Sweet Taste of Daddy. Warren Bisig. pap. 1.95 o.p. (ISBN 0-87682-260-X, 7260). Barclay Hse.

Sweet Temptation. Shannon Clare. (Superromances). 384p. 1982. pap. 2.50 (ISBN 0-373-70043-1, Pub. by Worldwide). Harlequin Bks.

Sweet Thursday. John Steinbeck. LC 54-7983. 1954. Viking Press.

Sweet Thursday. John Steinbeck. LC 78-1528. 1978. 1.95 (ISBN 0-14-004889-8). Penguin Books.

Sweet Tooth. Yves Navarre. LC 77-352250. 1976. 5.50 (ISBN 0-7145-3522-2). Calder.

Sweet Vengeance. large print ed. Laurey Bright. LC 82-11925. 1982. 12.95. G.K. Hall.

Sweet Victory. Jena Hunt. LC 82-17286. (Second Chance at Love). 11.95 (ISBN 0-89340-541-8). J. Curley.

Sweet Vixen. Maggie Mackeever. (Regency romance). 1979. 1.75 (ISBN 0-449-23902-0). Fawcett Crest Books.

Sweet Water: By Michael Cronin Pseud. Brendan Leo Cronin. LC 57-13425. (Chantecler mystery novel). 1957. Washburn.

Sweet Wild Wind. Joyce Verrette. (Orig.). 1982. pap. 3.95 (ISBN 0-440-17634-4). Dell.

Sweet Will. Eric Lawson Malpass. LC 73-87414. 1974. 6.95. St. Martin's Press.

Sweet William. Beryl Bainbridge. (Signet Book). 1977. 1.50 (ISBN 0-451-07525-0). New American Library.

Sweet William. Marguerite Bouvet. LC 12-30662. 1890. A.C. McClurg and Company.

Sweet William. Gwen Davis. (N3680). 1968. Bantam.

Sweet William. Gwen Davis. LC 67-22271. 1967. World Pub. Co.

Sweet William: A Novel. Beryl Bainbridge. LC 75-43672. 1976. 7.95 (ISBN 0-8076-0816-5). G. Braziller.

Sweetapple Cove. George Gray Van Schaick. LC 14-304173. 1914. Small, Maynard & Company.

Sweetbread. Translated from the French by Jean Stewart. Michelle Maurois. LC 59-7136. 1959. J. Messner.

Sweetbriar. Jude Deveraux. (Tapestry Romance Ser.). 1983. pap. 2.50 (ISBN 0-671-45035-2). PB.

Sweetbriar in Town: And Other Tales. David Christie Murray & Herman, Henry. LC 9-3856. (On cover: Seaside library. Pocket ed., no. 1256). 1889. G. Munro.

Sweetbrier and Thistledown: A Story. James Newton Baskett. LC 2-20981. 1902. W. A. Wilde Company.

Sweetcrab. Margaret Summerton. LC 70-150920. 1971. 4.95. Published for the Crime Club by Doubleday.

Sweeter Gwen & the Return of Gwendoline. Stanton. LC 76-8334. (Illus.). 1976. pap. 6.50 o.p. (ISBN 0-914646-06-0). Belier Pr.

Sweeter Music. Charlotte Vale Allen (ISBN 0-446-88187-2). Warner Books.

Sweeter Than. Mark Tryon. LC 55-16141.

Sweeter Than Candy. Cynthia Wilkerson. 272p. 1982. pap. 3.25 o.p. (ISBN 0-505-51856-2). Tower Bks.

Sweeter Than Honey. Arthur Applin. 1936. Green Circle Books.

Sweeter Than Wine, No. 78. Jena Hunt. 1982. pap. 1.75 (ISBN 0-515-06689-3). Jove Pubns.

Sweeter Woman. Louise Platt Hauck. LC 43-15961. 1943. Dodd, Mead & Company.

Sweetest Solace. John Randal. LC 7-7197. 1907. E. P. Dutton & Company.

Sweetest Stories Ever Told. W. H. Miller. (Stories That Win Ser.). 95p. 1927. pap. 0.95 o.p. (ISBN 0-8163-0061-5, 19791-3). Pacific Pr Pub Assn.

Sweetest Treasure. Ruth Burnett. 1981. pap. 6.95 (Avalon). Bouregy.

Sweetheart and Wife: A Novel ... 1882. G. W. Carleton & Co.; Etc., Etc.

Sweetheart Deal. Robert J Rosenblum. LC 75-34329. 8.95 (ISBN 0-399-11727-X). Putnam.

Sweetheart First Class. Vida Hurst. LC 43-870043. 1943. Gramercy Publishing Co.

Sweetheart for Somebody. A Novel. 1878. G. W. Carleton & Co.

Sweetheart Gwen; a Welsh Idyll. William Edwards Tirebuck. LC 8-26763. 1893. Longmans, Green, and Co.

Sweetheart Manette. Maurice Thompson. 1901. J. B. Lippincott Company.

Sweetheart of the Air. William Arthur Neubauer. LC 63-6691. 1963. Arcadia House.

Sweetheart, Sweetheart. Bernard Taylor. LC 77-9219. 8.95 (ISBN 0-312-78135-0). St. Martin's Press.

Sweetheart Tree. Hettie Grimstead. 3.95 o.p. Lenox Hill.

Sweethearts. Aron M. Krich. LC 82-17972. 14.95 (ISBN 0-517-54744-9). Crown Publishers.

Sweethearts. Emmett Williams. LC 68-15089. 1967. 15.00 (ISBN 0-89366-064-7); pap. 2.95 o.p. (ISBN 0-89366-065-5). Ultramarine Pub.

Sweethearts and Friends: A Novel. LC 8-32311. 1897. D. Appleton and Company.

Sweethearts and Friends: A Novel. LC 8-32310. (Half-title: Appletons' town and country library, no. 231). 1897. D. Appleton and Company.

Sweethearts and Wives: Stories of Life in the Navy. Anna Alexander Rogers. LC 99-1604. (Half-title: The ivory series). 1899. C. Scribner's Sons.

Sweethearts Unmet. Berta Ruck. LC 19-18080. 1919. 1.75. Dodd, Mead and Company.

Sweetman Curve. Howard Ashman. (Ace Original). 2.25 (ISBN 0-441-79132-8). Grosset Dunlap.

Sweetman Curve. Graham Masterton. 1979. pap. 2.50 (ISBN 0-441-79133-6). Ace Bks.

Sweetmeat Saga: The Epic of the Sixties. G. F. Gravenson. 1971. 6.95 o.p. (ISBN 0-87690-033-3). Dutton.

Sweetmeat Saga: The Epic Story of the Sixties. G F Gravenson. LC 77-149056. 1971. 6.95 (ISBN 0-87690-033-3). Outerbridge & Dienstfrey; Distributed by Dutton.

Sweets. J. J Savage. LC 77-6399. 1968. 1.75. Ophelia Press.

Sweet's Folly. Fiona Hill. (Berkley Medallion Book). 1978. 1.95 (ISBN 0-425-03587-5). Berkley Pub. Corp.

Sweet's Folly: A Novel. Fiona Hill. LC 76-22717. 8.95. Berkley Pub. Corp.: Distributed by Putnam.

Sweetsir. Helen Yglesias. LC 80-26041. 12.95 (ISBN 0-671-25092-2). Simon and Schuster.

Sweetwater. Jean Rikhoff. LC 76-10745. (Illus.). 1976. 8.95 (ISBN 0-8037-8436-8). Dial Press.

Sweetwater Point Motel. Peter Saab. LC 81-5733. 1981. 12.95 (ISBN 0-312-78141-5). St. Martin's Press.

Sweetwater Ranch. Harold Bindloss. LC 35-27301. 1935. Frederick A. Stokes Company.

Sweetwater Range. William Patterson White. LC 27-1994. 1927. Little, Brown, and Company.

Sweetwater Saga. Roxanne Dent. 1979. pap. 2.95 (ISBN 0-451-11979-7, AE1979, Sig). NAL.

Swell Jane. James Noble Gifford. LC 45-7761. 1945. Phoenix Press.

Swell Life at Sea: Or, Fun, Frigates, and Yachting; a Collection of Nautical Yarns. LC 8-20113. 1854. Stringer & Townsend.

Swell-Looking Babe. James Myers Thompson. LC 54-36459. (Lion book, 212). 1954. Lion Books by Arrangement with Cornell Pub. Corp.

Swell Looking Girl. Erskine Caldwell. 1965. pap. 0.50 o.p. (50-230). Manor Bks.

Swell Looking Girl. Erskine Caldwell. 128p. 1972. pap. 0.75 o.p. (T2603, GM). Fawcett World.

Swell Yokel. Philip Lindsay. 364p. Date not set. Repr. of 1955 ed. 6.95 o.s.i. (ISBN 0-85617-196-4). White Lion Pubs.

Swift Adventure. Jane Cardinal. LC 25-21268. George H. Doran Company.

Swift and Whiffy, and Other Children's Stories: A Picture Book Story for Kindergarten and First Grade Children. Celia Virginia Utley Conklin. (Illus.). 1973. 2.95. Vantage.

Swift Are the Shadows. Giuseppe Di Gioia. LC 41-211671. The Pyramid Press.

Swift Arrow. Josephine Cunnington Edwards. LC 67-17867. 116p. 1967. pap. 4.95 (ISBN 0-8163-0049-6, 19795-4). Pacific Pr Pub Assn.

Swift Arrow: An Historical Novel Based on the Sioux Indian Uprising. Alice Prendergast. 1958. T. S. Denison.

Swift As a Shadow. Elizabeth S Benoist. LC 80-132969. 9.95. Sunrise Pub. Co.

Swift Cloud. Sigrid De Lima. LC 52-7124. 1952. Scribner.

Swift Current. Florence McGraw McRaven. LC 54-198393. 1954. Press of the Schauer Print. Studio.

Swift Flows the River. Nard Jones. LC 40-5396. 1940. Dodd, Mead & Company.

Swift Flows the River: A Novel. Nard Jones. LC 48-10158. 1948. Binfords & Mort.

Swift: Gulliver's Travels. Ed. by Richard Gravil. 1981. pap. 20.00x (ISBN 0-333-14522-4, Pub. by Macmillan England). State Mutual Bk.

Swift Hour. Harriett Thurman. LC 41-36. Macrae-Smith Company.

Swift Lightning: A Story of Wild-Life Adventure in the Frozen North. James Oliver Curwood. LC 26-8388. 1926. Cosmopolitan Book Corporation.

Swift Runner. Frank O'Rourke. LC 72-77867. (Illus.). 1969. 6.95. Lippincott.

Swift Seasons. Helen Train Hilles. LC 53-8887. 1953. Coward-McCann.

Swift to Answer. Joye Hoekzema. LC 46-220769. 1946. Zondervan Publishing House.

Swift to Its Close. Simon Troy. LC 82-48393. (Fifty Classics of Crime Fiction, 1950-1975). 1982. 14.95 (ISBN 0-8240-4950-0). Garland Pub.

Swift to Its Close. Thurman Warriner. LC 69-20010. 1969. 4.95. Stein and Day.

Swift Water. Emilie Baker Loring. LC 29-221449. The Penn Publishing Company.

Swift Waters. Christine Whiting Parmenter. LC 37-213704. Thomas Y. Crowell Company.

Swifter Than Eagles: Bill White and the Battle of Athens, 1946: a Nonfiction Novel. Howard Cook. LC 80-69421. (Illus.). 15.00 (ISBN 0-938212-00-1). Friendly City Pub. Co.

Swiftest Eagle. Dwyer-Joyce, Alice. LC 79-5156. 1980. 8.95 (ISBN 0-312-78143-1). St. Martin's Press.

Swiftiana, 19 vols. Incl. Vol. 1. On the Tale of a Tub (ISBN 0-8240-1262-3); Vol. 2. Bickerstaffiana, & Other Early Materials on Swift (ISBN 0-8240-1263-1); Vol. 3. On Swift's Remarks on the Barrier Treaty, & His Conduct of the Allies (ISBN 0-8240-1264-X); Vol. 4. On the Drapier's Letters (ISBN 0-8240-1265-8); Vol. 5. Gulliver's Travels, One (ISBN 0-8240-1266-6); Vol. 6. Gulliver's Travels, Two (ISBN 0-8240-1267-4); Vol. 7. Gulliver's Travels, Three (ISBN 0-8240-1268-2); Vol. 8. Smedley on Swift (ISBN 0-8240-1269-0); Vol. 9. Biographical Satire (ISBN 0-8240-1270-4); Vol. 10. In Praise of Swift (ISBN 0-8240-1271-2); Vol. 11. Biography (ISBN 0-8240-1272-0); Vol. 12. Biography (ISBN 0-8240-1273-9); Vol. 13. Biography (ISBN 0-8240-1274-7); Vol. 14. Biography (ISBN 0-8240-1275-5); Vol. 15. Biography (ISBN 0-8240-1276-3); Vol. 16. Biography (ISBN 0-8240-1277-1); Vols. 17-19. Biography (ISBN 0-8240-1278-X). (Life & Times of Seven Major British Writers Ser). 1974. 47.00 ea. Garland Pub.

Swiftie the Magician: A Novel. Herbert Gold. LC 74-5020. 1974. 6.95 (ISBN 0-07-023645-3). McGraw-Hill.

Swiftly Now. Carolyn Stoloff. LC 81-11150. 52p. 1982. lib. bdg. 13.95x (ISBN 0-8214-0646-9, 82-84150); pap. 6.95 (ISBN 0-8214-0647-7, 80-84168). Ohio U Pr.

Swift's Gulliver's Travels. Jonathan Swift & Montgomery, Guy, Ed. LC 30-28639. 1930. R. R. Smith, Inc.

Swiftwater. Paul Annixter, pseud. LC 49-50439. 1950. Wyn.

Swiftwater: By Paul Annixter Pseud. Howard Allison Sturtzel. LC 49-50439. 1950. Wyn.

Swimmer. Eleanor Perry. 1968. pap. 0.60 o.p. (X1850). Pyramid Pubns.

Swimmer in the Secret Sea. William Kotzwinkle. 1975. pap. 2.25 (ISBN 0-380-00342-2, 55228). Avon.

Swimmer in the Secret Sea. William Kotzwinkle. 64p. 1981. pap. 2.25 (ISBN 0-380-55228-0, 55228, Bard). Avon.

Swimming Man Burning: A Rip-Roaring Novel of the American West. Terrence Kilpatrick. LC 76-45264. 1977. 8.50 (ISBN 0-385-12610-7). Doubleday.

Swimming Pool. Mary Roberts Rinehart. 1974. (pbk.) 1.25. Dell.

Swindler, and Other Stories. Ethel May Dell. LC 72-140329. (Short story index reprint series). 1970. Books for Libraries Press.

Swindler Named Zefano. C. H. Guenter. (Orig.). 1979. pap. 1.75 (ISBN 0-532-17225-6). Woodhill.

Swing. Edmund Schiddel. 1976. (pbk.) 1.95. Bantam Books.

Swing: A Novel. Edmund Schiddel. LC 74-23914. 1975. 9.95 (ISBN 0-671-21948-0). Simon and Schuster.

Swing Away, Climber: By Glyn Car Pseud. Showell Styles. LC 59-12254. 1959. Washburn.

Swing Full Circle. Chesley Wilson. LC 54-5252. 1954. Harcourt, Brace.

Swing Low. Barry Brissman. LC 72-79704. 1972. 5.95 (ISBN 0-06-010477-5). Harper & Row.

Swing Low. Edwin Augustus Peeples. LC 45-29368. 1945. Houghton Mifflin Company.

Swing Low, Sweet Harriet. George Baxt. (Signet mystery, P3425). 1968. New Amer. Lib.

Swing Low, Sweet Harriet. LC 67-13027. (Inner sanctum mystery). 1967. Simon and Schuster.

Swing Low, Swing Dead. Frank Gruber. (Johnny Fletcher Ser). (Osi). 1970. pap. 0.75 o.s.i. (B75-2039). Belmont-Tower.

Swing Low, Swing High. Helen Louise Williams. LC 68-14373. 1968. 4.00. Dorrance.

Swing Music Murder. Harlan Reed. LC 38-3241. 1938. E. P. Dutton & Company, Inc.

Swing of the Pendulum. Adriana Spadoni. LC 20-774. Boni and Liveright.

Swing of the Pendulum: A Novel. Frances Mary Peard. LC 7-33502. (On cover: Harper's Franklin square library, no. 742). 1894. Harper & Brothers.

Swing of Youth. Denise Robins. 1973. pap. 0.75 o.p. (94334). Beagle Bks.

Swing Old Adam. Libby Marsh Campbell. LC 64-22118. 1965. Dorrance.

Swing Shift. Grace Lois McDonald. LC 51-14553. 1951. Citadel Press.

Swing, Swing Together. Peter Lovesey. LC 77-350257. 1976. 2.95 (ISBN 0-333-19322-9). Macmillan.

Swing, Swing Together. Peter Lovesey. LC 77-3643. 1977. 9.95 (ISBN 0-89340-065-3). J. Curley & Associates.

Swing, Swing Together: A Novel of Suspense. Peter Lovesey. LC 76-14865. 6.95 (ISBN 0-396-07327-1). Dodd, Mead.

Swinger Who Swung by the Neck. Aaron Marc Stein. LC 75-107259. (Inner sanctum mystery). 1970. 4.95. Simon and Schuster.

Swinger Who Swung by the Neck. Hampton Stone, pseud. (Hampton Stone Mystery Ser). 1971. pap. 0.75 o.p. (ISBN 0-446-64763-2, 64-763-1). Paperback Lib.

Swinger Who Swung by the Neck. Hampton Stone, pseud. 1970. 4.95 o.p. (ISBN 0-671-20514-5). S&S.

Swingers. Carter Brown, pseud. (Orig.). 1980. pap. 1.75 (ISBN 0-505-51583-0). Tower Bks.

Swingers Three. Cherri Grant. (Orig.). 1974. pap. 1.95 (ISBN 0-87067-621-0, BH047). Holloway.

Swingers Three. Cherri Grant. 1974. (pbk.) 1.50 (ISBN 0-87067-449-8). Holloway House Pub. Co.

Swingin' Round the Cirkle. David R. Locke. LC 72-91085. (American Humorists Ser.). Repr. of 1867 ed. lib. bdg. 14.50 (ISBN 0-8398-1167-5). Irvington.

Swinging Caravan. Achmed Abdullah. LC 75-103485. (Short story index reprint series). 1969. Books for Libraries Press.

Swinging Caravan. Achmed Abdullah. LC 25-194261. Brentano's.

Swinging Goddess. Marjorie Chalmers Carleton. LC 26-9566. Small, Maynard & Company.

Swinging Marriage. (Illus.). pap. 5.00 (ISBN 0-910550-70-0). Centurion Pr.

Swinging Murder. Dudley Barker. LC 74-86965. 1969. 4.50. Walker.

Swinging Murder. 1st u.s. ed. Anthony Matthews, pseud. LC 74-86965. 1969. 4.50 o.p. (21056). Walker & Co.

Swinging Shutter. Cicely Fraser-Simson. LC 28-21191. E. P. Dutton & Company.

Swinging Singles. Mann Wright, Jr. (Orig.). pap. 0.95 o.p. (1116). Brandon.

Swinging Students. Garth Brandtson. pap. 1.95 o.p. (ISBN 0-87682-245-6, 7245). Barclay Hse.

Swirling Waters. Max Rittenberg. LC 13-18000. 1.25. G. W. Dillingham Company.

Swiss Abduction. Mark Denning. 1981. pap. 1.95 (ISBN 0-8439-0858-0, Leisure Bks). Nordon Pubns.

Swiss Account. Leslie Waller. LC 75-6274. 1975-1976. 8.95 (ISBN 0-385-09661-5). Doubleday.

Swiss Arrangement. William Fairchild. LC 73-87415. 1974. 6.95. St. Martin's Press.

Swiss Arrangement. William Fairchild. 1975. (pbk.) 1.50. Ballantine Books.

Swiss Conspiracy. Michael Stanley. 1976. (pbk.) 1.75 (ISBN 0-380-00492-5). Avon Books.

Swiss Family Manhattan... Christopher Darlington Morley. LC 31-28603. 1932. Doubleday, Doran & Company, Inc.

Swiss Legacy. Anne Armstrong Thompson. LC 74-11436. (Simon and Schuster novel of suspense). 1974. 6.95 (ISBN 0-671-21851-4). Simon and Schuster.

Swiss Secret. Jon Messmann. (Jefferson Boone handyman#4). 1974. (pbk.) 0.95. Pyramid Books.

Swiss Secret: Jefferson Boone, Handyman No. 4. Jon Messman. (Orig.). 1974. pap. 0.95 o.p. (ISBN 0-515-03490-8, N3490). BJ Pub Group.

Swiss Shot. Michael Bradley. (Adrano/for Hire 3). 1974. (pbk.) 1.25. Warner Paperback Library.

Swiss Sonata. Gwethalyn Graham Ericksen Brown. LC 38-10115. 1938. C. Scribner's Sons.

Swiss Sonata. Gwethalyn Graham. LC 38-10115. 1938. C. Scribner's Sons.

Swiss Summer. Stella Gibbons. LC 52-1851. 1951. Longmans, Green.

Switch. Mike Jahn. (Berkley Medallion Book). 1976. (pbk.) 1.25 (ISBN 0-425-03082-2). Berkley Publishing Corp.

Switch Bitch. Roald Dahl. LC 74-7731. 1974. 6.95. Knopf; Distributed by Random House.

Switcheroo. Emmett McDowell. LC 54-31826. (Ace double novel books, D-51). 1954. Ace Books.

Switzers. Carol Williams. LC 81-3131. (Orig.). 1981. 9.95 o.p. (ISBN 0-89865-170-0); pap. 6.95 (ISBN 0-89865-139-5). Donning Co.

Swoop! And Other Stories. Pelham Grenville Wodehouse & David A Jasen. LC 78-26758. (Continuum book). 1979. 9.95 (ISBN 0-8164-9350-2). Seabury Press.

Swoop of the Week: Or, The Treasure at "Ma's Legacy,". Louise Jackson Strong. LC 13-381545. Jennings and Graham.

Sword. Agnar OrArson. LC 77-125259. (Library of Scandinavian Literature, V. 7). 1972. 6.00. Twayne Publishers.

Sword. Agnar Thordarson. Tr. by Paul Schach from Icelandic. LC 77-125259. (Library of Scandinavian Literature: Vol. 7). 1970. 7.00x (ISBN 0-89067-016-1). Am Scandinavian.

Sword Above the Night. John Lymington, pseud. 1971. pap. 0.75 o.p. (75-398). Manor Bks.

Sword & Abyss: Short Stories. Keki N. Daruwalla. 1979. 7.95x (ISBN 0-7069-0680-2, Pub. by Vikas India). Advent NY.

Sword and Candle. Sidney Herschel Small. LC 27-6444. The Bobbs-Merrill Company.

Sword and Gown. author's ed. George Alfred Lawrence. LC 7-13228. 1859. Ticknor and Fields.

Sword and Gown. A Novel. George Alfred Lawrence. LC 7-3062. (On cover: Library of select novels. no. 213). 1859. Harper & Brothers.

Sword and Scalpel. 1st Ed. Frank Gill Slaughter. LC 57-6295. 1957. Doubleday.

Sword and the Distaff: Or, "Fair, Fat, and Forty". A Story of the South, at the Close of the Revolution. William Gilmore Simms. LC 8-13049. 1853. Lippincott, Grambo, & Co.

Sword and the Dove: Inspired by the Life of Sarah Bernhardt. Ruth Haig. LC 53-10294. Vantage Press.

Sword and the Net. Warren Stuart, pseud. LC 41-20734. 1941. W. Morrow and Company.

Sword and the Promise. 1st Ed. Siegel, Benjamin. LC 59-7534. 1959. Harcourt, Brace.

Sword & the Rose. Victor J. Banis. (Orig.). 1975. pap. 1.50 o.p. (A3596). BJ Pub Group.

Sword and the Rose. Catherine Elder. 1977. 1.75. Dell Pub. Co.

Sword and the Rose. Archibald William Smith. LC 38-27066. 1938. Little, Brown and Company.

Sword and the Scales. Hugh McLeave. LC 68-12584. 1968. Harcourt, Brace & World.

Sword & the Scimitar: The Saga of the Crusades. Ernle Bradford. (Illus.). 264p. 1974. 15.95 o.p. (ISBN 0-399-11375-4). Putnam Pub Group.

Sword and the Shadow. Sylvia Thorpe. 240p. 1977. pap. 1.50 (ISBN 0-449-22945-9, Crest). Fawcett.

Sword and the Shadow. Sylvia Thorpe. 1976. 1.50 (ISBN 0-449-22945-9). Fawcett Crest.

Sword & the Sorcerer. Norman Winski. 224p. (Orig.). 1982. pap. 2.50 (ISBN 0-523-41787-X). Pinnacle Bks.

Sword and the Soul: A Romance of the Civil War. William Rattle Plum. LC 18-7926. 1917. The Neale Publishing Company.

Sword and the Stallion. Michael Moorcock. (Chronicles of Corum). (Berkley medallion book: Vol. 6). 1974. (pbk.) 0.75 (ISBN 0-425-02548-9). Berkley Pub. Co.

Sword and the Sun: A Story of the Spanish Civil Wars in Peru. Gerald Green. LC 53-12314. 1953. Scribner.

Sword and the Swan. Roberta Gellis. LC 76-51629. 1977. 1.95. Playboy Press.

Sword Decides: A Chronicle of a Queen in the Dark Ages. Marjorie Bowen. LC 8-10858. 1908. The McClure Company.

Sword for Kregen. Dray Prescot. (Daw Science Fiction Ser.). (Orig.). 1979. pap. 1.95 (ISBN 0-87997-485-0, UE1485). Daw Bks.

Sword for the Empire. Gene Lancour. LC 77-11750. (Illus.). 1978. 6.95 (ISBN 0-385-13067-8). Doubleday.

Sword from Galway. Katherine Drayton Mayrant Simons. LC 48-5955. 1948. Appleton-Century-Crofts.

Sword Hand of Napoleon: A Romance of Russia and the Great Retreat. Cyrus Townsend Brady. LC 14-6800. 1914. 1.35. Dodd, Mead and Company.

Sword in the Mountains. Alice MacGowan. LC 10-25222. 1910. (Illus.). 1.35. G. P. Putnam's Sons.

Sword in the Soul. Roger Chauvire. Tr. by Boyd, Ernest Augustus. LC 29-195171. 1929. Longmans, Green and Co.

Sword in the Stone. Terence Hanbury White. LC 39-270144. 1939. G. P. Putnam's Sons.

Sword Is Forged. Evangeline Walton. 1983. 14.95 (ISBN 0-671-46490-6, Timescape). PB.

Sword Lily. Norman Lewis. LC 28-7947. Meador Publishing Company.

Sword Lover. John Frederick. LC 27-14966. 1927. Henry Waterson Company.

Sword Maker. 2d ed. Robert Barr. LC 42-8906. 1910. Frederick A. Stokes Company.

Sword Maker: By Robert Barr... Robert Barr. LC 10-14155. 1.25. Federick A. Stokes Company.

Sword of a Gascon. Tr. by William Hale. Hale, William. Tr. 1898. Howard Ainslee & Co.

Sword of Aldones. Marion Zimmer Bradley. LC 77-4513. (Darkover Ser.). (Gregg Press science fiction series (er)). 1977. Repr. of 1962 ed. lib. bdg. 10.95 o.p. (ISBN 0-8398-2367-3, Gregg). G K Hall.

Sword of Aldones. Marion Zimmer Bradley. 1976. 1.50. Ace.

Sword of Allah. Marc Olden. (Black Samurai). (Signet book: Vol. 7). 1975. (pbk.) 1.25. New American Library.

Sword of Bheleu. Lawrence Watt-Evans, pseud. 288p. 1983. pap. 2.50 (ISBN 0-345-30777-1, Del Rey). Ballantine.

Sword of Bussy: Or, The Word of a Gentleman; a Romance of the Time of Henry Iii. Robert Neilson Stephens & Nickerson, Herman. LC 12-25460. 1912. 1.25. L. C. Page & Company.

Sword of Chaos. Marion Zimmer Bradley. 1982. pap. 2.95 (ISBN 0-87997-722-1, UE1722). DAW Bks.

Sword of Conan. Robert E. Howard. LC 52-9402. (His The Hyborean Age). 1952. Gnome Press.

Sword of Damocles: A Story of New York Life. Anna Katharine Green Rohlfs. 1881. G. P. Putnam's Sons.

Sword of Damocles: A Story of New York Life. Anna Katharine Green Rohlfs. LC 17-130221. 1886. G. P. Putnam's Sons.

Sword of Damocles: A Story of New York Life. Anna Katharine Green Rohlfs. 1909. G. P. Putnam's Sons.

Sword of Desire. Robert W. Tracy. LC 52-2382. 1952. Arco Pub. Co.

Sword of Desire: By Robert Tracy Pseud. Alvin Schwartz. LC 52-2382. 1952. Arco Pub. Co.

Sword of Doom. 1st Ed. Sal Grimaldi. 1952. Pageant Press.

Sword of Dundee: A Tale of "Bonnie Prince Charlie". Theodora Agnes Peck. LC 3-17830. 1908. Duffield & Company.

Sword of Fire. Henry N. Hospers. 3.95 o.p. Carlton.

Sword of Gael. Andrew J. Offatt. 224p. 1981. pap. 2.25 (ISBN 0-441-79138-7). Ace Bks.

Sword of Garibaldi: A Story. Felicia Buttz Clark. LC 3-27970. 1903. Eaton & Mains.

Sword of God. Translated from the French by Humphrey Hare. 1st Ed. Rene Hardy. LC 54-8915. 1954. Doubleday.

Sword of Hachiman. Lynn Guest. LC 80-16232. 12.95 (ISBN 0-07-025108-8). McGraw-Hill.

Sword of Honor: Or, The Foundation of the French Republic; a Tale of the French Revolution. Eugene Sue & De Leon, Solon, Tr. LC 10-29412. 1910. New York Labor News Company.

Sword of Honour. David Beaty. LC 66-16313. 1966. bds., 3.95. Morrow.

Sword of Honour: The Final Version of the Novels: Men at Arms. 1952: Officers and Gentlemen. 1955: and The End of the Battle, 1962. 1st Amer. Ed. Evelyn Waugh. LC 66-25514. 1966. 7.95. Little.

Sword of Il Grande. William Long. LC 48-2609. 1948. Little, Brown.

Sword of Islam. Rafael Sabatini. LC 39-947. 1939. Houghton Mifflin Company.

Sword of Justice. Sheppard Stevens. LC 99-5136. 1899. Little, Brown and Company.

Sword of Monsieur Blakshirt. David Graeme, pseud. LC 36-29010. J. B. Lippincott Company.

Sword of Nemesis. Robert Archer Tracy. LC 73-18609. 1975. 24.50 (ISBN 0-404-11419-9). AMS Press.

Sword of Nemesis. Robert Archer Tracy. LC 20-13701. 1919. The Neale Publishing Company.

Sword of Orley. Stewart Farrar. LC 77-6. 1977. 8.95 (ISBN 0-312-78172-5). St. Martin's Press.

Sword of Pleasure: Being the Memoirs of the Most Illustrious Lucius Cornelius Sulla... 1st Ed. Peter Green, pseud. LC 58-9405. World Pub. Co.

Sword of Poyana. Gerald Earl Bailey. 1979. 1.75 (ISBN 0-425-04055-0). DAW.

Sword of Rhiannon. Leigh Brackett. 1975. (pbk.) 1.25. Ace Books.

Sword of Rhiannon. Leigh Brackett. LC 79-12236. (Gregg Press science fiction series). 1979. 9.95 (ISBN 0-8398-2522-6). Gregg Press.

Sword of Satan: A Novel by H. M. Mons. Translated by Richard Hanser. Hans Mahner-Mons. LC 52-12738. 1952. D. McKay Co.

Sword of Shandar. Victor Besaw. 1978. pap. 1.75 (ISBN 0-532-17195-0). Woodhill.

Sword of Shannara. Terry Brooks. LC 76-53925. (Del Rey Book.). (Illus.). 1978. 2.50 (ISBN 0-345-27444-X). Ballantine Books.

Sword of Skelos. Andrew J. Offutt. (Conan Ser.: No. 3). 1979. pap. 1.95 (ISBN 0-553-12970-8). Bantam.

Sword of Solomon: A Historical Novel. Robert S Easter. LC 62-21965. 1962. Macoy Pub. & Masonic Supply Co.

Sword of the Dawn. Michael Moorcock. (Illus.). 1977. 1.25 (ISBN 0-87997-310-2). DAW Books.

Sword of the Dawn: Runestaff Ser., No. 3. Michael Moorcock. (Science Fiction Ser). 1977. pap. 1.95 (ISBN 0-87997-631-4, UJ1631). DAW Bks.

Sword of the Demon. Richard A. Lupoff. 1978. pap. 1.75 (ISBN 0-380-01942-6, 37911). Avon.

Sword of the Demon: A Novel. Richard A. Lupoff. LC 76-5543. 7.95 (ISBN 0-06-012717-1). Harper & Row.

Sword of the Golden Stud. Ashley Carter, pseud. (Fawcett Gold Medal Book). 1977. 1.95 (ISBN 0-449-13842-9). Fawcett Pubns.

Sword of the Golem. Abraham Rothberg. 1973. 1.25. Bantam.

Sword of the Golem. Abraham Rothberg. LC 71-134477. 1971. 5.95. McCall Pub. Co.

Sword of the King: A Novel. Ronald Macdonald. 1900. The Century Co.

Sword of the Lamb. M. K. Wren, pseud. (Orig.). pap. 2.75 (ISBN 0-425-04746-6). Berkley Pub.

Sword of the Lictor. Gene Wolfe. LC 81-9427. (Wolfe, Gene. Book of the Sun: Vol. 3). 14.95 (ISBN 0-671-43595-7). Timescape Books: Distributed by Simon and Schuster.

Sword of the Lord: A Romance of the Time of Martin Luther. Joseph Hocking. LC 9-10031. 1.25. E. P. Dutton & Company.

Sword of the Nurlingas. Gerald Earl Bailey. 1979. 1.75 (ISBN 0-425-03954-4). Berkley Pub. Corp.

Sword of the Old Frontier: A Tale of Fort Chartres and Detroit; Being a Plain Account of Sundry Adventures Befalling Chevalier Raoul De Coubert, One Time Captain in the Hussars of Languedoc, During the Year 1763. Randall Parrish. LC 5-344733. 1905. A. C. McClurg & Co.

Sword of the Pyramids: A Story of Many Wars. Edward Lyman Bill. LC 10-103183. R. F. Fenno & Company.

Sword of the Spirit. Zephine Humphrey. LC 20-8516. E. P. Dutton & Company.

Sword of Tipu Sultan: A Historical Novel About the Life and Legend of Tipu Sultan of India. B. S Gidwani. LC 77-900292. 1976. 45.00. Allied Publishers.

Sword of Vengeance. Alexander Karol. (Belmont Tower Book). 1.50. Tower Pubns.

Sword of Vengeance. Alexander Karol. (Belmont Tower Book). 1.50. Tower Pubns.

Sword of Vengeance. Sylvia Thorpe. (Fawcett Crest Book.). 1977. 1.50. Fawcett Publicaions.

Sword of Vengence. Alexander Karol. 1977. pap. 1.50 o.s.i. (ISBN 0-505-51150-9). Tower Bks.

Sword of Wealth. Henry Wilton Thomas. LC 6-42369. 1906. G. P. Putnam's Sons.

Sword of Welleran & Other Wonder Tales. Lord Dunsany. (O.s.i.). 6.50 o.s.i. (ISBN 0-8159-6833-7). Devin.

Sword of Wood. Gilbert Keith Chesterton. 1928. lib. bdg. 8.50 (ISBN 0-8414-0902-1). Folcroft.

Sword of Youth... James Lane Allen. LC 15-4588. 1915. The Century Co.

Sword Peddler. Thomas Grant Springer. LC 28-6767. 1928. Cosmopolitan Book Corporation.

Sword Play. Charles B Stilson. LC 26-163333. 1926. G. H. Watt.

Sword Smith. Eleanor Arnason. LC 78-52972. 1978. pap. 1.95 o.s.i. (ISBN 0-89516-028-5). Condor Pub Co.

Sword Swallower. Ron Goulart. LC 68-27120. (Doubleday science fiction). 1968. 4.50. Doubleday.

Sword to the Heart. Barbara Cartland. (Barbara Cartland library, no. 13). 1974. (pbk.) 1.25. Bantam Books.

Sword Unsheathed. Helen Godfrey Pyke. LC 74-121862. (Crown book). 1970. Southern Pub. Association.

Sword Without Scabbard. Robin Estridge. LC 50-10371. 1950. Morrow.

Sword Woman. Robert E. Howard. (Orig.). 1979. pap. text ed. 1.95 (ISBN 0-425-04445-9). Berkley Pub.

Swordmaster. Alan Forrest. LC 76-366240. 1976. 6.75 (ISBN 0-86978-124-3). H. Timmins.

Swords Against Carthage. Friederich Donauer. Tr. by Cooper, Frederic Taber. LC 32-23717. 1932. Longmans, Green and Co.

Swords Against Darkness, No. 4. Andrew J. Offutt. 1981. pap. 2.50 (ISBN 0-89083-784-8). Zebra.

Swords Against Darkness Five. Andrew J. Offutt. 1981. pap. 2.50 (ISBN 0-89083-839-9). Zebra.

Swords Against Death. Fritz Leiber. LC 77-15548. (Leiber, Fritz, 1910-. The Fafhrd and the Gray Mouser Saga of Fritz Leiber: 2). (Illus.). 1977. 8.50 (ISBN 0-8398-2399-1). Gregg Press.

Swords Against Wizardry. Fritz Leiber. LC 77-15541. (Leiber, Fritz, 1910-. The Fafhrd and the Gray Mouser Saga of Fritz Leiber: 4). (Illus.). 1977. 8.50 (ISBN 0-8398-2401-7). Gregg Press.

Swords and Crowns and Rings. Ruth Park. LC 78-4005. 1978. 10.95 (ISBN 0-312-78178-4). St. Martin's Press.

Swords and Deviltry. Fritz Leiber. LC 77-15552. (Leiber, Fritz, 1910-. The Fafhrd and the Gray Mouser Saga of Fritz Leiber: 1). (Illus.). 1977. 8.50 (ISBN 0-8398-2398-3). Gregg Press.

Swords and Ice Magic. Fritz Leiber. 1977. 1.50 (ISBN 0-441-79166-2). Ace Books.

Swords and Ice Magic. Fritz Leiber. LC 77-15537. (Leiber, Fritz, 1910-. The Fafhrd and the Gray Mouser Saga of Fritz Leiber: 6). (Illus.). 1977. 8.50 (ISBN 0-8398-2403-3). Gregg Press.

Swords & Scepters, Coins & Cups. Alexander Fedoroff. Orig. Title: Rich Crowd. 1971. 7.95 o.p. (ISBN 0-525-21342-2). Dutton.

Swords & Scepters, Coins & Cups see Rich Crowd.

Swords and Scepters, Coins and Cups: A Novel. Alexander Fedoroff. LC 69-10296. 1971. 7.95 (ISBN 0-525-21342-2). Dutton.

Swords and Sorcery: Stories of Heroic Fantasy. (R-950). Pyramid.

Swords in the Mist. Fritz Leiber. LC 77-15482. (Leiber, Fritz, 1910-. The Fafhrd and the Gray Mouser Saga of Fritz Leiber: 3). (Illus.). 1977. 8.50 (ISBN 0-8398-2400-9). Gregg Press.

Swords in the North. Paul Lewis Anderson. LC 35-16481. 1935. D. Appleton-Century Company, Incorporated.

Swords of Anjou: A Novel. Mario Andrew Pei. LC 52-12686. 1953. J. Day Co.

Swords of Anjou: A Novel. Mario Andrew Pei. LC 77-7267. 3.95 (ISBN 0-89293-065-9). Beta Books.

Swords of Anjou, a Novel. Mario Andrew Pei. Repr. of 1953 ed. 15.00 o.p. Johnson Repr.

Swords of December. Robert York. LC 78-24026. 8.95. Scribner.

Swords of Lankhmar. Fritz Leiber. LC 77-15542. (Leiber, Fritz, 1910-. The Fafhrd and the Gray Mouser Saga of Fritz Leiber: 5). (Illus.). 1977. 8.50 (ISBN 0-8398-2402-5). Gregg Press.

Swords of Lankhmar. Fritz Leiber. 1974. (pbk.) 0.95. Ace Books.

Swords of Mars. Edgar Rice Burroughs. E. R. Burroughs, Inc.

Swords of Shahrazar. Robert E. Howard. (Berkley Medallion Book). 1978. 1.95 (ISBN 0-425-03709-6). Berkley Pub. Corp.

Swords of Shahrazar. Robert E. Howard & Michael William Kaluta. LC 76-16707. (Illus.). 12.95 (ISBN 0-913960-08-X). Fax Collector's Editions.

Swords of the Barbarians. Kenneth Bulmer. (O.s.i.). 1976. pap. 1.25 o.s.i. (BT50983). Belmont-Tower.

Swords of the Horseclans. Robert Adams. 1981. pap. 2.50 (ISBN 0-451-09988-5, E9988, Sig). NAL.

Swords of the Horseclans. Robert Adams. 1.25 (ISBN 0-523-00991-7). Pinnacle Books.

Swords on the Sea. Agnes Danforth Hewes. 1928. A. A. Knopf.

Swords Reluctant. Published in London Under the Title of "War and the Woman.". Max Pemberton. LC 12-15567. 1.25. G. W. Dillingham Company.

Swords Trilogy. Michael Moorcock. (ABerkley Medallion Book). 1977. 1.95 (ISBN 0-425-03468-2). Berkley Pub. Corp.

Swords Trilogy. Michael Moorcock. LC 80-16349. (Series: Gregg Press Science Fiction Series.). 1980. 17.95 (ISBN 0-8398-2623-0). Gregg Press.

Swordships of Scorpio. Alan Burt Akers. (Science Fiction Ser.). 1973. pap. 1.25 (ISBN 0-87997-231-9, UY1231). DAW Bks.

Swordsman. Ed. by William C. Heine. 1980. pap. 2.25 (ISBN 0-553-13190-7). Bantam.

Swordsman: By Jefferson Cooper Pseud. Gardner F Fox. LC 57-9607. (Cardinal edition, C-262. Fiction, 2). 1957. Pocket Books.

Swordsman of Napoleon and Alsace. Edgar Donald Lewis. LC 56-7543. 1956. Comet Press Books.

Swordsman of Warsaw: Or, Ralpho of the Iron Arm. Harlan Page Halsey. (secret service series, no. 19). 1889. Street & Smith.

Swordsmen & Supermen. Ed. by Donald M. Grant. (Time-Lost Ser.). 1973. pap. 0.75 o.p. (ISBN 0-87818-007-9). Centaur.

Swordswoman. Jessica A. Salmonson. 320p. (Orig.). 1982. pap. 2.75 (ISBN 0-523-48526-3). Pinnacle Bks.

Sworn Brothers: A Tale of the Early Days of Iceland, Tr. from the Danish of Gunnar Gunnarsson. Gunnar Gunnarsson. Tr. by Field C. LC 21-18948. 1921. A. A. Knopf.

Sworn to Silence: Or, Aline Rodney's Secret. Alexander McVeigh Miller. (On cover: The library of American authors, no. 21). 1890. G. Munro.

Sybaris & Other Homes. Edward Everett Hale. LC 70-155158. (Utopian Literature Ser). 1971. Repr. of 1869 ed. 13.00 (ISBN 0-405-03551-9). Ayer Co.

Sybaritic Death. Alexandra Roudybush. LC 72-175684. 1972. 4.95. Published for the Crime Club by Doubleday.

Sybelle. Roberta Gellis. 1983. pap. 3.50 (ISBN 0-515-07128-5). Jove Pubns.

Sybil. Louis Auchincloss. LC 51-8774. 1952-1951. Houghton Mifflin.

Sybil. Louis Auchincloss. LC 75-108840. 1971. (ISBN 0-8371-3728-4). Greenwood Press.

Sybil. Benjamin Disraeli. Ed. by Thom Braun. (English Library). 1980. pap. 5.95 (ISBN 0-14-043134-9). Penguin.

Sybil Brotherton. Emma Dorothy Eliza Nevitte Southworth. (arm chair library. no. 63). 1894. F. M. Lupton.

Sybil Brotherton. A Novel. Emma Dorothy Eliza Nevitte Southworth. LC 8-10837. T. B. Peterson & Brothers.

Sybil Knox: Or, Home Again; a Story of to-Day. Edward Everett Hale. LC 6-46200. Cassell Publishing Company.

Sybil Monroe the Forger's Daughter: Or, Out of the Shadow into the Sun. Martha Russell. LC 8-1343. 1859. L. P. Crown and Company.

Sybil: Or, The Two Nations. Benjamin Disraeli Beaconsfield. LC 64-54866. (Nelson classics). 1957. T. Nelson.

Sybil: Or, The Two Nations. new ed. Benjamin Disraeli Beaconsfield. LC 6-28835. G. Routledge and Sons.

Sybil: Or, The Two Nations. Benjamin Disraeli Beaconsfield. (Seaside library, v. 50, no. 1009). 1881. G. Munro.

Sybil: Or, The Two Nations. Benjamin Disraeli Beaconsfield. Ed. by Walter Sydney Sichel. LC 27-26169. (Half-title: The world's classics: 291). 1925. H. Milford, Oxford University Press.

Sybil: Or, The Two Nations. Benjamin Disraeli Beaconsfield. (In his The Bradenham edition of the novels and tales. New York, 1934? vol. IX). Alfred A. Knopf.

Sybil: Or, The Two Nations. Benjamin Disraeli Beaconsfield. Ed. by Richard Austen Butler. Thom Braun. LC 80-504740. (Penguin English library). 1980. 5.95 (ISBN 0-14-043134-9). Penguin Books.

Sybil: Or, the Two Nations. Benjamin Disraeli Beaconsfield. Ed. by Sheila Mary Smith. LC 80-40627. (World's classics). 1980. 7.95 (ISBN 0-19-281551-2). Oxford University Press.

Sybil, or the Two Nations. Benjamin Disraeli. (World's Classics Ser.). 11.95 (ISBN 0-19-250291-3). Oxford U Pr.

Sybil Trevyllian. Reginald Hughes. LC 7-5423. Ward & Drummond.

Sybille. Marion Meade. LC 82-18758. 1983. 15.95 (ISBN 0-688-00808-9). Morrow.

Sybilline Star War & Phaethon, Vol.1. Franz X. Kugler. Tr. by G. Kohler. 1980. pap. 12.00x (ISBN 0-917994-07-8). Kronos Pr.

Sybyll: The Dog Who Had All the Advantages. Illus. by Dick Moore. Bea Seidler. LC 66-21431. bds., 2.00. Pisani Pr.

Sycamore. Constance Wagner. LC 50-12352. 1950. Knopf.

Sycamore Bend, Population 1300. Frazier Hunt. LC 25-17418. Harcourt, Brace and Company.

Sycamore Men. David Taylor. LC 58-9533. 1958. Lippincott.

Sycamore Trail. Ellen Hayes. LC 29-23362. 1929. The Relay.

Sycamore Tree. Barbara K. Hodges. LC 34-7417. G. P. Putnam's Sons.

Sycamore Tree. 1st American Ed. Christine Brooke-Rose. LC 59-5753. 1959. Norton.

Sycamore Year. Mildred Lee, pseud. 1982. pap. 1.75 (ISBN 0-451-11357-8, AE1357, Vista). NAL.

Sycamores. Marcia Ford, pseud. (YA) 1972. 6.95 (Avalon). Bouregy.

Sycamores. Ruby Lorraine Radford. LC 52-11978. 1952. Bouregy & Curl.

Sydenham: Or, Memoirs of a Man of the World. W. Massie. LC 7-17806. 1833. E. L. Carey & A. Hart.

Sydney. A Novel. Georgiana Marion Craik May. (Franklin square library, no. 199). 1881. Harper & Brothers.

Sydney Carrington's Contumacy. X Lawson. LC 8-190985. F. Pustet & Co.

Sydney Carteret, Rancher. Harold Bindloss. LC 10-17324. 1911. 1.30. Frederick A. Stokes Company.

Sydney Clifton: Or, Vicissitudes in Both Hemispheres. A Tale of the Nineteenth Century... Theodore Sedgwick Fay. LC 6-88770. 1839. Harper & Brothers.

Sydney Duck. Frederick Ehrenfried Baume. LC 44-40336. 1944. Hutchinson & Co., Ltd.

Sydney-Side Saxon. Thomas Alexander Browne. 1891. Macmillan and Co.

Sydney Sovereign: And Other Tales. Jessie Catherine Huybers Couvreur. (On cover: Lovell's international series, no. 55). 1889. F. F. Lovell & Company.

Sydney, the Knight: An Historic Tale of Rustic and Religious Life in England in the Sixteenth Century. Ella Taylor Disosway. LC 7-3041. The American Sunday-School Union.

Sydnie Adriance: Or, Trying the World. Amanda Minnie Douglas. LC 6-33463. 1869. Lee and Shepard.

Sydnie Adriance: Or, Trying the World. Amanda Minnie Douglas. LC 6-33462. Lee and Shepard.

Syliva; a Novel: By Upton Sinclair. Upton Beall Sinclair. LC 13-10539. 1.20. The John C. Winston Comapny.

Sylph," a Nation's Honor in a Woman's Hands: The Romance and Intrigue of a Great Political Ring, by May Juneau Pseud.... May Fisher. LC 11-29234. W. R. Vansant.

Sylph: Or, The Organ-Grinder's Daughter. Lydia Louisa Anna Very. 1898. J. H. Earle.

Sylva: A Novel, by Vercors. Jean Bruller. LC 61-12749. 1962. Putnam.

Sylva the Mink. Ewan Clarkson. LC 68-25764. (Illus.). 1968. 4.95 o.p. (ISBN 0-525-21355-4). Dutton.

Sylvan Holt's Daughter. A Novel. Harriet Parr. (Harper's Franklin square library, no. 477). 1885. Harper & Brothers.

Sylvan Portal. Marie Mackin. LC 25-25552. 1925. Bismarck Book Company.

Sylvan Queen. A Novel. Eliza Tabor Stephenson. (Franklin square library, no. 109). 1880. Harper & Brothers.

Sylvandire. A Romance of the Reign of Louis Xiv. Alexandre Dukes & Maquet, Auguste. LC 6-43606. (Half-title: The romances of Alexandre Dumas. New series). 1897. Little, Brown, and Company.

Sylvester. Georgette Heyer. (Berkley medallion book). 1975. (pbk.) 1.50. Berkley.

Sylvester Night's Adventure. Heinrich Zschokke & W. M. B., Tr. 1884. R. Clarke & Co.

Sylvester; or, The Wicked Uncle. 2d american ed. Georgette Heyer. LC 72-151209. 1971. 5.95. Putnam.

Sylvester: Or, The Wicked Uncle. 1st American Ed. Georgette Heyer. LC 58-8059. 1957. Putnam.

Sylvester Romaine: A Novel. Charles Pelletreau. LC 7-36464. 1892. J. Pott & Co.

Sylvester Sound, the Somnambulist. Henry Cockton. LC 5-18488. 1894. G. Routledge & Sons, Limited.

Sylvia. Louise Platt Hauck. The Penn Publishing Company.

Sylvia: A Novel. Howard Melvin Fast. LC 60-13512. 1960. Doubleday.

Sylvia: A Novel. Upton Beall Sinclair. LC 79-115276. 1970. Scholarly Press.

Sylvia & Michael: The Later Adventures of Sylvia Scarlett. Compton Mackenzie. LC 19-5993. 1919. Harper & Brothers.

Sylvia Arden. A Novel. Oswald John Frederick Crawfurd. LC 6-31612. (On cover: Lovell's international series, no. 39). F. F. Lovell & Company.

Sylvia Lyndon: A Novel of England. Katherine Helen Maud Marshall Diver. LC 40-31872. 1940. Houghton Mifflin Company.

Sylvia of the Hills: A Gift Book. Anna Morris Clark. LC 37-1671. 1936. The Chronicle Shop.

Sylvia of the Minute. Helen Reimensnyder Martin. LC 27-2534. 1927. Dodd, Mead and Company.

Sylvia of the Stubbles. Jewell Bothwell Tull. LC 23-12441. The Reilly & Lee Co.

Sylvia Seabury: Or, Yankees in Japan: the Romantic Adventures of a Sailor-Boy. Justin Jones. LC 7-11899. H. Long & Brother.

Sylvia: The Story of an American Countess. Evelyn Emerson. LC 1-25681. 1901. Small, Maynard & Company.

Sylvia's Choice. A Novel. Georgiana Marion Craik May. (Seaside library. v. 25, no. 506). 1879. G. Munro.

Sylvia's Daughter. Ivy Valdes. (Rainbow Romance Edition). 1973. (pbk) 0.60. New American Lib.

Sylvia's Husband. Constance Cary Harrison. LC 4-2325. (On cover: Novelettes de luxe). 1904. D. Appleton & Co.

Sylvia's Lovers. Elizabeth Cleghorn Stevenson Gaskell. (Half-title: The world's classics, clvi, The novels and tales of Mrs. Gaskell--v). 1909. H. Frowde.

Sylvia's Lovers. with an introduction by dr. a. w. ward... ed. Elizabeth Cleghorn Stevenson Gaskell. Ed. by Adolphus William Ward. LC 6-43780. (Half-title: The works of Mrs. Gaskell... Knutsford ed. v. 6). 1906. G. P. Putnam's Sons; Etc., Etc.

Sylvia's Lovers. Elizabeth Cleghorn Stevenson Gaskell. Ed. by Andrew Sanders. LC 81-18871. (World's classics). 1982. 7.95 (ISBN 0-19-281571-7). Oxford University Press.

Sylvia's Lovers. To Which Is Added An Italian Institution. Elizabeth Cleghorn Stevenson Gaskell. LC 72-186543. (works of Mrs. Gaskell, v. 6). (Illus.). 1972. 24.00 (ISBN 0-404-07256-9). AMS Press.

Sylvia's Marriage: A Novel. Upton Beall Sinclair. LC 14-17806. 1.20. The John C. Winston Company.

Sylvia's World and Crimes Which the Law Does Not Reach. Sue Petigru Bowen. LC 6-16092. 1859. Derby & Jackson.

Sylvie and Bruno. Charles Lutwidge Dodgson. LC 41-405391. 1890. Macmillan and Co.

Sylvie: Recollections of Valois. Gerard De Nerval & Halevy, Ludovic. LC 7-17272. G. Routledge & Sons.

Sylvie: Recollections of Valois. Gerard De Nerval. LC 77-10266. 1981. 24.00 (ISBN 0-404-16318-1). AMS Press.

Symbol. Alvah Cecil Bessie. LC 66-21482. 1967. Random House.

Symbol Stories for Children of All Ages. Adolph Roeder. LC 10-4642. 1909. New Church Board of Publication.

Symozia: Voyage of Discovery. J. C. Symmes. LC 74-16520. (Science Fiction Ser). (Illus.). 248p. 1975. Repr. 17.00x (ISBN 0-405-06312-1). Ayer Co.

Sympathetic Medium: A Family Chronicle. Robina Sharpe Tucker. LC 26-8494. The Christopher Publishing House.

Sympathetic to Bare Feet. Jonathan Leonard. 1931. The Viking Press.

Symphonies. Mary Chavelita Bright. LC 6-25388. 1897.

Symphony for Two Players. Maynah Lewis. 1973. pap. 0.75 o.p. (26547-5-075). Beagle Bks.

Symphony in Murder. Amelia Reynolds Long. LC 44-5665. Ziff-Davis Publishing Company.

Symphony in Two Time. Alexander Irving, pseud. LC 48-8399. (Red badge detective). 1948. Dodd, Mead.

Symptoms for Murder. T. H. Wells. 4.95 o.p. Vantage.

Symzonia; a Voyage of Discovery. Adam Seaborn. LC 8-3387. 1820. Printed by J. Seymour.

Symzonia: A Voyage of Discovery, by Adam Seaborn, Pseud. A Facsim. Reproduction. Introd. by J. O. Bailey. John Cleves Symmes. LC 65-10000. 1965. 7.50. Scholars' Facsimiles.

Symzonia; Voyage of Discovery. John Cleves Symmes. LC 74-16520. (Science Fiction). (Illus.). 1975. 14.00 (ISBN 0-405-06312-1). Arno Press.

Syndic. Cyril M. Kornbluth. 256p. 1982. pap. 2.75 (ISBN 0-523-48543-3). Pinnacle Bks.

Syndic. 1st Ed. Cyril M Kornbluth. (Doubleday science fiction). 1953. Doubleday.

Syndicate Murders. William R Randall. LC 35-4005. Greenberg.

Syndicate Wife. John Racine. 192p. (Orig.). 1973. pap. 1.95 o.p. (ISBN 0-87056-290-8, 6290). Brandon.

Syndicate. 1st Ed. Denys Rhodes. 1960. Doubleday.

Synergy Saga: A South Seas Collage. Ardent Candor. 1973. 6.00. (ISBN 0-682-47724-9). Exposition Press.

Synnove Solbakken. Bjornstjerne Bjornson. Tr. by Julie Sutter. Edmund William Gosse. LC 79-38341. 1972. (ISBN 0-8369-6758-5). Books for Libraries Press.

Synopsis of the Yankee Drummer Abroad. Robert Cosby Rawlings. LC 9-17661. Press of Punton-Clark Pub. Co.

Synthajoy. David Guy Compton. LC 77-6800. (Gregg Press science fiction series). 1977. 12.50 (ISBN 0-8398-2373-8). Gregg Press.

Synthetic Gentleman. Channing Pollock. LC 34-19672. Farrar & Rinehart Incorporated.

Synthetic Man. Theodore Sturgeon. 1974. pap. 1.25 o.p. (ISBN 0-515-03344-8, N3344). BJ Pub Group.

Synthetic Men of Mars. Edgar Rice Burroughs. LC 40-7008. 1940. E. R. Burroughs,Inc.

Synthetic Philanthropist. James Harold Wallis. LC 43-9411. 1943. E. P. Dutton & Company, Inc.

Syringa Blossom: A Romantic Story of Durban in Days Gone by. Eunice Rosalie Boyer. LC 54-150175.

Syrinx. Lawrence North. LC 9-6851. 1909. Duffield & Company.

Syrinx: Or, A Sevenfold History. William Warner. LC 72-128939. (Series: Northwestern University Studies. Humanities Series, V. 26). (Illus.). 1970. AMS Press.

Syrup of the Bees... Tr. from the Original Manuscript. Francis William Bain. LC 14-17987. 1914. 1.25. G. P. Putnam's Sons.

System. William S. Ruben. 1977. pap. 1.75 (ISBN 0-532-17164-0). Woodhill.

System of Dante's Hell. Leroi Jones. 1965. 3.95 o.p. (GP351). Grove.

System of Dante's Hell: A Novel. Leroi Jones. LC 65-23858. 1965. Grove Press.

Systemic Shock. Dean Ing. 320p. (Orig.). 1981. pap. 2.50 (ISBN 0-441-79381-9). Ace Bks.

System's Hand. Mary Tupper Jones. LC 20-57776. 1920. Mid-West Publishing & Producing Co., Inc.

Syzgy. Frederik Pohl. 240p. 1981. pap. 3.50 (ISBN 0-553-20527-7). Bantam.

T

T As in Trapped. Lawrence Treat. LC 47-6505. 1947. W. Morrow.

T. H. E. M. G. C. Edmundson. LC 73-10968. 192p. 1974. 4.95 o.p. (ISBN 0-385-02532-7). Doubleday.

T. Macci Plauti Miles Gloriosus. Ed. by Mason Hammond et al. 1963. 4.95 o.p. Harvard U Pr.

T. Racksole & Daughter: Or, The Result of an American Millionaire Ordering Steak and a Bottle of Bass at the Grand Babylon Hotel, London. Arnold Bennett. LC 2-9452. 1902. New Amsterdam Book Company.

T. Tembarom. Frances Hodgson Burnett. LC 13-22758. 1913. The Century Co.

T. Tembarom. Frances Hodgson Burnett. LC 14-10511. 1914. The Century Co.

T. Tembarom. Frances Hodgson Burnett. LC 32-22587. 1915. A. L. Burt Company.

T. Thorndyke: Attorney-at-Law; the Romance of a Young Lawyer. Herbert Irvin Goss. LC 7-24769. 1907. C. M. Clark Publishing Company.

T. Thorndyke, Attorney-at-Law: The Romance of a Young Lawyer. Herbert Irvin Goss. LC 7-24032. 1907. The C. M. Clark Publishing Company.

T Zero. Italo Calvino. LC 76-14789. (Harbrace paperbound library; HPL 70). 1976. 2.25 (ISBN 0-15-692400-5). Harcourt Brace Jovanovich.

T Zero. Italo Calvino. LC 74-15982. 1970. Collier Books.

Ta. John Robert Russell. 1975. (pbk.) 1.25. Pocket Books.

Tabby Man. Lael Tucker Wertenbaker. LC 73-79367. 1970. 6.95 o.p. (.31195). Little.

Tabernacle on the Wissahickon: A Tale of the Early Days of Pennsylvania. Johann Adam Weishaar. LC 21-182499. 1921. Eden Publishing House.

Tabitha Ffoulkes. John Linssen. 1980. pap. 2.25 (ISBN 0-425-04458-0). Berkley Pub.

Tabitha Ffoulkes: A Novel. John Linssen. LC 78-57319. 8.95 (ISBN 0-87795-192-6). Arbor House.

Table for Five. Ron Renauld. 224p. (Orig.). 1983. pap. 2.50 (ISBN 0-523-42062-5). Pinnacle Bks.

Table for Four. Jack Iams. LC 39-8349. 1939. Simon and Schuster.

Table for Two. Maysie Greig. LC 47-17264. 1946. Random House.

Table for Two. Lawrence Nelson. LC 37-875416. 1937. Hillman Curl, Inc.

Table Forty-Seven. Rolaine A. Hochstein. LC 82-45570. 360p. 1983. 16.95 (ISBN 0-385-18242-2). Doubleday.

Table in a Roar, or, If You've Heard It, Try to Stop Me. James Ferguson. 303p. 1980. Repr. of 1933 ed. lib. bdg. 15.00 (ISBN 0-8495-1703-6). Arden Lib.

Table in the Wilderness. Norton S Parker. LC 47-756. 1947. Ziff-Davis Publishing Company.

Table Stakes: A Novel. Ernest Tidyman. LC 78-8773. 1978. 9.95 (ISBN 0-316-84512-4). Little, Brown.

Tableau: Or, Heaven As a Republic. John George Schwahn. LC 8-2056. 1892. Press of the Franklin Printing Company.

Tables of the Law. Thomas Mann. Tr. by Helen Tracy Lowe. LC 45-47191. 1945. A. A. Knopf.

Tables Turned: A Temperance Story. Mattie Talbert Fay. LC 14-15184. 1.00. The Roxburgh Publishing Company, Inc.

Tabletop. Eden Phillpotts. 1939. The Macmillan Company.

Tablets. A. Bronson Alcott. 1969. Repr. of 1868 ed. 10.00x (ISBN 0-87556-011-3). Saifer.

Tabloid Love. Patricia Lee. LC 37-15784. 1936. Godwin.

Tabloid Murders: Mystery Story in Startling New Technique. Clement Wood. LC 30-17940. The Macaulay Company.

Taboo. Wilbur Daniel Steele. LC 25-16651. Harcourt, Brace and Company.

Taboo: By Jack Woodford Pseud. & Gordon Greene. Josiah Pitts Woolfolk & Gordon Greene. 1953. Signature Press.

Taboo Love: A Novel. Joseph A Ngongwikuo. (Illus.). 1980. 10.00 (ISBN 0-682-49507-7). Exposition.

Taboo 2. LC 65-9214. (New Classics House original,e). 1965. New Classics House.

Tabula Rasa: A Constructivist Novel. Richard Kostelanetz. LC 78-61089. 1978. pap. 200.00 (ISBN 0-932360-27-0). RK Edns.

Tacey Cromwell. Conrad Richter. LC 74-84234. (Zia book). 1974. 2.45 (ISBN 0-8263-0361-7). University of New Mexico Press.

Tacey Cromwell. Conrad Richter. LC 42-21771. 1942. A. A. Knopf.

Tachi Tree. Lillian O'Donnell. LC 67-24831. (Raven book). 1968. Abelard-Schuman.

Tackling Matrimony: To the Men and Girls Who Love Each Other More Than Ease and Show and Sham. George Lee Burton. LC 13-498995. 1913. 1.00. Harper & Brothers.

Tacony Farm. Lawrence Ealy. LC 42-51969. 1942. Dorrance and Company.

Tactical Exercise. Evelyn Waugh. LC 78-167471. (Short story index reprint series). 1971. (ISBN 0-8369-3997-2). Books For Libraries Press.

Tactics. Jennifer Maiden. 1974. 9.95x (ISBN 0-7022-0944-9); pap. 4.95x (ISBN 0-7022-0947-3). U of Queensland Pr.

Tactics of Conquest. Barry N Malzberg. LC 73-21332. 1974. (pbk.) 0.95. Pyramid Books.

Tactics of Mistake. Gordon R Dickson. LC 75-139013. (Doubleday science fiction). 1971. 4.95. Doubleday.

Tactics: Or, Cupid in Shoulder-Staps. A West Piont Love Story. Jeannie H Grey. LC 6-45413. 1858. Carleton.

Tactics: Or, Cupid in Shoulder-Straps. A West Point Love Story. Jeannie H. Grey. LC 34-38283. 1863. Carleton.

Tacuara! Olga Rich. (Orig.). 1969. pap. 1.75 (ISBN 0-87067-181-2, BH181). Holloway.

Tad Potter. Asa Wilgus. LC 42-19132. 1942. Duell Sloan and Pearce.

Tadeuskund, the Last King of the Lenape. An Historical Tale. Nicholas Marcellus Hentz. LC 7-496399. 1825. Cummings, Hilliard & Co.

Tadpole Hall. Helen Ashton. LC 41-51771. 1941. The Macmillan Company.

Taffy: A Novel by Philip B. Kaye Pseud. Alger Adams. LC 50-10610. 1950. Crown Publishers.

Taffy Came to Cairo. Anne Duffield. LC 45-9511. 1945. Arcadia House, Inc.

Tag Murders. Carroll John Daly. LC 30-14392. E. J. Clode, Inc.

Tag: Or, The Chien Boule Dog. Valance J Patriarche. LC 9-26437. 1909. L. C. Page & Company.

Tagalong. M. Ekin. 4.00 o.p. (ISBN 0-8062-1170-9). Carlton.

Tagalong & His Handicap. G. S. Larrabee. 2.00 o.p. Carlton.

Tagati. Cynthia Stockley. LC 30-8794. 1930. G. P. Putnam's Sons.

Taggart. Louis L'Amour. LC 59-792278. (Bantam books, 1977. Western, 7). 1959. Bantam Books.

Tagget. Irving A Greenfield. LC 78-72920. 9.95 (ISBN 0-87795-209-4). Arbor House.

Tagget. Irving A Greenfield. LC 80-12655. 11.50 (ISBN 0-89340-275-3). J. Curley & Associates.

Taggy and Waggy. George Luzerne Hart. LC 26-5442. Dorrance and Company.

Tagore Testament. Rabindranath Tagore. Tr. by Indu Dutt. 1969. pap. 1.85 o.p. (ISBN 0-88253-188-3). InterCulture.

Tahiti Romance. Francis B. Gauss. 1968. 4.95 o.p. Vantage.

Tahiti (The Marriage of Loti) Julien Viaud & Bell, Mrs. Clara Courtenay (Poynter) 1834-1927, Tr. LC 27-651. 1925. Frederick A. Stokes Company.

Tahoe. Dorothy Dowdell. LC 77-76126. 1.95. Playboy Press.

Tahoe: Or, Life in California. A Romance. Sallie B Morgan. 1881. J. P. Harrison & Co.

Tai-Pan. James Clavell. LC 66-16356. 1966. 17.50 o.p. (ISBN 0-689-11068-5). Atheneum.

Tai-Pan. James Clavell. 1982. pap. 4.95 (ISBN 0-440-18462-2). Dell.

Tai-Pan. James Clavell. 1983. 19.95 (ISBN 0-440-08724-4). Delacorte.

Tai-Pan: A Novel of Hong Kong. James Clavell. LC 66-16356. 6.95. Atheneum.

Tai-Pan: A Novel of Hong Kong. James Clavell. (8462). 1967. Dell.

Tai-Pan: A Novel of Hong Kong. James Clavell. LC 66-16356. 1966. Atheneum.

Tail Job. Henry Kane. 1971. pap. 0.95 o.p. (ISBN 0-447-75180-8). Lancer.

Tail of a Guinea-Pig. Cicely Englefield. LC 38-8907. 1937. Oxford University Press.

Tailor & Ansty. 2nd ed. Eric Cross. 1964. pap. 4.50 (ISBN 0-85342-050-5). Irish Bk Ctr.

Tails & Tales. Nancy Price. Repr. of 1945 ed. 5.00 o.p. (ISBN 0-89987-111-9). Darby Bks.

Tailspin. Davis-Goff, Annabel. LC 79-17966. (Illus.). 11.95 (ISBN 0-698-11023-4). Coward, McCann & Geoghegan.

Taint. Patricia Wallace. 1983. pap. 2.95 (ISBN 0-8217-1174-1). Zebra.

Tain't Me, It's Democracy Speakin'. Arthur E Johnston. LC 48-1134. 1948. Christopher Pub. House.

Taint of Innocence. Marquis William Childs. LC 66-21716. 1967. Harper & Row.

Tainted: By Jack Woodford Pseud. & Conrad Carter. Josiah Pitts Woolfolk & Conrad Carter. LC 53-405182. 1953. Signature Press.

Tainted Power: A Race Williams Detective Story. Carroll John Daly. LC 31-3499. E. J. Clode, Inc.

Tainted Spring: A Woman's Search for Religious and Materital Fulfillment. 1st Ed. Sean O'Donnell. LC 60-527. 1960. Exposition Press.

Tainted Token. Kathleen Moore Knight. LC 38-34800. 1938. Pub. for the Crime Club, Inc., by Doubleday, Doran & Co., Inc.

Tainted Token. Kathleen Moore Knight. LC 40-3249. 1939. The Sun Dial Press, Inc.

Taipan and the Pillow Book: An Improbable Tale of Bibulous Bachelors, Convivial Clubs, and Lady Loves, Set in the World's Most Extraordinary Port City, Kobe, Japan. 1st Ed. Courtney Browne. LC 56-11123. 1956. C. E. Tuttle Co.

Taitu. Empress of Ethiopia. 1st Ed. Settimio Salbucci. LC 62-10598. 1962. Vantage Press.

Taka, the Man Who Would Be White. May Roberts Clark. LC 43-37794. 1938. The Rosicrucian Press, Ltd.

Take a Body. John Creasey. LC 75-185120. (Falcon's head mystery). 1972. 5.95 (ISBN 0-529-04480-3). World Pub.

Take a Deep Breath. Jane Chichester. 1962. 3.50 o.p. HM.

Take a Girl Like You. Kingsley Amis. 1960. 14.95 (ISBN 0-575-00252-2, Pub. by Gollancz England). David & Charles.

Take a Girl Like You. Kingsley Amis. 320p. 1976. pap. 1.95 o.p. (ISBN 0-14-001848-4). Penguin.

Take a Girl Like You. Kingsley Amis. 4.50 o.p. (ISBN 0-15-187839-0). HarBraceJ.

Take a Golden Spoon. Diana Julia Marr-Johnson. LC 73-85378. 1974. 6.95. St. Martin's Press.

Take a Golden Spoon. Diana Julia Marr-Johnson. LC 73-85378. 191p. 1974. 6.95 o.p. St Martin.

Take a Golden Spoon. Diana Julia Marr-Johnson. 1977. pap. 1.25 o.p. (ISBN 0-515-04394-X). BJ Pub Group.

Take a Number. Armando T Perretta. LC 57-13697. 1957. Morrow.

Take a Number in New York: Morrow. Armando T Perretta. LC 57-136974.

Take a Pair of Private Eyes. James Murdoch MacGregor. LC 68-31493. 1968. 3.95. Published for the Crime Club by Doubleday.

Take a Pair of Private Eyes. J. T. McIntosh. LC 68-31493. 1968. 3.95 o.p. Doubleday.

Take All to Nebraska. Sophus Keith Winther. LC 75-11672. 1976. 10.00 (ISBN 0-8032-0861-8) (ISBN 0-8032-5831-3). University of Nebraska Press.

Take All to Nebraska. Sophus Keith Winther. LC 36-27190. 1936. The Macmillan Company.

Take All You Can Get. Stephen Gould Fisher. LC 55-8142. 1955. Random House.

Take an Alternate Route. Paul Pierce. 160p. 1968. 2.95 o.p. (ISBN 0-8202-0093-X). Sherbourne.

Take Away the Darkness. John Edward Thompson. LC 44-478057. 1944. Murray & Gee, Inc.

Take Back the Heart. Vivien Grey. LC 47-31464. 1947. Arcadia House.

Take Care of My Little Girl. Peggy Goodin. LC 50-5361. (Illus.). 1950. Dutton.

Take Care of My Roses. Bessie Breuer. 1961. 3.95 o.p. Atheneum.

Take Five. D. Keith Mano. LC 81-43296. 1982. 17.95 (ISBN 0-385-04128-4). Doubleday.

Take Hands at Winter: A Novel. John Desmond Peter. LC 67-10978. 1967. Doubleday.

Take Heed of Loving. Dulcie Sancier. LC 38-32403. Carrick & Evans, Inc.

Take Heed of Loving Me. Dorothy Phoebe Ansle. LC 75-23949. 1976. 6.95 (ISBN 0-8415-0416-4). Saturday Review Press.

Take Heed of Loving Me. Laura Conway. 1976. 6.95 o.p. (ISBN 0-8415-0416-4). Dutton.

Take Heed of Loving Me. Elizabeth Gray Vining. LC 63-20398. 1964. Lippincott.

Take Her, Mr. Wesley. John W Drakeford. LC 72-84158. 1973. 4.95. Word Books.

Take It All. P. Jackson & G. Kalinsky. 1970. pap. 3.95 o.s.i. (ISBN 0-02-029190-6, Collier). Macmillan.

Take It Away, Sam!" The Story of Sam Hubbard's Career in Radio. Paul Wing. 1938. Dodd, Mead and Company.

Take It Crooked. Francis Beeding. LC 31-28681. 1932. Little, Brown, and Company.

Take It Easy. Damon Runyon. LC 38-31059. 1938. Frederick A. Stokes Company.

Take It Easy: Fourteen Stories... Damon Runyon. LC 45-7777. 1945.

Take It off- Mark Tryon. LC 53-657824. 1953. Vixen Press.

Take It or Leave It. Raymond Federman. LC 75-21556. 426p. 1976. 11.95 (ISBN 0-914590-22-7); pap. 4.95 (ISBN 0-914590-23-5). Fiction Coll.

Take It or Leave It: An Exaggerated Second-Hand Tale to Be Read Aloud Either Standing or Sitting. Raymond Federman. LC 75-21556. 11.95. (ISBN 0-914590-22-7) (ISBN 0-914590-23-5). Fiction Collective.

Take Me Back: A Novel. Richard Bausch. LC 80-25762. 11.95 (ISBN 0-8037-8487-2). Dial Press.

Take Me. By Jack Woodford Pseud. & Gordon Greene. Josiah Pitts Woolfolk & Gordon Green. LC 53-205128. 1953. Signature Press.

Take Me Like a Photograph. Chocolate Waters. (Illus.). 1977. pap. 4.00 o.p. (ISBN 0-935060-02-2). Eggplant Pr.

Take Me Out to the Ballgame. Gary Morgenstein. LC 79-22862. 10.95 (ISBN 0-312-78351-5). St. Martin's Press.

Take Me, Shame Me. Ken Taylor. 192p. (Orig.). 1972. pap. 1.95 o.p. (ISBN 0-87977-173-9, DBB-173). Dansk Blue Bk.

Take Me to My Friend: A Novel of Suspense. Hope Dahle Jordan. LC 62-20927. 1962. Lothrop, Lee and Shepard Co.

Take Me to Your Leader. Joseph Clifton Jones. LC 70-82023. 1969. Dorrance.

Take Me to Your President. Illus. by Ronald Wing. Leonard Wibberley. LC 57-6196. 1957. Putnam.

Take Me to Your President. Illus. by Ronald Wing. Leonard Patrick O'Connor Wibberley. LC 57-6196. 1957. Putnam.

Take Me Where the Good Times Are. Robert Cormier. 1981. 2.25 (ISBN 0-380-52662-X). Avon Books.

Take Me Where the Good Times Are: A Novel. Robert Cormier. LC 65-12005. 1965. Macmillan.

Take Murder. John William Wainwright. LC 80-28485. 9.95 (ISBN 0-312-78357-4). St. Martin's Press.

Take My Face. Peter Held. LC 57-8751. 1957. Mystery House.

Take My Heart. Besse Sprague. LC 38-17091. M. S. Mill Co., Inc.

Take My Life. Winston Graham. (S3790). 1968. Bantam.

Take My Life. Winston Graham. LC 67-10416. 1967. Doubleday.

Take My Place: By Frances Sarah Moore Pseud. Elsie Frances Wilson Mack. 1954. Avalon Books.

Take Nothing for Your Journey. Ann Schiear Steward. LC 43-14787. 1943. The Macmillan Company.

Take Now Thy Son: Novel. Mac Hyman. LC 65-21240. bds., 4.95. Random.

Take-off. William Ash. LC 74-103379. 1970. 4.50. Walker.

Take-off! Irwin R Franklyn. LC 30-22023. The Bobbs-Merrill Company.

Take One Ambassador. Alison Broinowski. LC 74-162637. 1973. 4.95 (ISBN 0-333-13946-1). Macmillan of Australia.

Take One Blood Red Rose. Mary J. Coleman. 1978. pap. 2.00 (ISBN 0-931122-10-4). West End.

Take Only As Directed. James Byrom. 1964. pap. 0.65 o.p. (ISBN 0-14-002126-4). Penguin.

Take or Destroy: A Novel of Alamein. John Harris. LC 76-364644. (Illus.). 1976. 3.95 (ISBN 0-09-126280-1). Hutchinson.

Take-Over. Louis Rossetto, Jr. 1974. 6.95 (ISBN 0-8184-0205-9). Lyle Stuart.

Take-Over: A Speculative and Otherwise Utterly Fictional Account of How Richard Milhous Nixon Will Usurp the Power of His Office, Take Over the Country, and Commit Other Heinous and Nasty Acts. Louis Rossetto. LC 74-81719. 1974. 6.95. Lyle Stuart.

Take the A Train. Michael Blankfort. LC 78-1434. 8.95. Dutton.

Take the A Train. Michael Blankfort. 1979. 1.95 (ISBN 0-440-18553-X). Dell Publishing.

Take the High Ground. 1st Ed. Everett C Marston. LC 54-5112. Little, Brown.

Take the Laughter. Karen De Wolf. LC 41-3534. The Bobbs-Merrill Company.

Take the Lightning. Nancy Wilson Ross. LC 40-30759. Harcourt, Brace and Company.

Take the Money & Die. Wynn Williams. (Raven House Mysteries Ser.). 224p. 1982. pap. 2.25 (ISBN 0-373-63024-7, Pub. by Worldwide). Harlequin Bks.

Take the War to Washington. Peter Van Greenaway. LC 74-18896. 1975. 8.95. St. Martin's Press.

Take These Hands. Anne Frances Eimselen. LC 39-6478. 1939. Macrae-Smith Company.

Take These Hands. Anne Paterson. LC 39-647827. 1939. Macrae-Smith Company.

Take This Child. Robert Liddell. LC 40-3357. The Greystone Press.

Take This Man. Frederick Busch. LC 81-3104. 1981. 12.00 (ISBN 0-374-27246-8). Farrar, Straus, Giroux.

Take This Woman. Lindsay Hayes. LC 47-31445. 1947. Macmillan Co.

Take Three Doctors. Elizabeth Seifert. LC 73-79151. 1973. 6.95. Aeonian Press.

Take Three Doctors. Elizabeth Seifert. LC 47-31050. 1947. Dodd, Mead.

Take Three Tenses: A Fugue in Time. Rumer Godden. LC 45-2392. 1945. Little, Brown and Company.

Take Three Tenses: A Fugue in Time. Rumer Godden. 1.50 (ISBN 0-380-00574-3). Avon.

Take Thy World. Mary Douglas. LC 55-13731. 1955. Bouregy & Curl.

Take Time. Vera Holding. 1966. cancelled o.p. (ISBN 0-89137-300-4). Quality Pubns.

Take to the Boats. George Hook Grant. LC 38-4883. 1938. Little, Brown and Company.

Take Twenty-Three: Short Stories Round the World. Ed. by John Keith Ewers. LC 72-180108. 1971. (ISBN 0-17-004944-2). Thomas Nelson (Australia.

Take up the Bodies. Kenneth Thomas Knobloch. LC 33-122370. 1933. Harper & Brothers.

Take What You Want. Faith Baldwin. LC 74-80369. 1970. 4.95 o.p. (ISBN 0-03-081839-7). HR&W.

Take What You Want. Faith Baldwin Cuthrell. LC 74-80369. 1970. 4.95. Holt, Rinehart and Winston.

Take What You Will. George Malko. (Orig.). 1975. pap. 1.75 o.p. (ISBN 0-515-03882-2). BJ Pub Group.

Take Your Choice. Maurice Walsh. LC 54-9420. 1954. Lippincott.

Taken Alive, and Other Stories: With an Autobiography. Edward Payson Roe. LC 7-40241. (On cover: Roe's works). Dodd, Mead, and Company.

Taken at the Flood. Mary Elizabeth Braddon Maxwell. (Seaside library. v. 30, no. 619). 1877. G. Munro.

Taken at the Flood. Mary Elizabeth Braddon Maxwell. (On cover: Seaside library. Pocket ed. no. 559). 1885. G. Munro.

Taken at the Flood. Mary Elizabeth Braddon Maxwell. (On cover: Lovell's library, no. 872). 1887. J. W. Lovell Company.

Taken at the Flood. George Woodman. LC 57-124585. 1957. Macmillan.

Taken at the Flood: A Story in Four Parts. Geraldine Bonner. LC 27-183782. The Bobbs-Merrill Company.

Taken at the Flood: The Human Drama As Seen by Modern American Novelists. Ed. by Ann Watkins. LC 46-7945. 1946. Harper & Brothers.

Taken by Siege. A Novel. Jeannette Leonard Gilder. LC 11-7160. 1887. J. B. Lippincott Company.

Taken by Siege: A Novel. Jeannette Leonard Gilder. LC 6-44056. 1897. C. Scribner's Sons.

Taken by Storm. Kay Robbins. (Second Chance at Love Ser.: No. 110). pap. 1.75 (ISBN 0-515-06874-8). Jove Pubns.

Taken by Storm, No. 31. Glenna Finley, pseud. 1982. pap. 2.25 (ISBN 0-451-11784-0, AE1784, Sig). NAL.

Taken Child. George Agnew Chamberlain. 1928. G. P. Putnam's Sons.

Taken Town. Dudley Carew. LC 47-2359. 1947. C. Scribner's Sons.

Takeoff. Randall Garrett & Polly Freas. LC 79-9140. (Starblaze editions). 1980. 4.95 (ISBN 0-915442-84-1). Donning Co.

Takeoff. 1st Ed. Cyril M Kornbluth. LC 52-7206. (Doubleday science fiction). 1952. Doubleday.

Takeover. Jonathan Evans. 416p. 1982. pap. 3.50 (ISBN 0-523-48044-X). Pinnacle Bks.

Takeover. Lawrence L. Goldman. (Orig.). 1973. pap. 0.95 o.p. (09206). Curtis.

Takeover. Herbert Schmertz & Larry Woods. LC 79-19069. 9.95 (ISBN 0-671-25137-6). Simon and Schuster.

Takeover. Muriel Spark. LC 76-17909. 1976. 8.95 (ISBN 0-670-69107-0). Viking Press.

Takeover. Muriel Spark. LC 76-378355. 1976. 3.95 (ISBN 0-333-19677-5). Macmillan.

Takeover. Muriel Spark. LC 78-314263. 1978. 2.50 (ISBN 0-14-004596-1). Penguin Books.

Takeover. Richard Edward Wormser. (Orig.). 1971. pap. 0.75 o.p. (T2420, GM). Fawcett World.

Takeover: A Novel. Niven Busch. LC 72-90388. 1973. 7.95 (ISBN 0-671-21368-7). Simon and Schuster.

Takeover Bid. Sarah Gainham. LC 73-102143. 1972. 5.95 (ISBN 0-03-084910-1). Holt, Rinehart & Winston.

Taker: By Daniel Carson Goodman. Daniel Carson Goodman. LC 19-11944. 1919. Boni and Liveright.

Takers. Robert C Ackworth. LC 77-76875. 1977-1978. 10.95 (ISBN 0-672-52298-5). Bobbs-Merrill.

Takers. Harald J. Taub. 1968. pap. 0.60 o.p. (X1925). Pyramid Pubns.

Takers of the City. Hoffman Reynolds Hays. LC 46-4248. 1946. Reynal & Hitchcock.

Takes: Stories from the Talk of the Town. Lillian Ross. 288p. 1983. 14.95 (ISBN 0-86553-074-2). Congdon & Weed.

Taking Care. Joy Williams. LC 81-11969. 246p. 1982. 12.50 (ISBN 0-394-52157-9). Random.

Taking Care of Mrs. Carroll. Paul Monette. 1979. 2.75 (ISBN 0-380-45161-1). Avon Books.

Taking Care of Mrs. Carroll: A Novel. Paul Monette. LC 77-14928. 8.95 (ISBN 0-316-57821-5). Little, Brown.

Taking Chances. Mary Lesta Skrine. LC 29-28508. 1930. J. B. Lippincott Company.

Taking Changes. Mary Nesta Skrine Keane. LC 29-28508.

Taking Gary Feldman. Stanley Cohen. LC 79-121945. (Red mask mystery). 1970. 4.95. Putnam.

Taking It Easy. Edward S Hyams. LC 60-4273. 1960. Longmans, Green.

Taking Liberty. Lawrence Dunning. LC 80-68430. 2.95 (ISBN 0-380-77297-3). Avon Books.

Taking of Kommand Group 8. C. J Floyd. (Assault,#2). 1975. (pbk.) 1.25. Award Books.

Taking of Lisa. Gil Babcock. pap. 1.95 o.s.i. (Venus). Grove.

Taking of Pelham One Two Three. Morton Freedgood. LC 72-92306. 1973. 6.95 (ISBN 0-399-11094-1). Putnam.

Taking of Pelham One Two Three. Morton Freedgood. (Dell book). 1974. (pbk.) 1.75. Dell.

Taking of Pelham One, Two Three. John Godey. (YA) 1973. 6.95 o.p. (ISBN 0-399-11094-1). Putnam.

Taking of Pelham 1-2-3. John Godey. 1982. pap 3.50. Dell.

Taking of Satcon Station. Barney Cohen & Jim Baen. 288p. (Orig.). 1982. pap. 2.95 (ISBN 0-523-48531-X). Pinnacle Bks.

Taking of the Gry. John Masefield. LC 34-341987. 1934. The Macmillan Company.

Taking off. Julia Percivall & Pixie Burger. 1975. (pbk.) 1.25 (ISBN 0-380-00212-4). Avon.

Taking Our Time. Red Ladder. 72p. (Orig.). 1981. pap. 4.95 (ISBN 0-86104-210-7). Pluto Pr.

Taking Sides. Norma Klein. 144p. 1982. pap. 1.95 (ISBN 0-380-00528-X, 60004-8, Flare). Avon.

Taking the Bastile: Or Six Years Later, a Sequel to "The Queen's Necklace". Alexandre Dumas & Maquet, Auguste. G. Routledge and Sons, Limited.

Taking the Count. Charles Emmett Van Loan. LC 19-146282. George H. Doran Company.

Takoma's Revenge. Craig Massey. 1970. pap. 0.95 o.p. Moody.

Talba: An Historical Romance. new and rev. ed. Anna Eliza Kempe Stothard Bray. LC 41-30721. 1884. Chapman and Hall, Limited.

Talba; or, Moor of Portugal. A Romance. By Mrs. Bray... Anna Eliza Kempe Stothard Bray. LC 6-18278. 1831. J. & J. Harper.

Talbot and Vernon. A Novel... John Ludlum McConnel. LC 7-15291. 1850. Baker and Scribner.

Talbot's Angles. Amy Ella Blanchard. LC 11-165622. D. Estes & Company.

Talbott Agreement. Richard M Garvin & Edmond G. Addeo. LC 68-55591. 1968. 4.95. Sherbourne Press.

Tale for Easter. Tasha Tudor. (Illus.). 1973. 1.50, +015 (ISBN 0-8098-1807-8). Walck.

Tale for Midnight. Frederic Prokosch. LC 76-178790. 1973. (ISBN 0-8371-6281-5). Greenwood Press.

Tale for Midnight. 1st Ed. Frederic Prokosch. LC 55-983353. 1955. Little, Brown.

Tale for the Bluebird. Gerald Clifford Weales. LC 60-10933. 1960. Harcourt, Brace.

Tale for the Fall of the Year. M. Stanley-Wrench. 1973. Repr. text ed. 4.95x o.s.i. (ISBN 0-8277-2109-9). British Bk Ctr.

Tale for the Mirror: A Novella and Other Stories. Hortense Calisher. LC 62-17952. 1962. Little, Brown.

Tale of a Hero. Stella Wilchek. LC 64-180843. 4.95. Harper.

Tale of a Hundred Years: The Story of Four Generations... Pattie Stone. 1922. The Brown Printing Company.

Tale of a Hundred Years: The Story of Four Generations... Pattie Wright Stone. LC 28-11929. 1922. The Brown Printing Company.

Tale of a Lonely Parish. Francis Marion Crawford. 1886. Macmillan and Co.

Tale of a Lonely Parish. Francis Marion Crawford. LC 32-336126. 1893. Macmillan and Co.

Tale of a Lonely Parish. Francis Marion Crawford. LC 16-19147. (Lettered on cover: Works of F. Marion Crawford). 1910. The Macmillan Company; London, Macmillan & Co., Ltd.

Tale of a Physician: Or, The Seeds and Fruits of Crime... Andrew Jackson Davis. LC 6-32497. 1869. W. White & Company.

Tale of a Tub. Jonathan Swift. Ed. by Edward Hodnett. (Illus.). Repr. of 1930 ed. 15.00 (ISBN 0-404-06308-X). AMS Pr.

Tale of a Tub. 5th ed. Jonathan Swift. Incl. Account of a Battle Between the Ancient & Modern Books in St. James's Library; Discourse Concerning the Mechanical Operation of the Spirit. 1975. Repr. of 1710 ed. text ed. 16.95x o.s.i. (ISBN 0-8277-3992-3). British Bk Ctr.

Tale of a Tub. Jonathan Swift. LC 71-170512. (Foundations of the Novel Ser). (O.s.i.: Vol. 8). 322p. 1973. Repr. of 1704 ed. lib. bdg. 50.00 o.s.i. (ISBN 0-8240-0520-1). Garland Pub.

Tale of a Tub. Jonathan Swift. 189p. leatherbound 45.00 o.p. (ISBN 0-913720-23-2, Sandstone). Beil.

Tale of a Tub. Jonathan Swift. Bd. with Battle of the Books & Other Stories. 3.95x o.p. (ISBN 0-460-00347-X, Evman). Dutton.

Tale of a Tub. Jonathan Swift. Incl. Battle of the Books & Other Stories. 1972. pap. 1.95 o.p. (ISBN 0-460-01347-5, Evman). Dutton.

Tale of a Tub: And An Account of a Battel Between the Ancient and Modern Books in St. James's Library, and A Discourse Concerning the Mechanical Operation of the Spirit. Jonathan Swift. LC 71-170512. (Foundations of the novel). 1972. (ISBN 0-8240-0520-1). Garland Pub.

Tale of a Tub & The Battle of the Books. Jonathan Swift. Ed. by Robert Folkenflik. LC 79-65738. (Mind of Man Ser.). (Illus.). 224p. 1979. 30.00x (ISBN 0-934710-00-7). J Simon.

Tale of a Whale. Kelly L. Segraves. (O.s.i.). 1974. pap. 3.49 with cassette o.s.i. Creation Sci.

Tale of a Whistling Shrimp. 1st Ed. Vladimir B Grinioff. LC 57-11632. 1957. Dutton.

Tale of an Amateur Adventuress. The Autobiography of Esther Gray. Elizabeth Kingsbury. LC 7-12157. 1898. The Editor Publishing Co.

Tale of an Empty House: And Bagnell Terrace. Edward Frederic Benson. LC 25-21917. George H. Doran Company.

Tale of an Old Castle. Bertha Behrens & Smith, Mrs. Mary Stuart (Harrison) 1834- Tr. LC 6-9425. (On cover: Seaside library. Pocket ed. no. 1175). G. Munro.

Tale of Ancient Egypt. Frederick C Heckel. LC 62-20872. 1963. Philosophical Library.

Tale of Ancient Times, Entitled Romulus. August Heinrich Julius Lafontaine. LC 4-22521. 1814. P. Mauro.

Tale of Asa Bean. Jack Matthews. LC 75-142092. 1971. 5.95 (ISBN 0-15-187982-6). Harcourt Brace Jovanovich.

Tale of Balain. Tr. by David E. Campbell from Fr. LC 72-77830. (Medieval French Texts). (O.s.i.) 144p. 1972. text ed. 8.95x o.s.i. (ISBN 0-8101-0385-0). Northwestern U Pr.

Tale of Bali. Vicki Baum. Tr. by Crighton, Basil. LC 38-27014. 1937. Doubleday, Doran & Co., Inc.

Tale of Brittany: Mon Frere Yves by Pierre Loti Pseud.; Translated from the French by W. P. Baines. Julien Viaud. Tr. by Baines, William Peter, 1878- LC 24-26329. 1924. Frederick A. Stokes Company.

Tale of Chole: An Episode in the History of Beau Beamish. George Meredith. LC 1-19365. (On cover: Lovell's Westminister series. no. 6). 1890. J. W. Lovell Company.

Tale of Christopher: A Fantasia. Abigail Colton. LC 17-286605. Purdy Publishing Company.

Tale of Csar Saltan: Or the Prince & the Swan Princess. Aleksandr Sergeevich Pushkin. Tr. by Patricia T. Lowe. LC 75-5655. 1975. 5.95 o.p. (ISBN 0-690-00792-2, TYC-J). Har-Row.

Tale of Exiles. John Coffee Yarbrough. LC 21-9371. The Roxburgh Publishing Company, Inc.

Tale of Genji. Shikibu Murasaki. Tr. by Arthur Waley. LC 55-2413. (Doubleday anchor books, A55). 1955. Doubleday.

Tale of Genji. Murasaki Shikibu. Tr. by Edward G. Seidensticker from Japanese. LC 76-13680. 1978. pap. 11.95 (ISBN 0-394-73530-7). Knopf.

Tale of Genji. Tr. by Arthur Waley. 8.95 (ISBN 0-394-60405-9). Modern Lib.

Tale of Genji, Vol. 2. Arthur Waley. (UNESCO Collection of Representative Works). 1935. pap. 10.50 (ISBN 0-04-823013-8). Allen Unwin.

Tale of Genji: A Novel. Shikibu Murasaki. LC 50-471326. Houghton Mifflin.

Tale of Genji: A Novel in Six Parts. Shikibu Murasaki. LC 60-52014. (Modern library of the world's best books. A Modern library giant, G-38). 1960. Modern Library.

Tale of Genji-One. Lady Murasaki. LC 50-47132. pap. 4.95 (ISBN 0-385-09275-X, Anch). Doubleday.

Tale of Gockel: Hinkel & Gackeliah. Translated from the German by Doris Orgel. Illustrated by Maurice Sendak. Clemens Maria Brentand. LC 61-7766. 1961. Random House.

Tale of Kieu: The Classic Vietnamese Verse Novel. Du Nguyen & Thong, Huynh-Sanh. 1973. pap. 1.95 o.p. (ISBN 0-394-71925-5, Vin). Random.

Tale of Mr. Tubbs. Annie Edith Foster Jameson. LC 19-8072. 1.50. George H. Doran Company.

Tale of Mr. Tubbs: A Story of a Knight Without Armour. Annie Edith Foster Jameson. LC 19-8742. 1918. Hodder and Stoughton.

Tale of One January: A Novel. Albert Maltz. 1966. 4.50 o.p. Fernhill.

Tale of Pausanian Love. Edward P. Warren. LC 78-22236. (Gay Experience). Repr. of 1927 ed. 16.50 (ISBN 0-404-61518-X). AMS Pr.

Tale of Poor Lovers: A Novel. Vasco Pratolini. LC 49-9486. 1949. Viking Press.

Tale of Reading Town: An Episode from the Plot Against Washington. James Bennett Nolan. LC 30-25380. 1930. A. & C. Boni.

Tale of Red Roses. George Randolph Chester. LC 14-17983. 0.50. The Bobbs-Merrill Company.

Tale of Sin, and Other Tales. Ellen Price Henry Wood Wood. (Seaside library, v. 52, no. 1054).

Tale of the Amazing Tramp. Dan Propper. LC 76-58849. 1977. pap. 2.50x (ISBN 0-916156-20-6). Cherry Valley.

Tale of the Big Computer see End of Man?.

Tale of the Big Computer: A Vision. Hanes Alfven. LC 68-11869. 1968. Coward-McCann.

Tale of the Big Computer: A Vision. Tr. by Naomi Walford. 1st Amer. Ed. Olof Johannesson. LC 68-118694. 1968. 4.00. Coward.

Tale of the Campaign of Igor. Tr. by Robert C. Howes. 1974. pap. text ed. 2.95x (ISBN 0-393-09310-7). Norton.

Tale of the Cumberland Mountains. The Wind-up of the Big Meetin' on No Bus'ness. William Eleazar Barton. LC 11-10542. 1887. Pub. for the Author by the Oberlin News.

Tale of the Death of King Arthur. Edited by Eugene Vinaver. Thomas Malory & Arthur, King (Romances, Etc.) Ed. by Eugene Vinaver. LC 55-14444. 1955. Clarendon Press.

Tale of the Four Dervishes of Amir Khusru. Amina Shah. LC 77-368963. 1976. 4.75 (ISBN 0-900860-44-8). Octagon Press.

Tale of the Genji. Murasaki Shikibu. Tr. by Edward G. Seidensticker. 1976. 35.00 o.s.i. (ISBN 0-394-48328-6). Knopf.

Tale of the Gypsies: A Powerful Human Drama, Extraordinary, Mysterious, Gripping and Entrancingly Beautiful. Arthur O Julin. LC 45-2496. 1945. The Sunset Press.

Tale of the Heike: Heike Monogatari. LC 75-325691. (Illus.). 47.00 (ISBN 0-86008-128-1). University of Tokyo Press.

Tale of the Heike: Heike Monogatari. 1977. (vol. 1) 6.95 (ISBN 0-86008-188-5) (ISBN 0-86008-189-3). University of Tokyo Press.

Tale of the House of the Wolfings and All the Kindreds of the Mark. William Morris. LC 78-105005. (Newcastle Forgotten Fantasy library; v. 16). 1978. 3.95 (ISBN 0-87877-115-8). Newcastle Pub. Co.

Tale of the House of the Wolfings and All the Kindreds of the Mark. William Morris. LC 80-19670. 1980. 10.95 (ISBN 0-87877-515-3). Borgo Press.

Tale of the Kansas Border. Charles C Lowther. LC 50-6918. 1950. Vantage Press.

Tale of the Kloster: A Romance of the German Mystics of the Cocalico by Brother Jabez Pseud. Ulysses Sidney Koons. LC 5-1181. 1904. Griffith & Rowland Press.

Tale of the Lady Ochikubo. Wilfred Whitehouse & Eizo Vanagisawa. LC 76-150935. (Orig.). 1971. pap. 1.95 o.p. (ISBN 0-385-03030-4, Anch). Doubleday.

Tale of the Lazy Dog: A Novel. Alan Williams. 1973. 0.95. (ISBN 0-671-20674-5). Pocket Books.

Tale of the Lazy Dog: A Novel. Alan Williams. LC 78-132203. 1970. 6.95. Simon and Schuster.

Tale of the Shore and Ocean: Or, The Heir of Kilfinnan. William Henry Giles Kingston. (On cover: Seaside library. Pocket ed., no. 117). 1883. G. Munro.

Tale of the Times. Jane West. LC 74-8110. (Feminist Controversy in England, 1788-1810). 1974. 22.00 (ISBN 0-8240-0886-3). Garland Pub.

Tale of the Town: Or, Philip Henson, M.D. George Hastings. (On cover: American series, no. 335). M. J. Ivers & Co.

Tale of the Twain. Samuel August Constantino. LC 46-7368. 1946. Harper & Brothers.

Tale of the Twin Cities. Lights and Shadows of the Street Car Strike in Minneapolis and St. Paul, Minnesota, Beginning April 11, 1889. Eva Gay. 1889.

Tale of the Unextinguished Moon: And Other Stories. Boris Andreevich Vogau. LC 67-17363. (Russian library). 1967. Washington Square Press.

Tale of the Village: Abridged. Francis Edward Paget. LC 7-35793. 1841. Protestant Episcopal Female Tract Society.

Tale of the West, or, Life with a Sister. Emma Carra. LC 9-1841. 1846. H. H. Brown, Printer.

Tale of the Widows' Sons (an Interlude of Faith) Robert Harris Gearhart. LC 44-12292. 1944. The Muhlenberg Press.

Tale of the World's Fair. Frank Tennyson Neely. LC 7-25788. (On cover: Neely's series. v. 2, no. 15). 1890. F. T. Neely.

Tale of the Wyo. and Mo. Valley... Asa Countryman. LC 13-2062. 1897. Democrat Print.

Tale of Three Cities: A Novel in Baroque. David Leslie Murray. LC 40-14082. 1940. A. A. Knopf.

Tale of Three Lions. Henry Rider Haggard. (On cover: Lovell's library. no. 1100). 1887. J. W. Lovell Company.

Tale of Triona. William John Locke. LC 22-18470. 1922. Dodd, Mead and Company.

Tale of Twenty-Five Hours. Brander Matthews & Jessop, George Henry, D. 1915, Joint Author. LC 7-24696. 1892. D. Appleton and Company.

Tale of Two Bad Mice. Beatrix Potter. LC 4-27991. 1904. F. Warne & Co.

Tale of Two Cities. Charles Dickens. LC 65-6514. (Perennial classic). 1965. Harper & Row.

Tale of Two Cities. Charles Dickens. (Washington Square Press Enriched Classics). (Illus.). 1973. (pbk.) 0.95. Pocket Books.

Tale of Two Cities. Charles Dickens. LC 64-15722. (Classics to grow on). 1966. Parents' Magazine's Cultural Institute.

Tale of Two Cities. Charles Dickens. LC 68-56081. (Cambridge classics library). (Illus.). 1968. Cambridge Book Co.

Tale of Two Cities. Charles Dickens. Ed. by George Woodcock. LC 76-882938. (Penguin English library). (Illus.). 1970 (ISBN 0-14-043054-7). Penguin.

Tale of Two Cities. Charles Dickens. LC 78-2806. 1969. 5.95. F. Watts.

Tale of Two Cities. Charles Dickens. Ed. by Whipple, Edwin Percy. LC 15-23138. (Half-title: Works of Charles Dickens. New illustrated library ed. vol. xx). Houghton Mifflin Company.

Tale of Two Cities. Charles Dickens. Ed. by Lang, Andrew. LC 4-16301. (Half-title: Gadshill edition. The works of Charles Dickens... vol. xxi). 1898. Chapman & Hall, Ltd.

Tale of Two Cities. Charles Dickens. (Half-title: Library of famous novels). 1898. G. P. Putnam's Sons.

Tale of Two Cities. Charles Dickens. Ed. by Kirk, Ella (Boyce) LC 99-5213. (Eclectic school readings). American Book Company.

Tale of Two Cities. Charles Dickens. Ed. by Moore, Hamilton Byron. LC 1-24593. (Heath's English classics). 1901. D. C. Heath & Co.

Tale of Two Cities. Charles Dickens. Ed. by Coult, Margaret. LC 5-749. (Standard literature series double no. 60). 1904. University Publishing Company.

Tale of Two Cities. Charles Dickens. Ed. by Witham, Rose Adelaide. LC 5-34697. (Riverside literature series. 161). Houghton, Mifflin and Company.

Tale of Two Cities. Charles Dickens. Ed. by Linn, James Weber. LC 6-30927. (Standard English classics). Ginn & Company.

Tale of Two Cities. Charles Dickens. Ed. by Baldwin, Edward Chauncey. LC 6-6261. (Lake English classics). 1906. Scott, Foresman & Company.

Tale of Two Cities. Charles Dickens. Ed. by Buehler, Huber Gray & Mason, Lawrence. LC 6-14228. (Macmillan's pocket American and English classics). 1906. The Macmillan Company.

Tale of Two Cities. Charles Dickens. LC 7-38601. (Half-title: The "prairie" classics). 1907. A. C. McClurg & Co.

Tale of Two Cities. Charles Dickens. (Half-title: Everyman's library, ed. by Ernest Rhys. Fiction. no. 102). 1908. J. M. Dent & Co.

Tale of Two Cities. Charles Dickens. Ed. by Abernethy, Julian Willis. LC 8-6987. (Merrill's English texts). C. E. Merrill Co.

Tale of Two Cities. Charles Dickens. Ed. by McComb, Ernest Hackett Kemper. LC 12-18505. (Half-title: English readings for schools). 1912. H. Holt and Company.

Tale of Two Cities. Charles Dickens. Ed. by Baldwin, Edward Chauncey. LC 29-30755. (Lake English classics). 1919. Scott, Foresman and Company.

Tale of Two Cities. Charles Dickens. Ed. by Baldwin, Edward Chauncey. LC 19-807655. (Half-title: The Lake English classics. General editor: L. T. Damon). Scott, Foresman and Company.

Tale of Two Cities. Charles Dickens. LC 22-4431. 1921. Cosmopolitan Book Corporation.

Tale of Two Cities. Charles Dickens. Ed. by Erwin, Edward J. LC 25-187011. (Half-title: University classics for high schools--colleges--universities). 1925. The University Publishing Company.

Tale of Two Cities. Charles Dickens. LC 25-27465. Dodd, Mead and Company.

Tale of Two Cities. Charles Dickens. LC 26-26546. (modern readers' series). 1926. The Macmillan Company.

Tale of Two Cities. Charles Dickens. LC 26-269932. (Rittenhouse classics). 1926. 2.25. G. W. Jacobs & Company.

Tale of Two Cities. Charles Dickens. LC 28-13795. (Western series of English and American classics). 1928. Harlow Publishing Company.

Tale of Two Cities. Charles Dickens. (Riverside library). Houghton Mifflin Company.

Tale of Two Cities. Charles Dickens. Ed. by Rutledge, Archibald Hamilton. LC 30-25383. (Lettered on cover: Laurel English classics). Laurel Book Company.

Tale of Two Cities. Charles Dickens. Ed. by Buehler, Huber Gray & Mason, Lawrence. Moffett, Harold Young. LC 30-10975. (New Pocket Classics). (Half-title: New pocket classics). The Macmillan Company.

Tale of Two Cities. Charles Dickens. LC 36-37100. (Half-title: Everyman's library, ed. by Ernest Rhys. Fiction. no. 102). 1931. J. M. Dent & Sons, Ltd.

Tale of Two Cities. Charles Dickens. LC 31-27059. (Golden books). 1931. D. McKay.

Tale of Two Cities. Charles Dickens. LC 36-22625. (Half-title: The modern library of the world's best books. no. 189). 1935. The Modern Library.

Tale of Two Cities. Charles Dickens. LC 38-33030. The Heritage Club.

Tale of Two Cities. Charles Dickens. (Universal library). 1940. Grosset & Dunlap.

Tale of Two Cities. Charles Dickens. LC 44-51608. 1944. Pocket Books, Inc.

Tale of Two Cities. Charles Dickens. LC 46-22837. (Half-title: The Living library). 1946. The World Publishing Company.

Tale of Two Cities. Charles Dickens. LC 49-9728. (Oxford illustrated Dickens). 1949. Oxford University Press.

Tale of Two Cities. Charles Dickens. Ed. by Rutledge, Archibald Hamilton. LC 25-16974. (Lettered on cover: The Windsor English classics). F. M. Ambrose Company.

Tale of Two Cities. Charles Dickens. LC 80-13314. (Classics in Large Print). 14.95 (ISBN 0-8161-3075-2). G. K. Hall.

Tale of Two Cities. Charles Dickens. (Arabic.). pap. 12.00x o.p. Intl Bk Ctr.

Tale of Two Cities. Charles Dickens & Benscoter, Grace A. LC 47-4396. (CEBCO classics for enjoyment). 1947. College Entrance Book Co.

Tale of Two Cities. Charles Dickens & Blackmore, Richard Doddridge. LC 42-460490. (Prose and poetry individualized program. The novel). 1942. The L. W. Singer Company.

Tale of Two Cities. Charles Dickens & Browne, Hablot Knight, 1815-1882, Illus. LC 42-50772. (On cover: Great illustrated classics). 1942. Dodd, Mead & Company.

Tale of Two Cities. Charles Dickens & Busoni, Rafaello, 1900- Illus. LC 48-1826. (Illustrated junior library). Grosset & Dunlap.

Tale of Two Cities. Charles Dickens & Holmes, Mabel Dodge. Globe Book Company.

Tale of Two Cities. Charles Dickens & Kincheloe, Isabella. LC 36-11554. (On cover: Stratford classics). Lyons & Carnahan.

Tale of Two Cities. Charles Dickens & John Steinbeck. Ed. by Edgar Howard Schuster & S. G. Eskin. LC 64-9642. (Noble's comparative classics). Noble and Noble.

Tale of Two Cities. Charles Dickens & Toomey, Elizabeth, 1901- LC 47-22236. (The Everyreader library). 1947. Webster Publishing Company.

Tale of Two Cities. Charles Dickens & Whipple, Edwin Percy. LC 6-37244. (Half-title: Works... New illustrated library ed. vol. xxii). 1877. Hurd and Houghton.

Tale of Two Cities. Lenore Mussoff & Barnes & Noble, Inc. New York. LC 66-30581. (Barnes & Noble book notes, 818). 1967. Barnes & Noble.

Tale of Two Cities see Classics Set.

Tale of Two Cities. Abridged, with Introd. and Notes, by Edith Carol Younghem. Drawings by John Moment. Charles Dickens & Edith Carol Younghem. LC 50-7818. 1950. Harcourt, Brace.

Tale of Two Cities: And Great Expectations. diamond ed. Charles Dickens. 1867. Ticknor and Fields.

Tale of Two Cities: And Great Expectations. illustrated household ed. Charles Dickens. LC 6-37065. 1870. Fields, Osgood & Co.

Tale of Two Cities: And The Mystery of Edwin Drood. Charles Dickens. Ed. by Dickens, Charles. Browne, Hablot Knight & Fildes, Sir Luke. LC 6-37063. 1896. Macmillan and Co.

Tale of Two Cities. Ed. by M. W. and G. Thomas. With Original Illus. by 'Phiz.' Charles Dickens. Ed. by Maurice Walton Thomas & Gladys Thomas. LC 66-6620. (Shorter classics). 1963. bds., 2.50. Ginn.

Tale of Two Cities: Ed. with a Life of Dickens, Notes, and Other Aids to the Study of the Book. Charles Dickens. Ed. by De Mille, Alban Bertram. LC 22-23717. (academy classics). Allyn and Bacon.

Tale of Two Cities. Hard Times for These Times. Four Volumes in One... Charles Dickens. LC 6-37035. 1867. Hurd and Houghton.

Tale of Two Cities. Sketches by Boz. Charles Dickens. LC 9-82255. Aldine Book Publishing Co.

Tale of Two Cities: With an Introd. by Edward Wagenknecht. Charles Dickens & France-History-Revolution-Ficiton. LC 50-12241. (Modern Library college editions, T9). 1950. Modern Library.

Tale of Two Clocks. James H Schmitz. LC 62-9978. (Torquil book). 1962. Distributed by Dodd, Mead.

Tale of Two Countries: Or, The Greater Love. pseud.... ed. Haratune Michaelyan. LC 46-595. 1945. Stratford House, Inc.

Tale of Two Countries: Or, The Greater Love. Haratune Michaelyan. LC 46-7660. 1946. Stratford House, Inc.

Tale of Two Families. Byron T. Sauls. (Illus.). 1976. 4.95 o.p. Valkyrie Pr.

Tale of Two Families. Dorothy Gladys Smith. LC 72-103381. 1970. 5.95. Walker.

Tale of Two Kings: A Modern Novelization of the Lives and Times of David and Saul, Kings of Israel, Whose Loves and Lusts, Triumphs and Defeats, Are Indelibly Engraved in the Annals of History. Saul Saphire & Winburg, Lew Earl, Joint Author. LC 36-11053. United Publishing Co.

Tale of Two Lovers. Enea S. Piccolomini. Tr. by Flora Grierson from Lat. LC 76-48452. (Library of World Literature Ser.). 1978. Repr. of 1929 ed. lib. bdg. 14.50 (ISBN 0-88355-598-0). Hyperion Conn.

Tale of Two Pities. Sydney N. Lord. 1978. 5.95 o.p. (ISBN 0-533-03051-X). Vantage.

Tale of Two Villages. Ethel Sidgwick. LC 31-28161. 1931. Harper & Brothers.

Tale of Valor. Vardis Fisher. 1976. Repr. of 1958 ed. lib. bdg. 22.80x (ISBN 0-89190-834-X). Am Repr-Rivercity Pr.

Tale of Warning: Or, The Victims of Indolence. Woodland. LC 6-631223. 1827. W. B. Gilley.

Tale of Wealth: Being the Personal Narrative of Chambers Rundel. James Paxton Voorhees. LC 8-32687. 1890. W. N. Morrison.

Tale of West and East. L. F Strauss. LC 14-17168. 1914. The Four Seas Company.

Tale That Is Told. Frederick John Niven. LC 20-17825. 1.90. George H. Doran Company.

Tale to Tell. Olive M Squair. LC 76-873409. 1970 (ISBN 0-902706-03-9). Club Leabhar Ltd.

Tale Whose Time Has Come. Robert Siegel & Karol Barske. LC 81-483177. (Illus.). 3.95 (ISBN 0-8256-3807-0). Hidden House/Flash Books.

Talent for Destruction. Sheila Radley. LC 82-10425. 1982. 10.95 (ISBN 0-684-17663-7). Scribner.

Talent for Love. Florence Stonebraker. LC 45-260. 1944. Phoenix Press.

Talent for Murder. John L Benton. LC 42-20323. 1942. Gateway Books.

Talent for Murder. John William Wainwright. LC 67-23105. 1967. Walker.

Talent for Murder. Anna Mary Wells. LC 42-15981. 1942. A. A. Knopf.

Talent for Murder. Anna Mary Wells. (Perennial Library). 1981. 2.50 (ISBN 0-06-080535-8). Harper & Row.

Talent for the Invisible. Ron Goulart. 1973. 0.95. DAW Books.

Talent for Trouble. Thomas W Shaw. LC 83-1973. 1983. 12.95 (ISBN 0-89340-604-X). J. Curley.

Talent for Trouble. Thomas W. Shaw. 224p. (Orig.). 1980. pap. 1.75 (ISBN 0-449-14362-7, GM). Fawcett.

Talent Scout. Romain Gary, pseud. LC 61-6214. 1961. Harper.

Talented Mr. Ripley. Patricia Highsmith. LC 55-10083. 1955. Coward-McCann.

Talented Wench: A Novel. Buena Vista Stine. LC 50-3309. 1950. Wetzel Pub. Co.

Tales. Honore De Balzac. Ed. by Georges Lannois. 1971. pap. 2.20 o.p. (ISBN 0-08-016378-5). Pergamon.

Tales. Wilhelm Hauff. LC 76-113675. (Short story index reprint series). 1970. Books for Libraries Press.

Tales. Nathaniel Hawthorne. Ed. by Carl Clinton Van Doren. LC 29-12622. (Half-title: The World's classics, CCCXIX). 1928. Oxford University Press, H. Milford.

Tales. Hermann Hesse. LC 7-12618. 1842. Hilliard, Gray and Company.

Tales. Leigh Hunt. LC 79-178441. (Short story index reprint series). (Treasure house of tales by great authors). (Illus.). 1971. (ISBN 0-8369-4042-3). Books for Libraries Press.

Tales. Leroi Jones. LC 67-27881. (Evergreen Bk. E-469). 1968. pap., 1.95. Grove.

Tales. Edgar Allan Poe. LC 65-11927. 1965. Whitman Pub. Co.

Tales. centenary ed.; with pictures in colours by e. l. blumenschein. ed. Edgar Allan Poe. LC 8-31689. Duffield & Company.

Tales. Edgar Allan Poe. LC 28-85211. 1927. Oxford University Press, H. Milford.

Tales. Edgar Allan Poe. Ed. by Williams, Blanche Colton. LC 28-28966. (modern readers' series). 1928. The Macmillan Company.

Tales. Edgar Allan Poe. LC 30-21181. 1930. The Lakeside Press.

Tales. Edgar Allan Poe. Ed. by Moffett, Harold Young. LC 30-10971. (Half-title: New pocket classics). The Macmillan Company.

Tales. G. Bernard Shaw. (Illus.). 1964. pap. 1.45 o.p. (ISBN 0-399-50232-7, 100, Cap). Putnam.

Tales About Temperaments. Pearl Mary Teresa Richards Craigie. (Appletons' town and country librry, no. 315). 1902. D. Appleton and Company.

Tales and Ballads. Caroline Howard Gilman. LC 6-44036. 1839. W. Crosby & Company.

Tales and Novels. Maria Edgeworth. LC 79-164752. (Illus.). 1967. AMS Press.

Tales and Novels. harper's stereotype ed. Maria Edgeworth. LC 6-26309. 1835-36. Harper & Brothers.

Tales and Sketches. Nathaniel Hawthorne. LC 81-20760. (Library of America). 25.00 (ISBN 0-940450-03-8). Literary Classics of the United States: Distributed by Viking Press.

Tales and Sketches. William Leggett. LC 7-13147. 1829. Printed by J. & J. Harper.

Tales and Sketches. Catharine Maria Sedgwick. LC 8-11245. 1835. Carey, Lea, and Blanchard.

TITLE INDEX TALES OF A TRAVELLER.

Tales and Sketches,--Such As They Are-- William Leete Stone. LC 8-16293. 1834. Harper & Brothers.

Tales and Sketches: From the Queen City. Benjamin Drake. LC 6-34230. 1838. E. Morgan and Co.

Tales and Sketches Illustrating the Character of the Irish Peasantry. William Carleton. LC 79-24474. (Ireland, from the Act of Union, 1800, to the Death of Parnell, 1891). 1979. 42.00 (ISBN 0-8240-3488-0). Garland Pub.

Tales & Sketches: Nathaniel Hawthorne. Ed. by Roy H. Pearce. LC 81-20760. 1504p. 1982. 27.50 (ISBN 0-940450-03-8). Literary Classics.

Tales and Stories. Hans Christian Andersen & Patricia Conroy. LC 80-50867. 14.95 (ISBN 0-295-95769-7). University of Washington Press.

Tales and Stories. Mary Wollstonecraft Godwin Shelley. LC 75-5677. (Gregg Press science fiction series). 1975. 18.00 (ISBN 0-8398-2311-8). Gregg Press.

Tales and Stories. Mary Wollstonecraft Godwin Shelley. LC 76-47547. (Illus.). 1976. 35.00 (ISBN 0-8414-7655-1). Folcroft Library Editions.

Tales and Stories for Black Folks. Ed. by Toni Cade Bambara. LC 79-144248. (Zenith anthologies). 1971. 3.95. Zenith Books.

Tales & Stories for Black Folks: Written by Black Authors. Ed. by Toni Cade Bambara. LC 79-144248. 3.95 o.p. (ISBN 0-385-06598-1). Doubleday.

Tales and Tangles. Maude Alexander Snyder. LC 30-30780. The Christopher Publishing House.

Tales Before Midnight. Stephen Vincent Benet. LC 39-27965. Farrar & Rinehart, Inc.

Tales Before Supper. Theophile Gautier et al. Tr. by Myndart Verelst. LC 79-113271. Repr. of 1888 ed. 19.50 (ISBN 0-404-05506-0). AMS Pr.

Tales Before Supper: From Theophile Guatier and Prosper Merimee. Gautier, Theophile, 1811-1872 & Merimee, Prosper, 1803-1870. LC 7-1505. 1887. Brentano's.

Tales Before Supper from Theophile Gautier and Prosper Merimee. Tr. by Myndart Verelst. Edgar Evertson Saltus. LC 79-113271. 1970. (ISBN 0-404-05506-0). AMS Press.

Tales by Douglas Jerrold. Douglas Jerrold. Repr. of 1891 ed. 25.00 (ISBN 0-89987-112-7). Darby Bks.

Tales by Edgar Allan Poe. Edgar Allan Poe. LC 1-26069. (Century classics). 1901. The Century Co.

Tales by the O'Hara Family, Eighteen Twenty-Five, 3 vols. John Banim & Michael Banim. Ed. by Robert L. Wolff. (Ireland Nineteenth Century Fiction - Ser. Two: Vol. 16). 1278p. 1979. lib. bdg. 96.00 (ISBN 0-8240-3465-1). Garland Pub.

Tales by the Way: A Little Book of Odd Stories. Willard Douglas Coxey. LC 6-28853. 1898.

Tales for a Rainy Night: The Fourteenth Mystery Writers of America Anthology. Edited by David Alexander. 1st Ed. Mystery Writers of America. Ed. by David Alexander. LC 61-15807. 1961. Holt, Rinehart and Winston.

Tales for a Stormy Night. Translations from the French... Ivan Sergeevich Turgenev et al. Tr. by Susan Walker Longworth et al. LC 8-20112. 1891. R. Clarke & Co.

Tales for All Seasons. George Andrew Wolfersberger. LC 4-35678. 1863. Crissy & Markley, Printers.

Tales for Christmas: And Other Seasons. Francois Coppee. Tr. by Jones, Myrta Leonora. LC 2601. 1900. Little, Brown, and Company.

Tales for Expectant Fathers. William F Van Wert. LC 82-9636. 1982. 13.95 (ISBN 0-385-27798-9). Dial Press.

Tales for Fifteen. James Fenimore Cooper. LC 59-6525. 1977. Repr. of 1823 ed. 35.00x (ISBN 0-8201-1247-X). Schol Facsimiles.

Tales for Frails. Ed. by Dorothy Sara. LC 46-22352. 1946. Cadillac Publishing Co., Inc.

Tales for the Journey. Swami Kriyananda. 1975. pap. 3.50 o.p. (ISBN 0-916124-08-8). Ananda.

Tales for the Marines. Henry Augustus Wise. LC 9-3038. 1855. Phillips, Sampson, & Company.

Tales for the Son of My Unborn Child: Berkeley, 1966-1969. Thomas Farber. 1971. 5.95 o.p. (ISBN 0-525-21365-1). Dutton.

Tales for Tots. Peggy Lockwood. (Illus.). 1974. 3.75. Vantage.

Tales for You: A Collection of Original and Selected Literature. LC 8-20111. 1841. J. J. Sharkey.

Tales from a Dugout. Arthur Guy Empey. LC 79-101808. (Short story index reprint series). (Illus.). 1969. Books for Libraries Press.

Tales from a Dugout. Arthur Guy Empey. LC 18-206635. 1918. The Century Co.

Tales from a Kings Book of Kings: Houghton Shah-Nameh Miniatures. LC 73-90026. (Illus.). pap. 1.00 o.p. (ISBN 0-87290-060-6). Corning.

Tales from a Kings Book of Kings: Houghton Shah-Nameh Miniatures. LC 73-90026. (Illus.). pap. 1.00 o.p. (ISBN 0-87290-060-6). Corning.

Tales from a Mother-of-Pearl Casket. Anatole France, pseud. LC 78-37542. (Short story index reprint series). 1972. (ISBN 0-8369-4101-2). Books for Libraries Press.

Tales from a Mother-of-Pearl Casket. Anatole France, pseud. Tr. by Pene Du Bois, Henri. LC 6-43274. 1896. G. H. Richmond & Co.

Tales from a Reservation Storekeeper. Raleigh E. Barker. Ed. by John Hicks. 64p. 1981. pap. 3.00 (ISBN 0-934996-01-6). Am Stud Pr.

Tales from a Rolltop Desk. Christopher Darlington Morley. LC 21-10609. 1921. Doubleday, Page & Company.

Tales from a Troubled Land. Alan Paton. LC 61-7209. 1961. Scribner.

Tales from Alfred de Mussett. E. D. Vermont. Repr. 10.00 (ISBN 0-8414-9196-8). Folcroft.

Tales from Balzac. Honore De Balzac. LC 74-138659. (Pergamon Oxford French series). (Commonwealth and international library). 1971. (ISBN 0-08-016378-5). Pergamon Press.

Tales from Balzac: With a Preface by George Saintsbury. Honore De Balzac. Bell, Mrs. Clara Courtenay (Poynter) 1834- Tr et al. LC 27-27928. 1927. Dodd, Mead and Company.

Tales from Bective Bridge. Mary Lavin. LC 42-132709. 1942. Little, Brown and Company.

Tales from Bernard Shaw: Told in the Jungle. Gwladys Evan Morris & Shaw, George Bernard, 1856- LC 29-21010. Frederick A. Stokes Company.

Tales from "Blackwood" Being the Most Famous Series of Stories Ever Published, Especially Selected from That Celebrated English Publication. series i ed. Blackwood's Edinburgh Magazine & Roberts, Chalmers, 1870- 1905. Doubleday, Page & Company.

Tales from 'Blackwood' Being the Most Famous Series of Stories Ever Published, Especially Selected from That Celebrated English Publication. Selected by H. Chalmers Roberts. Illus. by Jess. Emily Brangs. Blackwood's Magazine. Ed. by Chalmers Roberts. LC 57-52241. Leslie-Judge Co.

Tales from Bohemia. Robert Neilson Stephens. LC 8-26830. 1908. L. C. Page & Company.

Tales from Far and Near. Ed. by Ernest Rhys. Scott, Mrs. Catharine Amy (Dawson) Joint Ed. LC 30-24846. 1930. D. Appleton and Company.

Tales from Gavagan's Bar. expanded ed. Lyon Sprague De Camp & Fletcher Pratt. LC 78-55068. (Illus.). 1978. 13.00 (ISBN 0-913896-12-8). Owlswick Press.

Tales from Gavagan's Bar: By Fletcher Pratt and L. Sprague De Camp; Illustrated by Inga. Fletcher Pratt & Lyon Sprague De Camp. LC 53-124808. 1953. Twayne Publishers.

Tales from Gorky: Translated from the Russian with a Biographical Notice of the Author. 3d ed. Maksim Gorkii & Bain, Robert Nisbet, 1854-1909, Tr. LC 2-11732. 1902. Funk & Wagnall's Company.

Tales from Greenery Street. Denis George Mackail. LC 75-140335. (Short story index reprint series). 1970. Books for Libraries Press.

Tales from Grimm. Wanda Gag. 1981. pap. 5.95 (ISBN 0-698-20534-0, Coward). Putnam Pub Group.

Tales from Grimm. Jakob Ludwig Karl Grimm & Wilhelm Karl Grimm. LC 45-315936. 1945. E. P. Dutton & Co., Inc.

Tales from Hoffmann. Translated by Various Hands; Edited and with an Introd. by J. M. Cohen. With Illus. by Gavarni. Ernst Theodor Amadeus Hoffmann. LC 51-103835. 1951. Coward-McCann.

Tales from Jokai. 3d ed. Mor Jokai. Ed. by Robert Nisbet Bain. LC 76-163032. (Short story index reprint series). (Illus.). 1971. (ISBN 0-8369-3946-8). Books for Libraries Press.

Tales from McClure's; Adventure... McClure's Magazine et al. LC 8-28166. 1897. Doubleday & McClure Co.

Tales from McClure's; Humor... McClure's Magazine et al. LC 8-28167. 1897. Doubleday & McClure Co.

Tales from McClure's: Romance... McClure's Magazine et al. LC 8-28168. 1897. Doubleday & McClure Co.

Tales from McClure's: The West... McClure's Magazine et al. LC 8-18170. 1897. Doubleday & McClure Co.

Tales from McClure's: War Being True Stories of Camp and Battlefield... McClure's Magazine et al. LC 8-28169. 1898. Doubleday & McClure Co.

Tales from Modern India. Ed. by Natwar-Singh, K. LC 66-23791. 1966. Macmillan.

Tales from Moonshine Valley. Sam Woolford. Ed. by Crickett C. Waldroup. LC 72-92662. 300p. 1973. 2.95 o.p. (ISBN 0-88319-009-5). Shoal Creek Pub.

Tales from Pickwick: With The Five Sisters of York and the Baron of Grogzwig, from Nicholas Nickleby. Charles Dickens. LC 42-26799. 1888. G. Routledge and Sons.

Tales from Sacchetti. Franco Sacchetti. LC 76-48457. (Classics of European Literature). (Hyperion library of world literature). 1977. 12.95. (ISBN 0-88355-608-1) (ISBN 0-88355-609-X). Hyperion Press.

Tales from Shakespeare: By Charles and Mary Lamb; Illustrated by John C. Wonsetler. Charles Lamb & Shakespeare, William. Paraphrases, Tales, Etc. LC 50-12189. (New children's classics). 1950. Macmillan.

Tales from Southern Africa. A. C Jordan. LC 76-145787. (Perspectives on Southern Africa, 4). (Illus.). 1973. 9.00 (ISBN 0-520-01911-3). University of California Press.

Tales from Tartary. James Riordan & Krystyna Turska. LC 77-27871. (His Russian tales; v. 2). 1979. (ISBN 0-670-69156-9). Kestrel Books.

Tales from the Adirondack Foothills: Two-Page Yarns About the Foothills. Howard Thomas. 1956. 4.95 (ISBN 0-913710-03-2). Prospect.

Tales from the Argentine. Ed. by Waldo David Frank. LC 78-122706. (Short story index reprint series). (Illus.). 1970. Books for Libraries Press.

Tales from the Argentine. Ed. by Waldo David Frank. Tr. by Brenner, Anita. LC 30-24042. Farrar & Rinehart, Incorporated.

Tales from the Blue Stacks. Robert Bernen. LC 78-3742. 8.95 (ISBN 0-684-15540-0). Scribner.

Tales from the Bursh Country. Bunyan Blackwell. LC 63-21044. 1963. Naylor Co.

Tales from the Egean. Demetrios Bikelas. Tr. by Opdycke, Leonard Eckstein. LC 6-12783. 1894. A. C. McClurg and Company.

Tales from the Fjeld. Peter C. Asbjornsen. Tr. by George W. Dasent. LC 69-13232. (Illus.). 1969. Repr. of 1896 ed. 20.00 (ISBN 0-405-08217-7). Ayer Co.

Tales from the German: Comprising Specimens from the Most Celebrated Authors. Tr. by John Oxenford & C. A. Feiling. Musaus, Johann Karl August, 1735-1787 et al. LC 7-3057. (On cover: Library of select novels. no. 42). 1844. Harper & Brothers.

Tales from the German of Paul Heyse. Paul Johann Ludwig Von Heyse. LC 7-6607. (Half-title: Collection of foreign authors, no. xv.). 1879. D. Appleton and Company.

Tales from the Heptameron. Marguerite De Navarre. Ed. by H. P. Clive. (Athlone Renaissance Library). 1970. text ed. 19.50x (ISBN 0-485-13801-8, Athlone Pr); pap. text ed. 11.75x (ISBN 0-485-12801-2, Athlone Pr). Humanities.

Tales from the Heptameron. Marguerite de Navarre. Ed. by H. P. Clive. 1970. 6.00 o.p.; pap. 3.00 o.p. Oxford U Pr.

Tales from the High Sea. Ed. by Amy Hogeboom. LC 48-9073. 1948. Lothrop, Lee & Shepard Co.

Tales from the House of Mystery: Volume 2. Jack Oleck. 1973. (pbk) 0.95. Warner Paperback Library.

Tales from the Igloo. Ed. & tr. by Maurice Metayer. LC 76-54253. (Illus.). 1977. pap. 4.95 o.p. (ISBN 0-312-78418-X). St Martin.

Tales from the Land of Manana. G. Cunyngham Cunningham. LC 98-1310. 1898. The Editor Publishing Co.

Tales from the Masnavi. Celaleddin. Tr. by Arthur J. Arberry. 1961. 5.50 o.p. Hillary.

Tales from the New Age. R. Inwood. (Illus.). 1977. pap. 7.50 o.p. Porter.

Tales from the New Life with Meher Baba. Eruch et al. 191p. 1976. 8.95 (ISBN 0-940700-10-7); pap. 4.95 (ISBN 0-940700-09-3). Meher Baba Info.

Tales from the Newgate Calendar. Rayner Heppenstall. 256p. 1981. 40.00x (Pub. by Constable Pubs). State Mutual Bk.

Tales from the Nightside. Charles L Grant. LC 81-4851. 11.95 (ISBN 0-87054-091-2). Arkham House.

Tales from the Northern Sagas. Donald A. Mackenzie. Repr. ltd. ed. 17.50 (ISBN 0-8482-5171-7). Norwood Edns.

Tales from the Old French. Isabel Butler. LC 10-29516. 1910. Houghton Mifflin Co.

Tales from the Plum Grove Hills. Jesse Stuart. LC 46-7101. 1946. E. P. Dutton & Company, Inc.

Tales from the Rectory. Francis Clement Kelley. LC 43-6171. 1943. The Bruce Publishing Company.

Tales from the Skipper. Ed. by H. K. Rigg. LC 68-17072. 1968. 7.50. Barre Publishers.

Tales from the Sonoita. Frank M. Seibold. LC 73-21889. 1973. 4.95 (ISBN 0-8111-0523-7). Naylor Co.

Tales from the Spanish. Pedro Antonio De Alarcon. Ed. by Rodale, Jerome Irving. LC 48-8278. 1948. Story Classics.

Tales from the Thousand & One Nights. Tr. by N. J. Dawood. (Classics Ser.). (Orig.). 1973. pap. 3.95 (ISBN 0-14-044289-8). Penguin.

Tales from the Uncertain Country. Jacques Ferron. Tr. by Betty Bednarski from Fr. LC 71-190704. (Anansi Fiction Ser.: No. 19). 102p. 1972. pap. 3.95 (ISBN 0-88784-320-4, Pub. by Hse Anansi Pr Canada); study guide by Mary Ziroff 1.00x (ISBN 0-88784-053-1). U of Toronto Pr.

Tales from the Vulgar Unicorn. Robert L. Asprin. 1982. pap. 2.75 (ISBN 0-441-79577-3, Pub. by Ace Science Fiction). Ace Bks.

Tales from the White Hart. Arthur Charles Clarke. LC 56-128218. (Ballantine books, 186). 1957. Ballantine Books.

Tales from the White Hart. Arthur Charles Clarke. LC 76-95870. 1970. Harcourt, Brace & World.

Tales from the X-Bar Horse Camp: The Blue-Roan "Out Law" and Other Stories. William Croft Barnes. LC 20-126001. 1920. The Breeders' Gazette.

Tales from Third Street. Carol Jordan. (Illus.). 100p. 1980. pap. 3.50 (ISBN 0-9605360-0-0). C Jordan.

Tales from Toussaint. Miriam Monger. LC 45-4049. 1945. B. Humphries, Inc.

Tales from Two Hemispheres. Hjalmar Hjorth Boyesen. LC 78-98563. (Short story index reprint series). (Illus.). 1969. Books for Libraries Press.

Tales from Two Hemispheres. Hjalmar Hjorth Boyesen. LC 6-16078. 1877. J. R. Osgood and Company.

Tales from Underwood. David Henry Keller. LC 52-8576. 1952. Published for Arkham House by Pellegrini & Cudahy.

Tales I Tell My Mother: A Collection of Feminist Short Stories. Zoe Fairbairns et al. 161p. pap. 5.00 (ISBN 0-89608-111-7). Crossing Pr.

Tales I Told My Mother. Robert Nye. LC 72-86821. 1970. 4.95. Hill and Wang.

Tales in Tapa... Eleanor Rivenburgh. LC 10-133910. 1909. 1.00. Paradise of the Pacific.

Tales: Mini, Midi, and Maxi. Edith Bannister Dowling. LC 71-146957. (Illus.). 1970. 10.95. Peacock Press.

Tales: National and Revolutionary. Catherine Read Arnold Williams. LC 6-7134. 1830. H. H. Brown, Printer.

Tales, Now First Collected. facsimile ed. Leigh Hunt. LC 79-178441. (Short Story Index Reprint Ser.). Repr. of 1891 ed. 21.00 (ISBN 0-8369-4042-3). Ayer Co.

Tales of a Cruel Country. Charles Frederick Kenyon. LC 74-150546. (Short story index reprint series). 1971. (ISBN 0-8369-3843-7). Books for Libraries Press.

Tales of a Cruel Country. Charles Frederick Kenyon. LC 19-19358. Brentano's.

Tales of a Dalai Lama. Pierre Delattre. (Illus.). 1973. 1.25. New York.

Tales of a Dude Wrangler. enl. ed. Gene Hoopes. LC 63-18080. 1963. Naylor Co.

Tales of a Dude Wrangler: With an Introd. by Charles Franklin Parker and Illus. by George Phippen. Gene Hoopes. LC 52-6317. 1951. Exposition Press.

Tales of a Flier's Faith. 1st Ed. Ed Mack Miller. LC 58-55773. 1958. Doubleday.

Tales of a Garrison Town. Arthur Wentworth Hamilton Eaton & Betts, Craven Langstroth, Joint Author. LC 6-36814. 1892. D. D. Merrill Company.

Tales of a Grandfather. Walter Scott. LC 9-3047. (Standard literature series, no. 28). 1898. University Publishing Company.

Tales of a Grandfather: Being the History of Scotland, from the Earliest Period to the Close of the Regin of James the Fifth. Walter Scott. Ed. by Ginn, Edwin. LC 8-3046. (Classics for children). 1885. Ginn & Company.

Tales of a Greek Island. Julia D. Dragoumis. LC 76-110184. (Short story index reprint series). (Illus.). 1970. Books for Libraries Press.

Tales of a Greek Island. Julia D Dragoumis. LC 12-85698. 1912. Houghton Mifflin Company.

Tales of a Rambler. John Ellberg. LC 70-110185. (Short story index reprint series). (Illus.). 1970. Books for Libraries Press.

Tales of a Small Town: By One Who Lived There. Arthur Jerome Eddy. LC 7-30989. 1907. J. B. Lippincott Company.

Tales of a Talkative Doctor, Told Over the Hookah. George Grank Lydston. LC 7-14515. J. E. Potter & Company, Limited.

Tales of a Time and Place. Grace Elizabeth King. LC 69-11908. (American short story series, v. 67). 1969. Garrett Press.

Tales of a Time and Place. Grace Elizabeth King. LC 76-122593. 1970. AMS Press.

Tales of a Time and Place. Grace Elizabeth King. 1892. Harper & Brothers.

Tales of a Traveller. Washington Irving & Eaton, Margaret A., Ed. LC 7-19042. (On cover: Classic library). Educational Publishing Company.

Tales of a Traveller: With Selections from the Sketch Book. Washington Irving & Krapp, George Philip, 1872- Ed. LC 1-26060. (lake English classics). 1901. Scott, Foresman and Company.

Tales of a Voyager to the Arctic Ocean. Robert Pearse Gillies. LC 6-44042. 1827. H. C. Carey & I. Lea.

Tales of a Warrior: Sanguine but Not Sanguinary for Old-Time People. Charles Richardson. LC 7-16755. 1907. The Neale Publishing Company.

Tales of a Wayside Inn. Henry Wadsworth Longfellow. (Pocket Classics). 3.50 o.p. (ISBN 0-679-50092-8). McKay.

Tales of Adventure & Medical Life. Arthur Conan Doyle. pap. 1.95 o.p. Transatlantic.

Tales of Adventure. Edited by Irving Shepard. 1st Ed. Jack London. LC 56-5714. 1956. Hanover House.

Tales of Adventure from Modern French Authors. Ed. by Frederick Charles Roe. LC 37-9717. 1936. Longmans, Green and Co.

Tales of Adventurers. Geoffrey Household. LC 52-5869. 1952. Little, Brown.

Tales of Alexander the Macedonian. Rosalie Reich. 1973. 10.00 o.p. (ISBN 0-87068-179-6). Ktav.

Tales of Algeria: Or, Life Among the Arabs: from the Veloce of Alexandre Dumas. Alexandre Dumas. Tr. by Bache, Richard Meade. LC 6-43620. 1868. Claxton, Remsen & Haffelfinger.

Tales of Algernon Blackwood. Algernon Blackwood. LC 39-27302. 1939. E. P. Dutton & Co., Inc.

Tales of All Countries. Anthony Trollope. Ed. by N. John Hall. LC 80-1879. (Selected Works of Anthony Trollope Ser.). 1981. Repr. of 1861 ed. Vol. 1 First Ser. lib. bdg. 35.00x (ISBN 0-405-14138-6); Vol. 2 Second Ser. lib. bdg. 39.00x (ISBN 0-405-14139-4). Ayer Co.

Tales of All Countries. First Series. Anthony Trollope. LC 31-28508. (Half-title: The World's classics, CCCXXVII). 1931. H. Milford, Oxford University Press.

Tales of All Countries: First Series. reprint ed. / introduction by donald d. stone. ed. Anthony Trollope. LC 80-1879. (Trollope, Anthony, 1815-1882. Selections. 1981). 1981. 35.00 (ISBN 0-405-14138-6). Arno Press.

Tales of All Countries: Second Series. reprint ed. / introduction by donald d. stone. ed. Anthony Trollope. LC 80-1880. (Trollope, Anthony, 1815-1882. Selections. 1981). 1981. 39.00 (ISBN 0-405-14139-4) (ISBN 0-405-14138-6). Arno Press.

Tales of Amadou Koumba. Birago Diop. Tr. by Dorothy S. Blair. 1966. 4.50x o.p. (ISBN 0-19-913173-2). Oxford U Pr.

Tales of an American Landlord: Containing Sketches of Life South of the Potomac ... LC 8-25574. 1894. W. B. Gilley.

Tales of an Engineer, with Rhymes of the Rail. Cy Warman. LC 8-33723. 1895. C. Scribner's Sons.

Tales of an Evening. Founded on Facts. Ed. by Francis Murphy. LC 7-3063. 1815. Printed by James Winnard.

Tales of an Old Chateau. Marguerite Bouvet. LC 99-5797. 1899. A.C. McClurg and Co.

Tales of an Optician: A Collection of True Stories of Romance, Adventure, Comedy by Mrs. Frederick A. Airlie, Spectacle Maker. Albert Ernest Innes. 1903. F. Boger Pub. Co.

Tales of Appalachia. John B. Vaughan. 3.75 o.p. Carlton.

Tales of Army Life. Lev Nikolaevich Tolstoi & Maude, Mrs. Louise (Shanks) 1855- Tr. LC 36-271294. (Half-title: The world's classics. 208). 1935. H. Milford, Oxford University Press.

Tales of Army Life: By Leo Tolstoy; Translated by Louise and Aylmer Maude... Lev Nikolaevich Tolstoi. LC 36-27129. (Half-title: The World sclassics, 208) uContents omitted.). 1935. Oxford University Press.

Tales of Aroostook. Suzanne Reynolds. LC 40-5949. Fortuny's.

Tales of Aztlan: The Romance of a Hero of Our Late Spanish-American War; Incidents of Interest from the Life of a Western Pioneer, and Other Tales. rev. ed. George Hartmann. LC 9-16920. Broadway Publishing Company.

Tales of Beatnik Glory. Ed Sanders. LC 76-360314. 8.95 (ISBN 0-88373-029-4). Stonehill Pub. Co.

Tales of Bengal. Sita Chatterjee & Chatterjee, Santa. LC 23-10471. (Half-title: An Eastern library. no. 1). 1922. H. Milford, Oxford University Press.

Tales of Big Antlers. Pan Chia-Lin. 1967. 4.50 o.p. (ISBN 0-682-45799-X). Exposition.

Tales of Bolivar's Children. Edward Everett Chase. LC 15-23882. 1914. 1.00. Kennebec Journal Company.

Tales of California Yesterdays. Rose Lucile Ellerbe. LC 17-1331. 1.00. W.T. Potter.

Tales of Cedar River. William Murray Clark. LC 60-14595. 1960. D. McKay Co.

Tales of Chicago Streets. Ben Hecht. (Little blue book, no. 608, ed. by E. Haldeman-Julius)). Haldeman-Julius Company.

Tales of Chinatown. facsimile ed. Sax Rohmer. LC 75-178459. (Short Story Index Reprint Ser.). Repr. of 1922 ed. 19.50 (ISBN 0-8369-4060-1). Ayer Co.

Tales of Chinatown. Arthur Sarsfield Ward. LC 75-178459. (Short story index reprint series). 1971. (ISBN 0-8369-4060-1). Books for Libraries Press.

Tales of Chinatown. Arthur Sarsfield Ward. LC 22-20685. 1922. Doubleday, Page & Company.

Tales of Chinatown. Arthur Sarsfield Ward. LC 22-144201. 1922. Cassell and Company, Ltd.

Tales of Chinatown. Arthur Sarsfield Ward. LC 26-23560. A. L. Burt Company.

Tales of Chivalry and the Olden Time: Selected from the Works of Sir Walter Scott. Walter Scott. Ed. by Rolfe, William James. LC 3-30456. (English classics for school reading). 1887. Harper & Brothers.

Tales of Christmas from Near and Far. Ed. by Herbert Henry Wernecke. LC 63-10832. 1963. Westminster Press.

Tales of Cibola. Ramon Jose Sender. LC 64-55691. 1964. Las Americas Pub. Co.

Tales of Conan: By Robert E. Howard and L. Sprague De Camp. Robert E. Howard & Lyon Sprague De Camp. LC 55-12268. Gnome Press.

Tales of Crime & Detection. Retold by George F. Wear. (Tales Retold for Easy Reading Ser.). 1939. pap. text ed. 1.20x o.p. (ISBN 0-19-422243-8). Oxford U Pr.

Tales of D. H. Lawrence. David Herbert Lawrence. LC 73-145135. 1971. (ISBN 0-403-01068-3). Scholarly Press.

Tales of Dalai Lama. Pierre Delattre. LC 74-153958. (Illus.). 1971. 4.95 (ISBN 0-395-12707-6). Houghton Mifflin.

Tales of Darkest America. Fenton Johnson. LC 72-178477. (Black Heritage Library Collection). 1971. (ISBN 0-8369-8926-0). Books for Libraries Press.

Tales of Destiny. Elizabeth Garver Jordan. LC 79-103522. (Short story index reprint series). (Illus.). 1969. Books for Libraries Press.

Tales of Destiny. Elizabeth Garver Jordan. LC 2-16922. 1902. Harper & Brothers.

Tales of Detection & Mystery. Dorothy Leigh Sayers. 1967. pap. 0.60 o.p. (60-278). Manor Bks.

Tales of Dunstable Weir. Gwendoline Keats. LC 70-94736. (Short story index reprint series). 1969. Books for Libraries Press.

Tales of Dunstable Weir. Gwendoline Keats. LC 1-246496. 1901. C. Scribner's Sons.

Tales of East and West. Rudyard Kipling & Limited Editions Club, Inc., New York. LC 74-170451. (Illus.). 1973. Limited Editions Club.

Tales of East & West. Sax Rohmer. 1976. 6.50. Bookfinger.

Tales of East and West. Maurice Schneps. LC 61-4068. Cross Continent Co., in Ms.: Dist. Perkins Oriental Books, Los Angeles.

Tales of East and West: Thirteen Little Masterpieces of Death and Fear and Terror. Arthur Sarsfield Ward. LC 33-10973. 1933. Pub. for the Crime Club by Doubleday, Doran & Company, Inc.

Tales of Eastern Idaho. David L. Crowder. (Illus.). 150p. (Orig.). 1981. pap. text ed. 8.95 (ISBN 0-9607304-1-9). KID Broadcasting.

Tales of Eccentric Life. William Alexander Hammond. LC 7-1510. 1886. D. Appleton and Company.

Tales of Edgar Allan Poe. Edgar Allan Poe. LC 64-15721. (Classics to grow on). 1966. Parent's Magazine's Cultural Institute.

Tales of Edgar Allan Poe. Edgar Allan Poe. Ed. by Wilson, James Southall. LC 27-7510. (Half-title: The modern student's library). C. Scribner's Sons.

Tales of Edgar Allan Poe. Edgar Allan Poe. Ed. by Ati Forberg. LC 79-105826. (Golden Press classics library). (Illus.). 3.50 (ISBN 0-307-12227-1). Golden Press.

Tales of Espionage and Intrique: The Secret Agent in Literature. Arthur Liebman. LC 76-21875. (Masterworks of mystery series). 1976. 7.97 (ISBN 0-8239-0311-7). Richards Rosen Press.

Tales of European Life. LC 8-25572. 1870. Loring.

Tales of Fantasy. Larry Todd. (Troubador monster series). (Illus.). 1975. (pbk.) 2.00 (ISBN 0-912300-60-4). Troubador Press.

Tales of Fantasy and Fact. Brander Matthews. LC 73-98586. (Short story index reprint series). (Illus.). 1969. Books for Libraries Press.

Tales of Fantasy and Fact. Brander Matthews. 1896. Harper & Brothers.

Tales of Fear & Frightening Phenomena: An Anthology. Ed. by Helen Hoke. LC 82-7299. 11.50 (ISBN 0-525-66789-X). E. P. Dutton.

Tales of Flemish Life. Hendrik Conscience. LC 42-332301. 1857. Dix, Edwards & Co.

Tales of Fun & Flagellation. Lord Spanker & Lady Spanker. 1972. pap. 1.95 o.s.i. (V1092T, Venus). Grove.

Tales of Glauber-Spa. Ed. by William Cullen Bryant. LC 69-11880. (American short story series, v. 37-38). (Library of select novels, 27-28). 1969. Garrett Press.

Tales of Glauber-Spa. Ed. by William Cullen Bryant. LC 1-15462. (Library of select novels. 27-28). 1832. J. & J. Harper.

Tales of Good and Evil. Nikolai Vasilevich Gogol. LC 57-11419. (Doubleday anchor books, A120). 1957. Doubleday.

Tales of Gooseflesh and Laughter: By John Wyndham Pseud. John Beynon Harris. LC 56-12818. (Ballantine books, 182). Ballantine Books.

Tales of Great Dragons. John K. Anderson. (Illus.). 64p. 1980. pap. 3.50 (ISBN 0-88388-075-X). Bellerophon Bks.

Tales of Hashish. Ed. by Andrew Kimmens. (Illus.). 1977. 8.95 (ISBN 0-688-03194-3); pap. 4.95 (ISBN 0-688-08194-0). Morrow.

Tales of Hearsay. Joseph Conrad. LC 25-4859. 1925. Doubleday, Page & Company.

Tales of Henry James: Vol. 1, 1864-1869. Henry James. Ed. by Maqbool Aziz. (Illus.). 1973. 39.00x (ISBN 0-19-812457-0). Oxford U Pr.

Tales of Hoffman. William Hoffman. LC 61-18644. 1961. T. S. Denison.

Tales of Hoffmann. Ernst Theodor Amadeus Hoffmann. Ed. by Michael Bullock. LC 63-21988. 1963. Ungar.

Tales of Horror & Fantasy. Ambrose Gwinnett Bierce. 228p. Repr. of 1907 ed. lib. bdg. 13.55x (ISBN 0-89190-187-6). Am Repr-Rivercity Pr.

Tales of Horror and the Supernatural. Arthur Machen & Stern Philip Van Doren, 1900- Ed. LC 48-758919. 1948. A. A. Knopf.

Tales of Horror and the Supernatural: Introd. by Philip Van Doren Stern. Arthur Machen. Ed. by Philip Van Doren Stern. LC 64-57246. 6.00. J. Baker.

Tales of Horror and the Supernatural: The Occult in Literature. Ed. by Arthur Liebman. LC 73-84994. 1974. (lib. bdg.) 6.96 (ISBN 0-8239-0299-4). R. Rosen Press.

Tales of Horror and the Supernatural: The Occult in Literature. Ed. by Arthur Liebman. LC 73-94058. 1974. 6.96 (ISBN 0-8239-0299-4). R. Rosen Press.

Tales of Humour and Romance: Selected from Popular German Writers. Ed. by Richard Holcraft. Hoffmann, Ernst Theodor Wilhelm, 1776-1822 et al. LC 7-13308. 1829. J. Seymour, Etc.

Tales of India. Rudyard Kipling. LC 35-20672. (Wisdermere series). Rand, McNally & Company.

Tales of Insouciant Youth. George Brakeley White. LC 34-5794. 1933. H. S. Jacobs & Co., Inc.

Tales of Intrigue and Revenge. Stephen McKenna. LC 72-128738. (Short story index reprint series). 1970. Books for Libraries Press.

Tales of Intrigue and Revenge. Stephen McKenna. LC 25-7204. 1925. Little, Brown, and Company.

Tales of Ireland. William Carleton. Ed. by Robert L. Wolff. (Ireland Nineteenth Century Fiction - Ser. Two: Vol. 36). 384p. 1979. lib. bdg. 32.00 (ISBN 0-8240-3485-6). Garland Pub.

Tales of Irish Life and Character. Anna Maria Fielding Hall. LC 78-174395. 1971. B. Blom.

Tales of Irish Life and Character. Anna Maria Fielding Hall. LC 74-134964. (Short story index reprint series). (Illus.). 1970. (ISBN 0-8369-3694-9). Books for Libraries Press.

Tales of Japanese Justice. Saikaku Ihara. Tr. by Thomas M. Kondo & Alfred H. Marks. 1980. pap. text ed. 7.50x (ISBN 0-8248-0669-7). UH Pr.

Tales of John Oliver Hobbes Pseud. "Some Emotions and a Moral,""A Study in Temptations," "The Sinner's Comedy," "A Bundle of Life.". Pearl Mary Teresa Richards Craigie. LC 7-41412. F. A. Stokes Company.

Tales of Joujouka. Hamri. Ed. by Edouard Roditi. Tr. by Blanca Nyland. (Capra Chapbook Ser.: No. 35). (Illus.). 48p. (Orig.). 1975. pap. 2.50 o.p. (ISBN 0-88496-044-7). Capra Pr.

Tales of King Arthur. Thomas Malory & Michael Senior. LC 81-40412. (Illus.). 1981. 24.95 (ISBN 0-8052-3779-8). Schocken Books.

Tales of Labor. Albert Scott Ames. LC 36-35986. Welles Press.

Tales of Land & Sea. Joseph Conrad. (Illus.). 1953. 4.95 o.p. Doubleday.

Tales of Land and Sea: Illustrated by Richard M. Powers. Introd. by William McFee. Joseph Conrad. LC 53-12929. 1953. N. Y., Hanover House.

Tales of Lincolnshire. Herbert Rhoades Crocock. LC 26-13384. Printed by Wing & Co.

Tales of Love and Fury... By Irving Shulman and Others. Irving Shulman. LC 54-23522. (Avon, 549). 1953. Avon Publications.

Tales of Love & Hate. Arthur Conan Doyle. pap. 1.95 o.p. Transatlantic.

Tales of Love, Fantasy & Horror: A Taste of Poe in the Spanish-American Short Story. Gustavo Adolfo Becquer et al. Tr. by Russell C. Peterson. 1971. 4.00 o.p. (ISBN 0-682-47271-9). Exposition.

Tales of Love, Fantasy, and Horror: A Taste of Poe in the Spanish-American Short Story. Russell C. Peterson. LC 70-25120. 1971. 4.00 (ISBN 0-682-47271-9). Exposition Press.

Tales of Manhattan. Louis Auchincloss. (95-178). 1968. Popular Lib.

Tales of Manhattan. Louis Auchincloss. LC 67-12670. 1967. Houghton Mifflin.

Tales of Many Lands. Rose Anne Braendle. LC 7-2056. Press of Gibson Bros.

Tales of Mean Streets. Arthur Morrison. LC 78-128742. (Short story index reprint series). 1970. Books for Libraries Press.

Tales of Mean Streets... Arthur Morrison. LC 22-247810. 1895. Roberts Brothers.

Tales of Mean Streets. Arthur Morrison. R. F. Fenno & Company.

Tales of Mean Streets. Arthur Morrison. LC 22-15856. (Half-title: The modern library of the world's best books). Boni and Liveright.

Tales of Mean Streets. Lizerunt, Squire Napper, Without Visible Means, Three Rounds, and Others. Arthur Morrison. (On cover: Seaside library. Pocket ed. no. 2142). 1895. G. Munro's Sons.

Tales of Melvil's Mouser. Ed. by Paul S. Dunkin. LC 74-131911. (5 x 8 1/2. Here is a collection of 44 satirical essays on librarianship. Includes such topics as free access to information, education for librarianship, and the information explosion). (Illus.). 182p. 1970. 12.95 o.p. (ISBN 0-8352-0467-7). Bowker.

Tales of Men and Ghosts. Edith Newbold Jones Wharton. LC 10-23944. 1910. C. Scribner's Sons.

Tales of Military Life. 2d ed. George Robert Gleig. LC 6-43983. 1833. Key and Biddle.

Tales of Monterey. Ed. by Davis Dutton & Judy Davis. (Comstock Editions). (Orig.). 1974. pap. 1.50 o.p. (24075-8-150). Comstock Edns.

Tales of Moonlight and Rain: Japanese Gothic Tales. Akinari Ueda. LC 79-175064. (Illus.). 1972. 7.50 (ISBN 0-231-03631-0). Columbia University Press.

Tales of Moonlight & Rain: Japanese Gothic Tales. Akinari Uyeda. Tr. by Kengi Hamada from Japanese. LC 79-175064. (Illus.). 1972. 15.00x (ISBN 0-231-03631-0). Columbia U Pr.

Tales of My Landlord. First Series. Black Dwarf. Old Mortality... From the Last Revised Edition, Containing the Author's Final Corrections, Notes, &C. parker's ed. Walter Scott. LC 44-15523. (Waverley novels: library edition. Vol. v). 1855. Sanborn, Carter and Bazin.

Tales of My Native Town. Gabriele D' Annunzio. 1968. Greenwood Press.

Tales of My Native Town. Gabriele D' Annunzio. LC 30-6706. 1920. Doubleday, Page & Company.

Tales of My Native Town. Gabriele D'Annunzio. Tr. by Rafael Mantellini. LC 69-10065. Repr. of 1920 ed. lib. bdg. 17.75x (ISBN 0-8371-0056-9, DANT). Greenwood.

Tales of My Neighbourhood. Gerald Griffin. (Nineteenth Century Fiction Ser.: Ireland: Vol. 30). 956p. 1979. lib. bdg. 46.00 (ISBN 0-8240-3479-1). Garland Pub.

Tales of My People. Shalom Asch. LC 75-128752. (Short story index reprint series). 1970. Books for Libraries Press.

Tales of Mystery. Edgar Allan Poe. LC 4-1888. (Half-title: The unit books, no. 3). 1903. H. W. Bell.

Tales of Mystery. Ernest Rhys. Ed. by C. A. Dawson-Scott. Repr. 10.00 (ISBN 0-8414-7427-3). Folcroft.

Tales of Mystery. George Saintsbury. Repr. of 1891 ed. 10.00 (ISBN 0-8414-8173-3). Folcroft.

Tales of Mystery and Horror. Maurice Level & Macklin, Alys Eyre, Tr. LC 20-182553. 1920. R. M. McBride & Co.

Tales of Mystery and Imagination. Edgar Allan Poe. Ed. by Harry Clarke. LC 77-364949. (Illus.). 1977. 27.50 (ISBN 0-85636-000-7). Minerva Press.

Tales of Mystery and Imagination. Edgar Allan Poe. LC 33-24665. (Half-title: The world's classics. xxi). 1928. H. Milford, Oxford University Press.

Tales of Mystery & Imagination. Edgar Allan Poe. LC 36-271351. 1935. J. B. Lippincott Co.

Tales of Mystery & Imagination. With an Introd. by Vincent Starrett & Photogravures of the Original Aquatints by William Sharp. Edgar Allan Poe. LC 58-3546. 1958. Heritage Press.

Tales of Mystery & Immagination. Edgar Allan Poe. (Illus.). 384p. deluxe ed. 11.95 slipcased in half-linen with decorated sides o.p. (ISBN 0-89050-254-4). Heritage Conn.

Tales of Mystery and Melodrama. Leonard R. N. Ashley. LC 75-33668. 1975. 1.95 (ISBN 0-8120-0477-9). Barron's Educational Service.
Tales of Mystic India. Dampier-Bennett, MV. LC 77-364072. 1976. 3.00 (ISBN 0-7223-0874-4). Stockwell.
Tales of N. S. Leskov. Nikolai Semenovich Leskov. LC 76-23887. (Classics of Russian literature). (Hyperion library of world literature). 1977. 10.50. (ISBN 0-88355-499-2). Hyperion Press.
Tales of Neveryon. Samuel R. Delany. 1979. pap. 2.25 (ISBN 0-553-12333-5). Bantam.
Tales of New England. Sarah Orne Jewett. LC 77-110223. (Short story index reprint series). 1970. Books for Libraries Press.
Tales of New England. Sarah Orne Jewett. LC 5-2447. 1894. Houghton, Mifflin and Company.
Tales of New England. Sarah Orne Jewett. LC 12-23267. (Riverside school library). Houghton, Mifflin & Company; Etc., Etc.
Tales of O. Henry. O. Henry. 6.95 o.p. (ISBN 0-385-02877-6). Doubleday.
Tales of O. Henry. William Sydney Porter. LC 71-6700. 1969. International Collectors Library.
Tales of Old Cairo. Najib Mahfuz. pap. 5.50x Arabic (ISBN 0-86685-150-X). Intl Bk Ctr.
Tales of Old Flanders. Count Hugo of Craenhove, Wooden Clara and The Village Innkeeper. Three Tales. Hendrik Conscience. LC 6-28057. 1856. Murphy &Co.
Tales of Old Hawai'i. Russ Apple & Peg Apple. LC 77-78112. (Illus.). 1977. pap. 4.00 (ISBN 0-89610-040-5). Island Her.
Tales of Oliver Pig. 1980. lib. bdg. 5.89 (ISBN 0-8252-8736-7); pap. 1.95 (ISBN 0-8252-8737-5). Quist.
Tales of Our Coast. Samuel Rutherford Crockett. LC 70-116966. (Short story index reprint series). (Illus.). 1970. Books for Libraries Press.
Tales of Our Coast... Samuel Rutherford Crockett et al. LC 3-20109. 1896. Dodd, Mead and Company.
Tales of Our People: Great Stories of the Jew in America. Ed. by Jerry D. Lewis. LC 69-17510. 1969. 6.95. Bernard Geis Associates.
Tales of Padre Pio: The Friar of San Giovanni. John McCaffery. LC 81-43068. 224p. 1981. pap. 4.50 (ISBN 0-385-17739-9, Im). Doubleday.
Tales of Passion. Francis Barry Boyle St. Leger. LC 8-3723. 1829. J. & J. Harper.
Tales of Petrolea and Elsewhere. Edward Buell Bloss. LC 40-118152. Dorrance & Co., Inc.
Tales of Piracy, Crime and Ghosts. Daniel Defoe & Withers, Carl, Ed. LC 46-5468. (On cover: Penguin books, 554). 1945. Penguin Books.
Tales of Poindi. Jean Mariotti. Tr. by Averill, Esther. LC 38-38711. Dominio Press.
Tales of Power. Carlos Castaneda. 287p. 1975. pap. 4.95 (ISBN 0-671-22144-2, Touchstone Bks). S&S.
Tales of Rabbi Nachman. Martin Buber. Tr. by Maurice Friedman. 6.00 o.p. (ISBN 0-8446-1758-X). Peter Smith.
Tales of Rabbi Nachman. Martin Buber. Tr. by Maurice Friedman. 1968. 4.95 o.p. (ISBN 0-8180-1300-1). Horizon.
Tales of Raindrop, the Cloud Fairy. Barbara Scott. 2.95 o.p. Vantage.
Tales of Rollo. Daniel J. Smith. 3.50 o.p. Vantage.
Tales of Rudy Raccoon & Fritz Fox. William R. Zimmerman. 2.50 o.p. Vantage.
Tales of St. Augustine. Nina L. Smith. LC 8-9620. W. H. Wheeler.
Tales of Science and Sorcery. Clark Ashton Smith. LC 65-208. 4.00. Arkham.
Tales of Science Fiction. Ed. by Brian N. Ball. LC 71-549414. (Peacock books). 1968. Penguin.
Tales of Sea & Shore. Edward R. Snow. (Illus.). 1966. 4.50 o.p. (ISBN 0-396-05448-X). Dodd.
Tales of Secret Egypt. Sax Rohmer. 1976. Repr. of 1918 ed. lib. bdg. 16.85x (ISBN 0-89190-809-9). Am Repr-Rivercity Pr.
Tales of Secret Egypt. Arthur Sarsfield Ward. LC 21-3636. (Oriental mystery stories). 1920. R. M. McBride & Company.
Tales of Secret Egypt. Arthur Sarsfield Ward. LC 26-7491. 1920. McKinlay, Stone & Mackenzie.
Tales of Sherlock Holmes. Arthur Conan Doyle. LC 63-14835. (Macmillan classics, 24). (Illus.). 1963. Macmillan.
Tales of Sherlock Holmes. Arthur Conan Doyle. LC 6-28762. A. L. Burt Company.
Tales of Sherlock Holmes. Arthur Conan Doyle. LC 16-7020. 1915. Grosset & Dunlap.
Tales of Sherlock Holmes. Arthur Conan Doyle. LC 43-27405. 1932. National Home Library Foundation.
Tales of Sherlock Holmes. LC 63-14835. (Macmillan classics, 24). 1963. Macmillan.
Tales of Soldiers and Civilians. Ambrose Gwinnett Bierce. LC 70-121522. (Short story index reprint series). 1970. Books for Libraries Press.
Tales of Soldiers and Civilians. Ambrose Gwinnett Bierce. LC 11-10540. 1891. E. L. G. Steele.
Tales of Space and Time. Herbert George Wells. LC 72-3285. (Short story index reprint series). 1972. 12.75 (ISBN 0-8369-4166-7). Books for Libraries Press.
Tales of Space and Time. Herbert George Wells. LC 99-5480. 1899. Doubleday & McClure Co.
Tales of Student Life. Hermann Hesse. LC 75-35871. 1976. 8.95. Farrar, Straus and Giroux.
Tales of Suspense: Edited by Robert Ashley and Herbert Van Thal. Lithographs by Anne Scott. Wilkie Collins. LC 54-10162. 1954. Library Publishers.
Tales of Telal. Hanford Montrose Burr. LC 14-155671. 1914. The Seminar Publishing Company.
Tales of Ten Worlds. Arthur Charles Clarke. (Signet Books, Q5452). 1973. 0.95. New American Library.
Tales of Ten Worlds. Arthur Charles Clarke. LC 62-16730. 1962. Harcourt, Brace & World.
Tales of Terror. Ed. by Joseph Lewis French. LC 73-37269. (Short story index reprint series). (Illus.). 1971. (ISBN 0-8369-4080-6). Books for Libraries Press.
Tales of Terror. Ed. by Joseph Lewis French. LC 26-180. Small, Maynard & Company.
Tales of Terror & Darkness. Algernon Blackwood. 1978. 14.00 o.p. (ISBN 0-600-30347-0). Transatlantic.
Tales of Terror and Mystery. Arthur Conan Doyle. LC 75-36589. (Illus.). 1977. 7.95 (ISBN 0-385-11448-6). Doubleday.
Tales of Terror and Mystery. Arthur Conan Doyle. LC 78-21982. 3.95 (ISBN 0-14-004878-2). New York.
Tales of Terror & Mystery. Arthur Conan Doyle. pap. 1.95 o.p. Transatlantic.
Tales of Terror and the Supernatural. Wilkie Collins. LC 75-189974. 1972. 3.00 (ISBN 0-486-20307-7). Dover Publications.
Tales of Terror & the Supernatural. Ed. by Herbert Van Thal. 5.50 o.p. (ISBN 0-8446-4725-X). Peter Smith.
Tales of Terror & the Unknown. Algernon Blackwood. (Orig.). pap. 1.95 o.p. (ISBN 0-525-47166-9). Dutton.
Tales of Terror and the Unknown. Pref. by the Author. Algernon Blackwood. LC 65-2340. (D166). 1965. pap., 1.75. Dutton.
Tales of Terror & Tragedy. Edward R. Snow. LC 79-21872. (Illus.). 1979. 8.95 o.p. (ISBN 0-396-07775-7). Dodd.
Tales of Terror & Wonder. M. G. Lewis. 283p. 1980. Repr. of 1887 ed. lib. bdg. 30.00 (ISBN 0-8492-6304-2). R West.
Tales of Terror: Or, The Mysteries of Magic: a Selection of Wonderful and Supernatural Stories, Translated from the Chinese, Turkish, and German. Ed. by St. Clair, Henry. LC 4-35652. 1848. J. Harding.
Tales of Terror, Selected: With an Introduction. Ed. by Boris Karloff. LC 43-16438. 1943. The World Publishing Company.
Tales of the Argonauts. Bret Harte. 1875. Repr. lib. bdg. 25.00 (ISBN 0-8414-5014-5). Folcroft.
Tales of the Argonauts and Eastern Sketches. Bret Harte. LC 12-27751. (Half-title: The works of Bret Harte. Riverside edition... v 3). 1882. Houghton, Mifflin and Company.
Tales of the Argonauts, and Other Sketches. Bret Harte. LC 78-152943. (Short story index reprint series). 1971. (ISBN 0-8369-3802-X). Books for Libraries Press.
Tales of the Argonauts, and Other Sketches. Bret Harte. LC 3-29617. Houghton, Mifflin and Company.
Tales of the Bald Eagle Mountains in Central Pennsylvania. Henry Wharton Shoemaker. LC 13-312. The Bright Printing Company.
Tales of the Black Cat. Najib Mahfuz. pap. 5.50x Arabic (ISBN 0-86685-157-7). Intl Bk Ctr.
Tales of the Black Widowers. Isaac Asimov. LC 73-9010. 1974. 5.95. Doubleday.
Tales of the Black Widowers. Isaac Asimov. 1976. 1.50 (ISBN 0-449-22944-0). Fawcett Crest.
Tales of the Border. James Hall. LC 74-104471. 1970. (ISBN 0-8398-0756-2). Literature House.
Tales of the Border. James Hall. LC 7-314. 1835. H. Hall.
Tales of the Caddo. John Tomlin. LC 8-25980. 1849. Printed at the Office of "The Great West,
Tales of the Caravanserai. James Baillie Fraser. (Added t.-p.: The library of romance v. 7). 1833. Carey, Lea and Blanchard.
Tales of the Caribbean. 1st Ed. Garland Roark. LC 59-6271. 1959. Doubleday.
Tales of the Caucasus: The Ball of Snow, and Sultanetta. Alexandre Dumas & Pushkin, Aleksandr Sergrevich. LC 6-42315. (Half-title: The romances of Alexandre Dumas. Illustrated library ed. New series. v. 6). 1895. Little, Brown, and Company.
Tales of the Chesapeake. George Alfred Townsend. LC 8-29823. 1880. American News Company.
Tales of the City. Armistead Maupin. LC 77-11781. (Harper colophon book; CN654-). 5.95. Harper & Row.
Tales of the City Room. Elizabeth Garver Jordan. LC 70-116958. (Short story index reprint series). 1970. Books for Libraries Press.
Tales of the City Room. Elizabeth Garver Jordan. LC 7-11692. 1898. C. Scribner's Sons.
Tales of the Cloister. Elizabeth Garver Jordan. LC 76-110204. (Short story index reprint series). (Illus.). 1970. Books for Libraries Press.
Tales of the Cloister. Elizabeth Garver Jordan. LC 1-21983. (On cover: Harper's portrait collection of short stories. v. 4). 1901. Harper & Brothers.
Tales of the Cochiti Indians. Ruth Benedict. LC 80-54563. 256p. 1982. 12.95 (ISBN 0-8263-0569-5). U of NM Pr.
Tales of the Convict System: Selected Stories of Price Warung I.E. W. Astley. William Astley & B. G Andrews. LC 76-356503. 1975. 18.95 (ISBN 0-7022-0929-5). University of Queensland.
Tales of the Cthulhu Mythos. Ed. by August William Derleth. Howard Phillips Lovecraft. LC 72-14474. 1969. 7.50. Arkham House.
Tales of the Cthulhu Mythos. Howard Phillips Lovecraft et al. Ed. by August Derleth. 1969. 7.50 o.p. (ISBN 0-87054-030-0). Arkham.
Tales of the Cthulhu Mythos Vol. 1. Howard Phillips Lovecraft et al. 1971. pap. 0.95 o.p. (95080). Beagle Bks.
Tales of the Cthulhu Myths, Vol. 2. Howard Phillips Lovecraft et al. (Boxer Ser). 1971. pap. 0.95 o.p. (95124). Beagle Bks.
Tales of the Don. Mikhail Aleksandrovich Sholokhov. LC 62-8669. 1962. Knopf.
Tales of the Eskimo: Being Impressions of a Strenuous, Indominatable, and Cheerful Little People. With Photographs by the Author. Henry Toke Munn. LC 26-13385. 1925. W. & R. Chambers, Limited.
Tales of the Ex-Tanks: A Book of Hard-Luck Stories. Clarence Louis Cullen. LC 5016. 1900. Grosset & Dunlap.
Tales of the Ex-Tanks: A Book of Hard Luck Stories. Clarence Louis Cullen. LC 24-22230. Grosset & Dunlap.
Tales of the Fairies & of the Ghost World Collected from Oral Tradition in South-West Munster. Jeremiah Curtin. LC 71-110294. 1970. Repr. of 1895 ed lib bdg. 10.00 o.s.i. (ISBN 0-87696-005-0). Lemma.
Tales of the Fairies & the Ghost-World. Jeremiah Curtin. LC 75-152760. Repr. of 1895 ed. 14.00 (ISBN 0-405-08416-1, Blom Pubns). Ayer Co.
Tales of the Fireside. LC 8-25569. 1827. Hilliard, Gray, Little and Wilkins.
Tales of the Fish Patrol. Jack London. LC 72-4454. (Short story index reprint series). 1972. 10.50 (ISBN 0-8369-4181-0). Books for Libraries Press.
Tales of the Fish Patrol. Jack London. LC 67-29242. (Abercrombie & Fitch library). (Illus.). 1967. Arno Press.
Tales of the Fish Patrol. Jack London. LC 5-32831. 1905. The Macmillan Company.
Tales of the Five Towns. Arnold Bennett. LC 74-17131. (Collected works of Arnold Bennett). 1974. (ISBN 0-518-19158-3). Books for Libraries Press.
Tales of the Flying Mountains. Poul Anderson. LC 76-108145. 1970. Macmillan.
Tales of the French Revolution. Harriet Martineau. (On cover: Lovell's library, v. 7, no. 353). 1884. J. W. Lovell Company.
Tales of the Frightened. 3rd ed. Ed. by Boris Karloff & Michael Avallone. 1969. pap. 0.60 o.p. (1024). Belmont-Tower.
Tales of the Galactic Midway, No. 1: Sideshow. Mike Resnick. 1982. pap. 2.50 (ISBN 0-451-11848-0, AE1848, Sig). NAL.
Tales of the Galactic Midway, No. 2: The Three-Legged Hootch Dancer. Mike Resnick. (No. 2). 155p. 1983. pap. 2.50 (Sig). NAL.
Tales of the Garden of Kosciusko. Samuel Lorenzo Knapp. LC 7-142804. 1834. Printed by West & Trow.
Tales of the Good Woman. James Kirke Paulding. LC 7-34065. 1829. G. & C. & H. Carvill.
Tales of the Good Woman. James Kirke Paulding. Ed. by Paulding, William Irving. LC 7-34063. 1867. C. Scribner and Company.
Tales of the Great St. Bernard... George Croly. LC 6-32154. 1829. Printed by J. & J. Harper.
Tales of the Grotesque & Curious. Ryunosuke Akutagawa. Tr. by G. W. Shaw. 3.00 o.p. Japan Pubns.
Tales of the Heart. Roland Burke Hennessy. LC 7-41263. 1897. Meyer Brothers & Co.
Tales of the Home Folks in Peace and War. Joel Chandler Harris. LC 7-2894. 1898. Houghton, Mifflin and Company.
Tales of the Jazz Age. Francis Scott Key Fitzgerald. LC 22-18785. 1922. C. Scribner's Sons.
Tales of the Labrador. Wilfred Thomason Grenfell. LC 16-22895. 1916. Houghton Mifflin Company.
Tales of the Little Quarter. Jan Neruda. LC 76-49935. 1976. 17.50 (ISBN 0-8371-9344-3). Greenwood Press.
Tales of the Long Bow. Gilbert Keith Chesterton. LC 56-6130. (New world Chesterton). 1956. Sheed and Ward.
Tales of the Long Bow. Gilbert Keith Chesterton. LC 25-159899. 1925. Cassell and Company, Ltd.
Tales of the Long Bow. Gilbert Keith Chesterton. LC 25-20706. 1925. Dodd, Mead and Company.
Tales of the Maine Coast. Noah Brooks. LC 4-15069. 1894. C. Scribner's Sons.
Tales of the Malayan Coast. facs. ed. Rounsevelle Wildman. LC 72-90593. (Short Story Index Reprint Ser.). 1899. 17.00 (ISBN 0-8369-3076-2). Ayer Co.
Tales of the Malayan Coast: From Penang to the Philippines. Rounsevelle Wildman. LC 72-90593. (Short story index reprint series). (Illus.). 1969. Books for Libraries Press.
Tales of the Malayan Coast: From Penang to the Philippines. Rounsevelle Wildman. LC 99-1505. Lothrop Publishing Company.
Tales of the Mountains & the Steppes. Chinquiz Aitmatov. 280p. 1973. 6.95 (ISBN 0-8285-0937-9, Pub. by Progress Pubs USSR). Imported Pubns.
Tales of the Munster Festivals. Gerald Griffin. LC 78-12001. (Ireland, from the Act of Union, 1800, to the Death of Parnell, 1891). 1979. 42.00 (ISBN 0-8240-3476-7). Garland Pub.
Tales of the Natural and Supernatural. Mario Andrew Pei. LC 72-149813. (Illus.). 1971. 5.95. Devin-Adair Co.
Tales of the Niagara Frontier. Pt. 1-2. Jesse Walker. LC 9-3419. 1845. Steele's Press.
Tales of the Northwest. William Joseph Snelling. LC 75-7067. (Garland Library of Narratives of North American Indian Captivities; V. 45). 1976. 21.00 (ISBN 0-8240-1669-6). Garland Pub.
Tales of the Northwest. William Joseph Snelling. LC 70-180636. 1971. 10.00 (ISBN 0-87018-058-4). Ross & Haines.
Tales of the Occult. Ed. by Jack Wolf. LC 75-4340. (Fawcett Crest Book.). 1975. (pbk.) 1.75. Fawcett Publications.
Tales of the Ocean, and Essays for the Forecastle: Containing Matters and Incidents Humorous, Pathetic, Romantic, and Sentimental: Illustrated with Numerous Engravings... John Sherburne Sleeper. LC 20-23157. G. W. Cottrell.
Tales of the O'Hara Family, 3 vols. John Banim & Michael Banim. Ed. by Robert L. Wolff. (Ireland Nineteenth Century Fiction - Ser. Two: Vol. 18). 1080p. 1979. lib. bdg. 96.00 (ISBN 0-8240-3467-8). Garland Pub.
Tales of the Pampas. William Henry Hudson. LC 16-21712. 1916. A. A. Knopf.
Tales of the Pampas. William Henry Hudson. LC 79-26374. 5.95 (ISBN 0-916870-23-5). Creative Arts Book Co.
Tales of the Puritans. The Regicides.--The Fair Pilgrim.--Castine. Delia Salter Bacon. LC 6-15470. 1831. A. H. Malthy.
Tales of the Real Gypsy. Paul Kester. LC 77-142004. 1971. Gryphon Books.
Tales of the Real Gypsy. Paul Kester. 1897. Doubleday and McClure Company.
Tales of the Revolution. Mikhail Petrovich Artsybashev. LC 72-4417. (Short story index reprint series). 1972. (ISBN 0-8369-4168-3). Books for Libraries Press.
Tales of the Revolution. Mikhail Petrovich Artsybashev & Pinkerton, Percy E. LC 17-26653. 1917. B. W. Huebsch.
Tales of the Road. Charles Newman Crewdson. LC 5-30267. 1905. Thompson & Thomas.
Tales of the Sacred & the Supernatural. Mircea Eliade. LC 81-12924. 112p. 1981. pap. 7.95 (ISBN 0-664-24391-6). Westminster.
Tales of the Sandman. Kenneth B. Blois. 1975. 3.95 o.p. (ISBN 0-8059-2216-4). Dorrance.
Tales of the Sierras. Jeff W Hayes. LC 3878. 1900. F. W. Baltes and Company.
Tales of the South Pacific. James A Michener. LC 81-7022. 1981. 18.95 (ISBN 0-8161-3263-1). G.K. Hall.
Tales of the South Pacific. ed. is complete and unabridged ed. James Albert Michener. LC 67-6887. 1967. Macmillan.
Tales of the South Pacific. James Albert Michener. LC 47-301278. 1947. The Macmillan Company.
Tales of the South Pacific. James Albert Michener. (Crest Book, P1790). 1973. 1.25. Fawcett.
Tales of the South Seas. Thornton Jenkins Hains. LC 6-461627. 1894. Brown Thurston Company.

Tales of the Southern Border. Charles Wilkins Webber. LC 14-193491. 1853. Lippincott, Grambo & Co.

Tales of the Southern Border. Charles Wilkins Webber. LC 8-36746. 1868. J. B. Lippincott & Co.

Tales of the Southwest: A Western Story Bonanza... Barry Storm. LC 57-9454. 1958. Storm Pub. Associates.

Tales of the Spanish Seas. Henry William Herbert. LC 7-4296. 1847. Burgess, Stringer & Co.

Tales of the Spring Rain: Harusame Monogatari. Akinari Ueda & Barry Jackman. LC 75-330677. (Japan Foundation Translation Series). 10.50. University of Tokyo Press.

Tales of the Sun-Land: By Verner Z. Reed... Illustrated by L. Maynard Dixon... Verner Zevola Reed. LC 7-30946. 1897. Continental Publishing Co.

Tales of the Supernatural. Stephaine Dowrick. pap. 1.95 (Evman). Biblio Dist.

Tales of the Tatras: Foreword by Carl Carmer. Kazimierz Tetmajer & Kennedy, Harriette Eleanor, Tr. LC 43-185539. 1943. Roy.

Tales of the Tatterman. Doven Hayes. Ed. by Roberta Munro. (Illus.). 1977. pap. 3.95 (ISBN 0-918774-00-4). Fig Leaf.

Tales of the Telegraph: The Story of a Telegrapher's Life and Adventures in Railroad, Commercial, and Military Work. Jasper Ewing Brady. LC 99-4628. 1899. Doubleday & McClure Co.

Tales of the Thumb. Charles Louis Severance. LC 72-86863. 1972. 3.95 (ISBN 0-8059-1743-8). Dorrance.

Tales of the Town. Charles Belmont Davis. LC 78-167447. (Short story index reprint series). (Illus.). 1971. (ISBN 0-8369-3973-5). Books for Libraries Press.

Tales of the Town. Charles Belmont Davis. LC 11-19989. 1911. 1.30. Duffield and Company.

Tales of the Trail: Short Stories of Western Life. Henry Inman. 1898. Crane & Company.

Tales of the Tripod: Or, A Delphian Evening. Tabias Watkins. LC 8-36762. 1821. F. Lucas, Jr.

Tales of the Turf. Hugh S Fullerton. LC 22-15206. A. R. DeBeer.

Tales of the Uncanny and Supernatural. Algernon Blackwood. LC 50-105. 1949. P. Nevill.

Tales of the Undead, Vampires and Visitants. Ed. by Elinore Blaisdell. LC 47-3319. 1947. Thomas Y. Crowell Company.

Tales of the Village. Francis Edward Paget. LC 42-268901. 1844. D. Appleton & Co.

Tales of the Werewolf Clan, Vol. II. H. Warner Munn. 12.00 (ISBN 0-937986-29-1). D M Grant.

Tales of the West of Ireland. 3rd ed. James Berry. Ed. by Gertrude M. Horgan. (Yeats Cent. Papers Ser.: Vol. 8). 186p. 1975. text ed. 13.75x (ISBN 0-85105-285-1, Dolmen Pr); pap. text ed. 4.50x (ISBN 0-85105-286-X). Humanities.

Tales of the White Hills: And Sketches. Nathaniel Hawthorne. LC 7-3771. (On cover: Riverside literature series, no. 40). 1889. Houghton, Mifflin and Company.

Tales of the Wilderness. Boris Pilnyak. Tr. by F. O'Dempsey from Rus. LC 72-90306. (Soviet Literature in English Translation Ser.). 223p. 1973. Repr. of 1925 ed. 16.50 (ISBN 0-88355-017-2). Hyperion Conn.

Tales of the Wilderness. Boris Andreevich Vogau. LC 72-90306. 1973. 12.00 (ISBN 0-88355-017-2). Hyperion Press.

Tales of the Wilderness. Boris Andreevich Vogau. LC 72-169567. (Short story index reprint series). 1971. (ISBN 0-8369-4030-X). Books for Libraries Press.

Tales of the Wilderness. Boris Andreevich Vogau & O'Dempsey, F., Tr. LC 25-955737. 1925. A. A. Knopf.

Tales of the Woods and Fields. Anne Marsh-Caldwell. LC 8-33291. 1836. Harper & Brothers.

Tales of Three Centuries. Mikhail Nikolaevich Zagoskin & Curtin, Jeremiah, 1840-1906, Tr. LC 9-2206. 1891. Little, Brown, and Company.

Tales of Three Cities. Henry James. LC 7-7433. 1884. J. R. Osgood and Company.

Tales of Three Hemispheres. Edward John Moreton Drax Plunkett Dunsany. LC 76-381702. (Illus.). 1976. 9.00 (ISBN 0-913896-06-3). Owlswick Press.

Tales of Three Planets. Edgar Rice Burroughs. LC 64-15792. (Illus.). 1975. Repr. 10.00 (ISBN 0-940724-09-X). Canaveral.

Tales of to-Day. George Robert Sims. LC 8-9004. F. F. Lovell & Company.

Tales of to-Day and Other Days: From the French... Alfred De Musset et al. LC 8-20108. Cassell Publishing Company.

Tales of Today: Contemporary Stories of Breathless Adventure, Brave Deeds, & Humble Service. H. L. Gee. 1978. Repr. of 1942 ed. lib. bdg. 15.00 (ISBN 0-8492-0971-4). R West.

Tales of Tongue Fu. Paul Krassner. LC 80-16192. (Illus.). 130p. 1981. pap. 4.95 (ISBN 0-915904-55-1). And-or Pr.

Tales of Trail and Town. Bret Harte. LC 70-121562. (Short story index reprint series). 1970. Books for Libraries Press.

Tales of Trail and Town. Bret Harte. LC 7-3652. 1898. Houghton, Mifflin and Company.

Tales of Troy and Greece. Andrew Lang. LC 37-15471. 1936. Longmans, Green and Co.

Tales of Two Countries. Maksim Gorkii. LC 70-160933. (Short story index reprint series). 1971. (ISBN 0-8369-3912-3). Books for Libraries Press.

Tales of Two Countries. Maksim Gorkii. 1914. B. W. Huebsch.

Tales of Two Countries. facsimile ed. Maksim Gorkii. LC 70-160933. (Short Story Index Reprint Ser.). Repr. of 1914 ed. 15.00 (ISBN 0-8369-3912-3). Ayer Co.

Tales of Two Countries. Alexander Lange Kielland. LC 71-98580. (Short story index reprint series). (Illus.). 1969. Books for Libraries Press.

Tales of Two Countries. Alexander Lange Kielland & Archer, William, 1856- Tr. LC 5-2449. 1891. Harper and Brothers.

Tales of Unease. John Frederick Burke. LC 69-10966. 1969. 4.95. Doubleday.

Tales of Unrest. Joseph Conrad. LC 73-8283. 1974. 29.95. Gordon Press.

Tales of Unrest. Joseph Conrad. LC 77-372195. (Penguin modern classics). 1977. 1.95 (ISBN 0-14-003885-X). Penguin Books.

Tales of War. Mihail Sadoveanu. LC 61-185074. 1962. Twayne Publishers.

Tales of Wells Fargo. Frank Gruber. LC 58-7191. (Bantam books, 1726. Western, 6). 1958. Bantam Books.

Tales of Xavier. James Edward Walsh. LC 46-8524. 1946. Sheed & Ward.

Tales Out of Court. Frederick Trevor Hill. LC 20-18659. 1.60. Frederick A. Stokes Company.

Tales out of the East. Lafcadio Hearn. pap. 1.65 o.p. (ISBN 0-498-04016-X, Prpta). A S Barnes.

Tales Out of the East: Selected by J. I. Rodale Pictures by Jeanyee Wong. Lafcadio Hearn. LC 52-2444. 1952. Story Classics.

Tales Out of Time, Vol. 1: The Mad Compactor & Other Science Fiction Short Stories. Regina Rapier. 1980. 7.50. R C Rapier.

Tales the Boatman Told. Ed. by James Lee. LC 77-89270. (Illus.). 1977. 12.95 (ISBN 0-916838-08-0). Schiffer.

Tales to Be Told in the Dark. Ed. by Basil Davenport. 1953. 4.00 o.p. (ISBN 0-396-03453-5). Dodd.

Tales to Be Told in the Dark: A Selection of Stories from the Great Authors, Arranged for Reading and Telling Aloud. Ed. by Basil Davenport. LC 52-14111. 1953. Dodd, Mead.

Tales to Fill You with Fear & Trembling. Eleanor Sullivan. 348p. 1980. 9.95 (ISBN 0-8037-0392-9). Dial.

Tales to Tell. Larry G. Stenzel. 128p. (Orig.). 1979. pap. 4.50 (ISBN 0-910021-00-7). Samuel P Co.

Tales Told by Simpson. May Sinclair. LC 73-151228. (Short story index reprint series). 1971. (ISBN 0-8369-3859-3). Books for Libraries Press.

Tales Told by Simpson. May Sinclair. LC 30-22752. 1930. The Macmillan Company.

Tales Told in Palestine. James Edward Hanauer & Mitchell, Hinckley Gilbert Thomas, 1816-1920, Ed. LC 5-11353. Jennings and Graham.

Tales Worth Retelling: Adapted and Edited by Herzl Fife. Illustrated by Thomas G. Fraumeni. Ed. by Herzl Fife. LC 50-8007. 1950. Globe Book Co.

TaleSpinners I, 8 bks. Incl. Balloon Spies. Dudley Bromley. LC 80-65914 (ISBN 0-8224-6730-5); Better Than New. Douglas Hiller. LC 80-65915 (ISBN 0-8224-6731-3); Death Angel. Earle Rice, Jr. LC 80-65913 (ISBN 0-8224-6729-1); Dream Pirate. Jack Durish & Nicki Street. LC 80-65918 (ISBN 0-8224-6734-8); Golden God. Jeanne DuPrau. LC 80-65911 (ISBN 0-8224-6727-5); Johnny Tall Dog. Leo P. Kelley. LC 80-65917 (ISBN 0-8224-6733-X); Joker. Nicki Street & A. F. Oreshnik. LC 80-65916 (ISBN 0-8224-6732-1); Man in the Cage. Lisa Eisenberg. LC 80-65912 (ISBN 0-8224-6728-3). (gr. 7). 1981. complete set & tchr's guide 37.12 (ISBN 0-8224-6725-9); 4.64 ea. Pitman Learning.

Talfulano. Bill Rane. LC 75-27249. (Illus.). 1976. 4.00 (ISBN 0-912292-39-3). Smith.

Talien, a Spanish Princess. Edwin Styles Metcalf. LC 10-16326. 0.50. L'Ora Queta Publishing Company.

Taliput Leaves in the Path of the Sunrise. J. Thurber Wing. LC 22-7209. 1921. M. Kennerley.

Talis Qualis; or, Tales of the Jury Room. Gerald Griffin. (Nineteenth Century Fiction Ser.: Ireland: Vol. 31). 942p. 1979. lib. bdg. 46.00 (ISBN 0-8240-3480-5). Garland Pub.

Talisman. Cecily Crowe. LC 79-16342. 1979. 8.95 (ISBN 0-312-78426-0). St. Martin's Press.

Talisman. John Godey. (Berkley Medallion Book). 1977. 1.95 (ISBN 0-425-03492-5). Berkley Pub. Corp.

Talisman. Walter Scott. LC 72-195006. (Illus.). 1972. Heritage Press.

Talisman. Walter Scott. Ed. by Hollbrook, Dwight. (Classics for children). 1886. Ginn & Company.

Talisman. Walter Scott. LC 30-26384. 1929. Dodd, Mead and Company.

Talisman. Walter Scott. Ed. by Trendley, Frederick. Moffett, Harold Young. LC 20-188161. (Half-title: New pocket classics). The Macmillan Company.

Talisman. Walter Scott. Ed. by Maxfield, Ezra Kempton. LC 30-286320. (Half-title: Nelson's English series; general editor, E. Bernbaum). 1930. T. Nelson and Sons.

Talisman. Walter Scott. LC 36-37015. (Half-title: Everyman's library, ed. by Ernest Rhys. Fiction. no. 144). 1935. J. M. Dent & Sons, Ltd.

Talisman. Walter Scott. LC 43-51244. (On cover: Great illustrated classics). 1943. Dodd, Mead, & Company.

Talisman.--The Two Drovers. My Aunt Margaret's Mirror. The Tapestried Chamber. The Laird's Jock. Walter Scott. LC 8-5784. (Waverley novels. Illustrated library ed.). 1879. Houghton, Mifflin and Company.

Talisman: A Romance. Walter Scott. Ed. by Trendley, Frederick. LC 4-34125. (On verso of half-title: Macmillan's pocket American and English classics). 1904. The Macmillan Company.

Talisman. A Tale of the Crusaders. Walter Scott. (Franklin square library, no. 78). 1879. Harper & Brothers.

Talisman. A Tale of the Crusaders. Walter Scott. Ed. by Lang, Andrew. LC 15-28129. (On cover: Waverley novels). D. Estes & Company.

Talisman. A Tale of the Crusaders. Walter Scott. (On cover: Cronell series). A. L. Burt Company.

Talisman: A Tale of the Crusaders. Walter Scott. LC 27-203408. (Riverside book-shelf). 1927. Houghton Mifflin Company.

Talisman: A Tale of the Crusaders. Walter Scott. Ed. by Ball, Francis Kingsley. LC 28-132962. Ginn and Company.

Talisman: A Tale of the Crusaders. Walter Scott & Dewey, Julia M. LC 406. (Eclectic school readings). American Book Company.

Talisman: A Tale of the Crusaders, and Chronicles of the Canongate. Walter Scott. LC 8-3044. 1885. G. Routledge and Sons.

Talisman: A Tale of the Crusaders and The Chronicle of the Canongate. Walter Scott. (On cover: Lovell's library, no. 581). 1885. J. W. Lovell Company.

Talisman & Other Stories. Carlos Heard Baker. 192p. 1976. 7.95 o.p. (ISBN 0-684-14473-5). Scribner.

Talisman. Ed. by M. W. and G. Thomas. Illus. by Eric Thomas. Walter Scott. Ed. by Maurice Walton Thomas & Gladys - Thomas. LC 66-6329. (Shorter classics). 1966. bds., 2.50. Ginn.

Talisman of Kubla Khan, 1229-1298. Lititia Beryl Tucker Wingate. LC 29-14766. 1929. R. M. McBride & Company.

Talisman Ring. Georgette Heyer. 1976. 1.50 (ISBN 0-449-23003-1). Fawcett Crest.

Talisman Ring. Georgette Heyer. LC 67-20530. 1967. Dutton.

Talisman Ring. Georgette Heyer. LC 37-12764. 1937. Doubleday, Doran & Company, Inc.

Talismans and Other Stories. Carlos Heard Baker. LC 75-20366. 7.95 (ISBN 0-684-14473-5). Scribner.

Talitha: A Novel of the Old Southland. Ethel R Chavis. LC 63-8346. Greenwich Book Publishers.

Talitha Cumi: A Story of Freedom Through Christian Science. Annie Jefferson Holland. LC 4-326647. 1904. Lee and Shepard.

Talk. Linda Rosenkrantz. LC 68-17002. 1968. Putnam.

Talk. Emanie N. Sachs. LC 24-186742. 1924. Harper & Brothers.

Talk & Contact: Stories. Barbara Wilson. LC 77-52008. 1978. 3.00 (ISBN 0-931188-01-6). Seal Press.

Talk Down. Brian Lecomber. LC 78-5794. (Illus.). 1978. 8.95 (ISBN 0-698-10937-6). Coward, McCann & Geoghegan.

Talk Down. Brian Lecomber. 1979. 2.25 (ISBN 0-425-04196-4). Berkley Pub. Corp.

Talk in the Townlands. Dorothy Mabel Large. 1937. Longmans, Green and Co.

Talk of the Town. June Jennifer. LC 37-328543. 1937. Godwin.

Talk of the Town. Lynn Montross & Montross, Lois Seyster. LC 27-11717. 1927. Harper & Brothers.

Talk of the Town. Ann Pinchot. LC 41-8358. 1941. Houghton Mifflin Company.

Talk of the Town. Joan Smith. LC 78-70934. 1979. 8.95 (ISBN 0-8027-0622-3). Walker.

Talk of the Town. A Novel. James Payn. (On cover: Seaside library. Pocket ed. no. 343). 1885. G. Munro.

Talk of the Twon: A Neighborhood Novel. Elisa Armstrong Bengough. LC 2-25759. (Half-title: Naoelettes de luxe). 1902. D. Appleton & Co.

Talk Show. Noel Bertram Gerson. LC 76-142403. 1971. 6.95. Morrow.

Talk Show Murders. Steve Allen. LC 81-12473. 11.95 (ISBN 0-440-08471-7). Delacorte Press.

Talk Stories. Lillian Ross. (O.S.I.). 1966. 5.95 o.s.i. (ISBN 0-671-70210-6). S&S.

Talk to Me About England. Paul Ferris. LC 78-26797. 1979. 8.95 (ISBN 0-698-10969-4). Coward, McCann & Geoghegan.

Talk to Me About England. Paul Ferris. 1980. 1.95 (ISBN 0-445-04560-4). Fawcett Popular Library.

Talk United States! Robert Whitcomb. LC 35-5376. 1935. H. Smith and R. Haas, Inc.

Talker: A Story of to-Day, from the Play of Marion Fairfax. Arthur Hornblow & Fairfax, Marion. LC 12-21278. G. W. Dillingham Company.

Talkers. Robert William Chambers. LC 23-5521. 1.75. George. H. Doran Company.

Talking at the Boundaries. David Antin. LC 76-15374. 1976. 11.95 (ISBN 0-8112-0559-2); pap. 3.95 (ISBN 0-8112-0560-6, NDP388). New Directions.

Talking Clock. Frank Gruber. LC 40-29648. Farrar & Rinehart, Inc.

Talking Coffins of Cryo-City. Shirley Parenteau. LC 79-20760. 7.95 (ISBN 0-525-66666-4). Elsevier/Nelson Books.

Talking Horse. Thomas Anstey Guthrie. LC 79-103514. (Short story index reprint series). 1969. Books for Libraries Press.

Talking Horse. Thomas Anstey Guthrie. LC 3-21960. J. W. Lovell Company.

Talking Horse. Thomas Anstey Guthrie. LC 3-21959. (On cover: The Strathmore series). 1892. Chicago, United States Book Company.

Talking Image of Urur. Franz Hartmann. LC 7-36584. (On cover: Lovell's international ser. no. 76). J. W. Lovell Company.

Talking Pine. George Moore. LC 76-44812. 1976. Repr. of 1931 ed. lib. bdg. 8.50 (ISBN 0-8414-6059-0). Folcroft.

Talking Rifle. Glenn R Vernam. LC 73-81415. (Doubleday western). 1973. 4.95 (ISBN 0-385-08098-0). Doubleday.

Talking Room: A Novel. Marianne Hauser. LC 75-21557. 8.95. (ISBN 0-914590-20-0) (ISBN 0-914590-21-9). Fiction Collective: Distributed by G. Braziller.

Talking Sparrow Murders. Darwin Le Ora Teilhet. LC 34-20789. 1934. W. Morrow & Co.

Talking Trees. Sean O'Faolain. LC 74-121428. 1970. 6.95 o.p. (ISBN 0-316-63291-0). Little.

Talks with a Devil. P. D. Ouspensky. (O.s.i.). 1973. 5.95 o.s.i. (ISBN 0-394-48537-8). Knopf.

Talks with a Devil. P. D. Ouspensky. 1980. pap. 2.75 (ISBN 0-671-82574-7). PB.

Talks with a Devil. Petr Den'Ianovich Uspenskii. LC 73-4305. 1973-1974. 5.95 (ISBN 0-394-48537-8). Knopf; Distributed by Random House.

Talks with Barbara: Being an Informal and Experimental Discussion, from the Point of View of a Young Woman of to-Morrow, of Certain of the Complexities of Life, Particularly in Regard to the Relations of Men and Women. Elizabeth Knight Tompkins. LC 3127. 1900. G. P. Putnam's Sons.

Tall Against the Sky. Orville Steggerde. LC 61-20159. 1960. Zondervan Pub. House.

Tall and Short Stories. Gloria Jeannette Stanford. LC 77-356420. 1976. Bardac Group.

Tall, Balding & Thirty-Five see Limbo Affair.

Tall, Balding, Thirty-Five. Anthony Firth. LC 67-13701. 1967. Harper & Row.

Tall Baseball Stories. Jiggs Amarant. 1979. 6.95 (ISBN 0-89200-034-1). Atlantis-by-the-Sea.

Tall Baseball Stories. Julius J. Amarant. 1979. 6.95 (ISBN 0-89962-013-2). Todd & Honeywell.

Tall Boots & Yellow Legs. W. Eagen. 5.95 o.p. Carlton.

Tall Brigade: True Adventures of Tom McKay, Brigade Leader for the Early Hudson's Bay Company. Hermia Harris Fraser. LC 56-8827. 1956. Binfords & Mort.

Tall Captains. Bart Spicer. LC 57-5876. Dodd, Mead.

Tall, Dark and Dead. Kermit Jaediker. LC 47-121264. 1947. Mystery House.

Tall, Dark and Deadly. Harold Q. Masur. LC 56-14295. (Inner sanctum mystery). 1956. Simon and Schuster.

Tall, Dark and Deadly. Dark and Deadly. Harold Q Masur. LC 56-142957. (Inner sanctum mystery). 1956. Simon and Schuster.
Tall Dark Man. Anne Chamberlain. LC 55-6822. 1955. Bobbs-Merrill.
Tall Dolores. Michael Avallone. 1973. (pbk) 0.75. Curtis.
Tall Dolores: A Novel of Suspense. 1st Ed. Michael Avallone. LC 52-13071. 1953. Holt.
Tall Girl. Peggy O'More, pseud. (Contemporary Teens Ser.). 224p. (Orig.). 1981. pap. 2.25 (ISBN 0-89531-147-X, 0146-96). Sharon Pubns.
Tall Grass. Evelyn Murray Campbell. LC 33-7377. 1933. L. MacVeagh, Dial Press, Inc.
Tall Grew the Pines. Sigman Byrd. LC 36-14922. 1936. D. Appleton Century Company, Incorporated.
Tall Grey Gates. Theresa Thomas. LC 42-215. D. Ryerson, Inc.
Tall Headlines. Audrey Erskine Lindop. LC 50-9821. 1950. Macmillan.
Tall House Mystery. Archibald E. Fielding. LC 88-286701. 1933. H. C. Kinsey & Company, Inc.
Tall Houses in Winter. Doris Betts. LC 56-10222. 1957. Putnam.
Tall in the Saddle. Gordon Ray Young. LC 45-20694. The Sun Dial Press.
Tall in the Sight of God. Robert A Bowen. LC 58-93094. 1958. J. F. Blair.
Tall in the West. Vechel Howard, pseud. 1978. pap. 1.75 (ISBN 0-449-13898-4, GM). Fawcett.
Tall Ladder. Katharine Newlin Burt. LC 32-329153. 1932. Houghton Mifflin Company.
Tall Man. Gavin Douglas. LC 36-17481. 1936. G. P. Putnam's Sons.
Tall Man. Alfred Martin Harris. LC 58-13249. 1958. Farrar, Straus and Cudahy.
Tall Man Riding. Norman A Fox. LC 51-10447. (Silver star westerns). 1951. Dodd, Mead.
Tall Man Riding. Ray Hogan. (Signet Book). 1.95 (ISBN 0-441-82409-9). New American Library.
Tall Man Riding. Peter McCurtin. 1970. pap. 0.60 o.p. (B60-1079). Belmont-Tower.
Tall Man Walking; Murder--with Music by Wagner. Katherine Wolff. LC 36-35051. 1936. Pub. for the Crime Club, Inc., by Doubleday, Droran & Co., Inc.
Tall Marshal. James B. Kelly. 192p. (OSI). 1973. 4.95 o.s.i. Lenox Hill.
Tall Marshal. James B Kelly. 1973. 4.95. Lenox Hill Press.
Tall Men... Clay Fisher. LC 54-5702. 1954. Houghton Mifflin.
Tall Men. James Stuart Montgomery. LC 27-14798. 1927. The Literary Guild of America.
Tall Men:... by Clay Fisher Pseud. Henry Allen. LC 54-5702. 1954. Houghton Mifflin.
Tall One. Barbara Jefferis. LC 76-51741. 1977. 8.95 (ISBN 0-688-03144-7). Morrow.
Tall One. Barbara Jefferis. 1979. 1.95 (ISBN 0-445-04367-9). Popular Library.
Tall Ship on Other Naval Occasion. Lewis Anselm da Costa Ritchie. 1916. G. P. Putnam's Sons.
Tall Ship on Other Naval Occasions. Lewis Anselm Da Costa Ricci. LC 41-70778. 1938. Penguin Books Limited.
Tall Ship on Other Naval Occasions. Lewis Ainselm da Costa Ritchie. LC 41-7077. 1938. Penguin Books Limited.
Tall Ships. John Edward Jennings. LC 58-10872. 1958. McGraw-Hill.
Tall Stones. Moyra Caldecott. LC 77-23896. 1977. 7.95 (ISBN 0-8090-9120-8). Hill and Wang.
Tall Stories. Eric Duthie. Repr. of 1959 ed. 10.00 o.p. (ISBN 0-89987-114-3). Darby Bks.
Tall Stories. Eric Duthie. 1959. 15.00. Havertown Bks.
Tall Stranger. Louis L'Amour. LC 80-24975. (Series: Gregg Press Western Fiction Series.). 1981. 10.95 (ISBN 0-8398-2695-8). Gregg Press.
Tall Stranger. Dorothy Emily Stevenson. LC 57-10945. 1957. Rinehart.
Tall Stranger. Dorothy Emily Stevenson. 1978. 1.95 (ISBN 0-441-79621-4). Ace Books.
Tall Stranger see Complete L'Amour.
Tall Stranger see L'Amour Westerns.
Tall Tales. Fred W. Moore. 4.95 o.p. Vantage.
Tall Tales and Short. Ed. by Catharine Louise Bullard. Maus, Julia, Joint Ed. LC 38-4576. 1938. H. Holt and Company.
Tall Tales and Short. Ed. by Catherine Bullard & Maus, Julia. LC 38-4576. H. Holt and Company.
Tall Tales and Short. Edmund Ware Smith. LC 38-37551. The Derrydale Press.
Tall Tales from a Ranch. Illustrated by Walter A. McKinney. Annie M Boyce. LC 57-491557. 1957. Naylor Co.
Tall Tales from Grandma Norris. Minerva L. Norris. (Illus.). 1977. 4.50 o.p. (ISBN 0-533-02873-6). Vantage.
Tall Tales from Rogue River: The Yarns of Hathaway Jones. Hathaway Jones. Ed. by Stephen Dow Beckham. LC 73-16524. (Illus.). 1974. 6.50 (ISBN 0-253-18654-4). Indiana University Press.
Tall Tales from Texas. Mody Coggin Boatright. LC 34-246362. 1934. The Southwest Press.
Tall Tales of the Maritimes. Roland Harold Sherwood. LC 74-168971. 1972. 1.00. Lancelot Press.
Tall Tales of the Outdoors. Jim Goss. 1981. 4.95 (ISBN 0-8062-1739-1). Carlton.
Tall Tales of the Southwest. Ed. by Franklin Julius Meine. LC 30-104958. (On cover: American deserta). 1930. A. A. Knopf.
Tall Texan. Lee Floren. 0.50 o.p. (50-453). Manor Bks.
Tall Timber. George Goodchild. LC 25-3942. W. J. Watt & Co.
Tall Timber Valley. Donald B. Hobart. (Masked Rider Ser). (Orig.). 1971. pap. 0.60 o.p. (06145). Curtis.
Tall Villa. Mary St. Leger Kingsley Harrison. LC 20-3. George H. Doran Company.
Tall Woman. Wilma Dykeman. LC 62-11580. 1962. 8.95 (ISBN 0-03-030965-4). HR&W.
Tall Wyoming. Dan Cushman. LC 57-775122. (Dell first edition, A140). 1957. Dell Pub. Co.
Tallahassee Girl... Maurice Thompson. LC 8-19963. (On cover: Round-robin series). 1882. J. R. Osgood and Company.
Tallahassee Girl. 7th ed. Maurice Thompson. LC 41-31395. 1888. Ticknor and Company.
Tallant for Disaster. Christopher Nicole. LC 77-76963. 1978. 6.95 (ISBN 0-385-13284-0). Published for the Crime Club by Doubleday.
Tallant for Disaster. Andrew York. LC 77-76963. (Crime Club Ser.). 1978. 6.95 o.p. (ISBN 0-385-13284-0). Doubleday.
Tallant for Trouble. Christopher Nicole. LC 76-18377. 1977. 5.95 (ISBN 0-385-12355-8). Published for the Crime Club by Doubleday.
Tallant for Trouble. Andrew York. LC 76-18377. (Crime Club Ser.). 1977. 5.95 o.p. (ISBN 0-385-12355-8). Doubleday.
Taller Than Trees. John Gordon Davis. LC 75-13392. 1975. 6.95 (ISBN 0-385-11069-3). Doubleday.
Tallest Liar: A Novel. Cyrus Leo Sulzberger. LC 77-5649. 7.95 (ISBN 0-517-53141-0). Crown Publishers.
Talleyrand Maxim. Joseph Smith Fletcher. 1920. A. A. Knopf.
Tallien's Children. Hertha Pretorius, pseud. LC 61-7814. 1961. Appleton-Century-Crofts.
Tallulah and Jocassee: Or, Romance of Southern Landscape, and Other Tales. Thomas Addison Richards. 1852. Walker, Richards & Co.
Tallyman. Bill Knox. LC 69-12183. 1969. 3.95. Published for the Crime Club by Doubleday.
Talon: A Novel of Suspense. James Coltrane, pseud. LC 77-15436. 8.95 (ISBN 0-672-52391-4). Bobbs-Merrill.
Talons of the Hawk. Jeanne Hines. (Dell book). 1975. (pbk.) 0.95. Dell.
Talons of Time. Paul Twitchell. LC 74-21136. 1974. pap. 2.95 (ISBN 0-914766-23-6). IWP Pub.
Tam O' the Scoots. Edgar Wallace. LC 19-263443. Small, Maynard & Company.
Tama. Winnifred Eaton Babcock. LC 10-229801. 1910. Harper & Brothers.
Tama: The Diary of a Japanese School Girl. Ed. by Florence Wells. LC 19-170694. 1919. The Womans Press.
Tamam. Charles Chilton Moore. 1908. The Neale Publishing Company.
Tamar Curze. Alice Alberthe Robertson. LC 8-31157. R. F. Fenno & Company.
Tamara. Mary L. Dodge. (Orig.). 1969. pap. 0.60 o.p. (63-074). Paperback Lib.
Tamara. Eeva Kilpi. LC 77-18751. 8.95 (ISBN 0-440-08494-6). Delacorte Press/S. Lawrence.
Tamara: A Novel of Imperial Russia. Irina Skariatina. LC 42-3385. The Bobbs-Merrill Company.
Tamarac. Margaret Hutchison. LC 57-14608. 1957. St. Martin's Press.
Tamarack: A Novel. Edith Kneipple Roberts. LC 40-9594. The Bobbs-Merrill Company.
Tamarack Tree. Howard Breslin. LC 47-11149. 1947. Whittlesey House.
Tamara's Ecstasy. Sylvie F. Sommerfield. 1982. pap. 3.50 (ISBN 0-89083-998-0). Zebra.
Tamarind Seed. Evelyn Anthony. (YA) 1971. 6.95 o.p. (ISBN 0-698-10362-9). Coward.
Tamarind Seed: A Novel. Eve Stephens, pseud. (Dell book). 1973. (pbk) 1.50. Dell Pub. Co.
Tamarind Seed: A Novel. Eve Stephens, pseud. LC 76-153988. 1971. 6.95. Coward, McCann & Geoghegan.
Tamarisk. Claire Lorrimer. Date not set. pap. cancelled (ISBN 0-553-14739-0). Bantam.
Tamarisk Row. Gerald Murnane. LC 75-314734. 1974. (ISBN 0-85561-036-0). Heinemann.
Tamarisk Town. Sheila Kaye-Smith. 1919. Cassell and Company, Ltd.
Tamarisk Town. Sheila Kaye-Smith. LC 20-7297. E. P. Dutton & Company.
Tambay Gold. Samuel Hopkins Adams. LC 42-23560. 1942. J. Messner, Inc.
Tambo. James Francis Jenkins. LC 28-10299. 1928. R. M. McBride & Company.
Tambourine, Trumpet and Drum. Sheila Kaye-Smith. LC 43-13161. 1943. Harper & Brothers.
Tambourines to Glory. Langston Hughes. LC 58-13324. 1970. pap. 1.95 o.p. (ISBN 0-8090-0097-0, AmCen). Hill & Wang.
Tambourines to Glory: A Novel. Langston Hughes. LC 58-13324. 1958. J. Day Co.
Tambu. Robert L. Asprin. LC 80-100016. 4.95 (ISBN 0-441-79741-5). Ace Books.
Tamburas. Karlheinz Grosser. LC 67-19051. 1967. Holt, Rinehart and Winston.
Tamburas: Tr. by Kathleen Szasz. Karlheinz. Grosser. (8481). 1968. Dell.
Tame Surrender: A Story of the Chicago Strike. Charles King. LC 7-13216. (On cover: The lotus library). 1896. J. B. Lippincott Company.
Tamer. Nicolas Fokker. LC 78-2056. 10.00 (ISBN 0-06-011299-9). Harper & Row.
Tamer. Nicolas Fokker. LC 79-17962. 1980. 10.95 (ISBN 0-89340-227-3). J. Curley.
Tamer of the Wild. Max Brand. 1979. pap. 1.75 (ISBN 0-446-94334-7). Warner Bks.
Tamer of the Wild. Frederick Faust. 1975. (pbk.) 1.25. Warner Paperback Library.
Tamil Short Stories. Ed. by Ka N. Subramanyam. 1981. text ed. 15.00x (ISBN 0-7069-1241-1, Pub by Vikas India). Advent NY.
Taming a Vaquero. Lillian Gimblin Chester. 1909. Press Whitaker & Ray-Wiggin Co.
Taming of Amorette: A Comedy of Manners. Anne Warner French. LC 15-5557. 1915. 1.00. Little, Brown, and Company.
Taming of Calinga. C. L Carlsen. LC 16-230871. 1.35. E. P. Dutton & Company.
Taming of Carner Wilde. Bart Spicer. LC 54-5629. (Red badge detective). 1954. Dodd, Mead.
Taming of John Blunt. Alfred Ollivant. LC 11-264099. 1911. 1.20. Doubleday, Page & Company.
Taming of Nan. Ethel Holdsworth. LC 19-19359. E. P. Dutton and Company.
Taming of Nan. Ethel Holdsworth. LC 21-20618. 1920. E. P. Dutton and Company.
Taming of Red Butte Western. Francis Lynde. LC 10-9522. 1910. C. Scribner's Sons.
Taming of the Jungle. Charles William Doyle. 1899. J. B. Lippincott Company.
Taming of Zenas Henry. Sara Ware Bassett. LC 15-11871. 1.25. George H. Doran Company.
Tammany Boy: A Romance and a Political Career. Dermot Cavanagh. LC 28-21983. J. H. Sears & Company, Inc.
Tammy in Rome. Cid Ricketts Sumner. LC 65-108872. 4.50. Coward.
Tammy in Rome. Cid Ricketts Sumner. LC 65-10687. 1965. Coward-McCann.
Tammy Out of Time: A Novel. Cid Ricketts Sumner. 1948. Bobbs-Merrill Co.
Tammy, Tell Me True. Cid Ricketts Sumner. LC 59-14300. 1959. Bobbs-Merrill.
Tammy's Tales. Lucile M. Grey. 2.50 o.p. Vantage.
Tampico a Novel. Joseph Hergesheimer. LC 26-16351. 1926. A. A. Knopf.
Tampico: A Novel. Joseph Hergesheimer. LC 45-41678. 1926. A. A. Knopf.
Tamsie. Rosamond Napier Lawrence. LC 12-21599. 1912. Hodder & Stoughton.
Tamsie. Rosamond Napier. LC 12-215991. 1.35. Hodder & Stoughton, George H. Doran Company.
Tamzen. Jane Gilmore Rushing. LC 71-171319. 1972. 6.95. Doubleday.
Tan and Sandy Silence. John Dann MacDonald. LC 72-178011. (Travis McGee series). (Fawcett gold medal book). 1972. Fawcett Publications.
Tan and Sandy Silence. John Dann MacDonald. LC 78-24110. (Travis McGee series). 1979. 8.95 (ISBN 0-397-01343-4). Lippincott.
Tan and Sandy Silence. John Dann MacDonald. LC 82-15396. 1982. 12.95 (ISBN 0-8161-3381-6). G.K. Hall.
Tan-Faced Children. Frank Calkins. LC 78-18556. 1978. 7.95 (ISBN 0-385-14410-5). Doubleday.
Tan Ming, a Fantasy. 1st Ed. Lan Stormont. LC 54-12893. (Banner book). 1955. Exposition Press.
Tanamera. Noel Barber. LC 80-29570. 14.95 (ISBN 0-02-506840-7). MacMillan.
Tanaquil: A Novel. Donald Windham. LC 77-73864. 1977. 8.95 (ISBN 0-03-022566-3). Holt, Rinehart and Winston.
Tanaquil: Or, The Hardest Thing of All. Donald Windham. LC 73-167496. 1972. Printed by Stamperia Valdonega.
Tanar of Pellucidar. Edgar Rice Burroughs. LC 62-17749. (Illus.). 1962. Canaveral Press.
Tanar of Pellucidar. Edgar Rice Burroughs. LC 30-14877. Metropolitan Books.
Tanar of Pellucidar see Pellucidar Novels.
Tancred: Or, The New Crusade. new ed. london, longmans, green. ed. Benjamin Disraeli Beaconsfield. LC 77-107159. 1970. Scholarly Press.
Tancred: Or, The New Crusade. new ed. Benjamin Disraeli Beaconsfield. LC 79-98811. 1970. (ISBN 0-8371-3072-7). Greenwood Press.
Tancred: Or, The New Crusade. new ed. Benjamin Disraeli Beaconsfield. LC 6-28834. 1877. G. Routledge and Sons.
Tancred: Or, The New Crusade. Benjamin Disraeli Beaconsfield. LC 6-28849. (Seaside library, v. 45, no. 918). 1881. G. Munro.
Tancred: Or, The New Crusade. Benjamin Disraeli Beaconsfield. (In his The Bradenham edition of the novels and tales. New York, 1934? vol. x). Alfred A. Knopf.
Tancred: Or, the New Crusade. Benjamin Disraeli. LC 79-98811. Repr. of 1877 ed. lib. bdg. 19.00x (ISBN 0-8371-3072-7, BATA). Greenwood.
Tancred, Prince of Tiberias: A Tale of the Eleventh Century. Charles Guenot. Tr. by Freeman, Mary Julia. LC 7-153. 1884. J. Murphy & Co.
Tancredi: A Tale of the Opera. E. Allen Wood. 1888. G. W. Dillingham.
Tandem. Deborah Camp. (Orig.). 1980. pap. 1.95 (ISBN 0-532-23236-4). Woodhill.
Tandem. Violet Keppel Trefusis. LC 33-20287. 1933. G. P. Putnam's Sons.
Tang. Helen Bell. LC 21-4714. Small, Maynard & Company.
Tang of Life. Henry Herbert Knibbs. LC 18-16487. 1918. 1.50. Houghton Mifflin Company.
Tangent Factor. Lawrence Sanders. LC 77-21173. 9.95. Putnam.
Tangent Factor. Lawrence Sanders. (Berkley book). 1979. 2.25 (ISBN 0-425-04120-4). Berkley Pub. Corp.
Tangent Objective. Lawrence Sanders. (Berkley Medallion Book). 1977. 1.95. Berkley Pub. Corp.
Tangent Objective. Lawrence Sanders. LC 76-930. (ISBN 0-399-11750-4). Putnam.
Tangerine: Translated from the French by Norman Denny. 1st Ed. Christine De Rivoyre. LC 59-5011. 1959. Dutton.
Tangerines. Alice Bell. LC 13-17748. 1894. The Vance-Garrett Press.
Tangi. Witi Tame Ihimaera. LC 74-173974. 1973. Heinemann.
Tangier. William Bayer. LC 77-11150. 9.95. Dutton.
Tangier. William Bayer. (Dell Book.). 1979. 2.25 (ISBN 0-440-18643-9). Dell Pub. Co.
Tangier Buzzless Flies. John Hopkins. LC 75-167891. 1972. 7.95. Atheneum.
Tangled. A Novel. Rachel Carew. LC 6-22818. 1877. S. C. Griggs and Company.
Tangled Bank. Stanley Edgar Hyman. LC 62-11682. 1974. pap. text ed. 4.25x (ISBN 0-689-70513-1, 204). Atheneum.
Tangled Cord: By Frances and Richard Lockridge. 1st Ed. Frances Louise Davis Lockridge & Richard Lockridge. LC 57-6240. (Main line mysteries). 1957. Lippincott.
Tangled Emotions. Billie J. Longstreth et al. LC 82-80742. 357p. 1983. 10.95 (ISBN 0-9608142-0-5); pap. 2.95 (ISBN 0-9608142-1-3). Shamrock Pubns.
Tangled Evidence. Champion De Crespigny, Rose Key. LC 24-319073. 1924. Cassell and Company, Ltd.
Tangled Paths. Anna Hanson McKenney Dorsey. LC 6-337071. 1879. D. & J. Sadlier & Co.
Tangled Shadows. Flora Kidd. (Harlequin Presents Ser.). (Orig.). 1980. pap. 1.50 (ISBN 0-373-70833-5). Harlequin Bks.
Tangled Skein. Anna Gillilland Hopkins. LC 14-5510. 1.50. C.
Tangled Threads. Sallie Lee Bell. LC 68-16013. 1968. Zondervan Pub. House.
Tangled Threads. Eleanor Hodgman Porter. LC 19-16146. 1919. Houghton Mifflin Company.
Tangled Threads: By Rex Hopkins & Earl Shelton. Rex Hopkins & Earl Shelton. LC 50-2688. 1950. Chapman & Grimes.
Tangled Trail. Fred East. LC 47-925. 1947. Macrae-Smith-Co.
Tangled Trail. Roy Manning. LC 47-925. 1947. Macrae-Smith Company.
Tangled Trails. Peter Germano. LC 64-88. Arcadia House.
Tangled Trails. Roy Norton. LC 34-19653. E. J. Clode, Inc.
Tangled Trails. Willis Staton. LC 31-24651. 1931. Meador Publishing Company.
Tangled Trails: A Western Detective Story. William MacLeod Raine. LC 21-18579. 1921. 1.75. Houghton Mifflin Company.
Tangled Trinities. James Chapman Woods. LC 1-25038. 1901. Dodd, Mead & Company.
Tangled Tropics. Sam Mims. LC 39-25039. W. T. Tardy.
Tangled up in Beulah Land. Andrew Carpenter Wheeler. LC 2-22409. 1902. Doubleday, Page & Co.

Tangled Web. Anne Benson. LC 81-80078. 192p. 1981. pap. 1.95 (ISBN 0-87216-873-5). Playboy Pbks.
Tangled Web. Philippe Ganier-Raymond. (O.S.I.). 224p. pap. 0.95 o.s.i. (ISBN 0-446-65934-7, 65-934). Paperback Lib.
Tangled Web. Barbara Hazard. 224p. 1981. pap. 1.95 (ISBN 0-449-50177-9, Coventry). Fawcett.
Tangled Web. Giles A Lutz. LC 82-45614. (Double D western). 1983. 11.95 (ISBN 0-385-18433-6). Doubleday.
Tangled Web. Lucy Maud Montgomery. LC 31-28155. 1931. Frederick A. Stokes Company.
Tangled Web. C. G. Stevens. (Playbooks). 1.50 o.p. McKay.
Tangled Web. Lois A. Sunagel. 1979. pap. 1.75 (ISBN 0-89041-258-8). Major Bks.
Tangled Web: By Nicholas Blake Pseud. 1st Ed. Cecil Day-Lewis. LC 56-877592. 1956. Harper.
Tangled Web: Or, The Pale Countess. Hans Wachenhusen & Safford, Mary Joanna, Tr. LC 98-6732. (Globe library, v. 2, no. 292). 1898. Rand, McNally & Co.
Tangled Wedlock. Edgar Jepson. 1908. The McClure Company.
Tangled Wives. Peggy Smith Shane. LC 33-32242. C. Kendall.
Tangled Wood. Iris Bromige. (Orig.). 1974. pap. 0.75 o.p. (ISBN 0-345-20520-0). Beagle Bks.
Tangles. Mae G Chandler. LC 26-548.
Tangles: Tales of Some Droll Predicaments. Margaret H. C. Cameron. LC 12-235116. 1912. Harper & Brothers.
Tangles Unravelled. Evelyn Kimball Johnson. J. S. Ogilvie & Company.
Tangletown Letters: Being the Reminiscences, Observations, and Opinions of Timotheus Trap, Esq. Including a Report of the Great Mammothic Reform Convention. Elhanan Winchester Reynolds. LC 7-30598. 1856. Wanzer, McKim & Co.
Tangleweed. George William Willis. LC 43-159556. 1943. Doubleday, Doran and Company, Inc.
Tanglewood Murder. Lucille Kallen. 1981. pap. 2.25 (ISBN 0-345-29668-0). Ballantine.
Tanglewood Murder. Lucille Kallen. LC 80-25148. 325p. 1980. Repr. of 1980 ed. large print ed. 10.95x (ISBN 0-89621-257-2). Thorndike Pr.
Tanglewood Murder. 1980. 11.95 (ISBN 0-671-61018-X, Wyndham). S&S.
Tanglewood Tales: And Biographical Stories. Nathaniel Hawthorne. LC 7-3783. (Hawthorne's Works. Illustrated library edition). 1881. Houghton, Mifflin and Company.
Tango. George Mikes. text ed. 4.50x o.s.i. (ISBN 0-8277-0453-4). British Bk Ctr.
Tango: A Novel. Vida Hurst. J. H. Hopkins & Son.
Tango Briefing. Adam Hall, pseud. LC 73-79676. 288p. 1973. 6.95 o.p. (ISBN 0-385-04281-7). Doubleday.
Tango Briefing. Elleston Trevor. LC 73-79676. 1973. 6.95 (ISBN 0-385-04281-7). Doubleday.
Tango November. John Howlett. LC 76-53950. 1977. 8.95. Atheneum.
Tania. Tania. 1971. 8.95 o.p. (ISBN 0-394-47337-X). Random.
Tania see Dawn of Love.
Tank. Arch Whitehouse. 1973. pap. 0.95 o.p. (09089). Curtis.
Tank Fighters. S. W. Karl. 1978. pap. 1.50 (ISBN 0-532-15331-6). Woodhill.
Tank McNamara Chronicles. Jeff Millar & Bill Hinds. LC 78-67227. (Treasury Ser.). (Illus.). 1978. pap. 7.95 o.p. (ISBN 0-8362-1119-7). Andrews & McMeel.
Tank of Sacred Eels. Ivor Drummond. LC 75-40785. 7.95. St. Martin's Press.
Tank of Sacred Eels. Ivor Drummond. LC 76-374692. 1976. 3.50 (ISBN 0-7181-1466-3). Joseph.
Tank Tales. Stephen Foot & Wood, Eric, Joint Author. LC 20-5898. 1919. Funk & Wagnalls Company.
Tanka. Ida Henrietta Bean. LC 99-2068. (On cover: Neely's popular library, no. 137). 1899. F.T. Neely.
Tanker. Rayne Kruger. LC 52-3130. 1952. Longmans, Green.
Tanker Derbent. IUrii Solomonovich Krymov. LC 74-10086. (Illus.). 1975. 14.50 (ISBN 0-88355-173-X). Hyperion Press.
Tanker "Derbent," A Soviet Novel. IUrii Solomonovich Krymouv. Tr. by John S. Spink. LC 45-5087. (On cover: Penguin books. 466). 1944. Penguin Books.
Tannahill Tangle: A Fleming Stone Story. Carolyn Wells. LC 28-25629. 1928. J. B. Lippincott Company.
Tannenwiese: Or, A Happy Home. A Sequel to "Where Is Heaven?". Hedwig Prohl. Tr. by Butcher, M. P. LC 12-37748. (On cover: The fatherland series). Lutheran Publication Society.
Tansy Taniard. Myrtle Beatrice S Strode-Jackson. LC 45-35190. 1945. C. Scribner's Sons.
Tanta Is Not a Madame! Frita Roth Drapkin. LC 78-75763. 1969. 4.50. New Voices Pub. Co.
Tantalizing Locked Room Mysteries. Isaac Asimov & Charles Waugh. LC 80-54817. 1982. 12.95 (ISBN 0-8027-0680-0). Walker.
Tantalizing Locked Room Mysteries. Ed. by Martin Greenberg & Charles Waugh. LC 80-54817. 224p. 1982. 12.95 (ISBN 0-8027-0680-0). Walker & Co.
Tantalus. Dorothy Easton. LC 23-27433. 1923. 2.50. A. A. Knopf.
Tantalus. Mary Forward Kimmell. LC 10-7403. 1909. 1.50. The C. M. Clark Publishing Company.
Tantalus: A Novel, by Jo Van Ammers-Kuller... Jo Van Ammers-Kuller. Tr. by Renier, Gustaaf Johanes. E. P. Dutton & Co., Inc.
Tantchen Mohnhaupt. Johannes Schiaf & Gates, Clifford Elwood, 1893- Ed. LC 28-2511. (Half-title: Borzoi German texts). 1927. A. A. Knopf.
Tante. Anne Douglas Sedgwick. LC 12-48. 1911. The Century Co.
Tante. Anne Douglas Sedgwick. LC 31-272192. 1931. Houghton Mifflin Company.
Tantine: l'Histoire de Lucille Landry Augustine Gabrielle. Monica Landry & Julien Olivier. Tr. by Penny Anderson & Mary Granger. (Oral History Ser.). (Illus.). 45p. (Fr.). (gr. 9). 1981. pap. 2.00x (ISBN 0-911409-05-X). Natl Mat Dev.
Tao of Pooh. Benjamin Hoff. 1983. pap. 4.95 (ISBN 0-14-006747-7). Penguin.
Tao Tales. Henry Milner Rideout. LC 27-19781. 1927. Duffield and Company.
Taos: A Novel. Irwin R Blacker. LC 77-426. (Illus.). 1977. 8.95 (ISBN 0-912588-51-9). Brooke House.
Taos: A Novel. 1st Ed. Irwin R Blacker. LC 59-7749. 1959. World Pub. Co.
Taos Pueblo. 2nd rev ed. Phillip Reno. LC 72-78538. 36p. 1972. pap. 2.95 o.p. (ISBN 0-8040-0329-7, SB). Swallow.
Tap on the Shoulder. Morrison Dupree. LC 29-14763. 1929. Pub. for The Club, Inc., by Doubleday, Doran and Company, Incorporated.
Tap Roots. James Howell Street. LC 42-36265. 1942. The Dial Press.
Tapestry. Arthur Moore. (Orig.). 1979. pap. 2.50 (ISBN 0-89083-523-3). Zebra.
Tapestry of Death. Dorothy Mueller Bowick, pseud. LC 74-31922. 1975. 5.95 (ISBN 0-8027-5322-1). Walker.
Tapestry of Death. Dorothy Muller. LC 74-31922. 184p. 1975. 5.95 o.p. (ISBN 0-8027-5322-1). Walker & Co.
Tapestry of Love. Cathryn Ladd. (Adventures in Love Ser.: No. 32). 1982. pap. 1.75 (ISBN 0-451-11786-7, AE1786, Sig). NAL.
Tapestry of Magics. Brian Daley. 304p. 1983. pap. 2.95 (Del Rey). Ballantine.
Tapestry of Terror. Marianne Ruuth. (Ace gothic no. 7). 1975. (pbk.) 0.95. Ace Books.
Tapestry of Time. Isabell C Crawford. LC 27-15197. 1927. The Christopher Publishing House.
Tapestry Room Murder. Carolyn Wells. LC 29-74033. 1929. J. B. Lippincott Company.
Tappan's Burro: And Other Stories. Zane Grey. LC 23-15824. Harper & Brothers.
Tapping on the Wall: The College Faculty Prize Mystery. Helen Rose Hull. LC 60-11937. (Red badge detective). 1960. Dodd, Mead.
Taproots of Falconhurst. Ashley Carter, pseud. 1978. 2.25 (ISBN 0-449-14090-3). Fawcett Gold Medal Books.
Taps. Franz Adam Beyerlein. Tr. by Swickard, Charles. LC 15-26997. J. W. Luce & Company.
Taps: A Novel of War and Peace. Hector Lazo. LC 37-33117. B. Humphries, Inc.
Taps at Little Big Horn. John Benteen. (Sundance Ser.: No. 9). 1978. pap. 1.50 (ISBN 0-8439-0561-1, Leisure Bks). Nordon Pubns.
Taps at Little Big Horn. John Benteen. (Sundance Ser.: No. 9). 144p. 1981. pap. 1.75 (ISBN 0-8439-1048-8, Leisure Bks). Nordon Pubns.
Taps at Reveille. Francis Scott Key Fitzgerald. LC 35-4215. 1935. C. Scribner's Sons.
Taps for Private Tussie. Jesse Stuart. LC 74-83971. (Illus.). 1969. 6.95. World Pub. Co.
Taps for Private Tussie. Jesse Stuart. LC 43-163424. 1943. E. P. Dutton & Company, Inc.
Taps for Private Tussie. Jesse Stuart & Benton, Thomas Hart, 1889- Illus. LC 43-178384. 1943. Books, Inc., Distributed by E. P. Dutton & Company, Inc.
Taquisara. Francis Marion Crawford. LC 4-15095. 1895. Macmillan and Co.
Taquisara. Francis Marion Crawford. LC 44-22840. 1896. The Macmillan Company.
Tar: A Midwest Childhood. Sherwood Anderson. Ed. by Ray L. White. LC 69-17680. (Major Fiction of Sherwood Anderson Ser.). 1969. 7.50 o.p. (ISBN 0-8295-0159-2). Pr of Case WR.
Tar-Aiym Krang. Alan Dean Foster. 1982. pap. 2.50 (ISBN 0-345-30280-X, Del Rey). Ballantine.
Tar and Feathers. Victor Rubin. LC 23-11265. 1923. Dorrance.
Tar Baby. Jerome Charyn. LC 72-185228. 1973. 6.95. Holt, Rinehart and Winston.
Tar Baby. Toni Morrison. LC 81-6851. 1981. 15.95 (ISBN 0-8161-3293-3). G.K. Hall.
Tar-Heel Baron. Mabell Shippie Clarke Smith. LC 3-6139. 1903. J. B. Lippincott Company.
Tar Heel Ghosts. John Harden. xiv, 178p. 1980. 9.95 (ISBN 0-8078-0660-9); pap. 4.95 (ISBN 0-8078-4069-6). U of NC Pr.
Tar Heel Tales. Henry Edward Cowan Bryant. LC 72-6511. (Black Heritage Library Collection). (Illus.). 1972. (ISBN 0-8369-9162-1). Books for Libraries Press.
Tar Pit Murders: L6. Helen Jaskoski. Ed. by Jean McConochie. (gr. 7-12). 1982. pap. text ed. 2.25 (ISBN 0-88345-499-8, 21078). Regents Pub.
Tar, Pitch and Turpentine: A Novel of the South and Its People. Vinton M Dubberly. LC 44-47010. 1944. Dorrance & Company.
Tara. Deirdre Stiles. (Leisure Books). 1.95 (ISBN 0-8439-0491-7). Nordon Pubns.
Tara Kane. George Markstein. LC 77-91613. 1978. 9.95 (ISBN 0-8128-2474-1). Stein and Day.
Tara of the Twilight. Lin Carter. (Orig.). 1979. pap. 2.25 (ISBN 0-89083-428-8). Zebra.
Tarabas, a Guest on Earth. Joseph Roth. LC 34-38524. 1934. The Viking Press.
Tarakian. Ludovic Peters. LC 64-10279. (Raven book). 1964. Abelard-Schuman.
Tarantella: A Romance. Mathilde Blind. 1885. Roberts Brothers.
Tarantula. Don Luis De V. (Venus Bks). pap. 1.75 o.p. (V1002). Grove.
Tarantula. Don Luis De V. pap. 4.00 o.p. (Z1002, Zebra). Grove.
Tarantula Strike. (Nick Carter Ser.). 192p. (Orig.). 1980. pap. 1.95 (ISBN 0-441-79840-3, Pub. by Charter Bks). Ace Bks.
Taras Bulba. Nikolai Vasilevich Gogol. Tr. by Hapgood, Isabel Florence. LC 6-43745. T. Y. Crowell & Co.
Taras Bulba. Nikolai Vasilevich Gogol. Tr. by Hapgood, Isabel Florence. (On cover: Lovell's library, no. 1016). 1888. J. W. Lovell Company.
Taras Bulba. Nikolai Vasilevich Gogol. Repr. lib. bdg. 9.55 (ISBN 0-88411-138-5). Amereon Ltd.
Taras Bulba. Nikolai Vasilevich Gogol & Hapgood, Isabel Florence, 1850-1928, Tr. LC 45-26347. 1938. Foreign Language Book Co.
Taras Bulba. A Historyical Novel of Russia and Poland By Nikolai Vasilyevitch Gogol. Nikolai Vasilevich Gogol. Tr. by Curtin, Jeremiah. LC 6-43744. J. B. Alden.
Taras Bulba: A Tale of the Cossacks. Nikolai Vasilevich Gogol. Tr. by Hapgood, Isabel Florence. LC 15-20145. 1915. A. A. Knopf.
Taras Bulba & Other Stories. Nikolai Vasilevich Gogol. Tr. by Constance Garnett. (YA) (gr. 9 up). pap. 0.60 o.p. (W572). WSP.
Taras Bulba & Other Tales. Nikolai Vasilevich Gogol. 3.95x o.p. (ISBN 0-460-00740-8, Evman). Dutton.
Taras' Family: By Boris Gorbatov. Translated from the Russian by Elizabeth Donnelly. Boris Leont'Evich Gorbatov & Donnelly, Elizabeth, Tr. LC 46-215761. 1946. Cattell and Company, Inc.
Tara's Healing. Janice Holt Giles. (Fawcett crest, M2053). 1974. (pbk.) 0.95. Fawcett Publications.
Tara's Healing. Janice Holt Giles. LC 72-2428. 1972. 6.95 (ISBN 0-395-14099-4). Houghton Mifflin.
Tara's Healing. Janice Holt Giles. LC 51-14712. 1951. Westminster Press.
Tara's Song. Barbara Ferry Johnson. LC 78-58903. 1978. 2.25 (ISBN 0-380-39123-6). Avon Books.
Tare Harvest. Eleanor Peters. LC 36-221898. Reynal & Hitchcock.
Tarentella. Edith Macvane. LC 11-26405. 1911. Houghton Mifflin Company.
Target. William Wister Haines. LC 64-21482. 1964. Little, Brown.
Target: Charity Ross. Jack M Bickham. LC 68-27109. (DD western). 1968. 3.95. Doubleday.
Target: Daimler-Benz. Lawrence Cortesi, pseud. 1980. pap. 1.75 o.s.i. (ISBN 0-8439-0713-4, Leisure Bks). Nordon Pubns.
Target: Death. Colin R. Beeson. 1978. pap. 1.50 (ISBN 0-532-15384-7). Woodhill.
Target Delta V. James Good. (Sub Wars Ser.: No. 1). (Orig.). 1981. pap. 2.50 (ISBN 0-89083-892-5). Zebra.
Target: Doomsday Island. Nick Carter. (Nick Carter Killmaster Ser). 192p. (Orig.). 1973. pap. 0.95 o.p. (AN1075, Award). Univ Pub & Dist.
Target: Doomsday Island. Nick Carter. (Nick Carter/Killmaster Series). 1973. (pbk) 0.95. Award Books.
Target Five. Colin Forbes, pseud. 1973. 6.95 o.p. (ISBN 0-525-21430-5). Dutton.
Target Five. Raymond H. Sawkins. LC 73-82203. (Illus.). 1973. 6.95 (ISBN 0-525-21430-5). Dutton.
Target for Murder. Guy Elwyn Giles. LC 43-8246. 1943. W. Morrow & Company.
Target for Terror. S. A. Martinez. 176p. (Orig.). 1976. pap. 1.50 (ISBN 0-89041-101-8, 3101). Major Bks.
Target for Terror. Laura C. Raef. 1980. 6.95 (Avalon). Bouregy.
Target for Their Dark Desire. Alan Geoffrey Yates. LC 67-1959. (His The Carter Brown mystery series). 1966. New American Library.
Target for Tonight. Rod Gray. (New Lady from L.U.S.T. Ser). (O.s.i.: No. 3). (Orig.). 1975. pap. 1.25 o.s.i. (BT50805). Belmont-Tower.
Target for Tonight. Rod Gray. (Lady from L.U.S.T.). 1975. (pbk.) 1.25. Belmont Tower Books.
Target for Tragedy. Hugh Pentecost. LC 82-5088. (Red badge novel of suspense). 10.95 (ISBN 0-396-08079-0). Dodd, Mead.
Target for Tragedy: A Peter Styles Mystery Novel. Judson Pentecost Philips. LC 82-5088. 1982. 10.95 (ISBN 0-396-08079-0). Dodd.
Target in Taffeta: A Wade Paris Mystery. Ben Benson. LC 53-10942. 1953. M. S. Mill Co. and W. Morrow.
Target Island: A Novel. John Brophy. LC 44-6864. 1944. Harper & Brothers.
Target Luftwaffe: The Tragedy and the Triumph of the World War II Air Victory. William A Ong. LC 80-83828. (Illus.). 19.95 (ISBN 0-913504-60-2). Lowell Press.
Target Manhattan: A Novel. Drew Mallory. LC 74-30563. 1975. 7.95 (ISBN 0-399-11496-3). Putnam.
Target Mayflower. Richard Clark Hirschhorn. LC 77-73056. 8.95 (ISBN 0-15-187995-8). Harcourt Brace Jovanovich.
Target: Plutex. Paul Bryers. LC 75-18371. 1976. 7.95 (ISBN 0-385-11048-0). Doubleday.
Target Practice. Nicholas Meyer. LC 73-19959. 1974. 5.95 (ISBN 0-15-187997-4). Harcourt Brace Jovanovich.
Target Practice. Nicholas Meyer. 1975. (pbk.) 1.25 (ISBN 0-523-00680-2). Pinnacle Books.
Target Sixteen Hundred. David B. Charnay. 1980. 10.00 (ISBN 0-8184-0290-3). Lyle Stuart.
Target Star. K. H Scheer. (Perry Rhodan Series#92). 1976. (pbk.) 1.25. Ace Books.
Targets. Donald E McQuinn. LC 79-25493. 12.50 (ISBN 0-02-583710-9). Macmillan.
Tariro: Translated by Elsa Kruuse. Arvid Albrektson. LC 59-6667. 1959. Muhlenberg Press.
Tark and the Golden Tide. Colum MacConnell. (Leisure Books). 1977. 1.50 (ISBN 0-8439-0470-4). Nordon Pubns.
Tark & the Golden Tide. Colum MacDonnell. 1977. pap. 1.25 o.s.i. (ISBN 0-8439-0470-4, Leisure Bks). Nordon Pubns.
Tarn. Wyndham Lewis. LC 73-89681. 1973. 12.50 (ISBN 0-914300-00-8). Jubilee Books.
Tarnished: A Story of Love and Mystery, Published Serially Under the Title 'Little Miss Nobody' Vida Hurst. LC 31-13232. Grosset & Dunlap.
Tarnished Angel. Phyllis G Leonard. LC 79-20795. 10.95 (ISBN 0-698-10999-6). Coward, McCann & Geoghegan.
Tarnished Angel. Judson Pentecost Philips. LC 62-17927. (Red Badge detective). 1963. Dodd, Mead.
Tarnished Fame. Vera Brown. LC 34-4687. Grosset & Dunlap.
Tarnished Love. Gerry Travis, pseud. LC 42-7505. 1942. Phoenix Press.
Tarnished Rainbow, No. 82. Jocelyn Day. 1982. pap. 1.75 (ISBN 0-515-06693-1). Jove Pubns.
Tarnished Scalpel. Norman Daniels. (Orig.). 1968. pap. 0.75 o.p. (74-935). Lancer.
Tarnished Tower. Ann Marbut. LC 57-110792. 1957. D. McKay Co.
Tarot Murders. Mignon Warner. LC 78-51824. (Mw Suspense). 1978. 6.95 (ISBN 0-88331-094-5). D. McKay Co.
Tarot Spell. Willo Davis Roberts. 1970. pap. 0.95 o.s.i. (75-336). Lancer.
Tarotown. Bruce Jones. 240p. (Orig.). 1982. pap. 2.50 (ISBN 0-8439-1089-5). Leisure Bks CT.
Tarot's Tower. Jennie Melville, pseud. LC 77-19299. 8.95 (ISBN 0-671-22905-2). Simon and Schuster.
Tarpaper Palace. Lida Larrimore Thomas. LC 28-115369. 1928. Macrae Smith Company.
Tarpaper Palace. Lida Larrimore Thomas. LC 42-10317. 1942. Triangle Books.

Tarpaulin Muster. John Masefield. LC 73-132120. (Short story index reprint series). 1970. (ISBN 0-8369-3677-9). Books for Libraries Press.
Tarpaulin Muster. John Masefield. LC 8-10282. 1908. B. W. Dodge & Company.
Tarpaulin Muster. John Masefield. LC 20-17414. 1919. Dodd, Mead and Company.
Tarr. Wyndham Lewis. LC 18-13642. 1918. A. A. Knopf.
Tarrano the Conqueror. Ray Cummings. LC 75-400. (Garland Library of Science Fiction). 1975. 11.00 (ISBN 0-8240-1406-5). Garland Pub.
Tarrano the Conqueror. Ray Cummings. LC 30-107022. 1930. A. C. McClurg & Co.
Tarrant of Tin Spout. Henry Oyen. LC 22-9054. George H. Doran Company.
Tarrington Chase. Sylvia Thorpe. 1980. pap. 1.75 (ISBN 0-449-50055-1, Coventry). Fawcett.
Tarrington Chase. Sylvia Thorpe. (Fawcett Crest Book). 1976. (pbk.) 1.50. Fawcett.
Tarry and Be Hanged. Sara Woods, pseud. 1973. (pbk.) 0.95. Dell.
Tarry and Be Hanged. Sara Woods, pseud. LC 77-150970. (Rinehart suspense novel). 1971. 4.95 (ISBN 0-03-086022-9). Holt, Rinehart and Winston.
Tarry Flynn. Patrick Kavanagh. 189p. 1978. pap. 3.95 (ISBN 0-14-004553-8, Pub. by Penguin England). Irish Bk Ctr.
Tarry Flynn: A Novel. Patrick Kauvanagh. LC 49-11429. 1949. Devin-Adair Co.
Tarry Thou till I Come: Or, Salathiel, the Wandering Jew; by George Croly. thulstrup illustrated ed. George Crody. LC 1-31847. 1901. Funk & Wagnalls Company.
Tarry Thou till I Come: Or, Salathiel, the Wandering Jew, by George Croly. George Croly. LC 41-31311. 1902. Grosset & Dunlap.
Tart Is the Apple; a Novel. Joyce Varney. LC 73-1738. 1973. 6.95 (ISBN 0-672-51270-X). Bobbs-Merrill.
Tartar Slave. Oscar Doyle Johnson. LC 32-21676. The Stratford Company.
Tartar Steppe. Dino Buzzati. 1980. pap. 2.75 (ISBN 0-380-50252-6, 50252, Bard). Avon.
Tartar Steppe. Dino Buzzati. pap. 1.45 o.p. (N277, Noonday). FS&G.
Tartar Steppe. Translated by Stuart C. Hood. Dino Buzzati. LC 52-11813. 1952. Farrar, Straus and Young.
Tartarin of Tarascon & Tartarin on the Alps. Alphonse Daudet. 1969. Repr. of 1910 ed. 9.95 (Evman). Biblio Dist.
Tartarin of Tarascon... Revised Translation. Alphonse Daudet. LC 4-23586. 1895. T. Y. Crowell & Co.
Tartarin of Tarascon: Tartarin on the Alps; Artists' Wives. Alphonse Daudet. LC 26-26989. (Half-title: The novels and romances of Alphonse Daudet. Handy library edition). Little, Brown and Company.
Tartarin of Tarascon, Traveller, "Turk," and Lion-Hunter. Alphonse Daudet. LC 42-44641. 1887. G. Routledge and Sons.
Tartarin on the Alps: With Illustrations. Revised Translation. Alphonse Daudet. LC 11-17972. T. Y. Crowell & Co.
Tartarus Incident. William Greenleaf. 1983. pap. 2.50 (ISBN 0-441-79846-2, Pub. by Ace Science Fiction). Ace Bks.
Tarzan Alive. Philip Jose Farmer. LC 81-80084. 352p. 1981. pap. 2.75 (ISBN 0-87216-876-X). Playboy Pbks.
Tarzan & Shane Meet the Toad. limited ed. Gerald Locklin et al. 1975. 2.00 (ISBN 0-917554-01-9). Maelstrom.
Tarzan and the Ant Men. Edgar Rice Burroughs. LC 24-23085. 1924. A. C. McClurk & Co.
Tarzan and the Ant Men. Edgar Rice Burroughs. LC 33-780485. 1924. Grosset & Dunalp.
Tarzan & the Castaways. Edgar Rice Burroughs. 1980. pap. 1.95. Ballantine.
Tarzan & the Castaways. Edgar Rice Burroughs. LC 64-25826. (Illus.). 1975. Repr. 10.00 (ISBN 0-940724-10-3). Canaveral.
Tarzan and the City of Gold. Edgar Rice Burroughs. LC 33-24091. E. R. Burroughs, Inc.
Tarzan and the City of Gold: Illustrated by Jesse Marsh. Authorized Abridged Ed. Edgar Rice Burroughs. LC 56-233. (Whitman books for boys and girls). 1952. Whitman Pub. Co.
Tarzan and the Forbidden City. Edgar Rice Burroughs. LC 38-38071. E. R. Burroughs, Inc.
Tarzan and the Forbidden City: Illustrated by Jesse Marsh. Authorized Abridged Ed. Edgar Rice Burroughs. LC 53-232. (Whitman books for boys and girls). 1952. Whitman Pub. Co.
Tarzan and "The Foreign Legion.". Edgar Rice Burroughs. LC 47-62143. 1947. E. R. Burroughs, Inc.
Tarzan and the Golden Lion. Edgar Rice Burroughs. LC 23-6839. 1923. A. C. McClurg & Co.
Tarzan and the Jewels of Opar. Edgar Rice Burroughs. LC 65-4503. House of Greystoke.
Tarzan and the Jewels of Opar. Edgar Rice Burroughs. LC 18-848844. 1918. A. C. McClurg & Co.
Tarzan and the Jewels of Opar. Edgar Rice Burroughs. LC 28-16853. 1918. Grosset & Dunlap.
Tarzan & the Jewels of Opar, No. 5. Edgar Rice Burroughs. 160p. 1980. pap. 1.95 (ISBN 0-345-28917-X). Ballantine.
Tarzan & the Leopard Man. Edgar Rice Burroughs. 1980. pap. 1.95 (ISBN 0-345-28687-1). Ballantine.
Tarzan and the Leopard Men. Edgar Rice Burroughs. LC 35-194218. Edgar Rice Burroughs, Inc.
Tarzan and the Lion Man. Edgar Rice Burroughs. LC 34-299083. E. R. Burroughs, Inc.
Tarzan & the Lion Men. Edgar Rice Burroughs. 1980. pap. 1.95 (ISBN 0-345-28988-9). Ballantine.
Tarzan and the Lost Empire. frontispeice by a. w. sperry. ed. Edgar Rice Burroughs. LC 29-20009. Metropolitan Books.
Tarzan and the Madman. Edgar Rice Burroughs. LC 64-15789. 1964. Canaveral Press.
Tarzan and the Tarzan Twins. Edgar Rice Burroughs. LC 63-10779. (Illus.). 1963. Canaveral Press.
Tarzan at the Earth's Core. Edgar Rice Burroughs. LC 62-21543. 1962. Canaveral Press.
Tarzan at the Earth's Core. Edgar Rice Burroughs. LC 30-32136. Metropolitan Books, Inc.
Tarzan in the Forbidden City. authorized abridged ed., retold in 100 pages by edgar rice burroughs. ed. Edgar Rice Burroughs. LC 41-11008. (On cover: Bantam books. 28). Bantam Publications, Inc.
Tarzan, Lord of the Jungle. Edgar Rice Burroughs. LC 28-214162. 1928. A. C. McClurg & Co.
Tarzan of the Apes... Edgar Rice Burroughs. LC 14-11094. 1914. A. C. McClurg & Co.
Tarzan of the Apes. Edgar Rice Burroughs. LC 17-61034. A. L. Burt Company.
Tarzan of the Apes. Edgar Rice Burroughs. 1927. Grosset & Dunlap.
Tarzan of the Apes. Edgar Rice Burroughs. LC 73-9353. 1973. (lib. ed.) 4.99 (ISBN 0-448-13161-7). Grosset and Dunlap.
Tarzan of the Apes, No. 1. Edgar Rice Burroughs. 256p. 1979. pap. 1.95 (ISBN 0-345-28377-5). Ballantine.
Tarzan the Invincible. Edgar Rice Burroughs. LC 31-33380. E. R. Burroughs, Inc.
Tarzan the Magnificent. Edgar Rice Burroughs. LC 39-31537. Edgar Rice Burroughs, Inc.
Tarzan the Terrible. Edgar Rice Burroughs. LC 21-11024. 1921. A. C. McClurg & Co.
Tarzan the Untamed. Edgar Rice Burroughs. LC 30-7515. 1920. A. C. McClurg & Co.
Tarzan the Untamed. Edgar Rice Burroughs. 1922. Grosset & Dunlap.
Tarzan Triumphant. Edgar Rice Burroughs. LC 32-22545. E. R. Burroughs, Inc.
Tarzan's Quest. Edgar Rice Burroughs. LC 36-24404. E. R. Burroughs, Inc.
Tashkent Crisis. William Craig. 1971. 6.95 o.p. (ISBN 0-525-21435-6). Dutton.
Tashkent Crisis: A Novel. William Craig. LC 74-125549. 1971. 6.95 (ISBN 0-525-21435-6). Dutton.
Tasker Martin: A Novel. Diana Gaines. LC 50-7047. 1950. Random House.
Taskmakers. George Kibbe Turner. LC 74-22819. Repr. of 1902 ed. 18.50 (ISBN 0-404-58480-2). AMS Pr.
Taskmaster. Harold King. LC 77-3529. 7.95 (ISBN 0-698-10827-2). Coward, McCann & Geoghegan.
Taskmasters. George Kibbe Turner. LC 2-255202. 1902. McClure, Phillips & Co.
Tassels on Her Boots. Arthur Cheney Train. LC 40-30185. 1940. C. Scribner's Sons.
Taste for Blood. Ralph Hayes. (hunter#3). 1975. (pbk.) 1.25. Leisure Books.
Taste for Brillants. Noel Clad. LC 64-10015. (Random House mystery). 1964. Random House.
Taste for Death. Peter O'Donnell. LC 69-10993. 1969. 4.95. Doubleday.
Taste for Honey. Gerald Heard. LC 41-172503. The Vanguard Press.
Taste for Honey... Gerald Heard. LC 47-320985. (On cover: New Avon library. 108). 1946.
Taste for Power. Muriel Dobbin. LC 80-15547. 10.95 (ISBN 0-399-90095-0). R. Marek Publishers.
Taste for Violence. Davis Dresser. LC 49-783810. (Red badge mystery). 1949. Dodd, Mead.
Taste of Apples. Jennette Barbour Perry Lee. LC 13-19331. 1913. Dodd, Mead and Company.
Taste of Apples. John Rowlands. (O.s.i.). 1967. pap. 0.60 o.s.i. (A275, Award). Univ Pub & Dist.
Taste of Ashes. Howard Browne. LC 57-14050. (Inner sanctum mystery). 1957. Simon and Schuster.
Taste of Brass. Robert Donald Locke. LC 57-7474. (Dell first edition, A196). 1957. Dell Pub. Co.
Taste of Brine. Edith Noel Daniell Barclay. LC 14-18922. (Illus.). 1914. Hodder and Stoughton.
Taste of Death. Fenn McGrew. LC 52-12111. (Murray Hill mystery). 1953. Rinehart.
Taste of Eden. Abra Taylor. (Superromances Ser.). 384p. 1982. pap. 2.50 (ISBN 0-373-70012-1, Pub. by Worldwide). Harlequin Bks.
Taste of Fear: Thirteen Eerie Tales of Horror. Hugh Lamb. LC 76-8997. 1976. 8.95 (ISBN 0-8008-7549-4). Taplinger Pub. Co.
Taste of Glory: A Novel. Carleton Beals. LC 56-11370. 1956. Crown Publishers.
Taste of Honey. Eric Maschwitz. LC 25-265909. 1925. R. M. McBride & Company.
Taste of Infamy: The Adventure of John Killane, a Novel. Charles O Locke. LC 60-7582. 1960. Norton.
Taste of Paradise. Margaret Mayo. (Harlequin Romances Ser.). 192p. 1981. pap. 1.50 (ISBN 0-373-02439-8). Harlequin Bks.
Taste of Passion. Kay Martin. pap. 0.60 o.p. (60-324). Manor Bks.
Taste of Power. Tr. from Slovak by Paul Stevenson. Foreword by Max Hayward. Ladislav Mnacko. LC 67-20489. 1967. 5.95. Praeger.
Taste of Proof. Bill Knox. LC 65-14011. 1965. Published for the Crime Club by Doubleday.
Taste of Rabbit Tracks: Expedition into a Frozen Wilderness. Mike Shields. LC 78-320086. (Exposition-banner book). (Illus.). 10.50 (ISBN 0-682-49082-2). Exposition Press.
Taste of Red Onion. Paul D. Olejar. LC 81-50630. 240p. (Orig.). 1981. pap. 8.95x (ISBN 0-935834-04-4). Rainbow-Betty.
Taste of Sangria. Carlton Keith, pseud. 1969. pap. 0.60 o.p. (0502-06055-060). Curtis.
Taste of Sangria. Carlton Keith, pseud. LC 68-14211. 1968. 3.95 o.p. Doubleday.
Taste of Sangria. Keith Robertson. LC 68-14211. 1968. Published for the Crime Club by Doubleday.
Taste of Steel. Robert W. March. 224p. pap. 2.50 (ISBN 0-8439-2022-X, Kable Bks). Dorchester Pub Co.
Taste of Steel. Robert W. Marsh. 224p. 1982. pap. 2.50 o.s.i. (ISBN 0-8439-1155-7, Leisure Bks). Nordon Pubns.
Taste of Terror. Martha Albrand. LC 77-3446. 1977. 7.95 (ISBN 0-399-11965-5). Putnam.
Taste of the Lotus. Florine De Veer. 1979. 9.50 o.p. (ISBN 0-533-03915-0). Vantage.
Taste of Time. Ferol Egan. LC 76-48209. 9.95 (ISBN 0-07-019050-X). McGraw-Hill.
Taste of Treason: Brock Potter Novel. Arthur Maling. LC 82-48580. 14.50 (ISBN 0-06-015128-5). Harper & Row.
Taste of Treasure. Gordon Ashe, pseud. (Rinehart Suspense Novel). 1966. 3.95 o.p. (ISBN 0-03-060295-5). HR&W.
Taste of Treasure: By Gordon Ashe. 1st Ed. John Creasey. LC 66-21635. 1966. bds., 3.95. Holt.
Taste of Vengeance. Lavinia Riker Davis. LC 46-848492. 1947. Pub. for the Crime Club by Doubleday & Company, Inc.
Taste of War: A Novel. Charles Henry Johnson. LC 71-98958. 1969. 5.50. Exposition Press.
Tate. Dale Oldham. 1978. pap. 1.50 o.s.i. (ISBN 0-505-51306-4). Tower Bks.
Tatlin! Guy Davenport. (Illus.). 352p. 1974. 7.95 o.p. (ISBN 0-684-13783-6). Scribner.
Tatlin! Six Stories. Guy Davenport. LC 73-19359. (Illus.). 1974. 10.00. Scribner.
Tatlin! Six Stories. johns hopkins paperbacks ed. Guy Davenport. LC 81-48197. 1982. 7.95 (ISBN 0-8018-2800-7). Johns Hopkins University Press.
Tatoo, the Wicked Cross. Floyd Salas. 1981. PLB 15.95 (ISBN 0-531-07320-3, Pub. by Second Chance Pr). Watts.
Tatsuniyoyi Na Hausa see Hausa Tales & Traditions.
Tatter'd Loving. Phyllis Bottome. LC 30-24772. 1930. Houghton Mifflin Company.
Tatterdemalion. John Galsworthy. LC 20-5770. 1920. C. Scribner's Sons.
Tatterley: The Story of a Dead Man. Tom Gallon. (Half-title: Appletons' town and country library, no. 210). 1897. D. Appleton and Company.
Tatters: A Novel. Fanny D. Bates. (On cover: Good company series, no. 17). 1892. Lee and Shepard.
Tattle-Tales of Cupid. Paul Leicester Ford. LC 70-94720. (Short story index reprint series). 1969. (ISBN 0-8369-3099-1). Books for Libraries Press.
Tattle-Tales of Cupid, Told. Paul Leicester Ford. LC 98-1219. 1898. Dodd, Mead and Company.
Tatto, the Wicked Cross. Floyd Salas. 352p. 1982. pap. 8.95 (ISBN 0-531-07340-8, Pub. by Second Chance Pr). Watts.
Tattoo. A. Parry. 1971. pap. 1.50 o.p. (Collier). Macmillan.
Tattoo. Earl Thompson. LC 74-79668. 1974. 8.95 (ISBN 0-399-11328-2). Putnam.
Tattoo. Earl Thompson. LC 74-79668. (Signet book). 1975. (pbk.) 2.25. New American Library.
Tattoo: A Collection. Jack Cady. LC 78-11142. 1978. 5.75 (ISBN 0-931594-01-4). Circinatum Press.
Tattoo Mystery. William Le Queux. LC 27-3173. The Macaulay Company.
Tattoo the Wicked Cross. Floyd Salas. LC 67-20344. (Evergreen black cat bk., B156). 1968. pap., 1.25. Grove.
Tattoo the Wicked Cross. Floyd Salas. LC 67-20344. 1967. Grove Press.
Tattooed Arm. Isabel Egenton Ostrander. LC 22-141867. 1922. R. M. McBride & Company.
Tattooed Countess. Carl Van Vechten. LC 77-78307. 1981. 23.00 (ISBN 0-404-15127-2). AMS Press.
Tattooed Countess: A Romantic Novel with a Happy Ending. Carl Van Vechten. LC 24-21077. 1924. A. A. Knopf.
Tattooed Gun Hand. Charles Plumb. 1978. pap. 1.50 (ISBN 0-89041-213-8, 3213). Major Bks.
Tattooed Heart. Theodora Keogh. LC 53-61182. 1953. Farrar, Straus & Young.
Tattooed Innocent & the Raunchy Grandmother: An Adult Fairy Tale, Quite Grim. Robert F. Cline. LC 81-69430. 192p. (Orig.). 1983. pap. 7.95 (ISBN 0-9607082-0-0). Argos House.
Tattooed Rood. Kyle Onstott & Lance Horner. 384p. 1978. pap. 2.75 (ISBN 0-449-23619-6, Crest). Fawcett.
Tattooed Rood: By Kyle Onstott and Lance Horner. Kyle Onstott & Lance Horner. 1960. Denlinger's.
Tau Cross Mystery. Alfred Walter Stewart. LC 35-933297. 1935. Little, Brown, and Company.
Tau Zero. Poul Anderson. LC 78-97645. 1970. 4.95. Doubleday.
Taurua: Or, Written in the Book of Fate. Emily Syrena Loud. 1899. The Editor Publishing Co.
Taurus. George Wells. 1982. pap. 2.50 (ISBN 0-451-11553-8, AE1553, Sig). NAL.
Taurus Trip. Thomas Blanchard Dewey. LC 72-130470. (Inner sanctum mystery). 1970. 4.95 (ISBN 0-671-20699-0). Simon and Schuster.
Tauzero. Poul Anderson. (Berkley Medallion Book). 1976. 1.50 (ISBN 0-425-03210-8). Berkley.
Tavern. Marguerite Steen. LC 36-8264. The Bobbs-Merrill Company.
Tavern: A Novel. Irving Townsend. LC 78-23343. 10.95 (ISBN 0-89141-052-X). Presidio Press.
Tavern Girl. Watkins Eppes Wright. LC 48-10101. 1948. Phoenix Press.
Tavern House. Charlene Keel. (O.s.i.). 1976. pap. 1.95 o.s.i. (BT50956). Belmont-Tower.
Tavern House. Charlene Keel. Belmont Tower.
Tavern in the Town. Cecile Hulse Matschat. LC 42-25504. 1942. Farrar & Rinehart, Inc.
Tavern-Keepers Victims: Or, Six Nights with the Washingtonians. new and complete edition, with illustrations. ed. Timothy Shay Arthur & Cruikshank, George, 1792-1878, Illus. 1860. Leary, Getz & Co.
Tavern Knight. Rafael Sabatini. LC 27-128281. 1927. Houghton Mifflin Company.
Tavern Rogue. Robert Gordon Anderson. LC 34-25927. Farrar & Rinehart, Inc.
Tavern Wench. Sarah Farrant. LC 77-82761. 1979. 8.95 (ISBN 0-385-13064-3). Doubleday.
Taverna in Terrazzo. Millie J Ragosta. 1975. (pbk.) 0.95 (ISBN 0-345-26701-X). Ballantine Books.
Tavola Ritonda. Tr. by Anne Shaver from Fr. 1982. write for info. 0.00 (ISBN 0-86698-053-9). Medieval & Renaissance NY.
Taw & Other Thai Stories. Ed. by Jennifer Draskau. (Writing in Asia Ser.). 1975. pap. text ed. 6.50x (00215). Heinemann Ed.
Taw Jameson. May Davies Martenet. LC 52-12206. 1953. Knopf.
Tawi Tawi. Louis Dodge. LC 21-5080. 1921. C. Scribner's Sons.
Tawn Delaney. Anne Tedlock Brooks. 1955. Arcadia House.
Tawny. Donald Henderson Clarke. LC 36-772138. 1936. The Vanguard Press.
Tawny Gold Man. Amii Loren. 1980. pap. 1.75 (ISBN 0-440-18978-0). Dell.
Tawny Sands. new ed. Violet Winspear. (World of Romance Ser.). 192p. 1972. 4.95 o.p. (ISBN 0-529-04892-2, A4480). World Pub.
Tax Rolls from Karanis... Ed. by Herbert Chayyim Youtie. Schuman, Verne Brinson, Ed & Pearl, Orsamus Merrill, Ed. LC 37-27506. (Half-title: University of Michigan studies. Humanistic series. vol. ILII-). University of Michigan Press.
Taxi. Violette Leduc. LC 75-189339. 1972. 4.95 (ISBN 0-374-27253-0). Farrar, Straus & Giroux.
Taxi. Alice Duer Miller. LC 31-26804. 1931. Dodd, Mead & Company.
Taxi. Helen Potrebenko. 168p. pap. 3.95 (ISBN 0-919888-02-X). Crossing Pr.

Taxi: An Adventure Romance. George Agnew Chamberlain. LC 20-26439. The Bobbs-Merrill Company.
Taxi Dancer. Robert Terry Shannon. E. J. Clode, Inc.
Taxi Heaven. Patrick O'Mara. LC 32-13938. The Vanguard Press.
Taxi, Lady? Wright Williams. LC 38-221337. Phoenix Press.
Taxi, Lady? Watkins Eppes Wright. LC 38-22133. 1938. Phoenix Press.
Taxi to Dubrovnik. Whitfield Cook. LC 80-28003. 10.95 (ISBN 0-440-08693-0). Delacorte Press.
Tazia's Torment. Sylvie F. Sommerfield. (Orig.). 1981. pap. 2.95 (ISBN 0-89083-882-8). Zebra.
Tazia's Torment. Sylvie F. Sommerfield. 416p. (Orig.). 1980. pap. 2.50 (ISBN 0-89083-669-8). Zebra.
Tcherkesse Prince. Sophie Radford De Meissner. LC 7-25856. De. Wolfe, Fiske & Co.
Tchitchikoff's Journeys: Or, Dead Souls. Nikolai Vasilevich Gogol. Tr. by Hapgood, Isabel Florence. LC 6-437438. T. Y. Crowell & Co.
Te Illusion off Mr. and Mrs. Benssingham. LC 13-44. 1912. 1.25. John Lane.
Te Nine-Tenths: A Novel. James Oppenheim. LC 11-23868. 1911. 1.25. Harper & Brothers.
Tea-Shop in Limehouse. Thomas Burke. LC 77-103499. (Short story index reprint series). 1969. Books for Libraries Press.
Tea Shop in Limehouse. Thomas Burke. LC 31-6072. 1931. Little, Brown, and Company.
Tea Table Talk. Jerome Klapka Jerome. LC 3-26167. 1903. Dodd, Mead and Company.
Tea Tray Murders. Christopher Bush. LC 34-30548. 1934. W. Morrow & Company.
Tea with Mr. Timothy. Illus. by Nicholas Fisk. 1st Amer. Ed. Geoffrey Morgan. LC 66-12873. 3.75. Little.
Teach the Angry Spirit. Cornelia Jessey. LC 49-10547. Crown Publishers.
Teach the Angry Spirit. Sussman, Cornelia (Silver) LC 49-10547. 1949. Crown Publishers.
Teach Us to Outgrow Our Madness: Four Short Novels. Kenzaburo Oe. LC 76-54582. 1977. 10.00. (ISBN 0-8021-0133-X) (ISBN 0-8021-4042-4). Grove Press: Distributed by Random House.
Teach You a Lesson. 1st Ed. Jim Hollis, pseud. LC 54-12185. Harper.
Teacher. Alexandre Bryce. 288p. (Orig.). 1981. pap. 2.50 (ISBN 0-523-41012-3). Pinnacle Bks.
Teacher Lady. Mary Frances Morgan. LC 52-5536. (Illus.). 1952. Doubleday.
Teacher of the Violin and Other Tales. Joseph Henry Shorthouse. LC 8-7332. 1888. Macmillan and Co.
Teacher Was the Sea: The Story of Pacific High School. Michael S. Kaye. LC 72-89536. (Illus.). 1972. pap. 3.95 o.p. (ISBN 0-8256-3003-7, 030003, Pub. by Links Bks). Quick Fox.
Teachers. Susan Parrish. (Modern Career Girl Series). 1973. (pbk.) 1.25. Ace Books.
Teachers & Their Students. Deena Winters. 224p. pap. 1.95 o.p. (7129). Barclay Hse.
Teacher's Blood. Ivan T Ross, pseud. LC 64-11302. 1964. Published for the Crime Club by Doubleday.
Teacher's Husband. Henry Lieferant & Sylvia Saltzberg Lieferant. LC 41-249653. The Dial Press.
Teachers of Mad Dog Swamp. Khonkhai Khammaan. Tr. by Gehan Wijeyewardene from Thai. LC 81-14783. (Asian & Pacific Writing 18). 263p. 1982. text ed. 18.00 (ISBN 0-7022-1641-0); pap. 9.50 (ISBN 0-7022-1651-8). U of Queensland Pr.
Teacher's Report Card: And Other Inspiring Stories. Mary Vandermey. LC 77-2790. 1977. pap. 2.50 (ISBN 0-915134-42-X). Mott Media.
Teacup Club. Elisa Armstrong Bengough. LC 6-2432. 1897. Way and Williams.
Teahouse of the August Moon. Vern J. Sneider. LC 51-3768. 1951. Putnam.
Teak see Novella Box.
Team. Frank O'Rourke. LC 49-11084. (Barnes sports novel). 1949. Barnes.
Team Bells Woke Me, and Other Stories. Harold Lenoir Davis. LC 73-13321. 1974. 13.50 (ISBN 0-8371-7125-3). Greenwood Press.
Team Bells Woke Me: And Other Stories. Harold Lenoir Davis. LC 53-5338. 1953. Morrow.
Tear His Head off His Shoulders. Nell Dunn, pseud. LC 74-17768. 1975. 6.95 (ISBN 0-385-00888-0). Doubleday.
Tear in the Cup: And Other Stories. Opie Percival Read. (On cover: The library of choice fiction, no. 76). 1894. Laird & Lee.
Tear in the Silk. Louise O'Flaherty. (Orig.). 1976. pap. 1.25 o.p. (ISBN 0-515-03864-4). BJ Pub Group.
Tear-Stained Path of Glory: A Novel. Sara Mildred Gaines Snow. LC 59-8903. 1959. Greenwich Book Publishers.
Tear Stains. Peter Marsh. LC 35-938. Arcadia House.
Tears and Laughter.-- The Charles Dickens Parlor Album of Illustrations. Selected. Chronologically Arranged According to Their Original Publication. with a Table of Contents, Including the Artists' Names. Charles Dickens. LC 6-37062. 1879. G. W. Carleton & Co.
Tears & Smiles. Albert Hershcel Propper. LC 9-22184. 1.00. Broadway Publishing Company.
Tears & Stone. Donita K. Simpson. 1971. pap. 1.95 o.s.i. New Voices.
Tears Are for the Living. Margaret S Banister. 1.95 (ISBN 0-445-08536-3). Popular Library.
Tears Are for the Living. Margaret S Banister. LC 63-14183. 1963. Houghton, Mifflin.
Tears for a King. Ron Rendleman. 2.25. Bible Voice Inc.
Tears for Jessie Hewitt. Sherry, Edna. LC 58-5984. 1958. Dodd, Mead.
Tears for the Bride. Robert Lee Martin. LC 54-570783. (Red badge detective). 1954. Dodd, Mead.
Tears in Paradise. Jane Blackmore. (First published in Great Britain in 1959.). 1973. (pbk.) 0.95. Dell Pub. Co.
Tears in Paradise Intrigue. Jane Blackmore. 1979. pap. 1.25 (ISBN 0-440-18565-3). Dell.
Tears of Agony. John Shalhoub. 4.95 o.p. Vantage.
Tears of Autumn. Charles McCarry. LC 74-7419. 1975. 7.95 (ISBN 0-8415-0309-5). Saturday Review Press.
Tears of Gold. Laurie McBain. LC 79-50429. 1979. 2.50 (ISBN 0-380-41475-9). Avon Books.
Tears of Love. Barbara Cartland. (pbk.) 1.25. Bantam Books.
Tears on the Diadem: Or, The Crown and the Cloister. A Tale of the White and Red Roses. Anna Hanson McKenney Dorsey. LC 6-33706. 1846. E. Dunigan.
Tease. Richard Smithies. 1975. (pbk.) 1.25. New American Library.
Tease for Two. Aston Cantwell. 240p. (Orig.). 1983. pap. 2.75 (ISBN 0-446-30293-7). Warner Bks.
Teaser. Orrie Hitt. LC 56-38436. 1956. Woodford Press.
Teaser. Craig Shepard. LC 47-18673. 1947. Phoenix Press.
Teaser, by Richard Grant Pseud. Joseph Calvitt Clarke. LC 37-2062. 1937. Godwin.
Teaspoon of Honey. Bert Kruger Smith. LC 72-14769. 1970. 5.95. Aurora Publishers.
Teaspoonful of Freedom. LC 68-56608. American Hungarian Literary Guild.
Technicians of Death. Tony Williamson. LC 78-55426. 1978. Atheneum.
Technicolor Time Machine. Harry Harrison. LC 67-17726. (Doubleday sci. fic.). 1967. 3.95. Doubleday.
Technique of the Novel: A Handbook on the Craft of the Long Narrative. Thomas H. Uzzell. LC 47-890. 1947. J. B. Lippincott Company.
Technos. E. C. Tubb. (Dumarest of Terra Ser.: No. 7). 1982. pap. 2.25 (ISBN 0-441-79976-0, Pub. by Ace Science Fiction). Ace Bks.
Tecumseh. Paul J. Lederer. 1982. pap. 2.95 (ISBN 0-451-11410-8, AE1410, Sig). NAL.
Tecumseh. William Gilmore Simms. 1974. Repr. of 1878 ed. lib. bdg. 30.00 (ISBN 0-8414-8068-0). Folcroft.
Tecumseh! A Play. Allan W. Eckert. 1974. pap. 2.50 o.p. (ISBN 0-316-20872-8). Little.
Ted. Alexander L Johnson. LC 52-6936. 1952. Vantage Press.
Ted: And Some Other Stories. Louise Dunham Goldsberry. LC 18-12855. 1918. 1.50. The Gorham Press.
Ted Mark Reader. Ted Mark, pseud. (Orig.). 1969. pap. 0.60 o.p. (73-515). Lancer.
Ted River Guns. Donald B. Hobart. 1970. pap. 0.60 o.p. (0502-06083). Curtis.
Teddie: A Simple, Little Out-of-Door Story About a Child, in the Telling of Which a Promise to a Friend Is Redeemed. Frederic H Britton. LC 10-183834. 1910. F.B. Dickerson Co.
Teddy Bear. Georges Simenon. LC 72-175800. 1971. 1.50 (ISBN 0-241-02063-8). H. Hamilton.
Teddy Bear. Georges Simenon. LC 73-182332. 1972. (ISBN 0-15-188377-7). Harcourt Brace Jovanovich.
Teddy in Darkest Africa: Or, The Daring Exploits of Bwana-Tumbo; an Exciting Narrative of Thrilling Adventures, and Songs to Nature. Ovidio Giberga. LC 10-14149. 1910. 0.50.
Teddy in the Tree. Constantine FitzGibbon & Marjorie FitzGibbon. 5.70 (ISBN 0-385-09005-6) (ISBN 0-385-09011-0). Doubleday.
Tedos and Tisod: A Temperance Story. Ada Matilda Cole Bittenbender. LC 11-29661. Gilloa Book Company.
Teeftallow. Thomas Sigismund Stribling. LC 26-26291. 1926. Doubleday, Page & Company.
Teen-Age Detective Stories. Ed. by Abraham Loew Furman. Jack E Woolgar. LC 68-23983. (Teen-age library). 1968. 3.25. Lantern Press.
Teen Angel. Sonia Pilcer. LC 78-5376. 9.95 (ISBN 0-698-10941-4). Coward, McCann & Geoghegan.
Teen Angels. Sonia Pilcer. 1979. pap. 2.50 (ISBN 0-380-47662-2, 61689). Avon.
Teen Deviate '70. Geoffrey Kyle. pap. 1.95 o.p. (ISBN 0-87682-104-2, 7104). Barclay Hse.
Teen Idols. Martin A. Grove. (Orig.). 1979. pap. 1.95 (ISBN 0-532-19258-3). Woodhill.
Teen Sex Games. Gene North. LC 72-186009. (API, 106). 1.95. Nu-Triumph.
Teen Sex Slaves. Sterling Harkins. 192p. pap. 1.95 o.p. (7116). Barclay Hse.
Teenage Call Girls. Clark Gifford. pap. 1.95 o.p. (ISBN 0-87056-229-0, 6229). Brandon.
Teenage Ghost Stories: Volume 1. Tim Hallinan. (official Tiger Beat Publication). 1973. (pbk.) 0.95. New American Lib.
Teenage Harem. Thomas Shire. 192p. (Orig.). 1972. pap. 1.95 o.p. (ISBN 0-87682-276-6, 7276). Barclay Hse.
Teenage Hookers. Ellen Evans, pseud. (O.s.i.). 1976. pap. 1.50 o.s.i. (BT50958). Belmont-Tower.
Teenage Love Stories; Volume 4. Tim Hallinan. (Official Tiger Beat Publication). 1973. (pbk) 0.95. New American Lib.
Teenage Love Stories Volume 5. Louise Haynes. (official tiger beat publication.). 1973. (pbk.) 0.95. New American Library.
Teenage Love Stories Volume 6. Louise Haynes. (Official Tiger Beat Publication)). 1973. (pbk.) 0.95. New American Lib.
Teenage Runaway. John Benton. LC 76-12603. 1.50 (ISBN 0-8007-0770-2). F. H. Revell Co.
Teenage Seductresses. Ralph Benton. pap. 1.95 o.p. (ISBN 0-87682-231-6, 7231). Barclay Hse.
Teenage Sex Seducers. Stephen Jones. pap. 1.95 o.p. (ISBN 0-87682-237-5, 7237). Barclay Hse.
Teenage Swingers. Ellis. pap. 1.95 o.p. (ISBN 0-87682-190-5, 7190). Barclay Hse.
Teenagers. Jean Dor. 160p. pap. 1.95 o.p. (MP-115). Montmartre.
Teeth of the Dragon. David Lowry. F. T. Neely.
Teeth of the Tiger. Maurice Leblanc. Tr. by Teixeira De Mattos, Alexander Louis. LC 14-16469. 1914. 1.25. Doubleday, Page & Company.
Teeth of the Tiger. Maurice Leblanc. Tr. by Teixeira De Mattos, Alexander Louis. LC 21-8693. Grosset & Dunlap.
Teeth of the Wolf: A Novel. Alain Paris. LC 83-96. 15.95 (ISBN 0-283-98784-7). Holt, Rinehart, and Winston.
Teething Thirties. Maxine Carter. LC 68-19720. 1968. pap. 3.00 o.p. William-F.
Teething Thirties; a Young Girl's Search for Maturity During the Depression: A Novel. Maxine Carter. LC 68-19720. 1968. William-Frederick Press.
Teg's 1994: An Anticipation of the Near Future. Robert Theobald & J. M Scott. LC 70-150754. 1975. (pbk.) 1.25. Warner Books.
Teh Treasure of Sainte Foy. Donald W. Heiney. LC 79-23242. (Illus.). 1980. 11.95 (ISBN 0-689-11025-1). Atheneum.
Tehilla, and Other Israeli Tales: By S. J. Agnon and Others. Translated by I. M. Lask and Others. Samuel Joseph Agnon. LC 56-8049. (Ram's horn books). 1956. Abelard-Schuman.
Teitlebaum's Window. Wallace Markfield. LC 74-118712. 1970. 6.95. Knopf.
Tejanos! K. R. G. Granger. LC 55-8717. (Permabooks, M-3018). 1955. Permabooks.
Tejanos see Texas Outlaws.
Tejas Country: By Frank Miller Pseud. Noel M. Loomis. LC 54-12783. 1953. Avalon Books.
Tejedora de Suenos see Historia de una Escalera.
Tejera Secrets. Mary Orr, pseud. LC 74-4313. 1974. 7.95 (ISBN 0-8037-8587-9). Dial Press.
Tejera Secrets. Mary Orr, pseud. 1975. (pbk.) 1.50. Bantam Books.
Tekel: Or, Cora Glencoe. A Novel... Henry A Bragg. LC 6-17943. 1870. J. B. Lippincott & Co.
Tekla: A Romance of Love and War. Robert Barr. LC 98-1106. 1898. Frederick A. Stokes Company.
Telefair, the House on the Island. Craig Rice. LC 42-720318. 1942. The Bobbs-Merrill Company.
Telefon. Walter H Wager. LC 74-19402. 1975. 7.95 (ISBN 0-02-622430-5). Macmillan.
Telefon. Walter H Wager. LC 74-19402. 1976. (pbk.) 1.95. Warner Books.
Telegram from Heaven. Arnold Manoff. LC 42-21514. 1942. The Dial Press.
Telegraph Trail: By Chuck Stanley. Charles Stanley Strong. LC 57-59388. 1957. Arcadia House.
Telemann Touch: By William Haggard Pseud. 1st Ed. Richard Clayton. LC 58-11439. 1958. Little, Brown.
Telempath. Spider Robinson. LC 76-20495. 6.95. Berkley Pub. Corp.: Distributed by Putnam.
Telempath. Spider Robinson. (Berkley Medallion Book). 1977. 1.50 (ISBN 0-425-03548-4). Berkley Pub. Corp.
Teleny; or, the Reverse of the Medal. Oscar Wilde. 140p. 1972. pap. 1.95 o.p. (ISBN 0-87056-261-4, 6261). Brandon.
Telephone Book. Dorothy Kunhardt. 1975. 2.95 (ISBN 0-307-12144-5). Golden Press.
Telephone Connection. Rebecca Smith. 1981. pap. 1.50. Eldridge Pub.
Teles of Edgar Allan Poe: With an Introduction by Hervey Allen and Wood Engravings. Edgar Allan Poe. LC 44-6315. 1944. Random House.
Teles: The Cynic Teacher. Ed. by Edward N. O'Neil. LC 76-41800. (Society of Biblical Literature. Texts & Translantion - Graeco-Roman Religion Ser.). 1977. pap. 6.00 (ISBN 0-89130-092-9, 060211). Scholars Pr Ca.
Telespheres. Fereidoun M. Esfandiary. 1.75 (ISBN 0-445-04115-3). Popular Library.
Televising of Heller: A Novel. John Bartlow Martin. LC 79-7502. 1980. 10.00 (ISBN 0-385-15135-7). Doubleday.
Television Nurse. Florence Stonebraker. LC 68-2873. 1968. Arcadia House.
Telfair's Daughter. Jean Libman Block. LC 74-5081. 1974. Bantam Books.
Telfair's Daughter. Jean Libman Block. 1974. (pbk.) 1.25. Bantam.
Tell Bill Goodbye. Cecily Spaulding. LC 42-796972. 1942. Arcadia House, Inc.
Tell Death to Wait: A Story About a Murder. Anita Boutell. LC 39-2600. 1939. G. P. Putnam's Sons.
Tell England: A Study in a Generation. Ernest Raymond. LC 22-6029. 1922. 7.60. Cassell and Company, Ltd.
Tell England: A Study in a Generation. Ernest Raymond. LC 22-25805. 2.00. George H. Doran Company.
Tell Her It's Murder. Helen Kieran Reilly. LC 54-5392. 1954. Random House.
Tell Her the Judge Is a Bastard. Lee Rothchild. 125p. 1982. pap. 3.95 (ISBN 0-940978-05-9). Sharral Pub.
Tell It Again: Indian Stories. Jessie Colvin. 112p. 1974. pap. 2.00 o.p. (ISBN 0-89036-006-5). Hawkes Pub Inc.
Tell It As It Is. Theodore Carcich. LC 75-25225. (Stories That Win Ser). 1976. pap. 0.95 o.p. (ISBN 0-8163-0216-2, 20075-8). Pacific Pr Pub Assn.
Tell It on the Drums. Robert W Krepps. 1955. Macmillan.
Tell It on the Mountain. William R. Lasky & James F. Scheer. 1977. pap. 1.95 o.p. (ISBN 0-8007-8311-5, Spire). Revell.
Tell It to the Birds. James Hadley Chase. 1974. (pbk.) 0.95 (ISBN 0-671-77764-5). Pocket Books.
Tell It to the Laughing Stars: A Novel. Havill, Edward. LC 42-9121. 1942. Harper & Brothers.
Tell Me a Riddle. Tillie Olsen. (O.s.i.). 1978. 8.95 o.s.i. (ISBN 0-440-08654-X, Sey Lawr). Delacorte.
Tell Me a Riddle. Tillie Olsen. 1971. pap. 3.95 (ISBN 0-440-58573-2, Delta). Dell.
Tell Me a Story, an Anthology. 1st Ed. Ed. by Charles Laughton. LC 57-12586. 1957. McGraw-Hill.
Tell Me About Women. Harry Reasoner. LC 46-4258. 1946. B. Ackerman, Inc.
Tell Me Another Morning: A Novel. 1st Ed. Zdena Berger. LC 61-645658. 1961. Harper.
Tell Me Another Story. Ed. by Eileen Colwell. pap. 0.95 o.p. (ISBN 0-14-030210-7). Penguin.
Tell Me How Long the Train's Been Gone. James B. Baldwin. (O.s.i.). 1968. 9.95 o.s.i. (ISBN 0-8037-8579-8). Dial.
Tell Me Love: A Novel. Lucy Prince Scheidlinger. LC 66-24384. 1966. Astra Books.
Tell Me My Name. Mary Carter. LC 75-43671. 1976. 11.95 (ISBN 0-8161-6345-6). G. K. Hall.
Tell Me My Name: A Novel. Mary Carter. LC 75-8535. 1975. 7.95. W. Morrow.
Tell Me My Name: A Novel. Mary Carter. (Kangaroo Book). 1977. 1.75 (ISBN 0-671-80852-4). Pocket Books.
Tell Me No Lies. Mira Lederer. 1982. pap. 2.50 (ISBN 0-89083-945-X). Zebra.
Tell Me No Lies. Mira Lederer. (Orig.). 1980. pap. 2.50 (ISBN 0-89083-587-X). Zebra.
Tell Me Now, and Again. Richard Llewellyn. LC 77-80895. 1978. 8.95 (ISBN 0-385-12123-7). Doubleday.
Tell Me, Stranger. Charles Bracelen Flood. 1971. pap. 0.95 o.p. (B95-2113). Belmont-Tower.
Tell Me That You Love Me, Junie Moon. Marjorie Kellogg. 1973. (pbk) 0.95. Popular Library.
Tell Me That You Love Me, Junie Moon. Marjorie Kellogg. LC 68-24600. 1968. Farrar, Straus and Giroux.
Tell Morning This. Kylie Tennant, pseud. LC 68-85839. 1967. 3.75. Angus & Robertson.

TITLE INDEX TEMPTATION OF TORILLA.

Tell My Horse. Zora Neale Hurston. (New World Writing Ser). (Illus.). 296p. 1981. 17.95 o.p. (ISBN 0-913666-31-9); pap. 8.95. Turtle Isl Foun.
Tell No Man. Adela Rogers St. Johns. LC 66-11726. 1966. Doubleday.
Tell No Tales. Gina Day. LC 68-16422. 1968. Stein and Day.
Tell Sparta... Alexander Cameron Sedgwick. LC 45-2641. 1945. Houghton Mifflin Company.
Tell-Tale Clock Mystery: Stonewall Rountree's First Case. Jesse Carmack. LC 37-348. 1937. Frederick A. Stokes Company.
Tell-Tale Heart. Edgar Allan Poe. Ed. by Raymond Harris. (Jamestown Classics). (Illus.). 48p. (Orig.). 1982. pap. text ed. 2.00x (ISBN 0-89061-262-5, 467); tchr's ed. 3.00x (ISBN 0-89061-263-3, 469). Jamestown Pubs.
Tell-Tale or the Invisible Witness see Court & City Vagaries, or Intrigues, of Both Sexes.
Tell-Tale Watch (Der Lebende Hat Recht.) A Novel. From the German of George Hocker. Georg Hocker & De Vere, Meta, Tr. LC 44-18754. (Ledger library. No. 95). 1893. Robert Bonner's Sons.
Tell the Mischief. William Hawkins. LC 64-21988. 1964. Appleton-Century.
Tell the President. Harold C. Butt. 1977. 5.95 o.p. (ISBN 0-533-02748-9). Vantage.
Tell the Time to None. Helen Hudson. LC 66-13652. bds., 4.95. Dutton.
Tell Them What's-Her-Name Called. Mildred B Davis. LC 74-17137. 1975. 5.95 (ISBN 0-394-49509-8). Random House.
Tell Them What's-Her-Name Called. 1976. (pbk.) 1.50 (ISBN 0-671-80402-2). Pocket Books.
Tell Them Willie Boy Is Here. Harry Lawton. (O.s.i.). 1968. pap. 0.75 o.s.i. (AS944, Award). Univ Pub & Dist.
Tell Us, Jerry Silver: A Novel. Stanley Cohen. LC 73-1736. 1973. 5.95 (ISBN 0-672-51828-7). Bobbs-Merrill.
Tell Us of the Night. Coningsby William Dawson & Browne, Barton. LC 41-2703. 1941. Jefferson House.
Tell You What I'll Do. Henry Cecil. (O.S.I.). 1970. 4.95 o.s.i. (ISBN 0-671-20522-6). S&S.
Tell Your Sons: A Novel of the Napoleonic Era. Willa Gibbs. 1946. Farrar, Straus and Company, Inc.
Teller: a Story by Edward Noyes Westcott:... with the Letters of Edward Noyes Westcott. Edward Noyes Westcott. Ed. by Margaret Westcott Muzzey. Heermans, Forbes, 1856- LC 1-24451. 1901. D. Appleton and Company.
Teller in the Tale. Louis D. Rubin, Jr. LC 67-21197. 1967. 9.50 o.p. (ISBN 0-295-97871-6). U of Wash Pr.
Tellers of Tales: 100 Short Stories from the United States, England, France, Russia and Germany. Ed. by William Somerset Maugham. LC 39-20438. 1939. Doubleday, Doran & Company, Inc.
Tellier House. Tr. from French by Desmond Flower. Illus. by Charles Mozley. Guy De Maupassant. LC 65-110395. 1965. bds., 10.00. Potter.
Telling. Laura Riding Jackson. price not set o.p. (Athlone Pr). Humanities.
Telling: A Novel. John Weston. LC 66-137873. 4.50. McKay.
Tellings. Tacy Stokes Paxton. LC 28-196229. 1928. Doubleday, Doran & Company, Inc.
Telltale Lilac Bush & Other West Virginia Ghost Tales. Ruth A. Musick. LC 64-14000. (Illus.). 208p. 1976. pap. 6.50 (ISBN 0-8131-0136-0). U Pr of Ky.
Telltale Telegram. Helen Burnham. LC 32-6424. 1932. R. M. McBride & Company.
Teltase Idea: Or, Reform Working Backward. George K Coryell. LC 6-287222. (sunset library, v. i, no. 2). 1893. Sunset Publishing Company.
Telzey Toy. James H. Schmitz. 192p. 1982. pap. 2.25 (ISBN 0-441-80035-1). Ace Bks.
Telzey Toy. James H. Schmitz. (Science Fiction Ser.). 1973. pap. 0.95 o.p. (UQ1086). DAW Bks.
Telzey Toy. James H Schmitz. 1973. (pbk.) 0.95. Daw Books.
Temescal. Henry Herbert Knibbs. LC 25-7941. 1925. Houghton Mifflin Company.
Temper. Lawrence Henry Conrad. LC 74-22774. (Labor Movement in Fiction and Non-Fiction). 1976. 18.50 (ISBN 0-404-58414-4). AMS Press.
Temper. Lawrence Henry Conrad. LC 24-3531. 1924. Dodd, Mead and Company.
Temper Cure. Stanley Edwards Johnson. LC 1-29204. The Abbey Press.
Temper of the Days. William Maier. LC 61-6901. 1961. Scribner.
Temper the Wind. Clyde Brion Davis. LC 48-52672. 1948. J. B. Lippincott Co.
Temperamental Henry: An Episodic History of the Early Life and the Young Loves of Henry Calverly, 3rd. Samuel Merwin. LC 17-243965. 1917. 1.50. The Bobbs-Merrill Company.
Temperamental People. Mary Roberts Rinehart. LC 24-20550. George H. Doran Company.
Temperance Doctor. Mary Dwinell Chellis. LC 6-23355. 1868. National Temperance Society and Publication House.
Temperance Meeting in the Village of Tattertown. Founded on Fact. Lucius Manlius Sargent. LC 8-1822. (On cover: Temperance tales, v. 7, no. 21). 1843. W. S. Damrell.
Temperance Tales. new illustrated ed. Lucius Manlius Sargent. LC 1-21948. 1873. W. J. Holland & Co.
Temperance Tales: Or, Six Nights with the Washingtonians. Timothy Shay Arthur. LC 73-107158. (Illus.). 1971. (ISBN 0-403-00466-7). Scholarly Press.
Tempered Blade. Monte Barrett. LC 46-271420. 1946. The Bobbs-Merrill Company.
Tempered Steel: A Romance. Herbert Samuel Mallory. R. F. Fenno & Company.
Tempering. Charles Neville Buck. LC 20-577267. 1920. Doubleday, Page & Company.
Tempest. Arthur Moore. (Orig.). 1979. pap. 2.50 (ISBN 0-89083-521-7). Zebra.
Tempest. Christina Savage, pseud. (Orig.). 1982. pap. 3.50 (ISBN 0-440-18895-4). Dell.
Tempest and Sunshine. Mary Jane Hawes Holmes. Ed. by Donald A. Koch. LC 68-31705. (Popular American fiction). 1968. Odyssey Press.
Tempest and Sunshine. Mary Jane Hawes Holmes. LC 9-20136. Rand, NcNally & Company.
Tempest and Sunshine. Mary Jane Hawes Holmes. LC 9-8811. Rand, McNally & Company.
Tempest & Tenderness. Ann M. Wills. (Superromance Ser.). 295p. 1983. pap. 2.95 (ISBN 0-373-70062-8). Harlequin Bks.
Tempest at Summer's End. Julia Thatcher, pseud. LC 76-20642. (Zodiac gothic: gemini). 1976. 7.95 (ISBN 0-89340-011-4). J. Curley & Associates.
Tempest at Summer's End. Julia Thatcher, pseud. LC 76-6994. 1976. 1.25. Ballantine Books.
Tempest in a Tea-Cup. William Shand. LC 59-8446. Roy Publishers.
Tempest of Souls. Nevius Pase. Tr. by De Gennaro, Zeno. LC 31-34484. Walter F. Palase Co., Inc.
Tempest of the Heart. Mary Agatha Gray. 1912. 1.25. Benziger Brothers.
Tempest of Tombstone. Lee D. Willoughby. (Women Who Won the West Ser.: No. 1). (Orig.). 1982. pap. 2.95 (ISBN 0-440-08581-0, Bryans). Dell.
Tempest Over Scotland: The Story of John Knox. Norman Eugene Nygaard. LC 60-1443. 1960. Zondervan Pub. House.
Tempest-Tossed. A Romance. Theodore Tilton. LC 8-27025. 1874. Sheldon & Company.
Tempest-Tossed. A Romance. (new and rev. ed.) ed. Theodore Tilton. LC 8-26775. 1883. R. Worthington.
Tempest-Tossed. A Romance. (new and rev. ed.) ed. Theodore Tilton. LC 8-26776. (On cover: Lovell's library, v. 3, no. 94). 1883. J. W. Lovell Co.
Tempest Tossed: The Story of Seejungfer. Margaret Roberts. LC 42-31395. 1884. G. Routledge and Sons.
Tempest-Tost. William Robertson Davies. LC 52-5560. 1952. Rinehart.
Tempests of the Play Gods: A Novel. Janie E Stoddard. LC 4-9637. 1904. The Neale Publishing Company.
Tempestuous Eden. Heather Graham. (Candlelight Ecstasy Supreme Ser.: No. 1). 288p. (Orig.). 1983. pap. 2.95 (ISBN 0-440-18646-3). Dell.
Tempestuous Lovers. Suzanne Simmons. (Orig.). 1981. pap. 1.75 (ISBN 0-440-18551-3). Dell.
Tempestuous Petticoat. Mary Ann Gibbs, pseud. LC 77-439. 1977. 7.95 (ISBN 0-88405-386-5). Mason/Charter.
Tempestuous Petticoat. Mary Ann Gibbs, pseud. 1978. 1.50 (ISBN 0-449-23489-4). Fawcett Crest Books.
Temple. Edward Frederic Benson. LC 25-8119. George H. Doran Company.
Temple. Arkady Leokum. LC 75-93471. 1969. 6.95 o.p. (H0320, NAL). Norton.
Temple. Jerome Weidman. 448p. 1976. 9.95 o.p. (ISBN 0-671-22100-0). S&S.
Temple: A Novel. Robert Greenfield. LC 82-10555. 15.95 (ISBN 0-671-44735-1). Summit Books.
Temple: A Novel. Arkady Leokum. LC 75-93471. 1969. 6.95. World Pub. Co.
Temple: A Novel. Jerome Weidman. LC 75-19212. 1975. 9.95 (ISBN 0-671-22100-0). Simon and Schuster.
Temple: A Novel. Jerome Weidman. (Kangaroo Book). 1977. 1.95 (ISBN 0-671-81232-7). Pocket Books.
Temple at Ilumquh. Jack Laflin. (Adjusters Espionage Ser). (O.s.i.). 1970. pap. 0.60 o.s.i. (A646X, Award). Univ Pub & Dist.
Temple-Beau: Or, The Town Coquets. LC 74-17026. (Flowering of the Novel). 1974. (ISBN 0-8240-1141-4). Garland Pub.
Temple-Beau; or, the Town Coquets: A Novel, 1754. Ed. by Michael F. Shugrue. (Flowering of the Novel, 1740-1775 Ser: Vol. 42). 1974. lib. bdg. 50.00 (ISBN 0-8240-1141-4). Garland Pub.
Temple Builders... Ruth Harwood. LC 39-20165. Guilders Publishing Center.
Temple Dogs. Robert L. Duncan. LC 76-51781. 1977. 8.95 o.p. (ISBN 0-688-03181-1). Morrow.
Temple Dogs: A Novel. Robert Lipscomb Duncan. LC 76-51781. 1977. 8.95 (ISBN 0-688-03181-1). Morrow.
Temple House: A Novel. Elizabeth Drew Barstow Stoddard. LC 74-174745. 1971. Johnson Reprint Corp.
Temple House: A Novel. rev. ed. Elizabeth Drew Barstow Mrs. R. H. Stoddard Stoddard. LC 8-15672. Cassell & Company, Limited.
Temple Kent. D. G Devon. LC 81-22886. 1982. 2.75 (ISBN 0-345-29848-9). Ballantine Books.
Temple Light: A Story Which Kindles a Glowing Fire Upon the Altar of Human Hearts. G. Bayard Young. LC 29-11248. The Biola Book Room, Bible Institute of Los Angeles.
Temple of Amon Ra. Mary Tudor Gray. LC 45-2916. 1945. Margent Press.
Temple of Darkness. large print ed. William Edward Daniel Ross. LC 76-20648. (Zodiac gothic: Pisces). 1976. 7.95 (ISBN 0-89340-008-4). J. Curley.
Temple of Darkness: An Astrological Gothic Novel (Pisces) William Edward Daniel Ross. LC 75-40194. 1.25 (ISBN 0-345-24857-0). Ballantine Books.
Temple of Dawn. Yukio Mishima, pseud. LC 73-7277. (His The sea of fertility 3). 1973. 7.95 (ISBN 0-394-46614-4). Knopf; Distributed by Random House.
Temple of Fear. Nick Carter. (Nick Carter Ser.). (O.s.i.). 192p. (Orig.). 1968. pap. 1.25 o.s.i. (AQ1440, Award). Univ Pub & Dist.
Temple of Fire. Margaret Way. (Harlequin Romances Ser.). 192p. 1981. pap. 1.50 (ISBN 0-373-02429-0, Pub. by Harlequin). PB.
Temple of Gold. 1st Ed. William Goldman. LC 57-12073. 1957. Knopf.
Temple of the Golden Pavilion. Yukio Mishima, pseud. LC 59-7222. (Illus.). 1959. Knopf.
Temple of the Past. Stefan Wul, pseud. LC 72-10093. (Continuum book). 1973. 6.95 (ISBN 0-8164-9148-8). Seabury Press.
Temple of the Sun. Moyra Caldecott. LC 78-4611. (Her The Sacred Stones). 8.95 (ISBN 0-8090-9212-3). Hill and Wang.
Temple of the Sun. Jeanne Judson. 1973. pap. 0.75 o.s.i. (01-390). Lancer.
Temple of the Winds. Christopher Hyde. LC 65-19720. 1965. World Pub. Co.
Temple Rakes: or Innocence Preserved see Finished Rake: or Gallantry in Perfection.
Temple Servant: And Other Stories. E. R Morrough. LC 30-6554. 1930. Longmans, Green and Co.
Temple Shadows. Pearl R. Matthews. 1968. 3.95 o.p. Vantage.
Temple Tower. Herman Cyril McNeile. LC 29-10175. 1929. Pub. for the Crime Club, Inc., by Doubleday, Doran & Company, Inc.
Temple Tree. David Beaty. LC 78-159404. 1971. 5.95 (ISBN 0-395-12704-1). Houghton Mifflin.
Templeford Park: A Novel. Alice Acland. LC 55-7090. 1955. Coward-McCann.
Temples of Ayocan. Jeffrey Lord. (Richard Blade Ser., No. 14). 192p. 1975. pap. 1.75 (ISBN 0-523-40787-4). Pinnacle Bks.
Temples of Ayocan. Jeffrey Lord. (Richard Blade Series,#14). 1975. (pbk.) 1.25 (ISBN 0-523-00623-3). Pinnacle Books.
Temples of Tyranny. Cash Asher. LC 54-35678. 1954. Crusader Press.
Templeton Case. Victor Lorenzo Whitechurch. LC 24-21589. E. J. Clode, Inc.
Templeton Memoirs. easy eye ed. Dorothy Daniels. (Orig.). pap. 0.95 o.s.i. (75-224). Lancer.
Tempo Word Finds, No. 17. Michael Richards. (Illus.). 128p. 1982. pap. 1.50 (ISBN 0-448-17336-0, Pub. by Tempo). Ace Bks.
Temporal Power. Marie Corelli. pap. 4.95 (ISBN 0-910122-26-1). Amherst Pr.
Temporal Power" A Study in Supremacy. Marie Corelli. LC 2-21102. 1902. Dodd, Mead and Company.
Temporal Power" A Study in Supremacy. Marie Corelli. LC 6-20361. 1906. Dodd, Mead and Company.
Temporary Address: Reno. Faith Baldwin Cuthrell. LC 41-13057. Farrar & Rinehart, Inc.
Temporary Address: Reno. Faith Baldwin Cuthrell. 1974. (pbk.) 1.25. Warner Paperback Library.
Temporary Affair. Kay Clifford. (Harlequin Romances Ser.). 192p. 1982. pap. 1.50 (ISBN 0-373-02505-X). Harlequin Bks.
Temporary Answers: A Novel. Jai Nimbkar. LC 74-900547. 1974. lib. bdg. 4.00x (ISBN 0-8364-0472-6). South Asia Bks.
Temporary Kings. Anthony Dymoke Powell. LC 73-10237. 1973. 6.95 (ISBN 0-316-71547-6). Little, Brown.
Temporary Life. David Storey. LC 74-3632. 1974. 6.95 (ISBN 0-525-21495-X). Dutton.
Temporary Sanity: A Novel. Thomas Glynn. LC 76-4765. 8.95. (ISBN 0-914590-28-6) (ISBN 0-914590-29-4). Fiction Collective: Distributed by G. Braziller.
Temporary Wife. Carlotta Baker. LC 38-209852. Phoenix Press.
Temporary Wife. Elizabeth York Miller. LC 33-1491. 1932. G. H. Watt.
Temporary Wife. John Pasquarelli. LC 54-13287. 1954. New Voices Pub. Co.
Temporary Wife. Leona Slottman. LC 38-20985. 1938. Phoenix Press.
Temps n'a pas d'Odeur see Day Before Tomorrow.
Tempt Not This Flesh. Barbara Riefe. LC 79-88565. 400p. (Orig.). 1979. pap. 2.95 (ISBN 0-87216-938-3). Playboy Pbks.
Temptation. David Dresser. LC 38-190881. 1938. Godwin.
Temptation. David Dresser & Manheim, Ralph, 1907- Tr. LC 46-229115. 1946. Creative Age Press, Inc.
Temptation. Vincas Kreve. Tr. by Raphael Sealey. 1965. 3.00 o.p. (ISBN 0-87141-016-8). Manyland.
Temptation. Charlotte Lamb, pseud. (Harlequin Presents Ser.). 1979. pap. 1.50 (ISBN 0-373-70810-6, Pub. by Harlequin). PB.
Temptation: A Novel. Richard Bagot. 1907. The Macmillan Company.
Temptation: A Novel by John Pen Pseud. Translated from the Hungarian by Ralph Manheim and Barbara Tolnai. John Szekely. LC 51-688723. 1949. Citadel Press.
Temptation and Triumph, with Other Stories. Virginia Frances Townsend. LC 8-29816. 1863. Poe & Hitchcock.
Temptation: By Vincas Kreve. Tr. from Lithuanian by Raphael Sealey. Introd. by Charles Angoff. Vincas Kreve-Mickervicius. LC 65-170331. 3.00. Manyland.
Temptation for a King. 1st Ed. John H Secondari. LC 54-5603. 1954. Lippincott.
Temptation Game. John Gardner. signed ltd. ed. 45.00. New London Pr.
Temptation in a Private Zoo. Anthony Dekker. LC 70-95709. 1970. 5.95. Morrow.
Temptation of Adam. Helmut Gruber. LC 78-65530. 9.95 (ISBN 0-89696-036-6). Everest House.
Temptation of Angelique. Anne Golon. LC 70-97072. 1970. 6.95. Putnam.
Temptation of Archer Watson. Laurence Snelling. LC 74-8576. 1974. 6.95. Norton.
Temptation of Don Volpi. 1st Ed. Alfred Hayes. LC 60-11943. 1960. Atheneum.
Temptation of Eileen Hughes. Brian Moore. LC 81-4466. 10.95 (ISBN 0-374-27285-9). Farrar Straus Giroux.
Temptation of Friar Consol: A Story of the Devil, Two Saints & a Booke. Eugene Field. 1900. 25.00 (ISBN 0-932062-56-3). Sharon Hill.
Temptation of Jack Orkney and Other Stories. Doris May Lessing. 1974. (pbk.) 1.95. Bantam Books.
Temptation of Jack Orkney and Other Stories. Doris May Lessing. LC 72-2241. 1972. 6.95 (ISBN 0-394-48244-1). Knopf; Distributed by Random House.
Temptation of Katharine Gray. Mary Lowe Dickinson. 1895. A. J. Rowland.
Temptation of Olive Latimer. Elizabeth Thomasina Meade Smith. The Mershon Company.
Temptation of Roger Heriott. Edward Newhouse. LC 54-10198. 1954. Houghton Mifflin.
Temptation of Saint Anthony. Gustave Flaubert & Hearn, Lafcadio, 1850-1904, Tr. LC 43-63594. 1943. The Limited Editions Club.
Temptation of St. Anthony. Translated by Lafcadio Hearn. Illustrated by Mahlon Blaine. Gustave Flaubert. LC 50-4638. (Illustrated library). Halcyon House.
Temptation of Saint Antony. Gustave Flaubert & Kitty Mrosovsky. LC 80-70452. (Illus.). 1981. 17.50 (ISBN 0-8014-1239-0). Cornell University Press.
Temptation of St. Antony: Or, A Revelation of the Soul. Gustave Flaubert. LC 78-6700. 1978. 16.00. H. Fertig.
Temptation of the West. Andre Malraux. Tr. by Robert Hollander from Fr. LC 74-76607. Orig. Title: Tentation De L'occident. 122p. 1974. Repr. of 1961 ed. lib. bdg. 12.50x o.p. (ISBN 0-914300-03-2). Jubilee Bks.
Temptation of Torilla. Barbara Cartland. LC 77-156026. 1977. 6.95 (ISBN 0-87272-026-8). Duron Books.

Temptation of Wealth: Or, The Heir by Primogeniture. 2d ed. Emilia Smith Flygare Carlen. Tr. by Hebbe, Gustaf Clemens. LC 6-20141. 1846. C. Muller.

Temptation to Steal. Noel Bertram Gerson. 1973. 0.95. Popular Lib.

Temptation to Steal: A Novel. Noel Bertram Gerson. LC 79-171290. 1972. 5.95. Doubleday.

Temptations. Stewart Richardson. LC 81-18936. 1982. 12.00 (ISBN 0-688-01142-X). Morrow.

Temptations: A Book of Short Stories. David Pinsky. LC 74-163045. (Short story index reprint series). 1971. (ISBN 0-8369-3959-X). Books for Libraries Press.

Temptations: A Book of Short Stories. David Pinsky. Tr. by Isaac Goldberg. LC 19-801351. 1919. Brentano's.

Temptations of a Great City: Or, The Love That Lived Through All. Edna Winfield, pseud. LC 99-2371. (On cover: Holly library. no. 154)). 1899. The Mershon Co.

Temptations of Big Bear. Rudy Henry Wiebe. LC 77-360407. (New Canadian library; no. 122). 1976. 3.50 (ISBN 0-7710-9222-9). McClelland and Stewart.

Temptations of the Past. Paul Debreczeny. LC 82-3051. 6.50 (ISBN 0-938920-17-0). Hermitage.

Tempted of the Devil. Passages in the Life of a Kabbalist. August Becker & Macdowall, M. W., Tr. LC 6-9776. Cupples & Hurd.

Tempted To Love. Flora Kidd. (Harlequin Presents Ser.). 192p. 1983. pap. 1.95 (ISBN 0-373-10577-0). Harlequin Bks.

Tempter. Norbert Wiener. LC 59-10838. 1959. Random House.

Tempter and the Tempted. E C De Calabrella. LC 1-1517. (Brother Jonathan, Extra. v. 2, no. 8, Sug. 31, 1842). 1842. Wilson & Company.

Tempting Fate. Chelsea Q. Yarbra. 1982. pap. 3.95 (ISBN 0-451-11865-0, AE1865, Sig). NAL.

Tempting Fate. Chelsea Quinn Yarbro. LC 81-16714. 1982. 17.95 (ISBN 0-312-79087-2). St. Martin's Press.

Tempting of Father Anthony. George Horton. LC 1-24476. 1901. A. C. McClurg & Co.

Tempting of Pescara. Conrad Ferdinand Meyer. LC 75-4902. 1975. 10.00. H. Fertig.

Tempting of Pescara. Conrad Ferdinand Meyer. Tr. by Bell, Clara Courtney (Poynter) LC 7-25873. 1890. W. S. Gottsberger & Co.; Etc., Etc.

Tempting of Tavernake. Edward Phillips Oppenheim. LC 12-24241. 1912. 1.75. Little, Brown, and Company.

Tempting of Tavernake. Edward Phillips Oppenheim. LC 11-10863. 1911. Little, Brown, and Company.

Tempting Offer. Dora Delmar. (On cover: Library of American authors. no. 59). 1894. G. Munro's Sons.

Tempting Treasures Cookbook. Ed. by Gertrude Wright & Ralph D. Luedke. 1978. pap. 3.25 o.p. (ISBN 0-89542-606-4). Ideals.

Tempting Virtue. Madeleine Sharpe Buchanan. LC 33-16350. The Macaulay Company.

Temptress. Carter Brown, pseud. LC 60-3862. (Signet books, S1817). 1960. New American Library of World Literature.

Temptress. William Le Queux. LC 7-13133. F. A. Stokes Company.

Temptress. Sandra Shulman. pap. 0.95 o.p. (65-395-0). Paperback Lib.

Temptress. Josiah Pitts Wollfolk. LC 35-3358. W. Godwin, Inc.

Temptress: La Tierra De Todos. Vicente Blasco Ibanez & Ongley, Leo, Tr. LC 23-26840. E. P. Dutton & Company.

Ten Afternoons Over the Tea-Cup. A Composite Novelette in Ten Chapters by Ten Authors. De Pauw University. Author's Club. LC 16-19176. 1893. W. B. Burford, Printer.

Ten Against Caesar. K. R. G. Granger. LC 52-8518. 1952. Houghton Mifflin.

Ten Against the Third Reich. Stanley E Smith. LC 61-4748. (Belmont books, 229). 1961. Belmont Books.

Ten-Bay Summer. Janet Quin-Harkin. 1982. pap. 1.95 (ISBN 0-553-22519-7). Bantam.

Ten Beautiful Years: And Other Stories. Mary Knight Potter. LC 16-16718. 1916. 1.25. J. B. Lippincott Company.

Ten Boys Who Lived on the Road from Long Ago to Now. Jane Andrews. LC 13-93322. (On cover: Classics for home and school). 1893. Ginn & Company.

Ten by Bo. Carl B. Bocock. 1981. 7.95 (ISBN 0-533-04680-7). Vantage.

Ten Cent Love. Maysie Greig. LC 34-5970. 1934. Doubleday, Doran & Company, Inc.

Ten Commandments. Warwick Deeping. LC 31-23465. 1931. A. A. Knopf.

Ten Commandments: A Novel. Henry MacMahon. LC 24-19533. Grosset & Dunlap.

Ten Commandments: Ten Short Novels of Hitler's War Against the Moral Code. Ed. by Armin L. Robinson. Mann, Thomas, 1875- LC 43-513550. 1943. Simon and Schuster.

Ten Contemporary Polish Stories. Ed. by Edmund Ordon. LC 74-2842. 252p. 1974. Repr. of 1958 ed. lib. bdg. 16.25x (ISBN 0-8371-7436-8, ORPS). Greenwood.

Ten Contemporary Polish Stories: Translated by Various Hands. With an Introd. by Olga Scherer-Virski. Ed. by Edmund Ordon. LC 58-6988. 1958. Wayne State University Press.

Ten Days in August: A Novel. Bernard Frizell. LC 56-6667. 1956. Simon and Schuster.

Ten Days, Mister Cain? Brian Freeborn. LC 77-10311. 1978. 7.95 (ISBN 0-312-79090-2). St. Martin's Press.

Ten Days of Christmas. Gladys Bronwyn Stern. LC 50-10760. 1950. Macmillan.

Ten Days of Terror. Ethel I. Sullivan. 92p. 1975. 4.00 o.p. (ISBN 0-682-47765-6). Exposition.

Ten Days' Wonder. Muriel Hine Coxon. 1931. D. Appleton and Company.

Ten Days' Wonder. Ellery Queen, pseud. LC 48-4963. 1948. Little Brown.

Ten Day's Wonder. Ellery Queen, pseud. LC 82-4686. 1982. 14.95 (ISBN 0-89340-525-6). J. Curley.

Ten Degrees Backward. Ellen Thorneycroft Fowler. LC 15-190808. 1915. Hodder and Stoughton.

Ten Degrees Backward. Ellen Thorneycroft Fowler. LC 15-21425. 1915. 1.25. George H. Doran Company.

Ten Degrees by the Dial. Charles G Floyd. LC 56-13208. (Nobel book). 1956. Comet Press Books.

Ten Favorite French Stories. Joseph Stanislaus Galland. (Fr.). 1935. 12.50x (ISBN 0-89197-506-3); pap. text ed. 6.95x (ISBN 0-89197-962-X). Irvington.

Ten Favorite French Stories: Edited with Notes and Vocabulary. Ed. by Joseph Stanislaus Galland. LC 35-3687. 1935. F. S. Crofts & Co.

Ten-Foot Chain. facs. ed. Achmed Abdullah et al. LC 73-116924. (Short Story Index Reprint Ser). 1920. 11.00 (ISBN 0-8369-3426-1). Ayer Co.

Ten-Foot Chain: Or, Can Love Survive the Shackles? a Unique Symposium. Achmed Abdullah & Brand, Max. LC 20-174075. 1920. Reynolds Publishing Company, Inc.

Ten Foot Square Hut & Tales of Heike. Tr. by A. L. Sadler. LC 72-157261. (Illus.). 1971. pap. 5.95 (ISBN 0-8048-0879-1). C E Tuttle.

Ten for Kaddish. Israel Jacobs. LC 72-163370. 1972. 6.95 (ISBN 0-393-08665-8). Norton.

Ten German Novellas. Ed. by Harry Steinhauer. LC 73-86891. 1969. 2.45. Doubleday.

Ten Gifts. Elizabeth Goudge. Ed. by Mary Baldwin. LC 73-99287. 1969. 6.95. Coward-McCann.

Ten Grand. George G. Gilman, pseud. (Edge Ser.: No. 2). 160p. 1982. pap. 1.95 (ISBN 0-523-41868-X). Pinnacle Bks.

Ten Great Mysteries. Ed. by Howard Haycraft & John Beecroft. LC 59-12628. 1959. Doubleday.

Ten Green Bottles: Short Stories. Audrey Callahan Thomas. LC 67-18409. 1967. Bobbs-Merrill.

Ten Holy Horrors. Francis Beeding. LC 39-23987. 1939. Harper & Brothers.

Ten Hours. Constance I Smith. LC 21-15952. 1921. Harcourt, Brace and Company.

Ten Hours: A Mystery. Harry Stephen Keeler. LC 37-33902. E. P. Dutton & Company, Inc.

Ten Jataka Stories' Each Illustrating One of the Ten Paramita. Jatakas. Ed. by I. B. Horner. (With Pali Text). 1957. 5.00 o.p. Verry.

Ten Jewels. Patrick Wynnton. LC 31-15931. 1931. J. B. Lippincott Company.

Ten Little Indians. Agatha Miller Christie. LC 78-108821. (Greenway edition; 24). 1978. 6.95 (ISBN 0-396-07515-0). Dodd, Mead.

Ten Little Virgins. Paul Snow. LC 34-41060. W. Godwin, Inc.

Ten Million. Mark Hellinger. LC 34-35472. Farrar & Rinehart, Incorporated.

Ten Million Dollar Girl. Charles Miron. 1978. pap. 1.50 (ISBN 0-532-15359-6). Woodhill.

Ten Million Dollar Hostage. Cummings-Noorbergen. (Daybreak Ser.). 1981. pap. 3.95 (ISBN 0-8163-0438-6). Pacific Pr Pub Assn.

Ten Million Years to Friday. John Lymington, pseud. LC 72-89125. 1970. 4.50. Doubleday.

Ten Millions: Or, Uncle Jacob's Legacy. Harriette Newell Woods Baker. LC 6-6882. I. Bradley & Co.

Ten Minute Alibi. Anthony Armstrong Willis & Shaw, Herbert. (On cover: Penguin books. 131). 1940. Penguin Books Limited.

Ten Minute Stories. Algernon Blackwood. LC 72-103495. (Short story index reprint series). 1969. Books for Libraries Press.

Ten Minute Stories' C4. Godfrey Elton Elton. LC 26-10566. 1926. Houghton Mifflin Company.

Ten Modern Masters: An Anthology of the Short Story. Ed. by Robert Gorham Davis. LC 53-1755. 1953. Harcourt, Brace.

Ten Modern Masters: An Anthology of the Short Story. 2d ed. Ed. by Robert Gorham Davis. LC 59-7732. 1959. Harcourt, Brace.

Ten Modern Masters: An Anthology of the Short Story. 3d ed. Ed. by Robert Gorham Davis. LC 70-183244. 1972. (ISBN 0-15-590281-4). Harcourt Brace Jovanovich.

Ten Modern New Zealand Story Writers: Longer Stories and Linked Stories. Phoebe Churchill Norris Meikle. LC 77-366999. (Illus.). 1976. 4.95 (ISBN 0-582-71748-5). Longman Paul.

Ten Modern Short Novels. Ed. by Leo Hamalian & Edmond Loris Volpe. LC 58-6834. 1958. Putnam.

Ten Modern Stories. John Hampden. Repr. of 1931 ed. lib. bdg. 10.00 (ISBN 0-8414-4987-2). Folcroft.

Ten Must Die. Morgan Hill. (Orig.). 1981. pap. 1.95 (ISBN 0-440-18717-6). Dell.

Ten Nights in a Bar-Room: And What I Saw There. Timothy Shay Arthur. LC 4-8610. 1882. H. T. Coates & Co.

Ten Nights in a Bar-Room: And What I Saw There. Timothy Shay Arthur. LC 7-1631. 1855. J. W. Bradley.

Ten Nights in a Bar-Room: And What I Saw There. Timothy Shay Arthur. LC 6-27502. Porter & Coates.

Ten Nights in a Bar-Room, and What I Saw There. Ed. by Donald A. Koch. Timothy Shay Arthur. LC 64-25051. (John Harvard Lib.). 4.95. Belknap Pr. of Harvard.

Ten Nights in a Bar-Room: By T. S. Arthur, and In His Steps by Charles M. Sheldon. Ed. by C. Hugh Holman. Timothy Shay Arthur. Ed. by Clarence Hugh Holman. Charles Monroe Sheldon. LC 66-232566. (Popular Amer. fic.). 1966. pap., 1.50. Odyssey.

Ten Nights of Dream, Hearing Things, The Heredity of Taste. Soseki Natsume. LC 73-86136. 1974. 6.95 (ISBN 0-8048-1136-9). Tuttle.

Ten North Frederick. John O'Hara. LC 55-8167. 1955. Random House.

Ten O'clock Scholar. Marjorie Holmes. LC 48-5034. 1948. J.B. Lippincott Co.

Ten of Us: Original Stories and Sketches. Sigmund Bowman Alexander. LC 6-490. Laughton, Macdonald & Co.

Ten Old Maids: And Five of Them Were Wise, and Five of Them Were Foolish. A Novel. Julie P. Smith. LC 8-818253. 1874. G. W. Carleton & Co.; Etc., Etc.

Ten Plus One. Ed McBain. 1982. pap. 2.25 (ISBN 0-451-11923-1, AE1923, Sig). NAL.

Ten Plus One: An 87th Precinct Inner Sanctum Mystery, by Ed McBain Pseud. Evan Hunter. LC 63-10851. 1963. Simon and Schuster.

Ten Princes: Dandin's Dasha-Kumara-Charita. Ryder. Tr. by Arthur W. Ryder from Sanskrit. (Midway Reprint Ser). (O.s.i.). 240p. 1974. pap. 6.50x o.s.i. (ISBN 0-226-73250-9). U of Chicago Pr.

Ten-Second Jailbreak. Eliot Asinof et al. 1973. 6.95 o.p. (ISBN 0-03-001011-X). HR&W.

Ten Seconds from Now. Kay Cicellis. LC 58-5094. (Evergreen books, E-85). 1958. Grove Press.

Ten Seconds to Zero. Ken Stanton. (Aquanauts Ser). 1970. pap. 0.75 o.p. (75-388). Manor Bks.

Ten Short Novels, with General Introduction and Prefaces. Ed. by Thomas L. Ashton. LC 77-88714. 6.95 (ISBN 0-669-01029-4). Heath.

Ten Short Stories. R. T. Nasr. pap. text ed. 1.00x o.p. (ISBN 0-582-76006-2). Longman.

Ten Short Stories. Mary M Riley. LC 31-23458. Printed by P. M. Covi.

Ten Short Stories. Tasmanian Fellowship of Australian Writers. LC 67-74205. (Aus 66-2-137).

Ten Stories. Damon Runyon. LC 46-19943. (Avon modern short story monthly. 27). 1945. Avon Book Company.

Ten Tales. Francois Coppee. LC 76-86140. (Short story index reprint series). (Illus.). 1969. Books for Libraries Press.

Ten Tales. Francois Coppee. Tr. by Learned, Walter. LC 16-9388. Harper & Brothers.

Ten Tales. Francois Coppee. Tr. by Learned, Walter. LC 6-30861. 1891. Harper & Brothers.

Ten Tales from Shakespeare. Charles Lamb & Mary Ann Lamb. LC 69-20293. (Illus.). 1969. 5.95. F. Watts.

Ten Tall Tales & Other. David Kneeshaw. 2.75 o.p. Vantage.

Ten: The Hard Way, by Kelley Banks Pseud. 1st Ed. James E Eubank. LC 54-12651. 1955. Vantage Press.

Ten-Thirty from Marseille see Sleeping Car Murders.

Ten-Thirty on a Summer Night. Marguerite Duras. LC 61-11781. 1963. Grove Press.

Ten-Thirty on a Summer Night see Four Novels.

Ten Thousand a-Year. Samuel Warren. LC 3-24511. 1885. G. Routledge and Sons.

Ten Thousand a-Year. complete ed. Samuel Warren. LC 41-40529. 1887. G. Routledge and Sons.

Ten Thousand a-Year. Samuel Warren. 1894. Little, Brown, and Company.

Ten Thousand a Year. a new edition, with notes and illustrations. ed. Samuel Warren. LC 30-19191. H. T. Coates & Co.

Ten Thousand a Year. Samuel Warren. LC 15-17424. (Half-title: Handy library edition...). 1914. Little, Brown, & Co.

Ten Thousand a Year. Samuel Warren. LC 37-20890. 1932. A. L. Burt Company.

Ten Thousand a-Year. a new ed., carefully rev. with notes and illustrations... ed. Samuel Warren. LC 45-52357. 1881. F. D. Linn & Co.

Ten Thousand a-Year. Samuel Warren. LC 44-24887. E. P. Dutton and Co.

Ten-Thousand-Dollar Arm: And Other Tales of the Big League. Charles Emmett Van Loan. LC 12-35736. Small, Maynard and Company.

Ten-Thousand-Dollar Arm: And Other Tales of the Big League. Charles Emmett Van Loan. LC 16-140933. 1913. Small, Maynard and Company.

Ten Thousand Dollars Reward. Charles Wesley Sanders. LC 24-7119. (Famous authors series. no. 46). 1924. Garden City Publishing Co., Inc.

Ten Thousand Eyes. Richard Collier. pap. 0.75 o.p. (T1645). Pyramid Pubns.

Ten Thousand Goddam Cattle. Katie Lee. LC 75-43346. (Illus.). 208p. 1976. 12.50 o.p. (ISBN 0-87358-148-2); pap. 9.50 (ISBN 0-87358-206-3). Northland.

Ten Thousand Light Years from Home. James Tiptree. LC 76-10429. (Gregg Press science fiction series). 1976. 13.50. Gregg Press.

Ten Thousand Light-Years from Home. James Tiptree. 1973. (pbk.) 0.95. Ace Books.

Ten Thousand Miles in a Balloon! Earnest Markman. (On cover: The ten cent helper books. no. 1).

Ten Thousand One Hundred Thirty-Two. Otis Lee Spurgeon. LC 20-4215. R. G. Badger.

Ten Thousand Several Doors. Mary Craig. 1973. 5.95 o.p. Hawthorn.

Ten Thousand Several Doors. Mary Francis Shura, pseud. LC 73-347. 1973. 5.95. Hawthorn Books.

Ten Thousand Things. Maria Dermout. LC 82-21867. (Library of the Indies). 1983. 19.00 (ISBN 0-87023-384-X). University of Massachusetts Press.

Ten Thousand Things: A Novel. Maria Dermout. LC 58-5123. 1958. Simon and Schuster.

Ten Thousand Tom-Toms. Jens Larsen. 1956. pap. 2.25 o.p. (ISBN 0-8006-1716-9). Fortress.

Ten Thousand Tom-Toms: Illustrated by George L. Connelly. Jens Peter Mouritz Larsen. LC 52-14180. 1952. Muhlenberg Press.

Ten Times One Is Ten - the Possible Reformation: A Story in Nine Chapters. Edward Everett Hale. LC 76-42803. Repr. of 1871 ed. 15.50 (ISBN 0-404-60069-7). AMS Pr.

Ten to One in Sweden. Paddy Sylvanus. LC 29-275252. 1929. D. Appleton and Company.

Ten to Seventeen: A Boarding-School Diary. Josephine Dodge Daskam Bacon. LC 8-2943. 1908. Harper & Brothers.

Ten Toes up. Anthony Armstrong Willis. LC 35-18236. Godwin.

Ten-Tola Bars. Burton Wohl. LC 75-14458. 1975. 7.95 (ISBN 0-440-05977-1). Delacorte Press.

Ten Tombstones. George G. Gilman, pseud. (Edge Ser.: No. 18). 192p. 1976. pap. 1.95 (ISBN 0-523-41773-X). Pinnacle Bks.

Ten Tombstones. Gilman, George G. (Edge Series#18). 1976. (pbk.) 1.25 (ISBN 0-523-00856-2). Pinnacle Books.

Ten Tomorrows. Roger Elwood. (Gold medal, M2820). 1973. (pbk.) 0.95. Fawcett.

Ten Tomorrows (Original Science Fiction Anthology) Ed. by Roger Elwood. 224p. (Orig.). 1973. pap. 0.95 o.p. (M2820, GM). Fawcett World.

Ten Top Stories. Ed. by David A Sohn. LC 64-25021. (Bantam pathfinder editions. FP74). 1964. Bantam Books.

Ten Years--Ten Days: Translated from the German of Walther Von Hollander. Walther Georg Heinrich Von Hollander & Wonderley, Lilian, Tr. LC 33-29649. 1933. The Macmillan Company.

Ten Years a Cowboy. Charles Clement Post. LC 7-30619. 1896. Rhodes & McClure Publishing Company.

Ten Years a Police Court Judge. A. A Putnam. LC 7-42399. (On cover: Standard library, no. 122). 1884. Funk & Wagnalls.

Ten Years in Cossack Slavery: Or, Black Russia. Julian Jasiencyk. Tr. by Mankowaki, Mary De. LC 1-29741. The Abbey Press.

Ten Years of His Life. E. H. Hough. LC 7-7142. (On cover: Munro's library, v. 1, no. 56). 1883. N. L. Munro.

Ten Years of Torture: Or, Sutten's Death-Bed Confession of How He Married Miss Martha Morton, an Accomplished Young Lady of Baltimore, with the Hellish Design of Torturing Her to Death... Charles Wesley Alexander. 1871. C. W. Alexander.

Ten Years' Tenant, and Other Stories. library ed. Walter Besant & Rice, James. LC 3-27826. 1888. Dodd, Mead & Company.

Tenacious Miss Tamerlane. Kasey Michaels. 192p. 1982. pap. 2.25 (ISBN 0-380-79889-1, 79889). Avon.

Tenant. Roland Topor. LC 66-11181. 1966. Doubleday.

Tenant for Death. Alfred Alexander Gordon Clark. LC 37-160706. 1937. Dodd, Mead & Company.

Tenant for the Tomb. Anthony Gilbert, pseud. 1971. pap. 0.95 o.p. (95173). Beagle Bks.

Tenant for the Tomb. Anthony Gilbert, pseud. 1971. 4.95 o.p. (ISBN 0-394-46325-0). Random.

Tenant for the Tomb. Lucy Beatrice Malleson. LC 76-140705. 1971. 4.95 (ISBN 0-394-46325-0). Random House.

Tenant of Wildfell Hall. Anne Bronte. LC 62-5682. (Harcourt library of English and American classics). 1962. Harcourt, Brace & World.

Tenant of Wildfell Hall. Anne Bronte. LC 73-3127. (Bronte, Charlotte, 1816-1855. Life & Works of the Sisters Bronte: Vol. 6). (Illus.). 1973. 25.00 (ISBN 0-404-08836-8). AMS Press.

Tenant of Wildfell Hall. Anne Bronte. LC 6-24367. 1848. Harper & Brothers.

Tenant of Wildfell Hall. Anne Bronte. LC 6-17957. 1855. Harper & Brothers.

Tenant of Wildfell Hall. Anne Bronte. Estes and Lauriat.

Tenant of Wildfell Hall. Anne Bronte. Ed. by May Sinclair. (Half-title: Everyman's library, ed. by Ernest Rhys. Fiction. no. 685). 1914. J. M. Dent & Sons, Ltd.

Tenant of Wildfell Hall. Anne Bronte. LC 79-4122. 1979. 4.95 (ISBN 0-912800-70-4). Woodbridge Press Pub. Co.

Tenant of Wildfell Hall and Agnes Grey. Anne Bronte. LC 45-408378. (Half-title: The novels of Charlotte, Emily, & Anne Bronte). 1922. J. M. Dent & Sons Ltd.

Tenant of Woodfell. A Story of Fate. Martha McCulloch Williams. (Once a week library no. 20). 1892. P. F. Collier.

Tenant. Tr. from French by Francis K. Price. Roland Topor. LC 66-11181. 3.95. Doubleday.

Tenants. Bernard Malamud. LC 71-165400. 1971. 6.95 (ISBN 0-374-27290-5). Farrar, Straus and Giroux.

Tenants: An Episode of the '80s. Mary Stanbery Watts. LC 8-11081. 1908. The McClure Company.

Tenants of Malory: A Novel. Joseph Sheridan Le Fanu. LC 76-5276. (Le Fanu, Joseph Sheridan, 1814-1873. Works. 1976). (Works. 1976.). 1976. (3vols.) 53.00 (ISBN 0-405-09233-4). Arno Press.

Tenants of Malory. A Novel. Joseph Sheridan Le Fanu. LC 34-37781. 1867. Harper & Brothers.

Tenants of Moonbloom. Edward Lewis Wallant. LC 63-13501. (Harbrace paperbound lib. HLP59). 1973. 1.85 (ISBN 0-15-688535-2). Harcourt.

Tenants of the Earth. Sandra Paretti. (Kangaroo Book). 1977. 1.95 (ISBN 0-671-80941-5). Pocket Books.

Tenants of the Earth. Sandra Paretti. LC 75-44424. (ISBN 0-87131-190-9). M. Evans.

Tenants Were Corrie & Tennie. Kent Thompson. LC 72-90482. 1973. 7.95 o.p. St Martin.

Tendencies: A Novel. Timothy Cohrs. LC 82-17042. 12.95 (ISBN 0-312-79099-6). St. Martin/Marek.

Tender Age, a Novel. Thacher, Russell. LC 52-12575. 1952. Macmillan.

Tender & the Savage. Paula Fairman. 384p. (Orig.). 1980. pap. 2.75 (ISBN 0-523-41006-9). Pinnacle Bks.

Tender Betrayal. Jennifer Blake. 1979. pap. 2.95 (ISBN 0-445-04429-2). Popular Lib.

Tender Buns. P. N. Dedeaux. pap. 1.95 o.p. (ISBN 0-87056-252-5, 6252). Brandon.

Tender Cheeks. Wolfe Kaufman. LC 34-31989. Covici, Friede.

Tender Ecstasy. Janelle Taylor. (Orig.). 1983. pap. 3.75 (ISBN 0-8217-1212-8). Zebra.

Tender Evil: By George Kramer Pseud. George Kravitz. LC 53-246149. 1953. Woodford Press.

Tender Fugitive. Jennifer Roberts. (Orig.). 1980. pap. 2.50 o.s.i. (ISBN 0-505-51504-0). Tower Bks.

Tender Fugitives. Jennifer Roberts. 2.50 (ISBN 0-505-51504-0). Tower Books.

Tender Herb. Clara Bernice Miller. LC 68-12026. 1968. Herald Press.

Tender Is the Knife: By Joan Shepherd Pseud. B J Buchanan. LC 56-14362. 1956. Washburn.

Tender Is the Night. Francis Scott Key Fitzgerald. LC 78-109644. 1978. 15.00 (ISBN 0-684-15151-0) (ISBN 0-684-71763-8). Scribner.

Tender Is the Night: A Romance. Francis Scott Key Fitzgerald. LC 51-13789. 1951. Scribner.

Tender Is the Night: A Romance. Francis Scott Key Fitzgerald. LC 34-8347. 1934. C. Scribner's Sons.

Tender Is the Night: A Romance: with the Author's Final Revision. Francis Scott Key Fitzgerald. LC 75-305177. 1974. Penguin.

Tender Is the Night Notes. Carol H Poston. 1974. (pbk.) 1.25 (ISBN 0-8220-1241-3). Cliffs Notes.

Tender Killer. Stanley Bennett Hough. Ed. by J. Barzun & W. H. Taylor. LC 81-47399. (Crime Fiction 1950-1975 Ser.). 191p. 1982. lib. bdg. 14.95 (ISBN 0-8240-4967-5). Garland Pub.

Tender Killer. Stanley Bennett Hough. 1977. 5.20 o.p. State Mutual Bk.

Tender Leaves. Robert Mason. LC 50-4004. (Jay library).

Tender Leaves. Essie Summers. 192p. 1982. pap. 1.50 (ISBN 0-373-02453-3, Pub. by Harlequin). PB.

Tender Love. Sandra Morris. LC 78-50085. 1978. pap. 1.50 o.p. (ISBN 0-87216-442-X). Playboy.

Tender Loving Care. Joni Moura & Jackie Sutherland. 5.95 o.p. Delacorte.

Tender Meaning. Lia Sanders. (Candlelight Ecstasy Ser.: No. 41). (Orig.). 1982. pap. 1.75. Dell.

Tender Melody. Albert Quandt. LC 49-592. 1948. Arcadia House.

Tender Men. Willa Gibbs. LC 48-5369. 1948. Farrar, Straus.

Tender Mercies. Rosellen Brown. LC 78-1315. 1978. 10.00 (ISBN 0-394-42741-6). Knopf.

Tender Mercy. Lenard Kaufman. LC 49-7338. 1949. Creative Age Press.

Tender Moments. Ed. by Ben Whitley. (Illus.). 1975. Repr. of 1970 ed. 3.50 o.p. (ISBN 0-87529-196-1). Hallmark.

Tender Offer. Alexandra Marshall. LC 80-23233. 1981. 10.95 (ISBN 0-394-50757-6). Knopf.

Tender Offer. large print ed. Alexandra Marshall. LC 81-9083. 10.95 (ISBN 0-89621-305-6). Thorndike Press.

Tender Offers. Peter Engel. 384p. 1983. 14.95 (ISBN 0-312-79093-7). St Martin.

Tender Offers. Peter H Engel. LC 83-2935. 1983. 14.95 (ISBN 0-312-79093-7). St. Martin's Press.

Tender Passions. Kathleen Drymon. (Orig.). 1982. pap. 3.50 (ISBN 0-8217-1032-X). Zebra.

Tender Poisoner. John Michael Ward Bingham. LC 53-5524. (Red badge detective). 1953. Dodd, Mead.

Tender Recollections of Irene Macgillicuddy. Also, Parkwater; or, Told in the Twilight. Laurence Oliphant & Wood, Ellen (Price) "Mrs. Henry Wood.". (Seaside library, v. 12, no. 234). 1878. G. Munro.

Tender Rhapsody. Judith Duncan. (Superromances Ser.). 384p. 1983. pap. 2.50 (ISBN 0-373-70051-2, Pub. by Worldwide). Harlequin Bks.

Tender Season. Lorena A. Olmsted. 1982. pap. 6.95 (Avalon). Bouregy.

Tender Shoot & Other Stories. Sidonie Gabrielle Colette. Tr. by Antonia White from Fr. 404p. 1975. 10.00 (ISBN 0-374-27310-3); pap. 7.95 (ISBN 0-374-51258-2). FS&G.

Tender Shoot: And Other Stories. Sidonie Gabrielle Colette. Tr. by Antonia White. 1975. pap. 6.95 o.p. (ISBN 0-374-51258-2). FS&G.

Tender Shoot: And Other Stories. Tr. from French by Antonia White. Sidonie Gabrielle Colette. (Signet bk. D1947). 1961. New American Lib.

Tender Talons: A Novel. Helen Reimensnyder Martin. LC 30-240533. 1930. Dodd, Mead & Company.

Tender Taming. Heather Graham. (Candlelight Ecstasy Ser.: No. 125). (Orig.). 1983. pap. 1.95 (ISBN 0-440-18803-2). Dell.

Tender Temptation. Elaine Castellano. 1978. 3.50 o.p. (ISBN 0-8059-2498-1). Dorrance.

Tender Time. Denise C. Brookman. (Willow Bks). 1971. pap. 0.75 o.p. (JT50). Pyramid Pubns.

Tender to Danger. Eliot Reed, pseud. LC 51-14723. 1951. Published for the Crime Club by Doubleday.

Tender Torment. Jane Archer. 1978. 1.95 (ISBN 0-441-80040-8). Ace Books.

Tender Torment. Alicia Meadows. (Orig.). 1980. pap. 2.25 (ISBN 0-446-92179-3). Warner Bks.

Tender Triumph. large print ed. Jasmine Craig. LC 82-4633. (Second Chance at Love). 1982. 11.95 (ISBN 0-89340-530-2). J. Curley.

Tender Victory. Taylor Caldwell. LC 55-11559. 1974. (pbk.) 1.50. Popular Library.

Tender Victory. Taylor Caldwell. 1978. 2.25 (ISBN 0-445-08298-4). Popular Library.

Tender Warrior. Fern Michaels. 384p. (Orig.). 1983. pap. 3.50 (ISBN 0-345-30358-X). Ballantine.

Tender Wilderness. Christine H. Cott. (Superromances Ser.). 384p. 1982. pap. 2.50 (ISBN 0-373-70030-X, Pub. by Worldwide). Harlequin Bks.

Tender Yearnings. Elaine Chase. (Candlelight Ecstacy Ser.: No. 19). (Orig.). 1981. pap. 1.50 (ISBN 0-440-18552-1). Dell.

Tenderfoot. Robert Ames Bennet. LC 28-238710. 1928. A. C. McClurg & Co.

Tenderfoot. Max Brand. Orig. Title: Outlaw's Gold. 1976. pap. 1.95 (ISBN 0-446-90653-0). Warner Bks.

Tenderfoot. Zane Grey. (Belmont Tower Book). 1977. 1.50 (ISBN 0-505-51191-6). Tower Pubs.

Tenderfoot. William H. B Kent. LC 42-18664. 1942. The Macmillan Company.

Tenderfoot. George Brydges Rodney. LC 33-23929. E. J. Clode, Inc.

Tenderfoot Abroad. Justine Grayson. LC 8-438. 1907. W. A. Butterfield.

Tenderfoot at Bar X. Myrtle Mosher Perdew. LC 42-51781. 1942. The Caxton Printers, Ltd.

Tenderfoot Bill. Archie Joscelyn. Phoenix Press.

Tenderfoot Bride: Tales from an Old Ranch. Clarice Estabrook Richards. LC 20-21005. Fleming H. Revell Company.

Tenderfoot: By Max Brand Pseud. Frederick Faust. LC 53-9598. (Silver star western). Dodd Mead.

Tenderfoot Comes West. Roy P. McLaughlin. (Illus.). 1968. 5.00 o.p. (ISBN 0-682-46765-0). Exposition.

Tenderfoot Kid. Peter Field. LC 39-31265. W. Morrow & Company,

Tenderfoot Kid. Peter Field. LC 49-9077. (Triple-A western classic). 1949. Jefferson House.

Tenderfoot Trail. Syl MacDowell. LC 36-341659. J. Messner, Inc.

Tenderfoots. Francis Lynde. LC 27-1238. 1925. C. Scribner's Sons.

Tenderloin. Samuel Hopkins Adams. LC 59-5702. Random House.

Tenderloin. Arline De Haas. LC 28-14830. Grosset & Dunlap.

Tenderloin. Andrew Wylie. 1971. pap. 2.00 o.s.i. (ISBN 0-915890-40-2, Telegraph). Dynamic Learn Corp.

Tenderly. My Love. Mary Savage. LC 60-10591. (Torquil book). 1960. Distributed by Dodd, Mead.

Tending Upward. Mary B Willey. LC 8-36922. 1893. The American Sunday-School Union.

Tendre comme le Souvenir. Guillaume Apollinaire. 11.95. French & Eur.

Tenement Girl. Joseph Calvitt Clarke. LC 35-5434. 1935. Godwin.

Tenement Girl. Joseph Calvitt Clarke. LC 35-6534. 1935. Godwin.

Tenement of Dreams: A Novel of 1915. 1st Ed. Joseph William Meagher. LC 56-9068. 1956. Little, Brown.

Tenement Tales of New York. James William Sullivan. LC 8-17666. (On cover: Buckram series). 1895. H. Holt and Company.

Tengo. Nicholas Guillen. Tr. by Richard Carr. 1974. 7.25; pap. 4.25 (ISBN 0-910296-29-4). Broadside.

Tengu. Graham Masterton. (Tor Bks.). 384p. (Orig.). 1983. pap. 3.50 (ISBN 0-523-48061-X). Pinnacle Bks.

Tengu Child. Kikuo Itaya. LC 82-5876. (Illus.). 243p. 1983. 15.95 (ISBN 0-8093-1081-3). S Ill U Pr.

Tennessean: A Novel, Founded on Facts. Anne Newport Royall. LC 35-33412. 1827. The Author.

Tennessee Blue. Patricia Browning Griffith. LC 80-25626. 9.95 (ISBN 0-517-54187-4). C.N. Potter: Distributed by Crown Publishers.

Tennessee Hazard. Maristan Chapman. LC 52-13737. 1953. Lippincott.

Tennessee Judge: A Novel. Opie Percival Read. (On cover: The library of choice fiction, no. 68). 1893. Laird & Lee.

Tennessee Mountaineers in Type: A Collection of Stories. John Thurman Essary. LC 10-27738. 1910. Chochrane Publishing Company.

Tennessee Poppy: Or, Which Way Is Westminister Abbey? Frances Kirkwood Crane. LC 22-17262. Farrar & Rinehart, Incorporated.

Tennessee Shad, Chronicling the Rise and Fall of the Firm of Doc. Macnooder and the Tennessee Shad. Owen McMahon Johnson. LC 11-11563. (His Lawrenceville stories). 1911. The Baker & Taylor Company.

Tennessee Sketches. Louisa Preston Looney. LC 79-169558. (Short story index reprint series). 1971. (ISBN 0-8369-4020-2). Books for Libraries Press.

Tennessee Sketches. Louisa Preston Looney. LC 1-23047. 1901. A. C. McClurg & Co.

Tennessee Smash. Don Pendleton. (Executioner Ser.: No. 32). 1978. pap. 1.95 (ISBN 0-523-41096-4). Pinnacle Bks.

Tennessee Smith. James E Hitt. LC 78-20976. 10.95 (ISBN 0-525-21546-8). Dutton.

Tennessee Todd: A Novel of the Great River. George Washington Ogden. LC 3-269601. 1903. A. S. Barnes & Company.

Tennessee Williams: Eight Plays. Tennessee Williams. LC 80-110574. 1979. 8.95. N. Doubleday.

Tennessee's Partner. Bret Harte & Armes, William Dallam. LC 7-32155. (Half-title: Western classics no, 3). P. Elder and Company.

Tennis Hustler. J. R. Pici. 1978. pap. 1.95 (ISBN 0-89041-187-5, 3187). Major Bks.

Tennis Player and Other Stories. Kent Nelson. LC 77-10449. (Illinois short fiction). 7.50. (ISBN 0-252-00678-X) (ISBN 0-252-00677-1). University of Illinois Press.

Tennis Players. Lars Gustafsson. LC 82-22559. 13.00 (ISBN 0-8112-0861-3) (ISBN 0-8112-0862-1). New Directions.

Tension. Edmee Elizabeth Monica De La Pasture. LC 20-17523. 1920. The Macmillan Company.

Tent of Grace. Adelina Cohnfeldt Lust. LC 99-1710. 1899. Houghton, Mifflin and Company.

Tent of Miracles. Jorge Amado. LC 78-142957. 1971. 7.95 (ISBN 0-394-44826-X). Knopf.

Tent of the Wicked. Robert Switzer. LC 56-997959. (Signet book, 1313). 1956. New American Library.

Tent on Corsica. Martin Quigley. LC 49-9131. 1949. J. B. Lippincott Co.

Tent Peg: A Novel. Aritha Van Herk. LC 81-125119. 14.95 (ISBN 0-7710-8702-0). McClelland and Stewart.

Tent Peg: A Novel. Aritha Van Herk. LC 81-52072. 1982. (ISBN 0-87223-751-6). Seaview Books.

Tent Peg: A Novel. Aritha Van Herk. LC 81-52072. 1982. 11.50. (ISBN 0-87223-751-6). Seaview Books.

Tent Peg: A Novel. Aritha Van'Herk. LC 81-52072. 1982. (ISBN 0-87223-751-6). Seaview Books.

Tent Show. Peggy Gaddis, pseud. LC 44-327240. 1944. Arcadia House, Inc.

Tent Show Summer. August William Derleth. LC 63-7419. 5.95 (ISBN 0-88361-069-8). Stanton & Lee.

Tent Show Summer. August William Derleth. 4.95 o.s.i. (ISBN 0-88451-039-5). Edco-Vis Assoc.

Tentacles. Martha Kinross. LC 26-15958. 1926. Harper & Brothers.

Tentacles. Mabel Dana Lyon. LC 49-50361. 1950. Harper.

Tentacles of Dawn. Robert Wilson. 1978. pap. 1.75 (ISBN 0-89041-222-7, 3222). Major Bks.

Tentation de l'Occident. Andre Malraux. pap. 6.95. French & Eur.

Tentation De L'occident see Temptation of the West.

Tentation de Saint Antoine. Gustave Flaubert. (Coll. Prestige). 9.95 o.p. French & Eur.

Tenterhooks. Ada Leverson. 1972. pap. 0.75 o.p. (07249). Curtis.

Tenth Commandment. Lawrence Sanders. 1981. pap. 3.95. Berkley Pub.

Tenth Commandment. Lawrence Sanders. 1980. 12.95. Putnam Pub Group.

Tenth Commandment: A Novel. Lawrence Sanders. LC 80-13002. 11.95. Putnam.

Tenth Commandment: A Novel. Lawrence Sanders. LC 81-4795. 1981. 16.95 (ISBN 0-8161-3208-9). G.K. Hall.

Tenth Home: By F. O. Bennett. Francis Oswald Bennett. LC 67-109439. 1966. bds., 5.25. Blackwood & Janet Paul.

Tenth Life. Richard Lockridge. LC 77-6673. 8.95 (ISBN 0-397-01237-3). Lippincott.

Tenth Life. Richard Lockridge. LC 79-10637. 1979. 11.95 (ISBN 0-8161-6717-6). G. K. Hall.

Tenth Man. Edward Francis Murphy. LC 72-4647. (Black Heritage Library Collection). 1972. 11.50 (ISBN 0-8369-9114-1). Books for Libraries Press.

Tenth Man. Edward Francis Murphy. LC 37-426631. 1937. The Dolphin Press.

Tenth Measure. Brenda Lesley Segal. LC 80-14387. (Illus.). 14.95 (ISBN 0-312-79110-0). St. Martin's Press.

Tenth Month. Laura Z. Hobson. 1972. pap. 2.25 (ISBN 0-440-18605-6). Dell.

Tenth Month: A Novel. Laura Keane Zametkin Hobson. LC 70-130480. 1971. 6.95. Simon and Schuster.

Tenth Moon. Dawn Powell. LC 32-216873. Farrar & Rinehart, Incorporated.

Tenth Pan Book of Horror Stories. Ed. by H. Van Thal. 1982. pap. 10.00x (ISBN 0-330-02369-1, Pub. by Pan Bks). State Mutual Bk.

Tenth Planet. Edmund Cooper. 1973. 12.50 (ISBN 0-399-11187-5). Ultramarine Pub.

Tenth Planet: A Novel. Edmund Cooper. LC 73-78642. 1973. 5.95 (ISBN 0-399-11187-5). Putnam.

Tenth Point. Thomas Walsh. LC 65-11974. (Inner sanctum mystery). 1965. bds., 3.50. S. & S.

Tenth Symphony. Mark Aleksandrovich Aldanov. Tr. by Golubeff, Gregory. LC 48-8603. 1948. C. Scribner's Sons.

Tenth Victim. Robert Sheckley. (Science Fiction Ser.). 1978. lib. bdg. 9.95 o.p. (ISBN 0-8398-2440-8, Gregg). G K Hall.

Tenth Year of the Ship. 1st American Ed. Norman Lewis. LC 62-10496. (Helen and Kurt Wolff book). 1962. Harcourt, Brace & World.

Tenthragon. Constance Savery. LC 30-19830. 1930. A. H. King.

Tenting at Stony Beach. Maria Louise Pool. 1888. Houghton, Mifflin and Company.

Tentmaker: A Novel Based on the Life of Saint Paul. Julius Berstl. LC 52-5558. 1952. Rinehart.
Tents Against the Sky. Robert Brainerd Ekvall. LC 78-67642. 4.95 (ISBN 0-89107-161-X). Good News Publishers.
Tents Against the Sky: A Novel of Tibet. Robert Brainerd Ekvall. LC 54-568521. Farrar, Straus & Young.
Tents of Jacob. Hyman Cohen. LC 26-10314. 1926. R. M. McBride & Company.
Tents of Shem.". Grant Allen. LC 6-483. (On cover: Seaside library. Pocket ed. no. 1221). G. Munro.
Tents of Wickedness. Miriam Coles Harris. LC 7-31979. 1907. D. Appleton and Company.
Tents of Wickedness. Mella Russell McCallum. LC 28-21581. 1928. The Century Co.
Teodoro: The Sage. Luigi Lucatelli. Tr. by Bishop, Morris. LC 23-5824. Boni and Liveright.
Tequila. Margaret Page Hood. LC 50-9817. 1950. Coward-McCann.
Teran X 500. Stuart J. Byrne. LC 76-8574. (Star Man Ser.: No. 1). 1977. pap. cancelled (3173). Major Bks.
Terapia De Muerte. new ed. Richard Sapir & Warren Murphy. Tr. by Margarita O. Castro from Eng. (Compadre Collection Ser.: el Destructor: No. 6). Orig. Title: Death Therapy. (Illus.). 160p. (Span.). 1975. pap. 0.95 (ISBN 0-88473-406-4). Fiesta Pub.
Terassa of Spain. Horace Fish. LC 23-9242. 1923. M. Kennerley.
Terence. Bithia Mary Sheppard Croker. LC 1092. 1900. F. M. Buckles & Company; Etc., Etc.
Terence O'Rourke: Gentlemen Adventurer. Louis Joseph Vance. 1905. A. Wessels Company.
Teresa. Les Savage. LC 54-7510. (First edition, 23). 1954. Dell Pub. Co.
Teresa of Watling Street. Arnold Bennett. LC 74-17051. (Collected Works of Arnold Bennett: Vol. 78). 1976. Repr. of 1904 ed. 16.75 (ISBN 0-518-19159-1). Ayer Co.
Teresita, la Ardiente. new ed. Terray Duncan. (Pimienta Collection Ser). (Illus.). 160p. (Span.). 1975. pap. 1.25 o.p. (ISBN 0-88473-233-9). Fiesta Pub.
Tereza Batista: Home from the Wars. Jorge Amado. LC 74-21313. 1975. 10.00 (ISBN 0-394-48752-4). Knopf: Distributed by Random House.
Tereza Batista: Home from the Wars. Jorge Amado. (Bard Book). 1977. 2.95 (ISBN 0-380-01752-0). Avon Books.
Terhoven File: A Novel. Robert Pick. LC 44-7512. 1944. J. B. Lippincott Company.
Term of Silence. Forrest Halsey. LC 13-22446. Desmond FitzGerald, Inc.
Terminal Bar. Larry Mitchell. 220p. (Orig.). 1982. pap. 6.00 (ISBN 0-930762-05-3). Calamus Bks.
Terminal Beach. J. G. Ballard. 1977. pap. 1.95 o.p. (ISBN 0-14-002499-9). Penguin.
Terminal Connection. Robin Moore. Ace.
Terminal Leave. Thomas C. Stimson. 100p. (Orig.). 1982. pap. 4.95 (ISBN 0-940978-02-4). Sharral Pub.
Terminal Man. Michael Crichton. LC 73-136320. (Illus.). 1972. 6.95 (ISBN 0-394-44768-9). Knopf.
Termination Order. Philip Friedman. 1979. 9.95 o.s.i. (ISBN 0-8037-8625-5, J Wade). Dial.
Termination Order: A Novel. Philip Friedman. LC 78-31945. 9.95 (ISBN 0-8037-8625-5). The Dial Press.
Terminations. Henry James. LC 71-134966. (Short story index reprint series). 1970. Books for Libraries Press.
Terminations: The Death of the Lion, The Coxon Fund, The Middle Years, The Altar of the Dead. Henry James. LC 7-7432. 1895. Harper & Brothers.
Terminator: Mercenary Kill, No. 1. John Quinn. 208p. (Orig.). 1982. pap. 2.25 (ISBN 0-523-41695-4). Pinnacle Bks.
Terminators. Donald Hamilton. (Matt Helm Ser.). 224p. 1978. pap. 1.95 (ISBN 0-449-14035-0, GM). Fawcett.
Terminators. Donald Hamilton. (New Matt Helm). (Fawcett gold medal book: Vol. 16). 1975. (pbk.) 1.25. Fawcett.
Terminators. Berkely Mather. LC 70-162788. 1971. (ISBN 0-684-12608-7). Scribner.
Terminus. Peter Edwards. LC 75-29133. 1976. 8.95. St. Martin's Press.
Terms of Conquest. Howard Vincent O'Brien. LC 23-17474. 1923. Little, Brown, and Company.
Terms of Endearment. Larry McMurtry. (Signet book). 1976. 1.95. New American Library.
Terms of Endearment. Larry McMurtry. (O.s.i.). 448p. 1975. 9.95 o.s.i. (ISBN 0-671-22102-7). S&S.
Terms of Endearment: A Novel. Larry McMurtry. LC 75-16399. 1975. 9.95 (ISBN 0-671-22102-7). Simon and Schuster.
Terms of Surrender. Louis Tracy. LC 13-208246. E. J. Clode.
Terra Amata. Jean Marie Gustave Le Clezio. LC 69-15510. 1969. 5.95. Atheneum.
Terra Data. E. C. Tubb. (Science Fiction Ser.). 1980. pap. 1.75 (ISBN 0-87997-533-4, UE1533). Daw Bks.
Terra Incognita. Nancy Dorer & Frances Dorer. (Orig.). 1980. pap. 1.95 (ISBN 0-532-23178-3). Woodhill.
Terra Nostra. Carlos Fuentes. LC 76-18238. 1976. 15.00 (ISBN 0-374-27327-8). Farrar, Straus, Giroux.
Terra SF: The Year's Best European Sf. Ed. by Richard D. Nolane. (Science Fiction Ser.). 1981. pap. 2.25 (ISBN 0-87997-595-4, UE1595). Daw Bks.
Terrace. Louise Andrews Kent. 1934. Houghton Mifflin Company.
Terrace. Margaret Elizabeth Sangster. LC 37-203209. Greenberg.
Terrace of Mon Desir: A Novel of Russian Life. Sophie Radford De Meissner. Cupples, Upham and Company.
Terrace Roses. A Romance. Celia Emmeline Gardner. LC 7-312. 1878. G. W. Carleton & Co.
Terrace Roses. A Romance. Celia Emmeline Gardner. LC 6-4638. (On cover: Madison square library, no 54). G. W. Dillingham Co.
Terrace Suicide Mystery. Leonard Reginald Gribble. LC 29-18966. 1929. Pub. for the Crime Club, Inc., by Doubleday, Doran & Company, Inc.
Terrania: Or, The Feminization of the World. Columbus Bradford. LC 20-4724. The Christopher Publishing House.
Terrarium. Lee Head. LC 75-43650. 7.95 (ISBN 0-399-11644-3). Putnam.
Terrarossa, a Novel. Translated from the Italian by Elizabeth Ellman. Saverio Strati. LC 62-13798. 1962. Abelard-Schuman.
Terressa: A Thrilling Western Romance. Gemes L'Mon Hamrick. LC 12-620152. 1911. Times Print.
Terrible Beauty. Arthur J Roth. LC 58-5186. 1958. Farrar, Straus and Cudahy.
Terrible Door. George Sims. LC 64-22592. 1964. Horizon Press.
Terrible Family. Florence Alice Price James. LC 7-7973. (On cover: The author's library, no. 1). 1893. The International News Company.
Terrible Hobby of Sir Joseph Londe, Bart. Edward Phillips Oppenheim. LC 27-949. 1927. Little, Brown, and Company.
Terrible Inheritance. Grant Allen. LC 50-494941.
Terrible Island. Beatrice Ethel Grimshaw. LC 20-19507. 1920. The Macmillan Company.
Terrible Island. Beatrice Ethel Grimshaw. LC 19-13156. The Ridgway Company.
Terrible Love Life of Dudley Cornflower. Kin Platt. LC 76-9962. 8.95 (ISBN 0-87888-108-5). Bradbury Press.
Terrible Ones. Nick Carter. (Nick Carter Killmaster Ser.). (O.s.i.). (Orig.). 1968. pap. 0.60 o.s.i. (A310X, Award). Univ Pub & Dist.
Terrible People. Edgar Wallace. LC 26-12717. 1926. Doubleday, Page & Company.
Terrible Pictures. Ben Healey. LC 67-10493. 1967. Harper & Row.
Terrible Secret. John Russell Coryell & Hungerford, Margaret Wolfe (Hamilton) 1855?-1897. Beatrix. LC 6-39919. (On cover: Munro's library, v. 1, no. 336). 1885. N. L. Munro.
Terrible Secret. John Russell Coryell & Hungerford, Margaret Wolfe (Hamilton) 1855?-1897. Beatrix. LC 6-39918. (On cover: Lovell's library, no. 1266). 1888. John W. Lovell Company.
Terrible Secret. Geraldine Fleming & Hungerford, Mrs. Margaret Wolfe (Hamilton) 1855?-1897. LC 6-39919. (On cover: Munro's library, v. 1, no. 336). 1885. N. L. Munro.
Terrible Secret. Geraldine Fleming & Hungerford, Mrs. Margaret Wolfe (Hamilton) 1855?-1897. LC 6-39918. (On cover: Lovell's library, no. 1266). 1888. J. W. Lovell Company.
Terrible Secret: Suppression of the Truth about Hitler's "Final Solution". Walter Ze'Er Laqueur. 1982. pap. 5.95 (ISBN 0-14-006136-3). Penguin.
Terrible Sexy Secret of Castle McNab. Barry Sterling. 1974. (pbk.) 1.25. Warner Paperback Library.
Terrible Swift Swoard: A Novel. Arthur Steuer. LC 56-11522. 1956. Coward-McCann.
Terrible Tangle. M. B. Smith. (On cover: Munro's library, no. 671). 1886. N. L. Munro.
Terrible Teague Bunch. Gary Jennings. LC 74-23338. (Illus.). 1975. (ISBN 0-393-08706-9). Norton.
Terrible Temptation. Charles Reade. LC 49-37128. (works of Charles Reade. Library ed.). 1895. Metropolitan Pub. Co.
Terrible Temptation. Charles Reade. (On cover: Seaside library. Pocket ed., no. 213). 1884. G. Munro.
Terrible Temptation. Charles Reade. (On cover: Lovell's library, v. 19, no. 914). 1887. J. W. Lovell Company.
Terrible Temptation: A Story of the Day. library ed. Charles Reade. LC 75-321025. (His The works of Charles Reade; v. 8). (Illus.). 1970. AMS Press.
Terrible Temptation. A Story of to-Day. Charles Reade. LC 3-28180. 1871. J. R. Osgood and Company.
Terrible Ten. Mallory T. Knight. (Man from T.O.M.C.A.T. Ser). (O.s.i.). (Orig.). 1967. pap. 0.60 o.s.i. (A249X, Award). Univ Pub & Dist.
Terrible Thing Has Happened to Miss Dupont. Polly Hobson. LC 73-96305. 1970. 4.50. McCall Pub. Co.
Terrible Tide. Alisa Craig. LC 82-45867. (Crime Club Ser.). 192p. 1983. 11.95 (ISBN 0-385-18700-9). Doubleday.
Terrible Time to Die. Anthony Scaduto. LC 78-5223. 7.95 (ISBN 0-399-12233-8). Putnam.
Terrible Tuesday. Don Pendleton. (Executioner: No. 34). 1979. pap. 2.95 (ISBN 0-523-41765-9). Pinnacle Bks.
Terrible Twins. Edgar Jepson. LC 13-212574. 1.25. The Bobbs-Merrill Company.
Terrible Twos. Ishmael Reed. LC 81-21504. 11.95 (ISBN 0-312-79199-2). St. Martin's Press/Marek.
Terrible Voyage. Edwin Palmer Hoyt. 1976. (pbk.) 1.25 (ISBN 0-523-00811-2). Pinnacle Books.
Terribly Strange Tales. Elizabeth Hough Sechrist. LC 67-26976. 1967. Macrae Smith Co.
Terribly Wild Flowers. Gerald Kersh. 1981. 18.95x (Pub. by Remploy England). State Mutual Bk.
Terridae. E. C. Tubb. (Science Fiction Ser.). 1981. pap. 2.25 (ISBN 0-87997-662-4, UE1662). DAW Bks.
Terrific Timothys. Margaret Parsons Drake. LC 55-140085. 1954. Avalon Books.
Terrified. James W. Covington. 1979. pap. 1.75 (ISBN 0-532-17206-X). Woodhill.
Terrified Heart. Alicia Grace. 1976. pap. 1.25 o.p. (LB383ZK, Leisure Bks). Nordon Pubns.
Terrified Heart. Alicia Grace. (O.s.i.). Orig. Title: Terrified Target. 1973. pap. 0.95 o.s.i. (BT50508). Belmont-Tower.
Terrified Heart. Alicia Grace. 1976. 1.25. Leisure Books.
Terrified Society. Hildegarde Tolman Teilhet. LC 47-5254. 1947. Doubleday.
Terrified Starlet. Gilbert Kilgore. 192p. pap. 1.95 o.p. (ISBN 0-87977-132-1, DBB132). Dansk Blue Bk.
Terrified Target. Alicia Grace. 1978. pap. 1.25 (ISBN 0-532-12537-1). Woodhill.
Terrified Target see Terrified Heart.
Terriford Mystery. Marie Adelaide Belloc Lowndes. LC 24-12761. 1924. Doubleday, Page & Company.
Territorial Rights. Muriel Spark. LC 78-24146. 1979. 8.95 (ISBN 0-698-10929-5). Coward, McCann & Geoghegan.
Terror. Michael D. Albers. (Orig.). 1980. pap. 2.25 (ISBN 0-532-23311-5). Woodhill.
Terror. John Creasey. 1966. large print 7.50 o.p. (ISBN 0-8027-5173-3). Walker & Co.
Terror. Arthur Machen. (Seagull Lib. of Mystery & Suspense Ser). 1965. 4.50 o.p. (ISBN 0-393-08501-5). Norton.
Terror. Arthur Machen & Richard Garnett. (Fantasy Classics, 1). (Illus.). 1973. (pbk.) 1.95. Fantasy House.
Terror. M J Reynolds. LC 30-21417. 1930. The Macmillan Company.
Terror: A Fantasy. Introd. by Vincent Starrett. Arthur Machen. LC 65-9495. (Seagull lib. of mystery and suspense). 3.95. Norton.
Terror: A Mystery. Arthur Machen. LC 17-25086. 1917. R. M. McBride & Company.
Terror: A New Novel. Robert Bloch. LC 63-34106. 1962. Belmont Books.
Terror: A Romance of the French Revolution. Felix Gras. Tr. by Janvier, Catharine Ann (Drinker) 1898. D. Appleton and Company.
Terror: A Romance of the French Revolution. Felix Gras. Tr. by Janvier, Catharine Ann (Drinker) LC 4-17516. 1899. D. Appleton and Company.
Terror Alliance. Jack D. Hunter. 1980. pap. 2.75 (ISBN 0-8439-0808-4). Nordon PUbns.
Terror at Compass Lake. Tech Davis. LC 35-206777. 1935. Pub. for the Crime Club, Inc., by Doubleday, Doran & Company, Inc.
Terror at Hillcrest. Shannon Graham. LC 77-88490. 1978. pap. 1.95 o.s.i. (ISBN 0-89516-019-6). Condor Pub Co.
Terror at Marbury Hall. Marilyn Ross. (queen-size gothic). 1975. (pbk.) 1.25. Popular Library.
Terror at Nelson Woods. Susan Richard. (Paperback Library gothic). 1973. (pbk.) 0.95. Warner Paperback Library.
Terror at Octagon House. Ardis Coffman. (Orig.). 1979. pap. 1.95. Woodhill.
Terror at Sea. Dean W Ballenger. 2.50 (ISBN 0-451-09670-3). Signet Books.
Terror at Seacliff Pines. Florence Hurd. 240p. 1976. pap. 1.25 (ISBN 0-532-12368-9). Woodhill.
Terror at Stamps House. Frank King. LC 30-19637. 1929. G. H. Watt.
Terror at Tansey Hill. Suzanne Roberts. (Candlelight gothic). 1975. (pbk.) 0.75. Dell.
Terror at Tolliver Hall. Juanita Tyree Osborne. (YA) 1981. 6.95 (Avalon). Bouregy.
Terror by Gaslight: More Victorian Tales of Terror. Hugh Lamb. LC 75-27980. 1976. 8.95 (ISBN 0-8008-7559-1). Taplinger Pub. Co.
Terror by Night. Richard Day Bunnell. LC 57-13725. 1957. Naylor Co.
Terror by Night. R. Chetwood-Hayes. 1976. pap. 1.25 o.p. (ISBN 0-515-03924-1). BJ Pub Group.
Terror by Night. Norman Klein. Farrar & Rinehart, Incorporated.
Terror by Night. Ware Torrey. LC 38-370084. 1938. E. P. Dutton & Co., Inc.
Terror by Night & Day. M. Egetkaroff. (Destiny Ser.). 1980. pap. 4.95. Pacific Pr Pub Assn.
Terror by Twilight: A Margot Blair Mystery. Kathleen Moore Knight. LC 42-17151. 1942. Published for the Crime Club by Doubleday, Doran and Co., Inc.
Terror Chronicle. Bob Sang & Dusty Sang. 1979. pap. 2.25 (ISBN 0-932844-01-4). R H Sang & Son.
Terror Factor. Eva-Lis Wuorio. 1970. pap. 0.75 o.p. (ISBN 0-447-74710-X). Lancer.
Terror for Three. Patricia Kershaw. 192p. (YA) 1973. pap. 1.25 o.p. (9765P). Zondervan.
Terror in Eagle Basin. Cliff Farrell. LC 73-18911. 1974. 4.95 (ISBN 0-385-03096-7). Doubleday.
Terror in Room Two-O-One. Tom Mitcheltree. (Orig.). 1980. pap. 1.75 o.s.i. (ISBN 0-505-51475-3). Tower Bks.
Terror in Taormina. Alice Hesse. 1978. 5.00 (ISBN 0-682-49151-9). Exposition.
Terror in Technicolor. Mary F. Ford. (YA) 1973. 4.95 o.p. (Avalon). Bouregy.
Terror in the Bay. Ione F. Turek. 1971. pap. 0.75 o.p. (07181). Curtis.
Terror in the High Sierras. Bob Wright. (Perspective I Novel Ser.). 48p. 1982. 2.50 (ISBN 0-87879-300-3). Acad Therapy.
Terror in the Modern Vein: An Anthology. 1st Ed. Ed. by Donald A. Wollheim. LC 55-6488. 1955. Hanover House.
Terror in the Mountains. Helen L. Dell. (Griffons Ser). (Orig.). 1969. pap. 0.50 o.p. (Golden Pr). Western Pub.
Terror in the Sunlight: A Novel of Romantic Suspense. Amanda McAllister. 1977. 1.50. Playboy Press.
Terror in the Town. Edward Sidney Aarons. LC 47-1338. 1947. David McKay Company.
Terror in the Town. Edward Sidney Aarons. 160p. 1974. pap. 0.95 (ISBN 0-532-15266-2). Woodhill.
Terror in the Town. Edward Sidney Aarons. 1971. pap. 0.75 o.p. (75-414). Manor Bks.
Terror Keep. Edgar Wallace. LC 27-152046. 1927. Doubleday, Page & Company.
Terror Lurks in Darkness. 1st Ed. Dolores Birk Hitchens. LC 53-8349. 1953. Published for the Crime Club by Doubleday.
Terror of Heartbreak House. Dorien K. Miles. (YA) 1979. 6.95 (Avalon). Bouregy.
Terror of Peru. Meade Minnigerode. LC 40-115568. Farrar & Rinehart, Inc.
Terror of St. Trinian's. D. B. Lewis, pseud. 1977. 6.05 o.p. State Mutual Bk.
Terror of Stormcastle. Audrey Leech. (Paperback Library gothic). 1973. (pbk.) 0.95. Warner Paperback Lib.
Terror of the Handless Corpse. William Dale. LC 40-8743. 1939. Gateway Books.
Terror of the Twin. Dorothy Daniels. (Berkley Medallion Book). 1976. (pbk.) 1.25 (ISBN 0-425-03120-9). Berkley Publishing Corp.
Terror on Broadway. David Alexander. LC 54-664963. 1954. Random House.
Terror on Planet Ionus. Allen Adler. LC 57-12153. Orig. Title: Mach One. 1969. pap. 0.60 o.p. (63-048). Paperback Lib.
Terror on the Island. John Alexander Ferguson. LC 42-9119. 1942. The Vanguard Press.
Terror on the Mountain. Charles Ferdinand Ramuz. LC 68-12597. 1968. Harcourt, Brace & World.
Terror or Love? Bommi Baumann's Own Story of His Life As a West German Urban Guerrilla. Michael Baumann. LC 78-73031. 1979. 6.95 o.p. (ISBN 0-394-50718-5, GP822). Grove.
Terror Over Bluehaven. Nell Marr Dean. 1975. 4.95. Avalon Books.
Terror Syndicate. Donald Seaman. LC 76-25011. 1976. 7.95 (ISBN 0-698-10791-8). Coward, McCann & Geoghegan.
Terror: The Return of Dr. Palfrey. John Creasey. LC 66-169216. bds., 3.50. Walker.
Terror Touches Me. Stanton Forbes, pseud. LC 66-11735. 1966. Published for the Crime Club by Doubleday.
Terror Trap. Willo Davis Roberts. 1971. pap. 0.75 o.p. (ISBN 0-447-74761-4). Lancer.
Terror Under the Sun. Lillian O'Donnell. 1973. pap. 0.75 o.p. (94387-075). Beagle Bks.

Terrorist Summit. Don Pendleton. (Executioner Ser.). 192p. 1982. pap. 1.95 (ISBN 0-373-61044-0, Pub. by Worldwide). Harlequin Bks.

Terrorists. Maj Sjowall & Per Wahloo. LC 76-9987. 7.95 (ISBN 0-394-48532-7). Pantheon Books.

Terrorists. Maj Sjowall & Per Wahloo. LC 77-3192. 1978. 1.65 (ISBN 0-394-72452-6). Vintage Books.

Terrorizers. Donald Hamilton. (Fawcett Gold Medal Book). 1977. 1.75 (ISBN 0-449-13865-8). Fawcett Pubns.

Terrors. Charles L. Grant. LC 81-85822. 224p. (Orig.). 1982. pap. 2.50 (ISBN 0-86721-138-5). Playboy Pbks.

Terror's Cradle. Duncan Kyle. LC 74-81239. 1974. 7.50. Saint Martin's Press.

Terrors of Dr. Treviles: A Romance. Peter Redgrove & Penelope Shuttle. LC 75-300150. 1974. 8.75 (ISBN 0-7100-7919-2). Routledge and K. Paul.

Terrors, Torments & Traumas. Ed. by Helen Hoke. LC 78-2406. 1978. Repr. 7.95 o.p. (ISBN 0-525-66600-1). Lodestar Bks.

Terrors, Torments, and Traumas: An Anthology. Ed. by Helen Hoke. LC 78-2406. 6.95 (ISBN 0-8407-6600-9). T. Nelson.

Terry. Harriet Theresa Smith Comstock. LC 43-12690. 1943. Doubleday, Doran & Co., Inc.

Terry. Peggy O'More, pseud. LC 49-118715. 1949-1948. Arcadia House.

Terry: A Tale of the Hill People. Charles Goff Thomson. LC 21-5542. 1921. The Macmillan Company.

Terry & the Pirates: China Journey. 1977. pap. 6.95 (ISBN 0-517-23320-7). Crown.

Terry's Call: A Novel. Ethel Symonds Low. LC 43-10071. Zondervan Publishing House.

Terse Tales. Clarence H Murphy. LC 17-17620. 1917. Point Pleasant Printing and Publishing Co.

Tertarin of Tarascon. Alphonse Daudet. Tr. by Le Clereq, Jacques Georges Clemenceau. LC 30-24077. 1930. The Limited Editions Club.

Tesoro de los Modocs. new ed. John Benteen. Tr. by John T. Diaz from Eng. (Compadre Collection, Sundance Ser: No. 5). (Illus.). 160p. (Span.). 1975. pap. 0.95 (ISBN 0-88473-535-4). Fiesta Pub.

Tess Harcourt. Rosamond Napier Lawrence. LC 13-23027. 1913. Hodder and Stoughton.

Tess Harcourt. Rosamond Napier. LC 13-23027. 1913. Hodder and Stoughton.

Tess of the D'Urbervilles. Thomas Hardy. LC 55-421929. (Pocket library, PL25). 1955. Pocket Books.

Tess of the D'Urbervilles. Thomas Hardy. (Washington Square Press Enriched Classics). (Illus.). 1973. (pbk.) 0.95. Pocket Books.

Tess of the D'Urbervilles. Thomas Hardy. LC 60-707. (Riverside editions, B47). 1960. Houghton Mifflin.

Tess of the D'Urbervilles. Thomas Hardy. LC 32-17678. (Half-title: The modern library of the world's best books). 1932. The Modern Library.

Tess of the D'Urbervilles: A Pure Woman Faithfully Presented. Thomas Hardy. LC 66-1435. 1960. Dolphin Books.

Tess of the D'Urbervilles: A Pure Woman Faithfully Presented. Thomas Hardy. 1892. Harper & Brothers.

Tess of the D'Urbervilles: A Pure Woman Faithfully Presented. new and rev. ed. Thomas Hardy. LC 21-4147. 1892. Harper & Brothers.

Tess of the D'Urbervilles: A Pure Woman Faithfully Presented. new and completely rev. ed. Thomas Hardy. LC 7-1902. 1893. Harper & Brothers.

Tess of the D'Urbervilles: A Pure Woman Faithfully Presented. Thomas Hardy. LC 12-21681. Harper & Brothers.

Tess of the D'Urbervilles: A Pure Woman Faithfully Presented. Thomas Hardy. 1899. Harper & Brothers.

Tess of the D'Urbervilles: A Pure Woman Faithfully Presented. Thomas Hardy. LC 32-19525. 1906. Harper & Brothres.

Tess of the D'Urbervilles: A Pure Woman Faithfully Presented. Thomas Hardy. LC 23-8609. A. L. Burt Company.

Tess of the D'Urbervilles: A Pure Woman Faithfully Presented. Thomas Hardy. Harper & Brothers.

Tess of the D'Urbervilles: A Pure Woman Faithfully Presented. Ed., Introd., Notes, by Arnold Kettle. Standard Ed. Thomas Hardy. Ed. by Arnold Kettle. LC 66-16604. (Perennial classic, P3066E). 1966. Harper.

Tess of the D'Urbervilles, a Pure Woman Faithfully Presented. Introd. by Robert Cantwell. Illustrated with Wood Engravings by Agnes Miller Parker. Thomas Hardy. LC 56-19674. 1956. Limited Editions Club.

Tess of the D'Urbervilles, a Pure Woman Faithfully Presented: Introd. by Carl J. Weber. Thomas Hardy. LC 51-2271. (Modern Library college editions, T46). 1951. Modern Library.

Tess of the D'Urbervilles: A Pure Woman. Thomas Hardy. LC 80-22884. (His The New Wessex edition). 1981. 2.95 (ISBN 0-312-79347-2). St. Martin's.

Tess of the D'Urbervilles: A Pure Woman. Thomas Hardy & Weber, Carl Jefferson. LC 35-8028. (Harper's modern classics). Harper & Brothers.

Tess of the D'Urbervilles: An Authoritative Text. 2d ed. Thomas Hardy & Scott Elledge. LC 78-16891. (Norton critical edition). 4.95 (ISBN 0-393-09044-2). Norton.

Tess of the D'Urbervilles: An Authoritative Text; Hardy and the Novel; Criticism. Thomas Hardy. Ed. by Scott Elledge. LC 65-22075. (Norton critical edition). 1965. W. W. Norton.

Tess of the D'Urbervilles. Introd. by Albert J. Guerard. Thomas Hardy. (Collateral Classic, CC511). 1966. Washington Sq.

Tess of the Storm Country. Grace Miller White. LC 9-29254. W. J. Watt & Company.

Tessa of Destiny. Leigh Ellis. 1979. pap. 2.50 (ISBN 0-380-75028-7, 75028). Avon.

Tessa Wadsworth's Discipline. Jennie Maria Drinkwater Conklin. LC 6-30415. 1879. R. Carter & Brothers.

Tessie Moves Along. Robert Leicester Wagner. LC 28-1999. 1928. J. H. Sears & Company, Inc.

Tessie, the Hound of Channel One. Shepherd Mead. LC 51-9267. 1951. Doubleday.

Test. Howard Rockey. LC 27-1848. Macrae Smith Company.

Test. Burnell Van Dalsem. LC 40-326270. Dorrance and Company.

Test: A Novel. Mary Tappan Wright. LC 4-73301. 1904. C. Scribner's Sons.

Test for Nurse Barbi. Adelaide Humphries. 1975. 4.95. Avalon Books.

Test Match Murder. 1981. 18.95x (Pub. by Remploy England). State Mutual Bk.

Test of Courage. Henry M Ross. LC 8-6032. 1908. Benziger Brothers.

Test of Donald Norton. Robert Eugene Pinkerton. LC 24-747712. The Reilly & Lee Co.

Test of Heritage: A Russian Class-War Novel. Louis Joseph Gallagher. LC 38-32627. 1938. Benziger Brothers.

Test of Love: "The Trail of the Serpent") Third and Last Series. Emma Dorothy Eliza Nevitte Southworth. LC 12-38905. (On cover: Southworth library. no. 152). 1907. Street & Smith.

Test of Loyalty. James M Hiatt. LC 73-39089. (Black Heritage Library Collection). 1972. (ISBN 0-8369-9027-7). Books for Libraries Press.

Test of Loyalty. James M Hiatt. LC 7-4752. 1864. Merrill and Smith.

Test of Scarlet, a Romance of Reality. Coningsby William Dawson. LC 19-15578. 1919. John Lane Company.

Test of Valor: A Story of the Olympic Games. James Wesley Ingles. LC 53-5305. 1953. Westminster Press.

Test of Virtue. Davis Dresser. LC 34-120273. 1934. W. Godwin, Inc.

Test: Or, Mother Bertrand's Reward. Mary Genevieve Kilpatrick. LC 7-32844. C.

Test. Translated by Xan Fielding. Pierre Boulle. LC 57-122520. 1957. Vanguard Press.

Test-Tube Babies. Noel Jackson. 1974. 8.00 o.p. (ISBN 0-682-47920-9). Exposition.

Test Tube Baby. Samuel Michael Fuller. LC 36-36000. 1936. Godwin.

Testament. Ray Coryton Hutchinson. 1963. Repr. of 1938 ed. 8.95 o.p. (ISBN 0-7156-0333-7). Dufour.

Testament. David Morrell. 1976. 1.95 (ISBN 0-449-23033-3). Fawcett Crest.

Testament. Elie Wiesel. 1982. pap. 3.95. Bantam.

Testament: A Novel. Ray Coryton Hutchinson. LC 38-334083. Farrar & Rinehart, Inc.

Testament: A Novel. Elie Wiesel. LC 80-27251. 13.95 (ISBN 0-671-44833-1). Summit Books.

Testament of Caspar Schultz. Jack Higgins, pseud. 1978. pap. 1.75 (ISBN 0-449-13963-8, GM). Fawcett.

Testament of Caspar Schultz. Henry Patterson. LC 62-8281. (Raven book). 1962. Abelard-Schuman.

Testament of Israel Potter. William Doreski. LC 76-8902. (Illus.). 72p. 7.95 (ISBN 0-913282-06-5); signed limited ed. 60.00 (ISBN 0-913282-08-1); pap. 3.75 (ISBN 0-913282-07-3). Seven Woods Pr.

Testament of Paul Keller. Jose Alejandrino. 1981. 7.95 (ISBN 0-533-04819-2). Vantage.

Testament of the Lost Son. Soma Morgenstern. LC 50-4468. 1950. Jewish Publication Society of America.

Testament of Theophilus. Leonard Wibberley. 1973. 7.95 o.p. (ISBN 0-688-00149-1). Morrow.

Testament of Theophilus: A Novel of Christ and Caesar. Leonard Patrick O'Connor Wibberley. LC 72-14252. 1973. 7.95 (ISBN 0-688-00149-1). W. Morrow.

Testament XXI. Guy Snyder. (Daw sf Books, no. 64). (Illus.). 1973. (pbk.) 0.95. Daw Books.

Testamento "Nueva Vida". Orig. Title: New Life Testament. 600p. (Span.). 1981. pap. 6.50 (ISBN 0-311-48712-2). Casa Bautista.

Tested! A Sequel to "Robin's Heritage". Amy Le Feuvre. LC 11-24969. 1911. Heidelberg Press.

Tested by Fire. Merrill Womach et al. 1982. pap. 2.95 (ISBN 0-8007-8433-2, Spire Bks). Revell.

Tested: Or, Hope's Fruition. A Story of Woman's Constancy. Celia Emmeline Gardner. LC 7-311. 1874. G. W. Carleton & Co.; Etc., Etc.

Testimonies. Patrick O'Brian. LC 52-9854. (Secker and Warburg) has title: Three bear witness.). 1952. Harcourt, Brace.

Testimony and Demeanor. John Casey. LC 78-20599. 1979. 8.95 (ISBN 0-394-50097-0). Knopf.

Testimony by Silence. Doris Miles Disney. (Signet book). 1974. (pbk.) 0.95. New American Library.

Testimony by Silence. Doris Miles Disney. LC 48-869844. 1948. Pub. for the Crime Club by Doubleday.

Testimony of Two Men. Taylor Caldwell. LC 68-13137. 1968. Doubleday.

Testimony of Two Men. Taylor Caldwell. 1977. 2.25 (ISBN 0-449-23212-3). Fawcett Pub. Co.

Testing Fire. Alexander Corkey. LC 12-1163. 1.25. The H. K. Fly Company.

Testing Ground. Jean Weatherford Strong. LC 81-80178. (Illus.). 4.95 (ISBN 0-914766-66-X). IWP Pub.

Testing of Diana Mallory. Mary Augusta Arnold Humphry Ward Ward. 1908. Harper & Brothers.

Testing of Janice Day. Helen Beecher Long. LC 15-19473. 1.25. Sully and Kleinteich.

Testing of Olive Vaughan. Percy James Brebner. LC 9-7141. 1909. C. H. Doscher & Co.

Testing Time. David P Allison. LC 38-133333. 1938. Wm. B. Eerdmans Publishing Co.

Testore, the Romance of an Italian Fiddle-Maker. Pat Candler. LC 19-4792. 1916. E. P. Dutton & Company.

Tet. Don Oberdorfer. LC 73-160887. (Illus.). 1971. 7.95 o.p. (ISBN 0-385-08571-0). Doubleday.

Tete Coupable see Frere Ocean.

Tete Jaune Cache. 1st Ed. John Spencer Owen. LC 53-8111. 1953. Pageant Press.

Tether. Ezra Selig Brudno. 1908. J. B. Lippincott Company.

Tether: Una Grey's Story. Front. by Eleanore Claire. Kunigunde Duncan. LC 53-12854. 1953. L. C. Page.

Tethered: A Novel. David Lozell Martin. LC 79-4368. 9.95 (ISBN 0-03-048241-0). Holt, Rinehart and Winston.

Tethered Bubble. Fanny Lee Weyant. LC 30-5409. The Century Co.

Tether's End. Margery Allingham. LC 58-12029. 1974. (pbk.) 0.95. Manor Books.

Tether's End. 1st Ed. Margery Allingham. LC 58-12029. 1958. Doubleday.

Tetherstones. Ethel May Dell. LC 23-13943. 1923. G. P. Putnam's Sons.

Tetramachus Collection. Philippe Van Rjndt. LC 76-20522. 8.95 (ISBN 0-399-11781-4). Putnam.

Tetramachus Collection. Philippe Van Rjndt. (Berkley Medallion Book). 1978. 1.95 (ISBN 0-425-03516-6). Berkley Pub. Corp.

Tetrarch. Alexander Comfort. LC 79-67684. (Illus.). 1980. 12.95 (ISBN 0-87773-175-6). Shambhala.

Tetrasomy Two. Oscar Rossiter. LC 73-83666. (Doubleday science fiction). 1974. 5.95 (ISBN 0-385-07732-7). Doubleday.

Tetrasomy Two. Oscar Rossiter. 1975. (pbk.) 1.50. Bantam Books.

Tette. Theodora H. Wood. 3.50 o.p. Carlton.

Teville Obsession. Caroline Stafford, pseud. LC 78-1429. 8.95 (ISBN 0-671-24032-3). Simon and Schuster.

Tevye's Daughters. Sholom Aleichem. 1959. 2.98 o.p. (ISBN 0-517-03053-5). Crown.

Tex. Clarence Edward Mulford. (Hopalong Cassidy Ser). 1976. Repr. of 1922 ed. lib. bdg. 16.85x (ISBN 0-88411-226-8). Amereon Ltd.

Tex" How Tex Ewalt, Two-Gun Man, Philosopher, Poet, and One-Time Companion of Hopalong Cassidy Turned a Whole Community Upside Down, and Dealt Retributive Justice to Several of Windsor's Leading Citizens, for the Sake of a Girl He Loved. Clarence Edward Mulford. LC 76-28253. 1976. 6.95 (ISBN 0-88411-226-8). Aeonian Press.

Tex" How Tex Ewalt, Two-Gun Man, Philosopher, Poet, and One-Time Companion of Hopalong Cassidy Turned a Whole Community Upside Down, and Dealt Retributive Justice to Several of Windsor's Leading Citizens, for the Sake of a Girl He Loved. Clarence Edward Mulford. LC 22-720432. 1922. A. C. McClurg & Co.

Tex Thorne Comes Out of the West. Zane Grey. 300p. Repr. of 1937 ed. lib. bdg. 15.95x (ISBN 0-89190-761-0). Am Repr-Rivercity Pr.

Texan. Herbert Arthur, pseud. LC 46-39293. 1946. R. M. Mc-Bride & Company.

Texan. John Thomas Edson. 192p. (Orig.). 1983. pap. 2.25 (ISBN 0-425-05858-1). Berkley Pub.

Texan. Herbert Shappiro. LC 46-3293. 1946. R. M. McBride & Company.

Texan: A Story of the Cattle Country. James Beardsley Hendryx. LC 28-485097. 1918. A. L. Burt Company.

Texan: A Story of the Cattle Country. James Beardsley Hendryx. LC 18-223638. 1918. G. P. Putnam's Sons.

Texan, a Tale of Texas. Lee Mays Taylor. LC 9-96756. 1908.

Texan Bravo: Or, The Lone Star of Texas. A Tale of Early Life in the Southwest. John Hovey Robinson. LC 7-42167. (owl library, no. 3). 1892. G. W. Studley.

Texan Captain and the Female Smuggler. A Mexican Tale of Land and Water. Lorry Luff. LC 7-14737. 1850. W. F. Burgess.

Texan from Montana. Al Cody, pseud. (Montana Ser.: No. 1). 192p. 1976. pap. 1.25 o.p. (ISBN 0-532-12370-0). Woodhill.

Texan from Montana. Al Cody, pseud. Ed. by Alice Sachs. 1970. 3.95 o.p. Lenox Hill.

Texan from Montana. Al Cody, pseud. (Montana Ser.: No. 1). 192p. 1976. pap. 1.25 o.p. (ISBN 0-532-12370-0). Manor Bks.

Texan Rides Alone. Lauran Paine. LC 59-22531. (Foulsham western story). 1958. W. Foulsham.

Texan Scouts: A Story of the Alamo and Golaid. Joseph Alexander Altsheler. LC 22-145369. 1921. D. Appleton and Company.

Texan Scouts: The Story of the Alamo and Goliad. Joseph Alexander Altsheler. 1913. D. Appleton and Company.

Texan Star: The Story of a Great Fight for Liberty. Joseph Alexander Altsheler. LC 12-21954. 1912. Appleton and Company.

Texan Triumph: A Romance of the San Jacinto Campaign. Joseph Alexander Altsheler. LC 13-20342. 1913. D. Appleton and Company.

Texan Virago: Or, The Tailor of Gotham, and Other Tales. Charles Wilkins Webber. LC 22-5137. (Tales of the southern border. part II). 1852. Lippincott, Grambo & Co.

Texana, a Novel. Robert F Mirvish. LC 54-5805. 1954. W. Sloane Associates.

Texans. Dwight Bennett. LC 78-22788. (Double D western). 1979. 7.95 (ISBN 0-385-14422-9). Doubleday.

Texan's Antic-Dotes. Fred J Tarrant. LC 54-21572. 1954. Naylor Co.

Texar the Southerner. Jules Verne. 3.95. Assoc Bk.

Texar's Vengenace: Or, North Versus South. Jules Verne & Kendall, Mrs. Laura E., Tr. LC 1-9847. (On cover: Seaside library. Pocket ed. no. 1011). G. Munro.

Texas Bank Robbing Company. Giles Tippette. (Wilson Young Adventure Ser.: No. 6). (Orig.). 1982. pap. 1.95 (ISBN 0-440-18847-4). Dell.

Texas Blood. Bradford Scott. 1969. pap. 0.50 o.p. (R2025). Pyramid Pubns.

Texas, Blood Red. Shepard Rifkin. LC 56-6010. (Dell first edition, 82). Dell Pub. Co.

Texas' Bloodless Revolution. Melissa Allen Castle. Tardy Publishing Company.

Texas Breed. easy eye ed. James D. Sayers. pap. 0.60 o.p. Lancer.

Texas Bride. Catherine Creel. (Orig.). 1982. pap. 3.50 (ISBN 0-8217-1050-8). Zebra.

Texas Brigade. Ray Hogan. (Shaw Starbuck). (Signet brand western: Vol. 18). 1974. (pbk.) 0.95. New American Library.

Texas Celebrity Turkey Trot. Peter Gent. 1979. 2.25 (ISBN 0-688-03334-2). Berkley Publishing Corp.

Texas Celebrity Turkey Trot: A Novel. Peter Gent. LC 78-17286. 1978. 8.95 (ISBN 0-688-03334-2). Morrow.

Texas Cowman. Lee Floren. LC 47-30784. 1947. Phoenix Press.

Texas Cowman. Lee Thomas. LC 47-30784. 1947. Phoenix Press.

Texas Empire. Peter McCurtin. (Sundance Ser.: No. 43). 208p. (Orig.). 1982. pap. 2.25 (ISBN 0-8439-1124-7, Leisure Bks). Nordon Pubns.

Texas Fever. Jordan Allen. 224p. (Orig.). 1980. pap. 1.95 (ISBN 0-89083-664-7). Zebra.

Texas Fever. W. F Bragg. LC 82-14825. (Atlantic large print). (Atlantic series). 1983. 11.95 (ISBN 0-89340-463-2). Chivers Press.

Texas Fever. William Frederick Bragg. LC 53-13063. 1953. Areadia House.

Texas Fever. Donald Hamilton. LC 81-69104. 9.95 (ISBN 0-8027-4002-2). Walker.

Texas Flame. Catherine Creel. 1981. pap. 2.75 (ISBN 0-89083-797-X). Zebra.

Texas Fury: By John Callahan Pseud. Joseph Chadwick. LC 50-11225. 1950. Avalon Books.

Texas Gold. John Henry Reese. LC 74-12705. 1975. 4.95 (ISBN 0-385-08550-8). Doubleday.

Texas Gold. John Henry Reese. 1976. 1.25. Belmont Tower Books.

Texas Gun. Leslic Charles Ernenwein. LC 51-27095. (Gold medal books, 156). 1951. Fawcett Publications.

Texas Gun. Lessie Charles Ernenwein. 1975. (pbk.) 0.95. Leisure Books.
Texas Guns. Robert J Hogan. LC 54-850231. (Silver star westerns). 1954. Dodd, Mead.
Texas Hellion. Ben Thompson. (Belmont Tower Book). 1.50 (ISBN 0-505-51376-5). Tower Publications Inc.
Texas Hellion: The True Story of Ben Thompson. Jaime Harrysson Plenn. (Signet book, 1174). 1955. New American Library.
Texas-Israeli War: Nineteen Ninety-Nine. Howard Waldrop & Jake Saunders. 224p. 1982. pap. 2.25 (ISBN 0-345-30508-6, Del Rey). Ballantine.
Texas Jack: The White King of the Pawnees. Edward Zane Carroll Judson. LC 7-11454. (sea and shore series--no. 28). 1891. Street & Smith.
Texas Land Grab. Johnny Nelson. 1979. pap. 1.25 o.s.i. (ISBN 0-8439-0671-5, Leisure Bks). Nordon Pubns.
Texas Lawman. Ray Hogan. pap. 0.50 o.p. Lancer.
Texas Lawyer. 1st Ed. Ben Richards. LC 53-100716. 1953. Pageant Press.
Texas Lost Mines. Jesse Rascoe. 1974. (pbk.) 3.50. Frontier Book.
Texas Man. Robert Ames Bennet. LC 34-300491. 1934. I. Washburn, Inc.
Texas Man. William MacLeod Raine. LC 28-23099. Doubleday, Doran & Company, Inc.
Texas Matchmaker. Andy Adams. LC 4-9634. 1904. Houghton, Mifflin and Company.
Texas Medico: By Len Turner Pseud. Lee Floren. 1954. Arcadia House.
Texas Men. Paul Evan Lehman. Green Circle Books.
Texas Night Riders. Ray Slater. 176p. 1982. pap. 1.95 o.s.i. (ISBN 0-8439-1063-1, Leisure Bks). Nordon Pubns.
Texas Night Riders. Ray Slater. 176p. pap. 1.95 (ISBN 0-8439-2023-8, Kable Bks). Dorchester Pub Co.
Texas: Or, The-Broken Link in the Chain of Family Honors; a Romance of the Civil War. Fannie Eoline Atkinson Selph. LC 5-20442.
Texas Outlaw. Richard Jessup. pap. 0.60 o.p. (R2495, GM). Fawcett World.
Texas Outlaws. easy eye ed. K. R. G. Granger. Orig. Title: Tejanos. 1969. pap. 0.75 o.p. (74998). Lancer.
Texas Pistol: By James Keene Pseud. Will Cook. LC 55-8151. 1955. Random House.
Texas Pride. Charles Morris Martin. (Graphic books, 86). 1954. Graphic Pub. Co.
Texas Range Rider. George M Johnson. LC 33-305643. E. J. Clode, Inc.
Texas Ranger. Napoleon Augustus Jennings. LC 99-2118. 1899. C. Scribner's Sons.
Texas Ranger. William MacLeod Raine. LC 11-189758. G. W. Dillingham Company.
Texas Ranger. Herman Toepperwein. pap. 1.50 (ISBN 0-910722-10-2). Highland Pr.
Texas Ranger Justice. Jesse Edward Grinstead. LC 41-5371. Dodge Publishing Company.
Texas Rapture. Jalynn Friends. (Orig.). 1983. pap. 3.50 (ISBN 0-8217-1195-4). Zebra.
Texas Red: By Lynn Westland Pseud. Archie Joscelyn. LC 50-9983. 1950. Phoenix Press.
Texas Renegade. Walker A Tompkins. LC 54-7152. (Bull's-eye western). 1954. Macrae Smith Co.
Texas Rider. Buck Billings. LC 35-3046. G. H. Watt.
Texas Rider. Claude Rister. LC 35-3046. G. H. Watt.
Texas Rising. D. S Phantom. LC 78-62122. (Illus.). 3.95. S & S Press.
Texas Shepherd Girl. Fannie J. Mooney Anderson. LC 43-1017. The Story Book Press.
Texas Sheriff: A Novel of 'the Territory' Eugene Cunningham. LC 34-349770. 1934. Houghton Mifflin Company.
Texas Sheriff: A Novel of 'the Territory,' Eugene Cunningham. LC 44-7847. 1944. Triangle Books.
Texas Sheriff: By Burt Arthur. Herbert Arthur, pseud. LC 56-13506. 1956. Avalon Books.
Texas Showdown. Johnston McCulley. LC 53-7219. 1953. Arcadia House.
Texas Showdown. Dick Stivers. (Able Team Ser.). 192p. 1982. pap. 1.95 (ISBN 0-373-61203-6, Pub. by Worldwide). Harlequin Bks.
Texas Spurs. Johanas L. Bouma. 1981. pap. 1.95 (ISBN 0-505-51731-0). Tower Bks.
Texas Spurs. Johanas L. Bouma. (O.s.i.). 1975. pap. 0.95 o.s.i. Tower.
Texas Spurs. Charles Horace Snow. LC 35-159267. Loring & Mussey.
Texas Spurs: A Western Novel. Johanas L Bouma. LC 55-328303. (Popular Library eagle books, EB41). 1955. Popular Library.
Texas Storm. Don Pendleton. (Executioneer,#18). 1974. (pbk.) 1.25 (ISBN 0-523-00353-6). Pinnacle Books.
Texas Talbert. Lee Floren. LC 45-21691. 1945. Phoenix Press.
Texas Talbert. Lee Thomas. LC 45-21691. 1945. Phoenix Press.
Texas Titan: The Story of Sam Houston. John Milton Oskison. LC 29-898635. 1929. Doubleday, Doran and Company, Inc.
Texas Trail. Jesse Edward Grinstead. LC 39-15956. Phoenix Press.
Texas Triggers. Eugene Cunningham. LC 38-3422. 1938. Houghton Mifflin Company.
Texas Trilogy. Preston Jones. 338p. 1976. pap. 8.95 (ISBN 0-8090-1236-7, Mermaid). Hill & Wang.
Texas Tumbleweed. Walker A Tompkins. LC 43-13711. 1943. Phoenix Press.
Texas Twister. Lauran Paine. LC 66-31659. 1966. Arcadia House.
Texas Wildflower: Laurian Kane. Kitt Brown. (Frontier Woman Saga Ser.: No. 3). 1982. pap. 2.95 (GM). Fawcett.
Texas Wind. James M. Reasoner. (Orig.). 1980. pap. 1.95 (ISBN 0-532-23201-1). Woodhill.
Texican. Dane Coolidge. 1911. 1.35. A. C. McClurg & Co.
Text of the Canterbury Tales, 8 Vols. Geoffrey Chaucer. Ed. by John M. Manly & Edith Rickert. (O.s.i.). (Illus.). 1967. Set. 160.00x o.s.i. (ISBN 0-226-50321-6). U of Chicago Pr.
Texts of Festival. Mick Farren. 1975. (pbk.) 1.25 (ISBN 0-380-00444-5). Avon.
Textures of Life. Hortense Calisher. (A novel). 1963. 4.95 o.p. (ISBN 0-316-12460-5). Little.
Textures of Life: A Novel. Hortense Calisher. LC 63-8956. 1963. Little, Brown.
Th Sign of the Praying Tiger. Drawings by Alice Caddy. Ben Lucien Burman. LC 66-177274. 4.95. New Amer. Lib.
Thackeray. Gordon Norton Ray. LC 72-8078. (Illus.). 1972. (2 vol.) 45.00 (ISBN 0-374-96722-9). Octagon Books.
Thackeray: Vanity Fair. Ed. by Arthur Polland. 1981. pap. 20.00x (Pub. by Macmillan England). State Mutual Bk.
Thackeray's Henry Esmond. William Makepeace Thackeray & Bissell, Walter Lewis, 1879- Ed. LC 8-5580. (Eclectic English classics). American Book Company.
Thaddeus of Warsaw... Jane Porter. LC 1-13955. 1832. J. C. Gerrish.
Thaddeus of Warsaw. Jane Porter. LC 17-491. 1860. Derby & Jackson.
Thaddeus of Warsaw. Jane Porter. LC 1-13950. 1868. J. B. Lippincott & Co.
Thaddeus of Warsaw. new and rev. ed., with the addition of new notes, etc., by the author. ed. Jane Porter. (On cover: Seaside library. Pocket ed. no. 698). G. Munro.
Thaddeus of Warsaw. Jane Porter. LC 2-17281. (Library of famous books by famous authors. 241). 1898. H. M. Caldwell Company.
Thaddeus of Warsaw: A Tale Founded on Polish Heroism. Jane Porter. LC 20-19335. (Lettered on cover: The home library). A. L. Burt Company.
Thais. Anatole France, pseud. Tr. by Hall, Arthur D. LC 6-43276. (On cover: Lakeside series. v. 1. no. 1). M. C. Smith Publishing Company.
Thais. Anatole France, pseud. Tr. by Tristan, Ernest. LC 26-4069. (Half-title: The modern library of the world's best books). The Modern Library.
Thais. Anatole France, pseud. LC 33-1968. (guild classics). The Literary Guild of America.
Thais. Anatole France, pseud. Tr. by Douglas, Robert Bruce. LC 29-15330. (modern readers' series). 1929. The Macmillan Company.
Thais. Anatole France & Basia Gulati. LC 75-20893. 10.00 (ISBN 0-226-25988-9). University of Chicago Press.
Thais see Romans et Contes.
Thais & Rotisserie. Anatole France, pseud. 1959. 9.50 o.p. French & Eur.
Thais: Or, The Vengeance of Venus; a Novel. Anatole France, pseud. Tr. by Pierson, Ernest De Lancey. LC 6-43275. (On cover: Romantic series. no. 10). 1892. The Minerva Publishing Company.
Thais: The Crime of Sylvestre Bonnard. Anatole France, pseud. (companion classics). W. J. Black, Inc.
Thais: The Crime of Sylvestre Bonnard. Anatole France, pseud. LC 43-789045. (On cover: Classics club library). 1943. Pub. for the Classics Club by W. J. Black.
Thalassa"! Gertrude M. Robins Reynolds. 1907. Brentano's.
Thalia. Frances Faviell. LC 57-12155. 1957. Farrar, Straus and Cudahy.
Thamar and the Destruction of Jerusalem. Charles Henry Rohe & Ireland, Mrs. Mary Eliza (Haines) 1834- Tr. LC 19-3219. Lutheran Book Concern.
Thamilla (The Turtle-Dove) a Story of the Mountains of Algeria. Ferdinand Duchene & May, Isabelle, Tr. LC 27-20027. Fleming H. Revell Company.
Than This World Dreams of... Ruby Mildred Ayres. LC 34-41290. 1935. Doubleday, Doran & Company, Inc.
Thanatos. Frank Hilaire. 1973. 1.25 (ISBN 0-671-78283-5). Pocket Books.
Thanatos. Frank Hilaire. LC 76-148474. 1971. 6.95 (ISBN 0-525-21550-6). Dutton.
Thank God It's Friday. Robert Gardner. LC 78-65836. 1978. pap. 4.95 (ISBN 0-8323-0310-0). Binford.
Thank You, Doctor. Ethel McCrossin Orr. LC 40-33128. 1940. Winningway Pub. Co.
Thank You, Jeeves! Pelham Grenville Wodehouse. LC 34-271033. 1934. Little, Brown, and Company.
Thank You, Mr. Moto. John Phillips Marquand. LC 36-102353. 1936. Little, Brown, and Company.
Thank You, Mr. Moto & Mr. Moto Is So Sorry: From the Saturday Evening Post. John Phillips Marquand. LC 77-90931. 5.95. Curtis Pub. Co.
Thank You, Mr. Moto & Mr. Moto Is So Sorry from the Saturday Evening Post. John Phillips Marquand. LC 77-90931. 320p. 1977. 5.95 (ISBN 0-89387-016-1, Co-Pub. by Sat Eve Post). Curtis Pub Co.
Thank You, Stranger. Jean Tanner. LC 53-6483. 1953. Vantage Press.
Thankful Blossom: A Romance of the Jerseys, 1779. Bret Harte. LC 39-19463. 1877. G. Routledge and Sons.
Thankful Blossom: A Romance of the Jerseys, 1779. Bret Harte. LC 4-26867. Houghton, Mifflin and Company.
Thankful Blossom: A Romance of the Jerseys, 1779. Bret Harte. LC 34-305757. 1877. J. R. Osgood and Company.
Thankful Blossom, and Other Eastern Tales and Sketches. Bret Harte. LC 72-37546. (Short story index reprint series). (Illus.). 1972. (ISBN 0-8369-4105-5). Books for Libraries Press.
Thankful Blossom: And Other Eastern Tales and Sketches. Bret I. E. Francis Bret Harte. LC 12-24358. (Half-title: Standard library edition. The writings of Bret Harte... vol. xi). Houghton, Mifflin and Company; Etc., Etc.
Thankful Spicers. Agnes Mary Brownell. LC 21-14547. 1921. C. Scribner's Sons.
Thankfulness: A Narrative: Comprising Passages from the Diary of the Rev. Allan Temple. Charles Benjamin Tayler. LC 8-20123. (On cover: C. B. Tayler's works). 1851. Stanford and Swords.
Thankfulness: A Narrative: Comprising Passages from the Diary of the Rev. Allan Temple. Charles Benjamin Tayler. 1853. Stanford and Swords.
Thankful's Inheritance. Joseph Crosby Lincoln. LC 15-13471. 1915. 1.35. D. Appleton and Company.
Thankful's Inheritance. Joseph Crosby Lincoln. LC 21-13937. 1918. A. L. Burt Company.
Thankless Child... Frank Arthur Swinnerton. LC 42-25367. 1942. Doubleday, Doran and Company, Inc.
Thankless Child. Frank Arthur Swinnerton. LC 42-25507. 1942. Hutchinson & Co. Ltd.
Thanks, Angel. Anne Brooks. LC 45-216903. 1945. Gramercy Publishing Co.
Thanks for the Ride. Ralph A Graves. 1949. J. B. Lippincott Co.
Thanks for the Rubies, Now Please Pass The Moon. Jill Schary. 1972. 7.95 o.p. Dial.
Thanks for the Rubies, Now Please Pass the Moon. Jill Robinson. LC 73-163590. 1972. 7.95. Dial Press.
Thanks, Miss O'Brien. Edward C Malewitz. LC 77-156210. 6.95 (ISBN 0-533-02851-5). Vantage Press.
Thanks to Murder. Joseph Krumgold. LC 35-7170. The Vanguard Press.
Thanks to the Saint. Leslie Charteris. LC 57-13016. 1957. Published for the Crime Club by Doubleday.
Thanksgiving. Robert Jordan. LC 70-158591. 1971. 6.95 (ISBN 0-525-21553-0). Dutton.
Thanksgiving: A Novel in Celebration of America. Terry Coleman. LC 81-13635. 14.95 (ISBN 0-671-42570-6). Simon and Schuster.
Thanksgiving Day in Modern Story. Ed. by Maud Van Buren. Bemis, Katharine Isabel, Joint Ed. LC 28-236580. The Century Co.
Thanksgiving Visitor. Truman Capote. 1968. 12.95 (ISBN 0-394-44824-3). Random.
Thanos Island. Lucy Casselman. 1978. pap. 1.75 (ISBN 0-532-17192-6). Woodhill.
Tharlane. Dorothy Cottrell. LC 30-13095. 1930. Houghton Mifflin Company.
Tharon of Lost Valley. Vingie Eve Roe. LC 19-149414. 1919. Dodd, Mead and Company.
Tharrus Three. Catherine Macdonald Maclean. LC 43-101760. 1943. The Macmillan Company.
That Affair at Elizabeth. Burton Egbert Stevenson. LC 7-34779. 1907. H. Holt and Company.
That Affair at Portstead Manor. Gladys Edson Locke. LC 14-13880. 1914. 1.25. Sherman, French & Company.
That Affair at St. Peter's. Edna Adelaide Brown. Lothrop, Lee & Shepard Co.
That Affair at "The Cedars". Lee Thayer, pseud. LC 21-1896. 1921. Doubleday, Page & Company.
That Affair in Philadelphia. Sarah Darby. Broadway Publishing Co.
That Affair Next Door. Anna Katharine Green Rohlfs. LC 7-40752. (The Hudson library, no. 17). 1897. G. P. Putnam's Sons.
That American Woman. Alec Waugh. Farrar & Rinehart, Incorporated.
That Angelic Woman: A Story. James Meeker Ludlow. LC 7-14723. 1892. Harper & Brothers.
That Artful Vicar. The Story of What a Clergyman Tried to Do for Others and Did for Himself. Eustace Clare Grenville Murray. (Franklin square library, no. 52). 1879. Harper & Brothers.
That Awful Mess on Via Merulana: A Novel. Tr. from Italian and Introd. by William Weaver. Carlo Emilio Gadda. LC 65-19320. 5.95. Braziller.
That Awful Mess on Via Merulana: A Novel. LC 65-19320. 1965. G. Braziller.
That Band from Indiana. Charlie Davis. (Illus.). 1982. 12.00 (ISBN 0-930000-19-6); pap. 8.95 (ISBN 0-930000-20-X). Mathom.
That Beautiful Wretch. A Brighton Story. William Black. LC 6-129413. (Seaside library, no. 49). G. Munro.
That Bennington Mob. Henry Barnard Safford. LC 35-4220. J. Messner, Incorporated.
That Betty. Harriet Elizabeth Prescott Spofford. LC 3-21012. 1903. F. H. Revell Company.
That Boy O' Mine. Nina Hill Robinson. 1908. Publishing House M. E. Church, South, Smith & Lamar, Agents.
That Bright Heat. George O'Neil. LC 28-8411. 1928. Boni and Liveright.
That Callahan Spunk. Francis H Ames. LC 65-19909. 4.50. Doubleday C.
That Callahan Spunk! Francis H Ames. 1976. 1.50. Ace Books.
That Carolina Summer. Janet Dailey. (Harlequin Presents Ser.). 192p. 1982. pap. 1.75 (ISBN 0-373-10488-X, Pub. by Harlequin). PB.
That Certain Summer. Emma Bennett. (Candlelight Ecstasy Ser.: No. 120). (Orig.). 1983. pap. 1.95 (ISBN 0-440-18579-3). Dell.
That Child.". Margaret Roberts. LC 44-25677. 1886. T. Whittaker.
That Cold Day in the Park. Richard Miles, pseud. LC 64-13651. 3.95. Delacorte Pr. Dist. Dial.
That Cold Day in the Park. Richard Miles. 1974. (pbk.) 1.25 (ISBN 0-515-03425-8). Pyramid Books.
That Collison Woman. Deirdre Stiles. (Leisure Books). 1977. 1.95 (ISBN 0-8439-0501-8). Nordon Pubns.
That Dakota Girl. Stella Lucile Gilman. LC 8-11268. United States Book Company.
That Dakota Girl. Stella Lucile Gilman. LC 4276. (Eagle library, no. 171). 1900. Street & Smith.
That Dark Inn. Sarah Nichols. (Orig.). 1973. pap. 0.95 o.p. (09220). Curtis.
That Darn Cat. Mildred Gordon & Gordon Gordon. Orig. Title: Undercover Cat. 212p. 1973. 5.95 o.p. (ISBN 0-385-08391-2). Doubleday.
That Day Shall Come. William H Yancey. LC 60-893. (Milestone book). 1959. Comet Press Books.
That Dinner at Bardolph's. Robert Alfred John Walling. LC 28-1742. 1928. W. Morrow & Company.
That Dreadful Boy: An American Novel. Kate Tannatt Woods. LC 8-37534. 1886. De Wolfe, Fiske and Company.
That Duel at the Chateau Marsanac. Walter Pulitzer. LC 99-42982. Funk & Wagnalls Company.
That Dumbest Okie: And Other Short Stories... By H. P. Charles Pseud. Henry Charles Dougherty. LC 54-20971. 1952. Wetzel Pub. Co.
That Dying Tree. Capitolina Donselaar. LC 31-13801. The Stratford Company.
That Egyptian Woman. Noel Bertram Gerson. LC 56-9056. 1956. Doubleday.
That Enchantress. Doris Oppenheim Leslie. 1973. 0.95. Popular Lib.
That Eurasian. Aleph Bey. (On cover: Neely's international library). F. T. Neely.
That Evening in Shanghai. Paul Thorne. LC 31-10367. The Penn Publishing Company.
That Fair False Woman: A Novel. Michael Angelo Holmes. (On cover: The Marguerite series, no. 14). E. A. Weeks & Company.
That Family on Archer Street. Craig Massey. LC 58-47880. 1958. Zondervan Pub. House.
That Far Paradise. Gene Markey. LC 60-7115. (Illus.). 1960. McKay.
That Fatal Year & Selected Stories. Henry M. Ross. 1968. 4.50 o.p. (ISBN 0-682-46791-X). Exposition.
That Fellow Perceval. Anne Green. LC 35-2542. E. P. Dutton & Co., Inc.
That First Affair, and Other Sketches. John Ames Mitchell. LC 77-98587. (Short story index reprint series). (Illus.). 1969. Books for Libraries Press.

TITLE INDEX THAYENDANEGEA.

That First Affair: And Other Sketches. 4th ed. John Ames Mitchell. LC 24-11860. 1898. C. Scribner's Sons.

That Flannigan Girl. Patsy Ruth Miller. LC 39-23529. 1939. W. Morrow and Company.

That Fool Moffett. Ellen Corrigan Scott. LC 26-142. 1926. B. Herder Book Co.

That Fool of a Woman: And Four Other Sombre Tales. Millicent Fanny St. Clair-Erskine Sutherland-Leveson-Gower Sutherland. LC 25-15636. 1925. G. P. Putnam's Sons.

That Fortune. Charles Dudley Warner. LC 73-104590. 1970. Literature House.

That Fortune. A Novel. Charles Dudley Warner. LC 99-2985. 1899. Harper & Brothers.

That Fortune: A Novel. Charles Dudley Warner. (American Studies). Repr. of 1899 ed. 23.00 (ISBN 0-384-65870-9). Johnson Repr.

That French Girl: By Joseph Hilton Pseud. Joseph Hilton Smyth. LC 60-6221. 1960. Fell.

That Frenchman! A Novel. Archibald Clavering Gunter. LC 7-133. 1889. The Home Publishing Company.

That Gay Deceiver! Linn Boyd Porter. (Dillinghamhs American authors library. no. 46). 1899. G. W. Dillingham Co.

That Gay Nineties Murder: Or, A Victorian Crime. Foxhall Daingerfield. LC 28-12310. 1928. Pub. for the Crime Club, Inc., by Doubleday, Doran & Company, Inc.

That Girl. Jeanne Bowman, pseud. (Starlight Romance Ser). 160p. 1972. pap. 0.75 o.p. Manor Bks.

That Girl. Jacques Deval, pseud. Tr. by Morris, Lawrence Shackelford. 1932. The Viking Press.

That Girl. Peggy O'More, pseud. LC 43-165234. 1943. Grammercy Publishing Co.

That Girl from Bogata: A Novel. Clarice Irene Clinghan. LC 6-29734. 1896. The Home Publishing Company.

That Girl from Boston. Robert H. Rimmer. LC 80-15312. 1980. 12.50 (ISBN 0-8290-0226-X). Irvington Publishers.

That Girl from Boston. 1st Ed. Robert H Rimmer. LC 62-170589. 1962. Challenge Press.

That Girl from Memphis. Wilbur Daniel Steele. LC 45-545687. 1945. Doubleday, Doran and Company, Inc.

That Girl from Memphis. Wilbur Daniel Steele. LC 46-18011. 1946. The Sun Dial Press.

That Girl from New York. Allene Soule Corliss. LC 32-200449. Farrar & Rinehart, Incorporated.

That Girl from Texas: A Novel. Jeannette Ritchie Hadermann Walworth. LC 8-331282. Belford, Clarke & Co.

That Girl in Black: And, Bronzie. Mary Louisa Stewart Molesworth. (On cover: Lovell's library. no. 1381). J. W. Lovell Company.

That Girl in the Alley. Mary Kelly. LC 73-93932. 192p. 1974. 5.95 o.p. (ISBN 0-8027-5301-9). Walker & Co.

That Girl, Jennifer! Rona Randall. LC 47-1745. 1946. Arcadia House, Inc.

That Girl March. W. H Rainsford. LC 20-20431. 1920. John Lane.

That Girl Montana. Marah Ellis Martin Ryan. LC 1-25436. 1901. Rand, McNally & Company.

That Girl of Johnson's. Jean Kate Ludlum. LC 7-14723. (Street & Smith's select series, no. 53). 1890. Street & Smith.

That Girl of Mine. Maurice Frances Egan. LC 6-37568. T. B. Peterson & Brothers.

That Girl on the River: An Historical Novel. Edward Seccomb Fox. LC 55-32833. (Popular Library eagle book, EB38). 1955. Popular Library.

That Girl on the River. An Historical Novel. Ted Fox, pseud. LC 55-328837. (Popular Library eagie book, EB36). 1955. Popular Library.

That Good Between Us. Howard Barker. 1981. pap. 9.95 (ISBN 0-7145-3765-9). Riverrun NY.

That Grail Song, Sam, One More Time. George V. Packard. LC 69-17745. 1969. 4.95. Gambit.

That Hagen Girl. Edith Kneipple Roberts. LC 46-766792. 1946. Doubleday & Company, Inc.

That Hastings Girl. Ethel Powelson Hueston. LC 33-2850. The Bobbs-Merrill Company.

That Hideous Strength see Space Trilogy.

That Hideous Strength: A Modern Fairy-Tale for Grownups. Clive Staples Lewis. LC 68-7663. 1968. 5.95. Macmillan.

That Hideous Strength: A Modern Fairy-Tale for Grown-Ups. Clive Staples Lewis. LC 46-377331. 1946. The Macmillan Company.

That Horrid Girl ... LC 8-27757. 1877. G. W. Carleton & Co.

That Husband of Mine. Mary Andrews Denison. LC 6-33981. 1877. Lee and Shepard.

That Husband of Mine. Mary Andrews Denison. LC 6-12131. (On cover: Library of popular fiction, no. 36). Lothrop, Lee & Shepard Co.

That Incredible First Day. Jon L. Joyce. (Orig.). 1980. pap. 2.00 (ISBN 0-937172-15-4). JLJ Pubs.

That Island. Archibald Marshall. LC 27-962855. 1927. Dodd, Mead and Company.

That Island: A Political Romance. Samuel Crocker. LC 76-42807. Repr. of 1892 ed. 15.50 (ISBN 0-404-60065-4). AMS Pr.

That Island, That Summer. Belle Thorne. (Candlelight Ecstasy Ser.: No. 35). (Orig.). 1982. pap. 1.75 (ISBN 0-440-18725-7). Dell.

That Lass O' Lowrie's. Frances Hodgson Burnett. LC 5-2772.

That Lass O' Lowrie's. 3d thousand. ed. Frances Hodgson Burnett & Fredericks, Alfred, Illus. LC 42-26161. Scribner, Armstrong & Company.

That Lass O'Lowrie's. Frances Hodgson Burnett. LC 7-13286. C. Scribner's Sons.

That Last Infirmity. Charles Brackett. LC 26-163350. 1926. The John Day Company.

That Last Rehearsal," And Other Stories. Margaret Wolfe Hungerford & Edwards, Amelia Ann Blandford, 1831-1892. (On cover: The seaside library. Pocket ed, no. 136). 1884. G. Munro.

That Late Unpleasantness. Norval Richardson. LC 24-24692. Small, Maynard & Company.

That Lofty Sky. Henry Beetle Hough. LC 41-17251. 1941. Doubleday, Doran and Company, Inc.

That Loring Woman. Edith Kneipple Roberts. LC 50-5998. 1950. Doubleday.

That Mainwaring Affair. Anna Maynard Barbour. LC 1-29007. 1901. J. B. Lippincott Company.

That Mainwaring Affair. Anna Maynard Barbour. LC 16-19142. 1908. J. B. Lippincott Company.

That Man. George J. Abrams. 1977. pap. 1.95 (ISBN 0-532-19142-0). Woodhill.

That Man. Pritam Amrita. 1975. (ISBN 0-88253-778-4). Sterling Pub.

That Man Bolt! Peter Crowcroft. 1974. (pbk.) 0.95 (ISBN 0-671-77750-5). Pocket Books.

That Man Cartwright: A Novel. Dorothy Tait. LC 76-130317. 1970. 7.95. Crown.

That Man Donaleitis. A Story of the Coal Regions. Margaret Rebecca Himes Seebach. LC 9-26961. (John Rung prize series). Lutheran Publication Society.

That Man from Smyrna: An Historical Novel. Bernard Martin. LC 78-17647. 9.95. Jonathan David Publishers.

That Man from Texas. Steven C. Lawrence, pseud. 1972. pap. 0.75 o.p. (07242). Curtis.

That Man Gull. Julian Anthony Stuart Hale. LC 78-67777. 1979. 8.95 (ISBN 0-87795-204-3). Arbor House.

That Man Gull. Anthony Stuart, pseud. 224p. 1981. pap. 1.95 (ISBN 0-445-04637-6). Popular Lib.

That Man Is Here Again: The Adventures of a Hollywood Agent. Arthur Kober. LC 46-8274. 1946. Random House.

That Man Is Mine. Faith Baldwin. 1976. Repr. of 1937 ed. lib. bdg. 16.60x (ISBN 0-88411-613-1). Amereon Ltd.

That Man Is Mine. Faith Baldwin Cuthrell. LC 74-82153. 1975. (ISBN 0-88411-613-1). Aeonian Press.

That Man Is Mine. Faith Baldwin Cuthrell. LC 37-5313. Farrar & Rinehart, Incorporated.

That Man Is Mine. Faith Baldwin Cuthrell. 1973. (pbk) 0.95. Paperback Lib.

That Man Lafayette: A Historical Novel. 1st Ed. William Schoeler. LC 56-12302. 1957. Vantage Press.

That Man of Mine. Patricia Lee. LC 38-353957. 1938. Hillman-Curl, Inc.

That Man on Beta: A Novel. Addison E Steele. (Buck Rogers;2). (Illus.). 1979. 1.95 (ISBN 0-440-10948-5). Dell Pub. Co.

That Man's Daughter.". Henry M Ross. LC 5-11604. 1905. Benziger Brothers.

That Marriage Bed of Procrustes: And Other Stories. Daniel Curley. LC 57-9950. 1957. Beacon Press.

That Minister's Boy: Or, Was He As Black As They Painted Him? Fred Harwood; or, Turned Out of His Home. Washington Wells Hooper. LC 2-19728. 1902. Brooklyn Eagle Press.

That Mrs. Renney. Donald Henderson Clarke. LC 27-7076. 1937. The Vanguard Press.

That Mrs. Renney. Donald Henderson Clarke. LC 47-6421. 1947. Triangle Books.

That Murdering Bootlegging Friend of Mine. James E. Lewis. 2.00 o.p. Carlton.

That Nairobi Affair. Betty Leslie-Melville. LC 75-6158. 1975. 6.95 (ISBN 0-385-01185-7). Doubleday.

That Nairobi Affair. Betty Leslie-Melville. (A Kangaroo Book.). 1977. 1.75. (ISBN 0-671-80930-X). Pocket Books.

That New World Which Is the Old. Elizabeth Powell. LC 25-11368. 1924. The Norman, Remington Co.

That New York Girl: By Carol Holliston Pseud. James Noble Gifford. LC 52-148537. 1952. Arcadia House.

That Nice Young Couple. Francis Hackett. LC 25-10470. 1925. Boni & Liveright.

That Night. Jane Blackmore. 1973. pap. 0.95 o.s.i. (75-479). Lancer.

That Night, and Other Satires. Freeman Tilden. LC 15-19194. 1915. Hearst's International Library Co.

That Night It Rained. Hillary Waugh. LC 61-6525. 1961. Published for the Crime Club by Doubleday.

That Noble Mexican. Thomas Bernard Joseph Connery. LC 6-30682. (On cover: Neely's popular library no. 101). 1897. F.T. Neely.

That None Should Die. Frank Gill Slaughter. LC 75-31752. 1975-1976. 9.95 (ISBN 0-89190-286-4). American Reprint Co.

That None Should Die. Frank Gill Slaughter. LC 41-455465. 1941. Doubleday, Doran and Company, Inc.

That Notorious Lola Paget. Jane Littell. LC 32-5298. 1932. L. MacVeagh, Dial Press, Inc.

That Office Boy. Francis James Finn. LC 15-22543. 1915. Benziger Brothers.

That Old College Try: A Novel. Willard Temple. LC 66-26171. 1967. Crown Publishers.

That One Mistake: A Novel. Ferenc Kormendi. Tr. by Amy Allen. LC 47-3635. 1947. Philosophical Library.

That Other Hand Upon the Helm. Charles Frederic Goss. LC 10-25215. 0.75. Jennings and Graham.

That Other Love. Geoffrey McNeill-Moss. LC 30-14663. 1930. Doubleday, Doran & Company.

That Other Person. A Novel... Margaret Hunt. (On cover: The seaside library. Pocket ed. no. 915). 1887. G. Munro.

That Other Woman. Annie Hall Thomas Cudlip. (On cover: Lovell's international ser. no. 31). F. F. Lovell & Company.

That Other Woman. Annie Hall Thomas Cudlip. (On cover: Seaside library. Pocket ed. no. 1219). 1889. G. Munro.

That Other Woman. Amelia Appleton Prendergast Hawes. LC 99-2065. 1899. F. T. Neely.

That Other World. Harriet Chaffey Payne. 1973. 5.95 (ISBN 0-533-00628-7). Vantage.

That Passing Laughter: Stories of the Southland. Flo H. Scott. (Cloth ed. 6.95 o.p.). 1966. pap. 4.95 o.s.i. (ISBN 0-87651-004-7). Southern U Pr.

That Plot That Thickened. P. G. Wodehouse. 340p. 1974. Repr. lib. bdg. 8.95 o.p. (ISBN 0-8161-6186-0, Large Print Bks). G K Hall.

That Pretty Young Girl: A Novel. Laura Jean Libbey. LC 7-14314. 1889. The American News Company.

That Printer of Udell's. Harold Bell Wright. LC 11-34743. 1911. The Book Supply Company.

That Printer of Udell's: A Story of the Middle West. Harold Bell Wright. LC 3-10203. 1903. The Book Supply Company.

That Printer of Udell's: A Story of the Middle West. Harold Bell Wright. LC 21-139421. 1911. A. L. Burt Company.

That Prosser Kid. Lloyd Pye. LC 77-79528. 8.95 (ISBN 0-87795-165-9). Arbor House.

That Pup. Ellis Parker Butler. LC 8-30251. 1908. The McClure Company.

That Quisset House. Jennie Maria Drinkwater Conklin. R. Carter & Brothers.

That Reek of Sin. Elery A Lay. LC 51-842. 1951. Vantage Press.

That Ridiculous Woman. Leonard Rossiter. LC 27-13521. 1927. E. P. Dutton & Company.

That Romanist" A Novel. Adella R MacArthur. LC 7-15273. 1896. Arena Publishing Company.

That Royle Girl. Edwin Balmer. LC 25-15387. 1925. 2.00. Dodd, Mead and Company.

That Sandhiller, a Novel. Malvina Sarah Black Clark Waring Waring. LC 4-15002. 1904. The Neale Publishing Company.

That Saxon Place. Marcia Marcoux. (Orig.). 1969. pap. 1.75 o.p. (63061). Brandon.

That Skipper from Stonington. Theda Kenyon. LC 47-213. 1946. J. Messner, Inc.

That Spanish Woman. Frank Wilson Kenyon. 1978. pap. 1.95 o.s.i. (ISBN 0-505-51301-3). Tower Bks.

That Special Kiss. Elsie W. Strother. 1982. pap. 6.95 (Avalon). Bouregy.

That Stick. Charlotte Mary Yonge. LC 9-1208. 1892. Macmillan and Co.

That Strange Sylvester Affair. Lee Thayer, pseud. LC 38-258783. 1938. Dodd, Mead & Company.

That Summer. Allen Drury. (8663). 1967. Dell.

That Summer. Mary Raymond. (Orig.). 1974. pap. 0.75 o.p. (26607-2-075). Beagle Bks.

That Summer: A Novel 1st Amer. Ed. Allen Drury. LC 66-10425. 1966. bds., 4.95. Coward.

That Summer in Connecticut. Isabel Moore. (Orig.). 1970. pap. 0.95 o.p. (ISBN 0-447-75125-5). Lancer.

That Sweet Enemy. Katharine Tynan Hinkson, pseud. LC 3-11498. (On cover: Lippincott's series of select novels). 1901. J. B. Lippincott Company.

That Terrible Man. William Edward Norris et al. (Seaside Library. Pocket Ed.). (On cover: Seaside library. Pocket ed. no. 355: No. 355). 1885. G. Munro.

That Terrible Man: A Novel. William Edward Norris. LC 7-33283. (Harper's handy series, no. 1). 1885. Harper & Brothers.

That Terrible Man: A Novel. William Edward Norris. (On cover: Lovell's library, no. 592). 1885. J. W. Lovell Company.

That They May Be One. Blanche Bayliss. LC 29-192509. The Stratford Company.

That They Might Know Thee. Illustrated by Adell Reese Palmfr. Frances Carter Yost. LC 65-28838. 1965. Deseret Book Co.

That Thin Red Line: Fire. Stephen Barlay. 1976. pap. 3.95 o.p. (ISBN 0-09-125711-5, Pub. by Hutchinson). Merrimack Bk Serv.

That Uncertain Feeling. Kingsley Amis. LC 56-5331. 1956. Harcourt, Brace.

That Vanderbilt Woman. Philip Van Rensselaer. LC 78-17513. 10.00 (ISBN 0-87223-502-5). Playboy Press.

That Vanderbilt Woman. Philip Van Rensselaer. 1980. 2.75 (ISBN 0-87216-787-9). Playboy Paperbacks.

That Was a Time. Harriet Gift Castlen. LC 37-1712. 1937. E. P. Dutton & Co., Inc.

That Was Yesterday. Margaret Storm Jameson. LC 32-26062. 1932. A. A. Knopf.

That Was Yesterday. Storm Jameson. (Berkley Medallion Book). 1976. (pbk.) 1.50 (ISBN 0-425-03074-1). Berkley Publishing Corp.

That Washington Affair. James Hay. LC 26-2812. 1926. Dodd, Mead and Company.

That Which Hath Wings: A Novel of the Day. Clotilde Inez Mary Graves. LC 18-16897. 1918. G. P. Putnam's Sons.

That Which Is Crooked. Doris Miles Disney. LC 48-671347. 1948. Pub. for the Crime Club by Doubleday.

That Which Is Hidden: A Novel. Robert Smythe Hichens. LC 40-6911. 1940. Doubleday, Doran & Company, Inc.

That Which Is Passed. G Murray Atkin. LC 23-13452. Thomas Y. Crowell Company.

That Wife of Mine. Mary Andrews Denison. LC 6-33986. 1877. Lee and Shepard.

That Wild Wheel: A Novel. Frances Eleanor Ternan Trollope. 1892. Harper & Brothers.

That Wilder Woman. Barry Jay Kaplan. 1983. pap. 3.50 (ISBN 0-553-22922-2). Bantam.

That Williams Boy. Thomas Morris Longstreth. LC 61-7058. 1961. Macmillan.

That Winter. Merle Miller. LC 48-517102. 1948. W. Sloane Associates.

That Winter Night: Or, Love's Victory. Robert Williams Buchanan. LC 6-19877. (Harper's handy series, no. 103). 1886. Harper & Brothers.

That Winter Night: Or, Love's Victory. Robert Williams Buchanan. (On cover: Seaside library. Pocket ed., no. 892). 1886. G. Munro.

That Young Man. Charles Richard Tuttle. LC 8-323082. 1878. N. H. Whitney & Co.

That's Hollywood: The Love Goddesses, No. 2. George Carpozi, Jr. 1978. pap. 1.95 (ISBN 0-532-19191-9). Woodhill.

That's Incredible! Wendy Jeffries. (That's Incredible Ser.: Vol. 5). (Illus.). 192p. (Orig.). 1981. pap. 2.50 (ISBN 0-515-06172-7). Jove Pubns.

That's Jazz! Stephanie R. Sorine. LC 81-15639. (Illus.). 48p. 1982. PLB 9.99 (ISBN 0-394-95049-6); pap. 6.95 o.p. (ISBN 0-394-85049-1). Knopf.

That's Me in the Middle. Donald Jack. LC 72-79396. 1973. 7.95 (ISBN 0-385-04901-3). Doubleday.

That's My Boy: By Francis Wallace. Francis Wallace. LC 32-24277. Farrar & Rinehart, Incorporated.

That's No Way to Die. Lamar Kelley. (Orig.). 1970. pap. 0.60 o.p. (X2148). Pyramid Pubns.

That's the House, There. Loren Singer. LC 73-79710. 1973. 5.95 (ISBN 0-385-05514-5). Doubleday.

That's the Spirit. Mary Violet Heberden. LC 50-7831. 1950. Published for the Crime Club by Doubleday.

That's the Way the Money Goes. Sigmund Stephen Miller. LC 62-11800. 1962. Crown Publishers.

That's Why They Call Me Johnny Valentine. Bruce White. 22p. 1981. pap. 2.00 (ISBN 0-939924-08-0). Expedition Pr.

Thaw. Simone J. Press. pap. 1.95 o.p. (ISBN 0-8180-1572-1). Horizon.

Thaw. Translated by Manya Harari. Ilya Grigorevich Ehrenburg. LC 55-40732. 1955. H. Regnery Co.

Thawing of Mara. Janet Dailey. (Harlequin Presents). (Orig.). 1980. pap. 1.50 (ISBN 0-373-10349-2, Pub. by Harlequin). PB.

Thayendanegea: The Scourge; or, The War-Eagle of the Mohawks. A Tale of Mystery Ruth, and Wrong. Edward Zane Carroll Judson. LC 7-12841. F. A. Brady.

Thayendanegea, the Scourge: Or, The War-Eagle of the Mohawks. A Tale of Mystery, Ruth, and Wrong. Edward Zane Carroll Judson. LC 7-12841. F. A. Brady.

The Black Arab, and Other Stories: By Mikhail Rishvin, Translated from the Russian by David Magarshack. Mikhail Mikhailovich Prishvin & Magarshack, David, Tr. LC 47-20166. 1947. Hutchinson International Authors, Limited.

The Black Automatic. William Byron Mowery. LC 37-3523. 1937. Little, Brown, and Company.

The Camberwell Miracle. John Davys Beresford. LC 41-7792. (On cover: Penguin books. 224). 1939. Penguin Books Limited.

The Constant Heart. Ruby Mildred Ayres. 1941. Doubleday, Doran and Company, Inc.

The Fate of Fay Delroy. John Wilstach. LC 33-19971. The Macaulay Company.

The Food of the Gods, and How It Came to Earth. Herbert George Wells. LC 4-25110. 1904. C. Scribner's Sons.

The Invisible Glass. Lawrence Madalena. LC 50-6075. 1950. Greenberg.

The Last of the Mohicans: A Narrative of 1757. James Fenimore Cooper. Ed. by Strunk, William. LC 4370. (English classics--Star series). Globe School Book Company.

The Man in Ratcatcher, and Other Stories. Herman Cyril McNeile. LC 22-7103. George H. Doran Company.

The Market Place. Berry Fleming. LC 38-27859. Harcourt, Brace and Company.

The Modern Haga. A Novel. rev. ed... ed. Charlotte Clark. LC 6-25354. 1883. Pub. by the Author.

The Other Room. Borden Deal. LC 73-81429. 1974. 7.95 (ISBN 0-385-03700-7). Doubleday.

THe Return of Joan. Joseph McCord. LC 37-2025. 1937. Macrae Smith Company.

The Supernatural (The) Selected by the Eds. of Playboy. Playboy Editors. LC 67-14552. (BA0119). 1968. Playboy.

The Voice Form the Void: The Great Wireless Mystery. William Le Queux. LC 23-4010. 1922. Cassell and Company, Ltd.

THe Voice Form the Void: The Great Wireless Mystery. William Le Queux. LC 23-6149. The Macaulay Company.

The Whipping Boy see Scapegoat.

Thea. Margaret Maddocks. 1973. (pbk.) 0.75. Ace Books.

Thea. Nancy Brysson Morrison. LC 62-11211. 1962. Vanguard Press.

Theater in My Head. Dan Chefetz. 1971. pap. 2.95 o.p. (ISBN 0-316-13842-8). Little.

Theater Nurse. Ruth McCarthy Sears. 1973. 4.95. Lenox Hill Press.

Theatre. William Somerset Maugham. LC 75-25365. (Maugham, William Somerset, 1874-1965. Works. 1976). 1976. 15.00 (ISBN 0-405-07823-4). Arno Press.

Theatre see Oeuvres Completes.

Theatre: A Novel. William Somerset Maugham. LC 37-2832. 1937. Doubleday, Doran and Company, Inc.

Theatre, a Novel... William Somerset Maugham. LC 44-51245. (New Avon library. 56). 1944.

Theatre of Love: A Collection of Novels. LC 74-17469. (Flowering of the Novel). 1974. (ISBN 0-8240-1151-1). Garland Pub.

Theatre of Love: A Collection of Novels, 1759. Ed. by Michael F. Shugrue. (Flowering of the Novel, 1740-1775 Ser: Vol. 52). 1974. lib. bdg. 50.00 (ISBN 0-8240-1151-1). Garland Pub.

Theatre Terrible: A Creation, Presenting Various Aspects of the Greater Drama. Charles Edwin Hewes. LC 10-26174. 1910. 1.50. The Egerton-Palmer Press.

Theban Mysteries. Amanda Cross, pseud. (Kate Fansler novel). 1973. 0.95. Warner Paperback Lib.

Theban Mysteries. Amanda Cross, pseud. LC 70-136346. 1971. 5.95 (ISBN 0-394-41108-0). Knopf.

Theban Mysteries. Amanda Cross, pseud. 1979. 1.75 (ISBN 0-380-45021-6). Avon Books.

Theban Mysteries. large print ed. Amanda Cross, pseud. LC 82-5469. 1982. 11.95 (ISBN 0-89621-362-5). Thorndike Press.

Thee Children of Shiny Mountain. Dvorkin David. (Kangaroo Book). 1977. 1.75 (ISBN 0-671-80954-7). Pocket Books.

Thee Children of Shiny Mountain. Dvorkin David. (Kangaroo Book). 1977. 1.75 (ISBN 0-671-80954-7). Pocket Books.

Theft & The Man Who Was Left Behind. Rachel Ingalls. LC 73-118212. 1970. 4.95. Gambit.

Theft of Magna Carta. John Creasey. LC 72-11127. 200p. 1973. 5.95 o.p. (ISBN 0-684-13265-6). Scribner.

Theft of Magna Carta: The 42nd Story of Roger West. John Creasey. LC 72-11127. (His Superintendent West stories). 1973. 5.95 (ISBN 0-684-13265-6). Scribner.

Theft of the Heart. Barbara Cartland. 1974. pap. 1.25 o.p. (ISBN 0-515-03388-X, V3388). Pyramid Pubns.

Theft of the Heart, No. 67. Barbara Cartland. 1977. pap. 1.25 o.p. (ISBN 0-515-04316-8). BJ Pub Group.

Theft of the Magna Carta. John Creasey. (O.s.i.). 1976. pap. 1.50 o.s.i. (ISBN 0-441-80554-X, Award). Univ Pub & Dist.

Thefts of Nick Velvet. Edward D. Hoch. LC 77-20721. 1978. 10.00. (ISBN 0-89296-035-3). Mysterious Press.

Their Ancient Grudge. Harry Harrison Kroll. LC 46-632512. 1946. The Bobbs-Merrill Company.

Their Broken Promise. Rose Kiss Vargo. LC 19-14082. Sold Only by the Author.

Their Child see Collected Works.

Their Children.". Henry Steele Clarke. LC 6-21376. 1875. D. Lothrop & Co.

Their Choice: A Novel. Henrietta Channing Dana Skinner. LC 13-2571. 1913. Benziger Brothers.

Their Christmas Golden Wedding. Caroline Abbot Stanley. LC 13-18721. 1913. Thomas Y. Crowell Company.

Their Day Was Yesterday. Vergilius Ture Anselm Ferm. LC 54-13163. 1954. Library Publishers.

Their Dusty Hands. Marjorie Chalmers Carleton. LC 25-3549. 1924. B. J. Brimmer Company.

Their Evil Ways. John William Wainwright. LC 82-17054. 1983. 10.95 (ISBN 0-312-79526-2). St. Martin's Press.

Their Eyes Were Watching God: A Novel. Zora Neale Hurston. LC 70-88437. 1969. Negro Universities Press.

Their Eyes Were Watching God: A Novel. Zora Neale Hurston. J. B. Lippincott Company.

Their Eyes Were Watching God: A Novel. Zora Neale Hurston. LC 77-18230. 1978. 3.95 (ISBN 0-252-00686-0). University of Illinois Press.

Their Family. Warren Fine. LC 78-171125. 1972. 3.50 (ISBN 0-394-47219-5). Knopf.

Their Fathers' God. Ole Edvart Rolvaag. LC 82-17636. 1983. 7.95 (ISBN 0-8032-8911-1). University of Nebraska Press.

Their Fathers' God. Ole Edvart Rolvaag & Ager, Trygve M., Tr. LC 31-29967. 1931. Harper & Brothers.

Their Fathers' God: A Novel. Ole Edvart Rolvaag. LC 73-11847. 1973. 13.75 (ISBN 0-8371-7068-0). Greenwood Press.

Their Fathers' God: A Novel. Ole Edvart Rolvaag. Tr. by Trygve M. Ager. LC 73-11847. 338p. 1974. Repr. of 1931 ed. lib. bdg. 25.00x (ISBN 0-8371-7068-0, ROFG). Greenwood.

Their First Formal Call. Grace MacGowan Cooke. 1906. Harper & Brothers.

Their Guns Were Fast. Harry Sinclair Drago. LC 55-6376. 1955. Dodd, Mead.

Their Hearts' Desire. Frances Foster Perry. LC 9-28204. 1909. 2.00. Dodd, Mead & Company.

Their Hearts to Keep. Peggy Gaddis, pseud. LC 39-80766. 1939. Arcadia House, Inc.

Their High Adventure. John Oxenham, pseud. LC 11-30044. Hodder and Stoughton.

Their Hopes Were High. Horace Clyde Filley. LC 77-238322. (Illus.). 1969. Johnson Pub. Co.

Their Husbands' Wives. Ed. by William Dean Howells & Henry Mills Alden. Clemens, Samuel Langhorne et al. LC 9-8311. (Harper's novelettes). 1906. Harper & Brothers.

Their Immortal Hearts. x ed. Ed. by Bruce McAllister. 1980. pap. 5.00 (ISBN 0-915596-24-5). West Coast.

Their Island Home: The Later Adventures of the Swiss Family Robison. Jules Verne & Metcalfe, Cranstoun, Tr. LC 24-196631. 1924. G. H. Watt.

Their Land: An Anthology of Ukrainian Short Stories. Pref. by Clarence A. Manning. Introd. by Luke Luciw. Biog. Sketches by Bohdan Krawciw. Ed. by Michael Luchkovich. LC 65-383. 1964. 5.00. Svoboda Pr.

Their Love Led to Paradise. Byrle Payne. LC 81-90274. 110p. 1982. 8.95 (ISBN 0-533-05134-7). Vantage.

Their Majesties' Bucketeers. L. Neil Smith. 176p. (Orig.). 1981. pap. 2.25 (ISBN 0-345-29244-8, Del Rey). Ballantine.

Their Man in the White House. Tom Ardies. LC 71-144246. (Illus.). 1971. 5.95. Doubleday.

Their Mutual Child. Pelham Grenville Wodehouse. LC 19-27525. 1919. Boni and Liveright.

Their Nearest and Dearest. Bernice Carey Martin. LC 52-13380. 1953. Published for the Crime Club by Doubleday.

Their Nearest and Dearest. 1st Ed. Bernice Carey. LC 52-13380. 1953. Published for the Crime Club by Doubleday.

Their Own Country. Valma Clark. LC 34-30245. G. P. Putnam's Sons.

Their Own Country. Alice Tisdale Nourse Hobart. LC 40-27270. The Bobbs-Merrill Company.

Their Own Desire. Sarita Fuller. LC 29-17658. 1929. Doubleday, Doran and Company, Inc.

Their Own Wedding. Louise Sarah Hotchkiss. 1900. G. H. Ellis.

Their Pilgrimage. Charles Dudley Warner. LC 4-15175. 1887. Harper & Brothers.

Their Shadows Before: A Story of the Southampton Insurrection. Pauline Carrington Rust Bouve. LC 72-39078. (Black Heritage Library Collection). 1972. (ISBN 0-8369-9016-1). Books for Libraries Press.

Their Shadows Before: A Story of the Southampton Insurection. Pauline Carrington Rust Bouve. LC 99-5796. 1899. Small, Maynard & Company.

Their Ships Were Broken. Constance Wright. LC 38-27146. E. P. Dutton & Co., Inc.

Their Silver Wedding Journey: A Novel. William Dean Howells. LC 4-15458. 1900. Harper & Brothers.

Their Son, The Necklace. Eduardo Zamacois & England, George Allan, 1877-1936, Tr. LC 19-18640. (Penguin series). 1919. Boni and Liveright.

Their Story Runneth Thus. L. W Reilly. LC 7-306526. (Catholic library. v. 26). 1898. C. Wildermann.

Their Town. 1st Ed. Wilbur Daniel Steele. LC 52-10042. 1952. Doubleday.

Their Tradition. Guy Rawlence. LC 27-23260. 1927. Little, Brown, and Company.

Their Wedding Journey. William Dean Howells. LC 7-5760. 1872. J. R. Osgood and Company.

Their Wedding Journey. William Dean Howells. LC 7-5759. 1888. Houghton, Mifflin and Company.

Their Wedding Journey. William Dean Howells. LC 7-5758. 1895. Houghton, Mifflin and Company.

Their Wedding Journey. large paper ed. William Dean Howells. LC 7-5757. 1895. Printed at the Riverside Press.

Their Wedding Journey. William Dean Howells. LC 99-5419. 1899. Houghton, Mifflin and Company.

Their Word of Honor, and Other Stories ... LC 40-34006. Review and Herald Publishing Association.

Their Yesterdays. Harold Bell Wright. LC 12-207943. 1912. The Book Supply Company.

Their Yesterdays. Harold Bell Wright. LC 21-139459. 1918. A. L. Burt Company.

Theirs Be the Guilt: A Novel of the War Between the States. rev. ed. Upton Beall Sinclair. LC 59-14631. 1959. Twayne Publishers.

Theirs Was the Kingdom. Ronald Frederick Delderfield. LC 76-155426. (Illus.). 1971. 8.95 (ISBN 0-671-21024-6). Simon and Schuster.

Thekla: A Story of Viennese Musical Life. William Armstrong. LC 11-7166. 1887. J. B. Lippincott Company.

Thelma. Marie Corelli. LC 2-25318. 1902. R. F. Fenno & Company.

Thelma. Marie Corelli. LC 12-220748. R. E. Fenno & Company.

Thelma. Marie Corelli. LC 24-28545. 1922. Grosset & Dunlap.

Thelma. Marie Corelli. LC 43-42363. Grosset & Dunlap.

Thelma. A Norweigian Princess. Marie Corelli. LC 32-33597. (Lettered on cover: The home library). A. L. Burt.

Thelma: A Society Novel. Marie Corelli. LC 12-19591. W. L. Allison & Company.

Thelma: By Dean and Walter Nielson. 1st Ed. Dean Nielson & Walter Nielson. LC 53-8804. 1953. Pageant Press.

Thelma Ledge. March Hastings. (Orig.). 1969. pap. 0.95 o.p. (B95-1015). Belmont-Tower.

Thelma Svane. Flora Sandstrom. LC 34-517338. 1934. H. C. Kinsey & Company, Inc.

Thelma. 1st Ed. Vera Caspary. LC 52-9079. 1952. Little, Brown.

T.H.E.M. G. C Edmondson. LC 73-10968. (Doubleday science fiction). 1974. 4.95 (ISBN 0-385-02532-7). Doubleday.

Them. Robert French. (Orig.). 1979. pap. 1.95 (ISBN 0-532-23156-2). Woodhill.

Them. Joyce Carol Oates. LC 74-89660. 1969. 6.95. Vanguard Press.

Them. 256p. (Orig.). 1981. pap. 2.95 (ISBN 0-553-13650-X). Bantam.

Him/Them... Gene DeWeese & Robert Coulson. LC 74-33677. 1975. 5.95 (ISBN 0-385-05624-9). Doubleday.

Him/Them... Gene DeWeese & Robert Coulson. LC 76-2630. 1976. 8.95 (ISBN 0-8161-6358-8). G. K. Hall.

Theme and Variation in the Short Story. John de Lancey Ferguson & Blaine, Harold Ario, Joint Ed. LC 38-19921. The Cordon Company.

Theme for Ballet. Vicki Baum. 1979. 1.95 (ISBN 0-445-04352-0). Popular Library.

Theme for Ballet. 1st Ed. Vicki Baum. LC 58-9380. 1958. Doubleday.

Theme for Reason. Elisabeth Ogilvie. LC 73-132348. 1970. 6.95. McGraw-Hill.

Theme Is Love. James Noble Gifford. LC 41-9277. 1941. Gramercy Pub. Co.

Theme Is Love. Carol Holliston. LC 41-9277. Gramercy Publishing Co.

Theme Is Murder. Charles Rodda. LC 40-2313. 1939. Simon and Schuster.

Theme Is Murder: An Anthology of Mysteries. Miriam Allen De Ford. LC 67-13459. 1967. Abelard-Schuman.

Themes in Science Fiction: A Journey into Wonder. Ed. by Leo P. Kelly. LC 73-160714. (Patterns in literary art). 1972. (ISBN 0-07-033504-4). Webster Division, McGraw-Hill.

Then. Carroll Arnett. 1965. pap. 3.00 (Pub. by Elizabeth Pr). SBD.

Then Again June. Elizabeth Bishop Reeves. LC 41-22073. Farrar & Rinehart, Inc.

Then Again, Maybe I Won't. Judy Blume. pap. 1.95 (ISBN 0-440-98659-1, LFL). Dell.

Then Am I Strong. Francena Harriet Arnold. 1969. pap. 3.95 (ISBN 0-8024-0060-4). Moody.

Then Am I Strong: Illustrated by James E. Jarrett. Francena Harriet Arnold. LC 52-6076. 1951. Moody Press.

Then, and Not 'til Then. A Novel. Clara Nevada McLeod. LC 7-20434. Authors' Publishing Association.

Then and Now. William Somerset Maugham. LC 46-4126. 1946. Doubleday & Company, Inc.

Then and Now: A Novel. William Somerset Maugham. LC 75-25364. (Maugham, William Somerset, 1874-1965. Works. 1976). 1977. 15.00 (ISBN 0-405-07822-6). Arno Press.

Then and Now: Or, Hope's First School. by Zillah Raymond Pseud. Lou H Frayser. LC 6-43142. 1883. Jackson & Bell.

Then Came Bronson. William Johnston. (Orig.). 1969. pap. 0.75 o.p. (T2106). Pyramid Pubns.

Then Came Bronson, No. 2: Ticket, No. 2# Ticket. Chris Stratton. (Orig.). 1970. pap. 0.75 o.p. (T2213). Pyramid Pubns.

Then Came Bronson, No. 3: Rock, No 3# Rock. Chris Stratton. (Orig.). 1970. pap. 0.75 o.p. (T2259). Pyramid Pubns.

Then Came Molly. Harriet Verona Cadwalader Ogden. LC 22-10018. 1922. The Penn Publishing Company.

Then Came Romance. Adelaide Humphries. LC 44-958151. 1944. Arcadia House, Inc.

Then Came the Test... Margaret Bass Pedler. LC 42-7502. 1942. Doubleday, Doran & Company, Inc.

Then Came Violence. John Dudley Ball. LC 79-8047. 1980. 8.95 (ISBN 0-385-15726-6). Published for the Crime Club by Doubleday.

Then Cometh the Devil: A Story of Life and Love in the Sportiest Town on the River. John MacLeod Sutherland. LC 7-25074. L. H. Higley.

Then Gilded Dust. John Shirley Hurst. LC 43-51077. 1943. The Bobbs-Merrill Company.

Then I'll Come Back to You. Larry Evans. LC 15-25507. 1.35. The H. K. Fly Company.

Then It Happened: Stories of Unforgettable Moments. Ed. by Wilma McFarland. LC 52-13040. 1952. F. Watts.

Then King Down Came. Richard Johnson. (Orig.). 1970. pap. 2.00 (ISBN 0-932264-14-X). Trask Hse Bks.

Then Ninth Vibration, & Other Stories. Lily Moresby & Adams Beck. Ed. by R. Reginald & Douglas Menville. LC 75-46251. (Supernatural & Occult Fiction Ser.). 1976. Repr. of 1922 ed. lib. bdg. 18.00x (ISBN 0-405-08111-1). Ayer Co.

Then, Now, and Forever. Carmelino John Rapisardi. LC 77-22082. 1977. 8.95 (ISBN 0-89554-000-2). Brasch & Mulliner.

Then, Now & Forever, My Dr. Sovatta. Annette Millard. 1977. pap. 2.95 o.p. (ISBN 0-8059-2422-1). Dorrance.

Then Pity, Then Embrace. Nancy W Bartlett. LC 67-24285. 1967. Macmillan.

Then Shall the Dust Return. Julien Green. Tr. by Whitall, James. LC 41-7859. Harper & Brothers.

Then There Grew up a Generation... Thyra Ferre Bjorn. LC 74-117285. 1970. 4.95. Holt, Rinehart and Winston.

Then There Were Three... Daniel Mainwaring. LC 38-34546. 1938. W. Morrow & Co.

Then We Shall Hear Singing: A Fantasy in C Major. Margaret Storm Jameson. LC 42-22992. 1942. The Macmillan Company.

Theo. Frances Hodgson Burnett. LC 6-17248. C. Scribner's Sons.

Theo." A Love Story. Frances Hodgson Burnett. LC 6-17249. T. B. Peterson & Brothers.

Theo Waddington: A Novel. Julian Wyndham. (On cover: Carlyle's bi-monthly series, no. 1). 1892. United Publishing Company.

Theodor Fontane, the Major Novels. Alan Bance. LC 81-21688. (Anglica Germanica. Series 2). 1982. 44.50 (ISBN 0-521-24532-X). Cambridge University Press.

Theodora. Caroline Arnett, pseud. (Fawcett Crest Book). 1977. 1.50 (ISBN 0-449-23347-2). Fawcett Books.

Theodora. Caroline Arnett, pseud. LC 79-1221. 1979. 10.95 (ISBN 0-89340-194-3). J. Curley.

Theodora: A Home Story. Phebe Fuller McKeen. LC 7-19984. A. D. F. Randolph & Company.

Theodora: A Novel. Noel Bertram Gerson. LC 69-11067. 1969. 6.95. Prentice-Hall.

TITLE INDEX THESE AMERICANS IN MOCCASINS.

Theodora and the Emperor: The Drama of Justinian. 1st Ed. Harold Lamb. LC 52-8750. 1952. Doubleday.
Theodora: Or, Star by Star ... LC 8-27751. 1880. J. B. Lippincott & Co.
Theodora, the Courtesan of Constantinople. Clara Underhill. Sears Publishing Company, Inc.
Theodore. A Story About Baptism. Annie Ketchum Dunning. Presbyterian Board of Publication.
Theodore, the Child of the Sea: Or, The Adopted Son of Lafitte. A Sequel to "Lafitte, the Pirate of the Gulf.". Joseph Holt Ingraham. R. M. De Witt.
Theodosia. Jean Anne Bartlett. (torment of Aaron Burr;). 1977. 1.50 (ISBN 0-445-03219-7). Popular Library.
Theodosia Ernest: Or, The Heroine of Faith. Amos Cooper Dayton. LC 6-32945. 1857. Graves, Marks & Rutland.
Theodosin: Daughter of Aaron Burr. Anne Colver. LC 41-3684. Farrar & Rinehart, Inc.
Theologian. William Harrison. LC 65-213806. 1965. 4.95. Harper.
Theophano: The Crusade of the Tenth Century: a Novel. Frederic Harrison. LC 4-29186. 1904. Harper & Brothers.
Theophile Gautier. Theophile Gautier & Ives, George Burnham, 1856- Tr. (Half-title: Little French masterpieces... III). 1903. G. P. Putnam's Sons.
Theophile Gautier. Theophile Gautier & Ives, George Burnham, 1856- Tr. LC 41-268848. (Little French masterpieces, ed. by Alexander Jessup III). 1909. G. P. Putnam's Sons.
Theophile Gautier's Short Stories. Theophile Gautier. Tr. by George B. Ives. LC 73-122710. (Short Story Index Reprint Ser). 1903. 15.00 (ISBN 0-8369-3543-8). Ayer Co.
Theophilus North. Thornton Niven Wilder. LC 74-573. 1974. 14.95 (ISBN 0-8161-6193-3). G. K. Hall.
Theophilus North. Thornton Niven Wilder. 1974. (pbk.). 1.75. Avon.
Theophilus Wallop: A Romantic History of a Country Neighborhood. John R East. LC 6-36387. 1890. J. B. Alden.
Theophrastus Such. George Eliot. (Lovell's library, v. 5, no. 202). 1883. J.W. Lovell Company.
Theory & Practice of Hell. Eugen Kogan. 1975. pap. 2.95 (ISBN 0-425-02932-8, Windhover). Berkley Pub.
Therapy in Dynamite. Victor B Miller. 1975. (pbk.) 1.25 (ISBN 0-671-78865-5). Pocket Books.
There Ain't No Justice. James Curtis. LC 37-229680. 1937. A. A. Knopf.
There and Back a Story. George Macdonald. LC 7-18785. D. Lothrop Company.
There and Back Again: The Story of a Family. Mary Crosbie. LC 27-20818. J. H. Sears & Company, Inc.
There and Then. Christine Goutiere Weston. LC 47-31104. 1947. C. Scribner's Sons.
There Are Brothers. Fannie Heaslip Lea. LC 40-4664. 1940. Dodd, Mead & Company.
There Are Dead Men in Manhattan: A Jigger Moran Story. John Roeburt. LC 46-184633. 1946. Mystery House.
There Are Moments in Life: Adventure Stories. 1st Ed. Jacob Schmitt. LC 54-8272. 1954. Exposition Press.
There Are No Madmen Here. Gina Valdes. Ed. by Pedro Gutierrez & Herbert O. Espinoza. LC 81-81828. 152p. (Orig.). 1981. pap. 7.95x (ISBN 0-939558-01-7). Maize Pr.
There Are Thirteen. Francis Bedding. LC 46-2153. 1946. Harper & Brothers.
There Are Victories. Charles Yale Harrison. LC 33-32231. Covici, Friede.
There Came a Day: A Novel. Harvey Hinton. LC 7-4685. (On cover: The waytown series, no. 1). 1895. Allen & Co.
There Comes a Moment. Elinor Maxwell. LC 38-3533. Arcadia House.
There Comes a Time. Thomas Bell. LC 46-540823. 1946. Little, Brown and Company.
There Comes a Time. Charles E Mercer. LC 55-10096. 1955. Putnam.
There Glass Lady. Asa Bordages. LC 32-33985. 1932. W. Godwin, Inc.
There Goes Davey Cohen. Wendy Owen. LC 66-26526. 1967. Coward-McCann.
There Goes Lona Henry: A Novel. Polan Banks. LC 41-19300. 1941. W. Morrow & Company.
There Goes Shorty Higgins. Jack Karney. LC 45-10195. 1945. W. Morrow and Company.
There Goes the Bride. Margaretta Brucker. LC 40-238196. Gramercy Publishing Co.
There Goes the Groom. Gordon Arthur Smith. LC 22-134535. E. P. Dutton & Company.
There Goes the Queen. Geoffrey Uther Ellis. LC 35-300572. 1935. W. Morrow & Co.
There Have to Be Six: A True Story About Pioneering in the Midwest. Amelia Mueller. LC 66-159272. 3.50. Herald Pr.
There Is a Book. Madelyn Galbraith. LC 75-147021. 1971. 6.25 (ISBN 0-8309-0043-8). Herald Pub. House.
There Is a Happy Land. Albert Isaac Bezzerides. LC 42-11113. 1942. H. Holt and Company.
There Is a Season. Barbara Bennett. LC 76-377135. 1976. 3.50 (ISBN 0-434-06110-7). Heinemann.
There Is a Season. Alice Mary Ross Colver. LC 56-6830. 1957. Dodd, Mead.
There Is a Season: A Novel. Faith Baldwin Cuthrell. LC 66-10288. 1966. Holt, Rinehart and Winston.
There Is a Serpent in Eden. Robert Bloch. (Orig.). 1979. pap. 2.25 (ISBN 0-89083-514-4). Zebra.
There Is a Tide. Agatha Miller Christie. 1974. (pbk.) 0.95. Dell.
There Is a Tide. Agatha Miller Christie. (Dell Book). 1977. 1.50 (ISBN 0-440-18692-7). Dell Pub. Co.
There Is a Tide. Agatha Miller Christie. LC 48-614963. (Red badge detective). 1948. Dodd, Mead.
There Is a Tide. John Collis Snaith. LC 24-7947. 1924. D. Appleton and Company.
There Is a Tide. Percival Wilde. Harcourt, Brace and Company.
There Is a Tree More Ancient Than Eden. Leon Forrest. LC 72-11426. 1973. 5.95. Random House.
There Is a Tyrant in Every Country. Gilbert Neiman. LC 47-4506. 1947. Harcourt, Brace.
There Is Always Love. Emilie Baker Loring. LC 76-42215. 1976. 6.95 (ISBN 0-88411-363-9). Aeonian Press.
There Is Always Love. Emilie Baker Loring. LC 40-907638. 1940. Little, Brown and Company.
There Is Always Love. Emilie Baker Loring. LC 83-24. 1983. 15.95 (ISBN 0-8161-3518-5). G.K. Hall.
There Is Another Heaven. Robert Nathan. The Bobbs-Merrill Company.
There Is Confusion. Jessie Redmon Fauset. LC 73-18575. 1974. (ISBN 0-404-11386-9). AMS Press.
There Is Confusion. Jessie Redmon Fauset. LC 24-7317. 1924. Boni and Liveright.
There Is My Heart. Peter Neagoe. LC 36-8138. Coward-McCann, Inc.
There Is No Armour, a Novel. Howard Spring. LC 49-7710. Harper.
There is No Darkness. Joe Haldeman & Jack C. Haldeman, II. Date not set. pap. price not set (Pub. by Ace Science Fiction). Ace Bks.
There Is No Devil". Mor Jokai. Tr. by Steinitz, F. LC 7-11928. Cassell Publishing Company.
There Is No Justice. R. B Dominic. LC 76-171268. 1971. 4.95. Published for the Crime Club by Doubleday.
There Is No Return: An Adelaide Adams Story. Anita Blackmon Smith. LC 38-21861. 1938. Pub. for the Crime Club, Inc., by Doubleday, Doran & Company, Inc.
There Is No Such Place As America. Peter Bichsel. 1971. 4.95 o.p. (8710-6, Sey Lawr). Delacorte.
There Is Today. Josephine Lawrence. LC 42-23976. 1942. Little, Brown and Company.
There Lies a Tale. Ernest Ellis. LC 71-162031. 1971. 4.95. Eerdmans.
There May Be Heaven. Elisabeth Ogilvie. LC 63-23461. 1964. McGraw-Hill.
There May Be Heaven. Elisabeth Ogilvie. 1976. (pbk.) 1.50 (ISBN 0-380-00640-5). Avon.
There Must Be a Pony. James Kirkwood. 1976. pap. 2.75 (ISBN 0-380-00689-8, 56317). Avon.
There Must Be a Pony! A Novel. 1st Ed. Jim Kirkwood, pseud. LC 60-6536. 1960. Little, Brown.
There Must Be Love: By Frances Sarah Moore Pseud. Elsie Frances Wilson Mack. LC 53-10531. 1953. Avalon Books.
There Must Be More to Love Than Death: Three Short Novels. Charles Hamilton Newman. LC 76-17743. 8.95 (ISBN 0-8040-0748-9). Swallow Press.
There None Embrace. Frederick B Shroyer. LC 74-82065. 1974. 5.95 (ISBN 0-8402-1360-3). Nash Pub.
There Oughta Be a Law. Harry Shorten. (O.s.i.). 1976. pap. 1.25 o.s.i. (BT50918). Belmont-Tower.
There Shall Be Laughter. Asa Bordages. LC 34-11659. 1934. W. Godwin, Inc.
There She Blows! a Whaling Yarn. James Cooper Wheeler. LC 13-17999. E. P. Dutton & Company.
There Should Have Been Castles. Herman Raucher. LC 78-14364. 9.95 (ISBN 0-440-09038-5). Delacorte Press.
There Was. James L. Weil. 1969. pap. 4.00 o.p. (Pub. by Elizabeth Pr). SBD.
There Was a Crooked Man. David King. (Orig.). 1970. pap. 0.60 o.p. (63-522). Paperback Lib.
There Was a Crooked Man. Kelley Roos. LC 45-350037. 1945. Dodd, Mead & Company.
There Was a Crooked Man". George Worthing Yates. LC 36-169361. 1936. W. Morrow and Company.
There Was a Crooked Man,". George Worthing Yates. LC 41-3916. 1940. Triangle Books.
There Was a Crooked Man. Cover Painting by Ray Johnson. Day Keene. (Gold medal books, 405). 1954. Fawcett Publications.
There Was a King in Egypt. Norma Octavia Lorimer. LC 18-187418. 1918. Brentano's.
There Was a King in Egypt. Norma Octavia Lorimer. LC 26-7518. 1919. Brentano's.
There Was a Lady. Sarah Litsey. LC 45-7025. 1945. The Bobbs-Merrill Company.
There Was a Little Girl. Josephine Moore Proffitt. LC 51-10839. (Illus.). 1951. Macmillan.
There Was a Little Man. Guy Pearce Jones & Jones, Constance (Bridges) Joint Author. LC 48-1163. 1948. Random House.
There Was a Man in Our Town: A Novel. Granville Hicks. LC 52-8545. 1952. Viking Press.
There Was a Man of Our Town. Keith Thomas. 1969. pap. 8.50x (ISBN 0-392-04957-0, ABC). Sportshelf.
There Was a Rustle of Black Silk Stockings. Robert McAlmon. LC 63-25387. 1963. Belmont Books.
There Was a Season: A Biographical Novel of Jefferson Davis. Theodore V Olsen. LC 68-22636. (Illus.). 1972. 7.95. Doubleday.
There Was a Ship: A Romance, with Frontispiece. Richard Le Gallienne. LC 30-7569. 1930. Doubleday, Dorane & Company, Inc.
There Was a Time. Taylor Caldwell. LC 75-701. 1975. 9.95 (ISBN 0-88411-157-1). Aeonian Press.
There Was a Time. Taylor Caldwell. LC 47-3322. 1947. C. Scribner's Sons.
There Was an Old Woman. Lou Ellen Davis. LC 70-131070. 1971. 4.50. Published for the Crime Club by Doubleday.
There Was an Old Woman. Eden Phillpotts. LC 47-5406. 1947. Hutchinson.
There Was an Old Woman: A Novel. Ellery Queen, pseud. LC 43-51064. 1943. Little, Brown and Company.
There Was an Old Woman: A Novel. Ellery Queen, pseud. LC 46-6604. 1946. The Sun Dial Press.
There Was Another. Ruby Mildred Ayres. LC 38-6972. 1938. Doubleday, Doran & Company, Inc.
There Was No Yesterday. John Stuart Arey. LC 41-3240. 1944. Doubleday, Doran and Co., Inc.
There Was Once a City. Godfrey Edmund Turton. LC 27-166753. 1927. A. A. Knopf.
There Was Once a Man. A Story. Robert Henry Newell. LC 7-32305. ("Our continent" library. v. 6). 1884. Fords, Howard, & Hulbert, for Our Continent Publishing Co.
There Were Giants. Victor E. Johnson. 120p. 1971. 1.25 o.p. (ISBN 0-913862-01-0). Aragorn Bks.
There Were Giants: A Story of Blood and Steel. Grover Jones & McNutt, William Slavens. LC 39-6117. M. S. Mill Co., Inc.
There Were No Heroes: A Personal Record of a Man's Beginning. George Washington Ogden. LC 40-170478. 1940. Dodd, Mead & Company.
There Were No Windows. Norah Hoult. LC 47-302213. 1947. Didier.
There Were Two Pirates: A Comedy of Division. James Branch Cabell & Cosgrave, John O'Hara, 1908- Illus. LC 46-6145. 1946. Farrar, Straus and Company, Inc.
There Will Be a Road. Dwight William Jensen. LC 77-90810. (Illus.). 1978. 7.95 (ISBN 0-385-14003-7). Doubleday.
There Will Be a Short Interval. Margaret Storm Jameson. LC 72-9171. (Cass Canfield book). 1973. 5.95 (ISBN 0-06-012173-4). Harper & Row.
There Will Be Fighting. Peadar O'Donnell. LC 31-7639. 1931. G. P. Putnam's Sons.
There Will Be Peace: A Story of the Civil War Days. Charles Theodore Davidson. LC 51-7624. 1951. White Wing Pub. House & Press.
There Will Be Time. Poul Anderson. LC 73-150721. 1972. 5.95. Doubleday.
There Will Be War. Jerry Pournelle. 320p. 1983. pap. 2.95 (ISBN 0-523-48555-7). Pinnacle Bks.
There You Are! Frederick Hugh Herbert. LC 25-185772. The Macaulay Company.
There You Are, but Where Are You? Robert F Mirvish. LC 64-12579. 1964. Dutton.
Thereby Hands the Tale: A Novel of the Twenties. Marguerite Langston. LC 60-9059. 1961. William- Frederick Press.
Thereby Hangs a Corpse: A Tony Lantz and Eddie Wright Mystery. Clarence Mullen. LC 46-19791. 1946. Mystery House.
Thereby Hangs the Tale: A Novel of the Roaring Twenties. Marguerite Langston. 1977. pap. 5.00 (ISBN 0-87164-062-7). William-F.
There's a Divinity. Marie Tello Phillips. LC 37-12213. Observer Press.
There's a Lot of It Going Around. Eric Nicol. LC 75-14833. 250p. 1976. 7.95 o.p. (ISBN 0-385-05410-6). Doubleday.
There's a Reason for Everything. Ernest Robertson Punshon. LC 46-2496. 1946. The Macmillan Company.
There's a Spot in My Heart. Frank Leslie. LC 47-19427. 1947. Simon and Schuster.
There's a Whip in My Valise. Angela Pearson. (Orig.). 1969. pap. 1.95 o.s.i. (OPH-170, Ophelia). Olympia.
There's Always a Payoff. Robert P Hansen. LC 59-113567. 1959. M. S. Mill Co. and W. Morrow.
There's Always a Rainbow. Eleanor Elliott Carroll. LC 36-7619. The Penn Publishing Company.
There's Always a Throgmorton: A Novel. Frederic O'Brady. LC 77-116507. 1970. 6.50. Simon and Schuster.
There's Always Annette. Lorena Carleton. LC 47-1681. 1946. Arcadia House, Inc.
There's Always Another Year. Martha Ostenso. LC 33-29800. 1933. Dodd, Mead & Company.
There's Always Tomorrow: A Historical Novel. Bessie Carroll. LC 51-3281. 1951. Exposition Press.
There's an Aardvark in My Ark. Kelly L. Segraves. (Young Reader Ser.). pap. 2.95 (ISBN 0-89293-075-6). Beta Bk.
There's Been Murder Done" A Novel of Crime, Police Work, and Punishment. Kenneth Thomas Knoblock. LC 31-38396. 1931. Harper & Brothers.
There's No Base Like Home. Harry Charles Witwer. LC 20-978491. 1920. Doubleday, Page & Company.
There's No Place Like Nome. Artis Palmer. LC 63-12635. 1963. Morrow.
There's No Return. Claudia Jones Holland. LC 38-394934. 1937. The Naylor Company.
There's Nothing in It. Jennie Bidwell. LC 6-13104. 1877. H. Keller & Co.
There's One Born Every Minute. Phineas Taylor Barnum. 60p. 1982. pap. 1.50 (ISBN 0-86541-011-9). Filter.
There's One in Every Family. Frances Eisenberg. LC 41-51800. J. B. Lippincott Company.
There's One in Every Town. 1st Ed. James Aswell. LC 51-10508. 1951. Bobbs-Merrill.
There's Only One. Alice Mary Ross Colver. LC 41-390319. 1941. Macrae-Smith-Company.
There's Only One. Alice Mary Ross Colver. LC 42-50416. 1942. Triangle Books.
There's Only One. Sophie Kerr. LC 36-907806. Farrar & Rinehart, Incorporated.
There's Time. Art Glogau. pap. 2.50 o.s.i. (ISBN 0-8181-0318-3). Pageant-Poseidon.
There's Trouble Brewing. Nicholas Blake. LC 81-47805. 224p. 1982. pap. 3.37i (ISBN 0-06-080569-2, P 569, PL). Har-Row.
There's Trouble Brewing. Cecil Day-Lewis. LC 37-6304. 1937. Harper & Brothers.
Theresa. Arthur Schnitzler. Tr. by William A. Drake. LC 70-175445. 460p. 1972. Repr. of 1928 ed. 27.50 (ISBN 0-404-05617-2). AMS Pr.
Theresa at San Domingo: A Tale of the Negro Insurrection of 1791. Armand Fresneau. Tr. by Magrath, Emma Geiger. LC 6-28745. 1889. A. C. McClurg and Company.
Theresa; the Chronicle of a Woman's Life. Arthur Schnitzler. LC 70-175445. 1971. 12.50 (ISBN 0-404-05617-2). AMS Press.
Theresa: The Chronicle of a Woman's Life. Arthur Schnitzler. Tr. by Drake, William A. LC 28-23659. 1928. Simon and Schuster.
Theresa's Choice. Rachel MacCarthy Cecil. LC 59-16201. Dodd, Mead.
Therese. Francois Mauriac & Sutton, Eric, Tr. LC 28-14827. 1928. Boni & Liveright.
Therese: A Portrait in Four Parts. Francois Mauriac. Tr. by Gerard Hopkins. LC 47-31392. 1947. H. Holt.
Therese, a Portrait in Four Parts. Translated by Gerald Hopkins. Francois Mauriac. LC 56-81993. (Doubleday anchor book, A79). 1956. Doubleday.
Therese & Angelica. Tr. by Paul Anhalt. 1968. pap. 1.75 o.p. (3031). Brandon.
Therese & Angelica. Jean Baptiste De Boyer Argens & Arles De Montigny. LC 77-143. (Brandon House library edition). 1968. 1.75. Brandon House.
Therese and Isabelle. Violette Leduc. LC 67-13389. 1967. Farrar, Straus & Giroux.
Therese De Quilliane: Or, On the Convent's Threshold; from the French of Leon De Tinseau. Leon De Tinseau & Gray, Frances S., Tr. LC 8-26766. 1892. J. Ireland.
Therese Dunoyer. A Novel. Eugene Sue & H, J. S., Tr. LC 8-17671. J. Winchester.
Therese Raquin. Emile Zola. LC 62-5008. (Penguin classics, L120). 1962. Penguin Books.
Therese Raquin. A Novel. Emile Zola & Sherwood, Mrs. Mary (Neal) Tr. LC 9-130274. T. B. Peterson & Brother.
Thermal Thursday. Don Pendleton. (Executioner Ser.: No. 36). (Orig.). 1979. pap. 2.25 (ISBN 0-523-41854-X). Pinnacle Bks.
These Americans in Moccasins. Bonnie Hunter. 1968. 2.95 o.p. Vantage.

These Are My Children. Antoinette Spitzer. LC 35-186943. The Macaulay Company.
These Are My Jewels. Lily Bess Campbell. W. W. Norton & Company, Inc.
These Are My Jewels. Ella Booker Cook. LC 45-7300. 1945. Dorrance & Company.
These Are My People. Ruth Burr Sanborn. LC 41-23969. 1941. Thomas Y. Crowell Company.
These Are My Sisters. Lara Jefferson. LC 73-82256. 200p. 1975. pap. 2.50 o.p. (ISBN 0-385-08444-7, Anch). Doubleday.
These Are the Times: A Novel. Clare Jaynes. LC 44-40108. 1944. Random House.
These Arrows Point to Death. William O'Farrell. LC 51-2019. (Bloodhound mystery). 1951. Duell, Sloan and Pearce.
These Bars of Flesh. Thomas Sigismund Stribling. LC 38-101247. 1938. Doubleday, Doran & Company, Inc.
These Bright Young Dreams. Clyde R Bulla. LC 41-8919. The Penn Publishing Company.
These Changing Years. Elisabeth Stancy Payne. LC 42-27373. A. L. Burt Company, Pub. by Arrangement with The Penn Publishing Co.
These Changing Years. Elisabeth Stancy Payne. LC 31-30600. The Penn Publishing Company.
These Charming People: Being a Tapestry of the Fortunes, Follies, Adventures, Gallantries and General Activities of Shelmerdene That Lovely Lady:, Lord Tarylon, Mr. Michael Wagstaffe, Mr. Ralph Wyndham Trevor and Some Others of Their Friends of the Lighters Sort. Michael Arlen. LC 24-6734. George H. Doran Company.
These Cliffs Are Dangerous. Lindsay March. LC 72-90397. (Simon and Schuster novel of suspense). 1973. 5.95 (ISBN 0-671-21456-X). Simon and Schuster.
These Elder Rebels: A Novel. Helen Raymond Abbott Beals. LC 35-131719. 1935. Frederick A. Stokes Company.
These Foolish Things. Michael Sadleir. LC 37-165372. 1937. G. P. Putnam's Sons.
These Frantic Years. James Warner Bellah. LC 27-7181. 1927. D. Appleton & Company.
These Generations. Elinor Mordaunt, pseud. LC 30-25303. 1930. Brewer and Warren Inc.
These Go in Flight. Martha Richford-Roberts. 1970. 4.00 (ISBN 0-8233-0150-8). Golden Quill.
These Golden Pleasures. Valerie Sherwood. 512p. (Orig.). 1977. pap. 3.95 (ISBN 0-446-30761-0). Warner Bks.
These I Have Loved... Stuart Petre Brodie Mais. LC 34-1368. Putnam.
These I Like Best: The Favorite Novels and Stories of Kathleen Norris,Chosen by Herself. Kathleen Thompson Norris. LC 41-2437. 1941. Doubleday, Doran and Company, Inc.
These Innocents: Illustrated by the Author. Winant Johnston. LC 51-841. Vantage Press.
These Items of Desire. Louis A Brennan. LC 53-5015. 1953. Random House.
These Lonely Victories. Elliot West. LC 78-188723. 1972. 6.95. Putnam.
These Lord's Descendants. Gloria Goddard. LC 30-3354. 1930. Frederick A. Stokes Company.
These Lovers Fled Away. 1st Ed. Howard Spring. LC 55-8049. 1955. Harper.
These Low Grounds. Waters Edward Turpin. LC 73-76121. 1969. McGrath Pub. Co.
These Low Grounds. Godfrey Edmund Turton. LC 37-19647. 1937. Harper & Brothers.
These Lynnekers. John Davys Beresford. LC 16-66460. 1916. Cassell and Company, Ltd.
These Lynnekers. John Davys Beresford. LC 16-8462. 1.50. George H. Doran Company.
These Married People. Corinne Running. LC 52-12108. 1953. Rinehart.
These Men: Thy Friends. Edward John Thompson. Harcourt, Brace and Company.
These, My People. Bertha B. Moore McCurry. LC 42-20806. 1942. Wm. B. Eerdmans Publishing Company.
These Old Shades. Georgette Heyer. LC 66-251245. 1966. 4.95. Dutton.
These Old Shades. Georgette Heyer. (SB4004). 1967. Bantam.
These Old Shades. Georgette Heyer. LC 26-19346. Small, Maynard & Company.
These People Mine. Merle Good. LC 73-6196. (Illus.). 1973. (pbk.) 1.25 (ISBN 0-8361-1718-2). Herald Press.
These Restless Heads, a Trilogy of Romantics. James B. Cabell. 1971. Repr. of 1932 ed. 22.00 o.p. (ISBN 0-403-00541-8). Scholarly.
These Restless Heads: A Triology of Romantics. James Branch Cabell. LC 70-131654. (Illus.). 1971. (ISBN 0-403-00541-8). Scholarly Press.
These Same Hills. E. R. Zietlow. LC 60-12384. 1960. Knopf.
These Songs Without Music. Walter J. Sepaniac. 1975. 2.95 o.s.i. (ISBN 0-8181-0334-5). Pageant-Poseidon.
These Stories Went to Market: Successful "First" Stories Published in Collier's, Saturday Evening Post, Harper's Bazaar... Ed. by Vernon McKenzie. LC 35-7024. R. M. McBride & Company.
These Thousand Hills. Alfred Bertram Guthrie. LC 56-13458. 1956. Houghton Mifflin.
These Thousand Hills. Alfred Bertram Guthrie. LC 79-16716. (Series: Gregg Press Western Fiction Series.). (Illus.). 1979. 9.95 (ISBN 0-8398-2584-6). Gregg Press.
These Three. Ward Hudson Parry. LC 30-2693. R. G. Badger.
These Tigers' Hearts. Jane Land. LC 77-12865. 1978. 7.95 o.p. (ISBN 0-385-12970-X). Doubleday.
These Twain. Arnold Bennett. LC 76-372220. 1976. 2.25 (ISBN 0-14-003886-8). Penguin.
These Twain. Arnold Bennett. LC 74-17052. (Collected works of Arnold Bennett). 1974. (ISBN 0-518-19160-5). Books for Libraries Press.
These Twain. Arnold Bennett. LC 15-26713. George H. Doran Company.
These Unlucky Deeds. Richard Martin Stern. LC 61-6902. 1961. Scribner.
These Were Brethren. Carl Harry Claudy. LC 47-29260. 1947. Temple Publishers.
These Were the Brontes. Dorothy Helen Cornish. LC 40-302750. 1940. The Macmillan Company.
These Were the Young. Mary Nicholson. LC 38-38335. 1938. Longmans, Green and Co.
These White Hands. Warwick Deeping. LC 37-272636. 1937. R. M. McBride & Company.
These Will Chill You: Twelve Terrifying Tales of Malignant Evil. Ed. by Lee Wright & Richard G. Sheehan. LC 67-12255. (Bantam's tales of supernatural horror). 1967. Bantam Books.
These Women. Ed. by Mary MacArthur et al. (Illus.). 1978. pap. 3.50 (ISBN 0-916300-15-3). Gallimaufry.
These Young Rebels. Frances Roberta Sterrett. LC 21-130602. 1921. D. Appleton and Company.
These, Your Children: By Bruno Lessing and Others. Ed. by Harold Uriel Ribalow. LC 52-13604. 1952. Beechhurst Press.
These 13, Stories. William Faulkner. LC 31-24896. J. Cape & H. Smith.
These 13; Stories: Stories. William Faulkner. LC 45-34615. 1931. J. Cape & H. Smith.
Theseus: Hero of Attica. A Novel. Sylvanus Cobb. (On cover: The popular series, no. 27). 1892. R. Bonner's Sons.
Thespian Quest: A Novel. Charles Edmund Williams. LC 73-80954. 1973. 7.95. T. Gaus' Sons.
Theta Syndrome. Elleston Trevor. LC 76-55904. 1977. 7.95 (ISBN 0-385-07463-8). Doubleday.
Theta Syndrome. Elleston Trevor. 1978. 1.95 (ISBN 0-449-23668-4). Fawcett Crest Books.
They. Rudyard Kipling. LC 24-168881. 1904. C. Scribner's Sons.
They. Marya Mannes. LC 68-22514. 1968. 4.95 o.p. Doubleday.
They: A Novel. Marya Mannes. LC 68-22514. 1968. 4.95. Doubleday.
They All Bleed Red. Richard Sted. LC 54-12831. (Inner sanctum mystery). 1954. Simon and Schuster.
They All Called It Tropical: True Tales of the Romantic Everglades, Cape Sable, & the Florida Keys. Charles M. Brookfield & Oliver Griswold. (O.s.i). (Illus.). 1977. pap. 2.25 o.s.i. (ISBN 0-916224-25-2). Banyan Bks.
They All Ran Away. Edward Sidney Aarons. 1970. Repr. pap. 0.75 o.p. (75-307). Manor Bks.
They Also Serve. Peter Bernard Kyne. LC 27-18549. 1927. Cosmopolitan Book Corporation.
They Always Come Home. Henry Lieferant & Sylvia Saltzberg Lieferant. LC 42-570498. 1942. E. P. Dutton & Co., Inc.
They and I. Jerome Klapka Jerome. LC 9-24947. 1909. Dodd, Mead and Company.
They" and The Brushwood Boy. Rudyard Kipling & Townsend, Frederick Henry, 1868-1920, Illus. LC 27-15322. 1926. Doubleday, Page & Company.
They Are People: Modern Short Stories of Nuns, Monks and Priests... Ed. by Mariella Gable. LC 43-15505. 1943. Sheed & Ward.
They Ask for Bread: A Novel. Rebecca Pegues Rogers. LC 47-297. 1946. Rockport Press, Inc.
They Blocked the Suez Canal. Arthur Durham Divine. LC 36-8616. 1936. Green Circle Books.
They Blocked the Suez Canal. Arthur Durham Divine. LC 36-8616. 1936. Green Circle Books.
They Both Were Naked. Philip Wylie. LC 65-22585. 1965. Doubleday.
They Both Were Naked. Philip Wylie. 1974. (pbk.) 1.75. Manor Books.
They Brought Their Guns: Stories. Thomas Thompson. LC 54-9669. Ballantine Books.
They Brought Their Women. Edna Ferber. LC 70-110188. (Short Story Index Reprint Ser.). 1936. 17.00 (ISBN 0-8369-3339-7). Ayer Co.
They Brought Their Women: A Book of Short Stories. Edna Ferber. LC 70-110188. (Short story index reprint series). (Illus.). 1970. Books for Libraries Press.
They Brought Their Women: A Book of Short Stories. Edna Ferber. LC 33-27164. 1933. Doubleday, Doran & Company, Inc.
They Brought Their Women: Sophisticated Short Stories. Edna Ferber. LC 44-47317. (On cover: Avon modern short story monthly. No. 19). 1944. Avon Book Company.
They Buried a Man. Mildred Davis. (Kangaroo Book). 1977. 1.50. Pocket Books.
They Buried a Man. Mildred B Davis. LC 53-8190. (Inner sanctum mystery). 1953. Simon and Schuster.
They Burn the Thistles. Yashar Kemal. LC 76-54763. 1977. 10.95 o.p. (ISBN 0-688-03164-1). Morrow.
They Burn the Thistles. Yasar Kemal. LC 76-54763. 1977. 10.95 (ISBN 0-688-03164-1). Morrow.
They Call It Love. Frank Frankfort Moore. LC 7-25301. (On cover: Lippincott's select novels. no. 168). 1895. J. B. Lippincott Company.
They Call It Love: A Novel. Louis Joseph Vance. LC 27-21017. 1927. J. B. Lippincott Company.
They Call It Patriotism. Bruno Brehm. Tr. by Goldsmith, Margaret Leland. LC 32-26201. 1932. Little, Brown, and Company.
They Call It Sin. Alberta Stedman Eagan. LC 33-222593. The Macaulay Company.
They Call It T.L.C. L. E. Ogle. 3.00 o.p. Carlton.
They Call Me Carpenter: A Tale of the Second Coming. Upton Beall Sinclair. LC 22-209621. Boni and Liveright.
They Call Me Sunny. Helen Duttweiler & Elizabeth Cain. LC 73-92389. (Illus.). 76p. 1974. 9.50 o.p. (ISBN 0-915082-01-2, Project Pr). Proj Pub & Des.
They Call Me the Mercenary: Bush Warfare, No. 10. Axel Kilgore. (They Call Me the Mercenary Ser.). (Orig.). 1982. pap. 2.50 (ISBN 0-8217-1023-0). Zebra.
They Call Me the Mercenary: Death Lust, No. 11. (Orig.). 1982. pap. 2.50 (ISBN 0-8217-1056-7). Zebra.
They Call Me the Mercenary, No. 13: Naked Blade, Naked Gunn. Axel Kilgore. 1983. pap. 2.50. Zebra.
They Call Me the Mercenary, No. 14: The Silberian Alternative. Axel Kilgore. (Orig.). 1983. pap. 2.50 (ISBN 0-8217-1194-6). Zebra.
They Call Me the Mercenary, No. 5: Canadian Killing Ground. Axel Kilgore. (Orig.). pap. 2.50 (ISBN 0-89083-829-1). Zebra.
They Call Me the Mercenary: The Terror Contract, No. 9. Axel Kilgore. (They Call Me the Mercenary Ser.). 1982. pap. 2.50 (ISBN 0-89083-985-9). Zebra.
They Called Her Charity. Wenzell Brown. LC 51-14143. 1951. Appleton-Century-Crofts.
They Called Her "Sin" for Short. Vida Hurst. LC 37-23924. M. S. Mill Co., Inc.
They Called Him Blue Blazes. William MacLeod Raine. LC 41-9245. 1941. Houghton Mifflin Company.
They Called Him Death. John Victor Turner. 1935. D. Appleton-Century Company, Incorporated.
They Called Him Deathwind. M. P. King. 1981. 5.75 (ISBN 0-8062-0650-0). Carlton.
They Called Him Doctor: By Marsh Morrison Pseud. Morris Marsh. LC 56-114953. 1956. F. Fell.
They Called Him Joseph. by joseph n. cole. ed. Joseph N Cole. LC 66-20849.
They Called Him Shifta. Dick Bohrer. LC 95-28. 320p. 1981. pap. 4.95 (ISBN 0-8024-7910-3). Moody.
They Came from Outer Space: 12 Classic Science Fiction Tales That Became Major Motion Pictures. Jim Wynorski. LC 80-2249. (Illus.). 11.95 (ISBN 0-385-18502-2). Doubleday.
They Came from the Sea. E. V. Timms. 1967. Repr. pap. 1.60 o.s.i. Tri-Ocean.
They Came Like Swallows. William Maxwell. LC 37-6382. 1937. Harper & Brothers.
They Came Like Swallows. Slight Revisions Have Been Made by the Author. William Maxwell. LC 60-894. (Milestone book). 1960. Vintage Books.
They Came to a River. Allis McKay. LC 41-517492. 1941. The Macmillan Company.
They Came to a Valley. Bill Gulick, pseud. LC 81-587. (Series: Gregg Press Western Fiction Series.). 1981. 16.95 (ISBN 0-8398-2683-4). Gregg Press.
They Came to a Valley: By Bill Gulick. 1st Ed. Grover C Gulick. LC 66-20983. 1966. 5.95. Doubleday.
They Came to Baghdad. Agatha Miller Christie. LC 51-10011. (Red badge detective). 1951. Dodd, Mead.
They Came to Baghdad. Dame Agatha Miller Christie. 1974. (pbk.) 0.95. Dell.
They Came to Cordura. Glendon Fred Swarthout. LC 58-5264. 1958. Random House.
They Came to Kill. Margaret Scherf. LC 42-18287. 1942. G. P. Putnam's Sons.
They Came to London. Paul Tabor. LC 43-17977. 1943. The Macmillan Company.
They Came to Sacandaga: The Story of Godfrey Shew, Fish House Patriot. Donald J Sawyer. LC 75-27827. (Illus.). 6.50 (ISBN 0-913710-06-7). Prospect Books.
They Came to the Castle. Anthony Bertram. LC 32-10935. E. P. Dutton & Co., Inc.
They Can Only Kill You Once. Dan Brennan. 1977. pap. 1.50 o.s.i. (ISBN 0-8439-0455-0, Leisure Bks). Nordon Pubns.
They Can't All Be Guilty. Mary Violet Heberden. LC 47-2974. 1947. Pub. for the Crime Club by Doubleday & Company, Inc.
They Can't Hang Me! Jacqueline Mallet. LC 74-4860. 1974. 6.95 (ISBN 0-06-012801-1). Harper & Row.
They Can't Hang Me. James Ronald. LC 38-25511. 1938. Pub. for the Crime Club, Inc., by Doubleday, Doran & Company, Inc.
They Change Their Skies. Letitia Preston Osborne. LC 45-3708. 1945. J. B. Lippincott Company.
They Come and They Go. Venetia Savile. LC 40-30761. 1940. W. Morrow & Company.
They Come from Baghdad. Agatha Miller Christie. 1977. 1.50 (ISBN 0-440-18700-1). Dell Pub. Co.
They Conspired to Kill. Leonard Gribble. 1975. 7.95 (ISBN 0-09-123370-4, Pub. by Hutchinson). Merrimack Pub Cir.
They Could Not Sleep. Maxwell Struthers Burt. LC 28-9650. 1928. C. Scribner's Sons.
They Couldn't Say No. Harvey Fulton. LC 31-659778. J. Cape & H. Smith.
They Couldn't Say No. Matt Harding, pseud. 1971. pap. 0.75 o.p. (75-370). Manor Bks.
They Cried a Little. Sonya Schulberg. LC 37-23918. 1937. C. Scribner's Sons.
They Cry for Love. John N. Kamp. 1968. 3.95 o.p. Vantage.
They Cry for Mercy. 1st Ed. Eugene Janas. LC 56-12915. 1957. Vantage Press.
They Dare Not Go a-Hunting. Dorothea Cornwell. LC 44-8550. 1944. Dodd, Mead & Company.
They Dared to Be Different. Hugh Steven. LC 76-42174. 1976. pap. 2.95 o.p. (ISBN 0-89081-029-X, 029X). Harvest Hse.
They Dared to Breathe. John Tortorello. 3.75 o.p. Vantage.
They Deal in Death. Robert Terrall. LC 43-4736. 1943. Simon and Schuster.
They Did Not Fear. Philip E Singer. LC 52-12034. 1952. Beechhurst Press.
They Did Not Pass. A. Belodorodov. 80p. 1970. pap. 1.20 o.p. (ISBN 0-8285-0504-7, Pub. by Progress Pubs USSR). Imported Pubns.
They Died in Darkness. Lacy A. Dillon. 1976. 9.95 o.p. (ISBN 0-87012-230-4). McClain.
They Died Laughing. Alan Baer Green. LC 52-10085. (Inner sanctum mystery). 1952. Simon and Schuster.
They Died with Their Boots on: Reissue. Thomas Ripley. (6165). 1964. Pocket Bks.
They Do It in Church. Topsy Gregory. LC 71-160794. 1971. 4.95 (ISBN 0-687-41651-5). Abingdon Press.
They Do It with Mirrors. Agatha Miller Christie. (Greenway Edition). 1969. 8.95 (ISBN 0-396-06067-6). Dodd.
They Do It with Mirrors. Jim Conaway. (Belmont Tower Book). 1977. 1.50 (ISBN 0-505-51190-8). Tower Pubns.
They Do It with Mirrors. Carol White. LC 77-20113. 8.95 (ISBN 0-698-10873-6). Coward, McCann & Geoghegan.
They Do Not: The Letters of a Nonprofessional Lady Arranged for Public Consumption. Colin Campbell Clements. LC 26-18169. Small, Maynard & Company.
They Don't Dance Much. James Ross. LC 74-23650. (Lost American fiction). 1975. 8.95 (ISBN 0-8093-0714-6). Southern Illinois University Press.
They Don't Dance Much. James Ross. (Lost American Fiction Series). 1976. (pbk.) 1.50. Popular Library.
They Don't Dance Much. James Ross. LC 40-32624. 1940. Houghton Mifflin Company.
They Don't Dance Much: A Novel. James Ross. LC 74-23650. (Lost American Fiction Ser.). 308p. 1975. 8.95 (ISBN 0-8093-0714-6). S Ill U Pr.
They Don't Make Them Like Daddy Anymore. E. M. Hull. 4.00 o.p. (ISBN 0-8062-0707-8). Carlton.
They Don't Make Them Like That Any More. James Leasor. LC 74-84392. 1970. 5.95. Doubleday.
They Don't Shoot Cowards. John Henry Reese. LC 73-79703. 1973. 4.95 (ISBN 0-385-05577-3). Doubleday.
They Dream of Home. Niven Busch. LC 44-991796. 1944. D. Appleton-Century Company Incorporated.
They Emerged from the Shade. Thelma Hoffmann Tyler Arceneaux. LC 74-80408. 1974-1975. 6.95. Harlo.

TITLE INDEX THIEF OF LOVE.

They Fell from God's Hands. Translated from the German by Geoffrey Sainsbury. 1st Ed. Hans Werner Richter. LC 56-629752. 1956. Dutton.
They Fell in Love: A Novel. Harold Norling Swanson. LC 32-21673. Harcourt, Brace and Company.
They Fought for Liberty. Marshall Adams. LC 37-197589. The Dodge Publishing Company.
They Found Atlantis. Dennis Yates Wheatley. 1979. 9.95 (ISBN 0-09-044612-7, Pub. by Hutchinson). Merrimack Pub Cir.
They Found Atlantis: A Novel. Dennis Yates Wheatley. LC 36-134611. J. B. Lippincott Company.
They Found Him Dead. Georgette Heyer. LC 72-93958. 1973. 5.95 (ISBN 0-525-21675-8). Dutton.
They Found Him Dead: The Most Amusing, and One of the Most Exciting Mysteries of the Year. Georgette Heyer. LC 37-18250. 1937. Pub. for the Crime Club, Inc., by Doubleday, Doran & Company, Inc.
They Found Him Dead: The Most Amusing, and One of the Most Exciting Mysteries of the Year. Georgette Heyer. LC 39-258. 1938. The Sun Dial Press, Inc.
They Found the Buried Cities. Robert Wauchope. LC 65-24433. 392p. 1974. pap. text ed. 4.50 o.s.i. (ISBN 0-226-87633-0, P463, Phoen). U of Chicago Pr.
They Gave Him a Gun. William Joyce Cowen. LC 36-1738. 1936. H. Smith & R. Haas.
They Got What They Wanted. Phyllis Raphael. 1973. 0.75. Popular Lib.
They Got What They Wanted. Phyllis Raphael. LC 78-38838. 1972. (ISBN 0-393-08668-2). Norton.
They Had to Honeymoon. Alice Marjorie Howe. 1928. A. M. Howe.
They Had to See Paris. Homer Croy. LC 34-865019. 1926. Grosset & Dunlap.
They Had to See Paris. Homer Croy. 1926. Harper & Brothers.
They Hanged My Saintly Billy. Robert Graves. LC 80-18535. 1980. 14.95 (ISBN 0-89733-030-7) (ISBN 0-89733-029-3). Academy Chicago.
They Hanged My Saintly Billy: The Life and Death of Dr. William Palmer. Robert Graves. LC 57-7283. 1957. Doubleday.
They Have Bodies: A Realistic Novel in Eleven Chapters and Three Acts. Barney Allen. LC 29-12404. 1929. The Macaulay Company.
They Have Bodies: A Realistic Novel in Eleven Chapters and Three Acts. Sol Barney Allen. LC 29-12404. 1929. Macaulay Co.
They Hunted a Fox. Alice Ormond Campbell. LC 40-30398. 1940. C. Scribner's Sons.
They Know Not. George Sanford Foster. LC 39-14383. The Christopher Publishing House.
They Left the Land. Naomi Ellington Jacob. LC 40-35093. 1940. The Macmillan Company.
They Lifted Their Eyes. Allan Bethel. LC 51-5187. 1951. Humphries.
They Lived: A Bronte Novel. Elsie Prentys Thornton-Cook. LC 35-18073. 1935. C. Scribner's Sons.
They Love Not Poison. Sara Woods, pseud. LC 72-78132. (Rinehart suspense novel). 1972. 4.95 (ISBN 0-03-001451-4). Holt, Rinehart and Winston.
They Loved Too Young. Mabel Margaret Clark. LC 30-9731. 1930. Harper & Brothers.
They Meant to Marry. Helena Grose. LC 34-167155. The Macaulay Company.
They Met at Mrs. Bloxom's: A Novel. Hayden Norwood. LC 38-32419. 1938. Rodale Press.
They Met by Chance: A Society Novel. Olive Logan Sikes Logan. LC 11-7159. Adams, Victor & Co.
They Move with the Sun. Daniel Edward Schneider. LC 48-8506. 1948. Farrar, Straus.
They Must All Die. J. M. Newby. 4.00 o.p. (ISBN 0-8062-0576-8). Carlton.
They Never Came Home. Lois Duncan. 192p. 1980. pap. 1.95 (ISBN 0-380-50229-1, 62026X). Avon.
They Never Come Back: A Novel by William Plomer. William Charles Franklyn Plomer. LC 32-3190. Coward-McCann, Inc.
They Never Get Tired. Catharine Macadam. LC 37-19460. 1937. Frederick A. Stokes Company.
They Never Had It So Good. Joseph Gies. LC 49-7367. 1949. Harper.
They Never Looked Inside. easy eye ed. Michael Francis Gilbert. 1968. pap. 0.75 o.p. (74-922). Lancer.
They Never Say When. Peter Cheyney. LC 45-1822. 1945. Dodd, Mead & Company.
They of the High Trails. Hamlin Garland. LC 16-10307. 1916. Harper & Brothers.
They of the High Trails see Collected Works.
They Opened the West: An Anthology. Western Writers of America. Ed. by Thomas Wakefield Blackburn. LC 67-10418. 1967. Doubleday.
They Ran for Their Lives. 1st Ed. John Brick. LC 54-9830. 1954. Doubleday.
They Return at Evening: A Book of Ghost Stories. Herbert Russell Wakefield. LC 28-17214. 1928. D. Appleton and Company.
They Ride with Rifles. Lee Floren. (O.s.i.). 1976. pap. 0.95 o.s.i. (BT50964). Belmont-Tower.
They Rode the Shining Hills. Norman A. Fox. LC 68-24028. 1968. Dodd, Mead.
They Rose Above It. Bob Considine, pseud. 1978. pap. 1.75 (ISBN 0-449-23417-7, Crest). Fawcett.
They Sailed for Senegal: An Historical Novel. David Wilson MacArthur. LC 38-669432. 1938. Frederick A. Stokes Company.
They Sailed on a Friday. Thomas Camborne Paynter. LC 28-253532. 1928. Longmans, Green and Co.
They Saw the Second Coming: An Explosive Novel About the End of the World! Douglas Clark. LC 78-71427. 1979. 6.95 o.p. (ISBN 0-89081-196-2); pap. 4.95 (ISBN 0-89081-190-3); pap. 2.95 mass sales (ISBN 0-89081-260-8). Harvest Hse.
They Seek a Country. Francis Brett Young. LC 37-24571. Reynal & Hitchcock.
They Seldom Speak. Leland Hall. Harcourt, Brace and Company.
They Shall Call Me Trask. Allen Trask. LC 81-80158. 160p. 1983. pap. 7.95 (ISBN 0-86666-008-9). GWP.
They Shall Come Again. Ruth Comfort Mitchell. LC 44-461186. 1944. D. Appleton-Century Company, Incorporated.
They Shall Inherit the Earth. Morley Callaghan. LC 35-19988. 1935. Random House.
They Shall Inherit the Earth. Morley Callaghan. LC 39-15718. 1937. Modern Age Books, Inc.
They Shall Not Hurt nor Destroy. 1st Ed. Mary Hostetler Murray. LC 55-9528. 1955. Vantage Press.
They Shall Not Pass: A Novel of the Spanish Civil War. Bruce Palmer. LC 77-139051. (Illus.). 1971. 8.95. Doubleday.
They Shall Not Pass Unseen. Ivan Southall. 1967. Repr. pap. 1.60 o.s.i. Tri-Ocean.
They Shoot Horses, Don't They? Horace McCoy. LC 35-10855. 1935. Simon and Schluster.
They Shoot Horses Don't They? Horace McCoy. (S S 10). Avon.
They Shouldn't Make you Promise That. Lois Simmie. 1982. pap. 2.50 (ISBN 0-451-11866-9, AE1866, Sig). NAL.
They Sought a Country. Norman Eugene Nygaard. LC 50-5476. 1950. Longmans, Green.
They Sought for Paradise. Stuart David Engstrand. LC 39-278808. 1939. Harper & Brothers.
They Stay for Death. Sara Woods, pseud. LC 79-27321. 8.95 (ISBN 0-312-79983-7). St. Martin's Press.
They Still Fall in Love. Jesse Lynch Williams. LC 29-6352. 1929. C. Scribner's Sons.
They Still Say No. Wells Lewis. LC 39-10239. Farrar & Rinehart, Incorporated.
They Stoned Ma Hayden. John Irby Koon. LC 40-33704. Pegasus Publishing Company.
They Stood & Watched. L. Dan Sheridan, Jr. 560p. 1972. 11.50 o.p. (ISBN 0-682-47358-8). Exposition.
They Stooped to Folly: A Comedy of Morals. Ellen Anderson Gholson Glasgow. LC 61-3703. (Dolphin pooks). 1961. Doubleday.
They Stooped to Folly: A Comedy of Morals. Ellen Anderson Gholson Glasgow. LC 29-17854. 1929. Doubleday, Doran & Company, Inc.
They Talk and Walk: By Ray Brown. Raymond Barrington Brown. LC 66-29481. Magna Carta Press.
They Talked of Poison. March Everman. LC 38-133292. 1938. The Macmillan Company.
They Tell No Tales. Manning Coles, pseud. LC 42-733732. 1942. Published for the Crime Club by Doubleday, Doran & Co., Inc.
They Tell No Tales. Lee Thayer, pseud. LC 30-1703. Sears Publishing Company, Inc.
They That Go Down in Ships. Marguerite Steen. LC 31-6794. 1931. Cosmopolitan Book Corporation.
They That Remain: A Story of the End Times. Dayton A Manker. LC 41-19194. Zondervan Publishing House.
They That Sit in Darkness: A Story of the Australian Never-Never. John Mackie. LC 7-19411. Frederick A. Stokes Company.
They That Take the Sword-- Nicholas Kalashnikoff. LC 39-217853. 1939. Harper & Brothers.
They That Took the Sword. Nathaniel Wright Stephenson. LC 1-7322. 1901. John Lane.
They That Walk in Darkness" Ghetto Tragedies. Israel Zangwill. LC 70-116969. (Short story index reprint series). (Illus.). 1970. (ISBN 0-8369-3473-3). Books for Libraries Press.
They That Walk in Darkness" Ghetto Tragedies. Israel Zangwill. LC 99-5157. 1899. The Macmillan Company.
They Thirst. Robert R. McCammon. 554p. 1981. pap. 2.95 (ISBN 0-380-77180-2, 77180). Avon.
They Thought They Could Buy It. Dorothy Walworth. LC 30-25908. 1930. Doubleday, Doran and Company, Inc.
They: Three Parodies of H. Rider Haggard's She. R. Reginald & Douglas Alver Menville. LC 77-84277. (Lost Race and Adult Fantasy Fiction). 1978. 37.00 (ISBN 0-405-11015-4). Arno Press.
They Took the High Road: The Lady of Gurtha and the Catamount O' the North The Princess Yleria and the Mac-in-Sagart, The Puritan Woman and the Scots Cavalier, The Virginia Girl and Washington's Rifle Man; Romances of the Shaws of Scotland and America. Gurthie Shaw Patch. LC 47-957. 1946. The Dietz Press, Incorporated.
They Used Dark Forces. Dennis Yates Wheatley. 1978. 10.95 (ISBN 0-09-072262-0, Pub. by Hutchinson). Merrimack Pub Cir.
They Waited for the Night. Virginia Dale. LC 39-8478. 1939. Doubleday, Doran & Company, Inc.
They Walk Again: An Anthology of Ghost Stories. Ed. by Colin De La Mare. De La Mare, Walter John. LC 31-29823. E. P. Dutton & Co., Inc.
They Walk Again: An Anthology of Ghost Stories. Ed. by Colin De La Mare. De La Mare, Walter John, 1873- LC 43-6805. 1942. E. P. Dutton & Co., Inc.
They Walk in Darkness. Ellen Catt Philtine. LC 45-5600. 1945. Liveright Publishing Corporation.
They Walk in the City: The Lovers in the Stone Forest. John Boynton Priestley. LC 76-165447. 1972. (ISBN 0-8371-6224-6). Greenwood Press.
They Walk in the City: The Lovers in the Stone Forest. John Boynton Priestley. LC 36-18147. 1936. Harper & Brothers.
They Walked Like Men. Clifford D. Simak. 1979. 1.95 (ISBN 0-380-42861-X). Avon.
They Wanted to Live. Cecil Roberts. LC 39-6123. 1939. The Macmillan Company.
They Went. Norman Douglas. LC 21-4164. 1921. Dodd, Mead and Company.
They Went by Too Fast. Stanley B. Russell. 4.95 o.p. Vantage.
They Went on Together. Robert Nathan. LC 41-231793. 1941. A. A. Knopf.
They Went Thataway. Dee Alexander Brown. LC 60-8466. (Illus.). 1960. Putnam.
They Went Thataway. James Horwitz. 1976. 8.95 o.p. (ISBN 0-525-21683-9). Dutton.
They Were Dreamers: A Saga of the Irish in North America. James F. Murphy. LC 81-69138. 1983. 14.95 (ISBN 0-689-11250-5). Atheneum.
They Were Married. Walter Besant & Rice, James. (Lovell's library, v. 1. no. 18). 1882. J. W. Lovell Company.
They Were Seven (a Mystery) Eden Phillpotts. LC 45-2568. 1944. Pub. for the Crime Book Society by Hutchinson & Co., Ltd.
They Were Seven (a Mystery) Eden Phillpotts. LC 45-6198. 1945. The Macmillan Company.
They Were Sisters. Dorothy Whipple. LC 44-4328. 1944. The Macmillan Company.
They Were So Young. Abdullah, Achmed. LC 29-8834. Payson & Clarke ltd.
They Were There. Wesley H Hager. LC 66-18725. bds., 2.95. Eerdmans.
They Who Have... Reita Lambert. LC 37-19887. 1936. Doubleday, Doran & Co., Inc.
They Who Love: Four Stories. Faith Baldwin Cuthrell. LC 48-3777. 1948. Rinehart.
They Who Paddle. Rosalind Webster. LC 28-12082. E. P. Dutton & Company.
They Who Question... Sarah Macnaughton. LC 14-15366. 1914. The Macmillan Company.
They Winter Abroad. James Aston, pseud. 1973. pap. 0.75 o.p. (07274). Curtis.
They Won't Demolish Me! Roch Carrier. Tr. by Sheila Fischman from Fr. (Anansi Fiction Ser.: No. 30). 134p. (Orig.). 1974. pap. 6.95 (ISBN 0-88784-328-X, Pub. by Hse Anansi Pr Canada). U of Toronto Pr.
They Wouldn't Be Chessmen: A M. Hanaud Story. Alfred Edward Woodley Mason. LC 35-14570. 1935. Pub. for the Crime Club, Inc., by Doubleday, Doran & Co., Inc.
They Wouldn't Be Chessmen: A M. Hanaud Story. Alfred Edward Woodley Mason. LC 37-14579. 1937. The Sun Dial Press, Inc.
They'd Rather Be Right. Mark Clifton & Frank Wilbert Riley. LC 81-5384. 4.95 (ISBN 0-89865-165-4). Donning Co.
They'd Rather Be Right: By Mark Clifton and Frank Riley. 1st Ed. Mark Clifton & Frank Wilbert Riley. LC 57-14670. 1957. Gnome Press.
They'll Never Make a Movie Starring Me. Alice Bach. 1975. pap. 1.75 (ISBN 0-440-96111-4, LFL). Dell.
They're Coming to Kill You, Jane! Kirby Carr. (Hitman # 4). 1974. (pbk.) 1.50 (ISBN 0-89014-120-7). Canyon Books.
They're Going to Kill Me. 1st Ed. Kathleen Moore Knight. LC 55-11345. 1955. Published for the Crime Club by Doubleday.
They're Not Home Yet. Stanton Forbes, pseud. LC 62-7677. 1962. Published for the Crime Club by Doubleday.
They're Not Home Yet. 1st Ed. Forbes Rydell, pseud. LC 62-7677. 1962. Published for the Crime Club by Doubleday.
They've Killed Anna. Marc Olden. (Signet Book). 1977. 1.25 (ISBN 0-451-07368-1). New American Library.
They've Shot the President's Daughter! Edward Stewart. LC 72-97275. 1973. 6.95 (ISBN 0-385-04236-1). Doubleday.
Thibaults. Martin Du Gard, Roger. LC 26-21458. Boni & Liveright.
Thibaults. Martin Du Gard, Roger. Tr. by Stuart Gilbert. LC 39-272606. 1939. The Viking Press.
Thick Blue Sweater. Pete Fry. 2.95 o.p. Roy.
Thick Blue Sweater. Clifford King. LC 64-15753. 1964. Roy Publishers.
Thicker Than Water. Vera Caspary. LC 32-21670. Liveright, Inc.
Thicker Than Water. Richard Dorso. LC 79-3357. 10.95 (ISBN 0-15-189586-4). Harcourt Brace Jovanovich.
Thicker Than Water. Madeleine A Polland. LC 65-15058. (Rinehart suspense novel). 3.50. Holt.
Thicker Than Water: A Father Dowling Mystery. Ralph M McInerny. LC 81-10432. 9.95 (ISBN 0-8149-0858-6). Vanguard Press.
Thicker Than Water. A Novel. James Payn. (Harper's Franklin square library, no. 331). 1883. Harper & Brothers.
Thicker Than Water: A Novel. James Payn. (On cover: Lovell's library, no. 187). 1883. J. W. Lovell Company.
Thicker Than Water. A Novel. James Payn. (Seaside library. v. 85, no. 1711). 1883. G. Munro.
Thicker Than Water: A Story of Hashknife Hartley. Wilbur C Tuttle. LC 27-19186. 1927. Houghton Mifflin Company.
Thicker Than Water: Stories of Family Life, Edited by W. Robert Wunsch and Edna Albers for the Commission on Human Relations. Ed. by William Robert Wunsch. Lerner, Edna (Albers) 1913- Joint Ed. LC 39-9819. (Half-title: Progressive education association publications. Commission on human relations). D. Appleton-Century Company, Incorporated.
Thicket. Patricia Gallagher. 1977. pap. 1.75 (ISBN 0-380-01578-1, 33316). Avon.
Thicket of Terror. Georgia M. Shewmake. (YA) 1981. 6.95 (Avalon). Bouregy.
Thief. Frank Hokimer. 224p. Date not set. pap. 2.50 (ISBN 0-87216-862-X). Playboy Pbks.
Thief. Archie Joscelyn. LC 58-752820. 1958. Augustana Press.
Thief. Leonid Maksimovich Leonov & Butler, Hubert, Tr. LC 31-29200. 1931. L. MacVeagh, The Dial Press.
Thief. Doris Born Monthan. LC 61-5703. 1961. New Authors Guild.
Thief: And Other Tales. Anton Pavlovich Chekhov. LC 64-55863. 1964. Vantage Press.
Thief & the Dogs. Najib Mahfuz. (Arabic.). pap. 5.50x (ISBN 0-86685-158-5). Intl Bk Ctr.
Thief at the Villa le Grotte. Elizabeth Wallace. (Orig.). 1979. pap. 1.95 (ISBN 0-532-23246-1). Woodhill.
Thief Hunt. William Oliver Turner. LC 72-86231. (Double D western). 1973. 4.95. Doubleday.
Thief Hunt. William Oliver Turner. 1974. (pbk.) 0.95. Manor Books.
Thief in the Brown Van. Bob Wright. (Tom & Ricky Mystery Ser.: No. 2). (Illus.). 48p. 1983. pap. 2.00 (ISBN 0-87879-339-9). Acad Therapy.
Thief in the Night. Jim Grant. 128p. 1974. pap. 2.95 (ISBN 0-8024-8688-6). Moody.
Thief in the Night. Harriet Elizabeth Prescott Spofford. LC 8-14051. 1872. Roberts Brothers.
Thief in the Night. another issue ed. Harriet Elizabeth Prescott Spofford. 1872. Roberts Brothers.
Thief in the Night. Thomas Walsh. LC 62-17981. (Inner sanctum mystery). 1962. Simon and Schuster.
Thief in the Night: Further Adventures of A. J. Raffles, Cricketer and Cracksman. Ernest William Hornung. LC 5-33029. 1905. C. Scribner's Sons.
Thief of Bagdad. Achmed Abdullah. LC 24-18677. The H. K. Fly Company.
Thief of Bagdad. Achmed Abdullah & Thomas, Elton. LC 42-26789. 1924. A. L. Burt Company.
Thief of Copper Canyon. Elizabeth Graham, pseud. (Harlequin Presents Ser.). 192p. (Orig.). 1981. pap. 1.50 (ISBN 0-373-10403-0, Pub. by Harlequin). PB.
Thief of Hearts. Nell Marr Dean. LC 50-3442. 1950. Gramercy Pub. Co.
Thief of Kalimar. Graham Diamond. 1979. pap. 1.95 (ISBN 0-449-14214-0, GM). Fawcett.
Thief of Love. Barbara Cartland. 1974. pap. 1.25 o.p. (ISBN 0-515-03277-8, V3272). Pyramid Pubns.

Thief of Love. Barbara Cartland. 1975. pap. 1.25 o.p. (ISBN 0-515-03905-5). BJ Pub Group.
Thief of Love: Bengali Tales from Court & Village. Ed. & tr. by Edward C. Dimock, Jr. LC 63-11396. xiv, 306p. 1975. pap. 3.95 (ISBN 0-226-15236-7, P624, Phoen). U of Chicago Pr.
Thief of Thoth see Doomsman.
Thief of Time. John William Wainwright. LC 77-94461. 1978. 8.95 (ISBN 0-312-79989-6). St. Martin's.
Thief of Virtue. Eden Phillpotts. LC 10-7479. 1910. John Lane Company.
Thief or Two. Sara Woods, pseud. LC 77-76659. 1977. 7.95 (ISBN 0-312-79994-2). St. Martin's Press.
Thief River. Nelson Coral Nye. LC 51-9643. (Silver star westerns). 1951. Dodd, Mead.
Thief. Translated by Hubert Butler. Leonid Maksimovich Leonov. LC 60-31953. (Vintage Russian library, R-1005). 1960. Vintage Books.
Thief Who Came to Dinner. Terrence Lore Smith. LC 78-139062. 1971. 4.95. Doubleday.
Thief Who Was Robbed: Or, A Dose of His Own Medicine. Nick Carter & Dey, Frederic Van Rensselaer. LC 34-382772. (On cover: New magnet library. no. 848). Street & Smith.
Thief's Journal. Jean Genet. LC 64-24077. 1964. Grove Press.
Thieftaker. J. G Jeffreys, pseud. LC 72-80528. 1972. 4.95 (ISBN 0-8027-5260-8). Walker.
Thieftaker. J. G. Jeffreys. Ed. by Lois D. Cole. LC 72-80528. 144p. 1972. 4.95 o.p. (ISBN 0-8027-5260-8). Walker & Co.
Thieves. T. A Noton. LC 78-67232. 6.95 (ISBN 0-914850-41-5). Impact Books.
Thieves: A Novel. Pseud Aix. LC 11-5476. 1911. Duffield & Company.
Thieves' Brand. Giles A Lutz. LC 80-2905. 1981. 9.95 (ISBN 0-385-17487-X). Doubleday.
Thieves' Hole. David Armine Howarth. LC 54-5396. 1954. Rinehart.
Thieves' Honor. Sinclair Gluck. 1925. 2.00. Dodd, Mead & Company.
Thieves in the Night. Arthur Koestler. 1967. 12.95 o.s.i. (ISBN 0-02-565670-8). Macmillan.
Thieves in the Night: Chronicle of an Experiment. Arthur Koestler. LC 46-7678. 1946. The Macmillan Company.
Thieves in the Night: Chronicle of an Experiment. New Postscript by the Author. Arthur Koestler. LC 67-15779. (Danube ed.). 1967. 5.95. Macmillan.
Thieves in the Schoolhouse. Lawrence Moores. LC 78-50636. 1979. 13.95 (ISBN 0-87949-119-1). Ashley Bks.
Thieves Like Us. Edward Anderson. 1974. (pbk.) 1.25. Avon.
Thieves Like Us: A Novel. Edward Anderson. LC 37-9667. 1937. Frederick A. Stokes Company.
Thieves' Market. Albert Isaac Bezzerides. LC 49-8004. 1949. C. Scribner's Sons.
Thieves' Nights: The Chronicles of De Lancey, King of Thieves. Harry Stephen Keeler. LC 29-221460. E. P. Dutton & Co., Inc.
Thieves of Tumbutu. 1st Ed. Harris Greene. LC 68-18095. 1968. 5.95. Doubleday.
Thieves' Picnic. Leslie Charteris. LC 38-2972. 1937. Pub. for the Crime Club, Inc., by Doubleday, Doran & Co., Inc.
Thieves' Picnic. Leslie Charteris. LC 39-8128. 1939. The Sun Dial Press, Inc.
Thieves' Road. Rene Sussan. LC 61-9559. 1961. Doubleday.
Thieves to Flesh. Salvatore Farinella. 32p. 1977. pap. 2.50 o.p. (ISBN 0-914852-09-4). Manifest Destiny.
Thieves World. Robert L. Asprin. 320p. 1981. pap. 2.75 (ISBN 0-441-80579-5, Pub. by Ace Science Fiction). Ace Bks.
Thieves'wit: An Everyday Detective Story. Hulbert Footner. LC 18-17998. George H. Doran Company.
Thin Air. Howard Browne. LC 54-6671. (Inner sanctum mystery). 1954. Simon and Schuster.
Thin Air. George E Simpson & Neal R. Burger. (Dell Book). 1978. 1.95 (ISBN 0-440-18709-5). Dell Pub. Co.
Thin Air: A Yellowthread Street Mystery. William Leonard Marshall. LC 77-20786. (Rinehart suspense novel). 1978. 6.95 (ISBN 0-03-021071-2). Holt, Rinehart and Winston.
Thin Air: A Yellowthread Street Mystery. William Leonard Marshall. LC 81-22642. 1982. 2.95 (ISBN 0-14-006137-1). Penguin Books.
Thin Air: An Anthology of Ghost Stories. Alan C. Jenkins. Repr. of 1966 ed. lib. bdg. 10.00 o.p. Folcroft.
Thin Edge of Violence: A Novel of Suspense. William O'Farrell. LC 49-4673. 1949. Duell, Sloan and Pearce.
Thin Ghost and Others. Montague Rhodes James. LC 74-167454. (Short story index reprint series). 1971. (ISBN 0-8369-3980-8). Books for Libraries Press.
Thin Ghost and Others. Montague Rhodes James. LC 20-14895. 1919. Longmans, Green & Co.
Thin Ice. Gary Cartwright. 1976. (pbk.) 1.75. Fawcett.
Thin Ice & Other Stories. Barbara Wilson. LC 81-4713. 128p. (Orig.). 1981. pap. 4.95 (ISBN 0-931188-09-1). Seal Pr WA.
Thin Ice. 1st American Ed. Compton Mackenzie. LC 56-102378. Putnam, C.
Thin Line. Roy Doliner. 1982. pap. 2.95 (ISBN 0-425-05289-3). Berkley Pub.
Thin Line: A Novel. Roy Doliner. LC 80-12750. 11.95 (ISBN 0-517-54171-8). Crown Publishers.
Thin Line. 1st American Ed. Edward Selim Atiyah. LC 52-5414. 1952. Harper.
Thin Man. Dashiell Hammett. LC 34-689. 1934. A. A. Knopf.
Thin Man. Dashiell Hammett. LC 46-5257. 1946. A. A. Knopf.
Thin Man. Dashiell Hammett. LC 81-89. 1981. 12.95 (ISBN 0-89340-329-6). J. Curley.
Thin Men of Haddam. Charles William Smith. LC 73-7187. 1973. 7.95 (ISBN 0-670-70039-8). Grossman.
Thin Mountain Air. Paul Horgan. LC 77-3983. 10.00 (ISBN 0-374-27466-5). Farrar, Straus and Giroux.
Thin Red Line. James Jones. LC 62-12099. 1962. Scribner.
Thin Red Line. James Jones. LC 62-12099. 1975. (pbk.) 1.95. Avon.
Thin Santa Claus: The Chicken Yard That Was a Christmas Stocking. Ellis Parker Butler. LC 9-25816. 1909. Doubleday, Page & Company.
Thin Seam: And Other Stories. Sid Chaplin. LC 68-26940. (Pergamon English Library). 1968. (ISBN 0-08-012860-2). Pergamon Press.
Thin Volume. Jacob Randolph Perkins. LC 17-28080. Saalfield Pulishing Company.
Thin White Line. Rayanne Moore. (American Romance Ser.). 192p. 1983. pap. 2.25 (ISBN 0-373-16008-9). Harlequin Bks.
Thine Enemy. Ralph Webster Neighbour. LC 63-15735. 1963. Zondervan Pub. House.
Thine Enemy. A Novel. Philip Hamilton Gibbs. LC 50-10833. 1950. M. McBride Co.
Thine Is the Glory. Samuel A. Schreiner. LC 74-18163. 1975. 8.95 (ISBN 0-87795-101-2). Arbor House.
Thine Is the Glory. Samuel Agnew Schreiner. 1976. 1.95 (ISBN 0-449-22887-8). Fawcett Crest.
Thine Is the Kingdom. James Hogg Hunter. LC 51-11555. 1951. Zondervan Pub. House.
Thing. Alan Dean Foster. 1982. pap. 2.75 (ISBN 0-553-20477-7). Bantam.
Thing. J. J. Madison. 1978. pap. 1.50 o.s.i. (ISBN 0-505-51235-1). Tower Bks.
Thing About Clarissa. Roberta St. Clair Cook. LC 58-9155. 1958. Bobbs-Merrill.
Thing Apart. Lucy Stone Terrill. LC 21-8832. The Bobbs-Merrill Company.
Thing at the Door. Henry Slesar. LC 74-8225. 1974. 5.95 (ISBN 0-394-49007-X). Random House.
Thing at the Door. Slesar, Henry. 1976. (pbk.) 1.50 (ISBN 0-671-80427-8). Pocket Books.
Thing at Their Heels. Eden Phillpotts. LC 23-12869. 1923. The Macmillan Company.
Thing Desired. Lalage Pulvertaft. LC 57-9491. 1957. Viking Press.
Thing from the Lake. Eleanor Marie Ingram. LC 75-46281. (Supernatural and Occult Fiction). 1976. 18.00 (ISBN 0-405-08140-5). Arno Press.
Thing from the Lake. Eleanor Marie Ingram. LC 21-21550. 1921. J. B. Lippincott Company.
Thing in the Brook. Philip Van Doren Stern. LC 37-3369. 1937. Simon and Schuster.
Thing in the Night... Katharine Virden. LC 30-25378. 1930. Pub. for the Crime Club, Inc., by Doubleday, Doran & Company, Inc.
Thing in the Woods. Harper Williams. LC 24-289599. 1924. R. McBride & Company.
Thing King. Charles E. Eaton. 104p. 1982. 9.95 (ISBN 0-8453-4743-8). Cornwall Bks.
Thing of Beauty. Archibald Joseph Cronin. LC 56-5923. 1956. Little, Brown.
Thing of It Is. William Goldman. LC 67-11967. 1967. Harcourt, Brace & World.
Thing of Nought. Hilda Vaughan. LC 35-20670. 1935. C. Scribner's Sons.
Thing That Happens to You. Evelyn Berckman. LC 64-11427. Dodd, Mead.
Thing to Love. Geoffrey Household. LC 63-13454. 1963. Little, Brown.
Things. Francis Ponge. Tr. by Cid Corman. (Pap. ed. 4.95 o.p.). (Illus.). 1971. 12.95 (Pub. by Mushinsha Bks). SBD.
Things. Francis Ponge. (Mushinsha Bks). 1971. pap. 4.95 o.p. (ISBN 0-670-70057-6, Grossman). Penguin.
Things About to Disappear: Stories. Allen Wier. LC 78-9819. 1978. 7.95 (ISBN 0-8071-0471-X). Louisiana State University Press.
Things & Other Things: Tales of the Diabolic. Harold W. Hartl. 107p. 1972. 4.50 o.p. (ISBN 0-682-47636-6). Exposition.
Things As They Are. Paul Horgan. LC 64-12769. 1964. Farrar, Straus.
Things As They Are, a Novel in Three Parts. Gertrude Stein. LC 50-4312. Banyan Press.
Things by Their Right Names; a Novel. Printed by Munroe & Francis, Published by Them at Cornhill, and by Edward Cotton, Marlboro'-Street.
Things Common and Uncommon. Mary Dwinell Chellis. LC 31-35212. Congregational Publishing Society.
Things Fall Apart. Chinua Achebe. LC 59-7114. McDowell.
Things Gone and Things Still Here. Paul Frederic Bowles. LC 77-8030. 1977. 10.00. (ISBN 0-87685-342-4) (ISBN 0-87685-341-6) (ISBN 0-87685-343-2). Black Sparrow Press.
Things Greater Than He. Luciano Zuccoli. Tr. by Parkhurst, Eloise. LC 26-10201. 1926. H. Holt and Company.
Things Greater Than He. Luciano Zuccoli & Parkhurst, Eloise, Tr. LC 26-10201. H. Holt and Company.
Things He Wrote to Her. Richard Wightman. LC 14-5815. 1914. The Century Co.
Things in Place. Jerry Bumpus. LC 75-10744. 8.95. (ISBN 0-914590-14-6) (ISBN 0-914590-15-4). Fiction Collective: Distributed by G. Braziller.
Things in the Driver's Seat. Harry R. Huebel. 1972. pap. 12.95 (ISBN 0-395-30633-7). HM.
Things Is Going As Usual. Jane Baldwin Cotton. LC 28-12962. Marshall Jones Company.
Things My Mother Told Me. Ellen J. Kennedy. 1975. 5.00 o.p. (ISBN 0-8283-1605-8). Branden.
Things Past. Malcolm Muggeridge. Ed. by Ian A. Hunter. LC 78-71376. 1979. 9.95 o.p. (ISBN 0-688-03445-4). Morrow.
Things She Wrote to Him. Richard Wightman. LC 30-9488. The Century Co.
Things That Are Caesar's: A Novel. Reginald Wright Kauffman. LC 2-21094. 1902. D. Appleton and Company.
Things That Count. Laurence Eyre. LC 14-18919. 1914. 1.25. Little, Brown, and Company.
Things That Go Bump in the Night. Louis C. Jones. (Illus.). 207p. 1959. pap. 6.95 o.p. (ISBN 0-8090-1336-3). Hill & Wang.
Things That Matter. Francis Henry Gribble. LC 6-45416. (The Hudson library, v. 13). 1896. G. P. Putnam's Sons.
Things to Come. Herbert George Wells. 184p. 1975. Repr. of 1935 ed. lib. bdg. 12.50 (ISBN 0-8398-2318-5, Gregg). G K Hall.
Things to Come and Go: Three Stories. Bette Howland. LC 82-48724. 1983. 11.95 (ISBN 0-394-53032-2). Knopf: Distributed by Random House.
Things We Are: A Novel. John Middleton Murry & Leary, Daniel Bell. LC 30-7678. E. P. Dutton and Co., Inc.
Things Were Different. Elisabeth Fagan. LC 28-23465. 1928. L. MacVeagh, The Dial Press.
Things Which Belong-- Constance Holme. LC 38-29099. (Oxford book shelf). 1938. Oxford University Press.
Thinis. Patricia. (Illus.). 330p. (Orig.). 1980. sprial bdg. 7.95 (ISBN 0-935146-12-1). Morningland.
Think a Bit. Carrie Leighton Adams. LC 31-33684. Printed by A. J. Lenon Co.
Think and Thank: A Tale. Samuel Williams Cooper. LC 6-30879. 1890. The Jewish Publication Society of America.
Think Fast, Mr. Moto. John Phillips Marquand. LC 37-8750. 1937. Little, Brown and Company.
Think of a Number. Anders Bodelsen. LC 69-15287. (Joan Kahn-Harper novel of suspense). 1969. 4.95. Harper & Row.
Think of Death. Richard Lockridge & Frances Louise Davis Lockridge. LC 47-2226. 1947. J. B. Lippincott Company.
Think of Tea. Agnes Repplier. 208p. 1981. Repr. of 1932 ed. lib. bdg. 20.00 (ISBN 0-8495-4644-3). Arden Lib.
Thinking Bayonet. James Kendall Hosmer. LC 7-7153. 1865. Walker, Fuller, and Company.
Thinking Girl. Norma Meacock. 1974. (pbk.) 1.25. Avon.
Thinking Girl: A Novel. Norma Meacock. LC 70-163581. 1972. 5.95. Dial Press.
Thinking Machine: Being a True and Complete Statement of Several Intricate Mysteries Which Came Under the Observation of Professor Augustus S. F. X. Van Dusen, PH. D., LL. D., F. R. S., M. D., Etc. Jacques Futrelle. LC 7-9843. 1907. Dodd, Mead & Company.
Thinking Machine on the Case. Jacques Futrelle. LC 8-9816. 1908. D. Appleton and Company.
Thinking of You. Jeanette Nabile. 1982. pap. 1.95 (ISBN 0-553-22516-2). Bantam.
Thinking Reed. Rebecca West. LC 36-271883. 1936. The Viking Press.
Thinking Reed. Rebecca West. LC 78-18920. 1978. 4.95 (ISBN 0-14-004749-2). Penguin Books.
Thinking Reed. Rebecca West. LC 75-41294. 1980. 28.00 (ISBN 0-404-14630-9). AMS Press.
Thinking Seat. Peter Tate. LC 70-78739. 1969. 4.95. Doubleday.
Thinly Veiled. Mannix Walker. LC 48-8722. 1948. Dodd, Mead.
Thiodolf the Icelander. A Romance. Friedrich Heinrich Karl La Motte-Fouque. LC 7-3080. J. Miller.
Third Act. Frederick Jackson. LC 13-24398. Desmond FitzGerald, Inc.
Third Act in Venice. Sylvia Thompson. LC 36-894637. 1936. Little, Brown, and Company.
Third Angel: A Novel. 1st Ed. Jerome Weidman. LC 53-9140. 1953. Doubleday.
Third Annual Club Adam Swingers Dictionary. 1974. pap. 2.00 o.p. (BH458). Holloway.
Third Arm. Kenneth Royce. LC 79-28330. 10.95 (ISBN 0-07-054169-8). McGraw-Hill.
Third Assembling: An Annual of Otherwise Unpublishable Imaginative Work, No. 3. annual Ed. by Richard Kostelanetz et al. (Illus.). 300p. (Orig.). 1972. pap. 4.95. Assembling Pr.
Third Avenue. James Fritzhand. LC 78-70784. 1979. 2.25 (ISBN 0-515-05112-8). Jove/HBJ.
Third Avenue, New York. John McNulty. LC 46-3682. 1946. Little, Brown and Company.
Third Bank of the River & Other Stories. Joao Guimaraes Rosa. (Port). 1968. 5.95 o.p. (ISBN 0-394-44840-5). Knopf.
Third Bank of the River: And Other Stories. Joao Guimaraes Rosa. LC 68-12682. 1968. 5.95. Knopf.
Third Battle. E. F. Miller, pseud. 1978. pap. 1.50 (ISBN 0-532-15333-2). Woodhill.
Third Body. Sam Dann. 1.75 (ISBN 0-445-04458-6). Popular Library.
Third Book About Achim. Uwe Johnson. LC 67-12273. 1967. Harcourt, Brace & World.
Third Bullet: And Other Stories. John Dickson Carr. LC 54-6008. 1954. Harper.
Third Child. Aeleta Nichols. (Orig.). 1971. pap. 0.75 o.p. (T2426). Pyramid Pubns.
Third Choice. 1st Ed. Elizabeth Janeway. 1959. Doubleday.
Third Cicle. A Deal in Wheat, and Other Stories of the New and Old West. Frank Norris. LC 67-3233. (His Complete works, v. 4). 1967. Kennikat Press.
Third Circle. Frank Norris. LC 9-15089. 1909. 1.50. J. Lane Company; Etc., Etc.
Third Crime Lucky. Anthony Gilbert, pseud. Orig. Title: Prelude to Murder. 192p. 1972. Repr. of 1939 ed. 5.95 o.s.i. (ISBN 0-85617-550-1). White Lion Pubs.
Third Cross. Avin Harry Johnson. LC 61-14868. 1961. Zondervan Pub. House.
Third Daughter: A Story of Chinese Home Life. Lu Wheat. LC 6-1568. Oriental Publishing Co.
Third Day. Joseph Arnold Hayes. (Crest bk., t816). 1965. Fawcett.
Third Day. Joseph Arnold Hayes. LC 64-19212. 1964. McGraw-Hill.
Third Day. George Manning-Sanders. LC 30-13878. 1930. H. Liveright.
Third Deadly Sin. Lawrence Sanders. LC 80-26325. 13.95 (ISBN 0-399-12614-7). Putnam.
Third Deadly Sin. Lawrence Sanders. LC 82-9222. 1982. 17.95 (ISBN 0-8161-3405-7). G.K. Hall.
Third Degree. Charles Ross Jackson. G. W. Dillingham.
Third Degree. Joe Barry Lake. LC 43-16764. 1943. Mystery House.
Third Degree. Joe Barry Lake. LC 44-47611. (Prize mystery novels. No. 12). 1944. Crestwood Publishing Co., Inc.
Third Degree: A Narrative of Metropolitan Life. Charles Klein & Hornblow, Arthur. LC 9-29769. 1.50. G. W. Dillingham Company.
Third-Degree Rape. James Kerstetter. pap. 1.95 o.s.i. (OPH-235, Ophelia). Olympia.
Third Diamond. John Breckenridge Ellis. LC 13-21479. 1.25. R. G. Badger.
Third Ear. Curt Siodmak. 1974. (pbk.) 1.25 (ISBN 0-523-00345-5). Pinnacle Books.
Third Ear. Curt Siodmak. LC 75-163415. 1971. 5.95. Putnam.
Third Encounter. Woods, Sara, pseud. LC 63-16534. 1963. Harper & Row.
Third Estate. Marjorie Bowen. LC 18-26817. 1918. E. P. Dutton and Company.
Third Eye. Etienne Leroux. LC 69-18123. 1969. 4.95. Houghton Mifflin Co.
Third Eye. T. Rampa. pap. 2.95. Weiser.
Third Eye. Ethel Lina White. LC 37-6308. 1937. Harper & Brothers.
Third Eye: The Autobiography of a Tibetan Lama. Rampa T. Lobsang. LC 57-6296. 1957. Doubleday.
Third Factory. Viktor Borisovich Shklovskii. Ed. & tr. by Richard Sheldon. 1977. 12.95 (ISBN 0-88233-132-9); pap. 3.50 o.p. (ISBN 0-88233-133-7). Ardis Pubs.
Third Figure. Collin Wilcox. LC 68-15410. (Red badge mystery). 1968. Dodd, Mead.
Third Flight of the Starfire. Edwin Mumford. 1972. 4.00 (ISBN 0-682-47503-3). Exposition.
Third Fontana Book of Great Ghost Stories. Ed. by Robert Aickman. 1971. pap. 0.95 o.p. (95156). Beagle Bks.

Third Generation. Chester B. Himes. 1973. Repr. of 1954 ed. 8.95x o.p. (ISBN 0-911860-37-1). Chatham Bkseller.
Third Generation. 1st Ed. Chester B Himes. LC 52-18247. 1954. World Pub. Co.
Third Ghost Book. Ed. by Cynthia Asquith. 1970. pap. 0.95 o.p. (95019). Beagle Bks.
Third Girl. Agatha Miller Christie. LC 67-22196. 1967. Dodd, Mead.
Third Girl. Agatha Miller Christie. 1979. 2.25 (ISBN 0-671-83151-8). Pocket Books.
Third Grave. David Case. LC 80-26818. (Illus.). 10.95 (ISBN 0-87054-089-0). Arkham House.
Third Half. Mildred B Davis. LC 69-20006. 1969. 4.50. Published for the Crime Club by Doubleday.
Third Hand High: A Novel. W. N Murdock. LC 7-31843. 1893. Lee and Shepard.
Third Haven. James Noble Giffford. LC 41-15916. 1941. Arcadia House.
Third Haven. Warren Howard. LC 41-159161. 1941. Arcadia House, Inc.
Third Hour. Geoffrey Household. LC 38-104659. 1938. Little, Brown and Company.
Third Identity. Rosemary Gatenby. LC 79-16081. 8.95 (ISBN 0-396-07727-7). Dodd, Mead.
Third Level. Jack Finney. LC 57-9626. 1957. Rinehart.
Third Life of Grange Copeland. Alice Walker. LC 77-3427. (Harvest/HBJ book). 1977. 2.95 (ISBN 0-15-689960-4). Harcourt Brace Jovanovich.
Third Life of Grange Copeland. Alice Walker. LC 79-117577. 1970. (ISBN 0-15-189905-3). Harcourt, Brace, Jovanovich.
Third Life of Per Smevik. Ole Edvart Rolvaag. LC 71-172872. 1971. 5.95 (ISBN 0-87518-045-0). Dillon Press.
Third Man. Graham Greene. 1974. (pbk.) 1.25 (ISBN 0-671-78393-9). Pocket Books.
Third Man. Graham Greene. LC 50-6976. 1950. Viking Press.
Third Man, Loser Takes All. Graham Greene. 208p. 1983. 18.75 (ISBN 0-670-70084-3). Viking Pr.
Third Man: And, The Fallen Idol. Graham Greene. LC 72-184805. 1971. 0.25 (ISBN 0-14-003278-9). Penguin.
Third Messenger. Patrick Wynnton. LC 27-817. George H. Doran Company.
Third Miss Wenderby. Mabel Sarah Barnes Grundy. LC 11-266088. 1911. 1.35. The Baker & Taylor Company.
Third Mississippi Regiment - C.S.A. Dale Greenwell. LC 72-95852. (Illus.). Printed by Lewis Print. Services.
Third Murderer. Carroll John Daly. LC 31-21541. Farrar & Rinehart Incorporated.
Third Mystery Companion. Ed. by Abraham Louis Furman. LC 45-10366. 1945. Gold Label Books.
Third Notch and Other Stories. Shahnon Ahmad. LC 81-178491. (Writing in Asia Series). 1981. 5.50. Heinemann Educational Books (Asia)
Third of Life. Perriton Maxwell. LC 21-16807. Small, Maynard & Company.
Third One. Russell Mead. (Raven House Mysteries Ser.). 224p. 1983. pap. cancelled (ISBN 0-373-63056-5, Pub. by Worldwide). Harlequin Bks.
Third Owl. Robert Joseph Casey. LC 34-10331. The Bobbs-Merrill Company.
Third Owl. Robert Joseph Casey. LC 44-5953. (Prize mystery novels). 1944. Crestwood Publishing Co., Inc.
Third Part of the Countesse of Pembrokes Yuychurch. Ed. by Gerald Snare. (Renaissance Editions Ser.: No. 8). 1975. 8.00 o.p. CSUN.
Third Parties. Laura Cunningham. LC 80-13305. 10.95 (ISBN 0-698-11040-4). Coward, McCann & Geoghegan.
Third Party. Frederic Arthur Stanley. LC 15-16339. 1915. The Macaulay Company.
Third Passenger. Caroline Crane. LC 82-19923. 1983. 10.95 (ISBN 0-396-08132-0). Dodd, Mead.
Third Passenger. Cleo M. Stephens. 1973. pap. 0.75 o.s.i. (01-377). Lancer.
Third Pillar. Soma Morgenstern. LC 55-8462. 1955. Farrar, Straus and Cudahy.
Third Planet from Altair. Edward Packard. 128p. 1981. pap. 1.95 (ISBN 0-553-22000-4). Bantam.
Third Policeman. Flann O'Brien. 1976. pap. 4.95 (ISBN 0-452-25350-0, Z5350, Plume). NAL.
Third Policeman. Flann O'Brien. 1970. pap. 0.95 o.p. (ISBN 0-447-75145-X). Lancer.
Third Policeman. Flann O'Brien. 1967. 4.95 o.p. Walker & Co.
Third Policeman. Brian O'Nolan. LC 67-23112. 1968. 4.95. Walker.
Third Power. Neville Frankel. LC 80-21723. 13.95 (ISBN 0-8253-0026-6). Beaufort Books.
Third Rider. Barry Cord. 1978. pap. 1.25 o.s.i. (ISBN 0-505-51318-8). Tower Bks.
Third Sex. Ernst Ludwig Wolzogen Und Neuhaus & Colbron, Grace Isabel, Tr. LC 14-17485. 1914. The Macaulay Company.
Third Side of the Coin. Francis Clifford. (YA) 1965. 3.95 o.p. Coward.
Third Side of the Coin. Arthur Leonard Bell Thompson. LC 65-20400. 1965. Coward-McCann.
Third Side of the Coin: By Francis Clifford. Pseud., 1st Amer. Ed. Arthur Leonard Bell Thompson. LC 65-204006. 3.95. Coward.
Third Skin. John Michael Ward Bingham. LC 54-8496. (Red badge detective). 1954. Dodd, Mead.
Third Skin. John Michael Ward Bingham Clanmorris. LC 54-8496. (Red badge detective). 1954. Dodd, Mead.
Third Son. Margaret Culkin Banning. LC 34-516339. 1934. Harper & Brothers.
Third Spectre. William Edward Daniel Ross. LC 67-6622. 1967. Arcadia House.
Third Statue: A Professor Challis Adventure. Shane Martin. LC 59-5775. 1959. Morrow.
Third Sunday Singing. 1st Ed. Colquitt Bray. LC 54-41709. 1954. W. C. Bray Enterprises.
Third Time Lucky. Stanley Mann. LC 78-4008. 1978. 6.95 (ISBN 0-312-80032-0). St. Martin's Press.
Third Time Lucky. Berta Ruck. 1958. Dodd, Mead.
Third Tongue: A Narrative in Two Parts, Pt. 1- Louise M Simes. LC 27-23278. The Author.
Third Tower. Alice Abbott. (Ace Gothic). 1974. (pbk.) 0.95. Ace Books.
Third Truth. Michael Bar-Zohar. LC 73-5833. 1973. 5.95 (ISBN 0-395-15458-8). Houghton Mifflin.
Third Truth. Michael Bar-Zohar. 1974. (pbk.) 1.50. Ballantine Books.
Third Victim. Collin Wilcox. Dell.
Third Violet,. Stephen Crane. LC 72-104433. 1970. Literature House.
Third Violet. Stephen Crane. 1897. D. Appleton and Company.
Third Volume. by fergus hume... ed. Fergus Hume. LC 7-5844. The Cassell Publishing Co.
Third Ward, Newark. Curtis Lucas. LC 46-8619. 1946. Ziff-Davis Publishing Company.
Third Warning. Augustus Muir. LC 25-21591. The Bobbs-Merrill Company.
Third Weaver. Emily Calvin Blake. LC 29-21926. 1929. Willett, Clark & Colby.
Third Wedding. Costas Taktsis. LC 76-409421. 1969. Penguin.
Third Wedding. Costas Taktsis. LC 79-155440. 1971. 6.95 (ISBN 0-87376-018-2). Red Dust.
Third Wife. Jeanne Hines. 1977. 1.95 (ISBN 0-445-08615-7). Popular Library.
Third Window. Anne Douglas Sedgwick. LC 2-10315. 1920. Houghton Mifflin Company.
Third Woman. Aloyzas Baronas. Tr. by Nola M. Zobarskas. LC 68-54593. Orig. Title: Trecioji Moteris. 1968. 5.00 o.p. (ISBN 0-87141-025-7). Manyland.
Third Woman. Henryk Sienkiewicz & Babad, Nathan M., Tr. LC 13-17732. (Peerless series, no. 107). 1898. J. S. Ogilvie Publishing Company.
Third World: A Tale of Love and Strange Adventure. Henry Clay Fairman. 1896. The Trans-Atlantic Publishing Company.
Third World War. John Hackett et al. 1980. pap. 3.50 (ISBN 0-425-05019-X). Berkley Pub.
Thirlby Hall. A Novel. William Edward Norris. (Harper's Franklin square library, no. 356). 1884. Harper & Brothers.
Thirlby Hall. A Novel. William Edward Norris. (On cover: Seaside library. Pocket ed. no. 184). 1884. G. Munro.
Thirst! Charles Eric Maine. 1978. 1.95 (ISBN 0-441-80676-7). Charter Communications.
Thirst: A Novel. Charles Lee Robinson. LC 47-11232. 1947. J. Day Co.
Thirst for Love. Yukio Mishima, pseud. 1971. pap. 1.95 (ISBN 0-425-03430-5, Medallion). Berkley Pub.
Thirst for Love. Yukio Mishima, pseud. (O.s.i). 1969. 10.95 o.s.i. (ISBN 0-394-44844-8). Knopf.
Thirst for Love. Yukio Mishima, pseud. Tr. by Alfred H. Marks. (The Perigee Japanese Library). 224p. 1981. pap. 4.95 (ISBN 0-399-50494-X, Perige). Putnam Pub Group.
Thirst for the Unknown. Sequel to "The Parisian Sultana". Adolphe Belot. (Seaside library, v. 51, no. 1036). G. Munro.
Thirsty Day & Permanent Wave. Kathleen Aguero & Miriam Goodman. LC 76-55615. 88p. 1977. pap. 4.95 (ISBN 0-914086-17-0). Alicejamesbooks.
Thirsty Earth. Francis Rhodes Farmer. LC 34-39367. 1934. Longmans, Green and Co.
Thirsty Earth. William Henry Robinson. LC 37-2868. J. Messner, Inc.
Thirsty Evil. Philip Maitland Hubbard. LC 73-91624. 1974. 5.95 (ISBN 0-689-10594-0). Atheneum.
Thirsty Evil. facs. ed. Gore Vidal. LC 72-140345. (Short Story Index Reprint Ser). 1956. 11.00 (ISBN 0-8369-3737-6). Ayer Co.
Thirsty Evil: Seven Short Stories. Gore Vidal. LC 72-140345. (Short story index reprint series). 1970. Books for Libraries Press.
Thirsty Evil: Seven Short Stories. Gore Vidal. LC 56-11329. 1956. Zero Press.
Thirsty Evil: Seven Short Stories. Gore Vidal. LC 81-6719. 20.00 (ISBN 0-917342-83-6) (ISBN 0-917342-84-4). Gay Sunshine Press.
Thirsty Land. Norman A. Fox. LC 49-819613. (Silver star westerns). 1949. Dodd, Mead.
Thirsty Oak. M. Janet Becker. LC 50-7040. 1950. Coward-McCann.
Thirsty Range. Edward Beverly Mann. LC 35-558. 1935. W. Morrow & Co.
Thirsty Sword: A Story of the Norse Invasion of Scotland (1262-1263. Robert Leighton. LC 7-14310. 1892. C. Scribner's Sons.
Thirteen. Frederick Britten Austin. LC 25-200239. 1925. Doubleday, Page & Company.
Thirteen. Ernest Temple Thurston. LC 12-8137. 1912. Dodd, Mead and Company.
Thirteen & Ready. Ann Griffin. pap. 1.95 o.p. (8068). Cameo.
Thirteen at Dinner. Agatha Miller Christie. LC 33-296437. 1933. Dodd, Mead & Company.
Thirteen Castle Walk. DeWitt Bodeen. LC 75-15081. 1975. 1.25 (ISBN 0-515-03912-8). Pyramid Books.
Thirteen Clocks. James Thurber. (Illus.). 1977. pap. 3.95 (ISBN 0-671-22944-3, Fireside). S&S.
Thirteen Clues for Miss Marple. Agatha Miller Christie. 1983. pap. 2.95 (ISBN 0-440-18755-9). Dell.
Thirteen Clues for Miss Marple: A Collection of Mystery Stories. Agatha Miller Christie. LC 66-22905. 3.50. Dodd.
Thirteen Crimes of Science Fiction. Ed. by Isaac Asimov et al. LC 78-22762. 1979. 14.95 (ISBN 0-385-15220-5). Doubleday.
Thirteen Famous Ghost Stories. Peter Underwood. (Everyman paperback). (Everyman's library; 1749). 1977. Dent.
Thirteen Famous Ghost Stories. Ed. by Peter Underwood. (Everyman paperback). (Everyman's library; 1749). 1977. Dent.
Thirteen Famous Ghost Stories: Haunting Tales to Keep You from Your Sleep. Ed. by Peter Underwood. 1977. pap. 2.25x (ISBN 0-460-01749-7, Evman). Biblio Dist.
Thirteen for the Kill. Peter Buck. (Mercenary Ser.: No. 1). (Orig.). 1981. pap. 2.25 (ISBN 0-451-09893-5, E9893, Sig). NAL.
Thirteen French Science-Fiction Stories: Edited by Damon Knight. Ed. by Damon Francis Knight. LC 65-15738. 1965. Bantam Books.
Thirteen Great Modern Stories, a New Anthology. Frederick Faust. LC 44-47803. (On cover: Avon modern short story monthly. No. 15). 1944. Avon Book Company.
Thirteen Great Stories: By Felipe Alfau and Others. Ed. by Daniel Talbot. LC 56-8074. (Dell first edition, D99). Dell Pub. Co.
Thirteen Great Stories from the Long Valley. John Steinbeck. LC 44-753097. (Avon modern short story monthly, no. 9). 1943. Avon Book Company.
Thirteen Guests. Joseph Jefferson Farjeon. LC 38-312914. 1938. The Bobbs-Merrill Company.
Thirteen Hours by Air. Wallace West & Rogers, Bogart. LC 36-9380. Lynn Publishing Co., Inc.
Thirteen Ivenrow. P. Lehman. 4.00 o.p. (ISBN 0-8062-1101-6). Carlton.
Thirteen Men. William Alexander Fraser. LC 72-4423. (Short story index reprint series). 1972. 12.00 (ISBN 0-8369-4176-4). Books for Libraries Press.
Thirteen Men. William Alexander Fraser. LC 6-36036. 1906. D. Appleton and Company.
Thirteen Men. Tiffany Thayer & Blaine, Mahlon, Illus. 1930. C. Kendall.
Thirteen Men in the Mine. Pierre Hubermont & Titterton, L. H., Tr. LC 31-31225. 1931. The Macmillan Company.
Thirteen Millionaires: A Novel. A. L Dabney. LC 78-70589. 8.95. Harlo.
Thirteen O'clock: Stories of Several Worlds. Stephen Vincent Benet. LC 78-152935. (Short story index reprint series). 1971. (ISBN 0-8369-3793-7). Books for Libraries Press.
Thirteen O'clock: Stories of Several Worlds. Stephen Vincent Benet. LC 37-28740. Farrar & Rinehart, Inc.
Thirteen Problems. Agatha Miller Christie. (Greenway Edition). 1981. 8.95 (ISBN 0-396-06818-9). Dodd.
Thirteen Satires of Juvenal, 2 Vols. Decimus J. Juvenalis. Ed. by J. E. Major. Set. 44.80 o.p. Adler.
Thirteen Seconds That Rocked the World: Or, The Mentator. John Joseph Meyer. LC 35-1690. R. D. Henkle.
Thirteen Steps. Elwyn Whitman Chambers. LC 35-36176. 1935. Doubleday, Doran & Company, Inc.
Thirteen Stories. Robert Bontine Cunninghame Graham. LC 78-103511. (Short story index reprint series). 1969. Books for Libraries Press.
Thirteen Stories: Selected, Introd. by Ruth M. Vande Kieft. Eudora Welty. LC 65-14703. (Harvest bk.; HB89). pap., 1.65. Harcourt.
Thirteen Tales of Terror. Les Daniels & Diane Thompson. LC 76-42252. (Scribner student paperbacks). 4.95 (ISBN 0-684-14845-5). Scribner.
Thirteen Tales of Terror. Jack London. 1978. pap. 3.75 (ISBN 0-445-04254-0). Popular Lib.
Thirteen Thirteenth Street. Natalie Sumner Lincoln. LC 32-16254. 1932. D. Appleton and Company.
Thirteen Thirty Nine or So: Being an Apology for a Pedlar. Nicholas Seare, pseud. LC 75-11732. (Illus.). 184p. 1975. 7.95 o.p. (ISBN 0-15-189935-5). HarBraceJ.
Thirteen Towers. Celeste Caldwell. 1978. pap. 1.50 o.s.i. (ISBN 0-505-51286-6). Tower Bks.
Thirteen Towers. Celeste Caldwell. 1974. (pbk.) 0.95. Belmont Tower Books.
Thirteen Toy Pistols... Eugene E. Halleran. LC 45-6335. 1945. David McKay Company.
Thirteen Travellers. Hugh Walpole. LC 21-15428. George H. Doran Company.
Thirteen Trumpeters. Laurence Walter Meynell. LC 77-17996. (Jubilee mystery). 1978. 7.95 (ISBN 0-8128-2423-7). Stein and Day.
Thirteen Ways to Dispose of a Body: An Anthology. Ed. by Basil Davenport. LC 66-16564. (Red badge mystery). bds., 4.00. Dodd.
Thirteen Ways to Dispose of a Body: An Anthology. Ed. by Basil Davenport. LC 66-16564. (Red badge mystery). 1966. Dodd, Mead.
Thirteen Ways to Kill a Man: An Anthology. Ed. by Basil Davenport. LC 65-16822. (Red badge detective). bds., 4.00. Dodd.
Thirteen Women. Tiffany Thayer. LC 32-5595. C. Kendall.
Thirteen Years of Proof: The Story of a Boy: His Real Life and His Dream Life. 1st Ed. Olive K Neilson. LC 59-127051. 1959. Greenwich Book Publishers.
Thirteenth Apostle. Richard A Johns. LC 66-19908. 1966. Broadman Press.
Thirteenth Apostle. Eugene Vale. LC 59-11660. 1959. Scribner.
Thirteenth Bed in the Ballroom. Fonseca, Esther Haven. LC 37-4274. 1937. Pub. for the Crime Club, Inc., Doubleday, Doran & Company. Inc.
Thirteenth Commandment. Rupert Hughes. LC 22-14550. 1916. A. L. Burt Company.
Thirteenth Commandment: A Novel. Rupert Hughes. LC 16-15151. 1916. Harper & Brothers.
Thirteenth District. Brand Whitlock. (Muckrakers Ser.). Repr. of 1902 ed. lib. bdg. 13.50 (ISBN 0-8398-2163-8). Irvington.
Thirteenth Gun. A. L. Cahill. (Orig.). 1981. pap. 1.75 o.s.i. (ISBN 0-505-51587-3). Tower Bks.
Thirteenth Hour. Everett A. Bell & John A. Rush. 190p. 1976. pap. 2.75 o.p. (ISBN 0-920124-03-8). Humanity Pubns.
Thirteenth Hour. John Lee. LC 77-82768. 1978. 10.00 (ISBN 0-385-12992-0). Doubleday.
Thirteenth Hour. John Lee. 1979. 2.50. Dell Pub. Co.
Thirteenth Juror: A Tale Out of Court. Frederick Trevor Hill. LC 13-20823. 1913. 1.20. The Century Co.
Thirteenth Letter. Natalie Sumner Lincoln. LC 24-5108. 1924. D. Appleton and Company.
Thirteenth Man. Mary Jean Hickling Gwynne Kernahan. LC 10-27192. G. W. Dillingham Company.
Thirteenth Outpost. S. W. Karl. 1978. pap. 1.50 (ISBN 0-532-15376-6). Woodhill.
Thirteenth Pan Book of Horror Stories. Ed. by H. Van Thal. 1982. pap. 10.00x (ISBN 0-330-23331-9, Pub. by Pan Bks). State Mutual Bk.
Thirteenth Summer: A Novel. Virginia Oakey. LC 55-7165. 1955. A. A. Wyn.
Thirteenth Sun. Worker Daniachew. (African writers series, 125). 1975. (ISBN 0-435-90125-7). Heinemann.
Thirteenth Sun. Daniachew Worku. (African Writers Ser.). 1973. pap. text ed. 2.50x (ISBN 0-435-90125-7). Heinemann Ed.
Thirteenth Tribe. Arthur Koestler. 1978. pap. 2.95 (ISBN 0-445-04242-7). Popular Lib.
Thirteenth Tribe. Jenette Norris. LC 51-10069. 1951. Vantage Press.
Thirteenth Trick. Russell Braddon. LC 73-665. 1973. 5.95 (ISBN 0-393-08375-6). Norton.
Thirteenth Valley. John M. Del Vecchio. LC 81-70920. (Illus.). 606p. 1982. 15.95 (ISBN 0-553-05022-2). Bantam.
Thirteenth Woman & Other Stories. Lydia Davis. 1976. pap. 3.00 (Pub. by Living Hand). SBD.
Thirtieth Piece of Silver. Lilian Hayes. LC 70-125217. (Short story index reprint series). 1970. Books for Libraries Press.
Thirtieth Piece of Silver. Lilian Hayes. LC 24-24944. 1924. The Macmillan Company.
Thirtieth Year. Ingeborg Bachman. LC 63-9139. 1964. Knopf.
Thirty. Howard Vincent O'Brien. LC 15-177631. 1915. 1.35. Dodd, Mead and Company.
Thirty Acres. Philippe Pannetoa & Walter, Felix, Tr. LC 40-27711. 1940. The Macmillan Company.
Thirty Clocks Strike the Hour: And Other Stories. Victoria Mary Sackville-West. LC 32-266659. 1932. Doubleday, Doran & Company, Inc.

Thirty Days Hath July. Alice Brennan. 1975. (pbk.) 0.95 (ISBN 0-380-00379-1). Avon.

Thirty Days Hath September. Dorothy Cameron Disney & Perry, George Sessions, 1910- Joint Author. LC 42-25511. 1942. Random House.

Thirty Days Hath September. Owen John. LC 67-11364. 1967. Dutton.

Thirty Days in Eden. Peggy Gaddis, pseud. LC 38-190713. 1938. Arcadia House.

Thirty Days to Live. Lucy Beatrice Maleson. LC 44-9740. 1944. Smith & Durrell.

Thirty-Eight Calibur. William Ard. LC 52-8738. (Murray Hill mystery). 1952. Rinehart.

Thirty-Eight Short Stories: An Introductory Anthology. 2d ed. Ed. by Michael Timko. LC 78-10668. 7.95 (ISBN 0-394-32182-0). Knopf.

Thirty-Eight Short Stories: An Introductory Anthology. 2nd ed. Ed. by Michael Timko. 1978. pap. text ed. 8.95 (ISBN 0-394-32182-0). Knopf.

Thirty-Eight Short Stories: An Introductory Anthology, Ed. by Michael Timko, Clinton F. Oliver. Ed. by Michael Timko. LC 68-121185. 1968. pap., 4.75. Knopf.

Thirty-Eighth Floor. Clifford Irving. LC 65-20974. bds., 5.95. McGraw.

Thirty Fables in Slang. George Ade & Bacon, Peggy, 1895- Illus. Arrow Editions.

Thirty-First Bullfinch. Helen Kieran Reilly. LC 30-17889. 1930. Pub. for The Crime Club, Inc., by Doubleday, Doran & Company, Inc.

Thirty-First Floor. Per Wahloo. (YA) 1967. 4.95 o.p. Knopf.

Thirty-First Floor: By Peter Wahloo. Tr. from Swedish by Joan Tate. 1st Amer. Ed. Per Wahloo. LC 67-11145. 1967. bds., 4.95. Knopf.

Thirty-First of February. Nelson Slade Bond. LC 78-121524. (Short story index reprint series). 1970. Books for Libraries Press.

Thirty-First of February. Julian Symons. 1978. pap. 1.95 o.p. (ISBN 0-06-080460-2, P 460, PL). Har-Row.

Thirty-First of February. Julian Symons. 1971. pap. 0.95 o.p. (95139). Beagle Bks.

Thirty Five-Cent Thrills. Joyce Thompson. (Lynx House Press Fiction Ser.). 1978. pap. 3.50 (ISBN 0-89924-014-3). Lynx Hse.

Thirty for a Harry: A John Denson Mystery. Richard Hoyt. LC 81-7847. 192p. 1981. 8.95 (ISBN 0-87131-357-X). M Evans.

Thirty for Time. Kenneth Lohf. 2.00 o.p. Branden.

Thirty for Tonight. John Richard Finch. LC 41-282953. Printed by the Advertiser Publishing Co., Ltd.

Thirty-Four Charlton. Rene Leilani Kuhn. LC 45-35082. 1945. D. Appleton-Century Co. Incorporated.

Thirty-Four East. Alfred Coppel. LC 73-20346. 1974. 7.95 (ISBN 0-15-189950-9). Harcourt Brace Jovanovich.

Thirty-Four East. Alfred Coppel. 1975. (pbk.) 1.95. Popular Library.

Thirty-Four Short Stories. Katherine Mansfield. (Standard Classic Ed.). 4.95 o.p. (ISBN 0-00-421577-X, JC577). Collins-World.

Thirty-Four Years. An American Story of Southern Life. John Marchmont. LC 7-20445. 1878. Claxton, Remsen & Haffelfinger.

Thirty Manhattan East. Hillary Waugh. 1978. pap. 1.75 o.s.i. (ISBN 0-505-51311-0). Tower Bks.

Thirty Manhattan East. Hillary Waugh. (Homicide North Ser). (Osi). 1971. pap. 0.95 o.s.i. (B95-2081). Belmont-Tower.

Thirty Manhattan East. Hillary Waugh. (O.s.i.). 1973. pap. 0.95 o.s.i. (BT40150). Belmont-Tower.

Thirty Manhattan East: A Case for Homicide North. Hillary Waugh. LC 68-17819. 1968. Doubleday.

Thirty-Nine Steps. John Buchan. LC 15-22677. G. H. Doran Company.

Thirty-Nine Steps. John Buchan & Ardizzone, Edward, 1900- Illus. LC 64-56217. (Children's illustrated classics, no. 64). 1964. Dent.

Thirty-Nine Steps: And The Power-House. John Buchan. LC 25-8744. 1922. T. Nelson and Sons. Ltd.

Thirty-Nine Steps in Du Maurier, Daphne, 1907- Jamaica Inn... Edited and Abridged by Jay E. Greene. John Buchan. LC 51-7131. 1951. Globe Book Co.

Thirty North One Sixty-Five East. Paul Justin Stam. LC 78-55377. 1978. 1.75 (ISBN 0-380-01965-5). Avon.

Thirty Notches see Maverick Marshall.

Thirty Notches: By Brad Ward Pseud. Samuel Anthony Peeples. LC 56-106230. 1956. Macmillan.

Thirty-One Families Under Heaven. Georg Fink & Hummel, Lillie C., Tr. LC 31-9859. H. Liveright.

Thirty-One Stories by Thirty & One Authors. Ed. by Ernest Rhys. Scott, Mrs. Catharine Amy (Dawson) Joint Ed. LC 23-149143. 1923. D. Appleton and Company.

Thirty-One Stories: Edited by Michael R. Booth and Clinton S. Burhans, Jr. Ed. by Michael R Booth & Clinton S. Burhans. LC 60-6501. 1960. Prentice-Hall.

Thirty-Second Day: By Charles O'Neal, Victor Trivas. Charles O'Neal. (Signet bk., T2711). 1965. New Amer. Lib.

Thirty Seconds Over New York. Robert Buchard. LC 73-100559. 1970. 5.95. Morrow.

Thirty' Seen a Lot. Evangelina Vigil. LC 81-68073. 88p. (Orig.). 1982. pap. 5.00 (ISBN 0-934770-13-1). Arte Publico.

Thirty Signing off - Jefferson Adams & Other Stories. Harry McDermott. 1970. 3.50 o.p. Vantage.

Thirty Stories. Kay Boyle. LC 57-860113. (New Directions paperbook, 62). 1957. J. Laughlin.

Thirty Stories. Kay Boyle. LC 46-118455. 1946. Simon and Schuster.

Thirty Stories I Like to Tell. Margaret White Eggleston. LC 49-7725. 1949. Harper.

Thirty Strange Stories. Herbert George Wells. LC 72-103531. (Short story index reprint series). 1969. Books for Libraries Press.

Thirty Strange Stories. Herbert George Wells. LC 5-2458. 1897. E. Arnold.

Thirty Strange Stories. Herbert George Wells. LC 20-15629. Harper & Brothers.

Thirty Tales & Sketches. Robert Bontine Cunninghame Graham. LC 76-125213. (Short story index reprint series). 1970. Books for Libraries Press.

Thirty Tales & Sketches. Robert Bontine Cunninghame Graham. Ed. by Garnett, Edward. LC 29-19240. 1929. The Viking Press.

Thirty Thousand Dollar Bequest: And Other Stories. Samuel Langhorne Clemens. LC 6-24649. Harper & Brothers,

Thirty Thousand Dollar Bequest: And Other Stories. Samuel Langhorne Clemens. LC 28-4844. 1917. Harper & Brothers.

Thirty Thousand on the Hoof. Zane Grey. (Kangaroo Book). 1977. 1.50 (ISBN 0-671-80820-6). Pocket Books.

Thirty Thousand on the Hoof. Zane Grey. LC 40-14076. Harper & Brothers.

Thirty Thousand on the Hoof. Zane Grey. 240p. 1982. pap. 2.25 (ISBN 0-671-44715-7). PB.

Thirty-Three Brand. Frank Roderus. LC 77-77639. 1977. 6.95 (ISBN 0-385-13312-X). Doubleday.

Thirty-Three Brand. Frank Roderus. 1979. pap. 1.75 (ISBN 0-441-80845-X). Ace Bks.

Thirty-Three Sardonics I Can't Forget. Ed. by Tiffany Thayer. LC 46-5746. 1946. Philosophical Library.

Thirty Two Votes Before Breakfast: Politics at the Grass Roots. Jesse Stuart. LC 73-18049. 1974. 7.95 (ISBN 0-07-062299-X). McGraw-Hill.

Thirty Years Ago: Or The Memoirs of a Water Drinker. William Dunlap. LC 6-35866. 1836. Bancroft & Holley.

Thirty Years from Now. Robert C Emery. LC 34-327517.

Thirty Years Peace. Peter O Chotjewitz. LC 80-24472. 1981. 12.95 (ISBN 0-394-50182-9). Knopf.

Thirty Years with the Wind Machine. Clinton Shaffer. LC 79-139948. 1971. 3.95 (ISBN 0-8059-1524-9). Dorrance.

This--Is Murder! Cortland Fitzsimmons & Adams, Gerald, Joint Author. LC 41-20048. 1941. Frederick A. Stokes Company.

This Above All. Eric Mowbray Knight. LC 41-51668. Harper & Brothers.

This Above All. Eric Mowbray Knight. LC 41-22069. 1941. Harper & Brothers.

This Above All. Eric Mowbray Knight. LC 42-16506. 1942. Grosset & Dunlap.

This Above All. Matthew Phipps Shiel. LC 33-12043. The Vanguard Press.

This Above All. Harold Speakman. LC 24-21399. The Bobbs-Merrill Company.

This Ancient Evil. easy eye ed. Dorothy Daniels. (Orig.). 1968. pap. 0.75 o.p. (74-971). Lancer.

This and No More. Benedict Freedman & Nancy Mars Freedman. LC 50-2686. 1950. Harper.

This Angry Loving Land. Jean K. Freeman. 184p. (Orig.). 1981. pap. 3.95 (ISBN 0-87123-568-4, 210568). Bethany Hse.

This Angry, Loving Land. Jean Lenore Kenny. LC 81-10245. 3.95 (ISBN 0-87123-568-4). Bethany House.

This Animal Is Mischievous. David Benedictus. LC 66-11366. 1966. 4.95. New Amer. Lib.

This Awakening. Margaret Witter Fuller. LC 48-6162. 1948. Westminister Press.

This Awful Age. Florence Ryerson & Clements, Colin Campbell, 1894- Joint Author. LC 30-21866. 1930. D. Appleton and Company.

This Barangay: a Novel. J. C. Laya. 1970. Repr. of 1954 ed. 8.75 o.p. Cellar.

This Bed Not for Sleeping. Hans Melcher. (Orig.). 1969. pap. 1.95 o.p. (6041). Brandon.

This Bed Thy Centre. Pamela Hansford Johnson. LC 35-153196. Harcourt, Brace and Company.

This Belongs to You. 1st Ed. Robert Dehart. LC 53-386. 1952. Pageant Press.

This Best Possible World, a Novel. Frederick L Hackbenburg. LC 34-12883. 1934. R. O. Ballou.

This Bittersweet Love. Barbara Andrews. (Candlelight Ecstasy Ser.: No. 127). (Orig.). 1983. pap. 1.95 (ISBN 0-440-18797-4). Dell.

This Blessed Shore. Thomas Bruce Morgan. LC 66-172533. 4.95. Shorecrest Dist. Shorewood.

This Blessed Shore. Thomas Bruce Morgan. LC 66-17253. 1966. Shorecrest.

This Blessed Spot. Barbara Woollcott. LC 61-9573. Doubleday,

This Body the Earth. Paul Green. LC 35-19876. 1935. Harper & Brothers.

This Bread. Rosemary Buchanan. LC 45-6098. 1945. The Bruce Publishing Company.

This Bright Summer. Richard Warner Hatch. LC 33-814928. 1933. Covici, Friede.

This Bright Sword. Donald Barr Chidsey. LC 57-8766. 1957. Crown Publishers.

This Brittle Glory. Stella Morton. LC 50-14109. 1950. Morrow.

This Burning Flesh. Marsha Alexander. pap. 1.25 o.p. (2047). Brandon.

This Burning Harvest. Gloria Goldreich. 1983. pap. 3.50 (ISBN 0-425-06078-0). Berkley Pub.

This Business of Bomfog. Madelaine Duke. LC 69-15202. (Doubleday science fiction). 1969. 4.50. Doubleday.

This Calder Range. large print ed. Janet Dailey. LC 82-19534. 1983. 13.95 (ISBN 0-89621-420-6). Thorndike Press.

This Calder Range. Janet Dailey. (Orig.). 1982. pap. 3.50 (ISBN 0-671-45960-0). PB.

This Calder Sky. Janet Dailey. 1982. pap. 3.50 (ISBN 0-671-43856-5). PB.

This Can't Be Love. Peggy Gaddis, pseud. LC 40-8131. Gramercy Publishing Co.

This Chequered Floor. Francis Bamford. LC 41-28668. 1941. Longmans, Green and Co.

This Child's Gonna Live. Sarah E Wright. (Laurel edition). 1975. (pbk.) 1.25. Dell.

This Child's Gonna Live. Sarah E Wright. LC 69-19438. 1969. 5.95. Delacorte Press.

This Circle of Flesh. Lloyd R. Morris. LC 32-6435. 1932. Harper & Brothers.

This City Is Ours. Denis Pitts. LC 75-1378. 1975. 7.95 o.p. (ISBN 0-88405-101-3). Mason Charter.

This City Is Ours: A Novel. Denis Pitts. LC 75-5881. 1975. 7.95 (ISBN 0-88405-101-3). Mason/Charter.

This City Is Ours: A Novel. Denis Pitts. 1978. 1.95 (ISBN 0-380-01851-9). Avon.

This Company of Men. William Pearson. LC 63-18761. 1963. St Martin's Press.

This Crooked Way. Elizabeth Spencer. LC 52-7349. 1952. Dodd, Mead.

This Crooked Way. Elizabeth Spencer. LC 68-20058. 1968. McGraw-Hill.

This Crowded Earth. Robert Bloch. Bd. with Ladies' Day. (Orig.). 1968. pap. 0.60 o.p. (B60-080). Belmont-Tower.

This Cruel Beauty. Trevor Meldal-Johnsen. 368p. (Orig.). 1983. pap. 3.50 (ISBN 0-380-81851-5). Avon.

This Dark Enchantment. Rosalind Carson. (Superromances Ser.). 384p. 1982. pap. 2.50 (ISBN 0-373-70016-4, Pub. by Worldwide). Harlequin Bks.

This Dark Monarchy. Francis W Leary. LC 49-6694. 1949. E. P. Dutton.

This Darkening Universe. Lloyd Biggle, Jr. LC 75-11070. 1975. 5.95 (ISBN 0-385-08676-8). Doubleday.

This Darkling Love. LC 66-5424. 1966. Acardia House.

This Day and Time. Anne Wetzell Armstrong. LC 30-21771. 1930. A. A. Knopf.

This Day and Time. With a Personal Reminiscence by David McClellan. Anne Wetzell Armstrong. LC 76-627812. 1970. 3.95. Research Advisory Council, East Tennessee State University.

This Day of Love. Constance Robinson. (Orig.). 1979. pap. 4.95 (ISBN 0-934796-00-9). Footsteps.

This Day's Death. John Rechy. 1970. 6.95 o.p. (GP620, GP620). Grove.

This Day's Death: A Novel. John Rechy. LC 72-111018. 1970. 6.95. Grove Press.

This Day's Job. Peggy Gaddis, pseud. LC 42-254374. 1942. Phoenix Press.

This Day's Madness... Adelaide Champneys. LC 26-24285. The Bobbs-Merrill Company.

This Day's Madness... Miss Tiverton Goes Out, Author of. LC 26-24285. The Bobbs-Merrill Company.

This Day's Madness. Frederic Franklyn Van De Water. LC 57-6605. 1957. Washburn.

This Day's Rapture. Frances Park. LC 33-19973. 1933. A. H. King.

This Deadly Dark. Lee Wilson. LC 46-7308. 1946. Dodd, Mead & Company.

This Deadly Grief. Patricia Power. LC 70-171313. 1972. 4.95. Published for the Crime Club by Doubleday.

This Dear Encounter. Catherine Hutter. LC 52-6627. 1952. Holt.

This Death Was Murder. March Everman. LC 40-318732. 1940. The Macmillan Company.

This Delicate Creature. Con O'Leary. LC 29-2130. 1929. E. Holt.

This Demi-Paradise: A Westchester Diary. Margaret Halsey. LC 60-10975. 1960. Simon and Schuster.

This Desirable Bachelor. Maysie Greig. LC 41-139352. 1941. Doubleday, Doran and Company, Inc.

This Dog-Gone World. Kim Allison. 1965. 3.00 o.p. (ISBN 0-8059-0013-6). Dorrance.

This Dog-Gone World. Ruth Garbisch. LC 64-7623. 1965. Dorrance.

This Double Thread. Walter Starcke. pap. 2.50 o.p. (RD64, HarpR). Har-Row.

This Downhill Path. Anna Clarke. LC 77-77541. (MW suspense). 1977. 7.95 (ISBN 0-679-50771-X). McKay.

This Dying Land. James Earl Johnson. LC 75-139947. 1971. 3.00 (ISBN 0-8059-1525-7). Dorrance.

This Dynasty of Doctors. Rhoda Truax. LC 40-13810. The Bobbs-Merrill Company.

This Eager Heart. Clare Jaynes, pseud. LC 47-4912. 1947. Random House.

This Eager Pace. Vada Rutherford. LC 51-5970. 1951. Humphries.

This Earth, My Brother: An Allegorical Tale of Africa. Kofi Awoonor. LC 74-187898. 1972. 1.45. Anchor Books.

This Earth, My Brother: An Allegorical Tale of Africa. Kofi Awoonor. LC 75-131066. 1971. 5.95. Doubleday.

This Ecstasy. Elizabeth Gertrude Levin Stern. LC 37-6806. J. H. Sears & Company, Inc.

This Edge of the Night. John Prebble. LC 48-630649. 1948. W. Sloane Associates.

This Fatal Writ. Sara Woods, pseud. 1982. 15.00x (ISBN 0-333-25963-7, Pub. by Macmillan England). State Mutual Bk.

This Fearful Paradise. Maysie Greig. LC 53-5020. 1953. Random House.

This Festive Season. Jeanne Florence Goodstein Singer. LC 43-16081. 1943. Harcourt, Brace and Company.

This Fiery Night. Joan Vatsek. LC 59-1928. 1959. Harper.

This Fiery Night. Joan Vatsek. LC 58-12472. (Illus.). 1959. Harper.

This Fiery Promise. Joan Van Every Frost. 1978. pap. 2.25 o.s.i. (ISBN 0-8439-0582-4, Leisure Bks). Nordon Pubns.

This Fifty Years of Exile: Israel Potter) Introd. by Lewis Leary. Herman Melville. LC 57-9765. (American century series, S-13). 1957. Sagamore Press.

This Finer Shadow. Harlan Cozad McIntosh. LC 41-4716. 1941. The Dial Press.

This Flesh: A Cinematic Novel. Wythe Williams. LC 31-10082. 1931. R. M. McBride & Company.

This Flower Only Blooms Every Hundred Years. Sherril Jaffe. LC 78-27461. 1979. 4.50. (ISBN 0-87685-417-X) (ISBN 0-87685-418-8). Black Sparrow Press.

This Fool, Passion. Carlos Keith. LC 34-6832. 1934. The Vanguard Press.

This for Caroline. Doris Leslie. 1973. 0.95. Popular Lib.

This Fortress. Manning Coles, pseud. LC 42-222694. 1942. Doubleday, Doran & Company, Inc.

This Fortress World. James Edward Gunn. (Berkley book). 1979. 1.75. Berkley Pub. Corp.

This Fortress World. 1st Ed. James Edward Gunn. LC 55-12188. 1955. Gnome Press.

This Freedom. Arthur Stuart-Menteth Hutchinson. LC 22-175572. 1922. 2.50. Little, Brown, and Company.

This Freedom. Arthur Stuart-Menteth Hutchinson. LC 22-26760. 1922. Little, Brown, and Company.

This Generation Shall Not Pass till All These Things Be Fulfilled,". Alvin Pender Cummins. LC 39-17646. 1939. Wm. B. Eerdmans Publishing Co.

This Girl Is Mine. Mary Munro, pseud. Ed. by Gene DeRoin. (Aston Hall Presents Ser.). (Orig.). 1980. pap. 1.50 (ISBN 0-89936-017-3). Aston Hall.

This Giving in Marriage. Grace Stair. LC 32-7597. 1932. L. MacVeagh, Dial Press, Inc.

This Golden Land. Louise O'Flaherty. 416p. (Orig.). 1982. pap. 2.95 (ISBN 0-345-28346-5). Ballantine.

This Golden Valley. Francine Rivers. 416p. 1983. pap. text ed. 3.50 (ISBN 0-515-06823-3). Jove Pubns.

This Grass, This Gun. Lee Floren. 1978. pap. 1.25 (ISBN 0-532-12531-2). Woodhill.

This Great People Has Said "Enough". (Illus.). 38p. 0.50 o.p. Peoples Pr.

This Green and Pleasant Land. 1st American Ed. Dudley Barker. LC 56-7723. 1956. Holt.

This Green Thicket World. Howell Vines. LC 34-9619. 1934. Little, Brown, and Company.

This Gun for Hire. Graham Greene. LC 35-13041. 1936. Doubleday, Doran & Company, Inc.

This Gun for Hire see Three by Graham Greene.

This Gun for Justice. Robert Engle. 160p. 1974. pap. 1.50 o.p. (ISBN 0-89014-117-7, CB-117). Canyon Bks.

This Gun for Justice. Robert Engle. 1974. (pbk.) 1.25. Canyon Book.

This Gun for Justice. V. J Santiago. 1978. 1.50. Pinnacle Books.

This Happy Rural Seat. 1st Ed. George Lanning. LC 52-5160. 1953. World Pub. Co.

This Haunted Land. Bruce Roberts. pap. 2.50 o.p. McNally.

This Healing Passion. Benjamin Siegel. (Pocket Book.). 1978. Pocket Books.

This Heart, This Hunter. Hallie Southgate Burnett. LC 52-13072. 1953. Holt.

This Hero Business. Hal Hode. LC 44-47151. 1944. Gold Label Books Inc.

This House Is Burning. Mona Goodwyn Williams. LC 77-88794. 8.95 (ISBN 0-89256-045-2). Rawson Associates Publishers.

This House Is Burning. Mona Goodwyn Williams. (Signet Book). 1979. 2.25 (ISBN 0-451-08695-3). New American Library.

This Hunger... Anais Nin. LC 45-9829. Gemor Press.

This Immortal. Roger Zelazny. LC 75-443. (Garland Library of Science Fiction). 1975. 11.00 (ISBN 0-8240-1445-6). Garland Pub.

This Is Adam. Brainard Cheney. 1958. 7.95 (ISBN 0-8392-1116-3). Astor-Honor.

This Is Adam: A Novel. Brainard Cheney. LC 58-12579. 1958. McDowell, Obolensky.

This Is America. Don Finney. LC 48-174220. 1948. Ozark Pub. & Distribution Co.

This Is Beverly. Hope Bishop Colket. LC 45-5195. 1945. J. B. Lippincott Company.

This Is for Always. Gladys Bagg Taber. LC 38-3232. 1938. Macrae Smith Company.

This Is for Real. Rene Raymond. LC 67-23111. 1967. Walker.

This Is Goodbye. Betty Baur. LC 46-3588. 1946. J. B. Lippincott Company.

This Is Happy. Peggy Gaddis, pseud. LC 47-481469. 1947. Arcadia House.

This Is It: Michael Shayne by Brett Halliday Pseud. Davis Dresser. LC 50-6521. (Red badge mystery). 1950. Dodd, Mead.

This Is Kate. Margaret Steel Hard. LC 44-5431. 1944. H. Holt and Company.

This Is Lagos & Other Stories. Flora Nwapa. 3.50 o.p. Panther Hse.

This Is Life. Paul Hutchens. LC 38-676726. 1937. W. B. Eerdmans Publishing Co.

This Is Me, Kathie: A Novel. Julia Truitt Yenni. LC 38-18392. Reynal & Hitchcock.

This Is Me, Kathie: A Novel. Julia Truitt Yenni. LC 42-254823. 1942. Triangle Books.

This Is Mr. Fortune. Henry Christopher Bailey. LC 38-276591. 1938. Pub. for the Crime Club, Inc., by Doubleday, Doran & Co., Inc.

This Is Moscow Speaking: And Other Stories. IUlii Markovich Daniel. LC 68-59615. (Illus.). 1969. 4.95. Dutton.

This Is Moscow Speaking & Other Stories. Yuli Daniel. 1969. 4.95 o.p. Dutton.

This Is Moscow Speaking & Other Stories. Yuli Daniel. 1970. pap. 1.25 o.p. (05019, Collier). Macmillan.

This Is Murder. Erle Stanley Gardner. LC 35-8407. 1935. W. Morrow.

This Is Murder. Charles J Kenny. LC 35-8407. 1935. W. Morrow & Co.

This Is Murder, Mr. Herbert: And Other Stories. Day Keene. LC 48-10749. 1948. Avon Pub. Co.

This Is Murder, Mr. Jones. Timothy Fuller. 1943. Little, Brown and Company.

This Is My Body. Margery Latimer. LC 30-4852. J. Cape, H. Smith.

This Is My Brother. Louis Paul. LC 43-17138. 1943. Crown Publishers.

This Is My God. Herman Wouk. 1980. pap. 3.95 (ISBN 0-671-41512-3). PB.

This Is My Man. William Babington Maxwell. LC 33-3927. 1933. Dodd, Mead & Company.

This Is My Son. Elizabeth Alexander. LC 43-15761. 1943. Doubleday, Doran and Co., Inc.

This Is My Son. Clarence Budington Kelland. LC 49-731707. 1948. Harper.

This Is Not for You. Jane Rule. LC 72-96310. 1970. 6.95. McCall Pub. Co.

This Is the Castle. Nicolas Freeling. LC 68-28225. 1968. 4.95. Harper & Row.

This Is the Hour. Lion Feuchtwanger. LC 51-10602. 1951. Viking Press.

This Is the House. Deborah Hill. (Signet Book). 1977. 1.95 (ISBN 0-451-07610-9). New American Library.

This Is the House. Deborah Hill. LC 75-26844. (ISBN 0-698-10704-7). Coward, McCann & Geoghegan.

This Is the Life. Helen Chappell White. LC 54-9834. 1955. Doubleday.

This Is the Schoolroom. Nicholas Monsarrat. LC 40-32086. 1940. A. A. Knopf.

This Is the Story of The Legacy. Elbert Hubbard. LC 7-5399. 1896. Printed at the Roycroft Printing Shop.

This Is the Town. James Warner Bellah. LC 37-17239. 1937. D. Appleton-Century Company, Incorporated.

This Is the Way That It All Happened. 1st Ed. Lena F Kirkpatrick. LC 59-12274. Greenwich Book Publishers.

This Is the Year. Feike Feikema, pseud. LC 47-2430. 1947. Doubleday & Company, Inc.

This Is the Year. Frederick Feikema Manfred. LC 47-2430. 1947. Doubleday.

This Is the Year. Frederick Feikema Manfred. LC 79-14446. (Series: Gregg Press Western Fiction Series.). 1979. 14.95. Gregg Press.

This Is What Happened. Tod Claymore. LC 39-30881. 1939. Simon and Schuster.

This Is Your Day. Edward Newhouse. LC 37-1713. 1937. L. Furman, Inc.

This Is Your Death. Dominic Devine. LC 82-5564. 10.95 (ISBN 0-312-80052-5). St. Martin's Press.

This Island, Now. Peter Abrahams. LC 66-22422. 1967. 5.95 o.p. Knopf.

This Island Earth. 1st Ed. Raymond F Jones. LC 53-5746. Shasta Publishers.

This Isn't the End. Margaret Widdemer. LC 36-34167. Farrar & Rinehart, Incorporated.

This January Tale. Bryher. LC 66-23808. (Helen & Kurt Wolff Bk). 1966. 4.95 o.p. (ISBN 0-15-190058-2). HarBraceJ.

This January Tale: By Bryher. 1st Ed. Winifred Bryher. LC 66-23808. 1966. 4.50. Harcourt.

This Journey. James Wright. 91p. 1982. 10.00 (ISBN 0-394-52365-2). Random.

This Kind of Woman: Ten Stories by Japanese Women Writers, 1960-1976. Yukiko Tanaka & Elizabeth Hanson. LC 81-51332. 1982. 18.75 (ISBN 0-8047-1130-5). Stanford University Press.

This Labyrinthine Life: A Tale of the Arizona Desert. George Alexander Fischer. LC 7-11590. 1907. B.W. Dodge & Co.

This Land Fulfilled. 1st Ed. Charles Andrew Brady. LC 58-9591. 1958. Dutton.

This Land I Hold. Virginia Myers. LC 50-10146. 1950. Bobbs-Merrill.

This Land Is Mine. Hess Harley. (Orig.). 1980. pap. 1.75 (ISBN 0-532-23227-5). Woodhill.

This Land Is Mine! Tex Holt, pseud. 1963. Arcadia House.

This Land Is Mine. Frances Casey Kerns. LC 74-9990. (Illus.). 1974. 7.95 (ISBN 0-690-00589-X). Crowell.

This Land Is Ours. Louis Zara. LC 40-27418. 1940. Houghton Mifflin Company.

This Land, These People: By Howard Fast and Others. Ed. by Harold Uriel Ribalow. LC 50-11139. Beechhurst Press.

This Land Turns Evil Slowly. Mary L. Roby. Bd. with Dig a Narrow Grave. 1978. pap. 2.50 (ISBN 0-451-11696-8, AE1696, Sig). NAL.

This Little World. Florence Olmstead. 1921. C. Scribner's Sons.

This Little World. Francis Brett Young. LC 34-32948. 1934. Harper & Brothers.

This Little World: A Novel. David Christie Murray. LC 7-31825. (Half-title: Appleton's town and country library, no. 236). 1898. D. Appleton and Company.

This Lonely House. John R. Milton. 1968. 3.75 o.s.i. (ISBN 0-911506-08-X). Thueson.

This Love to Hold. Neubauer, William Arthur. LC 66-2954. 1966. Arcadia House.

This Loving Torment. Valerie Sherwood. 1977. 1.95 (ISBN 0-446-89415-X). Warner Books.

This Mad Ideal: A Novel. Floyd Dell. LC 25-77523. 1925. A. A. Knopf.

This Magic Dust. Constance Cassady. LC 37-257603. The Bobbs-Merrill Company.

This Magic Dust. Constance Wagner. LC 37-25760. The Bobbs-Merrill Company.

This Magnificent World. John Mayo Goss. LC 48-106313. 1948. Rinehart.

This Man. Maurice B Gardner. LC 37-166444. 1937. Meador Publishing Company.

This Man Adams: The Man Who Never Died. Samuel McCoy. 1928. 17.50 o.p. (ISBN 0-8274-3597-5). R West.

This Man & This Woman. Jim Bishop. 320p. 1975. pap. 1.50 (ISBN 0-532-15161-5, 532-15161-150). Woodhill.

This Man & This Woman. Jim Bishop. Orig. Title: Honeymoon Diary. 320p. 1973. pap. 1.25 o.p. (532-12152-125). Manor Bks.

This Man and This Woman. Katharine Brush. LC 44-8991. The Blakiston Company.

This Man and This Woman. James Thomas Farrell. LC 51-13556. 1951. Vanguard Press.

This Man and This Woman. Florence Bingham Livingston. LC 28-9653. 1928. Doubleday, Doran & Company, Inc.

This Man and This Woman. Donald Stauffer. LC 30-472279. 1930. H. Liveright.

This Man Did I Kill? John Creasey. LC 74-78516. 1974. 5.95 (ISBN 0-8128-1714-1). Stein and Day.

This Man Is My Brother. Myron Brinig. LC 32-2661. Farrar & Rinehart, Incorporated.

This Man Is Yours. Rob Eden. LC 38-668989. M. S. Mill Co., Inc.

This Man Joe Murray. William Corcoran. LC 37-23642. 1937. Little, Brown and Company.

This Man Lives. 1st Ed. Jettie Irving Felps. LC 51-14968. Pageant Press.

This Man's Art. Walton Hall Smith. LC 31-15554. 1931. Doubleday, Doran & Company, Inc.

This Man's Wife: A Story of Woman's Faith. George Manville Fenn. LC 6-39390. 1887. J. W. Lovell Company.

This Man's World. Irvin Shrewsbury Cobb. LC 29-5955. 1929. Cosmopolitan Book Corporation.

This Man's World. Will Levington Comfort. LC 21-19387. 1921. Doubleday, Page & Company.

This Marriage. Edith Kneipple Roberts. LC 41-3614. The Bobbs-Merrill Company.

This Marrying. Margaret Culkin Banning. LC 20-5228. 1.75. George H. Doran Company.

This Misery of Boots. Herbert George Wells. 1907. lib. bdg. 7.50 (ISBN 0-8414-9416-9). Folcroft.

This Mortal Coil. Ed. by Cynthia Mary Evelyn Charteris Asquith. LC 47-18968. 1947. Arkham House.

This Mrs. Kingi. Frances Cleary. 1972. 5.40 o.s.i. (ISBN 0-535-00025-1). Tri-Ocean.

This Much and More. Michael Drury. 1973. 0.95. Pocket Books.

This Much Is Mine! Nola Henderson. LC 34-3088. 1934. H. Smith & R. Haas.

This Murderous Shaft. Helen Joan Hultman. LC 46-2504. 1946. Phoenix Press.

This, My Brother. John Rood. LC 36-359749. 1936. Midwest Federation of Arts and Professions.

This, My Brother: A Novel. Argye M Briggs. LC 50-7008. 1950. W. B. Eerdmans Pub. Co.

This, My House. Nelia Gardner White. LC 33-64793. 1933. Frederick A. Stokes Company.

This, My Island. Lisl Beer, pseud. LC 63-7374. 1963. Bruce Humphries.

This, My Son" (Les Noellets) Rene Basin. Tr. by Angelo Solomon Rappoport. LC 9-6572. 1909. C. Scribner's Sons.

This Mysterious River. Melvin Richard Ellis. (Laurel-leaf library). 1973. 0.95. Dell.

This Mysterious River. Melvin Richard Ellis. LC 74-182753. 1972. 5.95 (ISBN 0-03-091347-0). Holt, Rinehart and Winston.

This Naughty World. 1st Ed. William Engel. LC 54-11293. 1954. Pageant Press.

This Nettle, Danger: A Novel. Philip Hamilton Gibbs. LC 39-27187. 1939. Doubleday, Doran & Company, Inc.

This New Madness. Joseph Bercovici. LC 35-2888. The Macaulay Company.

This Night Called Day. Edward J Edwards. LC 46-892220. 1945. The Bruce Publishing Company.

This Old, Evil House. Laura Frances Brooks. (Ace gothic no. 16). 1975. (pbk.) 0.95. Ace Books.

This One Kindness. Ethel Powelson Hueston. LC 42-156922. 1942. The Bobbs-Merrill Company.

This One Night. Denise Robins. 1975. (pbk.) 0.95 (ISBN 0-380-00410-0). Avon.

This Other Eden. Marilyn Harris. LC 76-25236. 8.95. Putnam.

This Other Eden. Marilyn Harris. 1978. 2.25 (ISBN 0-380-01840-3). Avon.

This Our Exile. David Burnham. LC 31-6083. 1931. C. Scribner's Sons.

This Our Heritage: A Novel. Desemea Wilson. E. P. Dutton & Co., Inc.

This Outcast Generation. Luminous Moss. Taijun Takeda. LC 67-20951. (Library of Japanese literature). 1967. C. E. Tuttle Co.

This Outward Angel. Alanna Knight. (Orig.). 1972. pap. 0.95 o.p. (75-359). Lancer.

This Paris. Barry Devlin. LC 55-436744. 1955. Vixen Press.

This Passing Night. 1st Ed. Clive T Miller. LC 62-145595. 1962. Harper & Row.

This Passion Never Dies. Sophus Keith Winther. LC 38-11080. 1938. The Macmillan Company.

This Passover or the Next I Will Never Be in Jerusalem. Hilton Obenzinger. LC 80-20986. 1980. lib. bdg. 12.50x (ISBN 0-917672-13-5); pap. 4.95x (ISBN 0-917672-12-7). Momos.

This Pen for Hire. John Leonard. LC 72-92597. 384p. 1973. 7.95 o.p. (ISBN 0-385-03923-9). Doubleday.

This People. Ludwig Lewisohn. LC 33-65790. 1933. Harper & Brothers.

This Perfect Day. Ira Levin. 1979. pap. 2.25 (ISBN 0-440-18704-4). Dell.

This Perfect Day: A Novel. Ira Levin. LC 70-102346. 1970. 6.95. Random House.

This Pleasant Lea. Anne Crone. LC 51-6678. 1951. Scribner.

This Poor Player. Shirley Watkins. LC 29-8002. Macrae-Smith Company.

This Porcelain Clay. Naomi Ellington Jacob. LC 39-27735. 1939. The Macmillan Company.

This Pounding Wheel: A Novel. Albert Benjamin Cunningham. LC 47-353185. 1947. E. P. Dutton & Company, Inc.

This Precious Dust: A Novel. Rita Kissin. LC 48-775. 1948. Ziff-Davis Pub. Co.

This Promised Land. Gloria Goldreich. 448p. 1982. pap. 3.50 (ISBN 0-425-05464-0). Berkley Pub.

This Promised Land: A Novel of California. Robert Olney Easton. LC 82-1255. 1982. 18.00 (ISBN 0-88496-183-4). Capra Press.

This Proud Heart... Pearl Sydenstricker Buck. LC 38-27051. Reynal & Hitchcock.

This Proud Land: The Blue Ridge Mountains. John F. West & Bruce Roberts. LC 74-20051. (Illus., Orig.). 1974. pap. 4.50 (ISBN 0-87461-960-2). McNally.

This Pure Young Man. Irving Fineman. LC 30-27770. 1930. Longmans, Green and Co.

This Range Is Mine. Willis Todhunter Ballard. LC 75-19102. 1975. 0.95. Ballantine Books.

This Range Is Mine. Paul Evan. (YA) 1973. 4.95 o.p. (Avalon). Bouregy.

This Range Is Mine. Paul Evan Lehman. LC 53-7475. 1953. Bouregy & Curl.

This Ravaged Heart. Barbara Riefe. LC 76-51626. 416p. 1977. pap. 2.95 (ISBN 0-87216-890-5). Playboy Pbks.

This Rebel Hunter. Lynn Le Mon. 2.50 (ISBN 0-671-83560-2). Pocket Books.

This Remembered Glory. By Joan Garrison Pseud. William Arthur Neubauer. LC 56-10913. 1956. Arcadia House.

This Right I Claim. Doris M Hume. LC 42-14393. 1942. Macrae Smith Company.

This Rough Magic. Edith Pargeter. 1981. 18.95x (Pub. by Remploy England). State Mutual Bk.

This Rough Magic. Mary Stewart. LC 64-21158. 1964. M. S. Mill Co.; Distributed by Morrow.

This Russian Land. George Alexis Bankoff. LC 43-6282. 1943. Hutchinson.

This Russian Land. George Borodin. LC 43-6282. 1943. Hutchinson & Co., Ltd.

This Same Flower. Jeannette Covert Nolan. LC 48-4617. Appleton-Century-Crofts.

This Savage Land. Burt Womack. (Fawcett Gold Medal Book). 1977. 1.75. (ISBN 0-449-13793-7). Fawcett Publications.

This Scheming World. Saikaku Ihara. LC 65-17850. (Tut Book). (Library of Japanese literature). 1973. (pbk.) 2.95 (ISBN 0-8048-1115-6). Tuttle.

This Scheming World. Tr. by Masanori Takatsuka, David C. Stubbs. Saikaku Ihara. LC 65-17850. (Lib. of Japanese lit.). 3.50. Tuttle.

This Sentient Earth. Trevor Hoyle. (Orig.). 1979. pap. 1.95 (ISBN 0-89083-473-3). Zebra.

This Shrouded Night. Dana Fuller Ross. 1975. (pbk.) 0.95 (ISBN 0-671-77954-0). Pocket Books.

This Side Idolatry: A Novel Based on the Life of Charles Dickens. Carl Eric Bechhofer Roberts. LC 28-21370. The Bobbs-Merrill Company.

This Side Jordan. Margaret Laurence. LC 76-377653. (New Canadian library; no. 126). 1976. 2.95 (ISBN 0-7710-9226-1). McClelland and Stewart.

This Side Jordan: A Novel. Margaret Laurence. LC 60-13874. 1960. St. Martin's Press.

This Side of Glory. Gwen Bristow. 1961. Grosset & Dunlap.

This Side of Glory. Gwen Bristow. LC 40-27259. 1940. Thomas Y. Crowell Company.

This Side of Heaven. Anne Tedlock Brooks. LC 43-145684. 1943. Arcadia House, Inc.

This Side of Heaven. Alexandra Scott. (Harlequin Romances Ser.). 192p. 1982. pap. 1.50 (ISBN 0-373-02514-9). Harlequin Bks.

This Side of Innocence. Taylor Caldwell. 1974. (pbk.) 1.50. Popular Library.

This Side of Innocence. Taylor Caldwell. LC 46-250923. 1946. C. Scribner's Sons.

This Side of Jordan. Roark Bradford. LC 29-36605. 1929. Harper & Brothers.

This Side of Land: An Island Epic. Elizabeth Hollister Frost. LC 42-363196. 1942. Coward-McCann, Inc.

This Side of Love. Paula Christian. LC 78-103687. 1978. 4.50 (ISBN 0-931328-01-2). Timely Books.

This Side of Paradise. Francis Scott Key Fitzgerald. LC 25-7167. 1920. A. L. Burt Company.

This Side of Paradise. Francis Scott Key Fitzgerald. LC 29-643025. 1920. C. Scribner's Sons.

This Side of Paradise. Francis Scott Key Fitzgerald. LC 22-5177. 1921. C. Scribner's Sons.

This Side of Paradise. Kay Thorpe. (Harlequin Presents Ser.). (Orig.). 1980. pap. 1.50 (ISBN 0-373-70836-X, Pub. by Harlequin). PB.

This Side of Regret. Clarissa Fairchild Cushman. LC 37-11440. 1937. Little, Brown and Company.

This Side of Sin. James Noble Gifford. LC 40-35999. 1940. Phoenix Press.

This Side of Sin. John Saxon. LC 40-359995. Phoenix Press.

This Side of the Sky. James Barlow. LC 64-17500. 1964. Simon and Schuster.

This Side of the Stars. 1st Ed. Louise Bailey Burgess. LC 57-13419. 1958. Borden Pub. Co.
This Side of Tomorrow. Ruth Livingston Hill. 1972. 1.25. Zondervan.
This Side of Tomorrow. Ruth Livingston Hill Munce. LC 63-1860. Zondervan Pub. House.
This Side, the Other Side. Minh C Hoai Trinh. LC 80-81781. 1980. 8.95 (ISBN 0-911050-48-5). Occidental Press.
This Simian World. Clarence Day. 1968. 4.50 o.p. Knopf.
This Solid Flesh: A Novel of Intermarriage Between East and West. Bradford Smith. LC 37-8398. The Bobbs-Merrill Company.
This Son of Vulcan. library ed. Walter Besant & Rice, James. LC 3-28171. 1888. Dodd, Mead & Co.
This Sorching Earth: A Novel. Donald Richie. LC 55-10624. 1956. Tuttle.
This Sorry Scheme. Bruce Marshall. LC 25-4206. Harcourt, Brace and Company.
This Splendid Breed. Denis Meadows. LC 46-1634. 1945. J. Long Limited.
This Splendid Earth. Victor J Banis. LC 77-10283. 1978. 10.00. St. Martin's Press.
This Splendid Land. Chet Cunningham. (Leisure book). 1.95 (ISBN 0-8439-0638-3). Nordon Pubns.
This Splendid Peril. Rosemary Fitzgerald. (Orig.). 1982. pap. 3.50 (ISBN 0-440-18810-5). Dell.
This Sporting Life. David Storey. LC 60-12956. 1960. Macmillan.
This Spring of Love. Charles Henry Mergendahl. LC 48-7019. 1948. Doubleday.
This Stage of Fools. Leonard Merrick. LC 13-8080. 1913. M. Kennerly.
This Stony Ground. Vera Minshall. LC 69-11641. 1969. 2.95. Zondervan Pub. House.
This Strange Adventure. Mary Roberts Rinehart. LC 29-262710. 1929. Doubleday, Doran & Company, Inc.
This Strange Love. Phyllis Gordon Demarest. LC 39-271531. The Macaulay Company.
This Stranger, My Son. Louise Wilson. pap. 2.50 (ISBN 0-451-11301-2, AE1301, Sig). NAL.
This Stranger My Son: A Mother's Story. Louise Wilson. 1968. 6.95 (ISBN 0-399-10797-5). Putnam Pub Group.
This Suitcase Is Going to Explode. Tom Ardies. LC 79-180054. 1972. 5.95. Doubleday.
This Summer's Dolphin. Maurice Shadbolt. LC 69-15515. 1969. 4.95. Atheneum.
This Sunday. Jose Donoso. LC 67-18600. 1967. Knopf.
This Sweet and Bitter Earth. Alexander Cordell, pseud. LC 78-4009. 1978. 9.95 (ISBN 0-312-80067-3). St. Martin's Press.
This Sweet Sickness. Patricia Highsmith. 250p. 1982. pap. 3.50 (ISBN 0-14-003469-2). Penguin.
This Sweet Sickness. Patricia Highsmith. 1970. pap. 0.75 o.p. (75-290). Manor Bks.
This Sweet Sickness. 1st Ed. Patricia Highsmith. LC 59-133124. 1960. Harper.
This Tangled Web: By Maxine Dale Pseud. Alice Lent Covert. LC 52-11976. 1952. Bouregy & Curl.
This Thing Called Freedom. Howard Rockey. LC 32-21424. The Macaulay Company.
This Thing Called Love. Elizabeth Carfrae, pseud. LC 34-3733. 1934. G. P. Putnam's Sons.
This Thing Called Love. Elizabeth Carfrae, pseud. LC 42-117041. 1941. Triangle Books.
This Thing Called Love. Louis Arthur Cunningham. LC 30-24354. 1929. L. Carrier & Co.
This Thing Called Love: A Collection of Stories Edited by Marc Slonim and Havey Breit. Ed. by Mark L'Vovich Slonim & Harvey Breit. LC 55-11507. (Signet books, 1234). 1955. New American Library.
This Thing Don't Lead to Heaven. Harry Crews. LC 78-103712. 1970. 5.95. Morrow.
This Time a Better Earth: A Novel by Ted Allan... Ted Allan. LC 39-4904. 1939. W. Morrow & Co.
This Time Forever. Alice Lent Covert. LC 32-10650. 1952. Bouregy & Curl.
This Time Forever. Elaine Lowell. 256p. (YA) 1972. 6.95 (Avalon). Bouregy.
This Time Forever: A Romance. Stanley Kauffmann. LC 45-2912. 1945. Doubleday, Doran and Company, Inc.
This Time Forever: By Eleanor Browne... Eleanor Browne. LC 35-5370. 1935. Arcadia House.
This Time in Twilight. Anthony Tuttle. LC 66-17257. 5.95. New Amer. Lib.
This Time It's Love. Barbara Cartland. 1977. pap. 1.25 o.p. (ISBN 0-515-03994-2). BJ Pub Group.
This Time Next Year. Anne N. Stallworth. 1973. pap. 1.25 o.p. Curtis.
This Time Next Year. Anne Nall Stallworth. LC 74-155672. 288p. 1972. 10.95 (ISBN 0-8149-0704-0). Vanguard.
This Time Next Year: A Novel. Anne Nall Stallworth. LC 74-155672. 1972. 6.95 (ISBN 0-8149-0729-6). Vanguard Press.
This Time of Morning. Nayantara Pandit Sahgal. 221p. 1969. pap. 1.95 (ISBN 0-88253-079-8). Ind-US Inc.
This Time of Morning: A Novel. Nayantara Pandit Sahgal. LC 65-25939. 1966. bds., 4.50. Norton.
This, Too, Is Love. Georgia Craig. 1967. pap. 0.60 o.p. (60-295). Manor Bks.
This, Too, Is Love. Peggy Gaddis, pseud. LC 50-5186. 1949. Arcadia House.
This Towering Passion. Valerie Sherwood. 512p. (Orig.). 1978. pap. 3.95 (ISBN 0-446-30770-X). Warner Bks.
This Town Needs a Doctor. Libbie Block. LC 75-132501. 1971. 6.95. Doubleday.
This Traitor Moon. Amanda J. Jarrett. 320p. 1983. pap. 3.50 (ISBN 0-440-08813-5, Bryans). Dell.
This Triumphant Fire. Anne Carsley. 352p. 1982. pap. 2.95 (ISBN 0-380-79632-5, 79632). Avon.
This Troublesome World. Elizabeth Thomasina Meade Smith. LC 8-86556. 1893. Macmillan Co.
This Uncertain Love. William Edward Daniel Ross. 1982. 6.95 (Avalon). Bouregy.
This Very Day. David F. Barr. LC 76-48111. 1977. 7.95 (ISBN 0-8361-1803-0). Herald Press.
This Very Earth. Erskine Caldwell. LC 48-7977. 1948. Duell, Sloan and Pearce.
This Very Sun. Edith Heal. LC 44-47197. 1944. Crown Publishers.
This Very Tree. Josephine Young Case. LC 69-19566. (Illus.). 1969. 4.95. Houghton Mifflin.
This Violent Land: A Novel. William H Jacobs. LC 59-7891. 1959. F. Fell.
This Wanderer. Louis Golding. LC 35-1598. Farrar & Rinehart, Inc.
This Was a Man"... A Romance. Hattie Horner Louthan. LC 6-453553. 1906. The C. M. Clark Publishing Co.
This Was Alaska. Mary Muckala Parker. LC 50-58264. 1950. Tewkesbury.
This Was Ivor Trent. Claude Houghton Oldfield. LC 35-447. 1935. Doubleday, Doran & Company, Inc.
This Was Lidice. Gustav Holm & Abbott, Elisabeth, Tr. LC 43-51291. 1943. G. P. Putnam's Sons.
This Was Life. James Weber Linn. LC 36-3330. The Bobbs-Merrill Company.
This Was Sandra. Beren Van Slyke. LC 38-29535. 1938. Funk & Wagnalls Company.
This Was Their Land. Alma Estelle Lloyd. LC 43-13076. 1943. Harper & Brothers.
This Was Tomorrow. Thane, Elswyth. LC 51-10411. 1951. Duell, Sloan and Pearce.
This Was Tomorrow. Elswyth Thane. LC 76-5517. 1976. (ISBN 0-88411-962-9). Aeonian Press.
This Was Tomorrow. Elswyth Thane. LC 80-25604. 1981. 14.95 (ISBN 0-8161-3161-9). G. K. Hall.
This Way for Love: By Joan Garrison Pseud. William Arthur Neubauer. LC 57-979809. 1957. Arcadia House.
This Way for the Gas, Ladies and Gentlemen: And Other Stories. Tadeusz Borowski. LC 67-21889. 1967. Viking Press.
This Way for the Gas, Ladies and Gentlemen. Tadeusz Borowski. (Writers from the other Europe). 1976. 2.95. Penguin Books.
This Way Out". Paul Hutchens. LC 36-762537. 1935. W. B. Eerdmans Publishing Co.
This Way Out. Frederic Stewart Isham. LC 17-251205. The Bobbs-Merrill Company.
This Way Out. Philip Littell. LC 28-211822. 1928. Coward-McCann, Inc.
This Way Out. James Ronald. LC 41-12024. J. B. Lippincott Company.
This Way Out. Anna McClure Sholl. LC 15-246691. 1915. Hearst's International Libarary Co.
This Way to Happiness. Maysie Greig. LC 32-24678. 1932. L. MacVeagh, Dial Press, Inc.
This Way to Happiness. Clyde Narramore. 1969. pap. 0.95 o.p. (FN1965). Pyramid Pubns.
This Way to Hell. Harry Sinclair Drago. LC 33-7561. The Macaulay Company.
This Way to the Stars. Elizabeth Carfrae, pseud. LC 37-39118. G. P. Putnam's Sons.
This Way up. Solita Solano. LC 27-193195. 1927. G. P. Putnam's Sons.
This Week's Short-Short Stories. Edited, with an Introd. and an Essay, How to Write a Short-Short Story, by Stewart Beach. This Week Magazine. Ed. by Stewart Beach. LC 53-5607. 1953. Random House.
This Week's Stories of Mystery and Suspense: Edited, with a Pref., Notes, and an Essay, 'How to Write the Mystery and Suspense Story,' by Stewart Beach. Introd. by Alfred Hitchcock. This Week Magazine. Ed. by Stewart Beach. LC 57-10038. 1957. Random House.
This Whiskey Room and Other Stories. Jackie A Moore. LC 64-8206. 1964. William-Frederick Press.
This Wild Heart. Margarett McKean. (Second Chance at Love Ser.: No. 91). 1982. pap. 1.75. Jove Pubns.
This Wild Land: A Novel. Cody Kennedy. 1979. 1.95 (ISBN 0-446-89675-6). Warner Books.
This Willing Passion. Patricia Cloud. LC 77-18048. 9.95. Putnam.
This Winged World: An Anthology of Aviation Fiction. Ed. by Thomas Collison. LC 43-160901. 1943. Coward-McCann, Inc.
This Witch. Wilson Tucker. LC 70-157630. 1971. Published for the Crime Club by Doubleday.
This Woman. Howard Rockey. LC 24-510333. The Macaulay Company.
This Woman and This Man. Katharine Newlin Burt. LC 34-33671. 1934. C. Scribner's Sons.
This Woman Is Death. Stephen Frances. (John Gail Ser.). (O.s.i.: No. 1). 1969. pap. 0.60 o.s.i. (A512X, Award). Univ Pub & Dist.
This Woman Wanted. Elinore Denniston. LC 76-136503. (Red badge novel of suspense). 1971. 4.95 (ISBN 0-396-06285-7). Dodd, Mead.
This Woman Wanted. Rae Foley. 1971. 4.95 o.p. (ISBN 0-396-06285-7). Dodd.
This World & Nearer Ones: Essays Exploring the Familiar. Brian Wilson Aldiss. LC 81-9179. (Illus.). 261p. 1981. pap. 6.95 (ISBN 0-87338-261-7). Kent St U Pr.
This World Does Not Belong to the Old Ladies. Elizabeth Fisher. 28p. (Orig.). 1976. pap. 5.00. Iron Mtn Pr.
This World Is Mine. Luigi Creatore. LC 47-1211. 1947. Rinehart & Company, Inc.
This World Is Ours. Kathleen Rollins. LC 37-16933. Arcadia House.
This World of Ours. Jane Werner Watson. (Giant little golden book). 1959. Golden Press.
This Wound. August William Derleth. 3.50 o.p. Arkham.
This Wounded Passion. Jess Wilcox. 1978. pap. 2.25 (ISBN 0-532-22121-4). Woodhill.
This Year in Jerusalem. Joel Gross. 304p. 1983. 14.95 (ISBN 0-399-12812-3, Putnam). Putnam Pub Group.
This Year: Next Year Sometime-- Berta Ruck. LC 32-12519. 1932. Dodd, Mead & Company.
This Year's Death. John Godey. (Berkley medallion book). 1974. (pbk.) 0.95 (ISBN 0-425-02538-1). Berkley Pub. Co.
This Year's Death: By John Godey Pseud. 1st Ed. Morton Freedgood. LC 52-13385. 1953. Published for the Crime Club by Doubleday.
This Year's Sin. Florence Stonebraker. LC 45-8586. 1945. Phoenix Press.
This'll Kill You. Marie Freid Rodell. LC 40-32862. H. Holt and Company.
Thistle & the Rose. Hester W. Chapman. 1972. pap. 1.25 o.p. (ISBN 0-515-02860-6, V2860). Pyramid Pubns.
Thistle and the Rose. Eleanor Hibbert. LC 73-76152. 1973. 6.95 (ISBN 0-399-11196-4). Putnam.
Thistle and the Rose. Eleanor Hibbert. (Berkley Medallion book). 1974. (pbk.) 1.50 (ISBN 0-425-02634-5). Berkley Pub. Co.
Thistle Down. Jeannea O'Casey. 1976. 3.95 o.p. (ISBN 0-8059-2326-8). Dorrance.
Thistle Sifters. Charles Russell Burke. LC 6-18656. F. T. Neely.
Thistles & Roses. Iain Crichton Smith. 1961. 4.95 o.p. Dufour.
Thistles of the Baragan... Panalt Istrati & Le Clercq, Jacques Georges Clemenceau, 1896- Tr. The Vanguard Press.
Thomas. H B Creswell. LC 19-4113. 1918. R. M. McBride & Company.
Thomas: A Novel of the Life, Passion, and Miracles of Becket. Shelley Smith Mydans. (Signet bk., Q3111). New Amer. Lib.
Thomas: A Novel of the Life, Passion, and Miracles of Becket. Shelley Smith Mydans. LC 65-14012. (Illus.). 1965. Doubleday.
Thomas Berryman Number. James Patterson. LC 75-38617. (ISBN 0-316-69361-8). Little, Brown.
Thomas Boobig. A Complete Enough Account of His Life and Singular Disapperance. Narration of His Scribe. Luther Marshall. Lee and Shepard.
Thomas Carlyle. A History of the First Forty Years of His Life, 1795-1835. James Anthony Froude. LC 21-15358. (Seaside library, v. 63, no. 1277). 1882. G. Munro.
Thomas Forty: A Novel. Edward Stanley. LC 47-11829. 1947. Duell, Sloan and Pearce.
Thomas Hard, Priest. William H. Lewis. LC 7-14363. A.D.F. Randolph & Company.
Thomas Hardy Omnibus. Thomas Hardy. LC 78-20727. 1979. 15.00 (ISBN 0-312-80157-2). St. Martin's Press.
Thomas Hardy Selected Stories. Thomas Hardy. 1980. pap. 3.95 (ISBN 0-312-71119-0). St Martin.
Thomas Hardy's The Return of the Native. Thomas Hardy. Ed. by Haworth, Irene M. LC 31-10088. (Modern literature series). Ginn and Company.
Thomas Holcroft and the Revolutinary Novel. by rodney m. baine. ed. Rodney M Baine. LC 65-24599. (University of Georgia Monographs, No. 13). 1965. University of Georgia Press.
Thomas L'imposteur. Ed. by Bernard Garniez. Jean Cocteau. LC 64-11034. (Macmillan mod. French lit. ser., 32309). pap., 1.95. Macmillan.
Thomas Mason: Adventurer. Henry Pleasants. LC 34-238088. The John C. Winston Co.
Thomas of Reading; or, the Sixe Worthy Yeomen of the West. Thomas Deloney. 1975. text ed. 7.50x o.s.i. (ISBN 0-8277-3800-5); pap. text ed. 4.95x o.s.i. (ISBN 0-8277-2181-1). British Bk Ctr.
Thomas Onetwo. Ernest M Robson. LC 70-28038. (Illus.). 1971. (ISBN 0-87110-074-6). Something Else Press.
Thomas Ruffin. A Novel. Edward Winslow Gilliam. LC 6-44045. 1896. Nichols, Killam & Maffitt.
Thomas Rutherton: Anovel. John Henton Carter. LC 6-228059. H. C. Nixon.
Thomas the Fish. Diana Morgan. LC 76-381831. 1976. 2.95 (ISBN 0-09-127310-2). Hutchinson.
Thomas the Imposter. Jean Cocteau. Tr. by Galantiere, Lewis. LC 25-2660. 1925. D. Appleton and Company.
Thomas the Impostor: A Story. Jean Cocteau & Galantiere, Lewis, Tr. LC 25-2660. 1925. D. Appleton and Company.
Thomas the Lambkin: Gentleman of Fortune; Authorized Translation from the French. Claude Farrere. Tr. by Ongley, Leo. LC 24-22266. E. P. Dutton & Co.
Thomas the Obscure. Maurice Blanchot. LC 73-85970. 1973. 8.50. D. Lewis.
Thomas-Thomas-Ancil-Thomas. Robert Peter Tristram Coffin. LC 41-604692. 1941. The Macmillan Company.
Thomas Wingfold, Curate. George Macdonald. LC 4-16310. 1876. G. Routledge and Sons.
Thomas Wingfold, Curate. George Macdonald. (Seaside library, v. 30, no. 627). 1879. G. Munro.
Thomas Wingfold, Curate. George Macdonald. LC 12-18322. 1911. D. McKay.
Thomasheen James. Maurice Walsh. LC 41-522629. 1941. Frederick A. Stokes Company.
Thomasheen James Gets His Hair Cut. & Other Stories. Maurice Walsh. LC 64-22182. 1964. Lippincott.
Thomasina. Paul Gallico. 1981. 2.25 (ISBN 0-380-53009-0). Avon Books.
Thomasina: The Cat Who Thought She Was God. Paul Gallico. LC 57-13018. 1957. 5.95 o.p. (ISBN 0-385-04804-1). Doubleday.
Thompson Street Poker Club: From "Life"... Henry Guy Carleton. LC 11-10549. 1888. White and Allen.
Thompson's Progress. Charles John Cutcliffe Wright Hyne. LC 3-15227. 1903. The Macmillan Company.
Thongor and the Dragon City. Lin Carter. (Berkley Medallion Book). 1976. (pbk.) 0.95 (ISBN 0-425-03068-7). Berkley Publishing Corp.
Thongor and the Wizard of Lemuria. Lin Carter. (Berkley Medallion Book). 1976. (pbk.) 0.95 (ISBN 0-425-03042-3). Berkley Publishing Corp.
Thongs. Alexander Trocchi. LC 77-286398. (Brandon House library edition, 2038). 1967. Brandon House.
THorace Everett: A Novel. Clara Hammond Lanza. LC 11-15094. 1897. G. W. Dillingham Co.
Thora's Sacrifice. Kurt Brand. (Perry Rhodan, 70). (Illus.). 1975. (pbk.) 1.25. Ace Books.
Thord Firetooth. Alice Alison Lide & Margaret Alison Johansen. LC 37-13966. 1937. Lothrop, Lee and Shepard Company.
Thoreau: People, Principles, & Politics. Henry D. Thoreau. Ed. by Milton Meltzer. 235p. 1963. 4.95 o.p. (ISBN 0-8090-9350-2). Hill & Wang.
Thorgils. Maurice Henry Hewlett. LC 17-51278. 1917. 1.35. Dodd, Mead and Company.
Thorley Weir. Edward Frederic Benson. LC 13-21027. 1913. 1.35. J. B. Lippincott Company.
Thorn. Fred Saberhagen. 1980. pap. 2.75 (ISBN 0-441-80744-5). Ace Bks.
Thorn. Lois Worbois. 128p. 1977. pap. 3.25 (ISBN 0-89367-005-7). Light & Life.
Thorn-Apple Tree. Grace MacLennan Grant Campbell. LC 43-51037. 1943. Duell, Sloan and Pearce.
Thorn Birds. Colleen McCullough. LC 76-26271. 9.95 (ISBN 0-06-012956-5). Harper & Row.
Thorn Birds. Colleen McCullough. LC 78-7340. 1978. 21.95 (ISBN 0-8161-6580-7). G. K. Hall.
Thorn Bush Blooms. Rosalyn Alsobrook. 304p. (Orig.). 1981. pap. 2.95 (ISBN 0-505-51753-1). Tower Bks.
Thorn for the Flesh. Robert Boston. LC 72-9763. 1973. 6.95 (ISBN 0-06-010406-6). Harper & Row.
Thorn in Her Heart. Charlotte Mary Brame. LC 44-38087. (On cover: Seaside library. Pocket ed. No. 1008). G. Munro.

Thorn in Her Heart: A Novel. Charlotte Mary Brame. LC 5200. (Bertha Clay library, no. 25). 1900. Street & Smith.
Thorn in His Side. Shelby Steger. Orig. Title: Desire in the Ozarks. 1972. pap. 0.75 o.p. (532-00463-075). Manor Bks.
Thorn in the Flesh: A Dramatic Novel. Ida Josephine Scott. LC 46-12926. 1945. Meador Publishing Company.
Thorn in the Flesh: A Novel. Grace Brown. 1968. 3.95 o.p. Vantage.
Thorn in the Nest. Martha Finley. LC 6-41218. Dodd, Mead & Company.
Thorn in the Rose. Maye Barrett. 192p. (Orig.). 1980. pap. 1.75 (ISBN 0-515-05631-6). Jove Pubns.
Thorn of Arimathea. Frank Gill Slaughter. LC 59-6372. 1959. Doubleday.
Thorn of Arimathea. Frank Gill Slaughter. LC 75-38767. 1975. 9.95 (ISBN 0-89190-288-0). American Reprint Co.
Thorn of Arimathea. Frank Gill Slaughter. (Kangaroo Book). 1977. 1.95 (ISBN 0-671-80899-0). Pocket Books.
Thorn of Arimithea. Frank Gill Slaughter. 1976. Repr. of 1959 ed. lib. bdg. 16.60x (ISBN 0-89190-288-0). Am Repr-Rivercity Pr.
Thorn Tree: A Novel. Nelia Gardner White. LC 55-7375. 1955. Viking Press.
Thorn Trees. John McIntosh. LC 67-11970. 1967. Harcourt, Brace & World.
Thornblossoms. Margaret Rebecca Lay. LC 48-7552. 1949. Rinehart.
Thorne Smith Three-Bagger: The Glorious Pool, Skin and Bones, Topper. Thorne Smith. LC 43-8704. 1943. Doubleday, Doran and Company, Inc.
Thorne Smith Triplets: Illustrated by Roese. Thorne Smith. LC 39-17660. 1938. Doubleday, Doran and Company, Inc.
Thorne Smith 3-Decker. Thorne Smith. LC 36-6320. 1936. Doubleday, Doran and Company, Inc.
Thorne Theatre Mystery. Joshua Willard. LC 38-16695. Phoenix Press.
Thorney. Alexander Black. LC 13-499256. 1913. 1.25. McBride, Nast & Company.
Thornley Colton: Blind Detective. Clinton Holland Stagg. LC 24-19326. 1923. G. H. Watt.
Thorns. Robert Silverberg. LC 69-13671. 1969. 4.95. Walker.
Thorns and Orange Blossoms. Charlotte Mary Brame. LC 11-10521. J. S. Ogilvie & Company.
Thorns and Orange Blossoms. Charlotte Mary Brame. LC 44-38283. (On cover: Lovell's library, v. 17, no. 800). 1886. John W. Lowell Company.
Thorns & Roses. Ruby A. Newman. LC 79-92510. 140p. 1981. pap. 3.50 (ISBN 0-932964-05-2). MN Pubs.
Thorns in the Flesh. A Romance of the War and Ku-Klux Periods. A Voice of Vindication from the South in Answer to "A Fool's Errand" and Other Slanders... Nicholas Jackson Floyd & Gregory, Edward S. LC 6-27478. 1884. Hubbard Bros.
Thorns in the Flesh. A Romance of the War and Ku-Klux Periods.) A Voice of Vidication from the South in Answer to "A Fool's Errand" and Other Slanders... Edward S. Gregory & Gregory, Edward S., 1843-1884. LC 43-445473. 1884. J. P. Bell & Co.
Thorns in Your Sides. Harriette A Keyser. 1884. G. P. Putnam's Sons Etc.
Thorns of Defense. Bruce Merrill. LC 55-9798. 1955. Comet Press Books.
Thorns of Love. Joan Doller. LC 65-872. 1965. 4.95. De Tanko Pubs., Riverside Dr.
Thorns of Love. Joan Doller. LC 65-872. 1964. De Tanko Publishers.
Thorns of Pleasure. Bernard B. Shively. 3.50 o.p. Carlton.
Thornton Wilder Trio: The Cabala, The Bridge of San Luis Rey. The Woman of Andros. Introd. by Malcolm Cowley. Thornton Niven Wilder. LC 56-11401. 1956. Criterion Books.
Thorny Path (Per Aspera) Georg Moritz Ebers. Tr. by Clara Courtenay Bell. LC 6-43721. 1892. D. Appleton and Company.
Thornycroft Grange. A Novel. Rett Winwood. LC 8-37128. (On cover: The idle hour series. no. 16). 1892. The F. M. Lupton Publishing Company.
Thorofare. Christopher Darlington Morley. LC 42-36384. 1942. Harcourt, Brace and Company.
Thorough Bohemienne. Henriette Etiennette Fanny Arnaud Reybaud. LC 7-30927. (Appletons' new handy-volume series v. 27)). 1879. D. Appleton and Company.
Thoroughbred. William McClellan Ferguson. LC 35-1984. Phoenix Press.
Thoroughbred. Edith Macvane. G. W. Dillingham Company.
Thoroughbred. Henry Kitchell Webster. LC 17-357515. The Bobbs-Merrill Company.
Thoroughbreds. William Alexander Fraser. LC 2-25516. 1902. McClure, Phillips & Co.
Thoroughbreds. Michael Geller. 1981. pap. 2.75 (ISBN 0-8439-0901-3, Leisure Bks). Nordon Pubns.
Thoroughly Decent People: A Folktale. Glenys Ann Tomassetti. LC 77-359363. (Illus.). 1976. (ISBN 0-86914-001-9). McPhee Gribble.
Thorpe. Mary Dutton. LC 67-22272. 1967. World Pub. Co.
Thorpe: A Quiet English Town, and Human Life Therein. William Mountford. LC 7-26095. 1852. Ticknor, Reed, and Fields.
Thorpe of the Hole-in-the-Wall Country: A Story of Wyoming and the Cattle Country, Written Around One of the Most Thrilling and Dramatic Incidents in the History of the West--the "Rustler War" of 1892. Ford Douglas. LC 16-11384. (On cover: Railroad series, no. 111). J. S. Ogilvie Publishing Company.
Thorpe's Way. Morley Roberts. LC 11-69552. 1911. The Century Co.
Thor's Gold: A Novel Depicting Real Life in the Northwest from Pioneer Days... Elias Rachie. LC 27-1231. 1927.
Thorson of Thunder Gulch. Norman A Fox. LC 45-1423. 1945. Dodd, Mead & Company.
Thorton Cove. Anne Hall. 1977. pap. 1.95 (ISBN 0-532-19159-5). Woodhill.
Those About Trench. Edwin Herbert Lewis. LC 16-4390. 1916. The Macmillan Company.
Those Almost Happy Years. Willard Temple. LC 65-15837. 1965. Crown Publishers.
Those Barren Leaves. Aldous Leonard Huxley. LC 49-7993. (P3079). 1968. Harper.
Those Barren Leaves. Aldous Leonard Huxley. LC 49-7993. 1948. Harper.
Those Barren Leaves. Aldous Leonard Huxley. LC 25-2661. George H. Doran Company.
Those Black Diamond Men: A Tale of the Anthrax Valley. William Futhey Gibbons. LC 74-22785. (Labor Movement in Fiction and Non-Fiction). (Illus.). 1977. 23.50 (ISBN 0-404-58431-4). AMS Press.
Those Black Diamond Men: A Tale of the Anthrax Valley. William Futhey Gibbons. LC 2-16452. 1902. F. H. Revell Company.
Those Brewster Children. Florence Morse Kingsley. LC 10-7481. 1910. Dodd, Mead & Company.
Those Crazy Bartletts. Peggy Gaddis, pseud. LC 45-214025. 1945. Arcadia House, Inc.
Those Dale Girls. Frances Weston Carruth Prindle. LC 99-2761. 1899. A. C. McClurg & Co.
Those Delightful Americans. Sara Jeannette Duncan Cotes. LC 2-14852. 1902. D. Appleton and Company.
Those Dexters. Edwin Grey Rust. 1929. The Michie Co., Printers.
Those Difficult Years. Faith Baldwin Cuthrell. LC 25-9822. Small, Maynard & Company.
Those First Affections. Dorothy Graffe Van Doren. LC 38-279748. 1938. Houghton Mifflin Company.
Those Fitzenbergers. Helen Reimensnyder Martin. LC 17-7923. 1917. 1.35. Doubleday, Page & Company.
Those Gentle Voices: A Promethean Romance of the Spaceways. George Alec Effinger. 1976. (pbk.) 1.25 (ISBN 0-446-86113-8). Warner Books.
Those Gillespies. William John Hopkins. LC 16-10881. 1916. 1.35. Houghton Mifflin Company.
Those Girls. Henrietta Eliza Vaughan Stannard. LC 8-27080. United States Book Company.
Those Girls. Henrietta Eliza Vaughan Stannard. LC 2-12481. (Sea shore & mountain series). 1902. Street & Smith.
Those Good Normans. Sibylle Gabrielle Marie Antoinette De Riquetti De Mirabeau Martel De Janville. Tr. by Jussen, Marie. LC 7-24381. 1896. Rand, McNally & Company.
Those Good Normans. Sybille Gabrielle Marie Antoinette De Riquetti De Mirabeau Martel De Janville. Tr. by Marie Jussen. LC 7-24381. 1896. Rand, McNally & Company.
Those Harper Women: A Novel. Stephen Birmingham. LC 64-17564. 1964. McGraw-Hill.
Those Hitch Hikers. Booth Jameson. LC 30-27765. The Bobbs-Merrill Company.
Those Idiots from Earth: Ten Science-Fiction Stories. Richard Wilson. LC 57-14678. (Ballantine books, 237). 1957. Ballantine Books.
Those Little Things: Fictionized Recollections of a Congenial Family. 1st Ed. Gwen E Owens. LC 57-4539. 1957. Exposition Press.
Those of His Own Household (Madame Corentine) Rene Basin. Tr. by L. M. Leggatt. LC 14-18079. 1914. The Devin-Adair Company.
Those of His Own Household (Madame Corentine) Rene Bazin. Tr. by Lillian Marian Phillips Leggatt. LC 14-18079. 1914. The Devin-Adair Company.
Those Orphans: Or, The Trials of a Stepmother. Jennie Cooper. LC 8-29696. 1883. O. W. W. Williams.
Those Other People. Mary Paula King O'Donnell. LC 46-886. 1946. Houghton Mifflin Company.
Those Preston Twins: A Story by Lzola Forrester... Illustrated by Chase Emerson. Izola Louise Forrester. LC 10-27862. W. A. Wilde Company.
Those Pretty St. George Girls. A Society Novel... Lucy Hamilton Jones Hooper. LC 8-29693. T. B. Peterson & Brothers.
Those Queer Browns. Florence Morse Kingsley. LC 7-25050. 1907. Dodd, Mead and Company.
Those Seven Alibis. Charles Gordon Booth. LC 32-343753. 1932. W. Morrow & Company.
Those S.O.B.'s at Tarryall, and Other Tales of the Rockies. Fred Huston. LC 74-79252. (Mesquite collector series, no. 5). (Illus.). 1974. 4.95 (ISBN 0-89015-061-3). Nortex Press.
Those Subtle Weeds. Jo Ann Lordahl. 1974. (pbk.) 0.95. Ace Books.
Those the Sun Has Loved. Rose Jourdain. LC 77-82952. 1978. 10.95 (ISBN 0-385-13028-7). Doubleday.
Those Times and These. Irvin Shrewsbury Cobb. LC 72-5862. (Short story index reprint series). 1972. (ISBN 0-8369-4201-9). Books for Libraries Press.
Those Times and These. Irvin Shrewsbury Cobb. LC 17-16321. George H. Doran Company.
Those Torn from Earth. Frederick Hollander. LC 41-9497. Liveright Publishing Corporation.
Those Van Der Meer Women: A Novel. Joy Darlington. LC 78-14839. 8.95 (ISBN 0-399-12174-9). Putnam.
Those Were the Good Old Days. Edgar R. Jones. (Fireside Paperback Ser). 1971. pap. 7.95 (ISBN 0-671-21073-4, Fireside). S&S.
Those Westerton Girls. Florence Alice Price James. LC 7-7974. (On cover: Lovell's Westminister series, no. 34). 1891. J. W. Lovell Company.
Those Who Come After. Henry Legend. LC 34-68371. 1933. Dial Press, Inc.
Those Who Dare: Short Stories of the Midwest. Norman Rowcliff. 1970. pap. 1.50 o.p. Rowcliff.
Those Who Enter Here. Michael Rubin. 1970. 6.95 o.p. (ISBN 0-07-054188-4). McGraw.
Those Who Go Against the Current. Shirley Seifert. LC 43-14822. 1943. J. B. Lippincott Company.
Those Who Love. Denise Robins. 1972. pap. 0.75 o.p. (94251). Beagle Bks.
Those Who Love. Irving Stone. LC 65-19900. 1965. 11.95 (ISBN 0-385-00157-6). Doubleday.
Those Who Love. Irving Stone. pap. 2.50 (ISBN 0-451-07871-3, E7871, Sig). NAL.
Those Who Love: A Biographical Novel of Abigail and John Adams. Irving Stone. LC 65-19900. 1965. Doubleday.
Those Who Perish. Edward Dahlberg. LC 75-41071. 1977. 11.00 (ISBN 0-404-14528-0). AMS Press.
Those Who Perish. Edward Dahlberg. LC 34-28620. The John Day Company.
Those Who Remain. Eileen Marie Wade. LC 42-191599. 1942. Hutchinson & Co., Ltd.
Those Who Return (L'ombre) Maurice Level & Drillien, Berengere, Tr. LC 23-17270. 1923. R. M. McBride & Company.
Those Who Stayed Behind. Eleanor Hyde. 1981. pap. 2.95 (ISBN 0-451-11069-2, AE1109, Sig). NAL.
Those Who Walk Away. Patricia Highsmith. LC 67-11292. 1967. Published for the Crime Club by Doubleday.
Those Who Walk in Darkness. Perley Poore Sheehan. LC 17-25514. 1917. George H. Doran Company.
Those Who Watch. Robert Silverberg. 1983. pap. 2.25 (ISBN 0-451-12022-1, AE2022, Sig). NAL.
Those Without Shadows. Francoise Quoirez. LC 57-12105. 1974. (pbk.) 0.95. Popular Library.
Those Without Shadows. Francoise Sagan, pseud. Tr. by Frances Frenaye. 1957. 3.95 o.p. (ISBN 0-525-21831-9). Dutton.
Those Without Shadows: By Francoise Sagan Pseud. Translated from the French by Frances Frenaye. 1st Ed. Francoise Quoirez. LC 57-12105. 1957. Dutton.
Thou Art Peter. Lawrence Eugene Claire Joers. LC 52-4939. 1952. Vantage Press.
Thou Art the Man. Richard Blaker. LC 37-194566. R. M. McBride and Company.
Thou Art the Man. A Suggestion Story for the Christian Church. Frederic Werden Pangborn. LC 3361. Wright & Company.
Thou Fool. John Joy Bell. LC 8-235303. 1908. TheBaker & Taylor Company.
Thou Israel. Charles Francis Stocking. LC 22-2005. 1921. The Maestro Co.
Thou My Beloved... Elisabeth Stancy Payne. LC 33-29801. 1933. Dodd, Mead & Company.
Thou Shalt Not. Elsie Kendrick. LC 35-32205. Authors' Association.
Thou Shalt Not... Linn Boyd Porter. LC 7-37764. 1889. G. W. Dillingham.
Thou Shalt Not Love. Georgia Craig. LC 36-17365. G. H. Watt, Inc.
Thou Shalt Not Love. Peggy Gaddis, pseud. LC 36-1736. G. H. Watt.
Thou Shalt Not Love. Alma Sioux Scarberry. LC 37-540631. M. S. Mill Co., Inc.
Thou Shalt Not (New Series) Linn Boyd Porter. LC 7-37763. (On cover: The albatross novels). 1896. G. W. Dillingham Co.
Thou Shell of Death. Nicholas Blake. 1977. pap. 1.95i (ISBN 0-06-080428-9, P428, PL). Har-Row.
Thou Worm Jacob. Mark Mirsky. LC 67-12339. 1967. Macmillan.
Though Given in Vain, The Mysterious Egg and A Berkshire Story. Charles A Gunnison. LC 7-134. Press of Commercial Publishing Company.
Though He Slay Me. Ella M Noller. LC 41-12277. 1941. Wm. B. Eardmans Publishing Co.
Though He Slay Me. 1st Ed. Arthur Ayers. LC 56-5535. 1956. Vantage Press.
Though Hearts Resist. Meg Hudson. (Superromance Ser.). 295p. 1983. pap. 2.95 (ISBN 0-373-70064-4, Pub. by Worldwide). Harlequin Bks.
Though I Know She Lies. Sara Woods, pseud. LC 75-183536. (Rinehart suspense novel). 1972. 4.95 (ISBN 0-03-091407-8). Holt, Rinehart and Winston.
Though Life Us Do Part. Elizabeth Stuart Phelps H. D. Ward Ward. LC 8-26679. 1908. Houghton Mifflin Company.
Though the Gods and the Years Relent: Or, The Romance of Two Women. F. A. H. Morgan. (On cover: Modern novelists' series no. 8). Home Book Company.
Though the Heavens Fall.". Irene Wakeham. LC 73-108959. (Crown book). 1970. Southern Pub. Association.
Though They Go Wandering. Nona Coxhead. LC 45-2839. 1945. C. Scribner's Sons.
Though This Be Madness. Robert Keable. LC 28-21058. 1928. G. P. Putnam's Sons.
Though Time Be Fleet. Louise Andrus. LC 37-4096. 1937. Lothrop, Lee and Shepard Company.
Though Young. Leighton Barret. LC 38-13328. Random House.
Though Your Sins Be As Scarlet: A Story. Marie Florence Giles. LC 6-44050. 1898. F. T. Neely.
Thought-Reading Machine. Andre Maurois. Tr. by James Whitall. LC 38-13105. 1938. Harper & Brothers.
Thoughtful Cathy. Ethel V Pryor. (Illus.). 1974. 3.75 (ISBN 0-533-01182-5). Vantage Press.
Thoughtless Yes. Helen Hamilton Chenoweth Gardener. (On cover: Belford American novel series. no 29). Belford Company.
Thoughts in Springtime. Lewis Walton. 1979. pap. 1.25 (ISBN 0-8163-0247-2). Pacific Pr Pub Assn.
Thoughts to Live by. Maxwell Maltz. 1981. pap. 2.75 (ISBN 0-671-43999-5). PB.
Thousand. Murray Carlin. 1969. pap. 1.40x o.p. (ISBN 0-19-644085-8). Oxford U Pr.
Thousand. Murray Carlin. 1969. pap. 1.40x o.p. (ISBN 0-19-644085-8). Oxford U Pr.
Thousand a Year. E. M Bruce. LC 6-17214. 1866. Lee & Shepard.
Thousand and First Night. Grant Martin Overton. LC 24-28975. George H. Doran Company.
Thousand and One Afternoons in Chicago. Ben Hecht. LC 22-23966. 1922. Covici-McGee.
Thousand and One Nights: Or, The Arabian Nights' Entertainments. a new ed. LC 31-38226. 1881. Porter & Costes.
Thousand and Second Night: An Arabesque. Gunnar Serner & Bjorkman, Edwin August, 1866- Tr. LC 25-14714. Thomas Y. Crowell Company.
Thousand Clowns. Herb Gardner. 1962. 7.95 o.p. (ISBN 0-394-40777-6, BYR). Random.
Thousand Clowns. Herb Gardner. 126p. 1983. pap. 4.95 (ISBN 0-14-048202-4). Penguin.
Thousand Cranes. Yasunari Kawabata. LC 80-39964. (Illus.). 1981. 3.95 (ISBN 0-399-50526-1). Perigee Books.
Thousand Cranes. Translated by Edward G. Seidensticker. 1st American Ed. Yasunari Kawabata. LC 59-6220. 1959. Knopf.
Thousand Days in the Attic. Valerie Kent & Robert G Kent. LC 77-363098. Coach House Press.
Thousand Deaths of Mr. Small. 1st Ed. Gerald Kersh. LC 50-9372. 1950. Doubleday.
Thousand Diamonds in Your Backyard. George Dickinson. LC 79-88821. (Stories That Win Ser.). 1979. pap. 0.95 o.p. (ISBN 0-8163-0329-0, 20397-6). Pacific Pr Pub Assn.
Thousand Doors. Abraham Rothberg. LC 65-103074. 4.95. Holt.
Thousand Doors. Abraham Rothberg. LC 65-10307. 1965. Holt, Rinehart and Winston.

Thousand Errors. Phyllis Nichols. (Orig.). 1980. pap. 1.95 (ISBN 0-532-23121-X). Woodhill.
Thousand Eugenias and Other Stories. Cecily Ullmann Sidgwick. LC 2-25930. 1902. Longmans, Green, and Co.
Thousand Fires. Anne Powers, pseud. LC 57-9356. 1957. Bobbs-Merrill.
Thousand Fires. Anne Powers, pseud. (Belmont Tower Book). 2.25 (ISBN 0-505-51291-2). Tower Publications.
Thousand for Sicily. Geoffrey Trease. LC 66-16981. 1966. 3.95. Vanguard.
Thousand for the Cariboo. Bill Gulick, pseud. 1969. pap. 0.60 o.p. (63-193). Paperback Lib.
Thousand for the Cariboo: By Bill Gulick. Grover C Gulick. LC 54-8135. 1954. Houghton Mifflin.
Thousand Francs Reward. Emile Gaboriau. Tr. by Safford, Mary Joanna & Kendall, Laura E. Merimee, Prosper. (On cover: Seaside library. Pocket ed. no. 1015). 1887. G. Munro.
Thousand Happiness. Berta LaVan Barker. (YA) 1978. 6.95 (Avalon). Bouregy.
Thousand Hour Day. W. S. Kuniczak. LC 66-24263. 1966-1967. Dial Press.
Thousand Imitations. Florence Bonime. LC 67-16090. 1967. Harcourt, Brace & World.
Thousand Leggers. Catherine Winspear Moss. LC 9-16438. 1909. The C. M. Clark Publishing Company.
Thousand Miles an Hour. Robert C Givins. LC 13-17972. 0.25. Maclear & Marcus.
Thousand Miles to Belton: A Texas Frontier Romance. Winifred Lowe Baggett Fox. LC 52-14708. 1952. Naylor Co.
Thousand Pardons. Katinka Loeser. LC 82-45173. 1982. 12.95 (ISBN 0-689-11310-2). Atheneum.
Thousand Pieces of Gold: A Biographical Novel. Ruthanne Lum McCunn. LC 81-68270. (Illus.). 10.95 (ISBN 0-932538-08-8). Design Enterprises of San Francisco.
Thousand Quotations, Bk. 1. John Newlander. LC 77-70322. 1980. pap. 4.95 (ISBN 0-89485-009-1). EdMart Intl.
Thousand Secrets. John Selborne. LC 15-6452. (Lettered on cover: Mitchell Kennerley's railroad novels) $1.00). 1915. M. Kennerley.
Thousand Springs: A Collection of Short Stories. Mary Gray Hughes. LC 70-27310. 1971. Puckerbrush Press.
Thousand Summers. Garson Kanin. LC 73-79679. 1973. 6.95 (ISBN 0-385-06973-1). Doubleday.
Thousand Summers. Garson Kanin. LC 73-22423. 1974. 8.95 (ISBN 0-8161-6192-5). G. K. Hall.
Thousand Summers. Garson Kanin. 1974. (pbk.) 1.75. Bantam Books.
Thousand Thousand Mornings: A Novel. John Bart Gerald. LC 64-11227. 1964. Viking Press.
Thousandstar. Anthony Piers. 304p. 1980. pap. 2.75 (ISBN 0-380-75556-4, 80259). Avon.
Thousandth Case. George Dilnot. LC 33-27117. 1933. Houghton Mifflin Company.
Thousandth Man. Ruby Mildred Ayres. LC 39-201693. 1939. Doubleday, Doran & Company, Inc.
Thousandth Woman. Ernest William Hornung. LC 13-22448. The Bobbs-Merrill Company.
Thouse-Mates. John Davys Beresford. Cassell and Company, Ltd.
Thracian Sea" A Novel. John Helston. LC 14-155608. 1914. 1.35. The Macmillan Company.
Thrail of Leif the Lucky: A Story of Viking Days. Ottilia Adelina Liljencrantz. LC 6-14751. Small, Maynard & Co.
Thrall of Leif the Lucky: A Story of Viking Days. Ottilia Adelina Liljencrantz. LC 2-9134. 1902. A. C. McClurg & Co.
Thrall of Love. Riva Carles. (Berkley Medallion Book). 1977. 1.75 (ISBN 0-425-03405-4). Berkley Pub.Corp.
Thralls of the Dragon's Heart. Elizabeth Boyer. 304p. 1982. pap. 2.75 (ISBN 0-345-30236-2, Del Rey). Ballantine.
Thread of Faith. Rintha V. Scott. 1979. 12.98; pap. 10.98. CLCB Pr.
Thread of Flame. Basil King. LC 20-14599. 1920. Harper & Brothers.
Thread of Gold. Lucie Dayton Phillips. LC 7-36059. 1893. American Baptist Publication Society.
Thread of Scarlet. Percy J King. LC 29-7402. 1928. Brentano's Ltd.
Thread of Scarlet. Ben Ames Williams. LC 39-27164. 1939. Houghton Mifflin Company.
Thread That Is Spun. Margaret Horner Clyde. LC 15-27931. 1915. 1.20. Sherman, French & Company.
Threads. Frank Stayton. LC 21-17010. 1921. 1.90. The Century Co.
Threads. Roger E Swaybill. LC 80-17011. 9.95 (ISBN 0-440-08190-4). Delacorte Press.
Threads Cable-Strong: William Faulkner's Go Down, Moses. Dirk Kuyk. LC 81-72030. 22.50 (ISBN 0-8387-5037-0). Bucknell University Press.
Threads of Destiny. Jean Lyttle. LC 61-9821. 3.00 o.p. Garrett-Helix.
Threads of Intrigue. Lynn Williams. (Candlelight mystery, 122). 1973. (pbk.) 0.75. Dell.
Threads of Life. Clara Harriot Sherwood Rollins. LC 7-40758. 1897. Lamson, Wolffe and Company.
Threads of Time: Three Original Novellas of Science Fiction. Ed. by Robert Silverberg. LC 74-11290. 1974. 6.50 (ISBN 0-8407-6402-2). T. Nelson.
Threat. Richard Jessup. LC 80-52001. 1981. 12.95 (ISBN 0-670-70618-3). Viking Press.
Threat of Dragons. Lavinia Riker Davis. LC 48-841436. 1948. Pub. for the Crime Club by Doubleday.
Threat of Love. Maye Barrett. (Orig.). pap. 1.75 (ISBN 0-515-05727-4). Jove Pubns.
Threatening Shadows. Victor G. Vecki. LC 31-648510. The Stratford Company.
Three. Ann Quin. LC 66-25350. 1966. 3.95. Scribners.
Three. William Sansom. LC 47-310527. 1947. Reynal & Hitchcock.
Three--Legged Hootch Dancer. Mike Resnick. (Tales of the Galactic Midway: No. 2). 160p. 1983. pap. 2.50 (ISBN 0-451-12082-5, Sig). NAL.
Three-a-Day. Dorothy Hartzell Kuhns Heyward. LC 30-10242. 2.50. The Century Co.
Three: A Novel. Sylvia Ashton-Warner. 1974. (pbk.) 1.25. Warner Paperback Library.
Three: A Novel. Ashton-Warner, Sylvia. LC 70-106622. 1970. 5.95. Knopf.
Three: A Novel. Pamela Frankau. LC 29-176861. 1929. Doubleday, Doran & Company, Inc.
Three Aces: A Nero Wolfe Omnibus. Rex Stout. LC 70-151262. 1971. 8.95 o.p. (ISBN 0-670-70622-1). Viking Pr.
Three-Act Special: 3 Complete Mystery Novels: A Wreath for Rivera. Spinsters in Jeopardy. Night at the Vulcan. Ngaio Marsh. LC 60-9354. 1960. Little, Brown.
Three Adventure Novels: She, King Solomon's Mines and Allan Quatermain. Each Complete and Unabridged. Henry Rider Haggard. LC 60-20211. Dover Pblications.
Three Against Fate: A Tale of 1917. Mary Agnes Adamson Hamilton. LC 30-3353. 1930. Houghton Mifflin Company.
Three Against the Witch World. Andre Norton, pseud. LC 77-23202. (Norton, Andre. The Witch World Novels of Andre Norton). 1977. 7.95 (ISBN 0-8398-2358-4). Gregg Press.
Three Against the World. Sheila Kaye-Smith. LC 32-33619. 1929. E. P. Dutton & Co., Inc.
Three Amateurs. Michael Arthur Lewis. LC 29-11582. 1929. Houghton Mifflin Company.
Three and a Half Husbands. Dorothy Fuldheim. LC 76-15221. 6.95 (ISBN 0-671-22321-6). Simon and Schuster.
Three and a Half Husbands. Dorothy Fuldheim. (Signet Book). 1977. 1.75 (ISBN 0-451-07793-8). New American Library.
Three-and-Twenty. Jennie Maria Drinkwater Conklin. LC 6-306579. 1895. A. I. Bradley & Co.
Three Apprentices of Moon Street. From the French of Georges Montorgueil. With Illustrations by Louis Le Reverend and Paul Steck. Georges Montorgueil. LC 7-31123. T. Y. Crowell & Company.
Three Arrows. Iris Murdoch. Bd. with Servants & the Snow. 1974. 10.00 o.s.i. (ISBN 0-670-70638-8). Viking Pr.
Three Arrows: The Young Buffalo Hunter. Egerton Ryerson Young. LC 32-6894. Friendship Press.
Three at the Angel. 1st Ed. Maurice Procter. LC 58-6173. 1958. Harper.
Three at the Wedding. Loula Grace Erdman. LC 53-102112. 1953. Dodd, Mead.
Three at Wolfe's Door: A Nero Wolfe Threesome. Rex Stout. LC 60-9225. 1960. Viking Press.
Three at Wolfe's Door: A Nero Wolfe Threesome. Rex Stout. 1974. (pbk.) 0.95. Bantam Books.
Three Bags Full. Roger Burlingame. LC 36-199752. Harcourt, Brace and Company.
Three Bamboos. Digby George Gerahty. LC 42-24039. 1942. The Macmillan Company.
Three Barrels of Steam. James E. Boynton. LC 73-77544. (Illus.). 1973. 14.50 o.s.i. (ISBN 0-911760-13-X). Glenwood.
Three Bears. Bertha B. Moore McCurry. LC 38-21321. 1938. Wm. B. Eerdmans Publishing Co.
Three Beds in Manhattan. Georges Simenon. LC 64-10560. 1964. Doubleday.
Three Beds in Manhattan. Georges Simenon. LC 76-372631. 1976. 2.95 (ISBN 0-241-89326-7). Hamilton.
Three Bernices: Or, Ansermo of the Crag. Amanda Metcalf Bright. LC 6-182559. 1869. Claxton, Remsen & Haffelfinger.
Three Black Bags. Marion Polk Angellotti. LC 22-17454. 1922. The Century Co.
Three Black Lambs: A Modern Grecian Drama. Peter H Kellar. LC 37-20750. 1937. Meador Publishing Company.
Three Black Pennys. Joseph Hergesheimer. LC 30-30714. 1930. A. A. Knopf.
Three Black Pennys: A Novel. Joseph Hergesheimer. LC 17-25287. 1917. A. A. Knopf.
Three Blind Mice. Adele Seifert. LC 42-3384. 1942. W. Morrow and Company.
Three Blind Mice. James Wood. LC 73-188691. 1973. 5.95 (ISBN 0-8149-0705-9). Vanguard Press.
Three Blind Mice & Other Stories. Agatha Miller Christie. 1980. pap. 2.50 (ISBN 0-440-15867-2). Dell.
Three Blossoms of Chang-an. Kenneth Westmacott Lane. 1946. The Macmillan Company.
Three Blows: Or, Love, Pride and Revenge. Karl Drury. (select ser. no. 77). 1891. Street & Smith.
Three Brass Elephants. Herman Landon. LC 30-48498. 1930. H. Liveright.
Three Brides. Charlotte Mary Yonge. (On cover: Seaside library. Pocket ed. no. 275). 1884. G. Munro.
Three Brides, Love in a Cottage: And Other Tales. Francis Alexander Durivage. LC 42-26574. 1856. Sanborn, Carter & Bazin.
Three Bright Pebbles. Zenith Jones Brown. LC 38-34810. Farrar & Rinehard, Inc.
Three Brothers. catholic literary foundation ed. Michael McLaverty. LC 48-8111. 1948. Macmillan Co.
Three Brothers. Eden Phillpotts. LC 9-204347. 1909. The Macmillan Company.
Three Brothers. William Townend. LC 55-419972. 1955. Rich and Cowan.
Three Brothers and Seven Daddies. Harry Harrison Kroll. LC 32-237202. 1932. R. Long and R. R. Smith, Inc.
Three Bummers: And Other Stories of War. C. W. Ecob. (On cover: Lovell's library. no. 967). J. W. Lovell Company.
Three by Box. Edgar Box, pseud. 1978. 12.95 (ISBN 0-394-50117-9). Random.
Three by Box: The Complete Mysteries of Edgar Box I.E. G. Vidal. Gore Vidal. LC 78-57100. 12.95 (ISBN 0-394-50117-9). 1962. Random House.
Three by Flannery O'Connor: Wise Blood, the Violent Bear It Away, a Good Man Is Hard to Find. Flannery O'Connor. 1980. pap. 2.95 (ISBN 0-451-09792-0, E9792, Sig). NAL.
Three by Graham Greene. Graham Greene. Bd. with This Gun for Hire; Confidential Agent; Ministry of Fear. 1936-43. 5.95 o.p. (ISBN 0-670-70680-9); pap. 2.75 o.p. (ISBN 0-670-00221-6, C221, Comp). Viking Pr.
Three by Heinlein. The Puppet Masters; Waldo; Magic, Inc. Robert Anson Heinlein. LC 65-23797. 1965. 5.95. Doubleday.
Three by Irving. John Irving. LC 79-26607. 1980. 17.95 (ISBN 0-394-50983-8). Random House.
Three by Peter Handke. Peter Handke. LC 76-52801. (Band Book). 1977. 2.25 (ISBN 0-380-00968-4). Avon Books.
Three by Tey. Josephine Tey. (O.s.i.). 1954. 8.95 o.s.i. (ISBN 0-02-617180-5). Macmillan.
Three by Tey: Miss Pym Disposes: The Franchise Affair and Brat Farrar. Elizabeth Mackintosh. LC 54-12125. (Cock Robin mystery). 1954. Macmillan.
Three by Three: Stairway to the Sea. Jones, Thomas Firth. LC 61-11771. 1962. Grove Press.
Three Came to Ville Marie. Alan Sullivan. LC 42-2916. 1941. Oxford University Press.
Three Came to Ville Marie. Alan Sullivan. LC 43-2269. 1943. Coward-McCann, Inc.
Three Came Unarmed. Eileen Arbuthnot Robertson. LC 33-16068. Garden City Publishing Company, Inc.
Three Came Unarmed. Eileen Arbuthnot Robertson. LC 30-839. 1930. Doubleday, Doran & Company, Inc.
Three Can Love. Leslie Scott. LC 52-5792. 1952. Arco Pub. Co.
Three Cases for Mr. Campion. 1st Ed. Margery Allingham. LC 61-65125. 1961. Published for the Crime Club by Doubleday.
Three Cases of Shomri Shomar. Henry Klinger. LC 68-54557. 1968. 6.50. Trident Press.
Three Chapters in the Lascivious Life of Mr. Howard. Charles Sackville. 1972. pap. 1.95 o.s.i. (V1116T, Venus). Grove.
Three Cheers and a Tiger. Edwin McDowell. LC 66-18769. 1966. Macmillan.
Three Cheers for Me, the Journals of Bartholomew Bandy, R. F. C. Edited and Adapted, and with an Introd. by Donald Lamont Jack. Donald Lamont Jack. LC 62-11928. 1962. Macmillan.
Three Cheers for Nothing. Peter Kinsley. LC 64-23216. 1964. Dutton.
Three Cheers for the Paraclete. Thomas Keneally. LC 69-15651. 1969. 4.95. Viking Press.
Three Cheers for War in General. John D. Spooner. LC 68-14742. 1969. pap. 0.75 o.p. (ISBN 0-446-64998-8, 64-068). Paperback Lib.
Three Cheers for War in General: A Novel of the Army Reserve. John D Spooner. LC 68-14742. 1968. Little, Brown.
Three Chevaliers. A Sequel to "Helene Sainte Maur.". Luman Allen. LC 6-49. (On cover: The Melbourne series, no. 17). E. A. Weeks & Company.
Three Children of the Holocaust. Sol Chaneles. LC 76-353555. 1974. 1.25 (ISBN 0-380-00118-7). Avon.
Three Christie Crimes: Starring Hercule Poirot. An Omnibus Containing The Murder of Roger Ackroyd, Murder in the Calais Coach and Thirteen at Dinner, Complete and Unabridged. Agatha Miller Christie. LC 38-36747. 1937. Grosset & Dunlap.
Three Cities: A Trilogy. Shalom Asch. Tr. by Muir, Willa. LC 43-13042. 1943. G. P. Putnam's Sons.
Three Cities: A Trilogy. Shalom Asch & Muir, Mrs. Willa, Tr. LC 33-273246. 1933. G. P. Putnam's Sons.
Three Cities. I. Lourdes. new ed., rev. and cor. ed. Emile Zola & Vizetelly, Ernest Alfred, 1853-1922, Tr. LC 3-14795. 1897. The Macmillan Company.
Three Clerks. Anthony Trollope. LC 80-1876. (Trollope, Anthony, 1815-1882. Selections). 1981. 105.00 (ISBN 0-405-14126-2). Arno Press.
Three Clerks. dover ed. Anthony Trollope. LC 80-69483. 1981. 6.00 (ISBN 0-486-24099-1). Dover Publications.
Three Clerks, 3 vols. Anthony Trollope. Ed. by N. John Hall. LC 80-1876. (Selected Works of Anthony Trollope Ser.). 1981. Repr. of 1858 ed. lib. bdg. 105.00 (ISBN 0-405-14126-2). Ayer Co.
Three Clerks. Anthony Trollope & Shore, William Teighmouth, 1865-1932, Ed. (Half-title: The world's classics. cxl. The works of Anthony Trollope. 1). 1929. H. Milford, Oxford University Press.
Three Clerks. Anthony Trollope & Thorold, Algar Labouchere, Ed. LC 12-39452. (Half-title: The new pocket library. vol. xxi). 1904. John Lane.
Three Clerks. A Novel. Anthony Trollope. LC 8-28874. 1874. Harper & Brothers.
Three Coffins. John Dickson Carr. LC 35-15618. 1935. Harper & Brothers.
Three Coffins. John Dickson Carr. LC 79-690. (Gregg Press Mystery Series). 1979. 9.95 (ISBN 0-8398-2533-1). Gregg Press.
Three Companion Pieces. Margery Sharp. LC 41-23676. 1941. Little, Brown and Company.
Three Complete Novels. avenel 1981 ed. Frederick Forsyth. LC 81-2081. 1981. 6.98 (ISBN 0-517-34346-0). Avenel Books: Distributed by Crown Publishers.
Three Complete Novels and Five Short Stories. Daphne Du Maurier. LC 81-12891. 1981. 6.98 (ISBN 0-517-34917-5). Avenel Books: Distributed by Crown.
Three Comrades. Gustav Frenssen. Tr. by Winstanley, L. LC 7-20513. D. Estes & Company; Etc., Etc.
Three Comrades: Translated from the German. Erich Maria Remarque & Wheen, Arthur Wesley, Tr. LC 37-5987. 1937. Little, Brown and Company.
Three-Cornered Cover. George Marton & Christopher Felix. LC 72-78114. 1972. 6.95 (ISBN 0-03-001371-2). Holt, Rinehart and Winston.
Three-Cornered Halo: By Christianna Brand Pseud. Mary Christianna Milne Lewis. LC 57-12356. 1957. Scribner.
Three-Cornered Hat. Pedro Antonio De Alarcon & Fassett, Jacob Sloat, 1889- Tr. LC 18-12856. (The Borzoi Spanish translations). 1918. A. A. Knopf.
Three-Cornered Hat. Pedro Antonio De Alarcon & Springer, Mary, Tr. LC 5-42176. Cassell Publishing Company.
Three-Cornered Hat. Pedro De Alarcon. Tr. by Harriet De Onis from Span. 1958. pap. 2.50 (ISBN 0-8120-0207-5). Barron.
Three-Cornered Hat. Pedro A. De Alarcon. 1959. 2.50 o.p. Hillary.
Three-Cornered Hat, and Other Stories. Alarcon, Pedro Antonio De. LC 76-371763. (Penguin classics). 1975. 1.95 (ISBN 0-14-044314-2). Penguin.
Three-Cornered Hat. El Sombrero De Tres Picos.,Translation by Harriet De Onis. Introd. by William E. Colford. Pedro Antonio de Alarcon. LC 58-325894. 1958. Barron's Educational Series.
Three Cornered Hat. Newly Translated from the Spanish by William H. Warden. Pedro Antonio de Alarcon. LC 52-11889. Vantage Press.
Three-Cornered Hat: The True History of an Affair Current in Certain Tales and Ballads and Here Written Down As and How It Befel. Pedro Antonio De Alarcon & Armstrong, Martin Donisthorpe, 1882- Tr. LC 28-6761. 1928. Simon & Schuster.

Three-Cornered Hat: The True History of an Affair Current in Certain Tales and Ballads, Here Written Down As & How It Befell. Now Translated Out of the Spanish by Martin Armstrong, with an Introd. by Gerald Brenan & Illustrated by Roger Duvoisin. Pedro Antonio De Alarcon & Duvoisin Roger Antoine, 1904- Illus. LC 60-105549. 1959. Printed for the Members of the Limited Editions Club at the Plantin Press.
Three-Cornered Hat. Tr. from Spanish by H. F. Turner. Pedro Antonio De Alarcon. LC 65-7418. 1965. 3.50. J. Calder.
Three-Cornered Heart. Anne Fremantle. 1972. pap. 0.95 o.p. (09153). Curtis.
Three-Cornered House. Kathleen Ford. LC 68-13882. 1968. McGraw-Hill.
Three Cornered Love. Nancy Hoyt. 1932. Doubleday, Doran & Company, Inc.
Three Cornered Murder. Jean Leslie. LC 47-3320. 1947. Pub. for the Crime Club by Doubleday & Co., Inc.
Three Cornered Sun: A Historical Novel. Linda Ty-Casper. 1979. pap. 8.75x (New Day). Cellar.
Three Cornered World. Soseki Natsume. LC 67-28480. (UNESCO Collection of Representative Works: Japanese Series). 1967. H. Regnery Co.
Three-Cornered World. Natsume Soseki. Tr. by Alan Turney from Japanese. (Perigee Japanese Library). 184p. 1982. pap. 4.95 (ISBN 0-399-50607-1, Perige). Putnam Pub Group.
Three Cornered-World. Natsume Soseki. Tr. by Alan Turney. LC 67-28480. 1970. 3.95 o.p. (71830); pap. 1.95 o.p. (6143). Regnery.
Three-Cornered Wound. George Dyer. LC 31-11278. 1931. Houghton Mifflin Company.
Three Corners to Nowhere. Martin Caidin. 1975. (pbk.) 1.75. Bantam Books.
Three-Corpse Trick. Miles Burton. 1977. 5.80 o.p. State Mutual Bk.
Three Corsican Stories. Gabrielle Melies. LC 20-13975. 1920. P. G. Melies.
Three Couriers. Compton Mackenzie. LC 29-10480. 1929. Doubleday, Doran & Company, Inc.
Three Courts. Joseph Hadley Davis. LC 6-32478. Johnson & Kiergan, Printing.
Three Cousins. James A Maitland. LC 7-16597. 1860. T. B. Peterson & Brothers.
Three Cousins Die: By John Rhode. Cecil John Charles Street. LC 60-6172. (Red badge detective). 1960. Dodd, Mead.
Three Creeks to Cross: By M. Fran Engels Pseud. Madyne Frances Engelhardt. LC 56-7543. 1956. Comet Press Books.
Three Cries of Terror. Ann Ashton. LC 79-7664. (Romantic Suspense Ser.). 1980. 8.95 o.p. (ISBN 0-385-15379-1). Doubleday.
Three Cries of Terror. John M. Kimbro. LC 79-7664. 1980. 8.95 (ISBN 0-385-15379-1). Doubleday.
Three Crimson Days. Harrison Eastman Patten. LC 11-467. 1910. 0.75. The Neale Publishing Company.
Three Cross & Deputy of Violence. Ray Hogan. (Orig.). 1978. pap. 2.50 (ISBN 0-451-11604-6, AE1604, Sig). NAL.
Three Crosses. Federigo Tozzi & Capellero, R., Tr. LC 22-26323. 1921. Moffat, Yard & Company.
Three Crowns. Jean Plaidy. LC 76-55937. 1977. 8.95 (ISBN 0-399-11892-6). Putnam Pub Group.
Three Cups of Coffee. Ruth Feiner. LC 40-33700. J. B. Lippincott Company.
Three-D. Patrick Dennis, pseud. 224p. 1972. 6.95 o.p. (ISBN 0-698-10450-1). Coward.
Three D. Patrick Dennis, pseud. 1973. pap. 1.25 o.p. (01053). Curtis.
Three Daggers: A Detective Story. Cecil Freeman Gregg. LC 29-19251. 1929. L. MacVeagh, The Dial Press.
Three Daughters. Manfred Bieler. LC 77-76627. 10.00 (ISBN 0-312-80245-5). St. Martin's Press.
Three Daughters. Jane Dashwood. LC 29-19247. 1929. Houghton Mifflin Company.
Three Daughters. Ruth Eleanor McKee & Sturgis, Alice Fleenor, Joint Author. LC 33-13182. 1938. Doubleday, Doran & Company, Inc.
Three Daughters of Madame Liang. Pearl Sydenstricker Buck. (John Day Bk.). 1969. 9.95i (ISBN 0-381-98055-3, A79000). T Y Crowell.
Three Daughters of Madame Liang: A Novel. Pearl Sydenstricker Buck. LC 75-77010. 1969. 6.95. John Day Co.
Three Daughters of the Confederacy: The Story of Their Loves and Their Hatreds, Their Joys and Their Sorrows, During Many Surprising Adventures on Land and Sea, by Cyrus Townsend Brady... Cyrus Townsend Brady. LC 5-26943. 1905. G. W. Dillingham Company.
Three Day Alliance. Howard R. Simpson. LC 75-144298. 1971. 4.95. Published for the Crime Club by Doubleday.
Three Day Pass. Leslie Waller. LC 45-8412. 1945. The Viking Press.
Three Days. Robert King Atwell. LC 40-11868. The Saravan House.
Three Days. Stephen Longstreet. LC 47-1673. 1947. J. Messner.
Three Days. Don Robertson. LC 59-8025. 1959. Prentice-Hall.
Three Days. A Midsummer Love-Story. Samuel Williams Cooper. 1889. J. B. Lippincott Company.
Three Days and a Child. Abraham B Yehoshua. LC 73-103786. 1970. 5.95. Doubleday.
Three Days in November. T. H Althof. LC 78-3982. 1978. 10.95 (ISBN 0-312-80248-X). St. Martin's Press.
Three Days' Terror. Joseph Smith Fletcher. LC 28-9468. E. J. Clode, Inc.
Three Days to Live. Robert Charles, pseud. LC 68-8326. 1969. 3.95 o.p. Roy.
Three Days to Live. Robert Charles Smith. LC 68-8326. 1968. 3.95. Roy Publishers.
Three Days to Tucson. Erle Adkins. 1981. pap. 1.95 (ISBN 0-89083-744-9). Zebra.
Three Dead Men. Paul McGuire. LC 32-11946. 1932. Brentano's.
Three Degrees of Glory. Melvin J. Ballard. pap. 0.75 o.p. (ISBN 0-87747-501-6). Deseret Bk.
Three Dervishes. Reuben Levy. Repr. of 1923 ed. lib. bdg. 10.00 o.p. Folcroft.
Three Desires of the Happy Life: A Novel. James T Duncan. LC 28-4773. The Gordon Company.
Three Detective Novels: Including The Arabian Nights Murder; The Burning Court; The Problem of the Wire Cage. John Dickson Carr. LC 59-6006. 1959. Harper.
Three Detective Stories. English Language Services. (Collier-Macmillan English Readers). pap. 1.40 (ISBN 0-02-971440-0). Macmillan.
Three Die at Midnight. John Hunter. LC 37-7716. 1937. E. P. Dutton & Co., Inc.
Three Died Beside the Marble Pool. Carl Mattison Chapin. LC 36-10747. 1936. Pub. for the Crime Club, Inc., by Doubleday, Doran & Company, Inc.
Three Died Variously: A Mystery Novel. Guy Elwyn Giles. LC 43-17039. (Black cat detective series. No. 1). 1943. Crestwood Publishing Co., Inc.
Three Died Variously: A New Mystery. Guy Elwyn Giles. LC 41-24076. Reynal & Hitchcock, Inc.
Three Dimensional. Edward Everett Tanner. LC 72-76667. 1972. 6.95 (ISBN 0-698-10450-1). Coward, McCann & Geoghegan.
Three Doors to Death: A Nero Wolfe Threesome. Rex Stout. LC 50-6707. 1950. Viking Press.
Three Down Vulnerable: A Beau and Pogy Murder Mystery. Zola Helen Ross. LC 47-24204. 1946. The Bobbs-Merrill Company.
Three Dukes. G Ystridde. LC 5-1490. 1904. G. P. Putnam's Sons.
Three Early American Novels. Ed. by William S. Kable. LC 72-95305. (Charles E. Merrill literary texts). 1970. C. E. Merrill.
Three Edwards. Thomas Bertram Costain. (Plantagenets Ser: Vol. 3). 1976. pap. 2.95 (ISBN 0-445-08513-4). Popular Lib.
Three Eerie Tales from 19th Century German. Edward Mornin. LC 75-2178. 1975. 7.50. (ISBN 0-8044-2637-6) (ISBN 0-8044-6520-7). F. Ungar Pub. Co.
Three Eighteenth Century Novels: Moll Flanders, Joseph Andrews, the Vicar of Wakefield. Intro. by Erica Jong. 1982. pap. 3.95 (ISBN 0-451-51612-5, CE1612, Sig Classics). NAL.
Three Eighteenth Century Romances. Ed. by Harrison Ross Steeves. LC 78-31092. (Scribner library emblem editions). 1971. 3.95 (ISBN 0-684-12479-3). Scribner.
Three Eighteenth Century Romances: The Castle of Otranto; Vathek; The Romance of the Forest, with an Introduction. Ed. by Harrison Ross Steeves. Walpole, Horace & Beckford, William. LC 31-24442. (Half-title: The modern student's library). C. Scribner's Sons.
Three Eleven Congress Court: 1st Ed. Richard Sullivan. LC 53-898390. 1953. Holt.
Three Englishmen: A Romance of Married Lives. Frankau, Gilbert. LC 35-7384. 1935. E. P. Dutton & Co., Inc.
Three Eras of a Woman's Life: The Maiden, the Wife, and the Mother. Timothy Shay Arthur. LC 6-34242. 1855. J. W. Bradley.
Three Eras of Woman's Life. Elizabeth Elton Smith. LC 8-8635. 1836. Harper & Brothers.
Three Exemplary Novels. Miguel de Unamuno. Tr. by Angel Flores. Incl. Marquis of Lumbria; Two Mothers; Nothing Less Than a Man. 1956. pap. 3.95 o.p. (ISBN 0-394-17203-5, E30, Ever). Grove.
Three Exemplary Novels. Miguel De Unamuno Y Jugo. LC 56-5729. (evergreen book, E-30). Grove Press.
Three Exemplary Novels and a Prologue. Unamuno y Jugo, Miguel De & Flores, Angel, Tr. LC 31-5120. 1930. A. and C. Boni.
Three Exemplary Novels: Translated by Samuel Putnam. Illustrated by Luis Quintanilla. 1st Ed. Miguel de Cervantes de Saavedra. Tr. by Samuel Putnam. LC 50-10034. 1950. Viking Press.
Three Exotic Tales. Philip Freund. LC 45-6155. 1945. Pilgrim House.
Three Experiments of Living: Living Within the Means. Living up to the Means. Living Beyond the Means... Hannah Farnham Sawyer Lee. LC 7-12619. (On cover: Stories from real life. no. 1). 1837. W. S. Damrell, and B. H. Greene.
Three Experiments of Living: Living Within the Means, Living up to the Means, Living Beyond the Means... Hannah Farnham Sawyer Lee. LC 10-5688. 1837. W. S. Damrell and B. H. Greene.
Three Experiments of Living: Living Within the Means, Living up to the Means, Living Beyond the Means... Hannah Farnham Sawyer Lee. LC 8-30890. (On cover: Stories from real life. 1). 1837. W. S. Damrell, S. Colman.
Three Experiments of Living: Living Within the Means, Living up to the Means, Living Beyond the Means. Hannah Farnham Sawyer Lee. LC 6-35398. 1847. E. G. Taylor.
Three-Eyes. Stuart Gordon. (DAW Books no. 171). 1975. (pbk.) 1.50. DAW Books.
Three Eyes. Maurice Leblanc. Tr. by Teixeira De Mattos, Alexander Louis. LC 21-8517. The Macaulay Company.
Three-Eyes: Science Fiction. Stuart Gordon. LC 77-354926. (Illus.). 1976. 3.95 (ISBN 0-283-98231-4). Sidgwick and Jackson.
Three Faces of Eve. Corbett Thigpen & Hervey M. Cleckley. 24.50 (ISBN 0-911238-51-4). Regent House.
Three Faces of Eve. Corbett H. Thigpen & Hervey M. Cleckley. 1974. pap. 2.25 (ISBN 0-445-08137-6). Popular Lib.
Three Faces of Love. Faith Cutherell Baldwin, pseud. LC 57-839474. 1974. (pbk.) 0.95. Warner Paperback Library.
Three Faces of Love. Faith Baldwin Cuthrell. LC 57-8394. 1957. Rinehart.
Three Faces of Love. Emile Zola. LC 67-29442. 1968. 4.95. Vanguard Press.
Three Fair Philanthropists. Alice M Muzzy. The Abbey Press.
Three Famous Murder Novels. 4.95 o.p. (G66); PLB 3.89 o.p. Modern Lib.
Three Famous Murder Novels, Complete and Unabridged in One Volume. Before the Fact. Cerf, Bennett Alfred, 1808- & Cox, Anthony Berkeley, 1893- Before the Fact. LC 41-13491. Random House.
Three Famous Short Novels. William Faulkner. LC 58-6368. (Modern library paperbacks, P36). 1958. Random House.
Three Famous Spy Novels, Complete and Unabridged in One Volume. The Great Impersonation. Cerf, Bennett Alfred, 1898- Ed & Oppenheim, Edward Phillips, 1866- The Great Impersonation. LC 42-18722. 1942. Random House.
Three Farms. John Matter. LC 13-7079. 1913. H. Holt and Company.
Three Farms: A Story of South Africa. Cynthia Stockley. LC 25-21774. 1925. G. P. Putnam's Sons.
Three Fates. Francis Marion Crawford. LC 6-33037. 1892. Macmillan and Co.
Three Fates: By F. Marion Crawford... Francis Marion Crawford. LC 33-174932. 1898. Macmillan and Co.
Three Fears. Jonathan Stagge, pseud. LC 49-7409. 1949. Pub. for the Crime Club by Doubleday.
Three Feathers. William Black. (On cover: Lovell's library, v. 5, no. 213). J. W. Lovell Co.
Three Feathers. A Novel. William Black. (On cover: Seaside library. Pocket ed. no. 121). G. Munro.
Three Feathers: A Novel. library ed. William Black. LC 4-165013. Harper & Brothers.
Three Fevers. Leo Walmsley. LC 32-18948. 1932. A. A. Knopf.
Three Fields to Cross: An Historical Novel. Frances Tysen Nutt. LC 47-123339. 1947. Stephen-Paul.
Three Fires: A Story of Ceylon. Amelia Josephine Burr. LC 22-18551. 1922. The Macmillan Company.
Three Fishers. Francis Beeding. LC 31-18589. 1931. Little, Brown, and Company.
Three Flights up. Sidney Coe Howard. LC 24-25527. 1924. C. Scribner's Sons.
Three for a Wedding: A Novel. Patte Wheat Mahan, pseud. LC 65-14962. 1965. D. McKay Co.
Three for All. Marcus Van Heller, pseud. (Orig.). 1968. pap. 1.75 o.s.i. (126, Ophelia). Olympia.
Three for an Orgy. F. W. Paul. pap. 0.60 o.p. Lancer.
Three for Bedroom C: And Key to Two Hundred and Sixteen Exercises. Goddard Lieberson. LC 47-629. 1947. Doubleday & Company, Inc.
Three for McGee: By John D. MacDonald. 1st Ed. John Dann Macdonald. LC 67-26537. 1967. 5.95. Doubleday.
Three for the Chair. Rex Stout. 160p. 1981. pap. 1.95 (ISBN 0-553-14449-9). Bantam.
Three for the Chair, a Nero Wolfe Threesome. Rex Stout. LC 57-7222. 1957. Viking Press.
Three for the Money. James McConnaughey. LC 54-55443. 1954. Sloane.
Three for the Money: A New Mystery Novel by Joe Barry Pseud. Joe Barry Lake. LC 50-24475. (Handi-book mystery). 1950. Handi-Book Editions.
Three for Tomorrow: Three Original Novellas of Science Fiction. Robert Silverberg & Roger Zelazny. LC 70-85419. 1969. 5.95. Meredith Press.
Three Freshmen: Ruth, Fran, and Nathalie. Jessie Anderson Chase. 1898. A. C. McClurg & Company.
Three Friends. Norman Collins. LC 36-7000. 1936. Doubleday, Doran and Company, Inc.
Three from the Legion. Jack Williamson. 1980. 2.95 (ISBN 0-671-83372-3). Pocket Books.
Three Furlongers. Sheila Kaye-Smith. LC 14-11042. 1914. 1.25. J. B. Lippincott Company.
Three Gals a Week. Adelaide Humphries. LC 42-24965. 1942. Phoenix Press.
Three Gals a Week. Token West, pseud. LC 42-249652. 1942. Phoenix Press.
Three Gay Tales from Grimm. Jakob Ludwig Karl Grimm & Wilhelm Karl Grimm. LC 43-51302. 1943. Coward-McCann.
Three Generations. Sarah Anna Emery. LC 6-37827. 1872. Lee and Shepard.
Three Gentlemen... Alfred Edward Woodley Mason. LC 32-25729. 1932. Doubleday, Doran & Company, Inc.
Three Gentlemen from New Caledonia. Richard D'Oyly Hemingway & Halsalle, Henry De, 1872- Joint Author. LC 14-216267. 1915. G.P. Putnam's Sons.
Three Girls in a Flat. Enid Yandell & Loughborough, Jean, Joint Author. LC 9-3434. Knight, Leonard & Co.
Three Girls Lost. Robert Douglas Andrews, pseud. LC 30-19829. Grosset & Dunlap.
Three Go Back. James Leslie Mitchell. LC 32-11460. The Bobbs-Merrill Company.
Three Godfathers. Peter Bernard Kyne. LC 13-25608. George H. Doran Company, Publishers in America for Hodder & Stoughton.
Three Gorgeous Hussies. Josiah Pitts Wollfolk. LC 36-202405. Godwin.
Three Gorgeous Hussies. Josiah Pitts Woolfolk. LC 48-10607. (Novel library, 1). 1948. Novel Publications.
Three Gothic Novels. William Beckford. Incl. Castle of Otranto. Horace Walpole; Vampyre. J. Polidori (ISBN 0-8446-2749-6); Vathek. W. Beckford (ISBN 0-8446-1621-4). 8.00 o.p. Peter Smith.
Three Gothic Novels. Ed. by Everett Franklin Bleiler. Bd. with Castle of Otranto. 2nd ed. Horace Walpole; Vathek. William Beckford. Tr. by Samuel Henley; Fragment of a Novel. George G. Byron. xl, 291p. 1966. pap. 2.00 o.p. (ISBN 0-486-21232-7). Dover.
Three Gothic Novels. Ed. by Peter Fairclough. LC 77-368199. (Penguin English library). (Illus.). 1968. Penguin.
Three Graces. Jane Ashford. 1982. pap. 2.25 (ISBN 0-451-11418-3, AE1418, Sig). NAL.
Three Graces. Polly Hobson. LC 76-146323. 1971. 4.95 o.s.i. (ISBN 0-8277-0250-7). British Bk Ctr.
Three Graces. Concordia Merrel. LC 30-288409. Doubleday, Doran & C.
Three Graces: A Novel. Margaret Wolfe Hungerford. LC 7-9053. 1895. J. B. Lippincott Company.
Three Graces at College: A Sequel to Three Graces. Gabrielle Emilie Snow Jackson. LC 4-25106. 1904. D. Appleton and Company.
Three Great American Novels, 3 bks. in 1. Incl. Farewell to Arms. Ernest Hemingway; Great Gatsby. F. Scott Fitzgerald; Ethan Frome. Edith Wharton. (Modern Standard Authors Ser). 370p. 1967. Repr. text ed. 5.95 o.p. (ISBN 0-684-41458-9). Scribner.
Three Great American Novels: The Great Gatsby by F. Scott Fitzgerald. with an Introd. by Malcolm Cowley. A Farewell to Arms by Ernest Hemingway, with an Introd. by Robert Penn Warren. Ethan Frome by Edith Wharton, with an Introd. by Edith Wharton. Francis Scott Key Fitzgerald & Ernest Hemingway. LC 67-24030. (Modern standard authors). 1967. 4.95. Scribners.
Three Great Classics. Ed. by Fred Honig. Incl. Peter Schlemihl. Adalbert Von Chamisso; Misunderstanding. Prosper Merimee; Wife for Sale. Anton Chekhov. LC 64-10916. 1964. lib. bdg. 4.50 o.p. (ISBN 0-668-01158-0). Arco.
Three Great Irishmen: Shaw, Yeats, Joyce. With Portraits by Augustus John. Arland Ussher. LC 53-10682. 1953. Devin-Adair.

Three Greatest Novels of Anatole France... Anatole France, pseud. Tr. by Evans, Arthur William & Hearn, Lafcadio. Doubleday, Doran & Company, Inc.
Three Greek Romances. Ed. by Moses Hadas. LC 53-10378. 1964. text ed. 18.50x (ISBN 0-672-51090-1). Irvington.
Three Greek Romances. Tr. by Moses Hadas. Incl. Daphnis & Chloe. Longus; Ephesian Tale. Xenophon; Hunters of Euboia. Dio Chrysoston. LC 53-10378. 1964. 6.60 o.p. (ISBN 0-672-51090-1, LLA201); pap. 3.40 o.p. (ISBN 0-672-60442-6, LLA201). Bobbs.
Three Green Bottles. Dominic Devine. LC 72-76150. 1972. 4.95 (ISBN 0-385-00121-5). Published for the Crime Club by Doubleday.
Three Guardsmen. Alexandre Dumas & Auguste Maquet. LC 45-50941. 1846. Taylor, Wilde and Company.
Three Guardsmen: Or, The Queen's Musketeers. Alexandre Dumas & Maquet, Auguste. LC 6-42124. (American series. no. 296). M. J. Ivers & Co.
Three Guardsmen: Or, The Three Mousaquetaires. Alexandre Dumas & Maquet, Auguste. (Seaside library. v. 13, no. 244). G. Munro.
Three Guineas. Virginia Woolf. LC 38-27681. 1963. pap. 2.95 (ISBN 0-15-690177-3, Harv). HarBraceJ.
Three Guns from Colorado: A Powder Valley Western. Peter Field. LC 52-5057. 1952. Jefferson House.
Three Guns North. Burt Arthur & Budd Arthur. 1979. pap. 1.25 o.s.i. (ISBN 0-505-51349-8). Tower Bks.
Three Half Moons. Sue Walcott Burtin. LC 30-16241. 1930. R.M. McBride & Company.
Three Harbours. Francis Van Wyck Mason. (Berkley medallion book). 1975. (pbk.) 1.95 (ISBN 0-425-02946-8). Berkley Pub. Co.
Three Harbours. Francis Van Wyck Mason. LC 38-33742. J. B. Lippincott Company.
Three Harbours. Francis Van Wyck Mason. LC 40-3968. 1939. J. B. Lippincott Company.
Three-Headed Angel. Roark Bradford. LC 37-5565. 1937. Harper & Brothers.
Three Hearts and Three Lions. Poul Anderson. (Berkley Book). 1978. 1.75 (ISBN 0-425-03680-4). Berkley Pub. Corp.
Three Histories. The History of an Enthusiast. The History of a Nonchalant. The History of a Realist. Maria Jane Jewsbury. LC 7-9739. 1831. Perkins & Marvin.
Three Hostages. John Buchan. LC 64-9899. (Nelson classics). 1963. Nelson.
Three Hostages. John Buchan. LC 24-18767. 1924. Houghton Mifflin Company.
Three Hostages. John Buchan. 1973. 0.95. Popular Lib.
Three Hours till Midnight. Emmett Thurmon & Atherton, Paull, Joint Author. LC 38-36514. 1938. Atlas Printing & Engraving Co.
Three Hundred & Nine East & a Night of Levitation. Bianca Van Orden. LC 57-12371. 1957. Harcourt,Brace.
Three Hundred & Sixty-Six Goodnight Stories. Illus. by Esme Eve & Gwyneth Mamlock. (Illus.). 1969. 4.95 o.p. (ISBN 0-307-15568-4, Golden Pr). Western Pub.
Three Hundred Dollar Man. John B Sanford. LC 67-13967. 1967. Prentice-Hall.
Three Hundred Five East: A Novel. Paul Gillette. LC 72-94017. 9.50 (ISBN 0-87795-082-2). Arbor House: Distributed by E. P. Dutton.
Three Hundred Sixty-Five Days. Ed. by Kay Boyle & Vail, Laurence. LC 36-34618. Hancourt, Brace and Company.
Three Hundred Sixty-Five Nights in Hollywood. Jimmy Starr. LC 26-12137. 1926. David Graham Fischer Corporation.
Three Hundred Sixty-One. Donald E Westlake. LC 62-8444. (Random House mystery). 1962. Random House.
Three Hundred Thirty-Four. Thomas M Disch. LC 76-9057. (Gregg Press science fiction series). 1976. 12.50 (ISBN 0-8398-2331-2). Gregg Press.
Three Hundred Thirty-Four. Thomas M. Disch. (Science Fiction Ser.). 288p. 1976. Repr. of 1974 ed. lib. bdg. 12.50 o.p. (ISBN 0-8398-2331-2, Gregg). G K Hall.
Three Hundred Thirty Three: A Bibliography of the Science Fantasy Novel. Joseph H. Crawford et al. LC 74-15959. (Science Fiction Ser). 82p. 1965. Repr. 10.00x (ISBN 0-405-06324-5). Ayer Co.
Three Hundred Years Ago: Or, The Martyr of Brentwood. William Henry Giles Kingston. LC 7-12527. 1868. Lutheran Board of Publication.
Three Hundred Years Hence. Mary Griffith. LC 75-5793. (Gregg Press science fiction series). 1975. 8.00 (ISBN 0-8398-2303-7). Gregg Press.
Three Hundred Years Hence: With Introd. and Notes by Nelson F. Adkins. Mary Griffith. LC 52-2043. (Prime Press series of reprints of early American Utopian novels, no. 2). 1950. Prime Press.
Three Imposters. Arthur Machen. 1965. 3.50. John Baker.
Three Impostors. Arthur Machen. 1923. A. A. Knopf.
Three Impostors: Or, The Transmutations. Arthur Machen. LC 7-19997. (On cover: Keynotes series no. 18). 1895. Roberts Bros.; Etc., Etc.
Three in a Bed. Frank Owen. LC 32-5864. 1932. W. Godwin, Inc.
Three in One. Hammond Innes. LC 77-118710. 1970. 8.95. Knopf.
Three in the Attic. Stephen H Yafa. (Signet bk., T3568). 1968. New Amer. Lib.
Three Indelicate Ladies. Hawthorne Hurst. LC 33-19896. 1933. W. Godwin, Inc.
Three Indian Chiefs. Alphonse Maria Grussi. LC 33-11625. The Christopher Publishing House.
Three into Two Won't Go. Andrea Newman. LC 68-20838. 1968. Doubleday.
Three Is a Family. Edna Pettigrew. LC 59-10685. (Illus.). 1959. Doubleday.
Three Journeys: An Automythology. Paul Zweig. LC 75-36386. 176p. 1976. 10.00 o.p. (ISBN 0-465-08610-1). Basic.
Three Jumps Ahead of the Squirrels. Gladys Mae Walter. LC 79-157453. 1971. 4.50 (ISBN 0-8309-0051-9). Herald Pub. House.
Three Just Men. Edgar Wallace. LC 29-9875. 1929. Pub. for The Crime Club, Inc., by Doubleday, Doran & Company, Inc.
Three Just Men. Edgar Wallace. LC 40-37538. 1930. Doubleday, Doran & Company, Inc.
Three Keys. Frederic Van Rensselaer Dey. LC 9-16439. 1909. W. J. Watt & Company.
Three Killers. Eli Colter. LC 32-28969. A. H. King, Inc.
Three Kingdoms. Margaret Storm Jameson. LC 26-6640. 1926. A. A. Knopf.
Three Kings of Cologne. Joannes Of Hildesheim. Ed. by C. Horstmann. (EETS, OS Ser.: No. 85). Repr. of 1886 ed. 17.00 (ISBN 0-527-00083-3). Kraus Repr.
Three Kings. 1st Ed. Richard Sullivan. LC 56-9139. 1956. Harcourt, Brace.
Three Knaves. Saul G Greenleef. LC 12-246843. 1.25. R. F. Fenno & Company.
Three Knots: A Mystery. Richard Parker. LC 24-23483. The Macaulay Company.
Three Laws and the Golden Rule. Morgan Robertson. LC 70-86152. (Short story index reprint series). 1969. Books for Libraries Press.
Three Layers of Guilt. Jeffrey Ashford, pseud. 185p. 1983. pap. 2.95 (ISBN 0-8027-3016-7). Walker & Co.
Three Legends. The Snow Goose, The Small Miracle, Ludmila, by Paul Gallico. Illus. by Reisie Lonette. Paul Gallico. (75237). 1967. Pocket Bks.
Three Legends: The Snow Goose, The Small Miracle, Ludmila. Illus. by Reisie Lonette. Paul Gallico. LC 66-1686. 1966. 3.95. Doubleday.
Three Legions. Gregory Solon. LC 56-5211. Random House.
Three Lights from a Match. Leonard Hastings Nason. LC 27-11488. George H. Doran Company.
Three Lights from a Match. Leonard Hastings Nason. LC 37-144050. 1937. The Sun Dial Press, Inc.
Three Lights Went Out... Robert George Dean. LC 37-132690. 1937. Pub. for the Crime Club, Inc., by Doubleday, Doran & Co., Inc.
Three Lilies Vert, a Novel. first ed. Herman P Cook. 1973. 7.50 (ISBN 0-533-00840-9). Vantage Press.
Three Little Kittens, with New Pictures. Wiese, Kurt, 1887- Illus. LC 28-21643. (happy hour books). 1928. The Macmillan Company.
Three Little Women's Success: A Story for Girls. Gabrielle Emilie Jackson. LC 10-26228. 1.00. The John C. Winston Company.
Three Little Words. Florence Faulkner. 1976. 4.95. Avalon Books.
Three Live Ghosts. Frederic Stewart Isham. LC 18-22739. The Bobbs-Merrill Company.
Three Lives. Gertrude Stein. LC 33-293501. (Half-title: The modern library of the world's best books). The Modern Library.
Three Lives. Gertrude Stein. LC 44-39873. (New classics). 1941. New Directions.
Three Lives of Elizabeth. Seifert, Shirley. LC 52-5087.
Three Lives of Sharon Spence. Elizabeth Frances Corbett. LC 79-91009. 1969. 5.95. Meredith Press.
Three Lives: Stories of the Good Anna, Melanctha, and the Gentle Lena. Gertrude Stein. LC 9-20912. 1909. The Grafton Press.
Three Loaves. Archibald Joseph Cronin. 1981. 29.00x (ISBN 0-575-00069-4, Pub. by Gollancz England). State Mutual Bk.
Three Love Stories, 12 bks. 544p. 1981. pap. 2.95 ea. o.p. (100). Playmore & Prestige.
Three Lovers. Ross Sloane. LC 35-2182. Godwin.
Three Lovers. Frank Arthur Swinnerton. LC 22-26983. George H. Doran Company.
Three Lovers: A Novel. Julia O'Faolain. LC 76-146078. 1971. 5.95. Coward, McCann & Geoghegan.
Three Loves. Max Brod & Hartmann, Jacob Wittmer, 1881- Tr. LC 29-15287. 1929. A.A. Knopf.
Three Loves. Alice Mary Ross Colver. LC 34-32217. 1934. Dodd, Mead & Company.
Three Loves. Archibald Joseph Cronin. LC 32-90362. 1932. Little, Brown, and Company.
Three Loves. John R. Graves. 1970. 2.95 o.p. (ISBN 0-8059-1469-2). Dorrance.
Three Loves Are Mine. Alice Mary Ross Colver. LC 46-8402. 1946. Macrae-Smith-Company.
Three Loves Claim Victor Hugo. Clarence V Crockett. LC 64-23331. 1964. Liveright Pub. Corp.
Three Loves for Cecily. Frances D. Hancock. (Valentine Ser). Orig. Title: Flowering Vine. 1970. pap. 0.60 o.p. (ISBN 0-447-73873-9). Lancer.
Three Loving Ladies. Mary Frances Harriet Borthwick Dowdall. LC 21-26725. 1921. Houghton Mifflin Company.
Three McMahons. Al Cody, pseud. 1977. pap. 1.25 (ISBN 0-532-12517-7). Woodhill.
Three Maidens: A Novel. Eden Phillpotts. LC 30-113809. 1930. R. R. Smith Inc.
Three Marchen of E. T. A. Hoffmann. Ernst Theodor Amadeus Hoffmann. LC 76-120580. (Illus.). 1971. (ISBN 0-87249-188-9). University of South Carolina Press.
Three Marias. Rachel De Queiroz. LC 63-17615. 1963. University of Texas Press.
Three Martian Novels. Edgar R. Burroughs. Incl. Thuvia, Maid of Mars. Repr. of 1920 ed; Chessmen of Mars. Repr. of 1922 ed; Master Mind of Mars. Repr. of 1928 ed. vi, 499p. pap. 6.00 (ISBN 0-486-20039-6). Dover.
Three Martian Novels. Edgar R. Burroughs. Incl. Thuvia, Maid of Mars; Chessmen of Mars; Master Mind of Mars. 10.00 (ISBN 0-8446-1779-2). Peter Smith.
Three Martian Novels: Thuvia, Maid of Mars. The Chessmen of Mars. The Master Mind of Mars. Edgar Rice Burroughs. LC 62-3086. (Illus.). 1962. Dover Publications.
Three Megaton Gamble. D. Terman. LC 78-59875. 5.95 (ISBN 0-915248-21-2). Vermont Crossroads Press.
Three Men and a Maid. Pelham Grenville Wodehouse. LC 22-8940. George H. Doran Company.
Three Men and a Maid. Pelham Grenville Wodehouse. LC 37-828029. A. L. Burt Company.
Three Men and a Woman. A Story of Life in New York. Robert Harrison Parker Miles. LC 1-30609. 1901. G. W. Dillingham Co.
Three Men and Diana. Kathleen Thompson Norris. LC 34-16177. 1934. Doubleday, Doran & Company, Inc.
Three Men and Maid. Robert Fraser. LC 7-16753. 1907. E. J. Clode.
Three Men Die. Sarah Gertrude Liebson Millin. LC 34-33286. 1934. Harper & Brothers.
Three Men for Libby D. Russell Trainer. pap. 0.95 o.p. (1163). Brandon.
Three Men in a Boat. Jerome Klapka Jerome. 1977. 9.95x (ISBN 0-460-00118-3, Evman); pap. 2.95x (ISBN 0-460-01118-9, Evman). Biblio Dist.
Three Men in a Boat. Jerome Klapka Jerome. Ed. by David A. Jasen. (Continuum Classic of Humor Ser.). 208p. 1980. 11.95 (ISBN 0-8264-0018-3). Continuum.
Three Men in a Boat. Jerome Klapka Jerome. 1978. pap. 2.95 (ISBN 0-14-001213-3). Penguin.
Three Men in a Boat. Jerome Klapka Jerome. (Illus.). 1978. 14.00 o.p. (ISBN 0-600-38767-4). Transatlantic.
Three Men in a Boat. Jerome Klapka Jerome. (Illus.). 3.00 o.p. (ISBN 0-00-422558-9). Collins-World.
Three Men in a Boat, Also, Diary of a Pilgrimage; and, Three Men on the Bummel. Jerome Klapka Jerome. LC 78-311978. (Illus.). 1977. 8.50 (ISBN 0-600-38767-4). Spring Books.
Three Men in a Boat: To Say Nothing of the Dog! Jerome Klapka Jerome. LC 77-23999. 1971. u.s.) 0.95. Penguin Books.
Three Men in a Boat: To Say Nothing of the Dog. Jerome Klapka Jerome. LC 4-22823. (The home library). A. L. Burt.
Three Men in a Boat: To Say Nothing of the Dog. Jerome Klapka Jerome. LC 4-16323. 1890. H. Holt and Company.
Three Men in a Boat: To Say Nothing of the Dog. Jerome Klapka Jerome. LC 4867. W. B. Conkey Company.
Three Men in a Boat: To Say Nothing of the Dog. Jerome Klapka Jerome. LC 42-18156. 1942. C. Scribner's Sons.
Three Men in a Boat (to Say Nothing of the Dog) Jerome Klapka Jerome. LC 80-16728. (Series: Continuum Classic of Humor.). 1980. 11.95 (ISBN 0-8264-0018-3). Continuum.
Three Men in a Boat: To Say Nothing of the Dog. Jerome Klapka Jerome. LC 81-8748. (Time Reading Program Special Edition). 1981. 12.95 (ISBN 0-8094-3694-9) (ISBN 0-8094-3695-7). Time-Life Books.
Three Men in Her Life. Barry Caldwell. LC 38-5868. 1938. Godwin.
Three Men in New Suits. John Boynton Priestley. LC 45-7058. 1945. Harper & Brothers.
Three Men Murdered. Archie Joscelyn. LC 37-30402. Phoenix Press.
Three Men on the Bummel. Jerome Klapka Jerome. 1978. 9.95x (ISBN 0-460-00188-4, Evman); pap. 2.95x (ISBN 0-460-01188-X, Evman). Biblio Dist.
Three Men on the Bummel. Jerome Klapka Jerome. 192p. 1982. pap. text ed. 4.25x (ISBN 0-86299-029-7, Pub. by Sutton England). Humanities.
Three Men on the Left Hand. 1st Ed. Ilka Chase. LC 60-8857. 1960. Doubleday.
Three Men on Wheels. Jerome Klapka Jerome. LC 2534. 1900. Dodd, Mead and Company.
Three Men Out. A Nero Wolfe Threesome. Rex Stout. LC 54-7052. 1954. Viking Press.
Three Mesquiteers. William Colt MacDonald. LC 44-492445. 1944. Doubleday, Doran & Co., Inc.
Three Midnight Stories. Alexander Wilson Drake. LC 16-24203. 1916. 5.00. The Century Co.
Three Miles Square. Paul Corey. LC 39-27721. The Bobbs-Merrill Company.
Three Mint Lollipops. Robert Sabatier. LC 73-79569. 1974. 7.95 (ISBN 0-525-21855-6). Dutton.
Three Minutes to Midnight. Mildred Davis. (Dell book). 1973. (pbk) 1.25. Dell Pub. Co.
Three Minutes to Midnight. Mildred B Davis. LC 76-162390. 1971-1972. 5.95 (ISBN 0-394-47316-7). Random House.
Three Miss Graemes. Sarah Broom Macnaughton. LC 9-35443. 1908. E. P. Dutton and Company.
Three Miss Kings. Ada Cambridge Cross. (On cover: Seaside library. Pocket ed. no. 2139). 1895. G. Munro's Sons.
Three Months Later: A Novel of the Communist Coup in Czechoslovakia. Presented and Prefaced by Adam Keneth. 1st Ed. Algue Eger. LC 57-66596. 1957. Greenwich Book Publishers.
Three Months Under the Snow. Jean Jacques Porchat. LC 42-273007. (On cover: Young peoples series). 1892. Hunt & Eaton.
Three Moral Girls. Susie M Chamberlin. LC 10-151940. 1.00. C.
Three More Novels. Ronald Firbank. Incl. Caprice; Inclinations; Vainglory. LC 55-9910. 1951. 6.50 o.s.i. (ISBN 0-8112-0277-1). New Directions.
Three Motives for Murder. Roy Winsor. (Fawcett Book). 1976. 1.25. Fawcett.
Three Musketeers. Alexandre Dumas. (W-1004). 1961. Washington Sq. Pr. Dist. Affiliated Pubs.
Three Musketeers. Alexandre Dumas. Tr. by William Robson. (Illus.). 1975. (pbk.) 4.95 (ISBN 0-8055-1157-1). Hart Publishing Co.
Three Musketeers. Alexandre Dumas. (Rainbow classics). (Illus.). 1957. World Pub. Co.
Three Musketeers. Alexandre Dumas. LC 50-5390. (Modern library of the world's best books). 1950. Modern Library.
Three Musketeers... Alexandre Dumas. LC 1-519. 1894. Drallop Pub. Co.
Three Musketeers. Alexandre Dumas. LC 18-20848. T. Y. Crowell Company.
Three Musketeers. Alexandre Dumas. (Half-title: Everyman's library, ed. by Ernest Rhys. Fiction. no. 81). 1909. J. M. Dent & Co.
Three Musketeers. Alexandre Dumas. LC 20-15705. 1920. Dodd, Mead and Company.
Three Musketeers. Alexandre Dumas. Tr. by Allen, Philip Schuyler. LC 23-12714. (Windermere series). Rand, McNally & Company.
Three Musketeers. Alexandre Dumas. Ed. by Shattuck, Marquis E. LC 25-240604. (The modern readers series). 1925. The Macmillan Company.
Three Musketeers. Alexandre Dumas. LC 30-26383. 1929. Dodd, Mead & Company.
Three Musketeers. Alexandre Dumas. LC 31-26979. (golden books). 1930. D. McKay.
Three Musketeers. Alexandre Dumas. Ed. by Higgins, Violet Moore. LC 31-20924. The John C. Winston Company.
Three Musketeers. Alexandre Dumas. LC 37-2947. (Immortal masterpieces of literature, vol. 1). The Spencer Press.
Three Musketeers. Alexandre Dumas. LC 40-27070. 1940. Garden City Publishing Co., Inc.
Three Musketeers. Alexandre Dumas. LC 49-49546. (World's greatest literature). 1949. Fountain Press.
Three Musketeers. Alexandre Dumas & Bond, A. Curtis, D. 1923, Tr. LC 1-519. (On cover: Fleur de lys series). Drallop Publishing Co.

Three Musketeers. Alexandre Dumas & Carlin, Jerome, 1913- LC 47-6519. 1947. Globe Book Co.

Three Musketeers. Alexandre Dumas & Reg Craig. LC 65-7014. 1964.

Three Musketeers. Alexandre Dumas & Maquet, Auguste. LC 6-42123. 1888. Little, Brown and Company.

Three Musketeers. Alexandre Dumas & Auguste Maquet. LC 9-21713. Little, Brown, & Company.

Three Musketeers... Alexandre Dumas & Maquet, Auguste. LC 20-156283. Little, Brown, and Company.

Three Musketeers... Alexandre Dumas & Maquet, Auguste. LC 4-17499. (Half-title: The romance of Alexandre Dumas. Handy library edition. The D'Artagnan romances...). 1893. Little, Brown and Company.

Three Musketeers. Alexandre Dumas & Maquet, Auguste. LC 6-42132. (Half-title: The romances of Alexandre Dumas. Illustrated library ed. v. 12-13). 1893. Little, Brown, and Company.

Three Musketeers. Alexandre Dumas & Maquet, Auguste. LC 6-42140. T. Y. Crowell & Company.

Three Musketeers. Alexandre Dumas & Maquet, Auguste. Tr. by Robson, William. 1895. D. Appleton & Co.

Three Musketeers. Alexandre Dumas & Maquet, Auguste. Tr. by Robson, William. LC 13-23593. 1911. D. Appleton and Company.

Three Musketeers. Alexandre Dumas & Maquet, Auguste. LC 21-27481. (Rittenhouse classics). 1921. G. W. Jacobs & Company.

Three Musketeers. Alexandre Dumas & Maquet, Auguste. Tr. by Robson, William. 1922. D. Appleton and Company.

Three Musketeers. Alexandre Dumas & Maquet, Auguste. Ed. by Shepard, Odell. LC 28-21822. (modern readers' series). 1928. The Macmillan Company.

Three Musketeers. Alexandre Dumas & Maquet, Auguste. LC 36-37091. (Half-title: Everyman's library, ed. by Ernest Rhys. Fiction. no. 81). 1931. J. M. Dent & Sons, Ltd.

Three Musketeers. Alexandre Dumas & Auguste Maquet. LC 45-25339. 1940. The Book League of America.

Three Musketeers... Alexandre Dumas & O'Neil, James. LC 4695. H. M. Caldwell Co.

Three Musketeers. Alexandre Dumas & William Robson. LC 77-152301. (Illus.). 1976. 10.00. (ISBN 0-8055-0204-1) (ISBN 0-8055-1157-1). Hart Pub. Co.

Three Musketeers: A New Translation by Jacques Le Clercq, Edited and Abridged by the Translator Especially for the Illustrated Junior Library. Illustrated by Norman Price and E. C. Van Swearingen. Alexandre Dumas. Ed. by Jacques Georges Clemenceau Le Clercq. LC 53-3493. (Illustrated junior library). 1953. Grosset &Dunlap.

Three Musketeers: Being the First of the D'Artagnan Romances. Alexandre Dumas & Auguste Maquet. LC 3-27813. G. Routledge and Sons, Limited.

Three Musketeers: Decorations by Valenti Angelo. Alexandre Dumas. LC 36-7717. 1935. The Three Sirens Press.

Three Musketeers. Illustrated by C. Walter Hodges. Introd. by May Lamberton Becker. Alexandre Dumas. LC 57-7408. 1957. World Pub. Co.

Three Musketeers: Introd. by Thomas Layman. Alexandre Dumas. LC 53-1236. 1952. Fine Editions Press.

Three Musketeers or the Three Guardsman. Alexandre Dumas. (Illus.). 592p. Date not set. pap. price not set (ISBN 0-86649-067-1). Twentieth Century.

Three Musketeers. The Translation by William Robson, with an Introd. by Ben Ray Redman & Illus. by Edy Legrand. Alexandre Dumas. LC 50-8474. 1950. Heritage Press.

Three Musketeers: Translated by Isabel Ely Lord; Designed for Modern Reading. Illustrated by Daniel Rasmusson. Alexandre Dumas. LC 52-7847. 1952. Doubleday.

Three Musketeers. Translated by William Robson; Illustrated by Hookway Cowles. Alexandre Dumas. LC 50-109237. (Macdonald illustrated classics, 15). 1950. Coward-McCann.

Three Musketeers. With Illus. by Edy Legrand and a Pref. by the Author. Translated from the French. Alexandre Dumas. LC 60-2842. 1960. bxd. 6.00. Heritage Press Dist. Dial Press.

Three Mustangeers. Will James. LC 33-30565. 1933. C. Scribner's Sons.

Three Names for Murder. Harriette Russell Campbell. Harper & Brothers.

Three Nice Smelling Skunks. Dennis Provencher. 3.95 o.p. Vantage.

Three Nights in a Lager Beer Saloon. A Tale of American Life, Being the Counterpart to T. S. Arthur's "Ten Nights in a Barroom". H. A Wilkens & Marxhausen, C., Joint Author. 1876.

Three Nights of Love. Leona Slottman. LC 46-1786. 1946. Phoenix Press.

Three Nights of Love. LC 46-1786. 1946. Phoenix Press.

Three Nineteenth-Century Novels. Intro. by Victoria Glendinning. Incl. Pride & Prejudice. Austen; Wuthering Heights. Bronte; Silas Marner. Eliot. 1979. pap. 2.95 (ISBN 0-451-51241-3, CE 1241, Sig Classics). NAL.

Three Nineteenth-Century Novels. LC 79-87934. (Signet classic). 1979. 2.95 (ISBN 0-451-51241-3). New American Library.

Three-Notch Cameron. William Colt MacDonald. LC 52-10996. (Double D western). Doubleday.

Three Novellas. Ivan Sergeevich Turgenev. Tr. by Marion Mainwaring from Rus. LC 69-13741. 208p. 1969. 5.95 (ISBN 0-374-27672-2). FS&G.

Three Novellas: Punin and Baburin, The Inn, The Watch. Ivan Sergeevich Turgenev. LC 69-13741. 1969. 5.95. Farrar, Straus & Giroux.

Three Novels. Mariano Azuela & Frances Kellam Hendricks. LC 78-68663. 1979. 15.00 (ISBN 0-911536-78-7). Trinity University Press.

Three Novels. Samuel Beckett. Incl. Molloy; Malone Dies; Unnamable. 1965. pap. 4.95 (ISBN 0-394-17299-X, B78, BC). Grove.

Three Novels. Joseph Conrad. LC 70-18842. 1970. 0.75. Washington Square Press.

Three Novels. Charles Dickens. LC 78-312488. (Illus.). 1977. 9.75 (ISBN 0-600-32930-5). Spring Books.

Three Novels. Shelby Foote. Incl. Follow Me Down; Jordan County; Love in a Dry Season. 252p. 1964. 7.50 o.p. (ISBN 0-8037-8840-1). Dial.

Three Novels. Witold Gombrowicz. LC 78-55104. (Evergreen book). 1978. 9.95 (ISBN 0-8021-4210-9). Grove Press: Distributed by Random House.

Three Novels. bulfinch ed. Ed. by Edward J. Gordon & Virginia T. Wilkinson. (gr. 7 up). 1967. text ed. 4.36 o.p. Ginn.

Three Novels. Ernest Hemingway. LC 62-9455. (Modern standard authors). 1962. Scribner.

Three Novels. Vidiadhar Surajprasad Naipaul. LC 82-47819. 1982. 18.95 (ISBN 0-394-52847-6). Knopf.

Three Novels. Harriet B. Stowe. Ed. by Kathryn K. Sklar. Bd. with Uncle Tom's Cabin, or Life among the Lowly; Minister's Wooing; Oldtown Folks. LC 81-18629. (Illus.). 1488p. 1982. 25.00 (ISBN 0-940450-01-1, Pub. by Library of America). Literary Classics.

Three Novels: Bibliotheca Neerlandica Ser. William Elsschot. Incl. Soft Soap; Leg; Will-O'-the Wisp. 1965. 10.00x o.s.i. (ISBN 0-8277-0377-5). British Bk Ctr.

Three Novels: Bibliotheca Neerlandica Ser. William Elsschot. Incl. Soft Soap; Leg; Will-O'-the Wisp. 1965. 10.00x o.s.i. (ISBN 0-8277-0377-5). British Bk Ctr.

Three Novels: Blue Voyage, Great Circle, King Coffin by Conrad Aiken.Pref. by Conrad Aiken. Conrad Potter Aiken. LC 65-25145. 1966. pap., 2.25. McGraw.

Three Novels by Mariano Azuela. Mariano Azuela. Tr. by Frances K. Hendricks & Beatrice Berler. LC 78-68663. 373p. 1979. 15.00 (ISBN 0-911536-78-7). Trinity U Pr.

Three Novels: Ferdydurke, Pornografia, & Cosmos. Witold Gombrowicz. Tr. by Eric Mosbacher & Alastair Hamilton. 1978. pap. 9.95 (ISBN 0-394-17067-9, E720, Ever). Grove.

Three Novels: Follow Me Down; Jordan County; Love in a Dry Season. Shelby Foote. LC 64-20281. 1964. Dial Press.

Three Novels from Ancient India. Banabhatta. 500p. 1982. text ed. 37.50x (ISBN 0-7069-1347-7, Pub. by Vikas India). Advent NY.

Three Novels from Ancient India: Dandin's Dashakumaracharita, Subandhu's Vasavadatta, Banabhatta's Kadambari. Vishwanath S Naravane & Dandin. LC 81-905535. 37.50 (ISBN 0-7069-1347-7). Vikas Pub. House.

Three Novels: Harriet Beecher Stowe. Ed. by Kathryn F. Sklar. LC 81-18629. 1448p. 1982. 27.50 (ISBN 0-940450-01-1). Literary Classics.

Three Novels: Headlong Hall, Nightmare Abbey, Crotchet Castle. Thomas Love Peacock. LC 41-11196. (Nelson classics). 1940. T. Nelson and Sons, Ltd.

Three Novels: Hordubal, An Ordinary Life and Meteor. omnibus ed. Karel Capek. Tr. by Weatherall, Marie. LC 49-7788. 1948. A. A. Wyn.

Three Novels: Molloy. Malone Dies. The Unnamable. Tr. from French. Samuel Beckett. LC 65-5000. (Evergreen black cat bk., BC-78). 1965. pap., 1.45. Grove.

Three Novels: Rule Golden, Natural State, and The Dying Man. Damon Francis Knight. LC 67-10420. 1967. Doubleday.

Three Novels: Soft Soap: The Leg: Will-O'-the-Wisp. by Willem Elsschot. Tr by A. Brotherton. Alfons De Ridder, pseud. LC 65-24360. (Bibliotheca Neerlandica. 12). 1965. 5.95. London House.

Three Novels: The Europeans, The Spoils of Poynton, The Sacred Fount. Introd. by Tony Tanner. Henry James. LC 68-2500. (Perennial classic, P 3077). 1968. pap., 1.45. Harper.

Three Novels: The Europeans, The Spoils of Poynton, The Sacred Fount. Henry James. LC 68-2500. (Perennial classic, P3077). 1968. Harper & Row.

Three Novels: The Great Gatsby. Francis Scott Key Fitzgerald. LC 53-11657. (Modern standard authors). 1953. Scribner.

Three Novels: The Great Gatsby; Tender Is the Night; & the Last Tycoon. Francis Scott Key Fitzgerald. 1953. pap. text ed. 10.95x (ISBN 0-684-16245-8, ScribC). Scribner.

Three Novels: Uncle Moses, Chaim Lederer's Return, Judge Not-- Shalom Asch & Krauch, Elsa, Tr. LC 38-29527. 1938. G. P. Putnam's Sons.

Three Novels: Vainglory; Inclinations; Caprice. With an Introd. by Ernest Jones. Arthur Annesley Ronald Firbank. LC 51-9910. 1951. New Directions.

Three Nuns. Sara Harris. 224p. 1976. 8.95 o.p. (ISBN 0-679-50613-6). McKay.

Three Nuns. Sara Harris. 224p. 1976. 8.95 o.p. (ISBN 0-679-50613-6). McKay.

Three Nuns: An Intimate Story. Sara Harris. LC 76-23305. 8.95 (ISBN 0-679-50613-6). McKay.

Three O'clock Dinner. Josephine Pinckney. LC 45-8451. 1945. The Viking Press.

Three of a Kind. James Mallahan Cain. LC 43-431294. 1943. A. A. Knopf.

Three of a Kind. Merritt Clifton. 20p. 1979. pap. 1.00. Samisdat.

Three of a Kind. Illus. by Gustaf Tenggren. LC 73-76031. (Golden Book). (Illus.). 1973. (pbk) 1.45. Golden Pr.

Three of a Kind: And The Haunting of Jack Burnham. Herman Cyril McNeile. LC 26-6909. George H. Doran Company.

Three of a Kind: The Story of an Old Musician, a Newsboy and a Cocker Dog. Richard Burton. LC 8-26676. 1908. Little, Brown, and Company.

Three of Clubs. Valentine Williams. LC 24-17906. 1924. Houghton Mifflin Company.

Three of Diamonds. 1st ed. Kathleen Moore Knight. LC 53-9346. 1953. Published for the Crime Club by Doubleday.

Three of Hearts. Berta Ruck. LC 17-21877. 1917. Dodd, Mead and Company.

Three of Us. Joyce Elbert. LC 72-94016. 1973. 7.95 (ISBN 0-87795-052-0). Arbor House.

Three of Us, Barney. Cossack. Rex. Izora Cecilia Chandler. LC 6-23127. 1895. Hunt & Eaton.

Three Old Maids in Hawaii. Ellen Blackmar Maxwell. LC 7-18758. 1896. Eaton & Mains.

Three on a Honeymoon. Frances Kerry, pseud. LC 42-19758. 1942. Gramercy Publishing Co.

Three on a Match. H. Robert Mason. LC 47-24301. 1947. Meador Publishing Company.

Three Ought to Be a Law: And Other Stories. Nunnally Johnson. LC 31-6491. 1931. Doubleday, Doran & Company, Inc.

Three Outsiders: Pascal, Kierkegaard, Simon Weil. Diogenes Allen. 120p. (Orig.). 1983. pap. 6.00 (ISBN 0-936384-08-5). Cowley Pubns.

Three Over the Frontier. Jean Bekessy. Tr. by Eric Sutton. LC 39-4491. 1939. Dodd, Mead & Company.

Three Pairs of Silk Stockings: A Novel of the Life of the Educated Class Under the Soviet. Panteleimon Sergeevich Romanov. LC 72-90308. 1973. (ISBN 0-88355-019-9). Hyperion Press.

Three Pairs of Silk Stockings: A Novel of the Life of the Educated Class Under the Soviet. Panteleimon Sergeevich Romanov. Tr. by Leonid Sergeevich Zarin. Graham, Stephen, 1884- Ed. LC 31-12121. 1931. C. Scribner's Sons.

Three Partners, and Other Tales. Bret Harte. LC 76-37547. (Short story index reprint series). (Illus.). 1972. (ISBN 0-8369-4106-3). Books for Libraries Press.

Three Partners: Or, The Big Strike on Heavy Tree Hill. Bret Harte. LC 41-38125. 1897. Houghton Mifflin Company.

Three Parts Earth. Edna Frederikson. LC 78-161348. 1971. 6.95. Threshold Books.

Three Parts Earth. Edna Frederikson. 1974. (pbk.) 1.25. Popular Library.

Three Passions. Cosmo Hamilton. LC 28-23046. 1928. G. P. Putnam's Sons.

Three: Pebbles and Well Water: A Flower Blooming in the Land. The Church in the Dale. Harry Barba. LC 67-27073. 1967. Harian Press.

Three Penny Land: A Novel. Fielding Dawson. LC 80-27344. 20.00 (ISBN 0-87685-447-1) (ISBN 0-87685-446-3). Black Sparrow Press.

Three Penny Lane. Fielding Dawson. 150p. (Orig.). 1981. signed ed. 20.00 (ISBN 0-87685-447-1); pap. 5.00 (ISBN 0-87685-446-3). Black Sparrow.

Three-Penny Novel. Bertolt Brecht. LC 73-156489. (Penguin modern classics). 1972. 0.45 (ISBN 0-14-001515-9). Penguin.

Three per Cent a Month: Or, The Perils of Fast Living. Charles Burdett. LC 6-18667. 1856. Derby & Jackson.

Three Perils of Man: War, Women, and Witchcraft. James Hogg. LC 73-4593. 1973. 12.50 (ISBN 0-87471-182-7). Rowman and Littlefield.

Three Pilgrims and a Tinker: A Novel. Mary Borden. LC 24-27433. 1924. A. A. Knopf.

Three-Pipe Problem. Julian Symons. LC 74-20421. 1975. 6.95 (ISBN 0-06-014193-X). Harper & Row.

Three Pirates: Or, The Virgin of the Islet. Justin Jones. LC 7-11900. 1853. H. Long & Brother.

Three Plays. Eugene Ionesco. Tr. by Donald Watson from Fr. Incl. Amedee; New Tenant; Victims of Duty. 1958. pap. 3.95 (ISBN 0-394-17212-4, E119, Ever). Grove.

Three Plots for Asey Mayo. Phoebe Atwood Taylor. LC 42-236683. 1942. W. W. Norton & Company, Inc.

Three Potato, Four. Wilfred Greatorex. LC 76-22718. 8.95 (ISBN 0-698-10764-0). Coward, McCann & Geoghegan.

Three Predatory Women. Sydney Loch. LC 70-125230. (Short story index reprint series). 1970. Books for Libraries Press.

Three Predatory Women. Sydney Loch. LC 26-3572. George H. Doran Company.

Three Pretty Girls. Vida Hurst. Gramercy Publishing Co.

Three Prisoners, a True Story of Adventure. William Henry Shelton. (The East and West series). 1904. A. S. Barnes & Company.

Three Prize Murders. Murder for Tea. by c. s. wallace. ed. Edith Howie & Marguerite Pearman McIntre. LC 41-17551. Farrar & Rinehart, Inc.

Three Problems for Solar Pons. August William Derleth. LC 52-14844. 1952. Mycroft & Moran.

Three Profiteers. Ulysses Samuel Leah. LC 34-14225. The Stratford Company.

Three Prophetic Novels. Herbert George Wells. Incl. When the Sleeper Wakes; Story of the Days to Come; Time Machine. 8.75 (ISBN 0-8446-3151-5). Peter Smith.

Three Prophetic Novels of H. G. Wells. Herbert George Wells. Ed. by E. F. Bleiler. pap. 5.00 (ISBN 0-486-20605-X). Dover.

Three Prophetic Novels. Selected and with an Introd. by E.F. Bleiler. Herbert George Wells. LC 59-14229. 1960. Dover Publications.

Three Racketeers. 1st Ed. Anthony Giancol. LC 55-7182. 1955. Vantage Press.

Three Ranches West. C. S. Adams & T. E. Brown, Sr. 10.95 o.p. Carlton.

Three Recruits, and the Girls They Left Behind Them. A Novel. Joseph Hatton. (Franklin square library, no. 145). 1880. Harper & Brothers.

Three Red Roses. Henrietta Hamilton Diehl. (Illus.). 1974. 3.50 (ISBN 0-533-01058-6). Vantage Press.

Three Religious Rebels: Forefathers of the Trappists. Raymond. LC 44-8993. (His The saga of Citeaux. 1st epoch). 1944. P. J. Kenedy & Sons.

Three Renaissance Classics. Ed. by Burton A. Milligan. 1971. pap. 3.95 Lyceum Ed. o.p. (ISBN 0-684-12478-5, SL299). Scribner.

Three Rich Men. Sidney Herschel Small. LC 32-10334. Covici, Friede.

Three Richard Whalens: A Story of Adventure. James Knapp Reeve. LC 7-30934. (Twentieth century series). F. A. Stokes Company.

Three-Ring Psychus. John Shirley. 240p. (Orig.). 1980. pap. 1.95 (ISBN 0-89083-674-4). Zebra.

Three Rivers. Walter C. Kidney. (Illus.). 80p. 1982. pap. 7.95 (ISBN 0-916670-07-4). Pitt Hist & Landmks Found.

Three Rivers. Roberta Latow. LC 81-153081. 1981. 12.95 (ISBN 0-531-09560-6). D. Elliott: Distributed by F. Watts.

Three Rivers South, the Story of Young Abe Lincoln: Illustrated by Thomas Hart Benton. Virginia Louise Snider Eifert. LC 53-7784. 1953. Dodd, Mead.

Three Rivers to Run. Albert Butler. 1981. 1.95 (ISBN 0-505-51672-1). Tower Publications Inc.

Three Roads. Kenneth Millar. 1974. (pbk.) 1.25. Bantam Books.
Three Roads. Kenneth Millar. LC 48-7047. 1948. A. A. Knopf.
Three Roads: Great Novels of Courage, Adventure and Romance: Blackcock's Feather, The Road to Nowhere, Green Rushes. Maurice Walsh. LC 36-285062. 1936. Frederick A. Stokes Company.
Three Roads to a Star. David Garth. LC 54-104827. Putnam.
Three Roads to Valhalla. Catherine Pomeroy Stewart. LC 48-8080. 1948. C. Scribner's Sons.
Three Rode North. Al Conroy. 1978. pap. 1.25 (ISBN 0-440-18852-0). Dell.
Three Roman Girls. A Tale of the Catacombs. Mary Ellen Bamford. LC 12-30675. American Baptist Publication Society.
Three Roses. Vicente Blasco Ibanez & Grummon, Stuart Edgar, Tr. LC 32-22554. 1932. E. P. Dutton & Co., Inc.
Three Royal Magi: Or, The Journey to Bethlehem. By the Author of "The Blind Orphan Boy.". Blumenthal, Carl E., Tr. LC 1-1693. 1850. H. Perkins.
Three R's... Martin Louis Alan Gompertz. LC 31-8421. Pub. for the Crime Club, Inc., by Doubleday, Doran & Company, Inc.
Three Sapphires. William Alexander Fraser. LC 18-22251. George H. Doran Company.
Three Science-Fiction Novels. John Taine, pseud. Incl. Time Stream; Greatest Adventure; Purple Sapphire. 5.00 o.p. (ISBN 0-8446-0933-1). Peter Smith.
Three Score and Ten. Angela Mackail Thirkell & Carolina Alice Lejeune. LC 62-11048. 1962. Knopf.
Three Score and Ten. Alec Waugh. LC 30-7791. 1930. Doubleday, Doran & Company, Inc.
Three Seasons at Askrigg. Clare Rossiter. LC 77-109. 1977. 7.95 (ISBN 0-312-80307-9). St. Martin's Press.
Three Secret Seeds. Joyce Reason. 1964. pap. 1.50 (ISBN 0-87508-766-3). Chr Lit.
Three Secrets: A Story of Portugal. Minna Josephine Smith. LC 41-4268. 1941. The Macmillan Company.
Three Secrets: Based on a Screenplay by Martin Rackin and Gina Kaus. Margaret Lee Runbeck & Three Secrets (Motion Picture) LC 51-15544. (Gold medal book, 128). 1950. Fawcett Publications.
Three Selected Short Novels. Booth Tarkington. LC 47-5078. 1947. Doubleday.
Three Sentimental Novels. Ed. by Albert J. Kuhn. LC 75-94349. (Rinehart editions). 1969. Holt, Rinehart and Winston.
Three Sentimental Novels. (Rinehart Editions). pap. price not set o.p. (HoltC). HR&W.
Three Sentinels. Geoffrey Household. LC 74-186961. 1972. 6.95. Little, Brown.
Three, Seven, Ace: And Other Stories. Vladimir Tendryakov. Tr. by David Alger et al from Rus. LC 72-8319. 252p. 1973. 6.95 o.p. (ISBN 0-06-014242-1, HarpT). Har-Row.
Three Sevens: A Story of Ancient Initiations. William P Phelon. LC 7-36085. 1889. The Hermetic Publishing Company.
Three Sevens: A Story of Ancient Initiation. William P. Phelon & Phelon, Mira M. LC 39-993314. The Philosophical Publishing Co.
Three Shades of Lace. Frances V. Wilkes. 1970. 4.50 o.p. Carlton.
Three Shall Be One. Francena Harriet Arnold. LC 53-134455. 1953. Moody Press.
Three Shapes of Love. Marian L Wells. LC 76-55759. 5.95 (ISBN 0-8024-8749-1). Moody Press.
Three-Sheet. Tiffany Thayer. LC 32-258448. 1932. Liveright, Inc.
Three Sheets in the Wind. Guy Gilpatric. 1936. Dodd, Mead & Company.
Three Ships and Three Kings. Georgia Sallaska. LC 69-10948. (Illus.). 1969. 6.95. Doubleday.
Three Ships in Azure. Irvin Anthony. LC 26-14986. 1926. The Penn Publishing Company.
Three Short Biers. Jimmy Starr. LC 45-7195. 1945. Murray & Gee, Inc.
Three Short Novels. Kay Boyle. LC 58-2140. (Beacon paperback no. 55). 1958. Beacon Press.
Three Short Novels. Kay Boyle. LC 81-21034. 1982. 5.95 (ISBN 0-14-006109-6). Penguin Books.
Three Short Novels. Jean Bruller & Sutton, Eric, Tr. LC 47-2784. 1947. Little, Brown and Company.
Three Short Novels. Fairbairn, Douglas. LC 61-10673. 1961. Random House.
Three Short Novels. Ivan Sergeevich Turgenev. 303p. 1974. 5.45 (ISBN 0-8285-1064-4, Pub. by Progress Pubs USSR). Imported Pubns.
Three Short Novels: By Dostoevsky. Tr. by Andrew R. MacAndrew. Fedor Mikhailovich Dostoevskii. LC 66-14716. (Bantam classic, NC293). 1966. Bantam.
Three Short Novels from Here Today and Gone Tomorrow. Louis Bromfield. LC 44-47314. (On cover: Avon modern short story monthly. No. 13). 1944. Avon Book Company.
Three Short Novels from Papua New Guinea. Benjamin Umba et al. Ed. by Mike Greicus. (Illus.). 1975. text ed. 12.00x (ISBN 0-582-71437-0); pap. 6.50x (ISBN 0-582-71436-2). Longman.
Three Short Novels of Dostoyevsky. Fyodor Dostoyevsky. Ed. by Avrahm Yarmolinsky. Tr. by Constance Garnett. Incl. Double; Notes from the Underground; Eternal Husband. LC 60-57341. pap. 6.95 (ISBN 0-385-09435-3, A193, Anch). Doubleday.
Three Short Romances, Written on Planes, a Train & Elsewhere. Carlos Anne Phelps. LC 78-934. (Illus.). 5.50 (ISBN 0-87770-195-4). Ye Galleon Press.
Three Short Stories. Robert Musil. Ed. by Hugh Sacker. (Clarendon German Ser). 1970. pap. 7.95x (ISBN 0-19-832467-7). Oxford U Pr.
Three Short Stories. Pauline D. Wilson. 3.00 o.p. Carlton.
Three Shorter Novels of Herman Melville: With Critical and Biographical Material by Joseph Schiffman. Herman Melville. LC 62-9481. (Harper's modern classics). 1962. Harper.
Three Sides of the Mirror: A Novel. Robert Watson. LC 66-22468. 1966. Putnam.
Three Sides to the River. Estelle Carruth. LC 63-15618. 1963. Naylor Co.
Three Silences. Catherine Isabel Dodd. LC 27-17806. George H. Doran Company.
Three Silver Birches. Ruth McCarthy Sears. (Candlelight romance). 1975. (pbk.) 0.75. Dell.
Three Sirens. Irving Wallace. 1971. pap. 3.50 (ISBN 0-451-11359-4, AE1359, Sig). NAL.
Three Sisters. May Sinclair. LC 14-18337. 1914. The Macmillan Company.
Three Sisters and Three Fortunes: Or, Rose, Blanche, and Violet. George Henry Lewes. LC 7-3531. (On cover: Library of select novels. no.118). 1848. Harper & Brothers.
Three Sisters Flew Home. Mary Fitt. LC 36-13189. 1936. Doubleday, Doran & Company,Inc.
Three Sisters Flew Home. Kathleen Freeman. LC 36-13189. 1936. Doubleday, Doran.
Three Sisters of Briarwick. Katheryn Kimbrough. (Queen-size gothic: large easy-to-read type). 1973. (pbk.) 0.95. Popular Lib.
Three Sisters of Sz. Kok Seng Tan. (Writing in Asia Ser.). 1978. pap. text ed. 3.95x (00241). Heinemann Ed.
Three Sisters: Or Sketches of a Highly Original Family. Elsa de'Esterre Keeling. LC 7-11427. (On cover: Seaside library. Pocket ed. no. 382). G. Munro.
Three Sisters: The Story of the Soong Family of China. Cornelia Spencer, pseud. The John Day Company.
Three Sisters: The Story of the Soong Family of China. Grace Yankey & Wiese, Kurt, 1887-Illus. LC 39-27472. 1939. The John Day Company.
Three Sixteenth-Century Conteurs. Ed. by A J Krailsheimer. Marguerite D'Angouleme, Queen of Navarre, 1492-1549. L'Heptameron et al. LC 66-77494. (Clarendon French Ser.: B66-14520). 1966. Oxford U.P.
Three Sixteenth-Century Conteurs. Ed. by A J Krailsheimer. LC 66-9511. (Clarendon French series). 1966. Oxford University Press.
Three Soldiers. John Dos Passos. LC 21-26886. George H. Doran Company.
Three Soldiers. John Dos Passos. LC 32-331547. (Half-title: The modern library of the world's best books). The Modern Library.
Three Soldiers. John Dos Passos. LC 37-5368. 1937. The Sun Dial Press, Inc.
Three Soldiers. John Dos Passos. 1947. Houghton, Mifflin, Co.
Three Solid Stones. Martha Mvungi. (Africa Writers Series; 159). 1975. (ISBN 0-435-90159-1). Heinemann.
Three Sons. large print ed.. ed. Ursula Bloom. LC 82-19830. 1983. 12.95 (ISBN 0-89340-489-6). J. Curley & Associates.
Three Sons and a Mother. Gilbert Cannan. LC 16-6608. 1916. 1.50. George H. Doran Company.
Three Sons of Adam Jones. John S. Daniels, pseud. (Orig., Osi). 1969. pap. 0.50 o.s.i. (B50-1020). Belmont-Tower.
Three Spaniards. A Romance. George Walker. LC 8-33289. (On back of cover: Lovell library). J. W. Lovell Company.
Three Speeds Forward: An Automobile Love Story with One Reverse. Lloyd Osbourne. LC 6-31657. 1906. D. Appleton and Company.
Three Stages of Clarinda Thorbald. William T Hamilton. LC 24-4582. Dorrance.
Three Stances of Modern Fiction: A Critical Anthology of the Short Story. Ed. by Stephen Minot. LC 72-184369. 1972. (pbk) 4.50 (ISBN 0-87626-875-0). Winthrop Publishers.
Three Star Mystery Book: The Old Dark House, by J. B. Priestley. Was It Murder? John Boynton Priestley & James Hilton. LC 42-16050. 1942. Harper & Brothers.
Three Steeples: A Tragedy of Earth. Le Roy MacLeod. LC 31-5755. Covici, Friede.
Three Stigmata of Palmer Eldritch. Philip K Dick. LC 65-11537. (Doubleday sci. fic.). 1965. 4.95. Doubleday.
Three Stigmata of Palmer Eldritch. Philip K Dick. LC 79-18572. (Gregg science fiction series). 1979. 14.95 (ISBN 0-8398-2479-3). Gregg Press.
Three Stones. Cloyd Criswell. 1955. 2.00 (ISBN 0-8233-0016-1). Golden Quill.
Three Stories. Max Apple. 1983. signed limited ed. 55.00 (ISBN 0-939722-11-9). Pressworks.
Three Stories. Robert Verlin Cassill. LC 82-82012. 75p. (Orig.). 1982. pap. 4.50 (ISBN 0-9605008-1-2). Hermes Hse.
Three Stories. William Fitzgerald Jenkins & Jack Williamson. LC 67-11801. (Doubleday science fiction). 1967. Doubleday.
Three Stories. limited ed. Leon & Rochester Folk Art Guild. LC 76-16165. 1969. Rochester Folk Art Guild.
Three Stories. The Busted Ex-Texan. How Deacon Tulman and Parson Whitney Celebrated New Years, The Leaf of Red Rose. William Henry Harrison Murray. LC 7-32493. Printed by C. W. Calkins & Co.
Three-Stranded Yarn: The Wreck of the Lady Emma. William Clark Russell. LC 8-1807. E. A. Weeks & Company.
Three Strange Lovers. Victor Francis Calverton & O'Brien, Edward Joseph Harrington, 1890- LC 30-5239. The Macaulay Company.
Three Straw Men. August William Derleth. 5.95 (ISBN 0-88361-071-X). Stanton & Lee.
Three Straw Men. August William Derleth. 4.95 o.s.i. (ISBN 0-88451-040-9). Edco-Vis Assoc.
Three Street. Will Stevens. LC 62-11317. 1962. Doubleday.
Three Street. Will Stevens. LC 62-11317. 1962. Doubleday.
Three Strings. Natalie Sumner Lincoln. LC 18-215313. 1918. D. Appleton and Company.
Three Strong Women: A Tall Tale from Japan. Claus Stamm. (Viking Seafarer Book). (Illus.). 1974. (pbk.) 0.95 (ISBN 0-670-05095-4). Viking Press.
Three Students. Haldane Macfall. LC 26-12241. 1926. A. A. Knopf.
Three Suitors: A Novel. Richard Jones. LC 68-13967. 1968. Little, Brown.
Three Suitors for Cassandra. Jane Seth-Smith. LC 56-22597. 1955. Hurst & Blackett.
Three Summers with Pop. Gertrude Finnegan Cable. LC 40-7567. The Pyramid Press.
Three Supernatural Novels of the Victorian Period. Everett Franklin Bleiler. LC 74-82204. 1975. 4.00 (ISBN 0-486-22571-2). Dover Publications.
Three Tales. Paul Frederic Bowles. LC 75-18063. 24p. (Minimum order: 3 copies). 1975. pap. 3.50 (ISBN 0-916228-10-X). Phoenix Bk Shop.
Three Tales. Paul Frederic Bowles. LC 75-18063. 1975. pap. 3.50 (Pub. by F Hallman). SBD.
Three Tales. Gustave Flaubert & McDowell, Arthur Sydney, 1877-1933, Tr. LC 43-46669. (Borzoi pocket books).
Three Tales. Gustave Flaubert & McDowell, Arthur Sydney, 1877-1933, Tr. LC 45-7848. (New classics). 1944. New Directions.
Three Tales. Johann Wolfgang Von Goethe. Ed. by C. A. Russ. (Clarendon German Ser). (Ger). 1964. 2.25x o.p. (ISBN 0-19-832440-5). Oxford U Pr.
Three Tales. Johann Wolfgang Von Goethe. Ed. by C. A. Russ. (Clarendon German Ser.). 128p. 1964. pap. 2.50x o.p. (ISBN 0-19-500327-6). Oxford U Pr.
Three Tales. Frank O'Connor, pseud. 56p. 1971. Repr. of 1942 ed. 11.00x (ISBN 0-7165-1395-1, Pub. by Cuala Press Ireland). Biblio Dist.
Three Tales: Christine Van Amberg, Resignation, and The Village Doctor: by the Countess D'Arbouville. Sophie De Bexancourt Loyre D'Arbouville & Field, Maunsell Bradhurst, 1823-1875, Ed. and Tr. LC 26-164679. 1853. Harper & Brothers.
Three Tales: The Ghost, The Brazen Android, The Carpenter. William Douglas O'Connor. LC 8-16598. 1892. Houghton, Mifflin and Company.
Three Taps: A Detective Story Without a Moral. Ronald Arbuthnott Knox. LC 27-40653. 1927. Simon and Schuster.
Three Teachers. Gino Montenero. LC 67-11988. 1967. Philosophical Library.
Three Telltale Allegories. Keith J. Anderson. 5.95 o.p. Vantage.
Three-Ten to Anywhere. Leo Calvin Rosten. LC 75-26771. 204p. 1976. 8.95 (ISBN 0-07-053982-0, GB). McGraw.
Three Tetons: A Story of the Yellowstone. Alice Wellington Rollins. LC 7-40756. Cassell & Company, Limited.
Three Things: The Forge in Which the Soul of a Man Was Tested. Mary Raymond Shipman Andrews. LC 15-24856. 1915. Little, Brown, and Company.
Three Thirds of a Ghost. Timothy Fuller. LC 40-35814. 1941. Little, Brown, and Company.
Three Thirty Park. Stanley Cohen. LC 76-53027. 8.95 (ISBN 0-399-11901-9). Putnam.
Three-Thirty Park. Stanley Cohen. 1978. pap. 1.95 (ISBN 0-425-03874-2, Dist. by Putnam). Berkley Pub.
Three Thirty Park. Stanley Cohen. 1977. 8.95 o.p. (ISBN 0-399-11901-9). Putnam Pub Group.
Three: This Gun for Hire: The Confidential Agent, The Ministry of Fear. Graham Greene. LC 52-9618. 1952. Viking Press.
Three Thousand Dollars. Anna Katharine Green Rohlfs. LC 9-29770. 1910. R. G. Badger.
Three Thousand Years. 1st Ed. Thomas Calvert McClary. LC 54-5691. (FP science fiction). 1954. Fantasy Press.
Three-Time Losers. Aaron Marc Stein. LC 58-5955. 1958. Published for the Crime Club by Doubleday.
Three Times and Out. Mary Lowe Dickinson. 1895. Hunt & Eaton.
Three Times Dead: Or, The Secret of the Heath... Mary Elizabeth Braddon Maxwell. (Seaside library. v. 30, no. 629). 1879. G. Munro.
Three Times I Bow. Carl Glick. LC 43-12358. 1943. Whittlesey House, McGraw-Hill Book Company, Inc.
Three Times I Bow. Carl Glick. LC 45-5727. 1945. Hurst & Blackett Ltd.
Three Times Sin. Florence Stonebraker. LC 49-1188. 1949. Phoenix Press.
Three Times Three: Mystery Omnibus. Ed. by Howard Haycraft & John Beecroft. LC 64-16225. 1964. Doubleday.
Three to Be Read: Containing The Smuggled Atom Bomb, Sporting Blood, and the Experiment in Crime. Philip Wylie. LC 52-7156. Rinehart.
Three to Conquer. Eric Frank Russell. LC 56-13295. 1956. Avalon Books.
Three to Dorsai! Three Novels from the Childe Cycle. Gordon R Dickson. LC 75-330595. N. Doubleday.
Three to Get Ready. Margaret Guion Herzog. LC 38-8219. 1938. Doubleday, Doran & Co., Inc.
Three to Make Merry see You Better Believe It.
Three to Make Murder. Victor Patrick. LC 47-17764. 1947. Mystery House.
Three to Make Ready. Catherine Isabel Hackett Turlington & Archibald Douglas Turnbull. LC 49-11818. 1948. Vanguard Press.
Three to Show: A Trilogy. Dick Francis. LC 70-88643. 1969. 8.95. Harper & Row.
Three Tomorrows: American, British & Soviet Science Fiction. John Griffiths. 217p. 1980. 23.50x (ISBN 0-389-20008-5); pap. 8.95x (ISBN 0-389-20009-3). B&N Imports.
Three Trapped Tigers. Cabrera Infante, Guillermo. LC 70-148427. (Illus.). 1971. 8.95 (ISBN 0-06-010594-1). Harper & Row.
Three Trapped Tigers. Guillermo Cabrera Infante. (Harper Colophon books). 1978. 5.95 (ISBN 0-06-090636-7). Harper & Row.
Three Trials of Manirema. Jose J Veiga. LC 79-79320. 1970. 4.95. Knopf.
Three Trips in Time and Space. Larry Niven & John Brunner. (Laurel leaf library). 1974. (pbk.) 0.95. Dell.
Three Trips in Time & Space: Original Novellas of Science Fiction. Larry Niven et al. 224p. 1973. 5.95 o.p. Hawthorn.
Three Trips in Time and Space: Original Novellas of Science Fiction. LC 72-4917. 1973. 5.95. Hawthorn Books.
Three Trumps: A Nero Wolfe Omnibus. Rex Stout. LC 72-9601. 1973. 6.95 (ISBN 0-670-71031-8). Viking Press.
Three Verdicts. A Story. Frances I Katzenberger. LC 98-2088. 1898. The Editor Publishing Co.
Three Victorian Detective Novels. Everett Franklin Bleiler. LC 77-91266. 1978. 4.50 (ISBN 0-486-23668-4). Dover Publications.
Three Virgins. Kathryn G. Wilkie. 7.50 o.p. Vantage.
Three Virgins. Kathryn G. Wilkie. Date not set. 7.50 o.p. Vantage.
Three Vocatios. Caroline Frances Little. LC 7-19403. 1888. The Young Churchman Co.
Three-Way Affair. Carolyn Westergren. 1977. pap. 1.75 o.p. (ISBN 0-515-04246-3). BJ Pub Group.
Three-Way Affair. Carolyn Westergren. (Pyramid Book). 1977. 1.75 (ISBN 0-515-04246-3). Pyramid Publications.
Three Way Swap. Richard E. Geis. pap. 1.95 o.p. Barclay Hse.
Three Wayfarers. Thomas Hardy. LC 44-3618. 1979. Repr. of 1893 ed. lib. bdg. 25.00x (ISBN 0-8201-1206-2). Schol Facsimiles.
Three Ways to Mecca. Edwin Corle. LC 47-4555. 1947. Duell, Sloan and Pearce.

Three Wayward Girls. Florence Alice Price James. LC 7-7972. The International News Company.
Three Weeks. Elinor Sutherland Glyn. LC 7-21536. 1907. The Business Press.
Three Weeks. Elinor Sutherland Glyn. LC 8-11007. 1907. Duffield & Company.
Three Weeks in October. Yael Dayan. LC 78-10970. 8.95 (ISBN 0-440-07992-6). Delacorte Press/E. Friede.
Three Weeks in Politics. John Kendrick Bangs. 1973. Repr. of 1894 ed. 7.45 o.p. R West.
Three Went Armed. Jacland Marmur. LC 33-29999. 1933. L. MacVeagh, Dial Press, Inc.
Three Were Thoroughbreds. Kenneth Perkins. LC 39-135432. 1939. Doubleday, Doran & Company, Inc.
Three Wheels to Baja. Jane S Fredricks. (Illus.). 1973. 5.00 (ISBN 0-682-47639-0). Exposition Pr.
Three White Horses. Fingul Rosenquist. LC 47-1304. 1947. Little, Brown and Company.
Three Who Died: A Judge Peck Mystery. August William Derleth. LC 33-3815. Loring & Mussey.
Three Who Loved. Edita Morris. LC 45-1872. 1945. The Viking Press.
Three Who Were Strong. Barbara Webb. LC 33-165822. 1933. Doubleday, Doran & Company, Inc.
Three Widows. Bernice Carey Martin. LC 52-5113. 1952. Published for the Crime Club by Doubleday.
Three Widows. 1st Ed. Bernice Carey. LC 52-5113. 1952. Published for the Crime Club by Doubleday.
Three: Williwaw. A Thirsty Evil. Julian the Apostate. Gore Vidal. LC 62-4993. (Signet books, T2131). 1962. New American Library.
Three Wise Guys: And Other Stories. Damon Runyon. LC 47-20914. (On cover: New Avon library. 102). 1946.
Three Wise Men of Gotham." A "New" Reading of an Old Rhyme. Marie Corelli. LC 6-28738. 1896. J. B. Lippincott Company.
Three Wishes for Jamie. Charles O'Neal. LC 79-66116. 1980. 12.50 (ISBN 0-933256-08-6) (ISBN 0-933256-09-4). Second Chance Press.
Three Wishes of Jamie McRuin. Charles O'Neal. LC 49-10831. 1949. J. Messner.
Three, with Blood. Aaron Marc Stein. LC 50-5999. 1950. Published for the Crime Club by Doubleday.
Three Witnesses. Rex Stout. 192p. 1981. pap. 2.25 (ISBN 0-553-14451-0). Bantam.
Three Witnesses: A Nero Wolfe Threesome. Rex Stout. LC 56-6283. 1956. Viking Press.
Three Witnesses: A Novel. Sjoerd Leiker & Auer, Johanna Cornelia Fagginger, Tr. LC 46-22639. 1946. Querido.
Three Wives. Beatrice Kean Stapleton Seymour. LC 27-185452. 1927. A. A. Knopf.
Three Wives: By Alex Fraser Pseud. Henry Brinton. LC 58-12106. 1958. Roy Publishers.
Three Wives: Translated from the Swedish. Ragnar Af Geijerstam. Tr. by Ekstrom, Arne H. LC 42-15424. 1942. The Greystone Press.
Three Wogs. Alexander Theroux. LC 75-137019. 1972. 5.95 (ISBN 0-87645-055-9). Gambit.
Three Women. Jennie Maria Drinkwater Conklin. Bradley & Woodruff.
Three Women. Faith Baldwin Cuthrell. LC 26-17629. 1926. Dodd, Mead & Company.
Three Women. Faith Baldwin Cuthrell. 1973. (pbk.) 0.95. Warner Paperback Library.
Three Women. Firth Haring. (Inflation Fighter Ser.). 176p. 1982. pap. 1.50 (ISBN 0-8439-1096-8, Leisure Bks). Nordon Pubns.
Three Women. Hazel Hawthorne. 1938. E. P. Dutton & Co., Inc.
Three Women. Rachel Swete Macnamara. LC 43-109093. 1943. Arcadia House, Inc.
Three Women Alone. Betty Lyons. (O.s.i.). 224p. (Orig.). 1975. pap. 1.50 o.s.i. (AD1473, Award). Univ Pub & Dist.
Three Women at the Waters' Edge. Nancy Thayer. LC 80-2879. 1981. 14.95 (ISBN 0-385-17299-0). Doubleday.
Three Women for Curt. Rex Weldon, pseud. (Orig.). 1968. pap. 1.25 o.p. (2077). Brandon.
Three Women in Black. Helen Kieran Reilly. LC 41-22074. Random House.
Three Women of Annam. Cl Chivas-Baron & Chipperfield, Faith, Tr. LC 25-17058. 1925. Frank-Maurice, Inc.
Three Women-the Bronx & Petitio Principii: A Novel of Tempered Sex. George Injayan. 1978. 6.50 (ISBN 0-87164-050-3). William-F.
Three Works. Shigeharu Nakano. LC 79-128951. (Cornell University. Cornell University East Asia Papers: No. 21). 5.00. Cornell China-Japan Program.
Three Worlds of Johnny Handsome. Morton Freedgood. (Paperback Lib., 75-165). 1973. 0.95. Warner Paperback Lib.
Three Worlds of Johnny Handsome. Morton Freedgood. LC 72-188894. 1972. 5.95 (ISBN 0-394-47406-6). Random House.
Three Worlds of Johnny Handsome. John Godey. 1972. 5.95 o.p. (ISBN 0-394-47406-6). Random.
Three Worlds to Conquer. Poul Anderson. 1974. pap. 1.25 o.p. (ISBN 0-515-03541-6, N3541). BJ Pub Group.
Three Years. Josephine Elizabeth Felicitas Schwerin. Tr. by Safford, Mary Joanna. LC 8-2060. 1889. Rand, McNally & Company.
Three Years Behind the Guns: The True Chronicles of a "Diddybox". Lien Tisdale. LC 8-251212. 1908. The Century Co.
Three Years in a Man-Trap. Timothy Shay Arthur. LC 6-3425. 1872. J. M. Stoddart & Co.
Three Years to Play. Colin MacInnes. LC 71-125157. 1970. 6.95. Farrar, Straus & Giroux.
Three Years with Counterfeiters, Smuglers & Boodle Carriers. George P. Burnham. Repr. of 1875 ed. 24.00 o.s.i. Finch Pr.
Three, 1964: Going the Other Way. Robert Houston Robinson. LC 64-11987. 1964. Random House.
Three: 1971. Arthur Gould et al. 1971. 5.95 o.p. (ISBN 0-394-46219-X). Random.
Three: 1971: The Good Professor Who Murdered the Bad Little Girl. LC 72-140416. 1971. 5.95 (ISBN 0-394-46219-X). Random House.
Threepenny Novel. Translated from the German by Desmond I. Vesey. Verses Translated by Christopher Isherwood. Bertolt Brecht. LC 56-109580. (Evergreen books, E-42). Grove Press.
Threepenny Novel. Translated from the German by Desmond I. Vesey; Verses Translated by Christopher Isherwood. Bertolt Brecht. LC 57-611. 1956. Grove Press.
Threepersons Hunt. Brian Wynne Garfield. LC 73-87704. 1974. 6.95 (ISBN 0-87131-140-2). M. Evans.
Three's a Crowd. Doris Miles Disney. 1975. (pbk.) 1.25. Ace Books.
Three's a Crowd. Doris Miles Disney. LC 79-139014. 1971. 4.50. Published for the Crime Club by Doubleday.
Three's a Crowd: An Anglo-American Comedy. William Caine. LC 17-30732. 1917. 1.50. Houghton Mifflin Company.
Three's a Shroud. Richard S. Prather. (Shell Scott Ser). 1969. pap. 0.60 o.p. (R2188, GM). Fawcett World.
Three's Are Wild. Zeke Masters, pseud. 1981. pap. 1.95 (ISBN 0-671-43907-3). PB.
Three's Company. Alfred Leo Duggan. LC 57-13159. 1958. Coward-McCann.
Threescore and Ten. Walter Ernest Allen. LC 59-74043. 1959. W. Morrow.
Threesome: Including These Outstanding Novels: Impatient Virgin, Confidential and Millie's Daughter. Donald Henderson Clarke. 1947. Sun Dial Press.
Thresher. Herbert Krause. LC 47-417. 1946. The Bobbs-Merrill Company.
Threshing Floor: A Novel. Joseph Coyne. LC 56-102475. 1957. Putnam.
Threshold. Marjorie Benton Cooke. LC 18-66923. 1918. Doubleday, Page & Company.
Threshold. Judith Singer. 1975. (pbk.) 1.25. Bantam Books.
Threshold. Karin Von Wahl. LC 48-6775. 1948. Houghton Mifflin Co.
Threshold: A Novel. Evelyn Campbell. LC 21-20039. 1921. R. M. McBride & Company.
Threshold: A Novel. Cornelio Penna. LC 75-1911. 1975. 7.95 (ISBN 0-87133-042-3). Franklin Pub. Co.
Threshold of Enchantment. Edward Joseph Burns. LC 52-10591. 1952. Christopher Pub. House.
Threshold of Fear. Arthur John Rees. LC 25-17621. 1925. Dodd, Mead and Company.
Threshold of Spring. Jou-Shih. LC 81-184532. (Illus.). 1980. 2.95 (ISBN 0-8351-0809-0). Foreign Languages Press.
Threshold of Spring. Rou Shi. 1981. pap. 2.95 (ISBN 0-8351-0809-0). China Bks.
Threshold. Translated from the German by Moura Budberg and Tania Alexander. 1st American Ed. Dorothea Rutherford. LC 55-10765. Little, Brown.
Thresholds. Faith Baldwin Cuthrell. LC 25-19117. Small, Maynard & Company.
Thrice a Pioneer. A Story of Forests, Plains and Mountains. Peter M Hannibal. LC 1-271042. 1901. Danish Luth. Publ. House, Printers.
Thrice Armed. Harold Bindloss. LC 8-33157. F. A. Stokes Company.
Thrice Lost, Thrice Won. May Agnes Early Fleming. LC 3668. (On cover: Eagle library, no. 168). 1900. Street & Smith.
Thrice Thorned Rose. Philip R. Smith. 1969. 2.95 o.p. (ISBN 0-8059-1356-4). Dorrance.
Thrice Told Tales: Thirteen Re-Prints of Stories. Blanche Colton Williams & Columbia University. Extension Dept. 1924. Dodd, Mead and Company.
Thrice Wedded, but Only Once a Wife. Sarah Elizabeth Forbush G. S. Downs Downs. LC 7-363616. (select series. no. 80). 1891. Street & Smith.
Thrifty Abe: Or, From the Bottom to the Top... Harlan Page Halsey. (Old Sleuth's own, no. 118). The Parlor Car Publishing Co.
Thrifty Stock: And Other Stories. Ben Ames Williams. LC 23-103563. E. P. Dutton & Company.
Thrill. Barbara Petty. (Dell Book). (Illus.). 1977. 1.95 (ISBN 0-440-15295-X). Dell Pub. Co.
Thrill a Minute with Jack Albany. Morton Freedgood. LC 67-12919. (Inner sanctum mystery). 1967. Simon and Schuster.
Thrill a Minute with Jack Albany. John Godey. LC 67-12919. (Inner sanctum mystery). 1967. Simon and Schuster.
Thrill Circus. Stephen A Jones. 1973. (pbk.) 1.95. Barclay House.
Thrill of Horror: Twenty-Two Terrifying Tales. Ed. by Hugh Lamb. LC 75-8200. 222p. 1975. 8.50 (ISBN 0-8008-7683-0). Taplinger.
Thrill of Horror: 22 Terrifying Tales. Hugh Lamb. LC 75-8200. 1975. 8.50 (ISBN 0-8008-7683-0). Taplinger Pub. Co.
Thrillers, Chillers, & Killers: An Anthology. Ed. by Helen Hoke. LC 79-4502. 6.95 (ISBN 0-525-66633-8). Elsevier/Nelson Books.
Thrillers, Startling Tales. Herbert George Wells. LC 30-18564. 1929. E. J. Clode, Inc.
Thrilling Adventures of the Prisoner of the Border. Peter Hamilton Myers. LC 7-23120. 1860. Derby & Jackson.
Thrilling Escapes by Night. Albert Lee. 296p. 6.95. Rod & Staff.
Thrilling Mystery. Harlan Page Halsey. LC 7-1176. (On cover: The calumet series, no. 25). G. Munro's Sons.
Thrilling Scenes on the Ocean: Or, Swell Life at Sea. A Collection of Nautical Yarns. Gould, John W & Hannay, James, 1827-1873. LC 8-30857. 1860. Derby & Jackson.
Thrillingly Yours--Judy. Octave Foerster Schully. LC 37-3443. 1937. Hillman Curl, Inc.
Thrills, Chills, and Sorrow: A Novel. 1st Ed. Stella Rybacki. LC 54-7047. Exposition Press.
Thro' Lattice-Windows. William James Dawson. LC 6-32247. 1897. Doubleday and McClure Co.
Thro' Space. James Rock. LC 9-28247. 1909. New England Druggist Publishing Co.
Throckmorton: A Novel. Molly Elliot Seawell. LC 8-64320. (On cover: Appletons' town and country library, no. 55). 1890. D. Appleton and Company.
Throne of Ashes: A Narrative Interpretation of the Life of Job. George Raymond Stoner. LC 51-25843. 1951.
Throne of David. Joseph Holt Ingraham. LC 99-5422. (New Sabbath Library, v. 2, no. 9). 1899. D. C. Cook Pub. Co.
Throne of David: from the Consecration of the Shepherd of Bethlehem, to the Rebellion of Prince Absalom... In a Series of Letters Addressed by an Assyrian Ambassador... to This Lord and King on the Throne of Nineveh... Joseph Holt Ingraham. 1860. G. G. Evans.
Throne of David; from the Consecration of the Shepherd of Bethlehem to the Rebellion of Prince Absalom... In a Series of Letters Addressed by an Assyrian Ambassador... to His Lord and King on the Throne of Nineveh... Joseph Holt Ingraham. LC 7-10524. 1887. Roberts Brothers.
Throne of David: From the Consecration of the Shepherd of Bethlehem to the Rebellion of Prince Absalom... in a Series of Letters Addressed by an Assyrian Ambassador... to His Lord and King on the Throne of Nineveh... Joseph Holt Ingraham. LC 7-10525. 1896. Roberts Brothers.
Throne of Saturn. Sydney Fowler Wright. LC 50-5482. 1949. Arkham House.
Throne of Saturn: A Novel of Space and Politics. Allen Drury. LC 73-138928. 1971. 7.95. Doubleday.
Throne of the World. Louis De Wohl. LC 49-1262. 1949. J. B. Lippincott Co.
Through a Dark Curtain. Peter Saxon. (Orig.). pap. 0.60 o.p. (73-714). Lancer.
Through a Glass Darkly. Val Henry Gielgud. LC 63-16756. 1963. Scribner.
Through a Glass, Darkly. Helen McCloy. LC 50-7488. 1950. Random House.
Through a Glass Darkly. Kathleen Thompson Norris. LC 57-11317. 1970. Repr. of 1957 ed. 10.50x o.p. (ISBN 0-7182-0818-8). Intl Pubns Serv.
Through a Glass Darkly. Kathleen Thompson Norris. (Kathleen Norris Romance Ser). 1971. pap. 0.95 o.p. (65-740). Paperback Lib.
Through a Window in My Garden I Look Far Across a Restless Sea. Sam J. Stransky. 1975. 2.95 o.s.i. (ISBN 0-8181-0338-8). Pageant-Poseidon.
Through a Woman's Eyes: By Zsolt De Harsanyi. Zsolt Harsanyi. Tr. by Muir, Willa. LC 40-308854. G. P. Putnam's Sons.
Through an Unknown Isle: A Story of New Guinea. Charles Phillips Chipman. 1903. The Sallfield Publishing Company.
Through Beds of Stone. Minnie Louise Haskins. LC 29-691. 1928. A. A. Knopf.
Through Blazes for Love. Lee Klareich. Ed. by Lasky, Joseph. LC 37-18104. 1937. Printed by Ginsberg Linotyping Co.
Through Blood and Iron: A Story of the French-German War. Rudolph Leonhart. LC 7-13206. 1871. E. Luft & Co., Book and Job Printers.
Through Caverns Infinite. Becky L. Weyrich. 1978. pap. 2.25 (ISBN 0-532-22124-9). Woodhill.
Through Christian Eyes: A Novel of Christian Ethics. Florence Hood. LC 51-8663. 1951. Vantage Press.
Through Clouds of Flame. Richard H. Curtis. (Skymasters Ser.: No. 9). 1983. pap. 3.25 (ISBN 0-440-08765-1). Dell.
Through Deserts of Snow. Lawrence Fixel. LC 75-316456. (Capra chapbook series; no. 30). (Illus.). 1975. 10.00 (ISBN 0-88496-028-5) (ISBN 0-88496-027-7). Capra Press.
Through Devil's Gate. Deta Petersen Neeley & Neeley, Nathan Glen. LC 41-191916. 1941. Meador Publishing Company.
Through Dooms of Love. Maxine W Kumin. LC 64-25665. 1965. Harper & Row.
Through Dooms of Love: A Novel. Karl Stern. LC 60-7627. 1960. Farrar, Straus and Cudahy.
Through Envious Eyes and Slanderous Tongues. John Lanning. LC 73-88864. 1974. 8.95 (ISBN 0-8059-1954-6). Dorrance.
Through Eyes of Evil. Alpha Blair. (Leisure book). 1981. 2.50 (ISBN 0-8439-0865-3). Norden Publications, Inc.
Through Four Seasons. Edith M. Patch. 1933. Repr. 15.00 o.p. Finch Pr.
Through Gates of Splendor. Elisabeth Elliot. 1970. pap. 0.95 o.p. (N2358). Pyramid Pubns.
Through Glass. Henry Alley. LC 79-21296. (American Land Ser.: Vol. 1). 191p. (Orig.). 1979. 12.95 (ISBN 0-916078-06-X); pap. 7.95 (ISBN 0-916078-07-8). Iris Pr.
Through Golden Meadows. Sallie Lee Bell. LC 51-11551. 1951. Zondervan Pub. House.
Through Golden Meadows. Sallie Lee Bell. LC 72-146582. 1971. 0.95. Zondervan Pub. House.
Through Green Glasses. Andy Merrigan's Great Discovery and Other Irish Tales. Edmund Downey. LC 6-34247. 1887. D. Appleton & Company.
Through Hell to Alaska: A Novel. C. V Myers. LC 55-8210. 1955. Exposition Press.
Through Iran in Disguise. Sarah Hobson. 189p. 1982. pap. 5.95 (ISBN 0-89733-024-2). Academy Chi Ltd.
Through John's Eyes. Huntly Robertson. LC 22-651381. 1.90. George H. Doran Company.
Through Lands of Yesterday: A Story of Romance and Travel. Charles H Curran. LC 11-8101. 1911. 1.50. Chapple Publishing Company, Limited.
Through Many Waters. Netta Muskett. 1975. pap. 1.25 o.p. (ISBN 0-515-03626-9, V3626). BJ Pub Group.
Through Many Windows. Arthur Gordon. LC 82-12308. 10.95 (ISBN 0-8007-1319-2). F.H. Revell.
Through Midnight Streets. 1st Ed. Joseph William Meagher. LC 54-51032. Little, Brown.
Through Mighty Waters Saved. A Romance of the Johnstown Destruction, May 31,. 1889. Duke Bailie. (pastime series, v. 29). 1889. Laird & Lee.
Through Mocking Bird Gap. Helen Bagg. LC 21-6031. 1921. The Penn Publishing Company.
Through Night to Light: A Novel. author's ed.... ed. Friedrich Spielhagen. Tr. by Maximilian Schele De Vere. LC 3-22353. 1870. Leypoldt & Holt.
Through Night to Light: A Novel. author's ed.... ed. Friedrich Spielhagen. Tr. by Maximilian Schele De Vere. LC 3-22354. (Leisure moment series. no. 95). 1888. H. Holt and Company.
Through Old Rose Glasses and Other Stories. Mary Tracy Earle. LC 70-128732. (Short story index reprint series). 1970. Books for Libraries Press.
Through Old Rose Glasses: And Other Stories. Mary Tracy Earle. 1900. Houghton, Mifflin and Company.
Through One Administration. Frances Hodgson Burnett. LC 67-29260. (Americans in fiction). 1967. Gregg Press.
Through One Administration. Frances Hodgson Burnett. LC 68-55390. 1969. Johnson Reprint Corp.
Through One Administration. Frances Hodgson Burnett. LC 6-17247. 1883. J. R. Osgood and Company.
Through One Administration. Frances Hodgson Burnett. LC 4-15421. 1901. C. Scribner's Sons.
Through One Administration. Frances Hodgson Burnett. LC 17-7984. 1914. C. Scribner's Sons.
Through Other Eyes. Amy McLaren. LC 14-5168. 1914. G. P. Putnam's Sons.

Through Pain to Peace: A Novel. Sarah Doudney. (On cover: Broadway series, no. 14). 1892. J. A. Taylor and Company.

Through Purple Glass. Letitia Preston Osborne. LC 46-5415. 1946. J. B. Lippincott Company.

Through Shadow to Sunshine. H. F. Fitch. LC 6-40729. 1885. Gazette-Journal Company.

Through Stained Glass: A Novel. George Agnew Chamberlain. LC 15-5598. 1915. 1.30. The Century Co.

Through Streets Broad and Narrow: By Gabriel Fielding Pseud. Alan Gabriel Barnsley. LC 60-8109. 1960. Morrow.

Through Stress and Storm: The Stars in Their Courses. Gregory Brooke. LC 1-29447. 1900. The Abbey Press.

Through the Bering Strait: Part Two of the Fur Country. Jules Verne. 3.95. Assoc Bk.

Through the Dark and Hairy Wood. Shaun Herron. LC 72-2907. 1972. 5.95 (ISBN 0-394-47473-2). Random House.

Through the Dark Corridors. John Michael. 1959. 3.95 o.p. Commonsense.

Through the Desert. Henryk Sienkiewicz & Artois, Mary Webb, 1852- Tr. LC 12-1474. 1912. Benziger Brothers.

Through the Doors of Brass. Fitzroy Davis. 350p. 1974. 6.95 o.p. (ISBN 0-396-06946-0). Dodd.

Through the Doors of Brass: A Novel of Hollywood. Fitzroy Davis. LC 74-100. 1974. 6.95 (ISBN 0-396-06946-0). Dodd, Mead.

Through the Earth. Clement Fezandie. LC 80-23960. 1980. 8.95. Borgo Press.

Through the Earth: A Story. Clement Fezandie. 1898. The Century Co.

Through the Eye of a Needle. Hal Clement. LC 78-17511. 1978. 1.75 (ISBN 0-345-25850-9). Ballantine Books.

Through the Eye of a Needle: Shop Sketches. Translated from the Yiddish by M. Spiegel. Menashe Zinkin. LC 55-57331. 1955. I. W. Biderman.

Through the Eye of the Needle: A Romance, with an Introduction. William Dean Howells. 1907. Harper & Brothers.

Through the Eye of the Needle: A Romance, with an Introduction. William Dean Howells. LC 78-9572. 1977. 15.00 (ISBN 0-404-11548-9). AMS Press.

Through the Eye of Time. Trevor Hoyle. (Q Ser.: No. 2). 192p. 1982. pap. 2.25 (ISBN 0-441-80843-3, Pub. by Ace Science Fiction). Ace Bks.

Through the Eyes of the Judge. Graham Montague Jeffries. LC 30-14660. 1930. J. B. Lippincott Company.

Through the Fields of Clover. Peter De Vries. 1974. (pbk.) 1.50. Popular Library.

Through the Finger Goggles: Stories. Peter Schneeman. LC 81-69834. (Breakthrough Ser.: No. 37). 112p. pap. 6.95 (ISBN 0-8262-0360-4). U of Mo Pr.

Through the First Gate. John Craig Stewart. LC 50-6534. 1950. Dodd, Mead.

Through the Fog. second printing. ed. Ivar Spector. LC 35-19424. 1935. Uraitha.

Through the Fog: A Russian Novel Written in English. Ivar Spector. LC 31-5881. 1930. Uraitha Publishing Co.

Through the Gates of Old Romance. Weymer Jay Mills. 1903. J. B. Lippincott Company.

Through the Gates of Understanding: A Novel of Los Angeles--of the Yesterday and Today. Frances Marian Mitchell. LC 26-20763. 1926. The Strickland Publishing Corporation.

Through the Golden Gate. Sara Giffin. LC 74-78808. 1974. 3.50 (ISBN 0-8059-2030-7). Dorrance.

Through the Hoop. Michel Del Castillo. LC 62-8695. 1963. Knopf.

Through the House Door. Helen Rose Hull. LC 40-275745. Coward-McCann, Inc.

Through the Invisible: A Love Story. with illustrations by ella f. pell. ed. Paul Tynder. LC 8-32295. 1897. Continental Publishing Co.

Through the Lattice. Evelyne Close. LC 29-12532. Rae D. Henkle Co., Inc.

Through the Lens: A Thornton Zane Story. Morrell Massey. The Penn Publishing Company.

Through the Long Nights. Elizabeth Lynn Linton. (On cover: Seaside library. Pocket ed. no. 1109). 1888. G. Munro.

Through the Long Nights: A Novel. Elizabeth Lynn Linton. (On cover: Harper's Franklin square library. no. 625). 1888. Harper & Brothers.

Through the Looking Glass. Lewis Carroll. 1979. pap. 1.95x (ISBN 0-460-01018-2, Evman). Biblio Dist.

Through the Looking Glass. giant illus ed. Lewis Carroll. LC 76-62759. 1977. pap. 4.95 o.p. (ISBN 0-312-80377-X). St Martin.

Through the Narrows. Myrtle Louie Bodle Roe. LC 12-151. 1912. Sherman, French & Company.

Through the Night: Translated by Elisabeth Abbott. Hans Scholz. LC 59-125491. 1959. Crowell.

Through the Postern Gate: A Romance in Seven Days. 75th thousand. ed. Florence Louisa Charlesworth Barclay. LC 14-13584. 1912. G. P. Putnam's Sons.

Through the Postern Gate: A Romance of Seven Days. Florence Louisa Charlesworth Barclay. LC 11-11737. 1911. 1.25. G. P. Putnam's Sons.

Through the Reality Warp. Donald J Pfeil. LC 75-35833. 1976. 1.50 (ISBN 0-345-25377-9). Ballantine Books.

Through the Red-Litten Windows, and The Old River House. Theodor Hertz-Garten. LC 7-43105. ("unknown" library. v. 11). Cassell Publishing Company.

Through the Shadows. Cyril Argentine Alington. LC 22-993520. 1922. The Macmillan Company.

Through the Storm: A Novel. Philip Hamilton Gibbs. LC 46-1603. 1945. Hutchinson & Co., Ltd.

Through the Storm: A Novel. Philip Hamilton Gibbs. LC 46-264154. 1946. Doubleday & Company, Inc.

Through the Storm: Pictures of Life in Armenia. Avetis Nazarbek. Tr. by Elton, Letitia (MacColl) Oliver Eton. 1899. Longmans, Green & Co.

Through the Swinging Doors of Hell. R. D. Price. 3.50 o.p. Carlton.

Through the Thorns to the Stars. I. Lazutin. 342p. 1979. 7.95 (ISBN 0-8285-1570-0, Pub. by Progress Pubs USSR). Imported Pubns.

Through the Turf Smoke. facs. ed. Seumas Macmanus. LC 72-81273. (Short Story Index Reprint Ser.). 1899. 16.00 (ISBN 0-8369-3025-8). Ayer Co.

Through the Turf Smoke: The Love, Lore, and Laughter of Old Ireland. Seumas MacManus. 1899. Doubleday & McClure Co.

Through the Valley. Frances M. Swan. LC 78-73254. (Orig.). 1978. pap. 3.95 (ISBN 0-9602126-1-2). F M Swan.

Through the Valley of Death. E. M. Allison. (Crime Club Ser.). 192p. 1983. 11.95 (ISBN 0-385-18462-X). Doubleday.

Through the Visograph. John Walter Chancellor. LC 28-11709. The Christopher Publishing House.

Through the Wall. Cleveland Moffett. LC 75-32768. (Literature of Mystery and Detection). (Illus.). 1976. 23.00 (ISBN 0-405-07887-0). Arno Press.

Through the Wall. Cleveland Moffett. 1909. D. Appleton and Company.

Through the Wall. Patricia Wentworth. 1982. pap. 2.25 (ISBN 0-553-22837-4). Bantam.

Through the Wall. Patricia Wentworth. (O.S.I.). 1973. pap. 0.95 o.s.i. (ISBN 0-515-03118-6). Pyramid Pubns.

Through the Wall. 1st Ed. Patricia Wentworth. LC 50-9571. (Her A Miss Silver mysery). 1950. Lippincott.

Through the Wheat. Thomas Alexander Boyd. LC 23-80588. 1923. C. Scribner's Sons.

Through the Wheat. Thomas Alexander Boyd. LC 27-21877. 1927. C. Scribner's Sons.

Through the Wheat: A Novel. Thomas Alexander Boyd. LC 77-11635. (Lost American fiction). 1978. 8.95 (ISBN 0-8093-0855-X). Southern Illinois University Press.

Through the Wilderness, and Other Stories. Dan Jacobson. LC 69-10188. 1968. Macmillan.

Through the Wilderness: Or, The Deserted Children. Sophronia Currier. LC 6-31717. 1887. T. Whittaker.

Through the Woods. Carroll Arnett. 1971. 10.00 (Pub. by Elizabeth Pr); pap. 5.00. SBD.

Through the Years. Irl Leslie Allison. LC 25-8666. 1925. Schroeder and Gunther, Inc.

Through These Fires. Grace Livingston Hill. LC 43-150613. 1943. J. B. Lippincott Company.

Through Time and Space with Ferdinand Feghoot: The First Forty-Five Feghoot Adventures with Five More Never Previously Heard of. Grendel Briarton, pseud. LC 63-886. 1962. Paradox Press.

Through Time & the Valley. John R. Erickson. (Illus.). 260p. 1983. pap. 7.95 (ISBN 0-9608612-1-1). Maverick Bks.

Through-Traffic. Russell Wheeler Davenport. LC 30-31487. 1930. Doubleday, Doran & Company, Inc.

Through-Traffic. Russell Wheeler Davenport. LC 30-31487. 1930. Doubleday, Doran & Company, Inc.

Through Troubled Waters. A Story Founded on Fact. From the French. Tr. by Lizzie Townsend Darr. LC 6-33066. 1895. Town Topics Publishing Company.

Through War to Peace. Benjamin F Mason. 1891. Pacific Press Publishing Co. Pub. for the Author.

Through Welsh Doorways. Jeannette Augustus Marks. LC 78-167463. (Short story index reprint series). (Illus.). 1971. (ISBN 0-8369-3989-1). Books for Libraries Press.

Through Welsh Doorways. Jeannette Augustus Marks. LC 9-7949. 1909. Houghton Mifflin Company.

Through Winding Ways. LC 47-217. 1946. Fleming H. Revell Company.

Through Winding Ways. A Novel. Ellen Warner Olney Kirk. LC 7-125084. 1880. J. B. Lippincott & Co.

Through Wooden Eyes. John G. Bussell. Repr. of 1956 ed. 11.00 o.s.i. Finch Pr.

Throughout the Year. Mary Elizabeth Walsh. LC 8-33261. Knight, Leonard & Co.

Throughout the Year. Mary Elizabeth Walsh. LC 8-33259. D. H. McBride & Co.

Throught the Wall. Cleveland Moffett. LC 20-188098. 1920. D. Appleton and Company.

Throw. Anthony Bloomfield. LC 65-21481. 1965. Scribner.

Throw Away the Key. Max Hampton. 1966. 5.95 o.p. Bobbs.

Throw His Saddle Out. Charles Newcomb. LC 70-132697. (Illus.). 1970. 8.50 o.p. Northland.

Throw Love Away. Ann Lawrence. LC 34-364030. W. Godwin, Inc.

Throw Wide the Door. Emilie Baker Loring. LC 63-2150. Grosset & Dunlap.

Throw Wide the Door. Emilie Baker Loring. LC 79-10585. 1979. 12.50 (ISBN 0-8161-6728-1). G. K. Hall.

Throwback: A Romance of the Southwest. Alfred Henry Lewis. LC 14-10508. A. L. Burt Company.

Throwback: A Romance of the Southwest. Alfred Henry Lewis. LC 6-11306. 1906. The Outing Publishing Company.

Throwbacks. Roger A. Caras. LC 60-1064. 1969. Repr. pap. 0.60 o.p. (B60-1064). Belmont-Tower.

Thrown on the World. Charlotte Mary Brame. LC 44-382884. (On cover: Lovell's library, v. 19, no. 928). J. W. Lovell Company.

Thrown on the World: Or, The Discarded Wife. Charlotte Mary Brame. LC 11-10522. ("New York weekly series" no. 1). 1877. G. W. Carleton & Co.

Thru the Dust. Jennie Slowe Carlson. LC 52-32075. 1952. Christopher Pub. House.

Thrush Green. Read. 224p. 1959. 10.95 o.p. (ISBN 0-7181-0370-X, Pub. by Michael Joseph). Merrimack Pub Cir.

Thrush Green. Miss Read. 1982. Repr. lib. bdg. 16.95 (ISBN 0-89966-435-0). Buccaneer Bks.

Thrust. C. S. Vanek. (Orig.). 1969. pap. 1.95 o.s.i. (TC-467, Travellers Comp). Olympia.

Thruway West see Naked Range.

Thudbury, an American Comedy. 1st Ed. Clyde Brion Davis. LC 52-9534. 1952. Lippincott.

Thugs & Bottles. San Antonio. Tr. by Cyril Buhler. 1970. pap. 0.60 o.p. (63-306). Paperback Lib.

Thumb-Nail Sketches of Australian Life. Charles Haddon Chambers. LC 6-23341. Tait, Sons & Company.

Thumb Tripping. Donald Grant Mitchell. LC 77-117031. 1970. 5.95. Little, Brown.

Thumbcap Weir. Frances Gillmor. LC 29-5706. 1929. Minton, Balch & Company.

Thumbing: Our Adventures As Hitchhikers. Diane & Brenda. 1974. (pbk.) 1.25 (ISBN 0-523-00298-X). Pinnacle Books.

Thumbs Down. Jean Louis D'Esque. LC 37-2459. Abbott House.

Thump's Client. R. L Gilbert. LC 6-44064. The Authors' Publishing Company.

Thunder Above: By A. J. Wallis and Charles F. Blair, Jr. 1st Ed. Arthur James Wallis & Charles F. Blair. LC 56-10505. 1956. Holt.

Thunder Above the Sea. Heinrich Hauser & Kirwan, Patrick, Tr. H. Liveright.

Thunder and the Shouting. Christopher Nicole. LC 78-78686. 1969. 5.95. Doubleday.

Thunder at Bushwhack. Russell Kidd. LC 67-5894. 1967. Arcadia House.

Thunder at Dawn. Alan Evans. LC 78-1195. 1979. 8.95. Doubleday.

Thunder at Dawn: A Novel. Jack Hoffenberg. LC 65-11609. 1965. Dutton.

Thunder at Sunset. John Masters. LC 73-15357. 1974. 7.95 (ISBN 0-385-09030-7). Doubleday.

Thunder Beach. Lee Belvedere, pseud. 1973. pap. 0.75 o.s.i. (01-385). Lancer.

Thunder Before Seven. Anna Brand. LC 41-440525. 1941. Doubleday, Doran and Company, Inc.

Thunder Below. Daniel Joseph Clinton. LC 31-23672. 1931. Farrar & Rinehart, Incorporated.

Thunder Bird. Bertha Muzzy Sinclair. 1919. Little, Brown, and Company.

Thunder Birds. Orson Falk. LC 42-177978. 1942. Randon House.

Thunder Birds. Orson Falk. LC 43-38694. Sun Dial Press.

Thunder Castle. Veronica Smith. 1981. pap. 2.95 (ISBN 0-89083-795-3). Zebra.

Thunder Creek Range. Paul Evan Lehman. 1971. pap. 0.60 o.p. (60-473). Manor Bks.

Thunder Creek Range: By Paul Evan Pseud. Paul Evan Lehman. LC 57-12664. 1957. Avalon Books.

Thunder Dragon Gate. Talbot Mundy. LC 37-4538. 1937. D. Appleton-Century Company, Incorporated.

Thunder from the Sea. Willowdean Chatterson Handy. LC 73-80210. (Illus.). 1973. 8.50 (ISBN 0-8248-0284-5). University Press of Hawaii.

Thunder God: A Romantic Story of Love, Hatred and Adventure. Peter Bernard Kyne. LC 30-2368. Grosset & Dunlap.

Thunder Heights. Phyllis A Whitney. LC 60-6170. 1960. Appleton, Century, Crofts.

Thunder Hill. Dean Owen. 256p. 1981. pap. 1.95 (ISBN 0-441-80854-9). Ace Bks.

Thunder in Heaven. Armine Von Tempski. LC 42-22721. 1942. Duell, Sloan and Pearce.

Thunder in January. Harry O Austin. LC 52-9675. 1952. Vantage Press.

Thunder in the Dust. Alan Le May. Farrar & Rinehart, Incorporated.

Thunder in the Earth. Jacob Benjamin. (Orig.). 1979. pap. 2.25 (ISBN 0-532-23169-4). Woodhill.

Thunder in the Earth. Edwin Moultrie Lanham. LC 41-181132. Harcourt, Brace and Company.

Thunder in the Egg. Flav Farrow. LC 75-16786. (Illus.). 7.95. Papillon Books.

Thunder in the Heart. John Lee Weldon. LC 54-539053. Random House.

Thunder in the Kerk. Ann Marlowe. LC 79-9808. 8.95 (ISBN 0-396-07672-6). Dodd, Mead.

Thunder in the Room. Harris Downey. LC 56-10961. 1956. Macmillan.

Thunder in the Sun. Frank O'Rourke. LC 54-7424. 1954. Ballantine Books.

Thunder in the West. Frank Chester Robertson. LC 34-21299. (Tired business man's library of adventure, detective, and mystery novels). 1934. D. Appleton-Century Company, Incorporated.

Thunder in the Wind. June L. Shiplett. 448p. 1983. pap. 3.50 (ISBN 0-451-11995-9, Sig). NAL.

Thunder in the Winderness. Harry Hamilton. LC 49-7492. 1949. Bobbs-Merrill Co.

Thunder Island. Lewis Erle Jones. LC 40-3851. The Saravan House.

Thunder la Boom. Anne Steinhardt. LC 73-6087. (Richard Seaver Books). (O.s.i.). 192p. 1974. 6.95 o.s.i. (ISBN 0-670-71129-2). Viking Pr.

Thunder La Boom: A Novel. Anne Steinhardt. LC 73-6087. 1974. 6.95 (ISBN 0-670-71129-2). Viking Press.

Thunder-Maker. John Creasey. LC 75-32833. 192p. 1976. 6.95 o.p. (ISBN 0-8027-5324-8). Walker & Co.

Thunder Maker: A New Dr. Palfrey Adventure. John Creasey. LC 76-372421. 6.95 (ISBN 0-8027-5324-8). Walker.

Thunder Moon. Max Brand. 160p. 1982. pap. 1.95 (ISBN 0-671-41567-0). PB.

Thunder Moon. Frederick Faust. LC 69-16206. (Dodd, Mead silver star westerns). 1969. Dodd, Mead.

Thunder Moon. D. M. Peters. 3.95 o.p. Vantage.

Thunder Moon Strikes. Max Brand. LC 82-5087. (Silver Star Western Ser.). 1982. 12.95 (ISBN 0-396-08081-2). Dodd.

Thunder Moon's Challenge. Max Brand. LC 82-5023. (Silver Star Western). 1982. 9.95 (ISBN 0-396-08077-4). Dodd, Mead.

Thunder Mountain. Zane Grey. LC 35-6200. 1935. Harper & Brothers.

Thunder Mountain. Zane Grey. LC 81-15116. 1982. 13.95 (ISBN 0-89340-383-0). J. Curley & Associates.

Thunder Mountain. Zane Grey. LC 82-3083. 1982. 12.95 (ISBN 0-8161-3353-0). G.K. Hall.

Thunder Mountain. Harley Hess. (Orig.). 1979. pap. 1.75 (ISBN 0-532-23181-3). Woodhill.

Thunder of Her Heart. Elisabeth Beresford. LC 77-94494. 1978. pap. text ed. 1.50 o.s.i. (ISBN 0-89559-018-2). Dale Books Inc.

Thunder of Hoofs. Tex Holt, pseud. LC 47-19190. 1947. Arcadia House.

Thunder of Hoofs. Claude Rister. LC 47-191906. 1947. Arcadia House.

Thunder of the Roses: A Detective Novel. Manuel Peyrou. LC 71-181009. 1972. 5.95 (ISBN 0-665-00010-3). Herder and Herder.

Thunder of the Roses: A Detective Novel. Manuel Peyrov. Tr. by Donald A. Yates from Span. LC 71-181009. 1972. 5.95 o.p. (ISBN 0-665-00010-3). McGraw.

Thunder on St. Paul's Day: By Jane Lane Pseud. Elaine Kidner Dakers. LC 54-12448. 1954. Newman Press.

Thunder on Sunday. Karen Campbell, pseud. LC 72-80798. (Black Bat Mystery Ser). 1972. 4.95 o.p. (ISBN 0-672-51737-X). Bobbs.

Thunder on the Buckhorn. Frank O'Rourke. LC 49-9852. 1949. Random House.

Thunder on the Buckhorn see Ambuscade.

Thunder on the Chesapeake. Arthur Durham Divine. LC 61-8108. 1961. Macmillan.

Thunder on the Left... Christopher Darlington Morley. LC 36-9351. 1936. Doubleday, Doran & Company, Inc.

Thunder on the Mountain. Frederick Perry. LC 72-87467. (Illus.). 1973. 5.95 o.p. (ISBN 0-8059-1751-9). Dorrance.

Thunder on the Mountain. 1st Ed. Gifford Paul Cheshire. LC 60-11378. (ADouble D western Americana). 1960. Doubleday.
Thunder on the Mountains. Frederick E. Perry. LC 72-87467. (Illus.). 1973. 5.95 (ISBN 0-8059-1751-9). Dorrance.
Thunder on the Range. Henry Leyford Gates. LC 35-6770. 1935. R.M. McBride & Company.
Thunder on the Range. Frank Chester Robertson. LC 38-11788. 1938. E. P. Dutton & Co., Inc.
Thunder on the Right. Mary Stewart. LC 58-8008. 1958. M. S. Mill, and W. Morrow.
Thunder on the River. Charlton Grant Laird. 1949. Little, Brown.
Thunder Over Black Mountain. Dorothy Mitchell. (YA) 1972. 4.50 o.p. (Avalon). Bouregy.
Thunder Over the Bronx. Arthur Kober. LC 35-177715. 1935. Simon and Schuster.
Thunder Over White Horse. James Lyon Rubel. LC 39-258733. Phoenix Press.
Thunder Ridge. Ben Thompson. 1978. pap. 1.50 o.s.i. (ISBN 0-8439-0580-8, Leisure Bks). Nordon Pubns.
Thunder Road. Hilton Obenzinger. 1970. pap. 1.00 o.s.i. Siamese Banana.
Dream/Thunder Road: Stories and Dreams, 1955-1965. Fielding Dawson. LC 72-6937. 1972. (ISBN 0-87685-113-8) (ISBN 0-87685-112-X). Black Sparrow Press.
Thunder Rock. Anita Allen, pseud. (Berkley large-type gothic). 1974. (pbk.) 0.95. Berkley Pub. Co.
Thunder Shield. Frederic Franklyn Van De Water. LC 33-25971. The Bobbs-Merrill Company.
Thunder Shower. Bellamy Partridge. LC 36-11734. Arcadia House.
Thunder Stone. Sylvia Cooper. LC 55-5947. 1955. Simon and Schuster.
Thunder to the West. Al Cody, pseud. 1980. pap. 1.75 (ISBN 0-8439-0848-3). Nordon Pubns.
Thunder Trail. Norman Daniels. 1972. pap. 0.75 o.s.i. (74-791). Lancer.
Thunder Trail. Bradford Scott. (Orig.). 1967. pap. 0.45 o.p. (K1705). Pyramid Pubns.
Thunder Valley see Burnt Wagon Ranch.
Thunder Valley: By Burt Arthur. 1st Ed. Herbert Arthur, pseud. LC 51-11268. (Double D western). 1951. Doubleday.
Thunder Without Rain. Clifton Cuthbert. LC 33-110793. 1933. W. Godwin, Inc.
Thunderball. Ian Fleming. LC 61-7275. 1961. Viking Press.
Thunderbird. David Garth. LC 42-109660. 1942. H. C. Kinsey & Company, Inc.
Thunderbird Range. Ford Bowne, pseud. 192p. (OSI). 1971. 3.95 o.s.i. Lenox Hill.
Thunderbird Range. W. C Tuttle. (Avalon westerns). 1974. 4.50. Avalon Books.
Thunderbird Range. Wilbur C Tuttle. LC 54-718956. 1953. Avalon Books.
Thunderbird Song. Carl M. Beall. 1970. 5.50 (ISBN 0-682-47055-4). Exposition.
Thunderbird Trail. William Colt MacDonald. LC 46-7343. 1946. Doubleday & Company, Inc.
Thunderboats, Ho! Rutherford George Montgomery. LC 45-1820. 1945. David McKay Company.
Thunderbolt. Howard Vincent O'Brien. LC 23-9244. 1923. A. C. McClurg & Co.
Thunderbolt. Gertrude Weaver. LC 20-7061. 1920. T. Seltzer.
Thunderbolt: A Novel of Ancient Israel. Sallie Lee Bell. Zondervan Pub. House.
Thunderbolt & Lightfoot. Joe Millard, pseud. (O.s.i.). 160p. 1975. pap. 1.25 o.s.i. (AQ1465, Award). Univ Pub & Dist.
Thunderer: A Romance of Napoleon and Josephine. Lily Moresby Adams Beck. LC 27-19113. 1927. Dodd, Mead and Company.
Thundergust Trail. Walker A Tompkins. LC 42-254841. 1942. Phoenix Press.
Thunderhawk: A Tale of the Wabash Flatwoods, by. David Wulf Anderson. LC 26-23682. 1926. Doubleday, Page & Company.
Thunderhead see Day Before Forever: Science Fiction.
Thunderhead: A Novel. Mary Ture-Vasa. LC 43-9419. 1943. J. B. Lippincott Company.
Thunderhead Lady. by william j. wilson. ed. Anna Fuller & Read, Brian. LC 13-12280. 1913. 1.00. G. P. Putnam's Sons.
Thunderhead Range. 1st Ed. Frederick Tillinghast. LC 56-5526. 1956. Vantage Press.
Thundering Herd. Zane Grey. LC 25-883. 1925. Harper & Brothers.
Thundering Herd. large print ed. Zane Grey. LC 81-2827. 1981. 10.95 (ISBN 0-89621-276-9). Thorndike Press.
Thundering Hills. Al Cody, pseud. 256p. (YA) 1973. 6.95 (Avalon). Bouregy.
Thundering Hills: By Al Cody Pseud. Archie Joscelyn. LC 52-13527. 1952. Bouregy & Curl.
Thundering Hoofs. Charles Horace Snow. LC 37-25383. The Greystone Press.
Thundering Trail. Norman A Fox. LC 44-379242. 1944. Dodd, Mead & Company.
Thunders of Silence. Irvin Shrewsbury Cobb. LC 18-7923. 0.50. George H. Doran Company.
Thunderstorm. John Neely Rhoads. LC 4-35334. 1904. Ferris & Leach.
Thunderstorm. Gladys Bronwyn Stern. LC 25-11589. 1925. A. A. Knopf.
Thunderworld. Zach Hughes. (Orig.). 1982. pap. 2.25write for info. (ISBN 0-451-11290-3, AE1290, Sig). NAL.
Thurb Revolution. Alexei Panshin. 1978. 1.75 (ISBN 0-441-80855-7). Ace Books.
Thurber Album. James Thurber. 1965. pap. 4.95 o.p. (ISBN 0-671-21015-7, Fireside). S&S.
Thurber Country. James Thurber. 1960. pap. 2.95 o.p. (ISBN 0-671-72901-2, Fireside). S&S.
Thurber Dogs. James Thurber. 1963. pap. 2.95 (ISBN 0-671-21031-9, Fireside). S&S.
Thurley Ruxton. Philip Verrill Mighels. LC 11-9151. 1911. D. Fitz Gerald, Inc.
Thurlston Tales. Robert Pearse Gillies. LC 6-439893. 1835. E. L. Carey & A. Hart.
Thurman Lucas. Harlan Eugene Read. LC 29-9794. 1929. The Macmillan Company.
Thursday April. Alberta Pierson Hannum. LC 31-19086. 1931. Harper & Brothers.
Thursday at Dawn: By Werner J. Luddecke. Tr. by Harald O. Dyrenforth. Werner Jorg Luddecke. LC 65-238000. 3.50. Pub. for the Crime Club by Doubleday.
Thursday Island. Maud Keck & Orbison, Olive. LC 32-30514. 1932. I. Washburn.
Thursday, My Love. Robert H. Rimmer. (Signet novel, Y5237). 1973. (pbk.) 1.25. New American Lib.
Thursday, My Love. Robert H. Rimmer. LC 70-183524. 1972. 6.95. New American Library; Distributed by Norton.
Thursday the Rabbi Walked Out. Harry Kemelman. LC 78-8466. 1978. 8.95 (ISBN 0-688-03362-8). Morrow.
Thursday the Rabbi Walked Out. Harry Kemelman. 1979. 2.25 (ISBN 0-449-24070-3). Fawcett Crest.
Thursday the Rabbi Walked Out. Harry Kemelman. LC 78-26798. 1979. 13.95 (ISBN 0-8161-6663-3). G. K. Hall.
Thursday Turkey Murders. Craig Rice. LC 43-17232. 1943. Simon and Schuster.
Thursday Woman. Muriel Davidson. LC 77-18388. 1979. 9.95 (ISBN 0-689-10884-2). Atheneum.
Thursday's Blade. Frederick Clyde Davis. LC 47-1992. 1947. Pub. for the Crime Club by Doubleday & Company, Inc.
Thursday's Child. Faith Baldwin. LC 75-18668. 1976. 7.95 o.p. (ISBN 0-03-014916-9). HR&W.
Thursday's Child. Faith Baldwin Cuthrell. LC 75-18668. 7.95 (ISBN 0-03-014916-9). Holt, Rinehart, and Winston.
Thursday's Child. Faith Baldwin Cuthrell. LC 76-19788. 1976. 10.95 (ISBN 0-8161-6387-1). G. K. Hall.
Thursday's Child. Donald Macardle. LC 41-188980. Frederick A. Stokes Company.
Thursday's Child. Victoria Poole. 288p. 1981. pap. 2.95 (ISBN 0-445-04656-2). Popular Lib.
Thursday's Child. Arthur Tofte. (Orig.). 1981. pap. 2.25 (ISBN 0-8439-8017-6, Tiara Bks). Nordon Pubns.
Thursday's Child. Mary Wiltshire. LC 25-171214. 1925. Dodd, Mead & Company.
Thursday's Child, No. 3. Ed. by Edward Robbin. 200p. (Orig.). 1982. pap. 4.95x (ISBN 0-9603518-3-3). Glen Pr.
Thursday's Child No. 2. Ed. by Edward Robbin. LC 80-83893. (Anthology of Short Stories Ser.). (Illus.). 300p. (Orig.). 1980. pap. 5.95 (ISBN 0-9603518-2-5). Glen Pr.
Thursday's Folly: A Peter Styles Mystery Novel, by Judson Philips. Judson Pentecost Philips. LC 67-19228. (Red badge mystery). 1967. Dodd, Mead.
Thursdays 'til 9: A Novel. Jane Trahey. LC 79-3366. (Illus.). 9.95 (ISBN 0-15-190261-5). Harcourt Brace Jovanovich.
Thurston House. Danielle Steel. (Orig.). 1983. pap. 7.95 (ISBN 0-440-58655-0, Dell Trade Pbks). Dell.
Thurston of Orchard Valley. Harold Bindloss. LC 10-5055. 1910. 1.20. Frederick A. Stokes Company.
Thurstons of the Old Palmetto State: or, Varieties of Southern Life. Illustrated in the Fortunes of a Distinguished Family of South Carolina. By Rev. John H. Caldwell... John H. Caldwell. LC 43-27402. 1861. J. Russell.
Thus Am I Slayn.". Howard Clewes. LC 48-904. 1948. E. P. Dutton.
Thus Doctor Mallory. Elizabeth Seifert. LC 73-79136. 1973. 5.95. Aeonian Press.
Thus Doctor Mallory. Elizabeth Seifert. LC 40-613007. 1940. Dodd, Mead & Company.
Thus Far. John Collis Snaith. 1925. D. Appleton and Company.
Thus He Took His Pilgrimage. Floyd Melvin Barton. LC 46-575. 1945. Dorrance & Company.
Thus Spake the Kings. Walter H. Marx. (Illus.). 1978. pap. text ed. 5.50x (ISBN 0-88334-106-9). Ind Sch Pr.
Thus Was Adonis Murdered. Sarah Caudwell. LC 81-8594. 1981. 16.95 (ISBN 0-684-17294-1). Scribner.
Thus Was Adonis Murdered. Sarah Caudwell. LC 82-12258. 1982. 11.95. Penguin.
Thuvia, Maid of Mars. Edgar Rice Burroughs. LC 20-195799. 1920. A. C. McClurg & Co.
Thuvia, Maid of Mars see Three Martian Novels.
Thuvia, Maid of Mars, and The Chessmen of Mars. Edgar Rice Burroughs. LC 73-152514. 1972. Doubleday.
Thuvia, Maid of Mars: By Edgar Rice Burroughs... Illustrated by J. Allen St. John. Edgar Rice Burroughs. LC 27-161489. 1921. Grosset & Dunlap.
THX One Thousand One Hundred Thirty-Eight. Benjamin Bova et al. (Orig.). 1971. pap. 0.75 o.p. (64-624). Paperback Lib.
Thy Brother Leonidas. Sarah Wilder Pratt. LC 1641. 1900. Universal Truth Publishing Co.
Thy Brother's Blood. Larry Ward. LC 61-11188. 1961. Cowman Publications.
Thy Brother's Wife. large print ed. Andrew M. Greeley. LC 82-12151. 1982. 15.95 (ISBN 0-8161-3416-2). G.K. Hall.
Thy Brother's Wife. Andrew M. Greeley. LC 81-16239. 1982. 3.95. Warner Books.
Thy Dark Freight. Vere Hutchinson. LC 29-42064. 1929. H. Liveright.
Thy Daughter's Nakedness. Myron S. Kaufmann. LC 68-24134. 1968. 8.95. Lippincott.
Thy Kingdom Come. John J Kirvan. LC 77-14826. (Emmaus books). 1.95 (ISBN 0-8091-2077-1). Paulist Press.
Thy Men Shall Fall. Sidney Moss & Moss, Samuel, Joint Author. LC 48-831222. 1948. Ziff-Davis Pub. Co.
Thy Name Is Woman: A Novel. Olive Beatrice Muir. 1894. G. W. Dillingham, Successor to G. W. Carleton & Co.
Thy Name Is Woman. From the French of Dubut De Laforest. Jean Louis Dubut De Laforest & Howe, Frank Howard, Tr. LC 6-34627. (On cover: The Belford American novel series, no. 12). Belford Company.
Thy Neighbor's Wife. Linn Boyd Porter. LC 7-37762. (On cover: The albatross novels). 1892. G. W. Dillingham.
Thy Neighbor's Wife: Twelve Original Variations on the Theme of Adultery. James Turner & Denys Val Baker. LC 68-17322. 1968. Stein and Day.
Thy Neighbour's Wife. Liam O'Flaherty. LC 24-5104. Boni and Liveright.
Thy Wedded Husband. Mary Garland O'Connor. 1958. Houghton Mifflin.
Thy Will Be Done- - -". 1st. ed. G. Wallace Banks. 1974. 5.95. Vantage.
Thyra: A Romance of the Polar Pit. Robert Ames Bennet. LC 1-24977. 1901. H. Holt and Company.
Thyra: A Romance of the Polar Pit. Robert Ames Bennet. LC 77-84199. (Lost Race and Adult Fantasy Fiction). (Illus.). 1978. 20.00 (ISBN 0-405-10957-1). Arno Press.
Thyra Varrick: A Love Story. Amelia Edith Huddleston Barr. LC 3-10202. 1903. J. F. Taylor & Company.
Thyrza: A Tale. George Robert Gissing. LC 74-500. 1974. 18.00 (ISBN 0-8386-1544-9). Fairleigh Dickinson University Press.
Thyrza: A Tale. George Robert Gissing. LC 72-75984. 1969. AMS Press.
Ti-Coyo and His Shark: An Immoral Fable. Clement Richer. LC 51-11057. 1951. Knopf.
Tia Tula (by Unamuno) E. D'Entremont. 1974. pap. text ed. 4.50 o.p. (ISBN 0-13-522466-7). P-H.
Tiajuana Susie. Columbia Sileo. LC 51-17389. 1950. Rockport Press.
Tianitolka: Povesti. Vladimir Maramzin. 200p. (Rus.). 1981. 16.95 (ISBN 0-88233-510-3); pap. 7.50 (ISBN 0-88233-511-1). Ardis Pubs.
Tiara Tahiti. Geoffrey Cotterell. 1962. 4.95 o.p. (ISBN 0-397-00248-3). Lippincott.
Tibb's Flooders: A Tale of the Ohio River Flood of 1937. Elizabeth Peck. LC 41-267423. 1941. House of Field, Inc.
Tiber Was Silver. 1st Ed. Michael Novak. LC 61-125642. 1961. Doubleday.
Tiberius Smith: As Chronicled by His Right-Hand Man, Billy Campbell. Hugh Pendexter. 1907. Harper & Brothers.
Tibetan Inroads. Stephen Lowe. 50p. 1982. pap. 5.95 (ISBN 0-413-48710-5, NO. 3611). Methuen Inc.
Tibetan Venus. Morton, John Bingham. LC 51-8195. 1951. Sheed and Ward.
Tibubon: A Novel. Vicki Baum. LC 56-356621. 1956.
Tiburon, a Novel. Vicki Baum. LC 56-356623. 1956.
Tick of Death. Peter Lovesey. LC 74-3781. (Red badge novel of suspense). 1974. 5.95 (ISBN 0-396-06972-X). Dodd, Mead.
Tick of Death. Peter Lovesey. (Penguin crime fiction). 1976. 1.95 (ISBN 0-14-003770-5). Penguin Books.
Tick of the Clock. Herbert Asbury. LC 28-5643. 1928. Macy-Masius.
Ticker Khan. Bamber Gascoigne. LC 74-26902. (Illus.). 1975. 3.95 (ISBN 0-671-21963-4). Simon and Schuster.
Ticker-Tape Murder. Milton Morris Propper. LC 30-709741. 1930. Harper & Brothers.
Ticket for a Seamstitch: By Henry W. Wiggen, but Polished for the Printer by Mark Harris. 1st Ed. Mark Harris. LC 57-564959. 1957. Knopf.
Ticket That Exploded. William S. Burroughs. LC 66-28732. 1967. Grove Press.
Ticket to Buffalo. 1st Ed. Amber Dean. LC 51-9250. 1951. Published for the Crime Club by Doubleday.
Ticket to Fleet Street. Samuel Andrew Wood. LC 57-438455. 1957. Macmillan.
Ticket to Oblivion. Robert B Parker. LC 50-6314. 1950. Rinehart.
Ticket to Ride. Ritchie Perry. LC 74-5366. (Midnight novel of suspense). 1974. 5.95 (ISBN 0-395-19412-1). Houghton Mifflin.
Ticket to Ride Number Three. Ritchie Perry. 192p. 1981. pap. 2.25 (ISBN 0-345-29057-7). Ballantine.
Ticket to Romance. Neubauer, William Arthur. LC 65-7473. 1961. Arcadia House.
Ticket to Romance. Neubauer, William Arthur. LC 64-57490. 1961. Arcadia House.
Ticket to the Stars. Vasilii Pavlovich Aksenov. LC 63-24949. (Signet books, P2315). 1963. New American Library.
Tickets. Richard P Brickner. LC 80-22683. 12.95 (ISBN 0-671-41209-4). Simon and Schuster.
Tickets for Death: A Michael Shayne Story. Davis Dresser. LC 41-4261. H. Holt and Company.
Tickets to the Devil. Richard Pitts Powell. LC 68-27777. 1968. Scribner.
Ticking Clock: By Frances and Richard Lockridge. Frances Louise Davis Lockridge & Richard Lockridge. LC 62-11349. (Main line mysteries). 1962. Lippincott.
Ticking Heart. Dolores Birk Hitchens. LC 40-31456. 1940. Pub. for the Crime Club by Doubleday, Doran and Co., Inc.
Ticking Is in Your Head. Leonard Daventry. 1970. pap. 0.75 o.p. (0502-07065). Curtis.
Ticking Terror Murders. Darwin Le Ora Teilhet. LC 35-349203. 1935. Pub. for the Crime Club, Inc., by Doubleday, Doran & Company, Inc.
Tickling Heart. Dolores Birk Olsen. LC 40-314561. 1940. Pub. for the Crime Club by Doubleday, Doran and Co., Inc.
Ticonderoga: Or The Black Eagle. A Romance of Days Not Far Distant. George Payne Rainsford James. LC 7-10527. (On cover: Library of select novels, no. 191). 1854. Harper & Brothers.
Tid Bits: Humorous Stories of Home People. Clara A Lynn. LC 25-19115. The Rumford Press.
Tidal Forest. Geoff Wyatt. 1974. 14.95x (ISBN 0-7022-0892-2); pap. 7.95x (ISBN 0-7022-0891-4). U of Queensland Pr.
Tidal News. John Curl. 108p. (Orig.). 1982. pap. 5.00 (ISBN 0-938392-02-6). Homeward Pr.
Tidal Wave. Ethel May Dell. LC 19-5814. 1919. 1.00. G. P. Putman's Sons.
Tidal Wave. Martin Wallace Tyler. 1975. (pbk.) 1.50. Leisure Books.
Tidal Wave, and Other Stories. Ethel May Dell. LC 20-21292. 1920. G. P. Putnam's Sons.
Tidal Wave: And Other Stories. Ethel May Dell. LC 22-613. 1921. Grosset & Dunlap.
Tidal Wave: La Mort De Belle, Translated by Louise Varese; Le Fond De la Bouteille, Translated by Cornelia Schaeffer; Les Freres Rico, Translated by Ernst Pawel. 1st Ed. Georges Simenon. LC 54-5717. 1954. Doubleday.
Tiddledywink Tales. John Kendrick Bangs. LC 6-6118. 1891. R. H. Russell & Son.
Tiddling Tennis Theorem. Arthur Hoppe. 1977. 7.95 o.p. (ISBN 0-670-71251-5). Viking Pr.
Tiddling Tennis Theorem. Arthur Hoppe. 1977. 7.95 o.p. (ISBN 0-670-71251-5). Viking Pr.
Tiddly Winks: The Topless Cartoon Book. John Drummond. pap. 1.00 o.p. (01021). Brandon.
Tide. Mildred Cram. LC 24-28671. 1924. A. A. Knopf.
Tide. Vincent Sheean. LC 33-29349. 1933. Doubleday, Doran & Company, Inc.
Tide: A Novel of Catastrophe. Hugh Zachary. LC 73-93733. 1974. 5.95 (ISBN 0-399-11358-4). Berkley Pub. Corp; Distributed by Putnam.
Tide Always Rises. Elisabeth Stancy Payne. LC 37-23641. 1937. Dodd, Mead & Company.
Tide Can't Wait. Louis Trimble. LC 57-12688. 1957. Mystery House.
Tide House: A Novel. Maude Caldwell Perry. LC 29-200087. Harcourt, Brace and Company.
Tide Marks. Margaret Westrup. LC 13-212941. 1913. The Macmillan Company.
Tide Mill. Dorothy Daniels. (Queen-size gothic). 1975. (pbk.) 1.25. Popular Library.
Tide of Destiny: A Story with a Purpose... A Popular Adaptation of the Great Fraternal Story Our Brother's Child. William Hampton Reynolds. LC 10-17995. 1910. Mayhew Publishing Company.

Tide of Empire. Peter Bernard Kyne. LC 28-17815. 1928. Cosmopolitan Book Corporation.
Tide of Empire. 1st Ed. John Edward Jennings. LC 52-11040. 1952. Holt.
Tide of Life. Catherine Cookson. 288p. 1976. 8.95 o.p. (ISBN 0-688-03032-7). Morrow.
Tide of Life: A Novel. Catherine Cookson. LC 76-3596. 1976. 7.95 (ISBN 0-688-03032-7). Morrow.
Tide of Terror. Ed. by Hugh Lamb. LC 73-150894. 1972. 2.50 (ISBN 0-491-00833-3). W. H. Allen.
Tide of Terror: An Anthology of Rare Horror Stories. Ed. by Hugh Lamb. LC 73-6181. 1973. 6.95 (ISBN 0-8008-7695-4). Taplinger Pub. Co.
Tide of Time. Edgar Lee Masters. LC 37-20208. Farrar & Rinehart, Incorporated.
Tide Rips. James Brendan Connolly. LC 22-7410. 1922. C. Scribner's Sons.
Tide-Rode. Adelyn Bushnell. LC 47-4401. 1947. Coward-McCann.
Tidefall: A Novel. Thomas Head Raddall. LC 53-9329. 1953. Little, Brown.
Tidehawks. Jeanne Hines. (queen-size gothic). 1974. (pbk.) 1.25. Popular Library.
Tides. Eduard Heinrich Nikolaus Graf Von Keyserling & Ashton, Arthur Jacob, 1855- Tr. LC 29-11572. 1929. The Macaulay Company.
Tides. Ada Hilt Street & Street, Julian Leonard, 1879- Joint Author. LC 26-22066. 1926. Doubleday, Page & Company.
Tides of Barnegat. Francis Hopkinson Smith. LC 6-27705. 1906. C. Scribner's Sons.
Tides of Dawn. Emma Louise Mally. LC 49-7761. 1949. W. Sloane Associates.
Tides of Ecstasy. Luanne Walden. 1981. pap. 3.25 (ISBN 0-89083-769-4). Zebra.
Tides of Fremannion. Kathleen A Shoesmith. (Ace Gothic). 1973. (pbk.) 0.95. Ace Books.
Tides of Kregen. Alan Burt Akers. (Science Fiction Ser.). 1976. pap. 1.25 o.p. (UY1247). DAW Bks.
Tides of Love. Patricia Matthews. LC 82-115943. 1981. 5.95 (ISBN 0-553-01328-9). Bantam Books.
Tides of Lust. Samuel R Delany. 1973. 1.50. Lancer Books.
Tides of Malvern. Francis Griswold. LC 30-23091. 1930. W. Morrow & Company.
Tides of Mont St. Michel. Roger Vercel & Mont St. Michel. France--Fiction. LC 38-27611. Random House.
Tides of Mont St.-Michel. Roger Vercel. LC 78-100213. 1970. (ISBN 0-8371-4052-8). Greenwood Press.
Tides of the Tantramar. Louis Arthur Cunningham. The Penn Publishing Company.
Tides of Time: Translated from the French by Mary Glasgow. Emile Danoen. LC 52-14045. 1952. Ballantine Books.
Tide's Rise. June Strader. LC 73-86776. 1973. 5.95 (ISBN 0-87716-049-X). Moore Pub. Co.
Tidewater. Clifford Dowdey. LC 43-13074. 1943. Little, Brown and Company.
Tidewater. Margaret Maitland, pseud. (Belmont Tower Book). 1977. 1.95 (ISBN 0-505-51168-1). Tower Pubns.
Tidewater: By Warren Howard Pseud. James Noble Gifford. LC 54-13351. 1954. Arcadia House.
Tidewater Dynasty: The Lees of Stratford Hall. Carey Roberts & Rebecca Seely. LC 80-29276. (ISBN 0-15-190294-1). Harcourt Brace Jovanovich.
Tidewater Dynasty: The Lees of Stratford Hall. Carey Roberts & Rebecca Seely. LC 80-8758. (Illus.). 13.95 (ISBN 0-15-190294-1). Harcourt Brace Jovanovich.
Tidewater Sprig. Robert Emmett McDowell. LC 60-153903. 1961. Crown Publishers.
Tidewater Valley: A Story of the Swiss in Oregon. Jo Evalin Lundy. (Land of the Free series). 1949. Winston Co.
Tideway. Francis Browning Drew Bickerstaffe-Drew. LC 18-652429. 1918. Benziger Brothers.
Tidings. Translated from the German by Marie Heynemann and Margery B. Ledward. Ernest Emil Wiechert. LC 59-6296. 1959. Macmillan.
Tidoon. Robert L. Olivier. LC 70-18934. 96p. 1972. 5.95 (ISBN 0-911116-62-1). Pelican.
Tidoon, a Story of the Cajun Teche. Robert L. Olivier. LC 70-189734. 1972. 3.95 (ISBN 0-911116-62-1). Pelican Pub. Co.
Tie and Trick. A Novel. Hawley Smart. (Harper's Franklin square library, no. 442). 1885. Harper & Brothers.
Tie-Fast Hombre. Charles Morris Martin. LC 36-21197. 1936. Greenberg.
Tie That Binds. Eleanor Hodgman Porter. LC 19-161471. 1919. Houghton Mifflin Company.
Tie That Binds: A Story of the North and the South. Willie Walker Caldwell. LC 6-21868. 1895. The Editor Publishing Co.
Tied for Murder. Cortland Fitzsimmons. LC 43-10421. 1943. J. B. Lippincott Company.
Tied to a Leopard. Dorris M. Blough. 125p. (Orig.). 1982. pap. 2.75 (ISBN 0-87178-845-4). Brethren.
Tied up in Tinsel. Ngaio Marsh. LC 72-5107. 1972. 9.95 (ISBN 0-8161-6042-2). G. K. Hall.
Tied up in Tinsel. Ngaio Marsh. LC 77-183854. 1972. 6.95. Little, Brown.
Tierra Amarilla; Stories of New Mexico... Sabine R Ulibarri. LC 75-153942. 1971. 3.45 (ISBN 0-8263-0154-1). University Of New Mexico Press.
Tierras Flacas see Lean Lands.
Ties--Human and Divine. Benjamin Leopold Farjeon. LC 6-38764. (Lovell's international series, no. 167). 1891. J. W. Lovell Company.
Tieta, the Goat Girl: Or, The Return of the Prodigal Daughter: Melodramatic Serial Novel in Five Sensational Episodes, with a Touching Epilogue, Thrills and Suspense! Jorge Amado. LC 78-11470. 1979. 12.95 (ISBN 0-394-50139-X). Knopf: Distributed by Random House.
Tieta: The Goat Girl, or the Return of the Prodigal Daughter, a Melodramatic Serial Novel in Five Sensational Episodes, with a Touching Epilogue: Thrills and Suspense: Jorge Amado. (Bard book). 1980. 4.95 (ISBN 0-380-50815-X). Avon Books.
Tiffany Caper. Joseph Purtell. LC 73-93770. 1974. 6.95 (ISBN 0-698-10596-6). Coward, McCann & Geoghegan.
Tiffany Street. Jerome Weidman. LC 73-5041. 1974. 6.95 (ISBN 0-394-47281-0). Random House.
Tiffany Thayer's Three Musketeers. Tiffany Thayer & Dumas, Alexandre, 1802-1870. Les Trois Mousquetaires. LC 39-30763. 1939. The Dial Press.
Tiger. Bud Blake. LC 78-84744. (Tempo books). 1969. 0.60. Grosset & Dunlap.
Tiger. Max Brand. 1981. 18.95x (Pub. by Remploy England). State Mutual Bk.
Tiger. James Gilman, pseud. LC 79-50899. pap. 2.25 o.s.i. (ISBN 0-89516-085-4). Condor Pub Co.
Tiger. Sterling North. LC 33-10967. The Reilly & Lee Co.
Tiger Among Us. 1st Ed. Leigh Brackett. LC 57-5533. 1957. Published for the Crime Club by Doubleday.
Tiger Bayou. Nevil Gratiot Henshaw. LC 31-23474. A. H. King.
Tiger by the Tail. Hunter Adams. (Man from Planet X#2). 1975. (pbk.) 1.50 (ISBN 0-523-00646-2). Pinnacle Books.
Tiger by the Tail... Lawrence L. Goldman. LC 46-4961. 1946. David McKay Company.
Tiger Claws. Frank Lucius Packard. LC 28-25961. 1928. Pub.for the Crime Club, Inc. by Doubleday, Doran & Company, Inc.
Tiger Comes to Amityville. Clarence P Milligan. LC 47-5636. 1947. Christopher Pub. House.
Tiger Eye. Bertha Muzzy Sinclair. LC 30-18189. 1930. Little, Brown, and Company.
Tiger Hill. Ardath Wise. LC 74-34120. 1975. 4.95 (ISBN 0-517-52163-6). Lenox Press.
Tiger in Red Weather. John Wyllie. LC 79-6285. 1980. 8.95 (ISBN 0-385-15954-4). Published for the Crime Club by Doubleday.
Tiger in Summer. 1st Ed. Michael Keon. LC 52-11688. 1953. Harper.
Tiger in the Bed. Max Catto. LC 63-13218. 1963. Morrow.
Tiger in the Garden. Speed Lamkin. LC 50-5403. 1950. Houghton Mifflin.
Tiger in the Honeysuckle. Elliott Chaze. LC 65-115854. 4.95. Scribners.
Tiger in the Kitchen, & Other Strange Stories. facs. ed. Villi Sorensen. Tr. by Maureen Neiiendam. LC 74-87737. (Short Story Index Reprint Ser). 1957. 15.00 (ISBN 0-8369-3060-6). Ayer Co.
Tiger in the Kitchen: And Other Strange Stories. Villy Srensen. LC 74-87737. (Short story index reprint series). 1969. Books for Libraries Press.
Tiger in the Kitchen, and Other Strange Stories. Translated from the Danish by Maureen Neiiendam. With an Introd. by Angus Wilson. Villy Sorensen. LC 57-583089. 1957. Abelard-Schuman.
Tiger in the Mountains. Franklin M. Proud & Alfred F. Eberhardt. LC 76-25849. (Illus.). 8.95. St. Martin's Press.
Tiger in the Night: An Original Novel. Robert Kyle, pseud. LC 55-11393. (Dell first edition, 66). 1955. Dell Pub. Co.
Tiger in the Smoke. Margery Allingham. 223p. Repr. of 1952 ed. lib. bdg. 13.25x (ISBN 0-89190-198-1). Am Repr-Rivercity Pr.
Tiger in the Smoke. Margery Allingham. (1973 ed. 0.95 o.p.). 1975. pap. 1.50 (ISBN 0-532-95247-2). Woodhill.
Tiger in the Smoke. Margery Allingham. LC 52-10048. 1968. pap. 0.60 o.p. (60-344). Manor Bks.
Tiger Island. Patrick Clay. (Sgt. Hawk Ser.: No. 4). 240p. 1982. pap. 2.50 (ISBN 0-8439-1104-2, Leisure Bks). Nordon Pubns.
Tiger Island. Gouverneur Morris. LC 34-8992. E. P. Dutton & Co., Inc.
Tiger Juan. Perez De Ayala, Ramon. Tr. by Starkie Walter Fitswilliam. LC 33-17004. 1933. The Macmillan Company.
Tiger Kittens. Albert Zuckerman. LC 72-84958. 1973. 4.95 (ISBN 0-385-02440-1). Published for the Crime Club by Doubleday.
Tiger Lil. Roy Booth. LC 35-353751. Godwin.
Tiger-Lilies: A Novel. Sidney Lanier. LC 73-89948. (Southern literary classics series). 1969. University of North Carolina Press.
Tiger-Lilies. A Novel. Sidney Lanier. LC 7-14081. 1867. Hurd and Houghton.
Tiger Lily: A Story of a Woman. George Manville Fenn. The Cassell Publishing Co.
Tiger Lily, and Other Stories. Julia Thompson Von Stosch Schayer. LC 70-98593. (Short story index reprint series). 1969. Books for Libraries Press.
Tiger Lily: And Other Stories. Julia Thompson Von Stosch Schayer. LC 8-2026. 1883. C. Scribner's Sons.
Tiger-Lily: Or, The Woman Who Came Between. Alexander McVeigh Miller. (On cover: The library of American authors, no. 43). 1892. G. Munro.
Tiger Love. Robert Terry Shannon. LC 32-14015. E. J. Clode, Inc.
Tiger Love: A Novel. Eustace Hale Ball. LC 26-199613. Grosset & Dunlap.
Tiger Man. George Owen Baxter. LC 29-12129. The Macaulay Company.
Tiger Man. Frederick Faust. LC 29-12129. 1929. The Macaulay Company.
Tiger Man. Female Jordan. 192p. 1982. pap. 1.75 (ISBN 0-373-10477-4, Pub. by Harlequin). PB.
Tiger Milk. David Garth. LC 41-5368. 1941. H. C. Kinsey & Company, Inc.
Tiger of Baragunga. J. Inman Emery. LC 25-21073. 1925. G. P. Putnam's Sons.
Tiger of Cloud River. Ridgwell Cullum. LC 29-133660. 1929. J. B. Lippincott Company.
Tiger of Muscovy. Frederick J Whishaw. 1904. Longmans, Green, and Co.
Tiger of Wrath. Ramos. 224p. (Orig.). 1980. pap. 1.95 (ISBN 0-87067-684-9). Holloway.
Tiger Rag. Kit Reed, pseud. LC 73-79987. 1973. 6.95 (ISBN 0-525-21988-9). Dutton.
Tiger Rag. Kit Reed, pseud. (Fawcett Crest Book). 1977. 1.75 (ISBN 0-449-23173-9). Fawcett Pubns.
Tiger River. Arthur O Friel. LC 23-4293. 1923. Harper & Brothers.
Tiger Shark. Ken Stanton. (Operation Sea Monster Ser.). 1978. pap. 1.25 o.p. (ISBN 0-532-12543-6). Woodhill.
Tiger Shark. Ken Stanton. (Operation Sea Monster Ser.). 1978. pap. 1.25 o.p. (ISBN 0-532-12543-6). Manor Bks.
Tiger-Slayer. A Tale of the Indian Desert. rev. and ed. by percy b. st. john. ed. Gustave Aimard & St. John, Percy Bolingbroke, 1821-1889, Ed. LC 5-42194. (On cover: Lovell's library, no. 1032). 1887. J. W. Lovell Company.
Tiger Sniffs the Rose. Helen Grace Carlisle. LC 58-7350. 1958. Doubleday.
Tiger Standish... Sydney Horler. LC 33-481. 1933. Pub. for the Crime Club, Inc., by Doubleday, Doran & Company, Inc.
Tiger Street. Elleston Trevor. LC 54-318551. (Lion original, 207). 1954. Lion Books.
Tiger Street. Trevor, Elleston. LC 51-33990. 1951. T. V. Boardman.
Tiger Ten. William D. Blakenship. (Berkley Medallion Book). 1978. 1.95 (ISBN 0-425-03674-X). Berkley Pub. Corp.
Tiger Ten. William D Blankenship. LC 75-29127. 7.95 (ISBN 0-399-11679-6). Putnam.
Tiger Tiger. Charles William White. LC 40-33109. Duell, Sloan and Pearce.
Tiger, Tiger. Charles William White. LC 46-21221. 1946. The Blakiston Company.
Tiger Valley. Reginlad Campbell. LC 31-21902. 1931. R. R. Smith, Inc.
Tiger Waits: A Novel. Anton Myrer. LC 72-10355. 1973. 7.95 (ISBN 0-393-08672-0). Norton.
Tiger with the Bright Blue Eyes & Other Stories. Ed. by Lewis Jones. (Readers Ser.: Stage 2). 1981. pap. text ed. 1.95 (ISBN 0-88377-137-3). Newbury Hse.
Tigerman of Terrahpur see Hombre Tigre De Terrahpur.
Tigers & Traitors. Jules Verne. 1959. 3.95 o.p. Assoc Bk.
Tigers Are Better-Looking: With a Selection from The Left Bank: Stories. Jean Rhys. LC 72-9175. 1974. 6.95 (ISBN 0-06-013561-1). Harper & Row.
Tigers Are Better-Looking: With a Selection from the Left Bank. Jean Rhys. 1976. (pbk.) 1.50. Popular Library.
Tigers Are Burning. Martin Caidin. (Illus.). 1980. pap. 2.75 (ISBN 0-523-41816-7). Pinnacle Bks.
Tigers Are Hungry. Charles Early. LC 67-25320. 1967. Morrow.
Tiger's Chance. H. V. Elkin. (Cutler Ser.: No. 6). (Orig.). 1980. pap. 1.95 o.s.i. (ISBN 0-505-51559-8). Tower Bks.
Tiger's Claw. Albert Payson Terhune. LC 24-22003. George H. Doran Company.
Tiger's Coat. Elizabeth Dejeans. LC 17-7810. 1.50. The Bobbs-Merrill Company.
Tiger's Daughter. Bharati Mukherjee. LC 77-162011. 1972. 5.95 (ISBN 0-395-12715-7). Houghton Mifflin Co.
Tiger's Gold. George G. Gilman, pseud. (Edge Ser.: No. 14). 192p. 1975. pap. 1.95 (ISBN 0-523-41772-1). Pinnacle Bks.
Tigers Is Only Cats. Sophie Kerr. LC 29-226938. Farrar & Rinehart Incorporated.
Tiger's Mate. Wallace Smith. LC 28-22139. 1928. G. P. Putnam's Sons.
Tigers of Justice. Gar Wilson. (Phoenix Force Ser.). 192p. 1983. pap. 1.95 (Pub. by Worldwide). Harlequin Bks.
Tigers of Subtopia, and Other Stories. Julian Symons. LC 82-8596. 1983. 14.95 (ISBN 0-670-71283-3). Viking Press.
Tiger's Whiskers. Tr. from the French by Frances Frenaye. Harold Talbott. Jean Caran. 4.50. Walker.
Tiger's Woman. Celeste De Blasis. LC 80-23285. 14.95 (ISBN 0-440-08819-4). Delacorte Press.
Tight Corner. Sam Ross. LC 56-61604. 1956. Farrar, Straus and Cudahy.
Tight Lines. Jeff D. Marion. 42p. (Orig.). 1981. pap. 12.50 (ISBN 0-931182-04-2). Iron Mtn Pr.
Tight Little Island. Compton Mackenzie. LC 50-10385. 1950. Houghton Mifflin.
Tight Rope. Allison L Burks. LC 45-7203. 1945. Duell, Sloan and Pearce.
Tight Rope. Tom Wilson. LC 81-19298. 66p. 1981. pap. 6.95 (ISBN 0-942020-00-6). K B S Pr.
Tight Squeeze: Or, The Adventures of a Gentleman, Who, on a Wager of Ten Thousand Dollars, Undertook to Go from New York to New Orleans in Three Weeks, Without Money, As a Professional Tramp. William Staats. LC 8-13888. 1879. Lee and Shepard.
Tight White Collar. Grace Metalious. LC 60-710455. 1960. Messner.
Tight White Collar: A Novel. John L'Heureux. LC 72-171303. 1972. 5.95. Doubleday.
Tightrope. Stanley Kauffmann. LC 52-11571. 1952. Simon and Schuster.
Tightrope: A Novel of Intrigue in the Paris Underworld. Jean Legaret. LC 76-108949. 1970. 5.95. Little, Brown.
Tightrope Men. Desmond Bagley. LC 72-96226. 1973. 6.95 (ISBN 0-385-04827-0). Doubleday.
Tightrope Men. Desmond Bagley. LC 73-15999. 1973. 11.95 (ISBN 0-8161-6163-1). G. K. Hall.
Tightrope Minor: A Novel. Tom Topor. LC 74-150921. 1971. 5.95. Doubleday.
Tightrope Walker. Arden Fleetwood. LC 74-77471. 1976. 7.95 (ISBN 0-87949-029-2). Ashley Books.
Tightrope Walker. Dorothy Gilman. LC 78-20006. 1979. 7.95 (ISBN 0-385-14959-X). Doubleday.
Tightrope Walker. Dorothy Gilman. LC 79-25273. 1980. 12.95 (ISBN 0-8161-3026-4). G. K. Hall.
Tigranes: A Tale of the Days of Julian the Apostate. Giovanni Giuseppe Franco. LC 6-43153. ("Messenger series", no. 6). 1874. P. F. Cunningham & Son.
Tigress. Anne Warner French. LC 16-13510. 1.25. W. J. Watt & Company.
Tigress in the Village. Frank Arthur Swinnerton. LC 59-800156. 1959. Doubleday.
Tigress of the Harem. Ram Narain. LC 30-7425. The Macaulay Company.
Tike and Five Stories. Jonathan Strong. LC 69-16964. 1969. 5.75. Little, Brown.
Til Death. Evan Hunter. (Signet book). 1975. (pbk.) 1.25. New American Library.
Til Death. Ed McBain. 1959. 1.50 o.p. (ISBN 0-671-73030-4). S&S.
Til Death: By Ed McBain Pseud. Evan Hunter. LC 59-13127. 1959. Simon and Schuster.
Til Death You Do Pay. Muriel Davidson. LC 81-4052. 13.95 (ISBN 0-399-90131-0). R. Marek.
Til Night Is Gone. Phyllis Primmer. 1980. pap. 1.95 mass mkt. o.p. (ISBN 0-310-26342-5). Zondervan.
Tilbury Nogo: Or, Passages in the Life of an Unsuccessful Man. George John Whyte-Melville. (seaside library. v. 74, no. 1507). 1883. G. Munro.
Tilbury Nogo: Or, Passages in the Life of an Unsuccessful Man. new ed. George John Whyte-Melville. LC 42-29941. (On cover: Select library of fiction). 1904. Ward, Lock, and Co.
Tilda. Mark Van Doren. LC 43-473019. 1943. H. Holt and Company.
Tiler's Jewel. Harlan Hoge Ballard. LC 21-2818. 1921. The Stratford Company.
Till A' the Seas Gang Dry. John Innes. E. P. Dutton & Company.
Till Death Do Us Part: A Dr. Fell Mystery Story. John Dickson Carr. LC 44-766673. 1944. Harper & Brothers.

Till Death Do Us Part or Something Else Comes Up. Zane Alexander, pseud. LC 76-16851. (O.s.i.). 1976. pap. 4.50 o.s.i. (ISBN 0-664-24750-4). Westminster.

Till Death Do Us Part or Something Else Comes Up. Zane Alexander, pseud. LC 76-16851. (O.s.i.). 1976. pap. 4.50 o.s.i. (ISBN 0-664-24750-4). Westminster.

Till Death Us Do Part. A Novel. Lilian Headland Spender. (Harper's Franklin square library. no. 238). 1882. Harper & Brothers.

Till Heaven Cracks. Micheline Keating. LC 35-67205. The Hartney Press.

Till I Come Back to You. Thomas Bell. LC 43-8538. 1943. Little, Brown and Company.

Till Life Us Do Part. Elisabet Petertzen. LC 70-889877. 1970 (ISBN 0-85523-002-9). Wingate.

Till Morning Comes: A Novel. Suyin Han. LC 81-19150. (Illus.). 1982. 15.95 (ISBN 0-553-05011-7). Bantam Books.

Till Passion Dies. Sidney Herbert Daukes. LC 34-11266. 1934. H. C. Kinsey & Company, Inc.

Till the Boys Come Home. Elizabeth Head Fetter. LC 44-7912. 1944. Harper & Brothers.

Till the Clock Stops. John Joy Bell. LC 17-4710. Hodder and Stoughton.

Till the Clock Stops. John Joy Bell. 1917. 1.35. Duffield & Co.

Till the Day Dawn. George Franklin Allee. LC 44-39874. Zondervan Publishing House.

Till We Have Faces. C. S. Lewis. (O.s.i.). 1964. pap. 2.95 o.s.i. (ISBN 0-8028-6019-2). Eerdmans.

Till We Have Faces. Clive Staples Lewis. (O.s.i.). 1964. pap. 2.95 o.p. (ISBN 0-8028-6019-2). Eerdmans.

Till We Have Faces: A Myth Retold. Clive Staples Lewis. LC 79-24272. (Harvest/HBJ book). 1980. 3.95. Harcourt Brace Jovanovich.

Till We Have Faces: A Myth Retold. 1st American Ed. Clive Staples Lewis. LC 56-11300. 1957. Harcourt, Brace.

Till You Find Love. Louise Marks Clancy. LC 37-5756. Greenberg.

Tillers of the Soil. John Edward Patterson. LC 11-3241. 1911. 1.30. Duffield & Company.

Tillicum Tales. Seattle, Writers Club. LC 7-37714. 1907. Lowman & Hanford.

Tillie, a Mennonite Maid. Helen Reimensnyder Martin. LC 68-20018. (Americans in Fiction Ser.). (Illus.). lib. bdg. 16.00 (ISBN 0-8398-1251-5); pap. text ed. 5.95x (ISBN 0-89197-966-2). Irvington.

Tillie, a Mennonite Maid: A Story of the Pennsylvania Dutch. Helen Reimensnyder Martin. LC 68-20018. (Americans in Fiction). (Illus.). 1968. Gregg Press.

Tillie, A Mennonite Maid: A Story of the Pennsylvania Dutch. Helen Reimensnyder Martin. LC 4-3734. 1904. The Century Co.

Tillie, a Mennonite Maid: A Story of the Pennsylvania Dutch. Helen Reimensnyder Martin. LC 16-25041. 1916. The Century Co.

Tillie's Punctured Romance. Leeds. 5.95 o.p. (ISBN 0-87690-047-3). Dutton.

Tilly. Catherine Cookson. LC 80-16627. 384p. 1980. 12.95 (ISBN 0-688-03715-1). Morrow.

Tilly. Catherine Cookson. 1981. pap. 3.50 (ISBN 0-671-42604-4). PB.

Tilly Alone. Catherine Cookson. LC 81-11203. 272p. 1982. 13.50 (ISBN 0-688-00455-5). Morrow.

Tilly Trotter Wed see Tilly Wed.

Tilly Wed. Catherine Cookson. Orig. Title: Tilly Trotter Wed. 384p. 1980. 11.95 (ISBN 0-688-00188-2). Morrow.

Tilly Wed. Catherine Cookson. 1982. pap. 3.50 (ISBN 0-671-42605-2). PB.

Tilly Wed: A Novel. Catherine Cookson. LC 80-26306. 1981. 11.95 (ISBN 0-688-00188-2). Morrow.

Tilly Widowed. Catherine Cookson. LC 81-11203. 1982. 12.95 (ISBN 0-688-00455-5). Morrow.

Tillyloss Scandal. James Matthew Barrie. LC 77-98560. (Short story index reprint series). 1969. Books for Libraries Press.

Tillyloss Scandal. James Matthew Barrie. LC 6-8639. (On cover: The Belmore series. no. 17). Lovell, Coryell & Company.

Tillyloss Scandal. James Matthew Barrie. LC 24-27956. (Lettered on cover: Little leather library. no 57). 1918. Little Leather Library Corporation.

Tilsit Inheritance. Catherine Gaskin. LC 63-12979. 1963. Doubleday.

Tilsit Inheritance. Catherine Gaskin. 1973. (pbk) 1.25. Fawcett Crest.

Tilt. Dave Morice. 1972. pap. 1.00 o.p. (ISBN 0-915124-00-9). Toothpaste.

Tilting at Windmills: A Story of the Blue Grass Country. Emma M Connelly. LC 6-30691. D. Lothrop Company.

Tim. Colleen McCullough. 1.75 (ISBN 0-445-03168-9). Popular Library.

Tim. Colleen McCullough. 1977. 1.95 (ISBN 0-445-08545-2). Popular Library.

Tim: A Novel. Colleen McCullough. LC 73-14318. 1974. 6.95 (ISBN 0-06-012891-7). Harper & Row.

Tim: A Novel. Colleen McCullough. LC 74-12177. 1974. (lib. bdg.) 10.95 (ISBN 0-8161-6233-6). G. K. Hall.

Tim, a Story. Jesse Stuart. LC 68-23552. Kentucky Writers' Guild, Harvest Press.

Tim: A Story of School Life... Howard Overing Sturgis. LC 8-16864. 1891. Macmillan and Co.

Tim: A Story of School Life. Howard Overing Sturgis. LC 78-63996. (Gay Experience). Repr. of 1891 ed. 26.50 (ISBN 0-404-61514-7). AMS Pr.

Tim & His Mother. Richard B. Long. 192p. (Orig.). 1973. pap. 1.95 o.p. (ISBN 0-87682-344-4, 7344). Barclay Hse.

Tim and Jim: A Modern Fad in Practical Operation. George Lindley Young. LC 27-5842. R. G. Badger.

Tim Kane's Treasure. C M Bennett. LC 31-17600. E. P. Dutton & Co., Inc.

Tim Whosoever. Jerome Hines. 1970. 3.95 o.p. (ISBN 0-8007-0382-0). Revell.

Timbal Gulch Trail. Max Brand. LC 34-687168. 1934. Dodd, Mead & Company.

Timbal Gulch Trail. Frederick Faust. LC 34-687. 1934. Dodd, Mead & Company.

Timber". Harold Titus. LC 22-740726. Small, Maynard & Company.

Timber". Harold Titus. LC 25-155034. 1922. A. L. Burt.

Timber: A Novel of Pacific Coast Loggers. Roderick Langmere Haig Haig-Brown. LC 42-36058. 1942. W. Morrow & Company.

Timber Beast. Archie Binns. LC 44-4725. 1944. C. Scribner's Sons.

Timber Beasts: A Malloy of the Royal Mounted Story. Charles Stoddard. LC 45-9778. 1945. Arcadia House, Inc.

Timber Beasts: A Malloy of the Royal Mounted Story. Charles Stanley Strong. LC 45-9778. 1945. Arcadia House.

Timber Jack. Maribelle Cormack. LC 52-14565. 1952. F. Watts.

Timber Lane. Warren Murphy. (Destroyer Ser.: No. 42). 192p. (Orig.). 1980. pap. 2.25 (ISBN 0-523-41767-5). Pinnacle Bks.

Timber Line. Gene Fowler, pseud. 1981. Repr. lib. bdg. 15.95x (ISBN 0-89966-424-5). Buccaneer Bks.

Timber Line. Gene Fowler, pseud. 1956. 4.95 o.p. Doubleday.

Timber Pirate. Charles Christopher Jenkins. LC 22-19604. 1.75. George H. Doran Company.

Timber Town Nurse. Annie L. Gelsthorpe. 1972. pap. 0.75 o.s.i. (01-361). Lancer.

Timber-Wolf. Jackson Gregory. LC 23-124331. 1923. C. Scribner's Sons.

Timber Wolves. Bernard Cronin. LC 21-36317. 1921. The Macmillan Company.

Timberline: A Novel by the Ozarks. Wesley Albert Shanholtzer. LC 29-24080.

Timbers of the Western Gate. Mary Goodrich. LC 32-16258. 1932. Goodhue-Kitchener Printing Company.

Timbertwist. 1st Ed. Thomas Allen Mussaeus. LC 56-125813. 1957. Pageant Press.

Time After Time: A Novel. Karl Alexander. LC 78-27386. 9.95 (ISBN 0-440-08900-X). Delacorte Press.

Time Against the Sky: 19th Century Days in Philadelphia. Mary Paul Caner. LC 66-19599. 1966. Dresser, Chapman & Grimes.

Time and a Place: Stories. William Humphrey. LC 68-31608. 1968. 4.95. Knopf.

Time and Again. Jack Finney. LC 71-101873. (Illus.). 1970. 7.95. Simon and Schuster.

Time and Again. Clifford D Simak. LC 51-10314. (A Science-fiction adventure). 1951. Simon and Schuster.

Time and Again. Clifford D. Simak. 1975. (pbk.) 1.25. Ace Books.

Time and Again. Clifford D. Simak. 1976. 1.75. Ace Books.

Time & Chance. Brian Barnes. 336p. (Orig.). 1982. pap. 3.25 (ISBN 0-505-51815-5). Tower Bks.

Time and Chance: A Novel. Anna Wibberley. LC 73-13579. 1974. 7.95 (ISBN 0-671-21611-2). Simon and Schuster.

Time and Chance: A Romance and a History: Being the Story of the Life of a Man. Elbert Hubbard. LC 99-3143. 1899. The Roycrofters.

Time and Chance: A Romance and a History: Being the Story of the Life of a Man. rev. ed. Elbert Hubbard. LC 1-23036. 1901. T. P. Putnam's Sons.

Time and Chance: A Romance and a History; Being the Story of the Life of a Man. Elbert Hubbard. LC 22-2103. Printed at the Roycroft Shops.

Time and Circumstance: A Novel of Puritan New England (Period, 1655-56) Philip Jerome Simon. LC 77-84548. 7.50 (ISBN 0-911180-01-X). Priam Press.

Time and Eternity, a Tale of Three Exiles. Gilbert Cannan. LC 20-7039. 1920. 1.90. George H. Doran Company.

Time and Place. Bryan Woolley. LC 76-58873. 8.95 (ISBN 0-525-21991-9). E. P. Dutton.

Time and Space in the Novels of Samuel Richardson. John Samuel Bullen. LC 65-65258. (Utah. State University of Agriculture and Applied Science, Logan. Monograph Ser.: Vol. 12, No. 2). 1965. Utah State University Press.

Time and Stars. Poul Anderson. LC 64-1129. (Doubleday science fiction). 1964. Doubleday.

Time and Stars. Poul Anderson. (Berkley Medallion Book). 1978. 1.50 (ISBN 0-425-03621-9). Berkley Pub. Corp.

Time and the Gods. Edward John Moreton Drax Plunkett Dunsany. LC 76-113659. (Short story index reprint series). (Illus.). 1970. Books for Libraries Press.

Time & the Hour. Faith Baldwin. 1974. 6.95 o.p. HR&W.

Time & the Hour. Faith Baldwin. (Adult Ser). 410p. 1974. Repr. lib. bdg. 10.95 o.p. (ISBN 0-8161-6251-4, Large Print Bks). G K Hall.

Time and the Hour. Faith Baldwin Cuthrell. LC 73-12856. 1974. 6.95 (ISBN 0-03-012231-7). Holt, Rinehart and Winston.

Time and the Hour. Faith Baldwin Cuthrell. (Kangaroo Book). 1977. 1.50 (ISBN 0-671-81139-8). Pocket Books.

Time and the Hour. Faith Baldwin Cuthrell. LC 74-18283. 1974. (ISBN 0-8161-6251-4). G. K. Hall.

Time and the Hour. Edith Austin Holton. LC 46-4904. 1946. G. P. Putnam's Sons.

Time and the Hour. Robert Howard Spring & Full Name: Robert Howard Spring. LC 58-5426. Harper.

Time and the Place: A Novel. Robert Paul Smith. LC 52-6529. 1952. Simon and Schuster.

Time and the Riddle: Thirty-One Zen Stories. Howard Melvin Fast. LC 75-18095. 12.95 (ISBN 0-378-06375-8). Ward Ritchie Press.

Time and the Riddle: Thirty-One Zen Stories. Howard Melvin Fast. LC 79-24981. 1980. 6.95 (ISBN 0-395-29180-1). Houghton Mifflin.

Time & the Rivers. Florence Kerigan. LC 60-13115. 1960. Concordia Pub. House.

Time and the Wind. Erico Verissimo. LC 51-12487. 1951. Macmillan.

Time and the Wind. Erico Verissimo. LC 78-88995. 1969. Greenwood Press.

Time and the Woman: A Novel. Richard Pryce. LC 13-35469. 1913. R. F. Fenno & Company.

Time and Tide. Ruby R Krider. LC 68-8350. 1968. 4.00. Dorrance.

Time and Time Again. James Hilton. LC 53-7314. 1953. Little, Brown.

Time at Her Heels. Dorothy Aldis. LC 37-8022. 1937. Houghton Mifflin Company.

Time Bandits: The Movie Script. Terry Gilliam & Michael Palin. LC 81-43117. 216p. 1981. pap. 9.95 (ISBN 0-385-17732-1, Dolp). Doubleday.

Time Before This. Nicholas Monsarrat. LC 62-16649. 1962. W. Sloane Associates.

Time Between. Gale Wilhelm. LC 42-22991. 1942. W. Morrow & Co.

Time Bomb. James D. Atwater. LC 77-5825. 1977. 7.95 (ISBN 0-670-26116-5). Viking Press.

Time Bomb. James D. Atwater. LC 78-8046. 1978. 12.95 (ISBN 0-8161-6595-5). G. K. Hall.

Time Bomb. James D. Atwater. LC 78-25593. 1979. 1.95 (ISBN 0-14-005023-X). Penguin Books.

Time Bomb. Wilson Tucker. LC 55-8008. 1955. Rinehart.

Time Cannot Dim. Malachy Gerard Carroll. LC 56-135797. 1955. H. Regnery Co.

Time-Catcher. Caslav V. Stanojevic. LC 74-78671. 1974. 6.95 (ISBN 0-8059-2020-X). Dorrance.

Time Clock of Death. Nick Carter. (Nick Carter Ser.). (O.s.i.). 192p. (Orig.). 1970. pap. 1.25 o.s.i. (AQ1370, Award). Univ Pub & Dist.

Time Connection. Thomas F. Monteleone. 192p. 1982. pap. 2.50 (ISBN 0-445-00417-7). Popular Lib.

Time Dweller. Michael Moorcock. (Daw Science Fiction Ser.). 1979. pap. 1.75 (ISBN 0-87997-489-3, UE1489). Daw Bks.

Time Echo. Robert Lionel, pseud. 1970. Repr. pap. 0.60 o.p. (60-459). Manor Bks.

Time Element, and Other Stories. John O'Hara. LC 72-5133. 1972. 6.95 (ISBN 0-394-48211-5). Random House.

Time Enough. Emily Kimbrough. LC 74-1823. (Cass Canfield book). (Illus.). 1974. 7.95 (ISBN 0-06-012364-8). Harper & Row.

Time Enough for Love. Robert Anson Heinlein. 1974. pap. 2.75 (ISBN 0-425-04684-2, Medallion). Berkley Pub.

Time Enough for Love: The Lives of Lazarus Long. Robert Anson Heinlein. (Berkley medallion book). 1974. (pbk) 1.95 (ISBN 0-425-02493-8). Putnam.

Time Enough Later. Kylie Tennant, pseud. LC 43-1681. 1943. The Macmillan Company.

Time Enough to Die. Peter Rabe. LC 60-706. (Gold medal books, 969). 1959. Fawcett Publications.

Time Exile. Reinhold Millers. 1972. 3.00 (ISBN 0-912852-01-1). Echo Publishers.

Time Expired: By G. C. O'Donnell. Gus C O'Donnell. LC 67-204221. 1967. bds., 8.25. Leksand Pr.

Time Exposure. Parkhurst Whitney. LC 31-324107. Farrar & Rinehart, Incorporated.

Time Flew by, a Novel. Juanita M Whisenant. LC 51-10976. 1951. Exposition Press.

Time for a Murder. John Russell Warren. LC 41-3425. Sheridan House.

Time for Awakening. Richard J. Aielli. 5.00 o.p. Carlton.

Time for Deceit. Elsie W. Strother. 1981. pap. 6.95 (Avalon). Bouregy.

Time for Desire. June Wetherell. 1977. 1.95. Pinnacle Books.

Time for Dreaming. John O. Crosby. 2.75 o.p. Carlton.

Time for Frankie Coolin. Bill Griffith. LC 81-19247. 13.50 (ISBN 0-394-52123-4). Random House.

Time for Giving. Jill Briscoe. Ed. by James A. Kuse. 1979. pap. 5.95 (ISBN 0-89542-069-4). Ideals.

Time for Glory. Robert O'Neil Bristow. LC 68-30867. 1968. 5.95. W. Morrow.

Time for Incest. Tom Young. pap. 1.95 o.p. (ISBN 0-87056-198-7, 6198). Brandon.

Time for Laughter. Jessica Wellner. LC 48-1190. 1948. Simon and Schuster.

Time for Living. Gertrude Schleier. LC 61-15298. (Torquil book). 1961. Distributed by Dodd, Mead.

Time for Love. Ramona Herdman. LC 36-66647. 1936. Harper & Brothers.

Time for Love. LC 47-18224. 1947. Arcadia House.

Time for Loving. Anne Starr. (Adventures in Love Ser.: No. 27). 1982. pap. 1.75 (ISBN 0-451-11706-9, AE1706, Sig). NAL.

Time for Loving. Herbert Tarr. LC 72-2733. 1973. 5.95 (ISBN 0-394-46158-4). Random House.

Time for Miss Boo. Margaret Lee Runbeck. LC 49-4495. 1949. Appleton-Century-Crofts.

Time for Outrage. Amelia Bean. LC 67-19116. 1967. Doubleday.

Time for Paris. George J. W Goodman. LC 57-12466. 1957. Doubleday.

Time for Passion. William Arthur Neubauer. LC 51-9013. 1950. Phoenix Press.

Time for Pirates. Gavin Black. LC 79-144193. (Novel of Suspense Ser). 1971. 5.95 o.p. (ISBN 0-06-010372-8, HarpT). Har-Row.

Time for Pirates. Oswald Wynd. LC 79-144193. 1971. 5.95 (ISBN 0-06-010372-8). Harper & Row.

Time for Rejoicing. Elizabeth Renier. 1973. (pbk.) 0.75. Ace Books.

Time for Roses. Agatha D. Anastasi. (Orig.). 1982. pap. 3.50 (ISBN 0-89083-946-8). Zebra.

Time for Silence. Andre Maurois. Tr. by Edith Johannsen. 1942. D. Appleton Century Company, Incorporated.

Time for Sleeping. James Moffat. 1974. pap. 0.75 o.p. (LB00067). Leisure Bks.

Time for Tea. John Coates. LC 50-6193. 1950. Macmillan.

Time for the Stars. Robert Anson Heinlein. (Del Rey Bk.). Date not set. pap. cancelled (ISBN 0-345-29389-4). Ballantine.

Time for Titans. Vina Delmar. LC 73-18499. 1974. 7.95 (ISBN 0-15-190445-6). Harcourt Brace Jovanovich.

Time for Treason. Olga Hesky. LC 68-13601. (Red badge mystery). 1968. Dodd, Mead.

Time for Trusting. Christina Abbey. (Candlelight Romance). 1975. (pbk.) 0.75. Dell.

Time for Truth. Hans Hellmut Kirst. LC 74-8127. 1974. 7.95 (ISBN 0-698-10624-5). Coward, McCann & Geoghenan.

Time for Us. Arlene Hale. LC 76-45207. 1977. 8.95 (ISBN 0-89340-049-1). J. Curley & Associates.

Time for Us. Arlene Hale. LC 72-754. 1972. (ISBN 0-316-33874-5). Little, Brown.

Time for Vengeance. Giles A Lutz. 1977. 1.50 (ISBN 0-441-81132-9). Ace Books.

Time for Vengeance. Kingley West. LC 61-10652. (Double D western). 1961. Doubleday.

Time for Violence. Anthea Goddard. (O.s.i.). 1978. 7.95 o.s.i. (ISBN 0-8027-5369-8). Walker & Co.

Time for Violence: A Novel. Noel M Loomis. LC 60-12177. 1960. Macmillan.

Time Forgotten. David Houston. (Tales of Tomorrow Ser.: No. 5). (Illus.). 208p. (Orig.). 1982. pap. 2.50 o.s.i. (ISBN 0-8439-1170-0, Leisure Bks). Nordon Pubns.

Time, Forward! Valentin Petrovich Kataev. LC 76-11933. 1976. 12.50 (ISBN 0-253-36018-8) (ISBN 0-253-20204-3). Indiana University Press.

Time, Forward!... Authorized Translation from the Russian. Valentin Petrovich Kataev. Tr. by Malamuth, Charles. LC 33-324173. Farrar & Rinehart, Incorporated.

Time Gate. John W. Jakes. LC 72-175546. 1972. 4.75 (ISBN 0-664-32510-6). Westminster Press.

Time Gladiator. Mack Reynolds. pap. 0.75 o.p. Lancer.

Time-Hoppers. Robert Silverberg. (S372). 1968. Avon.

Time Hoppers. Robert Silverberg. (Leisure Book). 1977. 1.50 (ISBN 0-8439-0512-3). Nordon Pubns.

Time-Hoppers. Robert Silverberg. LC 67-12893. 1967. Doubleday.

Time in Advance: By William Tenn Pseud. Philip Klass. LC 58-8495. (Bantam book, A1786). 1958. Bantam Books.

Time in Its Flight. Susan Fromberg Schaeffer. LC 77-15181. 1978. 12.95 (ISBN 0-385-13335-9). Doubleday.

Time in Its Flight. Susan Fromberg Schaeffer. 1979. 2.95 (ISBN 0-671-82677-8). Pocket Books.

Time in September. Isobel Stewart. Ed. by Gene DeRoin. (Aston Hall Presents Ser.). (Orig.). 1979. pap. 1.50 (ISBN 0-89936-002-5). Aston Hall.

Time in the Sun. Jane Barry. (H2754). 1965. Bantam.

Time in the Sun. 1st Ed. Jane Barry. LC 62-11313. 1962. Doubleday.

Time Is a Gentleman. Charles Goff Thomson. LC 28-24475. 1928. The Macmillan Company.

Time Is a River: The Story of a Strange Adventure. Beatrice Hermann. LC 45-8635. 1945. The Folio Club.

Time Is an Enemy. Sidney J Baker. LC 58-9127. 1958. Mystery House.

Time Is Coming. W. B Bolmer. LC 6-10370. 1896. G. W. Dillingham Co.

Time Is Forever. Helen Partridge. LC 38-131811. 1938. Arcadia House.

Time Is Noon. Pearl Sydenstricker Buck. (John Day Bk.). 1967. 8.95 o.p. (ISBN 0-381-98056-1, A79800, TYC-T). T Y Crowell.

Time Is Noon: A Novel. Pearl Sydenstricker Buck. LC 67-10824. 1967. John Day Co.

Time Is Now. Maxwell Maltz. LC 74-16020. 1975. 8.95 (ISBN 0-671-21859-X). Simon and Schuster.

Time Is Now. Marjorie Bartholomew Paradis. LC 53-6810. 1953. Abelard Press.

Time Is Ripe. Walter Greenwood. LC 35-3662. 1935. Doubleday, Doran & Company, Inc.

Time Is the Simplest Thing. Clifford D Simak. LC 61-9554. (Doubleday science fiction). 1961. Doubleday.

Time Is Whispering. Elizabeth Robins. LC 23-7984. Harper & Brothers.

Time It Never Rained. Elmer Kelton. LC 73-79680. 1973. 6.95 (ISBN 0-385-05075-5). Doubleday.

Time-Jump. John Brunner. 1973. (pbk.) 0.95. Dell Pub. Co.

Time Lay Asleep. Carman Dee Barnes. LC 46-7495. 1946. Harper & Brothers.

Time Lock. Charles Edmonds Walk. LC 12-23066. 1912. A. C. McClurg & Co.

Time Machine. Herbert George Wells. LC 64-5500. 1964. Heritage Press.

Time Machine. Herbert George Wells. LC 64-4964. 1964. Limited Editions Club.

Time Machine. Herbert George Wells. LC 66-1485. (Berkley highland book). 1965. Berkley Pub. Corp.

Time Machine see Three Prophetic Novels.

Time Machine; The War of the Worlds. a critical ed. / edited by frank d. mcconnell. ed. Herbert George Wells. LC 76-42672. (Illus.). 1977. 4.00 (ISBN 0-19-502164-9). Oxford University Press.

Time Machine: An Invention. Herbert George Wells. LC 71-183141. 1971. (ISBN 0-8376-0403-6). R. Bentley.

Time Machine, an Invention. Herbert George Wells. (Buckram series). 1895. H. Holt and Company.

Time Machine, an Invention. Herbert George Wells. LC 20-18818. H. Holt and Company.

Time Machine: An Invention. Herbert George Wells. LC 24-304563. 1922. H. Holt and Company.

Time Machine: An Invention by H. G. Wells. Herbert George Wells. 1966. 6.50 o.p. (ISBN 0-434-85202-3). Dufour.

Time Masters. Wilson Tucker. LC 53-5357. 1953. Rinehart.

Time Must Have a Stop. Aldous Leonard Huxley. LC 66-114. (Harper perennial classic, HP6050L). 1965. bds., 1.95. Harper.

Time Must Have a Stop. Aldous Leonard Huxley. LC 44-7463. 1944. Harper & Brothers.

Time Must Have a Stop. Aldous Leonard Huxley. LC 47-6418. 1947. Sun Dial Press.

Time No Longer. Taylor Caldwell. LC 41-15452. 1941. C. Scribner's Sons.

Time No Longer. Taylor Caldwell & Max Reiner. LC 75-633. 1975. 11.95 (ISBN 0-88411-161-X). Aeonian Press.

Time nor Tide: A Novel. William Delligan. LC 81-17352. 15.50 (ISBN 0-525-24104-3). Dutton.

Time O' Day. Doris Egerton Jones. LC 15-9204. 1915. 6.00. Cassell and Company, Ltd.

Time O' Day. Doris Egerton Jones. LC 15-9697. 1915. 1.25. G. W. Jacobs & Company.

Time of Adam; Stories. Elizabeth Cullinan. LC 72-125649. 1971. 5.95. Houghton Mifflin.

Time of Changes. Robert Silverberg. LC 75-26203. 1971. N. Doubleday.

Time of Changes. Robert Silverberg. LC 75-318599. (Panther science fiction). 1975. 0.50 (ISBN 0-586-03995-3). Panther.

Time of Changes. Robert Silverberg. (Berkley book). 1979. 1.95 (ISBN 0-425-04051-8). Berkley Pub. Corp.

Time of Death. Dobrica Cosic. LC 77-73047. 10.95 (ISBN 0-15-190448-0). Harcourt Brace Jovanovich.

Time of Desecration. Alberto Moravia. LC 80-14438. 1980. 12.95 (ISBN 0-374-27781-8). Farrar, Straus & Giroux.

Time of Dreaming. Josephine Edgar. 1974. (pbk.) 0.95 (ISBN 0-671-77758-0). Pocket Books.

Time of Drums: A Novel. John Ehle. LC 78-108944. 1970. 6.95. Harper & Row.

Time of Fallen Blossoms. Allan Stephen Clifton. LC 51-9538. (Illus.). 1951. Knopf.

Time of Fear: A Novel. Roderick MacLeish. LC 58-5971. 1958. Viking Press.

Time of Fortune. Benjamin Appel. LC 63-12001. 1963. Morrow.

Time of Friendship: A Volume of Short Stories by Paul Bowles. 1st Ed. Paul Frederic Bowles. LC 67-15664. 1967. 4.95. Holt.

Time of Fury. Norton Parker & Kallie Norton. 1980. pap. 2.25 (ISBN 0-8439-0791-6). Nordon Pubns.

Time of Gold. Desemea Wikson. LC 32-763. E. P. Dutton & Co., Inc.

Time of Growing. Ed. by Jean Van Leeuwen. 1967. Random House.

Time of Her Life. Cornell George Hopley-Woolrich. LC 31-4332. 1931. H. Liveright.

Time of Her Life. Cornell Woolrich, pseud. H. Liberight.

Time of Heroes. Steve. Damion. pap. 0.50 o.p. (52-888). Paperback Lib.

Time of Hope. Charles Percy Snow. LC 61-954. (His Strangers and brothers, 3; Scribner lib. SL130). 1966. pap., 1.65. Scribners.

Time of Hope. Snow, Charles Percy. LC 50-8342. (His Strangers and brothers, 3). 1950. Macmillan.

Time of Illusion. Johnathan Schell. 1976. pap. 4.95 (ISBN 0-394-72217-5, 72217, Vin). Random.

Time of Indifference. Alberto Moravia. LC 53-70821. 1974. (pbk.) 1.50. Manor Books.

Time of Indifference. Alberto Moravia. LC 75-25264. 1975. 15.50 (ISBN 0-8371-8383-9). Greenwood Press.

Time of Indifference. Alberto Moravia. LC 70-874458. (Penguin books). 1970 (ISBN 0-14-003123-5). Penguin.

Time of Indifference: By Alberto Moravia Pseud. Translated by Angus Davidson. Alberto Pincherle. LC 53-7082. 1953. Farrar, Straus and Young.

Time of Killing. William M Hardy. LC 62-9719. 1962. Dodd, Mead.

Time of Lust. John Fountain. 192p. pap. 1.95 o.p. (2000). Intimate Lib.

Time of Man. Elizabeth Madox Roberts. (Signet giant S1133). 1954. New American Library.

Time of Man. Elizabeth Madox Roberts. LC 35-27140. (Half-title: The modern library of the world's best books). The Modern Library.

Time of Man: A Novel. Elizabeth Madox Roberts. 1926. The Viking Press.

Time of Man: A Novel. Elizabeth Madox Roberts. LC 82-40178. (Illus.). 23.00 (ISBN 0-8131-1467-5) (ISBN 0-8131-0152-2). University Press of Kentucky.

Time of Man: A Novel. Elizabeth Madox Roberts & Leighton, Clare Veronica Hope, 1900- Illus. LC 46-442. 1945. The Viking Press.

Time of Miracles: A Legend. Borislav Pekic. LC 76-21876. 10.95 (ISBN 0-15-190464-2). Harcourt Brace Jovanovich.

Time of Music: A Time of Magic. Joseph L. S Terrell. LC 72-83188. 1972. 6.95 (ISBN 0-910244-68-5). J. F. Blair.

Time of Night. Ruth Swazee. 1979. pap. 1.50 (ISBN 0-532-15387-1). Woodhill.

Time of Parting. Anton Donchev. Tr. by Marguerite Alexieva. 1968. 5.95 o.p. Morrow.

Time of Passage: SF Stories About Death and Dying. Joseph D Olander & Martin Harry Greenberg. LC 77-76727. 1977. 9.95 (ISBN 0-8008-7733-0). Taplinger Pub. Co.

Time of Peace: September 26, 1930-December 7, 1941. Ben Ames Williams. LC 42-36338. 1942. Houghton Mifflin Company.

Time of Predators. Joseph N Gores. LC 69-16470. 1969. 4.95. Random House.

Time of Rebellion: A Novel. Olive Church. LC 68-19629. 1968. Herald House.

Time of Reckoning. Walter H Wager. LC 77-22548. 8.95 (ISBN 0-87223-495-9). Playboy Press.

Time of Soldiers: A Novel. Andrew Jolly. LC 75-33121. 1976. (ISBN 0-525-21995-1). Dutton.

Time of Soldiers: A Novel. Andrew Jolly. 1977. 1.75 (ISBN 0-380-00959-5). Avon Books.

Time of Temptation: 1st Amer. Ed. Pierre Audemars. LC 66-16933. 3.50. Pub. for the Crime Club by Doubleday.

Time of Terror. Hugh Pentecost. (Red Badge Novel of Suspense). 194p. 1975. 5.95 o.p. (ISBN 0-396-07123-6). Dodd.

Time of Terror. Judson Pentecost Philips. LC 75-4817. (Red badge novel of suspense). 1975. 5.95 (ISBN 0-396-07123-6). Dodd, Mead.

Time of Terror. 1st Ed. Lionel White. LC 60-12114. 1960. Dutton.

Time of Testing. Jon R Littlejohn. LC 65-28173. 3.95. Concordia.

Time of the Angels. Iris Murdoch. LC 66-24208. 1966. bds., 5.00. Viking.

Time of the Butcherbird. Alex La Guma. LC 79-670199. (African writers series; 212). (H.E.B. paperback). 1979. 2.95 (ISBN 0-435-90212-1). Heinemann Educational.

Time of the Dark. Barbara Hambly. LC 81-22836. (Illus.). 1982. 2.50 (ISBN 0-345-29669-9). Ballantine.

Time of the Dragon. Dorothy Eden. LC 75-22243. 1975. 8.95 (ISBN 0-698-10699-7). Coward, McCann & Geoghegan.

Time of the Dragons. Robert Shea. (Shike Ser.). 488p. 1982. 14.95 (ISBN 0-399-12728-3). Putnam Pub Group.

Time of the Dragons Shike, Bk. I. Robert Shea. 464p. (Orig.). 1981. pap. 3.50 (ISBN 0-515-07119-6). Jove Pubns.

Time of the Emergency. Peter Rand. LC 77-75388. 1977. 5.95 (ISBN 0-385-07033-0). Doubleday.

Time of the Fire: By Marc Brandel Pseud. Marcus Beresford. LC 54-5968. 1954. Random House.

Time of the Fourth Horseman. Chelsea Q. Yarbo. 256p. 1981. pap. 2.25 (ISBN 0-441-81181-7). Ace Bks.

Time of the Fourth Horseman. Chelsea Q. Yarbo. LC 75-41677. 192p. 1976. 5.95 o.p. (ISBN 0-385-11076-6). Doubleday.

Time of the Fourth Horseman. Chelsea Quinn Yarbro. LC 75-41677. 1976. 5.95 (ISBN 0-385-11076-6). Doubleday.

Time of the Gringo. Elliott Arnold. LC 52-6402. 1953. Knopf.

Time of the Hawk. Andrew Tully. LC 67-11637. 1967. Morrow.

Time of the Hawklords. Michael Moorcock & Michael Butterworth. 1976. 1.50 (ISBN 0-446-78986-0). Warner Books.

Time of the Hero. Mario Vargas Llosa. (Harper Colophon books). 1979. 5.95 (ISBN 0-06-090652-9). Harper & Row.

Time of the Hero. Tr. from Spanish by Lysander Kemp. Mario Vargas Llosa. LC 65-14204. 5.95. Grove.

Time of the Juggernaut. Herbert Steinhouse. LC 58-8772. 1958. Morrow.

Time of the Leonids. Christine Bruckner. LC 81-38536. 1982. 13.95 (ISBN 0-89182-040-X). Charles River Books.

Time of the Peacock: Stories, by Mena Abdullah, Ray Mathew. Mena Abdullah & Ray Mathew. LC 65-9181. bds., 2.95. Angus and Robertson.

Time of the Peacock: Stories, by Mena Abdullah, Ray Mathew. Mena Abdullah & Ray Mathew. LC 67-25635. 1968. bds., 3.50. Roy.

Time of the Sign. Richard A. Coffen. (Flame Ser.). 48p. 1975. pap. text ed. 0.95 (ISBN 0-8127-0306-5). Review & Herald.

Time of the Singing of Birds. Grace Livingston Hill. LC 44-8708. 1944. J. B. Lippincott Company.

Time of the Unicorn. Barbara Jefferis. LC 73-20468. 1974. 6.95 (ISBN 0-688-00249-8). Morrow.

Time of the Young Soldiers. Hans Peter Richter. LC 76-379464. 1976. 2.50 (ISBN 0-7226-5122-8). Kestrel Books.

Time of Their Coming. Bertha B. Moore McCurry. LC 43-578338. 1943. Wm. B. Eerdmans Publishing Company.

Time of Understanding: Stories of Girls Learning to Get Along with Their Parents. Helen Josephine Ferris. LC 63-11555. 1963. F. Watts.

Time of War. Ralph L. Lowenstein. 320p. 1973. pap. 1.25 o.s.i. (78-736). Lancer.

Time of Wrath. Luis Spota. LC 62-11459.

Time off for Death: By George Braddon Pseud. George Alexis Bankoff. LC 58-7548. 1958. Roy Publishers.

Time off for Murder. Zelda Popkin. LC 40-28126. J. B. Lippincott Company.

Time on Earth. Vilhelm Moberg. LC 65-17110. 1965. Simon and Schuster.

Time on Earth. Tr. from Swedish by Naomi Walford. Wilhelm Moberg. LC 65-17110. bds., 4.50. S. & S.

Time on the Sun. M. J. Scott. 4.50 o.p. Vantage.

Time Ot the Hawklords. Michael Moorcock & Michael Butterworth. LC 76-380783. 1976. 3.80 (ISBN 0-85628-030-5). A. Ellis.

Time Out. David Ely. LC 68-20108. 1968. 4.95. Delacorte Press.

Time Out. Ronald Forman. LC 31-21536. The Macaulay Company.

Time Out for Eternity. Jane Annixter, pseud. LC 38-6581. 1938. Dutton.

Time Out for Eternity. Jane Levington Comfort, pseud. LC 38-6581. 1938. E. P. Dutton & Co., Inc.

Time Out from Texas. John Thom Spach. LC 74-99318. 1969. 5.95. J. F. Blair.

Time Out of Joint. Philip K Dick. LC 79-4400. (Gregg Press science fiction series). (Illus.). 1979. 19.95 (ISBN 0-8398-2480-7). Gregg Press.

Time Out of Mind. Richard Cowper, pseud. (Orig.). 1981. pap. 2.25 (ISBN 0-671-83580-7, Timescape). PB.

Time Out of Mind. Rachel Lyman Field. LC 35-4871. 1935. The Macmillan Company.

Time Out of Mind. Colin Murry. 1981. 2.25 (ISBN 0-671-83580-7). Pocket Books.

Time Out of Mind, and Other Stories. Pierre Boulle. LC 66-26792. 1966. Vanguard Press.

Time Out of Mind: Trekking the Hindu Kush. Lynda W. Schmidt. (Illus.). viii, 158p. (Orig.). 1979. pap. 5.95 (ISBN 0-931474-11-6). TBW Bks.

Time Outworn. Val Mulkerns. 4.95 (ISBN 0-8159-6905-8). Devin.

Time Outworn: A Novel. Val Mulkerns. LC 52-13184. 1952. Devin-Adair Co.

Time Piece. Naomi Ellington Jacob. LC 37-1663. 1937. The Macmillan Company.

Time Piece. Peter Neill. LC 76-106297. 1970. 5.95. Grossman.

Time, Place, and Idea: Essays on the Novel. John Henry Raleigh. LC 68-10116. (Crosscurrents: modern critiques). 1968. Southern Illinois University Press.

Time Probe: The Sciences in Science Fiction. Ed. by Arthur Charles Clarke. LC 66-12704. 1966. Delacorte Press.

Time Remembered. Laurie Hillyer. LC 45-9825. 1945. The Macmillan Company.

Time Right Deadly. Sarah Gainham. 1962. pap. 0.95 o.p. (02031, Collier). Macmillan.

Time Rogue. Leo P. Kelley. (Orig.). 1970. pap. 0.75 o.p. (ISBN 0-447-74627-8). Lancer.

Time Running Out. Kage Booton. LC 68-22614. 1968. 3.95. Published for the Crime Club by Doubleday.

Time Safari. David Drake. 288p. (Orig.). 1982. pap. 2.75 (ISBN 0-523-48541-7). Pinnacle Bks.

Time Shall Try. A Novel. Frances Eliza Millett Notley. (Franklin square library, no. 21). 1878. Harper & Brothers.

Time Shifters. Sam Merwin, Jr. 1973. pap. 0.75 o.p. (74-776). Lancer.

Time Slave. John Norman. (Science Fiction Ser). 1975. pap. 1.95 (ISBN 0-87997-322-6, UJ1322). DAW Bks.

Time Spirit: A Romantic Tale. John Collis Snaith. LC 18-122191. 1918. D. Appleton and Company.

Time Storm. Gordon R Dickson. LC 76-62762. 10.00 (ISBN 0-312-80517-9). St. Martin's Press.

Time Story. Stuart Gordon. (Science Fiction Ser.). 1973. pap. 0.95 o.p. (UQ1047). DAW Bks.

Time Story. Gordon Stuart. 1973. 0.95. Daw Books.

Time Stream. Eric Temple Bell. LC 75-437. (Garland Library of Science Fiction). 1975. 11.00 (ISBN 0-8240-1439-1). Garland Pub.

Time Stream. Eric Temple Bell. LC 77-176354. 1971. 1.75 (ISBN 0-486-22738-3). Dover Publications.

Time Stream. Eric Temple Bell. LC 46-11123. 1946. Buffalo Book Company and G.H.E.

Time Stream. John Taine, pseud. Ed. by Lester Del Ray. LC 75-437. (Library of Science Fiction). 1975. lib. bdg. 15.00 (ISBN 0-8240-1439-1). Garland Pub.

Time Stream. John Taine, pseud. Bd. with Greatest Adventure. Repr. of 1929 ed; Purple Sapphire. Repr. of 1924 ed. (Illus.). v, 532p. Repr. of 1932 ed. pap. 2.50 o.p. (ISBN 0-486-21180-0). Dover.

Time Stream see Three Science-Fiction Novels.

Time Stream: A Science-Fiction Novel. John Taine. (Illus.). 186p. 1931. pap. 1.75 o.p. (ISBN 0-486-22738-3). Dover.

Time Stream. The Greatest Adventure. The Purple Sapphire. Eric Temple Bell. LC 64-13464. 1964. Dover Publications.

Time-Swept City. Thomas F. Monteleone. 288p. 1982. pap. 2.75 (ISBN 0-445-04081-5). Popular Lib.

Time That Was Then. Harry Roskolenko. 1971. 8.95 o.p. Dial.

Time, the Place and the Girl. Harry Byron Magill. 1908. Yellowstone Park Publishing Co.

Time, the Place and the Girl: From the Play of Will M. Hough and Frank R. Adams. John William Harding & Hough, Will M. G. W. Dillingham Company.

Time: the Present: A Book of Short Stories. Tess Slesinger. LC 35-10856. Simon and Schuster.

Time to Be Born. David Bell. LC 74-14648. 1975. 5.95 (ISBN 0-688-00332-X). Morrow.

Time to Be Born. David Bell. (Dell Book). 1.95 (ISBN 0-440-18799-0).,C.

Time to Be Born. Dawn Powell. LC 42-210786. 1942. C. Scribner's Sons.

Time to Be Happy. 1st Ed. Nayantara Pandit Sahgal. LC 58-5358. 1958. Knopf.

Time to be Re-Born. William Maestri. LC 82-24336. 147p. (Orig.). 1983. pap. 5.95 (ISBN 0-8189-0447-X). Alba.

Time to Be Young. Martin Yoseloff. LC 66-25038. 1967. A. S. Barnes.

Time to Change Hats. Margot Bennett. LC 46-3951. 1946. Pub. for the Crime Club by Doubleday & Company, Inc.

Time to Choose. Tana Reiff. LC 78-75225. (LifeTimes Ser.). 1979. pap. 3.32 (ISBN 0-8224-4322-8). Pitman Learning.

Time to Come. Ed. by August William Derleth. pap. 0.75 o.p. (T2012). Pyramid Pubns.

Time to Come: Science-Fiction Stories of to-Morrow. Ed. by August William Derleth. LC 54-7307. 1954. Farrar, Straus and Young.

Time to Dance, and Other Stories. Bernard MacLaverty. LC 82-4342. 1982. 10.95 (ISBN 0-8076-1045-3). G. Braziller.

Time to Die. Hilda Lawrence. LC 45-181512. 1945. Simon and Schuster.

Time to Die. Kap Pothan. LC 67-109821. 1967. bds., 4.75. Jacaranda.

Time to Die. Kap Pothan. LC 67-100821. 1967. aust. 3.25. Jacaranda.

Time to Dream: By Gay Rutherford Pseud. James Noble Gifford. 1956. Arcadia House.

Time to Embrace. Lilli Palmer. LC 80-13014. 12.95. Macmillan.

Time to Fantasize. May K. Davenport. LC 80-69294. (Illus.). 130p. (Orig.). (gr. 5-12). 1980. pap. 4.50x (ISBN 0-9603118-7-4). Davenport.

Time to Go. Renee Shann. LC 38-5601. G. P. Putnam's Sons.

Time to Go Home. 1st Ed. William C Fridley. LC 51-11432. 1951. Dutton.

Time to Hate. Seldon Truss, pseud. LC 62-7689. 1962. Published for the Crime Club, by Doubleday.

Time to Heal. Ford. pap. 2.95 (ISBN 0-425-04693-1). Berkley Pub.

Time to Heal: A Novel. Claire Rayner. LC 75-167702. 1972. 7.95 (ISBN 0-671-21131-5). Simon and Schuster.

Time to Keep, and Other Stories. George Mackay Brown. LC 70-78882. 1970. Harcourt, Brace & World.

Time to Kill. Rearden Conner, pseud. LC 36-19981. 1936. A.A. Knopf.

Time to Kill. Geoffrey Household. LC 51-11781. 1951. Little, Brown.

Time to Kill. Miriam Lynch. (Mystery Puzzler Ser.: No. 15). (Illus., Orig.). 1979. pap. 1.95 (ISBN 0-89083-435-0). Zebra.

Time to Kill. Wallace Reed. LC 40-7251. Phoenix Press.

Time to Kill. David Michael Winser. LC 39-10374. 1939. Longmans, Green and Co.

Time to Kill... a Time to Die: A Novel. Jack Pearl, pseud. LC 78-155326. 1971. 5.95 (ISBN 0-393-08648-8). Norton.

Time to Kill...a Time to Die. Jack Pearl, pseud. 208p. 1972. pap. 0.95 o.p. (ISBN 0-532-95206-5). Woodhill.

Time to Kill...a Time to Die. Jack Pearl, pseud. 208p. 1972. pap. 0.95 o.p. (ISBN 0-532-95206-5). Manor Bks.

Time to Laugh. Rhys Davies. LC 38-2492. Stackpole Sons.

Time to Laugh. Laurence Victor Thompson. LC 54-677742. 1954. J. Messner.

Time to Live. Michael Blankfort. LC 43-552461. 1943. Harcourt, Brace and Company.

Time to Live. Dorothy Boone Kidney. LC 79-67785. 2.25 (ISBN 0-88270-399-4). Logos International.

Time to Lose. Hugh Preston. LC 76-62790. 1977. 7.95 (ISBN 0-312-80526-8). St. Martin's Press.

Time to Love. Mary Pace. pap. 4.00. Crossroads Prods.

Time to Love a Time to Die. Leopold Lowenstein. 1973. pap. 1.25 o.p. (ISBN 0-515-02917-3, V2917). Pyramid Pubns.

Time to Love and a Time to Die. Erich Maria Remarque. LC 54-7899. 1954. Harcourt, Brace.

Time to Murder & Create. Lawrence Block. 192p. 1983. pap. 2.95 (ISBN 0-515-06801-2). Jove Pubns.

Time to Murder and Create. Lawrence Block. 1.25. Dell.

Time to Pass Over. Drawings by Barbara Remington. Henry Gordon Green. LC 62-118985. 1962. Morrow.

Time to Prey. Frances Keinzley. LC 70-104647. 1970. 4.95. Stein and Day.

Time to Remember. Don Jennings. 1975. 3.00 (ISBN 0-87069-127-9). Wallace-Homestead.

Time to Remember. Leane Zugsmiht. LC 36-19251. Random House.

Time to Retreat. Brian Cooper. 1963. 3.95 o.p. (ISBN 0-8149-0044-5). Vanguard.

Time to Run: Worldwide Pictures. Allan Sloane. 140p. 1973. pap. 1.50 o.p. (ISBN 0-87123-538-2, Dimension Bks). Bethany Hse.

Time to Sow. Evans Wall. LC 32-21423. The Macaulay Company.

Time to Stop Running. George Burton. 1978. pap. 1.50 o.p. (ISBN 0-8007-8293-3, Spire). Revell.

Time to Stop Running. George Burton. 1978. pap. 1.50 o.p. (ISBN 0-8007-8293-3, Spire). Revell.

Time to Strike: Or, Our Nation's Curse. Alpin Marshall Bowes. LC 8-31829. Pentecostal Publishing Company.

Time to Teleport-Delusion World. Gordon R. Dickson. 256p. 1981. pap. 2.50 (ISBN 0-441-81237-6). Ace Bks.

Time Together: A Novel. Marian Seldes. LC 81-7661. 1981. 12.95 (ISBN 0-395-31264-7). Houghton Mifflin.

Time Too Soon. Edward Ernest Smith. LC 67-11633. 1967. W. Morrow.

Time Traders. Andre Norton, pseud. 1979. lib. bdg. 9.95 (ISBN 0-8398-2421-1, Gregg). G K Hall.

Time Traders Series. Andre Norton, pseud. 1979. 35.00 (Gregg). G K Hall.

Time Trap: A Science Fiction Novel. Keith Laumer. LC 75-102646. 1970. 4.50. Putnam.

Time Trap of Ming. Alex Raymond. (Flash Gordon Ser). 1976. Repr. of 1974 ed. lib. bdg. 5.95 (ISBN 0-89190-111-6). Am Repr-Rivercity Pr.

Time Traveler's Strictly Cash. Spider Robinson. 208p. 1982. pap. 2.25 (ISBN 0-441-81277-5). Ace Bks.

Time Trip. Rob Swigart. LC 78-31271. 1979. 8.95. (ISBN 0-395-27756-6) (ISBN 0-395-27757-4). Houghton Mifflin.

Time Untamed. Isaac Asimov et al. (O.s.i.). 1972. pap. 0.75 o.s.i. (BT 50245). Belmont-Tower.

Time Was... John Selby. LC 56-57224. 1956. Rinehart.

Time Was. John Foster West. LC 65-10458. 4.95. Random.

Time Will Come. Rachel McBrayer Varble. LC 41-533. 1940. Doubleday, Doran & Company, Inc.

Time Will Darken It. William Maxwell. LC 48-8331. 1948. Harper.

Time Will Run Back: A Novel About the Rediscovery of Capitalism. rev. ed. Henry Hazlitt. LC 66-23142. 1966. Arlington House.

Time Will Tell. Leonora Dorothy Rivers Cook Mackesy. LC 47-24313. 1947. Arcadia House.

Time-Worn Town. Joseph Smith Fletcher. LC 24-26924. A. A. Knopf.

Time Zone. Satty. 1973. pap. 5.95 o.p. (ISBN 0-87932-067-2, 102067). Quick Fox.

Time: 110100. Leo P Kelley. LC 71-186186. 1972. 5.95 (ISBN 0-8027-5551-8). Walker.

Timebertwist. 1st Ed. Thomas Allen Mussaeus. LC 56-12581. 1957. Pageant Press.

Timed for Love. Glenna Finley, pseud. (Orig.). 1979. pap. 1.95 (AJ1494, Sig). NAL.

Timejumper. William Greenleaf. 1981. pap. 1.95 (ISBN 0-8439-0867-X). Nordon Pubns.

Timeless Land. Eleanor O'Reilly Dark. LC 41-18613. 1941. The Macmillan Company.

Timeless Moment. Christina Rainsford. 1962. 3.00 o.p. (ISBN 0-8233-0084-6). Golden Quill.

Timeless Place. Ellen Bromfield Geld. LC 72-152789. 1971. 5.95. Doubleday.

Timeless Serpent. Roger Fuller, pseud. (O.S.I.). 4.95 o.s.i. (ISBN 0-671-73320-6). Trident.

Timeless Stories for Today and Tomorrow. 1st Ed. Ed. by Ray Bradbury. LC 52-64152. (Bantam giant, A944). 1952. Bantam Books.

Timelock. Desmond Cory, pseud. (Johnny Fedora Ser., No. 3). (O.s.i.). 1968. pap. 0.75 o.s.i. (A343S, Award). Univ Pub & Dist.

Timelock. Shaun McCarthy. LC 67-23099. 1967. Walker.

Timelock: By Desmond Cory. Shaun McCarthy. (Award Bks. A343S). 1968. Universal Pub. & Dist.

Time's Corner. Nancy Wilson Ross. LC 52-9581. 1952. Random House.

Time's Dark Laughter. James Kahn. 1982. pap. 2.75 (Del Rey). Ballantine.

Time's Door. Esther Hallam Moorhouse Meynell. LC 35-13506. 1935. The Macmillan Company.

Time's Fool. Grant Carrington. LC 79-8558. 1981. 9.95 (ISBN 0-385-15288-4). Doubleday.

Times Four: Four Science Fiction Tales. Herbert George Wells et al. Ed. by Virginia F. Allen. (Falcon Bks). (YA) 1968. Set Of 42 Copies Of 8 Pbks. pap. 37.50 set o.p. (ISBN 0-8372-9637-4); teachers' notes avail. o.p. (ISBN 0-8372-8939-4). Bowmar-Noble.

Times Four: The Short Story in Depth, Ed. by Donald S. Heines. Ed. by Donald S Heines. (Prentice English lit. ser.). 1968. 3.95. Prentice.

Times Have Changed. Elmer Holmes Davis. LC 23-8059. 1923. R. M. McBride & Company.

Times Last Gift. Philip Jose Farmer. (Del Rey Bks). 1977. pap. 1.50 (ISBN 0-345-25843-6). Ballantine.

Time's Laughter in Their Ears: A Novel. Murrell Edmunds. LC 46-3955. 1946. The Beechhurst Press, B. Ackerman Incorporated.

Times Like These. Gwyn Jones. 1980. 13.95 o.p. (ISBN 0-575-02740-1, Pub. by Gollancz England); pap. 5.95 o.p. (ISBN 0-575-02741-X). David & Charles.

Time's Lonely One. K. H Scheer. (Perry Rhodan,#42). 1974. (pbk.) 0.75. Ace Books.

Times of Alchemy. Zakarias Topelius. (surgeon's stories. (cycle 6)). 1884. Jansen, McClurg, & Company.

Times of Battle and of Rest. Zakarias Topelius. (surgeon's stories. (cycle 2)). 1883. Jansen, McClurg, & Company.

Times of Charles XII. Zakarias Topelius. LC 8-29977. (surgeon's stories) (cycle 3)). 1884. Jansen, McClurg, & Company.

Times of Frederick I. Zakarias Topelius. LC 8-29974. (surgeon's stories.) (cycle 4)). 1884. Jansen, McClurg, & Company.

Times of Gustaf Adolf. Zakarias Topelius. LC 8-29979. (surgeon's stories. (cycle 1)). 1883. Jansen, McClurg & Company.

Times of Life: Prayers and Poems. Huub Oosterhuis & N. D Smith. LC 79-89653. 5.95 (ISBN 0-8091-2245-6). Paulist Press.

Times of Linnaeus. Zakakias Topelius. LC 8-29980. (surgeon's stories. (cycle 5)). 1884. Jansen, McClurg & Company.

Times of London Anthology of Detective Stories. Ed. by Agatha Miller Christie et al. LC 73-7406. 252p. 1973. 6.95 o.p. (ISBN 0-381-98254-8). John Day.

Times of London Anthology of Detective Stories. LC 73-173403. 1973. 6.95 (ISBN 0-381-98254-8). John Day Co.

Time's Revenges: A Novel. David Christie Murray. LC 7-31824. 1892. Harper & Brothers.

Time's Scythe. Nellie J Meeker. LC 7-25861. Cassell & Company, Limited.

Times Square. Cornell Woolrich, pseud. LC 29-993833. 1929. H. Liveright.

Times Square Connection. Frank Scarpetta. (O.s.i.). 1976. pap. 1.25 o.s.i. (BT50919). Belmont-Tower.

Times Square Connection. Frank Scarpetta. 1976. (pbk.) 1.25. Belmont Tower Books.

Time's Ungentle Tide. Dudley Winthrop Moore. (Library of select novels). 1876. The American News Company.

Times Without Number. John Brunner. 224p. 1983. pap. 2.50 (ISBN 0-345-30679-1, Del Rey). Ballantine.

Times Without Number. John Brunner. 1975. (pbk.) 0.95. Ace Books.

Timescape. Gregory Benford. LC 79-27298. 11.95 (ISBN 0-671-25327-1). Simon and Schuster.

Timetable. Amos Elon. LC 79-6861. 1980. 10.95 (ISBN 0-385-15795-9). Doubleday.

Timetipping. Jack Dann. LC 78-20067. 1980. 8.95 (ISBN 0-385-14338-9). Doubleday.

Timid Adventures of a Window Washer. Georges Michel. LC 69-12239. 1969. 4.95. Doubleday.

Timid Brave. The Story of an Indian Uprising. William Justin Harsha. LC 7-2865. (On cover: Standard library. no. 138). 1886. Funk & Wagnalls.

Timid Woman. Ann Du Pre. LC 33-176731. The Macaulay Company.

Timoleon: A Friend of Paul; Being the Romantic Adventures of a Waif of Tarsus, Together with a Setting Forth of the Great Apostle's Journeys. Mabel Ansley Murphy. LC 21-8366. American Sunday-School Union.

Timothy: A Novel. John Leslie Palmer, pseud. LC 32-3749. 1932. Doubleday, Doran & Company, Inc.

Timothy Baines. John H. Culp. 1969. 6.95 o.p. (ISBN 0-03-081843-5). HR&W.

Timothy Baines: A Novel. John H Culp. LC 79-80338. 1969. 6.95. Holt, Rinehart, and Winston.

Timothy Larkin. Jane Hutchens. LC 42-9578. 1942. Doubleday, Doran & Company, Inc.

Timothy Sprinklebritches. Bill Erin. LC 48-847545. 1948. Dorrance.

Timothy Stand-by: The Sunday-School Man. Joseph Clark. 1904. The Sunday School Times Co.

Timothy, the Young Elder. Mary Helm Clarke. LC 74-76621. 1969. 3.95. Herald Press.

Timothy Winebruiser. James Nestor Gallagher. LC 33-182201. 1933. Naylor Printing Company.

Timothy Winebruiser: A Narrative in Prose and Verse. James Nestor Gallagher. LC 6-44489. 1886. San Antonio Light Print.

Timothy's People. Carma Rossi. LC 73-75396. 1973. 4.95 (ISBN 0-88290-018-8). Horizon Publishers.

Timothy's Quest: A Story for Anybody, Young or Old, Who Cares to Read It. Kate Douglas Smith Wiggin. LC 8-37036. Houghton, Mifflin and Company.

Timothy's Quest: A Story for Anybody, Young or Old, Who Cares to Read It. Kate Douglas Smith Wiggin. LC 4-15183. 1895. Houghton, Mifflin and Company.

Timothy's Quest: A Story for Anybody, Young or Old, Who Cares to Read It. Kate Douglas Smith Wiggin. LC 24-22212. Hougton Mifflin Company.

Timothy's Second Wife. Isla May Hawley Mullins. LC 23-192. Fleming H. Revell Company.

Timpanogos Cave Story. George V. Martin. 1973. pap. 2.00 o.p. (ISBN 0-89036-022-7). Hawkes Pub Inc.

Tim's Place. Eva Knox Witte. LC 50-9460. 1950. Putnam.

Tim's Place: Illustrated: By Bruno Frost. Eva Knox Evans. LC 50-9460. 1950. Putnam.

Tin Angel. Ron Goulart. (Daw sf Books, no. 80). (Illus.). 1973. (pbk.) 0.95. Daw Books.

Tin Can Tree. Tyler, Anne. LC 65-18762. 1965. Knopf.

Tin Can Tree. Anne Tyler. 1977. 1.95 (ISBN 0-445-08617-3). Popular Library.

Tin Cop. F. G. Clinton. 240p. 1983. pap. 2.50 (ISBN 0-523-41923-6). Pinnacle Bks.

Tin Cowrie Dass: A Story. Henry Milner Rideout. LC 18-22738. 1918. 1.25. Duffield & Company.

Tin Cravat: A Novel. Jack D Hunter. LC 80-5770. 10.95 (ISBN 0-8129-0962-3). Times Books.

Tin Cravat: A Novel. Jack D Hunter. LC 81-47356. 11.50 (ISBN 0-06-038004-7). Harper & Row.

Tin Diskers: The Story of an Invasion That All but Failed. Lloyd Osbourne. H. Altemus Company.

Tin Drum. Gunter Grass. LC 62-14256. 1963. Pantheon Books.

Tin Flute: By Gabrielle Roy. Gabrielle Carbotte Roy. Tr. by Josephson, Hannah (Geffen) LC 47-30245. 1947. Reynal & Hitchcock.

Tin God of Twisted River. Wilbur C Tuttle. LC 41-51906. 1941. Houghton Mifflin Company.

Tin Gods: An Adventure of Jonathan Laidlow. Edith Bryat. 3.95 o.p. Vantage.

Tin Hats. Frederick John MacIsaac. LC 27-8553. Chelsea House.

Tin Kitchen. J. Hatton Weeks. T. Y. Crowell & Company.

Tin Lizzie Troop. Glendon Fred Swarthout. 1973. (pbk) 1.25 (ISBN 0-671-78302-5). Pocket Books.

Tin Lizzie Troop. Glendon Fred Swarthout. LC 71-184918. 1972. 5.95. Doubleday.

Tin Men: 1st Amer. Ed. Michael Frayn. LC 66-103703. 1966. bds., 4.95. Atlantic-Little.

Tin Soldier. Temple Bailey. 1918. The Penn Publishing Company.

Tin Soldier. Temple Bailey. LC 19-50481. 1919. The Penn Publishing Company.

Tin Soldier. Temple Bailey. LC 33-28350. 1921. Grosset & Dunlap.

Tin Soldier. Temple Bailey. LC 28-17926. 1926. The Penn Publishing Company.

Tin Soldiers: A Novel. Robert Wohlfarth. LC 34-161781. A. H. King.

Tin-Star Target. Jackson Cole, pseud. 1975. (pbk.) 0.95. Popular Library.

Tin Sword. Malcolm Stuart Boylan. LC 50-9683. 1950. Little, Brown.

Tin Trumpet of China. George Charles Appell. LC 50-9615. 1950. Duell, Sloan and Pearce.

Tin-Types Taken in the Streets of New York: A Series of Stories and Sketches Portraying Many Singular Phases of Metropolitan Life. Lemuel Ely Quigg. Cassell Publishing Company.

Tin Wedding. Margaret Leech. LC 26-18171. 1926. Boni and Liveright.

Tin Whistle Tune Book. William E. White. LC 79-26872. 1980. pap. 1.50 (ISBN 0-87935-051-2). Williamsburg.

Tin Woodman. David F. Bischoff & Dennis R. Bailey. LC 78-62599. 1979. 7.95 (ISBN 0-385-12785-5). Doubleday.

Tin Woodman of Oz. Lyman Frank Baum. 272p. 1981. pap. 2.25 (ISBN 0-345-28234-5, Del Rey). Ballantine.

Tina. Robert W Taylor. LC 54-430905. (Lion book, 226). 1954. Lion Books by Arrangement with Margood Pub. Corp.

Tina, the Little Lace-Maker of Brussels. Sarah Elizabeth Forbush G. S. Downs Downs. LC 6-45954. (On cover: The select series. no. 99). 1892. Street & Smith.

Tinbadge. Drake C Denver, pseud. LC 41-924041. Phoenix Press.

Tinder-Box. Maria Thompson Daviess. LC 18-23494. 1913. The Century Co.

Tinfish Run. Ronald Bassett. LC 76-50167. 1977. 8.95 o.p. (ISBN 0-06-010233-0, HarpT). Har-Row.

Tinhorn. Arthur N Jacobs. LC 27-16144. 1927. Sexton Press.

Tinhorn Tommie: A Western Story. Frank M Benedict. F. M. Benedict.

Tinker of Bedford: A Historical Fiction on the Life & Times of John Bunyan. William S. Deal. 1977. pap. 2.95. Crusade Pubs.

Tinker, Tailor, Soldier, Spy. John Le Carre. LC 74-5084. 1974. (ISBN 0-394-49219-6). Knopf; Distributed by Random House.

Tinker, Tailor, Soldier, Spy. John Le Carre. LC 74-18372. 1974. (ISBN 0-8161-6241-7). G. K. Hall.

Tinker, Tailor, Soldier, Spy. John Le Carre. (Adult Ser). 670p. 1974. Repr. lib. bdg. 13.95 o.p. (ISBN 0-8161-6241-7, Large Print Bks). G K Hall.

Tinker Two: Further Adventures of the Admirable Tinker. Edgar Jepson. LC 6-34688. 1906. McClure, Phillips & Co.

Tinkering with School. Virginia Delancey & Mark DeLancey. LC 77-94642. (Africa Sketches Series). (Illus.). 1.95 (ISBN 0-89253-107-X). InterCulture Associates.

Tinker's Leave. Maurice Baring. LC 28-3168. 1928. Doubleday, Doran & Company, Inc.

Tinkler Gypsies. Andrew McCormick. LC 77-19203. 1907. 45.00 (ISBN 0-8414-6235-6). Folcroft.

Tinkling Cymbals. Milton George Nicola. LC 34-15717. D. Ryerson.

Tinkling Cymbals: A Novel. Edgar Fawcett. LC 6-38778. 1884. J. R. Osgood and Company.

Tinkling Cymbals: A Novel of Tolerance. Renzo Dee Bowers. LC 29-18554. The Four Seas Company.

Tinkling Symbol: An Asey Mayo Mystery. Phoebe Atwood Taylor. LC 67-5688. 1967. Norton.

Tinkling Symbol: An Asey Mayo Mystery of Cape Cod. Phoebe Atwood Taylor. LC 35-312175. W. W. Norton & Company.

Tinonc, Son of the Cajun Teche. Robert L. Olivier. LC 74-23826. 1974. 3.95 (ISBN 0-88289-054-9). Pelican Pub. Co.

Tinsel. Charles Hanson Towne. LC 26-3568. 1926. D. Appleton and Company.

Tinsel: A Novel. William Goldman. LC 78-31943. 10.95 (ISBN 0-440-08735-X). Delacorte Press.

Tinsel Affair see Love Betrayed.

Tinsel and Gold. Dion Clayton Calthrop. LC 10-9697. 1.50. G. W. Dillingham Company.

Tinsley's Bones. Percival Wilde. LC 42-194315. 1942. Random House.

Tinted Vapours. A Nemesis. James Maclaren Cobban. (On cover: Seaside library. Pocket ed. no. 485). 1885. G. Munro.

Tinted Venus: A Farcical Romance. Thomas Anstey Guthrie. LC 7-23663. (On cover: Lovell's library. v. 12, no. 616). 1885. J. W. Lovell Company.

Tintin in America. Herge. LC 79-64865. (Adventures of Tintin Ser.). 1979. pap. 3.95 (ISBN 0-316-35852-5, Pub. by Atlantic-Little Brown). Little.

Tintinnabulations of Boos & Applause. David Kalugin. (Illus.). 1979. pap. 4.95 (ISBN 0-933586-05-1). Book Promo Unltd.

Tintype of a Lady. Kathleen Shepard. LC 36-510631. The Macaulay Company.

Tiny Carteret... Herman Cyril McNeile. LC 30-15622. 1930. Pub. for the Crime Club, Inc., by Doubleday, Doran & Company, Inc.

Tiny Diamond. Charlotte Murray Russell, pseud. LC 37-6530. 1937. Pub. for the Crime Club, Inc., by Doubleday, Doran & Company, Inc.

Tiny Luttrell: By Ernest William Hornung... Ernest William Hornung. LC 7-13205. Cassell Publishing Company.

Tiny Makes a Promise. Merle Lien. 1966. 4.00 o.p. (ISBN 0-682-44010-8). Exposition.

Tio Pepe. Mary Lasswell. LC 63-10562. (Illus.). 1963. Houghton Mifflin.

Tioba: And Other Tales. Arthur Willis Colton. LC 3-5938. 1903. H. Holt and Company.

Tioga's Pigs. E A Krewson. LC 56-230692. 1955. Binfords & Mort.

Tiomane: A Girl of Berck. (Vaillante--Ce Que Femme Veut. Angele Dussaud Bary d'Arnex & Tracy, Sara C., Tr. LC 8-19784. (On cover: Globe library, v. 1, no. 173). 1892. Rand, McNally & Company.

Tip on a Dead Jockey: And Other Stories. Irwin Shaw. LC 57-5382. 1957. Random House.

Tippecanoe: Being a True Chronicle of Certain Passages Between David Larrance & Antoinette O'Bannon of the Battle of Tippecanoe in the Indiana Wilderness and of What Befell Thereafter in Old Corydon and Now First Set Forth. Samuel McCoy. LC 16-6763. The Bobbs-Merrill Company.

Tipping Point. Lou Cameron. 1971. pap. 0.95 o.p. (ISBN 0-447-75169-7). Lancer.

Tipple Bell. Hilary H Milton. LC 77-110763. (Illus.). 1970. 5.95. R. B. Luce.

Tippy Locklin: A Novel. John William Meagher. LC 59-5283. 1960. Little, Brown.

Tiradora Infalible. new ed. Glen Chase, pseud. Tr. by Jacinto De Torres from Eng. (Pimienta Collection Ser.: Cereza Delicias: No. 5). Orig. Title: Crack Shot. 160p. (Span.). 1975. pap. 1.00 (ISBN 0-88473-228-2). Fiesta Pub.

Tirana Assignment. Christopher Portway. 1975. (pbk.) 1.25 (ISBN 0-523-00578-4). Pinnacle Books.

Tired Captains. Kent Curtis. LC 28-4068. 1928. D. Appleton and Company.

Tired Gun. Lewis B Patten. LC 72-89339. 1973. 4.95 (ISBN 0-385-07509-X). Doubleday.

Tired of Picasso & Other Stories. J. D. Stanley. 128p. 1982. 7.95 (ISBN 0-89962-282-8). Todd & Honeywell.

Tired Spy. David Stone. LC 61-5712. 1961. Putnam.

Tiroirs De L'inconnu. Marcel Ayme. (Coll. Soleil). 1960. 9.95. French & Eur.

Tirra Lirra by the River. Jessica Anderson. 142p. 1983. pap. 3.95 (ISBN 0-14-070085-4). Penguin.

Tirreno and Other Stories. Stanley D Burchard. LC 28-1193. The Christopher Publishing House.

Tirzah Ann's Summer Trip: And Other Sketches. Marietta Holley. LC 71-166755. 1971. (ISBN 0-403-01437-9). Scholarly Press.

Tirzah Ann's Summer Trip, and Other Sketches. Marietta Holley. LC 7-6041. (On cover: The idle hour series. no. 1). The F. M. Lupton Publishing Company.

Tis Folly to Be Wise: Or, Death and Transfiguration of Jean-Jacques Rousseau, a Novel. Translated by Frances Fawcett. Lion Feuchtwanger. LC 58-832189. 1953. J. Messner.

Tis Sweet & Sad in an Irish Cottage. Patrick Tarrant. 152p. 1982. pap. 4.00 (ISBN 0-9608850-0-5). Tarrant.

Tisa. Helga Moray. LC 52-13714. 1952. D. McKay Co.

Tish. Cissie Miller. LC 81-43049. 1982. 10.95 (ISBN 0-385-17468-3). Doubleday.

Tish. Mary Roberts Rinehart. LC 16-15840. 1916. Houghton Mifflin Company.

Tish Marches on. Mary Roberts Rinehart. LC 37-28472. 1937. Farrar & Rinehart, Inc.

Tish Plays the Game. Mary Roberts Rinehart. LC 26-19724. George H. Doran Company.

Tish: The Chronicle of Her Escapades and Excursions. Mary Roberts Rinehart. LC 19-11339. 1916. A. L. Burt Company.

Tit for Tat: A Novel. Matthew Estes. LC 72-38649. (Black Heritage Library Collection). 1972. (ISBN 0-8369-9007-2). Books for Libraries Press.

Tit for Tat. A Novel. Matthew Estes. LC 5-2559. Garret & Company; Etc., Etc.

Tit for Tat: A Teutonic Adventure. Clara Hammond Lanza. LC 7-13838. 1880. G. P. Putnam's Sons.

Titan. Theodore Dreiser. LC 49-54858. 1946. World Pub. Co.

Titan. Theodore Dreiser. LC 14-9767. 1914. John Lane Company.

Titan. John Varley. LC 78-23865. (Illus.). 9.95. Berkley Pub. Corp.: Distributed by Putnam.

Titan: A Romance. Johann Paul Friedrich Richter & Brooks Charles Timothy 1818-1883 Tr. LC 41-34809. 1864. Ticknor and Fields.

Titan Agonistes: The Sotry of an Outcast. LC 8-26760. 1867. G. W. Carleton & Co.; Etc., Etc.

Titan and Volcan: A Story Woven into the Lives of Two Young Men; the Fate of Peter Shaw; Depicting Volcan Island and the Unsolved Mysteries of Its People. Alexis Francois Gillet. LC 34-447. 1933. Meador Publishing Company.

Titan, Son of Saturn: The Coming World Emperor. Joseph Birkbeck Burroughs. LC 5-20774. 1905. The Emeth Publishers.

Titan. 1st Ed. Peter Schuyler Miller. LC 53-18614. 1952. Fantasy Press.

Titanic: A Novel. Robert Friedlaender. Tr. by McArthur, Erna. LC 40-7415. 1940. E. P. Dutton & Co., Inc.

Titanic Hotel Mystery. John Hawk. LC 28-170962. 1928. Pub. for The Crime Club, Inc., by Doubleday, Doran & Company, Inc.

Titans. Charles Guernon. LC 23-4360. 1922. Duffield & Company.

Titans. John W. Jakes. LC 76-17349. (Jakes, John W. 1932-. The American Bicentennial Ser.). 1976. 1.95 (ISBN 0-515-04046-0). Pyramid Books.

Titans. book club ed.. ed. John W. Jakes. LC 78-105289. (His The Kent chronicles; v. 5). ((Series: Jakes, John W., 1932-). (American Bicentennial series; v. 5.). (Illus.). 1977. 3.99. N. Doubleday.

Titans see Kent Family Chronicles.

Titan's Daughter. James Blish. 128p. 1981. pap. 1.95 (ISBN 0-380-56929-0, 56929). Avon.

Titans of the Universe. James Harvey. 1978. pap. 1.50 (ISBN 0-532-15371-5). Woodhill.

Tithe Proctor: Being a Tale of the Tithe Rebellion in Ireland. William Carleton. Ed. by Robert L. Wolff. (Ireland Nineteenth Century Proctor Fiction - Ser. Two: Vol. 43). 304p. 1979. lib. bdg. 32.00 (ISBN 0-8240-3492-9). Garland Pub.

Title--Rejected. A Novel. Adella Octavia Clouston. LC 7-304. 1894. G. W. Dillingham.

Title Counterfeiter: Or, The American Detective in France. John Russell Coryell. (On cover: Secret service series, no. 56). 1892. Street & Smith.

Title Is Murder... Hugh Lawrence Nelson. LC 47-1196. 1947. Rinehart & Company, Inc.

Title Market. Emily Price Post. LC 9-25632. 1909. Dodd, Mead and Company.

Title-Mongers. William Farquhar Payson. 1898. Dodd, Mead and Company.

Titled Maiden. Caroline Atwater Mason. LC 7-25576. (On cover: Pilgrim prize series. no. 2). Congregational Sunday-School and Publishing Society.

Titles. Peter Evans. LC 78-4204. 1978. 10.00 (ISBN 0-345-27719-8). Ballantine Books.

Tito. William Henry Carson. LC 3-4670. 1903. C. M. Clark Publishing Company.

Tittlebat Titmouse: Abridged from Dr. Samuel Warren's Famous Novel, Ten Thousand a Year. Samuel Warren & Brady, Cyrus Townsend, 1861-1920. LC 3-25206. 1903. Funk & Wagnalls Company.

Titus: A Comrade of the Cross. Florence Morse Kingsley. LC 14-5753. David C. Cook Publishing Company.

Titus, a Comrade of the Cross: A Novel. Florence Morse Kingsley. 1895. D. C. Cook Publishing Company.

Titus, a Comrade of the Cross. A Tale of the Christ for the Christmas Tide. Florence Morse Kingsley. LC 19-12055. (Sabbath library. v. 7, no. 284). David C. Cook Publishing Co.

Titus Alone. rev. ed. Mervyn Laurence Peake. LC 67-26054. (Illus.). 1968. 0.95. Ballantine Books.

Titus Alone. revised ed. Mervyn Laurence Peake. LC 72-882089. (Penguin modern classics). 1970 (ISBN 0-14-003091-3). Penguin.

Titus Gamble. Peter Gentry. (Fawcett Gold Medal Book). 1.95 (ISBN 0-449-13790-2). Fawcett Pubns.

Titus Gamble. Peter Gentry. (Fawcett Gold Medal Book). 1.95 (ISBN 0-449-13790-2). Fawcett Pubns.

Titus Groan. rev. ed. Mervyn Laurence Peake. LC 67-26052. (Illus.). 1968. 0.95. Ballantine Books.

Titus Groan: A Gothic Novel. Mervyn Laurence Peake. LC 46-7865. 1946. Reynal & Hitchcock.

Tiverton Tales. Alice Brown. LC 67-29259. (Americans in Fiction). 1967. Gregg Press.

Tiverton Tales. Alice Brown. LC 99-1940. 1899. Houghton, Mifflin and Company.

Tlooth. 1st Ed. Harry Mathews. LC 66-20984. 1966. 3.95. Doubleday.

TNT Cowboy... Frank Morton Archer. LC 19-7079.

TNT Cowboy... Frank Morton Archer. LC 19-9536.

To a Blindfold Lady: A Mystery Novel. Joseph Purtell. LC 42-181582. 1942. Reynal & Hitchcock.

To a Dubious Salvation: A Trilogy of Fantastical Novels. Etienne Leroux. LC 73-174373. (Penguin modern classics). 1972. 0.75 (ISBN 0-14-003473-0). Penguin.

To a God Unknown. John Steinbeck. LC 76-22543. 1976. 1.50 (ISBN 0-14-004233-4). Penguin Books.

To a God Unknown. John Steinbeck. LC 33-30144. 1933. R. O. Ballou.

To a High Place. Teo Savory. LC 78-134748. 1972. (ISBN 0-87775-023-8). Unicorn Press.

To a Silent Valley. Howard R Simpson. LC 61-14194. 1961. Knopf.

To Abide in the Shadows. Shirley Yates Merz. LC 72-90483. 1973. 2.95 (ISBN 0-8059-1772-1). Dorrance.

To All Generations. Clara Bernice Miller. LC 77-24926. 1977. 6.95 (ISBN 0-8361-1825-1). Herald Press.

To an Early Grave. Wallace Markfield. (O.S.I.). 1964. 4.50 o.s.i. (ISBN 0-671-73410-5). S&S.

To Arkon! Kurt Mahr. (Perry Rhodan). (Ace SF: 30). 1973. (pbk.) 0.75. Ace.

To Arms! La Veillee Des Armes) An Impression of the Spirit of France. Marcelle Tinayre & Humphrey, Lucy Henderson, 1869- Tr. LC 18-2412. E. P. Dutton & Company.

To Be... Harold Flender. 256p. 1972. pap. 0.95 (ISBN 0-532-95199-9). Woodhill.

To Be a Hero. James P. McCague. LC 62-117988. 1962. Crown Publishers.

To Be a King. Robert De Maria. LC 75-30771. 1976. 10.00 o.p. (ISBN 0-672-52201-2). Bobbs.

To Be a King: A Novel About Christopher Marlowe. Robert De Maria. LC 75-30771. 7.95 (ISBN 0-672-52201-2). Bobbs-Merrill.

To Be a Man. William Decker. LC 67-23829. 1975. (pbk.) 0.95 (ISBN 0-671-77993-1). Pocket Books.

To Be a Man: A Novel. William Decker. LC 67-23829. 1967. Little, Brown.

To Be a Pilgrim. Joyce Cary. (First Trilogy, Vol. 2). 1970. pap. 1.45 o.p. (ISBN 0-06-080130-1, P130, PL). Har-Row.

To Be a Pilgrim: A Novel. Joyce Cary. LC 49-849103. 1949. Harper.

To Be Free: a Novel. Edilberto K. Tiempo. 1972. wrps. 5.75 o.p. Cellar.

To Be Hanged... Bruce Hamilton. LC 30-20595. 1930. Pub. for The Crime Club, Inc., by Doubleday, Doran & Company, Inc.

To Be Loved Again. Mrs. Lewis Cox. 1973. 0.75. Pocket Books.

To Be My Wedded Wife. Rose Meadows. 1974. (pbk.) 0.95 (ISBN 0-671-77721-1). Pocket Books.

To Be or Not to Be. Sue Byfield. (Harlequin Romances Ser.). 192p. 1983. pap. 1.50 (ISBN 0-373-02529-7). Harlequin Bks.

To Be Somebody. Zan Skelton. 1967. 2.95 o.p. Moody.

To Beaucock, with Love. Thomas E Doremus. LC 61-11406. 1961. C. N. Potter.

To Bedlam and Back Again: And Other Stories. Frank Houghton. LC 7-7140. (On cover: Lovell's modern novelists series, no. 6). Home Book Company.

To Begin Tomorrow: Translated from the French by Mary Glasgow. Francoise Des Ligneris. LC 52-424. 1951. Staples Press.

To Begin with Love. Kristin Michaels. 160p. 1975. pap. 1.25 (ISBN 0-451-07732-6, Y7732, Sig). NAL.

To Begin with Love. Kristin Michaels. 1975. (pbk.) 0.95. New American Library.

To Borrow Trouble. Miriam Borgenicht. LC 65-22586. 1965. Published for the Crime Club by Doubleday.

To Bring a Sword. Jon L. Joyce. (Orig.). 1981. pap. 2.00 (ISBN 0-937172-23-5). JLJ Pubs.

To Brooklyn with Love. Gerald Green. LC 67-23587. 1967-1968. 5.95. Trident.

To Build a Dream. Jan Vlachos Westcott. 288p. 1973. 6.95 o.p. Putnam.

To Build a Ship. new ed. Don Berry. LC 60-5835. 1977. pap. 2.50 (ISBN 0-89174-029-5). Comstock Edns.

To Build a Ship: A Novel. Don Berry. LC 63-12360. 1963. Viking Press.

To Burgundy and Back. Dorothy Mackie Low. 1973. (pbk) 0.95. Ace Books.

To Byzantium: Stories. Andrew Fetler. LC 76-13854. (Illinois short fiction). 6.95. (ISBN 0-252-00583-X) (ISBN 0-252-00584-8). University of Illinois Press.

To Cache a Millionaire. Margaret Scherf. LC 78-180106. 1972. 4.95. Published for the Crime Club, by Doubleday.

To Call Her Mine. A Novel. Walter Besant. (On cover: Seaside library. Pocket ed., no. 980). 1887. G. Munro.

To Call Her Mine. A Novel. Walter Besant. (On cover: Lovell's librry; no. 1002). 1887. J. W. Lovell Company.

To Catch a Bird. Jay Williams. (O.s.i.). 1968. 3.95g o.s.i. (ISBN 0-02-793040-8, CCPr). Macmillan.

To Catch a Bride. Glenna Finley, pseud. (Signet Book). 1977. 1.50 (ISBN 0-451-07742-3). New American Library.

To Catch a Dream. Marsha Manning. (Cameo Romance). (Fawcett gold medal book). (Cameo Romance). 1974. (pbk.) 0.95. Fawcett.

To Catch a King. Harry Patterson, pseud. 1980. pap. 2.95 (ISBN 0-449-24323-0, Crest). Fawcett.

To Catch a King: A Novel. Jack Higgins, pseud. LC 79-22680. 1979. 10.95 (ISBN 0-8161-3011-6). G. K. Hall.

To Catch a King: A Novel. Henry Patterson. LC 79-13298. 1979. 9.95 (ISBN 0-8128-2676-0). Stein and Day.

To Catch a Man: By Rehna 'Tiny' Cloete. With Illus. by the Author. Rehna Cloete. LC 57-10794. 1957. Houghton Mifflin.

To Catch a Rainbow. Estelle Thompson. LC 80-7564. 1980. 9.95 (ISBN 0-8027-0652-5). Walker.

To Catch a Rainbow. Estelle Thompson. LC 80-24246. 1980. 9.95 (ISBN 0-89621-251-3). Thorndike Press.

To Catch a Shadow. Bradshaw-Jones, Malcolm Henry. LC 77-98280. 1970. 4.50. Bobbs-Merrill.

To Catch a Shadow. Bradshaw Jones. LC 77-98280. 1970. 4.50 o.p. (50958). Bobbs.

To Catch a Spy. Bruce Sanders. LC 59-8448. Roy Publishers.

To Catch a Spy. Chris Scott. LC 77-21953. 1977. 8.95 (ISBN 0-670-71663-4). Viking Press.

To Catch a Spy. Chris Scott. LC 79-386. (Penguin crime fiction). 1979. 1.95 (ISBN 0-14-005169-4). Penguin Books.

To Catch a Spy: An Anthology of Favourite Spy Stories. Ed. by Eric Ambler. LC 65-15044. 1965. Atheneum.

To Catch a Thief. David Dodge. LC 52-5136. 1952. Random House.

To Catch a Thief... Craig Rice. LC 43-7382. 1943. The Dial Press.

To Catch a Thief: A Mystery Novel. Craig Rice. LC 44-6009. (Handi-book mysteries). 1944. Quinn Publishing Co., Inc.

To Catch a Viper. John Wyllie. LC 76-23809. 1977. 5.95 (ISBN 0-385-12155-5). Published for the Crime Club by Doubleday.

To Catch the Wild Wind. Jo Calloway. (Candlelight Ecstasy Ser.: No. 82). (Orig.). 1982. pap. 1.95 (ISBN 0-440-11126-9). Dell.

TITLE INDEX

TO LOVE THE UNLOVELY.

To Challenge Chaos. Brian M. Stableford. 160p. (Orig.). 1972. pap. 0.95 o.p. (UQ1007). Daw Bks.
To Come to Have Become. Theodore Enslin. 1966. pap. 8.00 (Pub. by Elizabeth Pr). SBD.
To Conquer Chaos. John Brunner. 1981. 1.95 (ISBN 0-87997-596-2). DAW Books.
To Conquer the Earth: A Novel. Stephen Delrosso. LC 51-385. 1950. Exposition Press.
To Construct a Clock. John Taggart. 1971. 10.00 o.p. Elizabeth Pr.
To Control the Stars. Robert Hoskins. LC 76-56166. 1977. 1.50 (ISBN 0-345-25253-5). Ballantine Books.
To-Day: A Novel. Richard Parker & Broadhurst, George H. LC 14-92852. 1914. 1.25. The Macaulay Company.
To-Day: a Romance. Richard Burleigh Kimball. LC 7-12233. 1870. Carleton; Etc., Etc.
To-Days and Yesterdays. Carrie Adelaide Cooke. LC 6-28090. D. Lothrop & Company.
To-Day's Daughter. Josephine Dodge Daskam Bacon. LC 14-307219. 1914. 1.35. D. Appleton and Company.
To-Day's Daughter. Berta Ruck. LC 30-23663. Dodd, Mead & Company.
To-Day's to-Morrow. Walter Simeon Martin. LC 35-17496. The Christopher Publishing House.
To Deadwood & Beyond. Dorothy Gill & Harry S. Gill. LC 81-71713. (Illus.). 1982. pap. 7.95 (ISBN 0-87482-114-2). Wake-Brook.
To Defend - to Destroy. James Reston, Jr. LC 78-128036. 1971. 5.95 o.p. (ISBN 0-393-08621-6). Norton.
To Die a Branded Man. D. L. Winkle. 256p. (Orig.). 1981. pap. 1.95 (ISBN 0-440-18710-9). Dell.
To Die a Little. Hamilton Jobson. LC 78-69744. 7.95 (ISBN 0-312-80656-6). St. Martin's Press.
To Die Elsewhere. Theodore Wilden. LC 76-21748. 7.95 (ISBN 0-15-190480-4). Harcourt Brace Jovanovich.
To Die for a Golden Leaf. Robert P. Hilldrup. (Orig.). 1980. pap. 1.95 (ISBN 0-532-23217-8). Woodhill.
To Die in Beverly Hills. Gerald Petievich. 256p. 1983. 14.50 (ISBN 0-87795-487-9). Arbor Hse.
To Die in California. Newton Thornburg. LC 72-13857. 1973. 6.95 (ISBN 0-316-84388-1). Little, Brown.
To Die in California. Newton Thornburg. 1974. (pbk.) 1.50. Avon.
To Die in Italbar. Roger Zelazny. (Science Fiction Ser). 176p. 1974. pap. 1.50 (ISBN 0-87997-439-7, UT1439). DAW Bks.
To Die in Italbar. Roger Zelazny. LC 72-96269. 192p. 1973. 4.95 o.p. (ISBN 0-385-02020-1). Doubleday.
To Disembark. Gwendolyn Brooks. 63p. 1981. 8.95 (ISBN 0-88378-101-8); pap. 4.25 (ISBN 0-88378-102-6). Third World.
To Distant Shores. Jill Gregory. 1980. pap. 2.50 (ISBN 0-441-81465-4). Ace Bks.
To Drain the Sea. Tr. from Polish by H. C. Stevens. Jan Dobraczynski. LC 66-1012. 1966. bds., 5.00. Heinemann.
To Dream Again. John Fisher. LC 34-376270. 1933. H. Holt and Company.
To Dream of Evil. Ralph Comer. Orig. Title: Mirror of Dionysos. 1971. pap. 0.75 o.p. (A905S, Award). Univ Pub & Dist.
To Dusty Death. Translated from the German by Constantine Fitzgibbon. Manes Sperber. LC 53-33968. 1952. Wingate.
To Dwell in Shadows. Nancy C. Smith. 1978. pap. 1.50 o.s.i. (ISBN 0-505-51305-6). Tower Bks.
To Each a Penny. Francis Plummer. LC 34-31647. 1934. Lothrop, Lee & Shepard Company.
To Each Her Dream. Adeline McElfresh. LC 61-13144. 1961. Bobbs-Merrill.
To Each His Dream. Sara Ware Bassett. LC 55-7654. 1955. Doubleday.
To Each His Own. Letty M. Shaw. 1978. 7.95 o.p. (ISBN 0-533-03697-6). Vantage.
To End the Night: A Novel. Alex Gaby. LC 52-9475. 1952. McKay.
To Escape the Stars. Robert Hoskins. LC 78-61809. 1978. 1.75 (ISBN 0-345-25856-8). Ballantine Books.
To Every Man a Penny: A Novel. Bruce Marshall. LC 49-11479. 1949. Houghton Mifflin Co.
To Every Man His Work. Etta Florence Stock. LC 19-5846. 1919. The Four Seas Company.
To Fame Unknown. Clifford Lindsey Alderman. LC 54-10706. 1954. Appleton-Century-Crofts.
To Fathoms in Hell & Back. William W. Bartlett. 208p. 1981. 9.00 (ISBN 0-682-49790-8). Exposition.
To Fear a Painted Devil. Ruth Rendell. LC 65-22041. 1965. Published for the Crime Club by Doubleday.
To Fear a Painted Devil. Ruth Rendell. LC 76-24851. 1976. 7.95. J. Curley.
To Find a Killer. 1st Ed. Lionel White. LC 54-10916. (Guilt edged mystery). 1954. Dutton.
To Find a Man. S. J. Wilson. LC 69-11723. 1969. 4.95. Viking Press.
To Find My Son. Ron Putterman. 192p. (Orig.). 1981. pap. 2.50 (ISBN 0-380-78980-9, 78980). Avon.
To Follow a Flag. Will Henry, pseud. LC 53-5012. 1953. Random House.
To Follow a Flag: By Will Henry Pseud. Henry Allen. LC 53-5012. 1953. Random House.
To Follow a Star: Nine Science Fiction Stories About Christmas. Ed. by Terry Carr. LC 77-2727. 1977. 6.95 (ISBN 0-8407-6573-8). T. Nelson.
To Forget Palermo. Edmonde Charles-Roux. Tr. by Helen Eustis. LC 68-10376. 1968. 5.95 o.p. Delacorte.
To Forget Palermo. Tr. by Helen Eustis. Charles-Roux, Edmonde. LC 68-10376. 1968. bds., 5.95. Delacorte.
To Get Along with the Beautiful Girls. Bruce Cassiday. (Bold Ones, No. 3). 192p. (Orig.). 1974. pap. 1.25 o.p. (532-12215-125). Manor Bks.
To Get Along with the Beautiful Girls. Bruce Cassiday. (Bold Ones,#3). 1974. (pbk.) 1.25. Manor Books.
To Glory We Steer. Alexander Kent. LC 68-25444. (Illus.). 1968. Putnam.
To Glory We Steer. Alexander Kent. (Berkley Book). 1978. 1.95 (ISBN 0-425-04016-X). Berkley Pub. Co.
To Go to Rome. Con Downey. LC 73-94157. (Contemporary Poets of Dorrance Ser.). 112p. 1974. 3.95 o.p. (ISBN 0-8059-1992-9). Dorrance.
To God Alone, a Novel. Minns Sledge Robertson. LC 56-4984. 1956. College Pub. Co.
To God Be the Glory. Ed. by James Kuse & Ralph D. Luedke. 1977. pap. 2.95 o.p. (ISBN 0-89542-862-8). Ideals.
To Guard the Right. Hugh Zachary. (Raven House Mysteries Ser.). 224p. 1981. pap. 2.25 (ISBN 0-373-63008-5, Pub. by Worldwide). Harlequin Bks.
To Guide & Guard. A. Hasluck. 1967. pap. 10.00x o.p. (ISBN 0-85564-009-X, Pub by U of W Austral Pr). Intl Schol Bk Serv.
To Hang a Witch. Ruth Wissmann. 1974. (pbk.) 1.25 (ISBN 0-446-76644-5). Warner Paperback Library.
To Have and Have Not. Ernest Hemingway. LC 37-23935. (SL 132). 1966. pap., 1.65. Scribners.
To Have and Have Not. Ernest Hemingway. 1937. C. Scribner's Sons.
To Have & to Hold. Lori Herter. (Candlelight Ecstasy Ser.: No. 118). (Orig.). 1983. pap. 1.95 (ISBN 0-440-18861-X). Dell.
To Have and to Hold. Mary Johnson. LC 31-30505. 1931. Houghton Mifflin Company.
To Have and to Hold. Mary Johnston. LC 1124. 1900. Houghton, Mifflin and Company.
To Have and to Hold. Mary Johnston. LC 20-16472. Houghton Mifflin Company.
To Have and to Hold. Mary Johnston. LC 30-12317. 1901. Houghton, Mifflin and Company.
To Have and to Hold. Mary Johnston & Schoonover, Frank Earle, 1877- Illus. LC 31-30505. 1931. Houghton Mifflin Company.
To Have and to Hold. Mary Johnston & Shoup, Grace. LC 34-312884. (Riverside literature series). Houghton Mifflin Company.
To Have and to Kill. Robert Lee Martin. LC 60-123332. (Red badge detective). 1960. Dodd, Mead.
To Have Eyes. Geoffrey Holloway. 1972. pap. 1.00 (Pub. by Anvil Pr); pap. 2.50 signed ltd. ed. SBD.
To Have, to Keep. Jane Ludlow Drake Abbott. LC 30-15959. J. B. Lippincott Company.
To Heaven on Horseback: The Romantic Story of Narcisse Whitman. Paul Cranston. LC 52-10011. 1952. Messner.
To Hell for Half-A-Crown. James A. Cross. 1967. 3.95 o.p. Random.
To Hell for Half-a-Crown. Hugh Jones Parry. LC 66-22255. 1967. Random House.
To Hell with Hollywood. Horace Atkisson Wade. LC 31-88031. 1931. L. MacVeagh, The Dial Press.
To Hide a Rogue. Thomas Walsh. LC 64-14425. (Inner sanctum mystery). 1964. Simon and Schuster.
To Him That Endureth, a Romance of the Salmon River Country. James A Herndon. LC 29-17787. 1929. The Caxton Printers, Ltd.
To Him That Hath. Leroy Scott. 1907. Doubleday, Page & Company.
To Him That Hath: A Novel of the West of Today. Charles William Gordon. LC 21-201123. 1.75. George H. Doran Company.
To Him That Knocketh. Margery Land May. LC 25-22381. Printed by Zincograph Company.
To Him That Overcometh. Franklin Pierce Johnson. LC 15-700. 1.50. International Literary Bureau.
To Him Who Waits. Mary McMaster. Ed. by Gene DeRoin. (Aston Hall Presents Ser.). (Orig.). 1979. pap. 1.50 (ISBN 0-89936-012-2). Aston Hall.
To His Own Master. A Novel. Frances Bridges Marshall. LC 7-24395. 1893. Cleveland Publishing Company.
To Hold Against Famine. Kathleen Coyle. 1942. E. P. Dutton & Co., Inc.
To Keep a Promise. Stefania Benvenuti. LC 67-21088. 1967. Dorrance.
To Keep a Promise. Fred Starr. LC 79-91802. 1969. 3.95. Christopher Pub. House.
To Keep Him. B. De Meo. 4.50 o.p. Carlton.
To Keep My Love. Vivien Grey. LC 45-5129. 1945. Arcadia House, Inc.
To Keep or Kill. Wilson Tucker. LC 47-30845. 1947. Rinehart.
To Keep Our Honor Clean. Edwin McDowell. LC 79-56025. 10.95 (ISBN 0-8149-0831-4). Vanguard Press.
To Keep The Ship. A. Bertram Chandler. 1978. 1.75 (ISBN 0-87997-385-4). DAW Books.
To Keep This Oath. Hebe Weenolsen. LC 58-10045. 1958. Doubleday.
To Keep Us Free. Marguerite Allis. LC 52-9827. 1953. Putnam.
To Kill a Cat. William John Burley. LC 77-126118. 1970. 4.95. Walker.
To Kill a Cop. Robert Daley. LC 76-26924. 8.95 (ISBN 0-517-52753-7). Crown Publishers.
To Kill a Dead Man. Charles W. Runyon. LC 75-40777. 176p. 1976. pap. 1.25 (ISBN 0-89041-061-5, 3061). Major Bks.
To Kill a House. Suzanne Roberts. 1973. pap. 0.95 o.s.i. (75-455). Lancer.
To Kill a Judge. George Ogan. (Raven House Mysteries Ser.). 224p. 1981. pap. 2.25 (ISBN 0-373-63005-0, Pub. by Worldwide). Harlequin Bks.
To Kill a Mockingbird. Harper Lee. LC 60-7847. 1960. Lippincott.
To Kill a Snowman. Charles Miron. 1978. pap. 1.75 (ISBN 0-532-17182-9). Woodhill.
To Kill a Witch. Alice Brennan. (Orig.). 1972. pap. 0.95 o.s.i. (75-401). Lancer.
To Kill a Witch. Bill Knox. LC 70-171399. 1972. 4.95. Published for the Crime Club by Doubleday.
To Kill or to Die: By Jeremy York 1st Amer. Ed. John Creasey. LC 65-21062. (Cock Robin mystery). 1965. 3.95. Macmillan.
To Kiss Earth Goodbye. Ingo Swann. 1975. 10.00 o.p. (ISBN 0-8015-7774-8). Hawthorn.
To Kiss or Kill. Day Keene. 1968. pap. 0.60 o.p. (60-334). Manor Bks.
To Kiss the Crocodile. Ernest Milton. LC 28-12305. 1928. Harper & Brothers.
To Know Is to Die. C. H. Guenter. (Mr. Dynamite Ser.). 1977. pap. 1.25 (ISBN 0-532-12528-2). Woodhill.
To Know Love. Kathleen Pieper. 1979. 6.95 (Avalon). Bouregy.
To Know What Dream. Millie Sherwood. LC 55-7602. 1955. Dorrance.
To Know You Care... Frank Vitto. 1974. 5.95 (ISBN 0-533-01157-4). Vantage.
To Last a Lifetime. Jennifer Blair. (Candlelight Romance). 1977. 0.95 (ISBN 0-440-18243-3). Dell Pub. Co.
To Lay a Hearth. Myra Scovel. 4.50 o.p. (HarpR). Har-Row.
To Leave Before Dawn. Julien Green. LC 67-19199. 1967. Harcourt, Brace & World.
To Leeward. Francis Marion Crawford. LC 6-30884. 1893. Macmillan and Co.
To Leeward. Francis Marion Crawford. LC 6-30885. 1884. Houghton, Mifflin and Company.
To Let. John Galsworthy. LC 75-8418. (His The Forsyte chronicles, v. 3). (Scribner library, SL207). 1969. 1.95. Scribner.
To Let. John Galsworthy. LC 21-15554. 1921. C. Scribner's Sons.
To Life Anew: A Novel. Christine Hunter, pseud. LC 68-22836. 1968. Zondervan Pub. House.
To Linger Is to Die. Lilya Wagner. LC 75-18349. (Crown book). 2.95 (ISBN 0-8127-0102-X). Southern Pub. Association.
To Live Again. Catherine Marshall. 1969. pap. 0.95 o.p. (M1226, Crest). Fawcett World.
To Live Again. Robert Silverberg. LC 76-78743. (Doubleday science fiction). 1969. 4.95. Doubleday.
To Live Again. Robert Silverberg. 1978. 1.95 (ISBN 0-425-03774-6). Berkley Pub. Corp.
To Live Again. Anamarie Trenchi De Bottazzi. LC 78-5029. 1978. 8.95 o.p. (ISBN 0-396-07570-3). Dodd.
To Live Alone. D. Michael Kaye. LC 33-31150. 1933. Frederick A. Stokes Company.
To Live and Die in Dixie. Theodore Roscoe. LC 61-13359. 1961. Scribner.
To Live As We Wish: Translated from the Russian by Nicholas Wreden. 1st Ed. Mark Aleksandrovich Aldanov. LC 52-8256. 1952. Dutton.
To Live Forever. Jack Vance, pseud. LC 56-121235. 1956. Ballantine Books.
To Live Forever: By Jack Vance Pseud. Henry Kuttner. LC 56-12123. 1956. Ballantine Books.
To Live with Love: A Novel. Margaret Gorman Nichols. LC 43-246959. 1943. Macrae-Smith-Company.
To London Town. Arthur Morrison. LC 99-4273. 1899. Herbert S. Stone & Company.
To London, with Love. Sandra Lawrence. (Illus., Orig.). pap. 0.50 o.p. (72-167). Lancer.
To Look & Pass. Taylor Caldwell. 288p. 1978. pap. 2.25 (ISBN 0-449-14055-5, GM). Fawcett.
To Look & Pass. Taylor Caldwell. 288p. (Orig.). 1973. 6.95 o.s.i. White Lion Pubs.
To Look and Pass. Taylor Caldwell. (Gold medal, P2772). 1973. (pbk.) 1.25. Fawcett.
To Love a Mermaid. Ruth Burnett. (YA) 1979. 6.95 (Avalon). Bouregy.
To Love a Queen: Walter Raleigh and Elizabeth R. Lawrence L Schoonover. LC 72-8887. 1973. 7.95 (ISBN 0-316-77461-8). Little, Brown.
To Love a Stranger. Hayton Monteith. (Candlelight Ecstasy Ser.: No. 62). (Orig.). 1982. pap. 1.75 (ISBN 0-440-14798-0). Dell.
To Love a Stranger. Lorena Ann Olmsted. LC 64-9206. 1964. Avalon Books.
To Love a Stranger. Barbara Paul. (General Ser.). 1980. lib. bdg. 14.95 (ISBN 0-8161-3169-4, Large Print Bks). G K Hall.
To Love a Stranger. Barbara Paul. LC 78-19429. 1979. 8.95 o.p. (ISBN 0-312-80688-4). St Martin.
To Love a Stranger. Barbara Vstedal. LC 78-19429. 8.95 (ISBN 0-312-80688-4). St. Martin's Press.
To Love a Stranger. Barbara Vstedal. LC 80-22070. 1980. 14.95 (ISBN 0-8161-3169-4). G. K. Hall.
To Love a Stranger. Marjorie Warby. Ed. by Gene DeRoin. (Aston Hall Presents Ser.). (Orig.). 1979. pap. 1.50 (ISBN 0-89936-003-3). Aston Hall.
To Love Again. Dorothy DePuy. 2.50 o.p. Carlton.
To Love Again. Joanne Kaye. LC 81-85176. (Garment Center Ser.). 224p. (Orig.). 1982. pap. 2.50 (ISBN 0-86721-095-8). Playboy Pbks.
To Love Again. Helen Murray. (Orig.). pap. 1.75 (ISBN 0-8439-8014-1, Tiara Bks). Nordon Pubns.
To Love Again. Denise Robins. 1970. pap. 0.75 o.p. (T2297, GM). Fawcett World.
To Love Again. Danielle Steel. LC 81-6783. 1981. 14.95 (ISBN 0-8161-3219-4). G.K. Hall.
To Love and Be Wise. Elizabeth Mackintosh. LC 51-2359. 1951. Macmillan.
To Love and Be Wise. Elizabeth Mackintosh. (Berkley medallion book). (Large-type edition). 1975. (pbk.) 1.25 (ISBN 0-425-02898-4). Berkley Pub. Co.
To Love and Be Wise. Elizabeth Mackintosh. (Kangaroo Book)). 1977. 1.75 (ISBN 0-671-80931-8). Pocket Books.
To Love & Be Wise. large type ed. Josephine Tey. 1975. pap. 1.25 (ISBN 0-425-02898-4, Medallion). Berkley Pub.
To Love & Be Wise. Josephine Tey. 208p. 1982. pap. 2.95 (ISBN 0-671-44191-4). PB.
To Love and Beyond. Therese Martini, pseud. 1977. 1.95 (ISBN 0-445-04092-0). Popular Library.
To Love and Corrupt. Joseph Viertel. LC 62-8456. 1962. Random House.
To Love & Honor. Daisy H. Thomson. 1974. pap. 0.95 o.p. (ISBN 0-515-03476-2, N3476). BJ Pub Group.
To Love and to Be Loved. A Story. Azel Stevens Roe. LC 7-40218. 1851. D. Appleton & Company.
To Love and to Cherish. Elizabeth Carfrae, pseud. LC 38-152251. 1938. G. P. Putnam's Sons.
To Love and to Cherish. Elizabeth Carfrae, pseud. LC 42-114461. 1942. Triangle Books.
To Love and to Cherish. Mabel Margaret Clark. LC 32-9935. Farrar & Rinehart, Incorporated.
To Love and to Cherish. Eliza Caroline Calvert Obenchain. LC 11-11278. 1911. 1.00. Little, Brown, and Company.
To Love and to Cherish. Emma Marr Petersen. LC 56-31364. Bookcraft.
To Love and to Honor. Emilie Baker Loring. LC 50-10612. 1950. Little, Brown.
To Love and to Honor. Emilie Baker Loring. 1974. (pbk.) 0.95. Bantam Books.
To Love and to Honor. Emilie Baker Loring. LC 77-6771. 1977. 9.95 (ISBN 0-89340-085-8). J. Curley.
To Love & Yet to Die. Stephen Frances. (O.s.i.). 176p. 1973. pap. 0.95 o.s.i. (AN1196, Award). Univ Pub & Dist.
To Love by Candlelight. Philip Lindsay. LC 56-2172. Avon Publications.
To Love Is Not to Lose. Lauren Randall. (Illus.). 96p. 1981. pap. 1.95 (ISBN 0-380-78337-1, 78337). Avon.
To Love Is to Be Happy With. Barry N. Kaufman. 1978. pap. 3.75 (ISBN 0-449-23475-4, Crest). Fawcett.
To Love Is to Listen: A Novel. Jane Kesner Morris Ardmore. LC 67-17680. 1967. Norton.
To Love the Unlovely. Thelma Leuang. 4.50 o.p. Vantage.

To Luna with Love. H. U. Bevis. Ed. by Alice Sachs. 1971. 3.95 o.p. Lenox Hill.
To M. L. G. Or He Who Passed. Alice Muriel Livingston Williamson. LC 12-1475. 1912. Frederick A. Stokes Company.
To Make a Life. Dan Styk. 1980. pap. 3.50 (ISBN 0-917652-21-5). Confluence Pr.
To Make a World. Theodore Morrison. LC 57-6432. 1957. Viking Press.
To Make a World: A Novel. Gideon Clark. LC 51-32664. 1951. Rich and Cowan.
To Make an Underworld. Joan Margaret Fleming. LC 76-46513. 1977. 7.95 (ISBN 0-89340-059-9). J. Curley.
To Make an Underworld. Joan Margaret Fleming. LC 77-360273. (crime club). 1976. 2.95 (ISBN 0-00-231834-2). Collins for the Crime Club.
To Make an Underworld. Joan Margaret Fleming. LC 76-14808. (Red mask mystery). 6.95. Putnam.
To Make My Bread. Grace Lumpkin. LC 32-21426. The Macaulay Company.
To Make the Wounded Whole. Matsu Crawford. LC 67-17242. 1967. Zondervan Pub. House.
To Man Alone. Dorothy Clewes. LC 45-1345. 1945. Arcadia House, Inc.
To Market. Harvey J Sconce. LC 28-28965. The Stratford Company.
To Market, to Market. Allen Richards. pap. 0.95 o.p. (02479, Collier). Macmillan.
To Market, to Market: By Allen Richards Pseud. Richard Rosenthal. LC 61-12702. (Cock Robin mystery). 1961. Macmillan.
To Marry A Tiger, The Tartan Touch, Cadence of Portugal. Isobel Chace. (Harlequin Romances Ser.). 576p. 1982. pap. 3.50 (ISBN 0-373-20065-X). Harlequin Bks.
To Mars Via the Moon: An Astronomical Story. Mark Wicks. LC 74-16526. (Science Fiction Ser). (Illus.). 352p. 1975. Repr. 19.00x (ISBN 0-405-06318-0). Ayer Co.
To Mary, with Love. Richard Sherman. LC 36-27158. 1936. Little, Brown, and Company.
To Meet Mr. Stanley. Dorothy Johnson. LC 26-18323. 1926. 2.00. Longmans, Green and Co., Ltd.
To Meet Mr. Stanley. Dorothy Johnson. LC 27-2158. 1926. Longmans, Green and Co.
To Michael with Love. Mary S Sheridan. (Avalon Books). 4.95. Thomas Bouregy.
To-Morrow? Vivian Cory. LC 4-14150. 1904. The W. Scott Publishing Co., Ltd.
To-Morrow and to-Morrow... A Novel. Stephen McKenna. LC 24-230862. 1924. Little, Brown, and Company.
To-Morrow Morning. Anne Parrish. LC 27-647192. Harper & Brothers.
To-Morrow Morning: Chronicle of the New Eve and the Same Old Adam. Edith Barnard Delano. LC 17-25434. 1917. 1.35. Houghton Mifflin Company.
To-Morrow Never Comes: A Novel. Robert Luther Duffus. LC 29-972473. 1929. Houghton Mifflin Company.
To-Morrow's Rainbow. Allene Albrecht. LC 35-162041. 1935. Concordia Publishing House.
To-Morrow's Tangle. Margaret Bass Pedler. LC 26-3796. George H. Doran Company.
To Mother. 1971. 3.95 (ISBN 0-88088-540-8). Peter Pauper.
To My Beloved: The Heart Letters of a Woman... LC 14-16208. George H. Doran Company.
To My Sons. Harold B. Wright. 261p. 1977. Repr. of 1934 ed. lib. bdg. 14.65x (ISBN 0-89966-267-6). Buccaneer Bks.
To Next Year in Jerusalem: A Novel. David Marcus. LC 55-3909. 1954. St. Martin's Press.
To-Night and Forever. Ruth Tracy Millard. LC 39-107582. The Penn Publishing Company.
To Open. Samuel Menashe. LC 73-17680. 728p. 1974. 6.95 o.p. (ISBN 0-670-71766-5). Viking Pr.
To Open the Sky. Robert Silverberg. LC 77-4407. (Gregg Press science fiction series). (Illus.). 1977. 11.00 (ISBN 0-8398-2382-7). Gregg Press.
To Pay the Piper. 1968. pap. 1.95 o.p. (6004). Brandon.
To Play the Fox. M. S Craig. LC 82-7442. 9.95 (ISBN 0-396-08099-5). Dodd, Mead.
To Prime the Pump. A. Bertram Chandler. (Orig.). 1971. pap. 0.75 o.p. (07116). Curtis.
To Protect the Guilty. Roderic Jeffries. LC 73-120401. 1970. 4.95. Walker.
To Quebec & the Stars. Howard Phillips Lovecraft. 15.00 (ISBN 0-937986-30-5). D M Grant.
To Raise a Nation: Historical Novel of Hawaii. Mary Cooke. LC 72-20717. (Illus.). 1.95.
To Raise These Halt. Fred Rothermell. LC 36-218274. L. Furman, Inc.
To Ravish Rani. Nadine McGuyer. (Orig.). 1979. pap. 1.95 (ISBN 0-532-23273-9). Woodhill.
To Reach a Dream. Nathan C Heard. (Signet, Y5490). 1973. (pbk.) 1.25. New American Lib.
To Reach a Dream. Nathan C Heard. LC 72-37440. 1972. 5.95. Dial Press.
To Remember at Midnight. Michael Foster. LC 38-34541. 1938. W. Morrow & Company.
To Remember Tina. Bettie Wysor. LC 74-26903. 1975. 7.95 (ISBN 0-8128-1795-8). Stein and Day.
To Remember Tina. Bettie Wysor. (Signet Book). 1976. 1.75. New American Library.
To Remember, to Forget: A Novel. Ben-Amotz, Dan. LC 73-10756. 7.95 (ISBN 0-8276-0041-0). Jewish Publication Society of America.
To Ride Pegasus. Anne McCaffery. 1973. (pbk.) 1.25 (ISBN 0-345-23417-0). Ballantine Books.
To Ride Pegasus. Anne McCaffrey. (Del Rey Bk.). Date not set. pap. 2.25 (ISBN 0-345-28507-7). Ballantine.
To Ride the River with. William MacLeod Raine. LC 36-19988. 1936. Houghton Mifflin Company.
To Right the Wrong. A Novel. Ada Ellen Bayly. LC 6-10290. 1894. Harper & Brothers.
To Risks Unknown. Douglas Reeman. LC 73-97073. (Illus.). 1970. 5.95. Putnam.
To Rouse a Lion see Pentagon Tapes.
To Russia with Lust. Rod Gray. (The Lady from L.U.S.T. Ser.). (O.s.i.). 1973. pap. 0.95 o.s.i. (BT50628). Belmont-Tower.
To Save His Life. Kelley Roos. LC 68-26154. (Red badge mystery). 1968. 3.95. Dodd, Mead.
To Save Their Souls. Bessie Lewis. LC 39-3409. The Christopher Publishing House.
To Savor the Past. Irving A Greenfield. (Berkley Medallion Book). 1975. (pbk.) 1.25 (ISBN 0-425-02959-X). Berkley Pub. Co.
To See a Fine Lady. Norah Lofts. 1.75 (ISBN 0-449-22890-8). Fawcett Crest.
To See a Fine Lady. Norah Robinson Lofts. LC 46-59444. 1946. A. A. Knopf.
To See a Stranger: By Margaret Lynn Pseud. 1st Ed. Gladys Starkey Battye. LC 62-11426. 1962. Published for the Crime Club by Doubleday.
To See Ourselves. Rachel Lyman Field & Pederson, Arthur, Joint Author. LC 37-339092. 1937. The Macmillan Company.
To See the Dream. Jessamyn West. LC 56-11961. 1957. 3.95 o.p. (ISBN 0-15-190599-1). HarBraceJ.
To See You Again. Alice Boyd Adams. (Contemporary American Fiction Ser.). 312p. 1983. pap. 5.95 (ISBN 0-14-006483-4). Penguin.
To See You Again: Stories. Alice Boyd Adams. LC 81-15621. 1982. 13.50 (ISBN 0-394-52335-0). Knopf: Distributed by Random House.
To Seek a Star. Suzanne Ebel. 1975. (pbk.) 0.95. Fawcett.
To Seize a Dream. Virginia Davis Hersch. LC 48-9092. 1948. Crown Publishers.
To Seize the Passing Dream. Ted Berkman. 1973. pap. 1.50 o.s.i. (71-343). Lancer.
To Seize the Passing Dream: A Novel of Whistler, His Women, and His World. Ted Berkman. LC 73-176345. 1972. 7.95. Doubleday.
To Seize the Rainbow. Jo Calloway. (Orig.). 1980. pap. 1.50 (ISBN 0-440-18754-0). Dell.
To Serve Them All My Days. Delderfield, Ronald Frederick. 1973. (pbk.) 1.75 (ISBN 0-671-78616-4). Pocket Books.
To Serve Them All My Days. Ronald Frederick Delderfield. LC 72-81349. 1972. 8.95 (ISBN 0-671-21371-7). Simon and Schuster.
To Set One's Heart: Belief & Teaching in the Church. Sara Little. LC 82-49020. 160p. 1983. pap. 7.50 (ISBN 0-8042-1442-5). John Knox.
To Sing with the Angels. Maurice Gerschon Hindus. LC 41-980271. 1941. Doubleday, Doran and Company, Inc.
To Sir With Love. Edward R. Braithwaite. 1982. pap. 1.75 (ISBN 0-451-11533-3, AE1533, Sig). NAL.
To Sir, with Love. Edward R. Braithwaite. pap. 0.75 o.p. (HT700). Pyramid Pubns.
To Sit on a Horse. Albert Morgan. LC 64-15169. 1964. Morrow.
To Slay the Dreamer. Alexander Cordell, pseud. LC 80-14397. 1980. 10.95 (ISBN 0-312-80741-4). St. Martin's Press.
To Smithereens. Rosalyn Drexler. LC 76-175196. 1972. 5.95. New American Library.
To Smithereens, a Novel. Rosalyn Drexler. 1972. 5.95 o.p. (NAL). Norton.
To Soar with Eagles. (Skymasters Ser.). 1982. pap. 2.95 (ISBN 0-440-08571-3). Dell.
To Span a Continent. Illus. by Anne Merriman Peck. Winnie Crandall Saunders. LC 65-18663. 4.50. Caxton.
To Speak of Many Things. Eunice Osgood & Phillips Endicott Osgood. LC 67-19666. 1967. T. S. Denison.
To Spit Against the Wind: A Novel. Benjamin H Levin. LC 76-111697. 1970. 7.95. Citadel Press.
To Spite Her Face. Hildegarde Dolson. LC 78-11074. 1979. 9.95 (ISBN 0-89340-182-X). J. Curley.
To Spite Her Face: A Mystery Novel. Hildegarde Dolson. LC 70-141907. 1971. 5.95. Lippincott.
To Step Aside: Seven Long Short Stories... Noel Pierce Coward. LC 44-6797. (Avon modern short story monthly. No. 3). Avon Book Company.
To Step Aside: Seven Stories. Noel Pierce Coward. LC 39-29438. 1939. Doubleday, Doran & Co., Inc.
To Still Live on: A Novel. Thomas E Ray. LC 53-122736. 1953. Dorrance.
To Still the Guns. James W. Smith. 1971. pap. 0.75 o.p. (T2583). Pyramid Pubns.
To Sting the Child. Robert Baylor. LC 64-15651. 1964. Bobbs-Merrill.
To Struggle, to Laugh. Samuel Marko. LC 47-286848. 1947. Chapman & Grimes.
To Suffer in Silence. Patricia Rae. 1981. pap. 2.75 (ISBN 0-89083-748-1). Zebra.
To Take a Wife: A Collection of Exotic Stories, by Colin Ross Pseud. Harry Roskolenko. LC 52-28543. 1952. Woodford Press.
To Tame a Land. Louis L'Amour. LC 80-24985. (Series: Gregg Press Western Fiction Series.). 1981. 11.95 (ISBN 0-8398-2697-4). Gregg Press.
To Tame a Land see Complete L'Amour.
To Tame a Land see L'Amour Westerns.
To Teach the Senators Wisdom: Or, An Oxford Guide-Book. John Cecil Masterman. LC 52-12877. 1952. Oxford University Press.
To Tell You the Truth. Leonard Merrick. LC 22-22701. (Half-title: The works of Leonard Merrick). E. P. Dutton and Company.
To the Bitter End. Johannes Mario Simmel. LC 70-107453. 1970. McGraw-Hill.
To the Bitter End. A Novel. Mary Elizabeth Braddon Maxwell. (Seaside library. v. 4, no. 69). 1877. G. Munro.
To the Bitter End: A Novel. stereotyped ed. Mary Elizabeth Braddon Maxwell. (On cover: Lovell's library, no. 588). 1885. J. W. Lovell Company.
To the Bitter End. A Novel. Mary Elizabeth Braddon Maxwell. (On cover: Seaside library. Pocket ed. no. 557). 1885. G. Munro.
To the Bright and Shining Sun. James Lee Burke. LC 73-106552. 1970. 5.95. Scribner.
To the Castle. Dorothea Malm. LC 57-8470. 1957. Appleton-Century-Crofts.
To the Castle. Dorothea Malm. (Ace gothic). 1974. (pbk.) 0.95. Ace Books.
To the Cleveland Station. Carol Anne Douglas. LC 81-22449. 1982. 6.95. Naiad Press.
To the Coral Strand; a Novel. 1st Ed. John Masters. LC 62-14558. 1962. Harper & Row.
To the Credit of the Sea. Lawrence Mott. LC 78-150555. (Short story index reprint series). (Illus.). 1971. (ISBN 0-8369-3852-6). Books for Libraries Press.
To the Credit of the Sea. Lawrence Mott. LC 7-17361. 1907. Harper & Brothers.
To the Dark Tower. Lyda B. Long. 1973. pap. 0.95 o.s.i. (75-478). Lancer.
To the Dark Tower: Being Gerard Linton's Account of All That Happened at the House of Jacques Cournot in the Summer of Nineteen Hundred and Seven... Mark Stanislaus Gross. LC 23-118. P. J. Kenedy & Sons.
To the Devil-a Daughter. Dennis Yates Wheatley, pseud. (Black magic ser.). 1972. 1.50. Ballantine.
To the Eagle's Nest. Joseph DiMona. LC 79-25496. 1980. 10.95 (ISBN 0-688-03653-8). Morrow.
To the Edge of Morning. James Ivor Jackson. LC 65-9552. 1964. Baxter Pub. Co.
To the End of the World. Blaise Cendrars. LC 68-21263. 1968. Grove Press.
To the End of the World. Helen Constance White. LC 39-30365. 1939. The Macmillan Company.
To the End of Time. William Olaf Stapledon & Basil Davenport. LC 75-5744. (Gregg Press science fiction series). 1975. 35.00 (ISBN 0-8398-2312-6). Gregg Press.
To the End of Time: The Best of Olaf Stapledon. Selection and Introd. by Basil Davenport. William Olaf Stapledon. Ed. by Basil Davenport. LC 53-6981. 1953. Funk & Wagnalls.
To the Far Blue Mountains. Louis L'Amour. LC 75-29190. 6.95. Saturday Review Press.
To the Far Blue Mountains. Louis L'Amour. LC 77-4748. 1977. 12.95 (ISBN 0-8161-6484-3). G. K. Hall.
To the Far Mountains. Wayne D Overholser. LC 63-16120. Macmillan.
To the Farthest Island. Ann Helming. LC 69-13195. 1969. 4.95. Coward-McCann.
To the Finland Station. Edmund Wilson. 1973. pap. 7.95 o.p. (ISBN 0-374-51045-8, N441). FS&G.
To the Front: A Sequel to Cadet Days. Charles King. LC 8-5578. 1908. Harper & Brothers.
To the Gallows I Must Go. Thomas Stanley Matthews. LC 31-930101. 1931. A. A. Knopf.
To the Hanging Gardens. Leo E. Litwak. 1966. pap. 0.75 o.p. (75-137). Manor Bks.
To the Hanging Gardens: 1st Ed. Leo E Litwak. LC 64-12467. 1964. World Pub. Co.
To the Healing of the Sea: A Novel. Edward James Catell. LC 3875. 1900. D. Biddle.
To the Highest Bidder. Florence Morse Kingsley. LC 11-84896. 1911. Dodd, Mead and Company.
To the Hilt. Percival Christopher Wren. LC 37-198802. 1937. Houghton Mifflin Company.
To the Honor of the Fleet. Robert H Pilpel. LC 78-3215. (Illus.). 1979. 12.95 (ISBN 0-689-10932-6). Atheneum.
To the Honor of the Fleet: By Robert H. Pilpel. Robert H Pilpel. (Illus.). (ISBN 0-445-04576-0)., C.
To the Honorable Miss S: And Other Stories. Ret Marut. (Illus.). 151p. 1981. 10.00 (ISBN 0-88208-130-6); pap. 5.95 (ISBN 0-88208-131-4). Lawrence Hill.
To the Honourable Miss S- and Other Stories. B Traven. LC 81-7222. 1981. 10.00 (ISBN 0-88208-130-6) (ISBN 0-88208-131-4). L. Hill.
To the Indies. Cecil Scott Forester. LC 40-10294. 1940. Little, Brown and Company.
To the Islands. Stow, Randolph. LC 59-11881. 1958. Little, Brown.
To the Islands: A Novel. rev. ed. Randolph Stow. LC 81-21407. 1982. 9.95 (ISBN 0-8008-7739-X). Taplinger Pub. Co.
To the Isthmus. Barbara Compton. LC 65-10384. 1965. 5.50. S. & S.
To the Land of the Electric Angel. William Rotsler. LC 75-34417. 1976. 1.50 (ISBN 0-345-24517-2). Ballantine Books.
To the Last Man. Zane Grey. W. J. Black.
To the Last Man. Zane Grey. LC 36-29345. (Home library edition). McKinlay, Stone & Mackenzie.
To the Last Man. Zane Grey. LC 78-2626. 1978. 9.95 (ISBN 0-89340-137-4). J. Curley & Associates.
To the Last Man: A Novel. Zane Grey. LC 33-28336. Grosset & Dunlap.
To the Last Man: A Novel. Zane Grey. LC 22-14573. 1922. Harper & Brothers.
To the Last Man: A Novel. Zane Grey. Grosset & Dunlap.
To the Last Penny. Edwin Lefevre. LC 17-10667. 1917. Harper & Brothers.
To the Lighthouse. Virginia Stephen Woolf. LC 27-10646. Harcourt, Brace & Company.
To the Lighthouse. Virginia Stephen Woolf. LC 37-28677. (Half-title: The modern library of the world's best books. 217). 1937. The Modern Library.
To the Manner Born. John Seymour Chaloner. LC 79-21559. (Illus.). 1980. 8.95 (ISBN 0-312-80750-3). St. Martin's Press.
To the Manor Born. Peter Spence. LC 80-14396. 1980. 8.95 (ISBN 0-312-80752-X). St. Martin's Press.
To the Manor Born. Peter Spence. LC 80-25231. 1980. 8.95 (ISBN 0-312-80752-X). St. Martin's Press.
To the Minute, Scarlet and Black: Two Tales of Life's Perplexities. Anna Katharine Green Rohlfs. LC 16-20555. 1916. G. P. Putnam's Sons.
To the Moment of Triumph. 1st American Ed. Pamela Frankau. LC 52-11684. Harper.
To the Mountain. Bradford Smith. LC 36-7369. The Bobbs-Merrill Company.
To the Mountain's Height: And Other Poems. Ruby MacRae Strahman. LC 56-11599. 1956. Exposition Press.
To the North. Elizabeth Bowen. LC 33-3924. 1933. A. A. Knopf.
To the Opera Ball. Sarah Gainham. LC 76-2773. 1977. 8.95 (ISBN 0-385-12133-4). Doubleday.
To the Opera Ball. Sarah Gainham. 1978. 2.25 (ISBN 0-446-82592-1). Warner Books.
To the Precipice. Judith Rossner. LC 66-249614. 1966. 5.95. Morrow.
To the Precipice. Judith Rossner. LC 66-24961. 1976. (pbk.) 1.75. Popular Library.
To the Queen's Taste: The First Supplement to 101 Years' Entertainment, Consisting of the Best Stories Published in the First Four Years of Ellery Queen's Mystery Magazine. Ellery Queen & Queen, Ellery, Pseud., Ed. 101 Years' Entertainment. LC 46-5985. 1946. Little, Brown and Company.
To the Slaughterhouse. Jean Giono. 13.50 (ISBN 0-7206-3602-7). Dufour.
To the Stars: Eight Stories of Science Fiction. Ed. by Robert Silverberg. LC 76-132555. 1971. 5.95. Hawthorn Books.
To the Sun. Edward Fisher. LC 29-7718. 1929. Cosmospolitan Book Corporation.
To the Sun? Jules Verne. Tr. by Edward Roth. Bd. with Off on a Comet. pap. 2.50 o.p. (ISBN 0-486-20634-3). Dover.
To the Sun! A Journey Through Planetary Space. From the French of Jules Verne... Jules Verne & Roth, Edward, 1826-1911, Tr. LC 41-42131. D. McKay.
To the Sun! Off on a Comet! Translated by Edward Roth. Jules Verne. LC 60-50100. (His Space novels). 1960. Dover Publications.
To the Swift: A Novel. Anne Hawkins. LC 49-7696. 1949. Harper.

To the Throne from the Sheepcotes. William Schoeler. LC 22-605. 1921. The Roxburgh Publishing Company, Inc.
To the Tune of Murder. Helen Mabry Ballard. LC 52-5786. 1952. M. S. Mill Co. and W. Morrow.
To the Turn of the Tide. Jonathan Powell. (Family at War). (Signet book: Vol. 2). 1975. (pbk.) 1.50. New American Library.
To the Unknown Hero. Hans Erich Nossack. LC 73-85729. 1974. 6.95 (ISBN 0-374-27838-5). Farrar, Straus and Giroux.
To the Valiant. Norah C James. LC 30-3866. 1930. W. Morrow & Company.
To the Vanquished. Ida Alexa Ross Wylie. LC 34-16904. 1934. Doubleday, Doran & Company, Inc.
To the Victor- Henry Von Rhau. 1931. Longmans, Green and Co.
To the Victor: A Novel. Herbert Byer. LC 36-30061. 1936. Doubleday, Doran & Company, Inc.
To the Victor, and Selected Stories. Natalie Shipman. LC 52-9206. 1952. Bouregy & Curl.
To the Victors the Spoils. Colin MacInnes. LC 68-76153. 1966. Penguin.
To Thee I Come. Mildred E. Reeves. 220p. 1975. 7.50. Prairie Pub.
To These Also. Bertha B. Moore McCurry. LC 40-8748. 1940. Wm. B. Eerdmans Publishing Company.
To These Also. Bertha B Moore. LC 40-874857. 1940. Wm. B. Eerdmans Publishing Company.
To Those Who Dare. Lydia Lancaster. 464p. (Orig.). 1982. pap. 2.95 (ISBN 0-446-90579-8). Warner Bks.
To Tojo from Billy-Bob Jones: A Novel. William Allen. LC 77-23228. 1977. 7.95 (ISBN 0-395-25376-4). Houghton Mifflin.
To Touch a Dream. Christina Crokett. (Super Romances Ser.). 384p. 1983. pap. 2.95 (ISBN 0-373-70055-5, Pub. by Worldwide). Harlequin Bks.
To Touch a Star. Garnett A. Schultz. 1971. 3.75 o.p. (ISBN 0-8059-1552-4). Dorrance.
To Trust a Stranger. Lorena A. Olmsted. (YA) 1973. 4.95 o.p. (Avalon). Bouregy.
To Trust a Stranger. Lorena Ann Olmsted. (Avalon romances). 1973. 4.50. Avalon Books.
To Turn You on: 39 Sex Fantasies for Women. J Aphrodite, pseud. LC 75-10490. 8.00 (ISBN 0-8184-0217-2). L. Stuart.
To Wake the Dead. John Dickson Carr. LC 38-5759. 1938. Harper & Brothers.
To Walk in the Light. Effie E. Sanders. 1970. 5.00 o.p. (ISBN 0-682-46838-X). Exposition.
To Walk the Line: A Novel. David Quammen. LC 77-111255. 1970. 5.95. Knopf.
To Walk the Night. Kathryn Kilby Borland & Helen Ross Speicher. LC 75-45166. 1976. 1.25 (ISBN 0-345-25007-9). Ballantine Books.
To Walk the Night. William Milligan Sloane. LC 54-12515. 1954. Dodd, Mead.
To Walk the Night: A Novel. William Milligan Sloane. LC 37-14931. 1937. Farrar & Rinehart, Incorporated.
To Warm the Heart. Caroline Eyring Miner. 1.95 o.p. (ISBN 0-87747-278-5). Deseret Bk.
To Wed a Doctor. Elizabeth Seifert. LC 68-16879. 1968. Dodd, Mead.
To What Dread End. Mary Violet Heberden. LC 44-1338. 1944. Pub. for the Crime Club, by Doubleday, Doran and Company, Inc.
To What Green Altar? William Babington Maxwell. LC 30-25202. 1930. Doubleday, Doran & Company, Inc.
To Whom Else? Robert Graves. LC 77-4107. Repr. of 1931 ed. lib. bdg. 10.00 (ISBN 0-8414-4555-9). Folcroft.
To Whom Else. Robert Graves. 10.00 o.s.i. Ridgeway Bks.
To Whom It May Concern: And Other Stories. James Thomas Farrell. LC 44-526805. 1944. The Vanguard Press.
To Whom It May Concern & Other Stories. Laura J. Wright. 1972. 3.50 o.p. (ISBN 0-682-47409-6). Exposition.
To Win the Love He Sought. The Great Awakening. Edward Phillips Oppenheim. LC 15-4863. 1912. P. F. Collier & Son.
To Windward: The Story of a Stormy Course. Henry Cottrell Rowland. LC 4-6881. 1904. A. S. Barnes & Company.
To Worlds Beyond: Stories of Science Fiction. Robert Silverberg. LC 65-14889. 3.95. Chilton.
To You, Girls. Kate Stanley. LC 60-16449. 1961. St. Paul Editions.
To You with Love. Terry Rowe. (Signet book). (Illus.). 1975. (pbk.) 1.25. New American Library.
To Your Scattered Bodies Go. Philip Jose Farmer. LC 80-13176. (Gregg Press science fiction series). 1980. 12.95 (ISBN 0-8398-2620-6). Gregg Press.
To Your Scattered Bodies Go see Philip Jose Farmer: The Complete Riverworld Novels.
To Your Scattered Bodies Go: A Science Fiction Novel. Philip Jose Farmer. LC 77-136810. 1971. 4.95. Putnam.
Toads of War. Eddie Iroh. LC 79-670372. (African writers series; 213). (H.E.B. paperback). 1979. 3.95 (ISBN 0-435-90213-X). Heinemann.
Toast Me with Bread, Charlie. E. Knox Kitzes. (O.s.i.). (Orig.). 1968. pap. 0.60 o.s.i. (A284X, Award). Univ Pub & Dist.
Toast of the Town. Alice Chetwynd Ley. LC 77-14524. 1978. 7.95 (ISBN 0-89340-113-7). J. Curley.
Toast to Lady Mary. Doris Leslie. 0.95. Popular Lib.
Toast to the King. Elizabeth Jane Coatsworth & Orr, Forrest, W., Illus. LC 40-35992. Coward McCann, Inc.
Toast to Tomorrow. Manning Coles, pseud. LC 53-10172. (Twenty-fifth anniversary Crime Club classic). 1953. Published for the Crime Club by Doubleday.
Toast to Tomorrow. Manning Coles, pseud. LC 41-6171. 1941. Pub. for the Crime Club by Doubleday, Doran and Company, Inc.
Toasted Blonde. Reeve, Christopher. LC 30-22436. 1930. W. Morrow & Company.
Toasted English. Marghanita Laski. LC 49-7933. 1949. Houghton Mifflin Co.
Tobacco Auction Murders. Robert Harry Turner. LC 54-318567. (Ave double novel books, D-55). 1954. Ace Books.
Tobacco Men: A Novel Based on Notes. Borden Deal & Theodore Dreiser. LC 65-12002. 1965. Holt, Rinehart and Winston.
Tobacco Road. Erskine Caldwell. LC 57-13977. 1957. Grosset & Dunlap.
Tobacco Road. Erskine Caldwell. LC 32-50231. 1932. C. Scribner's Sons.
Tobacco Road. Erskine Caldwell. LC 40-347423. Duell, Sloan and Pearce.
Tobacco Road. Erskine Caldwell. LC 78-55752. 1978. 10.00 (ISBN 0-8376-0422-2). R. Bentley.
Tobacco Road. Erskine Caldwell & Bourke-White, Margaret. LC 74-84334. (Illus.). 1974. Beehive Press.
Tobacco Tiller: A Tale of the Kentucky Tobacco Fields. Sarah Bell Hackley. LC 9-24896. 1909. 1.50. The C. M. Clark Publishing Company.
Tobey's First Case: A Novel. Clara Louise Root Burnham. LC 26-15574. 1926. Houghton Mifflin Company.
Tobias. Patrick Ross. 1977. pap. 1.95 (ISBN 0-8423-7250-4). Tyndale.
Tobias: A Cherokee's Search for Manhood. Patrick Ross. LC 76-47280. (Illus.). 1977. 1.95 (ISBN 0-8423-7250-4). Tyndale House.
Tobias: A Story of the Northwest. Hans Andersen Foss. Tr. by Skordalsvold, John Jenson. LC 99-2532. 1899. H. Petersen and Company.
Tobias and the Angel. Frank Yerby. LC 75-2153. 1975. 8.95 (ISBN 0-8037-5967-3). Dial Press.
Tobias Brandywine: A Novel. Dan Wickenden. LC 48-6542. 1948. W. Morrow.
Tobias O' the Light: A Story of Cape Cod. James A Cooper, pseud. G. Sully & Company.
Tobias Wilson: A Tale of the Great Rebellion. Jeremiah Clemens. LC 6-21356. 1865. J. B. Lippincott & Co.
Toby: A Novel of Kentucky. Credo Fitch Harris. LC 12-10648. Small, Maynard and Company.
Toby Alone. Robbie Branscum. 96p. 1980. pap. 1.75 (ISBN 0-380-50781-1, 50781). Avon.
Toby and Johnny Joe. avon books, ed. Robbie Branscum. 1.75 (ISBN 0-380-52670-0).
Toby Lived Here. Hilma Wolitzer. (YA) 1980. pap. 1.75 (ISBN 0-553-13133-8). Bantam.
Tockwotton Eclectics. Michael James McHugh. LC 34-25914. The Oxford Press.
Tod. 1st Ed. John Kiddell. LC 68-31697. 1968. 4.95, 4.75 lib. ed. Chilton.
Today and Forever: Stories of China. Pearl Sydenstricker Buck. LC 40-278365. The John Day Company.
Today in Paradise. Lorol E. Toy. 115p. 1957. 3.00 o.s.i. (ISBN 0-910348-03-0). Channel Pub.
Today Is Enough. Ruth Lininger Dobson. LC 39-27064. 1939. Dodd, Mead & Company.
Today Is Forever. Ramona Herdman. LC 37-408747. 1937. Harper & Brothers.
Today Is Ours. Netta Muskett. 1975. pap. 1.25 o.p. (ISBN 0-515-03761-3). BJ Pub Group.
Today Is Tonight: A Novel. Foreword by Arthur Landau. Introd. by Ezra Goodman. Jean Harlow. LC 65-23416. 1965. 5.00. Grove.
Today Is Yours. Emilie Baker Loring. 1938. Little, Brown and Company.
Today Is Yours. Emilie Baker Loring. LC 43-103052. 1943. The Sun Dial Press.
Today the Sun Rises. Eileen Jeanette Lyttle Garrett. LC 42-21968. 1942. Creative Age Press.
Today We Choose Faces. Roger Zelazny. LC 78-14249. (Gregg Press science fiction series). 1978. 10.00 (ISBN 0-8398-2407-6). Gregg Press.
Today We Choose Faces. Roger Zelazny. (Signet book, Q5435). 1973. (pbk) 0.95. New American Library.
Today, We're Free! 1st Ed. Rossie C Allen. LC 54-100235. 1954. Pageant Preses.
Today's Children: A Story of Modern American Life. Pillsbury Flour Mills Co., Minneapolis. LC 37-137085. Pillsbury Flour Mills Company.
Today's Frontier: The Oregon Country. 1st Ed. Iva Baker Wilson. LC 53-12704. 1953. Pageant Press.
Today's Game: A Novel. Martin Peter Quigley. LC 65-16901. 1965. Viking Press.
Today's Stories from Seventeen: A Fiction Anthology. Ed. by Babette Rosmond. LC 76-165096. 1971. 5.95. Macmillan.
Today's Virtue. Faith Baldwin Cuthrell. LC 31-607991. 1931. Dodd, Mead & Company.
Todd Dossier. Collier Young. LC 70-84908. 1969. 4.95. Delacorte Press.
Toddie: The Romance of a Woman Hater. Gilbert Watson. LC 11-241293. 1911. The Century Co.
Toddler on the Run: A Novel. Shena Mackay. LC 66-113382. 1966. 2.95. S. & S.
Toe: And Other Tales. Alexander Harvey. LC 73-125215. (Short story index reprint series). 1970. Books for Libraries Press.
Toe: And Other Tales. Alexander Harvey. LC 13-26608. 1913. 1.25. M. Kennerley.
Toff Among the Millions. John Creasey. LC 76-13798. 1976. 6.95 (ISBN 0-8027-5349-3). Walker.
Toff and Old Harry. John Creasey. LC 73-126117. 1970. 4.95. Walker.
Toff and the Curate. John Creasey. LC 71-86399. 1969. 4.50. Walker.
Toff & the Deadly Parson. John Creasey. 1970. pap. 0.75 o.p. (ISBN 0-447-74674-X). Lancer.
Toff and the Deep Blue Sea. John Creasey. LC 67-13219. 1967. Walker.
Toff and the Fallen Angels. John Creasey. LC 73-103384. 1970. 4.50. Walker.
Toff and the Golden Boy. John Creasey. LC 69-15716. 1969. 4.50. Walker.
Toff and the Great Illusion. John Creasey. LC 67-23648. 1967. Walker.
Toff and the Kidnapped Child: 1st Amer. Ed. John Creasey. LC 65-18633. 1965. bds. 3.50. Walker.
Toff and the Lady. John Creasey. LC 75-24718. 1975. 6.95 (ISBN 0-8027-5336-1). Walker.
Toff and the Runaway Bride. John Creasey. 1973. Popular Lib.
Toff & the Sleepy Cowboy. John Creasey. LC 74-21731. 1974. 5.95 o.p. (ISBN 0-8027-5313-2). Walker & Co.
Toff and the Sleepy Cowboy: The 56th Book of the Toff. John Creasey. LC 74-21731. 1975. 5.95 (ISBN 0-8027-5313-2). Walker.
Toff and the Spider. John Creasey. (R-1815). 1968. Pyramid.
Toff and the Spider. John Creasey. LC 66-12662., C.
Toff and the Stolen Tresses. John Creasey. LC 65-14362. 1973. (445-01583-075) 0.75. Popular Library.
Toff and the Stolen Tresses: First Amer. Ed. John Creasey. LC 65-14362. 1965. bds., 3.50. Walker.
Toff and the Terrified Taxman. John Creasey. LC 73-83307. 1973. 5.95 (ISBN 0-8027-5281-0). Walker.
Toff and the Toughs. John Creasey. LC 68-14001. 1968. 3.95. Walker.
Toff and the Trip-Trip-Triplets. John Creasey. LC 72-80532. 1972. 4.95 (ISBN 0-8027-5264-0). Walker.
Toff at Butlin's. John Creasey. LC 76-24556. (Illus.). 1976. 6.95 (ISBN 0-8027-5358-2). Walker.
Toff at the Fair. John Creasey. LC 68-27370. 1968. 3.95. Walker.
Toff Down Under. John Creasey. LC 77-86395. 1969. 4.50. Walker.
Toff Goes to Market. John Creasey. LC 67-23647. 1967. bds., 3.95. Walker.
Toff in New York. u.s. ed. John Creasey. LC 64-55927. 1964. Pyramid Books.
Toff in Town. rev. ed. John Creasey. LC 77-80630. 1977. 6.95 (ISBN 0-8027-5380-9). Walker.
Toff in Wax. John Creasey. LC 66-16922. bds., 3.50. Walker.
Toff in Wax. John Creasey. (R1801). 1968. Pyramid.
Toff Is Back. John Creasey. LC 73-93928. 175p. 1974. 5.95 o.p. (ISBN 0-8027-5295-0). Walker & Co.
Toff on Board. rev. ed. John Creasey. LC 72-95759. 1973. 4.95 (ISBN 0-8027-5270-5). Walker.
Toff on Fire. John Creasey. LC 66-24076. 1966. Walker.
Toff Proceeds. John Creasey. LC 68-13570. 1968. Walker.
Toff Takes Shares. John Creasey. 1972. 4.95 o.p. (ISBN 0-8027-5244-6). Walker & Co.
Together. Margaretta Brucker. LC 45-905299. 1945. Arcadia House, Inc.
Together. Robert Herrick. LC 62-5384. (Premier classics of American realism, (181). 1962. Fawcett Publications.
Together. Robert Herrick. LC 72-84657. 1976. (ISBN 0-403-03198-2). Scholarly Press.
Together. Robert Herrick. LC 8-20019. 1908. The Macmillan Company.
Together. Robert Herrick. LC 16-6612. 1913. The Macmillan Company.
Together. Hugh Phillips. LC 28-14002. 1928. D. Appleton and Company.
Together. Ellen Roddick. LC 78-21362. 8.95 (ISBN 0-312-80768-6). St. Martin's Press.
Together. Ellen Roddick. 1980. 2.25 (ISBN 0-671-83278-6). Pocket Books.
Together Again. Helen Grace Carlisle. LC 30-31038. J. Cape & H. Smith.
Together Again. Janet Doran. LC 43-11963. 1943. Gramercy Publishing Company.
Together Again. Flora Kidd. (Harlequin Romance Ser.). (Orig.). 1979. pap. 1.50 (ISBN 0-373-70827-0). Harlequin Bks.
Together and Apart. Margaret Kennedy. LC 37-4385. Random House.
Together Brothers. Jim Robinson. (O.s.i.). 160p. (Orig.). 1974. pap. 0.95 o.s.i. (AN1272, Award). Univ Pub & Dist.
Together for Good. Ann Harvey. LC 40-11868. 1940. Wm. B. Eerdmans Publishing Co.
Together Reader's Choice Treasury. Selected by the Readers and Editors of Together Magazine. Intro. by Leland D. Case. Leland Davidson Case. (SP410) Bible.). 1965. Popular Lib.
Together We'll Do It. Dorothy Clark Haskin. LC 58-627. Zondervan Pub. House.
Toil & Trouble. 2nd ed. Thomas Brooks. (O.s.i.). 1971. 10.95 o.s.i. (ISBN 0-440-08975-1). Delacorte.
Toil of Men. I Querido. Tr. by Arnold, F. S. LC 9-32366. 1909. G. P. Putnam's Sons.
Toil of the Brave. Inglis Clark Fletcher. LC 52-976. 1951. Garden City Books.
Toil of the Brave. Inglis Clark Fletcher. LC 77-16344. 1976-1977. 15.95 (ISBN 0-89244-010-4). Queens House.
Toil of the Brave. Inglis Clark Fletcher. LC 46-19480. 1946. The Bobbs-Merrill Company.
Toilers and Idlers: A Novel. John Robert McMahon. LC 7-33200. Wilshire Book Company.
Toilers of Babylon: A Novel. Benjamin Leopold Farjeon. LC 6-387633. (On cover: Harper's Franklin square library. no. 638). 1889. Harper & Brothers.
Toilers of the Hills. Vardis Fisher. LC 28-23667. 1928. Houghton Mifflin Company.
Toilers of the Hills. Vardis Fisher. LC 34-75. 1933. The Caxton Printers, Ltd.
Toilers of the Sea. library ed.... ed. Victor Marie Hugo. LC 7-5849. 1888. Little, Brown, and Company.
Toilers of the Sea. Victor Marie Hugo. Tr. by Isabel Florence Hapgood. LC 4-16884. T. Y. Crowell & Co.
Toilers of the Sea. Victor Marie Hugo. (On cover: Sea and shore series, no. 35). 1891. Street & Smith.
Toilers of the Sea. Victor Marie Hugo. LC 41-200879. T. Nelson and Sons.
Toilers of the Sea. Victor Marie Hugo & Thomas, William Moy, 1828-1910, Tr. LC 21-20582. (Lettered on cover: Victor Hugo's novels. vol. iii). 1886. G. Routledge and Sons.
Toilers of the Sea. Victor Marie Hugo & Thomas, William Moy, 1828-1910, Tr. (On cover: Seaside library. Pocket ed., no. 2149). 1895. G. Munro's Sons.
Toilers of the Sea. Victor Marie Hugo & Thomas, William Moy, 1828-1910, Tr. (Half title: Everyman's library, ed. by Ernest Rhys. Fiction. no. 509). 1911. J. M. Dent & Sons, Ltd.
Toilers of the Sea. A Novel. Victor Marie Hugo. LC 7-5847. 1866. Harper & Brothers.
Toilers of the Sea. A Novel. Victor Marie Hugo. LC 7-5848. Harper & Brothers.
Toilers of the Trails. George Tracy Marsh. LC 22-533. 1921. The Penn Publishing Company.
Toiling and Hoping: The Story of the Little Hunchback. Jenny Marsh. 1856. Derby and Jackson.
Toinette. A Novel. Albion Winegar Tourgee. 1874. J. B. Ford and Company.
Token. Louis Tracy. LC 24-10301. E. J. Clode.
Token of Evil. Elizabeth Grayson. 192p. 1974. pap. 0.95 o.p. (ISBN 0-532-95356-8). Woodhill.
Token of Evil. Elizabeth Grayson. 192p. 1974. pap. 0.95 o.p. (ISBN 0-532-95356-8). Manor Bks.
Tokolosh. Illustrated by David Marais. London. Ronald Segal. LC 62-37638. 1960. Sheed and Ward.
Tokyo Romance. Earnest Hoberecht. LC 47-30828. 1947. Didier.
Tokyo Undercover. Dan Ivan. Ed. by Rick Shively. LC 75-24804. (Ser. F1-2). (Illus.). 1976. pap. text ed. 3.50 o.p. (ISBN 0-89750-056-3). Ohara Pubns.

Tola. Anna Walker Robinson. LC 47-11125. 1947. W. A. Wilde Co.
Tolbecken. 1st Ed. Samuel Shellabarger. LC 56-10651. 1956. Little, Brown.
Told After Supper. Jerome Klapka Jerome. LC 7-9922. (On Cover: Altemus' Idle Hour Series, No. 2). H. Altemus.
Told Around the Campfire. Henry Van Hoevenbergh. LC 68-553. (Illus.). 1967. North Country Books.
Told at Tuxedo. A. M Emory. LC 6-37826. 1887. G. P. Putnam's Sons.
Told by an Idiot. Rose Macaulay. LC 24-289427. Boni and Liveright.
Told by the Camp Fire. Frank Hobart Cheley. LC 14-9283. 1914. 0.75. Association Press.
Told by the Colonel. William Livingston Alden. LC 72-166644. (Illus.). 1971. (ISBN 0-403-01435-2). Scholarly Press.
Told by the Colonel. William Livingston Alden. LC 6-498. 1893. J. S. Tati & Sons.
Told by the Death's Head: A Romantic Tale. Mor Jokai. Tr. by Boggs, Sara Elisabeth (Siegrist) LC 2-17857. 1902. The Saalfield Publishing Company.
Told by Two: A Romance of Bermuda. Harriet Louise Lynch. LC 11-20585. M. A. Donohue & Co.
Told by Uncle Remus: New Stories of the Old Plantation. Joel Chandler Harris. LC 76-39087. (Black Heritage Library Collection). (Illus.). 1972. (ISBN 0-8369-9025-0). Books for Libraries Press.
Told in a French Garden, August, 1914. Mildred Aldrich. LC 76-110176. (Short story index reprint series). (Illus.). 1970. Books for Libraries Press.
Told in a French Garden, August, 1914. Mildred Aldrich. LC 16-230861. 1916. Small, Maynard & Company.
Told in Norway: An Introduction to Modern Norwegian Fiction. Ed. by Hanna Astrup Larsen. LC 72-3366. (Series: Scandinavian Classics, V. 29.). (Short story index reprint series). 1972. (ISBN 0-8369-4152-7). Books for Libraries Press.
Told in Norway: An Introduction to Modern Norwegian Fiction. Ed. by Hanna Astrup Larsen. Tr. by Orbeck, Anders. LC 28-5982. (Half-title: Scandinavian classics, vol. xxix). 1927. The American-Scandinavian Foundation.
Told in the Coffee House. Turkish Tales. Cyrus Adler & Ramsay, Allan, Joint Author. LC 5-42180. 1898. The Macmillan Company.
Told in the East. Talbot Mundy. LC 20-21184. The Bobbs-Merrill Company.
Told in the Hills. Marah Ellis Martin Ryan. LC 4-35660. 1891. Rand, McNally & Company.
Told in the Rockies. A Pen Picture of the West. Anna Maynard Barbour. LC 6-7215. Rand, McNally & Company.
Told in the Smoker. James Perry Johnston. LC 8-27498. Thompson & Thomas.
Told in the Twilight. LC 12-3600. 1912. Benziger Brothers.
Told in Whispers: From the Lately Discovered Mss. of Lawrence Fleet, D.C.L. Leigh Hadley Irvine. (On cover: The Crown library. v. 3, no. 1). The Crown Pub. Co.
Told on the King's Highway. Eleanore Myers Jewett & Lawson, Marie (Abrams) Illus. LC 43-173958. 1943. The Viking Press.
Told Out of School. Abraham B. Shiffrin. LC 38-29561. 1938. Little, Brown and Company.
Told with a Drum. Edward Harris Heth. LC 37-2317. 1937. Houghton Mifflin Company.
Toledo Bend. Sam Mims. LC 74-186988. 1972. 6.95 (ISBN 0-911116-57-5); pap. 4.95 (ISBN 0-911116-70-2). Pelican.
Tolerance. Lincoln Potter. LC 32-15194. The Christopher Publishing House.
Toleration: A Novel. Andreas Christian Nygaard. LC 9-14214. 1909. R. G. Badger.
Tolkien. John Ronald Reuel Tolkien. (Includes: The Hobbit, The Fellowship Of The Ring, The Two Towers, The Return Of The King). 1982. pap. 10.00 boxed set (ISBN 0-345-27493-8). Ballantine.
Tolkien Compass. Ed. by Jared Lobdell. LC 74-20681. 1975. 18.50 (ISBN 0-87548-316-X); pap. 6.50 (ISBN 0-87548-303-8). Open Court.
Tolkien Reader: By J. R. R. Tolkien. 1st Ed. John Ronald Reuel Tolkien. LC 66-806566. 1966. Ballantine.
Toll. Marie Louise Fowler. LC 40-313378. 1938. House of Field, Inc.
Toll. Michael Mewshaw. LC 73-14804. 1974. 6.95. Random House.
Toll Bar. Annie Edith Foster Jameson. LC 12-15638. 1912. G. P. Putnam's Sons.
Toll for the Brave. by jack higgins. ed. Henry Patterson. (Fawcett Gold Medal Book). 1976. (pbk.) 1.50. Fawcett.
Toll-Gate. Georgette Heyer. LC 54-104832. 1954. Putnam.
Toll-Gate. 2d american ed. Georgette Heyer. LC 72-79523. 1972. 6.95 (ISBN 0-399-11029-1). Putnam.
Toll House Murder. Robert McNair Wilson. LC 35-159927. J. B. Lippincott Company.
Toll Mountain. Robert J McCaig. LC 53-852659. (Silver star westerns). 1953. Dodd, Mead.
Toll of the Bush. William Satchell. LC 6-16643. 1905. Macmillan and Co., Limited.
Toll of the Road. Marion Hill. LC 18-9883. 1918. D. Appleton and Company.
Toll of the Sands. Paul De Laney. LC 20-1. The Smith-Brooks Printing Company.
Toll of the Sea. Roy Norton. LC 9-16419. 1909. D. Appleton and Company.
Toll of Victory. Annette Reid. LC 79-144169. (Short story index reprint series). 1971. (ISBN 0-8369-3784-8). Books for Libraries Press.
Toll of Victory... Annette Reid. LC 27-11035. 1926. D. Appleton and Company.
Tolla: A Tale of Modern Rome. Edmond Francois Valentin About. LC 9-2690. 1836. Whittemore, Niles, and Hall.
Tollenkar's Lair. (Fantasy Trip Ser.). 1980. pap. write for info. (ISBN 0-88074-500-2). Metagam.
Tolliver on the Trail. Charles Stanley Strong. LC 47-6260. 1947. Phoenix Press.
Tollivers. Mateel Howe Farnham. LC 44-8362. 1944. Dodd, Mead & Company.
Tolstoy's Tales of Courage and Conflict. Tolstoi, Lev Nikolaevich. Ed. by Neider, Charles. LC 58-5957. 1958. Hanover House.
Toltec Cup: A Romance of Immediate Life in New York City. Andrew Carpenter Wheeler. 1890. L. Vanderpoole Publishing Company.
Tom. Don Prince. LC 40-145378. J. Messner, Inc.
Tom Akerley: His Adventures in the Tall Timber and at Gaspard's Clearing on the Indian River. Roberts Theodore Goodridge. 1923. L. C. Page and Company (Incorporated.
Tom and Jerry: Or, The Double Detectives. Harlan Page Halsey. LC 7-1175. (secret service sereis, no. 15). 1889. Street & Smith.
Tom and Joe. Two Farmer Boys in War and Peace and Love. A Louisiana Memory. Clarence B Collins. 1890. E. Waddey.
Tom and Kitty: A Story of Mobile Bay. Prescott Alphonso Parker. LC 8-37355. P. A. Parker.
Tom and Sylvia: Or, How to Live in Style on Twenty-Five Hundred a Year. Thomas Murray. LC 7-31822. Evening Post Job Print.
Tom and the Squatter's Son: A Stirring Tale of Adventures in the Pioneer Days for Boys from 7 to 60. Opie Percival Read. LC 10-52198. 0.50. Laird & Lee.
Tom Anderson, Dare-Devil: A Young Virginain in the Revolution. Edward Mostyn Lloyd. LC 16-22901. 1916. 1.50. Houghton Mifflin Company.
Tom Barber: Young Tom, The Retreat and Uncle Stephen. Forrest Reid, pseud. LC 55-10277. 1955. Pantheon Books.
Tom Beauling. Gouverneur Morris. LC 1-25455. 1901. The Century Co.
Tom Blinn's Temperance Society: And Other Tales. Timothy Shay Arthur. LC 6-3423. 1870. National Temperance Society and Publication House.
Tom Bone. Charles Burnet Judah. LC 44-5210. 1944. W. Morrow & Company.
Tom Brown at Oxford. new ed. Thomas Hughes. 1881. Macmillan and Co.
Tom Brown at Oxford. new ed. Thomas Hughes. LC 3-27257. 1889. Macmillan and Co.
Tom Brown at Oxford, 3 vols. in 2. Thomas Hughes. LC 79-8137. Repr. of 1861 ed. Set. 84.50 (ISBN 0-404-61927-4). Vol. 1 (ISBN 0-404-61928-2). Vol. 2 (ISBN 0-404-61929-0). AMS Pr.
Tom Brown at Oxford: A Sequel to School Days at Rugby. Thomas Hughes. LC 7-5418. 1861. Ticknor and Fields.
Tom Brown at Oxford: A Sequel to School Days at Rugby. Thomas Hughes. LC 27-136548. (On cover: Oxford edition). Lovell, Coryell & Company.
Tom Brown's School Days. Thomas Hughes. 1881. Macmillan and Co.
Tom Brown's School-Days. Thomas Hughes. LC 4-17295. 1902. Macmillan and Co., Limited.
Tom Brown's Schooldays. Ed. by M. W. and G. Thomas. Illus. by Ernest Shepard. Thomas Hughes. Ed. by Maurice Walton Thomas & Gladys Thomas. LC 66-6331. (Shorter classics). 1965. bds., 2.50. Ginn.
Tom Burke of "Ours,". Charles James Lever. LC 41-29095. G. Routledge and Sons.
Tom Burke of "Ours.". Charles James Lever. LC 8-77042. G. Munro's Sons.
Tom Burke of "Ours". Charles James Lever. LC 16-70086. G. Routledge and Sons.
Tom Burke of "Ours.". Charles James Lever. LC 4-16547. (On cover: Military novels). 1901. Little, Brown and Company.
Tom Burke of "Ours,". Charles James Lever. LC 45-45010. G. Routledge and Sons.
Tom Burke of "Ours." A Novel. Charles James Lever. (Seaside library, v. 15, no. 296). 1878. G. Munro.
Tom Burton: Or, The Days of '61. Nathaniel James Walter Le Cato. LC 7-12779. Belford, Clarke & Company.
Tom Chips. Inje Elidert Dickenga & Ashworth, T. M. LC 6-36829. 1871. J. B. Lippincott & Co.
Tom Clingstone's Letters to the Editor. Benjamin Franklin Cobb & Bar Association of Dallas. LC 6600. 1900. The Radford Review Co.
Tom Cringle's Log. new ed. Michael Scott. LC 8-2909. (On cover: Lovell's library. v. 4, no. 171). 1883. J. W. Lovell Company.
Tom Cringle's Log. Michael Scott. LC 4-15332. 1895. Macmillan and Co.
Tom Cringle's Log. Michael Scott. LC 99-4992. (Famous novels of the sea). 1899. Charles Scribner's Sons.
Tom Cringle's Log. Michael Scott. (Half-title: Everyman's library, ed. by Ernest Rhys. Fiction). J. M. Dent & Sons, Ltd.
Tom Cringle's Log. Michael Scott. McFee, William. LC 27-21144. 1927. Dodd, Mead and Company.
Tom Croly's Word. George W Hamilton. LC 7-95020. The Standard Publishing Co.
Tom Fool. Fryniwyd Tennyson Jesse. LC 26-27437. 1926. A. A. Knopf.
Tom Grogan. Francis Hopkinson Smith & Reinhart, Charles Stanley, 1844-1896, Illus. 1900. Houghton, Mifflin and Company.
Tom Hanson, the Avenger: A Tale of the Backwoods: Embracing the History, Legends, and Romance of the "Country Around the Head of the Ohio"... Samuel Young. LC 9-2216. 1847. J. W. Cook.
Tom Harris. Stefan Themerson. LC 68-12672. 1968. Knopf.
Tom Henry of Wahoo County: A Story of the Ozarks. Henry Hamby. LC 11-19413. 1911. The Westminster Press.
Tom Horn. Tom Horn. (Orig.). 1980. pap. 1.75 o.s.i. (ISBN 0-505-51563-6). Tower Bks.
Tom Huston's Transformation. 2d ed. Margaret Brown Love. LC 1-30117. The Abbey Press.
Tom Johnson. Robert L Rogers. LC 48-445433. F. T. Neely.
Tom Jones. Henry Fielding. (YA) 1950. pap. 4.50x (ISBN 0-394-30915-4, T15, Mod LibC). Modern Lib.
Tom Jones. Henry Fielding. pap. 2.95 (ISBN 0-451-51634-6, CE1634, Sig Classics). NAL.
Tom Jones. Henry Fielding. Ed. by Reg Mutter. (English Library Ser.). 1966. pap. 3.95 (ISBN 0-14-043009-1). Penguin.
Tom Jones. Henry Fielding. (O.s.i.). pap. 1.25 o.s.i. (ISBN 0-671-48137-1). WSP.
Tom Jones. Henry Fielding. 1982. Repr. lib. bdg. 23.95x (ISBN 0-89966-398-2). Buccaneer Bks.
Tom Jones. Henry Fielding. 1982. pap. 10.00x (ISBN 0-330-20027-5, Pub. by Pan Bks). State Mutual Bk.
Tom Jones. Henry Fielding. 2.95 o.p. (185). Modern Lib.
Tom Jones. Henry Fielding. (Illus.). 1964. boxed 10.00 o.p. (ISBN 0-394-44898-7). Random.
Tom Jones. Henry Fielding. gift classic 9.95 o.p. (ISBN 0-00-423529-0, CL529). Collins Pubs.
Tom Jones: An Authoritative Text, Contemporary Reactions, Criticism. Henry Fielding. Ed. by Sheridan Warren Baker. LC 72-7320. (Norton critical edition). 1973. 17.50 (ISBN 0-393-04359-2) (ISBN 0-393-04359-2). Norton.
Tom Mix Died for Your Sins. Darryl Ponicsan. (Dell Book). 1979. 1.95. Dell Pub. Co.
Tom Mix Died for Your Sins: A Novel Based on His Life. Darryl Ponicsan. LC 75-15555. (Illus.). 1975. 8.95 (ISBN 0-440-05969-0). Delacorte Press.
Tom Northway. Marshall Terry. LC 68-12600. 1968. Harcourt, Brace & World.
Tom Roper:: a Story of Travel and Adventure. Samuel Greene Wheeler Benjamin. LC 7-3438. Daughaday & Becker.
Tom Sawyer... Samuel Langhorne Clemens. LC 47-15248. 1946.
Tom Sawyer. Samuel Langhorne Clemens & Berglund, Albert Olaf. LC 49-49011. 1949. Scott, Foresman.
Tom Sawyer. Mark Twain. Incl. Huckleberry Finn. 1954. 6.00x o.p. (ISBN 0-460-00976-1, Evman); pap. 3.25 o.p. (ISBN 0-460-01976-7, EP1976, Evman). Dutton.
Tom Sawyer. Mark Twain. Bd. with Huckleberry Finn. (Standard Classic Ed). 4.95 o.p. (ISBN 0-00-421669-5, JC669). Collins-World.
Tom Sawyer Abroad. Samuel Langhorne Clemens. LC 67-16065. (Golden Press classics library). 1967. Golden Press.
Tom Sawyer Abroad. Samuel Langhorne Clemens & Mark Twain. (Golden Press classics library). (Illus.). 1967. Golden Press.
Tom Sawyer Abroad. Mark Twain. Bd. with Tom Sawyer, Detective. LC 81-40325. (Mark Twain Library). (Illus.). 160p. 1982. 13.50 (ISBN 0-520-04560-2); pap. 2.95 (ISBN 0-520-04561-0, CAL 557). U of Cal Pr.
Tom Sawyer Abroad. Mark Twain. Bd. with Tom Sawyer Detective. 1962. pap. 0.65 o.p. (04571, Collier). Macmillan.
Tom Sawyer Abroad, and Tom Sawyer, Detective: By Mark Twain Pseud Illus. by Gerald McCann. Samuel Langhorne Clemens. (Laurel leaf lib., 8943). Dell.
Tom Sawyer Abroad, and Tom Sawyer, Detective: By Mark Twain Pseud. Illustrated by Gerald McCann. Samuel Langhorne Clemens. LC 62-21645. 1962. Collier Books.
Tom Sawyer Abroad: By Huck Finn Pseud. Ed. by Mark Twain Pseud. with Illustrations by Dan Beard. Samuel Langhorne Clemens. LC 6-21351. 1894. C. S. Webster & Company.
Tom Sawyer Abroad: By Mark Twain. Illus. by Gerald McCann. Samuel Langhorne Clemens. LC 65-17196. (Companion lib. of classics). 1965. 1.25. Grosset.
Tom Sawyer Abroad. Tom Sawyer, Detective, and Other Stories, Etc., Etc. Samuel Langhorne Clemens. LC 7-3332. 1896. Harper & Brothers.
Tom Sawyer Abroad: Tom Sawyer, Detective, and Other Stories, Etc., Etc. Samuel Langhorne Clemens. LC 28-16813. 1917. Harper & Brothers.
Tom Sawyer & Huckelberry Finn. Mark Twain. 1982. pap. 10.00x (ISBN 0-330-30046-6, Pub. by Pan Bks). State Mutual Bk.
Tom Sawyer & Huckleberry Finn. Mark Twain. 1972. 9.95x (ISBN 0-460-00976-1, Evman); pap. 2.25x (ISBN 0-460-01976-7, Evman). Biblio Dist.
Tom Sawyer & Huckleberry Finn. Mark Twain. 1954. 6.00x o.p. (ISBN 0-460-00976-1, Evman); pap. 3.95 o.p. (ISBN 0-460-01976-7, Evman). Biblio Dist.
Tom Sawyer Comes Home. Dorothy Hight Richardson Kissling. LC 73-78123. 1973. 7.95 (ISBN 0-913676-02-0). Traumwald Press.
Tom Sawyer Comes Home. Dorothy Langley. LC 73-78123. 1973. 7.95 (ISBN 0-913676-02-0). Traumwald Pr.
Tom Sawyer, Detective see Tom Sawyer Abroad.
Tom Sawyer Detective, and Other Stories. Samuel Langhorne Clemens. (Companion library). 1961. Grosset & Dunlap.
Tom Sawyer, Detective: By Mark Twain. Illus. by Gerald McCann. Samuel Langhorne Clemens. LC 65-17197. (Companion lib.). 1965. 1.25. Grosset.
Tom Sawyer Grows up. Clement Wood. LC 39-207758. The World Syndicate Publishing Company.
Tom Sawyer Tycoon. Hazel Bussey. LC 78-65542. 55p. 1980. 4.95 (ISBN 0-533-04094-9). Vantage.
Tom Swindel: Or, The Adventures of a Boomer. John Lewis Peyton. LC 7-36155. 1893. G. L. Bolen.
Tom Sylvester: A Novel. Thomas Russell Sullivan. LC 8-17661. 1893. C. Scribner's Sons.
Tom the Young Explorer: Or, A Magnificent Reward. A Tale to Read. Harlan Page Halsey. LC 98-355. (Old Sleuth's own, no. 109). 1898. The Parlor Car Pub. Co.
Tom Thumb: The Tragedy of Tragedies. rev. & enl. ed. Henry Fielding. 1974. text ed. 15.00x o.s.i. (ISBN 0-8277-3829-3); pap. text ed. 6.95x o.s.i. (ISBN 0-8277-2192-7). British Bk Ctr.
Tom Tiddler's Ground. Edward Shanks. LC 34-22372. The Bobbs-Merrill Company.
Tom-Toms Speak. Alfred Lo Cascio. LC 40-10772. 1940. Meador Publishing Company.
Tom Tracy: The Trials of a New York Newsboy. Horatio Alger, Jr. (Illus.). 208p. 1978. Repr. of 1888 ed. 21.00. G K Westgard.
Tom-Walker: A New Novel. Mari Sandoz. LC 47-304093. 1947. Dial Press.
Tom Wilkins: A Story of School Management and Supervision. Jesse Thomas Gibbs. LC 14-114. 1913. 0.75. J. T. Gibbs.
Tomahawk. Lee Deighton. 156p. 1981. pap. 1.75 (ISBN 0-345-29431-9). Ballantine.
Tomahawk. Donald Clayton Porter. LC 83-166. (White Indian series; bk. 6). ((Series: Porter, Donald Clayton.). (Colonization of America series; bk. 6.). 1983. 18.95 (ISBN 0-8161-3451-0). G.K. Hall.
Tomahawk. (White Indian Ser.: No. 6). 1981. pap. 3.95. Bantam.
Tomahawk: By Lee Leighton Pseud. Wayne D Overholser. LC 58-8344. (Ballantine books, 255). 1958. Ballantine Books.
Tomahawk Rights. Hal George Evarts. LC 29-141049. 1929. Little, Brown, and Company.
Tomalyn's Quest: A Novel. George Brown Burgin. LC 6-18658. 1897. Harper & Brothers.
Tomaso's Fortune: And Other Stories. Hugh Stowell Scott. LC 4-77083. 1904. C. Scribner's Sons.
Tomatoes in the Treetops: Collected Tales of Harry Rhine. Ben E. Kitchens. LC 82-16980. 73p. 1982. pap. 5.95 (ISBN 0-943054-39-7). Thornwood Bk.
Tomb & Other Tales. Howard Phillips Lovecraft. 1982. pap. 2.25 (ISBN 0-345-30230-3, Del Rey). Ballantine.
Tomb & Other Tales. Howard Phillips Lovecraft. (Orig.). 1971. pap. 0.95 o.p. (95032-095). Beagle Bks.

Tomb for Boris Davidovic: A Novel. Danilo Kis. LC 77-15004. 1978. 6.95. Harcourt Brace Jovanovich.
Tomb for Boris Davidovich. Danilo Kis. (Penguin Writers from the Other Europe Ser.). 1980. pap. 3.95 (ISBN 0-14-005452-9). Penguin.
Tomb of the Twelfth Imam. Richard W Bulliet. LC 79-1800. 10.00 (ISBN 0-06-010519-4). Harper & Row.
Tombolo. Nicholas Fersen. LC 53-9252. 1954. Houghton Mifflin.
Tomboy Bride. Harriet F. Backus. LC 79-80764. (Illus.). 1977. pap. 6.50 (ISBN 0-87108-512-7). Pruett.
Tomboy in Lace. Berta Ruck. LC 47-366179. 1947. Dodd, Mead & Company.
Tomboy. With an Introd. by Fredric Wertham. Hal Ellson. LC 50-8423. 1950. Scribner.
Tombs of Atuan. Ursula K. Le Guin. 160p. 1975. pap. 2.50 (ISBN 0-553-14946-6, B13594-5). Bantam.
Tombs of Blue Ice. Ron Faust. LC 74-6523. (Black bat mystery). 6.50 (ISBN 0-672-52011-7). Bobbs-Merrill.
Tombstone. Matthew Braun. 224p. 1981. pap. 1.95 (ISBN 0-671-82033-8). PB.
Tombstone, Arizona Silver Camp. Robert L. Spude. (Illus.). 1979. 1.95 (ISBN 0-913814-23-7). Nevada Pubns.
Tombstone for a Trouble-Shooter. William C. MacDonald. 1982. 18.00x (ISBN 0-86025-173-X, Pub. by Ian Henry Pubns England). State Mutual Bk.
Tombstone for a Trouble Shooter. William C. MacDonald. 1978. pap. 1.25 o.s.i. (ISBN 0-505-51308-0). Tower Bks.
Tombstone for a Troubleshooter. William C. MacDonald. 1969. pap. 0.60 o.p. (B60-1025). Belmont-Tower.
Tombstone for a Troubleshooter: A Gregory Quist Story. 1st Ed. William Colt MacDonald. LC 60-6462. 1960. Lippincott.
Tombstone Pistollers. Graham Cassidy. Phoenix Press.
Tombstone Showdown. Leslie Scott. LC 57-9797. 1957. Arcadia House.
Tombstone Stage. William L Hopson. LC 48-10100. 1948. Phoenix Press.
Tombstone Trail. Ray Hogan. (Shawn Starbuck). (Signet brard western: Vol. 17). 1974. (pbk.) 0.95. New American Library.
Tombstone. 1st Ed. Clarence Budington Kelland. LC 53-5373. 1953. Harper.
Tomcat. Thom Racina. (Orig.). 1981. pap. 2.95 (ISBN 0-441-81651-7). Ace Bks.
Tomcat in Tights. Jack Hanley. LC 36-117338. Godwin.
Tomek, the Sculptor. Adelaide Eden Phillpotts. LC 27-3150. 1927. Little, Brown, and Company.
Tomfool's Pike. 1st Ed. William Kendall Clarke. LC 60-115045. 1960. Holt, Rinehart and Winston.
Tomioka Stories: From the Japanese Occupation. Martin Bronfenbrenner. 138p. 1975. 6.00 o.p. (ISBN 0-682-48150-5). Exposition.
Tommorrow's Hero. Mary Howard, pseud. LC 42-171483. 1942. Doubleday, Doran & Company, Inc.
Tommy. Chigger. 96p. 1976. 5.00 o.p. (ISBN 0-682-48185-8). Exposition.
Tommy & Co. Jerome Klapka Jerome. LC 4-24490. 1904. Dodd, Mead and Company.
Tommy and Grizel. James Matthew Barrie. LC 18-10542. 1917. C. Scribner's Sons.
Tommy and Grizel. James Matthew Barrie. LC 5652. 1900. C. Scribner's Sons.
Tommy & Grizel: A Novel. James Matthew Barrie. LC 43-51130. 1943. The Press of the Readers Club.
Tommy Atkins of the Ramchunders. Robert Blatchford. LC 6-13838. E. Arnold.
Tommy Gallagher's Crusade. James Thomas Farrell. LC 39-25041. The Vanguard Press.
Tommy Lee Feathers. Ed Bell. LC 38-10324. Farrar & Rinehart, Incorporated.
Tommy of the Voices. Reynolds Knight. LC 18-176075. 1918. 1.40. A. C. McClurg & Co.
Tommy Wideawake. Henry Howarth Bashford. LC 3-11674. 1903. John Lane.
Tommy's Money: Adventures in New York and Elsewhere. John Russell Coryell. LC 11-26250. 1911. 0.60. Harper & Brothers.
Tomoe Gozen. Jessica A. Salmonson. 272p. 1982. pap. 2.50 (ISBN 0-441-81652-5). Ace Bks.
Tomorrow! Philip Wylie. LC 53-10924. Rinehart.
Tomorrow: A Science Fiction Anthology. Ed. by Bernard C. Hollister. 124p. (Orig.). 1974. pap. 3.80 o.p. (ISBN 0-8278-0037-1, 00371); pap. text ed. 2.85 o.p. Pflaum-Standard.
Tomorrow About This Time. Grace Livingston Hill. LC 23-110803. 1923. J. B. Lippincott Company.
Tomorrow About This Time. (Grace Livingston Hill Ser: No. 52). 1978. pap. 1.95 (ISBN 0-553-14769-2, 12928-7). Bantam.
Tomorrow Achieved: A Novel. William R Furr. LC 50-16254. 1946. Chapman Publishers.
Tomorrow & Forever. Francesca Macklem. 256p. (Orig.). Date not set. pap. cancelled o.p. (ISBN 0-505-51839-2). Tower Bks.
Tomorrow & Tomorrow. Hunt Collins, pseud. 1970. pap. 0.60 o.p. (X2250). Pyramid Pubns.
Tomorrow and Tomorrow, and The Fairy Chessmen: Two Science Fiction Novels, by Lewis Padgett Pseud. 1st Ed. Henry Kuttner. LC 51-14785. Gnome Press.
Tomorrow, and Tomorrow, and Tomorrow... Ed. by Bonnie L. Heintz. LC 73-18429. 1974. 3.95 (ISBN 0-03-011806-9). Holt, Rinehart and Winston.
Tomorrow & Tomorrow & Tomorrow. Aldous Leonard Huxley. 1956. 4.95 o.p. (ISBN 0-06-012110-6, HarpT). Har-Row.
Tomorrow and Tomorrow: Ten Tales of the Future. Ed. by Damon Francis Knight. LC 73-2152. 1973. 7.95 (ISBN 0-671-65210-9). Simon and Schuster.
Tomorrow & Yesterday. Heinrich Boll. 1957. 5.95 o.p. (ISBN 0-87599-018-5). S G Phillips.
Tomorrow and Yesterday. Translated from Haus Ohne Huter. Heinrich Boll. LC 57-8261. 1957. Criterion Books.
Tomorrow Began Yesterday. Sarah Holland. (Harlequin Presents Ser.). 192p. 1982. pap. 1.75 (ISBN 0-373-10536-3). Harlequin Bks.
Tomorrow Come Sunrise. E. E. Elliott. LC 69-15273. 1970. 6.95. Harper & Row.
Tomorrow Comes Never. Eleanore Browne. 1939. Arcadia House.
Tomorrow Comes the Sun. Elizabeth Renier. 224p. 1981. pap. 1.75 (ISBN 0-441-81655-X). Ace Bks.
Tomorrow Fair. Winifred Halsted. LC 43-606. 1943. Dodd, Mead & Company.
Tomorrow File. Lawrence Sanders. LC 75-13994. 9.95 (ISBN 0-399-11511-0). Putnam.
Tomorrow File. Lawrence Sanders. (Berkley medallion book). 1976. 1.95 (ISBN 0-425-03200-0). Berkley.
Tomorrow for Sale. Helen Barham Shipman. LC 41-6945. 1941. Appellate Law Printers, Inc.
Tomorrow I Die. Mickey Spillane, pseud. LC 82-60903. 260p. 1983. 13.95 (ISBN 0-89296-061-2); write for info. limited ed. (ISBN 0-89296-062-0). Mysterious Pr.
Tomorrow I'll Be Happy. Dorothy Clark Haskin. LC 54-33268. 1954. Zondervan Pub. House.
Tomorrow, Inc. SF Stories About Big Business. Martin Harry Greenberg & Joseph D Olander. LC 76-11057. 1976. 9.95 (ISBN 0-8008-7746-2). Taplinger.
Tomorrow Is a River. Peggy Hanson Dopp & Barbara Fitz Vroman. LC 76-52054. 1978. 10.95 (ISBN 0-931762-00-6). J. Phunn.
Tomorrow Is Another Day. Henrietta Henkle. LC 34-23287. R. D. Henkle.
Tomorrow Is Another Day. Dorothy Quentin. LC 46-376956. 1946. Arcadia House, Inc.
Tomorrow Is Another Day. Annie Lucile White White. LC 42-201889. Dorrance and Company.
Tomorrow Is Another Day: A Comedy of Manners. Martha Byrd Spruill Porter. LC 52-11674. 1952. Exposition Press.
Tomorrow Is Another Day: A Novel by Anne Marie Selinko. Annemarie Selinko & Lindsay, Mary H., Tr. LC 39-31680. 1939. Alliance Book Corporation, Longmans, Green and Co.
Tomorrow Is for the Living: A Romantic Novel. 1st Ed. Thoburn Starkey. LC 55-11834. 1955. Exposition Press.
Tomorrow Is for Weeping. Judith MacEachron. LC 79-63106. 8.95 (ISBN 0-914338-04-8). Regmar Pub. Co.
Tomorrow Is Forever. Gwen Bristow. LC 43-17449. 1943. Thomas Y. Crowell Company.
Tomorrow Is Mine. Rebecca Salsbury James. LC 77-25597. 1979. 10.00 (ISBN 0-385-12675-1). Doubleday.
Tomorrow Is Murder. Carter Brown, pseud. LC 60-3142. (Signet books, S1806). 1960. New American Library of World Literature.
Tomorrow Is Ours. Louise Redfield Peattie. 1937. G. P. Putnam's Sons.
Tomorrow Is So Far from Now. David Kalugin. (Illus.). 1979. pap. 4.95 (ISBN 0-933586-01-9). Book Promo Unltd.
Tomorrow Is Theirs. Anne Duffield. 1974. (pbk.) 1.25 (ISBN 0-425-02713-9). Berkley Pub Co.
Tomorrow Is Too Far. James White. 192p. 1981. pap. 2.25 (ISBN 0-345-30153-6, Del Rey). Ballantine.
Tomorrow Is Yesterday: A Novel. Kastus Akula. LC 73-356992. (Illus.). 1968. 5.00. Pahonia Pub.
Tomorrow Knight. Michael Kurland. (Daw Science Fiction Book no. 183). 1976. (pbk.) 1.25. Daw Books.
Tomorrow Lies in Ambush. Bob Shaw. 1973. (pbk) 0.95. Ace Books.
Tomorrow May Be Even Worse. John Brunner. (Boskone Book). (Illus.). 1978. fine bound o.s.i. 43.00 (ISBN 0-915368-80-3); pap. 4.00 (ISBN 0-915368-15-3). NESFA Pr.
Tomorrow May Be Fair. Gladys Bagg Taber. LC 35-15731. Coward-McCann.
Tomorrow Might Be Different. Mack Reynolds. 1975. (pbk.) 1.25. Ace Books.
Tomorrow Never Comes. Ursula Bloom. 1979. pap. 2.25 (ISBN 0-89041-268-5, 3268). Major Bks.
Tomorrow Never Comes. Thomas Walter Gilkyson. LC 33-33265. Sears Publishing Company, Inc.
Tomorrow Never Comes: By Helen St. Bernard. Helen St. Bernard. LC 36-4462. C.
Tomorrow Now Occurs Again. Robert Gover. LC 75-6142. 1975. pap. 4.95 (ISBN 0-915520-00-1). Ross-Erikson.
Tomorrow Once Again. Edward L McKenna. LC 31-6601. Farrar & Rinehart, Incorporated.
Tomorrow Revealed. John Alfred Atkins. LC 56-8332. Roy Publishers.
Tomorrow Sometimes Comes. Elizabeth Carfrae, pseud. LC 44-510410. 1945. G. P. Putnam's Sons.
Tomorrow the Accolade... Marion Rolfe Johnson Deitrick. LC 37-38875. 1937. Doubleday, Doran and Company, Inc.
Tomorrow the Harvest. Viola Isabel Paradise. LC 52-9700. 1952. Morrow.
Tomorrow the New Moon. 1st Ed. Shirley Barker. LC 55-6820. Bobbs-Merrill.
Tomorrow, the Stars: A Science Fiction Anthology. Robert Anson Heinlein. LC 52-5218. 1952. Doubleday.
Tomorrow to Life. William Herber. LC 57-145246. 1958. Coward-McCann.
Tomorrow Today. Ed. by George Zebrowski. LC 73-82547. (Planet series, # 1). 1975. 6.95 (ISBN 0-913300-33-0) (ISBN 0-913300-31-4). Unity Press.
Tomorrow-Tomorrow. Philip Louis Gabriel. LC 72-165943. 1971. 5.95. Whitmore Pub. Co.
Tomorrow Trap. Miriam Borgenicht. LC 69-12357. 1969. 3.95. Doubleday.
Tomorrow We Part: A Novel. Gina Kaus. LC 33-36072. 1933. R. Long & R. R. Smith, Inc.
Tomorrow We Reap. James Howell Street & Childers, James Saxon. LC 49-9319. 1949. Dial Press.
Tomorrow Will Always Come. Clara Rosa De Lima. LC 65-15409. 1965. I. Obolensky.
Tomorrow Will Always Come. Clara Rosa De Lima. 1965. 7.95 (ISBN 0-8392-1141-4). Astor-Honor.
Tomorrow Will Always Come. Obolensky. Clara Rosa De Lima. LC 65-15409. bds., 4.50. World.
Tomorrow Will Be Better. large print ed. Betty Smith. LC 81-23780. 1982. 13.95 (ISBN 0-8161-3302-6). G.K. Hall.
Tomorrow Will Be Different. Larry Barretto. LC 36-7256. Farrar & Rinehart, Incorporated.
Tomorrow Will Be Fair. Rosamond Neal Du Jardin. LC 46-6025. 1946. Macrae-Smith-Company.
Tomorrow Will Be Monday. Melba Balmat Grimes Marlett. LC 46-5414. 1946. Doubleday & Company, Inc.
Tomorrow Will Be Monday: Stories About Parents and Children. Katinka Loeser. LC 64-14924. 1964. Atheneum.
Tomorrow Will Be Sunday. Harold Norwood. LC 65-19893. 1966. Doubleday.
Tomorrow Will Sing. Elliott Arnold. LC 45-1136. 1945. Duell, Sloan and Pearce.
Tomorrow You Die. Reona Peterson. 1976. 2.95. Bible Voice.
Tomorrow's Alternatives. Ed. by Roger Elwood. (O.s.i.). 192p. 1973. 5.95 o.s.i. Macmillan.
Tomorrow's Alternatives, Vol. 1. Ed. by Roger Elwood. (O.s.i.). 192p. 1973. pap. 1.50 o.s.i. (ISBN 0-02-019800-0, Collier). Macmillan.
Tomorrow's Alternatives; Original Science Fiction. Ed. by Roger Elwood. LC 73-6060. (Frontiers, 1). 1973. 1.50. Collier Books.
Tomorrow's Another Day. William Riley Burnett. LC 45-9319. 1945. A. A. Knopf.
Tomorrow's Bread. Beatrice Bisno. LC 38-2493. 1938. The Jewish Publication Society of America.
Tomorrow's Bride. Delaine Tucker. LC 81-69966. (Serenade Romance; 3). (Illus.). 2.95 (ISBN 0-671-44359-3). Wallaby Books: Distributed by Pocket Books.
Tomorrow's Children: 18 Tales of Fantasy and Science Fiction. Ed. by Isaac Asimov. LC 66-8099. (Illus.). 1966. Doubleday.
Tomorrow's Eve. Villiers De L'Isle-Adam. LC 82-13411. 17.95 (ISBN 0-252-00942-8). University of Illinois Press.
Tomorrow's Fire. Jay Williams. LC 64-22104. 1964. Atheneum.
Tomorrow's Ghost. Anthony Price. LC 78-22234. 1979. 8.95 (ISBN 0-385-14029-0). Published for the Crime Club by Doubleday.
Tomorrow's Harvest. Albert Root. 3.50 o.p. Vantage.
Tomorrow's Here. Kathryn Cotten. LC 54-13430. 1954. Naylor Co.
Tomorrow's Heritage. Juanita Coulson. (Children of the Stars Ser.: Bk. 2). 1982. pap. 2.75 (ISBN 0-345-26235-2, Del Rey). Ballantine.
Tomorrow's Horizon. George Edward Meagher. LC 47-24295. 1947. Dorrance.
Tomorrow's House: Or, The Tiny Angel. George O'Neil. LC 30-20208. 1930. E. P. Dutton & Co. Inc.
Tomorrow's Love. Kathleen Shepard. LC 33-16585. A. H. King.
Tomorrow's Memories: By Don O'Donnell Pseud. 1st Ed. Windsor Howard O'Donnell. LC 53-12638. 1953. Pageant Press.
Tomorrow's Miracle. Frank Gill Slaughter. LC 62-11427. 1962. Doubleday.
Tomorrow's Nurse. Teresa Holloway. 192p. (YA) 1973. 4.95 o.p. (Avalon). Bouregy.
Tomorrow's Promise. Temple Bailey. LC 38-22135. 1938. The Penn Publishing Company.
Tomorrow's Promise. Cecily Bowman. LC 47-30663. 1947. Arcadia House.
Tomorrow's Promise. Sandra Brown. (American Romance Ser.). 192p. 1983. pap. 2.25. Harlequin Bks.
Tomorrow's Promise. 1947. Arcadia House.
Tomorrow's Rapture. Ruth Lyons. LC 34-18692. The Macaulay Company.
Tomorrow's Roses. Peggy Gaddis, pseud. LC 36-868711. Arcadia House.
Tomorrow's Silence. Nicholas Goller. LC 79-5330. 10.00 (ISBN 0-312-80891-7). St. Martin's Press.
Tomorrow's Son. Robert Hoskins. LC 76-2782. 1977. 6.95 (ISBN 0-385-12100-8). Doubleday.
Tomorrow's Tangle. Geraldine Bonner. LC 3-25716. 1903. The Bobbs-Merrill Company.
Tomorrow's Voyage. Leonard Hess. LC 29-20655. 1929. I. Wash Burn.
Tomorrow's World. Hunt Collins, pseud. LC 56-13301. 1956. Avalon Books.
Tomorrow's World: By Hunt Collins Pseud. Evan Hunter. LC 56-13301. 1956. Avalon Books.
Tomorrow's Worlds. Robert Anson Heinlein et al. Ed. by Robert Silverberg. (O.s.i.). 1971. pap. 0.95 o.s.i. (A793N, Award). Univ Pub & Dist.
Tomorrow's Worlds. Ed. by Robert Silverberg. (O.s.i.). 1977. pap. 1.50 o.s.i. (AD1666, Award). Univ Pub & Dist.
Tomorrow's Worlds: Ten Stories of Science Fiction. Ed. by Robert Silverberg. LC 69-16298. 1969. 4.95. Meredith Press.
Tomorrow's Yesterday. Alfred Mortimer Stanley. LC 50-5018. 1949. Dorrance.
Tompkins and Other Folks: Stories of the Hudson and the Adirondacks. Philander Deming. LC 68-55673. (American short story series, v. 13). 1969. Garrett Press.
Tompkins and Other Folks: Stories of the Hudson and the Adirondacks. Philander Deming. LC 72-8157. (American short story series, v. 13). 1972. (ISBN 0-8422-8039-1). MSS Information Corp.
Tompkins: And Other Folks; Stories of the Hudson and the Adirondacks. Philander Deming. LC 6-34004. 1885. Houghton, Mifflin and Company.
Tompkinsville Folks: A Story of the Central States' Village Life. Nettie Stevens. 1909. 1.50. The C. M. Clark Publishing Company.
Tom's Heathen. Josephine R Baker. LC 6-6878. 1879. H. Hoyt & Co.
Tom's Last Forage. John Trotwood Moore. LC 26-22412. Cokesbury Press.
Tom's Wife! And How He Managed Her. George Douglas Tallman. 1877. G. W. Carleton & Co.; Etc. Etc.
Tom's Wife and How He Managed Her. George Douglas Tallman. LC 8-25563. (Dillingham's globe library, no. 12). 1896. G. W. Dillingham.
Tonda: A Story of the Sioux. Warren King Moorehead. 1904. The R. Clark Company.
Tondo for Short. Peter Inchbald. LC 81-43484. 1982. 10.95 (ISBN 0-385-18012-8). Published for the Crime Club by Doubleday.
Tone King: A Romance of the Life of Mozart. From the German of Heribert Rau... Herbert Rau. Tr. by Rae, Julia E. St. Quintin. LC 3-11819. 1900. Dodd, Mead & Company.
Tong in Cheek see Para China con Amor.
Tongking. Dan Cushman. LC 54-7025. (Ace double novel books, D-49). 1954. Ace Books.
Tongue of the Dumb. Dominic Mulaisho. (African Writers Ser.). 1971. pap. text ed. 4.00x (ISBN 0-435-90098-6). Heinemann Ed.
Tongue-Tied Canary. Nicolas Bentley. LC 49-5161. (A Bloodhound mystery). 1949. Duell, Sloan and Pearce.
Tongues of Conscience. Robert Smythe Hichens. LC 75-178440. (Short story index reprint series). 1971. (ISBN 0-8369-4041-5). Books for Libraries Press.
Tongues of Conscience. Robert Smythe Hichens. LC 5974. Frederick A. Stokes Company.
Tongues of Fallen Angels. Selden Rodman. LC 73-89485. (Illus.). 288p. 1974. 12.00 (ISBN 0-8112-0528-2); pap. 3.75 (ISBN 0-8112-0529-0, NDP373). New Directions.
Tongues of Fire. Peter Abrahams. LC 82-1390. 312p. 1982. 12.95 (ISBN 0-87131-374-X). M Evans.
Tongues of Fire: And Other Stories. Algernon Blackwood. LC 25-4769. E. P. Dutton & Company.

Tongues of Flame. Peter Clark Macfarlane. LC 24-11653. 1924. Cosmopolitan Book Corporation.
Tongues of Men. John Schultz. LC 69-13382. (A Big table book). 1969. Big Table Pub. Co.
Tongues of the Monte. J. Frank Dobie. (Illus.). 319p. 1980. pap. 6.95 (ISBN 0-292-78035-4). U of Tex Pr.
Tongues of the Moon. Philip Jose Farmer. 1978. pap. 1.50 (ISBN 0-515-04595-0). Jove Pubns.
Tongues of the Moon. Philip Jose Farmer. 1970. pap. 0.75 o.p. (T2260). Pyramid Pubns.
Toni & Her Brothers. Hammond. pap. 1.95 o.p. (ISBN 0-87056-175-8, 6175). Brandon.
Toni Diamonds. Gordon Latta. LC 31-19573. 1931. L. MacVeagh, The Dial Press.
Tonia. Iurii Pavlovich German & Garry, Stephen, Tr. LC 38-5126. 1938. A. A. Knopf.
Tonight Josephine: And Other Undiscovered Letters. Michael Green. 1982. 14.95 (ISBN 0-395-32112-3). HM.
Tonight or Never. Lewis Allen Browne & Hatvany, Lili, Barono. LC 32-144462. Grosset & Dunlap.
Tonight They Die to Mendelssohn. Fritz Gordon. (Schuyler Townsend Ser, No. 2). (O.s.i.). (Orig.). 1968. pap. 0.60 o.s.i. (A357X, Award). Univ Pub & Dist.
Tonio, Son of the Sierras: A Story of the Apache War. Charles King. LC 6-197773. 1906. G. W. Dillingham Company.
Toni's Kin-&-Sin Experiments. Clarke Hammond. pap. 1.95 o.p. (ISBN 0-87056-199-5, 6199). Brandon.
Toni's Tale. Marjorie B. McCune. 2.50 o.p. Carlton.
Tono-Bungay. Herbert George Wells. LC 59-47185. (Modern library of the world's best books, 197). 1959. Modern Library.
Tono-Bungay. Herbert George Wells. Ed. by Bergonzi, Bernard. LC 66-31882. 1966. Houghton Mifflin.
Tono-Bungay. Herbert George Wells. LC 60-23472. 1960. Printed for the Members of the Limited Editions Club.
Tono-Bungay. Herbert George Wells. LC 13-12912. 1908. Duffield & Company.
Tono-Bungay. Herbert George Wells. LC 27-16360. 1927. Duffield and Company.
Tono-Bungay. Herbert George Wells. LC 32-261567. (Half-title: The modern library of the world's best books). 1931. The Modern Library.
Tono-Bungay. Herbert George Wells. LC 77-28027. (Illus.). 1978. 13.95 (ISBN 0-8032-4702-8) (ISBN 0-8032-9701-7). University of Nebraska Press.
Tono-Bungay: A Novel. Herbert George Wells. LC 9-5520. 1909. Duffield & Company.
Tono-Bungay: A Novel. Herbert George Wells. LC 24-149332. 1923. Duffield & Company.
Tonopah Lady. Zola Helen Ross. LC 50-7205. 1950. Bobbs-Merrill.
Tonopah Nevada Silver Camp. Stanley W. Paher. (Illus.). 1978. pap. 1.95 (ISBN 0-913814-18-0). Nevada Pubns.
Tontine. Thomas Bertram Costain. 1975. (pbk.) 1.95 (ISBN 0-380-00543-3). Avon.
Tontine: A Ncvel. Thomas Bertram Costain. LC 55-9978. (Illus.). 1955. Doubleday.
Tonto Kid. Henry Herbert Knibbs. LC 36-187585. 1936. Houghton Mifflin Company.
Tonto Riley. Lee E Wells. LC 50-9570. 1950. Rinehart.
Tonto Trails. Gracie Scott Phillips. LC 50-126372. 1949. Humphries.
Tony. Stephen Hudson. LC 24-10842. 1924. A. A. Knopf.
Tony. Edward Everett Tanner. LC 65-19970. Dutton.
Tony. Elizabeth Vernon. LC 38-635029. R. M. McBride and Company.
Tony and the Revolution. Doris Overland. LC 39-5221. L. Furman, Inc.
Tony Butler. A Novel. Charles James Lever. LC 7-14478. 1865. Harper & Brothers.
Tony from America. Katharine Haviland Taylor. LC 24-391651. Harcourt, Brace and Company.
Tony: The Life & Times of a Charming Scoundrel Who Lived on Love. Patrick Dennis, pseud. 1965. 4.95 o.p. Dutton.
Tony, the Maid: A Novelette. Blanche Willis Howard Von Teuffel. LC 8-25951. 1887. Harper & Brothers.
Tony: The Story of a Waif. Laisdell Mitchell. LC 7-31100. 1894. C. H. Banes.
Tonya Baby. Jack Vast. pap. 1.95 o.p. (8038). Cameo.
Tonya. 1st Ed. Gregory Boyington. LC 60-135924. 1960. Bobbs-Merrill.
Tony's Wife. George Fort Gibbs. LC 10-95209. 1910. 1.50. D. Appleton and Company.
Too Beautiful. Sylvia Thalberg. LC 33-36945. J. Messner, Inc.C.
Too Black for Heaven. Day Keene. 1967. pap. 0.50 o.p. (50-399). Manor Bks.
Too Busy to Die. Henry Wisdom Roden. LC 44-7213. 1944. W. Morrow and Company.
Too Close Apart. Jean G. Howard, pseud. LC 77-92190. (Illus., Ltd. ed. 550 trade, 35 deluxe). 1977. 12.50 (ISBN 0-930954-01-7); deluxe ed. 50.00 (ISBN 0-930954-02-5). Tidal Pr.
Too Curious. Edward John Goodman. (On cover: Seaside library Pocket ed. no. 1081). 1888. G. Munro.
Too Dangerous. James Noble Gifford. LC 48-447899. 1948. Phoenix Press.
Too Dangerous to Be Free: By James Hadley Chase. Rene Raymond. LC 51-9949. (A Bloodhound mystery). 1951. Duell, Sloan and Pearce.
Too Dear for My Possessing. Pamela Hansford Johnson. LC 40-120333. 1940. Carrick and Evans, Inc.
Too Dear for My Possessing: A Novel. Pamela Hansford Johnson. LC 72-2007. 1973. 7.95 (ISBN 0-684-13052-1). Scribner.
Too Deep, Too Late. S. W. Karl. 1978. pap. 1.25 (ISBN 0-532-12578-9). Woodhill.
Too Early Lilac. Martha Edith Almedingen. LC 73-155661. 1974. 6.95 (ISBN 0-8149-0694-X). Vanguard Press.
Too Early to Tell. Jerome Weidman. LC 46-806357. 1946. Reynal & Hitchcock.
Too Far to Go. John Updike. 1979. pap. 2.50 (ISBN 0-449-24002-9, Crest). Fawcett.
Too Far to Walk. John Richard Hersey. LC 66-13500. 1966. Knopf.
Too Fat to Fight. Rex Ellingwood Beach. LC 19-3218. 1919. Harper & Brothers.
Too Few for Drums. Ronald Frederick Delderfield. LC 78-162712. 1971. 5.95 (ISBN 0-671-65195-1). Simon and Schuster.
Too Friendly, Too Dead: Michael Shayne's 45th Case. Davis Dresser. LC 63-9296. (Torquil book). 1963. Distributed by Dodd, Mead.
Too Good Looking: The Romance of Flossidoodle Darlo. Gelett Burgess. LC 36-9695. The Bobbs-Merrill Company.
Too Good to Be True. John Creasey. LC 71-85123. (Cock robin mystery). 1969. Macmillan.
Too Good to Be True. Kyle Hunt, pseud. Ed. by Alan Rinzler. (Cock Robin Mystery Ser). 1970. 4.50 o.p. (55742). Macmillan.
Too Hot for Hell. Wayne Lawrence. (Orig.). pap. 0.95 o.p. (1112). Brandon.
Too Hot to Handle. Anne Hampson. (Harlequin Presents Ser.). 192p. 1982. pap. 1.75 (ISBN 0-373-10516-9). Harlequin Bks.
Too Hot to Handle. Frank G Presnell. LC 51-12080. 1951. M. S. Mill Co., and W. Morrow.
Too Hot to Handle: A Marshal Pedley Novel, by Stewart Sterling Pseud. Prentice Winchell. LC 61-12152. (Random House mystery). 1961. Random House.
Too Late. Stephen Dixon. LC 77-6887. 8.95 (ISBN 0-06-010053-2). Harper & Row.
Too Late for Tears. Harry Carmichael. 1975. 6.95 o.p. (ISBN 0-8415-0350-8). Dutton.
Too Late for Tears. Roy Huggins. LC 47-30603. 1947. W. Morrow.
Too Late for Tears. Leopold Horace Ognall. LC 74-1596. 1975. 6.95 (ISBN 0-8415-0350-8). Saturday Review Press.
Too Late the Hero. Con Sellers. LC 71-24188. 1970. 0.75. Pyramid Books.
Too Late the Phalarope. Alan Paton. LC 53-11549. 1953. Scribner.
Too Late to Cry. Kathryn Williams. LC 73-80759. 1973. 4.95 (ISBN 0-8059-1880-9). Dorrance.
Too Late! Too Late! the Maiden Cried. Joan Margaret Fleming. LC 75-12733. 1975. 7.95 (ISBN 0-399-11539-0). Putnam.
Too Late! Too Late! the Maiden Cried. Joan Margaret Fleming. LC 76-46517. 1977. 9.95 (ISBN 0-89340-055-6). J. Curley & Associates.
Too Like the Lightning: A New Jim Steele Mystery. Albert Leffingwell. LC 39-24226. 1939. The Dial Press.
Too Little Love. Robert David Quixano Henriques. LC 50-8217. 1950. Viking Press.
Too Lively to Live. Anne Damer & Scott, Jack Denton, 1915- Joint Author. LC 46-405. 1945. Pub. for the Crime Club by Doubleday, Doran & Company, Inc.
Too Long Endured. Thayer, Lee, pseud. LC 50-10051. (Red badge mystery). 1950. Dodd, Mead.
Too Long in the West. Balachandra Rajan. LC 62-7542. 1962. Atheneum.
Too Loose. Leona Slottman. LC 46-8292. 1946. Phoenix Press.
Too Many Beaus. Alma Sioux Scarberry. LC 36-854554. J. H. Hopkins & Son, Inc.
Too Many Boats. Charles L Clifford. LC 34-2906. 1934. Little, Brown, and Company.
Too Many Bones. Ruth Otis Sawtell Wallis. LC 43-140900. 1943. Dodd, Mead & Company.
Too Many Bottles. Elisabeth Sanxay Holding. LC 51-10209. (Inner sanctum mystery). 1951. Simon and Schuster.
Too Many Clients. Rex Stout. 192p. 1981. pap. 2.25 (ISBN 0-553-20038-0). Bantam.
Too Many Clients: A Nero Wolfe Threesome Novel. Rex Stout. 1960. 2.95 o.p. (ISBN 0-670-72010-0). Viking Pr.
Too Many Cooks. Rex Stout. LC 75-46002. (Fifty Classics of Crime Fiction, 1900-1950; 45). 1976. 12.00 (ISBN 0-8240-2394-3). Garland Pub.
Too Many Cooks: A Nero Wolfe Mystery. Rex Stout. LC 38-20123. Farrar & Rinehart, Incorporated.
Too Many Cousins. Douglas Gordon Browne. LC 53-12561. 1953. Macmillan.
Too Many Crooks. Richard S. Prather. (Shell Scott Ser). 1969. pap. 0.60 o.p. (R2173, GM). Fawcett World.
Too Many Crooks. E. J Rath. LC 18-22896. W. J. Watt & Company.
Too Many Crooks Spoil the Caper. Frank Norman. LC 80-14392. 9.95 (ISBN 0-312-80899-2). St. Martin's Press.
Too Many Doctors. Holly Roth. LC 63-7125. (Random House mystery). 1963. Random House.
Too Many Doors. Ware Tarrey. LC 41-5983. E. P. Dutton & Co., Inc.
Too Many Enemies. Richard Clayton. LC 79-161115. 1972. 4.95 (ISBN 0-8027-5233-0). Walker.
Too Many Enemies. William Haggard. LC 79-161115. (Walker Mystery Ser). 1972. 4.95 o.p. (ISBN 0-8027-5233-0). Walker & Co.
Too Many Innocents. Otto Beeby. LC 73-163260. 1972. 3.50 (ISBN 0-09-109990-0). Hutchinson of Australia.
Too Many Magicians. Randall Garrett. LC 78-10722. (Gregg Press Science Fiction Series). (Double science fiction). 1978. Repr. 12.50 (ISBN 0-8398-2497-1). Gregg Press.
Too Many Magicians. 1st Ed. Randall Garrett. LC 67-22473. 1967. 4.95. Doubleday.
Too Many Murderers. George Childerness. LC 44-501990. 1944. Phoenix Press.
Too Many Sinners. Sheldon Stark. LC 55-16494. (Ace double novel books, D-81). 1954. Ace Books.
Too Many Suspects... Cecil John Charles Street. LC 45-3113. 1945. Dodd, Mead & Company.
Too Many Widows. Vince Ducette. 192p. (Orig.). 1973. pap. 1.95 o.p. (ISBN 0-87056-356-4, 6356). Brandon.
Too Many Widows. Vince Ducette. 1973. (pbk.) 1.95 (ISBN 0-87056-356-4). Brandon House.
Too Many Women. Maysie Greig. LC 41-181097. 1941. Doubleday, Doran & Company, Inc.
Too Many Women. Maysie Greig. LC 42-504396. 1942. The Sun Dial Press.
Too Many Women. Maysie Greig. LC 45-3284. 1944. Triangle Books, the Blakiston Company.
Too Many Women. Rex Stout. LC 47-11318. 1947. Viking Press.
Too Many Women: A Bachelor's Story. Duncan Schwann. LC 10-14152. 1910. 1.25. Frederick A. Stokes Company.
Too Many Yesterdays. Edward Rogers Knowlton. LC 42-16181. 1942. M. S. Mill Co., Inc.
Too Mini Murders. Patrick Morgan. (Operation Hang Ten Ser). (O.s.i.). 1969. pap. 0.75 o.s.i. (532-75258-075). Manor Bks.
Too Much Alike: Er, The Three Calendars. John Lang. LC 7-13869. (On cover: Humorous books, no. 3). 1882. Rhodes & McClure.
Too Much Alike: Or, The Three Calendars. John Lang. LC 7-13868. Rhodes & McClure.
Too Much Efficiency. E. J Rath. LC 17-4472. 1.35. W. J. Watt & Company.
Too Much Flesh and Jabez. Coleman Dowell. LC 77-1631. 1977. 5.95 (ISBN 0-8112-0658-0). New Directions Pub. Corp.
Too Much Java. Elinor Mordaunt, pseud. LC 28-27586. 1928. Payon & Clarke, Ltd.
Too Much Love of Living, a Novel. Robert Smythe Hichens. LC 47-447951. 1947. Macrae-Smith Co.
Too Much of Everything. Philip Wylie. LC 36-182642. Farrar & Rinehart, Incorporated.
Too Much of Water. Bruce Hamilton. LC 81-47348. 1983. 14.95 (ISBN 0-8240-4958-6). Garland.
Too Much of Water. Bruce Hamilton. LC 82-48242. (Perennial library; P/635). 1983. 2.95 (ISBN 0-06-080635-4). Harper & Row.
Too Much of Water. Bruce Hamilton. Ed. by J. Barzun & W. H. Taylor. LC 81-47348. (Crime Fiction 1950-1975 Ser.). 272p. 1982. lib. bdg. 14.95 (ISBN 0-8240-4958-6). Garland Pub.
Too Much Poison. Anne Van Melborn Rowe. LC 44-47199. 1944. M. S. Mill Co., Inc.
Too Much Sun: A Novel. Lee Olds. LC 60-9724. 1960. Vanguard Press.
Too Much to Ask. Fern Rives. LC 47-2144. 1947. G. P. Putnam's Sons.
Too Much Together. Ruby Mildred Ayres. LC 36-10495. 1936. Doubleday, Doran & Comapny, Inc.
Too Much Together. Ruby Mildred Ayres. LC 37-19765. 1937. The Sun Dial Press, Inc.
Too Much, Too Soon. Frank Barrymore & D. Barrymore. 1981. Repr. lib. bdg. 21.95 (ISBN 0-89966-425-3). Buccaneer Bks.
Too Near the Flame. Vera Abriel. LC 82-61844. 222p. (Orig.). 1983. pap. 1.75 (ISBN 0-943654-00-9). New Paradise Bks.
Too Near the Sun. Aimee Duvall. LC 82-14971. (Second Chance at Love). 1983. 11.95 (ISBN 0-89340-540-X). J. Curley & Associates.
Too Near the Sun. Gordon Forbes. LC 55-6846. 1955. Rinehart.
Too Near the Throne. Molly Costain Haycraft. LC 59-6703. 1974. (pbk.) 1.25. New American Library.
Too Near the Throne: A Novel Based on the Life of Lady Arbella Stuart. 1st Ed. Molly Costain Haycraft. LC 59-6703. 1959. Lippincott.
Too Old at Fifty: By Adjutant Wallace Pseud. 1st Ed. R W Herdman. LC 53-8107. 1953. Pageant Press.
Too Old for Dolls. Anthony Mario Ludovici. LC 21-74087. 1921. G. P. Putnam's Sons.
Too Old to Die. Gretchen Travis. LC 68-25461. (Red mask mystery.). 1968. Putnam.
Too Rich: A Romance After the German of Adolph Streckfuss. Adolf Streckfuss & Wister, Mrs. Annie Lee (Furness) 1830-1908, Tr. LC 6-743. 1906. J. B. Lippincott Company.
Too Rich to Be Poor. Souleika M. Lawrence. Ed. by Mosezelle N. White et al. 237p. (Orig.). 1982. pap. 9.95x (ISBN 0-936026-17-0). R&M Pub Co.
Too Saucy with the Gods. Paddy Sylvanus. LC 31-29815. 1931. D. Appleton and Company.
Too Small for His Shoes: A Novel of Detection. Laurence Payne. LC 63-16121. (Cock Robin mystery). 1963. Macmillan.
Too Small for Stove Wood, Too Big for Kindling. John V. Kelleher. 1980. pap. text ed. 10.50x (ISBN 0-85105-312-2, Dolmen Pr). Humanities.
Too Smart for Love. Davis Dresser. LC 37-612361. 1937. Hillman-Curl, Inc.
Too Soon to Die. Henry Wade. pap. 0.95 o.p. (02639, Collier). Macmillan.
Too Soon to Die: By Henry Wade Pseud. Henry Lancelot Aubrey-Fletcher. LC 53-13506. 1954. Macmillan.
Too Swift the Tide. Frankie Lee Griggs Zelley. LC 60-14540. 1960. Morrow.
Too Tough to Die. George Bruce. LC 37-2943. The William Caslon Company, Inc.
Too Tough to Die. Gordon D Shirreffs. (Belmont Tower Book). 1977. 1.25 (ISBN 0-505-51147-9). Tower Pubns.
Too Tough Too Die. Gordon D. Shirreffs. 1977. pap. 1.25 o.s.i. (ISBN 0-505-51147-9). Tower Bks.
Too True. A Story of to-Day. LC 8-29973. 1868. G. P. Putnam & Son.
Too Well Beloved. Dorothy Phoebe Ansle. LC 79-102910. 1979. 7.95 (ISBN 0-525-22086-0). Dutton.
Too Well Beloved. Laura Conway. 1979. 7.95 o.p. (ISBN 0-525-22086-0). Dutton.
Too Wise to Marry. Alma Sioux Scarberry. LC 35-701940. J. H. Hopkins & Son.
Too Young to Be a Grandfather. Willard Temple. LC 63-21125. 1964. Crown Publishers.
Too Young to Die. Lionel White. LC 58-426062. (Gold medal books, 786). 1958. Fawcett Publications.
Too Young to Die: By Robert O. Saber Pseud. Milton K Ozaki. LC 34-417131. (Graphic books, 90). 1954. Graphic Pub. Co.
Too Young to Live. 1st. ed. Ray Radford. LC 64-24800. 1964. Vantage Press.
Too Young to Marry. Margaret Culkin Banning. LC 38-279042. 1938. Harper & Brothers.
Too Young, Too Evil. Dave Price. 192p. pap. 1.95 o.p. (2003). Intimate Lib.
Tool Book. (Illus.). 36p. 0.75 o.s.i. Peoples Pr.
Tool of the Trade. F. W. Paul. (Orig.). 1969. pap. 0.60 o.p. (73-811). Lancer.
Toomey and Others. Shackleton, Robert. 1900. C. Scribner's Sons.
Tooner Schooner. Mary Lasswell. LC 53-9255. (Illus.). 1953. Houghton Mifflin.
Tooth Ane the Nail. William Sanborn Ballinger. LC 55-6564. 1955. Harper.
Tooth Merchant. Cyrus Leo Sulzberger. LC 72-88881. 288p. 1973. 7.95 o.p. (ISBN 0-8129-0268-8). Times Bks.
Tooth Merchant: A Novel. Cyrus Leo Sulzberger. LC 72-88881. 1973. 7.95 (ISBN 0-8129-0268-8). Quadrangle Books.
Toothsome Tales Told in Slang. Oliver Victor Limerick. LC 1-24575. 1901. Street & Smith.
Toothsome Tales Told in Slang. Oliver Victor Limerick. LC 1-24575. 1901. Street & Smith.
Top Assignment. 1st Ed. George Harmon Coxe. LC 55-755705. 1955. Knopf.
Top Bloody Secret. Henry Stanley Hyland. LC 77-81285. 1969. 5.00. Bobbs-Merrill.
Top Detective Annual. Ed. by Manners, David X. LC 51-31890. Best Books.
Top Dog. 1st Ed. Mary Cobb. LC 60-5917. 1960. Doubleday.
Top Drawer, Random Recollections by One Who Was Born in It. LC 28-3172. 1928. Doubleday, Doran & Company, Inc.
Top-Floor Idyl. illustrated by chase emerson. ed. George Gray Van Schaick. LC 17-23651. Small, Maynard & Company.

Top Floor Killer. Walter Adolphe Roberts. LC 73-18604. 1976. 24.50 (ISBN 0-404-11414-8). AMS Press.
Top Gun. Gordon Donalds, pseud. LC 57-13555. 1957. Avalon Books.
Top Gun. Gordon D Shirreffs. (Belmont Tower Book). 1977. 1.25 (ISBN 0-505-51176-2). Tower Pubns.
Top Gun from the Dakotas. Merle Constiner. 1980. pap. 1.75 (ISBN 0-441-81754-8). Ace Bks.
Top Hand. Charles Stanley Strong. LC 48-262419. 1948. Phoenix Press.
Top Hand: By Dwight Bennett Pseud. Dwight Bennett Newton. LC 55-10038. (Permabooks, M-3023,3). 1955. Permabooks.
Top Hand with a Gun. A Crest Reprint of the Novel Guardians of the Sage. Cover Painting by Walter Baumhofer. Complete and Unabridged. Harry Sinclair Drago. LC 55-12706. (Crest book, 116). 1955. Fawcett Publications.
Top Kick. Leonard Hastings Nason. LC 28-23048. 1928. Doubleday, Doran and Company, Inc.
Top Level Death. Hugh Zachary. (Raven House Mysteries Ser.). 224p. 1982. pap. cancelled (ISBN 0-373-63044-1, Pub. by Worldwide). Harlequin Bks.
Top Man with a Gun. Lewis B. Patten. 1979. pap. 1.75 (ISBN 0-449-14191-8, GM). Fawcett.
Top Man with a Gun. Lewis B. Patten. 1970. pap. 0.60 o.p. (R2210, GM). Fawcett World.
Top O' the Mornin' Seumas MacManus. LC 20-170814. Frederick A. Stokes Company.
Top O' the World. Charlotte Margaret Kruger Bryant. LC 51-21603. 1951. Zondervan.
Top of the Heap. Erle Stanley Gardner. LC 52-5061. 1952. Morrow.
Top of the Hill. Irwin Shaw. LC 79-17339. 9.95 (ISBN 0-440-08976-X). Delacorte Press.
Top of the Morning. Juliet Wilbor Tompkins. LC 10-3293. 1910. The Baker & Taylor Company.
Top of the World. Ethel May Dell. LC 20-12814. 1920. Cassell and Company, Ltd.
Top of the World. Ethel May Dell. LC 20-130654. 1920. 2.00. G. P. Putnam's Sons.
Top of the World. Hans Ruesch. LC 50-5806. 1950. Harper.
Top Sail Joins the Navy. Claude V Holland. (wide world of seanuts, v. 3). (Illus.). 1973. (pbk.) 1.25. Hol-Land Books and Posters.
Top Seal. Alfred Tack. 1970. pap. 0.75 o.p. (0502-07084). Curtis.
Top Secret Mission. Madelaine Duke. LC 55-7836. 1955. Criterion Books.
Top Soil, Rich in Wit and Humor, Relating the Happenings to One "Sandy Loam" a Simon Pure Hoosier Character. Ezra Fremont Kendall. LC 9-16001. 1909. The Cleveland News Co. Etc.
Top Steal. Alfred Tack. LC 68-22536. 1968. 4.50. Doubleday.
Top Story Murder... Anthony Berkeley Cox. LC 31-333282. Pub. for the Crime Club, Inc., by Doubleday, Doran & Company, Inc.
Topanga's Woman. Thomas Monroe Helm. LC 74-15784. 1975. 4.95 (ISBN 0-385-09903-7). Doubleday.
Topaz. rev. ed. Leon M. Uris. 416p. 1981. pap. 3.50 (ISBN 0-553-14845-1). Bantam.
Topaz: A Novel. Leon M. Uris. LC 67-11336. 1967. McGraw-Hill.
Topaz for My Lady Fair. Jane Jenke Toombs. LC 75-22286. (Birthstone gothic; 11). 1975. 1.25 (ISBN 0-345-24640-3). Ballantine Books.
Toper's End. George Douglas Howard Cole & Margaret Isabel Postgate Cole. LC 42-222931. 1942. The Macmillan Company.
Topham's Folly. George Stevenson. LC 13-3753. 1913. 1.30. John Lane Company.
Topless. Andrew Blake. (Orig.). 1968. pap. 0.75 o.p. (B75-225). Belmont-Tower.
Topless Dancer Hangup. Patrick Morgan. (Illus.). 1971. pap. 0.75 o.p. (532-75425-075). Manor Bks.
Topless Kitties. Sean O'Shea, pseud. (Valentine Flynn Ser., No. 6). (Orig.). 1968. pap. 0.60 o.p. (B60-086). Belmont-Tower.
Topless Towers: A Romance of Morningside Heights. Margaret Eliza Ashmun. LC 21-17909. 1921. The Macmillan Company.
Topology of a Phantom City. Robbe-Grillet, Alain. 1977. 8.95 (ISBN 0-8021-4100-5). Grove Press: Distributed by Random House.
Topper. Thorne Smith. Repr. lib. bdg. 15.95x (ISBN 0-89190-448-4). Am Repr-Rivercity Pr.
Topper. Thorne Smith. 208p. 1980. pap. 2.25 (ISBN 0-345-28722-3, Del Rey). Ballantine.
Topper: A Ribald Adventure. Thorne Smith. LC 36-8692. 1933. Grosset & Dunlap.
Topper: An Improbable Adventure. Thorne Smith. LC 26-58286. 1926. R. M. McBridge & Company.
Topper Takes a Trip. Thorne Smith. LC 32-12603. 1932. Doubleday, Doran & Company, Inc.
Topper Takes a Trip. Thorne Smith. LC 36-8693. 1935. Doubleday, Doran & Company, Inc.
Topper Takes a Trip. Thorne Smith. LC 37-2759. 1937. The Sun Dial Press, Inc.
Tops and Bottoms. Noel Streatfeild. LC 33-23918. 1933. Doubleday, Doran & Company, Inc.
Topsy. Alan Patrick Herbert. 1930. Doubleday, Doran & Company, Inc.
Topsy and Evil. George Baxt. LC 68-12163. (Inner sanctum mystery). 1968. Simon and Schuster.
Topsy-Turvy. Vernon Bartlett. LC 77-110179. (Short story index reprint series). (Illus.). 1970. Books for Libraries Press.
Topsy Turvy Spring. V. Tendryakov. 413p. 1978. pap. 5.45 (ISBN 0-8285-1052-0, Pub. by Progress Pubs USSR). Imported Pubns.
Tor: A Street Boy of Jerusalem. Florence Morse Kingsley. LC 5-1486. H. Altemus Company.
Tora, Tora, Tora. Gordon W. Prange. 1971. 12.50 o.p. (ISBN 0-07-050669-8). McGraw.
Torbeg. Grace MacLennan Grant Campbell. LC 52-12648. 1953. Duell, Sloane and Pearce.
Torch. Tom Biracree. 240p. 1983. pap. 2.95 (ISBN 0-515-05622-7). Jove Pubns.
Torch. Herbert Muller Hopkins. LC 3-25725. 1908. The Bobbs-Merrill Company.
Torch. Zsigmond Moricz & Lengyel, Emil, Tr. LC 31-13088. 1931. A. A. Knopf.
Torch. Wilder Penfield. LC 60-9349. (Illus.). 1960. Little, Brown.
Torch. Glover Wright. LC 80-13761. 10.95 (ISBN 0-399-12479-9). Putnam.
Torch and Other Tales. Eden Phillpotts. LC 71-144167. (Short story index reprint series). 1971. (ISBN 0-8369-3782-1). Books for Libraries Press.
Torch and Other Tales. Eden Phillpotts. LC 29-20785. 1929. The Macmillan Company.
Torch Bearer. Reina Melcher Marquis. LC 14-12212. 1914. 1.30. D. Appleton and Company.
Torch Bearer: A Camp Fire Girls' Story. Ida Treadwell Thurston. LC 13-13541. Fleming H. Revell Company.
Torch Bearers: A Novel. Bernard Victor Dryer. LC 67-25390. 1968. Simon and Schuster.
Torch Bearers: A Tale of Cavalier Days. Bernard G Marshall. LC 23-129638. 1923. D. Appleton and Company.
Torch-Bearers of Bohemia. V I Kryzhanovskaia. Tr. by Soskice, Juliet M. LC 17-11467. 1917. 1.40. R. M. McBride & Company.
Torch for a Dark Journey: A Novel. Lionel S. B. Shapiro. LC 50-953760. 1950. Doubleday.
Torch Murder: A New Leighton Swift Detective Story. Charles Reed Jones. LC 30-17936. E. P. Dutton & Co., Inc.
Torch of Life. Rene Dubos. (O.s.i.). 1962. 3.95 o.s.i. (ISBN 0-671-73920-4). S&S.
Torch of Life. Rachel Swete Macnamara. LC 14-9279. 1914. G. P. Putnam's Sons.
Torch of Life. Bertha Scher. LC 26-16201. Gem Publishing Company.
Torch Singer. William Arnold. 1970. pap. 0.75 o.p. (75-362). Manor Bks.
Torch Singer. Charles Grant. LC 32-32763. A. H. King, Inc.
Torch Song. Gerald Foster. LC 42-18489. 1942. J. Swift, Incorporated.
Torch Song. Anne Richardson Roiphe. LC 76-42209. 1977. 8.95 (ISBN 0-374-27848-2). Farrar, Straus and Giroux.
Torch Song. Anne Richardson Roiphe. (Signet Book). 1978. 1.95 (ISBN 0-451-07901-9). New American Library.
Torch Song. Anita Blackmon Smith. LC 35-3359. W. Goodwin, Inc.
Torch to Burn. Alan Lampe. LC 35-5374. C. Kendall & W. Sharp, Inc.
Torchbearer. Sallie Lee Bell. LC 56-26172. Zondervan Pub. House.
Torchbearers. Kamala Krishna. LC 25-22112. 1925. Solar Logos Publishing Co.
Torches Flare. Stark Young. LC 28-12078. 1928. C. Scribner's Sons.
Torches of Desire. Rochelle Larkin. (Signet book). 1979. 2.25 (ISBN 0-451-08511-6). New American Library.
Torches Through the Bush. Charles William Gordon. LC 34-37244. 1934. Dodd, Mead & Company.
Torchlight. Constance Leonie Caroline Borgstrom Aminoff. LC 21-17982. 1921. J. M. Dent & Sons, Ltd.
Torchlight. Constance Leonie Caroline Borgstrom Aminoff. LC 22-8048. E. P. Dutton & Company.
Torchlight Procession. Helen Douglas-Irvine. LC 46-219068. 1945. Longmans, Green and Co.
Torchlight Procession. Helen Douglas-Irvine. LC 46-3289. 1946. Doubleday & Company, Inc.
Torchlight to Valhalla. Gale Wilhelm. LC 75-12358. (Homosexuality). 1975. 9.00 (ISBN 0-405-07381-X). Arno Press.
Torchlight to Valhalla. Gale Wilhelm. LC 38-19633. Random House.
Torchy. Sewell Ford. LC 11-9899. 1.25. E. J. Clode.
Torchy and Vee. Sewell Ford. LC 19-17746. E. J. Clode.
Torchy As a Pa. Sewell Ford. E. J. Clode.
Torchy, Private Sec. Sewell Ford. LC 15-25937. E. J. Clode.
Torguemada Principle. Jerrold Morgulas. 1983. pap. 2.95 (ISBN 0-553-14514-2). Bantam.
Torguts. Walter Leslie River. LC 39-279405. 1939. Frederick A. Stokes Company.
Tories of the Hills. Wesley Sylvester Thompson. LC 53-442805. 1953. Christopher Pub. House.
Tories of the Hills. civil war centennial ed. Wesley Sylvester Thompson. LC 60-50939. 1960. Parcil Press.
Torment. With Illus. by Charles Mozley. Translated from the Spanish by J. M. Cohen. Benito Perez Galdos. LC 53-2043. (Illustrated novel library). 1953. Farrar, Straus & Young.
Tormented. Dorothy Daniels. 1971. pap. 0.75 o.p. (64-617). Paperback Lib.
Tormented. Theodore Pratt. LC 50-12088. (Gold medal book, 119). 1950. Fawcett Publications.
Tormented: A Biographical Novel of Paul Verlaine by Rogier Van Aerde Pseud. Translated from the Dutch by Elfriede Zaeyen. 1st American Ed. Adolf Josef Hubert Frans Van Rijen. LC 60-6903. 1960. Doubleday.
Tormented: A Novel. Carolyn Weston. LC 56-112605. 1956. Surrey House.
Tormented Playgirl. Bella Dietrich. 192p. pap. 1.95 o.p. (ISBN 0-87977-121-6). Dansk Blue Bk.
Tormented Virgin. Harvey Rodd. 1.95 o.p. (DBB108). Dansk Blue Bk.
Tormenting Flame. Nancy John. 192p. (Orig.). 1980. pap. 1.50 (ISBN 0-671-57017-X). S&S.
Tormentor. William Romaine Paterson. LC 7-34076. 1897. C. Scribner's Sons.
Tormentors. Pierre Stephen Robert Payne. LC 50-5255. 1950. Sloane.
Torn Asunder. Ann Cristy. 192p. 1982. pap. 1.75 (ISBN 0-515-06660-5). Jove Pubns.
Torn Covenants. Lois Swann. LC 80-15319. 12.95 (ISBN 0-684-16634-8). Scribner.
Torn Letter. Edwin Balmer. LC 41-122406. 1941. Dodd, Mead & Company.
Torn Sails: A Tale of a Welsh Village. Beynon Puddincombe. LC 8-659940. 1898. D. Appleton and Company.
Torn Sails: A Tale of a Welsh Village. Beynon Puddincombe. LC 8-661. (Half-title: Appleton's town and country library, no. 241). 1898. D. Appleton and Company.
Tornado. Juanita Tyree Osborne. LC 54-33885. (Ace double novel books, D-65). 1954. Ace Books.
Tornado Alley. William Tuning. 1979. 1.95 (ISBN 0-441-81765-3). Ace Books.
Toro. Henry Morgan. (Belmont Tower Books). (Illus.). 1977. 1.95 (ISBN 0-505-51178-9). Tower Pubns.
Toro! Toro! Toro! William Hjortsberg. LC 74-4314. 1974. 5.95 (ISBN 0-671-21798-4). Simon and Schuster.
Toro! Toro! Toro! William Hjortsberg. 1975. (pbk.) 1.50. Ballantine Books.
Toronto: No Mean City. 2nd ed. Eric R. Arthur. LC 65-3814. (Illus.). 1974. 35.00 (ISBN 0-8020-2139-5). U of Toronto Pr.
Toronto Short Stories. Douglas Daymond & Morris Wolfe. LC 76-52898. 1977. 5.95 (ISBN 0-385-12848-7). Doubleday Canada.
Toronto Short Stories. Ed. by Morris Wolfe & Douglas Daymond. LC 76-52898. 1977. softbound 5.95 o.p. (ISBN 0-385-12849-5). Doubleday.
Toronto Short Stories. Ed. by Morris Wolfe & Douglas Daymond. LC 76-52898. 1977. softbound 5.95 o.p. (ISBN 0-385-12849-5). Doubleday.
Torontonians; a Novel. 1st Ed. Phyllis Brett Young. LC 61-1115. 1960. Longmans, Green.
Toros Negros. new ed. John Benteen. Tr. by Jacinto De Torres from Eng. (Compadre Collection Ser., Fargo: No. 6). Orig. Title: Black Bulls. (Illus.). 160p. (Span.). 1975. pap. 0.95 (ISBN 0-88473-516-8). Fiesta Pub.
Torpedo! Harry Homewood. 272p. 1982. 12.95 (ISBN 0-07-029698-7). McGraw.
Torpedo Run. Douglas Reeman. LC 81-9623. 1981. 11.95 (ISBN 0-688-00133-5). W. Morrow.
Torpedo! Stories of the Royal Navy. Gilbert Hackforth-Jones. LC 43-6283. 1943. W. Morrow and Company.
Torpedoes Away! By Robert I. Olsen and David Porter. Robert I Olsen & David Uena Porter. LC 57-7446. 1957. Dodd, Mead.
Torquemada: A Novel. Howard Melvin Fast. LC 66-11756. 3.95. Doubleday.
Torquemada: A Novel. Howard Melvin Fast. LC 66-11756. 1966. Doubleday.
Torquemada Principle. Jerrold Morgulas. LC 79-67639. 1980. 10.95 (ISBN 0-89256-124-6). Rawson Wade.
Torquil's Success. Muriel Hine Coxon. LC 21-219427. 1921. John Lane Ltd.
Torquil's Success. Muriel Hine Coxon. 1922. John Lane Company.
Torre Siniestra. new ed. Errol Lecale, pseud. Tr. by John A. Reed from Eng. (Compadre Collection, el Artifice: No. 1). Orig. Title: Castledoom. 160p. (Span.). 1974. pap. 0.85 (ISBN 0-88473-621-0). Fiesta Pub.
Torrent. Burris Atkins Jenkins. LC 32-24985. The Bobbs-Merril Company.
Torrent: A Novel. Joseph Abruquah. 1968. pap. text ed. 2.50x (ISBN 0-582-64009-1). Humanities.
Torrent: Entre Naranjos. Isaac Goldberg & Goldberg, Isaac, 1887- Tr. LC 21-21763. E. P. Dutton & Company.
Torrent of Faces. James Blish & Norman L. Knight. LC 67-22474. (Doubleday science fiction). 1967. Doubleday.
Torrent of Faces: By James Blish, Norman L. Knight. James Blish & Norman L Knight. (Ace sci. fic. A-29). 1968. Ace.
Torrent of the Willows; an Historical Novel. Lewis Christopher Warden. LC 54-102533. 1954. Vantage Press.
Torrents. Marie-Anne Desmarest. Tr. by Lowell Blair. (Signet Book). 1977. 1.75 (ISBN 0-451-07614-1). New American Library.
Torrents. Josiah Pitts Woolfolk. 1951. Woodford Press.
Torrents of Spring. Ernest Hemingway. (Pap. ed. 2.95 o.p.). 90p. 1972. 5.95 (ISBN 0-684-13088-2, ScribT). Scribner.
Torrents of Spring. Pierre Stephen Robert Payne. LC 46-25146. 1946. Dodd, Mead and Company.
Torrents of Spring. Ivan Sergeevich Turgenev. LC 75-10351. (His Novels, v. 11). 1970. AMS Press.
Torrents of Spring: A Romantic Novel in Honour of the Passing of a Great Race. Ernest Hemingway. LC 66-76948. (B 66-10108). 1966. Penguin.
Torrents of Spring: A Romantic Novel in Honor of the Passing of a Great Race. Ernest Hemingway. LC 72-192513. 1972. 5.95 (ISBN 0-684-13088-2) (ISBN 0-684-12957-4). Scribner.
Torrents of Spring: A Romantic Novel in Honor of the Passing of a Great Race. Ernest Hemingway. LC 26-14154. 1926. C. Scribner's Sons.
Torrents of Spring, Etc. Ivan Sergeevich Turgenev. Tr. by Constance Black Garnett. LC 76-150489. (Short story index reprint series). 1971. (ISBN 0-8369-3830-5). Books for Libraries Press.
Torrents of War. Translated from the German by Eric Mosbacher. The U. S. Edition Contains Minor Additions and Restorations by Elsie Stern of Certain Passages Omitted from the Basic Translation. Igor Sentjurc. LC 62-16721. 1962. D. McKay Co.
Torri Mi: By Grace A. Kenelty. 1st Ed. Kenelty, Grace Antoinette. LC 63-22041. American Press.
Torrid Teens: By David O. Wilderness Pseud. Peter S Brody. LC 53-12126. 1954. Vantage Press.
Torrid Women for the Young Boys. Samantha Lasch. pap. 1.95 o.p. (ISBN 0-87056-195-2). Brandon.
Torthorwald. James Grant. (Seaside library, v. 54, no. 1097). G. Munro.
Tortilla Flat. John Steinbeck. 1977. 1.50. Penguin Books.
Tortilla Flat. John Steinbeck. LC 35-7569. Covici, Friede.
Tortilla Flat. John Steinbeck. LC 37-28675. (Half-title: The modern library of the world's best books. 216). 1937. The Modern Library.
Tortilla Flat. new illus. ed. John Steinbeck & Worthington, Peggy, Illus. LC 47-11796. 1947. Viking Press.
Tortilla Flat see Short Novels of John Steinbeck.
Tortoise. Edward Frederic Benson. LC 17-17423. 1.35. George H. Doran Company.
Tortoise: A Novel. Mary Borden. LC 21-15949. 1921. A. A. Knopf.
Tortoise and the Hare: A Novel. Elizabeth Jenkins. LC 54-11485. 1954. Coward-McCann.
Tortoise by Candlelight. Nina Bawden. LC 63-10608. 1963. Harper & Row.
Tortoises, a Novel. Translated by Antonia White. Loys Masson. LC 62-18042. 1962. Channel Press.
Tortoiseshell Cat: A Novel. Naomi Gwladys Royde-Smith. LC 25-23588. 1925. Boni & Liveright.
Tortuga. Rudolfo A. Anaya. LC 79-89689. 1979. pap. 5.50 (ISBN 0-915808-34-X). Editorial Justa.
Torture Contract. Frank Scarpetta. (Marksman#18). 1975. (pbk.) 1.25. Belmont Tower Books.
Torture Garden. Octave Mirbeau. Tr. by Alvah Cecil Bessie. LC 31-10983. 1931. C. Kendall.
Torture Garden. Octave Mirbeau & Bessie, Alvah Cecil, 1904- Tr. LC 49-195. 1949. Citadel Press.
Torture Garden. Tr. from French. Foreword by James Hunter. Octave Mirbeau. pap., 3.95. John Amslow, Box.

Torture Island. I R G Hart. LC 28-14319. 1928. Simon and Schuster.
Torture Machine. Paul Tabori. (Orig.). 1969. pap. 0.60 o.p. (X2057). Pyramid Pubns.
Torture Trail. Max Brand. 1978. 9.95 o.p. (ISBN 0-86025-081-4). State Mutual Bk.
Torture Trail. Frederick Faust. LC 65-15619. 1975. (pbk.) 1.25. Warner Paperback Library.
Torture Trail: By Max Brand Pseud. Frederick Faust. LC 65-15619. (Silver star westerns). 1965. bds., 3.50. Dodd.
Tortured & the Damned. Robert Payne. LC 76-54409. (Illus.). 1978. 9.95 (ISBN 0-8180-0624-2). Horizon.
Tortured Angel. David Garth. LC 48-2475. 1948. G. P. Putnam's Sons.
Tortured Earth: A Novel of the Russian Front. Gert Ledig. LC 56-8245. 1956. H. Regnery Co.
Tortured Heart: "The Trail of the Serpent") Second Series. Emma Dorothy Eliza Nevitte Southworth. LC 12-389029. (On cover: Southworth library. no. 151). Street & Smith.
Tortured Path. Kendell Foster Crossen. (O.S.I.). 1971. pap. 0.75 o.s.i. (ISBN 0-446-64706-3, 64-706-3). Paperback Lib.
Tortured Path. 1st Ed. Kendell Foster Crossen. LC 57-8518. 1957. Dutton.
Torturer's Horse. Robert Inman. LC 65-26512. 1965. Bobbs-Merrill.
Torvick Affair. Mauri Sariola. LC 72-80729. 1973. 4.95 (ISBN 0-8027-5268-3). Walker.
Tory House Mystery. Eleanor Wheeler. LC 35-233116. 1935. H. Smith and R. Haas.
Tory Lover. Sarah Orne Jewett. LC 72-84614. (Illus.). 1974. (lib. ed.) 16.50 (ISBN 0-403-02994-5). Scholarly Press.
Tory Lover. Sarah Orne Jewett. LC 1-20948. 1901. Houghton, Mifflin and Company.
Tory Lover. Sarah Orne Jewett. 1978. Repr. of 1901 ed. lib. bdg. 30.00 (ISBN 0-8495-2730-9). Arden Lib.
Tory Lover see Collected Works.
Tory Lover see Yankee Ranger.
Tory Maid: Being an Account of the Adventures of James Frisby of Fairlee, in the County of Kent, on the Eastern Shore of the State of Maryland, and Sometime an Officer in the Maryland Line of the Continental Army During the War of the Revolution. Herbert Baird Stimpson. LC 7-32328. 1899. Dodd, Mead and Company.
Tory Oath. Tim Pridgen. LC 41-7801. 1941. Doubleday, Doran and Company, Inc.
Tory Tavern. Henry Barnard Safford. LC 42-1435. 1942. Wm. Penn Publishing Corp.
Tory's. William Snyder. 384p. 1981. pap. 2.75 (ISBN 0-380-76547-0, 76547). Avon.
Tory's Daughter: A Romance of the North-West, 1812-1813. Albert Gallatin Riddle. LC 4-41436. 1888. G. P. Putnam's Sons.
Tosa Diary. Kino Tsurayuki. Tr. by William N. Porter from Japanese. LC 80-51194. 160p. 1981. Repr. of 1912 ed. 9.75 (ISBN 0-8048-1371-X). C E Tuttle.
Total Beast: A Novel. Mack Thomas. LC 72-101884. 1970. 6.95. Simon and Schuster.
Total Eclipse. John Brunner. LC 73-14042. 1974. 5.95 (ISBN 0-385-09598-8). Doubleday.
Total Eclipse. Christopher Hampton. 80p. 1982. pap. 6.95 (ISBN 0-571-18048-5). Faber & Faber.
Total Strangers. Terence Winch. LC 82-19278. 1982. 7.50 (ISBN 0-915124-77-7). Toothpaste Press.
Totaled. Frances Rickett & Steven McGraw. LC 81-1480. 1981. 10.95 (ISBN 0-688-00622-1). W. Morrow.
Totally Free Man: An Unauthorized Autobiography of Fidel Castro: a Novel. John Krich. LC 82-103035. (Illus.). 15.00 (ISBN 0-916870-41-3) (ISBN 0-916870-38-3). Creative Arts Book Co.
Totem. Blyden Jackson. LC 74-82729. 1974. 8.95 (ISBN 0-89388-172-4). Okpaku Communications.
Totem: A Novel. David Morrell. LC 79-15088. 8.95 (ISBN 0-87131-298-0). M. Evans.
Totem Dream. Alexander Knox. LC 72-11064. (Illus.). 1973. 6.95 (ISBN 0-670-72100-X). Viking Press.
Totem of Black Hawk: A Tale of Pioneer Days in North Western Illinois and the Black Hawk War. Everett McNeil. LC 14-18651. 1914. A. C. McClurg & Co.
Totem Tales of Old Seattle. Gordon Newell & Don Sherwood. 1974. pap. 1.50 o.p. (ISBN 0-89174-026-0). Comstock Edns.
Totempole. Sanford Friedman. LC 65-199485. 1965. 5.95. Dutton.
Totempole. Sanford Friedman. (Signet bk., Q3023). 1966. New Amer. Lib.
Totemwell. George Payson. LC 7-33759. 1854. Riker, Thorne & Co.
T'other Dear Charmer. Helen Buckingham Mathers Reeves. LC 7-30673. J. W. Lovell Company.
Toto, the Human Wonder Dog. Reed Lawton. 3.00 o.p. Carlton.
Tottie: A Tale of the Sixties. Sarah Aldridge. 1975. (pbk.) 4.50. Naiad Press.
Touch. Katia Baden. LC 29-212165. Dorrance and Company.
Touch. Daniel Keyes. LC 68-20069. 1968. Harcourt, Brace & World.
Touch. Patricia Rae. (Orig.). 1980. pap. 2.75 o.s.i. (ISBN 0-505-51580-6). Tower Bks.
Touch a Star. Barbara Cartland. (Barbara Cartland Ser.: No. 92). (Orig.). 1981. pap. 1.95 (ISBN 0-515-05961-7). Jove Pubns.
Touch & Die. Jess Cloud. 240p. 1981. pap. 2.25 (ISBN 0-8439-0987-0, Leisure Bks). Nordon Pubns.
Touch and Go. Victoria Berne. LC 39-13756. 1939. Harper & Brothers.
Touch and Go. Cyril Northcote Parkinson. LC 77-7665. (Illus.). 1977. 7.95 (ISBN 0-395-25592-9). Houghton Mifflin.
Touch and Go. Cyril Northcote Parkinson. LC 78-7276. (Illus.). 1978. 12.95 (ISBN 0-8161-6592-0). G. K. Hall.
Touch and Go. Cyril Northcote Parkinson. LC 80-81002. (Illus.). 1980. 2.25 (ISBN 0-87216-713-5). Playboy Press Paperbacks.
Touch and Go. Patricia Wentworth. J. B. Lippincott Company.
Touch Experiment. Pat Tierney. (Orig.). 1971. pap. 0.95 o.p. (A871N, Award). Univ Pub & Dist.
Touch Me Not: Four Write of a Curt Picaresque. Vincent McHugh. LC 30-183141. J. Cape & H. Smith.
Touch Me with Fire. Patricia Phillips. 416p. 1982. pap. 3.50 (ISBN 0-515-05908-0). Jove Pubns.
Touch Not the Cat. Mary Stewart. LC 76-4562. 1976. 8.95 (ISBN 0-688-03059-9). Morrow.
Touch Not the Cat. Mary Stewart. LC 76-40990. 1976. 13.50 (ISBN 0-8161-6403-7). G. K. Hall.
Touch Not the Cat. Mary Stewart. (Fawcett Crest Book). 1977. 1.95 (ISBN 0-449-23201-8). Fawcett Pubns.
Touch of Abner. Hiram Alfred Cody. LC 19-15672. 1.50. George H. Doran Company.
Touch of Acid. George Brandon Saul. 27p. 1971. 8.50 o.s.i. (ISBN 0-88216-024-9). Walton Pr.
Touch of Color: And Other Tales. Alvin Saunders Johnson. LC 63-18755. 1963. Atheneum.
Touch of Danger. James Jones. LC 72-97092. (Illus.). 1973. 7.95 (ISBN 0-385-04700-2). Doubleday.
Touch of Daniel. Peter Tinniswood. LC 69-20092. 1969. 5.95. Doubleday.
Touch of Darkness. John Crowe, pseud. 192p. 1974. pap. 1.25 (ISBN 0-532-12229-1). Woodhill.
Touch of Darkness. Dennis Lynds. LC 72-3617. (His A Buena Costa County mystery). (Illus.). 1972. 4.95 (ISBN 0-394-47543-7). Random House.
Touch of Darkness. Dennis Lynds. 1974. (pbk.) 1.25. Manor Books.
Touch of Death. John Creasey. LC 74-86397. 1969. 4.50. Walker.
Touch of Death. Cover Painting by Saul Tepper. Charles Williams. LC 55-15734. (Gold medal books, 434). 1954. Fawcett Publications.
Touch of Earth. Lella Warren. LC 26-159561. 1926. Simon and Schuster.
Touch of Eternity. Clark Darlton. (Perry Rhodan#57). (Illus.). 1974. (pbk.) 0.95. Ace.
Touch of Evil. Lydia Colby. 1977. 1.50. Playboy Press.
Touch of Fantasy: A Romance for Those Who Are Lucky Enough to Wear Glasses. Arthur Henry Adams. LC 12-11408. 1912. John Lane.
Touch of Frost. Willo Davis Roberts. 256p. (Orig.). 1981. pap. 2.25. Bantam.
Touch of Glory. Frank Gill Slaughter. LC 45-34515. 1945. Doubleday, Doran and Company, Inc.
Touch of Heaven. Tess Holloway. (Candlelight Ecstasy Ser.: No. 105). (Orig.). 1982. pap. 1.95 (ISBN 0-440-18931-4). Dell.
Touch of Human Hands: A Novel. Joseph Robert Linney. LC 47-254702. 1947. Dorrance.
Touch of Infinity. Howard Fast. (Science Fiction Ser). 1974. pap. 0.95 o.p. (UQ1137). DAW Bks.
Touch of Infinity: Thirteen New Stories of Fantasy and Science Fiction. Howard Melvin Fast. LC 72-135. 1973. 5.95 (ISBN 0-688-00180-7). Morrow.
Touch of Infinity: Thirteen New Stories of Fantasy and Science Fiction. Howard Melvin Fast. LC 73-17429. 1973-1974. 7.95 (ISBN 0-8161-6168-2). G. K. Hall.
Touch of Infinity: Thirteen New Stories of Fantasy and Science Fiction. Howard Melvin Fast. 1974. (pbk.) 0.95. DAW Books.
Touch of Infinity: 13 New Stories of Fantasy & Science Fiction. Howard Fast. 1973. 5.95 o.p. (ISBN 0-688-00180-7). Morrow.
Touch of Jonah: A Father Bredder Mystery Novel. by Leonard Holton. Leonard Patrick O'Connor Wibberley. LC 68-23091. (Red badge mystery). 1968. 3.95. Dodd.
Touch of Joshua. 1st Ed. Cecilia Bartholomew. LC 60-15168. 1960. Doubleday.
Touch of Love. Barbara Cartland. LC 77-670159. 1977. 6.95. Duron Books.
Touch of Magic. Elizabeth Hunter. 192p. 1981. pap. 1.50 o.s.i. (ISBN 0-671-57065-X). S&S.
Touch of Midas. Jan Carew. LC 58-103804. 1958. Coward-McCann.
Touch of Myrrh. Charlotte Hunt. (Ace gothic). 1974. (pbk.) 0.95. Ace Books.
Touch of Nutmeg: And More Unlikely Stories. John Collier. LC 44-40019. The Press of the Readers Club.
Touch of Passion. James Noble Gifford. LC 44-1470. 1944. Phoenix Press.
Touch of Passion. Lynda Ward. (Superromances Ser.). 384p. 1982. pap. 2.50 (ISBN 0-373-70033-4, Pub. by Worldwide). Harlequin Bks.
Touch of Polly Tucker. Bertha B. Moore McCurry. LC 50-8492. 1950. Eerdmans.
Touch of Portugal: Or, The Little Count of Villa Moncao. Mary Woodman. LC 11-131019. 1910. Atlantic Printing Company.
Touch of Rot: By Lewis Lester Pseud. Louis Lazowick. LC 52-3391. 1952. Woodford Press.
Touch of Sadness. Gerald W. Hines. 1976. 1.50 (ISBN 0-915626-04-7). Yellow Jacket.
Touch of Sadness. James R. Knutz. 3.75 o.p. Vantage.
Touch of Stage Fright. Jocelyn Davey, pseud. pap. 0.65 o.p. (ISBN 0-14-001880-8). Penguin.
Touch of Stage Fright. Chaim Raphael. LC 63-6596. (Penguin books, Penguin crime). 1963. Penguin Books.
Touch of Strange. Theodore Sturgeon. (Science Fiction Ser). 1978. pap. 1.95 o.p. (ISBN 0-87997-373-0, UJ1373). DAW Bks.
Touch of Strange. Edward Hamilton Waldo, pseud. LC 58-10044. 1958. Doubleday.
Touch of Strange. Edward Hamilton Waldo, pseud. LC 70-121565. (Short story index reprint series). 1970. Books for Libraries Press.
Touch of Strange. Edward Hamilton Waldo, pseud. 1978. 1.95. DAW Books.
Touch of Sun: And Other Stories. Mary Hallock Foote. LC 69-11892. (American short story series, v. 50). 1969. Garrett Press.
Touch of Sun, and Other Stories. Mary Hallock Foote. LC 72-4422. (Short story index reprint series). 1972. (ISBN 0-8369-4175-6). Books for Libraries Press.
Touch of Sun, and Other Stories. Mary Hallock Foote. LC 72-8385. (American short story series, v. 50). 1972. (ISBN 0-8422-8046-4). MSS Information Corp.
Touch of Sun: And Other Stories. Mary Hallock Foote. LC 3-28135. 1903. Houghton, Mifflin and Company.
Touch of Terror. Sarah Farrant. LC 78-19424. 8.95 (ISBN 0-312-80977-8). St. Martin's Press.
Touch of the Devil. Anne Weale. (Harlequin Presents Ser.). 192p. 1982. pap. 1.75 (ISBN 0-373-10511-8). Harlequin Bks.
Touch of the Dragon. Hamilton Basso. LC 64-12229. 1964. Viking Press.
Touch of the Sun: Stories. William Sansom. LC 57-142442. 1958. Reynal.
Touch of the Witch. June Wetherell. 1976. pap. 1.25 (ISBN 0-532-12442-1). Woodhill.
Touch of the Witch. June Wetherell. 1969. pap. 0.75 o.p. (74-576). Lancer.
Touch of the Witch. June Wetherell. 1972. pap. 1.65 o.s.i. (70-406). Lancer.
Touch of Thunder. Brian Cooper. (O.s.i.). 3.95 o.s.i. (ISBN 0-8149-0045-3). Vanguard.
Touch of Venom. Angela D'Amico. 96p. 1975. 5.00 o.p. (ISBN 0-682-48241-2). Exposition.
Touch People. Froma Sand. 1973. (pbk.) 1.25. Warner Paperback Library.
Touch the Devil. Jack Higgins, pseud. LC 82-40080. 1982. 14.95 (ISBN 0-8128-2872-0). Stein and Day.
Touch the Devil. large print ed. Jack Higgins, pseud. LC 82-23202. 1983. 16.95 (ISBN 0-8161-3484-7). G.K. Hall.
Touch the Fire. Grania Beckford. LC 78-19421. 10.00 (ISBN 0-312-80983-2). St. Martin's Press.
Touch the Lion's Paw. Derek Lambert. LC 75-12504. 1975. 7.95 (ISBN 0-8415-0391-5). Saturday Review Press.
Touch the Sun. Kaye Wilson Klein. LC 74-139037. 1971. 5.95. Doubleday.
Touch the Sun. Cynthia Wright. LC 78-60700. 1978. 2.25 (ISBN 0-345-27512-8). Ballantine Books.
Touch the Water, Touch the Wind. Amos Oz. LC 74-12178. 1974. 6.95 (ISBN 0-15-190873-7). Harcourt Brace Jovanovich.
Touch the Wind. Janet Dailey. 1979. 2.25 (ISBN 0-671-82517-8). Pocket Books.
Touch Us Gently. Harriet Henry, pseud. LC 33-152372. 1933. W. Morrow & Company.
Touchable. Leslie Scott. LC 51-14879. 1951. Arco Pub. Co.
Touchdown Glory. Joseph Archibald. LC 49-48151.
Touchdowns. Lawrence Perry. LC 24-225671. (His The fair play series). 1924. C. Scribner's Sons.
Touched by the Seasons. Ed. by James Kuse & Ralph D. Luedke. 1978. pap. 3.95 o.p. (ISBN 0-89542-056-2). Ideals.
Touched by the Thorn: A Novel. Maura Laverty. LC 43-15469. 1943. Longmans, Green and Co.
Touched with Fire. John William Tebbel. LC 52-5317. 1952. Dutton.
Touchfeather. Jimmy Sangster. 1969. 4.95 o.p. (ISBN 0-393-08428-0). Norton.
Touchfeather, Too. Jimmy Sangster. LC 70-103970. 1970. 4.95. Norton.
Touching. Gwen Davis. LC 79-132502. 1971. 5.95. Doubleday.
Touching. Fred B. Holmberg. (Illus., Orig.). 1973. pap. 2.95 (ISBN 0-911764-11-9). Durrell.
Touching. John Neufeld. LC 76-125867. 1970. 4.95. S. G. Phillips.
Touching Evil. Norma Stahl Rosen. LC 78-78879. 1969. Harcourt, Brace & World.
Touching Hand, and Six Short Stories. Sallie Bingham. LC 67-11825. 1967. Houghton Mifflin Co.
Touching the Clouds. Maysie Greig. LC 36-12311. 1936. Doubleday, Doran and Co., Inc.
Touching the Clouds. Maysie Greig. LC 37-19764. 1937. The Sun Dial Press, Inc.
Touchlings: The Adventures of the Fantasy Creatures That Who Live on Love, Sunshine & Giving. Michael W. Fox. LC 80-27959. 64p. 1981. 7.95 (ISBN 0-87491-293-8). Acropolis.
Touchstone. Lillian Janet. LC 47-2665. 1947. Rinehart & Company, Inc.
Touchstone. Edith Newbold Jones Wharton. LC 76-80628. 1969. AMS Press.
Touchstone. Edith Newbold Jones Wharton. LC 78-3645. 1968. Scholarly Press.
Touchstone. Ben Ames Williams. LC 30-12994. 1930. E. P. Dutton & Co., Inc.
Touchstone: A Story. Edith Newbold Jones Wharton. LC 2667. 1900. C. Scribner's Sons.
Touchstone of Fortune: Being the Memoir of Baron Clyde, Who Lived, Thrived, and Fell in the Doleful Reign of the So Called Merry Monarch, Charles II. Charles Major. LC 12-6556. 1912. The Macmillan Company.
Touchstone of Life. Ella MacMahon. LC 7-20427. F. A. Stokes Company.
Touchstone of Peril. A Novel of Anglo-Indian Life, with Scenes During the Mutiny. Robert Edward Forrest. LC 6-40376. (Harper's Franklin square library, no. 547). 1886. Harper & Brothers.
Touchstone of Peril. A Novel of Anglo-Indian Life, with Scenes During the Mutiny. Robert Edward Forrest. LC 6-40877. (On cover: The seaside library. Pocket ed. no. 879). 1886. G. Munro.
Touchstones. Sallie Phillips-McClenahan. LC 82-11454. (Illus.). 300p. (Orig.). 1982. pap. 8.95 (ISBN 0-87233-066-4). Bauhan.
Toucoutou. Edward Larocque Tinker. LC 28-11172. 1928. Dodd, Mead & Company.
Tough and Tenderfoot. Robert Claiborne Pitzer. LC 42-17837. 1942. Phoenix Press.
Tough and the Tender. Mina Lewiton. LC 50-10395. 1950. F. Watts.
Tough and the Tender. Angus MacLeod. LC 60-118438. 1960. Roy Publishers.
Tough and the Tender. Mina Lewiton Simon. LC 50-10395. 1950. F. Watts.
Tough Bullet. John Benteen. (Carmody Ser., No. 3). 1974. pap. 0.95 o.p. (LB136NK). Leisure Bks.
Tough Company: By Clem Colt. Nelson Coral Nye. LC 52-8983. (Silver star westerns). 1952. Dodd, Mead.
Tough Cookie. Lillian Sparks. 1981. pap. 4.95 (ISBN 0-88270-516-4, Pub. by Logos). Bridge Pub.
Tough Cop. John Roeburt. LC 49-956782. (Inner sanctum mystery). 1949. Simon and Schuster.
Tough Doll. Gail Jordan. 1970. pap. 0.75 o.p. (75-347). Manor Bks.
Tough Get Going. George Bagby, pseud. LC 76-56263. 1977. 6.95 o.p. (ISBN 0-385-12938-6). Doubleday.
Tough Get Going. Aaron Marc Stein. LC 76-56263. 1977. 6.95 (ISBN 0-385-12938-6). Published for the Crime Club by Doubleday.
Tough Guys. Mickey Spillane, pseud. 1970. pap. 1.75 (ISBN 0-451-09225-2, E9225, Sig). NAL.
Tough Hand. Wayne D Overholser. LC 54-7267. 1954. Macmillan.
Tough Justice. Frederic Dard. LC 69-13187. 1969. 4.50. Norton.
Tough Justice. San Antonio. 1969. 4.50 o.p. (ISBN 0-393-08417-5). Norton.
Tough Justice. San Antonio. Tr. by Cyril Buhler. (San Antonio Ser). 1970. pap. 0.60 o.p. (63-287). Paperback Lib.
Tough Little Trollop. Helen Adams. LC 35-13173. 1935. The Hartney Press.
Tough Luck L. A. Murray Sinclair. 256p. (Orig.). 1980. pap. 2.50 (ISBN 0-523-41140-5). Pinnacle Bks.
Tough One to Lose. Tony Kenrick. LC 72-7481. 1972. 9.95 (ISBN 0-8161-6048-1). G. K. Hall.
Tough One to Lose. Tony Kenrick. LC 75-187011. 1972. 5.95. Bobbs-Merrill.

Tough Ones: A Collection of Realistic Short Stories, Edited by Whit and Hallie Burnett. Ed. by Whit Burnett & Hallie Southgate Burnett. LC 55-17012. (Popular library eagle book, EB28). 1954. Popular Library.

Tough Saddle. Llewellyn Perry Holmes. LC 77-14568. 1978. 8.95 (ISBN 0-89340-117-X). J. Curley.

Tough Saddle: By Matt Stuart Pseud. Llewellyn Perry Holmes. LC 59-11759. (Silver star westerns). 1959. Dodd, Mead.

Tough Sod: A Novel by E. R. Eastman. Edward Roe Eastman & American Agriculturist. LC 45-266. 1944. American Agriculturist, Inc.

Tough Texan. Paul Evan Lehman. 1979. pap. 1.25 o.s.i. (ISBN 0-8439-0635-9, Leisure Bks). Nordon Pubns.

Tough Trip Through Paradise. Andrew Garcia. LC 66-14758. 1976. pap. 3.95 (ISBN 0-89174-008-2). Comstock Edns.

Tough Trip Through Paradise. Andrew Garcia. 1972. 1.25 o.p. (ISBN 0-345-02652-7). Comstock.

Toughest of Them All. Glenn Shirley. (Illus.). 1953. 3.50 o.p. (ISBN 0-8263-0093-6). U of NM Pr.

Toughest of Them All. Stories. Glenn Shirley. LC 53-63456. 1953. University of New Mexico Press.

Toujours Forever. Ren Glasser & Block, Jean Libman, Joint Author. LC 63-12060. 1963. Crown Publishers.

Tour. David Ely. (8979). 1968. Dell.

Tour. David Ely. LC 67-14995. 1967. Delacorte Press.

Tour. Aldo Lucchesi, pseud. (Orig.). 1969. pap. 1.25 o.p. (T125-1). Tower.

Tour. Aldo Lucchesi, pseud. (O.s.i.). 1975. pap. 1.25 o.s.i. (BT50867). Belmont-Tower.

Tour. Michael Perkins. pap. 1.95 o.p. (0118). Essex Hse.

Tour: A Story of Ancient Egypt. Louis Marie Anne Couperus. Tr. by Teixeira De Mattos, Alexander Louis. LC 20-10054. 1920. Dodd, Mead and Company.

Tour and a Romance. Alice E Robbins. LC 11-12711. 1911. 1.50. The Baker and Taylor Company.

Tour De Force. Christianna Brand, pseud. LC 81-47808. 192p. 1982. pap. 2.84i (ISBN 0-06-080572-2, P 572, PL). Har-Row.

Tour De Force. Christianna Brand, pseud. 1979. 15.00 (ISBN 0-86025-114-4, Pub. by Ian Henry Pubns England). State Mutual Bk.

Tour De Force. Kenneth Philip Hubert Cleife. LC 76-144195. 1971. 5.95 (ISBN 0-06-010204-7). Harper & Row.

Tour De Force: By Christianna Brand Pseud. Mary Christianna Milne Lewis. LC 55-967523. 1955. Scribner.

Tour du Monde en 80 Jours. Jules Verne. pap. 3.95. French & Eur.

Tour for Seven. Ruby A Newman. LC 77-75506. (Alton series; book 3). (Illus.). R. A. N. Publishers.

Tour of Duty, a Novel: 1st Ed. Walter J Sheldon. LC 50-13075. 1959. Lippincott.

Tour of Love. Sharon Wagner. (Adventures in Love Ser.). 160p. 1983. pap. 2.25 (ISBN 0-451-12015-9, Sig). NAL.

Tour of the World in Eighty Days. Verne, Jules. LC 1-9853. 1873. J. R. Osgood and Company.

Tour of the World in Eighty Days... Jules Verne. LC 1-9855. (On cover: Lovell's library, v. 4, no. 134). 1883. J. W. Lovell Company.

Tour of the World in Eighty Days. Jules Verne. LC 4-17514. A. L. Burt Company.

Tour to Romance. Lee Priestley. (YA) 1979. 6.95 (Avalon). Bouregy.

Touring. Page Edwards. LC 73-16567. 1974. 7.95 (ISBN 0-670-72217-0). Grossman Publishers.

Tourist. Gerald Green. LC 73-83592. 1973. 8.95 (ISBN 0-385-04284-1). Doubleday.

Tourist Cabins. Peggy O'More, pseud. Gramercy Publishing Co.

Tourist Season. Frances Oliver. LC 79-306889. 1978. 10.95 (ISBN 0-370-30083-1). Bodley Head, Apr.

Tourist Tales of California. Sara Isaman. LC 7-39997. 1907. The Author.

Tourist Tales of California. Sara Isaman. LC 10-1691. The Reilly & Britton Co.

Tourist Third. Ruth Hammitt Kauffman. LC 33-7687. The Penn Publishing Company.

Tourist Trap. Ted Stratton. LC 75-21827. (Red mask mystery). 6.95 (ISBN 0-399-11608-7). Putnam.

Tourists & Colonials. Ed. by Betty J. Breyer. LC 80-54162. (Anthony Trollope: the Complete Short Stories: Vol. III). 260p. 1981. 17.50 (ISBN 0-912646-62-4). Tex Christian.

Tourmaline: A Novel. Randolph Stow. LC 82-50910. 1983. 10.95 (ISBN 0-8008-7797-7). Taplinger Pub. Co.

Tourmalin's Time Cheque. Thomas Anstey Guthrie. LC 3-28160. 1893. D. Appleton and Company.

Tourmalin's Time Cheques. Thomas Anstey Guthrie. LC 9-8354. 1891. D. Appleton and Company.

Tournament. Shelby Foote. LC 49-10678. 1949. Dial Press.

Tournament. Herbert B Livesey & Ron Hamlin. LC 79-7870. 1980. 10.00 (ISBN 0-385-15159-4). Doubleday.

Tournament. Peter Vansittart. LC 61-10749. 1961. Walker.

Tournament: A Novel. Olive Wadsley. LC 33-898516. 1933. Dodd, Mead & Company.

Tournament of Shadows. Nicholas Carnac. LC 79-51163. (Illus.). 9.95 (ISBN 0-684-16148-6). Scribner.

Tournament of Thorns. Thomas Burnett Swann. (Science Fiction Special, 8). Ace.

Toute la Tendresse du Monde. Christine H. Cott. (Harlequin Seduction Ser.). 332p. 1983. pap. 3.25 (ISBN 0-373-45015-X). Harlequin Bks.

Tova & Esty. 1982. pap. 1.95 (ISBN 0-87306-247-7). Feldheim.

Tova & Esty's Purim Surprise. 1982. pap. 1.95 (ISBN 0-87306-248-5). Feldheim.

Tow Men and a Maid. A Tale. Harriett Jay. LC 7-7572. (Seaside library, v. 61, no. 1244). G. Munro.

Toward a New Light. Caryl Porter. LC 80-26824. 1981. 9.95 (ISBN 0-8164-0495-X). Seabury Press.

Toward Infinity: 9 Science Fiction Tales. Ed. by Damon Francis Knight. LC 68-28914. 1968. 4.95. Simon & Shuster.

Toward Love's Horizon: The Loves of Angela Carlyle, Vol. III. Michele DuBarry. 320p. 1981. pap. 2.50 (ISBN 0-8439-0957-9, Leisure Bks). Nordon Pubns.

Toward Romance. Rollo Walter Brown. Coward-McCann, Inc.

Toward Silence. Edward Lucie-Smith. 1968. pap. 2.75x o.p. (ISBN 0-19-211273-2). Oxford U Pr.

Toward the End: A Novel. Elizabeth Savage. LC 79-27364. 10.95 (ISBN 0-316-77156-2). Little, Brown.

Toward the Glory Gate: A Story of Soul Growth. Julia MacNair Wright. (Green fund book, no. 12 b.). The Union Press.

Toward the Goal: A Story. Sophia Nordling. LC 22-933. Printed by Carlen & Jonsson.

Toward the Horizon. Charles Angoff. LC 76-21600. 9.95 (ISBN 0-498-02015-0). A. S. Barnes.

Toward the Morning. Harvey Allen. LC 48-3507. 1948. Rinehart.

Toward the Stars. Barbara Cartland. (Orig.). 1975. pap. 1.25 o.p. (ISBN 0-515-03922-5). BJ Pub Group.

Toward the Stars. Barbara Cartland. 1977. pap. 1.50 o.p. (ISBN 0-515-04384-2). BJ Pub Group.

Toward What Bright Land. Thomas Walter Gilkyson. LC 47-30644. 1947. C. Scribner's Sons.

Towards a Better Life: Being a Series of Epistles or Declamations. 2d ed. Kenneth Burke. LC 66-13268. 1966. University of California Press.

Towards a Better Life: Being a Series of Epistles, or Declamations. Kenneth Burke. LC 32-3292. Harcourt, Brace and Company.

Towards Morning. Ida Alexa Ross Wylie. LC 18-16376. 1918. John Lane Company.

Towards the Dawn. Conor Galway. LC 21-4552. 1920. Frederick A. Stokes Company.

Towards the Gulf: A Romance of Louisiana. LC 72-3107. (Black Heritage Library Collection). 1972. 13.50 (ISBN 0-8369-9084-6). Books for Libraries Press.

Towards the Gulf: A Romance of Louisiana... LC 8-29833. 1887. Harper & Brothers; Etc., Etc.

Towards the Sunset. Muriel Elwood. LC 47-6518. 1947. C. Scribner's Sons.

Towards the West. Maurice Constantin-Weyer. LC 31-4181. The Macaulay Company.

Towards Victory. Roy Russell. (Family at War). (Signet book: Vol. 3). 1975. (pbk.) 1.50. New American Library.

Towards Zero... Agatha Miller Christie. LC 44-4960. 1944. The Blakiston Company; Distributed by Dodd, Mead & Company, New York.

Towards Zero see Death in the Clouds.

Towboat Pilot. Elston Joseph Melton. LC 48-5545. 1948. Caxton Printers.

Tower. Philip Maitland Hubbard. LC 67-14329. 1967. Atheneum.

Tower. Marguerite Steen. LC 60-7884. 1960. Doubleday.

Tower. Richard Martin Stern. LC 73-76565. 1973. 7.95. McKay.

Tower. Richard Martin Stern. 1974. (pbk.) 1.75. Warner Paperback Library.

Tower: A Novel. Mary Tappan Wright. LC 6-12137. 1906. C. Scribner's Sons.

Tower Abbey: A Novel of Suspense. Isabelle Holland. LC 77-77889. 8.95. Rawson Associates Publishers.

Tower Abbey: A Novel of Suspense. Isabelle Holland. 1979. 1.95 (ISBN 0-449-24044-4). Fawcett Crest Books.

Tower and the Dream. Jan Vlachos Westcott. LC 72-97312. 1974. 7.95 (ISBN 0-399-11128-X). Putnam.

Tower and the Town. Grace MacLennan Grant Campbell. LC 50-6027. 1950. Duell, Sloan and Pearce.

Tower Anthology of the San Jose Movement in Fiction, Vol. II. Jon Ilgen et al. Ed. by Merritt Clifton. (Illus.). 1976. pap. 1.00 o.p. Samisdat.

Tower Anthology of the San Jose Movement in Fiction. Tom Suddick et al. (Illus.). 1974. pap. 1.25 o.p. Samisdat.

Tower at the Edge of Time. Lin Carter. 1978. pap. 1.50 (ISBN 0-505-51224-6). Tower Bks.

Tower at the Edge of Time. Lin Carter. (Inflation Fighter Ser.). 144p. 1982. pap. 1.50 (ISBN 0-8439-1097-6, Leisure Bks). Nordon Pubns.

Tower by the Sea: Illustrated by Barbara Comfort. 1st Ed. Meindert De Jong. LC 50-10021. 1950. Harper.

Tower in the Desert. Virginia Durant Young. LC 9-1194. 1896. Arena Publishing Company.

Tower in the Forest. Jean Francis Webb. LC 51-8423. 1951. Bouregy & Curl.

Tower in the Sea: A Gothic Novel. Julia Thatcher, pseud. 1979. 1.75 (ISBN 0-445-04437-3). Popular Library.

Tower in the West. 1st Ed. Frank Callan Norris. LC 57-5903. Harper.

Tower Is Everywhere. Richard Jones. LC 79-149461. 1971. 6.95. Little, Brown.

Tower of Babel: A Novel. Morris L. West. LC 68-14801. (Illus.). 1968. Morrow.

Tower of David: A Book of Stories for the Program of Women's Organizations. Elma C. Ehrlich Levinger & National Council of Jewish Women. LC 25-4611. 1924. Bloch Publishing Company.

Tower of Evil. Cecil John Charles Street. LC 38-32015. 1938. Dodd, Mead & Company.

Tower of Flame: An Oil Fields Story: Jaragu of the Lost Islands, a High Seas Story. Rex Ellingwood Beach. (On cover: Bantam books. 19). 1940. Bantam Publications Inc.

Tower of Glass. Robert Silverberg. LC 75-123835. 1970. 5.95. Scribner.

Tower of Ivory. Gertrude Franklin Horn Atherton. LC 10-5308. 1910. The Macmillan Company.

Tower of Kilraven. Cecily Crowe. LC 65-22451. 1965. Holt, Rinehart and Winston.

Tower of London: A Historical Romance. a new ed. William Harrison Ainsworth & Cruikshank, George, 1792-1878, Illus. LC 4-16449. 1908. D. Appleton & Company.

Tower of Myriad Mirrors. Tung-Yueh. 1979. pap. 5.95 (ISBN 0-89581-501-X). Lancaster-Miller.

Tower of Oblivion. Oliver Onions. LC 21-198461. 1921. The Macmillan Company.

Tower of Percemont. A Novel. From the French of George Sand. George Sand. LC 6-35671. (Half-title: Collection of foreign authors. no. 4). 1877. D. Appleton and Company.

Tower of Percemont. Also, Marianne. George Sand. LC 6-35670. (On cover: Lovell's library, v. 4, no. 135). J. W. Lovell Company.

Tower of Sand & Other Stories. Wilbur Daniel Steele. LC 29-21555. 1929. Harper & Brothers.

Tower of Steel. Josephine Lawrence. LC 43-157823. 1943. Little, Brown and Company.

Tower of Taddeo. Louise De La Ramee. LC 6-33305. (On cover: The metropolitan series. no. 9). 1892. Hovendon Company.

Tower of Taddeo. Louise De La Ramee. 1901. Street & Smith.

Tower of Terror. Joseph Ivers Lawrence. LC 34-13899. The Macaulay Company.

Tower of Terror. Don Pendleton & Dick Stivers. (Able Team Ser.). 192p. 1982. pap. 1.95 (ISBN 0-373-61201-X, Pub. by Worldwide). Harlequin Bks.

Tower of Terzel. Pierre Van Paassen. LC 48-8721. 1948. Dial Press.

Tower of the Crow. Dora Polk. LC 74-25726. 1975. 7.95 (ISBN 0-679-50479-6). D. McKay Co.

Tower of the Dark Light. Elizabeth Erin Mande. 1973. (pbk) 0.95. Popular Library.

Tower of the Elephant. Robert E. Howard. Ed. by Grace Shaw. LC 78-59789. (Illus.). 1978. pap. 6.95 o.p. (ISBN 0-448-16238-5, G&D). Putnam Pub Group.

Tower of the Old Schloss. Jean Porter Rudd. LC 8-958. 1896. G. P. Putnam's Sons.

Tower of Treason: Hotel Destiny Four - New York. Zachary Hughes. (Orig.). 1982. pap. 2.95 (ISBN 0-515-06048-8). Jove Pubns.

Tower of Wye; a Romance. William Henry Babcock. LC 1-31251. 1901. H. T. Coates & Co.

Tower of Zanid. Lyon Sprague De Camp. 1972. pap. 0.75 o.p. (532-75467-075). Manor Bks.

Tower Room. Dorothy Daniels. (Orig.). pap. 0.60 o.p. (73-530). Lancer.

Tower Room. Mary Linn Roby. LC 74-341. 1974. 6.95 (ISBN 0-8015-7840-X). Hawthorn Books.

Tower Room. Mary Linn Roby. 1975. (pbk.) 1.25 (ISBN 0-523-00684-5). Pinnacle Books.

Tower Room. Julia Trevelyan. 1979. pap. 1.75 (ISBN 0-451-08711-9, E8711, Sig). NAL.

Towers Along the Grass: A Novel. Ellen Du Poise Taylor. LC 28-29242. 1928. Harper & Brothers.

Towers at the Edge of a World. Virgil Burnett. LC 80-14391. 1980. 10.95 (ISBN 0-312-81151-9). St. Martin's Press.

Towers in the Midst. Elizabeth Goudge. 386p. 1979. Repr. lib. bdg. 15.95x (ISBN 0-89966-109-2). Buccaneer Bks.

Towers in the Mist. Elizabeth Goudge. LC 38-27411. Coward-McCann, Inc.

Towers Inheritance: A Novel. 1st Ed. Catherine Rodgers. LC 58-5954. N. Y.

Towers of Illium. Ethelyn Leslie Huston. LC 16-20589. 1.35. George H. Doran Company.

Towers of Love. 1st Ed. Stephen Birmingham. LC 61-14549. 1961. Little, Brown.

Towers of Melnon. Jeffrey Lord. (Blade Ser. No. 15). 192p. 1975. pap. 2.25 (ISBN 0-523-41722-5). Pinnacle Bks.

Towers of Melnon. Jeffrey Lord. (Blade Heroic Fantasy Series, 15). 1975. (pbk.) 1.25 (ISBN 0-523-00688-8). Pinnacle Books.

Towers of St. Nicholas: A Story of the Days of "Good Queens Bess,". Mary Agatha Gray. LC 14-1108. 0.75. P. J. Kenedy & Sons.

Towers of Silence. Paul Scott. 1979. 2.50 (ISBN 0-380-44198-5). Avon.

Towers of Silence: A Novel. Paul Scott. LC 79-166355. 1972. 8.95. Morrow.

Towers of Trebizond. Rose Macaulay. LC 57-5921. 1957. Straus and Cudahy.

Towers with Ivy. Minnie Hite Moody. LC 37-9865. J. Messner, Inc.

Towhead: The Story of a Girl. Sarah Pratt McLean Greene. LC 6-45566. 1883. A. Williams and Company.

Town. William Faulkner. LC 57-6656. 1957. Random House.

Town. Conrad Richter. LC 50-6331. 1950. Knopf.

Town. Conrad Richter. 1975. (pbk.) 1.25. Bantam Books.

Town see Snopes: A Trilogy.

Town and Dr. Moore. Agnes Brooks Young. LC 66-11067. bds., 5.95. S. & S.

Town and Gown. Lynn Montross & Lois Seyster Montross. LC 70-132122. (Short story index reprint series). 1970. (ISBN 0-8369-3679-5). Books for Libraries Press.

Town and Gown. Lynn Montross & Montross, Lois Seyster. LC 23-3553. 2.00. George H. Doran Company.

Town & Square: From the Agora to the Village Green. Paul Zucker. (Illus.). 1970. pap. 4.95 o.p. (ISBN 0-262-74005-2, MIT-152). MIT Pr.

Town & the City. John Kerouac. 1970. pap. 7.95 (ISBN 0-15-690790-9, Harv). HarBraceJ.

Town & the City. 1st Ed. John Kerouac. LC 50-5679. 1950. Harcourt, Brace.

Town and the Trust. Harrison Eastman Patten. LC 10-233203. 1910. 1.25. The Neale Publishing Company.

Town Below. Roger Lemelin. Tr. by Putnam, Samuel. LC 48-665684. 1948. Reynal & Hitchcock.

Town Beyond the Wall. Elie Wiesel. LC 81-16546. 1982. 5.95 (ISBN 0-8052-0697-3). Schocken Books.

Town Beyond the Wall. new ed. Eliezer Wiesel. LC 67-27829. 1967. Holt, Rinehart and Winston.

Town Bull. 1971. pap. 1.45 o.p. (Z1072Q, Zebra). Grove.

Town Bull: Or, The Elysian Fields. LC 70-162821. (Zebra books, Z-1072-Q). 1970. 1.45. Grove Press.

Town Burning. Thomas Williams. 1959. Macmillan.

Town Burning. Thomas Williams. LC 70-102327. 1970. 6.95. Random House.

Town Called Charity: And Other Stories About Decisions. Blaine M. Yorgason & Brenton G Yorgason. LC 80-67358. 1980. 5.50 (ISBN 0-88494-408-5). Bookcraft.

Town Called Yellowdog. John Thomas Edson. 192p. (Orig.). 1981. pap. 1.95 (ISBN 0-425-04850-0). Berkley Pub.

Town Cried Murder. Zenith Jones Brown. LC 39-278743. 1939. C. Scribner's Sons.

Town from the Treetop. Dan Potter. LC 64-136536. bds., 3.95. Delacorte Pr. Dist. Dial.

Town Girl. Elizabeth Carfrae, pseud. LC 36-362. G. P. Putnam's Sons.

Town House. Norah Robinson Lofts. (Crest bk., P1756). (Illus.). 1972. 1.25. Fawcett.

Town House. Evelyn Gaurley Marley. LC 39-24446. 1939. R. R. Smith.

Town House: The Building of the House. 1st Ed. Norah Robinson Lofts. LC 59-13680. 1959. Doubleday.

Town in Bloom. 1st Amer. Ed. Dorothy Gladys Smith. LC 65-15239. bds., 4.95. Atlantic-Little.

Town Is Born: An American Christmas Story of Today. Tom Sayres. LC 38-34144. 1938. The Macmillan Company.

Town Is Drowning: Novel by Frederik Pohl and C. M. Kornbluth. Frederik Pohl & Cyril M. Kornbluth. LC 55-12407. Ballantine Books.

Town Is Full of Rumors. Ruth Wilson & Wilson, Alexander, 1898- Joint Author. LC 41-140617. 1941. Simon and Schuster.
Town Landing. Mabel Adelaide Farnum. LC 24-1492. 1923. P. J. Kenedy & Sons.
Town Like Alice. Nevil Shute. 1982. pap. 2.75 (ISBN 0-345-30565-5). Ballantine.
Town Like Alice; Pied Piper; The Far Country; The Chequer Board; No Highway. Nevil Shute Norway. LC 77-369233. 1976. 3.95 (ISBN 0-7064-0574-9). Heinemann: Octopus Books.
Town Like Any Other. Gerard Smith. LC 72-86861. 1972. 5.95 (ISBN 0-8059-1745-4). Dorrance.
Town of Blood. W. L. Fieldhouse. (Klaw Ser.: No. 2). (Orig.). 1981. pap. 1.75 (ISBN 0-505-51671-3). Tower Bks.
Town of Masks. Dorothy Salisbury Davis. LC 52-1691. 1952. Scribner.
Town of Tombarel. William John Locke. LC 71-150548. (Short story index reprint series). 1971. (ISBN 0-8369-3845-3). Books for Libraries Press.
Town of Tombarel. William John Locke. LC 30-860347. 1930. Dodd, Mead & Company.
Town on the Hill: A Novel. Melesina Mary Blount. LC 28-28682. 1928. Benziger Brothers.
Town on Trial, a Novel of Racial Violence in a Southern Town. 1st Ed. Nathaniel Hooks. LC 59-3594. 1959. Exposition Press.
Town Pump: An American Comedy. Charles Ellsworth Grapewin & Hillyer, Anthony. LC 33-18222. 1933. T. P. Stricker.
Town Tales of Times Past. Julius Buscher. 3.50 o.p. Carlton.
Town Tamer. Parker Bonner. (Orig.). 1968. pap. 0.50 o.p. (62-021). Paperback Lib.
Town Tamer. Peter Germano. 1976. pap. 1.25 o.p. (ISBN 0-532-12446-4). Woodhill.
Town Tamer. Peter Germano. 1976. pap. 1.25 o.p. (ISBN 0-532-12446-4). Manor Bks.
Town Tamer. Frank Gruber. LC 58-5117. 1958. Rinehart.
Town Tamer. Ray Hogan. 1981. pap. 1.95 (ISBN 0-451-11083-8, AJ1083, Sig). NAL.
Town That Saw No Evil. Harry Kantor. 1977. pap. 1.75 (ISBN 0-89041-148-4, 3148). Major Bks.
Town to Tame. Joseph Chadwick. 1979. pap. 1.50 (ISBN 0-449-14234-5, GM). Fawcett.
Town Traveller. George Robert Gissing. LC 68-54268. 1968. AMS Press.
Town Traveller. George Robert Gissing. LC 98-235. Frederick A. Stokes Company.
Town Without Pity: Translated by Robert Brain. Manfred Gregor. LC 61-12159. 1961. Random House.
Townman. Hilma Inman. LC 35-183. Ruth Hill.
Townsend Murder Mystery. Octavus Roy Cohen. LC 33-20522. 1933. D. Appleton Century Company, Incorporated.
Townsman. Pearl Sydenstricker Buck. 1945. 8.95 o.p. (ISBN 0-381-98058-8, A81800). John Day.
Townsman. John Sedges, pseud. LC 45-350928. 1945. The John Day Company.
Towser, Sheep Dog. 1st American Ed. Henry George Lamond. LC 56-5262. 1956. Dutton.
Toxar: A Romance. Joseph Shield Nicholson. LC 7-23127. (On cover: Harper's Franklin square library. no. 676). 1890. Harper & Brothers.
Toxin: A Story of Venice. Louise De La Ramee. LC 6-33303. (Twentieth century series). Frederick A. Stokes Company.
Toy. Kage Booton. LC 74-25093. 1975. 5.95 (ISBN 0-385-06992-8). Published for the Crime Club by Doubleday.
Toy. Gertrude Sanborn. LC 22-21803. 1922. M. A. Donohue & Company.
Toy Goes West. Patricia Clapton. (Signet, Q5528). 1973. (pbk.) 0.95. New American Lib.
Toy Shop, and Other Stories. Valeria L Burns. LC 53-29497. 1953. New Voices Pub. Co.
Toy Soldiers. Wayne A. Baker. 4.50 o.p. Vantage.
Toy Soldiers. Wayne A Baker. 1973. 4.50 (ISBN 0-533-00360-1). Vantage Press.
Toy Sword. Elizabeth Cadell. LC 62-11899. 1962. Morrow.
Toy Tragedy: A Story of Children. Elizabeth Bonham De La Pasture. LC 7-25668. 1906. E. P. Dutton and Company.
Toya the Unlike. Eleanor Mercein Kelly. LC 13-13540. 1.00. Small, Maynard and Company.
Toyko-Montana Express. Richard Brautigan. (O.s.i.). 1980. 10.95 o.s.i. (ISBN 0-440-08770-8, Sey Lawr); pap. 2.50 o.s.i. (ISBN 0-440-03725-5). Delacorte.
Toyland. Mark Smith. LC 65-20749. 1965. Little, Brown.
Toymaker. Jones. 5.00; pap. 2.00. Fantasy Pub Co.
Toymaker. 1st Ed. Raymond F Jones. LC 51-2678. 1951. Fantasy Pub. Co.
Toymakers. Charles Felton Pidgin. LC 7-15921. 1907. The C. M. Clark Publishing Co.
Toyman. E. C. Tubb. (Dumerest of Terra Ser.). 160p. 1982. pap. 1.95 (ISBN 0-441-81973-7). Ace Bks.
Toys of Peace: And Other Papers. Hector Hugh Munro. Ed. by Reynolds, Rothay. LC 19-7080. 1919. John Lane.
TR. Noel Bertram Gerson. LC 69-17863. 1970. 6.95. Doubleday.
Trace of Footprints. Ruth Wolff. LC 68-11298. (John Day Bk.). 1968. 6.50 o.p. (ISBN 0-381-98203-3, A8200). T y Crowell.
Trace of Footprints: A Novel. Ruth Wolff. LC 68-11298. 1968. John Day Co.
Trace of Red. Edward Hannibal. LC 81-15268. 13.95 (ISBN 0-385-27220-0). Dial Press.
Tracer of Lost Persons. Robert William Chambers. 1906. D. Appleton and Company.
Tracer: The Search for Missing Persons. Ed Goldfader. LC 72-107861. 1970. 5.95 o.p. (ISBN 0-8402-1134-1, 1134). Nash Pub.
Traceries. Olive Wadsley. LC 28-226618. 1928. Dodd, Mead & Company.
Traces. Patricia Wallace. 1982. pap. 2.95 (ISBN 0-8217-1007-9). Zebra.
Traces of Brillhart. Herbert Brean. 1965. pap. 0.95 o.p. (01777, Collier). Macmillan.
Traces of Brillhart: A Novel of Suspense, Detection, and a Curious Immortality. Herbert Brean. LC 60-7552. 1960. Harper.
Traces of Merrilee. Herbert Brean. 1966. bds., 3.95. Morrow.
Track of a Killer. Stephen Overholser. LC 82-60309. 1982. 10.95 (ISBN 0-8027-4013-8). Walker.
Track of a Killer. Stephen Overholser. 1982. 10.95 (ISBN 0-8027-4013-8). Walker & Co.
Track of a Storm. H. H. Lusk. LC 7-18775. 1896. J. B. Lippincott Company.
Track of the Albatross. Rudolph Mellard. (Illus.). 1974. 10.00x. A Jones.
Track of the Beast. Ralph Hayes. (Hunter#4). 1975. (pbk.) 1.25. Leisure Books.
Track of the Cat: A Novel. Walter Van Tilburg Clark. 1949. Random House.
Track of the Hunter. Lewis B Patten. LC 80-24615. 1981. 11.50 (ISBN 0-89340-307-5). J. Curley.
Track of the Snake. Gene Shelton. (Belmont-Tower books). 1979. 1.75 (ISBN 0-505-51387-0). Tower Pubns.
Track the Man Down. Bob Haning, pseud. LC 74-31215. 1974-1975. (ISBN 0-517-52119-9). Lenox Hill Press.
Track the Man Down. Theodore V Olsen. LC 74-27450. 1975. 5.95 (ISBN 0-385-09957-6). Doubleday.
Track to Bralgu. B Wongar. LC 77-18774. (Illus.). 6.95 (ISBN 0-316-95158-7). Little, Brown.
Trackdown. Arthur Moore. (Orig.). 1980. pap. 1.75 o.s.i. (ISBN 0-505-51501-6). Tower Bks.
Trackdown. Dean Owen. (Latigo Ser.: Vol. I). 224p. 1981. pap. 1.95 (ISBN 0-445-04644-9). Popular Lib.
Tracked by Wireless. William Le Queux. LC 23-6696. 1922. Moffat, Yard & Company.
Tracked to the West: Or, Nat Ridley at the Magnet Mine. Nat Jr Ridley. LC 26-12839. (His Nat Ridley series--2). 1926. Garden City Publishing Co., Inc.
Tracker. Tom Brown & William J. Watkins. 1979. pap. 2.50 (ISBN 0-425-04222-7). Berkley Pub.
Tracker. David Wagoner. LC 75-6812. 1975. 7.95 (ISBN 0-316-91700-1). Little, Brown.
Tracking the Bar-J Gold. Robert E. Trevathan. (YA) 1978. 6.95 (Avalon). Bouregy.
Tracking the Wolfpack. J. Farragut Jones. (Silent Service Ser.: No. 5). (Orig.). 1981. pap. 2.95 (ISBN 0-440-18589-0). Dell.
Trackless Death. Armstrong Livingston. LC 30-109789. The Bobbs-Merrill Company.
Tracks. Malaki. LC 78-11120. (Illus.). 1979. cloth 15.50 (ISBN 0-916906-17-5); signed ed. 35.00 (ISBN 0-916906-18-3); pap. 10.00 (ISBN 0-916906-16-7). Konglomerati.
Track's End: Being the Narratives of Judson Pitcher's Strange Winter Spent There As Told by Himself and Edited. Hayden Carruth. LC 11-23058. 1911. Harper & Brothers.
Tracks in the Snow. Ruthven Todd. LC 76-51349. (English Literature Ser, No. 33). 1977. lib. bdg. 37.95x (ISBN 0-8383-2159-3). Haskell.
Tracks in the Snow, by Lord Charnwood... Godfrey Rathbone Benson Charnwood. LC 28-2383. 1928. L. MacVeagh, The Dial Press.
Tracks on the River: A Novel. Olive Carr. LC 51-11836. 1951. Exposition Press.
Tracks We Tread. Edith J. Lyttleton. LC 7-28459. 1907. Doubleday, Page & Company.
Tract Number 3377: A Romance of the Oil Region. George Henry Higgins & Haffey, Margaret (Higgins) LC 9-25185. 1909. 1.50. The C. M. Clark Publishing Company.
Tract of Time. Smith Hempstone. LC 66-11226. 4.95. Houghton.
Tract of Time. Smith Hempstone. (Crest bk., R964). Fawcett.
Tracy Diamonds. Mary Jane Hawes Holmes. LC 99-4224. 1899. G. W. Dillingham Co.
Tracy's Tiger. William Saroyan. LC 51-13965. 1951. Doubleday.
Trade. William H Hallahan. LC 80-22248. 1981. 12.95 (ISBN 0-688-00103-3). Morrow.
Trade Imperial. Alan Lloyd. LC 78-26239. 1979. 10.95 (ISBN 0-698-10970-8). Coward, McCann & Geoghegan.
Trade-off. Victor B Miller. 1975. (pbk.) 1.25 (ISBN 0-671-80045-0). Pocket Books.
Trade-off. G. F Newman. (Dell Book). 1979. 1.95 (ISBN 0-440-18642-0). Dell Pub. Co.
Trade Secrets. Gabrielle Hughes. 288p. (Orig.). 1983. pap. 2.95 (ISBN 0-523-48049-0). Pinnacle Bks.
Trade Squares: The Last of the Roving Horse Traders, a Novel. David Maltom. LC 51-4760. 1951. Exposition Press.
Trade Wind. Mary Margaret Kaye. LC 64-1307. 1964. Coward McCann.
Trade Wind. Mary Margaret Kaye. LC 80-28302. 15.00 (ISBN 0-312-81226-4). St. Martin's Press.
Trade Wind Tales. Wade Warren Thayer. LC 55-44866. 1955. Printed by the Honolulu Star-Bulletin, Ltd.
Trade Wind Tales. Wade Warren Thayer. LC 44-7076. 1944. Tongg Publishing Company.
Trade Winds Over Kokio. G. Laura Raef. (Orig.). 1979. pap. 1.75 (ISBN 0-532-17246-9). Woodhill.
Tradegy That Wins: And Other Short Stories. Ed. by John Francis Xavier O'Conor. LC 5-20444. 1905. J. J. McVey.
Trademark of a Traitor. Kathleen Moore Knight. LC 43-101743. 1943. Pub. for the Crime Club by Doubleday, Doran and Co., Inc.
Tradeoffs. Jane Adams. Ed. by Pat Golbitz. 372p. 1983. 14.95 (ISBN 0-688-01366-X). Morrow.
Trader Ike & the Lost Gold Mine: As Told by Native Boy, Sam John, Vol. 2. Ira Weisner. LC 74-78073. (Illus.). 200p. 1974. 7.95 o.p. (ISBN 0-8059-2026-9). Dorrance.
Trader to the Stars. Poul Anderson. (Berkley Medallion Book). 1976. 1.25 (ISBN 0-425-03199-3). Berkley.
Traders. Marjel Jean De Lauer. 384p. (Orig.). 1981. pap. 2.75 (ISBN 0-440-18586-6). Dell.
Trader's Cat. Rebecca Stratton. (Harlequin Romances Ser.). 192p. 1980. pap. 1.25 (ISBN 0-373-02376-6, Pub. by Harlequin). PB.
Trader's Wife. Jean Kenyon Mackenzie. LC 30-7297. 1930. Coward-McCann, Inc.
Tradesman's Boast. Ann Sophia Winterbotham Stephens. LC 6-24373. 1846. Gleason's Publishing Hall.
Trading Post. Milton Krims. LC 32-690028. The Macaulay Company.
Trading up. Joan Lea. LC 75-10983. 1975. 8.95 (ISBN 0-689-10680-7). Atheneum.
Trading up. joan lea. ed. Joan Lea. 1976. 1.95 (ISBN 0-449-23014-7). Fawcett Crest.
Trading West: A Novel. Joseph Hudson Plumb. LC 41-733119. B. Humphries, Inc.
Tradition. George Frederick Hummel. LC 36-20256. 1936. Coward-McCann.
Tradition. Marie Van Vorst. LC 21-164315. Small, Maynard & Company.
Tradition of Pride. Janet Dailey. (Harlequin Presents Ser.). 192p. 1981. pap. 1.50 (ISBN 0-373-10421-9, Pub. by Harlequin). PB.
Traditional Indian Stories About Bhaskarananda see India & Her Miracle Feast-Come & Enjoy Yourself.
Traditional Indian Stories About Devadas Maharaj see India & Her Miracle Feast-Come & Enjoy Yourself.
Traditional Indian Stories About Shayama Charan Lahiri see India & Her Miracle Feast-Come & Enjoy Yourself.
Traditional Indian Stories About Troilanga Swami see India & Her Miracle Feast-Come & Enjoy Yourself.
Traditional Tales of the English and Scottish Peasantry. Allan Cunningham. LC 6-32175. (Half-title: Morley's universal library. v. 56). 1887. G. Routledge and Sons.
Traditionary Stories and Legendary Illustrations. Andrew Picken. 1833. E. C. Mielke.
Traditions. Alan Ebert & Janice Rotchstein. 1983. pap. 3.95 (ISBN 0-671-22838-2). Bantam.
Traditions: A Novel. Alan Ebert & Janice Rotchstein. LC 81-5045. 14.95 (ISBN 0-517-54492-X). Crown.
Traditions of Palestine: Or, Scenes in the Holy Land in the Days of Christ. Moses H. Sargent. LC 8-1824.
Traditions of the Tigris. Dikran Spear. LC 46-20366. 1946.
Trafalgar: A Tale. Benito Perez Galdos. Tr. by Bell, Clara Courtenay (Poynter) LC 7-36349. 1884. W. S. Gottsberger.
Trafalgar Rose. Clare F. Holmes. 160p. (Orig.). 1981. pap. 1.95 (ISBN 0-553-20100-X). Bantam.
Trafalgar Square. Claire Rayner. Orig. Title: Strand. 320p. 1982. pap. 3.25 o.s.i. (ISBN 0-8439-1152-2, Leisure Bks). Nordon Pubns.
Traffic in Souls: A Novel of Crime and Its Cure. Eustace Hale Ball. LC 14-698799. G. W. Dillingham Company.
Traffic, the Story of a Faithful Woman. Ernest Temple Thurston. LC 6-29093. 1906. G. W. Dillingham Company.
Traffic with Evil. 1st Ed. Johns, Avery. LC 62-12921. 1962. Published for the Crime Club by Doubleday.
Traffics and Discoveries. Rudyard Kipling. LC 4-27127. 1904. Doubleday, Page & Company.
Traffics and Discoveries. Rudyard Kipling. LC 41-42428. (Half-title: The pocket Kipling). 1909. Doubleday, Page & Company.
Traffics and Discoveries. Rudyard Kipling. LC 18-21827. 1914. Doubleday, Page & Company, for Review of Reviews Co.
Traffics and Discoveries. Rudyard Kipling. LC 28-1674. 1920. Doubleday, Page & Company.
Traffics and Discoveries. Actions and Reactions. Rudyard Kipling. LC 52-485173. (Mandalay edition of the works of Rudyard Kipling). 1925. Doubleday, Page.
Traficante. Frank Hilaire. LC 79-27313. 8.85 (ISBN 0-312-81327-9). St. Martin's Press.
Traficante Treasure. easy eye ed. Daoma Winston. (Orig.). pap. 0.60 o.p. (73-723). Lancer.
Traficante Treasure. Daoma Winston. 1976. (pbk.) 1.50 (ISBN 0-671-80435-9). Pocket Books.
Trafton Helen. Jonathan Leonard. LC 32-21191. 1932. Houghton Mifflin Company.
Tragedies of Life: Takes Place in the United States. Gertrude Pitts. LC 39-25324.
Tragedy at Beechcroft. Archibald E. Fielding. LC 35-154657. 1935. H. C. Kinsey & Company, Inc.
Tragedy at Chualar. Ernesto Galarza. 1979. pap. 4.00 (ISBN 0-87461-022-2). McNally.
Tragedy at Freyne. Lucy Beatrice Malleson. LC 27-9863. 1927. L. MacVeagh, The Dial Press.
Tragedy at Law. Cyril Hare. (Perennial Library). 1980. 2.25 (ISBN 0-06-080522-6). Harper & Row.
Tragedy at Ravensthorpe. Alfred Walter Stewart. LC 28-5169. 1928. Little, Brown, and Company.
Tragedy at the Beach Club. William Andrew Johnston. LC 22-4085. 1922. 1.75. Little, Brown, and Company.
Tragedy at the Unicorn. Cecil John Charles Street. LC 28-20603. 1928. Dodd, Mead & Company.
Tragedy at Twelvetrees. Arthur John Rees. LC 31-29491. 1931. Dodd, Mead & Company.
Tragedy at Wembley: A Tale of Inspector Higgins. Cecil Freeman Gregg. LC 36-34843. The Dial Press.
Tragedy in Blue. Marion Bramhall. LC 45-506578. 1945. Pub. for the Crime Club by Doubleday, Doran & Co., Inc.
Tragedy in E Flat. Leonard Reginald Gribble. LC 39-32051. 1939. Hillman-Curl, Inc.
Tragedy in Paradise. Henry Holm. 1960. Dorrance.
Tragedy in Pewsey Chart. Hilda Willett. LC 29-176609. 1929. Longmans, Green and Co.
Tragedy in the Hollow. Freeman Wills Crofts. LC 39-22445. 1939. Dodd, Mead & Company.
Tragedy in the Imperial Harem at Constantinople. Adriana Piazzi & Colston, Raleigh Edward. 1825-1896, Tr. LC 7-35923. 1883. W. S. Gottsberger.
Tragedy in the Imperial Harem at Constantinople. Adriana Delcambre Piazzi. Tr. by Colston, Raleigh Edward. LC 7-35923. 1883. W. S. Gottsberger.
Tragedy in the Rue De la Paix. Adolphe Belot. LC 6-11350. (On cover: Sea and shore series, no. 37). 1891. Street & Smith.
Tragedy in Turquoise. Louis Trimble. LC 42-196894. 1942. Phoenix Press.
Tragedy in Whiskers. Harold Thayer Davis. LC 18-2603. 1917. Apex Book Co.
Tragedy of a Widow's Third. Anna Christy Fall. LC 98-231. 1898. I. P. Fox.
Tragedy of Ages. Isabella M. Witherspoon. LC 8-37127. 1897. F. T. Neely.
Tragedy of an Indiscretion. John William Brodie-Innes. LC 16-13748. 1916. John Lane.
Tragedy of Baden. Cary Hamilton Wilkinson. LC 6-24577. 1906. The Neale Publishing Ocmpany.
Tragedy of Brinkwater: A Novel. Martha Livingston Moodey. LC 7-262226. (On cover: Cassell's sunshine series of choice fiction. v. 1, no. 13). 1888. Cassell & Company, Limited.
Tragedy of Errors. Arleigh Lee Darby. LC 54-834219. 1954. Vantage Press.
Tragedy of Ida Noble: A Novel. William Clark Russell. LC 8-1808. (On cover: Appletons' town and country library, no. 82). 1891. D. Appleton and Company.
Tragedy of Jane Shore. Nicholas Rowe. 1975. text ed. 15.95x o.s.i. (ISBN 0-8277-3954-0); pap. text ed. 8.50x o.s.i. (ISBN 0-8277-2351-2). British Bk Ctr.
Tragedy of Love and Hate: Or, A Woman's Vow. Bertha M. Clay. LC 48-445464. (Bertha Clay library, no. 153). 1902. Street & Smith.

TITLE INDEX TRAIL SMOKE.

Tragedy of Pudd'nhead Wilson. Samuel Langhorne Clemens. LC 65-9623. (Harper perennial classic). Harper & Row.
Tragedy of Pudd'nhead Wilson: And the Comedy Those Extraordinary, Twins. Samuel Langhorne Clemens. LC 6-21348. 1894. American Publishing Company.
Tragedy of Richard the Second. Robert J. Myers. LC 73-13017. 128p. 1973. 4.95 o.p. (ISBN 0-87491-371-3); pap. 4.95 o.p. (ISBN 0-87491-372-1). Acropolis.
Tragedy of the Chinese Mine. Ian Greig. LC 31-800. H. Holt and Company.
Tragedy of the Deserted Isle: A Chronicle of the Burr and Blennerhassett Conspiracy. Warren Wood. 1909. The C. M. Clark Publishing Company.
Tragedy of the Korosko. Arthur Conan Doyle. LC 80-67706. (Conan Doyle Centennial Ser.). (Illus.). 202p. 1983. 11.95 (ISBN 0-934468-47-8). Gaslight.
Tragedy of the Korosko. Arthur Conan Doyle. 5.95 o.p. (ISBN 0-7195-0381-7). Transatlantic.
Tragedy of the Korosko. Arthur Conan Doyle. 5.95 o.p. (ISBN 0-7195-0381-7). Transatlantic.
Tragedy of the Moon. Isaac Asimov. 1978. pap. 1.50 (ISBN 0-440-18999-3). Dell.
Tragedy of the Mountains: Or, The White Rocks. A Thrilling Tale of the Allegheneis. Alonzo F. Hill. LC 7-49423. (On cover: Columbian library. no. 1). 1890. Columbian Publishing Company.
Tragedy of the Unexpected: And Other Stories. Nora Perry. LC 7-36174. 1880. Houghton, Mifflin and Company.
Tragedy of the White Medicine: A Story of Indian Mystery, Revenge, and Love. Charles Edmund DeLand. LC 14-616. 1913. 1.00. The Neale Publishing Company.
Tragedy of Wild River Valley. Martha Finley. LC 6-41217. Dodd, Mead & Company.
Tragedy of X. Ellery Queen, pseud. LC 76-50693. (Mystery Library: Vol. 7). (Illus.). 1978. Repr. of 1932 ed. 10.95 o.p. (ISBN 0-89163-031-7). Pubs Inc.
Tragedy of X: A Drury Land Mystery. Ellery Queen. LC 32-7351. 1932. The Viking Press.
Tragedy of Y: A Drury Lane Mystery. Ellery Queen. LC 32-23140. 1932. The Viking Press.
Tragedy of Z: A Drury Lane Mystery. Ellery Queen, pseud. LC 33-6791. 1933. The Viking Press.
Tragedy on the Line. Cecil John Charles Street. LC 31-588016. 1931. Dodd, Mead & Company.
Tragedy Trail. Max Brand. 1982. pap. 2.25 (ISBN 0-671-41563-8). PB.
Tragedy Trail. Max Brand. 1982. 18.00x (ISBN 0-86025-149-7, Pub. by Ian Henry Pubns England). State Mutual Bk.
Tragg's Choice. Clifton Adams. LC 69-15578. (DD western). 1969. 3.95. Doubleday.
Tragic Bride: By Francis Brett Young. Francis Brett Young. LC 21-554357. E. P. Dutton & Company.
Tragic Comedians. George Meredith. LC 74-29508. (Modern Jewish Experience). 1975. 10.00 (ISBN 0-405-06735-6). Arno Press.
Tragic Comedians: A Study in a Well-Known Story. author's ed. George Meredith. Ed. by Clement King Shorter. LC 1-19372. 1892. Roberts Brothers.
Tragic Comedians: A Study in a Well-Known Story. rev. ed. George Meredith. LC 1-19375. 1898. C. Scribner's Sons.
Tragic Curtain. Stanley Hart Page. LC 35-19871. The Dial Press, Inc.
Tragic Fall of Chimpanza: Or, The Perils of Example. Alexander D Penfold. LC 42-26423. 1911. The Knickerbocker Press.
Tragic Forest: Tales of the Forest of Tombolo. John A Schillace. LC 51-12081. 1951. Exposition Press.
Tragic Ground. autograph ed. Erskine - Caldwell. 1961. Grosset & Dunlap.
Tragic Ground & Trouble in July. Erskine Caldwell. LC 79-110362. (Plume book). 1979. 4.95 (ISBN 0-452-25204-0). New American Library.
Tragic Idyl. Paul Charles Joseph Bourget. LC 6-14922. 1896. C. Scribner's Sons.
Tragic Innocents: A Novel. Rene Barjavel. LC 49-9301. 1949. Rinehart.
Tragic Magic: A Novel. Wesley Brown. LC 78-57136. 7.95 (ISBN 0-394-50224-8). Random House.
Tragic Muse. Henry James. LC 74-13067. (Apollo editions, A-385). 1975. 5.95 (ISBN 0-8152-0376-4). Crowell.
Tragic Muse. Henry James. LC 77-158786. (Scribner reprint editions). 1975. 13.50 (ISBN 0-678-02807-9) (ISBN 0-678-02808-7). A. M. Kelley.
Tragic Muse. Henry James. LC 7-7431. 1890. Houghton, Mifflin and Company.
Tragic Muse. Introd. by Leon Edel. Henry James. (Harper torchbooks, TB1017. The Academy library). 1960. Harper.
Tragic Muse. With an Introd. by R. P. Blackmur. Henry James. LC 61-425093. (Laurel Henry James, LX133). 1961. Dell Pub. Co.
Tragic Mystery: From the Diary of Inspector Byrnes. Julian Hawthorne & Byrnes, Thomas F., 1847?- LC 9-2211. Cassell & Company, Limited.
Tragic Mystery: From the Diary of Inspector Byrnes. Julian Hawthorne & Byrnes, Thomas F., 1847?- (On cover: Cassell's "rainbow" series, no. 24). 1888. Cassell & Company, Limited.
Tragic Target. 1st Ed. Mary Violet Heberden. LC 52-5537. 1952. Published for the Crime Club by Doubleday.
Tragicall Historye of Romeus & Juliet. Arthur Broke. LC 78-26035. (English Experience Ser.: No. 134). 168p. 1969. Repr. of 1562 ed. 21.00 (ISBN 90-221-0134-7). Walter J Johnson.
Trago. Frank Bonham. 192p. 1981. pap. 1.95 (ISBN 0-425-05041-6). Berkley Pub.
Trail. Sallie Lee Bell. LC 65-25951. 1966. Zondervan Pub. House.
Trail a Boy Travels, and Other Stories. Hervey Smith McCowan. 1916. Association Press.
Trail and Self-Discipline. Sarah Savage. LC 9-945. (Added t.-p.: Scenes and characters illustrating Christian truth ed. by H. Ware no. I). 1835. J. Munroe and Company.
Trail Back. Will McCann. Ed. by Alice Sachs. 1970. 3.95 o.p. Lenox Hill.
Trail Boss. Peter Dawson. 192p. (Orig.). 1981. pap. 1.95 (ISBN 0-553-12968-6). Bantam.
Trail Boss. John Thomas Edson. 1980. 1.95 (ISBN 0-425-04624-9). Berkley Books.
Trail Boss. Walter Gann. LC 37-17660. 1937. Houghton Mifflin Company.
Trail Boss. Jonathan H. Glidda. LC 43-2618. 1943. Dodd, Mead & Company.
Trail Boss from Texas. Barry Cord. 1979. pap. 1.25 o.s.i. (ISBN 0-505-51337-4). Tower Bks.
Trail Boss from Texas. Peter Germano. LC 48-2648. 1948. Phoenix Press.
Trail Builders. Leslie Scott. LC 56-129334. 1956. Arcadia House.
Trail Drive. Peter McCurtin. (Sundance Ser.: No. 36). 1981. pap. 1.95 (ISBN 0-8439-0878-5, Leisure Bks). Nordon Pubns.
Trail Drive: A True Narrative of Cowboy Life from Andy Adams' Log of a Cowboy. Ed., Illus. by Glen Rounds. Andy Adams. Ed. by Glen Rounds. LC 65-7571. (Includes all the trial episodes, which comprised about three-quarters of the original bk.). 3.95. Holiday House.
Trail Driver. Zane Grey. LC 36-418. 1936. Harper & Brothers.
Trail Driver. Zane Grey. LC 78-2625. 1978. 9.95 (ISBN 0-89340-136-6). J. Curley.
Trail Dust... Harry Sinclair Drago. LC 47-1014. 1947. Dodd, Mead & Company.
Trail Dust. large type ed. Clarence E. Mulford. Repr. lib. bdg. 16.60x (ISBN 0-88411-240-3). Amereon Ltd.
Trail Dust. Clarence Edward Mulford. 311p. 1974. Repr. of 1934 ed. lib. bdg. 16.60x large type ed. (ISBN 0-88411-212-8). Amereon Ltd.
Trail Dust, Hopalong Cassidy and the Bar 20 with the Trail Herd. Clarence Edward Mulford. LC 73-89659. 1973. 6.95. Aeonian Press.
Trail Dust: Hopalong Cassidy and the Bar 20 with the Trial Herd. Clarence Edward Mulford. LC 34-27135. 1934. Doubleday, Doran & Company, Inc.
Trail Eater: A Romance of the All-Alaska Sweepstakes. Florance Barrett Willoughby. LC 29-12915. 1929. G. P. Putnam's Sons.
Trail End. 1st Ed. Tom J Hopkins. LC 52-11618. (Double D western). 1952. Doubleday.
Trail from Devil's Country. Albert M Treynor. LC 26-6335. 1926. Dodd, Mead and Company.
Trail from Needle Rock: A Powder Valley Western. Peter Field. LC 47-183717. 1947. Jefferson House.
Trail from Texas. Dale Homer. LC 56-13311. Avalon Books.
Trail-Hardened. John G Lees. 1974. 4.95. Lenox Hill Press.
Trail Herd. Bradford Scott. LC 44-5987. 1944. Arcadia House, Inc.
Trail Herd. Strong, Charles Stanley. LC 51-12285. 1951. Phoenix Press.
Trail Horde. Charles Alden Seltzer. LC 20-161616. 1920. A. C. McClurg & Co.
Trail-Hunter. A Tale of the Far West. rev. and ed. by percy b. st. john. ed. Gustave Aimard & St. John, Percy Bolingbroke, 1821-1889, Ed. LC 5-42192. (On cover: Lovell's library, v. 11, no 567). 1885. J. W. Lovell Company.
Trail-Makers of the Middle Border. Hamlin Garland. Ed. by Donald Pizer. LC 70-96601. (American Authors Ser., Collected Works of Hamlin Garland, 45 Vols). 1969. Repr. of 1926 ed. lib. bdg. 19.75 o.s.i. (ISBN 0-512-00264-9). Garrett Pr.
Trail Markers of the Middle Border see Collected Works.
Trail Mates. Ney N Geer. LC 37-39115. Covici-Friede.
Trail North. Gordon Cortis Baldwin. LC 57-3330. 1957. Arcadia House.
Trail North. Al Cody, pseud. 160p. 1974. pap. 0.95 o.p. (532-95351-095). Manor Bks.
Trail North. Hawk Greenway. (Illus.). 180p. (Orig.). 1981. pap. 7.50 (ISBN 0-933280-04-1). Island CA.
Trail of a Gunfighter. Joseph Caruso. LC 61-5947. 1961. Macmillan.
Trail of a Sourdough: Life in Alaska. May Kellogg Sullivan. LC 10-225391. R. G. Badger.
Trail of a Tenderfoot. Stephen Chalmers. LC 11-1645. 1911. Outing Publishing Company.
Trail of Billy the Kid. Robert E. Alter. (O.s.i.). (Orig.). 1975. pap. 0.95 o.s.i. (BT50830). Belmont-Tower.
Trail of Blame: Stories of the Philippines. William J. Pomeroy. LC 71-188759. (New World paperbacks). 1971. 1.50. International Publishers.
Trail of Blood. Jeremy Potter. LC 74-139526. 1971. 5.95 (ISBN 0-8415-0063-0). McCall Pub. Co.
Trail of Conflict. Emilie Baker Loring. LC 22-19046. 1922. The Penn Publishing Company.
Trail of Danger. William MacLeod Raine. LC 34-24629. 1934. Houghton Mifflin Company.
Trail of Danger. William MacLeod Raine. 1973. (pbk.) 0.75. Popular Lib.
Trail of Deceit. Wilbur C Tuttle. LC 51-4544. 1951. Houghton Mifflin.
Trail of Desire. Robert E. Mills. (Kansan Ser.: No. 7). 208p. (Orig.). 1981. pap. 2.25 (ISBN 0-8439-1017-8, Leisure Bks). Nordon Pubns.
Trail of Destiny. Frank Henspeter. LC 53-12117. 1953. Pageant Press.
Trail of Fear. Anthony Armstrong Willis. LC 27-2001. Macrae Smith Company.
Trail of Fu Manchu. Sax Rohmer. 1970. pap. 0.60 o.p. (X2192). Pyramid Pubns.
Trail of Fu Manchu. Sax Rohmer. 1976. pap. 1.25 o.p. (ISBN 0-515-04070-3). BJ Pub Group.
Trail of Fu Manchu. Arthur Sarsfield Ward. LC 34-33268. 1934. Pub. for the Crime Club, Inc., by Doubleday, Doran & Company, Inc.
Trail of Glory. Leroy Scott. LC 26-9753. 1926. Houghton Mifflin Company.
Trail of Gold. Dane Coolidge. LC 37-5300. 1937. E. P. Dutton & Co., Inc.
Trail of Guns & Gold. Bradford Scott. 1973. pap. 0.75 o.p. (ISBN 0-515-03064-3, T3064). Pyramid Pubns.
Trail of Innocents see Vigilante Guns.
Trail of Lost Men. Tex Holt, pseud. LC 45-4045. 1945. Arcadia House.
Trail of Love. Taria Hayford. LC 81-51151. (Serenade Romance). (Illus.). 2.95 (ISBN 0-671-43701-1). Simon & Schuster: Distributed by Pocket Books.
Trail of McCallister. Matt Chisholm, pseud. 1971. pap. 0.75 o.p. (94048-075). Beagle Bks.
Trail of Tears. Williams Forrest. LC 58-12882. 1959. Crown Publishers.
Trail of the Apache Kid. Lewis B Patten. LC 78-22738. 1979. 7.95 (ISBN 0-385-15216-7). Doubleday.
Trail of the Apache Kid. Lewis B Patten. LC 80-19290. 1980. 10.95 (ISBN 0-8161-3130-9). G. K. Hall.
Trail of the Axe: A Story of the Red Sand Valley. Ridgwell Cullum. LC 10-27581. 1.50. G. W. Jacobs & Company.
Trail of the Axe: A Story of the Red Sand Valley. Ridgwell Cullum. LC 11-12262. 1.25. G. W. Jacobs & Company.
Trail of the Barrow: Or, The Brother's Revenge. James Mooney. LC 7-26217. (Mooney and Boland detective series, no. 1). 1888. J. S. Ogilvie & Company.
Trail of the Barrow: Or, The Brother's Revenge. James Mooney. LC 2032. (On cover: Magnet detective library, no. 124). 1900. Street & Smith.
Trail of the Beast. Achmed Abdullah. LC 19-10683. 1919. James A. McCann Company.
Trail of the Black King. Anthony Armstrong Willis. LC 31-1921. Macrae Smith Company.
Trail of the Buffalo Wolves: With Short Stories and Poems. Elwood Haines Ocain. LC 52-28518. 1952. Printed by Seward and Flood Print. Co.
Trail of the Cthulhu. Howard Phillips Lovecraft & August Derleth. (Boxer Ser). 1971. pap. 0.95 o.p. (95108). Beagle Bks.
Trail of the Elk. Mikkjel Fonhus & Weedon, Fru Sara Helene (Peterson) 1875-Tr. LC 23-9245. 1923. The Century Co.
Trail of the Fresno Kid. Ray Hogan. 1976. 1.25. Ace.
Trail of the Golden Girl. Rex Dolphin. (Sexton Blake Ser). 1969. pap. 0.60 o.p. (60-407). Manor Bks.
Trail of the Golden Horn. Hiram Alfred Cody. LC 23-133169. George H. Doran Company.
Trail of the Golden Skull. Ford Bowne, pseud. LC 67-5892. 1967. Arcadia House.
Trail of the Goldseekers. Hamlin Garland. Ed. by Donald Pizer. LC 75-96579. (American Authors Ser). 1970. lib. bdg. 15.95 o.s.i. (ISBN 0-512-00242-8). Garrett Pr.
Trail of the Goldseekers: A Record of Travel in Prose and Verse. Hamlin Garland. LC 99-2536. 1899. The Macmillan Company.
Trail of the Grand Seigneur. Olin Linus Lyman. LC 3-8899. 1903. New Amsterdam Book Company.
Trail of the Grand Seigneur. Olin Linus Lyman. LC 26-20068. The Corse Press.
Trail of the Gray Dragoon. Harry Edmund Danford. LC 28-30260. 1928. H. Vinal, Ltd.
Trail of the Gypsy Eight. Virginia Fairfax. LC 33-11634. (Her The girl scouts mystery series). A. L. Burt Company.
Trail of the Hawk: A Comedy of the Seriousness of Life. Sinclair Lewis. LC 15-17979. 1.35. Harper & Brothers.
Trail of the Innocents. Archie Joscelyn. 1964. Arcadia House.
Trail of the Jackal. Glenn R. Vernam. (Orig.). 1979. pap. 1.95 (ISBN 0-532-23261-5). Woodhill.
Trail of the Loathsome Missions. Willis Ocker. LC 54-8373. 1954. Vantage Press.
Trail of the Lonesome Pine. John Fox. LC 20-18827. 1912. C. Scribner's Sons.
Trail of the Lonesome Pine. John Fox. LC 21-13711. 1920. Grossett & Dunlap.
Trail of the Lonesome Pine. John Fox. LC 24-25021. 1923. Grosset & Dunlap.
Trail of the Lonesome Pine. John Fox. LC 38-8839. 1936. Grosset & Dunlap.
Trail of the Lost Electric. Florence Spaulding Pike. LC 14-11310. The Allen Publishing Company.
Trail of the Lotto. Anthony Armstrong Willis. LC 30-2369. 1930. Macrae Smith Company.
Trail of the Macaw: Soldiers of Fortune in Banana Land. Eugene Cunningham. LC 35-3086. 1935. Houghton Mifflin Company.
Trail of the Maverick. Al Cody, pseud. 192p. 1974. pap. 0.95 o.p. (532-95326-095). Manor Bks.
Trail of the Maverick. Al Cody. 1974. (pbk.) 0.95. Manor Books.
Trail of the Maverick. Archie Joscelyn. 1972. 4.95. Lenox Hill Press.
Trail of the Plow: An Historical Novel. Marie Miller Gofflin. LC 40-29647. Binfords & Mort.
Trail of the Reaper. Peter F Fox. LC 83-2949. 1983. 11.95 (ISBN 0-312-81366-X). St. Martin's Press.
Trail of the Rio Kid. C. William Harrison. (Orig.). 1971. pap. 0.60 o.p. (06141). Curtis.
Trail of the Serpent. Cedric Worth. LC 40-346021. 1940. E. P. Dutton & Co., Inc.
Trail of the Sioux. Lauran Paine. LC 56-12451. 1956. Arcadia House.
Trail of the Siouz. LC 56-12451. 1956. Arcadia House.
Trail of the Spanish Bit. Don Coldsmith. LC 80-15913. 1980. 8.95 (ISBN 0-385-15178-0). Doubleday.
Trail of the Spanish Bit. Don Goldsmith. LC 79-8559. 1980. 8.95 (ISBN 0-385-15178-0). Doubleday.
Trail of the Squid. Harvey Wickham. LC 24-3534. E. J. Clode.
Trail of the Sword. Gilbert Parker. LC 12-37863. 1894. D. Appleton and Company.
Trail of the Sword. Gilbert Parker. 1896. D. Appleton and Company.
Trail of the Vanishing Ranches. Stephen Payne. (Ace double western). 1974. (pbk.) 0.95. Ace Books.
Trail of the Waving Palm. Page Philips. LC 15-38681. 1915. 1.25. The Macaulay Company.
Trail of the White Knight. Graham Montague Jeffries. LC 27-3372. George H. Doran Company.
Trail of the White Mule. Bertha Muzzy Sinclair. LC 22-172204. 1922. Little, Brown, and Company.
Trail of Vengeance. Louis Kretschman. (Berkley Medallion Book). 1977. 1.25 (ISBN 0-425-03461-5). Berkley Pub. Corp.
Trail of Vengeance: By Arthur Henry Gooden... Arthur Henry Gooden. LC 30-314176. Phoenix Press.
Trail of '98: A Northland Romance. Robert William Service. LC 11-847. 1911. Dodd, Mead and Company.
Trail of '98: A Northland Romance. Robert William Service. LC 14-10506. 1911. Dodd, Mead and Company.
Trail Rider: A Romance of the Kansas Range. George Washington Ogden. LC 24-4504. 1924. 2.00. Dodd, Mead and Company.
Trail Rider & His God & Other Stories. Eva G. Frankill. 3.50 o.p. Carlton.
Trail Smoke. Ernest Haycox. LC 74-5107. 1974. 8.95. G. K. Hall.
Trail Smoke. Ernest Haycox. LC 36-10496. 1936. Doubleday, Doran & Company, Inc.
Trail Smoke. Ernest Haycox. LC 36-35241. 1936. The Sun Dial Press.

Trail Smoke. Ernest Haycox. (Signet Brand Western). 1974. (pbk.) 0.95. New American Library.

Trail South from Powder Valley. Peter Field. LC 42-2087. 1942. W. Morrow & Company.

Trail Through Tascosa. Peter Field. LC 63-11062. (His A Powder Valley western). 1963. Jefferson House.

Trail to Apacaz. Eugene Cunningham. LC 24-20551. 1924. 2.00. Dodd, Mead and Company.

Trail to Bang-Up. Archie Joscelyn. 1943. Phoenix Press.

Trail to Boot Hill. James Wesley. 1981. pap. 6.95 (Avalon). Bouregy.

Trail to Devil's Slide: A True Story of the Days When the West Was Young. 1st Ed. G R Hickok. LC 59-10106. 1959. Greenwich Book Publishers.

Trail to Dismal River. Archie Joscelyn. 1975. 4.95. Avalon Books.

Trail to El Dorado. Joseph Mills Hanson. LC 13-230231. 1913. A.C. McClurg & Co.

Trail to High Pine. Lee Floren. 224p. 1974. pap. 0.95 o.p. (532-95317-095). Manor Bks.

Trail to High Pine: By Wade Hamilton Pseud. Lee Floren. LC 56-7021. 1956. Arcadia House.

Trail to Lometa. Leroy Donald. 1976. 4.95. Avalon Books.

Trail to Lost Horse Ranch. Archie Joscelyn. (Avalon Books). 1977. 4.95. Thomas Bouregy.

Trail to Montana. Archie Joscelyn. LC 43-15063. 1943. Phoenix Press.

Trail to Ogallala. Benjamin Capps. (Signet bk. D2633). 1965. New Amer. Lib.

Trail to Ogallala. Benjamin Capps. LC 64-12432. Duell, Sloan and Pearce.

Trail to Paradise. Jackson Gregory. LC 30-22754. Dodd, Mead & Company.

Trail to San Triste: A Western Story. George Owen Baxter. LC 27-27941. 1927. Chelsea House.

Trail to Sundown: By Barry Cord Pseud. Peter Germano. LC 53-856590. 1953. AroadiaHouse.

Trail to the Hearts of Men: A Story of East and West. Abram Edward Cory. LC 16-21932. 1916. 1.35. Fleming H. Revell Company.

Trail to Timberline. Charles Stanley Strong. LC 47-258480. 1947. Phoenix Press.

Trail to Troublesome. Peter Field. (Jefferson House Western). 1959. 2.95 o.p. Morrow.

Trail to Troublesome: A Powder Valley Western. Peter Field. 1973 (ISBN 0-671-55131-0). Pocket Bks.

Trail to Yesterday. Charles Alden Seltzer. LC 13-217416. 1913. Outing Publishing Company.

Trail to Yesterday. Charles Alden Seltzer. LC 29-307721. 1915. A. L. Burt Company.

Trail Town. Ernest Haycox. LC 41-12690. 1941. Little, Brown and Company.

Trail Town. Ernest Haycox. LC 43-4980. 1943. The Sun Dial Press.

Trail Town. Ernest Haycox. LC 81-20117. 1982. 13.95 (ISBN 0-8161-3250-X). G.K. Hall.

Trail Trouble. Harry Sinclair Drago. LC 38-3524. Green Circle Books.

Trailblazer. 1981. pap. text ed. write for info. (ISBN 0-88074-020-5). Metagam.

Trailer Camp Woman. Doug Duperrault. pap. 0.75 o.p. (75-240). Manor Bks.

Trailer Doctor. Carlton Williams. LC 41-5148. The Penn Publishing Company.

Trailer Park. James M. Ballowe. 1981. 5.95 (ISBN 0-533-04783-8). Vantage.

Trailerpark. Russell Banks. LC 81-7662. 11.95 (ISBN 0-395-31547-6). Houghton Mifflin.

Trailers: A Novel. Ruth Little Mason Rice. LC 9-5525. Fleming H. Revell Company.

Trailers of the North... William Lewis Lockwood. LC 6-1905. Broadway Publishing Company.

Trailers of the Sage. John Keith Bassett. LC 36-826926. Greenberg.

Trailin'! Max Brand. LC 20-663716. 1920. G. P. Putnam's Sons.

Trailin'. Max Brand. 1975. (pbk.) 0.95 (ISBN 0-446-75342-4). Warner Paperback Library.

Trailin'! Frederick Faust. LC 20-6637. 1920. G. P. Putnam's Sons.

Trailing Back. Charles Alden Seltzer. LC 74-21540. 1974. (ISBN 0-88411-107-5). Aeonian Press.

Trailing on. Harry H. Halsell. LC 46-1716. 1945. The Author.

Trailing the Teepees. Montana Helena Weyer. LC 68-6376. 1968. Vantage Press.

Trails by Night. 1st Ed. Tom J Hopkins. LC 50-5165. (Double D western). 1950. Doubleday.

Trail's End. Ida Geneva Gibson McPherren. LC 39-185041. 1938. Prairie Publishing Co.

Trail's End. George Washington Ogden. LC 21-17372. 1921. A. C. McClurg & Co.

Trail's End. William MacLeod Raine. LC 40-12738. 1940. Houghton Mifflin Company.

Trail's End: A Tale of the Royal Canadian Mounted Police in the Catholic Land of Evangeline. William Leo Murphy. LC 41-10146. 1941. Catholic Literary Guild.

Trail's End at 'Dobie Town. K. R. G. Granger. 1971. pap. 0.75 o.p. (ISBN 0-447-74760-6). Lancer.

Trail's End: By Wade Hamilton Pseud. Lee Floren. LC 54-749456. 1954. Arcadia House.

Trails Meet. Bertha Muzzy Sinclair. LC 33-977. 1933. Little, Brown, and Company.

Trails of Adventure: A Story of Canons and Flowers in the Hills Near Pasadena. Mary Frances Kellogg. LC 28-2240. Post Printing & Binding Co.

Trails of Cthulhu. Ed. by August William Derleth. 4.00 o.p. Arkham.

Trails of Rage. Willis Todhunter Ballard. LC 75-6150. 1975. 5.95 (ISBN 0-385-09941-X). Doubleday.

Trails of Rage. Willis Todhunter Ballard. LC 76-101. 1976. 8.95 (ISBN 0-8161-6351-0). G. K. Hall.

Trails of Rage. Willis Todhunter Ballard. 1977. 1.50. Ace.

Trails of the Front Range. L. Kenofer. LC 72-75321. pap. 4.95 (ISBN 0-87108-048-6). Pruett.

Trails to Glory. Robert C. Barnes. (Orig.). 1982. pap. 3.25 (ISBN 0-440-08891-7). Dell.

Trails to Two Moons. Robert Welles Ritchie. LC 20-17007. 1920. 1.75. Little, Brown, and Company.

Trailsman, No. 10: Slave Hunter. Jon Sharpe. Date not set. pap. 2.25 (ISBN 0-451-11465-5, AE1465, Sig). NAL.

Trailsman, No. 12: Condor Pass. Jon Sharpe. 176p. Date not set. pap. 2.50 (ISBN 0-451-11837-5, AE1837, Sig). NAL.

Trailsman, No. 3: Blood Chase. Jon Sharpe. 1982. pap. 2.50 (ISBN 0-451-11927-4, AE1927, Sig). NAL.

Trailsman, No. 8: Six Gun Drive. Jon Sharpe. Date not set. pap. 2.50 (ISBN 0-451-12172-4, AE2172, Sig). NAL.

Trailway Tale. Noni Clack Bailey. LC 45-10591. 1945. The Christopher Publishing House.

Train. Vera Fedorovna Panova & Budberg, Marie, Tr. LC 49-8213. 1949. A A. Knopf.

Train see Adam & the Train.

Train from Katanga: A Novel. Wilbur A Smith. LC 64-18480. 1965. Viking Press.

Train in the Meadow. Robert Nathan. LC 53-6846. 1953. Knopf.

Train Leaves at Midnight. Waclaw Solski. LC 51-12803. 1951. Crown Publishers.

Train Ride. Peter Loughran. (75-193). 1968. Macfadden.

Train Ride. 1st Ed. in the U. S. A. Peter Loughran. LC 66-18618. 1966. 4.50. Doubleday.

Train Robberies, Train Robbers, & the Holdup Men. William A. Pinkerton. LC 74-15748. (Popular Culture in America Ser.). (Illus.). 88p. 1975. Repr. of 1907 ed. 10.00 (ISBN 0-405-06383-0). Ayer Co.

Train to Pakistan. Khushwant Singh. LC 75-15688. 1975. 11.50 (ISBN 0-8371-8226-3). Greenwood Press.

Train to Pakistan (Mano Majra) Khushwant Singh. LC 80-8920. 192p. (YA) (gr. 9 up). 1981. pap. 3.25 (ISBN 0-394-17887-4, B456, BC). Grove.

Train Was on Time. Translated by Richard Graves. 531st Ed. Heinrich Boll. 1956. Criterion Books.

Train Whistle Guitar. Albert Murray. LC 73-20086. 1974. 8.95 (ISBN 0-07-044087-5). McGraw-Hill.

Train Wreck! Jeremiah Jack. 192p. (Orig.). 1975. pap. 1.25 (ISBN 0-532-12287-9). Woodhill.

Training of Rachel Haller: By the Author of "The Family of the Black Forest.". Maria Frances Hill Anderson. LC 1-31121. 1900. American Baptist Pub. Society.

Training of Rachel Haller, by the Author of "The Family of the Black Forest."... L.M.N & N., L.M. LC 1-31121. American Baptist Publication Society.

Training of Silas. E J Devine. LC 7-2759. 1906. Benziger Brothers.

Trains That Met in the Blizzard: A Composite Romance; Being a Chronicle of the Extraordinary Adventure of a Party of Twelve Men and One Woman in the Great American Blizzard, March 12, 1888. Robert Pitcher Woodward. LC 8-37241. 1896. Salmagundi Publishing Company.

Train's Trust: A Western Story. George Owen Baxter. LC 27-27942. 1925. A. L. Burt Company.

Traipsin' Woman. Jeannette Bell Thomas. LC 33-186583. E. P. Dutton & Co., Inc.

Traitor. W. Howard Baker. (Orig.). pap. 0.60 o.p. (73-646). Lancer.

Traitor. Lavr Divomlikoff. LC 72-96234. 1973. 5.95 (ISBN 0-385-01472-4). Doubleday.

Traitor. Lavr Divomlikoff. 1976. 1.75. Popular Library.

Traitor. George Markstein. 192p. 1981. pap. 2.75 (ISBN 0-345-28609-X). Ballantine.

Traitor. William Lawrence Shirer. LC 50-10771. 1950. Farrar, Straus.

Traitor: A Story of the Fall of the Invisible Empire. Thomas Dixon. LC 7-24587. 1907. Doubleday, Page & Company.

Traitor: A Story of the Fall of the Invisible Empire. Thomas Dixon. LC 24-28521. Grosset & Dunlap.

Traitor and Loyalist: Or, The Man Who Found His Country. Henry Kitchell Webster. LC 4-25680. 1904. The Macmillan Company.

Traitor Betrayed. Osmington Mills. LC 65-23812. 1966. bds., 2.95. Roy.

Traitor Betrayed: By Osmington Mills. Vivian Collin Brooks. LC 65-23812. 1966. Roy Publishers.

Traitor Blitz. Johannes Mario Simmel. Tr. by Catherine Hutter from Ger. 1980. pap. 2.75 (ISBN 0-445-04512-4). Popular Lib.

Traitor: By Sydney Horler. Sydney Horler. LC 36-6819. 1936. Little, Brown, and Company.

Traitor Game. Dougal McLeish. LC 68-21738. 1968. Houghton, Mifflin.

Traitor in London. Fergus Hume. 1900. F. M. Buckles & Company; Etc., Etc.

Traitor in My Arms. Vivian Lord. 448p. 1982. pap. 2.75 (ISBN 0-449-14130-6, GM). Fawcett.

Traitor: Or, The Fate of Ambition. Emerson Bennett. LC 7-63490. U. P. James.

Traitor to the Living. Philip Jose Farmer. 1973. (pbk.) 1.25 (ISBN 0-345-23613-0). Ballantine Books.

Traitors. James Forman. LC 68-23747. (Bell bk.). 1968. 3.95. Farrar.

Traitors. William Stuart Long. (Australians Ser.: No. III). (Orig.). 1981. pap. 3.95 (ISBN 0-440-18131-3). Dell.

Traitors. Edward Phillips Oppenheim. LC 3-6461. 1903. Dodd, Mead & Company.

Traitors: A Novel. John Briley. LC 78-81568. 1969. 6.95. Putnam.

Traitors' Doom. John Creasey. (Doctor Palfrey Ser). (O.s.i.). 192p. 1972. pap. 0.95 o.s.i. (AN1029, Award). Univ Pub & Dist.

Traitors' Doom: A Story of Dr. Palfrey. John Creasey. LC 70-126119. 1970. 4.95 (ISBN 0-8027-5216-0). Walker.

Traitors' Gate. Catherine Irvine Gavin. LC 76-28031. 8.95. St. Martin's Press.

Traitor's Gate. Edgar Wallace. LC 27-20256. 1927. Doubleday, Page & Company.

Traitor's Moon. Robert Neill. LC 52-10991. 1952. Doubleday.

Traitor's Mountain. Showell Styles. LC 45-9828. 1945. Selwyn & Blount Ltd.

Traitor's Mountain. Showell Styles. LC 46-5533. 1946. The Macmillan Company.

Traitors of Bosworth. Robert Farrington. LC 78-337. 1978. 8.95 (ISBN 0-312-81378-3). St. Martin's Press.

Traitors' Pass. David Duff. LC 55-5922. Roy Publishers.

Traitor's Purse. Margery Allingham. LC 41-3900.

Traitor's Road. Dorothy Daniels. pap. 0.60 o.p. Lancer.

Traitor's Son. Constance Heaven. 1.75. Dell.

Traitor's Son: A Novel. Ruth Shartel McVoy. LC 15-245482. 1915. The Neale Publishing Company.

Traitor's Way. Bruce Hamilton. LC 39-6263. The Bobbs-Merrill Company.

Traitor's Way. Sidney Kilner Levett-Yeats. LC 1-25448. F. A. Stokes Company.

Traitor's Wife. 1st Ed. David Montross, pseud. LC 62-11442. 1962. Doubleday.

Traitors'Pass. David Duff. LC 54-41710. 1954. Staples Press.

Traits & Confidences. Emily Lawless. Ed. by Robert L. Wolff. (Ireland Nineteenth Century Fiction - Ser. Two: Vol. 75). 280p. 1979. lib. bdg. 32.00 (ISBN 0-8240-3524-0). Garland Pub.

Traits and Stories of the Irish Peasantry. William Carleton. LC 79-163022. (Short story index reprint series). (Illus.). 1971. (ISBN 0-8369-3936-0). Books for Libraries Press.

Traits and Stories of the Irish Peasantry... William Carleton. LC 6-19903. (On cover: Lovell's library. v. 17, no. 820-829). J. W. Lovell Company.

Traits and Stories of the Irish Peasantry. William Carleton. LC 78-27826. (Ireland, from the Act of Union, 1800, to the Death of Parnell, 1891; No. 34). 1979. 42.00 (ISBN 0-8240-3483-X). Garland Pub.

Traits and Stories of the Irish Peasantry. William Carleton. LC 79-9573. (Ireland, from the Act of Union, 1800, to the Death of Parnell, 1891; No. 34). 1979. 42.00 (ISBN 0-8240-3483-X). Garland Pub.

Traits and Stories of the Irish Peasantry. William Carleton. LC 79-19150. (Series: Irish Heritage Series (Wilmington, Del.). 1980. 42.00 (ISBN 0-934204-07-1). M. P. Browne.

Traits and Stories of the Irish Peasantry, Second Series. William Carleton. LC 78-27826. (Ireland, from the Act of Union, 1800, to the Death of Parnell, 1891; No. 35). 1979. 42.00 (ISBN 0-8240-3484-8). Garland Pub.

Traits & Stories of the Irish Peasantry: Second Series, 3 vols. William Carleton. Ed. by Robert L. Wolff. (Ireland Nineteenth Century Fiction - Ser. Two: Vol. 35). 1412p. 1979. lib. bdg. 96.00 (ISBN 0-8240-3484-8). Garland Pub.

Traits & Stories of the Irish Peasantry: With Illustrations by Phiz, Wrightson Lee & Others, 4 vols. facsimile ed. William Carleton. LC 79-163022. (Short Story Index Reprint Ser.). (Illus.). Repr. of 1853 ed. Set. 80.00 (ISBN 0-8369-3936-0). Ayer Co.

Traits and Trials of Early Life. Letitia Elizabeth Landon. LC 7-14305. 1837. E. L. Carey & A. Hart.

Traits of American Life. Sarah Josepha Hale. 1835. E. L. Carey & A. Hart.

Trajan: the History of a Sentimental Young Man: With Some Episodes in the Comedy of Many Lives' Errors. A Novel. Henry Francis Keenan. 1885. Cassell & Company, Limited.

Trammelings, and Other Stories. Georgina Pell Curtis. 1909. 1.50. B. Herderf Etc., Etc.

Tramp. Jack London. (Illus.). 22p. 1975. Repr. of 1905 ed. pap. 1.00 o.p. (ISBN 0-915046-20-2). Wolf Hse.

Tramp. W Townend. LC 27-20345. 1927. I. Washburn.

Tramp Abroad. Mark Twain. 1978. pap. 1.95 o.p. (ISBN 0-06-080453-X, P 453, PL). Har-Row.

Tramp Abroad: Mark Twain; Abridged and Edited with an Introduction by Charles Neider, with Illustrations by the Author. Samuel Langhorne Clemens. (Perennial library). (Illus.). 1978. 1.95 (ISBN 0-06-080453-X). Harper & Row.

Tramp and His Woman. Dorothy Charques. LC 37-3097. 1937. The Macmillan Company.

Tramp in Armor. Raymond H. Sawkins. LC 73-108888. 1970. 5.95. Dutton.

Tramp in Armour. Colin Forbes, pseud. 1970. 5.95 o.p. (ISBN 0-525-22205-7). Dutton.

Tramp in Society. Robert H Cowdrey. LC 6-28861. 1891. F. J. Schulte & Company.

Tramp Steamers. Meme Black. LC 81-37. (Illus.). 1981. pap. 6.95 (ISBN 0-201-03776-9). A-W.

Tramping Methodist. Sheila Kaye-Smith. LC 22-21486. 1922. E. P. Dutton & Company.

Trample an Empire Down. Mack Reynolds. 1978. pap. 1.50 o.s.i. (ISBN 0-8439-0585-9, Leisure Bks). Nordon Pubns.

Tramplers: A Novel by Jason Manor Pseud. Oakley M Hall. LC 56-5648. 1956. Viking Press.

Trampling of the Lilies. Rafael Sabatini. LC 26-15375. 1926. Houghton Mifflin Company.

Tramp's Daughter. M. B. Smith. (On cover: Munro's library, no. 674). 1886. N. L. Munro.

Tramp's Love... William Lee Popham. LC 10-145848. 0.50.

Trancas. Adriana Rowan. LC 79-4884. (ISBN 0-87223-557-2). Seaview Books.

Trance. Joy Fielding. LC 77-26673. 8.95 (ISBN 0-671-16969-6). Playboy Press.

Trance. Joy Fielding. (Jove/HBJ Book). 1978. 1.95 (ISBN 0-515-04702-3). Jove Publications, Inc.

Tranquility House. Augusta Huiell Seaman. LC 23-13451. 1.75. The Century Co.

Tranquillity Base and Other Stories. Asa Baber. LC 79-89138. 5.00 (ISBN 0-931362-01-6). Fiction International.

Trans-America Dragon Flight. Thomas DeCutler. 1978. pap. 3.00 o.s.i. New Albion.

Trans-Siberian Express. Warren Adler. LC 76-30634. 8.95 (ISBN 0-399-11895-0). Putnam.

Trans-Siberian Express. Warren Adler. (Kangaroo Book). 1978. 2.50 (ISBN 0-671-81736-1). Pocket Books.

Transaction in Hearts. Edgar Evertson Saltus. LC 68-54294. Repr. of 1889 ed. 17.50 (ISBN 0-404-05515-X). AMS Pr.

Transaction in Hearts: An Episode. Edgar Evertson Saltus. LC 68-54294. 1968. AMS Press.

Transaction in Hearts: An Episode. Edgar Evertson Saltus. LC 8-5793. (On cover: The household library. no. 18, v. 4). Belford, Clarke & Co.

Transactions of Lord Louis Lewis. Roland Pertwee. LC 18-2907. 1918. 1.50. Dodd, Mead and Company.

Transactions of Oliver Prince. Robert Erstone Forbes. LC 24-194181. 1924. H. Holt and Company.

Transactions of the Antiseptic Club. Albert Abram. LC 5-42583. 1895. E. B. Trent; Etc., Etc.

Transatlantic Blues. Wilfrid Sheed. LC 77-24629. 9.95 (ISBN 0-525-22226-X). Dutton.

Transatlantic Blues. Wilfrid Sheed. 1979. 2.25 (ISBN 0-380-42259-X). Avon Books.

Transatlantic Chatelaine a Novel. Helen Choate Pratt Prince. LC 7-300924. 1897. Houghton, Mifflin and Company.

Transatlantic Ghost... Dorothy Gardiner. LC 33-194004. 1933. Pub. for the Crime Club, Inc., by Doubleday, Doran & Company, Inc.

Transatlantic Stories: Selected from the Transatlantic Review. The Transatlantic Review, Paris. LC 26-4068. 1926. L. MacVeagh, The Dial Press.

Transatlantic Tunnel, Hurrah! Harry Harrison. 256p. 1981. pap. 2.50 (ISBN 0-523-48505-0). Pinnacle Bks.

Transatlantic Wife. Peggy Hopkins Joyce. LC 33-815153. The Macaulay Company.

Transatlantics. Frederick W Wendt. LC 2624. 1899. Brentano's.

Transcendent Man. Jerry Sohl. LC 52-135777. 1953. Rinehart.

Transcendental Meditation. Marharishi Mahesh Yogi. 320p. 1973. pap. 3.95 (ISBN 0-451-12184-8, AE2184, Sig). NAL.

Transcendental Murder. Jane Langton. LC 63-21455. Harper & Row.

Transcendental Murder. Jane Langton. 1974. (pbk.) 2.95. Lincoln Press.

Transcendental Wild Oats. Louisa May Alcott. LC 76-355426. (Illus.). 92p. (YA) 1981. 8.95 (ISBN 0-916782-21-2). Harvard Common Pr.

Transcendental Wild Oats and Excerpts from the Fruitlands Diary. Louisa May Alcott. LC 76-355426. (Illus.). Harvard Common Press.

Transcript. Tom Ahern. 1972. pap. 1.00 (ISBN 0-930900-38-3). Burning Deck.

Transfer. Silvano Ceccherini. LC 66-20533. 1967. G. Braziller.

Transfer. Thomas Palmer. LC 82-5518. 1982. 13.95 (ISBN 0-89919-130-4). Ticknor & Fields.

Transfer Point. Kathryn McLean. LC 47-11415. 1947. Harcourt, Brace.

Transfer to Yesterday. Isidore Haiblum. LC 80-2248. 1981. 9.95 (ISBN 0-385-17136-6). Doubleday.

Transfer to Yesterday. Isidore Haiblum. 1973. (pbk.) 1.25 (ISBN 0-345-23418-9). Ballantine Books.

Transference. Ella Smith. LC 81-81982. 320p. (Orig.). 1982. pap. 2.95 (ISBN 0-87216-940-5). Playboy Pbks.

Transfiguration. Sergeev-TSenskii, Sergei Nikolaevich. LC 72-90312. 1973. (ISBN 0-88355-022-9). Hyperion Press.

Transfiguration of Miss Philura. Florence Morse Kingsley. LC 1-31879. 1901. Funk & Wagnalls Company.

Transfiguration of Miss Philura. 13th ed. Florence Morse Kingsley. LC 15-231158. (hour-glass stories). 1902. Funk & Wagnalls Company.

Transfiguration of Miss Philura. Florence Morse Kingsley. LC 11-25082. 1911. Funk & Wagnalls Company.

Transfiguration: Translated from the Russian by Marie Budberg. Sergiei Nikolaevich Sergieev-Tsenskii & Budberg, Marie, Tr. LC 26-198252. 1926. R. M. McBride & Company.

Transfigurations. Michael Bishop. LC 79-11025. 1979. 10.95 o.p. (ISBN 0-399-12379-2). Putnam Pub Group.

Transformation. Joy Fielding. LC 76-1707. 320p. 1976. pap. 2.95 (ISBN 0-86721-116-4). Playboy Pbks.

Transformation. Joy Fielding. LC 76-1707. 1978. pap. 1.95 o.p. (ISBN 0-87216-316-4, E16316). Playboy.

Transformation. George B. Leonard. 288p. 1972. 7.95 o.p. (ISBN 0-440-09031-8). Delacorte.

Transformation. John Herman Wishar. LC 11-20591. 1911. The Reynard Press.

Transformation of Job: A Tale of the High Sierras. Frederick Vining Fisher. LC 70-137729. (American fiction reprint series). (Illus.). 1970. Books for Libraries Press.

Transformation of Job: A Tale of the High Sierras. Frederick Vining Fisher. LC 72-11757. 1973. Scholarly Press.

Transformation of Job: A Tale of the High Sierras. Frederick Vining Fisher. LC 29-82572. 1900. D. C. Cook Publishing Company.

Transformation of Krag. Eugene Percy Lyle. 1911. Doubleday, Page & Company.

Transformation of Mrs. Arthur. Flora Armitage. LC 66-18345. 1966. Dodd, Mead.

Transformation or the Romance of Monte Beni. Nathaniel Hawthorne. 374p. 1981. Repr. of 1914 ed. lib. bdg. 25.00 (ISBN 0-89987-366-9). Darby Bks.

Transformations. John Mella. LC 75-18961. 8.95 (ISBN 0-914090-16-X). Chicago Review Press: Distributed by Swallow Press.

Transfusion: Or, The Orphans of Unwalden. William Godwin. LC 6-43750. 1837. G. Dearborn & Co.

Transgressing the Law. A Novel. Frederick Whittaker. (On cover: Ledger library, no. 84). 1893. R. Bonner's Sons.

Transgression: A Novel. Y. Esther Livingston. LC 45-7904. 1945. The Hobson Book Press.

Transgression of Andrew Vane, a Novel. Guy Wetmore Carryl. LC 4-10539. 1904. H. Holt and Company.

Transgression of Terence Clancy: A Novel. Harold Vallings. LC 8-30865. (On cover: Harper's Franklin square library, no. 741). 1893. Harper & Brothers.

Transgressor. Harmon Bellamy. LC 34-42181. 1933. G. H. Watt.

Transgressor. Anthony Richardson. LC 28-23917. 1928. Dodd, Mead & Company.

Transgressor. Frank Thompson. LC 20-5891. R. G. Badger.

Transgressor: Published Anonymously) and Other Stories, Showing the Effects of Liquor Upon Society; and Its Coalition of Evil Sequalae! Ansley DeForest White. LC 9-18949. 1909. The Inter-State Prohibition Publishing Association.

Transgressor. Translated by Anne Green. Julien Green. LC 57-102342. 1957. Pantheon.

Transgressors: Story of a Great Sin. A Political Novel of the Twentieth Century. Francis Alexandre Adams. Independence Pub. Co.

Transient Guest: And Other Episodes. Edgar Evertson Saltus. LC 76-116007. 1970. (ISBN 0-404-05509-5). AMS Press.

Transient Guest, and Other Episodes. Edgar Evertson Saltus. LC 8-3746. Belford, Clarke & Co.; Etc., Etc.

Transient Hour. Marcel Ayme & Sutton, Eric. LC 48-196065. 1948. A. A. Wyn.

Transient Lady. Octavus Roy Cohen. LC 34-28966. 1934. D. Appleton Century Company, Incorporated.

Transients. Mark Van Doren. LC 35-560. 1935. W. Morrow & Company.

Transit. easy eye ed. Edmund Cooper. pap. 0.60 o.p. (73-690). Lancer.

Transit. Netty Reiling Radvanyi. Tr. by Galston, James Austin. LC 44-3969. 1944. Little, Brown.

Transit. Neville H. Romain & Robin More. LC 79-50901. pap. 2.25 o.s.i. (ISBN 0-89516-084-6). Condor Pub Co.

Transit of Earth. Playboy Editors. LC 70-136574. 1971. pap. 0.75 o.p. (16102). Playboy.

Transit of Earth. LC 70-136574. (Playboy science fiction). 0.75. Playboy Press.

Transit of Venus. Shirley Hazzard. LC 79-21754. 1980. 10.95 (ISBN 0-670-72426-2). Viking Press.

Transit of Venus. John Philip Sousa. LC 20-3062. Small, Maynard & Company.

Transit to Scorpio. Alan Burt Akers. (Science Fiction Ser). (Orig.). 1972. pap. 1.25 o.p. (ISBN 0-87997-169-X, UY1169). DAW Bks.

Transit: Translated from the German. Anna Seghers & Galston, James Austin, 1881- Tr. LC 44-3969. 1944. Little, Brown and Company.

Transit U. S. A. A Novel. Walter Leslie River. LC 40-323685. 1940. Frederick A. Stokes Company.

Transition. John L Hill. LC 9-18368. Broadway Publishing Company.

Transition: A Novel. Emma Frances Brooke. LC 6-19390. 1895. J. B. Lippincott Company.

Transition of Titus Crow. Brian Lumley. (Science Fiction Ser). 1975. pap. 1.50 (ISBN 0-87997-173-8, UW1173). DAW Bks.

Transition Stories: Twenty-Three Stories from "Transition". Ed. by Eugene Jolas. LC 78-37569. (Short story index reprint series). 1972. (ISBN 0-8369-4128-4). Books for Libraries Press.

Transition Stories: Twenty-Three Stories from "Transition". Transition & Jolas, Eugene, 1894- Ed. LC 29-2249. 1929. W. V. McKee.

Translation: A Novel. Stephen Marlowe. LC 75-38984. 7.95 (ISBN 0-13-930354-5). Prentice-Hall.

Translation of a Savage. Gilbert Parker. LC 7-34991. 1893. D. Appleton and Company.

Translation of a Savage. new ed. enl. ed. Gilbert Parker. LC 7-34990. 1898. D. Appleton and Company.

Translation of a Savage. new ed., enl. ed. Gilbert Parker. LC 34-37793. 1903. D. Appleton and Company.

Translation: the Story of Saint John in New Testament Times. Julian J Joyce. LC 73-92158. (Illus.). 1974. John Press.

Translations from the Siamese. With Illus. by Sheila Hawkins. Warren Chetham-Strode. 1958. McGraw-Hill.

Translator. Pat Goodheart. LC 78-14171. 6.95 (ISBN 0-03-043011-9). Holt, Rinehart and Winston.

Transmaniacon. John Shirley. (Orig.). 1979. pap. 1.95 (ISBN 0-89083-417-2). Zebra.

Transmigration of Bishop Timothy Archer. Philip K. Dick. 1982. write for info. (Timescape). PB.

Transmigration of Timothy Archer. Philip K Dick. LC 81-23182. 2.95 (ISBN 0-671-44066-7). Timescape Books: Distributed by Simon and Schuster.

Transmigration of Timothy Archer. Philip K. Dick. 1983. pap. 2.95 (Timescape). PB.

Transmission: A Novel. Fred Wallace Lawrence. 1900. The Editor Publishing Co.

Transmission Error. Michael Kurland. (Orig.). 1970. pap. 0.75 o.p. (T2379). Pyramid Pubns.

Transpacific Flight. Deck Morgan. LC 38-676817. J. H. Hopkins, Inc.

Transpacific Wings. Kay Karl Endow. LC 36-232628. 1935. Wetzel Publishing Co., Inc.

Transparent Eye-Ball and Other Stories. Dallas E Wiebe. LC 81-21583. 15.00 (ISBN 0-930900-91-X) (ISBN 0-930900-92-8). Burning Deck.

Transparent Things. Vladimir Vladimirovich Nabokov. 160p. 1974. pap. 1.25 o.p. (P2035, Crest). Fawcett World.

Transparent Things: A Novel. Vladimir Vladimirovich Nabokov. LC 72-3989. 1972. 5.95 (ISBN 0-07-045734-4). McGraw-Hill.

Transplant. Kathryn Jessup. LC 82-60721. (Karen Evans, M.D. Ser.: No. 4). 256p. 1983. pap. 2.75 (ISBN 0-86721-239-X). Playboy Pbks.

Transplant. Margaret Jones. LC 68-30947. 1968. 5.95. Stein and Day.

Transplanted. Gertrude Franklin Horn Atherton. 1919. lib. bdg. 15.00 (ISBN 0-8414-3097-7). Folcroft.

Transplanted. May Cummings. LC 18-8164. 1918. Saulsbury Publishing Company.

Transplanted. Brand Whitlock. LC 27-181430. 1927. D. Appleton & Company.

Transplanted: A Novel, by Gertrude Atherton... Gertrude Franklin Horn Atherton. LC 19-14473. 1919. 1.60. Dodd, Mead and Company.

Transplanted: A Story of Dixie Before the War. Mary Ann Harris Gay. LC 7-33195. 1907. The Neale Publishing Company.

Transplanted Lily: A Novel. Sydney J Wilson. LC 99-3878. (On cover: Dillingham's American authors library. no. 53). 1899. G. W. Dillingham Co.

Transplanted Rose: A Story of New York Society. Mary Elizabeth Wilson Sherwood. LC 8-112679. (Half-title: Harper's Franklin square library, no. 722). 1892. Harper & Brothers.

Transplanted Rose: A Story of New York Society. Mary Elizabeth Wilson Sherwood. LC 44-15328. 1882. Harper & Brothers.

Transplanted. Tr. from German by Lili Krakowski. Fridel Stoetzner. LC 66-264931. 1966. bds., 5.95. McGraw.

Transport. Isa Glenn. LC 29-26168. 1929. A. A. Knopf.

Transports & Disgraces. Robert Henson. LC 80-19131. (Illinois Short Fiction Ser.). 140p. 1980. 11.95 (ISBN 0-252-00840-5); pap. 4.95 (ISBN 0-252-00841-3). U of Ill Pr.

Transposed Heads: A Legend of India. Thomas Mann. Tr. by Helen Tracy Lowe. LC 41-7867. 1941. A. A. Knopf.

Transposed Man. Dwight V Swain. LC 55-42207. (Ace double novel books. D-113). 1955. Ace Books.

Transvection Machine. Edward D. Hoch. 1973. 0.95 (ISBN 0-671-77640-1). Pocket Books.

Transvection Machine. Edward D. Hoch. LC 78-161120. 1971. 5.95 (ISBN 0-8027-5539-9). Walker.

Trap. Jenifer Beckett. LC 74-15224. 1975. 8.95. St. Martin's Press.

Trap. Jenifer Beckett. LC 76-365311. 1976. 3.90 (ISBN 0-434-05360-0). Heinemann.

Trap. Jenifer Beckett. 1978. 1.95 (ISBN 0-445-04318-0). Popular Library.

Trap. Delfino Cinelli & Van Doren, Carl Clinton, 1885- LC 30-22433. The John Day Company.

Trap. Maximilian Foster. LC 20-14214. 1920. D. Appleton and Company.

Trap. Elizabeth Garver Jordan. LC 37-14573. 1937. D. Appleton-Century Company, Incorporated.

Trap. H. H Matteson. LC 22-7533. W. J. Watt & Company.

Trap. Lewis B Patten. 1976. 1.25. Belmont Tower Books.

Trap. Daoma Winston. 1973. 0.95. Popular Library.

Trap: A Novel. Tord Hubert. LC 76-52556. (MW suspense). 1977. 6.95 (ISBN 0-679-50755-8). D. McKay Co.

Trap: A Novel. Dan Jacobson. LC 55-5245. (Illus.). 1955. Harcourt, Brace.

Trap Angel. Frederick H Christian. (Angel series,#4). 1974. (pbk.) 0.95 (ISBN 0-523-00452-4). Pinnacle Books.

Trap for a Tease. J. J. Montague. 192p. pap. 1.95 o.p. (ISBN 0-87977-155-0, DBB155). Dansk Blue Bk.

Trap for Buchanan. Jonas Ward. 144p. 1978. pap. 1.50 (ISBN 0-449-14082-2, GM). Fawcett.

Trap for Cinderella. Sebastien Japrisot. LC 64-17283. (Inner sanctum mystery). 1964. Simon and Schuster.

Trap for Cinderella. Jean Baptiste Rossi. LC 79-19756. 1979. 3.50 (ISBN 0-14-005364-6). Penguin Books.

Trap for Cinderella. Tr. from French by Helen Weaver. Sebastien Japrisot. (Inner sanctum mystery, 50145). 1965. Pocket Bks.

Trap for Sam Dodge, and Valley of Savage Men. Harry Whittington. 1975. (pbk.) 1.25. Ace Books.

Trap Girl. Richard Kammer. pap. 1.95 o.p. (8064). Cameo.

Trap Line. William D Montalbano & Carl Hiaasen. LC 82-45553. 1982. 12.95 (ISBN 0-689-11307-2). Atheneum.

Trap No. 6. Stephen Ransome. (Crime Club Ser). 1971. 4.95 o.p. (ISBN 0-385-03710-4). Doubleday.

Trap the Baron. John Creasey. LC 76-142848. 1971. 4.95 (ISBN 0-8027-5229-2). Walker.

Trap the Baron. Anthony Morris, pseud. 1971. 4.95 o.p. (ISBN 0-8027-5229-2). Walker & Co.

Trap to Catch a Sunbeam. Matilda Anne Mackarness. LC 7-16431. 1849. J. Munroe and Company.

Trap: 1st Amer. Ed. John Knowler. LC 65-111051. 1965. bds., 4.95. Knopf.

Trapped. Louise Henry Cowan. The Christopher Publishing House.

Trapped. Innes Ralph Hammond. LC 40-32081. 1940. G. P. Putnam's Sons.

Trapped. Richard Hayward. LC 56-1168. (Gold medal book 558). 1956. Fawcett Publications.

Trapped. Hammond Innes. LC 40-320811. G. P. Putnam's Sons.

Trapped by Love. Rob Eden. LC 36-4464. J. H. Hopkins & Son, Inc.

Trapper. Thomas York. LC 80-70558. 1981. 15.95 (ISBN 0-385-17587-6). Doubleday Canada Ltd.

Trapper of Rat River: A "Malloy of the Mounted" Story. Charles Stoddard. LC 42-2915. 1941. Arcadia House, Inc.

Trapper of Rat River: A Malloy of the Mounted Story. Charles Stanley Strong. LC 42-2915. 1941. Arcadia House.

Trappers and Shawnees on the War Path. 1st Ed. Arnold H Schroeder. LC 54-10029. 1954. Pageant Press.

Trappers & Traders. Jane V. Barker & Sybil Downing. (Colorado Heritage Ser.: Bk. 3). (Illus.). 45p. (gr. 3-4). 1979. pap. text ed. 3.50x (ISBN 0-87108-214-4); tchr's. ed. 3.00x (ISBN 0-87108-216-0). Pruett.

Trapper's Bride: A Tale of the Rocky Mountains. St. John, Percy Bollingbroke. LC 8-3719. E. Ferrett & Co.

Trapper's Bride: Or, Spirit of Adventure. Charles Augustus Murray. LC 7-25480. 1848. Stratton and Barnard.

Trapper's Bride: Or, Spirit of Adventure. Charles Augustus Murray. LC 7-25479. U. P. James.

Trapper's Daughter: A Story of the Rocky Mountains. rev. and ed. by percy b. st. john. ed. Gustave Aimard & St. John, Percy Bolingbroke, 1821-1889, Ed. LC 5-42590. (On cover: Lovell's library, no. 1021). 1887. J. W. Lovell Company.

Trapper's Last Shot. John Yount. LC 72-11433. 1973. 6.95 (ISBN 0-394-46378-1). Random House.

Trapper's Niece. A Sketch of Western Life... Sophronia Currier. LC 11-10570. (Half-Title: New 8500 Prime Series). 1871. D. Lothrop & Co.

Trappers of Arkansas. A Narrative. rev. and ed. by percy b. st. john. ed. Gustave Aimard & St. John, Percy Bolingbroke, 1821-1889, Ed. LC 5-42201. (On cover: Lovell's library, no. 1045). 1887. J. W. Lovell Company.

Trappers' Rendezvous. Archie Joscelyn. LC 54-9133. 1954. Avalon Books.

Trappings. Elizabeth R Edwards. LC 75-6185. 4.95. Zondervan Pub. House.

Trappings of Gold. Manoje Basu. Tr. by S. L. Ghosh. 176p. 1969. pap. 2.00 (ISBN 0-88253-013-5). Ind-US Inc.

Trapp's Peace. Brian Callison. LC 79-57373. 1980. 9.95 (ISBN 0-525-22230-8). Dutton.

Trapp's War. Brian Callison. LC 75-23947. 1976. 6.95 (ISBN 0-8415-0414-8). Saturday Review Press.

Traps Need Fresh Bait. A. A. Fair, pseud. 1967. 4.50 o.p. Morrow.

Traps Need Fresh Bait: By A. A. Fair. Erle Stanley Gardner. LC 67-15158. 1967. bds., 3.95. Morrow.

Traps, Traps. Caryl Churchill. 52p. (Orig.). 1981. pap. 4.95. Pluto Pr.

Trash Dragon of Shensi. Andrew Glaze. (Illus., Orig.). 1978. pap. 4.50 (ISBN 0-914278-15-0). Copper Beech.

Trash Stealer. Jean Potts. LC 68-11539. 1968. Scribner.

Trashing. Ann Fettaman, pseud. LC 70-141474. 1970. 4.95. Straight Arrow Books; Distributed by the World Pub. Co., Cleveland.

Trashing. Ann Fetterman, pseud. 1972. pap. 0.95 o.p. (BT50226). Belmont-Tower.

Trask. Don Berry. LC 60-5835. 376p. 1976. pap. 2.25 (ISBN 0-89174-001-5). Comstock Edns.

Trask: A Novel. Don Berry. LC 60-5835. 1960. Viking Press.

Trauma Nurse. Patricia Rae. (Orig.). 1982. pap. 2.95 (ISBN 0-8217-1036-2). Zebra.

Traumerei. Leona Dalrymple. LC 12-12377. 1912. 1.35. McBride, Nast & Company.

Travail see Quatre Evangiles.

Travail. Labor; a Novel. Emile Zola. LC 1-31582. 1901. Harper & Brothers.

Travail of Gold. Edward Frederic Benson. LC 33-14403. 1933. Doubleday, Doran & Company, Inc.

Travel and Adventure: Comprising Some of the Most Striking Parratives on Record. Ed. by Davis Wasgatt Clark. LC 6-25352. (Fireside series). 1856. Swormstedt & Poe.

Travel Ideals. (Illus., Orig.). 1980. pap. 2.95 o.p. (ISBN 0-89542-333-2). Ideals.

Travel Letters from New Zealand, Australia & Africa see Collected Works.

Travel Notes. Stanley Crawford. LC 68-12165. (O.S.I.). 1968. 4.50 o.s.i. (74195). S&S.

Travel Notes (from Here-to There) A Book. Stanley G. Crawford. LC 68-12165. 1968. Simon and Schuster.

Travel Tales of Mr. Joseph Jorkens. Edward John Moreton Drax Plunkett Dunsany. LC 31-23456. G. P. Putnam's Sons.

Traveler and the Grapes. John Cranmer Baird. LC 8-2611. Broadway Publishing Co.

Traveler from Altruria. Introd. by Howard Mumford Jones. William Dean Howells. LC 57-12436. (American century series, S-16). 1957. Sagamore Press.

Traveler from Alturia. William Dean Howells. LC 7-5756. 1894. Harper & Brothers.

Traveler from Alturia. William Dean Howells. LC 7-5678. (On cover: Harper's Franklin square library. new ser. no. 757). 1895. Harper & Brothers.

Traveler in Time. Alison Uttley. LC 64-21478. (Illus.). 1964. Viking Press.

Traveler in Time. Alison Uttley. LC 40-32370. G. P. Putnam's Sons.

Travelers. Ruth Prawer Jhabvala. LC 72-9765. 256p. (YA) 1973. 8.95 o.p. (ISBN 0-06-012193-9, HarpT). Har-Row.

Travelers. Ruth Prawer Jhabvala. 1977. pap. 2.25 o.p. (ISBN 0-06-080432-7, P432, PL). Har-Row.

Travelers. Jonathan Leon. (Berkley Medallion Book). 1977. 1.75 (ISBN 0-425-03289-2). Berkley Pub. Corp.

Travelers: A Novel. Andrew Fetler. LC 65-12972. 1965. Houghton Mifflin.

Traveler's Companion, Orig see Double-Bellied Companion.

Traveler's End. Louise Platt Hauck. LC 43-12125. 1943. Dodd, Mead & Company.

Travelers Five Along Life's Highway: Jimmy, Gideon Wiggan, the Clown, Wexley Snathers, Bap. Sloan. Annie Fellows Johnston. LC 11-29656. 1911. L. C. Page & Company.

Travelers in Time: Strange Tales of Man's Journeyings into the Past and the Future. Ed. by Philip Van Doren Stern. LC 47-525543. 1947. Doubleday.

Travelers of Space. Introduced by Willy Ley; Illustrated by Edd Cartier. Special Feature: Science Fiction Dictionary; Introd. by Samuel Anthony Peeples. Special Story for Illus. by David Kyle. 1st Ed. Ed. by Martin Greenberg. LC 52-6494. (Adventures in science fiction series). Gnome Press.

Travelers' Rest. Ben Robertson. LC 38-11642. The Cottonfield Publishers.

Traveler's Samples: Stories and Tales. Michael O'Donovan. LC 51-10860. 1951. Knopf.

Travelers: Stories of Americans Abroad. Ed. by L. M. Schulman. LC 70-175600. 1972. 5.95. Macmillan.

Travelin' Woman. Katherine Gibbs. (Orig.). 1980. pap. 1.95 o.s.i. (ISBN 0-8439-0728-2, Leisure Bks). Nordon Pubns.

Traveling Companion. Norman Walker. 1934. Longmans, Green and Co.

Traveling Corpses. Rudolf Kagey. LC 43-12460. (On cover: A Crime novel selection. No. 2). Select Publications, Inc.

Traveling Grave: And Other Stories. Leslie Poles Hartley. LC 48-6751. 1948. Arkham House.

Traveling Light. Mary Joyce Capps. (Family library). 1973. (pbk.) 0.95 (ISBN 0-515-03091-0). Pyramid Publications.

Traveling Light. Lionel Mitchell. LC 79-67609. 10.95 (ISBN 0-87223-584-X). Seaview Books.

Traveling Lonesome Roads. J. L. Holland, Jr. 1979. pap. 7.98 (ISBN 0-932700-01-2). Centaur Pubn VA.

Traveling Men. William George Dowsley. LC 27-1351. 1926. Frederick A. Stokes Company.

Traveling Saleswoman. Silvia Gold. (Orig.). 1969. pap. 1.25 o.p. (2094). Brandon.

Traveling Secretary. Conchita C. de Carlo. LC 44-7130. 1944. Meador Publishing Company.

Traveling Sex Hunters. Cynthia Marshall. 192p. (Orig.). 1972. pap. 1.95 o.p. (ISBN 0-87682-283-9, 7283). Barclay Hse.

Traveling Thirds. Gertrude Franklin Horn Atherton. 1905. lib. bdg. 25.00 (ISBN 0-8414-3098-5). Folcroft.

Traveling Through the Dark. William Stafford. 1962. 6.95 o.p. (ISBN 0-06-013965-X, HarpT). Har-Row.

Traveling Woman: A Novel. John Barrington Wain. LC 59-10162. 1959. St. Martin's Press.

Traveller & the Deserted Village. Oliver Goldsmith. Ed. by Murison. text ed. 1.25 o.p. Cambridge U Pr.

Traveller from Altruria. William Dean Howells. 1959. 4.00 o.p. (ISBN 0-8446-2280-X). Peter Smith.

Traveller from Altruria. Romance. William Dean Howells. LC 15-17406. 1908. Harper & Brothers.

Traveller in the Fur Cloak. Stanley John Weyman. LC 24-9128. 1924. Longmans, Green, and Co.

Travellers. Jean Stubbs. LC 63-18943. 1963. St. Martin's Press.

Travellers by Land and Sea. Laura R Balgue. LC 43-13641. 1943. Balgue Publishing Company.

Travellers by Land & Sea. Mikhail A. Kuzmin. Tr. by John Barnstead from Rus. 140p. 1983. 15.00 (ISBN 0-88233-810-2); pap. 5.00 (ISBN 0-88233-811-0). Ardis Pubs.

Travellers by Night. Ed. by August William Derleth. LC 67-5887. 1967. Arkham House.

Traveller's Joy: A Novel. Ernest Frederic Pierce. LC 7-37555. 1907. E. P. Dutton & Company.

Travellers' Library: Containing Interesting Stories. Laughable Anecdotes, and Enjoyable Reading of a Select and Varied Nature. B. L. G. Yalcrabb. 1875. Barclay & Co.

Travellers' Tales. Enid Maud Dinnis. LC 72-5908. (Short story index reprint series). 1972. (ISBN 0-8369-4211-6). Books for Libraries Press.

Travelling Companions. Henry James. LC 75-37552. (Short story index reprint series). 1972. (ISBN 0-8369-4111-X). Books for Libraries Press.

Travelling Companions. Henry James. LC 19-26578. 1919. Boni and Liveright.

Travelling Grave, & Others. Leslie Poles Hartley. 3.00 o.p. Arkham.

Travelling Kind. Janet Dailey. (Harlequin Presents Ser.). 192p. 1981. pap. 1.50 (ISBN 0-373-10427-8, Pub. by Harlequin). PB.

Travelling Soul. Hugh C Rae. LC 77-93537. 1.50 (ISBN 0-380-01854-3). Avon Books.

Travelling Thirds. Gertrude Franklin Horn Atherton. LC 5-32853. 1905. Harper & Brothers.

Travels and Adventures of Benjamin the Third. Shalom Jacob Abramowitz. LC 49-9256. (Schocken library, 18). 1949. Schocken Books.

Travels and Adventures of Edward Brown, Esq. John Campbell & Edward Brown. LC 75-170599. (Foundations of the Novel). (Illus.). 1973. (ISBN 0-8240-0582-1). Garland Pub.

Travels and Adventures of Monsieur Violet: In California, Sonora, and Western Texas. Frederick Marryat. LC 42-299384. G. Routledge and Sons.

Travels and Adventures of Monsieur Violet. Frederick Marryat. LC 73-104523. (Illus.). 1970. (ISBN 0-8398-1250-7). Literature House.

Travels and Surprising Adventures of Baron Munchausen. Munchausen. English. LC 42-26177. Hurst & Co.

Travels by Sea and Land of Alethitheras. Laughton Osborn. LC 8-31905. 1868. Moorhead, Simpson & Bond.

Travels in a Donkey Trap. Daisy Baker. (Inspirational Ser). 1975. Repr. lib. bdg. 7.95 o.p. (ISBN 0-8161-6273-5, Large Print Bks). G K Hall.

Travels in History. Samuel Langhorne Clemens & Kendall, Calvin Noyes, 1858-1921, Ed. LC 10-17996. 1910. 0.75. Harper & Brothers.

Travels in Nihilon. Alan Sillitoe. LC 72-1187. (Illus.). 1972. 6.95 (ISBN 0-684-13004-1). Scribner.

Travels into Several Remote Nations of the World. Jonathan Swift. LC 1-16696. T. Y. Crowell & Co.

Travels into Several Remote Nations of the World. In Four Parts. Jonathan Swift & Darton, Frederick Joseph Harvey, Ed. LC 20-299831. Printed for Benj. Motte.

Travels into Several Remote Nations of the World, Vol. III (1727) and Memoirs of the Court of Lilliput (1727). LC 72-4431. (Gulliveriana, 3). (Illus.). 1972. (ISBN 0-8201-1101-5). Scholars' Facsimiles & Reprints.

Travels of a Lady's Maid. B. A. LC 8-28634. 1908. L. C. Page & Company.

Travels of Baron Munchausen. Munchausen. English. Ed. by Van Doren, Carl Clinton. Limited Editions Club, Inc., New York. LC 31-227. 1929. The Limited Editions Club.

Travels of Cyrus. To Which Is Annexed, A Discourse Upon the Theology and Mythology of the Pagans. Andrew Michael Ramsay. 1795. Printed by Manning & Loring, for S. Hall, W. Spotswood, J. White, Thomas & Andrews, D. West, E. Larkin, W. P. Blake, and J. West.

Travels of Jaimie McPheeters. Robert Lewis Taylor. LC 57-7831. 1958. Doubleday.

Travels of James Dolphin. James Dolphin. LC 78-5959. (Garland Library of Narratives of North American Indian Captivities; V. 33). 1979. 29.50 (ISBN 0-8240-1657-2). Garland Pub.

Travels of Jamie McPheeters. Robert L. Taylor. 544p. 1981. pap. 3.50 (ISBN 0-441-82269-X). Ace Bks.

Travels of Lemuel Gulliver into Several Remote Regions of the World. Jonathan Swift. (On cover: Farm and fireside library, no. 6). 1881. Farm and Fireside Company.

Travels of Maudie Tipstaff. Margaret Forster. LC 67-26415. 1967. Stein and Day.

Travels of Mr. John Gulliver, Son to Capt. Lemuel Gulliver (1731) Pierre Francois Guyot Desfontaines & Jonathan Swift. LC 72-162479. (Gulliveriana, 2). 1971. (ISBN 0-8201-1098-1). Scholars' Facsimiles & Reprints.

Travels of Phoebe Ann. Alberta Chamberlain Lawrence. 1908. The C. M. Clark Publishing Company.

Travels to the Enu: The Story of a Shipwreck. Jakov Lind. LC 81-21457. 1982. 11.95 (ISBN 0-312-81630-8). St. Martin's Press.

Travels with a Duchess. Menna Gallie. LC 68-15974. 1968. Harper & Row.

Travels with Charley in Search of America. John Steinbeck. 1980. pap. 2.95 (ISBN 0-14-005320-4). Penguin.

Travels with Marcy. Marcus Van Heller, pseud. (Orig.). 1969. pap. 1.95 o.s.i. (TC-466, Travellers Comp). Olympia.

Travels with My Aunt. Graham Greene. LC 78-302096. 1977. 1.95 (ISBN 0-14-003221-5). Penguin Books.

Travels with My Aunt: A Novel. Graham Greene. LC 72-94848. 1969. 5.95. Viking Press.

Travels with Myself. Christine Elizabeth Townend. LC 77-367026. 1976. (ISBN 0-909331-21-9). Wild & Woolley.

Travers, a Mystery Story. Roger Beard Siddall. LC 52-8134. 1952. Beard, Francis.

Travers: A Story of the San Francisco Earthquake. Sara Dean. LC 7-24768. 1908. F. A. Stokes Company.

Traverse of the Gods. Bob Langley. LC 80-12004. 1980. 10.95 (ISBN 0-688-03651-1). Morrow.

Travesty. John Hawkes. LC 75-26764. 1976. 5.95 (ISBN 0-8112-0597-5). New Directions Pub. Corp.

Travesty. Clare Thornton. LC 27-19218. 1927. Cosmopolitan Book Corporation.

Trawler. James Brendan Connolly. LC 14-19619. 1914. C. Scribner's Sons.

Trax. R. L. Hawke. 208p. (Orig.). 1983. pap. 2.25 (ISBN 0-523-41880-9). Pinnacle Bks.

Tray Upstairs. Mary L. Frances. 208p. 1975. 7.50 o.p. (ISBN 0-682-48341-9). Exposition.

Treacherous Ground: By Johan Bojer... Johan Bojer & Muir, Jessie, Tr. LC 20-478369. 1920. Moffat, Yard and Company.

Treacherous Heart. Angela Alexie. 1980. 1.95 (ISBN 0-449-14312-0). Fawcett Gold Medal Books.

Treacherous Road. Henry Gibbs. LC 67-13221. 1967. Walker.

Treacherous Road. Simon Harvester. 1967. pap. 0.60 o.p. (60-300). Manor Bks.

Treacherous Road. Simon Harvester. 1967. large print ed. 7.50 o.p. (ISBN 0-8027-5197-0). Walker & Co.

Treacherous Road: By Simon Harvester. Henry Gibbs. (60-300). Macfadden.

Treacherous Time Machine. Merlin Mesmer Merlino. 1973. 5.95 (ISBN 0-533-00771-2). Vantage Press.

Treacherous Woman. H. C. Hoffman. (On cover: Munro's library, popular novels. v. 1. no. 391). 1885. N. L. Munro.

Treachery in Trieste: By Charles L. Leonard Pseud. Mary Violet Feberden. LC 54-31245. (Ace double novel books, gWith, as issued. Fieischman, A. S. Counterspy express. New York 1954). 1954. Ace Books.

Treachery in Trieste: By Charles L. Leonard Pseud. 1st Ed. Mary Violet Heberden. LC 51-10453. 1951. Published for the Crime Club by Doubleday.

Treachery in Type. Josephine Bell. LC 79-67548. 1980. 8.95 (ISBN 0-8027-5402-3). Walker.

Treachery on the Double. H. Eugene Barfield. 1979. 7.00 (ISBN 0-682-49263-9). Exposition.

Treachery Trail. Cliff Farrell. LC 69-17864. (D D western). 1969. 4.50. Doubleday.

Treacle Story Series, Vol. 1, Nos. 1-4. Tom Ahern et al. LC 76-43558. (Illus.). 172p. 1976. 10.00 (ISBN 0-914232-14-2). McPherson & Co.

Tread Gently, Death. Robert Portner Koehler. LC 45-374521. 1945. Phoenix Press.

Tread Lightly, Angel. 1st Ed. Frederick Clyde Davis. LC 52-5229. 1952. Published for the Crime Club by Doubleday.

Tread of the Longhorns. Walter Ganna. LC 49-11450. 1949. Naylor Co.

Tread Softly. Frances Rickett. LC 64-13606. (Inner sanctum mystery). 1964. Simon and Schuster.

Tread Softly in Love. Renee Shann. 1972. pap. 0.75 o.p. (94282). Beagle Bks.

Tread Softly in Love see Right Man for Julie.

Tread Softly in the Sun. Annette Eyre. LC 78-465476. 1969. 3.00. Hutchinson of Australia.

Tread Softly in This Place. Brian Talbot Cleeve. LC 73-175476. 1973. 7.95 (ISBN 0-381-98247-5). John Day Co.

Treading the Winepress. Charles William Gordon. LC 25-23220. George H. Doran Company.

Treading Water. Robert Strobos. LC 79-24208. 1980. 9.95 (ISBN 0-8071-0682-8). Louisiana State University Press.

Treadmill. Lola Jean Simpson. LC 29-9291. 1929. The Macmillan Company.

Trean: Or, The Mormon's Daughter. A Romantic Story of Life Among the Latter-Day Saints. Alvah Milton Kerr. LC 7-10820. (On cover: The household library. v. 4. no. 30). Belford, Clarke & Company; Etc.,Etc.

Treason. Robert Gessner. LC 44-2104. 1944. C. Scribner's Sons.

Treason Game. Nick Carter. (Nick Carter Ser.). (Illus.). 224p. 1982. pap. 2.50 (ISBN 0-441-82348-3, Pub. by Charter Bks). Ace Bks.

Treason Line. John Branfroot Simpson Pedler. LC 74-87962. (A Stein and Day mystery). 1969. 4.95. Stein and Day.

Treason Line. Dominic Torr. 1969. 4.95 o.p. (ISBN 0-8128-1243-3). Stein & Day.

Treasure. Robert Daley. 1977. 10.00 (ISBN 0-394-41271-0). Random.

Treasure. Paul Webster Eaton. LC 9-29425. 1.50. R. F. Fenno & Company.

Treasure. A. E Hotchner. LC 77-102337. (Illus.). 1970. 6.95. Random House.

Treasure. Selma Ottiliana Lovisa Lagerlof. LC 73-86275. 1973. 3.00 (ISBN 0-913780-01-4). Daughters, Inc.

Treasure. Selma Ottiliana Lovisa Lagerlof. Tr. by Chater, Arthur G. LC 25-26436. 1925. Doubleday, Page & Company.

Treasure. Larry Levine. 1.75 (ISBN 0-449-14115-2). Fawcett Gold Medal.

Treasure. Kathleen Thompson Norris. LC 14-2353. 1914. 1.00. The Macmillan Company.

Treasure. LC 15-266590. George H. Doran Company.

Treasure. Gordon Ray Young. LC 28-135633. 1928. Doubleday, Doran & Company, Inc.

Treasure and Trouble Therewith: A Tale of California. Geraldine Bonner. LC 17-21974. 1917. 1.50. D. Appleton and Company.

Treasure and Undertow: Two Complete Novels. Kathleen Thompson Norris. LC 37-32426. 1937. The Sun Dial Press, Inc.

Treasure Below. Edward Ellsberg. (O.s.i.). 305p. 1976. Repr. of 1940 ed. lib. bdg. 10.50x o.s.i. Queens Hse.

Treasure Beyond Taurus. Gene Farrell. LC 55-23672. 1955. Van Kampen Press.

Treasure Book of Fairy Tales. Women'S Day Magazine. Ed. by A. McGovern. pap. 0.40 o.p. (K754, GM). Fawcett World.

Treasure by Degrees. David Williams. LC 77-76658. 1977. 7.95 (ISBN 0-312-81643-X). St. Martin's Press.

Treasure Chest. Glen Chase, pseud. (Cherry Delight Ser). (O.s.i.: No. 17). 1974. pap. 1.25 o.s.i. (LB220ZK, Leisure Bks). Nordon Pubns.

Treasure Chest of Sea Stories. Ed. by Max John Herzberg. LC 48-9315. 1948. J. Messner.

Treasure Chest of Sport Stories. Ed. by Max John Herzberg. LC 51-10064. 1951. Messner.

Treasure Cruise: And Other Crunch and Des Stories. Philip Wylie. LC 56-7481. 1956. Rinehart.

Treasure Divers: A Boy's Adventures in the Depths of the Sea. Charles Frederick Holder. LC 98-741. 1898. Dodd, Mead and Company.

Treasure for Treasure. Justin Scott. LC 73-93030. (McKay-Washburn suspense). 1974. 5.95 (ISBN 0-679-50444-3). D. McKay Co.

Treasure Found--a Bride Won: A Novel. George E Gardner. LC 7-309. (choice series. no. 122). 1895. R. Bonner's Sons.

Treasure Found--a Bride Won: A Novel. George E Gardner. LC 7-3089. 1895. R. Bonner's Sons.

Treasure House of Martin Hews. Edward Phillips Oppenheim. LC 29-3183. 1929. Little, Brown, and Company.

Treasure Hunt. Frederick Buechner. LC 77-4743. 1977. 8.95 (ISBN 0-689-10800-1). Atheneum.

Treasure Hunt. Tom Pace. LC 70-123993. 1970. 4.95. Harper & Row.

Treasure Hunters. Burt Wetanson & Thomas Hoobler. LC 82-60692. 240p. 1983. pap. 2.95 (ISBN 0-86721-235-7). Playboy Pbks.

Treasure in Hell's Canyon. Grover C Gulick. LC 78-20235. 1979. 7.95 (ISBN 0-385-09848-0). Doubleday.

Treasure in Oklahoma's Green Country. Violet McClain. LC 74-3485. 1974. 8.95 (ISBN 0-8111-0520-2). Naylor Co.

Treasure in Oklahoma's Green Country. Violet McClain. LC 74-3485. 1974. (ISBN 0-8111-0520-2). Naylor Co.

Treasure in the Hills. John Tedman & Alison Tedman. (New Oxford Supplementary Readers Ser). (Illus.). 96p. 1970. pap. text ed. 0.80x o.p. (ISBN 0-19-422469-4). Oxford U Pr.

Treasure in the West: Illustrated by Louis Macouillard. Margit Strom Heppenstall. LC 54-12687. 1954. Pacific Press Pub. Association.

Treasure Is Love. Barbara Cartland. LC 79-13511. 1980. 6.95 (ISBN 0-87272-079-9). Duron Books.

Treasure Island. Ed. by William A. Kottmeyer. 1972. text ed. 5.76 o.p. (ISBN 0-07-034020-X, W). McGraw.

Treasure Island. Robert Louis Stevenson. (Signet classic, CD272) Bibl.). 1965. New Amer. Lib.

Treasure Island. Robert Louis Stevenson. (Large type ed. Keith Jennison bk.). 1966. 6.95. Watts.

Treasure Island. Robert Louis Stevenson. LC 57-12790. (Children's classics). 1957. Winston.

Treasure Island. Robert Louis Stevenson. LC 62-19978. 1962. Collier Books.

Treasure Island. Robert Louis Stevenson. LC 63-6747. (World's classics, 295). 1955. Oxford University Press.

Treasure Island. Robert Louis Stevenson. LC 66-3845. (Scribner illustrated classics). Scribner.

Treasure Island. Robert Louis Stevenson. LC 63-14827. (Macmillan classics, 8). 1963. Macmillan.

Treasure Island. Robert Louis Stevenson. LC 65-6562. (Perennial library). 1965. Harper & Row.

Treasure Island. Robert Louis Stevenson. LC 65-11929. (Whitman classics library). 1965. Whitman Pub. Co.

Treasure Island. Robert Louis Stevenson. (Washington Square Press enriched classics.). (Illus.). 1974. (pbk.) 0.75. Pocket Books.

Treasure Island. Robert Louis Stevenson. (Macmillan classics, 8). (Illus.). 1963. Macmillan.

Treasure Island. Robert Louis Stevenson. LC 50-41964. 1883. Cassell.

Treasure Island. Robert Louis Stevenson. LC 50-41391. 1884. Roberts Bros.

Treasure Island. Robert Louis Stevenson. LC 48-4245. (Lippincott classics). 1948. J. B. Lippincott Co.

Treasure Island. Robert Louis Stevenson. LC 48-10611. (Prose and Poetry Individualized Program. The Novel). 1948. L. W. Singer Co.

Treasure Island. Robert Louis Stevenson. LC 49-4123. 1949. Random House.

Treasure Island. Robert Louis Stevenson. LC 17-23020. The Mershon Company.

Treasure Island. Robert Louis Stevenson. (On cover: Lovell's library, no. 819). 1886. J. W. Lovell Company.

Treasure Island. Robert Louis Stevenson. (On cover: Seaside library. Pocket ed. no. 888). 1886. G. Munro.

Treasure Island. Robert Louis Stevenson. LC 4924. W. B. Conkey Company.

Treasure Island. new ed., with original illustrations by wal paget. ed. Robert Louis Stevenson. 1902. C. Scribner's Sons.

Treasure Island. Robert Louis Stevenson. LC 5-16630. (Half-title: The biographical edition of the works of Robert Louis Stevenson). 1905. C. Scribner's Sons.

Treasure Island. Robert Louis Stevenson. LC 9-18058. Educational Publishing Company.

Treasure Island. Robert Louis Stevenson. Ed. by Baker, Franklin Thomas. (Merrill's English texts). 0.40. C. E. Merrill Co.

Treasure Island. Robert Louis Stevenson. LC 10-28494. (Half-title: The Scribner English classics). 0.25. C. Scribner's Sons.

Treasure Island. Robert Louis Stevenson. Ed. by Gaston, Charles Robert. LC 11-27847. 0.40. D. C. Heath & Company.

Treasure Island. Robert Louis Stevenson. LC 11-25047. 1911. C. Scribner's Sons.

Treasure Island. Robert Louis Stevenson. LC 11-25046. 1911. G. W. Jacobs and Company.

Treasure Island. Robert Louis Stevenson. Ed. by Blanchard, Ferdinand Quincy. LC 13-23418. (Half-title: The Barnes English texts. General editor: E. Fairley). 1913. The A. S. Barnes Company.

Treasure Island. Robert Louis Stevenson. Ed. by Lewis, William Dodge. LC 16-376. (academy classics). Allyn and Bacon.

Treasure Island. Robert Louis Stevenson. Rand, McNally & Company.

Treasure Island. Robert Louis Stevenson. (Every boy's library--Boy scout edition). 1915. Grosset & Dunlap.

Treasure Island. Robert Louis Stevenson. LC 15-23639. 1915. Harper & Brothers.

Treasure Island. Robert Louis Stevenson. LC 18-16895. 1918. C. Scribner's Sons.

Treasure Island. Robert Louis Stevenson. Ed. by Broadus, Edmund Kemper. LC 19-11566. (Half-title: The Lake English classics. General editor: L. T. Damon). Scott, Fore-Man and Company.

Treasure Island. Robert Louis Stevenson. Ed. by Signor, Florence R. LC 22-6610. (excelsior literature series. no. 69). F. A. Owen Publishing Company.

Treasure Island. Robert Louis Stevenson. Ed. by Herzberg, Max John. LC 23-468. (Riverside literature series). 0.60. Houghton Mifflin Company.

Treasure Island. Robert Louis Stevenson. LC 23-130112. 1923. The Macmillan Company.

Treasure Island. Robert Louis Stevenson. Ed. by Blakely, Gilbert Sykes. LC 25-2140. (Lettered on cover: The Winston clear-type popular classics). The John C. Winston Company.

Treasure Island. Robert Louis Stevenson. LC 25-2846. (Lettered on cover: Mayflower series). The Saalfield Publishing Co.

Treasure Island. Robert Louis Stevenson. Ed. by Searson, James William. LC 26-12596. (Half-title: University classics for high schools--colleges--universities). 1926. The University Publishing Company.

Treasure Island. Robert Louis Stevenson. Ed. by Hadsell, Sardis Roy & Wells, George C. LC 28-6085. (western series of English and American classics). 1926. Harlow Publishing Co.

Treasure Island. Robert Louis Stevenson. Ed. by Blanchard, Ferdinand Quincy. LC 28-974. (Laidlaw English classics). Laidlaw Brothers, Incorporated.

Treasure Island. Robert Louis Stevenson. Ed. by Hubbell, Jay Broadus. LC 27-22658. (modern readers' series). 1927. The Macmillan Company.

Treasure Island. Robert Louis Stevenson. LC 29-1569. (father and son library). J. H. Sears & Company, Inc.

Treasure Island. Robert Louis Stevenson. Ed. by Vance, Hiram Albert. Moffett, Harold Young. LC 29-205925. (Half-title: New pocket classics). The Macmillan Company.

Treasure Island. Robert Louis Stevenson. Ed. by Baker, Franklin Thomas. LC 29-30554. (Merrill's English texts). Charles E. Merrill Company.

Treasure Island. Robert Louis Stevenson. LC 30-263850. 1930. Garden City Publishing Company, Inc.

Treasure Island. Robert Louis Stevenson. LC 33-270449. (Windermere series). 1932. Rand, McNally & Company.

Treasure Island. Robert Louis Stevenson. Ed. by Lewis, William Dodge. LC 37-162268. (academy classics). Allyn and Bacon.

Treasure Island. Robert Louis Stevenson. LC 40-6580. 1940. McLoughlin Brothers, Inc.

Treasure Island. Robert Louis Stevenson. Limited Editions Club, Inc., New York. LC 41-8492. 1941. The Limited Editions Club.

Treasure Island. Robert Louis Stevenson. LC 43-27341. (Reader's library). J. H. Sears & Company, Inc.

Treasure Island. Robert Louis Stevenson. LC 42-49312. (Jacket library. 1). 1932. National Home Library Foundation.

Treasure Island. Robert Louis Stevenson. LC 43-5931. (Newbery classics). 1942. David McKay Company.

Treasure Island... Robert Louis Stevenson. LC 46-23133. 1946.

Treasure Island. Robert Louis Stevenson. LC 46-5531. (Half-title: Rainbow classics. General editor: May L. Becker). 1946. The World Publishing Company.

Treasure Island. Robert Louis Stevenson. Ed. by Vance, Hiram Albert. LC 3-546. (Macmillan's pocket American and English classics). 1902. The Macmillan Company.

Treasure Island. Robert Louis Stevenson. Ed. by Blakely, Gilbert Sykes. LC 25-10772. (Winston companion classics). The John C. Winston Company.

Treasure Island. Robert Louis Stevenson & Brown, Eleanor. LC 37-22389. 1937. Minnesota School for the Deaf.

Treasure Island. medallion ed. Robert Louis Stevenson & Harvey, Alexander. LC 6-42924. 1906. Current Literature Publishing Co.

Treasure Island. Robert Louis Stevenson & Livingston, Mary Georgia. LC 48-11090. 1948. Globe Book Co.

Treasure Island. illus. by alexander key and ernie king. ed. Robert Louis Stevenson & Moderow, Gertrude. LC 49-57912. 1949. Scott, Foresman.

Treasure Island. Robert Louis Stevenson & Price, Norman, 1877- Illus. LC 47-27064. (Illustrated junior library). 1947. Grosset & Dunlap.

Treasure Island: A Story of the Spanish Main. Robert Louis Stevenson. LC 50-5584. (World's greatest literature). 1949. Fountain Press.

Treasure Island: A Story of the Spanish Main. Robert Louis Stevenson. A. L. Burt Company.

Treasure Island. A Story of the Spanish Main. Robert Louis Stevenson. LC 41-35144. (Cornell series). 1898. A. L. Burt Company.

Treasure Island. Ed. by M. W. and G. Thomas. Illus. by Rosemary Grimble. Robert Louis Stevenson. Ed. by Maurice Walton Thomas & Gladys Thomas. LC 66-6327. (Shorter classics.). bds., 2.50. Ginn.

Treasure Island: Illustrated by Henry C. Pitz. Robert Louis Stevenson. LC 54-144661. 1954. Junior Deluxe Editions.

Treasure Island: Illustrated by John C. Wonsetler. Robert Louis Stevenson. LC 54-13484. (New children's classics). 1954. Macmillan.

Treasure Island: Illustrated by Paul Frame. Robert Louis Stevenson. LC 55-224354. (Whitman famous classics). 1955. Whitman Pub. Co.

Treasure Island: Kidnapped. Robert Louis Stevenson. LC 37-30974. (Half-title: Everyman's library, d. by Ernest Rhys. Fiction. no. 763). 1931. J. M. Dent & Sons, Ltd.

Treasure Island. New Arabian Nights. Edited and Introduced by M. R. Ridley. Robert Louis Stevenson. Ed. by Maurice Roy Ridley. LC 62-51246. (Everyman's library, 768. Fiction). 1962. Dent.

Treasure Island: Notes by Thomas A. Duff, Austin Fowler. Edit. Bd. of Consultants: Stanley Cooperman, Charles Leavitt, Unicio J. Violi. (Monarch notes and study guides, 726-O) Bibl.). pap., 1.00. Monarch Pr.

Treasure Island: The Black Arrow. Robert Louis Stevenson. LC 24-22219. (works of Robert Louis Stevenson. v. 8). 1910. The Jefferson Press.

Treasure Island. With Biographical Illus. and Drawings Reproduced from Early Editions, Together with an Introductory Biographical Sketch of the Author and Captions by Basil Davenport. Robert Louis Stevenson. LC 56-3902. (Great illustrated classics). Dodd, Mead.

Treasure Map. Adam Hardy. (Fox series,#4). 1974. (pbk.) 0.95 (ISBN 0-523-00294-7). Pinnacle Books.

Treasure Mountain. Louis L'Amour. LC 73-14811. 1973. 8.95 (ISBN 0-8161-6162-3). G. K. Hall.

Treasure Mountain: Or, The Young Prospectors. Edwin Legrand Sabin. LC 13-187341. Thomas Y. Crowell Company.

Treasure Mountains. Robert Randell. LC 38-1962. Dorrance and Company.

Treasure Nobody Saw. (Meg Mystery Ser.). 1981. 6.08 (ISBN 0-307-61515-4). Western Pub.

Treasure of Aspen Canyon. Charles Horace Snow. LC 35-174976. Loring & Mussey.

Treasure of Atlantis. J. Allan Dunn. (Time-Lost Ser.). (Illus.). 1971. 5.00 (ISBN 0-87818-006-0); pap. 0.75 (ISBN 0-87818-002-8). Centaur.

Treasure of Big Waters. Ridgwell Cullum. LC 30-281764. 1930. J. B. Lippincott Company.

Treasure of Caricar. Roy W Hinds. LC 27-131235. H. Altemus Company.

Treasure of Drowning River: A Tale of the Far North. Carl Burgess Glasscock. LC 33-18228. 1933. Roland Swain Company.

Treasure of Fan-Tan Flat. William Oliver Turner. LC 61-9203. (Double D western). 1961. Doubleday.

Treasure of Fan-Tan Flat. William Oliver Turner. (Berkley medallion book). 1975. (pbk.) 0.95 (ISBN 0-425-02758-9). Berkley Pub. Co.

Treasure of Fan-Tan Flat. William Oliver Turner. 1978. 1.25 (ISBN 0-425-03625-1). Berkley Pub. Corp.

Treasure of Happiness: Decorations by J. McA. Smiley. Jacob Keel. LC 49-37672. 1949.

Treasure of Heaven: A Romance of Riches. Marie Corelli. 1906. Dodd, Mead & Company.

Treasure of Heaven: A Romance of Riches. Marie Corelli. LC 35-33423. 1928. A. L. Burt Company.

Treasure of Hidden Valley. Willis George Emerson. LC 15-13842. 1915. 1.25. Forbes & Company.

Treasure of Ho. Lily Moresby Adams Beck. LC 24-9127. 1924. Dodd, Mead and Company.

Treasure of Hope. Hugh Zachary. (Sierra Leone Ser.: No. 3). (Orig.). 1982. pap. 2.75 (ISBN 0-440-08528-4). Dell.

Treasure of Matecumbe. Robert Lewis Taylor. 1.95 (ISBN 0-671-80609-2). Pocket Books.

Treasure of Montezuma. Rudolph Leonhart. LC 11-15096. 1888. Cassidy, Book and Job Printer.

Treasure of Painted Mountain. 1st Ed. Will Wagner. LC 53-13053. 1953. Pageant Press.

Treasure of Pearls. A Romance of Adventures in Californa. Gustave Aimard. LC 5-42200. (On cover: Lovell's library, no. 1145). 1888. J. W. Lovell Company.

Treasure of Peyre Gaillard: Being an Account of the Recovery, on a South Carolina Plantation, of a Treasure, Which Had Remained Buried and Lost in a Vast Swamp for Over a Hundred Years... John Bennett. LC 6-36431. 1906. The Century Co.

Treasure of Pleasant Valley. Frank Yerby. LC 55-9940. 1955. Dial Press.

Treasure of Pleasant Valley. Frank Garvin Yerby. 1973. 1.50. Dell.

Treasure of Rio Verde. Ralph Hayes. 1973. 4.95. Lenox Hill Pr.

Treasure of Russian Short Stories: 1900-1966. Tr. by Selig O. Wassner. Ed. by Selig O Wassner. LC 68-10800. 1968. 6.95. Fell.

Treasure of Sainte-Foy. MacDonald Harris. LC 79-23242. 1980. 11.95 o.p. (ISBN 0-689-11025-1). Atheneum.

Treasure of Seacliff Manor. Yvonne Norman. (Avalon Books). 4.95. Thomas Bouregy.

Treasure of Shag Rock: An Adventure Story. Robert Lloyd. LC 2-19881. Lothrop Publishing Company.

Treasure of Sierra Madre. Ed. by James Naremore. LC 78-53298. (Screenplay Ser.). (Illus.). 206p. 1979. 17.50 (ISBN 0-299-07680-6); pap. 6.95t (ISBN 0-299-07684-9). U of Wis Pr.

Treasure of Silver Dragon. Hamilton Thompson. (Microquest Ser.: No. 4). 1980. pap. write for info. (ISBN 0-88074-084-1). Metagam.

Treasure of the Brasada. Les Savage. LC 47-2904. 1947. Simon and Schuster.

Treasure of the Bucoleon. Arthur Douglas Howden Smith. LC 23-12339. Brentano's.

Treasure of the Chisos. John H. Culp. LC 79-80338. 1971. 5.95 o.p. (ISBN 0-03-085058-4). HR&W.

Treasure of the Chisos: A Novel. John H Culp. LC 78-102139. 1971. 5.95 (ISBN 0-03-085058-4). Holt, Rinehart and Winston.

Treasure of the Heart. Glenna Finley, pseud. (Orig.). 1971. pap. 1.25 (ISBN 0-451-07324-X, Y7324, Sig). NAL.

Treasure of the Heart. Pat Louis. (Superromances Ser.). 384p. 1982. pap. 2.50 (ISBN 0-373-70014-8, Pub. by Worldwide). Harlequin Bks.

Treasure of the Lake. Henry Rider Haggard. LC 26-12322. 1926. Doubleday, Page & Company.

Treasure of the Lost City. Aaron Fletcher. 1976. pap. 1.25 o.p. (LB391, Leisure Bks). Nordon Pubns.

Treasure of the Lost City. Aaron Fletcher. Leisure Books.

Treasure of the Sierra Madre. B Traven. LC 67-23519. 1967. Hill and Wang.

Treasure of the Sierra Madre. B Traven. LC 79-4018. (Modern Library books, 389). 1969. 2.45. Modern Library.

Treasure of the Sierra Madre. B Traven. LC 35-9050. 1935. A. A. Knopf.

Treasure of the Sierra Madre. B Traven. LC 79-10456. 1979. 10.00 (ISBN 0-8376-0436-2). R. Bentley.

Treasure of the Sierra Madre. B. Traven. LC 81-9086. (Time Reading Program Special Edition). 1981. (deluxe: set of 2) 12.95. Time-Life Books.

Treasure of the Sun. Adeline Attwood. LC 53-8531. 1954. Houghton Mifflin.

Treasure of Unicorn Gold. H. Thompson. (Microquest Ser.: No. 6). 1981. pap. write for info. (ISBN 0-88074-086-8). Metagam.

Treasure of Wonderwhat. Bill Starr. LC 76-13474. (Farstar & son novel; 2). 1977. 1.50 (ISBN 0-345-25157-1). Ballantine Books.

Treasure Preserved. David Williams. 224p. 1983. 10.95 (ISBN 0-312-81647-2). St Martin.

Treasure Ranch. Charles Alden Seltzer. LC 40-344291. 1940. Doubleday, Doran and Company, Inc.

Treasure Ranch. Charles Alden Seltzer. LC 74-21544. 1974. (ISBN 0-88411-110-5). Aeonian Press.

Treasure Royal: Being the Romance of a Modern Hunt for Treasure and an Adventure of James Drew, Detective. William A Garrett. LC 26-8008. 1926. D. Appleton and Company.

Treasure Seekers. Paul Roan. 192p. (Orig.). 1973. pap. 1.95 o.p. (ISBN 0-87056-352-1, 6352). Brandon.

Treasure Tower, a Story of Malta. Virginia Wales Johnson. (On cover: Globe library, v. 1, no. 167). 1892. Rand, McNally & Company.

Treasure Trail. Frederick John Niven. LC 23-13953. 1923. Dodd, Mead and Company.

Treasure Trail. Roland Pertwee. LC 25-4776. 1924. A. A. Knopf.

Treasure Trail. Frank Lillie Pollock. LC 6-18588. 1906. L. C. Page & Company.

Treasure Trail. Van W Tilford. 1981. 1.75 (ISBN 0-505-51673-X). Tower Publications Inc.

Treasure Trail. Van W Tilford. LC 81-15169. 1982. 11.95 (ISBN 0-89340-404-7). J. Curley & Associates.

Treasure Trail: A Romance of the Land of Gold and Sunshine. Marah Ellis Martin Ryan. LC 43-26671. 1918. Grosset & Dunlap.

Treasure Trail: A Romance of the Land of Gold and Sunshine. Marah Ellis Martin Ryan. LC 18-21164. 1918. A. C. McClurg & Co.

Treasure Train. Robert A. McGuire. 224p. (Orig.). 1982. pap. 2.25 (ISBN 0-8439-1030-5, Leisure Bks). Nordon Pubns.

Treasure Train: Adventures of Craig Kennedy, Scientific Detective, Which Ultimately Take Him Abroad. Arthur Benjamin Reeve. LC 17-15286. 1917. Harper & Brothers.

Treasure Train: Adventures of Craig Kennedy, Scientific Detective, Which Ultimately Take Him Abroad. Arthur Benjamin Reeve. LC 20-12452. 1919. Grosset & Dunlap.

Treasure Trove. Catharine Amy Dawson Scott. LC 9-10787. 1909. Duffield & Company.

Treasure up in Smoke. David Williams. LC 78-4010. 1978. 7.95 (ISBN 0-312-81648-0). St. Martin's Press.
Treasure Valley. Mary Esther Macgregor. LC 8-32386. G. H. Doran Company.
Treasure Vault of Atlantis. Olof W Anderson. LC 77-84194. (Lost Race and Adult Fantasy Fiction). (Illus.). 1978. 20.00 (ISBN 0-405-10952-0). Arno Press.
Treasure Vault of Atlantis: Giving an Account of a Very Remarkable Discovery of an Ancient Temple of Wealth... Olof W Anderson. LC 25-975722. 1925. Midland Publishing Co.
Treasure Worth Seeking. Rachel Ryan. (Candlelight Ecstasy Ser.: No. 59). (Orig.). 1982. pap. 1.75 (ISBN 0-440-18558-0). Dell.
Treasures from Hell. John Tominsky. 1981. 5.75 (ISBN 0-8062-1695-6). Carlton.
Treasures in the Marshes. Charlotte Mary Yonge. LC 9-1207. T. Whittaker.
Treasures of Darkness. Cornelia Jessey. LC 53-12569. 1953. Noonday Press.
Treasures of Darkness. Sussman, Cornelia (Silver) LC 53-12569. 1953. Noonday Press.
Treasures of Mayville. Otto John Schuster. LC 19-18837. Hayworth Publishing House.
Treasures of the Alhambra. 2d ed. Washington Irving & F Monfort. LC 79-66157. (Illus.). 1980. 5.98 (ISBN 8-474-24085-9). Crescent Books.
Treasures of the Kingdom; Stories of Faith, Hope and Love. Ed. by Thomas Everett Harre. 1947. Rinehard & Company, Inc.
Treasures of the Oregon Country: No. II. Maynard C. Drawson. 1974. pap. 8.95 o.p. (ISBN 0-934476-01-2). Dee Pub Co.
Treasures of Time. Penelope Lively. LC 79-8434. 1980. 8.95 (ISBN 0-385-15813-0). Doubleday.
Treasures of Tranicos. Robert E. Howard & L. Sprague de Camp. (Illus.). 1980. pap. 2.50 (ISBN 0-441-82245-2). Ace Bks.
Treasures on Earth. Carter Wilson. 256p. 1983. pap. 3.95 (ISBN 0-380-63305-1, Bard). Avon.
Treasures on Earth: A Novel. Carter Wilson. LC 80-29626. 1981. 11.95 (ISBN 0-394-51936-1). Knopf: Distributed by Random House.
Treasures Upon Earth. Frank David Higham. LC 31-15089. 1931. Doubleday, Doran & Company, Inc.
Treasury Alarm. Jocelyn Davey, pseud. LC 80-52081. 1981. 10.95 (ISBN 0-8027-5431-7). Walker.
Treasury of American Indian Tales. Theodore Whitson Ressler. LC 57-5046. 1957. Association Press.
Treasury of American Jewish Stories. Ed. by Harold Uriel Ribalow. LC 58-13736. 1958. T. Yoseloff.
Treasury of American Short Stories. Nancy Sullivan. LC 80-2438. 1981. 16.95 (ISBN 0-385-17139-0). Doubleday.
Treasury of Cat Stories. Ed. by Era Zistel. Bacon, Peggy, 1895- Illus. LC 44-40074. 1944. Greenberg.
Treasury of Contentment. James Kavanaugh. 10.00 o.s.i. (ISBN 0-671-27024-9). Trident.
Treasury of Doctor Stories by the World's Great Authors. Ed. by Noah Daniel Fabricant. Werner, Heinz, 1901- Joint Comp. LC 46-810744. 1946. F. Fell.
Treasury of Fantasy: Heroic Adventures in Imaginary Lands. avenel 1981 ed. Cary Wilkins. LC 81-434. (Illus.). 6.98 (ISBN 0-517-33629-4). Avenel Books: Distributed by Crown Publishers.
Treasury of Fishing Stories. Ed. by Charles Eliot Goodspeed. 1946. A. S. Barnes and Company.
Treasury of Gambling Stories. Robert Kendrick Brunner. LC 46-8526. 1946. Ziff-Davis Publishing Company.
Treasury of Gothic and Supernatural. avenel 1981 ed. LC 81-10787. 6.98 (ISBN 0-517-34802-0). Avenel Books : Distributed by Crown.
Treasury of Great Mysteries, 2 Vols. Ed. by Howard Haycraft & John Beecroft. LC 57-6099. 1969. 7.95 o.p. (ISBN 0-385-08043-3). Doubleday.
Treasury of Great Mysteries: Edited by Howard Haycraft and John Beecroft. Ed. by Howard Haycraft & John Beecroft. LC 57-6099. 1957. Simon and Schuster.
Treasury of Great Russian Short Stories: Pushkin to Gorky. Ed. by Avrahm Yarmolinsky. LC 44-1281. 1944. The Macmillan Company.
Treasury of Great Science Fiction, 2 Vols. Ed. by Anthony Boucher. 1959. 5.95 o.p. Doubleday.
Treasury of Great Science Fiction. William Anthony Parker White. LC 58-9379. 1959. Doubleday.
Treasury of Horse Stories. new ed. Ed. by Margaret C. Self. LC 72-92321. 1977. pap. 5.95 o.p. (ISBN 0-668-04205-2). Arco.
Treasury of Horse Stories. Margaret Cabell Self. LC 72-92321. (Illus.). 1945. 6.95 o.p. (ISBN 0-668-02828-9). Arco.
Treasury of Jewish Sea Stories. Ed. by Samuel Sobel. LC 64-8427. 5.95. J. David.
Treasury of Jewish Sea Stories. Ed. by Samuel Sobel. LC 64-8427. 1965. J. David.
Treasury of Modern Asian Stories. Ed. by William Clifford & Daniel Milton. pap. 2.95 (ISBN 0-452-25052-8, Z5052, Plume). NAL.
Treasury of Modern Asian Stories: Edited by Daniel L. Milton and William Clifford. Ed. by Daniel L Milton. LC 61-9137. (Mentor book, MD329). 1961. New American Library.
Treasury of Modern Fantasy. Terry Carr & Martin Harry Greenberg. LC 80-69603. 1981. 8.95 (ISBN 0-380-77115-2). Avon.
Treasury of Modern Mysteries. LC 73-77298. 1973. 8.95. Doubleday.
Treasury of Mountaineering Stories. Ed. by Daniel Talbot. LC 54-10505. 1954. Putnam.
Treasury of New England Short Stories from Yankee Magazine. Ed. by Laurie Hillyer. LC 74-83984. 1974. 6.95 (ISBN 0-911658-64-5). Yankee.
Treasury of New England Short Stories. 2nd ed. Ed. by C. Silitch & L. Hillyer. LC 74-83984. 324p. 1979. pap. 6.95 (ISBN 0-911658-94-7). Yankee Bks.
Treasury of Nurse Stories by World Famous Authors. Ed. by Sonia Barry. LC 61-17226. 1962. F. Fell.
Treasury of Russian and Soviet Short Stories. Ed. by Y. Ivanov. LC 75-159579. (Fawcett premier book, M519). 1971. 0.95. Fawcett Publications, Inc.
Treasury of Science Fiction. Ed. by Groff Conklin. LC 79-26154. 1980. 5.98 (ISBN 0-517-30618-2). Bonanza Books.
Treasury of Sea Stories. Ed. by Gordon Christian Aymar. LC 48-935550. 1948. A. S. Barnes.
Treasury of Sherlock Holmes: Selected and with an Introd. by Adrian Conan Doyle. Arthur Conan Doyle. LC 55-5930. Harover House.
Treasury of Short Stories. Rudyard Kipling. LC 57-8075. (Bantam books, S1609 9). 1957. Bantam Books.
Treasury of Short Stories: Favorites of the Past Hundred Years from Turgenev to Thurber, from Balzac to Hemingway; with Biographical Sketches of the Authors. Ed. by Bernardine Kielty Scherman. LC 48-5015. 1947. Simon and Schuster.
Treasury of Short Stories: Favorties of the Past Hundred Years from Turgenev to Thurber, from Balzac to Hemingway. Ed. by Kielty, Bernardine. LC 48-5015. 1947. Simon and Schuster.
Treasury of Tales: Containing One Hundred Choice Stories by the Best American and Foreign Authors. Ed. by William Swinton. LC 15-218607. 1885. Caxton Book Co.
Treasury of Terror. Christopher Lee. (Illus., Orig.). pap. 0.50 o.p. (R1498). Pyramid Pubns.
Treasury of Verse, for Little Children. Madalen G Edgar. Thomas Y. Crowell Company.
Treasury of Victorian Detective Stories. Everett Franklin Bleiler. LC 78-26908. 1982. 9.95 (ISBN 0-684-17640-8). Charles Scribner's Sons.
Treasury of Victorian Ghost Stories. Everett Franklin Bleiler. LC 81-13614. 16.95 (ISBN 0-684-17299-2). Scribner.
Treasury of Yiddish Stories. Ed. by Irving Howe. (Illus.). 1973. (pbk.) 4.50 (ISBN 0-8052-0400-8). Schocken Books.
Treasury of Yiddish Stories: Ed. by Irving Howe, Eliezer Greenberg. Authorized Abridgment. Ed. by Irving Howe & Eliezer Greenberg. (Premier bk., m 376). 1968. Fawcett.
Treasury of Yiddish Stories: Ed. by Irving Howe, Eliezer Greenberg. Drawings by Ben Shahn. Ed. by Irving Howe & Eliezer Greenberg. (Compass bk. c173). 1965. pap., 2.25. Viking.
Treasury of Yiddish Stories Edited: By Irving Howe and Eliezer Greenberg. With Drawings by Ben Shahn. Ed. by Irving Howe & Eliezer Greenberg. LC 58-8528. (Meridian books, MG13). 1958. Meridian Books.
Treasury of Yiddish Stories: With Drawings by Ben Shahn. Ed. by Irving Howe & Eliezer Greenberg. LC 54-9599. 1954. Viking Press.
Treatment: A Novel. Anthony Charles H Smith. LC 76-377281. 1976. 3.50 (ISBN 0-297-77073-X). Weidenfeld and Nicolson.
Treatment Man. William George Wiegand. LC 59-13220. 1959. McGraw-Hill.
Treats. Christopher Hampton. 62p. 1976. pap. 3.95 (ISBN 0-571-10967-5). Faber & Faber.
Treble Clef. Edward Charles Booth. LC 24-25642. 1924. 2.50. Dodd, Mead and Company.
Trecioji Moteris see Third Woman.
Tredici Novelle Moderne. Ed. by Kathleen Theresa Blake Butler. Reynolds, Barbara, Joint Ed. LC 47-6251. 1947. Univ. Press.
Tree: A Novel. F. Sionil Jose. 133p. 1979. pap. 6.00x o.p. (Pub. by Solidaridad Pub Hse Philippines). Cellar.
Tree and Its Fruits: Or, Narratives from Real Life. Phoebe Hinsdale Brown. LC 28-17912. 1836. E. Collier.
Tree and Leaf: 1st Amer. Ed. John Ronald Reuel Tolkien. LC 65-105335. 1965. 4.00. Houghton.
Tree Between Two Walls. limited ed. Jose E. Pacheco. pap. 5.00 signed ed. o.p. (ISBN 0-87685-070-0). Black Sparrow.
Tree Burns Green & Other Stories. Dianne S. Peters. 1978. 6.00 (ISBN 0-682-49193-4). Exposition.
Tree Drops a Leaf. Ruby Mildred Ayres. LC 38-372534. 1938. Doubleday, Doran & Company, Inc.
Tree-Dwellers. Katharine E. Dopp. 1930. Repr. 11.00 o.s.i. Finch Pr.
Tree Falls South. Wellington Roe. LC 37-925830. G. P. Putnam's Sons.
Tree: Four, Raa. Ed. by David Meltzer. (Illus., Orig.). pap. 4.00. Tree Bks.
Tree Frog. Martin Woodhouse. (YA) 1966. 4.95 o.p. (ISBN 0-698-10377-7). Coward.
Tree Frog. 1st Amer. Ed. Martin Woodhouse. LC 66-16581. 1966. bds., 4.95. Coward.
Tree Full of Stars. Davis Grubb. LC 65-23984. bds., 3.50. Scribners.
Tree Grown Straight. Percy Marks. LC 36-5633. 1936. Frederick A. Stokes Company.
Tree Grows in Brooklyn. Betty Smith. LC 43-121494. 1943. Harper & Brothers.
Tree Grows in Brooklyn. Betty Smith. LC 82-882. 1982. 21.95 (ISBN 0-8161-3301-8). G.K. Hall.
Tree Grows in Brooklyn: A Novel. Betty Smith. LC 47-11189. 1947. Harper.
Tree Has Roots. Mary Jane Ward. LC 37-5559. E. P. Dutton & Co., Inc.
Tree House Confessions. James McConkey. LC 78-13160. 9.95. Dutton.
Tree House Mystery. Bob Wright. (Tom & Ricky Mystery Ser.: No. 2). (Illus.). 48p. 1983. pap. 2.00 (ISBN 0-87879-338-0). Acad Therapy.
Tree in the Garden. Harvey S. Rusk. Ed. by Clifford A. Bennett & Literary Services Agency. 130p. (Orig.). 1982. pap. 5.00x (ISBN 0-917188-19-5). Nationwide Pr.
Tree May Fall. Jonah Jones. LC 80-513887. 1980. 10.95 (ISBN 0-370-30320-2). Bodley Head.
Tree of Arrows. Louis A Brennan. LC 64-20740. 1964. Macmillan.
Tree of Dark Reflection. Rocco Fumento. 1962. 5.95 o.p. Knopf.
Tree of Dreams, and Other Stories. Mika Toimi Waltari. LC 65-13299. 1965. Putnam.
Tree of Dreams: And Other Stories Tr. from Finnish. Mika Toimi Waltari. LC 65-13299. bds., 4.95. Putnam.
Tree of Evil. June Whetherell. (Orig.). 1970. pap. 0.75 o.p. (ISBN 0-447-74671-5). Lancer.
Tree of Heaven. Robert William Chambers. LC 7-173863. 1907. D. Appleton and Company.
Tree of Heaven. May Sinclair. LC 18-1225. 1917. Cassell and Company, Ltd.
Tree of Heaven. May Sinclair. LC 18-520. 1917. The Macmillan Company.
Tree of Heaven. May Sinclair. LC 18-30240. 1918. The Macmillan Company.
Tree of Horror. Elvira Steaves. 1975. pap. 2.95 o.p. (ISBN 0-8059-2235-0). Dorrance.
Tree of Horror. Elvira Steaves. 1975. pap. 2.95 o.p. (ISBN 0-8059-2235-0). Dorrance.
Tree of Knowledge. Baroja y Nessi, Pio. LC 74-4486. 1974. 12.50. H. Fertig.
Tree of Knowledge. Baroja y Nessi, Pio. Tr. by Bell, Aubrey Fitz Gerald. LC 28-18501. 1928. A. A. Knopf.
Tree of Knowledge see Author of Beltraffio.
Tree of Knowledge: A Document by a Woman. Pio Baroja Y Nessi. LC 8-14958. 1908. The Stuyvesant Press.
Tree of Liberty. Elizabeth Page. LC 39-27095. Farrar & Rinehart, Inc.
Tree of Liberty. Elizabeth Page. LC 39-17502. Farrar & Rinehart, Inc.
Tree of Life. Netta Syrett. LC 8-255841. 1897. J. Lane.
Tree of Light. James Augustin Brown Scherer. LC 21-17080. Thomas Y. Crowell Company.
Tree of Man. Patrick White. 1955. 13.95 (ISBN 0-670-72875-6). Viking Pr.
Tree of Night: And Other Stories. Truman Capote. LC 49-7722. 1949. Random House.
Tree of Solace: Illustrated by the Author. Ray W Iserman. LC 51-14116. 1951. Vantage Press.
Tree of the Folkungs. Verner Von Heidenstam & Chater, Arthur G., Tr. 1925. A. A. Knopf.
Tree of the Garden. Edward Charles Booth. LC 23-3441. 1923. D. Appleton and Company.
Tree of the Sun. Wilson Harris. LC 78-314415. 1978. 10.95 (ISBN 0-571-11181-5). Faber and Faber.
Tree on Fire. Alan Sillitoe. LC 68-22699. 1968. Doubleday.
Tree Outside the Window. Ellen C. Rose. LC 76-44671. 1976. 16.00 o.p. (ISBN 0-8357-0189-1, IS-00018, Pub. by U Press of New England). Univ Microfilms.
Tree-Pilot. Bertha Seavey Saunier. LC 7-33210. Jennings and Graham.
Tree: Six, Messiah. Ed. by David Meltzer. (Illus., Orig.). pap. 4.00. Tree Bks.
Tree: Tales in Psycho-Mythology. Marvin Spiegelman. LC 74-81034. 9.95. (ISBN 0-89031-008-4) (ISBN 0-89031-021-1). Phoenix House.
Tree Within. Ira Victor Morris. LC 48-8539. 1948. Doubleday.
Treehaven. Kathleen Thompson Norris. LC 46-457194. 1946. Triangle Books, the Blakiston Company.
Treehaven. Kathleen Thompson Norris. LC 32-25595. 1932. Doubleday, Doran & Company, Inc.
Treehouse. James Morrison. 1973. (pbk) 1.25. Dell.
Treehouse. James Morrison. LC 75-37449. 1972. 5.95. Dial Press.
Treeless Eden. Francine Findley. LC 34-569139. 1934. A. H. King.
Trees. Conrad Richter. (Bantam pathfinder editions). 1975. (pbk.) 1.25. Bantam Books.
Trees. Conrad Richter. LC 40-27179. 1940. A. A. Knopf.
Trees for the Forest: A Collection of Myths. Patricia Cast. LC 78-102914. (Illus.). 5.95 (ISBN 0-88347-096-9). T. More Press.
Trees of Heaven. Jesse Stuart. 1940. E. P. Dutton & Co., Inc.
Trees of Heaven. Jesse Stuart. LC 80-51020. (Illus.). 17.50 (ISBN 0-8131-1446-2) (ISBN 0-8131-0150-6). University Press of Kentucky.
Trees of Zharka. Nancy Mackenroth. 1975. (pbk.) 0.95. Popular Library.
Trees Went Forth. Walter O'Meara. LC 47-1335. 1947. Crown Publishers.
Tregaron's Daughter. Madeleine Brent. LC 78-150878. 1971. 5.95. Doubleday.
Trek or Treat. 1977. pap. 2.95 (ISBN 0-345-25679-4). Ballantine.
Trek to Florida: A Novel. Broome Stringfellow. LC 73-173047. (Illus.). 1972. 1.95 (ISBN 0-8200-1024-3). Great Outdoors Pub. Co.
Trek to the King's Mountain. Elery A. Lay. LC 76-46777. 7.95 (ISBN 0-87716-077-5). Moore Pub. Co.
Trelawny. Holman Freeland. LC 3-24815. 1903. E. J. Clode.
Trelawny. large print ed. Isabelle Holland. LC 81-18425. 1982. 11.95 (ISBN 0-89621-337-4). Thorndike Press.
Trelawny: A Novel. Isabelle Holland. LC 74-81692. 1974. 7.95 (ISBN 0-679-40122-9). Weybright and Talley.
Trellised Lane. Fiona Hill. 1977. pap. 1.50 (ISBN 0-425-03776-2, Medallion). Berkley Pub.
Trellised Lane. Fiona Hill. (Berkley Large Type Gothic). (Berkley medallion book). 1975. (pbk.) 0.95 (ISBN 0-425-02794-5). Berkley Pub. Co.
Treloars. Mary Fisher. Thomas Y. Crowell Company.
Tremaine of Texas. W. D Hoffman. LC 31-30511. 1931. A. C. McClurg & Co.
Tremayne Case. Alan Ernest Wentworth Thomas. LC 30-9312. 1930. J. B. Lippincott Company.
Tremaynes and the Masterful Monk: A Most Hateful and Lovable Tale. Owen Francis Dudley. LC 40-32860. (His Problems of human happiness. vi). 1940. Longmans, Green and Co.
Tremayne's Wife. Charlotte Hunt. (Ace Gothic). 1974. (pbk.) 0.95. Ace Books.
Tremble of a Hand. Richard Pierce. 1977. pap. 1.50 (ISBN 0-532-15250-6). Woodhill.
Tremble of a Hand. Richard Pierce. (Orig.). 1969. pap. 0.75 o.p. (74-993). Lancer.
Trembling Earth. Dale Van Every. 1975. (pbk.) 1.25. Popular Library.
Trembling Earth. Dale Van Every. LC 53-10515. 1953. J. Messner.
Trembling Earth Contract. Philip Atlee. (Contract Ser). (Orig.). 1969. pap. 0.60 o.p. (R2181, GM). Fawcett World.
Trembling Flame. Louis Joseph Vance. LC 31-15932. 1931. J. B. Lippincott Company.
Trembling Hills. Phyllis A Whitney. LC 56-10609. 1956. Appleton-Century-Crofts.
Trembling Land. 1st Ed. Robert Christie. LC 59-106622. 1959. Doubleday.
Trembling of a Leaf. John Colleton. 1981. pap. 2.50 (ISBN 0-671-41612-X). PB.
Trembling of a Leaf. William Somerset Maugham. LC 75-26136. (Maugham, William Somerset, 1874-1965. Works. 1976). 1977. 15.00 (ISBN 0-405-07857-9). Arno Press.
Trembling of a Leaf. William Somerset Maugham. LC 39-24307. 1939. Doubleday, Doran & Company, Inc.
Trembling of a Leaf... William Somerset Maugham. LC 47-20646. (On cover: Avon modern short story monthly, no. 35).
Trembling of a Leaf: Little Stories of the South Sea Islands. William Somerset Maugham. LC 21-16317. George H. Doran Company.
Trembling of the Sea. Barbara Lucas, pseud. LC 36-72571. 1936. Harper & Brothers.
Trembling Years. Elsie Marion Oakes Barber. LC 49-8317. 1949. Macmillan Co.
Tremendous Adventures. Dion Clayton Calthrop. LC 22-13775. 1922. Hodder and Stoughton, Ltd.

TITLE INDEX TRIANGLE.

Tremendous Adventures. Dion Clayton Calthrop. LC 22-14576. Frederick A. Stokes Company.
Tremendous Adventures of Bernie Wine. Ron Goulart. 1975. (pbk.) 1.50 (ISBN 0-446-78416-8). Warner Paperback Library.
Tremendous Event. Maurice Leblanc. Tr. by Teixeira De Mattos, Alexander Louis. LC 22-19605. The Macaulay Company.
Tremendous Trifles. Gilbert Keith Chesterton. 1927. 25.00 (ISBN 0-8414-9128-3). Folcroft.
Tremendous Trifles. Gilbert Keith Chesterton. 1968. 8.95 o.p. (ISBN 0-8023-1147-4). Dufour.
Tremolo. Ernest Boreman. LC 48-6896. 1948. Harper.
Tremor of Forgery. Patricia Highsmith. LC 69-12241. 1969. 4.95. Doubleday.
Tremor of Intent. Anthony Burgess. 1977. 4.95 (ISBN 0-393-08539-2, Norton Lib); pap. 4.95 1977 (ISBN 0-393-00416-3). Norton.
Tremor of Intent: By Anthony Burgess. John Anthony Burgess Wilson. LC 66-186262. 1966. bds., 4.95. Norton.
Tremor of Intent: By Anthony Burgess. John Anthony Burgess Wilson. (U6111). 1967. Ballantine.
Tremor of Intent. By Anthony Burgess. John Anthony Burgess Wilson. (N416). 1967. pap., 1.65. Norton.
Tremor Violet. David Lippincott. LC 75-955. 1975. 7.95 (ISBN 0-399-11519-6). Putnam.
Tremor Violet. David Lippincott. (Signet Book). 1976. (pbk.) 1.75. New American Library.
Tremorra Towers. Helen York. LC 75-36616. 1976. 5.95 (ISBN 0-385-11417-6). Published for the Crime Club by Doubleday.
Trempealeau Mountain. George Henry Willett. LC 14-14362. The Abingdon Press.
Trenck: The Love Story of a Favourite. Bruno Frank. Tr. by Paul, Eden. LC 28-217371. 1928. A. A. Knopf.
Trend. William Arkwright. LC 14-10075. 1914. John Lane.
Trenhawk. Mary Williams. LC 81-21450. 322p. 1982. 13.95 (ISBN 0-312-81766-5). St Martin.
Trent Intervenes. Edmund Clerihew Bentley. LC 38-23212. 1938. T. Nelson and Sons, Ltd.
Trent Intervenes. Edmund Clerihew Bentley. LC 38-279553. 1938. A. A. Knopf.
Trent Intervenes. Edmund Clerihew Bentley. LC 80-69482. 1981. 4.00 (ISBN 0-486-24098-3). Dover Publications.
Trent Trail. Wyndham Martyn. LC 30-29248. 1930. R. M. McBride & Company.
Trente-Trois Contes et Nouvelles. Michael Pargment. (Rinehart Editions). 1929. 6.10 o.p. (ISBN 0-03-016055-3, HoltC). HR&W.
Trent's Case Book. Edmund Clerihew Bentley. (YA) 1953. 6.95 o.p. Knopf.
Trent's Case Book: Comprising Trent's Last Case, Trent's Own Case, with H. Warner Allen and Trent Intervenes. With an Introd. by Ben Ray Redman. Edmund Clerihew Bentley. LC 52-12213. 1953. Knopf.
Trent's Last Case. Edmund Clerihew Bentley. LC 75-44955. (Fifty Classics of Crime Fiction, 1900-1950; 4). (Illus.). 12.00 (ISBN 0-8240-2353-6). Garland Pub.
Trent's Last Case. Edmund Clerihew Bentley. LC 30-973595. 1930. A. A. Knopf.
Trent's Last Case. Edmund Clerihew Bentley. LC 42-470998. 1929. A. A. Knopf.
Trent's Last Case... Edmund Clerihew Bentley. LC 45-13593. 1944.
Trent's Last Case. Edmund Clerihew Bentley. LC 76-50690. (Mystery Library; 5). (Illus.). 6.95 (ISBN 0-89163-030-9). University Extension, University of California, San Diego.
Trent's Own Case. Edmund Clerihew Bentley & Allen, Herbert Warner. LC 36-19980. 1936. A. A. Knopf.
Trent's Trust: And Other Stories. Bret Harte. LC 8-11675. 1903. Houghton, Mifflin and Company.
Trepleff. MacDonald Harris. 1969. 5.95 o.p. (ISBN 0-03-081850-8). HR&W.
Trepleff. Donald W. Heiney. LC 74-80342. 1969. 5.95. Holt, Rinehart and Winston.
Tres a la Vez. new ed. Rogelio Rios. (Pimienta Collection Ser). (Illus.). 160p. (Spanish.). 1975. pap. 1.25 (ISBN 0-88473-231-2). Fiesta Pub.
Tres Cuentistas Hispanoamericanos. Donald A. Yates et al. 1969. pap. text ed. 8.95x (ISBN 0-02-430840-4). Macmillan.
Tres Novelas. Ivan Sergeevich Turgenev. 269p. (Span.). 1980. 5.95 (ISBN 0-8285-1344-9, Pub. by Progress Pubs USSR). Imported Pubns.
Tres Novelas Valencianas. Vicente Blasco Ibanez. Bd. with Arroz y Tartana; Barraca; Canas y Barro. lea. bdg. 9.95 o.s.i.; 7.50 o.s.i. French & Eur.
Tres Relatos. Chinguiz Aitmatov. 280p. (Span.). 1978. 4.95 (ISBN 0-8285-1327-9, Pub. by Progress Pubs USSR). Imported Pubns.
Tresillian Court. A Novel. Harriet Lewis. (On cover: The choice series, no. 86). 1893. R. Bonner's Sons.
Trespass. Alice Dudeney. LC 9-28117. 1909. 1.25. Small, Maynard & Company.
Trespass. Fletcher Knebel. LC 71-78731. 1969. 6.95. Doubleday.
Trespass. 1st Ed. Eugene Brown. LC 52-10397. 1952. Doubleday.
Trespasser. David Herbert Lawrence. LC 70-145134. 1971. (ISBN 0-403-01067-5). Scholarly Press.
Trespasser. David Herbert Lawrence & Elizabeth Mansfield. LC 80-41663. (Laurence, David Herbert, 1885-1930. Ambridge Edition of the Letters and Works of D.H. Laurence: 1981). (Works.). 1981. 42.50 (ISBN 0-521-22264-8) (ISBN 0-521-29424-X). Cambridge University Press.
Trespasser. Gilbert Parker. LC 3-21951. 1893. D. Appleton and Company.
Trespasser. Gilbert Parker. 1897. D. Appleton and Company.
Trespasser. Melvin Weiser. 288p. 1981. pap. 2.95 (ISBN 0-380-77735-5, 77735). Avon.
Trespasser: Novelized. Harry Sinclair Drago & Goulding, Edmund. LC 29-20656. A. L. Burt Company.
Trespassers. Andrew Coburn. LC 74-10942. 1974. 6.95 (ISBN 0-395-19429-6). Houghton Mifflin.
Trespassers. Giles A. Lutz. 1980. pap. 1.75 (ISBN 0-345-29118-2). Ballantine.
Trespassers. Charles E Mercer. LC 64-18011. 1964. Putnam.
Trespassers: A Novel. Laura Keane Zametkin Hobson. LC 43-51230. 1943. Simon and Schuster.
Trespasses. Paul Bailey. LC 77-123979. 1971. 5.95 o.p. (ISBN 0-06-010183-0, HarpT). Harper & Row.
Tressider's Sister: A Novel. Isabel Constance Clarke. 1921. Benziger Brothers.
Tressilian and His Friends. Robert Shelton Mackenzie. LC 7-16304. 1859. J. B. Lippincott & Co.
Tresury of Short Stories. Rudyard Kipling. LC 57-8075. (Bantam books, S1609 9). 1957. Bantam Books.
Trevayne: A Novel. Robert Ludlum. LC 72-5354. 1973. 7.95. Delacorte Press.
Trevayne: A Novel. Jonathan Ryder. 1973. (pbk.) 1.50. Dell.
Treveryan. Angela Du Maurier. LC 42-23594. 1942. Doubleday, Doran & Company, Inc.
Trevor Case. Natalie Sumner Lincoln. LC 20-4961. 1912. A. L. Burt Company.
Trevor Case. Natalie Sumner Lincoln. LC 12-6227. 1912. 1.30. D. Appleton and Company.
Trevor Lordship. Edith Noel Daniell Barclay. LC 11-493123. 1911. 1.20. The Macmillan Company.
Trevy: The River. Leslie Reid. LC 28-608668. 1928. E. P. Dutton & Co.
Trey of Swords. Andre Norton, pseud. 192p. 1982. pap. 2.25 (ISBN 0-441-82349-1). Ace Bks.
Trey O'hearts: A Motion Picture Melodrama. Louis Joseph Vance. LC 14-20854. Grosset & Dunlap.
Tri Knigi: Nechistaia Sila, Panteon Sovetov Molodym Liudiam, Deti. Arkadii Averchenko. LC 79-65800. (Rus.). pap. 6.95 o.p. (ISBN 0-89830-009-6). Russica Pubs.
Triad. Mary Leader. LC 72-87585. 1973. 6.95 (ISBN 0-698-10496-X). Coward, McCann & Geoghegan.
Triad. Mary Leader. 1974. (pbk.) 1.50. Bantam Books.
Triad. Richard H Rohmer. LC 81-38466. (Illus.). 14.95 (ISBN 0-8253-0083-5). Beaufort Books.
Triad Imperative. Dwight Martin. LC 82-80217. 288p. 1982. pap. 2.95 (ISBN 0-86721-151-2). Playboy Pbks.
Triad Imperative: A Novel. Dwight Martin. LC 80-67860. 1980. 10.95 (ISBN 0-312-92829-7). Congdon & Lattes.
Triage. Leonard C Lewin. 1973. (pbk) 1.25. Warner.
Triage. Leonard C Lewin. LC 79-38901. 1972. 5.95. Dial Press.
Trial. Linda DuBreuil. 1975. pap. 1.50 o.p. (LB245DK, Leisure Bks). Nordon Pubns.
Trial. Linda DuBreuil. 1975. (pbk.) 1.50. Leisure Books.
Trial. William Harrington. LC 70-101200. 1970. 6.95. McKay.
Trial. Franz Kafka. LC 72-8032. 1973. (ISBN 0-394-70484-3). Vintage Books.
Trial. definitive ed. Franz Kafka. LC 68-59195. (Illus.). 1968. 1.95. Schocken Books.
Trial. Franz Kafka. Tr. by Muir, Willa. LC 37-250721. 1937. A. A. Knopf.
Trial & Error. Anthony Berkeley, pseud. 1981. pap. 2.25 (ISBN 0-440-18766-4). Dell.
Trial and Error. Anthony Berkeley Cox. LC 38-774. 1937. Doubleday, Doran & Co., Inc.
Trial and Error. Anthony Berkeley Cox. LC 39-30696. 1939. The Sun Dial Press, Inc.
Trial & Terror. Phil Conrad. 1978. 7.95 o.p. (ISBN 0-533-03620-8). Vantage.
Trial and Terror. Joan Kahn. LC 73-9954. 1973. 8.95 (ISBN 0-395-17208-X). Houghton Mifflin.
Trial and Terror. Lawrence Treat. LC 49-9910. (A Morrow mystery). 1949. W. Morrow.
Trial & the Fire. Leroy L. Ramsey. 1967. 4.00 o.p. (ISBN 0-682-45701-9). Exposition.
Trial & Triumph: A Novel About Maimonides, by Lester M. Morrison, Richard G. Hubler. Lester M Morrison & Richard Gibson Hubler. LC 65-15842. 5.95. Crown.
Trial at Apache Junction. Lewis B Patten. LC 80-27836. 1981. 11.50 (ISBN 0-89340-309-1). J. Curley & Associates.
Trial at Apache Junction. Lewis B Patten. (Signet Book). 1977. 1.25 (ISBN 0-451-07404-1). New American Library.
Trial at Bannock. Jesse Bier. LC 62-16728. 1963. Harcourt, Brace & World.
Trial at Topah. John M. Murray. Ed. by Alice Sachs. 1971. 3.95 o.p. Lenox Hill.
Trial Balance: And Other Stories About Schools. Charles William Bardeen. LC 14-2134. C. W. Bardeen.
Trial Balance: The Collected Short Stories of William March. William Edward March Campbell. LC 77-110818. 1970. (ISBN 0-8371-3221-5). Greenwood Press.
Trial Balance: The Collected Short Stories of William March Pseud. William Edward March Campbell. LC 45-9325. 1945. Harcourt, Brace and Company.
Trial Begins. Andrei Donatevich Siniavskii. LC 60-11760. 1960. Pantheon Books.
Trial Begins. Abram Tertz, pseud. Tr. by Max Hayward & George Dennis. Bd. with On Socialist Realism. pap. 1.95 (ISBN 0-394-70750-8, V-750, Vin). Random.
Trial Begins, & On Socialist Realism. Andrei Donatevich Siniavskii. LC 65-21265. (Vintage Russian library, V-750). 1965. Vintage Books.
Trial Begins: & On Socialist Realism. Andrei Donatevich Siniavskii & Terts, Abram. LC 65-21265. (Vintage Russian library, V-750). 1965. Vintage Books.
Trial Begins, & On Socialist Realism. Abram Pseud Terts & Abram Pseud. On Socialist Realism Terts. LC 65-212650. (Vintage Russian lib., V-750). 1965. pap., 1.65. Random.
Trial Begins. Translated by Max Hayward. 1st American Ed. Abram Tertz, pseud. LC 60-11760. 1960. Pantheon Books.
Trial by Ambush: By Leslie Ford Pseud. Zenith Jones Brown. LC 62-9950. 1962. Scribner.
Trial by Battle. David Piper. LC 65-26088. (Illus.). 1965. Chilmark Press.
Trial by Darkness: A Novel. Charles O Gorham. LC 52-10096. 1952. Dial Press.
Trial by Fire. Fay Morgan. (Second Chance at Love Ser.: No. 104). Date not set. pap. 1.75 (ISBN 0-515-06868-3). Jove Pubns.
Trial by Fire: A Novel. Charles Elliott. LC 57-5582. 1957. Putnam.
Trial by Fire: A Tale of the Great Lakes. Richard Matthews Hallet. LC 16-14052. 1.25. Small, Maynard and Company.
Trial by Fury. Craig Rice. LC 41-218891. 1941. Simon and Schuster.
Trial by Gunsmoke. Vernon L. Fluharty. LC 49-9678. (Dutton Diamond D western). 1949. E.P. Dutton.
Trial by Love. William Arthur Neubauer. LC 68-2872. 1968. Arcadia House.
Trial by Murder. Grace Hoster. LC 44-3318. 1944. Farrar & Rinehart, Inc.
Trial by Ordeal: By Osmington Mills. Brooks, Vivian Collin. LC 62-10703. Roy Publishers.
Trial by Slander. Travis Macrae, pseud. LC 60-5337. 1960. Rinehart.
Trial by Terror. 1st Ed. Paul Gallico. LC 52-5666. 1952. Knopf.
Trial by Water. Hulbert Footner. LC 31-155605. 1931. Farrar & Rinehart Incorporated.
Trial Driver. Zane Grey. 1982. 18.00x (ISBN 0-86025-186-1, Pub. by Ian Henry Pubns England). State Mutual Bk.
Trial Flight. Adelaide Humphries. LC 38-34799. 1938. Arcadia House.
Trial for Tennihan. Steven C Lawrence. 1976. (pbk.) 1.50. Ace Books.
Trial Honeymoon. Millicent Kent. LC 36-359986. 1936. Godwin.
Trial in the Upper Room: A Heavenly Novel. Paul Sann. LC 80-22106. 12.95 (ISBN 0-517-54284-6). Crown Publishers.
Trial Marriage. Frank Frankfort Moore. LC 8-19570. Empire Book Company.
Trial: More Links of The Daisy Chain. Charlotte Mary Yonge. LC 9-1206. 1864. D. Appleton & Co.
Trial: More Links of The Daisy Chain. Charlotte Mary Yonge. LC 4-16599. 1902. Macmillan and Co., Limited.
Trial of Adolf Hitler. Philippe Van Rjndt. LC 78-10641. 1978. 9.95 o.p. (ISBN 0-671-40028-2). Summit Bks.
Trial of Adolf Hitler: A Novel. Philippe Van Rjndt. LC 78-10641. 9.95 (ISBN 0-671-40028-2). Summit Books.
Trial of Alvin Boaker. John Reywall. LC 48-1038. Random House.
Trial of Billy Peale. Wayne D Overholser. LC 62-18382. 1962. Macmillan.
Trial of Callista Blake. Edgar Pangborn. LC 61-13391. 1962. St. Martin's Press.
Trial of Christopher Okigbo. Ali AlAmin Mazrui. LC 78-180662. 1972. 5.95 (ISBN 0-89388-024-8) (ISBN 0-89388-025-6). Third Press.
Trial of Cristopher Okigbo. Ali Al Amin Mazrui. LC 78-180662. 160p. 1972. 6.95 (ISBN 0-89388-024-8). Okpaku Communications.
Trial of Father Dillingham. John Broderick. 224p. 1981. 14.95 (ISBN 0-7145-2747-5, Pub. by M Boyars). Merrimack Pub Cir.
Trial of Gideon, and Countess Almara's Murder. Julian Hawthorne. LC 7-3880. 1886. Funk & Wagnalls.
Trial of Gregor Kaska. Fred Andreas & Ray, Winifred, Tr. LC 32-5866. H. Holt and Company.
Trial of Helen McLeod. Alice Beal Parsons. 1938. Funk & Wagnalls Company.
Trial of Honor: A Novel. William Pearson. LC 67-27436. 1967. New American Library.
Trial of Judas Wiley. Lewis B Patten. LC 79-171310. (DD western). 1972. 4.95. Doubleday.
Trial of Lee Harvey Oswald: Based Upon the Teleplay. Robert E Thompson. LC 78-104447. (Illus.). 1977. 1.95. Ace Books.
Trial of Martin Ross. Alfred Kern. LC 72-140755. 1971. 6.95 (ISBN 0-393-08637-2). Norton.
Trial of Mary Dugan, from the Play by Bayard Veiller, by William Almon Wolff. William Almon Wolff & Veiller, Byard. LC 28-905591. 1928. Doubleday, Doran & Company, Inc.
Trial of Scotland Yard. Stuart Martin. LC 30-211698. 1930. Harper & Brothers.
Trial of Soren Qvist. Janet Lewis, pseud. LC 47-2419. 1947. Doubleday & Company, Inc.
Trial of the Lonesome Pine. John Fox. 1908. C. Scribner's Sons.
Trial of the Spanish Horse. James Willard Schultz. LC 22-17722. 1922. Houghton Mifflin Company.
Trial of Vincent Doon. William Charles Oursler. LC 41-8175. 1941. Simon and Schuster.
Trial of Vivienne Ware: A Radiodrama. Kenneth M Ellis. LC 31-3685. Grosset & Dunlap.
Trial Run. Dick Francis. LC 78-20204. 10.00 (ISBN 0-06-011383-9). Harper & Row.
Trial Through Tascosa. Peter Field. (Kangaroo Book.). 1977. 1.25. (ISBN 0-671-80905-9). Pocket Books.
Trial to Abilene. Charles Horace Snow. LC 37-182589. 1937. Macrae Smith Company.
Trial. Translated from the German by Willia and Edwin Muir; Rev., and with Additional Materials Translated by E. M. Butler. Definitive Ed. Franz Kafka. LC 57-12574. (Modern library of the world's best books 318). 1961. Modern Library.
Trial. Translated from the German by Willa and Edwin Muir; Rev., and with Additional Materials Translated by E. M. Butler. Illustrated by George Salter. Definitive Ed. Franz Kafka. LC 57-12574. 1957. Knopf.
Trial. 1st Ed. Don M Mankiewicz. LC 54-12190. Harper.
Trials; a Tale. Mary Ann Kelty. LC 7-10980. 1824. A. Small.
Trials and Trails. Herman August Schroeder. LC 33-354792. 1933. Concordia Publishing House.
Trials and Tribulations of Aaron Amsted. Kenneth A Lapatine. LC 73-93681. 1974. 6.95 (ISBN 0-8027-0446-8). Walker.
Trials of a Respectable Family see Two Novels of the Mexican Revolution.
Trials of an Actress: Or, General Utility. Florence Blackburn White Schoeffel. LC 3946. (On cover: Eagles library. no. 169). 1900. Street & Smith.
Trials of Commander McTurk. Charles John Cutcliffe Wright Hyne. LC 6-35943. 1906. E. P. Dutton & Company.
Trials of Life. Elizabeth Caroline Grey. LC 6-45411. 1829. W. B. Gilley.
Trials of Ralph Haddelsey. John Cuckson. LC 1-30719. 1901. Cambridge, Printed, J. Wilson & Son.
Trials of Rumpole. John Clifford Mortimer. LC 80-460133. 1979. 2.95 (ISBN 0-14-005162-7). Penguin Books.
Trials of the Human Heart, 4 vols. in two. Susanna Haswell Rowson. LC 78-64091. Repr. of 1795 ed. 75.00 set (ISBN 0-404-17360-8). AMS Pr.
Trials of Windhaven. Marie De Jourlet. (Orig.). 1980. pap. 3.50 (ISBN 0-523-42013-7). Pinnacle Bks.
Triangle. Arlene DeMarco. (Signet novel, Y5058). 1973. (pbk.) 1.25. New American Library.
Triangle. Arlene DeMarco. LC 70-169064. 1971. 5.95. New American Library.
Triangle. Heiman Jacob Elkin. LC 11-9970. Steeg Printing and Publishing Company.
Triangle. L. F. Fieser. 1962. 1.95 o.p. Van Nos Reinhold.
Triangle. Sondra Marshak & Myrna Culbreath. (Orig.). 1983. pap. 2.50 (ISBN 0-671-83399-5, Timescape). PB.
Triangle. Teri White. 352p. (Orig.). 1982. pap. 3.25 (ISBN 0-441-82419-6, Pub. by Charter Bks). Ace Bks.

Triangle Cupid. Charles Alden Seltzer. 1912. Outing Publishing Company.
Triangle Man. George Fort Gibbs. LC 39-17098. 1939. D. Appleton-Century Company Incorporated.
Triangle of Death. Jon Hart. LC 80-71034. (Mercenaries Ser.). 128p. 1981. pap. 2.95 (ISBN 0-87754-228-7). Chelsea Hse.
Triangle of Hate. Glenn A. Williams. 3.50 o.p. Carlton.
Triangles. Nicholas Drake. LC 22-23918. Southern Progress Publishing Co.
Triangle's End: A Novelette. 1st Ed. William H Jones. LC 54-5750. 1954. Exposition Press.
Tribal Scars. Sembene Ousmane. (African Writers Ser.). 1974. pap. text ed. 1.95x o.p. (ISBN 0-435-90142-7). Heinemann Ed.
Tribal Scars, and Other Stories. Sembene Ousmane. LC 73-21642. 1974. (ISBN 0-87953-015-4). INSCAPE.
Tribe. Bari Wood. LC 80-26247. 13.95 (ISBN 0-453-00393-1). New American Library.
Tribe of Woman. Translated from the French by Richard Howard. Herve Bazin. LC 58-7509. 1958. Simon and Schuster.
Tribe of Women. Herve-Bazin, Jean Pierre Marie. LC 58-7509. 1958. Simon and Schuster.
Tribe That Lost Its Head. Nicholas Monsarrat. LC 56-90183. 1956. W. Sloane Associates.
Tribesmen of Gor. John Norman. (Science Fiction Ser.). 1976. pap. 2.25 (ISBN 0-87997-473-7, UE1473). DAW Bks.
Trible Candle. Louise Louis. 74p. 1977. pap. 4.95 (ISBN 0-941242-08-0). Pen-Art.
Tribulaciones De una Familia Decente. Mariano Azuela. Ed. by F. K. Hendricks & B. Berler. 1966. pap. text ed. 2.95x o.p. (ISBN 0-02-305060-8). Macmillan.
Tribulations of a Boy. Conrad Ferdinand Meyer. Tr. by E. M. Huggard from Ger. (Harrap's Bilingual Ser.). 83p. 1955. 5.00 (ISBN 0-911268-43-X). Rogers Bk.
Tribulations of a Chinaman in China. From the French of Jules Verne. Jules Verne & Lord, Grace Virginia, D. 1865, Tr. LC 1-9859. 1880. Lee and Shepard.
Tribulations of a Chinese Gentleman. Jules Verne. 3.95. Assoc Bk.
Tribulations of a Princess... Marguerite De Godart Cunliffe-Owen. LC 1-15288. 1901. Harper & Brothers.
Tribulations of Veneguay. Jim Stickter. LC 78-53364. (Illus.). 1978. 7.50 (ISBN 0-930770-08-0). Hemisphere House Books.
Tribune Prize War Stories. The Story of Our Mess by E. W. Gurley and Other Stories of the War. New York Tribune. (On cover: Lovell's library, no. 966). J. W. Lovell Company.
Tribune War Stories. A Series of Twenty-Five in Competition for Prizes. New York Tribune. LC 5-21863. (Tribune monthly. vol. III. April, 1891, no. 4). 1891. The Tribune Association.
Trick. Robert J. Stout. 1979. 3.00. Juniper Pr WI.
Trick Baby: The Biography of a Con Man. Robert Beck. LC 67-31580. 1967. Holloway House Pub. Co. Distributed by All American Distributors Corp.
Trick Baby: The Biography of a Con Man. Slim Iceberg. LC 67-31580. 1967. Holloway House.
Trick or Treat. Doris Miles Disney. LC 54-7667. 1955. Published for the Crime Club by Doubleday.
Tricks and Treats. Joseph N Gores & Bill Pronzini. LC 75-40727. 1976. 5.95 (ISBN 0-385-11416-8). Published for the Crime Club by Doubleday.
Tricks of the Trade. Robert L. Fish. (Red Mask Mystery Ser.). 205p. (YA) 1972. 4.95 o.p. (ISBN 0-399-10818-1). Putnam.
Tricks of the Trade: A Kek Huuygens Novel. Robert L Fish. LC 70-179026. (Red mask mystery). 1972. 4.95. Putnam.
Trickshot. Randolph Harris. (Orig.). 1974. pap. 1.50 (ISBN 0-87067-448-X, BH448). Holloway.
Tricky Dick & His Pals. Joseph Wortis. LC 73-92230. (Illus.). 24p. 1974. pap. 3.95 o.p. (ISBN 0-8129-0445-1). Times Bks.
Tricky Ground. Indira Parthasarthy. (Indian Novels Ser.). 191p. 1975. 9.50 (ISBN 0-89253-014-6). Ind-US Inc.
Tricolour. Mark Logan. LC 75-40796. 1976. 8.95 o.p. (ISBN 0-312-81830-0). St Martin.
Tricolour: A Novel of the French Revolution. Christopher Nicole. LC 75-40796. 8.95. St. Martin's Press.
Tricotrin: The Story of a Waif and Stray. Louise De La Ramee. LC 6-33302. 1869. J. B. Lippincott & Co.
Trident. Joel Hammil. 1982. pap. 2.95 (ISBN 0-8217-1017-6). Zebra.
Trident and the Net: A Novel. Marguerite De Godart Cunliffe-Owen. LC 5-29530. 1905. Harper & Brothers.
Trident Brand. G. Clifton Wisler, pseud. LC 81-43153. 1982. 10.95 (ISBN 0-385-17430-6). Doubleday.
Trident Hijacking. Dan Streib. (Counterforce Ser.: No. 2). 208p. (Orig.). 1983. pap. 2.50 (ISBN 0-449-12388-X, GM). Fawcett.
Tried and the Tempted. Timothy Shay Arthur. LC 6-3426. 1851. Lippincott, Grambo & Co.
Tried and the Tempted. Timothy Shay Arthur. LC 6-3427. (On cover: Lovell's library, v. 11, no. 585). J. W. Lovell Company.
Tried and True: Or Love and Loyalty; a Story of the Great Rebellion. Bella Zilfa Spencer. LC 8-16313. 1866. W. J. Holland.
Tried and True: Or Love and Loyalty; a Story of the Great Rebellion. Bella Zilfa Spencer. LC 8-16312. 1869. W. J. Holland.
Tried for Her Life. A Sequel to "Cruel As the Grave.". Emma Dorothy Eliza Nevitte Southworth. 1871. T. B. Peterson & Brothers.
Tried in the Fire. Isabel Anderson. LC 60-19394. 1960. Moody Press.
Trieste. Desmond Cory, pseud. (Johnny Fedora Ser., No. 5). (O.s.i.). 1968. pap. 0.60 o.s.i. (A394X, Award). Univ Pub & Dist.
Trifeton Papers. Warren Tilton & Crafts, William Augustus, 1819- Joint Author. LC 8-27024. 1856. Whittemore, Niles and Hall.
Trifler: A Love Comedy. Archibald Eyre. LC 3-26363. 1903. The Smart Set Publishing Co.
Triflers. Frederick Orin Bartlett. LC 17-10201. 1917. 1.40. Houghton Mifflin Company.
Triflers. Frederick Orin Bartlett. LC 22-4742. 1917. Grosset & Dunlap.
Trigger Finger Law. Nelson Coral Nye. LC 40-30524. Phoenix Press.
Trigger Gospel. Harry Sinclair Drago. LC 35-522. The Macaulay Company.
Trigger Gospel. Specially Rev. by the Author for This New Ed. Harry Sinclair Drago. LC 55-42187. (Ace double novel books, D-112). 1955. Ace Books.
Trigger Justice. Leslie Charles Ernenwein. 1977. pap. 1.25 o.s.i. (ISBN 0-8439-0447-X, Leisure Bks). Nordon Pubns.
Trigger Justice. Clement Yore. LC 28-17199. The Macaulay Company.
Trigger Lady. Phyllis Smith. 1980. pap. 1.75 o.s.i. (ISBN 0-8439-0714-2, Leisure Bks). Nordon Pubns.
Trigger Man. Richard Posner. (Fawcett gold medal book). 1974. (pbk.) 0.95. Fawcett.
Trigger Man from Nevada. Burt Arthur, pseud. (O.s.i.). 1976. pap. 0.95 o.s.i. (BT50924). Belmont-Tower.
Trigger Mortis. Frank Kane. LC 58-625679. 1958. Rinehart.
Trigger of Conscience. Isabel Egenton Ostrander. LC 21-15332. 1921. R. M. McBride & Company.
Trigger Pardners. Buck Billings. LC 36-1543. G. H. Watt, Inc.
Trigger Pardners. Claude Riter. LC 36-1543. G. H. Watt, Inc.
Trigger Points. Martin Mayer. LC 78-20212. 9.95 (ISBN 0-06-013019-9). Harper & Row.
Trigger Slammer. T. W. Ford. LC 46-590. 1946. Phoenix Press.
Trigger Slim. Clement Yore. LC 34-81393. TheMacaulay Company.
Trigger Talk. Nelson Coral Nye. LC 42-199410. 1942. Phoenix Press.
Trigger Trail. George C Henderson. LC 38-537044. Phoenix Press.
Trigger Trail. William Colt Macdonald. LC 36-33710. Covici-Friede.
Trigger Trail: A Western Novel. Willis Todhunter Ballard. LC 55-42720. (Popular library, 680). 1955. Popular Library.
Trigger Trail: A Western Novel. Fred East. LC 45-2792. 1945. Macrae-Smith-Co.
Trigger Trail: A Western Novel. Roy Manning. LC 45-2792. 1945. Macrae-Smith Company.
Trigger Trouble: By Chuck Stanley Pseud. Charles Stanley Strong. LC 57-114632. 1957. Arcadia House.
Trigger Tyrant. Tom West. (Orig.). 1979. pap. 1.95 (ISBN 0-89083-533-0). Zebra.
Trigger Vengeance. A Double D Western. John Trace. LC 40-31459. 1940. Doubleday, Doran and Company, Inc.
Triggerfish: Tales of the Florida Keys: By Betty Brothers. Illustrated by Netannis Kline. Betty Miller Brothers. LC 65-18406. 1965. Wake-Brook House.
Triggerfish: Tales of the Florida Keys. Illus. by Netannis Kline. Betty Miller Brothers. LC 65-18406. 3.00. C.
Triggerman. Bruno Rossi, pseud. (Sharpshooter Ser: No. 11). 1975. pap. 0.95 o.p. (LB229NK, Leisure Bks). Nordon Pubns.
Triggernometry. Eugene Cunningham. LC 41-1849. (Illus.). 1941. 12.95 (ISBN 0-87004-032-4). Caxton.
Triggers for Six. Clem Colt, pseud. LC 41-16486. Phoenix Press.
Triggers for Six. Nelson Coral Nye. LC 41-16486. Phoenix Press.
Trilby. George Louis Palmella Busson Du Maurier. 2.45 o.p. (520). W Collins.
Trilby, a Novel. Daphne Du Maurier. 1977. Repr. of 1895 ed. lib. bdg. 25.00 (ISBN 0-8414-1857-8). Folcroft.
Trilby: A Novel. George Louis Palmella Busson Du Maurier. LC 4-15308. 1894. Harper & Brothers.
Trilby: A Novel. George Louis Palmella Busson Du Maurier. LC 9-3010. 1895. Harper & Brothers.
Trilby: A Novel. (special limited ed.) ed. George Louis Palmella Busson Du Maurier. LC 278. (On cover: Standard series of paper novels, no. 6). 1899. International Book and Publishing Company.
Trilby: A Novel. George Louis Palmella Busson Du Maurier. (Half-title: Everyman's library, ed. by Ernest Rhys. Fiction). 1931. J. M. Dent & Sons, Ltd.
Trilby May Crashes in. Sewell Ford. LC 22-184031. 1922. Harper & Brothers.
Trilby: The Fairy of Argyle. 1st. ed. Charles Nodier & Dole, Nathan Haskell, 1852-1935, Tr. LC 44-333636. 1895. Estes and Lauriat.
Trilce. Cesar Vallejo. Tr. by David Smith. LC 73-80811. (Mushinsha Bks). 1974. pap. 5.95 o.p. (ISBN 0-670-73060-2, Grossman). Penguin.
Trillium Cup. Jacquelyn Aeby. (Candlelight Romance). 1975. (pbk.) 0.75. Dell.
Trilogy. Georgia H Ethridge. LC 74-76110. 1974. 6.95 (ISBN 0-8059-1998-8). Dorrance.
Trilogy. Diane Wakoski. LC 73-10548. 192p. 1974. pap. 3.95 (ISBN 0-385-09010-2). Doubleday.
Trilogy; an Experiment in Multimedia. Truman Capote & Eleanor Perry. LC 70-90221. (Illus.). 1969. Macmillan.
Trilogy of Desire. Theodore Dreiser. 15.00 o.p. (ISBN 0-529-04682-2, A4104). World Pub.
Trilogy of Desire: The Financier, the Titan, the Stoic. Theodore Dreiser. LC 72-81585. 1972. 15.00 o.p. (ISBN 0-690-00369-2). T Y Crowell.
Trilogy of Desire: Three Novels. Theodore Dreiser. LC 72-81585. 1972. 15.00 (ISBN 0-529-04682-2). World Pub.
Trilogy of Desire, Vol. 1: The Financier. Theodore Dreiser. 504p. 1974. pap. 4.95 o.p. (ISBN 0-8152-0360-8, CA-360). Apollo Eds.
Trilogy of Desire, Vol. 2: The Titan. Theodore Dreiser. 544p. 1974. pap. 4.95 o.p. (ISBN 0-8152-0367-5, CA-367). Apollo Eds.
Trilogy of Desire, Vol. 3: The Stoic. Theodore Dreiser. 320p. 1974. pap. 4.95 o.p. (ISBN 0-8152-0368-3, A-368). Apollo Eds.
Trimblerigg: A Book of Revelation. Laurence Housman. LC 75-145094. (Illus.). 1971. (ISBN 0-403-01032-2). Scholarly Press.
Trimblerigg: A Book of Revelation. Laurence Housman. LC 25-4342. 1925. A. & C. Boni.
Trimmed Lamp: And Other Stories of the Four Million. William Sydney Porter. LC 7-16486. 1907. McClure, Phillips & Co.
Trimmed Lamp: And Other Stories of the Four Million. William Sydney Porter. LC 15-174098. 1912. Doubleday, Page & Company.
Trimmed Lamp: And Other Stories of the Four Million. William Sydney Porter. 1919. Doubleday, Page & Company.
Trimmed Lamp: And Other Stories of the Four Million. William Sydney Porter. LC 22-14574. 1919. Doubleday, Page & Company, for Review of Reviews Co.
Trimmed Lamp: And Other Stories of the Four Million. William Sydney Porter. Ed. by Arthur Wilson Page. LC 24-27963. 1922. Doubleday, Page & Company.
Trimmed with Red. Wallace Irwin. LC 20-6843. George H. Doran Company.
Trimming of Goosie. James Marie Hopper. LC 9-24264. 1909. 1.10. Moffat, Yard and Company.
Trina. 1st Ed. Inga Hansen Dickerson. LC 55-123678. 1956. Comet Press Books.
Trinity. Leon M. Uris. LC 75-14844. (Illus.). 1976. 10.95 (ISBN 0-385-03458-X). Doubleday.
Trinity. Leon M. Uris. LC 77-365300. (Illus.). 1976. 5.25 (ISBN 0-233-96834-2). Deutsch.
Trinity. Leon M. Uris. LC 77-371949. (Illus.). 1976. Franklin Library.
Trinity Bells: A Tale of Old New York. Amelia Edith Huddleston Barr. 1899. J. F. Taylor and Company.
Trinity Factor. Sean Flannery, pseud. 418p. (Orig.). 1981. pap. 2.95 (ISBN 0-441-82402-1, Pub. by Charter Bks). Ace Bks.
Trinity Implosion. Robin Moore & Lewis Perdue. 1978. pap. 2.25 (ISBN 0-532-22117-6). Woodhill.
Trinity of Terror. William Doran. 48p. (Orig.). 1980. pap. 2.95 (ISBN 0-89288-045-7). Maverick.
Trinity Sketches. Selections from "The Trinity Tablet" 1887-1894... Ellis, George William, 1870- Ed & Paddock, Robert Louis, Joint Ed. LC 2-8384. 1894. Press of the Case Lockwood & Brainard Company.
Trinity Town. Norman Collins. LC 37-231670. 1937. Harper & Brothers.
Trio. Dorothy Dodds Baker. LC 77-5686. 1977. 16.50 (ISBN 0-8371-9647-7). Greenwood Press.
Trio. Dorothy Dodds Baker. LC 43-9798. 1943. Houghton Mifflin Company.
Trio Feliz. new ed. Jairo Ibero. (Pimienta Collection Ser). 160p. (Span.). 1974. pap. 1.00 o.p. (ISBN 0-88473-202-9). Fiesta Pub.
Trio for Blunt Instruments: A Nero Wolfe Threesome. Rex Stout. LC 64-15163. 1964. Viking Press.
Trio for Blunt Instruments: A Nero Wolfe Threesome. Rex Stout. 1974. (pbk) 1.25. Bantam Books.
Trio for Blunt Instruments: A Nero Woolfe Threesome. Rex Stout. Bd. with Kill Now, Pay Later; Murder Is Corny; Blood Will Tell. 256p. 1964. 3.50 o.p. (ISBN 0-670-73076-9). Viking Pr.
Trio in G. Al Glover. (Illus.). 92p. (Orig.). 1971. pap. 3.00. Frontier Press Calif.
Trio in Three Flats. Eileen Dewhurst. LC 81-43008. (Crime Club Ser.). 192p. 1981. 10.95 (ISBN 0-385-17647-3). Doubleday.
Trio: The Revolting Intellectuals Organization, a Novel. Patrick D Wall. LC 64-251998. 4.95. Potter Dist. Crown.
Trip Back: A Novel. Walter Sturdivant. LC 77-139662. 1971. 5.95 (ISBN 0-671-20847-0). Simon and Schuster.
Trip to Czardis. Edwin Granberry. LC 66-24830. 1966-1967. Trident Press.
Trip to London: Short Stories. Rhys Davies. LC 46-7210. 1946. Howell, Soskin.
Trip to Mars. Fenton Ash. LC 74-15948. (Science Fiction). (Illus.). 1975. 18.00 (ISBN 0-405-06274-5). Arno Press.
Trip to Mars. Marcianus Filomeno Rossi. LC 20-22794. Smith McKay.
Trip to the Center of the Earth. Jules Verne. LC 50-13085. 1950. Didier.
Trip to the Moon see Gulliveriana, No. 1.
Trip to the Moon: By Carol Holliston Pseud. James Noble Gifford. LC 55-140375. 1955. Arcadia House.
Trip to the Moon: Containing an Account of the Island of Noibla, 2 vols. in 1. Francis Gentleman. Ed. by Michael F. Shugrue. (Flowering of the Novel, 1740-1775 Ser.: Vol. 68). 1974. lib. bdg. 50.00 (ISBN 0-8240-1167-8). Garland Pub.
Trip to the Moon (1728) Murtagh McDermot. LC 73-133329. (Gulliveriana, 1). 1970. (ISBN 0-8201-1084-1). Scholars' Facsimiles & Reprints.
Trip to the North Pole: Or, The Discovery of the Ten Tribes As Found in the Arctic Ocean, and Published. Otto Julius Swenson Lindelof. LC 4-71. 1903. Tribune Printing Company.
Trip to the West Indies see Collected Works.
Trip to Venus: A Novel. John Munro. LC 75-10665. (Classics of science fiction). 1976. 11.95. (ISBN 0-88355-360-0) (ISBN 0-88355-460-7). Hyperion Press.
Trip Trap. Julian Rathbone. LC 72-81496. 1972. 5.95. St. Martin's Press.
Trip with Father. Katharine Hotchkiss. pap. 2.25 o.p. Calif Hist.
Triplanetary: A Tale of Cosmic Adventure. Edward Elmer Smith. LC 48-6988. 1948. Fantasy Press.
Triple. Ken Follett. 1980. pap. 9.95 (ISBN 0-8161-3099-X, Large Print Bks). G K Hall.
Triple. Ken Follett. 1980. pap. 3.95 (ISBN 0-451-12429-4, AE2429, Sig). NAL.
Triple. Ken Follett. 1980. 10.95 o.p. (ISBN 0-87795-223-X). Arbor Hse.
Triple: A Novel. Ken Follett. LC 79-21607. 1979. (ISBN 0-8161-3005-1). G. K. Hall.
Triple: A Novel. Ken Follett. LC 78-73869. 10.95 (ISBN 0-87795-223-X). Arbor House.
Triple Alliance. Henry Watson Clapp. LC 24-210731. Phelps Publishing Co.
Triple Cross. Nick Carter. (Nick Carter Ser). (O.s.i.). 1976. pap. 1.50 o.s.i. (AD1636, Award). Univ Pub & Dist.
Triple Cross. Carlos Fuentes et al. Tr. by Suzanne J. Levine & Hallie D. Taylor. 1972. 8.95 o.p. (ISBN 0-525-22280-4). Dutton.
Triple Cross. (Nick Carter Ser.). 208p. (Orig.). 1980. pap. 1.95 (ISBN 0-441-82407-2, Pub. by Charter Bks). Ace Bks.
Triple Cross: A Mystery Novel. abridged ed. Joe Barry Lake. LC 47-25467. (Handi-book mysteries, 52). 1946. Quinn Pub. Co.
Triple Cross: A Rush Henry Mystery. Joe Barry Lake. 1946. Mystery House.
Triple Cross at Trinidad. Edward London Foreman. (BT Brand western). 1974. (pbk.) 0.95. Belmont Tower Books.
Triple Cross at Trinidad. Leonard London Foreman. LC 78-150894. (Doubleday western). 1971. 4.95. Doubleday.
Triple Cross: Holy Place. LC 78-179856. 1972. 8.95 (ISBN 0-525-22280-4). E. P. Dutton.
Triple Cross Murders... Amelia Reynolds Long. LC 43-16387. 1943. Ziff-Davis Publishing Company.
Triple Cross Trail. Edwin Booth. (Berkley medallion book). 1974. (pbk.) 0.95 (ISBN 0-425-02557-8). Berkley Pub. Co.
Triple Cross Trail. Al Cody, pseud. 1977. pap. 1.25 (ISBN 0-532-12519-3). Woodhill.

Triple Detente. Piers Anthony, pseud. (Science Fiction Ser). 176p. (Orig.). 1974. pap. 0.95 o.p. (ISBN 0-87997-130-4, UQ1130). DAW Bks.
Triple Entanglement. Constance Cary Harrison. LC 99-1299. 1899. J. B. Lippincott Company.
Triple Espera: Novelas Cortas De Hispanoamerica. Ed. by Djelal Kadir. 235p. (Spanish.). 1976. pap. text ed. 9.95 (ISBN 0-15-592353-6, HC). HarBraceJ.
Triple Exposure, Containing Glass Triangle, Jade Venus & Fifth Key. George Harmon Coxe. 1959. 3.95 o.p. Knopf.
Triple Flirtation. Louis Michael Elshemus. LC 1-29914. The Abbey Press.
Triple Fugue. Osbert Sitwell. LC 74-134980. (Short story index reprint series). 1970. Books for Libraries Press.
Triple Fugue. Osbert Sitwell. LC 25-166106. 1925. George H. Doran Company.
Triple Hoax. Carolyn Keene, pseud. (Nancy Drew Ser.: No. 57). (Illus.). 192p. (gr. 3-7). 1979. 8.95 (ISBN 0-671-95490-3); pap. 2.95 (ISBN 0-671-95512-8). Wanderer Bks.
Triple Indemnity. Judith Richards. LC 82-72060. 14.95 (ISBN 0-87795-421-6). Arbor House.
Triple Jeopardy: A Nero Wolfe Threesome. Rex Stout. LC 52-8408. 1952. Viking Press.
Triple Mirror. Leigh James. 192p. 1975. pap. 1.25 (ISBN 0-532-12306-9). Woodhill.
Triple Mirror: Translated from the French of Le Puits Aux Trois Verites, by Mervyn Savill. Jean Jacques Gautier. LC 54-6810. Roy Publishers.
Triple Murder. Carolyn Wells. LC 29-24590. 1929. J. B. Lippincott Company.
Triple Mystery. Adele Luehrmann. LC 20-7518. 1920. Dodd, Mead and Company.
Triple Platinum. Stephen Holden. 1979. 2.50 (ISBN 0-440-18650-1). DellPublishing Co., Inc.
Triple Pursuit: A Graham Greene Omnibus. Graham Greene. 1971. 6.95 o.p. (ISBN 0-670-73126-9). Viking Pr.
Triple Target. Dean Owen. 1975. (pbk.) 0.95. Ace Books.
Triple Threat; Exploits of Three Famous Detectives: Hercule Poirot, Harley Quin and Tuppence. Agatha Miller Christie. LC 44-5990. 1943. Dodd, Mead & Company.
Triple Threat: Three Jeff and Haila Troy Mysteries. Kelley Roos. LC 49-110275. 1949. A. A. Wyn.
Triple Threat: Three Novels. Helen MacInnes. LC 72-79921. (Illus.). 1973. 8.95 (ISBN 0-15-191155-X). Harcourt Brace Jovanovich.
Triple Zeck: A Nero Wolfe Omnibus. Rex Stout. LC 73-19104. 1974. 8.95 (ISBN 0-670-73130-7). Viking Press.
Triplets. Joyce Rebeta-Burditt. (O.s.i.). 1981. 15.95 o.s.i. (ISBN 0-440-08943-3, Sey Lawr). Delacorte.
Tripoli Documents. Henry Kane. LC 76-19789. 7.95 (ISBN 0-671-22334-8). Simon and Schuster.
Tripoli Documents. Henry Kane. (Kangaroo Book). 1977. 1.95 (ISBN 0-671-81413-3). Pocket Books.
Tripper. Jocelyn. 144p. 1973. 5.00 o.p. (ISBN 0-682-47708-7, Banner). Exposition.
Tripper: A Novel. Jocelyn. LC 73-79362. (Exposition-banner book). 1973. 5.00 (ISBN 0-682-47708-7). Exposition Press.
Trippings in Author-Land. Emily Chubbuck Judson. 1846. Paine and Burgess.
Trips in Time: Nine Stories of Science Fiction. Robert Silverberg. LC 77-24213. 6.95 (ISBN 0-8407-6574-6). Nelson.
Trips with His Aunt. Thomas H. Hilton. 192p. pap. 1.95 o.p. (ISBN 0-87056-312-2, 6312). Brandon.
Trips with His Aunt. Thomas H Hilton. 1973. (pbk.) 1.95 (ISBN 0-87056-312-2). Brandon Books.
Tripticks. Ann Quin. 160p. 1979. 9.95 (ISBN 0-7145-0816-0, Pub. by M Boyars). Merrimack Pub Cir.
Triptych. Dora Landey & Elinor Klein. LC 82-15874. 1983. 16.95 (ISBN 0-395-33126-9). Houghton Mifflin.
Triptych. Claude Simon. LC 75-46560. 1976. 8.95 (ISBN 0-670-73136-6). Viking Press.
Triptych: A Novel. Claude Simon. Tr. by Helen R. Lane. LC 75-46560. (Richard Seaver Books). 192p. 1976. 8.95 o.p. (ISBN 0-670-73136-6). Viking Pr.
Triptych for the Atomic Age. John W. Andrews. 5.25 o.s.i. (ISBN 0-8283-1281-8). Branden.
Tripwire. Brian Wynne Garfield. LC 72-92637. 1973. 5.95. McKay.
Tristan. Herve Bazin. LC 71-154090. (O.s.i.). 1971. 7.95 o.s.i. (ISBN 0-671-20994-9). S&S.
Tristan. Hannah Priebsch Closs. LC 67-29445. 1968. Vanguard Press.
Tristan. Maria Kuncewicz. LC 73-86262. 228p. 1974. 7.95 (ISBN 0-8076-0726-6). Braziller.
Tristan: A Novel. Herve-Bazin, Jean Pierre Marie. LC 71-154090. (Illus.). 1971. 7.95 (ISBN 0-671-20994-9). Simon and Schuster.
Tristan and Isolde, Restoring Palamede. John Erskine. LC 32-33964. The Bobbs-Merrill Company.
Tristan Tristan; D, El Pesimismo: A Novel. Palacio Valdes, Armando & Reid, Jane Brewster, 1862- Tr. LC 25-7068. 1925. The Four Seas Company.
Tristana. Translated from the Spanish by R. Selden Rose. Benito Perez Galdos. LC 61-145741. 1961. R. R. Smith.
Triste Deleytacion: An Anonymous Fifteenth Century Castilian Romance. Ed. by E. Michael Gerli. LC 82-15742. 160p. (Orig., Span. & Eng.). 1983. lib. bdg. 14.95 (ISBN 0-87840-086-9). Georgetown U Pr.
Triste Historia De Mi Vida Oscura: A Peticion Popular. Armando Couto. LC 78-70332. 1978. pap. 5.95 (ISBN 0-89729-196-4). Ediciones.
Tristram Bent. Henry Barnard Safford. LC 40-6705. Coward-McCann, Inc.
Tristram Lacy: Or, The Individualist. William Hurrell Mallock. LC 99-2290. 1899. The Macmillan Company.
Tristram Lloyd: A Novel. Patrick Augustine Sheehan & Gaffney, Michael Henry, 1895- Ed. LC 28-25624. 1928. Longmans, Green and Co.
Tristram of Blent: An Episode in the Story of an Ancient House. Anthony Hope Hawkins. LC 1-17656. 1901. McClure, Philips & Co.
Tristram of Blent: An Episode in the Story of an Ancient House. Anthony Hope Hawkins. LC 8-26629. 1902. New Amsterdam Book Company.
Tristram of Lyonesse: The Story of an Immortal Love. Ruth Collier Sharpe. 1949. Greenberg.
Tristram's Salvation: A Novel. William Richard Bird. 1957. T. Bouregy.
Triton. Samuel R Delany. LC 77-5013. (Gregg Press science fiction series; 3). 1977. 15.00 (ISBN 0-8398-2371-1). Gregg Press.
Triton. Samuel R Delany. 1976. (pbk.) 1.95. Bantam.
Triton. Hubbard. 1972. 7.00 o.p. Fantasy Pub Co.
Triton: And Battle of Wizards. La Fayette Ronald Hubbard. LC 49-49235. 1949. Fantasy Pub. Co.
Triton Brig. Dudley Pope. LC 69-12242. 1969. 5.95. Doubleday.
Triton Ultimatum. Laurence Delaney. LC 77-1290. 8.95 (ISBN 0-690-01490-2). Crowell.
Tritonian Ring. Lyon Sprague De Camp & Jim Cawthorn. LC 76-56969. (Illus.). 1977. 12.50. Owlswick Press.
Tritonian Ring: And Other Pusadian Tales. Lyon Sprague De Camp. LC 53-12783. 1953. Twayne Publishers.
Tritons. Edwin Lassetter Bynner. LC 6-16405. 1878. Lockwood, Brooks and Company.
Tritons. Edwin Lassetter Bynner. (On cover: Lovell's library, v. 3. no. 102). 1883. J. W. Lovell Company.
Triumpal Entry. Thomas P. Baird. 1962. 4.95 o.p. HarBraceJ.
Triumph. Constance Leonie Caroline Borgstrom Aminoff. LC 26-3118. (Her Torchlight series of Napoleonic romances. vi). 1926. E. P. Dutton & Company.
Triumph. Helen Marion Edginton. LC 24-5802. 1924. H. Holt and Company.
Triumph. John K. Galbraith. 1968. 4.95 o.p. (ISBN 0-395-07710-9). HM.
Triumph. Arthur Moore. (Orig.). 1979. pap. 2.50 (ISBN 0-89083-522-5). Zebra.
Triumph. Frederick John Niven. LC 34-13509. E. P. Dutton & Co., inc.
Triumph. Arthur Stanwood Pier. LC 3-12521. 1903. McClure, Phillips & Co.
Triumph. John Wilmot Wiley. LC 26-7121. 1926. Minton, Balch & Company.
Triumph. Philip Wylie. LC 63-7705. 1963. Doubleday.
Triumph: A Novel. William Nathaniel Harben. LC 17-222971. Harper & Brothers.
Triumph: A Novel of Modern Diplomacy. John Kenneth Galbraith. LC 68-16480. 1968. Houghton Mifflin.
Triumph & Defeat. Gladys Martin & Donnis Martin. LC 72-189365. 336p. 1972. 5.95 o.p. (ISBN 0-8158-0280-3). Chris Mass.
Triumph and Defeat: The Triumph of Christianity Over Paganism, the Loss of Rome to the Goths. Donnis Martin & Gladys Martin. LC 72-189365. (Illus.). 1972. 5.95. Christopher Pub. House.
Triumph of a Fool. John Ressich. LC 26-108491. 1926. Cassell and Company, Ltd.
Triumph of Andrea. Katherine Sargent. 256p. 1982. pap. 2.75 (ISBN 0-449-14457-7, GM). Fawcett.
Triumph of Death. Gabriele D' Annunzio. Tr. by Arthur Hornblower. LC 9-34523. (His The rmoances of the rose). 1896. G. H. Richmond & Co.
Triumph of Death. David Rudkin. 60p. 1982. pap. 6.95 (ISBN 0-413-49110-2, NO. 3645). Methuen Inc.
Triumph of Death, from the Italian of Gabriele D'Annunzio. Gabriele D' Annunzio. LC 75-1254. 1975. 13.50. H. Fertig.
Triumph of Destiny. Julia Helen Watts Twells. LC 8-32303. 1896. J. B. Lippincott Company.
Triumph of Evil. Paul Kavanagh. LC 77-145834. 1971. 5.95. World Pub. Co.
Triumph of Failure. Patrick Augustine Sheehan. LC 75-467. (Victorian Fiction: Novels of Faith and Doubt). 1976. 35.00 (ISBN 0-8240-1545-2). Garland Pub.
Triumph of Gallio. Walter Lionel George. LC 24-206132. 1924. Harper & Brothers.
Triumph of John Kars: A Story of the Yukon. Ridgwell Cullum. LC 17-30120. G. W. Jacobs & Company.
Triumph of Life: A Novel. William Farquhar Payson. LC 3-9339. 1903. Harper & Brothers.
Triumph of O'Rourke. Brian Talbot Cleeve. LC 73-150882. 1972. 6.95. Doubleday.
Triumph of the Egg: A Book of Impressions from American Life in Tales and Poems. Sherwood Anderson. LC 21-21097. 1921. B. W. Huebsch, Inc.
Triumph of the Scarlet Pimpernel. Emmuska Orczy. LC 23-1202. 1.75. George H. Doran Company.
Triumph of the Spider Monkey. Joyce Carol Oates. 1979. pap. 2.25 (ISBN 0-449-23817-2, Crest). Fawcett.
Triumph of the Spider Monkey: A First-Person Confession by the Maniac Bobbie Gotteson. Joyce Carol Oates. LC 76-50134. 1976. 10.00. (ISBN 0-87685-291-6) (ISBN 0-87685-292-4) (ISBN 0-87685-290-8). Black Sparrow Press.
Triumph of Tim. Horace Annesley Vachell. George H. Doran Company.
Triumph of Time. James Blish. LC 58-475569. (Avon original T-279). 1958. Avon Publications.
Triumph of Vice. George William Target. LC 76-380092. 1976. 4.95 (ISBN 0-7156-1107-0). Duckworth.
Triumph of Virginia Dale. John Francis. LC 21-13066. 1921. The Page Company.
Triumph of Willie Pond. Caroline Beach Slade. LC 40-7253. The Vanguard Press.
Triumph of Yankee Doodle. Gilson Willets. LC 98-1171. (On cover: Neely's universal library. no. 31). F. T. Neely.
Triumph of Youth. Jakob Wassermann. LC 27-10821. 1927. Boni & Liveright.
Triumph Over Ashes. 1st Ed. Leonard Boyd. LC 51-844. 1951. De Vorss.
Triumph, the Undoing of Rafferty, Ward Heeler. Charles Francis Coe. LC 29-238802. J. H. Sears & Company, Inc.
Triumphal Entry. 1st Ed. Thomas P Baird. LC 62-14464. 1962. Harcourt, Brace World.
Triumphant Clay. Rupert Hughes. LC 51-34725. 1951. House-Warven.
Triumphant Footman: A Farcical Fable. Edith Olivier. LC 30-21168. 1930. The Viking Press.
Triumphant Rider. Frances Forbes-Robertson Harrod. LC 26-15265. 1926. Boni and Liveright.
Triumphs of Ephraim. James Ephraim McGirt. LC 79-39093. (Black Heritage Library Collection). (Illus.). 1972. (ISBN 0-8369-9031-5). Books for Libraries Press.
Triumphs of Eugene Valmont. Robert Barr. LC 6-96238. 1906. D. Appleton & Company.
Triumvirate. Oliver Robinson. LC 43-13676. 1943. B. Humphries, Inc.
Triumvirate. H. Baldwin Taylor. LC 66-11744. 1966. Published for the Crime Club by Doubleday.
Triune Man. Richard A. Lupoff. LC 75-26867. 6.95 (ISBN 0-399-11680-X). Berkley Pub. Corp.: Distributed by Putnam.
Trixey, the Manicure Girl. Margaret Redic Lyons. LC 8-18726. Broadway Publishing Co.
Trixie. Wallace Grayes. LC 77-79341. 1969. 6.95. Knopf.
Trixy. Elizabeth Stuart Phelps Ward. LC 4-26116. 1904. Houghton, Mifflin and Company.
Trixy: Or, The Shadow of a Crime. Sarah Elizabeth Forbush G. S. Downs Downs. LC 6-45956. (select series. no. 43). 1890. Street & Smith.
Trixy: Or, The Shadow of a Crime. A Novel. Sarah Elizabeth Forbush G. S. Downs Downs. (On cover: The Manhattan series. v 1, no. 4). A. L. Burt.
Trobadour Tales. Evaleen Stein. LC 29-269093. 1929. L. C. Page and Company.
Trocadero. Leslie Waller. (O.s.i.). 1978. 12.95 o.s.i. (ISBN 0-440-09073-3). Delacorte.
Trocadero: A Novel. Leslie Waller. LC 77-14174. 9.95 (ISBN 0-440-09073-3). Delacorte Press.
Trocadero: A Novel. Leslie Waller. 1979. 2.50 (ISBN 0-440-18613-7). Dell Publishing Co.
Trodden Gold. Howard Vincent O'Brien. LC 23-4895. 1923. 2.00. Little, Brown, and Company.
Trodden Paths. Jacqueline Gilbert. (Harlequin Romances Ser.). 192p. 1982. pap. 1.50 (ISBN 0-373-02492-4). Harlequin Bks.
Troika. David Gurr. LC 79-10534. 1979. 9.95 (ISBN 0-458-94210-3). Methuen.
Troika. David Montross, pseud. LC 63-19846. 1963. Published for the Crime Club by Doubleday.
Troika Belle. Ira J Morris. (Fawcett crest book). 1974. (pbk.) 1.50. Fawcett.
Troika Incident: A Tetralogue in Two Parts. James Cooke Brown. LC 70-103734. (Doubleday projections books). 1970. Doubleday.
Troilus & Criseyde. Geoffrey Chaucer. Tr. by R. M. Lumiansky. LC 52-4669. (Illus.). 1952. 9.95 o.p. (ISBN 0-87249-041-6). U of SC Pr.
Trois Contes. Gustave Flaubert. (Coll. GF). 1963. pap. 2.95 (1958). French & Eur.
Trois Contes. Gustave Flaubert. Ed. by Maynial. (Class. Garnier). pap. 6.95. French & Eur.
Trois Contes. Gustave Flaubert. Ed. by Maynial. (Coll. Prestige). 27.95. French & Eur.
Trois Mousquetaires. Alexandre Dumas. Ed. by Samaran. (Coll. Prestige). 35.00. French & Eur.
Trois Mousquetaires. Alexandre Dumas. Ed. by R. Hawkins. 1926. pap. 2.96 o.p. HR&W.
Trois Villes, 3 pts. Emile Zola. Incl. Lourdes; Rome; Paris. 7.95 ea. French & Eur.
Trojan. Noel Bertram Gerson. pap. 0.60 o.p. (53-825). Paperback Lib.
Trojan Brothers. Pamela Hansford Johnson. LC 45-4837. 1945. The Macmillan Company.
Trojan Cow: A Novel. Giles Tippette. LC 72-139468. 1971. Macmillan.
Trojan Gold. Sheila Cudahy. LC 79-14728. 8.95 (ISBN 0-06-010934-3). Harper & Row.
Trojan Horse. Christopher Darlington Morley. LC 37-34172. 1937. J. B. Lippincott Company.
Trojan Horse. Paul Nizan. LC 75-2170. 1975. 12.00. H. Fertig.
Trojan Mule. June Drummond. 159p. 1982. 17.50 o.p. (ISBN 0-575-03135-2, Pub. by Gollancz England). David & Charles.
Trojan War. 1981. pap. text ed. write for info. (ISBN 0-88074-251-8). Metagam.
Trojans. Wirt Williams. LC 66-21990. 1966. Little, Brown.
Troll Garden. Willa Sibert Cather. LC 5-10180. 1905. McClure, Phillips and Co.
Trolley Folly. Henry Wallace Phillips. 1909. 1.25. The Bobbs-Merrill Company.
Trolley Song. Sheila Raescild. (Orig.). 1981. pap. 3.50 (ISBN 0-89083-889-5). Zebra.
Tron. Brian Daley. 1982. pap. 2.75 (ISBN 0-345-30352-0, Del Rey). Ballantine.
Trooper Galahad. Charles King. LC 99-813. 1899. J. B. Lippincott Company.
Trooper MacLean. Charles Stoddard. LC 38-297193. The William Caslon Company, Inc.
Trooper MacLean. Charles Stanley Strong. LC 38-29793. 1937. W. Caslon Co.
Trooper of the Empress. Clinton Ross. LC 8-674. (Half-title: Appleton's town and country library, no. 240). 1898. D. Appleton and Company.
Trooper O'Neill: A Story of the North-West Mounted Police. George Goodchild. LC 23-16821. 1923. G. H. Watt.
Trooper Peter Halket of Mashonaland. Olive Schreiner. 1897. Roberts Brothers.
Trooper Ross and Signal Butte. Charles King. LC 7-12219. 1896. J. B. Lippincott Company.
Trooper Ross and Signal Butte. Charles King. LC 26-13537. 1908. J. B. Lippincott Company.
Trooper Tales. Will Levington Comfort. 1976. Repr. of 1899 ed. lib. bdg. 14.10x (ISBN 0-89190-853-6). Am Repr-Rivercity Pr.
Trooper Tales: A Series of Sketches of the Real American Private Soldier. Will Levington Comfort. LC 70-106271. (Short story index reprint series). (Illus.). 1970. Books for Libraries Press.
Trooper Tales: A Series of Sketches of the Real American Private Soldier. Will Levington Comfort. LC 99-5812. Street & Smith.
Troopers Three: From the Scenario by Guy Empey. Harry S Hart & Empey, Arthur Guy. LC 30-3071. A. L. Burt Company.
Troopers West. Forbes Parkhill & Santee, Ross, 1889- Illus. LC 45-269298. 1945. Farrar & Rinehart, Inc.
Tropic Death. Eric Walrond. LC 76-123460. (American Library). 1972. 1.95. Collier Books.
Tropic Death. Eric Walrond. LC 26-181643. 1926. Boni & Liveright.
Tropic Flower. Helen Marion Edginton. The Macaulay Company.
Tropic Gardens. Judith Cabot Priest. LC 52-4463. 1952. Woodford Press.
Tropic Moon. Georges Simenon & Gilbert, Stuart, Tr. LC 43-8276. 1943. Harcourt, Brace and Company.
Tropic Night. Inez Nichols. LC 32-4113. Sears Publishing Company, Inc.
Tropic of Cancer. Henry Miller. 7.95 (ISBN 0-394-60435-0). Modern Lib.
Tropic of Cancer. Henry Miller. (Rus. & Eng.). 1961. 7.50 o.p. (GP333); rus. ed. 7.50 o.p. Grove.
Tropic of Cancer. new ed. Henry Miller. 1975. pap. 4.95 o.p. (ISBN 0-394-17897-1, E664, Ever). Grove.

Tropic of Capricorn. Henry. Miller. 1963. 7.50 o.p. (GP259). Grove.
Tropic of Capricorn. Henry Miller. 1962. pap. 1.95 o.p. (ISBN 0-394-17295-7, B59, BC). Grove.
Tropic of Capricorn. new ed. Henry Miller. 1975. pap. 4.95 o.p. (ISBN 0-394-17898-X, E669, Ever). Grove.
Tropic of Desire. Antoinette Beaudry. 1978. 2.25 (ISBN 0-523-40344-5). Pinnacle Books.
Tropic of Doubt: A Novel. Susanne McConnaughey. LC 53-921055. 1953. Westminster Press.
Tropic Seed. Alec Waugh. LC 33-175167. Farrar & Rinehart, Incorporated.
Tropical Deathpact. Nick Carter. (Nick Carter Ser.). 256p. (Orig.). 1979. pap. 1.95 o.p. (ISBN 0-441-82417-X). Charter Bks.
Tropical Detective Story: The Flower Children Meet the Voodoo Chiefs. Raymond Mungo. LC 73-179844. 1972. 4.95 (ISBN 0-525-22328-2). E. P. Dutton.
Tropical Fruit: A Novel. Alfred Harding. LC 28-21493. 1928. Duffield & Company.
Tropical Knight. Lynsey Stevens. (Harlequin Romances Ser.). 192p. 1982. pap. 1.50 (ISBN 0-373-02507-6). Harlequin Bks.
Tropical Murder. Louis Williams. (Orig.). 1981. pap. 2.50 o.s.i. (ISBN 0-505-51667-5). Tower Bks.
Tropical Paradise. Robert Sylvester. LC 60-5520. 1960. Random House.
Tropical Winter. Joseph Hergesheimer. 1933. A. A. Knopf.
Tropisms. Tr. from French by Maria Jolas. Nathalie Sarraute. LC 67-182119. 1967. 3.50, 1.95 pap.,. Braziller.
Tros of Samothrace. Talbot Mundy. LC 58-8768. 1958. Gneme Press.
Tros of Samothrace. Talbot Mundy. LC 39-31693. 1938. D. Appleton-Century Company, Incorporated.
Trosy: Or, The Wreck of the Chesapeake. Eva Louise Dunning. LC 14-204994. 0.25. E. L. Dunning.
Trotecillos Del Pueblo. Corielle Vogel. (Illus.). 1973. pap. 1.25 o.p. (ISBN 0-913456-58-6). Interbk Inc.
Trotsky Dead. Bernard Wolfe. LC 74-29809. 1975. 8.95 (ISBN 0-88381-012-3). Wollstonecraft: Distributed by Price/Stern/Sloan Publishers.
Trotsky's Run. Richard Hoyt. LC 82-6343. 1982. 12.50 (ISBN 0-688-01311-2). Morrow.
Trotter Ross: A Novel. James Hoggard. LC 81-586. 12.00 (ISBN 0-914476-89-0). Thorp Springs Press.
Trottie True. Doris Caroline Abrahams & Skidelsky, Simon Jasha, Joint Author. LC 47-11421. 1947. J. B. Lippincott Co.
Troubadour. Louis Charles Vaczek. LC 60-14494. 1960. W Sloane Associates.
Troubadour of the Stars: The Romantic Life of Johannes Kepler. Olaf Saile & Galston, James Austin, 1881- Tr.
Troubadour Tales. Evaleen Stein. LC 3-17015. 1903. The Bobbs-Merrill Company.
Trouble! Graham Montague Jeffries. LC 29-13365. 1929. J. B. Lippincott Company.
Trouble at Breakdam. Ben Smith. LC 57-11735. 1957. Macmillan.
Trouble at Choctaw Bend. James D. Sayers. LC 52-7003. 1952. Bouregy & Curl.
Trouble at Double Triangle. Tex Holt, pseud. LC 44-7574. 1944. Arcadia House.
Trouble at Double Triangle. Claude Rister. LC 44-7574. 1944. Arcadia House, Inc.
Trouble at Glaye. Gertrude M. Robins Reynolds. LC 36-185483. 1936. Pub. for the Crime Club, Inc., by Doubleday, Doran & Company, Inc.
Trouble at Gunsight. Louis Trimble. 1974. 0.95. Ace Books.
Trouble at Hungerfords. 1st Ed. Cyril Harris. LC 52-12645. 1953. Little, Brown.
Trouble at Moon Pass. Burt Arthur, pseud. (Belmont Tower book). 1978. 1.25 (ISBN 0-505-51257-2). Tower Pubns.
Trouble at Moon Pass. Herbert Shappiro. LC 43-18065. 1943. Phoenix Press.
Trouble at Moon Pass: By Herbert Shappiro. Herbert Arthur, pseud. LC 43-15065. 1943. Phoenix Press.
Trouble at Pinelands: A Detective Story. Ernest M Poate. LC 22-246868. 1.75. Chelsea House.
Trouble at Shaplinch. David Emerson. 1981. 18.95x (Pub. by Remploy England). State Mutual Bk.
Trouble at Sudden Creek. Al Cody, pseud. 144p. 1975. pap. 0.95 (ISBN 0-532-95427-0). Woodhill.
Trouble at Sudden Creek. Al Cody, pseud. 1970. Repr. pap. 0.60 o.p. (60-451). Manor Bks.
Trouble at Tall Pine, by Brad Ward: Pseud. 1st Ed. Samuel Anthony Peeples. LC 54-582474. (Dutton Diamond D western). 1954. Dutton.
Trouble at the Lazy-K. James Wesley. (YA) 1978. 6.95 (Avalon). Bouregy.
Trouble at the Top. Charles Bracelen Flood. LC 76-178924. 1972. 6.95 (ISBN 0-07-021332-1). McGraw-Hill.
Trouble at Tragedy Springs. Edwin Booth. (Berkley medallion book). 1974. (pbk.) 0.95 (ISBN 0-425-02556-X). Berkley Pub. Co.
Trouble at Tulley's Run. George Charles Appell. LC 58-8468. 1958. Macmillan.
Trouble at Turkey Hill. Kathleen Moore Knight. LC 46-316074. 1946. Pub. for the Crime Club by Doubleday & Company, Inc.
Trouble at Wrekin Farm. Doris Bell Ball. LC 42-21769. 1942. Longmans, Green and Co.
Trouble Busters. John Thomas Edson. (Orig.). 1982. pap. 1.95 (ISBN 0-425-05227-3). Berkley Pub.
Trouble Comes Double. Robert P Hansen. 1954. M. S. Mill Co., and W. Morrow.
Trouble Country. Luke Short. LC 76-48273. 1977. 7.95 (ISBN 0-89340-039-4). J. Curley.
Trouble Country. Luke Short. 1976. (pbk.) 1.25. Bantam Books.
Trouble Follows Me. Kenneth Millar. LC 46-629442. 1946. Dodd, Mead & Company.
Trouble for Ben Melody. 2nd ed. Edward Beverly Mann. Orig. Title: Shootin' Melody. 1970. pap. 0.60 o.p. (B60-1089). Belmont-Tower.
Trouble for Lucia. Edward Frederic Benson. LC 39-277751. 1939. Doubleday, Doran & Company, Inc.
Trouble for Tallon. John Dudley Ball. LC 80-1983. 1981. 9.95 (ISBN 0-385-17329-6). Published for the Crime Club by Doubleday.
Trouble from Texas. Oscar Schisgall. LC 38-362561. 1938. The Macaulay Company.
Trouble Grabber. Frank Chester Robertson. LC 32-27069. 1932. I. Washburn.
Trouble in Burma: By Van Wyck Mason. 1st Ed. Francis Van Wyck Mason. LC 62-11377. 1962. Doubleday.
Trouble in Hunter Ward. Doris Bell Collier Ball. LC 76-53947. 1977. 6.95 (ISBN 0-8027-5361-2). Walker and Co.
Trouble in July. Erskine Caldwell. LC 40-27204. Duell, Sloan & Pearce.
Trouble in Paradise. Nick Carter. (Nick Carter Ser.). 192p. 1978. pap. 1.75 o.p. (ISBN 0-441-82460-9). Charter Bks.
Trouble in Paradise. Lorena Ann Olmsted. 1974. 4.50. Avalon.
Trouble in Paradise: A Captain Jose Da Silva Novel. Robert L Fish. LC 74-10498. 1975. 5.95 (ISBN 0-385-00479-6). Doubleday.
Trouble in Peaceful Valley. Peter Germano. LC 68-1541. 1968. Arcadia House.
Tròuble in the Flesh. Max Wylie. LC 59-7006. 1959. Doubleday.
Trouble in the Glen. Maurice Walsh. LC 51-944151. 1951. Lippincott.
Trouble in the Saddle. Arthur Henry Gooden. LC 48-584494. 1948. Houghton Mifflin Co.
Trouble in Thor: By Jo Valentine Pseud. Charlotte Armstrong. LC 53-5780. 1953. Coward-McCann.
Trouble in Tombstone. 1st Ed. Tom J Hopkins. LC 51-14165. (Double D western). 1951. Doubleday.
Trouble in Triplicate: A Nero Wolfe Threesome. Rex Stout. LC 49-1340. 1949. Viking Press.
Trouble in Twin Buttes. James Edward Hoskins. LC 65-8410. 1965. Arcadia House.
Trouble in Ward J. Neubauer, William Arthur. LC 64-7365. 1964. Arcadia House.
Trouble Is My Business. Raymond Chandler. pap. 2.25 (ISBN 0-345-28862-9). Ballantine.
Trouble Is My Business. Jay Flynn. 1976. pap. 1.25 o.p. (LB384ZK, Leisure Bks). Nordon Pubns.
Trouble Is My Business: Four Stories from The Simple Art of Murder. Raymond Chandler. LC 57-3881. (Pocketbook, 2823. Mystery, 3). 1957. Pocket Books.
Trouble Is My Master. Darwin Le Ora Teilhet. LC 42-9586. 1942. Little, Brown and Company.
Trouble Is: Stories of Social Dilemma. Angus & Curtin. 1973. pap. text ed. 7.95 o.p. Dickenson.
Trouble Is: Stories of Social Dilemma. Ed. by Sylvia Angus. LC 73-75039. (Illus.). 1973. 3.95 (ISBN 0-8221-0088-6). Dickenson Pub. Co.
Trouble I've Seen. Martha Gellhorn. LC 36-20249. 1936. W. Morrow and Company.
Trouble Kid. Max Brand. LC 81-932. 1981. 11.95 (ISBN 0-89340-322-9). J. Curley & Associates.
Trouble Kid. Frederick Faust. LC 72-107774. 1970. 3.95. Dodd, Mead.
Trouble Maker. Edward Roe Eastman. LC 25-19727. 1925. The Macmillan Company.
Trouble Makers. Celia Fremlin, pseud. LC 63-12829. 1963. Lippincott.
Trouble of It Is. David McCheyne Newell. LC 77-74976. (Illus.). 1978. 8.95 (ISBN 0-394-40413-0). Knopf: Distributed by Random House.
Trouble of Living Alone. A Novel. Frederick B Hofman. LC 8-36887. 1894. Arena Publishing Company.
Trouble of One House. Brendan Gill. LC 50-9905. 1950. Doubleday.
Trouble on Big Cat. Glenn Corbin. LC 54-8057. (Dell first edition, 25). 1954. Dell Pub. Co.
Trouble on East Green Street: A Novel. 1st Ed. Ivan Jontez. LC 56-10299. 1956. Exposition Press.
Trouble on Funeral Range. Walker A Tompkins. LC 44-236071. 1944. Phoenix Press.
Trouble on the Hill: And Other Stories. Michael Glenn. LC 79-88413. 156p. (Orig.). 1979. pap. 3.95 (ISBN 0-930720-61-X). Lake View Pr.
Trouble on the Hill & Other Stories. Michael Glenn. LC 79-88413. 1979. pap. 3.95 (ISBN 0-930720-61-X). Liberator Pr.
Trouble on the Rimrock. Will Kirkland, pseud. (YA) 1973. 4.95 o.p. (Avalon). Bouregy.
Trouble on the Trail. Charles H. Cooke. 3.00 o.p. Carlton.
Trouble Ranch. George M Johnson. LC 32-140171. E. J. Clode, Inc.
Trouble Range. Charles Wesley Sanders. LC 25-11076. 1925. G. H. Watt.
Trouble Rider. Thomas Thompson. LC 54-7560. 1954. Ballantine Books.
Trouble Rides Tall. William L. Hopson. (Belmont Tower book). 1979. 1.25 (ISBN 0-505-51359-5). Tower Pubns.
Trouble Rides Tall. William L. Hopson. 1976. (pbk.) 1.25. Award Books.
Trouble Rides Tall. Harry Whittington. LC 58-65842. 1958. Abelard-Schuman.
Trouble Rides Tall. Cover Painting by Frank McCarthy. William L Hopson. LC 55-42206. (Gold medal books, 501). 1955. Fawcett Publications.
Trouble Rides the Wind. Bertha Muzzy Sinclair. LC 35-9333. 1935. Little, Brown, and Company.
Trouble Shooter. Ernest Haycox. LC 37-1606. 1937. Doubleday, Doran & Company, Inc.
Trouble Shooter. Ernest Haycox. LC 38-6243. 1938. The Sun Dial Press, Inc.
Trouble Shooter. Ernest Haycox. LC 43-4981. 1943. The Sun Dial Press.
Trouble Shooter. large print ed. Ernest Haycox. LC 81-6218. 1981. 13.95 (ISBN 0-8161-3251-8). G.K. Hall.
Trouble Shooter. Ernest Haycox. (Signet brand western). 1975. (pbk.) 0.95. New American Library.
Trouble Town: By Burt Arthur. 1st Ed. Herbert Arthur, pseud. LC 50-5537. (Double D western). 1950. Doubleday.
Trouble Trail. Max Brand. LC 37-112363. 1937. Dodd, Mead & Company.
Trouble Trail. Fred East. 1946. E. P. Dutton & Company, Inc.
Trouble Trail. Frederick Faust. LC 37-1123. 1937. Dodd, Mead & Company.
Trouble Trailer. Wilbur C Tuttle. LC 46-3635. 1946. Houghton Mifflin Company.
Trouble Twisters. Poul Anderson. LC 66-174032. (Doubleday sci. fic.). 1966. 3.95. Doubleday.
Trouble Valley. Lee Hoffman. LC 75-38992. 1976. 0.95 (ISBN 0-345-24871-6). Ballantine Books.
Trouble Valley. Ward West, pseud. LC 35-27749. Greenberg.
Trouble with Being Born. E. M. Cioran. Ed. by Richard Howard. LC 75-33639. (Richard Seaver Book). 160p. 1976. 8.95 o.p. (ISBN 0-670-73262-1). Viking Pr.
Trouble with Eden. Jill Emerson. LC 72-95561. 1973. 7.95 (ISBN 0-399-11133-6). Putnam.
Trouble with Eden. Jill Emerson. (Berkley medallion book). 1974. (pbk.) 1.50 (ISBN 0-425-02517-9). Berkley Pub. Co.
Trouble with Fidelity. George Malcolm-Smith. LC 57-11315. 1957. Published for the Crime Club by Doubleday.
Trouble with Gumballs. James Nelson. 1956. 3.50 o.p. (76350). S&S.
Trouble with Gumballs: The Story of an Expensive Venture into Free Enterprise. James Carmer Nelson. LC 56-11185. 1956. Simon and Schuster.
Trouble with Harry. Jack Trevor Story. LC 50-9442. 1950. Macmillan.
Trouble with Harry. Jack Trevor Story. LC 49-29074. 1949. T. V. Boardman.
Trouble with Heaven. Leland Frederick Cooley. LC 66-12824. 1966. Doubleday.
Trouble with Heroes. Martin Dibner. LC 74-131071. 1971. 6.95. Doubleday.
Trouble with Lichen. John Beynon Harris. LC 74-86389. 1969. 4.95. Walker.
Trouble with Lichen. John Wyndham, pseud. 160p. 1982. pap. 2.25 (ISBN 0-345-30289-3, Del Rey). Ballantine.
Trouble with Lichen. John Wyndham, pseud. LC 74-86389. 1969. 4.95 o.p. Walker & Co.
Trouble with Murder. pseud. 1st ed. Paul Winterton. LC 48-7511. 1948. Harper.
Trouble with Paradise. Roy Chanslor. LC 54-663801. 1954. Crown Publishers.
Trouble with Series Three. Michael Kenyon. LC 67-21732. 1967. Morrow.
Trouble with Tigers. William Saroyan. LC 38-34537. Harcourt, Brace and Company.
Trouble with Tribbles. David Gerrold. pap. 2.25 (ISBN 0-345-27671-X). Ballantine.
Trouble with Tycho. Clifford D. Simak. pap. 2.50 (ISBN 0-441-82443-9, Pub. by Ace Science Fiction). Ace Bks.
Trouble with Tycoons. H. Baldwin Taylor. 1969. pap. 0.60 o.p. (0502-06029-060). Curtis.
Trouble with Tycoons: By H. Baldwin Taylor. 1st Ed. H. Baldwin Taylor. LC 67-14128. 1967. 3.95. Pub. for the Crime Club by Doubleday.
Trouble with You Earth People. Katherine MacClean. LC 79-15246. (Starblaze editions). 1979. 4.95 (ISBN 0-915442-95-7). Donning.
Trouble with You Earth People. Katherine Maclean. Ed. by Polly Freas & Kelly Freas. LC 79-15246. (Illus.). 1980. pap. 5.95 (ISBN 0-915442-95-7, Starblaze). Donning Co.
Trouble Woman. Clara Morris. LC 4-6734. (The Hour-glass stories, VII). 1904. Funk & Wagnalls Company.
Troublecross. Jessica Mann. LC 73-79952. 1973. 4.95. D. McKay Co.
Troubled Air. Irwin Shaw. LC 51-11045. 1951. Random House.
Troubled Border. 1st Ed. T. D. Allen, pseud. LC 54-6007. 1954. Harper.
Troubled Deaths. Roderic Jeffries. LC 78-4388. 1978. 7.95 (ISBN 0-312-81994-3). St. Martin's Press.
Troubled Empire. (Westward Rails Ser.: No. 4). (Orig.). 1982. pap. 2.95 (ISBN 0-440-08615-9, Bryans). Dell.
Troubled Grass: A Story of the Old Southwest. Lee Floren. LC 52-13333. 1952. Abelard Press.
Troubled Heart. Jean Z Owen. LC 55-11316. Muhlenberg Press.
Troubled Heritage. Jeanne Wilson. LC 76-50035. 8.95 (ISBN 0-87131-231-X). M. Evans.
Troubled Heritage. Jeanne Wilson. (Kangaroo Books). 1978. 1.95. Pocket Books.
Troubled House. Kage Booton. LC 57-12126. (Red badge detective). 1958. Dodd, Mead.
Troubled House. Kage Booton. 1974. (pbk.) 0.95. Dell.
Troubled Journey. Richard Lockridge. LC 73-82667. 1970. 4.95. J. B. Lippincott Co.
Troubled Midnight: A Novel. John Gunther. LC 45-1394. 1945. Harper & Brothers.
Troubled Midnight. 1st American Ed. Rodney Garland. LC 55-7779. 1955. Coward-McCann.
Troubled Range. John Thomas Edson. 160p. (Orig.). 1981. pap. 1.95 (ISBN 0-425-05071-8). Berkley Pub.
Troubled Range. 2nd ed. Paul Evan Lehman. 1974. pap. 0.95 (ISBN 0-532-95370-3). Woodhill.
Troubled Range. Paul Evan Lehman. 1973. pap. 0.75 o.p. (532-75491-075). Manor Bks.
Troubled Range. Edward Beverly Mann. LC 40-14427. 1940. W. Morrow and Company.
Troubled Sleep. Jean Paul Sartre. LC 72-3997. 1973. 11.95. Vintage Books.
Troubled Sleep. Tr. from French by Gerard Hopkins. Jean Paul Sartre. (Modern classic, NY 4015). 1968. Bantam.
Troubled Sleep. 1st American Ed. Translated from the French by Gerard Hopkins. Jean Paul Sartre. LC 50-58029. (His The roads to freedom, 8). 1951-1950. Knopt.
Troubled Spring. John Brick. LC 50-7264. 1950. Farrar, Straus.
Troubled Star. Bernard Augustine De Voto. LC 39-105224. 1939. Little, Brown and Company.
Troubled Star. Bernard Augustine De Voto. LC 39-10522. 1939. Little, Brown and Company.
Troubled Star. George Oliver Smith. LC 57-12683. 1957. Avalon Books.
Troubled Vision: An Anthology of Contemporary Short Novels and Passages. Ed. by Jerome Charyn. LC 72-109448. 1970. Collier Books.
Troubled Waters. Peter Health Fine. 192p. (Orig.). 1981. pap. 2.25 (ISBN 0-523-41213-4). Pinnacle Bks.
Troubled Waters. Elizabeth Lemarchand. LC 81-71195. (Illus.). 1982. 11.95 (ISBN 0-8027-5474-0). Walker.
Troubled Waters. Daniel Pratt Mannix. (Illus.). 1969. 6.95 o.p. (ISBN 0-525-22358-4). Dutton.
Troubled Waters. William MacLeod Raine. LC 25-171516. 1925. Doubleday, Page & Company.
Troubled Waters: A Novel. Roger Vercel & Wells, Warre Bradley, 1892- Tr. LC 40-27673. Randon House.
Troubled Waters. A Problem of to-Day. Beverley Ellison Warner. 1885. J. B. Lippincott Company.
Troublemaker. Birstein, Ann. LC 55-6193. 1955. Dodd, Mead.
Troublemaker. Joseph Hansen. LC 75-6368. 1975. 6.95 (ISBN 0-06-011758-3). Harper & Row.
Troublemaker. Robert McKay. 1972. pap. 1.50 (ISBN 0-440-99122-6, LFL). Dell.
Troublemaker. Jean Potts. LC 72-1197. 1972. 5.95 (ISBN 0-684-12975-2). Scribner.
Troublemaker: A Dave Brandstetter Mystery. Joseph Hansen. LC 81-4820. 1981. 3.50. Holt, Rinehart, and Winston.
Troubles. James Gordon Farrell. 1971. 6.95 o.p. (ISBN 0-394-47202-0). Knopf.

Troubles. Naomi May. 1979. 11.95 (ISBN 0-7145-3555-9); pap. 5.95 (ISBN 0-7145-3606-7). Riverrun NY.
Troubles: A Novel. Naomi May. LC 76-382647. 1976. 5.95 (ISBN 0-7145-3555-9). Calder.
Troubleshooter. Frank Anvic, pseud. 192p. (Orig.). 1973. pap. 1.95 o.p. (ISBN 0-87056-348-3, 6348). Brandon.
Troubleshooter. David Dodge. LC 79-122295. 1970. 6.95. Macmillan.
Troublesome Cowhand. Archie Joscelyn. LC 44-9901. 1944. Phoenix Press.
Troublesome Daughters. Lucy Bethia Colquhoun Walford. (On cover: Lovell's library. no. 1058). 1887. J. W. Lovell Company.
Troublesome Girl. Margaret Wolfe Hungerford & Errol, Josephine. LC 7-9052. (On cover: Lovell's international series, no. 23). 1889. F. F. Lovell and Company.
Troublesome Name. Catharine S Holmes. LC 7-6113. 1894. Cranston & Curts.
Troubling of a Star. Walt Sheldon. LC 52-10937. 1953. Lippincott.
Troupers: A Novel. Olive Harris Welch. LC 55-729179. 1955. Exposition Press.
Trousers of Taffeta: A Novel of the Child Mothers of India. Margaret Wilson. LC 29-21551. 1929. Harper & Brothers.
Trout Fishing in America. Richard Brautigan. Bd. with Pill Versus the Springhill Mine Disaster; In Watermelon Sugar. (Illus.). 156p. 1968. 14.95 o.s.i. (ISBN 0-440-07436-3, Sey Lawr). Delacorte.
Trout Fishing in America: A Novel. Richard Brautigan. LC 67-19577. (Writing 14). 1967. Four Seasons Foundation; Distributed by City Light Books.
Trout in the Milk. John Michael Evelyn. LC 72-80526. 1972. 5.95 (ISBN 0-8027-5258-6). Walker.
Trout in the Milk: A Sheriff Macready Detective Story. Hugh Holman. LC 45-4808. (On cover: Circle Mill mysteries). 1945. M. S. Mill Co., Inc.
Trout Inn Myster. Winifred Greenleaves. LC 29-20024. 1929. L. MacVeagh, The Dial Press.
Trout Madness. Robert Traver. 192p. Repr. of 1960 ed. 10.95 (ISBN 0-87905-067-5). Peregrine Smith.
Trout. Tr. from French by Peter Wiles. Roger Vailland. LC 65-19947. 1965. 4.50. Dutton.
Trovata. M. F Seymour. (On cover: Globe library, v. 1, no. 124). 1890. Rand McNally & Company.
Trove. Peter Smalley. LC 78-13654. 1978. 8.95 (ISBN 0-393-08835-9). Norton.
Troy and the Maypole. Winston David Armstrong Clewes. LC 50-7366. 1950. Knopf.
Troy Chimneys. Margaret Kennedy. 1972. pap. 0.95 o.p. (95212). Beagle Bks.
Troy Chinmeys. Margaret Kennedy. LC 52-9603. 1952. Rinehart.
Truant from Heaven. Mabel Hotchkiss Robbins. LC 12-3378. 1.00. R. G. Badger.
Truants: A Novel. Ron Carlson. LC 80-23781. 10.95 (ISBN 0-393-01383-9). Norton.
Truants: A Novel. Alfred Edward Woodley Mason. LC 4-268779. 1904. Harper & Brothers.
Truce. Mario Benedetti. LC 76-88642. 1969. 5.95. Harper & Row.
Truce: And Other Stories. Mary Tappan Wright. LC 9-1478. 1895. C. Scribner's Sons.
Truce for Love. Daisy H. Thomson. 1974. pap. 0.95 o.p. (ISBN 0-515-03517-3, N3517). BJ Pub Group.
Truce of God. Mary Roberts Rinehart. LC 20-219667. George H. Doran Company.
Truce of God: A Tale of the Eleventh Century. George Henry Miles. LC 7-18718. 1871. J. Murphy & Co.
Truce: Or, On and off Soundings. A Tale of the Coast of Maine. Joseph Holt Ingraham. 1847. Williams Brothers.
Truce with Life. Louise Platt Hauck. LC 36-30707. The Penn Publishing Company.
Truck. Katherine Dunn. 1974. (pbk.) 1.25. Avon.
Truck. Katherine Dunn. LC 78-144190. 1971. 6.95 (ISBN 0-06-011133-X). Harper & Row.
Truck (a Dance) Mary Ashley. 1972. pap. 5.00 (ISBN 0-930900-39-1). Burning Deck.
Truckful of Gold. S. Joshua L Zake. LC 79-92078. 16.95 (ISBN 0-89526-678-4). Regnery/Gateway.
Truckstop. Indiana Nelson. LC 79-16540. 1979. 9.95 (ISBN 0-312-82052-6). St. Martin's Press.
Trucos De Eva: La Ninta De G.O.C.E. new ed. Rod Gray. Tr. by Jairo Ibero. (Pimienta Collection Ser.). (Illus.). 160p. (Span.). 1975. pap. 1.25 (ISBN 0-88473-232-0). Fiesta Pub.
True Adventures of Huckleberry Finn. John D Seelye & Samuel Langhorne Clemens. LC 70-96907. 1970. (ISBN 0-8101-0290-0). Northwestern University Press.
True Adventures on Westward Trails: Illustrated by Lorence F. Bjorklund. 1st Ed. Alfred Powers. LC 54-8298. (True adventure library). 1954. Little, Brown.
True American: A Folk Fable. Melvin Van Peebles. LC 74-25128. 1976. 6.95 (ISBN 0-385-00598-9). Doubleday.
True: And Other Stories. George Parsons Lathrop. LC 7-13854. (On cover: Standard library. no. 128). 1884. Funk & Wagnalls.
True Aristocrat. Sarah Elizabeth Forbush G. S. Downs Downs. LC 6-45958. (select series. no. 44). 1890. Street & Smith.
True Aristocrat. A Novel. Sarah Elizabeth Forbush G. S. Downs Downs. (On cover: The Manhattan series. no. 10). 1889. A. L. Burt.
True As Steel. A Novel. Mary Virginia Terhune. LC 8-26065. 1872. G. W. Carleton & Co.
True As Steel. A Novel. Mary Virigina Terhune. LC 1358. (Madison square library, no. 3). 1900. G. W. Dillingham Co.
True Bearing. David Fairbank White. LC 80-19540. 9.95 (ISBN 0-8362-6113-5). Andrews and McMeel.
True Bills. George Ade. LC 4-29360. 1904. Harper & Brothers.
True by the Sun. Lida Larrimore Thomas. LC 34-354744. 1934. Macrae-Smith Company.
True Confections: A Novel. Sondra Gotlieb. LC 79-19441. 1980. 8.95 (ISBN 0-448-22369-4). Paddington Press.
True Confessions. John Gregory Dunne. 1981. pap. 3.50 (ISBN 0-671-42228-6). PB.
True Confessions: A Novel. John Gregory Dunne. LC 77-22126. 8.95 (ISBN 0-525-22365-7). Dutton.
True Confessions Anthology: Sixty Years of Sin, Suffering & Sorrow. Ed. by Florence Moriarity. 1979. 12.95 (ISBN 0-671-24957-6, Fireside); pap. 5.95 (ISBN 0-671-24745-X). S&S.
True Confessions, 1919-1979: Sixty Years of Sin, Suffering, & Sorrow: from the Pages of True Confessions, True Story, True Experience, True Romance, True Love, Secrets, Modern Romance. Florence Moriarty. LC 79-16605. (Fireside book). (Illus.). 10.00 (ISBN 0-671-24957-6) (ISBN 0-671-24745-X). Simon and Schuster.
True Cross, 1177-1192. Carlo Scarfoglio. LC 55-10285. (Illus.). 1956. Pantheon.
True Cross: 1177-1192: Translated by Frances Frenaye. Carlo Scarfoglio. LC 55-10285. 1956. Pantheon.
True Daughter of Hartenstein. A Novel. Tr. from the German of E. Vely, Pseud. Fran Emma Simon & Safford, Mary Joanna, Tr. (choice series, no. 62). 1892. R. Bonner's Sons.
True Deceivers. Hans Wilhelm Rosenhaupt. LC 54-11232. 1954. Dodd, Mead.
True Detective Stories. Maurice Moser. (On cover: Lovell's detective series, no. 6). J. W. Lovell Company.
True Detective Stories from the Archives of the Pinkertons. Cleveland Moffett. LC 12-369793. 1897. Doubleday & McClure Co.
True Detective Stories from the Archives of the Pinkertons. Cleveland Moffett. LC 16-6992. G. W. Dillingham Co.
True Floridians & Other Passing Attractions. Bob Morris. LC 81-84640. (pbk.) 5.95. Soggy Cracker Press.
True for Love's Sake. Dora Delmar. (On cover: Library of American authors. no. 70). 1897. G. Munro's Sons.
True Friend: A Novel. Adeline Sergeant. LC 8-68623. (On cover: Lovell's international series, no. 68). 1890. F. F. Lovell Company.
True Gold of Tennessee: A Romance of the English-Speaking World. Ernest Hugh Fitzpatrick. LC 22-18161. Clarke-McElroy Publishing Company.
True Grit: A Novel. Charles Portis. LC 68-14844. 1968. Simon and Schuster.
True Heart. Sylvia Townsend Warner. 1929. The Viking Press.
True Hearts & Purple Heads. Jim Klobuchar, pseud. pap. 2.95 (ISBN 0-87018-037-1). Ross.
True History of Astronaut Abbott. Brian Douglas Roiry. LC 67-15312. 1967. 5.50. Elizabethan Pr.
True History of Joshua Davidson. Elizabeth Lynn Linton. LC 75-1524. (Victorian Fiction: Novels of Faith and Doubt). 1975. 35.00 (ISBN 0-8240-1596-7). Garland Pub.
True History of Joshua Davidson: Communist. Elizabeth Lynn Linton. LC 7-16045. 1873. J. B. Lippincott & Co.
True Knight. Arthur D Hall & Downing, Robert L. LC 7-325. (On cover: Edgemore series, v.1. no. 1). 1892. Edgemore Publishing Co.
True Life of Sweeney Todd: A Collage Novel) Cozette De Charmoy. LC 77-1288. (Da Capo paperback). 1977. 5.95 (ISBN 0-306-80060-8). Da Capo Press.
True Life of Sweeney Todd: A Novel in Collage. Cozette De Charmoy. (Paperback Ser.). (Illus.). 1977. pap. 5.95 (ISBN 0-306-80060-8). Da Capo.
True Life Story of Jody McKeegan: A Novel. Don Carpenter. LC 74-15127. 1975. 7.95 (ISBN 0-525-22377-0). Dutton.
True Light. Joseph Calvitt Clarke. LC 35-23305. 1935. Arcadia House.
True Love. Herbert Gold. LC 82-72063. 1982. 14.50 (ISBN 0-87795-425-9). Arbor Hse.
True Love. Allan Noble Monkhouse. LC 20-13704. 1920. 1.75. H. Holt and Company.
True Love: A Comedy of the Affections. Edith Franklin Wyatt. LC 3-5532. 1903. McClure, Phillips & Co.
True Love and Its Consequences. James Edwards. 1881. Traynor's Publishing and Printing House.
True Love and Real Romance. Lynda Schor. LC 79-13135. 1979. 9.95 (ISBN 0-698-11004-8). Coward, McCann & Geoghegan.
True Love Is Forever: Filipina Rose. E. Ernest Bower. LC 73-83481. 1973. 5.98 (ISBN 0-8059-1897-3). Dorrance.
True Love Rewarded. A Tale. Azel Stevens Roe. LC 11-15084. 1877. G. W. Carleton & Co.; Etc., Etc.
True Love Story. Joseph Strano. 3.00 o.p. Carlton.
True Love, True Love. 1st Ed. Richard Gibson Hubler. LC 59-13738. 1959. Duell, Sloan and Pearce.
True Magdalen. Charlotte Mary Brame. (On cover: Lovell's library. v. 17. no. 806). J. W. Lovell Company.
True Marriage. A Novel. Emily Spender. (Franklin square library. no. 39). 1879. Harper & Brothers.
True Marriage. A Novel. Emily Spender. LC 8-15520. (Seaside library, v. 43, no. 888). 1880. G. Munro.
True Memoirs of Charley Blankenship: A Novel. Benjamin Capps. LC 79-39637. 1972. (ISBN 0-397-00760-4). Lippincott.
True or False? Miriam Borgenicht. LC 82-5657. 10.95 (ISBN 0-312-82055-0). St. Martin's Press.
True Patriot. Henry Fielding. LC 72-10055. (English Literature Ser., No. 33). 1972. Repr. of 1964 ed. lib. bdg. 66.95x (ISBN 0-8383-1597-6). Haskell.
True Riches. Adrian R Apple. LC 31-182726. A. R. Apple.
True Riches. Francois Coppee. LC 6-30860. 1893. D. Appleton and Company.
True Riches, and Other Tales. Timothy Shay Arthur. LC 44-15482. 1857. W. Bradley.
True Son of Liberty: Or, The Man Who Would Not Be a Patriot. Frank Purdy Williams. (On cover: The Waldorf series, no. 7). Saalfield & Fitch.
True Spirit Stories. Ed. by S. Robb. pap. 0.75 o.p. (T1974). Pyramid Pubns.
True Stories. Margaret Eleanor Atwood. 1982. 13.50 (ISBN 0-671-45271-1); pap. 4.95 (ISBN 0-671-45971-6). S&S.
True Stories of American Wars: From Old Records and Family Traditions ... D. Lothrop Company.
True Stories of Ashtabula. Ed. by Mary Stevenson. 1971. price not set o.p. (ISBN 0-912462-05-1). Foun Hist Rest.
True Stories of 1941- True Story Magazine & Ballou, Robert Oleson, 1892- Ed. LC 42-23429. Bartholomew House, Inc.
True Story. Stephen Hudson. LC 30-93077. 1930. A. A. Knopf.
True Story. Sydney Schiff. LC 65-8311. 1965. J. M. Dent.
True Story: By Stephen Hudson Pseud. Sydney Schiff. bds., 6.95. Dutton.
True Story Classics... True Story Magazine & Macfadden Publications, Inc., Pub. LC 29-20444. 1929. Macfadden Publications, Inc.
True Story of a Drunken Mother. Nancy Lee Hall. LC 74-79918. 1974. 3.00 (ISBN 0-913780-05-7). Daughters, Inc.
True Story of a Mud Marine. Richard W. Watkins. 4.50 o.p. Vantage.
True Story of Ah Q. 1969. pap. 2.25 (ISBN 0-8351-0408-7). China Bks.
True Story of an English Woman: With Five Different Occupations. T. J Deakin. 1889. Scholl Brothers' Electric Printing House.
True Story of Ida Johnson. Sharon Riis. LC 77-370713. Women's Press.
True Story of Master Gerard. Anna Theresa Sadlier. LC 404. 1900. Benziger Brothers.
True Story of the Lost Shackle: Or, Seven Years with the Indians. Owen P Dabney. LC 6-32228. Capital Printing Co.
True Tales of the South Seas: Selected, Ed. by A. Grove Day, Carl Stroven. 1st Ed. Ed. by Arthur Grove Day. LC 66-19999. 1966. 5.95. Appleton.
True Tales of Three Steers: Mentoro, Bravando, and Imppo, with Beauvena Heiffer and Beau Bumly. John Cornelius Sherbno. LC 76-169245. 1972. 4.75 (ISBN 0-8022-2062-2). Philosophical Library.
True Tall Tales of Stormalong: Sailor of the Seven Seas. Harold W. Felton. LC 68-22880. (Illus.). 1968. 4.95. Prentice-Hall.
True Tilda. Arthur Thomas Quiller-Couch. 1909. C. Scribner's Sons.
True Tiny Tales of Terror. Ann Hodgman. (Illus.). 1982. 4.95 (ISBN 0-399-50631-4, Perige). Putnam Pub Group.
True to Her Oath. A Tale of Love and Misfortune. Pedro Antonio De Alarcon & Montblanc, Ramiro, Tr. LC 99-2060. J. S. Ogilvie Publishing Company.
True to Herself. A Novel. Jeannette Ritchie Hadermann Walworth. (On cover: Manhattan series, no. 5). A. L. Burt.
True to Herself. A Novel. Jeannette Ritchie Hadermann Walworth. (select series, no. 52). 1890. Street & Smith.
True to Him Ever: A Novel. Fannie W Rankin. LC 26-235612. 1874. T. W. Carleton & Co.
True to the End: A Story of the Swiss Reformation. Henry Sweetser Burrage. LC 6-16390. American Baptist Publication Society.
True to the Last: Or, Alone on a Wide Wide Sea. Azel Stevens Roe. LC 7-402193. 1858. Derby & Jackson.
True to Themselves: A Psychological Study. Alexander Johnston Chalmers Skene. (On cover: Neely's library of choice literature, no. 72). 1897. F. T. Neely.
True Womanhood: A Tale. John Neal. LC 7-23107. 1859. Ticknor and Fields.
Truegate of Mogador. facs. ed. Sewell Ford. LC 76-142261. (Short Story Index Reprint Ser). 1906. 18.00 (ISBN 0-8369-3745-7). Ayer Co.
Truegate of Mogador: And Other Cedarton Folks. Sewell Ford. LC 76-142261. (Short story index reprint series). (Illus.). 1970. (ISBN 0-8369-3745-7). Books for Libraries Press.
Truegate of Mogador: And Other Cedarton Folks. Sewell Ford. LC 7-35042. 1906. C. Scribner's Sons.
Trueheart Margery. Norma Bright Carson. LC 17-296230. 1.35. George H. Doran Company.
Trufflers: A Story. Samuel Merwin. LC 16-21399. The Bobbs-Merrill Company.
Truimph of Count Ostermann. Jessie Hope. LC 3-68663. 1903. H. Holt and Company.
Trullion: Alastor Two Thousand, Two Hundred & Sixty-Two. Jack Vance, pseud. 1981. pap. 2.25 (ISBN 0-87997-590-3, UE1590). Daw Bks.
Trullion: Alastor 2262. Jack Vance. 1973. (pbk) 1.25. Ballantine.
Truly Married Woman: And Other Stories. Illus. by J. H. Vandi. Abioseh Nicol. LC 66-573. (Three crowns bk.). pap., 1.05. Oxford.
Truly Married Woman, and Other Stories. Abioseh Nicol. LC 66-573. (Three crowns book). 1965. Oxford University Press.
Trumbull Park, a Novel. Frank London Brown. LC 59-8460. 1959. Regnery.
Trumpet and the Rose. George Charles Appell. LC 60-12169. 1960. Macmillan.
Trumpet at the Gates. Jeanne Anna Ayres Widgery. LC 77-107463. 1970. 6.95. Doubleday.
Trumpet for a Walled City. Dolores Pala. LC 73-19542. 1974. 7.95 (ISBN 0-06-013263-9). Harper & Row.
Trumpet for a Walled City. Dolores Pala. 1979. 1.75 (ISBN 0-449-23913-6). Fawcett Crest.
Trumpet in the City. Helen Topping Miller. LC 48-8290. 1948. Bobbs-Merrill Co.
Trumpet in the Dust. Gene Fowler, pseud. LC 46-22496. 1946. The Sun Dial Press.
Trumpet in the Dust. Constance Holme. LC 38-3954. 1936. Oxford University Press.
Trumpet in the Dust: A Newspaper Story. Gene Fowler, pseud. LC 44-5941. New Avon Library.
Trumpet in the Wilderness. Robert S Harper. LC 40-33105. M. S. Mill Co., Inc.
Trumpet in Zion see Lost City.
Trumpet-Major. Thomas Hardy. (Seaside library, v. 43, no. 890). 1880. G. Munro.
Trumpet-Major. Thomas Hardy. (On cover: Seaside library. Pocket ed., no. 945). 1887. G. Munro.
Trumpet-Major. Thomas Hardy. (Lovell's library, no. 1354). 1889. J. W. Lovell Company.
Trumpet-Major; a Novel. Thomas Hardy. LC 24-28514. (Leisure hour series. no. 118). 1880. H. Holt and Company.
Trumpet Major & Robert His Brother. Thomas Hardy. (Pap ed. 2.25 o.p.). 1880. 10.95 o.p. (ISBN 0-312-82145-X, Papermac). St Martin.
Trumpet-Major & Robert His Brother. Thomas Hardy. (gr. 10-12). 1936. text ed. 1.60 o.p. (T78800). St Martin.
Trumpet-Major: John Loveday, a Soldier in the War with Buonaparte and Robert His Brother, First Mate in the Merchant Service, a Tale. Thomas Hardy. (Papermac P61). 1966. 2.50, 1.50 pap., lib. ed.,. St Martin's.
Trumpet-Major, John Loveday: A Soldier in the War with Buonaparte, and Robert His Brother, First Mate in the Merchant Service. Thomas Hardy. LC 16-9381. 1895. Harper & Brothers.
Trumpet-Major: John Loveday, a Soldier in the War with Buonaparte, and Robert His Brother, First Mate in the Merchant Service. Thomas Hardy. LC 1-21254. 1896. Harper & Brothers.

Trumpet-Major: John Loveday, a Soldier in the War with Buonaparte, and Robert His Brother, First Mate in the Merchant Service: a Tale. Thomas Hardy. LC 80-24489. (Hardy, Thomas, 1840-1928. The New Wessex Edition). 1981. 2.95. St. Martin's Press.
Trumpet of God. 1st Ed. David Duncan. LC 56-8094. 1956. Doubleday.
Trumpet of Jubilee: A Novel. Ludwig Lewisohn. LC 37-5562. 1937. Harper & Brothers.
Trumpet Shall Sound. Henry Major Tomlinson. LC 57-6459. 1957. Random House.
Trumpet to Arms. Bruce Lancaster. LC 76-40933. 1976. 6.95 (ISBN 0-88411-681-6). Aeonian Press.
Trumpet to Arms. Bruce Lancaster. LC 44-5271. 1944. Little, Brown and Company.
Trumpet to the World. Mark Harris. LC 46-3135. 1946. Reynal & Hitchcock.
Trumpet Unblown. 1st Ed. William Hoffman. LC 55-11601. 1955. Doubleday.
Trumpeter Fred: A Story of the Plains. Charles King. LC 7-12220. (Neely's prismatic library). 1896. F. T. Neely.
Trumpeter of Krakow. new ed. Eric Philbrook Kelly. LC 66-16712. 1966. Macmillan.
Trumpeter of Krakow. Eric Philbrook Kelly. LC 66-16712. (Collier Books). 1973. (pbk.) 0.95. MacMillan.
Trumpeter of Krakow: A Tale of the Fifteenth Century. Eric Philbrook Kelly. LC 28-217396. 1928. The Macmillan Company.
Trumpeter, Sound! David Leslie Murray. LC 34-7141. 1934. A. A. Knopf.
Trumpeter Swan. Temple Bailey. LC 28-1644. Grosset & Dunlap.
Trumpeter Swan. Temple Bailey. LC 20-17175. 1920. The Penn Publishing Company.
Trumpets at Dawn. Cyril Harris. LC 38-27729. 1938. C. Scribner's Sons.
Trumpets Calling. Dora Aydelotte. LC 38-27000. 1938. D. Appleton-Century Company, Incorporated.
Trumpets in the Dawn. Charles N. Heckelmann. 320p. 1982. pap. 2.95 (ISBN 0-445-04045-9). Popular Lib.
Trumpets in the Dawn. 1st Ed. Charles N Heckelmann. LC 58-132819. 1958. Doubleday.
Trumpets in the Morning. Lon Riley Woodrum. LC 61-728. 1960. Zondervan Pub. House.
Trumpets of Company K. William Chamberlain. LC 54-7561. 1954. Ballantine Books.
Trumpets of Dawn. Ruby I. Kingswood. 5.95 o.p. Vantage.
Trumpets of November. Wesley S Thurston. LC 66-23601. 1967. B. Geis Associates; Distributed by Random House.
Trumpets of November: By Wesley S. Thurston. Wesley S Thurston. (Signet bk., Q-3302). 1967. New Amer. Lib.
Trumpets Sound No More. Francis Van Wyck Mason. LC 75-12702. (Illus.). 1975. (ISBN 0-316-54931-2). Little, Brown.
Trumpets West. Elmer Theodore Peterson. LC 34-7925. Sears Publishing Company.
Trumps: A Collection of Short Stories. The Community Workers of the New York Guild for the Jewish Blind, Comp & Ade, George. LC 26-18099. 1926. G. P. Putnam's Sons.
Trumps. A Novel. George William Curtis. LC 16-9386. Harper & Brothers.
Trunk. Elizabeth Jane Coatsworth. LC 41-51623. 1941. The Macmillan Company.
Trunk-Call Mystery. Joseph Jefferson Farjeon. LC 32-220320. 1932. L. MacVeagh, Dial Press, Inc.
Trusia, a Princess of Krovitch. Davis Brinton. LC 6-35622. 1906. G.W. Jacobs and Company.
Truss, Seldon. A Mystery Story. LC 29-1679. 1929. Coward-McCann, Inc.
Trust. Cynthia Ozick. (Kangaroo Book.). 1977. 2.50 (ISBN 0-671-81084-7). Pocket Books.
Trust: A Novel. Cynthia Ozick. LC 66-172586. 7.95. New Amer. Lib.
Trust a Woman? Elinore Denniston. LC 72-9932. (Red badge novel of suspense). 1973. 4.95 (ISBN 0-396-06759-X). Dodd, Mead.
Trust a Woman? Rae Foley. LC 72-9932. 184p. 1973. 4.95 o.p. (ISBN 0-396-06759-X). Dodd.
Trust a Woman? Rae Foley. 1974. (pbk.) 0.95. Dell.
Trust an Englishman. John Knowler. LC 72-93147. 1973. 5.95 o.p. (ISBN 0-15-191317-X). HarBraceJ.
Trust in Chariots. Thomas Savage. LC 61-12442. 1961. Random House.
Trust Me. A Novel. Lilian Headland Spender. (Harper's Franklin square library. no. 523). 1886. Harper & Brothers.
Trust Me with Your Heart Again. Norton Stillman. (O.s.i.). 1973. pap. 3.95 o.s.i. (ISBN 0-671-21667-8, Fireside). S&S.
Trust No One at All. Amanda McAllister. LC 76-24250. (Amanda McAllister Ser.: No. 4). 1976. pap. 1.50 o.p. (ISBN 0-87216-352-0). Playboy.
Trust Not a Dream. Rob Eden. LC 48-3913. 1948. Gramercy Pub. Co.
Trust the Saint. Leslie Charteris. 1966. pap. 0.60 o.p. (60-253). Manor Bks.
Trust the Saint: Stories. 1st Ed. Leslie Charteris. LC 62-158660. (His The Saint series). 1962. Published for the Crime Club by Doubleday.
Trust Wesley! Bernard Louis Jacot De Boinod. LC 29-16826. 1929. Little, Brown, and Company.
Trust Your Trigger: By Otto Vloto Pseud. Forbes Parkhill. LC 56-11703. 1956. Arcadia House.
Trusted Like the Fox. Sara Woods, pseud. LC 64-25135. 1965. Harper & Row.
Trusted Outlaw. Johnston McCulley. LC 35-304327. 1934. G. H. Watt.
Trustee from the Toolroom. Nevil Shute Norway. LC 76-18891. 1976. 7.50 (ISBN 0-89244-016-3). Queens House.
Trustee from the Toolroom. Nevil Shute Norway. LC 60-9545. 1960. Morrow.
Trustee from the Toolroom. Nevil Shute. 311p. 1976. Repr. of 1960 ed. lib. bdg. 17.95x (ISBN 0-89244-016-3). Queens Hse.
Trustee from the Toolroom: By Nevil Shute Pseud. Nevil Shute Norway. (U5121). 1967. Ballantine.
Trusting & the Maimed. James Plunkett. 6.50 (ISBN 0-8159-6909-0). Devin.
Trusting and the Maimed: And Other Irish Stories. Wood Engravings by John De Pol. James Plunkett. LC 55-77418. 1955. Devin-Adair Co.
Trusty Five-Fifteen. George Frank Lydston. LC 22-654. 1921. Burton Publishing Company.
Trusty Knaves. new ed. Eugene Manlove Rhodes. LC 76-160503. (Western frontier library, v. 49). (Illus.). 1971. (ISBN 0-8061-0975-0). University of Oklahoma Press.
Trusty Knaves. Eugene Manlove Rhodes. LC 33-31756. 1933. Houghton Mifflin Company.
Trusty Servant. Gerturde Violet McFadden. 1920. John Lane.
Truth, a Novel. Louis De Villeneuve. LC 3-32704. 1894. The Author.
Truth About Camilla. Gertrude Hall Brownell. LC 13-22277. 1913. The Century Co.
Truth About Claire Veryan. 1st Ed. Seldon Truss, pseud. LC 57-9514. 1957. Published for the Crime Club by Doubleday.
Truth About Dragons: an Anti-Romance. Hazard Adams. LC 70-134569. 1971. 6.50 (ISBN 0-15-191320-X). Harcourt Brace Jovanovich.
Truth About Dragons: An Anti Romance. Hazard Adams. LC 70-134569. 179p. 1971. 6.50 (ISBN 0-15-191320-X). HarBraceJ.
Truth About It: And Other Sketches. Eloise Matilda Daniel. LC 6-33166. 1897. Dispatch Job Printing Company.
Truth About John Steinbeck and the Migrants. Goerge Thomas Miron. LC 40-886243. Haynes Corporation.
Truth About Lovers. Margaret Widdemer. LC 31-17275. Farrar & Rinehart, Incorporated.
Truth About Peter Harley. James Mills. LC 79-16640. 10.95 (ISBN 0-525-22393-2). Dutton.
Truth About the Cannonball Kid. Lee Hoffman. 1975. (pbk.) 0.95. Dell.
Truth About the Case: The Experiences of M. F. Goron, Ex-Chief of the Paris Detective Police. Marie Francois Goron. Ed. by Keyzer, Albert. LC 7-17362. 1907. J. B. Lippincott Company.
Truth About Them. Jose Yglesias. LC 79-159588. 1971. 7.95. World Pub.
Truth About Tolna. Bertha Runkle. LC 6-4241. 1906. The Century Co.
Truth About Tristem Varick: A Novel. Edgar Evertson Saltus. LC 74-95394. 1969. AMS Press.
Truth About Tristrem Varick: A Novel. Edgar Evertson Saltus. LC 8-5794. Belford, Clarke & Co.
Truth About Unicorns. Bonnie Jones Reynolds. LC 72-81211. 1972. 7.95 (ISBN 0-8128-1509-2). Stein and Day.
Truth About Vignolles. Albert Kinross. LC 22-919512. 1922. The Century Co.
Truth and a Woman. Anna Robeson Brown Burr. LC 3-135929. 1903. H.S. Stone & Company.
Truth and Consequence. Mary Slattery Stolz. LC 53-7746. 1953. Harper.
Truth and Fancy: Tales Legendary, Historic, and Descriptive. Mary Jane Windle. LC 8-37778. 1850. C. Sherman, Printer.
Truth Came Out. Ernest Robertson Punshon. 1934. Houghton Mifflin Company.
Truth Comes Limping. Alfred Walter Stewart. LC 38-8558. 1938. Little, Brown and Company.
Truth Dexter. illustrated ed. Mary Fenollosa. 1906. Little, Brown, and Company.
Truth Dexter: A Novel. Mary Fenollosa. LC 1-311982. 1901. Little, Brown, and Company.
Truth Game. Anne Betteridge, pseud. 1973. pap. 0.75 o.p. (ISBN 0-345-20729-7). Beagle Bks.
Truth Game. Douglas Hurd. LC 72-78183. 1972. 5.95. St. Martin's Press.
Truth in Romances. A German Story. Henry Allen Tupper. LC 8-32685. 1887. H.M. Wharton and Company.
Truth in the Night. Michael McLaverty. LC 51-12038.
Truth Is for Strangers: A Novel About a Soviet Poet. Efraim Sevela. LC 75-36580. 1976. 6.95 (ISBN 0-385-01704-9). Doubleday.
Truth Is Not Sober. Winifred Holtby. LC 77-121564. (Short story index reprint series). 1970. Books for Libraries Press.
Truth Is Not Sober. Winifred Holtby. LC 34-37447. 1934. The Macmillan Company.
Truth Is Stranger Than Fiction. Jennie W. Gould. LC 6-27642. 1891. W. Lansing & Son.
Truth Is Stranger Than Fishin'. Beatrice Gray Cook. 1955. Morrow.
Truth Lover. John Herdman. LC 73-177871. 1973. 1.30 (ISBN 0-900036-58-3). Akros Publications.
Truth Machine. Christopher Cerf & Sharon Lerner. LC 77-70857. 1977. 2.95. (ISBN 0-394-93575-6). Random House.
Truth or Dare. Jacqueline Wilson. LC 73-81125. 1974. 5.95 (ISBN 0-385-07895-1). Doubleday.
Truth: Or, Scenes from Real Life. Ed. by H. Waren. LC 9-943. (Added t.-p., Scenes and characters illustrating Christian truth ed. by H. Waren no. iv). 1835. J. Munroe and Company.
Truth-Tellers: A Novel. Henrietta Eliza Vaughan Stannard. LC 8-27031. (On cover: Lippincott's select novels. no. 183). J. B. Lippincott Company,
Truth That Makes Men Free; a Novel. 1st Ed. Thomas Playfair Ward. LC 55-11983. 1955. Pageant Press.
Truth to Tell. Alice Grant Rosman. LC 37-274512. G. P. Putnam's Sons.
Truth Verite. Emile Zola. 1903. J. Lane.
Truthful Jane. Florence Morse Kingsley. LC 7-5685. 1907. D. Appleton and Company.
Truxton Cipher. Henry Gruppe. LC 73-8027. (Simon and Schuster novel of suspense). 1973. 6.95 (ISBN 0-671-21573-6). Simon and Schuster.
Truxton King: A Story of Graustark. George Barr McCutcheon. LC 9-24451. 1909. Dodd, Mead & Company.
Truxton King: A Story of Graustark. George Barr McCutcheon. LC 16-6825. 1911. Dodd, Mead & Company.
Try and Hold Me. Norma Patterson. LC 37-2320. Farrar & Rinehart, Inc.
Try Another Country: Three Short Novels. Barbara Rees. LC 69-14849. 1969. Harcourt, Brace & World.
Try Another World: A Saga Coursing Its Way Through the Six Adventures of Joe Shaun Which Thrilled the Village of Caryldale. John Joseph Meyer. LC 42-20656. 1942. The Business Bourse.
Try Anything Twice. Peter Cheyney. LC 48-776010. (Red badge detective). 1948. Dodd, Mead.
Try Me Again. Rex Weldon, pseud. (Orig.). pap. 0.95 o.p. (1124). Brandon.
Try the Sky. Francis Stuart. LC 33-15008. 1933. The Macmillan Company.
Try to Forget Me. Virginia Nielsen, pseud. LC 42-7342. 1942. Doubleday, Doran and Company, Inc.
Tryant, Elizabeth Bonham De La Pasture. 1910. E.P. Dutton & Company.
Trying It on the Dog. Maurice Switzer. The Bobbs-Merrill Company.
Trying Out Torchy. Sewell Ford. LC 12-21398. 1.25. E. J. Clode.
Tryout. George Abbott. LC 79-15083. 9.95 (ISBN 0-87223-527-0). Playboy Press: Trade Distribution by Simon and Schuster.
Tryphena. Eden Phillpotts. LC 29-15571. 1929. The Macmillan Company.
Tryphena in Love. Walter Raymond. LC 4-15330. (On cover: Iris series). 1895. Macmillan and Co.
Tryphena's Summer. William Owen. LC 75-312104. 326p. 1975. 10.00x (ISBN 0-8002-0486-7). Intl Pubns Serv.
Tryst. Grace Livingston Hill. LC 21-9593. 1921. J. B. Lippincott Company.
Tryst. Grace Livingston Hill. 1975. (pbk.) 0.95. Bantam.
Tryst. Elswyth Thane. LC 74-4544. 1974. 6.95. Aeonian Press.
Tryst. Elswyth Thane. LC 48-6868. 1948. Duell, Sloan & Preach.
Tryst with Terror. Wilma Winthrop. 1972. pap. 0.95 o.s.i. (75-389). Lancer.
Tryst with the Stars. Kathleen Rollins. LC 38-7782. Arcadia House.
Trysting Tower. Catherine Ross, pseud. LC 66-76447. 1966. Joseph.
Tsaddick of the Seven Wonders. Isidore Haiblum. LC 81-65663. (Science Fiction Ser.). 192p. 1981. 10.95 (ISBN 0-385-17137-4). Doubleday.
Tsaddik of the Seven Wonders. Isidore Haiblum. LC 81-65663. (Doubleday Science Fiction). 1981. 10.95. Doubleday.
Tsali. Denton R Bedford. LC 72-91136. (Illus.). 1972. Indian Historian Press.
Tsantsa. Isabel Lhevinne. LC 32-23879. Brentano's.
Tsar's Window. Lucy Hamilton Jones Hooper. LC 74-164566. (American fiction reprint series). (No name series). 1971. (ISBN 0-8369-7043-8). Books for Libraries Press.
Tsar's Window... Lucy Hamilton Jones Hooper. LC 7-5262. (On cover: No name series). 1881. Roberts Brothers.
Tschiffely's Ride. A. Tschiffely. 1976. lib. bdg. 34.95 (ISBN 0-8490-2777-2). Gordon Pr.
Tselane. Jacqueline Louw Van Wijk. LC 60-53312. 1961. Houghton Mifflin.
Tsimmis in Tangier. Mallory T. Knight. (Man from T.O.M.C.A.T. Ser.). 160p. pap. 0.60 o.p. (A328X, Award). Univ Pub & Dist.
Tsing-Boom! Nicolas Freeling. LC 69-17290. 1969. 4.95. Harper & Row.
T.S.K.H. Tickle, Snug, Kiss, Hug. Elizabeth May. LC 77-70643. 1977. 10.00 o.p. (ISBN 0-8091-0226-9); pap. 6.95 (ISBN 0-8091-2022-4). Paulist Pr.
Tsolo. Mary Lake. LC 46-818830. 1946. The Hobson Book Press.
Tsotsi: A Novel. Athol Fugard. LC 80-5416. 8.95 (ISBN 0-394-51384-3). Random House.
Tsuga's Children. Thomas Williams. LC 76-53466. (Illus.). 7.95 (ISBN 0-394-49731-7). Random House.
Tsurezure Gusa see Miscellany of a Japanese Priest.
Tsushima: Grave of a Floating City. hyperion reprint ed. Novikov-Priboi, Aleksei Silych. LC 75-39005. (Early Soviet literature in English translation). (Illus.). 1978. 23.50 (ISBN 0-88355-408-9). Hyperion Press.
TThevizier's Elephant: Three Novellas. Translated from the Serbo-Croat by Drenka Willen. 1st Ed. Ivo Andric. LC 62-19586. 1962. Harcourt, Brace & World.
Tu Tze-Chun. Ryunosuke Akutagawa. Tr. by Dorothy Britton. LC 65-12283. (Illus.). 64p. 1965. 10.50 (ISBN 0-87011-013-6). Kodansha.
Tu-Tze's Tower: A Novel. Louise Betts Edwards. LC 3-11492. 1903. H. T. Coates & Co.
Tubal Cain. Joseph Hergesheimer. LC 22-15854. 1922. A. A. Knopf.
Tubie's Monument. 1st ed. Peter Keveson. LC 56-7638. 1956. Dutton.
Tuckahoe: A Collection of Indian Stories and Legends. Frances Elizabeth Scott Bagby. LC 7-18592. Broadway Publishing Co.
Tuckahoe: An Old-Fashioned Story of an Old-Fashioned People. Joseph William Eggleston. LC 3-245331. 1903. The Neale Publishing Company.
Tucker. Louis L'Amour. 192p. (Orig.). 1981. pap. text ed. 2.25 (ISBN 0-553-20393-2). Bantam.
Tucker. Louis L'Amour. 1978. pap. 1.95 (ISBN 0-553-14092-2). Bantam.
Tucker's People. Ira Wolfert. LC 43-6908. 1943. L. B. Fischer.
Tuckers Tune in. Hilda Morris. LC 43-9414. 1943. G. P. Putnam's Sons.
Tudor Agent. Robert Farrington. LC 73-89278. 1974. 6.95. St. Martin's Press.
Tudor Green. William Babington Maxwell. LC 36-6897. 1936. D. Appleton-Century Company, Incorporated.
Tudor Rose. Margaret Campbell Barnes. LC 53-7889. 1953. Macrae Smith.
Tudor Sunset. Josephine Mary Hope-Scott W. P. Ward Ward. LC 32-23878. 1932. Longmans, Green and Co.
Tudor Underground. Denis Meadows. LC 50-13666. 1950. Devin-Adair.
Tudor Wench. Elswyth Thane. Repr. lib. bdg. 19.95x (ISBN 0-88411-972-6). Amereon Ltd.
Tuen, Slave and Empress. Kathleen Gray Nelson. 1898. E. P. Dutton & Company.
Tuesday Blade: A Novel. Bob Ottum. LC 76-23439. 1977. 7.95 (ISBN 0-671-22400-X). Simon and Shuster.
Tuesday Blade: A Novel. Bob Ottum. 1978. 2.50 (ISBN 0-446-81362-1). Warner Books.
Tuesday Club Murders. Agatha Miller Christie. 1933. Dodd, Mead and Company.
Tuesday Club Murders. Dame Agatha Miller Christie. 1975. (pbk.) 1.25. Dell.
Tuesday Club Murders. 192p. 1982. pap. 2.95 (ISBN 0-440-19136-X). Dell.
Tuesday Never Comes. Lida Larrimore Thomas. LC 38-95. 1937. Macrae-Smith Company.
Tuesday the Rabbi Saw Red. Harry Kemelman. LC 73-78968. 1974. 6.95 (ISBN 0-525-63007-4). A. Fields Books.
Tuesday the Rabbi Saw Red. Harry Kemelman. LC 74-10502. 1974. (lib. bdg.) 11.95 (ISBN 0-8161-6230-1). G. K. Hall.
Tuesday to Bed. Francis Sill Wickware. LC 48-11051. 1948. Bobbs-Merrill Co.
Tuesday, Wednesday, Thursday. Dudley Carew. LC 27-7723. 1927. Frank-Maurice, Inc.
Tuesdays and Thursdays. Abby Mann. LC 76-2809. 1978. 8.95 (ISBN 0-385-08764-0). Doubleday.
Tuesdays and Thursdays. Abby Mann. 1979. 2.50 (ISBN 0-671-82506-2). Pocket Books.
Tuesday's Child. Hettie Grimstead. (Fawcett Gold Medal Book). 1975. (pbk.) 0.95. Fawcett.
Tug of the Millstone. Clarence E Hatfield. LC 15-181030. 1.25. R. G. Badger; Etc., Etc.

Tug of War. Sue Peters. (Harlequin Romances Ser.). 192p. 1981. pap. 1.25 (ISBN 0-373-02423-1). Harlequin Bks.

Tug of War. Joe Richards. LC 78-26470. 10.00 (ISBN 0-679-51351-5). McKay.

Tugboat Annie. Norman Reilly Raine. LC 34-5170. Minton, Balch & Company.

Tugboat Annie, Great Stories from the Saturday Evening Post. Norman Reilly Raine. LC 77-78985. 320p. 1977. 5.95 (ISBN 0-89387-010-2, Co-Pub. by Sat Eve Post). Curtis Pub Co.

Tugman's Passage. Edward Hoagland. 224p. 1983. pap. 5.95 (ISBN 0-14-006685-3). Penguin.

Tüileries. A Tale. Catherine Grace Frances Moody Gore. LC 6-27510. 1831. J. & J. Harper.

Tularemia Gambit. Steve Perry. 224p. (Orig.). 1981. pap. 2.25 (ISBN 0-449-14411-9, GM). Fawcett.

Tule Lake. Edward T. Miyakawa. Ed. by Carol S. Van Strum. (Orig.). 1979. 12.95; pap. 7.95. Hse by the Sea.

Tule Marsh Murder. Nancy Barr Mavity. LC 29-2736. 1929. Pub. for the Crime Club, Inc., by Doubleday, Doran & Company, Inc.

Tule Marsh Murder. Nancy Barr Mavity. LC 31-239. 1930. Grosset & Dunlap.

Tulip Place: A Story of New York. Virginia Wales Johnson. LC 7-10792. (Harper's handy series, no. 65). 1886. Harper & Brothers.

Tulip Tree. Mary Ann Gibbs. 1979. pap. 1.75 (ISBN 0-449-50000-4, Coventry). Fawcett.

Tulip Tree. Howard Rigsby. 1970. pap. 0.75 o.p. (64-373). Paperback Lib.

Tullus and the Ransom Gold. LC 74-75544. (Illus.). 1974. (pbk.) 1.25 (ISBN 0-912692-33-2). David C. Cook Pub. Co.

Tullus and the Vandals of the North. LC 74-81664. (Illus.). 1974. (pbk.) 1.25 (ISBN 0-912692-44-8). David C. Cook Pub. Co.

Tullus in the Deadly Whirlpool. LC 74-75546. (Illus.). 1974. (pbk.) 1.25 (ISBN 0-912692-34-0). David C. Cook Pub. Co.

Tulpa. J. N. Williamson. 1980. pap. 1.95 (ISBN 0-8439-0799-1). Nordon Pubns.

Tumbleberry and Chick. William John Hopkins. LC 25-4214. 1925. Houghton Mifflin Company.

Tumbled Wall. Dixie Browning. 192p. (Orig.). 1980. pap. 1.50 (ISBN 0-671-57038-2). S&S.

Tumbledown Farm. Alan Muir. (On cover: Seaside library. Pocket ed. no. 346). 1885. G. Munro.

Tumblefold. Joseph Whittaker. LC 19-5141. 1919. E. P. Dutton & Company.

Tumbleweed. Alice Marguerite Colter. LC 16-18908. 1.25. The Bobbs-Merrill Company.

Tumbleweed. Janwillem Van De Wetering. 1976. 6.95 (ISBN 0-395-24352-1). HM.

Tumbleweed. Janwillem Van de Wetering. 1981. pap. 2.50 (ISBN 0-671-43526-4). PB.

Tumbleweed: A Novel. Janwillem Van De Wetering. LC 76-1865. 1976. 6.95 (ISBN 0-395-24352-1). Houghton Mifflin.

Tumbleweed: A Novel. Janwillem Van De Wetering. (Kangaroo Book). 1977. 1.95 (ISBN 0-671-81339-0). Pocket Books.

Tumbleweed Drifter. V N White. LC 51-12930. 1951. Phoenix Press.

Tumbleweed Trail. George Brydges Rodney. LC 41-23066. Phoenix Press.

Tumbleweeds. Hal George Evarts. LC 23-12010. 1923. Little, Brown, and Company.

Tumbleweeds. Marta Roberts. LC 40-135549. G. P. Putnam's Sons.

Tumbleweeds. Tom K. Ryan. (Tumbleweed Ser.). (Illus.). 144p. 1981. pap. 1.75 (ISBN 0-449-13756-2, GM). Fawcett.

Tumbleweeds & Company. Tom K. Ryan. (Tumbleweed Ser.). (Illus.). 1979. pap. 1.75 (ISBN 0-449-14198-5, GM). Fawcett.

Tumbleweeds Roundup! Tom K. Ryan. (Tumbleweed Ser.). (Illus.). 128p. 1982. pap. 1.95 (ISBN 0-449-13814-3, GM). Fawcett.

Tumbleweeds. 1st Ed. Ralph W Palmer. LC 53-11954. 1953. Pageant Press.

Tumbling in the Hay: A Novel. Oliver St. John Gogarty. LC 39-16779. Reynal & Hitchcock.

Tumbling Mustard. Harold A Loeb. LC 29-12055. 1929. H. Liveright.

Tumbling Range Woman. Steve Frazee. LC 56-970248. (Permabooks, M-3049. Western, 9). 1956. Permabooks.

Tumbling River Range. Wilbur C Tuttle. LC 35-19880. 1935. Houghton Mifflin Company.

Tumult and the Joy. Mildred Gordon & Gordon Gordon. LC 79-151764. 1971. 6.95. Doubleday.

Tumult & the Joy. Mildred Gordon & Gordon Gordon. LC 79-151764. 1971. 6.95 o.p. (ISBN 0-385-01419-8). Doubleday.

Tumult and the Shouting. Katherine Ursula Parrott. LC 33-31881. 1933. Longmans, Green and Co.

Tumulto. Brad Williams. 1974. (pbk.) 1.25. Avon.

Tun-Huang: A Novel. Yasushi Inoue. LC 77-75969. (Illus.). 1978. 8.95 (ISBN 0-87011-314-3). Kodansha International.

Tunc: A Novel. Lawrence Durrell. LC 79-11706. 1979. 3.95 (ISBN 0-14-005184-8). Penguin Books.

Tundra Trail. Charles Stoddard. LC 47-3349. 1947. Arcadia House.

Tundra Trail. Charles Stanley Strong. LC 47-3349. 1947. Arcadia House.

Tune in on Love. Herman Irving Bloom. LC 40-114863. Gramercy Publishing Co.

Tune in the Tree. Nelia Gardner White. LC 29-5945. The Penn Publishing Company.

Tune That They Play. William Clive. LC 73-8479. (pbk.) 1.50 (ISBN 0-671-78871-X). Pocket Books.

Tuned for Murder. Kenneth Robeson, pseud. (Avenger Ser, No. 9). 160p. (Orig.). 1973. pap. 0.75 o.p. (ISBN 0-446-74025-X). Paperback Lib.

Tuned for Murder. Kenneth Robeson. (Avenger, #3). 1973. (pbk) 0.75 (ISBN 0-446-74025-X). Warner Paperback Library.

Tuned Higher Than the Race. Michael Reepmaker. LC 23-13033. Times-Mirror Press.

Tuned Out. Maja Wojciechowska. 1969. pap. 1.50 (ISBN 0-440-99139-0, LFL). Dell.

Tunes of Glory. James Kennaway. LC 57-6151. Harper.

Tungus Event. Rupert Furneaux. 1979. pap. 1.50 o.s.i. (ISBN 0-8439-0619-7, Leisure Bks). Nordon Pubns.

Tunnel. Anthony Bristowe. (Orig.). 1969. pap. 0.60 o.p. (B6-2025). Belmont-Tower.

Tunnel. Robert Byrne. (Dell book). 1979. 1.95 (ISBN 0-440-18609-9). Dell Pub. Co.

Tunnel. Bernhard Kellermann. LC 15-8824. 1915. 1.25. The Macaulay Company.

Tunnel. Baynard Hardwick Kendrick. LC 49-111224. 1949. C.Scribner's Sons.

Tunnel. Maureen Lawrence. LC 69-20094. 1969. 4.95. Doubleday.

Tunnel. Dorothy Miller Richardson. LC 19-14018. (Her Pilgrimage pt. IV). 1919. A. A. Knopf.

Tunnel: A Novel. Hal Friedman. LC 78-32072. 1979. 9.95 (ISBN 0-688-03439-X). Morrow.

Tunnel at Loibl Pass. Andre Lacaze. 608p. 1982. pap. 3.95 (ISBN 0-553-22584-7). Bantam.

Tunnel from Calais. Arthur Durham Divine. LC 42-50860. 1942. Collins.

Tunnel from Calais. Arthur Durham Divine. LC 42-50769. 1943. The Macmillan Company.

Tunnel Hill. Harlan Henthorne Hatcher. LC 31-10358. The Bobbs-Merrill Company.

Tunnel in the Sky. Robert Anson Heinlein. 1955. Scribner.

Tunnel Mystery. J. C Lenechan. LC 31-30610. 1931. The Mystery League, Inc.

Tunnel of Darkness. Rebecca N. Winstead. 160p. (Orig.). 1975. pap. 1.25 o.p. (ISBN 0-89014-119-3, CB-119). Canyon Bks.

Tunnel of Darkness. Rebecca N. Winstead. (original Canyon book). 1974. (pbk.) 1.25. Canyon Books.

Tunnel of Love. Peter De Vries. LC 81-13978. 1982. 3.95 (ISBN 0-14-002200-7). Penguin Books.

Tunnel of Love. Peter De Vries. 1982. pap. 3.95 (ISBN 0-14-002200-7). Penguin.

Tunnel of Love. 1st Ed. Peter De Vries. LC 54-6879. 1954. Little, Brown.

Tunnel Through the Deeps. Harry Harrison. LC 79-186650. 1972. 5.95 (ISBN 0-399-10918-8). Putnam.

Tunnel Thru the Air: Or, Looking Back from 1940. William D Gann. LC 27-23956. Financial Guardian Publishing Co.

Tunnel War. Lou Cameron. (Orig.). 1969. pap. 0.75 o.p. (74-526). Lancer.

Tunnel War. Joe Poyer, pseud. LC 79-63628. (Illus.). 1979. 12.95 (ISBN 0-689-11009-X). Atheneum.

Turbo. James Douglas Rutherford McConnell. LC 80-14237. 1980. 9.95 (ISBN 0-312-82332-0). St. Martin's Press.

Turbott Wolfe. William Charles Franklyn Plomer. LC 26-12143. Harcourt, Brace and Company.

Turbott Wolfe. Introd. by Laurens Van der Post. William Charles Franklyn Plomer. LC 65-58004. 4.50. Morrow.

Turbulent Duchess. Percy James Brebner. LC 14-309795. 1915. 1.30. Little, Brown, and Company.

Turbulent Pendrayles. Tobias Wagner. LC 37-4377. 1937. Little, Brown and Company.

Turbulent Times. Frank Wells. 3.95 o.p. Carlton.

Turbulent Waters: Lone Warriors in Colombia. Jane Livingstone. LC 59-337. (Pinebrook book club selection). 1958. Moody Press.

Turgenev. Lev Shestov. 110p. (Rus.). 1981. 14.50 (ISBN 0-88233-504-9); pap. 6.00 (ISBN 0-88233-505-7). Ardis Pubs.

Turistas Eroticos. Danilo Cesto. (Pimienta Collection Ser). (Illus.). 1976. pap. 1.25 (ISBN 0-88473-251-7). Fiesta Pub.

Turk. Beatrice Bliss. 1976. 6.95 (ISBN 0-914558-03-X); pap. 3.95 (ISBN 0-914558-06-4). Georgetown Pr.

Turk" A Novel. Opie Percival Read. LC 4-19873. Laird & Lee.

Turkey Bowman. Homer Croy. LC 20-16795. Harper & Brothers.

Turkey Hash. Craig Nova. LC 77-156564. 192p. 1972. 6.95 o.p. (ISBN 0-06-013224-8, HarpT). Har-Row.

Turkey Knob Line: A Novel of the Ozarks. 1st Ed. William George Hall. LC 54-7287. 1954. Exposition Press.

Turkey Mountain. Belva Clayton. 2.00 o.p. Carlton.

Turkey Red: A Novel of the Frontier. Frances Gilchrist Wood. LC 32-22991. 1932. D. Appleton and Company.

Turkey-Track Rampage. Bob Haning. 1974. 4.95. Lenox Hill Press.

Turkish Bloodbath. Nick Carter. (Nick Carter Ser.). 224p. (Orig.). 1982. pap. 2.25 (ISBN 0-441-82726-8, Pub. by Charter Bks). Ace Bks.

Turkish Captive. A Novel. Louis Ferdinand Lehmanowsky. LC 7-13149. 1853. A. Hart.

Turkish Delight. Jan Wolkers. LC 74-8821. 1974. 8.95 (ISBN 0-440-06094-X). Delacorte Press/S. Lawrence.

Turkish Delights. A. Degranamour. pap. 1.95 o.s.i. (Venus). Grove.

Turkish Mafia Conspiracy. Ralph Hayes. (Agent for Cominsec,#3). 1974. (pbk.) 0.95. Belmont Tower Books.

Turkish Rondo. Anne Stevenson, pseud. LC 81-3967. 1981. 10.95 (ISBN 0-688-00638-8). Morrow.

Turkish Spies Ali Abubeker Kaled and Zenobia Marrita Mustapha: Or, The Mohammedan Prophet of 1854. A True History of the Russo-Turkish War. Maturin Murray Ballou. LC 6-6093. 1855. A. R. Orton.

Turkish White. Mel Arrighi. LC 76-54620. 7.95 (ISBN 0-15-191390-0). Harcourt Brace Jovanovich.

Turmoil. Louise Ruland Eaves. LC 73-83483. 1973. 3.95 (ISBN 0-8059-1891-4). Dorrance.

Turmoil. 2nd ed. Arthur Moore. 1979. pap. 2.25 (ISBN 0-89083-490-3). Zebra.

Turmoil. Booth Tarkington & Baker, Elizabeth Whitemore, Ed. LC 29-22142. (Harper's modern classics). Harper & Brothers.

Turmoil: A Novel. Booth Tarkington. LC 15-3643. 1915. Harper & Brothers.

Turmoil: A Novel. Booth Tarkington. LC 21-4145. 1915. Grosset & Dunlap.

Turmoil at Brede. Seldon Truss, pseud. LC 31-5886. 1931. The Mystery League, Inc.

Turn About Eleanor. Ethel May Kelley. LC 17-23983. The Bobbs-Merrill Company.

Turn About Tales. Alice Caldwell Hegan Rice & Rice, Cale Young, 1872- Joint Author. LC 20-16343. 1920. The Century Co.

Turn Again Home. Herbert Harker. LC 76-53487. 8.95 (ISBN 0-394-41152-8). Random House.

Turn Again Home. Herbert Harker. (Signet Book). 1979 (ISBN 0-451-08556-6). New American Library.

Turn Again Tiger. Samuel Selvon. 1959. St. Martin's Press.

Turn-Around. Vladimir. Volkoff. LC 80-2630. 1981. 14.95 (ISBN 0-385-17071-8). Doubleday.

Turn Around Twice. Elisabeth Ogilvie. Repr. lib. bdg. 10.85x (ISBN 0-88411-339-6). Amereon Ltd.

Turn Back the Leaves. Edmee Elizabeth Monica De La Pasture. LC 30-672549. 1930. Harper & Brothers.

Turn Back the River. William George Hardy. LC 38-6978. 1938. Dodd, Mead & Company.

Turn but a Stone. Muriel Merritt. LC 70-145796. 1973. 1.95 o.p. Stewart.

Turn East, Turn West. Luella Sanders Bruce Creighton. LC 54-5663. 1954. Dodd, Mead.

Turn Ever Northward. Margaret Barrington. LC 39-31054. 1939. A. A. Knopf.

Turn Home. Eleanor R Mayo. LC 45-214773. 1945. W. Morrow & Company.

Turn in the Dark Wood. Edward Carl Stephens. LC 67-19128. 1967. Doubleday.

Turn Killer. Brian Lecomber. 1976. (pbk.) 1.95 (ISBN 0-671-80464-2). Pocket Books.

Turn Killer: A Novel. Brian Lecomber. LC 74-34338. (Simon and Schuster novel of suspense). 1975. 7.95 (ISBN 0-671-21994-4). Simon and Schuster.

Turn Left for Murder: By Stephen Marlowe Pseud. Milton Lesser. LC 55-225431. (Ace double novel books, D-69). 1955. Ace Books.

Turn Loose the Dragon. George C Chesbro. LC 81-22888. 1982. 2.95 (ISBN 0-345-29029-1). Ballantine Books.

Turn Loose Your Wolf. Bennett Foster. LC 48-10245. (Triple-A western classic). 1948. Jefferson House.

Turn Loose Your Wolf: A Novel of the West. Bennett Foster. LC 38-33001. 1938. W. Morrow & Co.

Turn, Magic Wheel. Dawn Powell. LC 36-484187. Farrar & Rinehart, Incorporated.

Turn Me On. Jack W. Thomas. (Orig.). 1969. pap. 2.25 (ISBN 0-553-14410-3, 13251-2). Bantam.

Turn of a Day. Catharine Amy Dawson Scott. LC 25-7199. 1925. H. Holt and Company.

Turn of a Pang. Nicole Brossard. LC 77-365030. (Coach House Quebec translations). Coach House.

Turn of a Wheel. Anne Van Melborn Rowe. LC 30-5178. 1930. The Macaulay Company.

Turn of Life's Tide. Ursula Bloom. LC 76-367715. 1976. 3.45 (ISBN 0-09-125910-X). Hutchinson.

Turn of the Balance. Brand Whitlock. LC 76-104765. 1970. University Press of Kentucky.

Turn of the Balance. Brand Whitlock. LC 7-10046. 1907. The Bobbs-Merrill Company.

Turn of the Balance. Brand Whitlock. LC 24-213953. The Bobbs-Merrill Company.

Turn of the Cards. Georgina Grey, pseud. (Regency romance). 1979. 1.75 (ISBN 0-449-23969-1). Fawcett Crest Books.

Turn of the Century. Jill Downie. 1982. pap. 3.50 (ISBN 0-380-80861-7, 80861). Avon.

Turn of the Dial. Chard Powers Smith. LC 43-3203. 1943. C. Scribner's Sons.

Turn of the Road. Eugenia Brooks Frothingham. LC 1-30742. 1901. Houghton, Mifflin and Company.

Turn of the Screw see Aspern Papers.

Turn of the Screw & Other Short Fiction. Henry James. (Bantam Classics Ser.). 416p. (Orig.). (gr. 9-12). 1981. pap. text ed. 1.95 (ISBN 0-553-21059-9). Bantam.

Turn of the Screw & Other Short Novels. Henry James. (Orig.). pap. 1.95 (ISBN 0-451-51669-9, CJ1669, Sig Classics). NAL.

Turn of the Screw & Other Stories. Henry James. 1970. pap. 1.95 (ISBN 0-14-003026-3). Penguin.

Turn of the Screw, The Lesson of the Master. Henry James. Ed. by Broun, Heywood Campbell. LC 30-26388. (Half-title: The modern library of the world's best books). 1930. The Modern Library.

Turn of the Sword. Charles Maclean Savage. 1913. F. G. Browne & Co.

Turn of the Tide. Horace Annesley Vachell. LC 8-31822. Cupples & Leon Company.

Turn of the Tide: A Story of Humble Life by the Sea. Mary Agatha Gray. LC 10-22798. 1910. Benziger Brothers.

Turn of the Tide: The Story of How Margaret Solved Her Problem. Eleanor Hodgman Porter. LC 8-31684. W. A. Wilde Company.

Turn of the Wheel. Roger Vailland. LC 77-20080. 1978. 14.50 (ISBN 0-313-20014-9). Greenwood Press.

Turn of Traitors. Palma Harcourt. LC 81-9336. 10.95 (ISBN 0-684-17346-8). Scribner.

Turn off the Sunshine: Tales of Los Angeles on the Wrong Side of the Tracks. Timothy Gilman Turner. LC 42-50916. 1942. The Caxton Printers, Ltd.

Turn on the Heat. A. A. Fair, pseud. LC 40-2120. 1940. W. Morrow and Company.

Turn on the Heat. A. A. Fair, pseud. LC 40-2120. 1940. W. Morrow.

Turn South at the Second Bridge. Leon Hale. LC 80-5517. 224p. 1980. Repr. of 1965 ed. 12.95 (ISBN 0-89096-100-X). Tex A&M Univ Pr.

Turn the Other Sheik. Troy Conway, pseud. (Coxeman Ser). (Orig.). 1970. pap. 0.75 o.p. (64-439). Paperback Lib.

Turn the Tigers Loose. Walter Lasly. LC 56-13479. 1956. Ballantine Books.

Turn to the Right. Bennet Musson & Smith, Winchell. LC 17-18357. 1917. Duffield and Company.

Turn to the Sun. Anne Duffield. LC 44-40869. 1944. Arcadia House, Inc.

Turn to the Table. Jonathan Stagge, pseud. LC 40-33294. 1940. Pub. for the Crime Club by Doubleday, Doran & Co., Inc.

Turn Toward Home. Michael P Arnold. LC 69-15204. 1969. 5.95. Doubleday.

Turnabout. Thorne Smith. LC 31-29016. 1931. Doubleday, Doran & Company, Incorporated.

Turnabout. Thorne Smith. LC 33-15505. 1933. Doubleday, Doran & Company, Incorporated.

Turnabout. Thorne Smith. 1934. Doubleday, Doran & Company, Incorporated.

Turnabout. Thorne Smith. LC 37-2032. 1936. Doubleday, Doran & Company, Incorporated.

Turnabout. Thorne Smith. LC 36-8022. 1935. Doubleday, Doran & Company, Incorporated.

Turnaround. Giles A. Lutz. 1979. pap. 1.75 (ISBN 0-671-82822-3). PB.

Turnaround: A Novel. Don Carpenter. LC 80-28069. 13.95 (ISBN 0-671-25353-0). Simon and Schuster.

Turnbulls. Taylor Caldwell. LC 75-565. 1975. 11.95 (ISBN 0-88411-155-5). Aeonian Press.

Turnbulls. Taylor Caldwell. LC 43-512621. 1943. C. Scribner's Sons.

Turncoat. Nick Carter. (Nick Carter Ser.). (O.s.i.). (Orig.). 1976. pap. 1.25 o.p. (AQ1581, Award). Univ Pub & Dist.

Turncoat. Jack Lynn. LC 75-31896. 8.95 (ISBN 0-440-09133-0). Delacorte Press.

Turncoat. Jack Lynn. (Dell Book). 1977. 1.95 (ISBN 0-440-18590-4). Dell Pub. Co.

Turned from the Door. A Christmas Story for 1869-70. Henry Morford. LC 7-26201. 1869. The American News Company.

Turned Loose on Irdra. Phyllis MacLennan. LC 73-89128. 1970. 3.95. Doubleday.
Turned on to L. U. S. T. Rod Gray. (Lady from L. U. S. T. Ser., No. 17). (Orig., Osi). 1971. pap. 0.95 o.s.i. (B95-2170). Belmont-Tower.
Turned on to L.U.S.T. Rod Gray. (The Lady from L.U.S.T. Ser.). (O.s.i.). 1974. pap. 0.95 o.s.i. (BT50692). Belmont-Tower.
Turner Diaries. 2d ed. Andrew Macdonald. LC 80-82692. 1980. 4.95 (ISBN 0-937944-02-5). National Alliance.
Turner's Wife: A Novel. Norman Garbo. LC 82-14221. 400p. 1983. 16.50 (ISBN 0-393-01521-1). Norton.
Turning Back the Pages of Time. Rodman Jolly. 3.00 o.p. Carlton.
Turning Islands. Paul Hastings Wilson. LC 76-48381 (ISBN 0-380-00861-0). Avon.
Turning Leaves. Ellen Eggleston Proctor. LC 42-24674. 1942. Dodd, Mead & Comapny.
Turning of the Road. Agnes Horsch Hofmaster. LC 30-21770. 1930. Mission Press.
Turning of the Tide. Samuel Lewin. Tr. by Joseph Leftwich. 8.95 (ISBN 0-8453-2087-4). Cornwall Bks.
Turning of the Tide. Jonathan Scofield, pseud. (Freedom Fighters Ser.: No. 7). (Orig.). 1981. pap. 2.95 (ISBN 0-440-08490-3, Bryans). Dell.
Turning of the Tide: A Novel. Samuel Lewin. LC 77-89644. 8.95 (ISBN 0-498-02087-8). A. S. Barnes.
Turning of the Wheel. Mary Dwinell Chellis. LC 6-23354. 1887. The National Temperance Society and Publication House.
Turning on: Thirteen Stories. Damon Francis Knight. LC 66-174386. (Doubleday sci. fic.). 3.50. Doubleday.
Turning Point. Hugh Clevely. LC 55-9477. 1955. Morrow.
Turning Point. Edward E. Fitzgerald. LC 48-8997. (Barnes sport novel). 1948. A. S. Barnes.
Turning Point. Arthur Laurents. (Signet Book). (Illus.). 1977. 1.95 (ISBN 0-451-07707-5). New American Library.
Turning Point. Louis Tracy. LC 23-122202. E. J. Clode.
Turning Sword: A Van Kill Novel of Detection. Spencer Bayne. LC 41-7645. Harper & Brothers.
Turning Tide. Sara Ware Bassett. The Penn Publishing Company.
Turning Tide. Evelyn Ward McDonald. LC 55-13921. D. McKay Co.
Turning Wheels. Stuart Cloete. LC 37-23233. 1937. Houghton Mifflin Company.
Turnover: A Tale of New Hampshire. LC 8-32319. 1853. J. French Etc.
Turnover Club. Tales Told at the Meetings of the Turnover Club, About Actors and Actresses. William T Hall. LC 7-1215. (On cover: The illustrated series, no. 11). 1890. Rand, McNally & Company.
Turnpike. Helen Van Valkenburgh. LC 33-1844. Pegasus Publishing Company.
Turnpike Lady: Beartown, Vermont, 1768-1796. Sarah Norcliffe Cleghorn. LC 7-308316. 1907. H. Holt and Company.
Turns & Movies & Other Tales in Verse. Conrad Potter Aiken. LC 73-18103. Repr. of 1916 ed. lib. bdg. 17.50 (ISBN 0-8414-2947-2). Folcroft.
Turnstile. Alfred Edward Woodley Mason. LC 12-14457. 1912. C. Scribner's Sons.
Turnstile of Night. William Allison. 1920. Doubleday, Page & Company.
Turpin. Stephen Jones. LC 68-23065. 1968. Macmillan.
Turquoise. Anya Seton. LC 46-25006. 1946. Houghton Mifflin Company.
Turquoise. Anya Seton. LC 47-6426. 1947. Sun Dial Press.
Turquoise Canon. Joseph Allan Elphinstone Dunn. LC 20-5121. 1920. Doubleday, Page & Company.
Turquoise Cup and The Desert. Arthur Cosslett Smith. LC 3-5535. 1903. C. Scribner's Sons.
Turquoise Hazard. Alfred Betts Caldwell. LC 36-13190. 1936. Pub. for the Crime Club, Inc., by Doubleday, Doran & Co., Inc.
Turquoise Lament. John Dann MacDonald. LC 73-14806. (His The Travis McGee stories). 1973. 5.95 (ISBN 0-397-00987-9). Lippincott.
Turquoise Lament. John Dann MacDonald. LC 82-9168. 1982. 12.95 (ISBN 0-8161-3383-2). G.K. Hall.
Turquoise Mask. Phyllis A. Whitney. LC 73-10823. 1974. 6.95 (ISBN 0-385-08514-1). Doubleday.
Turquoise Mask. Phyllis A. Whitney. LC 74-4122. 1974. (lib. bdg.) 11.95 (ISBN 0-8161-6200-X). G. K. Hall.
Turquoise Shop. Frances Kirkwood Crane. LC 41-17318. J. B. Lippincott Company.
Turquoise Talisman. Marilyn Marshall. (Adventures in Love Ser.: No. 38). 1982. pap. 1.95 (ISBN 0-451-11931-2, AJ1931, Sig). NAL.
Turquoise Talisman. Sharon Wagner. LC 75-22287. (Birthstone gothic; 12). 1975. 1.25 (ISBN 0-345-24663-2). Ballantine Books.
Turquoise Trail. Shirley Seifert. LC 50-6798. 1950. Lippincott.
Turret Room. Charlotte Armstrong. (Crest bk., R1077). 1967. Fawcett.
Turret Room. Charlotte Armstrong. LC 65-13276. 1965. Coward-McCann.
Turtle's Flying Lesson. Diane Redfield Massie. LC 71-190370. (Thistle Book). (Illus.). 1973. 4.95 (ISBN 0-448-21459-8). Grosset and Dunlap.
Turtles of Tasman. Jack London. LC 16-18916. 1916. The Macmillan Company.
Turuoise and Silver. Mina Morris Scott. LC 40-35264. H. Harrison.
Turvey: A Military Picaresque. rev. ed. Earle Birney. LC 76-363786. 1976. 8.95 (ISBN 0-7710-1412-0). McClelland & Stewart.
Turvey: A Picaresque Novel. Earle Birney. 1958. Abelard-Schuman.
Tuscan Spring: A Novel About Sandro Botticelli (1444-1510. James Cleugh. LC 39-27114. Reynal & Hitchcock.
Tuscany Terror. (Executioner Ser.). 192p. 1983. pap. 1.95 (ISBN 0-373-61052-1, Pub. by Worldwide). Harlequin Bks.
Tuscarora Tales: 29 Rare Stories. Robert B. Vale. LC 58-17570. 1957.
Tuscon Temptress. Chet Cunningham. (Agent Brad Spear Ser.: No. 3). (Orig.). 1981. pap. 2.25 (ISBN 0-440-09140-3, Banbury). Dell.
Tussy Is Me: A Novel of Fact. Michael Hastings. LC 74-145801. 1971. 7.95. Delacorte Press.
Tut, Tut! Mr. Tutt. Arthur Cheney Train. LC 23-12673. 1923. C. Scribner's Sons.
Tutankhamon: A Novel of Ancient Egypt. Paul Startzman. 1979. 9.00 (ISBN 0-682-49218-3, Banner). Exposition.
Tutor. Ed. by P. N. Dedeaux. 1971. pap. 1.95 o.p. (V1023, Venus). Grove.
Tutor: Being the Reminiscences of Thomasina Wragg. P. N Dedeaux. LC 77-171035. (Venus Library, V-1023-T). 1971. 1.95. Grove Press.
Tutor Laughter: The Joy & Adventure in Remedial Tutoring. Treb Sona. 1980. pap. 4.50 (ISBN 0-930480-02-3). R H Barnes.
Tutored Soul. Estelle Zinkhan Huselton. LC 16-204371. 1916. 1.25. Sherman, French & Company.
Tutors' Lane. Wilmarth Lewis. LC 22-19606. 1922. A. A. Knopf.
Tutor's Secret. Victor Cherbuliez. LC 6-26963. (On cover: Appletons' town and country library, no. 120). 1893. D. Appleton and Company.
Tutor's Story: An Unpublished Novel. Charles Kingsley & Harrison, Mrs. Mary St. Leger (Kingsley) 1852-1931. LC 16-15663. 1916. Dodd, Mead and Company.
Tutt and Mr. Tutt. Arthur Cheney Train. LC 20-6289. 1920. C. Scribner's Sons.
Tutt and Mr. Tutt. Arthur Cheney Train. LC 43-99312. 1943. Triangle Books.
Tutt for Tutt. Arthur Cheney Train. LC 34-71499. 1934. C. Scribner's Sons.
Tuxedo Avenue to Water Street: Being the Story of a Transplanted Church. Amos Russell Wells. LC 6-185874. 1906. Funk and Wagnalls Company.
TV Dancer. Regina Llewellyn Jones Woody. LC 67-1806. (Doubleday signal books). (Illus.). 1967. Doubleday.
TV Dancer. Regina Llewellyn Jones Woody. (Doubleday signal books). (Illus.). 1967. Doubleday.
TV Man. Rodrick Bradley. LC 80-13326. 12.95 (ISBN 0-03-056701-7). Holt, Rinehart, and Winston.
Twain Shall Meet. James P Leynse. LC 55-124545. 1955. Creative Press.
Twain Tradition. 1st Ed. Irene Perrot. LC 52-14516. 1952. Pageant Press.
Twain Unabridged. Mark Twain. Ed. by Lawrence Teacher. LC 76-43094. (Illus.). 1250p. (Orig.). 1976. lib. bdg. 19.80 (ISBN 0-914294-53-9); pap. 9.95 (ISBN 0-914294-54-7). Running Pr.
Twain Unabridged Two. Mark Twain. Ed. by Lawrence Teacher. LC 79-9576. 1979. 21.50 o.p.; lib. bdg. 19.80 (ISBN 0-89471-087-7); pap. 9.95 (ISBN 0-89471-086-9). Running Pr.
Twas a Most Remarkable Year- 1st Ed. Oscar Haukenes. LC 56-5807. 1956. Vantage Press.
Twas in Trafalgar's Bay: A Story. Walter Besant & Rice, James. LC 7-3326. (On cover: Harper's half-hour series v. 90). 1879. Harper & Brothers.
Twas in Trafalgar's Bay: And Other Stories. library ed. Walter Besant & Rice, James. LC 3-22885. 1888. Dodd, Mead & Company.
Twas Love's Fault: Or, A Young Girl's Trust. Charles Garvice. (On cover: Laurel library, no. 23). 1895. G. Munro's Sons.
Tweak the Devil's Nose. Richard Deming. LC 53-5358. (Murray Hill mystery). 1953. Rinehart.
Twee. Suzanne Heller. LC 75-114235. (Illus.). 1970. 3.50 o.p. (ISBN 0-396-06236-9). Dodd.
Tweed: A Story of the Old South. S. M Swales. LC 11-28686. Broadway Publishing Co.
Tweedie: The Story of a True Heart. Isla May Hawley Mullins. LC 19-4407. 1919. The Page Company.
Tween Snow and Fire: A Tale of the Last Kafir War. Bertram Mitford. (On cover: Cassell's sunshine series, no. 128). Cassell Publishing Company.
Twelfth: An Amethyst. Olive Katharine Parr. LC 29-201201. 1929. 2.50. Longmans, Green and Co.
Twelfth Gun. Ronald Watson. (Leisure book). 1.50 (ISBN 0-8439-0643-X). Nordon Pubns.
Twelfth Hour. Ada Iverson. 1972. pap. 0.75 o.p. (07234). Curtis.
Twelfth. Illustrated by V. H. Drummond. John Keith Stanford. LC 57-14049. 1957. Vt., Countryman Press.
Twelfth Juror. Mary Harriott Large. 1908. The C. M. Clark Publishing Company.
Twelfth Mile. Ernest G. Perrault. LC 77-157616. 264p. 1972. 5.95 o.p. (ISBN 0-385-06625-2). Doubleday.
Twelfth Mile. Ernest G. Perrault. 1974. pap. 1.25 o.p. (ISBN 0-515-03109-7, V3109). Pyramid Pubns.
Twelfth Physician. Willa Gibbs. LC 54-7311. 1954. Farrar, Straus and Young.
Twelfth Power of Evil. Jerrold Morgulas. LC 81-50325. 13.95 (ISBN 0-87223-704-4). Seaview Books.
Twelfth Step. Thomas Randall. LC 57-11665. 1957. Scribner.
Twelth Pan Book of Horror Stories. Ed. by H. Van Thal. 1982. pap. 10.00x (ISBN 0-330-02761-1, Pub. by Pan Bks). State Mutual Bk.
Twelve Against the Law. Edward D Radin. LC 46-7100. 1946. Duell, Sloan and Pearce.
Twelve Angels from Hell. David Wilkerson. (Pap. ed. 1.25 o.p.). 1965. 3.95 o.p. (ISBN 0-8007-0326-X). Revell.
Twelve Best Short Stories in the English Language. Ed. by Adam Luke Gowans. LC 21-14625. (Half-title: Gowan's cosmopolitan library. no. 1. English section). 1920. Gowans & Gray, Ltd.
Twelve Best Short Stories in the French Language. Auguste Dorchan. Repr. of 1920 ed. 10.00 o.p. (ISBN 0-89987-117-8). Darby Bks.
Twelve Best Short Stories in the German Language. Richard M. Meyer. Repr. of 1926 ed. 10.00 o.p. Folcroft.
Twelve Best Tales by English Writers. Ed. by Adam Luke Gowans. LC 11-28699. 0.75. Thomas Y. Crowell Company.
Twelve Chairs. Ilia Arnoldovich Ilf & Evgenii Petrovich Petrov. LC 61-2146. (Vintage Russian library, V-727). 1961. Vintage Books.
Twelve Chases on West Ninety-Ninth Street. Roy Bongartz. LC 65-10965. 1965. 4.00. Houghton.
Twelve Chinks and a Woman. James Hadley Chase. LC 41-145421. Howell, Soskin.
Twelve Chinks and a Woman. James Hadley Chase. LC 41-14542. 1941. Howell, Soskin.
Twelve Christmas Stories. Charles Dickens. Ed. by Gordon, Jane. LC 4-10924. (Eclectic school readings). 1904. American Book Company.
Twelve Contemporary Russian Stories. Vytas Dukas. LC 74-4969. 10.00 (ISBN 0-8386-1491-4). Fairleigh Dickinson University Press.
Twelve Crimes of Christmas. Ed. by Carol-Lynn R. Waugh et al. 256p. (Orig.). 1981. pap. 2.50 (ISBN 0-380-78931-0, 78931). Avon.
Twelve Dancing Princesses, and Other Fairy Tales. Ed. by Alfred David. LC 73-16517. (Illus.). 1974. 7.95 (ISBN 0-253-36100-1) (ISBN 0-253-36100-1). Indiana University Press.
Twelve Deaths of Christmas. Marian Babson. LC 81-142. 1981. 11.50 (ISBN 0-8161-3183-X). G.K. Hall.
Twelve Disguises. Francis Beeding. LC 42-16141. 1942. Harper & Brothers.
Twelve Dreams. James Lapine. LC 82-81974. 55p. 1982. pap. 3.95 (ISBN 0-933826-33-8). Performing Arts.
Twelve German Novellas. Ed. by Harry Steinhauer. LC 75-7204. (Campus; 176). 5.95 (ISBN 0-520-03002-8). University of California Press.
Twelve Girls in the Garden. Shane Martin. LC 57-8559. 1957. W. Morrow.
Twelve Great Classics of Science Fiction. Ed. by Groff Conklin. 1970. pap. 0.60 o.p. (R2192, GM). Fawcett World.
Twelve Great Classics of Science Fiction. Ed. by Groff Conklin. 192p. 1973. pap. 0.75 o.p. (T2749, GM). Fawcett World.
Twelve Great Diamonds. A Novel. Jane Goodwin Austin. LC 6-3854. (On cover: Idle hour series. no. 4). The F. M. Lupton Publishing Company.
Twelve Great Modern Stories: A New Collection ... LC 45-16241. (Avon modern short story monthly. 20). Avon Book Company.
Twelve Great Stories. James Thomas Farrell. LC 45-16235. N.Y.
Twelve Great Stories, a New Anthology ... LC 46-21100. (Avon modern short story monthly, no. 31). 1946. Avon Book Company.
Twelve Grindstones. John Gould. 1979. pap. 3.95 (ISBN 0-89272-058-1). Down East.
Twelve Grindstones. John Gould. 1970. 6.95 o.p. (ISBN 0-316-32178-8). Little.
Twelve Inches. Karl Flinders. (Orig.). 1970. pap. 1.95 o.s.i. (OHH-183, Ophelia). Olympia.
Twelve Inches Around the World. Karl Flinders. pap. 1.95 o.s.i. (OPH-237, Ophelia). Olympia.
Twelve Inches in Peril. Karl Flinders. 1972. pap. 1.95 o.s.i. (OPH-4012, Ophelia). Olympia.
Twelve Inches with a Vengeance. Karl Flinders. LC 70-27136. 1970. 1.95. Ophelia Press.
Twelve Maidens: A Novel of Witchcraft. Stewart Farrar. LC 73-77753. 1974. 6.95. St. Martins Press.
Twelve Maidens: A Novel of Witchcraft. Stewart Farrar. 1975. (pbk.) 1.50. Bantam Books.
Twelve Men. Theodore Dreiser. LC 74-144985. 1971. (ISBN 0-403-00914-6). Scholarly Press.
Twelve Must Die: A Horror Mystery Straight from the Devil's Notebook. Harold Ward. LC 80-8666. (Pulp classics; no. 19). 1980. 11.95 (ISBN 0-89370-083-5) (ISBN 0-89370-082-7). Borgo Press.
Twelve O'clock High! Beirne Lay & Sy Bartlett. LC 79-7278. (Flight, Its First Seventy-Five Years). 1980. 20.00 (ISBN 0-405-12187-3). Arno Press.
Twelve O'clock High! Beirne Lay & Sy Bartlett. LC 80-16525. (Five Great Classic Stories of World War II). 5.95 (ISBN 0-396-07867-2). Dodd, Mead.
Twelve O'clock High! Beirne Lay & Sy Bartlett. LC 81-728. 1981. 12.95 (ISBN 0-89340-332-6). J. Curley.
Twelve O'clock High. Beirne Lay & Bartlett, Sy, 1903- Joint Author. 1948. Harper.
Twelve of the World's Great Humor Stories. Ed. by Marjorie Barrows. Eaton, George, Joint Comp. LC 45-5274. Consolidated Book Publishers.
Twelve Pictures: A Novel. Edith Simon. LC 55-5771. 1955. Putnam.
Twelve Ravens. Howard Rose. Ed. by R. Marek. (O.s.i.). 1970. 6.95 o.s.i. (ISBN 0-02-604880-9). Macmillan.
Twelve Ravens: A Novel. Howard Rose. LC 78-75905. 1969. Macmillan.
Twelve Saints. Ruth Manning-Sanders. LC 26-6260. E. J. Clode, Inc.
Twelve Short Novels. Ray J Sherer. LC 75-34327. 6.95 (ISBN 0-03-012151-5). Holt, Rinehart and Winston.
Twelve Short Stories. Edited and with Commentaries by Marvin Magalaner and Edmond L. Volpe. Ed. by Marvin Magalaner & Edmond Loris Volpe. 1961. Macmillan.
Twelve Short Stories, Second Ser. Ed. by Edmond Loris Volpe & Edmond L. Volpe. (Orig.). 1969. pap. text ed. 3.50x o.p. (37469). Macmillan.
Twelve Short Stories, Second Series. Ed. by Marvin Magalaner. LC 69-10360. 1969. Macmillan.
Twelve Stories. Steen Steensen Blicher. Repr. of 1945 ed. 21.00 o.s.i. (ISBN 0-527-08950-8). Kraus Repr.
Twelve Stories and a Dream. Herbert George Wells. LC 72-152963. (Short story index reprint series). (Illus.). 1971. (ISBN 0-8369-3878-X). Books for Libraries Press.
Twelve Stories and a Dream. Herbert George Wells. LC 5-11349. 1905. C. Scribner's Sons.
Twelve Stories and a Dream. Herbert George Wells. LC 24-27882. 1924. C. Scribner's Sons.
Twelve Stories by Steen Steensen Blicher. Steen Steensen Blicher & Larsen, Hanna Astrup, 1873-1945, Tr. LC 46-871. 1945. Princeton University Press for the American-Scandinavian Foundation, New York.
Twelve Tales. Albert Engstrom. Tr. by Harold Borland from Swedish. (Bilingual Ser.). 1949. 5.00 (ISBN 0-911268-47-2). Rogers Bk.
Twelve Tales of Suspense and the Supernatural. Davis Grubb. LC 64-13272. 1964. Scribner.
Twelve Tales of the Life and Adventures of Saint Imaginus: Retold from the Collection Made by His Brethren of the Order of Saint Simplicitas, with Additional Stories Now Published for the First Time. Frances Margaret Cheadle McGuire. LC 47-31155. 1947. Sheed & Ward.
Twelve Ten from San Antone: Only the Swift. Kirk Hamilton. (Orig.). 1980. pap. 2.25 o.s.i. (ISBN 0-8439-0741-X, Leisure Bks). Nordon Pubns.
Twelve Tens. Victoria S. Morris. 1978. pap. 1.00 (ISBN 0-914318-08-X). V S Morris.
Twelve Trains to Babylon. Alfred Connable. LC 71-154957. 1971. 6.95. Little, Brown.
Twelve-Twenty p.m. William Gilmore Beymer. LC 44-991626. 1944. Wittlesey House, McGraw-Hill Book Company, Inc.
Twelve Years: An American Boyhood in East Germany. Joel Agee. LC 80-68233. 1980. 8.95 (ISBN 0-374-27958-6). Farrar Straus Giroux.

TITLE INDEX TWENTY THOUSAND LEAGUES UNDER

Twentieth Century Athenians. Ray Robinson. LC 18-4151. 1918. The Gorham Press.
Twentieth-Century Chinese Stories. Ed. by Chih-Tsing Hsia. LC 72-173986. (Companions to Asian Studies). 1971. 10.00 (ISBN 0-231-03589-6) (ISBN 0-231-03590-X). Columbia University Press.
Twentieth-Century Church and Club: Or, Facts Stranger Than Fiction. Edwin Horea. LC 1-30903. 1900. R. R. Donnelley & Sons Co.
Twentieth Century Discovery. Isaac Asimov. 1976. pap. 2.25 (ISBN 0-441-83227-X). Ace Bks.
Twentieth Century English Short Stories. Ed. by Tina Pierce & Edward Cochrane. 1981. 20.00x (ISBN 0-237-50143-0, Pub. by Evans Bros). State Mutual Bk.
Twentieth Century Fables. Lamar Strickland Payne. 1903. Broadway Publishing Co.
Twentieth Century Goslings: A Modern Love Story. Frances Mead Seager. LC 6-62627. Broadway Publishing Company.
Twentieth Century Interpretations of Molloy, Malone Dies, The Unnamable: A Collection of Critical Essays. Ed. by James Donald O'Hara. LC 77-126824. (Twentieth century interpretations). (Spectrum book). 1970. 4.95 (ISBN 0-13-599555-8). Prentice-Hall.
Twentieth Century Interpretations of Native Son: A Collection of Critical Essays. Ed. by Houston A. Baker, Jr. LC 72-8136. (Twentieth century interpretations). (Spectrum book). 1972. 4.95 (ISBN 0-13-609982-3) (ISBN 0-13-609982-3). Prentice-Hall.
Twentieth Century Interpretations of Poe's Tales: A Collection of Critical Essays. Ed. by William L. Howarth. LC 69-15337. (Twentieth century interpretations). (Spectrum book.). 1971. 4.95 (ISBN 0-13-684654-8). Prentice-Hall.
Twentieth Century Interpretations of Robinson Crusoe: A Collection of Critical Essays. Ed. by Frank Hale Ellis. LC 69-15338. (Twentieth century interpretations). (Spectrum book.). 1969. Prentice-Hall.
Twentieth Century Odyssey. Rev. Ed. Stephen G Prokopoff. LC 64-15614. 3.75. Christopher Pub.
Twentieth Century Short Stories. Ed. by Sylvia Chatfield Bates. LC 33-8544. Houghton Mifflin Company.
Twentieth Century Spanish-American Novel: A Bibliographic Guide. David W. Foster. LC 75-25787. 1975. 11.00 (ISBN 0-8108-0871-4). Scarecrow.
Twentieth Century Woman Toward the Reconstructive Movement. Matilde Juana Berra. LC 4-13281. 1904. Press Appeal Publishing Company.
Twentieth Door. Charles Monroe Sheldon. LC 8-5095. Congregational Sunday-School and Publishing Society.
Twentieth Meridian: A Novel. Robert John Travers. LC 51-11591. 1951. Norton.
Twentieth Son of Ornon. Mike Sirota. (Orig.). 1980. pap. 1.95 (ISBN 0-89083-685-X). Zebra.
Twenty. William Brinkley. LC 81-65283. 1981. 13.95 (ISBN 0-670-69751-6). Viking Press.
Twenty Best Short Stories in Ray Long's Twenty Years As an Editor. Ed. by Ray Long. LC 32-10110. 1932. R. Long & R. R. Smith, Inc.
Twenty Dollars a Week. Rob Eden. LC 31-190903. Grosset & Dunlap.
Twenty-Eight Humorous Stories: Old and New, by Twenty and Eight Authors. Ed. by Ernest Rhys. Scott, Mrs. Catharine Amy (Dawson) Joint Ed. LC 26-21006. 1926. D. Appleton and Company.
Twenty-Eight Science Fiction Stories. Herbert George Wells. LC 52-13264. 1952. Dover Publications.
Twenty-Eight Science Fiction Stories. Herbert George Wells. 9.95 (ISBN 0-8446-3152-3). Peter Smith.
Twenty-Eight Stories. Frances Gray Patton. LC 76-75201. 1969. 7.50. Dodd, Mead.
Twenty Eighth Day of Elul. Richard M. Elman. 1967. 4.95 o.p. (ISBN 0-684-10142-4). Scribner.
Twenty Eighty-Four, Vol. 1. Davida Gaida. LC 82-62540. (Orig.). 1983. pap. 7.95 (ISBN 0-88100-022-1). Ringa Pr.
Twenty-Fifth Hour. Herbert Best. LC 40-6586. Random House.
Twenty-Fifth Hour. Mary Kelly. LC 77-167286. 1972. 4.95 (ISBN 0-8027-5242-X). Walker.
Twenty-Fifth Hour. Lawrence Russell. 48p. (Orig.). 1981. pap. 2.50 (ISBN 0-914580-11-6). Angst World.
Twenty-Fifth Hour: By C. Virgil Gheorghiu. Tr. from Romanian by Rita Eldon. Constantin Virgil Gheorghiu. LC 66-258416. 1966. 6.50. Regnery.
Twenty-Fifth Hour: Translated from the Romanian by Rita Eldon. 1st American Ed. Constantin Virgil Gheorghiu. LC 50-14872. 1950. Knopf.
Twenty-Fifth Reunion. David M. Camerer. LC 67-18266. 1967. D. McKay Co.
Twenty-First Burr. Victor Lauriston. LC 22-19684. 2.00. George H. Doran Company.
Twenty-First Pan Book of Horror Stories. Ed. by H. Van Thal. 1982. pap. 10.00x (ISBN 0-330-26192-4, Pub. by Pan Bks). State Mutual Bk.
Twenty-Five Finest Short Stories. Ed. by Edward Joseph Harrington O'Brien. LC 31-10084. 1931. R. R. Smith, Inc.
Twenty Five Ghost Stories. Ed. by West Bob Holland. (On cover: Peerless series, no. 145). 1904. J. S. Ogilvie Publishing Company.
Twenty Five Ghost Stories. Ed. by West Bob Holland. LC 42-10679. 1941. Illustrated Editions Company.
Twenty-Five Welsh Stories. Ed. by Gwyn Jones. LC 75-863889. (Oxford paperbacks, 247). 1971. 0.65 (ISBN 0-19-281099-5). Oxford University Press.
Twenty-Five Years in Jackville, a Romance in the Days of "the Golden Circle," and Selected Poems. James Buchanan Elmore. LC 4-10078. 1904. The Author.
Twenty-Four by Twelve. Merritt Clifton. LC 79-84618. 92p. 1980. pap. 4.00 (ISBN 0-930012-26-7). Bandanna Bks.
Twenty-Four Eyes. Sakae Tsuboi. Tr. by Akira Miura from Japanese. LC 82-51098. Orig. Title: Nijushi no Hitomi. 256p. 1983. pap. 6.50 (ISBN 0-8048-1462-7). C E Tuttle.
Twenty-Four Hours. Louis Bromfield. LC 30-269444. 1930. Frederick A. Stokes Company.
Twenty-Four Hours a Day. Faith Baldwin. 1976. Repr. of 1937 ed. 16.30x (ISBN 0-88411-605-0). Amereon Ltd.
Twenty-Four Hours a Day. Faith Baldwin Cuthrell. LC 73-86740. 1973. Aeonian Press.
Twenty-Four Hours a Day. Faith Baldwin Cuthrell. LC 37-28594. Farrar & Rinehart, Inc.
Twenty-Four Hours a Day. Faith Baldwin Cuthrell. LC 65-989. 1972. Warner Paperback Lib.
Twenty-Four Hours at Le Mans: A Novel. Translated from the French by Bryen Gentry. 1st American Ed. Jean Albert Gregoire. LC 58-7469. 1958. J. Day Co.
Twenty-Four Hours Leave. Renee Shann. LC 43-1884. 1943. Random House.
Twenty-Four Love Songs. Edward Dorn. 1969. pap. 2.00. Frontier Press Calif.
Twenty-Four Stories by Premchand. Ed. by Nandini Nopany & P. Lal. 208p. 1981. text ed. 17.95x (ISBN 0-7069-1199-7, Pub by Vikas India). Advent NY.
Twenty-Four Vagabond Tales. John Gibbons. LC 32-258552. 1932. E. P. Dutton & Co., Inc.
Twenty-Fourth Horse. Judson Pentecost Philips. LC 40-33365. 1940. Dodd, Mead & Company.
Twenty-Fourth Level. (Red Badge Suspense Novel Ser.). 1970. 4.50 o.p. (ISBN 0-396-06074-9). Dodd.
Twenty-Fourth of June, Midsummer's Day. Grace Louise Smith Richmond. LC 14-14574. 1914. Doubleday, Page & Company.
Twenty-Fourth of June, Midsummer's Day. Grace Louise Smith Richmond. LC 21-74142. A. L. Burt Company.
Twenty Good Stories. Opie Percival Read. LC 20-18826. J. S. Ogilvie.
Twenty Good Stories. Opie Percival Read. (sunnyside series, no. 24). 1891. J. S. Ogilvie.
Twenty Grand Short Stories. Ed. by Ernestine Taggard. (gr. 6-12,RL 5). pap. 2.50 (ISBN 0-553-14947-4, B13618-6). Bantam.
Twenty Great Tales of Murder, by Experts of the Mystery Writers of America. Mystery Writers of America & Helen Ed McCloy. LC 51-12105. 1951. Random House.
Twenty Miles Out: Indiscretions of a Commuter's Wife. LC 25-21912. 1925. Little, Brown, and Company.
Twenty Miles to Terror. Eddie Stone. 1978. 1.75 (ISBN 0-87067-532-X). Holloway House Pub. Co.
Twenty Million Ransom: A Story of the Future. Frederick Augustus Mitchel. LC 7-31110. 1890. The "Journalist,
Twenty Minutes to Kill. Arthur Minturn Chase. LC 36-1120. 1936. Dodd, Mead & Company.
Twenty Months in Auschwitz. Pelagia Lewinska. Tr. by Albert Teichner. 1968. 4.95 (ISBN 0-8184-0090-0). Lyle Stuart.
Twenty-Nine Chats and One Scolding. Frederic Charles O'Neill. LC 5-2434. 1905. Christian Press Associaton Publishing Company.
Twenty-Nine Herriott Street. John Hutton. LC 79-53473. 1980. 10.95 (ISBN 0-312-82423-8). St. Martin's Press.
Twenty-Nine Herriott Street. John Hutton. 1980. 2.95 (ISBN 0-425-04799-7). Berkley Publishing Corp.
Twenty-Nine Love Stories: Old and New, by Twenty and Nine Authors. Ed. by Ernest Rhys. LC 25-24586. 1925. D. Appleton and Company.
Twenty-Nine Short Stories: An Introductory Anthology. Ed. by Michael Timko. LC 74-31093. 1975. 4.95 (ISBN 0-394-31910-9). Knopf: Distributed by Random House.
Twenty-Nine Stories. Ed. by William Harwood Peden. LC 59-65354. 1960. Houghton Mifflin.
Twenty-Nine Stories. 2d ed. Ed. by William Harwood Peden. LC 67-5311. 1967. Houghton Mifflin.
Twenty Nine Stories: Introductory Anthology. Michael Timko. 1975. pap. text ed. 6.95 o.p. (ISBN 0-394-31910-9). Knopf.
Twenty-Nine Tales from the French. Tr. by Alys Eyre Macklin. LC 72-157785. (Short story index reprint series). 1971. (ISBN 0-8369-3897-6). Books for Libraries Press.
Twenty Notches. Max Brand. LC 32-171428. 1932. Dodd, Mead & Company.
Twenty Notches. Frederick Faust. LC 32-17142. 1932. Dodd, Mead & Company.
Twenty Novelettes. LC 8-319169. (On cover: Love's international series, no. 53). 1889. F. F. Lovell & Company.
Twenty of Their Swords. Holmes Moss Alexander. LC 30-33334. Dorrance & Company.
Twenty-One Billionth Paradox. Leonard Daventry. LC 75-157582. (Doubleday science fiction). 1971. 4.95. Doubleday.
Twenty-One Clues. Alfred Walter Stewart. LC 41-7660. 1941. Little, Brown and Company.
Twenty-One Fifty A.D. Thea Alexander. 281p. (Orig.). 1971. pap. 4.25 (ISBN 0-913080-03-9). Macro Bks.
Twenty-One Great Stories. Ed. by Abraham Lass & Norma Tasman. (Orig.). 1969. pap. 2.25 (ISBN 0-451-62066-6, ME2066, Ment). NAL.
Twenty-One Great Stories. Ed. by Abraham Harold Lass. LC 69-17923. (Mentor book, MQ905). 1969. 0.95. New American Library.
Twenty-One Million Dollar Bank Note: And Other New Stories. Samuel Langhorne Clemens. LC 6-21354. 1893. C. L. Webster & Company.
Twenty-One Stories. Samuel Joseph Agnon. Ed. by Nahum Norbert Glatzer. LC 71-108902. 1970. 6.50. Schocken Books.
Twenty-One Stories. Graham Greene. 200p. 1981. pap. 3.50 (ISBN 0-14-003093-X). Penguin.
Twenty-One Stories. Graham Greene. 1962. 4.00 o.p. (ISBN 0-670-73475-6). Viking Pr.
Twenty-One Texas Short Stories. Ed. by William Walace Peery. LC 54-7339. 1954. University of Texas Press.
Twenty-One Variations on a Theme. Ed. by Donald Webster Cory. LC 52-10869. 1953. Greenberg.
Twenty Pebbles, and Other Stories. 1st Ed. Franklin Millard Webber. 1955. Pageant Press.
Twenty per Cent. 1st Ed. Travis Macrae, pseud. LC 61-17087. (Rinehart suspense novel). 1961. Helt, Rinehart and Winston.
Twenty Plus Two: A Novel of Suspense. 1st Ed. Frank Gruber. LC 61-6003. 1961. Dutton.
Twenty-Seventh Ride. Arthur Dorman Welton. LC 32-13342. Sears Publishing Company, Inc.
Twenty Short Stories. R. T. Nasr. pap. text ed. 1.25x o.p. (ISBN 0-582-76007-0). Longman.
Twenty Short Stories You'll Remember, Adventure, Romance, Humor: Favorites from Progressive Farmer Fiction. The Progressive Farmer. Ed. by Eugene Butler. LC 65-4372. 1964.
Twenty-Six Adventure Stories: Old and New, by Twenty and Six Authors. Ed. by Ernest Rhys. Scott, Mrs. Catharine Amy (Dawson) Joint Ed. LC 29-2250. 1929. D. Appleton and Company.
Twenty-Six and One, and Other Stories. Maksim Gorkii. LC 72-11935. (Short story index reprint series). 1973. (ISBN 0-8369-4233-7). Books for Libraries Press.
Twenty-Six & One: And Other Stories. Maksim Gorkii. LC 72-11935. (Short Story Index Reprint Ser.). 1973. Repr. of 1902 ed. 15.00 (ISBN 0-8369-4233-7). Ayer Co.
Twenty-Six and One: And Other Stories from the Vagabond Series. Maksim Gorkii. LC 2-11615. 1902. J. F. Taylor & Company.
Twenty-Six Clues. Isabel Egenton Ostrander. LC 19-3704. W. J. Watt & Company.
Twenty-Six Men and a Girl: And Other Stories. Maksim Gorkii. LC 74-103510. (Short story index reprint series). 1969. Books for Libraries Press.
Twenty Six Men & a Girl & Other Stories. Maksim Gorkii. LC 74-103510. (Short Story Index Reprint Ser.). 1902. 19.00 (ISBN 0-8369-3252-8). Ayer Co.
Twenty-Six Mystery Stories: Old and New, by Twenty and Six Authors. Ed. by Ernest Rhys. Scott, Mrs. Catharine Amy (Dawson) Joint Ed. LC 27-205852. 1927. D. Appleton and Company.
Twenty Stories: Selected, with an Introduction. Stephen Crane & Van Doren, Carl Clinton. LC 40-30097. 1940. A. A. Knopf.
Twenty-Third Web. Richard Himmel. LC 76-53464. 8.95 (ISBN 0-394-41089-0). Random House.
Twenty Thousand Leagues Under the Sea. Jules Verne. LC 56-2609. 1956. Junior Deluxe Editions.
Twenty Thousand Leagues Under the Sea. Jules Verne. LC 57-135888. 1957. Heritage Press.
Twenty Thousand Leagues Under the Sea. Jules Verne. LC 57-2751. 1957. Fine Editions Press.
Twenty Thousand Leagues Under the Sea. Jules Verne. LC 62-18394. (Macmillan classics, 40). 1962. Macmillan.
Twenty Thousand Leagues Under the Sea. Jules Verne. LC 64-15710. (Classics to grow on). 1966. Parents' Magazine's Cultural Institute.
Twenty Thousand Leagues Under the Sea. Jules Verne. (Classics to grow on). 1966. Parents' Magazine's Cultural Institute.
Twenty Thousand Leagues Under the Sea. Jules Verne. (Great illustrated classics). (Illus.). 1952. Dodd, Mead.
Twenty Thousand Leagues Under the Sea. Jules Verne. LC 79-93038. (Signet classic, CT489). 1969. 0.75. New American Library.
Twenty Thousand Leagues Under the Sea. Jules Verne. LC 16-9962. 1916. C. Scribner's Sons.
Twenty Thousand Leagues Under the Sea. Jules Verne. LC 17-10162. Grosset & Dunlap.
Twenty Thousand Leagues Under the Sea. Jules Verne. LC 25-21265. 1925. C. Scribner's Sons.
Twenty Thousand Leagues Under the Sea. Jules Verne. LC 32-31009. The John C. Winston Company.
Twenty Thousand Leagues Under the Sea. Jules Verne. LC 35-16476. The Saalfield Publishing Company.
Twenty Thousand Leagues Under the Sea. Jules Verne & Wiese, Kurt, 1887- Illus. LC 46-5467. (Half-title: Rainbow classics; general editor: May Lamberton Becker). 1946. The World Publishing Company.
Twenty-Thousand Leagues Under the Sea: Abridged & adapted to grade 2 reading level. Jules Verne. Ed. by Andrea M. Clare. LC 73-80399. (Pacemaker Classics Ser.). 1973. pap. 4.92 (ISBN 0-8224-9233-4); tchrs' manual free. Pitman Learning.
Twenty Thousand Leagues Under the Sea: And Around the Moon. Jules Verne & Jules Verne. LC 65-15193. (Platt & Munk great writers collection). 1965. Platt & Munk.
Twenty Thousand Leagues Under the Sea: Adapted by Gertrude Moderow. Design, Cover, Map by Ray Martin. Jules Verne & Gertrude Moderow. LC 55-2925. 1955. Scott, Foresman.
Twenty Thousand Leagues Under the Sea. A Definitive Modern Tr. by Walter James Miller, Assist. by Judith Ann Tirsch. Afterword by Damon Knight. Illus. by Walter Brooks. Jules Verne. (Reader's enrichment ed., RE709). Washington Sq.
Twenty Thousand Leagues Under the Sea. A Definitive Mod. Tr. by Walter James Miller, Judith Ann Tirsch. Afterword by Damon Knight. Illus. by Walter Brooks. Jules Verne. LC 65-25245. 1966. 3.95. Washington Sq.
Twenty Thousand Leagues Under the Sea and The Blockade Runners. Jules Verne. LC 37-5397. (Immortal masterpiece of literature, vol. vi). The Spencer Press.
Twenty Thousand Leagues Under the Sea: And The Blockade Runners. Jules Verne & Jules Verne. LC 50-3414. (World's greatest literature). 1950. Fountain Press.
Twenty Thousand Leagues Under the Sea. Introd. by Charles Angoff. Jules Verne. LC 97-2751. 1957. Fine Editions Press.
Twenty Thousand Leagues Under the Seas: Or, The Marvellous and Exciting Adventures of Pierre Aronnax, Conseil His Servant, and Ned Land, a Canadian Harpooner. Jules Verne. LC 1-9861. 1874. G. M. Smith & Co.
Twenty Thousand Leagues Under the Sea: Translated by Anthony Bonner, with a Special Introd. by Ray Bradbury. Jules Verne. LC 64-23657. (Bantam pathfinder editions) "HP84."). 1964. Bantam Books.
Twenty Thousand Leagues Under the Sea. The English Version Made from the French by Mercier Lewis, with a New Introd. by Fletcher Pratt, and with Hand-Colored Illus. by Edward A. Wilson. Jules Verne. LC 57-15359. 1956. Printed for the Members of the Limited Editions Club at the Plantin Press.
Twenty Thousand Leagues Under the Sea. The English Version Made from the French by Mercier Lewis, with a New Introd. by Fletcher Pratt, and with Hand-Colored Illus. by Edward A. Wilson. Jules Verne. LC 57-13588. 1957. Heritage Press.
Twenty Thousand Leagues Under the Sea: The Marvelous and Exciting Adventures of Pierre Aronnax, Consiel, His Servant, and Ned Land, a Canadian Harpooner. Jules Verne. LC 4-17515. A. L. Burt Company.
Twenty Thousand Leagues Under the Sea. With Biographical Illus. and Drawings Reproduced from Early Editions, Together with an Introductory Biographical Sketch of the Author and Anecdotal Captions by Allen Klots, Jr. Jules Verne. LC 53-8076. (Great illustrated classics). 1952. Dodd, Mead.

Twenty Thousand Leagues Under the Sea: With Four Colour Plates and Line Drawings in the Text by William McLaren. Jules Verne. LC 66-66050. (C.I.C. ser., no. 71). 1966. 3.50. Dent.

Twenty-Three and a Half Hours' Leave. Mary Roberts Rinehart. LC 18-211667. George H. Doran Company.

Twenty-Three Modern Stories. Ed. by Barbara Howes. LC 63-7652. 1963. Vintage Books.

Twenty-Three Stories. Ernest Rhys & Scott, Mrs. Catherine Amy Dawson Joint Ed. LC 24-28114. 1924. D. Appleton and Company.

Twenty-Three Tales. Lev Nikolaevich Tolstoi. 7.95 o.p. (ISBN 0-19-250072-4). Oxford U Pr.

Twenty-Three Tales. Lev Nikolaevich Tolstoi & Maude, Mrs. Louise (Shanks) 1855- Tr. LC 39-2495. (Half-title: The world's classics, 72). 1936. H. Milford, Oxford University Press.

Twenty-Twenty Vision. Jerry Pournelle. 256p. 1980. pap. 2.25 (ISBN 0-449-24302-8, Crest). Fawcett.

Twenty-Two Fires. Jerome Agel & Eugene Boe. 1977. 1.95 (ISBN 0-553-11631-2). Bantam Books.

Twenty-Two Great Modern Short Stories from Jackpot. Erskine Caldwell. LC 44-7917. (On cover: Avon modern short story monthly. No. 14). 1944. Avon Book Company.

Twenty-Two Malaysian Stories. Lloyd Fernando. (Writing in Asia Ser.). 1968. pap. text ed. 5.50x (00229). Heinemann Ed.

Twenty-Two Strange Stories. John L. Hardie. Repr. of 1945 ed. 12.50 o.p. (ISBN 0-89987-119-4). Darby Bks.

Twenty Years After. Alexandre Dumas & Maquet, Auguste. (Seaside library, v. 15, no. 283). G. Munro.

Twenty Years After. Alexandre Dumas & Maquet, Auguste. LC 6-421275. (On cover: Seaside library. Pocket ed. no. 75). G. Munro.

Twenty Years After. Alexandre Dumas & Maquet, Auguste. LC 6-42128. (On cover: Lovell's library v. 16. no. 786). J. W. Lovell Company.

Twenty Years After. Alexandre Dumas & Maquet, Auguste. LC 6-42129. 1888. Little, Brown, and Company.

Twenty Years After. Alexandre Dumas & Maquet, Auguste. LC 4-21714. Little, Brown, & Company.

Twenty Years After... Alexandre Dumas & Maquet, Auguste. LC 4-17500. (Half-title: The romances of Alexandre Dumas, Handy library edition. The D'Artagnan romances...). 1893. Little, Brown and Company.

Twenty Years After. Alexandre Dumas & Maquet, Auguste. LC 6-42131. (Half-title: The romances of Alexandre Dumas. Illustrated library ed. v. 14-15). 1893. Little, Brown, and Company.

Twenty Years After. Alexandre Dumas & Maquet, Auguste. T. Y. Crowell & Company.

Twenty Years After. Alexandre Dumas & Maquet, Auguste. 1899. Little, Brown, and Company.

Twenty Years After. Alexandre Dumas & Maquet, Auguste. LC 23-17114. 1923. Dodd, Mead and Company.

Twenty Years After. Alexandre Dumas & Maquet, Auguste. LC 28-26951. (Rittenhouse classics). 1928. Macrae Smith Company.

Twenty Years After. Alexandre Dumas & Maquet, Auguste. LC 36-37231. (Half-title: Everyman's library, ed. by Ernest Rhys. Fiction no. 175). 1930. J. M. Dent & Sons. Ltd.

Twenty Years After: A Historical Romance... Alexandre Dumas. Tr. by Williams, Henry Llewellyn. LC 852. (On cover: Arrow library, no. 99). 1899. Street & Smith.

Twenty Years After. A Historical Romance. Alexandre Dumas & Maquet, Auguste. LC 6-42130. (American series. no. 297). M. J. Ivers & Co.

Twenty Years After: A Sequel to "The Three Musketeers,". Alexandre Dumas & Maquet, Auguste. LC 3-27815. G. Rutledge and Sons.

Twenty Years After: Or, The Further Feats and Fortunes of a Gasson Adventurer. Being a Sequel to "The Three Guardsmen.". Alexandre Dumas & Maquet, Auguste. Tr. by Barrow, William. LC 6-42126. 1850. W. F. Burgess.

Twenty Years After. With Illus. by Edy Legrand and an Introd. by Ben Ray Redman. Translated from the French. Alexandre Dumas. LC 60-2838. 1960. bxd. 6.00. Heritage Press Dist. Dial Press.

Twenty Years Ago: And Now. Timothy Shay Arthur. LC 6-3428. 1860. J. W. Bradley.

Twenty Years in Siberia: And Leaves from My Russian Diary. M. De Packh. LC 8-294240. Guarantee Publishing Co.

Twenty Years in the Tropics. A Novel. Mathias P. Greensword. LC 6-44863. 1887. W. F. Boshart, Printer.

Twenty Years of Stanford Short Stories: Ed. by Wallace Stegner, Richard Scowcroft with Nancy Packer. Ed. by Wallace Earle Stegner & Richard Scowcroft. LC 66-25958. 1966. 2.95 pap., 6.95. Stanford Univ. Pr.

Twenty Years of Stanford Short Stories. Ed. by Wallace Earle Stegner & Richard Scowcroft. 1966. 15.00x (ISBN 0-8047-0394-9). Stanford U Pr.

Twenty Years of the Magazine of Fantasy and Science Fiction. Ed. by Edward L. Ferman. LC 70-105597. 1970. 5.95. G. P. Putnam's Sons.

Twentyfour Times Twelve. Merritt Clifton. 1975. pap. 1.00 o.p. Samisdat.

Twentymen. Philip Purser. LC 67-13940. 1967. 3.95. Walker.

Twice Adopted: A Romance, Rev. for General Circulation. Thomas R. Vernon. LC 22-21211. The Vernon Company.

Twice American. Eleanor Marie Ingram. LC 17-28801. 1917. J. B. Lippincott Company.

Twice-Born. Cecily Crowe. 1975. (pbk.) 1.25. Dell.

Twice-Born. Cecily Crowe. LC 72-1058. 1972. 5.95 (ISBN 0-394-47554-2). Random House.

Twice Born. Rose Franken. LC 35-4223. 1935. C. Scribner's Sons.

Twice Born Twice Dead: A Novel. Kartar S. Duggal. 1980. text ed. 10.00x (ISBN 0-7069-0714-0, Pub. by Vikas India). Advent NY.

Twice Brightly. Harry Secombe. LC 74-17428. 1975. 7.95. St. Martin's Press.

Twice Crowned. A Story of the Days of Queen Mary. Harriet Burn McKeever. LC 7-16313. 1873. Claxton, Remsen & Haffelfinger.

Twice Dead. Larry D Names. (Leisure Book). 1978. 1.75 (ISBN 0-8439-0601-4). Nordon Publications, Inc.

Twice Dead! Marilyn Ross. (Stewarts of Stormhaven-10). 1978. 1.75 (ISBN 0-445-04252-4). Popular Library.

Twice Dead: By John Rhode. Cecil John Charles Street. LC 60-11927. (Red badge detective). 1960. Dodd, Mead.

Twice Defeated: Or, The Story of a Dark Society in Two Countries. Rollin Edwards. LC 6-36593. 1877. J. B. Lippincott & Co.

Twice Freed. St. John, Patricia Mary. LC 79-143476. 1971. 3.95. Moody Press.

Twice Have I Loved. Denise Robins. (Beagle romance#37). 1975. (pbk.) 0.95 (ISBN 0-345-26668-4). Ballantine Books.

Twice in Time. Manly Wade Wellman. LC 57-12672. 1957. Avalon Books.

Twice Lost. Phyllis Paul. LC 60-5848. 1960. Norton.

Twice Lost. A Story of Shipwreck, and of Adventure in the Wilds of Australia. William Henry Giles Kingston. LC 42-29441. 1884. T. Nelson and Sons.

Twice Loyal: A Novel. Mary K White. LC 17-25977. 1917. The Neale Publishing Company.

Twice Retired. Richard Lockridge. LC 73-105547. 1970. 4.95. Lippincott.

Twice Shy. Dick Francis. LC 81-15814. 13.95 (ISBN 0-399-12707-0). Putnam.

Twice Shy. David Morrice Low. LC 34-2064. Harcourt, Brace and Company.

Twice So Fair. Nedra Tyre. LC 78-159384. 1971. 5.95 (ISBN 0-394-47186-5). Random House.

Twice Taken: An Historical Romance of the Maritime British Provinces. Charles Winslow Hall. LC 7-320. 1867. Lee and Shepard.

Twice Ten Thousand Miles: A Novel. Frances Lynch. LC 73-92056. 1974. 7.95. St. Martin's Press.

Twice the New Moon. Katharine Dunlap. LC 55-6372. 1955. Morrow.

Twice They Lived. I. B Ezra. LC 65-172149. 4.95. A. S. Barnes.

Twice Told Tales. Hilton Brown. Repr. of 1929 ed. 10.00 o.p. (ISBN 0-89987-120-8). Darby Bks.

Twice Told Tales. Hilton Brown. 1946. 10.00. Havertown Bks.

Twice-Told Tales. Nathaniel Hawthorne. Ed. by Stegner, Wallace Earle. Limited Editions Club, Inc., New York. LC 67-9047. 1966. Printed for the Members of the Limited Editions Club.

Twice-Told Tales. Nathaniel Hawthorne. (On cover: Lovell's library, v. 7, no. 370). 1884. J. W. Lovell Company.

Twice-Told Tales. Nathaniel Hawthorne. LC 9-8358. (Half-title: Riverside ed. The complete works of Nathaniel Hawthorne... vol. i). 1893. Houghton, Mifflin and Company.

Twice-Told Tales. Nathaniel Hawthorne. LC 7-3769. (On cover: Standard literature series, no. 15). 1896. University Publishing Company.

Twice-Told Tales... Nathaniel Hawthorne. LC 7-3768. (On cover: Maynard's English classic series, no. 188, 189). Maynard, Merrill & Co.

Twice-Told Tales. Nathaniel Hawthorne. LC 4718. W. B. Conkey Company.

Twice-Told Tales. Nathaniel Hawthorne. Ed. by Robert Herrick. LC 3-28138. (lake English classics). 1903. Scott, Foresman and Company.

Twice-Told Tales. Nathaniel Hawthorne & Bates, Katherine Lee, 1859- LC 4720. T. Y. Crowell & Co.

Twice-Told Tales. Nathaniel Hawthorne & Herrick, Robert, 1868- Ed. LC 19-18645. (Half-title: The Lake English classics, general editor L. T. Damon...). Scott, Foresman and Company.

Twice-Told Tales. Nathaniel Hawthorne & Scott, John Hubert, Ed. LC 7-36413. (Riverside literature series no. 82, quadruple numer). Houghton, Mifflin and Company.

Twice-Told Tales: An Anthology of Short Fiction. Gerard A. Barker. LC 78-69561. 1979. pap. text ed. 12.50 (ISBN 0-395-26635-1); instr's. manual 1.00 (ISBN 0-395-26636-X). HM.

Twice-Told Tales: And Other Short Stories. With an Introd. by Quentin Anderson. New Ed. Nathaniel Hawthorne. LC 60-694. (Washington Square Press book, W580). 1960. Washington Square Press.

Twice-Told Tales. Selected, Introduced by Wallace Stegner. Illus. by Valenti Angelo. Nathaniel Hawthorne. Valenti Angelo. 1967. bds., 7.50. Heritage Pr.

Twice Told Tales: Short Stories Broadcast by the B. C. Hilton Brown. 64p. 1982. Repr. of 1946 ed. lib. bdg. 20.00 (ISBN 0-8495-0080-X). Arden Lib.

Twice Tried: Or, Asa Warren's Metal. Martha Williams Lewis. LC 4590. (On cover: The Silver line series). The Silver Line Publishing Co.

Twice Trodden Ground. Barbara Y. Main. (Illus.). 96p. 1972. 5.00 o.s.i. (ISBN 0-7016-0369-0); pap. 3.00 o.s.i. Tri-Ocean.

Twice Turned Tales. Donald B. Miller. LC 77-88730. (Illus.). 1977. pap. 3.50 o.p. (ISBN 0-930918-00-2). Vitality Assocs.

Twice Twenty-Two. Ray Bradbury. LC 66-10615. (Science Fiction Ser.). 1966. 14.95 (ISBN 0-385-05594-3). Doubleday.

Twice Twenty-Two: The Golden Apples of the Sun. A Medicine for Melancholy. Drawings by Joe Mugnaini. Ray Bradbury. LC 66-10615. 1966. 4.95. Doubleday.

Twice Upon a Time. Carolyn Jones. LC 78-140569. 1971. 6.95 (ISBN 0-671-27074-5). Trident Press.

Twiddledum Twaddledum. Peter Spielberg. LC 74-77779. 1974. 7.95 (ISBN 0-914590-04-9); pap. 3.95 (ISBN 0-914590-05-7). Fiction Coll.

Twiddledum Twaddledum: A Novel. Peter Spielberg. LC 74-77779. 1974. 7.95 (ISBN 0-914590-04-9) (ISBN 0-914590-04-9). Fiction Collective; Distributed by G. Braziller.

Twiddleham & Other Tales. G. E. Booker. 2.75 o.p. Carlton.

Twig Is Bent. Estelle Thompson. LC 60-13627. Abelard-Schuman.

Twila. Harry Price Sturm. 1975. write for info. o.p. (ISBN 0-87012-248-7). McClain.

Twilight. Julia Davis Frankau. LC 16-4750. 1916. 1.35. Dodd, Mead and Company.

Twilight. Eduard Heinrich Nikolaus Graf Von Keyserling. LC 27-3360. The Macaulay Company.

Twilight at Monticello. William Harwood Peden. LC 72-9020. 1973. 5.95 (ISBN 0-395-15462-6). Houghton Mifflin.

Twilight at the Elms. Dorothy Daniels. (Signet Book). 1976. 1.25. New American Library.

Twilight at the Well of Souls: The Legacy of Nathan Brazil. Jack L. Chalker. (Saga of the Well World: Vol. 5). 320p. 1980. pap. 2.25 (ISBN 0-345-28368-6). Ballantine.

Twilight Candelabra. William J Craddock. LC 70-180120. (Doubleday projections book). 1972. 2.95. Doubleday.

Twilight Cheats. Grace Perkins Oursler. LC 39-25867. Farrar & Rinehart, Inc.

Twilight Comes Early. Louis Berg. LC 39-626286. L. Furman, Inc.

Twilight Embrace, No. 86. Jennifer Rose, pseud. 1982. pap. 1.75 (ISBN 0-515-06697-4). Jove Pubns.

Twilight for Taurus. Miriam Lynch. (Berkley Medallion Book). 1976. (pbk.) 1.25 (ISBN 0-425-03091-1). Berkley Publishing Co.

Twilight for the Gods. Ernest Kellogg Gann. LC 56-10744. 1956. W. Sloans Associates.

Twilight for the Heroes. Alla Bozarth. LC 66-25047. 1966. Christopher Pub. House.

Twilight Forest. Clare H. Lawless. (Orig.). 1973. pap. 1.25 o.p. (ISBN 0-515-03178-X, V3173). Pyramid Pubns.

Twilight Hour. Novelle Richards. 1970. 4.95 o.p. Vantage.

Twilight in Delhi. 2nd ed. Ahmed Ali. 290p. 1974. pap. 3.00 (ISBN 0-88253-281-2). Ind-US Inc.

Twilight in Delhi: A Novel. 2nd ed. Ahmed Ali. (Champak Library). 1966. 5.00x o.p. (ISBN 0-19-211346-1). Oxford U Pr.

Twilight in Delhi: A Novel. 2nd Ed. Ahmed Ali. LC 67-892197. 1966-1967. 3.40. Oxford Univ. Pr.

Twilight in Djakarta. Mochtar Lubis. Tr. by Claire Holt. LC 64-16196. 1964. 7.95 o.s.i. (ISBN 0-8149-0148-4). Vanguard.

Twilight Journey. Leslie Purnell Davies. LC 68-18097. 1968. Doubleday.

Twilight Man. Frank Gruber. LC 67-11375. 1967. Dutton.

Twilight Men. Otto Basil. Orig. Title: If Only the Fuehrer Knew. 1968. 6.95 o.p. (ISBN 0-696-84938-0). Hawthorn.

Twilight Men. Andre Tellier. LC 48-4636. 1948. Greenberg.

Twilight Men. Andre Tellier. LC 31-4813. Greenberg.

Twilight Men: A Novel. Otto Basil. LC 68-9517. 1968. 6.95. Meredith Press.

Twilight of a Poet, and Other Stories. Dominador Paulo Dizon. LC 63-4050. (Regal series, 4). 1962. Regal Pub. Co.

Twilight of a World. Franz V. Werfel. Tr. by Helen Tracy Porter Lowe. LC 37-427818. 1937. The Viking Press.

Twilight of Briareus. Richard Cowper, pseud. (Science Fiction Ser). 1975. pap. 1.50 o.p. (ISBN 0-87997-183-5, UW1183). DAW Bks.

Twilight of Briareus. Richard Cowper, pseud. LC 73-19470. 256p. 1974. 6.95 o.p. (ISBN 0-381-98270-X). John Day.

Twilight of Briareus. Richard Cowper, pseud. (Science Fiction Ser). 1975. pap. 1.50 o.p. (ISBN 0-87997-183-5, UW1183). DAW Bks.

Twilight of Briareus. Colin Murry. LC 73-19470. 1974. 6.95 (ISBN 0-381-98270-X). John Day Co.

Twilight of Honor. Jan S. Paul. 1977. pap. 1.25 o.p. Echo Pubs.

Twilight of the City. Charles Platt. 1978. pap. 1.75 (ISBN 0-425-03832-7, Medallion). Berkley Pub.

Twilight of the City: A Novel of the Near Future. Charles Platt. LC 76-40913. 8.95 (ISBN 0-02-597620-6). Macmillan.

Twilight of the Day. Mervyn Jones. LC 74-6137. 1974. 8.95 (ISBN 0-671-21815-8). Simon and Schuster.

Twilight of the Dragoon. Graham Montague Jeffries. 1954. Putnam.

Twilight of the Elephant. Elio Vittorini. LC 51-10545. (Direction, 21). 1951. J. Laughlin.

Twilight of the Gods. Florizel Von Reuter. (Illus.). 1962. 9.50x (ISBN 0-910476-02-0). Cultural Pr.

Twilight of the Gods: And Other Tales. new and augm. ed. Richard Garnett. LC 3-17945. 1903. J. Lane.

Twilight of the Gods, and Other Tales: With an Introduction by T. E. Lawrence. Richard Garnett & Lawrence, Thomas Edward, 1888-1935, Ed. (Half-title: Blue jade library). 1926. A. A. Knopf.

Twilight of the Souls. Louis Marie Anne Couperus & Teixeira De Mattos, Alexander Louis, 1865-1921, Tr. LC 17-25859. 1917. Dodd, Mead and Company.

Twilight on the Danube. Franz Carl Weiskopf & Marx, Olga, 1894- Tr. 1946. A. A. Knopf.

Twilight on the Floods: A Sequel to "The Sun in My Undoing.". Marguerite Steen. LC 49-9801. 1949. Doubleday.

Twilight on the River. Ilanon Moon. LC 77-14241. 1977. 9.50 (ISBN 0-88319-031-1). Shoal Creek Publishers.

Twilight Return. John M. Kimbro. LC 76-45204. (Zodiac gothic: Cancer). 1977. 9.95 (ISBN 0-89340-012-2). J. Curley & Associates.

Twilight Return: An Astrological Gothic Novel: Cancer. John M. Kimbro. LC 76-6995. 1.25. Ballantine Books.

Twilight Sleep. Edith Newbold Jones Wharton. LC 27-112091. 1927. D. Appleton and Company.

Twilight Star. William Arthur Neubauer. LC 51-1592. 1951. Arcadia House.

Twilight Strangler. Charles Miron. (Airport Cop Ser.: No. 2). 192p. 1975. pap. 1.25 o.p. (ISBN 0-532-12271-2). Woodhill.

Twilight Strangler. Charles Miron. (Airport Cop Ser.: No. 2). 192p. 1975. pap. 1.25 o.p. (ISBN 0-532-12271-2). Manor Bks.

Twilight Tales: Twenty-Four Stories of Love and Romance from Real Life. Margaret Elizabeth Munson Sangster. LC 12-17512. The Christian Herald.

Twilight Tapestry. Frieda Bair. 1977. 3.95 o.p. (ISBN 0-8059-2470-1). Dorrance.

Twilight Web. William Edward Daniel Ross. LC 68-4042. 1968. Arcadia House.

Twilight Woman. Leslie Scott. LC 52-14892. (Arco sophisticate). 1952. Arco.

Twilight World. Poul Anderson. 256p. (Orig.). 1983. pap. 2.75 (ISBN 0-523-48561-1). Tor Bks.

Twilight World. Poul Anderson. LC 64-6098. (Torquil book). 1961. Distributed by Dodd, Mead.

Twilight Zone Companion. Marc S. Zicree. 512p. 1982. pap. 9.95 (ISBN 0-553-01416-1). Bantam.

Twilight Zone Revisited. Rod Serling. LC 64-24432. 1964. Grosset & Dunlap.

Twilighters. Noel M. Loomis. LC 55-1106. 1955. Macmillan.

Twilights and Dawn: Four Allegorical Myths. Hidalgo-Briceno, Miguel. LC 76-170950. 1971. 7.50. Julian Press.

Twilight's Last Gleaming: A Novel. Leon Arden. LC 75-185076. 1972. 5.95. Crown Publishers.

Twin: A Novel. Andrew Blumley. LC 76-104643. 1970. 4.95. Stein and Day.

Twin Adventures: The Adventures of William Saroyan, a Diary. The Adventures of Wesley Jackson, a Novel. William Saroyan & Saroyan, William. LC 50-6550. 1950. Harcourt, Brace.

Twin Athletes: Or, Always on Top. A Tale of Wonderful Surprises. Harlan Page Halsey. (Old Sleuth's own, no. 104). 1898. The Parlor Car Publishing Co.

Twin Beds. Edward Salisbury Field. LC 13-17415. 0.75. W. J. Watt & Company.

Twin Bussars. Frank West Rollins. (American series no. 238). 1891. M. J. Ivers & Co.

Twin Buttes. Minnie O. Byxbe. 5.75 o.p. Carlton.

Twin Colts. Morgan Hill. (Orig.). 1980. pap. 1.95 (ISBN 0-440-18620-X). Dell.

Twin Cousins, a Novel. 1st Ed. Oriana Torrey Atkinson. LC 51-12434. 1951. Bobbs-Merrill.

Twin Detectives: Or, The Robbers of the Tomb. K. F Hill. (secret service series--no. 4). 1888. Street & Smith.

Twin Gods: A Novel. John Joseph Cosgrove. LC 17-7809. 1.00. The Technical Book Publishing Company.

Twin Killing. Aaron Marc Stein. LC 47-24073. 1947. Pub. for the Crime Club by Doubleday & Company, Inc.

Twin Lieutenants: Or, The Soldier's Bride. Alexandre Dumas. LC 6-43614. (On cover: Seaside library. Pocket ed. No. 2075). G. Munro.

Twin Lights. Sara Ware Bassett. LC 32-216917. The Penn Publishing Company.

Twin Mavericks. William L. Hopson. 1978. pap. 1.25 o.s.i. (ISBN 0-505-51277-7). Tower Bks.

Twin Oaks. Earl W. Hammond. 1975. 6.95 o.s.i. (ISBN 0-8181-0335-3). Pageant-Poseidon.

Twin Pines and Other Highlights in the Lives of the Horace W. Osbornes. Harvey Hassall Smith. LC 47-30653. 1947. C. Scribner's Sons.

Twin Planets. Philip E. High. (Orig.). pap. 0.50 o.p. (52-392). Paperback Lib.

Twin Roses. A Narrative. Anna Cora Ogden Mowatt Ritchie. LC 7-41659. 1857. Ticknor and Fields.

Twin Satyrs. Salambo Forest. (Orig.). 1968. pap. 1.75 o.s.i. (127, Ophelia). Olympia.

Twin Serpents: A Novel of Suspense. Ronald Scott Thorn, pseud. LC 65-18464. 1965. Macmillan.

Twin Sisters. A Love Story. Florence Nightingale Craddock. LC 6-31145. (Dillingham's metropolitan library, no. 11). 1895. G. W. Dillingham.

Twin Sisters: A Novel. Justus Miles Forman. LC 16-66069. 1916. Harper & Brothers.

Twin Sisters of Martigny: A Story of Italian Life Forty Years Ago... Joel Foote Bingham.

Twin Sombreros. Zane Grey. LC 41-51902. C.

Twin Sombreros. Zane Grey. 1976. (pbk.) 1.50 (ISBN 0-671-80447-2). Pocket Books.

Twin Soul. Charles Mackay. (On cover: Lovell's library, no. 1137). 1888. J. Lovell Company.

Twin Souls. Jeannie Wormley Blackburn Moran. LC 22-12395. The Christopher Publishing House.

Twin Starrs: A Novel. John Breckenridge Ellis. LC 8-11704. 1908. Mayhew Publishing Company.

Twin Strangers. Sinclair Tousey. G. H. Watt.

Twin Tales: Are All Men Alike and The Lost Titian. Arthur John Arbuthnott Stringer. LC 21-19199. The Bobbs-Merrill Company.

Twin Trouble. Phyllis Sweet White. LC 43-20233. 1941. Institute Press, Wood, Wood and Wood.

Twin Valley. Charles Roy Cox. LC 55-37562. 1955. American Book Concern.

Twinkle. James Eldridge. (Illus.). 64p. (Orig.). 1980. pap. 3.25 (ISBN 0-938900-00-5). Creations Unltd.

Twinkle, Twinkle, "Killer" Kane. William Peter Blatty. (Signet Book, Y5850). 1973. (pbk.) 1.25. New American Library.

Twinkle, Twinkle, "Killer" Kane! William Peter Blatty. LC 66-12825. 1966. Doubleday.

Twinkle, Twinkle Little Star. Ben Barzman. LC 60-11429. 1960. Putnam.

Twinkle Twinkle Little Star see Echo X.

Twinkletoes: A Tale of Limehouse. Thomas Burke. 1918. R. M. McBride & Company.

Twins. Mark Dunster. LC 75-192367. (Rin Ser.: Pt. 35). 1975. 4.00 (ISBN 0-89642-036-1). Linden Pubs.

Twins. Bari Wood & Jack Geasland. 1978. pap. 3.50 (ISBN 0-451-09886-2, E9886, Sig). NAL.

Twins: A Domestic Novel. Martin Farquhar Tupper. LC 42-35210. (Half-title: Wiley and Putnam's library of choice reading). 1845. Wiley & Putnam.

Twins: A Novel. Bari Wood & Jack Geasland. LC 76-52948. 8.95 (ISBN 0-399-11866-7). Putnam.

Twins: A Novel. Bari Wood & Jack Geasland. (Signet Book). 1978. 2.50 (ISBN 0-451-08015-7). New American Library.

Twins & Other Stories. M. Krichevsky. 4.50 o.p. (ISBN 0-8062-0444-3). Carlton.

Twins & Supertwins. Amram Scheinfeld. 1973. pap. 2.25 o.p. (ISBN 0-14-021512-3, Pelican). Penguin.

Twins Have Mother. Peggy Swenson, pseud. pap. 1.95 o.p. (ISBN 0-87682-248-0, 7248). Barclay Hse.

Twins in Twain. Rose Taylor Loveridge. 1909. 1.50. F. W. Brown.

Twins of Nuremberg: A Novel. Hermann Kesten & Basch, Ernst, Tr. LC 46-4717. 1946. L. B. Fischer.

Twins of Suffering Creek. Ridgwell Cullum. LC 12-985513. G. W. Jacobs & Co.

Twins of Table Mountain: And Other Stories. Bret Harte. LC 7-23538. Houghton, Mifflin and Company.

Twins or Triplets? Grace C Carney. LC 38-11475. 1938. Meador Publishing Company.

Twist of Fate. Charlotte Lamb, pseud. (Harlequin Presents). (Orig.). 1980. pap. 1.50 (ISBN 0-373-10358-1, Pub. by Harlequin). PB.

Twist of Lemon. Edward Carl Stephens. LC 58-9375. Doubleday,

Twist of Sand. Jeffrey Jenkins. (Keith Jennison Large Type Bks). 8.95 o.p. (ISBN 0-531-00299-3). Watts.

Twist of Sand: A Novel. Geoffrey Jenkins. LC 60-5836. 1960. Viking Press.

Twist of the Knife. Victor Canning. LC 55-6905. 1955. W. Sloane Associates.

Twist of Yarn. 1st Ed. Emmitt Lookabee. LC 56-127595. 1956. Pageant Press.

Twisted Clay. Frank Walford. LC 34-169074. C. Kendall.

Twisted Drives of Victoria Mac Call. Tony Trelos, pseud. 1968. pap. 1.75 o.p. (3042). Brandon.

Twisted Eglantine. Henry Brereton Marriott Watson. LC 5-35294. 1905. D. Appleton and Company.

Twisted Face. Frederic Arnold Kummer. LC 38-22207. 1938. Dodd, Mead & Company.

Twisted Foot. Henry Milner Rideout. 1910. 1.20. Houghton Mifflin Company.

Twisted Foot. William Patterson White. LC 24-19025. 1924. Little, Brown, and Company.

Twisted Heart, a Novel. Mary MacLaren. LC 52-8636. 1952. Exposition Press.

Twisted Kicks. Tom Carson. LC 81-22901. 5.95 (ISBN 0-915904-62-4). And/Or Press.

Twisted Mirror. Leonard Lee. LC 47-6187. 1947. Ziff-Davis Pub. Co.

Twisted Ones. Tom Foran. LC 63-21019. Beacon-Signal Books.

Twisted Ones. Jerome Warr. (Orig.). 1969. pap. 1.25 o.p. (2097). Brandon.

Twisted People: A Peter Styles Mystery. Judson Pentecost Philips. LC 65-200525. (Red badge detective). bds., 3.50. Dodd.

Twisted Saber: A Biographical Novel of Benedict Arnold. Philip Vail. LC 63-14958. 1963. Dodd, Mead.

Twisted Skein. Florence Elise Hyde. LC 43-1999. The Paebar Company.

Twisted Skein. Ralph Delahaye Paine. LC 15-18108. 1915. 1.35. C. Scribner's Sons.

Twisted Tales. Frank DuGan. 64p. 1975. 4.00 o.p. (ISBN 0-682-48331-1). Exposition.

Twisted Tales from Shakespeare. R. Armour. pap. 4.95 (ISBN 0-07-002251-8). McGraw.

Twisted Tendril: A Story of Eighteen Sixty-Five. Alice Glasgow & Booth, John Wilkes. LC 28-7867. 1928. Frederick A. Stokes Company.

Twisted Thing. Frank Morrison Spillane. LC 66-10062. 1966. Dutton.

Twisted Threads. Mary Dummett Nauman Robinson. LC 7-23111. 1870. Claxton, Remsen & Haffelfinger.

Twisted Tracks. Donald A Plankel. LC 52-6938. 1952. Vantage Press.

Twisted Trail. Paul Evan Lehman. 1971. pap. 0.60 o.p. (60-471). Manor Bks.

Twisted Trails. Henry Oyen. LC 21-50813. George H. Doran Company.

Twisted Triangle. Stan Mitchell. 176p. pap. 1.95 o.p. (6100). Brandon.

Twisted Wire. Richard Falkirk, pseud. 1971. 5.95 o.p. (ISBN 0-385-08151-0). Doubleday.

Twisted Wire. Richard Falkirk. 1973. pap. 0.95 o.p. (ISBN 0-515-03016-3, N3016). Pyramid Pubns.

Twisted Wire. Derek Lambert. LC 71-131073. 1971. 5.95. Doubleday.

Twister. Jack M Bickham. LC 75-46444. 1976. 8.95 (ISBN 0-385-11499-0). Doubleday.

Twister. Jack M Bickham. (Kangaroo Book). 1978. 1.95 (ISBN 0-671-81971-2). Pocket Books.

Twister. David Hagberg. 1975. (pbk.) 1.25. Dell.

Twister. Edgar Wallace. LC 29-7298. 1929. Pub. for The Crime Club, Inc., by Doubleday, Doran & Company, Inc.

Twister Man. Keith Zerkle. LC 78-50634. 1979. 8.95 (ISBN 0-87949-129-9). Ashley Books.

Twists and Turns of Love. Barbara Cartland. LC 77-486. 1978. 6.95. Duron Books.

Twits. Roald Dahl. 96p. 1982. pap. 1.95 (ISBN 0-553-15167-3). Bantam.

Twittering Bird Mystery. Henry Christopher Bailey. LC 37-25761. 1937. Pub. for the Crime Club. Inc., by Doubleday, Doran & Company, Inc.

Twittering Bird Mystery. Henry Christopher Bailey. LC 39-121. 1938. The Sun Dial Press, Inc.

Twixt Heaven and Earth. Genie Holtzmeyer Johnson Rosenfeld. (On cover: United service library. v. 1, no. 4). 1889. The United Service Publishing Company.

Twixt Land and Sea. Joseph Conrad. LC 12-27196. Hodder & Stoughton, George H. Doran Company.

Twixt Love and Duty: A Novel. Tighe Hopkins. LC 7-5242. (Harper's handy series, no. 52). 1886. Harper & Brothers.

Twixt Love and Duty. A Novel. Tighe Hopkins. LC 7-5241. (On cover: Seaside library. Pocket ed. no. 714). G. Munro.

Twixt Love and Law: A Novel. Annie Jenness Miller. LC 7-25973. (On cover: The household library, v. 4, no. 9). 1888. Belford, Clarke & Company.

Twixt Shade and Shine. Annabel Gray. (Seaside library, v. 74, no. 1505). 1883. G. Munro.

Twixt Smile and Tear. Charlotte Mary Brame. (On cover: Lovell's library. v. 20 no. 984). J. W. Lovell Company.

Twixt Smile and Tear. Charlotte Mary Brame. (On cover: Seaside library. Pocket ed. no. 924). G. Munro.

Twixt Smile and Tear. Charlotte Mary Brame. LC 44-11672. (On cover: Seaside library. Pocket ed. No. 924). G. Munro.

Twixt Wind and Water: A Novel. Leona Rasmussen Phillips. LC 80-12218. 1982. 10.95 (ISBN 0-87949-179-5). Ashley Books.

Twnety Thousand Leagues Under the Sea. Jules Verne & Darlene Geis. LC 58-3523. Grosset & Dunlap.

Two. Eric Jourdan. LC 63-4452. 1963. Pyramid Publications.

Two. 192p. 1982. pap. 3.50 (ISBN 0-553-22658-4). Bantam.

Two: A Novel. Martin Boris. LC 78-19607. 8.95 (ISBN 0-8129-0783-3). Times Books.

Two: A Phallic Novel. Alberto Moravia. 1973. (pbk.) 1.50 (ISBN 0-374-28005-3). Manor Books.

Two; a Phallic Novel. Alberto Moravia. LC 76-183232. 1972. 7.95 (ISBN 0-374-28005-3). Farrar, Straus and Giroux.

Two Admirals. James Fenimore Cooper. LC 99-4892. (Famous novels of the sea). 1899. Charles Scribner's Sons.

Two Admirals. A Tale. James Fenimore Cooper. LC 2-3955. 1842. Lea and Blanchard.

Two Admirals. A Tale. James Fenimore Cooper. (Added t.-p.: The works of J. Fenimore Cooper). 1852. G. P. Putnam.

Two Admirals. A Tale. new ed. James Fenimore Cooper. LC 6-29673. 1852. Stringer and Townsend.

Two Admirals. A Tale. James Fenimore Cooper. LC 26-246948. (Half-title: The choice works of Cooper. Revised and corrected series. v. 16). 1856. Stringer & Townsend.

Two Admirals: A Tale. James Fenimore Cooper. LC 8-7684. 1872. Hurd and Houghton.

Two Admirals: A Tale. James Fenimore Cooper. 1874. D. Appleton and Company.

Two Admirals. A Tale. James Fenimore Cooper. LC 12-195923. Houghton, Mifflin and Company.

Two Admirals. A Tale. James Fenimore Cooper. LC 4-19564. 1896. D. Appleton and Company.

Two Admirals. A Tale of the Sea. James Fenimore Cooper. (Seaside library. v. 29, no. 590). 1879. G. Munro.

Two Admirals: A Tale of the Sea. James Fenimore Cooper. (On cover: Lovell's library. no. 484). 1885. J. W. Lovell Company.

Two Admirals. A Tale of the Sea. James Fenimore Cooper. (On cover: Seaside library. Pocket ed. no. 349). 1885. G. Munro.

Two Adolescents. Alberto Moravia. LC 81-82970. 240p. 1982. pap. 2.95 (ISBN 0-86721-001-X). Playboy Pbks.

Two Adolescents: The Stories of Agostino and Luca. Alberto Moravia. LC 75-25266. 1975. 14.50 (ISBN 0-8371-8392-8). Greenwood Press.

Two Adolescents: The Stories of Agostino and Luca. Alberto Pincherle. LC 50-8597. 1950. Farrar, Straus.

Two African Tales. Abioseh Nicol. 1965. text ed. 4.50x (ISBN 0-521-05826-0). Cambridge U Pr.

Two After Malic. Ludovic Peters. LC 66-22498. 1966. Walker.

Two Against Fate. Louella Annette Woolfolk. LC 35-7022. Arcadia House.

Two Against Scotland Yard. Zenith Jones Brown. LC 31-33900. Farrar & Rinehart, Incorporated.

Two Against the North: A Story of Huskie and Spareribs. Bertrand Leslie Shurtleff. LC 49-10423. 1949. Bobbs-Merrill Co.

Two Against the Western Ocean. Patrick Ellan & Colin Mudie. 1972. pap. 0.75 o.p. (07213). Curtis.

Two Altheas. Edith E Horsman. LC 7-7160. Estes and Lauriat.

Two, and Bits of Life. Edith Smith Davis. LC 6-32495. 1888. Burr Printing House.

Two and the Town. Henry Gregor Felsen. LC 52-9116. 1952. Scribner.

Two-and-Twenty. Cecil Scott Forester. LC 31-21754. 1931. D. Appleton & Company.

Two and Twenty: A Collection of Short Stories. Ed. by Ralph H Singleton. LC 62-11702. 1962. St. Martin's Press.

Two & Two. Henrik Tjele. pap. 1.50 o.p. (Z1053D, Zebra). Grove.

Two and Two Make Twenty-Two. Gwen Bristow & Manning, Bruce, Pseud., Joint Author. LC 32-574477. 1932. The Mystery League, Inc.

Two Apaches of Paris. Alice J. De C. Leake Askew & Askew, Claude Arthur Cary, Joint Author. LC 11-16563. 1911. W. Rickey & Company.

Two Bad Blue Eyes: A Novel. Eliza M. J. Humphreys. (On cover: Lovell's library, no. 1144). 1888. J. W. Lovell Company.

Two Bad Brown Eyes. Harriet Louise Lynch. LC 8-3403. The Merriam Company.

Two Banks of the Seine: Les Deux Rives. Fernand Vanderem & Raffalovich, George, 1880- Tr. (Half-title: The library of French fiction, ed. by B. J. Beyer) $1.90). 1919. E. P. Dutton & Company.

Two Barbaras. A Novel. M. B. Stuart. LC 8-16874. 1876. G. W. Carleton & Co.; Etc., Etc.

Two Baronesses: A Romance. Hans Christian Andersen. LC 49-39437. 1870. Hurd and Houghton.

Two Baronesses: A Romance. Hans Christian Andersen. LC 44-32801. 1876. Hurd and Houghton.

Two Beds for Liz. Peter Kanto. (Orig.). pap. 0.95 o.p. (1168). Brandon.

Two Billions of Miles: Or, The Story of a Trip Through the Solar System. Milton Worth Ramsey. (Nation library. v. 7, no. 4). 1900.

Two Bishops. Agnes Sligh Turnbull. LC 80-22819. 1980. 14.95 (ISBN 0-8161-3173-2). G. K. Hall.

Two-Bit Rancher. 1st Ed. Charles N Heckelmann. LC 50-5034. (Double D Western). 1950. Doubleday.

Two Bites at a Cherry: With Other Tales. Thomas Bailey Aldrich. LC 69-11877. (American short story series, v. 34). 1969. Garrett Press.

Two Bites at a Cherry: With Other Tales. Thomas Bailey Aldrich. LC 4-15061. 1894. Houghton, Mifflin and Company.

Two Bites at a Cherry, with Other Tales. Thomas Bailey Aldrich. 1972. Repr. of 1894 ed. lib. bdg. 24.00 (ISBN 0-8422-8002-2). Irvington.

Two Bites at a Cherry, with Other Tales. Thomas Bailey Aldrich. 1894. 25.00 o.p. (ISBN 0-403-04318-2). Somerset Pub.

Two Bites at a Cherry, with Other Tales. Thomas Bailey Aldrich. Ed. by Clarence Gohdes. LC 69-11877. (American Short Stories Ser. Vol. 34). 1969. Repr. of 1894 ed. lib. bdg. 9.95 o.s.i. (ISBN 0-512-00006-9). Garrett Pr.

Two Bits in Change. Otis D. Richardson. 6.95 o.p. Vantage.

Two Black Crows in the A.E.F. Charles E Mack. LC 23-21379. The Bobbs-Merrill Company.

Two Black Sheep. Warwick Deeping. LC 33-23671. 1933. A. A. Knopf.

Two Black Sheep. Harry Leon Wilson. LC 31-29814. 1931. Cosmopolitan Book Corporation.

Two Blocks Down. Jina Delton. 1982. pap. 1.50 (ISBN 0-451-11477-9, AW1477, Vista). NAL.

Two Blondes. Albert Scott Hickman. 1.35. R. G. Badger; Etc., Etc.

Two Bottles of Relish: A Book of Strange and Unusual Stories. Ed. by Whit Burnett. Petrina, Carlotta, 1901- Illus. LC 43-511658. 1943. Dial Press.

Two Boys. Charles W. Shlimbaum. 3.75 o.p. Vantage.

Two Brides. A Tale. Bernard O'Reilly. LC 7-23187. 1879. G. W. Carleton & Co.; Etc., Etc.

Two Brothers. Honore De Balzac. Tr. by Katharine Prescott Wormeley. LC 3-23195. (Half-title: The comedy of human life... Scenes from provincial life). 1887. Roberts Brothers.

Two Brothers. Honore De Balzac. Tr. by Katherine Prescott Wormeley. LC 3-23196. (Half-title: The comedy of human life... Scenes from provincial life). 1889. Roberts Brothers.

Two Brothers. James McKinley Bryant. LC 69-17331. 1974. pap. 5.50. J M Bryant.

Two Brothers. 1982. pap. 1.95 (ISBN 0-87306-242-6). Feldheim.

Two Brothers and Their Animals Friends... Lois Lenski. LC 29-18031. 1929. Frederick A. Stokes Company.

Two Brothers (Pierre et Jean) Guy De Maupassant. Tr. by Clara Bell. LC 7-25593. (On cover: Lovell's series of foreign literature, no. 4). J. W. Lovell Company.

Two Bubbles. John Temple Jr. Graves. LC 20-5890. 1920. The Stratford Company.

Two by Francis. Dick Francis. LC 82-48488. 1983. 13.44 (ISBN 0-06-015126-9). Harper & Row.

Two by Two. Bo Beskow. 128p. 1981. pap. 2.95 (ISBN 0-380-55210-8, 55210, Bard). Avon.

Two by Two. Mary Slattery Stolz. LC 54-6813. 1954. Houghton Mifflin.

Two by Two: A Story of Survival. David Garnett. LC 63-22036. 1964. Atheneum.

Two Came by Sea. William Standish Stone. LC 53-5217. 1953. Morrow.

Two Came Calling. Nancy Dorer & Frances Dorer. (Orig.). 1980. pap. 1.95 (ISBN 0-532-23226-7). Woodhill.

Two Came to Town. Simeon Strunsky. LC 47-11426. 1947. E. P. Dutton.

Two Can Play. Josiah Pitts Woolfolk. LC 52-3785. 1952. Signature Press.

Two Captains. Veniamin Aleksandrovich Kaverin. Tr. by Swan, Edith Leda (Straznik) LC 42-10425. 1942. Modern Age Books.

Two Captains. William Clark Russell. LC 4-31668. Dodd, Mead & Company.

Two Captains. William Clark Russell. LC 8-18098. 1897. Dodd, Mead & Company.

Two Captains: A Romance of Bonaparte and Nelson. Cyrus Townsend Brady. LC 5-3790. 1905. The Macmillan Company.

Two-Car Funeral. John T Hough. LC 73-5647. 1973. 5.95 (ISBN 0-316-37392-3). Little, Brown.

Two Carnations. Marjorie Bowen. LC 13-2376. 1913. P. R. Reynolds.

Two Cheers for Democracy. Edward Morgan Forster. Ed. by Oliver Stallybrass. (Abinger Edition of E. M. Forster Ser.). 1978. text ed. 11.50x (ISBN 0-8419-5808-4). Holmes & Meier.

Two Chefs of Dunboy: Or, An Irish Romance of the Last Century. James Anthony Froude. LC 42-31390. 1889. C. Scribner's Sons.

Two Chiefs of Dunboy: Or, An Irish Romance of the Last Century. James Anthony Froude. (On cover: Seaside libary. Pocket ed., no. 1180). 1889. G. Munro.

Two Children of the Foothills. Elizabeth Harrison. LC 2-25761. Sigma Publishing Co.

Two Children's Stories for Physicians and Other Wise Men. Georg Dahl. LC 73-80769. (Illus.). 1973. (ISBN 0-912922-03-6). Bell Museum of Pathobiology, University of Minnesota Medical School.

Two Circuits. A Story of Illinois Life. James L Crane. LC 6-30869. 1877. Jansen, McClurg & Co.

Two Clues: The Clue of the Runaway Blonde. The Clue of the Hungry Horse. Erle Stanley Gardner. LC 47-2600. 1947. W. Morrow & Company.

Two Coeval Evils. John Joseph Link. LC 41-28064. 1941. Meador Publishing Company.

Two College Friends. Frederick Wadsworth Loring. LC 7-14763. Loring.

Two Comrades. Ellen Hayes. LC 12-16079. 1912. 0.60. E. L. Grimes Company.

Two Conspiracies. C L Patterson. LC 28-2243. The Christopher Publishing House.

Two Coronets. Mary Agnes Tincker. LC 8-26771. 1889. Houghton, Mifflin and Company.

Two Countesses. Ebner Von Eschenbach, Marie & Waugh, Mrs. Ellen, Tr. LC 6-26324. ("unknown" library. no. 27). Cassell Publishing Company.

Two Coyotes. David Grew. LC 24-7806. 1924. T. Seltzer.

Two Crossings of Madge Swalue. Henri Davignon. LC 19-10148. 1918. John Lane.

Two Crossings of Madge Swalue. Henri Davignon. Tr. by Cammaerts, Mme. Tita (Brand) 1918. John Lane.

Two Crows Came. Jonni Dolan. LC 80-18252. 156p. 1980. pap. 5.95 (ISBN 0-914718-53-3). Pacific Search.

Two Daughters of One Race. Tr. by D. M. Lowery & Mrs. D. M. Lawrey. LC 6-9424. 1889. Worthington Co.

Two Days. Jay Wheeler Dow. LC 6-34406. (On cover: Hammock stories). Fords, Howard, & Hulbert.

Two Days, Two Nights. Per Olof Sundman. LC 69-15470. 1969. 4.95. Pantheon Books.

Two Dead Men: Tr. from the Danish of Jens Anker Pseud. Robert Hansen & Toksvig, Frithjof, Tr. LC 22-12089. 1922. A.A. Knopf.

Two Deaths of Christopher Martin. William Gerald Golding. LC 57-10059. 1957. Harcourt, Brace.

Two Deaths of Christopher Martin see Pincher Martin.

Two Deaths of Quincas Wateryell. Jorge Amado & Antonucci, Emil, Illus. LC 65-21553. 1965. Knopf.

Two Demands. Fannie Sydnor Cartmell. LC 9-29426. 1909. The Roycrofters.

Two Destinies. A Novel. Wilkie Collins. LC 3-27265. 1876. Harper & Brothers.

Two Dianas. Alexandre Dumas & Paul Meurice. 1891. Little, Brown, and Company.

Two Dianas. Alexandre Dumas & Meurice, Paul. LC 6-43624. (Half-title: The romances of Alexandre Dumas. Illustrated library ed. vol. i-iii). 1893. Little, Brown, and Company.

Two Dianas. Alexandre Dumas & Meurice, Paul. LC 8-26660. 1894. Little, Brown, and Company.

Two Dianas. An Historical Romance. Alexandre Dumas & Meurice, Paul. LC 42-28438. (Seaside library, v. 30, no. 616). G. Munro.

Two Dianas. An Historical Romance. Alexandre Dumas & Paul Meurice. LC 6-43622. (On cover: Seaside library. Pocket ed. no. 3110). G. Munro.

Two Dianas... By Alexandre Dumas. Alexandre Dumas & Meurice, Paul. D. Estes & Company.

Two Died at Three: A Tale of Inspector Higgins. Cecil Freeman Gregg. LC 44-51106. 1944. Mystery House.

Two Divided by One: A Novel. Norah Cordner James. LC 36-19092. The Macaulay Company.

Two Doctors: A Novel, by Elizabeth Cambridge Pseud. Barbara K. Hodges. LC 37-1870. 1937. G. P. Putnam's Sons.

Two Doctors and a Girl. Elizabeth Seifert. LC 76-26166. 1976. 6.95 (ISBN 0-396-07352-2). Dodd, Mead.

Two Doctors and a Girl. Elizabeth Seifert. LC 78-3818. 1978. 9.95 (ISBN 0-89340-146-3). J. Curley.

Two Doctors, Two Loves. Elizabeth Seifert. LC 82-7436. 1982. 10.95 (ISBN 0-396-08101-0). Dodd, Mead.

Two Dreams. Justin Masse. Tr. by Frederick Arthur. LC 17-17617. 1.25. The Devin-Adair Company.

Two Drovers: A Short Story. Walter Scott. LC 75-164412. (Illus.). 1971. Kindle Press.

Two Duchesses. A Story of to-Day... Emile Zola & Cooney, Myron A., Tr. (Brookside library, no. 375). 1884. F. Tousey.

Two Duchesses: From the French of A. Mathey Pseud. Arthur Arnould & Clark, Frank Pinckney, Tr. (On cover: Lovell library). J. W. Lovell Company.

Two-Edged Vengeance. Willis Todhunter Ballard. LC 51-9979. 1951. Macmillan.

Two-Eyes. Stuart Gordon. 1974. (pbk.) 1.25. Daw Books.

Two Fables: Translated by Christopher Morley. Ed. by Christopher Darlington Morley. Mussel, Aldred De, 1810-1857. Histoire D'un Merle Blanc & Hauff, Wilhelm, 1802-1827. LC 25-16654. 1925. Doubleday, Page & Company.

Two-Faced. Graham Montague Jeffries. LC 77-374837. 1977. 8.95 (ISBN 0-09-128220-9). Hutchinson.

Two-Faced Man. Frederic Van Rensselaer Dey. LC 18-9489. 1918. 1.40. The Macaulay Company.

Two Faced Murder. Jean Leslie. LC 46-39440. 1946. Pub. for the Crime Club by Doubleday & Company, Inc.

Two Faces see Aspern Papers.

Two Faces of Dr. Collier. Elizabeth Seifert. LC 72-7752. 1973. 5.95 (ISBN 0-396-06708-5). Dodd, Mead.

Two Faces of Dr. Collier. Elizabeth Seifert. (Signet Book, Q5799). 1974. (pbk.) 0.95. New American Library.

Two Faces of Doctor Collier. Elizabeth Seifert. LC 76-20661. 1976. 8.95 (ISBN 0-89340-045-9). J. Curley.

Two Faces of Fear. Julie Wellsley. 1971. pap. 0.75 o.p. (ISBN 0-447-74758-4). Lancer.

Two Faces of January. Highsmith, Patricia. LC 64-18704. 1964. Published for the Crime Club by Doubleday.

Two Faces of Love: Lust for Life and Immortal Wife. Irving Stone. LC 62-11465. 1962. Doubleday.

Two Faces of Robert Just. Kay Dick. LC 80-14206. 1980. 9.95 (ISBN 0-688-03621-X). W. Morrow.

Two Faces of Tomorrow. James P. Hogan. 1979. pap. 1.95 (ISBN 0-345-27517-9, Del Rey Bks). Ballantine.

Two Families. first ed. Milton Bromfield. 1972. 4.95 (ISBN 0-533-00311-3). Vantage.

Two Families. Milton T. Bromfield. 4.95 o.p. Vantage.

Two Families. Archibald Marshall. LC 31-3371. 1931. Dodd, Mead & Company.

Two Family Mothers. Marie Sofle Birath Schwartz. Tr. by Borg Selma. LC 8-2062. 1872. Lee and Shepard.

Two Fathers. An Unpublished Original Spanish Work. Antonio Diodoro De Pasonal. Tr. by Edgar, Henry. LC 7-34086. 1852. Stringer & Townsend.

Two Feet from Heaven. Percival Christopher Wren. LC 41-42. 1941. Macrae-Smith Company.

Two Femmes in Fairyland. Elliot Storm. LC 35-35379. Godwin.

Two Filipino Women. F. Sionil Jose. 104p. 1981. pap. 7.25x. New Day NY.

Two-Fisted Banana: Electric & Gothic. Mary Beach. LC 79-14957. 1980. pap. 4.00x (ISBN 0-916156-35-4). Cherry Valley.

Two-Fisted Cowpoke. Nelson Coral Nye. LC 36-21200. Greenberg.

Two Flappers in Paris. A Cantab. LC 77-6845. (Venus library). 1969. Grove Press.

Two Flights up. Mary Roberts Rinehart. LC 28-18123. 1928. Doubleday, Doran and Company, Inc.

Two for Joy. E. Morchard Bishop. LC 39-315382. 1938. C. Scribner's Sons.

Two for Joy. Oliver Stonor. LC 39-31538. 1938. Scribner.

Two for Texas. James Lee Burke. 167p. (Orig.). 1982. pap. 1.95 (ISBN 0-671-44112-4). PB.

Two for the Money. Jerry Oliver. LC 73-155606. 1972. 1.95. Greenleaf Classics.

Two for the Price of One. Tony Kenrick. LC 73-22006. 1974. (lib. bdg.) 10.95 (ISBN 0-8161-6185-2). G. K. Hall.

Two for the Price of One. Tony Kenrick. LC 73-10701. 1974. 6.95 (ISBN 0-672-51888-0). Bobbs-Merrill.

Two for the the Road. F. Raphael. 1967. 4.50 o.p. (ISBN 0-03-064650-2). HR&W.

Two for Vengeance. Lewis B Patten. (Signet Brand Western). 1974. (pbk.) 0.75. New American Library.

Two For Vengeance see Redskin.

Two Forsyte Interludes: A Silent Wooing, Passers by. John Galsworthy. LC 28-3685. 1938. C. Scribner's Sons.

Two Friends, and Other Stories. Ivan Sergieevich Turgenev. Tr. by Constance Garnett. LC 21-103982. (novels of Ivan Turgenev. xvi). 1921. The Macmillan Company; Etc., Etc.

Two Frigates: Or, Captain Bisset's Legacy. George Cupples. LC 44-43126. 1859. Routledge, Warnes, and Routledge.

Two from Galilee. Marjorie Holmes. 1974. (pbk.) 1.50. Bantam Books.

Two from Galilee: A Love Story. Marjorie Holmes. LC 73-9948. 1973. (lib. bdg.) 10.95 (ISBN 0-8161-6131-3). G. K. Hall.

Two Gay Sleuths. H. R. Kaye, pseud. (Orig.). 1969. pap. 1.75 o.p. (3066). Brandon.

Two Generations. Lev Nikolaevich Tolstoi. LC 8-25989. ((Seaside library. Pocket ed., no. 1073)). 1888. G. Munro.

Two Generations, and Other Stories. Lev Nikolaevich Tolstoi. (On cover: Lovell's library, no. 1124). 1888. J. W. Lovell Company.

Two Gentlemen and a Lady. Alexander Woollcott. LC 79-134984. (Short story index reprint series). (Illus.). 1970. (ISBN 0-8369-3714-7). Books for Libraries Press.

Two Gentlemen of Boston: A Novel. Caroline C. Field. LC 6-41189. 1887. Ticknor and Company.

Two Gentlemen of Gotham. Arthur Winslow Bot & Coghill, Howard. (On cover: Cassell's sunshine series, v. 1, no. 12). 1888. Cassell & Company, Limited.

Two Gentlemen of Gotham. Arthur Winslow Cabot & Coghill, Howard. LC 6-21885. Cassell & Company, Limited.

Two Gentlemen of Hawaii. A Novel. Seward W Hopkins. (choice series, no. 114). 1894. R. Bonner's Sons.

Two Gentlemen of Hawaii. A Novel. Seward W Hopkins & Burstenbinder, Elisabeth, 1838-1918. The Stolen Vail. LC 7-8470. (Ledger library). 1894. Robert Bonner's Sons.

Two Gentlemen of Kentucky. James Lane Allen. LC 99-5565. (Little books by famous writers). 1899. Harper & Brothers.

Two Gentlemen of Virginia: A Novel of the Old Regime in the Old Dominion. George Cary Eggleston. LC 8-22541. 1908. Lothrop, Lee & Shepard Co.

Two Girls. Amy Ella Blanchard. LC 12-81114. 1894. J. B. Lippincott Company.

Two Girls Abroad. Nelli M Carter. 1888. R. Carter and Brothers.

Two Girls on a Barge: By V. Cecil; with Forty-Four Illustrations by F. H. Townsend. V. Cecil Cotes. LC 7-1236. 1891. D. Appleton and Company.

Two Gods... by Walter S. Cramp... Walter Samuel Cramp. LC 12-27193. 1.25. R. G. Badger.

Two Green Bars. Boris Stankevich. LC 67-19892. 1967. Harcourt, Brace & World.

Two Guests for Swedenborg. March Cost, pseud. LC 74-155664. 7.95 o.s.i. (ISBN 0-8149-0695-8). Vanguard.

Two Guests for Swedenborg. Peggy Morrison, pseud. LC 74-155664. 1971. 5.95 (ISBN 0-8149-0695-8). Vanguard Press.

Two Gun Fury. Charles Morris Martin. (O.s.i.). 1975. pap. 0.95 o.s.i. (Leisure Bks). Nordon Pubns.

Two-Gun Harney. Buck Billings. LC 33-482. 1932. G. H. Watt.

Two-Gun Harney. Claude Rister. LC 33-482. 1932. G. H. Watt.

Two-Gun Kid. Clement Yore. LC 32-16252. TheMacaulay Company.

Two-Gun Law. Robert J Hogan. LC 50-10683. (Silver star westerns). 1950. Dodd, Mead.

Two-Gun Law. easy eye ed. James D. Sayers. pap. 0.60 o.p. Lancer.

Two-Gun Law. Cover Painting by Leslie Ross. Clifton Adams. LC 54-38660. (Gold medal books, 422). 1954. Fawcett Publications.

Two-Gun Man... Robert Ames Bennet. LC 24-9264. 1924. A. C. McClurg & Co.

Two-Gun Man. Charles Alden Seltzer. LC 11-27805. 1911. Outing Publishing Company.

Two-Gun Man. Charles Alden Seltzer. LC 29-30771. 1913. A. L. Burt Company.

Two-Gun Parson. James Lyon Rubel. LC 36-7591. Phoenix Press.

Two-Gun Quaker. Amos Moore. LC 38-73249. I. Washburn, Inc.

Two-Gun Rio Kid. Davis Dresser. LC 41-17247. 1941. W. Morrow & Company.

Two-Gun Rio Kid: By Don Davis Pseud. Davis Dresser. LC 51-9002. (Triple-A western classic). 1951. Jefferson House.

Two-Gun Sue. Isabel Egenton Ostrander. LC 22-107714. 1922. R. M. McBride & Company.

Two-Gun Vengeance. Archie Joscelyn. 1968. pap. 0.50 o.p. (62-029). Paperback Lib.

Two-Headed Reader: By Richard Condon, Being His Two Most Celebrated Novels: The Oldest Confession, The Manchurian Candidate. Complete, Unabridged. Richard Condon. LC 65-12956. 1966. 5.95. Random.

Two-Headed Reader: The Oldest Confession, & the Manchurian Candidate. Richard Condon. 1966. 8.95 o.p. (ISBN 0-394-44966-5). Random.

Two Heads Are Better. Elliott Lewis. (Bennett Ser.: No. 1). 224p. (Orig.). 1980. pap. 1.95 (ISBN 0-523-41462-5). Pinnacle Bks.

Two Hearts Adrift. Wendy Martin, pseud. 1976. 4.95. Avalon Books.

Two Hearts Doubled. Watkins Eppes Wright. LC 43-2624. 1943. Arcadia House, Inc.

Two Hearts in a Melting Pot. Paul Kolesar. 104p. 1983. 8.95x (ISBN 0-87141-074-5). Manyland.

Two Hemispheres: A Romance. From the German of Otto Rupius ! Otto Rupplus. Tr. by W., C. L. LC 8-967. 1870. Claxton, Remsen & Haffelfinger.

Two Heroes and a Violin. An Extravaganza. D Biagi. LC 99-3736. (Neely's universal library. no. 77). 1899. F. T. Neely.

Two Heroines of Plumplington. Anthony Trollope. Ed. by John K. Shannon. (Harting Grange Library). (Illus.). 116p. 1980. lib. bdg. 10.95 (ISBN 0-932282-48-2); pap. 5.95 (ISBN 0-932282-49-0). Caledonia Pr.

Two Hours on Sunday. Joseph Pillitteri. LC 77-150406. 1971. 5.95. Dial Press.

Two Hours to Darkness. Antony Trew. LC 63-7124. (Illus.). 1963. Random House.

Two Hours with Ivanhoe... Walter Scott. LC 7-16377. (nutshell library, ed. by S. Cody). The Old Greek Press.

Two Hours with Pickwick... Charles Dickens. LC 7-15594. (nutshell library; ed. by S. Cody). The Old Greek Press.

Two Hours with Vanity Fair... William Makepeace Thackeray. LC 7-15593. (nutshell library; ed. by S. Cody). The Old Greek Press.

Two Houses. Elizabeth Henderson McRobie Calvert. LC 18-19985. The Roxburgh Publishing Company, Inc.

Two Humorous Novels: A Diverting Dialogue Between Scipio & Bergansa & the Comical History of Rinconete & Cortadillo. Miguel de Cervantes de Saavedra. Tr. by Robert Goadby. LC 80-2474. Repr. of 1741 ed. 39.50 (ISBN 0-404-19106-1). AMS Pr.

Two Hundred and Other Stories. Natalie Rice Wahl. LC 32-7118. 1932. Metropolitan Press.

Two Hundred Fifty Thousand Dollars. Edward M. Cohen. 1967. 4.95 o.p. (ISBN 0-399-10823-8). Putnam.

Two Hundred Fifty Thousand Dollars: By Edward M. Cohen. Edward M. Cohen. LC 67-231212. 1967. 4.95. Putnam.

Two-Hundred Million A.D. Alfred Elton Van Vogt. 1978. pap. 1.75 (ISBN 0-89083-357-5). Zebra.

Two-Hundred Million A.D. Alfred Elton Van Vogt. Orig. Title: Book of Ptath. 1971. pap. 0.50 o.p. (ISBN 0-446-62718-6, 62-718). Paperback Lib.

Two Hundred Nine Thriller Road. Sam North. LC 79-27177. 8.95 (ISBN 0-312-82688-5). St. Martin's Press.

Two Hundred Seventy-Two Maple Avenue. Winthrop Bushnell Palmer. LC 44-51003. 1944. Harbinger House.

Two Hundred Twenty-One A Baker Street: The Adamantine Sherlock Holmes. Hapi. LC 74-169161. (Yellow-breeched philosopher, 2). (Illus.). 1974. 2.95. Kanthaka Press.

Two Hundred Years of Great American Short Stories. Ed. by Martha Foley. LC 75-1107. 960p. 1975. 14.95 (ISBN 0-395-20447-X). HM.

Two Husbands: Or, Buried Secrets. Harriet Lewis. (On cover: The choice series, no. 52). 1892. R. Bonner's Sons.

Two I Love. Ruth Rosemary Corby. LC 41-154372. 1941. Arcadia House, Inc.

Two If by Sea. Ernest Savage. LC 81-21273. 11.95 (ISBN 0-684-17435-9). Scribner.

Two If by Sea. Paul Winterton. LC 49-503360. 1949. Harper.

Two If by Sea or the Magic of Three: Episode Number. 1st. ed. Inez Sandelin Criss. (Illus.). 1974. 4.00 (ISBN 0-682-47835-0). Exposition Press.

Two IIa Duo. LC 64-8876. 1964. Skylight Press.

Two in Italy. Maud Howe Elliott. LC 5-33979. 1905. Little, Brown, and Company.

Two in Tampa: By Carol Holliston Pseud. James Noble Gifford. LC 54-113374. 1954. Arcadia House.

Two in the Bush. George Bagby. LC 75-21208. (Crime Club Ser.). 192p. 1976. 5.95 o.p. (ISBN 0-385-11438-9). Doubleday.

Two in the Bush. Aaron Marc Stein. LC 75-21208. 1976. 5.95 (ISBN 0-385-11438-9). Published for the Crime Club by Doubleday.

Two in the Wilderness. Jackson Gregory. LC 42-18362. 1942. Dodd, Mead & Company.

Two Inches of Gold. Joseph Papaleo. LC 72-121430. 1970. 5.95 o.p. (690317). Little.

Two Is Company. Peggy O'More, pseud. LC 45-466443. 1945. Grammercy Publishing Co.

Two Is Lonely: A Sequel to The I-Shaped Room and The Backward Shadow. Lynne Reid Banks. LC 73-20755. 1974. 7.95 (ISBN 0-671-21732-1). Simon and Schuster.

Two Keys: Or, Margaret Houghton's Heroism. Sarah Elizabeth Forbush G. S. Downs Downs. (On cover: The select series. no. 89). 1891. Street & Smith.

Two Keys to a Cabin. Lida Larrimore Turner Thomas. LC 36-21830. 1936. Macrae-Smith Company.

Two Kids & the Three Bears. John D. Brown. LC 75-40538. (Lucky Heart Bks.). 40p. 1975. pap. 3.00 (ISBN 0-913198-10-2). Salt Lick.

Two Kingdoms: A Novel of Islandia. Mark Saxton. LC 79-10771. (Illus.). 1979. 9.95 (ISBN 0-395-28152-0). Houghton Mifflin.

Two Kisses. Hawley Smart. Loring.

Two Kisses: A Tale of a Very Modern Courtship. Oliver Onions. LC 13-23492. 1.25. George H. Doran Company, Publishers in America for Hodder & Stoughton.

Two Kisses, and, Like No Other Love. Charlotte Mary Brame. LC 44-11143. (On cover: Seaside library. Pocket ed. No. 307). G. Munro.

Two Kisses: Or, To Wed or Not to Wed. Hawley Smart. T. B. Peterson & Brothers.

Two Ladies in Verona see Lady Is a Spy.

Two-Lane Blacktop. Will Cory. (O.s.i.). (Orig.). pap. 0.95 o.s.i. (A897N, Award). Univ Pub & Dist.

Two Leaves and a Bud. Mulk Raj Anand. LC 54-31290. 1954. Liberty Press.

Two Legacies. Georgina Lowell Putnam. LC 8-31907. 1863. Printed at the Riverside Press.

Two-Legged Wolf: A Romance. Nikolai Nikolevich Karazin. Tr. by Lanin, Boris. 1894. Rand, McNally & Company.

Two-Legs. Carl Ewald. Tr. by Teixeira De Mattos, Alexander Louis. LC 6-323643. 1906. C. Scribner's Sons.

Two Lessons in Love: Master of Hearts. Mr. Lowell and the Goddess. Paul Eldridge. LC 46-20586. 1946. The Beechurst Press.

Two Life-Paths. A Romance. Klara Muller Mundt. Tr. by Greene, Nathaniel. LC 7-25470. (On cover: Library of choice reading, no. 5). 1869. D. Appleton and Company.

Two Little Children and How They Grew. Doris Miles Disney. 1975. (pbk.) 1.50. Ace Books.

Two Little Children and How They Grew. Doris Miles Disney. LC 78-84393. 1969. 4.50. Published for the Crime Club by Doubleday.

Two Little Devils. Robert E. Holt. 1979. 6.95 (ISBN 0-682-49362-7). Exposition.

Two Little Maids; a Tale of South Florida. And Conchita; a Mexican Romance. Marguerite Louise Verdier. LC 8-30201. W. L. Allison Company.

Two Little Parisians (Caillou and Tili) Authorised Translation from the French of Pierre Mille. Pierre Mille & Drillien, Berengere, Tr. LC 13-23886. 1913. John Lane.

Two Little Rich Girls. Mignon Good Eberhart. 1973. Popular Lib.

Two Little Rich Girls. Mignon Good Eberhart. LC 74-159340. 1971. 4.95 (ISBN 0-394-47180-6). Random House.

Two Little Savages. Ernest Thompson Seton. (Illus.). 9.50 (ISBN 0-8446-2909-X). Peter Smith.

Two Little Savages. Ernest Thompson Seton. (Illus.). 1959. 4.95 o.p. (ISBN 0-385-05315-0). Doubleday.

Two Little Wooden Shoes. Louise De La Ramee. LC 6-33299. 1897. J. B. Lippincott Company.

Two Lives of An-Marie: A Novel. Muriel Molland Jernigan. LC 57-12825. 1957. Crown Publishers.

Two Lives: Or, To Seem and to Be. Maria Jane McIntosh. LC 7-16450. 1846. D. Appleton & Co.

Two Lives: Or, To Seem and to Be. 2d rev. ed. Maria Jane McIntosh. LC 18-4336. 1847. D. Appleton & Company.

Two Lives: Or, To Seem and to Be. Maria Jane McIntosh. LC 7-16449. 1865. D. Appleton and Company.

Two Lives, Two Lands. Ruth Freeman Solomon. LC 75-27417. 1975. 8.95 (ISBN 0-399-11672-9). Putnam.

Two Living and One Dead. Sigurd Wesley Christiansen. LC 73-22751. 1975. 14.25 (ISBN 0-8371-7348-5). Greenwood Press.

Two Living and One Dead. Sigurd Wesley Christiansen & Bjorkman, Edwin August, 1866- Tr. LC 32-9034. 1932. Liveright, Inc.

Two L.O. Walter S Masterman. LC 28-5402. E. P. Dutton & Company.

Two Lost Tribes. Sheldon Greene. LC 78-71789. 4.95 (ISBN 0-9602318-0-3). Kinur Pub.

Two Lovely Beasts, and Other Stories. Liam O'Flaherty. LC 50-8649. 1950. Devin-Adair.

Two Loves. Elliott Arnold. LC 34-202181. 1934. Greenberg.

Two Loves. Suyin Han. LC 62-17587. 1962. Putnam.

Two Loves. Vincent A. McCrossen. LC 78-61110. 1979. 12.50. Philos Lib.

Two Loves. Denise Robins. 1975. (pbk.) 1.25. Bantam Books.

Two Loves Have I. Vida Hurst. LC 50-9956. 1950. Gramercy Pub. Co.

Two Loves I Have: The Romance of William Shakespeare. Clara De Longworth Chambrun. LC 34-6600. 1934. J. B. Lippincott Company.

Two Loves: Mary Magdalene, Judas Iscariot. Vincent A McCrossen. LC 78-61110. 12.50. (ISBN 0-8022-2237-4). Philosophical Library.

Two Loyal Lovers: A Romance. Elizabeth Winthrop Johnson. 1890. F. A. Stokes Company.

Two Magics: The Turn of the Screw, Covering End. Henry James. LC 98-746. 1898. The Macmillan Company.

Two Major Novels: The Master of Ballantrae. weir of hermiston. with an introd. by morton dauwen zabel. ed. Robert Louis Stevenson. LC 60-50773. (Bantam classic, FC76). 1960. Bantam Books.

Two Make a World. Peter Bernard Kyne. LC 32-25888. 1932. H. C. Kinsey & Company, Inc.

Two Man Woman. Linda Roberts. LC 34-15492. 1934. G. H. Watt.

Two Marriages. Dinah Maria Mulock Craik. (On cover: Seaside library. Pocket ed., no. 1018). G. Munro.

Two Marriages. Dinah Maria Mulock Craik. LC 16-9358. (Lettered on cover: Miss Mulock's works). 1904. Harper & Brothers.

Two Marriges. Dinah Maria Mulock Craib. LC 6-31070. Harper & Brothers.

Two Measures of Rice. Thakazhi S. Pillai. Tr. by M. A. Shakoor. 1967. pap. 2.10 o.p. (ISBN 0-88253-169-7). InterCulture.

Two Men: A Novel. rev. ed. philadelphia, h. t. coates, 1901. ed. Elizabeth Drew Barstow Stoddard. LC 78-174746. 1971. Johnson Reprint Corp.

Two Men. A Novel. rev. ed. Elizabeth Drew Barstow Stoddard. LC 8-15671. Cassell & Company, Limited.

Two Men: A Novel. rev. ed. Elizabeth Drew Barstow Stoddard. LC 4-22016. 1901. Henry T. Coates & Co.

Two Men: A Romance of Sussex. Alfred Ollivant. Doubleday, Page & Company.

Two Men and Some Women: A Novel. Walter Marion Raymond. The Abbey Press.

Two Men in Me. Daniel-Rops, Henry. LC 76-163024. (Short story index reprint series). 1971. (ISBN 0-8369-3938-7). Books for Libraries Press.

Two Men in Me. Henry Daniel-Rops. Tr. by Meynier, Gil. LC 31-13349. 1931. Thomas S. Rockwell Company.

Two Men in Twenty. Maurice Procter. LC 64-18089. 1964. Harper & Row.

Two Men of the World. A Novel. Harriet True Bates. LC 6-9080. 1891. G. W. Dillingham.

Two Men Round the Moon. 1st. ed. Ray Lewis. (Illus.). 1974. 4.00 (ISBN 0-682-47930-6). Exposition Press.

Two Merchants: Or, Solvent and Insolvent. Timothy Shay Arthur. LC 6-3429. T. B. Peterson.

Two Million Dollar Blueprint. Charles Miron. 1978. pap. 1.75 (ISBN 0-532-17175-6). Woodhill.

Two-Minute Warning. George La Fountaine. LC 74-16642. 1975. 6.95 (ISBN 0-698-10633-4). Coward, McCann & Geoghegan.

Two Minutes of Silence: Selected Short Stories. Tr. from Danish by Vera Lundholm Vance, Introd. by Richard B. Vowles. Hans Christian Branner. LC 66-228651. (Nordic tr. ser.). 1966. 5.00. Univ. of Wis. Pr.

Two Mirrors. Peter De Polnay. LC 46-249099. 1946. Creative Age Press.

Two Miss Flemings. A Novel. (Franklin square library, no. 75). 1879. Harper & Brothers.

Two Miss Flemings. A Novel. (On cover: Seaside library. Pocket ed. no. 784). 1886. G. Munro.

Two Mistresses: Emmeline; The Son of Titian; Frederick and Bernerette; Pierre and Camille... Alfred De Musset. Tr. by Fosdick, Gertrude (Christian) LC 6026. (Half-title: Roman contemporain. Romancists. v. 5). G. Barrie & Son.

Two Modern Women: A Novel. Catherine Boott Gannett Wells. LC 8-36648. 1890. J. B. Lippincott Company.

Two Mothers see Three Exemplary Novels.

Two Mrs. Abbotts: A New Buncle Book. Dorothy Emily Stevenson. LC 43-18202. 1943. Farrar & Rinehart, Inc.

Two Much. Donald E Westlake. (Fawcett Crest Book). 1976. (pbk.) 1.75. Fawcett.

Two Names for Death. Fenwick, E. P. 1945. Farrar & Rinehart, Inc.

Two No-Trump: A Novel of Apartment-Hotel Life. Gertrude Myers. LC 23-16273. 1923. Convici-McGee Co.

Two Noble Women. Susan Parkman. LC 7-34730. American Tract Society.

Two Novellas. Julia Markus & Barbara Reid. 1977. lib. bdg. 17.50 o.s.i. (ISBN 0-918222-03-6); pap. 2.95 o.p. (ISBN 0-918222-04-4). Apple Wood.

Two Novellas: A Patron of the Arts & the Tears of San Lorenzo. 2nd ed. Julia Markus & Barbara Reid. 96p. 1981. pap. 4.95 (ISBN 0-918222-23-0). Apple Wood.

Two Novels. Ronald Firbank. Incl. Flower Beneath the Foot; Prancing Nigger. LC 62-17271. 1962. pap. 1.90 o.p. (ISBN 0-8112-0049-3, NDP128). New Directions.

Two Novels. Alain Robbe-Grillet. LC 65-16711. (Evergreen black cat book, BC-69). 1965. Grove Press.

Two Novels see Insight: English Literature.

Two Novels of Mexico: The Flies. The Bosses. Mariano Azuela. LC 56-4372. 1956. University of California Press.

Two Novels of the Mexican Revolution. Mariano Azuela. Tr. by Frances K. Hendricks & Beatrice Berler. Bd. with Trials of a Respectable Family; Underdogs. 267p. 1963. 6.00 o.p. (ISBN 0-911536-00-0). Trinity U Pr.

Two Novels of the Victorian Underground. Incl. Power of Mesmerism; Laura Middleton. 7.50 o.p. (X1011); pap. 1.75 o.p. (Z1040, Zebra). Grove.

Two Novels: The Flower Beneath the Foot and Prancing Nigger. Arthur Annesley Ronald Firbank. LC 62-17271. (New Directions paperbook, no. 128). 1962. New Directions.

Two Novels: Though You Be Far and When Summer, Returning. Katherine Ursula Parrott. LC 36-20144. 1936. Longmans, Green and Co.

Two Novels. Tr. from French by Richard Howard. Alain Robbe-Grillet. LC 65-16711. (Evergreen black cat bk., BC-69). pap., 1.65. Grove.

Two Novels: Venusberg. Agents & Patients. Anthony Dymoke Powell. LC 52-12524. 1952. Periscope-Holliday.

Two Nuns. Anne Hure. LC 64-16123. 1964. Sheed and Ward.

Two Nymphs Named Melissa. John Colleton. 1979. pap. 2.75 (ISBN 0-451-09945-1, E9945, Sig). NAL.

Two O'clock Courage. Gelett Burgess. LC 34-1304. The Bobbs-Merrill Company.

Two O'clock Sun. Cairns, Robert. LC 64-14842. 1964. Random House.

Two Odd Girls: Or, Douglas Rock's Secret. John A Peters. LC 8-4781. 1898. G. W. Dillingham Co.

Two of a Kind. Vereen Bell. LC 43-161. 1943. Little, Brown and Company.

Two of a Kind. Patrick Cauvin. (O.s.i.). 1980. 8.95 o.s.i. (ISBN 0-440-08670-1). Delacorte.

Two of a Kind. George G. Gilman, pseud. 160p. 1980. pap. 2.25 (ISBN 0-523-42031-5). Pinnacle Bks.

Two of a Kind: A Love Story. Patrick Cauvin. LC 80-10961. 8.95 (ISBN 0-440-08670-1). Delacorte Press.

Two of a Trade. Martha McCulloch Williams. (On cover: Tait's Kenilworth series, no. 4). 1894. J. S. Tait and Sons.

Two of the Guests. Kate Gertrude Prindiville. LC 5-9061. 1905. J. Pott & Company.

Two of Them. James Matthew Barrie. LC 6-8636. Lovell, Coryell & Company.

Two of Them. Joanna Russ. LC 77-26137. 8.95 (ISBN 0-399-12149-8). Berkley Pub. Corp.: Distributed by Putnam.

Two of Us. Claude Berri. LC 68-54412. (Illus.). 1968. 4.95. Morrow.

Two of Us. Maysie Greig. pap. 0.50 o.p. (50-289). Manor Bks.

Two of Us. Alberto Moravia. LC 74-189113. 1974. 0.50 (ISBN 0-586-03838-8). Panther.

Two Offenders. Louise De La Ramee. LC 6-33298. 1894. J. B. Lippincott Company.

Two Old Cronies. Ward Macauley. LC 14-18462. 1914. Duffield & Company.

Two Old Letters. 2d ed. John Singleton Thomas. LC 6-4635. 1905. The Foley Railway Printing Company.

Two Old Men's Tales. The Deformed, and The Admiral's Daughter... Anne Caldwell Marsh-Caldwell. LC 7-19682. 1834. Harper & Brothers.

Two Oldest Professions. Garth Brandtson. 1973. (pbk.) 1.95. Barclay House.

Two on a Tower. new wesser ed. Thomas Hardy. LC 77-70263. (Illus.). 1977. 2.95 (ISBN 0-312-82742-3). St. Martin's Press.

Two on a Tower. Thomas Hardy. (Lovell's library v. 2, no. 43). 1882. J. W. Lovell Company.

Two on a Tower. Thomas Hardy. LC 16-13096. 1895. Harper & Brothers.

Two on a Tower: A Novel. Thomas Hardy. LC 7-1903. (On cover: Leisure hour series. no. 142). 1882. H. Holt and Company.

Two on Galley Island. A Thrilling Tale of the Sea. Frederick Eames. (On cover: Once a week library, v. 10, no. 21). 1893. P. F. Collier.

Two on Safari: A Novel. George Agnew Chamberlain. LC 35-1985. The Bobbs-Merrill Company.

Two on the Trail: A Story of the Far Northwest. Hulbert Footner. LC 11-1969. 1911. Doubleday, Page & Company.

Two or Three Graces: And Other Stories. Aldous Leonard Huxley. LC 26-10804. George H. Doran Company.

Two Orphans. Adolphe Philippe Dennery. (On cover: Seaside library. v. 17, no. 332). 1878. G. Munro.

Two Orphans. Adolphe Philippe Dennery. (On cover: Seaside library. Pocket ed. no. 242). 1884. G. Munro.

Two Passions: An Every Day Tale of Love. Emma Ridley Collins. 1891. R. M. Collins.

Two Paths. Louisa Dalton. LC 6-33177. (On cover: Premium library). 1892. H. L. Kilner & Co.

Two Paths. Marie Watson. LC 8-31928. 1897. A. C. Clark.

Two Paycheck Marriage. Caroline Bird. 1980. pap. 3.50 (ISBN 0-671-83037-6). PB.

Two Penny Lane. Fielding Dawson. LC 77-12548. 1977. 15.00 (ISBN 0-87685-315-7) (ISBN 0-87685-314-9). Black Sparrow Press.

Two People. Alice Boyd. 1973. 1.25. Dell.

Two People. Alan Alexander Milne. LC 31-24493. 1931. E. P. Dutton & Company, Inc.

Two People: A Novel. Donald Wildham. LC 65-20405. 1965. Coward-McCann.

Two per Cent Fear. John Burgan. LC 47-31054. 1947. Farrar, Straus.

Two Pictures: Or, What We Think of Ourselves and What the World Thinks of Us. Maria Jane McIntosh. LC 72-39094. (Black Heritage Library Collection). 1972. (ISBN 0-8369-9032-3). Books for Libraries Press.

Two Pictures: Or, What We Think of Ourselves, and What the World Thinks of Us. Maria Jane McIntosh. LC 7-16448. 1864. D. Appleton Anc Company.

Two Pinches of Snuff. A Novel. William Westall. (Harper's Franklin square library, no. 539). 1886. Harper & Brothers.

Two Planets. Kurd Lasswitz. Ed. by Erich Lasswitz. Tr. by Hans Rudnick from Ger. LC 78-156776. Orig. Title: Auf Zwei Planeten. 1971. 10.00x o.p. (ISBN 0-8093-0508-9). S Ill U Pr.

Two Planets. Auf Zwei Planeten. Kurd Lasswitz & Erich Lasswitz. LC 78-156776. 1971. 10.00 (ISBN 0-8093-0508-9). Southern Illinois University Press.

Two Planets. Auf Zwei Planeten: A Novel. Kurd Lasswitz & Erich Lasswitz. 1973. Popular Lib.

Two Plus Two. Alan Cochran. LC 79-8964. 1980. 10.95 (ISBN 0-385-15603-0). Doubleday.

Two Plus Two Equals Minus Seven. John Festus Adams. LC 73-75392. (Cock Robin mystery). 1969. Macmillan.

Two Point Zero. Anne Snyder & Louis Pelletier. 1982. pap. 1.75 (ISBN 0-451-11476-0, AE1476, Vista). NAL.

Two Prisoners. Lajon Zilahy & Zeitlin, Ida; Joint Tr. LC 31-16450. 1931. Doubleday, Doran & Company, Inc.

Two Prisoners. Lajos Zilahy. LC 68-29590. (Great Novels and Memoirs of World War I, 4). 1969. 8.95. Stackpole Books.

Two Qualms & a Quirk. Richard De Mille. (Capra Chapbook Ser.). (Cloth ed. 10.00: No. 7). (Orig.). 1973. pap. 2.50 o.p. (ISBN 0-912264-64-0). Capra Pr.

Two Qualms & a Quirk. Richard DeMille. (Capra Chapbook Ser.). (Cloth ed. 10.00 o.p.: No. 7). (Orig.). 1973. pap. 2.50 o.p. (ISBN 0-912264-64-0). Capra Pr.

Two Qualms & a Quirk: Three Stories. Richard De Mille. LC 75-316989. (Yes! Capra chapbook series; no. 7). (Illus.). 1973. 2.50 (ISBN 0-912264-65-9) (ISBN 0-912264-64-0). Capra Press.

Two Rails West. Walker A. Tompkins. 1972. pap. 0.60 o.p. (06155). Curtis.

Two Ravens. Cecelia Holland. LC 76-49833. 1977. 7.95 (ISBN 0-394-49988-3). Knopf.

Two Reel Gay Girls. Jack Donne. (Illus., Orig.). pap. 0.95 o.p. (1166). Brandon.

Two Renwicks. Marie Agnes Davidson. LC 99-3757. (On cover: Neely's imperial library. no. 42). 1899. F. T. Neely.

Two Rivers Meet in Concord. Thomas Morris Longstreth. LC 46-230. 1946. The Westminster Press.

Two Roads to Guadalupe. Robert Lewis Taylor. LC 64-17916. 1964. Doubleday.

Two Rode Together. Will Cook. 1979. pap. 1.50 (ISBN 0-553-13044-7). Bantam.

Two Royal Foes. Eva Annie Madden. 1907. The McClure Company.

Two Rubles to Times Square. 1st Ed. Guy Richards. LC 56-5921. Duell, Sloan and Pearce.

Two Runaways and Other Stories. Harry Stillwell Edwards. LC 72-8707. (American short story series, v. 47). 1972. 14.00 (ISBN 0-8422-8042-1). MSS Information Corp.

Two Runaways and Other Stories. Harry Stillwell Edwards. LC 69-11889. (American short story series, v. 47). (Illus.). 1969. Garrett Press.

Two Runaways: And Other Stories. Harry Stillwell Edwards. LC 6-36577. The Century Co.

Two Russian Idyls. Marcella. Esfira. LC 8-32300. (On cover: Appletons' new handy-volume series no. 57). 1880. D. Appleton and Company.

Two Salomes: A Novel. Maria Louise Pool. LC 7-38170. 1893. Harper & Brothers.

Two Saps: And Fourteen Other Stories. James Walter Clark. LC 42-11705. 1942. DeVorse & Co.

Two Schools: A Moral Tale. Mary Robson Hughs. LC 31-195045. 1835. F. Lucas, Jr.

Two Selves of Jessica Throckmorton: An Aesthetic Realism Lesson. Eli Siegel. 1971. pap. 1.50x (ISBN 0-911492-10-0). Aesthetic Realism.

Two Serious Ladies. Jane Auer Bowles. LC 43-5575. 1943. A. A. Knopf.

Two Sets to Murder. Ludovic Peters. LC 64-17968. 1964. Coward-McCann.

Two Shall Be Born. Roberts Theodore Goodridge. LC 13-8319. 1913. 1.25. Cassell & Company.

Two Shall Be Born. Marie Conway Oemler. LC 22-18851. 1922. The Century Co.

Two Shall Be Born: A Novel. Ralston Robinson Price. LC 54-833165. 1954. Vantage Press.

Two Sided Triangle. Gus Stevens. (Orig.). pap. 0.95 o.p. (1165). Brandon.

Two Sides of a Story: And Other Stories... George Parsons Lathrop. LC 7-13855. (On cover: Cassell's sunshine series of choice fiction. v. 1. no. 33). 1889. Cassell & Company, Limited.

Two Sides of Evil. Clarence J. Lincoln. 4.50 o.p. Vantage.

Two Sides of the Face: Midwinter Tales. Arthur Thomas Quiller-Couch. LC 3-28290. 1903. C. Scribner's Sons.

Two Sides of the Shield. Charlotte Mary Yonge. (On cover: Seaside library. Pocket ed. no. 563). 1885. G. Munro.

Two Sieges of Paris: Or, A Girl of the Commune. George Alfred Henty. LC 41-34803. R. F. Fenno & Company.

Two Sinners. David George Ritchie. LC 15-163368. E. P. Dutton & Company.

Two Sisters. Herbert Ernest Bates. LC 26-19720. 1926. The Viking Press.

Two Sisters. Rose Holzman Stein. LC 35-182351. Covici, Friede.

Two Sisters. Count Valieur. pap. 1.95 o.p. (V1043T, Venus). Grove.

Two Sisters. Virginia Belle Terhune Van De Water. LC 14-9081. 1914. Hearst's International Library Co.

Two Sisters: A Memoir in the Form of a Novel. Gore Vidal. LC 71-117027. 1970. 5.95. Little, Brown.

Two Sisters: And A Confession. Paul Charles Joseph Bourget. Tr. by Winnie Barber Millard. LC 12-9857. 1.10. H. W. Kimber.

Two Sisters: Or, Virginia and Magdalene. Emma Dorothy Eliza Nevitte Southworth. LC 12-38906. T. B. Peterson & Brothers.

Two Sofas in the Parlor. 1st Ed. David Cornel De Jong. LC 52-5115. 1952. Doubleday.

Two Soldiers. Paxton Davis. LC 56-7490. 1956. Simon and Schuster.

Two Soldiers and a Lady: By H. S. Reid. Hilda Stewart Reid. LC 32-255899. E. P. Dutton & Co., Inc.

Two Soldiers, and a Politician. Clinton Ross. LC 18-4335. 1893. G. P. Putnam's Sons.

Two Soldiers, and Dunraven Ranch. Two Novels. Charles King. LC 16-13114. 1907. J. B. Lippincott Company.

Two Solitudes. Hugh MacLennan. LC 45-1344. 1945. Duell, Sloan and Pearce.

Two Solitudes. Martha Ellen Wright Shakespeare. LC 40-31639. 1940. The Penn Publishing Company.

Two Solitudes. Martha Ellen Wright. LC 40-31639. The Penn Publishing Company.

Two Sought Adventure: Exploits of Fafhrd and the Gray Mouser. Fritz Leiber. LC 57-7112. 1957. Gnome Press.

Two Spanish Picaresque Novels. Tr. by Michael Alpert. Incl. Lazarillo De Tormes; Swindler. Francisco Quevedo. (Classics Ser). (Orig.). 1969. pap. 3.50 (ISBN 0-14-044211-1). Penguin.

Two Spanish Picaresque Novels. LC 70-413395. (Penguin classics L 211). 1969. Penguin.

Two Spruce Lane. Gretchen Travis. LC 74-30587. 1975. 7.95 o.p. (ISBN 0-399-11514-5). Putnam Pub Group.

Two Standards. William Francis Barry. LC 75-466. (Victorian Fiction: Novels of Faith and Doubt; 20). 1975. 35.00 (ISBN 0-8240-1544-4). Garland Pub.

Two Standards. William Francis Barry. LC 96-2145. 1898. The Century Co.

Two-Star Pigeon. Michael Wolfe, pseud. LC 74-5804. 1975. 6.95 (ISBN 0-06-014715-6). Harper & Row.

Two Stolen Idols. Frank Lucius Packard. LC 27-21145. George H. Doran Company.

Two Stories. Alan Swallow. pap. 0.50 o.p. Swallow.

Two Stories & a Memory. Giuseppe Di Lampedusa. Tr. by Archibald Colguhoun. (Illus.). 1968. pap. 2.45 o.p. (ISBN 0-448-00227-2, UL). G&D.

Two Stories High. Zulie Butck. 96p. 1976. 3.50 o.s.i. (ISBN 0-8181-0357-4). Pageant-Poseidon.

Two Stories: The Missouri Rattler and Sam and Charlie. Ronald L Caruso. LC 74-78670. 1974. 4.95 (ISBN 0-8059-2019-6). Dorrance.

Two Strand River. Keith Maillard. LC 77-354672. 1976. 8.95 (ISBN 0-88878-088-5). Press Porcepic.

Two Strange Adventurers: Or, A Marvellous Coincidence... Kinahan Cornwallis. (On cover: Neely's popular library, on. 85). 1897. F. T. Neely.

Two Strangers. Margaret Oliphant Wilson Oliphant. LC 7-32500. R. F. Fenno & Company.

Two Strings to His Bow. Walter Mitchell. LC 7-31089. 1894. Houghton, Mifflin and Company.

Two Strings to My Bow: By Jeanne Bowman Pseud. Peggy O'More, pseud. 1955. Arcadia House.

Two Strokes of the Bell: A Strange Story. Charles Howard Montague. LC 7-31811. 1886. W. I. Harris & Co.

Two Summer Girls and I. Theodore Burt Sayre. LC 98-2117. 1898. G. A. S. Wieners.

Two Summer Sequences. Gerald Locklin. 1979. 2.50 (ISBN 0-917554-10-8). Maelstrom.

Two Susans: A Novel. William Brinkley. LC 62-12728. 1962. Random House.

Two Suspicious Girls. Katie Mitchell. 1973. pap. 1.95 o.p. (Z409, Zebra). Grove.

Two Symphonies. Andre Paul Guillaume Gide. LC 77-4750. 1977. 2.45 (ISBN 0-394-72454-2). Vintage Books.

Two Symphonies: Isabelle and The Pastoral Symphony. Andre Paul Guillaume Gide. LC 49-9194. 1949. Knopf.

Two Symphonies: Translated from the French of Andre Gide. Andre Paul Guillaume Gide. Tr. by Bussy, Dorothy. LC 31-13096. 1931. A. A. Knopf.

Two Tales. Y. Agnon. Incl. Betrothed; Edo & Enam. LC 65-25414. 1966. 4.95x (ISBN 0-8052-3271-0). Schocken.

Two Tales. Charlotte Bronte & William V Holtz. LC 77-11182. (Illus.). 1978. 28.00 (ISBN 0-8262-0232-2). University of Missouri Press.

Two Tales and Eight Tomorrows. Harry Harrison. LC 68-19247. 1968. 0.50. Bantam Books.

Two Tales by Charlotte Bronte: "The Secret" & "Lily Hart". Ed. by William Holtz. LC 77-11182. 1978. 28.00x (ISBN 0-8262-0232-2); limited 65.00x (ISBN 0-8262-0245-4). U of Mo Pr.

Two Tales for Autumn. Berry Fleming. LC 79-88065. 1979. 9.95. Cotton Lane Press.

Two Tales: Man Who Would Be King & Without Benefit of Clergy. Rudyard Kipling. pap. 2.50 (ISBN 0-8283-1460-8, 2, IPL). Branden.

Two Tales of the Occult. Mircea Eliade. LC 77-127872. 1970. 5.00. Herder and Herder.

Two Theives and a Puma. John Henry Reese. LC 79-7806. 1980. 7.95 (ISBN 0-385-15372-4). Doubleday.

Two Thieves. Manuel Komroff. LC 31-2976. 1931. Coward-McCann, Inc.

Two Thieves. Theodore Francis Powys. LC 79-167466. (Short story index reprint series). 1971. (ISBN 0-8369-3992-1). Books for Libraries Press.

Two-Thirds of a Ghost. Helen McCloy. LC 56-880010. 1956. RandomHouse.

Two Thousand A. D. Illustrations from the Golden Age of Science Fiction. Jacques Sadoul. LC 75-13242. (Illus.). 176p. 1975. 17.95 o.p. (ISBN 0-8092-8298-4); pap. 7.95 o.p. (ISBN 0-8092-8117-1). Contemp Bks.

Two Thousand & Eighteen, A.D. (or the King Kong Blues) Sam J. Lundwall. (Science Fiction Ser). 1975. pap. 1.25 o.p. (UY1161). DAW Bks.

Two-Thousand & One: A Space Odyssey. Arthur C. Clarke. 1980. 7.95 (ISBN 0-453-00269-2, H269). NAL.

Two Thousand & One: A Space Odyssey. Arthur C. Clarke. 1972. pap. 2.95 (ISBN 0-451-11864-2, AE1864, Sig). NAL.

Two Thousand & Ten: Odyssey Two. Arthur C. Clarke. 320p. 1982. 14.95 (ISBN 0-345-30305-9, Del Rey). Ballantine.

Two Thousand Eight Hundred Ninety-Four of, the Fossil Man: A Mid-Winter Night's Dream. Walter Browne. LC 6-17219. 1894. G. W. Dillingham.

Two-Thousand-Eighteen A.D. Sam J. Lundwall. (Science Fiction Ser). pap. 1.25 (ISBN 0-87997-161-4, UY1161). Daw Bks.

Two Thousand One Hundred & Fifty A. D. Thea Alexander. 288p. (Orig.). 1976. pap. 2.95 (ISBN 0-446-33056-6). Warner Bks.

Two Thousand per Cent Rule. Edward A. Pollitz. LC 73-11790. 1974. 6.95 (ISBN 0-672-51909-7). Bobbs-Merrill.

Two, Three, Many More. Nicholas Von Hoffman. LC 69-20164. 256p. 1969. 5.95 o.p. (ISBN 0-8129-0110-X). Times Bks.

Two, Three, Many More: A Novel. Nicholas Von Hoffman. LC 69-20164. 1969. 5.95. Quadrangle Books.

Two Ticket Puzzle. Alfred Walter Stewart. LC 30-20810. 1930. Little, Brown, and Company.

Two Tickets for Tangier. F. Van Wyck Mason. 1976. Repr. of 1955 ed. lib. bdg. 15.45x (ISBN 0-89190-354-2). Am Repr-Rivercity Pr.

Two Tickets for Tangier: A Colonel North Story. Francis Van Wyck Mason. LC 75-34056. 1975. 9.95 (ISBN 0-89190-354-2). American Reprint Co.

Two Tickets for Tangier. 1st Ed. Francis Van Wyck Mason. LC 55-5250. (Colonel North story). 1955. Doubleday.

Two Tickets to Destruction. Gladys S. Foster. 140p. 1975. 6.00 o.p. (ISBN 0-682-48178-5). Exposition.

Two Tickets West. Elliot Storm. LC 34-30041. W. Godwin, Inc.

Two-Time Girl. Florence Stonebraker. LC 45-548186. 1945. Phoenix Press.

Two-Time Woman. Wright Williams. LC 37-16814. Phoenix Press.

Two-Time Woman. Watkins Eppes Wright. LC 37-16814. 1937. Phoenix Press.

Two to Conquer: A Darkover Novel. Marion Zimmer Bradley. (Science Fiction Ser.). (Orig.). 1980. pap. 2.50 (ISBN 0-87997-651-9, UE1651). DAW Bks.

Two to Make a Wife. Louise Braden. LC 41-3112. Modern Age Books.

Two Together. Louise Platt Hauck. LC 32-6425. The Penn Publishing Company.

Two Towers. John Ronald Reuel Tolkien. 1967. 11.95 (ISBN 0-395-08255-2). HM.

Two Towers: Being the Second Part of The Lord of the Rings. silver anniversary ed. John Ronald Reuel Tolkien. LC 81-166148. (Tolkien, John Ronald Reuel, 1892-1973. Lord of the Rings: Pt. 2). (Illus.). 1981. 11.95 (ISBN 0-395-31266-3). Houghton Mifflin.

Two Trails to Bannack. Peter Grady. LC 56-13299. 1956. Avalon Books.

Two True California Stories. Augusta Dane; or, The Influence of Circumstances. Mary Morton; or, The Result of a Fashionable Education. Jonathan Vinton Webster. LC 8-36742. 1883. P. J. Thomas.

Two Under the Covers. Jean MacCready & Vicki Quade. (Illus., Orig.). 1981. pap. 2.95 (ISBN 0-9602604-1-2). V Quade.

Two Under the Indian Sun. Jon Godden & Rumer Godden. (O.s.i.). 1966. 5.50 o.s.i. (ISBN 0-670-73740-2). Viking Pr.

Two Undertakers. Francis Beeding. LC 33-974. 1933. Little, Brown, and Company.

Two Valleys. Howard Melvin Fast. LC 33-29998. 1933. Dial Press, Inc.

Two Vanrevels. Booth Tarkington. LC 2-22845. 1902. McClure, Phillips & Co.

Two Vanrevels. Booth Tarkington. LC 20-156072. 1913. Doubleday, Page & Company.

Two Vanrevels. Booth Tarkington. LC 22-16006. 1920. Doubleday, Page & Company.

Two Views. Uwe Johnson. LC 66-23811. (Illus.). 1966. Harcourt, Brace & World.

Two Villages. Louisa Brannan. LC 11-29731. Every Where Publishing Co.

Two Virginities. Herbert S Gorman. LC 26-17609. 1926. The Macaulay Company.

Two Virgins. Kamala Markandaya, pseud. LC 73-4293. (John Day Bk.). 256p. 1973. 10.53i (ISBN 0-381-98244-0). T Y Crowell.

Two Virgins: A Novel. Kamala Markandaya, pseud. LC 73-4293. 1973. 7.95 (ISBN 0-381-98244-0). John Day Co.

Two Voices. Henry Harland. LC 7-18967. Cassell & Company, Limited.

Two Walk Together. Barbara Cooper. LC 35-29679. 1935. T. Nelson and Sons, Ltd.

Two Washington Belles. A Story of to-Day. Lester M Del Garcia. LC 98-573. F. T. Neely.

Two-Way Arrow Pointing to Right Arrow Pointing to Left Traffic. Joel Lieber. LC 76-171304. 1972. 6.95. Doubleday.

Two Way Mistress. Mark Savage. (Orig.). pap. 0.95 o.p. (1152). Brandon.

Two Way Swinger. Frank G. Harris. (Orig.). pap. 1.25 o.p. (2053). Brandon.

Two-Way Traffic. Joel Lieber. LC 76-171304. 1972. 6.95 o.p. (ISBN 0-385-09031-5). Doubleday.

Two Ways Meet: Stories of Migrants in Australia. Ed. by Louise Elizabeth Rorabacher. LC 66-5080. 1966. bds., 2.95. F. W. Cheshire.

Two Ways Meet: Stories of Migrants in Australia. Ed. by Louise Elizabeth Rorabacher. LC 66-5080. 1963. F. W. Cheshire.

Two Ways to Die. Emma Redington Lee Thayer. LC 59-8299. (Red Badge detective). 1959. Dodd, Mead.

Two Ways to Matrimony: Or, False Pride. (On cover: Peterson's dollar series). T. B. Peterson & Brothers.

Two Weeks in Another Town. Irwin Shaw. LC 60-5560. 1960. Random House.

Two Weeks to Find a Killer. Charles Davis. 2.50 o.p. Carlton.

Two Wessex Tales. Thomas Hardy. LC 19-18227. (Half-title: International pocket library, ed. by E. R. Brown). The Four Seas Company.

Two White Elephants. Arthur Henry Veysey. LC 99-858. 1899. G. W. Dillingham Co.

Two White Slaves: Or, The Creole Orphans. A Tale of the Power of Virtue Over Dishonor. James S Peacocke. (On cover: Columbian publishing company. no 3). 1890. Columbian Publishing Company.

Two Wilderness Voyagers: A True Tale of Indian Life. Franklin Welles Calkins. 1902. F. H. Revell Company.

Two Witnesses. Maurice E Taylor. LC 67-28916. 1968. Dorrance.

Two Witnesses: Or, A Story of Yesterday, Today and Tomorrow. Norma Page. LC 32-7600. The Evangelical Press.

Two Wives. George Frederick Myddleton Cornwallis-West. LC 30-2779. 1929. G. P. Putnam's Sons.

Two Wives. George Frederick Myddleton Cornwallis-West. LC 30-75709. 1930. G. P. Putnam's Sons.

Two Wives. M. B. Smith. (On cover: Munro's library, no. 673). G. Munro.

Two Wives: A Tale in Four Parts. Frank Arthur Swinnerton. LC 40-27288. 1940. Doubleday, Doran & Company, Inc.

Two Wives: Or, Lost and Won. Timothy Shay Arthur. LC 6-34303. (On cover: Lovell's library, v. 10, no. 507). J. W. Lovell Company.

Two Women. Justus George Frederick. LC 23-18373. 1924. N. L. Brown.

Two Women. Peggy Gaddis, pseud. LC 36-149303. Godwin.

Two Women. Majorie Lee. 1978. pap. 1.95 (ISBN 0-89041-180-8, 3180). Major Bks.

Two Women. Alberto Moravia. 1974. (pbk.) 1.50. Manor Books.

Two Women. Harry Mulisch. LC 79-41752. 1980. 11.95 (ISBN 0-7145-3810-8). J. Calder.

Two Women: A Moral Blot. Sigmund B Alexander. (On cover: The pastime series, no. 50). 1897. Laird & Lee.

Two Women. A Novel. Georgiana Marion Craik May. (Franklin square library, no. 114). 1880. Harper & Brothers.

Two Women & a Fool. Hobart Chatfield Chatfield-Taylor. LC 6-234320. 1895. Stone & Kimballk.

Two Women and Their Man: A Novel. Mervyn Jones. LC 81-18212. 1982. 10.95 (ISBN 0-312-82754-7). St Martin's Press.

Two Women: By Alberto Moravia Pseud. Translated from the Italian by Angus Davidson. Alberto Pincherle. LC 58-743950. 1958. Farrar, Straus and Cudahy.

Two Women in Black: The Marvelous Career of a Noted Forger. John W Postgate. LC 7-30315. (Moooney & Boland detective series no. 2). 1886. Belford, Clarke & Co.

Two Women: Or, "Over the Hills and Far Away,". Lida Ostrom Vanamee. LC 8-30238. The Merriam Company.

Two Women: The One: a Fog in Santone; the Other: a Medley of Moods. William Sydney Porter. LC 10-30733. Small, Maynard and Company.

Two Women, Two Worlds. Robert F Mirvish. LC 60-11708. 1960. W. Sloane Associates.

Two Worlds. Poul Anderson. LC 78-726. (Gregg Press Science Fiction Series). (Worlds of Poul Anderson; 7). 1978. 9.95 (ISBN 0-8398-2429-7). Gregg Press.
Two Worlds. David Daiches. 1971. 8.50x (ISBN 0-85621-001-3, Pub. by Scottish Academic Pr Scotland). Columbia U Pr.
Two Worlds. Ivan Molek. Tr. by Mary Molek from Slovene. LC 77-88259. Orig. Title: Dva svetova. 166p. 3.45x o.s.i. (ISBN 0-9603142-2-9). M Molek Inc.
Two Worlds: A Novel of the Near Past. Aaron Chait. LC 62-681326. 1962.
Two Worlds and Their Ways. Ivy Compton-Burnett. LC 49-916937. 1949. A. A. Knopf.
Two Worlds: Dva Svetova. Ivan Molek. LC 77-88259. 1978. 3.45. M. Molek.
Two Worlds of Johnny Truro. reprinted ed. George Sklar. LC 48-217248. 1948. Sun Dial Press.
Two Worlds of Johnny Truro. George Sklar. LC 47-165018. 1947. Little, Brown and Company.
Two Worlds of Kamau. Gary P Ferraro. LC 77-94639. (Africa Sketches Series). (Illus.). 1.95 (ISBN 0-89253-106-1). InterCulture Associates.
Two Worlds of Noriko: By Vivian Breck. Vivian Gurney Breckenfeld. 1966. 3.25. Doubleday.
Two Worlds of Peggy Scott. Dorothy Daniels. LC 77-3719. 1977. 7.95 (ISBN 0-89340-079-3). J. Curley.
Two Worlds of Peggy Scott. Dorothy Daniels. 1974. (pbk.) 0.95 (ISBN 0-671-77768-8). Pocket Books.
Two Years. Alberto Albertini & Livingston, Arthur, 1883- Tr. LC 46-290063. 1936. The Viking Press.
Two Years Ago. Charles Kingsley. LC 7-12149. 1857. Ticknor and Fields.
Two Years Ago. Charles Kingsley. LC 41-31112. 1882. Macmillan and Co.
Two Years Ago. Charles Kingsley. LC 4-18687. 1890. Macmillan and Co.
Two Years Before the Mast. Charles H. Dana. (Regents Illustrated Classics Ser.). (gr. 7-12). 1982. pap. text ed. 2.25 (ISBN 0-88345-482-3). Regents Pub.
Two Years Before the Mast. Richard Dana. 1981. Repr. lib. bdg. 18.95x (ISBN 0-89966-426-1). Buccaneer Bks.
Two Years Before the Mast. Richard H. Dana. 1972. 8.95x (ISBN 0-460-00588-X, Evman); pap. 3.50x (ISBN 0-460-01588-5, Evman). Biblio Dist.
Two Years Before the Mast. Richard H. Dana, Jr. Date not set. pap. 3.50 (ISBN 0-451-51764-4, CE1764, Sig Classics). NAL.
Two Years in My Afternoon. Elisabeth Ayrton. LC 72-79564. 1972. 5.95 (ISBN 0-87645-060-5). Gambit.
Two Young Brides: Translated from the French of Honore De Balzac by the Lady Mary Loyd, with a Critical Introduction by Henry James... Honore De Balzac. Tr. by Lady Mary Sophia Hely-Hutchinson Loyd. LC 2-21101. (Half-title: A century of Franch romance. Parisian ed. vol. ii). 1902. D. Appleton & Co.
Two Zany Americans in Pre-War Japan. Heiji Vere. 5.95 o.p. Vantage.
Twofold Life. Wilhelmine Birch Von Hillern & S., M., Tr. LC 7-4676. 1873. J. B. Lippincott & Co.
Twofold Vibration. Raymond Federman. LC 81-47831. 10.95 (ISBN 0-253-18989-6). Indiana University Press.
Twopence Coloured. Patrick Hamilton. LC 28-19134. 1928. Little, Brown.
Two's Company. Margaret Guion Herzog. LC 34-4568. 1934. W. Morrow and Company.
Twospot. Bill Pronzini & Collin Wilcox. LC 78-1969. 8.95. Putnam.
Twyborn Affair. Patrick White. LC 79-26242. 1980. 10.95 (ISBN 0-670-73789-5). Viking Press.
Twyborn Affair. Patrick White. LC 81-4769. 1981. 4.95 (ISBN 0-14-005544-4). Penguin Books.
Twyla. Pamela Walker. (Berkley Medallion Book). 1976. (pbk.) 0.95 (ISBN 0-425-03076-8). Berkley Publishing Corp.
Tycoon. Richard Posner. (Orig.). 1983. pap. 3.50 (ISBN 0-440-18856-3). Dell.
Tycoon. Charles Elbert Scoggins. LC 34-4194. Thomas Y. Crowell Company.
Tycoon for Ann. Glenna Finley, pseud. Orig. Title: Career Wife. 1969. pap. 0.60 o.p. (73-852). Lancer.
Tyger! Tyger! R. C. K Ginn. LC 68-17515. 1968. Macmillan.
Tyler, Georgie Vere. (On cover: Sergel's Columbian library, v. l, no. 6). 1890. C. H. Sergel & Co.
Tyler of Barnet. Bernard Gilbert. LC 23-12097. ("Old England" series, vol. iii). Small, Maynard & Company.
Tyler's Row. Miss Read, pseud. (Adult Ser.). 366p. 1973. Repr. lib. bdg. 8.95 o.p. (ISBN 0-8161-6113-5, Large Print Bks). G K Hall.
Tyler's Row. Dora Jessie Saint. LC 72-6730. (Illus.). 1973. 5.95 (ISBN 0-395-15480-4). Houghton Mifflin.
Tyler's Row. LC 73-6829. (Illus.). 1973. 8.95 (ISBN 0-8161-6113-5). G. K. Hall.
Tyll Ulenspiegel's Merry Pranks. Moritz Adolf Jagendorf & Eulenspiegel. LC 38-9511. 1938. The Vaguard Press.
Tyne Folk: Masks, Faces and Shadows. Joseph Parker. LC 7-34986. 1896. F. H. Revell Company.
Tynedale Daughters. Norma Lee Clark. LC 80-54482. 1981. 9.95 (ISBN 0-8027-0676-2). Walker.
Type-High: A Novel. Paul Dayton Bailey. LC 37-30667. Suttonhouse, Ltd.
Typee. Herman Melville. LC 57-13622. Grosset & Dunlap.
Typee. Herman Melville. LC 51-5640. Dodd, Mead.
Typee. Herman Melville. LC 33-73840. (The companion classics). W. J. Black, Inc.
Typee: A Narrative of the Marquesas Islands. Herman Melville. LC 22-5075. (Half-title: Everyman's library, edited by Ernest Rhys. Fiction. no. 180). 1921. J. M. Dent & Sons, Ltd.
Typee: A Narrative of the Marquesas Islands. Herman Melville. LC 32-26362. (Aventine classics). 1931. Aventine Press.
Typee: A Peep at Polynesian Life. Herman Melville. Ed. by George Woodcock. LC 72-188906. (Penguin english library). (Illus.). 1972. (0.35, 1.65 u.s.) (ISBN 0-14-043070-9). Penguin.
Typee: A Peep at Polynesian Life; Omoo: a Narrative of Adventures in the South Seas; Mardi: and a Voyage Thither. Herman Melville. Ed. by G. Thomas Tanselle. LC 81-18600. (Library of America). 25.00 (ISBN 0-09-404500-3). Literary Classics of the United States: Distributed by the Viking Press.
Typee: A Peep at Polynesian Life During a Four Months' Residence in a Valley of the Marquesas. Herman Melville. LC 63-2556. West Virginia Pulp and Paper Co.
Typee: A Peep at Polynesian Life, During a Four Months' Residence in a Valley of the Marquesas. by herman melville. ed. Herman Melville. 1857. Harper & Brothers.
Typee, a Peep at Polynesian Life: During a Four Months' Residence in a Valley of the Marquesas; the Rev. Ed., with a Sequel The Story of Toby. Herman Melville. LC 3-27255. Harper & Brothers.
Typee: A Real Romance of the South Sea. With an Introd. by C. Merton Babcock. Herman Melville. LC 58-59811. (Harper's modern classics) 'Bibliographical note': p. xv.). 1959. Harper.
Typee: A Romance of the South Seas. Herman Melville. Ed. by Leonard, Sterling Andrus. LC 20-13343. Harcourt, Brace and Howe.
Typee: A Romance of the South Seas. Herman Melville. Ed. by Leonard, Sterling Andrus. LC 26-22322. Harcourt, Brace and Howe.
Typee: By Herman Melville. Herman Melville. (Half-title: The World's classics. cclxxiv). 1924. H. Milford.
Typee: By Herman Melville Illustrations by Mead Schaeffer. Herman Melville. LC 23-26933. Dodd, Mead and Company.
Typee: Life in the South Seas. Herman Melville. Ed. by Trent, William Peterfield. (On cover: Heath's home and school classics. The young reader's series). 1902. D. C. Heath & Co.
Typee, Omoo, Mardi: Herman Melville. Ed. by G. T. Tanselle. LC 81-18600. 1344p. 1982. 27.50 (ISBN 0-940450-00-3). Literary Classics.
Typee: Or, A Peep at Polynesian Life. Herman Melville. (golden books). 1930. D. McKay.
Types of English Fiction. Ed. by Hardin Craig & Dodds, John Wendell. LC 40-34867. (Types of English literature: Hardin Craig, general editor). 1940. The Macmillan Company.
Types of Men and Women (As Studied Through Ideality) Mary McArthur Thompson Tuttle. LC 7-38026.
Types of Prose Fiction. Ed. by George P Elliott. LC 63-18281. Random House.
Types of Short Fiction. 2d ed. Ed. by Roy R Male. LC 75-87240. 1969. Wadsworth Pub. Co.
Typewriter Girl. Grant Allen. (Arrow library, no. 101). 1900. Street & Smith.
Typewriter in the Sky. Fear. Two Novels. 1st Ed. La Fayette Ronald Hubbard. LC 51-3763. 1951. Gnome Press.
Typewriter's Conquests. Emma D. Mills. Manas Publishing Company.
Typhaines Abbey: A Tale of the Twelfth Century. Joseph Arthur Gobineau. Tr. by Meigs, Charles Delucena. 1869. Claxton, Remsen and Haffelfinger.
Typhaines Abbey: A Tale of the Twelfth Century. Joseph Arthur Gobineau. Tr. by Meigs, Charles Delucena. (On cover: Lovell's library, no. 434). 1884. J. W. Lovell Company.
Typhon's Beard. John Vasseur. LC 27-14059. George H. Doran Company.
Typhoon. Joseph Conrad. LC 2-21481. 1902. G. P. Putnam's Sons.
Typhoon. John G. Davis. 1979. 10.95 o.p. (ISBN 0-525-22555-2, Thomas Congdon Book). Dutton.
Typhoon. John G. Davis. 320p. 1982. pap. 3.25 (ISBN 0-445-04721-6). Popular Lib.
Typhoon: A Novel. John Gordon Davis. LC 79-1366. 10.95 (ISBN 0-525-22555-2). Dutton.
Typhoon: A Story of New Japan. J. W McConaughy & Lengyel, Menyhert. LC 13-4353. The H. K. Fly Company.
Typhoon, and Other Stories. Joseph Conrad. LC 26-14837. 1926. Doubelday, Page & Company.
Typhoon, and Other Stories. Joseph Conrad. LC 38-32637. 1938. The Sun Dial Press, Inc.
Typhoon & Other Tales. Joseph Conrad. pap. 3.95 (ISBN 0-451-51779-2, CE1779, Sig Classics). NAL.
Typhoon & Other Tales. Joseph Conrad. (Illus.). 1972. 5.50 o.p. (ISBN 0-396-04805-6). Dodd.
Typhoon Shipments. Kevin Klose & Philip A. McCombs. LC 74-4141. 1974. 6.95 (ISBN 0-393-08693-3). Norton.
Typhoon Shipments. Kevin Klose & Philip A. McCombs. 1976. (pbk.) 1.75 (ISBN 0-515-03865-2). Pyramid Books.
Typhoon's Eye: A Novel. Preston Schoyer. LC 59-7176. (Illus.). 1959. J. Day Co.
Typhoon's Secret. Solomon Neill Sheridan. LC 20-7516. 1920. Doubleday, Page & Company.
Typoo: A Novel. Earl Conrad. LC 76-76292. (Illus.). 1969. 3.95. P. S. Eriksson.
Typoo: A Typographical Novel. Earl Conrad. LC 76-76292. (Illus.). 1969. 3.95 o.p. (ISBN 0-8397-8450-3). Eriksson.
Tyranny of Distance. Geoffrey Blainey. pap. 3.95 o.s.i. Tri-Ocean.
Tyranny of Love. Colin Spencer. LC 68-28267. 6.75. Weybright & Talley.
Tyranny of Power. Daniel Thomas Curtin. LC 23-594865. 1923. 2.00. Little, Brown, and Company.
Tyranny of Power: A Romance of Two Notable Wars of the United States, Before the Rebellion, an American Story for Americans. Charles Summer Clark. LC 10-36345. 1910. 1.50. The C.M. Clark Publishing Company.
Tyranny of Prohibition: A Novel. Joseph Warren Fabian. LC 24-24698. The Independent Author's Library.
Tyranny of Sex: The Case of Mr. Crump. Ludwig Lewisohn. LC 48-1961. (Penguin books, 649). 1947. Penguin Books.
Tyranny of the Dark. Hamlin Garland. LC 72-84709. 1974. (ISBN 0-403-02283-5). Scholarly Press.
Tyranny of the Dark. Hamlin Garland. 1905. Harper & Brothers.
Tyranny of the Dark see Collected Works.
Tyranny of Weakness. Charles Neville Buck. LC 17-206650. W. J. Watt & Company.
Tyrant in White. Henry Berman. 1.50. F. F. Lovell Company.
Tyrant of Bagdad: By Glenn Pierce Pseud. 1st Ed. Glenn S Dumke. LC 55-107692. 1955. Little, Brown.
Tyrant of Time. 1st Ed. Lloyd Arthur Eshbach. LC 55-14065. (Science fiction)gShort stories.). Fantasy Press.
Tyrant: Tirano Banderas) a Novel of Warm Lands. Ramon Del Valle-Inclan & Pavitt, Margarita, Tr. LC 29-23493. H. Holt and Company.
Tyrants. Charles E. Jarvis. LC 77-78167. (Illus.). 1977. pap. text ed. 2.95 (ISBN 0-915940-02-7). Ithaca Pr Ma.
Tyrants Destroyed & Other Short Stories. Vladimir Vladimirovich Nabokov. Tr. by Dmitri Nabokov from Rus. LC 74-19209. 252p. 1975. 8.95 (ISBN 0-07-045739-5, GB). McGraw.
Tyrants of North Hyben. Frank Dilnot. LC 4-12974. 1904. J. Lane.
Tyrants. Translated by Naomi Walford. Richard Borge Thomsen. LC 55-566978. Putnam.
Tyree Legend. William Kelley. LC 78-23927. 12.50 (ISBN 0-671-22544-8). Simon and Schuster.
Tyrone of Kentucky. Clark McMeekin. LC 54-71562. 1954. Appleton-Century-Crofts.
Tyrrell of the Cow Country. Robert Ames Bennet. LC 23-13373. 1923. 1.90. A. C. McClurg & Co.
Tyrst. Elswyth Thane. LC 39-27213. Harcourt, Brace and Company.
Tysons (Mr. and Mrs. Nevill Tyson) May Sinclair. LC 6-17002. 1906. B. W. Dodge & Company.
Tzvika's Class: The Big Suprise, Vol. 3. 1982. pap. 1.19 (ISBN 0-87306-227-2). Feldheim.
Tzvika's Class: The Outing, Vol. 5. pap. 1.19. Feldheim.
Tzvika's Class: The Rosh Chodesh Party, Vol. 4. 1982. pap. 1.19 (ISBN 0-87306-228-0). Feldheim.
Tzvika's Class: The Snow, Vol. 1. 1982. pap. 1.19 (ISBN 0-87306-188-8). Feldheim.
Tzvika's Class: The Traffic Accident, Vol. 2. 1982. pap. 1.19 (ISBN 0-87306-226-4). Feldheim.
T13 White Tulips. Frances Kirkwood Crane. LC 53-5022. 1953. Random House.

U

U-Five Hundred Five. Daniel V. Gallery. 1967. pap. 2.25 (ISBN 0-446-32012-9). Warner Bks.
U. P. Trail. large print ed. Zane Grey. LC 82-711. 1982. 11.95 (ISBN 0-89621-348-X). Thorndike Press.
U. P. Trail: A Novel. Zane Grey. LC 18-2607. 1918. Harper & Brothers.
U. P. Trail: A Novel. Zane Grey. LC 21-13686. 1918. Grosset & Dunlap.
U. P Trail: A Novel. Zane Grey. LC 22-247791. 1920. Grosset & Dunlap.
U. S. A. The Land & the People. Robert James Dixson. (Illus.). 1959. pap. text ed. 1.50 o.p. (ISBN 0-88345-164-6, 17432). Regents Pub.
U. S. A. y Yo. Miguel Delibes, pseud. Ed. by F. L. Gordon. LC 77-117216. 1970. pap. 4.50 o.p. (ISBN 0-672-63133-4). Odyssey Pr.
U S Incorporated. William F Steuber. LC 53-5238. 1953. Bobbs-Merrill.
U. S. S. Paradise. 1st Ed. Hawes C Harris. LC 55-11736. 1955. Comet Press Books.
U-237 in the Devil's Triangle. John M Jones. LC 75-4195. 1975. 1.25 (ISBN 0-914042-03-3). Neptune Books.
Uarda: A Romance of Ancient Egypt... popular uniform ed. Georg Moritz Ebers. Tr. by Bell, Clara Courtenay (Poynter) LC 16-15713. (historical romances of Georg Ebers. vol. ii). 1915. D. Appleton and Company.
Ubik. Philip K Dick. LC 69-15205. (Doubleday science fiction). 1969. 4.50. Doubleday.
Ubik. Philip K Dick. LC 79-4123. (Gregg Press science fiction series). (Reprint of the ed. published by Doubleday, Garden City, N.Y., in series: Doubleday science fiction.). 1979. 18.95 (ISBN 0-8398-2478-5). Gregg Press.
Ubiquitos Yank: Or, The Weird Narrative of a Lost Man. An Exciting Story of Detective Adventure in the Far West. Harlan Page Halsey. (On cover: The calumet series, no. 4). G. Munro.
Udara, Prince of Bidur: A Romance of India. Arthur Joseph Westermayr. LC 13-8395. G. W. Dillingham Company.
UFO: Encounters of the Fourth Kind. Art Gatti. (Orig.). 1978. pap. 2.25 (ISBN 0-89083-336-2). Zebra.
UFO-1, Flesh Hunters. Robert Miall. 1973. (pbk) 0.95. Warner Paperback Lib.
UFO-2: Sporting Blood. Robert Miall. 1973. (pbk.) 0.95. Warner Paperback Lib.
Ugly American. E. Burdick & W. J. Lederer. 1977. pap. 2.75 (ISBN 0-449-24201-3, Crest). Fawcett.
Ugly American. William J. Lederer. LC 58-7388. 1958. Norton.
Ugly Barrington. Margaret Wolfe Hungerford & Broughton, Rhoda, 1860- (On cover: The seaside library. Pocket ed., no. 862). 1886. G. Munro.
Ugly Club. Tom Lockwood. (O.s.i.). (Orig.). pap. 0.60 o.s.i. (A174X, Award). Univ Pub & Dist.
Ugly Duchess. Lion Feuchtwanger & Muir, Willa, Tr. LC 28-1190. 1928. The Viking Press.
Ugly Duckling. Illus. by Adrienne Adams. LC 65-21364. (Illus.). 1982. pap. 2.95 (ISBN 0-689-70748-7, A-123, Aladdin). Atheneum.
Ugly Duckling. Hans Christian Andersen. LC 6-39755. 1905. Moffat, Yard & Company.
Ugly Duckling. Hans Christian Andersen. New York, The Saalfield Publishing Company.
Ugly Face. Carolina Litowich. LC 32-30024. The Christopher Publishing House.
Ugly Frontier. David Shears. (Illus.). 1970. 6.95 o.p. (ISBN 0-394-45010-8). Knopf.
Ugly Heroine. A Novel of Domestic Life. Christine Faber. LC 6-37856. 1883. J. B. Lippincott & Co.
Ugly Idol: A Development. Claud Nicholson. LC 7-32298. (On cover: Keynotes series, 28). 1896. Roberts Bros.; Etc., Etc.
Ugly Prince. Tempest, Jan. LC 50-11196. 1950. Arcadia House.
Ugly Swans. Arkady Strugatsky & Arkadii Natanovich Strugatskii. Tr. by Alexander Nakhimovsky. 1979. 10.95 o.s.i. (ISBN 0-02-615190-1). Macmillan.
Ugly Swans. Arkady Strugatsky & Arkadii Natanovich Strugatskii. Tr. by Alexander Nakhimovsky & Alice Nakhimovsky. 1980. pap. 2.95 o.s.i. (ISBN 0-02-007240-6, Collier). Macmillan.
Ugly Unicorn. Russell Rinehart. LC 79-84875. 1979. pap. 2.00 (ISBN 0-934020-01-9). Illusive Unicorn.
Ugly Woman. William O'Farrell. (A Bloodhound mystery). 1948. Duell, Sloan and Pearce.
Uharna. Gerve Baronti. LC 27-286026. Dorrance and Company.

Ujamaa Wa Kiafrika. William Tordoff. (Swahili). 1965. pap. 0.75 o.p. (Pub. by East African Publ Hse). Northwestern U Pr.
Ukiyo: Stories of Post War Japan. Ed. by Jay Gluck. (Orig.). pap. 2.65 o.p. (ISBN 0-448-00114-4, UL). G&D.
Ukiyo: Stories of "The Floating World" of Postwar Japan. Ed. by Jay Gluck. LC 63-21851. 1965. Vanguard Press.
Ulcerated Milkman. William Sansom. 224p. 1979. 7.95 o.p. (ISBN 0-7012-0220-3, Pub. by Chatto Bodley Jonathan). Merrimack Pub Cir.
Uller Uprising. H. Beam Piper. 1983. pap. 2.75 (ISBN 0-441-84292-5, Pub. by Ace Science Fiction). Ace Bks.
Ullman Code: A Novel. Robert Bernhard. LC 74-16575. 1974. 6.95 (ISBN 0-399-11417-3). Putnam.
Ulric the Jarl: A Story of the Penitent Thief. William Osborn Stoddard. LC 99-4701. 1899. Eaton & Mains.
Ulrick the Ready: A Romance of Elizabethan Ireland. Standish O'Grady. LC 7-32495. 1896. Dodd. Mead and Company.
Ulterior Motives. David Garnett. LC 67-10761. 1967. Harcourt, Brace & World.
Ultima: A Novel. Robin Moore & Susan Deitz. LC 75-40495. 1976. 1.95 (ISBN 0-345-25375-2). Ballantine Books.
Ultima Thule. Henry Handel Richardson. LC 29-18422. 1929. W. W. Norton.
Ultimate. James Lund. LC 76-382847. 1976. 3.95. (ISBN 0-7145-3595-8) (ISBN 0-7145-3596-6). Calder.
Ultimate Act. Lawrence Paul Bachmann. LC 71-190396. 1972. 5.95. Atheneum.
Ultimate Code. Nick Carter. (Nick Carter Ser). (O.s.i.). 176p. (Orig.). 1975. pap. 1.50 o.s.i. (ISBN 0-441-84308-5, AQ1486, Award). Univ Pub & Dist.
Ultimate Dare. Sonya Jones. 1975. 2.50 o.s.i. (ISBN 0-917938-01-1). Vanity.
Ultimate Enemy. Fred Saberhagen. 1979. pap. 2.25 (ISBN 0-441-84316-6). Ace Bks.
Ultimate Flower. Miguel Serrano. (Colophon bks., CN285). (Illus.). 1972. 1.95. Harper.
Ultimate Flower. Miguel Serrano. LC 69-19629. (Illus.). 1970. 8.95. Schocken Books.
Ultimate Frog: An Unforgettable Story of a Strange Quest. Roy Dickinson. LC 40-1225. 1939. The Vanguard Press.
Ultimate Game. John W. Cummings, Jr. 176p. (Orig.). 1976. pap. 1.50 (ISBN 0-89041-098-4, 3098). Major Bks.
Ultimate Game. Ralph Glendinning. 1982. pap. 3.50. Jove Pubns.
Ultimate Game: A Novel. Ralph Glendinning. LC 80-27952. 13.95 (ISBN 0-671-42016-X). Wyndham Books.
Ultimate Good Luck. Richard Ford. LC 80-22069. 1981. 9.95 (ISBN 0-395-30373-7). Houghton Mifflin.
Ultimate Issue. George Markstein. 336p. (Orig.). 1982. pap. 2.75 (ISBN 0-345-29031-3). Ballantine.
Ultimate Moment. William Rheem Lighton. LC 3-28966. (Illus.). 1903. Harper & Brothers.
Ultimate Passion: A Novel. Philip Verrill Mighels. LC 5-15689. 1905. Harper & Brothers.
Ultimate Retreat. Richard Erno. LC 71-147343. (Illus.). 1971. 4.95 o.p. Crown.
Ultimate Revolution. Walter Starcke. LC 73-85058. 1973. pap. 3.95 o.p. (ISBN 0-06-067524-1, RD65, HarpR). Har-Row.
Ultimate Sex. Linda DuBreuil. 1976. pap. 1.50 o.p. (ISBN 0-8439-0347-3, Leisure Bks). Nordon Pubns.
Ultimate Solution. Eric Norden. 1973. (pbk.) 0.95 (ISBN 0-446-75154-5). Warner Paperback Library.
Ultimate Threshold: A Collection of the Finest in Soviet Science Fiction. Ed. by Mirra Ginsburg. LC 79-80362. 1970. 5.95. Holt, Rinehart and Winston.
Ultimate Threshold: A Collection of the Finest in Soviet Science Fiction. Ed. by Mirra Ginsburg. LC 78-2250. 1978. 2.50. Penguin Books.
Ultimate Triumph. Ruth Freeman Solomon. LC 73-87207. 1973. 8.95 (ISBN 0-399-11225-1). Putnam.
Ultimate Weapon. John Wood Campbell. (Ace Great Years Series). 1976. (pbk.) 1.25. Ace Books.
Ultimate Weapon. Edward Grant. 1976. (pbk.) 1.25 (ISBN 0-523-00832-5). Pinnacle Books.
Ultimate World. Hugo Gernsback. LC 73-161119. 1972. 5.95 (ISBN 0-8027-5542-9). Walker.
Ultimate World War. Joyce F. Kenney. (Illus., Orig.). 1980. pap. 2.95 o.p. (ISBN 0-89260-172-8). Hwong Pub.
Ultimatum. William Craig. 1970. 5.95 o.p. (ISBN 0-87777-026-3). R W Baron.
Ultimatum. Antony Trew. LC 76-5379. 8.95. St. Martin's Press.
Ultimatum: PU 94. Uri Dan & Peter Mann. Orig. Title: Nuclear Terror Novel. 1977. pap. 1.95 o.s.i. (ISBN 0-8439-0523-9, Leisure Bks). Nordon Pubns.
Ultimax Man. Keith Laumer. LC 77-10282. 7.95 (ISBN 0-312-82851-9). St. Martin's Press.
Ultimte Weapon. Anne Walters. 1966. pap. 1.00x (ISBN 0-88020-076-6). Coach Hse.
Ultra: A Story of Pre-Natal Influence. Laura Shellabarger Hunt. LC 23-12440. 1923. Times-Mirror Press.
Ultra Goes to War. Ronald Lewin. 1981. pap. 3.95 (ISBN 0-671-44531-6, 82844). PB.
Ultra-Violet Tales. Silvio Villa. LC 27-19220. 1927. The Macmillan Company.
Ultramarine: A Novel. 1st American Ed. Malcolm Lowry. LC 62-15207. 1962. Lippincott.
Ultraviolet Widow. Frances Kirkwood Crane. LC 56-8816. 1956. Random House.
Ultus, the Man from the Dead. William Reginald Hodder & Pearson, G. LC 16-14837. 0.50. George H. Doran Company.
Ultus, the Man from the Dead (Adapted from the Gaumont Co.'s Cinema Play of G. Pearson and T. A. Welsh) by Reginald Hodder... William Reginald Hodder & Pearson, G. LC 16-14597. 1916. Hodder and Stoughton.
Ulysse and the Sorcerers: Or, The Golden Legend of a Black. Marius Leblond & Leblond, Ary. Tr. by Miall, Bernard. LC 27-7673. 1927. Frederick A. Stokes Company.
Ulysses. James Augustine Aloysius Joyce. LC 76-151567. (Illus.). 1976. Franklin Library.
Ulysses. new ed. reprinted; with, "ulysses: a short history," by richard ellmann. ed. James Augustine Aloysius Joyce. LC 77-426586. (Penguin modern classics 3000). 1969. Penguin.
Ulysses. James Augustine Aloysius Joyce. LC 76-151567. (Illus.). 1976. Franklin Library.
Ulysses. James Augustine Aloysius Joyce. LC 49-29073. Random House.
Ulysses. James Augustine Aloysius Joyce. LC 34-2348. Random House.
Ulysses. a limited ed. James Augustine Aloysius Joyce. LC 78-108435. (Greatest Books of the Twentieth Century). (Illus.). 1978. 39.00. Franklin Library.
Ulysses, "Cyclops," "Nausicaa," & "Oxen of the Sun" A Facsimile of Page Proofs for Episodes 12-14. James Augustine Aloysius Joyce. LC 77-14655. (Joyce, James, 1882-1941. The James Joyce Archive). (Illus.). 1978. 85.00 (ISBN 0-8240-2819-8). Garland.
Ulysses, "Oxen of the Sun" & "Circe" A Facsimile of Drafts, Manuscripts, & Typescripts for Episodes 14 & 15 (Part I) James Joyce & Michael Groden. LC 77-22764. (Joyce, James, 1882-1914. The James Joyce Archive). (Illus.). 1977. 85.00 (ISBN 0-8240-2824-4). Garland Pub.
Ulysses, 'Telemachus,' 'Nestor,' 'Proteus,' Calypso,' 'Lotus Eaters,' & A Facsimile of Page Proofs for Episodes 1-6. James Augustine Aloysius Joyce. LC 77-14620. (Joyce, James, 1882-1941. The James Joyce Archive). (Illus.). 1978. 85.00 (ISBN 0-8240-2816-3). Garland.
Ulzana. James Robert Olson. LC 73-7916. 1973. 6.95 (ISBN 0-395-17123-7). Houghton Mifflin.
Umbertina. Helen Barolini. LC 79-4874. 10.95 (ISBN 0-87223-536-X). Seaview Books.
Umberto's Circus. Eduard Bass. LC 51-3901. 1951. Farrar, Straus.
Umbilical Connection. Shirley A. White. 96p. (Orig.). 1981. pap. 3.95 (ISBN 0-933362-06-4). Assoc Creative Writers.
Umbrage. Gae Rusk. LC 81-85569. 192p. 1983. pap. 4.95 (ISBN 0-86666-053-4). GWP.
Umbrella-Maker's Daughter. Janet Caird. LC 79-6563. 10.95 (ISBN 0-312-82855-1). St. Martin's Press.
Umbrella Mender. Beatrice Harraden. LC 13-17729. (Sunnyside series. no. 81). 1894. J. S. Ogilvie Publishing Company.
Umbrella Murder. Carolyn Wells. LC 31-314539. 1931. J. B. Lippincott Company.
Umbrella of Aesculapius. Thomas Meyer. LC 75-21930. 1975. 17.50x (ISBN 0-912330-31-7, Dist. by Inland Bk); pap. 7.50 (ISBN 0-912330-32-5). Jargon Soc.
Umbrella Steps. Julie Goldsmith Gilbert. 1973. (pbk.) 1.25. Paperback Lib.
Umbrella Steps. Julie Goldsmith Gilbert. LC 73-37041. 1972. 4.95 (ISBN 0-394-47945-9). Random House.
Umbrella Thorn. Peter De Polnay. LC 47-1832. 1947. Creative Age Press.
Umbrellas to Mend. Margaret Thomson Janvier. LC 6-1020. 1905. R. G. Badger.
Umilta. Louise De La Ramee & Piper, Anne Ellis. (seaside library. v. 33, no. 676). 1880. G. Munro.
Un-American Activities: A Novel. Richard Kluger. LC 81-43440. 1982. 19.95 (ISBN 0-385-13506-8). Doubleday.
Un-Americans. 1st Ed. Alvah Cecil Bessie. LC 57-1776. 1957. Cameron Associates.
Un Ami, C'est Quelqu'un Qui T'aime. Traduit Par Anne Carter. Joan Walsh Anglund. LC 65-14113. 1.95. Harcourt.
Un-Chri stian Jew. Lawrence Sterner. LC 17-31027. 1917. 1.50. The Neale Publishing Company.
Un de Beaumugnes see Oeuvres Romanesques.
Un-Easy. James L. Weil. 1969. pap. 4.00 o.p. (Pub. by Elizabeth Pr). SBD.
Un Mystere (A Mystery) Alice Marie Celeste Durand. Tr. by Alford, Harvey C. (On cover: Dearborn series, no. 18). 1890. Donohue, Heneberry & Co.
Un Ze Studio." An Idyl of the Housetops. Dora Higbee Geppert. 1895. The Franklin Printing and Publishing Co.
Unabridged Jack London. Jack London. LC 81-4383. 19.80 (ISBN 0-89471-123-7) (ISBN 0-89471-124-5). Running Press.
Unabridged Mark Twain. Samuel Langhorne Clemens. LC 76-43094. 1976. 15.90. (ISBN 0-914294-53-9) (ISBN 0-914294-54-7). Running Press.
Unaccompanied Sonata & Other Stories. Orson Scott Card. LC 80-20448. (Quantum book). 10.95 (ISBN 0-8037-9175-5). Dial Press.
Unafraid. Eleanor Marie Ingram. LC 13-21028. 1913. 1.25. J. B. Lippincott Company.
Unaltered Cat. Albert Lewin. LC 67-23689. 1967. Scribner.
Unambo, a Novel of the War in Israel: Translated by Ludwig Lewisohn. Max Brod. LC 52-5797. 1952. Farrar, Straus and Young.
Unanointed: A Novel. Laurene Chambers Chinn. LC 58-12877. 1959. Crown Publishers.
Unapparent Wounds. Gloria Nagy. LC 81-1487. 320p. 1981. 12.95 (ISBN 0-688-00623-X). Morrow.
Unappointed Rounds. Doris Miles Disney. LC 56-8093. 1956. Published for the Crime Club by Doubleday.
Unarmed in Paradise. Ellen Marsh. LC 58-13304. 1959. Macmillan.
Unarmed Killer. C. William Harrison. LC 57-9614. (Permabooks, M-3093, Western, 3). 1957. Permabooks.
Unarmed Warrior. Joe Wisong. 7.95 o.p. Vantage.
Unashamed. Peggy Gaddis, pseud. LC 45-21684. 1945. Phoenix Press.
Unasked Questions: Seven Stories & a Novella. Harry A. Hargrave. 1980. 6.00 o.p. (ISBN 0-682-49254-X). Exposition.
Unavoidable Delay, and Other Stories. 1st Ed. Dinan Athill. 1962. Doubleday.
Unbaited Trap. Catherine Cookson. (Signet book). 1974. (pbk.) 1.50. New American Library.
Unbaited Trap. Catherine Marchant, pseud. 1971. pap. 0.95 o.p. (95050). Beagle Bks.
Unbeaten. Giles A Lutz. 1975. (pbk.) 0.95. Leisure Books.
Unbeaten. Giles A Lutz. LC 76-175389. 1972. 4.95. Doubleday.
Unbecoming Habits. Tim Heald. LC 73-81792. 1973. 6.95 (ISBN 0-8128-1612-9). Stein and Day.
Unbecoming Habits. 192p. 1980. pap. 1.95 (ISBN 0-345-28902-1). Ballantine.
Unbegotten: A Doctor Palfrey Thriller. John Creasey. LC 79-183920. 1972. 4.95 (ISBN 0-8027-5246-2). Walker.
Unbeheaded King. Lyon Sprague De Camp. LC 82-16466. 1983. 9.95 (ISBN 0-345-30773-9). Ballantine Books.
Unbeheaded King. Lyon Sprague De Camp. 1983. 9.95 (ISBN 0-345-30773-9, Del Rey). Ballantine.
Unbeliever. Leo Francis Reardon. LC 28-13452. 1928. The Bunker Press.
Unbeliever: A Novel. Lillian Sailer. 96p. 1972. 4.00 o.p. (ISBN 0-682-47449-5). Exposition.
Unbelievers Downstairs. Maude Phelps McVeigh Hutchins. LC 67-19241. 1967. W. Morrow.
Unbelieving Wife. Margaret Echard. LC 55-7678. 1955. Longmans, Green.
Unbidden. R. Chetwynd-Hayes. 1975. pap. 1.25 o.p. (ISBN 0-515-03589-0, V3589). Pyramid Pubns.
Unbidden Guest. Frances Cooke. 1909. Benziger Brothers.
Unbidden Guest. Silvio Villa. LC 77-142280. (Short story index reprint series). (Illus.). 1970. (ISBN 0-8369-3764-3). Books for Libraries Press.
Unbidden Guest. Silvio Villa. LC 22-204243. 1922. The Macmillan Company.
Unbidden Guests. Lael Tucker Wertenbaker. LC 73-79367. 1970. 6.95. Little, Brown.
Unbirthday. A. M. Stephenson. 112p. 1982. pap. 1.95 (ISBN 0-380-79418-7, 79418, Flare). Avon.
Unblessed. Berneice Lunday. LC 78-15244. (Orion). 1.59 (ISBN 0-8127-0200-X). Southern Pub. Association.
Unblessed. Paul Richards. (Orig.). 1982. pap. 2.95 (ISBN 0-89083-949-2). Zebra.
Unborn. David Shobin. LC 80-18333. 1981. 11.95 (ISBN 0-671-25626-2). Linden Press/Simon & Schuster.
Unbottled Poison. Ruth J. Buntain. 32p. 1973. pap. 0.75 o.p. (ISBN 0-8163-0078-X, 21040-1). Pacific Pr Pub Assn.
Unbranded Thirty. Claude Rister. LC 44-699036. 1944. Arcadia House, Inc.
Unbreakable Mrs. Doll. Grace Perkins Oursler. LC 38-8557. Farrar & Rinehart, Incorporated.
Unbroken Heart. Robert Speaight. LC 46-3768. 1946. The Basilian Press.
Unbroken Lines. Harriet Theresa Smith Comstock. LC 19-18299. 1919. Doubleday, Page & Company.
Unbroken Reed: The Story of a Heart's Faithfulness to God. Blancha Lee Miller. LC 57-153458. 1956. Zondervan Pub. House.
Unbroken Web. Richard Adams. 1982. pap. 3.95 (ISBN 0-345-30368-7). Ballantine.
Unbroken Web. Richard Adams. (Illus.). 144p. 1980. 12.95 (ISBN 0-517-54231-5). Crown.
Uncalled. Paul Laurence Dunbar. LC 70-104443. 1970. Literature House.
Uncalled: A Novel. Paul Laurence Dunbar. LC 70-76104. 1969. McGrath Pub. Co.
Uncalled: A Novel. Paul Laurence Dunbar. LC 70-100262. 1969. Negro Universities Press.
Uncalled: A Novel. Paul Laurence Dunbar. LC 71-81116. 1969. Mnemosyne Pub. Inc.
Uncalled, a Novel. Paul Laurence Dunbar. LC 78-164804. 1972. (ISBN 0-404-00042-8). AMS Press.
Uncalled: A Novel. Paul Laurence Dunbar. LC 98-1206. 1898. Dodd, Mead and Company.
Uncalled: A Novel. Paul Laurence Dunbar. LC 6-40786. 1901. International Association of Newspapers and Authors.
Uncanny House. Mary Lucy Pendered. LC 29-19455. International Fiction Library.
Uncanny Stories. May Sinclair. LC 23-131923. 1923. The Macmillan Company.
Uncanny Tales. Mary Louisa Stewart Molesworth. LC 75-46294. (Supernatural & Occult Fiction). (Illus.). 1976. 13.00 (ISBN 0-405-08155-3). Arno Press.
Uncanny Tales. Mary Louisa Stewart. Ed. by R. Reginald & Douglas Menville. LC 75-46294. (Supernatural & Occult Fiction Ser.). 1976. Repr. of 1896 ed. lib. bdg. 13.00x (ISBN 0-405-08155-3). Ayer Co.
Uncanonized: A Romance of English Monachism. Margaret Horton Potter. LC 5119. 1900. A. C. McClurg & Co.
Uncas Island Murders. Francis Woolsey Bronson. LC 42-14363. 1942. Farrar & Rinehart, Inc.
Uncensored Mad. (Mad Ser.: No. 55). 192p. (Orig.). 1980. pap. 1.75 (ISBN 0-446-94462-9). Warner Bks.
Uncertain April. Celia Page. LC 40-301793. 1940. Doubleday, Doran and Company, Inc.
Uncertain Feast. Solita Solano. LC 24-28670. 1924. 2.00. G. P. Putnam's Sons.
Uncertain Glory. Henry Francis Prevost Battersby. LC 14-14922. 1914. 1.30. John Lane.
Uncertain Glory. Adelaide Humphries. LC 43-78651. 1943. Arcadia House, Inc.
Uncertain Glory,". Herb Meadow & Vadnay, Laszlo. LC 44-3951. 1944. Grossett & Dunlap.
Uncertain Glory. illustrated by h. weston taylor. ed. Harriet Lummis Smith. LC 26-11856. L. C. Page & Company.
Uncertain Heart. Alice Mary Ross Colver. LC 48-5909. 1948. Macrae-Smith-Co.
Uncertain Heart. Denise Robins. LC 76-52875. 1977. 1.25 (ISBN 0-380-00963-3). Avon Books.
Uncertain Irene. Katharine Holland Brown. LC 11-27110. 1911. 1.20. Duffield & Company.
Uncertain Journey. Oscar Lewis. LC 45-7529. 1945. A. A. Knopf.
Uncertain Memory. Laura Basse. LC 81-16798. 1982. 13.50 (ISBN 0-688-00749-X). Morrow.
Uncertain Sound. Roy Lewis. LC 79-27316. 1980. 8.95 (ISBN 0-312-82858-6). St. Martin's Press.
Uncertain Sound: A Novel. Herman Cromwell Gilbert. LC 70-103166. 1969. 6.00. Path Press.
Uncertain Traveller. John Fisher. LC 31-481462. 1931. W. Morrow & Company.
Uncertain Treasure. Helen Woodbury. LC 28-6713. 1928. Little, Brown, and Company.
Uncertain Trumpet. Arthur Stuart-Menteth Hutchinson. LC 29-200197. 1929. Little, Brown, and Company.
Uncertain Voyage. Dorothy Gilman Butters. LC 67-20921. 1967. Doubleday.
Uncertain Voyage. Dorothy Gilman. LC 67-20921. 1967. Doubleday.
Uncertain Voyage. Arthur Walcott. LC 36-36429. 1936. Atwood & Knight.
Uncertainty Principle. Dmitrii Aleksandrovich Bilenkin. LC 78-9620. 7.95 (ISBN 0-02-510770-4). Macmillan.
Unchanging Quest. Philip Hamilton Gibbs. LC 26-2545. George H. Doran Company.
Unchaperoned: A Novel. Helen Reimensnyder Martin. (On cover: Summer series, no. 46). 1896. R. F. Fenno & Company.
Uncharted Island. Sydney Muller Parkman. 1936. Harper & Brothers.
Uncharted Romance. Mary Howard, pseud. 1941. Doubleday, Doran and Company, Inc.
Uncharted Seas. Robert Adger Bowen. LC 13-67706. 1.35. Small, Maynard and Company.

Uncharted Seas. Emilie Baker Loring. LC 32-23568. The Penn Publishing Company.
Uncharted Seas. (Romance Ser.: No. 31). 256p. 1982. pap. 2.50 (ISBN 0-553-22671-1). Bantam.
Uncharted Spaces. Monica Selwin-Tait. LC 33-287354. 1933. Longmans, Green and Co.
Uncharted: The Tale of an Island and a Ship. Webb Waldron. The Greystone Press.
Unclaimed Letter. Anna McClure Sholl. LC 21-15110. Dorrance and Company, Inc.
Unclassed. George Robert Gissing. LC 75-29851. 1976. 18.50. Fairleigh Dickinson University Press.
Unclassed. rev. ed. George Robert Gissing. LC 77-362950. (Society and the Victorians; No. 26). 1976. 5.95 (ISBN 0-85527-054-3). Harvester Press.
Unclassed. George Robert Gissing. LC 68-54269. (Illus.). 1968. AMS Press.
Unclassed. George Robert Gissing. LC 6-43975. R. F. Fenno & Company; Etc., Etc.
Unclay. Theodore Francis Powys. LC 76-145247. 1976. 21.00 (ISBN 0-403-01162-0). Scholarly Press.
Unclay. Theodore Francis Powys. LC 32-6429. 1932. The Viking Press.
Uncle. Margaret Abrams. LC 62-14187. 1962. Houghton Mifflin.
Uncle. Julia Markus. (Literary Fellowship Award Novel Ser.). 1978. 7.95 (ISBN 0-395-27098-7). HM.
Uncle: A Novel. Julia Markus. LC 78-6858. 1978. 7.95 (ISBN 0-395-27098-7). Houghton Mifflin.
Uncle: A Novel. Julia Markus. 1979. 1.95 (ISBN 0-445-04469-1). Popular Library.
Uncle Abe's Miss Ca'line. Elizabeth Jones Boykin. LC 24-2076. The Roxburgh Publishing Company, Inc.
Uncle Abner, Master of Mysteries. Melville Davisson Post. LC 62-19630. (Collier mystery classics, AS417). 1962. Collier Books.
Uncle Abner: Master of Mysteries. Melville Davisson Post. LC 18-16373. 1918. D. Appleton and Company.
Uncle Abner, Master of Mysteries: A Collection of Classic Detective Stories. Melville Davisson Post. LC 75-11279. 1975. 2.75. (ISBN 0-486-23202-6). Dover Publications.
Uncle Amos, Politician. Philip Mallory Conley. LC 40-35161. West Virginia Publishing Co.
Uncle & Other Stories. Joan Shaw. Ed. by Angela Jaffray. LC 82-70936. 101p. 1983. pap. 6.00 (ISBN 0-932274-31-5); signed 15.00 (ISBN 0-932274-32-3). Cadmus Eds.
Uncle Anghel. Panait Istrati & White, Maude Valerie, 1855- Tr. LC 27-19173. 1927. A. A. Knopf.
Uncle Bernac: A Memory of the Empire. Arthur Conan Doyle. 1897. D. Appleton and Company.
Uncle Bernac: A Memory of the Empire. Arthur Conan Doyle. 9.95 (ISBN 0-7195-0392-2). Transatlantic.
Uncle Bijah's Ghost. Jennette Barbour Perry Lee. LC 22-651934. 1922. C. Scribner's Sons.
Uncle Billy: The Curious Cobbler. Clarence Hawkes. LC 39-32378. Chapman & Grimes.
Uncle Bob and Aunt Becky's Strange Adventures at the World's Great Exposition. Wilbur Herschel Williams. LC 4-16172. Laird & Lee.
Uncle Bob's Baby. An Autobiography. Wilbur Fisk Brown. LC 6-172377. (On cover: The seven ages series). 1894. G. W. Dillingham.
Uncle Bud's Acres, a Mystery Tale of the Ozarks. Elinora Richardson. LC 49-419111. 1949. New Age Pub. Co.
Uncle By Gosh of Old South County. Jennie R Partelow. LC 29-23793. The Christopher Publishing House.
Uncle Caleb's Niece. Lida Larrimore Thomas. LC 39-275530. 1939. Macrae Smith Company.
Uncle Carl. C. E. True. LC 8-15881. 1908. The Neale Publishing Company.
Uncle Charlie's Story Book. Fun, Fact, and Fancy. (Fiftieth Birthday Souvenir.) Lovingly Dedicated to Old Friends and New. Charles Noel Douglas. LC 13-19422. 0.30. C. N. Douglas.
Uncle Daniels' Story of "Tom" Anderson and Twenty Great Battles. McElroy, John, 1846-1929, Supposed Author. 1886. A. R. Hart & Co.
Uncle Danny's Neighbors. Francis Bail Pearson. LC 19-18028. The Bobbs-Merrill Company.
Uncle Earle's Monopoly. Anne Frances Cole. LC 42. 1899. The Editor Publishing Company.
Uncle Ezra Holds Prayer Meeting in the White House. Mae C. Turnor. 1970. pap. 2.00 o.p. (ISBN 0-682-47067-8). Exposition.
Uncle Fred in the Springtime. Pelham Grenville Wodehouse. LC 72-4717. (P. G. Wodehouse classic). 1969. 4.95. Simon and Schuster.
Uncle Fred in the Springtime. Pelham Grenville Wodehouse. LC 39-277011. 1939. Doubleday, Doran & Co., Inc.
Uncle Fred in the Springtime. Pelham Grenville Wodehouse. LC 40-32569. 1940. The Sun Dial Press.
Uncle from India (A Bargain in Souls) An Impossible Story. Ernest De Lancey Pierson. LC 7-35900. (On cover: The pastime series, no. 57). 1897. Laird & Lee.
Uncle Gabe Tucker: Or, Reflection, Song, and Sentiment in the Quarters. John Alfred Macon. 1883. J. B. Lippincott & Co.
Uncle Gideon. Nettie Bisbee Fanning. LC 32-25727. The Stratford Company.
Uncle Gregory. George Sandeman. LC 9-6275. 1909. G. P. Putnam's Sons.
Uncle Herschel, Dr. Padilsky, and the Evil Eye: A Novel of Old Brooklyn. Isador S Young. LC 72-91842. 1973. 6.95 (ISBN 0-15-192690-5). Harcourt Brace Jovanovich.
Uncle Hosie: The Yankee Salesman. Phillips Haynes Lord. LC 30-28846. 1930. Simon and Schuster.
Uncle Jack. by f. anstey, pseud. ed. Walter Besant & Guthrie, Thomas Anstey. (On cover: Seaside library. Pocket ed., no. 137). 1884. G. Munro.
Uncle Jack, and Other Stories. Walter Besant & Pollock, Walter Herries. LC 6-12401. (Harper's handy series, no. 16). 1885. Harper & Brothers.
Uncle Jack and Other Stories. Walter Besant & Pollock, Walter Herries. (On cover: Lovell's library, v. 12, no. 634). 1885. J. W. Lovell Company.
Uncle Jack's Executors. Annette Lucile Noble. LC 7-33475. 1880. G. P. Putnam's Sons.
Uncle James' Shoes. Doris Webster & Webster, Samuel, Joint Author. LC 23-124318. 1923. The Century Co.
Uncle Jed, Caddle-Master. Joseph Chapman. LC 34-181922. J. Chapman.
Uncle Jed's Country Letters. Hilda Brenton. 1902. H. A. Dickerman & Son.
Uncle Jeremiah at the Panama-Pacific Exposition: Strange, Startling and Amazing Adventures of the Famous Farmer Philosopher and His Friends Amid the Gorgeous Scenes at the Golden Gate. Charles McClellan Stevens. LC 15-14444. 0.25. The Hamming Whitman Company.
Uncle Jim: A Modern Roman. T. A. Fagan. LC 7-2174. 1893. E. P. Hutchings.
Uncle Jim; a Pioneer Tale. Louis Addison Bone. LC 26-18170. The Christopher Publishing House.
Uncle John: A Novel. George John Whyte-Melville. LC 1-20254. 1900. Longmans, Green & Co.
Uncle Julius and the Angel with Heartburn. Ethel Clifford Rosenberg. LC 51-10307. 1951. Simon and Schuster.
Uncle Lancy for President. Ethel Powelson Hueston. LC 40-6129. The Bobbs-Merrill Company.
Uncle Lisha's Outing. Rowland Evans Robinson. LC 7-42179. 1897. Houghton, Mifflin and Company.
Uncle Lisha's Outing: The Buttles Gals and Along Three Rivers; Foreword by Edward D. Collins; Introduction. Rowland Evans Robinson & Perkins, Llewellyn Rood, Ed. LC 35-6767. The Tuttle Company.
Uncle Lisha's Shop. Rowland Evans Robinson. LC 79-96892. 1969. Literature House.
Uncle Lisha's Shop and A Danvis Pioneer. Rowland Evans Robinson. Ed. by Llewellyn Rood Perkins. Fisher, Mrs. Dorothea Frances (Canfield) 1870- LC 34-2032. The Tuttle Company.
Uncle Lisha's Shop. Life in a Corner of Yankeeland. Rowland Evans Robinson. LC 7-42180. 1887. Forest and Stream Publishing Co.
Uncle Louie. C. J. Matthews. 4.50 o.p. Carlton.
Uncle Mark's Amaranths. Anne Gardner Hale. LC 6-46164. D. Lothrop & Company.
Uncle Mary: A Novel for Young or Old. Isla May Hawley Mullins. LC 22-11788. 1922. The Page Company.
Uncle Max. Rosa Nouchette Carey. (On cover: Seaside library. Pocket ed. no. 930). G. Munro.
Uncle Max. Rosa Nouchette Carey. LC 4-15425. (On cover: The home library). A. L. Burt.
Uncle Max. Rosa Nouchette Carey. LC 4-19038. 1902. Macmillan and Co., Limited.
Uncle Moses: A Novel. Shalom Asch & Goldberg, Isaac, 1887- Tr. LC 20-21189. E. P. Dutton & Co.
Uncle Nathan's Farm: A Novel. Mary Ann Mann Cornelius. LC 98-1947. 1898. Laird & Lee.
Uncle Ned's Cabin. A Son of the South. LC 23-10102. 1922. E. S. Upton Printing Co.
Uncle Ned's Cabin: Or, The Little Angel Comforter. Also, "Twixt Cup and Lip. Adah M Howard. (On cover: Munro's library. v. 1. no. 128). N. L. Munro.
Uncle Ned's White Child. Mary Edwards Bryan. (On cover: The library of American authors, no. 13). 1889. G. Munro.
Uncle Noah's Christmas Inspiration. Leona Dalrymple. LC 12-25841. 1912. 0.50. McBride, Nast & Company.
Uncle Noah's Christmas Inspiration. Leona Dalrymple. LC 41-31102. 1913. McBride, Nast & Company.
Uncle Noahs Christmas Inspiration. Leona Dalrymple. LC 14-18307. 1914. 1.00. McBride, Nast & Company.
Uncle Noah's Christmas Party. Leona Dalrymple. LC 14-18306. 1914. 1.00. McBride, Nast & Company.
Uncle of an Angel: And Other Stories. Thomas Allibone Janvier. LC 73-98578. (Short story index reprint series). (Illus.). 1969. Books for Libraries Press.
Uncle of an Angel and Other Stories. Thomas Allibone Janvier. LC 7-10336. (Harper's Franklin square library, no. 707). 1891. Harper & Brothers.
Uncle of an Angel: And Other Stories. Thomas Allibone Janvier. LC 7-10335. 1891. Harper & Brothers.
Uncle Peel. Irving Bacheller. LC 33-10154. 1933. Frederick A. Stokes Company.
Uncle Phil: A Novel. 2d and rev. ed. Josephine Russell Clay. LC 1-31841. The Abbey Press.
Uncle Piper of Piper's Hill. Jessie Catherine Huybers Couvreur. LC 70-397098. (Nelson's Australasian paperbacks). (Illus.). 1969. 1.95. Nelson (Australia.
Uncle Piper of Piper's Hill: An Australian Novel. Jessie Catherine Huybers Couvreur. (On cover: Harper's Franklin square library, no. 652). 1889. Harper & Brothers.
Uncle Piper of Piper's Hill: An Australian Novel. Jessie Catherine Huybers Couvreur. (On cover: Lovell's international series, no. 33). 1889. F. F. Lovell & Company.
Uncle Piper of Piper's Hill: An Australian Novel. Jessie Catherine Huybers Couvreur. (On cover: Seaside library. Pocket ed., no. 1217). 1889. G. Munro.
Uncle Remus, His Songs and His Sayings. New and Rev. Ed; with 112 Illus. Joel Chandler Harris & Frost, Arthur Burdett, 1851-1928, Illus. LC 47-5732. 1947. D. Appleton-Century Co.
Uncle Remus, His Songs and His Sayings. Joel Chandler Harris & Robert E. Hemenway. LC 82-7482. (Penguin American Library). 1982. 4.95 (ISBN 0-14-039014-6). Penguin Books.
Uncle Remus: His Songs and His Sayings; the Folk-Lore of the Old Plantation. Joel Chandler Harris. LC 7-2896. 1881. D. Appleton and Company.
Uncle Remus; Tales. Joel Chandler Harris. LC 74-76980. (Illus.). 1974. Beehive Press.
Uncle Robin in His Cabin in Virginia: And Tom Without One in Boston. John W Page. LC 7-24117. 1853. J. W. Randolph.
Uncle Robin in His Cabin in Virginia, & Tom Without One in Boston. John W. Page. 1853. 12.00 o.p. (ISBN 0-404-04615-0). AMS Pr.
Uncle Sam. Louise Crittenden Case. LC 12-284042. 1.50. Broadway Publishing Company.
Uncle Sam. Martha Sawyer Gielow. LC 13-22289. 0.50. Fleming H. Revell Company.
Uncle Sam: And the Negro in 1920. Edward Winslow Gilliam. LC 7-8215. 1906. J. P. Bell Company, Inc.
Uncle Sam, Detective. William Atherton Du Puy. LC 16-16259. 1916. Frederick A. Stokes.
Uncle Sam of Freedom Ridge. Margaret Prescott Montague. LC 20-11895. 1920. Doubleday, Page & Company.
Uncle Sam's Bad Boys: Or, Leaves from a Diary of a Post Office Inspector. Byron D Adsit. (Globe detective series. no 9). 1888. The Eagle Publishing Co.
Uncle Sam's Bible: Or, Bible Teachings About Politics. James Booth Converse. LC 116. 1899. The Schulte Publishing Company.
Uncle Sam's" Cabins. A Story of American Life, Looking Forward a Century. Benjamin Rush Davenport. (On cover: Mascot library, no. 8). 1895. The Mascot Publishing Co.
Uncle Sam's Children: Story of Life in the Philippines. Oscar Phelps Austin. LC 6-39754. 1906. D. Appleton and Company.
Uncle Sam's Dreams. S. A. De Armond. (On cover: The enterprise series, no. 89). 1896. E. A. Weeks & Company.
Uncle Sam's Emancipation: Earthly Care, a Heavenly Discipline, and Other Sketches. Harriet Elizabeth Beecher Stowe. LC 76-92442. Negro History Press.
Uncle Sam's Emancipation: Earthly Care a Heavenly Discipline; and Other Tales and Sketches. Harriet Elizabeth Beecher Stowe. LC 74-133163. (Black Heritage Library Collection). (Illus.). 1970. (ISBN 0-8369-8719-5). Books for Libraries Press.
Uncle Sam's Emancipation: Earthly Care, a Heavenly Discipline; and Other Sketches. Harriet Elizabeth Beecher Stowe. LC 8-16113. 1853. W. P. Hazard.
Uncle Sam's Farm Fence. A. D Milne. LC 7-254511. 1854. C. Shepard & Co.
Uncle Sam's Palace: Or, The Reigning King. Emma Wellmont. LC 8-36651. 1853. B. B. Mussey and Company.
Uncle Sam's Star Route: A Romance of a Rural Mail Route and the New Parcel Post, of Michigan's "Iron Country" and Its Southern Sand Hills, of the Glorious Farm Lands to the South and the West of Lake Michigan, and of Love, Politics and Personal Efficiency Everywhere. Jenness Mae Braden. LC 14-1766. 1913. 1.45. The Twentieth Century Publishing Company of Chicago.
Uncle Scipio: A Story of Uncertain Days in the South. Jeannette Ritchie Hadermann Walworth. R. F. Fenno & Company.
Uncle Seth's Will. Jennie Maria Drinkwater Conklin. 1886. Presbyterian Board of Publication.
Uncle Silas. Joseph Sheridan Le Fanu. (Seaside library. v. 16, no. 316). 1878. G. Munro.
Uncle Silas. Joseph Sheridan Le Fanu. (Victorian gothic novel of mystery). 6.50 (ISBN 0-8446-2444-6). Peter Smith.
Uncle Silas. Joseph Sheridan Le Fanu & Longford, Christine, Countess of, Ed. (On cover: Penguin books. 279). 1940. Penguin Books.
Uncle Silas: A Tale of Bartram-Haugh. Joseph Sheridan Le Fanu. LC 76-5278. (Le Fanu, Joseph Sheridan, 1814-1873. Works. 1976). 1976. (3 vols.) 62.00 (ISBN 0-405-09237-7). Arno Press.
Uncle Silas: A Tale of Bartram-Haugh. Joseph Sheridan Le Fanu. LC 66-13830. 1966. Dover Publications.
Uncle Silas: A Tale of Bartram-Haugh. New Introd. by Frederick Shroyer. Joseph Sheridan Le Fanu. (Dover bk. rebound). 1967. 4.00. P. Smith.
Uncle Sim. Fred Perrine Lake. 1909. The C. M. Clark Publishing Co.
Uncle Snowball. Frances Mary Frost. LC 40-27127. Farrar and Rinehart, Inc.
Uncle Snowball. Frances Mary Frost. LC 40-27127. Farrar and Rinehart, Inc.
Uncle Stephen. Forrest Reid, pseud. LC 70-145256. 1971. (ISBN 0-403-01171-X). Scholarly Press.
Uncle Terry: A Story of the Maine Coast. Charles Clark Munn. LC 1-29090. 1900. Lee and Shepard.
Uncle Tom Andy Bill: A Story of Bears and Indian Treasure. Charles Major. LC 8-28633. 1908. The Macmillan Company.
Uncle Tom of the Old South: A Story of the South in Reconstruction Days. M. F. Surghnor. LC 72-3108. (Black Heritage Library Collection). 1972. 16.50 (ISBN 0-8369-9082-X). Books for Libraries Press.
Uncle Tom of the Old South. A Story of the South in Reconstruction Days. M. F Surghnor. LC 15-6326. 1897. L. Graham & Son, Ltd.
Uncle Tom's Adventure in a Hollow Log. Thomas Halpin. The Halpin.
Uncle Tom's Cabin. Harriet Elizabeth Beecher Stowe. LC 66-6111. (Signet classic, CT322). 1966. New American Library.
Uncle Tom's Cabin. Harriet Elizabeth Beecher Stowe. LC 75-31408. (Illus.). 10.00. (ISBN 0-8055-1180-6) (ISBN 0-8055-0243-2). Hart Pub. Co.
Uncle Tom's Cabin. Harriet Elizabeth Beecher Stowe. LC 74-92333. (Charles E. Merrill program in American literature). (Charles E. Merrill standard editions.). (Illus.). 1969. C. E. Merrill Pub. Co.
Uncle Tom's Cabin. Harriet Elizabeth Beecher Stowe. (Half title: Everyman's library, ed. by Harriet Rubys. For young people 361). 1909. J. M. Dent & Co.
Uncle Tom's Cabin. Harriet Elizabeth Beecher Stowe. LC 26-2547. (modern readers' series). 1926. The Macmillan Company.
Uncle Tom's Cabin. Harriet Elizabeth Beecher Stowe. LC 36-37181. (Half-title: Everyman's library, ed. by Ernest Rhys. For young people. no. 371). 1929. E. P. Dutton & Co.
Uncle Tom's Cabin. Harriet Elizabeth Beecher Stowe & Daugherty, James Henry, 1889- LC 29-23126. 1929. Edward McCann Co.
Uncle Tom's Cabin. Harriet Elizabeth Beecher Stowe & Anne Terry White. LC 66-20534. (Venture book). (Illus.). 1966. G. Braziller.
Uncle Tom's Cabin. Harriett B. Stowe. (Arabic.). pap. 7.95x o.p. (ISBN 0-86685-270-0). Intl Bk Ctr.
Uncle Tom's Cabin" Contrasted with Buckingham Hall, the Planter's Home: Or, A Fair View of Both Sides of the Slavery Question. Robert Criswell. LC 72-950. (Illus.). 1973. 6.50 (ISBN 0-404-00254-4). AMS Press.
Uncle Tom's Cabin" Contrasted with Buckingham Hall, the Planter's Home: Or, A Fair View of Both Sides of the Slavery Question. Robert Criswell. LC 6-31603. 1852. D. Fanshaw.
Uncle Tom's Cabin: Introd. by Charles Angoff. Harriet Elizabeth Beecher Stowe. LC 57-2697. 1957. Fine Editions Press.

Uncle Tom's Cabin of to-Day. Andasia Kimbrough Bruce. LC 72-6488. (Black Heritage Library Collection). 1972. (ISBN 0-8369-9161-3). Books for Libraries Press.

Uncle Tom's Cabin of to-Day. Andasia Krmbrough W. L. Bruce Bruce. LC 6-46250. 1906. The Neale Publishing Company.

Uncle Tom's Cabin, or, Life Among the Lowly; The Minister's Wooing; Oldtown Folks. Harriet Elizabeth Beecher Stowe. LC 81-18629. (Library of America). (Illus.). 25.00 (ISBN 0-940450-01-1). Literary Classics of the United States: Distributed by the Viking Press.

Uncle Tom's Cabin: Or, Life Among the Lowly, by Harriet Beecher Stowe. Harriet Elizabeth Beecher Stowe. (Alpha library). Rand, McNally and Company.

Uncle Tom's Cabin: Or, Life Among the Lowly, by Harriet Beecher Stowe; with an Introduction by the Author, a Biographical Sketch; a Bibliography of the Work by George Bullen... and One Hundred and Six Illustrations. Harriet Elizabeth Beecher Stowe & Bullen, George, 1816-1894. Houghton, Mifflin and Company.

Uncle Tom's Cabin: Or, Life Among the Lowly. Harriet Elizabeth Beecher Stowe. LC 62-9431. (John Harvard Library). 1962. Belknap Press.

Uncle Tom's Cabin: Or, Life Among the Lowly. Harriet Elizabeth Beecher Stowe. LC 62-1966. 1962. Heritage Press.

Uncle Tom's Cabin: Or, Life Among the Lowly. Harriet Elizabeth Beecher Stowe. LC 65-9109. (Classic Collier books). 1962. Collier Books.

Uncle Tom's Cabin: Or, Life Among the Lowly. Harriet Elizabeth Beecher Stowe. LC 65-6529. (Perennial classic). 1965. Harper & Row.

Uncle Tom's Cabin: Or, Life Among the Lowly. Harriet Elizabeth Beecher Stowe. LC 51-48701. 1887. Houghton, Mifflin.

Uncle Tom's Cabin: Or, Life Among the Lowly. Harriet Elizabeth Beecher Stowe. LC 16-3413. 1852. J. P. Jewett & Company.

Uncle Tom's Cabin: Or, Life Among the Lowly. Harriet Elizabeth Beecher Stowe. LC 12-15048. 1852. John P. Jewett & Company.

Uncle Tom's Cabin: Or, Life Among the Lowly. 30th thousand. ed. Harriet Elizabeth Beecher Stowe. LC 18-16942. 1852. J. P. Jewett & Company.

Uncle Tom's Cabin: Or, Life Among the Lowly. illustrated ed... original designs by billings; engraved by baker and smith. ed. Harriet Elizabeth Beecher Stowe. LC 19-18265. 1853. J. P. Jewett and Company.

Uncle Tom's Cabin: Or, Life Among the Lowly. Harriet Elizabeth Beecher Stowe. (Added t.-p.: The writings of Harriet Beecher Stowe.: vol. 1-11). 1896. Houghton, Mifflin and Company.

Uncle Tom's Cabin: Or, Life Among the Lowly. Harriet Elizabeth Beecher Stowe. LC 12-39186. T. Y. Crowell & Company.

Uncle Tom's Cabin: Or, Life Among the Lowly. Harriet Elizabeth Beecher Stowe. LC 99-4324. 1899. Houghton, Mifflin and Company.

Uncle Tom's Cabin: Or, Life Among the Lowly. Harriet Elizabeth Beecher Stowe. LC 4791. (Altemus' young people's library). 1900. H. Altemus Company.

Uncle Tom's Cabin: Or, Life Among the Lowly. Harriet Elizabeth Beecher Stowe. LC 4-19035. 1904. R. F. Fenno & Company.

Uncle Tom's Cabin: Or, Life Among the Lowly. Harriet Elizabeth Beecher Stowe. LC 43-28882. Houghton Mifflin Company.

Uncle Tom's Cabin: Or, Life Among the Lowly. new ed., with illustrations, and a bibliography of the work by george bullen... together with an introductory account of the work. ed. Harriet Elizabeth Beecher Stowe & Bullen, George, 1816-1894. LC 8-16112. 1879. Houghton, Osgood and Company.

Uncle Tom's Cabin: Or Life Among the Lowly. aldine ed. Harriet Elizabeth Beecher Stowe & Higginson, Thomas Wentworth, 1823-1911. LC 99-582. (Half-title: The world's great books). 1898. D. Appleton and Company.

Uncle Tom's Cabin, or, Life Among the Lowly. Harriet Elizabeth Beecher Stowe & Weaver, Raymond Melbourne, 1888- LC 39-14273. The Limited Editions Club,

Uncle Tom's Cabin, or Life among the Lowly see Three Novels.

Uncle Tom's Cabin. With 16 Full-Page Illus. Including Reproductions from Previous Editions Together with Introductory Remarks and Captions by Langston Hughes. Harriet Elizabeth Beecher Stowe. LC 52-12396. (Great Illustrated Classics). 1952. Dodd, Mead.

Uncle Tom's Children. Richard Wright. LC 76-86656. 1969. 5.00. Harper & Row.

Uncle Tom's Children: Five Long Stories. Richard Wright. LC 40-29877. Harper & Brothers.

Uncle Tom's Children: Four Novellas. Richard Wright. LC 38-7794. 1938. Harper & Brothers.

Uncle Tom's Mansion. William Grant Burleigh. LC 31-15083. Wm. B. Eerdmans Publishing Co.

Uncle Valentine and Other Stories: Willa Cather's Uncollected Short Fiction, 1915-1929. Willa Sibert Cather. LC 72-83755. 1973. 6.95 (ISBN 0-8032-0820-0). University of Nebraska Press.

Uncle Wash: His Stories. John Trotwood Moore. LC 10-268221. 1910. The John C. Winston Co.

Uncle Whiskers. Philip Brown. 1976. pap. 2.95 (ISBN 0-446-87108-7). Warner Bks.

Uncle Will and the Fitzgerald Curse. John Dennis Fitzgerald. LC 61-7908. 1961. Bobbs-Merrill.

Uncle William, the Man Who Was Shif'less. Jennette Barbour Perry Lee. LC 42-28975. 1906. A. L. Burt Company.

Uncle William, the Man Who Was Shif'less. Jennette Barbour Perry Lee. LC 6-7774. 1906. The Century Co.

Uncle Zeek and Aunt Liza: A Tale of Episodes. Henry C Fox. LC 6-2546. Mayhew Publishing Company.

Unclean and Spotted from the World. Nellie Sims William Beckman. Beckman. LC 6-14753. 1906. The Whitaker & Ray Company (Incorporated).

Uncles & Nieces. Jack Benjamin. 224p. pap. 1.95 o.p. (7128). Barclay Hse.

Uncloseted Skeleton. Lucretia Peabody Hale & Bynner, Edwin Lassetter, 1842-1893, Joint Author. LC 6-46206. Ticknor and Company.

Unclothed: A Novel. Daniel Carson Goodman. LC 12-103145. 1912. 1.30. M. Kennerley.

Unclouded Summer: A Love Story. Alec Waugh. LC 48-5604. 1948. Farrar, Straus.

Uncoffin'd Clay. Gladys Mitchell. LC 82-5586. 1982. 9.95 (ISBN 0-312-82857-8). St. Martin's Press.

Uncollected Poems of Henry Timrod. Henry Timrod. Ed. by Guy A. Cardwell, Jr. LC 42-6215. 121p. 1942. 9.00 (ISBN 0-8203-0194-9). U of Ga Pr.

Uncollected Short Stories. Sarah Orne Jewett. Ed. by Richard Cary. 408p. 1971. 12.50 o.p. (ISBN 0-910394-10-5). Colby.

Uncollected Short Stories of Sarah Orne Jewett. Sarah Orne Jewett. Ed. by Richard Cary. LC 79-31367. 1971. Colby College Press.

Uncollected Stories of William Faulkner. Ed. by Joseph Blotner. LC 78-21803. 1979. 17.95 (ISBN 0-394-40044-5). Random.

Uncollected Stories of William Faulkner. William Faulkner & Joseph Leo Blotner. LC 78-21803. 17.95 (ISBN 0-394-40044-5). Random House.

Uncollected Stories of William Faulkner. William Faulkner & Joseph Leo Blotner. LC 80-6120. 1981. 7.95 (ISBN 0-394-74656-2). Vintage Books.

Uncomfortable Inn. Dachine Rainer. LC 60-117465. 1960. Abelard-Schuman.

Uncommercial Traveler. Charles Dickens. 1970. 5.00x o.p. (ISBN 0-460-00536-7, Evman). Biblio Dist.

Uncommercial Traveller. Charles Dickens. 1866. Hurd and Houghton.

Uncommercial Traveller. Charles Dickens. LC 6-37057. 1869. Hurd and Houghton.

Uncommercial Traveller. Charles Dickens. (On cover: Lovell's library. v. 5, no. 282). 1883. J. W. Lovell Company.

Uncommercial Traveller. Charles Dickens. (Half-title: Everyman's library, ed. by Ernest Rhys. Fiction). 1909. J. M. Dent & Co.

Uncommercial Traveller. Charles Dickens. Ed. by Dickens, Charles. LC 6-37241. 1896. Macmillan and Co.

Uncommercial Traveller. And Additional Christmas Stories. diamond ed. Charles Dickens. LC 6-37056. 1867. Ticknor and Fields.

Uncommercial Traveller: And Additional Christmas Stories. Charles Dickens. LC 6-37060. 1870. Field, Osgood & Co.

Uncommercial Traveller: And Additional Christmas Stories. Charles Dickens. (Half-title: Works.. New illustrated library ed. vol. xxvi). 1877. Hurd and Houghton.

Uncommercial Traveller: Master Humphrey's Clock, New Christmas Stories, General Index of Characters and Their Appearances, Familiar Sayings. Charles Dickens. LC 6-37034. 1869. Hurd and Houghton.

Uncommitted Man: A Novel of Suspense. Robert Easton Pickering. LC 67-20670. 1967. Farrar, Strauss and Giroux.

Uncommitted Man: A Suspense Novel. Robert Easton Pickering. (X1594). 1968. Berkley.

Uncommon People: Short Stories. Helen Rose Hull. LC 36-813606. Coward-McCann, Inc.

Uncommon Reader. Harper's Bazaar & Morris, Alice S., Ed. II. Title. LC 65-5623. (Avon book, NS4). 1965. Avon Books.

Unconfessed. Mary Hastings Bradley. LC 34-29554. 1934. D. Appleton-Century Company, Incorporated.

Unconquerable Survivor of 2055 A.D: A Novel. first ed. Victor S Lyons. 1973. 7.00 (ISBN 0-682-47842-3). Exposition Press.

Unconquerables: Translated from the Slovak by Andrew Bachleda. 1st Ed. Jozef Pauco. LC 58-59467. 1958. Vantage Press.

Unconquered. William Somerset Maugham. LC 45-1828. (The Crown octavos. No. 8). 1944. House of Books, Ltd.

Unconquered. Bertrice Small. 1982. pap. 6.95 (ISBN 0-345-28712-6). Ballantine.

Unconquered. Jeffrey M. Wallman. 1977. pap. 1.75 o.s.i. (ISBN 0-8439-0442-9, Leisure Bks). Nordon Pubns.

Unconquered. Ben Ames Williams. LC 52-141157. 1953. Houghton Mifflin.

Unconquered: A Novel of the Pontiac Conspiracy. Neil Harmon Swanson. LC 49-1721. 1948. Sun Dial Press.

Unconquered: A Novel of the Pontiac Conspiracy. Neil Harmon Swanson. LC 47-12222. 1947. Doubleday.

Unconquered: A Romance. Katherine Helen Maud Marshall Diver. LC 17-237562. 1917. G. P. Putnam's Sons.

Unconquered: Europe Fights Back. Robert Carse. LC 42-50213. 1942. R. M. McBride & Company.

Unconquered Sun. Ralph Dulin. LC 63-9337. 1963. Macmillan.

Unconscious Comedians. Caroline King Duer. 1901. Dodd, Mead & Company.

Unconscious Crime. E. O. Tilburn. (On cover: The library of choice fiction, no. 14). 1891. Laird & Lee.

Unconscious Crusader. Sidney Clark Williams. LC 20-4708. Small, Maynard & Company.

Unconscious Sinner. Vivian Cory. LC 30-33615. The Macaulay Company.

Unconscious Victorious & Other Stories. Stanley Berne. LC 69-20442. (Archives of Post-Modern Literature). (Illus.). 1969. pap. 7.00 (ISBN 0-913844-04-7). Am Canadian.

Unconscious Victorious & Other Stories. Stanley Berne. 304p. 1973. pap. 6.00 (ISBN 0-8180-0616-1). Horizon.

Unconscious Victorious & Other Stories. Stanley Berne. (Illus.). 1969. pap. 8.00 o.p. (ISBN 0-8150-0016-2). Wittenborn.

Unconscious Witness. Richard Austin Freeman. LC 42-6283. 1942. Dodd, Mead & Company.

Unconsidered: By Gregor Lang Pseud. With Illus. by Raymond Lufkin. Faber Birren. LC 55-112604. 1955. Citadel Press.

Unconventional: By Jack Woodford Pseud. & Gordon. Greene. Josiah Pitts Woolfolk & Gordon Greene. LC 52-681087. 1952. Signature Press.

Unconventional Joan ... LC 22-23906. Bungalow Book Company.

Uncorrupted. Robert Harmon. LC 67-30165. 1967. National Book Co.

Uncovered Wagon. Hart Stilwell. LC 47-308772. 1947. Doubleday.

Uncrowned King. Harold Bell Wright. LC 10-23317. 1910. The Book Supply Company.

Uncrowned King: A Romance of High Politics. Hilda Caroline Gregg. LC 2-20404. 1896. G. P. Putnam's Sons.

Uncrowned King: A True Romance of the '60's Now First Put on Record. Emmuska Orczy. LC 35-10039. G. P. Putnam's Sons.

Uncrowned Prince: Or, The Mystery of the Yellow Manse. Joseph J Farrington. 1900.

Undaunted. John Harris. LC 53-9340. 1953. W. Sloane Associates.

Undaunted... Alan Hart. LC 36-869049. 1936. W. W. Norton & Company, Inc.

Undaunted, a Novel. Nathan Hoffman. LC 38-1822. N. Hoffman.

Undaunted River. Richard Hubert Francis Cox. 1966. pap. 1.00x (ISBN 0-88020-080-4). Coach Hse.

Undead. Ed. by James Dickie. 1976. (pbk.) 1.95 (ISBN 0-671-80465-0). Pocket Books.

Undefeated. Keith Laumer. 1974. (pbk.) 0.95. Dell.

Undefeated. John Collis Snaith. LC 19-5272. 1919. D. Appleton and Company.

Undefeated. George Wolfenden, pseud. LC 41-18120. Greenberg.

Undefeated. Ida Alexa Ross Wylie. LC 57-5360. 1957. Random House.

Undefiled: A Novel of to-Day. Frances Aymar Mathews. LC 6-29094. 1906. Harper & Brothers.

Undelivered. Olive Ruth Brown Pattison. LC 73-85311. 1969. 4.95. Revell.

Under a Ban. Harriet Lodge. (On cover: The seaside library. Pocket ed. no. 174). 1884. G. Munro.

Under a Calculating Star. John Morressy. LC 75-907. (Doubleday science fiction). 1975. 5.95 (ISBN 0-385-09635-6). Doubleday.

Under a Calculating Star. John Morressy. 1978. 1.50 (ISBN 0-445-04240-0). Popular Library.

Under a Charm. A Novel. Elisabeth Burstenbinder. Tr. by Tyrrell, Christina. (Seaside library, v. 72, no. 1453). 1882. G. Munro.

Under a Cloud. Hilda Van Siller. LC 44-7028. 1944. Pub. for the Crime Club by Doubleday, Doran and Co., Inc.

Under a Cloud. Hilda Van Siller. LC 44-7028. 1944. Pub. for the Crime Club by Doubleday, Doran and Co., Inc.

Under a Cloud. A Novel. Jean Kate Ludlum. (choice series, no. 40). 1891. R. Bonner's Sons.

Under a Dancing Star. Ethel M Comins. (Avalon Books). 4.95. Thomas Bouregy.

Under a Glass Bell. Anais Nin. LC 82-72155. 101p. 1948. pap. 4.25 (ISBN 0-8040-0302-5). Swallow.

Under a Glass Bell, and Other Stories. Anais Nin. LC 48-605. 1948. E. P. Dutton.

Under a Shadow. Charlotte Mary Brame. LC 44-11261. (On cover: Lovell's library, v. 19, no. 1029). John W. Lovell Company.

Under a Shadow. Charlotte Mary Brame. LC 44-111427. (Primrose series. No. 26). Street & Smith.

Under a Shadow. A Novel. Charlotte Mary Brame. LC 11-10523. 1882. G. W. Carleton & Co.

Under a Thousand Eyes. Florence Bingham Livingston. LC 23-7724. 1923. Cosmopolitan Book Corporation.

Under a Willow Tree. Arthur Raymond Macdougall. LC 47-628. 1946. Coward-McCann, Inc.

Under-Age Lover. George H. Paul. pap. 1.95 o.p. (8021). Cameo.

Under an Alias. A Story of War, of Love and of Colorado. Howard B Jeffries. LC 7-10192. 1883. Times Steam Printing House.

Under Angels' Wings. Dorothea Mary Bolton. LC 56-34764.

Under Angels' Wings. Dorothea Mary Bolton. LC 51-17397. 1950.

Under Brazillian Skies. Bettie Freshwater Pool. LC 8-346031. 1908. G. P. E. Hart.

Under Calvin's Spell: A Tale of the Heroic Times in Old Geneva. Deborah Alcock. LC 10-24714. 1910. F. H. Revell Company.

Under Canadian Skies: A French-Canadian Historical Romance. Joseph P Choquet. LC 22-12896. The Oxford Press.

Under Capricorn. Helen De Guerry Simpson. LC 38-27033. 1938. The Macmillan Company.

Under Castle Walls. Henry Christopher Bailey. LC 6-25688. 1906. D. Appleton and Company.

Under Cover. Wyndham Martyn. LC 14-14915. 1914. Little, Brown, and Company.

Under Cover Man. John Wilstach. LC 31-15093. 1931. W. Morrow & Co.

Under Cover of Darkness. Donald Smith. 1981. pap. 2.50 (ISBN 0-8439-0903-X, Leisure Bks). Nordon Pubns.

Under Crimson Sails. Lynna Lawton. 352p. 1983. pap. 3.50 (ISBN 0-8439-2002-5, Leisure Bks). Dorchester Pub Co.

Under-Currents. Margaret Wolfe Hungerford. (On cover: Seaside library. Pocket ed., no. 1123). 1888. G. Munro.

Under-Currents of Wall-Street. A Romance of Business. Richard Burleigh Kimball. LC 7-12234. 1862. G. P. Putnam.

Under Dog. Francis Hopkinson Smith. LC 3-13055. 1903. C. Scribner's Sons.

Under Dog, and Other Stories. Agatha Miller Christie. LC 51-12402. (Red badge detective). 1951. Dodd, Mead.

Under Dog, and Other Stories. Agatha Miller Christie. 1975. (pbk.) 0.95. Dell.

Under Dogs. Mariano Azuela. Tr. by Munguia, Enrique. LC 20-181517. 1929. Brentano's.

Under Dogs. Hulbert Footner. LC 25-19121. George H. Doran Company.

Under Drake's Flag: A Tale of the Spanish Main. George Alfred Henty & Browne, Gordon Frederick, 1858- Illus. LC 4-17540. Blackie & Son, Limited.

Under Egyptian Skies: Or, Masked in Mystery. St. George Rathborne. (On cover: Eagle library, no. 147). Street & Smith.

Under False Pretences: A Novel. Adeline Sergeant. LC 8-6863. (Lovell's international series, no. 6). F. F. Lovell & Company.

Under Fate's Wheel. Emma Murdoch Van Deventer. LC 1-30547. (On cover: Pinkerton detective series, no. 46). Laird & Lee.

Under Fire. Charles King. LC 7-12221. 1895. J. B. Lippincott Company.

Under Fire. Richard Parker & Megrue, Roi Cooper. LC 16-6437. 1916. 1.25. The Macaulay Company.

Under Fire: A Tale of New England Village Life. Frank Andrew Munsey. 1897. F. A. Munsey.

Under Fire. A Tale of the Shenandoah Valley. T P James. (On cover: Flag series, no. 5). Street & Smith.

Under Fire: The Story of a Squad. Henri Barbusse. Tr. by W. Fitzwater Wray. LC 17-23964. E. P. Dutton & Co.

Under Fire: The Story of a Squad. Henri Barbusse. Tr. by W. Fitzwater Wray. (Half-title: Everyman's library, ed. by Ernest Rhys. Fiction. No. 800 E). 1928. E. P. Dutton & Co.

Under Fire: The Story of a Squad (Le Feu. Henri Barbusse. Tr. by W. Fitzwater Wray. LC 17-30722. 1917. E. P. Dutton & Co.

TITLE INDEX UNDER THE SAME STARS.

Under Five Lakes: Or, The Cruise of the "Destroyer.". Charles Bertrand Lewis. (On cover: Library of American authors, no. 56). G. Munro.
Under Five Lakes: Or, The Cruise of the "Destroyer,". Charles Bertrand Lewis. (On cover: Seaside library. Pocket ed., no. 852). 1886. G. Munro.
Under Friendly Caves. Olive E Dana. LC 6-33167. 1894. Burleigh & Flynt.
Under Frozen Stars. George Tracy Marsh. LC 28-23460. The Penn Publishing Company.
Under Gemini. Rosamunde Pilcher. LC 72-26192. 8.95. St. Martin's Press.
Under God's Umbrella. Jose L. Valencia. 1978. pap. 6.00x (Pub. by New Day). Cellar.
Under Golden Skies: or, In the New Eldorado: A Story of Southern Life. D C Osborne. LC 7-23180. 1898. Edwards & Broughton, Printers.
Under Goliath. Peter Carter. LC 77-5656. 1977. 7.95 (ISBN 0-19-271405-8). Oxford University Press.
Under Green Apple Boughs. Helen Stuart Campbell. LC 6-21484. ("Our continent" library, v. 1). 1882. Fords, Howard & Hulbert.
Under Green Apple Boughs. Lucile Grebenc. LC 36-27327. 1936. Doubleday, Doran & Company, Inc.
Under Groove: A Novel. Arthur John Arbuthnott Stringer. LC 8-13274. 1908. The McClure Company.
Under Handicap: A Novel. Jackson Gregory. LC 14-8241. 1914. 1.35. Harper & Brothers.
Under Heaven's Bridge. Michael Bishop & Ian Watson. 224p. 1982. pap. 2.50 (ISBN 0-441-84481-2). Ace Bks.
Under His Thumb: Or, The Rival Detectives' Clews. Donald J McKenzie. (On cover: Secret service series, no. 26). 1889. Street & Smith.
Under Life's Key: And Other Stories. Mary Cecil Hay. (Franklin square library, no. 160). 1881. Harper & Brothers.
Under Life's Key: And Other Stories. Mary Cecil Hay. (Seaside library, v. 46, no. 935). 1881. G. Munro.
Under Lock and Key, a Story. Thomas Wilkinson Speight. LC 8-15508. Turner Brothers & Co.
Under Lock & Key: A Story, 3 vol. in 1. Thomas Wilkinson Speight. LC 75-32785. (Literature of Mystery & Detection). 1976. Repr. of 1869 ed. 47.00x (ISBN 0-405-07900-1). Ayer Co.
Under Mad Anthony's Banner. James Ball Naylor. LC 3-18746. 1903. The Saalfield Publishing Co.
Under My Own Roof. Adelaide Louise Rouse. LC 2-7124. 1902. Funk & Wagnalls Company.
Under My Wings Everything Prospers. Curtis Harnack. LC 76-42334. 1977. 7.95 (ISBN 0-385-12501-1). Doubleday.
Under Northern Stars. William MacLeod Raine. LC 32-300227. 1932. Houghton Mifflin Company.
Under Northern Stars. William MacLeod Raine. LC 42-20804. 1942. Triangle Books.
Under Oath. An Adirondack Story. Jean Kate Ludlum. (choice series, no. 26). 1890. R. Bonner's Sons.
Under One Roof. Josephine Lawrence. LC 75-12972. 1975. 7.95 (ISBN 0-15-192803-7). Harcourt Brace Jovanovich.
Under One Roof. Ruth Eleanor McKee. LC 36-33979. 1936. Doubleday, Doran & Company, Inc.
Under One Roof. Emma Wilson. LC 55-54837. 1955. W. Funk.
Under One Roof: An Episode in a Family History. A Novel. James Payn. (Franklin square library, no. 53). 1879. Harper & Brothers.
Under One Roof. An Episode in a Family History... James Payn. (Seaside library. v. 26, no. 502). 1879. G. Munro.
Under One Roof: An Episode in a Family History. new ed. James Payn. LC 41-42507. Chatto and Windus.
Under Orders: Not His Own Master. Isabel Edis G. S. Reaney. 1900. Advance Publishing Co.
Under Orion. Janice Law, pseud. LC 78-6685. 1978. 7.95 (ISBN 0-395-26484-7). Houghton Mifflin.
Under Palmetto and Pine: Series of Stories. John Wesley Carhart. LC 99-2642. 1899. Editor Pub. Co.
Under Pike's Peak: Or, Mahalma, Child of the Fire Father. Charles L McKesson. LC 11-348. (On cover: Neely's continental library, 1898, no. 8). F. T. Neely.
Under Plowman's Floor. Richard A Watson. LC 78-16386. 1978. 7.95 (ISBN 0-914264-25-7). Zephyrus Press.
Under Plowman's Floor: A Novel. Richard A. Watson. LC 78-16386. 244p. 1978. 9.50 (ISBN 0-914264-25-7). Cave Bks MO.
Under Plum Lake. Lionel Davidson. LC 80-7628. 8.95 (ISBN 0-394-51252-9). Knopf.
Under Pontius Pilate: Being a Part of the Correspondence Between Caius Claudius Proculus in Judea and Lucius Domintius Ahenobarbus at Athens in the Years 28 and 29 A. D. William Schuyler. LC 6-36184. 1906. Funk & Wagnalls Company.
Under Pressure. Frank Herbert. 224p. 1981. pap. 2.50 (ISBN 0-345-29859-4, Del Rey). Ballantine.
Under Pressure. Frank Herbert. 208p. 1981. pap. 5.95 (ISBN 0-345-29829-2, Del Rey). Ballantine.
Under Pressure. Lily Conrad Theodoli. LC 8-277522. 1892. Macmillan & Co.
Under Pressure: A Novel. George Agnew Chamberlain. LC 36-17533. The Bobbs-Merrill Company.
Under Purple Skies. Virginia K Smiley. (Cameo romance). 1975. (pbk.) 0.95. Fawcett.
Under Red Pillars. Ada M Kennicott. 1902. The Abbey Press.
Under Rocking Skies. Lewis Frank Tooker. LC 5-28381. 1905. The Century Co.
Under Running Laughter. David Joseph Manners. LC 42-50770. 1943. E. P. Dutton & Co., Inc.
Under Sealed Orders. Grant Allen. LC 6-484. (On cover: Once a week library, v. 12, no. 10-11). P. F. Collier.
Under Sealed Orders. Hiram Alfred Cody. LC 17-286002. 1917. 1.35. George H. Doran Company.
Under Sealed Orders. Robert Peterson. 1976. pap. 2.50 (Pub. by Cloud Marauder). SBD.
Under Secret Orders. Tr. from Swedish by L. W. Kingsland. 1st Amer. Ed. Harry Kullman. LC 68-251866. 1968. 3.50. Harcourt.
Under Side of Things: A Novel. Lilian Lida Bell. LC 6-11705. 1896. Harper & Brothers.
Under Slieve-Ban: A Yarn in Seven Knots. Robert Edward Francillon. (Leisure hour series, no. 119). 1881. H. Holt and Company.
Under the Apple Tree. Dan Wakefield. 1983. pap. 3.95 (ISBN 0-440-19402-4). Dell.
Under the Apple Tree. Dan Wakefield. (General Ser.). 1983. lib. bdg. 16.50 (ISBN 0-8161-3474-X, Large Print Bks). G K Hall.
Under the Apple Tree: A Novel. Dan Wakefield. LC 81-19502. 13.95 (ISBN 0-440-09222-1). Delacorte Press/Seymour Lawrence.
Under the Arch. Isabella Caroline Somers-Cocks Somerset. LC 6-7346. 1906. Doubleday, Page & Company.
Under the Arctic Rind: A Story of the North. Sturdivant, R H. LC 51-14654. 1951. Dorrance.
Under the Auroras. A Marvellous Tale of the Interior World... W. J. Shaw. LC 8-5087. Excelsior Publishing House.
Under the Badge. Charles Hall Thompson. LC 57-700003. (Dell first edition, A132). 1957. Dell Pub. Co.
Under the Ban: A South Carolina Romance. Teresa Hammond Strickland. LC 8-16880. Rand, McNally & Company.
Under the Bells: A Romance. Leonard Kip. LC 7-12542. 1879. G. P. Putnam's Sons.
Under the Berkeley Oaks: Stories by Students of the University of California. University of California Magazine. Editorial Staff. LC 1-30407. 1901. A. M. Robertson.
Under the Big Dipper. Desiderius George Dery. 1916. Brentano's.
Under the Boardwalk. Norman Rosten. LC 68-26738. 1968. 4.95. Prentice-Hall.
Under the Bowdoin Pines: A Second Collection of Short Stories of Life at Bowdoin College. Ed. by John Clair Minot. LC 12-937. 1907. Kennebec Journal Print.
Under the Brutchstone: By J. M. Denwood and S. Fowler Wright, with a Preface by Hugh Walpole. Jonathan M Denwood & Wright, Sydney Fowler. LC 31-289181. 1931. Coward-McCann, Inc.
Under the Cactus Flag: A Story of Life in Mexico. Nora Archibald Smith. LC 99-401714. 1899. Houghton, Mifflin and Company.
Under the Cedars: Or, What the Years Brought. Alice J Hatch. LC 7-2636. 1872. Lee and Shepard.
Under the Christmas Stars. Grace Louise Smith Richmond. LC 13-23022. 1913. Doubleday, Page & Company.
Under the Circumstances. Kimon Lolos. LC 62-14557. 1962. Harper & Row.
Under the City of Angels. Jerry E. Brown. 304p. (Orig.). 1981. pap. 1.95 (ISBN 0-553-14605-X). Bantam.
Under the Colors. Milovan Djilas. LC 76-134576. 1971. 9.75 o.p. (ISBN 0-15-153470-5). HarBraceJ.
Under the Colors. Milovan Ilas. LC 76-134576. 1971. (ISBN 0-15-153470-5). Harcourt, Brace, Jovanovich.
Under the Corsican: A Novel. Emily Howland Hoppin. LC 7-523619. J. S. Tait and Sons.
Under the Cottonwoods: A Sketch of Life on a Prairie Homestead. Oren Frederic Morton. LC 1-29770. 1900. The Acme Publishing Company.
Under the Country Sky. Grace Louise Smith Richmond. LC 16-10118. 1916. Doubleday, Page & Company.
Under the Covenant: A Story of the Mormons by John C. Murdock. John C Murdock. LC 65-29083. 1966. Vantage Press.
Under the Crescent. Helen Barham Shipman. LC 15-15295. Grosset & Dunlap.
Under the Crust. Thomas Nelson Page. LC 7-372691. 1907. C. Scribner's Sons.
Under the Cuban Flag: Or, The Cacique's Treasure. Frederick Albion Ober. Estes & Lauriat.
Under the Deodars. Rudyard Kipling. LC 9-3025. F. F. Lovell Company.
Under the Deodars. Rudyard Kipling. LC 4877. H. M. Caldwell Company.
Under the Deodars: The Phantom Rickshaw, Wee Willie Winkee. new ed., rev. with additions. ed. Rudyard Kipling. LC 7-12350. 1895. Macmillan and Co.
Under the Deodars. The Phantom 'rickshaw, Wee Willie Winkie. copyright ed. Rudyard Kipling. LC 99-3033. 1899. Doubleday & McClure Co.
Under the Deodars: The Phantom 'rickshaw, Wee Willie Winkie. Rudyard Kipling. LC 28-1673. 1920. Doubleday, Page & Company.
Under the Deodars. The Works of Rudyard Kipling. Rudyard Kipling. LC 9-16371. 1909. The Nottingham Society.
Under the Eagle's Wing. Sara Miller. LC 15576. 1899. The Jewish Publication Society of America.
Under the Eaves of Shanghai: Shanghai Wuyansya, an Annotated Chinese Play. Ed. by Richard F. Chang. 1974. 5.50. Far Eastern Pubns.
Under the Empire: Or, The Story of Madelon. James Barron Hope. LC 7-5258. 1878. J. B. Hope & Co.
Under the Eye of Night. Robert E. Mills. 1980. pap. 2.25 o.s.i. (ISBN 0-8439-0718-5, Leisure Bks). Nordon Pubns.
Under the Eye of the Storm. John Richard Hersey. (N3579). 1968. Bantam.
Under the Eye of the Storm: By John Hersey. 1st Ed. John Richard Hersey. LC 67-14363. 1967. 4.95. Knopf.
Under the Fifth Sun: A Novel of Pancho Villa. Earl Shorris. LC 80-15714. 14.95 (ISBN 0-440-09388-0). Delacorte Press.
Under the Fig Leaf. Edwin Greenwood. LC 38-1069. 1937. Doubleday, Doran & Company, Inc.
Under the Flag of the Cross. James Hamilton Sedberry. LC 8-60308. 1908. The C. M. Clark Publishing Co.
Under the German Eagle. Franz Kruger. (Orig.). pap. 1.25x o.p. (SpS). Soccer.
Under the Goal Posts. Edwin Dooley. LC 33-28939. 1933. J. L. Pratt.
Under the Green Star. Lin Carter. (Science Fiction Ser.). (Orig.). 1972. pap. 1.50 (ISBN 0-87997-433-8, UY1433). DAW Bks.
Under the Greenwood Tree. Thomas Hardy. (wayfarer's library). 1914. J. M. Dent & Sons Ltd.
Under the Greenwood Tree. Thomas Hardy. LC 43-27333. (Jacket library. 11). 1932. National Home Library Foundation.
Under the Greenwood Tree: A Rural Painting of the Dutch School. Thomas Hardy. LC 1-21953. 1896. Harper and Brothers.
Under the Greenwood Tree: Or, The Mellstock Quire, a Rural Painting of the Dutch School. Thomas Hardy. LC 58-812. (St. Martin's library). 1957. Macmillan.
Under the Greenwood Tree: Or, The Mellstock Quire; a Rural Painting of the Dutch School. Thomas Hardy. LC 66-8902. (Papermac, P62). 1966. St. Martin's Press.
Under the Greenwood Tree or the Mellstock Quire. Thomas Hardy. 1872. 7.50 o.p.; pap. 1.25 o.p St Martin.
Under the Greenwood Tree; or, The Mellstock Quire. 1872. 7.50 o.p. (ISBN 0-312-82985-X); pap. 1.95 o.p. (ISBN 0-312-82950-7, Papermac). St Martin.
Under the Harrow. Ellis Meredith. LC 7-12976. 1907. Little, Brown and Company.
Under the Hermes: And Other Stories. Clotilde Inez Mary Graves. LC 70-121554. (Short story index reprint series). 1970. Books for Libraries Press.
Under the Hermes: And Other Stories. Clotilde Inez Mary Graves. LC 20-123558. 1917. Dodd, Mead and Company.
Under the Hill. Aubrey Vincent Beardsley & John Glassco. 1968. pap. 0.95 o.p. (Z1024, Zebra). Grove.
Under the Hog, an Historical Novel. Patrick Carleton. LC 36-14892. 1938. E. P. Dutton & Co., Inc.
Under the Influence of Mae. Gerard H. Shyne. LC 79-16921. 1979. 3.00 (ISBN 0-914772-00-7). Inwood Press.
Under the Influence. 1st American Ed. Geoffrey Kerr. LC 54-5592. 1954. Lippincott.
Under the Jack-Staff. Chester Bailey Fernald. LC 3-25878. 1903. The Century Co.
Under the Levee. Edward Earl Sparling. LC 25-6858. 1925. C. Scribner's Sons.
Under the Lilies and Roses. Florence Marryat Church Lean. LC 7-13226. (On cover: Lovell's library. v. 19. no. 950). 1887. J. W. Lovell Company.
Under the Linden Tree: An Interlude. Thames Ross Williamson. LC 35-5812. 1935. Doubleday, Doran & Company, Inc.
Under the Lion's Claw. John N Clarke. 1898. F. T. Neely.
Under the Live Oaks. Tryphena Matilda Archer Browne. LC 6-17220. 1893. T. Whittaker.
Under the Magnolias. Lyman W Denton. LC 6-33975. 1888. Funk and Wagnalls.
Under the Man-Fig. Mary Evelyn Moore Davis. 1895. Houghton, Mifflin and Company.
Under the Maples: A Story of Village Life. Walter N Hinman. LC 7-4684. 1888. Belford, Clarke & Co.
Under the Mesa Rim. Chandler Whipple. LC 54-34202. (Ace double novel books, D-64). 1954. Ace Books.
Under the Mesa Rim. A Double D Western. Chandler Whipple. LC 40-6547. 1940. Doubleday, Doran & Co., Inc.
Under the Moons of Mars: A History and Anthology of "the Scientific Romance" in the Munsey Magazines, 1912-1920. Ed. by Samuel Moskowitz. LC 72-80355. 1970. 7.95. Holt, Rinehart and Winston.
Under the Moorish Wall: Adventures in Andalusia. Peter Luke. 176p. 1980. text ed. 18.75x (ISBN 0-85105-371-8, Dolmen Pr). Humanities.
Under the Mulberry Trees: A Romance of the Old 'forties. Theron Brown. LC 9-29776. 1909. 1.50. R. C. Badger.
Under the Net. Iris Murdoch. 1977. pap. 3.95 (ISBN 0-14-001445-4). Penguin.
Under the Net: A Novel. Iris Murdoch. LC 54-705362. 1954. Viking Press.
Under the Northern Lights. Florence Gannon Hanfeld J. C. Ward Ward. LC 9-25635. 1909. A. Wessles.
Under the Old Elms. Mary Bucklin Davenport Claflin. LC 6-25377. T.Y. Crowell & Co.; Etc., Etc.
Under the Palmetto in Peace and War. Richard Meade Bache. LC 6-5034. 1880. Claxton, Remsen, & Haffelfinger.
Under the Pruning-Knife. A Story of Southern Life. Mary Tucker Magill. LC 7-20268. Presbyterian Board of Publication and Sabbath-School Work.
Under the Puppet's Crown: An Historical Novel. Lawrence Ealy. LC 39-21566. 1939. Meador Publishing Company.
Under the Quiet Water. Frances Shelley Wees. LC 49-8093. 1949. Macrae-Smith-Co.
Under the Raging Moon. Joan Hunter. 1975. (pbk.) 0.95 (ISBN 0-671-77996-6). Pocket Books.
Under the Rainbow. Lawrence R. Roszkowiak. LC 80-68893. 94p. (Orig.). 1980. pap. 3.95 (ISBN 0-9604986-0-5). Brandywine Bks.
Under the Rainbow Sky. Alice Mary Ross Colver. LC 26-149852. 1926. The Penn Publishing Company.
Under the Red Flag. Mary Elizabeth Braddon Maxwell. (Lovell's library, no. 266). 1883. J. W. Lovell Company.
Under the Red Flag. A Novel. Mary Elizabeth Braddon Maxwell. (On cover: Seaside library. Pocket ed. no. 110). 1883. G. Munro.
Under the Red Robe. Stanley John Weyman. LC 3-244883. 1894. Longmans, Green, and Co.
Under the Red Robe. Stanley John Weyman. LC 26-24699. 1926. Longmans, Green, and Co.
Under the Redwoods. Bret Harte. LC 72-113674. (Short story index reprint series). (Illus.). 1970. Books for Libraries Press.
Under the Redwoods. Bret Harte. LC 1-31541. 1901. Houghton, Mifflin and Company.
Under the Riviera Sun: A Novel; with Six Songs, Lyrics and Music, by the Author. Zeilke, Herta. LC 52-9244. 1952. Exposition Press.
Under the Robe. Dean Coffin. LC 73-103317. 1970. 6.95 (ISBN 0-87426-019-1). Whitmore Pub. Co.
Under the Rose. Frederic Stewart Isham. 1903. The Bown-Merrill Company.
Under the Rose. Arthur Johnson. LC 20-15533. Harper & Brothers.
Under the Rose Garden. Croft-Cooke, Rupert. LC 79-560909. 1971. 1.50 (ISBN 0-491-00136-3). W. H. Allen.
Under the Rose Short Stories. Ellen Wood. LC 8-37566. 1878. G. W. Carleton & Co.; Etc., Etc.
Under the Sabbath Lamp: Stories of Our Time for Old and Young. Abram Samuel Isaacs. LC 19-10462. 1919. The Jewish Publication Society of America.
Under the Same Stars. Dean Hughes. LC 79-10472. 1979. 5.95 (ISBN 0-87747-750-7). Deseret Book Co.

Under the Saucer's Shadow. Elna Kenney. 4.50 o.p. Vantage.
Under the Second Renaissance; a Novel. Florence Trail. LC 7-32331. 1894. C. W. Moulton.
Under the Shadow of a Cross and Other Tales. Mary Raymond. Sisters of St. Dominic.
Under the Shadow of Etna: Sicilian Stories from the Italian of Giovanni Verga. Giovanni Verga & Dole, Nathan Haskell, 1852- Ed. and Tr. LC 8-3007. (On cover: Round table library). 1896. Joseph Knight Company.
Under the Shadow of the Wigwam. Newton W Gaines. LC 28-30067. The Christopher Publishing House.
Under the Sign of Saturn. Susan Sontag. 300p. 1980. 10.95 (ISBN 0-374-28076-2). FS&G.
Under the Skin. Nina Bawden. LC 64-18071. 1964. Harper & Row.
Under the Skin. Dorothea Bennett. LC 62-7239. 1962. M. S. Mill Co.
Under the Skin. Kathleen MacNeal Clarke. LC 29-7086. 1929. The Macaulay Company.
Under the Skin. Warren Leslie. LC 73-97589. 1970. 5.95. B. Geis Associates; Distributed by World Pub. Co.
Under the Skin. William F Vassall. LC 23-17846. F. Stone Williams Co.
Under the Skin: A Novel. 1st Ed. Phyllis Bottome. LC 50-6760. 1950. Harcourt, Brace.
Under the Skylights. Henry Blake Fuller. LC 68-55675. (American short story series, v. 15). 1969. Garrett Press.
Under the Skylights. Henry Blake Fuller. LC 1-27439. 1901. D. Appleton and Company.
Under the Skylights see Collected Works.
Under the Southern Cross. Elizabeth Robins. LC 7-360936. 1907. F. A. Stokes Company.
Under the Spell. A Novel. Frederick William Robinson. (seaside library, v. 77, no. 1570). 1883. G. Munro.
Under the Spell of the Firs. Annabell Jerome. LC 15-403. 1.50. Broadway Publishing Co.
Under the Stars. Howard Agg. LC 61-15109. 1961. C. N. Portter.
Under the Stars and Bars: Or, A Wearing of the Gray. A Thrilling Story of Tennessee. Maurice C. Walsh. (War library Pocket ed. no. 3). 1883. Novelist Publishing Co.
Under the Stars and Stripes... E. M Reeves. LC 7-30683. 1891. The Author.
Under the Stars of Druufon. Clark Darlton. (Perry Rhodan#68). (Illus.). 1975. (pbk.) 1.25. Ace Books.
Under the Storks' Nest. A Romance. From the German of A. E. Katsch. Adolf Katsch. Tr. by Steinestel, Emily R. LC 7-11673. 1875. J. B. Lippincott & Co.
Under the Storks' Nest. A Romance. From the German of A. E. Sic Katsch. Adolf Katsch & MacNamara, Emily R. (Steinestel) Tr. LC 7-11673. 1875. J. B. Lippincott & Co.
Under the Storm: Or, Steadfast's Charge. Charlotte Mary Yonge. (On cover: Seaside library. Pocket ed. no. 1024). 1887. G. Munro.
Under the Sun. Dane Coolidge. LC 27-9862. E. P. Dutton & Company.
Under the Sun. George Junghanns. 1969. 4.50; pap. 2.45. Gauntlet Bks.
Under the Sun of Satan: A Novel. Georges Bernanos. LC 49-10776. 1949. Pantheon.
Under the Sun: Or, The Passing of the Incas. A Story of Old Peru. Charles William Buck. LC 2-27940. 1902. Sheltman & Company.
Under the Sun: Tales of Love and Death. Grace C. Hodgson Flandrau. LC 36-293053. 1936. C. Scribner's Sons.
Under the Sunset... Ed. by William Dean Howells & Alden, Henry Mills. LC 6-16645. (Harper's novelettes). 1906. Harper & Brothers.
Under the Sunset. Bram Stoker. Ed. by R. Reginald & Douglas Menville. LC 80-19564. (Newcastle Forgotten Library Ser.: Vol. 17). 190p. 1980. Repr. of 1978 ed. lib. bdg. 11.95x (ISBN 0-89370-516-0). Borgo Pr.
Under the Sunset. Bram Stoker. (Forgotten Fantasy Library: Vol. 17). 1978. pap. 4.95 (ISBN 0-87877-116-6, F-116). Newcastle Pub.
Under the Surface. Emma M Connelly. LC 11-10561. 1873. J.B. Lippincott & Co.
Under the Sweetwater Rim. Louis L'Amour. 1979. pap. 1.95 (ISBN 0-553-13779-4, Y13779-4). Bantam.
Under the Sword of Damocles: A Novel. Anatolijus Kairys. LC 79-91233. 10.00. Lithuanian Literary Associates.
Under the Thatch. Beynon Puddicombe. LC 10-9265. 1910. 1.50. Dodd, Mead and Company.
Under the Tonto Rim. Grey, Zane. LC 63-6981. (Great western edition, 43). 1963. Grosset & Dunlap.
Under the Tonto Rim. Zane Grey. LC 26-22063. 1926. Harper & Brothers.
Under the Tonto Rim. Zane Grey. 1976. (pbk.) 1.50 (ISBN 0-671-80448-0). Pocket Books.
Under the Tree of Heaven. Olive Amelia Smith. LC 54-64113. 1954. Bruce Humphries.
Under the Tricolor: Or, The American Colony in Paris. A Novel. Lucy Hamilton Jones Hooper. LC 7-5261. 1880. J. B. Lippincott & Co.
Under the Tricolour. Pierre Mille & Drillien, Berengere, Tr. LC 15-38731. 1915. John Lane.
Under the Triple Suns. 1st Ed. Stanton Arthur Coblentz. LC 54-569418. 1955. Fantasy Press.
Under the Vierkleur: A Romance of a Lost Cause. Benjamin Johannis Viljoen. 1904. Small, Maynard & Company.
Under the Volcano. Malcolm Lowry. LC 47-1776. 1947. Reynal & Hitchcock.
Under the Volcano. Introd. by Stephen Spender. Malcolm Lowry. LC 65-11640. 1965. bds., 5.95. Lippincott.
Under the Wall. Nick Carter. (Nick Carter Series). (O.s.i.). Date not set. pap. 1.50 o.s.i. (AD1673, Award). Univ Pub & Dist.
Under the Wall. (Killmaster Spy Chiller. Nick Carter.). 1978. 1.75 (ISBN 0-441-84499-5). Charter Communications.
Under the War Flags of 1861. A Romance of the South. William Lowndes Pickard. LC 7-35921. 1895. C. T. Dearing.
Under the Wheel. Hamlin Garland. 1890. lib. bdg. 6.95 o.s.i. (ISBN 0-512-00228-2). Garrett Pr.
Under the White Boar. Mary Dodgen Few. LC 70-161090. (Illus.). 219p. 1973. 6.95 (ISBN 0-87667-069-9). Carolina Edns.
Under the Will: And Under Life's Key. Mary Cecil Hay. (On cover: Lovell's library, v. 9, no. 466). 1884. J. W. Lovell Company.
Under the Willows: Or, The Three Countesses. Elizabeth Van Loon. LC 8-302188. T. B. Peterson & Brothers.
Under the Winter Moon. Teresa Brooke. LC 58-8083. 1958. Doubleday.
Under the Witches' Moon: A Romantic Tale of Mediaeval Rome. Nathan Gallizier. LC 17-25744. 1917. 1.50. The Page Company.
Under the Yoke. Ivan Minchov Vazov. LC 70-146052. 1971. Twayne Publishers.
Under the Yoke. Ivan Minchov Vazov & Margarita Aleksieva. LC 76-370313. (Bulgaria 1300 years). 1976. Sofia Press.
Under the Yoke: A Book with a Purpose. Frank Dalton O'Sullivan. LC 22-1450. Lansing, Ltd.
Under the Yoke: And Other Tales. Julia MacNair Wright. LC 9-520. 1871. Western Tract and Book Society.
Under Topsils and Tents. Cyrus Townsend Brady. LC 1-31412. 1901. C. Scribner's Sons.
Under Trail. Anna Alice Chapin. LC 12-10239. 1912. 1.25. Little, Brown, and Company.
Under Tropic Skies. Louis Becke. LC 73-113650. (Short story index reprint series). 1970. Books for Libraries Press.
Under Tropic Skies. Louis Becke. LC 5-40808. 1905. T. F. Unwin.
Under Tropic Skies. Louis Becke. LC 26-27690. J. B. Lippincott Company.
Under Twenty. Ed. by May Lamberton Becker. LC 32-26334. Harcourt, Brace and Company.
Under Twenty. Ed. by May Lamberton Becker. LC 39-20784. 1937. Harcourt, Brace and Company.
Under Twenty. Abigail Wells Cowley. LC 46-2975. 1946. Meador Publishing Company.
Under Two Flags. Louise De La Ramee. LC 8-76802. A. L. Burt.
Under Two Flags. Louise De La Ramee. LC 2-23594. 1902. H. M. Caldwell Company.
Under Two Flags. Louise De La Ramee. LC 24-14944. 1923. Grosset & Dunlap.
Under Two Flags: A Novel. De la Ramee, Louise. LC 66-24804. (Doughty library, no. 3). 1967. Stein and Day.
Under Two Flags. A Novel. Louise De La Ramee. LC 6-35187. 1876. J. B. Lippincott & Co.
Under Two Flags: A Novel. Louise De La Ramee. LC 6-33296. 1896. J. B. Lippincott Company.
Under Western Eyes. Joseph Conrad. LC 26-26988. 1925. Doubleday, Page & Company.
Under Western Eyes: A Novel. Joseph Conrad. LC 11-26602. 1911. Harper & Brothers.
Under Western Eyes. Introd. by Morton Dauwen Zabel. Joseph Conrad. LC 51-12422. (New classics series). 1951. New Directions.
Under Which King? A Novel. Compton Reade. (Harper's Franklin square library, no. 440). 1885. Harper & Brothers.
Under Which King? A Novel. Compton Reade. (On cover: Seaside library. Pocket ed., no. 340). 1885. G. Munro.
Under Which Lord? Elizabeth Lynn Linton. LC 75-482. (Victorian Fiction: Novels of Faith and Doubt; 35). 1976. 35.00 (ISBN 0-8240-1559-2). Garland Pub.
Under Which Lord? A Novel, 1879. Elizabeth Lynn Linton. LC 75-482. (Victorian Fiction Ser). 1975. lib. bdg. 66.00 (ISBN 0-8240-1559-2). Garland Pub.
Under Whose Wings. Zenobia Bird. LC 28-194567. Biola Book Room.
Under Whose Wings. Zenobia Bird. LC 83-329162. Fleming H. Revell Company.
Under Whose Wings. Zenobia Bird. LC 28-19456. 1928. Biola Book Room.
Under Whose Wings. Zenobia Bird. LC 33-32916. 1933. Fleming H. Revell Company.
Underbrush Boys. Patrick Doyle. 192p. pap. 1.95 o.p. (6127). Brandon.
Undercover Cat see That Darn Cat.
Undercover Cat: By the Gordons. Mildred Gordon & Gordon Gordon. LC 63-16265. 1963. Doubleday.
Undercover Cat Prowls Again: By the Gordons. 1st Ed. Mildred Gordon & Gordon Gordon. LC 66-20. 1966. 4.50. Doubleday.
Undercover Cop. Jose L. Guzman & Carl Fick. (Orig.). 1979. pap. 2.25 (ISBN 0-89083-488-1). Zebra.
Undercover Deputy. Benjamin Hilton. LC 75-32272. 1978. pap. 1.50 (ISBN 0-89041-214-6, 3214). Major Bks.
Undercover Girl. Carole Halston. LC 82-15635. 1982. 7.95 (ISBN 0-8161-3461-8). G.K. Hall.
Undercover Woman. Dorothy Herzog. LC 37-231848. The Macaulay Company.
Undercurrent. Robert Grant. LC 4-27986. 1904. C. Scribner's Sons.
Undercurrent. Barbara Jefferis. LC 53-6232. 1953. Sloane.
Undercurrent. Bill Pronzini. LC 73-1931. 1973. 4.95 (ISBN 0-394-48265-4). Random House.
Underdog on Strike. (Illus.). 10p. 0.25 o.p. Peoples Pr.
Underdog. 1st Ed. William Riley Burnett. LC 57-564876. 1957. Knopf.
Underdogs. Mariano Azuela. Tr. by E. Munguia, Jr. (Orig.). pap. 2.50 (ISBN 0-451-51741-5, CE1741, Sig Classics). NAL.
Underdogs see Two Novels of the Mexican Revolution.
Underdogs of War: A Novel Panorama. Ronald Shero. LC 48-17880. 1948. Wetzel Pub. Co.
Undergraduate Syndrome. Anne Worthington. LC 73-86371. 1975. Golden Triangle Pub. Co.
Underground. Bryn Beorse. (O.s.i.). 180p. 1976. pap. 1.95 o.s.i. (ISBN 0-912852-18-6). Echo Pubs.
Underground. Joseph Jefferson Farjeon. LC 28-250239. 1928. L. MacVeagh, The Dial Press.
Underground. Mario Tobino. LC 64-19278. 1966. Doubleday.
Underground Cities Contract. Philip Atlee. (Joe Gallo). (Fawcett Gold Medal: Vol. 18). 1974. (pbk.) 0.95. Fawcett.
Underground City. Harold Louis Humes. LC 58-6734. 1958. Random House.
Underground Game. Mallet-Joris, Francoise. LC 74-30249. 1975. 8.95 (ISBN 0-525-22587-0). Dutton.
Underground Game. Mallet-Joris, Francoise. LC 75-305562. 1974. W. H. Allen.
Underground: In Pursuit of B. Traven and Kenny Love. Jonah Raskin. LC 77-15429. 1978. 8.95 (ISBN 0-672-52382-5). Bobbs-Merrill.
Underground Man. Edward F. Abood. LC 72-97331. 189p. 1973. pap. 6.95 (ISBN 0-88316-048-X). Chandler & Sharp.
Underground Man. Ross MacDonald. LC 70-38100. 1971. Repr. lib. bdg. 8.95 o.p. (ISBN 0-8161-6005-8, Large Print Bks). G K Hall.
Underground Man. Ross MacDonald. (YA) 1971. 5.95 o.p. (ISBN 0-394-43467-6). Knopf.
Underground Man. Milton Meltzer. (Laurel Leaf library). 1974. (pbk.) 0.95. Dell.
Underground Man. Kenneth Millar. LC 76-136337. 1971. 5.95 (ISBN 0-394-43467-6). Knopf.
Underground Man. Kenneth Millar. LC 70-38100. 1971. 8.95 (ISBN 0-8161-6005-8). G. K. Hall.
Underground Man. Gabriel Tarde. Tr. by C. Bereton from Fr. LC 73-13268. (Classics of Science Fiction Ser.). 206p. 1974. 11.50 (ISBN 0-88355-122-5); pap. 2.95 (ISBN 0-88355-151-9). Hyperion Conn.
Underground Retreat. Maribelle Cormack & Bytovetzski, Pavel L., Joint Author. LC 46-65463. 1946. Reynal & Hitchcock.
Underground Shadows. Valery Oistenau. 1977. pap. 1.50 (ISBN 0-9601870-0-6). Pass.
Underground Stream: An Historical Novel of a Moment in the American Winter. Albert Maltz. 1940. Little, Brown and Company.
Underground Woman. Kay Boyle. LC 72-186008. 1975. 7.95 (ISBN 0-385-07047-0). Doubleday.
Undergrowth. Francis Brett Young. LC 20-190502. 1920. E. P. Dutton & Company.
Underhandover. Kenneth O'Hara. LC 63-13129. (Cock Robin mystery). 1963. Macmillan.
Underlay. Harry N. Malzberg. 1974. (pbk.) 1.50. Avon.
Undersea. Paul Hazel. LC 82-12649. (Hazel, Paul. The Finnbranch: Vol. 2). 14.95 (ISBN 0-316-35261-6). Little, Brown.
Undersea Quest. Frederik Pohl & Jack Williamson. 160p. 1982. pap. 1.95 (ISBN 0-345-30701-1, Del Rey). Ballantine.
Undershirts & Other Stories. Cathy Cockrell. 1982. pap. 4.00 (ISBN 0-914610-30-9). Hanging Loose.
Understanding American Politics Through Fiction. 2d ed. Ed. by Myles L. Clowers. Lorin Letendre. LC 76-18872. 4.95 (ISBN 0-07-011450-1) (ISBN 0-07-011451-X). McGraw-Hill.
Understanding Heart. Peter Bernard Kyne. LC 26-148388. 1926. Cosmopolitan Book Corporation.
Understanding Heart. 1966. 3.95 (ISBN 0-88088-554-8). Peter Pauper.
Understanding Men. Adeline Morrow. LC 34-28464. 1934. Meador Publishing Company.
Understrike. John E Gardner. LC 65-192661. bds., 3.95. Viking.
Understrike. John E Gardner. (Crest bk., D1126). 1968. Fawcett.
Understudies. facs. ed. Mary Eleanor Wilkins Freeman. LC 70-86141. (Short Story Index Reprint Ser.). 1901. 17.00 (ISBN 0-8369-3045-2). Ayer Co.
Understudies: Short Stories. Mary Eleanor Wilkins Freeman. LC 70-86141. (Short story index reprint series). (Illus.). 1969. Books for Libraries Press.
Understudies: Short Stories. Mary Eleanor Wilkins Freeman. LC 1-31689. 1901. Harper & Bros.
Understudy. Elia Kazan. LC 74-78538. 1976. (pbk.) 1.95. Warner Books.
Understudy. Berta Ruck. LC 33-6703. 1933. Dodd, Mead & Company.
Understudy: A Novel. Elia Kazan. LC 74-78538. 1975. 8.95 (ISBN 0-8128-1731-1). Stein and Day.
Understudy: A Novel of the West End Stage. Donald Landels Henderson. LC 45-8812. 1945. Hurst & Blackett, Ltd.
Undertaker. Jake Quinn. (Shannon Ser.). (O.s.i.: No. 1). 1974. pap. 0.95 o.s.i. (LB203NK, Leisure Bks). Nordon Pubns.
Undertaker Wind. Whit Masterson, pseud. LC 72-12539. (Red badge novel of suspense). 1973. 4.95 (ISBN 0-396-06773-5). Dodd, Mead.
Undertaker's Gone Bananas. Paul Zindel. (gr. 6-12). 1979. pap. 2.25 (ISBN 0-553-20172-7). Bantam.
Undertow. Anne Tedlock Brooks. LC 43-41348. 1943. Arcadia House, Inc.
Undertow. Arthur Hamilton Gibbs. LC 32-266486. 1932. Little, Brown, and Company.
Undertow. Howard Maier. LC 45-9768. 1945. Doubleday, Doran & Co., Inc.
Undertow. Henry Kingdon Marks. LC 23-11925. Harper & Brothers.
Undertow. Kathleen Thompson Norris. LC 17-11464. 1917. Doubleday, Page & Company.
Undertow: A Tale of Both Sides of the Sea. Robert Edward Knowles. LC 6-38396. F. H. Revell Company.
Undertow: A Thrilling Romantic Tale of Love and Sacrifice, Based on the Motion Picture Story. Wilbur Daniel Steele. LC 30-14004. Jacobsen Publishing Company, Inc.
Underwater: A Novel. Joan Winthrop. LC 74-79482. 1974. 6.95 (ISBN 0-399-11369-X). Putnam.
Underwood Mystery. Charles Judson Dutton. 1921. 1.90. Dodd, Mead and Company.
Underworld: The Story of Robert Sinclair, Miner. James C. Welsh. LC 20-17082. Frederick A. Stokes Company.
Underworld U.S.A. Joseph Francis Dinneen. LC 56-7819. 1956. Farrar, Straus & Cudahy.
Undesirable Alien. Regis Debray. LC 77-28775. 1978. 9.95 (ISBN 0-670-74066-7). Viking Press.
Undesirable Company. Francis Ryck. LC 74-80463. 1974. 5.95 (ISBN 0-8128-1709-5). Stein and Day.
Undesirable Governess. Francis Marion Crawford. LC 13-12926. 1909. The Macmillan Company.
Undesirable Governess. Francis Marion Crawford. LC 10-9511. 1910. The Macmillan Company.
Undesired Princess. Lyon Sprague De Camp. pap. 1.50 o.p. (Pub. by Fantasy Pub Co). Borden.
Undesired Princess. 1st Ed. Lyon Sprague De Camp. LC 51-24859. 1951. Fantasy Pub. Co.
Undetective. Graham Montague Jeffries. LC 63-19218. (A London House mystery). 1963. London House & Maxwell.
Undine. Friedrich Heinrich Karl La Motte-Fouque. LC 7-140999. 1868. Hurd and Houghton.
Undine. Friedrich Heinrich Karl La Motte-Fouque. Tr. by Courtney, William Leonard. 1909. W. Heinemann.
Undine. Friedrich Heinrich Karl La Motte-Fouque. Tr. by Gosse, Edmund William. Limited Editions Club, Inc., New York. LC 30-24045. 1930. The Limited Editions Club.
Undine. Olive Schreiner. LC 75-38698. (Belles lettres in English). (Illus.). 1972. Johnson Reprint Corp.
Undine. Olive Schreiner. Ed. by Cronwright-Schreiner, Samuel Cron. LC 29-694. 1928. Harper & Brothers.
Undine. Phyllis Brett Young. LC 64-21156. 1964. Putnam.
Undine: A Legend. Friedrich Heinrich Karl La Motte-Fouque. LC 11-18064. 0.35. McLoughlin Brothers.
Undine, a Romance. Frederich Heinrich Karl La Motte-Fouque. Tr. by Upton, George Putnam. LC 8-23095. (Half-title: Life stories for young people). 1908. A. C. McClurg & Co.

TITLE INDEX UNHOLY CHILD.

Undine: A Tale. La Motte-Fouque, Friedrich Heinrich Karl. Tr. by Edmund William Gosse. LC 76-48431. (Classics of European Literature). (Hyperion library of world literature). 1977. 11.50. (ISBN 0-88355-558-1) (ISBN 0-88355-559-X). Hyperion Press.
Undine, a Tale. Friedrich Heinrich Karl La Motte-Fouque. Tr. by Alger, Abby Langdon. LC 7-14101. (On cover: Home and school library). 1897. Ginn & Company.
Undine; an Experience. Clarine Stephenson. LC 11-27809. 0.50. Broadway Publishing Co.
Undine & Other Stories. Fouque La Motte. 25.00 (ISBN 0-89987-122-4). Darby Bks.
Undine and Other Stories: From the German of La Motte Fouque. Friedrich Heinrich Karl La Motte-Fouque. Tr. by Edmund William Gosse. LC 33-7203. (Half-title: The World's classics. cdviii). 1932. H. Milford, Oxford University Press.
Undine, and Other Tales. Friedrich Heinrich Karl La Motte-Fouque. Tr. by Bunnett, Fanny Elizabeth. LC 4-16864. (On cover: The home library). A. L. Burt.
Undine and Other Tales by Friedrich, Baron De La Motte Fouque. Undine, The Two Captains, Aslauga's Knight, Sintram and His Companions. Friedrich Heinrich Karl La Motte Fouque. LC 4-21609. (Riverside classics). 1889. Houghton, Mifflin and Company.
Undine, and Sintram and His Companions. Friedrich Heinrich Karl La Motte-Fouque. Tr. by Tracy, Thomas. LC 17-22985. (Half-title: Wiley and Putnam's library of choice reading). 1845. Wiley and Putnam.
Undine, and Sintram and His Companions. new ed.... ed. Friedrich Heinrich Karl La Motte-Fouque. Tr. by Tracy, Thomas. LC 7-16066. 1852. G. P. Putnam.
Undine and The Two Captains. Friedrich Heinrich Karl La Motte-Fouque. LC 7-14100. (On cover: Lovell's library. v. 14. no. 711). J. W. Lovell Co.
Undiplomatic Exit. 1st Ed. Sherwood, John. LC 58-12054. 1958. Published for the Crime Club by Doubleday.
Undiscoverables, and Other Stories. Ralph Bates. LC 42-957319. 1942. Random House.
Undiscovered Country. William Dean Howells. LC 71-129976. 1970. Scholarly Press.
Undiscovered Country. William Dean Howells. LC 8-190964. Houghton Mifflin Company.
Undiscovered Country. William Dean Howells. LC 7-5677. 1880. Houghton, Mifflin and Company.
Undiscovered Country. Julian Mitchell. LC 75-78365. 1969. 5.95. Grove Press.
Undiscovered Country. Jay Walz & Audrey Walz. LC 58-6764. 1958. Duell, Sloan and Pearce.
Undismayed: The Story of a Yankee Chaplain's Family in the Civil War. Elizabeth Eaton Hincks. LC 52-2332. 1952. Priv. Print.
Undoing of Miss Abigail Wrigley: A Country Mystery. Christine Hathorn. 1973. 4.95 (ISBN 0-533-00368-7). Vantage.
Undream'd of Shores. Frank Harris. LC 24-11139. Brentano's.
Undue Fulfillment. Kathleen Coyle. LC 34-33287. 1934. W. Morrow & Co.
Undying Fire. Fletcher Pratt. LC 53-7621. 1953. Ballantine Books.
Undying Fire: A Contemporary Novel. Herbert George Wells. LC 19-8465. 1919. The Macmillan Company.
Undying Grass. Yasar Kemal. 1978. 10.95 o.p. (ISBN 0-688-03306-7). Morrow.
Undying Monster. Jessie Douglas Kerruish. (O.s.i.). 1968. pap. 0.75 o.s.i. (A758S, Award). Univ Pub & Dist.
Undying Monster: A Tale of the Fifth Dimension. Jessie Douglas Kerruish. LC 37-1673. 1936. The Macmillan Company.
Undying Past. Dorothy Phoebe Ansle. LC 79-54042. 1980. 8.95 (ISBN 0-525-22595-1). Dutton.
Undying Past. Laura Conway. 1980. 8.95 o.p. (ISBN 0-525-22595-1). Dutton.
Undying Past. 1st Ed. Ed. by Orville Prescott. LC 61-9544. 1961. Doubleday.
Undying Wizard. Andrew J. Offutt. 240p. 1982. pap. 2.25 (ISBN 0-441-84514-2). Ace Bks.
Undying World. Jeffrey Lord. (Richard Blade Ser., No. 8). 192p. (Orig.). 1973. pap. 1.50 (ISBN 0-523-40438-7). Pinnacle Bks.
Une' Edinburg: A Plantation Echo. Thomas Nelson Page. LC 7-35794. 1895. C. Scribner's Sons.
Unearth People. Kris Neville. 1968. pap. 0.50 o.p. (B50-843). Belmont-Tower.
Unearthly. Dorothy Daniels. 1971. pap. 0.75 o.p. (ISBN 0-447-74723-1). Lancer.
Unearthly. Robert Smythe Hichens. 1926. Cosmopolitan Book Corporation.
Unearthly Kingdom. Verner Meurice Whitney. LC 30-9478. The Grafton Press.
Uneasy Lies the Dead. M. E. Chaber, pseud. (Milo March Ser). 1970. pap. 0.60 o.p. (63-328). Paperback Lib.
Uneasy Money. Pelham Grenville Wodehouse. LC 16-63924. 1916. D. Appleton and Company.
Uneasy Spring. Robert Molloy. LC 46-119922. 1946. The Macmillan Company.
Uneasy Street. Wade Miller, pseud. LC 48-7954. 1948. Farrar, Straus.
Uneasy Street. Arthur Somers Roche. 1920. Cosmopolitan Book Corporation.
Uneasy Sun. Michael Butterworth. LC 70-103737. 1970. 4.50. Published for the Crime Club by Doubleday.
Uneasy Survivors: Five Women Writers. Jeri Parker. LC 75-37705. 1975. 5.95 (ISBN 0-87905-061-6). Peregrine Smith.
Uneasy Terms... Peter Cheyney. LC 47-1013. 1947. Dodd, Mead & Company.
Uneasy Virtue. Originally Titled Make with the Brains, Pierre. Dana Wilson. LC 48-10568. (Avon monthly novel, 5). 1948. Avon Editions.
Uneasy Years. Forrest Rosaire. LC 50-13188. 1950. Knopf.
Uneducating Mary. Kathleen Thompson Norris. LC 24-6458. (On cover: Famous authors series. no. 30). 1923. Garden City Publishing Co., Inc.
Unenchanted Circle. Rupert Latimer. LC 33-197033. 1933. D. Appleton-Century Company, Incorporated.
Unenchanted Circle. Algernor Victor Mills. LC 33-19703. 1933. D. Appleton-Century Company, Incorporated.
Unequal Conflict. Godfrey Winn. LC 32-184341. 1932. W. Morrow & Company.
Unequal to Song: A Novel. Charles Martin. LC 36-32646. 1936. Stackpole Sons.
Unequal Yoke. Joseph Stephen Ziegler. LC 56-12121. (Reflection book). 1956. Comet Press Books.
Unequal Yoke (1886) A Novel. a facsim. reproduction / with an introd. by james d. woolf. ed. Edmund William Gosse. LC 75-31652. 1975. 12.00 (ISBN 0-8201-1163-5). Scholars' Facsimiles & Reprints.
Uneven Struggle. Maurie T Prillaman. LC 53-121514. 1954. Vantage Press.
Unexamined Wife. Sherril Jaffe. 150p. 1983. 14.00 (ISBN 0-87685-570-2); pap. 8.50 (ISBN 0-87685-569-9); signed ed. 25.00 (ISBN 0-87685-571-0). Black Sparrow.
Unexpected. Ed. by Bennett Alfred Cerf. LC 48-3644. 1948. Bantam Books.
Unexpected Affinities: A Serio-Comedy. Susan Taber. LC 13-672870. 1918. Duffield & Company.
Unexpected Corpse. E Louise Cushing. LC 57-7720. Arcadia House.
Unexpected Death. Elizabeth Linington. LC 74-108332. 1970. 5.95. Morrow.
Unexpected Death. Dell Shannon. 1970. 5.95 o.p. Morrow.
Unexpected Guest. Bernadette Murphy. LC 34-327531. G. P. Putnam's Sons.
Unexpected Holiday. Libby Mansfield, pseud. 1978. pap. 1.50 (ISBN 0-440-19208-0). Dell.
Unexpected Journey & Other Stories. Mary Verdick. pap. 2.40x o.p. (G6, RRS, 2-48252). HM.
Unexpected Mrs. Pollifax. Dorothy Gilman. LC 66-12241. 3.95. Pub. for the Crime Club by Doubleday.
Unexpected Night. Elizabeth Daly. LC 40-723800. Toronto, Farrar & Rinehart, Inc.
Unexpected Peace. Jack Kelly. LC 69-13266. 1969. 5.95. Gambit Inc.
Unexpected Twist Series. Paul J. Payack. (Illus.). 1976. pap. 1.00. Chthon Pr.
Unexpected Uncle. Eric Hatch. LC 41-3331. Farrar & Rinehart, Inc.
Unexpected Warrior. Eric Hatch. LC 47-760. 1947. Rinehart & Company, Inc.
Unexpected Wedding. Edna G Young Reed. LC 54-25577. 1954. Pentecostal Pub. Co.
Unexploded Man. Leslie Watkins. LC 78-59604. 1978. 8.95 o.p. (ISBN 0-688-03369-5). Morrow.
Unexpurgated Diary of Mata Hari. Tr. by Adrian Y. Meadows. pap. 1.95 o.p. (ISBN 0-87056-231-2). Brandon.
Unfair Gods: Novel. 1st Ed. Winifred Greer. LC 55-12393. 1955. Pageant Press.
Unfairly Won. A Novel. Nannie Power O'Donoghue. (Harper's Franklin square library, no. 504). 1885. Harper & Brothers.
Unfairly Won. A Novel. Nannie Power O'Donoghue. (On cover: Seaside library. Pocket ed., no. 718). 1886. G. Munro.
Unfairness of Easter & Other Stories. David Cornel De Jong. LC 59-8069. (Illus.). 1959. 5.00 o.p. Talisman.
Unfaitful Wife: A Lurid Tale of Passion and Jealousy. Charles Paul De Kock. Tr. by Lukenow. (On cover: Fox's sensational series, no. 10). R. K. Fox.
Unfaithful? Peggy Gaddis, pseud. LC 34-41058. W. Godwin, Inc.
Unfaithful. Evald Mand. LC 54-7586. 1954. Muhlenberg Press.
Unfaithful. Craig Saunders. (O.s.i.). (Orig.). pap. 1.25 o.s.i. (A893Q, Award). Univ Pub & Dist.
Unfaithful by John Baxter Pseud. An Avon 1st Ed. Howard Hunt. LC 55-405217. (Avon, 647). Avon Publications.
Unfaithful Lady. Charles Pettit. LC 48-21611. (New Avon library, 155). 1948. Avon Book Co.
Unfaithful Wife. Translated from the French by J. Robert Loy. 1st Ed. Jules Roy. LC 56-8912. 1956. Knopf.
Unfamiliar Faces. Alice Grant Rosman. LC 38-275080. 1938. G. P. Putnam's Sons.
Unfamiliar Territory. Robert Silverberg. LC 73-3914. 1973. 5.95 (ISBN 0-684-13432-2). Scribner.
Unfamiliar Territory. Robert Silverberg. 1978. 1.95 (ISBN 0-425-03882-3). Berkley Publishing Corporation.
Unfeeling Sky. Peter Saxon. 1971. pap. 0.75 o.p. (94034-075). Beagle Bks.
Unfettered: And Dorlan's Plan. Sutton Elbert Griggs. LC 79-144623. 1971. (ISBN 0-404-00168-8). AMS Press.
Unfinished Building. Henry J. Ambers. LC 74-19535. 400p. 1974. 8.95 (ISBN 0-9600874-2-7). Edelweiss Pr.
Unfinished Business. John Erskine. LC 31-33120. The Bobbs-Merril Company.
Unfinished Business. Lester A. Fiedler. LC 72-81820. 1972. pap. 2.95 (ISBN 0-8128-1482-7). Stein & Day.
Unfinished Business. Cary Lucas. LC 47-4995. 1947. Simon and Schuster.
Unfinished Business. Michael Rubin. LC 74-24752. 1975. 7.95 (ISBN 0-399-11518-8). Putnam.
Unfinished Business. Maggie Scarf. 1981. pap. 3.95 (ISBN 0-345-29791-1). Ballantine.
Unfinished Business: A Novel of South Africa. Sheila Gordon. LC 74-30395. 1975. (ISBN 0-517-51905-4). Crown Publishers.
Unfinished Cathedral. Thomas Sigismund Stribling. LC 34-27137. 1934. Doubleday, Doran & Company, Inc.
Unfinished Clue. Georgette Heyer. LC 76-104781. 1970. 4.95. E. P. Dutton.
Unfinished Clue. Georgette Heyer. LC 34-116675. 1934. Longmans, Green and Co.
Unfinished Clue... Georgette Heyer. LC 37-127055. 1937. Pub. for the Crime Club, Inc., by Doubleday, Doran & Co., Inc.
Unfinished Crime... Elisabeth Sanxay Holding. LC 35-1092. 1935. Dodd, Mead & Company.
Unfinished Crime. Helen McCloy. LC 54-745488. 1954. Random House.
Unfinished Day. Alberta Stedman Eagan. LC 34-1048. The Macaulay Company.
Unfinished Divorce: Or, Her Better Self. Francis Dawson Gallatin. LC 9-10489. 1909. Cochrane Publishing Co.
Unfinished Portrait. 1st ed. Agatha Miller Christie. LC 34-41055. 1934. Doubleday, Doran.
Unfinished Portrait. Mary Westmacott. LC 34-41055. 1934. Doubleday, Doran & Company, Inc.
Unfinished Portrait: A Novel of Romance and Suspense. Agatha Miller Christie. LC 73-184885. 1972. 6.95 (ISBN 0-87795-029-6). Arbor House.
Unfinished Revolution. Lenore Mummy. 3.75 o.p. Carlton.
Unfinished Symphony. Sylvia Thompson. LC 33-270718. 1933. Little, Brown, and Company.
Unfinished Symphony: A Novel. Florence Elise Hyde. LC 35-12575. B. Humphries, Inc.
Unfinished Symphony: A Story-Life of Franz Schubert. David Ewen. LC 31-7178. 1931. Modern Classics Publishers, Inc.
Unfinished Tale: Or, The Daughter of the Mill. A Romance of Lake George. F Clairborne. LC 6-25376. 1881. W.L. Allison & Son.
Unfinished Tales. John Ronald Reuel Tolkien. Ed. by Christopher Tolkien. (Illus.). 368p. 1980. 15.95 (ISBN 0-395-29917-9). HM.
Unfinished Tales. John Ronald Reuel Tolkien. 1982. pap. 8.25 (ISBN 0-395-32441-6). HM.
Unfinished Tales of Numenor and Middle-Earth. John Ronald Reuel Tolkien & Christopher Tolkien. LC 80-83072. 1980. 15.00 (ISBN 0-395-29917-9). Houghton Mifflin.
Unfinished Tales of Numenor and Middle-Earth. John Ronald Reuel Tolkien & Christopher Tolkien. LC 80-40617. (Illus.). 1980. 7.50 (ISBN 0-04-823179-7). Allen & Unwin.
Unfinished Tapestry. Georgia Atwood White. LC 41-5217. Liveright Publishing Corporation.
Unfinished Things. Eleanor Fischer. LC 75-28246. 1976. 6.95 (ISBN 0-688-03005-X). Morrow.
Unfinished Thunder. Robert Peck. 1979. pap. 2.95 (ISBN 0-89185-178-X). Anthelion Pr.
Unforbidden Fruit. Warner Fabian. LC 28-148811. 1928. Boni and Liveright.
Unforeseen. Mary Stewart Doubleday Cutting. LC 10-23673. 1910. 1.20. Doubleday, Page & Company.
Unforeseen. Dorothy Macardle. LC 46-25192. 1946. Doubleday & Company, Inc.
Unforeseen. John Collis Snaith. LC 30-200708. 1930. D. Appleton & Company.
Unforeseen. A Novel. Alice O'Hanlon. (Harper's Franklin square library, no. 497). 1885. Harper & Brothers.
Unforeseen. A Novel. Alice O'Hanlon. (On cover: Seaside library. Pocket ed., no. 634). 1885. G. Munro.
Unforgetable: A Sensational African Novel. Mario Cardillo. LC 36-10755. The Cardillo Publishing Co.
Unforgivable Mistake. Maurits Ignatius Boas. LC 68-18144. 1968. 6.95. F. Fell.
Unforgiven... Anna C Ellis. LC 6-37573. 1882. R. P. Studley & Co., Printers.
Unforgiven. Petr Nikolaevich Krasnov. Tr. by Olga Vitali. Brooke, Vera, Joint Tr. LC 28-8143. 1928. Duffield and Company.
Unforgiven. Alan Le May. LC 57-6269. 1957. Harper.
Unforgiven. Alan Le May. LC 78-14529. 1978. 9.95 (ISBN 0-8398-2465-3). Gregg Press.
Unforgiven. Maynah Lewis. (Ace Gothic#24). 1976. (pbk.) 0.95. Ace Books.
Unforgiving. Eva Zumwalt. 336p. (Orig.). 1982. pap. 2.95 (ISBN 0-505-51804-X). Tower Bks.
Unforgiving Offender. John Reed Scott. LC 13-9286. 1913. 1.25. J. B. Lippincott Company.
Unforgiving Wind. John Harris. 1964. 4.95 o.p. (Sloane Assocs). Morrow.
Unforgotten. Dorothy Phoebe Ansle. LC 76-182487. 1972. 5.95 (ISBN 0-8415-0162-9). Saturday Review Press.
Unforgotten. Laura Conway. LC 76-182487. 1972. 5.95 o.p. (ISBN 0-8415-0162-9). Dutton.
Unforgotten Prisoner. Ray Coryton Hutchinson. LC 34-215340. Farrar & Rinehart.
Unfortunate Fursey: A Novel. Mervyn Wall. LC 47-17700. 1947. Crown Publishers.
Unfortunate Man. Frederick Chamier. LC 6-23330. 1835. Harper & Brothers.
Unfortunate Murderer. Richard Henry Sampson. LC 42-683818. 1942. J. Messner, Inc.
Unfortunate Sensibility: Or, The Life of Mrs. L, Written by Herself, in a Series of Sentimental Letters, Dedicated to Mr. Yorick in the Elysian Fields. LC 74-34238. (Sterneiana ; 17-18). (Life & times of seven major British writers). 1975-1976. 28.00 (ISBN 0-8240-1333-6). Garland Pub.
Unfortunate Traveller: Or, The Life of Jack Wilton. Newly Edited, with an Intord., by John Berryman. With 6 Original Illus, by Michael Ayrton. Thomas Nash. LC 59-12690. (Capricorn books, CAP16). 1960. Putnam.
Unfound Door. Al Hine. LC 51-13954. 1951. Little, Brown.
Unfrozen. Ernst Dreyfuss. 1970. pap. 0.60 o.p. (T060-11). Tower.
Unfulfilled. William George Hardy. LC 51-8664. 1952. Appleton-Century-Crofts.
Ungodly: A Novel of the Donner Party. Richard Rhodes. LC 72-95170. (Illus.). 1973. 8.95. Charterhouse.
Unguarded. Dorothy Daniels. (Orig.). 1968. pap. 0.60 o.p. (73-762). Lancer.
Unguarded Hour. Arthur Williams Marchmont. LC 18-193038. 1918. Cassell and Company, Ltd.
Unguarded Moment. L. F. James. 1977. pap. 1.50 o.s.i. (ISBN 0-8439-0438-0, Leisure Bks). Nordon Pubns.
Unguarded Moment. L. F James. (Leisure Books). 1.50. Nordon Publications.
Unguarded Moment. L. F James. (Leisure Books). 1.50. Nordon Publications.
Unhallowed Harvest. Homer Greene. LC 17-8465. 1917. G. W. Jacobs & Company.
Unhappy Hooligan. 1st Ed. Stuart Palmer. LC 55-10714. 1956. Harper.
Unhappy in Thy Daring. Una Maud Lyle Smyth. LC 16-11228. 1916. 1.35. G. P. Putnam's Sons.
Unhappy New Year. Carroll Cox Estes. LC 52-13561. 1953. Published for the Crime Club by Doubleday.
Unhappy Rendezvous. Anne Nash. LC 46-7932. 1946. Pub. for the Crime Club by Doubleday & Company, Inc.
Unhappy Returns. Elizabeth Lemarchand. 175p. 1983. pap. 2.95 (ISBN 0-8027-3007-8). Walker & Co.
Unhappy Wind. Nelson Antrim Crawford. LC 30-28185. 1930. Coward-McCann, Inc.
Unhatched Egghead. Ted Mark, pseud. (Orig.). 1976. pap. 1.50 o.p. (ISBN 0-532-15194-1). Woodhill.
Unhatched Egghead. Ted Mark, pseud. pap. 0.60 o.p. Lancer.
Unhatched Egghead. Ted Mark, pseud. (Orig.). 1976. pap. 1.50 o.p. (ISBN 0-532-15194-1). Manor Bks.
Unheard Music. Eleanor Cameron. LC 50-7533. 1950. Little, Brown.
Unheard Music. Ursula Perrin. LC 81-9678. 13.95 (ISBN 0-385-27201-4). Dial Press.
Unholy. Alex A. Niebrensky. 1982. pap. 2.95 (ISBN 0-451-11863-4, AE1863, Sig). NAL.
Unholy Child. Catherine Breslin. 1980. pap. 3.95 (ISBN 0-451-12378-6, AE2378, Sig). NAL.

Unholy Child: A Novel. Catherine Breslin. LC 79-17219. 12.95 (ISBN 0-8037-9261-1). Dial Press.
Unholy City. Charles Grandison Finney. LC 37-13858. 1937. The Vanguard Press.
Unholy Desires. Stephanie Blake. LC 80-82849. 368p. (Orig.). 1981. pap. 2.95 (ISBN 0-87216-785-2). Playboy Pbks.
Unholy Goddess. Baker Stein. (Orig.). 1981. pap. 2.95 (ISBN 0-89083-846-1). Zebra.
Unholy Hymnal. Albert Eugene Kahn. LC 78-159132. (O.s.i.). 1971. 5.95 o.s.i. (ISBN 0-671-21116-1). S&S.
Unholy Loves. Joyce Carol Oates. 320p. 1981. pap. 2.95 (ISBN 0-449-24457-1, Crest). Fawcett.
Unholy Loves. Joyce Carol Oates. LC 79-64396. 1979. 12.95 (ISBN 0-8149-0813-6). Vanguard.
Unholy Loves: A Novel. Joyce Carol Oates. LC 79-64396. 10.95 (ISBN 0-8149-0813-6). Vanguard Press.
Unholy Mourning. David Lippincott. (Orig.). 1982. pap. 3.50 (ISBN 0-440-19224-2). Dell.
Unholy Pilgrim. R. F. Tapsell. LC 68-23963. 1968. 5.95. Knopf.
Unholy Smile. Gregory Douglas. 1981. pap. 2.50 (ISBN 0-89083-796-1). Zebra.
Unholy Three. Clarence Aaron Robbins. LC 17-24206. 1917. 1.40. John Lane Company.
Unholy Trinity: Three Short Novels of Gothic Terror. Ray Russell. LC 67-12253. (Bantam's tales of supernatural horror). 1967. Bantam Books.
Unholy Trio see Better Wed Than Dead.
Unholy Uproar. 1st Ed. Clyde Brion Davis. LC 57-10873. 1957. Lippincott.
Unholy Virgins. Edna Walker Malcoskey. LC 29-92183. The Century Co.
Unholy Wedlock. Idabel Williams. LC 36-23907. 1936. Godwin.
Unholy Wish. Ellen Price Henry Wood Wood. (On cover: Seaside library. Pocket ed. no. 508). 1885. G. Munro.
Unholy Writ. David Williams. LC 76-62800. 1977. 7.95. St. Martin's Press.
Unhooked. Ed. by James R. Adair. (Orig.). 1971. 3.95 o.p. (ISBN 0-8010-0018-1); pap. 1.25 direction bks o.p. (ISBN 0-8010-0017-3). Baker Bk.
Unhurried Chase That Ended at L'abri. Betty Carlson. 1975. pap. 1.95 (ISBN 0-8423-7801-4). Tyndale.
Unhurrying Chase. Hilda Frances Margaret Prescott. LC 55-1792. 1955. Macmillan.
Unhurrying Chase. Hilda Frances Margaret Prescott. LC 25-17149. 1925. Dodd, Mead and Company.
UNIAD. Jay Williams. LC 68-17294. 1968. Scribner.
Unicorn. Iris Murdoch. 1963. 5.00 o.p. (ISBN 0-670-74077-2). Viking Pr.
Unicorn. Marguerite Steen. LC 32-5301. 2.50. The Century Co.
Unicorn. Martin Walser. 283p. 1981. pap. 7.95 (ISBN 0-7145-0886-1, Pub. by M Boyars). Merrimack Pub Cir.
Unicorn: A Novel. Iris Murdoch. LC 63-11857. 1963. Viking Press.
Unicorn and Other Tales. Dallas Stivens. LC 77-368277. 1976. (ISBN 0-909331-22-7). Wild & Woolley.
Unicorn Caper. James W. Lampp. 1980. pap. 1.95 (ISBN 0-8439-0817-3). Nordon Pubns.
Unicorn Creed. Elizabeth Scarborough. 352p. 1983. pap. 3.95. Bantam.
Unicorn Girl. Caroline Glyn. LC 67-15273. 1967. Coward-McCann.
Unicorn Girl. Michael Kurland. 1969. pap. 0.95 o.p. (X1990). Pyramid Pubns.
Unicorn Girl. Michael Kurland. 1974. pap. 0.95 o.p. (ISBN 0-515-03391-X, N3391). BJ Pub Group.
Unicorn Group. Lee R Bobker. LC 78-23545. 1979. 8.95. W. Morrow.
Unicorn Murders. John Dickson Carr. LC 35-30052. 1935. W. Morrow & Co.
Unicorns! Jack Dann & Gardener Dozois. 320p. 1982. pap. 2.75 (ISBN 0-441-85441-9). Ace Bks.
Unidentified Woman. Mignon Good Eberhart. LC 43-51328. Random House.
Unidentified Woman. Mignon Good Eberhart. 1975. (pbk.) 0.95. Popular Library.
Uniform of Glory. Percival Christopher Wren. LC 41-15921. 1941. Macrae-Smith-Company.
Uninhabited. Audre Du Bouchet. 1976. pap. 3.00 (Pub. by Living Hand). SBD.
Uninhibited. Tr. by Paul Anhalt. pap. 1.95 o.p. (6019). Brandon.
Uninhibited Happening. Dick Winfield. pap. 0.60 o.p. (B60-075). Belmont-Tower.
Unintentional Gigolo. A. Cassata. 3.00 o.p. Carlton.
Uninterrupted Sky: A Novel. Paul Hutchens. LC 49-50152. 1949. Van Kampen Press.
Uninvited. John Farris. LC 82-2426. 15.95 (ISBN 0-440-09217-5). Delacorte Press.
Uninvited. William W. Johnstone. (Orig.). 1982. pap. 2.95 (ISBN 0-89083-933-6). Zebra.
Uninvited. Dorothy Macardle. LC 42-18493. 1942. Doubleday, Doran and Company, Inc.
Uninvited. Dorothy Macardle. LC 77-10424. 1977. 11.50 (ISBN 0-89244-068-6). Queens House.
Uninvited Guest. George Harmon Coxe. LC 53-6840. 1953. Knopf.
Uninvited Guest. Barbara Kennedy. 256p. 1981. pap. 2.50 (ISBN 0-449-14421-6, GM). Fawcett.
Union: A Story of the Great Rebellion. John Roy Musick. LC 7-33324. (On cover: Columbian historical novel. v. 12). 1894. Funk & Wagnalls Company.
Union Club Mysteries. Isaac Asimov. 216p. 1983. 13.95 (ISBN 0-385-18806-4). Doubleday.
Union Down: A Signal of Distress. Frederick William Davis. LC 6-32490. 1893. Arena Publishing Company.
Union Dues. John Sayles. 1977. 9.95 (ISBN 0-316-77231-3, Atlantic-Little, Brown). Little.
Union Dues. John Sayles. 1978. pap. 2.50 (ISBN 0-671-82109-1). PB.
Union Dues: A Novel. John Sayles. (Kangaroo Book). 1978. 2.50. Pocket Books.
Union for Shabbos, and Other Stories of Jewish Life in America. Ed. by Max Rosenfeld. Shalom Asch. LC 67-22185. (Illus.). 1967. Sholom Aleichem Club Press.
Union Forever: An Historical Story of the Turbulent Years, 1854-1865, in the Lincoln Country and the Kansas-Missouri Border of the Old Central West, Based on Contemporary Records, Documents and Letters of Lewis Hanback, Hitherto Unpublished. Muriel Culp Barbe & Hanback, Lewis. LC 49-6110. 1949. Barbe Associates.
Union Onion. John A. Ryan. 1970. pap. 1.50. White Rabbit.
Union Square. Albert Halper. LC 33-5479. 1933. The Viking Press.
Union Station Massacre. Merle Clayton. 1977. pap. 1.50 o.s.i. (ISBN 0-8439-0430-5, Leisure Bks). Nordon Pubns.
Unique Heritage. Herman Bernard Sheffield. LC 41-23272. 1941. Bloch Publishing Co.
Unique Tales. Ludwig Nicolovius. LC 1-11753. The Abbey Press.
Unique World of Women: In Bible Times & Now. Eugenia Price. (Inspirational Ser.). 322p. 1974. Repr. lib. bdg. 9.95 o.p. (ISBN 0-8161-6218-2, Large Print Bks). G K Hall.
Unisave. Axel Madsen. Ed. by Jim Baen. 1980. pap. 1.95 (ISBN 0-441-84569-X). Ace Bks.
Unit Lamp. Radclyffe Hall. LC 80-39856. 1981. 5.95 (ISBN 0-8037-9171-2). Dial Press.
Unit Pride. John McAleer & Billy Dickson. LC 80-1066. 1981. 13.95 (ISBN 0-385-15925-0). Doubleday.
United: A Novel. Carlos Pena Romulo. LC 51-11704. 1951. Crown Publishers.
United Planets. Victor Wadey. LC 67-1321. 1967. Arcadia House.
United States of Both Americas: A Novel. Alberto Cora Collazo. LC 50-10257. 1950. Meador Pub Co.
U. S. Stories: Regional Stories from the Forty-Eight States. Ed. by Martha Foley & Rothberg, Abraham. LC 49-2904. 1949. Hendricks House-Farrar Straus.
U. S. Stories: Regional Stories from the Forty-Eight States. Ed. by Martha Foley & Rothberg, Abraham. LC 49-8267. 1949. Hendricks House-Farrar Straus.
United They Stand. Henry Lieferant & Sylvia Saltzberg Lieferant. LC 40-409557. 1940. E. P. Dutton & Co., Inc.
Unity. John Davys Beresford. LC 24-226778. The Bobbs-Merrill Company.
Unity,". Elias John George. LC 42-25487. 1942. Meador Publishing Company.
Unity's Children. Thomas L Sterling. LC 62-17279. 1962. Atheneum.
Universal Baseball Association, Inc., J. Henry Waugh, Prop. Robert Coover. LC 68-14517. 1968. Random House.
Universal Genius: Or, The Coming Man. Marmion W. Savage. 1860. D. W. Evans & Company.
Universal History of Infamy. Jorge Luis Borges. LC 72-82717. 1972. 6.95 (ISBN 0-525-22670-2). Dutton.
Universal Knights. Anthony V Mandekic. LC 37-16222. 1937. The Saunders Studio Press.
Universal Peace: Or, The Crowning Work of Two Lives. Samuel Harry Wood. LC 14-4060. 1914. Uintaland Publishing Company.
Universal Station. Beth Brown. LC 44-476142. 1944. Regent House.
Universe Against Her. James H. Schmitz. 192p. 1982. pap. 2.25 (ISBN 0-441-84576-2, Pub. by Ace Science Fiction). Ace Bks.
Universe Aganist Her. James H. Schmitz. LC 80-24990. (Series: Gregg Press Science Fiction Series.). 1981. 9.95 (ISBN 0-8398-2597-8). Gregg Press.
Universe Between. Alan Edward Nourse. LC 65-24489. 3.95. McKay.
Universe Eight. Ed. by Terry Carr. LC 77-82932. 1978. 7.95 o.p. (ISBN 0-385-12479-1). Doubleday.
Universe Eleven. Ed. by Terry Carr. LC 80-2790. (Science Fiction Ser.). 192p. 1981. 10.95 (ISBN 0-385-17226-5). Doubleday.
Universe Maker. Alfred Elton Van Vogt. 1974. (pbk.) 0.95. Ace Books.
Universe Makers. Alfred Elton Van Vogt. (Orig.). 1979. pap. 2.50 (ISBN 0-671-83145-3, Timescape). PB.
Universe Makers. Donald A. Wollheim. LC 75-123973. 1971. 4.95 o.p. (ISBN 0-06-014727-X, HarpT). Har-Row.
Universe of Smith Americana. A. P. Faretra. LC 75-135739. 1971. 3.75 (ISBN 0-8283-1303-2). Branden Press.
Universe Six. Ed. by Terry Carr. LC 75-21216. (Science Fiction Ser.). 192p. 1976. 5.95 o.p. (ISBN 0-385-11413-3). Doubleday.
Universe Spi, Inc. 1982. pap. 10.95 (ISBN 0-553-01433-1). Bantam.
Universe Ten. Ed. by Terry Carr. LC 79-6534. (Double Science Fiction Ser.). 1980. 10.95 (ISBN 0-385-15477-1). Doubleday.
Universe Thirteen. Ed. by Terry Carr. LC 82-45351. (Science Fiction Ser.). (Illus.). 192p. 1983. 11.95 (ISBN 0-385-18288-0). Doubleday.
Universe Twelve. Ed. by Terry Carr. LC 81-43900. (Double D Science Fiction Ser.). 192p. 1982. 10.95 (ISBN 0-385-17923-5). Doubleday.
Universe 3. Ed. by Terry Carr. LC 73-5053. 1973. 5.95 (ISBN 0-394-48181-X). Random House.
Universe 4. Ed. by Terry Carr. LC 73-17302. 1974. 5.95 (ISBN 0-394-48182-8). Random House.
Universe 5. Ed. by Terry Carr. LC 74-9090. 1974. 6.95 (ISBN 0-394-48562-9). Random House.
Universe 7. Ed. by Terry Carr. LC 76-28556. 1977. 7.95 (ISBN 0-385-11414-1). Doubleday.
Universe 9. Ed. by Terry Carr. LC 78-14679. 1979. 7.95 (ISBN 0-385-13649-8). Doubleday.
University. Roger Coan. 224p. 1973. 6.50 o.p. Exposition.
University: A Novel. Roger Coan. 1973. 6.50 (ISBN 0-682-47685-4). Exposition Pr.
University Nurse. Arlene Hale. 1974. (pbk.) 0.75. Ace Books.
University of Intelligence. Manuel Eisenberg. LC 73-176519. 1973. 9.95. Mindbuilder Publishers.
University on the Heights. Ed. by Wesley First. LC 68-29645. 1969. 4.95 o.p. Doubleday.
Univited Guests. Joseph Jefferson Farjeon. LC 25-109673. 1925. L. MacVeagh, The Dial Press.
Unjust Steward: Or, The Minister's Debt. Margaret Oliphant Wilson Oliphant. LC 7-32501. 1896. J. B. Lippincott Company.
Unkind Star. Nancy Hoyt. LC 27-14954. 1927. A. A. Knopf.
Unkind Word: And Other Stories. Dinah Maria Mulock Craik. LC 70-101278. (Short story index reprint series). 1969. Books for Libraries Press.
Unkind Word: And Other Stories. Dinah Maria Mulock Craik. 1870. Harper & Brothers.
Unkind Word & Other Stories. facsimile ed. Dinah Maria Mulock Craik. LC 70-101278. (Short Story Index Reprint Ser.). 1870. 19.50 (ISBN 0-8369-3215-3). Ayer Co.
Unkissed Bride. Berta Ruck. LC 29-184193. 1929. Dodd, Mead & Co.
Unkist, Unkind! A Novel. Violet Hunt. LC 7-9381. 1898. Harper & Brothers.
Unknown. Ed. by Donald R. Bensen. 1970. pap. 0.75 o.p. (T2326). Pyramid Pubns.
Unknown. A Prize Tale. Pierce C Grace. 1849. Chambers and Knapp.
Unknown Ajax. Georgette Heyer. (Berkley medallion book). 1974. (pbk.) 1.25 (ISBN 0-425-02516-0). Putnam.
Unknown Angel. Lewis Kruglick. 24p. 1970. pap. 1.50 o.p. Christopher-Tree.
Unknown Angel: By March Cost Pseud. Peggy Morrison, pseud. LC 55-10459. 1955. Lippincott.
Unknown Artist. Veniamin Aleksandrovich Kaverin. LC 72-14052. 1973. (ISBN 0-88355-006-7). Hyperion Press, Inc.
Unknown Blond. Laura Lou Brookman. LC 34-227714. Grosset & Dunlap.
Unknown Country. Coningsby William Dawson. LC 15-534532. 0.50. Heart's International Library Co.
Unknown Disciple. Francesco Perri. LC 50-6703. 1950. Macmillan.
Unknown Garden. Rupert Holloway. LC 41-13499. 1941. The Bobbs-Merrill Company.
Unknown God. J. F. Coppola. 10.00 o.p. Vantage.
Unknown God. Bertram Lenox Simpson. 1911. Dodd, Mead and Company.
Unknown Goddess: A Novel. Ruth Cross. LC 26-9262. 1926. Harper & Brothers.
Unknown Heart. Barbara Cartland. (Barbara Cartland Ser.: No. 11). 176p. (Orig.). 1981. pap. 1.75 (ISBN 0-515-05859-9). Jove Pubns.
Unknown Heart. Barbara Cartland. 1971. pap. 1.25 o.p. (ISBN 0-515-02577-1, V2577). BJ Pub Group.
Unknown Isle. LC 11-125069. 1911. Cassell and Company, Ltd.
Unknown Lady: A Novel. Justus Miles Forman. LC 11-1961. 1911. Harper & Brothers.
Unknown Lands: The Story of Columbus. Vicente Blasco Ibanez & Livingston, Arthur, 1883- Tr. LC 29-618363. E. P. Dutton & Co., Inc.
Unknown Lover. Jessie Bell Vaizey. LC 13-115367. 1913. G. P. Putnam's Sons.
Unknown Man: No. 89. Elmore Leonard. 1977. 8.95 o.s.i. (ISBN 0-440-09216-7). Delacorte.
Unknown Man No. 89: A Novel. Elmore Leonard. LC 76-41221. 8.95 (ISBN 0-440-09216-7). Delacorte Press.
Unknown Man, Seen in Profile. Kenneth O'Hara. 1981. 15.00x (ISBN 0-86025-165-9, Pub. by Ian Henry Pubns England). State Mutual Bk.
Unknown Master: And Other Stories. Joseph Aloysius Murphy. LC 16-13047. 1916. 1.15. The Pilot Publishing Co.
Unknown Mission. 1st. amer. ed. John Creasey. LC 73-81179. 1973. 4.95. David McKay.
Unknown Mr. Kent. Roy Norton. LC 16-217040. 1.25. George H. Doran Company.
Unknown: Or, The Mystery of Raven Rocks. Emma Dorothy Eliza Nevitte Southworth. LC 8-14258. (Ledger library, no. 2). R. Bonner's Sons.
Unknown Path. Lucy Beatrice Malleson. LC 50-6700. (Faber and Faber) has title: The draper of Edgecumbe.). 1950. Random House.
Unknown Path: A Tale of Men, Women and Great Horses. Bertram Atkey. LC 27-3175. 1927. D. Appleton and Company.
Unknown Patriot: A Story of the Secret Service. Frank Samuel Child. 1899. Houghton, Mifflin and Company.
Unknown Quality. Gertrude Hall Brownell. LC 10-5304. 1910. H. Holt and Company.
Unknown Quantity. Edgar Oakes Achorn & Teall, Edward Nelson, Joint Author. LC 19-138880. 1919. Marshall Jones Company.
Unknown Quantity. Hermann Broch & Muir, Mrs. Willa, Tr. LC 35-6536. 1935. The Viking Press.
Unknown Quantity. Ethel May Dell. LC 24-276440. 1924. 2.00. G. P. Putnam's Sons.
Unknown Quantity. Mignon Good Eberhart. LC 52-95826. 1953. Random House.
Unknown Quantity. Mignon Good Eberhart. LC 52-9582. 1974. (pbk.) 0.95. Popular Library.
Unknown Quantity. Gerard Hopkins. LC 23-4004. E. P. Dutton & Company.
Unknown Quantity: A Book of Romance and Some Half-Told Tales. Henry Van Dyke. LC 12-23517. 1912. C. Scribner's Sons.
Unknown Quantity: A Novel. Hermann Broch. LC 75-22400. 1975. 12.00. H. Fertig.
Unknown Sea. Francois Mauriac & Hopkins, Gerard, 1892- Tr. LC 48-8557. 1948. H. Holt.
Unknown Sector: Milky Way. Kurt Mahr. (Perry Rhodan,#45). 1974. (pbk.) 0.95. Ace Books.
Unknown Seven: A Detective Story. Harry Coverdale. LC 23-11449. Chelsea House.
Unknown Shores: The Saga of the Steeles, Vol. II. Joseph Csida. (Richard Galen Bks.). (Orig.). 1981. pap. 3.50 (ISBN 0-671-83136-4). PB.
Unknown Soldier. Vernon Bartlett. LC 30-18194. 1930. Frederick A. Stokes Company.
Unknown Soldier. Coningsby William Dawson. LC 29-12485. 1929. Doubleday, Doran & Company, Inc.
Unknown Soldier: A Novel. Translated from the Finnish. Vaino Linna. LC 56-10235. 1957. Putnam.
Unknown Soldiers. John Rolfe Gardiner. LC 76-30635. 8.98 (ISBN 0-525-22675-3) (ISBN 0-525-22675-3). Dutton.
Unknown to History. Charlotte Mary Yonge. LC 27-20583. Harper & Brothers.
Unknown to History. A Story of the Captivity of Mary of Scotland. Charlotte Mary Yonge. (Harper's Franklin square library, no. 263). 1882. Harper & Brothers.
Unknown to History: A Story of the Captivity of Mary of Scotland. Charlotte Mary Yonge. LC 4-16855. 1882. Macmillan and Co.
Unknown to History: A Story of the Captivity of Mary of Scotland. Charlotte Mary Yonge. (Seaside library, v. 65, no. 1311). 1882. G. Munro.
Unknown to History: A Story of the Captivity of Mary of Scotland. Charlotte Mary Yonge. LC 4-16600. 1901. Macmillan Co.
Unknown Volunteer. Patrick William McCora. LC 37-22391. 1937. Meador Publishing Company.
Unknown Welshman: An Historical Novel. Jean Stubbs. LC 75-187519. (Illus.). 1972. 7.95 (ISBN 0-8128-1474-6). Stein and Day.
Unknown Woman. Ruth Cranston. LC 12-6584. 1912. John Lane Company.

Unknown Woman. Frederic Morton. LC 75-45476. 1976. 8.95 o.p. (ISBN 0-316-58531-9, Pub. by Atlantic Monthly Pr). Little.

Unknown Woman: A New Novel. Frederic Morton. LC 75-45476. 8.95 (ISBN 0-316-58531-9). Little, Brown.

Unknown Wrestler. Hiram Alfred Cody. LC 18-199271. 1.50. George H. Doran Company.

Unlamented. Dorothy Daniels. LC 77-3178. 1977. 9.95 (ISBN 0-89340-082-3). J. Curley & Associates.

Unlamented. Dorothy Daniels. 1975. (pbk.) 1.25 (ISBN 0-671-77946-X). Pocket Books.

Unlatched Door. Lee Thayer, pseud. LC 20-91393. 1920. The Century Co.

Unlawful Occasions. Henry Cecil. 1974. 5.95 o.s.i. (ISBN 0-8277-3343-7). British Bk Ctr.

Unleashed. Leon Orr. LC 79-13290. (Orion). 2.95 (ISBN 0-8127-0230-1). Southern Pub. Association.

Unleashed: By Jack Woodford Pseud. & Bruce McFarlane. Josiah Pitts Woolfolk & Bruce McFarlane. LC 54-818108. 1953. Signature Press.

Unleashed Powers. Kurt Brand. (Perry Rhodan Series#90). 1976. (pbk.) 1.25. Ace Books.

Unleashed Will: By Christopher Clark. Christopher Clark. LC 47-2900. 1947. Little, Brown and Company.

Unleavened Bread. Robert Grant. LC 68-20014. (Americans in Fiction). 1968. Gregg Press.

Unleavened Bread. Robert Grant. LC 2992. 1900. C. Scribner's Sons.

Unless I Marry. Gladys Bronwyn Stern. LC 59-13361. 1959. Macmillan.

Unless I See. John W. Bowman. LC 76-42859. (Illus.). 1977. pap. 4.00 (ISBN 0-89430-002-4). Morgan-Pacific.

Unless She Burn. Francine Mezo. 2.25 (ISBN 0-380-76968-9). Avon Books.

Unless the Wind Turns. Mildred Walker, pseud. LC 41-51949. Harcourt, Brace and Company.

Unless Two Be Agreed. Margaret Bass Pedler. LC 47-3257. 1947. R. M. McBride & Company.

Unless You Die Young. Gladys H. Carroll. 1977. 8.95 o.p. (ISBN 0-393-08776-X). Norton.

Unless You Die Young: A Novel. Gladys Hasty Carroll. LC 76-57781. 8.95 (ISBN 0-393-08776-X). Norton.

Unlighted House: A Novel. James Hay. LC 21-409015. 1921. Dodd, Mead and Company.

Unlikeliest Hero. Booton Herndon. (Destiny Ser.). 199p. 1982. pap. 4.95 (ISBN 0-8163-0527-7). Pacific Pr Pub Assn.

Unlikeliest Hero. Booton Herndon. LC 67-26302. 199p. 1967. pap. 2.95 o.p. (21449-4). Pacific Pr Pub Assn.

Unlikely Ghosts. James Turner. LC 71-82688. 1969. 4.95. Taplinger Pub. Co.

Unlikely Meeting see Sentimental Talks.

Unlikely Rivals. Megan Daniels. 1981. pap. 2.25 (ISBN 0-451-11076-5, AE1076, Sig). NAL.

Unlimited Dream Company. J. G. Ballard. LC 79-9806. 288p. 79. 10.95 (ISBN 0-03-052431-8). HR&W.

Unlit Fire. Denise Robins. 1972. pap. 0.75 o.p. (94269). Beagle Bks.

Unlit Lamp. Radclyffe Hall. LC 29-19025. 1929. J. Cape.

Unlit Lamp: A Novel. Radclyffe Hall. LC 74-145067. (Series: Florin Books.). 1972. (ISBN 0-403-01010-1). Scholarly Press.

Unlit Lamp: A Study on Interactions. Elisabeth Sanxay Holding. LC 22-18233. E. P. Dutton & Company.

Unlived Life of Little Mary Ellen. Ruth McEnery Stuart. LC 10-277140. The Bobbs-Merrill Company.

Unlocked Door. Mary MacCracken. 1973. price not set o.p. (ISBN 0-397-00994-1). Lippincott.

Unloved: By Dolan Birkley Pseud. Dolores Birk Hitchens. LC 65-19048. 1965. 3.50. Pub. for the Crime Club by Doubleday.

Unloved One. A Domestic Story. Barbara Wreaks Hoole Hofland. 1844. Harper & Brothers.

Unloved Wife. A Novel. Emma Dorothy Eliza Nevitte Southworth. LC 8-142598. (Ledger library, no. 28). 1891. R. Bonner's Sons.

Unlucky Break. Osmington Mills. LC 57-7085. 1957. Roy Publishers.

Unlucky Break: By Osmington Mills. Vivian Collin Brooks. LC 57-7085. 1957. Roy Publishers.

Unlucky Family. Elizabeth Bonham De La Pasture. LC 8-81014. 1908. E. P. Dutton & Company.

Unlucky for Pringle: Unpublished and Other Stories. Wyndham Lewis. LC 73-172813. 1973. 7.95. D. Lewis.

Unlucky Hero. With Illus. from the Century Magazine. Frank Robert Donovan. LC 63-16840. 1963. Duell, Sloan and Pearce.

Unlucky Seed. Paul Ritchie. LC 62-58924. 1962. Cassell.

Unmade Bed. Francoise Quoirez. LC 78-17568. 9.95 (ISBN 0-440-09212-4). Delacorte Press/E. Friede.

Unmade Bed. Francoise Quoirez. 1979 (ISBN 0-440-19258-7). Dell Publishing Co.

Unmade Bed. Francoise Sagan, pseud. 1978. 9.95 o.p. (ISBN 0-440-09212-4, E Friede). Delacorte.

Unmaking a King. Oscar Newman. LC 81-1506. (Illus.). 10.95 (ISBN 0-02-588890-0). Macmillan.

Unman. Vadim Sergeevich Shefner. LC 80-36763. (Series: Macmillan's Best of Soviet Science Fiction.). 9.95 (ISBN 0-02-610060-6). Collier Books.

Unman-Kovrigin's Chronicles. Vadim Sergeevich Shefner. Tr. by Antonina Bouis et al from Rus. (Best of Soviet Science Fiction Ser.). 192p. 1982. 3.95 (ISBN 0-02-025230-7). Macmillan.

Unman Kovrigin's Chronicles. Vadim Sergeevich Shefner. Tr. by Antonina Bouis et al. 1980. 9.95 o.s.i. (ISBN 0-02-610060-6). Macmillan.

Unmarried Couple. Maysie Creig. 1972. pap. 0.75 o.p. (94220). Beagle Bks.

Unmarried Couple. Maysie Greig. LC 40-6581. 1940. Doubleday, Doran & Company, Inc.

Unmarried Father. Floyd Dell. LC 27-208172. George H. Doran Company.

Unmarried Man: A Novel. Darryl Ponicsan. LC 79-22163. 8.95 (ISBN 0-440-00104-8). Delacorte Press.

Unmarried Mother. Florence Edna May. LC 18-220307. J. S. Ogilvie Publishing Co.

Unmarried Wife. Abraham Loew Furman. LC 33-22466. 1933. The Macaulay Company.

Unmarried Woman: A Novel. Carol DeChallis Hill. 1978. 1.75 (ISBN 0-380-01834-9). Avon.

Unmistakable Flirtation. Louis Garner. LC 6-40715. 1879. G. W. Carleton & Co.

Unmoral. Josiah Pitts Woolfolk. LC 33-6573. 1933. W. Godwin, Inc.

Unnamable. Samuel Beckett. Tr. by Samuel Beckett from Fr. 1958. 10.00 (ISBN 0-394-47528-3, GP639). Grove.

Unnamable see Three Novels.

Unnatural Bondage. Charlotte Mary Brame. (On cover: Lovell's library. no. 1051). J. W. Lovell Company.

Unnatural Bondage. Bertha M. Clay. LC 44-122461. (On cover: Lovell's library, no. 1051). J. W. Lovell Company.

Unnatural Bondage: And, That Beautiful Lady. Charlotte Mary Brame. (On cover: Seaside library. Pocket ed. no. 995). G. Munro.

Unnatural Bondage: And, That Beautiful Lady. Charlotte Mary Brame. LC 44-392374. (On cover: Seaside library. Pocket ed. No. 995). G. Munro.

Unnatural Causes. P. D James. LC 67-24924. 1975. (pbk.) 1.25. Popular Library.

Unnatural Causes. P. D James. LC 76-381835. (fingerprint book). 1976. 3.50 (ISBN 0-241-89365-8). Hamilton.

Unnatural Causes. P. D James. LC 80-17904. 1980. 12.95 (ISBN 0-8161-3106-6). G. K. Hall.

Unnatural Causes: By P. D. James. P. D. James. LC 67-24924. 1967. Scribner.

Unnatural Death. Dorothy Leigh Sayers. LC 79-10661. 1979. 14.95 (ISBN 0-8161-6723-0). G. K. Hall.

Unnatural Death-(The Dawson Pedigree) Dorothy Leigh Sayers. LC 56-8785. Harper.

Unnatural Scenery. Vincent Canby. LC 78-7562. 1978. 8.95 (ISBN 0-394-50148-9). Knopf.

Unnecessary Woman. Mollie Vesey. 1980. 2.25 (ISBN 0-505-51503-2). Belmont Tower Books.

Unneutral Murder. Hulbert Footner. LC 44-5766. 1944. Harper & Brothers.

Uno Who: A Story. Elizabeth Stoughton Gale White. LC 1-31396. The Abbey Press.

Unoffical Love-Story. Albert Hickman. LC 9-28112. 1909. 1.00. The Century Co.

Unoffical Wife. Ruby Mildred Ayres. LC 38-157538. 1937. Doubleday, Doran & Company, Inc.

Unoffical Wife. Ruby Mildred Ayres. LC 39-7923. 1939. The Sun Dial Press, Inc.

Unofficial Breath. Marie Buchanan. (Fawcett crest book). 1975. (pbk.) 1.25. Fawcett.

Unofficial Breath: A Novel. Marie Buchanan. LC 73-77761. 1973. 5.95. St. Martin's Press.

Unofficial Honeymoon. Dolf Wyllarde. LC 11-27916. 1911. John Lane Company.

Unofficial Patriot. Helen Hamilton Chenoweth Gardener. 1894. Arena Publishing Company.

Unofficial Rose. Iris Murdoch. 1962. 4.95 o.p. (ISBN 0-670-74150-7). Viking Pr.

Unofficial Rose: A Novel. Iris Murdoch. LC 62-116699. 1962. Viking Press.

Unofficial Rose: A Novel. Iris Murdoch. 1973. 1.25. Warner Paperback Lib.

Unofficial Secretacy. Mary Ridpath Mann. LC 12-13895. 1912. A. C. McClurg & Co.

Unofficial Wife. Ruby Mildred Ayres. LC 42-47089. 1940. Triangle Books.

Unoriginal Sinner & the Ice-Cream God. John R Powers. LC 77-75850. 8.95 (ISBN 0-8092-7929-0). Contemporary Books.

Unorthodox Sex Education of Billy Joe. Max Hopper. LC 74-28560. (Traveller's companion series, TC 473). 1.95. Traveller's Companion, Inc.

Unpaid Debt. Ethel Almaz Stout. 1929. G. P. Putnam's Sons.

Unpaid Piper. Peggy Smith Shane. LC 27-22841. 1927. C. Scribner's Sons.

Unpardonable Liar. Gilbert Parker. 1900. C. H. Sergel Company.

Unpardonable Sin. Lowery Davis. 10p. pap. text ed. 1.00x (ISBN 0-8134-1455-5, 1455). Interstate.

Unpardonable Sin. Rupert Hughes. LC 22-14540. 1919. A. L. Burt Company.

Unpardonable Sin. Gladys Brace Vilsack. LC 16-7233. Broadway Publishing Co.

Unpardonable Sin. Arthur Dudley Vinton. LC 8-32698. (On cover: The red cover series, no. 68). J. S. Ogilvie.

Unpardonable Sin: A Novel. Rupert Hughes. LC 18-12228. Harper & Brothers.

Unpath'd Waters. Frank Harris. LC 78-122714. (Short story index reprint series). 1970. Books for Libraries Press.

Unpath'd Waters. Frank Harris. LC 13-115382. 1913. 1.25. M. Kennerley.

Unpleasant Profession of Jonathan Hoag. Robert Anson Heinlein. (Berkley Medallion Book). 1976. (pbk.) 1.50 (ISBN 0-425-03052-0). Berkley Publishing Corp.

Unpleasant Profession of Jonathan Hoag. Robert Anson Heinlein. LC 77-365306. 1976. 0.70 (ISBN 0-450-02886-0). New English Library.

Unpleasant Profession of Jonathan Hoag. 1st Ed. Robert Anson Heinlein. LC 59-15188. Gnome Press.

Unpleasantness at the Bellona Club. Dorothy Leigh Sayers. LC 28-19623. Payson & Clarke, Ltd.

Unpleasantness at the Bellona Club. Dorothy Leigh Sayers. LC 79-10522. 1979. 13.95 (ISBN 0-8161-6724-9). G. K. Hall.

Unpolished Diamond: A Romance. Roland Hill Nelson. LC 30-238983. J. W. Stowell Printing Co.

Unpopular Planet. Evelyn E Smith. 1975. (pbk.) 1.25. Dell.

Unpopular Public and Louis. Lillian E. Sommers. LC 8-10217. (On cover: Globe library, no. 82). 1889. Rand McNally & Co.

Unpossessed. Yvonne Dufour. LC 33-20293. 1933. E. P. Dutton & Co., Inc.

Unpossessed. Tess Slesinger. LC 34-12024. 1934. Simon and Schuster.

Unprecedented Heart. Louise Ingeborg Ohlers. LC 66-24282. 1966. T. Gaus' Sons.

Unpredictable Adventure: A Comedy of Woman's Independence. Claire Myers Spotswood. LC 35-17680. 1935. Doubleday, Doran & Company, Inc.

Unpredictable Bride. Barbara Cartland. 1969. pap. 0.95 o.p. (HN2146). Pyramid Pubns.

Unpredictable Bride. Barbara Cartland. 1975. pap. 1.25 o.p. (ISBN 0-515-03906-3). BJ Pub Group.

Unpredictable Wind. Charles Brandon Rummer & Bill Brown. 80p. 1972. pap. 2.95 (ISBN 0-8407-5578-3, Co-Pub Thomas Nelson). Aragorn Bks.

Unpretenders. Ruth Cranston. LC 16-5186. 1916. 1.20. John Lane Company.

Unprofessional. Rudyard Kipling. LC 30-24060. 1930. Doubleday, Doran & Company, Inc.

Unprofessional Spy. John Michael Evelyn. LC 64-21253. 1964. Published for the Crime Club by Doubleday.

Unprofessional Spy. Michael Underwood. 1977. 5.30 o.p. State Mutual Bk.

Unpromised Land, a Novel. Burton Edwards Martin. LC 48-5714. 1948. I. Washburn.

Unpublishable Memoirs. Abraham Simon Wolf Rosenbach. LC 17-30280. 1917. M. Kennerley.

Unpublished True Stories from the Private Files of True Story Magazine. True Story Magazine. LC 39-5766. 1939. Macfadden Book Company Inc.

Unquenchable Fire. Joan Sutherland. LC 26-23890. 1927. Harper & Brothers.

Unquenchable Flame. Arthur John Rees. LC 26-956. 1926. Dodd, Mead and Company.

Unquenched Fire: A Novel. Alice Gerstenberg. LC 12-10649. 1.25. Small, Maynard and Company.

Unquiet. Joseph Gollomb. LC 35-194197. 1935. Dodd, Mead & Company.

Unquiet Autumn. Hildred S. Reynolds. 3.75 o.p. Carlton.

Unquiet Field. Beatrice Kean Stapleton Seymour. LC 40-117552. 1940. The Macmillan Company.

Unquiet Grave. Cyril Connolly. 156p. 1982. cancelled 12.95 (ISBN 0-89255-074-0); pap. 5.95 (ISBN 0-89255-058-9). Persea Bks.

Unquiet Grave. John S. Strange. 1971. pap. 0.75 o.p. (07145). Curtis.

Unquiet Grave. Dorothy Stockbridge Tillet. LC 49-50125. 1949. Published for the Crime Club by Doubleday.

Unquiet Night: A Novel. Albrecht Goes. LC 51-12153. 1951. Houghton Mifflin.

Unquiet Seed: A Novel. Jane Cuddeback. LC 47-20010. 1947. Pellegrini & Cudahy.

Unquiet Sleep. William Haggard. 1962. 3.50 o.p. Washburn.

Unquiet Sleep: By William Haggard Pseud. Richard Clayton. LC 62-17390. 1962. Washburn.

Unquiet Spirit: A Tale. 1st American Ed. Marguerite Steen. LC 56-76600. 1956. Doubleday.

Unraveling a Mystery. Emma Josephine Smith. LC 12-46. 1911. The Cosmopolitan Press.

Unraveling of a Tangle. Marion Ames Taggart. LC 3-5935. 1903. Benziger Brothers.

Unravelled Knots. Emmuska Orczy. LC 26-2544. George H. Doran Company.

Unready Heart. Richard Sherman. LC 44-3947. 1944. Little, Brown and Company.

Unreal Estate: Short Stories. Brian Swann. LC 82-2799. (Illus.). 1982. 30.00 (ISBN 0-915124-39-4) (ISBN 0-915124-40-8). Toothpaste Press.

Unreal People. Martin Siegel. 1973. pap. 1.25 o.s.i. (78-763). Lancer.

Unreasonable Man. Henrie Mayne. LC 77-364186. 1976. 4.50 (ISBN 0-7043-2117-3). Quartet Books.

Unreasonable Summer. Dixie Browning. 192p. (Orig.). 1980. pap. 1.50 (ISBN 0-671-57012-9). S&S.

Unreasoning Heart. Constance Beresford-Howe. 1946. Dodd, Mead & Company.

Unreasoning Mask. Philip Jose Farmer. LC 81-8677. 12.95 (ISBN 0-399-12673-2) (ISBN 0-399-12676-7). Putnam.

Unrelenting, a Novel of Suspense. 1st Ed. Constance Woodbury Dodge. LC 50-5157. 1950. Doubleday.

Unrepentant. Conrad Phillips. LC 58-692021. 1958. Roy Publishers.

Unrepentant Women. Judith Burnley. LC 82-42836. 210p. 1983. 14.95 (ISBN 0-8128-2914-X). Stein & Day.

Unrequited Loves. Elliott Baker. LC 73-85659. 1973. 6.95 (ISBN 0-399-11242-1).

Unrest: A Story of the Struggle for Bread. Walter Robinson Parr. LC 15-19416. 1.25. R. G. Badger; Etc., Etc.

Unresting Year. Alice Massie. LC 26-218972. 1926. Cassell and Company, ltd.

Unresting Year. Alice Massie. LC 26-218986. H. Holt and Company.

Unrestrained. Peggy Gaddis, pseud. LC 38-380681. 1998. Godwin.

Unripe Fruit. Marie Louise Fowler. LC 45-2263. 1944. The Hobson Book Press.

Unsanctified: A Novel. Audrey Banta. LC 51-4405. 1951. Exposition Press.

Unseemly Adventure. Ralph Straus. LC 24-19422. 1924. H. Holt and Company.

Unseemly Adventure. Ralph Straus. LC 41-70792. (On cover: Penguin books. 167). 1939. Penguin Books Limited.

Unseemly End. Roderic Jeffries. LC 81-88372. 210p. 1982. 9.95 (ISBN 0-312-83372-5). St Martin.

Unseemly End: An Inspector Alvarez Novel. Jeffrey Ashford, pseud. LC 81-21474. 1982. 9.95 (ISBN 0-312-83372-5). St. Martin's Press.

Unseen! Albert Payson Terhune. LC 37-844. 1937. Harper & Brothers.

Unseen. Ethel L. White. 1969. pap. 0.60 o.p. (ISBN 0-446-63189-2, 63-189). Paperback Lib.

Unseen Bridegroom: Or, Wedded for a Week. May Agnes Early Fleming. LC 6-39941. (On cover: The library of American authors, no. 48). 1892. G. Munro.

Unseen Bridegroom: Or, Wedded for a Week. May Agnes Early Fleming. LC 131. (On cover: Eagle library, no. 136). 1899. Street & Smith.

Unseen Commander: A Novel. Zillah Marshall Loepke. LC 33-21929. The Marshall Company.

Unseen Ear. Natalie Sumner Lincoln. LC 21-2971. 1921. D. Appleton and Company.

Unseen Enemy. Christopher Landon. LC 57-8300. 1957. Published for the Crime Club by Doubleday.

Unseen Hand. Stopford James Ram. LC 8-209. 1863. J. R. Hawley.

Unseen Hand: Adventures of a Diplomatic Free Lance. Clarence Herbert New. LC 18-6695. 1918. Doubleday, Page & Company.

Unseen Hands. Isabel Egenton Ostrander. LC 20-10735. 1920. R. M. McBride & Co.

Unseen Harbor. Frank Laskier. LC 47-312623. 1947. J. B. Lippincott Co.

Unseen Influences. Dick Sutphen, pseud. (Orig.). 1982. 2.75 (ISBN 0-671-82604-2). PB.

Unseen Jury: A Novel. Edward Clary Root. LC 7-95468. 1907. F. A. Stokes Company.

Unseen Torment. Katheryn Kimbrough. (Queen-size Gothic). 1974. (pbk.) 0.95. Popular Library.

Unshaken Loyalty. Denise Robins. 1979. 1.75 (ISBN 0-380-47258-9). Avon Books.

Unsheltered. Dewey Comstock Ward. LC 62-8462. 1963. Random House.

Unsinkable Mrs. Jay: A Novel. Lewis Graham & Olmstead, Edwin. LC 34-18186. Covici, Friede.

Unsleeping Eye. D. G Compton. 1974. (pbk.) 1.25. DAW Books.
Unsleeping Eye. David Guy Compton. 1980. pap. 2.25 (ISBN 0-671-83077-5, Timescape). PB.
Unsleeping Eye. David Guy Compton. (Science Fiction Ser). pap. 1.25 o.p. (UY1110). DAW Bks.
Unsocial Socialist. George Bernard Shaw. LC 2-21204. 1901. Brentano.
Unsocial Socialist. George Bernard Shaw. LC 29-25297. (Half-title: The Modern library of the world's best books). 1917. The Modern Library.
Unsocial Socialist. George Bernard Shaw. LC 29-441. (Half-title: The modern library of the world's best books). The Modern Library.
Unsocial Socialist: A Novel. George Bernard Shaw. LC 77-131830. 1970. Scholarly Press.
Unsocial Socialist: A Novel. George Bernard Shaw. LC 72-6639. (Norton library). 1972. 2.95 (ISBN 0-393-00660-3). Norton.
Unsolved. Graham Montague Jeffries. LC 32-46355. 1932. J. B. Lippincott Company.
Unsought Adventure. Howard Angus Kennedy. LC 30-17421. 1929. L. Carrier & Co.
Unspeakable Gentleman. John Phillips Marquand. LC 22-10170. 1922. C. Scribner's Sons.
Unspeakable Perk. Samuel Hopkins Adams. LC 16-15844. 1916. Houghton Mifflin Company.
Unspeakable Practices, Unnatural Acts. Donald Barthelme. LC 68-14918. 1968. Farrar, Straus and Giroux.
Unspeakable Skipton. Pamela Hansford Johnson. LC 80-26139. 1981. 10.95 (ISBN 0-684-16336-5). Scribner.
Unspeakable Skipton. 1st American Ed. Pamela Hansford Johnson. 1959. Harcourt, Brace.
Unspeakables: A Tale of Lombardy. Laverne Gay. LC 45-9482. 1945. C. Scribner's Sons.
Unspecified Disasters and Other Good Times. Jack Philbrick. LC 75-17331. 5.95. T. Gaus' Sons.
Unspotted from the World. Mary Stewart. LC 8-15689. R. L. Weed Company.
Unstrung Bow: A Story of Conquest. David Oren Batchelor. LC 10-23630. 1910. 1.20. Sherman, French & Company.
Unsubstantial Castle. Robert Rushmore. LC 76-91279. 1969. 4.95. Dodd, Mead.
Unsuccessful Man. Torben Nielsen. LC 76-5550. 6.95 (ISBN 0-06-013201-9). Harper & Row.
Unsuitable Attachment. Barbara Pym. LC 82-70741. 12.50 (ISBN 0-525-24117-5). E.P. Dutton.
Unsuitable Englishman. Desmond Stirling Stewart. LC 54-5688. 1954. Farrar, Straus & Young.
Unsuitable Job for a Woman. P. D. James. LC 72-11140. 1973. 5.95 (ISBN 0-684-13280-X). Scribner.
Unsuitable Job for a Woman. P. D. James. LC 80-21837. 1980. 13.95 (ISBN 0-8161-3149-X). G. K. Hall.
Unsung Road. Simon Harvester. (Dorian Silk Espionage Adventure No. 4). 1968. pap. 0.60 o.p. (60-326). Manor Bks.
Unsuspected. Charlotte Armstrong. Repr. lib. bdg. 11.15x (ISBN 0-88411-567-4). Amereon Ltd.
Unsuspected. Charlotte Armstrong. (Berkley Medallion Book). 1976. (pbk.) 0.95. Berkley Publishing Corp.
Unsuspected: A Novel. Charlotte Armstrong. LC 46-1108. 1946. Coward-McCann, Inc.
Unsuspected Chasm... John Innes Mackintosh Stewart. LC 46-1871. 1946. Dodd, Mead & Company.
Unsuspected Isle. Rebecca Rosse. (Orig.). 1980. pap. 1.95 (ISBN 0-532-23323-9). Woodhill.
Untamed. Max Brand. 1919. 1.50. G. P. Putnam's Sons.
Untamed. Frederick Faust. LC 19-4517. 1919. G. P. Putnam's Sons.
Untamed. Frederick Faust. LC 78-12681. (Gregg Press Western Fiction Series). 1978. 10.95 (ISBN 0-8398-2462-9). Gregg Press.
Untamed. Helga Moray. LC 50-6366. 1950. Putnam.
Untamed. Helga Moray. 1973. (pbk) 1.25 (ISBN 0-671-78306-8). Pocket Books.
Untamed. Andre Pezon. 160p. pap. 1.95 o.p. (MP-118). Montmartre.
Untamed: A Bilingual Edition of the Slovene Classic. Prezihov Voranc. 1982. pap. 8.00 (ISBN 0-934158-01-0). Zalozba Prometej.
Untamed Breed. Gordon D. Shirreffs. 352p. 1981. pap. 2.75 (ISBN 0-449-14387-2, GM). Fawcett.
Untamed: By Jack Woodford Pseud. & Gordon Greene. Josiah Pitts Woolfolk & Gordon Greene. 1953. Signature Press.
Untamed Heart. Julia Greene. 1978. pap. 2.25 o.s.i. (ISBN 0-505-51321-8). Tower Bks.
Untamed Heart. Alexis Hill. 416p. (Orig.). 1980. pap. 2.75 (ISBN 0-515-04863-1). Jove Pubns.
Untamed Heart. Elda Minger. (Harlequin American Romance). 256p. 1983. pap. 2.50 (ISBN 0-373-16012-7). Harlequin Bks.
Untamed Philosopher at Home and with the Plugonians of Plugolia: Being a Tale of Hens and Some Other People. Frank Warren Hastings. 1906. The C. M. Clark Publishing Co.
Untamed Wilderness. William Stanislaus Hoffman. LC 31-14548. 1931. Spinner Publishing Co.
Untamed Witch. Patricia Lake. (Harlequin Presents Ser.). 192p. 1981. pap. 1.75 (ISBN 0-373-10465-0, Pub. by Harlequin). PB.
Untarnished. Louise Platt Hauck. LC 31-246568. The Penn Publishing Company.
Untempered Wind. Joanna E Wood. LC 8-37552. (On cover: Tait's illustrated series, no. 4). 1894. J. S. Tait and Sons.
Unterrified. Constance Noyes Robertson. LC 46-25188. 1946. H. Holt and Company.
Unthinkable. Francis H Sibson. LC 33-28400. 1933. H. Smith and R. Haas.
Untidy Gnome. Stella Gibbons. LC 36-8059. 1935. Longmans, Green & Co.
Untidy Murder: A Mr. & Mrs. North Mystery. Frances Louise Davis Lockridge & Richard Lockridge. LC 47-12327. 1947. J. B. Lippincott Co.
Untidy Pilgrim: A Novel. 1st Ed. Eugene Walter. LC 53-5417. 1954. Lippincott.
Untie the Winds. Jean Clark. LC 75-31595. (Illus.). 8.95 (ISBN 0-02-525780-3). Macmillan.
Until Death. Suzanne Somers, pseud. 1973. pap. 0.95 o.p. (09213). Curtis.
Until Death Do Us Part. Mary McMullen. LC 82-45398. 1982. 11.95 (ISBN 0-385-18295-3). Published for the Crime Club by Doubleday.
Until He Comes Again: A Novel Based on the Life of Jesus. William Andrew Boerger. LC 52-5695. 1952. Exposition Press.
Until I Close My Eyes. Allen Robert Taft. LC 34-8055. R. O. Ballou.
Until I Find-- A Novel of Boyhood. Edgcumb Pinchon. LC 36-7598. 1936. A. A. Knopf.
Until I Find Her. Tempest, Jan. LC 50-9009. 1950. Arcadia House.
Until Love Happens. Margaret Gorman Nichols. LC 48-189471. 1948. Triangle Books.
Until Love Happens. Margaret Gorman Nichols. LC 46-839722. 1946. Macrae-Smith-Company.
Until Proven Guilty. Charles W Calhoun. LC 17-14188. 1917. Western Publishing Company.
Until Seventy Times Seven: A Story. LC 3-10204. 1903. T. Whittaker.
Until She Screams. Mason Hoffenberg. 1968. 3.95 o.s.i. (Travellers Comp); pap. 1.25 o.s.i. (2216). Olympia.
Until She Screams. Faustino Perez. pap. 1.75 o.p. (3008). Brandon.
Until Summer. Frances E. Wilson. 1981. pap. 6.95 (Avalon). Bouregy.
Until Temptation Do Us Part. Alan Geoffrey Yates. LC 67-4008. (Carter Brown mystery series). 1967. New American Library.
Until That Day. Kressmann Taylor. LC 42-19761. 1942. Duell, Sloan & Pearce.
Until the Colors Fade. Tim Jeal. (Dell Book). 1977. 2.25 (ISBN 0-440-19260-9). Dell Pub. Co.
Until the Colors Fade: A Novel. Tim Jeal. LC 76-17621. (ISBN 0-440-09299-X). Delacorte Press.
Until the Colours Fade. Tim Jeal. LC 77-356363. 1976. 4.50 (ISBN 0-241-89484-0). H. Hamilton.
Until the Day Break. Mercedes De Acosta. 1928. Longmans, Green and Co.
Until the Day Break. Sallie Lee Bell. 244p. 1972. pap. 2.50 (ISBN 0-310-21062-3). Zondervan.
Until the Day Break. Louis Bromfield. LC 42-15035. 1942. Harper & Brothers.
Until the Day Break. A Novel. Alice Elinor Bowen Bartlett. LC 6-9404. (On cover: International series ef new approved novels). Porter and Coates.
Until the Day Break: A Novel. Robert Burns Wilson. LC 4808. 1900. C. Scribner's Sons.
Until the Day Break: A Novel of the Time of Christ. Sallie Lee Bell. LC 50-6002. 1950. Zondervan.
Until the Day Breaks. A Novel. Emily Spender. (Harper's Franklin square library. no. 514). 1886. Harper & Brothers.
Until the Day Breaks. A Novel. Emily Spender. (On cover: The seaside library. Pocket ed. no. 735). 1886. G. Munro.
Until the Daybreak. Walter Lionel George. LC 13-1307. 1913. Dodd, Mead and Company.
Until the Greyhound Comes. Garrett Anderson. LC 76-378598. 1976. 3.95 (ISBN 0-214-20132-5). Barrie & Jenkins.
Until the Jaguar Sings. Tina Green. (Avalon Books). 1977. 4.95. Thomas Bouregy.
Until the Phoenix: A Novel. Fa-Shun Chang. LC 52-9614. 1952. J. Day Co.
Until the Real Thing Comes Along. Noel Clad. LC 61-12158. 1961. Random House.
Until the Shearing. Anne Miller Downes. LC 40-33581. 1940. Frederick A. Stokes Company.
Until the Sun Dies. Robert Jastrow. 1980. pap. 4.95 (ISBN 0-446-97348-3). Warner Bks.
Until the Sun Falls. Cecelia Holland. LC 68-58527. (Illus.). 1969. 7.95. Atheneum.
Until They Scream. J. J. Montague. 192p. pap. 1.95 o.p. (ISBN 0-87977-159-3, DBB159). Dansk Blue Bk.
Until We Meet Again. Ann Farrington. 1977. pap. 1.50 (ISBN 0-532-15288-3). Woodhill.
Until You Are Dead. S. E Ellacott. LC 72-4463. 1972. 2.50 (ISBN 0-200-71914-9). Abelard-Schuman.
Until You Are Dead. Henry Kane. LC 50-11040. (Inner sanctum mystery). 1951. Simon and Schuster.
Until You Come Back. Peggy Gaddis. LC 42-7195. Gramercy Publishing Co.
Untilled Field. George Moore. LC 70-125233. (Short story index reprint series). 1970. Books for Libraries Press.
Untilled Field. George Moore. LC 3-11146. 1903. J. B. Lippincott Company.
Untimely Death. Cyril Hare. LC 58-11300. 1980. pap. 2.25i (ISBN 0-06-080514-5, P 514, PL). Har-Row.
Untimely Death: By Cyril Hare Pseud. Alfred Alexander Gordon Clark. LC 58-11300. (Cock Robin mystery). 1958. Macmillan.
Unto a Good Land. Vilhelm Moberg. (Emigrants Saga: No. 2). 1971. pap. 2.95 (ISBN 0-445-08542-8). Popular Lib.
Unto a Good Land: A Novel; Translated from the Swedish by Gustaf Lannestock. Vilhelm Moberg. LC 54-9057. 1954. Simon and Schuster.
Unto Caesar. Emmuska Orczy. LC 14-7730. George H. Doran Company.
Unto Death. Amos Oz. LC 75-16239. (Illus.). 1975. 6.95 (ISBN 0-15-193095-3). Harcourt Brace Jovanovich.
Unto Death. Amos Oz. LC 77-15963. (Harvest/HJB book). (Illus.). 1978. 2.95 (ISBN 0-15-693170-2). Harcourt Brace Jovanovich.
Unto Death: "Crusade" & "Late Love". Amos Oz. LC 75-16239. (Helen & Kurt Wolff Bk.). (Illus.). 167p. 1975. 6.95 (ISBN 0-15-193095-3). HarBraceJ.
Unto the End. Isabella Macdonald Alden. LC 2-13612. 1902. Lothrop Publishing Company.
Unto the Fourth Generation: One Solution of the Negro Problem. Elizabeth Seal Blakely. LC 13-23596. 1894. H. H. Bevis.
Unto the Heights of Simplicity. Johannes Reimers. LC 3935. 1900. L. C. Page & Company (Incorporated.
Unto the Hills. Julia Lestarjette Glover. LC 41-28077. The Wartburg Press.
Unto the Hills: A Novel. Leslie A Outterson. LC 51-12. 1950. Vantage Press.
Unto the Hills: A Story of the Blue Ridge Mountains. Neville Calmes. Fleming H. Revell Company.
Unto the Hills: An Idyl of Missouri Ozarks... Ann Hendrix. LC 34-243570. Burton Publishing Company.
Unto the Third and Fourth Generation. Helen Stuart Campbell. LC 6-21485. 1880. Fords, Howard & Hulbert.
Unto the Uttermost. Sallie Lee Bell. LC 54-32783. 1954. Zondervan Pub. House.
Unto the Uttermost. Wade H. Horton. 1973. 4.95 o.p. (ISBN 0-87148-876-0); pap. 3.95 o.p. (ISBN 0-87148-877-9). Pathway Pr.
Unto Zeor, Forever. Jacqueline Lichtenberg. LC 77-12871. 1978. 7.95 (ISBN 0-385-13566-1). Doubleday.
Unto Zeor Forever. Jacqueline Lichtenberg. 1980. 2.25 (ISBN 0-87216-598-1). Playboy Press Paperbacks.
Unto Zeor, Forever. Mary Lieber. 1980. 2.25 (ISBN 0-87216-598-1). Playboy Press.
Untold Glory: A Novel. Based on the Diaries and Letters of Felicia Lee Cary Thornton Shover. Cothburn O'Neal. LC 57-12817. 1957. Crown Publishers.
Untold Millions: A Novel. Laura Keane Zametkin Hobson. LC 81-47587. 10.95 (ISBN 0-06-014924-8). Harper & Row.
Untold Millions: A Novel. Laura Keane Zametkin Hobson. LC 82-9167. 1982. 15.95 (ISBN 0-8161-3406-5). G.K. Hall.
Untold Story of Gretchen. C. A. Perry. 3.95 o.p. Vantage.
Untold Tale. Will Phillip Hooper & Savage, Richard Henry, 1846-1903. (On cover: The welcome series, no. 23). The Home Publishing Company.
Untold Tales of the Past. Beatrice Harraden. LC 7-2849. 1897. Dodd, Mead and Company.
Untouchable. Mulk Raj Anand. (Mayfair Paperbacks Ser.). 226p. 1981. pap. 3.00 (ISBN 0-86578-068-4). Ind-US Inc.
Untouchable. Mulk Raj Anand. 181p. 1974. pap. 2.75 (ISBN 0-88253-280-4). Ind-US Inc.
Untouchable, a Novel. Mulk Raj Anand. 1971. 5.95 o.p. (ISBN 0-8180-0611-0). Horizon.
Untouchable Juli. James Aldridge. LC 75-25807. 6.95 (ISBN 0-316-03122-4). Little, Brown.
Untouchables. Eliot Ness & Oscar Fraley. (O.s.i.). 192p. 1975. pap. 1.50 o.s.i. (ISBN 0-441-84672-6, AD1484, Award). Univ Pub & Dist.
Untouched by Human Hands: Thirteen Stories. Robert Sheckley. LC 54-7987. 1954. Ballantine Books.
Untouched Wife. Rachel Lindsay. (Harlequin Presents Ser.). 192p. 1981. pap. 1.75 (ISBN 0-373-10467-7). Harlequin Bks.
Untrodden Show. Denise Robins. 1972. pap. 0.75 o.p. (94194). Beagle Bks.
Unused Perfume. Angel Martinez. 1982. pap. 3.95 (ISBN 0-8054-5189-7). Broadman.
Unusual Seder. Gershon Kranzler, pseud. saddle-stitched 3.00 (ISBN 0-87559-136-1). Shalom.
Unvanquished. Howard Melvin Fast. LC 42-16612. 1942. Duell, Sloan and Pearce.
Unvanquished. indian ed. Howard Melvin Fast. LC 47-8034. 1944. Duell, Sloan and Pearce.
Unvanquished. William Faulkner. LC 38-7091. Rendom House.
Unvanquished: A Novel. Howard Melvin Fast. LC 45-948975. (Half-title: The Modern library of the world's best books). 1945. The Modern Library.
Unvanquished: Reissue Drawings by Edward Shenton. William Faulkner. LC 38-271619. 4.95. Random.
Unvarnished Facts and Unvarnished Yarns of Unvarnished Dry Goods Men. Albert E Hiles. LC 7-4940. 1889. Evening Express Co., Printers.
Unveiled. Beatrice Kean Stapleton Seymour. LC 25-9293. 1925. T. Seltzer.
Unveiled Heart: A Simple Story. LC 8-32291. 1835. J. Allen and Co.
Unveiling. Grace Visher Payne. LC 50-3159. Westminster Press.
Unveiling Hearts. Lorain Wakefield Barton. LC 52-6728. B. Humphries.
Unvexed to the Sea: A Novel of the Vicksburg Campaign. Gerry Morrison. LC 60-898433. 1961. St. Martin's Press.
Unwanted. Christiaan Neethling Barnard & Siegfried Stander. LC 75-16236. 1975. 9.95 o.p. (ISBN 0-679-50567-9). McKay.
Unwanted see Let Us Not Forget.
Unwanted: A Novel. Christiaan Neethling Barnard & Siegfried Stander. LC 75-12696. 1975. 9.95 (ISBN 0-679-50567-9). McKay.
Unwanted Breed. Robert Hussa. 1978. pap. 5.00 (ISBN 0-89502-019-X). FEB.
Unwanted Bride. Anne Hampson. (Harlequin Presents Ser.). 192p. 1982. pap. 1.75 (ISBN 0-373-10515-0). Harlequin Bks.
Unwanted Child: A Novel Founded on the Play of the Same Name. Florence Edna May. LC 23-18390. J. S. Ogilvie Publishing Company.
Unwanted Children. Jonathon Le Mire & Helk, Ellie M., 1940-Joint Author. LC 49-9964. 1949. B. Humphries.
Unwanted Legacy. Carrie E. Myers Gruhn. LC 53-13508. 1953. Van Kampen Press.
Unwanted Nina. 1st Ed. Mary Styrska Carlton. LC 59-14292. 1960. Vantage Press.
Unwanted: Translated from the Italian by Frances Frenaye. Dante Arfelli. LC 51-5375. 1951. Scribner.
Unweave a Rainbow: A Sentimental Fantasy. Edgar Johnson. LC 31-982. 1931. Doubleday, Doran & Company, Inc.
Unwed Mother. Philip Basvic. LC 71-167823. 1972. 5.95 (ISBN 0-8059-1606-7). Dorrance.
Unwed Mother. Mike Phillips. 1972. 5.95 o.p. (ISBN 0-8059-1606-7). Dorrance.
Unwed Widow. Julia Sorel. 1975. (pbk.) 1.50 (ISBN 0-345-24123-1). Ballantine Books.
Unwedded Wife. Genevieve Kirke. (On cover: Idylwild series, v. 1, no. 15). 1892. Morrill, Higgins & Co.
Unwelcome Corpse. Barbara Frost. LC 47-30247. 1947. Coward-McCann, Inc.
Unwelcome Man: A Novel. Waldo David Frank. LC 17-2340. 1917. 1.50. Little, Brown, and Company.
Unwilling Actress. Bella Dietrich. 192p. pap. 1.95 o.p. (ISBN 0-87977-115-1). Dansk Blue Bk.
Unwilling Adventurer. Richard Austin Freeman. LC 13-21362. Hodder and Stoughton.
Unwilling Bride: A Novel. Michael Angelo Holmes. (On cover:The Marguerite series, no. 15). E. A. Weeks & Company.
Unwilling Bride: Or, The Curse of Rosser. M. P Green. (On cover: The laurel library, no. 1). 1891. G. Munro.
Unwilling Dictator. Jules Verne. 3.95. Assoc Bk.
Unwilling Enchantress. Lydia Gregory. (Candlelight Ecstasy Ser.: No. 103). (Orig.). 1982. pap. 1.95 (ISBN 0-440-19185-8). Dell.
Unwilling God. Percy Marks. LC 29-21552. 1929. Harper & Brothers.
Unwilling Guest. Grace Livingston Hill. LC 2-15861. 1902. American Baptist Publication Society.
Unwilling Heiress. Sandra Heath. (Orig.). 1981. pap. 1.95 (ISBN 0-451-09771-8, J9771, Sig). NAL.
Unwilling Journey. Clarence Pendleton Lee. LC 40-271501. 1940. The Macmillan Company.

Unwilling Maid: Being the History of Certain Episodes During the American Revolution in the Early Life of Mistress Betty Yorke, Born Wolcott. Jeanie Thomas Gould Lincoln. LC 7-20110. 1897. Houghton, Mifflin and Company.

Unwilling Mistress. Alma Werdon. 192p. pap. 1.95 o.p. (ISBN 0-87977-119-4). Dansk Blue Bk.

Unwilling Model. Paula Tarrant. 192p. (Orig.). 1973. pap. 1.95 o.p. (ISBN 0-87977-192-5). Dansk Blue Bk.

Unwilling Rebel. Mirium Lynch. 1975. pap. 1.25 o.p. (ISBN 0-515-03748-6). BJ Pub Group.

Unwilling Sinner. Josiah Pitts Woolfolk. LC 33-13043. 1933. W. Godwin, Inc.

Unwilling Vestal. Edward Lucas White. LC 42-47098. 1937. E. P. Dutton & Co., Inc.

Unwilling Vestal: A Tale of Rome Under the Caesars. Edward Lucas White. LC 18-7033. 1918. E. P. Dutton & Company.

Unwilling Witness. Teresa Holloway. 192p. (YA) 1974. 4.95 o.p. (Avalon). Bouregy.

Unwilling Witness. Teresa Holloway. (Avalon romances). 1974. 4.50. Avalon Books.

Unwritten History; Life Among the Modocs. Joaquin Miller. LC 72-197934. 1972. 2.95. Orion Press.

Unwritten History: Life Amongst the Modocs. Joaquin Miller. LC 68-57540. (American novels of muckraking, propaganda, and social protest). (Illus.). 1968. Gregg Press.

Up. Ronald Sukenick. LC 68-14993. Orig. Title: Sentence of Death. 1968. 4.95 o.p. (92533). Dial.

Up Above the World: A Novel. Paul Frederic Bowles. LC 66-11958. 1966. Simon and Schuster.

Up Against It. Frederic Van Rensselaer Dey. LC 20-15062. The Macaulay Company.

Up Against It. Mike Royko. 1971. pap. 1.95 o.p. (ISBN 0-8092-9725-6). Regnery.

Up and Coming. Nalbro Isadorah Bartley. LC 23-400650. 1923. 1.90. G. P. Putnam's Sons.

Up & Coming. Troy Conway, pseud. (Coxeman Ser., No. 30). 1972. pap. 0.75 o.p. (ISBN 0-446-65805-7). Paperback Lib.

Up and Coming Man: A Novel. Frank Branston. LC 76-62751. 1977. 7.95 (ISBN 0-312-83378-4). St. Martin's Press.

Up and Down. Edward Frederic Benson. LC 18-174124. 1.50. George H. Doran Company.

Up and Down the Sands of Gold. Mary Devereux. LC 1-25037. 1901. Little, Brown, and Company.

Up at the Villa. William Somerset Maugham. LC 75-25366. (Maugham, William Somerset, 1876-1965. Works. 1976). 1977. 15.00 (ISBN 0-405-07824-2). Arno Press.

Up at the Villa. William Somerset Maugham. LC 41-51121. 1941. Doubleday, Doran & Company, Inc.

Up at the Villa. LC 29-20439. 1929. D. Appleton & Company.

Up Broadway: And Its Sequel. A Life Story. Eleanor Maria Easterbrook Ames. LC 7-19407. 1870. Carleton; Etc., Etc.

Up Country: A Story of the Vanguard. Louise Redfield Peattie & Peattie, Louise (Redfield) LC 28-4073. 1928. D. Appleton and Company.

Up Daddy. Karl Flinders. pap. 1.95 o.s.i. (TC-508, Travellers Comp). Olympia.

Up Eel River. Margaret Prescott Montague. LC 77-150552. (Short story index reprint series). (Illus.). 1971. (ISBN 0-8369-3849-6). Books for Libraries Press.

Up Eel River. Margaret Prescott Montague. LC 28-106230. 1928. The Macmillan Company.

Up Ferguson Way. Louis Bromfield. LC 81-85856. (Illus.). 64p. 1982. 9.95 (ISBN 0-941660-06-0); pap. 4.95 (ISBN 0-941660-07-9). Still Point Pr.

Up for Grabs. A. A. Fair, pseud. 1964. 3.95 o.p. Morrow.

Up for Grabs. Erle Stanley Gardner. 1964. Morrow.

Up from Agony: A Novel of Americanization. John Harms. LC 72-91294. 1969. 5.95 (ISBN 0-910014-04-3). Acorn Press.

Up from Never. Joseph N. Sorrentino. 1973. pap. 1.25 (ISBN 0-532-12156-2, 532-12156-125). Woodhill.

Up from Nowhere. Walter Olesky. (Tom Delos & the Guardians Novel). (Illus.). 192p. 1982. pap. 1.95 (ISBN 0-448-16831-6, Pub. by Tempo). Ace Bks.

Up from Seltzer. Peter Hochstein & Sandy Hoffman. LC 80-54617. (Illus.). 96p. 1981. pap. 3.95 (ISBN 0-89480-145-7). Workman Pub.

Up from the Cape. A Plea for Republican Simplicity... Hezekiah Butterworth. 1883. Estes and Lauriat.

Up from the Valley. W. E. Nabers. 2.75 o.p. Vantage.

Up-Grade. George Fort Gibbs. LC 27-175735. 1927. D. Appleton and Company.

Up Grade. Wilder Goodwin. LC 10-147094. 1910. 1.50. Little, Brown, and Company.

Up Hill, Down Dale: A Volume of Short Stories. 2d ed. Eden Phillpotts. LC 79-150558. (Short story index reprint series). 1971. (ISBN 0-8369-3855-0). Books for Libraries Press.

Up Hill, Down Dale: A Volume of Short Stories. 2d ed. Eden Phillpotts. LC 26-26288. 1926. The Macmillan Company.

Up Home. Ardyth Kennelly. LC 55-8103. 1955. Houghton Mifflin.

Up in Ardmuirland. Michael Barrett. LC 12-28405. 1912. 1.25. Cincinnati Etc. Benziger Brothers.

Up in Heaven. Pierre LaTour. 1970. pap. 1.45 o.p. (V1014Q, Venus). Grove.

Up in Mamie's Diary. John Colleton. (Orig.). 1975. pap. 2.25 (ISBN 0-451-09230-9, E9230, Sig). NAL.

Up in Mamie's Diary. John Colleton. (Signet book). 1975. (pbk.) 1.50. New American Library.

Up in the Hills. Edward John Moreton Drax Plunkett Dunsany. LC 36-4842. G. P. Putnam's Sons.

Up into the Singing Mountain. Richard Llewellyn. 1960. Doubleday.

Up Jumped the Devil. Cleve Franklin Adams. LC 43-735775. 1943. Reynal & Hitchcock.

Up Jumped the Devil... Cleve Franklin Adams. LC 45-3436. (Handi-book mysteries. 33).

Up My Mother's Flagpole. Danah Zohar. LC 73-90696. 1974. 6.95 (ISBN 0-8128-1655-2). Stein and Day.

Up My Mother's Flagpole. Danah Zohar. 1976. 1.95 (ISBN 0-14-004134-6). Penguin Books.

Up North. William H. Bowden. 3.00 o.p. Carlton.

Up North. William H. Bowden. 4.95 o.p. Vantage.

Up North. William H. Bowden. 1973. 4.95 (ISBN 0-533-00640-6). Vantage.

Up North. John S. Wade. (WNJ: No. 12). 1979. 10.00; signed ed. 20.00; pap. 4.50. Juniper Pr WI.

Up She Rises. David Garnett. LC 76-62770. 1977. 8.95 (ISBN 0-312-83387-3). St. Martin's Press.

Up Terrapin River. Opie Percival Read. (On cover: The Rialto series, no. 13). 1889. Rand, McNally & Company.

Up the Down Road. Cecil Coffey. LC 77-155181. 63p. 1971. pap. 0.95 (ISBN 0-8163-0063-1, 21650-7). Pacific Pr Pub Assn.

Up the Down Staircase. Bel Kaufman. LC 64-24258. (Illus.). 1965. Prentice-Hall.

Up the Grade. David William Edwards. LC 9-29971. 1909. The C. M. Clark Publishing Company.

Up the Hill and Over. Isabel Ecclestone Macpherson Mackay. LC 17-101640. George H. Doran Company.

Up the Junction. Drawings by Susan Benson. Nell Dunn, pseud. LC 66-25408. 1966. bds., 3.95. Lippincott.

Up the Junction. Drawings by Susan Benson. Nell Dunn, pseud. (Mod bk., U5098). 1967. Ballantine.

Up the Line. 4th ed. Robert Silverberg. (Del Rey Bks). 256p. 1978. pap. 2.50 (ISBN 0-345-29696-6). Ballantine.

Up the Matterhorn in a Boat. Marion Manville Pope. 1897. The Century Co.

Up, the Rebels! James Owen Hannay. LC 19-15676. George H. Doran Company.

Up the Republic! A Novel of the Irish Easter Rebellion. James Meade. LC 52-7655. 1952. Exposition Press.

Up the Republic! A Novel of the Irish Easter Rebellion. James Meade. LC 52-7655. 1952. Exposition Press.

Up the Rito. Helen Bagg. LC 25-15269. 1925. The Penn Publishing Company.

Up the Road with Sallie. Frances Roberta Sterrett. LC 15-18280. 1915. 1.25. D. Appleton and Company.

Up the Sandbox! Anne Richardson Roiphe. LC 79-130488. 1970. 4.95 (ISBN 0-671-20704-0). Simon and Schuster.

Up the Walls of the World. James Tiptree. LC 77-24470. 8.95 (ISBN 0-399-12083-1). Berkley Pub. Corp.: Distributed by Putnam.

Up the Walls of the World. James Tiptree. (Berkley book). 1979. 1.95 (ISBN 0-425-03880-7). Berkley Pub. Corp.

Up the Witch Brook Road: A Summer Idyl. Kate Upson Clark. LC 2-28412. 1902. J. F. Taylor & Company.

Up There the Stars: A Novel. Ralph Corsel. LC 68-19126. 1968. 5.95. Citadel Press.

Up This Crooked Way: A Sheriff Macready Detective Story. Hugh Holman. LC 46-8413. 1946. M. S. Hill Co., Inc.

Up Tight. Carl Ross. (Orig.). 1968. pap. 1.75 o.s.i. (128, Ophelia). Olympia.

Up-Tight. Dick Winfield. Orig. Title: Doolie's Private Goddess. 1967. pap. 0.50 o.p. (52-605). Paperback Lib.

Up to Calvin's". Laura Elizabeth Howe Richards. LC 10-24027. 1.25. D. Estes & Company.

Up-to-Date Courtship. Clara Parrish Wright. LC 10-114351. 1909. Cochrane Publishing Co.

Up-to-Date Pauper. Helen Maude Wheeler. LC 7-40000. 1907. The C. M. Clark Publishing Co.

Up to Her Neck: A Novel of Suspense. John Newton Chance. LC 55-1599. (Popular library, 646). 1955. Popular Library.

Up to No Good. Aaron Marc Stein. LC 41-13944. 1941. Pub. for the Crime Club by Doubleday, Doran and Company, Inc.

Up to Now. Martin Shaw. (Illus.). 218p. 1980. Repr. of 1929 ed. lib. bdg. 20.00 (ISBN 0-89984-404-9). Century Bookbindery.

Up to the Hilt. Anne Van Melborn Rowe. LC 45-9491. 1945. M. S. Mill Co., Inc.

Up Where I Used to Live. Max Schott. LC 78-11619. (Illinois Short Fiction Ser.). 1978. 11.95 (ISBN 0-252-00719-0); pap. 4.95 (ISBN 0-252-00720-4). U of Ill Pr.

Up Your Ante. Glen Chase, pseud. (Cherry Delight Ser.: No. 4). 1975. pap. 1.25 o.p. (LB4072K, Leisure Bks). Nordon Pubns.

Up Your Asteroid! a Science Fiction Farce. C. Everett Cooper. LC 77-866. 1977. lib. bdg. 9.95x (ISBN 0-89370-106-8); pap. 3.95x (ISBN 0-89370-206-4). Borgo Pr.

Up Your Banners. Donald E. Westlake. 1970. pap. 0.95 o.p. (ISBN 0-447-75156-5). Lancer.

Up Your Banners: A Novel. Donald E Westlake. LC 78-76326. 1969. Macmillan.

Upas Tree. Florence Louisa Charlesworth Barclay. LC 12-25325. 1912. G. P. Putnam's Sons.

Upas Tree. Robert McMurdy. LC 12-23932. F. J. Schulte & Company; Etc., Etc.

Upas Tree: A Christmas Story for All the Year. Florence Louisa Charlesworth Barclay. LC 12-25384. 1912. 1.00. G. P. Putnam's Sons.

Upas Tree: A Novel. Eva Hanagan. LC 79-22926. 8.95 (ISBN 0-312-83397-0). St. Martin's Press.

Upbeat. Irving Shulman. 224p. 1973. pap. 1.25 o.s.i. (78-734). Lancer.

Upfold Farm Mystery. Archibald E. Fielding. LC 33-1257. 1932. H. C. Kinsey & Company, Inc.

Upheaval. Lena Ellen McKay. LC 54-102455. 1955. Rvantage Pess.

Uphill Climb. Bertha Muzzy Sinclair. LC 13-807917. 1913. Little, Brown, and Company.

Uphill into the Sun. Fred Trump. LC 73-17245. (Illus.). 1973. 7.95 (ISBN 0-8111-0498-2). Naylor Co.

Uphill Road. Ruby Mildred Ayres. LC 22-3961. W. J. Watt & Company.

Uphill Struggle from the Poorhouse to the Resthome. Mabel Wood. 2.50 o.p. Carlton.

Upland Mystery: A Tragedy of New England. Mary R. Platt Hatch. LC 7-2637. Laird & Lee.

Uplands: A Novel. Frances Davis Baker. 1898. G. M. Hausauer.

Uplands and Lowlands: Or, Three Chapters in a Life. Rose Porter. LC 7-37423. A. D. F. Randolph & Company.

Uplands of Dream. Edgar Evertson Saltus. Ed. by Charles Honce. LC 78-93776. Repr. of 1925 ed. 17.50 (ISBN 0-404-05550-8). AMS Pr.

Upon a Cast. Charlotte Dunning Wood. LC 9-510. 1885. Harper & Brothers.

Upon the Head of the Goat. Aranka Siegal. 192p. 1983. pap. 2.25 (ISBN 0-451-12084-1, Sig Vista). NAL.

Upon the Sweeping Flood. Joyce Carol Oates. LC 66-16632. 12.95 (ISBN 0-8149-0172-7). Vanguard.

Upon the Sweeping Flood: And Other Stories. Joyce Carol Oates. LC 66-166322. bds., 4.95. Vanguard.

Upon the Willows & Other Stories. Rowena T. Torrevillas. 192p. 1980. pap. 6.00x. Cellar.

Upon the Winds of Yesterday. George Barr. 25.00 o.p. D M Grant.

Upon Their Shoulders: A Novel; with a Foreword by Miles E. Carey. Ota, Shelley Ayame Nishimura. LC 51-6976. 1951. Exposition Press.

Upon This Rock: A Novel of Simon Peter, Prince of the Apostles. Frank Gill Slaughter. LC 63-15534. 1963. Coward-McCann.

Upon This Rock: A Tale of Peter. John Cosgrove. LC 77-94404. 4.95 (ISBN 0-87973-775-1). Our Sunday Visitor, Inc.

Upon Thy Doorposts. Jennie Rosenholtz. LC 36-11055. 1936. Bloch Publishing Company.

Upper Berth. Francis Marion Crawford. LC 11-10574. (Half-title: Autonym library v. 1). 1894. G. P. Putnam's.

Upper Case: A Novel. Mollie Merrick. LC 36-20139. I. Washburn, Inc.

Upper Crust. Charles Sherman. LC 13-928755. The Bobbs-Merrill Company.

Upper Empire: A Story of American Business and Politics. Daniel Maurice Robins. LC 28-11314. Dorrance and Company.

Upper Hand. John William Corrington. LC 66-20271. 1967. Putnam.

Upper Hand. Emerson Gifford Taylor. 1906. A S. Barnes & Company.

Upper Pleasure Garden. Gordon M. Williams. LC 73-117223. 1970. 6.95. Morrow.

Upper Room. Robert Hugh Benson. 1956. pap. 0.85 o.p. McKay.

Upper Room Disciplines. 1977. pap. 2.00 o.s.i. (UR348); pap. 1.80 ea. 10 or more o.s.i. (UR293). Upper Room.

Upper Ten. A Novel of the Snobocracy. William Hosea Ballou. LC 6-6087. (On cover: American novelists' series, no. 54). United States Book Company.

Upper Ten Thousand: Sketches of American Society. Charles Astor Bristed. LC 6-18248. 1852. Stringer & Townsend.

Upper Ten Thousand: Sketches of American Society. Charles Astor Bristed. LC 45-49953. 1852. Stringer & Townsend.

Upper Trail. Mary A MacIvor. LC 12-13465. 1.50. The Roxburgh Publishing Company, Incorporated.

Upps of Suffolk Street. Wilma Pollock. LC 37-198920. E. P. Dutton & Company, Inc.

Upright Love: A Novel. Phyllis Speshock. LC 59-48814. 1959. Zondervan Pub. House.

Uproar in the Village. Oskar Jellinek. Tr. by Stamper, Evelyn B. G. LC 33-27088. 1933. R. M. McBride & Company.

Uprooted. 2nd enl. ed. Oscar Handlin. 1973. 9.95 (ISBN 0-316-34301-3, Pub. by Atlantic Monthly Pr); pap. 6.95 (ISBN 0-316-34313-7, Pub. by Atlantic Monthly Pr). Little.

Uprooted. Brand Whitlock. LC 26-5384. 1926. D. Appleton and Company.

Uprush of Mayhem. Jack S Scott, pseud. LC 81-21298. 1982. 10.95 (ISBN 0-89919-095-2). Ticknor & Fields.

Ups and Downs. An Every-Day Novel. Edward Everett Hale. LC 6-462031. 1873. Roberts Brothers.

Ups and Downs in the Life of a Distressed Gentleman. William Leete Stone. LC 7-3067. 1836. Leavitt, Lord & Co.

Ups and Downs" of a Virginia Doctor. Clarence Archibald Bryce. LC 4-33218. 1904. Ashland Printing Company.

Upshur Hall: Or, The Power of Influence. Cornelia Holroyd Bradley. LC 7-12334. American Baptist Publication Society.

Upside Down in the Magnolia Tree. Mary Bancroft. LC 52-5520. (Illus.). 1952. Little, Brown.

Upside Down Murder. Hugh Austin Evans. LC 38-12698. The Sun Dial Press, Inc.

Upside Down Murders. Hugh Austin. LC 37-638402. 1937. Pub. for the Crime Club, Inc., by Doubleday, Doran & Company, Inc.

Upside Down Murders. Hugh Austin. LC 38-12698. 1938. The Sun Dial Press, Inc.

Upside Down Murders. Hugh Austin Evans. LC 37-6384. 1937. Pub. for the Crime Club, Inc., by Doubleday, Doran & Company, Inc.

Upside-Down Tree. Hardy Kruger. LC 77-5843. 8.95. Citadel Press.

Upside Downside. Ron Goulart. 1982. pap. 2.25 (ISBN 0-87997-697-7, UE1697). DAW Bks.

Upsidonia. Archibald Marshall. 1917. Dodd, Mead and Company.

Upstairs at the Bull Run. Moira Pearce. LC 74-139384. 1971. 6.95 (ISBN 0-393-08630-5). Norton.

Upstairs, Downstairs. John Hawkesworth. LC 79-20434. 1980. 13.95 (ISBN 0-8161-6794-X). G. K. Hall.

Upstairs, Downstairs. John Hawkesworth. 1973. (pbk) 1.50. Dell.

Upstairs Room. Johanna Reiss. (Pathfinder Ser.). 176p. (gr. 5-8). 1973. pap. 1.95 (ISBN 0-553-12754-3, Y14425-1). Bantam.

Upstart. Henry Morrow Hyde. LC 6-34689. 1906. The Century Co.

Upstart. Edison Marshall. 1945. Farrar & Rinehart, Inc.

Upstart. Piers Paul Read. LC 73-653. 1973. 7.95 (ISBN 0-397-00966-6). Lippincott.

Upstart. Piers Paul Read. 1974. (pbk.) 1.50. Bantam Books.

Upstart. avon books, ed. Piers Paul Read. 2.25 (ISBN 0-380-49023-4).

Upstream. Martin Jerome Scott. LC 29-22801. P. J. Kenedy & Sons.

Uptown--Downtown. Thomas Grant Springer. LC 36-14925. Greenberg.

Uptown & Downtown. Fischler. pap. 8.95 (ISBN 0-8015-8196-6, 0869-260, Hawthorn). Dutton.

Upward Guide: By Ian Jefferies Pseud. Peter Hays. LC 60-9112. 1960. Harper.

Upward Spiral: A Novel. Dilip Kumar Roy. LC 50-26029. 1949. Jaico Pub. House.

Upward to Glory. Anna Ziak. LC 48-2647. 1948.

Upward Trail. Dinch Bikis. LC 38-6348. Wm. B. Eerdmans Publishing Co.

Upward Trail. Edith Nicholl Ellison. LC 18-9773. 1.35. Rowland & Ives.

Upwinds. Anders Otterland & Sunnergren Lennart. pap. 3.50 o.p. (ISBN 0-8407-5599-6). Nelson.

Urada: A Romance of Ancient Egypt. Georg Ebers. Tr. by Clara Courtnay Bell. LC 21-21461. (Manhattan library. vol. i. no. 3). 1891. A. L. Burt.

Urada: A Romance of Ancient Egypt. authorized ed... ed. Georg Moritz Ebers. Tr. by Clara Courtenay Bell. LC 6-43634. 1880. W. S. Gottsberger.

Urada. A Romance of Ancient Egypt. Georg Moritz Ebers. Tr. by Clara Courtenay Bell. (Seaside library, v. 35, no. 712). 1880. G. Munro.
Urada: A Romance of Ancient Egypt. authorized ed...rev., cor. and enl. from the latest german ed. Georg Moritz Ebers. Tr. by Clara Courtenay Bell. 1881. W. S. Gottsberger.
Urada. A Romance of Ancient Egypt. Georg Moritz Ebers. Tr. by Clara Courtenay Bell. (On cover: Seaside library. Pocket ed., no. 983). 1887. G. Munro.
Urada: A Romance of Ancient Egypt. Georg Moritz Ebers. Tr. by Clara Courtenay Bell. LC 4-16861. 1901. D. Appleton and Company.
Urada. A Romance of Ancient Egypt. Georg Moritz Ebers. LC 17-26997. (On cover: The home library). 1916. A. L. Burt Company.
Urania. Camille Flammarion & Robins, E. P., Tr. (On cover: The optimus series, no. 17). Donohue, Henneberry & Co.
Urania. Camille Flammarion & Stetson, Augusta Rice, Tr. LC 6-39543. Estes and Lauriat.
Uranian Fantasies. Aurora Armstrong. 1977. 2.95 o.p. (ISBN 0-8059-2377-2). Dorrance.
Uranie. Camille Flammarion. Tr. by Mary Jane Serrano. LC 7-3007. Cassell Publishing Company.
Uranie. Camille Flammarion. Tr. by Mary Jane Serrano. LC 7-3008. (On cover: Cassell's sunshine series. no. 46). 1890. Cassell Publishing Company.
Uranie. Camille Flammarion. Tr. by Mary Jane Serrano. (On cover: Cassell's sunshine series, no. 46). The Cassell Publishing Co.
Uranium! Bernard Brunner. LC 68-9261. 1968. 6.95. F. Fell.
Uranium Murders. John E Barry. LC 52-16434. 1951. J. Long.
Uranium 235. John E Muller. LC 67-3715. 1967. Arcadia House.
Uranus. Marcel Ayme. (Coll. Soleil). 1962. 13.50. French & Eur.
Urban Affair. Daniel Stern. 288p. (Orig.). 1982. pap. 2.75 (ISBN 0-380-57919-7, 57919). Avon.
Urban Affair: A Novel. Daniel Stern. LC 80-15495. 10.95 (ISBN 0-671-41226-4). Simon and Schuster.
Urban Cowboy. Aaron Latham. 1980. pap. 2.50 (ISBN 0-553-13826-X). Bantam.
Urbane and His Friends. Elizabeth Payson Prentiss. LC 7-30121. A. D. F. Randolph & Company.
Urbane and His Friends. Familiar Talks on Subjects Relating to the Spiritual Life. new and enl. ed. Elizabeth Payson Prentiss. LC 7-30120. A. D. F. Randolph & Company.
Urbane and His Friends. Familiar Talks on Subjects Relating to the Spiritual Life. new and enl. ed. Elizabeth Payson Prentiss. LC 98-163720. A. D. F. Randolph Company.
Urban's Boys. Sigmund H Uminski. LC 70-131212. (Illus.). 1970. 3.00. Polish Publication Society of America.
Urdag: The Aleut. Marvyn Jay Bigelow. LC 54-118761. Vantage Press.
Urge for Justice. John William Wainwright. LC 82-5757. 1982. 10.95 (ISBN 0-312-83527-2). St. Martin's Press.
Urith. A Tale of Dartmoor. authorized ed. Sabine Baring-Gould. LC 6-7198. (On cover: Lovell's international series, no. 143). United States Book Company.
Urkey Island. Wilbur Daniel Steele. LC 26-7016. Harcourt, Brace and Company.
Urshurak. The, Brothers Hildebrandt & Jerry Nichols. 1979. pap. 8.95 (ISBN 0-553-01166-9). Bantam.
Ursula. Honore De Balzac. Tr. by Katharine Prescott Wormeley. LC 3-23197. (Half-title: The comedy of human life... Scenes from provincial life). 1891. Roberts Brothers.
Ursula: A Novel. Robert J. Williams. 4.95 o.p. Ross.
Ursula: A Novel. by Bob Williams. 1st Ed. Robert J Williams. LC 66-29007. 1966. 4.95. Dillon Pr.
Ursula Finch: A Novel. Isabel Constance Clarke. 1920. Benziger Brothers.
Ursula Trent. Walter Lionel George. LC 21-169261. 1921. Harper & Brothers.
Ursula Vivian: The Sister-Mother. american ed. Annie S Swan Smith. LC 8-8622. 1890. Cranston and Stowe.
Ursule Mirouet. Honore De Balzac. Tr. by Donald Adamson. LC 77-455640. (Penguin classics). 1976. 2.95 (ISBN 0-14-044316-9). Penguin.
Ursus Major. Roberta Smoodin. LC 79-22743. 1980. 8.95 (ISBN 0-394-50973-0). Knopf: Distributed by Random House.
Ursus of Ultima Thule. Avram Davidson. (Avon science-fiction). 1973. (pbk.) 0.95. Avon Books.
Us". Kate Mayhew Speake Penney. LC 34-38187. Dorrance & Company, Inc.
US. 288p. 1981. pap. 2.95 (ISBN 0-553-14552-5). Bantam.
Us Fellers. James Dean Mackey. LC 52-13091. 1953. Dorrance.
Us Fellers" Text by Izola L. Forrester, Pictures by B. Cory Kilvert. Izola Louise Forrester. LC 7-320325. 1907. G. W. Jacobs & Company.
Us He Devours: By James B. Hall. James B Hall. LC 64-16821. 1964. New Directions-San Francisco Review.
Us or Them War. William Garner. LC 69-18174. 1969. 5.95. Putnam.
Us Three Women. Roger Wiley & Wood, Helen McGloin, Joint Author. LC 37-7990. The Penn Publishing Company.
U.S.A. Dos Passos, John. LC 63-16593. (Illus.). 1963. Houghton Mifflin.
U.S.A. Dos Passos, John. LC 74-162129. (Penguin modern classics). 1973. 1.35 (ISBN 0-14-002418-2). Penguin.
U.S.A. A Book Devoted to the Younger Writers. Glicksberg, Charles Irving, 1901- Ed. LC 48-1171.
U.S.A. I. The 42nd Parallel. II. Nineteen Nineteen. III. The Big Money. John Dos Passos. LC 39-216774. 1939. The Modern Library.
U.S.A. 1. The 42nd Parallel. 2. Nineteen Nineteen. 3. The Big Money. John Dos Passos. LC 38-27019. Harcourt, Brace and Company.
U.S.A. 1. The 42nd Parallel. 2. Nineteen Nineteen. 3. The Big Money. John Dos Passos. LC 40-375219. 1938. Harcourt, Brace and Company.
Use & Abuse, Repr. Of 1849 Ed. Felicia Mary Frances Skene. Ed. by Robert L. Wolff. Bd. with Hidden Depths. Repr. of 1866 ed. LC 75-474. (Victorian Fiction Ser.). 1975. lib. bdg. 66.00 (ISBN 0-8240-1552-5). Garland Pub.
Use of Riches. John Innes Mackintosh Stewart. (Phoenix Fiction Ser.). 246p. 1957. pap. 6.95 (ISBN 0-226-77403-1). U of Chicago Pr.
Use of Riches: A Novel 1st Ed. John Innes Mackintosh Stewart. LC 57-11242. 1957. Norton.
Useful Lady. Evan John David. The Macaulay Company.
Useless Cowboy. Alan Le May. LC 43-126913. 1943. Farrar & Rinehart, Inc.
Useless Day. Janine Bregeon. LC 68-22017. 1968. 3.50. Grove Press.
Useless Hands. Charles Bargone. LC 74-15969. (Science Fiction Ser). 300p. 1975. Repr. of 1926 ed. 19.00x (ISBN 0-405-06289-3). Ayer Co.
Useless Hands. Claude Farrere. LC 74-15969. (Science Fiction). 1975. 17.00 (ISBN 0-405-06289-3). Arno Press.
Useless Hands. Claude Farrere. Tr. by Abbott, Elisabeth. LC 26-17606. E. P. Dutton & Company.
Users. Joyce Haber. LC 76-22551. 8.95 (ISBN 0-440-09220-5). Delacorte Press.
Uses. James L. Weil. 1974. wrappers 4.00 o.p. (Pub. by Elizabeth Pr). SBD.
Uses & Pleasures of the Rod. Lady Lovebirch. pap. 2.25 o.s.i. (Venus). Grove.
Usha, the Mouse-Maiden. Mehlli Gobhai. LC 69-10913. (Illus.). 1969. 4.25. Hawthorn Books.
Ushaba. Jordan K Ngubane. LC 74-18755. 1974. (ISBN 0-914478-03-6) (ISBN 0-914478-04-4). Three Continents Press.
Ushaba: The Hurtle to Blood River. rev. ed. Jordan K. Ngubane. LC 74-18755. 1979. 15.00 (ISBN 0-914478-80-X); pap. 7.00 (ISBN 0-914478-81-8). Three Continents.
U.S.S. Mudskipper: The Submarine That Wrecked a Train; a Novel. William M Hardy. LC 67-12714. 1967. Dodd, Mead.
Usual Lunacy. David Guy Compton. LC 78-14953. 1978. 3.95 (ISBN 0-89370-225-0). Borgo Press.
Usurper. Harry Harrison Kroll. LC 41-51636. The Bobbs-Merrill Company.
Usurper. William John Locke. LC 1-25427. 1902. J. Lane.
Usurper: An Episode in Japanese History. Judith Gautier. Alger, Abby Langdon, 1850- Tr. LC 7-18761. 1884. Roberts Brothers.
Utah Blaine. Louis L'Amour. LC 79-21612. (Gregg Press Western Fiction Series). (Illus.). 1980. 9.95 (ISBN 0-8398-2693-1). Gregg Press.
Utah Blaine see Complete L'Amour.
Utah Sims. George Parker Milne. LC 40-4223. Phoenix Press.
Utah Spring. Elaine Stienon. LC 79-15774. 8.00 (ISBN 0-8309-0242-2). Herald House.
Utah Vengeance. John Earl Lewis. (YA) 1981. 6.95 (Avalon). Bouregy.
Ute Pass. W J Reynolds. LC 58-696. 1958. Arcadia House.
Ute Revenge. Paul Ledd. 1981. pap. 2.25 (ISBN 0-89083-818-6). Zebra.
Ute's Last Stand. Al Look. (O.s.i.). Orig. Title: Last Massacre. (Illus.). 1972. 5.95 o.s.i. (ISBN 0-87315-055-4). Golden Bell.
Uther and Igraine. Warwick Deeping. LC 3-26168. 1903. The Outlook Company.
Uther and Igraine. Warwick Deeping. LC 28-11712. (Blue jade library). 1928. A. A. Knopf.
Utinam: A Glimmering of Goddesses. William Arkwright. LC 17-13362. 1917. John Lane.
Utmost Fish! ' Hugh Wray McCann. LC 65-125916. 1965. 5.95. S. & S.
Utmost Island. Henry Myers. LC 51-6679. 1951. Crown Publishers.
Utopia. Thomas More. Tr. by Paul Turner. (Classics Ser.). (Orig.). 1965. pap. 2.50 (ISBN 0-14-044165-4). Penguin.
Utopia. Thomas More. Tr. by Peter K. Marshall. pap. 2.25 (ISBN 0-671-42462-9). WSP.
Utopia. Thomas More. Ed. by Edward Surtz. (Selected Works of St. Thomas More Ser.: No. 2). (Illus., Orig.). 1964. 17.50x (ISBN 0-300-00980-1); pap. 4.95x (ISBN 0-300-00238-6, Y119). Yale U Pr.
Utopia Achieved. Herman Hine Brinsmade. LC 74-154431. (Utopian Literature). 1971. (ISBN 0-405-03514-4). Arno Press.
Utopia Achieved: A Novel of the Future. Herman Hine Brinsmade. LC 12-8414. Broadway Publishing Co.
Utopia, Inc. Herman Everett Gieske. LC 41-1056. Forhary. Publishers.
Utopia Three. George Alec Effinger. LC 80-80986. 192p. 1980. pap. 1.95 (ISBN 0-87216-677-5). Playboy Pbks.
Utopia 3. George Alec Effinger. 1980. 1.95 (ISBN 0-87216-677-5). Playboy Press.
Utopian Fantasy, Study of English Utopian Fiction Since the End of the Nineteenth Century. Richard Gebber. 1955. 12.50 o.p. Folcroft.
Utopian Literature, 41 Bks. Ed. by Arthur Orcutt Lewis, Jr. 1971. Set. 688.00 (ISBN 0-405-03510-1). Ayer Co.
Utter Failure: A Novel. Miriam Coles Harris. LC 7-3002. 1891. D. Appleton and Company.
Utter Zoo Alphabet. Edward Gorey. (Illus.). 1967. 4.95 o.p. (ISBN 0-8015-8268-7, Hawthorn). Dutton.
Utterly Depraved. Crosseux Egout. 160p. pap. 1.95 o.p. (MP-113). Montmartre.
Utterly Mistaken. Annie Hall Thomas Cudlip. LC 6-31158. Cassell Publishing Company.
Utterly Wrecked: A Novel of American Coast Life. Henry Morford. LC 8-30892. The American News Company.
Uttermost Farthing. R. Austin Freeman. 1974. 6.50. Bookfinger.
Uttermost Farthing. Marie Adelaide Belloc Lowndes. LC 10-2605. 1910. M. Kennerley.
Uttermost Farthing: A Savant's Vendetta. Richard Austin Freeman. LC 14-623313. 1.20. The John C. Winston Company.

V

V. Thomas Pynchon. 1968. pap. 2.95 (ISBN 0-553-10689-9, 13370-5). Bantam.
V. A Novel. Thomas Pynchon. LC 63-8634. 1963. Lippincott.
V As in Victim. Lawrence Treat. LC 45-9735. 1945. Duell, Sloan and Pearce.
V for Vengeance. Dennis Yates Wheatley. LC 42-15554. 1942. Hutchinson & Co., Ltd.
V for Vengeance. Dennis Yates Wheatley. LC 42-21517. 1942. The Macmillan Company.
V-J Day. Alan Fields, pseud. (Dell Book.). 1978. 2.25 (ISBN 0-440-19250-1). Dell Pub.Co.
V Plan. Graham Seton Hutchison. LC 41-23671. 1941. Smith & Durrell, Inc.
V. V.'s Eyes. Henry Sydnor Harrison. 1913. Houghton Mifflin Company.
V. V.'s Eyes. Henry Sydnor Harrison. LC 16-1256. 1913. Grosset & Dunlap.
Vacancy. Patrick Mann, pseud. 320p. (YA) 1973. 7.95 o.p. (ISBN 0-399-11204-9). Putnam.
Vacancy. Patrick Mann. (Berkley medallion book). 1974. (pbk.) 1.50. Putnam.
Vacancy: A Novel. Leslie Waller. LC 73-78592. 1973. 7.95 (ISBN 0-399-11204-9). Putnam.
Vacancy on India Street: A Novel. Barbara Rex. LC 67-15825. 1967. Norton.
Vacancy with Corpse. Miles Burton. LC 41-6065. 1941. Pub. for the Crime Club by Doubleday, Doran & Company, Inc.
Vacant Niche: Or, Land of Gold... Clarence E Bennett. LC 28-118180. Robson and Adee.
Vacant Throne. David Hanna. (Belmont Tower books). 1979. 2.25. Tower Pubns.
Vacation in a Buggy. Maria Louise Pool. LC 7-381693. 1887. G. P. Putnam's Sons.
Vacation in Space. Leo P. Kelley. LC 78-68232. (Galaxy 5 Ser.: Bk. 3). 1979. pap. 4.24 (ISBN 0-8224-3203-X). Pitman Learning.
Vacation of the Kelwyns: An Idyl of the Middle Eighteen-Seventies. William Dean Howells. LC 20-16794. Harper & Brothers.
Vadim. Mikhail IUrevich Lermontov. Ed. & tr. by Helena Goscilo. 100p. 1983. 15.00 (ISBN 0-88233-682-7). Ardis Pubs.
Vaexande Hot see Growing Terror.
Vagabond. Adam Badeau. LC 6-5038. 1859. Rudd & Carleton.
Vagabond. Sidonie Gabrielle Colette. LC 77-178785. 1973. 10.00 (ISBN 0-8371-6293-9). Greenwood Press.
Vagabond. Frederick Palmer. 1903. C. Scribner's Sons.
Vagabond. A Novel. George Walker. LC 7-3034. 1800. Printed for West and Greenleaf, No., and John West, No., Cornhill, From the Press of John Russell.
Vagabond Cavalry. James Leo Phelan. LC 51-8425. 1951. T. V. Boardman.
Vagabond City. Winifred Boggs. LC 11-254311. 1911. G. P. Putnam's Sons.
Vagabond Fiddler. Darling Simons. LC 34-463194. Robin-Wilder and Company.
Vagabond Hall: A Novel. Arthur Mabb Plyer. LC 44-508. 1943. The Welrad Corporation.
Vagabond Lady. Frank Owen. LC 34-898985. The Macaulay Company.
Vagabond Lover. by charleson gray, from the scenario by james a. creelman, illustrated with scenes from the radio picture starring rudy vallee. ed. Charleston Gray & Creelman, James A. A. L. Burt Company.
Vagabond Lover. Eliza M. J. Humphreys. (On cover: Seaside library. Pocket ed., no. 1237). 1889. G. Munro.
Vagabond Lover: A Novel. Eliza M. J. Humphreys. (On cover: Lovell's international series, no. 15). 1889. F. F. Lovell & Company.
Vagabond of Space. Clark Darlton. (Perry Rhodan Series#93). 1976. (pbk.) 1.25. Ace Books.
Vagabond Path. James Gray. LC 41-21888. 1941. The Macmillan Company.
Vagabond Path. Iris Origo. 1973. 10.95 o.p. (ISBN 0-684-12951-5). Scribner.
Vagabond Tales. Hjalmar Hjorth Boyesen. D. Lothrop Company.
Vagabond. Translated by Enid McLeod. Sidonie Gabrielle Colette. LC 55-5832. 1955. Farrar, Straus and Young.
Vagabonde. Sidonie Gabrielle Colette. 1957. pap. 3.95 (283). French & Eur.
Vagabondia: A Love Story. Frances Hodgson Burnett. LC 6-17246. 1884. J. R. Osgood and Company.
Vagabondia: A Love Story. Frances Hodgson Burnett. LC 6-17245. 1889. C. Scribner's Sons.
Vagabondia: A Love Story. Frances Hodgson Burnett. LC 16-25047. 1909. C. Scribner's Sons.
Vagabonds. Knut Hamsun & Gay-Tifft, Eugene, Tr. LC 30-29561. 1930. Coward-McCann, Inc.
Vagabonds a Novel. Margaret Louisa Bradley Woods. LC 8-37242. 1894. Macmillan and Co.
Vagabond's Way: The Story of Francois Villon. 1st Ed. in the U. S. A. Doris Oppenheim Leslie. LC 62-158871. 1962. Doubleday.
Vagabunden: Three Modern German Stories. Ed. by Wolfgang Paulsen. B. Die Geschichte Eines Amerikanischen Seemanns Traven et al. Ed. by Fred Louis Fehling. LC 50-13114. 1950. Holt.
Vagaries. Florence Brooks Emerson. LC 1-29181. 1900. Small, Maynard & Company.
Vagaries Malicieux. Djuna Barnes. LC 75-5248. 1974. 15.00 o.p. F Hallman.
Vagaries Malicieux: Two Stories. Djuna Barnes. LC 76-355569. 1974. F. Hallman.
Vagaries Malicievex. Djuna Barnes. 1974. 15.00 (Pub. by F Hallman). SBD.
Vagaries of Tod and Peter. Lizzie Allen Harker. LC 23-12444. 1923. C. Scribner's Sons.
Vagor: Or, Vicissitudes of a Vagabond. Joseph McVittie. LC 7-20276. 1891. A. M. Eddy.
Vagrant and Other Tales. Vladimir Galaktionovich Korolenko. Tr. by Delano, Aline P, (Kvz'michova) LC 7-14117. T. Y. Crowell & Co.
Vagrant Duke. George Fort Gibbs. LC 21-976. 1921. D. Appleton and Company.
Vagrant Tune. Bryan T Holland. LC 22-133967. Small, Maynard and Company.
Vagrant Wife. Florence Alice Price James. (On cover: Seaside library. Pocket ed., no. 482). 1885. G. Munro.
Vail's Gate. Joan Cabot. Ed. by Alice Sachs. 1970. 3.95 o.p. Lenox Hill.
Vail's Gate. Jane Corby. 1973. pap. 0.95 o.p. (ISBN 0-532-95245-6). Woodhill.
Vail's Gate: A Gothic Novel. Jane Corby. 1973. (pbk) 0.95. Manor Books.
Vain and the Vainglorious. Katrinka Blickle. LC 80-2324. 1981. 13.95. Doubleday.
Vain Citadels: A Novel. Brian Stanford Morgan. LC 47-12529. 1948. Little, Brown.
Vain Forebodings. Bernahardine Schulze-Smidt. Tr. by Wister, Annie Lee (Furness) LC 8-2054. 1885. J. B. Lippincott Company.
Vain Fortune. George Moore. LC 7-25298. 1892. C Scribner's Sons.
Vain Goddess. Laura Lou Brookman. LC 29-130662. Grosset & Dunlap.
Vain Oblations. Katharine Fullerton Gerould. LC 14-4741. 1914. 1.35. C. Scribner's Sons.
Vain Pantomime: A Novel. Desemea Wilson. E. P. Dutton & Co., Inc.
Vain Shadow: A Romantic Biography of the Discoverer of the Amazon. Hartzell Spence. LC 47-3537. 1947. Whittlesey House, McGraw-Hill Book Company, Inc.

Vainglory. Arthur Annesley Ronald Firbank. LC 25-19902. Brentano's.
Vainglory see Three More Novels.
Vaiti of the Islands. Beatrice Ethel Grimshaw. LC 8-30710. 1908. A. Wessels Company.
Val-Maria. A Romance of the Time of Napoleon I. Francese Hubbard Litchfield Turnbull. LC 8-32320. 1893. J. B. Lippincott Company.
Val of Paradise. Vingie Eve Roe. LC 21-4162. 1921. Dodd, Mead and Company.
Val Sinestra. Martha Morton. LC 25-760. E. P. Dutton & Company.
Val Strange. A Story of the Primrose Way. David Christie Murray. (Harper's Franklin square library, no. 286). 1882. Harper & Brothers.
Val the Tomboy. Florence Blackburn White Schoeffel. (On cover: The laurel library, no. 8). 1892. G. Munro.
Val Verde. Judith Polley. LC 74-13210. 1974. 6.95 (ISBN 0-440-06092-3). Delacorte Press.
Valadero Ranch. Anna Johnson. 1.00. American Tract Society.
Valago Crest. Jean Anne Bartlett. 1.75 (ISBN 0-445-04471-3). Popular Library.
Valao of the South Seas. Jeanne Larson. (Crown Ser.). 128p. 1975. pap. text ed. 3.50 o.p. Review & Herald.
Valao of the South Seas. Jeanne Larson. (Crown Ser.). 128p. 1975. pap. text ed. 3.50 o.p. Southern Pub.
Valarie Scorby and the Big Port: A Novel. Roy Bradford. LC 60-378245. 1960. Lone Star Pub. Co.
Valcour Meets Murder: A Lieutenant Valcour Mystery... Rufus King. LC 32-32767. Pub. for the Crime Club, Inc, by Doubleday, Doran & Company, Inc.
Valdepenas. Richard Lortz. LC 79-66114. 1980. 12.50 (ISBN 0-933256-06-X) (ISBN 0-933256-07-8). Second Chance Press.
Valdez Horses. 1st Ed. Lee Hoffman. LC 67-15208. 1967. 3.95. Doubleday.
Valdez Is Coming. Elmore Leonard. 144p. 1981. pap. 1.75 (ISBN 0-553-13758-1). Bantam.
Valdez Is Coming. Elmore Leonard. (Orig.). 1970. pap. 0.60 o.p. (R2328, GM). Fawcett World.
Valdez Marriage. Violet Winspear. (Harlequin Presents Ser.). 1979. pap. 1.25 (ISBN 0-373-70788-6, Pub. by Harlequin). PB.
Valdez, the Pirate: Or, Scenes off Long Island. Jack Brace. H. Long & Brother.
Valdoro's Mistress. Evelyn Stewart Armstrong. LC 77-356883. (Troubadour). 1976. 3.75 (ISBN 0-354-04050-2). Macdonald and Jane's.
Vale of Aragon. Fred McLaughlin. LC 29-17917. The Bobbs-Merrill Co.
Vale of Cedars: Or, The Martyr. Grace Aguilar. LC 31-19529. 1850. D. Appleton and Company.
Vale of Cedars: Or, The Martyr. Grace Aguilar. LC 7-1627. 1851. D. Appleton & Company.
Vale of Illusion. Lorraine Catlin Brower. LC 15-7365. 1915. The Reilly & Britton Co.
Vale of Laughter. Peter De Vries. LC 67-11236. 1967. Little, Brown.
Vale of Shadows. Alexandre Erixon. LC 8-31156. Broadway Publishing Company.
Vale of Tyranny. 1st Ed. Suzanne Butler. LC 54-8279. 1954. Little, Brown.
Valedictory. Frank Rooney. LC 74-8371. 1974. 6.95. Harcourt Brace Jovanovich.
Valencia. Leon Tahcheechee. Coward-McCann.
Valencia's Garden. Mary Bradford Crowninshield. LC 1-7288. 1901. McClure, Phillips & Co.
Valentin and Number Seventeen. new ed. with a frontispiece by r. caton woodville. ed. Henry Kingsley. LC 6-13687. 1899. Longmans, Green & Co.
Valentin Mankin. V. Kukushkin. 48p. 1979. pap. 2.95 (ISBN 0-8285-1752-5, Pub. by Progress Pubs USSR). Imported Pubns.
Valentina. Fern Michaels. 1981. pap. 2.75 (ISBN 0-345-29580-3). Ballantine.
Valentina: By Evelyn Anthony. 1st Ed. in the U.S.A. Eve Stephens, pseud. LC 66-20986. 1966. 4.50. Doubleday.
Valentine. Grant I. E. Franklin Thomas Grant Richards. LC 13-22099. 1913. Houghton Mifflin Company.
Valentine: A Novel. Leon Gozlan. Tr. by Mead, Leon. LC 6-27647. (On cover: United service library of original fiction. v. 1, no. 2). 1889. The United Service Publishing Company.
Valentine Estate. Stanley Ellin. LC 68-28541. 1968. 5.95. Random House.
Valentine for Noel. Emmett Williams. LC 73-78692. 1973. pap. 10.00 (ISBN 0-87110-107-6). Ultramarine Pub.
Valentine M'Clutchy, the Irish Agent. William Carleton. LC 78-14007. (Ireland, from the Act of Union, 1800, to the Death of Parnell, 1891). (Illus.). 1979. 32.00 (ISBN 0-8240-3489-9). Garland Pub.
Valentine M'Clutchy, the Irish Agent: The Chronicles of Castle Cumber Property, with the Pious Aspirations of Solomon M'Slime, 3 vols. in 2. William Carleton. LC 79-8247. Repr. of 1845 ed. 84.50 set (ISBN 0-404-61807-3). AMS Pr.
Valentine Strange. A Story of the Primrose Way. David Christie Murray. (On cover: Seaside library. Pocket ed., no. 691). 1886. G. Munro.
Valentine Victim. Dougal McLeish. LC 69-12443. 1969. 4.95. Houghton Mifflin.
Valentine Vox. Henry Cockton. LC 42-35612. The Walter Scott Publishing Co., Ld.
Valentino. An Historical Romance of the Sixteenth Century in Italy. William Waldorf Astor Astor. LC 6-4534. 1885. C. Scribner's Sons.
Valerie. Valerie Chronis. pap. 3.00. Anhinga Pr.
Valerie. Winifred Mary Scott. LC 36-5873. 1938. Doubleday, Doran and Co., Inc.
Valerie. Joan Smith. 224p. 1981. pap. 1.95 (ISBN 0-449-50193-0, Coventry). Fawcett.
Valerie. An Autobiography. Frederick Marryat. LC 7-24676. (Seaside library. v. 55. no. 1116). 1881. G. Munro.
Valerie Aylmer. A Novel. Frances Christine Tiernan. LC 9-2482. 1870. D. Appleton and Company.
Valerie Hathaway. Claudius Gregory. LC 34-446. 1934. Sears Publishing Company.
Valerie Trent. Vida Hurst. 1949. Gramercy Pub. Co.
Valerie's Fate. Annie French Hector. (On cover: Lovell's library, v. 7, no. 349). 1884. J. W. Lovell Company.
Valerie's Fate. Annie French Hector. (On cover: Seaside library. Pocket ed., no. 189). 1884. G. Munro.
Valerie's Wilderness Adventure. Regina Lambert. LC 78-9027. 1978. 2.95 (ISBN 0-8024-3936-5). Moody.
Valerius: A Roman Story... John Gibson Lockhart. 1821. Wells and Lilly.
Valery, Jeune Poete. 1 Ed. Charles G Whiting. LC 60-50663. 1960. Yale University Press.
Valga Krusa. Charles Potts. LC 77-76164. 1977. pap. 7.77 (ISBN 0-915214-19-9). Litmus.
Valhalla. Newton Thornburg. LC 80-20985. 10.95 (ISBN 0-316-84393-8). Little, Brown.
Valhalla: A Novel. Jere Peacock. LC 61-5706. Putnam.
Valhalla Exchange. Henry Patterson. LC 76-44293. (Illus.). 1976. 8.95 (ISBN 0-8128-1932-2). Stein and Day.
Valhalla Exchange. Henry Patterson. LC 77-9599. 1977. 11.95 (ISBN 0-8161-6496-7). G. K. Hall.
Valhalla Exchange. Henry Patterson. (Fawcett Crest Book). (Illus.). 1978. 2.25 (ISBN 0-449-23449-5). Fawcett Pub.
Valhalla Seven: Women's Fiction. Ed. by Rochelle H. Dubois. (Illus.). 55p. (Orig.). 1981. pap. 2.50 o.p. (ISBN 0-934536-05-8). Merging Media.
Valhalla Six Lifespan. Ed. by Rochelle H. Dubois & Diane C. Erdmann. (Literary Magazine Ser.). (Illus.). 1980. pap. 3.50 o.p. (ISBN 0-934536-02-3). Merging Media.
Valiant. Sigman Byrd & John E. Sutherland. LC 55-8607. 1955. Jason Press.
Valiant and the Damned. Roy Clews. (Signet Book). 1977. 1.75 (ISBN 0-451-07539-0). New American Library.
Valiant and the Wasted. Leo O Miller. 1975. (pbk.) 1.25 (ISBN 0-523-00530-X). Pinnacle Books.
Valiant: By William MacLeod Raine. William MacLeod Raine. LC 30-9313. 1930. Doubleday, Doran & Company.
Valiant Coward. Y. Esther Livingston. LC 51-1776. Dorrance.
Valiant Dust. Helen Genung & Hayes, Caryl May. LC 36-21345. L. Furman, Inc.
Valiant Dust. Katharine Fullerton Gerould. LC 22-22699. 1922. C. Scribnerhs Sons.
Valiant Dust. Percival Christopher Wren. LC 32-24663. 1932. Frederick A. Stokes Company.
Valiant Dust: A Novel. Margaret Mackprang Mackay. LC 41-21403. The John Day Company.
Valiant Gentleman: By M. J. Stuart Pseud. Kathleen Mary Aguller. LC 25-1964. Small, Maynard & Company.
Valiant Heart. Eva Mabel Tenison. LC 21-978. 1920. E. S. Gorham.
Valiant Heart: By George Blake. George Blake. LC 40-6199. 1940. A.A. Knopf.
Valiant Hearts. Albert Boardman Kerr. LC 36-12317. The Stratford Company.
Valiant Is the Word for Carrie. Barry Benefield. LC 35-19873. Reynal & Hitchcock.
Valiant Lady: A Novel. Kathleen Henrietta Nash-Webber Sinclair. LC 48-5167. 1948. Doubleday.
Valiant Lady: A Novel. 1st American Ed. Brigid Knight. LC 48-5167. 1948. Doubleday.
Valiant Libertine. John Gordon Bryson. LC 42-10684. 1942. D. Appleton-Century Company, Incorporated.
Valiant Ones. Norman A Fox. LC 57-12131. (Silver star westerns). 1957. Dodd, Mead.
Valiant Papers. Calvin Miller. LC 81-19724. (Illus.). 5.95 (ISBN 0-310-29291-3). Zondervan Pub. House.
Valiant Runaways. Gertrude Franklin Horn Atherton. LC 98-1179. 1898. Dodd, Mead and Company.
Valiant Sailors. V. A. Stuart. (Hazard: No. 1). 1979. pap. 1.75 (ISBN 0-523-40481-6). Pinnacle Bks.
Valiant Virginians. James Warner Bellah. LC 53-11281. (Illus.). 1953. Ballantine Books.
Valiant Wife. Margaret Wilson. LC 34-5692. 1934. Doubleday, Doran & Company, Inc.
Valiant Wings. Rebecca Drury. (Women at War Ser.: No. 13). (Orig.). 1983. pap. 3.25 (ISBN 0-440-09243-4). Dell.
Valiant Woman. Sheila Kaye-Smith. LC 38-32230. 1938. Harper & Brothers.
Valiant Women. Dorothy Jeanne Williams. LC 80-133823. (Arizona Saga; V. 1). 2.75 (ISBN 0-671-82536-4). Pocket Books.
Valiants of Virginia. Hallie Erminie Rives. LC 26-22313. A. L. Burt Company.
Valiants of Virginia. Hallie Erminie Rives. LC 12-271942. The Bobbs-Merrill Company.
Valid for All Countries. Desmond O'Grady. 1979. 14.95x (ISBN 0-7022-1368-3); pap. 7.95x (ISBN 0-7022-1369-1). U of Queensland Pr.
Valid for All Countries: Stories. Desmond O'Grady. LC 79-322495. 1979. 9.75 (ISBN 0-7022-1368-3) (ISBN 0-7022-1369-1). University of Queensland Press.
Valis. Philip K. Dick. 240p. (Orig.). 1981. pap. 2.25 (ISBN 0-553-14156-2). Bantam.
Valkyrie Encounter. Stephen Marlowe. LC 77-11177. 7.95 (ISBN 0-399-12068-8). Putnam.
Valkyrie Encounter. Stephen Marlowe. (Jove/HBJ Book). 1978. 1.95 (ISBN 0-515-04705-8). Jove Publications.
Valkyrie Mandate. Robert Vaughan. LC 73-16880. 1974. 6.95 (ISBN 0-671-27116-4). Simon and Schuster.
Valkyrie Mandate. Robert Vaughan. 1975. (pbk.) 1.50 (ISBN 0-671-78870-1). Pocket Books.
Valkyrie Project. Michael Kilian. LC 81-8823. 1981. 13.95 (ISBN 0-312-83607-4). St. Martin's Press.
Valla: The Story of a Sea Lion. Dean Southern Jennings. LC 74-85933. (Illus.). 1970. 4.95. World Pub. Co.
Vallejo Kitty. Ann Knox. LC 29-17218. 2.50. The Century Co.
Vallency Tradition. Gordon Merrick. LC 55-984754. 1955. J. Messner.
Vallette Heritage. Louisa Bronte. LC 77-91250. (Jove/HBJ Book). 1978. 2.25 (ISBN 0-515-04309-5). Jove Pub.
Valley. Eric Alter. 496p. (Orig.). 1982. pap. 2.95 (ISBN 0-446-90086-9). Warner Bks.
Valley. Nathan Asch. LC 35-14573. 1935. The Macmillan Company.
Valley. Elizabeth Clarke. 1971. 3.95 o.p. (ISBN 0-571-09140-7, Pub. by Faber & Faber). Merrimack Pub Cir.
Valley. Joel Kotkin. (Orig.). pap. 8.95 (ISBN 0-88496-189-3). Capra Pr.
Valley: A Novel. Joel Kotkin. LC 82-4301. 1982. 15.95 (ISBN 0-88496-185-0). Capra Press.
Valley: A Novel. 1st Ed. Clifford Irving. LC 61-11651. 1961. McGraw-Hill.
Valley Below. Brett Hagen. 3.75 o.p. Vantage.
Valley Beyond. William Byron Mowery. LC 38-25513. 1938. Doubleday, Doran and Company, Inc.
Valley Beyond. William Byron Mowery. LC 40-12431. 1940. The Sun Dial Press.
Valley Beyond Time. William Vaughan Wilkins. LC 55-9053. 1955. St. Martin's Press.
Valley Boy. Theodore Pratt. LC 46-25055. 1946. Duell, Sloan and Pearce.
Valley Called Disappointment. Robert Bell. 128p. 1982. pap. 1.95 (ISBN 0-345-30076-9). Ballantine.
Valley Far. Carlisle C. Smith. 192p. 1975. 7.50 o.p. (ISBN 0-682-48320-6). Exposition.
Valley Forge. MacKinlay Kantor. 1976. 1.95 (ISBN 0-345-25270-5). Ballatine Books.
Valley Forge. James Alvin Sullivan. LC 64-15902. 1964. Dorrance.
Valley Forge: A Novel. MacKinlay Kantor. LC 75-20057. 1975. 9.95 (ISBN 0-87131-197-6). M. Evans: Distributed by Lippincott.
Valley Forge: A Tale. Alden Walker Quimby. Eaton & Mains.
Valley Gold. Harold Bindloss. LC 34-4067. 1934. Frederick A. Stokes Company.
Valley in Arms: A Novel of the Settlement of Connecticut. by earl schenck miers. ed. Earl Schenck Miers. LC 43-5802. 1943. The Westminster Press.
Valley is Bright. Nell Collins & Mary Beth Moster. 102p. 1983. pap. 4.95 (ISBN 0-8407-5835-9). Nelson.
Valley of a Thousand Hills. F. E. Mills Young. LC 14-183095. 1914. John Lane Company.
Valley of Adventure. Jackson Gregory. LC 35-2776. 1935. Dodd, Mead & Company.
Valley of Adventure: A Romance of California Mission Days. George Washington Ogden. LC 26-154734. 1926. A. C. McClurg & Co.
Valley of Areana. Arthur Preston Hankins. LC 23-13004. 1923. Dodd, Mead and Company.
Valley of Bones. Anthony Dymoke Powell. LC 64-17472. (His The music of time). 1964. Little, Brown.
Valley of Content. Blanche Upright. LC 22-12631. W. J. Watt & Company.
Valley of Creation. Edmond Hamilton. (Orig.). pap. 0.60 o.p. (73-577). Lancer.
Valley of Creeping Men. Rayburn Crawley. LC 30-14875. 1930. Harper & Brothers.
Valley of Death. by herbert shappiro. ed. Herbert Arthur, pseud. LC 42-2913. 1941. Areadin House.
Valley of Death. Stuart Jason. (Butcher,#11). 1974. (pbk.) 0.95 (ISBN 0-523-00332-3). Pinnacle Books.
Valley of Death. Herbert Shappiro. LC 42-2913. 1941. Arcadia House, Inc.
Valley of Decision. Marcia Gluck Davenport. LC 42-235934. 1942. C. Scribner's Sons.
Valley of Decision. Marcia Gluck Davenport. LC 78-74648. 1979. 15.00 (ISBN 0-8376-0427-3). R. Bentley.
Valley of Decision. Margaret Flint. LC 37-233493. 1937. Dodd, Mead & Company.
Valley of Decision: A Novel. Edith Newbold Jones Wharton. LC 74-8770. Scholarly Press.
Valley of Decision: A Novel. Edith Newbold Jones Wharton. LC 79-126661. 1970. (ISBN 0-404-06914-2). AMS Press.
Valley of Decision: A Novel. Edith Newbold Jones Wharton. LC 2-60765. 1902. C. Scribner's Sons.
Valley of Desire. 1st Ed. Adel Pryor, pseud. LC 67-172282. 1967. bds., 2.50. Zondervan.
Valley of Dry Bones. Arthur Henry Gooden. LC 45-1078. 1945. Houghton Mifflin Company.
Valley of Eagles: A Novel. Dexter Allen. LC 57-7053. 1957. Coward-McCann.
Valley of Exile. Lilian Faith Loveday Prior. LC 40-7425. 1940. Harrison-Hilton Books, Inc.
Valley of Eyes Unseen. Gilbert Collins. LC 23-17119. 1923. Duckworth and Co.
Valley of Fear. Arthur Conan Doyle. LC 76-27106. (Illus.). 1977. 7.95 (ISBN 0-385-12284-5). Doubleday.
Valley of Fear. Arthur Conan Doyle. LC 76-27106. 1977. 7.95 o.p. (ISBN 0-385-12284-5). Doubleday.
Valley of Fear: A Sherlock Holmes Novel. Arthur Conan Doyle. LC 15-26136. George H. Doran Company.
Valley of Fear: A Sherlock Holmes Novel. Arthur Conan Doyle. LC 21-13708. 1920. A. L. Burt Company.
Valley of Getians. Margaret Rome. (Harlequin Romances Ser.). 192p. 1982. pap. 1.50 (ISBN 0-373-02513-0). Harlequin Bks.
Valley of Ghosts. Edgar Wallace. LC 23-133227. Small, Maynard & Company.
Valley of God. Irene Patai. LC 56-5205. 1956. Random House.
Valley of Gold. Earle E Perrenot. LC 50-538006. 1949. Phoenix Press.
Valley of Gold: A Tale of the Saskatchewan. David Howarth. LC 21-21367. Fleming H. Revell Company.
Valley of Golden Tombs. Warren T. Longtree. (Ruff Justice Ser.: No. 5). Date not set. pap. 2.50 (ISBN 0-451-11563-5, AE1563, Sig). NAL.
Valley of Grim Men. Clement Yore. LC 34-38721. The Macaulay Company.
Valley of Guns. Wayne D Overholser. LC 53-5925. 1953. Macmillan.
Valley of Guns. Wayne D Overholser. 1974. (pbk.) 0.95. Dell.
Valley of Headstrong Men. Joseph Smith Fletcher. LC 23-1208. 1921. Hodder and Stoughton.
Valley of Headstrong Men. Joseph Smith Fletcher. LC 24-9357. 1924. George H. Doran Company.
Valley of Horses: Earth's Children. Jean M. Auel. 512p. 1982. 15.95 (ISBN 0-517-54489-X). Crown.
Valley of Hunted Men. Paul Evan Lehman. Green Circle Books.
Valley of Judgment. Kenneth West. LC 25-4602. The Roxburgh Publishing Company, Incorporated.
Valley of Lebanon. Helen Saunders Smith Wright. LC 16-15661. 1916. R. J. Shores.
Valley of Light. 1st Ed. Glennie V Patterson. LC 55-718055. 1955. Vantage Press.
Valley of Love... William Lee Popham. LC 10-23668. 0.50. Printed by Westerfield-Bonte Co.
Valley of Missing Men. Lynn Gunnison. LC 25-18056. 1925. 2.00. A. C. McClurg & Co.
Valley of Night: Being an Episode in the Career of Jasper Shrig of Bow Street, with Particulars of His Highly Original Methods in the Wrybrook Case, Set Down. Jeffery Farnol. LC 42-21965. 1942. Doubleday, Doran and Company, Inc.

Valley of Peace. Lida Lavinia Coghlan. LC 25-3. 1925. B. Herder Book Co.
Valley of Power. Eleanor Buckles. LC 45-8891. 1945. Creative Age Press.
Valley of Regret. Adelaide Holt. LC 11-11218. 1911. 1.50. John Lane.
Valley of Revenge. Jackson Cole, pseud. LC 43-22858.
Valley of Revenge. Oscar Schisgall. LC 43-22858. 1944. Arcadia House, Inc.
Valley of Romance. Jean Woodward. 1976. 4.95. Avalon Books.
Valley of St. Ives. Arthur Herbert Bryant. LC 49-7214.
Valley of Secrets. Elizabeth Renier. 208p. 1981. pap. 1.95 (ISBN 0-441-85912-7). Ace Bks.
Valley of Shadows. Francis Grierson. Ed. by Harold P. Simonson. (Masterworks of Literature Ser.). 1970. 6.00x (ISBN 0-8084-0309-5); pap. 3.45x (ISBN 0-8084-0310-9, M28). Coll & U Pr.
Valley of Shadows. easy eye ed. Delphine C. Lyons. (Orig.). 1968. pap. 0.75 o.p. (74-929). Lancer.
Valley of Shadows. Delphine C. Lyons. (Orig.). 1972. pap. 0.95 o.s.i. (75-358). Lancer.
Valley of Shenandoah: Or, Memoirs of the Graysons. George Fox Tucker. LC 70-123106. (Southern literary classics series). 1970. (pbk) 4.25. University of North Carolina Press.
Valley of Shenandoah: Or, Memoirs of the Graysons... 2d ed. George Fox Tucker. 1828. O. A. Roorbach.
Valley of Shenandoah or the Memoirs of the Graysons. George Fox Tucker. (Southern Literary Classics Ser). (Orig.). 1970. 7.95x o.p. (ISBN 0-8078-1143-2). U of NC Pr.
Valley of Silent Men: A Story of the Three River Country. James Oliver Curwood. LC 20-15535. 1920. Cosmopolitan Book Corporation.
Valley of Silent Men: A Story of the Three River Country. James Oliver Curwood. LC 31-18075. 1923. Grosset & Dunlap.
Valley of Silent Men: A Story of the Three River Country. James Oliver Curwood. LC 43-2715. 1943. Triangle Books.
Valley of Skulls. John Benteen. (Fargo Ser.: No. 8). 160p. 1982. pap. 1.95 (ISBN 0-505-51803-1). Tower Bks.
Valley of Skulls. John Benteen. (Fargo No. Eight Ser). (Orig.). 1970. pap. 0.75 o.p. (B75-2057). Belmont-Tower.
Valley of Skulls. John Benteen. (Fargo Ser.). (O.s.i.). 1972. pap. 0.75 o.s.i. (BT 50249). Belmont-Tower.
Valley of Smugglers: A Napoleon Bonaparte Story. Arthur William Upfield. LC 60-11392. 1960. Published for the Crime Club by Doubleday.
Valley of Strife. Marshall R Hall. LC 25-11039. Small, Maynard & Company.
Valley of Suspicion. John Ulrich Giesy. LC 27-13658. (On cover: Western series. no. 15). 1927. Garden City Publishing Co., Inc.
Valley of the Assassins. Ian MacAlister. (Fawcett Gold Medal Book). 1976. (pbk.) 1.25. Fawcett.
Valley of the Brave. Maulsby N. Blackman. 1966. 6.00 o.p. (ISBN 0-8059-0033-0). Dorrance.
Valley of the Dolls. Jacqueline Susann. (Q3597). 1967. pap., 1.25. Bantam.
Valley of the Dolls: A Novel. Jacqueline Susann. LC 66-13705. bds., 5.95. Geis; Dist. Random.
Valley of the Dolls: A Novel. special 15th anniversary ed.. ed. Jacqueline Susann. LC 81-204091. 1981. 5.95 (ISBN 0-937858-02-1). Newmarket Home Library.
Valley of the Giants. Peter Bernard Kyne. LC 18-188878. 1918. Doubleday, Page & Company.
Valley of the Giants. Peter Bernard Kyne. LC 21-17628. 1920. Grosset & Dunlap.
Valley of the Giants. Peter Bernard Kyne. LC 44-784419. 1944. Triangle Books.
Valley of the Hunted Men: Calamity Range. Paul Evan Lehman. (Double Western Ser.). 1979. pap. 2.25 o.s.i. (ISBN 0-8439-0679-0, Leisure Bks). Nordon Pubns.
Valley of the Kings. Arthur Henry Gooden. LC 35-15466. 1935. H. C. Kinsey & Company, Inc.
Valley of the Kings... Marmaduke William Pickthall. LC 26-27440. 1926. A. A. Knopf.
Valley of the Kings: A Novel of Tutankhamun. Elizabeth Eliot Carter. LC 77-5157. 7.95. Dutton.
Valley of the Moon. Jack London. LC 75-19138. (His Jack London centennial series; no. 1). 1975. 10.95 (ISBN 0-87905-050-0) (ISBN 0-87905-051-9). Peregrine Smith.
Valley of the Moon. Jack London. LC 75-19137. (His Jack London centennial series; no. 1). 1975. (ISBN 0-87905-051-9). Peregrine Smith.
Valley of the Moon. Jack London. LC 13-22812. 1913. The Macmillan Company.
Valley of the Moon. Jack London. LC 29-25269. Grosset & Dunlap.
Valley of the Passions. Paula Fairman. 352p. (Orig.). 1982. pap. 3.25 (ISBN 0-523-41749-7). Pinnacle Bks.
Valley of the Poor. Wertie Clarice Weaver. LC 45-6560. 1945. Wetzel Publishing Co., Inc.
Valley of the Ravens. Nancy Buckingham. LC 73-7179. 1973. 5.95. Hawthorn Books.
Valley of the Ravens. Nancy Buckingham. 1976. (pbk.) 1.25 (ISBN 0-523-00838-4). Pinnacle Books.
Valley of the Shadow. Brian Wynne Garfield. LC 75-89115. (Doubleday western). 1970. 4.50. Doubleday.
Valley of the Shadow. Charles Marquis Warren. LC 48-8339. 1948. Doubleday.
Valley of the Silent Men. James O. Curwood. 1976. Repr. of 1920 ed. lib. bdg. 15.95x (ISBN 0-88411-857-6). Amereon Ltd.
Valley of the Sky. Hobert Douglas Skidmore. LC 44-6671. 1944. Houghton Mifflin Company.
Valley of the Squinting Windows. Brinsley MacNamara. LC 19-806797. 1919. Brentano's.
Valley of the Squinting Windows. A. E. Weldon. LC 19-8067. 1919. Brentano's.
Valley of the Squinting Windows. By Brinsley MacNamara Pseud. A. E. Weldon. 1966. pap., 1.25. Anvil Bks.
Valley of the Stars. Louis Arthur Cunningham. LC 38-3531. The Penn Publishing Company.
Valley of the Stars. Charles Alden Seltzer. LC 26-9323. The Century Co.
Valley of the Sun. Clarence Budington Kelland. LC 40-27716. Harper & Brothers.
Valley of the Sun. William K McCoy. LC 22-13324. H. K. Fly Company.
Valley of the Tyrant. Dick Pearce, pseud. LC 51-20340. (Handi-book western, 125). 1951. Quinn Pub. Co.
Valley of the Vanished Men. C. William Harrison. (Orig.). 1973. pap. 0.75 o.p. (07290). Curtis.
Valley of the Vanishing Men. Max Brand. 1981. pap. 1.95 (ISBN 0-671-83310-3). PB.
Valley of the Vapours. Janet Dailey. LC 77-357207. 1976. 1.95 (ISBN 0-263-06097-7). Mills & Boon.
Valley of the Vines: A Novel. Joy Petersen Packer. LC 55-11318. 1956-1955. Lippincott.
Valley of Thunder. Rex Ellingwood Beach. LC 39-25044. Farrar & Rinehart, Inc.
Valley of Time. Gregory Wilson, pseud. LC 66-12242. 1967. Doubleday.
Valley of Twisted Trails. Wilbur C Tuttle. LC 31-20654. 1931. Houghton Mifflin Company.
Valley of Vanishing Herds: A Hashknife Hartley Story. Wilbur C Tuttle. LC 42-19560. 1942. Houghton Mifflin Company.
Valley of Vanishing Men. Frederick Faust. 1973. (pbk.) 0.75. Pocket Books.
Valley of Vanishing Riders. Norman A Fox. LC 46-3591. 1946. Dodd & Mead & Company.
Valley of Violence: A Western Novel. Louis Trimble. LC 48-8405. 1948. Macrae-Smith-Co.
Valley of Vision. Sarah Comstock. LC 19-5818. 1919. Doubleday, Page & Company.
Valley of Vision. Vardis Fisher. 3.95 o.p.; pap. 1.95 o.p. (13). Swallow.
Valley of Vision: A Book of Romance, and Some Half-Told Tales. Henry Van Dyke. LC 19-4519. 1919. C. Scribner's Sons.
Valley of Vision: A Novel of King Solomon and His Time. 1st Ed. Vardis Fisher. LC 51-10836. 1951. Abelard Press.
Valley of Voices. George Tracy Marsh. LC 24-23084. 1924. The Penn Publishing Company.
Valley of Vultures: John Eagle, Expeditor No. 5. Paul Edwards. (Orig.). 1973. pap. 0.95 o.p. (N3183). Pyramid Pubns.
Valley of Vye-Vye: A Novel. Rufus M. Reed. 1979. 8.50 o.p. (ISBN 0-682-49483-6). Exposition.
Valley of Wanted Men. Edward Beverly Mann. LC 32-222073. 1932. W. Morrow & Co.
Valley of Wild Horses. Grey, Zane. (Great western edition 45). 1962. Grosset & Dunlap.
Valley of Wild Horses. Zane Grey. LC 72-1475. 1972. 9.95 (ISBN 0-8161-6036-8). G. K. Hall.
Valley of Wild Horses. Zane Grey. LC 47-39285. 1947. Harper & Brothers.
Valley of Wolves. Laurie York Erskine. LC 40-14689. 1940. D. Appleton-Century Company, Incorporated.
Valley of Yesterday. Cleo M. Stephens. LC 63-6706. 1963. Avalon Books.
Valley of Yesterday: A Novel of Our Pioneers. Stella Rybacki. LC 70-145973. (Illus.). 1971. 3.50. William-Frederick Press.
Valley of Yesterday: A Novel of Our Pioneers. LC 58-8472. 1960. William-Frederick Press.
Valley Path. William Allen Dromgoole. LC 6-34216. 1898. Estes and Lauriat.
Valley People. Frances Marion. LC 70-144161. (Short story index reprint series). 1971. (ISBN 0-8369-3776-7). Books for Libraries Press.
Valley People... Frances Marion. LC 35-10851. Reynal & Hitchcock.
Valley Ranch. Archie Joscelyn. LC 43-11847. 1943. Phoenix Press.
Valley Road. Mary Hallock Foote. LC 15-18105. 1915. Houghton Mifflin Company.
Valley Thieves. large print ed. Max Brand. LC 81-2048. 1981. 11.95 (ISBN 0-89340-323-7). J. Curley.
Valley Vixen. Ben Ames Williams. LC 48-3947. (New Avon library, 153). 1948. Avon Book Co.
Valley Vultures. Max Brand. LC 32-174936. 1932. Dodd, Mead & Company.
Valley Vultures. Max Brand. (Paperback Lib. western 64-987). 1972. Warner Paperback Lib.
Valley Vultures. Frederick Faust. LC 32-1749. 1932. Dodd, Mead & Company.
Valley Waters. Charles David Stewart. LC 22-20877. E. P. Dutton & Company.
Valley Where Time Stood Still. Lin Carter. LC 73-22803. 1974. 4.95 (ISBN 0-385-04232-9). Doubleday.
Valleys Beyond. E. V. Timms. 1975. pap. 1.25 o.p. (ISBN 0-515-03611-0, V3611). BJ Pub Group.
Valleys Beyond. E. V. Timms. 1968. pap. 1.80 o.s.i. Tri-Ocean.
Valleys of Destiny. Dorothy Yates Wilson. LC 67-30759. (Illus.). 1968. Dorrance.
Valmond the Crank. The Forbidden Book. Samuel E. Wells. The Original Publishing Company.
Valor of Francesco D'amini. Dominic N. Certo. (Orig.). 1979. pap. 2.25 (ISBN 0-532-23111-2). Woodhill.
Valor of the Range. Laurie York Erskine. LC 25-17342. 1925. D. Appleton and Company.
Valor. 1st Ed. Denys Arthur Rayner. Holt.
Valour: A Novel. Warwick Deeping. LC 34-270722. 1934. R. M. McBride & Company.
Valparaiso. Nicolas Freeling. LC 65-14662. 1965. Harper & Row.
Valse Macabre. 1st Ed. Kathleen Moore Knight. LC 52-11008. 1952. Published for the Crime Club by Doubleday.
Valserine: And Other Stories. Marguerite Audoux. LC 73-110178. (Short story index reprint series). 1970. Books for Libraries Press.
Valserine & Other Stories. facsimile ed. Marguerite Audoux. LC 73-110178. (Short Story Index Reprint Ser.). 1912. 16.00 (ISBN 0-8369-3329-X). Ayer Co.
Value of Nothing: A Novel. John Weitz. LC 75-87957. 1970. 6.95 (ISBN 0-8128-1275-1). Stein and Day.
Vamos a Ver. Helena Valenti. 1972. pap. 4.95 (ISBN 0-912022-31-0). EMC.
Vamp till Ready. Paul R Milton. LC 31-29957. 1931. The Mohawk Press, Inc.
Vamp till Ready: 1st Ed. Terry Rieman. LC 54-10081. 1954. Harper.
Vampire. Hanns Heinz Ewers. Tr. by Sallagar, Fritz. LC 34-30867. The John Day Company.
Vampire and Other Stories. Lavinia Leitch Hynd. LC 27-23508. The Christopher Publishing House.
Vampire Cameo. easy eye ed. Dorothea Nile, pseud. (Orig.). pap. 0.60 o.p. (73-706). Lancer.
Vampire Chase. Stephen Brett. (Orig.). 1979. pap. 1.75 (ISBN 0-532-17217-5). Woodhill.
Vampire Curse. Daoma Winston. (Orig.). 1971. pap. 0.60 o.p. (ISBN 0-446-63031-4, 63-031). Paperback Lib.
Vampire: His Kith & Kin. Ed. by Montague Summers. 7.95 o.p. (ISBN 0-8216-0039-7). Univ Bks.
Vampire of Curitiba and Other Stories. Dalton Trevisan. LC 72-2246. 1972. 7.95 (ISBN 0-394-46645-4). Knopf.
Vampire of Mons. Desmond Stewart. 1977. 1.50 (ISBN 0-380-01681-8). Avon.
Vampire of Mons. Desmond Stirling Stewart. LC 76-372789. 1976. 3.50 (ISBN 0-241-89402-6). Hamilton.
Vampire of N'Gobi. Ridgwell Cullum. J. B. Lippincott Company.
Vampire Tapes. Arabella Randolphe. (Berkley Medallion Book.). 1977. 1.75. Berkley Pub. Corp.
Vampire Tapestry. Suzy McKee Charnas. LC 80-237. 10.95 (ISBN 0-671-25415-4). Simon and Schuster.
Vampire Tapestry. Suzy M. Charnos. 1981. pap. 2.75 (ISBN 0-671-83484-3). PB.
Vampire Women. Victor Samuels. 1973. (pbk.) 0.95. Popular Library.
Vampires. John Rechy. LC 70-155123. 1971. 6.95 (ISBN 0-394-47585-2). Grove Press.
Vampires and the Witch. Lee Falk. (Adventures of the Phantom). 1974. (pbk.) 0.95. Avon.
Vampires at Midnight. Ed. by Peter Hainig. Orig. Title: Midnight People. 1970. Repr. of 1968 ed. 4.95 o.p. (1986). G&D.
Vampires at Midnight: Seventeen Brilliant and Chilling Tales of the Ghastly Bloodsucking Undead. Ed. by Peter Haining. LC 76-119041. 1970. 4.95. Grosset & Dunlap.
Vampires Ltd. Stories of Science and Fantasy. Tr. from Czech by Iris Urwin. Josef Nesvadba. LC 65-648. (Artia pocket bks.). pap., 1.40. Artia.
Vampires; Mademoiselle Reseda. Julie Grinnell Storrow Cruger. LC 6-31183. 1891. J. B. Lippincott Company.
Vampire's Moon. Peter Saxon. 1970. pap. 0.75 o.p. (B75-1095). Belmont-Tower.
Vampires of the Andes. Henry Carew. LC 77-84206. (Lost Race and Adult Fantasy Fiction). 1978. 20.00 (ISBN 0-405-10962-8). Arno Press.
Vampires of the Nightworld. David F. Bischoff. (Orig.). 1981. pap. 2.25 (ISBN 0-345-28763-0, Del Rey). Ballantine.
Vampires: Stories of the Supernatural. Aleksei Konstantinovich Tolstoi. LC 69-12958. (Illus.). 1969. 4.95. Hawthorn Books.
Vampires, Werewolves & Other Monsters. Compiled by Roger Elwood. 1974. pap. 0.95 o.p. (09260). Curtis.
Vampyr. Jan Jennings. 304p. (Orig.). 1981. pap. 2.95 (ISBN 0-523-48010-5). Pinnacle Bks.
Vampyre. John W. Polidori. (Illus.). 42p. 1973. 11.00x (ISBN 0-85263-244-4). Intl Pubns Serv.
Vampyre see Castle of Otranto (Three Gothic Novels).
Vampyre see Three Gothic Novels.
Van Alens: First Family of a Nation's First City. Samuel Agnew Schreiner, Jr. LC 80-70222. 448p. 1981. 12.95 (ISBN 0-87795-311-2). Arbor Hse.
Van Alens: First Family of a Nation's First City. Samuel Agnew Schreiner, Jr. 1982. pap. 3.50 (ISBN 0-8217-1000-1). Zebra.
Van Alstinc Case: By the Author of "Nick Carte,". John Russell Coryell. LC 99-1530. (On cover: Magnet detective library, no. 77). 1899. Street & Smtih.
Van Beck Will: A Novel. Henry Wynans Jessup. LC 28-25625. 1928. W. Neale.
Van Bibber and Others. Richard Harding Davis. LC 72-5865. (Short story index reprint series). (Illus.). 1972. (ISBN 0-8369-4208-6). Books for Libraries Press.
Van Bibber, and Others. Richard Harding Davis. 1892. Harper & Brothers.
Van Bibber and Others. Richard Harding Davis. LC 16-7543. Harper & Brothers.
Van Bibber, and Others. Richard Harding Davis. (Half-title: Harper's Franklin square library, no. 749, extra). 1894. Harper & Brothers.
Van Bibber and Others. Richard Harding Davis. LC 4-15444. 1903. Harper & Brothers.
Van Cleve. Mary Stanbery Watts. LC 13-217444. 1913. The Macmillan Company.
Van Dreisen Affair. Holly Roth. LC 60-5534. 1960. Random House.
Van Dwellers: A Strenuous Quest for a Home. Albert Bigelow Paine. 1901. J. F. Taylor & Company.
Van Dyne Collection. Marianne D. Scott. 1973. pap. 0.95 o.s.i. (75-447). Lancer.
Van Gelder Papers: And Other Sketches. John Treat Riving. 1887. G. P. Putnam's Sons.
Van Gogh Field & Other Stories. William Kittredge. LC 77-26791. 1978. 9.00x o.p. (ISBN 0-8262-0248-9). U of Mo Pr.
Van Haavens. Caroll Brevoort Hilton-Turvey. LC 16-18560. 1.35. Small, Maynard & Company.
Van Hoff; or: The New Faust. Alfred Smythe. LC 8-10191. (On cover: Fortnightly series, no. 38). American Publishers Corporation.
Van Norton Murders. Charles Reed Jones. LC 31-32062. The Macaulay Company.
Van Patten. Bertha Muzzy Sinclair. LC 26-14384. 1926. Little, Brown, and Company.
Van Rensselaers of Old Manhattan. Weymer Jay Mills. LC 7-38597. 1907. F. A. Stokes Company.
Van Rhyne Heritage. Louisa Bronte. LC 78-61601. (Bronte, Louisa. The American Dynasty Ser.). 1979. 2.25 (ISBN 0-515-04310-9). Jove Publications.
Van Roon. John Collis Snaith. LC 22-17147. 1922. D. Appleton and Company.
Van Tassel and Big Bill. Henry Hastings Curran. LC 23-13317. 1923. C. Scribner's Sons.
Van, the Government Detective: Or, The Base Metal Coiners. Harlan Page Halsey. (secret service series, no. 3). 1888. Street & Smith.
Van Zanten's Happy Days: A Love Story from Pelli Island. Laurids Valdemar Bruun. Tr. by Pritchard, David. LC 22-5373. 1922. A. A. Knopf.
Vancouver Split. John Birmingham. LC 73-2312. 1973. 7.95 (ISBN 0-671-21519-1). Simon and Schuster.
Vandal: Or, Half a Christian; a Novel on Irish-American Life. William Jeremiah Luby. LC 9-25188. 1909. 1.25. J. S. Hyland and Company.
Vandal. 1st Ed. Richard O'Connor. LC 60-5940. 1960. Doubleday.
Vandals see Willis & His Friends Series.
Vandals of the Void. John Holbrook Vance. LC 52-8975. (Science fiction novel). 1953. Winston.
Vandals of the Void. John Holbrook Vance. LC 79-446. (Th Gregg Press science fiction series). (Illus.). 1979. 9.50 (ISBN 0-8398-2517-X). Gregg Press.
Vandals of the Void. James Morgan Walsh. LC 75-10671. (Classics of science fiction). 1976. 11.95. (ISBN 0-88355-353-8) (ISBN 0-88355-464-X). Hyperion Press.

Vandals of the Void: By Jack Vance Pseud. Jacket and Endpaper Designs by Alex Schomburg. 1st Ed. Henry Kuttner. LC 52-8975. (Science fiction novel). 1953. Winston.
Vandals of Treason House. Veglahn, Nancy. (Illus.). 1974. 4.95. Houghton Mifflin.
Vandameer's Road. John R Humphreys. LC 46-1795. 1946. C. Scribner's Sons.
Vandeleur: Or, Animal Magnetism. A Novel... Marianna Pisani. LC 7-39629. 1837. Carey, Lea and Blanchard.
Vandemark's Folly. Herbert Quick. LC 22-2739. The Bobbs-Merrill Company.
Vandenberg: A Novel. Oliver Lange. LC 77-144774. 1971. 6.95 (ISBN 0-8128-1358-8). Stein and Day.
Vanderdecken. Henry De Vere Stacpoole. LC 22-17065. 1922. R. M. McBride & Company.
Vanderheyde Manor-House. Mary Cruger. Worthington Company.
Vanderleigh Legacy. Betty Caldwell. (Orig.). 1981. pap. 2.75 (ISBN 0-89083-813-5). Zebra.
Vanderlyn's Adventure. Marie Adelaide Belloc Lowndes. LC 31-31661. J. Cape & H. Smith.
Vanderlyn's Kingdom. John Innes Mackintosh Stewart. LC 68-10886. 1968. Norton.
Vandover and the Brute. Frank Norris. LC 59-5421. 1959. Grove Press.
Vandover and the Brute. Frank Norris. LC 67-3235. (His Complete works, v. 5). 1967. Kennikat Press.
Vandover and the Brute. Frank Norris. LC 14-6799. 1914. Doubleday, Page & Company.
Vandover and the Brute. Frank Norris. LC 78-8537. 1978. 15.00 (ISBN 0-8032-3300-0) (ISBN 0-8032-8350-4) (ISBN 0-8032-8350-4). University of Nebraska Press.
Vane of the Timberland. Harold Bindloss. LC 11-14752. 1.25. Frederick A. Stokes Company.
Vanessa. Catherine Fellows. (Dell Book). 1978. 1.75 (ISBN 0-440-17181-4). Dell Pub. Co.
Vanessa. Peter Fraser. (Portrait Ser.). 176p. (Orig.). 1983. pap. 2.50 (ISBN 0-523-41817-5). Pinnacle Bks.
Vanessa. Ann Pinchot. LC 76-39717. 1977. 8.95 (ISBN 0-87795-157-8). Arbor Hse.
Vanessa. Hugh Walpole. 1933. 8.95x o.p. St Martin.
Vanessa. Sir Hugh Walpole. (Herries Saga #4). 1972. 1.25. Curtis Books.
Vanessa: A Novel. Kay Martin. LC 74-79659. 1974. 6.95 (ISBN 0-399-11393-2). Putnam.
Vanessa: A Novel. Hugh Walpole. LC 33-274146. 1933. Doubleday, Doran & Company, Inc.
Vangel Griffin. 1st Ed. Herbert Lobsenz. LC 61-6184. 1961. Harper.
Vanguard. Arnold Bennett. LC 27-249475. George H. Doran Company.
Vanguard. Edgar Beecher Bronson. LC 14-6191. 1.25. George H. Doran Company.
Vanguard: A Fantasia. Arnold Bennett. LC 74-17054. (Collected works of Arnold Bennett). 1974. (ISBN 0-518-19166-4). Books for Libraries Press.
Vanguard to Venus. Jeffery Lloyd Castle. LC 57-12127. 1957. Dodd, Mead.
Vanguards of Progress. Donald C. Birdsall. LC 69-19896. 1969. 3.00. Dorrance.
Vanguards of the Plains: A Romance of the Old Santa Fe Trail. Margaret Hill McCarter. LC 17-29178. 1917. Harper & Brothers.
Vanish in an Instant. Margaret Millar. 1974. (pbk.) 1.25. Avon.
Vanish in an Instant. Margaret Millar. LC 52-5144. 1952. Random House.
Vanished. Marjorie Chalmers Carleton. LC 55-637092. (A Morrow mystery). 1955. Morrow.
Vanished. Fletcher Knebel. LC 68-10591. 1968. Doubleday.
Vanished. Bill Pronzini. LC 72-8969. 1973. 4.95 (ISBN 0-394-48170-4). Random House.
Vanished Cities. Hermann Schreiber & Georg Schreiber. (Illus.). (YA) 1957. 7.95 o.p. (ISBN 0-394-45035-3). Knopf.
Vanished Emperor. Percy Andreae. LC 6-2456. 1896. Rand, McNally & Company.
Vanished Empire: A Tale of the Mound Builders. Waldo Hilary Dunn. LC 4-10888. 1904. The R. Clarke Company.
Vanished Helga. Elizabeth Frances Corbett. LC 18-18960. 1.50. George H. Doran Company.
Vanished Jet. James Blish. LC 68-10256. 1968. 4.50. Weybright and Talley.
Vanished Men. George Tracy Marsh. LC 39-21782. The Penn Publishing Company.
Vanished Messenger. Edward Phillips Oppenheim. LC 16-9369. 1915. Little, Brown, and Company.
Vanished Messenger. Edward Phillips Oppenheim. LC 21-13714. 1916. A. L. Burt Company.
Vanishing Acts. Linda Crawford. LC 81-84523. 13.50 (ISBN 0-87223-783-4). Seaview/Putnam.
Vanishing American. Grey, Zane. LC 62-53252. (Great western edition 46). Grosset & Dunlap.
Vanishing American. Zane Grey. LC 25-24588. 1925. Harper & Brothers.
Vanishing Animals & Other Stories. Mary Morris. LC 79-52637. (Illus.). 1979. 10.95. D. R. Godine.
Vanishing Corpse. Ellery Queen, pseud. Orig. Title: Ellery Queen, Master Detective. 1972. pap. 0.75 o.p. (T2615). Pyramid Pubns.
Vanishing Corpse. Ellery Queen, pseud. 1976. pap. 1.25 o.p. BJ Pub Group.
Vanishing Diary. Cecil John Charles Street. LC 61-11718. (Red badge detective). 1961. Dodd, Mead.
Vanishing Fleets. Roy Norton. 1908. D. Appleton and Company.
Vanishing Frontier. George Brydges Rodney. LC 35-287266. Greenberg.
Vanishing Gold Truck. Harry Stephen Keeler. LC 41-23263. 1941. E. P. Dutton & Co., Inc.
Vanishing Gun-Slinger. William Colt MacDonald. LC 43-14785. 1943. Doubleday, Doran and Co., Inc.
Vanishing Herds. Claude Rister. LC 36-487. E. J. Clode, Inc.
Vanishing Idol. George Fort Gibbs. LC 36-877476. 1936. D. Appleton-Century Company, Incorporated.
Vanishing Island: An Irish Entertainment. Charles C O Connell. LC 58-12622. 1958. Devin- Adair Co.
Vanishing Ladies. Ed McBain. 1982. pap. 2.25 (ISBN 0-451-11463-9, AE1463, Sig). NAL.
Vanishing Ladies: By Richard Marsten Pseud. Evan Hunter. LC 57-96137. (Permabooks, M-3097. Mystery, 7). 1957. Permabooks.
Vanishing Lady, & Other Stories. English Language Services. (English Readers Ser.). pap. 1.40 (ISBN 0-02-971310-2). Macmillan.
Vanishing Man: A Detective Romance. Richard Austin Freeman. LC 12-686. 1911. Dodd, Mead and Company.
Vanishing Men. Richard Washburn Child. LC 20-7298. E. P. Dutton & Company.
Vanishing Men. George McLeod Winsor. LC 28-3175. 1927. W. Morrow & Company.
Vanishing of Betty Varian. Carolyn Wells. LC 22-15213. George H. Doran Company.
Vanishing of Ira Bouck. David John Walsh. LC 36-34163. Printed by J. J. Little and Ives Company.
Vanishing Point. Victor Canning. LC 82-18845. 224p. 1983. 10.95 (ISBN 0-688-01107-1). Morrow.
Vanishing Point. Coningsby William Dawson. LC 22-72105. 1922. Cosmopolitan Book Corporation.
Vanishing Point. Pat Flower. LC 77-21129. 1977. 7.95 (ISBN 0-8128-2418-0). Stein and Day.
Vanishing Point. Patricia Wentworth. 1976. Repr. of 1953 ed. lib. bdg. 14.10x (ISBN 0-88411-742-1). Amereon Ltd.
Vanishing Point: A Miss Silver Mystery. 1st Ed. Patricia Wentworth. LC 53-8936. (Mainline mysteries). 1953. Lippincott.
Vanishing Points. Alice Brown. LC 71-106250. (Short story index reprint series). 1970. Books for Libraries Press.
Vanishing Points. Alice Brown. LC 13-37612. 1913. The Macmillan Company.
Vanishing Rider. Evelyn Murray Campbell. LC 32-207341. 1932. L. MacVeagh, Dial Press, Inc.
Vanishing Senator. Judson Pentecost Philips. LC 72-721. (His Peter Styles mysteries). (Red badge novel of suspense). 1972. 4.95 (ISBN 0-396-06579-1). Dodd, Mead.
Vanishing Shadow. Margaret Sutton. (Judy Bolton Mysteries). 1976. Repr. of 1932 ed. lib. bdg. 10.85x (ISBN 0-88411-714-6). Amereon Ltd.
Vanishing Ships. Phillip M Fisher. LC 43-15962. 1943. M. S. Mill Co., Inc.
Vanishing Smuggler. Stephen Chalmers. LC 9-24893. 1909. 1.50. E. J. Clode.
Vanishing Species. Chuck Sullivan. (Red Clay Reader: Vol. 10, No. 3). 1975. pap. 2.95 (ISBN 0-911692-06-1). Red Clay.
"Vanishing Swede" A Tale of Adventure and Pluck in the Pine Forests of Oregon. Mary Hamilton O'Connor. 1905. R. G. Cooke.
Vanishing Tower. Michael Moorcock. (Elric of Melnibone Ser.). (Illus.). 200p. 1981. slipcased 25.00 (ISBN 0-915822-38-5). Archival Pr.
Vanishing Tower. Michael Moorcock. (Science Fiction Ser). 1977. pap. 1.75 (ISBN 0-87997-553-9, VE1553). DAW Bks.
Vanishing Tower. Michael Moorcock. 1977. 1.25 (ISBN 0-87997-304-8). DAW Books.
Vanishing Vector. John P. Evans & John B. Mannion. 256p. (Orig.). 1981. pap. 2.50 (ISBN 0-449-14409-7, GM). Fawcett.
Vanishing Village. Will Rose. 350p. 1970. 5.50 (ISBN 0-9600350-0-1). Catskill Art.
Vanishing Virgin. Dan Gilbert. LC 35-223919. The Danielle Publishers.
Vanishing Virgin. (Illus.). 4.95 (ISBN 0-910550-65-4). Centurion Pr.
Vanitas: Polite Stories. Violet Paget. LC 7-35792. (On cover: Lovell's international series, no. 216). Lovell, Coryell & Company.
Vanitas: Polite Stories, Including the Hitherto Unpublished Story Entitled A Frivolous Conversion. 2d ed. Violet Paget. 1911. J. Lane.
Vanity Box. Charles Norris Williamon & Williamson, Mrs. Alice Muriel (Livingston) 1869- Joint Author. LC 11-5372. 1911. Doubleday, Page & Company.
Vanity Case. Carolyn Wells. 1926. G. P. Putnam's Sons.
Vanity Dies Hard. Ruth Rendell. 160p. 1980. pap. 1.25 (ISBN 0-345-29286-3). Ballantine.
Vanity Dies Hard. Ruth Rendell. (Orig.). 1971. pap. 0.95 o.p. (95029-095). Beagle Bks.
Vanity Fair. William Makepeace Thackeray. LC 65-6371. (Harper's modern classics). 1964. Harper & Row.
Vanity Fair. William Makepeace Thackeray. LC 57-14616. (Harper's modern classics). 1958. Harper.
Vanity Fair. William Makepeace Thackeray. LC 76-433622. (Penguin English library, EL35). 1968. Penguin.
Vanity Fair... William Makepeace Thackeray. LC 17-17436. (Harvard classics shelf of fiction, selected by C. W. Eliot. 5-6). P. F. Collier & Son.
Vanity Fair. William Makepeace Thackeray & Davenport, Basil, 1905- Ed. (Half-title: Great illustrated classics). 1943. Dodd, Mead & Company.
Vanity Fair, a Novel Without a Hero. William Makepeace Thackeray. LC 63-3850. (Riverside editions, B66). 1963. Houghton Mifflin.
Vanity Fair: A Novel Without a Hero. Thackeray, William Makepeace. LC 60-670. Random House.
Vanity Fair: A Novel Without a Hero. William Makepeace Thackeray. LC 50-11915. (Modern Library college editions, T33). (Illus.). 1950. Modern Library.
Vanity Fair: A Novel Without a Hero. William Makepeace Thackeray. LC 7-744. M. A. Donohue & Co.
Vanity Fair: A Novel Without a Hero. William Makepeace Thackeray. LC 31-262189. Caxton Publishing Co.
Vanity Fair: A Novel Without a Hero. William Makepeace Thackeray. LC 26-3647. (On cover: Holly library, no. 6). The Mershon Company.
Vanity Fair. A Novel Without a Hero. William Makepeace Thackeray. LC 8-27760. Harper & Brothers.
Vanity Fair. A Novel Without a Hero. William Makepeace Thackeray. LC 8-27761. 1865. Sever and Francis.
Vanity Fair: A Novel Without a Hero. household ed. William Makepeace Thackeray. 1869. Fields, Osgood & Co.
Vanity Fair: A Novel Without a Hero. William Makepeace Thackeray. LC 8-281221. (Added t.-p.: The works of William Makepeace Thackeray... vol. I-II). 1879. Smith, Elder, & Co.
Vanity Fair. A Novel Without a Hero. William Makepeace Thackeray. LC 8-28192. (On cover: Lovell's library, v. 4, no. 172). 1883. J. W. Lovell Company.
Vanity Fair. A Novel Without a Hero. William Makepeace Thackeray. LC 26-3659. Belford, Clarke & Company.
Vanity Fair: A Novel Without a Hero. William Makepeace Thackeray. (Half-title: Everyman's library, ed. by Ernest Rhys. Fiction. no. 298). 1909. J. M. Dent & Co.
Vanity Fair: A Novel Without a Hero... William Makepeace Thackeray. LC 13-23590. (Illustrated cabinet edition). 1912. D. Estes & Company.
Vanity Fair: A Novel Without a Hero. William Makepeace Thackeray. LC 33-5088. (international classics). 1924. Dodd, Mead and Company.
Vanity Fair: A Novel Without a Hero. William Makepeace Thackeray. LC 33-27302. (Half-title: The modern library of the world's best books). 1933. The Modern Library.
Vanity Fair: A Novel Without a Hero... William Makepeace Thackeray. LC 38-3247. (On cover: The works of William Makepeace Thackeray). 1937. Garden City Publishing Company, Inc.
Vanity Fair: A Novel Without a Hero. William Makepeace Thackeray. LC 40-111074. The Heritage Press.
Vanity Fair. A Novel Without a Hero. William Makepeace Thackeray. LC 44-25672. J. W. Lovell.
Vanity Fair: A Novel Without a Hero. William Makepeace Thackeray & Crombie, Charles, Illus. LC 39-17507. (The international classics). 1936. Dodd, Mead and Company.
Vanity Fair: A Novel Without a Hero. William Makepeace Thackeray & Herzberg, Max John, 1886- Ed. LC 26-4939. (modern readers' series). 1926. The Macmillan Company.
Vanity Fair: A Novel Without a Hero. William Makepeace Thackeray & More, Paul Elmer, 1864- Ed. LC 35-157473. (Half-title: The Doubleday-Doran series in literature, Robert Shafer, general editor). Doubleday, Doran & Company, Inc.
Vanity Fair: A Novel Without a Hero. William Makepeace Thackeray & Wells, John Edwin, 1875- Ed. LC 28-25349. (modern readers' series). 1928. The Macmillan Company.
Vanity Fair: A Novel Without a Hero and Lovel the Widower. William Makepeace Thackeray. LC 3-27790. (Thackeray's complete works. Sterling edition... v. 1-2). 1888. Estes and Lauriat.
Vanity Fair: A Novel Without a Hero, and Lovel the Widower. William Makepeace Thackeray. LC 13-208393. (Half-title: Illustrated library edition. The complete works of... Thackeray... vol. I). 1889. Houghton, Mifflin and Company.
Vanity Fair: A Novel Without a Hero. Illus. by the Author. William Makepeace Thackeray. LC 66-5489. (Macdonald illus. classics. 16). 1966. 3.50. Macdonald.
Vanity Fair. Introd. by John W. Dodds. William Makepeace Thackeray. LC 55-8418. (Rinehart editions, 76). 1955. Rinehart.
Vanity Girl. Compton Mackenzie. LC 20-16504. 1920. Cassell and Company, Limited.
Vanity Girl. Compton Mackenzie. LC 20-772497. Harper & Brothers.
Vanity Goes to Paris. Wallace G Young. LC 37-65205. Chapman & Grimes.
Vanity, My Beloved. Jess Wilcox, pseud. 1976. pap. 1.95. Woodhill.
Vanity of Duluoz: An Adventurous Education, 1935-46. John Kerouac. LC 68-11867. (Illus.). 1968. Coward-McCann.
Vanity of Duluoz: An Adventurous Education, 1935-46. John Kerouac. LC 77-18045. 1978. 3.95 (ISBN 0-399-50386-2). Putnam.
Vanity Row. 1st Ed. William Riley Burnett. LC 52-6403. 1952. Knopf.
Vanity Square: A Story of Fifth Avenue Life. Edgar Evertson Saltus. LC 73-113267. 1970. (ISBN 0-404-05538-9). AMS Press.
Vanity Square: A Story of Fifth Avenue Life. Edgar Evertson Saltus. LC 6-18354. 1906. J. B. Lippincott Company.
Vanity Under the Sun: A Novel. Dale Collins. 1928. Little, Brown, and Company.
Vanity's Daughter. Hawley Smart. (On cover: Mayflower library, no. 10). 1892. J. A. Taylor and Company.
Vanneck. Robert Grant. LC 27-14951. E. P. Dutton & Company.
Vanozza: A Novel of the Enigmatical Borgias of the Renaissance. K. T Wills. LC 68-10614. 1969. 6.95. A. S. Barnes.
Vanquish the Angel: A Novel by Diana and Meir Gillon. 1st American Ed. Diana Gillon & Meir Gillon. LC 56-5978. 1956. J. Day Co.
Vanquished. Brian Wynne Garfield. (Double D western). 1964. Doubleday.
Vanquished. A Novel. Agnes Leonard Scanland Hill. 1867. G. W. Carleton & Co.; Etc., Etc.
Vantage Ground. Thomas J. Dulack. LC 73-131174. 1970. 5.95. Dial Press.
Vantage Hall. Constance Gluyas. (O.s.i.). 1974. pap. 0.95 o.s.i. (LB206NK, Leisure Bks). Nordon Pubns.
Vantage Point. Hilda Morris. LC 40-104468. G. P. Putnam's Sons.
Vantine Diamonds... Austin J Small. LC 31-527. 1930. Pub. for the Crime Club, Inc., by Doubleday, Doran & Company, Inc.
Vanya. a Narrative. Laura Chase. LC 51-4168. Island Press Cooperative.
Vapor. Bryna Baroni. LC 76-619. 1976. 4.95x (ISBN 0-913426-03-2). Visual Impact.
Vaquero Guns. Jackson Cole. 1973. 0.75. Popular Lib.
Var the Stick. Piers Anthony, pseud. 1973. (pbk.) 0.95. Bantam Books.
Varanoff Tradition. Howard Rockey. LC 26-16906. Macrae Smith Company.
Vardy. John Harris. 1981. 18.95x (Pub. by Remploy England). State Mutual Bk.
Vardy: 1st Amer. Ed. John Harris. LC 63-17696. 1965. 4.95. W. Sloane Dist. Morrow.
Variable Man: And Other Stories. Philip K Dick. 1976. 1.50. Ace.
Variable Syndrome: A Science Fiction Story. Don McGregor. 144p. (Also including: Investigating "Decectives, Inc. & Marvel Comics -- a memoir). 1981. pap. 10.00 (ISBN 0-934882-05-3). Fictioneer Bks.
Variable Winds at Jalna. Mazo De La Roche. LC 54-11127. (Fawcett crest book). 1975. (pbk.) 1.50. Fawcett.
Variable Winds at Jalna. Whiteoak Ed. 1st Ed. Mazo De La Roche. LC 54-11127. 1954. Little, Brown.
Varied Narratives. Ed. by Warner Taylor. LC 32-227092. 1932. R. Long & R. R. Smith, Inc.
Varietes Modernes. Leon Verriest & M. L. Hall. LC 52-10905. (Fr.). 1952. text ed. 5.50 o.p. (ISBN 0-395-05498-2, 3-57665). HM.
Varieties of Love: Stories. Herbert Kubly. LC 58-7515. 1958. Simon and Schuster.

Variety. Richard Edward Connell. LC 25-8050. 1925. Minton, Balch & Company.
Variety of Fiction: A Critical Anthology. Ed. by Edward Alan Bloom. LC 75-79102. 1969. Odyssey Press.
Variety of People. Don Marquis. LC 29-22137. 1929. Doubleday, Doran and Company, Inc.
Variety of Short Stories. Ed. by John C. Schweitzer. (Also for Slow HS Students). (gr. 11-12). 1968. pap. text ed. 5.00 o.p. (ISBN 0-684-51556-3, SSP14, ScribC). Scribner.
Variety of Weapons. Rufus King. LC 43-11547. 1943. Pub. for the Crime Club by Doubleday, Doran & Company, Inc.
Various Short Stories. Ed. by Oliphant Gibbons. LC 38-3721. 1937. The Grotzka Press, Inc.
Various Temptations: Each Story Complete and Unabridged. An Avon Red and Gold Ed. LC 55-41996. (Avon, T-109). 1955. Avon Publications.
Varkaus Conspiracy. John Dalmas, pseud. 288p. (Orig.). 1983. pap. 2.95 (ISBN 0-523-48567-0). Tor Bks.
Varleigh Medallion. Sylvia Thorpe. LC 79-25367. 1980. 10.95 (ISBN 0-89340-245-1). J. Curley.
Varmints. Peggy Bennett. LC 46-8190. 1947-1946. A. A. Knopf.
Varney, the Vampire, or, the Feast of Blood, 3 vols. Thomas P. Prest. Ed. by Devendra P. Varma. LC 70-120557. (Gothic Novels). 933p. Repr. of 1847 ed. boxed 35.00 (ISBN 0-405-00801-5). Ayer Co.
Varney, the Vampyre: Or, The Feast of Blood. LC 70-188949. 1972. per vol. 5.00 (ISBN 0-486-22844-4) (ISBN 0-486-22845-2). Dover Publications.
Varsity Letter. Franklin Mering Reck. LC 42-10685. 1942. Thomas Y. Crowell Company.
Varvana & Other Short Stories. Maurice Sarfaty. 1967. 3.50 o.p. (ISBN 0-682-45755-8); pap. text ed. 1.96, s.p. 1.47 o.p.; teachers' manual. 1.96, s.p. 1.47, 6 readers, RL 2-6. 1.16 ea., s.p. 0.87 ea., teachers' manual for readers 1.16, s.p. 0.87 o.p. Exposition.
Varvara. Dennis Parry. LC 56-7598. 1956. Reynal.
Vasco. Marc Chadourne. Tr. by Sutton, Eric. LC 28-20838. Harcourt, Brace and Company.
Vasconiselos. William Gilmore Simms. 1974. Repr. of 1890 ed. lib. bdg. 30.00 (ISBN 0-8414-8069-9). Folcroft.
Vasconselos: a Romance of the New World. William Gilmore Simms. LC 70-116016. 1970. (ISBN 0-404-06037-4). AMS Press.
Vasconselos; a Romance of the New World. William Gilmore Simms. 1857. Redfield.
Vasconselos, a Romance of the New World. William Gilmore Simms. LC 8-110242. 1882. A. C. Armstrong & Son.
Vasconselos: a Romance of the New World. William Gilmore Simms. (On cover: Lovell's library, v. 13, no. 677). 1885. J. W. Lovell Company.
Vashti and the Strange God. Gladys Moon Cook. LC 74-29465. (Illus.). 1.50 (ISBN 0-912692-57-X). D. C. Cook Pub. Co.
Vashti: Or, "Until Death Us Do Part." A Novel. Augusta Jane Evans Wilson. LC 8-37103. 1897. G. W. Dillingham Co.
Vashti's Fate: Or, Purified by Fire. A Novel. Helen Corwin Pierce. (select series, no. 78). 1891. Street & Smith.
Vaskor, Son of Vaskor. Tanith Lee. 1978. 1.95 (ISBN 0-87997-350-1). DAW Books.
Vassalage. Adelaide Fuller Bell. LC 9-29255. 1909. 1.50. The C. M. Clark Publishing Company.
Vassall Morton. Francis Parkman. LC 78-104535. 1970. (ISBN 0-8398-1552-2). Literature House.
Vassall Morton. A Novel. Francis Parkman. 1856. Phillips, Sampson and Company.
Vassar Stories. Grace Margaret Gallaher. LC 71-113663. (Short story index reprint series). (Illus.). 1970. Books for Libraries Press.
Vassar Stories. Grace Margaret Gallaher. LC 49. 1900. R. G. Badger & Co.
Vassar Stories. rev. ed., profusely illustrated. cover design by i. b. hazelton. ed. Grace Margaret Gallaher. LC 7-2058. 1907. E. H. Bacon and Co.
Vassar Studies. Julia Augusta Schwartz. LC 99-2688. (The university series, no. 5). 1899. G. P. Putnam's Sons.
Vates. Tomas Blanco. LC 80-67415. (Obras completas de Tomas Blanco). 96p. 1981. pap. 3.75 (ISBN 0-940238-43-8). Ediciones Huracan.
Vathek. William Beckford & Redman, Ben Ray, 1896- LC 28-28675. 1928. The John Day Company.
Vathek see Castle of Otranto (Three Gothic Novels).
Vathek see Three Gothic Novels.
Vathek: An Arabian Tale. William Beckford. Ed. by William North. LC 22-24770. Pollard & Moss.
Vathek: An Arabian Tale from an Unpublished Manuscript. William Beckford. Tr. by Samuel Henley from Fr. 1975. text ed. 22.50x o.p. (ISBN 0-8277-3733-5); pap. text ed. 8.50x o.p. British Bk Ctr.
Vathek: an Oriental Romance. William Beckford. Ed. by Cyrus Redding. LC 7-3538. (Mirror library, new ser. no. 1). 1845. Morris, Willis & Fuller.
Vatican Rip. Jonathan Gash, pseud. LC 82-16478. 1983. 2.95 (ISBN 0-14-006431-1). Penguin Books.
Vatican Roulette. David Lodge. 1968. pap. 0.75 o.p. Lancer.
Vatican Swindle: Les Caves Du Vatican: Translated from the French of Andre Gide. by dorothy bussy. ed. Andre Paul Guillaume Gide. Tr. by Bussy, Dorothy. LC 25-22755. A. A. Knopf.
Vatican Target. Barry J Schiff & Hal Fishman. LC 78-21421. 1979. 8.95 (ISBN 0-312-83801-8). St. Martin's Press.
Vatican Vendetta. Nick Carter. (Nick Carter Ser.). (O.s.i.). 176p. (Orig.). 1974. pap. 0.95 o.s.i. (AN1263, Award). Univ Pub & Dist.
Vaudeville: A Novel. Aben Kandel. 1927. H. Waterson.
Vaudeville Marriage. Sandra Hochman. 1966. 3.95 o.p. (ISBN 0-670-74350-X). Viking Pr.
Vault of Horror. Jack Oleck et al. LC 73-6811. 1973. pap. 0.95. Bantam Books.
Vault of Night. Donald Von Raysdael Drenner. LC 52-67082. 1952. Zauberberg Press.
Vault of the Ages. Poul Anderson. 1978. pap. 1.95 (ISBN 0-425-04336-3, Medallion). Berkley Pub.
Vault of the Ages. Poul Anderson. 1979. lib. bdg. 9.50 (ISBN 0-8398-2521-8, Gregg). G K Hall.
Vawder's Understudy: A Study in Platonic Affection, by James Knapp Reeve; Illustrated by Louise L. Heustis. James Knapp Reeve. LC 7-30933. (Twentieth century series). 1896. F. A. Stokes Company.
Vayenne. Percy James Brebner. LC 8-7896. The J. McBride Co.
Vecinos. span. ed. Jim Kelly. (Small Star Stories). (O.s.i.). (Illus.). 1975. 5.95 o.s.i. (64547). Glencoe.
Vector. David R. Slavitt. LC 73-115698. 1970. 5.95. Bernard Geis Associates.
Vector. Henry Sutton, pseud. 1970. 5.95 o.p. (73-115698). Geis.
Vector for Seven. Josephine Saxton. 1970. 4.95 o.p. Doubleday.
Vector for Seven: The Weltanschaung of Mrs. Amelia Mortimer and Friends. Josephine Saxton. LC 70-123709. (Doubleday science fiction). 1970. 4.95. Doubleday.
Vector-Lee. Richard Cloke. LC 76-56063. 1977. 3.50 (ISBN 0-917458-02-8) (ISBN 0-917458-03-6). Kent Publications.
Vedettes, a Collection of Stories. Edward Loomis. LC 64-16117. 1964. A. Swallow.
Vedettes: A Collection of Stories. Edward Loomis. LC 82-72171. 112p. (Orig.). 1964. 6.50 (ISBN 0-8040-0309-2); pap. 3.50 (ISBN 0-8040-0310-6). Swallow.
Vegas. Max Franklin, pseud. 1978. pap. 1.75 (ISBN 0-345-28051-2). Ballantine.
Vegas: A Memoir of a Dark Season. John Gregory Dunne. LC 73-5034. 1973. 8.95 o.p. (ISBN 0-394-46165-7). Random.
Vegas Legacy: A Novel. Ovid Demaris, pseud. LC 82-13019. 15.95 (ISBN 0-440-09172-1). Delacorte Press.
Vegas Vendetta see Venganza En Las Vegas.
Vehement Flame: A Novel. Margaret Wade Campbell Deland. Harper & Brothers.
Vehement Flame: The Story of Stephen Escott. Ludwig Lewisohn. LC 48-9059. 1948. Farrar, Straus.
Veil: A Romance of Tunis. Ethel Stefana Stevens Drower. LC 9-22178. 1909. F. A. Stokes Company.
Veil Lifted. large type ed. J. Traill Taylor. (Illus.). pap. 4.95 (ISBN 0-910122-42-3). Amherst Pr.
Veil of Death. Roger Simons. LC 66-78047. 1966. bds., 3.50. Bles.
Veil of Glamour. Lilly Clive Nutt. LC 26-144921. The Bobbs-Merrill Company.
Veil of Loneliness. Radclyffe Hall. LC 28-30704. 1928. Covici Friede.
Veil of Sand. Ann Boyle. (Avalon Books). 4.95. Thomas Bouregy.
Veil of Silence. Aileen Seilaz. 1976. (pbk.) 1.25. Ace Books.
Veil of the Temple: Or, From Dark to Twilight. William Hurrell Mallock. LC 4-109276. 1904. G. P. Putnam's Sons.
Veil of Veronica. Gertrud Von Le Fort. LC 70-126667. 1970. (ISBN 0-404-03946-4). AMS Press.
Veil of Veronica. Gertrud F. Von Lefort, pseud. Tr. by Conrad M. Bonacina. LC 70-126667. Repr. of 1933 ed. 21.45 (ISBN 0-404-03946-4). AMS Pr.
Veiled Aristocrats. Gertrude Sanborn. LC 24-1182. The Associated Publishers.
Veiled Beyond: A Romance of the Adopta. Sigmund B Alexander. LC 11-8223. Cassell & Company, Limited.
Veiled Doctor: A Novel. Varina Anne Jefferson Davis. 1895. Harper & Brothers.
Veiled Fountain. Harry Hervey. LC 47-11674. 1947. G. P. Putnam's Sons.
Veiled Hand: A Novel of the Sixties, the Seventies, and the Eighties. Frederick Wicks. LC 8-362520. (Harper's Franklin square library, no. 730). 1893. Harper & Brothers.
Veiled Lady. Elwood Stokes Stewart. Holtz & Co.
Veiled Lady: And Other Men and Women. Francis Hopkinson Smith. LC 7-12697. 1907. C. Scribner's Sons.
Veiled Lady & Other Men & Women. Francis Hopkinson Smith. (Illus.). 295p. 1981. pap. write for info. (ISBN 0-86649-031-0). Twentieth Century.
Veiled Murder. Alice Ormond Campbell. LC 49-10148. 1949. Random House.
Veiled Sultan. Peggy Morrison, pseud. LC 76-99494. 1969. 5.95. Vanguard Press.
Veiled Victory. Otto Chester Brodhay. LC 41-220670. Dorrance and Company.
Veiled Woman: A Novel of West and East. Achmed Abdullah. LC 31-5696. H. Liveright.
Veiled Women. Marmaduke William Pickthall. LC 13-3757. 1913. Duffield and Company.
Veils. Robert Smythe Hichens. LC 44-914. 1943. Etc. Hutchinson & Co. Ltd.
Veils of Azlaroc. Fred Saberhagen. 1978. 1.95 (ISBN 0-441-86064-8). Ace Books.
Veils of Isis, and Other Stories. Frank Harris. 1.25. George H. Doran Company.
Vein of Iron. Ellen Anderson Gholson Glasgow. LC 35-272706. Harcourt, Brace and Company.
Vein of Riches. John Knowles. LC 77-10730. 9.95 (ISBN 0-316-49971-4). Little Brown.
Veinte Cuentos Espanoles Del Siglo Veinte. Ed. by Enrique Anderson-Imbert & Lawrence B. Kiddle. (Orig., Span.). (gr. 10-12). 1961. pap. text ed. 12.95 (ISBN 0-13-941567-X). P-H.
Veldt, the Lion Hunter: A Comic Opera Whirl. James M Reilly. LC 10-15399. 1910. Broadway Publishing Company.
Vella Vernell; or, An Amazing Marriage. Sumner Hayden. (On cover: Street & Smith's select series, no. 3). 1887. Street & Smith.
Velma. new ed. Clara Verner. 1973. 3.95 (ISBN 0-8341-0081-9). Beacon Hill.
Velocipede Handicap. Louise W King. 1973. 0.75. Curtis Books.
Velocipede Handicap. 1st Ed. in the U.S.A. Louise W King. LC 66-117577. 1966. 4.50. Doubleday.
Velvet Ape. Elinore Denniston. 1975. (pbk.) 0.95. Dell.
Velvet Ape. David C Holmes. LC 57-8727. 1957. Mystery House.
Velvet Black. Richard Washburn Child. E. P. Dutton & Company.
Velvet Bubble. Alice Winter. LC 65-16570. 1965. W. Morrow.
Velvet Claw. Adrian Y. Meadows. 192p. (Orig.). 1974. pap. 1.95 o.p. (ISBN 0-87056-375-0, 6375). Brandon.
Velvet Cushion... John William Cunningham. LC 6-31579. 1815. Green & Co.
Velvet Cushion... John William Cunningham. 1815. Publishing by Richard Scott, Pearl-Street.
Velvet Cushion... John William Cunningham. LC 6-31580. (With his A world without souls. Philadelphia, 1815). 1815. E. Earl.
Velvet Doublet: Condensed and Simplified for Quick Reading by James Street, Jr. James Howell Street. (Hanover House headliners). 1954.
Velvet Doublet. 1st Ed. James Howell Street. LC 52-133681. 1953. Doubleday.
Velvet Fleece. Lois Christine Eby & Fleming, John Chester, 1906- Joint Author. LC 47-31434. 1947. E. P. Dutton.
Velvet Glove. Hugh Stowell Scott. 1901. Dodd, Mead & Company.
Velvet Hammer. Faith Baldwin. LC 69-11798. 1969. 4.95 o.p. (ISBN 0-03-076385-1). HR&W.
Velvet Hammer. Faith Baldwin Cuthrell. LC 69-11798. 1969. 4.95 (ISBN 0-03-076385-1). Holt, Rinehart and Winston.
Velvet Hand. Helen Kieran Reilly. 1953. Random House.
Velvet Hand: New Madame Storey Mysteries. Hulbert Footner. LC 28-290771. 1928. Pub. for the Crime Club, Inc., by Doubleday, Doran & Company, Inc.
Velvet Horn. Andrew Nelson Lytle. LC 57-105187. 1957. McDowell, Obolensky.
Velvet Hours. Page B. Woods. 2.95 o.p. Vantage.
Velvet Jungle. Eugene Horowitz. Orig. Title: Mr. Jack & the Greenstalks. 1970. pap. 1.25 o.p. (ISBN 0-446-66459-6, 66-459). Paperback Lib.
Velvet Knife. 1st Ed. Shulman, Irving. LC 59-8272. 1959. Doubleday.
Velvet Promise. Jude Deveraux, pseud. (Richard Gallen Bks.). 416p. 1981. pap. 2.95 (ISBN 0-671-41785-1). PB.
Velvet Shadows. Andre Norton, pseud. 1978. pap. 1.95 (ISBN 0-449-23135-6, Crest). Fawcett.
Velvet Shadows. Andre Norton. (Fawcett Crest Book). (Illus.). 1977. 1.50 (ISBN 0-449-23135-6). Fawcett Publications.
Velvet Shadows of Justin Wood. Andrea Haley. 1982. pap. 2.25 (ISBN 0-89083-990-5). Zebra.
Velvet Song. Jude Deveraux. (Montgomery Annals Ser.: No. 3). (Orig.). 1983. pap. 2.95 (ISBN 0-671-45404-8). PB.
Velvet Target: By Genevieve Holden Pseud. 1st Ed. Genevieve Long Pou. LC 56-9846. (Crime Club selection). 1956. Published for the Crime Club by Doubleday.
Velvet Thorn. Angela Alexie. 320p. (Orig.). 1982. pap. 2.95 (ISBN 0-449-14502-6, GM). Fawcett.
Velvet Trap. Kirk Westley. (Orig.). 1971. pap. 0.95 o.p. (95-161). Manor Bks.
Velvet Vice: A Novel. Pearl Eytinge. LC 6-38129. (On cover: The Eytinge ser. no. 1). 1889. The Eytinge Publishing Company.
Velvet Vixen. Alan Geoffrey Yates. LC 64-6492. (Signet book). 1964. New American Library of World Literature.
Velvet Well. John Gearon. LC 46-5163. 1946. Duell, Sloan and Pearce.
Velvet Whip. 1st Ed. Leonard Snyder. LC 54-5718. 1954. Doubleday.
Velveteen Rabbit: Or How Toys Become Real. Margery Williams. (Camelot book). (Illus.). 1975. (pbk.) 1.50 (ISBN 0-380-00255-8). Avon.
Venables. Kathleen Thompson Norris. LC 41-13941. 1941. Doubleday, Doran & Co., Inc.
Venables: A Novel. Geoffrey Atheling Wagner. LC 52-8146. 1952. Simon and Schuster.
Venal Sin. Weldon Matthews. LC 34-486222. 1934. W. Godwin, Inc.
Vendetta. Honore De Balzac. LC 6-6299. (On cover: Redpath's books for the camp fires no. 3). J. Redpath.
Vendetta. Marie Corelli. pap. 4.95 (ISBN 0-910122-27-X). Amherst Pr.
Vendetta. Charles Durbin. LC 78-111432. 1970. 5.95. Coward-McCann.
Vendetta. Joseph Haas. 1976. pap. 1.75 o.p. (ISBN 0-515-04057-6). BJ Pub Group.
Vendetta. Joel D. Humphreys. LC 81-15605. 256p. 1982. 12.95 o.p. (ISBN 0-02-557150-8). Macmillan.
Vendetta. Joel D. Humphreys. 240p. 1983. 2.75 (ISBN 0-380-63644-1). Avon.
Vendetta. Leopold Horace Ognall. LC 63-15690. (Cock Robin mystery). 1963. Macmillan.
Vendetta. Nick Quarry. (Orig.). 1973. pap. 0.95 o.p. (M2737, GM). Fawcett World.
Vendetta: A Novel. Joseph Haas. LC 74-27810. 1975. 7.95 (ISBN 0-8092-8284-4). Regnery.
Vendetta Con Brio. Beth DeBilid. LC 72-9881. (Black bat mystery). 1973. 5.95 (ISBN 0-672-51791-4). Bobbs-Merrill.
Vendetta Con Brio. Beth De Bilio. LC 72-9881. (Black Bat Mystery Ser). 1973. 5.95 o.p. (ISBN 0-672-51791-4). Bobbs.
Vendetta Contract. Jon Messman. (Revenger). (Revenger#3: Vol. 3). 1974. (pbk.) 0.95. New American Library.
Vendetta of Silence. Ann Cornelisen. LC 76-161421. 1971. 6.95 o.p. (ISBN 0-316-15744-9, Pub. by Atlantic Monthly Pr). Little.
Vendetta of the Hills. Willis George Emerson. LC 17-9456. 1917. 1.35. The Chapple Publishing Company, Ltd.
Vendetta: Or, The Southern Heiress. Lucy Randall Comfort. LC 6-30215. (On cover: The library of American authors. no. 17). 1890. G. Munro.
Vendetta! Or, The Story of One Forgotten. Marie Corelli. LC 41-31308. William L. Allison Company.
Vendetta! Or, The Story of One Forgotten. Marie Corelli. (On cover: Seaside library. Pocket ed. no. 1068). 1888. G. Munro.
Vendetta! Or, The Story of One Forgotten. ...a new ed. Marie Corelli. LC 43-401259. (On cover: Lippincott's series of select novels...No. 78). 1890. J. B. Lippincott Company.
Vendor of Sweets. R. S. Morton. 1983. pap. 4.95 (ISBN 0-14-006258-0). Penguin.
Vendor of Sweets. R. K. Narayan. LC 66-23818. 1967. Viking Press.
Veneer: The Story of a Man. Ursula Bloom. LC 29-7491. G. H. Watt.
Veneerings: A Novel. Harry Hamilton Johnston. LC 22-5602. 1922. The Macmillan Company.
Venetia. new ed. Benjamin Disraeli Beaconsfield. LC 7-16067. G. Routledge and Sons.
Venetia. Georgette Heyer. 320p. 1981. pap. 1.95 (ISBN 0-515-05728-2). Jove Pubns.
Venetia. Georgette Heyer. 308p. 1973. 7.95 (ISBN 0-399-11171-9). Putnam Pub Group.
Venetia. Georgette Heyer. 320p. 1982. pap. 2.75 (ISBN 0-515-06878-0). Jove Pubns.
Venetia: A Novel. Benjamin Disraeli Beaconsfield. LC 6-28848. (Seaside library, v. 49, no. 999). 1881. G. Munro.
Venetia. 1st American Ed. Georgette Heyer. LC 59-6056. Putnam.

Venetian: A Novel. David Weiss. LC 76-18940. 1976. 9.95. Morrow.
Venetian Affair. Helen MacInnes. 352p. 1978. pap. 2.95 (ISBN 0-449-24196-3, Crest). Fawcett.
Venetian Blind: By William Haggard Pseud. Richard Clayton. LC 59-13740. (Chantecler novel of suspense). 1959. Washburn.
Venetian Blinds. Ethel Edith Mannin. LC 38-27191. 1933. A. A. Knopf.
Venetian Charade. Helen York. LC 77-92234. 1978. 7.95 (ISBN 0-385-12657-3). Doubleday.
Venetian Glass Nephew. Elinor Hoyt Wylie. LC 25-17616. 1925. George H. Doran Company.
Venetian Inheritance. Annette Eyre. (Signet book). 1975. (pbk.) 0.95. New American Library.
Venetian June. Anna Fuller. LC 4-16825. 1896. G. P. Putnam's Sons.
Venetian June. Anna Fuller. LC 13-21355. 3.00. G. P. Putnam's Sons.
Venetian Key. Allen Upward. LC 27-18317. 1927. J. B. Lippincott Company.
Venetian Life. William Dean Howells. Repr. of 1895 ed. lib. bdg. 25.00 (ISBN 0-8414-5179-6). Folcroft.
Venetian Lover: The Romance of Giorgione. Anton Noder. Tr. by Chambers, Whitaker. LC 31-32083. 1931. R. Long & R. R. Smith, Inc.
Venetian Masque: A Romance. Rafael Sabatini. LC 34-25930. 1934. Houghton Mifflin Company.
Venetian Moon. Clarissa Ross, pseud. (Original Historical Romance Ser.). 288p. 1980. pap. 2.75 (ISBN 0-515-04817-8). Jove Pubns.
Venetian Night. Louise W. Boothe. 3.95 o.p. Vantage.
Venetian Red. P. M Pasinetti. LC 60-7682. 1960. Random House.
Venetian Secret. Evelyn Bond. pap. 0.60 o.p. Lancer.
Venetian Spring. Sonia Phillips. 1978. pap. 1.25 (ISBN 0-532-12580-0). Woodhill.
Venetian Study in Black and White. Charles Edward Barns. LC 6-7218. 1889. W. Fracker & Co.
Venetians: A Novel. Mary Elizabeth Braddon Maxwell. LC 7-25295. 1892. Harper & Brothers.
Venganza En Las Vegas. new ed. Don Pendleton. Tr. by O. J. Blanco from Eng. (Compadre Collection: El Verdugo Ser, No. 9). Orig. Title: Vegas Vendetta. 160p. (Span.). 1974. pap. 0.75 (ISBN 0-88473-309-2). Fiesta Pub.
Vengeance. J. L Bouma. 1976. (pbk.) 0.95. Leisure Books.
Vengeance. Johanas L. Bouma. 160p. 1981. pap. 1.75 (ISBN 0-8439-0991-9, Leisure Bks). Nordon Pubns.
Vengeance. Johanas L. Bouma. (O.s.i.). (Orig.). 1976. pap. 0.95 o.s.i. (LB329NK, Leisure Bks). Nordon Pubns.
Vengeance: A Drama of the Congo--That Is Stirring in Its Intensity and Overwhelming in Its Power. A Great Story of Tropical Life--Vivid--Colorful --Dynamic, Based on the Motion Picture Story. Frederick Hugh Herbert. LC 30-14011. Jacobsen Publishing Company, Inc.
Vengeance Afoot. Virginia Whitman. LC 66-18941. bds., 2.95. Zondervan.
Vengeance Army. Axel Kilgore. (Call Me the Mercenary Ser.: No. 6). (Orig.). 1981. pap. 2.50 (ISBN 0-89083-872-0). Zebra.
Vengeance at Ventura. George G. Gilman, pseud. (Edge Ser.: No. 37). 160p. 1981. pap. 1.95 (ISBN 0-523-41448-X). Pinnacle Bks.
Vengeance Breed. Charley Barstow. 224p. (Orig.). 1982. pap. 2.25 (ISBN 0-505-51768-X). Tower Bks.
Vengeance Gun. Ray Hogan & Leonard London Foreman. (Ace double Western). 1973. (pbk.) 0.75. Ace.
Vengeance Gun. Bret Sanders. (Hawk Ser). (O.s.i.). 160p. (Orig.). 1974. pap. 0.95 o.p. (AN1258, Award). Univ Pub & Dist.
Vengeance Hunt. Charles R. Pike, pseud. LC 80-69218. (Jubal Cade Westerns Ser.). 128p. 1980. pap. 2.95 (ISBN 0-87754-234-1). Chelsea Hse.
Vengeance Is a Stranger. Cecil P. Lewis. LC 66-15440. (Double D western). 3.50. Doubleday.
Vengeance Is Mine. Andrew Balfour. LC 2054. 1900. New Amsterdam Book Company.
Vengeance Is Mine. Ralph Hayes. 1978. pap. 1.50 (ISBN 0-532-15344-8). Woodhill.
Vengeance Is Mine. John E Lewis. 1974. 4.95. Lenox Hill Press.
Vengeance Is Mine. Frank Morrison Spillane. LC 50-14876. (Guilt edged mystery). 1950. Dutton.
Vengeance Mountain. R. C. House. (Orig.). 1981. pap. cancelled (ISBN 0-505-51642-X). Tower Bks.
Vengeance, My Love. E. G. Fulton. 320p. (Orig.). 1982. pap. 2.95 (ISBN 0-523-48035-0). Pinnacle Bks.
Vengeance of a Jew. Charles Guenot. LC 7-152. 1867. E. Cummiskey.
Vengeance of Don Manuel: By Bernard Deleuze Pseud. Translated by Norman Cameron. Jean Sabran. LC 52-13640. 1953. Putnam.
Vengeance of Felix. Jose Joaquim de Campos da Costa Medeiros e Albuquerque. Ed. & tr. by Isaac Goldberg. (International Pocket Library). pap. 3.00. Branden.
Vengeance of Fortuna West. Ray Hogan. LC 82-45612. (D. D. Western Ser.). 192p. 1983. 11.95 (ISBN 0-385-18432-8). Doubleday.
Vengeance of Hurricane Williams. Gordon Ray Young. LC 25-221132. George H. Doran Company.
Vengeance of Jefferson Gawne. Charles Alden Seltzer. LC 17-25244. 1917. A. C. McClurg & Co.
Vengeance of Jefferson Gawne. Charles Alden Seltzer. LC 29-307707. 1917. Grosset & Dunlap.
Vengeance of Maurice Denalguez. Selina Dolaro. LC 6-33855. Belford, Clarke & Company; Etc., Etc.
Vengeance of Monsieur Blakshirt. David Graeme, pseud. LC 35-753. J. B. Lippincott Company.
Vengeance of the God. Lewis Arriola. 206p. 1981. 9.50 (ISBN 0-682-49687-1). Exposition.
Vengeance of the Gods, and Three Other Stories of Real American Color Line Life. William Pickens. LC 72-4612. (Black Heritage Library Collection). 1972. 8.50 (ISBN 0-8369-9120-6). Books for Libraries Press.
Vengeance of the Gods, and Three Other Stories of Real American Color Line Life. William Pickens. LC 73-18564. 1975. 7.50 (ISBN 0-404-11376-1). AMS Press.
Vengeance of the Gods: And Three Other Stories of Real American Color Line Life. William Pickens. LC 22-15210. The A. M. E. Book Concern.
Vengeance of the Golden Hawk. Joseph Rosenberger. (Death merchant# 14). 1976. (pbk.) 1.25 (ISBN 0-523-00796-5). Pinnacle Books.
Vengeance of the Ivory Skull. Marion Harvey. LC 23-8531. E. J. Clode.
Vengeance of Valdone. Betty Ferm. (Dell book). 1973. (pbk) 0.75. Dell.
Vengeance Platoon. Daniel T. Streib. (Orig.). 1979. pap. 1.50 (ISBN 0-532-15393-6). Woodhill.
Vengeance Rider. Gerald Drayson Adams. Orig. Title: Rawhide Killer. 192p. 1974. pap. 1.25 o.p. (ISBN 0-87056-376-9, 6376). Brandon.
Vengeance Rider. Dan Roberts. LC 66-8150. 1966. Arcadia House.
Vengeance Riders: A Western Novel by Jack Barton Pseud. Joseph Chadwick. LC 56-26166. (Popular library, 729). 1956. Popular Library.
Vengeance Rides West. A. A Baker. 1976. 4.95. Avalon Books.
Vengeance Seeker No. 2. Will C Knott. 1975. (pbk.) 0.95. Ace Books.
Vengeance: Short Story Collection. Leslie Caron. LC 81-43630. 192p. 1982. 12.95 (ISBN 0-385-17896-4). Doubleday.
Vengeance Spur. Tex Steele. 1980. pap. 1.75 (ISBN 0-8439-0833-5). Nordon Pubns.
Vengeance Street: By Robert Bloomfield Pseud. 1st Ed. Leslie Edgley. LC 52-10404. 1952. Published for the Crime Club by Doubleday.
Vengeance Ten. Joe Poyer, pseud. LC 80-65990. 1980. 13.95 (ISBN 0-689-11110-X). Atheneum.
Vengeance Trail. Max Brand. 1979. pap. 2.25 (ISBN 0-671-83034-1). PB.
Vengeance Trail. Dwight Bruckner. 128p. 1982. pap. 1.75 (ISBN 0-505-51764-7). Tower Bks.
Vengeance Trail. Frederick Faust. LC 41-19715. 1941. Dodd, Mead & Company.
Vengeance Trail. Charles N Heckelmann. LC 44-47009. 1944. Arcadia House, Inc.
Vengeance Trail. Kim Knight. LC 42-126391. 1942. Dodge Publishing Company.
Vengeance Trail. Dean Owen. (Latigo Ser.: Vol. 2). 224p. (Orig.). 1981. pap. 1.95 (ISBN 0-445-04663-5). Popular Lib.
Vengeance Trail. Lauran Paine. (Foulsham western story). 1958. W. Foulsham.
Vengeance Trail: By Ford Pendleton Pseud. Gifford Paul Cheshire. LC 58-9132. 1958. Avalon Books.
Vengeance Trail of Josey Wales. Forrest Carter. LC 75-41318. 6.95 (ISBN 0-440-09298-1). Delacorte Press/Eleanor Friede.
Vengeance Trial. Dwight Bruckner. (Belmont Tower Book). 1.25 (ISBN 0-505-51218-1). Tower Pubns.
Vengeance Valley. Allen Appel. 1979. pap. 1.75 o.s.i. (ISBN 0-505-51448-6). Tower Bks.
Vengeance Valley. Fred East. LC 46-814. 1946. Macrae-Smith-Co.
Vengeance Valley. Fred East. LC 47-23584. 1947. Triangle Books.
Vengeance Valley. Allan K. Echols. 1970. Repr. pap. 0.50 o.p. (50-490). Manor Bks.
Vengeance Valley. George G. Gilman, pseud. (Edge Ser.: No. 17). 160p. (Orig.). 1976. pap. 1.95 (ISBN 0-523-41838-8). Pinnacle Bks.
Vengeance Valley. Frederick Dilley Glidden. LC 75-26982. 1975. 8.95 (ISBN 0-8161-6328-6). G. K. Hall.
Vengeance Valley. Paul Evan Lehman. LC 50-39498. (Handi-book western, 119). 1950. Quinn Pub. Co.
Vengeance Valley. Roy Manning. LC 46-814. 1946. Macrae-Smith Company.
Vengeance Valley. Roy Manning. LC 47-235842. 1947. Triangle Books, the Blakiston Company.
Vengeance Valley. Luke Short. (Adult Ser.). 1975. Repr. lib. bdg. 8.95 o.p. (ISBN 0-8161-6328-6, Large Print Bks). G K Hall.
Vengeance Valley. Harry Whittington. LC 46-21220. 1946. Phoenix Press.
Vengeance Valley: By Luke Short Pseud. Frederick Dilley Glidden. LC 50-10633. 1950. Houghton Mifflin.
Vengeful Men. Ray Gaulden. LC 57-115708. (Permabooks, M-3110. Western, O). 1957. Permabooks.
Vengenance Trail. Max Brand. LC 41-197157. 1941. Dodd, Mead & Company.
Vengence Is Mine" A Story of Simple Faith. Hodge Mathes. LC 29-13683. 1928. David C. Cook Publishing Company.
Veni! Vidi!-----? Belle M Miller. LC 7-25972. Hann & Adair.
Venial Sin. Jewel Montreu. LC 34-39245. 1934. Meador Publishing Company.
Venice & the Fourth Crusade. Denton Whitson. 6.95 o.p. Moore Pub Co.
Venice Plot. Raymond Rudorff. LC 76-8168. 7.95 (ISBN 0-399-11803-9). Berkley Pub. Corp.: Distributed by Putnam.
Venice Plot. Raymond Rudorff. (Berkley Medallion Book). 1977. 1.75 (ISBN 0-425-03554-9). Berkley Pub. Corp.
Venice Train. Georges Simenon. LC 74-5759. 1974. 6.50 (ISBN 0-15-193506-8). Harcourt Brace Jovanovich.
Venison and a Breath of Sage: Tales of the San Juan Ranch. Edward Selden Spaulding. LC 68-1089. 1967. W.T. Genns.
Venna Hastings: Story of an Eastern Mormon Convert. Julia Farr. LC 19-856346. 1919. Zion's Printing and Publishing Company.
Venner Crime. Cecil John Charles Street. LC 34-692. 1934. Dodd, Mead & Company.
Venom. Alan Scholefield. LC 77-22600. 1978. 7.95 (ISBN 0-688-03250-8). Morrow.
Venom Business: A Novel. Michael Crichton. LC 69-18536. 1969. 5.95. World Pub. Co.
Venom House. Arthur William Upfield. LC 52-5120. 1952. Published for the Crime Club by Doubleday.
Venom in Eden. Marjorie Boniface. 1942. Published for the Crime Club by Doubleday, Doran & Company, Inc.
Venom of Argus. Richard Avery. (Expendables). (Gold Medal Book: Vol. 4) (ISBN 0-449-13586-1). Fawcett.
Ventian Secret. Evelyn Bond. 1977. pap. 1.50 (ISBN 0-532-15242-5). Woodhill.
Venture. Max Eastman. LC 27-24010. 1927. A. & C. Boni.
Venture: A Story of the Shadow World. Robert Norman Grisewood. LC 11-3476. 1.00. R. F. Fenno & Company.
Venture in Identity. Lucile Wand Caplinger Houghton. LC 11-29080. 1911. Doubleday, Page & Company.
Venture in the East. Bruce Lancaster. LC 51-3397. 1951. Little, Brown.
Venture into Darkness. Alice Tisdale Nourse Hobart. LC 55-7205. 1955. Longmans, Green.
Venture Inward. Hugh L. Cayce. pap. 0.95 o.p. (ISBN 0-06-080424-6, P424, PL). Har-Row.
Venture Once More: A Novel of Cornwall, 1790-1791. Winston Graham. LC 54-6780. 1954. Doubleday.
Venture's End. Karin Michaelis. Tr. by Colbron, Grace Isabel. LC 28-6305. Harcourt, Brace and Company.
Ventures in Common Sense see Collected Works.
Ventures into the Deep. Leonard Wibberly, pseud. (Illus.). 1962. 3.95 o.p. Washburn.
Ventures of Connie; or, Being Married. Dorothy S Day. LC 22-6935. 1922. The Stratford Company.
Venturing South. Illustrated by Ludmilla Monomachov. Roy White. LC 58-463544. 1958. Brethren Press.
Venturous Lady. George Harmon Coxe. LC 48-6066. 1948. A. A. Knopf.
Venus. Rena Oldfield Pettersen. LC 24-4580. Dorrance & Company.
Venus. Jean Vignaud & Shively, Mrs. Hilda, Tr. LC 29-11245. The Bobbs-Merrill Company.
Venus: A Novel Based on the Life of Anais Nin. Darwin Porter. LC 81-70031. 1982. 13.95 (ISBN 0-87795-366-X). Arbor Hse.
Venus and Cupid: Or, A Trip from Mount Olympus to London. Henry William Pullen. LC 7-42393. 1896. J. B. Lippincott Company.
Venus and the Voters. Gwyn Thomas. LC 47-12527. 1948. Little, Brown.
Venus Belt. L. Neil Smith. (Orig.). 1981. pap. 2.25 (ISBN 0-345-28721-5, Del Rey). Ballantine.
Venus Death. Ben Benson. LC 53-5411. 1953. M. S. Mill Co. and W. Morrow.
Venus Del Circo. new ed. Jairo Ibero. 160p. (Span.). 1974. pap. 1.00 o.p. (ISBN 0-88473-213-4). Fiesta Pub.
Venus Disarmed: A Novel. Jeremy Dole. LC 66-15113. 1966. Crown Publishers.
Venus Equilateral. George Oliver Smith. LC 75-426. (Garland Library of Science Fiction). 1975. 11.00 (ISBN 0-8240-1431-6). Garland Pub.
Venus Equilateral. George Oliver Smith. LC 47-31451. 1947. Prime Press.
Venus Examined. Robert Kyle, pseud. 320p. 1972. pap. 0.95 o.p. (M1761, Crest). Fawcett World.
Venus Examined: A Physiological Novel. Robert Kyle, pseud. LC 68-16152. 1968. B. Geis Associates; Distributed by Grove Press.
Venus Factor. Ed. by Vic Ghidalia & Roger Elwood. 1977. pap. 1.25 (ISBN 0-532-12475-8). Woodhill.
Venus Factor. 2nd ed. Ed. by Vic Ghidalia & Roger Elwood. 1972. pap. 0.95 o.p. (532-75462-075). Manor Bks.
Venus Fly-Trap. John William Wainwright. LC 79-22757. 8.95 (ISBN 0-312-83870-0). St. Martin's Press.
Venus in Furs. 2nd ed. Leopold Von Sacher-Masoch. 1968. pap. 0.75 o.p. (B75-220). Belmont-Tower.
Venus in Furs: By Leopold Von Sacher-Masoch Von Lemberg. Leopold Sacher-Masoch. LC 65-7008. 1964. pap., 3.00. John Amslow Box.
Venus in India. Charles Devereaux. (Orig.). 1967. pap. 1.95 (ISBN 0-87067-611-3, BH611). Holloway.
Venus in India. Charles Devereaux. 1967. pap. 1.25 o.p. (ISBN 0-87067-138-3, 88-138). Holloway.
Venus in Sparta. Louis Auchincloss. LC 58-9052. 1958. Houghton Mifflin.
Venus in the Country. LC 82-48000. (Grove Press Victorian library). 1982. 3.95 (ISBN 0-394-62420-3). Grove Press.
Venus in the East. Wallace Irwin. LC 18-22249. George H. Doran Company.
Venus in Transit. Audrey Louise Laski. LC 64-8737. 1965. bds., 4.95. McGraw.
Venus McFarland: A Novel. Adah Camilla Dodd Poince. LC 4298.
Venus of Cadiz: An Extravaganza. Rihard Henry Wilson. LC 5-18316. 1905. H. Holt and Company.
Venus of Ille & Other Stories. Prosper Merimee. Tr. by Jean Kimber. (Oxford Library of French Classics Ser). 1966. 6.50x o.p. (ISBN 0-19-255211-2). Oxford U Pr.
Venus of Ille: And Other Stories; Tr. by Jean Kimber; Introd. by A. W. Raitt. Prosper Merimee. LC 66-74874. (Oxford lib. of French classics). 1966. 4.00. Oxford.
Venus of Konpara. 1st Ed. John Masters. LC 60-755062. 1960. Harper.
Venus on the Half-Shell. Kilgore Trout. LC 77-360347. 1975. 1.25. Dell Publishing.
Venus on the Half-Shell. Kilgore Trout. 1975. (pbk.) 0.95. Dell.
Venus Over Lannery. Martin Donisthorpe Armstrong. LC 36-17530. Harcourt, Brace and Company.
Venus Plus X. Theodore Sturgeon. LC 76-10719. (Gregg Press science fiction series). 1976. 8.50 (ISBN 0-8398-2321-5). Gregg Press.
Venus Rising: A Novel. 1st Ed. Charles Grayson. LC 54-10692. 1954. Holt.
Venus School-Mistress. Pref. by M. Wilson. 1969. pap. 1.35 o.p. (Z1027Z, Zebra). Grove.
Venus: The Lonely Goddess. John Erskine. 1949. W. Morrow.
Venus Trap. James Michael Ullman. LC 66-21817. (Inner sanctum mystery). 1966. Simon and Schuster.
Venus Unarmed. Lawrence Treat. LC 61-14001. 1961. Published for the Crime Club by Doubleday.
Venus Unmasked. Evelyn Herbert. LC 52-8987. 1952. Dodd, Mead.
Venus Victrix: A Study of a Woman. Helen Buckingham Mathers Reeves. LC 7-30672. United States Book Company.
Venus with Pistol. Gavin Lyall. LC 74-83683. 1969. 5.95. Scribner.
Venus with Us: A Tale of the Caesar. William Moulton Marston. LC 32-198241. Sears Publishing Company.
Venusberg and Agents and Patients. Anthony Dymoke Powell. (Two early novels in one volume). 1965. 4.75 o.p. (ISBN 0-316-71540-9). Little.
Venusian Secret Science. Michael X. 1970. pap. 6.95. G Barker Bks.
Venus's Doves. A Novel. Ida Ashworth Taylor. LC 8-25665. (On cover: Seaside library. Pocket ed. no. 426). 1885. G. Munro.
Vera. Elizabeth. 1973. pap. 0.95 o.p. (09190). Curtis.
Vera. Elizabeth. 1973. (pbk) 0.95. Curtis.
Vera. Georg Kaiser. Tr. by Thomas, R. Willis. LC 39-31687. Alliance Book Corporation, Longmans, Green & Co.

Vera. Mary Annette Beauchamp Russell Russell. LC 21-18795. 1921. Doubleday, Page & Company.

Vera Dickson's Triumph. Sara Currie Palmer. LC 17-25814. The Bible Institute Colportage Ass'n.

Vera Gerard Case. Joseph Cottin Cooke. LC 37-12433. 1937. Manthorne & Burack, Inc.

Vera of the Strong Heart. Marion Mole. LC 10-14368. 1910. G. P. Putnam's Sons.

Vera the Medium. Richard Harding Davis. 1908. C. Scribner's Sons.

Vera Vorontzoff. Sof'Ia Vasil'Evna Kovalevskaia. LC 7-141645. Lamson, Wolffe and Co.

Verana: A Tale of Border Life. Carl Jaeger. The Abbey Press.

Veranilda: A Romance. George Robert Gissing. LC 68-54270. 1968. AMS Press.

Veranilda: An Unfinished Romance. George Robert Gissing. LC 38-10341. (Half-title: The world's classics, cccxlix). 1929. Oxford University Press, H. Milford.

Vera's Charge. Frances Christine Tiernan. The Ave Maria.

Verbalist. Alfred Ayers. 1911. 12.50 (ISBN 0-8274-3669-6). R West.

Verbena Camellia Stephanotis: And Other Stories. Walter Besant. LC 6-12400. (On cover: Harper's Franklin square library, no. 723). 1892. Harper &Brothes.

Verdi: a Novel of the Opera. Franz V. Werfel. Tr. by Helen Jessiman. 1925. Simon & Schuster.

Verdict. Hildegard Knef. LC 75-34174. 384p. 1976. 10.00 o.p. (ISBN 0-374-28322-2). FS&G.

Verdict. Hildegarde Neff. LC 75-34174. 10.00 (ISBN 0-374-28322-2). Farrar, Straus and Giroux.

Verdict. Barry C Reed. LC 79-27314. 10.95 (ISBN 0-671-25110-4). Simon & Schuster.

Verdict. Barry C Reed. LC 80-22825. 1980. 14.95 (ISBN 0-8161-3175-9). G. K. Hall.

Verdict in Question: An Eve Gill Story. 1st Ed. Selwyn Jepson. LC 60-9481. (Crime club selection). 1960. Published for the Crime Club by Doubleday.

Verdict of Bridlegoose. Llewelyn Powys. LC 26-12537. Harcourt, Brace and Company.

Verdict of the Gods. Sarath Kumar Ghosh. LC 5-9057. 1905. Dodd, Mead & Company.

Verdict of the Sea. Alan Sullivan. LC 28-333216. 1928. E. P. Dutton & Company.

Verdict of Thirteen. Ed. by Detection Club. 256p. 1980. pap. 2.25 (ISBN 0-345-28901-3). Ballantine.

Verdict of Thirteen: A Detection Club Anthology. Julian Symons & Detection Club. LC 78-69511. 9.95 (ISBN 0-06-014212-X). Harper & Row.

Verdict of Thirteen: A Detection Club Anthology. Julian Symons & Detection Club. LC 80-27323. 1981. 13.50 (ISBN 0-89340-300-8). J. Curley.

Verdict of Thirteen: A Detective Club Anthology. Ed. & intro. by Julian Symons. LC 78-69511. 1979. 9.95i (ISBN 0-06-014212-X, HarpT). Har-Row.

Verdict of Twelve. Raymond William Postgate. LC 67-6693. 1967. Knopf.

Verdict of Twelve. Raymond William Postgate. LC 40-11301. 1940. Pub. for the Crime Club, by Doubleday, Doran and Co., Inc.

Verdict of Twelve. Raymond William Postgate. LC 40-12661. 1940. Pub. for the Crime Club by Doubleday, Doran and Co., Inc.

Verdict of Twelve. Raymond William Postgate. LC 45-13282. 1944. Triangle Books, the Blakiston Company.

Verdict of You All. Henry Lancelot Aubrey-Fletcher. LC 27-4394. Payson & Clarke, Ltd.

Verdict Suspended. Helen Nielsen. 1970. pap. 0.60 o.p. (0502-06094). Curtis.

Verdict Suspended: A Mystery Novel. Helen Nielsen. LC 64-17614. 1964. Morrow.

Verena in the Midst: A Kind of a Story. Edward Verrall Lucas. LC 20-17824. 1.90. George H. Doran Company.

Verendorps: A Novel. Basil Verdendorp. LC 8-30202. 1880. C. M. Hertig.

Verge of Glory. 1st Ed. Frederick Stallknecht Wight. LC 56-11296. 1956. Harcourt, Brace.

Vergil's Lovers. Stanley Ward. 49p. (Orig.). 1982. pap. 4.00 (ISBN 0-942626-01-X). Quincunx.

Verite see Quatre Evangiles.

Verity. Brenda Jagger. LC 79-6656. 1980. 11.95 (ISBN 0-385-15887-4). Doubleday.

Verla Winters Story. Helen E Lumpp. 4.50. New Voices Pub. Co.

Verla Winters Story: By Helen E. Lumpp. Helen E Lumpp. LC 66-1462. 1966. New Voices Pub. Co.

Verlorene Koffer: Reader 1. Rita M. Walbruck. LC 80-22198. (Auf Heisser Spur Ser.). (gr. 9-12). 1981. pap. 1.95 (ISBN 0-88436-850-5). EMC.

Vermilion. Nathan Aldyne. 1980. pap. 2.75 (ISBN 0-380-76596-9, 81570-2). Avon.

Vermilion. Phyllis A. Whitney. LC 81-23524. 1982. 13.95 (ISBN 0-8161-3312-3). G.K. Hall.

Vermilion Box. Edward Verrall Lucas. LC 16-223002. George H. Doran Company.

Vermilion Bridge. Shelley Smith Mydans. LC 79-7804. 1980. 11.95 (ISBN 0-385-03547-0). Doubleday.

Vermilion: By Idwal Jones. Idwal Jones. LC 47-2544. 1947. Prentice-Hall, Inc.

Vermilion Gate. Lin Yutang. 439p. 1980. 7.95 (ISBN 0-89955-163-7, Pub. by Mei Ya China); pap. 6.50 (ISBN 0-89955-192-0). Intl Schol Bk Serv.

Vermilion Gate: A Novel of a Far Land. Lin Yutang. LC 53-6586. 1953. J. Day Co.

Vermilion Gate: A Novel of a Far Land. Lin Yutang. LC 70-138158. (Illus.). 1971. (ISBN 0-8371-5615-7). Greenwood Press.

Vermilion Gate: A Novel of a Far Land. Lon Yu-T'ang. LC 70-138158. 438p. 1972. Repr. of 1953 ed. lib. bdg. 18.25x (ISBN 0-8371-5615-7, LIVG). Greenwood.

Vermilion Pencil: A Romance of China. Homer Lea. 1908. The McClure Company.

Vermont Renaissance. Coral Crosman. (Illus.). 72p. 1976. pap. 2.50 (ISBN 0-913884-01-4). Porphyrion Pr.

Vermont Village Murder. B. Comfort. 192p. (Orig.). 1982. 4.00 (ISBN 0-9608726-0-4). Landgrove Pr.

Vernal Dune: In Which Is Shown the End of an Era. Eugene Hall. LC 13-18996. 1913. The Neale Publishing Company.

Vernal Equinox, a Novel in Four Parts. Olive Hamlin. LC 46-951. 1946. B. Humphries, Inc.

Verner's Pride. Ellen Price Henry Wood Wood. (Seaside library, v. 5, no. 83). 1877. G. Munro.

Vernon, an Anecdotal Novel. Osmond Beckwith. LC 81-65121. (Illus.). 10.00. Breaking Point.

Vernon: An Anecdotal Novel. Osmond Beckwith. LC 81-65121. (Illus.). 204p. 1981. 10.00 (ISBN 0-917020-02-2). Breaking Point.

Vernon Lonsdale. L. Clay Kilby. 1876. For the Author.

Vernon's Aunt: Being the Oriental Experiences of Miss Lavinia Moffat. Sara Jeannette Duncan Cotes. LC 7-3325. 1895. D. Appleton and Company.

Veronica. Martha Waddill Austin. LC 3-6969. 1903. Doubleday, Page & Company.

Veronica. Elisabeth Beresford. (Orig.). 1980. pap. 1.75 (ISBN 0-8439-8004-4, Tiara Bks). Nordon Pubns.

Veronica. Florence Morse Kingsley. LC 13-5074. 1913. D. Appleton and Company.

Veronica. Laura Pope. LC 51-5968. 1951. Longmans, Green.

Veronica: A Novel. Constance Loveland. LC 58-121939. 1958. Vanguard Press.

Veronica, a Novel. W Leon Sydnor. LC 56-871998. 1956. Exposition Press.

Veronica: A Novel. Frances Eleanor Ternan D. Trollope. LC 52-48516. 1870. Harper.

Veronica. A Novel. (seaside library. v. 73, no. 1475). 1883. G. Munro.

Veronica Died Monday. Geraldine Trotta. LC 52-7351. (Red badge detective). 1952. Dodd, Mead.

Veronica: Or, The Free Court of Aarau. Heinrich Zschokke & Spring, Samuel, Tr. 1845. Harper & Brothers.

Veronica Playfair. Maud Wilder Goodwin. 1909. 1.50. Little, Brown, and Company.

Veronica's Room: A Melodrama. Ira Levin. 1974. 5.95 (ISBN 0-394-49145-9). Random.

Veronique. Virginia Coffman. 1976. 1.75 (ISBN 0-449-22964-5). Fawcett Crest.

Veronique: A Novel. Virginia Coffman. LC 74-18162. 8.95 (ISBN 0-87795-107-1). Arbor House.

Veronique: A Novel. Virginia Coffman. LC 80-17940. 1980. 17.50 (ISBN 0-8161-3048-5). G. K. Hall.

Verstical City. Fannie Hurst. LC 22-5605. Harper & Brothers.

Vertical and Horizontal. Lillian Ross. LC 63-12570. 1963. Simon and Schuster.

Vertical Smile. Richard Condon. LC 74-163593. 1971. 6.95. Dial Press.

Verts: Or, The Three Creeds: a Novel. Charles Maurice Davies. LC 75-1506. (Victorian Fiction: Novels of Faith and Doubt; V. 56). 1975. 35.00 (ISBN 0-8240-1580-0). Garland Pub.

Verts; or, the Three Creeds, 1876. Charles Maurice Davies. Ed. by Robert L. Wolff. LC 75-1506. (Victorian Fiction Ser.). 1975. lib. bdg. 66.00 (ISBN 0-8240-1580-0). Garland Pub.

Veruchia. E. C. Tubb. (Dumarest of Terra Ser.: No. 8). 160p. 1982. pap. 2.25 (ISBN 0-441-86181-4, Pub. by Ace Science Fiction). Ace Bks.

Very Best People. Elizabeth Villars, pseud. LC 78-26160. 9.95 (ISBN 0-698-10980-5). Coward, McCann & Geoghegan.

Very Breath of Hell. George Beare. 1971. 4.95 o.p. (ISBN 0-395-12666-5). HM.

Very Breathe of Hell. George Beare. LC 74-151464. (Vic Stallard adventure). 1974. (pbk.) 1.25. Warner Paperback Lib.

Very Cagey Lady. Joyce Elbert. 1980. pap. 2.95 (ISBN 0-451-09936-2, E9936, Sig.). NAL.

Very Cold for May. William P. McGivern. LC 50-7786. (Red badge mystery). 1950. Dodd, Mead.

Very Dead of Winter. Sarah Nichols. (queen-size gothic). 1974. (pbk.) 1.25. Popular Library.

Very Deadly Game. Victor B Miller. (Kojak,#6). 1975. (pbk.) 1.25 (ISBN 0-671-78960-0). Pocket Books.

Very Dry with a Twist. Daniel Banko. LC 74-23232. 1975. 6.95. Saturday Review Press.

Very Dutiful Daughter. Elizabeth Hansfield. (Orig.). 1982. pap. 2.25 (ISBN 0-425-05226-5). Berkley Pub.

Very Dutiful Daughter. Elizabeth Mansfield, pseud. (Berkley book). 1979. 1.95 (ISBN 0-425-04084-4). Berkley Pub. Corp.

Very End & Other Stories. Osbert Burdett. 1973. lib. bdg. 15.00 (ISBN 0-8414-2546-9). Folcroft.

Very End & Other Stories. Osbert Burdett. 1977. Repr. of 1929 ed. lib. bdg. 10.00 (ISBN 0-8492-0394-5). R West.

Very End & Other Stories. Osbert Burdett. 1929. Repr. 20.00 o.p. R West.

Very Fall of the Sun. Samuel Hazo. 1978. 1.95 (ISBN 0-445-04209-5). Popular Library.

Very Far Away from Anywhere Else. Ursula K. Le Guin. (gr. 9-12). pap. 1.95 (ISBN 0-553-20081-X). Bantam.

Very Far Country. Martha Edith Almedingen. LC 58-7832. 1958. Appleton-Century-Crofts.

Very First Lady. Steve Dunleavy. LC 80-14544. 10.95 (ISBN 0-671-24691-7). Simon and Schuster.

Very Friendly Skies. Jan Kendrick. 1976. (pbk.) 1.50. Warner Books.

Very Good Hater: A Tale of Revenge. Reginald Hill. LC 82-8301. 1982. 12.95 (ISBN 0-914378-97-X). Countryman Press.

Very Good, Jeeves. Pelham Grenville Wodehouse. LC 30-17701. 1930. Doubleday, Doran & Company, Inc.

Very Good, Jeeves. Pelham Grenville Wodehouse. LC 35-28574. 1931. A. L. Burt Company.

Very Hard Cash. A Novel. Charles Reade. LC 13-9387. 1864. Harper & Brothers.

Very Hard Cash: By Charles Reade... Charles Reade. (On cover: Lovell's library, v. 19, no. 915). 1887. J. W. Lovell Company.

Very Heaven. Richard Aldington. LC 37-4272. 1937. Doubleday, Doran & Company, Inc.

Very House. Mazo De La Roche. 1937. Little, Brown and Company.

Very Like a Whale. Ferdinand Mount. 1967. 5.00 o.p. Weybright.

Very Like a Whale: A Novel. Ferdinand Mount. LC 67-20364. 1967. Weybright and Talley.

Very Little Person. Mary Marvin Heaton Vorse. LC 11-112169. 1911. Houghton Mifflin Company.

Very Naughty Angel. Barbara Cartland. 1975. (pbk.) 1.25. Bantam Books.

Very Nearest Room. Jane Logan. LC 73-1122. 1973. 6.95 (ISBN 0-684-13527-2). Scribner.

Very Private Chauffeur. Charles Stanley Strong. LC 41-786925. Phoenix Press.

Very Private Life. Michael Frayn. LC 68-26503. 1968. Viking Press.

Very Private Love. Monica Haviland. 1970. pap. 0.75 o.p. (75-295). Manor Bks.

Very Private Secretary... Gertrude M. Robins Reynolds. LC 33-10597. 1933. Pub. for the Crime Club, Inc., by Doubleday, Doran & Company, Inc.

Very Private Secretary. Karl Rockwood. 192p. 1972. pap. 1.95 o.p. (ISBN 0-87977-145-3, DBB145). Dansk Blue Bk.

Very Private Secretary. Alan West. 160p. 1974. pap. 1.95 o.p. (ISBN 0-87682-401-7, 7401). Barclay Hse.

Very Private Sin. Laurence Oliver Brown. LC 32-20051. 1932. Minton, Balch & Company.

Very Private War. Jon Cleary. LC 80-12006. 1980. 9.95 (ISBN 0-688-03648-1). Morrow.

Very Proper Widow. Laura Matthews. 1982. pap. 2.25 (ISBN 0-451-11919-3, AE1919, Sig). NAL.

Very Quiet Place. Andrew Garve. 1967. 4.50 o.p. (ISBN 0-06-011447-9, HarpT). Har-Row.

Very Quiet Place: By Andrew Garve. 1st Ed. Paul Winterton. LC 67-11337. 1967. bds., 4.50. Harper.

Very Rich Hours of Count Von Stauffenberg. Paul West. LC 79-2662. (Illus.). 9.95 (ISBN 0-06-014593-5). Harper & Row.

Very Short Walk: A Novel. Lawrance Holmes. LC 76-107050. 1970. Macmillan.

Very Simple Scheme. Rebecca Baldwin. (Coventry Romance Ser.: No. 173). 224p. 1982. pap. 1.50 (ISBN 0-449-50274-0, Coventry). Fawcett.

Very Small Person. Annie Hamilton Donnell. LC 6-388916. 1906. Harper & Brothers.

Very Small Remnant. Michael Whitney Straight. LC 63-9144. 1963. Knopf.

Very Small Remnant. Michael Whitney Straight. LC 76-21507. (Zia book). 1976. 2.95 (ISBN 0-8263-0433-8). University of New Mexico Press.

Very Special Agent. Bernard Glemser. LC 67-25418. 1967. Funk & Wagnalls.

Very Special Agent. G. Napier. 1967. 5.95 o.p. (760170). Funk & W.

Very Special Agent. Geoffrey Napier. 1970. pap. 0.75 o.p. (T1489, Crest). Fawcett World.

Very Special Yarmulka. 1982. pap. 2.50 (ISBN 0-87306-186-1). Feldheim.

Very Strange Family. Frederick William Robinson. (On cover: Lovell's international series, no. 63). 1890. F. F. Lovell & Company.

Very Tender Love. Katharine Newlin Burt. (Signet Book). 1975. (pbk.) 0.95. New American Library.

Very Thin Line. Miriam Borgenicht. LC 78-116191. 1970. 4.50. Published for the Crime Club by Doubleday.

Very Unusual" The Wonderful World of Mr. K. Nakamura. limited 1st ed. Manly Palmer Hall. LC 76-54369. (Illus.). 8.75 (ISBN 0-89314-537-8). Philosophical Research Society.

Very Welcome Death. 1st Ed. D. L. Mathews. LC 61-11306. 1961. Holt, Rinehart and Winston.

Very Woman (Sixtine) A Cerebral Novel. Remy De Gourmont. Tr. by Barrets, J. L. LC 22-161492. 1922. N. L. Brown.

Very Young Couple. Benjamin Leopold Farjeon. LC 6-387629. (On cover: Lovell's Westminister series. no. 18). 1890. United States Book Company.

Very Young Housewife. Del Tremens. LC 79-17808. (Bogus Bks). (Orig.). 1979. pap. 5.95 o.p. (ISBN 0-916782-18-2). Harvard Common Pr.

Very Young Man and the Angel-Child. Elisa Armstrong Bengough. LC 6571. Dodge Publishing Company.

Very Young Mrs. Poe. Cothburn O'Neal. LC 56-7186. Crown Publishers.

Veselie Rusi. Evgeny Popov. 156p. (Rus.). 1981. 16.00 (ISBN 0-88233-675-4); pap. 7.50 (ISBN 0-88233-676-2). Ardis Pubs.

Vesey Inheritance. Gwendoline Butler. LC 76-377016. 1976. 3.50 (ISBN 0-333-18628-1). Macmillan.

Vesna Fialte: Spring in Fialte. Vladimir Vladimirovich Nabokov. (Sobranie Rasskazov I Povestei: Vol. 3). (Rus.). 1978. 15.00 (ISBN 0-88233-383-6); pap. 7.00 (ISBN 0-88233-384-4). Ardis Pubs.

Vesper Bells. Betty Hale Hyatt. LC 67-5893. 1967. Arcadia House.

Vesper Service Murders... Francis Van Wyck Mason. LC 31-14329. Pub. for the Crime Club, Inc., by Doubleday, Doran & Company, Inc.

Vespers in Vienna. Bruce Marshall. LC 47-306693. 1947. Houghton Mifflin-Co.

Vesprie Towers: A Novel. 2d impression. ed. Theodroe Watts-Dunton. LC 17-745821. 1917. John Lane Company.

Vespucci Papers. Ben Healey. LC 72-8572. 1972. 6.95 (ISBN 0-8161-6054-6). G. K. Hall.

Vessel of Dishonor: A Novel. Paul Roche. LC 62-15274. 1962. Sheed and Ward.

Vessel of Sadness. William Woodruff. LC 74-102075. (Illus.). 1969. 5.95. Kallman Pub. Co.

Vessel of Sadness. William Woodruff. LC 77-18270. 1978. 8.95 (ISBN 0-8093-0875-4). Southern Illinois University Press.

Vessel of Wrath: Tr. from the French. Simon Gantillon & Chevalier, Haakon Maurice, 1902- Tr. LC 47-30673. G. P. Putnam's Sons.

Vesta: Or, The Hidden Cross. Florida Presley Reed. LC 7-39793. 1894. The Foote & Davies Co., Printers.

Vestal Fire. Compton Mackenzie. LC 27-231481. George H. Doran Company.

Vestal: Or, A Tale of Pompeii... Thomas Gray. LC 6-45540. 1830. Gray and Bowen.

Vestal Virgin. Arthur Meeker. LC 34-41927. G. P. Putnam's Sons.

Vestibule Limited Mystery. Alexander Robertson. LC 7-41679. (secret service series, no. 39). 1891. Street & Smith.

Vestige of Valor. Gene Marvin. 1973. 6.50 (ISBN 0-533-00614-7). Vantage Press.

Vestiges of Time. Richard C Meredith. LC 77-76254. 1978. 6.95 (ISBN 0-385-13174-7). Doubleday.

Vestiges of Time. Richard C Meredith. 1979. 1.95 (ISBN 0-87216-572-8). Playboy Press.

Vestigia. Julia Constance Fletcher. 1884. Roberts Brothers.

Vesty of the Basins: A Novel. Sarah Pratt McLean Greene. LC 1-888. 1892. Harper & Brothers.

Vesty of the Basins: A Novel. Sarah Pratt McLean Greene. LC 1-8805. (On cover: Harper's quarterly. no. 1). 1893. Harper & Brothers.

Vesty of the Basins: A Novel. Sarah Pratt McLean Greene. LC 6783. 1900. Harper & Brothers.

Vesuvius. Emmanuel Robles. LC 70-106345. (New library of French classics). 1970. 7.95. Prentice-Hall.
Veta Posse. Eugene C. Vories. 192p. 1974. 5.50 o.p. (ISBN 0-682-48009-6, Lochinvar). Exposition.
Veteran, District Thirteen. Hazel V. Denney. 1976. 6.95 o.p. (ISBN 0-8059-2331-4). Dorrance.
Veteran of the Grand Army. Cyrus Cobb & Darius Cobb. LC 1-3250. 1871. L. N. Richardson & Co.
Veteran of the Grand Army. A Novel. Cyrus Cobb & Darius Cobb. LC 1-3249. 1870. C. and D. Cobb.
Veterans of Chelsea Hospital. new ed. George Robert Gleig. LC 8-30422. 1857. G. Routledge & Co.
Vet's Daughter. Barbara Comyns. LC 81-9702. (Virago Modern Classic). 1981. 5.95 (ISBN 0-385-27190-5). Dial.
Veva: Or, The War of the Peasants, and The Conscript. Hendrik Conscience & Mayer, Brantz, 1809-1879, Tr. LC 6-28056. 1856. Murphy & Co.
Via Berlin. Crittenden Marriott. LC 17-28756. R. J. Shores.
Via Crucis: A Romance of the Second Crusade. Francis Marion Crawford. LC 98-1488. 1898. The Macmillan Co.
Via Crucis: A Romance of the Second Crusade. Francis Marion Crawford. LC 9-52083. 1899. The Macmillan Company.
Via Crucis: A Romance of the Second Crusade. Francis Marion Crawford. 1900. The Macmillan Company.
Via Lucis: A Novel. Magda Sindici. LC 7-4109. 1898. G. H. Richmond & Son.
Via Mala: A Novel. John Knittel. LC 34-399379. 1935. Frederick A. Stokes Company.
Via Manhattan. Hawthorne Hurst. LC 30-25813. A. H. King.
Via Negativa. Ed. by D. W. Dockrill & R. Mortley. 211p. 1983. pap. text ed. 23.25x (ISBN 0-85668-915-7, Pub. by Aris & Phillips England). Humanities.
Via P. & O. Jane Stocking. LC 14-6793. 1914. Dodd, Mead and Company.
Via Panama. Margaret Jepson. LC 34-20214. 1934. Harper & Brothers.
Via Vitae. Oella Azuba Thompson. LC 18-6921. The Roxburg Publishing Company, Inc.
Viaduct Murder. Ronald Arbuthnott Knox. LC 26-8067. 1926. Simon and Schuster.
Viaje a la Luna. Julio Verne. (Span.). 9.95 (ISBN 84-241-5635-8). E Torres & Sons.
Viajes de Gulliver. Jonathan Swift. (Span.). 9.95 (ISBN 84-241-5631-5). E Torres & Sons.
Vial of Vishnu: The Report of a Cycle of Events Following the Violation of the Command That the Vial Must Always Remain in the Possession of Its Rightful Owner. Austin Mann Drake. LC 16-554. 1915. 1.35. P. Roberts.
Viala. Elizabeth C McClintic. LC 45-5485. 1945. Dorrance & Company.
Vibrations--Appalachian. Gerald W. Covey. 4.75 (ISBN 0-8062-1023-0). Carlton.
Vibrations: Or, It Seemed Like a Good Idea at the Time: a Novel. Maxwell E Siegel. LC 79-13076. 1979. 7.95 (ISBN 0-688-03521-3). Morrow.
Vibrations: The Adventures & Musical Times of David Amram. David Amram. 1971. pap. 3.75 o.p. (ISBN 0-670-00324-7). Penguin.
Vic" The Autobiography of a Fox-Terrier. by marie more marsh. ed. Marie Louise More Marsh. LC 7-24671. F. J. Schulte & Company.
Vicar of Bullhampton. Anthony Trollope. LC 25-26590. (Half-title: The World's classics. cclxxii). 1924. H. Milford.
Vicar of Bullhampton. Anthony Trollope. LC 79-50727. (Illus.). 1979. 6.00 (ISBN 0-486-23824-5). Dover Publications.
Vicar of Bullhampton. A Novel. Anthony Trollope. LC 8-28873. 1870. Harper & Brothers.
Vicar of Christ. Walter F. Murphy. LC 78-26478. 12.95 (ISBN 0-02-588220-1). Macmillan.
Vicar of Christ. Walter F. Murphy. 1980. 2.95 (ISBN 0-345-28371-6). Ballantine Books.
Vicar of the Marches. Clinton Scollard. LC 10-29518. 1911. 1.20. Sherman, French & Company.
Vicar of Wakefield. Oliver Goldsmith. Ed. by Oswald Doughty. LC 73-16269. (Series: Scholartis Eighteenth Century Novels, No. 4.). 1973. 30.00. Folcroft Library Editions.
Vicar of Wakefield. Oliver Goldsmith. LC 48-36693. 1890. Macmillan.
Vicar of Wakefield. Oliver Goldsmith. LC 1-8251. (Half-Title: Young Folks' Series). D. Lothrop and Company.
Vicar of Wakefield. Oliver Goldsmith. LC 1-8252. 1888. Ginn & Company.
Vicar of Wakefield. Oliver Goldsmith. LC 1-8253. T. Y. Crowell & Co.
Vicar of Wakefield. Oliver Goldsmith. LC 1-8255. (Eclectic English classics). 1895. American Book Company.
Vicar of Wakefield. Oliver Goldsmith. LC 4853. W. B. Conkey Company.
Vicar of Wakefield. Oliver Goldsmith. Ed. by Hale, Edward Everett. LC 1-29047. (Standard Literature Series. No. 45). 1900. University Publishing Company.
Vicar of Wakefield. Oliver Goldsmith. Ed. by Edwards, George Clifton. LC 1-30750. (Johnson's English classics, no. 1). 1900. B. F. Johnson Publishing Company.
Vicar of Wakefield. Oliver Goldsmith. Ed. by Maitland, Louise. LC 4-21657. (Twentieth century text-books). 1904. D. Appleton and Company.
Vicar of Wakefield. Oliver Goldsmith. (Half-title: Everyman's library, ed. by Ernest Rhys. Fiction. no. 295). 1908. J. M. Dent & Co.
Vicar of Wakefield. Oliver Goldsmith. Ed. by Rutledge, Archibald Hamilton. LC 23-14120. Ginn and Company.
Vicar of Wakefield. Oliver Goldsmith. LC 27-26085. (Half-Title: The Series of English Idylls). 1926. 2.00. E. P. Dutton & Company.
Vicar of Wakefield. Oliver Goldsmith. Ed. by Raymond, Frederic Newton. LC 28-16167. (modern renders' series). 1928. The Macmillan Company.
Vicar of Wakefield. Oliver Goldsmith. (Half-title: The world's classics. 4). 1929. Oxford University Press, H. Milford.
Vicar of Wakefield. Oliver Goldsmith. LC 29-27453. 1929. David McKay Company.
Vicar of Wakefield. Oliver Goldsmith. Ed. by Jennings, Blandford. LC 31-15294. (Half-title: New pocket classics). The Macmillan Company.
Vicar of Wakefield, Oliver Goldsmith. Ed. by Turpin, Edna Henry Lee. LC 6-14553. (Maynard's English classic series. Special no.). (Illus.). 1906. Maynard, Merril, & Co.
Vicar of Wakefield. Oliver Goldsmith. LC 80-13171. (Classics in Large Print). 1980. 9.95 (ISBN 0-8161-3072-8). G. K. Hall.
Vicar of Wakefield. Oliver Goldsmith & Dobson, Austin. LC 4-18076. 1900. Macmillan & Co.
Vicar of Wakefield see Classics Set.
Vicar of Wakefield: A Tale. Oliver Goldsmith. LC 1-823332. 1772. Printed for William Mentz, and Sold by Most of the Booksellers in America.
Vicar of Wakefield: A Tale. Oliver Goldsmith. LC 34-32775. 1801. Printed by Joshua Cushing, for Cushing & Appleton.
Vicar of Wakefield. A Tale. Oliver Goldsmith. LC 4-220572. 1809. Printed and Published by William Duane, No., Market Street.
Vicar of Wakefield. A Tale. Oliver Goldsmith. LC 1-82360. 1812. Printed and Published by Cramer. Spear and Eichbaum.
Vicar of Wakefield: A Tale. Oliver Goldsmith. LC 1-8238. 1823. Deans and Force.
Vicar of Wakefield: A Tale. Oliver Goldsmith. LC 41-41838. 1830. J. Locken.
Vicar of Wakefield: A Tale. Oliver Goldsmith. LC 31-35201. (On cover: Putnam's choice library). 1848. G. P. Putnam.
Vicar of Wakefield: A Tale. Oliver Goldsmith. LC 1-8248. 1882. J. W. Lovell Company.
Vicar of Wakefield: A Tale. Oliver Goldsmith. LC 1-824958. (Half-Title: Classic Series). 1883. Roberts Brothers.
Vicar of Wakefield: A Tale. Oliver Goldsmith. LC 41-38134. 1888. Belford, Clarke & Co.
Vicar of Wakefield: A Tale. Oliver Goldsmith. Ed. by James, Henry. LC 6781. (Century classics). 1900. The Century Co.
Vicar of Wakefield: A Tale. Oliver Goldsmith. Ed. by Browne, William Hand. LC 2707. (English Classics--Star Series). Globe School Book Company.
Vicar of Wakefield: A Tale Supposed to Be Written by Himself. Oliver Goldsmith. LC 62-21360. 1963. Collier Books.
Vicar of Wakefield: A Tale Supposed to Be Written by Himself. Oliver Goldsmith. Ed. by Arthur Friedman. LC 74-171261. (Oxford English novels). 1974. 9.75 (ISBN 0-19-255345-3). Oxford University Press.
Vicar of Wakefield: A Tale Supposed to Be Written by Himself. Oliver Goldsmith. LC 1-8254. (Riverside Literature Series. No. 78). Houghton, Mifflin and Company.
Vicar of Wakefield: A Tale Supposed to Be Written by Himself. Oliver Goldsmith. Ed. by Morton, Edward Payson. LC 98-151. (Lake English classics). 1898. Scott, Foresman & Co.
Vicar of Wakefield: A Tale Supposed to Be Written by Himself. Oliver Goldsmith. Ed. by Boynton, Henry Walcott. LC 99-1685. (On verso of half-title: Macmillan's pocket English classics). 1899. The Macmillan Company.
Vicar of Wakefield: A Tale Supposed to Be Written by Himself. ed. for school use by edward p. morton... ed. Oliver Goldsmith. Ed. by Morton, Edward Payson. LC 20-5576. (Half-title: The Lake English classics, general editor, L. T. Danion...). 1920. Scott, Foresman and Company.
Vicar of Wakefield, and She Stoops to Conquer: Including the Author's Famous Essay "On the Theatre.". Oliver Goldsmith & Goldsmith, Oliver, 1728-1774. She Stoops to Conquer. LC 65-6534. (Perennial library). 1965. Harper & Row.
Vicar of Wakefield: And The Deserted Village. Oliver Goldsmith. LC 50-3300. (World's greatest literature). 1950. Fountain Press.
Vicar of Wakefield: And The Deserted Village. Oliver Goldsmith. LC 6-30925. (Eclestic English classics). American Book Company.
Vicar of Wakefield. Rasselas, Paul and Virginia... Oliver Goldsmith & Johnson, Samuel. LC 26-247072. G. Routledge and Sons.
Vicar of Wakefield. With an Introd. by Ernest Brennecke. Oliver Goldsmith. LC 56-14696. (Pocket library, PL54). 1957. Pocket Books.
Vicar of Wrexhill. Frances Milton Trollope. LC 70-162903. (Illus.). 1975. 27.50 (ISBN 0-404-54478-9). AMS Press.
Vicar of Wrexhill. Frances Milton Trollope. LC 75-486. (Victorian Fiction: Novels of Faith and Doubt; No. 39). 1975. 35.00 (ISBN 0-8240-1563-0). Garland Pub.
Vicarion. Henry Gardner Hunting. LC 26-165379. 1926. Unity School of Christianity.
Vicarious Years. John Van Druten. 1956. Scribner.
Vicar's Daughter. Emily Hilda Young. LC 28-24061. Harcourt, Brace and Company.
Vicar's Daughter: An Autobiographical Story. George Macdonald. LC 4-17597. G. Routledge & Sons, Limited.
Vicar's Daughter. An Autobiographical Study. George Macdonald. LC 12-183231. 1911. D. McKay.
Vicar's People. George Manville Fenn. (seaside library. vol. LVI. no. 1143). 1881. G. Munro.
Vice and Versa: By Jack Woodford Pseud. & Bruce McFarlane. Josiah Pitts Woolfolk & Bruce McFarlane. LC 53-4219. 1953. Signature Press.
Vice and Virture: A Story of Our Times. author's ed. William Gleeson. LC 13-18067. 1.50. W. F. Mecklenberg.
Vice Avenged: A Moral Tale. Lolah Burford. LC 78-136261. 1971. 5.95. Macmillan.
Vice Czar Murders. Cleve Franklin Adams. LC 41-13226. W. Funk, Inc.
Vice Isn't Private. Brian Talbot Cleeve. pap. 0.60 o.p. (73-621). Lancer.
Vice Isn't Private. By Brian Cleeve. Brian Talbot Cleeve. LC 66-21500. 1966. 3.95. Random.
Vice of Fools. Hobart Chatfield Chatfield-Taylor. LC 6-23431. 1897. H. S. Stone & Co.
Vice-President's Son. Dan Sytton. LC 29-25614. The Canterbury Press.
Vice Versa: A Novel. Josiah Pitts Woolfolk. Godwin.
Vice Versa: Or, A Lesson to Fathers. 2d ed. Thomas Anstey Guthrie. LC 41-30740. 1882. D. Appleton and Company.
Vice Versa: Or, A Lesson to Fathers. Thomas Anstey Guthrie. (Lovell's library. v. 1, no. 30). 1882. J. W. Lovell Company.
Vice Versa: Or, A Lesson to Fathers. Thomas Anstey Guthrie. (On cover: Seaside library. Pocket ed. no. 59). 1883. G. Munro.
Vice Versa: Or, A Lesson to Fathers. 7th ed. Thomas Anstey Guthrie. LC 4-16528. 1903. D. Appleton and Company.
Viceroy of Ouidah. Bruce Chatwin. pap. 5.15. Summit Bks.
Viceroys. Federico De Roberto. Tr. by Archibald Colquhoun. LC 62-10497. 1962. 5.95 o.p. (ISBN 0-15-193630-7). HarBraceJ.
Viceroys. Translated from the Italian by Archibald Colquhoun, with an Introd. by the Translator. 1st American Ed. Federico De Roberto. LC 62-10497. 1962. Brace & World.
Vicious Circle. Manning Long. LC 42-133844. 1942. Duell, Sloan and Pearce.
Vicious Circles. Julian Anthony Stuart Hale. LC 78-67769. 8.95 (ISBN 0-87795-205-1). Arbor House.
Vicious Circles. Anthony Stuart, pseud. 1979. 8.95 (ISBN 0-87795-205-1). Arbor Hse.
Vicious Circles. Anthony Stuart, pseud. 224p. 1981. pap. 1.95 (ISBN 0-445-04648-1). Popular Lib.
Vicious Circuit: A Novel. Franklin Coasten Langdon. LC 53-12555. 1953. Macmillan.
Vicious Pattern. Mary Violet Heberden. LC 45-10361. 1945. Pub. for the Crime Club by Doubleday, Doran and Co., Inc.
Vicious Virgin. John Furlong. (Orig.). pap. 0.95 o.p. (1140). Brandon.
Vicious Virtuoso. Louis Lombard. LC 10-163282. 1909. D. Estes & Company.
Vicious Viscount. rev. ed. Madeline Gibson. 176p. 1981. pap. 1.95 (ISBN 0-553-14812-5). Bantam.
Vicissitudes of Evangeline. Elinor Sutherland Glyn. (Barbara Cartland's Library of Love: Vol. 8). 182p. 1979. 12.95x (ISBN 0-7156-1385-5, Pub. by Duckworth England). Biblio Dist.
Vicissitudes of Evangeline: A Novel. Elinor Sutherland Glyn. LC 5-6946. 1905. Harper & Brothers.
Vicksburg. John T. Foster. 1981. pap. 2.95 (ISBN 0-89083-789-9). Zebra.
Vicky Van. Carolyn Wells. LC 18-55002. 1918. J. B. Lippincott Company.
Vicomte De Bragellone: The Son of Athos; or, Ten Years Later. A Continuation of "The Three Guardsmen" and "Twenty Years After". Alexandre Dumas & Maquet, Auguste. LC 6-42135. (American series. no. 298). M. J. Ivers & Co.
Vicomte De Bragelonne. Alexandre Dumas & Maquet, Auguste. LC 6-42134. (Half-title: The d'Artagnan romances). 1888. Little, Brown and Company.
Vicomte De Bragelonne... Alexandre Dumas & Maquet, Auguste. LC 4-17501. (Half-title: The romances of Alexandre Dumas. Handy library edition. The D'Artagnan romances...). 1893. Little, Brown and Company.
Vicomte De Bragelonne. Being the Continuation of the "Three Guardsmen" and "Twenty Years After,". Alexandre Dumas & Maquet, Auguste. LC 6-42137. (On cover: Seaside library. Pocket ed. no. 2064). G. Munro.
Vicomte De Bragelonne... By Alexandre Dumas. Alexandre Dumas & Maquet, Auguste. LC 36-37490. (Half-title: Everyman's library, ed. by Ernest Rhys. Fiction. no. 593-595). 1934-36. J. M. Dent & Sons, Ltd.
Vicomte De Bragelonne: Or, Ten Years After.". Alexandre Dumas & Maquet, Auguste. (Seaside library, v. 32, no. 664). G. Munroe.
Vicomte De Bragelonne: Or, Ten Years Later. Alexandre Dumas & Maquet, Auguste. LC 6-42138. (Half-title: The romances of Alexandre Dumas. Illustrated library ed. v. 16-21). 1893. Little, Brown, and Company.
Vicomte De Bragelonne; or Ten Years Later. By Alexandre Dumas... Alexandre Dumas & Maquet, Auguste. LC 4-22490. (Half-title: The D'Artagnan romances). 1901. Little, Brown, and Company.
Vicomte De Bragelonne: Or, Ten Years Later; Being the Completion of the "Three Musketeers," and "Twenty Years After.". Alexandre Dumas & Maquet, Auguste. LC 6-42133. 1857. G. Routledge & Co.
Vicomte De Bragelonne: Or Ten Years Later, Being the Completion of "The Three Musketeers" and "Twenty Years After". Alexandre Dumas & Maquet, Auguste. LC 3-27814. 1889. G. Routledge and Sons, Limited.
Vicomte De Bragelonne, the Son of Athos: Or, Ten Years Later. A Continuation of "The Three Musketeers". by alex dumas. a new revised translation by h. llewellyn williams. ed. Alexandre Dumas & Maquet, Auguste. Tr. by Williams, Henry Llewellyn, Jr. (On cover: The elite series, no. 17). The F. M. Lupton Publishing Company.
Vicomte's Bride. Amelie Claire Leroy. LC 8-20121. (On cover: Lovell's international series, no. 106). 1890. J. W. Lovell Company.
Victim. Doris Bell Collier Ball. LC 75-42827. 1976. 6.95 (ISBN 0-8027-5348-5). Walker.
Victim. Josephine Bell. 192p. 1983. pap. 2.95 (ISBN 0-8027-3021-3). Walker & Co.
Victim. Josephine Bell. LC 75-42827. (O.s.i.). 1976. 6.95 o.s.i. (ISBN 0-8027-5348-5). Walker & Co.
Victim. Saul Bellow. LC 47-120883. 1947. Vanguard Press.
Victim. U. Ludu Hla. LC 76-360166. 1976. 6.95 (ISBN 0-8027-5348-5). Ludu U Hla.
Victim: A Romance of the Real Jefferson Davis. Thomas Dixon. LC 14-12076. 1914. 1.35. D. Appleton and Company.
Victim: A Romance of the Real Jefferson Davis. Thomas Dixon. LC 31-195174. Grosset & Dunlap.
Victim and The Worm. Phyllis Bottome. LC 23-8183. George H. Doran Company.
Victim and Victor. John Rathbone Oliver. LC 28-28747. 1928. The Macmillan Company.
Victim for Hire. Pablo Morales. (Leisure book). 1.50 (ISBN 0-8439-0625-1). Nordon Pubns.
Victim Must Be Found see Epitaph for a Nurse.
Victim Must Be Found. 1st Ed. Mona Naomi Anne Hocking Messer. LC 59-6269. 1959. Published for the Crime Club by Doubleday.
Victim of a Crime. Weldon J Cobb. (On cover: The Melbourne series, no. 13). 1893. E. A. Weeks & Company.
Victim of Chancery: Or, a Debtor's Experience. Frederick Jackson. LC 5-2558. 1841. J. F. Trow, Printer.
Victim of Circumstance. Michael Underwood. LC 79-5332. 1980. 8.95 (ISBN 0-312-83951-0). St. Martin's Press.
Victim of Circumstances: A Novel. Geraldine Anthony. LC 1-31516. 1901. Harper & Bros.
Victim of Circumstances, and Other Stories. George Robert Gissing. LC 73-169551. (Short story index reprint series). 1971. (ISBN 0-8369-4013-X). Books for Libraries Press.

Victim of Circumstances: And Other Stories. George Robert Gissing. Ed. by Gissing, Alfred C. LC 28-2385. 1927. Houghton Mifflin Company.
Victim of Circumstances: Or, Nick Carter to the Rescue. Frederick William Davis. LC 6605. (On cover: Magnet detective library. no. 156). 1900. Street & Smith.
Victim of Excitement. The Bosom Serpent. Etc., Etc., Etc. Caroline Lee Whiting Hentz. LC 7-4140. 1853. A. Hart.
Victim of Good Luck: A Novel. William Edward Norris. (On cover: Appletons' town and country library, no. 151). 1894. D. Appleton and Company.
Victim of Gossip. F. Dionis Frankel. LC 6-43163. (Dillingham's metropolitan library, no. 31). 1897. G. W. Dillingham, Co.
Victim of His Clothes. Charles Witherle Hooke & Burton, Frederick Russell, 1861-1909, Joint Author. (sunnyside series, no. 12). 1890. J. S. Ogilvie.
Victim of Intrigue. A Tale of Burr's Conspiracy. James Wickes Taylor. 1847. Robinson & Jones.
Victim of Love. Lee Canaday. 1978. 1.25 (ISBN 0-440-19265-X). Dell Pub. Co.
Victim of Love. Dyan Sheldon. LC 82-20001. 1983. 14.75 (ISBN 0-670-74586-3). Viking Press.
Victim of Rape. Eddie Stone. (Orig.). 1976. pap. 1.95 (ISBN 0-87067-641-5, BH641). Holloway.
Victim of Rape. Eddie Stone. 1976. 1.50 (ISBN 0-87067-494-3). Holloway House.
Victim of the Aurora. Thomas Keneally. LC 77-84391. 7.95 (ISBN 0-15-193631-5). Harcourt Brace Jovanovich.
Victim of the Schoolboys. Pat Shannon. 192p. pap. 1.95 o.p. (ISBN 0-87977-135-6, DBB135). Dansk Blue Bk.
Victim: The Other Side of Murder. Gary Kinder. 1983. pap. 3.95 (ISBN 0-440-19704-X). Dell.
Victim Was Important by: Joe Rayter Pseud. Mary F McChesney. LC 54-5916. 1954. Scribner.
Victims. B. M Gill. LC 81-190440. 25.00 (ISBN 0-340-25353-3). Hodder and Stoughton.
Victims. Isidore Okpewho. 200p. (Orig.). 1979. 9.00 o.s.i. (ISBN 0-89410-115-3); pap. 5.00 o.s.i. (ISBN 0-89410-114-5). Three Continents.
Victims. Isidore Okpewho. LC 71-150931. (Africana Ser). (Orig.). 1971. pap. 1.95 o.p. (ISBN 0-385-02521-1, Anch). Doubleday.
Victims. new ed. Jack Pearl, pseud. (Osi). 1973. 4.95 o.s.i. (27094-X). Trident.
Victims. Jack Pearl. 1973. 0.95. Pocket Books.
Victims: A Novel. Arthur Maimane. LC 77-367758. 1976. 3.95 (ISBN 0-85031-162-4). Allison and Busby.
Victims: A Novel of Polygamy in Modern Africa. Isidore Okpewho. LC 71-150931. 1971. 1.95. Anchor Books.
Victims: A Tale from Fermanagh. Eugene McCabe. LC 77-354262. 1976. 3.20 (ISBN 0-575-02169-1). Gollancz.
Victims of an Unknown Wrath. Geraldine M. Leach. 440p. (Orig.). 1981. pap. 3.95 (ISBN 0-9605274-0-0). Albion Am Bks.
Victims of Circumstances: The Most Sensational, Illustrated Novel of the Century. Abel Cornelius Anthony. LC 47-24596. 1947. Mid-State Publications.
Victims of Duty see Three Plays.
Victims of Gaming; Being Extracts from the Diary of an American Physician. LC 8-328016. 1838. Weeks, Jordan & Company.
Victims of Mammon. Solon Doggett. (Solon Doggett's novels)). 1897. B. B. Russell.
Victims of Marriage... Levi D. Heller. LC 7-4113. 1890. The Heller Publishing Co.
Victims of Society. Marguerite Power Farmer Gardiner Blessington. LC 48-44544. 1837. Carey, Lee & Blanchard.
Victims-Story of a Teen-Age Hooker. James E. Able. Ed. by Sylvia Ashton. LC 78-53087. 1979. 12.95 (ISBN 0-87949-130-2). Ashley Bks.
Victims. 1st Ed. James F Lee. LC 59-65075. 1959. Vantage Press.
Victoire. Clare Darcy. LC 73-90389. 1974. 7.95 (ISBN 0-8027-0443-3). Walker.
Victoire. Clare Darcy. LC 78-2628. 1978. 9.95. J. Curley.
Victor. Richard Sill Holmes. LC 8-30535. 1.50. F. H. Revell Company.
Victor. Ellery Sinclair. LC 8-9007. Cassell & Company.
Victor and the Vanquished: By P. B. Abercrombie Pseud. Patricia Abercrombie Barnes. LC 57-7676. Vanguard Press.
Victor and Vanquished. Mary Cecil Hay. (On cover: Lovell's library, v. 20, no. 978). 1887. J. W. Lovell Company.
Victor and Vanquished. A Novel. Mary Cecil Hay. (On cover: Seaside library. Pocket ed., no. 716). 1886. J. W. Lovell Company.
Victor Hugo and His Time. Alfred Barbou. (Seaside library. v. 67, no. 1360). 1882. G. Munro.
Victor Hugo's Les Miserables; an Adaptation. Ettie Lee. LC 24-11019. Boni & Liveright, Inc.
Victor Hugo's Ninety-Three: A Tragic and Historic Poem in Prose; an Abridged Edition. Victor Marie Hugo & Chandler, Frank Randolph, 1840- Ed. LC 31-11094. National Advertising Co.
Victor La Tourette. A Novel. Edward Augustus Warriner. LC 8-33481. 1875. Roberts Brothers.
Victor Lescar. Maria M Grant. (Seaside library, v. 20, no. 398). G. Munro.
Victor Norman: Rector. Mary Andrews Denison. LC 6-33979. 1873. J. B. Lippincott & Co.
Victor of Salamis. William Stearns Davis. (O.s.i.). 1925. 5.95 o.s.i. (ISBN 0-02-530040-7). Macmillan.
Victor of Salamis: A Tale of the Days of Xerxes, Leonidas, and Themistocles. William Stearns Davis. LC 7-15591. The Macmillan Company.
Victor Ollnee's Disciple see Collected Works.
Victor Ollnee's Discipline. Hamlin Garland. LC 72-84718. 1974. (lib. ed.) 12.50 (ISBN 0-403-02970-8). Scholarly Press.
Victor Ollnee's Discipline. Hamlin Garland. LC 11-23899. 1911. Harper & Brothers.
Victor Serenus: A Story of the Pauline Era. Henry Wood. 1898. Lee and Shepard.
Victor Serenus: A Story of the Pauline Era. Henry Wood. LC 37-327927. 1900. Lee and Shepard.
Victor Victorious. Cecil Starr Johns. LC 16-2219. 1915. 1.25. John Lane.
Victoria. Reg Gadney. LC 74-30598. 1975. 7.95 (ISBN 0-698-10673-3). Coward, McCann & Geoghegan.
Victoria. Knut Hamsun & Chater, Arthur G., Tr. LC 23-7829. 1923. A. A. Knopf.
Victoria. Marie L. Henkels. 1979. pap. 1.75 (ISBN 0-532-17207-8). Woodhill.
Victoria. Martha Grace Pope. LC 15-13560. 1915. 1.35. Sherman, French & Company.
Victoria: A Love Story. Knut Hamsun. LC 69-11574. 1975. (pbk.) 1.75 (ISBN 0-380-00545-X). Avon.
Victoria and Albert. Eve Stephens, pseud. LC 58-6053. 1958. Crowell.
Victoria and Albert: A Novel. Eve Stephens, pseud. LC 58-6053. 1974. (pbk.) 1.25. New American Lib.
Victoria and Company. Terence Brady & Charlotte Bingham. LC 74-182427. 1974. 2.50 (ISBN 0-491-01700-6). W. H. Allen.
Victoria at Night, and Other Stories. Uli Beigel. LC 58-5265. 1958. Random House.
Victoria at Nine. Don Robertson. LC 78-19630. (Illus.). 1979. 8.95 (ISBN 0-345-28097-0). Ballantine Books.
Victoria, Four-Thirty. Cecil Roberts. LC 37-274005. 1937. The Macmillan Company.
Victoria Grandolet: A Novel. Henry Bellamann. LC 43-16087. 1943. Simon and Schuster.
Victoria: Or, The World Overcome. Caroline Chesebro' LC 6-24214. 1856. Derby and Jackson.
Victoria Pruitt Comes to Town. Ruth Gilbert Cochran. LC 41-6365. 1941. Mystery House.
Victoria Welles. Stephen Solomita. (Orig.). 1969. pap. 1.95 o.s.i. (TC457, Travellers Comp). Olympia.
Victoria Winters. Marilyn Ross. (Orig.). pap. 0.50 o.p. (52-421). Paperback Lib.
Victorian Album. Evelyn Berckman. LC 73-81412. 1973. 5.95 (ISBN 0-385-07815-3). Doubleday.
Victorian Album. Evelyn Berckman. 1975. (pbk.) 1.25. Dell.
Victorian Chaise Longue. Marghanita Laski. LC 54-5695. 1954. Houghton Mifflin.
Victorian Crown. Edwina Noone, pseud. 1970. pap. 0.75 o.p. (B75-2042). Belmont-Tower.
Victorian House. Dorothy Hewlett. LC 39-21298. The Bobbs-Merrill Company.
Victorian Nightmares. Hugh Lamb. LC 76-55901. 1977. 8.95 (ISBN 0-8008-7984-8). Taplinger Pub. Co.
Victorian Scandal. Ray Jenkins. 1976. pap. 1.75 o.p. (ISBN 0-515-04098-3). BJ Pub Group.
Victorian Tales of Terror. Ed. by Hugh Lamb. LC 74-20217. 1975. 8.50 (ISBN 0-8008-7986-4). Taplinger.
Victories of Wesley Castle. Charles Wesley Winchester. LC 6741. 1900. The Christian Literature Company.
Victorine. Maude Hutchins. LC 82-72197. 191p. 1959. 8.95 (ISBN 0-8040-0311-4); pap. 4.95 (ISBN 0-8040-0312-2). Swallow.
Victorine. Frances Parkinson Wheeler Keyes. LC 58-111562. 1958. J. Messner.
Victorine. Frances Parkinson Wheeler Keyes. (Kangaroo Book). 1977. 1.95 (ISBN 0-671-80898-2). Pocket Books.
Victorine. 1st American Ed. Maude Phelps McVeigh Hutchins. LC 60-1693. 1959. A. Swallow.
Victorious. Reginald Wright Kauffman. LC 19-687425. The Bobbs-Merrill Company.
Victorious Defeat: The Story of a Franchies. Charles Frederic Gilliam. LC 6-38355. The Roxburgh Publishing Company.
Victorious Knight. Estella M Kaiser. LC 31-25922. The Stratford Company.
Victorious Life: By Leonora B. Halsted: Frontispiece by H. Richard Boelan. Leonora B Halsted. LC 10-13585. 1910. The Metropolitan Press.
Victorious Troy: Or, The Hurrying Angel. John Masefield. LC 35-21573. 1935. The Macmillan Company.
Victors. Clement Pollock. LC 56-10950. 1956. Random House.
Victors: A Romance of Yesterday Morning & This Afternoon. Robert Barr. LC 1-32979. 1901. F. A. Stokes Company.
Victors and Vanquished. Francis Stuart. LC 59-12306. 1959. Pennington Press.
Victory. Constance Leonie Caroline Borgstrom Aminoff. LC 25-11396. (Her Torchlight series of Napoleonic romances. v). 1925. E. P. Dutton & Company.
Victory. Joseph Conrad. LC 22-10649. 1921. Doubleday, Page & Company.
Victory. Joseph Conrad. LC 32-26954. (Half-title: The modern library of the world's best books). 1932. The Modern Library.
Victory. Joseph Conrad. LC 37-5415. 1937. The Sun Dial Press, Inc.
Victory. Vincent McHugh. LC 47-31203. 1947. Random House.
Victory! Charles Elmo Robinson. LC 36-35054. Zondervan Publishing House.
Victory. Molly Elliot Seawell. LC 6-36051. 1906. D. Appleton and Company.
Victory. LC 72-1874. (Black Heritage Library Collection). 1972. 13.00 (ISBN 0-8369-9051-X). Books for Libraries Press.
Victory Also Ends. Fred W Booth. LC 52-5555. 1952. Rinehart.
Victory Among the Insane. Russ Madison. 1970. pap. 1.25 o.p. (B274, EverBC). Grove.
Victory Among the Insane: A Novel. Russ Madison. LC 68-22010. 1969. 6.95. Grove Press.
Victory: An Island Tale. Joseph Conrad. LC 15-633648. 1915. Doubleday, Page & Company.
Victory: an Island Tale. Joseph Conrad. LC 27-133883. 1926. Doubleday, Page & Company.
Victory: An Island Tale. Joseph Conrad. LC 33-18744. 1933. Garden City Publishing Company, Inc.
Victory at Dawn. Howard Carlton Emmons. LC 56-39658. 1956. Zondervan Pub. House.
Victory at Daybreak: A Christian Novel. Capwell Wyckoff. LC 45-8306. 1945. Wm. B. Eerdmans Publishing Company.
Victory Celebrations. Aleksandr Isaevich Solzhenitsyn. LC 83-1652. 1983. 12.50 (ISBN 0-374-28356-7). Farrar, Straus, and Giroux.
Victory Deane. A Novel. Cecil Griffith. (On cover: Seaside library. Pocket ed. no. 583). 1885. G. Munro.
Victory Deane: A Novel. Cecil Griffith. (On cover: Lovell's library. no. 732). 1886. J. W. Lovell Company.
Victory for Kregen. Dray Prescot. (Science Fiction Ser.). 1980. pap. 1.95 (ISBN 0-87997-532-6, UJ1532). Daw Bks.
Victory for Love. Winifred Mary Scott. LC 42-18726. 1942. H. C. Kinsey & Company, Inc.
Victory Law. Ruth Cranston. LC 14-5044. 1914. 1.30. John Lane Company; Etc., Etc.
Victory Lee: Her Story. Elsie Augusta Gerrish. LC 40-1224. News Job Print.
Victory Murders. Gilbert Vivian Seldes. LC 27-4325. 1927. The John Day Company.
Victory of Allan Rutledge: A Tale of the Middle West. Alexander Corkey. LC 11-1646. 1.50. The H. K. Fly Company.
Victory of Ezry Gardner. Imogen Clark. LC 6-24239. T. Y. Crowell & Company.
Victory of Mary Christopher: A Story of to-Morrow. Harvey Reeves Calkins. LC 29-25302. (On cover: Little books on practice). 1903. Jennings & Pye.
Victory of Paul Kent. Albert Benjamin Cunningham. LC 48-7536. 1948. E. P. Dutton.
Victory of the Vanquished. A Story of the First Century. Elizabeth Rundle Charles. LC 41-34736. (On cover: Schonberg-Cotta series). 1884. T. Nelson and Sons.
Victory on Janus. Alice Mary Norton. LC 66-5959. 1966. Harcourt, Brace & World.
Victory on West Hill: A Story. Robert Luther Duffus. LC 42-173567. 1942. The Macmillan Company.
Victory Pass. 1st Ed. Burgess Leonard. LC 50-14376. 1950. Lippincott.
Victory Summer. Dawn Lindsey. 304p. 1981. pap. 2.25 (ISBN 0-553-13647-X). Bantam.
Victory Was Slain. Hilde Abel. LC 41-236672. Alliance Book Corporation.
Vida. Marge Piercy. 480p. 1981. pap. 2.95 (ISBN 0-449-24409-1, Crest). Fawcett.
Vida. Marge Piercy. LC 79-19298. 412p. 1980. 12.95 (ISBN 0-671-40110-6). Summit Bks.
Vida. Marge Piercy. 480p. 1981. 15.00 (ISBN 0-671-40110-6). Ultramarine Pub.
Vida En Espana. William H. Marshall & Elena L. De Martin. 1977. pap. text ed. 3.75x (ISBN 0-88334-105-0). Ind Sch Pr.
Vida y Obras De Ermilo Abreu Gomez. Cecilia R. Silva De Rodriguez. 1975. 4.00 o.p. Tex Christian.
Vida's Story. (On cover: The seaside library, Pocket ed. no. 545). 1885. G. Munro.
Vidduy. 1982. pap. 2.25. Feldheim.
Videhi: A Novel of Indian Life. Charles Leslie Holden. LC 53-11164. 1953. St. Martin's Press.
Vidette: Or, the Girl of the Robber's Pass. A Tale of the Mexican War. Newton Mallory Curtis. 1848. Williams Brothers.
Vienna Dreams. Janette Radcliffe. (Orig.). 1982. pap. 3.50 (ISBN 0-440-19530-6). Dell.
Vienna Elephant. Edwin Leather. LC 77-22320. 7.95 (ISBN 0-396-07507-X). Dodd, Mead.
Vienna Nineteen Hundred: Games with Love & Death. Arthur Schnitzler. 365p. 1974. pap. 3.95 (ISBN 0-14-003759-4). Penguin.
Vienna Pursuit. Anthea Goddard. LC 75-42826. 1976. 6.95 (ISBN 0-8027-5346-9). Walker.
Vienna Summer. Nancy Buckingham. LC 79-4895. 1979. 8.95. (ISBN 0-312-84579-0). St. Martin's Press.
Vienna 1900 - Games with Love and Death: The Stories Which Formed the Basis of the BBC TV Serial... Arthur Schnitzler. LC 74-188252. 1973. 0.45 (ISBN 0-14-003759-4). Penguin.
Viennese Idylls. Arthur Schnitzler. LC 72-10811. (Short story index reprint series). 1973. (ISBN 0-8369-4226-4). Books for Libraries Press.
Viennese Love Die Freudlose Gases. Hugo Bettauer. Tr. by Lyon, Francis Hamilton. LC 29-11648. The Macaulay Company.
Viennese Medley. Edith Louise Coues O'Shaughnessy. LC 24-27996. 1924. B. W. Huebsch, Inc.
Viennese Novelettes. Arthur Schnitzler. LC 71-175578. (Illus.). 1974. 17.50 (ISBN 0-404-08278-5). AMS Press.
Viennese Novelettes. Arthur Schnitzler. LC 31-211782. 1931. Simon and Schuster.
Viento Del Pueblo see Rayo Que No Cesa.
Viera: A Romance 'twixt the Real and Ideal. Roman Ivanovitch Zubof. LC 8-37857. T. Y. Crowell & Co.
Viera: A Romance 'twixt the Real and Ideal. new ed., with life and portrait of the author... ed. Roman Ivanovitch Zubof & Hammond, Charles F. LC 8-377943. 1890. The American News Company.
Viet-Nam Story. H. J. M. Melaro. LC 68-20489. (Illus.). 1969. 5.95. Alexia Press.
View from a Hearse see Last Thing We Talk About.
View from a Height. Isaac Asimov. pap. 1.25 o.s.i. (33-020). Lancer.
View from a Window: A Novel. Florence Ruth Howard. LC 42-150042. 1942. W. Morrow & Company.
View from Another Shore: European Science Fiction. Ed. by Franz Rottensteiner. LC 73-78082. (Continuum book). 1973. 6.95 (ISBN 0-8164-9151-8). Seabury Press.
View from Calvary, and Other Stories. Patrick Boyle. LC 77-357273. 1976. 4.25 (ISBN 0-575-02129-2). Gollancz.
View from Chivo. Harry Allen Smith. LC 71-150722. 1971. 6.95 (ISBN 0-671-27082-6). Trident Press.
View from Daniel Pike. Edward Boyd & Bill Knox. LC 74-81227. 172p. 1974. 6.95 o.p. (ISBN 0-312-84595-2). St Martin.
View from Daniel Pike. Bill Knox & Edward Boyd. LC 74-81227. 1974. 6.95. St. Martin's Press.
View from Deacon Hill. Jack S Scott, pseud. LC 80-28532. 1981. 9.95 (ISBN 0-89919-033-2). Ticknor & Fields.
View from Eighty. Malcolm Cowley. 1982. pap. 3.95 (ISBN 0-14-006050-2). Penguin.
View from Pompey's Head. Hamilton Basso. LC 54-10767. 1954. Doubleday.
View from Pompey's Head. Hamilton Basso. LC 79-110821. (Illus.). 1970. (ISBN 0-8371-3207-X). Greenwood Press.
View from the Air. Hugh Fosburgh. LC 53-234. 1953. Scribner.
View from the Fortieth Floor. Theodore Harold White. LC 60-7412. 1960. W. Sloane Associates.
View from the Parsonage. 1st Ed. Sheila Kaye-Smith. LC 54-8960. 1954. Harper.
View from the Valley. Denys Val Batter. LC 77-355065. 1976. 3.25 (ISBN 0-7183-0234-6). Kimber.
View from Tower Hill. John Braine. LC 75-133079. 1971. 6.95. Coward-McCann.
View of Dawn in the Tropics. Cabrera Infante, Guillermo. LC 76-5134. 8.95 (ISBN 0-06-010622-0). Harper & Row.
View of My Own. Elizabeth Hardwick. 1962. pap. 1.65 o.p. (ISBN 0-374-50284-6, N242, Noonday). FS&G.
View of the Bay. Richard Scowcroft. LC 55-5048. 1955. Houghton Mifflin.

View of the Harbour. Elizabeth Taylor. LC 47-11276. 1947. A. A. Knopf.
View of the Sea. Elizabeth Fair. LC 55-11091. 1955. Funk & Wagnalls Co.
View of the Town: By Jan Hilliard Pseud. Hilda Kay Grant. LC 54-10224. 1954. Abelard - Schuman.
View of Vultures. Alan Scholefield. LC 66-23039. 4.95. Doubleday.
Viewless Winds. Morgan, Murray C. 1949. E. P. Dutton.
Viewpoints. Tunku Abdul Rahman. 1978. text ed. 21.50x (00122); pap. text ed. 7.95x (00123). Heinemann Ed.
Views. Roger Dean. (O.s.i.). (Illus.). 1978. pap. 10.95 o.s.i. (ISBN 0-905071-05-0). A & W Pubs.
Views. Enslin. 1973. 16.00 (Pub. by Elizabeth Pr); pap. 8.00. SBD.
Views and Vagabonds. R Macaulay. LC 12-35737. 1912. H. Holt and Company.
Views of a Nearsighted Cannoneer. Seymour Krim. 1968. pap. 1.95 o.p. (ISBN 0-525-47214-2). Dutton.
Viga-Glums Saga. 2nd ed. Ed. by Gabriel Truville-Petre. 1960. 6.00x o.p. (ISBN 0-19-811117-7). Oxford U Pr.
Vigil. Harold Begbie. LC 8-9173. 1908. Dodd, Mead & Company.
Vigil. Satinath Bhaduri. LC 65-16131. (UNESCO Collection of Representative Works: Indian Series). 1965. Asia Pub. House.
Vigil. Rodney Nelson. 1979. pap. 3.00 (ISBN 0-931498-10-4). DuBois Zone Pr.
Vigil (a Novel) Satinath Bhaduri. 6.50x o.p. (ISBN 0-210-22621-8). Asia.
Vigil: A Novel. Young-Bruehl, Elisabeth. LC 82-17160. 1983. 12.95 (ISBN 0-8071-1075-2). Louisiana State University Press.
Vigil of Emmeline Gore. Abele Rudolph Radama Von. LC 62-8145. 1962. Houghton Mifflin.
Vigil of Quebec. Fernand Dumont. LC 72-97423. 1974. 12.50x o.p. (ISBN 0-8020-1976-5); pap. 6.00 (ISBN 0-8020-6184-2). U of Toronto Pr.
Vigilante. Ray Hogan. (Signet Book). 1975. (pbk.) 1.25. New American Library.
Vigilante, a Novel. Richard Aldrich Summers. 1949. Duell, Sloan and Pearce.
Vigilante-Anybody? Henry W Bruckert. 1973. 6.95. Vantage.
Vigilante Girl. Jerome Hart. LC 10-89320. 1910. 1.50. A. C. McClurg & Co.
Vigilante Guns. Al Cody, pseud. Orig. Title: Trail of Innocents. 1969. pap. 0.60 o.p. (B60-1034). Belmont-Tower.
Vigilante Law. Charles Morris Martin. (O.s.i.). 1976. pap. 0.95 o.s.i. (BT50923). Belmont-Tower.
Vigilante of Alder Gulch. Hugh Pendexter. LC 55-14034. 1955. Arcadia House.
Vigilante: Twenty-First Century. Robert M. Williams. (Orig.). 1968. pap. 0.60 o.p. (73-644). Lancer.
Vigilante War in Buena Vista. Frank Chester Robertson. LC 42-105. 1942. E. P. Dutton & Co., Inc.
Vigilantes. Lee D. Willoughby. (Making of America Ser.: No. 25). (Orig.). 1982. pap. 2.95 (ISBN 0-440-08758-9, Bryans). Dell.
Vigilantes of Gold Gulch. Charles Horace Snow. LC 37-2249. 1937. Macrae Smith Company.
Viginia Comedian: Or, Old Days in the Old Dominion. John Esten Cooke. LC 12-19565. 1854. D. Appleton and Company.
Vignettes. Ella Benjamin. 3.95 o.p. Carlton.
Vignettes from the Late Ching: Bizarre Happenings Eyewitnessed Over Two Decades. Wo-Yao Wu. LC 76-2359. 1976. (ISBN 0-87075-125-5). St. John's University Press.
Vignettes of Manhattan. Brander Matthews. LC 70-90587. (Short story index reprint series). (Illus.). 1969. Books for Libraries Press.
Vignettes of Manhattan. Brander Matthews. LC 4-15136. 1894. Harper & Brothers.
Vignettes of Manhattan: Outlines in Local Color. Brander Matthews. LC 21-17369. 1921. C. Scribner's Sons.
Vignettes: Real and Ideal: Stories by American Authors. Ed. by Frederic Edward McKay. De Wolfe, Fiske & Co.
Vigorous Daunt: Billionaire. Ambrose Pratt. LC 8-20346. R. F. Fenno & Company.
Vikas Book of Modern Indian Love Stories. Ed. by Pritish Nandy. 1980. text ed. 12.50x (ISBN 0-7069-0799-X, Pub. by Vikas India). Advent NY.
Viking. Edison Marshall. LC 51-7196. 1951. Farrar, Straus and Young.
Viking Heart. Laura Goodman Salverson. LC 23-13449. George H. Doran Company.
Viking Prince: Or, The Adventures of Harold Trygvesen. Arthur Loring Mackaye. LC 28-13562. L. C. Page & Company.
Viking Process. Norman Hartley. LC 75-33859. 7.95 (ISBN 0-671-22198-1). Simon and Schuster.
Viking Romance. Mabel Lagerlof Manville. LC 58-4754. (Milestone book). 1958. Comet Press Books.
Viking Summer. Charles Andrew Brady. LC 56-13194. 1956. Bruce Pub. Co.
Vikings of the Far East. Kozuo Myamoto. 6.95 o.p. Vantage.
Viking's Rest: A Story of the Land of Evangeline. Frances Fenwick Williams. LC 24-19467. The Century Co.
Viking's Skull. John R Carling. LC 4-9121. 1904. Little, Brown, and Company.
Vikram & the Vampire: Tales of Hindu Deviltry. Richard F. Burton. (Illus.). 5.50 o.p. (ISBN 0-8446-0530-1). Peter Smith.
Vikrama's Adventures, or Thirty-Two Tales of the Throne, 2 Vols. Ed. by Franklin Edgerton. (Oriental Ser. Nos. 26 & 27). 1926. Set. 18.00 o.p. (ISBN 0-674-93885-2). Harvard U Pr.
Vikrama's Adventures; or, Thirty-Two Tales of the Throne: A Collection of Stories About King Vikrama, As Told by the Thirty-Two Statuettes That Supported His Throne, 2 pts. Vikrama. Ed. & tr. by Frank Edgerton. LC 23-26324. (Oriental Ser., Nos. 26 & 27). cxxi, 635p. 1926. Set. 18.00 o.p. (ISBN 0-674-93885-2). Harvard U Pr.
Vile Bodies. Evelyn Waugh. LC 30-7431. J. Cape, H. Smith.
Vile Bodies. Evelyn Waugh. LC 33-27415. (Half-title" The modern library of the world's best books). 1933. The Modern Library.
Villa Aurelia: A Riviera Interlude. Burton Egbert Stevenson. LC 32-24550. 1932. Dodd, Mead & Company.
Villa Bohemia. Mary Le Baron Andrews Urie. LC 8-31930. 1882. Kochendoerfer & Urie.
Villa by the Sea: A Novel. Isabel Constance Clarke. LC 25-805341. 1925. Benziger Brothers.
Villa by the Sea: By Ann Carter Pseud. Anne Tedlock Brooks. LC 52-14349. 1952. Arcadia House.
Villa Caprice. Irene Alexander. The Penn Publishing Company.
Villa Claudia. John Ames Mitchell. LC 4-12097. 1904. Life Publishing Company.
Villa Eden: The Country-House on the Rhine. Berthold Auerbach. Tr. by Shackford, Charles Chauncy. LC 9-3817. 1869. Roberts Brothers.
Villa Elsa: A Story of German Family Life. Stuart Oliver Henry. LC 20-2260. E. P. Dutton & Company.
Villa Golitsyn. Piers Paul Read. 208p. 1983. pap. 3.50 (ISBN 0-380-61929-6, Bard). Avon.
Villa Golitsyn: A Novel. Piers Paul Read. LC 81-47688. 10.95 (ISBN 0-06-014949-3). Harper & Row.
Villa in Brittany. Donald Moffat. LC 31-27004. 1931. Doubleday, Doran & Company, Inc.
Villa in Summer. Penelope Mortimer. LC 76-380178. 1976. 3.25 (ISBN 0-7278-0113-9). Severn House: Distributed by Hutchinson.
Villa in Summer. 1st American Ed. Penelope Mortimer. Harcourt Brace.
Villa Jane. Janet Laing. LC 29-18555. The Century Co.
Villa Milo. Xavier Domingo. LC 62-9934. 1962. 4.00 (ISBN 0-8076-0183-7). Braziller.
Villa Mimosa. Jerrard Tickell. LC 61-6522. 1961. Doubleday.
Villa of the Ferromonte. Lawrence B Eisenberg. LC 73-22332. 1974. 6.95 (ISBN 0-671-21765-8). Simon and Schuster.
Villa of the Peacock: And Other Stories. Clotilde Inez Mary Graves. 1921. George H. Doran Company.
Villa on the Palatine. Margot Arnold, pseud. (Berkley Book). 1978. 1.75 (ISBN 0-425-03656-1). Berkley Publishing Corporation.
Villa on the Palatine. Margot Arnold, pseud. LC 81-9860. 1981. 12.95 (ISBN 0-89340-358-X). J. Curley.
Villa on the Rhine. author's ed. new york, leypoldt & holt, 1869. ed. Berthold Auerbach. LC 72-11581. 1972-1973. (ISBN 0-403-02350-5). Scholarly Press.
Villa on the Rhine. Berthold Auerbach & Taylor, Bayard. 1869. Leypoldt & Holt.
Villa on the Rhine. author's ed. Berthold Auerbach & Taylor, Bayard. Tr. by Davis, James. 1911. Henry Holt and Company.
Villa on the Shore. Michael Butterworth. LC 73-9014. 1974. 4.95 (ISBN 0-385-08794-2). Published for the Crime Club by Doubleday.
Villa Rossignol: Or, The Advance of Islam. Maria Longworth Storer. LC 18-680219. 1918. B. Herder Book Co.
Villa Rubein. John Galsworthy. LC 8-20136. 1908. G. P. Putnam's Sons.
Villace to Authorized Translation from the Russian of Ivan Bunin. Ivan Alekseevich Bunin & Hapgood, Isabel Florence, 1850-1928, Tr. LC 23-9538. 1923. A. A. Knopf.
Village. Ivan Alekseevich Bunin & Hapgood, Isabel Florence, 1850-1928, Tr. LC 23-9538. 1923. A.A. Knopf.
Village. Ivan Alekseevich Bunin & Hapgood, Isabel Florence, 1850-1928, Tr. LC 33-27458. 1933. A. A. Knopf.
Village. Bruce Elliott. 592p. 1982. pap. 3.50 (ISBN 0-380-79020-3, 79020). Avon.
Village. Marghanita Laski. LC 52-1234. 1952. Houghton Mifflin.
Village Affairs. Read. LC 78-19137. (Illus.). 1978. 7.95 (ISBN 0-395-26482-0). Houghton Mifflin.
Village and Other Tales. Hannah More. 1851. D. Appleton & Co.
Village. Authorized Translation from the Russian of Ivan Bunin. Ivan Alekseevich Bunin. Tr. by Isabel Florence Hapgood. LC 74-4246. 1974. H. Fertig.
Village Belles. A Novel... Anne Manning. LC 16-19154. 1833. J. & J. Harper.
Village Beyond. Livingston Biddle. LC 56-10815. 1956. Lippincott.
Village by the Sea... William Lee Popham. LC 10-23669. 0.50. Printed by Westerfield-Bonte Co.
Village by the Yangtze: Imperial and Communist China and a Village Mission School Caught in the Web of Change and Espionage. Vincent Herbert Gowen. LC 72-87751. 1975. 7.95 (ISBN 0-913264-08-3). Douglas-West Publishers.
Village Centenary. Miss Read. 240p. 1981. 10.95 (ISBN 0-395-31262-0). HM.
Village Centenary. LC 81-6300. 1981. 10.95 (ISBN 0-395-31262-0). Houghton Mifflin.
Village Christmas. Miss Read. 1966. 2.95 o.p. (ISBN 0-395-08111-4). HM.
Village Christmas: By Miss Read. Dora Jessie Saint. LC 66-19843. 1966. 2.95. Houghton.
Village Commune. A Story. Louise De La Ramee. (seaside library. v. 45, no. 915). 1881. G. Munroe.
Village Daybook. August William Derleth. 7.95 (ISBN 0-88361-072-8). Stanton & Lee.
Village Detective. V. Lipatov. 419p. 1970. pap. 4.45 (ISBN 0-8285-1008-3, Pub. by Progress Pubs USSR). Imported Pubns.
Village Diary. Miss Read. 1957. 3.50 o.p.; repr. in prep o.p. HM.
Village Diary: By Miss Read Pseud. Illustrated by J. S. Goodall. Dora Jessie Saint. LC 57-9983. 1957. Houghton Mifflin.
Village Doctor. Lucy Agnes Hancock. LC 50-5790. 1950. Macrae-Smith-Co.
Village Doctor. Sheila Kaye-Smith. LC 28-3965. E. P. Dutton & Co., Inc.
Village Doctors: And Other Tales. Timothy Shay Arthur. LC 6-3431. 1843. Godey & McMichael.
Village Drama. Vesta S Simmons. LC 8-8994. (Half-title: The "unknown" library). The Cassell Publishing Co.
Village Girl. A. S. Shears. 1973. pap. 0.95 o.p. (09209). Curtis.
Village Had No Walls. Vyankatesh Digamber Madgulkar. 1972. pap. 4.25x (ISBN 0-210-31153-3). Asia.
Village Had No Walls. Vyankatesh Digamber Madgulkar. 1973. pap. 2.75x o.p. (ISBN 0-210-31153-3). Asia.
Village Had No Walls: By Vyankatesh Madgulkar; Tr. by Ram Deshmukh from the Marathi Novel 'Bangarwadi.' Vyankatesh Digambar Madgulkar. LC 67-86724. 1967. pap., 2.75. Asia Pub.
Village in August. Chun Hsiao. LC 74-3729. 1974. 14.25 (ISBN 0-8371-7458-9). Greenwood Press.
Village in August. Chun Hsiao. LC 50-40331. 1944. World Pub. Co.
Village in August. Chun Hsiao. LC 42-117072. 1942. Smith & Durrell.
Village in the Jungle. Leonard Sidney Woolf. LC 26-265198. 1926. Harcourt, Brace and Company.
Village in the Jungle. Leonard Sidney Woolf. LC 82-140134. (Oxford paperbacks). 1981. 6.95 (ISBN 0-19-281312-9). Oxford University Press.
Village in the Sun. Madelyn Galbraith. LC 73-87640. 1975. 7.50 (ISBN 0-8309-0109-4). Herald Pub. House.
Village in the Treetops. Jules Verne. 3.95. Assoc Bk.
Village in the Turkish Novel & Short Story 1920-1955. Carole Rathbun. (Near & Middle East Monographs Ser: No. 2). 192p. 1972. text ed. 46.25x (ISBN 90-2792-327-2). Mouton.
Village Mystery: And Through War to Peace. Benjamin F Mason. LC 11-311. Broadway Publishing Co.
Village of Fear. Frances Cowen. (Ace gothic). 1974. (pbk.) 0.95. Ace Books.
Village of Glass. Frances Mary Frost. LC 42-15550. 1942. Farrar & Rinehart, Inc.
Village of Stars. Paul Stanton. LC 60-12917. 1960. M. S. Mill Co. and W. Morrow.
Village of Vagabonds. Frank Berkeley Smith. LC 10-120972. 1910. Doubleday, Page & Company.
Village of Youth, and Other Fairy Tales. Bessie Hatton. LC 44-39961. 1895. Frederick A. Stokes Company.
Village on the Cliff. A Novel. Anne Isabella Thackeray Ritchie. LC 44-32799. (With her Old Kensington. New York. 1873. Copy 2). 1867. Harper & Brothers.
Village on the Yarra. Tom Luscombe. LC 76-352032. 1974. 6.95 (ISBN 0-17-005004-1). Nelson.
Village Ophelia. Anne Reeve Aldrich. LC 90-2061. 1899. G. W. Dillingham Co.
Village Photographs. Augusta Larned. LC 7-13842. 1887. H. Holt and Company.
Village Pomapadour. Joan Conquest. LC 32-9375. The Macaulay Company.
Village Rector. Honore De Balzac. Tr. by Katharine Prescott Wormeley. LC 3-23166. (Half-title: The comedy of human life... Scenes from country life). 1893. Roberts Brothers.
Village Romeo and Juliet. Gottfried Keller. LC 55-8747. (College Translations). 1955. Ungar.
Village Romeo and Juliet. Translated by Paul Bernard Thomas with the Collaboration of Bayard Quincy Morgan. Gottfried Keller. LC 61-4628. (Atlantic paperbacks, 2105). 1960. F. Ungar Pub. Co.
Village Shield: A Story of Mexico. Ruth Louise Gaines & Read, Georgia Willis. LC 17-136229. E. P. Dutton & Company.
Village Sketches: Or, Tales of Somerville ... LC 9-2688. 1825. Printed by D. Sower, Jr.
Village Steeple. Charles Guenot. Tr. by Murphy, Lady Blanche Elizabeth Mary Annunciata (Noel) LC 7-1517. Benziger Brothers.
Village Tale. John De Meyer. LC 38-7473. J. B. Lippincott Company.
Village Tale. Nancy Macdougall Kennedy. 1978. pap. 1.50 (ISBN 0-532-15369-3). Woodhill.
Village Tale. Philip Duffield Stong. LC 34-528817. Harcourt, Brace and Company.
Village, the City, and the World. Esma Rideout Booth. LC 66-14498. 4.95. McKay.
Village Virgin. Dean Fales. LC 31-13476. 1931. L. MacVeagh, The Dial Press.
Village Virtue. Harry Durant. LC 31-24143. 1931. The Knickerbocker Press.
Village Watch-Tower. Kate Douglas Smith Wiggin. LC 74-113696. (Short story index reprint series). 1970. Books for Libraries Press.
Village Watch-Tower. 13th thousand ed. Kate Douglas Smith Wiggin. LC 9-8360. 1895. Houghton, Mifflin and Company.
Village Wooing. Frank Lanzl. Date not set. 6.95 o.p. Vantage.
Village Wooing. Frank Lanzl. 1973. 6.95 (ISBN 0-533-00594-9). Vantage.
Villagers. Jack Oleck. LC 70-143211. 1971. 5.95. L. Stuart.
Villagers, and Other Stories... Inez M Porter. LC 43-12685. Printed by Niagara Frontier Publishing Co., Inc.
Villager's Son. Asenath B. Odaga. (Heinemann Secondary Readers Ser.). 1971. pap. text ed. 3.00x (ISBN 0-435-92501-6). Heinemann Ed.
Villain and the Virgin. Rene Raymond. LC 48-10601. (Avon monthly novel, 4). 1948. Avon Editions.
Villain of the Piece: A Novel. Lane Kauffmann. LC 72-11552. 1973. 7.95. Dial Press.
Villainous Company. Ruth Fenisong. (60-2279). 1968. Popular Lib.
Villainous Company: 1st Ed. Ruth Fenisong. LC 67-14129. 1967. 3.95. Pub. for the Crime Club by Doubleday.
Villains. Charlotte Keppel. 224p. 1982. 10.95 (ISBN 0-312-84681-9). St Martin.
Villains. John Rossiter. LC 75-36550. 1976. 7.95 (ISBN 0-8027-5339-6). Walker.
Villains: A Haunting Tale of the Marshes. Charlotte Keppel. LC 81-16728. 1981. 10.95 (ISBN 0-312-84681-9). St. Martin's Press.
Villains by Necessity. Sara Woods, pseud. LC 81-23211. 1982. 10.95 (ISBN 0-312-84683-5). St. Martin's Press.
Villains Galore. Gerard Bell. 1976. 1.75 (ISBN 0-671-80691-2). Pocket Books.
Villa's Rifles. Lewis B Patten. LC 77-79560. (Double D western). 1977. 6.95 (ISBN 0-385-13378-2). Doubleday.
Villeta Linden: Or, The Artist's Bride. Emerson Bennett. 1874. Claxton, Remsen & Haffel-Finger.
Villette. Charlotte Bronte. LC 62-5683. (Harcourt library of English and American classics). 1962. Harcourt, Brace & World.
Villette. Charlotte Bronte. LC 73-3129. (Bronte, Charlotte, 1816-1855. Life & Works of the Sisters Bronte: Vol. 3). (Illus.). 1973. 25.00 (ISBN 0-404-08833-3). AMS Press.
Villette. Charlotte Bronte. LC 73-131288. (Riverside editions, B119). 1971. (ISBN 0-395-11150-1). Houghton Mifflin.
Villette. Charlotte Bronte. LC 49-57558. 1859. Derby & Jackson.
Villette. Charlotte Bronte. (Half-title: Everyman's library, ed. by Ernest Rhys. Fiction. no. 351). 1909. J. M. Dent & Co.
Villette. Charlotte Bronte. LC 45-40839. (Half-title: The novels of Charlotte, Emily, & Anne Bronte). 1922. J. M. Dent & Sons Ltd.
Villette. Charlotte Bronte. LC 43-21549. (Half-title: The World's classics, XLVII. The novels of Charlotte, Emily, and Anne Bronte. IV). 1936. Oxford University Press, H. Milford.

Villette. Charlotte Bronte. Ed. by Geoffrey Tillotson. Donald Hawes. LC 78-25919. 1978. 21.00 (ISBN 0-8357-0347-9). University Microfilms International.

Villette. Charlotte Bronte. LC 79-670147. 1978. 9.95 (ISBN 0-7011-1240-9). Zodiac Press.

Villette. By Charlotte Bronte, "Currer Bell" Pseud.... Charlotte Bronte. (Seaside library, v. 22, no. 438). G. Munro.

Villiers Touch: A Novel. Brian Wynne Garfield. LC 77-121572. 1970. 6.95. Delacorte Press.

Vim and Ventures of Bolivar Hornet: The Alabama Doctor) with the Advice and Consent of David Rattlehead, M. D. Pseud.... Marcus Lafayette Byrn. (Rattlehead's humorous series, no. 5). Coast City Publishing Company.

Vincent: A Novel Based on the Life of Van Gogh. Joost Poldermans. LC 62-8869. 1962. Holt, Rinehart and Winston.

Vindication. Harriet Theresa Smith Comstock. LC 16-5582. 1916. 1.35. Doubleday, Page & Company.

Vindication: A Novel. Stephen McKenna. LC 24-865196. 1924. Little, Brown, and Company.

Vindication of Robert Creighton: A Tale of the Southwest. Daniel Frederick Fox. LC 21-21365. Fleming H. Revell Company.

Vindicator. John J. Dalton. (Orig.). 1979. pap. 1.95 (ISBN 0-532-19236-2). Woodhill.

Vindicator. Edward Phillips Oppenheim. LC 7-6767. 1907. Little, Brown, and Company.

Vine and the Olive. Margaret Culkin Banning. LC 64-14387. 1964. Harper & Row.

Vine of Sibmah: A Relations of the Puritans. Andrew Macphail. LC 6-17001. 1906. The Macmillan Company.

Vinegar Buyer; Sharp Sayings of Sharp People. Ezra Fremont Kendall. LC 9-28077. 1909. The Cleveland News Company Etc.

Vinegar Hill. Franklin Coen. LC 50-4294. 1950. Rinehart.

Vinegar Hill. Colin Free. LC 78-3131. 1978. 8.95 (ISBN 0-312-84685-1). St. Martin's Press.

Vinegar Saint. Hughes Mearns. LC 19-8808. 1919. The Penn Publishing Company.

Vines of Yarrabee. Dorothy Eden. LC 69-11054. 1969. 6.95. Coward McCann.

Vines of Yarrabee. Dorothy Eden. LC 78-6654. 1978. 8.95 (ISBN 0-698-10389-0). Coward, McCann & Geoghegan.

Vineta: The Phantom City. Elisabeth Burstenbinder. Tr. by Shaw, Frances A. (Cobweb series of choice fiction). 1877. Estes and Lauriat.

Vineta: The Phantom City. Elisabeth Burstenbinder. Tr. by Shaw, Frances. A. (On cover: Lovell's library, v. 14, no. 734). 1886. J. W. Lovell Company.

Vineyard. Pearl Mary Teresa Richards Craigie. LC 4-7332. 1904. D. Appleton and Company.

Vineyard. Idwal Jones. LC 42-24772. 1942. Duell, Sloan and Pearce.

Vineyard Chapel. Dorothy Daniels. 1976. (pbk.) 1.50 (ISBN 0-671-80459-6). Pocket Books.

Vineyard Keeper. Harry H. Fein. 1.50 o.p. (ISBN 0-8283-1385-7). Branden.

Vineyard Tales. Gale Huntington. LC 80-52793. 7.95 (ISBN 0-932384-13-7). Tashmoo Press.

Vingt Contes Favoris. Ed. by Foster E. Guyer & A. G. Bovee. 1941. 3.95 o.p. (ISBN 0-19-500902-9, OxfordC). Oxford U Pr.

Vingt et un Contes. 3rd ed. Leon P. Irvin & Donald L. King. 1964. pap. text ed. 12.50 scp (ISBN 0-06-043220-9, HarpC). Har-Row.

Vingt Mille Lieues sous les Mers. Jules Verne. pap. 4.50. French & Eur.

Vinh Long. Perry Oldham. 1977. 7.95 o.p. (ISBN 0-89002-168-6); pap. 2.95 o.p. (ISBN 0-89002-167-8). Northwoods Pr.

Vinnie. Albert T. Quandt. LC 52-652. Orig. Title: Cellar Club. 1968. pap. 0.50 o.p. (52-652). Paperback Lib.

Vinnie and the Flag-Tree, a Novel of the Civil War in Southern Illinois--America's Egypt. 1st Ed. Mabel Thompson Rauch. LC 59-6679. 1959. Duell, Sloan and Pearce.

Vinnie Ream and Mr. Lincoln. Freeman H Hubbard. LC 49-11038. 1949. Whittlesey House.

Vintage. Ursula Keir. LC 53-860455. 1953. Sloane.

Vintage. Anita Clay Kornfeld. LC 80-12652. 13.95. Simon and Schuster.

Vintage. Joseph William Sharts. LC 11-9152. 1911. Duffield & Company.

Vintage. Anthony P. West. LC 50-5012. 1950. Houghton Mifflin.

Vintage: A Romance of the Greek War of Independence. Edward Frederic Benson. LC 6-11337. 1898. Harper & Brothers.

Vintage Anthology of Science Fantasy. Ed. by Christopher Cerf. LC 66-13014. 1966. Vintage Books.

Vintage Bradbury: Ray Bradbury's Own Selection of His Best Stories. Introd. by Gilbert Highet. Ray Bradbury. LC 65-189366. (Vintage bk., V294). pap., 1.45. Random.

Vintage Murder. Ngaio Marsh. LC 72-193487. (Illus.). 1972. 5.95. Little, Brown.

Vintage Murder. Ngaio Marsh. LC 41-10144. (On cover: Penguin books. 253). 1940. Penguin Books.

Vintage of Spain. Janie Sawyer Smart. LC 11-1852. The C. M. Clark Publishing Company.

Vintage of Yon Yee. Louise Jordan Miln. LC 31-100871. 1931. Frederick A. Stokes Company.

Vintage Turgenev, Vol. 1. Ivan Turgenev. Incl. Smoke; Fathers & Sons; First Love. 1960. pap. 1.95 o.s.i. (ISBN 0-394-70711-7, V-711, Vin). Random.

Vintage Turgenev, Vol. 2. Ivan Turgenev. Incl. On the Eve; Rudin; Quiet Spot; Diary of a Superfluous Man. pap. 1.95 o.s.i. (ISBN 0-394-70712-5, V-712, Vin). Random.

Viola: A Novel. Katharine Read Lockwood. LC 36-6807. B. Humphries, Inc.

Viola Gwyn. George Barr McCutcheon. LC 22-17730. 1922. Dodd, Mead and Company.

Viola Hudson: A Novel. Isabel Constance Clarke. LC 23-120675. 1923. Benziger Brothers.

Viola: Or, Adventures in the Far South-West. Emerson Bennett. LC 14-22448. 1854. T. B. Peterson.

Viola; or, Life in the Northwest. Thomas Sharon. LC 8-4793. 1874. R. R. McCabe & Co., Printers.

Viola Tricolor. Theodor Storm. 2.75 o.p. (ISBN 0-592-04223-5). Transatlantic.

Viola Tricolor & Curator Carsten. Theodor Storm. LC 65-7498. 1956. pap. 2.45 o.p. (ISBN 0-8044-6881-8). Ungar.

Viola Tricolor, the Little Stepmother: Translated by Bayard Quincy Morgan. Curator Carsten, Translated by Frieda M. Voigt. Theodor Storm & Storm, Theodor, 1817-1888. Curator Carsten. Tr. by Bayard Quincy Morgan. LC 56-749891. (College Translations). 1956. F. Ungar Pub. Co.

Violated. Ashe Mannix. 1972. pap. 1.75 o.s.i. (V1095K, Venus). Grove.

Violated: A Novel. Vance Nye Bourjaily. LC 58-10571. 1958. Dial Press.

Violated One. Jack Hanley. Orig. Title: City Streets. pap. 0.60 o.p. (60-386). Manor Bks.

Violated Virgin. Ward Fulton. 192p. pap. 1.95 o.p. (ISBN 0-87977-114-3). Dansk Blue Bk.

Violation of Marcia Thomaston. A. Verge. 1972. pap. 1.95 o.s.i. (V1106T, Venus). Grove.

Violation of the Virgins and Other Stories. Hugh Garner. LC 78-163606. 1971. (ISBN 0-07-092931-9). McGraw-Hill Ryerson.

Violation of Vanessa. A. Degranamour. pap. 1.95 o.s.i. (Venus). Grove.

Violator. Henry Kane. 1974. (pbk.) 1.75. Warner Paperback Lib.

Violator. Lionel Webb. 1979. pap. 1.75 o.s.i. (ISBN 0-505-51335-8). Tower Bks.

Violator. Lionel Webb. (Orig.). 1970. pap. 0.95 o.p. (N2369). Pyramid Pubns.

Violators: Short Stories. Warren Kliewer. LC 64-253617. 1965. 3.00. M. Jones Co.

Violence. Anna Marcet Haldeman-Julius & Haldeman-Julius, Emanual, 1889- Joint Author. LC 29-17997. 1929. Simon and Schuster.

Violence. Festus Iyayi. 316p. (Orig.). 1979. 10.00 o.s.i. (ISBN 0-89410-105-6); pap. 5.00 o.s.i. (ISBN 0-89410-104-8). Three Continents.

Violence at Sundown. Frank O'Rourke. LC 53-500742. 1953. Random House.

Violence at Sundown. Frank O'Rourke. (Signet brand western). 1974. (pbk.) 0.95. New American Library.

Violence: By Cornell Woolrich Pseud. Cornell George Jopley-Woolrich. LC 58-107705. (Red badge detective). 1958.

Violence in Velvet: An Ed Noon Novel of Suspense. Michael Avallone. LC 56-7925. (Signet book, 1294). 1956. New American Library.

Violence Is Golden. Davis Dresser. (Mike Shayne mystery). 1973. (pbk.) 0.75. Dell.

Violence Is Golden: By C. H. Thames Pseud. Milton Lesser. LC 56-3580. 1956. Bouregy & Curl.

Violence Trail. George G. Gilman, pseud. (Edge Ser.: No. 25). 1978. pap. 1.95 (ISBN 0-523-41802-7). Pinnacle Bks.

Violent Air. Chris Renn. LC 80-14998. 1980. 10.95 (ISBN 0-312-84696-7). St. Martin's Press.

Violent Bear It Away. Flannery O'Connor. LC 60-6752. 1960. Farrar, Straus & Cudahy.

Violent Breed. Chuck Adams, pseud. 1979. pap. 1.50 o.s.i. (ISBN 0-8439-0680-4, Leisure Bks). Nordon Pubns.

Violent City: By John and Ward Hawkins. John Hawkins & Ward Hawkins. LC 57-126941. (Red badge detective). 1957. Dodd, Mead.

Violent Death of a Bitter Englishman. Brian Talbot Cleeve. LC 67-22673. 1967. Random House.

Violent Friends: A Novel. Winston David Armstrong Clewes. LC 45-20448. 1945. D. Appleton-Century Company.

Violent Hours. Frank Castle. LC 56-1211. (Gold medal books, 554). 1956. Fawcett Publications.

Violent Land. Jorge Amado. LC 65-15064. 1965. Knopf.

Violent Land. Wayne D Overholser. LC 54-12604. 1954. Macmillan.

Violent Land: By Jorge Amado, Translated from the Portuguese (Terras Do Sem Fim) by Samuel Putnam. Jorge Amado & Putnam, Samuel, 1892- Tr. LC 45-4925. 1945. A. A. Knopf.

Violent Land: Tales the Old Timers Tell. Robert Laxalt. LC 53-351676. 1953. Nevada Pub. Co.

Violent Man. Wayne C Lee. 1978. 1.75 (ISBN 0-441-86455-4). Ace Books.

Violent Man. Alfred Elton Van Vogt. LC 62-16951. 1962. Farrar, Straus and Cudahy.

Violent Man. e. van vogt. ed. Alfred Elton Van Vogt. (Kangaroo Book). 1978. 1.95 (ISBN 0-671-82004-4). Pocket Books.

Violent Maverick. Walt Coburn. 1970. pap. 0.60 o.p. (60-460). Manor Bks.

Violent Men. Ford Bowne, pseud. LC 67-1448. 1967. Arcadia House.

Violent Ones. Howard Hunt. LC 50-13511. (Gold medal book, 113). 1950. Fawcett Publications.

Violent Past. easy eye ed. Elizabeth Berridge. pap. 0.75 o.p. Lancer.

Violent Saturday. 1st Ed. William L Heath. LC 54-12183. 1955. Harper.

Violent Season. Robert Goulet. (O.s.i.). 1961. 4.50 o.s.i. (ISBN 0-8076-0143-8). Braziller.

Violent Shore. 1st Ed. Anton Myrer. LC 62-953935. 1962. Little, Brown.

Violent Streets. Don Pendleton. (Executioner Ser.). 192p. 1982. pap. 1.95 (ISBN 0-373-61041-6, Pub. by Worldwide). Harlequin Bks.

Violent Streets: The Story of a Gang's Girl. Introd. by Anna M. Kross. Dale Kramer. LC 55-9496. (Signet book, 1226). 1955. New American Library.

Violent Take It by Storm. Dorothy Mackinder. LC 39-105325. 1939. Sheed & Ward.

Violent Voyage. Arthur Nash. LC 57-8625. McGraw-Hill.

Violent Wedding. Robert James Collas Lowry. LC 76-110831. 1970. (ISBN 0-8371-2566-9). Greenwood Press.

Violent Wedding. 1st Ed. Robert James Collas Lowry. LC 53-5966. 1953. Doubleday.

Violent World of Hugh Greene: A Novel. Colin Wilson. LC 63-19132. 1963. Houghton Mifflin.

Violent World of Michael Shayne. Davis Dresser. LC 66-1993. 1965. Dell Pub. Co.

Violent World of Mike Shayne. Brett Halliday. 1974. (pbk.) 0.95. Dell.

Violet. Whitfield Cook. LC 42-25582. 1942. Coward-McCann, Inc.

Violet. Julia Magruder. LC 7-20128. 1896. Longmans, Green and Co.

Violet Clay. Gail Godwin. LC 77-12890. 1978. 10.00 (ISBN 0-394-49912-3). Knopf: Distributed by Random House.

Violet Douglas: Or, The Problems of Life. Emma Martin Marshall. LC 7-24665. (On cover: Household library, no. 10). D. Lothrop & Co.

Violet Flame: A Story of Armageddon and After. Frederick Thomas Jane. LC 74-16501. (Science Fiction). (Illus.). 1975. 14.00 (ISBN 0-405-06300-8). Arno Press.

Violet for Bonaparte. Geoffrey Trease. LC 77-357100. 1976. 2.95 (ISBN 0-333-21186-3). Macmillan.

Violet Gray: Or, From Ambition to Success. Sarah E Phipps. LC 7-36048. 1889. Funk & Wagnalls.

Violet Hour. Ilyea Darkas. LC 66-19976. 1966. Dorrance.

Violet Jermyn: Or, Tender and True. James Grant. LC 44-316286. 1883. G. Routledge and Sons.

Violet Keith: Or, Convent Life in Canada. Ellen McGregor Ross. LC 8-676. 1868. G. W. Carleton.

Violet Lisle. Charlotte Mary Brame. (On cover: The select series, no. 94). Street & Smith.

Violet Lisle. Bertha M. Clay. LC 44-116601. (On cover: The Select series, no. 94). Street & Smith.

Violet Moses. Leonard Merrick. LC 27-5952. (Half-title: The works of Leonard Merrick...). 1927. E. P. Dutton and Company.

Violet; or the Danseuse: A Portraiture of the Human Passions & Character, 2 vols. in 1. Marianne D. Malet. LC 79-8167. Date not set. Repr. of 1836 ed. 44.50 (ISBN 0-404-62018-3). AMS Pr.

Violet: Or, The Times We Live in. Harriet Cordelia Shubrick. LC 8-7323. 1858. J. B. Lippincott & Co.

Violet Vyvian, M. F. H. Maria Henrietta De La Cherois Crommelin. (On cover: Lovell's international series no. 1 91). 1890. J. W. Lovell Company.

Violets. Carrie D Beebe. LC 6-97669. 1873. "Banner of Liberty" Publishing House.

Violets. Doretta Klaber. (Illus.). 208p. 1976. 50.00 (ISBN 0-8386-7915-3). Fairleigh Dickinson.

Violets Are Blue. Gloria Lanius. 3.95 o.p. Carlton.

Violett: A Chronicle. Betsey Riddle Hutton Zum Stolzenberg. LC 4-3938. 1904. Houghton, Mifflin and Company.

Violetta: A Romance After the German of Ursula Zoge Von Manteuffel. Zoge Von Manteuffel, Ursula & Wister, Mr Annis Lee (Furness) 1830-1908. LC 7-20451. 1886. J. B. Lippincott Company.

Violetta and I. Maria Jane McIntosh. LC 7-16447. Loring.

Violetta & Other Stories. Amalia Georghiades. 1970. 3.50 o.p. Vantage.

Violette: A Story of Seeking and Finding. Maude Mary Butler. LC 17-12712. 1.25. Davis & Bond.

Violette of Pere Lachaise. Anna Strunsky Walling. LC 15-18827. 1915. Frederick A. Stokes Company.

Violin Lady. Daisy Rhodes Campbell. 1916. 1.25. The Page Company.

Violin Maker. Victor Martin Otto Denk. Tr. by Smith, Sara Trainer. LC 5-35789. 1905. Benziger Brothers.

Violin Obligato: And Other Stories. Margaret Crosby. LC 74-106283. (Short story index reprint series). 1970. Books for Libraries Press.

Violin Obligato: And Other Stories. Margaret Crosby. LC 6-31965. 1891. Roberts Brothers.

Violin Obligato & Other Studies. facsimile ed. Margaret Crosby. LC 74-106283. (Short Story Index Reprint Ser.). 1891. 17.00 (ISBN 0-8369-3320-6). Ayer Co.

Violin-Player. Bertha Thomas. (seaside library. v. 51, no. 1048). 1881. G. Munro.

Violin Solo: And Other Stories. Louisa Cutler Francis Curtis. LC 6-35455. 1906. The Milne Printery.

Violins at Dawn. Rachael Borne. LC 56-391755. 1956. Zondervan Pub. House.

Violins of Saint-Jacques. Patrick L. Fermor. LC 76-29863. 1977. 7.95 o.p. (ISBN 0-312-84700-9). St Martin.

Violins of Saint-Jacques: A Tale of the Antilles. 1st American Ed. Patrick Leigh Fermor. LC 53-10668. 1954. Harper.

Violins of Saint-Jacques: A Tale of the Antilles. Patrick Leigh Fermor. LC 76-29863. (Illus.). 1977. 7.95. St. Martin's Press.

V.I.P. A Novel. Elleston Trevor. LC 59-14091. 1960. Morrow.

Viper. Larry Pryor, pseud. LC 77-11779. 1978. 8.95 (ISBN 0-06-013449-6). Harper & Row.

Viper and the Hawk. Arthur Moore. (California Saga #3.). 1979. 1.95 (ISBN 0-445-04431-4). Popular Library.

Viper in the First. Herve-Bazin, Jean Pierre Marie. LC 51-1497. 1951. Prentice-Hall.

Viper of Milan. Marjorie Bowen. 1963. pap. 1.25 o.p. (ISBN 0-14-047018-2, PK18, Peacock). Penguin.

Viper of Milan: A Romance of Lombardy. Marjorie Bowen. LC 6-41272. 1906. McClure, Phillips & Co.

Viper of Milan: A Romance of Lombardy. Introd. Note by Graham Greene. Marjorie Bowen. LC 64-25494. 1965. 3.50. Dufour.

Viper Three. Walter H Wager. LC 75-142348. 1971. 5.95. Macmillan.

Viper's Bite. Jean DeWitt Fitz. LC 72-87226. 1969. 4.95. Geron-X.

Viper's Game. Robert S Hopkins. LC 74-3487. 1974. 6.95 (ISBN 0-440-08689-2). Delacorte Press.

Viper's Game. Robert S Hopkins. 1975. (pbk.) 1.50. Dell.

Vipers' Tangle. Translated by Warre B. Wells. Francois Mauriac. LC 57-3389. (Doubleday image book, D51). 1957. Image Books.

Virgen Insaciable. new ed. Jason Hytes. Tr. by Danilo Cesto from Eng. (Pimienta Collection Ser). Orig. Title: Part Time Virgin. (Illus.). 160p. (Span.). 1975. pap. 1.25 (ISBN 0-88473-244-4). Fiesta Pub.

Virgie, Goodbye. Nathan Rothman. LC 47-309142. 1947. Crown Publishers.

Virgil Drops His Cane: A Story of Boston in the Seventies, and the Great Fire. Frank Wright Pratt. LC 38-14379. The Christopher Publishing House.

Virgin. Susan Coon. 288p. 1981. pap. 2.50 (ISBN 0-380-77842-4, 77842). Avon.

Virgin. James Patterson. LC 80-11524. 9.95 (ISBN 0-07-048820-7). McGraw-Hill.

Virgin and the Gipsy. David Herbert Lawrence. LC 44-6437. 1944. The World Publishing Company.

Virgin and the Gipsy. David Herbert Lawrence. LC 30-305683. 1930. A. A. Knopf.

Virgin & the Gypsy. David H. Lawrence. 1968. pap. 2.50 (ISBN 0-553-14549-5, 12328-9). Bantam.

Virgin & the Monster. S. V. Baxter. pap. 1.95 o.s.i. (OPH-243, Ophelia). Olympia.

Virgin and the Swine: The Fourth Branch of the Mabinogi. Evangeline Walton. LC 38-882315. 1936. Willett, Clark & Company.

Virgin and the Vampire: A Novel. Robert John Myers. (Kangaroo Book). 1977. 1.75 (ISBN 0-671-81016-2). Pocket Books.

Virgin Fish of Babughat. Lokenath Bhattacharya. Tr. by Meenakshi Mukherjee from Bengali. (Indian Novels Ser.). 160p. 1975. 5.95 (ISBN 0-89253-016-2). Ind-US Inc.

Virgin Flame. Ernest Pascal. LC 28-17922. 1925. Grosset & Dunlap.
Virgin Flame: A Novel. Ernest Pascal. LC 25-4050. Brentano's.
Virgin Heart. Remy De Gourmont. Tr. by Huxley, Aldous Leonard. LC 27-26626. (Half-title: The modern library of the world's best books). 1927. The Modern Library.
Virgin Heart: A Novel. Remy De Gourmont. Tr. by Huxley, Aldous Leonard. LC 22-473161. 1921. N. L. Brown.
Virgin Hostage. William Horton. pap. 1.95 o.p. (8093). Cameo.
Virgin Huntress. Elisabeth Sanxay Holding. LC 51-8201. (Inner sanctum mystery). 1951. Simon and Schuster.
Virgin in Flames. Sax Rohmer. 1978. 6.50. Bookfinger.
Virgin in Judgment. Eden Phillpotts. LC 7-28960. 1907. P. R. Reynolds.
Virgin in Judgment. Eden Phillpotts. LC 8-29741. 1908. Moffat, Yard and Company.
Virgin in the Garden. Antonia Susan Drabble Byatt. LC 78-13653. 1979. 11.95 (ISBN 0-394-47325-6). Knopf: Distributed by Random House.
Virgin in the Ice: The Sixth Chronicle of Brother Cadfael. Ellis Peters. LC 82-14500. (Illus.). 1983. 11.95 (ISBN 0-688-01672-3). Morrow.
Virgin Kills. Raoul Whitfield. LC 32-4750. 1932. A. A. Knopf.
Virgin King: A Novel. Francis Watson. LC 36-35985. 1936. D. Appleton-Century Company, Incorporated.
Virgin Kisses. Gloria Nagy. 320p. 1982. pap. 2.95 (ISBN 0-446-90210-1). Warner Bks.
Virgin Kisses: A Novel. Gloria Nagy. LC 78-56873. 1978. 8.95. Chelsea House; Distributed by Atheneum.
Virgin Luck. Laurence Meynell. (G 1295). 1966. Avon.
Virgin Luck. Laurence Walter Meynell. 1964. 8.95 o.p. (ISBN 0-671-79020-X). S&S.
Virgin Market. C. Y. Lee. LC 64-15342. 1964. Doubleday.
Virgin No More. Maurice Laval. pap. 1.95 o.s.i. (Venus). Grove.
Virgin of Lontano. Helen Tucker. LC 73-80795. 1973. 6.95 (ISBN 0-8128-1606-4). Stein and Day.
Virgin of Lontano. Helen Tucker. (Signet book.). 1974. (pbk.) 1.50. New American Library.
Virgin of San Gil: A Novel. Paul Olsen. LC 65-20545. 1965. Holt, Rinehart and Winston.
Virgin of Skalholt. Gudmunder Kamban. Tr. by Ramsden, Evelyn Charlotte. LC 35-30572. 1935. Little, Brown, and Company.
Virgin of the Sun. Henry Rider Haggard. LC 22-11445. 1922. Doubleday, Page & Company.
Virgin of the Sun. Henry Rider Haggard. LC 22-6607. 1922. Cassell and Company, Limited.
Virgin of Yesterday. Dorothy Speare. LC 27-143449. George H. Doran Company.
Virgin Planet. Poul Anderson. 1970. pap. 0.60 o.p. (63-333). Paperback Lib.
Virgin Queene. Harford Willing Hare Powel. LC 28-11058. 1928. Little, Brown & Co.
Virgin Seducer. John Clarke. Bd. with Batchelor-Keeper; Voyage to Cacklagallinia. Samuel Brunt; Account of the State of Learning in the Empire of Lilliput. (Foundations of the Novel Ser.: Vol. 49). lib. bdg. 50.00 (ISBN 0-8240-0561-9). Garland Pub.
Virgin Sex Freaks. Ed. by John W. Fitzgerald. pap. 2.95 o.p. (ISBN 0-87964-108-8). Academy-Parliament.
Virgin Soil. translated with the author's sanction from the french version, by t. s. perry. ed. Ivan Sergeevich Turgenev. LC 13-12908. 1877. H. Holt and Company.
Virgin Soil. Ivan Sergeievich Turgenev & Perry, Thomas Sergeant, 1845- Tr. LC 13-12908. (Leisure hour series). 1877. H. Holt and Company.
Virgin Soil. Ivan Sergeievich Turgenev & Townsend, Rochelle S., Tr. (Half-title: Everyman's library, ed. by Ernest Rhys. Fiction). 1911. J. M. Dent & Sons, Ltd.
Virgin Soil: A Novel. Ivan Sergeevich Turgenev. LC 71-10271. (His Novels, v. 6-7). 1970. AMS Press.
Virgin Soil. Translated from the Russian by Constance Garnett. Ivan Sergeevich Turgenev. LC 56-910. (Evergreen book, E-27). 1956. Grove Press.
Virgin Soil Upturned. Translated from the Russian by Stephen Garry. Sholokhov, Mikhail Aleksandrovich. LC 59-4792. 1959. Knopf.
Virgin Soldiers. Thomas, Leslie. LC 66-11629. 1966. Little, Brown.
Virgin Stealers. Dan Streib. (Hawk Ser.: No. 12). (Orig.). 1981. pap. 1.95 (ISBN 0-515-06010-0). Jove Pubns.
Virgin to the Sun. Ethel Savage. 1968. 3.75 o.p. Vantage.
Virgin Wholly Marvelous. Ed. by Peter Brookby. LC 81-13928. (Illus.). 204p. 1981. 10.95 (ISBN 0-911218-18-1); pap. 6.95 (ISBN 0-911218-17-3). Ravengate Pr.
Virgin Widow: A Novel. Randal Charlton. LC 8-9522. 1908. G. W. Dillingham Company.
Virgin Widow. A Realistic Novel. Arthur Arnould. (On cover: Seaside library. Pocket ed. no. 1239). 1889. G. Munro.
Virgin with Butterflies. Tom Powers & Duvoisin, Roger Antoine, 1904- Illus. LC 45-4300. 1945. The Bobbs-Merrill Company.
Virgin with Child. Tom McDonough. LC 80-54083. 1981. 11.95 (ISBN 0-670-74721-1). Viking Press.
Virgin with Child. Tom McDonough. LC 82-5277. 1982. 4.95 (ISBN 0-14-006276-9). Penguin Books.
Virginia. Ellen Anderson Gholson Glasgow. LC 13-8758. 1913. Doubleday, Page & Company.
Virginia Belle. Sem Ralph. LC 8-207. (On cover: Satchel series, no. 29). W. B. Smith & Co.
Virginia Bohemians: A Novel. John Esten Cooke. LC 6-27185. (On cover: Harper's library of American fiction, no. 14). 1880. Harper & Brothers.
Virginia Clay. Meredith Rich. 320p. (Orig.). 1982. pap. 2.95 (ISBN 0-449-14505-0, GM). Fawcett.
Virginia Coffman Romances, 4 bks. Virginia Coffman. (Reader's Request Ser.). 1980. Set. lib. bdg. 60.00 (ISBN 0-8161-3140-6, Large Print Bks). G K Hall.
Virginia Comedians. John Esten Cooke. LC 68-23717. (Americans in Fiction Ser.). Repr. of 1854 ed. lib. bdg. 14.00 (ISBN 0-8398-0274-9). Irvington.
Virginia Comedians. John Esten Cooke. LC 68-23717. (Americans in Fiction Ser). 1968. Repr. of 1854 ed. lib. bdg. 11.50x o.p. (ISBN 0-8398-0274-9). Gregg.
Virginia Comedians: Or, Old Days in the Old Dominion. John Esten Cooke. LC 68-23717. (Americans in fiction). 1968. Gregg Press.
Virginia Comedians: Or, Old Days in the Old Dominion. John Esten Cooke. LC 11-10571. 1883. D. Appleton and Company.
Virginia Cousin, & Bar Harbor Tales. Constance Cary Harrison. LC 7-2889. 1895. Lamson, Wolffe and Co.
Virginia Cousin: &Bar Harbor Tales. Constance Cary Harrison. LC 74-96036. (Short story index reprint series). (Illus.). 1969. Books for Libraries Press.
Virginia Dare: A Romance of the Sixteenth Century. E. A. B. Shackelford. LC 8-4788. 1892. T. Whittaker.
Virginia Exiles. Elizabeth Gray Vining. LC 55-6300. 1955. Lippincott.
Virginia Feud: The Story of a Mountain Lassie. George Taylor Lee. LC 8-3519. 1908. The Neale Publishing Company.
Virginia Fly Is Drowning. Angela Huth. LC 72-96882. 1973. 4.95 (ISBN 0-698-10525-7). Coward, McCann & Geoghegan.
Virginia Graham: The Spy of the Grand Army. Justin Jones. Loring.
Virginia Heiress. May Agnes Early Fleming. LC 6-39940. (select series. no. 15). 1888. Street & Smith.
Virginia Inheritance: A Novel. Edmund Pendleton. LC 7-363702. (On cover: Appletons' town and country library. no. 6). 1888. D. Appleton and Company.
Virginia Lysle. Ida May Linkins Broughton. LC 36-4038. Chapman & Grimes.
Virginia of the Air Lanes. Herbert Quick. LC 9-26671. 1909. 1.50. The Bobbs-Merrill Company.
Virginia of Virginia: A Story. Amelie Rives Chanler Troubetzkoy. LC 9-1457. 1888. Harper & Brothers.
Virginia Randall. A Novel. Richard Burleigh Kimball. LC 7-12235. 1892. G. W. Dillingham, Successor to G. W. Carleton & Co.
Virginia Reels. William Hoffman. LC 78-16613. (Illinois Short Fiction Ser.). 1978. 11.95 (ISBN 0-252-00702-6); pap. 4.95 (ISBN 0-252-00703-4). U of Ill Pr.
Virginia Rose. Edward Reynolds Roe. (On cover: Dearborn series, no. 60). 1892. Donohue, Henneberry & Co.
Virginia Russell. Irene Dickson Schulder. LC 8-22542. 1908. Cochrane Publishing Company.
Virginia Woolf: To the Lighthouse. Ed. by Morris Beja. 1981. pap. 20.00x (ISBN 0-333-03689-1, Pub. by Macmillan England). State Mutual Bk.
Virginian. Owen Wister. LC 66-1480. (Western heritage library book). Popular Library.
Virginian: A Horseman of the Plains. Owen Wister. LC 65-6527. (Perennial classic). 1965. Harper & Row.
Virginian: A Horseman of the Plains. Owen Wister. LC 68-16182. (Great illustrated classics). (Illus.). 1968. Dodd, Mead.
Virginian: A Horseman of the Plains. Owen Wister. LC 2-14431. 1902. The Macmillan Company.
Virginian: A Horseman of the Plains. Owen Wister. LC 8-47715. 1902. The Macmillan Company.
Virginian: A Horseman of the Plains. Owen Wister. LC 4-8706. 1904. The Macmillan Company.
Virginian: A Horseman of the Plains. Owen Wister. LC 13-190306. (Half-title: Macmillan's standard library). Grosset & Dunlap.
Virginian: A Horseman of the Plains. Owen Wister. LC 21-12960. Grosset & Dunlap.
Virginian: A Horseman of the Plains. new ed., with illustrations by charles m. russell and drawings from western scenes by frederic remington. ed. Owen Wister. LC 11-264124. 1911. The Macmillan Company.
Virginian: A Horseman of the Plains. Owen Wister. LC 20-15625. 1916. Grosset & Dunlap.
Virginian: A Horseman of the Plains. Owen Wister. LC 28-17918. 1925. Grosset & Dunlap.
Virginian: A Horseman of the Plains. Owen Wister. LC 28-17915. 1925. The Macmillan Company.
Virginian: A Horseman of the Plains. Owen Wister. LC 30-12328. 1929. Grosset & Dunlap.
Virginian: A Horseman of the Plains. Owen Wister & Hosic, James Fleming, 1870- Ed. LC 17-24098. (On verso of half-title: Macmillan's pocket American and English classics). 1917. The Macmillan Company.
Virginian: A Horseman of the Plains. Owen Wister & Hosic, James Fleming, 1870- Ed. LC 30-10974. (Half-title: New pocket classics). The Macmillan Company.
Virginian: A Horseman of the Plains. Drawings from Western Scenes by Charles M. Russell. Owen Wister. LC 67-7676. 1967. 7.95. Macmillan.
Virginian, a Horseman of the Plains. With an Introdu. by Struthers Burt and Illus. by William Moyers. Owen Wister. LC 58-4204. 1958. Heritage Press.
Virginian Holiday. Anna Johnson. 1.00. American Tract Society.
Virginians. William Makepeace Thackeray. (Half-title: Everyman's library; ed. by Ernest Rhys. Fiction. no. 507-508). 1911. J. M. Dent & Sons, Ltd.
Virginians. William Makepeace Thackeray. LC 36-37328. (Half-title: Everyman's library, ed. by Ernest Rhys. Fiction. no. 507-508). 1925. J. M. Dent & Sons, Ltd.
Virginians: A Tale of the Eighteenth Century. William Makepeace Thackeray. LC 24-285517. (home library). 1923. A. L. Burt Company.
Virginians: A Tale of the Last Century. William Makepeace Thackeray. LC 31-260188. Caxton Publishing Co.
Virginians. A Tale of the Last Century. household ed. William Makepeace Thackeray. 1869. Fields, Osgood & Co.
Virginians: A Tale of the Last Century. William Makepeace Thackeray. LC 17-23008. (Half-title: The works of W. M. Thackeray). 1879. Smith, Elder & Co.
Virginians: A Tale of the Last Century. William Makepeace Thackeray. T. Y. Crowell & Company.
Virginians: A Tale of the Last Century. William Makepeace Thackeray. LC 4-16346. (Half-title: The biographical edition. The works of... Thackeray... vol. X). 1899. Harper & Brothers.
Virginians in Texas. A Story for Young Old Folks and Old Young Folks. William Mumford Baker. LC 6-6809. (On cover: Harper's library of American Section, no. 11). 1878. Harper & Brothers.
Virginia's Inheritance. Louisa Cooke Don-Carlos. LC 15-21793. 1.00. Davis & Bond.
Virginia's Married Life: A Sequel to Virginia Lysle. Ida May Linkins Broughton. LC 36-29303. Chapman & Grimes.
Virginia's Thing. Henry Woodfin. LC 68-29576. 1968. 4.95. Harper & Row.
Virginia's Wild Oats. Francis Evans Baily. LC 24-16807. The Bobbs-Merrill Company.
Virginie. Ernest James Oldmeadow. LC 8-4038. 1908. The McClure Company.
Virginie: Her Two Lives. John Hawkes. LC 81-48054. 256p. 1982. 13.41i (ISBN 0-06-014981-7, HarpT). Har-Row.
Virginie: Her Two Lives. John Hawkes. LC 81-48054. 256p. 1982. lmtd. ed 75.00 (ISBN 0-8112-0840-0). New Directions.
Virginie: Or, The Dawning of the World, a Novel. Joseph Majault. LC 73-91514. 1974. 5.95 (ISBN 0-517-51478-8). Crown.
Virginity: A Novel. Wilbur Finley Fauley. LC 31-161298. The Macaulay Company.
Virgins: A Novel. Jillian Becker. LC 76-363794. 1976. 3.50 (ISBN 0-575-02073-3). Gollancz.
Virgins & Cherry Lovers. Ed. by John W. Fitzgerald. pap. 2.95 o.p. (ISBN 0-87964-103-7). Academy-Parliament.
Virgin's Brand. Leo Perutz. Tr. by Stamper, Evelyn B. G. LC 35-4598. E. P. Dutton & Co., Inc.
Virgin's Destiny. Joseph Calvitt Clarke. LC 33-29198. 1933. W. Godwin.
Virgin's Destiny. Joseph Calvitt Clarke. LC 33-29196. 1933. W. Godwin, Inc.
Virgin's Holiday. Davis Dresses. LC 35-42916. W. Godwin, Inc.C.
Virgins in Cellophane: From Maker to Consumer Untouched by Human Hand. Bett Hooper & Flagg, James Montgomery, 1877- Illus. LC 32-25330. 1932. R. Long & R. R. Smith, Inc.
Virile Older Men & Willing Young Girls. J. P. Donaldson. pap. 1.95 o.p. (ISBN 0-87682-249-9, 7249). Barclay Hse.
Virility Factor. Henry Kane. LC 77-179348. 1971. 6.95. D. McKay Co.
Virility Factor: A Novel. Robert Merle. LC 76-58513. 9.95 (ISBN 0-07-041496-3). McGraw-Hill.
Virility Gene. Tully Zetford. 1976. (pbk.) 1.25 (ISBN 0-523-00800-7). Pinnacele Books.
Virtue of This Jest. James Stuart Montgomery. LC 29-16670. Greenberg.
Virtue OK'd. George Walker Clarke. LC 31-21628. 1931. Amour Press, Inc.
Virtue Takes a Holiday. Henry Leyford Gates. LC 33-708822. 1933. Grosset & Dunlap.
Virtues & Vices. Grania Beckford. LC 80-21892. 1981. 13.95 (ISBN 0-312-84954-0). St. Martin's Press.
Virtues of Hell. Pierre Boulle. LC 74-81811. 1974. 6.95 (ISBN 0-8149-0744-X). Vanguard Press.
Virtuous Courtesan. Jean Crooks Devanny. LC 35-13546. 1935. The Macaulay Company.
Virtuous Girl. Maxwell Bodenheim. LC 48-10570. (New Avon library 168). 1948. Avon Pub. Co.
Virtuous Girl. Maxwell Bodenheim. LC 30-15102. 1930. H. Liveright.
Virtuous Husband. Freeman Tilden. LC 25-12247. 1925. The Macmillan Company.
Virtuous Knight. Robert Emmet Sherwood. LC 31-226521. 1931. C. Scribner's Sons.
Virtuous Orphan. Pierre C. De Marivaux. Ed. by William H. McBurney & Michael F. Shugrue. Tr. by Mary Collyer. LC 65-10065. 1965. 12.50x o.p. (ISBN 0-8093-0162-8); pap. 4.00x o.p. (ISBN 0-8093-9705-6). S Ill U Pr.
Virtuous Orphan; or, the Life of Marianne, Countess of ---, 4 vols. Mary Mitchell Collyer. Ed. by Ronald Paulson. LC 78-60843. (Novel 1720-1805 Ser.). 1979. lib. bdg. 31.00 ea. (ISBN 0-8240-3652-2). Garland Pub.
Virtuous Orphan: Or, The Life of Marianne, Countess of. Pierre Carlet De Chamblain De Marivaux. LC 78-60843. (Novel, 1720-1805; 3). 1979. (4 vol. set) 112.00 (ISBN 0-8240-3652-2). Garland Pub.
Virtuous Villager. Charles De Fieux Mouhy. LC 74-34593. (Flowering of the Novel). 1975. 25.00 (ISBN 0-8240-1106-6). Garland Pub.
Virtuous Woman. Daphne Muir. LC 30-94733. 1929. Harper & Brothers.
Virtuous Women of Pont Clery: A Novel. 1st American Ed. Flora Sandstrom. LC 58-6351. 1958. John Day Co.
Virus Killer. Irwin Philip Sobel. (Fawcett Crest Book). 1976. (pbk.) 1.50. Fawcett.
Virus Killer. Irwin Philip Sobel. LC 74-24715. 1975. (ISBN 0-385-09563-5). Doubleday.
Visa for Avalon. Winifred Bryher. LC 65-16955. 1965. Harcourt, Brace & World.
Visa to France. Berry Fleming. LC 30-141892. 1930. Doubleday, Doran & Company, Inc.
Visa to Limbo. Richard Clayton. LC 79-52625. 1979. 8.95 (ISBN 0-8027-5412-0). Walker.
Visa to Limbo. William Haggard. (Walker Mystery Ser.). (O.s.i.). 1979. 8.95 o.s.i. (ISBN 0-8027-5412-0). Walker & Co.
Visa to Limbo. William Haggard. 202p. 1983. pap. 2.95 (ISBN 0-8027-3009-4). Walker & Co.
Viscous Circle. Piers Anthony, pseud. 272p. 1982. pap. 2.95 (ISBN 0-380-79897-2, 79897). Avon.
Vishnu: Or, The Planet of the Sevenfold Unity, an Autobiographical, Scientific and Mystical Romance. Walter William Strickland. LC 31-21306. 1928. B. Westermann Co., Inc.
Visibility Zero. Bernard Alvin Palmer. LC 44-411795. 1944. Zondervan Publishing House.
Visible and Invisible. Edward Frederic Benson. LC 24-7112. George H. Doran Company.
Visible Man. Gardner Dozois. (Berkley Medallion Book). 1977. 1.75 (ISBN 0-425-03595-6). Berkley Pub. Corp.
Visible Man. Dozois Gardner. 1977. pap. 1.75 (ISBN 0-425-03595-6, Medallion). Berkley Pub.
Vision. Richard J. Aielli. 3.50 o.p. Carlton.
Vision. Peter Arendson. 348p. (Orig.). 1982. 12.50. P Arendson.
Vision. Paul Hutchens. LC 41-123474. 1940. Wm. B. Eerdmans Publishing Company.
Vision. Dean Koontz. LC 77-7079. 8.95. Putnam.
Vision & the Dream. Marguerite Hargrove. 1980. pap. 2.25 (ISBN 0-8439-0811-4). Nordon Pubns.
Vision at the Savoy. Winifred Graham Cory. LC 6-1904. Fleming H. Revell Company.
Vision Beyond. Maurice Reidy. LC 26-21462. 1926. B. Herder Book Co.

Vision De Espana. Angel Del Rio & Margarita Ucelay. LC 68-13503. (Illus.). (gr. 9 up). 1968. text ed. 7.50 o.p. (ISBN 0-03-068810-8, HoltC); tapes avail. o.p. HR&W.
Vision House. Charles Norris Williamson & Alice Muriel Livingston Williamson. LC 21-9591. George H. Doran Company.
Vision in Verse & Three Ghosts. William H. Knapp. 1971. 3.95 o.p. (ISBN 0-8059-1546-X). Dorrance.
Vision Is Fulfilled. Kay L McDonald. LC 82-51303. 1983. 14.95 (ISBN 0-8027-4019-7). Walker.
Vision, Lest We Perish. Mary Barbara Koch Kemp. LC 48-223425. 1948. L. H. Kay.
Vision of Battlements. Anthony Burgess. 1966. 4.50 o.p. (ISBN 0-393-08416-7). Norton.
Vision of Battlements: By Anthony Burgess. John Anthony Burgess Wilson. (U5035). 1966. Ballantine.
Vision of Battlements: By AnthonyBurgess. John Anthony Burgess Wilson. LC 65-18780. 1966. bds., 4.50. Norton.
Vision of Desire. Margaret Bass Pedler. LC 22-23172. 1922. Hodder and Stoughton Ltd.
Vision of Desire. Margaret Bass Pedler. LC 23-3444. George H. Doran Company.
Vision of Elijah Berl. Nason, Frank Lewis. LC 5-9276. 1905. Little, Brown, and Company.
Vision of Empire. Enoch Anson More. LC 15-12992. R. G. Badger; Etc., Etc.
Vision of Hell. D. D. Owen. 1971. 17.50x (ISBN 0-7073-0160-2, Pub. by Scottish Academic Pr Scotland). Columbia U Pr.
Vision of Joy: Or, When "Billy" Sunday Came to Town; a Sequel to "The Victory of Allan Rutledge,". Alexander Corkey. LC 14-229. 1.25. The H. K. Fly Company.
Vision of Love. Elizabeth Graham, pseud. (Harlequin Presents Ser.). 192p. 1983. pap. 1.95 (ISBN 0-373-10583-5). Harlequin Bks.
Vision of Love: By Emily Noble Pseud. James Noble Gifford. LC 55-118723. 1955. Arcadia House.
Vision of Murder. J Maurice Brillant. LC 54-9553. 1954. Comet Press Books.
Vision of Stephen. Lolah Burford. LC 77-185142. (O.s.i.). 192p. 1972. 5.95 o.s.i. (ISBN 0-02-518120-3). Macmillan.
Vision of Stephen: An Elegy. Lolah Burford. 1974. (pbk.) 1.25. Bantam Books.
Vision of Tarot. Piers Anthony, pseud. 272p. 1982. pap. 2.50 (ISBN 0-425-05720-8). Berkley Pub.
Vision of Thady Quinlan. Michael M. McNamara. LC 73-91520. 1974. 5.95 (ISBN 0-517-51495-8). Crown Publishers.
Vision of the Eagle: A Novel. Kay L McDonald. LC 77-2579. 10.00 (ISBN 0-690-01491-0). Crowell.
Vision of Truth, the Soul's Awakening: A Story. Pub. by the Author, Adelaide Walther. Adelaide Richter Walther. LC 15-13209. 1915.
Vision Quest. Terry Davis. (Windstone Ser.). 204p. 1981. pap. 2.50 (ISBN 0-553-14815-X). Bantam.
Vision Quest: A Novel. Terry Davis. LC 79-10297. 1979. 8.95 (ISBN 0-670-74722-X). Viking Press.
Vision Splendid. Laurence Walter Meynell. LC 77-360364. 1976. 3.50 (ISBN 0-7091-5535-2). Hale.
Vision Splendid. Tom Ronan. LC 54-12753. 1954. Macmillan.
Vision Splendid: A Story of to-Day. William MacLeod Raine. LC 13-18223. 1.25. G. W. Dillingham Company.
Vision Splendid (Hardy, Housman) Neville H. Watts. LC 74-16122. 1974. Repr. of 1946 ed. lib. bdg. 20.00 (ISBN 0-8414-9548-3). Folcroft.
Visionaries. James Gibbons Huneker. LC 78-116979. (Short story index reprint series). 1970. Books for Libraries Press.
Visionaries. James Gibbons Huneker. LC 5-33500. 1905. C. Scribner's Sons.
Visionary: From the Papers of the Count De O--. A Tale from the German of Schiller. Johann Christoph Friedrich Von Schiller. LC 7-1650. (On cover: Library of German romance, no. 4). 1845. E. Ferrett & Co.
Visionary Novels: Lilith, Phantastes. Edited by Anne Fremantle, with an Introd. by W. H. Auden. George Macdonald. LC 54-117297. 1954. Noonday Press.
Visioning: A Novel. Susan Glaspell. LC 11-9941. 1911. Frederick A. Stokes Company.
Visions. Martin A. Grove. 496p. (Orig.). 1980. pap. 2.75 (ISBN 0-89083-695-7). Zebra.
Visions of Cody. John Kerouac. LC 72-3847. (Illus.). 1972. 8.95 (ISBN 0-07-034201-6). McGraw Hill.
Visions of Cody. John Kerouac. 1974. (pbk.) 3.95 (ISBN 0-07-034202-4). McGraw-Hill.
Visions of Esmaree. Elna Stone. LC 75-26201. 8.95. St. Martin's Press.
Visions of Gerard. John Kerouac. LC 63-16472. 1963. Farrar, Straus.
Visions of Gerard. John Kerouac. LC 76-14217. (McGraw-Hill paperbacks). (Illus.). 1976. 2.95 (ISBN 0-07-034204-0). McGraw-Hill.
Visions of Isabelle. William S Bayer. LC 75-30770. (Illus.). 7.95 (ISBN 0-440-09315-5). Delacorte Press.
Visions of Terror. William Katz. 288p. (Orig.). 1981. pap. 2.50 (ISBN 0-446-91347-2). Warner Bks.
Visions of the Damned. Jacqueline Marten. LC 79-88845. (Playboy Press paperback). 1980. 2.25 (ISBN 0-87216-529-9). Playboy Press.
Visions of Tomorrow: Six Journeys from Outer to Inner Space. David Samuelson. LC 74-16519. (Science Fiction). 1975. 25.00 (ISBN 0-405-06334-2). Arno Press.
Visions; Tales from the Russian. Il'Ia L'Vovich Tolstoi. LC 17-15284. 1917. J. B. Pond.
Visit. Friedrich Duerrenmatt. Ed. by Maurice Valency. 1958. 3.95 o.p. Random.
Visit. Ian Hamilton. 45p. cancelled o.s.i. (ISBN 0-571-09369-8, Pub. by Faber & Faber). Merrimack Pub Cir.
Visit After Dark. Daoma Winston. (Ace gothic). 1975. (pbk.) 1.25. Ace Books.
Visit From the Footbinder: And Other Stories. Emily Prager. 1982. 14.95 (ISBN 0-671-61013-9). S&S.
Visit of the Princess: A Romance of the Nineteen-Sixties. Ralph Hale Mottram. LC 46-17062. 1946. Hutchinson & Co. Ltd.
Visit to Pay. Isabella Holt. The Bobbs-Merrill Company.
Visit to the Bjorkheda Parsonage. Kristina Johanna Augusta Von Hofsten & Larsen, Carl, Tr. LC 7-6039. 1889. Cranston and Stowe.
Visitants: A Novel. Randolph Stow. LC 80-53710. 192p. 1981. 9.95 (ISBN 0-8008-8018-8). Taplinger.
Visitation. Rothayne Amare. 1977. pap. 1.75 (ISBN 0-89041-143-3, 3143). Major Bks.
Visited on the Children. A Novel. Theodora Havers Boulger. (Franklin square library, no. 192)). 1881. Harper & Brothers.
Visited on the Children. A Novel. Theodora Havers Boulger. (Seaside library, v. 53, no. 1088)). 1881. G. Munro.
Visiting Hours. Kent Rembo. 224p. (Orig.). 1982. pap. 2.50 (ISBN 0-523-41844-2). Pinnacle Bks.
Visiting Hours Are Over. Constance Bannister. 1968. pap. 1.00 (ISBN 0-671-10235-4, Fireside). S&S.
Visiting Moon. Ralph Hayes. Ed. by Alice Sachs. 1971. 3.95 o.p. Lenox Hill.
Visiting Nurse. Margaretta Brucker. LC 56-13290. 1956. Avalon Books.
Visiting Nurse. Kathleen Harris, pseud. LC 44-4533. 1944. Arcadia House, Inc.
Visiting Nurse. Adelaide Humphries. LC 44-4533. 1944. Arcadia House.
Visiting the Sin: A Tale of Mountain Life in Kentucky and Tennessee. Emma Rayner. LC 6453. 1900. Small, Maynard & Company.
Visiting Villain. Carolyn Wells. LC 34-28433. J. B. Lippincott Company.
Visitor. Jere Cunningham. LC 78-4011. 1978. 8.95 (ISBN 0-312-85055-7). St. Martin's Press.
Visitor. Jere Cunningham. (Berkley Book). 1979. 2.50 (ISBN 0-425-04210-3). Berkley Pub. Corp.
Visitor. Anthony Gilbert, pseud. 1971. pap. 0.95 o.p. (95136). Beagle Bks.
Visitor. Anthony Gilbert, pseud. 1967. 4.50 o.p. Random.
Visitor. Lucy Beatrice Malleson. LC 67-22677. 1967. Random House.
Visitor. Carl Randau & Zugsmith, Leane, 1903- Joint Author. LC 44-40042. 1944. Random House.
Visitors. Nathaniel Benchley. LC 64-7862. bds., 4.95. McGraw.
Visitors. Mary McMinnies. LC 58-10893. 1958. Harcourt, Brace.
Visitors. Clifford D. Simak. LC 79-2282. 1980. 9.95 (ISBN 0-345-28441-0). Ballantine Books.
Visitors at the Flower-Patch. Flora Klickmann. LC 31-15999. 1931. G. P. Putnam's Sons.
Visitors from Outer Space. L. B. Keefer. 3.50 o.p. Carlton.
Visitors to Hugo. Alice Grant Rosman. LC 29-16774. Minton, Balch & Company,
Visits of Elizabeth. Elinor Sutherland Glyn. 1901. J. Lane; Etc.
Visits of the Queen of Sheba. Miguel Serrano. LC 77-188030. (Harper colophon books, CN 315). (Illus.). 1973. 1.95 (ISBN 0-06-090315-5). Harper & Row.
Visits of the Queen of Sheba. 2nd ed. Miguel Serrano. LC 74-168866. (Illus.). 1972. 1.50 (ISBN 0-7100-7341-0) (ISBN 0-7100-7399-2). Routledge and K. Paul.
Visits of the Queen of Sheba. Foreword by C.G. Jung. Illustrated by Julio Escamez. Miguel Serrano. LC 61-3328. 1960. Asia Pub. House.
Vistas of New York. Brander Matthews. LC 70-37279. (Short story index reprint series). (Illus.). 1971. (ISBN 0-8369-4090-3). Books for Libraries Press.
Vistas of New York. Brander Matthews. LC 12-4767. 1912. Harper & Brothers.
Vita Inutil De Pito Perez. Jose Ruben Romero. Ed. by W. Cord. 1972. 6.95 o.p. (517045, Spec); pap. 5.95 o.p. (517037). P-H.
Vita Sexualis. Ogai Mori. LC 72-79020. 1972. 5.00 (ISBN 0-8048-1048-6). C. E. Tuttle Co.
Vital Parts. Thomas Berger. 448p. 1982. pap. 8.95 (ISBN 0-440-59378-6, Delta). Dell.
Vital Parts. Chelsea Farraday. 1979. pap. 2.25 o.s.i. (ISBN 0-505-51444-3). Tower Bks.
Vital Parts: A Novel. Thomas Berger. LC 73-108975. 1970. 6.95. R. W. Baron.
Vital Parts: A Novel. Thomas Berger. LC 82-5146. 1982. 16.95 (ISBN 0-440-09373-2). Delacorte Press/S. Lawrence.
Vital Question: Or, What Is to Be Done? Nikolai Gavrilovich Chernyshevskii & Dole, Nathan Howell, 1852- Tr. 1888. J. W. Lovell Company.
Vital Question: Or, What Is to Be Done? Nikolai Gavrilovich Chernyshevskii & Dole, Nathan Haskell, 1852- Tr. LC 8-25958. 1886. T. Y. Crowell & Co.
Vital Signs. Ralph Burrows. 256p. 1982. pap. 2.75 (ISBN 0-449-14472-0, GM). Fawcett.
Vital Signs. Michael A Weiner. LC 82-84738. 8.95 (ISBN 0-932238-20-3). Avant Books.
Vital Statistics. Thomas Chastain. LC 77-79024. 8.95 (ISBN 0-8129-0698-5). Times Books.
Vital Touch: A Story of the Power of Love. Frances Margaret Schnebly. LC 12-163223. 1.00. Laird & Lee.
Vittoria. author's ed. George Meredith. LC 9-3833. 1888. Roberts Brothers.
Vittoria. rev. ed. George Meredith. LC 1-18377. 1897. C. Scribner's Sons.
Vittoria Cottage. Dorothy Emily Stevenson. LC 71-160439. 1971. 5.95 (ISBN 0-03-080286-5). Holt, Rinehart and Winston.
Vittoria Cottage. Dorothy Emily Stevenson. LC 49-6496. 1949. Rinehart.
Vittorini Omnibus: The Twilight of the Elephant & Other Novels. Elio Vittorini. Tr. by Cinina Brescia et al from It. LC 73-78790. 320p. 1973. 9.50 (ISBN 0-8112-0498-7); pap. 3.75 (ISBN 0-8112-0499-5, NDP366). New Directions.
Vituous Orphan: Or The Life of Marianne, Countess of An Eighteenth-Century English Translation by Mary Mitchell Collyer, of Marivaux's La Vie De Marianne. Ed., Critical Introd. by William Harlin McBurney, Michael Francis Shugrue. Pierre Carlet De Chamblain De Marivaux. Ed. by William Harlin McBurney & Michael Francis Shugrue. LC 65-10065. 12.50. Southern Ill. Univ. Pr.
Viva. Mrs. Bridges. (On cover: Lovell's library, v. 18, no. 859). 1887. J. W. Lovell Company.
Viva. A Novel. Mrs. Bridges. 1878. J. B. Lippincott & Co.
Viva. A Novel. Mrs. Bridges. (On cover: Seaside library. Pocket ed. no. 734). 1886. G. Munro.
Viva Madison Avenue! 1st Ed. George Panetta. LC 57-6213. 1957. Harcourt Brace.
Viva Max. James Lehrer. LC 66-14952. 4.95. Duell Dist. Meredith.
Vivandiere! Phoebe Fenwick Gaye. LC 29-13065. H. Liveright.
Vivanti: A Paul Vivanti Story. Sydney Horler. LC 28-28168. 1927. George H. Doran Company.
Vive la France: A Narrative Founded on the Diary of Jeannette De Martigny. Emilie Benson Knipe. LC 19-14014. 1919. The Century Co.
Vive le Roy: A Novel. Ford Madox Ford. LC 36-7113. 1936. J. B. Lippincott Comapny.
Viver of Vivier, Longman & Company, Bankers: A Novel. William Cadwalader Hudson. LC 99-3951. (On cover: Magnet detective library, no. 94). 1899. Street & Smith.
Vivero Letter. Desmond Bagley. LC 68-10686. 1968. 4.95. Doubleday.
Vivette: Or, The Memoirs of the Romance Association... Gelett Burgess. 1897. Copeland & Day.
Vivia: Or, The Secret of Power. Emma Dorothy Eliza Nevitte Southworth. LC 12-38910. T. B. Peterson & Brothers.
Vivian. Henry Leyford Gates. LC 27-123977. 1927. Barse & Hopkins.
Vivian: A Story Written by Fourteen Wichita High School Yound Ladies. Wichita, Kan. High School.
Vivian Grey. new ed. Benjamin Disraeli Beaconsfield. LC 4-23589. G. Routledge and Sons.
Vivian Grey. Benjamin Disraeli Beaconsfield. (Seaside library, v. 20, no. 392). G. Munro.
Vivian Grey. Benjamin Disraeli Beaconsfield. (On cover: Seaside library. Pocket ed. no. 793). 1886. G. Munro.
Vivian Grey. Benjamin Disraeli Beaconsfield. LC 4-46494. 1901. Longmans, Green and Co.
Vivian Grey. Benjamin Disraeli Beaconsfield. LC 6-11547. (Half-title: The English Comedie humaine. 2d series). 1906. The Century Co.
Vivian Grey. Benjamin Disraeli. Ed. by Herbert Van Thal. (First Novel Library). 1969. 5.95 o.p. (ISBN 0-304-92622-1); pap. 3.95 o.p. Dufour.
Vivian Grey: A Romance of Youth. Benjamin Disraeli Beaconsfield. LC 76-12451. (Works of Benjamin Disraeli, Earl of Beaconsfield; v. 1-2). (Illus.). 1976. (ISBN 0-404-08800-7). AMS Press.
Vivian Inheritance. Jean Stubbs. LC 82-17020. 1982. 12.95 (ISBN 0-312-85068-9). St. Martin's Press.
Vivian of Cavendish Square. Kathryn Douglas, pseud. 416p. 1982. pap. 2.95 (ISBN 0-345-28923-4). Ballantine.
Vivian of Mackinac. William C Levere. LC 11-188404. 1911. Forbes & Company.
Vivian of Virginia: Being the Memoirs of Our First Rebellion. Hulbert Fuller. LC 6-31699. 1897. Lamson, Wolffe and Company.
Vivian the Beauty. Annie Edwards. (On cover: Seaside library. Pocket ed. no. 835). 1886. G. Munro.
Vivians. Edwin Barrett Hay. 1907. The Neal Publishing Company.
Vivid Night. Garroway Renfrew. LC 43-22856. 1943. The Christopher Publishing House.
Vivien. William Babington Maxwell. LC 5-35300. 1905. D. Appleton and Company.
Vivien. William Babington Maxwell. LC 5-28384.
Vivienne. Eliza M. J. Humphreys. (On cover: Lovell's library. no. 1153). 1888. J. W. Lovell Company.
Vivier, of Vivier, Longman & Company, Bankers: A Novel. William Cadwalader Hudson. LC 7-5644. Cassell Publishing Company.
Viviette. William John Locke. LC 16-101232. 1916. 1.00. John Lane Company.
Vivisector. Patrick White. LC 72-104137. 1970. 8.95. Viking Press.
Vivisector. Patrick White. LC 74-171252. (Penguin modern classics). 1973. 0.60 (ISBN 0-14-003693-8). Penguin.
Vixen. Mary Elizabeth Braddon Maxwell. LC 7-25294. (Seaside library. v. 25, no. 481). 1879. G. Munro.
Vixen. Mary Elizabeth Braddon Maxwell. (On cover: Seaside library. Pocket ed. no. 204). 1884. G. Munro.
Vixen: A Novel. Mary Elizabeth Braddon Maxwell. (On cover: Lovell's library, no. 766). 1886. J. W. Lovell Company.
Vixen in Velvet. Fern Michaels. LC 76-10609. 1976. 1.25 (ISBN 0-345-25174-1). Ballantine Books.
Vixen Zero Three. Clive Cussler. 1979. pap. 2.75 (ISBN 0-553-12810-8). Bantam.
Vixen 03. Clive Cussler. LC 78-63035. 1978. 9.95 (ISBN 0-670-74741-6). Viking Press.
Vixens see Friends & Lovers.
Vixens: A Novel. Frank Yerby. LC 47-3065. 1947. The Dial Press.
Vixen's Cub. Katharine Morris. LC 52-7802. 1952. Dutton.
Vixen's Revenge. Paula Allardyce, pseud. LC 79-89961. (Historical Romance Ser.). 208p. (Orig.). 1980. pap. 1.95 (ISBN 0-87216-607-4). Playboy Pbks.
Vizier of the Two-Horned Alexander. Frank Richard Stockton & Birch, Reginald Bathurst, 1856- Illus. LC 99-1700. 1899. The Century Co.
Vizier's Elephant: Three Novellas. Ivo Andric. Tr. by Drenka Willin. 1962. 4.75 o.p. HarBraceJ.
Vizier's Elephant: Three Novellas. Ivo Andric. LC 77-127924. 1970. pap. 2.45 o.p. (ISBN 0-8092-6142-1). Gateway Ed Ltd.
Vlemk, the Box-Painter. John Champlin Gardner. LC 79-91630. (Illus.). 1979. 15.00 (ISBN 0-935716-01-7). Lord John Press.
Voadica: A Romance of the Roman Wall. Ian Campbell Hannah. LC 28-11713. 1928. Longmans, Green and Co., Ltd.
Vocation of Edward Conway. Maurice Francis Egan. LC 6-37567. 1896. Benziger Brothers.
Vocations. Gerald O'Donovan. LC 22-7437. Boni and Liveright.
Voci Della Sera. Ed. by Natalia Ginzburg & Sergio Pacifici. (It). 1971. pap. text ed. 3.95 o.p. (ISBN 0-394-31222-8, RanC). Random.
Vocie from the Living. Marc Lovell, pseud. LC 77-92221. 1978. 6.95 (ISBN 0-385-14104-1). Published for the Crime Club by Doubleday.
Vodka on Ice. Hugh McLeave. LC 69-12041. 1969. Harcourt, Brace & World.
Voice. Margaret Wade Campbell Deland. LC 12-219537. 1912. Harper & Brothers.
Voice. Anthony Gilbert, pseud. 1971. pap. 0.95 o.p. (95183). Beagle Bks.
Voice. Paul Hutchens. LC 38-601112. Wm. B. Eerdmans Publishing Co.
Voice. Gabriel Okara. LC 76-90298. (African writers series, no. 68). 1970. 1.50. Africana Pub. Corp.
Voice and the Light. Edwin Fadiman. LC 49-6000. 1949. Crown Publishers.
Voice at Sea. Henry C Nichols. LC 48-11064. 1948. House of Edinboro.

Voice at the Back Door. Elizabeth Spencer. LC 56-11727. 1956. McGraw-Hill.
Voice: By Anthony Gilbert Pseud. Lucy Beatrice Malleson. LC 65-21246. (Random House mystery). 1965. bds., 3.95. Random.
Voice from Heaven. Ralph Webster Neighbour. LC 59-319081. Zondervan Pub. House.
Voice from the Dark. Eden Phillpotts. LC 25-48601. 1925. The Macmillan Company.
Voice from the Grave. Doris Miles Disney. LC 68-29496. 1968. 3.95. Published for the Crime Club by Doubleday.
Voice from the Grave. Clarissa Ross, pseud. 1971. pap. 0.75 o.p. (ISBN 0-447-74754-1). Lancer.
Voice from the Mess. Eva Lena Weeks. LC 51-6940. 1951. Story Book Press.
Voice from the Silence: A Story of the Ozarks. Howard Leslie Terry. LC 15-158. 1914. 1.25. The Palisades Press.
Voice from the Wings. Nancy Hallinan. LC 65-11103. 5.95. Knopf.
Voice in the Closet. Raymond Federman. LC 78-11233. (Illus.). 30.00. (ISBN 0-930956-04-4) (ISBN 0-930956-05-2). Coda Press.
Voice in the Closet. Herman Landon. LC 30-15097. 1930. H. Liveright.
Voice in the Closet: La Voix Dans le Cabinet De Debarras. Raymond Federman & Maurice Roche. LC 78-11233. (Illus., Fr.). 1979. limited ed. 30.00 (ISBN 0-930956-04-4); pap. 6.95 (ISBN 0-930956-05-2). Coda Pr.
Voice in the Darkness. Pamela Bennetts. LC 78-21423. 7.95 (ISBN 0-312-85079-4). St. Martin's Press.
Voice in the Darkness. Margaret James. LC 79-17580. 1979. 10.95 (ISBN 0-8161-6749-4). G. K. Hall.
Voice in the Desert. Pauline Bradford Mackie Cavendish. LC 3-9836. 1903. McClure, Phillips and Company.
Voice in the Desert. Pauline Bradford Mackie Hopkins. LC 3-9336. 1903. McClure, Phillips and Company.
Voice in the Fog. Harold MacGrath. LC 15-3418. 0.75. The Bobbs-Merrill Company.
Voice in the Night and Other Stories. Frederick Fairchild Hall. LC 12-286. 1911. The Sunday School Times Company.
Voice in the Night and Other Stories. Frederick Fairchild Hall. LC 29-12656. The Biola Book Room, Bible Institute of Los Angeles.
Voice in the Rice. Gouverneur Morris. LC 10-8533. 1910. Dodd, Mead and Company.
Voice in the Streets: A Novel. John William Tebbel. LC 54-8858. 1954. Dutton.
Voice in the Wilderness. Richard Blaker. LC 22-27463. 1922. George H. Doran Company.
Voice in the Wilderness. Grace Livingston Hill. Repr. lib. bdg. 18.80x (ISBN 0-89190-031-4). Am Repr-Rivercity Pr.
Voice in the Wilderness. Grace Livingston Hill. 1916. 2.95 o.p. (ISBN 0-448-05268-7). G&D.
Voice in the Wilderness: A Novel. Grace Livingston Hill. LC 16-18483. 1916. Harper & Brothers.
Voice in the Wilderness: A Novel. 1st Ed. Mina Moore McCrory. LC 54-13174. 1955. Exposition Press.
Voice Like Velvet. Donald Landels Henderson. LC 46-1792. 1946. Random House.
Voice of a Child. Sophie Bronson Titterington. LC 12-27599. American Tract Society.
Voice of a Flower. Emily Gerard. LC 7-15444. (On cover: Appleton's town and country library. no. 116). 1893. D. Appleton and Company.
Voice of Air. Evelyn Berckman. LC 72-107348. 1970. 4.95. Doubleday.
Voice of Allah. Edwin Palmer Hoyt. LC 77-89311. 1970. 8.95. John Day Co.
Voice of Armageddon. David Lippincott. LC 73-93179. 1974. 6.95 (ISBN 0-399-11326-6). Putnam.
Voice of Armageddon. David Lippincott. (Signet book). 1975. (pbk.) 1.50. New American Library.
Voice of Bugle Ann. MacKinlay Kantor. LC 35-27277. Coward-McCann, Inc.
Voice of Dashin: A Romance of Wild Mountains. Martin Louis Alan Gompertz. LC 27-816. George H. Doran Company.
Voice of Johnnywater. Bertha Muzzy Sinclair. LC 23-3439. 1923. Little, Brown and Company.
Voice of Love. William Arthur Neubauer. LC 52-10205. 1952. Arcadia House.
Voice of Love. Daisy H. Thomson. 1977. pap. 1.25 o.p. (ISBN 0-515-04208-0). BJ Pub Group.
Voice of Murder. Margaret Erskine, pseud. 1974. 0.95. Ace Books.
Voice of Murder: By Margaret Erskine Pseud. 1st Ed. Wetherby Williams. LC 56-5967. 1956. Published for the Crime Club by Doubleday.
Voice of My Beloved: A Novel. Phyllis Speshock. LC 58-15410. 1957. Zondervan Pub. House.
Voice of the Big Firs. Agnette Midgarden Lohn. LC 18-60267. Printed by the Pioneer Co.
Voice of the City. William Sydney Porter. LC 37-14406. 1937. The Sun Dial Press, Inc.
Voice of the City: Further Stories of the Four Million. William Sydney Porter. LC 8-17555. 1908. The McClure Company.
Voice of the City: Further Stories of the Four Million. William Sydney Porter. LC 15-17407. 1914. Doubleday, Page & Company.
Voice of the City: Further Stories of the Four Million. William Sydney Porter. LC 19-135214. 1919. Doubleday, Page & Company.
Voice of the City: Further Stories of the Four Million. William Sydney Porter. LC 22-14572. 1919. Doubleday, Page & Company, for Review of Reviews Co.
Voice of the City: Further Stories of the Four Million. William Sydney Porter. LC 25-215938. 1925. Doubleday, Page & Company.
Voice of the Clown. Brenda B. Canary. 288p. 1982. pap. 2.95 (ISBN 0-380-79624-4, 79624). Avon.
Voice of the Corpse. Max Murray. LC 47-11002. 1947. Farrar, Straus.
Voice of the Crab. Geraldine Halls. LC 74-1888. 1974. 5.95 (ISBN 0-06-012196-3). Harper & Row.
Voice of the Crab. Geraldine Halls. LC 74-32282. 1975. 8.95 (ISBN 0-8161-6270-0). G. K. Hall.
Voice of the Crab. Charlotte Jay, pseud. (Adult Ser.). 1975. Repr. lib. bdg. 8.95 o.p. (ISBN 0-8161-6270-0, Large Print Bks). G K Hall.
Voice of the Crab. Charlotte Jay, pseud. LC 74-1888. (Novel of Suspense). 160p. (YA) 1974. 5.95 o.p. (ISBN 0-06-012196-3, HarpT). Har-Row.
Voice of the Dolls. Dorothy Eden. 1977. 1.75. Ace.
Voice of the Dolphins: And Other Stories. Leo Szilard. LC 61-7014. 3.00. Simon and Schuster.
Voice of the Heart. Barbara Taylor Bradford. LC 81-47863. 1983. 21.95 (ISBN 0-385-15323-6). Doubleday.
Voice of the Heart: A Romance by Margaret Blake Pseud.... Illustrations by E. A. Furman. Lida Clara Schem. LC 13-8394. G. W. Dillingham Company.
Voice of the House. Margaret Erskine. (Ace gothic). 1975. (pbk.) 0.95. Ace Books.
Voice of the House. Wetherby Williams. LC 47-24304. 1947. Pub. for the Crime Club by Doubleday.
Voice of the Lobster. Robert Joseph Casey. LC 30-6728. The Bobbs-Merrill Company.
Voice of the Lord: A Novel. Laurene Chambers Chinn. LC 61-15797. 1961. Crown Publishers.
Voice of the Lute: A Romantic Novel. Skulda Vanadis Baner. LC 59-12745. 1959. Longmans, Green.
Voice of the Morning. Alan Livingstone Wilson. LC 68-22168. 1968. Zondervan.
Voice of the Murderer. Goodwin Walsh. LC 26-14632. 1926. G. P. Putnam's Sons.
Voice of the Night. Brian Coffey. LC 79-7327. 1980. 10.95 o.p. (ISBN 0-385-15258-2). Doubleday.
Voice of the Night. Brian Coffey. 1981. pap. 2.75 (ISBN 0-451-09966-4, E9966, Sig). NAL.
Voice of the Night. Dean Koontz. LC 79-7321. 1980. 10.95 (ISBN 0-385-15258-2). Doubleday.
Voice of the Pack. Edison Marshall. LC 20-26323. 1920. Little, Brown, and Company.
Voice of the People. Ellen Anderson Gholson Glasgow. LC 71-96882. 1969. Literature House.
Voice of the People. Ellen Anderson Gholson Glasgow. 1900. Doubleday, Page & Co.
Voice of the People. Ellen Anderson Gholson Glasgow. 1902. Doubleday, Page & Co.
Voice of the People. Ellen Anderson Gholson Glasgow. LC 24-285292. 1922. Doubleday, Page & Company.
Voice of the Pigeon. George Mysels. 5.95 o.p. Vantage.
Voice of the Seven Sparrows. Harry Stephen Keeler. LC 28-4667. E. P. Dutton & Company.
Voice of the Steppe. I. Kramov. 478p. 1981. 9.60 (ISBN 0-8285-2056-9, Pub. by Progress Pubs USSR). Imported Pubns.
Voice of the Stranger. Madge Reinhardt. LC 81-65402. (Illus.). 477p. 1982. 12.95 (ISBN 0-917162-05-6); pap. 7.50 (ISBN 0-917162-06-4). Back Row Pr.
Voice of the Street. Ernest Poole. LC 6-19774. 1906. A. S. Barnes & Company.
Voice of the Turtle. John Ankenbruck. LC 74-75071. (Illus.). 1974. 1.95. News Pub. Co.
Voice of Verdun. Elmer Naslund. LC 35-5818. The Elm Publishing Co.
Voice of Warning. Parley P. Pratt. 1974. pap. 3.50 (ISBN 0-89036-044-8). Hawkes Pub Inc.
Voice on the Mountain: A Story of Those Who Understand. Maria. LC 23-17847. 1923. A. A. Knopf.
Voice on the Southwind. Betty Dickens. Ed. by Barbara Holley. (Orig.). 1982. pap. 3.50 (ISBN 0-933494-15-7). Earthwise Pub.
Voice on the Telephone. Mildred B Davis. LC 64-10535. (Random House mystery). 1964. Random House.
Voice on the Wind. Dorothy Daniels. 1971. pap. 0.75 o.p. (64-599). Paperback Lib.
Voice on the Wire: A Novel of Mystery. Eustace Hale Ball. LC 15-15753. 1915. Hearst's International Library Co.
Voice Out of Darkness. Ursula Reilly Curtiss. LC 48-10246. (Red badge detective). 1948. Dodd, Mead.
Voice Outside. Ken Grimwood. LC 80-1808. 1982. 15.95 (ISBN 0-385-15744-4). Doubleday.
Voice That Fills the House: A Novel. Martin Mayer. LC 59-80530. 1959. Simon and Schuster.
Voice Through a Cloud. Denton Welch. LC 66-4918. 1966. Humanities Research Center University of Texas.
Voice Through a Cloud. Denton Welch. LC 80-17151. 1980. 9.95 (ISBN 0-8290-0249-9). Irvington Publishers.
Voiceless Ones. John Creasey. LC 73-93938. (His A Doctor Palfrey thriller). 1974. 5.95. Walker.
Voiceless Ones. Palfrey. LC 73-93938. 192p. 1974. 5.95 o.p. (ISBN 0-8027-5300-0). Walker & Co.
Voices. Elizabeth Maria Beskow. Tr. by Kjellstrand, August William. 1.25. Augustana Book Concern.
Voices. George J Brenn. LC 23-12432. 1923. 1.75. The Century Co.
Voices. I Lowenberg. LC 20-3263. 1920. H. Wagner Publishing Co.
Voices East & West: German Short Stories Since 1945. Ed. by Roger C. Norton. LC 81-70125. 250p. Date not set. 14.95 (ISBN 0-8044-2660-0); pap. 6.95 (ISBN 0-8044-6608-4). Ungar.
Voices from France: Ten Stories by French Nobel Prize Winners. Ed. by Miriam Morton. LC 78-79971. 1969. 3.95. Doubleday.
Voices from the Asylum. Michael Glenn. 1974. lib. bdg. 10.00x o.p. (ISBN 0-06-136137-2, TLE137, Torch Lib). Har-Row.
Voices from the Big House. Ed. by Frank Earl Andrews. 1974. (pbk.) 1.25. Pyramid Books.
Voices from the Big House. Ed. by Frank Earl Andrews. LC 72-86910. 1972. 7.00. Harlo Press.
Voices from the Bottom of the World: A Policeman's Journal. T. Mike Walker. LC 79-111017. 1970. 6.95. Grove Press.
Voices from the Dust. Jeffery Farnol. LC 32-26645. 1932. Little, Brown, and Company.
Voices from the Edge of Eternity. John Myers. 1970. pap. 0.95 o.p. (N2400). Pyramid Pubns.
Voices from the Forest. Lisel Mueller. (William N. Judson Ser.: No. 7). 1979. 10.00; pap. 4.50. Juniper Pr WI.
Voices from the Kenduskeag... Jame Sophia Appleton & Barrett, Mrs. Cornelia Crosby, Joint Ed. LC 1-571723. 1848. D. Bugbee.
Voices from the Plain of Jars: Life Under an Air War. Frederick Branfman. (Illus.). 160p. 1972. lib. bdg. 6.00x o.p. (ISBN 0-06-136091-0, TLE91, Torch Lib). Har-Row.
Voices from the Sky. Arthur C. Clarke. 1971. pap. 0.75 o.p. (T2396). Pyramid Pubns.
Voices in an Empty House. Joan Aiken. LC 74-14376. 1975. 7.95 (ISBN 0-385-07535-9). Doubleday.
Voices in an Empty Room. Philip Loraine. LC 73-20598. 1974. 5.95 (ISBN 0-394-48949-7). Random House.
Voices in the Catacombs. Ludwig Bauer. LC 51-5818. 1951. Christopher Pub. House.
Voices in the City. Anita Desai. (Orient Paperbacks Ser). 257p. 1973. pap. 1.60 o.p. (ISBN 0-88253-250-2). InterCulture.
Voices in the Dark. Mona Goodwyn Williams. 1968. 3.50 o.p. Doubleday.
Voices in the Evening. Natalia Ginzburg. LC 63-5817. 1963. Dutton.
Voices in the Fog. Kate Cameron, pseud. (Holderly Hall Ser: No. 3). 1975. pap. 0.95 o.p. (LB230NK, Leisure Bks). Nordon Pubns.
Voices in the Garden. Dirk Bogarde. LC 81-47494. 1981. 12.95 (ISBN 0-394-52156-0). Knopf: Distributed by Random House.
Voices in the Hills. Frederick Thaumazo. LC 14-228. 1913. Broadway Publishing Co.
Voices in the House: By John Sedges Pseud. Pearl Sydenstricker Buck. LC 52-12687. 1953. J. Day Co.
Voices in the Night: A Chromatic Fantasia. Flora Annie Webster Steel. LC 3280. 1900. The Macmillan Company.
Voices in the Square. George Abbe. LC 38-19256. 1938. Coward-McCann, Inc.
Voices in the Storm. Walter Kaufman. LC 73-162941. 1972. 1.95 (ISBN 0-7260-0104-X). Gold Star Publications.
Voices in the Wilderness. John Ressich. LC 79-152954. (Short story index reprint series). 1971. (ISBN 0-8369-3869-0). Books for Libraries Press.
Voices in the Wilderness. John Ressich. LC 24-4009. E. P. Dutton & Company.
Voices Long Hushed. Barbara Anne Pauley. LC 75-21240. 1976. 5.95 (ISBN 0-385-11362-5). Published for the Crime Club by Doubleday.
Voices of a Summer Day. Irwin Shaw. LC 65-13414. 1965. Distributed by the Dial Press.
Voices of Death. Edwin S. Shneidman. 224p. 1982. pap. 2.95 (ISBN 0-553-13997-5). Bantam.
Voices of Doom. Basil Copper. LC 79-5157. 1980. 10.00 (ISBN 0-312-85083-2). St. Martin's Press.
Voices of Glory. Davis Grubb. LC 62-17729. 1962. Scribner.
Voices of Loving. Anne Neville, pseud. (Starlight Romance Ser.). 144p. 1981. pap. cancelled (ISBN 0-553-14363-8). Bantam.
Voices of Masada. David Kossoff. LC 72-90762. (Illus.). 1973. 6.95. St. Martin's Press.
Voices of Others: A Novel. Ruth M Tabrah. LC 59-7805. 1959. Putnam.
Voices of the Dead: A Novel. Waldomiro Autran. Dourado. LC 81-4470. 1981. 10.95 (ISBN 0-8008-8030-7). Taplinger Pub. Co.
Voices of Things. Francis Ponge. Tr. by Beth Brombert from Fr. Orig. Title: Parti-Pris Des Choses. 180p. 1972. 5.95 o.p. (ISBN 0-07-073753-3). McGraw.
Voices That Endured: The Great Books & the Active Life. Stringfellow Barr. LC 70-138946. 1971. 5.95 o.p. (ISBN 0-13-943738-X). P-H.
Voices Under the Window. John Hearne. 164p. (Orig.). 1973. pap. 3.95 (ISBN 0-571-09985-8). Faber & Faber.
Voices, Voices. Stefan Grunwald. LC 80-20881. (Unilaw Library Book). 4.95. Donning.
Void Captain's Tale. Norman Spinrad. LC 81-21334. 15.50 (ISBN 0-671-43483-7). Timescape Books: Distributed by Simon and Schuster.
Volcanito, a Fairy Tale of Today. Flora N. De Muth. 2.50 o.p. Vantage.
Volcano. Shusaku Endo. Tr. by Richard A. Schuchert from Japanese. LC 79-23678. 175p. 1980. 8.95 (ISBN 0-8008-8032-3). Taplinger.
Volcano. Susan Heller & Douglas Wallin. (Orig.). 1981. pap. 3.25 (ISBN 0-440-19319-2). Dell.
Volcano. Cecil Roberts. LC 36-6314. 1936. D. Appleton-Century Company, Incorporated.
Volcano. Anant Gopal Sheorey. LC 65-29046. 1965. Pageant Press.
Volcano: A Frolic. Ralph Straus. LC 25-17700. 1925. H. Holt and Company.
Volcano: A Novel. Arthur Bullard. LC 30-730212. 1930. The Macmillan Company.
Volcano: A Novel. Shusaku Endo. LC 79-23678. 1980. 8.95 (ISBN 0-8008-8032-3). Taplinger Publishing Co.
Volcano Diggings: A Tale of California Law. Leonard Kip. LC 7-12544. 1851. J. S. Redfield.
Volcano House. Gunder E. Olson. (Illus.). 1974. pap. 4.50 o.p. (ISBN 0-912180-22-6). Petroglyph.
Volcano in Our Midst. 1st Ed. Arthur Joseph. LC 52-10972. 1952. Pageant Press.
Volcano Ogre. Lin Carter. (Zarkon Ser: No. 3). 1978. pap. 1.50 (ISBN 0-445-04310-5). Popular Lib.
Volcano Ogre. Lin Carter. LC 75-21217. 192p. 1976. 5.95 o.p. (ISBN 0-385-08807-8). Doubleday.
Volcanoes Above Us. Norman Lewis. LC 58-117742. Pantheon.
Volcanoes of San Domingo. Adam Hall, pseud. 1972. pap. 0.95 o.p. (N2709). Pyramid Pubns.
Volcanoes of San Domingo. Elleston Trevor. LC 64-10232. 1964. Simon and Schuster.
Volcano's Edge. Wilson Prichett. LC 46-8196. 1946. Goerge S. Ferguson Co.
Voleur de Maigret. Georges Simenon. pap. 3.95. French & Eur.
Voleurs D'or see Gold Robbers.
Volga Boatman. Konrad Bercovici. LC 72-131628. (Illus.). 1970. Scholarly Press.
Volga Boatman. Konrad Bercovici. Grosset & Dunlap.
Volga Falls to the Caspian Sea. Boris Pilnyak. LC 71-110428. Repr. of 1931 ed. 15.00 (ISBN 0-404-05047-6). AMS Pr.
Volga Falls to the Caspian Sea. Boris Andreevich Vogau. LC 71-110428. 1970. AMS Press.
Volga Falls to the Caspian Sea. Boris Andreevich Vogau & Malamuth, Charles, Tr. LC 31-19415. 1931. Cosmopolitan Book Corporation.
Volkhavaar. Tanith Lee. 1977. 1.50 (ISBN 0-87997-312-9). DAW Books.
Volney Randolph. A Novel. James Robertshaw. LC 7-41203. 1893. G. W. Dillingham.
Volonor. Glen Brion Winship. LC 25-20411. 1925. T. Selzter.
Voltaire Smile & Other Stories. Ron Harvie. 196p. (Orig.). 1982. pap. 6.95 (ISBN 0-9604724-1-X). Gay Pr NY.
Voltairian Narrative Devices As Considered in the Author's Contes Philosophiques. Dorothy Madeleine McGhee. LC 72-84997. 1973. 15.00. Russell & Russell.
Volteface. Mark Adlard. 1978. 1.50 (ISBN 0-441-86607-7). Ace Books.

Volunteer Nurse! The Lovely Young Martyrs of Memphis, Grenada, New Orleans, Shreveport! The Yellow Fever Plague in the South! Being the Romantic, Heart-Touching History of Two Lovely Young Ladies ... Who Nobly Volunteered to Go Nurse the Sick, and Who Died While Doing So ... LC 22-5147. The Old Franklin Publishing House.
Volunteer: Or, The Maid of Monterey. A Tale of the Mexican War. Edward Zane Carroll Judson. LC 7-12840. F. Gleason's Publishing Hall.
Volunteer Organist: A Novel Founded on the Famous Temperance Play of the Same Name. William B Gray. 1902. W. B. Gray & Company.
Volunteer with Pike: The True Narrative of One Dr. John Robinson and of His Love for the Fair Senorita Valloia. Robert Ames Bennet. LC 9-26328. 1909. A. C. McClurg & Co.
Volunteers for Glory. Jonathan Scofield, pseud. (Freedom Fighters Ser.: No. 10). (Orig.). 1981. pap. 2.95 (ISBN 0-440-09405-4, Bryans). Dell.
Voluptuaries. Betty E Ullman. LC 78-2187. 8.95 (ISBN 0-399-12084-X). Putnam.
Voluptuous. Albert Quandt. LC 49-596. 1948. Phoenix Press.
Voluptuous Duchess; or, The Romance of an Hour. Guy De Maupassant. LC 7-25592. (On cover: Lakeside series, v. 1). N. C. Smith Publishing Company.
Von Blumers. Thomas Lansing Masson. LC 6-41275. 1906. Moffat, Yard & Company.
Von Richtofen Sisters: The Triumphant & Tragic Modes of Love. Martin Burgess Green. LC 73-81037. 1974. 15.00 o.s.i. (ISBN 0-465-09050-8). Basic.
Von Ryan's Express. David Westheimer. LC 63-20513. 1964. Doubleday.
Von Ryan's Return. David Westheimer. LC 79-24078. 10.95 (ISBN 0-698-11003-X). Coward, McCann & Geoghegan.
Von Ryan's Return. David Westheimer. LC 80-24232. 12.95 (ISBN 0-89621-253-X). Thorndike Press.
Von Toodleburgs: Or, The History of a Very Distinquished Family. Francis Colburn Adams. LC 5-12955. 1868. Claxton, Remsen & Haffelfinger.
Vonda Rosegood. Richard Dohrman. LC 64-18075. 1965. Harper & Row.
Voodoo! A Chrestomathy of Necromancy. Bill Pronzini. LC 79-56021. 10.95 (ISBN 0-87795-262-0). Arbor House: Distributed by Dutton.
Voodoo, a Murder Mystery. Samuel Shellabarger. LC 30-6545. 1930. Pub. for The Crime Club, Inc., by Doubleday, Doran & Company, Inc.
Voodoo Die. Warren Murphy. (Destroyer Ser.: No. 33). (Orig.). 1978. pap. 1.75 (ISBN 0-523-40909-5). Pinnacle Bks.
Voodoo Drums. 1976. pap. 1.25 (ISBN 0-532-12443-X). Woodhill.
Voodoo Goat. Audrey Gaines. LC 42-317042. 1942. Thomas Y. Crowell Company.
Voodoo Kill. Rod Gray. (New Lady from L.U.S.T. Ser). (O.s.i.). (Orig.). 1975. pap. 1.25 o.s.i. (BT50829). Belmont-Tower.
Voodoo Kill. Rod Gray. (new lady from L.U.S.T.). 1975. (pbk.) 1.25. Belmont Tower Books.
Voodoo Mad. (Mad Ser.: No. 14). (Illus.). 192p. 1976. pap. 1.75 (ISBN 0-446-94391-6). Warner Bks.
Voodoo Moon. Nick Carter. (Orig.). 1970. pap. 0.60 o.p. (A597X, Award). Univ Pub & Dist.
Voodoo Planet see Star Hunter.
Voodoo Planet and Star Hunter. Andre Norton, pseud. LC 77-26231. (Norton, Andre. The Space Adventure Novels of Andre Norton). 1978. 7.95 (ISBN 0-8398-2417-3). Gregg Press.
Voodoo Queen: A Novel. Robert Tallant. LC 56-6496. Putnam.
Voodoo Slave. Norman Daniels. (Orig.). 1970. pap. 0.95 o.p. (63-350). Paperback Lib.
Voodoo'd. Kenneth Perkins. LC 31-496730. 1931. Harper & Brothers.
Voorloper. Andre Norton, pseud. 272p. 1981. pap. 2.95 (ISBN 0-441-86610-7). Ace Bks.
Vor. James Blish. 1958. pap. 1.95 (ISBN 0-380-44966-8, 44966). Avon.
Vorovich Affair. S. L Stebel. LC 75-12512. 1975. 8.95 (ISBN 0-670-74790-4). Viking Press.
Vorovich Affair. S. L Stebel. LC 76-55738. (Penguin crime fiction). 1977. 1.95 (ISBN 0-14-004380-2). Penguin Books.
Vortex. Jon Cleary. LC 77-26672. 1978. 8.95. Morrow.
Vortex. David Heller. 1.95 (ISBN 0-380-42762-1). Avon Books.
Vortex. Jose Eustasio Rivera. Tr. by E. K. Jones from Span. (Viper's Tongue Bks). 1979. pap. 6.95 (ISBN 0-931106-22-2). TVRT.
Vortex Blaster. Edward Elmer Smith. LC 60-4973. 1960. Gnome Press.
Vortex Blasters & Other Stories from Modern Masterpieces of Science Fiction. Ed. by Samuel Moskowitz. 1968. pap. 0.60 o.p. (60-325). Manor Bks.
Vortex: La Voragine. Jose Eustasio Rivera. LC 75-44095. 1976. H. Fertig.
Vortex; La Voragine. Jose Eustasio Rivera. Tr. by James, Earle Kenneth. LC 35-6195. G. P. Putnam's Sons.
Vospominaniia O Neproshedshem Vremeni. Raisa Orlova. 250p. (Rus.). 1983. 20.00 (ISBN 0-88233-725-4); pap. 13.50 (ISBN 0-88233-726-2). Ardis Pubs.
Voss. Patrick White. 1957. 13.95 (ISBN 0-670-74807-2). Viking Pr.
Votan. John James. LC 67-19165. 1967. New American Library.
Vote for Love. Arlene Hale. LC 81-3103. 1981. 11.95 (ISBN 0-89340-340-7). J. Curley & Associates.
Vote for Love. Arlene Hale. (Signet Book). 1977. 1.25 (ISBN 0-451-07505-6). New American Library.
Vote for Quimby-and Quick. Harry Miles Muheim. LC 77-28708. 8.95 (ISBN 0-02-587870-0) (ISBN 0-02-023120-2). Macmillan.
Vote for the Toff. John Creasey. LC 78-161112. 1971. 4.95 (ISBN 0-8027-5236-5). Walker.
Vote X for Treason. Brian Talbot Cleeve. LC 65-11290. (Random House mystery). 1965. 3.95. Random.
Vote X for Treason see Counterspy.
Votes for Quimby-and Quick! Harry Miles Muheim. LC 77-28697. 4.95 (ISBN 0-02-023120-2). Collier Books.
Vouivre. Marcel Ayme. (Illus.). deluxe ed. 61.25. French & Eur.
Vow. Maria Bontempi Fogelin. 272p. (Orig.). 1980. pap. 2.50 (ISBN 0-89083-653-1). Zebra.
Vow. Shunyo Yanagawa & Kihara, Tsunekichi, Tr. LC 35-6925. B. Humphries, Inc.
Vow: A Novel. Paul Trent. LC 11-2972. 1911. Frederick A. Stokes Company.
Vow of Love. Frances Y McHugh. 1972. 4.95. Lenox Hill Press.
Vow of Vengeance. Lewis B Patten. (Signet brand western). 1975. (pbk.) 0.95. New American Library.
Vow on the Heron. Jean Plaidy. LC 81-23438. (Plaidy, Jean, 1906-. Plantagenet Saga). 1982. 12.95 (ISBN 0-399-12708-9). Putnam.
Vows of the Peacock. 1st Ed. Alice Walworth Graham. LC 55-6479. 1955. Doubleday.
Voyage. Victor H. Johnson. LC 71-153182. 1971. 3.95 (ISBN 0-87212-004-X). Libra.
Voyage. Henri Legras & Goldsmith, Margaret Leland, 1894- Tr. LC 34-5694. Farrar & Rhinehart, Incorporated.
Voyage. Charles Morgan. LC 40-32622. 1940. The Macmillan Company.
Voyage: A Novel of 1896. Sterling Hayden. LC 76-40593. 12.95 (ISBN 0-399-11665-6). Putnam.
Voyage at Anchor. William Clark Russell. LC 99-4691. (Half-title: Appletons' town and country library, no. 274). 1899. D. Appleton and Company.
Voyage au Centre de la Terre. Jules Verne. pap. 3.95. French & Eur.
Voyage by Bus. Leonard Wibberly, pseud. 1971. 5.95 o.p. (ISBN 0-688-02716-4). Morrow.
Voyage d'Urien: Nouvelles. Andre Paul Guillaume Gide. pap. 4.95. French & Eur.
Voyage from Yesteryear. James P Hogan. LC 81-22890. 1982. 2.95 (ISBN 0-345-29472-6). Ballantine Books.
Voyage Home. Richard Church. 1966. 7.50 o.p. John Day.
Voyage Home. Margaret Storm Jameson. 1930. A. A. Knopf.
Voyage Home. Translated by Denver Lindley. 1st Ed. Ernest Schnabel. LC 58-5924. 1958. Harcourt, Brace.
Voyage Imaginaire: Une Anthologie De Fantaisie et D'imagination. L. J. Wang & S. E. Wang. 1970. pap. text ed. 7.95x o.p. (ISBN 0-02-424490-2). Macmillan.
Voyage in the Dark. Jean Rhys. 1975. (pbk.) 1.25. Popular Library.
Voyage in the Dark. Jean Rhys. LC 68-16564. 1968. W. W. Norton.
Voyage in the Dark. Jean Rhys. LC 35-32208. 1935. W. Morrow & Co.
Voyage in the Dark. Jean Rhys. LC 81-19024. 1982. 3.95 (ISBN 0-393-00083-4). W.W. Norton.
Voyage in, Voyage Out. Jean Rikhoff. LC 63-7851. 1963. Viking Press.
Voyage into Danger. Clara Lee Brown. (Illus.). 150p. 1972. 4.95 o.p. (ISBN 0-8158-0291-9). Chris Mass.
Voyage into Nowhere. James Wood. LC 67-29441. 1968. 4.95. Vanguard.
Voyage into Violence. Frances Louise Davis Lockridge & Richard Lockridge. 1975. Repr. of 1956 ed. lib. bdg. 12.05x (ISBN 0-89190-908-7). Am Repr-Rivercity Pr.
Voyage into Violence: A Mr. and Mrs. North Mystery. Frances Louise Davis Lockridge & Richard Lockridge. LC 76-213. 1976. (ISBN 0-89190-908-7). Rivercity Press.
Voyage into Violence: By Frances and Richard Lockridge. 1st Ed. Frances Louise Davis Lockridge & Richard Lockridge. LC 56-10814. (Their A Mr. and Mrs. North mystery). 1956. Lippincott.
Voyage No.39. Willard Christensen. LC 51-3773. 1951. Vantage Press.
Voyage of Argo. Appollonius of Rhodes. Tr. by Emil V. Rieu. (Classics Ser.). (Orig.). 1959. pap. 3.95 (ISBN 0-14-044085-2). Penguin.
Voyage of Captain Bart. John Erskine. 1943. J. B. Lippincott Company.
Voyage of Consolation (Being in the Nature of a Sequel to the Experiences of "An American Girl in London") by sara jeannette duncan (mrs. everard cotes)... ed. Sara Jeannette Duncan Cotes. LC 11-10514. 1898. D. Appleton and Company.
Voyage of Death. Mark Cruz. (Kill Squad Ser). 192p. (Orig.). 1975. pap. 1.25 o.p. (ISBN 0-532-12278-X). Woodhill.
Voyage of Death. Mark Cruz. (Kill Squad Ser). 192p. (Orig.). 1975. pap. 1.25 o.p. (ISBN 0-532-12278-X). Manor Bks.
Voyage of Desire. Ben Westfield. 304p. (Orig.). 1980. pap. 2.50 (ISBN 0-89083-622-1). Zebra.
Voyage of Discovery. Barbara Corrigan. LC 45-9987. 1945. C. Scribner's Sons.
Voyage of the Arrow to the China Seas. Its Adventures and Perils, Including Its Capture by Sea Vultures from the Countess of Warwick, As Set Down by William Gore, Chief Mate. Thornton Jenkins Hains. LC 6-14552. 1906. L. C. Page & Company (Incorporated.
Voyage of the Fleetwing: A Narrative of Love, Wreck and Whaling Adventures. Charles Martin Newell. LC 7-17276. (The Fleetwing series, v. 1). De Wolfe, Fiske & Co.
Voyage of the Franz Joseph. James Yaffe. LC 79-113519. 1970. 6.95. Putnam.
Voyage of the Golden Hind. Edmund Gilligan. LC 45-2841. 1945. C. Scribner's Sons.
Voyage of the Heart. Virginia Creed. LC 42-247682. 1942. Duell, Sloan and Pearce.
Voyage of the Investigator. K. A. Austin. (Illus.). 1964. 9.00 o.s.i.; pap. 1.50 o.s.i. Tri-Ocean.
Voyage of the Norman D., As Told by the Cabin-Boy. Barbara Newhall Follett. LC 28-9376. 1928. A. A. Knopf.
Voyage of the "Pulo Way" A Record of Some Strange Doings at Sea, by Carlton Dawe... Illustrated by J. Ambrose Walton. William Carlton Lanyon Dawe. LC 99-1055. R. F. Fenno & Company.
Voyage of the Rattletrap. Hayden Carruth. LC 6-24220. 1897. Harper & Brothers.
Voyage of the Secret Duchess. Florence Hurd. 1975. (pbk.) 0.95 (ISBN 0-380-00353-8). Avon.
Voyage of the Space Beagle. Alfred Elton Van Vogt. LC 50-14253. (A Science fiction adventure). 1950. Simon and Schuster.
Voyage of the Starfire to Atlantis. Edwin Mumford. 1973. 4.00 (ISBN 0-682-47692-7). Exposition.
Voyage of the Vagabond. Betty Frost. (Perspective I Novel Ser.). 48p. 1982. 2.50 (ISBN 0-87879-296-1). Acad Therapy.
Voyage of the Vagabond. Richard Thruelsen. LC 65-18730. 1965. Brace & World.
Voyage Out. Virginia Woolf. LC 20-8627. George H. Doran Company.
Voyage Out. Virginia Stephen Woolf. LC 68-6631. 1968. Harcourt, Brace & World.
Voyage Round My Father. John Clifford Mortimer. 1983. pap. 4.95 (ISBN 0-14-048169-9). Penguin.
Voyage Round the World. In Search of the Castaways: a Romantic Narrative of the Loss of Captain Grant of the Brig Britannia and of the Adventures of His Children and Friends in His Discovery and Rescue. Jules Verne. LC 11-10504. 1873. J. B. Lippincott & Co.
Voyage to a Dark Island. Edmund Keeley. 1972. pap. 0.75 o.p. (07239). Curtis.
Voyage to a Forgotten Sun. Donald J Pfeil. 1975. (pbk.) 1.25 (ISBN 0-345-24338-2). Ballantine Books.
Voyage to Arcturus. David Lindsay. LC 63-15669. (Macmillian's library of science fiction classics). 1963. Macmillan.
Voyage to Arcturus. David Lindsay. LC 77-8471. (Gregg Press science fiction series). 1977. 15.00 (ISBN 0-8398-2375-4). Gregg Press.
Voyage to Cacklagallinia see Virgin Seducer.
Voyage to Cacklogallinia see Gulliveriana, No. 4.
Voyage to Dari. Ian Wallace. (Science Fiction Ser). (Orig.). 1974. pap. 1.25 o.p. (UY1142). DAW Bks.
Voyage to Dari. Ian Wallace. 1974. (pbk.) 1.25. DAW Books.
Voyage to Eden. Bennie Caroline Hall. LC 50-5945. 1950. Arcadia House.
Voyage to Faremido. Capillaria. Frigyes Karinthy & Frigyes Karinthy. LC 66-17528. 1966. Living Books.
Voyage to Laputa, from Travels by Lemuel Gulliver. Jonathan Swift. LC 77-358706. (Illus.). 1976. Angelica Press.
Voyage to Love. Kristin Michaels. Bd. with Shadow of Love. 1981. pap. 2.50 (ISBN 0-451-11525-2, AE1525, Sig). NAL.
Voyage to Pagany. William Carlos Williams. LC 71-145373. 1972. (ISBN 0-403-01278-3). Scholarly Press.
Voyage to Pagany. William Carlos Williams. LC 76-122108. (New Directions book). 1970. 7.95. New Directions Pub. Corp.
Voyage to Pagany. William Carlos Williams. LC 28-21220. 1928. The Macaulay Company.
Voyage to Paradise. Dorothy Quentin. 1943. Arcadia House, Inc.
Voyage to Purilia. Elmer L. Rice. LC 30-71916. 1930. Cosmopolitan Book Corporation.
Voyage to Santa Fe. Janice Holt Giles. 1978. 1.75 (ISBN 0-380-00965-X). Avon.
Voyage to Somewhere. Sloan Wilson. LC 46-22910. 1946. A. A. Wyn, Inc.
Voyage to the Cape. William Clark Russell. LC 9-1490. (Harper's handy series, no. 99). 1886. Harper & Brothers.
Voyage to the Country of the Houyhnhnms, Being the 5th Part of the Travels into Several Remote Parts of the World by Lemuel Gulliver. Jonathan Swift. Ed. by Matthew Hodgart. 1970. 2.95 o.p. (ISBN 0-399-10848-3). Putnam.
Voyage to the First of December. Henry C. Carlisle. 253p. (YA) 1972. 6.95 o.p. (ISBN 0-399-10842-4). Putnam.
Voyage to the First of December: A Novel. Henry C. Carlisle. LC 76-175259. (Illus.). 1972. 6.95. Putnam.
Voyage to the Gold Coast: Or, Jack Bond's Quest. Frank H Converse. LC 3328. (On cover: Medal library, no. 55). 1900. Street & Smith.
Voyage to the Moon. Savinien Cyrano De Bergerac. Tr. by Lovell, A. Ed. by Page, Curtis Hidden. LC 99-1262. 1899. Doubleday & McClure Co.
Voyage to the Moon. George Fox Rucker. LC 75-5843. (Gregg Press science fiction series). 1975. 13.00 (ISBN 0-8398-2315-0). Gregg Press.
Voyage to Wonderland. Hubert Nicholson. 1973. lib. bdg. 12.50 o.p. Folcroft.
Voyage Unplanned. Frank Yerby. LC 73-21831. 1974. 8.95 (ISBN 0-8037-1411-4). Dial Press.
Voyagers. Ben Bora. 400p. 1982. pap. 3.50 (ISBN 0-553-22522-7). Bantam.
Voyagers. Benjamin Bova. LC 80-2836. 1981. 14.95 (ISBN 0-385-14890-9). Doubleday.
Voyagers. Vivian Lord. 448p. 1982. pap. 2.75 (ISBN 0-449-14358-9, GM). Fawcett.
Voyagers. Dale Van Every. LC 57-10427. 1957. Holt.
Voyagers in Time: Twelve Stories of Science Fiction. Ed. by Robert Silverberg. LC 67-20857. 1967. Meredith Press.
Voyages. 2d ed. Peter Najarian. LC 79-23722. (Illus.). 8.95 (ISBN 0-933706-12-X) (ISBN 0-933706-13-8). Ararat Press.
Voyages and Adventures of Captain Hatteras. Jules Verne. LC 62-57038. 1876. J. R. Osgood.
Voyages and Adventures of Captain Robert Boyle. William Rufus Chetwood & Benjamin Victor. LC 79-170565. (Foundations of the Novel). (Illus.). 1972. (ISBN 0-8240-0558-9). Garland Pub.
Voyages, Dangerous Adventures, and Imminent Escapes of Captain Richard Falconer. William Rufus Chetwood. LC 77-170543. (Foundations of the Novel). 1973. 22.00 (ISBN 0-8240-0544-9). Garland.
Voyages Out. Harry Hollins. LC 70-107969. 1970. 5.95. Outerbridge & Dienstfrey; Distributed by Dutton.
Voyages, Travels, and Adventures of William Owen Gwin Vaughan, Esq. William Rufus Chetwood. LC 76-170591. (Foundations of the Novel). (Illus.). 1972. (ISBN 0-8240-0573-2). Garland Pub.
Voyeur. Alain Robbe-Grillet. Tr. by Richard Howard from Fr. (Orig.). 1958. pap. 2.95 (ISBN 0-394-17117-9, B133, BC). Grove.
Voyeur. David R. Slavitt. LC 68-26006. 1969. 5.95. Bernard Geis Associates.
Voyeur. Henry Sutton, pseud. LC 68-26006. 1969. 5.95 o.p. Geis.
Voyeur. (Illus.). pap. 5.00 (ISBN 0-910550-63-8). Centurion Pr.
Voysey. Richard Orton Prowse. 1901. The Macmillan Company.
Vozvrashchenie Chorba. Vladimir Vladimirovich Nabokov. (Sobranie Rasskazov I Povestei). (Cloth ed. 15.00 o.p.: Vol. 1). (Rus.). 1976. pap. 7.00 o.p. (ISBN 0-88233-226-0). Ardis Pubs.
V.P. A Novel. George Merlis. LC 72-168480. 1971. 6.95. Morrow.
Vrag Naroda (Enemy of the People) Emeric Melius. LC 67-28992. (Illus.). 1967. New Century Pub. Firm.
Vril: the Power of the Coming Race. Edward George Earle Lytton Bulwer-Lytton Lytton. LC 71-183054. (Steinerbooks). 1972. 1.95. R. Steiner Publications.

Vrilles De la Vigne see Sido.
Vronina. Owen Vaughan. LC 8-22545. 1908. Dodd Mead and Company.
Vrouw Grobelaar and Her Leading Cases. Perceval Gibbon. LC 6-2542. 1906. McClure, Phillips & Co.
Vrouw Grobelar and Her Leading Cases. Perceval Gibbon. LC 73-142263. (Short story index reprint series). 1970. (ISBN 0-8369-3747-3). Books for Libraries Press.
Vulcan Bulletins. Sam Gulliver. (O.s.i.). 1974. 6.95 o.s.i. (ISBN 0-671-21665-1). S&S.
Vulcan Disaster. Nick Carter. (Nick Carter Ser.). (O.s.i.). (Orig.). 1976. pap. 1.25 o.s.i. (AQ1600, Award). Univ Pub & Dist.
Vulcan Rising. Ashley Aasheim. 320p. (Orig.). 1982. pap. 3.50 (ISBN 0-440-19348-6). Dell.
Vulcan's Hammer. Da Cruz, Daniel. LC 67-19166. 1967. New American Library.
Vulcan's Hammer. Philip K Dick. LC 79-17775. (Gregg Press science fiction series). (Illus.). 1979. 11.95 (ISBN 0-8398-2484-X). Gregg Press.
Vulgar Errors. Thomas Browne. 15.00 o.s.i. Finch Pr.
Vulgar Streak. Wyndham Lewis. LC 73-89682. 1973. 10.00 (ISBN 0-914300-01-6). Jubilee Books.
Vulgarians. Edgar Fawcett. 1903. The Smart Set Publishing Co.
Vulnerable. Dale Collins. LC 33-22158. The Bobbs-Merrill Company.
Vulture. Scott-Heron, Gil. LC 73-119019. 1970. 6.95. World Pub. Co.
Vulture Valley. Donald B. Hobart. 1970. pap. 0.60 o.p. (0502-06076). Curtis.
Vulture Valley: By Tom West Pseud. 1st Ed. Fred East. LC 51-9252. (Dutton Diamond D western). 1951. Dutton.
Vultures. Robert E. Howard. (Illus., Also including "Showdown at Hell's Canyon). 1973. 8.50 (ISBN 0-87707-115-2). Fictioneer Bks.
Vultures: A Novel. Hugh Stowell Scott. LC 2-20814. 1902. Harper & Brothers.
Vulture's Claw: A Tale of Rural Life. Charles Franklin Wimberly. LC 10-27580. 1910. R. F. Fenno & Company.
Vultures in the Sky. Todd Downing. LC 35-5196. 1935. Pub. for the Crime Club, Inc., by Doubleday, Doran & Company, Inc.
Vultures in the Sun. Brian Wynne Garfield. LC 63-9261. 1963. Macmillan.
Vultures of the Dark. Richard Edward Enright. LC 24-25416. Brentano's.
Vultures on Horseback. Paul Evan Lehman. (Leisure book). 1979. 1.25 (ISBN 0-8439-0645-6). Nordon Pubns.
Vultures: Or, The Secret of a Birth. A Story of Boston. Lavinia Stella Tyler Goodwin. (novelette, no. 119). Office American Union, Flag of Our Union, and Ballou's Monthly.
Vultures; Showdown at Hell's Canyon. Robert E. Howard. 1973. 5.95. Fictioneer Books.
Vulture's Vengeance. (Executioner Ser.). 192p. 1983. pap. 1.95 (ISBN 0-373-61051-3, Pub. by Worldwide). Harlequin Bks.
Vynes of Vyne Court. Humphrey Pakington. LC 55-3552. 1955. W. W. Norton.
Vyvyans: Or, The Mystery of the Rue Bellechasse. Annie Jane Terrant Harvey. (On cover: Globe library, v. 1, no. 179). 1893. Rand, McNally & Company.

W

W. H. Hudson's Tales of the Pampas. William Henry Hudson & Duvoisin, Roger A., Illus. LC 39-278020. 1939. A. A. Knopf.
W. I. L. One to Curtis. Philip Loraine. LC 67-12722. 1967. Random House.
W. L., Esquire. Eleanor M Fox. LC 77-84119. 8.95. Marando Press.
W Plan. Graham Seton Hutchison. 1930. Cosmopolitan Book Corporation.
W Plan. Graham Seton Hutchison. LC 41-6548. (On cover: Penguin books. 50). 1939. Penguin Books Limited.
W. Somerset Maugham: Four Short Stories. William Somerset Maugham. LC 77-124590. (Illus.). 1971. 2.50 o.p. (ISBN 0-87529-120-1). Hallmark.
W. W. and the Dixie Dancekings. Thomas Rickman. 1975. (pbk.) 1.25 (ISBN 0-671-78813-2). Pocket Books.
Wacousta; or, The Prophecy. An Indian Tale... rev. ed. John Richardson. LC 7-159289. Dewitt & Davenport.
Waddington Cipher. William Andrew Johnston. LC 23-132662. 1923. Doubleday, Page & Company.
Wade Inheritance. L. Virginia Brown. 1977. pap. 1.95 o.p. (ISBN 0-515-04254-4). BJ Pub Group.
Wads' & Gina's Songbook. Jim Kelly. (Small Star Stories). (Illus.). 1975. 3.96 o.p. (ISBN 0-02-645790-3, 64579). Glencoe.
Wage Slaves of New York.". Roy Larcom McCardell. LC 99-5435. (Dillingham's American authors' library, no. 56). 1899. G. W. Dillingham Co.
Wager. L McManus. 1902. F. M. Buckles & Company.
Wager: A Kek Huuygens Novel. Robert L Fish. LC 73-93180. (Red mask mystery). 1974. 5.95 (ISBN 0-399-11318-5). Putnam.
Wager, and Other Stories: Illustrated with Wood Engravings by Elizabeth Rivers. Daniel Corkery. LC 50-6340. 1950. Devin-Adair.
Wager for Love. Caroline Courtney. LC 79-24669. 1980. 13.95 (ISBN 0-8161-3020-5). G. K. Hall.
Wager for Love. Rachelle Edwards. 1980. pap. 1.75 (ISBN 0-449-50021-7, Coventry). Fawcett.
Wager of Battle: A Tale of Saxon Slavery in Sherwood Forest. Henry William Herbert. LC 7-42973. 1855. Mason Brothers.
Wagered Weekend. Jayne Castle. (Candlelight Ecstacy Ser.: No. 17). (Orig.). 1981. pap. 1.75 (ISBN 0-440-19413-X). Dell.
Wages. Mary Lanier Magruder. LC 24-48666. 1924. Harper & Brothers.
Wages of Fear: By Georges Arnaud Pseud. Translated from the French by Norman Dale. Henri Georges Charles Achille Girard. LC 52-5799. 1952. Farrar, Straus and Young.
Wages of Honor: And Other Stories. Katharine Holland Brown. LC 17-24278. 1917. 1.35. C. Scribner's Sons.
Wages of Sin. authorized ed. Mary St. Leger Kingsley Harrison. LC 12-12211. (On cover: Lovell's international series, no. 102). United States Book Company.
Wages of Sin. Mary St. Leger Kingsley Harrison. LC 2-19290. 1902. R. F. Fenno & Company.
Wages of Sin. A Novel. From the German. Tr. by A. Howard. 1891. G. W. Dillingham.
Wages of Sin: Stories. Gerald W Haslam. LC 80-65780. (Windriver book). 1980. 4.00 (ISBN 0-916918-11-4). Duck Down.
Wages of Virtue. Percival Christopher Wren. LC 17-31882. 1917. Frederick A. Stokes Company.
Wages Paid. James Carnegie. LC 77-354981. 1976. Casa De las Americas.
Waggeries and Vagaries: A Series of Sketches, Humorous and Descriptive. William Evans Burton. 1848. Carey & Hart.
Wagner, the Wehr-Wolf. George William McArthur Reynolds. LC 74-78971. (Illus.). 1975. 3.50 (ISBN 0-486-22005-2). Dover Publications.
Wagon and the Star. Lida Larrimore Thomas. LC 29-800527. Macrae Smith Company.
Wagon and the Star. Lida Larrimore Thomas. LC 47-20103. 1947. Triangle Books, the Blakiston Company.
Wagon Boss. Charles Stanley Strong. LC 50-5957. 1950. Phoenix Press.
Wagon Captain. Eugene E Halleran. LC 56-13473. 1956. Ballantine Books.
Wagon to a Star: By Jennifer Ames Pseud. Maysie Greig. LC 53-6602. 1953. Bouregy & Curl.
Wagon Train: By Chuck Stanley Pseud. Charles Stanley Strong. LC 55-118811. 1955. Arcadia House.
Wagon Train Westward. Archie Joscelyn. LC 44-9093. 1944. Phoenix Press.
Wagon Wheel. William Patterson White. LC 23-5947. 1923. Little, Brown, and Company.
Wagon Wheel Brand. Bill J Douglas. LC 57-9800. 1957. Arcadia House.
Wagon Wheel Gap. 1st Ed. Allan Vaughan Elston. LC 54-611557. 1954. Lippincott.
Wagons East. George G. Gilman, pseud. (Steele Ser.: No. 21). 192p. 1982. pap. 1.95 (ISBN 0-523-41454-4). Pinnacle Bks.
Wagons in the Wind, a Novel. 1st Ed. Jack Payne Jones. LC 53-6716. 1953. Exposition Press.
Wagons to Backsight. John Thomas Edson. 1980. 1.95 (ISBN 0-425-04625-7). Berkley Books.
Wagons to California. Thomas Albert Curry. (Orig.). 1973. pap. 0.75 o.p. (07300). Curtis.
Wagons to California. Tom Curry. (Rio Kid Western). 1973. (pbk) 0.75. Curtis.
Wagons to Tucson. Muriel Naomi Evans. LC 54-6865. 1954. Little, Brown.
Wagons to Wind River. Charles N. Heckelmann. (Orig.). 1982. pap. 2.75 (ISBN 0-445-04740-2). Popular Lib.
Wagons West. Archie Joscelyn. LC 51-12217. 1951. Bouregy & Curl.
Wagons West. Leslie Turner White. LC 64-11694. 1964. Doubleday.
Wagons Westward: The Old Trail to Santa Fe. Armstrong Sperry. LC 37-27088. The John C. Winston Company.
Wagontongue. Elmer Kelton. 1982. pap. 1.95 (ISBN 0-553-22525-1). Bantam.
Wagontongue Way. Harry Blocker. (Orig.). pap. 0.95 o.p. (1006). Brandon.
Wagtail. Alice Crew Gall & Fleming H. Crew. LC 66-10281. H.Z. Walck.
Waif -A Prince. facsimile ed. W. T. Andrews. LC 73-37581. (Black Heritage Library Collection). Repr. of 1895 ed. 18.50 (ISBN 0-8369-8957-0). Ayer Co.
Waif--a Prince: Or, A Mother's Triumph. An Egyptian Story of Fiction and Fact. W. T. Andrews. LC 6-2450. 1895. Publishing House Methodist Episcopal Church, South.
Waif-a Prince: Or, A Mother's Triumph. W. T. Andrews. LC 73-37581. (Black Heritage library collection). 1972. (ISBN 0-8369-8957-0). Books for Libraries Press.
Waif from Texas... By Kate Alma Orgain. Kate Alma Orgain. LC 1-31038. 1901. B. C. Jones & Co., Printers.
Waif in the Conflict of Two Civilizations. A Tale of the Great Civil War in America and the Last Days of Slavery. Augustin Thompson. LC 8-282643. 1892. The Rapid Printing Co.
Waif-O-the-Sea: A Romance of the Great Deep. Cyrus Townsend Brady. LC 18-19514. 1918. 1.40. A. C. McClurg & Co.
Waif of the Plains. Bret Harte. LC 7-3654. 1890. Houghton, Mifflin and Company.
Waif of the Plains: And Other Tales. Bret I. E. Francis Bret Harte. LC 12-27747. (Half-title: Standard library edition The writings of Bret Harte... vol. ix). Houghton, Mifflin Company; Etc., Etc.
Waif of the Sea. Charlotte M. Stanley McKenna. (On cover: Munro's library, v. 1, no. 112). 1884. N. L. Munro.
Waif of the Wreck," And Joe Gains. Charles Melvin Van Curen. LC 20-6495. Van Publishing Company.
Waif: Or, The Web of Life. A Novel. Emma Erichsen. 1883. J. P. Harrison & Co., Printers.
Waifs and Stray: Twelve Stories. William Sydney Porter. LC 19-17075. 1919. Doubleday Page & Company.
Waifs and Strays: Twelve Stories. William Sydney Porter. LC 25-237244. 1925. Doublday, Page & Company.
Waifs and Wanderings. A Novel. Samuel P Putnam. LC 7-42403. The Truth Seeker Company.
Waif's Progress. Rhoda Broughton. LC 18-11267. 1906. Macmillan and Co., Limited.
Waifwood. A Novel. Alexander Lovett Stimson. LC 8-15681. 1864. W. V. Spencer.
Waikiki Nurse. Laura C Raef. 1976. 4.95. Avalon Books.
Waikiki Widow. 1st Ed. Juanita Sheridan. LC 53-11653. 1953. Published for the Crime Club by Doubleday.
Wail for the Corpses: By Lawrence Treat. Lawrence Treat. LC 43-12655. (On cover: Best detective selection, no. 6). 1943. Select Publications Inc.
Wail of La Llorona. Paula G Paul. (Avalon Books). 4.95. Thomas Bouregy.
Wailing Mountain. Mihailo Lalic. LC 65-14708. 1965. Harcourt, Brace & World.
Wailing Rock Murders. Clifford Orr. LC 32-23429. Farrar & Rinehart, Incorporated.
Wailing Terror. Betty C. Mowery. 1981. pap. 6.95 (Avalon). Bouregy.
Wailing Woman. Dora Shuttuck. (Warner Paperback Lib. gothic). 1973. (pbk.) 0.95. Warner Paperback Lib.
Wailings of a Wife Hunter: Or The Mishaps and the Hithaps of My Courtships. Marcus Lafayette Byrn. ("Rattlehead's humorous series", no. 3). M. L. Byrn.
Waimea Summer. John D. Holt. (Illus.). 1976. text ed. 8.95 (ISBN 0-914916-12-2); pap. 3.50 (ISBN 0-914916-13-0). Topgallant.
Wainwright Inheritance. Elizabeth Frances Corbett. 1972. pap. 0.95 o.p. (95284). Beagle Bks.
Waist of the World... James Hampton Lee. LC 7-447. Broadway Publishing Company.
Wait and See... Susanna Paine. LC 7-35787. 1860. Printed by J. Wilson and Son.
Wait & Win: The Story of Jack Drumond's Fluck. Horatio Alger, Jr. (Illus.). 279p. 1979. Repr. of 1908 ed. 27.75. G K Westgard.
Wait for a Corpse. Max Murray. LC 57-134244. (Chantecler novel of suspense). 1957. Washburn.
Wait for Dawn. Anne Philipe. LC 68-15739. 1968. McGraw-Hill.
Wait for Death. Gordon Ashe, pseud. LC 70-161504. (Rinehart Suspense Novel Ser.). 1972. 4.95 o.p. (ISBN 0-03-086701-0). HR&W.
Wait for Death. John Creasey. (Patrick Dawlish mystery). 1973. 0.75. Popular Lib.
Wait for Death. John Creasey. LC 70-161504. 1972. 4.95 (ISBN 0-03-086701-0). Holt, Rinehart and Winston.
Wait for Love. Arlene Hale. LC 63-6739. 1963. Avalon Books.
Wait for Love. Arlene Hale. (Candlelight Romance#181). 1975. (pbk.) 0.75. Dell.
Wait for Love. William Arthur Neubauer. LC 45-11427. 1945. Gramercy Publishing Company.
Wait for Me. Olive Wadsley. LC 41-481616. 1941. Dodd, Mead & Company.
Wait for Me: A Novel. Lois Bailey Wills. LC 76-4264. 6.95 (ISBN 0-8158-0336-2). Christopher Pub. House.
Wait For Me & Other Stories. Seth W. Gilkerson. LC 82-82216. 144p. 1982. pap. write for info (ISBN 0-88100-014-0). Natl Writ Pr.
Wait for Me, Darling. James Noble Gifford. LC 44-506. 1944. Gramercy Pub. Co.
Wait for Me, Darling. Carol Holliston. LC 44-506903. 1944. Gramercy Publishing Co.
Wait for Me: Michael. Mary Slattery Stolz. LC 61-7329. 1961. Harper.
Wait for Me, Wendy. Jeanne Marie. 1974. 4.95 (ISBN 0-517-51804-X). Lenox Hill Press.
Wait for Mrs. Willard. Dorothy Langley. LC 44-2602. 1944. Simon and Schuster.
Wait for Mrs. Willard: A Novel by Dorothy Langley Pseud. Dorothy Langley. LC 44-2602. 1944. Simon and Schuster.
Wait for November. Hans Erich Nossack. LC 82-1395. 1982. 14.95 (ISBN 0-88064-004-9). Fromm International Pub. Corp.
Wait for the Dawn. Martha Albrand. LC 50-5756. 1950. Random House.
Wait for the Dawn. Heidi Huberta Freybe Loewengard. LC 50-5756. 1950. Random House.
Wait for the Day. Marguerite Nelson, pseud. pap. 0.50 o.p. (B50-658). Belmont-Tower.
Wait for the Day: By Claudia Hall Pseud. Lee Floren. LC 55-118841. 1955. Arcadia House.
Wait for the New Grass: A Novel. Henry Birne. LC 60-13880. 1961. St. Martin's Press.
Wait for the Storm. Jayne Bauling. (Harlequin Presents Ser.). 192p. 1982. pap. 1.75 (ISBN 0-373-10505-3, Pub. by Harlequin). PB.
Wait for the Sun. Maud McCurdy Welch. LC 45-4050. 1945. Arcadia House, Inc.
Wait for the Tide. Edith Austin Holton. LC 39-4204. The Penn Publishing Company.
Wait for the Wagon. Mary Lasswell. LC 51-7401. (Illus.). 1951. Houghton Mifflin.
Wait for the Wedding. Celia Fremlin, pseud. 1961. 3.95 o.p. Lippincott.
Wait for Tomorrow. Ethel E Bangert. LC 49-1193. 1948. Arcadia House.
Wait for Tomorrow. Denise Robins. 1973. pap. 0.75 o.p. (T2708, GM). Fawcett World.
Wait for Tomorrow. Robert Wilder. LC 50-6164. 1950. Putnam.
Wait for What Will Come. Barbara Mertz. LC 78-18319. 8.95 (ISBN 0-396-07577-0). Dodd, Mead.
Wait for What Will Come. Barbara Michaels. LC 79-13525. 1979. 12.95 (ISBN 0-8161-6720-6). G. K. Hall.
Wait, Just You Wait. Evelyn Berckman. LC 73-83615. 1974. 5.95 (ISBN 0-385-01640-9). Doubleday.
Wait, Just You Wait. Evelyn Berckman. (Dell Book). 1977. 1.25 (ISBN 0-440-19410-5). Dell Pub. Co.
Wait, Son, October Is Near. John Bell Clayton. LC 53-8478. 1953. Macmillan.
Wait till the Sun Shines, Nellie: A Novel. Audrey Gellen Maas. LC 66-26048. 1966. bds., 4.50. New Amer. Lib.
Wait Until Evening. Henrietta Buckmaster, pseud. LC 73-16398. 1974. 7.50 (ISBN 0-15-194125-4). Harcourt Brace Jovanovich.
Wait until Midnight. Virginia Pittinger. LC 78-58393. (Moonstone Gothic Ser.). 208p. 1978. pap. 1.75 (ISBN 0-87216-668-6). Playboy Pbks.
Wait Until Spring, Bandini. John Fante. (Orig.). 1983. 17.50 (ISBN 0-87685-555-9); signed ed. 25.00 (ISBN 0-87685-556-7); pap. 8.50 (ISBN 0-87685-554-0). Black Sparrow.
Wait Until Spring, Bandini: A Novel. John Fante. LC 38-32610. Stackpole Sons.
Wait Until the Evening. Hal Z. Bennett. LC 73-10855. 1974. 6.95 (ISBN 0-385-01022-2). Doubleday.
Wait until Tomorrow. Harriet M. Savitz. (Orig.). 1981. pap. 1.95 (ISBN 0-451-09780-7, J9780, Sig). NAL.
Waiter Syndrome. Richard Neely. 1970. 5.95 o.p. (ISBN 0-8415-0061-4). Sat Rev Pr.
Waiters. 1st ed. William Fisher. LC 52-13237. 1953. World Pub. Co.
Waiters on the Dance. Julian Jay Savarin. LC 78-2997. 1978. 8.95 (ISBN 0-312-85416-1). St. Martin's Press.
Waithera: The Soul of an African Girl. Anne Woodley. LC 42-511245. 1942. The Moody Press.
Waiting. Bonnie Melbourne Busch. LC 33-38220. 1933. The Acadia Press.
Waiting. Daniel F. Gerber. 1966. 2.50 o.p. (ISBN 0-8059-0099-3). Dorrance.
Waiting. Maude Farman Kempster. LC 27-6915. 1927. H. Vinal.
Waiting. Mary Napier. 240p. (Orig.). 1980. pap. 2.25 (ISBN 0-553-13477-9). Bantam.
Waiting. Karen Van der Zee. (Harlequin Presents Ser.). 192p. 1982. pap. 1.75 (ISBN 0-373-10544-4). Harlequin Bks.

Waiting Darkness. Willo Davis Roberts. (Orig.). 1970. pap. 0.75 o.p. (ISBN 0-447-74599-9). Lancer.
Waiting Eyes: An Astrological Gothic Novel: Aquarius. Morris Hershman. LC 75-34222. 1976. 1.25 (ISBN 0-345-24812-0). Ballantine Books.
Waiting for a Ship. Marcus Lauesen. Tr. by Chater, Arthur G. LC 33-270911. 1933. A. A. Knopf.
Waiting for a Tiger. Ben Healey. LC 65-21381. 1965. Harper & Row.
Waiting for Camilla. Elizabeth Montagu. LC 54-8745. 1954. Lippincott.
Waiting for Caroline. Amanda McAllister. LC 76-14023. (Amanda McAllister Ser.: No. 2). 1976. pap. 1.50 o.p. (ISBN 0-87216-328-8, C16328). Playboy.
Waiting for Cordelia. Herbert Gold. LC 76-29231. 8.95 (ISBN 0-87795-154-3). Arbor House.
Waiting for Love. 1st American Ed. Venetia Murray. LC 59-7794. 1959. Dutton.
Waiting for Nothing. Tom Kromer. LC 68-14793. (American century series, AC89). 1968. Hill & Wang.
Waiting for Sheila. John Braine. LC 79-24757. 9.95 (ISBN 0-416-00571-3). Methuen.
Waiting for Spring. R. P. Jones. LC 78-52925. 1978. pap. 4.00 (ISBN 0-931594-00-6). Circinatum Pr.
Waiting for Surabiel. Raja Proctor. (Asian & Pacific Writing Ser.). 238p. 1981. text ed. 18.00 (ISBN 0-7022-1566-X); pap. 9.75 (ISBN 0-7022-1567-8). U of Queensland Pr.
Waiting for the Barbarians. J. M. Coetzee. LC 81-19188. 1982. 3.95 (ISBN 0-14-006110-X). Penguin Books.
Waiting for the Earthquake. Lawrence Swaim. LC 76-48035. 1977. 8.95 (ISBN 0-316-82470-4). Little, Brown.
Waiting for the Mahatma. R. K. Narayan. LC 55-11689. (Illus.). 1955. Michigan State University Press.
Waiting for the News. Leo E. Litwak. LC 77-82956. 1969. 5.95. Doubleday.
Waiting for the Rain. Charles Mungoshi. (African Writers Ser.). 1975. pap. text ed. 3.00x (ISBN 0-435-90170-2). Heinemann Ed.
Waiting for the Signal: A Novel. Henry O Morris. The Schulte Publishing Co.
Waiting for the Verdict. Rebecca Harding Davis. LC 68-57520. (American novels of muckraking, propaganda, and social protest). (Illus.). 1968. Gregg Press.
Waiting for the Verdict. Rebecca Harding Davis. LC 7-123363. 1868. Sheldon & Company.
Waiting for Thursday. Hamilton Jobson. LC 77-10284. 1978. 7.95 (ISBN 0-312-85426-9). St. Martin's Press.
Waiting for Willa. Dorothy Eden. LC 77-96783. 1970. 5.95. Coward-McCann.
Waiting for Willy. Jack Houston. LC 51-9591. 1951. Rinehart.
Waiting for Winter. John O'Hara. 1966. 14.95 (ISBN 0-394-45082-5). Random.
Waiting for Winter: Stories. John O Hara. LC 66-214593. 1966. 5.95. Random.
Waiting for Winter: Stories. John O Hara. (N3537). 1967. Bantam.
Waiting Game. Diana Blayne. (Candlelight Ecstasy Ser.: No. 94). (Orig.). 1982. pap. 1.95 (ISBN 0-440-19570-5). Dell.
Waiting Game. A. Fullerton. 1962. 3.50 o.p. Washburn.
Waiting Game. Cynthia Harrod-Eagles. (Signet book). 1974. (pbk.) 1.25. New American Library.
Waiting Game. Michael Powell. LC 75-26189. (Illus.). 7.95. St. Martin's Press.
Waiting Game. Patrick Wayland. LC 65-15665. 1965. Published for the Crime Club by Doubleday.
Waiting Heart. Henrietta Hardy Hammond. LC 7-56274. (On cover: Munro's library. v. 1. no. 106). N. L. Munro.
Waiting Heart. Marcia Miller. 1963. Avalon Books.
Waiting in Line: Stories. David Walton. LC 75-317476. (Ardis fiction series; no. 1). 1975. 6.95. (ISBN 0-88233-088-8) (ISBN 0-88233-087-X). Ardis.
Waiting on God. Andrew Murray. 1961. pap. 1.95 (ISBN 0-87508-399-4). Chr Lit.
Waiting People. Illustrated by Mine Okubo. Peggy Billings. LC 62-784956. 1962. Friendship Press.
Waiting Sands. Susan Howatch. LC 72-80345. 1972. 6.95. Stein and Day.
Waiting Sands. Susan Howatch. (Fawcett crest book). 1975. (pbk.) 1.25. Fawcett.
Waiting Time. Maurade Glennon. LC 73-132506. 1971. 4.95. Doubleday.
Waiting to Hear from William. Babs H Deal. LC 74-31514. 1975. 5.95 (ISBN 0-385-00694-2). Doubleday.
Waiting with Alistair. Alistair Sampson. (Illus.). 176p. 1978. 9.95 (ISBN 0-916838-14-5). Schiffer.
Waiting Years. Fumiko Ueda Enchi. LC 72-158644. 1971 (ISBN 0-87011-159-0). Kodansha International.
Waitress. Cora Miller. pap. 1.95 o.p. (8037). Cameo.
Wakau. Orvel L. Trainer. 1970. 9.95 o.p. (ISBN 0-87108-036-2). Pruett.
Wake. Steve Allen. LC 72-83136. 1972. 5.95 (ISBN 0-385-07608-8). Doubleday.
Wake All the Dead. Sarah Kilpatrick. LC 79-116222. 1970. 4.50. Published for the Crime Club by Doubleday.
Wake and Find a Stranger. Eleanor Shaler. LC 34-16314. 1934. W. Morrow and Company.
Wake and Remember. James Gray. LC 36-201362. 1936. The Macmillan Company.
Wake for a Lady. Henry Wisdom Roden. LC 46-493072. 1946. W. Morrow & Company.
Wake in Darkness: A Novel. Donald E. McQuinn. 436p. 1982. 14.95 (ISBN 0-02-583730-3). Macmillan.
Wake in Ybor City. Jose Yglesias. LC 63-12608. 1963. Holt, Rinehart and Winston.
Wake Island. Duane Schultz. LC 79-52760. (W.W. II Ser.). 224p. 1981. pap. 2.50 (ISBN 0-86721-122-9). Playboy Pbks.
Wake Island. Duane Schultz. (War Bks.). 224p. 1983. pap. 2.50 (ISBN 0-86721-122-9). Jove Pubns.
Wake Me When It's Over. Howard Singer. LC 59-7804. 1959. Putnam.
Wake of a Lawyer. 1st Ed. Aubrey Holmes. LC 60-15060. 1960. Houston American Pub. Co.
Wake of Glory. John M Redding & Smith, Thor, Joint Author. LC 45-8452. 1945. The Bobbs-Merrill Company.
Wake of the Icarus. Nathaniel Benchley. LC 70-86551. 1969. 6.95. Atheneum.
Wake of the Prairie Schooner. Irene D. Paden. (Illus.). pap. 5.95 (ISBN 0-8093-0462-7). Patrice Pr.
Wake of the Red Witch. Garland Roark. LC 46-187845. 1946. Little, Brown and Company.
Wake of the Setting Sun. William Averill Stowell. LC 23-739589. 1923. D. Appleton and Company.
Wake the Sleeping Wolf: By Rae Foley Pseud. Elinore Denniston. LC 52-8078. (Red badge detective). 1952. Dodd, Mead.
Wake-up America. Robert L. Preston. 128p. 1972. pap. 3.95 (ISBN 0-89036-027-8). Hawkes Pub Inc.
Wake up and Love. June Jennifer. LC 37-19348. 1937. Hillman, Curl, Inc.
Wake-up and Open Your Eyes. Edward Muhire. LC 76-980727. 1976. 9.00. East African Pub. House.
Wake up Screaming: Sixteen Chilling Tales of the Macabre. Ed. by Lee Wright & Richard G. Sheehan. LC 67-12257. (Bantam's tales of supernatural horror). 1967. Bantam Books.
Wake up, Stupid. 1st Ed. Mark Harris. LC 59-9255. 1959. Knopf.
Wake up. We're Almost There. Chandler Brossard. LC 76-125552. 1971. 8.95 (ISBN 0-87777-028-X). R. W. Baron.
Wakefield House. Jan Deering. 1973. pap. 0.95 o.p. (09151). Curtis.
Wakefield Witches. Daoma Winston. 1975. (pbk.) 1.25 (ISBN 0-671-68021-8). Pocket Books.
Wakefield's Course. whiteoak ed. Mazo De La Roche. LC 41-17248. 1941. Little, Brown, and Company.
Wakefield's Course. Mazo De La Roche. (Jalna Ser.). 1977. pap. 1.95 (ISBN 0-449-23431-2, Crest). Fawcett.
Wakefield's Passion. Catherine Linden. 208p. 1981. pap. 2.25 (ISBN 0-380-78139-5, 78139). Avon.
Waking. Ed Cox. 48p. (Orig.). 1977. pap. 2.50 (ISBN 0-917342-56-9). Gay Sunshine.
Waking. Eva Figes. LC 81-14078. 7.95 (ISBN 0-394-52325-3). Pantheon.
Waking Bird. Barbara Goolden. LC 29-221344. The John Day Company.
Waking Slow. michael mewshaw. ed. Michael Mewshaw. 1.75 (ISBN 0-380-00804-1). Avon Books.
Waking Slow. Michael Mewshaw. LC 70-37067. 1972. 5.95 (ISBN 0-394-47593-3). Random House.
Waking up the Giant: The Strategy for American Victory and World Freedom. Stefan Thomas Possony. LC 74-1041. 1974. 12.95 (ISBN 0-87000-206-6). Arlington House.
Walda: A Novel. Mary Holland McNeish Kinkaid. LC 3-7655. 1903. Harper & Brothers.
Walden Two. Burrhus Frederic Skinner. LC 75-41339. 7.95 (ISBN 0-02-411521-5) (ISBN 0-02-411511-8). Macmillan.
Walden West. August William Derleth. LC 61-14127. 8.95 (ISBN 0-88361-073-6). Stanton & Lee.
Walden West. August William Derleth. 5.00 o.p. Arkham.
Walden West. August William Derleth. LC 61-14127. (Illus.). 262p. 1973. Repr. 7.95 o.s.i. (ISBN 0-88451-001-8). Edco-Vis Assoc.
Waldere. Ed. by Arne Zettersten. (Old & Middle English Texts Ser.). (Illus.). 40p. 1979. text ed. 15.00x (ISBN 0-06-497970-9). B&N Imports.
Waldo: A Novel. Paul Theroux. LC 66-12078. 1967. Houghton Mifflin.
Waldo: And Magic, Inc. Robert Anson Heinlein. LC 50-5838. (Doubleday science fiction). 1950. Doubleday.
Waldo and Magic, Inc. Robert Anson Heinlein. LC 79-12729. (Gregg Press science fiction series). (Illus.). 1979. 12.95 (ISBN 0-8398-2507-2). Gregg Press.
Waldo Trench see Collected Works.
Waldo. 1st Ed. Lane Kauffmann. LC 60-6395. 1960. Lippincott.
Waldorf. James Goldman. LC 65-19635. 1965. Random House.
Waldorf: Or, The Dangers of Philosophy. Sophia King. LC 73-22066. (Feminist Controversy in England, 1788-1810). 1974. (2 vols.) 44.00 (ISBN 0-8240-0871-5). Garland Pub.
Waldtraut: According to the Chronicle of the Pastor of Hinrichshagen. Minna Waack Rudiger. Tr. by Crook, Corinth Le Duc. LC 98-1884. 1898. H. S. Elliott.
Walewska. A Tale of the First Empire. Lina Bartlett Ditson. LC 6-33872. (On cover: Neely's popular library. no. 111). 1898. F. T. Neely.
Walford: A Novel. Ellen Warner Olney Kirk. LC 7-12509. 1890. Houghton, Mifflin and Company.
Walk a Black Wind. Michael Collins, pseud. (Dan Fortune Detective Ser.). 192p. 1978. pap. 2.25 (ISBN 0-87216-903-0). Playboy Pbks.
Walk a Black Wind. Michael Collins, pseud. LC 70-158342. 1971. 4.95 o.p. (ISBN 0-396-06370-5). Dodd.
Walk a Black Wind. Dennis Lynds. LC 70-158342. (Red Badge novel of suspense). 1971. 4.95 (ISBN 0-396-06370-5). Dodd, Mead.
Walk a Black Wind. Dennis Lynds. (Dan Fortune novel of suspense). 1978. 1.50 (ISBN 0-87216-478-0). Playboy Press.
Walk a Crooked Mile. Judson Pentecost Philips. LC 75-15998. (Red badge novel of suspense). 1975. 5.95 (ISBN 0-396-07137-6). Dodd, Mead.
Walk a Dark Road. Lynn Williams. (Candlelight romance#183). 1975. (pbk.) 0.75. Dell.
Walk a Narrow Trail. Steven C Lawrence. (Slattery#4). 1975. (pbk.) 0.95. Leisure Books.
Walk a Tightrope. Julie Ellis. 1975. (pbk.) 0.95. Dell.
Walk a Wicked Mile. Robert P Hansen. LC 55-712336. 1955. M. S. Mill Co., and W. Morrow.
Walk a Winter Beach. Sandy Johnson. LC 81-22205. 13.95 (ISBN 0-440-09353-8). Delacorte Press/Eleanor Friede.
Walk Across America. Peter Jenkins. 336p. (Orig.). 1981. pap. 2.95 (ISBN 0-449-24277-3, Crest). Fawcett.
Walk & Other Stories. Robert Walser. 1957. 2.00 o.p. Hillary.
Walk Around the Square. Daoma Winston. 1975. (pbk.) 1.25. Ace Books.
Walk at a Steady Pace. Norman Fisher. LC 75-161114. 1971. 4.95 (ISBN 0-8027-5237-3). Walker.
Walk at Night. David Craig. LC 76-150943. 1971. 5.95 o.p. (ISBN 0-8128-1384-7). Stein & Day.
Walk at Night. Allan James Tucker. LC 76-150943. 1971. 4.95 (ISBN 0-8128-1384-7). Stein and Day.
Walk Away from 'em. Elliot Chess. LC 41-15199. Coward-Mc-Cann, Inc.
Walk Away Slowly. Seamus Cullen. 1970. 4.95 o.p. Crown.
Walk Away Slowly: A Novel. Seamus Cullen. LC 76-108066. 1970. 5.95. Crown.
Walk by My Side. Sandra Field. (Harlequin Presents Ser.). 192p. 1983. pap. 1.75 (ISBN 0-373-10568-1). Harlequin Bks.
Walk, Don't Walk. Gordon M. Williams. LC 72-78179. 1972. 7.50. St. Martin's Press.
Walk Down Main Street: A Novel. Ruth Moore. LC 59-143252. 1960. Morrow.
Walk Egypt. Vinnie Williams. LC 60-7670. 1960. Viking Press.
Walk Gently This Good Earth. Margaret Craven. LC 78-7487. 1978. 9.95 (ISBN 0-8161-6585-8). G. K. Hall.
Walk Gently This Good Earth. Margaret Craven. 1979. 1.95 (ISBN 0-440-19484-9). Dell Publishing Co.
Walk Hard--Talk Loud: A Novel. Len Zinberg. LC 40-325701. The Bobbs-Merrill Company.
Walk Humbly. Barbara B Stevens. LC 35-18843. 1935. Houghton Mifflin Company.
Walk-in. Virgil Scott & Dominic Koski. LC 76-18220. 7.95 (ISBN 0-671-22327-5). Simon and Schuster.
Walk-in. Virgil Scott & Dominic Koski. 1979. 1.95 (ISBN 0-671-81356-0). Pocket Books.
Walk in a Tall Shadow. Amelia Elizabeth Walden. LC 68-24408. 1968. 3.95. Lippincott.
Walk in Beauty. Grace Jamison Breckling. LC 54-13160. 1955. Scribner.
Walk in Darkness. Jean Bekessy, pseud. Tr. by Hanser, Richard F. LC 48-8727. 1948. G. P. Putnam's Sons.
Walk in Dread: Twelve Classic Eerie Tales. Ed. by Dorothy Tomlinson. LC 72-2204. 1972. 6.95 (ISBN 0-8008-8037-4). Taplinger.
Walk in Shadow: A Novel. Julius Fast. LC 47-314316. 1947. Rinehart.
Walk in the City. Daniel Smith. LC 70-133477. 1974. (pbk.) 1.50. Manor Books.
Walk in the Dark. Jan Roffman. 1970. 4.50 o.p. Doubleday.
Walk in the Dark. Margaret Summerton. (Ace gothic read easy large type). 1973. (pbk.) 0.95. Ace.
Walk in the Dark. Margaret Summerton. LC 77-97685. 1970. 4.50. Published for the Crime Club by Doubleday.
Walk in the Dolomites. Caroline Neilson. LC 77-104000. 1970. 4.95. Scribner.
Walk in the Jungle. Glenn Canary. 1975. (pbk.) 1.25 (ISBN 0-523-00660-8). Pinnacle Books.
Walk in the Night & Other Stories. Alex La Guma. 1967. 11.95x (ISBN 0-8101-0399-0); pap. 4.95x (ISBN 0-8101-0139-4). Northwestern U Pr.
Walk in the Paradise Garden. Anne Maybury. LC 76-37066. 1972. 5.95 (ISBN 0-394-47881-9). Random House.
Walk in the Shadows. Peter Reichman. 5.50 o.p. Vantage.
Walk in the Spring Rain. Rachel Maddux. 2.95. Doubleday.
Walk in the Spring Rain. Rachel Maddux. 1978. 1.50 (ISBN 0-380-01833-0). Avon Books.
Walk in the Sun. Harry Peter M'Nab Brown. LC 44-52741. 1944. A. A. Knopf.
Walk in the Sun & Other Stories. Norman Donald Hunter. 1977. 4.00 o.p. (ISBN 0-682-48626-4). Exposition.
Walk in Wolf Wood. Mary Stewart. 192p. 1981. pap. 2.50 (ISBN 0-449-24433-4, Crest). Fawcett.
Walk in Wolf Wood: A Tale of Fantasy & Magic. Mary Stewart. LC 80-13010. (Illus.). 160p. 1980. o.s. 8.95 (ISBN 0-688-03679-1). Morrow.
Walk into Murder. Peter J Helm. LC 61-7214. 1961. Scribner.
Walk into My Parlor. Margaret Lane. LC 41-280630. Harper & Brothers.
Walk into My Parlor: Chapters from Inviting Books. Ed. by Betty Bandel. LC 76-158783. 1972. 5.00 (ISBN 0-8048-0920-8). C. E. Tuttle Co.
Walk into My Parlour. Pamela Frankau. LC 33-13330. 1933. W. Morrow & Company.
Walk into Yesterday. Mildred B Davis. LC 67-20922. 1967. Published for the Crime Club by Doubleday.
Walk Like a Man. Donald Honig. LC 61-5723. 1961. W. Sloane Associates.
Walk Like a Mortal. Dan Wickenden. LC 40-27192. 1940. W. Morrow & Co.
Walk of the Conscious Ants. Taylor Morris. (Illus.). (YA) 1972. 6.95 o.p. (ISBN 0-394-47425-2). Knopf.
Walk on Glass. Lisa Robinson. LC 82-2254. 14.95 (ISBN 0-937858-05-6). Newmarket Press.
Walk on the Blind Side. J. T. MacCargo. (Mannix Ser). (O.s.i.: No. 3). (Orig.). 1975. pap. 1.25 o.s.i. (BT50825). Belmont-Tower.
Walk on the Blind Side. J. T MacCargo. (Mannix#3). 1975. (pbk.) 1.25. Belmont Tower Books.
Walk on the Sky. Ruth Southworth Brown. LC 73-79437. 1973. 6.95. Pioneer Print & Stationery Co.
Walk on the Water. Ralph Leveridge. LC 51-9994. 1951. Farrar, Straus & Young.
Walk on the Water. Ralph Leveridge. LC 52-38416. (Signet book no. 940). 1952. New American Library.
Walk on the Wild Side. Nelson Algren. LC 56-8623. 1956. Farrar, Straus and Cudahy.
Walk on the Wild Side. Nelson Algren. LC 77-2393. 1977. 1.95 (ISBN 0-14-003565-6). Penguin Books.
Walk on the Wild Side. Nelson Algren. LC 78-509. 1979. 18.50 (ISBN 0-313-20294-X). Greenwood Press.
Walk Softly, Men Praying. Oswald Wynd. LC 67-11978. 1967. Harcourt, Brace & World.
Walk Softly on the Green: A Novel. Jack Cole. LC 80-52463. 1981. 8.95 (ISBN 0-938556-00-2). Taugus House.
Walk Softly, Witch. Carter Brown, pseud. Bd. with Wayward Wahine. 1980. pap. 1.75 (ISBN 0-451-09418-2, E9418, Sig). NAL.
Walk the Dark Bridge. William O'Farrell. LC 52-12353. 1952. Published for the Crime Club by Doubleday.
Walk the Dark Streets. William Krasner. LC 49-9259. 1949. Harper.
Walk the Dark Streets. Charles C. Thomas. 4.95 o.p. Vantage.

TITLE INDEX WALSH COLVILLE.

Walk the Night Unseen. Lucinda Baker. LC 76-57220. 8.95 (ISBN 0-399-11896-9). Putnam.
Walk the Path in the Hills. Carmel Lee Pritt. LC 74-20066. (Illus.). 1975. (ISBN 0-87012-201-0). Pritt.
Walk Through the Valley. Zelda Popkin. LC 49-7469. 1949. J. B. Lippincott Co.
Walk to Survival. D. J Arneson. 1973. (pbk) 0.95. Ace Books.
Walk to the End of the World. Suzy McKee Charnas. 1979. pap. 1.95 (ISBN 0-425-04239-1). Berkley Pub.
Walk to the Hills of the Dreamtime. Donald Gordon Payne. LC 79-96301. (Illus.). 1970. 5.50. Morrow.
Walk to the Paradise Gardens. 1st Ed. Charmian Clift. LC 60-5963. 1960. Harper.
Walk to the River. William Hoffman. LC 71-103756. 1970. 5.95. Doubleday.
Walk to Your Grave. N M Newland. LC 51-11750. 1951. Phoenix Press.
Walk Toward the Rainbow. John Bell Clayton. LC 54-12922. 1954. Macmillan.
Walk up Market Street: By Gay Rutherford Pseud. James Noble Gifford. LC 55-715545. 1955. Arcadia House.
Walk with a Separate Pride. Sheila Alexander. LC 47-20012. 1947. The Itasca Press, a Division of the Webb Publishing Company.
Walk with a Shadow. Juanita Tyree Osborne. 1982. 6.95 (Avalon). Bouregy.
Walk with a Stranger. W. J. Young. 3.00 o.p. Carlton.
Walk with Care. Patricia Wentworth. LC 33-182214. J. B. Lippincott Company.
Walk with Evil. Robert Wilder. 1970. pap. 0.75 o.p. (T2336, GM). Fawcett World.
Walk with Love & Death. Hans Koning. (O.s.i.). 1961. 3.50 o.s.i. (ISBN 0-671-79565-1). S&S.
Walk with Love and Death: A Novel. Hans Koningsberger. LC 61-5839. 1961. Simon and Schuster.
Walk with Me Tomorrow. Allene Soule Corliss. LC 40-300062. Farrar & Rinehart, Inc.
Walk with Peril. Dorothy V. S Jackson. LC 59-6171. 1959. Putnam.
Walk with Raschid, and Other Stories. Josephine Jacobsen. LC 78-4584. 1978. 10.00 (ISBN 0-917492-08-0). Jackpine Press.
Walk with the Devil. Elliott Arnold. 1973. pap. 1.25 o.p. (ISBN 0-515-03002-3, V3002). BJ Pub Group.
Walk with the Devil. 1st Ed. Elliott Arnold. LC 50-9934. 1950. Knopf.
Walkabout. James Vance Marshall. LC 61-9533. (Illus.). 1961. Doubleday.
Walkabout. Donald Gordon Payne. LC 61-9533. C.
Walkabout. rev. ed. Donald Gordon Payne. LC 72-131932. (Illus.). 1971. 5.95. Morrow.
Walkabout Long Canoe. Dennis Steley. LC 78-59309. (Destiny Ser.). 1979. pap. 4.95 o.p. (ISBN 0-8163-0248-0). Pacific Pr Pub Assn.
Walkabouts: A Family at Sea. Michael Saunders. LC 75-9849. (Illus.). 285p. 1975. 8.95 o.s.i. (ISBN 0-8128-1820-2). Stein & Day.
Walked Yard. Lionel White. 1978. pap. 1.95 (ISBN 0-532-19188-9). Woodhill.
Walker: And Other Stories. 1st Ed. Patrick O'Brian. LC 55-9376. 1955. Harcourt, Brace.
Walker in Shadows. Barbara Mertz. LC 79-9298. 1979. 8.95 (ISBN 0-396-07713-7). Dodd, Mead.
Walker in Shadows. Barbara Michaels. LC 79-27833. 1980. 12.95 (ISBN 0-8161-3060-4). G. K. Hall.
Walker of the Secret Service. Melville Davisson Post. LC 24-222711. 1924. Appleton and Company.
Walkers. Gary Brandner. 1.95 (ISBN 0-449-14319-8). Fawcett Gold Medal Books.
Walkers on the Sky. David J. Lake. (Science Fiction Ser.). 1976. pap. 1.25 o.p. (ISBN 0-87997-273-4, UY1273). DAW Bks.
Walkers on the Sky. David J Lake (ISBN 0-87997-273-4). Daw Books.
Walking Black and Tall. Omar Fletcher. 1977. 1.75 (ISBN 0-87067-513-3). Holloway House Pub. Co.
Walking Corpse. Margaret Isabel Postgate Cole & Cole, Mrs. Margaret Isabel (Postgate) 1893- Joint Author. LC 31-22142. 1931. W. Morrow & Company.
Walking Davis: A Novel. David Ely. LC 72-84217. 1972. 6.95. Charterhouse.
Walking Dead. Peter Dickinson. LC 77-5299. 6.95 (ISBN 0-394-42010-1). Pantheon Books.
Walking Dead Man. Hugh Pentecost. LC 72-12434. (Pierre Chambrun Mystery Novel Ser.). 194p. 1973. 4.95 o.p. (ISBN 0-396-06779-4). Dodd.
Walking Dead Man. Judson Pentecost Philips. LC 72-12434. (Red badge novel of suspense). 1973. 4.95 (ISBN 0-396-06779-4). Dodd, Mead.
Walking Deadman. Hugh Pentecost. 1974. pap. 0.95 o.p. (ISBN 0-515-03539-4, N3539). Pyramid Pubns.
Walking Delegate. Leroy Scott. LC 68-57549. (Illus.). 1969. Literature House.
Walking Doll: Or The Asters and Disasters of Society. Robert Henry Newell. LC 74-171061. 1973. (ISBN 0-404-03664-3). AMS Press.
Walking Doll: Or, The Asters and Disasters of Society. Robert Henry Newell. LC 7-23134. 1872. F. B. Felt & Company.
Walking Gentleman. James Prior. LC 8-23524. 1908. E. P. Dutton and Company.
Walking in God's Love. Patricia Missick. (Illus.). 1980. pap. 3.95 o.p. (ISBN 0-89260-167-1). Hwong Pub.
Walking Naked. Nina Bawden. LC 81-16713. 1982. 10.95 (ISBN 0-312-85456-0). St. Martin's Press.
Walking on Air. Pierre Delattre. LC 79-28637. 1980. 9.95 (ISBN 0-395-29118-6) (ISBN 0-395-29119-4). Houghton Mifflin Co.
Walking on Borrowed Land, a Novel. 1st Ed. William A Owens. LC 54-9491. 1954. Bobbs-Merrill Co.
Walking on Grass. Andrew Crozier. 1969. pap. 4.00 o.p.; ltd. signed ed. 11.00 o.p. Ferry Pr.
Walking on Grass. Andrew Crozier. 1969. pap. 11.00 signed ltd. ed. o.p. Ferry Pr.
Walking Papers. Sandra Hochman. LC 78-148149. 1971. 6.95 (ISBN 0-670-74892-7). Viking Press.
Walking Shadow. Lenore Glen Offord. LC 59-13141. (Inner sanctuam mystery). 1959. Simon and Schuster.
Walking Shadows. Modena Gelien. LC 77-91491. (Illus.). 2.95 (ISBN 0-916406-90-3). Accent Books.
Walking Shadows: Sea Tales and Others. Alfred Noyes. Frederick A. Stokes Company.
Walking Small. Lawrence J Davis. LC 74-75686. 1974. 6.95 (ISBN 0-8076-0748-7). G. Braziller.
Walking Stick. Winston Graham. (N3779). 1968. Bantam.
Walking Stick. Winston Graham. LC 67-14130. 1967. Doubleday.
Walking Stick. Charles Elbert Scoggins. LC 30-243433. The Bobbs-Merrill Company.
Walking-Stick Papers. Robert C. Holland. 1973. Repr. of 1918 ed. 15.00 (ISBN 0-8274-0253-8). R West.
Walking Tall; Part Two. Webster Carey. 1975. (pbk.) 1.50. Bantam.
Walking the Dusk. L. J. Webb. LC 32-237192. Coward-McCann, Inc.
Walking the Whirlwind. Brigid Knight. LC 41-3333. 1941. Crowell.
Walking the Whirlwind. Kathleen Henrietta Nash-Webber Sinclair. LC 41-3333. 1941. Thomas Y. Crowell Company.
Walking the Whirlwind. Knight Brigid Sinclair. LC 41-3333. 1941. Thomas Y. Crowell Company.
Walking Through the Fire: A Hospital Journal. Laurel Lee. 1978. pap. 2.25 (ISBN 0-553-14494-4). Bantam.
Walking Through Tigerland: Stories. Barry Oakley. LC 78-302801. 1978. 6.95 (ISBN 0-7022-1099-4) (ISBN 0-7022-1105-2). University of Queensland Press.
Walking Trip. Henrietta Buckmaster, pseud. LC 73-182324. 1972. 5.95 (ISBN 0-15-194189-0). Harcourt Brace Jovanovich.
Walking Vanilla. Susan Efros. LC 78-66433. 1978. pap. 5.00 (ISBN 0-932278-01-9). Waterfall Pr.
Walking Wind. Franklin M. Proud. LC 78-19430. 8.95 (ISBN 0-312-85459-5). St. Martin's Press.
Walking Wounded. Steven Phillip Smith. 1979. 9.95 (ISBN 0-399-12320-2). Putnam Pub Group.
Walking Wounded. Stephen J. Thorpe. LC 79-6892. 1980. 11.95 (ISBN 0-385-15900-5). Doubleday.
Walks Along the Croton Aqueduct: An Esstory. Dante Anthony Puzzo. LC 79-66385. 8.50. Randatamp Press.
Walks Far Woman. Clark Spurlock. LC 76-40694. 1976. 8.95 (ISBN 0-8037-9365-0). Dial Press.
Walks-Far Woman. Colin Stuart. (O.s.i.). (YA) 1976. 8.95 o.s.i. (ISBN 0-8037-9365-0). Dial.
Wall. Gwendolyn Brooks. (Broadside Ser., No. 19). broadsheet. 0.50 o.p. Broadside.
Wall. John Cournos. LC 21-26724. 1921. Methuen & Co., Ltd.
Wall. John Richard Hersey. LC 50-5697. 1950. Knopf.
Wall. Mary Roberts Rinehart. LC 38-27563. Farrar & Rinehart, Inc.
Wall. Mary Roberts Rinehart. LC 44-7839. 1944. Triangle Books.
Wall. Mary Roberts Rinehart. 1973. (pbk) 1.25. Dell.
Wall Against the Night. Shroyer, Frederick B. LC 57-12044.
Wall: And Other Stories. Jean Paul Sartre. Tr. by Alexander, Lloyd. LC 48-964293. New Directions.
Wall Around a Star. Frederik Pohl & Jack Williamson. 288p. (Orig.). 1983. pap. 2.95 (ISBN 0-345-28995-1, Del Rey). Ballantine.
Wall Between. Elsie Marion Oakes Barber. LC 46-6324. 1946. The Macmillan Company.
Wall Between. Sara Ware Bassett. LC 20-157026. 1920. 1.90. Little, Brown, and Company.
Wall Between. Ralph Delahaye Paine. LC 14-145676. 1914. C. Scribner's Sons.
Wall-Eyed Caesar's Ghost and Other Sketches. Jane Baldwin Cotton. LC 77-106281. (Short story index reprint series). (Illus.). 1970. Books for Libraries Press.
Wall-Eyed Caesar's Ghost, and Other Sketches. Jane Baldwin Cotton. LC 25-20145. Marshall Jones Company.
Wall for San Sebastian. William Barnaby Faherty. LC 62-20460. 1962. Academy Guild Press.
Wall of Eyes. Margaret Millar. 1943. Random House.
Wall of Eyes. Margaret Miller. 1974. (pbk.) 0.95 (ISBN 0-380-00067-9). Avon.
Wall of Guns: By Jim O'Mara Pseud. 1st Ed. Vernon L Fluharty. LC 50-5629. (Dutton Diamond D western). 1950. Dutton.
Wall of Masks. Brian Coffey. LC 74-17666. 192p. 1975. 6.95 o.p. (ISBN 0-672-51905-4). Bobbs.
Wall of Masks. Dean Koontz. LC 74-17666. 1975. 6.95 (ISBN 0-672-51905-4). Bobbs-Merrill.
Wall of Men. Margaret Hill McCarter. LC 12-240627. 1912. A. C. McClurg & Co.
Wall of Men. William Rollins. LC 38-5295. Modern Age Books, Inc.
Wall of Night. Elizabeth Rainbow. pap. 0.95 o.s.i. (75-283). Lancer.
Wall of Noise: A Novel. Daniel M Stein. LC 60-863296. 4.95. Crown Publishers.
Wall of Partition. Florence Louisa Charlesworth Barclay. LC 14-15178. 1914. 1.30. G. P. Putnam's Sons.
Wall of Reeds. David Peters. LC 80-103051. 1979. 8.75 (ISBN 0-86925-089-2). Galaxie Press.
Wall of Serpents. Lyon Sprague De Camp & Fletcher Pratt. (Adventures of Harold Shea Ser.). (Illus.). 1978. Repr. of 1960 ed. 12.00 o.p. (ISBN 0-932096-00-X). Phantasia Pr.
Wall Paper Code: And Other Stories. Isabel Weld Perkins Anderson. LC 27-10952. The Four Seas Company.
Wall Street: A Story of the Greatest Street in All the World, with Its Intrigues, Plots, Counter-Plots, Its Gains--Its Losses--Its Hopes--Its Despairs. Jack Karkland & Gangelen, Paul. LC 30-14010. Jacobson Publishing Company, Inc.
Wall Street Girl. Frederick Orin Bartlett. LC 16-18329. 1916. 1.35. Houghton Mifflin Company.
Wall Street Haul: Or, A Bold Stroke for a Fortune. John Russell Coryell. (On cover: The secret service series, no. 18). 1889. Street & Smith.
Wall Street Murders. Douglas Meade Hoffecker. LC 36-7586. (The J. Gordon Drexel series). Fortuny's.
Wall Street Stories. Edwin Lefevre. LC 75-150478. (Short story index reprint series). 1971. (ISBN 0-8369-3819-4). Books for Libraries Press.
Wall Street Stories. Edwin Lefevre. LC 77-75578. 1969. Greenwood Press.
Wall Street Stories. Edwin Lefevre. 1901. McClure, Phillips & Co.
Wall Street Stories. Edwin Lefevre. LC 16-148116. 1916. Harper & Brothers.
Wall to Wall, a Novel. Douglas Woolf. LC 61-12765. 1962. Grove Press.
Wall-to-Wall Trap, a Novel. Morton Freedgood. LC 57-622995. 1957. Simon and Schuster.
Wall. With Twelve Aquatints by William Sharp and with an Introd. by George N. Shuster. John Richard Hersey. LC 57-58278. 1957. Printed at the Marchbanks Press for the Members of the Limited Editions Club.
Wall Within the Orbit. Grace Fox Perry. LC 53-121485. 1954. Vantage Press.
Wallace-Crabbe Reads from His Own Work. Chris Wallace-Crabbe. (O.s.i.). 1973. pap. 1.25x o.s.i. (ISBN 0-7022-0876-0); record 7.25x o.s.i. (ISBN 0-7022-0877-9). U of Queensland Pr.
Wallace Rhodes: A Novel. Norah Davis. LC 9-9508. 1909. 1.50. Harper & Brothers.
Walled City. Marcel Clouzot. LC 73-80169. 1973. 8.95 (ISBN 0-87131-128-3). M. Evans.
Walled City. Elspeth Joscelin Grant Huxley. LC 48-9605. 1949. J. B. Lippincott.
Walled in. Elizabeth Stuart Phelps Ward. LC 7-33590. 1907. Harper & Brothers.
Walled Parrot. John Weston. LC 75-9978. 1975. 7.95 (ISBN 0-07-069478-8). McGraw-Hill.
Wallet of Kai Lun. Ernest Bramah Smith. LC 23-26923. 1923. George H. Doran Company.
Wallet of Kai Lung. Ernest Bramah, pseud. 337p. 1977. lib. bdg. 15.95x (ISBN 0-89966-269-2). Buccaneer Bks.
Wallet of Kai Lung. Ernest Bramah, pseud. 1920. 4.50 o.p. Verry.
Wallet of Kai Lung: By Ernest Bramah Pseud. with an Introd. by Grant Richards. Ernest Bramah Smith. 1966. 4.50. G. Richards Ltd.
Wallflowe. Ruby Mildred Ayres. LC 40-110176. 1940. Doubleday, Doran and Co., Inc.
Wallflower at the Orgy. Nora Ephron. 176p. (Orig.). 1980. pap. 2.50 (ISBN 0-553-13119-2). Bantam.
Wallflower Season. Jeannette Bruce. LC 62-7607. 1962. Doubleday.
Wallflowers. Temple Bailey. LC 27-20249. 1927. The Penn Publishing Company.
Wallflowers. Nigel Waldo. The Hannis Jordan Company.
Walling Omnibus... The Corpse in the Coppice, The Corpse with the Grimy Glove, The Corpse with the Floating Foot. Robert Alfred John Walling. LC 40-5671. 1939. Blue Ribbon Books.
Wallingford: A Story of American Life... Eugene Coleman Savidge. LC 12-12214. 1887. J. B. Lippincott Company.
Wallingford and Blackie Daw. George Randolph Chester. LC 13-21357. 1.00. The Bobbs-Merrill Company.
Wallingford in His Prime. George Randolph Chester. LC 13-9792. 1.00. The Bobbs-Merrill Company.
Wallington Case. Montague Jon. LC 81-8837. 1981. 10.95 (ISBN 0-312-85461-7). St Martin's Press.
Wallops. Harry Durant. LC 7-40045. 1907. Dissell Publishing Co.
Wallpaper Fox: A Novel. Morris H. Philipson. LC 76-15582. 7.95 (ISBN 0-684-14773-4). Scribner.
Walls Against the Wind. Frances Park. LC 35-422204. 1935. Houghton Mifflin Company.
Walls Are High. Joseph Van Raalte. The Vanguard Press.
Walls Came Tumbling Down. Babs H Deal. LC 68-10592. 1968. Doubleday.
Walls Came Tumbling Down. Jo Eisinger. LC 43-16886. 1943. Coward-McCann, Inc.
Walls of Fire. Marc Worth. LC 26-138. 1925. Cosmopolitan Publishing Co.
Walls of Glass. Larry Barretto. LC 26-14385. 1926. Little, Brown, and Company.
Walls of Glass. Phyllis Bottome. LC 59-12393. Vanguard Press.
Walls of Gold. Kathleen Thompson Norris. LC 33-27068. 1933. Doubleday, Doran & Company, Inc.
Walls of Heaven. Robert McLaughlin. LC 61-70134. 1961. Simon and Schuster.
Walls of Heaven: A Novel. Jonathan Scott. LC 67-10963. 1967. Putnam.
Walls of Jericho. Rudolph Fisher. LC 69-18590. (American Negro, His History and Literature). (Illus.). 1969. Arno Press.
Walls of Jericho. Rudolph Fisher. LC 28-188993. 1928. A. A. Knopf.
Walls of Jericho. Joseph McCord. LC 42-572. 1942. Macrae-Smith Company.
Walls of Jericho. Paul Iselin Wellman. LC 56-58402. 1956. Doubleday.
Walls of Jericho. Paul Iselin Wellman. 1948. Sun Dial Press.
Walls of Jericho. Paul Iselin Wellman. LC 47-575. 1947. J. B. Lippincott Company.
Walls of Jolo: By Alan Caillou Pseud. Alan Lyle-Smythe. LC 60-130675. 1960. Appleton-Century- Crofts.
Walls of Silence. Dean Hawkins. LC 43-17347. 1943. Pub. for the Crime Club by Doubleday, Doran & Co., Inc.
Walls of Zion. Addie Spaulding Stowell. LC 53-3192. 1953. Herald House.
Walls Rise up... George Sessions Perry. LC 39-9209. 1939. Doubleday, Doran & Co., Inc.
Walls Rise up... George Sessions Perry. LC 45-3131. 1945. Whittlesey House, McGraw-Hill Book Company, Inc.
Walls Rise up. Hold Autumn in Your Hand. Two Novels. Foreword by John Mason Brown. George Sessions Perry. LC 59-106841. 1959. Doubleday.
Wally: A Story of the West. Guy Steely. LC 11-24679. 1911. 1.25. Dodd, Mead and Company.
Wally, Die Zweiflerin: A Translation from the German of Karl Gutzkow. Ed. by Ruth-Ellen Boetcher-Joeres. (Germanic Studies in America: Vol. 19). 130p. 1974. write for info. (ISBN 3-261-01086-X). P Lang Pubs.
Wally Laughs-Easy. Dane Coolidge. LC 39-20965. 1939. E. P. Dutton & Co., Inc.
Walnut Door. John Richard Hersey. LC 77-1148. (Illus.). 1977. 7.95 (ISBN 0-394-41742-9). Franklin Library.
Walnut Grove. Jane Gilmore Rushing. LC 64-16227. 1964. Doubleday.
Walnut Grove. Jane Gilmore Rushing. 1979. 1.95 (ISBN 0-380-44164-0). Avon.
Walpurgis III. Mike Resnick. 166p. 1982. pap. 2.25 (ISBN 0-451-11572-4, AE1572, Sig). NAL.
Walsh Colville: Or, A Young Man's First Entrance into Life. Anna Maria Porter. LC 73-22074. (Feminist Controversy in England, 1788-1810). 1974. 22.00 (ISBN 0-8240-0876-6). Garland Pub.

Walsh Girls. Elizabeth Janeway. LC 43-157622. 1943. Doubleday, Doran and Company, Inc.
Walshingham Woman. Jan Vlachos Westcott. LC 53-5678. 1953. Crown Publishers.
Walsingham: Or, The Pupil of Nature. Mary Darby Robinson. LC 73-22068. (Feminist Controversy in England, 1788-1810). 1974. (4 vol. set) 22.00 ea. (ISBN 0-8240-0878-2). Garland Pub.
Walsingham: The Gamester. Frederick Chamier. LC 41-33230. 1838. Carey, Lea and Blanchard.
Walt and Vult, or The Twins. Tr. from the Flegeljahre of Jean Paul Pseud. Johann Paul Friedrich Richter & Lee, Eliza (Buckminster) 1794-1864, Tr. LC 7-41236. 1846. J. Munroe and Company.
Walt Coburn's Action Novels: Four Western Novels... Story Heads. Walt Coburn. Fiction House, Inc.
Walt Disney Presents Legends of America. Jane Werner Watson. Disney (Walt) Productions. LC 79-7375. (Illus.). 1969. 1.95. Golden Press.
Walter: A Tale of the Times of Wesley. Emma Leslie. LC 7-14495. (Church history stories, 2d ser., v. 5). 1880. Phillips & Hunt.
Walter Ashwood. A Love Story. Albert Mathews. 1860. Rudd & Carleton.
Walter Harmsen. A Tale of Reformation-Times in Holland. By E. Rdes. Gerdes. Eduard Gerdes. Tr. by Van Pelt, Daniel. LC 6-44238. Presbyterian Board of Publication.
Walter Lorimer, and Other Tales. a new ed. Elizabeth Missing Sewell. LC 8-6877. 1853. D. Appleton & Company.
Walter March: Or, Shoepac Recollections. 3d ed. Orlando Bolivar Wilcox. LC 11-3201. 1857. J. French and Company.
Walter of Tiverton. Bernard G Marshall. LC 23-8404. 1923. D. Appleton and Company.
Walter Ogilby. A Novel. Juliette Augusta Kinzie. LC 7-12537. 1869. J. B. Lippincott & Co.
Walter Pieterse: A Story of Holland. Eduard Douwes Dekker. Tr. by Evans, Hubert. LC 5-748. 1904. Frederici & Gareis.
Walter Syndrome. Richard Neely. LC 79-122149. 1970. 5.95. McCall Pub. Co.
Walter Warren: Or, The Adventurer of the Northern Wilda. Owen Duffy. LC 9-1835. Stringer & Townsend.
Walters of the Flying W. Bradford Scott. LC 43-14819. 1943. Arcadia House, Inc.
Waltham. A Novel. LC 1-158373. (Added t.-p.: The library of romance v. 3). 1833. Carey, Lea and Blanchard.
Walther P.38. John William Wainwright. LC 76-371484. 1976. 2.95 (ISBN 0-333-18630-3). Macmillan.
Walton Experience. Travis Walton. 1978. pap. 1.95 (ISBN 0-425-03675-8, Medallion). Berkley Pub.
Waltons. Robert Weverka. (Bantam pathfinder editions.). 1974. (pbk.) 0.95. Bantam Books.
Waltons: The Easter Story. Robert Weverka. 1976. (pbk.) 1.25. Bantam Books.
Waltons: Trouble on the Mountain. Robert Weverka. 1975. (pbk.) 0.95. Bantam Books.
Waltz Across Texas. Max Crawford. LC 74-26604. 1975. 8.95 (ISBN 0-374-28628-0). Farrar, Straus, Giroux.
Waltz Across Texas. Max Crawford. 1978. 1.95 (ISBN 0-380-01856-X). Avon.
Waltz, and Other Stories. Felix Marti Ibanez. 5.00. Potter.
Waltz Contest. Berta Ruck. LC 41-353983. 1941. Dodd, Mead & Company.
Waltz into Darkness. Cornell George Hopley-Woolrich. LC 47-759. 1947. J. B. Lippincott Company.
Waltz Is Over. Hester Pine. LC 43-1377. 1943. Farrar & Rinehart, Inc.
Waltz of Death. P. B Maxon. LC 41-18899. Mystery House.
Waltz of Death. P. B Maxon. LC 45-1658. (Bart house books). 1944. Bartholomew House Inc.
Waltz of Hearts, No. 139. Barbara Cartland. 160p. (Orig.). 1981. pap. 1.95 (ISBN 0-553-14586-X). Bantam.
Waltz on the Wind. Ian Kavanaugh. (O'Donnells Ser.). (Orig.). 1983. pap. 3.50 (ISBN 0-440-09487-9). Dell.
Waltzer. Henry J. Ambers. LC 76-114002. 320p. 1970. 6.95. Edelweiss Pr.
Waltzer: A Novel. Henry J Ambers. LC 76-114002. 1970. T. Gaus' Sons.
Wampanaki Tales. James Howard Kunstler. 224p. 1980. pap. 1.95 (ISBN 0-345-28734-7). Ballantine.
Wampanaki Tales: A Novel. James Howard Kunstler. LC 78-18139. 1979. 8.95 (ISBN 0-385-14385-0). Doubleday.
Wampeters, Foma & Granfalloons. Kurt Vonnegut. 1975. pap. 2.95 (ISBN 0-440-58533-3, Delta). Dell.
Wampeters, Foma & Granfalloons. Kurt Vonnegut, Jr. 320p. 1974. 8.95 (ISBN 0-440-08717-1, Sey Lawr). Delacorte.
Wampeters, Foma & Granfalloons. Kurt Vonnegut, Jr. 320p. 1976. pap. 2.75 (ISBN 0-440-18533-5). Dell.
Wand and the Star. Pat Wallace, pseud. (Kangaroo Book). 1978. 1.95 (ISBN 0-671-81240-8). Pocket Books.
Wand of Noble Wood. Onuora Nzekwu. (African Writers Ser.). 1971. pap. text ed. 5.00x (ISBN 0-435-90085-4). Heinemann Ed.
Wand of Noble Wood. Onuora Nzekwu. (African Writers Ser.: No. 85). 208p. 1961. pap. text ed. 1.75x o.p. (ISBN 0-435-90085-4). Humanities.
Wanda. Joseph Calvitt Clarke. LC 33-37998. 1934. W. Godwin.
Wanda. Joseph Calvitt Clarke. LC 33-37996. 1934. W. Godwin, Inc.
Wanda, Countess Von Szalras. A Novel. Louise De La Ramee. (On cover: Lovell's library. v. 3, no. 112). 1883. J. W. Lovell Company.
Wanda Hickey's Night of Golden Memories and Other Disasters. Jean Shepherd. 1974. (pbk.) 1.25. Dell.
Wanda Hickey's Night of Golden Memories and Other Disasters. Jean Shepherd. (Doubleday Dolphin book). (Illus.). 1976. 3.95 (ISBN 0-385-11632-2). Dolphin Books.
Wanda Hickey's Night of Golden Memories, and Other Disasters. Jean Shepherd. LC 72-161317. (Illus.). 1971. 6.95. Doubleday.
Wander-Ships: Folk Stories of the Sea with Notes Upon Their Origin. Wilbur Bassett. LC 78-23905. 1978. Repr. of 1917 ed. lib. bdg. 20.00 (ISBN 0-8414-9900-4). Folcroft.
Wanderer. Henri Alain-Fournier. Date not set. pap. 2.75 (ISBN 0-451-51571-4, CE1571, Sig Classics). NAL.
Wanderer. Henri Alain-Fournier. Tr. by Francoise Delisle. 1958. pap. 1.95 o.p. (A14, Anch). Doubleday.
Wanderer. Ed. by A. J. Bliss & T. P. Dunning. (Methuesn's Old English Library Ser). (O.s.i.). 1969. text ed. 2.05 o.s.i. (ISBN 0-390-03379-0). Appleton.
Wanderer. Henry Lane Eno. LC 21-13093. 1921. Duffield and Company.
Wanderer. Alain Fournier. Tr. by Delisle, Francoise. Ed. by Ellis, Havelock. LC 28-29726. 1928. Houghton Mifflin Company.
Wanderer. Knut Hamsun. LC 75-5915. 1975. 7.95 (ISBN 0-374-28636-1). Farrar, Straus and Giroux.
Wanderer. Fritz Leiber. LC 70-426587. (Penguin science fiction, 2594). 1969. Penguin.
Wanderer. Fritz Leiber. LC 74-107004. 1970. 5.95. Walker.
Wanderer. Fritz Leiber. LC 80-23527. (Series: Gregg Press Science Fiction Series.). 1980. 15.95 (ISBN 0-8398-2642-7). Gregg Press.
Wanderer. LC 75-5547. (Flowering of the Novel). 1975. 25.00 (ISBN 0-8240-1173-2). Garland Pub.
Wanderer: A Novel. Frank Bruce Robinson. LC 47-22612. 1947. Psychiana.
Wanderer: A Novel of Dante and Beatrice. Nathan Schachner. LC 44-9331. 1944. D. Appleton-Century Company, Incorporated.
Wanderer (Le Grand Meaulnes) Alain Fournier. Tr. by Francoise Roussel Delisle. LC 74-128078. (Houghton Mifflin reprint editions). 1973. 13.50 (ISBN 0-678-03552-0). A. M. Kelley.
Wanderer: Le Grand Meaulnes. Alain Fournier. LC 53-12003. (Doubleday anchor books, A 14). 1953. Doubleday.
Wanderer of the Wasteland. Zane Grey. LC 28-796. Harper & Brothers.
Wanderer on a Thousand Hills. Edith Wherry. LC 17-11706. 1917. John Lane Company.
Wanderer: Or, The End of Youth (Le Grand Meaulnes. Alain Fournier. LC 72-165288. (Signet classic). 1971. 1.25. New American Library.
Wanderer Upon Earth. Jack Finegan. LC 55-6785. 1956. Harper.
Wanderers. Knut Hamsun & Worster, William John Alexander, 1882-1929, Tr. LC 22-5371. 1922. A. A. Knopt.
Wanderers. Mary Johnston. LC 17-24277. 1917. Houghton Mifflin Company.
Wanderers. Ingrid Rimland. LC 77-24290. 8.95 (ISBN 0-570-03266-0). Concordia Pub. House.
Wanderers: A Novel. Ezekiel Mphahlele. LC 73-117964. 1971. Macmillan.
Wanderers: A Novel. Richard Price. LC 73-22210. 1974. 6.95 (ISBN 0-395-18477-0). Houghton Mifflin.
Wanderers by Sea and Land: With Other Tales. Samuel Griswold Goodrich. LC 7-164058. 1855. D. Appleton and Co.
Wanderers Eastward, Wanderers West. Kathleen Winsor. (Signet bk., Y2822). 1966. pap., 1.25. New Amer. Lib.
Wanderers Eastward, Wanderers West. Kathleen Winsor. LC 65-11296. 1965. Random House.
Wanderer's End: The Odyssey of Don Paradise. Dennis D Cleugh. LC 30-9727. 1930. Doubleday, Doran & Company, Inc.
Wanderer's Eternity. Nadi Rehs. 113p. 1980. pap. 6.95 (ISBN 0-8059-2696-8). Dorrance.
Wanderers in the Mist: Translated from the German. Heinz Liepmann. Tr. by Burns, Emile. LC 31-7183. 1931. Harper & Brothers.
Wanderer's Necklace. Henry Rider Haggard. LC 14-2237. 1914. 1.35. Longmans, Green, and Co.
Wanderer's Return. Lucille Hunter. LC 68-12947. 1967. Zondervan Pub. House.
Wanderfoot: The Dream Ship. Cynthia Stockley. LC 13-22284. 1913. G. P. Putnam's Sons.
Wanderground: Stories of the Hill Women. Sally Miller Gearhart. LC 79-108682. (Illus.). 5.00 (ISBN 0-930436-02-4). Persephone Press.
Wandering. Hermann Hesse. Tr. by James Wright from Ger. 128p. 1972. pap. 5.95 (ISBN 0-374-50975-1, N420). FS&G.
Wandering Beauty: Or, The Temptations of a Great City. Florence Blackburn White Schoeffel. LC 8-2041. 1891. Munro's Publishing House.
Wandering Beggar: Or, The Adventures of Simple Shmerel. Solomon Simon & Simon, David, 1924- Tr. LC 42-16053. 1942. Behrman's Jewish Book House.
Wandering Dogies. Wilbur C Tuttle. LC 38-675488. 1938. Houghton Mifflin Company.
Wandering Eye. Hugh Massingham. LC 54-5212. 1954. Sloane.
Wandering Eye. Jean Semple. 3.95 o.s.i. (ISBN 0-8181-0178-4). Pageant-Poseidon.
Wandering Fires. Dolf Wyllarde. LC 21-18093. 1921. John Lane Company.
Wandering Ghosts. Francis Marion Crawford. LC 11-5409. 1911. The Macmillan Company.
Wandering Heart. Louis Arthur Cunningham. LC 48-123617. 1947. Gramercy Pub. Co.
Wandering Heath. Stories, Studies, and Sketches. Arthur Thomas Quiller-Couch. LC 6-29007. 1895. C. Scribner's Sons.
Wandering Heir. Charles Reade. LC 48-44539. (works of Charles Reade. Library ed.). 1895. Metropolitan Pub. Co.
Wandering Heir. Charles Reade. 1873. J. R. Osgood and Company.
Wandering Heir. A Novel. Charles Reade. LC 9-19673. 1873. Harper & Brothers.
Wandering in the Garden, Waking from a Dream: Tales of Taipei Characters. Hsien-Yung Pai & George Kao. LC 81-47165. (Chinese Literature in Translation). 1982. 25.00 (ISBN 0-253-19981-6) (ISBN 0-253-20276-0). Indiana University Press.
Wandering Jew. Eugene Sue. LC 8-17670. 1846. Harper & Brothers.
Wandering Jew. Eugene Sue. (Seaside library, v. 7, no. 129). 1877. G. Munro.
Wandering Jew. Eugene Sue. LC 9-2501. 1889. G. Routledge and Sons.
Wandering Jew. Eugene Sue. LC 4-17509. A. L. Burt Company.
Wandering Jew. Eugene Sue. LC 8-26622. 1903. The Century Co.
Wandering Jew. Eugene Sue. LC 40-27707. (Half-title: The modern library of the world's best books. Modern library giants). 1940. The Modern Library.
Wandering Jew in America. A Novel. William Macon Coleman. J. G. Hester.
Wandering Jews: By Eugene Sue... Reprinted from the Original Chapman and Hall Ed. Eugene Sue. LC 12-22073. T. Y. Crowell & Company.
Wandering Minstrel: The Life Story of Cagliardo Coraggioso. Cagliardo Coraggioso. LC 39-802337. 1938. Oxford University Press.
Wandering of Desire. 1st Ed. Marion Montgomery. LC 62-7900. Harper.
Wandering Osprey. Mackinder, Dorothy. LC 48-289586. 1948. Bruce Pub. Co.
Wandering Prince. Eleanor Hibbert. (Crest bk., M1771). 1972. 0.95. Fawcett.
Wandering Prince. Eleanor Hibbert. LC 74-174737. 1971. 6.95. Putnam.
Wandering Prince. Jean Plaidy. 1971. 6.95 o.p. (ISBN 0-399-10850-5). Putnam Pub Group.
Wandering Sea Gull. Brone Martin. Tr. by Jonas Zdanys from Lithuanian. 1979. 9.50 o.p. (ISBN 0-682-49436-4). Exposition.
Wandering Star. Shalom Rabinowitz. LC 52-568584. 1952. Crown Publishers.
Wandering Stars: An Anthology of Jewish Fantasy and Science Fiction. Ed. by Jack Dann. LC 73-4146. (Illus.). 1974. 6.95 (ISBN 0-06-010944-0). Harper & Row.
Wandering Stars: An Anthology of Jewish Fantasy and Science Fiction. Ed. by Jack Dann. 1975. (pbk.) 1.50. Pocket Books.
Wandering Stars: Together with The Lover. Winifred Ashton. 1924. The Macmillan Company.
Wandering Through Winter. Edwin W. Teale. LC 65-23773. (Illus.). 1965. 10.00 o.p. (ISBN 0-396-05190-1). Dodd.
Wandering Unicorn: A Novel. Manuel M. Lanez. Tr. by Mary Fitton from Span. LC 82-19598. 1983. 16.95 (ISBN 0-8008-8041-2). Taplinger.
Wandering Widows: By E. X. Ferrars Pseud. 1st American Ed. Morna Doris MacTaggart Brown. LC 62-15945. 1962. Published for the Crime Club by Doubleday.
Wandering Women. John Cournos. LC 30-25823. (Paper books). 1930. C. Boni.
Wanderings. Robert Herrick. LC 25-16720. Harcourt, Brace and Company.
Wanderings. Chaim Potok. 576p. 1980. pap. 3.95 (ISBN 0-449-24270-6, Crest). Fawcett.
Wanderings see Collected Works.
Wanderings and Adventures of Reuben Delano: Being a Narrative of Twelve Years' Life in a Whale Ship. Now First Published ... 1846. H. Long & Brother.
Wanderings and Fortunes of Some German Emigrants. Friedrich Wilhelm Christian Gerstacker. Tr. by Black, David. LC 6-44072. 1848. D. Appleton & Company.
Wanderings of a Vagabond. An Autobiography. John O'Connor. 1873. The Author.
Wanderings of French Ed: And Other Stories. Joseph Adelard Rene. 1899. Wright & Company.
Wanderings of William: Or The Inconstancy of Youth. Being a Sequel to The Farmer of New-Jersey. A Tale. John Davis. LC 6-39310. 1801. Printed for R. T. Rawle.
Wanderlight. Ernest Raymond. LC 24-18098. 1924. Cassell and Company, Ltd.
Wander's Voyage. Roland Green. LC 79-51253. 1979. 1.95 (ISBN 0-380-44271-X). Avon.
Wandorer. Mika Toimi Waltari. LC 51-13622. 1951. Putnam.
Wandor's Flight. Roland Green. 368p. 1981. pap. 2.75 (ISBN 0-380-77834-3, 77834). Avon.
Wandor's Journey. Roland Green. 1975. (pbk.) 0.95 (ISBN 0-380-00328-7). Avon.
Wandor's Ride. Roland Green. 1973. pap. 1.95 (ISBN 0-380-00575-1, 45658). Avon.
Wandor's Voyage. Roland Green. 1975. pap. 1.95 (ISBN 0-380-44271-X, 44271). Avon.
Wane of an Ideal: A Novel. Maria Antoinette Torelli-Viollier & Courtenay, Mrs. Clara (Poynter) 1834-1927, Tr. 1885. W. S. Gottsberger.
Wang the Ninth: The Story of a Chinese Boy. Bertram Lenox Simpson. LC 20-16797. Dodd, Mead and Company.
Wanita: A Novel by Mrs. Laura Gwyn... Laura Gwyn. LC 6-46691. 1880. Walker, Evans & Cogswell.
Wanneta, the Sioux: By Warren K. Moorehead... with Illustrations from Life. Warren King Moorehead. LC 7-17262. Dodd. Mead and Company.
Want Ad Heiress. Rob Eden. LC 35-472444. J. H. Hopkins & Son.
Wanted! Ed. by Eric Seidman. 1980. pap. 8.95 (ISBN 0-553-01224-X). Bantam.
Wanted--a Chaperon. Paul Leicester Ford. 1902. Dodd, Mead & Company.
Wanted--a Match Maker. Paul Leicester Ford. 1900. Dodd, Mead & Company.
Wanted--a Pedigree. Martha Finley. LC 11-7152. W.B. Evans & Co.
Wanted--a Sensation: A Saratoga Incident. Edward Sims Van Zile. LC 8-30214. (On cover: Cassell's "rainbow" series of original novels, no. 21). Cassell & Company.
Wanted--a Sensation: A Saratoga Incident. Edward Sims Van Zile. LC 8-30213. (On cover: Cassell's "rainbow" series of original novels, no. 21). 1889. Cassell & Company, Limited.
Wanted--a Sensation: A Saratoga Incident. Edward Sims Van Zile. (On cover: Princess series, no. 15). Street & Smith.
Wanted--a Wife (Lo Cerco Moglie) Alfredo Panzini & Cooper, Frederic Taber, 1864- Tr. LC 22-17456. 1922. N. L. Brown.
Wanted--Dead or Alive! Gordon Ray Young. LC 49-8977. (Double D western). 1949. Doubleday.
Wanted--Love. Ethelda Bedford. LC 32-23136. Grosset & Dunlap.
Wanted, a Copyist. William Henry Brearley. LC 6-17931. (Half-title: The "unkown" library v. 33). The Cassell Publishing Co.
Wanted; a Husband: A Novel. Samuel Hopkins Adams. LC 20-7140. 1920. Houghton Mifflin Company.
Wanted; a Murderess. Marion Holbrook. LC 43-14289. 1943. Dodd, Mead & Company.
Wanted a Tortoise Shell. Peter Blundell. LC 17-30355. 1917. John Lane.
Wanted: Dead Men. M. E. Chaber, pseud. (Milo March Mysteries). 1970. pap. 0.60 o.p. (63-460). Paperback Lib.
Wanted: Dead Men. M. E. Chaber, pseud. (Rinehart Suspense Novel). 1965. 3.50 o.p. (ISBN 0-03-051155-0). HR&W.
Wanted: Dead Men: A New Milo March Adventure. Kendell Foster Crossen. LC 65-14448. 1965. Holt, Rinehart and Winston.
Wanted for Killing. John Brennan. LC 67-10080. (Rinehart suspense novel). 1967. Holt, Rinehart and Winston.
Wanted for Killing. John Welcome, pseud. (Rinehart Suspense Novel Ser). 1967. 3.95 o.p. (ISBN 0-03-060305-6). Hr&W.
Wanted for Murder. George G. Gilman, pseud. (Steele Ser.: No. 20). 192p. 1982. pap. 1.95 (ISBN 0-523-41453-6). Pinnacle Bks.
Wanted for Murder. Nancy Rutledge. 1956. Random House.

Wanted for Murder: The Further Adventures of Simon Templar... Leslie Charteris. LC 31-22902. Pub. for the Crime Club, Inc., by Doubleday, Doran & Company, Inc.
Wanted Man. Henry Cecil. 1974. 6.95 o.s.i. (ISBN 0-8277-3346-1). British Bk Ctr.
Wanted: The Heart of a Red-Headed Woodpecker: An Anthology of Stories on Eastern Oklahoma. 2nd ed. Claire Woodward. LC 81-90659. (Illus.). 60p. (Orig.). 1982. pap. 3.95 (ISBN 0-9606812-0-5). C Woodward.
Wanting Factor. Gene DeWeese. LC 80-82212. 304p. 1980. pap. 2.50 (ISBN 0-87216-693-7). Playboy Pbks.
Wanting of Levine. Michael Halberstam. LC 78-2650. 1978. 10.00 (ISBN 0-397-01093-1). Lippincott.
Wanting of Levine. Michael Halberstam. (Berkley book). 1979. 2.25 (ISBN 0-425-04088-7). Berkley Pub. Corp.
Wanting Seed. Anthony Burgess. LC 76-365107. (Norton library; N808). 1976. 2.95. Norton.
Wanting Seed. John Anthony Burgess Wilson. LC 63-15877. 1963. W. W. Norton.
Wanton Boys. Michael Sidney Tyler-Whittle. LC 59-14417. 1959. Doubleday.
Wanton Boys. 1st American Ed. Mark Oliver, pseud. LC 59-14417. 1959. Doubleday.
Wanton Fires. Meriol Trevor. LC 79-55174. 1979. 8.95 (ISBN 0-525-22982-5). Dutton.
Wanton Mally. Booth Tarkington. LC 32-28094. 1932. Doubleday, Doran & Company, Inc.
Wanton Princess. Dennis Yates Wheatley. 1979. 9.95 (ISBN 0-09-105330-7, Pub by Hutchinson). Merrimack Pub Cir.
Wanton Shack-Up. Jackson Harmon. (Orig.). pap. 0.95 o.p. (1129). Brandon.
Wanton Summer Air. Samuel Hazo. LC 82-81479. 224p. 1982. 15.50 (ISBN 0-86547-085-5). N Point Pr.
Wanton Venus. Maurice Leblanc. Tr. by Ross, Patience. LC 35-31970. The Macaulay Company.
Wanton Way. Norah C James. LC 31-28023. 1931. W. Morrow & Co.
Wantons. Marcus Van Heller, pseud. pap. 1.75 o.p. (3006). Brandon.
Wapiti Pete: The Story of an Elk. Hal Glen Borland. LC 38-27846. Farrar & Rinehart, Incorporated.
Wapoose. Zack Cartwright. LC 28-749722. H. Holt and Company.
Wapshot Chronicle. John Cheever. LC 56-11100. (Perennial Lib., P295). (Illus.). 1973. (pbk.) 1.25 (ISBN 0-06-080295-2). Harper.
Wapshot Chronicle, the Wapshot Scandal. John Cheever. LC 79-1806. 1979. 15.00 (ISBN 0-06-010741-3). Harper & Row.
Wapshot Scandal. John Cheever. (S2882). 1965. Bantam.
Wapshot Scandal. Cheever, John. LC 63-20301. (Perennial Lib., P296). 1973. (pbk.) 1.25 (ISBN 0-06-080296-0). Harper.
Wapsipinicon Tales. Jay G Sigmund. LC 27-10728. The Prairie Publishing Company.
War. Jean Marie Gustave Le Clezio. LC 72-94243. 1973. 6.95 (ISBN 0-689-10547-9). Atheneum.
War. Arnold Friedrich Vieth von Golssenau. LC 29-15288. 1929. Dodd, Mead & Company.
War Above the Timberline. Jesse Edward Grinstead. LC 39-24575. Dodge Publishing Company.
War Against the Chtorr, Vol. 1: A Matter for Men. David Gerrold. 1983. 16.95 (ISBN 0-671-46493-0, Timescape); pap. 6.95 (ISBN 0-671-46494-9, Timescape). PB.
War Against the Mafia. Don Pendleton. (Executioner Ser.: No. 1). 192p. 1982. pap. 2.25 (ISBN 0-523-41065-4). Pinnacle Bks.
War Against the Rull. Alfred Elton Van Vogt. LC 59-13144. 1959. Simon and Schuster.
War Among Ladies. Eleanor Scott. LC 28-17206. 1928. Little, Brown, and Company.
War and After. first ed. Terrence Hill. 1972. 3.95 (ISBN 0-533-00271-0). Vantage.
War and Consequences. 1st Ed. George T Nagengast. LC 58-14880. 1958. Pageant Press.
War & Passion. Leslie Arlen. (Borodins Ser.: No. 2). 368p. (Orig.). 1981. pap. 2.75 (ISBN 0-515-05481-X). Jove Pubns.
War and Peace. Lev Nikolaevich Tolstoi. LC 68-31472. (Signet classic CJ404). 1968. 1.95. New American Library.
War and Peace. Tolstoi, Lev Nikolaevich. LC 56-10503. (Bantam books, S1497 7). Bantam Books)
War and Peace. Lev Nikolaevich Tolstoi. LC 62-1889. 1962. Heritage Press.
War and Peace. Lev Nikolaevich Tolstoi. LC 49-38009. Carlton House.
War and Peace. Lev Nikolaevich Tolstoi. Ed. by Maugham, William Somerset. LC 49-11244. (Ten Greatest Novels of the World). 1949. Winston.
War & Peace. Lev Nikolaevich Tolstoi. (Half-title: Everyman's library, ed. by Ernest Rhys. Fiction. (no. 525-527)). 1911. J. M.Dent & Sons, Ltd.
War & Peace, Vol. I. Lev Nikolaevich Tolstoi. 1976. 9.95x (ISBN 0-460-00525-1, Evman). Biblio Dist.
War & Peace, Vol. II. Lev Nikolaevich Tolstoi. 1976. 9.95x (ISBN 0-460-00526-X, Evman). Biblio Dist.
War & Peace, Vol. III. Lev Nikolaevich Tolstoi. 1976. 9.95x (ISBN 0-460-00527-8, Evman). Biblio Dist.
War & Peace. Lev Nikolaevich Tolstoi. Tr. by Garnett Constance. 1931. 9.95 (ISBN 0-394-60475-X). Modern Lib.
War & Peace. Lev Nikolaevich Tolstoi. Tr. by Ann Dunnigan. (Orig.). 1968. pap. 4.95 (ISBN 0-451-51661-3, CE1661, Sig Classics). NAL.
War & Peace. Lev Nikolaevich Tolstoi. 14.95 o.p. (ISBN 0-19-250898-9). Oxford U Pr.
War & Peace, 1 vol. ed. Lev Nikolaevich Tolstoi. 1982. pap. 8.95 (ISBN 0-14-044417-3). Penguin.
War & Peace. Lev Nikolaevich Tolstoi. Tr. by Constance Garnett. LC 76-6103. (Apollo Eds.). 1976. pap. 6.95i (ISBN 0-8152-0397-7, A397). T Y Crowell.
War & Peace. abr. ed. Lev Nikolaevich Tolstoi. Ed. by Ernest J. Simmons. 656p. (gr. 10 up). pap. 3.95 (ISBN 0-671-41893-9). WSP.
War & Peace. Lev Nikolaevich Tolstoi. 1982. pap. 10.00x (ISBN 0-330-02950-9, Pub. by Pan Bks). State Mutual Bk.
War & Peace. Lev Nikolaevich Tolstoi. 4.95 o.p. (ISBN 0-448-01072-0). G&D.
War & Peace. Lev Nikolaevich Tolstoi. Ed. by Alfred Neumann et al. (Illus.). 6.50 o.p. (ISBN 0-261-61789-3). Dufour.
War & Peace. Lev Nikolaevich Tolstoi. (Vol. 2). 3.95x o.p. (ISBN 0-460-00526-X, Evman). Dutton.
War & Peace. Lev Nikolaevich Tolstoi. (Rus.). 1945. 12.00 o.p. (ISBN 0-8236-6785-5). Intl Univs Pr.
War and Peace. Lev Nikolaevich Tolstoi & Dole, Nathan Haskell, 1852-1935, Tr. T. Y. Crowell & Co.
War and Peace. Lev Nikolaevich Tolstoi & Constance Black Garnett. LC 76-6103. 1976. 10.00. (ISBN 0-690-01108-3) (ISBN 0-8152-0397-7). Crowell.
War and Peace. Lev Nikolaevich Tolstoi & Garnett, Mrs. Constance (Black) 1862- LC 11-14411. 1911. John Lanecompany.
War and Peace. Lev Nikolaevich Tolstoi & Garnett, Mrs. Constance (Black) 1862- Tr. LC 31-281641. (Half-title: The modern library of the world's best books). 1931. The Modern Library.
War and Peace. Lev Nikolaevich Tolstoi & Maude, Louise (Shanks) 1855-1939, Tr. LC 44-8544. 1943. The Heritage Press.
War and Peace. Lev Nikolaevich Tolstoi & Maude, Mrs. Louise (Shanks) 1855-1939, Tr. LC 42-36201. Simon and Schuster.
War & Peace, Vol. 1. rev. ed. Lev Nikolaevich Tolstoi. Tr. by Rosemary Edmonds from Rus. (Classics Ser). 1978. pap. 4.95 (ISBN 0-14-044062-3). Penguin.
War & Peace, Vol. 2. rev. ed. Lev Nikolaevich Tolstoi. Tr. by Rosemary Edmonds from Rus. (Classics Ser). 1978. pap. 4.95 (ISBN 0-14-044063-1). Penguin.
War and Peace: A Historical Novel. Lev Nikolaevich Tolstoi & Bell, Clara, Tr. 1886. W. S. Gottsberger.
War and Peace. A Historical Novel. Lev Nikolaevich Tolstoi & Bell, Mrs. Clara Courtenay (Poynter) 1834- Tr. (Harper's Franklin square library, no. 508, 521, 521a). 1886. Harper & Brothers.
War and Peace: A Novel. Lev Nikolaevich Tolstoi. LC 52-78279. (World's classics, 233). 1951. Oxford University Press.
War and Peace: A Novel. Lev Nikolaevich Tolstoi & Napoleon I--Invasion of Russia, 1812--Fiction. LC 24-4706. (Half-title: The world's classics, CCXXXIII CCXXXIV, CCXXXV). 1922-23. H. Milford, Oxford University Press.
War and Peace: A Novel, Translated from the Russian by Constance Garnett. Tolstoi, Lev Nikolaevich. LC 56-58633. (Modern library of the world's best books). Random House.
War and Peace: Novel. Tolstoi, Lev Nikolaevich. LC 58-396. (Penguin classics, L62-63). 1957. Penguin Books.
War and Peace. Translated by Constance Garnett. The Authoritative Modern Abridgment by Edmund Fuller. Lev Nikolaevich Tolstoi. LC 55-117593. (Dell book, F53). 1955. Dell Pub. Co.
War & Rememberance. Herman Wouk. LC 78-16490. 1978. 17.50 (ISBN 0-316-95501-9). Little.
War and Remembrance. Herman Wouk. LC 78-17746. 15.00 (ISBN 0-316-95501-9). Little, Brown.
War and Remembrance. Herman Wouk. 3.95 (ISBN 0-671-81638-1).
War and the Woman. Max Pemberton. LC 12-13489. 1912. 1.25. Cassell and Company, Ltd.
War and War. Frederick Barthelme. LC 70-100045. (Doubleday projections books). (Illus.). 1971. 3.50. Doubleday.
War Babies. Gwen Davis. LC 66-13116. 1966. Coward-McCann.
War Beneath the Sea. Frank Bonham. LC 62-12811. 1962. Crowell.
War Between Men & Women. Henry Clemons. 1972. pap. 0.75 o.p. (07230). Curtis.
War Between the Tates. Alison Lurie. LC 73-20437. 1974. 6.95 (ISBN 0-394-46201-7). Random House.
War Bonnet: A Novel of Mountain Man War and Arapaho Intrigue Along the Old Medicine Road, by Clay Fisher Pseud. Henry Allen. LC 52-11830. 1953. Houghton Mifflin.
War Bonnet; a Novel of Mountain Man War and Arapaho Intrigue Along the Old Medicine Road. Clay Fisher. LC 52-11830. 1953. Houghton Mifflin.
War Bonnet Pass: By Logan Stewart Pseud. Les Savage. LC 51-17379. (Gold medal book, 137). 1950. Fawcett Publications.
War Breaks Down Doors. John Nesmith Greely. LC 29-25613. Hale, Cushman & Flint.
War Brides. Lois Battle. LC 82-7347. 13.95 (ISBN 0-89621-374-9). Thorndike Press.
War Bride's Adventure: An Interview with St. Peter. Florence Marie Telmany Von Kubinyi. LC 17-24799. 1916. 0.75. The Seemore Co.
War Cache. Wilfrid Douglas Newton. LC 18-454980. 1918. D. Appleton and Company.
War Casualty. Emil Dionne. LC 51-1524. Story Book Press.
War Chief. Edgar Rice Burroughs. LC 27-21142. 1927. A. C. McClurg & Co.
War Chief. Edgar Rice Burroughs. LC 78-13062. (Gregg Press Western Fiction Series). 1978. 9.95 (ISBN 0-8398-2453-X). Gregg Press.
War Chief. Donald Clayton Porter. LC 83-169. (White Indian series; bk. 3). ((Series: Porter, Donald Clayton.). (Colonization of America series; bk. 3.). 1983. 19.95 (ISBN 0-8161-3448-0). G.K. Hall.
War Chief. Donald Clayton Porter. (Colonization of America Ser.). 384p. (Orig.). 1980. pap. 2.95 (ISBN 0-553-14069-8). Bantam.
War Chief. Donald Clayton Porter. (Readers Request Ser.). 1983. lib. bdg. 19.95 (ISBN 0-8161-3448-0, Large Print Bks). G K Hall.
War Chiefs: A Story of the Spanish Conquerors in Santo Domingo. Frederick Albion Ober. LC 4-21655. 1904. E. P. Dutton and Company.
War Comes to Castle Rising. Phyllis Cradock. LC 78-60715. 1978. 9.95 (ISBN 0-525-23009-2). E. P. Dutton.
War Country. William Oliver Turner. LC 57-11339. 1957. Houghton Mifflin.
War Crisis on Horseback. Stephen Longstreet. Repr. lib. bdg. 18.30x (ISBN 0-89190-143-4). Am Repr-Rivercity Pr.
War Cry. Donald Clayton Porter. 1983. pap. 3.50. Bantam.
War Cry of the Sioux: A Historical Romance from the Sioux Outbreak of 1862. Eddy E Billberg. The Christopher Publishing House.
War Cry of the South: A Historical Novel of the Construction and Battles of the Rebel Ram, Abermarle. 1st Ed. W Frank Landing. LC 59-4266. Exposition Press.
War Dance Home. Richard Jessup. 1970. price not set o.p. Little.
War Detective: Or, The Plotters at Washington. A Tale of Booth's Conspiracy. A F Grant. LC 6-44742. (War library Pocket ed. no. 1). 1883. Novelist Publishing Co.
War Detective: Or, The Plotters at Washington. A Tale of Booth's Conspiracy. By Major A. F. Grant Pseud. Thomas Chalmers Harbaugh. LC 6-44742. (War library Pocket ed. no.1). 1883. Novelist Publishing Co.
War Drums. Herbert Ravenel Sass. LC 28-12651. 1928. Doubleday, Doran & Company, Inc.
War Eagle: A Contemporary Novel. William James Dawson. LC 18-163713. 1918. John Lane Company.
War Eternal. Jacob Jankelson. LC 34-37087. 1934. Meador Publishing Company.
War for Independence. Everett Titsworth Tomlinson. (Stories of colony and nation.). Silver, Burdett and Company.
War from the Clouds. Nick Cater. 224p. (Orig.). 1980. pap. 2.25 (ISBN 0-441-87192-5, Pub. by Charter Bks). Ace Bks.
War Game. Anthony Price. LC 77-354920. 1976. 3.75 (ISBN 0-575-02211-6). Gollancz.
War-Gamers' World. Hugh Walker. (Science Fiction Ser.). 1978. pap. 1.50 o.p. (ISBN 0-87997-416-8, UW1416). DAW Bks.
War Games. David F. Bischoff. (Orig.). 1983. pap. 2.95 (ISBN 0-440-19387-7). Dell.
War Games. Karl Hansen. LC 80-85104. 288p. (Orig.). 1981. pap. 2.50 (ISBN 0-87216-837-9). Playboy Pbks.
War Games. Wright Morris. LC 72-175327. 1972. (ISBN 0-87685-109-X) (ISBN 0-87685-108-1). Black Sparrow Press.
War Games. Wright Morris. LC 78-5603. 1978. 9.95 (ISBN 0-8032-0950-9) (ISBN 0-8032-5878-X). University of Nebraska Press.
War Games. James Park Sloan. LC 77-124357. 1971. 4.95. Hougton Mifflin.
War Games of Zelos. Richard Avery. (Expendables). (Fawcett Gold Medal Book: Vol. 3). 1975. (pbk.) 1.25. Fawcett.
War God. Frederick Escreet Smith. 336p. (Orig.). 1981. pap. 2.75 (ISBN 0-553-13663-1). Bantam.
War Goes on. Shalom Asch & Muir, Mrs. Willa, Tr. LC 36-285413. 1936. G. P. Putnam's Sons.
War Horses. Bill Bragg. 1.75 (ISBN 0-505-51511-3). Belmont Tower Books.
War Hound & the World's Pain. Michael Moorcock. 1982. pap. 2.50 (Timescape). PB.
War Hound and the World's Pain, a Fable. Michael Moorcock. LC 81-9030. 12.95 (ISBN 0-671-43708-9). Timescape Books.
War in Heaven. Philip Barry. LC 38-37582. Coward McCann.
War in Heaven. Charles Williams. LC 49-100111. 1949. Pellegrini & Cudahy.
War in Heaven see Novels.
War in Sandoval County. Wayne D Overholser. LC 60-5056. (Bantam western, 2032/2). 1960. Bantam Books.
War in the Air: And Particularly How Mr. Bert Smallways Fared While It Lasted. Herbert George Wells. LC 8-30615. 1908. The Macmillan Company.
War in the Air, in the Days of the Comet & the Food of the Gods. Herbert George Wells. 4.00 o.p. Peter Smith.
War in the Golden Weather. Stephen Longstreet. LC 65-13994.
War in the Golden Weather: A Novel. Stephen Longstreet. LC 65-139946. 5.95. Doubleday.
War in the Golden Weather: A Novel. LC 65-13994.
War in the Painted Buttes: A Powder Valley Western. Peter Field. LC 54-101959. 1954. Jefferson House.
War in the Panhandle. Roe Richmond. (Orig.). 1979. pap. 1.50 (ISBN 0-532-15392-8). Woodhill.
War Is Heaven! D. Keith Mano. LC 75-97671. 1970. 5.95. Doubleday.
War Is War. Ex-Private X. LC 30-17510. 1930. E. P. Dutton & Co., Inc.
War Journey. Fred Grove. LC 77-144269. (Doubleday western). 1971. 4.95. Doubleday.
War Lightning. Richard R. Ackley. 124p. 1975. 5.00 o.p. (ISBN 0-8059-2197-4). Dorrance.
War Lover. John Richard Hersey. LC 59-13177. 1959. Knopf.
War Machines of Kalinth. Gene Lancour. LC 76-40883. 1977. 5.95 (ISBN 0-385-12660-3). Doubleday.
War, Madame... Paul Geraldy. Tr. by Blake, Barton. LC 17-8886. 1917. C. Scribner's Sons.
War Maker: A Novel. Hillgarth, Alan. LC 26-24564. 1926. T. Nelson & Sons, Ltd.
War Memorial. Martin Russ. LC 67-11993. 1967-1966. Atheneum.
War Nurse: The True Story of a Woman Who Lived, Loved and Suffered on the Western Front. LC 30-11615. 1930. Cosmopolitan Book Corporation.
War of Camp Omongo. Burt Blechman. LC 63-9348. 1963. Random House.
War of Dreams. Angela Carter. LC 74-1157. 1974. 6.95. Harcourt Brace Jovanovich.
War of Dreams. Angela Carter. (Bard Book)). 1977. 1.95 (ISBN 0-380-00933-1). Avon Books.
War of Nerves. Paul Brickhill. 1963. 3.95 o.p. Morrow.
War of Nerves. Robert Graham. (Attar the Merman, #2). 1975. (pbk.) 0.95 (ISBN 0-671-77989-3). Pocket Books.
War of Powers: In the Shadow of Omizatrim, Bk. 5. Robert E. Vardeman & Victor Milan. 224p. 1981. pap. 2.50 (ISBN 0-87216-999-5, Playboy). Putnam Pub Group.
War of Shadows. William Stanley Moss. LC 52-8992. (Illus.). 1952. Macmillan.
War of the Buttons. Louis Pergaud. LC 68-28352. 1968. 5.95. Walker.
War of the Cybernauts. Alex Raymond. (Flash Gordon no. 6). 1975. (pbk.) 0.95 (ISBN 0-380-00206-X). Avon.
War of the Dons. Peter Rabe. (Orig.). 1972. pap. 0.95 o.p. (M2592, GM). Fawcett World.
War of the Running Fox. Robert Langley. LC 78-15445. 8.95 (ISBN 0-684-15918-X). Scribner.
War of the Wenuses. Charles Larcom Graves & Edward Verrall Lucas. LC 74-15979. (Science Fiction). 1975. 8.00 (ISBN 0-405-06293-1). Arno Press.
War of the Wing-Men. Poul Anderson. 1973. (pbk) 0.95. Ace Books.
War of the Wing-Men. Poul Anderson. LC 76-10743. (Gregg Press science fiction series). 1976. 9.00 (ISBN 0-8398-2326-6). Gregg Press.
War of the Worlds. Herbert George Wells. LC 66-1310. (Airmont classic). Airmont Pub. Co.
War of the Worlds. Herbert George Wells. LC 64-5499. 1964. Heritage Press.
War of the Worlds. Herbert George Wells. LC 64-5024. 1964. Limited Editions Club.

War of the Worlds. Herbert George Wells. LC 60-13060. (Looking glass library, 21). (Illus.). 1960. Epstein and Carroll Associates; Distributed by Random House.
War of the Worlds. Herbert George Wells. LC 24-22215. 1922. Harper & Brothers.
War of the Worlds & the Time Machine. Herbert George Wells. pap. 1.95 o.p. (ISBN 0-385-08274-6, Dolp). Doubleday.
War of the Worlds and the Time Machine. Adapted. Herbert George Wells. LC 56-14695. 1956. Globe Book Co.
War of the Worlds: By H. G. Wells... Herbert George Wells. LC 20-16467. Harper & Brothers.
War of the Worlds, The Time Machine, and Selected Short Stories. complete and unabridged. ed. Herbert George Wells. LC 63-14325. (Great writers collection). 1963. Platt & Munk.
War of the Xromabids: The MHT Alternative. John Hunter-Blair. 1974. 5.95 (ISBN 0-533-00950-2). Vantage Press.
War of Time. Alejo Carpentier. LC 70-98667. 1970. 4.95. Knopf.
War of Women. Alexandre Dumas. LC 16-9384. (Half-title: The romances of Alexandre Dumas. Handy library edition). Little, Brown, and Company.
War of 1938. Sydney Fowler Wright. LC 36-5513. G. P. Putnam's Sons.
War on Alkali Creek. Lee Floren. 1970. pap. 0.50 o.p. (50-502). Manor Bks.
War on Alkali Creek: By Will Watson Pseud. Lee Floren. LC 51-13759. 1951. Phoenix Press.
War on Charity Ross. Jack M Bickham. LC 67-21848. 1967. Doubleday.
War on Charity Ross. Jack M Bickham. 1976. (pbk.) 1.25. Ace Books.
War on the Cimarron. Frederick Dilley Glidden. LC 40-30408. 1940. Doubleday, Doran and Company, Inc.
War on the Cimarron. Luke Short. LC 76-48107. 1977. 8.95 (ISBN 0-89340-037-8). J. Curley.
War on the Cimarron. Luke Short. LC 40-30408. 1940. Doubleday, Doran and Company, Inc.
War on the Lazy K. William K Reilly, pseud. LC 46-2502. 1946. Phoenix Press.
War on the Range. Jesse Edward Grinstead. LC 41-5496. Dodge Publishing Company.
War on the Saddle Rock: By Will Ermine Pseud. Harry Sinclair Drago. LC 53-9783. (Triple-A western classic). 1953. Jefferson House.
War on the Webfoot Saloon & Other Tales of Feminine Adventures. Malcolm Clark, Jr. & Kenneth W. Porter. (Illus.). 54p. 1969. pap. 2.95 (ISBN 0-87595-023-X). Oreg Hist Soc.
War on Wishbone Range. Charles Alden Seltzer. LC 74-21539. 1974. (ISBN 0-88411-106-7). Aeonian Press.
War on Wishbone Range. Charles Alden Seltzer. LC 32-200471. 1932. Doubleday, Doran & Company, Inc.
War: Or What Happens When One Loves One's Enemy. John Luther Long. LC 13-7524. 1.30. The Bobbs-Merrill Company.
War Outside Ireland: A Novel. Michael Joyce. LC 82-80497. 8.50. Tinkers Dam Press.
War Paint. Dane Coolidge. LC 29-224578. E. P. Dutton & Company, Inc.
War Paint and Rouge. Robert William Chambers. LC 31-24773. 1931. D. Appleton and Company.
War Party. John Benteen. (Sundance Ser.: No. 14). 1974. pap. 1.50 o.p. (ISBN 0-8439-1009-7, Leisure Bks). Nordon Pubns.
War Party. John Benteen. (Sundance: No. 14). 208p. 1981. pap. 1.95 (ISBN 0-8439-1009-7). Leisure Bks CT.
War Party. Max Brand. LC 81-38502. 1981. 12.50 (ISBN 0-8376-0460-5). R. Bentley.
War Party. John S. Daniels, pseud. Bd. with Crossing. 1979. pap. 1.95 (ISBN 0-451-08761-5, J8761, Sig). Norton.
War Party. Frederick Faust. LC 72-7754. (Silver star westerns). 1973. 4.95 (ISBN 0-396-06741-7). Dodd, Mead.
War Party. Louis L'Amour. 1975. (pbk.) 0.95. Bantam Books.
War Phases According to Maria. Anna Eichberg Lane. LC 17-6332. 1917. 1.00. John Lane.
War Prayer. Mark Twain. (Illus.). 1971. pap. 1.25 o.p. (ISBN 0-06-080221-9, P221, PL). Har-Row.
War Prayer. Mark Twain. pap. 1.50 o.p. (ISBN 0-06-090197-7, CN197, CN). Har-Row.
War Reporter. Warren Edwards. (On cover: Flag ser. no. 7). Street & Smith.
War Song. M. J. Naparsteck. (Orig.). 1980. pap. 1.75 o.s.i. (ISBN 0-8439-0729-0). Nordon Pubns.
War? Stories. Ed. by Alex Austin. LC 57-590636. (Signet book. S1478). 1957. New American Library.
War! Stories. Ed. by Alex Austin. LC 57-59063. (Signet book. S1478). 1957. New American Library.
War Stories. Ed. by Roy Joseph Holmes. Starbuck, Arward, 1881- Joing Ed. LC 19-8805. Thomas Y. Crowell Company.
War Story. Gordon McGill. LC 79-28169. 8.95 (ISBN 0-440-09325-2). Delacorte Press.
War Story. Jim Morris. LC 78-14547. 12.95 (ISBN 0-87364-147-7). Sycamore Island Books.
War Terror: Further Adventures with Craig Kennedy, Scientific Detective. Arthur Benjamin Reeve. LC 15-6340. Hearst's International Library Co.
War Terror: Further Adventures with Craig Kennedy, Scientific Detective. Arthur Benjamin Reeve. LC 24-222105. 1922. Harper & Brothers.
War Tide. Anor Lin. LC 43-16876. 1943. The John Day Company.
War Tiger: Or, Adventures and Wonderful Fortunes of the Young Sea Chief and His Lad Chow: a Tale of the Conquest of China. William Dalton. LC 42-1412. J. Miller.
War Tiger: Or, Adventures and Wonderful Fortunes of the Young Sea Chief and His Lad Chow; a Tale of the Conquest of China... William Dalton. LC 1-29027. (Medal library, no. 76). 1900. Street & Smith.
War-Time in Our Street: The Story of Some Companies Behind the Firing Line. Annie Edith Foster Jameson. LC 17-307212. 1917. Hodder and Stoughton.
War-Time Wooing: A Story. Charles King. 1888. Harper & Brothers.
War-Time Wooing: A Story. Charles King. LC 16-7573. Harper & Brothers.
War to End Wars. Mollie Hardwick. LC 79-20283. 1980. 13.95 (ISBN 0-8161-6797-4). G. K. Hall.
War to End Wars. Mollie Hardwick. (Upstairs Downstairs#IV). 1975. (pbk.) 1.50. Dell.
War Toys: A Novel. Hampton Howard. LC 82-40008. 1983. 14.95 (ISBN 0-8128-2876-3). Stein and Day.
War Trail. John Benteen. 1976. pap. 1.25 o.s.i. (LB373ZK, Leisure Bks). Nordon Pubns.
War Trail. John Benteen. Leisure Books.
War-Trail Fort: Further Adventures of Thomas Fox and Pitamakan. James Willard Schultz. LC 21-15330. 1921. 1.75. Houghton Mifflin Company.
War Train: A Novel of 1916. Brown Meggs. LC 79-55612. (Illus.). 1981. 13.95 (ISBN 0-689-11052-9). Atheneum.
War Under Water. Serrano, Mrs. Mary Jane (Christie) D. 1923, Tr. (Cassell;s sunshine series, no. 122). Cassell Publishing Company.
War Was Better. Miodrag Bulatovic. 420p. 1972. 7.95 o.p. (ISBN 0-07-008846-2). McGraw.
War Wife. Renee Shann. LC 41-22670. Carlton House.
War Wife. Renee Shann. LC 42-50217. 1942. Triangle Books.
War Wings for Carol. Patricia O'Malley. LC 43-9190. 1943. Dodd, Mead & Company.
War with the News. Karel Capek. LC 75-5698. (Gregg Press science fiction series). 1975. 15.00 (ISBN 0-8398-2301-0). Gregg Press.
War with the Newts. Karel Capek. LC 75-41049. 1978. 19.00 (ISBN 0-404-14649-X). AMS Press.
War with the Newts. Karel Capek. (Berkley Medallion). 1.50 (ISBN 0-425-03168-3). Berkley.
War with the Robots. Harry Harrison. 1968. pap. 0.60 o.p. (X1898). Pyramid Pubns.
War-Workers. Edmee Elizabeth Monica De La Pasture. LC 18-18545. 1918. A. A. Knopf.
Warbonnet Law. Frank O'Rourke. Date not set. pap. 1.95 (ISBN 0-451-11131-1, AJ1131, Sig). NAL.
Ward Eight. Joseph Francis Dinneen. LC 76-6335. (Irish-Americans). 1977. 20.00 (ISBN 0-405-09331-4). Arno Press.
Ward Eight. Joseph Francis Dinneen. LC 36-22621. 1936. Harper & Brothers.
Ward I. Philip John Kent. LC 58-52357. (Milestone book). 1957. Comet Press Books.
Ward in Chancery: A Novel. Annie French Hector. (On cover: Appletons' town and country library, no. 134). 1894. D. Appleton and Company.
Ward of King Canute: A Romance of the Danish Conquest. Ottilia Adelina Liljencrantz. LC 6-14750. Small, Maynard & Co.
Ward of King Canute: A Romance of the Danish Conquest. Ottilia Adelina Liljencrantz. 1903. A. C. McClurg & Co.
Ward of Tecumseh. Crittenden Marriott. LC 14-179840. 1914. 1.25. J. B. Lippincott Company.
Ward of the King: A Romance. Katharine Sarah Gadsden Macquoid. LC 99-5288. 1899. F. M. Buckles & Company; Etc, Etc.
Ward of the Redskins. Sheba Hargreaves. LC 29-17826. 1929. Harper & Brothers.
Ward of the Sun King. Mildred Allen Butler. LC 79-100650. 1970. 4.95. Funk & Wagnalls.
Ward Seven. Valeriy Tarsis. Tr. by Katya Brown. pap. 1.25 o.p. (ISBN 0-525-47183-9). Dutton.
Ward Six & Other Short Novels. Anton Pavlovich Chekhov. Tr. by Ann Dunnigan. (Orig.). 1965. pap. 3.50 (ISBN 0-451-51690-7, CE1690, Sig Classics). NAL.
Ward Six: And Other Stories. Anton Pavlovich Chekhov. LC 66-279. (Signet classic, CT290). 1965. New American Library.
Ward Tales. Ellen Chivers Davies. LC 20-103692. (Half-title: On active service series). 1920. John Lane.
Ward Twenty. James Warner Bellah. LC 46-409. 1946. Doubleday & Company, Inc.
Ward 402. Ronald J Glasser. LC 73-79048. 1973. 6.95 (ISBN 0-8076-0691-X). G. Braziller.
Ward 7: An Autobiographical Novel. Tr. by Katya Brown. Valerii Tarsis. LC 65-240364. 3.50. Dutton.
Warden. Anthony Trollope. LC 56-2871. 1956.
Warden. Anthony Trollope. LC 51-8. 1950. Doric Books.
Warden. Anthony Trollope. (His The chronicies of Barsetshire, 1). 1962. Harcourt, Brace & World.
Warden. Anthony Trollope. LC 1-11831. 1862. Dick and Fitzgerald.
Warden. Anthony Trollope. LC 1-118321. (On cover: The seaside library. Pocket ed. no. 621). 1885. G. Munro.
Warden. Anthony Trollope. LC 4-24968. (On cover: The chronicles of Barsetshire. i). 1903. Dodd, Mead & Company.
Warden. Anthony Trollope. (Half-title: Everyman's library, ed. by Ernest Rhys. Fiction). 1907. J. M. Dent & Co.
Warden. Anthony Trollope. LC 31-281656. 1931. Houghton Mifflin Company.
Warden. Anthony Trollope. LC 38-16876. (Half-title: Everyman's library, ed. by Ernest Rhys. Fiction. no. 182). 1936. J. M. Dent & Sons, Ltd.
Warden. Anthony Trollope. LC 42-47282. 1931. The Book League of America.
Warden. Anthony Trollope & Gay, Robert Malcolm, 1879- Ed. LC 35-6277. (Half-title: The Doubleday-Doran series in literature, R. Shafer, general editor). Doubleday, Doran & Company, Inc.
Warden. Anthony Trollope & Myers, Jessie Du Val, Ed. LC 26-2816. (The Macmillan pocket classics). 1926. The Macmillan Company.
Warden. Anthony Trollope & David Skilton. LC 79-41035. (World's classics). 1979. 2.95 (ISBN 0-19-281506-7). Oxford University Press.
Warden. Anthony Trollope & Stevens, Edward Francis, 1866- Ed. LC 32-28183. 1932. Printed for Libraries.
Warden. Anthony Trollope & Thorold, Algar Labouchere, Ed. LC 12-39454. (new pocket library, vo. iv). 1902. John Lane.
Warden, and Barchester Towers. Anthony Trollope. Ed. by Louis Auchincloss. LC 67-1487. (Riverside editions, B97). 1966. Houghton Mifflin.
Warden: And Barchester Towers. Anthony Trollope. LC 36-10756. (Half-title: The modern library of the world's best books). The Modern Library.
Warden and Barchester Towers. Ed., Introd. by Louis Auchincloss. Anthony Trollope. (B97). pap., 1.95. Houghton.
Warden and Barchester Towers: With Contemporary Illus. from Trollope's Barsetshire Novels and a List of His Works Together with an Introd. and Anecdotal Captions by Marion E. Dodd. slightly abridged ed. Anthony Trollope. LC 48-9212. (Great Illustrated Classics). 1948. Dodd, Mead.
Warden of the Marches. Hilda Caroline Gregg. LC 3-136247. 1902. L. C. Page & Company.
Warden of the Marches: A Tale of Adventure on the Chinese Frontier of Tibet. Louis Margrath King. 1938. Houghton Mifflin Company.
Warden of the Smoke and Bells. 1st Ed. Richard Llewellyn. LC 56-11503. 1956. Doubleday.
Warden. With an Introd. by Ronald Knox. Illus. by Edward Ardizzone. Anthony Trollope. LC 52-148194. (Oxford Trollope. Crown ed.). 1952. Oxford University Press.
Wardens. Clark Howard. 1981. 2.75 (ISBN 0-425-04670-2). Berkley Publishing Corp.
Wardens: A Novel. Clark Howard. LC 78-13296. 9.95 (ISBN 0-399-90032-2). R. Marek.
Ward's Land: A Story of the Wards in Kansas in the Days of the Civil War. Jessica LaForge Bell. LC 67-26029. 1967. 10.00. Naylor.
Ward's Land: A Story of the Wards in Kansas in the Days of the Civil War. Jessica LaForge Bell. LC 67-26029. 1967. Naylor Co.
Wards of Liberty. Myra Kelly. LC 74-140332. (Short story index reprint series). (Illus.). 1970. Books for Libraries Press.
Wards of Liberty. Myra Kelly. 1907. The McClure Company.
Wards of Plotinus. A Novel. Eliza Meadows Shepherd Thorpe Hunt. LC 7-22748. (Franklin square library. no. 165). 1881. Harper & Brothers.
Wardship of Steepcoombe. Charlotte Mary Yonge. LC 9-34314. 1896. T. Whittaker.
Ware Case. George Pleydell. LC 13-8391. Hodder & Stoughton, George H. Doran Company.
Wares of Edgefield. Eliza Orne White. LC 9-25973. 1909. Houghton Mifflin Company.
Warfares of the Heart: Stories of the South. Allen Polk Houston. LC 18-518. The Branch Publishing Co.
Warfield Syndrome. Henry Denker. LC 80-29012. 12.95 (ISBN 0-399-12612-0). Putnam.
Wargrave Trust. Frances Christine Tiernan. LC 11-28367. 1912. Benziger Brothers.
Warhawk Patrol. Rutherford George Montgomery & Knight, Clayton, 1891- Illus. LC 44-852656. 1944. David McKay Company.
Warhead. F. Robert Baker. 304p. (Orig.). 1981. pap. 2.50 (ISBN 0-553-14790-0). Bantam.
Warhead. Noel Bertram Gerson. LC 78-103747. 1972. (445-00134-125) 1.25. Popular Lib.
Warhead. Noel Bertram Gerson. LC 78-103747. 1970. 6.95. Doubleday.
Warhorse. John M. Cunningham. 1972. pap. 0.95 o.p. (09130). Curtis.
Warhorse: A Novel of the Old West. John M. Cunningham. LC 56-729695. 1956. Macmillan.
Warhunter, No. 3: The Great Salt Lake Massacre. Scott Siegel. 1981. pap. 2.25 (ISBN 0-89083-785-6). Zebra.
Waring's Peril. Charles King. LC 16-13117. 1900. J. B. Lippincott Company.
Warleggan. Winston Graham. (Poldark Ser.: No. 4). 1977. pap. 1.95 (ISBN 0-345-26003-1). Ballantine.
Warleggan, 2 vols. Winston Graham. (Reader's Request Ser.). 1979. Set. lib. bdg. 17.95 (ISBN 0-8161-6679-X, Large Print Bks). G K Hall.
Warlock. J. M Flynn. 1976. (pbk.) 1.50. Pocket Books.
Warlock. Oakley M Hall. LC 58-9649. 1958. Viking Press.
Warlock. Oakley M Hall. LC 79-25080. 1980. 6.95 (ISBN 0-8032-7206-5). University of Nebraska Press.
Warlock. James Harrison. LC 81-9796. 6.95 (ISBN 0-440-59462-6). Delacorte Press/S. Lawrence.
Warlock. Dean R. Koontz. 1972. pap. 0.95 o.p. (75-386). Lancer.
Warlock. Ernest T. Martin. Ed. by David Kirkland. (Illus.). 352p. (Orig.). 1983. 9.50 o.p.; pap. 4.95 (ISBN 0-910759-00-6). Mars Pubns.
Warlock. Marc Olden. (Black Samurai). (Signet book: Vol. 6). 1975. (pbk.) 1.25. New American Library.
Warlock. Wilson Tucker. LC 67-12539. 1967. Published for the Crime Club by Doubleday.
Warlock: A Novel. James Harrison. LC 81-9796. 13.95 (ISBN 0-440-09462-3). Delacorte Press/S. Lawrence.
Warlock in Spite of Himself. Christopher Stasheff. LC 75-433. (Garland Library of Science Fiction). 1975. 11.00 (ISBN 0-8240-1436-7). Garland Pub.
Warlock O' Glenwarlock. A Homely Romance. George Macdonald. LC 9-4967. 1881. Lothrop, Lee & Shepard Co.
Warlock O' Glenwarlock. A Homely Romance. George Macdonald. (Franklin square library, no. 203). 1881. Harper & Brothers.
Warlock of the Witch World. Andre Norton, pseud. LC 77-23201. (Norton, Andre. The Witch Would Novels of Andre Norton). (Illus.). 1977. 7.95 (ISBN 0-8398-2359-2). Gregg Press.
Warlock of the Witch World. Andre Norton. 1974. (pbk.) 1.25. Ace Books.
Warlock Unlocked. Christopher Stasheff. 288p. (Orig.). 1982. pap. 2.75 (ISBN 0-441-87325-1). Ace Bks.
Warlocks and Warriors. Ed. by Lyon Sprague De Camp. LC 70-128629. (Illus.). 1970. 4.95. Putnam.
Warlock's Daughter. Angela Gray, pseud. (Orig.). 1972. pap. 0.95 o.s.i. (75-366). Lancer.
Warlock's Gift. Ardath Mayhar. LC 81-43149. 1982. 10.95 (ISBN 0-385-17359-8). Doubleday.
Warlord. Jason Frost. 1983. pap. 3.50 (ISBN 0-8217-1189-X). Zebra.
Warlord of Azatlan. Robert Payne. (Able Team Ser.). 192p. 1983. pap. 2.25 (ISBN 0-373-61206-0, Pub. by Worldwide). Harlequin Bks.
Warlord of Ghandor. Del Dowdell. (Illus.). 1.50 (ISBN 0-87997-315-3). DAW Books.
Warlord of Mars. Edgar Rice Burroughs. LC 19-154863. 1919. 4.40. A. C. McClurg & Co.
Warlord of Mars. Edgar Rice Burroughs. LC 24-285314. 1920. Grosset & Dunlap.
Warlord of the Air. Michael Moorcock. 1978. 1.50 (ISBN 0-87997-380-3). DAW Books.
Warlords. Malcolm J. Bosse. LC 82-19696. 717p. 1983. 17.95 (ISBN 0-671-44332-1). S&S.
Warlords. Bob Langley. LC 80-20572. 1981. 9.95 (ISBN 0-688-00069-X). Morrow.
Warlords of Nin. Stephen R. Lawhead. 488p. 1983. pap. 7.95 (ISBN 0-89107-278-0, Crossway Bks). Good News.

Warlord's World. Christopher Anuil. (Science Fiction Ser). pap. 1.25 o.p. (ISBN 0-87997-201-7, UY1201). DAW Bks.
Warlord's World. Christopher Anvil. 1975. (pbk.) 1.25. DAW Books.
Warm and Golden War. Nicholas Luard. LC 67-13319. 1968. Pantheon Books.
Warm Bed in Reno. Jason Morgan. (Orig.). 1968. pap. 0.60 o.p. (73-785). Lancer.
Warm Bodies: A Novel. Donald R Morris. LC 57-10981. (Illus.). 1957. Simon and Schuster.
Warm December. Raymond Giles. 1973. (pbk) 0.95. Lancer Books.
Warm Feeling. Merle Miller. LC 67-21515. 1968. Coward-McCann.
Warm Flesh, Hot Lead. Robert E. Mills. (Kansan: No. 5). 176p. 1981. pap. 1.95 (ISBN 0-8439-0978-1, Leisure Bks). Nordon Pubns.
Warm on a Cold Night. G. E. Lapington. LC 80-14909. 1980. 11.95 (ISBN 0-312-85618-0). St. Martin's Press.
Warm Rooms & Cold. Lars Gustafsson. Tr. by Yvonne Sandstroem. (Orig.). 1975. pap. 3.50 (ISBN 0-914278-05-3). Copper Beech.
Warm Summer. Craig Massey. 1968. 3.50 o.p. (50-9225). Moody.
Warm Weather. Joyce Eliason. LC 74-1881. 1974. 6.95 (ISBN 0-06-011241-7). Harper & Row.
Warm Wind, West Wind. Anne Irwin Matthew. LC 56-11368. 1956. Crown Pub.
Warm Wine: An Idyll. John Updike. LC 74-158479. (Albondocani Press publication no. 16). 1973. Albondocani Press.
Warmaster. Philip McCutchan. 1964. 3.95 o.p. John Day.
Warmth of Summer. Ed. by James A. Kuse. (Illus.). 1979. pap. 4.95 (ISBN 0-89542-065-1). Ideals.
Warn Angel. Frederick H Christian. (Angel Series#8). 1975. (pbk.) 0.95 (ISBN 0-523-00761-2). Pinnacle Books.
Warners: An American Story of Today. Gertrude Potter Daniels. LC 1-31277. 1901. Jamieson-Higgins Co.
Warning. George Hirthler. LC 81-17225. 144p. (Orig.). 1981. pap. 4.95 (ISBN 0-87784-841-6). Inter-Varsity.
Warning: A Novel. Winifred Mary Scott. LC 24-7730. 1924. Frederick A. Stokes Company.
Warning Call. Robert G. Keller. 1981. pap. 1.95 (ISBN 0-8439-0890-4, Leisure Bks). Nordon Pubns.
Warning from Mars. Edward Whiteside. LC 48-7165. 1948. Inter-Planetary Publications.
Warning Hill. John Phillips Marquand. LC 30-5243. 1930. Little, Brown, and Company.
Warning of the Wailing Phantom. Thomas J. Saunders. 4.75 o.p. Vantage.
Warning or the Ambassador's Dream: A Political Tale of Our Time. Martin Rosse. 1978. 5.95 (ISBN 0-533-03525-2). Vantage.
Warning to Lovers: & "Sauce for the Goose Is Sauce for the Gander,". Paul Leicester Ford. LC 6-52073. 1906. Dodd, Mead & Company.
Warning to Wantons: A Fantastic Romance Setting Forth the Not Undeserved but Awful Fate Which Befell a Minx. Mary Mitchell. LC 34-5606. 1934. Doubleday, Doran, & Company, Inc.
Warning to Wives. Hester Eloise Hosford. LC 24-1967. 1924. The Stratford Co.
Warp and Woof. Anna Hanson McKenney Dorsey. LC 6-33705. 1887. J. Murphy & Co.
Warp and Woof. Anna Hanson McKenney Dorsey. LC 43-466672. John Murphy Company.
Warp and Woof: Or, New Frames for Old Pictures. Frances Hartson Wood & Kitchel, Eva Paine, Joint Author. LC 8-37562. 1890. F. H. Wood.
Warp War. 1977. pap. write for info. (ISBN 0-88074-004-3). Metagam.
Warpaint. Les Wayne. 208p. (Orig.). 1982. pap. 2.25 (ISBN 0-8439-1042-9, Leisure Bks). Nordon Pubns.
Warpath. Oliver Payne. (Northwest Territory Ser.: No. 1). 432p. (Orig.). 1982. pap. 3.50 (ISBN 0-425-05738-0). Berkley Pub.
Warrant for a Wanton. Michael Gillian. LC 52-9692. 1952. M. S. Mill Co., and W. Morrow.
Warrant for X. Philip MacDonald. LC 38-6016. 1938. Pub. for the Crime Club, Inc., by Doubleday, Doran & Co., Inc.
Warrant for X. Philip MacDonald. LC 39-17659. 1939. The Sun Dial Press, Inc.
Warrant for X. Philip MacDonald. LC 41-7301. 1941. Triangle Books.
Warren Hyde. Helen Reimensnyder Martin. LC 7-25981. 1897. R. F. Fenno & Company.
Warren Wagontrain Raid: The First Complete Account of an Historic Indian Attack and Its Aftermath. Benjamin Capps. LC 73-19673. (Illus.). 1974. 8.95. Dial Press.
Warrens of Virginia: A Novel. George Cary Eggleston & De Mille, William Churchill, 1878- LC 8-22798. G. W. Dillingham Company.
Warrielaw Jewel. Winifred Peck. LC 33-23182. E. P. Dutton & Co., Inc.
Warring Sky. Peter Saxon. 1971. pap. 0.75 o.p. (94036-075). Beagle Bks.
Warrior. Wade Everett. 160p. 1981. pap. 1.75 (ISBN 0-345-29432-7). Ballantine.
Warrior. Thomas Ryan. LC 41-25262. 1941. P. Davies.
Warrior. Frank Gill Slaughter. (Kangaroo Book). 1977. 1.95 (ISBN 0-671-81076-6). Pocket Books.
Warrior & the Wizard. Jeffrey Dillow & Craig Fisher. 1980. 14.95 o.p. (ISBN 0-8359-8531-8); pap. 12.95 o.p. (ISBN 0-8359-8530-X). Reston.
Warrior Basin. Leslie Charles Ernenwein. LC 59-11590. 1959. Doubleday.
Warrior Creek. Llewellyn Perry Holmes. LC 77-14108. 1978. 7.95 (ISBN 0-89340-121-8). J. Curley.
Warrior Creek: By Matt Stuart Pseud. Llewellyn Perry Holmes. LC 60-119341. (Silver star westerns). 1960. Dodd, Mead.
Warrior Enchained. Sharon Green. 352p. 1983. pap. 2.95 (ISBN 0-87997-789-2). NAL.
Warrior Gap. A Story of the Sioux Outbreak of '68. Charles King. LC 7-13217. F. T. Neely.
Warrior King. Berhane Marian Sahle Sellassie. LC 75-513452. (African writers series; 163). (H.E.B. paperback). 1974-1975. 2.50 (ISBN 0-435-90163-X). Heinemann Educational.
Warrior of Mars. Edward P. Bradbury, pseud. pap. 0.50 o.p. (72-118). Lancer.
Warrior of Scorpio. Alan Burt Akers. (Science Fiction Ser.). 1975. pap. 1.25 (ISBN 0-87997-212-2, UY1212). DAW Bks.
Warrior of Scorpio. Alan Burt Akers. (Daw sf Books, no. 65). (Illus.). 1973. (pbk.) 0.95. Daw Books.
Warrior of the Dawn: The Adventures of Tharn. Howard Browne. LC 43-5946. 1943. Reilly & Lee.
Warrior of World's End. Lin Carter. (Science Fiction Ser). pap. 1.50 (ISBN 0-87997-420-6, UW1420). DAW Bks.
Warrior of World's End. Lin Carter. (Gondwane Epic, 1). 1974. (pbk.) 0.95. DAW Books.
Warrior Queen. James Sinclair. LC 77-10291. (Illus.). 1978. 8.95 (ISBN 0-312-85626-1). St. Martin's Press.
Warrior Queen. James Sinclair. 1979. 2.25 (ISBN 0-425-03947-1). Berkley Pub. Corp.
Warrior Range. Donald B. Hobart. 1970. pap. 0.60 o.p. (06103). Curtis.
Warrior Road. Fred Grove. LC 74-9253. 1974. (ISBN 0-385-03649-3). Doubleday.
Warrior the Untamed: The Story of an Imaginative Press Agent. William Henry Irwin. LC 9-24019. 1909. Doubleday, Page & Company.
Warrior Within. Sharon Green. 1982. pap. 2.50 (ISBN 0-87997-707-8, UE1707). DAW Bks.
Warrior Wives. Anne Eliot Crompton. 320p. (Orig.). 1982. pap. 2.95 (ISBN 0-523-41524-9). Pinnacle Bks.
Warrior. 1st Ed. Frank Gill Slaughter. LC 56-11506. 1956. Doubleday.
Warriors. John W. Jakes. LC 77-71698. (Jakes, John W. 1932-. The American Bicentennial Ser.). 1977. 2.25 (ISBN 0-515-04047-9). Pyramid Books.
Warriors. book club ed.. ed. John W. Jakes. LC 78-105294. (His The Kent chronicles; v. 6). ((Series: Jakes, John W., 1932-). (American Bicentennial series; v. 6.). (Illus.). 3.99. N. Doubleday.
Warriors. Joaquim Jaquiera & Manuel B. Mansa. Tr. by Jan Feidel. (Illus.). 1972. 8.50 (Pub. by Mushinsha Bks); pap. 3.95. SBD.
Warriors. Joaquim Jaquiera & Manuel B. Mansa. Tr. by Ernest Barge & Jan Feidel. LC 72-81311. (Mushinsha Bks). 1972. pap. 3.95 o.p. (ISBN 0-670-74995-8, Grossman). Penguin.
Warriors. Sol Yurick. LC 65-144471. 1965. 3.95. Holt.
Warriors see Kent Family Chronicles.
Warrior's Blood. Richard McEnroe. 320p. (Orig.). 1981. pap. 2.50 (ISBN 0-441-87333-2). Ace Bks.
Warriors of Dawn. M. A. Foster. (Science Fiction Ser.). pap. 1.95 (ISBN 0-87997-573-3, UE 1573). DAW Bks.
Warriors of Dawn. M. A. Foster. (Science Fiction Ser). 1975. pap. 1.25 o.p. (UY1152). DAW Bks.
Warriors of Dawn. M. A Foster. 1975. (pbk.) 1.25. Daw Books.
Warriors of Day. James Blish. (Orig.). 1968. pap. 0.60 o.p. (73-580). Lancer.
Warriors of Terra. John Faucette. (Peacemakers Ser.: Vol. 1). 1970. pap. 0.75 o.p. (B75-2002). Belmont-Tower.
Warrior's Path. Louis L'Amour. LC 80-29455. 1981. 13.95 (ISBN 0-8161-3145-7). G. K. Hall.
Warrior's Rest. Christiane Rochefort. LC 59-12272. 1959. D. McKay Co.
Warrior's Return. Ted Pittenaer. LC 55-11509. (Signet books, 1289). 1955. New American Library.
Warrior's Woman. Phyllis G Leonard. LC 77-4822. 1977. 9.95 (ISBN 0-698-10843-4). Coward, McCann & Geoghegan.
Warrior's Woman. Phyllis G. Leonard. (Jove/HBJ Book). 1978. 2.25 (ISBN 0-515-04620-5). Jove Publications.
Warrior's World. Richard McEnroe. 320p. (Orig.). 1981. pap. 2.50 (ISBN 0-441-87338-3). Ace Bks.
Wars. Timothy Findley. (O.s.i.). 1977. 8.95 o.s.i. (ISBN 0-440-09397-X, Sey Lawr). Delacorte.
Wars. Timothy Findley. 1983. pap. 3.95 (ISBN 0-440-39239-X, LE). Dell.
Wars of Love. Mark Schorer. LC 82-61041. 176p. 1982. Repr. of 1954 ed. 16.95 (ISBN 0-933256-34-5). Second Chance.
Wars of Love: A Novel. Mark Schorer. LC 53-7878. 1954. McGraw-Hill.
Wars of Pardon: A Novel. Robert R. Kirsch. LC 65-11165. S. & S.
Wars of Peace: A Novel. Anne Florence Wilson. LC 3-11814. 1903. Little, Brown, and Company.
Warsaw Document. Adam Hall, pseud. LC 77-139027. 1971. 5.95 o.p. (ISBN 0-385-04268-X). Doubleday.
Warsaw Document. Adam Hall, pseud. 1972. pap. 1.25 o.p. (ISBN 0-515-02763-4, V2763). Pyramid Pubns.
Warsaw Document. Elleston Trevor. LC 77-139027. 1971. 5.95. Doubleday.
Wartime. Milovan Djilas. LC 80-16174. 1980. 7.95 (ISBN 0-15-694712-9, Harv). HarBraceJ.
Wartime. Adrian Mitchell. LC 72-84934. 1975. 6.95 (ISBN 0-385-08195-2). Doubleday.
Warts & All. Paul Szep. LC 79-92213. 1980. pap. 6.95 o.p. (ISBN 0-8362-6206-9). Andrews & McMeel.
Warwhoop: Two Short Novels of the Frontier. MacKinlay Kantor. LC 52-9578. 1952. Random House.
Warwick. A Novel. Mansfield Tracy Walworth. (On cover: Madison square series, no. 10). 1897. G. W. Dillingham Co.
Warwick of the Knobs: A Story of Stringtown County, Kentucky. John Uri Lloyd. LC 1-25456. 1901. Dodd, Mead & Company.
Warwick, the King Maker. Kendall. 1968. pap. 2.95 o.p. (ISBN 0-448-00222-1, UL). G&D.
Warwyck's Choice. Rosalind Laker. LC 79-7803. 1980. 10.95 (ISBN 0-385-15649-9). Doubleday.
Warwyck's Choice. Rosalind Laker. 1981. pap. 2.50 (ISBN 0-451-09664-9, E9664, Sig). NAL.
Warwyck's Choice. Barbara Vstedal. LC 79-7803. 1980. 10.95 (ISBN 0-385-15649-9). Doubleday.
Warwyck's Woman. Rosalind Laker. LC 77-82955. 1978. 8.95 o.p. (ISBN 0-385-13448-7). Doubleday.
Warwyck's Woman. Rosalind Laker. 1979. pap. 2.25 (ISBN 0-451-08813-1, E8813, Sig). NAL.
Warwyck's Woman. Barbara Vstedal. LC 77-82955. 1978. 8.95 (ISBN 0-385-13448-7). Doubleday.
Wary Trangressor: By Raymond Marshall Pseud. Rene Raymond. LC 53-17124. 1952. Jarrolds.
Was der Grossmutter Lehre Bewirkt. Johanna Heusser Spyri & Barrows, Sarah Tracy, 1870- Ed. LC 10-20404. (Heath's modern language series). 1910. D. C. Heath & Co.
Was: Erskine Caldwell's Treatment of Racial Themes. William Alfred Sutton. LC 74-5389. 1974. 6.00 (ISBN 0-8108-0723-8). Scarecrow Press.
Was Ever Woman in This Humor Wooed? Charles Gibbon. (On cover: Lovell's international series, no. 48). F. F. Lovell & Company.
Was He Guilty? Eliza Ann Dupuy. LC 3-35704. T. B. Peterson & Brothers.
Was He Successful? A Novel. Richard Burleigh Kimball. 1864. Carleton; Etc., Etc.
Was It a Murder? or, Who Is the Heir? Le Bac. Fortune Du Boisgobey & H., A. D., Tr. LC 6-34409. 1883. Rand, McNally & Co.
Was It Love. Paul Charles Joseph Bourget. Tr. by Camden Curwen. LC 43-44550. (On cover: The Rose library). 1891. Worthington Co.
Was It Murder? James Hilton. LC 75-44984. (Fifty Classics of Crime Fiction, 1900-1950; 27). 1976. 12.00 (ISBN 0-8240-2376-5). Garland Pub.
Was It Murder? James Hilton. LC 35-27148. 1935. Harper & Brothers.
Was It Murder? Glen Trevor. LC 33-27267. 1933. Harper & Brothers.
Was It Right to Forgive? A Domestic Romance. Amelia Edith Huddleston Barr. LC 99-4622. 1899. H. S. Stone and Company.
Was It the Woman's Fault? Wilhelmina A Saville. LC 48-32261. (Deaborn Series, No. 44). Donohue, Henneberry.
Was It Too Late? & Other Stories. Adria E Booker. LC 54-1611. 1954. Meador Pub. Co.
Was She? A Novel. Cola Amanda Barr Craig. LC 6-19001. 1906. The Neale Publishing Company.
Was She Engaged? J L. Collins. LC 6-25418. 1871. J. B. Lippincott & Co.
Was She His Wife? Edwin S Deane. (On cover: Leisure-time series, no. 17). 1892. W. D. Rowland.
Was She Wife of Widow: A Novel. Malcolm Bell. LC 6-11708. (Ledger library, no. 55). 1892. R. Bonner's Sons.
Wash Me on Home Mama. Peter Najarian. 86p. 1978. pap. 3.00 (ISBN 0-917658-10-8). Berkeley Poets.
Wash Us and Comb Us: Stories. Barbara Deming. LC 78-184479. (Illus.). 1972. 8.95 (ISBN 0-670-75003-4). Grossman Publishers.
Washed in the Blood. Carolyn Flynn. LC 81-84525. 352p. 1983. 16.95 (ISBN 0-399-31018-5, Seaview Bks). Putnam Pub Group.
Washed in the Blood: A Novel. Carol Houlihan Flynn. LC 82-19214. 1983. 16.95. Seaview Books.
Washer of the Ford: Legendary Moralities and Barbaric Tales. William Sharp. LC 4-17817. 1896. Stone & Kimball.
Washington! Dana Fuller Ross. (Wagons West Ser.). 1982. pap. 3.50 (ISBN 0-553-20919-1). Bantam.
Washington! Dana Fuller Ross. (General Ser.). 1983. lib. bdg. 15.95 (ISBN 0-8161-3507-X, Large Print Bks). G K Hall.
Washington and Baltimore: Stories. Julian Mazor. LC 68-14883. 1968. Knopf.
Washington and His Generals: Or, Legends of the Revolution. George Lippard. LC 70-164570. (American fiction reprint series). 1971. (ISBN 0-8369-7047-0). Books for Libraries Press.
Washington Bachelor. A H Berzen. LC 56-18685. (Ace books, S-126). 1955. Ace Books.
Washington Calling! Marquis William Childs. LC 37-8399. W. Morrow & Co.
Washington, D. C. A Novel. 1st Ed. Gore Vidal. LC 67-15707. 1967. 6.95. Little.
Washington, D.C. Robert J Hensler (ISBN 0-671-80826-5). Pocket Books.
Washington, D.C. Gore Vidal. 1.95 (ISBN 0-345-25651-4). Ballantine.
Washington, D.C. A Novel. Gore Vidal. LC 75-42768. 1976. 12.50 (ISBN 0-394-40689-3). Random House.
Washington Diary: Characters and Events of the. Joseph Quayle Bristow. 1954. Exposition Press.
Washington Fringe Benefit: A Novel. Elizabeth L Ray. LC 77-352950. 1976. 1.75. Dell Pub. Co.
Washington Game. William Wright. 1974. 8.95 o.p. (ISBN 0-8415-0340-0). Dutton.
Washington: I.O.U. see Deuda De Sangre.
Washington Jitters. Dalton Trumbo. LC 36-23523. 1936. A. A. Knopf.
Washington Legation Murders: Captain North's Ninth Case. Francis Van Wyck Mason. LC 35-36177. 1935. Pub. for the Crime Club, Inc., by Doubleday, Doran & Company, Inc.
Washington Legation Murders: Captain North's Ninth Case. Francis Van Wyck Mason. LC 46-30072. 1941. Triangle Books.
Washington Monument Romance. William Lee Popham. LC 11-324172. 1.00. The World Supply Company.
Washington Payoff. Howard Hunt. 1975. (pbk.) 1.25 (ISBN 0-523-00535-0). Pinnacle Books.
Washington Playland. Edmund Griffen & Daniel Dodge. 1976. pap. 1.95 o.p. (LB403, Leisure Bks). Nordon Pubns.
Washington Randolphs and Their Friends: Extracts from the Diary of a Lady of Old Virginia, Selected and Edited by T. M. Anna Mary MacLeod & T. M. LC 16-1106. 1915. J. P. Bell Company, Inc.
Washington Shadows. Ada Mixon. LC 42-24493. 1942. Dorrance and Company.
Washington Slept Here. Stephanie Jackson, pseud. 192p. 1975. pap. 1.25 (ISBN 0-532-12300-X). Woodhill.
Washington Square. Henry James. LC 50-6046. 1950. Doric Books.
Washington Square. Henry James. Ed. by Gerald Willen. LC 69-13264. (Crowell critical library). 1970. Crowell.
Washington Square. Henry James. Limited Editions Club., Inc., New York. LC 73-30209. (Illus.). 1971. Printed for the Members of the Limited Editions Club at the Thistle Press.
Washington Square. Henry James. LC 7-7430. 1881. Harper & Brothers.
Washington Square. Henry James. LC 80-13183. (Classics in Large Print). 1980. 11.95 (ISBN 0-8161-3071-X). G. K. Hall.
Washington Square. Henry James & Mark Le Fanu. LC 82-8079. (World's classics). (Oxford paperbacks). 1982. 4.95 (ISBN 0-19-281611-X). Oxford University Press.
Washington Square see Classics Set.
Washington Square: A Novel. Henry James. LC 8-12805. Harper & Brothers.
Washington Square, and Daisy Miller. With an Introd. by Oscar Cargill. Henry James. LC 56-6981. (Harper's modern classics). 1956. Harper.
Washington Square Enigma: A Mystery Novel. Harry Stephen Keeler. LC 33-11403. 1933. E. P. Dutton & Co., Inc.

Washington Square Ensemble. Madison Smartt Bell. LC 82-40372. 1983. 16.75 (ISBN 0-670-75005-0). Viking Press.
Washington Square. Introd. by Clifton Fadiman. Henry James. LC 50-7693. (Modern library of the World's best books, 269). 1950. Modern Library.
Washington Story. Joseph Jay Deiss. LC 50-6462. 1950. Duell, Sloan and Pearce.
Washington Symphony. Esther Gracie Lawrence Wheeler. LC 8-360511. 1893. G. P. Putnam's Sons.
Washington, USA. Faith Baldwin Cuthrell. LC 43-1892. 1943. Farrar & Rinehart, Inc.
Washington Whispers Murder: By Leslie Ford Pseud. Zenith Jones Brown. LC 53-69926. 1953. Scribner.
Washington Winter. Madeleine Vinton Dahlgren. LC 6-32178. 1883. J. R. Osgood and Company.
Washingtonians. Pauline Bradford Mackie Hopkins. LC 1-25662. 1902. L. C. Page & Company.
Washingtons. Pauline Bradford Mackie Cavendish. LC 1-25662. 1902. L. C. Page & Company.
Washington's Lady. Elswyth Thane. 1976. Repr. of 1954 ed. lib. bdg. 16.60x (ISBN 0-88411-957-2). Amereon Ltd.
Washoe Giant in San Francisco. Mark Twain. LC 73-8919. 1928. lib. bdg. 25.00 (ISBN 0-8414-2683-X). Folcroft.
Wasp. Ursula Reilly Curtiss. LC 63-11543. (Red badge detective). 1963. Dodd, Mead.
Wasp. Ursula Reilly Curtiss. 1975. (pbk.) 1.25. Dell.
Wasp. Roberts Theodore Goodridge. LC 14-2354. 1914. 1.25. G. W. Dillingham Company.
W.A.S.P. Julius Horwitz. (N3859). 1968. Bantam.
W.A.S.P. Julius Horwitz. LC 67-16542. 1967. Atheneum.
Wasp. Eric Frank Russell. LC 57-12689. 1957. Avalon Books.
Waste. Robert Herrick. LC 76-1280. (Chicano Heritage). 1976. 20.00 (ISBN 0-405-09507-4). Arno Press.
Waste. Robert Herrick. LC 24-8369. Harcourt, Brace and Company.
Waste see Collected Works.
Waste Corner. Ruth Manning-Sanders. LC 28-12545. E. J. Clode, Inc.
Waste Heritage. Irene Baird. LC 39-29432. Random House.
Waste of Shame: A Novel. Edward T. McNamara. LC 67-25423. 1967. Vanguard Press.
Waste of Timelessness, and Other Early Stories. Anais Nin. LC 74-28648. 7.95 (ISBN 0-8027-0569-3). Magic Circle Press.
Waste of Timelessness: And Other Early Stories. Anais Nin. LC 74-28648. 105p. 1980. 7.95 (ISBN 0-8027-0569-3, 82-87716). Ohio U Pr.
Wasted Crime: A Novel. David Christie Murray. (On cover: Harper's Franklin square library, no. 734). 1893. Harper & Brothers.
Wasted Generation. Owen McMahon Johnson. LC 21-16375. 1921. Little, Brown and Company.
Wasted Island. Eimar O'Duffy. LC 20-16927. 1920. Dodd, Mead and Company.
Wasted Love. A Novel. (On cover: Seaside library. Pocket ed. no. 1028). 1887. G. Munro.
Wasted on the Young. Ralph Schoenstein. LC 73-11795. 1974. 4.95 (ISBN 0-672-51839-2). Bobbs-Merrill Co.
Wasted Pride. Poppy Nottingham. 1.75 (ISBN 0-441-87355-3). Ace Books.
Wasted Salt. George Washington Ogden. LC 30-4851. 1930. Dodd, Mead & Company.
Wasteland. LC 46-1556. 1946. Harper & Brothers.
Wasteland. LC 47-6435. 1947. Sun Dial Press.
Wastelands. Robert James Cosgriff. LC 28-18570. Wetzel Publishing Company.
Wasters. Bill Williams, pseud. 192p. 1971. pap. 1.25 o.p. Manor Bks.
Wastrel. David Maclure. LC 32-15437. 1932. Meador Publishing Company.
Wastrel. Arthur Douglas Howden Smith. LC 11-362623. 1911. Duffield and Company.
Wastrel. Frederic Wakeman. LC 49-7446. 1949. Rinehart.
Wastrels. Leslie Gladson. 1970. pap. 0.95 o.p. (ISBN 0-447-75154-9). Lancer.
Wat Tyler: Or, The Bondman. An Historical Novel of the Times of Richard the Second. O'Neill. 1848. Burgess, Stinger & Co.
Watch. Carlo Levi. LC 51-11404. 1951. Farrar, Straus & Young.
Watch and Ward. Henry James. LC 10-4181. 1878. Houghton, Osgood and Company.
Watch and Ward. Henry James. LC 79-15759. 1979. 3.95 (ISBN 0-394-17097-0). Grove Press: Distributed by Random House.
Watch Below. James White. LC 69-14241. 1969. 4.50. Walker.
Watch Dog: A Story of to-Day. Arthur Hornblow. LC 15-11873. G. W. Dillingham Company.
Watch-Dog of the Crown: A Romance of the Tower of London. John Knipe. LC 20-22450. 1920. John Lane.
Watch for Me on the Mountain. Forrest Carter. (O.s.i.). 1978. 9.95 o.s.i. (ISBN 0-440-02202-9, E Friede). Delacorte.
Watch for Me on the Mountain. Forrest Carter. 1983. pap. 3.95 (ISBN 0-440-39065-6, LE). Dell.
Watch for Romance. William Arthur Neubauer. LC 51-14525. 1951. Arcadia House.
Watch for the Dawn. Stuart Cloete. LC 39-276. 1939. Houghton Mifflin Company.
Watch for the Morning. Elisabeth Macdonald. LC 77-13662. 9.95. Scribner.
Watch Fora Tall White Sail: A Novel. Margaret Elizabeth Bell. LC 48-540823. 1948. W. Morrow.
Watch in the Night. Helen Constance White. LC 33-8303. 1933. The Macmillan Company.
Watch It, Dr. Adrian. Boyd Litzinger. LC 77-4312. 7.95 (ISBN 0-399-12015-7). Putnam.
Watch-Key. A Novel. Hannah Courtney Pinnix. LC 7-39642. 1889. Edwards & Broughton.
Watch Mc Lean. George Goodchild. 1973. lib. bdg. 5.95 o.s.i. (ISBN 0-85617-896-9). White Lion Pubs.
Watch Night. Walter B Lowrey. LC 53-6174. 1953. Scribner.
Watch of Evil. Pierre Le Bailly. LC 65-250. 1964. Exposition Press.
Watch on the Bridge. David Garth. 1967. pap. 0.60 o.p. (53-606). Paperback Lib.
Watch on the Bridge: A Novel. David Garth. LC 59-5681. 1959. Putnam.
Watch on the Wall. Hallie Southgate Burnett. bds., 5.95. Morrow.
Watch Out for the Mules. 1st Ed. Kaye Starbird. LC 68-125996. 1968. 4.95. Harcourt.
Watch Out for the Wind. C. J. Mize. (Orig.). 1980. pap. 2.25 o.s.i. (ISBN 0-505-51555-5). Tower Bks.
Watch Out for Willie Carter. Theodore Naidish. LC 44-6793. 1944. C. Scribner's Sons.
Watch Sinister. Marie Blizard. LC 51-5972. 1951. M. S. Mill Co. and W. Morrow.
Watch That Ends the Night. Hugh MacLennan. LC 59-6069. 1959. Scribner.
Watch the Curves. Richard Hoffmann. LC 34-1687. Farrar & Rinehart, Incorporated.
Watch the North Wind Rise. Robert Graves. LC 49-7959. 1949. Creative Age Press.
Watch the Stars Immortal. Samuel Milton Elam. LC 31-29963. 1931. Harper & Brothers.
Watch the Wall, My Darling. Jane Aiken Hodge. LC 66-17398. 4.95. Doubleday.
Watch Us Grow. Harry Hamilton. LC 40-4191. The Bobbs-Merrill Company.
Watch Your Step. Ann Lawrence. 1938. Godwin.
Watchdog. Faith Sullivan. LC 81-17163. 11.95 (ISBN 0-07-062355-4). McGraw-Hill.
Watchdog of Thunder River. Harry Sinclair Drago. LC 41-21400. 1941. W. Morrow & Company.
Watchdog of Thunder River: By Will Ermine Pseud. Harry Sinclair Drago. LC 50-14112. (Triple-A western classic). 1950. Jefferson House.
Watchdogs. John Weisman. LC 82-10857. 1983. 15.75 (ISBN 0-670-75022-0). Viking.
Watchdogs of Abaddon: A Novel. Ib Melchior. LC 78-69507. 8.95 (ISBN 0-06-012967-0). Harper & Row.
Watcher. Renate Chapman. (YA) 1974. 4.95 o.p. (Avalon). Bouregy.
Watcher. Renate Chapman. (Avalon romances). 1974. 4.50. Avalon Books.
Watcher. Kay Nolte Smith. LC 79-2366. 8.95 (ISBN 0-698-11006-4). Coward, McCann & Geoghegan.
Watcher. Collin Wilcox. LC 77-13898. 6.95 (ISBN 0-394-41256-7). Random House.
Watcher & Other Stories. Italo Calvino. LC 75-9829. (Harbrace paperbound library; HPL 65). 1975. 5.95 (ISBN 0-15-694952-0). Harcourt Brace Jovanovich.
Watcher & Other Stories. Italo Calvino. LC 75-134573. 1971. Harcourt Brace Jovanovich.
Watcher and Other Weird Stories. Joseph Sherridan Le Fanu. LC 76-5279. (collected works of Joseph Sheridan Le Fanu). 20.00 (ISBN 0-405-09241-5). Arno Press.
Watcher & the Red Deer. Richard Perry. (Illus.). 1971. 4.95 (ISBN 0-7153-5385-3). David & Charles.
Watcher & the Watched. Thomas Peachum. pap. 1.75 o.s.i. (301, Travellers Comp). Olympia.
Watcher at the Door. Geoffrey Holiday Hall. LC 54-5007. (Inner sanctum mystery). 1954. Simon and Schuster.
Watcher by the Threshold. John Buchan. LC 18-18337. 1.40. George H. Doran Company.
Watcher in the Shadows. Geoffrey Household. (Crime Ser). 1977. pap. 2.95 (ISBN 0-14-001962-6). Penguin.
Watcher in the Shadows. Geoffrey Household. 1982. 18.00x (Pub. by Ian Henry Pubns England). State Mutual Bk.
Watcher in the Shadows. Marcia Miller. (Avalon Books). 4.95. Thomas Bouregy.
Watcher in the Shadows: A Novel. 1st Ed. Geoffrey Household. LC 60-653158. 1960. Little, Brown.
Watcher of the Skies. Gustave Frederick Mertins. LC 11-20312. 1911. 1.25. Thomas Y. Crowell Company.
Watcher of Windcliff. J. H. Rhodes. (YA) 1980. 6.95 (Avalon). Bouregy.
Watcher on the Heights. August William Derleth. LC 66-10488. 5.95 (ISBN 0-88361-074-4). Stanton & Lee.
Watcher on the Heights. August William Derleth. 1966. 3.50 o.p. Hawthorn.
Watcher on the Heights. August William Derleth. 4.95 o.s.i. (ISBN 0-88451-041-7). Edco-Vis Assoc.
Watchers. Maud Louise Hudnut Chapin. LC 31-25770. 1931. Duffield and Green.
Watchers. Van Siller. 1970. pap. 0.60 o.p. (0502-06120). Curtis.
Watchers. Van Siller. LC 69-12243. (Crime Club Novel). 1969. 4.50 o.p. Doubleday.
Watchers. Hilda Van Siller. LC 69-12243. 1969. 4.50. Published for the Crime Club by Doubleday.
Watchers: A Novel. Alfred Edward Woodley Mason. LC 99-529137. F. A. Stokes Company.
Watchers of the Dark. Lloyd Biggle, Jr. LC 66-17440. (Doubleday sci. fic.). 4.50. Doubleday.
Watchers of the Plains: A Tale of the Western Prairies. Ridgwell Cullum. LC 9-8569. 1909. G. W. Jacobs & Company.
Watchers on the Longships. A Tale of Cornwall in the Last Century. from the 8th london ed. James Francis Cobb. LC 6-20724. T. Y. Crowell & Co.
Watchers on the Shore. Stan Barstow. LC 67-16794. 1967. Doubleday.
Watchers Out of Time, and Others. Howard Phillips Lovecraft & August William Derleth. LC 73-88394. (Illus.). 1974. Arkham House.
Watchfires. Louis Auchincloss. LC 81-2698. 1982. 13.95 (ISBN 0-395-31546-8). Houghton Mifflin.
Watchful at Night... Julius Fast. LC 45-8441. 1945. Farrar & Rinehart, Inc.
Watchful Gods: And Other Stories. Walter Van Tilburg Clark. (Signet bk., D1907). 1961. New American Library.
Watchful Gods, and Other Stories. Walter Van Tilburg Clark. LC 50-9687. 1950. Random House.
Watchgod's Cargo. Brian M. Stableford. pap. 0.95 o.p. (UQ1007). Daw Bks.
Watching at the Window. 1st Ed. Charlotte Payne Johnson. LC 55-753447. Bobbs-Merrill.
Watching Eye. Alicen White. (Dell Book). 1977. 1.50 (ISBN 0-440-16675-6). Dell Pub. Co.
Watching Me, Watching You. Fay Weldon. LC 81-9156. 13.50 (ISBN 0-671-44817-X). Summit Books.
Watching the Sun Go Down. Donald Caswell. pap. 3.00. Anhinga Pr.
Watchmaker. Alexandre Dumas. LC 6-42305. (On cover: Seaside library. Pocket ed. no. 2062). G. Munro's Sons.
Watchmaker's Wife: And Other Stories. Frank Richard Stockton. LC 4-15162. 1893. C. Scribner's Sons.
Watchman. G. R. Conrad. LC 72-184046. (New Cambridge Series of American Writers, No. 5). 1971. 4.75 o.s.i. Identity.
Watchman. Davis Grubb. LC 61-72062. 1961. Scribner.
Watchman. James A. Maitland. LC 7-16596. 1855. H. Long & Brother.
Watchman's Stone. Rona Randall. LC 75-7693. 1975. 8.95 (ISBN 0-671-22060-8). Simon and Schuster.
Watchstar. Pamela Sargent. (Orig.). 1980. pap. 2.25 (ISBN 0-671-83159-3, Timescape). PB.
Watchtower. Elizabeth A Lynn. LC 78-12602. (Illus.). 8.95 (ISBN 0-399-12272-9). Berkley Pub. Corp.: Distributed by Putnam.
Watchtower Chaos. Valerie Tomsett. 1974. pap. 1.50 o.p. (ISBN 0-87508-536-9). Chr Lit.
Water. Ruth Comfort Mitchell. LC 31-5711. 1931. D. Appleton and Company.
Water! Albert Payson Terhune. LC 28-65221. 1928. Harper & Brothers.
Water and the Sound. Gillian Tindall. LC 62-7717. 1962. Morrow.
Water-Babies. Charles Kingsley. (Legacy Library Ser). 1966. Repr. of 1863 ed. 4.95 o.p. (LL02001). Univ Microfilms.
Water-Bearer. Joseph Allan Elphinstone Dunn. LC 24-3536. 1924. Dodd, Mead and Company.
Water-Bug's Mittens. James Dickey. 25.00 (ISBN 0-89723-021-3). Bruccoli.
Water Castle. Ingeborg Lauterstein. LC 80-15515. 1980. 12.95 (ISBN 0-395-29471-1). Houghton Mifflin.
Water Circle. James Broughton. 1977. pap. 1.50. Man-Root.
Water Dancer. Jenifer Levin. LC 82-479. 15.95 (ISBN 0-671-44764-5). Poseidon Press.
Water Devil. Crittenden Marriott. LC 24-7120. (Famous authors series. no. 47). 1924. Garden City Publishing Co., Inc.
Water Gators in Hell. Douglas F. MacKenzie. 1977. 4.50 o.p. (ISBN 0-533-02936-8). Vantage.
Water Ghost. John Kendrick Bangs. Repr. of 1894 ed. lib. bdg. 15.50 (ISBN 0-8414-1672-9). Folcroft.
Water Ghost and Others. John Kendrick Bangs. LC 68-55662. (American short story series, v. 2). (Illus.). 1968. Garrett Press.
Water Ghost: And Others. John Kendrick Bangs. LC 6-6116. 1894. Harper & Brothers.
Water Gipsies. Alan Patrick Herbert. 1976. 8.95 (ISBN 0-09-126590-8, Pub. by Hutchinson). Merrimack Pub Cir.
Water Goats, and Other Troubles. Ellis Parker Butler. LC 10-143651. 1910. Doubleday, Page & Company.
Water, Grass, and Gunsmoke. Llewellyn Perry Holmes. LC 49-10246. (Double-D western). 1949. Doubleday.
Water Gypsies. Alan Patrick Herbert. 1930. Doubleday, Doran & Company, Inc.
Water in the Pearl. Carol Cox. 1982. pap. 4.50 (ISBN 0-914610-28-7). Hanging Loose.
Water in the Wine. April Oursler Armstrong. LC 63-14256. 1963. McGraw-Hill.
Water Is Wide. Martin Donisthorpe Armstrong. LC 27-220473. 1927. Harper & Brothers.
Water Is Wide. Ursula K. Le Guin. LC 77-153013. (Illus.). (ISBN 0-914010-03-4). Pendragon Press.
Water-Method Man. John Irving. LC 75-37055. 1972. 6.95 (ISBN 0-394-47332-9). Random House.
Water-Method Man. John Irving. 1978. 2.50 (ISBN 0-671-82254-3). Pocket Books.
Water Music. T. Coraghessan Boyle. 1983. pap. 6.95 (ISBN 0-14-006550-4). Penguin.
Water Music. Bianca Van Orden. LC 58-10887. 1958. Harcourt, Brace.
Water Music. Bianca Van Orden. LC 58-10887. 1958. 3.95 o.p. (ISBN 0-15-195015-6). HarBraceJ.
Water Music: A Novel. T. Coraghessan Boyle. LC 81-12423. 15.95 (ISBN 0-316-10467-1). Little, Brown.
Water of Gall: A Novel of Quaker Settlers in California. 1st Ed. Dorothy Fargo. LC 55-86834. (Exposition-Lochinvar book). 1955. Exposition Press.
Water of Kane. Oswald A Bushnell. LC 80-5463. 12.95 (ISBN 0-8248-0714-6). Published for the Friends of the Library of Hawaii by the University Press of Hawaii.
Water of Life. Glenn Clark. LC 33-332194. 1931. The Macalester Park Company.
Water of Life. Henry Morton Robinson. 1978. 2.25 (ISBN 0-441-87373-1). Ace Books.
Water of Life: A Novel. Henry Morton Robinson. 1960. Simon and Schuster.
Water of the Wondrous Isles. William Morris. LC 72-31088. (Adult fantasy). 1971. 1.25. Ballantine Books.
Water of the Wondrous Isles. William Morris. LC 4-15327. 1897. Longmans, Green, and Co.
Water on the Brain. Compton Mackenzie. LC 33-325916. 1933. Doubleday, Doran & Company, Inc.
Water Over the Dam. Marguerite Allis. LC 47-1829. 1947. G. P. Putnam's Sons.
Water Pourer: An Unpublished Chapter from The Origin of the Brunists. Robert Coover. LC 72-172738. 1972. Bruccoli-Clark.
Water Tramps: Or, the Cruise of the "Sea Bird." A Story. George Herbert Bartlett. LC 6-9402. 1895. G. P. Putnam's Sons.
Water Under the Bridge. Sumner Locke Elliott. 1977. 9.95 o.p. (ISBN 0-671-22823-4). S&S.
Water Under the Bridge: A Novel. Sumner Locke Elliott. LC 77-8447. 9.95 (ISBN 0-671-22823-4). Simon and Schuster.
Water Under the Bridge: A Novel. Sumner Locke Elliott. (jove/HBJ book). 1978. 1.95 (ISBN 0-515-04722-8). Jove Pubns.
Water Under the Dam. 1st Ed. Clarence Rowley Van Sant. LC 55-108653. 1955. Vantage Press.
Water Weed. Alice Ormond Campbell. LC 29-23881. Farrar & Rinehart, Incorporated.
Water Wheel. Julian L Shapiro. LC 37-55641. (Half-title: The dragon series). The Dragon Press.
Water-Witch. James Fenimore Cooper. (Seaside library. v. 28, no. 585). 1879. G. Munro.
Water Witch. Cynthia Felice & Connie Willis. 256p. (Orig.). 1982. pap. 2.50 (ISBN 0-441-87379-0). Ace Bks.
Water-Witch, by J. Fenimore Cooper: Condensed for Use in Schools with an Introduction and Explanatory Notes. James Fenimore Cooper. LC 6-296703. (Standard literature ser. Double no. 27). University Publishing Company.
Water-Witch: Or, The Skimmer of the Seas. James Fenimore Cooper. LC 77-109397. (Illus.). 1970. AMS Press.
Water-Witch: Or, The Skimmer of the Seas. James Fenimore Cooper. Ed. by Cooper, Susan Fenimore. LC 12-31522. (On cover: J. Fenimore Cooper's works. Household ed.). Houghton, Mifflin and Company.

Water-Witch: Or, The Skimmer of the Seas. James Fenimore Cooper. LC 4-15437. (In his Works. Mohawk ed.). 1896. G. P. Putnam's Sons.

Water-Witch: Or, The Skimmer of the Seas. A Tale. James Fenimore Cooper. LC 6-29668. 1831. Carey & Lea.

Water-Witch: Or, The Skimmer of the Seas. A Tale. James Fenimore Cooper. LC 4-19006. 1898. D. Appleton and Company.

Water-Witch: Or, The Skimmer of the Seas. A Tale. a new ed. James Fenimore Cooper. LC 42-47068. 1836. Carey, Lea, & Blanchard.

Water-Witch: Or, The Skimmer of the Seas. A Tale. James Fenimore Cooper & Darley, Felix Octavius Carr, 1822-1888, Illus. LC 43-31958. (With Farjeon, B. L. At the sign of the Silver flagon. New York, 1875). 1874. D. Appleton and Company.

Water-Witch: Or, The Skimmer of the Seas. A Tale. By J. Fenimore Cooper... With the Latest Revision and Corrections of the Author. James Fenimore Cooper. LC 26-24689. (Half-title: The choice works of Cooper. Revised and corrected series. v. 1). 1856. Stringer & Townsend.

Water with Berries. George Lamming. LC 72-78097. (Illus.). 1972. 6.95 (ISBN 0-03-001406-9). Holt, Rinehart and Winston.

Water World. William Appel. 224p. (Orig.). 1983. pap. 2.75 (ISBN 0-449-12537-8, GM). Fawcett.

Waterfall. Margaret Drabble. 1977. 1.95. Popular Library.

Waterfall. Margaret Drabble. LC 72-79321. 1969. 5.95. Knopf.

Waterfall. Averil Mackenzie-Grieve. LC 50-4298. 1950. Hutchinson.

Waterfalls of Slunj. Tr. by Eithne Wilkins, Ernst Kaiser. 1st Ed. Heimito Von Doderer. LC 66-23805. 1966. 6.95. Harcourt.

Waterflowers. Edward Gorey. (Illus.). 64p. 1982. 6.95 (ISBN 0-312-92928-5). Congdon & Weed.

Waterfront. John Brophy. LC 34-134299. 1934. The Macmillan Company.

Waterfront. Budd Schulberg. LC 79-11704. 1979. Repr. of 1955 ed. lib. bdg. 12.50x (ISBN 0-8376-0434-6). Bentley.

Waterfront, a Novel. Budd Schulberg. LC 55-5804. 1955. Random House.

Waterfront: A Novel. Budd Schulberg. LC 79-11704. 1979. 10.00 (ISBN 0-8376-0434-6). R. Bentley.

Waterfront: By Ferguson Findley Pseud. Charles Weiser Frey. LC 51-1076. 1951. Duell, Sloan and Pearce.

Waterfront Mark. John V Craven. LC 32-237257. 1932. A. A. Knopf.

Waterfront Reporter. Felix Riesenberg. LC 50-10281. 1950. Rand McNally.

Waterfront Waitress. Charles Stanley Strong. LC 38-11888. Phoenix Press.

Watering Place. Lyla Kessler. 1969. 5.50 o.p. (ISBN 0-394-40787-3). Random.

Waterloo. Emile Erckmann & Chatrian, Alexandre, 1826-1890, Joint Author. LC 5-24860. 1905. H. Holt and Company.

Waterloo. Emile Erckmann & Chatrian, Alexandre, 1826-1890, Joint Author. LC 29-11996. (Heath's modern language series). D. C. Heath and Company.

Waterloo: A Novel. Manuel Komroff. LC 36-16506. Coward-McCann.

Waterloo: A Sequel to The Conscript of 1813. Emile Erckmann & Chatrian, Alexandre, 1826-1890, Joint Author. LC 6-38163. (Half-title: Erckmann-Chatrian national novels). 1889. C. Scribner's Sons.

Waterloo: A Sequel to the The Conscript of 1813. Emile Erckmann & Chatrian, Alexandre I.E. Louis Gratien Charles Alexandre, 1826-1890, Joint Author. 1869. C. Scribner and Co.

Waterloo: Sequel to The Conscript of 1813. Emile Erckmann & Chatrian, Alexandre, 1826-1890, Joint Author. LC 98-1213. 1898. C. Scribner's Sons.

Waterlook. Emile Erckmann & Chatrian, Alexandre, 1826-1890, Joint Author. LC 12-26488. (Heath's modern language series). 1893. D. C. Heath & Co.

Watermeads: A Novel. Archibald Marshall. LC 16-194594. 1916. Dodd, Mead and Company.

Watermen. James A. Michener. (Illus.). 1979. 12.95 (ISBN 0-394-50660-X). Random.

Watermen. James A. Michener. 193p. 1979. 12.95. Md Hist.

Watermen: Selections from Chesapeake. James Albert Michener & John Moll. LC 79-14119. 12.95 (ISBN 0-394-50660-X). Random House.

Waters & the Wild. Leslie Paul. LC 75-9493. 181p. 1976. 6.95 o.p. (ISBN 0-312-85785-3). St Martin.

Waters Dark & Deep. Renate Chapman. 1982. 6.95 (Avalon). Bouregy.

Waters Dark & Deep. J. Farragut Jones. (Orig.). 1981. pap. 2.75 (ISBN 0-440-19470-9). Dell.

Water's Edge & Other Stories. Krishnan Srinivasan. 120p. 1981. text ed. 5.95x (ISBN 0-86590-009-4, Pub. by Writers Workshop India). Apt Bks.

Waters of Caney Fork: A Romance of Tennessee. Opie Percival Read. LC 7-36497. Rand, McNally & Company.

Waters of Cantaurus. Rosel George Brown. 1972. pap. 0.95 o.p. (75-278). Lancer.

Waters of Centaurus. Rosel George Brown. LC 73-103735. (Doubleday science fiction). 1970. 4.95. Doubleday.

Waters of Contradiction. Anna Catherine Minogue. LC 13-311. P. J. Kenedy & Sons.

Waters of Death. Irving A. Greenfield. 1976. pap. 1.25 (ISBN 0-532-12159-7). Woodhill.

Waters of Death. Irving A. Greenfield. 1970. pap. 0.75 o.p. (ISBN 0-447-74655-3). Lancer.

Waters of Decision. Warren Adler. (Berkley Medallion Book). 1976. (pbk.) 1.75 (ISBN 0-425-03075-X). Berkley Publishing Corp.

Waters of Hercules. A Novel. Emily Gerard & Longard De Longgarde, Dorothea (Gerard) (Harper's Franklin square library, no. 486). 1885. Harper & Brothers.

Waters of Hercules: A Novel... Emily Gerard & Longard De Longgarde, Dorothea (Gerard) LC 6-44242. (Harper's handy series, no. 12). 1885. Harper & Brothers.

Waters of Hercules: A Novel. Emily Gerard & Longard De Longgarde, Dorothea (Gerard) (On cover: Seaside library. Pocket ed., no. 512). 1885. G. Munro.

Waters of Kronos. 1st Ed. Conrad Richter. LC 60-7297. 1960. Knopf.

Waters of Life and Death. Aleksandr Konstantinovich Voronskii. LC 74-10094. 1975. 18.50 (ISBN 0-88355-180-2). Hyperion Press.

Waters of Marah. John Hill. (On cover: The seaside library. Pocket ed., no. 112). 1883. G. Munro.

Waters of Strife. Robert Ames Bennet. LC 22-2606. W. J. Watt & Company.

Waters of Strife. Francis Lynde. LC 30-25159. 1930. C. Scribner's Sons.

Waters of Strife. George Vane. LC 20-12603. 1920. John Lane.

Waters of the End. Charles Ingle. 1953. Lippincott.

Waters of the Wilderness. Shirley Seifert. 1976. Repr. of 1941 ed. lib. bdg. 9.95 (ISBN 0-89190-142-6). Am Repr-Rivercity Pr.

Waters of the Wilderness: A Novel. Shirley Seifert. LC 41-15454. J. B. Lippincott Company.

Waters on a Starry Night. Elisabeth Ogilvie. LC 68-11236. 1968. McGraw-Hill.

Waters Over the Dam. Harry Harrison Kroll. LC 44-20856. 1944. The Bobbs-Merrill Company.

Waters Plant. Patricia Wentworth. 1976. Repr. of 1951 ed. lib. bdg. 14.40x (ISBN 0-88411-741-3, 741). Amereon Ltd.

Waters Re-Born. Neeli Cherkovski. 1975. pap. 2.50 (Pub. by Red Hill). SBD.

Waters Under the Earth. John Cecil Moore. LC 65-205886. 6.95. Lippincott.

Waters Under the Earth. Martha Ostenso. LC 30-298272. 1930. Dodd, Mead & Company.

Watership Down. Richard Adams. 1975. pap. 4.95 (ISBN 0-380-00428-3, 614995). Avon.

Watership Down. Richard Adams. LC 73-6044. 429p. 1974. 12.95 (ISBN 0-02-700030-3, 70003). Macmillan.

Watership Down. deluxe ed. Richard Adams. (O.s.i). 448p. 1975. slipcase 14.95 o.s.i. (50020). Macmillan.

Watership Down Film Picture Book. Richard Adams. LC 78-24456. (Illus.). 1978. 16.95 o.s.i. (ISBN 0-02-500260-0); pap. 8.95 o.s.i. (ISBN 0-02-016060-7). Macmillan.

Watersplash. 1st Ed. Patricia Wentworth. LC 52-5094. (Her A Miss Silver mystery). Lippincott.

Watersprings. Arthur Christopher Benson. LC 13-21708. 1913. 1.35. G. P. Putnam's Sons.

Waterview Manor. Elisabeth Welles. 1.50 (ISBN 0-671-80689-0). Pocket Books.

Waterway. Eleanor O'Reilly Dark. LC 38-18391. 1938. The Macmillan Company.

Waterworks. Paul Violi. 1972. pap. 2.00 o.p. (ISBN 0-915124-06-8). Toothpaste.

Watling Green. Mollie Panter-Downes. LC 43-16878. 1943. C. Scribner's Sons.

Watling's: A Novel. Horace Annesley Vachell. LC 25-7945. 1925. Frederick A. Stokes Company.

Watseka: America's Most Extraordinary Case of Possession and Exorcism. St. Clair, David. LC 77-13665. 8.95. Playboy Press.

Watsons. Jane Austen & John Coates. LC 72-9808. 1973. 13.00 (ISBN 0-8371-6598-9). Greenwood Press.

Watsons. Jane Austen & John Coates. (S ignet Book). (Illus.). 1977. 1.95 (ISBN 0-451-07522-6). New American Library.

Watsons. Jane Austen & Oulton, L. LC 23-6147. 1923. D. Appleton and Company.

Watson's Choice. Gladys Mitchell. LC 76-24988. 1976. 6.95 (ISBN 0-679-50658-6). McKay.

Watsons: Jane Austen's Fragment Continued and Completed by John Coates. Jane Austen & John Coates. LC 59-5248. 1958. Crowell.

Watson's Revenge. Richard Mallett. LC 75-316699. (Illus.). 1974. 4.00. Aspen Press.

Watt. Samuel Beckett. LC 58-9097. 1959. Grove Press.

Watter's Mou' Bram Stoker. LC 8-37876. 1894. T. L. De Vinne & Co.

Watter's Mou' Bram Stoker. LC 14-1818. 1895. D. Appleton and Company.

Wattersons: A Novel of American Life. William Mara Bell. LC 7-19040. The Author.

Wau-Nan-Gee: Or, The Massacre at Chicago. A Romance of the American Revolution. John-Richardson. 1852. H. Long and Brother.

Wave. Christopher Hyde. LC 81-80090. 272p. 1981. pap. 2.95 (ISBN 0-87216-848-4). Playboy Pbks.

Wave. Morton Rhue. LC 81-70394. 10.95 (ISBN 0-440-09822-X). Delacorte Press.

Wave. Evelyn Scott. LC 29-14106. J. Cape and H. Smith.

Wave: A Novel. Christopher Hyde. LC 78-22328. 1979. 8.95 (ISBN 0-385-14762-7). Doubleday.

Wave; an Egyptian Aftermath. Algernon Blackwood. LC 16-242012. E. P. Dutton & Company.

Wave Hangs Dark. Alan Dipper. LC 72-82648. 1969. 4.95. Morrow.

Wave High the Banner: A Novel Based on the Life of Davy Crockett. Dee Alexander Brown. LC 42-11114. 1942. Macrae-Smith Company.

Wave of Destiny. Martha Melahn. 320p. 1981. pap. 2.75 (ISBN 0-380-79152-8, 79152). Avon.

Wave of Fear. Ed. by Hugh Lamb. LC 73-178542. 1973. 2.50 (ISBN 0-491-01241-1). W. H. Allen.

Wave of Fear: A Classic Horror Anthology. Ed. by Hugh Lamb. LC 74-186389. 1974. 7.95 (ISBN 0-8008-8063-3). Taplinger Pub. Co.

Wave of Fear: A Classic Horror Anthology. Ed. by Hugh Lamd. LC 74-1963. 1974. 7.95 o.p. (ISBN 0-8008-8063-3). Taplinger.

Wave of Life: A Novel. Clyde Fitch & M.J.M., Ed. LC 12-322393. M. Kennerley.

Wave Without a Shore. C. J. Cherryh. (Science Fiction Ser.). 176p. 1981. pap. 2.25 (ISBN 0-87997-646-2, UE1646). DAW Bks.

Wavelengths. Daniel M Klein. LC 80-2866. 1982. 14.95 (ISBN 0-385-17445-4). Doubleday.

Waverley. Walter Scott. (Premier world classic, M257). Fawcett.

Waverley. Walter Scott. LC 64-7311. (Nelson classics). 1963. Nelson.

Waverley. Walter Scott. LC 72-186964. (Penguin English Library). (Illus.). 1972. (0.50, 2.45 u.s.) (ISBN 0-14-043071-7). Penguin.

Waverley Novels. abbotsford ed. Walter Scott. LC 8-5765. 1857. J. B. Lippincott & Co.

Waverley Novels. illustrated excelsior ed.... ed. Walter Scott. 1872. Excelsior Publishing Company.

Waverley Novels. standard ed.... ed. Walter Scott. LC 47-42665. 1896. The Gebbie Publishing Company, Limited.

Waverley Novels. Walter Scott & Browne, William Hardcastle. LC 2-18735. P. F. Collier & Son.

Waverley Novels. Charles A. Young. 136p. 1980. Repr. of 1907 ed. lib. bdg. 22.50 (ISBN 0-8495-6100-0). Arden Lib.

Waverley Novels: Printed from the Latest English Editions, Embracing the Author's Last Corrections, Prefaces, and Notes. abbotsford ed. Walter Scott. LC 52-52927. 1852-66. Lippincott, Grambo.

Waverley: Or, 'Tis Sixty Years Since. Walter Scott. (Seaside library. v. 42, no. 857). 1880. G. Munro.

Waverley: Or, 'Tis Sixty Years Since. Walter Scott. LC 41-40520. Porter & Coates.

Waverley: Or 'Tis Sixty Years Since. Walter Scott. (On cover: Lovell's library, no. 502). 1885. J. W. Lovell Company.

Waverley: Or, 'Tis Sixty Years Since... Walter Scott. Ed. by Lang, Andrew. LC 8-4807. 1893. Estes and Lauriat.

Waverley: Or, 'Tis Sixty Years Since. Walter Scott. Ed. by Bouton, Archibald Lewis. (Standard literature series, double no. 50). 1902. University Pub. Co.

Waverley: Or, 'Tis Sixty Years Since. Walter Scott. (Half-title: Everyman's library, ed. by Ernest Rhys. Fiction). 1906. J. M. Dent & Co.

Waverley: Or, 'Tis Sixty Years Since. Walter Scott & Claire Lamont. LC 79-41313. 1980. 58.00 (ISBN 0-19-812643-3). Clarendon Press.

Waverley; or, 'Tis Sixty Years Since... From the Last Rev. Ed., Containing the Author's Final Corrections, Notes, &C. parker's ed. Walter Scott. LC 8-5785. (Waverley novels: Library ed. v. 1). Bazin & Ellsworth.

Waverley: Or, 'Tis Sixty Years Since. With an Introductory Essay by Andrew Lang and Illus. by Robert Ball. Walter Scott. LC 62-294811. 1961. Printed for the Members of the Limited Editions Club.

Waverley: Or, 'Tis Sixty Years Sonc. Walter Scott. LC 8-3041. 1835. Gaylord's Corrected Stereotype Ed.

Waves. M. A. Foster. (Science Fiction Ser.). 1980. pap. 2.25 (ISBN 0-87997-569-5, UE1569). DAW Bks.

Waves. Virginia Stephen Woolf. LC 31-306081. Harcourt, Brace and Company.

Waves. Virginia Stephen Woolf. LC 77-92142. (Harvest/HBJ book). 1978. 3.95 (ISBN 0-15-694960-1). Harcourt Brace Jovanovich.

Waves of Destiny. Margaret Bass Pedler. LC 24-25178. George H. Doran Company.

Waves of Night, and Other Stories. Harry Mark Petrakis. LC 74-81382. 1969. 5.95. McKay.

Waves of Terror. Michel Parry. 1976. 11.95 (ISBN 0-575-02184-5, Pub. by Gollancz England). David & Charles.

Waves of Terror: Weird Stories About the Sea. Michel Parry. LC 77-359601. 1976. 3.95 (ISBN 0-575-02184-5). Gollancz.

Wawona: An Indian Story of the Northwest. Ella Sterling Clark Mighels. LC 23-608. Harr Wagner Publishing Co.

Wax... Ethel Lina White. LC 35-145763. 1935. Pub. for the Crime Club, Inc., by Doubleday, Doran & Company, Inc.

Wax Apple. Mary Jane Ward. 1938. E. P. Dutton & Co., Inc.

Wax Apple. Donald E Westlake. LC 79-101335. 1970. 4.95. Random House.

Wax Boom. George Mandel. 1962. Random House.

Waxen Image. Rudy S. Apodaca. LC 77-73631. 1977. 7.95 (ISBN 0-9603314-0-9). Titan Pub Co.

Waxen Image: A Novel. Rudy S Apodaca. LC 77-73631. 1977. 7.95. Titan Pub. Co.

Waxman Production. John Hermansen. LC 73-4149. 1973. 6.95 (ISBN 0-06-011842-3). Harper & Row.

Waxwork. Peter Lovesey. LC 77-90420. 7.95 (ISBN 0-394-50066-0). Pantheon Books.

Waxwork. Peter Lovesey. LC 79-21740. 1980. 1.95 (ISBN 0-14-004887-1). Penguin Books.

Way. J. M Hartley. LC 44-40179. 1944. Thomas Y. Crowell Company.

Way. Emily Hyde. LC 7-9023. 1888. J. Murphy & Co.

Way. Thomas Liggert. 4.50 o.p. Vantage.

Way: A Story of Today. Caroline Hull. LC 11-30046. Crown Publishing Co.

Way Away Tales: From Away-off-from-Anywhere Land. Ed. by Edward Norman Harris. LC 40-29657. 1940. The Judson Press.

Way Back. A. Bertram Chandler. 1978. 1.50 (ISBN 0-87997-352-8). DAW Books.

Way Back; the Forceful: Lusty Story of the Rigorous Far North and the Virile Men Who Conquered It. J. Parks Harris. LC 53-12906. 1953. Naylor Co.

Way Beyond. Jeffery Farnol. LC 33-29193. 1933. Little, Brown, and Company.

Way Down East. A Romance of New England Life. Joseph Rhode Grismer & Parker, Lottie Blair. LC 8-21919. J. S. Ogilvie Publishing Companmy.

Way Down East: Or, Portraitures of Yankee Life. Seba Smith. LC 69-11916. (American short story series, v. 75). (Illus.). 1969. Garrett Press.

Way Down East: Or, Portraitures of Yankee Life. Seba Smith. LC 72-8151. (American short story series, v. 75). 1972. MSS Information Corp.

Way-Farer. Dennis Schmidt. 1978. 1.95 (ISBN 0-441-87625-0). Ace Books.

Way for a Sailor! Albert Richard Wetjen. LC 28-25548. The Century Co.

Way Hearts Go: A Social Comedy. Laurence Hayward. LC 17-3152. 1917. E. P. Dutton & Company.

Way Home. Basil King. LC 42-1106. 1913. A. L. Burt Company.

Way Home. Henrietta Richardson. LC 80-10981. W. W. Norton & Co., Inc.

Way Home. Henry Handel Richardson. LC 30-10981. 1930. W. W. Norton.

Way Home. Theodore Sturgeon. Ed. by Groff Conklin. 1969. pap. 0.60 o.p. (X2030). Pyramid Pubns.

Way Home: A Novel. Basil King. LC 13-19944. 1913. 1.35. Harper & Brothers.

Way Home, Stories of Science Fiction and Fantasy: By Theodore Sturgeon Pseud. Edward Hamilton Waldo, pseud. LC 55-5485. 1955. Funk & Wagnalls.

Way Homeward. Giles A Lutz. LC 76-26351. 1977. 5.95 (ISBN 0-385-12692-1). Doubleday.

Way Homeward. Giles A. Lutz. (Kangaroo Book). 1978. 1.50 (ISBN 0-671-82002-8). Pocket Books.

Way in: A Novel. Eugene Mirabelli. LC 68-22866. 1968. Viking Press.

Way It Is Now: Stories. Sallie Bingham. LC 70-176407. 1972. 6.50 (ISBN 0-670-75195-2). Viking Press.

Way It Is Now: Stories About Women. Sallie Bingham. (OSI). 1972. 6.50 o.s.i. (ISBN 0-670-75195-2). Viking Pr.

Way It Spozed to Be. James Herndon. LC 68-12171. 1968. 6.95 o.p. (ISBN 0-671-79846-4). S&S.
Way It Was. Stephen Sohmer. LC 66-21827. 1966. 4.95. S & S.
Way It Was with Them. Peadar O'Donnell. 1928. G. P. Putnam's Sons.
Way Life Is: A Novel. Tr. from French by Merloyd Lawrence. Genevieve Dormann. LC 66-129031. 5.00. Braziller.
Way O' the West. Ney N Geer. LC 40-79164. L. Furman, Inc.
Way of a Buccaneer. Davenport Steward. LC 56-7694. 1956. Dutton.
Way of a Gaucho. Herbert Childs. LC 48-836116. 1948. Printice-Hall.
Way of a Heart. William Arthur Neubauer. LC 51-12255. 1951. Arcadia House.
Way of a Man. Emerson Hough. LC 7-276152. 1907. The Outing Publishing Company.
Way of a Man. Joan Sutherland. LC 31-58873. 1931. Harper & Brothers.
Way of a Man: A Romance. Morley Roberts. (Half-title: Appleton's town and country library, no. 314). 1902. D. Appleton and Company.
Way of a Man: A Story of the New Woman. Thomas Dixon. LC 19-411118. 1919. D. Appleton and Company.
Way of a Man of Action. Fred De Armond. LC 73-143768. 160p. 1970. pap. 3.00 (ISBN 0-910998-16-7). Mycroft.
Way of a Man with a Maid... Frances Gordon Fane. LC 1-31291. 1901. G W. Dillingham Co.
Way of a Wanton. Richard S. Prather. (Shell Scott Ser). (Orig.). 1969. pap. 0.60 o.p. (R2086, GM). Fawcett World.
Way of a Woman: A Novel. Rina Ramsay. 1911. Dodd, Mead and Company.
Way of All Earth. Edith Barnard Delano. LC 25-8665. 1925. Boni and Liveright.
Way of All Flesh. Samuel Butler. LC 65-24086. (Harper perennial classic). 1964. Harper & Row.
Way of All Flesh. Samuel Butler. LC 72-186943. (Shrewsbury edition of the works of Samuel Butler, v. 17). (Illus.). 1968. AMS Press.
Way of All Flesh. Samuel Butler. LC 75-1540. (Victorian Fiction; Novels of Faith and Doubt; 87). 1975. (ISBN 0-8240-1611-4). Garland Pub.
Way of All Flesh. Samuel Butler. Ed. by James Cochrane. LC 66-78507. (Penguin English library, EL12). (Illus.). 1966. Penguin.
Way of All Flesh. Samuel Butler. LC 48-11522. (Rinehart editions). 1948. Rinehart.
Way of All Flesh. Samuel Butler. 1910. E. P. Dutton & Co.
Way of All Flesh. Samuel Butler. Ed. by Streatfeild, Richard Alexander. LC 16-13048. 1916. E. P. Dutton & Company.
Way of All Flesh. Samuel Butler. LC 25-25988. (Half-title: Modern readers' series. Ashley H. Thorndike, general editor). 1925. The Macmillan Company.
Way of All Flesh. Samuel Butler. Ed. by Streatfeild, Richard Alexander. (Half-title: Everyman's library, ed. by Ernest Rhys. Fiction. no. 800 a). 1927. E. P. Dutton & Co.
Way of All Flesh. Samuel Butler. LC 36-23009. (Half-title: The modern library of the world's best books. no. 13). The Modern Library.
Way of All Flesh. Samuel Butler. LC 33-27338. (Half-title: The world's classics. 438). 1936. H. Milford. Oxford University Press.
Way of All Flesh. Samuel Butler. LC 44-51607. 1941. Pocket Books, Inc.
Way of All Flesh. Samuel Butler. LC 36-7718. 1935. The Three Sirens Press.
Way of All Flesh. Samuel Butler & Durenceau, Andre, 1904- Illus. LC 47-23206. Doubleday & Company, Inc.
Way of All Flesh. Samuel Butler & Streatfeild, Richard Alexander. LC 13-25094. 1913. E. P. Dutton & Company.
Way of All Flesh. Samuel Butler & Streatfeild, Richard Alexander, 1866-1919, Ed LC 43-26004. (Half-title: Everyman's library, ed. by Ernest Rhys. Fiction. No. 895). 1933. J. M. Dent & Sons Ltd.
Way of All Flesh. Drawings by Donia Nachshen. Samuel Butler. 1965. bds., 3.95. Jonathan Cape.
Way of All Flesh. Ed. by James Cochrane. Introd. by Richard Hoggart. Samuel Butler. LC 66-746750. (Penguin Eng. lib., EL12). 1966. Penguin.
Way of All Flesh: Introd. by Morton Dauwen Zabel. Samuel Butler. LC 50-12237. (Modern Library college editions, T5). 1950. Modern Library.
Way of All Flesh Notes. Roger E Parsell. 1974. (pbk.) 1.25 (ISBN 0-8220-1373-8). Cliffs Notes.
Way of All Flesh: With an Introd. and Notes by George Moreby Acklom. Samuel Butler. LC 52-12153. (Everyman's library, 895A. Fiction). 1952. Dutton.
Way of All Flesh: With an Introd. by W. Y. Tindall. Samuel Butler. LC 50-6144. (Harper's modern classics). 1950. Harper.
Way of All Flesh. With Illus. of the Author, His Environment and the Setting of the Book. Samuel Butler. LC 57-12866. (Great illustrated classics). (Illus.). 1957. Dodd, Mead.
Way of Ambition. Robert Smythe Hichens. LC 13-184764. 1913. 1.35. Frederick A. Stokes Company.
Way of an Eagle. Ethel May Dell. LC 11-280765. 1911. 1.35. G. P. Putnam's Sons.
Way of an Eagle. Ethel May Dell. LC 20-1975. A. L. Burt Company.
Way of an Eagle. Ethel May Dell. LC 43-466681. A. L. Burt Company.
Way of an Eagle. Dan Potter. LC 72-104634. 1970. 4.95. Stein and Day.
Way of an Indian. bicentennial ed. Frederic Remington. LC 76-50438. (Illus.). 1976. 17.76 (ISBN 0-89436-000-0). Memento Publications.
Way of an Indian. Frederic Remington. LC 76-104548. (Illus.). 1970. (ISBN 0-8398-1755-X). Literature House.
Way of an Indian. Frederic Remington. LC 6-6263. 1906. Fox, Duffield & Company.
Way of Belinda. Frances Weston Carruth Prindle. LC 1-30877. 1901. Dodd, Mead & Co.
Way of Ecben: A Comedietta Involving a Gentleman. James Branch Cabell. LC 29-23485. 1929. R. M. McBride & Company.
Way of Escape. Margaret Georgina Todd. LC 2-16448. 1902. D. Appleton and Company.
Way of Fire. Ellen Blackmar Maxwell. LC 7-32309. 1897. Dodd, Mead and Company.
Way of Knowing: A Novel. Nolan Porterfield. LC 76-138792. 1971. 7.50 (ISBN 0-06-126550-0). Harper's Magazine Press.
Way of Life. Muriel De B Daly. LC 40-13012. 1940. D. Appleton-Century Company, Incorporated.
Way of Life. Arthur Hamilton Gibbs. LC 47-5148. 1947. Little, Brown.
Way of Life, Like Any Other. Darcy O'Brien. LC 77-11093. 7.95 (ISBN 0-393-08798-0). Norton.
Way of Love. Margaret G Fawcett. LC 33-233563. The Vanguard Press.
Way of Passion. Elizabeth Lee. 320p. 1981. pap. 2.75 (ISBN 0-380-78287-1, 78287). Avon.
Way of Passion. William Arthur Neubauer. LC 46-168157. 1946. Phoenix Press.
Way of Peace. William Trevelyan Browne. LC 18-43377. 1905. By Wynkoop Hallenbeck Crawford Co.
Way of Revelation: A Novel of Five Years. Wilfrid Herbert Gore Ewart. LC 22-2002. 1921. G. P. Putnam's Sons.
Way of Revelation: A Novel of Five Years. Wilfrid Herbert Gore Ewart. LC 22-10168. 1922. D. Appleton and Company.
Way of Revelation: A Novel of Five Years. Wilfrid Herbert Gore Ewart. LC 27-17355. 1927. D. Appleton & Company.
Way of Romance. Vivian Gilbert. LC 27-2303. 1927. D. Appleton and Company.
Way of Sequestered Places. Ewing Campbell. LC 79-87889. Date not set. cancelled o.s.i. (ISBN 0-918722-10-1). Nefertiti.
Way of Sequestered Places. Ewing Campbell. 1982. pap. text ed. 4.00 (ISBN 0-918722-11-X). Nefertiti.
Way of Sinners. Frederic Robert Buckley. LC 27-18772. 2.00. The Century Co.
Way of Some Flesh. Sally Chayes. LC 31-4961. 1931. H. Liveright.
Way of Stars: A Romance of Reincarnation. Lily Moresby Adams Beck. LC 25-8736. 1925. Dodd, Mead and Company.
Way of Stars: A Romance of Reincarnation. Lily Moresby Adams Beck. LC 40-5391. 1940. The Sun Dial Press.
Way of the Buffalo. Charles Alden Seltzer. LC 24-19416. The Century Co.
Way of the Bull. Leo F. Buscaglia. LC 73-83777. 176p. 1974. 9.95 (ISBN 0-913590-08-8). Slack Inc.
Way of the Bull. Leo F. Buscaglia. 192p. 1983. pap. 2.95 (ISBN 0-449-20090-6, Crest). Fawcett.
Way of the Burning Heart. Cecil Raymond Murrow. LC 34-22760. The Westminsters.
Way of the Cross. Roy Hession. 1974. pap. 1.75 (ISBN 0-87508-238-6). Chr Lit.
Way of the Dragon. Jillian Austen. LC 81-85172. 400p. (Orig.). 1982. pap. 3.50 (ISBN 0-86721-073-7). Playboy Pbks.
Way of the Four Winds. Yrjo Kokko. LC 52-13654. (Illus.). 1954. Putnam.
Way of the Gods. John Luther Long. LC 6-14549. 1906. The Macmillan Company.
Way of the Heart. Natalie Shipman & Worcester, Gurdon, Joint Author. LC 41-15920. The Greystone Press.
Way of the Lawless. Max Brand. 1978. 6.95 o.p. (ISBN 0-396-07552-5). Dodd.
Way of the Lawless. Max Brand. (gr. 7-12). 1979. lib. bdg. 12.95 o.p. (ISBN 0-8161-6747-8). G K Hall.
Way of the Lawless. Frederick Faust. LC 78-2354. (Silver star western). 1978. 6.95. Dodd, Mead.
Way of the Lawless. Frederick Faust. LC 79-16504. 1979. 12.95 (ISBN 0-8161-6747-8). G. K. Hall.
Way of the Magus. Maurus E. Mallon. 3.75 o.p. Carlton.
Way of the North... James Beardsley Hendryx. LC 45-720144. 1945. Doubleday, Doran & Co., Inc.
Way of the North: A Romance of the Days of Baranof. Warren Cheney. LC 5-9655. 1905. Doubleday, Page & Company.
Way of the Panther: A Romance of India. Denny C Stokes. LC 26-14106. 1926. Frederick A. Stokes Company.
Way of the Phoenix. Stephen McKenna. LC 32-187326. 1932. Dodd, Mead & Company.
Way of the Scarlet Pimpernel. Emmuska Orczy. LC 34-1475. 1934. G. P. Putnam's Sons.
Way of the Sea. Norman Duncan. LC 76-121537. (Short story index reprint series). (Illus.). 1970. Books for Libraries Press.
Way of the Shadows. first ed. Josephine Stephens Brown. 1973. 4.00 (ISBN 0-682-47737-0). Exposition Press.
Way of the Strong. Ridgwell Cullum. LC 14-7731. 1.35. G. W. Jacobs & Co.
Way of the Strong. Theodore Wayland Douglas. LC 44-957843. 1944. Macrae-Smith-Company.
Way of the Tamarisk. Anne Worboys. 1978. 1.95 (ISBN 0-441-87420-7). Ace Books.
Way of the Tamarisk: A Novel. Anne Worboys. LC 74-34285. 1975. 6.95 (ISBN 0-440-05990-9). Delacorte Press.
Way of the Tiger, the Sign of the Dragon: A Novel. Howard Lee. 1973. (pbk) 1.25. Warner Paperback Lib.
Way of the Transgressor. Andrew John West. LC 49-5078. 1948. West Pub. Co.
Way of the Walking Wounded. Bernard Fendig Borchardt. LC 24-15191. Dorrance & Company.
Way of the Wilderness. Mary C McLellan. LC 44-814141. 1944. Wm. B. Eerdmans Publishing Company.
Way of the Wind. Eugenia Brooks Frothingham. LC 17-632674. 1917. 1.40. Houghton Mifflin Company.
Way of the Wind. Zoe Anderson Norris. LC 11-30359. 1911. 1.00. The Author.
Way of the World. Katherine Von Der Lin. 1921. Times Mirror Printing & Binding House.
Way of the World.". David Christie Murray. (On cover: Seaside library. Pocket ed., no. 195). 1884. G. Munro.
Way of the World. A Novel. David Christie Murray. (Harper's Franklin square library, no. 376). 1884. Harper & Brothers.
Way of the World, and Other Stories. Anna Maria Fielding Hall. LC 42-34045. 1867. T. Nelson and Sons.
Way of the World and Other Ways: A Story of Our Set. Katherine Eleanor Conway. LC 6603. 1900. The Pilot Publishing Company.
Way of These Women. Edward Phillips Oppenheim. LC 13-2504. 1913. 1.30. Little, Brown, and Company.
Way of These Women. Edward Phillips Oppenheim. LC 15-18114. 1915. 1.35. Little, Brown, and Company.
Way of Ume. Edith Augusta Sawyer. LC 28-20571. 1928. W. E. Rudge.
Way Out. A. R. Bailey & D. G. Hull. (Illus.). 85p. 1980. pap. text ed. 6.95x (Pub. by Inst Res Pub Canada). Renouf.
Way Out. Edna Parthenia Halloran. LC 13-16998. R. G. Badger.
Way Out: A Story of the Cumberlands to-Day. Emerson Hough. LC 18-11147. 1918. D. Appleton and Company.
Way Out of Berkeley Square. Rosemary Tonks. LC 78-137017. 1971. 4.95 o.p. (ISBN 0-87645-038-9). Gambit.
Way Out World. John Nebel. pap. 0.50 o.p. (72-644). Lancer.
Way Some People Die. Ross Macdonald. LC 79-25495. 1980. 10.95 (ISBN 0-89340-250-8). J. Curley.
Way Some People Die. Kenneth Millar. LC 51-11053. 1951. Knopf.
Way Some People Live: A Book of Stories. John Cheever. LC 43-5522. 1943. Random House.
Way Station. Clifford D Simak. LC 63-12874. (Doubleday science fiction). 1963. Doubleday.
Way Station. Clifford D. Simak. 1973. (pbk) 0.95. Manor Books.
Way Station. Clifford D. Simak. LC 77-368916. (Methuen paperbacks). 1976. 0.65 (ISBN 0-413-36900-5). Eyre Methuen.
Way Station. Clifford D. Simak. LC 79-20182. 1979. 10.00 (ISBN 0-8376-0440-0). R. Bentley.
Way Station West. William E Vance. LC 56-16719. (Ace double novel books, D-128). 1955. Ace Books.
Way That Led Beyond. J Harrison. LC 4-32160. 1904. Benziger Brothers.
Way the Cookie Crumbles. James Hadley Chase. 1974. (pbk.) 0.95 (ISBN 0-671-77922-2). Pocket Books.
Way They Died. Leslie Charles Ernenwein. 1978. pap. 1.50 o.s.i. (ISBN 0-505-51275-0). Tower Bks.
Way Things Are. Edmee Elizabeth Monica De La Pasture. LC 28-39793. Harper & Brothers.
Way Things Are. Josephine Lawrence. LC 50-8916. 1950. McGraw-Hill.
Way Things Are: And Other Stories. Albert Maltz. LC 38-21701. International Publishers.
Way Through the Wood. Nigel Balchin. LC 51-6512. 1951. Houghton Mifflin.
Way to Dawnworld. Bill Starr. LC 75-22288. (His A Farstar & son novel; 1). 1975. 1.50. Ballantine Books.
Way to Dusty Death. Alistair MacLean. LC 73-17483. 1973. 8.95 (ISBN 0-8161-6169-0). G. K. Hall.
Way to Dusty Death. Alistair MacLean. (Fawcett crest book). 1974. (pbk.) 1.50. Fawcett.
Way to Fort Pillow. James Sherburne. 1972. 6.95 o.p. (ISBN 0-395-13525-7). HM.
Way to Fort Pillow: A Novel. James Sherburne. LC 70-173779. 1972. 6.95 (ISBN 0-395-13525-7). Houghton Mifflin.
Way to Glory: Or, The Last Night of the Holidays, a Love Story. John Dick Scott. LC 51-11973. 1952. Knopf.
Way to Go Home. E. D Pendry. LC 78-13502. 8.95. Norton.
Way to Peace. Margaret Wade Campbell Deland. LC 10-21750. 1910. Harper & Brothers.
Way to St. Ives. Sonia Gernes. LC 82-636. 13.95 (ISBN 0-684-17492-8). Scribner.
Way to Santiago. Arthur Calder-Marshall. LC 40-11293. Reynal & Hitchcock.
Way to Success: Or, Tom Randall. LC 5902. (On cover: Medal library, no. 72). 1900. Street & Smith.
Way to the Gold: A Novel. 1st Ed. Wilbur Daniel Steele. LC 55-7006. 1955. Doubleday.
Way to the Lantern. Audrey Erskine Lindop. LC 61-9529. 1961. Doubleday.
Way to the Old Sailors Home. Thomas P. Baird. LC 76-26260. 7.95 (ISBN 0-06-010173-3). Harper & Row.
Way to the Old Sailors Home. Thomas P. Baird. 1978. 1.75 (ISBN 0-380-39008-6). Avon Books.
Way to the Sun. Robert Beylen. LC 77-149458. 1972. Popular Lib.
Way to the Uncle Sam Hotel. William Brown. LC 68-1692. (Coyote books). (Illus.). Distributed by City Lights Books.
Way to Win. John W Ferguson. LC 10-1779. 1909. The Neale Publishing Company.
Way to Win. Ward Sprague. LC 8-14047. For the Author by C. C. Hall & Co.
Way up. Mary Patricia Willcocks. LC 10-14673. 1910. John Lane Company; Etc., Etc.
Way up: The Memoirs of Count Gramont; a Novel. Sanche De Gramont. LC 72-80340. 1972. 7.95 (ISBN 0-399-10978-1). Putnam.
Way Uptown in Another World. Shane Stevens. LC 70-149614. 1971. 6.95. Putnam.
Way We Die Now. Michael Z Lewin. LC 72-87619. (Red mask mystery). 1973. 5.95 (ISBN 0-399-11088-7). Putnam.
Way We Die Now. Michael Z Lewin. (Berkley book). 1979. 1.75 (ISBN 0-425-04028-3). Berkley Pub. Corp.
Way We Live Now. Anthony Trollope. LC 74-132935. (Library of literature). (Illus.). 1974. 12.00 (ISBN 0-672-51455-9) (ISBN 0-672-51455-9). Bobbs-Merrill.
Way We Live Now. Anthony Trollope. LC 50-10379. (Borzoi Trollope). 1950. Knopf.
Way We Live Now. Anthony Trollope. (Half-title: The World's classics. CCLXXXIV-CCLXXXV). 1941. Oxford University Press, H. Milford.
Way We Live Now. Anthony Trollope. LC 82-9474. 1982. 6.95 (ISBN 0-486-24360-5). Dover Publications.
Way We Live Now. Anthony Trollope & John Sutherland. LC 81-18729. (World's classics). 1982. 7.95 (ISBN 0-19-281576-8). Oxford University Press.
Way We Live Now. 1st Ed. Warren Miller. LC 58-7853. 1958. Little, Brown.
Way We Lived. Rems Nna Umeasiegbu. (African Writers Ser.). 1969. pap. text ed. 3.50x (ISBN 0-435-90061-7). Heinemann Ed.
Way We Were. Arthur Laurents. LC 70-181657. 1973. (pbk.) 1.25. Avon Books.
Way West. large type ed., complete and unabridged. ed. Alfred Bertram Guthrie. LC 68-31916. (Illus.). F. Watts.
Way West. Alfred Bertram Guthrie. 1949. W. Sloane Associates.
Way West. Alfred Bertram Guthrie. LC 78-12532. 1978. 14.00 (ISBN 0-89783-005-9). Larlin Corp.
Way with All Maidens. Mel Johnson. pap. 1.25 o.p. Lancer.
Way with Women. William Gwinn. LC 54-37054. (Lion book, 209). 1954. Lion Books by Arrangement with Classic Syndicate.

Wayfarer. Roy Purcell. LC 74-25836. (Illus.). 1975. pap. 4.95 o.p. (ISBN 0-89087-007-1). Celestial Arts.

Wayfarer. Natsume Soseki. Tr. by Beongcheon Yu. LC 66-26974. 326p. 1967. 12.95x (ISBN 0-8143-1318-3). Wayne St U Pr.

Wayfarer: A Novel. Kathleen Millay. LC 26-16046. 1926. W. Morrow and Company, Inc.

Wayfarer: A Novel. Shirley Seifert. LC 38-27996. M. S. Mill Co., Inc.

Wayfarer: Kojin. Soseki Natsume. LC 81-15429. 1982. 5.95 (ISBN 0-399-50612-8). Putnam.

Wayfarer. Kojin. Tr. from Japanese, with an Introd. by Beongcheon Yu. Soseki Natsume. LC 66-26974. 1967. 8.95. Wayne State Univ. Pr.

Wayfarers. William W Crain. LC 74-172251. 1972. 6.95 (ISBN 0-252-00199-0). University of Illinois Press.

Wayfarers. Mary Stewart Doubleday Cutting. LC 8-19022. 1908. The McClure Company.

Wayfarers. Knut Hamsun. LC 79-27034. 1980. 12.95 (ISBN 0-374-28672-8). Farrar, Straus Giroux.

Wayfarers. Dan Wickenden. LC 45-335343. 1945. W. Morrow and Company.

Wayfarers at the Angel's. Sara Ware Bassett. LC 17-28601. 1917. 1.25. George H. Doran Company.

Wayfarers of Fate: A Novel. John A Steinbacher. LC 55-10070. 1955. Dorrance.

Wayfares in Toodlume. Anne Moore. LC 39-30373. 1939. The Southworth-Anthoensen Press.

Wayfaring Men: A Novel. Ada Ellen Bayly. LC 6-10289. 1897. Longmans, Green and Co.

Wayferers. Dan Wickenden. LC 46-523343. 1945. W. Morrow and Company.

Waylaid by Wireless: A Suspicion, a Warning, a Sporting Proposition, and a Transatlantic Pursuit. Edwin Balmer. LC 9-15088. Small, Maynard and Company.

Waylaid in Boston: A Homer Evans Mystery. Elliot Harold Paul. LC 53-5005. Random House.

Wayne of the Flying W. Arthur Henry Gooden. LC 34-25154. 1934. H. C. Kinsey & Company, Inc.

Ways & Means. new ed. Henry Cecil. 1974. Repr. of 1952 ed. 5.95 o.s.i. (ISBN 0-8277-3348-8). British Bk Ctr.

Ways of Death. Hans C Owen. LC 37-309477. Green Circle Books.

Ways of Escape. Noel Forrest. LC 26-14984. 1926. Little, Brown, and Company.

Ways of Escape. Graham Greene. 288p. 1982. pap. 3.95 (ISBN 0-671-43820-4). WSP.

Ways of God and Men; Great Stories from the Bible in World Literature. Ed. by Ruth Selden. LC 50-10911. 1950. Stephen Daye Press.

Ways of God & Men: Great Stories from the Bible in World Literature. Ed. by Ruth Selden. text ed. 11.50 o.p. (ISBN 0-8044-2810-7, Pub. by Stephen Daye Pr). Ungar.

Ways of Jane: A Story with Which the Wise and Prudent Have No Concern. Mary Finley Leonard. 1917. Duffield and Company.

Ways of Laughter: A Comedy of Interferences. Harold Begbie. LC 22-3963. 1922. G. P. Putnam's Sons.

Ways of Life: Two Stories. Margaret Oliphant Wilson Oliphant. LC 7-32502. (The Hudson library, no. 22). 1897. G. P. Putnam's Sons.

Ways of Loving. Brendan Gill. LC 73-18497. 1974. 7.95 (ISBN 0-15-195312-0). Harcourt Brace Jovanovich.

Ways of Providence: Or, "He Doeth All Things Well.". Timothy Shay Arthur. LC 6-3432. (On cover: Lovell's library, v. 10, no. 538). J. W. Lovell Company.

Ways of Seeing. John Berger. (Richard Seaver Books). (Illus.). 1973. 8.95 o.p. (ISBN 0-670-75273-8). Viking Pr.

Ways of Sunlight. Samuel Selvon. LC 58-403612. St. Martin's Press.

Ways of the Hour. James Fenimore Cooper. LC 68-57518. (Muckrakers Ser.). Repr. of 1850 ed. lib. bdg. 16.00 (ISBN 0-8398-0277-3). Irvington.

Ways of the Hour: A Tale. James Fenimore Cooper. LC 68-57518. 1968. Gregg Press.

Ways of the Hour: A Tale. James Fenimore Cooper. (On cover: Lovell's library. no. 587). 1885. J. W. Lovell Company.

Ways of the Hour. A Tale. James Fenimore Cooper. 1887. D. Appleton and Company.

Ways of the Hour. A Tale. James Fenimore Cooper. (On cover: Seaside library. Pocket ed. no. 415). 1885. G. Munro.

Ways of the Service. Frederick Palmer. LC 70-106290. (Short story index reprint series). (Illus.). 1970. Books for Libraries Press.

Ways of the Service. Frederick Palmer. LC 1-31354. 1901. C. Scribner's Sons.

Ways of White Folks. Langston Hughes. LC 34-27175. 1934. A. A. Knopf.

Ways of Youth. Carl Gustaf Boberg & Lindborg, Olga E., Tr. LC 25-9755. The Covenant Book Concern.

Ways That Are Wary. Lemuel De Bra. LC 79-101796. (Short story index reprint series). 1969. Books for Libraries Press.

Ways That Are Wary. Lemuel De Bra. LC 25-7942. E. J. Clode, Inc.

Wayside Courtships. Hamlin Garland. LC 70-103509. (Short story index reprint series). 1969. Books for Libraries Press.

Wayside Courtships. Hamlin Garland. LC 6-407163. 1897. D. Appleton and Company.

Wayside Flower. Wynne May. (Harlequin Romance Ser.). 192p. 1983. pap. 1.75. Harlequin Bks.

Wayside Tavern. Norah Robinson Lofts. LC 80-954. 1980. 11.95 (ISBN 0-385-17201-X). Doubleday.

Wayside" The Waking Dream of a Soul Before an Open Wood Fire. Edward Allen Hall. 1914. Sherman, French & Company.

Wayside Waif. Marie Mackin. LC 29-14762. R. G. Badger.

Waysiders; Stories of Connacht. Seumas O'Kelly. LC 73-150480. (Short story index reprint series). (Illus.). 1971. (ISBN 0-8369-3821-6). Books for Libraries Press.

Waysiders: Stories of Connacht. Seumas O'Kelly. LC 18-16901. 1918. Frederick A Stokes Company.

Wayward and Searching. Betty A Amos. LC 73-93412. 1974. 5.95 (ISBN 0-87695-169-8). Aurora Publishers.

Wayward Angel. Verne Chute. LC 48-5301. 1948. A. A. Knopf.

Wayward Anne. Usan Richmond Lee. LC 10-5221. D. Estes & Company.

Wayward Bride. Liz Genell. (Orig.). pap. 0.95 o.p. (1121). Brandon.

Wayward Bus. John Steinbeck. LC 47-30085. 1947. The Viking Press.

Wayward Bus. John Steinbeck. LC 79-15163. 1979. 1.95 (ISBN 0-14-005001-9). Penguin Books.

Wayward Comrade and the Commissars. Translated from the Russian by Andrew R. MacAndrew. IUrii Olesha. LC 60-2643. (Signet books, S1799). 1960. New American Library.

Wayward Daughter. Mike Goldberg. 192p. pap. 1.95 o.p. (ISBN 0-87977-124-0). Dansk Blue Bk.

Wayward Dosia. Alice Marie Celeste Durand. (On cover: The pastime series, no. 43). 1890. Laird & Lee.

Wayward Feet. Arthur Rhys Goring-Thomas. LC 12-7188. 1912. 1.25. John Lane Company.

Wayward Gang. Wal Watkins. LC 65-191949. bds., 3.50. Rigby.

Wayward Gate: Science & the Supernatural. Philip Slater. LC 77-75445. 1977. 9.95 o.p. (ISBN 0-8070-2956-4). Beacon Pr.

Wayward Girl's Fate: A Story of the Wisconsin Dens. John A Fraser. (Globe detective series. v. 1, no. 19). 1890. The Eagle Publishing Co.

Wayward Head and Heart. Claude Prosper Jolyot De Crebillon. LC 63-24951. (Oxford library of French classics). 1963. Oxford University Press.

Wayward Head & Heart. Claude P. De Crebillon. Tr. by Barbara Bray. 1963. 2.40 o.p. Oxford U Pr.

Wayward Heart. Sallie Lee Bell. LC 57-36781. 1957. Zondervan Pub. House.

Wayward Heart. Alice Lent Covert. LC 50-6721. 1950. Avalon Books.

Wayward Heart. Brian Dyer, pseud. 1977. pap. 1.50 (ISBN 0-532-15296-4). Woodhill.

Wayward Heart. Jill Gregory. 480p. (Orig.). 1982. pap. 4.95 (ISBN 0-441-87630-7). Ace Bks.

Wayward Heart. Jill Gregory. 1982. pap. 4.95. Dell.

Wayward Life: Or, A Girl's Destiny. Anovel. LC 8-36753. 1886. G. W. Carleton & Co.

Wayward Nymph. Elisabeth Gill. pap. 0.60 o.p. (60-388). Manor Bks.

Wayward Ones. Sara Harris. LC 52-10774. 1952. Crown Publishers.

Wayward Pilgrims. Gerald Warner Brace. LC 36-27314. 1938. G. P. Putman's Sons.

Wayward Season. Virginia S Gunn. LC 79-7686. 1980. 10.00 (ISBN 0-385-15391-0). Doubleday.

Wayward Susan. Leona Slottman. LC 46-50492. 1946. Phoenix Press.

Wayward Teenagers. Sterling Harkins. 192p. pap. 1.95 o.p. (ISBN 0-87977-131-3, DBB131). Dansk Blue Bk.

Wayward Wahine see Walk Softly, Witch.

Wayward Widow, No. 81. Anne Mayfield. 1982. pap. 1.75 (ISBN 0-515-06692-3). Jove Pubns.

Wayward Wife. Alberto Moravia. Tr. by Angus Davidson from It. LC 60-5140. 224p. 1973. pap. 1.25 o.p. (532-12192-125). Manor Bks.

Wayward Wife: And Other Stories by Alberto Moravia Pseud. Selected and Translated from the Italian by Angus Davidson. Alberto Pincherle. LC 60-514085. bds., 3.95.,Farrar. Straus and Cudahy.

Wayward Wife, and Other Stories: By Alberto Moravia Pseud. Selected and Translated by Angus Davidson. Alberto Pincherle. LC 60-5140. 1960. Farrar, Straus and Cudahy.

Wayward Wife: And Other Stories by Alberto Moravia. Selected, Tr. by Angus Davidson. Alberto Pincherle. (A-23). 1968. Ace.

Wayward Wife: And Other Stories; Comp., Tr. from French by Angus Davidson. Alberto Pincherle. (Signet bk. D1926). 1961. New American Lib.

Wayward Winds. Evelyn Kahn. 576p. (Orig.). 1981. pap. 2.95 (ISBN 0-671-83128-3). PB.

Wayward Winds. Roger SeLegue. LC 80-52064. 464p. (Orig.). 1980. pap. 3.95x (ISBN 0-9604600-0-4). Rooney Pubns.

Wayward Winifred. Anna Theresa Sadlier. LC 5-36924. 1905. Benziger Brothers.

Wayward Woman. A Novel. Arthur George Frederick Griffiths. (Franklin square library. no. 113). 1880. Harper & Brothers.

Waywaya & Other Stories from the Philippines. F. Sionil Jose. (Writing in Asia Ser.). (Orig.). 1981. pap. text ed. 8.00x (00258). Heinemann Ed.

We. Evgeny Ivanovich Zamyatin. LC 73-183514. 1972. 6.95 (ISBN 0-670-75318-1). Viking Press.

We. Evgeny Ivanovich Zamyatin & Gregory Zilboorg. LC 75-5743. (Gregg Press science fiction series). 1975. 13.00 (ISBN 0-8398-2320-7). Gregg Press.

We. Evgeny Ivanovich Zamyatin & Zilboorg, Gregory. 1890- Tr. LC 25-761. E. P. Dutton & Company.

We Accept with Pleasure. Bernard Augustine De Voto. LC 34-306822. 1934. Little, Brown, and Company.

We Actor Folks: The Story of an Ugly Actress. Mary Asquith. LC 31-20403. White Squaw Press.

We Agnostics: On the Tightrope to Eternity. Bernard Basset. LC 67-25876. 1968. Herder & Herder.

We Ain't Going Back No More, No How, Vol. 2. Mike F. Holodnak. LC 77-71882. 1977. pap. 7.95 (ISBN 0-9601084-2-4). Jacek.

We All. Alice French. LC 4-16457. 1891. D. Appleton and Company.

We All Have Our Secrets. Berta Ruck. LC 55-620789. 1955. Dodd, Mead.

We All Killed Grandma. 1st Ed. Fredric Brown. LC 52-6647. (Guilt edged mystery). 1952. Dutton.

We All Live Through It. Harold MacGrath. LC 27-10318. 1927. Doubleday, Page & Company.

We Always Come Back. Paul Fassett Ader. LC 45-97341. 1945. P. Paul.

We Always Treat Women Too Well: A Novel. Raymond Queneau. LC 80-26462. (Illus.). 1981. 14.95 (ISBN 0-8112-0792-7) (ISBN 0-8112-0793-5). New Directions.

We and Our Neighbors: Or, The Records of an Unfashionable Street. (Sequel to "My Wife and I.") A Novel. Harriet Elizabeth Beecher Stowe. LC 8-16111. 1875. J. B. Ford & Company.

We and Our Neighbors: Or, The Records of an Unfashionable Street (Sequal to "My Wife and I") Harriet Elizabeth Beecher Stowe. LC 1-29829. (Half-title: The writings of Harriet Beecher Stowe... Riverside edition, v. 13). 1901. Houghton, Miffin and Company.

We Are All Legends. Darrell Schweitzer. LC 81-5041. (Starblaze editions). 4.95 (ISBN 0-89865-062-3). Donning Co.

We Are Besieged. Barbara Fitzgerald. LC 46-6364. 1946. G. P. Putnam's Sons.

We Are Betrayed. Vardis Fisher. 1935. Doubleday, Doran & Company, Inc.; and Caldwell, Id., The Caxton Printers, Ltd.

We Are Fires Unquenchable. Mary Speers. LC 42-12640. 1942. Murray & Gee.

We Are French.". Perley Poore Sheehan & Davis, Robert Hobart, 1869- Joint Author. LC 14-18338. George H. Doran Company.

We Are God's Utopia. Stefan Andres. Tr. by E. Walker Caspari. 1965. pap. 0.85 o.p. (6025, Gate). Regnery.

We Are Incredible. Margery Latimer. J. H. Sears & Company, Inc.

We Are Not Alone. James Hilton. LC 37-27105. 1937. Little, Brown and Company.

We Are Not Alone. Walter Sullivan. pap. 1.95 (ISBN 0-451-08168-4, J8168, Sig). NAL.

We Are One: A Story of American Life... Theo Welch. LC 8-36734. 1878. S. L. Ewing & Co.

We Are Seven. Decorations by Vasiliu. 1st Ed. Una Troy. LC 57-5328. 1957. Dutton.

We Are Spoiled. Phyllis Paul. LC 34-334. 1934. W. Morrow & Company.

We Are Ten. Fannie Hurst. LC 72-178442. (Short story index reprint series). 1971. (ISBN 0-8369-4043-1). Books for Libraries Press.

We Are Ten. Fannie Hurst. LC 37-215383. 1937. Harper & Brothers.

We Are the Living. Erskine Caldwell. LC 53-737809. 1953. Duell, Sloan and Pearce.

We Are the Living. Erskine Caldwell. LC 33-25381. 1933. The Viking Press.

We Are the Robbers. Edward Harris Heth. LC 47-11577. 1947. Harper.

We Ask So Little. Anne Wormser. LC 39-253223. 1939. Macrae Smith Company.

We Be Word Sorcerers: 25 Stories by Black Americans. Sonia Sanchez. (Bantam anthologies). 1973. (pbk.) 1.25. Bantam Books.

We Begin. Helen Grace Carlisle. LC 32-171521. 1932. H. Smith.

We Belong Together. Cecile Gilmore. LC 42-18724. 1942. H. C. Kinsey & Company, Inc.

We Bombed in New Haven: A Play. Joseph Heller. 1968. 4.95. Knoof.

We Brandons. Claretta Maxwell. LC 7-17045. Broadway Publishing Co.

We Can Begin Again Together. Dane Rudhyar. (O.s.i.). 1974. pap. 4.95 o.s.i. (ISBN 0-912358-45-9). Omen Pr.

We Can Build You. Philip K. Dick. (Science Fiction Ser.). 208p. (Orig.). 1972. pap. 0.95 o.p. (UQ1014). DAW Bks.

We Can Build You. Philip K. Dick. (Science Fiction Ser). 1975. pap. 1.25 o.p. (UY1164). DAW Bks.

We Can't All Be Blondes. Helen Jean Skillen Stone. LC 27-22838. 1927. H. Vinal, Ltd.

We Can't Breathe. Ronald L. Fair. LC 72-156560. 1972. 8.95 o.p. (ISBN 0-06-011216-6, HarpT). Har-Row.

We Can't Have Everything: A Novel. Rupert Hughes. LC 17-222999. Harper & Brothers.

We Can't Have Everything: A Novel. Rupert Hughes & Flagg, James Montgomery, 1877- Illus. LC 22-4735. 1917. A. L. Burt Company.

We Could Be Happy Together. Vivek Adarkar. 105p. 1973. 4.00x (ISBN 0-210-22370-7). Asia.

We Dance and Sing. Richard Dougherty. LC 72-139015. 1971. 6.95. Doubleday.

We Danced All Night. Barbara Cartland. 1972. pap. 1.25 o.p. (ISBN 0-515-04314-1, V4314). BJ Pub Group.

We Danced All Night. Barbara Cartland. 1977. pap. 1.25 o.p. BJ Pub Group.

We Fed Them Cactus. Fabiola Cabeza de Baca. LC 54-12881. (Zia Bks.). 208p. 1979. pap. 5.95 (ISBN 0-8263-0517-2). U of NM Pr.

We Few: A Novel. 1st Ed. H Frank Jones. LC 57-595464. 1957. Exposition Press.

We Few, We Happy Few: A Novel. David Albert Davidson. LC 73-90315. 1974. 6.95. Crown Publishers.

We Fished All Night. Willard Motley. LC 73-18875. 1974. 32.50 (ISBN 0-404-11370-2). AMS Press.

We Fished All Night. Willard Motley. LC 51-14180. 1951. Appleton-Century-Crofts.

We Fly Away. Robert Francis. LC 48-8497. 1948. Swallow Press.

We Forget Because We Must: A Story of Decades and Lustres. William Babington Maxwell. LC 26-251827. 1928. Doubleday, Doran and Company, Inc.

We Four Girls: A Summer Story, for Girls. Mary Greenleaf Darling. LC 99-3756. 1899. Lee and Shepard.

We Four Villagers. A Tale of Domestic Life in Pennsylvania. G Fort. LC 6-40375. 1861. J. S. McCalla.

We Gather Together. Sara Lucile Jenkins. LC 48-7581. 1948. Crowell.

We Gave at the Office: Or, What's a Girl to Do? Laura Mills & Pauline Burlick. (Fawcett gold medal book). 1974. (pbk.) 1.25. Fawcett.

We Go This Way but Once. Knox Quinn Lewis. LC 43-11845. 1943. Dorrance and Company.

We Had to Die to Live Forever. Stephen Cupchalk. 3.50 o.p. Carlton.

We Happy Few. Helen Huntington Howe. LC 46-170668. 1946. Simon and Schuster.

We Have All Gone Away. Curtis Harnack. LC 72-90970. 1973. 6.95 (ISBN 0-385-03260-9). Doubleday.

We Have All Gone Away. Curtis Harnack. LC 73-13813. 1973. 8.95 (ISBN 0-8161-6155-0). G. K. Hall.

We Have Always Lived in the Castle. Shirley Jackson. LC 62-17935. 1962. Viking Press.

We Have Been Warned: A Novel. Naomi Haldane Mitchison. LC 36-22624. 1936. The Vanguard Press.

We Have Changed All That. Herbert Quick & MacMahon, Elena Stepanoff. LC 28-8368. The Bobbs-Merrill Company.

We Have Met the Enemy. Ralph Mitchell Crosby & Perry, Oliver Hazard. LC 40-30526. The Bobbs-Merrill Company.

We Have Seen the Best of Our Times: Short Stories. Nancy A J Potter. LC 68-12676. 1968-1969. 4.95. Knopf.

We Have Your Daughter!". Frank Anvic, pseud. 1974. (pbk.) 1.95 (ISBN 0-87056-382-3). Brandon Books.

We Haven't Seen Her Lately. E. X. Ferrars, pseud. 1972. pap. 0.75 o.p. (07225). Curtis.

We Haven't Seen Her Lately: By E. X. Ferrars Pseud. 1st Ed. Morna Doris MacTaggart Brown. LC 56-809519. 1956. Published for the Crime Club by Doubleday.

We Hereby Certify--". Norman Wright Welsh. LC 43-102992. 1943. Harbinger House.
We in Captivity: A Novel. Kathleen Pawle. LC 36-7189. 1936. Dodd, Mead & Company.
We Inheritors. Mary Stuart Chamberlain. LC 37-17512. L. Furman, Inc.
We Joined the Navy. John Winton. LC 59-13836. 1959. St. Martin's Press.
We Kaytons. Steele Rudd. (O.s.i.). 188p. 1972. pap. 2.75x o.s.i. (ISBN 0-7022-0747-0). U of Queensland Pr.
We Killed Mangy-Dog & Other Stories. Luis Bernardo Honwana. (African Writers Ser.). 1969. pap. text ed. 3.00x (ISBN 0-435-90060-9). Heinemann Ed.
We Like It Here. Don Dabill. 72p. 1975. pap. 3.25. Country Print.
We Live but Once. Rupert Hughes. LC 27-114871. 1927. Harper & Brothers.
We Lived As Children. Kathryn Cavarly Hulme. LC 38-275425. 1938. A. A. Knopf.
We Love Glenda So Much, and Other Tales. Julio Cortazar. LC 82-48732. 1983. 11.95 (ISBN 0-394-53024-1). Knopf.
We Love Glenda So Much, and Other Tales. Julio Cortazar. LC 82-48718. 1983. 11.95 (ISBN 0-394-52493-4). Knopf.
We Love Glenda So Much & Other Tales. Julio Cortazar. Tr. by Gregory Rabassa from Span. LC 82-48732. 1983. 11.95 (ISBN 0-394-52493-4). Knopf.
We Loved Them Once. Ronda Rivers. LC 54-11899. Vantage Press.
We Met the Space People. Helen Mitchell & Betty Mitchell. 1967. pap. 1.00 o.p. Saucerian.
We Must Have a Trial. Margaret Leek. (Raven House Mysteries Ser.). 224p. 1983. pap. cancelled (ISBN 0-373-63050-6, Pub. by Worldwide). Harlequin Bks.
We Must March: A Novel of the Winning of Oregon. Honore McCue Willsie Morrow. LC 25-20630. 1925. Frederick A. Stokes Company.
We Need the Business,". Joseph E Austrian. LC 19-18832. Frederick A. Stokes Company.
We Never Make Mistakes" Two Short Novels. 2d ed. Aleksandr Isaevich Solzhenitsyn. LC 70-156226. 1971. 4.95 (ISBN 0-87249-090-4). University of South Carolina Press.
We Others: Stories of Fate, Love and Pity; Tr. from the French of Henri Barbusse... Henri Barbusse. Tr. by W. Fitzwater Wray. LC 18-20934. E. P. Dutton & Company.
We Parted at the Altar: A Novel. Laura Jean Libbey. (On cover: The choice series, no. 54). 1892. R. Bonner's Sons.
We Pass This Way. Charles A Cooper. LC 50-13055. 1950. Exposition Press.
We Pluck This Flower,. Thomas William Duncan. LC 37-3822. 1937. Coward-McCann, Inc.
We Real Cool. Gwendolyn Brooks. (Broadside Ser., No. 6). broadsheet. 0.50 o.p. Broadside.
We Ride the Gale! Emilie Baker Loring. LC 34-5283. The Penn Publishing Company.
We Sail Tomorrow. Frederick Hazlitt Brennan. LC 34-72947. 1934. Longmans, Green and Co.
We Sail with the Tide: A Novel. 1st Ed. George Thomas Whitson. LC 56-95723. 1956. Exposition Press.
We Sailed at Dawn. Thom Ditton. LC 55-38186. 1955. Christopher Pub. House.
We Saw Him Die. Aaron Marc Stein. LC 47-12129. 1947. Pub. for the Crime Club by Doubleday & Company, Inc.
We Saw the Sea. John Winton. LC 60-15876. 1960. St. Martin's Press.
We Shall March Again. Translated from the German by Anthony G. Powell. Gerhard Kramer. LC 55-822151. 1955. Putnam.
We Shall Stay Free. Taomie Stanfield. LC 45-54822. 1945. Dorrance & Company.
We Shook the Family Tree. Hildegarde Dolson. (Illus.). (YA) 1941. 5.95 o.p. (ISBN 0-394-45126-0). Random.
We Sing Diana. Wanda Fraiken Neff. 1928. Houghton Mifflin Company.
We Speak No Treason. Rosemary Hawley Jarman. 1973. 1.50. Popular Lib.
We Speak No Treason. Rosemary Hawley Jarman. LC 77-152400. (Illus.). 1971. 8.95. Little, Brown.
We Spend Our Years. Charlotte Margaret Kruger Bryant. LC 45-7905. 1945. Zondervan Publishing House.
We Spend Our Years. Charlotte Margaret Kruger. LC 45-7905. 1945. Zondervan Publishing House.
We Stood for Freedom. Iris Morley. LC 42-1111. 1942. W. Morrow & Company.
We That Are Left. Irene Kampen. LC 62-15873. 1963. Doubleday.
We, the Accused. Ernest Raymond. LC 81-8851. 1981. 12.95 (ISBN 0-312-85883-3). St. Martin's Press.
We, the Accused. Ernest Raymond. LC 81-19248. 1982. 12.95 (ISBN 0-14-006220-3). Penguin Books.
We, the Accused: A Novel. Ernest Raymond. LC 35-15166. 1935. Frederick A. Stokes Company.
We, the Accused: T. V. edition. Ernest Raymond. 1983. pap. 3.95 (ISBN 0-14-006220-3). Penguin.
We the Bereaved. Anna Clarke. LC 82-45539. (Crime Club Ser.). 192p. 1982. 11.95 (ISBN 0-385-18359-3). Doubleday.
We, the Few. John L Hawkinson. LC 51-11850. 1952. Exposition Press.
We the Living. Ayn Rand. LC 59-5735. 1959. Random House.
We the Living. Ayn Rand. LC 36-8275. 1936. The Macmillan Company.
We Three. Gouverneur Morris. LC 16-7500. 1916. D. Appleton and Company.
We Three: A Novel. Olga Ott & Ott, Estrid. Tr. by Van Sand, Albert. LC 24-23289. 1924. Minton, Balch & Company.
We Three: A Tale of the Erie Canal. Howard Preble Cotton. LC 11-1797. 1.50. The C. M. Clark Publishing Company.
We Three and Troddles. A Tale of London Life. A Barrett. LC 6-8649. 1895. H. Altemus.
We Too Are Drifting. Gale Wilhelm. LC 75-12359. (Homosexuality). 1975. 9.00 (ISBN 0-405-07380-1). Arno Press.
We Too Are Drifting. Gale Wilhelm. LC 35-128013. Random House.
We Took to the Woods. Louise D. Rich. (Illus.). 1975. pap. 5.95 (ISBN 0-89272-016-6). Down East.
We. Translated and with a Foreword by Gregory Zilboorg. Evgeny Ivanovich Zamyatin. LC 63-25202. (Dutton everyman paperback D39). 1959. Dutton.
We Two. William Woolfolk. LC 77-79427. 1977. 1.95. Playboy Press.
We Two: A Novel. Ada Ellen Bayly. LC 4-16493. 1902. D. Appleton and Company.
We Two Together. Denise Robins. 192p. 1973. pap. 0.75 o.p. (T2734, GM). Fawcett World.
We, Von Arldens. Clara Louise Root Burnham. 1881. H. A. Sumner & Company.
We Walk Alone. Harriet Henry, pseud. LC 35-157441. 1935. Harper & Brothers.
We Want That Range. Frank Chester Robertson. LC 31-14330. Barse & Co.
We Want to Live. Robert S. Crossley. LC 67-21859. 1967. pap. 0.95 o.p. (ISBN 0-87784-431-3). Inter-Varsity.
We Went Thataway. Harry Allen Smith. LC 49-11513. 1949. Doubleday.
We Were Once Beautiful Butterflies. Maria Kavanagh. (Orig.). 1982. pap. 2.95 (ISBN 0-89083-968-9). Zebra.
We Were Strangers. Robert Sylvester. LC 49-4494. (Signet books, 716). 1949. New American Library.
We Were Thirteen & Two Are Left. Josephine Jugar. 4.50 o.p. Vantage.
We Who Are About to. Joanna Russ. 1977. 1.50 (ISBN 0-440-19428-8). Dell Pub. Co.
We Who Died Last Night. Quentin Morrow Phillip. 1941. The Grail.
We Who Wait: They Also Serve Who Only Stand and Wait. Elizabeth Carfrae, pseud. LC 43-8186. 1943. G. P. Putnam's Sons.
We Will Not Meet Again. John Hawkins & Hawkins, Ward, Joint Author. LC 40-31522. The Dial Press, Inc.
We Won't Come Back to Oahu Anymore. Charles A. Snay. 4.95 o.p. Carlton.
We Wore Jump Boots & Baggy Pants. John Ospital. 1977. pap. 7.95 (ISBN 0-912450-15-0). Willow Hse.
Weak and the Strong. Gerald Kersh. LC 46-7278. 1946. Simon and Schuster.
Weak and Willing. John Saxon. 1942. Phoenix Press.
Weak-Eyed Bat. Margaret Millar. LC 42-7501. 1942. Published for the Crime Club, by Doubleday, Doran & Co., Inc.
Weak-Kneed Rogue: Or, A Misleading Clue. Frederic Van Rensselaer Dey. LC 44-202849. (On cover: New magnet library, no. 728). 1911. Street & Smith.
Weaker Than a Woman. Charlotte Mary Brame. (select series, no. 45). Street & Smith.
Weaker Than a Woman. Charlotte Mary Brame. (On cover: Columbus series). International Book Company.
Weaker Vessel. Edward Frederic Benson. LC 13-381224. 1913. 1.35. Dodd, Mead and Company.
Weaker Vessel. David Christie Murray. LC 44-155303. 1888. Macmillan and Co.
Weaker Vessel: A Novel. David Christie Murray. LC 7-25475. (On cover: Harper's Franklin square library, no. 637). 1889. Harper & Brothers.
Weaker Vessel. A Novel. David Christie Murray. (On cover: Seaside library. Pocket ed., no. 1162). 1889. G. Munro.
Weakfoot. Linda Cline. 1975. 5.95 o.p. (ISBN 0-688-41697-7); PLB 5.49 o.p. (ISBN 0-688-51697-1). Morrow.
Weakling, and The Enemy. Francois Mauriac. LC 52-5923. 1952. Pellegrini & Cudahy.
Wealth and Welfare. Albert Bitzius. LC 75-4947. 1975. 17.50. H. Fertig.
Wealth and Welfare. Albert Btizius. LC 6-12707. 1866. A. Strahan.
Wealth and Wine. Mary Dwinell Chellis. 1874. National Temperance Society and Publication House.
Wealth and Worth: Or, Which Makes the Man? ... LC 8-36752. 1842. Harper & Brothers.
Wealth of Mister Waddy. Herbert George Wells. Ed. by Harris Wilson. LC 78-76192. (Crosscurrents-Modern Fiction Ser.). 1969. 5.95 o.p. (ISBN 0-8093-0391-4). S Ill U Pr.
Wealth of Mr. Waddy: A Novel. Herbert George Wells. LC 78-76192. (Crosscurrents/modern fiction). 1969. 5.95. Southern Illinois University Press.
Wealth: The Passport to Sexual Excess. Clark Gifford. pap. 1.95 o.p. (ISBN 0-87682-261-8, 7261). Barclay Hse.
Weans. Robert Nathan. (O.s.i.). (Illus.). (YA) 1960. 6.95 o.s.i. (ISBN 0-394-45128-7). Knopf.
Weapon Heavy. John Henry Reese. LC 72-89344. 1973. 4.95 (ISBN 0-385-08950-3). Doubleday.
Weapon Makers. Alfred Elton Van Vogt. LC 52-5626. 1952. Greenberg.
Weapon Makers. Alfred Elton Van Vogt. LC 47-17966. 1947. Hadley Publishing Co.
Weapon Makers. Alfred Elton Van Vogt. 1.75 (ISBN 0-671-82267-5).
Weapon of Night. Nick Carter. (Nick Carter Killmaster Ser.). 160p. pap. 0.60 o.p. (A215X, Award). Univ Pub & Dist.
Weapon Shops of Isher. Alfred Elton Van Vogt. LC 54-318221. (Ace double novel books, D-53). 1954. Ace Books.
Weapon Shops of Isher. Alfred Elton Van Vogt. LC 51-11115. 1951. Greenberg.
Wear a Fast Gun. John W Jakes. LC 56-134435. 1956. Arcadia House.
Wear My Love Proudly. Laura Saunders. LC 53-6607. 1953. Bouregy; Curl.
Wear My Ring Again. Mildred Woodford. 1970. 2.95 o.p. (50-9300). Moody.
Weariest River. George S O'Neal. LC 35-8027. Greenberg.
Wearing of the Green.". Richard Ashe King. (On cover: Seaside library. Pocket ed., no. 344). 1885. G. Munro.
Wearing of the Green. A Novel. Richard Ashe King. (Harper's Franklin square library. no. 444). 1885. Harper & Brothers.
Wearithorne, or In the Light of to-Day. Marian Calhoun Legare Reeves. LC 7-30662. 1872. J. B. Lippincott & Co.
Weary Falcon. Tom Mayer. LC 75-132335. 1971. 4.95. Houghton Mifflin.
Weasel Hunt: A Novel of Suspense. James K MacDougall. LC 77-76881. 1977. 8.95 (ISBN 0-672-52337-X). Bobbs-Merrill.
Weather at Tregulla. Stella Gibbons. 288p. (O.S.I.). 1973. 5.95 o.s.i. (ISBN 0-85617-990-6). White Lion Pubs.
Weather Breeder. Sylvia Chatfield Bates. LC 48-6687. 1948. Duell, Sloan and Pearce.
Weather in Africa. Martha Gellhorn. LC 79-23763. 1980. 7.95 (ISBN 0-396-07781-1). Dodd, Mead.
Weather in Africa: Martha Gelhorn. Martha Gellhorn. (Bard Book.). 1981. 3.50 (ISBN 0-380-55855-6). Avon Books.
Weather in Middenshot: A Novel. 1st American Ed. Edgar Mittelholzer. LC 53-1289. 1953. J. Day Co.
Weather in the Streets. Rosamond Lehmann. LC 36-10357. Reynal & Hitchcock.
Weather of February. 1st Ed. Hollis Spurgeon Summers. LC 57-8215. 1957. Harper.
Weather of the Heart. Daphne Athas. LC 47-3621. 1947. D. Appleton-Century Company, Inc.
Weather Shelter. Erskine Caldwell. LC 73-83376. 1969. 5.50. World Pub. Co.
Weather Tomorrow: A Novel. John Sacret Young. LC 81-40227. 1981. 10.95 (ISBN 0-394-52149-8). Random House.
Weather Tree. Maristan Chapman. LC 31-285951. 1932. The Viking Press.
Weatherbeaten Man: A Tale of American Patriotism. William Velpeau Rooker. LC 11-8953. 1911. 1.50. Cochrane Publishing Company.
Weatherby Crisis. Bernard Lester. LC 56-13995. 1956. Twayne Publishers.
Weathercock. Constance Woodbury Dodge. LC 42-210876. 1942. Dodd, Mead & Company.
Weathercock. George Manville Fenn. LC 6-39509. United States Book Company.
Weatherhouse. Nan Shepherd. LC 30-12693. E. P. Dutton & Co., Inc.
Weathermakers. Benjamin Bova. LC 68-10078. 1967. Holt, Rinehart and Winston.
Weatherman Guy. Jon Burmeister. LC 75-9468. 1975. 7.95. St. Martin's Press.
Weathermonger. Peter Dickinson. (Science Fiction Ser). pap. 0.95 o.p. (UQ1112). DAW Bks.
Weathermonger. Peter Dickinson. 1974. (pbk.) 0.95. DAW Books.
Weave a Circle. Desemea Wilson. LC 38-324066. 1938. E. P. Dutton & Co., Inc.
Weave a Wicked Web. Paul Kruger. LC 67-16719. (Inner sanctum mystery). 1967. bds., 3.95. S.&S.
Weave It Like Nightfall. Ewing Campbell. LC 77-72760. 2.95. Nefertiti Head Press.
Weave of Women. E. M. Broner. 1982. pap. write for info. Bantam.
Weave of Women: A Novel. E. M Broner. LC 77-13609. 8.95 (ISBN 0-03-018461-4). Holt, Rinehart and Winston.
Weaver: A Collection of Fables. Robert K. Swisher. 1975. pap. 1.95x (ISBN 0-912852-05-4). Echo Pubs.
Weaver of Dreams. Myrtle Reed. LC 11-24126. 1911. G. P. Putnam's Sons.
Weaver of Dreams: A Love Story. Eleanor Elliott Carroll. LC 34-22036. Chelsea House.
Weaver of Tales: A Collection of Stories... Lee Marion Roussseau. LC 34-40093. Lion Press.
Weavers: A Tale of England and Egypt of Fifty Years Ago. Gilbert Parker. LC 7-30167. 1907. Harper & Brothers.
Weavers and Weft: Or, "Love That Hath Us in His Net.". Mary Elizabeth Braddon Maxwell. LC 7-25293. (On cover: Seaside library. Pocket ed. no. 943). 1887. G. Munro.
Weaver's Grave. Seumas O'Kelly. 1965. 2.50 o.p. (ISBN 0-900372-49-4). Irish Bk Ctr.
Weaving of Webs. Francis Wells Van Praag. LC 2-25598. 1902. R. F. Fenno & Company.
Web. Hugh Brooke. LC 34-30869. 1934. Doubleday, Doran and Company, Inc.
Web. Frederick Trevor Hill. LC 3-29278. 1903. Doubleday, Page & Co.
Web: A Novel. Frederic Arnold Kummer. LC 19-2187. 1919. The Century Co.
Web, a Trilogy of Novellas: Translated by Richard and Clara Winston. Illustrated by Selma Bluestein. 1st Ed. Fulop-Miller, Rene. LC 50-10880. 1950. Abelard Press.
Web and the Rock. Thomas Wolfe. LC 39-275749. 1939. Harper & Brothers.
Web Begun. Helen G. Farrar. (Orig.). 1971. pap. 0.75 o.p. (B75-2171). Belmont-Tower.
Web Between the Worlds. Charles Sheffield. LC 79-124282. 4.95 (ISBN 0-441-87862-8). Ace Books.
Web of Allyngrood. Francesca Chimenti. LC 76-56276. 1977. 6.95 (ISBN 0-385-12740-5). Doubleday.
Web of Angels. John M. Ford. (Orig.). 1980. pap. 2.25 (ISBN 0-671-82947-5, Timescape). PB.
Web of Darkness. Marion Zimmer Bradley. LC 80-22995. (Starblaze editions). 4.95 (ISBN 0-89865-032-1). Donning.
Web of Days. Edna L. Mooney Lee. LC 48-3511. 1948. Sun Dial Press.
Web of Days. Edna L. Mooney Lee. 1947. D. Appleton-Century Company, Inc.
Web of Deceit. Chester Alfred Smith. LC 58-110. (Milestone book). 1957. Comet Press Books.
Web of Deception. Francesca Chimenti. (Candlelight Intrigue). 1979. 1.25 (ISBN 0-440-19755-4). Dell Pub. Co.
Web of Desire. Jean Hager. (Candlelight Ecstasy Ser.: No. 31). 192p. (Orig.). 1981. pap. 1.75 (ISBN 0-440-19434-2). Dell.
Web of Desire: By Jack Woodford Pseud. & Evis Joberg. Josiah Pitts Woolfolk & Evis Joberg. LC 53-20872. 1953. Signature Press.
Web of Destiny. Mary Ann Lillibridge Bliven. LC 7-36918. Broadway Publishing Co.
Web of Destiny. Muriel Elwood. 1976. pap. 1.75 (ISBN 0-532-17147-0). Woodhill.
Web of Enchantment. Claudia Slack. Bd. with Outrageous Fortune. 1980. pap. 1.95 (ISBN 0-451-09357-7, J9357, Sig). NAL.
Web of Enchantment. Claudia Slack. (Signet Book.). 1977. 1.50. (ISBN 0-451-07471-8). New American Library.
Web of Everywhere. John Brunner. LC 74-5064. 1974. (pbk.) 1.25. Bantam Books.
Web of Evil. Lucille Emerick. LC 48-7662. 1948. Doubleday.
Web of Gold. Katharine Pearson Woods. T. Y. Crowell & Co.
Web of Guilt. Gene DeWeese. LC 76-44858. (Zodiac gothic: Scorpio). 1977. 8.95 (ISBN 0-89340-016-5). J. Curley & Associates.
Web of Gunsmoke: By Will Hickok Pseud. C. William Harrison. LC 55-11510. (Signet books, 1242). 1955. New American Library.
Web of Haefen. Juanita Tyree Osborne. 1982. pap. 6.95 (Avalon). Bouregy.
Web of Hate. Frederick Mayer. LC 61-10894. 1961. Whittier Books.
Web of Honey. Cecile Gilmore. LC 51-9327. 1951. Avalon Books.
Web of Intrigue. Barbara Cust. 1974. 4.95. Lenox Hill Press.
Web of Lace. Pascal Laine. 1977. 8.50 (ISBN 0-200-72453-3). Transatlantic.
Web of Lace: A Novel. Pascal Laine. LC 76-381327. 1976. 6.50 (ISBN 0-200-72453-3). Abelard-Schuman.
Web of Life. Robert Herrick. LC 75-104482. 1970. Literature House.
Web of Life. Robert Herrick. LC 388014. 1900. The Macmillan Company.

Web of Life. John H. Storer. LC 53-12063. (O.s.i.). (Illus.). 142p. pap. 5.95 o.s.i. (ISBN 0-8159-7203-2). Devin.
Web of Life see Collected Works.
Web of Light. Marion Zimmer Bradley. LC 82-23456. 12.95 (ISBN 0-89865-289-8). Donning.
Web of Light. Marion Zimmer Bradley. (Orig.). 1983. pap. 2.95 (ISBN 0-671-44875-7, Timescape). PB.
Web of Lucifer: A Novel of the Borgia Fury. Maurice Samuel. LC 47-2623. 1947. A. A. Knopf.
Web of Murder. Austin J Small. LC 29-4991. 1929. Pub. for the Crime Club, Inc., by Doubleday, Doran & Company, Inc.
Web of Our Life. Joseph Boxley Roberts. LC 56-112491. 1957. Bruce Humphries.
Web of Passion. Jacques Perdue. LC 56-26173. 1956. Castle Books.
Web of Peril. Dorothy Daniels. (Orig.). 1970. pap. 0.60 o.p. (X2180). Pyramid Pubns.
Web of Peril. Dorothy Daniels. 1974. pap. 0.95 o.p. (ISBN 0-515-03371-5, N3371). Pyramid Pubns.
Web of Salvage. Brian Callison. LC 73-91716. 192p. (YA) 1974. 5.95 o.p. (ISBN 0-399-11349-5). Putnam.
Web of Sand: Dumarest of Terra, No. 20. E. C. Tubb. (Science Fiction Ser.: No. 20). (Orig.). 1979. pap. 1.75 (ISBN 0-87997-479-6, UE1479). DAW Bks.
Web of Silence. C. H. Guenter. 1977. pap. 1.25 (ISBN 0-532-12525-8). Woodhill.
Web of Silk. Yvonne Whittal. (Harlequin Presents Ser.). 192p. 1983. pap. 1.95 (ISBN 0-373-10582-7). Harlequin Bks.
Web of Spies. Nick Carter. (Nick Carter Killmaster Ser.). (O.s.i.). pap. 0.60 o.s.i. (A288X, Award). Univ Pub & Dist.
Web of Starfire. Edwina Lindsay Travers. 1976. 5.00 (ISBN 0-682-48615-9). Exposition Press.
Web of Steel. Cyrus Townsend Brady. LC 16-8231. 1.35. Fleming H. Revell Company.
Web of the Chozen. Jack L Chalker. LC 77-25227. 1978. 1.75 (ISBN 0-345-27376-1). Ballantine Books.
Web of the Golden Spider. Frederick Orin Bartlett. LC 9-42965. 1909. 1.50. Small, Maynard and Company.
Web of the Spider. Andrew J. Offutt & Richard K. Lyon. (War of the Wizards Ser.: Part III). (Orig.). 1981. pap. 2.95 (ISBN 0-671-82680-8, Timescape). PB.
Web of the Witch World. Andre Norton, pseud. LC 77-23208. (Norton, Andre. The Witch World Novels of Andre Norton). (Illus.). 1977. 7.95 (ISBN 0-8398-2357-6). Gregg Press.
Web of Time. Christine Hunter, pseud. LC 78-2643. 1978. 3.95 (ISBN 0-89293-057-8). Beta Book Co.
Web of Time. Robert Edward Knowles. LC 8-31462. F. H. Revell Company.
Web of Time. 1st Ed. Josephine Lawrence. LC 53-106325. 1953. Harcourt, Brace.
Web of Youth. Wilheim Emmanuel Suskind & Campbell, Malcolm Hugh, 1895- LC 31-14625. 1931. Brewer and Warren Inc.
Webbing & Ashes. Charles W. Pratt. 2.50 o.p. Vantage.
Webs in the Sky. Marjorie Roberts. LC 40-32095. W. Funk Inc.
Webs of Everywhere. John Brunner. 192p. 1983. pap. 2.25 (ISBN 0-345-30680-5, Del Rey). Ballantine.
Webs of War in White and Black. Anneliza Carruthers Wilson. LC 13-24397. 1913. Broadway Publishing Co.
Webster--Man's Man. Peter Bernard Kyne. LC 17-251269. 1917. Doubleday, Page & Company.
Webster--Man's Man. Peter Bernard Kyne. LC 21-19132. 1919. Grosset & Dunlap.
Wed by Mighty Waves: A Thrilling Romance of Ill-Fated Galveston. Sue Greenleaf. (On cover: Library of choice fiction, no. 26). 1901. Laird & Lee.
Wed to a Lunatic. A Wild, Weird Yarn of Love... Frank Warren Hastings. LC 7-2633. 1896. L. W. Rowell.
Wedded and Parted. Charlotte Mary Brame. LC 44-112575. (On cover: Seaside library. Pocket ed. No. 79). G. Munro.
Wedded and Parted. Emma S Southworth. LC 50-40329. 1884. J. S. Ogilvie.
Wedded and Saved! Spreading the Toils, Cruelly Wronged, The Sport of Fortune, Her Mistake, A Secret Engagement. By the Author of "Under the Sword," "Over the Border," "The Fire Opal," Etc. Carrie L. Shove. LC 8-7328. 1882. Rhodes & McClure.
Wedded by Fate: Or, Sister Angela. Sarah Elizabeth Forbush G. S. Downs Downs. LC 6-45959. Dodd, Mead & Company.
Wedded for an Hour: Or, The Heiress of Heathcote. Emma Garrison Jones. LC 7-11906. (select series. no. 85). 1891. Street & Smith.
Wedded for Pique: A Novel. May Agnes Early Fleming. LC 6-39939. 1897. G. W. Dillingham Co.
Wedded Hands. A Novel. Charles Andrews. (On cover: The seaside library. Pocket ed. no. 628). 1885. G. Munro.
Wedded to Sport. Mary E. Kennard. National Book Company.
Wedded Unwooed. A Novel. Julia Howard Gatewood. 1892. G. W. Dillingham.
Wedded Widow: Or, The Love That Lived. Thomas W Hanshew. (On cover: Street & Smith's select series, no. 2). 1887. Street & Smith.
Weddin' Trimmin's. Mattie Virginia Harris. LC 49-2750. 1949. Exposition Press.
Wedding. Grace Lumpkin. LC 75-28481. (Lost American fiction). 1976. 8.95 (ISBN 0-8093-0767-7). Southern Illinois University Press.
Wedding. Grace Lumpkin. (Lost American fiction). 1977. 1.95 (ISBN 0-445-04090-4). Popular Library.
Wedding. Grace Lumpkin. LC 39-5402. L. Furman, Inc.
Wedding. Denis George Mackail. LC 35-19683. 1935. Doubleday, Doran & Company, Inc.
Wedding. Hana Stein. LC 50-7060. 1950. Wyn.
Wedding: A Novel. Grace Lumpkin. LC 75-28481. (Lost American Fiction Ser.). 325p. 1976. Repr. of 1939 ed. 8.95 (ISBN 0-8093-0767-7). S Ill U Pr.
Wedding: And Other Stories. Julie Grinnell Storrow Cruger. LC 6-31181. 1896. J. B. Lippincott Company.
Wedding Bargain. Agnes Sligh Turnbull. LC 66-24392. 1966. Houghton Mifflin.
Wedding Bells of Glendalough. Michael Earls. LC 13-11304. 1913. Benziger Brothers.
Wedding Bouquet. Natalie King. pap. 0.75 o.s.i. (01-405). Lancer.
Wedding Dance. Translated from the French by Mervyn Savill. Anne De Tourville. LC 53-7612. 1953. Farrar, Straus and Young.
Wedding Day. Helen Marion Edginton. LC 40-400013. The Penn Publishing Company.
Wedding Day. Edwa Moser. LC 44-4326. 1944. Duell, Sloan and Pearce.
Wedding Day: And Other Stories, Vol. 1. Kay Boyle. LC 72-4420. (Short Story Index Reprint Ser). Repr. of 1929 ed. 13.00 (ISBN 0-8369-4171-3). Ayer Co.
Wedding Day Deception, No. 151. Helen Tucker. 224p. 1981. pap. 1.50 (ISBN 0-449-50224-4, Coventry). Fawcett.
Wedding Eve Murder. Beulah Marie Dix. LC 41-5146. R. M. McBride and Company.
Wedding Feast & Two Novellas. Michael Brodsky. 1981. 15.00 (ISBN 0-916354-81-4); pap. 8.95 (ISBN 0-89396-002-0). Urizen Bks.
Wedding Garment. A Tale of the Life to Come. Louis Beauregard Pendleton. 1894. Roberts Brothers.
Wedding Gift: A Fishing Story. John Taintor Foote. LC 24-213551. 1924. D. Appleton and Company.
Wedding Gown Project: A Novel. first ed. F. T Klingenberg. 1973. 4.00 (ISBN 0-682-47612-9). Exposition Press.
Wedding Group. Elizabeth Taylor. LC 68-16077. 1968. Viking Press.
Wedding Guest. Ovid Williams Pierce. LC 73-81446. 1974. 7.95 (ISBN 0-385-08390-4). Doubleday.
Wedding Guest. David Wiltse. LC 81-12447. 11.95 (ISBN 0-440-09443-7). Delacorte Press.
Wedding Guest: A Friend of the Bride and Bridegroom. Timothy Shay Arthur. LC 6-3433. 1856. H. C. Peck & T. Bliss.
Wedding Guest Sat on a Stone. Dora Richards Shattuck. LC 63-9166. (Collier mystery classics). 1963. Collier Books.
Wedding Guest Sat on a Stone. Richard Shattuck. 1940. W. Morrow & Company.
Wedding in June. George S O'Neal. LC 35-75227. Greenberg.
Wedding Is Destiny. Cecile Gilmore. LC 52-8060. 1952. T. Bouregy.
Wedding Journey. Marjorie Eatock. (Orig.). 1980. pap. 1.25 (ISBN 0-440-19499-7). Dell.
Wedding Journey. Walter Dumaux Edmonds. LC 47-5530. 1947. Little, Brown.
Wedding March. Bjornstjerne Bjornson & Ford, Marian, Tr. (Seaside library, v. 73, no. 1480). 1882. G. Munro.
Wedding March. Berta Ruck. LC 38-3723. 1938. Dodd, Mead & Company.
Wedding March Murder. Monte Barrett. LC 33-2848. The Bobbs-Merrill Company.
Wedding Night... Peggy Gaddis, pseud. LC 34-18185. W. Godwin, Inc.
Wedding of Zein. Tayeb Salih. (African Writers Ser.). 1969. pap. text ed. 4.00x (ISBN 0-435-90047-1). Heinemann Ed.
Wedding of Zein. Tayeb Salih. Tr. by Denys Johnson-Davies from Arabic. 120p. (Orig.). 1978. 10.00 (ISBN 0-89410-200-1); pap. 5.00 (ISBN 0-89410-201-X). Three Continents.
Wedding of Zein & Other Stories. Tayeb Salih. Tr. by Denys Johnson-Davies. (African Writers Ser.: No. 47). (Orig.). 1969. pap. text ed. 2.00x o.p. (ISBN 0-435-90347-0). Humanities.
Wedding Portrait. Fiona Hill. 1977. pap. 1.25 (ISBN 0-425-03777-0, Medallion). Berkley Pub.
Wedding Ring. Beth Brown. LC 30-17935. 1930. Doubleday, Doran and Company, Inc.
Wedding Ring: A Tale of to-Day. Robert Williams Buchanan. LC 6-19876. Cassell Publishing Company.
Wedding Ring: With Drawings. Elizabeth Hollister Frost. LC 39-27795. Coward-McCann, Inc.
Wedding Rings. Grace Hayward & Pascal, Ernes. LC 30-33139. 1930. World Wide Publishing Co., Inc.
Wedding Song. David Burnham. 1934. The Viking Press.
Wedding Song. Ethel Watts Mumford Grant. LC 24-23489. 1924. Doubleday.
Wedding Train. 1st Ed. Margaret Scherf. LC 60-137462. 1960. Doubleday.
Wedding. Translated from the Spanish by Stephen Kaye. 1st Ed. Angel Maria De Lera. LC 62-7825. 1962. Dutton.
Wedding Trip. Pardo Bazan, Emilia. Tr. by Serrano, Mary Jane (Christie) LC 7-35608. Cassell Publishing Company.
Wedge. Clive Egleton. 1971. price not set o.p. Coward.
Wedge: A Novel of Mexico. Hermann Bacher Deutsch. LC 35-13554. 1935. Frederick A. Stokes Company.
Wedgwood Pitcher. Ruby Dell Baugher. LC 44-476156. 1944. The Hobson Book Press.
Wedlock. A. J. Langguth. 1973. 1.25. Ballantine.
Wedlock. A. J. Langguth. LC 73-154928. 1972. 6.95 (ISBN 0-394-47275-6). Knopf.
Wedlock. Jakob Wassermann & Lewisohn, Ludwig, 1882- Tr. LC 26-213003. 1926. Boni & Liveright.
Wednesday the Rabbi Got Wet. Harry Kemelman. LC 76-4106. 1976. 8.95 (ISBN 0-688-03060-2). Morrow.
Wednesday the Rabbi Got Wet. Harry Kemelman. LC 76-45788. 1976. 12.95 (ISBN 0-8161-6413-4). G. K. Hall.
Wednesday Visitors. James Broom Lynne. LC 68-11812. 1968. Doubleday.
Wednesday Wife. Juliette Gordon Smith. LC 21-16181. 1921. The Macmillan Company.
Wednesday's Child: A Tale of Love and Courage. Margaret Arbore Berg. LC 60-13905. 1960. Muhlenberg Press.
Wednesday's Wrath. Don Pendleton. (Executioner Ser.: No. 35). 1979. pap. 2.25 (ISBN 0-523-41801-9). Pinnacle Bks.
Wee Bit of Lace. Gladys M Schuldt. Dorrance and Company.
Wee Little Rhymes. Mary Dow Northam Brine. LC 15-258. Cassell & Company.
Wee Macgreegor. John Joy Bell. LC 3-11678. 1903. Harper & Brothers.
Wee Macgreegor. John Joy Bell. LC 3-11147. 1903. Street & Smith.
Wee Macgreegor Enlists. John Joy Bell. LC 16-127554. 1.00. Fleming H. Revell Company.
Wee Widow's Cruise in Quiet Waters. E M Cuttim. LC 6-32232. ("Unknown" library, v. 15). Cassell Publishing Company.
Wee Wifie. Rosa Nouchette Carey. LC 6-22806. (On cover: Lovell's library. v. 20. no. 959). J. W. Lovell Company.
Wee Willie Winkie: And Other Stories. Rudyard Kipling. LC 9-3026. F. F. Lovell Company.
Wee Willie Winkie: And Other Stories. Life's Handicap. Rudyard Kipling. LC 52-491676. (Mandalay edition of the works of Rudyard Kipling). 1925. Doubleday, Page.
Wee Willie Winkie: City of the Dreadful Night, American Notes. Rudyard Kipling. LC 9-16374. 1900. The Nottingham Society.
Wee Willie Winkie, The City of Dreadful Night, American Notes. Rudyard Kipling. LC 4878. H. M. Caldwell Company.
Weed by the Wall: By Kate Slaughter McKinney (Katydid)... Kate Slaughter McKinney. LC 11-322516. 1.25. R. G. Badger.
Weed in the Garden. 1st Ed. Leslie Winter Strom. LC 61-11882. 1961. Knopf.
Weeded and Parted: And, My Sister Kate. Charlotte Mary Brame. LC 44-38164. (On cover: Lovell's library, v. 13, no. 695). J. W. Lovell Company.
Weedkiller's Daughter. Harriette Louisa Simpson Arnow. LC 68-23960. 1970. 6.95. Knopf.
Weeds. Edith Summers Kelley. LC 72-75333. (Crosscurrents/Modern fiction). 1972. 7.95 (ISBN 0-8093-0587-9). Southern Illinois University Press.
Weeds. Edith Summers Kelley. LC 23-12959. Harcourt, Brace and Company.
Weeds: A Novel. Andrii Vasylovych Holovko. LC 77-364174. (Illus.). 1976. 1.33rub. Dnipro.
Weeds: A Novel. Edith Summers Kelley. LC 81-22061. 6.95 (ISBN 0-935312-01-3). Feminist Press.
Weeds of Violence. Earl Schenck. LC 49-9971. 1949. Doubleday.
Weedy Rough. Douglas C Jones. LC 80-28297. 13.95 (ISBN 0-03-050931-9). Holt, Rinehart and Winston.
Week. IUrii Nikolaevich Libedinskii. LC 72-90299. 1973. 12.00 (ISBN 0-88355-010-5). Hyperion Press.
Week. IUrii Nikolaevich Libedinskii. LC 72-90299. 1973. (ISBN 0-88355-010-5). Hyperion Press.
Week. IUrii Nikolaevich Libedinskii & Ransome, Arthur, 1884- Tr. LC 24-26029. 1923. B. W. Huebsch, Inc.
Week As Andrea Benstock. Jill Emerson. LC 74-18161. 1975. 7.95 (ISBN 0-87795-100-4). Arbor Hse.
Week at the Most. Louise Field Cooper. 1973. (pbk.) 1.25. Warner Paperback Lib.
Week at the Most: A Novel. Louise Field Cooper. LC 67-14237. 1967. 4.95. S. S.
Week Away from Time. Ed. by James Lodge. Fields, Annie (Adams) LC 7-1501. 1887. Roberts Brothers.
Week-End. Charles Brackett. LC 25-13518. 1925. R. M. McBride & Company.
Week-End. Philip Duffield Stong. C.
Week-End Book of Ghost Stories. Ed. by Hereward Carrington. LC 53-11373. I. Washburn.
Week-End Cruise. Marcia Bellowes. LC 32-2465. The Mohawk Press, Inc.
Week-End Girl. Warner Fabian. LC 32-127611. The Macaulay Company.
Week-End Husband. Peggy Gaddis, pseud. LC 43-13628. 1943. Phoenix Press.
Week-End in Baghdad: A Detective Story. Ruth Wadham. LC 59-5642. (Cock Robin mystery). 1959. Macmillan.
Week-End Make Believe. Octave Foerster Schully. LC 36-9341. Arcadia House.
Week-End Marriage. Faith Baldwin Cuthrell. LC 32-761. Farrar & Rinehart, Incorporated.
Week-End Murders. Archie Joscelyn. LC 39-5222. Phoenix Press.
Week-End Mystery. Robert Alfred Simon. LC 26-16328. 1926. G. H. Watt.
Week-End Pilot. Frank K. Smith. LC 74-5195. 1974. pap. 3.95 (ISBN 0-394-71069-X, Vin). Random.
Week-End Wife. Dolf Wyllarde. LC 31-322383. 1931. The Macaulay Company.
Week-End Wodehouse. Pelham Grenville Wodehouse. LC 39-27061. 1939. Doubleday, Doran & Co., Inc.
Week-End Wodehouse. Pelham Grenville Wodehouse. LC 40-13272. 1940. Garden City Publishing Co., Inc.
Week-End Woman. Ruby Mildred Ayres. LC 39-8615. 1939. Doubleday, Doran & Company, Inc.
Week Ends. Frederick William Thomas. LC 26-18633. 1925. G. P. Putnam's Sons.
Week in a French Country-House. Adelaide Kemble Sartoris. LC 3-2084. 1902. The Macmillan Company.
Week in Killarny. Margaret Wolfe Hungerford. LC 7-9050. (On cover: Lovell's library. v. 9, no. 477). 1884. J. W. Lovell Company.
Week in New York. Margaret Culkin Banning. LC 41-212718. Harper & Brothers.
Week in the Country. Ernest Gebler. LC 56-9392. 1957. Doubleday.
Week in Turenevo, and Other Stories. Aleksei Nikolaevich Tolstoi. LC 75-15693. 1975. 11.50 (ISBN 0-8371-8224-7). Greenwood Press.
Week in Turenevo, and Other Stories. Aleksei Nikolaevich Tolstoi. LC 57-6935. (Evergreen books E-89). 1958. Grove Press.
Week in Turenevo: And Other Stories. Tolstoi, Aleksei Nikolaevich, Graf. LC 57-6935. (Evergreen books E-89).
Week of Passion: Or, The Dilemma of Mr. George Barton the Younger. A Novel. Edward Jenkins. (Harper's Franklin square library, no. 461). Harper & Brothers.
Week of Passion: Or, The Dilemma of Mr. George Barton the Younger. A Novel. Edward Jenkins. LC 7-10204. (On cover: Seaside library. Pocket ed. no. 458). G. Munro.
Week of the Succubus. T. R. Austin. 1978. 7.95 o.p. (ISBN 0-533-03603-8). Vantage.
Week of the Wives. Sarah Elizabeth Rodger. LC 58-10757. 1958. Putnam.
Week to Kill. David Delman. LC 73-171286. 1972. 4.95. Published for the Crime Club by Doubleday.
Week with No Friday. Willard Marsh. LC 65-14663. 4.95. Harper.
Weekend. Tania Grossinger & Andrew Niederman. LC 79-26808. 12.95 (ISBN 0-312-86006-4). St. Martin's Press.
Weekend, & Other Short Stories. Aysn Aydin. 3.50 o.p. Vantage.
Weekend at Dunkirk. Robert Merle. LC 51-11083. 1951. Knopf.
Weekend at the Villa. Dorothy Quintano. LC 73-11718. 1974. 4.95. Published for the Crime Club by Doubleday.

Weekend at the Waldorf: A Film Classic Novelized. Charles Lee & Spewack, Samuel, 1899- LC 45-88677. (On cover: Grosset & Dunlap film classics library). 1945. Grosset & Dunlap.

Weekend Girls. John Frederick Burke. LC 67-12540. 1967. Published for the Crime Club by Doubleday.

Weekend Homo. William C. Spatari. (Orig.). 1968. pap. 1.75 o.p. (3037). Brandon.

Weekend in Dinlock. Clancy Sigal. LC 60-9148. 1960. Houghton Mifflin.

Weekend in Dinlock. Clancy Sigal. 1978. 1.95 (ISBN 0-445-04223-0). Popular Library.

Weekend Man. Richard Bruce Wright. LC 77-152242. 1971. 6.95 (ISBN 0-374-28740-6). Farrar, Straus & Giroux.

Weekend with Claude. Beryl Bainbridge. LC 81-17965. 1982. 10.95 (ISBN 0-8076-1031-3). G. Braziller.

Weekend with Death: A Mystery Novel. Patricia Wentworth. LC 41-4134. J. B. Lippincott Company.

Weekend Woman. Ruby Mildred Ayres. LC 49-12427. 1940. The Sun Dial Press.

Weekend '33. Bob Thomas. 1973. (pbk.) 1.50. Dell.

Weekend '33. Bob Thomas. LC 78-157627. 1972. 6.95. Doubleday.

Weep and Know Why. Elisabeth Ogilvie. 1976. (pbk.) 1.75 (ISBN 0-380-00621-9). Avon.

Weep and Know Why. Elisabeth Ogilvie. LC 70-39368. 1972. (ISBN 0-07-047619-5). McGraw-Hill.

Weep for a Blonde: By Brett Halliday Pseud. Davis Dresser. LC 57-7504. (Torquil book). 1957. Distributed by Dodd, Mead.

Weep for Her. Sara Woods, pseud. LC 80-53081. 9.95 (ISBN 0-312-86019-6). St. Martin's Press.

Weep for Love. Ruby Mildred Ayres. LC 40-6337. 1939. Doubleday, Doran & Company, Inc.

Weep for Me. Kathleen Shepard. LC 34-32940. A. H. King.

Weep for My Brother. Clifford Dowdey. LC 50-5304. 1950. Doubleday.

Weep for Willow Green. Paul Kruger LC 66-11957. (Inner sanctum mystery). bds., 3.50. S. & S.

Weep in the Sun. Jeanne Wilson. 1976. 1.95 (ISBN 0-671-80763-3). Pocket Books.

Weep in the Sun: An Island Chronicle. Jeanne Wilson. LC 76-375952. 1976. 4.25 (ISBN 0-333-18430-0). Macmillan.

Weep No More. Evelyn P. Burrell. 1.00 o.s.i. B Johns Pub.

Weep No More. Angela Du Maurier. LC 40-13626. 1940. Doubleday, Doran and Company, Inc.

Weep No More. Ward Greene. LC 32-3003. 1932. H. Smith.

Weep No More: A Novel. Janet Stevenson. LC 57-10578. 1957. Viking Press.

Weep No More My Brother: A Novel. Sterling Watson. LC 77-28354. 1978. 8.95 (ISBN 0-688-03311-3). Morrow.

Weep Not Child. Wa Thiongo Ngugi. (African Writers Ser.). 1964. pap. text ed. 3.00x (ISBN 0-435-90007-2). Heinemann Ed.

Weep Not, Child. Ngugi Wa Thiongo. LC 70-81547. (African/American library). 1969. 1.25. Collier Books.

Weep Not for Anger: A Novel of a Slavic-American Family in New England. J. G. Lohsen. 1979. 8.50 (ISBN 0-682-49219-1). Exposition.

Weep Not for Me. Gary G. Cohen & Catherine Runyon. LC 80-10773. (Illus.). 2.95 (ISBN 0-8024-4309-5). Moody Press.

Weep Not for Me. Milton K. Wallace. 5.95. Impress Hse.

Weep Not for Me... A Novel. Milton K Wallace. LC 72-94906. 1973. 5.95. Heath Cote Pub. Corp.

Weep Not for the Dead: Translated from the French for the First Time. Michel Matveev. Tr. by Desmond Flower. LC 35-4291. 1935. A. A. Knopf.

Weepers in Playtime. Beatrice Sands. 1908. J. Lane Company.

Weeping and the Laughter. Joachim Maass. LC 47-11081. 1947. A. A. Wyn.

Weeping and the Laughter. 1st Ed. Vera Caspary. LC 50-8522. 1950. Little, Brown.

Weeping Ash. Joan Aiken. LC 79-8431. 1980. 14.95 (ISBN 0-385-15719-3). Doubleday.

Weeping Bay. Joy Davidman. LC 50-6067. 1950. Macmillan.

Weeping Cross: An Unwordly Story. Henry Longan Stuart. LC 8-23103. 1908. Doubleday, Page & Company.

Weeping Cross: An Unwordly Story. Henry Longan Stuart. LC 33-15500. 1933. L. MacVeagh, Dial Press, Inc.

Weeping Cross: An Unworldly Story. Foreword by Paul K. Cuneo. Henry Longan Stuart. LC 53-13383. (Thomas More book to live). 1954. H. Regnery Co.

Weeping Is for Women. Donald Barr Chidsey. LC 36-24946. 1936. A. A. Knopf.

Weeping May Tarry. Raymond F Jones & Lester Del Rey. (Futorian Book). 1978. 1.75 (ISBN 0-523-40215-5). Pinnacle Books.

Weeping Tower. Christine Randell. 1971. pap. 0.60 o.p. (ISBN 0-446-63557-X, 63-557). Paperback Lib.

Weeping Willow Murders. Charles Koonce. LC 34-568536. Burton Publishing Company.

Weeping Wood. Vicki Baum. LC 78-156173. 1971. (ISBN 0-8371-6116-9). Greenwood Press.

Weeping Wood. Vicki Baum. LC 43-15655. 1943. Doubleday, Doran & Company, Inc.

Weevil in the Cotton. Samuel Milton Elam. LC 40-30178. 1940. Frederick A. Stokes Company.

Weiga of Temagami. facs. ed. Cy Warman. LC 76-140346. (Short Story Index Reprint Ser). 1908. 15.00 (ISBN 0-8369-3738-4). Ayer Co.

Weiga of Temagami, and Other Indian Tales. Cy Warman. LC 76-140346. (Short story index reprint series). (Illus.). 1970. Books for Libraries Press.

Weiga of Temagami, and Other Indian Tales. Cy Warman. LC 8-18370. H. M. Caldwell Co.

Weighed and Wanting. George Macdonald. LC 7-18786. D. Lothrop and Company.

Weighed and Wanting. A Novel. George Macdonald. (Harper's Franklin square library, no. 274). 1882. Harper & Brothers.

Weighed and Wanting. A Novel. George Macdonald. (Seaside library, v. 74, no. 1498). 1883. G. Munro.

Weighed in the Balance. Frances Christine Tierman. LC 3125. 1900. Marlier, Callanan, & Company.

Weigher of Souls. Andre Maurois. Tr. by Miles Hamish. LC 31-8219. 1931. D. Appleton and Company.

Weigher of Souls: & The Earth Dwellers. Andre Maurois. LC 63-13325. (Illus.). 1963. Macmillan.

Weight of Glory. Lon Riley Woodrum. LC 59-38516. 1959. Zondervan Pub. House.

Weight of the Cross. 1st Ed. Robert O Bowen. LC 51-2386. 1951. Knopf.

Weight of the Crown. Fred Merrick White. LC 8-8303. 1906. R. F. Fenno & Company; Etc., Etc.

Weight of the Evidence. John Innes Mackintosh Stewart. LC 43-14285. 1943. Dodd, Mead & Company.

Weight of the Name. Paul Charles Joseph Bourget. Tr. by George Burnham Ives. LC 8-9812. 1908. Little, Brown, and Company.

Weightless in Gaza. Fred Shannon. 1970. pap. 0.60 o.p. (T-060-12). Tower.

Weiland: Or The Transformation. Charles Brockden Brown. LC 9-2594. Printed by T. & J. Swords, for H. Caritat,

Weiland Treatment. Leslie Gladson. (Orig.). 1968. pap. 0.60 o.p. (73-742). Lancer.

Weir... Ruth Moore. LC 43-2351. 1943. W. Morrow & Co.

Weir: A Novel, by Jane Gillespie Pseud. 1st American Ed. Jane Shaw. LC 54-6534. 1954. Coward-McCann.

Weir House. Netta Muskett. 1974. pap. 0.75 o.p. (26560-2-075). Beagle Bks.

Weir of Herminston. The Misadventures of John Nicholson. The Story of a Lie. The Body-Snatcher. Robert Louis Stevenson. LC 6-18297. (Half-title: The biographical edition of the works of Robert Louis Stevenson). 1905. C. Scribner's Sons.

Weir of Hermiston: An Unfinished Romance. Robert Louis Stevenson. LC 78-150563. (Short story index reprint series). 1971. (ISBN 0-8369-3861-5). Books for Libraries Press.

Weir of Hermiston, and Other Stories. Robert Louis Stevenson & Paul Binding. LC 80-497333. (Penguin English library). 1980. 2.95 (ISBN 0-14-043138-1). Penguin Books.

Weird Adventures of the Shadow. Walter Brown Gibson. LC 66-20651. Grosset & Dunlap.

Weird Gathering & Other Tales. Ed. by Ronald Curran. 1979. pap. 2.50 (ISBN 0-449-23994-2, Crest). Fawcett.

Weird Heroes, Vol. 2. Ed. by Byron Preiss. 1975. pap. 1.50 o.p. (ISBN 0-515-04013-4). BJ Pub Group.

Weird Heroes, No. 6. Byron Preiss. 1977. pap. 1.50 o.p. (ISBN 0-515-04037-1). BJ Pub Group.

Weird Heroes: Nightshade, No. 4. King-Eachum. Ed. by Byron Preiss. (Orig.). 1976. pap. 1.50 o.p. (ISBN 0-515-04035-5). BJ Pub Group.

Weird Heroes: Quest of the Gypsy, No. 3. Ron Goulart. (Orig.). 1976. pap. 1.50 o.p. (ISBN 0-515-04034-7). BJ Pub Group.

Weird of the White Wolf. Michael Moorcock. (Science Fiction Ser.). 1977. pap. 1.95 (ISBN 0-87997-658-6, VJ1658). DAW Bks.

Weird of the White Wolf. 1977. Michael Moorcock. 1.25 (ISBN 0-87997-286-6).

Weird Ones (The) (L92-541). 1962. Belmont.

Weird Orient: Nine Mystic Talwes. Henry Iliowizi. LC 5979. 1900. H. T. Coates and Company.

Weird Picture. John R Carling. LC 5-14829. 1905. Little, Brown, and Company.

Weird Shadow Over Innsmouth: And Other Stories of the Supernatural. Howard Phillips Lovecraft. LC 44-6310. (Bart house books. 4). 1944. Bartholomew House, Inc.

Weird Show. Playboy Editors. (Orig.). 1971. pap. 0.95 o.p. (16138). Playboy.

Weird Show. LC 70-155837. 1971. 0.95. Playboy Press.

Weird Tales. Alistair Durie. 128p. 1981. 24.00x (Pub. by Jupiter England). State Mutual Bk.

Weird Tales. Ernst Theodor Amadeus Hoffmann. Ed. by John Thomas Bealby. LC 74-125218. (Short story index reprint series). 1970. Books for Libraries Press.

Weird Tales. Edgar Allan Poe. LC 12-37842. 1895. H. Altemus.

Weird Tales, No. 1. Ed. by Lin Carter. 288p. (Orig.). 1981. pap. 2.50 (ISBN 0-89083-714-7). Zebra.

Weird Tales, No. 2. Ed. by Lin Carter. 288p. (Orig.). 1981. pap. 2.50 (ISBN 0-89083-715-5). Zebra.

Weird Tales from Northern Seas: From the Danish of Jonas Lie. Jonas Lauritz Idemil Lie & Robert Nisbet Bain. LC 79-81272. (Short story index reprint series). (Illus.). 1969. Books for Libraries Press.

Weird Tales, No. 3. Ed. by Lin Carter. (YA) 1981. pap. 2.50 (ISBN 0-89083-803-8). Zebra.

Weird Tales Story. Ed. by Robert Weinburg. LC 77-73602. 1977. 17.50 o.p. (ISBN 0-913960-16-0). Fax Collect.

Weird, the Wild & the Wicked. Brad Steiger & John Pendragon. (Orig.). 1969. pap. 0.75 o.p. (T2077). Pyramid Pubns.

Weird World of Wes Beattie. John Norman Harris. LC 65-16532. 1963. Harper & Row.

Weird World of Wes Beattie. John Norman Harris. LC 64-41655. 1963. Macmillan of Canada.

Weirdies, Weirdies, Weirdies: A Horrifying Concatenation of the Super-Sur-Real or Almost or Not-Quite Real. Ed. by Helen Hoke. LC 73-14010. (Illus.). 1975. 5.90. F. Watts.

Weirdown Experiment. Edmund Wallace Hildick. LC 75-25085. 7.95 (ISBN 0-06-011889-X). Harper & Row.

Weirdown Experiment. Edmund Wallace Hildick. LC 77-361461. 1976. 3.50 (ISBN 0-241-89435-2). Hamilton.

Weirdstone of Brinsingamen. Alan Garner. 1981. pap. 1.95 (ISBN 0-345-29043-7, Del Rey). Ballantine.

Welchman's Hose. Robert Graves. 1925. 12.50 o.s.i. Ridgeway Bks.

Welcome. Hubert Creekmore. LC 48-9034. Appleton-Century-Crofts.

Welcome: A Romance of Jamaica. Isabel Constance Clarke. LC 43-78934. 1942. Hutchinson & Co., Ltd.

Welcome: A Romance of Jamaica. Isabel Constance Clarke. LC 43-14563. 1943. Longmans, Green and Co.

Welcome: A Romance of Jamaica. Isabel Constance Clarke. LC 44-71873. 1944. Longmans, Green and Co.

Welcome Back to Wayland. Frederick B. Shroyer. 1978. pap. 1.95 (ISBN 0-89041-182-4, 3182). Major Bks.

Welcome, Darkness. Leon Statham. LC 50-8169. 1950. Crowell.

Welcome Death. Glyn Edmund Daniel. LC 55-6208. (Red badge detective). 1955. Dodd, Mead.

Welcome for a Hero: A Novel. Robin Perry. LC 75-13949. 7.95 (ISBN 0-915772-01-9). Livingston Press.

Welcome Friend: Comprising a Choice Selection of Entertaining and Instructive Sketches. Now First Collected. LC 9-18143. 1858. H. C. Peck & T. Bliss.

Welcome Home. Alice Duer Miller. LC 28-8133. 1928. Dodd, Mead & Company.

Welcome Home, Johnny! Margaretta Brucker. LC 45-67265. 1945. Arcadia House, Inc.

Welcome Honorable Visitors: A Novel. Jean Raspail. LC 60-5270. 1960. Putnam.

Welcome Honourable Visitors: A Novel. Tr. from French by Jean Stewart. Jean Raspail. 1966. bds., 3.00. Hamish Hamilton.

Welcome Intruder. Charlotte Wisely. (Rapture Romance Ser.: No. 4). 1983. pap. 1.95 (ISBN 0-451-12007-8, AJ2007). NAL.

Welcome, My Dear, to Belfrey House. Stanton Forbes, pseud. 192p. 1974. pap. 0.95 o.p. (532-9532-095). Manor Bks.

Welcome, My Dear, to Belfry House. Stanton Forbes, pseud. LC 72-89821. 1973. 4.95 (ISBN 0-385-02734-6). Published for the Crime Club by Doubleday.

Welcome, Proud Lady. June Drummond. LC 68-10097. (Rinehart suspense novel). 1968. Holt, Rinehart and Winston.

Welcome, Sinner. Richard Posner. LC 73-93741. (Illus.). 1974. 8.95 (ISBN 0-399-11332-0). Putnam.

Welcome Soldier! Clark McMeekin. LC 42-7631. 1942. D. Appleton-Century Company, Incorporated.

Welcome Stranger. Virginia Lee Ward. LC 43-16346. 1943. Dorrance & Company.

Welcome, Stranger & Partners: The Story of God and the Man Who Succeeded Him: a Novel. Harry Pesin. LC 74-78884. (Illus.). 1974. 5.95. Perspective Publications.

Welcome Sundays: A Novel. Norman Keifetz. LC 78-23744. 8.95 (ISBN 0-399-12318-0). Putnam.

Welcome to Hard Times. E. L. Doctorow. LC 75-11408. 1975. 8.95 (ISBN 0-394-49833-X) (ISBN 0-394-73107-7). Random House.

Welcome to Mars. James Blish. 160p. 1983. pap. 2.50 (ISBN 0-380-63347-7). Avon.

Welcome to Mount Merry College. Carol Wallace & Mason Wiley. LC 81-15409. (Illus.). 4.95 (ISBN 0-399-50615-2). Putnam.

Welcome to Oblivion. Paul Petersen. 1975. (pbk.) 0.95 (ISBN 0-671-68016-1). Pocket Books.

Welcome to Our City: A Play in Ten Scenes. Thomas Wolfe & Richard S Kennedy. LC 82-20838. (Southern Literary Studies). 12.95 (ISBN 0-8071-1085-X). Louisiana State University Press.

Welcome to Paradise. Rose A. Forrest. (Illus.). 96p. 1981. pap. 1.95 (ISBN 0-380-76901-8, 76901). Avon.

Welcome to Teek-Wood. Roberta I. Newsome. 1970. 2.00 o.p. Carlton.

Welcome to the City: And Other Stories. Irwin Shaw. LC 42-5833. Random House.

Welcome to the Club. Clement Biddle Wood. (U6129). 1968. Ballantine.

Welcome to the Club. Clement Biddle Wood. LC 66-22300. 1966. McGraw-Hill.

Welcome to the Club. Clement Biddle Wood. LC 66-22300. 1966. McGraw-Hill.

Welcome to the Grand Hotel. Donald Thomas. 68p. 1975. 12.50 (ISBN 0-7100-8104-9). Routledge & Kegan.

Welcome to the Grave. Mary McMullen. LC 78-69660. 1979. 7.95 (ISBN 0-385-14535-7). Published for the Crime Club by Doubleday.

Welcome to the Monkey House. Kurt Vonnegut, Jr. 1968. 10.95 (ISBN 0-440-09440-2, Sey Lawr). Delacorte.

Welcome to the Monkey House. Kurt Vonnegut, Jr. pap. 2.95 (ISBN 0-440-19478-4). Dell.

Welcome to the Monkey House. Kurt Vonnegut, Jr. 1970. pap. 2.75 (ISBN 0-440-59434-0, Delta). Dell.

Welcome to the Monkey House: A Collection of Short Works. Kurt Vonnegut. LC 68-14979. 1968. Delacorte Press.

Welcome to Thebes. Glendon Fred Swarthout. LC 62-846352. 1962. Random House.

Welcome to Washington, Mr. Witherspoon. Tom Tiede. LC 79-13977. 1979. 10.95 (ISBN 0-688-03535-3). Morrow.

Welcome to Xanadu. Nathaniel Benchley. LC 68-16866. 1968. 5.95 o.p. (ISBN 0-689-10032-9). Atheneum.

Welcome Wilderness: A Novel. Grace Tomkinson. LC 46-7240. 1946. I. Washburn, Inc.

Welded Links. David P Allison. LC 39-225888. 1939. Wm. B. Eerdmans Publishing Company.

Welding. Lafayette McLaws. LC 7-34773. 1907. Little, Brown, and Company.

Weldman's Hose. Robert Graves. LC 76-30507. Repr. of 1925 ed. lib. bdg. 15.00 (ISBN 0-8414-4508-7). Folcroft.

Welfare Check. Ann W. Smith. 3.00 o.p. Carlton.

Welfare on Skid Row: A Novel. 1st. ed. Beatrice Garrett. 1974. 6.00 (ISBN 0-682-47611-0). Exposition Press.

Well. Jack Cady. LC 80-67623. 11.95 (ISBN 0-87795-287-6). Arbor House.

Well--Who Killed Him? Harry Vincent Dougherty. LC 22-209953. R. G. Badger.

Well: A Novel Tr. by Ruth Wisse. 1st Ed. Chaim Grade. LC 67-16186. 1967. 4.50. Jewish Pubn. Soc.

Well, After All-- Frank Frankfort Moore. LC 99-4572. 1899. Dodd, Mead & Company.

Well at the World's End: A Tale. William Morris. LC 70-17845. (Adult fantasy). 1970. per vol. 0.95. Ballantine Books.

Well at the World's End: A Tale. William Morris. 1896. Longmans, Green, and Co.

Well-Beloved: A Sketch of a Temperament. Thomas Hardy. LC 1-24729. 1897. Harper & Brothers.

Well-Beloved: A Sketch of a Temperament. Thomas Hardy. LC 77-79925. (His The New Wessex Edition). 1981. 2.95 (ISBN 0-312-86173-7) (ISBN 0-312-86172-9). St. Martin's Press.

Well-Born Corpse. Edla Benjamin. LC 39-186593. Random House.

We'll Come When It Rains. Yvette Nelson. LC 82-61649. (Minnesota Voices Project Ser.: No. 11). (Illus.). 70p. 1982. pap. 3.00 (ISBN 0-89823-043-8). New Rivers Pr.

Well Dressed for Murder. Laverne Rice. LC 38-365169. 1938. Pub. for the Crime Club, Inc., by Doubleday, Doran & Company, Inc.
Well-Dressed Skeleton. Brad Williams. LC 62-13615. 1962. M. S. Mill Co.
We'll Find Our Way: By Elaine Lowell Pseud. Alice Lent Covert. LC 51-12717. 1951. Bouregy & Curl.
Well Full of Leaves. Elizabeth Myers. LC 44-20108. 1944. W. Morrow & Company.
Well in the Desert. Adeline Knapp. LC 8-23557. 1908. The Century Co.
Well-Known Face: By Josephine Bell Pseud. Doris Bell Collier Ball. LC 60-133264. (Chantcler mystery novel). 1960. Washburn.
Well, Maybe Tomorrow. Sal Belloise. 1980. 6.95 (ISBN 0-533-04322-0). Vantage.
Well-Meaning Young Man. Louise King-Hall & King-Hall, Magdalen, 1904- Joint Author. LC 30-17417. 1930. D. Appleton and Company.
We'll Meet in England. Kitty Barne. LC 43-4374. 1943. Dodd, Mead & Company.
Well of Ararat. Emmanuel P Varandyan. LC 38-27062. 1938. Doubleday, Doran & Co., Inc.
Well of Compassion. David Alman. 1948. Simon and Schuster.
Well of Days. Ivan Alekseevich Bunin. Tr. by Gleb Struve & Hamish Miles. LC 74-4247. 1974. 12.50. H. Fertig.
Well of Days. Ivan Alekseevich Bunin & Struve, Gleb, Tr. 1934. A.A. Knopf.
Well of Fragrant Waters. Genevieve B. Wimsatt. (O.s.i.). 2.50 o.s.i. (ISBN 0-8283-1206-0). Branden.
Well of Gerar. Ruben Rothgiesser. Tr. by Harry Schneiderman from Ger. LC 53-7603. 1953. 3.00 o.p. (ISBN 0-8276-0165-4, 259). Jewish Pubn.
Well of Gerar: A Novel; Translated from the German Ms. by Harry Schneiderman. Ruben Rothgiesser. LC 53-7603. 1953. Jewish Publication Society of America.
Well of Loneliness. Radclyffe Hall. 448p. 1981. pap. 3.95 (ISBN 0-380-54247-1, 54247, Bard). Avon.
Well of Sacrifice. Donald Ediger. (Illus.). 1971. 10.00 o.p. (ISBN 0-385-00933-X). Doubleday.
Well of Saint Clare. Anatole France, pseud. LC 70-121549. (Short story index reprint series). 1970. Books for Libraries Press.
Well of Shiuan. C. J. Cherryh. (Science Fiction Ser). (Orig.). 1978. pap. 1.95 (ISBN 0-87997-371-4, UJ1371). DAW Bks.
Well of Shivan. C. J Cherryh. 1978. 1.95 (ISBN 0-87997-371-4). DAW Books.
Well of the Past. Charles Norman. LC 49-7965. 1949. N. Y., Doubleday.
Well of the Silent Harp: A Novel of the Life and Loves of Robert Burns. James Barke. LC 54-122927. (His Immortal memory). 1954. Macmillan.
Well of the Unicorn. George U Fletcher. Ed. by Lester Del Ray. LC 75-405. (Library of Science Fiction). 1975. lib. bdg. 15.00 (ISBN 0-8240-1410-3). Garland Pub.
Well of the Unicorn. Fletcher Pratt. LC 75-405. (Garland Library of Science Fiction). (Illus.). 1975. 11.00 (ISBN 0-8240-1410-3). Garland Pub.
Well of the Unicorn. Fletcher Pratt. LC 48-5093. 1948. W. Sloane Associates.
Well of Three Echoes. Ann Boyle. 1973. pap. 0.75 o.s.i. (01-371). Lancer.
Well Out of It: Six Days in the Life of an Ex-Teacher. John Habberton. LC 6-46673. (On cover: Mayflower library, no. 5). J. A. Taylor and Company.
We'll Sing One Song: A Novel. Olive Carruthers. LC 47-306073. 1947. Bobbs-Merrill Co.
Well Spring. Harriet S. Schiff. (Orig.). 1981. pap. 2.75 (ISBN 0-89083-721-X). Zebra.
Well-Spring of Immortality. A Tale of East Indian Life. S S Hewlett. LC 7-4664. A. D. F. Randolph & Company.
Well, There's Your Problem. Edward Koren. 112p. 1981. pap. 3.95 (ISBN 0-14-005967-9). Penguin.
Well-Told Lie. Christina Hobhouse. LC 72-8709. 1973. 6.95 (ISBN 0-394-48439-8). Knopf.
Well! Well! A Tale, Founded on Fact. 2d ed.... ed. M. A Wallace. LC 8-33280. 1863. D. & J. Sadlier & Co.
Well Won. copyright ed. Annie French Hector. (On cover: The Mayflower library, no. 1). 1891. J. A. Taylor & Company.
Wellesley Stories. Grace Louise Cook. 1901. R.G. Badger & Company.
Wellesley Stories. rev. ed., illustrated and enl. drawings by i. b. hazelton. ed. Grace Louise Cook. LC 4-3952. 1904. E. H. Bacon & Co.
Wellfields. A Novel. Jessie Fothergill. LC 21-139661. (Seaside library, v. 41, no. 840). 1880. G. Munro.
Wellington's. Marc Olden. (Signet Book). 1977. 1.95 (ISBN 0-451-07647-8). New American Library.
Wellmeadow: East Scots New Writers. Blairgowrie Library. LC 77-373071. (Illus.). 1976. 0.60 (ISBN 0-905452-00-3). Blairgowrie Library.
Wells Brothers: The Young Cattle Kings. Andy Adams. LC 11-4936. 1911. Houghton, Mifflin Company.
Wells Fargo Brand. Dan Roberts. LC 64-57225. 1964. Arcadia House.
Wells of Hell. Graham Masterton. 320p. 1982. pap. 2.95 (ISBN 0-523-48042-3). Pinnacle Bks.
Wells Without Water. Edith Snyder Pedersen. LC 43-10276. 1943. Wm. B. Eerdmans Publishing Co.
Wellspring. Janice Holt Giles. LC 75-15989. 1975. 8.95 (ISBN 0-395-20731-2). Houghton Mifflin.
Wellspring: A Novel. Edward H Hawkins. LC 68-57210. (Illus.). 1969. 4.95. Echo House.
Wellspring: Novel. Edward H Hawkins. LC 78-19057. (Illus.). 9.95 (ISBN 0-07-027295-6). McGraw-Hill.
Welsh Rarebit Tales. Harle Oren Cummins. LC 8-10614. The Mutual Book Company.
Welsh Short Stories. Gwyn Jones. Repr. of 1941 ed. 5.00 o.p. (ISBN 0-89987-123-2). Darby Bks.
Welsh Short Stories. Gwyn Jones. 1941. 10.00. Havertown Bks.
Welsh Witch: A Novel. Beynon Puddicombe. LC 2-17556. (Half-title: Appletons' town and country library, no. 312). 1902. D. Appleton and Company.
Wenatchee Bend: By Giff Cheshire. Gifford Paul Cheshire. LC 66-173957. (Double-D western). 3.50. Doubleday.
Wench Is Dead. Fredric Brown. LC 55-6847. (Guilt edged mystery). 1955. Dutton.
Wench Is Dead. 1st Ed. Ruth Fenisong. LC 53-69364. 1953. Published for the Crime Club by Doubleday.
Wench Is Willing. James Noble Gifford. 1948. Phoenix Press.
Wenderholme. A Story of Lancashire and Yorkshire. Phillip Hamerton. LC 29-25283. 1882. Roberts Brothers.
Wendy. Richard Hart. LC 78-72870. 1979. pap. 3.95 (ISBN 0-9602100-0-8). R Hart.
Wensley: A Story Without a Moral. Edmund Quincy. LC 7-42420. 1854. Ticknor and Fields.
Wensley: And Other Stories. Edmund Quincy. Ed. by Quincy, Edmund, D. LC 7-42421. 1885. J. R. Osgood and Company.
Went South: A Novel. Marianne Wiggins. LC 79-27309. 8.95 (ISBN 0-440-09420-8). Delacorte Press.
Wentworth. George C. Kohn. 4.50 o.p. Vantage.
Wentworth Hall. Anne O'Neill-Barna. (queen-size gothic). 1974. (pbk.). 0.95. Popular Library.
Wept of Wish-Ton-Wish. James Fenimore Cooper. LC 75-127081. (Charles E. Merrill program in American literature). (Charles E. Merrill standard editions.). (Illus.). 1970. Merrill.
Wept of Wish-Ton-Wish. James Fenimore Cooper. LC 74-38959. 1972. 18.00 (ISBN 0-404-01715-0). AMS Press.
Wept of Wish-Ton-Wish. Richard B. Davis. LC 75-127081. 1970. pap. text ed. 2.50x o.p. (ISBN 0-675-09298-1). Merrill.
Wept of Wish-Ton-Wish. Richard B. Davis. LC 75-127081. 1970. pap. text ed. 2.50x o.p. (ISBN 0-675-09298-1). Merrill.
Wept of Wish-Ton-Wish: A Tale. James Fenimore Cooper. LC 74-107169. 1970. (ISBN 0-403-00432-2). Scholarly Press.
Wept of Wish-Ton-Wish: A Tale. James Fenimore Cooper. 1829. Carey, Lea & Carey.
Wept of Wish-Ton-Wish: A Tale. James Fenimore Cooper. LC 41-28179. 1832. Carey, Lea & Carey.
Wept of Wish-Ton-Wish. A Tale. new ed. James Fenimore Cooper. LC 6-30203. 1852. Stringer and Townsend.
Wept of Wish-Ton-Wish. A Tale. new ed. James Fenimore Cooper. 1855. Stringer and Townsend.
Wept of Wish-Ton-Wish. A Tale. James Fenimore Cooper. LC 26-246888. (Half-title: The choice of Cooper. Revised and corrected series. v. 10). 1856. Stringer & Townsend.
Wept of Wish-Ton-Wish: A Tale. James Fenimore Cooper. LC 22-10827. 1859. W. A. Townsend and Company.
Wept of Wish-Ton-Wish: A Tale. James Fenimore Cooper. LC 8-7683. 1872. Hurd and Houghton.
Wept of Wish-Ton-Wish: A Tale. James Fenimore Cooper. (On cover: Lovell's library. no. 529). 1885. J. W. Lovell Company.
Wept of Wish-Ton-Wish. A Tale. James Fenimore Cooper. (On cover: Seaside library, Pocket ed. no. 400). 1885. G. Munro.
Wept of Wish-Ton-Wish. A Tale. James Fenimore Cooper. LC 4-19000. 1901. D. Appleton and Company.
Wept of Wish-Ton-Wish: A Tale. a new ed. James Fenimore Cooper. LC 42-48368. 1836. Carey, Lea, & Blanchard.
Were Death Denied. Cecil William Mercer. LC 46-8406. 1946. G. P. Putnam's Sons.
Were He a Stranger: A Novel of Suspense. Mary Francis Shura. LC 78-19073. 6.95 (ISBN 0-396-07590-8). Dodd, Mead.
We're Holding Your Son. Gordon R. McLean. LC 69-12297. 1969. 3.95 o.p. (ISBN 0-8007-0358-8). Revell.
Were I Thy Bride. Denise Robins. 1971. pap. 0.75 o.p. (T2546). Pyramid Pubns.
We're in the Money. Andrew Bergman. 1975. pap. 4.95xi (ISBN 0-06-131948-1, TB1948, Torch). Har-Row.
We're Not Out of the Woods Yet. G. B. Trudeau. 128p. 1980. pap. 1.75 (ISBN 0-553-13804-9). Bantam.
Were They Married? M. B. Smith. (On cover: Munro's library, no. 675). 1886. N. L. Munro.
Were They Sinners? A Novel. Charles Joseph Bellamy. (On cover: Authors library). 1890. Authors' Publishing Company.
Were This Wild Thing Wedded. Anna Wibberley. LC 76-13051. 7.95. St. Martin's Press.
Were This Wild Thing Wedded. Wibberley, Anna. (Fawcett Crest Book). 1977. 1.50 (ISBN 0-449-23377-4). Fawcett Books.
Were This Wild Thing Wedded. Anna Wibberley. LC 76-376263. 1976. 3.95 (ISBN 0-7181-1449-3). Joseph.
Were-Wolf. Clemence Housman. LC 75-46280. (Supernatural and Occult Fiction). 1976. 10.00 (ISBN 0-405-08138-3). Arno Press.
Were-Wolves & Will-O-the-Wisps: French Tales of Mackinac Retold. Dirk Gringhuis, pseud. (Illus.). 106p. (Orig.). 1974. pap. 2.50 (ISBN 0-911872-14-0). Mackinac Island.
Were You Ever Arrested? And Other Stories. Rebecca Steinhardt. LC 48-6251. 1948. International Press Associates.
Wereblood. Eric Iverson. (Belmont Tower book). 1.50 (ISBN 0-505-51354-4). Tower Pubns.
Werenight. Eric Iverson. (Belmont Tower Book). 1.50 (ISBN 0-505-51365-X). Tower Publications.
Werewolf. Clemence Housman & R. G Macready. (Fantasy classics, 2). (Illus.). 1973. (pbk.) 1.95. Fantasy House.
Werewolf. Bruce Lowery. LC 72-139981. 1972. 5.95 (ISBN 0-8149-0669-9). Vanguard Press.
Werewolf! Bill Pronzini. LC 78-72921. 8.95 (ISBN 0-87795-210-8). Arbor House.
Werewolf. Charles Lee Swem. LC 28-23275. 1928. Pub. for The Crime Club, Inc., by Doubleday, Doran & Company, Inc.
Werewolf Among Us. Dean R Koontz. (Ballantine science fiction). 1973. (pbk) 1.25 (ISBN 0-345-03055-9). Ballantine.
Werewolf of London. Carl Dreadstone & Robert Harris. (Berkley Medallion Book). (Illus.). 1977. 1.25 (ISBN 0-425-03413-5). Berkley Pub. Corp.
Werewolf of Paris. S. Guy Endore. LC 33-767723. Farrar & Rinehart, Incorporated.
Werewolf of Ponkert. H. Warner Munn. (Time-Lost Ser.). 162p. 1976. pap. 1.50 o.p. (ISBN 0-87818-012-5). Centaur.
Werewolf Pilot of the Eastern Shore and Other Stories: Five Stories. Karl B Knust. LC 72-87699. (Illus.). 1972. (pbk) 1.50.
Werewolf Principle. Clifford D. Simak. LC 67-23598. 1967. Putnam.
Werewolf Trace. John Gardner. LC 78-16508. 1978. 11.95 (ISBN 0-8161-6610-2). G. K. Hall.
Werewolf Trace. John E Gardner. LC 76-23761. 1977. 7.95 (ISBN 0-385-00543-1). Doubleday.
Werewolf: Varulven. Tr. from Norwegian by Gustaf Lannestock. Introd. by Harald S. Naess. Aksel Sandemose. LC 65-24188. (Nordic tr. ser.). 5.95. Univ. of Wis. Pr.
Werewolf Vs the Vampire Woman. Arthur N Scram. 1972. 1.50. Guild-Hartford.
Werewolf Walks Tonight. Michael Avallone. (Satan sleuth no. 2). 1974. (pbk.) 0.95. Warner Paperback Library.
Werewolves & Other Monsters. Thomas G. Aylesworth. (Illus.). 120p. (YA) 1973. lib. bdg. 5.95 o.p. (ISBN 0-8161-6071-6, Large Print Bks). G K Hall.
Werther's Younger Brother: The Story of an Attitude. Michael Fraenkel. LC 31-23457. Carrefour.
Wes Hardin's Gun. John Henry Reese. LC 75-3644. 1975. 5.95 (ISBN 0-385-08897-3). Doubleday.
Wesley Sheridan. Clayton Moore. (River Falls Series). (Berkley medallion book: Vol. 2). 1974. (pbk.) 1.25 (ISBN 0-425-02579-9). Berkley Pub. Co.
Wessex of Romance. Wilkinson Sherren. 1973. Repr. of 1903 ed. 30.00 (ISBN 0-8274-0450-6). R West.
Wessex Tales... Thomas Hardy. LC 1-21251. 1896. Harper & Brothers.
Wessex Tales and A Group of Noble Dames. Thomas Hardy & F. B Pinion. LC 80-24338. (His The New Wessex edition). (New Wessex edition of the stories of Thomas Hardy; v. 1). 1981. 2.95 (ISBN 0-312-86277-6). St. Martin's Press.
Wessex Tales, Strange, Lively, and Commonplace. Thomas Hardy. LC 7-1966. (On cover: Harper's Franklin square library, no. 621). 1888. Harper & Brothers.
West! Charles Alden Seltzer. LC 22-164754. 1922. The Century Co.
West and East: An Algerian Romance. Laura Coates Reed. LC 7-30947. (On cover: Sergel's international library, v. 1, no. 18). 1892. C. H. Sergel and Company.
West Broadway. Nina Wilcox Putnam. LC 21-18794. 1.75. George H. Doran Company.
West Country Short Stories. Lewis Wilshire. Repr. of 1949 ed. 6.50 o.p. (ISBN 0-89987-124-0). Darby Bks.
West Country Short Stories. Lewis Wilshire. 1949. 10.00. Havertown Bks.
West End Horror. Nicholas Meyer. 1977. 1.75. Ballantine Books.
West End Horror: A Posthumous Memoir of John H. Watson, M.D. Nicholas Meyer. LC 75-38776. 7.95 (ISBN 0-525-23102-1). E. P. Dutton.
West End Horror: A Posthumous Memoir of John H. Watson, M.D. Nicholas Meyer. 1977. 1.75 (ISBN 0-345-25411-2). Ballantine Books.
West End Nurse. Lucy Agnes Hancock. LC 43-728. 1943. Macrae-Smith-Company.
West from Abilene. Al Cody, pseud. 1978. pap. 1.25 (ISBN 0-532-12565-7). Woodhill.
West from Deadwood. Al Cody, pseud. 1980. pap. 1.95 (ISBN 0-8439-0850-5). Nordon Pubns.
West Goes the Road. Tim Pridgen. LC 44-5272. 1944. Doubleday, Doran and Company, Inc.
West India Lights. Henry St. Clair Whitehead. 1946. Arkham House.
West Indian Stories. Ed. by Andrew Salkey. 224p. (Orig.). 1968. pap. 4.95 (ISBN 0-571-08630-6). Faber & Faber.
West Lawn, and The Rector of St. Mark's. Mary Jane Hawes Holmes. LC 4-35647. 1876. G. W. Carleton & Co.
West Midland Underground: Stories. Michael Wilding. LC 76-357910. 1975. 7.90 (ISBN 0-7022-0990-2) (ISBN 0-7022-0069-7). University of Queensland Press.
West of Abilene. Vingie Eve Roe. LC 51-10625. 1951. Macrae Smith.
West of Apache Pass. Charles Alden Seltzer. LC 74-21541. 1974. (ISBN 0-88411-108-3). Aeonian Press.
West of Apache Pass. Charles Alden Seltzer. LC 34-32938. 1934. Doubleday, Doran & Company, Inc.
West of Appomattox. Harley Duncan. LC 61-17114. 1961. Appleton-Century Crofts.
West of Barbwire. Lee Floren. 1969. pap. 0.60 o.p. (60-427). Manor Bks.
West of Barter River. Robert Ormond Case. LC 41-8078. 1941. Doubleday, Doran and Company, Inc.
West of Cheyenne. Lee Hoffman. LC 69-10984. (DD western). 1969. 3.95. Doubleday.
West of Devil's Canyon. Richard Poole. 1970. pap. 0.60 o.p. (R2324, GM). Fawcett World.
West of Dodge. George Washington Ogden. LC 26-8010. 1926. Dodd, Mead and Company.
West of Fifth. Catharine Brody. LC 30-20812. 1930. Doubleday, Doran & Company, Inc.
West of Justice: By John Hunter Pseudd. Willis Todhunter Ballard. LC 54-5983. 1954. Houghton Mifflin.
West of Morning. August William Derleth. LC 60-16459. 4.95 (ISBN 0-88361-075-2). Stanton & Lee.
West of Morning. August William Derleth. 3.50 o.s.i. (ISBN 0-88451-023-9). Edco-Vis Assoc.
West of Omaha. Les Wayne. (Orig.). 1981. pap. 1.75 (ISBN 0-8439-0925-0, Leisure Bks). Nordon Pubns.
West of Owen Wister: Selected Short Stories. Owen Wister. LC 74-175805. 1972. 4.50 (ISBN 0-8032-0808-1). University of Nebraska Press.
West of Pike's Peak. Everett Bair. LC 55-9801. 1955. Comet Press Books.
West of Quarantine. Willis Todhunter Ballard. LC 52-9583. 1953. Houghton Mifflin.
West of Railhead. Dwight Bennett. LC 76-55683. 1977. 6.95 (ISBN 0-385-12151-2). Doubleday.
West of Railhead. Dwight Bennett. 1978. 1.50 (ISBN 0-445-04255-9). Popular Library.
West of Sundown. Al Cody, pseud. 1978. pap. 1.25 (ISBN 0-532-12544-4). Woodhill.
West of Sundown. Al Cody, pseud. 192p. 1973. pap. 0.75 o.p. (532-75495-075). Manor Bks.
West of Sundown. Archie Joscelyn. (YA) 1972. 4.50 o.p. (Avalon). Bouregy.
West of Texas Law. Walker A Tompkins. 1948. Macrae-Smith-Co.
West of the Hill. Gladys Hasty Carroll. LC 49-5190. 1949. Macmillan Co.
West of the Hill. Gladys Hasty Carroll. LC 81-15261. 1982. 13.95 (ISBN 0-89340-375-X). J. Curley.
West of the Law. Archie Joscelyn. LC 47-2863. 1947. Dodd, Mead & Company.
West of the Law. 1st Ed. Clarence Budington Kelland. 1958. Harper.

West of the Moon. Edith St. George. 192p. 1981. pap. 1.50 o.s.i. (ISBN 0-671-57069-2). S&S.
West of the Moon. Howard Simpson. 1968. 2.75 o.p. Vantage.
West of the Moon: A Romance. Anna Robeson Brown Burr. LC 26-19021. 1926. Duffield and Company.
West of the Nile: A Story of Saadia Gaon. Abraham Burstein & Simon, Howard, 1902- Illus. LC 42-222665. 1942. Hebrew Publishing Co.
West of the Pecos. Zane Grey. LC 37-969. 1937. Harper & Brothers.
West of the Pecos. Zane Grey. LC 78-2624. 1978. 9.95 (ISBN 0-89340-135-8). J. Curley.
West of the Pecos. Zane Grey. 1.50 (ISBN 0-671-80728-5). Pocket Books.
West of the Pecos: By Paul Evan Pseud. Paul Evan Lehman. LC 57-872666. 1957. Avalon Books.
West of the Rainbow. George Washington Ogden. LC 42-6761. 1942. Dodd, Mead & Company.
West of the Rimrock. Wayne D Overholser. LC 49-8367. 1949. Macmillan Co.
West of the Rimrock. Wayne D Overholser. 1974. (pbk.) 0.75. Dell.
West of the River. 1st Ed. Charlton Grant Laird. LC 52-12653. 1953. Little, Brown.
West of the Rockies. Daniel Fuchs. LC 70-142955. 1971. 5.95 (ISBN 0-394-46987-9). Knopf.
West of the Sabine: The Pioneers' Last Heritage. Robert Emmet Caudle. LC 39-1386. 1938. The Naylor Company.
West of the Sun. 1st Ed. Edgar Pangborn. LC 52-14193. (Doubleday science fiction). 1953. Doubleday.
West of the Sunset. James Denson Sayers. LC 40-1424. 1939. Hillman-Curl, Inc.
West of the Water Tower. Homer Croy. LC 23-798388. Harper & Brothers.
West of the Weather. Norma Patterson. LC 41-243828. Farrar & Rinehart, Inc.
West of the Wolverine. Paul Evan Lehman. LC 46-541323. 1946. S. Curl, Inc.
West of Washington. Holmes Moss Alexander. 1962. Fleet Pub. Corp.
West Pier. 1st American Ed. Patrick Hamilton. LC 52-10411. 1952. Doubleday.
West Point Cadet: Or, The Young Officer's Bride. A Romance in Real Life. pseud.... ed. Justin Jones. LC 44-15356. 1845. F. Gleason.
West Point Colors: A Novel. Anna Bartlett Warner. LC 3-27963. 1903. F. H. Revell Company.
West Point: Its Glamour and Its Grind. Harold Hammond. LC 10-7825. Cupples & Leon Company.
West Point Wooing: And Other Stories. Clara Louise Root Burnham. LC 99-775. 1899. Houghton, Mifflin and Company.
West Point Wooing & Other Stories. facsimile ed. Clara Louise Root Burnham. LC 79-94709. (Short Story Index Reprint Ser.). 1899. 16.00 (ISBN 0-8369-3088-6). Ayer Co.
West Quartet: Four Novels of Intrigue and High Adventure. Morris L. West. LC 81-4871. 1981. 14.95 (ISBN 0-688-00637-X). Morrow.
West Shore Mystery. Harlan Page Halsey. (On cover: The calumet series, no. 3). G. Munro.
West Side Story. Irving Shulman. (Orig.). (gr. 8 up). 1961. pap. 2.50 (ISBN 0-671-41853-X). PB.
West Side Story. abr. ed. Irving Shulman. Ed. by Virginia F. Allen & Francis Price. (Falcon Ser). 1969. Set Of 7 Copies Ea. Of 6 Pbks. pap. 37.50 set o.p. (ISBN 0-8372-9637-4). Bowmar-Noble.
West Side Story: A Novelization. Shulman, Irving. LC 61-65994. (Cardinal edition, GC-122). 1961. Pocket Books.
West to North. Compton Mackenzie. LC 41-516079. 1941. Dodd, Mead & Company.
West to Rising Sun. Julius W Butler. LC 30-12288. Jordan Publishing Company.
West to the Setting Sun. Harvey Chalmers. LC 65-871458. 6.00. Twayne.
West to the Sun. Cover Painting by Frank McCarthy. Noel M. Loomis. LC 55-351894. (Gold medal books, 485). 1955. Fawcett Publications.
West Virginian. Harry Edmund Danford. LC 26-22411. 1926. H. Vinal.
West We Go. Jules Loring. LC 46-4284. 1946. G. P. Putnam's Sons.
West Wind. Faith Baldwin Cuthrell. LC 62-12138. 1975. (pbk.) 1.25. Warner Paperback Library.
West Wind. Crosbie Garstin. LC 26-13575. 1926. Frederick A. Stokes Company.
West Wind: A Novel. Melvin Leighton Heimer. LC 64-16581. 1964. Trident Press.
West Wind: A Story of Red Men and White in Old Wyoming. Cyrus Townsend Brady. LC 12-21399. 1912. 1.35. A. C. McClurg & Co.
West Wind Drift. George Barr McCutcheon. LC 20-18655. 1920. Dodd, Mead and Company.
West Wind of Love. Compton Mackenzie. LC 40-31112. 1940. Dodd, Mead & Company.
West Wind Wild. Carolyn Vaughter. 416p. (Orig.). 1981. pap. 2.95 (ISBN 0-380-78691-5, 78691). Avon.
West Window. Leslie Poles Hartley. LC 45-8329. 1945. Doubleday, Doran and Co., Inc.
West with the Missouri. Cliff Farrell. LC 55-5808. 1955. Random House.
West with the Night. Beryl Markham. 304p. 1983. pap. 12.50 (ISBN 0-86547-118-5). N Point Pr.
West with the Vikings. 1st Ed. Edison Marshall. LC 61-12556. 1961. Doubleday.
Westbank Group. Henry Sackerman, pseud. 244p. 1970. 5.95 o.p. (ISBN 0-8202-0108-1). Sherbourne.
Westbrook Parsonage. Harriet Burn McKeever. LC 7-16312. 1870. Claxton, Remsen & Haffelfinger.
Westchester Bull. Sam Koperwas. LC 75-33716. 7.95 (ISBN 0-671-22199-X). Simon and Schuster.
Westcotes. Arthur Thomas Quiller-Couch. LC 2-2766. 1902. H. T. Coates & Co.
Westener. Zane Grey. Ed. by Loren Grey. (Belmont Tower Book). (Illus.). 1.25. Tower Pubns.
Westerby Inheritance. Marion Chesney. 352p. (Orig.). 1982. pap. 3.50 (ISBN 0-523-41276-2). Pinnacle Bks.
Westerfelt: A Novel. William Nathaniel Harben. LC 1-12822. 1901. Harper & Brothers.
Westering. 1st Ed. Irwin R Blacker. LC 58-10059. 1958. World Pub. Co.
Western. LC 82-463266. (No-Frills Book). 1981. 1.50 (ISBN 0-515-06245-6). Jove Publications.
Western: A Saga of the Great Plains. Frank Yerby. LC 81-19470. 1982. 17.95 (ISBN 0-385-27230-8). Dial Press.
Western Bonanza. Western Writers Of America Members. 1969. 6.95 o.p. (ISBN 0-385-01668-9). Doubleday.
Western Bonanza: Eight Short Novels of the West. Ed. by Willis Todhunter Ballard. Western Writers of America. LC 70-78684. 1969. 6.95. Doubleday.
Western Boy: Or the Road to Success. Horatio Alger. 1974. (pbk.) 1.25 (ISBN 0-89014-110-X). Canyon Books.
Western Circus. Rene de Goscinny. (Lucky Luke Series). (French.). 1976. 5.95x (ISBN 2-205-00425-5). Intl Learn Syst.
Western Classics from the Great Pulps. Damon Francis Knight. (Illus.). 1978. 2.95 (ISBN 0-06-465097-9). Barnes & Noble Books.
Western Clearings. Caroline Matilda Stansbury Kirkland. LC 69-11909. (American short story series, v. 68). 1969. Garrett Press.
Western Clearings. Caroline Matilda Stansbury Kirkland. LC 72-8160. (American short story series, v. 68). 1972. (ISBN 0-8422-8088-X). MSS Information Corp.
Western Clearings. Caroline Matilda Stansbury Kirkland. LC 9-15663. (Half-title: Wiley and Putnam's library of American books). Wiley and Putnam.
Western Coast. Paula Fox. LC 72-78452. 1972. (ISBN 0-15-195750-9). Harcourt Brace Jovanovich.
Western Express Robbery: Or, Nat Ridley and the Mail Thieves. Nat Jr Ridley. LC 27-7190. (His Nat Ridley series--15). 1927. Garden City Publishing Co., Inc.
Western Gateway: A Tale of the Birth Years of the Republic. Ray D Herrington. LC 45-4468. 1944. The Primavera Press, Inc.
Western Justice. James R Haning. 1973. 4.95. Lenox Hill Pr.
Western Merchant. A Narrative... John Beauchamp Jones. LC 8-7336. 1849. Grigg, Elliot & Co.
Western Romances. Peggy Simson Curry & Western Writers of America. (Gold medal book, M2913). 1974. (pbk.) 0.95. Fawcett.
Western Romances. Western Writers of America. Ed. by Peggy S. Curry. 192p. (Orig.). 1974. pap. 0.95 o.p. (449-02913-95, GM). Fawcett World.
Western Roundup. Ed. by Arnold Hano. LC 48-24431. (Bantam book, 256). 1948. Bantam Books.
Western Roundup, by Members of the Western Writers of America. Western Writers of America. Ed. by Nelson Coral Nye. LC 61-17161. 1961. Macmillan.
Western Scar: The Theme of the Been-to in West African Literature. William Lawson. LC 82-6372. x, 150p. 1982. lib. bdg. 18.95 (ISBN 0-8214-0649-3, 82-84184); pap. text ed. 11.95 (ISBN 0-8214-0695-7, 82-84648). Ohio U Pr.
Western Scenes; or, Life on the Prairie. A Series of Humorous Sketches Descriptive of Incidents and Character in the Wild West. To Which Are Added Other Miscellaneous Pieces. John S Robb. LC 7-41020. T. B. Peterson and Brothers.
Western Septet; Seven Stories of the American West. Henryk Sienkiewicz. LC 72-96321. 1973. 5.00 (ISBN 0-910366-15-2). Cherry Hill Books.
Western Septet: Seven Stories of the American West. new ed. Henryk Sienkiewicz. Ed. by Marion M. Coleman. LC 72-96321. (Illus.). 175p. 1973. pap. 5.00 (ISBN 0-910366-15-2). Alliance Coll.
Western Shore. Clarkson Crane. LC 25-61659. Harcourt, Brace and Company.
Western Stories... Ed. by Gene Autry. LC 47-208439. (On cover: A Dell book. 158). 1947.
Western Stories. Zane Grey. (O.s.i.). pap. 1.25 o.s.i. Belmont-Tower.
Western Stories: A Corral of Top-Hand Westerns. Ed. by William MacLeod Raine. LC 49-5794. (Dell book, 282). 1949. Dell Pub. Co.
Western Story Annual. LC 44-31052. Street & Smith Publications, Inc.
Western Story-Fact, Fiction, and Myth. Philip Durham & Everett L Jones. LC 74-27765. 1975. 4.95 (ISBN 0-15-595316-8). Harcourt Brace Jovanovich.
Western Story: Fact, Fiction & Myth. Philip Durham & Everett L. Jones. 384p. (Orig.). 1975. pap. text ed. 8.95 o.p. (ISBN 0-15-595316-8, HC). HarBraceJ.
Western Story Omnibus: A Collection of Short Stories. Ed. by William Targ. LC 45-2150. 1945. The World Publishing Company.
Western Thrillers: Edited and with an Introduction. Ed. by Leo Margulies. LC 35-36179. R. Speller, Inc.
Western Union. Zane Grey. LC 39-25440. 1939. Harper & Brothers.
Western Union. Zane Grey. 1974. (pbk.) 0.75 (ISBN 0-671-75839-X). Pocket Books.
Western Vengeance. Lauran Paine. LC 58-44393. 1958. W. Foulsham.
Western Vengeance. Orlando Rigoni. 1977. pap. 1.50 (ISBN 0-532-15291-3). Woodhill.
Western Warwick. Samuel George Blythe. LC 16-115877. George H. Doran Company.
Western Wind. Oliver B. Patton. 384p. 1981. pap. 2.95 (ISBN 0-445-04634-1). Popular Lib.
Western Writings of Stephen Crane. Bergon Frank. (Signet Classic). 1.95 (ISBN 0-451-51189-1). The New American Library.
Westerner. Zane Grey & Loren Grey. LC 80-24097. 1980. (ISBN 0-8161-3125-2). G. K. Hall.
Westerners. Stewart Edward White. LC 1-21940. 1901. McClure, Phillips & Co.
Westerns of the Forties. Ed. by Damon Francis Knight. LC 77-76880. 1977. 12.50 (ISBN 0-672-52036-2). Bobbs-Merrill.
Westfield. Roderick Thorp. LC 77-23372. 10.00 (ISBN 0-517-52972-6). Crown Publishers.
Westgate Mystery. St. John, Darby. LC 41-16600. Random House.
Westhaven. Frank Vandenberg. LC 43-4265. 1943. Wm. B. Eerdmans Publishing Co.
Westminster Disaster. Fred Hoyle & Geoffrey Hoyle. LC 77-11789. 8.95 (ISBN 0-06-012009-6). Harper & Row.
Westminster Mystery. Elaine Hamilton. LC 31-7378. 2.00. The Century Co.
Westminster One. Ted Willis. LC 74-30589. (YA) 1975. 7.95 o.p. (ISBN 0-399-11515-3). Putnam.
Westminster One. Ted Willis. (Berkley Medallion Book). 1976. (pbk.) 1.75 (ISBN 0-425-03112-8). Berkley Publishing Corp.
Weston Tragedy: A Golden Pilgrimage); a Novel. Clara Hammond Lanza. (On cover: The pastime series. no. 58). 1897. Laird & Lee.
Westover of Wanalah: A Story of Love and Life in Old Virginia. George Cary Eggleston. LC 10-16151. 1910. Lothrop, Lee & Shepard Co.
Westphal Empire. Al Fosbenner. (Orig.). 1980. pap. 2.75 (ISBN 0-440-19492-X). Dell.
Westport Landing. Homer Hatten. LC 51-27097. (Gold medal books, 157). 1951. Fawcett Publications.
Westward: A Tale of American Emigrant Life. Julia MacNair Wright.
Westward Ho! Charles Kingsley. LC 9-3017. (Manhattan library... v. 1, no. 12). 1891. A. L. Burt.
Westward Ho! Charles Kingsley & Oakley, Thornton, 1881- Illus. LC 20-26980. G. W. Jacobs & Co.
Westward Ho! A Narrativo Based Upon Episodes in the Life of Hiram Smith Holly. William Lockwood Smith. LC 50-11195. 1950. Dorrance.
Westward Ho! A Tale. James Kirke Paulding. LC 72-584. 1968. Scholarly Press.
Westward Ho! A Tale. James Kirke Paulding. LC 7-33782. 1832. J. & J. Harper.
Westward Ho! Ed. by M. W. and G. Thomas. Illus. by George W. Adamson. Charles Kingsley. Ed. by Maurice Walton Thomas & Gladys Thomas. LC 66-6650. (Shorter classics). 1963. bds., 2.50. Ginn.
Westward Ho! Illus. by Hookway Cowles. Charles Kingsley. (Macdonald illus. classics, 1). 1966. 3.50. Macdonald.
Westward Ho! Or, Amyas Leigh in the Spanish Main. Charles Kingsley & Hale, Edward Everett, 1863-1932, Ed. (Standard literature series, no. 33). University Publishing Company.
Westward Ho! Or, The Voyage and Adventures of Sir Amyas Leigh, Knight, of Burrough, in the County of Devon, in the Reign of Her Most Glorious Majesty Queen Elizabeth. Charles Kingsley & Wyeth, Nowell Convers, 1882- Illus. LC 20-18930. 1920. C. Scribner's Sons.
Westward Ho! Or, The Voyages and Adventures of Sir Amyas Leigh, Knight, of Burrough, in the County of Devon, in the Reign of Her Most Glorious Majesty, Queen Elizabeth, Rendered into Modern English, With 16 Full-Page Illus. Foreword by Basil Davenport. Charles Kingsley. (Great Illus. Classics; Titan Eds.). 1966. 4.50. Dodd.
Westward Ho! Or, The Voyages and Adventures of Sir Amyas Leigh, Knight, of Burrough, in the County of Devon, in the Reign of Her Most Glorious Majesty, Queen Elizabeth. Charles Kingsley. LC 4-16538. 1882. Macmillan and Co.
Westward Ho! Or, The Voyages and Adventures of Sir Amyas Leigh, Knight, of Burrough, in the County of Devon, in the Reign of Her Most Glorious Majesty, Queen Elizabeth. Charles Kingsley. 1886. Macmillan and Co.
Westward Ho! Or, The Voyages and Adventures of Sir Amyas Leight Knt. of Burrough, in the County of Devon, in the Reign of Her Most Glorious Majesty Queen Elizabeth. Charles Kingsley. (Half-title: Everyman's library, edited by Ernest Rhys. no. 20). 1906. J. M. Dent & Co.
Westward Ho! Or, The Voyages and Adventures of Sir Amyas Leigh, Knight, of Burrough, in the County of Devon, in the Reign of Her Most Glorious Majesty, Queen Elizabeth, Rendered into Modern English. Charles Kingsley. LC 28-20084. 1927. Dodd, Mead and Company.
Westward Ho! Or, The Voyages and Adventures of Sir Amyas Leigh, Knight, of Burrough, in the County of Devon, in the Reign of Her Most Glorious Majesty, Queen Elizabeth. Charles Kingsley & Gomme, Sir George Laurence, 1853-1916, Ed. (Half-title: Library of historical novels and romances, ed. by G. L. Gomme). 1898. Longmans, Green and Company; Etc., Etc.
Westward Ho! Or, The Voyages and Adventures of Sir Amyas Leigh, Knight of Burrough, in the County of Devon, in the Reign of Her Most Glorious Majesty, Queen Elizabeth. (abridged) ed. with an introduction and notes by sterling andrus leonard... ed. Charles Kingsley & Leonard, Sterling Andrus, 1858-1931, Ed. LC 19-1031. (Macmillan's pocket American and English classics). 1919. The Macmillan Company.
Westward Ho! Or, The Voyages and Adventures of Sir Amyas Leigh, Knight, of Burrough, in the County of Devon, in the Reign of Her Most Glorious Majesty Queen Elizabeth. Charles Kingsley & Moore, Mrs. Elizabeth C., Ed. LC 30-23184. (The Green and blue library). 1930. The Macmillan Company.
Westward Ho! The Voyages and Adventures of Sir Amyas Leigh, Knight, of Burrough, in the County of Devon, in the Reign of Her Most Glorious Majesty Queen Elizabeth. Charles Kingsley. LC 15-20286. 1855. Ticknor and Fields.
Westward Ho! The Voyages and Adventures of Sir Amyas Leigh, Knight, of Burrough, in the County of Devon, in the Reign of Her Most Glorious Majesty Queen Elizabeth. 4th ed. Charles Kingsley. LC 41-26691. 1857. Ticknor and Fields.
Westward Leading. John Tron. LC 42-23431. 1942. Wm B. Eerdmans Publishing Company.
Westward Love. Elizabeth Monterey. 416p. (Orig.). 1981. pap. 2.95 (ISBN 0-446-80677-3). Warner Bks.
Westward March of American Settlement see Collected Works.
Westward Passage: By Margaret Ayer Barnes. Margaret Ayer Barnes. LC 31-28424. 1931. Houghton Mifflin Company.
Westward the Dream. Frances Marion. LC 48-715120. 1948. Doubleday.
Westward the Monitors Roar. Willis Todhunter Ballard. LC 63-7700. (Double D western). 1963. Doubleday.
Westward the River. Dale Van Every. LC 45-6053. 1945. G. P. Putnam's Sons.
Westward the Sun. Geoffrey Cotterell. LC 52-13731. 1953. Lippincott.
Westward the Sun. Brigid Knight. LC 42-36172. 1942. Crowell.
Westward the Sun. Kathleen Henrietta Nash-Webber Sinclair. LC 42-36172. 1942. Thomas Y. Crowell Company.
Westward the Tide. Louis L'Amour. LC 77-9466. 1977. 11.95 (ISBN 0-8161-6498-3). G. K. Hall.
Westward the Tide. Harold Sinclair. LC 40-33068. 1940. Doubleday, Doran & Co., Inc.
Westward the Wagons. Burt Arthur & Budd Arthur. 1979. pap. 1.25 o.s.i. (ISBN 0-505-51396-X). Tower Bks.

Westward They Rode. Theodore V Olsen. 1976. 1.50. Ace Books.

Westward to Arthur. Richard Hoskins. 1977. pap. 6.95 (ISBN 0-906158-00-1). Pendragon Hse.

Westward to Chungking... Ching-Ch'Iu Kuo. LC 44-740953. 1944. D. Appleton-Century Company, Incorporated.

Westward to Destiny. Dorothy Bastien. 1973. 0.95. Curtis Books.

Westward to Laughter. Colin MacInnes. LC 76-95637. 1970. 5.95. Farrar, Straus & Giroux.

Westward to Paradise. W. D Hoffman. LC 27-22479. 1927. A. C. McClurg & Co.

Westward: Wagon Wheels! Mary Gray Mooers. LC 55-30076. 1955. Meador Pub. Co.

Westways: A Village Chronicle. Silas Weir Mitchell. LC 18-195059. 1913. The Century Co.

Westwind. James Nordhoff. LC 79-21116. 1980. 11.95 (ISBN 0-688-03590-6). Morrow.

Westwood Mystery. Archibald E. Fielding. LC 33-647759. 1933. H. C. Kinsey & Company, Inc.

Wet Clay. Seumas O'Kelly. LC 23-26858. 1923. Frederick A. Stokes Company.

Wet Parade. Upton Beall Sinclair. LC 31-23681. Farrar & Rinehart, Incorporated.

Wet Plates & Dry Gulches. Gilbert L. Campbell. LC 71-41602. (Wild & Woolly West Ser., No. 8). (Illus., Orig.). 1973. 7.00 (ISBN 0-910584-94-X); pap. 2.00 (ISBN 0-910584-11-7). Filter.

Wet Wash. Harding Upton. LC 26-19727. 1926. G. H. Watt.

Wet Weather. Hilary March. LC 27-15709. J. H. Sears & Company, Inc.

Wetback: A Novel. Claud Garner. LC 47-30955. 1947. Coward-McCann.

Wetback: An Original Novel. William O'Farrell. LC 56-119031. (Dell first edition, A120). 1956. Dell Pub. Co.

Wetherel Affair: By J. W. De Forest... John William De Forest. 1873. Sheldon and Company.

Wettermark. Elliott Chaze. LC 69-11567. 1969. 4.95. Scribner.

We've Been Waiting for You. Ethel M. Thornbury. LC 47-31214. 1947. Bobbs-Merrill Co.

Wexford. Julie Ellis. 1976. (pbk.) 1.50 (ISBN 0-671-80438-3). Pocket Books.

Weymouth Sands: A Novel. John Cowper Powys. LC 75-325260. 1973. 3.25 (ISBN 0-903747-04-9). Rivers Press Ltd.

Weymouth Sands: A Novel. John Cowper Powys. LC 34-353987. 1934. Simon and Schuster.

Whack the Cat. Bil Alvernaz. LC 75-17384. 1975. Knickered Midget Pub. Co.

Whacking Off. Michael Perkins. pap. 1.95 o.p. (0123). Essex Hse.

Whale. Jeremy Lucas. LC 81-9221. (Illus.). 11.95 (ISBN 0-671-43653-8). Summit Books.

Whale and the Grasshopper: And Other Fables. Seumas O'Brien. LC 16-22898. 1916. 1.35. Little, Brown, and Company.

Whale for the Killing. Farley Mowat. 224p. 1981. pap. 2.25 (ISBN 0-553-14702-1). Bantam.

Whale for the Killing. Farley Mowat. 1973. pap. 2.95 o.p. (ISBN 0-14-003728-4). Penguin.

Whaleman's Adventures in the Sandwich Islands and California. William Henry Thomes. LC 13-12915. (Added t.-p.: The Ocean life series). 1872. Lee and Shepard.

Whaleman's Adventures in the Sandwich Islands and California. William Henry Thomes. LC 15-21846. (American library. no. 6). 1883. Donnelley, Loyd & Co.

Whaleman's Adventures in the Sandwich Islands and California. William Henry Thomes. LC 12-11743. (Half-title: Ocean-life series). 1885. A. T. Loyd & Company.

Whaleman's Adventures in the Sandwich Islands and California. William Henry Thomes. (On cover: The detective and adventure library, no. 1). 1889. A. T. Loyd & Company.

Whaleman's Adventures in the Sandwich Islands and California. William Henry Thomes. (On cover: The library of choice fiction, no. 6). 1890. Larid & Lee.

Whaleman's Wife. Frank Thomas Bullen. LC 3-3746. 1903. D. Appleton and Company.

Whalers. Lee D. Willoughby. (Making of America Ser.: No. 37). (Orig.). 1983. pap. 3.25 (ISBN 0-440-09769-X). Dell.

Whalesong. Robert Siegel. LC 81-66610. 9.95 (ISBN 0-89107-219-5). Crossway Books.

Wham Bam Thank You, Ma'am Affair. Troy Conway, pseud. (Coxeman Ser). (Orig.). 1968. pap. 0.60 o.p. (53-692). Paperback Lib.

Whanau. Witi Tame Ihinera. LC 75-501632. 173p. 1974. 10.00x (ISBN 0-434-36502-5). Intl Pubns Serv.

Whangdoodles' Song. 1st Ed. Laura Billings Fox. LC 56-12842. 1957. Vantage Press.

Wharf by the Docks. A Novel. Florence Alice Price James. (On cover: The choice series, no. 130). 1896. R. Bonner's Sons.

Wharf Girl. William Manners. LC 54-42475. (Lion book, 219). 1954. Lion Books by Arrangementwith Prime Publications.

Wharf Sinister. Alicia Grace. 224p. 1976. pap. 1.25 (ISBN 0-532-12404-9). Woodhill.

Wharf Sinister. Alicia Grace. 1971. pap. 0.75 o.p. (ISBN 0-447-74765-7). Lancer.

What? Roman Polanski. LC 73-84632. (Illus.). 1973. (pbk.) 1.75 (ISBN 0-89388-121-X). Third Press.

What a Body. Alan Baer Greem. 1965. pap. 0.95 o.p. (02080, Collier). Macmillan.

What a Body. Alan Baer Green. LC 49-11698. (As Inner sanctum mystery). 1949. Simon and Schuster.

What a Life! Edward V. Lucas & George Morrow. LC 74-16979. (Illus.). 128p. (YA) 1975. pap. 2.50 (ISBN 0-486-23133-X). Dover.

What a Life. Lamar Vest. 1974. pap. 1.75 (ISBN 0-87148-904-X). Pathway Pr.

What a Man! Mattie Payne Blank. LC 46-21779. 1945. Mattie P. Blank.

What a Man Can See & Other Fables. Russell Edson. LC 60-9954. pap. 6.00 (ISBN 0-912330-13-9, Dist. by Inland Bk). Jargon Soc.

What a Man Wants. Charles Marriott. LC 13-24831. 1.30. The Bobbs-Merrill Company.

What a Man Wants: A Novel. Howard Vincent O'Brien. LC 25-185762. 1925. Doubleday, Page & Company.

What a Man Wills. Jessie Bell Vaizey. LC 15-6454. 1915. Cassell and Campany, Ltd.

What a Man Wills. Jessie Bell Vaizey. LC 15-8431. 1915. G. P. Putnam's Sons.

What a Man Wishes: A Novel. William Stanley Hill. LC 13-5691. The Morningside Press.

What a Way to Go. Glen Chase, pseud. (Cherry Delight Ser.: No. 15). 1974. pap. 1.25 o.p. (LB208ZK, Leisure Bks). Nordon Pubns.

What a Way to Go. Wright Morris. LC 78-26760. 1979. 14.50 (ISBN 0-8032-0915-0) (ISBN 0-8032-5862-3). University of Nebraska Press.

What a Way to Go. 1st Ed. Wright Morris. LC 62-172787. 1962. Atheneum.

What a Widow! Joseph Warren & Lovett, Josephine. LC 30-245183. Grosset & Dunlap.

What About Me? Gertie Evenhuis. (Puffin book). (Illus.). 1976. 1.25 (ISBN 0-14-030795-8). Penguin.

What About Tomorrow? Clyne W. Buxton. 1974. pap. 3.95 (ISBN 0-87148-903-1). Pathway Pr.

What All That Boy Won't Think of Next! Elizabeth McCarley Ryan. LC 72-168744. 1971. 4.95 (ISBN 0-8111-0421-4). Naylor Co.

What Allah Wills: A Romance of the Purple Sunset. Irwin Leslie Gordon. LC 17-25747. 1917. 1.35. The Page Company.

What Am I Bid? Geoffrey Johns. LC 61-9755. (Illus.). 1961. Doubleday.

What Answer? Anna Elizabeth Dickinson. LC 71-38646. (Black Heritage Library Collection). 1972. (ISBN 0-8369-9004-8). Books for Libraries Press.

What Answer. Anna Elizabeth Dickinson. LC 26-235463. 1869. Fields, Osgood, & Co.

What Answer: A Novel. Anna Elizabeth Dickinson. 1868. Ticknor and Fields.

What Are Friends for? John Jacob Clayton. LC 78-21014. 8.95 (ISBN 0-316-14719-2). Little, Brown.

What Are Little Girls Made of? Martin Yoseloff. LC 78-55452. 8.95 (ISBN 0-498-02217-X). A. S. Barnes.

What Are You Going to Do About It? Aldous Leonard Huxley. LC 77-3406. Repr. of 1936 ed. lib. bdg. 4.50 (ISBN 0-8414-4914-7). Folcroft.

What Became of Anna Bolton. Louis Bromfield. LC 44-3046. 1944. Harper & Brothers.

What Became of Eugene Ridgewood? A Novel. Paul James, pseud. LC 11-7153. 1883. G. W. Carleton & Co.; Etc., Etc.

What Became of Gunner Asch. Tr. from German by J. Maxwell Brownjohn 1st Amer. Ed. Hans Hellmut Kirst. LC 64-25129. 1965. 4.95. Harper.

What Became of Mr. Desmond. Constance Antonina Boyle. LC 22-212072. 1922. T. Seltzer.

What Beckoning Ghost? John Churchward. (Berkley Medallion Book). 1977. 1.50 (ISBN 0-425-03433-X). Berkley Pub. Corp.

What California Did to Betsy West. Olive Gardner. LC 30-8268. 1930. Wetzel Publishing Co., Inc.

What Came of It. A Novel. H. V Stitzel. 1878. G. H. Himes.

What Can She Do? Edward Payson Roe. LC 7-40242. Dodd, Mead, and Company.

What Can She Do? Edward Payson Roe. (On cover: Dodd, Mead & company's library of fiction, no. 16). Dodd, Mead, and Company.

What Can She Do? Edward Payson Roe. LC 7-402442. (On cover: Roe's works). Dodd, Mead and Company.

What Can She Do? Edward Payson Roe. LC 1-24828. 1898. Dodd, Mead and Company.

What Can You Do? James Leigh. LC 64-251309. 3.95. Harper.

What Cheer," The Sad Story of a Wicked Sailor. William Clark Russell. LC 13-17731. (On cover: The fortnightly library, v. 15, no. 8). 1896. P. F. Collier.

What Color Are Your Eyes? Hale Chatfield. 1979. signed ed. 20.00; 10.00; pap. 4.50. Juniper Pr WI.

What Comes Next. Jonathan Baumbach. LC 68-26545. 1968. 4.95. Harper & Row.

What Counts Is Life. Thiago De Mello. pap. 0.95 o.p. (ISBN 0-8278-4054-3, 14054). Pflaum-Standard.

What Crime Is It? 1st Ed. Dorothy Gardiner. LC 56-9848. 1956. Published for the Crime Club by Doubleday.

What Dark Secret. Dorothy Dudley & Sheridan, Juanita, Joint Author. LC 43-5800. 1943. W. Morrow & Company.

What David Did: Love Letters of Two Babies. Helen Smith Woodruff. LC 21-527179. Boni and Liveright.

What? Dead Again? Neil Shulman. LC 79-89932. 1980. 7.95 (ISBN 0-918784-52-2). Legacy Pub Co.

What Did Hattie See? Kelley Roos. LC 74-102730. (Red badge novel of suspense). 1970. 4.50. Dodd, Mead.

What Did I Do Tomorrow? Leslie Purnell Davies. LC 72-89300. 1973. 5.95 (ISBN 0-385-07807-2). Doubleday.

What Did It Mean. Angela Mackail Thirkell. 1973. pap. 1.25 o.p. (ISBN 0-515-03082-1, V3082). Pyramid Pubns.

What Did It Mean? 1st American Ed. Angela Mackail Thirkell. LC 54-8769. 1954. Knopf.

What Did You Do? Gladys D. Hunt. 5.95 o.p. Vantage.

What Do We Have for the Witnesses, Johnnie. new ed. Garry Trudeau, pseud. LC 74-5539. (Doonesbury Ser.). (Illus.). 128p. 1975. pap. 1.95. HR&W.

What Do Women Want? Dan Greenberg. 1983. pap. 3.95. PB.

What Do Women Want? A Novel. Dan Greenburg. LC 81-23118. 14.95 (ISBN 0-671-43793-3). Wyndham Books.

What Do You Do with an Artificial Lady? Carl Richards. 1978. pap. 1.75 (ISBN 0-532-17184-5). Woodhill.

What Do You Play on a Rainy Day? Joy Inman. 1972. pap. 1.95 o.s.i. (OPH-4269, Ophelia). Olympia.

What Do You Play on a Summer Day? Ethel Kessler & Leonard P. Kessler. 1977. 5.50 (ISBN 0-8193-0867-6). Parents' Magazine Press.

What Do You Play on a Summer Day? Ethel Kessler & Leonard P. Kessler. 1977. 5.50 (ISBN 0-8193-0867-6). Parents' Magazine Press.

What Do You Think? A Novel. Helen Burrell D'Apery. (Dillingham's American authors library, no. 2). 1895. G. W. Dillingham.

What Does WoMan Want. Timothy Leary. LC 78-61064. (Illus.). 237p. 1976. pap. 6.95 o.p. (ISBN 0-915238-27-6). Peace Pr.

What Doth It Profit a Man? Vincent Samuel Stevens. LC 45-372194. 1944. Dorrance & Company.

What Dread Hand. Christianna Brand, pseud. 1979. 15.00x (ISBN 0-86025-113-6, Pub. by Ian Henry Pubns England). State Mutual Bk.

What Dread Hand? A Benvenuto Brown Detective Story... Elizabeth Gill. LC 32-434260. Pub. for the Crime Club, Inc., by Doubleday, Doran & Company, Inc.

What Dreams May Come. Richard Matheson. 1979. pap. 2.25 (ISBN 0-425-04202-2). Berkley Pub.

What Dreams May Come: A Novel. Richard Matheson. LC 78-2817. 8.95. Putnam.

What Dreams May Come: A Study in Failure. Florence Nevill. LC 10-23670. 1910. 0.75. Sherman, French & Company.

What D'ya Know for Sure: A 20th Century-Fox Literary Fellowship Novel. Len Zinberg. LC 47-663. 1947. Doubleday & Company, Inc.

What Else Is There! A Novel. Inez Specking. LC 29-3186. 1929. B. Herder Book Co.

What End but Love. Gordon Webber. LC 59-11890. 1959. Little, Brown.

What Entropy Means to Me. George Alec Effinger. LC 72-182695. 1973. (pbk) 0.95. New American Library.

What Ever Became of the Bonner Boys. Campbell Geeslin. 1981. 11.95 o.p. (ISBN 0-671-42430-0). S&S.

What Ever Happened: A Novel of the Revolution. Boris Viktorovich Savinkov & Seltzer, Thomas, Tr. LC 18-6020. (On verso of half-title: The Borzoi Russian translations, XIII). 1917. A. A. Knopf.

What Ever Happened to Mavis Rooster? William Johnston. LC 72-108913. (Tempo books 5339). 1970. 0.75. Grosset & Dunlap.

What Everybody Wanted. Elsie Singmaster. LC 28-20602. 1928. Houghton Mifflin Company.

What Followed Was Pure Lesley. Mark Kelman. LC 73-76491. 1973. 5.95 (ISBN 0-8415-0262-5). Saturday Review Press.

What Frank Harris Did Not Say. Frank Harris & Alexander Trocchi. pap. 1.25 o.s.i. (207, Travellers Comp). Olympia.

What Gentleman Strangles a Lady? Robert George Dean. LC 36-214583. 1936. Pub. for the Crime Club, Inc., by Doubleday, Doran & Co., Inc.

What God Hath (Not) Joined. Russell Kelso Carter. LC 5-27398. Dodge Publishing Co.

What Greater Love. Dorothy E. Oldham. 50p. 1976. 4.00 o.p. (ISBN 0-682-48474-1). Exposition.

What Happened? Merle Miller. LC 79-28523. 1980. 10.95 (ISBN 0-312-86595-3). St. Martin's Press.

What Happened: A Novel. Merle Miller. LC 70-96000. 1972. 7.95 (ISBN 0-06-012962-X). Harper & Row.

What Happened at Andals? John Arnold. LC 30-4653. E. P. Dutton & Co., Inc.

What Happened at Hazelwood. Michael Innes, pseud. (Crime Ser.). 1976. pap. 2.95 (ISBN 0-14-002650-9). Penguin.

What Happened at Hazelwood. Michael Innes, pseud. 1969. pap. 0.95 o.p. (ISBN 0-14-002650-9). Penguin.

What Happened at Hazelwood? John Innes MacKintosh Stewart. LC 47-257. 1946. Dodd, Mead & Company.

What Happened at Quasi: The Story of a Carolina Cruise. George Cary Eggleston. LC 11-5991. 1911. Lothrop, Lee & Shepard Co.

What Happened in the Night, and Other Stories. James Marie Hopper. LC 13-199437. 1913. 1.10. H. Holt and Company.

What Happened in This. Betsey Riddle Hutten Zum Stolzenberg. LC 39-270830. 1939. E. P. Dutton & Company, Inc.

What Happened on the Mellisande. Phyllis Gordon Demarest. 1973. pap. 0.95 o.p. (09250). Curtis.

What Happened to Emily Goode After the Great Exhibition. Raylyn Moore. LC 78-2195. (Illus.). 1978. 4.95 (ISBN 0-915442-51-5). Starblaze Editions.

What Happened to Forester. Edward Phillips Oppenheim. LC 30-12740. 1930. Little, Brown, and Company.

What Happened to Mary: A Novelization from the Play and the Stories Appearing in the Ladies' World. Robert Carlton Brown. LC 13-18220. E.J. Clode.

What Happened to Sidney Granger: The Farm Boy. Philip George McManus. LC 37-8401. 1937.

What Happened to the Corbetts. Nevil Shute. 1982. 13.95 (ISBN 0-434-69905-5, Pub. by Heinemann). David & Charles.

What Happens Is: The Story of 'Hats by Clarice.' Illustrated by Marian Philips Stiteler. 1st Ed. Marie Colt Reece. LC 53-10081. 1953. Pageant Press.

What Happens Next? A Novel. Gilbert Rogin. LC 75-143826. 1971. 6.95 (ISBN 0-394-46088-X). Random House.

What Has Four Wheels and Flies? A Tale. Douglass Wallop. LC 58-13952. 1959. Norton.

What Hast Thou Done? A Novel. Joseph Fitzgerald Molloy. LC 7-19174. (Harper's Franklin square library, no. 325). 1883. Harper & Brothers.

What Hath a Man? Sarah Gertrude Liebson Millin. LC 38-13107. 1938. Harper & Brothers.

What He Least Expected. Harold Everett Porter. LC 17-8466. 1.50. The Bobbs-Merrill Company.

What Ho! Richard Edward Connell. LC 37-27297. G.P. Putnam's Sons.

What I Did with My Fifty Millions. George William Bagby. Ed. by Maurice, Caesar. LC 6-5022. 1874. J. B. Lippincott & Co.

What I Found Out in the House of a German Prince. Alice Muriel Livingston Williamson & An English-American Governess. LC 15-4827. 1915. Frederick A. Stokes Company.

What I Know About Ben Eccles. John Saunders Holt. LC 43-39052. 1869. J. B. Lippincott & Co.

What I Told Dorcas: A Story for Mission Workers. Mary Eliza Haines Ireland. LC 7-9718. 1895. E. P. Dutton and Company.

What If? Richard A Lupoff. 1981. 2.50 (ISBN 0-671-83190-9). Pocket Books.

What If...? A Selection of Social-Science Fiction. Ed. by Nelson W. Polsby. 224p. 1982. 12.95 (ISBN 0-86616-018-3). Greene.

What If This Friend... Richard O'Hanlon. LC 36-10613. C. Kendall and W. Sharp Inc.

What I'm Going to Do, I Think. l. woiwode. ed. L Woiwode. 1.75 (ISBN 0-380-00837-8). Avon Books.

What I'm Going to Do, I Think. Larry Woiwode. LC 69-13735. 1969. 5.95. Farrar, Straus and Giroux.

What is Blazers. Glenhall Taylor. 1980. pap. 1.50. Eldridge Pub.

What Is Christian Faith. Rudolph Norden. 1961. pap. 0.15 o.p. (13-1143). Concordia.

What Is Gentility? A Moral Tale... Margaret Smith. LC 17-492. 1828. P. Thompson.

What Is Love? Isaac Newton Stevens. LC 18-17493. 1918. Duffield & Company.

What Is the Stars? Arthur J Roth. LC 59-99606. 1959. Farrar, Straus and Cudahy.

What Is This Buzzing, Do You Hear It Too? Luigi Malerba. LC 74-85235. 1969. 5.95. Farrar, Straus & Giroux.

What Is to Be. John Collis Snaith. LC 26-7901. 1926. D. Appleton & Company.

What Is to Be Done. abr. ed. Nikolai Gaurilovich Chernyshevskii. Ed. by I. B. Turkerich. (Russian Library Ser). (Orig.). 1961. pap. 2.95 o.p. (ISBN 0-394-70723-0, V723, Vin). Random.

What Is to Be Done? Tales About New People. Introd. by E. H. Carr. The Benjamin R. Trucker Translation, Rev. and Abridged by Ludmila B. Turkevich. Nikolai Gaurilovich Chernyshevskii. LC 61-2225. (Vintage Russian library, V-723). 1961. Vintage Books.

What Is Truth? The Crucifixion of Christ As Seen Through Roman Eyes. Richard B Webb. LC 68-58964. 1968.

What It's All About. Vadim Grigorevich Frolov. 1968. Doubleday.

What Love Endures. Elizabeth Glenn. (Superromances Ser.). 384p. 1983. pap. 2.95 (ISBN 0-373-70067-9, Pub. by Worldwide). Harlequin Bks.

What Mad Pursuit. Jessie Douglas Fox. LC 30-25903. 1930. Brewer and Warren, Inc.

What Mad Pursuit: A Novel. Martha Gellhorn. LC 34-365502. 1934. Frederick A. Stokes Company.

What Mad Universe. Fredric Brown. LC 49-11544. 1949. Dutton.

What Maisie Knew. Henry James. LC 66-74137. (Penguin modern classics, 2448) 5/-). 1966. Penguin.

What Maisie Knew. Henry James. LC 54-4507. (Doubleday anchor books, A 43). 1954. Doubleday.

What Maisie Knew. Henry James. LC 6-37606. 1897. H. S. Stone & Co.

What Maisie Knew see Bodley Head Henry James.

What Maisie Knew & Other Stories. Henry James. 1908. 7.50 o.p. Scribner.

What Makes Sammy Run? Budd Schulberg. LC 41-5578. Random House.

What Makes Sammy Run? Budd Schulberg. LC 78-723. 1978. 1.95 (ISBN 0-14-004795-6). Penguin Books.

What Makes Sammy Run? Budd Schulberg. LC 79-10457. 1979. 10.00 (ISBN 0-8376-0435-4). R. Bentley.

What Makes Sammy Run? With a New Introd. by the Author. Budd Schulberg. LC 52-5877. (Modern library of the world's best books). 1952. Modern Library.

What Manner of Love: A Novel. Rita Weiman. LC 35-3207. 1935. Longmans, Green and Co.

What Manner of Man. Edna Kenton. LC 3-5182. 1903. The Bowen-Merrill Company.

What Men Live by. Lev Nikolaevich Tolstoi. Bd. with Where Love Is, There God Is. (gr. 7up). pap. 0.35 o.p. (L*P57). Pyramid Pubns.

What Men Live by, and Other Tales. Lev Nikolaevich Tolstoi & Maude, Mrs. Louise (Shanks) 1855- Tr. LC 19-19675. (Stratford universal library. (no. 4)). 1918. The Stratford Company.

What Men Live by: Russian Stories and Legends. Lev Nikolaevich Tolstoi & Maude, Louise (Shanks) 1855-1939, Tr. LC 43-51327. 1943. Pantheon Books Inc.

What Might Have Been Expected. Frank Richard Stockton. LC 2-28759. 1898. Dodd, Mead and Company.

What Mrs. McGillicuddy Saw! Agatha Miller Christie. LC 57-12135. (Red badge detective). 1957. Dodd, Mead.

What Mrs. McGillicuddy Saw! Agatha Miller Christie. 1973. (pbk.) 0.95 (ISBN 0-671-77684-3). Pocket Books.

What Mrs. McGuillicuddy Saw. Agatha Miller Christie. 1979. pap. 2.50 (ISBN 0-671-82422-8). PB.

What Necessity Knows. Lily Dougall. LC 6-33692. 1893. Longmans, Green, and Co.

What Never Happened: A Novel of the Revolution. Boris Savinkov & Seltzer, Thomas, Tr. LC 18-6020. (On verso of half-title: The Borzoi Russian translations, XIII). 1917. A. A. Knopf.

What Next? Provocative Tales of Faith and Morals. Laurence Housman. LC 77-167452. (Short story index reprint series). 1971. (ISBN 0-8369-3978-6). Books for Libraries Press.

What Nigel Knew. Evan Field. LC 81-5844. 10.95 (ISBN 0-517-54468-7). C.N. Potter: Distributed by Crown.

What Night Will Bring. Ruth Lenore Marting. LC 40-270494. 1939. Pub. for the Crime Club, by Doubleday, Doran & Company, Inc.

What Now My Love. Floyd Salas. LC 78-97156. 1969. 4.95. Grove Press.

What of Terry Conniston? Brian Wynne Garfield. (Fawcett crest book, M2044). 1974. (pbk.) 0.95. Fawcett Publications.

What of Terry Conniston? Brian Wynne Garfield. LC 72-133480. (Falcon's head suspense novel). 1971. 5.95. World Pub. Co.

What of the Night! Marie Adelaide Belloc Lowndes. LC 43-5350. 1943. Dodd, Mead & Company.

What Outfit Buddy? Thomas Howard Kelly. LC 20-3794. 1920. Harper & Brothers.

What People Live by. Lev Nikolaevich Tolstoi & Delano, Mrs. Aline P. Kuzmistchev, 1845- Tr. D. Lothrop and Company.

What People Said: A Novel. William Lindsay White. LC 38-7578. 1938. The Viking Press.

What Pierre Did with His Soul: From the French of Georges Ohnet. Georges Ohnet. Tr. by Robins, E. P. LC 7-32512. (On cover: The Belford American movel series, v. 2, no. 5). 1890. Belford Company.

What Price Fortitude: A Novel. 1st Ed. Will M Clower. LC 55-8380. 1955. Pageant Prss.

What Price Gloria! Geoffrey Clayton. LC 36-18153. 1936. H. C. Kinsey & Company, Inc.

What Price Love. Alice L. Covert. (Orig.). 1979. pap. 2.25 (ISBN 0-89083-491-1). Zebra.

What Price Murder. Cleve Franklin Adams. LC 42-14361. 1942. E. P. Dutton & Co., Inc.

What Price Paradise? Alan Hillgarth. LC 29-23245. 1929. Houghton Mifflin Company.

What Price Revolution. David J Krichevsky. LC 76-18448. 8.95 (ISBN 0-87881-052-8). Mojave Books.

What Price Youth: A Novel. Elizabeth Cooper & Stone, Lillian M. LC 29-3661. 1929. Frederick A. Stokes Company.

What Priests Never Tell. William Wilfrid Whalen. LC 27-25833. 1927. B. Herder Book Co.

What Really Happened. Clifford Irving. pap. 1.95 o.p. (Zebra). Grove.

What Really Happened. Marie Adelaide Belloc Lowndes. LC 26-19257. 1926. Doubleday, Page & Company.

What Really Happened: By Brett Halliday Pseud. Davis Dresser. LC 52-10158. (Red badge detective). 1952. Dodd, Mead.

What Rhymes With Cancer? Harry Brander. LC 82-81363. (Illus.). 54p. 1982. pap. 3.00 (ISBN 0-89823-038-1). New Rivers Pr.

What Rhymes with Murder? Jack Iams. LC 50-7624. 1950. Morrow.

What Rough Beast. John Trench. LC 57-108936. (Cock Robin mystery). 1957. Macmillan.

What Rough Beast. William J. Watkins. LC 79-89962. 192p. (Orig.). 1980. pap. 1.95 (ISBN 0-87216-608-2). Playboy Pbks.

What Shall I Cry. Anne Binkley, pseud. LC 68-12566. 1967. Harcourt, Brace & World.

What Shall We Steer by? Desemea Wilson. LC 36-10388. E. P. Dutton Co., Inc.

What She Came Through. Henrietta Keddie. (Seaside library, v. 72, no. 1458). G. Munro.

What Should You Know of Dying? Stanton Forbes, pseud. LC 67-10980. 1967. Published for the Crime Club by Doubleday.

What Should You Know of Dying? Tobias Wells. (60-2333). 1968. Popular Lib.

What Shy Men Dream. George Constable. LC 69-12031. 1969. 3.95. Harcourt, Brace & World.

What the Ancients Said. Lou D'Angelo. LC 71-139012. 1971. 5.95. Doubleday.

What the Crow Said. Robert Kroetsch. LC 79-303143. 1978. 12.95 (ISBN 0-7736-0067-1). General Pub. Co.

What the Spring Brought. Elisabeth Burstenbinder. Tr. by Smith, Mary Stuart (Harrison) (On cover: Seaside library. Pocket ed., no. 2074). 1894. G. Munro.

What the Spring Brought. A New Novel. Elisabeth Burstenbinder. Tr. by Smith, Mary Stuart (Harrison) LC 26-24717. (Seaside library. v. 50, no. 1020). 1881. G. Munro.

What the Swallow Sang: A Novel. Friedrich Spielhagen & S., M., Tr. LC 8-14062. (Leisure hour series v. 19). 1873. Holt & Williams.

What the Sweet Hell? Peter Chamberlain. LC 35-18998. H. Holt and Company.

What the Tallgrass Sats? David A. Evans. 120p. pap. 6.95 (ISBN 0-931170-17-6). Ctr Western Studies.

What the Trees Said. Stephen Diamond. 1971. 5.95 o.p. (9791-6, Sey Lawr). Delacorte.

What the Wind Forgets, a Woman's Heart Remembers. Helen Hyer. LC 75-32399. 1975. 4.95 (ISBN 0-87844-029-1). Sandlapper Pub Co.

What the World Made Them. Virginia Wales Johnson. LC 7-10793. 1871. G. P. Putnam & Sons.

What Then Is Love. Emilie Baker Loring. LC 77-6775. 1977. 9.95 (ISBN 0-89340-086-6). J. Curley.

What Then Is Love. 1st Ed. Emilie Baker Loring. LC 56-907280. 1956. Little, Brown.

What Then Must We Do? Leo Tolstoy. Tr. by Aylmer Maude from Rus. Bd. with Letter to Engelhardt. (World's Classics Ser: No. 281). 1975. 7.25 o.p. (ISBN 0-19-250281-6). Oxford U Pr.

What They Did to Miss Lily. Sonia Wolff. LC 80-8709. 12.95 (ISBN 0-06-014861-6). Harper & Row.

What Time Collects. James Thomas Farrell. LC 64-11695. 1964. Doubleday.

What Time Collects. James Thomas Farrell. 1974. (pbk.) 1.50. Manor Books.

What Time of Night Is It? Mary Slattery Stolz. (Ursula Nordstrom Bk). 1981. 9.89i (ISBN 0-06-026062-9, HarpT). Har-Row.

What Timmy Did. Marie Adelaide Belloc Lowndes. LC 22-14578. 1.75. George H. Doran Company.

What to Do About Alf. Henry Miller. 1978. 12.50 o.p. Porter.

What to Do About Molly. Marjorie Flack. LC 36-30844. 1936. Houghton Mifflin Company.

What to Do Until the Undertaker Comes. Stanton Forbes, pseud. LC 79-139073. 1971. 4.50. Published for the Crime Club by Doubleday.

What to Do Until the Undertaker Comes. Tobias Wells. LC 79-139073. (Crime Club Ser). 1971. 4.50 o.p. (ISBN 0-385-00114-2). Doubleday.

What Was Hiding Behind the Shrubbery? Tessie P. Hypes. 1980. 4.50 (ISBN 0-8062-1349-3). Carlton.

What Was His Duty? George Hyde Lee. 1900. The Neale Company.

What Way My Journey Lies. Frank Fenton. LC 46-3636. 1946. Duell, Sloan and Pearce.

What We Go by. Russell Hardin. LC 73-78029. (Illus.). (pbk.) 2.00. Latitudes Press.

What We Live by. Ernest Dimnet. 1978. Repr. of 1932 ed. lib. bdg. 15.00 (ISBN 0-8495-1035-X). Arden Lib.

What We Must See: Young Black Storytellers: An Anthology. Ed. by Orde Coombs. LC 77-154062. 1971. 5.95 (ISBN 0-396-06357-8). Dodd, Mead.

What We Talk About When We Talk About Love: Stories. Raymond Carver. LC 80-21752. 1981. 9.95 (ISBN 0-394-51684-2). Knopf: Distributed by Random House.

What We Talk About When We Talk About Love. Raymond Carver. LC 81-52447. 176p. pap. 2.95 (ISBN 0-394-75080-2, Vin). Random.

What Will He Do with It? by sir e. bulwer lytton... ed. Edward George Earle Lytton Bulwer-Lytton Lytton. LC 7-8458. 1859. Harper & Brothers.

What Will He Do with It? By Pisistratus Caxton. A Novel. the lord lytton ed. Edward George Earle Lytton Bulwer-Lytton Lytton. LC 8-30882. 1877. J. B. Lippincott & Co.

What Will He Do with It? By Pisistratus Caxton Pseud.... a new ed.... ed. Edward George Earle Lytton Bulwer-Lytton Lytton. LC 7-84578. G. Routledge and Sons.

What Will He Do with It? By Pisistratus Caxton Pseud.... Edward George Earle Lytton Bulwer-Lytton Lytton. LC 8-11030. G. Routledge and Sons.

What Will He Do with It? By Pisistratus Caxton Pseud. Edward George Earle Lytton Bulwer-Lytton Lytton. (Half-title: Novels of Sir Edward Bulwer Lytton. Library ed. The Caxton novels, vol. VII-IX). 1892. Little, Brown, and Company.

What Will People Say? A Novel. Rupert Hughes. LC 18-19399. 1914. Grosset & Dunlap.

What Will People Say? A Novel. Rupert Hughes. LC 14-7563. 1914. Harper & Brothers.

What Will She Do? A Romance of Southern Life. Margaret D Simms. LC 1-31376. The Abbey Press.

What Will Simon Say? Lila Sprague McGinnis. LC 73-89291. 1974. (pbk.) 2.50 (ISBN 0-88270-074-X) (ISBN 0-88270-074-X). Logos International.

What Will the World Say? A Novel. Charles Gibbon. (Seaside library, v. no. 1495). 1883. G. Munro.

What Will the World Say? A Novel of Every-Day Life. And, Only a Woman. Josephine Russell Clay. LC 6-21365. 1873. J. B. Lippincott & Co.

What Will the World Say? An American Tale of Real Life. Rhoda Elizabeth Waterman White. 1885. J. Duffy and Sons.

What Woman Wouldn't? Isabel Pallen Smith. (On cover: The optimus series, no. 9). 1891. Donohue, Henneberry & Co.

What Women Fear. Florence Riddell. LC 28-10631. 1928. J. B. Lippincott Company.

What Would Jesus Do? Wherein a New Generation Under- Takes to Walk in His Steps. Glenn Clark & Charles Monroe Sheldon. LC 51-3618. 1950. Macalester Park Pub. Co.

What Would One Have? A Woman's Confessions ... LC 6-18834. J. H. West Company.

What Would the World Think? A Novel. Adella Octavia Clouston. LC 7-303. The Dodworth Publishing House.

What Would You Have Done? Elias L. Macomb Bristol. LC 6-182466. 1895. Press of J.B. Watkins.

Whatever Gods. Maurice Samuel. LC 23-10691. 1923. Duffield and Company.

Whatever Goes Up. Troy Conway, pseud. (Coxeman Ser). (Orig.). 1969. pap. 0.60 o.p. (ISBN 0-446-63125-6, 63-125). Paperback Lib.

Whatever Goes up. Bertram Millhauser. LC 45-4812. 1945. Pub. for the Crime Club by Doubleday, Doran and Company, Inc.

Whatever Happened to Sandy Fowler? Gary Gabriel. Ed. by Jean McConochie. (Regents Readers Ser.). (gr. 7-12). 1982. pap. text ed. 1.95 (ISBN 0-88345-498-X, 20987). Regents Pub.

Whatever Happened to Uncle Albert? Sue Alexander. (Illus.). 128p. (gr. 3-6). 1980. 8.95 (ISBN 0-395-29104-6, Clarion); pap. 3.95 (ISBN 0-395-30061-4). HM.

Whatever Happens to Baby Animals? Bill Hall. LC 73-76029. (golden book). (Illus.). 1973. (pbk.) 1.45. Golden Press.

Whatever Is--Is Best. Wanda Pigott. 120p. 1975. 3.95 o.s.i. (ISBN 0-8181-0344-2). Pageant-Poseidon.

Whatever Isn't Glory: Short Stories. Thomas McAfee. LC 79-63586. (O.s.i.). 168p. 1980. 8.95 o.s.i. (ISBN 0-935896-00-7, Singing Wind); pap. 5.95 o.s.i. (ISBN 0-935896-07-4). K M Gentile.

Whatever Love Declares. Jascha Frederick Kessler. 1969. 10.00 o.p. Dawsons.

Whatever Love Is. Robert William Chambers. LC 33-23507. 1933. D. Appleton-Century Company, Incorporated.

Whatever Thou Art." A Novel. Wein Wilde. 1892. G. W. Dillingham.

Whatever We Do. Allan Eugene Updegraff. 1927. The John Day Company.

Whatever You Do, Don't Panic. Illustrated by John Huehnergarth. 1st Ed. Jean Doyle Mercier. LC 61-5975. 1961. Doubleday.

What'll We Do on Sunday? Gwen Dubov & Paul Dubov. LC 73-87175. 1974. 5.95 (ISBN 0-399-11281-2). Putnam.

What's a Heaven for? Percy Marks. LC 38-258794. 1938. Frederick A. Stokes Company.

What's Become of a Waring. Anthony Dymoke Powell. (A novel). 1963. 4.95 o.p. (ISBN 0-316-71541-7); pap. 1.95 o.p. (ISBN 0-316-71542-5). Little.

What's Become of Screwloose? and Other Inquiries. Ron Goulart. LC 76-143932. 1971. 4.95 (ISBN 0-684-12338-X). Scribner.

What's Become of Screwloose? and Other Inquiries. Ron Goulart. 1973. (pbk.) 0.95. DAW Books.

What's Bred in the Bone. Grant Allen. LC 4-8628. (On cover: Select series, no 32). 1902. R. F. Fenno & Company.

What's Clacking? A Novel by Emily Brinkerhoff Pseud. 1st Ed. Emily Brinkerhoff Vanderbeek Brogeler. LC 53-5145. 1953. Exposition Press.

What's for Dinner? James Schuyler. LC 78-16914. 1978. 10.00. (ISBN 0-87685-382-3) (ISBN 0-87685-383-1) (ISBN 0-87685-381-5). Black Sparrow Press.

What's Funny About Murder? Craig Cooper. LC 68-26889. 1968. 3.95. Roy Publishers.

What's He to Me? Arthur Asa Hill. LC 14-16482. 1914. 1.25. H. O. Bullard.

What's-His-Name. George Barr McCutcheon. LC 11-7738. 1911. Dodd, Mead and Company.

What's His Offence? A Novel... (On cover: Seaside library. Pocket ed. no. 637). 1885. G. Munro.

What's His Offence? A Novel. By the Author of "The Two Miss Flemings"... (Harper's Franklin square library, no. 498). 1885. Harper & Brothers.

What's in It for Me? Jerome Weidman. 1938. Simon and Schuster.

What's It All About, Charlie Brown? Jeffrey H. Loria. 160p. 1977. pap. 1.25 (ISBN 0-449-22696-4, Crest). Fawcett.

What's It Like Out There? And Other Stories. Edmond Hamilton. 1974. (pbk.) 0.95. Ace Books.

What's Left of April. 1st Ed. Robert James Collas Lowry. LC 56-9399. 1956. Doubleday.

What's Mine's Mine. George Macdonald. 1886. D. Lothrop & Company.

What's Mine's Mine. George Macdonald. LC 7-15862. G. Routledge and Sons.

What's Mine's Mine. A Novel. George Macdonald. (Harper's Franklin square library, no. 512). 1886. Harper & Brothers.

What's Mine's Mine. A Novel. George Macdonald. (On cover: Seaside library. Pocket ed., no. 722). 1886. G. Munro.

What's the Big Hurry? A Novel. 1st Ed. James Yaffe. LC 54-8286. 1954. Little, Brown.

What's the Matter? Josephine Jackson. LC 7-9469. (On cover: Satchel series. no. 27). The Author's Publishing Company.

TITLE INDEX WHEN I COME BACK.

What's the Matter with Helen. Richard Deming. (Orig.). 1971. pap. 0.95 o.p. Beagle Bks.
What's the World Coming to? Rupert Hughes. LC 20-8631. Harper & Brothers.
What's Wrong with My Plant? Chuck Crandall. 128p. 1980. pap. 2.50 (ISBN 0-380-45468-8, 45468). Avon.
Wheat and Tares. A Novel. Graham Claytor. LC 6-21361. 1889. J.B. Lippincott Company.
Wheat in the Ear. Louie Alien Baker. LC 6-687650. (The Hudson library, no. 30). 1898. G. P. Putnam's Sons.
Wheat Killing. Peter Tanous & Paul Rubinstein. LC 77-27682. 1979. 8.95 (ISBN 0-385-14233-1). Doubleday.
Wheat of Night. Oscar De Liso. LC 50-8911. 1950. Scribner.
Wheat Princess. Jean Webster. LC 5-28187. 1905. The Century Co.
Wheel. Alan White. LC 66-22290. 1967. Harcourt, Brace & World.
Wheel and the Hearth. Lucia Wilkins Moore. LC 53-5670. 1953. Ballantine Books.
Wheel is Fixed. James M. Fox. (Raven House Mysteries). 224p. 1982. pap. 2.25 (ISBN 0-373-63022-0, Pub. by Worldwide). Harlequin Bks.
Wheel Is Fixed: By James M. Fox Pseud. 1st Ed. James M. W. Knipscheer. LC 51-9027. 1951. Little, Brown.
Wheel O' Fortune. Louis Tracy. LC 8-25370. E. J. Clode.
Wheel O' Fortune. Louis Tracy. LC 7-25075. E. J. Clode.
Wheel of Destiny: A Story of Love and Adventure. Samuel Hyman Borofsky. LC 17-14176. R. G. Badger; Etc., Etc.
Wheel of Earth. Helga Sandburg. LC 58-6506. 1958. McDowell,Obolensky.
Wheel of Fire. Arlo Bates. LC 6-9083. 1885. C. Scribner's Sons.
Wheel of Fortune. Karen Campbell, pseud. LC 73-3909. (Black Bat Mystery Ser.). 176p. 1973. 5.95 o.p. (ISBN 0-672-51868-6). Bobbs.
Wheel of Fortune. Karen Campbell, pseud. LC 73-3909. (Black bat mystery)). 1973. 5.95. (ISBN 0-672-51868-6). Bobbs-Merrill Co.
Wheel of Fortune. Stephen Longstreet. 448p. (Orig.). 1981. pap. 2.75 (ISBN 0-523-40965-6). Pinnacle Bks.
Wheel of Fortune. Alberto Pincherle & Livingston, Arthur, 1883- Tr. LC 37-5983. 1937. The Viking Press.
Wheel of Fortune. Ruth McCarthy Sears. 1973. 4.95. Lenox Hill Pr.
Wheel of Fortune. 1st Ed. Marta Nanse. LC 55-125211. Pageant Press.
Wheel of Life. Ellen Anderson Gholson Glasgow. LC 6-156744. 1906. Doubleday, Page & Company.
Wheel of Life: A Novel. Herminia Zur Muhlen & Goldsmith, Margaret Leland, 1894- Tr. Title. LC 33-225945. 1933. Frederick A. Stokes Company.
Wheel of Love: And Other Stories. Joyce Carol Oates. LC 79-134661. 1970. 6.95. Vanguard Press.
Wheel of Misfortune: Or, The Victims of Lottery and Policy Dealers. A Yarn from the Web of New York Life. Edward Zane Carroll Judson. Garrett & Co.
Wheel of Time; Collaboration, Owen Wingreve. Henry James. LC 10-4180. 1893. Harper & Brothers.
Wheel Spins see Lady Vanishes.
Wheel Spins: A Novel. Ethel Lina White. LC 36-181458. 1936. Harper & Brothers.
Wheel That Turned... Kathleen Moore Knight. LC 36-23256. 1936. Pub. for the Crime Club, Inc., by Doubleday, Doran & Company, Inc.
Wheel That Turned... Kathleen Moore Knight. LC 31-383132. 1937. The Sun Dial Press, Inc.
Wheel Turns. Gian Daull. Tr. by Miall, Bernard. LC 37-9259. 1937. G. P. Putnam's Sons.
Wheel Turns. G. Ugo Nalato & Miall, Bernard, Tr. LC 37-9259. 1937. G. P. Putnam's Sons.
Wheelchair Corpse. William Levine. (On cover: Bart house mystery. 14). 1945.
Wheelchair Willie & Other Plays. Alan Brown. 1980. pap. 4.95 (ISBN 0-7145-3655-5). Riverrun NY.
Wheeler, Dealer! Carter Brown, pseud. ("A Signet Book"). 1975. (pbk.) 1.25. New American Library.
Wheeler Dealers. Ross Kenyon. 192p. (Orig.). 1974. pap. 1.95 o.p. (ISBN 0-87056-364-5, 6364). Brandon.
Wheeler Fortune. Alan Geoffrey Yates. (Signet Book, T5795). 1974. (pbk.) 0.75. New American Library.
Wheeler: Trail in the Dust. new braille ed. Richard Gibson Hubler. LC 70-91859. 772p. 1970. 9.95. Creek Hse.
Wheels. Arthur Hailey. LC 77-152790. 1971. 7.95. Doubleday.
Wheels. A Bicycle Romance. A. R. McArthur. (Dillingham's Metropolitan library, no. 16). 1896. G. W. Dillingham Co.
Wheels and Whims. An Etching. Florine Thayer McCray & Smith Esther Louise, Joint Author. LC 7-15417. 1884. Cupples, Upham & Company.
Wheels and Whims: An Outing. 2d ed. Florine Thayer McCray & Smith, Esther Louise, Joint Author. LC 7-15418. 1886. J. S. Browning.
Wheels in the Dust. William Colt MacDonald. LC 46-3352. 1946. Doubleday & Company, Inc.
Wheels in the Timber. Evelyn Voss Wise. LC 41-3616. 1941. D. Appleton-Century Company Incorporated.
Wheels of Chance: A Bicycling Idyll. Herbert George Wells. LC 3-10907. 1896. Macmillan and Co.
Wheels of Chance & the Time Machine. Herbert George Wells. 1969. Repr. of 1935 ed. 8.95x (ISBN 0-460-00915-X, Evman). Biblio Dist.
Wheels of Chance: & The Time Machine. Herbert George Wells & Herbert George Wells. LC 68-4976. (Everyman's library, 915. Fiction). 1961. Dent.
Wheels of Heaven. David E. Lawrence. LC 81-66612. 1981. pap. 4.95 (ISBN 0-89107-218-7, Crossway Bks). Good News.
Wheels of If, and Other Science-Fiction. Lyon Sprague De Camp. LC 49-80448. 1948-1949. Shasta Publishers.
Wheels of Terror. Sven Hassel. 1970. pap. 0.95 o.p. (ISBN 0-447-75117-4). Lancer.
Wheels of Time. Florence Louisa Charlesworth Barclay. LC 3-23556. 1908. T. Y. Crowell & Co.
Wheels of Time. Florence Louisa Charlesworth Barclay. LC 10-18656. 1910. 0.50. T. Y. Crowell & Co.
Wheels Within Wheels. Alec Waugh. LC 75-305800. 1974. 2.50 (ISBN 0-491-01341-8). W. H. Allen.
Wheels Within Wheels. Carolyn Wells. LC 23-134504. George H. Doran Company.
Wheels Within Wheels: A Novel of the LaNague Federation. Francis Paul Wilson. LC 78-3262. 1978. 7.95 (ISBN 0-385-14397-4). Doubleday.
Wheels Within Wheels: A Novel of the La Nague Federation. F. Paul Wilson. LC 78-3262. 1978. 7.95 o.p. (ISBN 0-385-14397-4). Doubleday.
Wheelworld. Harry Harrison. 192p. 1981. pap. 2.25 (ISBN 0-553-14339-5). Bantam.
Whelp of the Winds: A Dog Story. Rufus King. LC 26-10801. George H. Doran Company.
Whelps of the Winds: A Dog Story. Rufus King. 1927. A. L. Burt Company.
Whelps of the Wolf. George Tracy Marsh. LC 22-10016. 1922. The Penn Publishing Company.
When a Cobbler Ruled the King. Augusta Huiell Seaman. LC 11-7739. 1911. Sturgis & Walton Company.
When a Feller Needs a Friend. Clare A. Briggs. Repr. of 1914 ed. 11.00 o.s.i. Finch Pr.
When a Girl Loves. Ruth Dewey Groves. LC 29-7963. Grosset & Dunlap.
When a Girl's in Love. Helen Topping Miller. LC 41-122764. 1941. D. Appleton-Century Company, Incorporated.
When a Man Loves: The Story of a Deathless Passion Based on the Motion Picture Story Adapted by Bess Meredyth. Allie Lowe Miles & Meredyth, Bess. LC 27-12297. Grosset & Dunlap.
When a Man Marries. Mary E. Rackham Mann. LC 16-3768. Hodder and Stoughton.
When a Man Marries. Mary Roberts Rinehart. 1.50. The Bobbs-Merrill Company.
When a Man Marries. Mary Roberts Rinehart. LC 21-868413. Grosset & Dunlap.
When a Man Murders see Royal Flush: A Nero Wolfe Omnibus.
When a Man's a Man: A Novel. Harold Bell Wright. LC 16-16077. 1916. The Book Supply Company.
When a Man's a Man: A Novel. Harold Bell Wright. LC 21-139442. 1918. A. L. Burt Company.
When a Man's Single. James Matthew Barrie. LC 6-8636. (On cover: Seaside library. Pocket ed. no. 2101). 1895. G. Munro's Sons.
When a Man's Single: A Tale of Literary Life. James Matthew Barrie. LC 6-6637. (On cover: Harper's Franklin square library, no 636).
When a Man's Single: A Tale of Literary Life. James Matthew Barrie. LC 4-16490. (On cover: The Home library). A. L. Burt.
When a Nurse a Doctor see Lost Wolf River.
When a Nurse Needs a Doctor. Peggy O'More, pseud. LC 65-29980. Arcadia House.
When a Nurse Needs a Doctor see Nurse's Heritage.
When a Renegade Rides: By Brett Austin Pseud. Lee Floren. LC 52-14851. 1952. Arcadia House.
When a Woman Loves. Beatrice Marean. LC 7-20442. (On cover: The Marguerite series. no. 10). 1893. E. A. Weeks & Company.
When Adam Wept. Alan Robert Craig. LC 33-19079. 1933. Doubleday, Doran & Company, Inc.
When Adolf Came: A Novel. Martin Hawkins. LC 43-18236. 1943. Jarrold's Limited.
When Age Grows Young. Hyland Clare Kirk. LC 78-22204. (Aging and Old Age). 1979. 18.00 (ISBN 0-405-11819-8). Arno Press.
When Age Grows Young. A Romance. Hyland Clare Kirk. C. T. Dillingham.
When All Is Said and Done. David Bergelson. LC 76-25614. 13.50 (ISBN 0-8214-0360-5) (ISBN 0-8214-0392-3). Ohio Univesity Press.
When All the Woods Are Green: A Novel. Silas Weir Mitchell. LC 4-15140. 1894. The Century Co.
When All Was Lost. Wade Hampton. LC 35-4335. Giffen Publishing Company.
When and If: A Novel. Phillip Reynolds. LC 52-12145. 1952. Sloane.
When April Comes. Edna Allenbaugh. 1980. 8.95 (ISBN 0-533-04267-4). Vantage.
When Autumn's Here. Julia Shawell. LC 37-23346. 1937. Arcadia House.
When Bad Things Happen to Good People. Harold S. Kushner. 160p. 1983. pap. 3.50 (ISBN 0-380-60392-6, 60392-6). Avon.
When 'Bear Cat' Went Dry. Charles Neville Buck. LC 18-6022. 1.40. W. J. Watt & Company.
When Beggars Choose. Katharine Newlin Burt. LC 37-18257. 1937. Macrae Smith Company.
When Beggars Ride. George Agnew Chamberlain. LC 30-12134. 1930. G. P. Putnam's Sons.
When Blades Are Out and Love's Afield: A Comedy of Cross-Purposes in the Carolinas, by Cyrus Townsend Brady. Cyrus Townsend Brady. LC 1-31150. 1901. J. B. Lippincott Company.
When Boston Braved the King: A Story of Tea-Party Times. William Eleazar Barton. LC 99-1928. W. A. Wilde & Company.
When Boyhood Dreams Come True. James Thomas Farrell & Farrell, Hortense (Alden) LC 47-418. 1946. The Vanguard Press, Inc.
When Boyhood Dreams Come True: Further Short Stories. reprint ed. James Thomas Farrell & Farrell, Hortense (Alden) LC 48-2167. 1948. Sun Dial Press.
When Calls the Heart. Janette Oke. LC 82-24451. 4.95 (ISBN 0-87123-611-7). Bethany House.
When Carey Came to Town. Edith Barnard Delano. LC 16-67190. 1916. 1.00. Dodd, Mead and Company.
When Cattle Kingdom Fell. John Richard Stafford. LC 10-28493. 1910. 1.25. B. W. Dodge & Company.
When Cometh Peace! 1st Ed. Cranford, Mary Poole. LC 52-67084. 1952. Pageant Press.
When D'Artagnan Was Young. Lucien Pemjean. Tr. by Boyd, Madeleine Elise (Reynier) LC 32-11207. 1932. Doubleday, Doran & Company, Inc.
When Dead Men Tell Tales. Sidney Floyd Gowing. LC 28-7335. 1928. G. P. Putnam's Sons.
When Death Rode the Range. William West Winter. LC 26-22306. (On cover: A pocket copyright. no. 67). 1926. Garden City Publishing Co., Inc.
When Desire Cometh. A Novel. G Embe. (Dillingham's metropolitan library, no. 27). 1897. G.W. Dillingham Co.
When Did You Last See My Mother. Christopher Hampton. (Orig.). 1967. pap. 1.00 o.p. (E422, Ever). Grove.
When Doctors Disagree. Franken Meloney. LC 40-11555. Farrar & Rinehart, Inc.
When Doctors Marry. Elizabeth Seifert. LC 60-843830. 1960. Dodd, Mead.
When Doctors Marry. Elizabeth Seifert. LC 73-79178. 1974. 5.95. Aeonian Press.
When Dogs Meet People. Gladys Bagg Taber. LC 52-6765. 1952. Macrae Smith.
When Dorinda Dances: By Brett Halliday Pseud. Davis Dresser. LC 51-13039. (Red badge detective). 1951. Dodd, Mead.
When Dragons Dance. Elliot Tokson. 416p. (Orig.). 1982. pap. 3.25 (ISBN 0-380-79145-5, 79145). Avon.
When Dreams Came True: And Other Stories. William Hamilton Johnston. LC 12-282. 1911. 0.75. Publishing House of the M. E. Church, South, Smith & Lamar, Agents.
When Dreams Come True. Ritter Brown. LC 12-24629. 1.25. D. FitzGerald, Inc.
When Dreams Come True. Arlene Hale. (CandlelightRomance). 1977. 0.95 (ISBN 0-440-19161-X). Dell Pub. Co.
When Dreams Come True; a Story of Emotional Life: By Edgar Saltus... Edgar Evertson Saltus. LC 8-3748. (On cover: Once a week semi-monthly library. v. 12, no. 13). 1894. P. F. Collier.
When Dreams Come True: A Story of Emotional Life. Edgar Evertson Saltus. LC 78-115005. 1970. AMS Press.
When Dreams Come True: A Story of Emotional Life. Edgar Evertson Saltus. LC 8-3748. (On cover: Once a week semi-monthly library, v. 12, no. 13). 1894. P. F. Collier.
When Duty Calls. Margaret Isabel Burke. LC 66-24277. 1966. Dorrance.
When East Goes West. Lerona Rosamond Morris. LC 45-1021. Mathis, Van Nort & Company.
When Egypt Went Broke: A Novel. Holman Francis Day. LC 21-116349. 1921. Harper & Brothers.
When Eight Bells Toll. Alistair MacLean. LC 66-17439. 1966. Doubleday.
When Emmalynn Remembers. Edwina Marlow. 1976. 1.50. Ace.
When Eve Was Not Created: And Other Stories. Hervey White. LC 1-31937. 1901. Small, Maynard & Company.
When Father Christmas Was Late. Coningsby William Dawson. LC 29-22914. 1929. Doubleday, Doran & Company, Incorporated.
When Feathers Fall. Auggie Alviggi. 1981. 4.95 (ISBN 0-533-04973-3). Vantage.
When Folks Was Folks. Elizabeth Lee Blunt. LC 10-15098. 1910. Cochrane Publishing Company.
When Fools Rush in. William Richard Hereford. LC 13-20350. 1.00. The Bobbs-Merrill Company.
When Footsteps Echo: Tales of Terror and the Unknown. Basil Copper. LC 75-7658. 1975. 7.95 (ISBN 0-7091-4770-8). St. Martin's Press.
When for the Truth. A Novel of Reconstruction Days in South Carolina. 1st Ed. Thornwell Jacobs. LC 50-2565. 1950. Walker, Evans and Cogswell.
When Fortune Smiles. Florence Stonebraker. LC 48-117675. 1948. Arcadia House.
When Geronimo Rode. Forrestine Cooper Hooker. LC 24-673576. 1924. Doubleday, Page & Company.
When Ghost Meets Ghost. William Frend De Morgan. LC 14-4932. 1914. H. Holt and Company.
When Glory Departs. Dorothy E Stromberg. LC 45-864215. 1945. Wm. B. Eerdmans Publishing Company.
When God Laughs: And Other Stories. Jack London. LC 11-131128. 1911. 1.50. The Macmillan Company.
When God Made Baalam's Donkey Talk. Evelyn Marxhausen. 1980. pap. 0.89 (ISBN 0-570-06135-0, 59-1253, Arch Bk). Concordia.
When God Quit: A Story of the Days After the Bomb. 1st Ed. Blanche B Coggan. LC 55-12021. 1955. Greenwich Book Publishers.
When God Slept: By Peter Bourne Pseud. Graham Montague Jeffries. LC 56-6491. 1956. Putnam.
When God Walks the Road: And Other Missionary Stories. Ed. by Sara Estelle Haskin. LC 21-212043. 1921. Publishing House of the M. E Church, South.
When Greek Meets Greek. George Demetrios. LC 76-116949. (Short story index reprint series). (Illus.). 1970. Books for Libraries Press.
When Greek Meets Greek. George Demetrios. LC 47-3892. 1947. Houghton Mifflin Co.
When Greek Meets Greek: A Tale of Love and War. Joseph Hatton. LC 7-2203. 1896. J. B. Lippincott Company.
When Half-Gods Go: Being the Story of a Brief Wedded Life As Told in Intimate and Confidential Letters Written by a Bride to a Former College Mate. Helen Reimensnyder Martin. LC 11-29713. 1911. 1.00. The Century Co.
When He Came to Himself. Louis Tucker. LC 28-8591. The Bobbs-Merrill Company.
When He Found Himself. Dorothy Palatianos. LC 19-171. 1918. The Heer Press.
When He Shall Appear. Harold - Kampf. LC 54-5126. 1954. Little, Brown.
When He Was Free and Young and He Used to Wear Silks: Stories. Austin Chesterfield Clarke. LC 73-10276. 1973. 6.95 (ISBN 0-316-14694-3) (ISBN 0-316-14694-3). Little, Brown.
When Hearts Are Light Again. Emilie Baker Loring. LC 76-44003. 1976. 6.95 (ISBN 0-88411-365-5). Aeonian Press.
When Hearts Are Light Again. Emilie Baker Loring. LC 43-12650. 1943. Little, Brown and Company.
When Hearts Are Young. Vida Hurst. LC 46-496204. 1946. Gramercy Publishing Co.
When Hearts Were True. Willoughby Reade. 1907. The Neale Publishing Company.
When Hell Came Through. John Breck. LC 29-6670. 1929. Harper & Brothers.
When Hitler Lived in the United States. Jesse S. Hance. 1968. 3.50 o.p. Vantage.
When I Am Rich: A Novel. Roy Mason. LC 9-18059. G. W. Dillingham Company.
When I Come Back. Frank Ramsay Adams. LC 44-509417. 1944. R. M. McBride & Co.

When I Grow Rich. Joan Margaret Fleming. LC 64-22681. (Collier mystery classic). 1965. Collier Books.
When I Grow Rich. Ethel Sidgwick. LC 28-23921. 1928. Harper & Brothers.
When I Hug You My Toes Curl. Art Glogau. pap. 2.50 o.s.i. (ISBN 0-8181-0304-3). Pageant-Poseidon.
When I Lived in Bohemia: Papers Selected from the Portfolio of Peter--, Esq. Fergus Hume. LC 7-3522. Tait, Sons & Company.
When I Think: I Get Scared. Ed. by Gleeda McConahay. (Illus.). 1974. (pbk.) 2.50. Fun Publishing.
When I Was a Boy, 2 vols. Tim Hausman. (Illus., Orig.). pap. 1.95 ea. o.p. Vol. 1 (ISBN 0-8220-1624-9). Vol. 2 (ISBN 0-8220-1625-7). Cliffs.
When I Was a Boy in Boston. Charles Angoff. LC 70-132111. (Short story index reprint series). (Illus.). 1970. Books for Libraries Press.
When I Was a Boy in Boston. Charles Angoff. LC 47-4503. 1947. Beechhurst Press.
When I Was a Child. Translated by Gustaf Lannestock. 1st Ed. Wilhelm Moberg. LC 56-5773. 1956. Knopf.
When I Was A Father. Alvaro Cardona-Hine. LC 82-80604. (Minnesota Voices Project Ser.: No. 7). (Illus.). 73p. 1982. pap. 4.00 (ISBN 0-89823-036-5). New Rivers Pr.
When I Was a Little Girl. Zona Gale. LC 13-21026. 1913. 1.50. The Macmillan Company.
When I Was Last on Cherry Street. Harry Roskolenko. LC 65-14398. 1965. 4.95 o.p. (ISBN 0-8128-1197-6). Stein & Day.
When I Whistle. Shusaku Endo. Tr. by Van C. Gessel from Japanese. LC 79-13183. Orig. Title: Kuchibue wo Fuku Toki. 273p. 1980. pap. 3.95 (ISBN 0-8008-8244-X). Taplinger.
When Immortals Wed. Etta Udora Glines Snow. LC 7-27616. 1907. Rumford Printing Company.
When in Greece. Emma Lathen, pseud. LC 76-75871. (Inner sanctum mystery). 1969. 4.95. Simon and Schuster.
When in Greece: An Inner Sanctum Mystery. Emma Lathen, pseud. LC 71-39773. 1972. 9.95 (ISBN 0-8161-6026-0). G. K. Hall.
When in Rome. Ngaio Marsh. LC 72-135434. 1971. 5.95. Little, Brown.
When in the Course-- Harry Leon Wilson. LC 40-14539. 1940. H. C. Kinsey & Company, Inc.
When Is a Lady? Harriet Henry, pseud. LC 40-2694. 1940. E. P. Dutton & Co., Inc.
When Is Always? Coningsby William Dawson. LC 27-7087. 1927. Cosmopolitan Book Corporation.
When It Was Dark: The Story of a Great Conspiracy. Cyril Arthur Edward Ranger Gull. LC 4-5417. 1904. G. P. Putnam's Sons.
When Jeremiah Prophesied: Or, Asaph; an Historical Religious Novel. Alice Kingsbury Cooley. LC 3648. (On cover: Alliance library, no. 16). 1900. Street & Smith.
When Jesus Was Here Among Men: A Story. Nellie Lathrop Helm. LC 2-24477. 1902. F. H. Revell Company.
When Joy Begins: A Little Story of the Woman-Heart. Clara Elizabeth Laughlin. LC 5-35796. 1905. F. H. Revell Company.
When Kings Go Forth to Battle: A Novel. William Wallace Whitelock. LC 7-28962. 1907. J. B. Lippincott Company.
When Knighthood Was in Flower, or, the Love Story of Charles Brandon & Mary Tudor the King's Sister, & Happening in the Reign of His August Majesty, King Henry VIII. Edwin Caskoden. LC 77-145160. (Illus.). 310p. 1972. Repr. of 1898 ed. 14.00 (ISBN 0-403-01088-8). Scholarly.
When Knighthood Was in Flower: Or, The Love Story of Charles Brandon and Mary Tudor, the King's Sister, and Happening in the Reign of His August Majesty, King Henry VIII. Charles Major. LC 70-126656. (Illus.). 1970. AMS Press.
When Knighthood Was in Flower: Or, The Love Story of Charles Brandon and Mary Tudor, the King's Sister, and Happening in the Reign of... Henry VIII. Charles Major. LC 77-145160. (Illus.). 1972. (ISBN 0-403-01088-8). Scholarly Press.
When Knighthood Was in Flower: Or, The Love Story of Charles Brandon and Mary Tudor, the King's Sister, and Happening in the Reign of... Henry VIII; Rewritten and Rendered into Modern English from Sir Edwin Caskoden's Memoir. Charles Major. LC 98-1304. 1898. The Bowen-Merrill Company.
When Knighthood Was in Flower: Or, The Love Story of Charles Brandon and Mary Tudor, the King's Sister, and Happening in the Reign of... Henry VIII; Rewritten and Rendered into Modern English from Sir Edwin Caskoden's Memoir. Charles Major. LC 22-19585. The Bowen-Merrill Company.
When Knighthood Was in Flower: Or, The Love Story of Charles Brandon and Mary Tudor, the King's Sister, and Happening in the Reign of Henry VIII; Rewritten and Rendered into Modern English from Sir Edwin Caskoden's Memoir. Charles Major. LC 22-247756. 1898. The Bowen-Merrill Company.
When Knighthood Was in Flower: Or, The Love Story of Charles Brandon and Mary Tudor, the King's Sister, and Happening in the Reign of... Henry VIII; Rewritten and Rendered into Modern English from Sir Edwin Caskoden's Memoir. 62d thousand. ed. Charles Major. LC 22-24774. 1899. The Bowen-Merrill Company.
When Knighthood Was in Flower: Or, The Love Story of Charles Brandon and Mary Tudor, the King's Sister, and Happening in the Reign of... Henry VIII; Rewritten and Rendered into Modern English from Sir Edwin Caskoden's Memoir. 95th thousand. ed. Charles Major. LC 4-164619. 1899. The Bowen-Merrill Company.
When Knighthood Was in Flower: Or, The Love Story of Charles Brandon and Mary Tudor, the King's Sister, and Happening in the Reign of His August Majesty, King Henry VIII; Rewritten and Rendered into Modern English from Sir Edwin Caskoden's Memoir. 100th thousand. ed. Charles Major. LC 9-2677. 1899. The Bowen-Merrill Company.
When Knighthood Was in Flower: Or, The Love Story of Charles Brandon and Mary Tudor, the King's Sister, and Happening in the Reign of His August Majesty, King Henry the Eighth; Rewritten and Rendered into Modern English from Sir Edwin Caskoden's Memoir. theatre ed. Charles Major. LC 9-32295. Grosset & Dunlap.
When Knighthood Was in Flower: Or, The Love Story of Charles Brandon and Mary Tudor, the King's Sister, and Happening in the Reign of His August Majesty, King Henry VIII. Rewritten and Rendered into Modern English from Sir Edwin Caskoden's Memoir. Charles Major. LC 45-52363. 1899. The Bowen-Merrill Company.
When Knights Are Cold. Letty Bohanon & Clark, Carrie Bliss, Joint Author. LC 27-9306. The Christopher Publishing House.
When Last I Died. Gladys Mitchell. LC 42-9898. 1942. A. A. Knopf.
When Last Seen. Marion J. Herrick & Trumbull Rogers. 1978. pap. 2.25 (ISBN 0-532-22123-0). Woodhill.
When Last Seen. Arthur Maling & Mystery Writers of America. LC 77-3795. 10.95 (ISBN 0-06-012848-8). Harper & Row.
When Legends Die. Greg Hunt. (Orig.). 1982. pap. 1.95 (ISBN 0-440-19465-2). Dell.
When Life Tumbles In, Then What. Paul R. Dodd. 1970. 2.75 o.p. Carlton.
When Lightning Strikes. Jane Donnelly. (Harlequin Romances Ser.). 192p. 1981. pap. 1.25 (ISBN 0-373-02408-8, Pub. by Harlequin). PB.
When Lily Smiles. Ruth Burnett. 1982. pap. 6.95 (Avalon). Bouregy.
When London Sleeps: A Novelization of the Highly Successful Drama. Charles Darrell. LC 12-32099. (On cover: Drama series. no. 33). Street & Smith.
When Love Calls. Stanley John Weyman. 1899. Brown and Company.
When Love Calls Men to Arms: An Autobiography of Love and Adventure, Truthfully Set Down by Rorie Maclean, Laird of Kilellan, in the Seventeenth Century, and Here Rewritten from the Original Ms. into Clearer English. Stephen Chalmers. LC 10-15234. 1.50. Small, Maynard & Company.
When Love Flies Out O' the Window. Leonard Merrick. LC 14-11802. 1914. 1.20. M. Kennerley.
When Love Flies Out O' the Window. Leonard Merrick. LC 18-232303. (Half-title: The works of Leonard Merrick). 1918. Hodder & Stoughton.
When Love Is a Razor Blade: How to Stay Alive. Alexander K. Sumner. LC 81-65037. 100p. (Orig.). pap. 4.95x (ISBN 0-939122-00-6). April Pub.
When Love Is Done: A Novel. Ethel Davis. LC 6-32491. 1895. Estes and Laurist.
When Love Is King. Margaret Doyle Jackson. LC 5-7899. 1905. G. W. Dillingham Company.
When Love Is Love: A Novel. Kate Lee Langley Bosher. LC 4-2326. 1904. The Neale Publishing Company.
When Love Is Not Enough. Marian Wells. LC 79-4534. 3.50 (ISBN 0-87123-646-X). Bethany Fellowship.
When Love Is Strong". Grace Wallace Doonan. LC 7-17046. 1907. Benziger Brothers.
When Love Is Young: A Novel. Roy Rolfe Gilson. LC 1-27067. 1901. Harper & Brother.
When Love Remains. Victoria Pade. (Avon Romance Ser.). 384p. (Orig.). 1983. pap. 2.95 (ISBN 0-380-82610-0, 82610). Avon.
When Love Returns. Arlene Hale. LC 76-45198. 1977. 8.95 (ISBN 0-89340-053-X). J. Curley.
When Love Returns. Arlene Hale. LC 70-121427. 1970. 4.95. Little, Brown.
When Love Speaks. Glenna Finley, pseud. 1973. pap. 1.95 (ISBN 0-451-11799-9, AJ1799, Sig). NAL.
When Love Speaks. Will Payne. LC 6-40589. 1906. The Macmillan Company.
When Love Was Not Enough. Clifford Mason. LC 80-82853. 272p. (Orig.). 1981. pap. 2.50 (ISBN 0-87216-779-8). Playboy Pbks.
When Lovely Maiden Stoops to Folly: Or, "When Lovely Woman Stoops to Folly." A Novel. Laura Jean Libbey. LC 7-145172. The American News Company.
When McQueen Was King: A Novel of Railroading. 1st Ed. Harry David Lyons. LC 56-5812. 1956. Vantage Press.
When Malindy Sings. Paul Laurence Dunbar. LC 71-164805. (Illus.). Repr. of 1903 ed. 12.50 (ISBN 0-404-00039-8). AMS Pr.
When Malindy Sings. facs. ed. Paul Laurence Dunbar. LC 79-83916. (Black Heritage Library Collection Ser.). (Illus.). 1903. 12.25 (ISBN 0-8369-8568-0). Ayer Co.
When Mammoths Roamed the Frozen Earth. Heinrich Schutz. Tr. by Barnes, Frank. LC 29-22141. 1929. J. Cape and H. Smith.
When Mankind Was Young. Frederick Britten Austin. LC 71-125201. (Short story index reprint series). 1970. Books for Libraries Press.
When Mankind Was Young. Frederick Britten Austin. LC 27-814618. 1927. Doubleday, Page & Company.
When May Follows. Betty Neels. (Harlequin Romances Ser.). 192p. 1981. pap. 1.25 (ISBN 0-373-02415-0). Harlequin Bks.
When Mayflowers Blossom: A Romance of Plymouth's First Years. Albert Hale Plumb. LC 14-5472. Fleming H. Revell Company.
When Michael Calls. John Farris. LC 67-29391. 1967. Trident Press.
When Miss Tillie Was Here. Irma Dunn. 1965. 3.50 o.p. Vantage.
When Mother Was a Little Girl. Frances Stanton Brewster. LC 1-27392. (Illus.). 1901. G.W. Jacobs & Co.
When My Ship Comes Home. Clara Elizabeth Laughlin. 1.00. Fleming H. Revell Company.
When My Ship Comes in. Gouverneur Morris. LC 15-18109. 1915. C. Scribner's Sons.
When Nature Speaks: The Life of Dr. Forrest Shaklee. Georges Spunt. LC 77-9916. 1977. 8.95 o.p. (ISBN 0-8119-0279-X). Fell.
When Next I Wake. Frank Dorn. 1978. pap. 1.75 (ISBN 0-532-17199-3). Woodhill.
When Next We Love. Heather Graham. (Candlelight Ecstasy Ser.: No. 117). (Orig.). 1983. pap. 1.95 (ISBN 0-440-19588-8). Dell.
When Next We Meet. Reita Lambert. LC 42-14358. 1942. Macrae-Smith-Company.
When Next We Meet. Reita Lambert. 1943. Triangle Books.
When Night Descends. Edgar Calmer. LC 36-35018. Farrar & Rinehart, Incorporated.
When No One Is Looking. Tabler. 1977. pap. 1.50 (ISBN 0-448-14594-4, Pub. by Tempo). Ace Bks.
When Oil Ran Red: By Clay Randall Pseud. Clifton Adams. LC 53-5021. 1953. Random House.
When Pan Pipes: A Fantastic Romance. Mary Taylor Thornton. LC 16-22600. 1916. George H. Doran Company.
When Patty Went to College. Jean Webster. LC 3-7657. 1903. The Century Co.
When Patty Went to College. Jean Webster. LC 28-18125. 1927. Grosset & Dunlap.
When Polly Was Eighteen. Emma C Dowd. LC 21-151097. 1921. Houghton Mifflin Company.
When Pumpkins Blossomed. Dragoslav Mihailovic. LC 70-134577. 1971. 5.95 (ISBN 0-15-195962-5). Harcourt Brace Jovanovich.
When Rain Clouds Gather: A Novel. Bessie Head. LC 69-12089. 1969. 4.95. Simon and Schuster.
When Rome Reigned: A Story of the Dawn-Time of Christianity. Mabel Ansley Murohy. LC 26-14386. Fleming H. Revell Company.
When Sarah Saved the Day. Elsie Singmaster. LC 9-27449. 1909. Houghton Mifflin Company.
When Sarah Went to School. Elsie Singmaster. LC 10-25066. 1910. Houghton Mifflin Company.
When Seasons Change. Richard James Schotts. LC 57-102573. 1957. Vantage Press.
When Shadows Disappear. Francis Marion Hart. LC 33-10975. The Christopher Publishing House.
When Shadows Fall. Nathan C. Heard. LC 76-49399. 1977. pap. 1.95 o.p. (ISBN 0-87216-373-3, E 16373). Playboy.
When She Came Home from College. Marian Hurd McNeely & Wilson, Jean Bingham, Joint Author. LC 9-28147. 1909. Houghton Mifflin Company.
When She Came to Herself. Alison Brooke. American Baptist Publication Society.
When She Was Bad. Katharine Brush. LC 48-21619. (New Avon library, 154). 1948. Avon Book Co.
When She Was Good. Philip Roth. LC 67-12724. 1967. Random House.
When She Was Wild. D. V. Holloway. 192p. (Orig.). 1972. pap. 1.95 o.p. (ISBN 0-87977-172-0, DBB172). Dansk Blue Bk.
When Shiloh Came. Ambrose Lester Jackson. J. S. Ogilvie Publishing Company.
When Sisterhood Was in Flower. Florence King. LC 81-65284. 1982. 13.95 (ISBN 0-670-75998-8). Viking Press.
When Spain Was Young. Frank Callcott. LC 32-21899. 1932. R. M. McBride & Company.
When Spring Is Past. Paul B Frazier & Saylor, Lettie (Hoskins) Joint Author. LC 44-4990. 1944. The Hobson Book Press.
When Strangers Meet. Leslie Edgley. LC 56-9847. 1956. Published for the Crime Club of Doubleday.
When Stuart Came to Sikum: A Western Story. Arthur Murray Chisholm. LC 24-16571. 2.00. Chelsea House.
When Summer Ends. Arlene Hale. (Candlelight Romance). Dell Pub. Co.,,C.
When Summer Goes; a Novel. Mary F. S. Toy. LC 25-11322. 1925. The S. S. Scranton Company.
When Sunday Comes. Sylvana Gardner. LC 82-10935. 46p. 1983. 14.50 (ISBN 0-7022-1822-7); pap. 7.50 (ISBN 0-7022-1832-4). U of Queensland Pr.
When Texans Ride. Jesse Edward Grinstead. LC 38-6973. The Dodge Publishing Company.
When the Bamboo Sings. Illus. and Dust Jacket by Bill Parlane. Douglas Cecil Percy. LC 59-1599. 1959. Zondervan.
When the Birds Fly South. Stanton Arthur Coblentz. LC 45-20869. 1945. The Wings Press.
When the Birds Fly South. Stanton Arthur Coblentz. LC 77-84212. (Lost Race and Adult Fantasy Fiction). 1978. 15.00 (ISBN 0-405-10967-9). Arno Press.
When the Birds Fly South. Stanton Arthur Coblentz. LC 80-10177. (Newcastle Forgotten Fantasy library; v. 23). 1980. 10.95 (ISBN 0-87877-522-6) (ISBN 0-87877-122-0). Newcastle Pub. Co.
When the Birds Fly South. Stanton Arthur Coblentz. LC 80-23935. 1980. 10.95. Borgo Press.
When the Blood Burns. Ethel Winifred Savi. LC 20-22037. 1920. G. P. Putnam's Sons.
When the Bough Bends. Alice Terhune. Date not set. 3.95 o.p. Vantage.
When the Bough Breaks. Otis Carney. 1957. Houghton Mifflin.
When the Bough Breaks. Lois Duncan. LC 73-169415. 1973. N. Doubleday.
When the Bough Breaks. Lois Duncan. 1974. (pbk.) 0.95. Bantam Books.
When the Bough Breaks. Cecile Gilmore. LC 47-30065. 1946. S. Curl, Inc.
When the Bough Breaks. Stuart Rosenberg. 1977. 1.95 (ISBN 0-425-03388-0). Berkley Pub. Corp.
When the Bough Breaks. Adeline Rumsey. LC 40-30407. 1940. Simon and Schuster.
When the Bough Breaks: A Novel. 1st Ed. Richard Kluger. LC 64-16219. 1964. N. Y., Doubleday.
When the Bough Breaks, and Other Stories. Naomi Haldane Mitchison. LC 71-160944. (Short story index reprint series). (Illus.). 1971. (ISBN 0-8369-3923-9). Books for Libraries Press.
When the Bugle Called. Edith Tatum. LC 8-11078. 1908. The Neale Publishing Company.
When the Cat's Away. Gerald William Bullett. LC 40-296433. 1941. A. A. Knopf.
When the Century Was New. A Novel. Charles Conrad Abbott. LC 5-42987. 1897. J. B. Lippincott Company.
When the Clock Strikes Thirteen. David Hanna. 1976. pap. 1.50 o.p. (LB387, Leisure Bks). Nordon Pubns.
When the Clock Strikes 13. David Hanna. Leisure Books.
When the Cock Crows. Waldron Baily. LC 18-17611. 1918. Bedford Publishing Co.
When the Dark Man Calls. Stuart M. Kaminsky. 224p. 1983. 13.95 (ISBN 0-312-86668-2). St Martin.
When the Dead Walk: A Novel. Lavinia Walsh. LC 2-10106. 1902. Mutual Pub. Co.
When the Devil Was Sick. E. J. Rath. LC 26-9267. 1926. G. H. Watt.
When the Doors Break. James Carey. 1982. 7.75 (ISBN 0-8062-1870-3). Carlton.
When the Dream Dies. A. Bertram Chandler. LC 82-155100. (Rim World Series; V. 2). 1981. 12.95 (ISBN 0-85031-361-9). Allison & Busby.
When the Drumbeat Changes. Intro. by Carolyn Parker & Stephen Arnold. 293p. (Orig.). 1981. 22.00x (ISBN 0-89410-262-1); pap. 14.00x (ISBN 0-89410-263-X). Three Continents.

TITLE INDEX WHERE ANGELS FEAR TO

When the Emperor Dies. Mason McCann Smith. LC 81-40222. (Illus.). 13.95 (ISBN 0-394-51458-0). Random House.

When the Enemy Is Tired. Russell Braddon. LC 69-12669. 1969. 5.95. Viking Press.

When the Fight Begins. Holman Francis Day. LC 26-8188. 1926. Small, Maynard & Company.

When the Fire Reaches Us. Barbara Wilson Tinker. LC 78-108865. 1970. 6.95. Morrow.

When the Flag Drops. Jack Brabham & Elizabeth Hayward. LC 72-87578. (Illus.). 1972. 6.95 o.p. (ISBN 0-698-10502-8). Coward.

When the Forests Are Ablaze. Katharine Berry Judson. LC 12-21397. 1912. A. C. McClurg & Co.

When the Fuse is Lit. Molly Rankin. 128p. Date not set. pap. 4.95. Pacific Pr Pub Assn.

When the Gangs Came to London... Edgar Wallace. LC 32-2120. Pub. for the Crime Club, Inc., by Doubleday, Doran & Company, Inc.

When the Gates Lift up Their Heads: A Story of the Seventies. Payne Erskine. LC 1-31860. 1901. Little, Brown, and Company.

When the Gods Are Silent. Mikhail Soloviev. LC 74-27185. 1975. 22.50 (ISBN 0-8371-7891-6). Greenwood Press.

When the Gods Are Silent: Translated by Harry C. Stevens. Mikhail Soloviev. LC 52-147836. D. McKay Co.

When the Gods Laughed. Leslie Roberts. LC 31-7408. 1931. Sears Publishing Company, Inc.

When the Going Was Good. Evelyn Waugh. LC 75-16612. (Illus.). 318p. 1976. Repr. of 1946 ed. lib. bdg. 22.00 (ISBN 0-8371-8253-0, WAWG). Greenwood.

When the Green Star Calls. Lin Carter. (Science Fiction Ser.). pap. 1.25 (ISBN 0-87997-267-X, OY 1267). DAW Bks.

When the Green Star Calls. Lin Carter. (Daw sf Books, no. 62). (Illus.). 1973. (pbk.) 0.95. Daw Books.

When the Heart Is Young: A Novel. Nina Miller Elliott. LC 17-31030. Thos. W. Jackson Publishing Co.

When the Heart Strays. Kathleen Rollins. LC 38-7791. 1938. Arcadia House.

When the Highbrow Joined the Outfit. Nina Wilcox Putnam & Jacobsen, Norman. LC 17-13921. 1917. 1.00. Duffield & Company.

When the Husband's Away. James Noble Sifford. LC 44-410345. 1944. Phoenix Press.

When the Idols Walked. John W. Jakes. (Kangaroo Book). 1978. 1.50 (ISBN 0-671-81373-0). Pocket Books.

When the King Loses His Head: And Other Stories. Leonid Nikolaevich Andreev. LC 74-116927. (Short story index reprint series). 1970. Books for Libraries Press.

When the King Loses His Head, & Other Stories. facs. ed. Leonid Nikolaevich Andreev. Tr. by Archibald J. Wolfe. LC 74-116927. (Short Story Index Reprint Ser.). 1919. 17.00 (ISBN 0-8369-3429-6). Ayer Co.

When the Kissing Had to Stop. new american ed. Constantine Fitz Gibbon. LC 72-88593. 1973. 7.95 (ISBN 0-87000-199-X). Arlington House.

When the Lamp Is Shattered. Frances M. Hoover. LC 79-63517. 1979. 7.95 o.p. (ISBN 0-533-04270-4). Vantage.

When the Land Was Young: Being the True Romance of Mistress Antoinette Huguenin and Captain Jack Middleton in the Days of the Buccaneers. Lafayette McLaws. LC 1-21991. Lothrop Publishing Company.

When the Legends Die. Hal Glen Borland. LC 63-11753. 1963. Lippincott.

When the Lights Are Low. Walter Gifford. LC 39-30074. 1939. White-Thompson.

When the Lights Go up Again. Norma Patterson. LC 43-12689. 1943. Farrar & Rinehart, Inc.

When the Lilacs Bloom. Allen Percy De Long. LC 9-12876. Benton Publishing Company.

When the Lion Feeds. Wilbur A Smith. 1.95. Dell.

When the Lion Feeds: A Novel. Wilbur A Smith. LC 64-11225. Viking Press.

When the Living Strive. Richard Tracy LaPiere. LC 41-75063. Harper & Brothers.

When the Looms Are Silent: Translated from the French of Maxence Van der Meersch. Maxence Van Der Meersch. Tr. by Blossom, Frederick Augustus. LC 34-34023. 1934. W. Morrow and Company.

When the Melody Is Finished... Norman Towar Boggs. LC 30-28916. 1930. W. Heinemann Ltd.

When the Moon Became a Chinaman: And Other Stories. Milton McGovern. LC 24-19918. P. J. Kenedy & Sons.

When the Moon Laughs. William Arthur Neubauer. LC 48-239815. 1948. Gramercy Pub. Co.

When the Mountain Fell. Charles Ferdinand Ramuz & Scott, Sarah (Fisher) 1909- Tr. LC 47-11205. 1947. Pantheon Books.

When the Music Changed. Marie R Reno. LC 80-15424. 12.95 (ISBN 0-453-00384-2). New American Library.

When the Music Stops. Tom Morse & Bobbie Lauster. 1971. 3.95 o.p. (ISBN 0-8007-0463-0). Revell.

When the Offspring Have Sprung: Or, "Happiness Is Turning the Nursery into a Wine Cellar". William C Anderson. LC 77-26676. 7.95 (ISBN 0-517-53301-4). Crown Publishers.

When the Old Bell Rang. William David Redwine. 7.75 o.p. (ISBN 0-8062-0580-6). Carlton.

When the Owl Cries. Paul Bartlett. LC 60-9265. 1960. Macmillan.

When the Rattlesnake Sounds. Alice Childress. LC 75-10456. (Illus.). 1975. 5.95. (ISBN 0-698-20342-9). Coward, McCann & Geoghegan.

When the Red God Ruled: An Historical Novel of the Great War. Phae Noble Fryer. LC 33-38002. P. N. Fryer.

When the Red Gods Call. Beatrice Ethel Grimshaw. LC 11-11319. 1911. 1.35. Moffat, Yard & Company.

When the Santos Talked: A Retable of New Mexico Tales. Angelico Chavez. LC 76-53086. (Illus.). 1977. 12.50 (ISBN 0-88307-528-8). W. Gannon.

When the Ship Comes Home. Walter Besant & Rice, James. LC 6-20962. (On cover: Harper's half-hour series. v. 5). 1877. Harper & Brothers.

When the Ship Comes Home. A Novel. Walter Besant & James Rice. (On cover: Lovell's library, v. 5, no. 268). 1883. J. W. Lovell Company.

When the Ship Sank. 1st Ed. James Murdoch Macgregor. LC 59-106776. 1959. Doubleday.

When the Sky Burned. Benjamin Bova. LC 72-95800. 1973. 5.95 (ISBN 0-8027-5560-7). Walker.

When the Sky Burned: A Novel. Benjamin Bova. 1974. (pbk.) 1.25. Popular Library.

When the Sleeper Wakes. Herbert George Wells. LC 99-2363. 1899. Harper & Brothers.

When the Sleeper Wakes see Three Prophetic Novels.

When the Storm Hit. 1st Ed. Elbridge Wilkes Gillenwater. LC 53-12801. 1953. Pageant Press.

When the Sun Stood Still. Cyrus Townsend Brady. LC 17-12713. Fleming H. Revell Company.

When the Tax Man Calls: A Story of One Man's Ordeal with the Internal Revenue Service. Stephen W. Hagan. LC 68-13257. 1968. Exposition Press.

When the Tide Turns. Filson Young. LC 8-31828. 1908. D. Estes & Company: Etc., Etc.

When the Trail Calls; "a Story of the North Country Portraying the Loves and Perils of Canadian Mounted Police.". Adolph Philip Lehner. LC 34-509976. 1934. Meador Publishing Company.

When the Tree Flowered: An Authentic Tale of the Old Sioux World. John Gneisenau Neihardt. 1973. 1.25 (ISBN 0-671-78281-9). Pocket Bks.

When the Tree Flowered: An Authentic Tale of the Old Sioux World. John Gneisenau Neihardt. LC 51-6974. 1951. Macmillan.

When the Tree Flowered: The Fictional Biography of Eagle Voice, a Sioux Indian. John Gneisenau Neihardt. LC 75-116055. 1970. 1.65. University of Nebraska Press.

When the Tree Sings. Stratis Haviaras. LC 78-27684. (Illus.). 9.95 (ISBN 0-671-24754-9). Simon and Schuster.

When the Tree Sings. Stratis Haviaris. 1979. 9.95 o.p. (ISBN 0-671-24754-9). S&S.

When the Tree Sings. Stratis Hayiaras. 192p. 1981. pap. 2.95. Ballantine.

When the Turtles Sing: And Other Unusual Tales. Don Marquis. LC 28-230474. 1928. Doubleday, Doran & Company, Inc.

When the Turtles Sing & Other Unusual Tales. facsimile ed. Don Marquis. LC 70-130065. (Short Story Index Reprint Ser.). Repr. of 1928 ed. 15.00 (ISBN 0-8369-3664-7). Ayer Co.

When the Turtles Sing & Other Unusual Tales. Don Marquis. (Short Story Index Reprint Ser). 1928. 9.50 o.p. (ISBN 0-8369-3664-7). Bks for Libs.

When the Veil Is Rent. Francis Clement Kelley. LC 29-13783. 1929. P. J. Kenedy & Sons.

When the Veil Is Rent. Francis Clement Kelley. LC 43-343. 1942. St. Anthony Guild Press.

When the Waker Sleeps. Ron Goulart. (DAW Science Fiction Books no. 175). 1975. (pbk.) 1.25. DAW Books.

When the War Is Over. Stephen D. Becker. LC 78-85575. 1969. 5.95. Random House.

When the West Was Young. John Davis Freeman. LC 36-252840. Broadman Press.

When the Whippoorwill-. Marjorie Kinnan Rawlings. LC 74-153431. 1973. 10.95 (ISBN 0-910220-52-2). N. S. Berg.

When the Whippoorwill-- Marjorie Kinnan Rawlings. LC 40-27409. 1940. C. Scribner's Sons.

When the Whippoorwill-Short Stories. Majorie Kinnan Rawlings. LC 40-27409. 1973. 12.95 (ISBN 0-910220-53-0). Berg.

When the White Camel Rides. Abigail Hetzel Fitch. LC 36-801713. The Henkle-Yewdale House, Inc.

When the Wicked Man. Ford Madox Ford. LC 31-13477. H. Liveright, Inc.

When the Wind Blows. Alfred Alexander Gordon Clark. LC 75-44980. (Fifty Classics of Crime Fiction, 1900-1950; 24). 1976. 12.00 (ISBN 0-8240-2373-0). Garland Pub.

When the Wind Blows. Noel Bertram Gerson. LC 56-8828. 1956. Farrar, Straus and Cudahy.

When the Wind Blows. Cyril Hare. LC 75-44980. (Crime Fiction Ser). 1976. Repr. of 1949 ed. lib. bdg. 17.50 (ISBN 0-8240-2373-0). Garland Pub.

When the Wind Blows. Cyril Hare. 1978. pap. 1.95 o.p. (ISBN 0-06-080454-8, P 454, PL). Har-Row.

When the Wind Blows. Leon Phillips. LC 56-8828. 1956. Farrar, Straus and Cudahy.

When the Wind Blows. John Saul. (Orig.). 1981. pap. 3.50 (ISBN 0-440-19857-7). Dell.

When the Wind Cries. Cludette Nicole. (Orig.). 1976. pap. 1.25 o.p. (ISBN 0-515-03822-9). BJ Pub Group.

When the Wolves Howl. Aquilino Ribeiro. LC 63-15695. 1963. Macmillan.

When the World Shook: Account of the Great Adventure of Bastin, Bickley, & Arbuthnot. H. Rider Haggard. LC 74-15980. (Science Fiction Ser). (Illus.). 424p. 1975. Repr. 23.00x (ISBN 0-405-06296-6). Ayer Co.

When the World Shook: Being an Account of the Great Adventure of Bastin, Bickley, and Arbuthnot. Henry Rider Haggard. LC 74-15980. (Science Fiction). (Illus.). 1975. 23.00 (ISBN 0-405-06296-6). Arno Press.

When the World Shook: Being an Account of the Great Adventure of Bastin, Bickley and Arbuthnot. Henry Rider Haggard. 1919. 1.60. Longmans, Green and Co.

When the World Was Younger. Mary Elizabeth Braddon Maxwell. LC 7-25292. R. F. Fenno & Company.

When the Yule Log Burns: A Christmas Story. Leona Dalrymple. LC 16-23623. 1916. 0.60. R. A. McBride & Company.

When There Is Love. Alice Mary Ross Colver. LC 40-186259. Macrne-Smith Company.

When They Come from Space. Mark Clifton. pap. 0.50 o.p. (50-341). Manor Bks.

When They Come from Space. 1st Ed. Mark Clifton. LC 62-7613. 1962. Doubleday.

When They Kill Your Wife. John Crowe, pseud. (Buena Costa County Mystery-Red Badge Novel of Suspence Ser.). 1977. 6.95 o.p. (ISBN 0-396-07443-X). Dodd.

When They Kill Your Wife. Dennis Lynds. LC 77-6748. (Buena Costa County mystery). 6.95 (ISBN 0-396-07443-X). Dodd, Mead.

When They Love. Maurice Baring. LC 28-22042. 1928. Doubleday, Doran & Company, Inc.

When Thieves Fall Out. Basil Home Thomson. LC 38-104412. 1937. Pub. for the Crime Club, Inc., by Doubleday, Doran & Co., Inc.

When Thieves Fall Out. Basil Home Thomson. LC 39-7781. 1939. The Sun Dial Press, Inc.

When Things of the Spirit Come First: Five Early Tales. Simone De Beauvoir. Tr. by Patrick O'Brian. 256p. 1982. 13.95 (ISBN 0-394-52216-8). Pantheon.

When Things Were Doing. Charles Allen Steere. LC 8-977. 1908. C. H. Kerr & Company.

When This Cruel War Is Over. Roy W. Adams. 1970. 3.50 o.p. Vantage.

When Thoughts Will Soar: A Romance of the Immediate Future. Bertha Felicie Sophie Kinsky Suttner & Dole, Nathan Haskell, 1852-LC 14-11353. 1914. Houghton Mifflin Company.

When Tomorrow Comes. Marjorie A Pegram. LC 63-15729. 1963. Zondervan Pub. House.

When Tragedy Grins. Grace Miller White. LC 12-3379. W. J. Watt & Company.

When Turtles Sing: And Other Unusual Tales. Don Marquis. LC 70-130065. (Short story index reprint series). 1970. Books for Libraries Press.

When Tutt Meets Tutt. Arthur Cheney Train. LC 27-274633. 1927. C. Scribner's Sons.

When Two Worlds Meet. Robert M. Williams. 1970. pap. 0.75 o.p. (0502-07081). Curtis.

When Valmond Came to Pontiac: The Story of a Lost Napoleon. Gilbert Parker. LC 20-18836. Harper & Brothers.

When Valmond Came to Pontiac: The Story of a Lost Napoleon. Gilbert Parker. LC 4-15150. 1898. The Macmillan Company.

When Virginia Was Rent in Twain: A Romance of Love and War and Statecraft. Warren Wood. LC 14-112. Broadway Publishing Company.

When Walls Are High. Elizabeth V. Hamilton. LC 72-93195. 1973. 6.00 (ISBN 0-937684-09-0). Tradd St Pr.

When War Breaks Out: Being a Selection from the Letters of Andrew D. Jones, the London Correspondent of "Calner's Weekly," During the War Between Great Britain and the Allied Powers of France and Russia, September 21st, 1900, to January 1st, 1901. Herbert Wrigley Wilson & White, Arnold, Joint Author. LC 1-58145. 1898. Harper & Brothers.

When Waverly Was Young. Earle S Bailey. 1944. Indianapolis Printing Company.

When We Get Where We're Going: A Story of the Sullivan Family from Ireland to the West, by Bertha M. Blacker. Bertha M Blacker. LC 67-776673. 1967. pap., 4.00. Printed by Trade Printery.

When We Get Where We're Going: A Story of the Sullivan Family from Ireland to the West. Bertha M Blacker. LC 67-7766. (Illus.). 1967. Printed by Trade Printery.

When We Had Other Names. Gillian Tindall. LC 60-11586. 1960. Morrow.

When We Were Boys. William O'Brien. LC 79-19758. (Ireland, from the Act of Union, 1800, to the Death of Parnell, 1891). 1979. 42.00. Garland Pub.

When We Were Good. David J Skal. 1981. 2.25 (ISBN 0-671-83015-5). Pocket Books.

When West Was West. Owen Wister. LC 28-14000. 1928. The Macmillan Company.

When Wilderness Was King. Randall Parrish. 1976. lib. bdg. 17.25x (ISBN 0-89968-088-7). Lightyear.

When Wilderness Was King: A Tale of the Illinois Country, by Randall Parrish. Randall Parrish. LC 4-9114. 1904. A. C. McClurg & Co.

When William Came: A Story of London Under the Hohenzollerns. Hector Hugh Munro. LC 14-4068. 1914. John Lane.

When Windwagon Smith Came to Westport. Ramona Weeks & Tom Allen. LC 77-442. 1977. 5.95. (ISBN 0-698-20407-7). Coward, McCann & Geoghegan.

When Woman Proposes. Anne Warner French. LC 11-23898. 1911. 1.25. Little, Brown, & Company.

When Women Love. Edmee Elizabeth Monica De La Pasture. LC 38-30221. 1938. Harper & Brothers.

When Women Rule. Ed. by Samuel Moskowitz. LC 79-186188. 1972. 5.95 (ISBN 0-8027-5547-X). Walker.

When Worlds Collide. Edwin Balmer & Philip Wylie. LC 33-7382. 1933. Frederick A. Stokes Company.

When Worlds Collide. Edwin Balmer & Philip Wylie. LC 40-8475. 1939. Triangle Books.

When Worlds Collide. Philip Wylie & Edwin Balmer. 1970. pap. 0.75 o.p. (ISBN 0-446-64360-2, 64-360). Paperback Lib.

When Worlds Collide: By Edwin Balmer and Philip Wylie. Edwin Balmer & Philip Wylie. LC 50-9382. 1950. Lippincott.

When Yellow Leaves. Ethel Mary Young Boileau. LC 34-25530. E. P. Dutton & Co., Inc.

When You Go to Tonga. Edward Tremblay. (Illus.). 1954. 3.25 (ISBN 0-8198-0173-9). Dghtrs St Paul.

When You Have Found Me: By Elizabeth Hoy Pseud. Nina Conarain. LC 51-4812. 1951. Arcadia House.

When You Least Expect Love. Diane Jones. (Avalon Books). 4.95. Thomas Bouregy.

When You Think of Me. With Illus. by Louis Macouillard, 1st Ed. Erskine Caldwell. LC 59-11096. 1959. Little, Brown.

When You Were a Boy. Edwin Legrand Sabin. LC 5-33647. 1905. The Baker & Taylor Company.

When Your Lover Leaves. Susan Trott. LC 80-14197. 9.95. St. Martin's Press.

Whenabouts of Burr. Michael Kurland. 1975. (pbk.) 1.25. DAW Books.

Whence All but He Had Fled: A Novel. Lawrence J Davis. LC 68-11417. 1968. Viking Press.

Where All the Queens Strayed. Barbara Hanrahan. 1979. 12.00x (ISBN 0-7022-1299-7); pap. 6.00x (ISBN 0-7022-1305-5). U of Queensland Pr.

Where Am I Now-When I Need Me? George Axelrod. LC 75-142549. 1971. 5.95 (ISBN 0-670-76049-8). Viking Press.

Where Angels Fear to Tread. Edward Morgan Forster. LC 20-3575. 1920. A. A. Knopf.

Where Angels Fear to Tread: A Tale of Life on a Mexican Hacienda and Bits of Travel in Mexico. Marguerite Zearing. 1895. W. F. Robinson & Co.

Where Angels Fear to Tread" And Other Tales of the Sea. Morgan Robertson. LC 99-468958. 1899. The Century Co.

Where Angels Fear to Tread," And Other Tales of the Sea. autograph ed. Morgan Robertson. LC 16-11586. 1914. McClure's Magazine and Metropolitan Magazine.

Where Angels Fear to Tread, & Other Tales of the Sea. Morgan Robertson. LC 79-122733. (Short Story Index Reprint Ser). 1899. 12.50 (ISBN 0-8369-3566-7). Ayer Co.
Where Are the Children? Mary Higgins Clark. LC 74-1907. (Simon and Schuster novel of suspense). 1975. 7.95 (ISBN 0-671-21942-1). Simon and Schuster.
Where Are the Children? Mary Higgins Clark. 1976. (pbk.) 1.95. Dell.
Where Are the Customers' Yachts. rev ed. Fred Schwed, Jr. (O.s.i.). 1955. pap. 1.45 o.s.i. (ISBN 0-671-81351-X, Fireside). S&S.
Where Are the Russians? John Bentley. LC 68-10593. 1968. Doubleday.
Where Are the Stars in New York? Hank Heifetz. LC 73-76492. 1973. 7.95 (ISBN 0-8415-0264-1). Saturday Review Press.
Where Are They Now? Don Kearney. 1977. pap. 1.25 o.s.i. (ISBN 0-8439-0431-3, Leisure Bks). Nordon Pubns.
Where Are You. Ed. by Helen Bignell. (O.s.i.). (Illus.). 50p. (Orig.). 1972. pap. 1.25 o.s.i. (ISBN 0-913040-17-7). H M Gousha.
Where Are You? Steve Frazee. 1968. 3.95 o.p. Hawthorn.
Where Are You Going, Where Have You Been? Stories of Young America. Joyce Carol Oates. LC 74-81905. (Fawcett premier book). 1974. (pbk.) 1.50. Fawcett Publications.
Where Beauty Dwells. Emilie Baker Loring. LC 41-4133. 1941. Little, Brown and Company.
Where Black Swans Fly, Summer Mountain, Butterfly Montane. Dorothy Cork. (Harlequin Romances Ser.). 576p. pap. 3.50 (ISBN 0-373-20068-4). Harlequin Bks.
Where Bonds Are Loosed. Elliot Lovegood Grant Watson. LC 18-6025. 1918. A. A. Knopf.
Where Bracken Grows. Amber Illsley. 1982. 6.95 (ISBN 0-533-05137-1). Vantage.
Where Dead Men Walk. Henry Leverage. LC 20-121020. 1920. Moffat, Yard & Company.
Where Democracy Triumphs. Frank Paul Miceli. LC 31-7181. 1931. F. P. Miceli.
Where Did Everybody Go? Paul Molloy. 240p. 1982. pap. 2.95 (ISBN 0-446-30375-5). Warner Bks.
Where Did the Girls Go? Michel Cousin. LC 68-19567. 1969. 4.95. Stein and Day.
Where Did You Go?" "Out." "What Did You Do?" "Nothing." 1st Ed. Robert Paul Smith. LC 57-7139. 1957. W. W. Norton.
Where Do Bastards Go to Die? Verne Benedict. 1981. 9.95 (ISBN 0-533-04879-6). Vantage.
Where Do Goldfish Go? Claude Cattaert. LC 63-21113. 1963. Crown Publishers.
Where Do the MacDonalds Bury Their Dead? Ronald Sutherland. LC 77-363099. (Trend setter edition). 1976. 5.95. (ISBN 0-7736-0043-4) (ISBN 0-7737-7128-X). General Pub. Co.
Where Do We Go from Here? Ed. by Isaac Asimov. LC 75-142033. 1971. 6.95. Doubleday.
Where Do You Go from the Gutter? Vernon L. Colvin. 5.95 o.p. Vantage.
Where Dragons Dwell. Frederick King Poole. LC 72-138791. 1971. 6.95 (ISBN 0-06-126500-4). Harper's Magazine Press.
Where Duty Lies. Silas Kitto Hocking. LC 7-4955. 1892. F. Warne & Co.
Where Eagles Dare. Alistair MacLean. LC 71-408857. 1968. to members. 0.85. Readers Book Club in Association with the Companion Book Club, London.
Where Eagles Dare. Alistair MacLean. LC 67-20923. 1967. Doubleday.
Where Eagles Nest. Anne Hampson. 192p. (Orig.). 1980. pap. 1.50 (ISBN 0-671-57040-4, Pub. by Silhouette Bks). S&S.
Where Flows the Kennebec: More Tales About Dud Dean. Arthur Raymond Macdougall. LC 47-12252. 1947. Coward-McCann.
Where Glory Waits: The Romance of Mary Vining and Anthony Wayne. Gertrude Crownfield. LC 34-7140. 1934. J. B. Lippincott Company.
Where Goes the Bride. Maude Williamson. LC 40-7019. Farrar & Rinehart, Inc.
Where Have All the Sardines Gone? Randall A. Reinstedt. LC 79-101716. (Illus.). 168p. 1978. pap. 6.50 (ISBN 0-933818-05-X). Ghost Town.
Where He Leads: A Novel of the Arkansas Foot-Hills. Lillie Gilliland McDowell. LC 46-2482. 1946. Wm. B. Eerdmans Publishing Company.
Where He Went: Three Novels. Robert Paul Smith. LC 58-12374. 1958. Viking Press.
Where Helen Lies. Rae Foley. (Red Badge Novel of Suspense Ser.). 1976. 6.95 o.p. (ISBN 0-396-07311-5). Dodd.
Where Helen Lies. Margaret Lane. LC 44-512781. 1944. Duell, Sloan and Pearce.
Where Helen Lies: A Novel of Suspense. Elinore Denniston. LC 76-7083. 1976. (ISBN 0-396-07311-5). Dodd, Mead.
Where Highways Cross. Joseph Smith Fletcher. LC 6-41680. (Iris series). 1895. Macmillan and Co.
Where Honour Leads. Mary Louise Parmelee Peebles. LC 7-36470. Dodd, Mead & Company.
Where Is Bianca? Ellery Queen, pseud. LC 66-31763. 1966. Popular Library.
Where Is Dancer's Hill? Robert Schuler. (Outlaws Ser.: Vol. 2). 1979. pap. 3.00x (ISBN 0-917624-18-1); pap. 4.95x lmtd. signed ed. (ISBN 0-917624-16-5). Lame Johnny.
Where Is Home? Frank Blomberg. LC 72-90205. 1972. 5.95. Harlo.
Where Is Janice Gantry? John Dann MacDonald. LC 61-2787. (Gold medal book, s1076). 1961. Fawcett Publications.
Where Is Jenny Now? Frances Shelley Wees. LC 58-558344. 1958. Published for the Crime Club by Doubleday.
Where Is Mary Bostwick? Elinore Denniston. 1973. 0.75. Dell.
Where Is My Mother? Charles Gilmore Kerley. LC 34-1578. 1933. H. Smith and R. Haas.
Where Is My Wandering Boy Tonight? David Wagoner. LC 79-124178. 1970. Farrar, Straus & Giroux.
Where Is the Pope? Gerard Bessiere. LC 75-206. (priority edition). (Illus.). 1975. 2.95 (ISBN 0-87029-047-9). Abbey Press.
Where Is the Promise of His Coming. Elena Arquero. 1968. 5.50 o.p. (ISBN 0-682-46814-2). Exposition.
Where Is the Withered Man? 1st. american ed. John Creasey. LC 73-81176. (MW suspense.). 1974. 4.95 (ISBN 0-679-50421-4). D. McKay Co.
Where It Touches the Ground. Montanye Perry. LC 17-227022. The Abingdon Press.
Where Late the Sweet Bird Sang. Kate Wilhelm. LC 75-6379. 1976. 8.95 (ISBN 0-06-014654-0). Harper & Row.
Where Late the Sweet Birds Sang. Kate Wilhelm. 1.75 (ISBN 0-671-80912-1). Pocket Books.
Where Love Begins. Louise Holmes. LC 38-972873. M. S. Mill Co, Inc.
Where Love Begins: Or, The Adventures of Mr. Philip St. Clare. A Novel of Fashionable Life. Roman Ivanovitch Zubof. LC 8-37856. (On cover: Madison square series, no. 83). 1895. G. W. Dillingham.
Where Love Dwells. William Arthur Neubauer. LC 53-129243. 1953. Arcadia Houe.
Where Love Has Gone. Harold Robbins. 1977. pap. 3.95 (ISBN 0-671-82676-X). PB.
Where Love Has Gone. Harold Robbins. 1962. 4.95 o.p. (81375). Trident.
Where Love Has Gone: A Novel by Harold Robbins Pseud. Harold Rubin. LC 62-203188. 1962. Simon AndSchuster.
Where Love Is. Peggy Gaddis, pseud. pap. 0.50 o.p. (B50-661). Belmont-Tower.
Where Love Is: A Novel. William John Locke. 1903. J. Lane.
Where Love Is: By Peggy Dern. Peggy Gaddis, pseud. LC 51-21218. 1951. Arcadia House.
Where Love Is, There God Is see What Men Live by.
Where Love Is There God Is Also, and What Men Liveby. Lev Nikolaevich Tolstoi & Dole, Nathan Haskell, 1852-1935, Tr. LC 25-10299. Thomas Y. Crowell Company.
Where Love Leads. Dora Delmar. (On cover: Library of American authors. no. 68). 1896. G. Munro's Sons.
Where Magic Lies. Ainslie Meares. LC 70-397118. 1968. 4.95. Hawthorn Press.
Where Men Have Walked: A Story of the Lucayos. H. Henry Rhodes. LC 9-29430. 1909. The C. M. Clark Publishing Company.
Where Mist Clothes Dream and Song Runs Naked: By Sara Pseud. Sally Mirliss Blake. LC 64-662853. 4.50. McGraw.
Where Mist Clothes Dream and Song Runs Naked. Sally Mirliss Blake. LC 75-3982. 1975. 12.50 (ISBN 0-8371-7413-9). Greenwood Press.
Where Mist Clothes Dream & Song Runs Naked. Sara, pseud. LC 75-3982. 200p. 1976. Repr. of 1965 ed. lib. bdg. 15.00x (ISBN 0-8371-7413-9, BLWM). Greenwood.
Where Mountains Wait. Fran Wilson. LC 81-13224. 1981. 11.95 (ISBN 0-8161-3246-1). G.K. Hall.
Where My Love Lies Dreaming. Amanda J. Jarrett. (Southerners Ser.: No. 3). (Orig.). 1983. pap. 3.50 (ISBN 0-440-09292-2). Dell.
Where My Love Sleeps. Clifford Dowdey. LC 45-91613. 1945. Little, Brown and Company.
Where Nests the Water Hen: A Novel. Gabrielle Carbotte Roy. LC 51-13143. 1951. Harcourt, Brace.
Where No Birds Sing. Ida Alexa Ross Wylie. LC 47-24305. 1947. Random House.
Where No Flags Fly. Frederick Ayer, Jr. LC 60-14055. 1960. Regnery.
Where No Man Had Trod. Nancy Dorer & Frances Dorer. (Orig.). 1979. pap. 1.95 (ISBN 0-532-23155-4). Woodhill.
Where No Sun Shines. Leo P. Kelley. LC 78-68229. (Galaxy 5 Ser.: Bk. 5). 1979. pap. 4.24 (ISBN 0-8224-3205-6). Pitman Learning.
Where Nothing Ever Happens. Lee Shippey. LC 35-942. 1935. Houghton Mifflin Company.
Where Passion Waits. Virginia L. Hart. 416p. 1982. pap. 2.95 (ISBN 0-523-41474-9). Pinnacle Bks.
Where Peacocks Cry. Maureen E Wakefield. 1973. 4.95. Lenox Hill Pr.
Where Phantoms Stir: Ghost Stories. Mary Williams. LC 77-375425. 1976 (ISBN 0-7183-0374-1). Kimber.
Where Pigeons Go to Die. R. Wright Campbell. LC 77-94146. 6.95 (ISBN 0-89256-058-4). Rawson Associates Publishers.
Where Robot Mice & Robot Men Run Round in Robot Towns. Ray Bradbury. 1977. 6.95 (ISBN 0-394-42206-6). Knopf.
Where Sands Are Pink. Stanley M. Babson. 1968. 3.50 o.p. Vantage.
Where Satan Dwells. Florence Stevenson. (O.s.i.). Date not set. pap. 1.25 o.s.i. (AQ1678, Award). Univ Pub & Dist.
Where Shall He Find Her? From the French. Henriette Etiennette Fanny Reybaud & A., I. D., Tr. LC 7-39926. 1867. Crowen & Co.
Where She Brushed Her Hair: And Other Stories. Max Steele. LC 67-28821. 1968. Harper & Row.
Where Snow Is Sovereign: A Romance of the Glaciers. Rudolf Stratz & Safford, Mary Joanna, Tr. LC 9-25628. 1909. Dodd, Mead and Company.
Where Speech Ends: A Music Maker's Romance. Robert Haven Schauffler. 1906. Moffat, Yard & Co.
Where Strongest Tide Winds Blew. Robert McReynolds. LC 7-18596. 1907. Gowdy-Simmons Publishing Co.
Where the Action Is. Glen Chase, pseud. (Leisure Books). 1977. 1.50 (ISBN 0-8439-0495-X). Nordon Pubns.
Where the Air Is Clear. Carlos Fuentes. 1960. 4.95 o.p. FS&G.
Where the Apple Reddens. Isabel Constance Clarke. LC 44-692644. 1944. Longmans, Green and Co.
Where the Apple Reddens. Alexandra Phillips. G. P. Putnam's Sons.
Where the Atlantic Meets the Land. H Caldwell Lipsett. LC 7-19003. 1896. Roberts Bros.; Etc., Etc.
Where the Battle Was Fought: A Novel. Mary Noailles Murfree. LC 4-15143. 1884. J. R. Osgood and Company.
Where the Battle Was Fought: A Novel. Mary Noailles Murfree. LC 16-250443. Houghton Mifflin Company.
Where the Blue Begins. Christopher Darlington Morley. LC 22-21185. 1922. Doubleday, Page & Company.
Where the Boys Are. Glendon Fred Swarthout. LC 60-5521. 1960. Random House.
Where the Bright Lights Shine. Anne Nall Stallworth. LC 75-25145. 7.95 (ISBN 0-8149-0770-9). Vanguard Press.
Where the Cherries End up. Gail Henley. LC 79-83703. 9.95 (ISBN 0-316-35630-1). Little, Brown.
Where the Cobra Sings. Cosmo Forbes. LC 32-9372. The Macaulay Company.
Where the Dark Streets Go. Dorothy Salisbury Davis. LC 71-85261. 1969. 4.95. Scribner.
Where the Dark Streets Go. Dorothy Salisbury Davis. 1975. (pbk.) 1.25. Bantam Books.
Where the Desert Ends. William Le Queux. LC 23-182128. 1923. Cassell and Company, Ltd.
Where the Dreams Cross. Ellen Douglas, pseud. LC 68-17220. 1968. 5.65. Houghton Mifflin.
Where the Evil Dwells. Clifford D. Simak. LC 82-6839. 1982. 11.95 (ISBN 0-345-30770-4). Ballantine Books.
Where the Field Goes. Jeanne Lohmann. (Illus.). 1976. pap. 3.00 o.p. (ISBN 0-9607688-0-7). J A Lohmann.
Where the Girls Were Different. Erskine Caldwell. 1965. pap. 0.60 o.p. (60-218). Manor Bks.
Where the Girls Were Different: And Other Stories. Erskine Caldwell. LC 48-392917. (New York library, 151). 1948. Avon Book Co.
Where the Heart Goes. Alice Mary Ross Colver. LC 39-25962. 1939. Dodd, Mead & Company.
Where the Heart Is. Arlene Hale. LC 73-16100. 1974. 6.95 (ISBN 0-316-33876-1). Little, Brown.
Where the Heart Is. Arlene Hale. LC 76-45209. 1977. 9.95 (ISBN 0-89340-052-1). J. Curley & Associates.
Where the Heart Is. Ruth McCarthy Sear. (YA) 1973. 4.50 o.p. (Avalon). Bouregy.
Where the Heart Is. Pearl Senical. LC 55-760586. 1955. Dorrance.
Where the Heart Is. Natalie Shipman. LC 47-30064. 1946. S. Curl.
Where the Heart Is. Florence R. Wiggins. LC 75-45857. 144p. 1976. 5.95 o.p. (ISBN 0-915684-03-9). Christian Herald.
Where the Heart Is: Showing That Christmas Is What You Make It. William Henry Irwin. LC 12-24484. 1912. D. Appleton and Company.
Where the Heart Leads. Susan Evans McCloud. LC 79-54208. 5.50 (ISBN 0-88494-381-X). Bookcraft.
Where the High Winds Blow. David Harry Walker. LC 60-12509. 1960. Houghton Mifflin.
Where the Hummingbird Flies. 1st Ed. Frank Hercules. LC 61-6643. 1961. Harcourt, Brace.
Where the Jackals Howl, and Other Stories. Amos Oz. LC 80-8754. 12.95 (ISBN 0-15-196038-0). Harcourt Brace Jovanovich.
Where the James Flows: The Story of a Perfect Palship. Walter Marion Raymond. LC 28-3692. 1927. F. H. Hitchcock.
Where the Laborers Are Few. Margaret Wade Campbell Deland. LC 9-27265. 1909. Harper & Brothers.
Where the Land and Water Meet: A Novel. Julian Moynahan. LC 78-27462. 1979. 9.95 (ISBN 0-688-03446-2). Morrow.
Where the Lilies Bloom. Vera Cleaver & Bill Cleaver. 1974. pap. 1.95 (ISBN 0-451-12292-5, AJ2292, Sig). NAL.
Where the Long Grass Blows. Louis L'Amour. LC 77-19159. 1977. 9.95 (ISBN 0-8161-6544-0). G. K. Hall.
Where the Loon Calls. Harry Sinclair Drago. LC 28-192821. The Macaulay Company.
Where the Lost Aprils Are. Elisabeth Ogilvie. LC 75-4563. 1975. 8.95 (ISBN 0-07-047606-3). McGraw-Hill.
Where the Lost Aprils Are. Ogilvie, Elisabeth. 1.75 (ISBN 0-380-00864-5). Avon.
Where the Music Was: Fifteen Stories. Charles East. LC 65-21027. 3.95. Harcourt.
Where the Path Breaks. Charles Norris Williamson & Alice Muriel Livingston Williamson. LC 16-6475. 1916. The Century Co.
Where the Pavement Ends. John Russell. LC 73-144170. (Short story index series). (Illus.). 1971. (ISBN 0-8369-3785-6). Books for Libraries Press.
Where the Pools Are Bright & Deep. Dana Storrs Lamb. (Illus.). 192p. 1973. 8.95 o.p. (ISBN 0-87691-110-6). Winchester Pr.
Where the Rainbow Touches the Ground. John Henderson Miller. LC 6-44370. 1906. Funk & Wagnalls Company.
Where the Readers Are: The Second Teacher's Guide to Yearling Books. Charles F. Reasoner. 1972. pap. text ed. 1.00, free with order of 25 Yearling Bks. Dell.
Where the Red Fern Grows: The Story of Two Dogs and a Boy. Wilson Rawls. (Bantam pathfinder editions). 1974. (pbk) 1.25. Bantam Books.
Where the Red Fern Grows: The Story of Two Dogs and a Boy. Wilson Rawls. LC 61-9201. 1961. Doubleday.
Where the Red Volleys Poured: By Charles W. Dahlinger... Illustrations by Charles Grunwald. Charles William Dahlinger. LC 7-23305. 1907. G. W. Dillingham Company.
Where the River Bends. Jo Calloway. (Candlelight Ecstasy Ser.: No. 109). (Orig.). 1983. pap. 1.95 (ISBN 0-440-19650-7). Dell.
Where the Rivers Flow North. Howard Frank Mosher. LC 78-13499. 1978. 8.95 (ISBN 0-670-76131-1). Viking Press.
Where the Road Led: And Other Stories. Anna Theresa Sadlier. LC 5-37585. 1905. Benziger Brothers.
Where the Sage and Cactus Grow. Moree E. Von Hoogstraat. LC 3-2228. 1900. Scroll Publishing Company.
Where the Shamrock Grows: The Fortunes and Misfortunes of an Irish Family. George Henry Jessop. LC 12-16614. 1912. The Baker & Taylor Company.
Where the Snow Was Red. Judson Pentecost Philips. LC 49-9680. (Red badge mystery). 1949. Dodd, Mead.
Where the Sod Shanty Stood. Virgil Dillin Boyles & Coursey, Oscar William. LC 26-22408. S. D., Educator Supply Company.
Where the Soil Was Shallow. Translated by Anthony Kerrigan. Jose Maria Gironella. LC 57-10824. 1957. H. Regnery Co.
Where the Souls of Men Are Calling. Credo Fitch Harris. LC 18-7992. Britton Publishing Company.
Where the Souls of Men Are Calling: A Love Story Out of the War Zone. Credo Fitch Harris. LC 21-129558. A. L. Burt Company.
Where the Spies Are: Title Orig: Passport to Oblivion. James Leasor. (Signet bk., P2839). 1966. New Amer. Lib.
Where the Sugar Maple Grows: Idylls of a Canadian Village. Adeline Margaret Teskey. LC 1-24544. 1901. R. F. Fenno & Co.
Where the Sun Swings North. Florance Barrett Willoughby. LC 22-20174. 1922. G. P. Putnam's Sons.
Where the Tide Comes in a Novel. Lucy Meacham Kidd Thruston. LC 4-7711. 1904. Little, Brown, and Company.
Where the Tides Meet. Edward Payson Berry. LC 6-11314. 1893. Area Publishing Company.

Where the Trade-Wind Blows: West Indian Tales. Mary Bradford Crowninshield. LC 6-31950. 1898. The Macmillan Company.

Where the Trail Divides. William Otis Lillibridge. LC 7-98427. 1907. Dodd, Mead and Company.

Where the Turnpike Starts. Harriett H Carr. LC 55-14269. 1955. Macmillan.

Where the Twain Met. Herbert Grafton Woodworth. LC 25-5462. Small, Maynard & Company.

Where the Waters Turn. Theodore Von Ziekursch. LC 27-10730. 1927. Macrae Smith Company.

Where the Weak Grow Strong. Eugene Morehead Armfield. LC 38-38712. Covici-Friede.

Where the Wind Is Wild. Franklin Proud. 2.50. Pocket Books.

Where the Wolf Leads. Jane Arbor. (Harlequin Romances). 192p. 1981. pap. 1.25 (ISBN 0-373-02396-0, Pub. by Harlequin). PB.

Where the World Kneels: A Novel. Mary N Bernard. LC 6-11327. 1893. W. C. Phillips, Printer.

Where the Young Child Was: And Also The Spirit of the House, The Youngest Officer, Linden Goes Home, The Little Brown House, That Makes the World Go Round. Marie Conway Oemler. LC 21-16533. 1921. The Century Co.

Where There Are Vultures. Anthony Heckstall-Smith. 1958. Roy Publishers.

Where There's a Will. Anne Burton. (Raven House Mysteries Ser.). 224p. 1982. pap. 2.25 (ISBN 0-373-63037-9, Pub. by Worldwide). Harlequin Bks.

Where There's a Will. Edith Pargeter. LC 60-16846. 1960. Published for the Crime Club by Doubleday.

Where There's a Will. Mary Roberts Rinehart. LC 12-20563. The Bobbs-Merrill Company.

Where There's a Will. Rex Stout. LC 82-3015. 1982. 13.95 (ISBN 0-8161-3287-9). G.K. Hall.

Where There's a Will: A Nero Wolfe Mystery. Rex Stout. LC 40-986627. Farrar & Rinehart, Inc.

Where There's a Will. 1st American Ed. Ellis Peters. LC 60-168469. 1960. Published for the Crime Club by Doubleday.

Where There's Smoke. Evan Hunter. LC 74-28191. 1975. 6.95 (ISBN 0-394-49670-1). Random House.

Where There's Smoke. Ed McBain. 1975. 6.95 o.p. (ISBN 0-394-49670-1). Random.

Where There's Smoke. Prentice Winchell. LC 46-8108. 1946. J. B. Lippincott Company.

Where There's Smoke. 1st Ed. Clarence Budington Kelland. 1959. Harper.

Where Three Roads Meet. Ethel May Dell. LC 36-101120. G. P. Putnam's Sons.

Where Thunder Hides. Marion Hodgson. LC 79-63393. (Orig.). 1979. pap. 2.50 (ISBN 0-912848-05-7). Coll Kids Cook.

Where Time Winds Blow. Robert Holdstock. 1982. pap. 2.95 (Timescape). PB.

Where Town Begins. Richard R Werry. LC 51-9819. 1951. Greenberg.

Where Town Begins. Richard R Werry. LC 52-40864. (Signet book no. 938). 1952. New American Library.

Where Two or Three Are Gathered Together, Someone Spills His Milk. Tom Mullen. LC 72-96355. 1973. 3.95 o.p. (ISBN 0-87680-314-1). Word Bks.

Where Two Ways Meet. Sarah Doudney. (On cover: Seaside library. Pocket ed. no. 679). 1886. G. Munro.

Where Two Ways Met. Grace Livingston Hill. LC 47-212. 1947. J. B. Lippincott Company.

Where Two Ways Met. Grace Livingston Hill. LC 78-12836. 1981. 11.50 (ISBN 0-89340-161-7). J. Curley.

Where Visions Come True. Evangeline Morrey. LC 42-9581. 1942. DeVorss & Co.

Where Were You in '76? A Novel. Jean Rikhoff. LC 78-7955. 9.95 (ISBN 0-399-90021-7). R. Marek Publishers.

Where Were You Last Pluterday? Paul Van Herck. (Science Fiction Ser.). 160p. (Orig.). 1973. pap. 0.95 o.p. (UQ1051). DAW Bks.

Where Were You Last Pluterday? Paul Van Herck. Tr. by Dannt De Laet & Willy Magiels. (Daw's sf books, UQ1051). 1973. 0.95. Daw Books.

Where Will This Path Lead! A Tale of a Summer Trip. Six Weeks at the Seaside and What It Led to. S. K Donovan. LC 98-227. 1898. The Laning Printing Company.

Where You Goin, Girlie? Josephine Carson. LC 75-5849. 1975. 8.95 (ISBN 0-8037-9815-6). Dial Press.

Where You Gonna Put It? Ruth F. Deibert. 3.00 o.p. Carlton.

Where Your Heart Is. Beatrice Harraden. LC 18-21162. 1918. 1.50. Dodd, Mead and Company.

Where Your Treasure Is-- John Hastings Turner. LC 22-11084. 1922. C. Scribner's Sons.

Where Your Treasure Is: Being the Personal Narrative of Ross Sidney, Diver. Holman Francis Day. LC 17-17284. 1917. 1.50. Harper & Brothers.

Whereabouts Unknown... Gertrude M. Robins Reynolds. LC 31-16241. Pub. for the Crime Club, Inc., by Doubleday, Doran & Company, Inc.

Wheres. Robert Kelly. LC 78-109088. (Sparrow; 68). 1978. 0.75. Black Sparrow Press.

Where's Annie? Eileen Bassing. LC 63-9346. 1963. Random House.

Where's Daddy? William Roos. LC 63-7706. 1963. Doubleday.

Where's Emily? A Fleming Stone Story. Carolyn Wells. LC 27-21881. 1927. J. B. Lippincott Company.

Where's Poppa? Robert Klane. LC 76-85561. 1970. 4.95. Random House.

Where's the Kids, Herman? Jim Unger. LC 78-56101. 1978. pap. 2.50 (ISBN 0-8362-1105-7). Andrews & McMeel.

Wherever Dreams Live. Peter Harris. (Illus.). 88p. (Orig.). 1982. pap. 7.95 (ISBN 0-943510-00-7). Lifesigns.

Wherever I Choose. Eleanor Blake Atkinson Pratt. LC 38-131048. G. P. Putnam's Sons.

Wherever Lynn Goes. Beatrice Parker. 1975. (pbk.) 1.25. Dell.

Wherever She Goes. Richard Scowcroft. LC 66-23247. 1967. Lippincott.

Wherever the Grass Grows. Bosworth, Allan R. LC 41-5145. 1941. Doubleday, Doran and Co., Inc.

Wherever the Grass Grows. Allan R Bosworth. LC 42-17382. 1942. The Sun Dial Press.

Wherever We Step, the Land Is Mined: A Novel. Natalie Scott. LC 80-18492. 1980. 8.95 (ISBN 0-531-09939-3). F. Watts.

Whether We Live or Die. Emma Rosa Bond. LC 51-5687. 1951. Messenger Press.

Whether White or Black, a Man. Edith Smith Davis. LC 77-37590. (Black heritage library collection). (Illus.). 1972. (ISBN 0-8369-8966-X). Books for Libraries Press.

Whether White or Black, a Man. Edith Smith Davis. 1898. F. H. Revell Company.

Whetstone Walls. Lella Warren. LC 52-13952. 1952. Appleton-Century-Crofts.

Whetted Bronze. Manning Norvil. 1.50 (ISBN 0-87997-364-1). DAW Books.

Which--Innocent or Guilty? And Other Short Stories. Emerson S Clem. LC 55-8505. 1955. Comet Press Books.

Which Doctor? By Edward Candy Pseud. Alison Neville. LC 54-5889. 1954. Rienhart.

Which Grain Will Grow: By H. H. Lynde Pseud. Helen Huntington. LC 52-5677. 1952. Crown Publishers.

Which Grain Will Grow: Stories and Sketches of Childhood. Ed. by Don Marion Wolfe. New York. New School for Social Research. LC 51-9727. 1950. Cambridge Pub. Co.

Which Hope We Have: By Ruby E. Hines... Ruby E Hines. LC 14-2137. 1913. 0.50. Printing Department of Illinois State Reformatory.

Which I Never: A Police Diversion. Strong, Leonard Alfred George. LC 52-7091. 1952. Macmillan.

Which Is My Husband? Jules Claretie & Safford, Mary Joanna. Tr. LC 11-9901. 1911. D. Appleton and Company.

Which Is the Wiser: Or, People Abroad; a Tale for Youth. Mary Botham Howitt. 1842. D. Appleton.

Which Loved Him Best? Charlotte Mary Brame. LC 42-23961. (On cover: Lovell's library. v. 17 no. 907). J. W. Lovell Company.

Which Mother Is Mine? Joan Oppenheimer. (YA) (gr. 6-12). 1980. pap. 1.95 (ISBN 0-553-13685-2). Bantam.

Which Mrs. Bennett? Anne Littlefield. LC 59-6366. 1959. Published for the Crime Club by Doubleday.

Which of the Low-Tide: An Edwardian Melodrama. 1st Ed. John Dickson Carr. LC 61-6208. 1961. Harper.

Which One? Robert Ames Bennet. LC 12-24065. 1912. 1.35. A. C. McClurg & Co.

Which One of You Is Interracial? A Novelette and Other Stories. Ira Lunan Ferguson. LC 78-79431. 1969. 3.25. Lunan Ferguson Library.

Which One of You Is Interracial? & Other Stories. Ira Lunan-Ferguson. LC 78-79431. 1969. 4.25 (ISBN 0-911724-10-9). Lunan-Ferguson.

Which Shall It Be! Annie French Hector. (Seaside library, v. 20, no. 400). 1878. G. Munro.

Which Shall It Be! Annie French Hector. (On cover: Seaside library. Pocket ed., no. 236). 1884. G. Munro.

Which Shall It Be! Annie French Hector. (On cover: Lovell's library, v. 20, no. 995). 1887. J. W. Lovell Company.

Which Shall It Be! A Novel. Annie French Hector. (Leisure hour series. no. 17). 1874. H. Holt and Company.

Which Shall It Be? Or, Through Great Tribulations. M. B. W Parrish. (sunnyside series, no. 4). J. S. Ogilvie.

Which the Justice, Which the Thief. William Harrington. LC 63-18292. 1963. Bobbs-Merrill.

Which, the Right or the Left ... LC 8-36044. 1855. Garrett & Co.

Which Was the Greater Love! Le Calvaire De Cimiez--a Story of the French Riviera. Henry Bordeaux & Descaves, Lucian, 1861. LC 39-10092. 1930. Como Publishing Co.

Which Way? Theodora Benson. LC 32-2128. 1932. Doubleday, Doran & Company, Inc.

Which Way? Ralph Lockwood Hoffman & Hoffman, Dorothy May, Joint Author. LC 31-9626. J. R. Hoffman.

Which Way Out: Stories Based on the Experience of a Psychiatrist. Clarence Paul Oberndorf. LC 49-72581. 1949. International Universities Press.

Which Way the Wind. Hans Herlin. LC 78-4013. 1978. 10.00 (ISBN 0-312-86709-3). St. Martin's Press.

Which Way the Wind. Hans Herlin. 1980. 2.25 (ISBN 0-380-48306-8). Avon Books.

Which Way the Wind Blows. Mario Edlosi. 1979. pap. 3.95 (ISBN 0-89185-207-7). Anthelion Pr.

Which Wins? A Story of Social Conditions. Mary Hanford Finney Ford. LC 6-41395. (On cover: Good company series, no. 9). 1891. Lee and Shepard.

Whicharts. Noel Streatfeild. LC 32-14944. Brentano's.

Whiff of Death. Isaac Asimov. LC 68-13442. 1968. Walker.

Whiff of Madness. Ron Goulart. (Science Fiction Ser.). 1976. pap. 1.25 o.p. (UY1251). DAW Bks.

Whiffs. Malcolm Marmorstein. 1975. (pbk.) 0.95. Berkley Pub. Co.

Whigs of Scotland: Or The Last of the Stuarts. An Historical Romance of the Scottish Persecution ... LC 24-24993. 1833. J. & J. Harper.

While Caroline Was Growing. Josephine Dodge Daskam Bacon. LC 11-2970. 1911. 1.50. The Macmillan Company.

While Charlie Was Away. Edith Evelyn Jaffray Bigelow. LC 1-24552. (Half-title: Novelettes de luxe). 1901. D. Appleton & Co.

While Gods Are Falling. Earl Lovelace. LC 66-17746. 1966. bds., 4.95. Regnery.

While Gondolas Pass. Helen Gansevoort Edwards Mackay. LC 30-18198. 1930. D. Appleton & Company.

While He Lies Sleeping. Giro. (O.S.I.). 1964. 3.95 o.s.i. (81390). S&S.

While He Lies Sleeping. LC 64-12478. 1964. Simon and Schuster.

While Heaven Waited. Odessa Rippetoe. (Illus.). 1969. 4.95 o.p. (ISBN 0-8059-1378-5). Dorrance.

While Hopes Were Kindling. Mary Catherine Frances Walsh. 1901. P. Paul & Co.

While Murder Waits: Shudders and Chills in a Hair-Raising Story of Death in a Lighthouse. Samuel Shellabarger. LC 37-20437. 1937. Pub. for the Crime Club, Inc. by Doubleday, Doran & Company, Inc.

While My Guitar Gently Weeps: A Novel. Paul Breeze. LC 80-22065. 1981. 9.95 (ISBN 0-8008-8247-4). Taplinger Pub. Co.

While Paris Danced. Patricia Wright. LC 81-43376. 1982. 18.95 (ISBN 0-385-17898-0). Doubleday.

While Paris Laughed: Being Pranks and Passions of the Poet Tricotrin. Leonard Merrick. LC 18-14994. E. P. Dutton and Company.

While Paris Laughed: Being Pranks and Passions of the Poet Tricotrin. Leonard Merrick. LC 20-562032. 1919. E. P. Dutton and Company.

While Passion Sleeps. Shirlee Busbee. 496p. 3.95 (ISBN 0-380-82297-0). Avon.

While Rivers Flow. Glen Fleischmann. LC 63-12139. 1963. Macmillan.

While Rivers Run: A Novel. Maurice Walsh. LC 28-13561. 1928. Frederick A. Stokes Company.

While She Sleeps. Ethel L. White. 1969. pap. 0.60 o.p. (ISBN 0-446-63171-X, 63-171). Paperback Lib.

While She Sleeps! A Novel. Ethel Lina White. LC 40-866014. Harper & Brothers.

While Shepherds Watched: By Richard Aumerle Maher; Decorations by Charles R. Stevens. Richard Aumerle Maher. LC 17-28077. 1917. The Macmillan Company.

While Still We Live. Helen MacInnes Highet. LC 44-218253. 1944. Little, Brown and Company.

While Still We Live. Helen MacInnes. 448p. 1981. pap. 3.25 (ISBN 0-449-24054-1, Crest). Fawcett.

While Still We Live. Helen MacInnes. LC 44-2182. 1971. 7.50 o.p. (ISBN 0-15-196090-9). HarBraceJ.

While the Angels Sing. Gladys Hasty Carroll. LC 47-11768. 1947. Macmillan Co.

While the Bells Rang. Charles L Clifford. LC 41-139303. 1941. Pub. for the Crime Club by Doubleday, Doran and Company, Inc.

While the Bridegroom Tarried. Edna Bryner. LC 29-1194. E. P. Dutton & Co., Inc.

While the Crowd Cheers. Karl Tunberg. LC 35-18999. The Macaulay Company.

While the Earth Shook. Jean Schopfer. Tr. by Rochemont, Ruth De. LC 27-142067. 1927. Bard and Company.

While the Gods Grinned. John Hastings Turner. LC 28-17929. 1928. G. P. Putnam's Sons.

While the Patient Slept. Mignon Good Eberhart. LC 30-26182. 1930. Pub. for The Crime Club, Inc., by Doubleday, Doran & Company, Inc.

While the Patient Slept. Mignon Good Eberhart. LC 44-360919. 1943. Triangle Books.

While the Patient Slept. Mignon Good Eberhart. 1973. (pbk.) 0.95. Popular Library.

While the Wind Howled. Audrey Gaines. LC 40-325576. 1940. Thomas Y. Crowell Co.

While the World Slept. Elizabeth Z Zane. LC 8-37873. J. E. Winner.

While There's Life. Elinor Mordaunt, pseud. LC 19-26571. 1919. H. Holt and Company.

While We Wait. Patti Bard. 1972. Zondervan.

Whilomville Stories. Stephen Crane. LC 69-11886. (American short story series, v. 44). (Illus.). 1969. Garrett Press.

Whilomville Stories. Stephen Crane. LC 76-7988. (Illus.). Scholarly Press.

Whim to Kill. Elizabeth Linington. LC 77-125669. 1971. 5.95. Morrow.

Whimsical Collection. Jewell B Reeve. LC 68-2312. 1968. Vantage Press.

Whimsical Tales. Douglas William Jerrold & Daniel, Lewis C., 1901- Illus. LC 48-2018. 1948. Story Classics.

Whimsical Woman. Emilia Smith Flygare Carlen & Perce, Elbert. LC 6-20140. 1854. C. Scribner.

Whimsical Wooing. Antonio Giulio Barrili. Tr. by Bell, Clara Courtensy (Poynter) LC 6-9410. 1882. W. S. Gottsberger.

Whimsy Girl. Charlotte Canty. LC 13-22094. 1913. Dodd, Mead and Company.

Whin Fell. Erica Isobel Oxenham. LC 27-11965. 1927. Longmans, Green and Co., Ltd.

Whip. Martin Caidin. LC 75-40221. 1976. 7.95 (ISBN 0-395-20707-X). Houghton Mifflin.

Whip. Catherine Cookson. LC 83-121762. 14.95 (ISBN 0-671-43272-9). Summit Books.

Whip. Catherine Cookson. 384p. 1983. 14.95. Summit Bks.

Whip. Sara Elizabeth Mason. LC 47-12530. W. Morrow.

Whip. Richard Parker & Raleigh, Cecil. LC 13-12594. 1913. 1.25. The Macaulay Company.

Whip. Luke Short. LC 80-11285. 1980. 10.95 (ISBN 0-8161-3087-6). G. K. Hall.

Whip Angels. Selena Warfield. (Orig.). pap. 1.75 o.s.i. (TC2220, Travellers Comp). Olympia.

Whip Hand. Victor Canning. LC 65-20962. 1965. Morrow.

Whip Hand. Dick Francis. LC 79-3408. 9.95 (ISBN 0-06-011384-7). Harper & Row.

Whip Hand. Ian Gordon, pseud. LC 54-6640. 1954. Crown Publishers.

Whip Hand. Helen Reimensnyder Martin. LC 34-1298. 1934. Dodd, Mead & Company.

Whip Hand: A Tale of the Pine Country. Samuel Merwin. LC 3-25211. 1903. Doubleday, Page & Company.

Whip Justice: By Larry Lawson. Clarence O Lawson. LC 57-126765. 1957. Avalon Books.

Whip Mistress. Marcus Van Heller, pseud. (Orig.). 1969. pap. 1.75 o.s.i. (OPH152, Ophelia). Olympia.

Whip-Poor-Will Mystery. Hulbert Footner. 1935. Harper & Brothers.

Whip Ryder's Way: A Novel. Grant Taylor. LC 35-458866. J. B. Lippincott Company.

Whipmasters. Roger Cunningham. 1972. pap. 1.95 o.s.i. (V1110T, Venus). Grove.

Whipped Cream. Stephen Genet. 224p. pap. 1.95 o.p. (6124). Brandon.

Whipped Cream. Geoffrey McNeill-Moss. LC 26-8951. George H. Doran Company.

Whipped Women. Jean De Villiot. pap. 1.75 o.p. (Z1060K, Zebra). Grove.

Whipperginny. Robert Graves. LC 76-39795. Repr. of 1923 ed. lib. bdg. 12.50 (ISBN 0-8414-4512-5). Folcroft.

Whipping. Roy Catesby Flannagan. LC 30-185534. J.Cape & H. Smith.

Whipping Boy. Beth Holmes. 1979. pap. 2.50 (ISBN 0-515-04698-1). Jove Pubns.

Whipping Boy. Shirley E Pfoutz. LC 56-104546. 1956. E. Messner.

Whipping Girls. Will Henry, pseud. pap. 1.95 o.s.i. (Venus). Grove.

Whipping Star. Frank Herbert. LC 80-18662. (Series: Gregg Press Science Fiction Series.). 1980. 13.95. Gregg Press.

Whipping Star see Worlds Beyond Dune: The Best of Frank Herbert.

Whipping Star: A Science Fiction Novel. Frank Herbert. LC 71-108744. 1970. 4.95. Putnam.

Whipple's Castle. Thomas Williams. LC 68-58852. 1969. 6.95. Random House.

Whippoorwill: A Novel. Frances Torian Johnson. LC 52-11238. 1952. Exposition Press.
Whippoorwill Cabin. John Kadon. 1980. pap. 5.00 (ISBN 0-89502-061-0). FEB.
Whippoorwill House. Louise Platt Hauck. The Penn Publishing Company.
Whippoorwill's Cry. Barbara Webb. LC 36-181561. 1936. Doubleday, Doran & Company, Inc.
Whippoorwill's Cry. Barbara Webb. LC 37-19763. 1937. The Sun Dial Press, Inc.
Whips Incorporated. Angela Pearson. pap. 1.95 o.s.i. (OPH-236, Ophelia). Olympia.
Whips of Time. Arabella Kenealy. LC 9-7440. 1909. Little, Brown, and Company.
Whirl: A Romance of Washington Society. Molly Elliot Seawell. LC 9-16108. 1909. Dodd, Mead & Company.
Whirl Asunder. Gertrude Franklin Horn Atherton. LC 6-4523. F. A. Stokes Company.
Whirl Asunder. Gertrude Franklin Horn Atherton. LC 2-23846. Frederick A. Stokes Company.
Whirligig. Robert L Fish. LC 76-105273. 1970. 5.95. World Pub. Co.
Whirligig. Edward Ballard Garside. LC 54-12028. 1955. Appleton-Century-Crofts.
Whirligig. Mayne Lindsay. 1901. Longmans, Green and Co.
Whirligig of Time. Lloyd Biggle, Jr. LC 78-1179. 1979. 8.95 (ISBN 0-385-13211-5). Doubleday.
Whirligig of Time. Dola De Jong. LC 64-22326. 1964. Published for the Crime Club by Doubleday.
Whirligig of Time. Wayland Wells Williams. LC 16-978135. Frederick A. Stokes Company.
Whirligig of Time: A Novel. Mary Britton Miller. LC 79-151023. 1971. 5.95. Crown Publishers.
Whirligigs. William Sydney Porter. LC 10-20844. 1910. Doubleday, Page & Company.
Whirligigs. William Sydney Porter. LC 15-17408. 1911. Doubleday, Page & Company.
Whirligigs. William Sydney Porter. LC 22-14573. 1919. Doubleday, Page & Company, for Review of Reviews Co.
Whirligigs. William Sydney Porter. LC 37-10652. 1937. The Sun Dial Press, Inc.
Whirling Around the World. Lillian Sutton Pelee. LC 27-104625. R. G. Badger.
Whirling Saws. Irene Welch Grissom. LC 42-21006. B. Humphries, Inc.
Whirling Shapes. Joan North. LC 67-19884. 1967. Farrar, Straus & Giroux.
Whirlpool. George Robert Gissing. LC 71-80632. 1969. AMS Press.
Whirlpool. 4th ed. George Robert Gissing. LC 1-30295. F. A. Stokes Company.
Whirlpool. Victoria Morton. LC 16-22402. E. P. Dutton & Company.
Whirlpool: A Novel. David Albert Lampson. LC 37-166519. 1937. C. Scribner's Sons.
Whirlpool of Reno. John Hamlin. LC 31-219001. 1931. L. MacVeagh, The Dial Press.
Whirlpool of Stars. Tully Zetford. (Hook,#1). 1975. (pbk.) 1.25 (ISBN 0-523-00528-8). Pinnacle Books.
Whirlpools: A Novel of Modern Poland. Henryk Seinkiewicz & Drezmal, Max Anthony, 1867-Tr. LC 10-134807. 1910. Little, Brown, and Company.
Whirlwind. Kuei Chiang. LC 78-304584. (Chinese Materials & Research Aids Service Center. Occasional Series: No. 26). (Illus.). 1977. 16.50. Chinese Materials Center.
Whirlwind. Eleanor Early. LC 30-211174. The White House.
Whirlwind. H. C. M Hardinge. LC 24-2256. 1923. G.P. Putnam's Sons.
Whirlwind. H. C. M Hardinge. LC 24-5201. 1924. G.P. Putnam's Sons.
Whirlwind. Margaret Kingery. 1979. pap. 1.00 o.p. Samisdat.
Whirlwind. Eden Phillpotts. 1907. McClure, Phillips & Co.
Whirlwind. Ann Shively. LC 81-48057. 13.94 (ISBN 0-06-014995-7). Harper & Row.
Whirlwind. A Stone. LC 23-173801. 1923. The A. Stone Foundation.
Whirlwind. Edna Worthley Underwood. LC 18-18190. Small, Maynard and Company.
Whirlwind: A Novel. by rupert hughes. ed. Rupert Hughes. LC 2-24251. 1902. Lothrop Publishing Company.
Whirlwind: An Historical Romance: Being the Story of the French Revolution As It Was Seen by Rene De Masac, Deputy to the National Assembly and General of the Republic. William Stearns Davis. LC 29-23882. 1929. The Macmillan Company.
Whirlwind Beneath the Sea. Ken Stanton. (Aquanauts Ser.). 1972. pap. 0.95 o.p. (ISBN 0-532-95194-8). Woodhill.
Whirlwind Beneath the Sea. Ken Stanton. (Aquanauts Ser.). 1972. pap. 0.95 o.p. (ISBN 0-532-95194-8). Manor Bks.
Whirlwind Courtship. Jayne Taylor. (Orig.). 1980. pap. 1.75 (ISBN 0-8439-8012-5, Tiara Bks). Nordon Pubns.
Whirlwind in Petticoats. Beril Becker. LC 47-31420. 1947. Doubleday.
Whirlwind of Desire. Dixie D. Trainer. (Orig.). 1980. pap. 2.50 (ISBN 0-440-19724-4). Dell.
Whisker of Hercules No. 103: The Man Who Was Scared. Kenneth Robeson, pseud. 208p. 1981. pap. 1.95 (ISBN 0-553-14616-5). Bantam.
Whiskey Jim & a Kid Named Billie. W. H. Hutchinson & R. N. Mullins. 5.00 o.p. Eakin Pubns.
Whiskey Man. Howell Raines. LC 77-9061. 1977. 8.95 (ISBN 0-670-76190-7). Viking Press.
Whiskey Room & Other Stories. Jackie A. Moore. 1975. 5.50 (ISBN 0-87164-058-9). William-F.
Whisky Drummer. Cy Martin. 1974. 4.95 (ISBN 0-517-51559-8). Lenox Hill Press.
Whisky Trail. George Washington Ogden. LC 36-59293. 1936. Dodd, Mead & Company.
Whisper Destiny. Jenifer Dalton. (Orig.). 1982. pap. 2.95 (Gallen). PB.
Whisper His Sin: By Vin Packer Pseud. Cover Painting by James Meese. Marijane Meaker. LC 54-4717. (Gold medal books, 426). 1954. Fawcett Publications.
Whisper in a Lonely Place. Gerald Sinstadt. 1977. 5.25 o.p. (ISBN 0-86025-013-X). State Mutual Bk.
Whisper in the Dark. Anne Maybury. 1977. 1.95. Ace Books.
Whisper in the Darkness. T. E Huff. (Dell Book). (Illus.). 1977. 1.25 (ISBN 0-440-15543-6). Dell Pub. Co.
Whisper in the Glen. Philip Maitland Hubbard. LC 73-175293. 1972. 4.95. Atheneum.
Whisper in the Gloom. Nicholas Blake. 1977. pap. 1.95 o.p. (ISBN 0-06-080418-1, P418, PL). Har-Row.
Whisper in the Gloom: By Nicholas Blake Pseyd. 1st Ed. Cecil Day-Lewis. LC 54-8944. 1954. Harper.
Whisper Murder! Vera Kelsey. LC 46-2493. 1946. Pub. for the Crime Club by Doubleday & Company, Inc.
Whisper My Name. Fern Michaels. 192p. 1981. pap. 1.50 (ISBN 0-671-57061-7, Pub. by Silhouette Bks). S&S.
Whisper My Name: A Novel. Burke Davis. LC 49-8667. 1949. Rinehart.
Whisper of a Name (Grand-Louis L'Innocent) Marie Le Franc & Shively, George Jenks, 1893- Tr. LC 28-23922. The Bobbs-Merrill Company.
Whisper of Danger. Clarissa Ross. (rose red romance, 142). 1974. (pbk.) 0.75. Bantam Books.
Whisper of Darkness. Margaret Lynn. pap. 0.50 o.p. (52-925). Paperback Lib.
Whisper of Darkness. Anne Mather. (Harlequin Presents Ser.). 192p. 1980. pap. 1.50 (ISBN 0-373-10376-X, Pub. by Harlequin). PB.
Whisper of Evil. Rosemary Gatenby. 1982. pap. 2.50 (ISBN 0-425-04673-7). Berkley Pub.
Whisper of Evil: A Novel of Suspense. Rosemary Gatenby. LC 78-19114. 6.95 (ISBN 0-396-07588-6). Dodd, Mead.
Whisper of Fear. Elna Stone. (Orig.). 1973. pap. 0.95 o.p. (345-26500-9-095). Beagle Bks.
Whisper of Glocken. Illus. by Imero Gobbato. Carol Kendall. LC 65-21698. 3.50. Harcourt.
Whisper of Heather. Lynn Benedict. (Ravenswood gothic). 1974. (pbk.) 0.95 (ISBN 0-671-77784-X). Pocket Books.
Whisper of My Heartbeats. Mildred S. Larsen. 3.50 o.p. Carlton.
Whisper of the Axe. Richard Condon. Date not set. pap. 2.25 (ISBN 0-345-28296-5). Ballantine.
Whisper of the Axe: A Novel. Richard Condon. LC 75-45310. 1976. 8.95 (ISBN 0-8037-9460-6). Dial Press.
Whisper on the Stair. Lyon Mearson. LC 24-192163. The Macaulay Company.
Whisper on the Water. Edmund P. Murray. 384p. (Orig.). 1982. pap. 3.25 (ISBN 0-441-88531-4). Ace Bks.
Whisper the Robin. Bernard Alvin Palmer. LC 78-180839. 1972. 3.95. Zondervan Pub. House.
Whisper Town. Judson Pentecost Philips. LC 60-11935. (Red badge detective). 1960. Dodd, Mead.
Whisper, Whisper. Katherine Court. LC 77-80150. 1977. 7.95 (ISBN 0-385-12652-2). Doubleday.
Whisper, Whisper. Katherine Court. 1978. 1.95 (ISBN 0-87216-498-5). Playboy Press.
Whisper Wind. large print ed. Sondra Stanford. LC 82-9235. 1982. 7.95 (ISBN 0-8161-3410-3). G.K. Hall.
Whispered Promise. Bonnie Drake. (Candlelight Ecstasy Ser.: No. 70). 1982. pap. 1.95 (ISBN 0-440-17673-5). Dell.
Whispered Sex. Kay Martin. pap. 0.60 o.p. (60-338). Manor Bks.
Whisperers. Robert Nicolson. LC 61-15042. 1961. Knopf.
Whispering Buddha. John Clifford Cowles. LC 32-34682. Hollyway Publishers.
Whispering Cannon: By Nelson and Shirley Wolford. Nelson Wolford & Shirley Wolford. LC 65-14013. (Double D western). 1965. Doubleday.
Whispering Canyon. John Mersereau. LC 26-2807. E. J. Clode, Inc.
Whispering Canyon. Louis Trimble. LC 55-14476. 1955. Avalon Books.
Whispering Caverns. Monroe Schere. LC 74-13205. (Simon and Schuster novel of suspense). 1974. 6.95 (ISBN 0-671-21882-4). Simon and Schuster.
Whispering Caverns. Monroe Schere. (Kangaroo Book). 1977. 1.75 (ISBN 0-671-80967-9). Pocket Books.
Whispering Chorus. Perley Poore Sheehan. LC 27-22158. 1927. G. H. Watt.
Whispering Creek. Alma E Henderson. LC 30-5070. 1926. Burton Publsihing Company.
Whispering Cup. Mabel Seeley. LC 40-9443. 1940. Pub. for the Crime Club by Doubleday, Doran and Company, Inc.
Whispering Cup. Mabel Seely. 1973. pap. 0.95 o.p. (N3001). Pyramid Pubns.
Whispering Dead. Alfred Ganachilly. LC 20-851919. (On verso of half-title: The Borzoi mystery stories, VIII). 1920. A. A. Knopf.
Whispering Death. Roy Vickers. LC 47-20014. 1947. Jefferson House.
Whispering Dust. Eldrid Reynolds. LC 14-1908. 1914. Frederick A. Stokes Company.
Whispering Ear. Clyde B Clason. LC 38-34801. 1938. Pub. for the Crime Club, Inc., by Doubleday, Doran & Company, Inc.
Whispering Gallery. Dan Ross, pseud. 1977. pap. 1.25 (ISBN 0-532-12508-8). Woodhill.
Whispering Gallery. Dan Ross, pseud. 1971. pap. 0.60 o.p. (60-463). Manor Bks.
Whispering Gallery. William Edward Daniel Ross. Ed. by Alice Sachs. 1970. 3.95 o.p. Lenox Hill.
Whispering Gallery. William Edward Daniel Ross. (Easy Read Gothics Ser). 176p. 1975. pap. 0.95 o.p. (532-95387-095). Manor Bks.
Whispering Gallery: Being Leaves from the Diary of an Ex-Diplomat. 1978. Repr. of 1926 ed. lib. bdg. 15.00 (ISBN 0-8495-0121-0). Arden Lib.
Whispering Gate. presented to the world at large by carex macphail... ed. Carex Macphail. LC 32-94272. The Bobbs-Merrill Company.
Whispering Ghost... Stephen Chalmers. LC 32-5024. Pub. for the Crime Club, Inc., by Doubleday, Doran & Company, Inc.
Whispering Hill. Martha Albrand. LC 47-3207. 1947. Random House.
Whispering Hill. Heidi Huberta Loewengard. LC 47-3207. 1947. Random House.
Whispering Hope. Iris Bancroft. 1983. pap. 3.50 (ISBN 0-553-22862-5). Bantam.
Whispering Island. Nelle McFather. (Ace Gothic). 1974. (pbk.) 0.95. Ace Books.
Whispering Lane. Fergus Hume. LC 25-76662. Small, Maynard & Company.
Whispering Leaves. Dorothy Collett. 1979. pap. 1.75 (ISBN 0-89041-227-8, 3227). Major Bks.
Whispering Man. Henry Kitchell Webster. LC 8-27494. 1908. D. Appleton and Company.
Whispering Master. Frank Gruber. LC 47-5592. 1947. Rinehart.
Whispering Pine. Sara Ware Bassett. LC 53-5595. 1953. Doubleday.
Whispering Pines: A Romance on a New England Hillside. Clara Endicott Sears. LC 30-21948. Priv. Print., Enterprise Press.
Whispering Range. Ernest Haycox. LC 75-35671. 1975. 9.95 (ISBN 0-89190-979-6). Rivercity Press.
Whispering Range. Ernest Haycox. LC 31-34062. Doubleday, Doran & Company, Inc.
Whispering Range. Haycox, Ernest. 1973. 0.75. Warner Paperback.
Whispering Range. Tom Roan. LC 34-345881. A. H. King.
Whispering River. Helen Topping Miller. LC 36-525712. 1936. D. Appleton-Century Company, Incorporated.
Whispering Runes. Doris Shannon. 1973. pap. 0.75 o.p. (94357-075). Beagle Bks.
Whispering Sage. Harry Sinclair Drago & Noel, Joseph, Joint Author. LC 22-18087. 1922. 1.75. The Century Co.
Whispering Sands. Erle Stanley Gardner & Charles Waugh. LC 81-19414. 1982. 12.95. J. Curley.
Whispering Sands: Stories of Gold Fever and the Western Desert. Erle Stanley Gardner & Charles Waugh. LC 80-29460. 1981. 11.95 (ISBN 0-688-00474-1). Morrow.
Whispering Smith. Frank Hamilton Spearman. LC 6-31385. 1906. C. Scribner's Sons.
Whispering Smith. Frank Hamilton Spearman. LC 16-341285. 1914. C. Scribner's Sons.
Whispering Smith. Frank Hamilton Spearman. LC 17-611885. 1916. C. Scribner's Sons.
Whispering Smith. Frank Hamilton Spearman. LC 24-222017. 1921. C. Scribner's Sons.
Whispering Smith. Frank Hamilton Spearman. LC 27-7339. Grosset & Dunlap.
Whispering Smith. Frank Hamilton Spearman. LC 43-9799. 1943. The Sun Dial Press.
Whispering Smith. Frank Hamilton Spearman. (Leisure book). 1979. 1.75 (ISBN 0-8439-0620-0). Nordon Pubns.
Whispering Tongues. Eric Andrew Simson. LC 34-5589. 1934. Doubleday, Doran & Company, Inc.
Whispering Valley. Robert Ormond Case. LC 32-22563. 1932. Doubleday, Doran & Company, Inc.
Whispering Willows. Dorothy Osborne. 1973. (pbk) 0.95. Popular Library.
Whispering Window. Cortland Fitzsimmons. LC 36-35049. 1936. Frederick A. Stokes Company.
Whispering Wires: Adapted from the Saturday Evening Post Story of the Same Title. Henry Leverage. LC 18-18546. 1918. Moffat, Yard and Company.
Whisperings. Rabindranath Tagore. Ed. by Lois Huffmon. LC 72-90378. (Illus.). 64p. 1973. 3.00 o.p. (ISBN 0-87529-329-8). Hallmark.
Whisperings Within. David Barash. 288p. 1981. pap. 4.95 (ISBN 0-14-005699-8). Penguin.
Whispers. Samuel Hopkins Adams. LC 40-5662. Liveright Publishing Corporation.
Whispers. Louis Dodge. LC 20-6862. 1920. C. Scribner's Sons.
Whispers. Dorothy Fletcher. 432p. (Orig.). 1980. pap. 2.50 (ISBN 0-89083-675-2). Zebra.
Whispers. Bernard Harper Friedman. LC 73-151219. 1972. (ISBN 0-87886-020-7). Ithaca House.
Whispers. Dean Koontz. LC 79-22858. 11.95 (ISBN 0-399-12351-2). Putnam.
Whispers. Stuart D. Schiff. LC 76-50307. 1977. 7.95 o.p. (ISBN 0-385-12568-2). Doubleday.
Whispers Four. Stuart D. Schiff. LC 82-45337. (Science Fiction Ser.). 192p. 1983. 11.95 (ISBN 0-385-18028-4). Doubleday.
Whispers in the Dark. Shyrle Hacker. 176p. 1976. pap. 1.25 (ISBN 0-89041-084-4, 3084). Major Bks.
Whispers in the Night. Ivan E. Painton. 1976. 2.95 o.p. (ISBN 0-8059-2324-1). Dorrance.
Whispers in the Night. William Edward Daniel Ross. Ed. by Alice Sachs. 1970. 3.95 o.p. Lenox Hill.
Whispers in the Sun. Maysie Greig. LC 49-11451. 1949. Random House.
Whispers in the Wind. Marsha Alexander. 1977. pap. 1.50 (ISBN 0-89041-174-3, 3174). Major Bks.
Whispers in the Wind. Ruth Wissman. LC 79-8947. 192p. 1980. 8.95 o.p. (ISBN 0-385-15778-9). Doubleday.
Whispers in the Wind. Ruth H Wissmann. LC 79-8947. 1980. 8.95 (ISBN 0-385-15778-9). Doubleday.
Whispers of Heavenly Death. Wally Coins. (Orig.). 1979. pap. 1.95 (ISBN 0-532-23152-X). Woodhill.
Whispers of the Hawk. Leigh F. James. 1981. pap. 2.95. Bantam.
Whispers of the Heart. Anne Shore. (Candlelight romance). 1978. 1.25 (ISBN 0-440-14541-4). Dell Pub. Co.
Whispers Three. Stuart D. Schiff. LC 80-2791. (Doubleday Science Fiction Ser.). (Illus.). 192p. 1981. 10.95 (ISBN 0-385-17162-5). Doubleday.
Whispers Two. Stuart D. Schiff. LC 78-22542. (Illus.). 1979. 10.95 (ISBN 0-385-14967-0). Doubleday.
Whistle. James Jones. LC 77-11980. 10.95 (ISBN 0-440-09548-4). Delacorte Press.
Whistle and I'll Come to You: An Idyll. Agnes Sligh Turnbull. LC 71-120832. 1970. 5.95. Houghton Mifflin.
Whistle, Daughter, Whistle. Herbert Best. LC 47-11391. 1947. Macmillan Co.
Whistle Down the Wind: A Modern Fable. Illus. by Oven Edwards. 1st Ed. Mary Hayley Bell, pseud. LC 59-11070. 1959. Dutton.
Whistle for a Wind: Maine 1820. Elisabeth Ogilvie. Repr. lib. bdg. 14.10x (ISBN 0-88411-340-X). Amereon Ltd.
Whistle for Me. Michael Jackson. LC 38-296423. 1933. W. Morrow & Co.
Whistle for the Crows. Dorothy Eden. 1977. pap. 2.25 (ISBN 0-441-88557-8). Ace Bks.
Whistle in the Wind. Dorothy Daniels. 1976. (pbk.) 1.25 (ISBN 0-671-80258-5). Pocket Books.
Whistle in the Wind: A Novel. John H Culp. LC 68-14924. 1968. Holt, Rinehart and Winston.
Whistle Me Home. Michael Rubin. LC 67-22964. 1967. McGraw-Hill.
Whistle Past the Graveyard. Richard Deming. LC 54-9127. (Murray Hill mystery). 1954. Rinehart.
Whistle Stop. Maritta Martin Wolff. LC 41-51795. Random House.
Whistle Stop Nurse. easy eye ed. Arlene Hale. (Orig.). 1968. pap. 0.60 o.p. (73-786). Lancer.
Whistle the Wild Wind. Geoffrey Bocca. LC 79-50895. Date not set. pap. 2.25 o.s.i. (ISBN 0-89516-080-3). Condor Pub Co.

Whistler: Three Western Novelettes. Edward Beverly Mann. LC 52-13108. 1953. Greenberg.

Whistler's Lane. Anthea Fraser. LC 76-8214. 1976. 9.95 (ISBN 0-8161-6372-3). G. K. Hall.

Whistler's Lane: A Novel of Suspense. Anthea Fraser. LC 75-12780. 1975. 6.95 (ISBN 0-396-07143-0). Dodd, Mead.

Whistlers Room. Paul Alverdes & Creighton, Basil, Tr. LC 30-3051. 1930. Covici, Friede.

Whistles of Silver and Other Stories. Helen Parry Eden. LC 72-152939. (Short story index reprint series). (Illus.). 1971. (ISBN 0-8369-3798-8). Books for Libraries Press.

Whistling Cat. Robert William Chambers. LC 32-7814. 1932. D. Appleton and Company.

Whistling Hangman. Baynard Hardwick Kendrick. LC 38-2819. 1937. Pub. for the Crime Club Inc., by Doubleday, Doran & Co., Inc.

Whistling in the Dark. Helen Knipe Carpenter & Gross, Laurence. LC 32-28829. 1932. Dodd, Mead & Company.

Whistling Lady: A Sheep's Sense of Fair Play, "Number Six". Robert James Thomas. LC 24-30782. 1923. Printed by Kennedy-Morris Corp.

Whistling Lead. Eugene Cunningham. LC 36-300631. 1936. Houghton Mifflin Company.

Whistling Legs. Roman McDougald. 1945. Simon and Schuster.

Whistling Man. Maximilian Foster. LC 13-16790. 1913. 1.30. D. Appleton and Company.

Whistling Shadow. Mabel Seeley. 1972. 0.95 o.p. (ISBN 0-515-02853-3, N2853). Pyramid Pubns.

Whistling Shadow: A Novel of Suspense. Mabel Seeley. LC 54-5365. 1954. Doubleday.

Whistling Woman. Robert Halifax. LC 12-40607. 1912. Frederick A. Stokes Company.

Whistling Zone. Herbert Kubly. LC 63-12574. 1963. Simon and Schuster.

White Acre Vs. Black Acre. A Case at Law. William MacCreary Burwell. LC 6-166892. 1856. J. W. Randolph.

White Acre Vs. Black Acre: A Case at Law. William MacCreary Burwell & J. G. LC 78-8668. 1969. Mnemosyne Pub. Co.

White Album. Joan Didion. (O.s.i.). 1979. 9.95 o.s.i. (ISBN 0-671-22685-1). S&S.

White Alley. Carolyn Wells. LC 15-10721. 1915. J. B. Lippincott Company.

White and Black. Hubert Anthony Shands. LC 22-5074. Harcourt, Brace and Company.

White and Gold Lady. Foxhall Daingerfield. LC 27-16476. George H. Doran Company.

White and the Blues. Alexandre Dumas. LC 6-43621. (Half-title: The romances of Alexandre Dumas. Illustrated library ed. vol. xli-xlii). 1894. Little, Brown, and Company.

White Apples: A Novella, Stories, and Fables. 1st Ed. Arno Karlen. LC 61-12249. (Keystone books, KB-29). 1961. Lippincott.

White Aprons: A Romance of Bacon's Rebellion: Virginia, 1676. Maud Wilder Goodwin. LC 6-31700. 1896. Little, Brown and Co.

White Aprons: A Romance of Bacon's Rebellion, Virginia, 1676. Maud Wilder Goodwin. LC 1-245416. 1901. Little, Brown, and Company.

White Arrow. Robert McNair Wilson. LC 32-63073. 1932. J. B. Lippincott Company.

White As Snow. Isabella Fyvie Mayo. LC 7-18484. 1870. A. D. F. Randolph & Co.

White Ashes. Sidney Robinson Kennedy & Noble, Alden Charles. LC 12-7967. 1912. 1.25. The Macmillan Company.

White Baby: A Novel. James Welsh. F. A. Stokes Company.

White Band, a Novel. Carter Brooke Jones. LC 59-12384. 1959. Funk & Wagnalls.

White Banners. Lloyd Cassel Douglas. LC 62-54. 1961. Grosset & Dunlap.

White Banners. Lloyd Cassel Douglas. LC 36-21188. 1936. Houghton Mifflin Company.

White Bears and Gold. Emmet Claire May. LC 32-332. 1931. R. G. Badger.

White Beeatomb: And Other Stories. William Charles Scully. LC 8-3388. 1897. H. Holt and Company.

White Betrayal: Translated by Derick Wulff. Hellmuth Unger & Wulff, Derick, Tr. LC 29-17922. Brentano's.

White Bikini. Alan Geoffrey Yates. LC 63-6091. (Signet book, S2275). 1963. New American Library of World Literature.

White Birch Abbey: A Characterization of Life at the Abbey. Kilian Beirne. LC 73-88993. (Illus.). 1973. 4.50. Novitiate Press.

White Birches: A Novel. Annie Eliot Trumbull. LC 8-28283. 1893. Harper & Brothers.

White Bird Flying. Bess Streeter Aldrich. 1961. Grosset & Dunlap.

White Bird Flying. Bess Streeter Aldrich. LC 75-29114. 1975. 6.95. Aeonian Press.

White Bird Flying. Bess Streeter Aldrich. LC 31-272093. 1931. S. Appleton and Company.

White Bird Flying. Bess Streeter Aldrich. LC 44-77112. 1944. The Sun Dial Press.

White Blackbird. Robert Aitken. LC 12-21730. 1912. Little, Brown, and Company.

White Blackbird: A Novel. Emma C Gradel. LC 32-318. Burton Publishing Company.

White-Blood. Vara A Majette. LC 24-215860. 1924. The Stratford Company.

White Blood: A Story of the South. Henry Marvin Wharton. LC 6-23162. 1906. The Neale Publishing Company.

White Boar. Marian Palmer. 1973. (pbk) 1.25. Popular Library.

White Boar. Marian Palmer. LC 68-11401. (Illus.). 1968. Doubleday.

White Book. Pavel Kohout. Tr. by Alex Page. LC 76-55846. 224p. 1977. 8.95 (ISBN 0-8076-0861-0). Braziller.

White Book: Adam Juracek, Professor of Drawing and Physical Education at the Pedagogical Institute in K., Vs. Sir Isaac Newton, Professor of Physics at the University of Cambridge: Reconstructed from Contemporary Records and Supplemented by Most Interesting Document. Pavel Kohout. LC 76-1201. 1977. 8.95 (ISBN 0-8076-0861-0). G. Braziller.

White Brigand. Edison Marshall. LC 37-20205. 1937. H. C. Kinsey & Company, Inc.

White Buck; Legend of the Border. Sarah Minier Sanborne Weaver. LC 57-14173. 1957. Naylor Co.

White Buffalo. Robert Ames Bennet. LC 35-16055. 1935. I. Washburn, Inc.

White Buffalo. Richard Sale. LC 75-11574. 1975. 7.95 (ISBN 0-671-22072-1). Simon and Schuster.

White Bull. Henry Blanchard. LC 47-5151. 1947. Doubleday.

White Bull: With Saul & Various Short Pieces. Voltaire. Tr. by C. E. Vulliamy. 1979. Repr. of 1929 ed. lib. bdg. 30.00 (ISBN 0-8495-5514-0). Arden Lib.

White Butterflies: And Other Stories. Kate Upson Clark. LC 75-103505. (Short story index reprint series). 1969. Books for Libraries Press.

White Butterflies and Other Stories. Kate Upson Clark. LC 2067. 1900. J. F. Taylor & Company.

White Cad Cross-up. William F. Nolan. LC 69-12921. (His The Bart Challis series). 1969. Sherbourne Press.

White Camelia. Francis Durham Grierson. LC 29-6666. E. J. Clode, Inc.

White Candles, Sex, & Michele Dubois. Danielle Bourde. 160p. 1975. 7.50 o.p. (ISBN 0-682-48337-0). Exposition.

White Castello. Marjorie McEvoy. Ed. by Alice Sachs. 1970. 3.95 o.p. Lenox Hill.

White Castle of Louisiana. Corfnelia Randolph Murrell. LC 3-32798. 1903. J. P. Morton & Company.

White Cat. Gelett Burgess. 1907. The Bobbs-Merrill Company.

White Charger. Elsa Triolet & Thielens, Gerrie (Ollier) 1909- Tr. LC 47-256. 1946. Rinehart & Company, Inc.

White Cherry Tree. Dorothy Worley. LC 56-13304. 1956. Avalon Books.

White Cheyenne. Frederick Faust. LC 60-66965. 1974. (pbk.) 0.95. Warner Paperback Library.

White Chief. Thomas Mayne Reid. LC 68-23726. (Americans in Fiction Ser.). (Illus.). lib. bdg. 16.00 (ISBN 0-8398-1752-5); pap. text ed. 4.95x (ISBN 0-89197-975-1). Irvington.

White Chief. Thomas Mayne Reid. (Americans in Fiction Ser: No. 66). 1968. Repr. of 1855 ed. lib. bdg. 11.50x o.p. (ISBN 0-8398-1752-5). Gregg.

White Chief Among the Red Men: Or, Knight of the Golden Melice; a Historical Romance. By the Author of "The Lost Hunter"... John Turvill Adams. 1859. Derby & Jackson.

White Christmas. Fannie Hurst. LC 42-249781. 1942. Doubleday, Doran and Co., Inc.

White Christopher: A Story. Annie Trumbull Slosson. LC 1-30828. 1901. J. Pott & Company.

White Church. A. C Pierson. LC 7-35902. 1887. Standard Publishing Co.

White Cipher. Henry Leverage. LC 19-10466. 1919. Moffat, Yard & Company.

White Circle. Carroll John Daly. LC 26-15708. E. J. Clode, Inc.

White Citadel. Charles Neider. LC 54-7519. 1954. Twayne Publishers.

White City. 1st Ed. Diane Seide. LC 55-10855. Vantage Press.

White Coat. Petr Nikolaevich Krasnov. Tr. by Vitali, Olga. Ed. by Brock, Henry Irving. LC 29-21546. 1929. Duffield and Company.

White Cockade. Charles James Louis Gilson. LC 23-12997. 1923. D. Appleton and Company.

White Cockade. Henry Farrand Griffin. LC 42-6832. The Greystone Press.

White Cockade: An Historical Novel. Vincent O'Brien. LC 63-11938. 1963. Abelard-Schuman.

White Cockade: Or, Faith and Fortitude. James Grant. LC 44-245580. G. Routledge and Sons.

White Cockades: An Incident of the "Forty-Five,". Edward Irenaeus Prime- Stevenson. 1887. C. Scribner's Sons.

White Cockatoo... Mignon Good Eberhart. LC 33-2219. 1933. Pub. for the Crime Club, Inc., by Doubleday, Doran & Company, Inc.

White Collar. Giacomo Patri. LC 75-9440. (Illus.). 1975. pap. 4.95 o.p. (ISBN 0-89087-101-9). Celestial Arts.

White Collar Girl. Faith Baldwin. 1976. Repr. of 1933 ed. lib. bdg. 16.30x (ISBN 0-88411-614-X). Amereon Ltd.

White Collar Girl. Faith Baldwin Cuthrell. LC 74-82155. 1975. (ISBN 0-88411-614-X). Aeonian Press.

White Collar Girl. Faith Baldwin Cuthrell. LC 33-11404. Farrar & Rinehart, Incorporated.

White Colors. Franklin D. Reeve. LC 73-81499. 1973. 7.95 (ISBN 0-374-28927-1). Farrar, Straus and Giroux.

White Colt. David Rook. LC 67-26601. (Illus.). 1967. Dutton.

White Columns. Cynthia Van Hazinga. (Orig.). 1980. pap. 2.75 (ISBN 0-440-19419-9). Dell.

White Company. Arthur Conan Doyle. (Illus.). 1975. (pbk.) 3.95. Hart.

White Company. Arthur Conan Doyle. LC 76-376204. (Illus.). 1975-1976. 9.50 (ISBN 0-7195-3225-6). J. Murray: Cape.

White Company. Arthur Conan Doyle. LC 62-9721. (Great illustrated classics). (Illus.). 1962. Dodd, Mead.

White Company. copyright ed. Arthur Conan Doyle. (On cover: Lovell's international ser. no. 176). J. W. Lovell Company.

White Company. Arthur Conan Doyle. LC 27-21618. (father and son library). J. H. Sears & Company, Inc.

White Company. Arthur Conan Doyle. LC 35-28572. Grosset & Dunlap.

White Company. Arthur Conan Doyle. 15.95 o.p. (ISBN 0-7195-3225-6). Transatlantic.

White Company. Arthur Conan Doyle & Bessey, Mabel Abbot, 1884- Ed. LC 27-12292. (Academy classics for junior high schools). Allyn and Bacon.

White Company. Arthur Conan Doyle & Wyeth, Newell Convers, 1882- Illus. LC 22-21570. 1922. Cosmopolitan Book Corporation.

White Company: A Novel. Arthur Conan Doyle. LC 16-7562. Harper & Brothers.

White Company: A Novel. Arthur Conan Doyle. LC 4-16521. 1894. Harper & Brothers,

White Company: A Novel. Arthur Conan Doyle. LC 25-154915. Harper & Brothers.

White Company: A Novel. Arthur Conan Doyle. LC 28-26942. 1929. Harper & Brothers.

White Company: A Novel. Arthur Conan Doyle. LC 43-5901. 1943. Garden City Publishing Co., Inc.

White Corn Sister. 2nd ed. Peter Blue Cloud. (Illus.). 1981. pap. 4.00 (ISBN 0-936574-02-X). Strawberry Pr NY.

White Cottage. Gwendoline Keats. LC 1-31551. 1901. C. Scribner's Sons.

White Cowl. Fannie Hewitt Harrison. LC 37-2321. Burney Brothers Publishing Co.

White Crane Has No Mourners. Han Shan. Tr. by Jim Hardesty & Art Tobias. Bd. with Honking Geese. Basho & Etsujin. Tr. by Etsuko Terasaki & Rich Jorgensen. 1978. pap. 3.00. Stone Pr Calif.

White Crash Helmet. Pete Fry. LC 70-79122. 1969. 3.95 o.p. Roy.

White Crash Helmet. Clifford King. LC 70-79122. 1969. 3.95. Roy Publishers.

White Crocus. Peter Packer. LC 47-30558. 1947. Whittlesey House.

White Crow. Philip MacDonald. LC 28-24949. 1928. L. MacVeagh, The Dial Press.

White Crown and Other Stories. Herbert Dickinson Ward. LC 8-36031. 1894. Houghton, Mifflin and Company.

White Cruiser: Or, The Fate of the Unheard-of. A Tale of Land and Sea; of Crime and Mystery. Edward Zane Carroll Judson. LC 7-11656. 1853. Garrett & Co.

White Dacoit. Berkely Mather. LC 74-9790. (Illus.). 1974. 6.95 (ISBN 0-684-13942-1). Scribner.

White Darkness: And Other Stories of the Great Northwest. Lawrence Mott. LC 74-150554. (Short story index reprint series). (Illus.). 1971. (ISBN 0-8369-3851-8). Books for Libraries Press.

White Darkness: And Other Stories of the Great Northwest. Lawrence Mott. LC 7-4162. 1907. The Outing Publishing Company.

White Dawn. Belle Hagen Winslow. LC 21-167693. 1920. Augsburg Publishing House.

White Dawn: A Legend of Ticonderoga. Theodora Agnes Peck. LC 14-16199. 1.25. Fleming H. Revell Company.

White Dawn: An Eskimo Saga. by james houston. drawings by the author ed. James A. Houston. (Signet novel, Y5280). (Illus.). 1972. 1.25. New American Lib.

White Dawn: An Eskimo Saga. James A. Houston. LC 72-134575. (Illus.). 1971. (ISBN 0-15-196115-8). Harcourt Brace Jovanovich.

White Death. Robert Sheckley. LC 63-19054. 1963. Bantam Books.

White Desert. Courtney Ryley Cooper. LC 22-2310. 1922. 1.75. Little, Brown and Company.

White Devil. Luis De Oteyza. Tr. by Cooper, Frederic Tabor. LC 30-284003. 1930. Frederick A. Stokes Company.

White Devil. rev. & enl. ed. John Webster. Ed. by F. L. Lucas. 1958. text ed. 5.00x o.p. Humanities.

White Devil of the Black Sea. Lewis Stanton Palen. LC 24-9682. 1924. Minton, Balch & Company.

White Devil of Verde. A Story of the West. Lucie France Pierce. LC 98-1761. 1898. G. W. Dillingham Co.

White Devil's Mate. Lewis Stanton Palen. LC 26-167058. 1926. Houghton Mifflin Company.

White Dog. Romain Gary, pseud. 1970. 6.95 o.p. (H0334, NAL). Norton.

White Dog. Ruth Ellen Allen Morris. 1974. 4.00 (ISBN 0-533-00999-5). Vantage Press.

White Dog. Fyodor Sologeib. Ed. by Isaac Goldberg. Tr. by John Cournos. (International Pocket Library). pap. 2.00 o.s.i. Branden.

White Dome. Laura Morrison. LC 30-13347. The Christopher Publishing House.

White Dominoes. Florence Mae Pettee. LC 21-5079. The Reilly & Lee Co.

White Dove. Helen Corse Berney. LC 56-12590. 1956. Crown.

White Dove. William John Locke. LC 16-191653. 1912. John Lane.

White Dove: A Novel. William John Locke. 1900. J. Lane.

White Dove in the Oak. M. Honora Zimmer. 1963. 5.00 o.p. (ISBN 0-87482-074-X). Wake-Brook.

White Dragon. Anne McCaffrey. LC 77-18913. (McCaffrey, Anne. The Dragonriders of Pern). (Illus.). 1978. 8.95 (ISBN 0-345-27567-5). Ballantine Books.

White Dragon. Anne McCaffrey. (Her The Dragonrirs of Pern; V.3). (Illus.). 1979. 2.25. Ballantine Books.

White Eagle. Mary Teresa Waggaman. LC 15-246681. The Ave Maria Press.

White Eagle, Dark Skies. Jean Karsavina. LC 73-1113. 1974. 9.95 (ISBN 0-684-13670-8). Scribner.

White Eagles, a Story of 1812 ... LC 29-23361. 1929. Houghton Mifflin Company.

White Eagles Over Serbia. Lawrence Durrell. LC 58-7779. 1958. 10.95 (ISBN 0-87599-030-4). S G Phillips.

White Elephant: A Story. Charles Reade. LC 7-39654. Gibson & King.

White Ensigns. Henry Taprell Dorling, pseud. LC 43-41804. 1943. G. P. Putnam's Sons.

White Eskimo. Harold Horwood. LC 72-76171. 264p. 1972. 5.95 o.p. (ISBN 0-385-04346-5). Doubleday.

White Face. Carl Ruthven Offord. LC 73-18596. 1975. 18.00 (ISBN 0-404-11407-5). AMS Press.

White Face. Carl Ruthven Offord. LC 43-8249. 1943. R. M. McBride & Company.

White Face... Edgar Wallace. LC 31-2441. Pub. for the Crime Club, Inc., by Doubleday, Doran & Company, Inc.

White Fang. Jack London. (Reader's enrichment ser., RE119). Washington Sq.

White Fang. Jack London. LC 37-18321. (works of Jack London). The Review of Reviews Company.

White Fang. Jack London. LC 5-37586. 1905. The Macmillan Company.

White Fang. Jack London. 1906. The Macmillan Company.

White Fang. Jack London. LC 21-4149. 1914. Grosset & Dunlap.

White Fang. Jack London. LC 16-13119. 1914. The Macmillan Company.

White Fang. Jack London & Limited Editions Club, Inc., New York. LC 74-171887. (Illus.). 1973. Printed at the Stinehour Press for the Members of the Limited Editions Club.

White Fang: And Other Stories. Jack London. LC 63-9542. (Great illustrated classics). (Illus.). 1963. Dodd, Mead.

White Fang. With Four Colour Plates and Line Drawings in the Text by Charles Pickard. Jack London. LC 68-86113. 1967. 3.95. Dent.

White Father. Julian Mitchell. LC 65-10512. 1965. bds., 4.95. Farrar.

White Feather. Jessie Catherine Huybers Couvreur. (On cover: Lovell's international series, no. 217). 1891. Lovell, Coryell & Company.

White Feather. Lechmere Worrall & Terry, J. E. Harold, Joint Author. LC 15-13208. E. J. Clode.

White Feathers." A Novel. William James Roe. LC 7-40733. 1885. J. B. Lippincott & Co.

White Figure, White Ground. Hugh Hood. LC 64-11081. 1964. Dutton.

White Fire. Charlotte H A Benton. LC 53-1658. 1953. Story Book Press.

White Fire. Rebecca Danton, pseud. 1982. pap. 2.75 (ISBN 0-449-24477-6, Crest). Fawcett.

White Fire. Edward J. Edwards. LC 43-17351. 1943. The Bruce Publishing Company.

White Fire. Jan MacLean. (Harlequin Romances Ser.). 192p. 1980. pap. 1.25 (ISBN 0-373-02348-0, Pub. by Harlequin). PB.
White Fire: A Novel. Louis Joseph Vance. LC 26-1955. E. P. Dutton & Company.
White Fires Burning. Catherine Dillon. (Signet Book). 1977. 1.75 (ISBN 0-451-07351-7). New American Library.
White Flag. Gene Stratton Porter. LC 23-13098. 1923. Doubleday, Page & Company.
White Flag. Stratton-Porter, Gene. LC 81-19054. 1982. 22.15 (ISBN 0-89190-943-5). American Reprint Co.
White Flag. Marcello Venturi. LC 70-79779. 1969. 5.95 (ISBN 0-8149-0004-6). Vanguard Press.
White Flame an Occult Story. Mary Ann Mann Cornelius. Stockham Publishing Co.
White Flesh for Black Markets. John G Garten. LC 77-78543. 9.95 (ISBN 0-89343-012-9). Ermine Publishers.
White Flower. Grace Livingston Hill. LC 27-21883. 1927. J. B. Lippincott Company.
White Flower. Stella Rybacki. LC 49-626. 1948. Christopher Pub. House.
White Flowers in the Snow. Penny Harter. LC 81-80549. (Illus.). 95p. 1981. pap. 3.00 (ISBN 0-89823-024-1). New Rivers Pr.
White Fog. Roxanne Dent. 1975. (pbk.) 0.95 (ISBN 0-380-00218-3). Avon.
White for a Shroud. Donald Clough Cameron. LC 47-31022. 1947. Pub. for Mystery House, by S. Curl.
White for Danger. David Stevens. LC 78-66260. 1979. 9.95 (ISBN 0-8128-2596-9). Stein and Day.
White Forest Battle. Harold Calin. (Leisure book). 1.75 (ISBN 0-8439-0624-3). Nordon Pubns.
White Fountain. Mildred McNaughton. LC 49-8389. 1949. Doubleday.
White Fox. Charles Elbert Scoggins. LC 28-55645. The Bobbs-Merrill Company.
White Gate. Warwick Deeping. LC 35-8189. 1935. R. M. McBride & Company.
White Ghost of Disaster: The Chief Mate's Yarn. Thornton Jenkins Hains. LC 12-12862. 1.25. G. W. Dillingham Company.
White Ghost of Fenwick Hall. Wharton, Althea. 1974. (pbk.) 0.95 (ISBN 0-671-77909-5). Pocket Books.
White Girl. Vera Caspary. LC 29-1200. J. H. Sears & Company, Inc.
White Girl of Spirit Island: A Story of Love and Adventure. George W Greene. LC 27-152161. The Christopher Publishing House.
White God of the Aztecs. William Arthur Berg. LC 60-15829. 1961. B. Humphries.
White Gods. Richard Friedenthal. Tr. by Lumley, Charles Hope. 1931. Harper & Brothers.
White God's Way. Stanley Shaw. LC 26-149199. Barse & Hopkins.
White Gold: A Mystery Romance of the Great Lakes. Myron David Orr. LC 36-21685. 1936. Capper, Harman, Slocum, Inc.
White Gold: A Rosicrucian Romance. John Pinckney Scott & Scott, Dorothy. LC 37-39104. The Langford Press.
White Gold Wielder. Stephen R Donaldson. LC 82-20640. (Second chronicles of Thomas Covenant; book 3). ((Series: Donaldson, Stephen R.). (Second chronicles of Thomas Covenant; book 3.). 1983. 14.95 (ISBN 0-345-30307-5). Ballantine Books.
White Guard. Mikhail Afanasevich Bulgakov. LC 75-26951. (McGraw-Hill paperbacks). 1975. (ISBN 0-07-008853-5). McGraw-Hill.
White Guard to Satan: Being an Account of Mine Own Adventures and Observation in That Time of the Trouble in Virginia Now Called Bacon's Rebellion, Which Same Did Take Place in... 1676. Alice Maude Ewell. LC 1-29037. 1900. Houghton, Mifflin and Company.
White Gulls Flying. Anne Tedlock Brooks. LC 53-621546. 1953. Arcadia House.
White Hand. A Story of Noblesse Oblige. Ella Farman Pratt. LC 21-13954. 1875. D. Lothrop & Co.
White Hand. A Story of Noblesse Oblige. Ella Farman Pratt. LC 20-193328. (On cover: The household library. no. 12). 1887. D. Lothrop & Co.
White Hand Murder Mystery. Mary Elizabeth Campbell. LC 37-10697. 1936. Renaissance Book Company.
White Hands. Arthur John Arbuthnott Stringer. LC 27-18769. The Bobbs-Merrill Company.
White Hare: A Novel. Francis Stuart. LC 36-23265. 1936. The Macmillan Company.
White Hart. Nancy Springer. 2.25. Pocket Books.
White Hart of Penlinton. Mair Unsworth. 1974. (pbk.) 0.75. Ace Books.
White Hawthorn. Lucille Papin Borden. LC 35-349162. 1935. The Macmillan Company.
White Heather. Mollie Dale. LC 38-5357. The Deseret News Press.
White Heather. A Novel. William Black. LC 6-13857. (Harper's Franklin square library, no. 496). Harper & Brothers.
White Heather. A Novel. William Black. LC 6-12415. (On cover: Lovell's library, v. 12, no. 678). 1885. J. W. Lovell Company.
White Heather: A Novel. William Black. (Seaside library, Pocket ed. no. 627). 1885. G. Munro.
White Heather: A Novel. William Black. 1886. Harper & Brothers.
White Hell. Jake Logan. LC 76-49402. (Jake Logan Ser.). 192p. (Orig.). 1977. pap. 1.95 (ISBN 0-87216-864-6). Playboy Pbks.
White Hell. Jake Logan. LC 76-49402. 1977. 1.25. Playboy Press.
White Hell of Pity. Norah Robinson Lofts. LC 37-28782. 1937. A. A. Knopf.
White Heron: A Novel of the Glades. Bernard Fendig Borchardt. LC 33-289348. The Author.
White Heron: And Other Stories. Sarah Orne Jewett. LC 7-9732. 1886. Houghton, Mifflin and Company.
White Heron: And Other Stories. 3d ed. Sarah Orne Jewett. LC 42-30334. 1887. Houghton, Mifflin and Company.
White Heron & Other Stories. Sarah Orne Jewett. Ed. by Donald Pizer. LC 71-96657. (American Authors Ser., Collected Works of Sarah Orne Jewett). 1970. Repr. of 1886 ed. lib. bdg. 15.95 o.s.i. (ISBN 0-512-00374-2). Garrett Pr.
White Heron & Other Stories see Collected Works.
White Hoods: A Tale of the Free City of Ghent; a Legend of the Fourteenth Century. John Sim. (On cover:The Marguerite series, no. 34). 1894. E. A. Weeks & Company.
White Horse and the Red-Haired Girl. Lorin Andrews Lathrop. LC 19-3998. 1.50. George H. Doran Company.
White Horse Inn. Georges Simenon. LC 79-3363. 7.95 (ISBN 0-15-196240-5). Harcourt Brace Jovanovich.
White Horse of Wootton. A Story of Love, Sport and Adventure in the Midland Counties of England and on the Frontier of America. Charles James Foster. LC 6-40370. Porter & Coates.
White Horse to Banbury Cross. Richard Llewellyn. 1973. 1.25 (ISBN 0-515-02963-7). Pyramid.
White Horse to Banbury Cross. Richard Llewellyn. LC 70-78681. 1970. 5.95. Doubleday.
White Horses. Alice Hoffman. LC 81-17789. 12.95 (ISBN 0-399-12709-7). Putnam.
White Hotel. D M Thomas. LC 80-52004. 1981. 11.95 (ISBN 0-670-76292-X). Viking Press.
White Hound. Frances Forbes-Robertson Harrod. LC 13-54158. 1913. 1.25. Dodd, Mead and Company.
White Hound: Stories. Ward Dorrance & Thomas Mabry. LC 59-9542. 1959. 10.00x o.p. (ISBN 0-8262-0000-1). U of Mo Pr.
White House: A Story. Agnes Vollmar. LC 22-21949. Augustana Book Concern.
White House Case: A Sequel to the Pentagon Case. Victor J. Fox, pseud. LC 68-20839. 1968. Fargo Press.
White House Massacre. Sam Victor. 192p. (Orig.). 1981. pap. 2.25 (ISBN 0-441-88567-5). Ace Bks.
White House Murder Case. Jules Feiffer. (Illus.). 1970. pap. 1.25 o.p. (ISBN 0-394-17173-X, B256, BC). Grove.
White Hunter, Black Heart. Peter Viertel. 1973. (pbk.) 1.50. Dell.
White Hunter, Black Heart. Peter Viertel. LC 53-5600. 1953. Doubleday.
White Indian. Donald Clayton Porter. LC 83-165. (White Indian series; bk. 1). ((Series: Porter, Donald Clayton.). (Colonization of America series; bk. 1.). 1983. 19.95 (ISBN 0-8161-3446-4). G.K. Hall.
White Indian. Edwin Legrand Sabin. LC 25-4212. G. W. Jacobs & Company.
White Indian Series. Donald Clayton Porter. LC 83-171. 1983. 19.95 (ISBN 0-8161-3446-4). G.K. Hall.
White Island. Nina Lansdale. LC 74-18157. 8.95 (ISBN 0-87795-104-7). Arbor House.
White Island. Michael Wood. LC 19-275991. E. P. Dutton & Company.
White Islander. Mary Hartwell Catherwood. LC 6-2074. 1893. The Century Co.
White Isles. Franklin Folsom Phillips. LC 12-7016. 1.50. The C. M. Clark Publishing Co.
White Jacket. Herman Melville. 1956. pap. 1.95 o.p. (E43, Ever). Grove.
White-Jacket. Herman Melville. (Rinehart Editions). 1967. pap. text ed. 2.00 o.p. (ISBN 0-03-063890-9, HoltC). HR&W.
White-Jacket: Or, The World in a Man-of-War. Herman Melville. LC 63-6558. 1950. L. C. Page.
White-Jacket: Or, The World in a Man-of-War. Herman Melville. Ed. by Humphreys, Arthur Raleigh. LC 66-78629. (Classic American texts). 1966. Oxford U.P.
White-Jacket: Or, The World in a Man-of-War. Herman Melville. LC 67-21603. (Writings of Herman Melville, v. 5). (Illus.). 1970. (ISBN 0-8101-0257-9) (ISBN 0-8101-0258-7). Northwestern University Press.
White-Jacket: Or, The World in a Man-of-War. Herman Melville. LC 42-30911. Harper & Brothers.
White-Jacket: Or, The World in a Man-of-War. Herman Melville. LC 7-17946. Harper & Brothers.
White-Jacket: Or, The World in a Man-of-War. Herman Melville. LC 7-258446. United States Book Company.
White-Jacket: Or, the World in a Man-of-War. Ed. by Hennig Cohen. Herman Melville. LC 67-15659. (Rinehart eds.). 1967. pap., 1.95. Holt.
White Jacket: Or, The World in a Man-of-War. With an Introd. by William Plomer. Herman Melville. LC 56-11220. (Evergreen books, E-43). 1956. Grove Press.
White Jade. Willo Davis Roberts. LC 74-14383. 1975. 5.95 (ISBN 0-385-09966-5). Published for the Crime Club by Doubleday.
White Jade Fox. Andre Norton, pseud. LC 74-23871. 1975. 7.95 (ISBN 0-525-42670-1). Dutton.
White Jade Fox. Andre Norton, pseud. (Fawcett Crest Book). 1976. 1.50. Fawcett.
White Kami: A Novel. Edward Alden Jewell. 1922. A. A. Knopf.
White Khan. Catherine Dillon. (Signet Book). 1978. 1.95 (ISBN 0-451-08043-2). New American Library.
White Kids. Michael Wolff. LC 79-9355. 10.95 (ISBN 0-671-40001-0). Summit Books.
White Kimono. 1st Ed. Joseph Emerson Newton. LC 57-830856. 1957. Pageant Press.
White King. Samuel Bertram Harrison. LC 50-5301. 1950. Doubleday.
White King of Africa: Or, The Mystery of the Ancient Fort. William Murray Graydon. LC 99-3779. (On cover: Medal library. no. 16). 1899. Street & Smith.
White King of Manoa. Joseph Hatton. LC 4-8705. R. F. Fenno & Company.
White King of Manoa: An Anglo-Spanish Romance. Joseph Hatton. 358p. 1981. Repr. of 1899 ed. lib. bdg. 35.00 (ISBN 0-89984-273-9). Century Bookbindery.
White Knight. Lachlan Jones. 1979. pap. 4.00 (ISBN 0-89502-035-1). FEB.
White Knight. Alexander L. Taylor. 1973. Repr. of 1952 ed. 20.00 o.p. R West.
White Ladies. Francis Brett Young. 1935. Harper & Brothers.
White Ladies of Worcester: A Romance of the Twelfth Century. Florence Louisa Charlesworth Barclay. LC 17-29028. 1917. 1.50. G. P. Putnam's Sons.
White Lady. Grace Livingston Hill. 1976. Repr. of 1930 ed. lib. bdg. 15.45x (ISBN 0-89190-025-X). Am Repr-Rivercity Pr.
White Lady. Malcolm Strauss. LC 32-3604. 1932. G.H. Watt.
White Lady of Khaminavatka: A Story of the Ukraine. Richard Henry Savage. (On cover: Rialto series, no. 84). 1898. Rand, McNally & Company.
White Land. William Dieter. LC 77-106616. 1970. 5.95. Knopf.
White Leopard. Inglis Clark Fletcher. 304p. 1976. Repr. of 1931 ed. lib. bdg. 16.95x (ISBN 0-89244-013-9). Queens Hse.
White Leopard: A Tale of the African Bush. Inglis Clark Fletcher & Kurt Wiese. LC 78-1718. 1978. 10.50. Queens House.
White Lie Assignment. Peter Driscoll. LC 72-688. 1975. 7.50. (ISBN 0-397-00904-6). Lippincott.
White Lie Assignment. Peter Driscoll. 1977. 1.95 (ISBN 0-445-08582-7). Popular Library.
White Lies. Charles Reade. LC 49-371291. (works of Charles Reade. Library ed.). 1895. Metropolitan Pub. Co.
White Lies. Charles Reade. (Seaside library, v. 3, no. 41). 1877. G. Munro.
White Lies. A Novel. Charles Reade. LC 25-15520. 1858. Ticknor and Fields.
White Lies. A Novel. household ed. Charles Reade. 1869. Fields, Osgood, & Co.
White Lies. A Novel. Charles Reade. LC 42-271325. 1870. Harper & Brothers.
White Light. Leonora Arent. LC 27-2990. The Christopher Publishing House.
White Lightning. Edwin Herbert Lewis. LC 23-969090. 1923. Covici-McGee.
White Lilly see Seeds of Life.
White Linen Nurses. Eleanor Hallowell Abbott. LC 13-212922. 1913. The Century Co.
White Lotus. John Richard Hersey. LC 65-11104. 1965. A. A. Knopf.
White Madness. Alice Alberthe Robertson. LC 28-29964. 1928. H. Vinal, Ltd.
White Madness. Alice Alberthe Robertson. LC 34-34435. 1934. Williams Publishing Company.
White Magic. Faith Baldwin. 1976. Repr. of 1939 ed. lib. bdg. 16.30x (ISBN 0-88411-615-8). Amereon Ltd.
White Magic. Faith Baldwin Cuthrell. LC 74-82156. 1975. 6.95 (ISBN 0-88411-615-8). Aeonian Press.
White Magic. Faith Baldwin Cuthrell. LC 39-27768. Farrar & Rinehart, Inc.
White Magic. Faith Baldwin Cuthrell. 1974. (pbk.) 0.95. Warner Paperback Lib.
White Magic. David Graham Phillips. (American Author Ser.). 1981. Repr. lib. bdg. 29.00. Scholarly.
White Magic. David Graham Phillips. 1910. lib. bdg. 19.75 o.s.i. (ISBN 0-512-00162-6). Garrett Pr.
White Magic: A Novel. David Graham Phillips. LC 72-84645. (Illus.). 1974. (lib. ed.) 19.75 (ISBN 0-403-02967-8). Scholarly Press.
White Magic: A Novel. David Graham Phillips. LC 10-7930. 1910. D. Appleton and Company.
White Mail. Cy Warman. LC 99-4130. 1899. C. Scribner's Sons.
White Mambo. Marilyn Allen. (Berkley Medallion Book). 1977. 1.50 (ISBN 0-425-03318-X). Berkely Pub. Corp.
White Man. George Agnew Chamberlain. LC 19-2324. 1.75. The Bobbs-Merrill Company.
White Man. Peter Freuchen. LC 46-6618. 1946. Rinehart & Company, Inc.
White Man a Tale of the West Indies and Other Stories. Cholly Aber-Nethy. (Illus.). 1974. 5.95 (ISBN 0-533-01101-9). Vantage Press.
White Man of God. Kenjo Jumbam. (African Writers Ser.). (Orig.). 1981. pap. text ed. 4.50x (ISBN 0-435-90231-8). Heinemann Ed.
White Mandarin. Dan Sherman. LC 81-66957. 352p. 1982. 15.25 (ISBN 0-87795-325-2). Arbor Hse.
White Man's Burden: A Satirical Forecast. Roger Sherman Tracy. LC 72-4597. (Black Heritage Library Collection). 1972. 14.50 (ISBN 0-8369-9130-3). Books for Libraries Press.
White Man's Burden; a Satirical Forecast. Roger Sherman Tracy. LC 15-5594. The Gorham Press; Etc., Etc.
White Man's Chance. Johnston McCulley. LC 27-131248. 1927. G. H. Watt.
White Man's Justice: Black Man's Grief. Donald Goines. 1973. (pbk) 1.50. Holloway House.
White Man's Road. Benjamin Capps. LC 78-85926. 1969. 6.95. Harper & Row.
White Marble Lady. Roi Ottley. LC 65-137278. bds., 4.95. Farrar.
White Marie: A Story of Georgian Plantation Life. William Nathaniel Harben. Cassell & Company.
White Mazurka. Bettina Boyers. LC 46-4934. 1946. Pub. for the Crime Club by Doubleday, & Company, Inc.
White Men, Red Men: And Mountain Men, by Bill Gulick. Grover C Gulick. LC 55-6129. 1955. Houghton Mifflin.
White Menace. Cecil John Charles Street. LC 26-24138. 1926. R. M. McBride & Company.
White Mice. Richard Harding Davis. LC 9-13544. 1909. C. Scribner's Sons.
White Midnight. Cillay Risku. LC 77-73436. 1977. 1.50. Playboy Press.
White Moll. Frank Lucius Packard. LC 20-8628. George H. Doran Company.
White Money: A Novel of the East Indies. Madelon Lulofs & Renier, Gustaaf Johannes, 1892- Tr. LC 33-13755. The Century Co.
White Monkey. John Galsworthy. LC 24-251821. 1924. C. Scribner's Sons.
White Monkey: And A Silent Wooing. John Galsworthy. LC 74-8099. ((His). (Scribner library.). (Forsyte chronicles, v.). (Contemporary classics.). 1969. 1.95. Scribner.
White Morning. Gertrude Franklin Horn Atherton. 1918. lib. bdg. 15.00 (ISBN 0-8414-3099-3). Folcroft.
White Morning: A Novel of the Power of the German Women in Wartime. Gertrude Franklin Horn Atherton. LC 18-3020. Frederick A. Stokes Company.
White Moth. Ruth Murray Underhill. LC 20-20002. 1920. Moffat, Yard and Company.
White Motley: A Novel. Max Pemberton. LC 11-11283. 1911. 1.30. Sturgis & Walton Company.
White Mouse. Anice Morris Stockton Terhune. LC 29-17392. 1929. Harper & Brothers.
White Mule. William Carlos Williams. LC 37-11249. 1937. New Directions.
White Mule: A Novel. William Carlos Williams. LC 67-3209. 1967. Published for J. Laughlin by New Directions Pub. Co.
White Narcissus: A Novel. Raymond Knister. LC 29-15565. Harcourt, Brace and Company.
White Nigger: A Story of the Old South. Winfield P Woolf & Orr, Angus Elgin, Joint Author. LC 38-25159. The Christopher Publishing House.
White Night, a Novel. Forrest Rosaire. LC 56-10809. 1956. Lippincott.

White Nights: And Other Stories. Fedor Mikhailovich Dostoevskii & Garnett, Mrs. Constance (Black) 1862- Tr. LC 19-411232. (Half-title: The novels of Fyodor Dostoevsky, vol. X). 1918. The Macmillan Company.

White Nights and Other Stories. Fedor Mikhailovich Dostoevskii & Garnett, Mrs. Constance (Black) 1862- Tr. LC 32-33164. (Half-title: The novels of Fyodor Dostoevsky. Vol. X). 1923. The Macmillan Company.

White Nights, Red Dawn. Frederick W. Nolan. LC 80-16653. 12.95 (ISBN 0-02-589850-7). Macmillan.

White Noon. Sigrid Van Sweringen. LC 39-31049. 1939. Benziger Brothers.

White Oak Farm. Elliott Crayton McCants. LC 28-24478. 1928. Longmans, Green and Co.

White Oak Heritage. Mazo De La Roche. 1974. (pbk.) 1.25. Fawcett.

White Oleander. Anne Wormser. LC 47-174444. 1947. Macrae-Smith-Company.

White on Black on White. Coleman Dowell. 251p. 1983. 14.95 (ISBN 0-88150-000-3). Countryman.

White Orchid. Henrietta Mason. LC 53-10841. 1953. Longmans, Green.

White Orchids. Grace Livingston Hill. LC 35-780921. J. B. Lippincott Company.

White Owl. Edmund Snell. LC 30-14659. 1930. J. B. Lippincott Company.

White Oxen: And Other Stories. Kenneth Burke. LC 25-1771. 1924. A. & C. Boni.

White Panther. Theodore J Waldeck & Wiese, Kurt, 1887- Illus. LC 41-226752. 1941. The Viking Press.

White Panthers. Derek Vane. LC 30-485613. 1930. The Macmillan Company.

White Pants Willie. Elmer Holmes Davis. LC 32-341027. The Bobbs-Merrill Company.

White Parade. Rian James. LC 34-23092. A. H. King.

White Paternoster, and Other Stories. Theodore Francis Powys. LC 70-178455. (Short story index reprint series). 1971. (ISBN 0-8369-4056-3). Books for Libraries Press.

White Path, a Novel. Eleanor Howard Waring. LC 7-41587. 1907. The Neale Publishing Company.

White Pavilion. Velda Johnston. LC 74-3342. 1974. 9.95 (ISBN 0-8161-6201-8). G. K. Hall.

White Pavilion: A Novel of Suspense. Velda Johnston. LC 73-7484. 1973. 5.95 (ISBN 0-396-06851-0). Dodd, Mead.

White Pavilion: A Novel of Suspense. Velda Johnston. (Signet book). 1979. 1.95 (ISBN 0-451-08700-3). New American Library.

White Peacock. David Herbert Lawrence. LC 65-23079. (Crosscurrents: modern fiction). 1966. Southern Illinois University Press.

White Peacock. Mary Linn Roby. LC 72-2143. 1972. 5.95. Hawthorn Books.

White Peacock: A Novel. David Herbert Lawrence. LC 11-1960. 1911. Duffield & Company.

White Pearl: A Romance. Samuel Field & Delano, Mrs. Edith (Barnard) LC 16-14562. 1916. 1.25. Duffield & Company.

White People. Frances Hodgson Burnett. LC 17-5128. 1917. 1.20. Harper & Brothers.

White Peril: The Secret Memoir of "Ralph Doubell". George Bartram. 1977. 1.95 (ISBN 0-445-04072-6). Popular Library.

White Petticoat. Eva McDonald. 1973. pap. 0.75 o.p. (07295). Curtis.

White Pierrot. Pamela Barrington, pseud. LC 31-7374. Sears Publishing Company, Inc.

White Pills: A Novel. Ted Carroll. LC 64-23804. 1964. Crown Publishers.

White Pine Mirage. Adelbert Alanson Alvord. LC 41-19188. Fortuny's.

White Piracy. James Warner Bellah. LC 33-27325. Farrar & Rinehart, Incorporated.

White Plague. Frank Herbert. LC 82-7586. 13.95 (ISBN 0-399-12721-6). Putnam.

White Plume. Samuel Rutherford Crockett. LC 6-34687. 1906. Dodd, Mead & Company.

White Plume. Samuel Edwards, pseud. 1971. pap. 0.95 o.p. (09114). Curtis.

White Plume. Noel Bertram Gerson. LC 61-13546. 1961. Morrow.

White Poppy. Helena Osborne. LC 76-58847. 1977. 7.95 (ISBN 0-698-10763-2). Coward, McCann & Geoghegan.

White Poppy. Helena Osborne. 1979. 1.95 (ISBN 0-671-81991-7). Pocket Books.

White Priory Murders. John Dickson Carr. LC 34-402963. 1934. W. Morrow and Company.

White Prophet. Hall Caine. LC 9-23731. 1909. D. Appleton and Company.

White Prophet. Hall Caine. LC 41-42330. 1909. Grosset & Dunlap.

White Python: Adventure and Mystery in Tibet. Mark Channing. LC 34-33675. J. B. Lippincott Company.

White Python: Adventure and Mystery in Tibet. Mark Channing. LC 77-84208. (Lost Race and Adult Fantasy Fiction). 1978. 20.00 (ISBN 0-405-10964-4). Arno Press.

White Quartz and Gold: Stories of the Mother Lode and The Boom Town Shylock. Roy Beach. LC 37-8783. Printed at the Davis Press.

White Queen. Betty Baur. LC 42-20809. 1942. The Viking Press.

White Queen. Frederic Fallon. 1973. (pbk) 1.50. Warner Paperback Library.

White Queen. Frederic Fallon. LC 75-175682. 1972. 6.95. Doubleday.

White Queen. Lesley J Nickell. LC 79-5039. 1979. 10.95 (ISBN 0-312-86785-9). St. Martin's Press.

White Queen: A Tale of the Youth of St. Louis, King of France. William Stearns Davis. The Macmillan Company.

White Quiver. Helen Fitzgerald Sanders. LC 13-13963. 1913. Duffield & Company.

White Rabbit. Kaye Dobkin. (Looking Glass Ser.: No. 3). (Orig.). 1983. pap. 3.50 (ISBN 0-440-09740-1). Dell.

White Rainbow. Alan Harrington. LC 81-8448. 13.95 (ISBN 0-316-34764-7). Little, Brown.

White Rajah. Nicholas Monsarrat. LC 61-13543. 1961. W. Sloane Associates.

White Rat: Short Stories. Gayl Jones. LC 77-6020. 7.95 (ISBN 0-394-49939-5). Random House.

White Reef. Martha Ostenso. LC 34-34436. 1934. Dodd, Mead & Company.

White Riband: Or, A Young Female's Folly. Fryniwyd Tennyson Jesse. LC 22-6515. 1.50. George H. Doran Company.

White Ribboner: Or, How Paul Hamilton Won the Victory. Horace G McDonald. LC 20-776. Bethel Publishing Company.

White Rider... Leslie Charteris. LC 30-24546. 1930. Pub. for the Crime Club, Inc., by Doubleday, Doran & Company, Inc.

White Rising: A Novel. Zane Kotker. LC 80-20011. 11.95 (ISBN 0-394-40776-8). Knopf: Distributed by Random House.

White River Pete Sez. Byron Bradfield. 1978. pap. 4.50 (ISBN 0-917624-08-4). Lame Johnny.

White River Raft: The Largely True Story of a Logging Trip into the Flooded Forests of Arkansas, Followed by an Eventful Voyage Down the Mississippi. Lewis Bennett Miller. LC 10-24481. D. Estes & Company.

White Roads. George Washington Ogden. LC 32-22210. 1932. Dodd, Mead & Company.

White Rock: A Novel. Denys Val Baker. LC 47-243121. 1947. D. Appleton-Century Company Inc.

White Rocks: A Novel. Edouard Rod. LC 7-39803. T. Y. Crowell & Company.

White Rocks: Or, The Robbers' Den. A Tragedy of the Mountains. Alonzo F. Hill. LC 7-4943. 1866. J. E. Potter.

White Rocks: Or, The Robbers' Den. A Tragedy of the Mountains. Alonzo F Hill. LC 42-26579. 1890. The Keystone Publishing Co.

White Rook. John Burland Harris-Burland. LC 18-139111. 1918. A. A. Knopf.

White Room. Leslie Purnell Davies. LC 69-20097. 1969. 4.50. Published for the Crime Club by Doubleday.

White Room: An Incredible Tale. Elizabeth Jane Coatsworth. (O.S.I.). (Illus.). 1958. 5.95 o.s.i. (ISBN 0-394-45177-5). Pantheon.

White Room. Illustrated by George W. Thompson. Elizabeth Jane Coatsworth. LC 58-609333. 1958. Pantheon Books.

White Rose. Alanna Knight. 1977. pap. 1.25 o.s.i. (ISBN 0-8439-0465-8, Leisure Bks). Nordon Pubns.

White Rose. Alanna Knight. 1974. (pbk.) 0.95 (ISBN 0-380-00183-7). Avon.

White Rose. Clare Rossiter. LC 77-12260. 1978. 7.95 (ISBN 0-312-86789-1). St. Martin's Press.

White Rose. B Traven. LC 78-24774. 8.95 (ISBN 0-88208-099-7). L. Hill.

White Rose. Jan Vlachos Westcott. LC 69-18199. 1969. 6.95. Putnam.

White Rose. George John Whyte-Melville. LC 7-258462. 1900. Longmans, Green & Co.

White Rose: And Other Stories... Josephine Earl Sheffield Porter. LC 7-33196. 1907. The Tuttle, Morehouse & Taylor Company.

White Rose of Memphis: A Novel. William C Falkner. LC 6-384222. 1881. G. W. Carleton & Co.; Etc., Etc.

White Rose of Memphis: A Novel; with an Introd. by Robert Cantwell. William C Falkner. LC 53-7415. 1953. Coley Taylor.

White Rose of the Miami. Mary David Ammerman. LC 11-14098. 1.50. Broadway Publishing Co.

White Rose of Winter. Anne Mather. (Presents Ser.). 1974. pap. 1.25 (ISBN 0-373-70565-4, 70565, Pub. by Harlequin). PB.

White Roses. Katharine Holland Brown. LC 10-23315. 1910. 1.20. Duffield and Company.

White Rover: Or, The Lovely Maid of Louisiana. A Romance of the Wild Forest. John Hovey Robinson. LC 7-42168. S. French.

White Russian Passport: A Novel. Del Frazier. LC 41-7326. Oxford Press.

White Sail. Sara Ware Bassett. LC 49-117842. 1949. Doubleday.

White Sails Crowding. Edmund Gilligan. LC 39-289793. 1939. C. Scribner's Sons.

White Sand of Shrahama. 1st Ed. Kenneth Church Lamott. LC 54-8282. 1954. Little, Brown.

White Sand. The Story of a Dreamer and His Dream. Marie Clothilde Balfour. LC 6-6322. The Merriam Company.

White Sand, Wild Sea. Diana Blayne. (Candlelight Ecstasy Ser.: No. 138). (Orig.). 1983. pap. 1.95 (ISBN 0-440-19627-2). Dell.

White Sapphire: A Mystery Romance. Lee Foster Hartman. LC 14-30184. 1914. Harper & Brothers.

White Satin and Homespun. Kate Nichols Trask. LC 8-29722. A. D. F. Randolph and Company.

White Satin Dress. Mary Raymond Shipman Andrews. LC 30-6535. 1930. C. Scribner's Sons.

White Savage. Arthur William Upfield. LC 61-9563. 1961. Published for the Crime Club by Doubleday.

White Savannahs. W. E. Collin. LC 73-92516. (Literature of Canada Ser.). 1975. pap. 7.50 (ISBN 0-8020-6241-5). U of Toronto Pr.

White Scalper. A Story. rev. and ed. by percy b. st. john. ed. Gustave Aimard & St. John, Percy Bolingbroke, 1821-1889, Ed. LC 5-42190. (On cover: Lovell's library, no. 1069). 1887. J. W. Lovell Company.

White Scourge. Edward Everett Davis. LC 40-10013. 1940. The Naylor Company.

White Sea-Bird. David Beaty. LC 79-25789. 1980. 10.95 (ISBN 0-688-03615-5). Morrow.

White Seahorse. Eleanor M. Fairburn. 1970. pap. 2.00 o.p. (ISBN 0-900372-33-8). Irish Bk Ctr.

White Seneca. William Walker Canfield. 1911. E. P. Dutton & Comany.

White Shadow. Max Evans. LC 77-85861. 1977. 7.95 (ISBN 0-89325-006-6). Joyce Press.

White Shadows. Guy Theodore Nunn. LC 47-3014. 1947. Reynal & Hitchcock.

White Shadows. Winifred Wadell. LC 47-24307. 1947. Arcadia House.

White Shaman. C. W. Nichol. 208p. 1980. pap. 2.50 (ISBN 0-553-14143-0). Bantam.

White Shaman: A Novel. Clive W. Nicol. LC 79-1305. 8.95 (ISBN 0-316-60650-2). Little, Brown.

White Shield. Caroline Atwater Mason. LC 4-21081. 1904. The Griffith & Rowland Press.

White Shield. Bertram Mitford. LC 8-30891. F. A. Stokes Company.

White Shield. Myrtle Reed. LC 12-22515. 1912. G. P. Putnam's Sons.

White Ship. Ian Cameron, pseud. (Illus.). 192p. 1976. 6.95 o.p. (ISBN 0-684-14597-9, ScribT). Scribner.

White Ship. Donald Gordon Payne. LC 75-40006. (Illus.). 6.95 (ISBN 0-684-14597-9). Scribner.

White Ship: Estonian Tales. facsimile ed. Aino J. Kallas. Tr. by Alex Matson from Finnish. LC 73-163034. (Short Story Index Reprint Ser.). Repr. of 1924 ed. 15.00 (ISBN 0-8369-3948-4). Ayer Co.

White Shore of Olinda. Sylvia Leao. LC 43-13340. 1943. The Vanguard Press.

White Shoulders. George Kibbe Turner. LC 21-13415. 1921. A. A. Knopf.

White Silence. George Tracy Marsh. LC 38-757222. The Penn Publishing Company.

White Sister. Francis Marion Crawford. LC 9-10790. 1909. The Macmillan Company.

White Slave. Fanny Howe. LC 79-52283. 4.95 (ISBN 0-380-45591-9). Avon.

White Slave: A Novel. Harry Coulter Todd. LC 13-18598. 1913. The Neale Publishing Company.

White Slave: Or, Memoirs of a Fugitive. Richard Hildreth. LC 71-82200. (Anti-Slavery Crusade in America). (Illus.). 1969. Arno Press.

White Slave: Or, Memoirs of a Fugitive... Richard Hildreth. LC 21-13951. 1852. Tappan and Whittemore.

White Snake: A Novel. Leon Whiteson. LC 81-17982. 13.95 (ISBN 0-8253-0095-9). Beaufort Books.

White Squadron. A Novel. Thomas Chalmers Harbaugh. (On cover: Clover series, no. 69). 1895. Street & Smith.

White Squaw: A Sequel to North of Saginaw Bay, by E. J. (Pete) Petersen. Ernest J Petersen. LC 54-28812. 1954. Tall Timber Press.

White Stacks: A Village Comedy. William Hewlett. LC 24-13709. 1924. Houghton Mifflin Company.

White Stone. Ruth Comfort Mitchell. LC 24-286684. 1924. D. Appleton and Company.

White Stone, a Novel. William Ross Fraser. LC 55-13981. 1955. Philosophical Library.

White Stone, a Novel. Translated from the French by Elizabeth Sutherland and Vera Bleuer. Carlo Coccioli. LC 60-12586. 1960. Simon and Schuster.

White Streak. Sinclair Gluck. LC 24-3537. E. J. Clode.

White Tails & Green Clover. Yolla Niclas. 4.50 o.p. Vantage.

White Terror: A Romance of the French Revolution and After; Tr. from the Provencal of Felix Gras... Felix Gras. Tr. by Janvier, Catharine Ann (Drinker) LC 139. 1899. D. Appaleton and Company.

White Terror and the Red: A Novel of Revolutionary Russia. Abraham Cahan. LC 74-27969. (Modern Jewish Experience). 1975. 26.00 (ISBN 0-405-06699-6). Arno Press.

White Terror and the Red: A Novel of Revolutionary Russia. Abraham Cahan. LC 5-5930. 1905. A. S. Barnes & Company.

White Terror of the Atlantic. Denison Halley Clift. LC 54-12720. 1954. Stackpole Co.

White Thighs. rev. ed. Alexander Trocchi. pap. 1.25 o.p. (2018). Brandon.

White Thorn. Francis M. Kercheville. 1971. 3.00 o.p. (ISBN 0-8059-1579-6). Dorrance.

White Thorntree: A Novel. Frank Dalby Davison. LC 71-394418. 1968. National Press.

White Thread: A Novel. Robert Halifax. LC 13-202050. 1913. Frederick A. Stokes Company.

White Thunder God. Pat Reid. LC 47-28819. 1947. P. Reid Publications.

White Tiger: By Henry Milner Rideout; with a Frontispiece by Gerorge Varian. Henry Milner Rideout. LC 15-199682. 1915. 1.00. Duffield & Company.

White Tower. James Ramsey Ullman. LC 45-7803. 1945. J. B. Lippincott Company.

White Trail's End. Theodore Von Ziekursch. LC 25-9492. 1925. Macrae Smith Company.

White Trumpets. Virginia Hamlet Harding. LC 72-79093. 1972. 5.95. McClure Press.

White Unicorn: A Novel. 1st Ed. Margaret Gray Blanton. LC 61-8380. 1961. R. S. Globus.

White Velvet. Arthur Sarsfield Ward. LC 36-34168. 1936. Doubleday, Doran & Company, Inc.

White Victory. Robert Ormond Case. LC 43-131605. 1943. Doubleday, Doran & Company, Inc.

White Violets. Edward Crandall. LC 54-5110. 1954. Little, Brown.

White Virgin. George Manville Fenn. LC 6-39512. (On cover: Globe library, v. 1, no. 239). 1896. Rand, McNally & Company.

White Virtue, a Tale of Equatiorial Africa. Hugh Kimber. LC 29-14108. 1929. Brentano's.

White Vision: A Novel. Carmine Esposito. LC 48-23640. 1948.

White Voyage. John Christopher. LC 61-5826. 1961. Simon and Schuster.

White Wampum: The Story of Kateri Tekakwitha. Frances Taylor Patterson. LC 34-32560. 1934. Longmans, Green and Co.

White Water. Penn Mullin. (Perspectives II Ser.). (Illus.). 48p. (Orig.). (gr. 7-12). 1982. pap. 2.50 (ISBN 0-87879-319-4). Acad Therapy.

White Water, a Novel. Robert Eugene Pinkerton. LC 26-18168. The Reilly & Lee Co.

White Water Love. Alyssa Morgan. (Candlelight Ecstasy Ser.: No. 58). (Orig.). 1982. pap. 1.95 (ISBN 0-440-19503-9). Dell.

White Waterfall. James Francis Dwyer. LC 12-268962. 1912. Doubleday, Page & Company.

White Widows. Sam Merwin. LC 53-5962. (Doubleday science fiction). 1953. Doubleday.

White Wind. Jacob Wendell Clark. LC 27-3819. J. H. Sears & Company, Inc.

White Wings: A Yachting Romance. William Black. LC 41-42367. 1880. Harper & Brothers.

White Wings. A Yachting Romance. William Black. LC 6-12412. (Lovell's library, v. 4, no. 146). J. W. Lovell Company.

White Witch. Elizabeth Ashton. (Harlequin Romances Ser.). 192p. 1982. pap. 1.50 (ISBN 0-373-02503-3). Harlequin Bks.

White Witch. Elizabeth Goudge. 1973. pap. 1.50 o.p. (ISBN 0-515-03113-5, A3113). Pyramid Pubns.

White Witch. Elizabeth Goudge. 1976. pap. 1.75 o.p. (ISBN 0-515-04160-2). BJ Pub Group.

White Witch. A Novel ... (Harper's Franklin square library, no. 447). 1885. Harper & Brothers.

White Witch. A Novel. (On cover: Seaside library. Pocket ed. no. 335). 1885. G. Munro.

White Witch Doctor. Louise A Stinetorf. LC 50-8709. 1950. Westminster Press.

White Witnesses. Helen Spalding. LC 48-8439. 1948. C. Scribner's Sons.

White Wolf. Max Brand. LC 26-159616. London.

White Wolf. Max Brand. LC 26-15961. 1926. G. P. Putnam's Sons.

White Wolf. Frederick Faust. LC 61-11717. 1975. (pbk.) 1.25. Warner Paperback Library.

White Wolf. Franklin Long Gregory. LC 41-16488. Random House.

White Wolf and Other Fireside Tales. Arthur Thomas Quiller-Couch. LC 2-23593. 1902. C. Scribner's Sons.

White Wolf's Pack: A Western Story. Hal Dunning. LC 30-13809. 1929. Chelsea House.

White Wolves. Bertha Muzzy Sinclair. LC 27-876. 1927. Little, Brown, and Company.

White Wool. Naomi Ellington Jacob. LC 44-5724. 1943. Hutchinson & Co. Ltd.
Whitebird Murders. Thomas B Black. LC 46-3064. 1946. Reynal & Hitchcock.
Whiteboy. Anna Maria Fielding Hall. LC 79-15125. (Ireland, from the Act of Union, 1800, to the Death of Parnell, 1891). 1979. 42.00 (ISBN 0-8240-3497-X). Garland Pub.
Whitechapel Mystery: A Psychological Problem. ("Jack the Ripper". E. O. Tilburn. (On cover: Globe detective series, no. 14). 1889. The Eagle Publishing Co.
Whitecoats Under Fire: With the Italian Expeditionary Corps in Russia-1941. Mark-Alan, Roy, pseud. LC 71-170800. (Illus.). 1972. 6.50. Helios Books.
Whitefire. Iris Summers. 1978. pap. 2.25 (ISBN 0-345-27712-0). Ballantine.
Whitehand of Athene. Jim Thorne. 1974. (pbk.) 1.25 (ISBN 0-523-00395-1). Pinnacle Books.
Whiteladies. A Novel. Margaret Oliphant Wilson Oliphant. (Seaside library, v. 69, no. 1396). 1882. G. Munro.
Whiteoak Brothers: Jalna-1923. Mazo De La Roche. (Jalna Ser, Whiteoak ed). 1953. 7.95 o.p. (ISBN 0-316-18011-4, Pub. by Atlantic Monthly Pr). Little.
Whiteoak Brothers: Jalna-1923. Whiteoak Ed. 1st Ed. Mazo De La Roche. LC 53-7333. 1953. Little, Brown.
Whiteoak Harvest. whiteoak ed. Mazo De La Roche. LC 36-27425. 1936. Little, Brown, and Company.
Whiteoak Harvest. Mazo De La Roche. (Jaina Ser.). 1978. pap. 1.75 (ISBN 0-449-23521-1, Crest). Fawcett.
Whiteoak Heritage. Mazo De La Roche. 1961. Grosset & Dunlap.
Whiteoak Heritage. whiteoak ed. Mazo De La Roche. LC 40-13042. 1940. Little, Brown and Company.
Whiteoak Heritage. Mazo de la Roche. 1979. pap. 1.95 (ISBN 0-449-22214-4, Crest). Fawcett.
Whiteoaks of Jalna. Mazo De La Roche. 1929. Little Brown, and Company.
Whiteoaks of Jalna. Mazo De La Roche. LC 35-12201. 1931. Grosset & Dunlap.
Whiteoaks of Jalna. whiteoak ed. Mazo De La Roche. LC 36-21012. 1935. Little, Brown, and Company.
Whiteout! Duncan Kyle. LC 76-10557. 7.95. St. Martin's Press.
Whiteout! Duncan Kyle. 1977. 1.75 (ISBN 0-380-01806-3). Avon.
Whitepaw Goes North: An Arctic Adventure. David Grew. LC 48-6808. 1948. D. McKay Co.
Whiter Than Snow. Willis B. Dowd. (On cover: Sunset ser. no. 104). J. S. Ogilvie Publishing Company.
Whiterock: A Story of the Ozarks. William E Landers. LC 34-5598. Burton Publishing Company.
Whites and the Blues. Alexandre Dumas. LC 8-7674. 1894. Little, Brown, and Company.
Whitest Man. Carrie Jane Makepeace. LC 6-748. 1905. R. G. Badger.
Whitewash. Ethel Watts Mumford Grant. LC 3-17016. 1903. D. Estes & Company.
Whitewash. Horace Annesley Vachell. LC 20-6712. 1920. Cassell and Company, Ltd.
Whitewash. Horace Annesley Vachell. LC 20-7763. George H. Doran Company.
Whitewater. Paul Horgan. LC 76-122830. 1970. 6.95. Farrar, Straus and Giroux.
Whitewater. Bill Knox. LC 74-4899. 1974. 4.95 (ISBN 0-385-05887-X). Published for the Crime Club by Doubleday.
Whitewater Dynasty: The Cumberland, No. 3. Helen L. Poole. (Whitewater Dynasty Ser.). 1982. pap. 2.95 (ISBN 0-89083-979-4). Zebra.
Whitey McAlpine: A Tale of Ambition. Ney, John. LC 62-14303. C. N. Potter.
Whitey; the Playboy of "Queen People" Runs Riot in Manhattan. Carroll Graham & Graham, Garrett. LC 31-2900. The Vanguard Press.
Whither. Dawn Powell. LC 25-55433. Small, Maynard & Company.
Whither? And Other Stories. Mordecai Zeeb Feierberg. LC 72-14057. (Masters of Modern Hebrew Literature). 1973. 4.95 (ISBN 0-8276-0014-3). Jewish Publication Society of America.
Whither I Must: A Novel. Bridget Dryden. LC 22-7813. 1932. Frederick A. Stokes Company.
Whither Millions? Swan Lindskold. LC 34-2560. The Christopher Publishing House.
Whither the Wind Bloweth. Elaine L. Schulte. 1982. pap. 2.25 (ISBN 0-380-79384-9, 79384-9, Flare). Avon.
Whither Thou Goest. Eleanor Dienstag. 1976. 7.95 o.p. (ISBN 0-525-23314-8). Dutton.
Whither Thou Goest. Ruth Beeghly Statler. LC 48-11826. 1948. Brethren Pub. House.
Whither Thou Goest: A Romance of the Clyde. John Joy Bell. F. H. Revell Company.
Whitney and Son. Inez Lopez. LC 41-215429. Coward-McCann, Inc.
Whittaker's Wife. Harry Bloom. LC 62-14274. 1962. Simon and Schuster.
Whitton's Folly. Pamela Hill. LC 74-83578. 1975. 7.95. St. Martin's Press.
Whitton's Folly. Pamela Hill. (Fawcett Crest Book). 1976. 1.75. Fawcett.
Whizz Fargo, Gunfighter. George C Henderson. LC 37-201944. Phoenix Press.
Who? Algis Budrys, pseud. LC 79-12951. (Gregg Press science fiction series). 1979. 10.95 (ISBN 0-8398-2492-0). Gregg Press.
Who? Elizabeth Kent. LC 12-22517. 1.25. G. P. Putnam's Sons.
Who Am I. Shirley M. Burgdorf. pap. 1.50 o.p. Pyramid Iowa.
Who Am ? Thirty Biographical Mysteries with Detachable Solutions. Mack W. Radstone. pap. 1.95 o.p. (ISBN 0-917306-02-3). Calif Pubns.
Who and What Am I? Marie E Hensley. LC 23-2887. The Christopher Publishing House.
Who Are the Violets Now? Auberon Waugh. LC 66-13849. 1966. 4.95. S. & S.
Who Bnnefits? Lee Thayer, pseud. LC 55-9926. (Red badge detective). 1955. Dodd, Mead.
Who Builds? A Romance... Dedicated to Brother Builders of the 32 and 33 of Ancient Scottish Rites and to Builders Yet More Ancient the World Throughout. Eveleen Laura Mason.
Who Came by Night. Nicholas Roland, pseud. LC 77-182751. 1972. 5.95 (ISBN 0-03-091389-6). Holt, Rinehart and Winston.
Who Can Buy the Stars? A Novel. 1st Ed. Antonia Pola. LC 57-112634. 1958. Vantage Press.
Who Can Deny Love? Barbara Cartland. LC 79-28822. 1980. 6.95 (ISBN 0-87272-086-1). Duron Books.
Who Can Replace a Man? Brian Wilson Aldiss. (Signet bk., P3311). 1967. New Amer. Lib.
Who Can Replace a Man? The Best Science-Fiction Stories of Brian W. Aldiss. 1st Amer. Ed. Brian Wilson Aldiss. LC 66-22272. 1966. 4.50. Harcourt.
Who Cares? a Story of Adolescence. Cosmo Hamilton. LC 19-772. 1919. 1.50. Little, Brown and Company.
Who Censored Roger Rabbitt? Gary A Wolf. LC 81-8861. 1981. 10.95 (ISBN 0-312-87001-9). St Martin's Press.
Who Could Love the Nightingale? Chester Eagle. LC 75-309389. 1973. Wren.
Who Cut the Colonel's Throat? William Laing Hay. LC 31-2834. 1931. Longmans, Green and Co.
Who Dare to Live. Ruth Lucas. LC 65-20220. 4.95. Houghton.
Who Did It? Mark Frazier. (On cover: Satchel series. no. 12). The Authors' Publishing Company.
Who Did It? A Novel. Robert N. Ogden. LC 9-930. 1870. Claxton, Remsen, and Haffelfinger.
Who Did It? The Last New York Mystery. Jose Francisco Godoy. LC 6-43757. 1883. The Bosqui Engraving and Printing Co.
Who Did What to Fedalia? Meredith Willson. 1952. Doubleday.
Who Dies There. Henry Kane. Orig. Title: Nobody Loves a Loser. 1969. pap. 0.75 o.p. (74-559). Lancer.
Who Do You Love? Maria Bontempi Fogelin. LC 66-11955. 5.95. S. & S.
Who Do You Think You Are? Oliver Gillie. 1976. 8.95 o.p. (ISBN 0-8415-0397-4). Dutton.
Who Do You Think You Are? Stories and Parodies. Malcolm Bradbury. LC 76-381291. 1976. 3.50 (ISBN 0-436-06503-7). Secker & Warburg.
Who Done It? Alice Laurance & Isaac Asimov. LC 80-10657. 1980. 9.95 (ISBN 0-395-29166-6). Houghton Mifflin.
Who Dwell with Wonder. Kathleen Coyle. LC 40-305255. E P Dutton & Co., Inc.
Who Eat up My People. Will Beale. LC 49-119101. 1949. Falmouth Pub. House.
Who Fears the Devil. Manly Wade Wellman. 4.00 o.p. Arkham.
Who Follows in Their Train?" A Syrian Romance. Mary Caroline Holmes. LC 17-31647. Fleming H. Revell Company.
Who Fought and Bled. Ralph Beebe. LC 41-7646. 1941. Coward-McCann, Inc.
Who Goes Hang? Henry Stanley Hyland. LC 59-829627. (Red badge detective). 1959. Dodd, Mead.
Who Goes Home? Richard Curle. LC 35-15472. The Bobbs-Merrill Company.
Who Goes Home. 1st American Ed. Maurice Edelman. LC 53-8922. 1953. Lippincott.
Who Goes Next? John William Wainwright. LC 76-28065. 7.95 (ISBN 0-312-87010-8). St. Martin's Press.
Who Goes Sailing? John Henry Robertson. LC 33-321911. 1933. Little, Brown, and Company.
Who Goes There! Robert William Chambers. LC 20-12352. A. L. Burt Company.
Who Goes There! Robert William Chambers. LC 15-60670. 1915. D. Appleton and Company.
Who Goes There? Lois Paxton. (Ace gothic). 1974. (pbk.) 0.95. Ace Books.
Who Goes There? Seven Tales of Science-Fiction. John Wood Campbell. LC 75-28850. (Classics of science fiction). 1976. 12.50. (ISBN 0-88355-365-1) (ISBN 0-88355-450-X). Hyperion Press.
Who Goes There? Seven Tales of Science-Fiction. John Wood Campbell. LC 48-7980. 1948. Shasta Publishers.
Who Goes There? Seven Tales of Science Fiction. John Wood Campbell. LC 75-28850. (Classics of Science Fiction Ser.). 230p. 1976. 16.50 (ISBN 0-88355-365-1); pap. 3.95 (ISBN 0-88355-450-X). Hyperion-Conn.
Who Goes There? Seven Tales of Science-Fiction. 2d Ed. John Wood Campbell. LC 51-6598. 1951. Shasta Publishers.
Who Goes There? The Story of a Spy in the Civil War. Blackwood Ketcham Benson. LC 6868. 1900. The Macmillan Company.
Who Guards the Prince? Reginald Hill. LC 81-48225. 1982. 12.95 (ISBN 0-394-52077-7). Pantheon Books.
Who Had Called Him Son: A Novel. 1st Ed. Samuel J Goldberg. LC 54-132116. 1954. Pageant Press.
Who Has Been Tampering with These Pianos? By Montagu O'Reilly Pseud. Wayne Andrews. LC 48-7190. (Direction, 4). 1948. New Directions.
Who Has Seen the Wind. William Ormond Mitchell. LC 47-30157. 1947. Little, Brown and Company.
Who Has Wilma Lathrop? Cover Painting by Barye Phillips. Day Keene. LC 55-381882. (Gold medal books, 494). 1955. Fawcett Publications.
Who Hath Not Sinned! Lillian Lawrence. LC 99-2669. Hub Publishing Co.
Who He?". Alfred Bester. LC 53-9322. 1953. Dial Press.
Who If I Cry Out. Gustavo Corcao. LC 67-64317. (Texas pan American series). 1967. University of Texas Press.
Who Is Angelina? A Novel. Al Young. LC 73-15460. 1975. 7.95 (ISBN 0-03-012271-6). Holt, Rinehart and Winston.
Who Is Carla Hart? A Novel. Joanna Barnes. LC 72-82170. 1973. 6.95 (ISBN 0-87795-039-3). Arbor House.
Who Is Guilty: A Novel. Philip Woolf. Cassell & Company.
Who Is Guilty: A Novel. Philip Woolf. (On cover: Cassell's "rainbow" series, v. 1, no. 4). 1889. Cassell & Company.
Who Is Hiding in My Hide-a-Bed I) Ann Warren Griffith. LC 58-11815. 1958. Simon and Schuster.
Who Is John Noman? Charles Henry Beckett. LC 6-97757. Cassell & Company, Limited.
Who Is Julia? Barbara S Harris. LC 70-188264. 1972. 6.95. D. McKay Co.
Who Is Lewis Pinder? Leslie Purnell Davies. (Signet bk., P3375). 1968. New Amer. Lib.
Who Is Lewis Pinder? By L. P. Davies. 1st Ed. in the U.S. Leslie Purnell Davies. LC 66-20987. 1966. 3.95. Pub. for the Crime Club by Doubleday.
Who Is Lucinda. Hermina Black. Bd. with Bitter Honey. 1977. pap. 2.95 (ISBN 0-451-11934-7, AE1934, Sig). NAL.
Who Is Lucinda? Hermina Black. (Signet T 5809). 1974. (pbk.) 0.75. New American Library.
Who Is Mary Stark? Lloyd Kropp. LC 73-79687. 1974. 6.95 (ISBN 0-385-05701-6). Doubleday.
Who Is My Neighbor? Nigel Balchin. LC 50-13899. 1950. Houghton Mifflin.
Who Is My Neighbor. John L Blanchard. LC 13-170980. R. G. Badger.
Who Is Nemo? Roy Douglas. LC 37-17087. J. B. Lippincott Company.
Who Is Responsible? A Story of American Western Life. William A Smith. D. Lothrop and Company.
Who Is Simon Warwick? Patricia Moyes. LC 78-53951. (Rinehart suspense novel). 6.95 (ISBN 0-03-044726-7). Holt, Rinehart, and Winston.
Who Is Sitting in Myra's Chair? Dorothy M. Williams. 3.00 o.p. Carlton.
Who Is Sylvia? Tom Clark. LC 79-19070. 1979. 15.00 (ISBN 0-912652-54-3); pap. 4.95 (ISBN 0-912652-53-5); signed & numbered cloth 25.00x (ISBN 0-912652-55-1). Blue Wind.
Who Is Sylvia? A Novel. Alice Price. (Harper's Franklin square library, no. 300). 1883. Harper & Brothers.
Who Is Teddy Villanova? Thomas Berger. LC 76-42227. 8.95 (ISBN 0-440-09546-8). Delacorte Press.
Who Is the Man! A Tale of the Scottish Border. James Selwin Tait. LC 8-25578. Tait, Sons & Company.
Who Is the Next? Henry Kitchell Webster. LC 75-46005. (Fifty Classics of Crime Fiction, 1900-1950; 48). 1976. 12.00 (ISBN 0-8240-2398-6). Garland Pub.
Who Is the Next? Henry Kitchell Webster. LC 31-31232. The Bobbs-Merrill Company.
Who Is the Next? Henry Kitchell Webster. LC 75-46005. (Fifty Classics of Crime Fiction 1900-1950; 48). 1981. 2.95. (ISBN 0-06-080539-0). Harper and Row.
Who Is This Girl? Helen Topping Miller. LC 41-549812. 1941. D. Appleton-Century Company, Incorporated.
Who Is This Man? Alice MacGowan & Newberry, Perry, 1870- Joint Author. LC 27-18261. 1927. Frederick A. Stokes Company.
Who Killed Aunt Maggie? Medora Field. LC 39-20248. 1939. The Macmillan Company.
Who Killed Aunt Maggie? Medora Field Perkerson. LC 39-20248. 1939. The Macmillan Company.
Who Killed Caldwell? Carolyn Wells. LC 42-2430. J. B. Lippincott Company.
Who Killed Cavelotti? Audrey Newell. LC 30-5402. The Century Co.
Who Killed Charmian Karslake! Annie Haynes. LC 30-6808. Dodd, Mead & Co.
Who Killed Cherokee McCadden? T. M. Landmark. pap. 1.95 o.s.i. (ISBN 0-918226-06-6). Acrobat.
Who Killed Chloe? Published Originally Under the Title, Dancers Inmourning. Margery Allingham. LC 44-7527. (Murder mystery monthly. No. 17). 1943. Avon Book Company.
Who Killed Cock Robin? Eden Phillpotts. LC 24-7110. 1924. The Macmillan Company.
Who Killed Coralie? The Aresbys. 1927. I. Washburn.
Who Killed Doc Robin? Robert E Meyer. LC 63-19835. 1963. T. Gaus' Sons.
Who Killed Doctor Sex? Alan Geoffrey Yates. LC 65-4784. (Carter Brown mystery series). 1964. New American Library of World Literature.
Who Killed Enoch Powell. Arthur Wise. LC 76-148431. (Novel of Suspense Ser). 1971. 5.95 o.p. (ISBN 0-06-014691-5, HarpT). Har-Row.
Who Killed Frankie Leash? Margaret Echard. 1973. pap. 0.75 o.p. (07316). Curtis.
Who Killed Gregory? Eugene Jones. LC 28-19625. 1928. Frederick A. Stokes Company.
Who Killed Honeybee. Craig Cooper. LC 69-12997. 1969. 3.95 o.p. Roy.
Who Killed Lady Poynder? Richard Marsh. LC 7-26342. 1907. D. Appleton and Company.
Who Killed Mister Crittenden: The Laura Fair Case. Kenneth Church Lamott. (Illus.). 1963. 4.95 o.p. McKay.
Who Killed Pretty Becky Low? 1st Ed. Albert Benjamin Cunningham. LC 51-11773. (Guilt edged mystery). 1951. Dutton.
Who Killed Robert Prentice? Dennis Yates Wheatley. LC 80-16735. 17.95. Mayflower Books.
Who Killed Sal Mineo? Susan Braudy. 1982. 14.95 (ISBN 0-671-61009-0, Wyndham Bks). S&S.
Who Killed Sal Mineo? A Novel. Susan Braudy. LC 81-19769. 16.50 (ISBN 0-671-61009-0). Wyndham Books.
Who Killed Stella Pomeroy? Divisional Superintendent Richardson's Sixth Case. Basil Home Thomson. LC 36-181446. 1936. Pub. for the Crime Club, Inc., by Doubleday, Doran & Co., Inc.
Who Killed Stella Pomeroy? Divisional Superintendent Richardson's Sixth Case. Basil Home Thomson. LC 37-32424. 1937. The Sun Dial Press, Inc.
Who Killed the Doctor? Miles Burton. LC 43-16889. 1943. Pub. for the Crime Club by Doubleday, Doran and Co., Inc.
Who Killed the Doctors? Alan Peters. 1934. Loring & Mussey.
Who Killed the Husband? Hulbert Footner. LC 41-9063. Harper & Brothers.
Who Killed the Pie Man? Phillips Lore. LC 79-88839. 192p. 1980. pap. 1.75 (ISBN 0-87216-587-6). Playboy Pbks.
Who Killed the Pie Man? Phillips Lore. 1975. 7.50 o.p. (ISBN 0-8415-0362-1). Dutton.
Who Killed the Pie Man? A Novel. Terrence Lore Smith. LC 74-23178. 1975. 7.50. Saturday Review Press.
Who Killed You, Candy Castle? Kirby Carr. (Hitman,#1). 1974. (pbk.) 1.50 (ISBN 0-89014-104-5). Canyon Books.
Who Knocks? Twenty Masterpieces of the Spectral for the Connoisseur. Ed. by August William Derleth. LC 46-2409. 1946. Rinehart & Company, Inc.
Who Knows. Irving A. Greenfield. 1977. pap. 1.95 (ISBN 0-532-19151-X). Woodhill.
Who Knows Julie Gordon? Kage Booton. LC 79-8498. 1980. 8.95 (ISBN 0-385-15819-X). Published for the Crime Club by Doubleday.
Who Laughs Last. Ashton Hilliers. LC 12-22592. 1912. 1.35. G. P. Putnam's Sons.
Who Lies? An Interrogation. Emil Blum & Alexander, Sigmund B., Joint Author. LC 6-14205. (On cover: Arean library, v. 1. no. 2). 1892. Arena Publishing Company.
Who Lies Here? Edith Pargeter. LC 65-12870. Morrow, C.

Who Lies Here? Ellis Peters. LC 65-128704. 1965. bds., 3.95. Morrow.

Who Love and Make a Lie. Willard L Brigner. LC 76-28948. 5.95 (ISBN 0-8283-1683-X). Branden Press.

Who Made the Lamb. Charlotte Painter. LC 64-236371. bds., 4.95. McGraw.

Who? Me?? Yoram Matmor. LC 70-107255. 1970. 4.95. Simon and Schuster.

Who Murdered Aikenhead? A Seventeenth Century Tragedy. Henry C Bogle. LC 73-75071. 1973. 7.95 (ISBN 0-8187-0011-4). Harlo.

Who Murdered Mary Rogers. Raymond Paul. (Illus.). 1971. 6.95 o.p. (ISBN 0-13-958306-8). P-H.

Who Owned the Jewels? Or, The Heiress of the Sandalwood Chest. Metta Victoria Fuller Victor. (On cover: The select series. no. 88). 1891. Street & Smith.

Who Pushed Paula. Akbar Del Piombo. 1968. pap. 1.95 o.s.i. (209, Travellers Comp). Olympia.

Who Rides a Tiger. Doris Miles Disney. LC 46-7654. 1946. Pub. for the Crime Club by Doubleday & Company, Inc.

Who Rides a Tiger. Doris Miles Disney. 1974. (pbk.) 0.95. Ace Books.

Who Rides on a Tiger. Marie Adelaide Belloc Lowndes. LC 35-566316. 1935. Longmans, Green and Co.

Who Rides with Wyatt: The Strange and Lonely Story of the Last of the Great Lawmen, by Will Henry Pseud. Henry Allen. LC 55-5802. 1955. Random House.

Who Rides with Wyatt: The Strange and Lonely Story of the Last of the Great Lawmen. Will Henry, pseud. LC 55-580256. 1955. Random House.

Who Saw Maggie Brown? Kelly Roos. LC 67-26144. (Red badge mystery). 1967. bds., 3.95. Dodd.

Who Says Get Married? Don Meredith. LC 81-16949. 176p. 1981. pap. 4.95 (ISBN 0-8407-5741-7). Nelson.

Who Shall Command Thy Heart? Thomas Hall Shastid. LC 24-25180. 1924. G. Wahr.

Who Shall Hand? Brian Hill. LC 29-14761. 1929. J. B. Lippincott Company.

Who Shall Live, Who Shall Die. Daniel Stern. LC 62-20057. 1963. Crown Publishers.

Who Shall Love, Who Shall Die. Daniel Stern. (Contempora Books). 1972. 1.50. Lancer.

Who Shot the Bull? Bill Knox. LC 79-111171. 1970. 4.50. Doubleday.

Who Spies, Who Kills? A Tim Corrigan Mystery. Ellery Queen, pseud. LC 67-2474. 1966. Popular Library.

Who Spoke Last? John Victor Turner. LC 33-3220. H. Holt and Company.

Who Started It? M C Wakimoto. LC 57-64. 1956. Meador Pub. Co.

Who Steals My Name. James Fraser, pseud. LC 75-40724. (Crime Club Ser.). 192p. 1976. 5.95 o.p. (ISBN 0-385-11589-X). Doubleday.

Who Steals My Name...? Alan White. LC 75-40724. 1976. 5.95 (ISBN 0-385-11589-X). Published for the Crime Club by Doubleday.

Who Steals My Name. Alan White. LC 76-365339. 1976. 2.95 (ISBN 0-214-20152-X). Barrie & Jenkins.

Who Steals My Name: A New Blake Morgan Adventure. Kendell Foster Crossen. LC 63-18986. 1964. Bobbs-Merrill.

Who Stole Sassi Manoon? Donald E Westlake. LC 69-16474. 1969. 4.95. Random House.

Who Stole Sassi Manoon? Donald E. Westlake. 1978. 1.95 (ISBN 0-441-88592-6). Charter.

Who Tempers the Wind. Mary Elizabeth Osborn. LC 63-11821. (Swallow paperbook). 1963. A. Swallow.

Who Told Clutha. Hugh Munro. LC 58-122471. (Chantecler mystery novel). 1958. Washburn.

Who Took the Gold Away. John Leggett. LC 69-16464. 1969. 6.95. Random House.

Who Took Toby Rinaldi. Gregory McDonald. 1981. pap. 3.50 (ISBN 0-440-19542-X). Dell.

Who Upset the Coach. Henry W. Coray. 1978. pap. 1.50 o.p. (ISBN 0-8007-8288-7, Spire). Revell.

Who Walk by Threes: By Ruth K. Baker and Jack L. Horlacher. Ruth K Baker & Jack L. Horlacher. LC 61-15450. 1961. Lothrop, Lee & Shepard.

Who Walk in Darkness. Chandler Brossard. LC 52-8562. 1952.

Who Walk in Pride. Helene Magaret. LC 45-1220. 1945. The Bruce Publishing Company.

Who Walk with the Earth. Dorsha Hayes. LC 74-26112. (Labor Movement in Fiction and Non-Fiction). 1977. 24.50 (ISBN 0-404-58438-1). AMS Press.

Who Walk with the Earth. Dorsha Hayes. LC 45-3287. 1945. Harper & Brothers.

Who Walks by Moonlight. Marjorie McEvoy. Ed. by Alice Sachs. 1969. lib. bdg. 3.50 o.p. Arcadia.

Who Walks by Moonlight? Marjorie McEvoy. pap. 0.75 o.s.i. (01-332). Lancer.

Who Wants to Live Forever? William MacLeod Raine. LC 45-6402. 1945. Houghton Mifflin Company.

Who Was Ellen Smith. Kaye Ayling. pap. 0.60 o.p. Lancer.

Who Was He? A Story of Two Lives. Metta Victoria Fuller Victor. LC 8-327900. Beadle and Company.

Who Was Julia? By Margaret and Dorothy Coligny. 1st Ed. Margaret Coligny & Dorothy Collgny. LC 56-9042. 1956. Vantage Press.

Who Was Lost and Is Found: A Novel. Margaret Oliphant Wilson Oliphant. LC 7-32498. 1895. Harper & Brothers.

Who Was She? or The Soldier's Best Glory. Cecilia L. Whiteley. LC 8-36555. 1871. Claxton, Remsen & Haffelfinger.

Who Was Sylvia? Judy Gardiner. LC 82-17048. 1983. 10.95 (ISBN 0-312-87030-2). St. Martin's Press.

Who Was That Masked Woman? Noretta Koertge. LC 80-28471. 1981. 11.95 (ISBN 0-312-87032-9). St. Martin's Press.

Who Was the Heir? John Russell Caryell. LC 6-39917. (On cover: Lovell's library, no. 1260). 1888. John W. Lovell Company.

Who Was the Heir? Geraldine Fleming. (On cover: Lovell's library, no. 1260). 1888. J. W. Lovell Company.

Who Was Then the Gentleman. Charles E. Israel. 1970. pap. 0.95 o.p. (M1500, Crest). Fawcett World.

Who Was Then the Gentleman? A Novel. Charles E Israel. LC 63-12573. 1963. Simon and Schuster.

Who Was This Woman? Two Photographs and the King of Hearts. Herman Cyril McNeile. LC 25-175403. George H. Doran Company.

Who Will Remember? Margaret Irwin. LC 24-20150. 1924. T. Seltzer.

Who Will Watch the Watchers. Edwin Fadiman. LC 71-103949. 1970. 5.95. Little, Brown.

Who Wins His Love. Natalie Shipman. LC 47-4754. 1947. S. Curl.

Who Wins? or, The Secret of Monkswood Waste. May Agnes Early Fleming. LC 6-39938. (On cover: The laurel library. no. 22). 1895. G. Munro's Sons.

Who Wins? or, The Secret of Monkswood Waste. May Agnes Early Fleming. LC 2817. (On cover: Eagle library, no. 157). 1900. Street & Smith.

Who Would Be Free. Marian Spitzer. LC 24-21924. 1924. Boni and Liveright.

Who Would Have Daughters? Marguerite Steen. 1972. 7.50x (ISBN 0-7182-0931-1). Intl Pubns Serv.

Who Would Have Thought It! A Novel... Henry S. Burton. LC 6-16702. 1872. J. B. Lippincott & Co.

Who Wrote the Book of Love? Thomas Farber. LC 77-22552. 6.95 (ISBN 0-393-08799-9). Norton.

Who Wrote the Book of Love? Thomas Farber. 1979. 1.95 (ISBN 0-380-41756-1). Avon.

Whoa! I Yelled Whoa! Loren L. Fenton. LC 78-50460. (Destiny Ser.). 1979. pap. 4.95 o.p. (ISBN 0-8163-0249-9). Pacific Pr Pub Assn.

Who'd Hire Brett? John Brett. LC 80-29008. 9.95 (ISBN 0-312-87038-8). St. Martin's Press.

Who'd Shoot a Genius? Sturges Mason Schley. LC 40-320964. Random House.

Who'd Want to Kill Old George. Robert Upton. 224p. 1982. pap. 2.50 (ISBN 0-523-41537-0). Pinnacle Bks.

Who'd Want to Kill Old George? Robert Upton. LC 76-44560. 1976. 7.95 o.p. (ISBN 0-399-11867-5). Putnam Pub Group.

Who'd Want to Kill Old George? A Novel. Robert Upton. LC 76-44560. 7.95 (ISBN 0-399-11867-5). Putnam.

Whodunit? Houdini? Otto Penzler. LC 76-3388. 288p. (YA) 1976. 13.41i (ISBN 0-06-013336-8, HarpT). Har-Row.

Whodunit? Houdini? Thirteen Tales of Magic, Murder, Mystery. Otto Penzler. LC 76-6866. 12.50 (ISBN 0-06-013336-8). Harper & Row.

Whoever I Am. Eileen Dewhurst. LC 82-45102. (Crime Club Ser.). 192p. 1983. 11.95 (ISBN 0-385-18185-X). Doubleday.

Whole Armor. Faith Baldwin Cuthrell. LC 51-9083. 1951. Rinehart.

Whole Creation. Theodore Morrison. LC 62-8195. 1962. Viking Press.

Whole Days in the Trees. Marguerite Duras. Tr. by Anita Barrows. 1981. 12.95 (ISBN 0-7145-3820-5); pap. 5.95 (ISBN 0-7145-3854-X). Riverrun NY.

Whole Family: A Novel by Twelve Authors: William Dean Howells, Mary E. Wilkins Freeman, Mary Heaton Vorse, Mary Stewart Cutting, Elizabeth Jordan, John Kendrick Bangs, Henry James, Elizabeth Stuart Phelps, Edith Wyatt, Mary R. Shipman Andrews, Alice Brown, Henry Van Dyke. William Dean Howells et al. LC 8-30253. 1908. Harper & Brothers.

Whole Heart. Helen Huntington Howe. LC 43-510263. 1943. Simon and Schuster.

Whole Hog. David Wagoner. LC 76-16526. 8.95 (ISBN 0-316-91702-8). Little, Brown.

Whole Land Brimstone. Translated by Peter Wiles. Anna Langfus. 1962. Pantheon Books.

Whole Loaf: Stories from Israel. Shalom Jacob Kahn. 1963. pap. 2.50 o.p. (ISBN 0-448-00150-0, UL). G&D.

Whole Loaf: Stories from Israel. 1st American Ed. Ed. by Sholom Jacob Kahn. LC 60-1219. 1960. T. Yoseloff.

Whole Man. John Brunner. LC 69-13670. 1969. 4.50. Walker.

Whole New Way of Being. Rainey Curtis. 4.95 o.p. Vantage.

Whole Prose Romances of Francois-Marie Arouet De Voltaire: Now First Completely Done into English. Francois Marie Arouet De Voltaire & Walton, William, Tr. LC 8-31917. (Half-title: The bibliophilist's library. 2d series. v. 1-3). 1897-98. Printed Only for Subscribers by G. Barrie.

Whole Story. Elizabeth Asquith Bibescu. LC 75-103493. (Short story index reprint series). 1969. Books for Libraries Press.

Whole Story. Elizabeth Asquith Bibescu. LC 26-6148. 1926. G. P. Putnam's Sons.

Whole Story. facsimile ed. Elizabeth Asquith Bibescu. LC 75-403493. (Short Story Index Reprint Ser.). 1926. 17.00 (ISBN 0-8369-3235-8). Ayer Co.

Whole Truth. J. H. Chadwick. Cassell & Company, Limited.

Whole Truth. Robert Daley. LC 67-14222. 5.95. New Amer. Lib.

Whole Truth. John Ehrlichman. LC 79-1377. 9.95 (ISBN 0-671-24358-6). Simon and Schuster.

Whole Truth: A Story. Willis Steell. LC 8-13424. H. Murray & Co.

Whole Voyald, and Other Stories. 1st Ed. William Saroyan. LC 56-10653. (Atlantic Monthly Press book). 1956. Little, Brown.

Whole World Is Outside. 1st Ed. Manuel Komroff. LC 67-18397. 1968. 5.95. Phaedra.

Whole World Is Watching. Al Morgan. LC 72-80766. 1974. (pbk.) 1.50. Popular Library.

Whole World Is Watching. Albert Morgan. LC 72-80766. 1972. 6.95 o.p. (ISBN 0-8128-1503-3). Stein & Day.

Who'll Burn the House Down? Robert Rushmore. LC 66-25888. 1967. World Pub. Co.

Whom God Hath Joined. Arnold Bennett. LC 74-17007. (Collected works of Arnold Bennett). 1974. (ISBN 0-518-19169-9). Books for Libraries Press.

Whom God Hath Joined. Arnold Bennett. 1911. G. H. Doran Company.

Whom God Hath Joined. Arnold Bennett. LC 79-4564. 1979. 12.95. (ISBN 0-915864-82-7) (ISBN 0-915864-81-9). Academy Chicago Ltd.

Whom God Hath Joined. A Novel. Frank Cahoon. (On cover: The pastime series, no. 54). 1891. Laird & Lee.

Whom God Hath Joined: A Novel. Elizabeth Gilbert Davis Martin. LC 7-24377. (Leisure hour series, no. 189). 1886. H. Holt and Company.

Whom God Hath Sundered. Oliver Onions. LC 26-13015. 1926. George H. Doran Company.

Whom Kathie Married. Amanda Minnie Douglas. 1883. Lee and Shepard.

Whom the Gods Destroy. Alfred Gordon Bennett. LC 47-5495. (Pharos books, 1).

Whom the Gods Destroy. Robert Baker Elder. LC 54-407611. Comet Press Books.

Whom the Gods Destroyed. Josephine Dodge Daskam Bacon. LC 70-116931. (Short story index reprint series). 1970. Books for Libraries Press.

Whom the Gods Destroyed. Josephine Dodge Daskam Bacon. 1902. C. Scribner's Sons.

Whom the Gods Would Destroy. Richard Pitts Powell. LC 71-120142. 1970. 6.95. Scribner.

Whom the Gods Would Slay. Ivar Jorgenson, pseud. (Orig.). 1968. pap. 0.50 o.p. (B50-849). Belmont-Tower.

Whom the Romans Call Mercury: A Tale of the Jews. James P Richardson. LC 22-9934. 1.00. Dorrance.

Whomsoever I Shall Kiss. Curt Siodmak. LC 52-10772. 1952. Crown Publishers.

Whoop-up Trail. Bertha Muzzy Sinclair. LC 33-347851. 1933. Little, Brown, and Company.

Whoop-up Trail. Bertha Muzzy Sinclair. LC 42-17352. 1942. Triangle Books.

Whooping Crane. 1st Ed. H. C Kreisheimer. LC 55-8796. 1955. Pageant Press.

Whoops Dearie! Peter Arno. LC 27-11210. Simon & Schuster.

Whore-Mother. Shaun Herron. LC 72-95976. 1973. 6.95 (ISBN 0-87131-112-7). M. Evans; Distributed in Association with Lippincott, Philadelphia.

Whoredaughter. Charlie Avery Harris. (Orig.). 1976. pap. 1.95 (ISBN 0-87067-654-7, BH654). Holloway.

Whores Before Descartes: Assorted Poetry & Sordid Prose. Stuart L. Burns. LC 80-54381. 96p. (Orig.). 1980. pap. 4.50 (ISBN 0-9605326-0-9). Wash Launderan.

Whoreson. Donald Goines. (Orig.). 1971. pap. 1.95 (ISBN 0-87067-642-3, BH046). Holloway.

Whoring Around. John Bryson. 154p. 1983. pap. 4.95 (ISBN 0-14-005906-7). Penguin.

Who's Afraid? Elisabeth Sanxay Holding. LC 40-14078. Duell, Sloan and Pearce.

Who's Been Sitting in My Chair? Charlotte Armstrong. (Ace gothics). 1974. (pbk.) 0.95. Ace Books.

Who's Calling? Helen McCloy. LC 42-95806. 1942. W. Morrow & Co.

Who's on First. William Frank Buckley. LC 79-55374. 1980. 9.95 (ISBN 0-385-15231-0). Doubleday.

Who's That Lady in the President's Bed? B. K Ripley. LC 79-39219. 1972. 6.95 (ISBN 0-396-06515-5). Dodd, Mead.

Who's That Pushy Bitch? Java Harris. 1981. 5.00. Jungle Garden.

Who's the Patriot? A Story of the Southern Confederacy. Flora McDonald Williams. LC 8-34354. 1886. Press of the Courier-Journal Job Printing Company.

Who's There? Patrick O'Mahony. 1973. pap. 0.95 (ISBN 0-532-95246-4). Woodhill.

Who's There Within? Louis Golding. LC 48-41806. 1942. Hutchinson.

Who's to Blame? Henry Fauntleroy. LC 6-38960. 1883. Southern Methodist Publishing House, Printed for the Author.

Who's Your Father? A Novel. Jack W Little. LC 51-4761. 1951. S. J. Bloch Pub. Co.

Whose Body? Dorothy Leigh Sayers. LC 49-3339. (New Avon library, 176). 1948. Avon Pub. Co.

Whose Body? Dorothy Leigh Sayers. LC 23-9239. Boni and Liveright.

Whose Body? Dorothy Leigh Sayers. LC 44-33113. (Murder mystery monthly, no. 14). Avon Book Company.

Whose Body? Dorothy Leigh Sayers. LC 79-10578. 1979. 11.95 (ISBN 0-8161-6722-2). G. K. Hall.

Whose Body A Lord Peter Wimsey Novel. Dorothy Leigh Sayers. LC 55-10716. 1956. Harper.

Whose Child Am I? Evelyn B Mersereau. LC 32-17155. Barnes Printing Company.

Whose Heaven, Whose Earth? Thomas Melville & Marjorie Melville. LC 70-118719. (Illus.). (YA) 1971. 6.95 o.p. (ISBN 0-394-45185-6). Knopf.

Whose Little Boy Are You? A Novel. Hanokh Bartov. LC 78-56551. 1978. 9.95 (ISBN 0-8276-0112-3). Jewish PUblication Society of America.

Whose Love Was the Greater? Undated Leaves from a Diary. John Francis Beckwith. LC 13-195071. 1913. The Shakespeare Press.

Whose Name Is Legion. Isabel Constance Clarke. LC 19-8469. 1919. Benziger Brothers.

Whose Soul Have I Now? A Novel. Mary Clay Knapp. 1896. Arena Publishing Company.

Whose Was the Crime? Gertrude Warden. LC 99-53541. (Eagle library no. 132). 1899. Street & Smith.

Whose Was the Hand? Mary Elizabeth Braddon Maxwell. (On cover: Lovel novel.). (Harper's Franklin square library, no. 457). J. W. Lovell Company.

Whose Wife Is She? Annie Lisle. (select series, no. 59). 1890. Street & Smith.

Whoso Findeth a Wife. Harry Sinclair Drago. LC 14-14924. 1914. The Macaulay Company.

Whoso Findeth a Wife. William Le Queux. LC 7-13132. Rand, McNally & Company.

Whosover Shall Offend. Francis Marion Crawford. LC 4-27352. 1904. The Macmillan Company.

Why? Albert Wass. LC 72-291317. 1952. Expert Print. Co.

Why? A Novel. Stephen M Gill. LC 77-360616. 1976. 3.25 (ISBN 0-919806-15-5). Vesta Publications.

Why and What Am I? The Confessions of an Inquirer. In Three Parts. Part 1. Heart-Experience; or, the Education of the Emotions. James Jackson Jarves. LC 7-103457. 1857. Phillips, Sampson and Company.

Why Are We in Vietnam? Norman Mailer. LC 77-354544. (Berkley Windhover book). 1977. 2.25 (ISBN 0-425-03306-6). Putnam: Distributed by Berkley Pub. Corp.

Why Are We in Vietnam? A Novel. Norman Mailer. (Medallion bk., N1557). 1968. Berkley.

Why Are We in Vietnam? A Novel. Norman Mailer. LC 67-23133. 1967. Putnam.

Why Are We in Vietnam? A Novel. Norman Mailer. LC 81-7261. 1982. 5.95 (ISBN 0-03-059977-6). Holt, Rinehart and Winston.

Why Are We So Blest? A Novel. Ayi Kwei Armah. (Anchor Book, AO-93). 1973. (pbk.) 2.95 (ISBN 0-385-07030-6). Anchor Pr./Doubleday.

Why Are We So Blest? A Novel. Ayi Kwei Armah. LC 70-175355. 1972. 6.95. Doubleday.

Why Call Them Back from Heaven? Clifford D. Simak. LC 67-10392. (Doubleday science fiction). 1967. Doubleday.

Why Can't We Live Together Like Civilized Human Beings? Stories. Maxine W. Kumin. LC 81-69967. 1982. 12.95 (ISBN 0-670-76553-8). Viking Press.

Why Did He Not Die? Or, The Child from the Ebraergang. After the German of Ad. Von Volckhausen. Adeline Volckhausen & Wister, Mrs. Annis Lee (Furness) 1830-1908, Tr. LC 8-32694. 1871. J. B. Lippincott & Co.

Why Did They Kill Charley? Carter Travis Young. LC 67-13786. 1967. Doubleday.

Why Didn't They Ask Evans? Agatha Miller Christie. LC 68-6296. (Greenway edition 6). 1968. 3.95. Dodd, Mead.

Why Doctor Dobson Became a Quack: And Other Stories. Parker Jewitt Noyes. LC 10-105808. 1910. 1.50. Cochrane Publishing Company.

Why Don't We Do Something Different? Carolyn C. Moore. 188p. 1973. pap. text ed. 4.95 o.p. (ISBN 0-87150-158-9, PWS1242). Prindle.

Why Frau Frohman Raised Her Prices & Other Stories. Anthony Trollope. Ed. by N. John Hall. LC 80-1900. (Selected Works of Anthony Trollope Ser.). 1981. Repr. of 1882 ed. lib. bdg. 45.00 (ISBN 0-405-14189-0). Ayer Co.

Why Frau Frohmann Raised Her Prices. Anthony Trollope. Ed. by John K. Shannon. (Harting Grange Library Ser.). (Illus.). 1978. lib. bdg. 9.95 (ISBN 0-932282-06-7); pap. 4.95 (ISBN 0-932282-05-9). Caledonia Pr.

Why Freud Fainted. Samuel Rosenberg. LC 77-25141. 1978. 10.00 (ISBN 0-672-52206-3). Bobbs-Merrill.

Why Girls Ride Sidesaddle. Dennis Lynds. LC 79-50801. (December Magazine: Vol. 21, No. 3-4). (Illus.). 5.00 (ISBN 0-913204-13-7). December Press.

Why I Am So Beat: A Novel. Nolan Miller. LC 54-5484. 1954. Putnam.

Why I Don't Write Like Franz Kafka. William S. Wilson. LC 77-71284. 1977. 7.95 (ISBN 0-912946-41-5). Ecco Press.

Why I Go to the Movies Alone. Richard Prince. (Illus.). 128p. (Orig.). 1982. 12.95 (ISBN 0-934378-37-1); pap. 5.95 (ISBN 0-934378-38-X). Tanam Pr.

Why I Left My Husband: And Other Human Documents of Married Life. Virginia Belle Terhune Van De Water. LC 12-23712. 1912. Moffat, Yard and Company.

Why I'm Single. Linn Boyd Porter. LC 7-37761. (On cover: The albatross novels). 1892. G. W. Dillingham.

Why Is a Crooked Letter. Harry Pesin. LC 77-82503. (Illus.). 1969. 5.95. Perspective Publications.

Why It Happened. Marie Adelaide Belloc Lowndes. LC 38-128455. 1938. Longmans, Green and Co.

Why Joan? Eleanor Mercein Kelly. LC 19-4788. 1919. 1.50. The Century Co.

Why Johnny Can't Run, Swim, Pull, Dig, Slither, Etc. Being a Fairytale for the Young at Mind. Jason Alexander & Deirdre J. G Porter. LC 78-58309. (Illus.). 5.95 (ISBN 0-931826-00-4). Sitnalta Press.

Why Johnny Can't Run, Swim, Pull, Dig, Slither, Etc. Jason Alexander. Ed. by Deirdre J. G. Porter. LC 78-58309. (Illus.). 206p. 1978. pap. text ed. 5.95 (ISBN 0-931826-00-4). Sitnalta Pr.

Why Kill a Butler. Percival Henry Powell. LC 57-708462. 1957. Roy Publishers.

Why Marry! The War on This Side. Farquson Johnson. LC 31-9711. The World Syndicate Publishing Co.

Why Me? Donald E. Westlake. 204p. 1983. 13.50 (ISBN 0-670-76569-4). Viking Pr.

Why Me? The Story of Jenny. Patric Dizenzo. LC 76-1489. 1.25. Avon.

Why Men Like Married Women: And Other Stories. Fannie Batchelder. LC 6-9092. 1894. G. W. Dillingham.

Why Murder? Judson Pentecost Philips. LC 79-1066. (Peter Styles mysteries). (Red badge novel of suspense). 7.95 (ISBN 0-396-07683-1). Dodd, Mead.

Why Murder the Judge? Claude Stuart Hammock. LC 30-11284. 1930. The Macmillan Company.

Why Must We Love? Alice Powers Weilbacher. LC 69-19906. 1969. 4.95. Dorrance.

Why Not. Florence Marryat Church Lean. LC 7-13227. (On cover: Lovell's library. v. 19. no. 931). 1887. J. W. Lovell Company.

Why Not? Myra Goodwin Plantz. Jennings & Pye.

Why Not? Margaret Widdemer. LC 24-14924. 1915. A. L. Burt Company.

Why Not? Margaret Widdemer. LC 15-18567. 1915. Hearst's International Library Co.

Why Not Everything: A Novel. Burt Hirschfeld. LC 77-28466. 1978. 9.95. Morrow.

Why Not Join the Giraffes? By Hope Campbell 1st Ed. Geraldine Wallis. LC 67-18685. 1968. bds., 3.75, 3.48 lib. ed.,. Norton.

Why Not? Or, Lawyer Truman's Story. William W Totheroh. LC 8-29970. W. Ward & Co.

Why? or, Kansas Girl's Query. Mary Ann Mann Cornelius. LC 3-29830. 1903. Authors' and Writers' Union.

Why? Or, Tried in the Crucible. D. S. Sherwin. LC 8-6419. J. H. Earle.

Why Rock the Boat: A Novel. William Weintraub. LC 61-12811. 1961. Little, Brown.

Why She Cries, I Do Not Know. Whit Masterson, pseud. LC 72-3142. (Red badge novel of suspense). 1972. 4.95 (ISBN 0-396-06615-1). Dodd, Mead.

Why Shoot a Butler? Georgette Heyer. LC 72-93959. 1973. 5.95 (ISBN 0-525-23375-X). Dutton.

Why Shoot a Butler? Georgette Heyer. LC 33-11086. 1933. Longmans, Green and Co.

Why Shoot a Butler? Featuring the Rudest Detective in Fiction. Georgette Heyer. LC 36-5515. 1936. Pub. for the Crime Club, Inc., by Doubleday, Doran & Company, Inc.

Why Slug a Postman. Seldon Truss, pseud. LC 50-7598. 1950. Published for the Crime Club by Doubleday.

Why So Dead? A Tim Corrigan Mystery. Ellery Queen, pseud. LC 66-31764. 1966. Popular Library.

Why Someone Had to Die. Jan Roffman. LC 75-13393. (Crime Club Ser.). 192p. 1976. 5.95 o.p. (ISBN 0-385-11153-3). Doubleday.

Why Someone Had to Die. Margaret Summerton. LC 75-13393. 1976. 5.95 (ISBN 0-385-11153-3). Published for the Crime Club by Doubleday.

Why Stay We Here! George Stanley Godwin. LC 30-102483. 1930. D. Appleton and Company.

Why the Chisholm Trail Forks: And Other Tales of the Cattle Country. Edited by Wilson M. Hudson. With Illus. by Malcolm Thurgood. Andy Adams. LC 56-11769. 1956. University of Texas Press.

Why the Chisholm Trail Forks, and Other Tales of the Cattle Country. Edited by Wilson M. Hudson. With Illus. by Malcolm Thurgood. Andy Adams. LC 56-117690. 1956. University of Texas Press.

Why the Robin's Breast Is Red. Emma Gellibrand. LC 6-18999. F. H. Revell Company.

Why, Theodora! Sarah Warder MacConnell. LC 15-269769. 1915. Small, Maynard & Company.

Why They Call Him The Buffalo Doctor. Jean Cummings. LC 82-79789. 309p. 1971. 10.95 (ISBN 0-8187-0035-1). Swallow.

Why Was It? A Novel. Lewis Benjamin. LC 7-34441. Belford, Clarke & Co.

Why Waterloo? Alan Patrick Herbert. LC 52-13376. 1953. Doubleday.

Why Won't My Teeter-Totter? Vicki Freeman & Suzy Adams. (Illus.). 48p. (YA) 1972. 2.50 (ISBN 0-8065-0269-X). Citadel Pr.

Wicca: The Way of the Witches. Hans Holzer. (Orig.). 1979. pap. 1.95 (ISBN 0-532-19254-0). Woodhill.

Wicked & the Whipped. Amy Gray. 192p. (Orig.). 1972. pap. 1.95 o.p. (ISBN 0-87977-177-1, DBB177). Dansk Blue Bk.

Wicked Angel. Taylor Caldwell. LC 65-25581. 1965. Fawcett Publications.

Wicked As the Devil. John Creasey. 1971. pap. 0.95 o.p. (95045-095). Beagle Bks.

Wicked As the Devil: By Kyle Hunt Pseud. John Creasey. LC 66-12640. (Cock Robin mystery). bds., 3.95. McAmillan.

Wicked City Chicago. Grant Eugene Stevens. LC 6-19933. 1906.

Wicked Cyborg. Goulart, Ron. 1978. 1.50 (ISBN 0-87997-411-7). DAW Books.

Wicked Designs. Lillian O'Donnell. LC 80-13306. 9.95 (ISBN 0-399-12523-X). Putnam.

Wicked Generation: A Novel. Donald Winks. LC 68-18875. 1968. Macmillan.

Wicked Girl. (authorized ed.) ed. Mary Cecil Hay. (On cover: Seaside library. Pocket ed., no. 849). 1886. G. Munro.

Wicked Girl. Mary Cecil Hay. (On cover: The advance library, no. 12). 1892. Springfield Publishing Co.

Wicked Girl: A Novel. Mary Cecil Hay. (Harper's handy series, no. 91). 1886. Harper & Brothers.

Wicked Guardian. Vanessa Gray, pseud. LC 81-1486. 1981. 12.95 (ISBN 0-89340-326-1). J. Curley.

Wicked Guardian. Elsie Lee. (Dell book). 1973. 0.95. Dell.

Wicked Is My Flesh. Stephanie Blake. LC 79-89965. 352p. (Orig.). 1980. pap. 2.50 (ISBN 0-86721-044-3). Playboy Pbks.

Wicked Lady. Inglis Clark Fletcher. LC 76-28469. 1976. 6.75 (ISBN 0-89244-009-0). Queens House.

Wicked Lady. Inglis Clark Fletcher. 1976. (pbk.) 1.50. Bantam Books.

Wicked Loving Lies. Rosemary Rogers. LC 76-41555 (ISBN 0-380-00776-2). Avon.

Wicked Marquis. Barbara Cartland. (Barbara Cartland Library#10). 1974. (pbk.) 1.25. Bantam Books.

Wicked Marquis. Marnie Ellingson. LC 81-71915. 1982. 11.95 (ISBN 0-8027-0707-6). Walker.

Wicked Marquis. Edward Phillips Oppenheim. LC 19-8565. 1919. 1.50. Little, Brown, and Company.

Wicked Pack of Cards. Rosemary Harris. LC 72-108617. 1970. 4.50. Walker.

Wicked Pack of Cards. Hugh R. Williamson. 1965. 3.95 o.s.i. Guild Pr Ltd.

Wicked Pavilion. Dawn Powell. 1954. Houghton Mifflin.

Wicked Sister. Helen Topping Miller. LC 45-24003. 1945. London, D. Appleton-Century Company, Incorporated.

Wicked Squire. Eva McDonald. (Orig.). 1973. pap. 0.75 o.p. (07286). Curtis.

Wicked Uncle. Patricia Wentworth. LC 47-11246. (Main line mysteries). 1947. J. B. Lippincott Co.

Wicked Village: A Story of Clochemerle. Translated from the French by Edward Hyams. Gabriel Chevallier. LC 56-6669. 1956. Simon and Schuster.

Wicked Water; an American Primitive. MacKinlay Kantor. LC 49-7139. 1948. Random House.

Wicked Way to Die. J. G Jeffreys. LC 73-83194. 1973. 5.95 (ISBN 0-8027-5284-5). Walker.

Wicked Way to Die. J. G. Jeffreys. (Jeremy Sturrock Ser). (O.s.i.). 256p. 1973. 5.95 o.s.i. (ISBN 0-8027-5284-5). Walker & Co.

Wicked Widow. Carter Brown, pseud. (Orig.). 1981. pap. 1.75 (ISBN 0-505-51610-1). Tower Bks.

Wicked Woman. Anne Austin. LC 33-259743. 1933. The Macmillan Company.

Wicked Woman: A Novel by Richard Marshe Pseud. Louis Philip De Saubleaux Warren. LC 50-13165. 1950. Woodford Press.

Wicked Women of Lobo Wells. Ray Gaulden. (Orig.). 1971. pap. 0.75 o.p. (B75-2122). Belmont-Tower.

Wicked Wynsleys. Alanna Knight. (Leisure Books). 1977. 1.50 (ISBN 0-8439-0472-0). Nordon Pubns.

Wickedest Man. Cover Painting by Lu Kimmel. Joseph Millard. LC 54-33176. (Gold medal books, 404). 1954. Fawcett Publications.

Wickedest Pilgrim. Donald Barr Chidsey. LC 60-15400. 1961. Crown Publishers.

Wicker Man. Robin Hardy & Schaffer, Anthony. 1979. 1.95 (ISBN 0-671-82671-9). Pocket Books.

Wicker Man: A Novel. Robin Hardy & Anthony Shaffer. LC 77-16229. 8.95 (ISBN 0-517-53259-X). Crown Publishers.

Wickford Point. John Phillips Marquand. (Little, Brown bk. rebound). 1966. 4.00. P. Smith.

Wickford Point. John Phillips Marquand. LC 39-27145. 1939. Little, Brown and Company.

Widder Doodle's Love Affair, and Other Stories. Marietta Holley. (people's hand book series. no. 23). 1893. F. M. Lupton.

Widderburn Horror. Warner R. Crozetti, pseud. 1974. pap. 0.75 o.p. (00028). Leisure Bks.

Widdershins. Oliver Onions. LC 75-46297. (Supernatural and Occult Fiction). 1976. 17.00 (ISBN 0-405-08157-X). Arno Press.

Widdershins. Oliver Onions. LC 41-10147. (On cover: Penguin books. 222). 1939. Penguin Books Limited.

Widdershins. Oliver Onions. Ed. by R. Reginald & Douglas Manville. LC 75-46297. (Supernatural & Occult Fiction Ser.). 1976. Repr. of 1911 ed. lib. bdg. 17.00x (ISBN 0-405-08157-X). Ayer Co.

Widdershins: The First Book of Ghost Stories. Oliver Onions. LC 77-20545. 1978. 3.00 (ISBN 0-486-23608-0). Dover Publications.

Widdicombe. Mary Patricia Willcocks. LC 12-399761. 1905. John Lane.

Wide Blade: A Comedy. Emily Wright. LC 38-180148. Chapman & Grimes, Inc.

Wide Courses. James Brendan Connolly. LC 12-897505. 1912. C. Scribner's Sons.

Wide Fields. Paul Green. LC 79-101911. 1970. AMS Press.

Wide Fields. Paul Green. LC 26-9651. 1928. R. M. McBride & Company.

Wide House. Taylor Caldwell. LC 75-632. 1975. 9.95 (ISBN 0-88411-156-3). Aeonian Press.

Wide House. Taylor Caldwell. LC 45-309654. 1945. C. Scribner's Sons.

Wide House. Taylor Caldwell. LC 46-4129. 1946. The Sun Dial Press.

Wide Is the Gate. Upton Beall Sinclair. LC 43-162. 1943. The Viking Press.

Wide Is the Gate. Loyd Oscar Thompson. LC 37-4013. The Macaulay Company.

Wide Is the Horizon. Illustrated by David Knight. 1st American Ed. Cecil Roberts. LC 62-17583. 1962. Coward-McCann.

Wide Is the Water. Jane Aiken Hodge. LC 81-3230. 12.95 (ISBN 0-698-11080-3). Coward, McCann & Geoghegan.

Wide Is the Water. Jane Aiken Hodge. LC 81-13185. 1981. 15.95 (ISBN 0-8161-3325-5). G.K. Hall & Co.

Wide Loop. Nelson Coral Nye. LC 52-10915. (Silver star westerns). 1952. Dodd, Mead.

Wide Net and Other Stories. Eudora Welty. LC 73-12880. (Harvest book, HB278). 1974. (pbk.) 2.75 (ISBN 0-15-696610-7). Harcourt.

Wide Net: And Other Stories. Eudora Welty. LC 44-1666. 1943. Harcourt, Brace and Company.

Wide Open. Jem Docteur. LC 73-162822. (Zebra books, Z-1071-Q). 1.45. Grove Press.

Wide Open. Jem. 1971. pap. 1.45 o.p. (Z1071Q, Zebra). Grove.

Wide Open Town. Myron Brinig. LC 31-6598. Farrar & Rinehart Inc.

Wide River, Wide Land. William Barnaby Faherty. LC 75-37091. (Illus.). 6.95 (ISBN 0-913656-15-1). Piraeus Publishers.

Wide Road Ahead: The Story of a Woman Bacteriologist. Anne Benson Fisher. LC 39-27127. E. P. Dutton & Co., Inc.

Wide Sargasso Sea. Jean Rhys. LC 75-329801. 1975. 0.50 (ISBN 0-14-002878-1). Penguin.

Wide Sleeve of Kwannon. Bruce Lancaster. (Illus.). 307p. 1975. Repr. of 1938 ed. lib. bdg. 13.10 (ISBN 0-89190-884-6). Am Repr-Rivercity Pr.

Wide Sleeve of Kwannon: A Novel. Bruce Lancaster. LC 75-31889. 1975. 9.95 (ISBN 0-89190-884-6). Rivercity Press.

Wide Sleeve of Kwannon: A Novel. Bruce Lancaster. LC 38-69759. 1938. Frederick A. Stokes Company.

Wide Waters. Aylward Edward Dingle. LC 24-21585. Brentano's.

Wide, Wide World. Susan Warner. LC 8-33694. 1888. J. B. Lippincott Comany.

Wide, Wide World. Susan Warner. LC 8-33693. 1892. J. B. Lippincott Company.

Wide, Wide World. Susan Warner. LC 5180. W. B. Conkey Company.

Wide, Wide World. Susan Warner. LC 4-16114. (On cover: The home library). A. L. Burt.

Wide, Wide World. Susan Warner. 1904. R. F. Fenno & Company.

Widecombe Fair. Eden Phillpotts. LC 13-733. 1913. 1.35. Little, Brown, and Company.

Wideness in God's Mercy. Gladys M. Ledbetter. 5.95 o.p. Vantage.

Widening Circle, a Chronicle. Townshend, Gladys Ethel Gwendolen Eugenie (Sutherst) Townshend. LC 20-12812. 1920. D. Appleton and Company.

Widening Gyre. Robert B. Parker. 192p. 1983. 13.95 (ISBN 0-440-08740-6, Sey Lawr). Delacorte.

Widening Path. Eleanor Thorne. LC 27-24012. The Avondale Press, Incorporated.

Widening Pool. Vera Murdock Stuart Jervis. LC 45-11420. 1946. Arcadia House, Inc.

Widening Stain. Morris Bishop. LC 42-4715. 1942. A. A. Knopf.

Widening Stain. W Bolingbroke Johnson. LC 42-4715. 1942. A. A. Knopf.

Widening Waters. Margaret Hill McCarter. LC 24-24693. 1924. Harper & Brothers.

Wider Way: A Novel. Desemea Wilson. LC 20-11891. E. P. Dutton & Company.

Wider Wings. Patricia O'Malley. LC 42-15036. 1942. The Greystone Press.

Widow. Charity Blackstock. 1978. pap. 1.95 o.s.i. (ISBN 0-505-51219-X). Tower Bks.

Widow. Charity Blackstock. 1970. pap. 0.75 o.p. (B75-2018). Belmont-Tower.

Widow. Charity Blackstock. 1967. 4.95 o.p. (ISBN 0-698-10401-3). Coward.

Widow. Nicolas Freeling. LC 79-1873. 8.95 (ISBN 0-394-50336-8). Pantheon Books.

Widow. Nicolas Freeling. LC 80-10634. 1980. 2.50 (ISBN 0-394-74467-5). Vintage Books.

Widow. Edward Mannix. LC 76-115811. 1970. World Pub. Co.

Widow. Jessamy Morrison. LC 73-153829. 1972. 1.95 (ISBN 0-491-00612-8). W. H. Allen.

Widow. Pierre Rey. (Berkley Book). 1978. 2.50 (ISBN 0-425-04010-0). Berkley Publishing Corp.

Widow: A Novel. Pierre Rey. LC 77-8995. 1977. 9.95. Putnam.

Widow and the Web. Robert Lee Martin. LC 54-10579. (Red badge detective). 1954. Dodd, Mead.

Widow Bedott Papers. Frances Miriam Berry Whitcher. LC 73-91096. (American humorists series). (Illus.). 1969. Literature House.

Widow Bedott Papers. Frances Miriam Berry Whitcher. (On cover: Lovell's library, v. 4, no. 194). 1883. J. W. Lovell Company.

Widow Bedott Papers. Frances Mirian Berry Whitcher. LC 42-26371. Hurst & Co.

Widow Bedott Papers. Frances Mirian Berry Whitcher & Haven, Mrs. Alice (Bradley) 1828-1863. LC 22-173483. 1874. Mason, Baker & Pratt.

Widow Bedott Papers: With an Introduction. Frances Miriam Whitcher & Haven, Mrs. Alice (Bradley) 1828-1863. LC 8-34349. 1858. Derby & Jackson.

Widow by Courtesy. Georgia Craig. LC 41-6366. 1940. Arcadia House, Inc.
Widow Cherry: Or, The Mystery of Roaring Meg. A Novel. Benjamin Leopold Farjeon. 1878. G. W. Carleton & Co.
Widow Creek. Warren T. Longtree. (Ruff Justice Ser.: No. 4). 1982. pap. 2.50 (ISBN 0-451-11422-1, AE1422, Sig). NAL.
Widow Gay. Arthur A Marcus. LC 48-206953. (Armchair mystery). 1948. D. McKay Co.
Widow Goldsmith's Daughter. Julie P. Smith. (On Cover: Madison Square Series, No. 23). 1897. G. W. Dillingham Co.
Widow Guthrie: A Nevel. Richard Malcolm Johnston. LC 7-10531. 1890. D. Appleton and Company.
Widow Had a Gun. 1st Ed. George Harmon Coxe. LC 51-9581. 1951. Knopf.
Widow Jones Monopoly: And Other Stories. Ada A M Pratt. LC 7-30293. A. D. F. Randolph Company.
Widow Julia. Margaret F. Csovanyos. 1978. pap. 5.50 (ISBN 0-682-49083-0). Exposition.
Widow Julia. Margaret F. Csovanyos. 1970. 3.75 o.p. Vantage.
Widow Julia. Margaret F Pirigyi. LC 48-7137. 1947. Psebar Co.
Widow Lamport. Sidney Kilner Levett-Yeats. LC 9-1223. R. F. Fenno and Company.
Widow Larouge. A Novel. Emile Gaboriau & Williams, Fred, Tr. LC 1-18037. (On cover: Osgood's library of novels. No. 28). 1873. J. R. Osgood and Company.
Widow Lerogue. Emile Gaboriau. LC 6-44498. (On cover: The secret service series, no. 49). 1891. Street & Smith.
Widow Lerouge. Emile Gaboriau. LC 75-32746. (Literature of Mystery and Detection). 1976. 9.00 (ISBN 0-405-07872-2). Arno Press.
Widow Lerouge: Tr. from the French... Illustrated by Louise L. Heustis. Emile Gaboriau. LC 2824. 1900. C. Scribner's Sons.
Widow Magoogin. John Joseph Jennings. LC 3025. 1900. G. W. Dillingham Co.
Widow-Makers. Michael Blankfort. LC 46-8185. 1946. Simon and Schuster.
Widow Man. Edgar Wolfe. LC 53-10234. 1953. Little, Brown.
Widow Melville's Boarding House... Dillon O'Brien. LC 7-33163. 1881. The Pioneer Press Print.
Widow, Nun & Courtesan: Three Novelettes from the Chinese. Lin Yu-T'ang. LC 75-112328. vi, 266p. Repr. of 1951 ed. lib. bdg. 15.00x (ISBN 0-8371-4716-6, LIWN). Greenwood.
Widow, Nun, and Courtesan: Three Novelettes from the Chinese. Tr. by Lin Yutang. LC 75-112328. 1971. (ISBN 0-8371-4716-6). Greenwood Press.
Widow, Nun and Courtesan: Three Novelettes from the Chinese, Translated and Adapted by Lin Yutang. Tr. by Lin Yutang. LC 51-10944. 1951. J. Day Co.
Widow of Bath. Anne Devon. (Second Chance at Love Ser.: No. 39). 192p. (Orig.). 1982. pap. 1.75 (ISBN 0-515-05968-4). Jove Pubns.
Widow of Bath. 1st Ed. Margot Bennett. LC 52-5238. 1952. Published for the Crime Club by Doubleday.
Widow of Ephesus: A Novel. Mary Granger. LC 26-18506. 1926. G. P. Putnam's Sons.
Widow of Ratchets. Owen Brookes. LC 78-12325. 9.95 (ISBN 0-03-040296-4). Holt, Rinehart and Winston.
Widow of Windsor. Eleanor Hibbert. LC 78-20391. (Illus.). 1978. 12.50 (ISBN 0-399-12282-6). Putnam.
Widow of Windsor. Jean Plaidy. 1979. pap. 1.95 (ISBN 0-449-24151-3, Crest). Fawcett.
Widow of Windsor. Jean Plaidy. LC 78-20391. 1978. 10.00 o.s.i. (ISBN 0-399-12282-6). Putnam Pub Group.
Widow of Windsor. Tyler-Whittle, Michael Sidney. LC 73-79337. 1973. 6.95. St. Martin's Press.
Widow Robinson: And Other Sketches. Benjamin W Williams. The Abbey Press.
Widow Rugby's Husband: A Night at the Ugly Man's and Other Tales of Alabama. Johnson Jones Hooper. LC 21-15397. 1851. A. Hart, Late Carey & Hart.
Widow Seymour: A Story for Youth and Age. William Elliott Smith Baker. LC 6-6871. 1876. J. A. Wagenseller.
Widow to Say Nothing of the Man. Helen Rowland. LC 8-18374. Dodge Publishing Company.
Widow Watchers. Frank Archer, pseud. 1969. pap. 0.60 o.p. (0502-06032-060). Curtis.
Widow Watchers: By Frank Archer Pseud. Richard O'Connor. LC 65-23801. 3.50. Pub. or the Crime Club by Doubleday.
Widow Wyse: A Novel... Helen Mary Bean. 1885. Cupples, Upham and Company.
Widowed Bride: Or, The Mystery of Glenhampton. Lucy Randall Comfort. LC 6-30216. (Street & Smith's select series. no. 75). 1891. Street & Smith.
Widowed Wife and Wedded Maid. Paul Perret. Tr. by Schonberg, James. LC 7-36187. Belford Company.
Widower. Georges Simenon. Tr. by Robert Baldick from Fr. LC 81-48256. 1982. 10.95 (ISBN 0-15-196644-3). HarBraceJ.
Widower. Hilda Van Siller. LC 58-8113. 1958. Published for the Crime Club by Doubleday.
Widower: Also, A True Account of Some Brave Frolics at Craigenfels. Julie P. Smith. LC 8-9615. 1871. G. W. Carleton & Co.; Etc., Etc.
Widower & Some Spinsters: Short Stories. Maria Louise Pool. LC 78-101288. (Short story index reprint series). (Illus.). 1969. Books for Libraries Press.
Widower & Some Spinsters: Short Stories. Maria Louise Pool & Hale, Amand M. LC 99-4977. 1899. H. S. Stone & Company.
Widower Indeed. Rhoda Broughton & Wetmore, Mrs. Elizabeth (Bisland) Joint Author. LC 6-18948. (On cover: Appleton's town and country library, no. 34). 1891. D. Appleton and Company.
Widower's Son. Alan Sillitoe. (Perennial library). 1978. 1.95 (ISBN 0-06-080465-3). Harper & Row.
Widowmaker. Maria Fagyas. LC 66-174583. 3.95. Pub. for the Crime Club by Doubleday.
Widowmaker. Maria Fagyas. (Signet bk., T3282). 1967. New Amer. Lib.
Widows. Ariel Dorfman. LC 82-48955. 1983. 10.95 (ISBN 0-394-52712-7). Pantheon Books.
Widows Are Dangerous. Vida Hurst. LC 44-699420. 1944. Gramercy Publishing Company.
Widow's Children. Paula Fox. LC 76-10211. 8.95 (ISBN 0-525-23377-6). Dutton.
Widow's Children. Paula Fox. 1978. 1.75 (ISBN 0-380-01791-1). Avon Books.
Widow's Cruise. Nicholas Blake. 1977. pap. 2.25i (ISBN 0-06-080399-1, P399, PL). Har-Row.
Widow's Cruise. Cecil Day-Lewis. (Perennial Library). 1977. 1.75 (ISBN 0-06-080399-1). Harper & Row.
Widow's Escort. Beth De Bilio. (Candlelight Intrigue.). 1979. 1.25 (ISBN 0-440-19498-9). Dell Pub. Co.
Widow's House: A Novel. Kathleen Coyle. LC 24-195290. E. P. Dutton & Company.
Widow's Might. Harford Willing Hare Powel. LC 35-15738. Greenberg.
Widow's Mite. Elisabeth Sanxay Holding. LC 53-6374. (Inner sanctum mystery). 1953. Simon and Schuster.
Widow's Necklace: A Novel. Ernest Davies. LC 13-20484. 1913. 1.35. The Devin-Adair Company.
Widow's Oats. Warner Fabian. LC 35-385862. The Macaulay Company.
Widows of Broome. Arthur William Upfield. LC 50-5145. 1950. Published for the Crime Club by Doubleday.
Widows of Thornton. 1st Ed. Peter Hillsman Taylor. LC 53-7839. 1954. Harcourt, Brace.
Widows Ought to Weep. Dolores Birk Hitchens. LC 47-4011. 1947. Ziff-Davis Publishing Company.
Widow's Peak. Harriet Henry, pseud. LC 40-13627. 1940. Dodd, Mead & Company.
Widow's Pique. Blair Treynor. LC 56-9413. 1956. M. S. Mill Co. and W. Morrow.
Widow's Pique. Blair Treynor. LC 57-3815. (Permabook M-3096. Mystery, 6). 1957. Permabooks.
Widows' Plight. 1st Ed. Ruth Fenisong. LC 55-550293. 1955. Published for the Crime Club by Doubleday.
Widow's Son. Albert E Potts. LC 56-19722. Christopher Pub. House.
Widow's Son. A Story of Jewish Life of the Past. I N Lichtenberg. Maccabean Publishing Co.
Widow's Tale: Or, The Indiscretions of Lettice. John Coates. LC 58-9369. 1958. W. Slone Associations.
Widow's Wager. Rose Ashleigh. LC 6-4529. (Street & Smith's select series, no. 9). 1888. Street & Smith.
Widow's Walk. Mary Bishop. 1975. (pbk.) 0.95. Dell.
Widow's Walk. Sarah Nichols. (Orig.). 1972. pap. 0.95 o.p. (09154). Curtis.
Widow's Walk. Margaret Tayler Yates & Bramlette, Paula, Joint Author. LC 45-6565. 1945. E. P. Dutton & Company, Inc.
Widow's War. Alan Williams. LC 79-67643. 1980. 8.95 (ISBN 0-89256-128-9). Rawson, Wade.
Widows Wear Weeds. Erle Stanley Gardner. LC 66-2983. 1966. W. Morrow.
Widows Wear Weeds. Erle Stanley Gardner. 1975. (pbk.) 1.25 (ISBN 0-671-78926-0). Pocket Books.
Widow's Web. Ursula Reilly Curtiss. LC 56-574291. (Red badge detective). 1956. Dodd, Mead.
Width of Waters. Alfred Kern. LC 58-9067. 1959. Houghton Mifflin.
Wieland: Or, The Transformation. Charles Brockden Brown. LC 63-24276. (His Novels, v. 1). (Illus.). 1963. Kennikat Press.
Wieland: Or, The Transformation. Charles Brockden Brown. LC 6-13647. 1827. S. G. Goodrich.
Wieland: Or, The Transformation. Charles Brockden Brown. LC 6-18967. (On cover: Library of standard romance, no. 1). 1846. W. Taylor & Co.
Wieland: Or, The Transformation. Charles Brockden Brown. LC 6-16395. 1857. M. Polock.
Wieland: Or, The Transformation. Charles Brockden Brown. LC 17-13039. (Half-title: Charles Brockden Brown's novels, vol. i). 1887. D. McKay.
Wieland: Or, The Transformation, an American Tale; Memoirs of Carwin, the Biloquist. Charles Brockden Brown. LC 78-15330. 4.75 (ISBN 0-87338-220-X). Kent State University Press.
Wieland; or, The Transformation, Together with Memoirs of Carwin the Biloquist, a Fragment. Edited with an Introd. by Fred Lewis Pattee. Charles Brockden Brown. LC 58-13328. (Hafner library of classics, no. 17). 1958. Hafner Pub. Co.
Wieland: Or, The Transformation, Together with Memoirs of Carwin, the Biloquist; a Fragment. Charles Brockden Brown. LC 79-7131. (Harbinger book). 1969. Harcourt, Brace & World.
Wieland: Or, The Transformation, Together with Memoirs of Carwin the Biloquist, a Fragment. Charles Brockden Brown & Pattee, Fred Lewis, 1863- Ed. LC 26-3794. (Half-title: American authors series, general editor, Stanley T. Williams). Harcourt, Brace and Company.
Wife. Judith Burnley. (O.s.i.). 1977. 6.95 o.s.i. (ISBN 0-617-22635-0). S&S.
Wife. Helen Grace Carlisle. LC 34-604531. Harcourt, Brace and Company.
Wife. Valentin Petrovich Kataev. LC 52-31441. 1946. Hutchinson International Authors.
Wife. Bharati Mukherjee. LC 75-2120. 1975. 7.95 (ISBN 0-395-20439-9). Houghton Mifflin.
Wife and Mother. Ruth Doan MacDougall. LC 75-34330. 7.95. Putnam.
Wife and Mother. Ruth Doan MacDougall. 1977. 1.75 (ISBN 0-380-01661-3). Avon Books.
Wife: And Other Stories. Anton Pavlovich Chekhov. Tr. by Garnett, Constance (Black) LC 18-10534. (Half-title: The tales of Chekhov, vol. v). 1918. The Macmillan Company.
Wife and the Wolf. Lee Jacquin. LC 42-19643. 1942. Phoenix Press.
Wife, and Woman's Reward... Caroline Sheridan Norton. LC 7-33178. 1835. Harper & Brothers.
Wife by Contract. Flora Kidd. (Harlequin Presents Ser.). 192p. 1980. pap. 1.50 (ISBN 0-373-10400-6). Harlequin Bks.
Wife by the Hour. Charles B Parmer. LC 32-7599. 1931. G. H. Watt.
Wife Decides: A Novel. Sydney Wharton. LC 11-599960. G. W. Dillingham Company.
Wife Exchange. Jud Blaine. (O.s.i.). (Orig.). 1969. pap. 0.60 o.s.i. (A402X, Award). Univ Pub & Dist.
Wife for a Year. Rachel Lindsay. (Harlequin Presents Ser.). 192p. (Orig.). 1981. pap. 1.50 (ISBN 0-373-10413-8). Harlequin Bks.
Wife for Sale. Anton Pavlovich Chekhov. 1959. 2.00 o.p. Hillary.
Wife for Sale. Kathleen Thompson Norris. LC 33-15493. 1933. Doubleday, Doran & Company, Inc.
Wife for Sale see Three Great Classics.
Wife Found Slain. Caroline Crane. LC 81-5501. 8.95 (ISBN 0-396-08026-X). Dodd, Mead.
Wife Found Slain. Caroline Crane. LC 82-1442. 1982. 12.95 (ISBN 0-89340-395-4). J. Curley.
Wife Hard Won. A Love Story. Julia MacNair Wright. LC 9-518. 1884. J. B. Lippincott & Co.
Wife in Name Only. Charlotte Mary Brame. (On cover: Seaside library. Pocket ed. no, 76). G. Munro.
Wife in Name Only. Charlotte Mary Brame. LC 36-29646. J. S. Ogilvie & Company.
Wife in Name Only. Charlotte Mary Brame. (On cover: Lovell's library. v.17 no. 812). J. W. Lovell Company.
Wife in Name Only: A Novel by Bertha M. Clay Pseud. Charlotte Mary Brame. LC 5340. (Bertha Clay library, no. 21). 1900. Street & Smith.
Wife into Wanton. Karl Flinders. LC 70-28567. (Traveller's companion series, TC-487). 1.95. Traveller's Companion.
Wife Lender. Dean McCoy. (O.s.i.). (Orig.). 1969. pap. 0.60 o.s.i. (A392X, Award). Univ Pub & Dist.
Wife of a Vain Man. Marie Sofle Birath Schwartz. Tr. by Borg, Selma & Shipley, Marie Adelaide (Brown) LC 8-2061. 1871. Lee and Shepard.
Wife of Bath. Vera Chapman. LC 78-66457. (Illus.). 1978 (ISBN 0-380-38976-2). Avon Books.
Wife of Bath. Vera Chapman. LC 78-66457. (Illus.). 1978 (ISBN 0-380-38976-2). Avon Books.
Wife of Bath's Prologue & Tale & the Clerk's Prologue & Tale. Geoffrey Chaucer. Ed. by Gloria Cigman. LC 75-17976. (London Medieval & Renaissance Ser.). 94p. 1976. text ed. 16.50x (ISBN 0-8419-0225-9); pap. 9.50x (ISBN 0-8419-0226-7). Holmes & Meier.
Wife of Colonel Hughes. Hubert Wales. 1909. P. R. Reynolds.
Wife of Colonel Hughes. Hubert Wales. LC 10-186583. 1910. The Stuyvesant Press.
Wife of Elias: A Mystery Novel. Eden Phillpotts. LC 37-22976. 1937. E. P. Dutton & Co., Inc.
Wife of His Youth. Charles Waddell Chesnutt. LC 76-29261. (Americans in Fiction Ser.). Repr. of 1899 ed. lib. bdg. 18.50 (ISBN 0-8398-0261-7). Irvington.
Wife of His Youth & Other Stories. Charles Waddell Chesnutt. (Illus.). 1968. pap. 5.95 (ISBN 0-472-06134-8, 134, AA). U of Mich Pr.
Wife of His Youth & Other Stories. Charles Waddell Chesnutt. (O.s.i.). 1968. 4.95 o.s.i. (ISBN 0-472-09134-4). U of Mich Pr.
Wife of His Youth: And Other Stories of the Color Line. Illus. by Clyde O. De Land. Charles Waddell Chesnutt. LC 67-29261. (Americans in Fic.). 1967. Gregg Pr.
Wife of His Youth: And Other Stories of the Color Line. Charles Waddell Chesnutt. LC 113. 1899. Houghton, Mifflin and Company.
Wife of His Youth, & Other Stories of the Color Line. Charles W. Chestnutt. (Illus.). 1968. Repr. of 1899 ed. 15.00 o.p. B Franklin.
Wife of Light. Diane Ackerman. LC 77-25297. 1978. 6.95 (ISBN 0-688-03286-9). Morrow.
Wife of Monte-Cristo. Being the Continuation of Alexander Dumas' Celebrated Novel of The Count of Monte-Cristo ... 1884. T. B. Peterson & Brothers.
Wife of Narcissus. Annulet Andrews. 1908. Moffat, Yard and Company.
Wife of Pilate. Translated by Marie C. Burhrle. Gertrud Von Le Fort. LC 57-10826. 1957. Bruce Pub. Co.
Wife of Pontius Pilate: A Story of the Heart of Procla. Agnes Sligh Turnbull. LC 28-19756. Fleming H. Revell Company.
Wife of Sir Isaac Harman. Herbert George Wells. LC 14-18457. 1914. The Macmillan Company.
Wife of Sir Isaac Harman. Herbert George Wells. LC 24-221997. 1915. The Macmillan Company.
Wife of Sir Isaac Harman. Herbert George Wells. LC 17-51303. 1916. The Macmillan Company.
Wife of Steffen Tromholt. Hermann Sudermann. Tr. by Eden Paul. Paul, Cedar, Joint Tr. LC 29-20441. 1929. H. Liveright.
Wife of the Century. Cyril Hume. LC 23-18374. George H. Doran Company.
Wife of the Red-Hared Man. 1st Ed. William Sanborn Ballinger. LC 57-614607. 1957. Harper.
Wife of the Secretary of State. Ella Middleton Tybout. LC 5-33977. 1905. J. B. Lippincott Company.
Wife of the Secretary of State. 3d ed. Ella Middleton Tybout. LC 9-20908. 1906. J. B. Lippincott Company.
Wife of Two Husbands. Marie Walsh. (On cover: Idylwild series, no. 6). 1892. Morrill, Higgins & Co.
Wife of Yesteryear: A Novel. 1st Ed. Loretto O'Brien Rhoades. LC 56-5539. 1956. Vantage Press.
Wife on Leave. Inez Sabastian. LC 33-2938. The Macaulay Company.
Wife on the Loose. Edward Hunt. (Orig.). 1971. pap. 0.95 o.p. (95-156). Manor Bks.
Wife or Death. Ellery Queen, pseud. LC 63-24842. 1963. Pocket Books.
Wife or Death. Ellery Queen. 1974. (pbk.) 0.95. New American Library.
Wife or Death & the Golden Goose. Ellery Queen, pseud. 1978. pap. 2.50 (ISBN 0-451-11305-5, AE1422, Sig). NAL.
Wife or Maid? Maurice Douglas Flattery. LC 98-729. F. T. Neely.
Wife or Mistress. Peggy Gaddis, pseud. LC 34-7028. 1934. W. Godwin, Inc.
Wife or Slave. Lenox Bell. LC 6-9416. (On cover: Munro's library, popular novels, v. l, no. 99). N. L. Munro.
Wife or Stenographer--Which? John Russell Coryell. LC 23-8366. (True story series. no. 2). 1923. Macfadden Publications, Inc.
Wife Out of Egypt. Norma Octavia Lorimer. 1914. Brentano's.
Wife-Ship Woman. Hugh Pendexter. LC 25-4339. The Bobbs-Merrill Company.
Wife-Swap Cruise. Jonathan Quist. pap. 2.25 o.s.i. (Venus). Grove.
Wife Swapping Society. Nora Saunders. pap. 2.45 o.p. (4021). Cameo.
Wife Swapping Spy. Robert H. Sheldon. pap. 1.95 o.p. (8082). Cameo.
Wife to Be. Albert Quandt. LC 49-119345. 1949. Arcadia House.

Wife to Caesar: A Novel of Washington. Berthe Knatvold Mellett. LC 32-14016. 1932. Brewer, Warren & Putnam.

Wife to Caliban. Louise Redfield Peattie. LC 34-230911. Minton, Balch & Company.

Wife to Henry V. 1st American Ed. Hilda Winifred Lewis. LC 57-55832. 1957. Putnam.

Wife to Hugo. Jessie Joy Baines. LC 31-10521. Sears Publishing Company, Inc.

Wife to Mr. Milton. Robert Graves. LC 79-9785. 1979. pap. 5.95 (ISBN 0-89733-009-9). Academy Chi Ltd.

Wife to Mr. Milton: The Story of Marie Powell. Robert Graves. LC 44-47871. 1944. Creative Age Press, Inc.

Wife to Mr. Milton: The Story of Marie Powell. Robert Graves. LC 78-9770. 1978. 18.50 (ISBN 0-374-93240-9). Octagon Books.

Wife to Mr. Milton: The Story of Marie Powell. Robert Graves. LC 79-9785. 1979. 11.95. (ISBN 0-89733-010-2) (ISBN 0-89733-009-9). Academy Chicago Ltd.

Wife to Order. Lucy Walker, pseud. 1980. pap. 1.75 (ISBN 0-345-29275-8). Ballantine.

Wife to Pilate. Mary Granger. LC 29-5415. 1929. Payson & Clarke Ltd.

Wife to the Bastard. Hilda Winifred Lewis. (95-192). 1968. Popular Lib.

Wife to the Bastard: By Hilda Lewis. 1st Amer. Ed. Hilda Winifred Lewis. LC 67-21217. 1967. 4.95. McKay.

Wife to the Kingmaker. Sandra Wilson. LC 74-81699. (Illus.). 1975. 6.95. St. Martin's Press.

Wife to Trade. Josiah Pitts Woolfolk. LC 36-9081. Godwin.

Wife Traders: A Tale of the North. Arthur John Arbuthnott Stringer. LC 36-3327. The Bobbs-Merrill Company.

Wife Vs. Secretary: Together with Two Complete Novelettes. Faith Baldwin Cuthrell. LC 36-16942. Grosset & Dunlap.

Wife Who Died Twice. Edgar Henry Bohle. LC 62-8963. (Random House mystery). 1962. Random House.

Wife Who Ran Away. Trina Mascott. 1975. (pbk.) 0.95. Dell.

Wifehood of Jessica. Louise Platt Hauck. LC 32-103356. The Penn Publishing Company.

Wife's Crime. Mary Grace Halpine. LC 7-1201. (On cover: Munro's library, v. 1., no. 406). N. L. Munro.

Wife's Engagement Ring. Timothy Shay Arthur. 1877. National Temperance Society and Publication House.

Wife's Eye View. Sophie Kerr. LC 47-38252. 1947. Rinehart & Company, Inc.

Wife's Honor. A Novel. Ernest A Young. G. W. Ogilvie.

Wife's Messengers: A Novel. M. B. Horton. LC 7-71566. 1869. J. B. Lippincott & Co.

Wife's Repentance: From the French of Georges Ohnet. Georges Ohnet. (On cover: The Melbourne series, no. 30). 1894. E. A. Weeks & Company.

Wife's Secret. A Novel. Bertha M. Clay. LC 47-39283. G. W. Ogilvie.

Wife's Secret. Also, Fair but False. Charlotte Mary Brame. (On cover: Seaside library. Pocket ed. no. 254). G. Munro.

Wife's Secret: Or, Gillian. Ann Sophia Winterbotham Stephens. LC 8-124042. T. B. Peterson & Brothers.

Wife's Tragedy. A Novel. May Agnes Early Fleming. LC 6-39937. 1881. G. W. Carleton & Co.

Wife's Trials; Married Life; Husbands and Wives. Emma Jane Worboise Guyton. LC 75-492. (Victorian Fiction: Novels of Faith and Doubt; 44). 1975. 35.00 (ISBN 0-8240-1568-1). Garland Pub.

Wife's Victory: And Other Nouvellettes. Emma Dorothy Eliza Nevitte Southworth. LC 8-14260. T. B. Peterson and Brothers.

Wifey. Judy Blume. 1981. pap. 2.95 (ISBN 0-671-83531-9). PB.

Wifey: An Adult Novel. Judy Blume. LC 78-6145. 8.95. Putnam.

Wig. Charles Wright. 1977. pap. 1.50 (ISBN 0-532-15253-0). Woodhill.

Wig: A Mirror Image. Charles Stevenson Wright. LC 66-11708. 1966. Farrar, Straus and Giroux.

Wigalois: The Knight of Fortune's Wheel. Wirnt Von Grafenberg. Tr. by J. W. Thomas. LC 76-44239. viii, 236p. 1977. 16.95x (ISBN 0-8032-0905-3). U of Nebr Pr.

Wigalois, the Knight of Fortune's Wheel. Wirnt Von Gravenburg & John Wesley Thomas. LC 76-44239. 10.95 (ISBN 0-8032-0905-3). University of Nebraska Press.

Wigwam and the Cabin. new and rev. ed. William Gilmore Simms. LC 72-116014. 1970. AMS Press.

Wigwam and the Cabin. William Gilmore Simms. LC 8-130470. (On cover: Wiley and Putnam's library of American books, no. 4, 12). 1845. Wiley and Putnam.

Wigwam and the Cabin. new and rev. ed. William Gilmore Simms. 1856. Redfield.

Wigwam and the Cabin. new and rev. ed. William Gilmore Simms. LC 8-11019. 1882. A. C. Armstrong & Son.

Wigwam and the Cabin. new and rev. ed. William Gilmore Simms. (On cover: Lovell's library, v. 13, no. 674). 1885. J. W. Lovell Company.

Wigwam and the Cabin. Life in America. William Gilmore Simms. LC 68-23729. (Illus.). 1968. Gregg Press.

Wilberforce Legacy. Doris Bell Collier Ball. LC 69-15714. 1969. 4.50. Walker.

Wilberforce Legacy. Josephine Bell. LC 69-15714. 1969. 4.50 o.p. Walker & Co.

Wilbur Crane's Handicap. John Maxwell Forbes. LC 18-18333. G. Sully & Company.

Wilbur: The Trusting Whippoorwill. August William Derleth. 4.95 (ISBN 0-88361-076-0). Stanton & Lee.

Wilburn: Or, The Heir of the Manor. A Romance of the Old Dominion. Walter Whitmore. LC 8-36550. R. E. Edwards.

Wilby Conspiracy. Peter Driscoll. LC 72-3629. 1973. (pbk.) 1.50. Popular Library.

Wild... Vera Brown. LC 33-190842. Grosset & Dunlap.

Wild. Carol Denny Hill. LC 27-183776. 1927. The John Day Company.

Wild Affair. Charlotte Lamb, pseud. (Harlequin Presents Ser.). 192p. 1982. pap. 1.75 (ISBN 0-373-10545-2). Harlequin Bks.

Wild and Outside. Allen Kim Lang. LC 66-15725. Chilton Books.

Wild & Tender Magic. Rose Marie Ferris. (Candlelight Ecstasy Ser.: No. 89). (Orig.). 1982. pap. 1.95 (ISBN 0-440-19411-3). Dell.

Wild and Willful: Or, To the Bitter End. Lucy Randall Comfort. LC 6-302174. (On cover: The library of American authors. no. 36). 1891. G. Munro.

Wild & Willing Hellcat. Roland Sanders. pap. 1.95 o.s.i. (Venus). Grove.

Wild and Wonderful. large print ed. Janet Dailey. LC 82-19813. 1983. 11.95 (ISBN 0-89340-487-X). Chivers Press.

Wild & Wonderful. Janet Dailey. (Harlequin Presents Ser.). 192p. 1981. pap. 1.50 (ISBN 0-373-10416-2). Harlequin Bks.

Wild & Woolly, Mostly Wild, Cass Thurner, Esquire. 1978. 9.00 o.p. (ISBN 0-915854-06-6); pap. 3.00 o.p. (ISBN 0-915854-10-4). Friend Freedom.

Wild Angels. Ursula K. Le Guin. (Capra Chapbook Ser.: No. 27). (Illus.). 48p. (Orig.). 1975. pap. 2.50 o.p. (ISBN 0-88496-030-7). Capra Pr.

Wild Animals at Home. Ernest Thompson Seton. 1978. Repr. of 1913 ed. lib. bdg. 25.00 (ISBN 0-8492-2555-8). R West.

Wild Animals. Illustrated by J. L. Vlasaty. Anna Ratzesberger. LC 56-6743. (Rand McNally giant book). 1956. Rand McNally.

Wild Apples: A California Story. Grace MacGowan Cooke & MacGowan, Alice. LC 18-18336. 1918. George H. Doran Company.

Wild Apples: A California Story. The Straight Road, Author of. LC 18-18336. George H. Doran Company.

Wild Apples I. Oliver Gogarty. 44p. 1971. Repr. of 1930 ed. 11.00x (ISBN 0-7165-1371-4, Pub. by Cuala Press Ireland). Biblio Dist.

Wild Are Among Us. Isidore Haiblum. LC 74-5526. (Doubleday science fiction). 1975. 5.95 (ISBN 0-385-08340-8). Doubleday.

Wild Artist in Boston. A Story of Love and Art in the Actual. James Bartlett Wiggin. LC 8-37038. 1888. J. B. Wiggin.

Wild Ass of a Man. Barry Oakley. LC 67-20060. 1967. aust. 3.25. Cheshire.

Wild Ass' Skin: The Chouans, and Other Stories. saintsbury ed. Honore De Balzac. Tr. by Ellen Marriage. LC 8-7686. 1899. The Gebbie Publishing Co., Ltd.

Wild Asses. James Gerald Dunton. LC 25-669833. Small, Maynard & Company.

Wild Ass's Skin. Honore De Balzac. Tr. by Ellen Marriage. LC 36-37076. (Half-title: Everyman's library, ed. by Ernest Rhys. Fiction. no. 26). 1938. J. M. Dent & Sons, Ltd.

Wild Ass's Skin. Introd. by Marcel Girard Tr. from French by Ellen Marriage. Honore De Balzac. (Everyman's lib. paperback, 26 1026). 1961. pap., 1.05. Dutton.

Wild Ass's Skin: La Peau De Chagrin) Honore De Balzac. Tr. by Herbert James Hunt. LC 78-302574. (Penguin classics). 1977. 2.95 (ISBN 0-14-044330-4). Penguin.

Wild Beauty: A Novel. Mateel Howe Farnham. LC 30-227560. 1930. Dodd, Mead & Company.

Wild Berry Wine. Joanna Cannan, pseud. LC 25-13306. 1925. Frederick A. Stokes Company.

Wild Bird. Katherine Helen Maud Marshall Diver. LC 29-11283. 1929. Houghton Mifflin Company.

Wild Bird. Hulbert Footner. LC 25-113971. George H. Doran Company.

Wild Bird. Denise Robins. LC 32-3602. 1932. G. H. Watt.

Wild Birds & Others. new ed. Wendy Long. LC 73-82533. (O.s.i.). 96p. 1974. pap. 3.95 o.s.i. (ISBN 0-912310-32-4). Celestial Arts.

Wild Blood. Frank Chester Robertson. LC 35-18234. Godwin.

Wild Blood. Gordon Ray Young. LC 21-17547. The Bobbs-Merrill Company.

Wild Blows the Heather. LC 56-7549. 1956. Comet Press Books.

Wild Boar Forest. Li Shau Chwun. pap. cancelled o.p. (ISBN 0-87359-008-2). Pendell Pub.

Wild Boar Forest. Li Shau Chwun. pap. cancelled o.p. (ISBN 0-87359-008-2). Pendell Pub.

Wild Body: A Soldier of Humour, and Other Stories. Wyndham Lewis. LC 70-137666. 1970. (ISBN 0-8383-1225-X). Haskell House.

Wild Body: A Soldier of Humour, and Other Stories. Wyndham Lewis. LC 28-7945. Harcourt, Brace and Company.

Wild Border Guns. Lee Floren. LC 53-7018. 1953. Arcadia House.

Wild Border Guns see Outlaw Breed.

Wild Boys. William Burroughs. 5.95 o.p. (ISBN 0-525-42745-7). Dutton.

Wild Boys: A Book of the Dead. William S. Burroughs. LC 78-155133. 1971. 5.95 (ISBN 0-394-47586-0). Grove Press.

Wild Breed. Carter Travis Young. LC 60-5951. 1960. Doubleday.

Wild Breed. Cover Painting by Barye Phillips. Ted Stratton. LC 55-205371. (Gold medal books, 443). 1954. Fawcett Publications.

Wild Bunch. Harry Sinclair Drago. LC 34-9399. A. L. Burt Company.

Wild Bunch. Brian Fox. (Orig.). 1969. pap. 0.60 o.p. (A464X, Award). Univ Pub & Dist.

Wild Bunch. Brian Fox. (O.s.i.). 1969. pap. 0.95 o.p. (AN1462, Award). Univ Pub & Dist.

Wild Bunch. Ernest Haycox. LC 75-31606. 1975. 9.95 (ISBN 0-89190-973-7). Rivercity Press.

Wild Bunch. Ernest Haycox. LC 43-16229. 1943. Little, Brown and Company.

Wild Bunch. Ernest Haycox. LC 47-20005. 1946. Triangle Books, the Blakiston Company.

Wild Bunch. Rick Walters, pseud. (Orig.). 1980. pap. 1.75 (ISBN 0-505-51601-2). Tower Bks.

Wild Calendar. Libbie Block. LC 45-10646. 1946. A. A. Knopf.

Wild Call of Love. Franklin Harrison. Orig. Title: Step Softly on the Beaver. 1972. pap. 0.95 o.p. (09137). Curtis.

Wild Card. Raymond Hawkey & Roger Bingham. LC 73-91858. 300p. 1974. 7.95 o.s.i. (ISBN 0-8128-1683-8). Stein & Day.

Wild Card: A Novel. Raymond Hawkey & Roger Bingham. LC 73-91858. 1974. 7.95 (ISBN 0-8128-1683-8). Stein and Day.

Wild Cat. Laura Black. LC 79-3115. 1979. 10.95 (ISBN 0-312-88001-4). St. Martin's Press.

Wild Cayuses. Charles Stanley Strong. LC 45-3742. 1945. Phoenix Press.

Wild Cherries. Dale Herd. 100p. (Orig.). 1980. pap. 5.00 (ISBN 0-939180-16-2). Tombouctou.

Wild Cherry Tree Road. 1st Ed. Bernice Kelly Harris. LC 51-13531. 1951. Doubleday.

Wild Child. Francois Trauffat & Jean Gruault. (Illus.). 1973. (pbk) 0.95 (ISBN 0-671-47893-1). Pocket Books.

Wild Conquest. 1st Ed. Peter Abrahams. LC 50-7364. 1950. Harper.

Wild Country. Louis Bromfield. 274p. Repr. of 1948 ed. lib. bdg. 15.15x (ISBN 0-88411-542-9). Amereon Ltd.

Wild Country. Louis Bromfield. 1.50 o.p. G&D.

Wild Country: A Novel. Louis Bromfield. LC 48-8800. 1948. Harper.

Wild Darrie. David Christie Murray & Herman, Henry. LC 41-31123. 1889. Longmans, Green, and Co.

Wild Darrie. David Christie Murray & Herman, Henry. (On cover: Seaside library. Pocket ed., no. 1214). 1889. G. Munro.

Wild Decembers: A Biographical Portrait of the Brontes. 1st Ed. Hilda White. LC 57-8985. 1957. Dutton.

Wild Deer: By R. Hernekin Baptist... R. Hernekin Baptist. LC 34-56903. The John Day Company.

Wild Desires. Kathleen Drymon. 1982. pap. 3.50 (ISBN 0-8217-1103-2). Zebra.

Wild Deuces. Robert E Larkin. LC 28-19292. The Macaulay Company.

Wild Dog Running. Alan Scholefield. 1973. (pbk) 0.95 (ISBN 0-671-77541-3). Pocket Books.

Wild Dog Running. Alan Scholefield. LC 79-135145. (Illus.). 1971. 5.95. Morrow.

Wild Dogs. Steve Maurer. 24p. (Orig.). 1981. pap. 2.50 (ISBN 0-940846-01-2). Hastings Bks.

Wild Drums Beat. Francis Van Wyck Mason. LC 54-19834. (Pocket book, 977). 1953. Pocket Books.

Wild Duck. Henrik Ibsen & Christopher Hampton. LC 81-126643. 1980. 7.50 (ISBN 0-571-11601-9). Faber and Faber.

Wild Duck Murders. Theodora McCormick Du Bois. LC 43-15966. 1943. Pub. for the Crime Club by Doubleday, Doran & Co., Inc.

Wild Earth's Nobility. Frank Waters. LC 35-691994. Liveright Publishing Corporation.

Wild Eelin: Her Escapades, Adventures, and Bitter Sorrows. illustrated by t. de thulstrup. ed. William Black. LC 98-219. 1898. Harper & Bros.

Wild Faun. George William Willis. LC 45-393102. 1945. Greenberg.

Wild Fawn. Mary Imlay Taylor. LC 20-7514. 1920. Moffat, Yard and Company.

Wild Fire. Cathie Linz. (Candlelight Ecstasy Ser.: No. 157). (Orig.). 1983. pap. 1.95 (ISBN 0-440-18953-5). Dell.

Wild Fire. Barbara Riefe. LC 80-83569. 1981. 2.95 (ISBN 0-87216-798-4). Playboy Paperbacks.

Wild Flowers and Elves. Elsie Jean Stern. LC 28-1286. 1927. T. Nelson and Sons.

Wild Freedom. Max Brand. LC 81-2676. (Silver Star Western). 8.95 (ISBN 0-396-07977-6). Dodd, Mead.

Wild Freedom. Max Brand. LC 81-23519. 1982. 12.95 (ISBN 0-8161-3305-0). Hall.

Wild Fruit. Harry Sinclair Drago. LC 26-19677. 1926. G. H. Watt.

Wild Geese. Eilis Dillon. LC 80-15630. 12.95 (ISBN 0-671-22852-8). Simon and Schuster.

Wild Geese. Ogai Mori. 1959. bds. 2.75 o.p. (ISBN 0-8048-0629-2). C E Tuttle.

Wild Geese. Martha Ostenso. LC 25-212147. 1925. Dodd, Mead and Company.

Wild Geese. Martha Ostenso. LC 33-17516. 1926. Dodd, Mead and Company.

Wild Geese. Stanley John Weyman. LC 9-4487. 1909. Doubleday, Page & Company.

Wild Geese Calling. Stewart Edward White. 1940. Doubleday, Doran & Company, Inc.

Wild Geese Coming to Pass by Night. Raphael Carse. 14p. 1972. pap. 0.50 o.p. Greenlf Bks.

Wild Girl. Day Keene. 1969. pap. 0.75 o.p. (75-274). Manor Bks.

Wild Girl of Nebraska. Charles Wilkins Webber. LC 22-4764. 1852. Lippincott, Grambo & Co.

Wild Goose. Gouverneur Morris. LC 19-15552. 1919. C. Scribner's Sons.

Wild Goose, Brother Goose. Mel Ellis. 1969. 5.95 o.p. (ISBN 0-03-081845-1). HR&W.

Wild Goose Chase. Edwin Balmer. LC 15-16634. 1915. Duffield & Company.

Wild-Goose Chase. Fannie Heaslip Lea. LC 29-5596. 1929. Dodd, Mead & Company.

Wild Goose Chase. Rex Warner. LC 38-34348. 1938. A. A. Knopf.

Wild Goose of Limerick. Achmed Abdullah. LC 26-16086. Brentano's.

Wild Grape. John Henry Hewlett. 1947. Whittlesey House.

Wild Grape: A Novel of the Ozarks. Louise Platt Hauck. LC 31-10363. The Penn Publishing Company.

Wild Grapes. Maurice Rutledge Hale. LC 13-13533. 1913. Moffat, Yard and Company.

Wild Grapes. Barbara Jefferis. LC 63-13220. 1963. W. Sloane Associates.

Wild Grass. Harry Sinclair Drago. LC 57-11175. (Permabooks, M-3085. Western, 5). 1957. Permabooks.

Wild Grow the Lilies. Christy Brown. LC 75-37905. 1976. 8.95 (ISBN 0-8128-1923-3). Stein and Day.

Wild Grow the Lilies. Christy Brown. (Scarborough Book). 1978. 4.95 (ISBN 0-8128-2470-9). Stein and Day Publishers.

Wild Grow the Lilies: An Antic Novel. Christy Brown. LC 76-363917. 1976. 3.90 (ISBN 0-436-07095-2). Secker & Warburg.

Wild Harp. Jacqueline La Tourrette. 576p. (Orig.). 1981. pap. 2.95 (ISBN 0-449-14408-9, GM). Fawcett.

Wild Harvest. Vingie Eve Roe. LC 41-5224. M. S. Mill Co., Inc.

Wild Harvest: A Novel of Transition Days in Odlahoma. John Milton Oskison. LC 25-157626. 1925. D. Appleton and Company.

Wild Heart. Isabelle Sandy. LC 26-8009. 1926. Houghton Mifflin Company.

Wild Hearts. Vingie Eve Roe. LC 32-172597. 1932. Doubleday, Doran & Company, Inc.

Wild Heather. Elizabeth Thomasina Meade Smith. LC 32-33583. 1909. Cassell and Company, Ltd.

Wild Honey. Paul Kavanagh. 1974. 9.95x (ISBN 0-7022-0943-0); pap. 4.95x (ISBN 0-7022-0948-1). U of Queensland Pr.

Wild Honey. Frederick John Niven. LC 27-23194. 1927. Dodd, Mead & Company.

Wild Honey. Cynthia Stockley. LC 71-150564. (Short story index reprint series). (Illus.). 1971. (ISBN 0-8369-3862-3). Books for Libraries Press.

Wild Honey: Some Pilgrims and Vagrants Going Our Way. Stories. Victoria Lincoln. LC 52-121076. 1953. Rinehart.

Wild Honey: Stories of South Africa. Cynthia Stockley. LC 14-13375. 1914. G. P. Putnam's Sons.

Wild Horizon. Francis Van Wyck Mason. (Berkley Medallion Book.). (Illus.). 1977. 1.95. (ISBN 0-425-03350-3). Berkley Pub. Corp.

Wild Horizon: By F. Van Wyck Mason. Drawings by Samuel H. Bryant. 1st Ed. Francis Van Wyck Mason. 1966. 6.95. Little.

Wild Horse. Les Savage. LC 50-13515. (Gold medal book, 111). 1950. Fawcett Publications.

Wild Horse Lightning: A Powder Valley Western. Peter Field. LC 56-7040. 1956. Jefferson House.

Wild Horse Mesa. Grey, Zane. (Great western edition 50). 1962. Grosset & Dunlap.

Wild Horse Mesa. Zane Grey. LC 28-23045. 1928. Harper & Brothers.

Wild Horse Mesa. Zane Grey. LC 81-4784. 1981. 12.95 (ISBN 0-8161-3239-9). G.K. Hall.

Wild-Horse Ranch: The Startling Experiences of Jack Harmon in the "Painted Canyon" of Arizona. Reginald Charles Barker. LC 27-17116. L. C. Page & Company.

Wild-Horse Ranch: The Startling Experiences of Jack Harmon in the "Painted Canyon" of Arizona. Reginald Charles Barker. LC 27-17116. 1937. L. C. Page & Company.

Wild Horse Range. Wayne D Overholser. LC 51-11474. 1951. Bouregy & Curl.

Wild Horse Roundup: A Collection of Stories by Members of Western Writers of America. Western Writers of America. (Short Story Index Reprint Ser.). Repr. of 1957 ed. 21.00 o.p. (ISBN 0-8369-4270-1). Ayer Co.

Wild Horse Shorty. Nelson Coral Nye. LC 44-7098. 1944. The Macmillan Company.

Wild Horse Valley: A 'Henry' Story. Wilbur C Tuttle. LC 38-186078. 1938. Houghton Mifflin Company.

Wild Horses: A Novel. Henry Herbert Knibbs. LC 24-4508. 1924. Houghton Mifflin Company.

Wild Horses, Turn of the Century Prairie Girlhood. Eva P. Henderson. LC 82-10631. (Illus.). 96p. (Orig.). 1983. pap. 8.95 (ISBN 0-86534-013-7). Sunstone Pr.

Wild Hunger: A Novel, by Fred Malloy Pseud. Holland E Nickerson. LC 53-37575. 1953. Woodford Press.

Wild Hunt. Harry Peter M'Nab Brown. LC 72-88803. 1973. 6.95 (ISBN 0-15-196720-2). Harcourt Brace Jovanovich.

Wild Hunt. Jill Tattersall. LC 73-13639. 1974. 6.95 (ISBN 0-688-00227-7). Morrow.

Wild in Limbo: Or, The Escape of Paul Clifford. Containing the Rescue of Dora, and The Adventures of Nibbling Joe. LC 22-5174. 1863. R. M. DeWitt.

Wild in the World. John Donovan. LC 74-159044. 1974. (pbk.) 0.95. Avon.

Wild Indian. George Frederick Miller. LC 42-6286. 1942. The Daylion Company.

Wild Irish Boy... Charles Robert Maturin. LC 18-11264. 1808. Printed for E. Sargeant and M. & W. Ward, By D. & G. Bruce.

Wild Irish Boy. Charles Robert Maturin. LC 77-2043. (Gothic Novels III). 1977. 60.00 (ISBN 0-405-10141-4). Arno Press.

Wild Irish Boy. Charles Robert Maturin. LC 78-20803. (Ireland, from Th Act of Union, 1800, to the Death of Parnell, 1891). 1979. 96.00 (ISBN 0-8240-3460-0). Garland Pub.

Wild Irish Girl. Sydney Owenson Morgan. LC 78-20968. (Ireland, from the Act of Union, 1800, to the Death of Parnell, 1891; No. 6). 1978. 96.00 (ISBN 0-8240-3455-4). Garland Pub.

Wild Irish Girl. Morgan S. Owenson. Ed. by Robert L. Wolff. (Ireland-Nineteenth Century Fiction, Ser. Two: Vol. 6). 1979. lib. bdg. 126.00 (ISBN 0-8240-3455-4); lib. bdg. 46.00 ea. Garland Pub.

Wild Irish Girl. Elizabeth Thomasina Meade Smith. LC 10-18956. Hurst & Company.

Wild Irish Girl: A National Tale. Sydney Owenson Morgan. LC 7-18741. 1807. Printed for Samuel F. Bradford, No. South Third Street.

Wild Irish Girl: A National Tale. Sydney Owenson Morgan. LC 42-28902. 1883. P. J. Kenedy.

Wild Is the Heart. Diana Summers. LC 77-15851. (Orig.). 1978. pap. 1.95 (ISBN 0-87216-450-0). Playboy Pbks.

Wild Is the River. Louis Bromfield. LC 41-51986. 1941. Harper & Brothers.

Wild Island: A Mystery. Antonia Fraser. 1978. 8.95 (ISBN 0-393-08831-6). Norton.

Wild Island Sands. Sonya T. Pelton. 1983. pap. 3.75 (ISBN 0-8217-1135-0). Zebra.

Wild Jack: Or, The Stolen Child: and Other Stories. Including the Celebrated Magnolia Leaves. Caroline Lee Whiting Hentz. LC 7-4141. 1853. A. Hart.

Wild Justice. James Owen Hannay. LC 30-9246. The Bobbs-Merrill Company.

Wild Justice. Lloyd Osbourne. LC 6-6742. 1906. D. Appleton and Company.

Wild Justice. Arthur Leonard Bell Thompson. LC 70-183556. 1973. (pbk.) 1.25. Pocket Books.

Wild Justice: A Novel of the Frontier West. Robert J McCaig. LC 59-6134. 1959. Macmillan.

Wild Justice: Stories of the South Seas. Lloyd Osbourne. LC 21-19482. 1921. D. Appleton and Company.

Wild Knight of Battersea: G. K. Chesterton. F. A. Lea. 1973. Repr. of 1945 ed. 25.00 (ISBN 0-8274-0321-6). R West.

Wild Lilac. Helen Topping Miller. LC 43-18852. 1943. D. Appleton-Century Company, Incorporated.

Wild Lone: The Story of a Pytchley Fox. Denys James Watkins-Pitchford. LC 38-28930. 1938. C. Scribner's Sons.

Wild Love. A Romance. Friedrich Heinrich Karl La Motte-Fouque. LC 7-3081. 1845. E. Ferrett and Company.

Wild Man. Margaret Rome. (Harlequin Romances Ser.). 192p. 1981. pap. 1.50 (ISBN 0-373-02428-2). Harlequin Bks.

Wild Margaret. John Russell Coryell. LC 4702. (On cover: Eagle series, no. 174). 1900. Street & Smith.

Wild Margaret. Geraldine Fleming. LC 4702. (On cover: Eagle series, no. 174). 1900. Street & Smith.

Wild Marriage. Benjamin Harrison Lehman. LC 25-5966. 1925. Harper & Brothers.

Wild Metal. Charles James Louis Gilson. LC 32-13191. The Bobbs-Merrill Company.

Wild Midnight Falls. M. E. Chaber, pseud. (Milo March Mystery, No. 5). 1970. pap. 0.60 o.p. (63-265). Paperback Lib.

Wild Midnight Falls. M. E. Chaber, pseud. LC 68-12202. (Rinehart Suspense Novel). 1968. 3.95 o.p. (ISBN 0-03-068070-0). HR&W.

Wild Midnight Falls. Kendell Foster Crossen. LC 68-12202. (Rinehart suspense novel). 1968. Holt, Rinehart and Winston.

Wild Money. Freeman Tilden. LC 27-4385. 1927. Doubleday, Page & Company.

Wild Mountain Thyme. Rosamunde Pilcher. LC 77-18456. 1978. 8.95 (ISBN 0-312-87981-4). St. Martin's Press.

Wild Mustard: A Seven Days Chronicle. William Jasper Nicolls. LC 14-16481. 1914. J. B. Lippincott Company.

Wild Nell, the White Mountain Girl. H. J Moore. LC 7-19171. 1860. Sheldon & Company.

Wild Night: By Rae Foley Pseud. Elinore Denniston. LC 66-14149. (Red badge mystery). bds., 3.50. Dodd.

Wild Night Company: Irish Stories of Fantasy and Horror. Ed. by Peter Haining. LC 70-147810. 1971. 5.95 (ISBN 0-8008-8335-7). Taplinger Pub. Co.

Wild Nights. Emma Tennant. LC 79-3365. 1980. 9.95 (ISBN 0-15-196725-3) (ISBN 0-15-696726-X). Harcourt Brace Jovanovich.

Wild North. Ion L. Idriess. pap. 1.60 o.s.i. Tri-Ocean.

Wild Oat. Joseph Smith Fletcher. LC 29-10738. 1929. Doubleday, Doran & Company, Inc.

Wild Oats. Alice Marie Celeste Durand. Tr. by Valentine, Ferdinand Charles. (On cover: Munro's library, popular novels, v. 1, no. 204). 1884. N. L. Munro.

Wild Oats. Jacob Epstein. LC 78-27743. 8.95 (ISBN 0-316-24570-4). Little, Brown.

Wild Oats. Jacob Epstein. 1980. 2.75 (ISBN 0-671-83393-6). Pocket Books.

Wild Oats. James Oppenheim. LC 10-15637. 1910. B. W. Huebsch.

Wild Ohio. Bart Spicer. LC 53-6320. 1953. Dodd, Mead.

Wild Olive. May Sutherland. LC 56-5447. Roy Publishers.

Wild Olive. Margaret Jessup Van Briggle. LC 49-496448. 1949. West Pub. Co.

Wild Olive: A Novel. Basil King. LC 10-12098. 1910. Harper & Brothers.

Wild One. Marianne Harvey. (Orig.). 1981. pap. 2.95 (ISBN 0-440-19207-2). Dell.

Wild One. Paul Kropp & Sandra Gulland. LC 82-12929. (Kropp, Paul. Encounters Ser.). EMC Pub.

Wild One. Amos Rank. 192p. (Orig.). 1974. pap. 1.95 o.p. (ISBN 0-87056-360-2, 6360). Brandon.

Wild One. John Henry Reese. 1981. pap. 1.75 (ISBN 0-449-13953-0, GM). Fawcett.

Wild Onion. Loren Carroll. LC 30-22758. 1930. Dodd, Mead and Company.

Wild Oranges. Joseph Hergesheimer. LC 22-158558. 1922. A. A. Knopf.

Wild Orchard. Dan Totheroh. LC 27-593963. George H. Doran Company.

Wild Orchard: A Story of Early Tasmania. Isabel Dick. LC 45-142542. 1945. Thomas Y. Crowell Company.

Wild Orchid. Sigrid Undset & Chater, Arthur G., Tr. LC 31-25413. 1931. A. A. Knopf.

Wild Palms. William Faulkner. LC 39-1750. Random House.

Wild Paradise. King Phillips. LC 27-750542. 1927. A. C. McClurg & Co.

Wild Party. John McPartland. pap. 0.60 o.p. (60-367). Manor Bks.

Wild Party. Terrence O'Neill. (O.s.i.). (Orig.). 1975. pap. 1.25 o.p. (AQ1412, Award). Univ Pub & Dist.

Wild Pastures. Rex Ellingwood Beach. LC 35-2777. Farrar & Rinehart, Incorporated.

Wild Patience Has Taken Me This Far: Poems 1978-1981. Adrienne Rich. 1981. 12.95 (ISBN 0-393-01494-0); pap. 4.95 (ISBN 0-393-00072-9). Norton.

Wild Peach. Claire Cave. LC 37-15888. Gramercy Publishing Co.

Wild Pitch. Alfred Bertram Guthrie. LC 72-4235. 1973. 5.95 (ISBN 0-395-15482-0). Houghton Mifflin.

Wild Pitch. Alfred Bertram Guthrie. LC 73-8513. 1973. 8.95 (ISBN 0-8161-6117-8). G. K. Hall.

Wild Proxy: A Tragic Comedy of to-Day. Lucy Lane Clifford. LC 6-207392. 1893. Cassell Publishing Company.

Wild Quarry. Giles A Lutz. (Ace western). 1974. (pbk.) 0.75. Ace Books.

Wild Queen. George Brandon Saul. LC 67-30726. (Illus.). 1967. J. F. Blair.

Wild Rhapsody. Shirley Hart. (Candlelight Ecstasy Ser.: No. 123). (Orig.). 1983. pap. 1.95 (ISBN 0-440-19545-4). Dell.

Wild Riding Runt. Frank Chester Robertson. LC 34-434735. 1934. I. Washburn.

Wild River. Anna Louise Strong. LC 43-15971. 1943. Little, Brown and Company.

Wild Rock: A Tale of Two Seasons. LC 8-33121. 1884. Printed for the Author.

Wild Rose. Clara Viola Fleharty. LC 11-16260. R. G. Badger.

Wild Rose. James Noble Gifford. LC 41-1233. 1941. Gramercy Pub. Co.

Wild Rose. Carol Holliston. LC 41-123341. Gramercy Publishing Co.

Wild Rose: A Tale of the Mexican Frontier. Francis Jr Francis. LC 6-43246. 1895. Macmillan and Co.

Wild Rose: A Tale of the Rockies. Howard Roscoe Driggs. LC 16-22847. University Publishing Company.

Wild Rose of Cherokee, or, Nancy War, "The Pocahontas of the West". A Story of the Early Exploration, Occupancy and Settlement of the State of Tennessee. A Romance, Founded on and Interwoven with History. E. Sterling King. 1895. University Press.

Wild Rose of Cherokee: Or, Nancy Ward, "The Pocahontas of the West." A Story of the Early Exploration, Occupancy and Settlement of the State of Tennessee; a Romance, Founded on and Interwoven with History. Elisha Sterling King. LC 38-32409. Myrtle K. Tatum.

Wild Rose of Gross-Stauffen. Nataly Von Eschstruth & Lathrop, Elise L., Tr. LC 6-38148. (On cover: Worthington's international library, no. 23). 1892. Worthington Company.

Wild Rose of the Beaver, and Tononqua, the Pride of the Wyandots. Two Border Tales of the 18th Century. Rudolph Leonhart. LC 7-12852. Printed by Werner & Lohmann.

Wild Roses. Julia Grice. 1980. pap. 2.95 (ISBN 0-380-75069-4, 78022). Avon.

Wild Roses. Sheila Paulos. (Candlelight Ecstasy Ser.: No. 108). (Orig.). 1983. pap. 1.95 (ISBN 0-440-19728-7). Dell.

Wild Roses: A Story Followed by a Love Letter. Jacques Ferron. LC 76-363937. 6.95 (ISBN 0-7710-3130-0). McClelland and Stewart.

Wild Runners. Mel Ellis. 1970. 4.95 o.p. (ISBN 0-03-085059-2). HR&W.

Wild Runs the River. Giles A Lutz. LC 68-11814. 1968. Doubleday.

Wild Rye. Muriel Hine Coxon. LC 32-1649. 1932. D. Appleton and Company.

Wild Scenes in the Forest and Prairie. Charles Fenno Hoffman. LC 76-104485. 1970. (ISBN 0-8398-0784-8). Literature House.

Wild Season. Allan W Eckert. LC 67-14449. 1967. Little, Brown.

Wild Seed. Octavia E Butler. LC 79-7596. 1980. 10.00 (ISBN 0-385-15160-8). Doubleday.

Wild Seed. Paige Mitchell, pseud. LC 79-8029. 1981. 14.95 (ISBN 0-385-14368-0). Doubleday.

Wild Song. Alice Mary Ross Colver. LC 35-277915. 1935. Dodd, Mead & Company.

Wild Southern Scenes. A Tale of Disunion! and Border War! John Beauchamp Jones. LC 7-11918. T. B. Peterson & Brothers.

Wild Stallion. Illustrated by William Moyers. Bud Murphy. LC 56-3495. (World junior library). World Pub. Co.

Wild Stallions. John Benteen. (Sundance Ser.: No. 7). 160p. 1981. pap. 1.75 (ISBN 0-8439-1046-1, Leisure Bks). Nordon Pubns.

Wild Storm of Heaven. June L. Shiplett. (Orig.). 1980. pap. 2.95 (ISBN 0-451-11247-4, AE1247, Sig). NAL.

Wild Strawberries: A Novel. Angela Mackail Thirkell. LC 34-272196. 1934. H. Smith & R. Haas.

Wild Streak. Margaret Emerson Bailey. LC 72-106245. (Short story index reprint series). 1970. (ISBN 0-8369-3281-1). Books for Libraries Press.

Wild Streak. Margaret Emerson Bailey. LC 32-24666. 1932. G. P. Putnam's Sons.

Wild Streets: Tales of the Frontier Towns. Western Writers of America. LC 73-113693. (Short story index reprint series). 1970. Books for Libraries Press.

Wild Streets: Tales of the Frontier Towns. Western Writers of America. LC 58-12058. 1958. Doubleday.

Wild Summit. Llewellyn Perry Holmes. 224p. 1982. pap. 1.95 (ISBN 0-445-00692-7). Popular Lib.

Wild Summit: By Matt Stuart Pseud. Llewellyn Perry Holmes. LC 58-107719. (Silver star westerns). 1958. Dodd, Mead.

Wild Swan. Margaret Kennedy. LC 57-5682. 1957. Rinehart.

Wild Swan: And Other Sketches; Illus. Ben Hur Lampman. LC 47-11339. 1947. T. Y. Crowell Co.

Wild Sweet Witch. Araby Scott. 336p. 1981. pap. 2.95 (ISBN 0-380-77339-2, 77339). Avon.

Wild Sweet Witch: A Novel. Philip Mason. LC 47-11009. 1947. Harcourt, Brace.

Wild Sweetness. Isobel Scott. (Circle of Love Ser.: No. 27). 192p. Date not set. 1.75 (ISBN 0-553-21543-4). Bantam.

Wild Talent. Wilson Tucker. LC 53-109215. 1954. Rinehart.

Wild Talents. Charles Fort. Ed. by Lester Del Ray. LC 75-409. (Library of Science Fiction). 1975. lib. bdg. 15.00 (ISBN 0-8240-1414-6). Garland Pub.

Wild Times. Brian Wynne Garfield. LC 78-15610. 10.95 (ISBN 0-671-24374-8). Simon and Schuster.

Wild Turkey. Roger Lichtenberg Simon. (O.s.i.). 1975. 6.95 o.s.i. (ISBN 0-671-21975-8, Straight Arrow). S&S.

Wild Turkey. Roger Lichtenberg Simon. 1976. 1.50 (ISBN 0-671-80309-3). Pocket Books.

Wild, Unwilling Wife. Barbara Cartland. LC 76-57981. 6.95. Dutton.

Wild Valley. Charlotte Paul. 1.95 (ISBN 0-441-88965-4). Ace Books.

Wild Violets. Ruth B. Field. 368p. (Orig.). 1980. pap. 2.50 (ISBN 0-89083-635-3). Zebra.

Wild Warringtons. A Family History. Arnold Gray. (Seaside library, v. 80, no. 1627). 1883. G. Munro.

Wild Wave. Kamelle Hess. (Orig.). 1979. pap. 1.95 (ISBN 0-532-23108-2). Woodhill.

Wild West. Bertrand William Sinclair. LC 26-6144. 1926. Little, Brown, and Company.

Wild Western Scenes. John Beauchamp Jones. LC 71-104501. (Illus.). 1970. (ISBN 0-8398-0958-1). Literature House.

Wild Western Scenes.-- Second Series. The War-Path: a Narrative of Adventures in the Wilderness: with Minute Details of the Captivity of Sundry Persons; Amusing and Perilous Incidents During Their Abode in the Wild Woods; Fearful Battle with the Indians: Ceremony of Adoption into an Indian Family; Encounters with Wild Beasts and Rattlesnakes, &C.... John Beauchamp Jones. LC 7-12850. 1856. J. B. Lippincott & Co.

Wild Western Scenes: A Narrative of Adventures in the Western Wilderness, Forty Years Ago; Wherein the Conduct of Daniel Boone, the Great American Pioneer, Is Particularly Described... John Beauchamp Jones. LC 18-17304. 1841. S. Coleman.

Wild Western Scenes: A Narrative of Adventure in the Western Wilderness, Forty Years Ago; Wherein in Conduct of Daniel Boone, the Great American Pioneer, Is Particularly Described. Also: Minute Accounts Are Given of Bear Hunts--Deer and Buffalo Hunts--Desperate Conflicts with the Savages--Wolf Hunts--Fishing and Fowling Adventures--Encounters with Serpents, Etc. Etc. John Beauchamp Jones. 1845. E. Ferrett & Co.

Wild Western Scenes: A Narrative of Adventures in the Western Wilderness, Wherein the Exploits of Daniel Boone, the Great American Pioneer, Are Particularly Described; Also, Accounts of Bear, Deer, and Buffalo Hunts--Desperate Conflicts with the Savages--Wolf Hunts--Fishing and Fowling Adventures--Encounters with Serpents, Etc. New Sterotype Ed., Altered, Rev., and Cor. John Beauchamp Jones. LC 7-11920. 1856. J. B. Lippincott & Co.

Wild Western Scenes: A Narrative of Adventures in the Western Wilderness, Wherein the Exploits of Daniel Boone, the Great American Pioneer, Are Particularly Described; Also, Accounts of Bear, Deer, and Buffalo Hunts--Desperate Conflicts with the Sabages--Wolf Hunts--Fishing and Fowling Adventures--Encoutners with Serpents, Etc. New Stereotype Ed., Altered, Rev., and Cor. John Beauchamp Jones. LC 7-11921. 1859. J. B. Lippincott & Co.

Wild Western Scenes: Or, The White Spirit of the Wilderness. Being a Narrative of Adventures, Embracing the Same Characters Portrayed in the Original "Wild Western Scenes"... John Beauchamp Jones. LC 7-12846. 1863. M. A. Malsby.

Wild Wheels. Carl Henry Rathjen. LC 65-21856. (Tempo books). 1965. Grosset & Dunlap.
Wild White Man of Badu. Ion L. Idriess. pap. 1.60 o.s.i. Tri-Ocean.
Wild White Woods: Or, A Winter Camp on the Canada Line. Russell Duryee Smith. 1.35. E. P. Dutton & Company.
Wild Widow. Gertie De S Wentworth-James. Empire Book Company.
Wild, Wild Women. Gene Curry. (Saddler Ser.: No. 5). (Orig.). 1980. pap. 1.75. Tower Bks.
Wild, Wildwood Flower & Other Deep South Tales. Olivia P. Solomon. LC 78-70631. 1979. 7.50 (ISBN 0-916620-23-9). Portals Pr.
Wild Willful Love. Valerie Sherwood. 576p. 1983. pap. 3.95 (ISBN 0-446-30850-1). Warner Bks.
Wild Wind. Temple Bailey. LC 30-23437. The Penn Publishing Company.
Wild Wind: A Novel. Marjorie Jane Putnam Sinclair. LC 50-6772. 1950. J. Day.
Wild Wind Westward. Vanessa Royall. (Orig.). 1982. pap. 3.50 (ISBN 0-440-19363-X). Dell.
Wild Winds of Love. Veronica Jason. 1982. pap. 3.50 (ISBN 0-451-11911-8, AE1911, Sig). NAL.
Wild Wine. Florence Jeannette Baier Ward. LC 32-28824. 1932. Macrae Smith Company.
Wild Women Don't Get the Blues. Barbara Emrys. 52p. 1977. 4.00 (ISBN 0-934816-00-X). Metis Pr Inc.
Wild Women of the West. Carl W. Breihan. 1982. pap. 2.50 (ISBN 0-451-11951-7, AE1951, Sig). NAL.
Wild Women" The Romance of a Flapper. Janet Lee. LC 22-12389. 1922. N. L. Brown.
Wild Work: The Story of the Red River Tragedy. Mary Edwards Bryan. LC 11-105574. 1881. D. Appleton and Company.
Wild Work: The Story of the Red River Tragedy. Mary Edwards Bryan. (On cover: The laurel library, no. 13). 1893. G. Munro's Sons.
Wild Yazoo. John Myers Myers. LC 47-301363. 1947. E. P. Dutton & Company, Inc.
Wild Young Fags. Jack Smith. pap. 1.95 o.p. (8005). Cameo.
Wild Youth, and Another. Gilbert Parker. LC 19-5850. 1919. J. B. Lippincott Company.
Wildcat. Sinclair Gluck. LC 32-80833. 1932. Dodd, Mead & Company.
Wildcat. William Heyliger. LC 37-184359. 1937. D. Appleton-Century Company, Incorporated.
Wildcat. Hugh Wiley. LC 20-15955. George H. Doran Company.
Wildcat Brand. William Frederick Bragg. LC 55-10194. 1955. Arcadia House.
Wildcat Woman. Curry, Gene. (belmont tower book). 1.75 (ISBN 0-505-51407-9). Tower Publications, Inc.
Wildcat 13. Tom Gill. LC 41-732910. G. P. Putnam's Sons.
Wildcats. John Thomas Edson. 192p. (Orig.). 1981. pap. 1.95 (ISBN 0-425-04755-5). Berkley Pub.
Wildcats of Tonto Basin. Drake C. Denber. LC 41-26002. 1941. Phoenix Press.
Wildcats of Tonto Basin. Drake C Denver, pseud. Phoenix Press.
Wildcatters. John Benteen. (Fargo Ser.: No. 5). (Orig.). 1980. pap. 1.50 (ISBN 0-505-51542-3). Tower Bks.
Wildcatters. John Benteen. 1970. pap. 0.60 o.p. (B60-1084). Belmont-Tower.
Wildcatters. Bryan Cooper. LC 77-357890. 1976. 3.75 (ISBN 0-356-08211-3). Macdonald and Jane's.
Wildcatters. (Making of America Ser.: No. 10). (Orig.). 1981. pap. 2.95 (ISBN 0-440-09830-0, Bryans). Dell.
Wildcatter's Woman. large print ed. Janet Dailey. LC 82-11922. 1982. 6.95 (ISBN 0-8161-3440-5). G.K. Hall.
Wildeblood's Empire. Brian M Stableford. 1977. 1.50 (ISBN 0-87997-331-5). DAW Books.
Wilder Curse. Kenneth Robeson. (Avenger,#23). 1974. (pbk.) 0.95. Warner Paperback Lib.
Wilder Shore. Daphne Clair. (Harlequin Presents Ser.). 192p. 1980. pap. 1.50 (ISBN 0-373-10385-9). Harlequin Bks.
Wilder Shores of Love. Leslie Blanch. 1970. pap. 3.95 o.p. (ISBN 0-671-20508-0, Touchstone Bks). S&S.
Wilder Stone. 1st Ed. John Leggett. LC 60-5907. Harper.
Wilderness. Noel Bertram Gerson. LC 59-7918. 1959. Doubleday.
Wilderness. Robert B. Parker. 1983. pap. price not set (ISBN 0-440-19328-1). Dell.
Wilderness. Carter A Vaughan, pseud. LC 59-7918. 1962. Doubleday.
Wilderness- Stone. 1st Ed. Robert Nathan. LC 60-53444. 1961. Knopf.
Wilderness: A Novel. Robert B. Parker. LC 79-12861. 8.95 (ISBN 0-440-09328-7). Delacorte Press/S. Lawrence.
Wilderness: A Story of the Hills, and of a Boy Who Suffered and Sacrificed. Pascal R Guntharp. Burton Publishing Company.
Wilderness: A Tale of the Civil War. Robert Penn Warren. LC 61-6248. 1961. Random House.
Wilderness Adventure. Elizabeth Page. LC 46-3221. 1946. Toronto, Rinehart & Company, Inc.
Wilderness & Gardens, an American Lady's Prospect. 1974. pap. 2.00 o.p. (ISBN 0-87423-011-X). Westburg.
Wilderness and the Rose: A Story of Michigan. Jerome James Wood. LC 8-37553. 1890. Wood Book Company.
Wilderness and the War Path. James Hall. LC 7-1217. 1849. J. Wiley.
Wilderness and the Warpath. James Hall. LC 68-55679. (American short story series, v. 20). 1969. Garrett Press.
Wilderness and the Warpath. James Hall. LC 72-8143. (American short story series, v. 20). 1972. (ISBN 0-8422-8069-3). MSS Information Corp.
Wilderness Brigade. 1st Ed. Phyllis Gordon Demarest. LC 56-10759. 1957. Doubleday.
Wilderness Castaways. Dillon Wallace. LC 13-18715. 1913. A. C. McClurg & Co.
Wilderness Cry: The Story of a Great Sacrifice. George Edward Day. LC 6-43786. 1906. The C. M. Clark Publishing Co.
Wilderness Dreams. 2nd ed. Wayne D. Thompson. (Illus.). 1982. pap. 4.95 (ISBN 0-914598-10-4). Padre Prods.
Wilderness Empire Seventeen Fifty-Five. Allan W. Eckert. 768p. 1980. pap. 3.50 (ISBN 0-553-13993-2). Bantam.
Wilderness House. Foxhall Daingerfield. LC 28-17811. 1928. D. Appleton and Company.
Wilderness Inn. Janet Louise Roberts (ISBN 0-671-80776-5). Pocket Books.
Wilderness Mine. Harold Bindloss. LC 20-14600. 1.90. Frederick A. Stokes Company.
Wilderness Nurse. Jane McCarthy. 192p. (YA) 1975. 4.95 o.p. (Avalon). Bouregy.
Wilderness Nurse. Jane McCarthy. 1975. 4.95. Avalon Books.
Wilderness Nurse. Marguerite Mooers Marshall. LC 49-996735. 1949. Macrae-Smith-Co.
Wilderness of Dreams. M. D. Parnell. 3.95 o.p. (ISBN 0-8062-0536-9). Carlton.
Wilderness of Four: Across the Far Mountain, No. 1. Niel Hancock. 256p. 1982. pap. 2.95 (ISBN 0-445-04705-4). Popular Lib.
Wilderness of Ice. Jules Verne. 3.95. Assoc Bk.
Wilderness of Mirrors. Tr. from German by Michael Bullock. 1st Amer. Ed. Max Frisch. 1966. bds., 6.00. Random.
Wilderness of Monkeys. Paige Mitchell, pseud. LC 65-15764. 1965. Dutton.
Wilderness of Monkeys. Paige Mitchell. 1974. (pbk.) 1.25. Popular Library.
Wilderness of Monkeys. Frederick Niven. LC 11-112191. 1911. 1.25. John Lane Company.
Wilderness of Spring. Pangborn, Edgar. LC 58-5139. 1958. Rinehart.
Wilderness of Stars. William F. Nolan. 1978. pap. 4.95 o.s.i. (ISBN 0-8202-5031-7). Sherbourne.
Wilderness of Stars. William F. Nolan. 288p. 1969. 5.95 o.p. (ISBN 0-8202-0111-1). Sherbourne.
Wilderness of Stars: Stories of Man in Conflict with Space. Ed. by William F. Nolan. LC 78-83562. 1969. 5.95. Sherbourne Press.
Wilderness of Vines. George Harold Bennett. LC 66-17441. 4.95. Doubleday.
Wilderness: Or, Braddock's Times. A Tale of the West... James McHenry. LC 7-16454. 1848. M. P. Morse; Allegheny, J. B. Kennedy.
Wilderness; or Braddock's Times: A Tale of the West, 2 vols. James McHenry. LC 78-64078. Repr. of 1823 ed. Set. 75.00 (ISBN 0-404-17270-9). AMS Pr.
Wilderness(Or, Braddock's Times: A Tale of the West. James McHenry. (American Historical Novel Ser). 1823. 13.50 o.s.i. (ISBN 0-512-00859-0). Garrett Pr.
Wilderness Orphan. Dorothy Wilkinson Cottrell. LC 40-326124. J. Messner, Inc.
Wilderness Passage. Forrester Blake. LC 52-7135. 1953. Random House.
Wilderness Patrol. Harold Bindloss. LC 23-13333. 1923. Frederick A. Stokes Company.
Wilderness Patrol. Charles Stoddard. LC 38-7571. The Dodge Publishing Company.
Wilderness Patrol. Charles Stanley Strong. LC 38-7571. 1938. Dodge Pub. Co.
Wilderness Reader. Frank Bergon. (Orig.). 1980. pap. 3.50 (ISBN 0-451-61902-1, ME1902, Ment). NAL.
Wilderness Road: A Romance of St. Clair's Defeat and Wayne's Victory. Joseph Alexander Altsheler. LC 1-8282. 1901. D. Appleton and Company.
Wilderness Seekers. Lou Cameron. (Dell Book). 1979. 2.50 (ISBN 0-440-09287-6). Dell Publishing Co.
Wilderness Speaks. Courtland Olmstead. LC 72-96460. 1973. 2.50 o.p. (ISBN 0-8059-1815-9). Dorrance.
Wilderness Track. Owen G. Irons. 224p. (Orig.). 1980. pap. 1.95 (ISBN 0-89083-659-0). Zebra.
Wilderness Trail. Francis William Sullivan. LC 13-15857. W. J. Watt & Company.
Wilderness Trek: A Novel of Australia. Zane Grey. LC 44-5520. 1944. Harper & Brothers.
Wilderness Walls. Jane Rolyat. LC 33-910028. E. P. Dutton & Co., Inc.
Wilderness War. Allan W. Eckert. LC 78-14862. 1978. 17.50 (ISBN 0-316-20875-2). Little.
Wilderness West. Jodi Rambo. LC 52-6267. 1951. Pageant Press.
Wilderness: Yuan-Yeh) Yu Tsao. LC 78-65981. (Chinese Literature in Translation). 1979. 12.50 (ISBN 0-253-17297-7). Indiana University Press.
Wilders Walk Away. Herbert Brean. LC 48-582828. 1948. W. Morrow.
Wildest Heart. Rosemary Rogers. 1974. pap. 3.50 (ISBN 0-380-00137-3, 79731). Avon.
Wildest Passion. Paula Fairman. 304p. (Orig.). 1982. pap. 3.25 (ISBN 0-523-42034-X). Pinnacle Bks.
Wildfire. Jack Foxx. LC 78-51082. 1978. 8.95 o.p. (ISBN 0-672-52214-4). Bobbs.
Wildfire. Zane Grey. LC 17-2028. 1917. 1.35. Harper & Brothers.
Wildfire. Zane Grey. LC 22-4733. 1917. Grosset & Dunlap.
Wildfire. Zane Grey. LC 21-13688. 1919. Grosset & Dunlap.
Wildfire. Zane Grey. LC 22-247787. Grosset & Dunlap.
Wildfire. Zane Grey. 1976. (pbk.) 1.50 (ISBN 0-671-80317-4). Pocket Books.
Wildfire: A Novel. Bill Pronzini. LC 78-51082. 8.95 (ISBN 0-672-52214-4). Bobbs-Merrill.
Wildfire at Midnight. Mary Stewart. LC 56-8470. 1956. Appleton-Century-Crofts.
Wildfire at Midnight. Mary Stewart. LC 61-65309. 1961. M. S. Mill Co., and W. Morrow.
Wildfire Encountered. Helen Bianchin. (Harlequin Presents Ser.). 192p. 1982. pap. 1.75 (ISBN 0-373-10527-4). Harlequin Bks.
Wildfire of Love. Glenna Finley, pseud. (Signet Book.). 1979. 1.75 (ISBN 0-451-08602-3). New American Library.
Wildfire Woman. Marianna Spring. 1978. 2.25 (ISBN 0-440-09579-4). Dell Pub. Co.
Wildfires, Bk. 4: The Story of Canada. Dennis Adair & Janet Rosenstock. 336p. 3.50 (ISBN 0-380-82313-6). Avon.
Wildflower. Jaroldeen Edwards. 608p. (Orig.). 1982. pap. 3.50 (ISBN 0-440-19374-5). Dell.
Wildflower. Grace Sourek. LC 28-29231. 1928. J. F. Sourek.
Wildflower. A Novel. Frederick William Robinson. (seaside library, v. 78, no. 1584). 1883. G. Munro.
Wildflowers. Pamela Redford Russell. LC 81-84526. 14.50 (ISBN 0-87223-777-X). Seaview Books.
Wildford's Daughter. Anne Rundle. LC 78-2636. 8.95. Putnam.
Wilding Graft: A Novel. Jack R Clemo. LC 48-9032. 1948. Macillan Co.
Wildings of Western. David J Lake. 1.50 (ISBN 0-87997-306-4). DAW Books.
Wildlife Heroes and Villains: Personality Portraits of Creatures Great and Small. Emiliian Stanev. LC 69-17639. (Illus.). 1969. 4.50. Stackpole Books.
Wildmoor. A Novel. Florence Burckett. LC 6-18669. 1875. J.B. Lippincott & Co.
Wildness Is Yours. Rose Thurburn. LC 50-8981. 1950. Morrow.
Wildon Affair. Roland DeForrest. (Erotica Ser.). 256p. 1983. pap. 2.75 (ISBN 0-446-30207-4). Warner Bks.
Wildwood. Jennie Maria Drinkwater Conklin. LC 6-30660. Presbyterian Board of Publication.
Wildwood. Josephine Winslow Johnson. LC 46-1199. 1946. Harper & Brothers.
Wildwood Romance. Charles Asbury Stephens. LC 35-3430. The Old Squire's Book Store.
Wildwoods and Wishes. Susan Berencsi. LC 80-3007. 1981. 10.95 (ISBN 0-385-17317-2). Doubleday.
Wildwoods & Wishes. Susan Berensci. LC 80-3007. (Starlight Romance Ser.). 192p. 1981. 10.95 (ISBN 0-385-17317-2). Doubleday.
Wiles of a Stranger. Joan Smith. (Coventry Romance Ser.: No. 195). 192p. 1982. pap. 1.50 (ISBN 0-449-50298-8, Coventry). Fawcett.
Wiles of Sexton Maginnis. Maurice Francis Egan. 1909. The Century Co.
Wiles of Women: From the Turkish. Tr. by Jean Adolphe Decourdemanche & Whitham, J. Mills. Makr I Zanan & Faraj-Ba'd-Shiddan. LC 30-15224. (Golden Dragon Library). (Half-title: The golden dragon library). 1929. L. MacVeagh, The Dial Press.
Wiley's Move. Lee Hoffman. (Dell book). 1973. (pbk) 0.95. Dell Publishing Co.
Wilfred: A Story with a Happy Ending. A. T Winthrop. (On cover: Spare-hour series). 1880. A. D. F. Randolph & Company.
Wilfred. A Story with a Happy Ending. A. T Winthrop. LC 8-37851. A. D. F. Randolph & Company.
Wilfred Glenn: Or, The Struggle with Wealth. Gilbert Romine Hammond. LC 11-31856. Printed by Drury Printing Co.
Wilfrid Cumbermede: An Autobiographical Story. George Macdonald. LC 7-15863. 1872. C. Scribner & Co.
Wilfrid Cumbermede: An Autobiographical Story. George Macdonald. LC 12-18326. 1911. D. McKay.
Wilful and Premeditated: An Inspector French Detective Story. Freeman Wills Crofts. LC 34-1291. 1934. Dodd, Mead & Company.
Wilful Heiress. Emma Scarr Booth. LC 6-15036. 1892. C. W. Moulton.
Wilful Lady. J. G Jeffreys. LC 75-330590. (Illus.). 1975. 6.95 (ISBN 0-8027-5332-9). Walker.
Wilhelm Meister's Apprenticeship. Johann Wolfgang Von Goethe. Tr. by Carlyle, Thomas. LC 17-17429. (Harvard classics shelf of fiction, selected by C. W. Eliot. 14). P. F. Collier & Son.
Wilhelm Meister's Apprenticeship and Travels. Johann Wolfgang Von Goethe. Tr. by Thomas Carlyle. LC 74-3190. (Carlyle, Thomas, 1795-1881. Works. 1974: Vols. 23-24). (Illus.). 1974. per vol. 17.50. AMS Press.
Wilhelm Meister's Apprenticeship and Travels. Johann Wolfgang Von Goethe. Tr. by Thomas Carlyle. LC 72-10629. (works of Thomas Carlyle, v. 23-24). 1972. Scholarly Press.
Wilhelm Meister's Years of Apprenticeship. Johann Wolfgang Von Goethe & H. M Waidson. LC 79-41173. 1980. 11.95 (ISBN 0-7145-3702-0). J. Calder.
Wilhelmina Changes Her Mind. Florence Morse Kingsley. LC 12-13892. Small, Maynard and Company.
Wilk Are Among Us. Isidore Haiblum. 1979. pap. 1.95 (ISBN 0-440-19817-8). Dell.
Wilk Are Among Us. Isidore Haiblum. LC 74-5526. 216p. 1975. 5.95 o.p. (ISBN 0-385-08340-8). Doubleday.
Wilk Are Among Us. Isidore Haiblum. LC 74-5526. 216p. 1975. 5.95 o.p. (ISBN 0-385-08340-8). Doubleday.
Will. Richard Martin Stern. LC 75-30460. 1976. 8.95 (ISBN 0-385-11084-7). Doubleday.
Will. Harvey Swados. LC 63-20240. 1963. World Pub. Co.
Will, a Modern Day Treasure Hunt. 2nd ed. Ronald Franks & Thomas Dowd. Date not set. pap. text ed. 6.95 (ISBN 0-9607132-0-4). Tricore Assoc.
Will: A Novel. authorized ed. rev. and cor. in the united states. ed. Ernst Eckstein & Bell, Clara, Tr. LC 6-35837. 1885. W. S. Gottsberger.
Will and Last Testament of Constance Cobble. Stanton Forbes, pseud. LC 79-8499. 1980. 7.95. Published for the Crime Club by Doubleday.
Will and the Deed. Dorothy Ogburn. LC 35-5305. 1935. Dodd, Mead & Company.
Will and the Way. James Maurice Scott. LC 49-682419. 1949. E. P. Dutton.
Will and the Way: A Guide to Self Help and Self Development... Leo Conrad Wende. W. B. Straube Print.
Will and the Way: A Novel. Susan M Belser. (John Rung prize series). Lutheran Publication Society.
Will and the Way Stories. Jessie Benton Fremont. LC 6-40027. D. Lothrop Company.
Will and the Wilful. Martha Tooke Webb. LC 68-57738. 1969. 3.95. Dorrance.
Will Anyone Who Saw the Accident... Roderic Jeffries. LC 64-12690. Harper and Row.
Will B. More Letters: Scenes in the Sunny South. author's ed. Honor Lupfer Wilhelm. LC 2482. 1900. The Mail Publishing Company.
Will Denbigh: Nobleman. Dinah Maria Mulock Craik. 1877. Roberts Brothers.
Will He Find Her? A Romance of New York and New Orleans. Winter Summerton. LC 8-17659. 1860. Derby & Jackson.
Will He Marry Her! A Domestic Drama for Home Reading. William P Peck. 1885. Rhodes & Mc-Clure Publishing Co.
Will in the Way. Miles Burton. LC 47-11089. 1947. Pub. for the Crime Club by Doubleday.
Will It March! The Progress of a Pilgrim of the Twentieth Century; or, The Life, Times, and Character of Paul Hampton, LITT. D. An Age-Long Epic with a Modern Phase and a Far-West Lilt. Incidentally More or Less Gratuitors Philosophy and Fugitive Criticism Attached. Joseph Ketchum Jones. LC 31-5220. Harr Wagner Publishing Co.
Will, My Son. Sarah Boston. pap. 4.95 (ISBN 0-86104-346-4). Pluto Pr.
Will O' the Mill. Robert Louis Stevenson. LC 9-1487. (On cover: Cosy corner series). 1895. J. Knight Company.
Will O' the Mill. Robert Louis Stevenson. LC 2-21401. 1902. H. M. Caldwell Co.
Will O' the Wasp: A Sea Yarn of the War of '12. Robert Cameron Rogers. LC 7-40736. 1896. G. P. Putnam's Sons.
Will-O'-the-Wisp. Patricia Wentworth. LC 28-25353. 1928. J. B. Lippincott Company.
Will-O'-the Wisp see Three Novels: Bibliotheca Neerlandica Ser.

Will of Allah. Kathlyn Rhodes. LC 9-85721. 1908. D. Estes & Company.

Will of Iron: A Novel. Isidore Rosen. LC 50-10046. 1950. Crown Publishers.

Will of Magda Townsend. Margaret Culkin Banning. LC 74-7295. 1974. 12.95 (ISBN 0-8161-6221-2). G. K. Hall.

Will of Magda Townsend: A Novel. Margaret Culkin Banning. LC 73-14306. (Cass Canfield book). 1974. 6.95 (ISBN 0-06-010206-3). Harper & Row.

Will of the Tribe. Arthur William Upfield. LC 62-12065. 1962. Published for the Crime Club by Doubleday.

Will Shakespeare: The Untold Story. John Clifford Mortimer. LC 77-11008. (Illus.). 8.95 (ISBN 0-440-09792-4). Delacorte Press.

Will She Win? Or, The Charmed Necklace. Emma Garrison Jones. LC 7-11907. (Street & Smith's select series--no. 8). 1888. Street & Smith.

Will the Real Renie Lake Please Stand Up? Barbara Morgenroth. 192p. 1982. pap. 1.95 (ISBN 0-449-70021-6, Juniper). Fawcett.

Will the Real Rod Please Stand Up. Troy Conway, pseud. (Coxeman, No. 21). (Orig.). 1970. pap. 0.60 o.p. (ISBN 0-446-64389-0, 64-389). Paperback Lib.

Will the Real Toulouse-Lautrec Please Stand up? Leslie Waller. LC 65-18394. 4.95. Doubleday.

Will There Really Be a Morning? Frances Farmer. 1982. pap. 3.50 (ISBN 0-440-19292-7). Dell.

Will to Die. Can Themba. (African Writers Ser.). 1972. pap. text ed. 3.00x (ISBN 0-435-90104-4). Heinemann Ed.

Will to Live. Mary Patricia Willcocks. LC 13-194999. 1913. The Macmillan Company.

Will to Live: Les Roquevillard); a Novel. Henry Bordeaux & Duffield, Pitts. LC 15-4586. 1915. Duffield & Company.

Will to Meaning. Victor Frankl. pap. 4.95 (ISBN 0-452-25277-6, Z5277, Plume). NAL.

Will to Survive. Elizabeth Salter. (Ace gothic). 1974. (pbk.) 0.95. Ace Books.

Will Tomorrow Ever Come? Elizabeth Szathmary. 1973. 3.75 (ISBN 0-533-00359-8). Vantage.

Will Warburton. George Robert Gissing. (Wayfarer's library). 1916. Dutton.

Will Warburton: A Romance of Real Life. George Robert Gissing. LC 71-98635. 1969. AMS Press.

Will Weatherhelm. The Yarn of an Old Sailor About His Early Life and Adventures. William Henry Giles Kingston. (On cover: Seaside library. Pocket ed., no. 761). 1886. G. Munro.

Will West. 2d ed. Paul C Metcalf. LC 73-180871. 1973. (pbk.) 2.95 (ISBN 0-912846-03-8). Bookstore Press.

Will West. 1st Ed. Paul C Metcalf. LC 56-43887. 1956. J. Williams.

Will You Love Me in September. Philippa Carr, pseud. LC 80-24326. 324p. 1981. 11.95 (ISBN 0-399-12590-6). Putnam Pub Group.

Will You Please Be Quiet, Please? Raymond Carver. (McGraw-Hill Paperbacks Ser.). 1978. pap. 4.95 (ISBN 0-07-010194-9, SP). McGraw.

Will You Please Be Quiet, Please? The Stories of Raymond Carver. Raymond Carver. LC 75-23333. 8.95 (ISBN 0-07-010193-0). McGraw-Hill.

Willa Cather's Collected Short Fiction. 1892-1912. Introd. by Mildred R. Bennett. Willa Sibert Cather. LC 65-10547. 8.50. Univ. of Neb. Pr.

Willard & His Bowling Trophies. Richard Brautigan. (gr. 10 up). 1978. pap. 1.95 (ISBN 0-671-82043-5). PB.

Willard & His Bowling Trophies. Richard Brautigan. 1977. pap. 2.95 o.p. (ISBN 0-671-22745-9, Touchstone Bks). S&S.

Willard and His Bowling Trophies: A Perverse Mystery. Richard Brautigan. LC 75-5991. 1975. 6.95 (ISBN 0-671-22065-9). Simon and Schuster.

Willard Crosby, Airman. Laura Zenobia Le Fevre. LC 44-5991. 1944. Fleming H. Revell Company.

Willful Gaynell: Or, The Little Beauty of the Passaic Cotton Mills... Laura Jean Libbey. LC 7-14516. 1890. N. L. Munro.

Willful Maid. A Love-Story. Charlotte Mary Brame. (On cover: Seaside library. Pocket ed. no. 323). G. Munro.

Willful Widow. Rebecca Ashley. (Candlelight Regency Ser.: No. 677). (Orig.). 1981. pap. 1.75 (ISBN 0-440-19177-7). Dell.

Willful Winnie: Or, The School-Girl's Secret. Harriet Sherburne. (Street & Smith's select series, no. 67). 1890. Street & Smith.

Willful Woman... Ladybird's Penitence... Her Own Deception... "We Kissed Again, with Tears"... Sophy Beckett. LC 27-13683. (Seaside library, v. 55, no. 1112). 1881. G. Munro.

Willful Young Woman: A Novel. Alice Price. (On cover: Lovell's library, no. 857). 1886. J. W. Lovell Company.

Willful Young Woman. A Novel. Alice Price. (On cover: Seaside library. Pocket ed. no. 903). 1886. G. Munro.

William. Emily Hilda Young. LC 26-189. 1925. Harcourt, Brace and Company.

William. Emily Hilda Young. LC 41-5985. The Press of the Readers Club.

William, an Englishman. Cicely Mary Hamilton. LC 20-8361. Frederick A. Stokes Company.

William and Bill. Grace MacGowan Cooke & Morrison, Caroline Wood. LC 14-1769. 1914. 1.25. The Century Co.

William and Dorothy. Helen Ashton. LC 38-29971. 1938. The Macmillan Company.

William and Mary: A Story. Penelope Farmer. LC 74-76272. 1974. 5.95 (ISBN 0-689-50005-X). Atheneum.

William and Matilda: A Mediaeval Historical Romance of William the Conqueror and His Wife, Matilda. Edward Joseph White. LC 25-11041. 1925. The Stratford Company.

William and Williamina. Frances Roberta Sterrett. LC 17-25816. 1917. 1.40. D. Appleton and Company.

William Blake. William Edward Heygate. LC 75-473. (Victorian Fiction: Novels of Faith and Doubt; 27). 1975. (ISBN 0-8240-1551-7). Garland Pub.

William by the Grace of God"-- 2d ed. Marjorie Bowen. LC 18-83. 1917. E. P. Dutton and Company.

William Cook: Antique Dealer. Clifford James Wheeler Hosken. LC 44-7845. (On cover: Penguin books). 1943. Penguin Books; Cairo, W. J. Eady.

William Edward March Ommibus. With an Introd. by Alistair Cooke. William Edward March Campbell. LC 56-563019. Rinehart.

William Faulkner: An Introduction and Interpretation. Lawrance Roger Thompson. LC 63-15356. (Amer. authors and critics ser., no. 10). 3.50, 1.50 pap.,. Barnes & Noble.

William Faulkner, the Short Story Career: An Outline of Faulkner's Short Story Writing from 1919 to 1962. Hans H. Skei. LC 82-144446. 1983. 17.00. Universitetsforlaget.

William Gilmore Simm's The Yemassee; a Romance of Carolina; Ed., with Introduction and Notes. William Gilmore Simms & Spencer, Matthew Lyle, 1881- Ed. (Johnson's English classics). B. F. Johnson Publishing Co.

William Jordan: Junior. John Collis Snaith. LC 8-6984. 1908. Moffat, Yard and Company.

William L. Locke's The Beloved Vagabond. William John Locke. Ed. by Lyman, Rollo La Verne. LC 31-14184. (Modern literature series). Ginn and Company.

William Pollok: And Other Tales. Gerald Grogan. LC 20-7728. 1919. John Lane.

William Saroyan Reader. William Saroyan. (Introduction by the author). 1958. 7.95 o.s.i. (ISBN 0-8076-0059-8). Braziller.

William the Conqueror. Lucie Delarue-Mardrus. Tr. by Trott, Josephine. LC 32-29095. 1932. Longmans, Green and Co.

William the Conqueror. A Historical Romance. Charles James Napier. Ed. by Napier, William Francis Patrick. LC 7-23116. 1858. G. Routledge & Co.

William the Dragon. Polly Donnison. LC 72-94138. (Animal picture books). (Illus.). 1973. (lib. ed.) 4.64 (ISBN 0-698-20258-9). Coward, McCann & Geoghegan.

William Updick: His Philosophy. William Henry Letterman Smith. LC 8-208587. 1908. The Neale Publishing Co.

William Wakefield. A Tale of the West. James Allan Ormar. LC 90-1884. 1899. Tribune Printing Company.

William Walter. Bentz Plagemann. LC 41-794619. The Greystone Press.

William Wilson. John Gardner. 1979. 9.95 (ISBN 0-89683-008-X); signed ltd. ed. 60.00 (ISBN 0-89683-007-1). New London Pr.

William Winston. Julia Williams Sheehy. LC 13-261011. Broadway Publishing Company.

Williams Mix. Bradbury Robinson. LC 77-132. 1977. (ISBN 0-917372-03-4). Coltsfoot Press.

Williams on Service. Hugh Samuel Johnson. LC 10-20899. 1910. 1.50. D. Appleton and Company.

William's Room. Alice Grant Rosman. LC 39-27505. 1939. G. P. Putnam's Sons.

Williams Sketches. Arthur Ketchum & Percival H. Truman. Ed. by Herbert Henry Lehman & Isaac H. Vrooman. LC 7-10823. 1898. J. B. Lyon Printer.

Williamsburg Christmas. Donna C. Sheppard. LC 80-7487. (World of Williamsburg Ser.). (Illus.). 84p. (Orig.). 1980. pap. 4.95 (ISBN 0-87935-054-7). Williamsburg.

Williamsburg Novels, 7 vols. Elswyth Thane. 1981. Set. lib. bdg. 105.00 (ISBN 0-8161-3177-5, Large Print Bks). G K Hall.

Willie Masters' Lonesome Wife. William H. Gass. LC 74-154912. (Tri-Quarterly. Supplement No. 2). (Illus.). 1971. 3.95 (ISBN 0-394-47245-4). Knopf.

Willie Masters' Lonesome Wife. William H. Gass. LC 77-21411. (Tri-Quarterly. Supplement: No. 2). (Illus.). 1968. 1.50. Northwestern University Press.

Willie Was Different: The Tale of an Ugly Thrushling. Molly Rockwell & Norman Rockwell. LC 69-18105. (Illus.). 1969. 3.95. Funk & Wagnalls.

Willie's Time: A Memoir. Einstein. pap. 2.50 (ISBN 0-425-04658-3). Berkley Pub.

Willing Horse: A Novel. John Hay Beith. LC 21-18479. 1921. Houghton Mifflin Company.

Willing Hostage. Marlys Millhiser. LC 75-43666. 7.95 (ISBN 0-399-11720-2). Putnam.

Willing Lips. Phil Carmichael. 192p. (Orig.). 1973. pap. 1.95 o.p. (ISBN 0-87682-328-2, 7328). Barclay Hse.

Willing Maid. Cicero T Ritchie. LC 56-591659. 1958. Abelard-Schuman.

Willing Nurses. Richard B Long. 1974. (pbk.) 2.25. Barclay House.

Willing Sisters. Myrle Kaye. pap. 1.95 o.p. (ISBN 0-87056-204-5, 6204). Brandon.

Willing to Die. Joseph Sheridan Le Fanu. LC 76-5280. (Le Fanu, Joseph Sheridan, 1814-1873. Works. 1976). 1976. (3 vols.) 59.00 (ISBN 0-405-09242-3). Arno Press.

Willing Transgressor: And Other Stories. Almira George Plympton. LC 7-38188. 1897. Roberts Brothers.

Willing Victim. Marsha Alexander. (Orig.). 1969. pap. 1.75 o.p. (3056). Brandon.

Willis & His Friends Series. Yves Jacot. Incl. Bow Bells (ISBN 0-8224-7425-5); Death in the Family; Grandma Cigar (ISBN 0-8224-7426-3); Messing up (ISBN 0-8224-7428-X); Pike's Peak Pack (ISBN 0-8224-7429-8); Prejudice (ISBN 0-8224-7430-1); Ser un Hombre (to Be a Man (ISBN 0-8224-7427-1); Vandals. 1974. pap. text ed. 1.88 ea. o.p. Fearon-Pitman.

Willis Peyton's Inheritance. The Story of a Claim. Emily Lee Sherwood Ragan. 1889. Universalist Publishing House.

Willitoft: Or, The Days of James I; a Tale ... LC 8-34350. 1851. J. Murphy & Co.

Williwaw: A Novel. Gore Vidal. 1946. E. P. Dutton & Company, Inc.

Willmoth the Wanderer: Or, The Man from Saturn. C. C Dail. LC 6-33194. Haskell Printing Co.

Willmoth, the Wanderer: Or, The Man from Saturn. C. C Dail. LC 6-33193. (peerless series. no. 47). 1891. J. S. Ogilvie.

Willo. Karen Snow. LC 76-15987. 1976. 5.95 (ISBN 0-914908-29-4). Street Fiction Press.

Willough Haven. Geraldine Killoran. (Ace Gothic#23). 1976. (pbk.) 1.25. Ace Books.

Willoughby Carter. 1st Ed. Humphrey Pakington. LC 54-6717. Norton.

Willoughbys. Alice Brown. LC 35-1699. 1935. D. Appleton-Century Company, Incorporated.

Willow and Cypress. Catherine M Verschoyle. LC 29-326936. 1929. Longmans, Green and Co.

Willow Cabin. Mary K Fiandt. LC 73-91883. 1974. 6.95 (ISBN 0-87131-144-5). M. Evans.

Willow Cabin. Pamela Frankau. LC 49-7916. 1949. Harcourt, Brace.

Willow Creek. Katharine Yirsa Reynolds. Grosset & Dunlap.

Willow Pattern: A Chinese Detective Story. 15 Illus. Drawn by the Author in Chinese Style. Robert Hans Van Gulik, pseud. LC 65-157835. 3.50. Scribners.

Willow Pattern: A Judge Dee Detective Story. Robert Van Gulik. LC 65-15783. 1974. (pbk.) 0.95. Warner Paperback Library.

Willow Pattern: A Judge Dee Mystery. Robert Van Gulik. 176p. 1981. pap. 2.50 (ISBN 0-684-17317-4, ScribT). Scribner.

Willow Run. Glendon Fred Swarthout. LC 43-9682. 1943. Thomas Y. Crowell Company.

Willow Smoke. Ethel Kirk Grayson. LC 28-299632. 1928. H. Vinal, Ltd.

Willow, the Wisp. Archie P McKishnie. LC 18-11826. 1918. Houghton Mifflin Company.

Willow Tree: By Rebecca Marsh Pseud. William Arthur Neubauer. LC 55-793820. 1955. Arcadia House.

Willow Weep. Dorothy Daniels. (Orig.). 1970. pap. 0.75 o.p. (T2374). Pyramid Pubns.

Willow Weep. Dorothy Daniels. 1974. pap. 0.95 o.p. (ISBN 0-515-03453-3, N3453). Pyramid Pubns.

Willowdale Handcar. Edward Gorey. LC 62-17515. (Illus.). 1979. 5.95 o.p. (ISBN 0-396-07767-6). Dodd.

Willowdale Handcar. Edward Gorey. (Illus.). 64p. 1982. pap. 5.95 (ISBN 0-312-92946-3). Congdon & Weed.

Willowood. Mollie Hardwick. 288p. 1981. pap. 2.50 (ISBN 0-445-04680-5). Fawcett.

Willowood. Mollie Hardwick. 322p. 1980. 10.95 o.p. (ISBN 0-312-88207-6). St Martin.

Willowwood. Mollie Hardwick. LC 80-14637. 1980. 10.95 (ISBN 0-312-88207-6). St. Martin's Press.

Willowwood. Elizabeth Savage. 1979. 2.25 (ISBN 0-425-04166-2). Berkley Pub. Corp.

Willowwood. Elizabeth Savage. LC 79-10579. 1979. 11.95 (ISBN 0-8161-6707-9). G. K. Hall.

Willowwood: A Novel. Mollie Hardwick. LC 80-27396. 1981. 16.95 (ISBN 0-8161-3154-6). G. K. Hall.

Willowwood: A Novel. Elizabeth Savage. LC 78-7866. 7.95 (ISBN 0-316-77138-4). Little, Brown.

Willy Burke: Or, The Irish Orphan in America. Mary Anne Madden Sadlier. LC 42-27064. 1850. P. Donahoe.

Willy Reilly and His Dear Cooleen ! Bawn. William Carleton. LC 6-24235. (On cover: Lovell's library, v. 4, no. 190). J. E. Potter and Company.

Willy Remembers. Irvin Faust. LC 79-157508. 1971. 6.95 (ISBN 0-87795-017-2). Arbor Hse.

Willy Remembers. Irvin Faust. LC 79-157508. (Priam Ser.). (F). 1980. pap. 5.95 (ISBN 0-87795-265-5). Arbor Hse.

Willy Remembers: A Novel. Irvin Faust. LC 79-157508. 1971. 6.95 (ISBN 0-87795-017-2). Arbor House.

Wilma Rogers. Sophia Belzer Engstrand. LC 41-139638. 1941. The Dial Press.

Wilmot's Child. Joseph Parker. LC 3-4382. 1895. Dodd, Mead & Company.

Wilsam. Susie Colyer Nethersole. LC 13-10048. 1913. 1.35. The Macmillan Company.

Wilson Freight. Robert Trimnell. (Loner Ser: No. 3). 192p. (Orig.). 1975. pap 0.95 o.p. (ISBN 0-532-95410-6). Woodhill.

Wilson Freight. Robert Trimnell. (Loner Ser: No. 3). 192p. (Orig.). 1975. pap. 0.95 o.p. (ISBN 0-532-95410-6). Manor Bks.

Wilson on the Mounted. Lionel E Sandford. LC 25-19123. L. E. Sandford.

Wilsons. Christopher La Farge. LC 41-51897. Coward-McCann, Inc.

Wilson's Gold. Giles Tippette. (Orig.). 1980. pap. 1.50 (ISBN 0-440-19677-9). Dell.

Wilson's Luck. Giles Tippette. (Orig.). 1980. pap. 1.95 (ISBN 0-440-19242-0). Dell.

Wilson's Revenge. Giles Tippette. (Orig.). 1981. pap. 1.95 (ISBN 0-440-19561-6). Dell.

Wilson's Tales of the Borders and of Scotland... John Mackay Wilson. LC 8-37780. Ward, Lock & Co.

Wilson's Woman. Giles Tippette. (Orig.). 1982. pap. 1.95 (ISBN 0-440-19636-1). Dell.

Wilt. Tom Sharpe. LC 76-373644. 1976. 3.50 (ISBN 0-436-45804-7). Secker and Warburg.

Wilt Alternative. Tom Sharpe. LC 79-27348. 1980. 10.00 (ISBN 0-312-88212-2). St. Martin's Press.

Wilt Thou Torchy. Sewell Ford. LC 77-122703. (Short story index reprint series). (Illus.). 1970. Books for Libraries Press.

Wilt Thou, Torchy. Sewell Ford. LC 17-5451. 1.35. E. J. Clode.

Wilton's. Eden Hughes. (Signet Book). 2.75 (ISBN 0-451-09520-0). New American Library.

Wiltons of Grand Prairie. Charles H Pearson. (On cover: Liddesdale series, no. 1.). J. S. Tait & Sons.

Wimsey Set II, 4 bks. Dorothy L. Sayers. Incl. Have His Carcase; Strong Poison; Five Red Herrings; Murder Must Advertise. 1980. lib. bdg. 60.00 set (ISBN 0-8161-3136-8, Large Print Bks). G K Hall.

Win--or Else- By D. J. Michael Pseud. Charles Einstein. LC 54-364636. (Lion book, 208). 1954. Lion Books.

Win, Lose or Draw. Morland G. Antoine. 1978. 6.50 o.p. (ISBN 0-533-03252-0). Vantage.

Win One for the Geezer. Mike Peters. LC 82-90325. (Illus.). 128p. 1982. pap. 4.50 (ISBN 0-553-01429-3). Bantam.

Win, Place, and Die! Lawrence Lariar. LC 53-6116. 1953. Appleton-Century-Crofts.

Winchester Connection. Margaret Scaroamp. (Perspectives II Ser.). (Illus.). 48p. (gr. 7-12). 1982. pap. 2.50 (ISBN 0-87879-314-3). Acad Therapy.

Winchester Cut: By Mark Sabin Pseud. Norman A Fox. LC 51-20936. (Gold medal book, 144). 1951. Fawcett Publications.

Winchester House. Anne Green. LC 36-4040. 1936. E. P. Dutton & Co., Inc.

Winchester Malory: A Facsimile. Thomas Malory. LC 77-361734. (Early English Text Society. Supplementary Series: No. 4). (Illus.). 1976. 99.00 (ISBN 0-19-722404-0). Oxford University Press for the Early English Text Society.

Winchester Quarantine. Carter Travis Young. LC 71-97654. 1970. 4.50. Doubleday.

Winchester Quarantine. Carter Travis Young. 1973. (pbk.) 0.95. Manor Books.

Winchester Wages. Lee Floren. LC 55-8983. 1955. Arcadia House.

Winckelmann. Wolfgang Leppmann. LC 70-118711. (Illus.). 1970. 10.00 o.p. (ISBN 0-394-45207-0). Knopf.

Wind. Dorothy Scarborough. LC 78-24225. (Eugene C. Barker Texas History Center Ser.: 4). 1979. 10.95 (ISBN 0-292-79012-0) (ISBN 0-292-79013-9). University of Texas Press.

Wind. Claude Simon. LC 59-8026. 1959. G. Braziller.
Wind Against Stone, a Texas Novel. Maude E Cole. LC 41-4916. Lymanhouse.
Wind Along the Waste. 4th ed. Maude Annesley. LC 11-4605. 1910. John Lane Company.
Wind Along the Waste. Gladys Etta Johnson. LC 21-5917. 1921. 2.00. The Century Co.
Wind Among the Pines. Isla P. Richardson. 1949. 2.75 o.p. (ISBN 0-8283-1561-2). Branden.
Wind and Fog, a Novel. George Earle Raiguel. LC 50-9601. 1950. Magee Press.
Wind & the Lion. John Milius. (O.s.i.). 176p. (Orig.). 1975. pap. 1.25 o.p. (AQ1468, Award). Univ Pub & Dist.
Wind & the Rain. Ed. by Joan Hollander & Harold Bloom. LC 72-8285. (Granger Index Reprint Ser). 1972. Repr. of 1961 ed. 18.00 (ISBN 0-8369-6388-1). Ayer Co.
Wind and the Rain. Joyce Mary Horner. LC 43-8213. 1943. Doubleday, Doran & Co., Incl.
Wind and the Rain. Johannes Mario Simmel. 1978. 1.95 (ISBN 0-445-04212-5). Popular Library.
Wind and the Rain: A Book of Confessions. Thomas Burke. LC 24-28112. 2.00. George H. Doran Company.
Wind and the Rain: Or, Camilla Grayson. Jack Eldredge. LC 42-2566. 1942. Meador Publishing Company.
Wind and Whirlwind: A Novel. Charles Wyllys Elliott. LC 6-327586. 1868. G.P. Putnam & Son.
Wind, Anonymous. Dorothy Scarborough. LC 26-137. 1925. Harper & Brothers.
Wind at Morning. James Vance Marshall. 1973. 5.95 (ISBN 0-688-02858-6). Morrow.
Wind at Morning. Donald Gordon Payne. LC 72-110. 1973. 5.95 (ISBN 0-688-00188-2). Morrow.
Wind at Morning. Donald Gordon Payne. LC 73-20266. 1974. (lib. bdg.). 8.95 (ISBN 0-8161-6175-5). G.K. Hall.
Wind at My Back: Three Short Novels. Victoria Lincoln. LC 46-7629. 1946. Rinehart & Company, Inc.
Wind at Winter's End. Deborah Lewis. (Orig.). 1979. pap. 1.95 (ISBN 0-89083-540-3). Zebra.
Wind Bandy Rode. Rebel M. Temple. 106p. 1982. pap. 2.25 (ISBN 0-89279-036-9). Graphic Pub.
Wind Before Dawn. Lois Seyster Montross. LC 32-17146. Liveright, Inc.
Wind Before Rain. John Downing Weaver. LC 42-7972. 1942. The Macmillan Company.
Wind Before the Dawn. Dell H Munger. LC 12-40585. 1912. 1.35. Doubleday, Page & Company.
Wind Between the Worlds. Alice Brown. LC 20-11071. 1920. The Macmillan Company.
Wind Blew West. Edwin Moultrie Lanham. LC 35-272786. 1935. Longmans, Green and Co.
Wind Bloweth. Donn Byrne. LC 22-19042. 1922. The Century Co.
Wind Bloweth. Donn Byrne. LC 42-43536. Grosset & Dunlap.
Wind Blows Death. Cyril Hare. LC 81-48171. 256p. 1982. pap. 2.84i (ISBN 0-06-080589-7, P 589, PL). Har-Row.
Wind Blows Death. Dale D Pierce. LC 77-90519. 1978. 4.95 (ISBN 0-89543-006-1). Grossmont Press.
Wind Blows Fair. William Arthur Neubauer. LC 48-183115. Gramercy Pub. Co.
Wind Blows Free. Frederick Feikema Manfred. LC 79-53217. 1979. 9.95 (ISBN 0-931170-09-5). Ctr Western Studies.
Wind Blows Free. Vian Smith. LC 67-13785. (Illus.). 1968. Doubleday.
Wind Blows Over. Walter John De La Mare. LC 71-113655. (Short story index reprint series). 1970. Books for Libraries Press.
Wind Blows Over. Walter John De La Mare. LC 36-210017. 1936. The Macmillan Company.
Wind Blows West. Christine Whiting Paramenter. LC 34-5826. Thomas Y. Crowell Company.
Wind Blows West. Bertha Muzzy Sinclair. LC 38-13335. 1938. Little, Brown and Company.
Wind Blows Wild. Bernard Alvin Palmer. LC 68-2777. 1968. Moody Press.
Wind Brings up the Rain. Eric Lawson Malpass. LC 80-52653. 1981. 10.95 (ISBN 0-312-88215-7). St. Martin's Press.
Wind Cannot Read: A Novel. Richard Lakin Mason. 1947. G. P. Putnam's Sons.
Wind Chaff. Mercedes De Acosta. LC 20-199171. 1920. Moffat, Yard & Company.
Wind Changes. Olivia Manning. LC 38-9621. 1938. A. A. Knopf.
Wind Child. R. M. Meluch. 202p. 1982. pap. 2.50 (ISBN 0-451-11528-7, AE1528, Sig). NAL.
Wind Chill Factor. Thomas Gifford. LC 74-16598. 1975. 8.95. (ISBN 0-399-11439-4). Putnam.
Wind Dancers. R. M. Meluch. (Orig.). 1981. pap. 2.25 (ISBN 0-451-09786-6, E9786, Sig). NAL.
Wind Driven. Jacland Marmur. LC 32-216802. 1932. L. MacVeagh, The Dial Press, Inc.
Wind Flower: A Novel. Caroline Atwater Mason. LC 99-1157. A. F. Rowland.
"Wind-Flower:" or, A Legend of the Ozarks. Harriet Townsend Foster. LC 6-40007. 1888. R. R. Donnelley & Sons.
Wind from a Burning Woman. Gregory Bear. LC 82-16395. (Illus.). 13.95 (ISBN 0-87054-094-7). Arkham House Publishers.
Wind from an Enemy Sky: A Novel. D'Arcy McNickle. LC 76-50450. 7.95 (ISBN 0-06-451050-6). Harper & Row.
Wind from Hastings. Morgan Llywelyn. LC 78-16918. 1978. 7.95 (ISBN 0-395-26474-X). Houghton Mifflin.
Wind from Nowhere. J. G. Ballard. 1976. pap. 1.95 o.p. (ISBN 0-14-002591-X). Penguin.
Wind from Nowhere. Oscar Micheaux. LC 72-4810. (Black Heritage Library Collection). 1972. 16.00 (ISBN 0-8369-9109-5). Books for Libraries Press.
Wind from the Main. Anne Osborne. 1974. pap. 1.50 (ISBN 0-89176-143-8, 6143). Mockingbird Bks.
Wind from the Main: A Novel. Anne Osborne. LC 72-86902. 1972. 6.95 (ISBN 0-87844-012-7). Sandlapper Press.
Wind from the Mountains. Trygve Gulbranssen. Tr. by Walford, Naomi. LC 37-27338. 1937. G. P. Putnam's Sons.
Wind from the Plain. Yashar Kemal. 1969. 5.95 o.p. (ISBN 0-396-05867-1). Dodd.
Wind from the Plain. Yasar Kemal. LC 72-75200. 1969. 5.95. Dodd, Mead.
Wind from the Sea. Ruth Blodgett. LC 30-243440. Harcourt, Brace and Company.
Wind from the South. Patricia O'Neill. LC 52-34941. 1952. Hutchinson.
Wind from the South: A Novel. El'Mar Grin. LC 51-18368. 1950. Foreign Languages Pub. House.
Wind from the Sun: Stories of the Space Age. by arthur c. clarke. ed. Arthur Charles Clarke. (Signet, Q5581). 1973. (pbk.) 0.95. New American Lib.
Wind from the Sun: Stories of the Space Age. Arthur Charles Clarke. LC 77-182325. 1972. (ISBN 0-15-196810-1). Harcourt Brace Jovanovich.
Wind from the West. Pamela Hinkson. LC 30-27924. 1930. The Macmillan Company.
Wind Gone Mad. L. Ron Hubbard. 1978. 11.00 (ISBN 0-917972-02-3). Theta Bks.
Wind in His Fists: A Novel of Ireland and Spain and Barbary, in the Middle of the Sixteenth Century: of the Struggle Between Christendom and Islam, the Power of the Turks in the Mediterranean, and the Terror of the 'Scourge of Allah.' 1557-1571. 1st Ed. John Edward Jennings. LC 55-10644. 1956. Holt.
Wind in Our Hands. Merle Duston. LC 66-289156. 1966. 4.95. Harlo Pr.
Wind in the Canyon. Edith Fox. LC 49-16170. Industrial Arts Press.
Wind in the Cypress. Ruth McCarthy Sear. 1975. pap. 1.25 o.p. (LB302ZK, Leisure Bks). Nordon Pubns.
Wind in the Door. Madeleine L'Engle. 208p. 1976. pap. 1.95 (ISBN 0-440-98761-X, LFL). Dell.
Wind in the East: A Romance. Anna Robeson Brown Burr. LC 33-13041. Duffield and Green.
Wind in the Forest. Inglis Clark Fletcher. 1975. (pbk.) 1.50. Bantam Books.
Wind in the Forest. Inglis Clark Fletcher. LC 77-10506. 1977-1976. 13.50 (ISBN 0-89244-011-2). Queens House.
Wind in the Forest. 1st Ed. Inglis Clark Fletcher. LC 57-8692. 1957. Bobbs-Merrill.
Wind in the Garden. F Hewes Lancaster. LC 19-7718. 1919. The Stratford Company.
Wind in the Rose-Bush and Other Stories of the Supernatural. Mary Eleanor Wilkins Freeman. LC 69-11895. (American short story series, v. 53). (Illus.). 1969. Garrett Press.
Wind in the Rose-Bush, and Other Stories of the Supernatural. Mary Eleanor Wilkins Freeman. LC 72-8198. (American short story series, v. 53). 1972. (ISBN 0-8422-8053-7). MSS Information Corp.
Wind in the Rose-Bush: And Other Stories of the Supernatural. Mary Eleanor Wilkins Freeman. LC 3-7170. 1903. Doubleday, Page & Company.
Wind in the Sage. Christine Bennett, pseud. (Contemporary Teens Ser.). 224p. (Orig.). 1981. pap. 2.25 (ISBN 0-89531-144-5, 0146-96). Sharon Pubns.
Wind in the Willows. Kenneth Grahame. LC 13-212531. 1913. C. Scribner's Sons.
Wind Is Rising. Robert Miskimon. LC 76-18024. 1977. 6.95 (ISBN 0-89185-021-X) (ISBN 0-89185-020-1). Anthelion Press.
Wind Is Rising. William Richard Russell. LC 50-14746. 1950. Scribner.
Wind Is Rising. Viola Wendt. LC 79-53723. 1979. pap. 4.50 (ISBN 0-916120-05-8). Carroll Coll.
Wind-Jammers. new and rev. ed. Thornton Jenkins Hains. LC 76-103516. (Short story index reprint series). 1969. Books for Libraries Press.
Wind-Jammers. Thornton Jenkins Hains. LC 90-925. 1899. J. B. Lippincott Company.
Wind-Jammers. new and rev. ed. Thornton Jenkins Hains. LC 3-2951. 1903. F. M. Buckles & Company.
Wind Leans West. August William Derleth. LC 70-76506. 1969. 5.75. Candlelight Press.
Wind Leaves No Shadow. Ruth Laughlin. LC 48-104258. 1948. Whittlesey House.
Wind Leaves No Shadow. Enl. Ed. Ruth Laughlin. LC 51-6677. 1951. Caxton Printers.
Wind Like a Bugle. Leonard Nathan. LC 54-9963. 1954. Macmillan.
Wind of Change. Gregory Allen Barnes. 1968. Lothrop, Lee & Shepard Co.
Wind of Change. Harold Klemp. LC 80-50516. (Illus.). 194p. 1980. 6.95 (ISBN 0-914766-54-6). Iwp Pub.
Wind of Change at Castle Rising. Phyllis Cradock. LC 79-54780. 1979. 10.95 (ISBN 0-525-23468-3). Dutton.
Wind of Complication. Susan Ertz. LC 27-1844. 1927. D. Appleton and Company.
Wind of Death. Mary Wilson. Dell.
Wind of Death. Oswald Wynd. LC 67-22858. (Illus.). 1967. Harper & Row.
Wind of Destiny. Arthur Sherburne Hardy. 1886. Houghton, Mifflin and Company.
Wind of Destiny: By Arthur Sherburne Hardy... Arthur Sherburne Hardy. LC 4-15450. Houghton, Mifflin and Company.
Wind of Morning. Thomas Camborne Paynter. LC 35-305743. Harcourt, Brace and Company.
Wind of Spring. Elizabeth Yates. 1945. Coward-McCann, Inc.
Wind off the Sea. David Beaty. LC 62-136179. 1962. Morrow.
Wind off the Water. Miriam Colwell. LC 45-4923. 1945. Random House.
Wind on the Dragon. Joyce Stranger, pseud. LC 72-83227. 1969. 4.95. Viking Press.
Wind on the Heath. Mrs. Essex Hope. LC 12-11409. 1912. John Lane Company.
Wind on the Pampas. Betty De Sherbinin. 1941. W. Morrow and Company.
Wind Over Rimfire. Wayne C Lee. 1973. 4.95. Lenox Hill Pr.
Wind Over the Citadel. Leslie Ames, pseud. 1973. pap. 0.75 o.s.i. (01-378). Lancer.
Wind Over Wisconsin. August William Derleth. LC 38-27410. 1938. C. Scribner's Sons.
Wind Over Wisconsin. August William Derleth. LC 42-210052. Grosset & Dunlap.
Wind River Outlaw. Harry Sinclair Drago. LC 36-32327. Green Circle Books.
Wind River Range: By Brett Austin Pseud. Lee Floren. LC 53-857014. 1953. Arcadia House.
Wind Rose. Helen Rose Hull. LC 58-7461. 1958. Coward-McCann.
Wind Scales. Keith Waldrop. (Treacle Story Ser.: No. 4). (Illus.). 36p. 1976. signed ed. 8.00 (ISBN 0-914232-13-4); pap. 2.50 (ISBN 0-914232-12-6). McPherson & Co.
Wind Shifting West. Shirley Ann Grau. LC 73-7290. 1973. 6.95 (ISBN 0-394-48890-3). Knopf.
Wind Shifting West. Shirley Ann Grau. 1977. 1.95 (ISBN 0-449-23349-9). Fawcett Pubns.
Wind Shifts. Alan Sharp. LC 68-14002. 1968. Walker.
Wind Stalker. Owen G. Irons. (Orig.). 1980. pap. 1.75 (ISBN 0-440-19076-2). Dell.
Wind-Swept: A Novel. Olga Moore. LC 37-1119. J. B. Lippincott Company.
Wind That Blows Is All That Anybody Knows. Henry D. Thoreau. (Stanyan Books Ser). (O.s.i.). 1970. 3.00 o.s.i. (ISBN 0-394-40490-4). Random.
Wind That Round the Fastnet Sweeps. John M. Feehan. LC 79-308537. 1978. 3.75 (ISBN 0-85342-550-7). Mercier Press.
Wind That Shakes the Barley: A Novel of the Life and Loves of Robert Burns. James Barke. LC 47-2788. 1947. The Macmillan Company.
Wind That Tramps the World: Splashes of Chinese Color. Frank Owen. LC 72-4426. (Short story index reprint series). 1972. 7.75 (ISBN 0-8369-4186-1). Books for Libraries Press.
Wind That Tramps the World: Splashes of Chinese Color. Frank Owen. LC 29-8268. 1929. The Lantern Press.
Wind Through the Heather. Jane Lane. 1971. pap. 1.25 o.p. (96027-125). Beagle Bks.
Wind Through the Heather. Jane Lane. 1965. 7.00 o.p. Intl Pubns Serv.
Wind 'til Sundown. Verna Moxley. LC 54-9102. (Illus.). 1954. Caxton Printers.
Wind-up Doll: The Carter Brown Mystery Series. Alan Geoffrey Yates. LC 64-3908. (Signet book). 1964. New American Library of World Literature.
Wind up the Willow. Alan Brown. 1981. 9.95 (ISBN 0-7145-3808-6); pap. 4.95. Riverrun NY.
Wind Whales of Ishmael. Philip Jose Farmer. 160p. 1981. pap. 1.95 (ISBN 0-441-89240-X). Ace Bks.
Wind Whales of Ishmael. Philip Jose Farmer. 1976. (pbk.) 1.25. Ace Books.
Wind Which Moved a Ship. Sophia Cleugh. LC 36-11967. 1936. Doubleday, Doran & Company, Inc.
Wind Without Rain. Herbert Krause. LC 39-270878. The Bobbs-Merrill Company.
Wind Without Rain. Shan Sedgwick. LC 30-24769. 1930. C. Scribner's Sons.
Wind Woman. Carol Hales. LC 53-165757. 1953. Woodford Press.
Windbells of Lovingwood. Juanita Tyree Osborne. 192p. (YA) 1974. 4.95 o.p. (Avalon). Bouregy.
Windblown. Paul Hutchens. LC 39-627311. 1939. Wm. B. Eerdmans Publishing Co.
Windblown. Lettie M Johnson. LC 52-968118. 1952. Vantage Press.
Windbreak. Garreta Helen Busey. LC 38-297917. 1938. Funk & Wagnalls Company.
Windchime Legacy. A. W Mykel. LC 80-14210. 1980. 13.95 (ISBN 0-312-88219-X). St. Martin's Press.
Windfall. Desmond Bagley. LC 82-10446. 14.95 (ISBN 0-671-43454-3). Summit Books.
Windfall. Aleen Leslie. LC 74-139585. 1970. 6.95. World Pub. Co.
Windfall. A. T Perry. LC 7-36181. The Authors' Publishing Company.
Windfall. Felix J Ring. LC 40-258. Dorrance and Company.
Windfall: A Novel. Mary Noailles Murfree. 1907. Duffield & Company.
Windfall Child. Louise Field Cooper. 1973. (pbk.) 1.25. Warner Paperback Lib.
Windfall Journal. Robert Richter. 83p. 1980. pap. 4.50 (ISBN 0-936204-10-9). Jelm Mtn.
Windfall's Eve: An Entertainment... Edward Verrall Lucas. LC 30-26563. 1930. J. B. Lippincott Company.
Windhaven Plantation. Marie De Jourlet. (Orig.). 1977. pap. 3.50 (ISBN 0-523-42006-4). Pinnacle Bks.
Windhaven Plantation. Marie De Jourlet. 1977. 1.95. Pinnacle Books.
Windhaven's Bounty. Marie De Jourlet. 512p. (Orig.). 1981. pap. 3.50 (ISBN 0-523-41110-3). Pinnacle Bks.
Windhaven's Crisis. Marie De Jourlet. 448p. (Orig.). 1981. pap. 3.50 (ISBN 0-523-41748-9). Pinnacle Bks.
Windhaven's Destiny. Marie De Jourlet. (Windhaven Saga Ser.: No. 12). 1983. pap. 3.75. Pinnacle Bks.
Windhaven's Fury. Marie De Jourlet. 448p. (Orig.). 1982. pap. 3.50 (ISBN 0-523-41112-X). Pinnacle Bks.
Windhaven's Peril. Marie De Jourlet. (Windhaven Ser.). 1979. pap. 3.50 (ISBN 0-523-41968-6). Pinnacle Bks.
Windhaven's Triumph. Marie De Jourlet. 448p. (Orig.). 1982. pap. 3.50 (ISBN 0-523-41111-1). Pinnacle Bks.
Windhorse. Ed. by Ronald M. Davidson. 126p. 1981. pap. 11.95 (ISBN 0-89581-461-7). Lancaster-Miller.
Winding Flows the River. Louis Reile. LC 75-2869. 1975. International Fine Arts Center of the Southwest.
Winding Lane. Philip Hamilton Gibbs. LC 31-8639. 1931. Doubleday, Doran & Company, Inc.
Winding Paths. Gertrude Page. LC 11-14102. 1911. D. Appleton and Company.
Winding Road. Jessie Bedford. LC 2-6077. 1902. H. Holt and Co.
Winding Road. Stephen Southwold. LC 34-296564. 1934. Little, Brown, and Company.
Winding Stair. Daphne Du Maurier. 1978. pap. 2.25 (ISBN 0-380-01848-9, 36459). Avon.
Winding Stair. Jane Aiken Hodge. LC 69-10985. 1969. 5.95. Doubleday.
Winding Stair. Douglas C Jones. LC 79-4195. (Illus.). 10.95. Holt, Rinehart, and Winston.
Winding Stair. large print ed. Douglas C Jones. LC 81-9023. 1981. 12.95 (ISBN 0-89621-303-X). Thorndike Press.
Winding Stair. Alfred Edward Woodley Mason. George H. Doran Company.
Winding Waters, the Story of a Long Trail and Strong Hearts. Frances Parker. LC 9-28206. 1909. 1.50. The C. M. Clark Publishing Company.
Winding Ways. Monica Selwin-Tait. LC 39-23525. The Ave Maria Press.
Windjammer World. Carstarphen. 1979. pap. 4.95 (ISBN 0-89272-066-2). Down East.
Windjammer's Half-Deck. Frank Coutis Hendry. (On cover: Penguin books. 241). 1940. Penguin Books.
Windless Cabins. Mark Van Doren. LC 40-271889. H. Holt & Company.
Windless Place. David Rottenberg. 1982. pap. 3.95 (ISBN 0-910291-00-4). Cedar Crest Bks.
Windless Sky. Fritz Faulkner. LC 37-5988. Covici, Friede.
Windlestraw. J. Mills Whitham. LC 25-16660. 1925. Boni and Liveright.

Windlestraws. Phyllis Bottome. LC 29-229202. 1929. Houghton Mifflin Company.

Windmill Circle. Jennings Rice. LC 43-7553. 1943. Harper & Brothers.

Windmill Mystery. Joseph Jefferson Farjeon. LC 34-94026. 1934. Pub. for the Crime Club, Ltd., by W. Colliuns, Sons & Co., Ltd.

Windmill on the Dune. Mary Ella Waller. LC 31-27017. 1931. Little, Brown, and Company.

Windmill Years. Vicky Martin. LC 77-10290. 8.95 (ISBN 0-312-88222-X). St. Martin's Press.

Windmills; a Book of Fables. Gilbert Cannan. LC 20-17654. 1920. B. W. Huebsch, Inc.

Windmills in Brooklyn. Prudencio De Pereda. LC 60-7774. 1960. Atheneum.

Windom's Way. James Ramsey Ullman. LC 52-5093. 1952. Lippincott.

Window. Alice Grant Rosman. LC 28-167187. 1928. Minton, Balch & Company.

Window: A Novel. Francis Henry King. LC 57-193761. 1957. Longmans, Green.

Window, and Short Stories. Guy De Maupassant. LC 10-7319. 1910. The Pearson Publishing Co.

Window at the White Cat. Mary Roberts Rinehart. LC 10-17597. The Bobbs-Merrill Company.

Window at the White Cat. Mary Roberts Rinehart. LC 24-149277. 1911. A. L. Burt Company.

Window-Gazer. Isabel Ecclestone Macpherson Mackay. LC 21-181671. 1.90. George H. Doran Company.

Window in Heaven. Margaret Bell Houston. LC 37-137026. 1937. D. Appleton-Century Company, Incorporated.

Window in the Dark. Frank O'Rourke. LC 60-14554. 1960. Morrow.

Window in the Fence. Harriet Brunkhurst. LC 16-95462. 1916. 1.25. George H. Doran Company.

Window in Thrums. 14th ed. london, hodder and stoughton, 1896. ed. James Matthew Barrie. LC 74-7895. Scholarly Press.

Window in Thrums. James Matthew Barrie. LC 6-8636. Lovell, Coryell & Company.

Window in Thrums. James Matthew Barrie. 1894. H. Altemus.

Window in Thrums. James Matthew Barrie. (On cover: Seaside library. Pocket ed. no. 2100). G. Munro's Sons.

Window in Thrums. James Matthew Barrie. LC 6-8633. 1896. Dodd, Mead and Company.

Window in Thrums. cameo ed. James Matthew Barrie. 1897. C. Scribner's Sons.

Window in Thrums. James Matthew Barrie. LC 4822. 1900. W. B. Conkey Co.

Window in Thrums. James Matthew Barrie. LC 43-20237. (On cover: Cassell's rainbow series... No. 110. May 5, 1892). 1892. Cassell Publishing Company.

Window on the Seine. Frances Y. McHugh. Ed. by Alice Sachs. 1969. lib. bdg. 3.50 o.p. Arcadia.

Window on the Square. Phyllis A. Whitney. 1978. pap. 2.50 (ISBN 0-449-23627-7, Crest). Fawcett.

Window on the Square. 1st Ed. Phyllis A Whitney. LC 62-8506. 1962. Appleton-Century-Crofts.

Window on the World. Joseph Gollomb. LC 47-31313. 1947. Harcourt, Brace.

Window Over the Way. Georges Simenon. LC 66-7639. 1966. Penguin Books.

Window Tree. Alexander Kuo. 1971. 4.00 o.p. (ISBN 0-911838-12-0). Windy Row.

Window with the Sleeping Nude. Robert Leslie Bellem. LC 50-39710. (Handi-book mystery, 118). 1950. Quinn Pub. Co.

Windows. David Guy Compton. LC 79-921. 9.95 (ISBN 0-399-12378-4). Berkley Pub. Corp.: Distributed by Putnam.

Windows. H. B. Gilmour. 1980. pap. 2.25 (ISBN 0-671-82863-0). PB.

Windows Facing West. Virginia MacFadyen. LC 25-177364. 1924. A. & C. Boni.

Windows into Tomorrow. Ed. by Robert Silverberg. 1975. (pbk.) 1.25 (ISBN 0-523-00520-2). Pinnacle Books.

Windows into Tomorrow: Nine Stories of Science Fiction. Ed. by Robert Silverberg. LC 73-10639. 1974. 6.95. Hawthorn Books.

Windows of Heaven. Blanche H. Nelsen & Gerald K. Hunter. (Illus.). 1963. 3.95 o.p. (ISBN 0-8158-0154-8). Chris Mass.

Windows of Heaven: A Novel. Elise Fraser. LC 54-12756. 1954. Van Kampen Press.

Windows of the Soul: A Novel. Ernest F MacDonald. LC 52-366. 1951. W. B. Eerdmans Pub. Co.

Winds, Blow Gently. Ronald De Levington Kirkbride. LC 45-35028. 1945. F. Fell.

Wind's End. Herbert Asquith. LC 24-165669. 1924. C. Scribner's Sons.

Winds of Altair. first ed. Benjamin Bova. LC 72-89836. 1973. 4.95 (ISBN 0-525-42945-X). Dutton.

Winds of April. I. D. Baharav. LC 65-17184. 1965. 3.95 (ISBN 0-911184-04-X). Primary.

Winds of April, a Novel. I. D Baharav. LC 65-171841. bds., 3.95. Primary Sources, Bleecker St.

Winds of April: A Novel by I. D. Baharav. I D Baharav. LC 65-17184. 1965. Primary Sources.

Winds of Chance. Rex Ellingwood Beach. LC 18-203254. 1918. Harper & Brothers.

Winds of Chance. Rex Ellingwood Beach. LC 24-27969. 1920. A. L. Burt Company.

Winds of Chance. Jeffery Farnol. LC 34-5408. 1934. Little, Brown, and Company.

Winds of Change and Other Stories. Isaac Asimov. LC 81-43912. 1982. 14.95 (ISBN 0-385-18099-3). Doubleday.

Winds of Darkover. Marion Zimmer Bradley. LC 78-21232. (Gregg Press science fiction series). (Illus.). 1979. 8.00 (ISBN 0-8398-2511-0). Gregg Press.

Winds of Desire. Louise Gerard. LC 29-8264. The Macaulay Company.

Winds of Desire. Marilyn Granbeck. LC 77-91233. (Jove / HBJ Book.). 1978. 1.95 (ISBN 0-515-04337-0). Jove Publications, Inc.

Winds of Desire. Jocelyn Haley. (Superromances Ser.). 384p. 1982. pap. 2.50 (ISBN 0-373-70031-8, Pub. by Worldwide). Harlequin Bks.

Winds of Desire: A Novel. Helen Marion Edginton. LC 46-4359. 1946. Macrae-Smith-Company.

Winds of Evil. Arthur William Upfield. LC 44-3158. 1944. Pub. for the Crime Club by Doubleday, Doran and Co., Inc.

Winds of Fear. Hodding Carter. LC 44-8269. 1944. Farrar & Rinehart, Inc.

Winds of Fear. Maysie Greig. LC 56-58071. 1956. Avalon Books.

Winds of Fire. Vyankatesh Digamber Madgulkar. Tr. by Pramod Kale from Marathi. 113p. 1975. pap. 1.95 (ISBN 0-88253-693-1). Ind-US Inc.

Winds of Gath. E. C. Tubb. (Dumarest of Terra Ser.: No. 4). 192p. 1982. pap. 2.50 (ISBN 0-441-89302-3, Pub. by Ace Science Fiction). Ace Bks.

Winds of Gobi. Robert Hyde. LC 30-8167. 1930. Brewer & Warren Inc., Payson & Clark Ltd.

Winds of God: A Tale of the North Country. Irving Bacheller. LC 41-19689. Farrar & Rinehart, Inc.

Winds of Heaven. Alice Lent Covert. LC 54-118143. 1954. Avalon Books.

Winds of Heaven. Monica Dickens. LC 55-10078. 1955. Coward-McCann.

Winds of Limbo. Michael Moorcock. LC 78-52885. 1978. pap. text ed. 1.95 o.s.i. (ISBN 0-89559-055-7). Dale Books Inc.

Winds of Limbo. Michael Moorcock. Orig. Title: Fireclown. 1969. pap. 0.60 o.p. (63-149). Paperback Lib.

Winds of Love. Virginia Myers. (Candlelight Romance). 1.25 (ISBN 0-440-19734-1). Dell Publishing Co.

Winds of Love. Hollister Noble. (Orig.). 1981. pap. 2.95 (ISBN 0-89083-899-2). Zebra.

Winds of Love. Hollister Noble. 480p. 1980. pap. 2.50 (ISBN 0-89083-599-3). Zebra.

Winds of Love. Agnes Sligh Turnbull. LC 77-1592. 1977. 8.95 (ISBN 0-395-25341-1). Houghton Mifflin.

Winds of Love. Agnes Sligh Turnbull. 1978. 1.75 (ISBN 0-449-23575-0). Fawcett Crest Books.

Winds of Love. Agnes Sligh Turnbull. LC 81-20328. 1982. 12.95 (ISBN 0-8161-3374-3). G.K. Hall.

Winds of Mitamura: A Novel. John Dudley Ball. LC 75-2291. 1975. 7.95 (ISBN 0-316-07951-0). Little, Brown.

Winds of Montauk. Ned Calmer. LC 79-67599. 10.95 (ISBN 0-87223-591-2). Seaview Books.

Winds of Morning. Harold Lenoir Davis. LC 52-5054. 1952. Morrow.

Winds of Morning. Harold Lenoir Davis. LC 77-138586. 1972. 13.50 (ISBN 0-8371-5785-4). Greenwood Press.

Winds of Morning. Laurie Marath, pseud. (Second Chance at Love Ser.: No. 13). 192p. (Orig.). 1981. pap. 1.75 (ISBN 0-515-05623-5). Jove Pubns.

Winds of Passion. Barbara A. Cooper. 1981. pap. 2.75 (ISBN 0-89083-778-3). Zebra.

Winds of Sinhala. Colin De'Silva. LC 80-2954. 1982. 17.95. Doubleday.

Winds of Springs. Walter Havighurst. LC 40-27325. 1940. The Macmillan Company.

Winds of Summer. Arlene Hale. LC 76-21817. 6.95 (ISBN 0-316-33854-0). Little, Brown.

Winds of Summer. Arlene Hale. LC 80-22074. 1980. 13.50 (ISBN 0-8161-3168-6). G. K. Hall.

Winds of Terror. Patricia Hagan Howell. 1975. (pbk.) 0.95 (ISBN 0-380-00460-7). Avon.

Winds of the Day: A Novel. Howard Spring. LC 64-25131. 1965. 4.95. Harper.

Winds of the Old Days. Betsy Aswad. LC 80-17446. 9.95 (ISBN 0-8037-9638-2). Dial Press.

Winds of the World. Ruby Mildred Ayres. LC 22-3960. W. J. Watt & Company.

Winds of the World. Talbot Mundy. LC 16-14726. 1916. Cassell and Company, Ltd.

Winds of the World. Talbot Mundy. LC 17-300412. 1.50. The Bobbs-Merrill Company.

Winds of Time. 1st Ed. Chad Oliver. LC 57-6711. (Doubleday science fiction). 1957. Doubleday.

Winds of War. Herman Wouk. 1973. 3.50 (ISBN 0-671-83312-X). Pocket Books.

Winds of War, a Novel. Herman Wouk. LC 72-161857. (Illus.). 1971. 10.00. Little, Brown.

Winds of War & War & Remembrance. Herman Wouk. 1978. 35.00 (ISBN 0-316-95502-7). Little.

Winds of War: T. V. tie-in edition. Herman Wouk. LC 77-70195. 1983. pap. 5.00 (ISBN 0-671-46319-5). PB.

Winds of Winter. Sandra Field. (Harlequin Romances). 192p. 1981. pap. 1.25 (ISBN 0-373-02398-7, Pub. by Harlequin). PB.

Winds over Manchuria. Alla Crone. (Orig.). 1983. pap. 3.50 (ISBN 0-440-18853-9). Dell.

Winds Over the Campus. James Weber Linn. LC 36-22178. The Bobbs-Merrill Company.

Wind's Twelve Quarters: Short Stories. Ursula K. Le Guin. LC 75-6372. 1975. 10.00 (ISBN 0-06-012562-4). Harper & Row.

Wind's Way. Mabel Cleland Widdemer. LC 39-32043. 1939. Aracdia House, Inc.

Wind's Will. Albert Britt. LC 13-380. 1912. Moffat, Yard and Company.

Wind's Will. Agnes Sweetman Castle & Castle, Egerton. LC 16-15504. 1916. Etc. Cassell and Company, Ltd.

Wind's Will: A Novel. Gerald Warner Brace. LC 64-17105. 1964. Norton.

Wind's Will: By Constance Posten and Anna Garrison Posten. 1st Ed. Constance Posten & Anna Garrison Posten. LC 53-19623. 1952. Pageant Press.

Windsinger. Frances Gillmor. LC 75-17380. (Zia book). 1976. 2.95 (ISBN 0-8263-0397-8). University of New Mexico Press.

Windsinger. Frances Gillmor. LC 30-282675. 1930. Minton, Balch & Company.

Windsong. Nicholas Gagarin. LC 75-115441. 1970. 5.95. W. Morrow.

Windsor Castle. William Harrison Ainsworth. LC 37-30954. (Half-title: Everyman's library, ed. by Ernest Rhys. Fiction. no. 709). 1933. J. M. Dent & Sons, Ltd.

Windsor Castle: An Historical Romance. a new ed. William Harrison Ainsworth. 1903. D. Appleton & Company.

Windsor Castle: An Historical Romance. William Harrison Ainsworth & Cruikshank, George, 1792-1878, Illus. LC 44-306272. 1885. G. Routledge and Sons.

Windsound. Doris Vallejo. (Orig.). 1981. pap. 2.25 (ISBN 0-425-04803-9). Berkley Pub.

Windstorm: A Novel of the Venezuelan Andes. Translated by Hugh Jencks. Luis Felipe Prato. LC 61-65750. 1961. Las Americas Pub. Co.

Windswept. Mary Ellen Chase. 1941. The Macmillan Company.

Windwagon Smith and Other Yarns. Wilbur Lang Schramm. LC 47-11419. 1947. Harcourt, Brace.

Windwalker. Blaine M. Yorgason. LC 78-75366. (Illus.). 4.50 (ISBN 0-88494-362-3). Bookcraft.

Windwalker. 2nd ed., rev. and enl., based on the story from the movie. ed. Blaine M. Yorgason & Brenton G Yorgason. LC 80-70130. (Illus.). 4.95 (ISBN 0-88494-415-8). Bookcraft.

Windward Crest. Anne Hampson. (Harlequin Presents Ser.). 192p. 1982. pap. 1.75 (ISBN 0-373-10494-4). Harlequin Bks.

Windward Goat. Robert H. Rodgers. 4.95 o.p. Vantage.

Windward Goat. Robert H Rodgers. (Illus.). 1973. 4.95 (ISBN 0-533-00599-X). Vantage Press.

Windward of Reason. Henry Gifford Irion. LC 54-7126. 1954. Dial Press.

Windward Passage. Mark Brewer. (O.s.i.). 1978. 10.00 o.s.i. (ISBN 0-517-53304-9). Crown.

Windward Passage: A Novel. Mark Brewer. LC 77-26675. 10.00 (ISBN 0-517-53304-9). Crown Publishers.

Windwood. Cynthia Adele Kreke. 240p. (Orig.). 1981. pap. 2.25 (ISBN 0-8439-1003-8, Leisure Bks). Nordon Pubns.

Windy City. Sam Ross. 1979. 12.50 o.p. (ISBN 0-399-12335-0). Putnam Pub Group.

Windy City: A Novel. Sam Ross. LC 78-27087. 10.00 (ISBN 0-399-12335-0). Putnam.

Windy Creek. Helen Stuart Thompson. LC 99-2695. 1899. C. Scribner's Sons.

Windy Hill. Helen Partridge. LC 36-446302. Arcadia House.

Windy Hill. Jennings Perry. LC 26-9830. 1926. Simon and Schuster.

Windy McPherson's Son. rev. ed. Sherwood Anderson. LC 40-5686. 1922. B. W. Huebsch, Inc.

Windy Macpherson's Son. Sherwood Anderson. LC 65-17280. (Chicago in Fiction Ser). 1965. pap. 2.45 (ISBN 0-226-01905-5, P250, Phoen). U of Chicago Pr.

Windy McPherson's Son. Introd. by Wright Morris. Sherwood Anderson. LC 65-17280. (Chicago in fic.). 1965. bds., 5.95. Univ. of Chic. Pr.

Windy McPherson's Son. Introd. by Wright Morris. Sherwood Anderson. (Phoenix bk., P250: Chicago in fic.). 1967. pap., 2.45. Univ. of Chicago Pr.

Windy McPherson's Sons. Sherwood Anderson. LC 16-18489. 1916. John Lane Company.

Windy Range. George Washington Ogden. LC 38-258826. 1938. Dodd, Mead & Company.

Windy Ridge: A Tale of the Tumbleweed Country. 1st Ed. Florence MacNaughton Butler. LC 57-6552. 1957. Greenwich Book Publishers.

Windy Side of the Law. Sara Woods, pseud. LC 65-27639. bds., 4.50. Harper.

Windyhaugh: A Novel. Margaret Georgina Todd. LC 99-535. 1899. D. Appleton and Company.

Windyjinn. Grace Kellogg Griffith. LC 32-652563. 1932. R. Long & R. R. Smith, Inc.

Windymere. Alice Mary Ross Colver. LC 31-24898. 1931. Dodd, Mead & Company.

Windyridge. William Riley. LC 13-35273. 1913. D. Appleton and Company.

Wine and the Music. William Edmund Barrett. LC 68-5532. 1968. 5.95. Doubleday.

Wine & the Music. David A. Kaufelt. 1982. pap. 3.95 (ISBN 0-440-19376-1). Dell.

Wine Cellar: Short Fiction. Edward Bonetti. LC 76-53794. 1977. 8.95 (ISBN 0-670-77210-0). Viking Press.

Wine Dark Sea: Homer's Heroic Epic of the North Atlantic. Henriette Mertz. LC 74-193168. (Illus.). Mertz.

Wine for My Brothers. Robert Emmett Higginbotham. LC 46-4127. 1946. Rinehart & Company, Inc.

Wine for the Living. Richard Hagopian. LC 56-5662. 1956. Scribner.

Wine for the Vintager. Elizabeth Perdix. LC 39-165176. 1939. L. Raley.

Wine Merchants. S. W. Karl. (Orig.). 1979. pap. 1.95 (ISBN 0-532-23271-2). Woodhill.

Wine O' the Winds. Keene Abbott. LC 20-103111. 1920. Doubleday, Page & Company.

Wine of Astonishment. Mary Hastings Bradley. LC 19-1774. 1919. 1.50. D. Appleton and Company.

Wine of Astonishment. Martha Gellhorn. LC 48-85755. 1948. C. Scribner's Sons.

Wine of Astonishment. Rachel MacKenzie. LC 73-14086. 1974. 5.95 (ISBN 0-670-77217-8). Viking Press.

Wine of Astonishment. Rachel MacKenzie. LC 74-18277. 1974. 8.95 (ISBN 0-8161-6249-2). G. K. Hall.

Wine of Endless Life: Taoist Drinking Songs from the Yuan Dynasty. Ed. by Shu-Sen Sui. Jerome B Seaton. LC 78-110701. Ardis.

Wine of Eternity: Short Stories from the Latvian. Translated by Ruth Speirs and Haralds Kundzins. Knuts Lesins. LC 57-13117. 1957. University of Minnesota Press.

Wine of Etna. Alexander Baron. LC 50-7398. 1950. Washburn.

Wine of Fury. Leigh Rogers. LC 24-12283. 1924. A. A. Knopf.

Wine of God's Anger. Kenneth Cook. LC 70-370756. 1968. Cheshire-Lansdowne.

Wine of Good Hope. Arthur Durham Divine. LC 39-27206. 1939. The Macmillan Company.

Wine of Illusion. Bruce Beddow. LC 24-580698. 1924. Cassell and Company, Ltd.

Wine of Life. William Redstreake. 3.95 o.p. Vantage.

Wine of Life. Arthur John Arbuthnott Stringer. LC 21-5918. 1921. A. A. Knopf.

Wine of Life: An Anthology of Short-Short Stories. Ed. by Julia Baldwin Hazelton. Los Angeles. Hollywood Evening High School. The Cloister Press of Hollywood.

Wine of Morning: A Novel of the First Century. Bob Jones. LC 50-11064. 1950. Van Kampen Press.

Wine of Paradise. Theresa Conway. 384p. (Orig.). 1982. pap. 2.95 (ISBN 0-449-24553-5, Crest). Fawcett.

Wine of Passion. Clarissa Ross, pseud. 1979. pap. 2.25 o.s.i. (ISBN 0-505-51390-0). Tower Bks.

Wine of San Lorenzo. Herbert Sherman Gorman. LC 45-2151. 1945. Farrar & Rinehart, Inc.

Wine of Satan: A Tale of Bohemond, Prince of Antioch. Laverne Gay. LC 49-7180. 1949. C. Scribner's Sons.

Wine of the Country. Hamilton Basso. LC 41-19301. 1941. C. Scribner's Sons.

Wine of the Country. J. Adin Mann. LC 52-13340. 1951. Bruce Humphries.

Wine of the Dreamers. Susannah Leigh. (Orig.). 1980. pap. 2.95 (ISBN 0-451-09157-4, E9157, Sig). NAL.

Wine of the Dreamers. John Dann MacDonald. LC 51-12736. 1951. Greenberg.

Wine of the Generals: A Novel. R. Page Jones. LC 78-19522. 1978. 1.95 (ISBN 0-515-04547-0). Jove/HBH.

Wine of Vengeance. Julie Wellsley. 1973. pap. 0.95 o.s.i. (75-481). Lancer.

Wine of Violence. Neil S Boardman. LC 64-17282. 1964. Simon and Schuster.

Wine of Violence. Lesley Egan, pseud. LC 69-15288. (Suspense Ser). 1969. 4.95 o.p. (ISBN 0-06-011159-3, HarpT). Har-Row.
Wine of Violence. Ralph McAllister Ingersoll. LC 51-2016. 1951. Farrar, Straus & Young.
Wine of Violence. Elizabeth Linington. LC 69-15288. 1969. 4.95. Harper & Row.
Wine of Youth. Robert Wilder. LC 55-5770. 1955. Putnam.
Wine on Desert. Max Brand. 1976. Repr. of 1940 ed. lib. bdg. 15.15x (ISBN 0-88411-511-9). Amereon Ltd.
Wine on the Desert: And Other Stories. Max Brand. LC 40-315157. 1940. Dodd, Mead & Company.
Wine on the Desert and Other Stories. Frederick Faust. LC 40-31515. 1940. Dodd, Mead & Company.
Wine on the Lees. John Alexander Steuart. LC 99-5469. 1899. Dodd, Mead & Company.
Wine-Press. Anna Robeson Brown Burr. LC 5-14827. 1905. D. Appleton and Company.
Wine Princes, a Novel. Margaret Mackprang Mackay. LC 58-7471. 1958. J. Day Co.
Wine Room Murder. Stanley Vestal. LC 35-4218. 1935. Little, Brown, and Company.
Wine with a Stranger. Louise Redfield Peattie. LC 32-246740. 2.00. The Century Co.
Wine, Women & Death. Walter Deptula. 1974. pap. 0.95 o.p. (09253). Curtis.
Wine, Women and War. Michael Jahn. (Six million dollar man,#1). 1975. (pbk.) 1.25 (ISBN 0-446-76833-2). Warner Paperback Library.
Winefred: A Story of the Chalk Cliffs. Sabine Baring-Gould. LC 5044. 1900. L. C. Page & Company.
Winemakers. Jack M Bickham. LC 76-56265. 1977. 10.00 (ISBN 0-385-12677-8). Doubleday.
Winemakers. Jack M Bickham. 1978. 2.50 (ISBN 0-671-82136-9). Pocket Books.
Winepress. Christine Beals. LC 13-1152. The Bookery Publishing Co.
Wines of Cyprien. Dorothy Daniels. 1977. pap. 1.75 o.p. (ISBN 0-515-04060-6). BJ Pub Group.
Winesburg, Ohio. Sherwood Anderson. LC 76-371719. 1976. 7.95 (ISBN 0-670-77236-4). Penguin Books.
Winesburg, Ohio. Sherwood Anderson. LC 77-364851. (100 Greatest Masterpieces of American Literature). (Illus.). 1976. Franklin Library.
Winesburg, Ohio. new ed. Sherwood Anderson. LC 60-10867. 1960. Viking Press.
Winesburg, Ohio: A Group of Tales of Ohio Small Town Life. Sherwood Anderson & Boyd, Ernest Augustus. LC 29-6851. (Half-title: The modern library of the world's best books). 1919. The Modern Library.
Winesburg, Ohio: Text and Criticism. Sherwood Anderson. Ed. by John H. Ferres. LC 66-25279. (Viking critical library). (Illus.). 1966. Viking Press.
Winespring Mountain. Charlton Ogburn. LC 73-5325. 1973. 6.95. Morrow.
Wing and the Thorn. Roxane Cotsakis. LC 52-7546. 1952. Tupper and Love.
Wing and the Yoke. 1st Ed. Francis Orville Mitchell. LC 53-7404. 1953. Smiths.
Wing-and-Win. James Fenimore Cooper.
Wing and Wing. James Fenimore Cooper. (Seaside library. v. 37, no. 761). 1880. G. Munro.
Wing and Wing. James Fenimore Cooper. (On cover: Lovell's library. no. 506). 1885. J. W. Lovell Company.
Wing-and-Wing: or, Le Feu-Follet. James Fenimore Cooper. LC 4-15438. (His works, Mohawk ed.). 1896. G. P. Putnam's Sons.
Wing-and-Wing, or, Le Feu-Follet: A Tale. James Fenimore Cooper. LC 6-29667. 1842. Lea and Blanchard.
Wing-and-Wing: Or, Le Feu-Follet. A Tale. new ed. James Fenimore Cooper. LC 6-29031. 1852. Stringer and Townsend.
Wing-and-Wing: or, Le Feu-Follet. A Tale. James Fenimore Cooper. LC 26-24683. (Half-title: The choice works of Cooper, Revised and corrected series. v. 17).
Wing-and-Wing: or, Le Feu-Follet. A Tale. household ed. James Fenimore Cooper. Ed. by Cooper, Susan Fenimore. LC 6-29030. Houghton, Mifflin Company.
Wing-and-Wing; or, Le Feu-Follet. A Tale. James Fenimore Cooper. LC 4-19575. 1894. D. Appleton and Company.
Wing-and-Wing: Or, Le Feu-Follet. A Tale. ...revised and corrected, with a new introduction, notes, &c., by the author. ed. James Fenimore Cooper. LC 44-153634. (Added t.-p.: The works of J. Fenimore Cooper). 1851. G. P. Putnam.
Wing-Men. Emsan Case. LC 79-65534. 2.50 (ISBN 0-380-47647-9). Avon Books.
Wing of Azrael. Mona Alison Caird. (On cover: Lovell's international series, no. 17). 1889. F. F. Lovell & Company.
Wing of Death. Rabindranath Tagore. Tr. by A. Bose. (Wisdom of the East Ser). 2.00 o.p. (ISBN 0-7195-1388-X). Paragon.
Wing of Fame: A Novel Based on the Life of James Smithson. Louise Wallace Hackney. LC 34-2648. 1934. D. Appleton-Century Company, Incorporated.
Wing of the Wind. A Nouvelette of the Sea. Joseph Holt Ingraham. 1845. Burgess, Stringer and Company.
Wingarden. Elsie Lee. LC 71-167744. 1971. 5.95 (ISBN 0-87795-019-9). Arbor House.
Winged Bull. Violet Mary Firth. LC 73-27457. 1971. 6.00 (ISBN 0-87728-110-6). S. Weiser.
Winged Chariot: An Allegory and Other Stories. Ben Boaz. LC 6-14195. 1858. A. B. Volney.
Winged Citadel. Kristmann Gudmundsson. Tr. by Mussey, June Barrows. LC 40-33362. H. Holt and Company.
Winged Darkness and Other Stories. William Heinesen. LC 82-10067. 1982. 19.50 (ISBN 0-8290-0990-6). Irvington.
Winged Destiny: Studies in the Spiritual History of the Gael. William Sharp. LC 72-87982. 1974. 17.50 (ISBN 0-87696-050-6). Lemma Pub. Corp.
Winged Escort. Douglas Reeman. LC 75-24969. 1975. 7.95 (ISBN 0-399-11635-4). Putnam.
Winged Helmet. Harold Steele MacKaye. LC 5-6287. 1905. L. C. Page & Company.
Winged Lion. Anne Carsley. 544p. (Orig.). 1981. pap. 2.95 (ISBN 0-440-19600-0). Dell.
Winged Lion. A Tale of Venice. Lina Bartlett Ditson. LC 99-28. F. T. Neely.
Winged Magic, No. 144. Barbara Cartland. 1981. pap. 1.95 (ISBN 0-553-14920-2). Bantam.
Winged Man. Alfred Elton Van Vogt & Edna Mayne Hull. 1980. 1.75 (ISBN 0-87997-524-5). DAW Books.
Winged Man: By A. E. Van Vogt. E. Mayne Hull. Alfred Elton Van Vogt & Edna Mayne Hull. (Doubleday sci. fic.). 1966. 3.95. Doubleday.
Winged Pharaoh. Joan Marshall Grant. LC 57-102492. 1957. Harper.
Winged Pharaoh. Joan Marshall Grant. LC 38-7207. 1938. Harper & Brothers.
Winged Pharaoh. Joan Marshall Grant. LC 78-20234. (Grant, Joan Marshall, 1907-. Works.). (Illus.). 1980. 26.00 (ISBN 0-405-11794-9). Arno Press.
Winged Pharoah. Joan Marshall Grant. 1977. pap. 1.75 (ISBN 0-425-03637-5, Medallion). Berkley Pub.
Winged Priestess. Joyce Verrette. 1980. 2.50 (ISBN 0-449-14329-5). Fawcett Gold Medal.
Winged Sword. Leslie Turner White. LC 55-10260. 1955. Morrow.
Winged Victory. Dan Brennan. 1978. pap. 1.50 o.s.i. (ISBN 0-505-51254-8). Tower Bks.
Winged Victory. Barbara Cartland. (Camfield Ser.: No. 2). (Orig.). 1982. pap. 1.95 (ISBN 0-515-06294-4). Jove Pubns.
Winged Victory. Sarah Grand. LC 16-18562. 1916. 1.50. D. Appleton and Company.
Winged Victory. Robert Morss Lovett. 1907. Duffield & Company.
Winged Victory. Claire Macfarlane. LC 54-12537. 1954. Mann Publishers.
Winged Victory. Victor M Yeates. LC 34-32205. 1934. H. Smith & R. Haas.
Winged Warrior. P. A Bechko. LC 77-76956. 1977. 6.95 (ISBN 0-385-13313-8). Doubleday.
Wingless Victory. 3d ed. M. P Willcocks. 1907. J. Lane Company.
Wingmaster. David Houston. 224p. (Orig.). 1981. pap. 2.25 (ISBN 0-8439-0945-5). Leisure Bks CT.
Wings. Ethel May Kelley. LC 24-214087. 1924. A. A. Knopf.
Wings. Arthur L. Kopit. 78p. 1978. 8.95 (ISBN 0-8090-9756-7, Mermaid); pap. 3.95 (ISBN 0-8090-1239-1). Hill & Wang.
Wings. John Saunders. LC 27-18767. Grosset & Dunlap.
Wings. Robert J Serling. LC 78-3182. (Illus.). 8.95 (ISBN 0-8037-9592-0). Dial Press.
Wings Above the Claypan. Arthur William Upfield. LC 43-7753. 1943. Pub. for the Crime Club by Doubleday, Doran & Co., Inc.
Wings Against the Sky. Richard Alexander Hough. LC 79-16570. 1979. 8.95. Morrow.
Wings for Carol. Patricia O'Malley. LC 41-3676. The Greystone Press.
Wings for Juliet. Marie Blizard. LC 42-14598. 1942. Arcadia House, Inc.
Wings for the Chariot. Arch Whitehouse. LC 72-93685. 260p. 1973. 5.95 o.p. (ISBN 0-385-01191-1). Doubleday.
Wings for the Chariots. Arthur George Joseph Whitehouse. LC 72-93685. 1973. 5.95 (ISBN 0-385-01191-1). Doubleday.
Wings North. Robert Ormond Case. LC 38-12837. 1938. Doubleday, Doran & Company, Inc.
Wings of a Butterfly: A Novel. Emmeline Morrison. LC 31-2165. 1930. L. MacVeagh, The Dial Press.
Wings of Adventure and Other Little Novels: By Philip Gibbs... Philip Hamilton Gibbs. LC 30-25905. 1930. Doubleday, Coran & Company, Inc.
Wings of Danger: A Novel. Arthur A Nelson. LC 15-19411. 1915. 1.35. R. M. McBride & Company.
Wings of Darkness. Pierre Audemars. 1970. pap. 0.60 o.p. (0502-06095). Curtis.
Wings of Darkness. Ellen Milburn. (Inflation Fighter Ser.). 192p. 1982. pap. cancelled o.s.i. (ISBN 0-8439-1121-2, Leisure Bks). Nordon Pubns.
Wings of Dawn. Guy Howard. LC 53-329083. 1953. Zondervan Pub. House.
Wings of Death. Marjorie Boniface. LC 46-3691. 1946. R. M. McBride & Company.
Wings of Death. Christopher Sloane. (Orig.). 1983. pap. 2.50 (ISBN 0-8217-1210-1). Zebra.
Wings of Desire. Maurice DeKobra, pseud. Tr. by Wainwright, Neal. LC 25-177033. The Macaulay Company.
Wings of Desire. Paula Dion. LC 78-66650. 1978. 2.25 (ISBN 0-345-27322-2). Ballantine Books.
Wings of Desire. Rita Wellman. LC 19-149126. 1919. Moffat, Yard & Company.
Wings of Desire. Mary Patricia Willcocks. LC 12-3793. 1912. John Lane Company.
Wings of Destiny. George Weston. LC 29-9994. 1929. Dodd, Mead & Company.
Wings of Destiny: Also Containing Phantom of the Desert, The Grey Shadow, The Hand, Hightide. Winnie Fields Moore. LC 30-15214. 1930. Wetzel Publishing Co., Inc.
Wings of Ecstasy. Barbara Cartland. (Barbara Cartland Ser.: No. 90). 192p. (Orig.). 1981. pap. 1.75 (ISBN 0-515-05955-2). Jove Pubns.
Wings of Fate. Leonard Noel Baker. LC 26-307708. The Curtiss Press.
Wings of Fear. Mignon Good Eberhart. LC 45-16623. 1945. Random House.
Wings of Great Desire. James Gray. LC 38-22280. 1938. The Macmillan Company.
Wings of Healing. Helen Reimensnyder Martin. LC 29-2969. 1929. Dodd, Mead & Company.
Wings of Hope. Hilda Mauck. LC 32-17510. C. Kendall.
Wings of Lead. Monica Selwin-Tait. LC 37-1985. The Ave Maria Press.
Wings of Learus: Being the Life of One Emilia Fletcher, As Revealed by Herself in Thirty-Five Letters, Written to Constance Norris Between July 18th, 188-, and March 26th of the Following Year; A Fragmentary Journal; A Postscript, by Laurence Alma Tadema. Laurence Alma-Tadema. LC 7-1496. 1894. Macmillan and Company.
Wings of Love. Barbara Cartland. 1971. pap. 1.25 o.p. (V2504). BJ Pub Group.
Wings of Love: The Love Story of a Girl Aviator. Vera Brown. LC 34-259373. Grosset & Dunlap.
Wings of Madness: A Novel of Charles Baudelaire. Geoffrey Atheling Wagner. LC 78-1039. 1978. 3.95 (ISBN 0-89370-220-X). Borgo Press.
Wings of Madness: A Peter Styles Mystery Novel. Judson Pentecost Philips. LC 66-23215. (Red badge mystery).
Wings of Night. 1st Ed. Thomas Head Raddall. LC 56-905973. 1956. Doubleday.
Wings of Peace. John Creasey. LC 77-95214. (Doctor Palfrey thriller). 1978. 7.95 (ISBN 0-8027-5388-4). Walker.
Wings of Pride. Louise Kennedy Mabie. LC 13-4991. 1913. Harper & Brothers.
Wings of Song. Georgiana L. Lahr. 3.75 (ISBN 0-533-00625-2). Vantage.
Wings of the Cardinal. Bertha Crowell. LC 17-25289. 1.35. George H. Doran Company.
Wings of the Dove. Henry James. LC 71-158798. (Scribner reprint editions). 1975. 12.50 (ISBN 0-678-02819-2) (ISBN 0-678-02820-6). A. M. Kelley.
Wings of the Dove. Henry James. LC 77-358074. (Penguin modern classics). 1976. 2.95 (ISBN 0-14-002320-8). Penguin.
Wings of the Dove. Henry James. LC 75-113743. (Charles E. Merrill standard editions). 1970. Merrill.
Wings of the Dove. Henry James. LC 2-20827. 1902. C. Scribner's Sons.
Wings of the Dove. Henry James. LC 45-983544. 1945. C. Scribner's Sons.
Wings of the Dove. Henry James & Joseph Donald Crowley. LC 77-19062. (Norton critical edition). 17.50 (ISBN 0-393-04478-5) (ISBN 0-393-09088-4). W. W. Norton.
Wings of the Dove see Bodley Head Henry James.
Wings of the Dove 2 Vols. Henry James. 1909. 7.50 ea. o.p. Scribner.
Wings of the Eagle. Nancy Dorer & Frances Dorer. (Orig.). 1979. pap. 1.95 (ISBN 0-532-23287-9). Woodhill.
Wings of the Eagle. Gilbert Vivian Seldes. LC 29-208855. 1929. Little, Brown, and Company.
Wings of the Falcon. Barbara Mertz. LC 77-24927. 8.95 (ISBN 0-396-07458-8). Dodd, Mead.
Wings of the Falcon. Barbara Michaels. LC 82-12149. 1982. 13.95 (ISBN 0-8161-3415-4). G.K. Hall.
Wings of the Hawk. Leigh F. James. (Colonization of America Ser.). 352p. (Orig.). 1981. pap. 2.95 (ISBN 0-553-14276-3). Bantam.
Wings of the Morning. David Beaty & Betty. Beaty. LC 81-19467. 1982. 14.95 (ISBN 0-698-11141-9). Coward, McCann & Geoghegan.
Wings of the Morning. Edward S Hyams. LC 39-14381. 1939. Little, Brown.
Wings of the Morning. Robert Bruce Thurber. LC 34-2640. Southern Publishing Association.
Wings of the Morning. Louis Tracy. LC 16-131200. 1903. E. J. Clode.
Wings of the Morning. Louis Tracy. 1903. Grosset & Dunlap.
Wings of the Morning. Louis Tracy. LC 24-22681. E. J. Clode.
Wings of the Morning. Louis Tracy. LC 28-31020. 1927. The John C. Winston Company.
Wings of the Morning. Frederic Franklyn Van De Water. LC 55-13944. 1955. Washburn.
Wings of the Tiger: A Novel. Carl Krueger. LC 66-27604. 1966. F. Fell.
Wings of the Wind. Credo Fitch Harris. LC 20-11301. 1.75. Small, Maynard & Company.
Wings of the Wind. Ed. by Robert M. Myers. (Children of Pride Ser.: Vol.5). 1977. pap. 1.95 (ISBN 0-445-04136-6). Popular Lib.
Wings of Time. Elizabeth Newport Hepburn. LC 21-17081. Frederick A. Stokes Company.
Wings of Victory. Richard Alexander Hough. LC 80-24111. 1980. 9.95 (ISBN 0-688-03758-5). Morrow.
Wings of Wax. Janet Hoyt. LC 29-7397. J. H. Sears & Company, Inc.
Wings of Youth. Helen Welshimer. LC 41-666075. 1941. Arcadia House, Inc.
Wings of Youth: A Novel. Elizabeth Garver Jordan. LC 18-6018. 1918. Harper & Brothers.
Wings on Her Heart. Peggy Gaddis, pseud. LC 42-17840. Gramercy Publishing Co.
Wings on My Feet: Black Ulysses at the Wars. Howard Washington Odum. LC 29-18983. The Bobbs-Merrill Company.
Wings on My Heart. Barbara Cartland. (Barbara Cartland Ser.: No. 47). 256p. 1981. pap. 1.95 (ISBN 0-515-05959-5). Jove Pubns.
Wings on My Heart. Barbara Cartland. 1975. pap. 1.25 o.p. (ISBN 0-515-03904-7). BJ Pub Group.
Wings Over Hawaii. Carlene Brien Myers. LC 40-3854. House of Field, Inc.
Wings, Tales of the Psychic. Achmed Abdullah. LC 20-9627. 1920. The James A. McCann Company.
Wings, the Vines. Katharyn M. Aal & ALice Fulton. (Illus.). 96p. 1982. 12.50 (ISBN 0-935526-06-4); pap. 6.50 (ISBN 0-935526-07-2). McBooks Pr.
Wings to the Sun. Edward Churchill. LC 40-8081. 1940. Gateway Books.
Wings Upon Heavens. 1976. 3.95 o.p. Ideals.
Wingtown Parson's Linen Duster. Isabella Pierpont Hopkins. 1903. Eaton & Mains.
Winifred. Doris Miles Disney. LC 75-25438. 1976. 5.95 (ISBN 0-385-11545-8). Published for the Crime Club by Doubleday.
Winifred Bertram: And the World She Lived in. Elizabeth Charles. LC 41-82200. Dodd, Mead & Company.
Winifred Bertram: And the World She Lived in. Elizabeth Rundle Charles. LC 6-24201. 1866. T. Nelson and Sons.
Winifred: Or, The Neglected Warning. Mary Kyle Dallas. LC 6-33178. (Street & Smith's select series, no. 27). Street & Smith.
Winifred Power. Joyce Darrell. LC 6-33064. (Lovell's library, v. 6, no. 315.). J. W. Lovell Company.
Winifrede's Journal of Her Life at Exeter and Norwich in the Days of Bishop Hall. Emma Martin Marshall. LC 7-24664. 1891. Macmillan and Co.
Winifred's Neighbors. Nina Rhoades. LC 3-15226. 1903. Lee and Shepard.
Winking at the Brim. Gladys Mitchell. LC 76-52572. 1977. 6.95 (ISBN 0-679-50732-9). D. McKay Co.
Winkles: Or, The Merry Monomaniacs. An American Picture with Portraits of the Natives. John Beauchamp Jones. LC 7-11924. 1855. D. Appleton and Company.
Winks & Wings. Paul A. Little. LC 72-103610. 1970. 3.00. Dorrance.
Winn. Taylor Alexander. LC 5-7379. M. A. Donohue & Company.
Winnapock Confectioner. Alfred W Miller. 1973. 4.50 (ISBN 0-533-00591-4). Vantage Press.
Winnebago Mysteries. Moira Crone. 144p. 1982. 10.95 (ISBN 0-914590-68-5); pap. 4.95 (ISBN 0-914590-69-3). Fiction Coll.
Winner. Borden Deal. LC 70-175363. 1973. 6.95 (ISBN 0-385-03699-X). Doubleday.
Winner. Borden Deal. 1974. (pbk.) 1.25 (ISBN 0-345-23700-5). Ballantine Books.

Winner. William Winter. LC 15-17135. The Bobbs-Merrill Company.

Winner on Satan's Doorstep: A Novel. Sam L Draper. LC 72-75824. 4.95. Windfall Press.

Winner Take All. Ruby Mildred Ayres. LC 39-478. 1938. The Sun Dial Press, Inc.

Winner Take All. Larry Evans. LC 24-780937. 1.75. The H. K. Fly Company.

Winner Take All. Gerard Fairlie. LC 53-522384. (Red badge detective). 1953. Dodd, Mead.

Winner Take Nothing. Ernest Hemingway. LC 83-31157. 1933. C.Scribner's Sons.

Winners. Poul Anderson. 288p. 1981. pap. 2.75 (ISBN 0-523-48507-7). Pinnacle Bks.

Winners. Julio Cortazar. LC 64-18305. 1965. Pantheon Books.

Winners. Judith H. Green. 240p. 1981. pap. 2.75. Ballantine.

Winners: A Love Story. Donna Ball. LC 81-18392. 13.95 (ISBN 0-312-88229-7). St. Martin's Press.

Winners: A Novel. Judith H Green. LC 79-3484. 1980. 8.95 (ISBN 0-394-50387-2). Knopf: Distributed by Random House.

Winners & Losers. Jodie Rhodes. 1982. pap. 2.95 (ISBN 0-515-06420-3). Jove Pubns.

Winners and Losers. Alice Caldwell Hegan Rice. LC 25-17662. The Century Co.

Winners and Losers; an Anthology of Great Sports Fiction. Ed. by L. M. Schulman. LC 68-24106. 1968. Macmillan.

Winners and Losers. 1st Ed. Martin Peter Quigley. LC 61-5993. 1961. Lippincott.

Winners: And Other Short Stories. 1st Ed. Raymond T Shafer. LC 54-12480. 1954. Exposition Press.

Winner's Circle. Charles P. Conn. 1980. pap. 2.50 (ISBN 0-425-04500-5). Berkley Pub.

Winner's Circle. Joseph Arnold Hayes. 1981. 2.95 (ISBN 0-440-19532-2). Dell Publishing Co., Inc.

Winner's Circle: A Novel. Joseph Arnold Hayes. LC 79-26844. 9.95 (ISBN 0-440-09538-7). Delacorte Press.

Winners Get Lost. Allan K Perry. LC 51-9074. 1950. Exposition Press.

Winners: Part II of Joyce Haber's The Users. Dominick Dunne & Joyce Haber. LC 81-23328. 12.95 (ISBN 0-671-24978-9). Simon and Schuster.

Winner's Share: A Novel About Power, Jealousy, and Suspicion. Roger Beardwood. LC 78-20024. 1980. 10.00 (ISBN 0-385-14426-1). Doubleday.

Winnetou. Karl Friedrich May. LC 77-14342. (collected works of Karl May; ser. 2, v. 1-2). 1977. 14.95. Seabury Press.

Winnie O'Wynn and the Wolves. Bertram Atkey. 1922. 1.75. Little, Brown, and Company.

Winnign Game. Sara Currie Palmer. LC 27-185365. The Bible Institute Colportage Ass'n.

Winning. Robin F. Brancato. (gr. 9-12). 1978. pap. 1.95 (ISBN 0-553-13693-3, Y13693-3). Bantam.

Winning a Fortune. Lewis William Klinker. LC 15-16636. 1.20. W. B. Conkey Company.

Winning a Wife & Other Stories. Peter Neagoe. LC 78-152951. (Short story index reprint series). 1971. (ISBN 0-8369-3866-6). Books for Libraries Press.

Winning a Wife & Other Stories. Peter Neagoe. LC 35-5699. Coward. McCann.

Winning Chance. Elizabeth Dejeans. 1909. J. B. Lippincott Company.

Winning Clue. James Hay. LC 19-10463. 1919. Dodd, Mead and Company.

Winning Game. Elizabeth Dejeans. LC 25-5382. 1925. Doubleday, Page & Company.

Winning Game. Madge Macbeth. LC 10-146461. 1910. Broadway Publishing Co.

Winning Hazard. Annie French Hector. (Half--title: Appletons' town and country library; no. 192). 1896. D. Appleton and Company.

Winning His Spurs. A Novel. James T Vallentine. (On cover: Clover series, no. 70). Street & Smith.

Winning Is Everything: A Novel. David Marlow. LC 82-21424. 15.95 (ISBN 0-399-12801-8). Putnam.

Winning Lady: And Others. Mary Eleanor Wilkins Freeman. LC 9-27999. 1909. Harper & Brothers.

Winning Line. Frederic Gregory Hartswick. LC 34-154916. Covici-Friede.

Winning of Aliene. Charles Elmo Robinson. LC 39-23190. Zondervan Publishing House.

Winning of Barbara Worth. Harold Bell Wright. LC 66-19498. 1966. Grosset & Dunlap.

Winning of Barbara Worth. Harold Bell Wright. LC 11-22022. 1911. The Book Supply Company.

Winning of Barbara Worth. Harold Bell Wright. LC 21-139501. 1913. A. L. Burt Company.

Winning of Kay Slade. Capwell Wyckoff. LC 51-14643. 1951. Zondervan Pub. House.

Winning of Lucia: A Love Story. Amelia Edith Huddleston Barr. LC 15-606690. 1915. 1.35. D. Appleton and Company.

Winning of Mickey Free. William Riley Burnett. LC 65-12773. (Bantam pathfinder editions, FP82). 1965. Bantam Books.

Winning of Opie. Dick Fleming. LC 78-7753. 1978. 7.95 (ISBN 0-385-14467-9). Doubleday.

Winning of the Valley: A Novel. David Taylor Robertson. LC 15-18286. 1.50. The Roxborough Publishing Company, Inc.

Winning of Westminster. Kurt Unkelbach. LC 66-23374. 1966. Prentice-Hall.

Winning Play. Ann K. Glasner. (YA) 1972. 4.50 o.p. (Avalon). Bouregy.

Winning Quest. Charles Pomeroy Sherman. Dorrance & Company, Inc.

Winning Side. Mary Dwinell Chellis. 1888. The National Temperance Society and Publication House.

Winning the Battle: Or, One Girl in Ten Thousand. Mary Von Erden Thomas. LC 8-27044. T. B. Peterson & Brothers.

Winning the Eagle Prize: Or, The Pluck of Billy Hazen. Samuel Richard Fuller. LC 10-10322. (His Five chums series). 1910. 1.25. Lothrop, Lee & Shepard Co.

Winning the Wilderness. Margaret Hill McCarter. LC 14-16470. 1914. A. C. McClurg & Co.

Winning Trick. Charles Neville Brand. LC 32-962. 1932. G. P. Putnam's Sons.

Winning, Wayward Woman. Chapters in the Heart History of Amelie Warden. Flora Adams Darling. LC 6-33068. (Judge's novels, no. 4). 1889. The Judge Publishing Co.

Winning Winds. A Novel. Willis George Emerson. LC 6-37831. 1885. G. W. Carleton & Co.

Winnipesaukee Whoppers: Fabulous Legends of the Lake Once Called Winnipiseogee. Elizabeth Crawford Wilkin. LC 60-11601. 1960. Wake-Brook House.

Winnowing. Robert Hugh Benson. LC 10-13389. 1910. B. Herder.

Winnowing Winds. Gerald Earl Bailey. 1967. 4.00 o.p. (ISBN 0-87141-020-6). Manyland.

Winnowing Winds. Ann Marlowe. LC 77-3881. 7.95 (ISBN 0-396-07445-6). Dodd, Mead.

Winnowing Winds. Ann Marlowe. (Signet Book). 1979. 1.95 (ISBN 0-451-08516-7). New American Library.

Winnowing Winds: A Novel. Gerald Earl Bailey. LC 67-28549. 1967. Manyland Books.

Winona: A Story of to-Day. Ella May Powell. LC 7-303128. A. Lovell & Co.

Winslow Plain. Sarah Pratt McLean Greene. LC 2-24932. 1902. Harper & Brothers.

Winsome but Wicked. Maude Meredith. LC 7-26227. (On cover: Dearborn series, no. 57). 1892. Donohue, Henneberry & Co.

Winsome Winnie, & Other New Nonsense Novels. facs. ed. Stephen B. Leacock. LC 74-140333. (Short Story Index Reprint Ser). 1920. 13.00 (ISBN 0-8369-3725-2). Ayer Co.

Winstle on the Wind. Shipley, Nan. LC 61-9274. 1961. F. Fell.

Winston Churchill. Warren Irving Titus. LC 63-17371. (Twayne's U.S. authors ser., 43). bds. qchurchill, winston. 1871-1947. 3.50. Twayne.

Winston Science Fiction Series for Young Adults. (Science Fiction Ser.). 1979. 50.00 o.p. (Gregg). G K Hall.

Winter. Friedrich Griese. Tr. by Hobman, D. L. Adler. LC 29-9490. 1929. 2.00. Longmans, Green and Co.

Winter: A Dance to the Music of Time, Vol. 4. Anthony Dymoke Powell. 1976. pap. 2.50 (ISBN 0-445-08448-0). Popular Lib.

Winter After This Summer. Stanley Ellin. 399p. 1981. pap. 4.95 (ISBN 0-914378-73-2, Foul Play). Countryman.

Winter Ambush. Eugene E Halleran. LC 54-62403. 1954. Macrae Smith Co.

Winter Amid the Ice: And Other Thrilling Stories. Jules Verne. LC 63-56363. 1877. World Pub. House.

Winter Away. Elizabeth Fair. LC 57-59259. 1957. St. Martin's Press.

Winter Bell. Henry Milner Rideout. LC 22-7408. 1922. Duffield and Company.

Winter Blood. John Roc. LC 70-162927. 1971. 7.95 (ISBN 0-671-27084-2). Trident Press.

Winter Bride. Carola Salisbury. 1978. 1.95 (ISBN 0-449-23838-5). Fawcett Crest Books.

Winter Cherry: A Novel of the T'ang Dynasty... Kenneth Westmacott Lane. LC 44-8404. 1944. The Macmillan Company.

Winter Circus. Peggy Gaddis, pseud. LC 48-15471. 1943. Arcadia House, Inc.

Winter Count. Chief Eagle, D. LC 67-5654. (Illus.). 1967. Dentan-Berkeland Printing Co.

Winter Count. Barry Holstun Lopez. LC 80-29454. (Illus.). 9.95 (ISBN 0-684-16817-0). Scribner.

Winter Drift. Carter Travis Young. LC 79-7886. 1980. 8.95 (ISBN 0-385-12327-2). Doubleday.

Winter Drift. Carter Travis Young. LC 82-839. 1982. 9.95 (ISBN 0-89621-352-8). Thorndike Press.

Winter Evening Tales. Amelia Edith Huddleston Barr. (On cover: The Christian herald library). The Christian Herald.

Winter Fire. Susannah Leigh. (Signet Book). 1978. 2.25 (ISBN 0-451-08011-4). New American Library.

Winter Fire. A Sequel to "Summer Drift-Wood". Rose Porter. A. D. F. Randolph & Company.

Winter Garden. Beryl Bainbridge. LC 80-70841. 1981. 8.95 (ISBN 0-8076-1011-9). Braziller.

Winter Harvest. Norah Lofts. LC 55-105129. (Fawcett Crest Book). 1973. (pbk) 1.25. Fawcett.

Winter Harvest. Norah Robinson Lofts. 288p. 1981. pap. 2.75 (ISBN 0-449-24466-0, Crest). Fawcett.

Winter Harvest: A Novel. Introd. by Stewart H. Holbrook. Norah Robinson Lofts. LC 55-10512. 1955. Doubleday.

Winter Heart: A Colorado Epic. Frances Casey Kerns. 1978. 2.50. Warner Books.

Winter House. 1st Ed. George Abbe. LC 57-13014. 1957. Doubleday.

Winter in a Dark Land. Miriam Lynch. (Candlelight Historical Romance, 201). Dell.

Winter in April. Robert Nathan. LC 38-270283. 1938. A. A. Knopf.

Winter in Geneva: And Other Stories. Anne Goodwin Winslow. 1945. A. A. Knopf.

Winter in Mallorca. Kenneth Thomas Knoblock. LC 34-24140. 1934. Harper & Brothers.

Winter in Moscow. Malcolm Muggeridge. LC 34-120255. 1934. Little, Brown, and Company.

Winter in Retirement: Or, Scattered Leaves. Hannah Blaney Washburn. LC 15-2. Frank Allaben Genealogical Company.

Winter in the Air: And Other Stories. Sylvia Townsend Warner. LC 56-7082. 1956. Viking Press.

Winter in the Air, and Other Stories. Sylvia Townsend Warner. LC 56-7082. 1956. Viking Press.

Winter in the Blood. James Welch. LC 74-5985. 1974. 6.95 (ISBN 0-06-452500-7). Harper & Row.

Winter in the Blood. James Welch. LC 75-9975. 1975. 8.95 (ISBN 0-8161-6299-9). G. K. Hall.

Winter in the Blood. James Welch. 1975. (pbk.) 1.75. Bantam.

Winter in the Blood. James Welch. 1981. 2.25 (ISBN 0-06-080537-4). Harper & Row.

Winter in the Heart: By E. M. Almedingen. Martha Edith Almedingen. 1960. Appleton-Century-Crofts.

Winter in the Hills. John Barrington Wain. LC 70-119783. 1970. 6.95. Viking Press.

Winter in the Sun. David Burnham. LC 37-4015. 1937. C. Scribner's Sons.

Winter in Thrush Green. Miss Read. 1982. Repr. lib. bdg. 16.95 (ISBN 0-89966-436-9). Buccaneer Bks.

Winter in Thrush Green. Miss Read. (Illus.). 1962. 3.75 o.p. HM.

Winter in Washington: Or, Memoirs of the Seymour Family... Margaret Smith. 1824. E. Bliss & E. White.

Winter Interlude. Kay Kirby. (Adventures in Love Ser.: No. 37). 1982. pap. 1.95 (ISBN 0-451-11930-4, AJ1930, Sig). NAL.

Winter Journey. Thomas Broughton. LC 79-16098. 10.95. Dutton.

Winter Journey. Eva Figes. LC 68-14781. 1968. Hill and Wang.

Winter Keeper. Jeanne Crecy. (Signet book). 1975. (pbk.) 0.95. New American Library.

Winter Kill. Stephen Gould Fisher. LC 46-1884. 1946. Dodd, Mead & Company.

Winter Kill. William Harrison. 1979. pap. 1.50 o.s.i. (ISBN 0-505-51441-9). Tower Bks.

Winter Kill. William Harrison. 1972. pap. 0.75 o.p. (BT50217). Belmont-Tower.

Winter Kill: By Len Turner Pseud. Lee Floren. LC 54-748353. 1954. Arcadia House.

Winter Kills. Richard Condon. LC 74-1163. 1974. 7.95 (ISBN 0-8037-8822-3). Dial Press.

Winter Kills. Richard Condon. 336p. 1975. pap. 2.25 (ISBN 0-440-16007-3). Dell.

Winter Lodge: Or, Vow Fulfilled, an Historical Novel, The Sequel to Simon Kenton. James Weir. LC 8-34348. 1854. Lippincott, Grambo, and Co.

Winter Lord. Jean B. Janowiak. 192p. 1983. pap. 2.95 (ISBN 0-451-12002-7, Sig). NAL.

Winter Love Song. Meredith Kingston. (Second Chance at Love, Contemporary Ser.: No. 2). 192p. (Orig.). 1981. pap. 1.75 (ISBN 0-515-05637-5). Jove Pubns.

Winter Meeting. Grace Zaring Stone. LC 46-552381. 1946. Little, Brown and Company.

Winter Morning. Nancy Bacon. (Love & Life Romance Ser.). 176p. (Orig.). 1982. pap. 1.75 (ISBN 0-345-29760-1). Ballantine.

Winter Murder Case: A Philo Vance Story. Willard Huntington Wright. LC 39-27933. 1939. C. Scribner's Sons.

Winter of Artifice. Anais Nin. LC 82-72288. 175p. (Orig.). 1961. pap. 5.95 (ISBN 0-8040-0322-X). Swallow.

Winter of Discontent. James Francis Barrett. LC 24-1494. P. J. Kenedy & Sons.

Winter of Our Discontent. John Steinbeck. LC 61-6793. 1961. Viking Press.

Winter of Our Discontent. John Steinbeck. LC 81-23442. 1982. 3.95 (ISBN 0-14-006221-1). Penguin Books.

Winter of the Coup. Carter Travis Young. LC 72-84956. 1972. 4.95 (ISBN 0-385-07559-6). Doubleday.

Winter of the First Summer. Mary L. Burks. 1980. 4.95 (ISBN 0-8062-1332-9). Carlton.

Winter of the White Seal. large print ed. Marie Herbert. LC 82-10339. 12.95 (ISBN 0-89621-378-1). Thorndike Press.

Winter of the World. Paul Anderson. Bd. with Queen of Air & Darkness. 1982. pap. 3.50 (ISBN 0-451-11940-1, AE1940, Sig). NAL.

Winter of the World. Poul Anderson. (Signet Book). 1976. (pbk.) 1.50. New American Library.

Winter Orchard, and Other Stories. Josephine Winslow Johnson. LC 35-13200. 1935. Simon and Schuster.

Winter People. Charles N. Barnard. LC 72-12435. (Illus.). 160p. 1973. 4.95 o.p. (ISBN 0-396-06780-8). Dodd.

Winter People. John Ehle. LC 81-47684. 13.42 (ISBN 0-06-014930-2). Harper & Row.

Winter People. Phyllis A. Whitney. LC 69-12244. 1969. 4.95. Doubleday.

Winter Picnic: The Story of a Four Months' Outing in Nassau, Told in the Letters, Journals, and Talk of Four Picnicers. J Dickinson & Dickinson, E. E. LC 6-37031. (Leisure hour series--no. 216). 1888. H. Holt and Company.

Winter Quarry. Paul Henissart. LC 77-357441. 1976. 3.95 (ISBN 0-09-126300-X). Hutchinson.

Winter Quarters. Alfred Leo Duggan. LC 56-10499. 1956. Coward-McCann.

Winter Quarters. Bennett Foster. LC 43-18241. The Sun Dial Press.

Winter Quarters. Pamela Hansford Johnson. LC 44-5302. 1944. The Macmillan Company.

Winter Quarters. Double D Western. Bennett Foster. LC 42-24962. 1942. Doubleday, Doran & Company, Inc.

Winter Range. Al Cody, pseud. 224p. 1975. pap. 0.95 (ISBN 0-532-95432-7). Woodhill.

Winter Range. Al Cody, pseud. 224p. 1973. pap. 0.95 o.p. (532-95301-095). Manor Bks.

Winter Range. Alan Le May. Farrar & Rinehart, Incorporated.

Winter Romance in Poppy Land. Una Nixson Hopkins. LC 10-29517. 1911. 1.25. R. G. Badger.

Winter Rooms. Danny L. Rendleman. 1975. pap. 3.50 (ISBN 0-87886-061-4, Pub. by Ithaca Hse). SBD.

Winter Rose. James Carver. LC 72-95771. 1973. 6.95 (ISBN 0-8027-0412-3). Walker.

Winter Rose. James Carver. 1974. (pbk.) 1.50. Dell.

Winter Rose. Barbara Daniels. 1978. pap. 1.95 o.s.i. (ISBN 0-505-51292-0). Tower Bks.

Winter Rose. Millie J Ragosta. LC 79-8562. 1982. 10.95 (ISBN 0-385-14891-7). Doubleday.

Winter Silk. James L. Stowe. 1980. 2.95 (ISBN 0-671-83401-0). Pocket Books.

Winter Solstice. Dorothy Cowlin, pseud. LC 43-103277. 1943. The Macmillan Company.

Winter Solstice: A Novel. Gerald Warner Brace. LC 60-9806. 1960. Norton.

Winter Sonata. Dorothy Edwards. 1930. E. P. Dutton & Co., Inc.

Winter Song. Roberta Gellis. LC 82-80218. 400p. (Orig.). 1982. pap. 3.50 (ISBN 0-86721-091-5). Playboy Pbks.

Winter Song. 1st Ed. Mary Roe. LC 52-143665. 1952. Pageant Press.

Winter Spy. Paul Henissart. LC 76-23332. 7.95 (ISBN 0-671-22375-5). Simon And Schuster.

Winter Spy. Paul Henissart. (Kangaroo Book). 1978. 1.95 (ISBN 0-671-81722-1). Pocket Books.

Winter Stalk. James L Stowe. LC 79-752. 9.95 (ISBN 0-671-24741-7). Simon and Schuster.

Winter Sun: By Gay Rutherford Pseud. James Noble Gifford. LC 56-7016. 1956. Arcadia House.

Winter Take All. Ruby Mildred Ayres. LC 37-153432. 1937. Doubleday, Doran and Company, Inc.

Winter Term. John Harriman. LC 40-522322. Howell, Soskin & Company.

Winter Thunder. Mari Sandoz. LC 54-94003. 1954. Westminster Press.

Winter Twilight. Charles Angoff. LC 71-81680. 1970. 6.95. T. Yoseloff.

Winter Visitors. Mary Therese McCarthy. LC 74-22445. 1970. Harcourt Brace Jovanovich.

Winter War: A Historical Novel. 1st Ed. William Wister Haines. LC 61-5731.

Winter Warriors. John Bertoli. (Orig.). 1979. pap. 1.95 (ISBN 0-532-23213-5). Woodhill.

Winter Wheat. Almey St. John Adcock. LC 26-12290. George H. Doran Company.

Winter Wheat. Mildred Walker, pseud. LC 44-40006. 1944. Harcourt, Brace and Company.

Winter Winds. Jackie Black. (Candlelight Ecstasy Ser.: No. 39). (Orig.). 1982. pap. 1.75 (ISBN 0-440-19528-4). Dell.

Winterborough. Eliza Orne White. 1892. Houghton, Mifflin and Company.

Winteredge Whispers. Dorinda Kamm. 1982. pap. 2.95 (ISBN 0-8217-1040-0). Zebra.

Winterflight: A Novel. Joseph Bayly. LC 81-51006. 8.95 (ISBN 0-8499-0297-5). Word Books.

Wintergreen. Margaret Reynolds. 1970. 4.95 o.p. Vantage.

Wintergreen: A Tale of the Reconstruction. Janet Laing. LC 22-16603. 1922. 1.75. The Century Co.

Wintering. Joan Williams. LC 78-134571. 1971. (ISBN 0-15-125225-4). Harcourt Brace Jovanovich.

Wintermind. Marvin Kaye & Parke Godwin. LC 81-43111. 1982. 12.95 (ISBN 0-385-17586-8). Doubleday.

Wintermute. Christopher Brookhouse. LC 77-22981. 7.95. Dutton.

Winterreise. Gerhard Roth. LC 79-21999. 9.95 (ISBN 0-374-29103-9). Farrar, Straus, Giroux.

Winter's Crimes, No. 13. Ed. by George Hardinge. 224p. 1982. 10.95 (ISBN 0-312-88239-4). St Martin.

Winter's Crimes Eight. Ed. by Hilary Watson. LC 76-28066. 1977. 8.95 o.p. (ISBN 0-312-88235-1). St Martin.

Winter's Crimes Eleven. George Hardinge. 1980. 9.95 o.p. (ISBN 0-312-88238-6). St Martin.

Winter's Crimes Fourteen. Hilary Watson. 224p. 1983. 11.95 (ISBN 0-312-88241-6). St Martin.

Winter's Crimes Nine. 9th, annual ed. Celia Dale et al. LC 77-83733. 1977. 8.95 o.p. (ISBN 0-312-88236-X). St Martin.

Winter's Crimes Ten. Ed. by Hilary Watson. LC 78-60975. 1979. 8.95 o.p. (ISBN 0-312-88237-8). St Martin.

Winters Heart. Cathryn Ladame. 192p. 1981. pap. 1.50 (ISBN 0-671-57055-2). S&S.

Winter's Love. Felicia Bryce. 1976. 4.95. Avalon Books.

Winter's Love. 1st Ed. Madeleine L'Engle. LC 57-68320. 1957. Lippincott.

Winter's Reckoning. Ellen Bromfield Geld. LC 73-9013. 1976. 7.95 (ISBN 0-385-03727-9). Doubleday.

Winter's Rose. Eleanor M Fairburn. LC 77-352626. 1976. 2.90 (ISBN 0-7091-5167-5). Hale.

Winter's Tale. Nathaniel Benchley. LC 63-20810. McGraw-Hill.

Winter's Tale. Jon Godden. 1961. 4.50 o.p. (ISBN 0-394-45221-6). Knopf.

Winter's Tale Twenty-Four. Ed. by A. D. Maclean. LC 78-62763. 1979. 8.95 o.p. (ISBN 0-312-88412-5). St Martin.

Winter's Tales. Karen Blixen. LC 70-169542. (Short story index reprint series). 1971. (ISBN 0-8369-4003-2). Books for Libraries Press.

Winter's Tales. Karen Blixen. LC 43-350. 1942. Random House.

Winter's Tales. Ed. by Caroline Hobhouse. 1980. 9.95 o.p. (ISBN 0-312-88375-7). St Martin.

Winter's Tales, Vols. 1-6, 8-13. Ed. by Alan Duart MacLean. price not set o.p. St Martin.

Winter's Tales, No. 27. Ed. by Edward Leeson. 224p. 1982. 11.95 (ISBN 0-312-88417-6). St Martin.

Winter's Tales Fourteen. 14th ed. Ed. by Kevin Crossley-Holland. LC 55-13894. 1969. 5.95 o.p. (W44836). St Martin.

Winter's Tales from Ireland. Ed. by Augustine Martin. LC 73-172706. (v. 1) 1.50 (ISBN 0-7171-0490-7). Gill and Macmillan.

Winter's Tales Nineteen. Ed. by Alan Duart MacLean. LC 55-13894. 270p. 1974. 6.95 o.p. (ISBN 0-312-88305-6). St Martin.

Winter's Tales: Number 21. Ed. by Alan Duart MacLean. 219p. 1975. 8.95 o.p. (ISBN 0-312-88375-7). St Martin.

Winter's Tales Seventeen. Ed. by Caroline Hobhouse. 1972. 6.95 o.p. (W44910). St Martin.

Winter's Tales Sixteen. Ed. by Alan Duart MacLean. LC 55-13894. 1971. 5.95 o.p. (W44900). St Martin.

Winter's Tales Twenty-Eight. Ed. by Alan Duart MacLean. 224p. 1983. 11.95 (ISBN 0-312-88421-4). St Martin.

Winter's Tales Twenty Three. Brian Wilson Aldiss et al. Ed. by Peter Collenette. LC 77-10374. 1977. 8.95 o.p. (ISBN 0-312-88411-7). St Martin.

Winter's Tales Twenty Two. Ed. by James Wright. 1977. 8.95 o.p. (ISBN 0-312-88410-9). St Martin.

Winter's Tales. 1- LC 55-13894. St. Martin's Press.

Winter's Tales. 10. Ed. by A. D. Maclean. Ed. by Alan Duart MacLean. LC 55-13894. 1965. bds., 4.95. St Martin's.

Winter's Tales: 11. LC 55-13894. 1966. bds., 4.95. St Martin's.

Winter'S Tales: 13. LC 55-13894. 1967. bds., 4.95. St. Martin's.

Winter's Tales 15. Ed. by Alan Duart MacLean. LC 55-13894. 1970. 5.95 o.p. (W44837). St Martin.

Winter's Tales 18. Ed. by D. A. Maclean. LC 55-13894. 270p. 1973. 6.95 o.p St Martin.

Winter's Tales 26. Ed. by Alan Duart MacLean. 224p. 1981. 11.95 (ISBN 0-312-88414-1). St Martin.

Winterscape. Anastasia Cleaver. 1976. (pbk.) 1.25. Ace Books.

Wintershade. Elaine Evans. 1974. (pbk.) 0.95. Popular Library.

Wintersmoon. Hugh Walpole. LC 28-4880. 1928. Doubleday, Doran & Company, Inc.

Winterspelt. Alfred Andersch. LC 76-56262. 1978. 8.95 (ISBN 0-385-01368-X). Doubleday.

Winterwood. Dorothy Eden. LC 67-10565. 1967. Coward-McCann.

Winthrop Covenant. Louis Auchincloss. LC 75-33042. 1976. 8.95 (ISBN 0-395-24081-6). Houghton Mifflin.

Winthrop Covenant. Louis Auchincloss. LC 77-370926. (Illus.). 1976. Franklin Library.

Winthrop Woman. Anya Seton. LC 58-5830. 1958. Houghton Mifflin.

Winthrops. Helen Sybil Norton Kestner Cournos. LC 27-23256. 1927. Brentano's.

Winwood: Or, The Fugitive of the Seas. Joseph Holt Ingraham. 1846. H. L. Williams.

Wipe Away the Tears. Patricia Lake. (Harlequin Presents Ser.). 192p. 1982. pap. 1.75 (ISBN 0-373-10521-5). Harlequin Bks.

Wipe Out the Brierlys. Ernest Haycox. 1977. pap. 1.25 o.s.i. (ISBN 0-505-51132-0). Tower Bks.

Wipe Out the Brierlys. Ernest Haycox. 1972. pap. 0.75 o.p. (BT40116). Belmont-Tower.

Wiped Out: Stories of the Foreign Legion... John Dimmock Newsom. LC 47-23568. (On cover: A Dell book, 165). 1947.

Wire Cutters: A Novel. Mary Evelyn Moore Davis. LC 99-696. 1899. Houghton, Mifflin and Company.

Wire Devils. Frank Lucius Packard. LC 18-9492. George H. Doran Company.

Wire God. Jack Willard. LC 53-5037. 1953. Doubleday.

Wire in the Wind: By Matt Stuart Pseud. 1st Ed. Llewellyn Perry Holmes. LC 52-8787. 1952. Lippincott.

Wire Tappers. Arthur John Arbuthnott Stringer. LC 6-16649. 1906. Little, Brown, and Company.

Wire Tappers. Arthur John Arbuthnott Stringer. LC 22-24220. The Bobbs-Merrill Company.

Wired. Harry Hellerstein. LC 81-21541. 11.95 (ISBN 0-312-88420-6). St. Martin's Press.

Wired Love: A Romance of Dots and Dashes. Ella Cheever Thayer. LC 8-27756. 1879. G. W. Carleton & Co.; Etc., Etc.

Wiretap! An Original Novel. Charles Einstein. LC 55-120304. (Dell first edition, 76). 1955. Dell Pub. Co.

Wirriyammu. Williams Sassine. Tr. by John Reed & Clive Wake. (African Writers Ser.). 148p. 1980. pap. 5.50x (ISBN 0-435-90199-0). Heinemann Ed.

Wisconsin Earth. August William Derleth. 5.00 o.p. Arkham.

Wisconsin Earth, a Sac Prairie Sampler. August William Derleth. LC 70-113065. (Illus.). 1971. (ISBN 0-8371-4696-8). Greenwood Press.

Wisconsin Earth: A Sac Prairie Sampler. August William Derleth. 1948. Stanton & Lee.

Wisconsin Ice Trade. Lee E. Lawrence. (Wisconsin Stories Ser.). 12p. pap. 1.25. State Hist Soc Wis.

Wisdom of Esau: A Novel. Robert Leonard Outhwaite & Chomley, Charles Henry. LC 1-31906. Cassell & Company, Limited.

Wisdom of Father Brown. Gilbert Keith Chesterton. LC 75-315511. (Penguin crime fiction). 1974-1975. 1.50 (ISBN 0-14-003118-9). Penguin.

Wisdom of Father Brown. Gilbert Keith Chesterton. 1914. Cassell and Company, Ltd.

Wisdom of Father Brown. Gilbert Keith Chesterton. LC 14-22553. 1915. John Lane Company.

Wisdom of Father Pecquet. Translated by Katherine Woods; Illus. by Doris Spiegel. 1st Ed. Omer Englebert. LC 51-12208. 1951. McKay.

Wisdom of Fools. Margaret Wade Campbell Deland. LC 72-98567. (Short story index reprint series). 1969. Books for Libraries Press.

Wisdom of Fools. Margaret Wade Campbell Deland. LC 6-45964. 1897. Houghton, Mifflin and Company.

Wisdom of Love. Jakob Schaffner. LC 30-465294. 1930. Coward-McCann, Inc.

Wisdom of the Sands. phoenix ed. Antoine De Saint Exupery. LC 79-15938. 1979. University of Chicago Press.

Wisdom of the Simple: A Tale of Lower New York. Owen Kildare. F. H. Revell Company.

Wisdom's Call. facs. ed. Sutton Elbert Griggs. LC 75-89411. (Black Heritage Library Collection Ser). 1911. 13.50 (ISBN 0-8369-8587-7). Ayer Co.

Wisdom's Child. Joseph Simons & Jeanne Reidy. 1969. 4.50 o.p. (M44510). Herder & Herder.

Wisdom's Daughter. Henry Rider Haggard. LC 77-84230. (Lost Race and Adult Fantasy Fiction). 1978. 25.00 (ISBN 0-405-10983-0). Arno Press.

Wisdom's Daughter: The Life and Love of a She-Who-Must-Be-Obeyed. Henry Rider Haggard. LC 23-7283. 1923. Doubleday, Page & Company.

Wisdom's Daughter: The Life & Love Story of She-Who-Must-Be-Obeyed. Henry Rider Haggard. Ed. by R. Reginald & Douglas Melville. LC 77-84230. (Lost Race & Adult Fantasy Ser.). 1978. Repr. of 1923 ed. lib. bdg. 25.00x (ISBN 0-405-10983-0). Ayer Co.

Wisdom's Folly: A Study in Feminine Development. Annie Victoria Dutton. 1896. H. Holt and Company.

Wisdom's Gate. Margaret Ayer Barnes. LC 35-27905. 1938. Houghton Mifflin Company.

Wise and the Foolish Virgins. Marguerite Steen. LC 32-289871. 1932. Little, Brown, and Company.

Wise and the Wayward: A Novel. George Slythe Street. 1896. J. Lane.

Wise As a Goose: A Novel of the California Redwood Country. Vernon Patterson. LC 39-312739. Lymanhouse.

Wise Blood. Flannery O'Connor. LC 52-6453. 1952. Harcourt, Brace.

Wise Blood. 2d Ed. Lannery O'Connor. LC 62-5776. Farrar, Straus and Cudahy.

Wise Brother. Isabelle Hughes. LC 54-44721. 1954. Ryerson Press.

Wise Child: A Novel. James Hughes. LC 69-16968. 1969. 5.95. Little, Brown.

Wise Children. Christine Goutiere Weston. LC 57-11666. 1957. Scribner.

Wise Folly. Dorothy Black. LC 33-10601. The Penn Publishing Company.

Wise Forget. Mary Howard, pseud. LC 45-824. 1945. Arcadia House, Inc.

Wise Heart: By Norma Newcomb Pseud. William Arthur Neubauer. LC 55-101968. 1955. Arcadia House.

Wise in Heart. Nancy Noon Kendall. LC 47-1652. 1947. Thomas Y. Crowell Company.

Wise Is the Heart. Anne Duffield. 1947. Arcadia House.

Wise Little Fool. Sylvia Parker. LC 36-89820. Phoenix Press.

Wise-Saws: Or, Sam Slick in Search of a Wife... Thomas Chandler Haliburton. LC 31-30206. 1855. Stringer & Townsend.

Wise Son. Charles Sherman. LC 14-45883. The Bobbs-Merrill Company.

Wise Virgin. Hebe Elsna. 1971. pap. 0.95 o.p. (95178). Beagle Bks.

Wise Virgins: A Story of Words, Opinions, and a Few Emotions. Leonard Sidney Woolf. LC 78-12830. 1978. 9.95. H. Fertig.

Wise Virgins: A Story of Words, Opinions, and a Few Emotions. Leonard Sidney Woolf. LC 79-1861. 1979. 9.95 (ISBN 0-15-197511-6). Harcourt Brace Jovanovich.

Wise Wife. Arthur Somers Roche. LC 28-2515. 1928. The Century Co.

Wise Woman: A Novel. Clara Louise Root Burnham. LC 4-15076. 1895. Houghton, Mifflin and Company.

Wise Woman & Other Fantasy Stories. George MacDonald. Ed. by Glenn G. Sadler. (Fantasy Stories of George MacDonald Ser.). 176p. 1980. pap. 2.95 (ISBN 0-8028-1860-9). Eerdmans.

Wise Women of Inverness. A Tale. William Black. LC 6-12419. (Lovell's library, v. 11, no. 584). J. W. Lovell Company.

Wise Women of Inverness. A Tale. William Black. (Seaside library. Pocket ed. no. 472). G. Munro.

Wiseguys: A Novel. Vincent Charles Teresa. LC 77-12575. 7.95. Dutton.

Wisest Fools. Michael Rossi. LC 83-2376. 1983. 9.95 (ISBN 0-8407-5285-7) (ISBN 0-8407-5842-1). T. Nelson.

Wish a Day. Berta Ruck. LC 56-6833. 1956. Dodd, Mead.

Wish: A Novel. Hermann Sudermann & Henkel, Lily, Tr. LC 7-29154. 1895. D. Appleton and Company.

Wish Child. Ina Seidel Seidel & Gribble, George Dunning, Tr. Farrar & Rinehart, Incorporated.

Wish for Love: No. One Hundred Sixty. Barbara Cartland. 160p. Date not set. 2.25 (ISBN 0-553-22822-6). Bantam.

Wish for Tomorrow. Ethel Owen. LC 41-1981. Robert Speller Publishing Corp.

Wish Her Safe at Home. Stephen Benatar. LC 82-5815. 11.95 (ISBN 0-312-88419-2). St. Martin's/Marek.

Wish on a Mountain. Virginia C Holmgren. (Avalon romances). 1964. Avalon Books.

Wishbone. Stirling Bowen. LC 30-973067. E. P. Dutton & Co., Inc.

Wishes Come True. Georgia Fraser. LC 26-4067. 1926. H. Vinal.

Wishing Carpet. Ruth Comfort Mitchell. LC 26-192506. 1926. D. Appleton and Company.

Wishing Gown. Peggy O'More, pseud. LC 38-32612. Phoenix Press.

Wishing Moon. Louise Elizabeth Dutton. LC 16-22296. 1916. 1.35. Doubleday, Page & Company.

Wishing-Ring Man. Margaret Widdemer. LC 17-25082. 1917. H. Holt and Company.

Wishing Star. Elizabeth Andrews. LC 81-8836. 1981. 13.95 (ISBN 0-312-88416-8). St. Martin's Press.

Wishing Star. Maysie Greig. LC 42-50442. 1942. Doubleday, Doran & Company, Inc.

Wishing Tree. Sandra Paretti. LC 76-62786. 10.00 (ISBN 0-312-88418-4). St. Martin's Press.

Wishing Tree. Sandra Paretti. 1977. 1.95 (ISBN 0-449-23604-8). Fawcett Crest.

Wisp of Bliss and Other Stories. Chwee Sian Heah. LC 82-134965. (Writing in Asia Series). 1982. 4.50. Heinemann Asia.

Wissy. A True Tale of Modern Theatrical Bohemia. James Paxton Voorhees. 1897. The B. S. Adams Press.

Wisteria Cottage. Robert Myron Coates. LC 48-8041. 1948. Harcourt, Brace.

Wistful Years. Roy Rolfe Gilson. 1909. 1.50. The Baker & Taylor Company.

Wistons: A Story in Three Parts. Ellen Melicent Cobden. LC 2-5220. 1902. C. Scribner's Sons.

Witch. Mary Johnston. LC 14-18425. 1914. Houghton Mifflin Company.

Witch. Barbara Mertz. LC 73-7492. 1973. 6.95 (ISBN 0-396-06838-3). Dodd, Mead.

Witch. Barbara Michaels. LC 73-7492. 288p. 1973. 6.95 o.p. (ISBN 0-396-06838-3). Dodd.

Witch. A Novel. Marie Madison. LC 7-20274. 1891. New Haven Publishing Company.

Witch: A Novel. St. James, Bernard, pseud. LC 79-1804. 8.95 (ISBN 0-06-013703-7). Harper & Row.

Witch and Cinderella. The Boom-Cat Kid, and Other Stories. Gabriel Conklyn Banks. LC 65-20518. Greenwich Book Publishers C.

Witch: And Other Stories. Anton Pavlovich Chekhov. Tr. by Garnett, Constance (Black) LC 18-10535. 1918. The Macmillan Company.

Witch and the Priest. Hilda Winifred Lewis. 1973. (pbk.) 1.50. Lancer Books.

Witch and the Priest. Hilda Winifred Lewis. LC 71-126059. 1970. 4.95. D. McKay Co.

Witch & the Weather Report. Susan Fromberg Schaeffer. LC 72-81233. 1972. pap. 2.75 (ISBN 0-913282-00-6). Seven Woods Pr.

Witch-Baiter. Charles Birkin. pap. 0.50 o.p. (52-468). Paperback Lib.

Witch Diggers. 1st Ed. Jessamyn West. LC 51-9108. 1951. Harcourt, Brace.

Witch Doctor. N. C. McDonald. LC 59-10384. (Ballantine books, 312K). 1959. Ballantine Books.

Witch-Doctors. Charles Beadle. LC 22-25807. 1922. Houghton Mifflin Company.

Witch Doctor's Holiday. Charles Ludwig. LC 45-4809. 1945. The Warner Press.

Witch Door. Elisabeth Ogilvie. LC 75-40381. 1976. (ISBN 0-88411-182-2). Aeonian Press.

Witch Door. 1st Ed. Elisabeth Ogilvie. LC 59-13212. 1959. McGraw-Hill.

Witch from the Sea. Philippa Carr, pseud. 1979. pap. 1.95 (ISBN 0-449-22837-1, Crest). Fawcett.

Witch from the Sea. Philippa Carr, pseud. LC 74-16582. 384p. 1975. 7.95 o.p. (ISBN 0-399-11427-0). Putnam Pub Group.

Witch from the Sea. Eleanor Hibbert. LC 74-16582. 1975. 7.95 (ISBN 0-399-11427-0). Putnam.

Witch from the Sea. Eleanor Hibbert. (Fawcett Crest Book). 1976. (pbk.) 1.95. Fawcett.

Witch Goddess. Robert Adams. (Horseclans Ser.: No. 9). 1982. pap. 2.50 (AE1792, Sig). NAL.

Witch Haven. Luanna Churchill. 1973. 4.95. Lenox Hill Pr.

Witch Hazel. Sarah Elizabeth Forbush G. S. Downs Downs. LC 6-45960. (On cover: The select series. no. 97). 1892. Street & Smith.

Witch-Herbalist of the Remote Town. Amos Tutuola. LC 82-670146. 1981. (u.s.) 15.95 (ISBN 0-571-11703-1) (ISBN 0-571-11704-X). Faber and Faber.

Witch Hill Murder: A Superintendent Capricorn Mystery. Pauline Glen Winslow. LC 76-28068. 7.95. St. Martin's Press.

Witch House. Evangeline Walton. LC 45-9458. 1945. Arkham House.

Witch in the Mill. Alfreda Marion Peel. LC 47-3873. 1947. The Dietz Press, Incorporated.

Witch in the Wilderness. Desmond Holdridge. LC 37-285146. Harcourt, Brace and Company.

Witch in the Wood. Terence Hanbury White. LC 39-31048. 1939. G. P. Putnam's Sons.

Witch Man". Margaret Bell Houston. LC 22-4440. Small, Maynard & Company.

Witch Miss Seeton. Heron Carvic. LC 78-135185. 1971. 4.95 (ISBN 0-06-010652-2). Harper & Row.

Witch of Bayou Pierre. Aida Mumford Gilvin & Mumford, James Everett. LC 40-6583. Southwest Press.

Witch of Belsen & Other Stories. L. C. Wheeler. 1981. 15.00x (ISBN 0-7223-1389-6, Pub. by Stockwell). State Mutual Bk.
Witch of Cumberland Gap. Bernard Stallard. (Illus.). 76p. 1981. pap. 5.95 (ISBN 0-9606908-0-8). B Stallard.
Witch of Endor. Frank Ales Gause. LC 52-6956. 1953. Vantage Press.
Witch of Endor. A. C. Webb. 1970. 3.00 o.p. Carlton.
Witch of Goblin's Acres. William Edward Daniel Ross. (O.s.i.). 1975. pap. 1.25 o.s.i. Belmont-Tower.
Witch of Goblin's Acres. William Edward Daniel Ross. 1974. 4.95. Lenox Hill Press.
Witch of Golgotha. Baruyr Pesh-Mal-Yan. LC 13-12279. 1913. 1.35. Sherman, French & Company.
Witch of Jamestown: A Story of Colonial Virginia. James T Bowyer. LC 44-27436. 1890. J. W. Randolph & English.
Witch of Murray Hill. Stephanie Hall. 1974. (pbk.) 0.95. Popular Library.
Witch of Plum Hollow. Thaddeus W H Leavitt. LC 7-15442. 1892. The Wells Publishing Co.
Witch of Prague: A Fantastic Tale. Francis Marion Crawford. LC 9-25028. 1891. Macmillan and Co.
Witch of Prague: A Fantastic Tale. Francis Marion Crawford. LC 13-204675. (On cover: The works of F. Marion Crawford). 1912. The Macmillan Company; Etc., Etc.
Witch of Ramoth: And Other Tales. Mark Van Doren. LC 50-8864. (Keepsake series, v. 8). 1950. Maple Press Co.
Witch of Salem. Benjamin Siegel. LC 53-33935. (Gold medal books, 307). 1953. Fawcett Publications.
Witch of Salem: Or, Credulity Run Mad. John Roy Musick. LC 7-33323. (On cover: Columbian historical novels v. 6). 1893. Funk & Wagnalls Company.
Witch of Spring. William Shore. LC 50-9196. 1950. Pellegrini & Cudahy.
Witch of the Dark Gate. John Jakes. (Orig.). 1972. pap. 0.95 o.s.i. (75-415). Lancer.
Witch of the Hills. Florence Alice Price James. (On cover: Lovell's library, no. 1309). 1888. J. W. Lovell Company.
Witch of the Nineteenth Century. William P Phelon. LC 7-36084. 1893. The Hermetic Publishing Company.
Witch of the Wave: Or, The Rover's Capture. A Story of Adventure. Henry P Cheever. (owl library, no. 2). 1892. G. W. Studley.
Witch of Turner's Bald. Edna C. Pierson. (Illus.). 1971. 5.00. Puddingstone.
Witch on Wheels: By Bill Boltin Pseud. Murray Boltinoff. LC 52-14497. 1952. Arco Pub. Co.
Witch or Wife: The Cartaret Affair. St. George Rathborne. (On cover: Library of choice fiction, no. 13). Laird & Lee.
Witch Power. Salambo Forest. pap. 1.95 o.s.i. (OPS-35). Olympia.
Witch Queen of Mongo. Alex Raymond. (Flash Gordon#5). 1974. (pbk.) 0.95 (ISBN 0-380-00180-2). Avon.
Witch Stone. Margaret Duncan. LC 75-24660. 1976. 7.95. St. Martin's Press.
Witch Tree. Lyda B. Long. 1971. pap. 0.75 o.p. (ISBN 0-447-74772-X). Lancer.
Witch Water. Helen Topping Miller. LC 52-10695. 1952. Bobbs-Merrill.
Witch Winnie at Shinnecock: Or, The King's Daughters in a Summer Art School. Elizabeth Williams Champney. LC 6-23133. Dodd, Mead & Company.
Witch Winnie at Versailles. Elizabeth Williams Champney. LC 6-20167. Dodd, Mead and Company.
Witch Winnie in Holland. Elizabeth Williams Champney. LC 6-20166. 1896. Dodd, Mead and Company.
Witch Winnie in Paris: Or, The King's Daughters Abroad. Elizabeth Williams Champney. LC 6-30168. Dodd, Mead & Company.
Witch Winnie in Spain. Elizabeth Williams Champney. LC 98-570. 1898. Dodd, Mead and Company.
Witch Winnie in Venice: And the Alchemist's Story. Elizabeth Williams Champney. LC 6-20169. 1897. Dodd, Mead and Company.
Witch Winnie: The Story of a "King's Daughter,". Elizabeth Williams Champney. LC 6-23323. White and Allen.
Witch Winnie: The Story of a "King's Daughter;". Elizabeth Williams Champney. Dodd, Mead & Company.
Witch Winnie's Mystery: Or, The Old Oak Cabinet; the Story of a King's Daughter. Elizabeth Williams Champney. LC 6-23132. Dodd, Mead and Company.
Witch Winnie's Studio: Or, The King's Daughter's Art Life. Elizabeth Williams Champney. LC 6-23131. Dodd, Mead & Company.
Witch-Woman: A Trilogy About Her. James Branch Cabell. LC 48-6952. 1948. Farrar, Straus.
Witch Wood. John Buchan. LC 27-171193. 1927. Houghton Mifflin Company.
Witch Wood. Frances Moyer Ross Stevens. LC 40-5400. 1940. Pub. for the Crime Club by Doubleday, Doran & Company, Inc.
Witch World. Andre Norton, pseud. 1974. (pbk.) 0.95. Ace Books.
Witch World. Andre Norton, pseud. LC 77-23209. (Norton, Andre. The Witch World Novels of Andre Norton). (Illus.). 1977. 7.95 (ISBN 0-8398-2355-X). Gregg Press.
Witch World Novels. Andre Norton, pseud. 1977. 62.50 (Gregg). G K Hall.
Witchcraft Reader. Ed. by Peter Haining. LC 70-131078. 1970. 4.95. Doubleday.
Witchdance in Bavaria. Bill Knox. LC 75-37818. 1976. 5.95 (ISBN 0-385-11225-4). Published for the Crime Club by Doubleday.
Witchdance in Bavaria. Noah Webster. LC 75-14846. (Crime Club Ser.). 1976. 5.95 o.p. (ISBN 0-385-11225-4). Doubleday.
Witchery Isle. Ella M Rea. LC 31-25042. 1931. Meador Publishing Company.
Witchery of an Oriental Lamp. John Fame. LC 23-783319. The Best Sellers Co.
Witchery of Rita: And Waiting for Tonti. William Henry Robinson. LC 20-649411. 1919. The Berryhill Co.
Witches. Francoise Mallet-Joris. Tr. by Herma Briffault from Fr. 1969. 6.95 o.p. (ISBN 0-374-29157-8). FS&G.
Witches. Francoise Mallet-Joris. Tr. by Herma Briffault from Fr. LC 74-82627. 1969. 6.95 o.p. (ISBN 0-374-29157-8). FS&G.
Witches. Jay Williams. LC 57-6464. 1957. Random House.
Witches' Brew. Nancy Faulkner. (Orig.). 1973. pap. 0.95 o.p. (09203). Curtis.
Witches' Brew. Ed. by Alfred Hitchcock. 1975. (pbk.) 0.95. Dell.
Witches' Circles. Kerstin Ekman. Tr. by June Bartlett from Swedish. Orig. Title: Haexringarna. 256p. (Orig.). 1983. pap. 7.95 (ISBN 0-940242-05-2). Fjord Pr.
Witches' Holiday. Miriam Lynch. 1971. pap. 0.75 o.p. (ISBN 0-447-74726-6). Lancer.
Witches of All Saints. Jill Tattersall. LC 74-22076. 1975. 7.95 (ISBN 0-688-02890-X). Morrow.
Witches of All Saints. Jill Tattersall. (Fawcett Crest Book). 1976. (pbk.) 1.50. Fawcett.
Witches of Brimstone Hill. Helen Arvonen. 160p. 1974. pap. 0.75 o.p. (T2910, GM). Fawcett World.
Witches of Karres. James H Schmitz. LC 66-25045. 4.95. Chilton.
Witches of Karres. James H. Schmitz. 1977. 1.95. Ace.
Witches of Omen. Audrey Leech. (Orig.). 1971. pap. 0.75 o.p. (T2411). Pyramid Pubns.
Witches' Poker Game & Other Stories. Carlos Montaner. Tr. by Robert Robinson from Sp. LC 73-84203. (Cloth ed. 3.95 o.p.). 171p. 1973. pap. 1.95 (ISBN 0-913480-18-5). Inter Am U Pr.
Witches' Pond. Florence Hurd. 1972. pap. 0.75 o.p. (532-75475-075). Manor Bks.
Witches Pond. Doris Siegel. LC 47-30930. 1947. Pub. for the Crime Club by Doubleday.
Witches' Sabbath. Paula Allardyce, pseud. 1970. pap. 0.60 o.p. (63-316). Paperback Lib.
Witches' Sabbath. Maurice Sachs. Tr. by Richard Howard. 316p. 1982. pap. 9.95 (ISBN 0-8128-6155-8). Stein & Day.
Witches' Sabbath. Ursula Torday. LC 62-8599. (Cock Robin mystery). 1962. Macmillian Sic.
Witches Three: Conjure Wife. John Ciardi. LC 52-12851. 1952. Twayne Publishers.
Witches: Three Tales of Sorcery. Mallet-Joris, Francoise. LC 74-82627. 1969. 6.95. Farrar, Straus and Giroux.
Witchfinder. Maurice Hilliard. LC 73-88542. 1974. 5.95 (ISBN 0-698-10575-3). Coward, McCann & Geoghegan.
Witchfinders. Stanley Hart Cauffman & Hopkins, Matthew, D. 1647--Fiction. LC 34-103321. The Penn Publishing Company.
Witchfinders. Ralph Comer. 1968. pap. 0.60 o.p. (A352X, Award). Univ Pub & Dist.
Witchfire. Andre Tellier. LC 31-23677. Greenberg.
Witchfires. Santana Arroyo. (Orig.). 1981. pap. 2.75 (ISBN 0-505-51707-8). Tower Bks.
Witching. Colin John. 336p. (Orig.). 1982. pap. 3.25 (ISBN 0-505-51806-6). Tower Bks.
Witching. Fritzen Ravenswood. 1982. pap. 2.95 (ISBN 0-89083-975-1). Zebra.
Witching Hill. Ernest William Hornung. LC 13-35065. 1913. C. Scribner's Sons.
Witching Hour. Sara Craven. (Harlequin Ser.). 192p. 1981. pap. 1.75 (ISBN 0-373-10459-6, Pub. by Harlequin). PB.
Witching Hour. Rona Randall. (Ace gothic). 1974. (pbk.) 0.95. Ace Books.
Witching Hour. Augustus Thomas. LC 8-30012. 1908. Harper & Brothers.
Witching Hour: And Other Stories. Margaret Wolfe Hungerford. (On cover: The seaside library. Pocket ed., no. 134). 1884. G. Munro.
Witching Lands: Tales of the West Indies. Hugh Barnett Cave. LC 63-10260. 1963. Doubleday.
Witching Night. C. S. Cody, pseud. 1968. pap. 0.60 o.p. (73-720). Lancer.
Witching Night. Leslie Waller. LC 52-5183. 1952. World Pub. Co.
Witching Night. Leslie Waller. 1973. (pbk.) 1.25. Lancer.
Witching Night. Leslie Waller. 1974. (pbk.) 1.50. Bantam Books.
Witching of Dracula. Robert Lory. (Dracula horror series,#6). 1974. (pbk.) 0.95 (ISBN 0-523-00398-6). Pinnacle Books.
Witching of Elspie: A Book of Stories. Duncan Campbell Scott. LC 70-37559. (Short story index reprint series). 1972. (ISBN 0-8369-4118-7). Books for Libraries Press.
Witching of Elspie: A Book of Stories. Duncan Campbell Scott. LC 23-166592. George H. Doran Company.
Witching Ship. Frederic Morton. LC 60-5522. 1960. Random House.
Witching Time: Tales for the Year's End. Ed. by Henry Norman. Dobson, Austin et al. LC 8-37844. 1887. D. Appleton and Company.
Witching Times. John William De Forest. LC 79-150941. (Monument edition, 4). 1972. 9.00. Bald Eagle Press.
Witching Times. John William De Forest. Ed. by Alfred Appel. LC 66-28602. (Masterworks of literature series). 1967. College & University Press.
Witchrock. Bill Knox. LC 77-11761. 1978. 6.95 (ISBN 0-385-13697-8). Published for the Crime Club by Doubleday.
Witch's Castle. George Howard Thorndyke. LC 3-24947. 1903. Life & Letters Co.
Witch's Cauldron. Eden Phillpotts. LC 33-13332. 1933. The Macmillan Company.
Witch's Crossing. Florence Stevenson. (Signet Book). 1975. 1.25. New American Library.
Witch's Curse. Harry Ludlam. (O.s.i.). 1977. pap. 1.25 o.s.i. (AQ1668, Award). Univ Pub & Dist.
Witchs Daughter. Nina Bawden. (O.s.i.). (gr. 4-6). 1974. pap. 0.95 o.s.i. (ISBN 0-671-29720-1). Archway.
Witch's Daughter. Nina Bawden. (Archway paperback). 1973. 0.75. Pocket Books.
Witch's Gold. Hamlin Garland. Ed. by Donald Pizer. LC 75-96587. (American Authors Ser., Collected Works of Hamlin Garland, 45 Vols). 1969. Repr. of 1906 ed. lib. bdg. 14.75 o.s.i. (ISBN 0-512-00250-9). Garrett Pr.
Witch's Gold: Being a New and Enlarged Version of "The Spirit of Sweetwater,". Hamlin Garland. LC 6-29770. 1906. Doubleday, Page & Company.
Witch's Hammer. Caroline Farr. Bd. with Granite Folly. 1978. pap. 2.50 (ISBN 0-451-11699-2, AE1699, Sig). NAL.
Witch's Head. A Novel. Henry Rider Haggard. (He seaside library. v. 99, no. 1995). 1885. G. Munro.
Witch's Holiday. Miriam Lynch. 1976. pap. 1.25 (ISBN 0-532-12423-5). Woodhill.
Witch's House. Charlotte Armstrong. LC 63-20757. 1963. Coward-McCann.
Witch's House. Charlotte Armstrong. (Berkley large-type edition). 1975. (pbk.) 0.95 (ISBN 0-425-02797-X). Berkley Pub. Co.
Witch's Moon. Giles Jackson. LC 41-11798. 1941. The Dial Press.
Witch's Moon. Albert Leffingwell. LC 41-11798. 1941. The Dial Press.
Witch's Song. Miriam Lynch. 1976. pap. 1.25 (ISBN 0-532-12433-2, 532-12433-125). Woodhill.
Witch's Suckling. Gimone Hall. 1976. pap. 1.25 (ISBN 0-532-12418-9). Woodhill.
Witch's Suckling. Gimone Hall. (Orig.). 1970. pap. 0.75 o.p. (75-365). Manor Bks.
Witch's Suckling. 2nd ed. Gimone Hall. 144p. 1973. pap. 0.95 o.p. (532-95282-095). Manor Bks.
Witch's Thorn. Ruth Park. LC 52-9591. 1952. Houghton Mifflin.
Witchstone. Victoria Graham. LC 73-17978. 1974. (pbk.). 1.25 (ISBN 0-515-03289-1). Pyramid Books.
Wite Lantern. Evan S. Connell. 1981. pap. 5.95. HR&W.
With a Bare Bodkin. Cyril Hare. (Perennial Library). 1980. 2.25 (ISBN 0-06-080523-4). Harper & Row.
With a Diploma: And The Whirlwind, by V. I. Nemirovitch-Dantchenko. Vasilii Ivanovich Nemirovich-Danchenko. Tr. by Pyper, W. J. Stanton. LC 16-6824. 1915. J. W. Luce & Company.
With a Face Like Mine. Sharon L. Berman. 160p. 1981. 8.95 (ISBN 0-87777-062-X, Pub. by R W Baron). Dutton.
With a Little Luck. Janet Dailey. (Harlequin Presents Ser.). 192p. 1982. pap. 1.75 (ISBN 0-373-10482-0). Harlequin Bks.
With a Vengeance. Gerald DiPego. LC 76-30472. 8.95 (ISBN 0-07-017012-6). McGraw-Hill.
With a Vengeance. Dell Shannon. 1970. pap. 0.75 o.p. (T2375). Pyramid Pubns.
With a Vengeance: By Dell Shannon. Elizabeth Linington. LC 66-23353. 1966. bds., 3.95. Morrow.
With All Her Heart. Florence Stonebraker. LC 48-991050. 1948. Arcadia House.
With All Its Thorns. Helen A Carey. LC 43-13942. 1943. Arcadia House, Inc.
With All My Heart. Margaret Campbell Barnes. 1973. 6.95. Macrae Smith.
With All My Heart. Margaret Campbell Barnes. (Signet Books, Y5387). 1973. 1.25. New American Library.
With All My Heart. Margaret Campbell Barnes. LC 51-13075. 1951. Macrae Smith.
With All My Heart. Sara Christy. J. H. Hopkins & Son.
With All My Heart. Vivien Grey. LC 47-408851. 1947. Arcadia House.
With All My Love. Ruth S. McGarity. 3.50 o.p. Carlton.
With All My Love. Mary Raymond. LC 36-226116. J. H. Hopkins & Son, Inc.
With All the World Away: A Novel. 1st Ed. Edwin Balmer. LC 58-12761. 1958. Longmans, Green.
With Banners. Emilie Baker Loring. LC 34-35892. The Penn Publishing Company.
With Bated Breath. Alice Ormond Campbell. LC 46-523481. 1946. Random House.
With Benefit of Clergy. Octavus Roy Cohen. LC 35-13899. 1935. D. Appleton Century Company, Incorporated.
With Benefit of Clergy. Florence Hackett. LC 24-122806. Boni and Liveright.
With Blood and Iron. Douglas Reeman. (75155). 1966. Pocket Bks.
With Blood in Their Eyes. Steven G. Lawrence. 1978. pap. 1.25 o.s.i. (ISBN 0-8439-0572-7, Leisure Books). Nordon Pubns.
With Bold Knife & Fork. M. F. Fisher. LC 79-15562. 1979. pap. 4.95 (ISBN 0-399-50397-8, Perige). Putnam Pub Group.
With Both Eyes Open. Paul Hyde Bonner. 1956. Scribner.
With British and Braves: Story of the War of 1812. L. K Parks. LC 7-34974. Curts & Jennings.
With Carrington on the Bozeman Road. Joseph Mills Hanson. LC 12-22565. ("Among the Sioux" series) $1.50). 1912. A.C. McClurg & Co.
With Carson and Fremont: Being the Adventures, in the Years 1842-'43-'44, on Trail Over Mountains and Through Deserts from the East of the Rockies to the West of the Sierras, of Scout Christopher Carson and Lieutenant John Charles Fremont, Leading Their Brave Company Including the Boy Oliver. Edwin Legrand Sabin. LC 12-24465. (Publisher's lettering: Trail blazers series). 1912. J. B. Lippincott Company.
With Costs. A Novel. Mary Wentworth Newman. LC 7-32303. (Franklin square library. no. 204). 1881. Harper & Brothers.
With Cradle and Clock. Knud Stowman. LC 46-25105. 1946. Harper & Brothers.
With Crooked Lines: A Novel. J M Hartley. LC 48-3928. 1948. Bruce Pub. Co.
With Cupid's Eyes. Florence Marryat Church Lean. LC 7-14289. (On cover: Lovell's library. v. 19. no. 910). 1887. J. W. Lovell Company.
With Daniel Boone on the Caroliny Trail. Alexander Key. LC 41-1126. The John C. Winston Company.
With Drake on the Spanish Main. Herbert Strang. LC 46-2764. 1944. Oxford University Press.
With Eastern Eyes. Ernest Poole. LC 26-17971. 1926. The Macmillan Company.
With Edge Tools. Hobart Chatfield Chatfield-Taylor. LC 6-23430. 1891. A. C. McClurg and Company.
With Edged Tools: A Novel. Hugh Stowell Scott. LC 13-2068. 1894. Harper & Brothers.
With Equal Grace. Rhoda Truax. LC 64-15663. 1964. Bobbs-Merrill.
With Essex in Ireland. Emily Lawless. LC 78-11884. (Ireland, from the Act of Union, 1800, to the Death of Parnell, 1891). (Illus.). 1979. 32.00 (ISBN 0-8240-3521-6). Garland Pub.
With Essex in Ireland: Being Extracts from a Diary Kept in Ireland During the Year 1599 by Mr. Henry Harvey, Sometime Secretary to Robert Devereux, Carl of Essex. Emily Lawless. LC 7-14085. (On cover: Lovell's international series. 97). 1890. J. W. Lovell Co.
With Every Loving Touch. Nell Kincaid. (Candlelight Ecstasy Ser.: No. 149). (Orig.). 1983. pap. 1.95 (ISBN 0-440-19661-2). Dell.
With Extreme Prejudice. Berkely Mather. LC 76-7291. 1976. 8.95 (ISBN 0-684-14628-2). Scribner.
With Eye & Ear. Kenneth Rexroth. LC 74-129675. 1972. 6.95 o.p. (ISBN 0-8164-9175-5, Continuum Bks). Seabury.
With Fate Against Him. Amanda Minnie Douglas. LC 11-16163. 1870. Sheldon & Company.

With Fate Conspire. Yvonne MacManus. (Dell book). 1974. (pbk.) 0.95. Dell.
With Fire and Sword: A Tale of the Past. Henryk Sienkiewicz. Tr. by Samuel Augustus Binion. LC 98-649. H. Altemus.
With Fire and Sword: A Tale of the Past. Henryk Sienkiewicz. Tr. by Samuel Augustus Binion. LC 5-20915. T. Y. Crowell & Co.
With Fire and Sword. An Historical Novel of Poland and Russia. popular ed. Henryk Sienkiewicz. Tr. by Jeremiah Curtin. LC 9-3436. 1890. Little, Brown, and Company.
With Fire and Sword. An Historical Novel of Poland and Russia. popular ed. Henryk Sienkiewicz. Tr. by Jeremiah Curtin. LC 4-16894. 1898. Little, Brown, and Company.
With Fortune Made: A Novel. Victor Cherbuliez. LC 6-26962. (Half-title: Appletons' town and country library, no. 205). 1896. D. Appleton and Company.
With Friends Like These... Liza Fosburgh. 1983. pap. 3.50. PB.
With Friends Like These... Alan Dean Foster. LC 77-6132. 1977. 1.75 (ISBN 0-345-25701-4). Ballantine Books.
With Gauge & Swallow, Attorneys. Albion Winegar Tourgee. LC 8-29836. 1889. J. B. Lippincott Company.
With God's Help: A Novel. Frances Gillham. LC 54-675067. 1954. Dorrance.
With Gold and Steel. Cecil Starr Johns. LC 17-28765. 1917. 1.40. John Lane.
With Grant at Vicksburg: A Boy's Story of the Siege of Vicksburg. James Otis Kaler. LC 10-23632. A. L. Burt Company.
With Guidons Flying: Tales of the U. S. Cavalry in the Old West. Western Writers Of America. Ed. by Charles N. Heckelmann. 1970. 5.95 o.p. Doubleday.
With Guidons Flying: Tales of the U.S. Cavalry in the Old West by Members of the Western Writers of America. Ed. by Charles N. Heckelmann. Western Writers of America. LC 77-103752. 1970. 5.95. Doubleday.
With Gyves of Gold. A Novel. Henry Athey & Bowers, A. Herbert. LC 6-103424. 1898. G. W. Dillingham Co.
With Harp and Crown: A Novel. library ed. Walter Besant & Rice, James. LC 3-27823. 1888. Dodd, Mead & Company.
With Harp and Crown: A Novel by the Authors of Readymoney Mortiboy. author's ed. from advance sheets. ed. Walter Besant & Rice, James. LC 51-54804. 1876. J. R. Osgood.
With Healing in His Wings. Orville Steggerde. LC 58-39435. 1958. Zondervan Pub. House.
With Healing in His Wings. Orville Steggerde. LC 75-146580. (Zondervan books). 1972. 0.95. Zondervan Pub. House.
With Hey, Ho & the Man with the Spats. John Cournos. 1963. 3.95 o.p. Twayne.
With His Own Hands: The Story of a Young Sabra Who Died That Israel Might Live. Moshe Shamir. Tr. by Joseph Schachter from Heb. (Institute for Translation of Hebrew Literature Ser). 253p. 1971. 5.00 o.p. (Pub. by Keter Inc). Intl Schol Bk Serv.
With Hitler in New York and Other Stories. Richard Grindal. LC 78-20695. 7.95 (ISBN 0-8008-8406-X). Taplinger Pub. Co.
With Hooks of Steel: A Tale of Old-Time Virginia. William Tunstall Townes. LC 14-110210. 1913. The Neale Publishing Company.
With Hoops of Steel. Florence Finch Kelly. LC 5987. The Bowen-Merrill Company.
With Hooves of Brass. 1st Ed. Robert S Close. LC 61-887814. 1961. Doubleday.
With Hope, Farewell. Alexander Baron. LC 52-132318. 1952. I. Washburn.
With in the Hollow Crown. Margaret Campbell Barnes. 336p. 1981. pap. 2.75 (ISBN 0-441-89457-7). Ace Bks.
With Intent. Laurence Henderson. LC 73-178863. 1971. 4.95. St. Martin's Press.
With Intent to Deceive. Manning Coles, pseud. LC 47-202673. 1947. Pub. for the Crime Club by Doubleday & Company, Inc.
With Intent to Destroy. Edward Rogers Knowlton. LC 44-47198. 1944. M. S. Mill Co., Inc.
With Intent to Kill. Elizabeth Linington. LC 72-97. 1972. 5.95. Morrow.
With Intent to Kill. Dell Shannon. 256p. 1972. 5.95 o.p. (ISBN 0-688-00058-4). Morrow.
With Intent to Kill: A Pierre Chambrun Mystery Movel. Hugh Pentecost. (Red Badge Novel of Suspense Ser.). 196p. 1982. 9.95 (ISBN 0-396-08042-1). Dodd.
With Juliet in England. Grace Louise Smith Richmond. LC 7-37713. 1907. Doubleday, Page & Company.
With Kisses Four. Charles Henry Mergendahl. LC 54-7106. 1954. Morrow.
With Kitchen Privileges.' Louise Andrews Kent. LC 53-102078. 1953. Houghton Mifflin.
With Land in Sight. Lois Seyster Montross. LC 39-171024. 1939. D. Appleton-Century Company, Incorporated.
With Land in Sight. Lois Seyster Montross. LC 42-508558. 1942. The Sun Dial Press.
With Lifted Heart. Agnes Cochran Bramblett. 3.00 o.p. (ISBN 0-8283-1202-8). Branden.
With Love & Elbow Grease. Elizabeth Browning. (O.s.i.). pap. 1.95 o.s.i. (ISBN 0-671-20655-9, Fireside). S&S.
With Love, from Jo. Jossy Ann Bolivar. Ed. by Josefa V. Bolivar. LC 80-13999. (Illus.). 120p. (Orig.). 1980. pap. 5.95 (ISBN 0-914598-01-5). Padre Prods.
With Love, Peter. Christopher Hollis. LC 48-5761. 1948. D.X. McMullen Co.
With Loving Tenderness. Gerald Drayson Adams. LC 76-350998. 1974. 6.50 (ISBN 0-7256-0112-4). Hawthorn Press.
With Lyon in Missouri. Byron Archibald Dunn. LC 10-21632. (young Missourians series). 1910. 1.25. A. C. McClurg & Co.
With Malice Toward All. Alberta Simpson Carter. (queen-size gothic). 1975. (pbk.) 1.25. Popular Library.
With Malice Toward All. Ed. by Robert L. Fish. pap. 1.25 o.p. (ISBN 0-14-003046-8). Penguin.
With Malice Toward All: An Anthology of Mystery Stories. Robert L. Fish. (YA) 1968. 5.95 o.p. (ISBN 0-399-10871-8). Putnam.
With Malice Toward All: An Anthology of Mystery Stories. Mystery Writers of America. Ed. by Robert L. Fish. LC 68-9584. (Red mask mystery). 1968. 4.95. Putnam.
With Malice Toward None. Honore McCue Willsie Morrow. LC 28-18115. 1928. W. Morrow & Company.
With Morgan on the Main... C M Bennett. LC 30-7099. E. P. Dutton & Co., Inc.
With Murder for Some. Howard C Huston. LC 53-6560. 1953. Macmillan.
With Murder in Mind. Jan Roffman. LC 63-17276. 1963. Published for the Crime Club by Doubleday.
With My Eyes Wide Open: The Story of Another Lost Soul. Marjorie Erskine Smith. LC 49-1575. 1949. Sheridan House.
With My Friends: Tales Told in Partnership. Brander Matthews. LC 72-3372. (Short story index reprint series). 1972. (ISBN 0-8369-4155-1). Books for Libraries Press.
With My Friends: Tales Told in Partnership. Brander Matthews et al. LC 4-15137. 1891. Longmans, Green, & Co.
With My Friends: Tales Told in Partnership; with an Introductory Essay on the Art & Mystery of Collaboration, Vol. 1. Brander Matthews. LC 72-3372. (Short Story Index Reprint Ser). Repr. of 1891 ed. 18.00 (ISBN 0-8369-4155-1). Ayer Co.
With My Knives I Know I'm Good. Julian Rathbone. LC 72-97089. (Red mask mystery). 1970. 4.50. Putnam.
With My Little Eye. Digby Durrant. LC 77-22953. 1978. 7.95 (ISBN 0-312-88605-5). St. Martin's Press.
With My Little Eye. Roy Fuller. LC 57-9366. (Murder revisited mystery novel, no. 18). 1957. Macmillan.
With Naked Foot. Emily Hahn. LC 34-30036. The Bobbs-Merrill Company.
With Night We Banish Sorrow. 1st Ed. Dorothy James Roberts. LC 60-6526. 1960. Little, Brown.
With No Crying. Celia Fremlin, pseud. LC 80-1034. 1981. 9.95 (ISBN 0-385-17206-0). Published for the Crime Club by Doubleday.
With One Stone: A Captain Heimrich Mystery. Richard Lockridge & Frances Louise Davis Lockridge. LC 61-6678. (Main line mysteries). 1961. Lippincott.
With Open Eyes. Ulrich Schaffer. LC 81-48213. (Illus., Orig.). 1982. 14.42 (ISBN 0-06-067073-8, RD 395, HarpR); pap. 9.57i (ISBN 0-06-067074-6). Har-Row.
With Option to Die: A Captain Heimrich Mystery. Richard Lockridge. LC 67-20287. (Main Line mysteries). 1967. Lippincott.
With or Without. Fannie Heaslip Lea. LC 26-5445. 1926. Dodd, Mead and Company.
With Other Eyes. Norma Octavia Lorimer. LC 20-8363. Brentano's.
With Pizarro in Peru. Stanislaus Jezewski & Lathrop, Elise L. LC 44-220134. 1892. Worthington Company.
With Rapture Bound. Mary Kay Simmons. (Kangaroo Book.). 1.95 (ISBN 0-671-81018-9). Pocket Books.
With Ring of Shield... Knox Magee. LC 6269. R. F. Fenno & Company.
With Rings on My Fingers. Dorothy Minnick. LC 51-9173. Dorrance.
With Ruth in Mind. Anselm Hollo. LC 79-28147. 50p. 1980. ltd., signed ed. 20.00 (ISBN 0-930794-19-2); pap. 4.45 (ISBN 0-930794-18-4). Station Hill Pr.
With Sherman to the Sea: A Boy's Story of General Sherman's Famous March and Capture of Savannah. James Otis Kaler. LC 11-120572. 1.00. A. L. Burt Company.
With Shuddering Fall. Joyce Carol Oates. LC 64-23317. 1964. Vanguard Press.
With Signs Following. 1st Ed. Jessie Benton Wise. 1954. Pageant Press.
With Silence My Companion. Shuntaro Tanikawa. Tr. by William I. Elliott & Kazuo Kawamura. LC 75-21399. 55p. 1975. 20.00 o.p. (ISBN 0-915986-01-9); pap. 5.00 (ISBN 0-915986-02-7). Prescott St Pr.
With Sincerest Regrets. Russell Edson. (Burning Deck Fiction Ser.). 30p. (Orig.). 1980. special signed ed. 25.00x (ISBN 0-930900-88-X); pap. 3.00 (ISBN 0-930900-87-1). Burning Deck.
With Sirens Screaming. Ernest Booth. LC 45-7801. 1945. New York, Doubleday, Doran and Company, Inc.
With Song or Sword. Clara Baldwin. LC 41-28292. 1941. The Black Faun Press, Compass Editions.
With Soul on Fire: A Novel by John Herman Randall. John Herman Randall. LC 19-15688. Brentano's.
With Soul So Dead. Gregory Mason. LC 56-11701. 1956. Arcadia House.
With Spurs. Edward Beverly Mann. LC 37-28769. 1937. W. Morrow & Company.
With Spurs of Gold: Heroes of Chivalry and Their Deeds. Frances Nimmo Greene & Kirk, Dolly Williams, Joint Author. LC 5-32829. 1905. Little, Brown, and Company.
With Sully into the Sioux Land. Joseph Mills Hanson. LC 10-268212. ("Among the Sioux" series) $1.50). 1910. A.C. McClurg & Co.
With Sun in Our Blood. Dorothy Myra Page. LC 50-10931. 1950. Citadel Press.
With Sword and Crucifix: Being an Account of the Strange Adventures of Count Louis De Sancerre, Companion of Sieur De la Salle, on the Lower Mississippi in... 1682. Edward Sims Van Zile. LC 793. 1900. Harper & Brothers.
With the Best Intention. Rudolph Edgar Block. LC 14-7690. 1914. 1.25. Hearst's International Library Co.
With the Best Intentions: A Midsummer Episode. Mary Virginia Terhune. 1890. C. Scribner's Sons.
With the Flag at Panama: A Story of the Building of the Panama Canal. Hugh Weir. LC 11-29726. W. A. Wilde Company.
With the Gilt off. Arthur St. John Adcock. LC 23-14806. 1923. G.P. Putnam's Sons.
With the Help of the Angels: A Novel. Wilfrid Woollam. LC 8-37236. (On cover: Harper's Franklin square library, no. 753). 1894. Harper & Brothers.
With the Immortals. Francis Marion Crawford. LC 75-46264. (Supernatural and Occult Fiction). 1976. 17.00 (ISBN 0-405-08122-7). Arno Press.
With the Immortals. Francis Marion Crawford. LC 3-22368. 1888. Macmillan and Co.
With the Immortals. Francis Marion Crawford. LC 38-174923. 1893. Macmillan and Co.
With the Indians in the Rockies. James Willard Schultz. LC 12-23115.
With the King at Oxford: A Tale of the Great Rebellion. Alfred John Church. LC 6-25399. (Harper's handy series. no. 66). 1886. Harper & Brothers.
With the Merry Austrians. Amy McLaren. LC 12-29983. 1912. G. P. Putnam's Sons.
With the Night Mail: A Story of 2,000 A.D. Together with Extracts from the Contemporary Magazine in Which It Appeared. Rudyard Kipling. LC 9-8570. 1909. Doubleday, Page & Company.
With the Procession see Collected Works.
With the Procession: A Novel. Henry Blake Fuller. LC 6-44576. 1895. Harper & Brothers.
With the Procession. New Introd. by Mark Harris. Henry Blake Fuller. LC 65-172880. (Chicago in fiction). bds., 4.95. Univ. of Chic. Pr.
With the Ring. Fannie Heaslip Lea. LC 25-38455. 1925. Dodd, Mead and Company.
With the Victors. Max Gallo. LC 73-10536. 1974. 8.95 (ISBN 0-385-05471-8). Doubleday.
With These Hands. Norman Katkov. LC 74-112. 1974. 6.95 (ISBN 0-671-21752-6). Simon and Schuster.
With These Hands. Norman Katkov. 1975. (pbk.) 1.75. Dell.
With These Two Hands. Josiah Pitts Woolfolk & John Burton Thompson. LC 51-10093. 1951. Arco Pub. Co.
With This Ring. Mignon Good Eberhart. LC 41-51988. Random House.
With This Ring. Mignon Good Eberhart & Gruber, Frank. The Mighty Blockhead. LC 42-19358. 1942. Detective Book Club.
With This Ring. Emilie Baker Loring. LC 61-4920. 1960. Grosset & Dunlap.
With This Ring. Emilie Baker Loring. LC 77-6773. 1977. 9.95 (ISBN 0-89340-088-2). J. Curley.
With This Ring. 1st Ed. Emilie Baker Loring. LC 59-110957. 1959. Little, Brown.
With Those That Were: Stories of Two Wars. Francis William Grattan. LC 9-9505. Broadway Publishing Co.
With Time & Tenderness. Rita Estrada. (Candlelight Ecstasy Ser.: No. 133). (Orig.). 1983. pap. 1.95 (ISBN 0-440-19587-X). Dell.
With Time Running Out. Leonard Wallace Robinson. (Signet bk., Y5242). 1973. 1.25. New American Lib.
With Trailing Banners. Estelle Aubrey Brown. LC 30-10096. 1930. Little Brown, and Company.
Withdraw Thy Foot. Cid Ricketts Sumner. LC 64-17967. 1964. Coward-McCann.
Withdrawing Room. Charlotte MacLeod. LC 80-920. 1980. 8.95 (ISBN 0-385-17181-1). Published for the Crime Club by Doubleday.
Withdrawing Room. Charlotte MacLeod. LC 81-17370. 1982. 12.95 (ISBN 0-89340-380-6). J. Curley & Associates.
Withered Heart. Timothy Shay Arthur. 1857. J. W. Bradley.
Withered Man. John Creasey. LC 73-81178. (MW suspense). 1974. 4.95 (ISBN 0-679-50377-3). McKay.
Withered Murder: By A. and P. Shaffer. Anthony Shaffer & Peter Shaffer. LC 56-13644. (Cock Robin mystery). 1956. Macmillan.
Withered Root. Rhys Davies. LC 28-11175. H. Holt and Company.
Within a Budding Grove. Marcel Proust. LC 74-22051. (His Remembrance of things past). 1970. 2.45 (ISBN 0-394-70595-5). Vintage Books.
Within a Budding Grove. Marcel Proust. Tr. by Scott-Moncrieff, Charles Kennet. LC 24-15190. (His Remembrance of things past. ii). 1924. T. Seltzer.
Within a Budding Grove. Marcel Proust. Tr. by Scott-Moncrieff, Charles Kenneth. LC 30-26832. (Half-title: The modern library of the world's best books). 1930. The Modern Library.
Within a Dark Wood. Jennifer Barr. LC 79-6976. 1979. 10.95 o.p. (ISBN 0-385-15228-0). Doubleday.
Within a Year: By Faith Baldwin. Faith Baldwin Cuthrell. LC 34-11261. Farrar & Rinehart, Incorporated.
Within an Inch of His Life. Emile Gaboriau. LC 6-44497. 1874. J. R. Osgood and Company.
Within an Inch of His Life: Tr. from the French of Emile Gaboriau. Emile Gaboriau. LC 13-7888. 1913. C. Scribner's Sons.
Within and Without: A Philosophical, Lego-Ethical and Religious Romance in 4 Parts. Part 1. Helen Ray's Narrative. Part 2. The Moody Revival of 1876. Part 3. The Unfinished Conflict. Part 4. Truth and the Law Triumphant. J Thompson Gill. LC 6-44049. 1887. J. T. Gill.
Within & Without the Mystery Circle. Gloria Howard. 1970. 2.00 o.p. Carlton.
Within Four Walls. Edith Baulsir. LC 21-15185. 1921. 1.90. The Century Co.
Within Me, Without You. Donita K. Simpson. 1973. pap. 1.95 o.s.i. New Voices.
Within Sea Walls: Or, How the Dutch Kept the Faith. Elizabeth Hely Walshe & Sargent, George Etell, D. 1883, Joint Author. LC 8-33258. I. Bradley & Co.
Within the Capes. Howard Pyle. LC 11-161593. 1885. C. Scribner's Sons.
Within the Capes. Howard Pyle. LC 42-28089. 1901. International Association of Newspapers and Authors.
Within the Clasp. A Story of the Yorkshire Jethunters. John Berwick Harwood. (Harper's Franklin square library, no. 429). 1884. Harper & Brothers.
Within the Clasp. A Story of the Yorkshire Jet-Hunters. John Berwick Harwood. (On cover: Seaside library. Pocket ed., no. 358). 1885. G. Munro.
Within the Hollow Crown. Margaret Campbell Barnes. 360p. 1971. 6.95 (ISBN 0-8255-1547-5). Macrae.
Within the Hollow Crown: A Novel. Margaret Campbell Barnes. LC 47-11910. 1947. Macrae-Smith Co.
Within the Law. Marvin Dana & Veiller, Bayard. LC 13-11965. 1.25. The H. K. Fly Company.
Within the Maze. Ellen Price Henry Wood Wood. (Seaside library, v. 6, no. 115). 1877. G. Munro.
Within the Maze. A Novel. Ellen Price Henry Wood Wood. LC 8-375658. T. B. Peterson & Brothers.
Within the Palace Gates: The Sotry of Nehemiah, Cupbearer to King Artaxerxes. Anna Pierpont Siviter. LC 33-96909. W. A. Wilde Company.
Within the Precincts. A Novel. Margaret Oliphant Wilson Oliphant. (Franklin square library, no. 44). 1879. Harper & Brothers.
Within the Shadow. Cornelia Holroyd Bradley. (On cover: V. I. F. series. no. 7). D. Lothrop and Company.
Within the Shadow. Cornelia Holroyd Bradley. LC 7-12335. (On cover: The household library, no. 3). 1886. D. Lothrop and Company.

Within the Tides: Tales. Joseph Conrad. LC 16-1892. 1916. Doubleday, Page & Company.
Within the Vault. Thayer, Lee, pseud. LC 50-5409. (Red badge mystery). 1950. Dodd, Mead.
Within the Walls. Agnes Carr Vaughan. LC 35-18416. 1935. The Macmillan Company.
Within the Web. Joan Sutherland. LC 32-16548. Farrar & Rinehart, Incorporated.
Within These Walls. Rupert Hughes. LC 23-9460. 1923. Harper & Brothers.
Within These Walls. Leonita Scheaffer. 160p. 1973. 5.50 o.p. (ISBN 0-682-47712-5). Exposition.
Within These Walls: A Novel. Leonita Serie Scheaffer. 1973. 5.50 (ISBN 0-682-47712-5). Exposition Pr.
Within These Walls: The Saga of a Family in Mormon Utah and in Tampa. 1st Ed. Freida Kerr Greene. LC 56-7466. 1956. Exposition Press.
Within This Present. Margaret Ayer Barnes. LC 38-32774. 1933. Houghton Mifflin Company.
Within Those Walls. Rose Holzman Stein. LC 31-34407. The Stratford Company.
Within White Walls. Allan Emory. LC 98-475. (On cover: Neely's continental library, no. 18). F. T. Neely.
Without a City Wall. Melvyn Bragg. LC 69-14733. 1969. 5.95. Knopf.
Without a Compass. A Novel. Frederick B Van Vorst. LC 12-176695. 1885. D. Appleton and Company.
Without a Doubt. Roy Naden. LC 75-32709. (Stories That Win Ser.). 1975. pap. 0.95 o.p. (ISBN 0-8163-0181-6, 23773-5). Pacific Pr Pub Assn.
Without a Grave. Poppy Nottingham. (Ace gothic no. 8). 1975. (pbk.) 0.95. Ace Books.
Without a Home. Edward Payson Roe. LC 28-4857. Dodd, Mead & Company.
Without a Home. Edward Payson Roe. LC 7-40245. (On cover: Dodd, Mead & company's library of fiction, no. 9). Dodd, Mead & Company.
Without a Home. Edward Payson Roe. LC 16-25018. Dodd, Mead and Company.
Without a Man of Her Own. Linda DuBreuil. (Orig.). 1975. pap. 1.50 o.p. (LB282DK, Leisure Bks). Nordon Pubns.
Without a Stair. Kathleen Wallace. LC 33-106003. 1933. Doubleday, Doran & Company, Inc.
Without a Stitch. Jens Bjorneboe. Tr. by Walter Barthold. (Illus.). 1969. 5.95 o.p. (GP579). Grove.
Without a Stitch. Jens Bjrneboe. LC 72-84894. 1969. 5.95. Grove Press.
Without a Stitch, No. 2. Jens Bjorneboe. Tr. by H. H. Bridge. 1971. pap. 1.75 o.p. (Z1087, Zebra). Grove.
Without a Stitch in Time: A Selection of the Best Humorous Short Stories. Peter De Vries. 1975. (pbk.) 1.50. Popular Library.
Without a Sword. Margaret Randolph Cate. LC 58-9810. 1958. Broadman Press.
Without a Trace. Beth Richardson Gutcheon. 384p. 1983. pap. 3.95 (ISBN 0-440-19496-2). Dell.
Without Armor. James Hilton. LC 34-4197. 1934. W. Morrow & Company.
Without Armor. James Hilton. LC 35-154617. 1935. W. Morrow & Company.
Without Armor. James Hilton. LC 42-17388. (Pocket books, 136). 1941. Pocket Books, Inc.
Without Barbarians. Jim Magnuson. LC 74-7457. 1974. 6.95 (ISBN 0-07-039506-3). McGraw-Hill.
Without Benefit of Clergy. Rudyard Kipling. 1899. Doubleday and McClure Company.
Without Benefit of Clergy: And Other Tales. Rudyard Kipling. LC 24-27958. (Little leather library. no. 4). Little Leather Library Corporation.
Without Benefit of Glamour. Ruth Rosemary Corby. LC 38-347955. 1938. Arcadia House.
Without Benefit of Headlines. Kathleen Harris, pseud. LC 41-6369. 1941. Arcadia House, Inc.
Without Benefit of Headlines. Adelaide Humphries. LC 41-6369. 1941. Arcadia House.
Without Blemish: To-Day's Problem. Jeannette Ritchie Hadermann Walworth. LC 72-3104. (Black Heritage Library Collection). 1972. 15.00 (ISBN 0-8369-9089-7). Books for Libraries Press.
Without Blemish: To-Day's Problem. Jeannette Ritchie Hadermann Walworth. LC 8-33127. 1886. Cassell & Company, Limited.
Without Blemish: To-Day's Problem. Jeannette Ritchie Hadermann Walworth. (On cover: Cassell's sunshine series, no. 8). 1888. Cassell & Company, Limited.
Without Charm Please! Louise Platt Hauck. LC 37-136929. The Penn Publishing Company.
Without Cherry Blossom. Panteleimon Sergeevich Romanov. LC 72-90310. 1973. 13.00 (ISBN 0-88355-020-2). Hyperion Press.
Without Cherry Blossom. Panteleimon Sergeevich Romanov. LC 78-142275. (Short story index reprint series). 1970. Books for Libraries Press.
Without Cherry Blossom. Panteleimon Sergeevich Romanov. Tr. by Leonid Sergeevich Zarin. Graham, Stephen, 1884- Ed. LC 32-5307. 1932. C. Scribner's Sons.
Without Clues. Jeannette Helm. LC 23-13262. Boni and Liveright.
Without Compromise. Lilian Bennet- Thompson & Hubbard, George, 1884- Joint Author. LC 22-467420. 1922. The Century Co.
Without Conditions. Agnes Mure Mackenzie. LC 23-17723. 1923. Doubleday, Page and Company.
Without Dogma. A Novel of Modern Poland. Henryk Sienkiewicz & Young, Iza, Tr. LC 8-68835. 1893. Little, Brown, and Comapny.
Without Excuse. Harry Jones. LC 78-63309. (Orig.). 1979. pap. 6.00x (ISBN 0-9601980-0-8). H Jones.
Without Gloves. James Beardsley Hendryx. LC 24-6685. 1924. G. P. Putnam's Sons.
Without Gloves. Fred S Kahre. LC 55-10067. Dorrance.
Without Judge or Jury. William North. LC 29-18268. 1929. L. MacVeagh, The Dial Press.
Without Lawful Authority. Manning Coles, pseud. LC 43-14089. 1943. Pub. for the Crime Club by Doubleday, Doran and Co., Inc.
Without Love. 1st Ed. Gerald Hanley. LC 57-820770. 1957. Harper.
Without Magnolias. Bucklin Moon. LC 49-8390. 1949. Doubleday.
Without Mercy. Sidney Floyd Gowing. LC 20-14762. 1920. G. P. Putnam's Sons.
Without Mercy. Leonard Jordan. (Orig.). 1981. pap. 2.95 (ISBN 0-89083-847-X). Zebra.
Without Music: A Novel. George Fox. LC 70-138872. 1971. 5.95 (ISBN 0-03-085989-1). Holt, Rinehart and Winston.
Without My Cloak. Kate O'Brien. LC 31-33550. 1931. Doubleday, Doran & Company, Inc.
Without Orders. Martha Albrand. LC 43-12148. 1943. Little, Brown.
Without Orders. Heidi Huberta Loewengard. LC 43-12148. 1943. Little, Brown and Company.
Without Passport. Joan Coons. LC 43-7751. 1943. The John Day Company.
Without Profit. Elizabeth FitzHugh Bartol. LC 53-64614. 1953. Vantage Press.
Without Regret. Frank Wilson Kenyon. LC 56-11117. 1956. Crowell.
Without Regrets: A Novel. Brian Dyer, pseud. LC 75-14274. 1975. 7.95 (ISBN 0-88405-115-3). Mason/Charter.
Without Respect of Persons. Colin Middleton. LC 7-25978. 1894. Pub. for the Author.
Without Restraint. Hampton Del Ruth. LC 37-466. Gideon & Stuyvesant.
Without Signposts. Kathleen Wallace. LC 41-10777. G. P. Putnam's Sons.
Without Sin. Jacques Roberti. Tr. by Putnam, Samuel. LC 32-24667. Covici, Friede.
Without Sin: A Novel. Augustus Moore. LC 7-26219. 1896. H. S. Stone & Company.
Without Sin: A Novel. Augustus Moore. 1896. W. Heinemann.
Without Sin Among You. Katherine Stapleton. (Orig.). 1979. pap. 2.50 (ISBN 0-89083-506-3). Zebra.
Without Sorcery: Thirteen Tales. Edward Hamilton Waldo, pseud. LC 49-13397. 1948. Prime Press.
Without the City. Charles C Fulton. LC 24-78077. The Christopher Publishing House.
Without the Cross. Elizabeth Beachley. LC 26-1459. 1925. Dorrance and Company.
Without Warning. Fern Michaels. (Orig.). 1981. pap. 2.50 (ISBN 0-671-83651-X). PB.
With's Gold see Collected Works.
Witling. Vernor Vinge. (Science Fiction Ser.). 1976. pap. 1.25 o.p. (ISBN 0-87997-215-7, UY1215). DAW Bks.
Witling. Vernor Vinge. (DAW science fiction books no. 179.). 1976. (pbk.) 1.25. DAW Books.
Witness. Jean Bloch-Michel. LC 49-5356. 1949. Pantheon.
Witness. Walter Cummins. 1975. pap. 2.00 o.p. Samisdat.
Witness. Grace Livingston Hill. 1976. Repr. of 1917 ed. lib. bdg. 17.45x (ISBN 0-89190-026-8). Am Repr-Rivercity Pr.
Witness. Grace Livingston Hill. 1917. 2.95 o.p. (ISBN 0-448-05273-3). G&D.
Witness. Dorothy Uhnak. LC 69-14286. (Inner sanctum mystery). 1969. 4.95. Simon and Schuster.
Witness. Dorothy Uhnak. LC 81-5361. 1981. 12.95 (ISBN 0-89340-349-0). J. Curley & Associates.
Witness: A Novel. Grace Livingston Hill. LC 76-41279. 1975-1976. 8.95 (ISBN 0-89190-026-8). American Reprint Co.
Witness: A Novel. Grace Livingston Hill. LC 17-29179. 1917. Harper & Brothers.
Witness at Large. Mignon Good Eberhart. LC 77-13544. 1978. 8.95 (ISBN 0-89340-099-8). J. Curley & Associates.
Witness at Large: By Mignon G. Eberhart. Mignon Good Eberhart. LC 66-11997. 1966. bds., 3.95. Random.
Witness at the Window. Charles Bryson. LC 28-4076. E. P. Dutton & Company.
Witness at the Window. Charles Bryson. LC 30-128358. 1929. Grosset & Dunlap.
Witness Before the Fact. E. X Ferrars, pseud. LC 79-7614. 1980. 7.95 (ISBN 0-385-15561-1). Published for the Crime Club by Doubleday.
Witness Before the Fact. E. X Ferrars, pseud. LC 80-23874. 1980. 11.95 (ISBN 0-8161-3126-0). G. K. Hall.
Witness for the Defence. Alfred Edward Woodley Mason. LC 13-266117. 1913. Hodder and Stoughton.
Witness for the Defence. Alfred Edward Woodley Mason. LC 14-142061. 1914. C. Scribner's Sons.
Witness for the Prosecution. Agatha Miller Christie. (Dell book). 1979. 1.95 (ISBN 0-440-19619-1). Dell Pub. Co.
Witness for the Prosecution, and Other Stories. Agatha Miller Christie. LC 48-8394. (Red badge detective). 1948. Dodd, Mead.
Witness My Hand: A Fenshire Story. LC 8-37125. (On cover: Cassell's "rainbow" series of original novels. v. 1, no. 2). 1887. Cassell & Company, Limited.
Witness of the Sun. Amelie Rives Chanler Troubetzkoy. LC 41-32224. 1889. J. B. Lippincott Company.
Witness of the Sun. Henry Smith Williams. LC 20-16495. 1920. Doubleday, Page & Company.
Witness to the Deed. George Manville Fenn. LC 6-39511. Cassell Publishing Company.
Witness to the Sacred: Mystical Tales of Primitive Hasidism. Alan A. Berger. (Illus.). 1977. pap. text ed. 4.00x (ISBN 0-914914-10-3). New Horizons.
Witness to the Wedding. Ethel Lockwood. Ed. by Alice Sachs. 1970. 3.95 o.p. Lenox Hill.
Witness to Treason. Millie J Ragosta. LC 76-50784. 1977. 6.95 (ISBN 0-385-12254-3). Doubleday.
Witness Tree. R. K Roberts. 1973. 4.95 (ISBN 0-517-51416-8). Lenox Hill Press.
Witnesses. Anne Holden. LC 71-156576. 1974. (pbk.) 1.25. Ballantine Books.
Witnesses: A Novel. Marcy Heidish. LC 80-10608. 1980. 10.95 (ISBN 0-395-29196-8). Houghton Mifflin.
Witnesses: A Novel, by M. W. Waring. M. W Waring. LC 67-25687. 1967. 7.95. Houghton.
Witnesses: A Novel by M. W. Waring. M. W Waring. (74001). 1968. pap., 1.25. Ballantine.
Witnesses to Jesus: The Stories of Five Who Knew Him. Mieczys Aw Malinski. LC 81-19440. 1982. 12.95 (ISBN 0-8245-0088-1). Crossroad.
Witnesses: Translated from the French by Moura Budberg, and The Watchmaker, Translated from the French by Norman Denny; Two Novels. 1st Ed. Georges Simenon. LC 56-6536. 1956. Doubleday.
Wits' End. Viola Isabel Paradise. LC 28-29960. E. P. Dutton & Co., Inc.
Witte Arrives. Elias Tobenkin. LC 68-57553. (Muckrakers Ser.). 1979. Repr. of 1916 ed. lib. bdg. 15.50 (ISBN 0-8398-1961-7). Irvington.
Witte Arrives: A Novel. Elias Tobenkin. LC 68-57553. (Illus.). 1968. Gregg Press.
Witte Arrives: A Novel. Elias Tobenkin. LC 16-166876. Frederick A. Stokes Company.
Witter Whitehead's Own Story About a Lucky Splash of Whitewash: Some Stolen Silver, and a House That Wasn't Vacant. Henry Gardner Hunting. LC 9-6843. 1909. 1.25. H. Holt and Company.
Wives and Daughters. Elizabeth Cleghorn Stevenson Gaskell. LC 75-319230. (Penguin English library). (Illus.). 1975. 3.95 (ISBN 0-14-043046-6). Penguin Books.
Wives and Daughters. Elizabeth Cleghorn Stevenson Gaskell. LC 75-468638. (Penguin English library). (Illus.). 1969. Penguin.
Wives and Daughters. Elizabeth Cleghorn Stevenson Gaskell. LC 33-34497. (Half-title: The novels and tales of Mrs. Gaskell--vi). H. Milford, Oxford University Press.
Wives and Daughters. A Novel. Elizabeth Cleghorn Stevenson Gaskell. LC 6-40385. 1866. Harper & Brothers.
Wives and Daughters: An Every-Day Story. Elizabeth Cleghorn Stevenson Gaskell. LC 72-186544. (works of Mrs. Gaskell, v. 8). (Illus.). 1972. 24.00 (ISBN 0-404-07258-5). AMS Press.
Wives and Daughters, an Every-Day Story. Elizabeth Cleghorn Stevenson Gaskell. Ed. by Adolphus William Ward. LC 7-5063. (Half-title: The works of Mrs. Gaskell... Knutsford ed. v. 8). 1906. G. P. Putnam's Sons; Etc., Etc.
Wives and Husbands. 1st Ed. David Duncan. LC 52-5190. 1952. World Pub. Co.
Wives and Lovers. Margaret Millar. LC 54-596102. 1954. Random House.
Wives and Mothers. Jean Rudd. LC 31-30608. 2.00. The Century Co.
Wives Are but Leaves. James P Leynse. LC 51-16294. (Gusto issues). 1950. House-Warven.
Wives Excuse, or, Cuckolds Make Themselves. new, critical ed. Thomas Southerne. Ed. by Ralph R. Thornton. (Illus.). 1974. 7.50x (ISBN 0-915180-19-7); pap. 3.50x (ISBN 0-915180-20-0). Harrowood Bks.
Wives in Exile: A Comedy in Romance. William Sharp. 1896. Lamson, Wolffe and Company.
Wives in Exile: A Comedy in Romance. William Sharp. LC 8-4800. 1896. Stone & Kimball.
Wives of High Pasture. Worth Tuttle Hedden. LC 44-6751. 1944. Doubleday, Doran & Co., Inc.
Wives of Men. David McCloud. 1930. Longmans, Green and Co.
Wives of the Prophet. Sydney Bell. LC 35-22392. The Macaulay Company.
Wives of the Prophet: A Novel. Opie Percival Read. (On cover: Library of choice fiction, no. 77). 1894. Laird & Lee.
Wives of the Wind. Marjorie Jarrett. LC 80-5200. 12.95 (ISBN 0-87223-612-9). Seaview Books.
Wives to Burn and Midnight Sailing. Lawrence Goldtree Blochman. LC 40-11292. Harcourt, Brace and Company.
Wives Who Swap. Sue Varian. 192p. pap. 1.95 o.p. (7140). Barclay Hse.
Wives Win. Florence Riddell. LC 31-225842. 1931. J. B. Lippincott Company.
Wiving of Lance Cleaverage. Alice MacGowan. 1909. G. P. Putnam's Sons.
Wizard. Henry Rider Haggard. LC 6-46154. 1896. Longmans, Green, and Co.
Wizard. John Varley. LC 79-24871. (Illus.). 10.95 (ISBN 0-399-12472-1). Berkley Pub. Corp.: Distributed by Putnam.
Wizard in Bedlam. Christopher Stasheff. LC 78-14711. 1979. 7.95 (ISBN 0-385-14497-0). Doubleday.
Wizard in Waiting. Robert D. Hughes. 208p. (Orig.). 1982. pap. 2.75 (ISBN 0-345-28574-3, Del Rey). Ballantine.
Wizard of Anharitte. Colin Kapp. (O.s.i.). 192p. (Orig.). 1972. pap. 0.95 o.s.i. (AN1156, Award). Univ Pub & Dist.
Wizard of Conlin: A Tale of an Election, Telling of Woman's Devotion and Man's Credulity. Thomas Edwin Smith. LC 421. La Velle Publishing Co.
Wizard of Death. Richard Forrest. (Kangaroo Book). 1978. 1.75 (ISBN 0-671-81799-X). Pocket Books.
Wizard of Death: A Novel of Suspense. Richard Forrest. LC 76-46226. 8.95 (ISBN 0-672-52238-1). Bobbs-Merrill.
Wizard of Earth Sea. Ursula K. Le Guin. (Illus.). 1975. (pbk.) 1.50. Bantam Books.
Wizard of Earthsea. Ursula K. Le Guin. 192p. (gr. 9-12). 1975. pap. 2.50 (ISBN 0-553-14863-X, 14863-X). Bantam.
Wizard of Granada. M. T. Caldor. (On cover: The idle hour series, no. 10). 1892. The F. M. Lupton Publishing Company.
Wizard of Id-Charge! Johnny Hart & Brant Parker. 1978. pap. 1.50 (ISBN 0-449-14046-6, GM). Fawcett.
Wizard of Linn. Alfred Elton Van Vogt. 1976. Repr. of 1962 ed. lib. bdg. 13.25x (ISBN 0-88411-976-9). Amereon Ltd.
Wizard of Linn. new ed. Alfred Elton Van Vogt. (1975 ed. 1.25 o.p.). 176p. 1977. pap. 1.50 (ISBN 0-532-15275-1). Woodhill.
Wizard of Linn. 2nd ed. Alfred Elton Van Vogt. 176p. 1974. pap. 0.95 o.p. (532-95319-095). Manor Bks.
Wizard of Loneliness. John Treadwell Nichols. LC 66-104766. 5.95. Putnam.
Wizard of Lonliness. John Treadwell Nichols. 2.75 (ISBN 0-671-82322-1)., C.
Wizard of Oz: The Critical Heritage. Lyman Frank Baum & W. W Denslow. LC 82-16953. (Critical heritage series). 1983. 19.95 (ISBN 0-8052-3812-3). Schocken Books.
Wizard of Storms. Dave Van Arnam. 1970. pap. 0.75 o.p. (B75-2015). Belmont-Tower.
Wizard of the Damavant: A Tale of the Crusades. Joseph Richardson Parke. LC 10-255802. 1910. 1.25. Professional Publishing Company.
Wizard of the Island: Or, The Vindication of Prof. Waldinger. Frank Stover Winger. LC 17-17079. 1917. Winger Publishing Co.
Wizard of Venus-Pirate Blood. Edgar Rice Burroughs. 256p. 1981. pap. 2.25 (ISBN 0-441-90194-8). Ace Bks.
Wizard of Winnfield. G. Dupre Litton. 1981. 6.95 (ISBN 0-8062-1751-0). Carlton.
Wizard of Zacna: A Lost City of the Mayas; Remarkable Adventures of an Ahmen, Wizard and Mystic of Yucatan, in an Unknown Country to Which the Ancient Mayas Had Fled, Leaving Their Great Stone Cities Silent and Desolate to Be Overgrown with Forest and Jungle. Theodore Arthur Willard. LC 29-28180. The Stratford Company.
Wizard of Zao. Lin Carter. 1978. 1.75 (ISBN 0-87997-383-8). DAW Books.
Wizard Tramp: Or, After the Race... Harlan Page Halsey. LC 7-1174. (Old Sleuth's own, no. 91). 1897. Parlor Car Publishing Co.

Wizards & Warlocks. Ed. by Vic Ghidalia. 1972. pap. 0.95 o.p. (532-95192-095). Manor Bks.
Wizard's Child. Helga Sandburg. LC 66-27394. 1967. 4.95. Dial.
Wizards' Country. Daphne Rooke. LC 57-714173. 1957. Houghton Mifflin.
Wizard's Daughter. Barbara Michaels. LC 80-15157. 9.95 (ISBN 0-396-07899-0). Dodd, Mead.
Wizard's Daughter. Barbara Michaels. LC 81-4841. 1981. 13.95 (ISBN 0-8161-3248-8). G.K. Hall.
Wizard's Daughter: And Other Stories. Margaret Collier Graham. LC 5-30272. 1905. Houghton, Mifflin and Company.
Wizard's Knot. William Francis Barry. LC 1-30947. 1901. The Century Co.
Wizard's Son. Margaret Oliphant Wilson Oliphant. (On cover: Lovell's library, v. 6, no. 326). 1883. J. W. Lovell Company.
Wizard's Wife: Or, Dora's Return to the Kitchen. A. A Cliffe. LC 19-15322. The Roller Pr. & Paper Co.
Wobble to Death. Peter Lovesey. 1974. (pbk.) 1.25. Dell.
Wobble to Death. Peter Lovesey. LC 77-1723. 1977. 7.95 (ISBN 0-89340-060-2). J. Curley & Associates.
Wobble to Death. Peter Lovesey. LC 70-121983. (Red badge novel of suspense). 1970. 4.50. Dodd, Mead.
Wobbles' Tour Around the World on a Bicycle. Edwin Ralph Collins. (On cover: The fireside series, no. 109). J. S. Ogilvie.
Wodehouse on Golf. Pelham Grenville Wodehouse. LC 40-30410. 1940. Doubleday, Doran & Company, Inc.
Woe Shirt. Paule Barton. Tr. by Howard Norman from Creole. LC 80-81728. (Illus.). 64p. 1980. 12.50x o.p. (ISBN 0-915778-37-8); deluxe ed. 40.00x (ISBN 0-915778-36-X). Penmaen Pr.
Woe to the Victors. Ephraim Kishon & Kariel Gardosh. 1969. 4.95 o.p. Bloch.
Wokosani Road: A Novel of Indian Lore in the Southwest. Jon Mockingbird. LC 63-4669. (Exposition-Lochinvar book). 1963. Exposition Press.
Wolf. James Harrison. LC 74-159131. 224p. 1973. pap. 1.25 o.p. (ISBN 0-532-12164-3). Woodhill.
Wolf. James Harrison. LC 74-159131. 224p. 1973. pap. 1.25 o.p. (ISBN 0-532-12164-3). Manor Bks.
Wolf. James Harrison. LC 74-159131. (O.s.i.). 1971. 5.95 o.s.i. (ISBN 0-671-21057-2). S&S.
Wolf. Richard Rose. 1982. pap. 2.50 (ISBN 0-89083-961-1). Zebra.
Wolf. Richard Rose. 288p. (Orig.). 1980. pap. 2.50 (ISBN 0-89083-657-4). Zebra.
Wolf. Charles Somerville & Walter, Eugene. LC 8-31821. G. W. Dillingham Company.
Wolf: A False Memoir, James Harrison. 1973. (pbk.) 1.25. Manor Books.
Wolf: A False Memoir. James Harrison. LC 74-159131. 1971. 5.95 (ISBN 0-671-21057-2). Simon and Schuster.
Wolf Among Wolves. Rudolf Ditzen, pseud. LC 38-279908. 1938. G. P. Putnam's Sons.
Wolf, an Inspector Silver Mystery... Henry Holt. LC 32-14330. Pub. for the Crime Club, Inc., by Doubleday Doran & Company, Inc.
Wolf and the Buffalo. Elmer Kelton. LC 79-8965. 1980. 12.95 (ISBN 0-385-14425-3). Doubleday.
Wolf & the Dove. Kathleen E. Woodiwiss. 1977. pap. 3.95 (ISBN 0-380-00778-9, 81919-8). Avon.
Wolf at Dusk, a Novel. Gwyn Thomas. LC 59-5641. 1959. Macmillan.
Wolf at the Door. Victoria Gordon. (Harlequin Romances Ser.). 192p. 1981. pap. 1.50 (ISBN 0-373-02433-9, Pub. by Harlequin). PB.
Wolf at the Door. John Yount. LC 66-21486. 1967. Random House.
Wolf at the Door: A Novel. Graham Shelby. LC 73-10973. (Illus.). 1975. 6.95 (ISBN 0-385-09437-X). Doubleday.
Wolf at the Door: La Grange Aux Trois Belles. Robert Francis. Tr. by Delisle, Francoise. Ellis, Havelock. LC 35-8406. (His Story of a family under the third republic). 1935. Houghton Mifflin Company.
Wolf Bell. Shirley R. Murphy. 176p. 1980. pap. 1.95 (ISBN 0-380-50666-1, 62216-5). Avon.
Wolf Brand and The Buzzards of Rocky Pass. L. P Holmes. 1976. (pbk.) 1.25. Ace Books.
Wolf Breed. Jackson Gregory. LC 17-258548. 1917. Dodd, Mead and Company.
Wolf by the Ears. Roy Lewis. LC 72-81106. (Falcon's head mystery). 1972. 5.95 (ISBN 0-529-04822-1). World.
Wolf Country. Jon Sharpe. (Trailsman Ser.: No. 7). (Orig.). 1981. pap. 2.25 (ISBN 0-451-09905-2, E9905, Sig). NAL.
Wolf-Cub: A Novel of Spain. Patrick Casey & Casey, Terence. LC 18-1388. 1918. 1.40. Little, Brown and Company.
Wolf Dog. Hal George Evarts. LC 35-521. 1935. Doubleday, Doran & Company, Inc.
Wolf Dog Range. Lee Floren. LC 47-158563. 1946. Phoenix Press.
Wolf Dog Range. Lee Floren. 1978. pap. 1.25 o.s.i. (ISBN 0-8439-0530-1, Leisure Books). Nordon Pubns.
Wolf Dog Town. Lee Thomas. 1970. pap. 0.60 o.p. (B60-2006). Belmont-Tower.
Wolf Dog Town: By Lee Thomas Pseud. Lee Floren. 1953. Arcadia House.
Wolf Howls "Murder,". Manning Lee Stokes. LC 45-559375. 1945. Phoenix Press.
Wolf Hunt. Mark Elder. LC 76-10847. 1976. 1.50 (ISBN 0-345-25264-0). Ballantine Books.
Wolf in Man's Clothing. Mignon Good Eberhart. 1974. (pbk.) 0.95. Popular Library.
Wolf in Man's Clothing. Mignon Good Eberhart. LC 42-36399. 1942. Random House.
Wolf in the Clouds. Ron Faust. LC 76-46165. 1977. 8.95 o.p. (ISBN 0-672-52244-6). Bobbs.
Wolf in the Clouds: A Novel of Suspense. Ron Faust. LC 76-46166. 8.95 (ISBN 0-672-52244-6). Bobbs-Merrill.
Wolf in the Fold. Duncan MacNeil. LC 77-76642. 1977. 8.95 o.p. (ISBN 0-312-88637-3). St Martin.
Wolf in the Fold: An 'Ogilvie' Novel. Philip McCutchan. LC 77-76642. 1977. 8.95 (ISBN 0-312-88637-3). St. Martin's Press.
Wolf in the Garden. Alfred Hoyt Bill. LC 31-25266. 1931. Longmans, Green and Co.
Wolf in the Garden. Alfred H. Bull. 144p. 1972. pap. 0.75 (ISBN 0-87818-008-7). Centaur.
Wolf Is Not Native to the South of France. William Wiser. LC 77-84396. 8.95 (ISBN 0-15-198023-3). Harcourt Brace Jovanovich.
Wolf Leader: Edited from the Translation of Alfred Allinson by L. Sprague De Camp. Illustrated by Mahlon Blaine. Alexandre Dumas. LC 50-962776. 1950. Prime Press.
Wolf-Lure. Agnes Sweetman Castle & Castle, Egerton. LC 17-24204. 1917. 1.50. D. Appleton and Company.
Wolf Man. Sandra Clark. (Harlequin Presents Ser.). 192p. 1982. pap. 1.75 (ISBN 0-373-10514-2). Harlequin Bks.
Wolf Man: The Were-Wolf. Alfred Machard. LC 25-10059. E. J. Clode, Inc.
Wolf Moon: A Romance of the Great Southwest. Joseph J Quinn. LC 24-1181. The Little Flower Press.
Wolf Mountain. Peter L. Sandberg. LC 74-33551. 1975. 8.95 (ISBN 0-87223-423-1). Playboy Press.
Wolf of Masada. John Fredman. LC 78-21586. 1979. 10.95 (ISBN 0-688-03415-2). Morrow.
Wolf of Purple Canyon: A Romance of the Southwest. Charles Kenmore Ulrich. LC 21-3627. 1921. The James A. McCann Company.
Wolf of the Mesas. Charles Horace Snow. LC 41-172535. 1941. Macrae-Smith-Company.
Wolf of the Pecos. Buck Billings. LC 34-421794. 1933. G. H. Watt.
Wolf of the Pecos. Claude Rister. LC 34-42179. 1933. G. H. Watt.
Wolf of Wall Street. Blake McVeigh & Anderson, Doris. LC 29-2725. Grosset & Dunlap.
Wolf of Wildcat Mountain. Oscar J Friend. LC 26-15471. 1926. A. C. McClurg & Co.
Wolf on the Fold. Nellise Child. LC 41-277146. 1941. Doubleday, Doran & Co., Inc.
Wolf Pack. Ridgwell Cullum. LC 27-9858. 1927. J. B. Lippincott Company.
Wolf Pack of Lobo Butte. Wilbur C Tuttle. LC 45-6996. 1945. Houghton Mifflin Company.
Wolf Pack Trail. Peter Field. (Powder Valley western). 1975. (pbk.) 0.95. Pocket Books.
Wolf Point: An Adventure in History. Leonard Dubkin. LC 53-8158. 1953. Putnam.
Wolf Solent: A Novel. John Cowper Powys. LC 75-145244. 1971. (ISBN 0-403-01159-0). Scholarly Press.
Wolf Solent: A Novel. John Cowper Powys. LC 29-116497. 1929. Simon and Schuster.
Wolf Solent: A Novel. John Cowper Powys. LC 33-36953. 1933. Garden City Publishing Company, Inc.
Wolf Song. Harvey Fergusson. LC 27-16585. 1927. A. A. Knopf.
Wolf Song. Harvey Fergusson. LC 78-13368. (Gregg Press Western Fiction Series). 1978. 8.95 (ISBN 0-8398-2471-8). Gregg Press.
Wolf Song. first bison book printing. ed. Harvey Fergusson. LC 81-3056. 1981. 5.50 (ISBN 0-8032-6855-6). University of Nebraska Press.
Wolf Streak. Richard Brister. LC 81-17369. (Atlantic series). 1982. 11.95 (ISBN 0-89340-402-0). J. Curley & Associates.
Wolf Strikes. John S. Morgan. 288p. (Orig.). 1981. pap. 2.25 (ISBN 0-505-51733-7). Tower Bks.
Wolf That Fed Us. Robert James Collas Lowry. LC 70-110832. 1970. (ISBN 0-8371-2611-8). Greenwood Press.
Wolf That Fed Us. Robert James Collas Lowry. LC 49-7962. 1949. Doubleday.
Wolf That Rode. Nelson Coral Nye. 1960. Macmillan.
Wolf, the Cat and the Nightingale. Stanley Hart Cauffman. 1926. The Penn Publishing Company.
Wolf: The Memoirs of a Cave-Dweller. Peter B McCord. LC 8-337823. 1908. B. W. Dodge & Company.
Wolf to the Slaughter. Ruth Rendell. LC 76-18875. 1976. 7.95. J. Curley.
Wolf to the Slaughter. Ruth Rendell. LC 68-14219. 1968. Published for the Crime Club by Doubleday.
Wolf Tracks. David Case. (Orig.). 1980. pap. 1.95 o.s.i. (ISBN 0-505-51485-0). Tower Bks.
Wolf Trail. Roger S Pocock. LC 23-953563. 1923. D. Appleton and Company.
Wolf Tree. 1st Ed. Helen Rucker. LC 60-652406. 1960. Little, Brown.
Wolf Willow: A History, a Story, and a Memory of the Last Plains Frontier. Wallace Earle Stegner. LC 79-18694. (Illus.). 1980. 18.50 (ISBN 0-8032-4109-7) (ISBN 0-8032-9108-6). University of Nebraska Press.
Wolf Woman: A Novel. Arthur John Arbuthnott Stringer. LC 28-14320. The Bobbs-Merrill Company.
Wolfbane. Cyril M. Kornbluth. Tr. by Frederik Pohl. LC 75-423. (Garland Library of Science Fiction). 1975. 11.00 (ISBN 0-8240-1428-6). Garland Pub.
Wolfbane. Frederik Pohl & C. M. Kornbluth. Ed. by Lester Del Ray. LC 75-423. (Library of Science Fiction). 1975. lib. bdg. 15.00 (ISBN 0-8240-1428-6). Garland Pub.
Wolfen. Whitley Streiber. LC 78-7482. 1978. (ISBN 0-688-03347-4). Morrow.
Wolfen. Whitley Strieber. 1979. pap. 2.50 (ISBN 0-553-20268-5). Bantam.
Wolfen. Whitley Strieber. LC 78-7482. 1978. 8.95 o.p. (ISBN 0-688-03347-4). Morrow.
Wolfenberg: A Novel. William Black. LC 6-124112. 1893. Harper & Brothers.
Wolfer. James B. Chaffin. 1980. pap. 1.50 o.s.i. (ISBN 0-505-51461-3). Tower Bks.
Wolfer. James B. Chaffin. (O.s.i.). 1972. pap. 0.75 o.s.i. (BT50209). Belmont-Tower.
Wolfer. Loren D. Estleman. 1981. pap. 1.95 (ISBN 0-671-42873-X). PB.
Wolfer. Frederick John Niven. LC 23-6949. 1923. 1.75. Dodd, Mead and Company.
Wolfe's Cloister. Bentz Plagemann. LC 74-8009. 1974. 6.95. Saturday Review Press.
Wolfhead. Charles L Harness. (Berkley Medallion Book). 1.75 (ISBN 0-425-03658-8). Berkley Pub. Corp.
Wolfine: a Romance in Which a Dog Plays on Honorable Part. X. LC 15-102842. 1915. Sturgis & Walton Company.
Wolfling: A Documentary Novel of the Eighteen-Seventies. Sterling North. LC 70-77916. (Illus.). 1969. 5.95. Dutton.
Wolfman. Carl Dreadstone & Siodmak, Curt. (Berkley Medallion Book). (Illus.). 1977. 1.25 (ISBN 0-425-03446-1). Berkley Pub. Corp.
Wolfnight. Nicolas Freeling. LC 81-48220. 1982. 12.50 (ISBN 0-394-52266-4). Pantheon Books.
Wolfpack. William M Hardy. LC 60-8439. 1960. Dodd, Mead.
Wolf's Candle. Dane Coolidge. LC 35-9051. 1935. E. P. Dutton & Co., Inc.
Wolf's Complete Book of Terror. Leonard Wolf. LC 79-448. 14.95 (ISBN 0-517-53634-X) (ISBN 0-517-53635-8). C. N. Potter: Distributed by Crown Publishers.
Wolf's Head. John Benteen. (Fargo Ser). (Orig.). 1970. pap. 0.60 o.p. (B60-2028). Belmont-Tower.
Wolfsbane. William W. Johnstone. (Orig.). 1982. pap. 2.95 (ISBN 0-8217-1070-2). Zebra.
Wolfsbane: A Novel. Craig Thomas. LC 78-5293. 8.95 (ISBN 0-03-022466-7). Holt, Rinehart, and Winston.
Wolfshead. Robert E. Howard. (Orig.). 1968. pap. 0.60 o.p. (73-721). Lancer.
Wolfshead. Robert E. Howard. 1972. Repr. pap. 0.95 o.p. Lancer.
Wolfshead. Jere Hungerford Wheelwright. LC 49-105823. 1949. C. Scribner's Sons.
Wolftrap. Eric Bercovici. LC 78-21598. 1979. 7.95 (ISBN 0-689-10949-0). Atheneum.
Wolfville. Alfred Henry Lewis. LC 69-11910. (American short story series, v. 69). (Illus.). 1969. (ISBN 0-512-00455-2). Garrett Press.
Wolfville. Alfred Henry Lewis. LC 72-8178. (American short story series, v. 69). 1972. (ISBN 0-8422-8090-1). MSS Information Corp.
Wolfville. Alfred Henry Lewis. LC 38-127604. Frederick A. Stokes Company.
Wolfville. Alfred Henry Lewis & Remington, Frederic, 1861-1909, Illus. LC 7-145041. Frederick A. Stokes Company.
Wolfville Days. Alfred Henry Lewis. LC 2-3924. 1902. F. A. Stokes Company.
Wolfville Folks. Alfred Henry Lewis. LC 24-11852. The Macaulay Company.
Wolfville Folks. Alfred Henry Lewis. LC 8-16469. 1908. D. Appleton and Company.
Wolfville Nights. Alfred Henry Lewis. LC 2-22665. 1902. F. A. Stokes Company.
Wolfville Nights. Alfred Henry Lewis. 1905. Grosset & Dunlap.
Wolheim's World's Best SF: Series II. Donald A. Wollheim. (Science Fiction Ser.). 1978. pap. 1.95 (ISBN 0-87997-427-3, UJ1427). DAW Bks.
Wollheim's World's Best Science Fiction: Series Four. Ed. by Donald A. Wollheim. (Science Fiction Ser.). pap. 2.25 (UE 1585). DAW Bks.
Wollheim's World's Best SF: Series Three. Ed. by Donald A. Wollheim. (Science Fiction Ser.). (Orig.). 1979. pap. 2.25 (ISBN 0-87997-507-5, UE1507). Daw Bks.
Wollheim's World's Best SF Series 1. Ed. by Donald A. Wollheim. (Science Fiction Ser). pap. 1.75 o.p. (UE1349). DAW Bks.
Wollow-Bender: A Novel. Helen Rich. LC 50-10862. 1950. Simon and Schuster.
Wolverine: A Romance of Early Michigan. Albert Lathrop Lawrence. LC 4-29789. 1904. Little, Brown, and Company.
Wolverton: Or the Modern Arena. D. A Reynolds. LC 7-30601. 1891. Rand, McNally & Company.
Wolves. Hans Hellmut Kirst. LC 68-11881. 1968. Coward-McCann.
Wolves. Guy Mazeline. Tr. by Eric Sutton. LC 34-30893. 1934. The Macmillan Company.
Wolves. Alden Walling Welch. LC 19-10523. 1919. A. A. Knopf.
Wolves Against the Moon. Julia Cooley Altrocchi. LC 57-9384. 1957. Pageant Book Co.
Wolves Against the Moon. Julia Cooley Altrocchi. LC 40-27372. 1940. The Macmillan Company.
Wolves and the Lamb. Joseph Smith Fletcher. LC 25-1018. 1925. A. A. Knopf.
Wolves at Cooking Lake and Other Stories. Gray McClintock. LC 32-12597. J. B. Lyon Company.
Wolves Came Down the Mountain. Michael Strong. (Walker Mystery Ser.). (O.s.i.). 1979. 7.95 o.s.i. (ISBN 0-8027-5414-7). Walker & Co.
Wolves of Chaos. Harold MacGrath. LC 29-6853. 1929. Doubleday, Doran and Company, Inc.
Wolves of Craywood. Jan Alexander, pseud. (Orig.). 1970. pap. 0.60 o.p. (ISBN 0-447-73868-2). Lancer.
Wolves of Craywood see Shadows.
Wolves of God: And Other Fey Stories. Algernon Blackwood & Wilfred Joint Author Wilson. LC 21-19123. 1921. E. P. Dutton & Company.
Wolves of the Chaparral. Paul Evan Lehman. LC 38-134041. Green Circle Books.
Wolves of the Sea: Being a Tale of the Colonies from the Manuscript of One Geoffry Carlyle, Seaman, Narrating Certain Strange Adventures Which Befell Him Aboard the Pirate Craft "Namur,". Randall Parrish. LC 18-18404. 1918. A. C. McClurg & Co.
Wolves of the Son. Gaston Leroux. LC 23-6286. The Macaulay Company.
Woman. Magdeleine Legendre Paz. Tr. by Seltzer, Adele Szold. LC 20-11894. 1920. T. Seltzer.
Woman a Day. Philip Jose Farmer. 1980. pap. 2.25 (ISBN 0-425-04526-9). Berkley Pub.
Woman: A Novel. Albert Payson Terhune & De Mille, William Churchill. LC 12-207932. The Bobbs-Merrill Company.
Woman About Town: A Novel. Allis McKay. LC 38-142677. 1938. The Macmillan Company.
Woman Accused. LC 33-4386. 1933. R. Long & R. R. Smith, Inc.
Woman Against the World. Evelyn Hanna. 480p. (Orig.). 1983. pap. 3.50 (ISBN 0-345-28931-5). Ballantine.
Woman Against Woman. Michael Angelo Holmes. (On cover: Lovell's library, v. 14, no. 709). 1886. J. W. Lovell Company.
Woman Against Woman. A Novel. Michael Angelo Holmes. LC 7-5178. G. W. Ogilvie.
Woman Alive. Susan Ertz. LC 36-9232. 1936. D. Appleton-Century Company, Incorporated.
Woman Alone. Lucy Lane Clifford. LC 6-213498. 1898. The Macmillan Company.
Woman Alone. Lucy Lane Clifford. 1901. D. Appleton and Company.
Woman Alone. Mabel Herbert Urner. LC 14-169472. 1914. Hearst's International Library Co.
Woman an Enigma: Or, Life and Its Revealings. Maria Jane McIntosh. LC 9-2507. 1843. Harper & Brothers.
Woman and Artist. Paul Blouet. LC 2205. 1900. Harper & Brothers.
Woman & Her Master. Jean DeVilliot. 1972. pap. 2.25 o.s.i. (V1097R, Venus). Grove.
Woman & Her Master. Jean De Villiot. (O.s.i.). 1968. pap. 0.95 o.s.i. (A316N, Award). Univ Pub & Dist.
Woman and the Puppet. Pierre Louys. LC 48-15314. (New Avon library, 135). 1947. Avon Book Co.
Woman and the Puppet. Pierre Louys. Tr. by Symons, Arthur. LC 36-7117. The Macaulay Company.
Woman & the Sea. Richard William Tregaskis. (Illus.). 6.50 (ISBN 0-910550-17-4). Elysium.

Woman and the Sea: Authorized Translation by Terrell Louise Tatum. Espina De Serna, Concha & Tatum, Terrell Louise, Tr. LC 34-19024. R. D. Henkle.

Woman and the Shadow; a Novel. Arabella Kenealy. LC 12-36158. Rand, McNally & Company.

Woman and the Sword. Rupert Lorraine. LC 47-35489. 1909. A. C. McClurg & Co.

Woman and the Whale: A Tale. Delmar Molarsky. LC 59-6476. 1959. Little, Brown.

Woman Astride. Nora Purtscher. LC 34-17971. 1934. D. Appleton-Century Company, Incorporated.

Woman at Bay. George Harmon Coxe. LC 45-9496. 1945. A. A. Knopf.

Woman at Bay (Una Donna) Rina Faccio. Tr. by Lannsdale, Maria Hornor. LC 8-30133. 1908. G. P. Putnam's Sons.

Woman at Otowi Crossing. Frank Waters. (O.s.i.). 1966. 12.95 o.s.i. (ISBN 0-8040-0324-6, SB). Swallow.

Woman at Otowi Crossing: A Novel. Frank Waters. LC 66-25961. 1966. A. Swallow.

Woman at the Door. Hugo Ballin. LC 25-21069. 1925. Authors Publishing Corporation.

Woman at the Door. Warwick Deeping. LC 37-25346. 1937. A. A. Knopf.

Woman at the Window: A Novel. Nelia Gardner White. LC 51-12543. 1951. Viking Press.

Woman at Thirty. Ernest Pascal. LC 34-29557. Harcourt, Brace and Company.

Woman Between Men. Elaine Green. 1979. pap. 1.75 (ISBN 0-532-17209-4). Woodhill.

Woman by Three. Evan S. Connell. 6.95 o.p. (ISBN 0-87465-037-2). Pacific Coast.

Woman Called Fancy. Frank Yerby. LC 51-3370. 1951. Dial Press.

Woman Called Fancy. Frank Yerby. LC 52-42177. 1952. Garden City Books.

Woman Called Fancy. Frank Yerby. 1975. (pbk.) 1.75. Dell.

Woman Called Moses: A Novel Based on the Life of Harriet Tubman. Marcy Heidish. LC 75-40240. 1976. (ISBN 0-395-21535-8). Houghton Mifflin.

Woman Called Scylla. David Gurr. LC 80-51998. 1981. 12.95 (ISBN 0-670-77775-7). Viking Press.

Woman Chief. Benjamin Capps. LC 78-22808. 1979. Doubleday.

Woman Clothed in Sun. Dorothy Jeanne Williams. LC 77-5652. 8.95 (ISBN 0-698-10838-8). Coward, McCann & Geoghegan.

Woman Clothed with the Sun: And Other Stories. Frank Laurence Lucas. LC 71-122731. (Short story index reprint series). 1970. Books for Libraries Press.

Woman Clothed with the Sun: And Other Stories. Frank Laurence Lucas. LC 38-25163. 1938. Simon and Schuster.

Woman Clothed with the Sun, & Other Stories. Frank Laurence Lucas. LC 71-122731. (Short Story Index Reprint Ser). 1938. 16.00 (ISBN 0-8369-3564-0). Ayer Co.

Woman Commands: Novelized. Guy Fowler & Foerster, Thilde. LC 32-32520. Gorsset & Dunlap.

Woman Day see Day of Timestop.

Woman Destroyed. Simone De Beauvoir. LC 69-15486. 1969. 5.95. Putnam.

Woman Destroyed. Simone De Beauvoir, pseud. 1969. 5.95 o.p. (ISBN 0-399-10875-0). Putnam.

Woman Doctor. Florence Haseltine & Yvonne Yaw. LC 76-26539. 1976. 8.95 (ISBN 0-395-24776-4). Houghton Mifflin.

Woman Errant: Being Some Chapters from the Wonder Book of Barbara, the Commuter's Wife. Mabel Wright. LC 4-15365. 1904. The Macmillan Company.

Woman Executive. Evelyn H Park. LC 77-80278. 1979. 7.95 (ISBN 0-87949-086-1). Ashley Books.

Woman for Mayor: A Novel of to-Day. Helen Maria Winslow. LC 9-16441. 1909. The Reilly & Britton Co.

Woman for President, Foundation of the Federation of the Goths, Stretching from Iran to Norway. H. Winky-Lotz. (Historical Novel, Europe About 175 B. C. to 95 B. C. Ser.: Vol. I). (Illus.). 312p. 1980. 14.55 (ISBN 0-936112-02-6); pap. 11.25 (ISBN 0-936112-09-3). Willyshe Pub.

Woman for President, the Roots of "Cinderella" of Our Fairy Tale. H. Winky-Lotz. (Historical Novel, Europe About 95 B. C. to 57 B. C. Ser.: Vol. II). (Illus.). 245p. 1980. 14.55 (ISBN 0-936112-08-5); pap. 11.25 (ISBN 0-936112-03-4). Willyshe Pub.

Woman Free. Ellis Ethelmer. 1893. Repr. 12.50 o.s.i. Finch Pr.

Woman from A.U.N.T. Brian Negulesco. 1970. 4.50 o.p. (ISBN 0-682-47089-9). Exposition.

Woman from "Outside" (on Swan River) Hulbert Footner. LC 21-184765. The James A. McCann Company.

Woman from Sarajevo. Ivo Andric. Tr. by J. Hitrec. 1965. 6.95 o.p. Knopf.

Woman from Sarajevo. Tr. from Serbo-Croatian by Joseph Hitrec 1st Amer. Ed. Ivo Andric. LC 64-19100. 5.95. Knopf.

Woman from Sicily. 1st Ed. Frank Arthur Swinnerton. LC 57-78302. 1957. Doubleday.

Woman from the Country. D'Arcy Niland. LC 59-534734. 1959. W. Sloane Associates.

Woman from the Glen. Chloe Gartner. LC 72-14278. 1973. 6.95. Morrow.

Woman from the Glen. Chloe Gartner. 1975. (pbk.) 1.50. Bantam Books.

Woman from Wolverton; a Story of Washington Life. Isabel Gordon Curtis. LC 12-35196. 1912. The Century Co.

Woman Gives, a Story of Regeneration. Owen McMahon Johnson. LC 16-17413. 1916. 1.40. Little, Brown, and Company.

Woman Handled. Robert Oliver. LC 36-8971. Phoenix Press.

Woman Hater. John Alexander Hugh Cameron. LC 12-24822. 1.25. Christian Press Association Publishing Company.

Woman-Hater. Charles Reade. (Seaside library, v. 1, no. 4). 1877. G. Munro.

Woman-Hater. A Novel. household ed. Charles Reade. LC 7-30653. 1877. Harper & Brothers.

Woman-Hater: A Novel. Charles Reade. (Harper's Franklin square library, Duodecimo ed.). 1883. Harper & Brothers.

Woman-Hater. A Novel. household ed. Charles Reade. LC 24-27986. 1900. Harper & Brothers.

Woman-Haters: A Yarn of Eastboro Twin-Lights. Joseph Crosby Lincoln. LC 25-8157. 1925. D. Appleton and Company.

Woman-Haters: A Yarn of Easthoro Twin-Lights. Joseph Crosby Lincoln. LC 11-141001. 1911. 1.25. D. Appleton and Company.

Woman He Chose. James Harold Wallis. LC 34-22035. E. P. Dutton & Co., Inc.

Woman He Desired. Louise Gerard. LC 22-14187. The Macaulay Company.

Woman He Kept. James Noble Gifford. LC 48-153818. 1948. Phoenix Press.

Woman Healer. Evelyn Whitell. LC 20-92789. The Master Mind Publishing Co.

Woman Herself. Ruth Holt Bouchicault. LC 9-12875. 1909. The Stuyvesant Press.

Woman Hunt. Francis Ryck. (Crest Book, M1881). 1973. (pbk.) 0.95. Fawcett.

Woman Hunt. Francis Ryck. LC 72-75510. 1972. 6.95 (ISBN 0-8128-1489-4). Stein and Day.

Woman Hunters. Arthur Somers Roche. LC 29-7502. The Century Co.

Woman I Am. Amber Lee, pseud. LC 25-6620. 1925. T. Seltzer.

Woman I Loved, and the Woman Who Loved Me. Isa Jane Blagden. LC 6-138544. (On cover: The seaside library. Pocket ed., no. 705). 1886. G. Munro.

Woman in Ambush. Rex Ellingwood Beach. LC 51-11401. 1951. Putnam.

Woman in Armor: Also Old Gargoyle, and The Man Who "Hadn't Time". Mary Hartwell Catherwood. LC 6-22284. 1875. G. W. Carleton & Co.; Etc., Etc.

Woman in Bed. Miles Tripp. LC 76-383145. 1976. 2.95 (ISBN 0-333-17807-6). Macmillan.

Woman in Black. Herbert Adams. LC 32-10111. 1932. J. B. Lippincott Company.

Woman in Black. Edmund Clerihew Bentley. LC 13-4761. 1913. 1.25. The Century Co.

Woman in Black. Zenith Jones Brown. LC 47-378029. 1947. C. Scribner's Sons.

Woman in Black. Monica Heath. (Signet book). 1974. (pbk.) 0.95. New American Library.

Woman in Chains. Elizabeth Alexander. LC 32-652219. Sears Publishing Company, Inc.

Woman in Exchange. Howard Buck. LC 36-18155. The Macaulay Company.

Woman in Exile. Horace Annesley Vachell. LC 26-15794. 1926. Frederick A. Stokes Company.

Woman in Flight. Fitz Percy Reck-Malleczewen. Tr. by Covan, Jenny. LC 28-14118. 1928. Boni & Liveright.

Woman in Her Prime. A. Konadu. (African Writers Ser.). 1967. pap. text ed. 4.00x (ISBN 0-435-90040-4). Heinemann Ed.

Woman in Her Prime: By S. A. Konadu. Samuel Asare Konadu. LC 67-91691. 1968. 3.00. Heinemann.

Woman in It: A Sketch of Feminine Misadventures. Eliza M. J. Humphreys. LC 7-5880. 1895. J. B. Lippincott Company.

Woman in Love. Kathleen Thompson Norris. 1971. pap. 0.75 o.p. (ISBN 0-446-64517-6, 64-517). Paperback Lib.

Woman in Love. Daisy H. Thomson. 1974. pap. 0.95 o.p. (ISBN 0-515-03493-2, N3493). BJ Pub Group.

Woman in Love. 1st Ed. Lucy Michaella Cores. LC 51-10389. 1951. Harper.

Woman in Marble. Carl Dekker, pseud. LC 72-80799. (Black bat mystery). 1972. 5.95. Bobbs-Merrill.

Woman in Pawn. Millicent Kent. Godwin.

Woman in Possession. Barbara Hedworth. LC 34-18839. E. P. Dutton & Co., Inc.

Woman in Possession. 1st Ed. Hallie Southgate Burnett. LC 51-9826. 1951. Dutton.

Woman in Purple Pajamas. Wilson Collison. LC 31-103704. 1931. R. M. McBride & Company.

Woman in Question. 2d ed. John Reed Scott. LC 9-19663. 1909. J. B. Lippincott Company.

Woman in Red. Lucy Beatrice Malleson. 1943. Smith and Durrell.

Woman in Residence. Michelle Harrison. 1983. pap. 5.95 (ISBN 0-14-006723-X). Penguin.

Woman in Revolt. Anne Lee. LC 13-24829. Desmond FitzGerald, Inc.

Woman in Silk and Shadows. Dorothy Daniels. (Signet Book). 1977. 1.25 (ISBN 0-451-07295-2). New American Library.

Woman in Space. Sara Cavanaugh. 1.75 (ISBN 0-8439-8023-0). C.

Woman in Sunshine. Frank Arthur Swinnerton. LC 44-9398. 1944. Hutchinson & Co., Ltd.

Woman in Sunshine... Frank Arthur Swinnerton. LC 45-2689. 1945. Doubleday, Doran and Company, Inc.

Woman in the Alcove. Jennette Barbour Perry Lee. LC 14-15747. 1914. C. Scribner's Sons.

Woman in the Alcove. Anna Katharine Green Rohlfs. LC 6-13935. 1906. The Bobbs-Merrill Company.

Woman in the Back Seat. Marguerite Steen. LC 59-9518. 1959. Doubleday.

Woman in the Case. Thomas Gifford. LC 75-34331. 1976. 8.95. Putnam.

Woman in the Case. Ellery Queen, pseud. LC 66-15960.

Woman in the Case. A Story. Bessie A Turner. LC 12-17302. 1875. G. W. Carleton & Co.; Etc., Etc.

Woman in the Case (Complices) A Novel. Hector Henri Malot & Maury, Max, Pseud.? Tr. (On cover: Library of choice fiction, no. 21). 1899. Laird & Lee.

Woman in the Case: Or, Debtor to the Devil... Fay P Rathburn. (peerless series, no. 48). 1891. J. S. Ogilvie.

Woman in the Dark: More Adventures of the Continental OP. Collected and Edited, with Introd., by Ellery Queen Pseud. Complete and Unabridged. Dashiell Hammett. LC 57-22163. L. E. Spivak.

Woman in the Dunes. Kobo Abe. LC 72-764. 1972. (ISBN 0-394-71814-3). Vintage Books.

Woman in the Dunes. Hiroshi Teshigahara. lib. bdg. 7.50x o.p. (ISBN 0-88307-266-1). Gannon.

Woman in the Hall. Gladys Bronwyn Stern. LC 39-27411. 1939. The Macmillan Company.

Woman in the House. William Edmund Barrett. LC 71-132500. 1971. 5.95. Doubleday.

Woman in the House. Robert Smythe Hichens. LC 45-9097. 1945. Macrae-Smith Company.

Woman in the Mirror. Winston Graham. LC 74-9451. 1975. 7.95 (ISBN 0-385-01235-7). Doubleday.

Woman in the Picture. Bernard Augustine De Noto. LC 44-210049. 1944. Little, Brown and Company.

Woman in the Sea. Nancy Bodington. LC 48-10786. 1948. Harper.

Woman in the Shadow. Louis Joseph Vance. LC 30-16944. 1930. J. B. Lippincott Company.

Woman in the Sky. James Hanley. LC 73-82070. 1973. 6.95 (ISBN 0-8180-0618-8). Horizon Press.

Woman in the Storm and Other Short Stories: Miscellany. A. C. St. V. Thurairajah. LC 76-904255. (Illus.). 1976. 8.50. S.N.

Woman in the White House. Herbert Arthur, pseud. LC 46-2011. 1945. Tech Books.

Woman in the White House. Herbert Shappiro. LC 46-2011. 1945. Tech Books, Inc.

Woman in the Window. Marcia Miller. 1975. 4.95. Avalon Books.

Woman in the Woods. Charity Blackstock. 1978. pap. 1.75 o.s.i. (ISBN 0-8439-0568-9, Leisure Books). Nordon Pubns.

Woman in the Woods. Ursula Torday. LC 58-5930. 1958. Published for the Crime Club by Doubleday.

Woman in the Wraparound Skirt. Anna E. Anderson. 1979. 7.50 (ISBN 0-682-49450-X). Exposition.

Woman in White. Wilkie Collins. LC 65-1. 1964. Heritage Press.

Woman in White. Wilkie Collins. LC 64-5445. 1964. Printed for the Members of the Limited Editions Club at the Elm Tree Press.

Woman in White. Wilkie Collins. Ed. by Kathleen Mary Tillotson. Anthea Trodd. LC 72-5304. (Riverside editions, B116). 1969. 1.95. Houghton Mifflin.

Woman in White. Wilkie Collins. LC 6-11544. (English Comedie humaine. 2d series). 1906. The Century Co.

Woman in White. Wilkie Collins. 1908. C. Scribner's Sons.

Woman in White. Wilkie Collins. (Half-title: everyman's library, ed. by Ernest Rhys. Fiction. no. 464). 1910. J. M. Dent & Sons, Ltd.

Woman in White. Wilkie Collins. LC 38-35047. (Half-title: The world's classics ccxxvi). 1932. H. Milford, Oxford University Press.

Woman in White. Wilkie Collins. LC 36-37320. (Half-title: Everyman's library, ed. by Ernest Rhys. Fiction. no. 464). 1932. J. M. Dent & Sons, Ltd.

Woman in White. Wilkie Collins. LC 32-26964. 1932. Harper & Brothers.

Woman in White. Wilkie Collins. LC 37-7816. (Classic romance of literature. vol. iv). The Spencer Press.

Woman in White. Wilkie Collins & Harvey Peter Sucksmith. LC 76-355695. 1975. 21.00 (ISBN 0-19-255347-X). Oxford University Press.

Woman in White. Wilkie Collins & Harvey Peter Sucksmith. LC 79-41334. (World's classics). 1980. 3.95. Oxford University Press.

Woman in White. Wilkie Collins & Julian Symons. LC 75-317695. (Penguin English library). 1974. 2.50 (ISBN 0-14-043096-2). Penguin.

Woman in White. A Novel. Wilkie Collins. LC 16-7539. (On verse of t-p.: Harper's illustrated library edition). 1873. Harper & Brothers.

Woman in White and The Moonstone,Adapted by Verda Evans. Wilkie Collins. LC 53-2308. 1953. Globe Book Co.

Woman in White. Ed. by M. W. & G. Thomas. Illus. by Patrick Stackhouse. Wilkie Collins. Ed. by Maurice Walton Thomas. Gladys Thomas. LC 66-6332. (Shorter classics). 1966. bds., 2.50. Ginn.

Woman in White. Introd. by Vincent Starrett. Illus. by Leonard Rosoman. Wilkie Collins & Leonard Illus Rosoman. LC 65-1. bds., 6.50. Heritage.

Woman in White: T. V. edition. Wilkie Collins. Ed. by Julian Symons. 1982. pap. 3.95 (ISBN 0-14-005980-6). Penguin.

Woman Intervenes: Or, The Mistress of the Mine. Robert Barr. LC 6-9067. 1896. F. A. Stokes Co.

Woman Is Witness; a Paris Diary. Ernst Lothar. Tr. by Mussey, June Barrows. LC 41-13939. 1941. Doubleday, Doran.

Woman Is Witness: A Paris Diary. Ernst Lothar. Tr. by Mussey, June Barrows. LC 41-13939. 1941. Doubleday, Doran & Company, Inc.

Woman Like Me. Marjorie Damsey Wilson. LC 32-3416. 1932. Farrar & Rinehart, Incorporated.

Woman Like That. Susan Richards Shreve. LC 76-50602. 1977. 8.95 (ISBN 0-689-10776-5). Atheneum.

Woman Like Us. Nicola Thorne, pseud. LC 79-2514. 8.95 (ISBN 0-312-88641-1). St. Martin's Press.

Woman (Malombra) 2d impression. ed. Antonio Fogazzaro. LC 7-32327. 1907. J. B. Lippincott Company.

Woman Marches: A Novel. Arthur A Gainess. LC 36-9231.

Woman Named Anne. Henry Cecil. LC 67-22513. 1967. Harper & Row.

Woman Named Anne. Henry Cecil. LC 67-22513. 1967. Harper & Row.

Woman Named Chaye: A Novel. 1st Ed. Rose Kluger Kornhauser Keil. LC 52-7653. 1952. Exposition Press.

Woman Named Smith. Marie Conway Oemler. LC 19-19357. 1919. The Century Co.

Woman Named Smith. Marie Conway Oemler. LC 22-537204. 1921. The Century Co.

Woman Named Solitude. Schwarz-Bart, Andre. LC 72-92614. 1973. 5.95. Atheneum.

Woman Named Solitude. Andre Schwarz-Bart. (Bantam book, X7880). 1974. (pbk.) 1.75. Bantam Books.

Woman Next Door. T. M. Wright. LC 81-47270. 256p. (Orig.). 1981. pap. 2.50 (ISBN 0-87216-912-X). Playboy Pbks.

Woman of Andros. Thornton Niven Wilder. LC 68-28228. (Bard book). 1975. (pbk.) 1.65 (ISBN 0-380-00308-2). Avon.

Woman of Andros. Thornton Niven Wilder. LC 30-5690. 1930. A. & C. Boni.

Woman of Bangkok: By Jack Reynolds Pseud. Jack Jones. LC 56-7236. 1956. Ballatine Books.

Woman of Boston. Alicia Meadows. (Woman's Destiny Ser.: No. 3). (Orig.). 1983. pap. 2.95 (ISBN 0-440-09750-9). Dell.

Woman of Character: A Novel. Julian Gloag. LC 72-12586. 1973. 6.95 (ISBN 0-394-48340-5). Random House.

Woman of Consequence. Sondra Gotlieb. LC 83-2950. 1983. 12.95 (ISBN 0-312-88643-8). St. Martin's Press.

Woman of Courage. Emily Newell Blair. LC 31-22576. Farrar & Rinehart, Incorporated.

Woman of Destiny. Grandin K. Hammell. (Orig.). 1981. pap. 3.25 (ISBN 0-89083-734-1). Zebra.

Woman of Destiny. Samuel Jesse Warshawsky. LC 37-28981. J. Messner, Incorporated.

Woman of Fashion. Marion Strobel. LC 31-14422. Farrar & Rinehart Incorporated.

Woman of Feeling. Louise Maunsell Field. LC 16-4749. 1916. 1.00. Dodd, Mead and Company.

Woman of Feeling. Violet Weingarten. 1975. (pbk.) 1.25. Dell.
Woman of Feeling. Violet Weingarten. (Kangaroo Book). 1977. 1.50 (ISBN 0-671-81050-2). Pocket Books.
Woman of Feeling. Violet Weingarten. LC 78-171133. 1972. 5.95 (ISBN 0-394-47353-1). Knopf.
Woman of Fire. Adolphe Belot. LC 6-113492. (On cover: Sea and shore series, no. 36). Street & Smith.
Woman of Fortune. Will Holt. 1981. pap. 3.50 (ISBN 0-451-11105-2, AE1105, Sig). NAL.
Woman of Fortune. A Novel. Frances Christine Tiernan. 1896. Benziger Brothers.
Woman of Forty. Desmond Hall. LC 48-8481. 1948. Dial Press.
Woman of Forty: A Monograph. Amelie Claire Leroy. LC 8-20120. 1893. D. Appleton and Company.
Woman of Fury. Constance Gluyas. 2.25 (ISBN 0-451-08075-0). New American Library.
Woman of Genius. Mary Hunter Austin. LC 76-51336. (Recovered Fiction by American Women). 1977. 22.00 (ISBN 0-405-10043-4). Arno Press.
Woman of Genius. Mary Hunter Austin. LC 12-20199. 1912. 1.35. Doubleday, Page & Company.
Woman of Genius. Mary Hunter Austin. LC 17-27748. 1917. 1.50. Houghton Mifflin Company.
Woman of Her Times. Gary J Scrimgeour. LC 81-15722. 14.95 (ISBN 0-399-12711-9). Putnam.
Woman of Honor. Henry Cuyler Bunner. LC 6-18671. 1883. J.R. Osgood and Company.
Woman of Honor: Or, False Friendships in Society. A Book for Women. Tr. from the French of Louis Enault, by Mrs. Rebecca L. Tutt.. Louis Enault & Tutt, Mrs. Rebecca L., Tr. LC 6-37821. T. B. Peterson & Brothers.
Woman of Ice. Adolphe Belot. LC 6-11348. 1891. The Price-McGill Publishing Co.
Woman of Impulse: A Novel. Justin Huntly McCarthy. LC 7-15174. (On cover: The Hudson library, no. 4). 1895. G. P. Putnam's Sons.
Woman of Independent Means. Elizabeth Forsythe Hailey. LC 77-28414. 1978. 9.95 (ISBN 0-670-77795-1). Viking Press.
Woman of Independent Means: A Novel. Elizabeth Forsythe Hailey. 1979. 2.50 (ISBN 0-380-42390-1). Avon Books.
Woman of It. Clare Ogden Davis. LC 29-16171. J. H. Sears & Company, Inc.
Woman of It. Mark Lee Luther. LC 12-213132. 1912. Harper & Brothers.
Woman of Jerusalem. 1st Ed. Elsie Frances Wilson Mack. LC 62-7659. 1962. Doubleday.
Woman of Justice. Georgia Di Donato. LC 78-20068. 1980. 10.95 (ISBN 0-385-14496-2). Doubleday.
Woman of Kali. Cover Painting by Herman Bischoff. Gardner F Fox. LC 55-15739. (Gold medal books, 438). 1954. Fawcett Publications.
Woman of Knockaloe. Hall Caine. LC 23-14273. 1923. Cassell and Company, Ltd.
Woman of Means. Taylor, Peter Hillsman. LC 50-7597. 1950. Harcourt, Brace.
Woman of My Age. Nina Bawden. LC 67-22109. 1967. Harper & Row.
Woman of My Life. Ludwig Bemelmans. LC 57-119902. 1957. Viking Press.
Woman of Mystery. Maurice Leblanc. LC 16-15596. 1916. The Macaulay Company.
Woman of Naples. Miklos Suranyi. LC 29-22051. 1929. Cosmopolitan Book Corporation.
Woman of Nerve: A Tale of the West. E. O. Tilburn. LC 6561. (pastime series. no. 98). 1900.
Woman of New Orleans. Rochel Denore. (Woman's Destiny Ser.: No. 2). (Orig.). 1983. pap. 2.95 (ISBN 0-440-09856-4, Banbury). Dell.
Woman of New York. Marcia Mager. (Woman's Destiny Ser.: No. 4). (Orig.). 1983. pap. 2.95 (ISBN 0-440-08968-9). Dell.
Woman of No Importance. Allen Crafton & Robert E. Gard. LC 74-82344. 1974. 8.95 (ISBN 0-88361-032-9). Stanton & Lee.
Woman of No Importance. Allen Crafton & Robert E. Gard. LC 74-82344. 1974. 8.95 o.s.i. (ISBN 0-88361-032-9). Wisconsin Hse.
Woman of No Importance: A Novel. Allen Crafton & Robert Edward Gard. LC 74-82344. 1974. 8.95 (ISBN 0-88361-032-9). Wisconsin House.
Woman of Property. Mabel Seeley. LC 47-310250. 1947. Doubleday.
Woman of Property. Sandra Wilson. 384p. 1981. pap. 2.95 (ISBN 0-449-24462-8, Crest). Fawcett.
Woman of Quality. Jan Vlachos Westcott. LC 78-17236. 1979. 8.95. Putnam.
Woman of Rome. Alberto Moravia. 1974. (pbk.) 1.75. Manor Books.
Woman of Rome. Alberto Pincherle. LC 49-10785. 1949. Farrar, Straus.
Woman of Samaria. James Wesley Ingles. LC 49-9158. 1949. Longmans, Green.
Woman of San Francisco. Lynn Erikson. (Woman's Destiny Ser.: No. 1). (Orig.). 1982. pap. 2.95 (ISBN 0-440-09845-9). Dell.
Woman of Shawmut: A Romance of Colonial Times. Edmund Janes Carpenter. LC 6-213475. 1891. Little, Brown and Company.
Woman of Sorek. Anthony Gould. LC 6-27640. The American News Company.
Woman of Spain: A Story of Old California. Scott O'Dell. LC 34-28775. 1934. Houghton Mifflin Company.
Woman of Straw. Catherine Arley. LC 57-10036. 1958. Random House.
Woman of Substance. Barbara Taylor Bradford. LC 77-9231. 1979. 12.95 (ISBN 0-385-12050-8). Doubleday.
Woman of Substance. Barbara Taylor Bradford. 1980. (ISBN 0-380-49163-X). Avon Books.
Woman of Texas. Reginald Thomas Staples. LC 79-7212. 1980. 10.95 (ISBN 0-385-15325-2). Doubleday.
Woman of Texas. R. T. Stevens. LC 79-7212. 1980. 11.95 o.p. (ISBN 0-385-15325-2). Doubleday.
Woman of the Avalon. Leonard London Foreman. (Dell first edition 57). 1955. Dell Pub. Co.
Woman of the Century. Eleanora Brownleigh. (Orig.). 1981. pap. 3.50 (ISBN 0-89083-862-3). Zebra.
Woman of the Dawn. Antonia Van-Loon. 1982. pap. 3.75 (ISBN 0-8217-1066-4). Zebra.
Woman of the Desert. Eric Moore Ritchie. LC 21-16004. 1921. Andrew Melrose, Ltd.
Woman of the Family: A Romantic Novel. Helen Marion Edgington. LC 36-3135. The Macaulay Company.
Woman of the Future. David Ireland. pap. 3.95. Bantam.
Woman of the Future: A Novel. David Ireland. LC 79-13297. 1979. 10.95 (ISBN 0-8076-0925-0). G. Braziller.
Woman of the Horizon. Gilbert Frankau. LC 23-9459. 1923. 2.00. The Century Co.
Woman of the Ice Age. Louis Pope Gratacap. LC 6-15110. 1906. Brentano's.
Woman of the People: A Novel. Benjamin Capps. LC 66-12607. bds., 4.95.
Woman of the Pepole. Benjamin Capps. 1966. 5.95 o.p. Hawthorn.
Woman of the Pharisees (La Pharisienne) Francois Mauriac. Tr. by Gerard Hopkins. LC 46-7273. 1946. H. Holt and Company.
Woman of the Rock. Hector Chevigny. LC 49-7789. 1949. A. A. Wyn.
Woman of the Shee and Other Stories. Donn Byrne. LC 32-192687. 2.00. The Century Co.
Woman of the Twilight: The Story of a Story. Marah Ellis Martin Ryan. LC 13-9142. 1913. A. C. McClurg & Co.
Woman of the World: An Every-Day Story. Frances Mabel Robinson. LC 8-4779. (On cover: Lovell's international series, no. 92). 1890. J. Lovell Company.
Woman of Thirty. Diana C Chang. LC 59-570947. 1959. Random House.
Woman of to-Day. ed. by james clarence harvey. ed. Margaret Crawford Jackson. Ed. by Harvey, James Clarence. LC 7-9468. (On cover: American author's series. no. 2). J. W. Lovell Company.
Woman of Uncertain Age. Mary Anne Berry. LC 9-12874. 1909. The Stuyvesant Press.
Woman of Valor. Allan Topol. LC 79-20186. 1980. 10.95 o.p. (ISBN 0-688-03578-7). Morrow.
Woman of Valor. Allan Topol. 256p. 1981. pap. 2.50 (ISBN 0-445-04669-4). Popular Lib.
Woman of Valor: A Novel. Allan Topol. LC 79-20186. 1980. 10.95 (ISBN 0-688-03571-X). Morrow.
Woman of War: And Other Stories. Felix Agnus. LC 6-2048. 1895. The American Job Printing Office.
Woman of War: And Other Stories. Felix Agnus. LC 8-12763. Kohn & Pollock, Inc.
Woman of Washington. Cornelius Vanderbilt. LC 37-1990. 1937. E. P. Dutton and Company, Inc.
Woman of Yesterday: A Novel. Caroline Atwater Mason. 1900. Doubleday, Page & Co.
Woman on a String. Thomas H. Hilton. 192p. (Orig.). 1972. pap. 1.95 o.p. (ISBN 0-87977-171-2, DBB171). Dansk Blue Bk.
Woman on Her Own. Jane Blackmore. (Ace gothic). 1974. (pbk.) 0.95. Ace Books.
Woman on Her Way. Faith Baldwin Cuthrell. LC 46-4733. 1946. Rinehart & Company, Inc.
Woman on Her Way. John Van Druten. LC 30-33144. 1930. G. P. Putnam's Sons.
Woman on Her Way. John Van Druten. LC 31-3682. 1931. A. A. Knopf.
Woman on the Beast: Viewed from Three Angles. Helen De Guerry Simpson. LC 33-32010. 1933. Doubleday, Doran & Company, Inc.
Woman on the Edge of Time. Marge Piercy. LC 75-36810. 1976. 10.00 (ISBN 0-394-49986-7). Knopf.
Woman on the Edge of Time. Marge Piercy. (Fawcett Crest Book). 1977. 2.25 (ISBN 0-449-23208-5). Fawcett Pubns.
Woman on the Pine Springs Road. Katie Daffan. LC 10-30576. 1910. 1.50. The Neale Publishing Company.
Woman on the Place. Harry Whittington. LC 56-28861. (Ace books, S-143). 1956. Ace Books.
Woman on the Roof. Mignon Good Eberhart. LC 77-13551. 1978. 7.95 (ISBN 0-89340-100-5). J. Curley,
Woman on the Roof. Helen Nielsen. LC 54-122192. 1954. Washburn.
Woman on the Roof: By Mignon G. Eberhart. Mignon Good Eberhart. LC 67-22626. 1968. bds., 4.50. Random.
Woman: Or, Ida of Athens. Sydney Owenson Morgan. LC 7-18739. Published by Bradford & Inskeep.
Woman Pays. Frederic Pierpont Ladd. M. Kennerley.
Woman Pharaoh. Burt Dean. 1978. 6.95 o.p. (ISBN 0-533-02908-2). Vantage.
Woman Power: A Novel. Gustaf Af Geijerstam. Tr. by Rapp, Esther. LC 28-5981. (Half-title: Scandinavian classics, vol. xxviii). 1927. The American-Scandinavian Foundation.
Woman Proposes; or, As It Should Be; a Story of to-Day. Charles E Leibold. LC 98-615. 1898. F. T. Nealy.
Woman Question. Dorothea Malm. LC 58-7393. Appleton-Century-Crofts.
Woman Reigns. Catherine McLaen New. 1896. The Bowen-Merrill Co.
Woman Scorned. Effie Adelaide Maria Albanesi. LC 1-30532. (On cover: Eagle series, no. 197). 1901. Street & Smith.
Woman Screamed. Robert Neumann. Tr. by Muir, Willa. LC 38-25693. 1938. The Dial Press.
Woman She Was. Lancelot De Giberne Sieveking. LC 34-18531. 1934. W. Morrow & Company.
Woman Soldier. Arnold Rodin. LC 56-1166. (Gold medal book 559). 1956. Fawcett Publications.
Woman Soldier see Blood on the Mountain.
Woman Soldier see Partisans.
Woman Space: Future & Fantasy Stories by Women. Ed. by Claudia M. Lamperti. 96p. (Orig.). 1981. pap. 4.95. New Victoria Pubs.
Woman Stealer. Harry Mills. LC 7-31115. (On cover: New York 10 cent library, no. 8). Katahdin Publishing Company.
Woman Taken in Adultery and The Poggenpuhl Family. Theodor Fontane. LC 78-31371. 1979. 14.00 (ISBN 0-226-25680-4). University of Chicago Press.
Woman Tamer. Stanley Shaw. LC 23-13887. The Macaulay Company.
Woman Tempted. Vera Fraser Cathcart. LC 26-982724. 1926. The Macaulay Company.
Woman That Was: Introd. by Jack Woodford. 1st Ed. Tommie Kane. LC 53-1942. 1952. Pageant Press.
Woman, the Man, and the Monster. William Carlton Lanyon Dawe. LC 9-14826. 1909. The Stuyvesant Press.
Woman Thing. rev. ed. Harriet Daimler. pap. 1.75 o.p. (2041). Brandon.
Woman Thing. Harriet Daimler. 1968. pap. 1.25 o.s.i. (2217, Travellers Comp). Olympia.
Woman Thou Art. Harry Sinclair Drago. LC 25-17702. The Macaulay Company.
Woman Thou Gavest Me: Being the Story of Mary 'Neill, Written. Hall Caine. LC 13-167872. 1913. J. B. Lippincott Company.
Woman Thou Gavest Me: Being the Story of Mary O'neill. Hall Caine. LC 17-13925. 1913. A. L. Burt Company.
Woman to Remember. Willie Belle Thompson. LC 54-7717. 1954. Comet Press Books.
Woman Triumphant (La Maja Desnuda) Vicente Blasco Ibanez & Keniston, Hayward, 1883- Tr. LC 20-72923. E. P. Dutton & Company.
Woman Trustee: And Other Stories About Schools. Charles William Bardeen. LC 5-4090. 1904. C. W. Bardeen.
Woman Under Glass, Saint Teresa of Avila. Virginia Davis Hersch. LC 30-24052. 1930. Harper & Brothers.
Woman Under the Mountain. Roman McDougald. LC 50-5799. (Inner sanctum mystery). 1950. Simon and Schuster.
Woman Ventures. David Graham Phillips. LC 78-104543. 1970. Literature House.
Woman Ventures: A Novel. David Graham Phillips. 1902. F. A. Stokes Company.
Woman Walks Alone. Ruth Putnam Mason. LC 31-8209. 1931. L. MacVeagh, The Dial Press.
Woman Who Commanded 500,000,000 Men. Charles Pettit. Tr. by Troubridge, Una Elena (Taylor) LC 29-14296. H. Liveright.
Woman Who Could Not Read, and Other Tales. Mikhail Mikhailovich Zoshchenko. LC 72-90319. 1973. 10.00 (ISBN 0-88355-028-8). Hyperion Press.
Woman Who Could Read the Minds of Dogs. Leslie Scalapino. 1976. pap. 3.25. Sand Dollar.
Woman Who Couldn't Die. Arthur John Arbuthnott Stringer. LC 29-8392. The Bobbs-Merrill Company.
Woman Who Dared. Richard Erdoes. (Fawcett Gold Medal Book). 1978. 1.95 (ISBN 0-449-13975-1). Fawcett Books.
Woman Who Dared: A Novel. Dale Drummond. LC 19-146228. Britton Publishing Company.
Woman Who Dares. Ursula Newell Gestefeld. LC 6-44070. Lovell, Gestefeld & Company.
Woman Who Did. Grant Allen. LC 6-485. (On cover: The keynotes series, v.8). 1895. Roberts Brothers; Etc., Etc.
Woman Who Did. Grant Allen & Boyd, Ernest Augustus, 1887- LC 26-16205. 1926. Little, Brown, and Company.
Woman Who Did Not. Vivian Cory. LC 6-31602. (On cover: Keynotes series no. 19). 1895. Roberts Bros.; Etc., Etc.
Woman Who Failed: And Others. Bessie Chandler. LC 6-23130. 1893. Roberts Brothers.
Woman Who Gathered Yarrow; The Box; Miss Vesey's Other Leg. Victor L Kaplan. LC 79-22650. 5.00 (ISBN 0-915306-18-2). Curbstone Press.
Woman Who Got on at Jasper Station, and Other Stories. Howard O'Hagan. LC 63-21869. (Swallow paperbook, 53). 1963. A. Swallow.
Woman Who Had Imagination: And Other Stories. Herbert Ernest Bates. LC 77-103239. (Short story index reprint series). 1969. Books for Libraries Press.
Woman Who Had Imagination: And Other Stories. Herbert Ernest Bates. LC 34-22748. 1934. The Macmillan Company.
Woman Who Had Imagination & Other Stories. facs. ed. Herbert Ernest Bates. LC 77-103239. (Short Story Index Reprint Ser.). 1934. 16.00 (ISBN 0-8369-3276-5). Ayer Co.
Woman Who Invented Love, La Donna Che Invento L'amore. Guido Da Verona & Sweet, Mrs. May McDaniel, 1865- Tr. LC 28-167173. E. P. Dutton & Company.
Woman Who Knocked Out Sugar Ray. Ralph Dranow. LC 81-70081. 4.50 (ISBN 0-9604152-5-4). Arrowhead Press.
Woman Who Lived in a Prologue. Nina Schneider. LC 79-18595. 1979. 12.95 (ISBN 0-395-28211-X). Houghton Mifflin.
Woman Who Lost Him: And Tales of the Army Frontier. Josephine Woempner Clifford McCrackin & James, George Wharton, 1858-1923. 1913. G. W. James.
Woman Who Loved John Wilkes Booth. Pamela Redford Russell. LC 77-18047. 6.95. Putnam.
Woman Who Loved John Wilkes Booth. Pamela Redford Russell. (Jove/HBJ book). 1979. 2.25 (ISBN 0-515-04869-0). Jove Pubns.
Woman Who Loved Paul: A Novel. Winthrop Neilson & Frances Fullerton Neilson. LC 77-12868. 1978. 6.95 (ISBN 0-385-13190-9). Doubleday.
Woman Who Loved the Moon & Other Stories. Elizabeth A. Lynn. 208p. (Orig.). 1981. pap. 2.25 (ISBN 0-425-05161-7). Berkley Pub.
Woman Who Never Did Wrong, and Other Stories. Katherine Eleanor Conway. LC 9-28697. T. J. Flynn & Company.
Woman Who Rode Away: And Other Stories. David Herbert Lawrence. LC 28-13907. 1928. A. A. Knopf.
Woman Who Serves. Myron Keats & Goulet, Edmund. LC 34-1470. Authors Publications, Inc.
Woman Who Slept with Demons. Eric Ericson. LC 80-51377. 1980. 9.95 (ISBN 0-312-88645-4). St. Martin's Press.
Woman Who Stole Everything, and Other Stories. Arnold Bennett. LC 74-17057. (Collected works of Arnold Bennett). 1974. (ISBN 0-518-19170-2). Books for Libraries Press.
Woman Who Stole Everything: And Other Stories. Arnold Bennett. LC 27-8463. George H. Doran Company.
Woman Who Trusted: A Story of Literary Life in New York. William Nathaniel Harben. H. Altemus Company.
Woman Who Was Changed, and Other Stories. Pearl Sydenstricker Buck. LC 78-69522. 8.95 (ISBN 0-690-01789-8). Crowell.
Woman Who Was No More: By Pierre Boileau and Thomas Narcejac; Translated from the French by Geoffrey Sainsbury. Pierre Boileau & Thomas Narcejac. LC 54-637435. 1954. Rinehart.
Woman Who Was Poor: A Contemporary Novel of the French 'eighties. Leon Bloy & Collins, I. J., Tr. LC 39-18660. 1939. Sheed & Ward.
Woman Who Went Away. Firth Haring. LC 80-28832. 12.95 (ISBN 0-03-059514-2). Holt, Rinehart and Winston.
Woman Will or Won't. Louise Platt Hauck. LC 42-23670. 1942. Dodd, Mead & Company.
Woman Wins. Robert Barr. LC 4-14890. 1904. F. A. Stokes Company.

Woman with a Future. Cecily Ullmann Sidgwick. LC 8-112643. ("The Newport series" of modern fiction). F. A. Stokes Company.
Woman with a Gun. George Harmon Coxe. LC 75-171135. 1972. 5.95 (ISBN 0-394-47441-4). Knopf.
Woman with a Past. Carlotta Baker. LC 40-33781. Phoenix Press.
Woman with a Past. Leona Slottman. LC 40-33781. 1940. Phoenix Press.
Woman with a Purpose. Anna Chapin Ray. LC 11-1856. 1911. 1.25. Little, Brown, and Company.
Woman with a Record. A Novel. Finley Anderson. LC 6-2451. 1896. G. W. Dillingham Co.
Woman with a Stone Heart: A Romance of the Philippine War. Oscar William Coursey. LC 14-11239. 0.75. The Educator Supply Company.
Woman with a Sword: Condensed and Simplified for Quick Reading by Ruth Adams Knight. Hollister Noble. LC 54-684782. (Hanover House headliners). 1954.
Woman with a Sword: The Biographical Novel of Anna Ella Carroll of Maryland. Hollister Noble. LC 48-7668. 1948. Doubleday.
Woman with a Thousand Children. Clara Viebig Cohn & Lunn, Brian, Tr. LC 30-9245. 1930. D. Appleton and Company.
Woman with Alabaster. Mabel Goode Frantz. LC 40-3962. Fleming H. Revell Company.
Woman with Good Intentions. Lottie Germaine. LC 7-18759. (Dillingham's American authors library, no. 12). 1896. G. W. Dillingham.
Woman with No Past: Translated from the French by Daphne Woodward. 1st American Ed. Serge Groussard. LC 54-109174. 1954. Dutton.
Woman with the Fan. Robert Smythe Hichens. LC 4-8273. 1904. F. A. Stokes Company.
Woman with the Little Fox, & Old Maid & the Dead Man, & Golden Buttons. Violette Leduc. Tr. by Derek Coltman. 1966. 4.95 o.p. FS&G.
Woman with the Little Fox: Three Novellas. Tr. from French by Derek Coltman. Violette Leduc. LC 66-25132. 1966. bds., 4.95. Farrar.
Woman with the Little Fox: Three Novellas. Tr. from French by Derek Coltman. Violette Leduc. (9649). 1968. Dell.
Woman with the Portuguese Basket. Eva-Lis Wuorio. LC 64-21915. (Rinehart suspense novel). 1964. Holt, Rinehart and Winston.
Woman with Two Smiles. Maurice Leblanc. LC 33-23361. The Macaulay Company.
Woman with White Eyes. Mary Borden. LC 30-320847. 1930. Doubleday, Doran & Company, Inc.
Woman Without a Country. Melbert Brinkerhoff Cary. LC 34-34583. 1934. Meador Publishing Company.
Woman Without Love. Andre Maurois. Tr. by Joan Charles. LC 45-8516. 1945. Harper & Brothers.
Woman Without Love. Frank Owen. LC 34-421753. 1933. G. H. Watt.
Woman Worth Winning. George Manville Fenn. LC 6-39510. (On cover: Globe library. vol. II. no. 280). 1898. Rand, McNally & Company.
Woman, 49. Francis Walton. LC 31-223999. Farrar & Rinehart, Incorporated.
Womanhunt. Harry Wilcox. LC 59-12458. 1959. Viking Press.
Woman's Age. Rachel Billington. LC 79-23723. 1980. 12.50 (ISBN 0-671-40115-7). Summit Books.
Woman's Atonement. Adah M Howard. N. L. Munro.
Woman's Courier: Being a Tale of the Famous Forty Conspiracy of 1696. William Joseph Yeoman. LC 11-7173. 1896. Stone & Kimball.
Woman's Doctor. Russell Boltar. LC 56-134977. (Ace double size books, D-163). 1956. Ace Books.
Woman's Doctor. Russell Boltar. LC 56-8691. 1956. J. Messner.
Woman's Doctor. Walter Lennox. LC 33-3084. 1933. W. Faro.
Woman's Doing. Jessie Hunter Brown. 1887. Standard Publishing Company.
Woman's Doing. Jessie Hunter Brown Pounds. LC 6-18935. 1887. Standard Publishing Company.
Woman's Duplicity: A Realistic Novel. Paul James Duff. (On cover: Nile 25c. series, v. 1). 1891. Nile Publishing Co.
Woman's Error. Charlotte Mary Brame. (On cover: Lovell's library. v. 17 no. 815). J. W. Lovell Company.
Woman's Evangel. Eva Kinney Griffith. LC 7-292. Woman's Temperance Publishing Association.
Woman's Eyes. Gus Weill. LC 74-19423. 1975. 7.95. Dial Press.
Woman's Face: Or, A Lakeland Mystery. Florence Alice Price James. (On cover: Lovell's library, no. 1180). 1888. J. W. Lovell Company.
Woman's Face: Or, A Lakeland Mystery. Florence Alice Price James. (On cover: Seaside library. Pocket ed., no. 1087). 1888. G. Munro.
Woman's Fault: Or, After Many Years. Evelyn Gray. (On cover: Munro's library, popular novels, v. 1, no. 58). G. Munro.
Woman's Freindship: A Story of Domestic Life. Grace Aguilar. LC 7-16182. 1852. D. Appleton & Company.
Woman's Friendship: A Story of Domestic Life. Grace Aguilar. LC 5-42980. 1857. D. Appleton & Company.
Woman's Hand: Or, Detective Wit Against Lawyer's Wiles. John Russell Coryell. (On cover: Secret service series, no. 37). 1890. Street & Smith.
Woman's Heart. A Novel. Annie French Hector. (On cover: Lovell's international series, no. 82). 1890. J. W. Lovell Company.
Woman's Heart: Manuscripts Found in the Papers of Katherine Peshconet and Edited by Her Executor Olive Ransom Pseud.... Kate Stephens. LC 6-11548. 1906. Doubleday, Page & Company.
Woman's Honor. Edith Pinero Green. (Dell Book.). 1977. 1.25. (ISBN 0-440-12800-5). Dell Pub. Co.
Woman's Honor. A Novel. Ernest A Young. (On cover: Lovell's library. v. 13, no. 691). 1885. J. W. Lovell Company.
Woman's House. Harry Lutf Verne Fletcher. LC 48-6205. 1948. J. Messner.
Woman's Inheritance. Amanda Minnie Douglas. LC 7-124269. 1886. Lee and Shepard.
Woman's Kingdom. A Love Story. Dinah Maria Mulock Craik. LC 6-31072. 1868. Harper & Brothers.
Woman's Life. Tr. from French Introd. by H. N. P. Sloman. Guy De Maupassant. LC 65-582611. (Penguin classics, L161). Penguin.
Woman's Love. Charlotte Mary Brame. LC 49-56142. (Calumet series, no. 5). Homewood Pub. Co.
Woman's Love Story. Alice Mangold Diehl. LC 6175. (On cover: Bertha Clay library, no. 29). 1900. Street & Smith.
Woman's Love-Story. Alice Mangold Diehl & Braene, Charlotte Monica. (On cover: Lovell's library, v. 19, no. 364). 1887. J. W. Lovell Company.
Woman's Man. Marjorie Patterson. LC 19-155711. 1.60. George H. Doran Company.
Womans' Mistake: Formerly Published Under the Title On a Margin. Julius Chambers. LC 6-23336. (On cover: Neely's popular library, no. 72). 1896. F. T. Neely.
Woman's Mistake: Or, Jacques De Trevannes. by mary neal sherwood, from the french of madame angele dussard... ed. Angele Dussaud Bary d'Arnex & Sherwood, Mrs. Mary (Neal) Tr. LC 6-392543. T. B. Peterson & Brothers.
Woman's Perils: Or, Driven from Home. James C. Cook. T.B. Peterson & Brothers.
Woman's Perpetual Love Calendar. Peggy Burke & Evan Burke. 192p. 1974. pap. 1.95 o.p. (ISBN 0-87056-381-5, 6381). Brandon.
Woman's Place. Anne Eliot Crompton. LC 78-598. (Illus.). 7.95 (ISBN 0-316-16144-6). Little, Brown.
Woman's Place. Ann Helming. LC 62-179946. 1962. Coward-McCann.
Woman's Place. Ed. by L. M. Schulman. (Adult Ser). 416p. 1974. Repr. lib. bdg. 10.95 o.p. (ISBN 0-8161-6244-1, Large Print Bks). G K Hall.
Womans Privilege: A Romantic Novel. Francis Evans Baily. LC 36-17714. 1936. The Macaulay Company.
Woman's Ransom. Frederick William Robinson. (Union square library. v. 4. no. 57). 1879. N. L. Munro.
Woman's Reason: A Novel. William Dean Howells. LC 16-75651. Houghton Mifflin Company.
Woman's Reason: A Novel. William Dean Howells. LC 7-5676. 1883. J. R. Osgood and Company.
Woman's Revenge. Robert Granger. LC 1-29712. The Abbey Press.
Woman's Revenge: Or, The Mystery of the Black Pines. A Popularnovel. J. F Reichhard. LC 7-30656. (sunnyside series, no. 49 i. e. 48). 1892. J. S. Ogilvie.
Woman's Rights and Woman's Mission. Mellisa Ann McCowat Lanier. LC 14-4931. 1908. McCowat-Mercer Printing Co.
Woman's Side. Frances Warren. LC 8-33688. 1890. The Manhattan Publishing Company.
Woman's Story. Brian Dyer, pseud. LC 76-41273. 1977. 7.95 (ISBN 0-88405-380-6). Mason/Charter.
Woman's Story: As Told by Twenty American Women; with Portraits and Sketches of the Authors. Ed. by Laura Carter Holloway Langford. LC 7-13871. 1889. J. B. Alden.
Woman's Talent: And Other Stories. Julia Morrell Hunt. LC 7-90432. (On cover: The Green paper series. no. 27). 1891. De Wolfe, Fiske & Co.
Woman's Temptation. A Novel. Charlotte Mary Brame. (On cover: Seaside library. Pocket ed. no. 951). G. Munro.
Woman's Temptation. A Novel. Charlotte Mary Brame. (primrose series, no. 9). 1890. Street & Smith.
Woman's Temptation. A Novel. Charlotte Mary Brame. LC 44-38285. (On cover: Seaside library. Pocket ed. No. 459). G. Munro.
Woman's Trials: Or, Tales and Sketches from the Life Around Us. Timothy Shay Arthur. LC 6-3833. (On cover: Lovell's library, no. 496). J. W. Lovell Company.
Woman's Vengeance. Michael Angelo Holmes. (Lovell's library, vo. 14, no. 743). 1886. J. W. Lovell Company.
Woman's Vengeance. A Novel. Michael Angelo Holmes. LC 7-5179. G. W. Ogilvie.
Woman's Victory: And Other Stories. Jozua Marius Willen Van Der Poorten Schwartz. LC 7-35218. 1907. D. Appleton and Company.
Woman's War. Charlotte Mary Brame. LC 44-382863. (On cover: Seaside library. Pocket ed. No. 295). G. Munro.
Woman's War. Charlotte Mary Brame. LC 44-378258. (On cover: Lovell's library, v. 20, no. 969). J. W. Lovell Company.
Woman's War. Charlotte Mary Brame. LC 44-378265. (On cover: Seaside library. Pocket ed. No. 952). G. Munro.
Woman's War: A Novel. Warwick Deeping. 1907. Harper & Brothers.
Woman's Way. Charles Garvice. LC 16-6480. 1914. Hodder and Stoughton.
Woman's Way: A Novel. Charles Somerville & Buchanan, Thompson, 1877- LC 9-28045. 1909. W. J. Watt & Company.
Woman's Web. A Novel. Christal V Maitland. LC 7-20124. 1884. G. W. Carleton & Co. Etc.
Woman's Whims: Or, The Female Barometer. Tr. from the French of X. B. Sainte... Joseph Xavier Boniface Known As Saintine & Robinson, Fayette, D. 1859, Tr. LC 8-373218. 1850. Baker and Scribner.
Woman's Will. Anne Warner French. LC 4-8268. 1904. Little, Brown, and Company.
Woman's Woman. Nalbro Isadorah Bartley. LC 19-132967. 1.75. Small, Maynard & Company.
Woman's Word; and How She Kept It. Virginia Frances Townsend. 1879. Lee and Shepard.
Woman's Word; and How She Kept It. Virginia Frances Townsend. Lothrop, Lee & Shepard Co.
Woman's Wrongs: A History of Mary and Fidelia. R. S Hume. 1872. Printed by B. Thurston and Company.
Womb to Let. Joseph Johnson. LC 74-171365. 1973. National Press.
Women. Mildred Barker. LC 70-183717. (Illus.). 1972. 5.95. Eakins Press.
Women. Charles Bukowski. LC 78-21998. 1978. 14.00. (ISBN 0-87685-391-2) (ISBN 0-87685-390-4) (ISBN 0-87685-392-0). Black Sparrow Press.
Women. Booth Tarkington. LC 74-178464. (Short story index reprint series). 1971. (ISBN 0-8369-4064-4). Books for Libraries Press.
Women. Booth Tarkington. LC 25-27730. 1925. Doubleday, Page & Company.
Women - Feminist Stories by New Fiction Authors. Photos by Mariette Ollier et al. 1971. 4.95 o.p.; pap. 2.50 o.p. Eakins.
Women Against Men. Margaret Storm Jameson. LC 33-3597. 1933. A. A. Knopf.
Women Also Dream. Ethel Edith Mannin. LC 37-166543. 1937. G. P. Putnam's Sons.
Women & Bestiality. Richard E. Geis. pap. 1.95 o.p. (ISBN 0-87682-181-6, 7181). Barclay Hse.
Women and Children First. Sally Benson. LC 44-40024. 1943. Random House.
Women & Men, Men & Women: An Anthology of Short Stories. William Smart. LC 74-23280. 1975. 4.95. St. Martin's Press.
Women and Men Together: An Anthology of Short Fiction. Dawson Gaillard & John Mosier. LC 77-78566. (Illus.). 7.50 (ISBN 0-395-25032-3). Houghton Mifflin.
Women and Monks. Iosif Kallinikov. Tr. by Kirwan, Patrick. LC 30-302264. Harcourt, Brace and Company.
Women and Peter: A Novel. Elissa Landi. LC 41-22070. 1941. Alliance Book Corporation.
Women and the Sun. Pierre Gascar, pseud. LC 76-54791. 1977. 16.00 (ISBN 0-8371-9360-5). Greenwood Press.
Women and the Sun. Stories Tr. from French by Merloyd Lawrence, Others. 1st Eng. Language Ed. Pierre Gascar, pseud. LC 64-17476. 1965. bds., 4.95. Atlantic-Little.
Women and Thomas Harrow. John Phillips Marquand. LC 58-10691. 1958. Little, Brown.
Women and Vodka: Edited by Mark Merrill Pseud. Ed. by David Markson. LC 56-4759. (Royal Pyramid book, R210). 1956. Pyramid Books.
Women and Wives. Harvey Fergusson. LC 24-107038. 1924. A. A. Knopf.
Women and Yamsey Loggers: A Novel. 1st Ed. Carl W Lange. LC 52-11670. 1953. Exposition Press.
Women Appeared to Me. Renee Vivien. LC 76-45689. (Illus.). 1976. 4.00. Naiad Press.
Women Are Born to Listen. Norah Cordner James. LC 37-2940. The Macaulay Company.
Women Are Devils. Nat Joseph Ferber. LC 32-9030. Farrar & Rinehart, Incorporated.
Women Are Difficult: A Kent Wilburn Romance. Maysie Greig. LC 34-37993. Doubleday, Doran & Company, Inc.
Women Are Freight. Roy Booth. LC 26-18132. Godwin.
Women Are Like That. Alice Elinor Lambert. LC 34-3288. The Vanguard Press.
Women Are Like That: Short Stories. Edmee Elizabeth Monica De La Pasture. LC 31-10645. 1930. Harper & Brothers.
Women Are Necessary: A Novel. John Held. LC 31-5699. The Vanguard Press.
Women Are Queer. Grace Sartwell Mason. LC 77-37278. (Short story index reprint series). 1971. (ISBN 0-8369-4089-X). Books for Libraries Press.
Women Are Queer. Grace Sartwell Mason. LC 32-16253. 1932. D. Appleton and Company.
Women Are Strange: And Other Stories. Frederick William Robinson. LC 7-42174. (Harper's Franklin square library, no. 394). 1884. Harper & Brothers.
Women at Pine Creek. A. McKay. (O.s.i.). 1966. 5.95 o.s.i. (ISBN 0-02-583460-6). Macmillan.
Women at Pine Creek. A. McKay. (O.s.i.). 1966. 5.95 o.s.i. (ISBN 0-02-583460-6). Macmillan.
Women at Pine Creek: A Novel. Allis McKay. LC 66-219806. 1966. 5.95. Macmillan.
Women at the Pump. Knut Hamsun. LC 78-5342. 10.00 (ISBN 0-374-29280-9). Farrar Straus Giroux.
Women at the Pump. Knut Hamsun & Chater, Arthur G., Tr. LC 28-22359. 1928. A. A. Knopf.
Women at Work. Kennedy, Margaret. LC 66-72249. (B 66-11635). 1966. Macmillan.
Women! From Mars. Christopher Langley. LC 76-15099. (Illus.). 8.95. Sun Light Press.
Women in Black. Kane Sullivan. LC 46-829198. 1946. Dorance & Company.
Women in Heat. Tony Trelos, pseud. 176p. pap. 1.95 o.p. (6107). Brandon.
Women in Love. David Herbert Lawrence. 1976. 2.95 (ISBN 0-14-004260-1). Penguin.
Women in Love. David Herbert Lawrence. LC 22-2278. 1922. T. Seltzer.
Women in Love. David Herbert Lawrence. LC 33-329259. 1933. Grosset & Dunlap.
Women in Love. David Herbert Lawrence. LC 37-274063. (Half-title: The modern library of the world's best books). 1937. The Modern Library.
Women in Love. Kathleen Thompson Norris. LC 35-1940. 1935. Douleday, Doran & Company, Inc.
Women in Love with Women. Karena Wilton. pap. 1.95 o.s.i. (OPS-39). Olympia.
Women in Passion. Jan Maat. 1975. pap. 2.00 (ISBN 0-87164-056-2). William-F.
Women in the Case. Louis Tracy. LC 28-12546. E. J. Clode, Inc.
Women in the Mirror. Pat M. Carr. LC 77-24965. (Iowa School of Letters Award for Short Fiction). 1977. 8.95. (ISBN 0-87745-081-1) (ISBN 0-87745-082-X). University of Iowa Press.
Women in the Shadows. Ann Bannon. LC 75-13751. (Homosexuality). 1975. 9.00 (ISBN 0-405-07407-7). Arno Press.
Women in the Shadows. facsimile ed. Ann Dannon. Ed. by Jonathan Katz. LC 75-13751. (Homosexuality Ser.). 1975. Repr. of 1959 ed. 9.00x (ISBN 0-405-07407-7). Ayer Co.
Women in the Sun. Benedict Thielen. LC 33-30005. The Bobbs-Merrill Company.
Women in the Wall. Julia O'Faolain. LC 75-1355. (Illus.). 1975. 7.95 (ISBN 0-670-77853-2). Viking Press.
Women in the Wall. Julia O'Faolain. 1976. (pbk.) 1.75 (ISBN 0-380-00592-1). Avon Books.
Women in the Wind. Francis Walton. LC 35-20111. Farrar & Rinehart, Incorporated.
Women in White. Peter Delius. LC 34-35695. J. B. Lippincott Company.
Women in White. Frank Gill Slaughter. LC 73-83673. 1974. 7.95 (ISBN 0-385-08568-0). Doubleday.
Women, Inc. Jane Kesner Morris. LC 46-67723. 1946. H. Holt and Company.
Women Like Men. Allan Leigh. LC 26-7839. The Macaulay Company.
Women Live Too Long. Vina Delmar. LC 32-9242. Harcourt, Brace and Company.
Women Love but Once. Mabel Dana Lyon. LC 33-19704. The Macaulay Company.
Women May Learn. Florence Jeannette Baier Ward. LC 33-31660. 1933. Macrae Smith Company.
Women Money Buys. Maysie Greig. LC 32-808. 1931. L. MacVeagh, Dial Press Inc.
Women Must Love. Leonora Baccante. LC 32-5022. 1932. The Vanguard Press.
Women Must Love. Julia Hart Lyon. LC 37-147349. 1937. E. P. Dutton & Co., Inc.

Women Must Weep. Ruth Adams Knight. LC 41-22358. Hale, Cushman & Flint.
Women Must Weep. Ruth Adams Yingling Knight. LC 41-22358. Hale, Cushman & Flint.
Women Must Weep: A Novel... Edgar Fawcett. LC 6-38777. (library of choice fiction). Laird & Lee.
Women Must Work: A Novel. Richard Aldington. LC 34-39748. 1934. Doubleday, Doran & Company, Inc.
Women of Brewster Place. Gloria Naylor. LC 82-24533. 1983. 5.95 (ISBN 0-14-006690-X). Penguin Books.
Women of Brewster Place: A Novel in Seven Stories. Gloria Naylor. LC 81-69969. 204p. 1982. 13.95 (ISBN 0-670-77855-9). Viking Pr.
Women of Champion City. Doris Davis. LC 51-7928. 1951. Sloane.
Women of Dallas. Burt Hirschfeld. (Dallas Ser.: Vol. 2). 288p. (Orig.). 1981. pap. 2.75 (ISBN 0-553-14497-9). Bantam.
Women of Eden. Marilyn Harris. LC 79-19757. 12.95 (ISBN 0-399-12478-0). Putnam.
Women of La Vina. Kay Richardson. LC 74-34011. 1975. 4.95 (ISBN 0-517-52164-4). Lenox Hill Press.
Women of Magliano: Translated by Archibald Colquhoun. Mario Tobino. LC 54-10491. 1954. Putnam.
Women of Peasenhall. R. J. White. LC 75-105242. (Novel of Suspense Ser). 1970. 4.95 o.p. (ISBN 0-06-014617-6, HarpT). Har-Row.
Women of the Family. Margaret Culkin Banning. LC 26-154723. 1926. Harper & Brothers.
Women of the Fatherland. Ludwig Alban Erbacher. LC 32-4220. Wetzel Publishing Co., Inc.
Women of the Plains. Kate Sullivan. (Leisure Books). 1977. 1.75. Nordon Pubns.
Women of the Shadows. Ann Cornelisen. (Illus.). 1976. 8.95 (ISBN 0-316-15745-7, Pub. by Atlantic Monthly Pr). Little.
Women of Wonder: Science Fiction Stories by Women About Women. Ed. by Pamela Sargent. LC 74-16044. 1975. (pbk.) 1.95 (ISBN 0-394-71041-X). Vintage Books.
Women on Horseback. William E. Barrett. 1970. pap. 0.95 o.p. (0502-09043). Curtis.
Women on the Porch. Caroline Gordon. LC 78-164524. 1971. (ISBN 0-8154-0393-3). Cooper Square Publishers.
Women on the Porch. Caroline Gordon. LC 44-45039. 1944. C. Scribner's Sons.
Women on the Wall. Wallace Earle Stegner. LC 49-50344. 1950. Houghton Mifflin.
Women on the Wall. Wallace Earle Stegner. LC 80-22461. 1981. 16.50 (ISBN 0-8032-4111-9) (ISBN 0-8032-9110-8). University of Nebraska Press.
Women: Or, Chronicles of the Late War. Mary Tucker Magill. 1871. Turnbull Brothers.
Women: Or, Pour et Contre. Charles Robert Maturin. LC 78-12330. (Ireland, from the Act of Union, 1800, to the Death of Parnell, 1891). 1978. 96.00 (ISBN 0-8240-3462-7). Garland Pub.
Women; or, Pour et Contre. A Tale. Charles Robert Maturin. LC 7-17590. 1818. Published by Moses Thomas (Johnson's Head) No. Chesnut-Street. G. Maxwell, Printer.
Women Plus Boys Equals Sex. Nora Saunders. pap. 2.45 o.p. (4023). Cameo.
Women Swore Revenge. Inez Haynes Irwin. LC 46-7071. 1946. Random House.
Women to Love: A Romance of the Underworld. Harry Sinclair Drago. LC 31-19274. Amour Press, Inc.
Women We Marry. Arthur Stanwood Pier. LC 14-5475. 1914. Houghton Mifflin Company.
Women Who Laugh. Ella May Powell. 1895. The Transatlantic Publishing Company.
Women Who Prey on Boys. James Rolland. 1972. pap. 1.95 o.s.i. (V1075T, Venus). Grove.
Women Who Seduce Boys. Beatrice Bartheleme. 225p. pap. 1.95 o.p. (7135). Barclay Hse.
Women Who Wait. Elaine Bissell. LC 78-2905. 8.95 (ISBN 0-87131-251-4). M. Evans.
Women Who Wait. Elaine Bissell. 1979. 1.95 (ISBN 0-445-04415-2). Popular Librar.
Women Who Went Away. Firth Haring. LC 80-28832. 228p. 1981. 12.95 (ISBN 0-03-059514-2). HR&W.
Women Will Be Doctors. Elizabeth Head Fetter. LC 40-27495. Random House.
Women Will Be Doctors. Hannah Lees, pseud. LC 40-274959. Random House.
Women with and Women Without: A Novel. Carol Murray. LC 82-2446. (American Dust Series; 14). 1982. 10.95 (ISBN 0-913218-81-2). Dustbooks.
Women with Nets. Richard Worthington Post. LC 32-6428. Brentano's.
Women with Wings: A Novel of the Modern Day Aviatrix. Genevieve Haugen. LC 35-8181. The Ganesha Publishers.
Women, Women, Everywhere. Gene Markey. (60-212). 1965. Macfadden.
Women Won't Let You. Alban Maurice Emley. LC 51-15541. (Gusto issues). 1950. House-Warven.
Women Writing. Denys Val Batter. LC 79-4842. 1979. 8.95 (ISBN 0-312-88787-6). St. Martin's Press.
Women's Barracks. Tereska Torres. LC 51-16296. (Gold medal book, 132). 1950. Fawcett Publications.
Women's Battalion. 2nd ed. W. A. Ballinger, pseud. 1969. pap. 0.75 o.p. (74-513). Lancer.
Women's Doctor. Frank Haskell. 1969. pap. 0.60 o.p. (60-401). Manor Bks.
Women's Gun. (Illus.). 1975. pap. 1.50 (ISBN 0-88447-030-X). Diana Pr.
Women's House. Arlene Stone. LC 78-25662. (Illus.). 1978. pap. 3.00 (ISBN 0-931588-05-7). Allegany Mtn Pr.
Women's Husbands. I. The Barber of Midas. II. The False Prince. III. Narciccus. LC 8-37115. 1880. J. B. Lip; Incott & Co.
Women's Room. Marilyn French. LC 77-24918. 10.95 (ISBN 0-671-40010-X). Summit Books.
Women's Tragedies. Henry Dawson Lowry. (On cover: Keynotes series no. 9). 1895. Roberts Bros.; Etc., Etc.
Women's Wiles: The 1979 Mystery Writers of America Anthology. Michele B. Slung & Mystery Writers of America. LC 79-1835. 9.95 (ISBN 0-15-198421-2). Harcourt, Brace, Jovanovich.
Women's Work: A Novel. Anne Tolstoi Wallach. LC 81-38417. 13.95 (ISBN 0-453-00403-2). New American Library.
Won and Not One. Emily Lucas Blackall. LC 6-131334. 1891. J. B. Lippincott Company.
Won at Last: A Novel. Beatrice Marean. LC 7-20441. 1892. Donohue, Henneberry & Co.
Won at West Point: A Romance of the Hudson. Williston Fish. LC 6-41214. 1883. Rand, McNally & Co.
Won by a Bicycle: Or, A Race for a Wife. Thomas Alexander Hyde. 1895. Greater Boston Publishing Co.
Won by a Woman La Maestrina Degli Operai: A Story from Life. Edmondo De Amicis. Tr. by Mantellini, Gaetano. LC 6-9412. Laird & Lee.
Won by Love: Or, They Heard His Voice. Seth S. Wood. American Tract Society.
Won by Waiting. Ada Ellen Bayly. (On cover: Seaside library. Pocket ed., no. 1173.). G. Munro.
Won on the Homestretch. A Novel. M. C. Williams. (On cover: The Manhattan series, no. 14). A. L. Burt.
Won on the Homestretch. A Novel. M. C. Williams. (select series, no. 60). 1890. Street & Smith.
Won Ton Ton: the Dog Who Saved Hollywood. E. M Corder. 1976. (pbk.) 1.50 (ISBN 0-671-80515-0). Pocket Books.
Won Under Protest. A Romance. Celia Emmeline Gardner. LC 7-310. 1896. G. W. Dillingham Co.
Wonder. John Davys Beresford. LC 17-820066. 1.40. George H. Doran Company.
Wonder Book: For Girls and Boys. Nathaniel Hawthorne. LC 4721. W. B. Conkey Company.
Wonder-Book of Horses. James A. Baldwin. LC 3-288477. 1903. The Century Co.
Wonder Book of Travellers' Tales. Henry C. Adams. (Black & Gold Lib). (Illus.). 1942. 6.95 (ISBN 0-87140-998-4). Liveright.
Wonder Cruise. Ursula Bloom. LC 34-4349. E. P. Dutton & Co., Inc.
Wonder Girl: A Tourist Tale of California. Anna E Satterlee. LC 15-27932. 1915. Sherman, French & Company.
Wonder Hero. John Boynton Priestley. LC 33-22935. 1933. Harper & Brothers.
Wonder Jungle: A Novel. Fran Podulka. LC 73-78600. 1973. 6.95 (ISBN 0-399-11198-0). Putnam.
Wonder Lady. Ella Lowery Moseley. LC 11-16258. 1911. Lothrop, Lee & Shepard Co.
Wonder of All the Gay World: A Novel of the Life and Loves of Robert Burns. James Barke. LC 50-8416. (His Immortal memory v. 3). (Illus.). 1950. Macmillan.
Wonder Tales from Baltic Wizards: From the German and English. Frances Jenkins Olcott. LC 28-24516. 1928. Longmans, Green and Co.
Wonder Tales: Pandora and the Mysterious Box; Midas, the King Who Turned Everything into Gold; Pegasus, the Winged Horse. Nathaniel Hawthorne & Stead, William Thomas, 1849-Ed. LC 8-23108. 1908. The Penn Publishing Company.
Wonder Winter. Robert Neill. 1970. pap. 0.75 o.p. (0502-07079). Curtis.
Wonder Woman. Mae Van Norman Long. LC 17-29137. 1917. The Penn Publishing Company.
Wonder-Worker. Dan Jacobson. LC 73-20406. 1974. 5.95 (ISBN 0-316-45562-8). Little, Brown.
Wonder-Worker. Dan Jacobson. 1977. 1.95 (ISBN 0-14-004077-3). Penguin Books.
Wonder-Worker. Dan Jacobson. LC 77-368604. 1977. 1.95 (ISBN 0-14-004077-3). Penguin.
Wonderflower of Utik. Kurt Mahr. (Perry Rhodan, 105). Ace.
Wonderful Adventures of Captain Priest: A Tale of but Few Incidents, and No Plot in Particular. With Other Legends. Samuel Adams Hammett. LC 76-166740. 1971. (ISBN 0-403-01374-7). Scholarly Press.
Wonderful Adventures of Captain Priest: A Tale of but Few Incidents, and No Plot in Particular. Samuel Adams Hammett. LC 7-932. 1855. Redfield.
Wonderful Adventures of Captain Priest; a Tale of but Few Incidents, and No Plot in Particular. With Other Legends. Samuel Adams Hammett. LC 7-932. 1855. Redfield.
Wonderful Adventures of Phra the Phoenician. Edwin Lester Linden Arnold. LC 41-42323. A. L. Burt Company.
Wonderful Adventures of Phra the Phoenician. Edwin Lester Linden Arnold. LC 20-265824. 1917. G. P. Putnam's Sons.
Wonderful Adventures of Phra the Phoenician. Edwin Lester Linden Arnold. LC 80-19173. (Newcastle Forgotten Fantasy library; v. 11). 1980. 10.95 (ISBN 0-87877-510-2). Borgo Press.
Wonderful Adventures of Phra the Phoenician. Retold by Edwin Lester Arnold... Edwin Lester Linden Arnold. LC 6-2068. (On cover: Harper's Franklin square library, no. 686). 1890. Harper & Brothers.
Wonderful Clouds. Francoise Sagan, pseud. LC 62-7805. 1974. (pbk.) 0.95. Popular Library.
Wonderful Country. Tom Lea. LC 79-9253. (Series: Gregg Press Western Fiction Series.). (Illus.). 1979. 9.95 (ISBN 0-8398-2587-0). Gregg Press.
Wonderful Country: A Novel. Tom Lea. LC 52-9093. (Illus.). 1952. Little, Brown.
Wonderful Dog and Other Tales. Mikhail Mikhailovich Zoshchenko. LC 72-90320. 1973. 10.00 (ISBN 0-88355-029-6). Hyperion Press.
Wonderful Flower of Woxindon. An Historical Romance of the Time of Queen Elizabeth. Joseph Spillmann. LC 8-140605. 1896. B. Herder.
Wonderful Gift. Clara McKinney Edwards. LC 27-21326. The Four Seas Company.
Wonderful History of Peter Schlemihl: The Man Who Lost His Shadow. Adelbert Von Chamisso. Tr. by Hedge, Frederic Henry. Ed. by Alger, William Rounseville. LC 99-3253. (On cover: Home and school library). 1899. Ginn & Company.
Wonderful History of Peter Schlemihl. original ed. Adelbert Von Chamisso. Tr. by Howitt, William. LC 6-23327. 1844. Burgess & Striger.
Wonderful Mrs. Ingram. Harlan Ware. LC 48-8548. 1948. Whittlesey House.
Wonderful Romance: From the French of Pierre De Coulevain Pseud.... Helene Favre De Coulevain & Ward, Alice Hall, Tr. LC 14-19688. 1914. 1.35. Dodd, Mead and Company.
Wonderful Scheme of Mr. Christopher Thorne. Harry Stephen Keeler. LC 36-296108. E. P. Dutton and Company, Inc.
Wonderful Sibleys. William Maier. LC 56-9471. 1956. Scribner.
Wonderful Summer. William Arthur Neubauer. 1946. Gramcery Publishing Co.
Wonderful Visit. Herbert George Wells. LC 8-36639. 1895. Macmillian and Co.
Wonderful Visit. Herbert George Wells. LC 77-84274. (Lost Race and Adult Fantasy Fiction). 1978. 18.00 (ISBN 0-405-11013-8). Arno Press.
Wonderful Way. 1st Ed. Frank A Clarvoe. LC 56-105084. 1956. Holt.
Wonderful Wheel: A Novel. Mary Tracy Earle. 1896. The Century Co.
Wonderful Year. William John Locke. LC 16-201116. 1916. John Lane Company.
Wondering Moon. George Weston. LC 26-12979. 1926. Dodd, Mead and Company.
Wonderland. Joyce Carol Oates. LC 72-155669. 12.95 (ISBN 0-8149-0659-1). Vanguard.
Wonderland: Novel. Joyce Carol Oates. LC 72-155669. 1971. 7.95 (ISBN 0-8149-0659-1). Vanguard Press.
Wonderland of John Devlin: A Novel. Clarence P Milligan. LC 45-2280. 1945. The Christopher Publishing House.
Wondermakers 2. Ed. by Robert Hoskins. LC 74-170296. (Fawcett premier book). 1974. (pbk.). 1.25. Fawcett Publications.
Wonders. Karen Snow. (Poets Ser.). 1980. pap. 6.95 (ISBN 0-14-042265-X). Penguin.
Wonders. Karen Snow. LC 79-20439. 79p. 1980. 11.95 (ISBN 0-670-77917-2). Viking Pr.
Wonders Will Never Cease: And Other Stories. Mary Xavier Queen. LC 7-42412. 1898. Gallery & McCann.
Wonderworks: Science Fiction & Fantasy Art. Michael Whelan. Ed. by Polly Freas & Kelly Freas. LC 79-12575. (Illus.). 1979. 13.95 o.p. (ISBN 0-915442-75-2, Starblaze); pap. 9.95 (ISBN 0-915442-74-4, Starblaze); collector's edition 30.00 (ISBN 0-915442-83-3). Donning Co.
Wondrous Gift: A Christmas Story. Daisy Newman. (Orig.). 1982. pap. text ed. write for info. (ISBN 0-941308-01-4). Religious Soc Friends.
Wondrous Moment Then. Rowena Rutherford Farrar. LC 68-10058. 1968. Holt, Rinehart and Winston.
Wondrous Strange: A Novel. Emma Newby. LC 7-261128. (On cover: Turners' select novels, no. 4). Turner Brothers & Co.
Wondrous Wife. Charles Marriott. LC 13-25052. The Bobbs-Merrill Company.
Wontus: Or, The Corps of Observation. William M Runkel. LC 8-96673. 1874. J. B. Lippincott & Co.
Wood and Stone: A Romance. John Cowper Powys. LC 15-23368. 1915. G. A. Shaw.
Wood and the Trees. Mary Elgin, pseud. 1976. (pbk.) 1.25. Bantam Books.
Wood and the Trees. Mary Elgin, pseud. LC 66-31994. 1967. M. S. Mill Co.; Distributed by Morrow.
Wood Beyond the World. William Morris. LC 71-189346. 1972. 3.50 (ISBN 0-486-22791-X). Dover Publications.
Wood Beyond the World. pocket ed.; new impression. ed. William Morris. LC 36-29352. (Longmans' pocket library). 1924. Longmans, Green and Co.
Wood-Carver of 'Lympus. Mary Ella Waller. 1904. Little, Brown, and Company.
Wood-Carver of 'Lympus. Mary Ella Waller. LC 25-715012. 1912. Little, Brown, and Company.
Wood-Carver of 'Lympus. Mary Ella Waller. LC 29-936756. 1929. Little, Brown, and Company.
Wood Fire in No. 3. Francis Hopkinson Smith. LC 76-94743. (Short story index reprint series). (Illus.). 1969. Books for Libraries Press.
Wood Fire in No. 3. Francis Hopkinson Smith. LC 5-34173. 1905. C. Scribner's Sons.
Wood, Hay and Stubble. Kate Waterman Hamilton. LC 7-948. Presbyterian Board of Publication.
Wood Heat. Allan A. Swenson. 1979. pap. 2.50 (ISBN 0-449-14248-5, GM). Fawcett.
Wood-Nymph. Eden Phillpotts. LC 37-6519. E. P. Dutton & Co., Inc.
Wood of the Hanging Templar: Le Bois Du Templier Pendu. Henri Beraud. Tr. by Sloan, Samuel. LC 30-258247. 1930. The Macmillan Company.
Wood-Pile Recollections. Charles Louis Olds. LC 7-33192. The Abbey Press.
Wood-Rangers: Or, The Trappers of Sonora. Louis De Bellemare. Tr. by Reid, Mayne. LC 12-37948. 1892. G. W. Dillingham.
Wood Rangers: Or, The Trappers of Sonora. Thomas Mayne Reid. LC 51-48704. M. A. Donohue.
Wood-Rangers: Or, The Trappers of Sonora. Thomas Mayne Reid. LC 44-43268. 1872. Carleton.
Wood Shed. Rayner Heppenstall. 1980. pap. 4.95 (ISBN 0-7145-0616-8). Riverrun NY.
Woodbridge, 1946. Martin Boris. 288p. 1981. pap. 3.25 (ISBN 0-441-90865-9). Ace Bks.
Woodburn Grange. William Howitt. LC 75-1511. (Victorian Fiction: Novels of Faith and Doubt; V. 61). 1975. 35.00 (ISBN 0-8240-1585-1). Garland Pub.
Woodcarver and Death. Tr. from Swedish by George C. Schoolfield. Hagar Olsson. LC 65-24187. (Nordic tr. ser.) Bibl.). 1965. 4.00. Univ of Wis. Pr.
Woodcarver of Tyrol. Edmund Aloysius Walsh. LC 35-23924. 1935. Harper & Brothers.
Woodchuck Hunt. Ulrich Becher. LC 77-3063. 10.00 (ISBN 0-517-51624-1). Crown Publishers.
Woodcliff. Harriet Burn McKeever. LC 7-16311. 1865. Lindsay & Blakiston.
Woodcraft. William Gilmore Simms. LC 44-32802.
Woodcraft. William Gilmore Simms. 1974. Repr. of 1882 ed. lib. bdg. 30.00 (ISBN 0-8414-8071-0). Folcroft.
Woodcraft. William Gilmore Simms. LC 68-20022. (Americans in Fiction Ser.). Repr. of 1856 ed. lib. bdg. 18.00 (ISBN 0-8398-1862-9). Irvington.
Woodcraft Girls in the City. Lillian Elizabeth Becker Roy. LC 18-118240. 1.25. George H. Doran Company.
Woodcraft; or, Hawks About the Devocote: A Story of the South at the Close of the Revolution. William Gilmore Simms. LC 61-8921. (Norton library, N507). 1961. Norton.
Woodcraft; or, Hawks About the Devocote: A Story of the South at the Close of the Revolution. new and rev. ed. William Gilmore Simms. LC 8-13046. 1854. Redfield.
Woodcraft: Or, Hawks About the Dovecote: a Story of the South at the Close of the Revolution. new and rev. ed. William Gilmore Simms. LC 76-9054. (Simms, William Gilmore, 1806-1870. Simms Revolutionary War Novels: Vol. 8). 1976. 21.00 (ISBN 0-87152-242-X). Reprint Co.

Woodcraft: Or, Hawks About the Dovecote; a Story of the South at the Close of the Revolution. William Gilmore Simms. LC 68-20022. (Americans in fiction). 1968. Gregg Press.

Woodcraft: Or, Hawks About the Dovecote, a Story of the South at the Close of the Revolution. new and rev. ed. William Gilmore Simms. LC 8-11011. 1882. A. C. Armstrong & Son.

Woodcraft; or, Hawks About the Dovecote. A Story of the South at the Close of the Revolution. new and rev. ed. William Gilmore Simms. (On cover: Lovell's library, v. 12, no. 684). 1885. J. W. Lovell Company.

Woodcutter Operation. Kenneth Royce. LC 74-19462. 1975. 7.95. Simon and Schuster.

Wooden Bottle. James Hogarth Dennis. LC 6-33976. 1887. R. H. Dennis.

Wooden Cow. T. Janakiraman. 1979. 4.00x (ISBN 0-8364-0567-6, Pub. by Sangam India). South Asia Bks.

Wooden Crosses. Roland Dorgeles, pseud. LC 21-3809. 1921. G. P. Putnam's Sons.

Wooden Gong: A Novel. Akpan, Ntieyong Udo. LC 68-4730. 1967. pap., 1.00. Longmans.

Wooden Guns: A Western Story. George Owen Baxter. LC 26-242942. Chelsea House.

Wooden Horseshoe. Leonard Sanders. LC 64-13871. 1964. Doubleday.

Wooden Horseshoe see Power Grab.

Wooden Indian. Carolyn Wells. J. B. Lippincott Company.

Wooden Ladder. Kelsey Ballou Sweatt. LC 27-12822. The Robinson Press.

Wooden Leg John: A Satire on Americans Living in Mexico. Garland F Clifton. LC 79-152280. 1971. 10.00 (ISBN 0-87012-098-0). Order from McClain Print. Co.

Wooden Nickels. Gerald Kaminski. LC 80-12997. 200p. 1984. pap. price not set (ISBN 0-914974-25-4). Holmgangers.

Wooden Pillow. Carl Fallas. LC 36-27079. 1936. The Viking Press.

Wooden Shepherdess. Richard Arthur Warren Hughes. LC 76-181656. (His The human predicament, 2). 1973. 7.50 (ISBN 0-06-011986-1). Harper & Row.

Wooden Shoe Hollow: A Novel. Charlotte Pieper. LC 51-6977. 1951. Exposition Press.

Wooden Spoil. Victor Rousseau Emanuel. LC 19-265681. George H. Doran Company.

Wooden Spoon. Llewelyn Wyn Griffith. LC 38-1048. E. P. Dutton & Co., Inc.

Wooden Star. William Tenn. 256p. (Orig.). 1981. pap. 2.25 (ISBN 0-345-29306-1, Del Rey). Ballantine.

Wooden Statue. Dorothy MacKinder. LC 52-11722. 1952. McMullen Books.

Wooden Sword. Edward Easton, pseud. (Orig.). 1970. pap. 0.95 o.p. (95-142). Manor Bks.

Wooden Swords. Jacques Deval, pseud. Tr. by Morris, Lawrence Shackelford. LC 30-17506. 1930. The Viking Press.

Wooden Wolf. John Kelly. LC 76-13476. (Illus.). 9.95. E. P. Dutton.

Wooden Woman. Alexander Townsend. LC 30-336117. 1930. Doubleday, Doran and Company, Inc.

Woodhouse Correspondence. George William Erskine Russell & Sichel, Edith Helen. LC 4-12100. 1904. Dodd, Mead and Company.

Woodhull. Pliny Berthier Seymour. LC 7-28977. 1907. The C. M. Clark Publishing Co.

Woodland Heritage & Other Poems. James G. King. 1968. 3.00 o.p. (ISBN 0-8059-0163-9). Dorrance.

Woodland Queen (Reine Des Bois) Andre Theuriet. LC 35-33424. 1910. Current Literature Publishing Company.

Woodland Wooing. Harriet Leonora Vose Bates. LC 6-9081. 1889. Roberts Brothers.

Woodlanders. library ed. Thomas Hardy. 1958. Macmillan.

Woodlanders. Thomas Hardy. (On cover: Lovell's library, v. 20, no. 956). 1887. J. W. Lovell Company.

Woodlanders. Thomas Hardy. (On cover: Seaside library. Pocket ed., no. 957). 1887. G. Munro.

Woodlanders. Thomas Hardy. LC 42-27364. Rand, McNally & Company.

Woodlanders. Thomas Hardy & Dale Kramer. LC 80-40057. 1980. 2.95 (ISBN 0-19-812504-6). Clarendon Press.

Woodlanders. A Novel. Thomas Hardy. LC 4-31669. (Harper's Franklin square library, no. 572). 1887. Harper & Brothers.

Woodlanders: A Novel. Thomas Hardy. LC 4-31667. 1887. Harper & Brothers.

Woodlanders: A Novel. Thomas Hardy. 1896. Harper & Brothers.

Woodlanders. With an Introd. by Carl J. Weber. Thomas Hardy. LC 57-146154. (Harper's modern classics). 1958. Harper.

Woodley Lane Ghost: And Other Stories. Madeleine Vinton Dahlgren. LC 6-32176. 1899. D. Biddle.

Woodman: A Novel. Quesnay De Beaurepaire, Jules. Tr. by Simpson, John. LC 7-42414. 1892. Harper & Brothers.

Woodneys: An American Family. John Breckenridge Ellis. LC 14-11241. 1914. 1.00. The Devin-Adair Company.

Woodreve Manor: Or, Six Months in Town. A Tale of American Life... Anna Hanson McKenney Dorsey. LC 6-33704. 1852. A. Hart.

Woodridge, 1946. Martin Boris. LC 79-27809. 10.95 (ISBN 0-517-54109-2). Crown Publishers.

Woodrow Wilson Dime. Jack Finney. LC 68-14837. (Illus.). 1968. Simon and Schuster.

Woods. David Plante. LC 81-70071. 160p. 1982. 8.95 (ISBN 0-689-11289-0). Atheneum.

Woods and River Tales: From the World of Roderick Haig-Brown. Haig-Brown, Roderick Langmere Haig. LC 80-484355. 1980. 12.95 (ISBN 0-7710-3768-6). McClelland and Stewart.

Woods Are Dark. Richard Laymon. 240p. (Orig.). 1981. pap. 2.75 (ISBN 0-446-90518-6). Warner Bks.

Woods Colt: A Novel of the Ozark Hills. Thames Ross Williamson. LC 33-28736. Harcourt, Brace and Company.

Woodshed. Rayner Heppenstall. 1968. pap. 6.95 (ISBN 0-214-15817-9). Dufour.

Woodsmoke. Susan K. Sibley. LC 76-53744. 8.95 (ISBN 0-910244-93-6). J. F. Blair.

Woodsmoke. Susan K. Sibley. 1979. 1.95 (ISBN 0-380-45435-1). Avon Books.

Woodsmoke. Francis Brett Young. LC 24-165640. E. P. Dutton & Company.

Woodstock: One More Time. Richard Hubbard. (O.s.i.). (Orig.). 1971. pap. 0.95 o.s.i. (A840N, Award). Univ Pub & Dist.

Woodstock: Or, The Cavalier. parker's ed. Walter Scott. (Waverley novels: Library ed. v. 19). 1832. Bazin & Ellsworth.

Woodstock: Or, The Cavalier. Walter Scott. LC 8-3040. (Eclectic English classics). 1894. American Book Company.

Woodstock: Or, The Cavalier; a Tale of the Year 1651. Walter Scott. LC 36-37082. (Half-title: Everyman's library, ed. by Ernest Rhys. Fiction). 1909. J. M. Dent & Co.

Woodstock: Or, The Cavalier, a Tale of the Year 1651. Walter Scott. LC 36-37082. (Half-title: Everyman's library, ed. by Ernest Rhys. Fiction. no. 72). 1926. J. M. Dent & Sons, Ltd.

Woodstock: Or, The Cavalier; a Tale of the Year Sixteen Hundred and Fifty-One. Walter Scott. (On cover: Lovell's library, no. 551). 1885. J. W. Lovell Company.

Woodville: Or, The Anchoret Reclaimed. Charles W. Todd. LC 9-929. 1832. Printed by F. S. Heiskell.

Woodworth's Cabinet of Curious Things. Francis Channing Woodworth. LC 15-10420. 1852. E. Darrow.

Wooed and Married. Rosa Nouchette Carey. (On cover: Lovell's library, v. 20 no. 960). J. W. Lovell Company.

Wooed and Married. A Novel. Rosa Nouchette Carey. LC 5-2551. F. M. Lupton.

Wooed and Married. A Novel. Rosa Nouchette Carey. LC 6-228079. 1876. J. B. Lippincott & Co.

Wooed and Married. A Novel. Rosa Nouchette Carey. LC 16-191409. 1910. J. B. Lippincott Company.

Wooed by a Sphinx of Aztlan: The Romance of a Hero of Our Late Spanish-American War and Incidents of Interest from the Life of a Western Pioneer. George Hartmann. LC 7-19593. 1907. G. Hartmann.

Wooers and Winners: Or, Under the Scars. A Yorkshire Story. Isabella Varley Banks. LC 21-139600. (Seadise library, v. 80, no. 1629). 1883. G. Munro.

Wooing a Widow. A Novel. Ewald August Koenig. Tr. by Robinson, Mary A. (choice series, no. 108). 1894. R. Bonner's Sons.

Wooing and Warring in the Wilderness: A Story of Canetuckey. Charles D Kirk. LC 7-13209. 1860. Derby & Jackson.

Wooing of a Recluse. George De Clyver Curtis. LC 14-6005. The Devin-Adair Company.

Wooing of Calvin Parks. Laura Elizabeth Howe Richards. LC 8-23552. D. Estes & Company.

Wooing of Folly. James Lauren Ford. LC 6-34804. 1906. D. Appleton and Company.

Wooing of Rosamond Fayre. Berta Ruck. LC 15-19628. 1915. 1.35. Dodd, Mead and Company.

Wooing of Sheila. Grace Little Rhys. LC 1-16992. 1901. H. Holt and Company.

Wooing of Tokala: An Intimate Tale of the Wild Life of the American Indian Drawn from Camp and Trail. Franklin Welles Calkins. LC 7-16943. F. H. Revell Company.

Wooing of Wistaria. Winnifred Eaton Babcock. LC 2-221702. 1902. Harper & Brothers.

Wooing O't, a Novel. Annie French Hector. (On verso of half--title: Macmillan's two shilling library. 11). 1899. Macmillan and Co., Limited.

Wooings of Jezebel Pettyfer: Being the Personal History of Jeehu Sennacherib Dyle, Commoonly Called Masheen Dyle; Together with an Account of Certain Things That Changed in the House of the Sorcerer, Here Set Down. Haldane Macfall. LC 25-18583. (Half-title: Blue jade library). 1925. A. A. Knopf.

Wooings of Judith. Sara Beaumont Cannon Kennedy. LC 2-23091. 1902. Doubleday, Page & Company.

Wool, Beef, and Gold: Sheep, Cattle, and Mining Stories of the West. Foreword by Velma Stevens Truett. Illustrated by Stewart Walters. Clel Evan Georgetta. LC 56-11826. 1956. Pacific Books.

Woolet Papers. A. Wellington Woolet. LC 450. 1899. Trade-Mark Record.

Woollen Dress. Davis, Ruth Helen, Tr. LC 12-22873. 1912. Duffield & Company.

Woolly Lamb of God. Bond, Frank Fraser. LC 33-29487. Fleming H. Revell Company.

Woolworth Madonna. Elizabeth Troop. LC 77-350499. 1976. 3.95 (ISBN 0-7156-1127-5). Duckworth.

Word. Irving Wallace. 1978. pap. 3.95 (ISBN 0-671-82216-0). PB.

Word: A Novel. Irving Wallace. LC 75-179586. 1972. 7.95 (ISBN 0-671-21153-6). Simon and Schuster.

Word and the Sword. Theo Lang. LC 74-3437. 1974. 10.00 (ISBN 0-440-08868-2). Delacorte Press.

Word and the Will. James Payn. (On cover: Lovell's international series, no. 121). J. W. Lovell Company.

Word Child. Iris Murdoch. LC 75-1418. 1975. 8.95 (ISBN 0-670-78236-X). Viking Press.

Word Finds with Themes, No. 4. Maura Jacobson. (Word Finds Ser.). 176p. (Orig.). 1982. pap. 1.95 (ISBN 0-86721-113-X). Playboy Pbks.

Word for Love. Alan Burgess. LC 68-12465. 1968. Dutton.

Word for World Is Forest. Ursula K. Le Guin. LC 75-37085. 6.95 (ISBN 0-399-11716-4). Berkley Pub. Corp.: Distributed by Putnam.

Word for World Is Forest. Ursula K. Le Guin. 1976. pap. 1.75 (ISBN 0-425-03910-2, K3279). Berkley Pub.

Word Hunt, No. 1. Ed. by Ann Mitchell. 128p. 1982. pap. 1.50 (ISBN 0-505-51791-4). Tower Bks.

Word Hunt, No. 2. Ed. by Ann Mitchell. 128p. 1982. pap. 1.50 (ISBN 0-505-51793-0). Tower Bks.

Word Hunt No. 3. 128p. 1982. pap. 1.50 (ISBN 0-505-51821-X). Tower Bks.

Word Lives on: A Treasury of Spiritual Fiction. Introd. by Halford E. Luccock. 1st Ed. Ed. by Frances Brentano. LC 51-10052. 1951. Doubleday.

Word of Honour. Herman Cyril McNeile. LC 27-299392. George H. Doran Company.

Word of Mouth. Jerome Weidman. LC 64-17938. 1964. Random House.

Word of Tomorrow. Patry Williams. LC 32-26576. The Penn Publishing Company.

Word Only a Word. popualr uniform ed. Georg Moritz Ebers. Tr. by Mary Joanne Stafford. LC 16-157096. (historical romances of Georg Ebers. vol. xiii). 1915. D. Appleton and Company.

Word, Only a Word: A Romance. Georg Moritz Ebers. Tr. by Mary Joanne Stafford. LC 6-43635. 1883. W. S. Gottsberger.

Wordarrow: Indians and Whites in the New Fur Trade. Gerald Robert Vizenor. LC 78-3202. 1981. 6.95 (ISBN 0-8166-0862-8). University of Minnesota Press.

Wordarrows: Indians and Whites in the New Fur Trade. Gerald Robert Vizenor. LC 78-3202. 7.95. (ISBN 0-8166-0859-8). University of Minnesota Press.

Wordboard. Jill Paton Walsh & Crossley-Holland, Kevin. LC 70-85364. 1969. 3.75. Farrar, Straus & Giroux.

Wordhoard: Anglo-Saxon Stories. Paton Walsh, Jill & Crossley-Holland, Kevin. LC 74-183335. (Puffin books). 1972. 0.20 (ISBN 0-14-030511-4). Penguin.

Words and Music. Eric Hatch. LC 43-1292. 1943. Farrar & Rinehart, Inc.

Words & the Music. Edward R. Eastman. (Illus.). 1959. 3.95 o.p. Interstate.

Words from My Soul. Guyvan B. Shirley. 3.95 o.p. Vantage.

Words Never to Be Forgotten and the Donkey. Paul Johann Von Heyse. Tr. by Fordyce, Abbie E. LC 7-6606. 1888. J. B. Hoff.

Words of Advice. Fay Weldon. LC 77-5987. 7.95 (ISBN 0-394-40547-1). Random House.

Words of Cheer for the Tempted: The Toiling, and the Sorrowing. Timothy Shay Arthur. LC 6-3832. T. Bliss & Co.

Words of My Roaring. Robert Kroetsch. LC 66-15326. 4.95. St. Martin's.

Words That Burn. A Romance. Lida Briggs Browne. 1900. D. B. Briggs.

Words to Say It: A Novel. Marie Cardinal. Tr. by Pat Goodheart from Fr. 320p. 1983. 14.95 (ISBN 0-941324-02-8). Van Vactor & Goodheart.

Words to That Effect. Charles Molesworth. LC 81-13587. 1981. 5.75 (ISBN 0-913282-23-5). Seven Woods Press.

Words to the Unwise. Kemper Campbell. LC 75-159126. (O.S.I.). 1971. 4.95 o.s.i. (ISBN 0-671-21022-X). S&S.

Wordy Gurdy, No. 1. United Features Syndicate. 160p. (Orig.). 1982. pap. 1.95 (ISBN 0-441-90895-0). Ace Bks.

Work. Stephen Dixon. LC 77-5627. 5.95 (ISBN 0-914908-30-8). Street Fiction Press.

Work: A Story of Experience. Louisa May Alcott. LC 76-48849. (Studies in the life of women). (Illus.). 1977. 10.50 (ISBN 0-8052-0563-2). Schocken Books.

Work: A Story of Experience. Louisa May Alcott. LC 76-51662. (Recovered Fiction by American Women). 1977. 22.00 (ISBN 0-405-10042-6). Arno Press.

Work & Days: With Prolegomena & Commentary. Hesiod. Ed. by M. L. West. 1978. text ed. 52.00x (ISBN 0-19-814005-3). Oxford U Pr.

Work and Wages: Or, Life in Service. A Continuation of "Little Coin, Much Care.". Mary Botham Howitt. LC 18-22557. (Half-title: Tales for the people and their children). 1843. D. Appleton & Co.

Work, for the Night Is Coming. Jared Carter. LC 80-24494. 1981. 10.95 (ISBN 0-02-522090-X) (ISBN 0-02-069290-0). Macmillan.

Work Is Innocent. Rafael Yglesias. LC 74-2530. 1976. 6.95 (ISBN 0-385-00965-8). Doubleday.

Work It Out for Yourself. Stevie Smith (ISBN 0-445-03164-6). Popular Library.

Work of an Ancient Hand. 1st Ed. Curtis Harnack. LC 60-6713. 1960. Harcourt, Brace.

Work of Art. Sinclair Lewis. LC 33-272683. 1934. Doubleday, Doran & Company, Inc.

Work of Darkness: A Novel. Jack Karney. LC 54-64923. Putnam.

Work of Our Hands. Hersilia A. Mitchell Copp Keays. LC 5-32858. 1905. McClure, Phillips & Co.

Work of Saint Francis. Illus. by Johannes Troyer. 1st Ed. MacKinlay Kantor. LC 58-9411. 1958. World Pub. Co.

Work Suspended: And Other Pieces Including Basil Seal Rides Again. Evelyn Waugh. LC 67-112384. 1967. Penguin.

Work, Wait, & Win. Opal Renfro. 288p. 1976. 8.00 o.p. (ISBN 0-682-48413-X). Exposition.

Work, Wait, and Win: A Novel. Ruth Buck Lamb. LC 76-353465. 8.00 (ISBN 0-682-48413-X). Exposition Press.

Work While Ye Have the Light. Lev Nikolaevich Tolstoi & Dillon, Emile Joseph, 1855- (On cover: Lovell's Westminster series, no. 22). 1890. United States Book Company.

Workaday Lady. Maysie Greig. LC 36-18263. 1936. Doubleday, Doran and Co., Inc.

Workaday Lady. Maysie Greig. LC 37-38260. 1937. The Sun Dial Press, Inc.

Worked Out Diggin's: A Tale of the Early Placer Mines of California. P. H Darrah. LC 43-169502. 1943. Dorrance and Company.

Workers. Audrey Lee. LC 76-81609. 1969. McGraw-Hill.

Workers in the Dawn. George Robert Gissing. LC 75-1527. (Victorian Fiction: Novels of Faith and Doubt; 75). 1975. 35.00 (ISBN 0-8240-1599-1). Garland Pub.

Workers in the Dawn... George Robert Gissing. LC 35-6765. (Half-title: The Doubleday-Doran series in literature, R. Shafer, general editor). Doubleday, Doran & Company, Inc.

Workers in the Dawn: A Novel. George Robert Gissing. LC 68-59358. 1968. AMS Press.

Working a Passage(or Life in a Liner. 2nd ed. Charles Frederick Briggs. Ed. by Elizabeth Weidman. LC 79-93594. (American Fiction Ser). 1970. Repr. of 1845 ed. lib. bdg. 8.95 o.s.i. (ISBN 0-512-00051-4). Garrett Pr.

Working Bullocks. Katharine Susannah Prichard. LC 27-9867. 1927. The Viking Press.

Working for the Man. Ralph Dennis. (Hardman#7). 1974. (pbk.) 0.95. Popular Library.

Working Girl. Hester Mundis. LC 81-3196. 12.95 (ISBN 0-698-11110-9). Coward, McCann & Geoghegan.

Working Girl. Kathleen Shepard. LC 31-14182. 1931. The Mohawk Press.

Working Girl. Florence Stonebraker. LC 41-25826. Gramercy Publishing Co.

Working Girl. Florence Stuart. LC 41-25826. Gramercy Publishing Co.

Working Girl. Marian Trump. LC 43-101876. 1942. Meador Publishing Company.

Working-Man's Loaf. Mary Dwinell Chellis. LC 6-23351. (On cover: Fife and drum series, no. 16). 1885. National Temperance Society and Publication House.

Working-Man's Way in the World: Being the Autobiography of a Journeyman Printer. Charles Manby Smith. LC 8-8627. 1854. Redfield.

Working Ten of the King's Daughters. Elizabeth Greenleaf. LC 6-45938. 1888. E. P. Dutton & Company.

Working Wives. Anne Gardner, pseud. LC 31-12017. Grosset & Dunlap.

Working Wives. Bernice Whittemore. LC 35-10053. Home Providers League, Inc.

Workingman Detective: Or, A Crime Against the Poor. Donald J McKenzie. LC 1138. (On cover: Magnet detective library. no. 110). 1899. Street & Smith.

Workingman's Paradise. William Lane. 324p. pap. 16.00 (Pub. by Sydney U Pr). Intl Schol Bk Serv.

Workingman's Wife: From the German of Friedrich Friedrich. Friedrich Friedrich. Tr. by Miller, Hettie E. LC 6-44726. (On cover: The Marguerite series. no. 26). 1894. E. A. Weeks & Company.

Workman and Soldier: A Tale of Paris Life During the Siege and the Rule of the Commune. James Francis Cobb. LC 6-26930. 1880. Griffith and Farran.

Workman's Confessions. Emile Souvestre. LC 8-12380. 1891. Hunt & Eaton.

Works. Ada Ellen Bably. LC 12-36391. A.L. Burt Company.

Works. Beryl Cook. 1980. pap. 5.95 (ISBN 0-14-005343-3). Penguin.

Works of A. Conan Doyle... Arthur Conan Doyle. LC 38-7476. 1937. Garden City Publishing Co., Inc.

Works of Aphra Behn, 6 Vols. Aphra Amis Behn. Ed. by Montague Summers. LC 67-22243. 1967. Repr. of 1915 ed. Set. 150.00 (ISBN 0-405-08253-3, Blom Pubns); 25.00 ea. Vol. 1 (ISBN 0-405-08254-1). Vol. 2 (ISBN 0-405-08255-X). Vol. 3 (ISBN 0-405-08256-8). Vol. 4 (ISBN 0-405-08257-6). Vol. 5 (ISBN 0-405-08258-4). Vol. 6 (ISBN 0-405-08259-2). Ayer Co.

Works of Balzac: Centenary Ed. Honore De Balzac. Tr. by Katharine Prescott Wormeley. Ives, George Burnham, 1856- Tr. LC 99-1794. 1899-19. Little, Brown and Company.

Works of Charles Dickens. Charles Dickens & George Cruikshank. LC 78-55407. (Illus.). 5.98 (ISBN 0-517-26311-4). Avenel Books.

Works of Charles Dickens. Excelsior Ed. Illustrated from Designs by Darley, Gilbert, Cruikshank, Etc.... Charles Dickens. LC 6-37247. 1870. Hurd and Houghton.

Works of Charles Dickens... With Introduction, Critical Comments, and Notes... Charles Dickens. LC 12-1799. P. F. Collier & Son.

Works of Gilbert Parker. imperial ed.... ed. Gilbert Parker. LC 12-27845. 1912-23. C. Scribner's Sons.

Works of God, and Other Stories: Translated from the Italian by Angus Davidson. Giuseppe Berto. LC 50-6841. (Direction, 16). 1950. New Directions.

Works of Guy De Maupassant... Guy De Maupassant. LC 41-42399. 1909. Bigelow, Brown & Co., Inc.

Works of Guy De Maupassant... Guy De Maupassant. Tr. by Albert M. C. McMaster. Henderson, A. E., Tr & Quesada, Mme. Louise Charlotte Garstin, 1864?- Tr. LC 12-456. Classic Publishing Company.

Works of Honore De Balzac... Honore De Balzac. LC 8-25846. The Kelmscott Society.

Works of Jack London. Jack London. LC 80-211. 5.98 (ISBN 0-517-30979-3). Avenel Books.

Works of Kathleen Norris... Kathleen Thompson Norris. LC 21-2972. 1920. Doubleday, Page & Company.

Works of L. E. Landon: In Two Volumes... Letitia Elizabeth Landon. LC 11-3205. 1847. J. Harding.

Works of Love. Wright Morris. LC 51-11978. 1952. Knopf.

Works of Malory. 2d ed. reprinted with corrections. ed. Thomas Malory & Eugene Vinaver. LC 77-8597. (Oxford paperbacks; 384). 1977. 5.95 (ISBN 0-19-281217-3). Oxford University Press.

Works of Morris & of Yeats in Relation to Early Saga Literature. Dorothy M. Hoare. LC 72-139476. 1971. Repr. of 1937 ed. 11.00x (ISBN 0-8462-1382-6). Russell.

Works of M.P. Shiel. Morse. 8.00 o.p. Borden.

Works of Mrs. Amelia Opie... Amelia Alderson Opie. LC 17-7992. 1835. J. & W. Sandford.

Works of Mrs. Amelia Opie: Complete in Three Volumes. Amelia Alderson Opie. LC 70-37706. (Women of letters). 1974. 75.00 (ISBN 0-404-56796-7). AMS Press.

Works of Mrs. Amelia Opie: Complete in Three Volumes... Amelia Alderson Opie. LC 7-24095. 1941. Crissy & Markley.

Works of Oscar Wilde. Oscar Wilde & V. Holland. (Cloth ed. 12.95 o.p.). imit. leather 19.95 (ISBN 0-00-410542-7, OW2). Collins Pubs.

Works of Satan. Richard Aumerle Maher. LC 21-14700. 1921. The Macmillan Company.

Works of Tobias Smollett. Tobias George Smollett & O. M Brack. LC 80-15167. 18.00 (ISBN 0-87413-121-9). University of Delaware Press.

Works of Tobias Smollett: Ed. by George Saintsbvry... with Illvstrations by Frank Richards. Tobias George Smollett. Ed. by Saintsbury, George Edward Bateman. LC 1-19419. 1895. Gibbings & Company, Lim.

Works of Wilkie Collins. Wilkie Collins. LC 77-124767. (Illus.). 1970. AMS Press.

Works of Wilkie Collins... Wilkie Collins. LC 42-46328. P. F. Collier.

Works of William Carleton. William Carleton. LC 77-106257. (Short story index reprint series). (Illus.). 1970. Books for Libraries Press.

Works of William Carleton... William Carleton. LC 31-240. (On cover: Carleton's works.). 1881. P. P. Collier.

Works of William Makepeace Thackeray... William Makepeace Thackeray. LC 8-27767. 1879-82. Smith, Elder, & Co.

Works: With Introductions by George Saintsbury, 18 vols. facsimile ed. Honore De Balzac. LC 78-150468. (Short Story Index Reprint Ser.). Repr. of 1901 ed. Set. 500.00 (ISBN 0-8369-3791-0). Ayer Co.

World Above. Abraham Polonsky. LC 51-9563. 1951. Little, Brown.

World According to Garp. John Irving. 1979. 2.75 (ISBN 0-671-82220-9). Pocket Books.

World According to Garp: A Novel. John Irving. LC 77-15564. 10.95 (ISBN 0-525-23770-4). E. P. Dutton.

World According to Two Feathers. David Warren. (Ithaca House Fiction Ser.). 71p. 1973. 4.95 (ISBN 0-87886-029-0); pap. 2.95 (ISBN 0-87886-030-4). Ithaca Hse.

World According to Two Feathers. David Warren. 80p. 1973. 4.95 (ISBN 0-87886-029-0, Pub. by Ithaca Hse); pap. 2.95 (ISBN 0-87886-030-4). SBD.

World According to Two-Feathers. David Warren. 1973. (pbk.) 2.95 (ISBN 0-87886-030-4). Ithaca House.

World Aflame. Gregory Kern. (Cap Kennedy, no. 13). 1974. (pbk.) 0.95. DAW Books.

World Against Her. Edward Reynolds Roe. LC 7-40250. (On cover: The pastime series, no. 68). 1891. Laird & Lee.

World Against Mary. Josef Maria Frank. Tr. by Frommer, Otto. LC 32-78093. E. P. Dutton & Co., Inc.

World and Julie. Gertrude Naugler. LC 55-9673. 1955. Scribner.

World & Other Places. Daniel M. Stokes. 1974. pap. 1.50. Chthon Pr.

World and Paradise: A Romance of the Thirty Years' War. Edgar Maass. LC 50-5798. 1950. Scribner.

World and Richard. Pauline Corley. LC 41-19641. Random House.

World and the Woman. Ruth Kimball Gardiner. LC 7-382650. 1907. A. S. Barnes & Company.

World and Thomas Kelly. Arthur Cheney Train. LC 17-29866. 1917. C. Scribner's Sons.

World and Thorinn. Damon Francis Knight. LC 79-21608. (Illus.). 12.95 (ISBN 0-399-12470-5). Berkley Pub.: Distributed by Putnam.

World and Winstow. Edith Henrietta Fowler. LC 1-100077. 1910. Dodd, Mead and Company.

World Asunder. Ian Wallace. (Science Fiction Ser.). 1976. pap. 1.50 o.p. (ISBN 0-87997-262-9, UW1262). DAW Bks.

World Asunder. Ian Wallace (ISBN 0-87997-262-9). Daw Books.

World at Bay: A Science Fiction Novel. Paul Capon. LC 54-7726. (Science fiction). 1954. Winston.

World at Christmas. j,5-8 ed. Charles House. (Illus.). 1969. 7.95 (80302). Glencoe.

World at My Feet: A Modern Novel of Sin and Penance. 1st Ed. Thomas M Robertson. LC 58-10333. 1958. Greenwich Book Publishers.

World at Six. Johan Wigmore Fabricius. LC 50-6782. 1950. Westminster Press.

World Before. Ruth Montgomery. 1977. pap. 2.50 (ISBN 0-449-23340-5, Crest). Fawcett.

World Before Our Own. Brad Steiger. 1979. pap. 2.25 (ISBN 0-425-04215-4). Berkley Pub.

World Below. Sydney Fowler Wright. LC 75-10672. (Classics of science fiction). 1976. 12.95. (ISBN 0-88355-350-3) (ISBN 0-88355-466-6). Hyperion Press.

World Below. Sydney Fowler Wright. LC 49-10510. (Library of classics). 1949. Shasta Publishers.

World Below. Sydney Fowler Wright. LC 30-9487. 1930. Longmans, Green and Co.

World Between. Norman Spinard. 1979. pap. 2.25 (ISBN 0-671-82876-2, Timescape). PB.

World Between. Norman Spinrad. 1979. 2.25 (ISBN 0-671-82876-2). Pocket Books.

World Between Them. Charlotte Mary Brame. LC 4978. (Bertha Clay library, no. 23). 1900. Street & Smith.

World Between Them. Charlotte Mary Brame. (On cover: Seaside library. Pocket ed. no. 821). G. Munro.

World Beyond. Ruth Montgomery. 176p. 1982. pap. 2.50 (ISBN 0-449-24085-1, Crest). Fawcett.

World Beyond. George E. Shirley. 2.50 o.p. Vantage.

World by the Tail. Marjorie Holmes. LC 43-7895. 1943. J. B. Lippincott Company.

World by the Tale. John Wood Campbell. 1970. pap. 0.75 o.p. (0502-07060). Curtis.

World Called Camelot. Arthur H. Landis. (Science Fiction Ser). pap. 1.75 (ISBN 0-87997-418-4, UE1418). DAW Bks.

World Called Camelot. Arthur H. Landis. (Science Fiction Ser). 1976. pap. 1.25 o.p. (UY1244). DAW Bks.

World Called Camelot. Arthur H Landis. (Daw Science Fiction 2). 1976. 1.25. Daw Books.

World Called Solitude. Stephen Goldin. LC 78-22611. 1981. 9.95 (ISBN 0-385-14375-3). Doubleday.

World Cannot Hear You: A Comedy of Ancient Desires. Thomas, Gwyn. LC 52-5862. 1952. Little, Brown.

World Champion. Joseph Morganstern. LC 69-12092. (O.S.I.). 1969. 4.95 o.s.i. (ISBN 0-671-20183-2). S&S.

World Champion: A Novel. Joseph Morgenstern. LC 69-12092. 1969. 4.95. Simon and Schuster.

World Champions. Paul Morand. Tr. by Miles, Hamish. LC 31-12372. Harcourt, Brace and Company.

World Class. Jane Boyar & Burt Boyar. LC 75-10257. 1975. 9.95 (ISBN 0-394-46053-7). Random House.

World Contrary. Zalman Feldman. LC 48-15201. 1947. Harbinger House.

World Cruise. Frances Malm. LC 60-6895.

World D. Harold Philip Trevarthen. LC 37-575913. 1935. Sheed & Ward, Inc.

World Decision see Collected Works.

World Elsewhere. 1st Amer. Ed. John Bowen. LC 66-14591. 1967. 4.50. Coward.

World Enough & Time. Robert Penn Warren. LC 78-23585. 1979. pap. 2.95 (ISBN 0-394-72818-1, Vin). Random.

World Enough and Time: A Romantic Novel. Robert Penn Warren. LC 50-7242. 1950. Random House.

World Enough and Time: A Romantic Novel. Robert Penn Warren. LC 78-23585. 1979. 4.95 (ISBN 0-394-72818-1). Vintage Books.

World-Famed Stories & Legends. Hamilton W. Mabie. Repr. of 1908 ed. 20.00 (ISBN 0-89987-125-9). Darby Bks.

World Fantasy Awards, Vol. 2. Stuart D. Schiff. Ed. by Fritz Leiber. LC 79-8034. (Double D Science Fiction Ser.). (Illus.). 224p. 1980. 12.95 (ISBN 0-385-15380-5). Doubleday.

World for Sale: A Novel. Gilbert Parker. LC 16-18027. 1916. Harper & Brothers.

World from Rough Stones. Malcolm MacDonald. LC 74-21296. (Illus.). 1975. 8.95 (ISBN 0-394-49434-2). Knopf: Distributed by Random House.

World from Rough Stones. Malcolm MacDonald. (Illus.). 1976. (pbk.) 1.95. New American Library.

World Full of Secrets. Allison Scott. LC 77-88152. 9.95 (ISBN 0-89256-039-8). Rawson Associates Publishers.

World Full of Secrets. Allison Scott. (Jove / HBJ Book). 1979. 2.25 (ISBN 0-515-04770-8). Jove Publications, Inc.

World Full of Strangers. David Alman. LC 74-29040. (Labor Movement in Fiction and Non-Fiction). 1977. 22.50 (ISBN 0-404-58521-3). AMS Press.

World Full of Strangers. David Alman. LC 49-9296. N. Y.

World Full of Strangers. Cynthia Freeman. LC 74-18154. 1975. 8.95 (ISBN 0-87795-102-0). Arbor Hse.

World Full of Strangers. Cynthia Freeman. 640p. 1976. pap. 3.50 (ISBN 0-553-20179-4, 20179-4). Bantam.

World Goes by: A Novel. 1st Ed. Maurice De Goumois. LC 56-114691. 1956. Pageant Press.

World Goes Smash. Samuel Hopkins Adams. LC 38-12952. 1938. Houghton Mifflin Company.

World Gone Mad. Clark Darlton. (Perry Rhodan, 29). (Illus.). 1973. (pbk.) 0.75. Ace.

World Healer. Paul M. Kourennoff. 1944. P. M. Kourennoff.

World I Left Behind Me. William Walling. LC 78-21425. 20.00 (ISBN 0-312-89050-8). St. Martin's Press.

World I Never Made. James Thomas Farrell. LC 36-24944. The Vanguard Press.

World I Never Made. James Thomas Farrell. LC 47-2417. 1947. The World Publishing Company.

World in a Glass: Selections from His Novels. John Dos Passos. 1966. 6.95 o.p. (ISBN 0-395-07624-2). HM.

World in a Grain of Sand. Erica Linton. LC 66-51243. 1965. 5.25x (ISBN 0-8002-0655-X). Intl Pubns Serv.

World in Eclipse. William Dexter. pap. 0.50 o.p. (52-338). Paperback Lib.

World in His Arms. Rex Ellingwood Beach. LC 46-5471. 1946. G. P. Putnam's Sons.

World in His Heart. Josephine Dodge Daskam Bacon. LC 41-146589. 1941. D. Appleton-Century Company, Incorporated.

World in Morning. Lewis Banci. 1978. pap. 1.95 o.s.i. (ISBN 0-505-51229-7). Tower Bks.

World in My Ears. Arthur T. Cushen. (Illus.). 204p. (Orig.). 1979. pap. 13.50x (ISBN 0-473-00019-9). Intl Pubns Serv.

World in Spell. Dorothy Emily Stevenson. LC 39-133567. Farrar & Rinehart, Inc.

World in the Attic. Wright Morris. LC 49-5058. 1949. C. Scribner's Sons.

World in the Evening. Christopher Isherwood. LC 54-5960. 1954. Random House.

World in the Evening. Christopher Isherwood. (Bard Book). 1978. 2.50 (ISBN 0-380-01857-8). Avon.

World in Tune. Elizabeth Gray Vining. LC 54-9007. 1968. 5.00x (ISBN 0-87574-066-9, 066). Pendle Hill.

World Inside. Robert Silverberg. LC 72-150918. (Doubleday science fiction). 1971. 4.95. Doubleday.

World Intervenes. Otto Viking. LC 64-3975. 1964. Exposition Press.

World Invisible. Walter Stahr. LC 54-25580. 1954. Christopher Pub. House.

World Is a Bridge. Christine Goutiere Weston. LC 50-6425. 1950. Scribner.

World Is a Comedy: A Tucholsky Anthology. Kurt Tucholsky. LC 58-16345. 1957. Sci-Art Publishers.

World Is a Wedding. Delmore Schwartz. LC 48-795743. 1948. New Directions.

World Is for the Young: And Other Stories. Blanche Girouard. LC 70-167450. (Short story index reprint series). 1971. (ISBN 0-8369-3976-X). Books for Libraries Press.

World Is Full of Divorced Women. Jackie Collins. 1981. 2.95. Warner Books.

World Is Full of Married Men. Jackie Collins. LC 68-29835. 1968. World Pub. Co.

World Is Like That. Kathleen Thompson Norris. LC 40-69133. 1940. Doubleday, Doran and Company, Inc.

World is Made of Glass. Morris L. West. 356p. 1983. 15.95 (ISBN 0-688-02031-3). Morrow.

World Is Mine: A Novel; a Dramatic Love Story of the Prize Ring. Pal Jesse Shoaf. LC 48-4316. 1948.

World Is Mine: The Story of a Modern Monte Cristo. William James Blech. LC 38-25698. 1938. Simon and Schuster.

World Is My Home. Evald Mand. LC 52-8591. 1952. Friendship Press.

World Is Not Enough. Zoe Oldenbourg. Tr. by Trask, Willard A. LC 48-6397. 1948. Pantheon Book.

World Is Not Enough: A Novel Tr. from French by Willard A. Trask Reissue. Zoe Oldenbourg. LC 48-6397. 1966. 6.95. Pantheon.

World Is Yours. Edith J. Lyttleton. 1934. D. Appleton-Century Company, Incorporated.

World Jones Made. Philip K Dick. LC 56-313627. (Ace double novel books, D-150). 1956. Ace Books.

World Jones Made. Philip K Dick. 1975. (pbk.) 1.25. Ace Books.

World Jones Made. Philip K Dick. LC 79-16811. (Gregg Press science fiction series). (Illus.). 1979. 12.95. Gregg Press.

World Light. Halldor Laxness, pseud. Tr. by Magnus Magnusson from Icelandic. LC 69-16109. (Nordic Translation Ser). Orig. Title: Heimsljos. 1969. 14.00 o.p. (ISBN 0-299-05191-9). U of Wis Pr.

World-Mender: A Novel. Mary Gleed Tuttiett. LC 16-14091. 1916. D. Appleton and Company.

World Menders. Lloyd Biggle. LC 75-139005. (Doubleday science fiction). 1971. 4.95. Doubleday.

World Next Door: By Fritz Peters. Arthur Anderson Peters. LC 49-10430. 1949. Farrar, Straus.

World of A. Alfred Elton Van Vogt. LC 48-1232. 1948. Simon and Schuster.

World of a Thousand Colors. Robert Silverberg. LC 82-72055. 1982. 14.95 (ISBN 0-87795-417-8, Pub. by Priam); pap. 6.95 (ISBN 0-87795-493-3). Arbor Hse.

World of Alphonse Allais. Ed. by Miles Kingston. 160p. 1978. 9.95 (ISBN 0-7011-2177-7, Pub. by Chatto Bodley Jonathan). Merrimack Pub Cir.

World of Apples. John Cheever. LC 72-11018. 1973. 5.95 (ISBN 0-394-48346-4). Knopf.

World of Blandings. Pelham Grenville Wodehouse. LC 76-377659. 1976. 4.95 (ISBN 0-214-20250-X). Barrie and Jenkins.

World of Cant. A Companion Book to "Robert Elsmere" ... (On cover: The fireside series, no. 67). J. S. Ogilvie.

World of Carrick's Cove: A Novel. Gerald Warner Brace. LC 57-10001. 1957. Norton.

TITLE INDEX WORLD'S GREAT ROMANCES.

World of Chance: A Novel. William Dean Howells. 1893. Harper & Brothers.
World of Difference. Bentz Plagemann. LC 70-77554. 1969. 4.95. Morrow.
World of Don Camillo. Giovanni Guareschi. 576p. 1982. 14.95 (ISBN 0-575-02933-1, Pub. by Gollancz England). David & Charles.
World of Dunnet Landing, a Sarah Orne Jewett Collection. Edited by David Bonnell Green. Sarah Orne Jewett. Ed. by David Bonnell Green. (Bison book, BB147). 1962. University of Nebraska Press.
World of Evelyn Waugh. Selected and Edited by Charles J. Rolo. 1st Ed. Evelyn Waugh. LC 58-7852. 1958. Little, Brown.
World of Fiction. Bernard De Voto. 1950. pap. 3.50 o.p. HM.
World of Gold. rev. ed. Timothy Green. (O.s.i.). 1969. pap. 2.45 o.s.i. (ISBN 0-671-20352-5, Touchstone Bks). S&S.
World of Good. Robert Gaffney. LC 70-103430. 1970. 5.95. Dial Press.
World of Great Stories. Ed. by Hiram Collins Haydn. Cournos, John, 1881- Joint Ed. LC 47-11447. 1947. Crown Publishers.
World of Great Stories: 115 Stories, the Best of Modern Literature. Ed. by Hiram Collins Haydn. John Cournos. LC 78-9909. 1978. 5.98 (ISBN 0-517-21662-0). Avenel Books.
World of Henry Orient: A Novel. Nora Johnson. LC 58-10682. 1958. Little, Brown.
World of Hurt: A Novel. Bo Hathaway. LC 80-18147. 1981. 11.95 (ISBN 0-8008-8586-4). Taplinger Pub. Co.
World of Idella May. Richard Sullivan. LC 46-8530. 1946. Doubleday & Company, Inc.
World of Japanese Fiction. Ed. by Yoshinobui Hakutani & Arthur O. Lewis. 1973. pap. 3.95 o.p. (ISBN 0-525-47342-4). Dutton.
World of Jeeves. Pelham Grenville Wodehouse. 1973. (pbk) 1.25. Manor Books.
World of Jeeves, Vol. 1. 2nd ed. P. G. Wodehouse. (1974 ed. 1.75 o.p.). 1976. pap. 1.95 (ISBN 0-532-19119-6). Woodhill.
World of Jeeves, Vol. 1. P. G. Wodehouse. 1973. pap. 1.25 o.p. (12161). Manor Bks.
World of Love. Elizabeth Bowen. 1978. 1.95 (ISBN 0-380-41350-7). Avon Books.
World of Love. 1st Ed. Elizabeth Bowen. LC 55-5209. 1955. Knopf.
World of Mr. Mulliner. Pelham Grenville Wodehouse. LC 74-5813. 1974-1975. 12.95 (ISBN 0-8008-8580-5). Taplinger Pub. Co.
World of Modern Fiction. Ed. by Steven Marcus. LC 66-26933. 1966. Simon and Schuster.
World of Mystery Fiction. Ed. by Elliot L. Gilbert. LC 78-2272. (Illus.). 1977. 14.95 o.p. (ISBN 0-89163-041-4); text ed. 7.95 o.p. (ISBN 0-89163-042-2); 4.95 o.p. study guide (ISBN 0-89163-043-0). Pubs Inc.
World of Nothing. Ronald L. Fair. LC 71-105237. 1970. 12.50 (ISBN 0-89366-096-5). Ultramarine Pub.
World of Nothing: Two Novellas. Ronald L Fair. LC 71-105237. 1970. 5.95. Harper & Row.
World of Null-A. Alfred Elton Van Vogt. (Orig.). 1982. pap. 2.25 (ISBN 0-425-05454-3). Berkley Pub.
World of Null-A. Alfred Elton Van Vogt. 1974. pap. 1.50 (ISBN 0-425-03322-8, Medallion). Berkley Pub.
World of Our Fathers. Irving Howe. LC 76-53818. 1977. pap. 6.95 (ISBN 0-671-22755-6, Touchstone). S&S.
World of Premchand: Selected Stories of Premchand. Dhanpat Rai Srivastava. Tr. by David George Rubin. LC 68-30793. (UNESCO Asian Fiction Series). 1969. 6.50. Indiana University Press.
World of Profit. Louis Auchincloss. LC 69-11213. 1968. 5.95. Houghton Mifflin.
World of Science Fiction. Cassill. Ed. by Robert P. Mills. 1970. pap. 0.75 o.p. (64-374). Paperback Lib.
World of Short Fiction. Ed. by Robert C. Albrecht. LC 69-11841. 1970. pap. text ed. 10.95 (ISBN 0-02-900335-0). Free Pr.
World of Short Fiction, an International Collection. Ed. by Thomas A. Gullason & Leonard Casper. LC 62-7145. 1962. Harper.
World of Strangers. Nadine Gordimer. LC 77-355320. 1976. 3.95 (ISBN 0-224-01274-6). Cape.
World of Sun & Snow & Other Stories. Marie E. Baker. 1978. 7.50 (ISBN 0-533-02764-0). Vantage.
World of Suzie Wong. Richard Lakin Mason. LC 57-9283. 1957. World Pub. Co.
World of the Short Story: Archetypes in Action. Ed. by Oliver Wendell Evans. LC 79-144004. 1971. (ISBN 0-394-31038-1). Knopf.
World of Tragedy. Ed. by John Kimmey & Ashley Brown. 1981. pap. 4.50 (ISBN 0-451-61991-9, ME1991, Ment). NAL.
World of Trouble. Robert E Toomey. 1973. (pbk) 1.25 (ISBN 0-345-03262-4). Ballantine Books.
World of Ukridge. P. G. Wodehouse. 1960. 13.95 o.s.i. (ISBN 0-8277-0237-X). British Bk Ctr.
World of William Clissold: A Novel at a New Angle. Herbert George Wells. LC 72-601. 1972. (ISBN 0-8371-6338-2). Greenwood Press.
World of William Clissold: A Novel at a New Angle. Herbert George Wells. LC 26-172457. George H. Doran Company.
World of Women. John Davys Beresford. LC 13-13964. 1913. 1.35. The Macaulay Company.
World of Wonder: An Introduction to Imaginative Literature. Ed. by Fletcher Pratt. LC 51-12260. 1951. Twayne Publishers.
World of Wonderful Reality. Ernest Temple Thurston. LC 19-14913. 1919. D. Appleton and Company.
World of Wonders. William Robertson Davies. LC 75-38778. 1976. 8.95 (ISBN 0-670-78812-0). Viking Press.
World of Wonders. William Robertson Davies. LC 76-39849. 1977. 1.95 (ISBN 0-14-004389-6). Penguin Books.
World of Yesterday. 1st Ed. Dorothea F Baker. LC 53-13193. 1953. Pageant Press.
World Out of Mind: By J. T. M'Intosh Pseud. 1st Ed. James Murdoch Macgregor. LC 53-6252. (Doubleday science fiction). 1953. Doubleday.
World Out of Time: A Novel. Larry Niven. LC 76-3373. 7.95 (ISBN 0-03-017776-6). Holt, Rinehart and Winston.
World Outside. Rudolf Ditzen, pseud. LC 34-39242. 1934. Simon and Schuster.
World Outside. Harold MacGrath. LC 23-7995. 1923. Doubleday, Page & Company.
World Over. Edith Newbold Jones Wharton. LC 36-9233. 1936. D. Appleton-Century Company, Incorporated.
World Over: Stories of Manifold Places and People.1st Ed. William Somerset Maugham. LC 52-11799. 1952. Doubleday.
World Set Free. Herbert George Wells. 1974. pap. 0.95 o.p. (LB0013X). Leisure Bks.
World Set Free: A Story of Mankind. Herbert George Wells. LC 14-5817. E. P. Dutton & Company.
World Shuffler. Keith Laumer. LC 70-108347. 1970. 4.95. Putnam.
World Shut Out. Norval Richardson. LC 19-15549. 1919. C. Scribner's Sons.
World So Fair. Karen Hansen Peyton. LC 63-17051. 1963. Chilton Books.
World So Wide. Sinclair Lewis. 256p. 1974. pap. 1.75 (ISBN 0-532-17113-6). Woodhill.
World So Wide: A Novel. Sinclair Lewis. LC 51-9716. 1951. Random Housa.
World Soul. Mikhail Tikhonovich Emtsev & Eremei Iudovich Paranov. LC 77-10908. 7.95 (ISBN 0-02-536020-5). Macmillan.
World, the Church, and the Devil. John Archibald Morison. LC 16-18486. R. G. Badger; Etc., Etc.
World: The Flesh, and Father Smith. Bruce Marshall. LC 57-215. (Doubleday image book, D47). 1957. Image Books.
World, the Flesh, and Father Smith. Bruce Marshall. LC 45-583928. 1945. Houghton Mifflin Company.
World, the Flesh and the Devil. authorized ed.... world the flesh and the devil ed. Mary Elizabeth Braddon Maxwell. (Lovell's international series, no. 165). J. W. Lovell Company.
World Their Own. George E. Shirley. 1965. 2.50 o.p. Vantage.
World They Wanted. Herbert D Kastle. LC 61-133924. 1961. St. Martin's Press.
World to Blame. A Novel. Waldorf Henry Phillips. LC 7-36057. 1874. Claxton, Remsen & Haffelfinger.
World to Live in. William Carey Wonderly. LC 18-21537. 1918. Moffat, Yard & Company.
World to Mend; the Journal of a Working Man. Margaret Pollock Sherwood. LC 20-17008. 1920. Little, Brown, and Company.
World to Win. Jack Conroy. LC 35-7312. Covici, Friede.
World to Win. Upton Beall Sinclair. LC 46-3965. 1946. The Viking Press.
World to Win. Upton Beall Sinclair. (His Lanny Budd series, no. 7). 1973. 1.50. Curtis Books.
World Turned Upside Down. William Rayner. LC 72-96302. 1970. 5.95. Morrow.
World War III. Brian House. (Orig.). 1982. pap. 2.75 (ISBN 0-671-44293-7). PB.
World War III. John Stanley. LC 75-24559. 1976. (pbk.) 1.95 (ISBN 0-380-00487-9). Avon.
World War III: Signs of the Impending Battle of Armageddon. John W. White. 1977. pap. 2.95 o.p. (ISBN 0-310-34362-3). Zondervan.
World Was Seventeen. Marie Sherman Cary. LC 31-6867. 1931. 2.00. The Century Co.
World We Do Not See. Judith Elizabeth Farley. LC 13-164423. 1912. 1.25. Broadway Publishing Company.
World We Live in. Louis Bromfield. LC 44-9147. 1944. Harper & Brothers.
World Well Lost. John Aiken. LC 74-131063. 1971. 4.95. Doubleday.
World Well Lost. Esther Robertson. LC 7-41680. 1898. Benziger Brothers.
World Went Mad. John Brophy. LC 34-42419. The Macmillan Company.
World Went Very Well Then. Walter Besant. (On cover: Lovell's library. v. 17, no. 812). 1887. J. W. Lovell Company.
World Went Very Well Then. A Novel. Walter Besant. (On cover: Seaside library. Pocket ed., no. 906). 1886. G. Munro.
World Went Very Well Then. A Novel. Walter Besant. (Harper's Franklin square library, no. 557). 1886. Harper & Brothers.
World Where Sex Was Born. Peter Kanto. (Orig.). 1968. pap. 1.75 o.s.i. (123, Ophelia). Olympia.
World with a Fence. Marian McCamy Sims. LC 36-594. J. B. Lippincott Company.
World Within These Walls. Desemea Wilson. LC 39-32375. 1939. E. P. Dutton & Co., Inc.
World Without End. Francine du Plessix Gray. LC 81-86255. 368p. 1982. pap. 3.50 (ISBN 0-86721-079-6). Playboy Pbks.
World Without End. Grant Martin Overton. LC 21-4319. 1921. Doubleday, Page & Company.
World Without End. Amber Reeves, pseud. LC 11-292364. 1911. 1.25. Sturgis & Walton Company.
World Without End: A Novel. Gilbert Frankau. LC 43-247310. 1943. E. P. Dutton & Co., Inc.
World Without End: A Novel. Francine Du Plessix Gray. LC 81-1493. 13.95 (ISBN 0-671-42786-5). Simon and Schuster.
World Without End, Amen. Jimmy Breslin. LC 73-384. 1973. 6.95 (ISBN 0-670-79020-6). Viking Press.
World Without End, Amen. Jimmy Breslin. 1974. (pbk.) 1.75. Avon.
World Without Heroes. Arthur C Fields. LC 50-7167. 1950. Whittlesey House.
World Without Raiment. Louise Dardenelle. LC 43-117423. Valiant Press.
World Without Souls... 4th american, from the 2d london ed. John William Cunningham. LC 6-31726. 1810. Published by John Kingston... Benjamin Edes, Printer..
World Without Souls... John William Cunningham. LC 6-31581. 1815. E. Earl..
World Without Visa. Jean Malaquais & Grant, Peter, Tr. LC 48-6934. 1948. Doubleday.
World Without Women. Virgilio Martini. LC 72-144379. 1971. 5.95. Dial Press.
World Wonders. Lloyd Biggle, Jr. (Science Fiction Ser). pap. 0.95 o.p. (UQ1015). DAW Bks.
World Wreckers. Marion Zimmer Bradley. LC 79-9385. (Gregg science fiction series). (Illus.). 1979. 9.50 (ISBN 0-8398-2515-3). Gregg Press.
Worldlings. Leonard Merrick. LC 6017. 1900. Doubleday, Page & Company.
Worldlings. Leonard Merrick. LC 20-5621. (Half-title: The works of Leonard Merrick). 1920. E. P. Dutton and Company.
Worldlings. Leonard Merrick. LC 21-4120. (Half-title: The works of Leonard Merrick). 1920. E. P. Dutton and Company.
Worldly Goods. Michael Korda. LC 81-40213. 15.95 (ISBN 0-394-51251-0). Random House.
Worldly Mental Calculations: An Annotated Translation of Ihara Saikaku's Seken Munezanyo. Saikaku Ihara. LC 70-635568. (California. University. University of California Publications: Occasional Papers: No. 5: Literature). 1976. (ISBN 0-520-09406-9). University of California Press.
Worldly Twin. The Heavenly Twins "Not in It.". 1893. G. W. Dillingham.
Worlds. Joe W. Haldeman. 1982. pap. 2.50 (ISBN 0-671-43594-9, Timescape). PB.
Worlds: A Novel of the Near Future. Joe W Haldeman. LC 80-51774. 1981. 12.95 (ISBN 0-670-78984-4). Viking Press.
Worlds Apart. Marthe Lucie Lahovary Bibesco. Tr. by Butler, Pierce. LC 35-13820. 1935. D. Appleton-Century Company, Incorporated.
Worlds Apart. Leo P. Kelley. LC 79-51076. (Space Police Bks.). 1979. pap. 4.24 (ISBN 0-8224-6378-4). Pitman Learning.
Worlds at War. Steven Caldwell. LC 79-52771. 3.98 (ISBN 0-517-29227-0). Crescent Books.
Worlds Beginning. Robert Ardrey. LC 45-1426. Duell, Sloan and Pearce.
World's Best Doctor Stories: Edited by Noah D. Fabricant and Heinz Werner. Ed. by Noah Daniel Fabricant. LC 51-13008. 1951. Garden City Books.
World's Best One Hundred Detective Stories (in Ten Volumes) Ed. by Eugene Thwing. LC 29-243793. Funk & Wagnalls Company.
World's Best Science Fiction: 1972. Ed. by Donald A. Wollheim. pap. 0.95 o.p. (UQ1005). Daw Bks.
World's Best Science Fiction: 1974 Annual. Ed. by Donald A. Wollheim. (Science Fiction Ser). pap. 1.25 o.p. (UY1109). DAW Bks.
World's Best Science Fiction: 1975 Annual. Ed. by Donald A. Wollheim. (Science Fiction Ser). pap. 1.50 o.p. (UW1170). DAW Bks.
World's Best Science Fiction: 1976 Annual. Ed. by Donald A. Wollheim. (Science Fiction Ser). pap. 1.50 o.p. (UW1232). DAW Bks.
World's Best Science Fiction 1977 Annual. Ed. by Donald A. Wollheim. (Science Fiction Ser.). 1977. pap. 1.75 (ISBN 0-87997-297-1, UE1297). DAW Bks.
World's Best Science Fiction, 1978 Edition. Ed. by Donald A. Wollheim. (Science Fiction Ser). (Orig.). 1978. pap. 1.95 (ISBN 0-87997-376-5, UJ1376). DAW Bks.
World's Best SF Annual 1979. Ed. by Donald A. Wollheim. (Science Fiction Ser.). 1979. pap. 2.25 (ISBN 0-87997-459-1, UE1459). DAW Bks.
World's Best SF, 1972 Annual. Ed. by Donald A. Wollheim. (Science Fiction Ser.). 304p. 1972. pap. 1.75 o.p. (UE1349). DAW Bks.
World's Best SF: 1973 Annual. Ed. by Donald A. Wollheim. (Science Fiction Ser.). (Orig.). 1973. pap. 0.95 o.p. (UQ1053). DAW Bks.
World's Best Short Short Stories. Ed. by Roger B. Goodman. (gr. 6-12,RL 6). pap. 1.95 (ISBN 0-553-13598-8, Y13598-8). Bantam.
World's Best Short Short Stories: Edited by Roger B. Goodman. Ed. by Roger B. Goodman. LC 67-17772. (Bantam pathfinder editions, FP172). 1967. Bantam Books.
Worlds Beyond Dune: The Best of Frank Herbert, 5 bks. Frank Herbert. Incl. Jesus Incident; Whipping Star; Destination: Void; Godmakers; Dosadi Experiment. 1982. Boxed Set. pap. 13.25 (ISBN 0-425-05836-0). Berkley Pub.
World's Daughter. Cyril Harcourt. LC 13-21068. 1913. John Lane.
World's Delight. Fulton Oursler. LC 29-16850. 1929. Harper & Brothers.
World's Desire. Henry Rider Haggard & Andrew Lang. LC 72-175455. (Ballantine adult fantasy series). 1972. 1.25 (ISBN 0-345-02467-2). Ballantine Books.
World's Desire: A Novel. Henry Rider Haggard & Lang, Andrew, 1844-1912, Joint Author. LC 6-46155. (On cover: Harper's Franklin square library. no. 684). 1890. Harper & Brothers.
World's Desire: By H. Rider Haggard, Andrew Lang. Illus. by Geoffrey Whittam. Henry Rider Haggard & Andrew Lang. LC 66-5454. 1966. bds., 2.95. Macdonald.
World's End. James Conaway. LC 78-11998. 1979. 9.95. Morrow.
World's End. Pamela Hansford Johnson. LC 38-5373. Carrick and Evans, Inc.
World's End. Upton Beall Sinclair. (Lanny Budd series, no. 1). 1973. 1.50. Curtis Bks.
World's End. Upton Beall Sinclair. LC 40-7427. 1940. The Viking Press.
World's-End. Amelie Rives Chanler Troubetzkoy. 1914. Frederick A. Stokes Company.
World's End and Other Stories. Paul Theroux. LC 80-12207. 1980. 9.95 (ISBN 0-395-29453-3). Houghton Mifflin.
Worlds' Ends. Jakob Wassermann & Galantiere, Lewis, 1895- Tr. LC 27-24344. Boni & Liveright.
World's Fair Murders. John Ashenhurst. LC 33-16242. 1933. Houghton Mifflin Company.
World's Fair Mystery. Weldon J Cobb. (On cover: American author's series, no. 1). 1892. Melbourne Publishing Company.
World's Fair Nineteen Ninety-Two. Robert Silverberg. 256p. 1982. pap. 2.50 (ISBN 0-441-90923-X, Pub. by Ace Science Fiction). Ace Bks.
World's Fifty Best Short Novels... Ed. by Grant Martin Overton. LC 29-16994. Funk & Wagnalls Company.
World's Finger: A London Mystery... Thomas W Hanshew. LC 1-31446. 1901. C.E. Irwin & Co.
World's Great Adventure Stories. one-volume ed. LC 79-163049. (Short story index reprint series). 1971. (ISBN 0-8369-3963-8). Books for Libraries Press.
World's Great Adventure Stories. one volume ed. LC 29-59693. W. J. Black, Inc.
World's Great Detective Stories. one volume ed. LC 29-930. W. J. Black, Inc.
World's Great Detective Stories: A Chronological Anthology. S. S. Van Dine, pseud. 1927. 12.50. Havertown Bks.
World's Great Detective Stories: A Chronological Anthology. Ed. by Willard Huntington Wright. LC 32-4641. Blue Ribbon Books.
World's Great Detective Stories: American and English Masterpieces, Edited, with an Introduction. Ed. by William Jacob Cuppy. LC 43-17450. 1943. The World Publishing Company.
World's Great Humorous Stories. LC 44-1894. 1944. The World Publishing Company.
World's Great Love Novels: Edited, with an Introduction. Ed. by Edwin Seaver. LC 44-7913. 1944. The World Publishing Company.
World's Great Romances. one volume ed. LC 29-796572. W. J. Black, Inc.

World's Great Short Stories: Masterpieces of American, English and Continental Literature. Ed. by Morris Edmund Speare. LC 42-20278. 1942. The World Publishing Company.
World's Great Short Stories: Masterpieces of American, English and Continental Literature. Ed. by Morris Edmund Speare. LC 47-420. 1946. The World Publishing Company.
World's Great Spy Stories Edited, with an Introduction. Ed. by Vincent Starrett. LC 44-8574. 1944. The World Publishing Company.
World's Great Tales of the Sea. Ed. by William McFee. LC 44-857345. 1944. The World Publishing Company.
World's Greatest Boxing Stories. Ed. by Harold Uriel Ribalow. LC 52-14183. 1952. Twayne Publishers.
World's Greatest Christmas Stories. Ed. by Eric Posselt. LC 49-50199. 1949. Ziff-Davis Pub. Co.
World's Greatest Detectives & Their Most Famous Cases. Bruce Henderson & Sam Summerlin. pap. 3.95 (ISBN 0-06-464023-X, BN). B&N NY.
World's Greatest Hoaxes. Richard Saunders. LC 79-89967. 192p. (Orig.). 1980. pap. 1.95 (ISBN 0-87216-606-6). Playboy Pbks.
World's Greatest Horse Stories. Ed. by J. N. Watson. LC 79-10676. (Illus.). 1979. 11.95 o.s.i. (ISBN 0-448-23171-9). Paddington.
World's Greatest True Stories. LC 42-5130. 1932. Macfadden Book Company, Inc.
World's Illusion. Jakob Wassermann & Lewisohn, Ludwig, 1882- Tr. LC 20-22159. (Half-title: The European library, ed. by J. E. Spingarn). 1920. Harcourt, Brace and Howe.
World's Illusion. Jakob Wassermann & Lewisohn, Ludwig, 1882- Tr. LC 26-16540. (Half-title: The European library, edited by J. E. Spingarn). 1926. Harcourt, Brace and Company.
World's Illusion. Jakob Wassermann & Lewisohn, Ludwig, 1882- Tr. LC 30-29996. 1930. Harcourt, Brace and Company.
Worlds in Collision. Immanuel Velikovsky. 1980. pap. 3.50 (ISBN 0-671-82717-0). PB.
World's Last Corner. Theodor Plivier. LC 51-2262. 1951. Appleton-Century-Crofts.
World's Mercy. Mary Gleed Tuttiett. LC 72-125239. (Short story index reprint series). 1970. Books for Libraries Press.
World's Mercy. Mary Gleed Tuttiett. LC 610.
World's Most Intriguing True Mysteries. Rupert Furneaux. LC 66-21117. (Illus.). 1969. pap. 2.00 o.p. (ISBN 0-668-01915-8). Arco.
Worlds of A. E. Van Vogt. Alfred Elton Van Vogt. 1974. (pbk.) 1.25. Ace Books.
Worlds of Color see Black Flame; a Trilogy.
Worlds of Fiction: Stories in Context. Ed. by T. Y. Greet et al. LC 64-2841. 1964. pap. text ed. 6.50 o.p. (3-19971). HM.
Worlds of Frank Herbert. Frank Herbert. LC 80-14583. (Series: Gregg Press Science Fiction Series.). 1980. 13.50 (ISBN 0-8398-2649-4). Gregg Press.
Worlds of Fritz Leiber. Fritz Leiber. LC 79-10247. (Gregg Press science fiction series). 1979. 15.00 (ISBN 0-8398-2477-7). Gregg Press.
Worlds of Fritz Leiber. Fritz Leiber. Ace.
Worlds of George O. George Oliver Smith. 352p. 1982. pap. 3.50 (ISBN 0-553-22532-4). Bantam.
Worlds of Jack Vance. Jack Vance. 1973. (pbk) 1.25. Ace.
Worlds of Maybe: Seven Stories of Science Fiction. Ed. by Robert Silverberg. 1974. (pbk.) 0.95. Dell.
Worlds of Maybe: Seven Stories of Science Fiction. Ed. by Robert Silverberg. LC 73-123115. 1970. 4.95. T. Nelson.
Worlds of Never: An Original Anthology. Ed. by R. Reginald & Douglas Alver Menville. LC 77-84278. (Lost Race & Adult Fantasy Ser.). (Illus.). 1978. lib. bdg. 28.00x (ISBN 0-405-11016-2). Ayer Co.
Worlds of Never: Three Fantastic Novels. Douglas Alver Menville & R Reginald. LC 77-84278. (Lost Race and Adult Fantasy Fiction). (Illus.). 1978. 28.00 (ISBN 0-405-11016-2). Arno Press.
Worlds of Poul Anderson. Poul Anderson. LC 78-319847. (Gregg Press Science Fiction Series). 1978. (4 vol. set) 56.00. Gregg Press.
Worlds of Poul Anderson. 1974. (pbk.) 1.25. Ace Books.
Worlds of Robert F. Young: Sixteen Stories of Science Fiction and Fantasy. Robert F Young. LC 65-11979. 1965. Simon and Schuster.
Worlds of Science Fiction. Ed. by Theodore W. Hipple & Robert G. Wright. (Literature Ser.). (gr. 7-12). 1979. pap. text ed. 6.52 (ISBN 0-205-06416-7, 4964160); tchrs'. ed. 3.44. Allyn.
Worlds of Science Fiction. Ed. by Robert P. Mills. LC 63-12175. 1963. Dial Press.
Worlds of the Imperium. Keith Laumer. (Berkley Medallion Book). 1977. 1.50 (ISBN 0-425-03466-6). Berkley Pub. Corp.
Worlds of the Imperium. Keith Laumer. 1973. (pbk.) 0.95. Ace Books.
Worlds of Tomorrow: Science-Fiction with a Difference. Ed. by August William Derleth. LC 52-12383. 1953. Pellegrini &Cudahy.
Worlds of Wonder: Sixteen Tales of Science Fiction. Ed. by Harry Harrison. LC 76-78664. 1969. 4.50. Doubleday.
Worlds of Wonder: Three Tales of Fantasy. William Olaf Stapledon. LC 49-50143. 1949. Fantasy Pub. Co.
World's One Hundred Best Short Stories... Ed. by Grant Martin Overton. LC 27-203469. Funk & Wagnalls Company.
World's Orphan. Boris De Tanko & Guerney, Bernard Gullbert, Tr. LC 31-25263. 1931. The Elf Publishers, Inc.
World's People. Julie Grinnell Storrow Cruger. LC 2-23411. 1902. J. F. Taylor & Company.
World's Rough Hand: Toil and Adventure at the Antipodes. Hubert Phelps Whitmarsh. 1898. The Century Co.
World's Shortest Stories: An Anthology. 1st Ed. Ed. by Richard Gibson Hubler. LC 61-8604. 1961. Duell, Sloan and Pearce.
World's Ten Greatest Novels. William Somerset Maugham. Orig. Title: Great Novelists & Their Novels. pap. 0.60 o.p. (R316, Prem). Fawcett World.
Worlds to Come. Ed. by Damon Francis Knight. 1970. pap. 0.75 o.p. (T2271, GM). Fawcett World.
Worlds to Come: Nine Science Fiction Adventures. Ed. by Damon Francis Knight. (Gold medal bk., R1942). 1968. Fawcett.
Worlds to Come: Nine Science Fiction Adventures. Ed. by Damon Francis Knight. LC 67-4153. 1967. Harper & Row.
World's Verdict: A Novel. Mark Hopkins. LC 7-5247. 1888. Ticknor and Company.
World's Warrant. Norah Davis. LC 7-13951. 1907. Houghton, Mifflin and Company.
Worldwide Machine: A Novel. Paolo Volponi. LC 66-26536. 1967. Grossman Publishers.
Worleys. Reese, Lizette Woodworth. LC 36-19223. Farrar & Rinehart, Incorporated.
Worm in the Bud. Ronald Pearsall. 1983. pap. 7.95 (ISBN 0-14-006343-9). Penguin.
Worm of Death. Nicholas Blake. 1976. pap. 2.25i (ISBN 0-06-080400-9, P400, PL). Har-Row.
Worm of Death. Nicholas Blake. 1962. pap. 0.95 o.p. (01679, Collier). Macmillan.
Worm of Death. Cecil Day-Lewis. (Perennial Library). (Illus.). 1976. 1.75 (ISBN 0-06-080400-9). Harper & Row.
Worm of Death. Day-Lewis, Cecil. LC 75-300061. 1973. 1.80 (ISBN 0-85617-304-5). White Lion Publishers.
Worm Ouroboros. Eric Rucker Eddison & Henderson, Keith, Illus. LC 26-267191. 1926. A. & C. Boni.
Worm Ouroboros: A Romance; Illustrated by Keith Henderson. With an Introd. by Orville Prescott. 1st Ed. Eric Rucker Eddison. LC 52-10432. 1952. Dutton.
Worm That Turned. William Robbins Gaut. LC 27-156042. 1927. Charleroi Publishing Company.
Worm Turns: By Stormy Pseud. 1st Ed. Willow M Stephan. LC 54-474. 1953. Pageant Press.
Worms Are Singing. Jerry Bumpus. 1979. 1.75 (ISBN 0-912824-22-0). Vagabond Pr.
Wormwood. Marie Corelli. pap. 4.95 (ISBN 0-910122-38-5). Amherst Pr.
Wormwood: A Drama of Paris. Marie Corelli. LC 36-29347. (On cover: The home library). A. L. Burt Company.
Worn Doorstep. Margaret Pollock Sherwood. LC 16-194205. 1916. Little, Brown, and Company.
Worn Doorstep. Margaret Pollock Sherwood. LC 17-269905. 1917. Little, Brown and Company.
Worse Than a Crime. Anne Burton. (Raven House Mysteries Ser.). 224p. 1982. pap. cancelled (ISBN 0-373-63046-8, Pub. by Worldwide). Harlequin Bks.
Worship of the Golden Calf. A Story of Wage-Slavery in Massachusetts. Charles Sheldon French. LC 8-23107. 1908. C. S. French.
Worship the Night. Mary Vigliante. 288p. (Orig.). 1982. pap. 2.95 (ISBN 0-505-51781-7). Tower Bks.
Worship the Wind. Mitchell Caine, pseud. 2.25 (ISBN 0-449-14178-0). Fawcett Gold Medal.
Worshipful Lucia. Edward Frederic Benson. LC 35-17484. 1935. Doubleday, Doran & Company, Inc.
Worshipful Society... John Galsworthy. LC 32-26054. 1932. C. Scribner's Sons.
Worshipped and the Damned. William Hegner. 1975. (pbk.) 1.75 (ISBN 0-671-78761-6). Pocket Books.
Worshipper of the Image. Richard Le Gallienne. LC 340. 1900. John Lane.
Worshippers: A Novel. Henry Berman. LC 6-4640. The Grafton Press.
Worst Enemies. Jack Scaparro. 352p. 1983. pap. 3.75 (ISBN 0-440-09590-5). Dell.
Worst Foe: A Temperance Novel. Grace Strong. LC 8-16877. 1885. W. G. Hubbard & Co.
Worst Foe: A Temperance Study. 5th ed. Grace Strong. LC 42-26108. 1886. W. G. Hubbard & Co.
Worst Foot Forward. Alison Kane. LC 65-25594. 3.95. Christopher Pub.
Worst Way to Die. Bruno Rossi. (Sharpshooter,#4). 1974. (pbk.) 0.95. Leisure Books.
Worth Avenue. John McIlvain. LC 82-19932. 16.95 (ISBN 0-399-31020-7). Coward, McCann & Geoghegan.
Worth Dale: A Novel. Jesse Gentry Hollingsworth. LC 51-5021. 1951. Exposition Press.
Worth of a Woman. David Graham Phillips. LC 75-96682. (American Authors Ser). 1970. lib. bdg. 12.50 o.s.i. (ISBN 0-512-00557-5). Garrett Pr.
Worth Remembering. Rhys James. LC 33-32009. 1933. Longmans, Green and Co.
Worth While. Frances Frederica Montresor. LC 41-40517. 1896. E. Arnold.
Worth While. And, Lady. Frances Frederica Montresor. LC 7-31124. 1896. E. Arnold.
Worth While: Or, Ships That Never Came in. Mary J Capron. LC 51-46671. Congregational Pub. Society.
Worthy Heart: By Joan Garrison Pseud. William Arthur Neubauer. LC 53-113090. 1953. Arcadia House.
Worthy Man: By Robert Standish Pseud. Digby George Gerahty. LC 52-12449. 1952. Macmillan.
Wotan Warhead. James Follett. LC 78-66261. 1979. 9.95 (ISBN 0-8128-2605-1). Stein and Day.
Would Any Man? Charles Peale Didier. LC 6-36833. 1898. Williams & Wilkins Company.
Would-Be Saint. Robin Jenkins. LC 79-9653. 207p. 1980. 9.95 (ISBN 0-8008-8710-7). Taplinger.
Would Christ Belong to a Labor Union! Or, Henry Fiedling's Dream. Cortland Myers. LC 1634. (On cover: Alliance library. no. 8). Street & Smith.
Would You Believe Love? Eliza McCormack. LC 78-162956. 1972. 1.25. New Amer. Lib.
Would You Have Left Her? William F Kip. LC 7-12545. 1888. G. P. Putnam's Sons.
Would You Kill Him? George Parsons Lathrop. LC 73-104507. 1970. (ISBN 0-8398-1151-9). Literature House.
Would You Kill Him? A Novel. George Parsons Lathrop. LC 7-13856. 1890. Harper & Brothers.
Wound. Malick Fall. Tr. by Clive Wake. (African Writers Series, 144). 1975. Heinemann.
Wound: Excerpts from the Second Novel of a Trilogy. William Richardson. LC 75-320677. (Yes! Capra chapbook series; no. 16). 1974. 10.00 (ISBN 0-912264-86-1) (ISBN 0-912264-85-3). Capra Press.
Wound Is Green: A Novel of Adventure. 1st Ed. Franklin Barnett. LC 56-8711. 1956. Exposition Press.
Wound of Love. Robert Verlin Cassill. LC 56-217495. (Avon 710). 1956. Avon Publications.
Wound-Stripes: Stories of After the War. Bertha Lippincott Coles. LC 21-21553. 1921. J. B. Lippincott Company.
Wounded by Love: A. C. Emmerick, 1774-1824. T. A. Rattler. 4.50 o.p. Vantage.
Wounded Cormorant, and Other Stories. Liam O'Flaherty. LC 73-14764. (Norton library, N704). 1973. 1.95 (ISBN 0-393-00704-9). Norton.
Wounded Face. Mabel Adelaide Farnum. LC 12-148. 1911. 1.00. Angel Guardian Press.
Wounded Heart. Kathleen Ross. (O.s.i.). 1973. pap. 0.75 o.s.i. (BT50551). Belmont-Tower.
Wounded Heart. Kathleen Ross. (O.s.i.). 1976. pap. 1.25 o.s.i. (BT50994). Belmont-Tower.
Wounded Heart. Kathleen Ross. 1976. 1.25. Belmont Tower.
Wounded Land: Book One of the Second Chronicles of Thomas Covenant. Stephen R. Donaldson. 512p. 1981. 12.95 (ISBN 0-345-28647-2); pap. 2.95 (ISBN 0-345-27831-3); 36 copy floor display. Ballantine.
Wounded Men, Broken Promises. Bob Klein. 300p. 1981. 13.95 o.s.i. (ISBN 0-02-563930-7). Macmillan.
Wounded Name. Dorothy Kathleen Broster. LC 23-9172. 1923. Doubleday, Page & Company.
Wounded Name. Charles King. LC 7-122242. F. T. Neely.
Wounded Planet. Ed. by Roger Elwood. 1974. (pbk.) 1.25. Bantam Books.
Wounded Souls. Philip Hamilton Gibbs. LC 20-26983. George H. Doran Company.
Wounds. Maureen Duffy. 1973. (pbk.) 1.50. Dell.
Wounds. Maureen Duffy. LC 76-79322. 1969. 4.95. Knopf.
Wounds in the Rain. Stephen Crane. LC 72-3294. (Short Story Index Reprint Ser). 1972. Repr. of 1900 ed. 22.00 (ISBN 0-8369-4145-4). Ayer Co.
Wounds in the Rain: A Collection of Stories Relating to the Spanish-American War of 1898. Stephen Crane. cancelled o.p. (ISBN 0-403-07780-X). Scholarly.
Wounds in the Rain: War Stories. Stephen Crane. LC 72-3294. (Short story index reprint series). 1972. (ISBN 0-8369-4145-4). Books for Libraries Press.
Wounds of Hunger. Translated and Edited by Barnaby Conrad. Luis Spota. LC 57-11129. 1957. Houghton Mifflin.
Woven in the Tapestry. Emily Price Post. LC 8-9525. 1908. Moffat, Yard and Company.
Woven Web. Pierre Audemars. LC 65-22587. 3.50. Pub. for the Crime Club by Doubleday.
Woven with the Ship: A Novel of 1865, Together with Certain Other Veracious Tales of Various Sorts. Cyrus Townsend Brady. LC 73-128722. (Short story index reprint series). (Illus.). 1970. Books for Libraries Press.
Woven with the Ship: A Novel of 1865, Together with Certain Other Veracious Tales of Various Sorts, by Cyrus Townsend Brady... Cyrus Townsend Brady. LC 2-23905. 1902. J. B. Lippincott Company.
Wow Factor. Robert Terrall. 1970. pap. 0.75 o.p. (T2274, GM). Fawcett World.
Wrack and Rune. Charlotte MacLeod. LC 81-43256. 1982. 10.95 (ISBN 0-385-17801-8). Published for the Crime Club by Doubleday.
Wrack and Rune. Charlotte MacLeod. LC 82-10009. 10.95 (ISBN 0-89621-372-2). Thorndike Press.
Wrack & Rune. Charlotte MacLeod. LC 81-43256. (Crime Club Ser.). 192p. 1982. 10.95 (ISBN 0-385-17801-8). Doubleday.
Wrack & Rune. Charlotte MacLeod. 208p. 1983. pap. 2.75 (ISBN 0-380-61911-3, 61911-3). Avon.
Wrack & Rune. large type ed. Charlotte Macleod. LC 82-10009. 322p. 1982. Repr. of 1982 ed. 10.95 (ISBN 0-89621-372-2). Thorndike Pr.
Wraith... Philip MacDonald. Pub. for the Crime Club, Inc., by Doubleday, Doran & Company, Inc.
Wraith of Knopf: And Other Stories. Howard James. Broadway Publishing Co.
Wraiths of Time. Andre Norton, pseud. 1978. pap. 1.95 (ISBN 0-449-23532-7, Crest). Fawcett.
Wraithwood. Luanna Churchill. 1973. 4.95. Lenox Hill Pr.
Wrangler on the Prod. Frank Chester Robertson. LC 50-8565. (Dutton Diamond D western). 1950. Dutton.
Wranglers. Lee D. Willoughby. (Making of America Ser.: No. 33). (Orig.). 1982. pap. 3.25 (ISBN 0-440-09838-6). Dell.
Wranglers and Rounders: The Cowboy Lore of Ross Santee. Ross Santee. LC 80-85229. (Illus.). 20.00 (ISBN 0-87358-284-5). Northland Press.
Wrap Her in Light. Sandra Adelson. LC 80-21014. 448p. 1981. 12.95 (ISBN 0-688-03753-4). Morrow.
Wrap It up. Amber Dean. LC 46-206402. 1946. Pub. for the Crime Club by Doubleday & Company, Inc.
Wrapped for Eternity. Mildred Pace. 1975. pap. 1.25 (ISBN 0-440-98886-1, LFL). Dell.
Wrath and the Wind: A Novel. Alexander Key. LC 49-7653. 1949. Bobbs-Merrill Co.
Wrath of Chane. Norman Gant. 1970. pap. 1.65 o.p. (ISBN 0-447-70401-X). Lancer.
Wrath of Fu Manchu. Sax Rohmer. (Daw Science Fiction#186). 1976. (pbk.) 1.50. Daw Books.
Wrath of Garde. Jerry LaPlante. (Chameleon Ser.: No. 1). 1979. pap. 1.95 (ISBN 0-89083-437-7). Zebra.
Wrath of God. James Graham, pseud. LC 70-144267. 1971. 5.95 o.p. (ISBN 0-385-09475-2). Doubleday.
Wrath of God. James Graham. 1974. (pbk.) 1.25. Dell.
Wrath of God. Henry Patterson. LC 70-144267. 1971. 5.95. Doubleday.
Wrath of the Eagles, a Novel of the Chetniks. Friedrich Heydenau & Mussey, June Barrows, 1910- Tr. LC 43-7868. 1943. E. P. Dutton & Co., Inc.
Wrath of the King. Walter C Utt. LC 65-29028. (Destiny book, D107). Pacific Press Pub. Association.
Wrath of the Lion. Jack Higgins. (Fawcett Gold Medal Book.). 1977. 1.50. (ISBN 0-449-13739-2). Fawcett Publications.
Wrath to Come. Edward Phillips Oppenheim. LC 24-767509. 1924. Little, Brown, and Company.
Wreath and a Curse. Donald Wetzel. LC 50-5252. 1950. Crown Publishers.
Wreath for Arabella. Doris Oppenheim Leslie. (Illus.). 1973. 0.95. Popular Lib.
Wreath for Arabella. Doris Oppenheim Leslie. LC 50-4717. 1948. Hutchinson.
Wreath for Jenny's Grave. Charlotte Hunt. 1975. (pbk.) 0.95. Ace Books.
Wreath for Rivera. Ngaio Marsh. LC 75-44993. (Fifty Classics of Crime Fiction, 1900-1950; 36). 1976. 12.00 (ISBN 0-8240-2385-4). Garland Pub.
Wreath for Rivers. Ngaio Marsh. LC 49-3021. 1949. Little, Brown.

Wreath for the Bride. Maria Lang. Tr. by Joan Tate. LC 68-31461. 1968. 3.95 o.p. (101849). Regnery.

Wreath for the Bride. Dagmar Lange. LC 68-31461. 1968. 3.95. H. Regnery Co.

Wreath for the Enemy. 1st Ed. Pamela Frankau. LC 54-6013. 1954. Harper.

Wreath for the Maidens. John Munonye. (African Writers Ser.). 1973. pap. text ed. 2.50x (ISBN 0-435-90121-4). Heinemann Ed.

Wreath for Udomo. Peter Abrahams. LC 77-160084. (American Library). 1971. 1.95. Collier Books.

Wreath for Udomo. 1st American Ed. Peter Abrahams. LC 56-576876. 1956. Knopf.

Wreath from Jessamine Lawn: Or, Free Grace the Flower That Never Fades. Harriet Livermore. LC 7-16058. 1831. Printed for the Authoress.

Wreath of Eve. Arthur Giles. LC 6-44054. F. T. Neely.

Wreath of Lords & Ladies. James Fraser, pseud. LC 75-5261. (Crime Club Ser). 192p. 1975. 5.95 o.p. (ISBN 0-385-11074-X). Doubleday.

Wreath of Lords and Ladies. Alan White. LC 75-19213. 1975. 5.95 (ISBN 0-385-11074-X). Published for the Crime Club by Doubleday.

Wreath of Orchids. Marjorie Shoebridge. LC 78-1247. 1978. 7.95 (ISBN 0-385-13130-5). Doubleday.

Wreath of Orchids. Marjorie Shoebridge. LC 80-81005. 1980. 1.95 (ISBN 0-87216-714-3). Playboy Press.

Wreath of Pale Roses. Erika Duncan. LC 76-53373. 1977. 6.95 (ISBN 0-8027-0570-7, Dist. by Walker & Co.); pap. 4.95 (ISBN 0-8027-7107-6). Magic Circle Press.

Wreath of Pale White Roses. Erika Duncan. LC 76-53373. 4.95 (ISBN 0-8027-7107-6) (ISBN 0-8027-0570-7). Magic Circle Press.

Wreath of Roses. John Blackburn. LC 65-22620. 1965. M. S. Mill Co.; Distributed by Morrow.

Wreath of Roses. Elizabeth Taylor. LC 49-7742. 1949. A. A. Knopf.

Wreath of Song. Robert C Broderick. LC 48-9689. Bruce Pub. Co.

Wreath of Stars. Louise Gerard. LC 12-103536. The Macaulay Company.

Wreath of Stars. Bob Shaw. LC 76-23797. 1977. 5.95 (ISBN 0-385-12463-5). Doubleday.

Wreathed Dagger. Margaret Young. LC 10-4046. 1909. Cassell and Company, Limited.

Wreck. Parley J Cooper. 1977. 1.95 (ISBN 0-441-91965-0). Ace Books.

Wreck. Thakura Ravindranatha. LC 21-10023. 1921. The Macmillan Company.

Wreck. Rabindranath Tagore. pap. 4.00x o.p. Verry.

Wreck of the Active: A Story of Adventure. Frank Vigor Morley. LC 36-27491. 1936. Houghton Mifflin Company.

Wreck of the: Cassandra. Frederic Prokosch. LC 66-144186. 4.95. Farrar.

Wreck of the Chancellor. Jules Verne. LC 1-9788. 1875. J. R. Osgood and Company.

Wreck of the Conemaugh: Being a Record of Some Events Set Down from the Notes of an English Baronet During the American War with Spain. Thornton Jenkins Hains. LC 6-2343. 1900. J. B. Lippincott Company.

Wreck of the Corsaire. William Clark Russell. LC 8-1810. C. H. Sergel Company.

Wreck of the Greyhound: Or, The Romantic Love of the Earl's Daughter. Charles Martin Newell. (Fleetwing series. v. 3). 1889. De Wolfe, Fiske & Co.

Wreck of the Grosvenor. William Clark Russell. LC 23-269319. 1923. Dodd, Mead and Company.

Wreck of the "Grosvenor." An Account of the Mutiny of the Crew and the Loss of the Shop When Trying to Make the Bermudas. William Clark Russell. (Harper's Franklin square library, no. 301). 1883. Harper & Brothers.

Wreck of the "Grosvenor" An Account of the Mutiny of the Crew and the Loss of the Ship When Trying to Make the Bermudas. William Clark Russell. LC 99-4984. (Famous novels of the sea). 1899. C. Scribner's Sons.

Wreck of the Grosvenor. With Portraits of the Author Pictures of Contemporary Scenes and Illus. Reporduced from Early Editions, Together an Introd. by Edouard A. Stackpole. William Clark Russell. LC 58-13087. (Great illustrated classics). 1959. Dodd, Mead.

Wreck of the Mary Deare. Hammond Innes. LC 57-4089. (Perma books, M-4079. Fiction, 9). 1957. Perma Books.

Wreck of the Mary Deare. Hammond Innes. LC 55-9262. 1956. Knopf.

Wreck of the Mary Deare: By Hammond Innes Pseud. 1st American Ed. Ralph Hammond-Innes. LC 55-9262. 1956. Knopf.

Wreck of the "Redwing". Beatrice Ethel Grimshaw. LC 27-169172. 1927. H. Holt and Company.

Wreck of the Running Gale. Garland Roark. LC 52-13570. 1953. Doubleday.

Wreck of the Titan. facs. ed. Morgan Robertson. LC 71-132125. (Short Story Index Reprint Ser). 1912. 13.00 (ISBN 0-8369-3682-5). Ayer Co.

Wreck of the Titan: Or, Futility. Morgan Robertson. LC 74-180261. (Illus.). 1974. 8.00 (ISBN 0-911962-09-3). C's Press.

Wreck of the Titan: Or, Futility. autograph ed. Morgan Robertson. LC 16-115843. 1914. McClure's Magazine and Metropolitan Magazine.

Wreck of the White Bear, East Indiaman. Ellen McGregor Ross. LC 8-677. 1870. G. W. Carleton.

Wreckage of Agathon. John Champlin Gardner. LC 71-122888. 1970. 6.95. Harper & Row.

Wrecked? A Novel. William Osborn Stoddard. LC 8-16300. White, Stokes and Allen,

Wrecked, but Not Lost. A Novel. Harriett Boomer Barber. 1880. J.B. Lippincott & Co.

Wrecked on Labrador. Winfrid Alden Stearns. LC 12-15059. T. Y. Crowell & Co.

Wrecker. Robert Louis Stevenson & Osbourne, Lloyd. LC 8-15699. 1892. C. Scribner's Sons.

Wrecker. Robert Louis Stevenson & Osbourne, Lloyd. LC 5-20450. (Half-title: The biographical edition of the works of Robert Louis Stevenson). 1905. C. Scribner's Sons.

Wrecker. Robert Louis Stevenson & Osbourne, Lloyd. LC 16-3410. 1914. C. Scribner's Sons.

Wrecker. Robert Louis Stevenson & Lloyd Osbourne. LC 82-9570. 1982. 6.50. Dover Publications.

Wreckers. Francis Lynde. LC 20-5584. 1920. C. Scribner's Sons.

Wreckers. A Social Study. George Thomas Dowling. LC 6-34404. 1886. J. B. Lippincott Company.

Wrecking Crew. Donald Hamilton. (Matt Helm Ser). 1979. pap. 1.75 (ISBN 0-449-14053-9, GM). Fawcett.

Wrecking of Offshore Five. Ronald Johnston. LC 68-12577. (Illus.). 1968. Harcourt, Brace & World.

Wrecks and Wreckers. A Tragedy and a Mystery. Sylvia Paul Jerman. LC 99-810. (Neely's booklet library. no. 6). 1899. F. T. Neely.

Wrecks in the Sea of Life. A Novel. Alexander Begg. LC 6-9756. (On cover: Lovell's library. v. 8, no. 423). J. W. Lovell Company.

Wrestler of Philippi: A Tale of the Early Christians. Fannie E Newberry. LC 15-12476. (Sabbath library, v. 9, no. 291). 1896. The David C. Cook Publishing Co.

Wrestler of Philippi: A Tale of the Early Christians. rev. ed. by fannie e. newberry. ed. Fannie E Newberry. LC 14-10425. David C. Cook Publishing Company.

Wrightsville Murders: An Ellery Queen Omnibus. Ellery Queen, pseud. LC 56-5625. Little, Brown.

Wrinkle in Time. Madeleine L'Engle. 192p. 1976. Repr. pap. 1.95 (ISBN 0-440-99805-0, LFL). Dell.

Wrinkle in Time. Madeleine L'Engle. (Yearling Book). 1973. 1.25. Dell.

Wrinkles. Charles Simmons. LC 78-9269. 1978. 7.95 (ISBN 0-374-29333-3). Farrar, Straus, and Giroux.

Wrist Mark. Joseph Smith Fletcher. LC 28-25956. 1928. Z. Z. Knopf.

Write It Murder: By Helen Arre Pseud. Zola Helen Ross. LC 56-10908. 1956. Arcadia House.

Write Me a Murder. Amanda Carter. (Mystery Puzzler Ser.: No. 19). (Illus., Orig.). 1979. pap. 1.95 (ISBN 0-89083-454-7). Zebra.

Write Murder Down. Richard Lockridge. LC 72-7334. 1972. 5.95 (ISBN 0-397-00946-1). Lippincott.

Write on Both Sides of the Paper. Mary Kelly. LC 77-111890. 1970. 4.50. London House & Maxwell.

Write Sorrow on the Earth. Charles Wertenbaker. LC 47-1902. 1947. H. Holt and Cómpany.

Writer & the Shaman. Elemire Zolla. Tr. by Raymond Rosenthal. LC 73-6632. (Helen & Kurt Wolff Bk.). 1973. 12.50 o.p. (ISBN 0-15-199560-5). HarBraceJ.

Writer of Books. Emily Morse Symonds. LC 15-23106. (Half-title: Appletons' town and country library. no. 256). 1899. D. Appleton and Company.

Writer of Fiction. Clive Holland. 1897. Copeland and Day.

Writer's Ant: A Collection of Short Stories. Ed. by Wallace Earle Stegner. LC 50-14822. 1950. Heath.

Writer's Art, a Collection of Short Stories. Wallace Earle Stegner. LC 74-148645. 358p. 1972. Repr. of 1950 ed. lib. bdg. 19.75x (ISBN 0-8371-6009-X, STWA). Greenwood.

Writer's Art: A Collection of Short Stories. Ed. by Wallace Earle Stegner & Richard Scowcroft. LC 74-148645. 1972. (ISBN 0-8371-6009-X). Greenwood Press.

Writer's Choice. Ed. by Rust Hills. John Barth. LC 74-82985. 1974. 9.95. (ISBN 0-679-50504-0) (ISBN 0-679-30270-0). D. McKay Co.

Writing Fiction. Arturo Vivante. The Writer, Inc.

Writing in General and the Short Story in Particular: An Informal Textbook. Rust Hills. LC 77-21224. 1977. 8.95 (ISBN 0-395-25715-8). Houghton Mifflin.

Writing on the Wall. Hilda Glynn Howard. LC 73-91563. (Social History of Canada, 20). 1974. 12.50 (ISBN 0-8020-2070-4) (ISBN 0-8020-2070-4). University of Toronto Press.

Writing on the Wall: A Novel Founded on Olga Nethersole's Play by William J. Hurlbut. Edward Marshall & Hurlbut, William J. LC 10-1230. 1.50. G. W. Dillingham Company.

Writings & Drawings. Bob Dylan. (Illus.). (YA) 1973. 8.95 o.p. (ISBN 0-394-48243-3). Knopf.

Writings of Herman Melville. Incl. Vol. 8. Israel Potter. 23.00 o.s.i. (ISBN 0-8101-0552-7); pap. 6.00 o.s.i. (ISBN 0-8101-0553-5); Vol. 9. Piazza Tales. 23.00 o.s.i. (ISBN 0-8101-0550-0); pap. 6.00 o.s.i. (ISBN 0-8101-0551-9); Vol. 10. Confidence-Man. 23.00 o.s.i. (ISBN 0-8101-0324-9); pap. 6.00 o.s.i. (ISBN 0-8101-0325-7). cancelled o.s.i. Northwestern U Pr.

Writings of Mark Twain Pseud. underwood ed. Samuel Langhorne Clemens. LC 8-20712. 1901-07. American Publishing Company.

Writings of Mark Twain Pseud. author's national ed. Samuel Langhorne Clemens. LC 20-19321. 1907. Harper and Brothers.

Writings of Mrs. Humphry Ward... Mary Augusta Arnold Humphry Ward Ward. LC 10-1255. 1909-12. Houghton Mifflin Company.

Written in Dust: A Mystery Story. Miles Burton. LC 40-488241. 1940. Pub. for the Crime Club by Doubleday, Doran & Co., Inc.

Written in Fire. Florence Marryat Church Lean. (On cover: Lovell's library. v. 19. no. 908). 1887. J. W. Lovell Company.

Written in Red: Or, The Conspiracy in the North Case. (A Story of Boston). Charles Howard Montague & Dyar, C. W. LC 7-31810. Cassell Publishing Company.

Written in Sand. Josephine Young Case. LC 45-1816.

Written in the Stars: A Novel. Alice Michalesi. LC 54-5417. Bruce Humphries.

Written in the Stars: A Novel About Albrecht Durer. Frances Hope Fisher. LC 51-10855. 1951. Harper.

Written Law. A. Thomas Thetford. LC 44-51243. 1944. Pepper Printing Co.

Written on the Wind: A Novel. Robert Wilder. LC 46-443. 1946. G. P. Putnam's Sons.

Written on Water. Vicki Baum. 256p. 1974. pap. 1.50 (ISBN 0-532-15131-3). Woodhill.

Written on Water. Vicki Baum. 1974. (pbk.) 1.50. Manor Books.

Written on Water: A Novel.,531st Ed. Vicki Baum. LC 56-11621. 1956. Doubleday.

Written on Water: Ecrit Sur De L'eau. Francis De Miomandre. LC 29-17529. 1929. Brentano's.

Wrong Angel. H. Moss. 1966. 4.95 o.p. (ISBN 0-02-587580-9). Macmillan.

Wrong Angel. Stanley Moss. 1969. 5.00 (Pub. by Anvil Pr); signed ed. 12.50; pap. 2.50. SBD.

Wrong Body. Arthur Hawthorne Carhart. LC 37-17080. 1937. A. A. Knopf.

Wrong Body. Lucy Beatrice Malleson. LC 51-12106. 1951. Random House.

Wrong Box. Robert Louis Stevenson & Lloyd Osbourne. LC 8-15698. 1889. C. Scribner's Sons.

Wrong Box: By Robert Louis Stevenson and Lloyd Osbourne. With an Introd. by Bernard Darwin. Robert Louis Stevenson & Osbourne, Lloyd. LC 55-1983. (World's classics, 540). 1954. Oxford University Press.

Wrong Box: By Robert Louis Stevenson and Lloyd Osbourne, with a Preface by Mrs. Stevenson. Robert Louis Stevenson & Osbourne, Lloyd. LC 5-30566. (Half-title: The biographical edition of the works of Robert Louis Stevenson). 1905. C. Scribner's Sons.

Wrong Case. James Crumley. LC 74-29598. 1975. 7.95 o.p. (ISBN 0-394-49618-3). Random.

Wrong Case: A Novel. James Crumley. LC 74-29598. 1975. 6.95 (ISBN 0-394-49618-3). Random House.

Wrong End of Time. John Brunner. (Daw sf Books, no. 61). (Illus.). 1973. (pbk.) 0.95. Daw Books.

Wrong End of Time. John Brunner. LC 74-175935. 1971. 4.95. Doubleday.

Wrong Girl. Rob Eden. LC 34-190274. Grosset & Dunlap.

Wrong Letter. Walter S Masterman. LC 26-153773. E. P. Dutton & Company.

Wrong Man. Henry Christopher Bailey. LC 45-8328. 1945. Pub. for the Crime Club by Doubleday, Doran & Company, Inc.

Wrong Man. Katrina Britt. (Harlequin Romances). 192p. 1981. pap. 1.25 (ISBN 0-373-02397-9, Pub. by Harlequin). PB.

Wrong Man: A Novel. Gertrude Gardenier. (On cover: Household library, v. 4, no. 5). Belford, Clarke & Co.

Wrong Man: A Novel. Dorothea Gerard Longard De Longgarde. LC 7-14784. (Half-title: Appletons' town and country library. no. 186). 1896. D. Appleton and Company.

Wrong Man in the Mirror. Philip Loraine. LC 75-12701. 1975. 6.95 (ISBN 0-394-49810-0). Random House.

Wrong Mr. Right: A Novel. Berta Ruck. LC 22-8595. 1922. Dodd, Mead and Company.

Wrong Move: A Romance. Anna Robeson Brown Burr. LC 23-5949. 1923. The Macmillan Company.

Wrong Murder. Craig Rice. LC 40-34598. 1940. Simon and Schuster.

Wrong Murder. Craig Rice. LC 45-6640. 1944. The World Publishing Company.

Wrong Murder Mystery. Charles Bryson. LC 33-8147. E. P. Dutton & Co., Inc.

Wrong Ones in the Dock. T. MofOlorynso Aluko. (African Writers Ser.: No. 242). 195p. 1982. pap. text ed. 6.00x (ISBN 0-435-90242-3). Heinemann Ed.

Wrong People. David Griffin. (Orig.). pap. 0.75 o.p. (54-493). Paperback Lib.

Wrong People. Robin Maugham. LC 78-146475. 1971. 6.95 (ISBN 0-07-040968-4). McGraw-Hill.

Wrong Plantagenet. Marian Palmer. 1973. (pbk) 0.95. Popular Library.

Wrong Plantagenet. Marian Palmer. LC 74-171309. (Illus.). 1972. 6.95. Doubleday.

Wrong Set: And Other Stories. Angus Wilson. LC 50-616967. 1950. Morrow.

Wrong Shadow. Harold Brighouse. LC 23-9853. 1923. R. M. McBride & Company.

Wrong Side of the Moon: By Francis and Stephen Ashton. Francis Leslie Ashton. LC 52-22911. 1952. T. V. Boardman.

Wrong Side of the Sky. Gavin Lyall. LC 61-11584. 1961. Scribner.

Wrong Side of the Tracks. LC 31-6989. The Bobbs-Merrill Company.

Wrong Slant of Red. Harley L Skalland. LC 67-14619. 1967. Dorrance.

Wrong Target. William Kaye. 208p. 1981. pap. 2.95 (ISBN 0-8439-0974-9, Leisure Bks). Nordon Pubns.

Wrong Target. John Wolfe. 1978. pap. 1.75 (ISBN 0-89041-200-6, 3200). Major Bks.

Wrong Turn: By Daniel Harper Pseud. Chandler Brossard. LC 54-364641. (Avon, 591). 1954. Avon Publications.

Wrong Turning. Charlotte Underwood. LC 47-1631. 1947. Harper & Brothers.

Wrong Twin. Harry Leon Wilson. 1921. Doubleday, Page & Company.

Wrong Venus. Charles Williams. LC 82-48818. 160p. pap. 2.84i (ISBN 0-06-080656-7, P 656, PL). Har-Row.

Wrong Verdict. Walter S Masterman. LC 38-5875. 1938. E. P. Dutton & Co., Inc.

Wrong-Way Camper & Other Stories. Jo Stanchfield. LC 72-92847. (Highway Holidays Ser). (gr. 3-6). 1973. pap. text ed. 3.54 o.p. (ISBN 0-8372-0796-7). Bowmar-Noble.

Wrong Way Down... Elizabeth Daly. 1946. Rinehart & Company, Inc.

Wrong Way Home. Alex T. Renck. LC 53-111165. 1954-1953. Lippincott.

Wrong Way Out. Oscar Du Breuil. 4.50 o.p. Vantage.

Wrong Wife. Arthur Somers Roche. LC 32-107675. Sears Publishing Company, Inc.

Wrong Woman. Glen Haley. LC 54-5662. 1954. Dodd, Mead.

Wrong Woman. Charles David Stewart. LC 12-934. 1912. Houghton Mifflin Company.

Wrong World. Louis Paul. LC 38-289878. 1938. Doubleday, Doran & Company, Inc.

Wronghand. Geraldine Tolman Wyatt. LC 49-9799. 1949. Longmans, Green.

Wrongs to Right. Charlotte Rebecca Woglom Bangs. 1892. H. B. Lonnsbury.

Wrostella's Weird. Helen Buckingham Mathers Reeves. Lovell, Coryell & Company.

Wroth. Agnes Sweetman Castle & Castle, Egerton. LC 7-36096. 1907. The Macmillan Company.

Wroth. Agnes Sweetman Castle & Castle, Egerton. LC 8-26197. 1908. The Macmillan Company.

Wu-Hsia. Liang Liang. (ChinAmerica book). 1975. 1.95(pbk.). ChinAmerica Enterprise.

Wulfheim. Sax Rohmer. 1972. 5.00. Bookfinger.

Wullie McWattie's Master. John Joy Bell. LC 10-118771. 0.60. Fleming H. Revell Company.

Wulnoth the Wanderer: A Story of King Alfred of England. Herbert Escott Inman. LC 9-73941. 1908. A. C. McClurg & Co.

Wulnoth the Wanderer: A Story of King Alfred of England. new ed., illustrated by james daugherty. ed. Herbert Escott Inman. LC 28-28676. 1928. Longmans, Green and Co.

Wunpost. Dane Coolidge. LC 20-10766. E. P. Dutton & Company.

Wuthering Heights. Emily Jane Bronte. Ed. by David Daiches. LC 65-29847. (Penguin English library, ELi). 1965. Penguin Books.

Wuthering Heights. Emily Jane Bronte. LC 65-6522. (Perennial classic). 1965. Harper & Row.

Wuthering Heights. Emily Jane Bronte. LC 73-3126. (Bronte, Charlotte, 1816-1855. Life & Works of the Sisters Bronte: Vol. 5). (Illus.). 1973. 25.00 (ISBN 0-404-08835-X). AMS Press.

Wuthering Heights. Emily Jane Bronte. (Signet classic, CP610). 1973. (pbk.) 0.60. New American Lib.

Wuthering Heights. Emily Jane Bronte. 1974. (pbk.) 0.95. Bantam Books.

Wuthering Heights. Emily Jane Bronte. Ed. by Ian Robert James Jack. Hilda Marsden. LC 76-378952. (Clarendon edition of the novels of the Brontes). 1976. 27.25 (ISBN 0-19-812511-9). Clarendon Press.

Wuthering Heights. Emily Jane Bronte. LC 68-56083. (Cambridge classics library). (Illus.). 1968. Cambridge Book Co.

Wuthering Heights. Emily Jane Bronte. LC 63-14838. (Macmillan classics, 25). (Illus.). 1963. Macmillan.

Wuthering Heights. Emily Jane Bronte. Ed. by Maugham, William Somerset. (Ten Greatest Novels of the World). 1949. Winston Co.

Wuthering Heights. Emily Jane Bronte. LC 17-23012. The Mershon Company.

Wuthering Heights. the haworth ed. Emily Jane Bronte. LC 4-16278. (Added t.-p.: Life and works of the sisters Bronte... vol. v). 1903. Harper & Brothers.

Wuthering Heights. Emily Jane Bronte. LC 6-12135. (Half-title: The English Comedie humaine. 2d series). 1906. The Century Co.

Wuthering Heights. Emily Jane Bronte. (Half-title: Everyman's library, ed. by Ernest Rhys. Fiction). 1907. J. M. Dent & Co,

Wuthering Heights. Emily Jane Bronte. LC 7-12273. 1907. Doubleday, Page & Company.

Wuthering Heights. Emily Jane Bronte. LC 25-26570. (Half-title: The modern library of the world's best books). The Modern Library.

Wuthering Heights. Emily Jane Bronte. Ed. by Paul Milton Fulcher. LC 29-11578. (modern readers' series). 1929. The Macmillan Company.

Wuthering Heights. Emily Jane Bronte. LC 31-26033. (Half-title: The travellers' library). 1930. J. Cape and H. Smith.

Wuthering Heights. Emily Jane Bronte. LC 31-30345. 1931. Random House.

Wuthering Heights. Emily Jane Bronte. Ed. by Heathcote William Garrod. LC 33-36090. (Half-title: The novels of Charlotte, Emily, and Anne Bronte.--II). 1932. H. Milford, Oxford University Press.

Wuthering Heights. Emily Jane Bronte. LC 36-37128. (Half-title: Everyman's library, ed. by Ernest Rhys. Fiction. no. 243). 1935. J. M. Dent & Sons. Ltd.

Wuthering Heights. Emily Jane Bronte. (Universal library). 1939. Grosset & Dunlap.

Wuthering Heights. Emily Jane Bronte. LC 45-40838. (Half-title: The novels of Charlotte, Emily, & Anne Bronte). 1922. J. M. Dent & Sons Ltd.

Wuthering Heights. Emily Jane Bronte. LC 43-18005. 1943. Random House.

Wuthering Heights. Emily Jane Bronte. LC 46-11857. (Illustrated modern library). 1946. Random House, Inc.

Wuthering Heights. Emily Jane Bronte. LC 47-30357. (Rainbow classics). 1947. World Pub. Co.

Wuthering Heights. Emily Jane Bronte. Ed. by Valentine Dobree. Bronte, Charlotte. LC 27-23868. (Borzol classics). 1927. A. A. Knopf.

Wuthering Heights. Emily Jane Bronte. LC 80-13315. (Classics in Large Print). 1980. 13.95 (ISBN 0-8161-3074-4). G. K. Hall.

Wuthering Heights. Emily Jane Bronte. Ed. by Ian Robert James Jack. LC 80-41510. (World's classics). 1981. 2.95 (ISBN 0-19-281543-1). Oxford University Press.

Wuthering Heights see Classics Set.

Wuthering Heights see Three Nineteenth-Century Novels.

Wuthering Heights. A Novel. Emily Jane Bronte. LC 6-24368. 1848. Harper & Brothers.

Wuthering Heights. Adapted by Ruby Withers; Edited by Mark Neville. Emily Jane Bronte. Adapted by Ruby Withers. LC 50-8473. 1950. Globe Book Co.

Wuthering Heights & Poems. Emily Jane Bronte. 1978. 8.95x (ISBN 0-460-00243-0, Evman); pap. 1.95x (ISBN 0-460-01243-6, Evman). Biblio Dist.

Wuthering Heights: By Emily Bronte; Ed. by Frederick T. Flahiff. Emily Jane Bronte. Ed. by Frederick T Flahiff. LC 68-21093. (Coll. classics in English). 1968. text, 1.80. Macmillan.

Wuthering Heights: Ed. by David Daiches. Emily Jane Bronte. (Penguin Eng. lib., 1) Bibl.). Penguin.

Wuthering Heights: Emily Bronte. Barbara Nathan Hardy. LC 64-545262. (Notes in Eng. lit.). 1964. Barnes & Noble.

Wuthering Heights. Introd. by Daphne Du Maurier. Illus. by W Stein. Emily Jane Bronte. LC 66-5487. (Macdonald illus. classics, 33). 1966. 3.50. Macdonald.

Wuthering Heights: Introd. by James William Johnson. Suggestions for Reading and Discussion by Roger K. Applebee. Emily Jane Bronte. LC 66-541. (Riverside lit. ser., R26). 1966. 1.48, .95 pap.,. Houghton.

Wuthering Heights. Introd. by Mark Schorer. Emily Jane Bronte. LC 50-5488. (Rinehart editions, 23). 1950. Rinehart.

Wuthering Heights: Introd. by Royal A. Gettmann. With Wood Engravings by Fritz Eichenberg. Emily Jane Bronte. LC 50-12235. (Modern Library college editions, T4). 1950. Modern Library.

Wuthering Heights. Pref. by Albert J. Guerard. Emily Jane Bronte. LC 60-42184. (Washington Square Press book, W-210). 1960. Washington Square Press.

Wuthering Heights: the Love Story of Catherine and Heathcliff. Emily Jane Bronte. Ed. by Peter S. Seymour. LC 74-157756. (Hallmark editions). (Illus.). 1971. 2.50 (ISBN 0-87529-213-5). Hallmark.

Wuthering Heights. With a New Introd. by Quentin Anderson. Emily Jane Bronte. LC 61-18554. (Classic Collier books, HS28). 1962. Collier Books.

Wuthering Heights: With an Introd. by Bruce McCullough. Emily Jane Bronte. LC 50-6221. (Harper's modern classics). 1950. Harper.

Wuthering Heights. With an Introd. by V. S. Pritchett. Emily Jane Bronte. LC 56-14017. (Riverside editions, B2). 1956. Houghton Mifflin.

WW II Historical Romance. Elizabeth Aspril. 1980. 7.95. E Keys.

Wyandotte; or, The Hutted Knoll. A Tale. new ed. James Fenimore Cooper. 1852. Stringer and Townsend.

Wyandotte; or, The Hutted Knoll. A Tale. James Fenimore Cooper. LC 22-10628. 1859. W. A. Townsend and Company.

Wyandotte; or, The Hutted Knoll: A Tale. James Fenimore Cooper. (On cover: Lovell's library, no. 512). 1885. J. W. Lovell Company.

Wyandotte: Or, The Hutted Knoll; a Tale. James Fenimore Cooper. (On cover: Seaside library. Pocket ed. no. 380). 1885. G. Munro.

Wyandotte; or, The Hutted Knoll. A Tale. James Fenimore Cooper. LC 4-19001. 1901. D. Appleton and Company.

Wyandotte, or, The Hutted Knoll: A Tale. James Fenimore Cooper & Thomas Philbrick. LC 81-1132. (Writings of James Fenimore Cooper). ((Series: Cooper, James Fenimore, 1789-1851.). (1981.). (Works.). 29.50 (ISBN 0-87395-414-9) (ISBN 0-87395-469-6). State University of New York Press.

Wyandotte, or, The Hutted Knoll. A Tale, by the Author of "The Pathfinder", "Deerslayer"... Etc. James Fenimore Cooper. LC 6-29027. 1843. Lea and Blanchard.

Wyatt's Hurricane. Desmond Bagley. LC 66-13195. 4.95. Doubleday.

Wyatt's Hurricane. Desmond Bagley. (75262). 1967. Pocket Bks.

Wych Hazel. Susan Warner & Anna Bartlett Warner. LC 8-33692. 1876. G. P. Putnam's Sons.

Wycherly Woman: By Ross Macdonald Pseud. 1st Ed. Kenneth Millar. LC 61-10295. 1961. Knopf.

Wychford Poisoning Case. Anthony Berkeley Cox. LC 30-13355. 1930. Pub. for The Crime Club, Inc., by Doubleday, Doran & Company, Inc.

Wychwood. Norma Johnston. LC 76-29706. 1977. 8.95 (ISBN 0-394-40016-X). Random House.

Wychwood. Nicole St. John. 320p. 1983. pap. 2.75 (ISBN 0-446-30819-6). Warner Bks.

Wycliffe and the Pea-Green Boat. William John Burley. LC 75-17480. 1975. 6.95. Walker.

Wycliffe and the Scapegoat. William John Burley. LC 78-22420. 1979. 7.95 (ISBN 0-385-15126-8). Doubleday.

Wycliffe and the Schoolgirls. William John Burley. LC 75-36548. 1976. 6.95 (ISBN 0-8027-5341-8). Walker.

Wycliffe in Paul's Court. William John Burley. LC 80-5449. 1980. 8.95 (ISBN 0-385-17208-7). Published for the Crime Club by Doubleday.

Wycliffe-Pepin Case: "Double Shooting at Merrile Court". Anthony Fane. LC 31-35111. 1931. Poe.

Wycliffe's Wild Goose Chase. W. J. Burley. LC 82-45350. (Crime Club Ser.). 192p. 1982. 11.95 (ISBN 0-385-18254-6). Doubleday.

Wyke Regis. Leonard, John. LC 66-15469. 1966. Delacorte Press.

Wylder's Hand. Joseph Sheridan Le Fanu. LC 77-84059. 1978. 4.50 (ISBN 0-486-23570-X). Dover Publications.

Wylder's Hand: A Novel. Joseph Sheridan Le Fanu. LC 76-5281. (Le Fanu, Joseph Sheridan, 1814-1873. Works. 1976). 1976. vols.) 59.00(3 (ISBN 0-405-09246-6). Arno Press.

Wylder's Hand: A Novel. Joseph Sheridan Le Fanu. LC 77-702. 1977. 85.00 (ISBN 0-8414-5814-6). Folcroft Library Editions.

Wylder's Hand. A Novel. Joseph Sheridan Le Fanu. LC 44-48097. 1865. Carleton.

Wyllard's Weird. A Novel. Mary Elizabeth Braddon Maxwell. (On cover: Seaside library. Pocket ed. no. 434). 1885. G. Munro.

Wyllard's Weird. A Novel. Mary Elizabeth Braddon Maxwell. (Harper's Franklin square library, no. 457). 1885. Harper & Brothers.

Wynastons. Hebron Baker. LC 12-1211. 19.50. Broadway Publishing Co.

Wyncote. Thomas Erskine. LC 6-38160. (Leisure hour ser. no. 49). 1875. H. Holt and Company.

Wyndham Lewis the Artist. Wyndham Lewis. LC 74-173843. (English Literature Ser., No. 33). 1971. Repr. of 1939 ed. lib. bdg. 45.95x (ISBN 0-8383-1348-5). Haskell.

Wyndham's Pal. Harold Bindloss. LC 19-16145. Frederick A. Stokes Company.

Wyndspelle. Aola Vandergriff. 1975. (pbk.) 1.50 (ISBN 0-446-78615-2). Warner Paperback Library.

Wyndspelle's Child. Aola Vandergriff. 1976. (pbk.) 1.50. Warner Books.

Wyndward Fury. Norman Daniels. 1979. 2.25 (ISBN 0-446-82991-9). Warner Books.

Wyndward Glory. Norman Daniels. 416p. (Orig.). 1981. pap. 2.95 (ISBN 0-446-90742-1). Warner Bks.

Wyndward Passion. Norman Daniels. 1978. 2.25 (ISBN 0-446-82669-3). Warner Books.

Wynema, a Child of the Forest. S. Alice Callahan. (On cover: The silver series, no. 1). 1891. H. J. Smith & Co.

Wynner. Mel Torme. LC 77-92714. 1978. 9.95 (ISBN 0-8128-2462-8). Stein and Day.

Wyoming. Zane Grey. 1978. 9.95 o.p. (ISBN 0-86025-110-1). State Mutual Bk.

Wyoming. Terry Treadway. LC 81-16733. 13.95 (ISBN 0-312-89527-5). St Martin's Press.

Wyoming: A Story of the Outdoor West. William MacLeod Raine. LC 8-20674. 1908. G. W. Dillingham Company.

Wyoming Bubble. 1st Ed. Allan Vaughan Elston. LC 55-10457. 1955. Lippincott.

Wyoming Glory. Jeanne Foster. (Eden Richards, The Frontier Women Saga Ser.: Vol. IV). 288p. (Orig.). 1982. pap. 2.95 (ISBN 0-449-14482-8, GM). Fawcett.

Wyoming Gun. Tom Roan. LC 55-419912. (Dell western 849). 1955. Dell Pub. Co.

Wyoming Gun Law. easy eye ed. Lee Floren. pap. 0.60 o.p. Lancer.

Wyoming Raiders. Walker A Tompkins. 1942. Phoenix Press.

Wyoming Range War. Dan Roberts. LC 67-1212. Arcadia House.

Wyoming Saddles. Lee Floren. 1977. pap. 1.25 (ISBN 0-532-12522-3). Woodhill.

Wyoming Showdown. Lee Floren. 1970. pap. 0.60 o.p. (ISBN 0-447-73208-0). Lancer.

Wyoming Summer. Mary O'Hara. LC 63-8297. 1963. Doubleday.

Wyoming Sun. Edward Bryant. (Illus.). 132p. 1980. deluxe ed. 15.50 signed (ISBN 0-936204-15-X); pap. 6.00 (ISBN 0-936204-12-5). Jelm Mtn.

Wyoming Trail. Walker A Tomkins. Phoenix Press.

Wyoming. 1st Ed. Zane Grey. LC 53-7735. 1953. Harper.

Wyrldmaker. Terry Bisson. 178p. (Orig.). pap. 2.25 (ISBN 0-671-83578-5, Timescape). PB.

Wyss Pursuit. Adam Hamilton. (Peacemaker). (Berkley medallion book: Vol. 4). 1975. (pbk.) 0.95. Berkley Pub. Co.

Wyst: Alastor 1716. Jack Vance, pseud. (Science Fiction Ser.). (Orig.). 1978. pap. 2.95 (ISBN 0-87997-593-8, YE1593). DAW Bks.

Wyszkowo, a Shtetl on the Bug River. Adele Mondry. LC 79-26259. (Illus.). 7.50 (ISBN 0-87068-657-7). Ktav Publishing House.

Wyvern Hall. Teddy's Luck. A Contrast. Three Stories. Anna Theresa Sadlier. (Catholic library. v. 18). 1898. C. Wildermann.

Wyvern Mystery: A Novel. Joseph Sheridan Le Fanu. LC 76-5282. (Le Fanu, Joseph Sheridan, 1814-1873. Works. 1976). 1976. (3 vols.) 53.00 (ISBN 0-405-09250-4). Arno Press.

X

X Factor: By Andre Norton Pseud. Alice Mary Norton. LC 65-17992. 3.25. Harcourt.

X. Jones of Scotland Yard. Harry Stephen Keeler. LC 36-10902. 1936. E. P. Dutton & Company, Inc.

X Marks the Dot. Muriel Stafford. LC 43-16940. 1943. Duell, Sloan and Pearce.

X Marks the Spot. Lee Thayer, pseud. LC 40-38566. 1940. Dodd, Mead & Company.

X Marks the Spot: A Symphony in Black in Four Movements. Michael Butterworth. LC 77-92207. 1978. 7.95 o.p. (ISBN 0-385-13686-2). Doubleday.

X-on. R. Martin Hunt. 1979. 6.95 (ISBN 0-533-04019-1). Vantage.

X-One: Experimental Fiction Project. Alvin Greenberg et al. Ed. by Harry Smith. LC 76-20256. (Illus.). 1976. pap. 5.00 (ISBN 0-912292-41-5). The Smith.

X-Rated Corpse. Michael Avallone. 1973. price not set o.p. Curtis.

X-Ray Murders. Milton Scott Michel. LC 42-51966. 1942. Coward-McCann, Inc.

X-Ray Murders... Milton Scott Michel. LC 45-3526. (Handi-book mysteries. 30).

X-1: Experimental Fiction Project. Harry Smith & Tom Tolnay. LC 76-20256. (Illus.). 1976. 5.00 (ISBN 0-912292-41-5). The Smith.

Xala. Sembene Ousmane. LC 75-41811. 1976. 5.95 (ISBN 0-88208-067-9). L. Hill & Co.

Xala. Sembene Ousmane. LC 77-368221. (African writers series; 175). (HEB papberback). (Illus.). 1976. 1.30 (ISBN 0-435-90175-3). Heinemann Educational.

Xala. Ousmane Sembene. Tr. by Clive Wake from Fr. (Illus.). 120p. 1983. pap. 6.95 (ISBN 0-88208-068-7). Lawrence Hill.

Xander Pursuit. Adam Hamilton. (Peacemaker). (Peacemaker,b3: Vol. 3). 1974. (pbk.) 0.95 (ISBN 0-425-02676-0). Berkley Pub. Co.

Xavier Affair: A Jose Da Silva Novel. Robert L Fish. LC 69-11459. (Red mask mystery). 1969. 4.50. Putnam.

Xelucha and Others. Matthew Phipps Shiel. LC 74-18654. 1975. 6.50 (ISBN 0-87054-069-6). Arkham House.

Xenia Repnina: A Story of the Russia of to-Day. Barbara MacGahan. LC 7-20007. G. Routledge and Sons, Limited.

Xerxes at Salamis. Peter Green, pseud. (Illus.). 1970. 10.00 o.p. Praeger.

Xingu: And Other Stories. Edith Newbold Jones Wharton. 1916. C. Scribner's Sons.

Xipehuz and The Death of the Earth. J. H. Rosny. LC 77-84283. (Lost Race and Adult Fantasy Fiction). 1978. 15.00 (ISBN 0-405-11020-0). Arno Press.

Xipehuz & the Death of the Earth (les Xipehuz & la Mort De la Terre, 2 vols. in 1. J. H. Rosynyaine. Ed. by R. Reginald & Douglas Melville. LC 77-84283. (Lost Race & Adult Fantasy Ser.). (Eng.). 1978. lib. bdg. 15.00x (ISBN 0-405-11020-0). Ayer Co.

XIth Commandment: A Novel. Halliwell Sutcliffe. LC 8-17655. 1896. New Amsterdam Book Company; Etc., Etc.

XPD. Len Deighton. LC 80-7629. 1981. 12.95 (ISBN 0-394-51258-8). Knopf: Distributed by Random House.

Xuala. 1st Ed. Estelle Davis. LC 56-12360. 1956. Pageant Press.

Xuan & the Girl from the Other Side. Paul A. Bergin. 1970. pap. 0.60 o.p. (T060-8). Tower.

XYY Man. Kenneth Royce. LC 76-126060. 1970. 4.95. McKay.

XYZ: A Detective Story. Anna Katharine Green Rohlfs. LC 9-1491. 1883. G. P. Putnam's Sons.

Y

Y. Cheung, Business Detective: A Mystery Novel. Harry Stephen Keeler. LC 39-14612. 1939. E. P. Dutton & Co., Inc.

Ya! & John-Juan. Douglas Woolf. LC 79-123990. 7.95 (ISBN 0-942296-03-6). Wolf Run Bks.

Ya! John-Juan; Two Novels. Douglas Woolf. LC 79-123990. 1971. 7.95. Harper & Row.

Yaalahn. Gustav Harders. Tr. by H. C. Nitz. 1953. 2.50 o.p. Northwest Pub.

Yaalahn: Translated by H. C. Nitz. Gustav Harders. LC 54-42477. 1954. Northwestern Pub. House.

Yagui: And Other Great Indian Stories. Zane Grey. Belmont Tower.

Yagui Gold: A Novel. Sewell Thomas. LC 63-21872. 1963. Sage Books.

Yahoo: A Novel of the Ex-G. I. on the Campus. James Wolf. LC 52-106164. 1952. William-Frederick Press.

Yakima: A Novel. 1st Ed. Inez Noelle Johnson. LC 54-13210. Pageant Press.

Yakuza. Leonard Schrader. 1975. (pbk.) 1.50. Warner Paperback Library.

Yale Tales. Ed. by Blakeman Quintard Meyer. Mason, Ray Murdoch & Fox, Edward Lyttleton. LC 2-204723. 1901.

Yale Yarns: Sketches of Life at Yale University. John Seymour Wood. LC 5-2459. 1895. G. P. Putnam's Sons.

Yaller Gal. Peggy Gaddis, pseud. LC 36-2214. Godwin.

Yama, the Hell-Hole: A New Translation by Nina N. Selivanova. Aleksandr Ivanovich Kuprin. LC 52-37803. (Pyramid giant, G50). 1952. Pyramid Books.

Yama: The Pit. Aleksandr Ivanovich Kuprin. Tr. by Bernard G. Guerney from Rus. LC 76-23883. (Classic of Russian Literature). 1977. 13.95 (ISBN 0-88355-493-3); pap. 5.50 (ISBN 0-88355-494-1). Hyperion Conn.

Yama: The Pit: a Novel in Three Parts. Aleksandr Ivanovich Kuprin. LC 76-23883. (Classics of Russian literature). (Hyperion library of world literature). 1977. 12.95. (ISBN 0-88355-493-3) (ISBN 0-88355-494-1). Hyperion Press.

Yamhills: An Indian Romance. Jacob Calvin Cooper. 1904. J. C. Cooper.

Yancey. Peter Dawson. 160p. 1981. pap. 1.95 (ISBN 0-553-20392-4). Bantam.

Yancey's War. William Hoffman. LC 65-172626. 4.95. Doubleday.

Yancey's War. William Hoffman. (Crest bk., t1079). 1967. Fawcett.

Yang and Yin: A Novel of an American Doctor in China. Alice Tisdale Nourse Hobart. LC 36-303207. The Bobbs-Merrill Company.

Yang Meridian. James Leasor. (YA) 1968. 4.95 o.p. (ISBN 0-399-10893-9). Putnam.

Yang Meridian: A Novel. James Leasor. LC 68-12101. 1968. Putnam.

Yangtze Skipper. Thomas Woodrooffe. LC 37-4264. Sheridan House.

Yank--the Crusader. Earl Christian Van Zandt. LC 19-14081. 1919. The Wahlgreen Publishing Company.

Yank in the R. A. F. Harlan C Thomas. LC 41-178754. Random House.

Yank on Piccadilly. C. L McDermott. LC 51-4521. 1951. Vantage Press.

Yankee. Dana Fuller Ross. (Orig.). 1982. pap. 3.50 (ISBN 0-440-19841-0). Dell.

Yankee. Jon Williams. LC 81-150717. (Privateers and Gentlemen; V. 2). 2.95 (ISBN 0-440-19779-1). Dell Pub. Co.

Yankee Among the Mermaids, and Other Waggeries and Vagaries. William Evans Burton. LC 12-6835. (On cover: Library of humorous American works). 1854. Getz & Buck.

Yankee Among the Nullifiers. Asa Greene. LC 72-104468. 1970. (ISBN 0-8398-0667-1). Literature House.

Yankee Among the Nullifiers: An Auto-Biography. Asa Green. LC 22-10841. 1833. W. Stodart.

Yankee Among the Nullifiers: An Auto-Biography. 2d ed. Asa Green. LC 6-45943. 1833. W. Pearson.

Yankee and the Belle. Catherine Creel. (Belmont Tower Book). 2.25 (ISBN 0-505-51432-X). Tower Publications,C.

Yankee Bob. Dovie Patterson Thomas. LC 49-48763. 1949. Exposition Press.

Yankee Bodleys: A Novel. Naomi Lane Babson. LC 36-271671. Reynal & Hitchcock.

Yankee Brig. Noel Bertram Gerson. LC 60-5949. 1960. Doubleday.

Yankee Brig. Carter A Vaughan, pseud. LC 60-5949. 1960. Doubleday.

Yankee Champion: Or, The Tory and His League. A Revolutionary Story of Land and Sea. Sylvanus Cobb. (On cover: Sea and shore series, no. 18). 1890. Street & Smith.

Yankee Cruiser: A Story of the War of 1812. Illustrative of Scenes in the American Navy. Charles Wheeler Denison. LC 9-3819. (American popular tales no. 2). 1848. J. E. Farwell & Co.

Yankee Crusoe: Or, The Golden Treasure of the Virgin Islands. Charles W. Willis. LC 6137. 1900. H. A. Dickerman & Son.

Yankee Dared: A Romance of Our Railroads. Frank J Nevins. LC 33-309911. 1933. The O'Sullivan Publishing House.

Yankee Doodle. Peter Farb. LC 74-130196. 1970. 6.95. Simon and Schuster.

Yankee Doodle Dandy: A Biographical Novel of John Hancock. Noel Bertram Gerson. LC 65-19945. 1965. Doubleday.

Yankee Doodle Dixie: Or, Love the Light of Life. An Historical Romance, Illustrative of Life and Love in an Old Virginia Country Home, and Also an Explanatory Account of the Passions, Prejudices, and Opinions Which Culminate in the Civil War. John Vincent Ryals. LC 8-1352. 1890. E. Waddey Co.

Yankee Driver: By W. E. Butterworth. William E Butterworth. LC 73-4453. (Thistle Book). 1973. (lib. ed.) 3.99 (ISBN 0-448-26221-5). Grosset and Dunlap.

Yankee Enterprise, or The Two Millionaires: And Other Thrilling Tales. LC 3-10905. 1855. Dayton and Wentworth.

Yankee Faith and Other Stories. Francescantonio Michele Daniele. Greenberg.

Yankee Flier Over Berlin. Rutherford George Montgomery. LC 44-52453. 1944. Grosset & Dunlap.

Yankee from Llanquihue (Yank-Key-Way) 1st Ed. Orr Hubbard. LC 57-9929. 1957. Pageant Press.

Yankee from Tennessee. Noel Bertram Gerson. LC 60-10671. 1960. Doubleday.

Yankee from the West: A Novel. Opie Percival Read. LC 98-1879. Rand, McNally & Company.

Yankee Girl. Ellen Argo. LC 80-14388. 1981. 12.95 (ISBN 0-399-12528-0). Putnam.

Yankee in London: Or, A Short Trip to America ... LC 9-1472. 1826. J. Carson.

Yankee Jack: Or, The Perils of a Privateersman. Justin Jones. LC 7-11901. H. Long & Brother.

Yankee Lawyer: The Autobiography of Ephraim Tutt... Arthur Cheney Train. LC 43-124551. 1943. C. Scribner's Sons.

Yankee Longstraw. Bill Burchardt, pseud. (Double D western). 3.50. Doubleday.

Yankee Middy: Or, The Two Frigates. A Romance of the Coast of Maine. William Robinson. LC 7-42189. H. Long & Brother.

Yankee Pasha: The Adventures of Jason Starbuck. Edison Marshall. LC 47-111168. 1947. Farrar, Straus.

Yankee Passional. Samuel Badisch Ornitz. LC 27-24492. 1927. Boni & Liveright.

Yankee Princess. Maggie Osborne. 1982. pap. 3.50 (ISBN 0-451-11820-0, AE1820, Sig). NAL.

Yankee Ranger. Sarah Orne Jewett. Orig. Title: Tory Lover. 1975. pap. 1.50 o.p. (LB300DK, Leisure Bks). Nordon Pubns.

Yankee Ranger. Sarah Orne Jewett. 1975. (pbk.) 1.50. Leisure Books.

Yankee Rascals. Noel Bertram Gerson. LC 63-11237. 1963. Doubleday.

Yankee Rookie. Edward E Fitzgerald. LC 52-8980. (Barnes sports novel series). 1952. A. S. Barnes.

Yankee Rookie. Edward E Fitzgerald. 1961. Grosset & Dunlap.

Yankee Rover, Being the Story of the Adventures of Jonathan Drew During His Travels in the South & Far West by Road, River and Trail in the Years 1824-29: Together with Some Account of the People He Met, White, Black, and Red, Good, Bad and Indifferent, His Friends and Enemies and What They Did or Tried to Do. As Taken Down. Christopher Ward. LC 32-25325. 1932. Simon and Schuster.

Yankee School-Teacher in Virginia. Lydia Wood Baldwin. LC 70-37583. (Black Heritage Library Collection). (Series: Standard library (New York, London, Funk & Wagnalls, 1880-) no. 124.). 1972. (ISBN 0-8369-8959-7). Books for Libraries Press.

Yankee School-Teacher in Virginia. A Tale of the Old Dominion in the Transition State. Lydia Wood Baldwin. LC 6-6856. (On cover: Standard library; no. 124). 1884. Funk & Wagnalls.

Yankee Should Never Be Black. Ann Husbands. LC 73-90721. 1973. Bascom Books.

Yankee Slave-Dealer: Or, An Abolitionist Down South. A Tale for the Times. LC 9-2228. 1860. The Author.

Yankee Stranger. Elswyth Thane. LC 76-5501. 1976. 6.95 (ISBN 0-88411-963-7). Aeonian Press.

Yankee Stranger. Elswyth Thane. LC 44-8139. 1944. Duell, Sloan and Pearce.

Yankee Stranger. Elswyth Thane. LC 80-25609. 1981. 16.95 (ISBN 0-8161-3166-X). G. K. Hall.

Yankee Tabernacle: A Novel. Paul W Pyle. LC 52-9749. 1952. Chapman & Grimes.

Yankee Tiger. Virginia Nielsen, pseud. (A fawcett gold medal book). 1.75 (ISBN 0-449-14020-2). Fawcett Publications.

Yankee Trader: A Novel. Stanley Morton. LC 47-62341. 1947. Sheridan House.

Yankee Viking: A Novel. Livingston Hartley. LC 51-10907. 1951. Exposition Press.

Yankee Volunteer. Mary Imlay Taylor. LC 98-1435. 1898. A. C. McClurg & Co.

Yankee Woman. Frederick Ehrenfried Baume. LC 45-313332. 1945. Dodd, Mead & Company.

Yankees on the Run. John Brick. 1961. 4.50 o.p. Hawthorn.

Yanko, the Musician and Other Stories. Henryk Sienkiewicz. Tr. by Jeremiah Curtin. 1893. Little, Brown, and Company.

Yanqui. Thomas Wakefield Blackburn. 1973. (pbk.) 0.75. Dell.

Yaqui Drums. Dane Coolidge. LC 40-6296. 1940. E. P. Dutton & Co., Inc.

Yarb and Cretine: Or, Rising from Bonds. George Banghart Henry Swayze. LC 72-4644. (Black Heritage Library Collection). 1972. (ISBN 0-8369-9128-1). Books for Libraries Press.

Yarb and Cretine: Or, Rising from Bonds. George Banghart Henry Swayze. LC 6-46774. 1906. The C. M. Clark Publishing Co.

Yarborough. Bernard Harper Friedman. LC 64-23377. 1964. World Pub. Co.

Yarcus: A Romance of Ancient Egypt. Ira C Fuller, pseud. LC 7-1610. 1899. Dawining Light Press.

Yard: A Novel. Horace Annesley Vachell. LC 23-268663. 1923. George H. Doran Company.

Yardstick Man. Arthur Frederick Goodrich. LC 10-21161. 1910. 1.50. D. Appleton and Company.

Yargo. Jacqueline Susann. 1979. pap. 2.50 (ISBN 0-553-12855-8). Bantam.

Yarn of Old Harbour Town. William Clark Russell. 1906. G. W. Jacobs.

Yarn Spinning. Andrew K Dutch. LC 70-175149. 1971. Landmark Syndicate.

Yarns. Tristan Jones. 250p. 1983. 14.95 (ISBN 0-914814-41-9). Sail Bks.

Yarns. Alice Turner Yardley. LC 21-8711. 1895. J. Murphy & Co.

Yarns & Tales from the Great Smokies. Joseph S. Hall. (Illus.). 80p. 1979. pap. 3.50 o.p. (ISBN 0-9600168-2-1). Hollywood.

Yarns of the Southwest. William Henry Robinson. LC 21-221021. The Berryhill Company.

Yarns: The Ludovic Zam Affair. Percy William Edward Hart. The Bibelot Brothers.

Yasmina's Daughter. Corinne Childs. 1981. pap. 2.50 (ISBN 0-8439-0838-6, Leisure Bks). Nordon Pubns.

Yates of Red Dog. Archie Joscelyn. LC 42-141192. 1942. Phoenix Press.

Yates Paul, His Grand Fights, His Tootings. James Baker Hall. LC 63-18584. 1963. World Pub. Co.

Yates Pride: A Romance. Mary Eleanor Wilkins Freeman. LC 12-26367. 1912. Harper & Brothers.

Yawning Heights. Aleksandr Aleksandrovich Zinovev. LC 78-21802. 1979. 15.00 (ISBN 0-394-42710-6). Random House.

Yawning Heights. Aleksandr Aleksandrovich Zinovev. LC 79-28215. 1980. 6.95 (ISBN 0-394-74374-1). Random House.

Yawning Heights. Aleksandr Aleksandrovich Zinovev. LC 79-3608. 1980. 6.95 (ISBN 0-394-74374-1). Random House.

Yaya Garcia: A Novel. Machado De Assis, Joaquim Maria. LC 76-376690. (UNESCO Collection of Representative Works: Brazilian Series). 1976. 4.25 (ISBN 0-7206-0394-3). P. Owen.

Yazoo. A Study. Will J Wheless. LC 8-36045. 1889. Printed at Murray's Steam Printing House.

Yazoo Mystery: A Novel. Irving Craddock. LC 19-15965. Britton Publishing Company.

Yazoo Stories. Beverly Carradine. LC 12-28424. 1.00. The Christian Witness Co.

Y'bird, Vol. 1 No. 1. Ishmael Reed. (Illus.). 1977. pap. 4.95 (ISBN 0-931676-00-2). Reed & Youngs Quilt.

Ye Drunken Damozel," The Travern in the Folly. Simon Jesty. LC 33-135567. 1932. H. Smith & R. Haas.

Ye Lyttle Salem Maide: A Story of Witchcraft. Pauline Bradford Mackie Cavendish. 1898. Lamson, Wolffe & Company.

Ye Lyttle Salem Maide: A Story of Witchcraft. Pauline Bradford Mackie Hopkins. 1898. Lamson, Wolffe & Company.

Ye Nexte Thynge. Eleanor Amerman Sutphen. LC 8-25652. F. H. Revell Company.

Ye Old Spye Inn. Stanley L Wojcik. LC 75-17065. (Illus.). 6.50. Amboy Press.

Ye Olde Bluebird: A Novelette. Marion Montgomery. LC 67-28672. 1967. New College Press.

Ye That Judge. Helen Reimensnyder Martin. LC 26-26079. 1926. Dodd, Mead and Company.

Year. David A. Billeci. LC 78-65690. 1979. 7.95 o.p. (ISBN 0-533-04114-7). Vantage.

Year. Daisye Kern Miller. LC 25-132993. 1925. Dorance and Company.

Year: A Novel. Suzanne Lange. LC 78-120787. 1970. 4.95. S. G. Phillips.

Year After Tomorrow: An Anthology of Science Fiction Stories Selected by Lester Del Rey, Cecile Matschat and Carl Carmer. Foreword by Lester Del Rey; Illustrated by Mel Hunter. 1st Ed. Ed. by Lester Del Rey. LC 52-8976. 1954. Winston.

Year and a Day: A Novel. 1st Ed. Gladys Seale Knight. LC 53-8097. 1953. Pageant Press.

Year As a Lion. Eric Roman. LC 78-7563. 1978. 9.95. Stein and Day.

Year at Brown. Frederick William Jones. LC 3-28165. 1903. Snow & Farnham.

Year Before Last. Kay Boyle. LC 74-76191. (Crosscurrents/modern fiction). 1969. 6.95. Southern Illinois University Press.

Year Between. Doris Egerton Jones. LC 19-7299. G. W. Jacobs & Company.

Year by Candlelight: A Novel. Carroll Leja Nichols & Hill, Liane, Joint Author. LC 41-6047. 1941. Minerva Books.

Year Growing Ancient. Irene Hunter Steiner. LC 78-14925. 8.95 (ISBN 0-312-89619-0). St. Martin's Press.

Year in Eden. Harriet Waters Preston. LC 7-30116. 1887. Roberts Brothers.

Year in Paradise. Sara Lucile Jenkins. LC 52-7033. 1952. Crowell.

Year in San Fernando. Michael Anthony. (Caribbean Writers Ser.). 1970. pap. text ed. 3.00x (ISBN 0-435-98031-9). Heinemann Ed.

Year in the Closet. William Carney. 1974. (pbk.) 1.50. Warner Paperback Library.

Year of August: A Novel. Anton Fereva. LC 55-5663. 1955. Putnam.

Year of August: A Novel of Intrigue. Mark Saxton. LC 43-188811. 1943. Farrar & Rinehart, Inc.

Year of Consent. Kendell Foster Crossen. LC 54-88714. (Dell first edition, 82). 1954. Dell Pub. Co.

Year of December; a Novel. Lucy Michaella Cores. LC 73-19675. 1974. 8.95 (ISBN 0-07-013128-7). McGraw-Hill.

Year of Decision. Anna L Schroeder. LC 63-1850. Zondervan Pub. House.

Year of Delight. Margaret Widdemer. LC 21-14548. 1921. Harcourt, Brace and Company.

Year of Living Dangerously. Christopher J. Koch. LC 78-19428. 1979. 10.00 (ISBN 0-312-89623-9). St. Martin's Press.

Year of Living Dangerously. Christopher J. Koch. LC 82-12259. 1983. 3.95 (ISBN 0-14-006535-0). Penguin Books.

Year of Living Dangerously: Movie tie-in edition. Christopher J. Koch. 1983. pap. 3.95 (ISBN 0-14-006535-0). Penguin.

Year of Love. Ethyl Wood Crouse, Research Assistant. Margaret Lee Runbeck. LC 55-9327. 1956. Houghton Mifflin.

Year of Miracle: A Tale of the Year One Thousand Nine Hundred. Fergus Hume. LC 7-5845. (On cover: Lovell's Westminster series. no. 41). J. W. Lovell Company.

Year of Monday Mornings. Charles Mohler. LC 59-6687. 1959. Beacon Press.

Year of the Angry Rabbit. 1st Amer. Ed. Russell Braddon. LC 65-18017. 1965. 3.95. Norton.

Year of the Ape. Lee Chang, pseud. (Kung Fu Ser: No. 8). 192p. (Orig.). 1975. pap. 1.25 o.p. (ISBN 0-532-12303-4). Woodhill.

Year of the Ape. Lee Chang, pseud. (Kung Fu Ser: No. 8). 192p. (Orig.). 1975. pap. 1.25 o.p. (ISBN 0-532-12303-4). Manor Bks.

Year of the Capricorn. David Austin. 1981. 9.95 (ISBN 0-533-04467-7). Vantage.

Year of the Cloud. Kate Wilhelm & Ted Thomas. 1970. 4.95 o.p. Doubleday.

Year of the Cock. C. K. Fong. (Kung Fu Ser.: No. 7). 192p. (Orig.). 1975. pap. 1.25 o.p. (ISBN 0-532-12277-1). Woodhill.

Year of the Cock. C. K. Fong. (Kung Fu Ser.: No. 7). 192p. (Orig.). 1975. pap. 1.25 o.p. (ISBN 0-532-12277-1). Manor Bks.

Year of the Cock. Salambo Forest. (Orig.). 1969. pap. 1.75 o.s.i. (OPH137, Ophelia). Olympia.

Year of the Cougar. Jesse Bier. LC 75-43776. 8.95 (ISBN 0-15-199736-5). Harcourt Brace Jovanovich.

Year of the Death. Reuben R Merliss. LC 65-10619. 4.95. Doubleday.

Year of the Dragon. Lee Chang, pseud. (Kung Fu Ser.: No. 4). 192p. 1974. pap. 1.25 o.p. (ISBN 0-532-12235-6). Woodhill.

Year of the Dragon. Lee Chang, pseud. (Kung Fu Ser.: No. 4). 192p. 1974. pap. 1.25 o.p. (ISBN 0-532-12235-6). Manor Bks.

Year of the Dragon. Lee Chang, pseud. (Kung Fu,#4). 1974. (pbk.) 1.25. Manor Books.

Year of the Dragon. Robert Daley. 1982. pap. 3.95 (ISBN 0-451-11817-0, AE1817, Sig). NAL.

Year of the Dragon: A Novel. Robert Daley. LC 81-8963. 14.95 (ISBN 0-671-41045-8). Simon and Schuster.

Year of the French: A Novel. Thomas J. B. Flanagan. LC 78-23539. (Illus.). 14.95 (ISBN 0-03-044591-4). Holt, Rinehart, and Winston.

Year of the Golden Ape. Raymond H. Sawkins. LC 74-12371. 1974. 7.95 (ISBN 0-525-23895-6). Dutton.

Year of the Gun: An Original Western. Gifford Paul Cheshire. LC 57-10339. (Dell first edition, A147). 1957. Dell Pub. Co.

Year of the Hare. Helen Luster. pap. 2.95. Man-Root.

Year of the Horse. Lee Chang, pseud. (Kung Fu Ser.: No. 5). 192p. (Orig.). 1975. pap. 1.25 o.p. (ISBN 0-532-12258-5). Woodhill.

Year of the Horse. Lee Chang, pseud. (Kung Fu Ser.: No. 5). 192p. (Orig.). 1975. pap. 1.25 o.p. (ISBN 0-532-12258-5). Manor Bks.

Year of the Horse. Lee Chang, pseud. (Kung Fu,#5). 1974. (pbk.) 1.25. Manor Books.

Year of the Horse: A Novel. Eric Hatch. LC 65-24331. bds., 3.95. Crown.

Year of the Horsetails. R. F. Tapsell. LC 67-18608. 1967. Knopf.

Year of the Intern. Robin Cook. LC 72-75414. 1972. (ISBN 0-15-199740-3). Harcourt Brace Jovanovich.

Year of the Lion: A Novel. Gerald Hanley. LC 54-1687. 1954. Macmillan.

Year of the Mongoose. William Hogan. LC 81-66022. 1981. 12.95 (ISBN 0-689-11209-2). Atheneum.

Year of the Quicksand. Paul P Mok. LC 67-23590. 1967. Trident Press.

Year of the Quiet Sun. Wilson Tucker. LC 79-10246. (Gregg Press science fiction series). 1979. 14.95 (ISBN 0-8398-2529-3). Gregg Press.
Year of the Rat. Lee Chang, pseud. (Kung Fu Ser.: No. 3). 192p. (Orig.). 1974. pap. 1.25 o.p. (ISBN 0-532-12218-6). Woodhill.
Year of the Rat. Lee Chang, pseud. (Kung Fu Ser.: No. 3). 192p. (Orig.). 1974. pap. 1.25 o.p. (ISBN 0-532-12218-6). Manor Bks.
Year of the Rat. Lee Chang, pseud. (Kung Fu,#3). 1974. (pbk.) 1.25. Manor Books.
Year of the Rat: A Chronicle. Mladin Zarubica. LC 64-18298. 1964. Harcourt, Brace & World.
Year of the Rats. Barbara Guignon Ricci. LC 72-95760. 1973. 6.95 (ISBN 0-8027-5557-7). Walker.
Year of the Rooster. Mary Kay Simmons. LC 79-10947. 1971. 5.95. Delacorte Press.
Year of the Rooster. Mary Kay Simmons. 1979. 1.95 (ISBN 0-671-81022-7). Pocket Books.
Year of the Rose. William M Hardy. LC 60-14092. 1960. Dodd, Mead.
Year of the Snake. Lee Chang, pseud. (Kung Fu Ser.: No. 2). 192p. (Orig.). 1974. pap. 1.25 o.p. (ISBN 0-532-12207-0). Woodhill.
Year of the Snake. Lee Chang, pseud. (Kung Fu Ser.: No. 2). 192p. (Orig.). 1974. pap. 1.25 o.p. (ISBN 0-532-12207-0). Manor Bks.
Year of the Snake. Lee Chang, pseud. (Kung Fu,#2). 1974. (pbk.) 1.25. Manor Books.
Year of the Tiger. John Bechtel. LC 46-80543. 1946. Moody Press.
Year of the Tiger. Henry Patterson. LC 64-10183. (Raven book). 1964. Abelard-Schuman.
Year of the Unicorn. Andre Norton, pseud. 1974. (pbk.) 0.95. Ace Books.
Year of the Unicorn. Andre Norton, pseud. LC 77-23221. (Norton, Andre The Witch World Novels of Andre Norton). (Illus.). 1977. 7.95 (ISBN 0-8398-2356-8). Gregg Press.
Year of the Uprising. Stanlake Samkange. LC 78-325260. (Afican writers series; 190). (H.E.B. paperback). 1978. 2.25 (ISBN 0-435-90190-7). Heinemann.
Year of the Waterbearer. Marguerite Dorian. LC 75-19447. 7.95 (ISBN 0-02-532180-3). Macmillan.
Year of the White Trees. Jane Rothschild Mayer. LC 58-5270. 1958. Random House.
Year of the Wood-Dragon. Achmed Abdullah. LC 26-10690. Brentano's.
Year of the Yahoo: A Novel. Victor Wartofsky. LC 72-2405. 1972. 6.95. J. Day Co.
Year of the Yield: By March Cost Pseud. Peggy Morrison, pseud. LC 65-26137. bds., 4.95. Vanguard.
Year of Wreck: A True Story. George Chittenden Benham. LC 1-21943. 1880. Harper & Brothers.
Year of Wreck: A True Story. George Chittenden Benham & A Victim. LC 75-38639. (Black Heritage Library Collection). 1972. (ISBN 0-8369-8997-X). Books for Libraries Press.
Year One. Elizabeth Delehanty. LC 46-2485. 1946. E. P. Dutton & Company, Inc.
Year One: A Page of the French Revolution... a Novel. John Edward Bloundelle-Burton. LC 6-16671. 1901. Dodd, Mead and Company.
Year or So with Edgar. George V. Higgins. LC 78-20206. 8.95 (ISBN 0-06-011873-3). Harper & Row.
Year Out of Life. Mary Ella Waller. LC 9-8571. 1909. D. Appleton and Company.
Year the Dreams Came Back. Anita M. Feagles. (gr. 7-9). 1978. pap. 1.25 o.p. (ISBN 0-671-29875-5). Archway.
Year the Lights Came on. Terry Kay. LC 76-15170. 1976. 6.95 (ISBN 0-395-24738-1). Houghton Mifflin.
Year the Lights Came on. Terry Kay. 1978. 1.75 (ISBN 0-553-10717-8). Bantam Books.
Year the Yankees Lost One Pennant: A Novel. 1st Ed. Douglass Wallop. LC 54-11922. 1954. Norton.
Year the Yankees Lost the Pennant: A Novel. Douglass Wallop. LC 64-18313. Norton.
Year to Live: The Silver Answer. Dorothy Richards Bryant. LC 43-208. 1942. Zondervan Publishing House.
Year to Remember: Signs of the Gathering Storm. 1st. ed. Leo Edward Schottland. 1974. 5.50 (ISBN 0-682-47948-9). Exposition.
Year Two Thousand. Harry Harrison. 1970. 4.95 o.p. (ISBN 0-385-09058-7). Doubleday.
Year Two Thousand Plus. K. Dobbs. 3.00 o.p. Carlton.
Year with Juliet. Elizabeth Frayne. LC 39-152057. 1938. Arcadia House.
Year with the Franklins: Or To Suffer and Be Strong. Eliza Jane Cate. LC 6-2291. 1846. Harper & Brothers.
Year with the Saints. Ray Goin. 1980. pap. 5.00 (ISBN 0-89502-037-8). FEB.
Year with Uncle Jack. W Thomas Carden. LC 13-17744. 1897. Printed for the Author.
Year Worth Living: A Story of a Place and of a People One Cannot Afford Not to Know. William Mumford Baker. LC 6-6870. 1878. Lee and Shepard.
Year 2000: An Anthology. Ed. by Harry Harrison. LC 70-97667. (Doubleday science fiction). 1970. 4.95. Doubleday.
Yearbook: A Novel. David Marlow. LC 76-39716. 8.95 (ISBN 0-87795-156-X). Arbor House.
Yearbook: A Novel. David Marlow. 1.95 (ISBN 0-449-23551-3). Fawcett Crest Books.
Yearbook: A Novel. David Murlow. (Illus.). 1978. 1.95 (ISBN 0-449-23551-3). Fawcett Crest.
Yearbook Killer. Tom Philbin. (Orig.). 1981. pap. 1.95 (ISBN 0-449-14400-3, GM). Fawcett.
Yearling. Marjorie Kinnan Rawlings. LC 39-27939. 1939. C. Scribner's Sons.
Yearling. Marjorie Kinnan Rawlings. LC 41-18616. C. Scribner's Sons.
Yearling: Decorations. Marjorie Kinnan Rawlings. LC 38-27280. 1938. C. Scribner's Sons.
Yearling: Decorations. Marjorie Kinnan Rawlings. LC 40-1013. 1940. C. Scribner's Sons.
Yearling: Decorations by Edward Shenton. Marjorie Kinnan Rawlings. (Large type ed., Keith Jennison bk.). 1966. 6.95. Watts.
Yearly Lease. Val Lewton. LC 48-106041. 1948. Triangle Books.
Yearly Lease. Val Lewton. LC 32-314587. 1932. The Vanguard Press.
Yearning Is Forever. Ameris Crane. LC 74-27223. 1975. 4.95 (ISBN 0-8059-2120-6). Dorrance.
Yearning Years. Eva Zumwalt. (Orig.). 1978. pap. 1.95 (ISBN 0-89041-170-0, 3170). Major Bks.
Years. Virginia Stephen Woolf. LC 37-27268. Harcourt, Brace & Company.
Years Are Even: A Novel. Hobert Douglas Skidmore. LC 52-7133. 1952. Random House.
Years Are So Long: A Novel. Josephine Lawrence. LC 34-18686. 1934. Frederick A. Stokes Company.
Years Are So Long: A Novel. Josephine Lawrence. LC 41-15918. 1941. Triangle Books.
Years Before the Flood. Marianne Steiff Finton Meisel. LC 45-8444. 1945. S. Scribner's Sons.
Year's Best Fantasy Stories. Lin Carter. 1980. 1.95 (ISBN 0-87997-510-5). DAW Books.
Year's Best Fantasy Stories. Ed. by Lin Carter. 1977. 1.50 (ISBN 0-87997-338-2). DAW Books.
Year's Best Fantasy Stories. Ed. by Lin Carter. 1975. (pbk.) 1.25. DAW Books.
Year's Best Fantasy Stories, No. 6. Lin Carter. 1980. 1.95 (ISBN 0-87997-578-4). DAW Books.
Year's Best Fantasy Stories, No. 7. Arthur W. Saha. (Science Fiction Ser.). 1981. pap. 2.25 (ISBN 0-87997-661-6, UE1661). DAW Bks.
Year's Best Fantasy Stories, No. 8. Arthur W. Saha. 192p. 1982. pap. 2.50. DAW Bks.
Year's Best Fantasy Stories: No. 2. Ed. by Lin Carter. (Science Fiction Ser.). 1976. pap. 1.25 o.p. (UY1248). DAW Bks.
Year's Best Horror Stories. Karl Edward. (Series X). 1982. pap. 2.50 (ISBN 0-87997-757-4, UE1757). DAW Bks.
Year's Best Horror Stories. Ed. by Gerald W. Page. 1977. 1.50 (ISBN 0-87997-311-0). DAW Books.
Year's Best Horror Stories. Ed. by Gerald W. Page. (Series VI). 1978. 1.75 (ISBN 0-87997-387-0). DAW Books.
Year's Best Horror Stories, No. IX. Karl Edward Wagner. (Science Fiction Ser.). 1981. pap. 2.50 (ISBN 0-87997-647-0, UE1647). DAW Bks.
Year's Best Horror Stories, No. VIII. Karl Edward Wagner. (Science Fiction Ser.). (Orig.). 1980. pap. 1.95 (ISBN 0-87997-549-0, UJ1549). DAW Bks.
Year's Best Horror Stories; Series II. Ed. by Richard Davis. 1974. (pbk.) 1.25. DAW Books.
Year's Best Horror Stories: Series 1. Richard Davis. (Science Fiction Ser). 1975. pap. 1.25 o.p. (UY1184). DAW Bks.
Year's Best Horror Stories: Series 2. Ed. by Richard David. 1974. pap. 1.25 o.p. (UY1119). DAW Bks.
Year's Best Horror Stories: Series 3. Richard Davis. (Science Fiction Ser). 1975. pap. 1.25 o.p. (UY1180). DAW Bks.
Year's Best Horror Stories: Series 4. Ed. by Gerald W. Page. (Science Fiction Ser.: Series 4). 1976. pap. 1.25 o.p. (ISBN 0-87997-263-7, UY1263). DAW Bks.
Year's Best Horror Stories: Series 5. Ed. by Gerald W. Page. (Science Fiction Ser.). 1977. pap. 1.50 (ISBN 0-87997-311-0, UW1311). DAW Bks.
Year's Best Horror Stories: Series 6. Ed. by Gerald W. Page. (Science Fiction Ser). (Orig.). 1978. pap. 1.75 o.p. (ISBN 0-87997-387-0, UE1387). DAW Bks.
Year's Best Horror Stories: Series 6. Ed. by Gerald W. Page. (Science Fiction Ser). (Orig.). 1978. pap. 1.75 o.p. (ISBN 0-87997-387-0, UE1387). DAW Bks.
Year's Best Horror Stories: VII. Ed. by Gerald W. Page. (Orig.). 1979. pap. 1.95 (ISBN 0-87997-476-1, UJ1476). DAW Bks.
Year's Best Horror Stories, Vol. 1. Ed. by Richard Davis. (Science Fiction Ser.). 176p. 1972. pap. 0.95 o.p. (UQ1013). DAW Bks.
Year's Best Mystery & Suspense Stories - 1982. Ed. by Edward D. Hoch. 228p. 1982. 12.95 (ISBN 0-8027-0713-0). Walker & Co.
Year's Best Science Fiction Novels. 1952-54. Ed. by Everett Franklin Bleiler. LC 52-13217. F. Fell.
Years Between: By William and Molly Burton. William A Burton & Molly Burton. LC 54-10865. 1957. B. Humphries.
Year's Finest Fantasy. Ed. by Terry Carr. LC 78-7133. 9.95. Berkley Pub. Corp.: Distributed by Putnam.
Year's Finest Fantasy 2. Ed. by Terry Carr. LC 79-965. 9.95 (ISBN 0-399-12327-X). Berkley Pub. Corp.: Distributd by Putnam.
Years for Rachel. Berta Ruck. LC 18-18536. 1918. 1.50. Dodd, Mead and Company.
Years in Ambush. Translated from the French by Linda Asher. Roger Grenier. LC 60-8589. half-cloth, 3.75. Knopf.
Years in Waiting. Oldrich Bohumil Sulek. LC 13-22824. Printed by Laurence Press Company.
Year's Letters. Algernon Charles Swinburne. LC 74-15290. (Illus.). 1974. 12.00 (ISBN 0-8147-7758-9). New York University Press.
Years of Achievement. Frances Roberta Sterrett. LC 32-28975. The Penn Publishing Company.
Years of Alison: A Novel. Warren Chetham-Strode. LC 61-8354. 1961. Putnam.
Years of Change. Mollie Hardwick. LC 79-20284. 1980. 14.95 (ISBN 0-8161-6796-6). G. K. Hall.
Years of Change. Mollie Hardwick. 1974. (pbk.) 1.50. Dell.
Years of Childhood. Sergey Aksakov. (Russian Library Ser). 1960. pap. 1.65 o.p. (ISBN 0-394-70708-7, V708, Vin). Random.
Years of Discretion. Frederic Hatton & Hatton, Fanny Locke, Joint Author. 1913. Dodd, Mead and Company.
Years of Eden. Gordon Webber. LC 51-9804. 1951. Little, Brown.
Years of Grace. Margaret Ayer Barnes. LC 30-170057. 1930. Houghton Mifflin Company.
Years of Grace. Margaret Ayer Barnes & Ben S Wohlberg. LC 77-364859. (Illus.). 1976. Franklin Library.
Years of Growth, 1861-1893... Harold Sinclair. LC 40-5192. 1940. Doubleday, Doran and Company, Inc.
Years of Illusion. Harold Sinclair. LC 41-52002. 1941. Doubleday,Doran and Company, Inc.
Years of Indiscretion. Maurice A Hanline. LC 34-39054. The Macaulay Company.
Years of Love. Margaret Widdemer. LC 33-73788. Farrar & Rinehart, Incorporated.
Years of Madness. W. E. Woodward. 312p. (Orig.). 1967. pap. 3.25. Frontier Press Calif.
Years of Our Days. Christine Hunter, pseud. LC 67-22681. 1967. Zondervan Pub. House.
Years of Peace. Le Roy MacLeod. LC 32-222022. The Century Co.
Years of Pilgrimage. Kenneth Sydney Davis. LC 48-5050. 1948. Doubleday.
Years of Protest: A Collection of American Writings of the 1930's, Ed. by Jack Salzman. Barry Wallenstein, Asst. Ed. Ed. by Jack Salzman. LC 67-13489. 1967. pap., 2.50. Pegasus.
Years of the City. George Rippey Stewart. LC 55-8102. 1955. Houghton Mifflin.
Years of the Eclipse: A Novel Translated from the Hungarian by Lawrence Wolfe. 1st Ed. Ferenc Kormendi. LC 51-5969. 1951. Bobbs-Merrill.
Years of the Hungry Tiger. John Gordon Davis. LC 73-83623. 1975. 10.00 (ISBN 0-385-06933-2). Doubleday.
Years of the Hungry Tiger. John Gordon Davis. (Kangaroo Book.). 1977. 1.95. (ISBN 0-671-80939-3). Pocket Books.
Years of the Locust. Loula Grace Erdman. LC 47-30737. 1947. Dodd, Mead.
Years of the Locust. Loula Grace Erdman. LC 79-16721. (Series: Gregg Press Western Fiction Series.). 1979. 10.95 (ISBN 0-8398-2595-1). Gregg Press.
Years of the Locust. Albert Payson Terhune. LC 18-5645. R. J. Shores.
Years of the Past. Chester E. Dobosz. LC 47-6284. 1947. Meador Pub. Co.
Years of the Sky Kings. Arch Whitehouse. 1972. pap. 0.95 o.p. (09126). Curtis.
Years of the Sky Kings. Arch Whitehouse. (O.s.i.). (Orig.). pap. 0.75 o.s.i. (A111, Award). Univ Pub & Dist.
Years of Their Lives. Ikbal Athar. LC 77-366801. 1976. 4.95 (ISBN 0-356-04703-2). Macdonald and Jane's.
Years of Turmoil: A Novel. Philip Harding Jordan. LC 45-102976. 1945. Enterprise Publishing Co., Inc.
Years Out. Ross Feld. LC 72-11020. 1973. 6.95 (ISBN 0-394-48138-0). Knopf.
Years That Answer. Maggie Anderson, pseud. LC 79-2610. 96p. 1980. pap. 4.95 o.p. (ISBN 0-06-090760-6, CN 760, HarpR). Har-Row.
Years That Are Told. Rose Porter. LC 7-37421. A. D. F. Randolph & Company.
Years That Crown. Gwendoline Frances Clear. LC 30-20459. 1930. Longmans, Green and Co.
Years That Take the Best Away. Barbara Noble. LC 30-14882. 1930. Doubleday, Doran and Company, Inc.
Years That the Locust Hath Eaten. Annie E Holdsworth. LC 7-6127. 1895. Macmillan and Co.
Year's Tragedy. Charles Quentin. LC 7-42413. 1893. Cleveland Publishing Company.
Yearwood. Paul Hazel. LC 79-28171. 10.95 (ISBN 0-316-35260-8). Little, Brown.
Yeast: A Problem. Charles Kingsley. (Half-title: Everyman's library, ed. by Ernest Rhys. Fiction. no. 611). J. M. Dent & Sons, Ltd.
Yeast: A Problem. Charles Kingsley. LC 7-12154. 1851. Harper & Brothers.
Yeast: A Problem. Charles Kingsley. LC 25-155024. 1871. Harper & Brothers.
Yeast: A Problem. Charles Kingsley. LC 4-21182. 1893. Macmillan and Co.
Yedidya & the Esrog Tree. 1982. pap. 2.50 (ISBN 0-87306-235-3). Feldheim.
Yees Man's Land. Harry Charles Witwer. LC 29-6856. 1929. G. P. Putnam's Sons.
Yehuda. Meyer Levin. LC 31-5213. J. Cape & H. Smith.
Yehudis Prepares for Shabbos. 1982. pap. 0.99. Feldheim.
Yekl. Abraham Cahn. Bd. with Imported Bridegroom & Other Stories of the New York Ghetto. xi, 240p. pap. 2.50 o.p. (ISBN 0-486-22427-9). Dover.
Yekl: A Tale of the New York Ghetto. Abraham Cahan. LC 6-21875. 1896. D. Appleton and Company.
Yekl and The Imported Bridegroom, and Other Stories of the New York Ghetto. Abraham Cahan. LC 71-91354. 1970. 2.50 (ISBN 0-486-22427-9). Dover Publications.
Yell Bloody Murder. Joseph Shallit. LC 51-11204. (Main line mysteries). 1951. Lippincott.
Yeller- Headed Summer. Francis Irby Gwaltney. LC 54-10961. 1954. Rinehart.
Yellow Angel. Mary Stewart Daggett. LC 14-9282. 1914. 0.75. Browne & Howell Company.
Yellow Angels. Henry Edward Helseth. LC 40-30886. Harper & Brothers.
Yellow Arrow Murders... Francis Van Wyck Mason. LC 32-101091. Pub. for the Crime Club, Inc., by Doubleday, Doran & Company, Inc.
Yellow Aster. A Novel. Kathleen Mannington Hunt Caffyn. (On cover: Seaside library. Pocket ed., no. 2083). G. Munro's Sons.
Yellow Back Radio Broke-Down. Ishmael Reed. LC 69-20100. 1969. (pbk) 1.95. Doubleday.
Yellow Back Radio Broke-Down: A Novel. Ishmael Reed. 1977. 1.95 (ISBN 0-380-01751-2). Avon Books.
Yellow Brick Road. Elizabeth Cadell. 1960. 4.95 o.p. Morrow.
Yellow Butterflies. Mary Raymond Shipman Andrews. LC 22-245820. 1922. C. Scribner's Sons.
Yellow Cat. 1st Ed. Clifford Knight. LC 50-5945. (Guilt edged mystery). 1950. Dutton.
Yellow Circle. Pearl Foley. LC 37-22500. J. B. Lippincott Company.
Yellow Circle. Charles Edmonds Walk. LC 9-26145. 1909. A. C. McClurg & Co.
Yellow Claw. Sax Rohmer. 1976. lib. bdg. 13.95x (ISBN 0-89968-142-5). Lightyear.
Yellow Claw. Arthur Sarsfield Ward. LC 15-800093. 1915. McBride, Nast & Company.
Yellow Claw. Arthur Sarsfield Ward. LC 21-4513. 1920. R. M. McBride & Company.
Yellow Corsair. James W Bennett. LC 27-183828. 1927. Duffield and Company.
Yellow Creek Gun. Lyman Lutes. LC 67-2533. 1967. Arcadia House.
Yellow Crystal. Robert McNair Wilson. LC 30-23186. 1930. J. B. Lippincott Company.
Yellow Danger: Or, What Might Happen If the Division of the Chinese Empire Should Estrange All European Countries. Matthew Phipps Shiel. LC 99-4313. 1899. R. F. Fenno & Company.
Yellow Diamond. George Fort Gibbs. LC 35-569676. 1935. D. Appleton-Century Company, Incorporated.
Yellow Document: Or, "Fantomas of Berlin,". Marcel Allain. LC 19-5848. (Fantomas detective novels). 1919. Brentanos.
Yellow Dog. Henry Irving Dodge. LC 18-109643. 1918. Harper & Brothers.
Yellow-Dog Contract. Ross Thomas. LC 76-15608. 1977. 8.95 (ISBN 0-688-03104-8). Morrow.
Yellow Dog Contract. Ross Thomas. 1977. 1.75 (ISBN 0-380-01828-4). Avon Books.
Yellow Dove. George Fort Gibbs. LC 15-21786. 1915. 1.25. D. Appleton and Company.
Yellow Dust. Charles De Verteuil. LC 54-702. 1953. Staples Press.
Yellow Eyes. Rutherford George Montgomery. LC 37-17497. 1937. The Caxton Printers, Ltd.

Yellow Face. Fred Merrick White. LC 8-4908. R. F. Fenno & Company; Etc., Etc.

Yellow Fever. Tr. from French by Xan Fielding. Jean Larteguy. LC 65-19969. 1965. 4.95. Dutton.

Yellow Fiend. Annie French Hector. LC 1-31737. 1901. Dodd, Mead and Company.

Yellow Fingers: A Novel. Gene Wright. LC 25-212628. 1925. J. B. Lippincott Company.

Yellow Flood. William Ashley Anderson. LC 32-28977. 1932. R. M. McBride & Company.

Yellow-Flower Moon. Jean Hager. LC 81-14503. 1981. 9.95 (ISBN 0-89621-312-9). Thorndike Press.

Yellow Flowers in the Antipodean Room. Janet Frame, pseud. LC 69-12802. 1969. 5.95. G. Braziller.

Yellow Frigate: Or, The Three Sisters. James Grant. LC 44-316297. G. Routledge and Sons.

Yellow Gentians and Blue. Zona Gale. LC 27-20431. 1927. D. Appleton and Company.

Yellow Gold of Tiryns. Helena Osborne. LC 77-81009. 1969. 5.95. Coward-McCann.

Yellow Hair: A Novel of Indian Warfare in the Arkansas Valley of 1868, and of the Fate-Foreshadowing, Willful Way of George A. Custer Eight Years Before an Engry History Caught up with Him on the Banks of Montana's Little Big Horn. Clay Fisher. LC 53-9246. 1953. Houghton Mifflin.

Yellow Hair: A Novel of Indian Warfare in the Arkansas Valley of 1868. And of the Fate-Foreshadowing, Willful Way of George A. Custer Eight Years Before an Angry History Caught up with Him on the Banks of Montana's Little Big Horn. Clay Fisher. 1973. (pbk.) 0.75. Bantam Books.

Yellow Hearse. Floyd Mahannah. LC 50-13321. 1950. Duell, Sloan and Pearce.

Yellow Holly. Fergus Hume. LC 3-25724. 1903. G. W. Dillingham Company.

Yellow Horde. Hal George Evarts. LC 21-679721. 1921. 1.75. Little, Brown, and Company.

Yellow Horn. Jack Micheline. 1975. pap. 2.50 (ISBN 0-935062-02-5, Pub. by Golden Mtn). SBD.

Yellow Horse. Dee Alexander Brown. 224p. 1981. pap. 1.95 (ISBN 0-553-14988-1). Bantam.

Yellow Horse: A Western Story. Arthur Murray Chisholm. LC 26-192633. Chelsea House.

Yellow House. Edward Phillips Oppenheim. LC 8-28315. C. H. Doscher & Co.

Yellow House: Master of Men. Edward Phillips Oppenheim. 1912. P. F. Collier & Son.

Yellow Is for Fear: And Other Stories. Dorothy Eden. 1976. (pbk.) 1.50. Ace Books.

Yellow Jersey. Ralph Hurne. LC 72-93513. 1973. 7.95 (ISBN 0-671-21499-3). Simon and Schuster.

Yellow Journalist. Miriam Michelson. LC 5-35296. 1905. D. Appleton and Company.

Yellow Kid in McFadden's Flats. Edward Waterman Townsend. LC 8-29827. (Dillingham's American authors library, no. 24). 1897. G. W. Dillingham Co.

Yellow Leaf. Mort Friedlander. LC 46-11906. 1946. Current Books Inc., A. A. Wyn.

Yellow Letter. William Andrew Johnston. LC 11-25739. 1.25. The Bobbs-Merrill Company.

Yellow Lola. Edward Dorn. LC 80-68260. 132p. 1981. signed ltd. ed. 20.00 (ISBN 0-932274-14-5); pap. 6.00. Cadmus Eds.

Yellow Lord. Will Levington Comfort. LC 19-806848. 1.50. George H. Doran Company.

Yellow Magic. Eugene Thomas. LC 34-899386. Sears Publishing Company, Inc.

Yellow Mask. Wilkie Collins. LC 7-1622. (The Keystone series of novels, no. 5). Strawbridge & Clothier.

Yellow Meads of Asphodel. Herbert Ernest Bates. LC 77-352863. 1976. 3.50 (ISBN 0-7181-1499-X). Joseph.

Yellow Men and Gold. Gouverneur Morris. LC 11-77421. 1911. Dodd, Mead and Company.

Yellow Men Sleep. Jeremy Lane. LC 19-13966. 1919. 1.00. The Century Co.

Yellow Mistletoe. Walter S Masterman. LC 30-257397. E. P. Dutton Company, Inc.

Yellow Moon. Rebecca Stratton. (Presents Ser.). 1975. pap. 1.25 (ISBN 0-373-70606-5, 70606, Pub. by Harlequin). PB.

Yellow Moon Lodge. Phyllis Yahnke. LC 56-117065. 1956. Arcadia House.

Yellow Munro. Gerard Fairlie. LC 29-14103. 1929. Little, Brown, and Company.

Yellow Music Kill. Walter J Sheldon. (Fawcett Gold Medal Book). 1974. (pbk.) 0.75. Fawcett.

Yellow Napoleon: A Romance of West Africa. Arthur Eustace Southon. LC 72-4613. (Black Heritage Library Collection). 1972. 11.50 (ISBN 0-8369-9127-3). Books for Libraries Press.

Yellow Napoleon: A Romance of West Africa. Arthur Eustace Southon. LC 29-8656. 1928. Fleming H. Revell Company.

Yellow Pages: A Novel. John Linssen. LC 78-73873. 9.95 (ISBN 0-87795-226-4). Arbor House.

Yellow Pearl: A Story of the East and the West. Adeline Margaret Teskey. LC 11-16564. Hodder and Stoughton, George H. Doran Company.

Yellow Peril" The Adventures of Sir John Weymouth-Smythe. Richard Jaccoma. 1980. 2.95 (ISBN 0-425-04556-0). Berkley Publishing Co.

Yellow Peril: The Adventures of Sir John Weymouth Smythe. 1980. pap. 2.95 (ISBN 0-425-04556-0). Berkley Pub.

Yellow Peril" The Adventures of Sir John Weymouth-Smythe: a Novel. Richard Jaccoma. LC 78-4069. 8.95 (ISBN 0-399-90007-1). Richard Marek Publishers.

Yellow Pigeon. Carmel Goldsmid Guest. LC 29-3265. 1929. L. MacVeagh, The Dial Press.

Yellow Pine Basin: The Story of a Prospector. Henry G Catlin. LC 6-22282. 1897. G. H. Richmond & Co.

Yellow Poppy. Dorothy Kathleen Broster. LC 22-26480. 1922. R. M. McBride & Company.

Yellow Primrose: Novel. Joan Frances Young. LC 28-21494. 1928. Longmans, Green and Co.

Yellow Robe: A Novel of the Life of Buddha. Pierre Stephen Robert Payne. LC 48-6038. 1948. Dodd, Mead.

Yellow Robe Murders. Lois Bull. LC 36-103917. The Macaulay Company.

Yellow Room. M. Le Comple Du Bouleau. pap. 1.75 o.s.i. (Venus). Grove.

Yellow Room... Mary Roberts Rinehart. LC 45-6796. 1945. Farrar & Rinehart, Inc.

Yellow Room. George Shipway. LC 79-150917. 1971. 5.95. Doubleday.

Yellow Room. George Shipway. 1973. (pbk) 1.25. Manor Books.

Yellow Rose. Shana Carrol, pseud. 1982. pap. 3.50 (ISBN 0-515-05557-3). Jove Pubns.

Yellow Rose. Shana Carrol, pseud. Date not set. pap. 3.50. Berkley Pub.

Yellow Rose of New Orleans. A Novel. Nevada McNeill. (On cover: The southern rose series). 1895. G. W. Dillingham.

Yellow Roses. Elizabeth Cullinan. LC 76-49132. 1977. 8.95 (ISBN 0-670-79387-6). Viking Press.

Yellow Scarf. Florence Stonebraker. LC 51-9301. 1950. Arcadia House.

Yellow Seven. Edmund Snell. LC 23-12434. 1923. 1.90. The Century Co.

Yellow Shadows. Arthur Sarsfield Ward. LC 26-10562. 1926. Doubleday, Page & Company.

Yellow Snake. Edgar Wallace. 192p. 1973. lib. bdg. 5.95 o.s.i. (ISBN 0-85617-380-0). White Lion Pubs.

Yellow Soap. Katharine Haviland Taylor. LC 20-10312. 1920. Doubleday, Page & Company.

Yellow Souls. Dorota Flatau. LC 18-157196. George H. Doran Company.

Yellow Spider. John Charles Beecham. LC 21-6036. W. J. Watt & Company.

Yellow Stockings. David Wilson MacArthur. LC 26-9577. 1925. Cassell and Company, Ltd.

Yellow Storm. Ch'ing Ch'un Shu. Tr. by Pruitt, Ida. LC 51-9088. Harcourt, Brace.

Yellow Streak. Valentine Williams. LC 22-8943. 1922. Houghton Mifflin Company.

Yellow Streak: And Other Stories About Schools. Charles William Bardeen. LC 12-20560. C. W. Bardeen.

Yellow Submarine. Max Wilk. Tr. by Douglass Parker. Lee Minoff. LC 75-4967. (Illus.). 1968. 1.95. New American Library.

Yellow Summer. Suzanne Prou. LC 70-156565. 1972. 5.95 (ISBN 0-06-013432-1). Harper & Row.

Yellow Tapers for Paris. Bruce Marshall. LC 46-252698. 1946. Houghton Mifflin Company.

Yellow Taxi. Jonathan Stagge, pseud. LC 42-13335. 1942. Published for the Crime Club by Doubleday, Doran & Company, Inc.

Yellow Trail (a Story of Salmon River Gold) Elias Manchester Boddy. LC 23-1442. Times-Mirror Press.

Yellow Trousers. Clifford King. LC 63-13372. 1963. Roy Publishers.

Yellow Turban. Charlotte Jay, pseud. LC 55-10710. 1968. pap. 0.60 o.p. (63-046). Paperback Lib.

Yellow Turban: By Charlotte Jay Pseud. 1st Ed. Geraldine Jay. LC 55-10710. 1955. Harper.

Yellow Typhoon. Harold MacGrath. LC 19-155505. Harper & Brothers.

Yellow Van. Richard Whiteing. 1903. The Century Co.

Yellow Villa. Suzanne Blanc. LC 64-13103. 1964. Published for the Crime Club by Doubleday.

Yellow Violet. Frances Kirkwood Crane. LC 42-517838. 1942. J. B. Lippincott Company.

Yellow Wall Paper. Charlotte Perkins Stetson Gilman. LC 8-27769. 1899. Small, Maynard & Company.

Yellow Wallpaper. Charlotte Perkins Stetson Gilman. LC 73-5795. (Feminist Press reprint no. 3). 1973. (pbk.) 1.25 (ISBN 0-912670-09-6). Feminist Press.

Yellowhawk. Jane Stuart. LC 72-10001. 1973. 6.95 (ISBN 0-07-062196-9). McGraw-Hill.

Yellowhorse. Dee Alexander Brown. LC 79-181019. 256p. 1972. 4.95 o.p. (ISBN 0-395-13577-X). HM.

Yellowhorse: A Novel of the Cavalry in the West. Dee Alexander Brown. LC 56-9209. 1956. Houghton Mifflin.

Yellowleaf. Sacha Gregory. LC 19-155649. 1919. J. B. Lippincott Company.

Yellowplush Papers. William Makepeace Thackeray. LC 47-36811. Henry Altemus Company.

Yellowstone Kelly. Clay Fisher. LC 57-6945. 1957. Houghton Mifflin.

Yellowstone Nights. Herbert Quick. LC 11-11898. 1.25. The Bobbs-Merrill Company.

Yellowstone Park Romance. William Lee Popham. LC 11-32420. 1.00. The World Supply Company.

Yellowthread Street. William Leonard Marshall. 1977. 1.50 (ISBN 0-445-04109-9). Popular Library.

Yemasse. William Gilmore Simms. 1974. Repr. of 1882 ed. lib. bdg. 30.00 (ISBN 0-8414-8072-9). Folcroft.

Yemassee. William Gilmore Simms & Cowie, Alexander, 1896- Ed. LC 37-4083. (Half-title: American fiction series; general editor, H. H. Clark). American Book Company.

Yemassee: A Romance of Carolina. William Gilmore Simms. Ed. by Holman, Clarence Hugh. LC 61-66407. (Riverside editions, A65). 1961. Houghton Mifflin.

Yemassee: A Romance of Carolina. William Gilmore Simms. LC 62-10274. (Twayne's United States classics series). 1964. Twayne Publishers.

Yemassee; a Romance of Carolina. new and rev. ed. William Gilmore Simms. 1853. Redfield.

Yemassee, a Romance of Carolina. new and rev. ed. William Gilmore Simms. LC 8-11013. 1882. A. C. Armstrong & Sons.

Yemassee: a Romance of Carolina. new and rev. ed. William Gilmore Simms. (On cover: Lovell's library, v. 12, no. 653). 1885. J. W. Lovell Company.

Yemenite Girl. Curt Leviant. 1978. 1.95 (ISBN 0-380-41293-4). Avon.

Yemenite Girl: A Novel. Curt Leviant. LC 78-52741. 8.95 (ISBN 0-672-52263-2). Bobbs-Merrill.

Yenan Seeds and Other Stories. LC 77-365036. (Illus.). 1976. Foreign Languages Press.

Yenan Seeds & Other Stories. 1976. pap. 1.95 o.p. (ISBN 0-8351-0444-3). China Bks.

Yenan Seeds & Other Stories. 1976. pap. 1.95 o.p. (ISBN 0-8351-0444-3). China Bks.

Yennycott Folks: Or, The Planting of Southold. An Historical Romance of the Pioneer Days of Long Island, Touching Upon Such Well-Known Families As the Hallock, Terry, Yonges, Horton, Tuttle, Salmon, Conkelyne, Goldsmith, Moore, Akerly, Booth, Herbert, Benjamin, Miller, King, Brown, Elton, Case, Tucker, Wines, Haynes, Corey and Payne Families. Metta Horton Cook. LC 10-169787. J. S. Ogilvie Publishing Company.

Yeoman: A Novel. Charles Kennett Burrow. LC 4-6883. 1904. J. Lane.

Yeoman Fleetwood. Mary E. Sweetman Blundell. LC 5-603. 1900. Longmans, Green, and Co.

Yeoman's Daughter: A Novel. 1st Ed. Julia Luker. LC 53-97911. 1953. Exposition Press.

Yeoman's Hopspital. Helen Ashton. LC 45-183173. 1945. The Viking Press.

Yeoman's Progress. Douglas Reed. LC 46-1385. 1946. The Bobbs-Merrill Company.

Yermah the Dorado. Frona Eunice Wait Smith Colburn. LC 8-32827. 1897. W. Doxey.

Yermakov Tranfer. Derek Lambert. 1974. 7.95 o.p. (ISBN 0-8415-0326-5). Dutton.

Yermakov Transfer. Derek Lambert. LC 74-1103. 1974. 7.95. Saturday Review Press.

Yermakov Transfer. Derek Lambert. 1975. (pbk.) 1.75. Bantam Books.

Yerney's Justice. Ivan Cankar & Adamie, Louis, Tr. LC 26-165386. Vanguard Press.

Yes. Bibi Wein. LC 69-12050. 1969. Harcourt, Brace & World.

Yes and Back Again: A Novel. Richard Grenier. LC 67-11235. 1967. Little, Brown.

Yes, Farewell. Michael Burn. LC 47-1780. 1947. The Macmillan Company.

Yes from No Man's Land. Bernard Kops. 1968. pap. 0.60 o.p. (73-652). Lancer.

Yes from No-Man's Land: 1st Amer. Ed. Bernard Kops. LC 65-13274. 4.50. Coward.

Yes, Helen, there were Dinosaurs. Lewis S. Brown. Ed. by Lena M. Brown. (Illus.). 152p. (Orig.). 1982. pap. 7.95 (ISBN 0-9608542-0-7). L S Brown Pub.

Yes I Remember. Jessie Ivey. 21p. Date not set. pap. 2.00. Ivey Pubns.

Yes Is Better Than No. Byrd Bayler. 1980. pap. 1.95 (ISBN 0-380-50625-4, 50625). Avon.

Yes, My Darling Daddy. Carter Sprague. 192p. (Orig.). 1973. pap. 1.95 o.p. (ISBN 0-87682-292-8, 7292). Barclay Hse.

Yes, Yes, Yes. Anne Biggs. 1977. 6.95 o.p. (ISBN 0-533-02849-3). Vantage.

Yes, You Can! Art Linkletter. 224p. 1982. pap. 2.95 (ISBN 0-515-06442-4). Jove Pubns.

Yeshiva. Chaim Grade. LC 76-11608. 1976. 12.50 (ISBN 0-672-52264-0). Bobbs-Merrill.

Yeshua's Diary. Wesley Shrader. LC 67-11498. 1967. Judson Press.

Yesterday: An American Novel. Elizabeth Winthrop Johnson. (On cover: Leisure hour series no. 137). 1882. H. Holt and Company.

Yesterday & Tomorrow. Jules Verne. 3.95. Assoc Bk.

Yesterday at the Seventh Hour. Jeanne Hale. (Orig.). 1976. pap. 1.50 o.p. (ISBN 0-88368-076-9). Whitaker Hse.

Yesterday Framed in to-Day: A Story of the Christ, and How to-Day Received Him. Isabella Macdonald Alden. LC 90-178903. 1898. Lothrop Pub. Co.

Yesterday in Ireland. Eyre Evans Crowe. 1829. Printed by J. & J. Harper.

Yesterday Is Dead. Dallas Barnes. (Signet Book). 1976. (pbk.) 1.50. New American Library.

Yesterday Is Real. Endpapers by the Author. 1st Ed. Irma Laraway Dunn. LC 53-10539. 1953. Exposition Press.

Yesterday Morning. Parker Hoysted Fillmore. LC 31-5128. 2.00. The Century Co.

Yesterday Rider. Ray Hogan. (Signet Book). 1977. 1.25 (ISBN 0-451-07500-5). New American Library.

Yesterday Rider. Ray Hogan. LC 75-36627. 1976. 5.95 (ISBN 0-385-11683-7). Doubleday.

Yesterday Rider. Ray Hogan. LC 78-7329. 1978. 8.95 (ISBN 0-8161-6579-3). G. K. Hall.

Yesterday, Today & Forever. Jeane Dixon. 1977. pap. 3.50 (ISBN 0-553-20446-7, 20446-7). Bantam.

Yesterday Was Doomsday. Translated from the German by Norman Denny. Michael Horbach. LC 61-12150. 1961. Random House.

Yesterday Will Return. Tom Hanlin. LC 46-7344. 1946. The Viking Press.

Yesterdays. Harold S. Ladoo. LC 74-75919. (Anansi Fiction Ser.: No. 29). 110p. 1974. 10.95 (ISBN 0-88784-431-6, Pub. by Hse Anansi Pr Canada); pap. 4.95 (ISBN 0-88784-329-8). U of Toronto Pr.

Yesterday's Burdens. Robert Myron Coates. LC 74-23583. (Lost American fiction). 1975. 7.95 (ISBN 0-8093-0717-0). Southern Illinois University Press.

Yesterday's Burdens. Robert Myron Coates. LC 33-34142. The Macaulay Company.

Yesterday's Child. Helene Brown. 1977. pap. 2.50 (ISBN 0-451-11300-4, AE1300, Sig). NAL.

Yesterday's Child. Janet Kern. 1962. 4.95 o.p. Lippincott.

Yesterday's Child. Barbara Wood. LC 78-20010. 1979. 8.95 (ISBN 0-385-14132-7). Doubleday.

Yesterday's Child. Barbara Wood. 1981. 2.50 (ISBN 0-380-50765-X). Avon Books.

Yesterday's Children. David Gerrold. LC 76-29042. 1976 (ISBN 0-88411-193-8). Aeonian Press.

Yesterday's Daughter. Reita Lambert. LC 41-5110. 1941. Macrae-Smith-Company.

Yesterday's Dreams. trans- lated from the german by norman alexander. ed. Ruth Feiner & Alexander, Norman, Tr. LC 39-15267. J. B. Lippincott Company.

Yesterday's Enemy. Richard Clayton. LC 76-24557. 1976. 6.95 (ISBN 0-8027-5351-5). Walker.

Yesterday's Enemy. Richard Clayton. LC 77-357699. 1976. 3.75 (ISBN 0-304-29727-5). Cassell.

Yesterday's Enemy. William Haggard. 1976. 6.95 o.p. (ISBN 0-8027-5351-5). Walker & Co.

Yesterday's Enemy. Simon Harvester. 204p. 1983. pap. 2.95 (ISBN 0-8027-3011-6). Walker & Co.

Yesterday's Evil. Lydia Benson Clark. (Ace gothic). 1974. (pbk.) 0.95. Ace Books.

Yesterday's Evil. Dorothy Daniels. (Orig.). 1979. pap. 1.75 (ISBN 0-451-08567-1, E8567, Sig). NAL.

Yesterday's Glory. Dorothy Quentin. 1944. Arcadia House, Inc.

Yesterday's Harvest. Margaret Bass Pedler. LC 27-204433. 1926. George H. Doran Company.

Yesterday's Harvest. Margaret Bass Pedler. LC 33-174809. 1928. Grosset & Dunlap.

Yesterday's Hero. Otis Carney. LC 59-12183. 1959. Houghton Mifflin.

Yesterday's House. Nancy Gardiner. (Avalon Books). 1977. 4.95. Thomas Bouregy.

Yesterdays in Paris. A Sketch from Real Life. William Bradford. LC 6-15197. (On cover: Satchel series, no. 26). The Authors' Publishing Company.

Yesterday's Lesson. Sharon Isabell. LC 74-8354. 1974. Women's Press Collective.

Yesterday's Lessons. Sharon Isabell. LC 74-7829. (Illus.). 1974. (pbk.) 2.50. Women's Press Collective.

Yesterday's Lily. Jeff Jones. (Illus.). 80p. 1980. pap. 8.95 (ISBN 0-8256-9552-X, Quick Fox). Putnam Pub Group.

Yesterday's Love. Faith Baldwin Cuthrell. 1973. (pbk.) 0.95. Warner Paperback Library.

Yesterday's Love. abr. ed. Marsha Manning. Ed. by Alice Sachs. (Orig.). 1970. Repr. of 1969 ed. 3.95 o.p. Lenox Hill.

Yesterday's Love: And Eleven Other Stories. James Thomas Farrell. LC 48-3991. (New Avon library, 157). 1948. Avon Book Co.

Yesterday's Madness. Marian Cockrell. LC 43-464046. 1943. Harper & Brothers.

Yesterday's Prelude. Lucille H. Bednarczyk. 1979. 6.95 o.p. (ISBN 0-533-02521-4). Vantage.

Yesterday's Promise. Mary Badger Wilson. LC 34-1303. The Penn Publishing Company.

Yesterday's Rain. Paul Hutchens. LC 38-34540. Wm. B. Eerdmans Publishing Co.

Yesterday's Scars. Carole Mortimer. (Harlequin Presents Ser.). 192p. 1980. pap. 1.50 (ISBN 0-373-10383-2, Pub. by Harlequin). PB.

Yesterday's Sin: A Nudist Novel. Harry A Keller. LC 34-58235. The Macaulay Company.

Yesterday's Son. William Edward Wilson. LC 41-11015. Farrar and Rinehart, Inc.

Yesterday's Spy. Len Deighton. LC 75-12609. 1975. 7.95 (ISBN 0-15-199753-5). Harcourt Brace Jovanovich.

Yesterday's Spy. Len Deighton. 1976. 1.95. Warner Books.

Yesterday's Streets. Silvia Tennenbaum. LC 81-1119. 15.95 (ISBN 0-394-51478-5). Random House.

Yesterday's Tears. Susannah Leigh. 1982. pap. 3.50 (ISBN 0-451-11764-6, AE1764, Sig). NAL.

Yesterday's Thrall. Edith Austin Holton. Thomas Y. Crowell Company.

Yesterday's Tomorrow. Ursula Bloom. 1978. pap. 1.95 (ISBN 0-89041-188-3, 3188). Major Bks.

Yesterday's Tomorrow. Bernard Edelman. 225p. 1972. 5.00 o.p. (ISBN 0-912852-02-X). Echo Pubs.

Yesterday's Tomorrow. Olive Wadsley. LC 30-24144. 1929. Dodd, Mead & Company.

Yesterday's Tomorrow: Anonymous. Herman Alfred Kasen. LC 35-33. 1933. G. H. Watt.

Yesterday's Tomorrows: Favorite Stories from Forty Years as a Science Fiction Writer. Ed. by Frederik Pohl. 1982. pap. 8.95 (ISBN 0-425-05648-1). Berkley pub.

Yesterday's Woman. Nancy L. Vogler. (Orig.). 1979. pap. 1.95 (ISBN 0-532-23322-0). Woodhill.

Yesteryear Phantom. William Edward Daniel Ross. Ed. by Alice Sachs. 1971. 3.95 o.p. Lenox Hill.

Yesteryear Phantom. William Edward Daniel Ross. (Avon gothic). 1974. (pbk.) 0.95 (ISBN 0-380-00056-3). Avon.

Yesteryears of Texas. John Earl Brown. LC 36-18550. 1936. The Naylor Company.

Yet Do Not Grieve. Conal O'Connell O'Riordan. LC 28-29240. 1928. C. Scribner's Sons.

Yet He Was a Gentleman. Grace Jewett Austin. LC 40-25691. Printed by Pantagraph Press.

Yet Other Waters. James Thomas Farrell. LC 52-11116. 1952. Vanguard Press.

Yet She Loved Him. Kate Vaughn. LC 8-30207. (Ledger library, no. 112). 1894. R. Bonner's Sons.

Yet She Must Die. Sara Woods, pseud. LC 73-3744. (Rinehart suspense novel). 1974. 4.95 (ISBN 0-03-010816-0). Holt, Rinehart and Winston.

Yet Speaketh He. Gertrude Capen Whitney. LC 10-951313. 1910. Sherman, French & Comapny.

Yetta Segal. Horace J Rollin. LC 7-40753. 1898. G. W. Dillingham Co.

Yiddish Tales. Ed. by Helena Frank. LC 74-29531. (Modern Jewish Experience). 1975. 36.00 (ISBN 0-405-06755-0). Arno Press.

Yiddish Tales. Ed. by Helena Frank. LC 12-11712. 1912. 1.50. The Jewish Publication Society of America.

Yiddish Tales. facsimile ed. Ed. by Moses Rischin. Tr. by Helena Frank from Yiddish. LC 74-29531. (Modern Jewish Experience Ser.). (Eng.). 1975. Repr. of 1912 ed. 36.00x (ISBN 0-405-06755-0). Ayer Co.

Yieger's Cabinet. Spiritual Vampirism: the History of Etherial Softdown, and Her Friends of the "New Light". Charles Wilkins Webber. LC 8-367457. 1853. Lippincott, Grambo & Co.

Yield to the Night. Joan Henry. LC 54-9831. 1954. Doubleday.

Yielded Heart. Irene Murray, pseud. LC 60-17197. 1959. Zondervan Pub. House.

Yisroel: The First Jewish Omnibus. Ed. by Joseph Leftwich. LC 52-14417. 1952. Beechhurst Press.

Yisroel: The First Jewish Omnibus. rev. ed. Ed. by Joseph Leftwich. LC 61-15264. 1963. T. Yoseloff.

Ylana of Callisto. Lin Carter. (Callisto Books; 7). 1977. 1.50 (ISBN 0-440-14244-X). Dell Pub. Co.

Yngling. John Dalmas, pseud. (Orig.). 1971. pap. 0.75 o.p. (T2466). Pyramid Pubns.

Yo Soy Cereza, Vuela Conmigo. new ed. Glen Chase, pseud. Tr. by J. De Torres from Eng. (Pimienta Collection, Cereza Delicias Ser: No. 6). 160p. (Span.). 1975. pap. 1.25 (ISBN 0-88473-236-3). Fiesta Pub.

Yo-Yo. Diane Balson. LC 75-25723. 1976. 7.95 (ISBN 0-688-02979-5). Morrow.

Yo-Yo. Diane Balson. (Kangaroo Book). 1977. 1.75 (ISBN 0-671-80919-9). Pocket Books.

Yobbo Nowt. John McGrath. 72p. (Orig.). 1981. pap. 4.95 (ISBN 0-904383-76-8). Pluto Pr.

Yodogima, in Feudalistic Japan. I. William Adams. LC 11-208116. 1911. The Mikilosch Press.

Yogi of Cockroach Court. Frank Waters. LC 72-91922. 1972. 2.75 (ISBN 0-8040-0613-X). Sage Books.

Yogi of Cockroach Court. Frank Waters. LC 47-1900. 1947. Rinehart & Company, Inc.

Yoke. Hubert Wales. 1908. The Stuyvesant Press.

Yoke: A Romance of the Days When the Lord Redeemed the Children of Israel from the Bondage of Egypt. Elizabeth Jane Miller. LC 4-3581. 1904. The Bobbs-Merrill Company.

Yoke and Burden. Issac Remson Blauvelt. 1869. United States Publishing Company.

Yoke & the Star. Tana De Gamez, pseud. 1969. pap. 0.95 o.p. (B95-106). Belmont-Tower.

Yoke and the Star: A Novel of the Cuban Revolution. Tana De Gamez. LC 66-22670. 1975. (pbk.) 1.75 (ISBN 0-345-24414-1). Ballantine Books.

Yoke and the Star: A Novel of the Cuban Revolution. Tana De Gamez. LC 66-22670. 5.95. Bobbs.

Yoke of Life. Frederick Philip Grove, pseud. LC 30-28641. 1930. R. R. Smith, Inc.

Yoke of Pity: L'ordination. Julien Benda. Tr. by Cannan, Gilbert. LC 13-17156. 1913. 1.00. H. Holt and Company.

Yoke of Silence. Amy McLaren. LC 11-254343. 1911. G. P. Putnam's Sons.

Yoke of Stars. Frances Mary Frost. LC 38-290955. 1939. Farrar & Rinehart.

Yoke of the Thorah. Henry Harland. LC 75-104474. 1970. Literature House.

Yoke of the Thorah. Henry Harland. LC 77-139741. (Series in American studies). 1971. Johnson Reprint Corp.

Yoke of the Thorah. Henry Harland. LC 7-1897. Cassell & Company, Limited.

Yoke of the Thorah. Henry Harland. (On cover: Cassell's sunshine series, no. 62). The Cassell Publishing Co.

Yoked with a Lamb: And Other Stories. Helen Reimensnyder Martin. LC 76-152948. (Short story index reprint series). 1971. (ISBN 0-8369-3807-0). Books for Libraries Press.

Yoked with a Lamb and Other Stories. Helen Reimensnyder Martin. LC 30-3539. 1930. Dodd, Mead and Company.

Yokefellow. Ralph Boardman Davisson. LC 8-37185. 1908. The C. M. Clark Publishing Co.

Yoket the Star. Tana de Gamez. 1977. pap. 1.95 o.s.i. (ISBN 0-8439-0475-5, Leisure Books). Nordon Pubns.

Yokohama, California. Short Stories. Toshio Mori. LC 49-8320. 1949. Caxton Printers.

Yokohama Hood. J. R. Fernandes. 2.50 o.p. Vantage.

Yolan, a Tale of Love and Mystery Beside the Blue Danube. Jerrard Tickell. LC 29-3187. 1929. G. P. Putnam's Sons.

Yolanda & the Strange Objects. Lezley Saar. LC 78-64740. (Illus.). 1978. pap. 6.95 (ISBN 0-918408-10-5). Reed & Cannon.

Yolanda, Maid of Burgundy. Charles Major. LC 5-33630. 1905. The Macmillan Company.

Yolanda: The Girl from Erosphere. Dominique Verseau. 1975. pap. 1.50 o.p. (D9452, Dist. by Dell). Grove.

Yolande. William Black. LC 6-124109. (Lovell's library, v. 4. no. 136). 1883. J. W. Lovell Co.

Yolande. A Novel. William Black. (Harper's Franklin square library. no. 319). Harper & Brothers.

Yolande. A Novel. William Black. (Seaside library. Pocket Ed. no. 1). G. Munro.

Yollop. George Barr McCutcheon. LC 22-4206. 1922. Dodd, Mead and Company.

Yomah--and After. F. C Hendry. LC 32-263724. 1932. H. Holt and Company.

Yonah. 1982. pap. 6.95. Feldheim.

Yonder. Margaret Bell Houston. LC 55-7233. 1955. Crown Publishers.

Yonder Comes the Train. Lance Phillips. (Illus.). 1965. 7.98 o.p. (ISBN 0-498-06303-8, Encore). A S Barnes.

Yonder Grow the Daisies. William R. Lipman. LC 29-20649. 1929. I. Washburn.

Yonder Lies Jericho. Samuel Bertram Harrison. LC 33-19693. D. Appleton-Century Company, Incorporated.

Yonder Sails the Mayflower. Honore McCue Willsie Morrow. LC 34-42183. 1934. W. Morrow and Company.

Yonder: Stories of Fantasy and Science Fiction. Charles Beaumont. LC 58-6415. (Bantam giant, A1759). 1958. Bantam Books.

Yondering. Louis L'Amour. (Orig.). 1980. pap. 1.95 (ISBN 0-553-13829-4). Bantam.

Yonderville. George Abbe. LC 68-28487. (New England heritage book). 1968. 2.50 (ISBN 0-8283-1004-1). Branden Press.

Yone Santo, a Child of Japan. Edward Howard House. LC 7-7137. Belford, Clark and Co.

Yonnondio. Tillie Olsen. 1979. pap. 3.95 (ISBN 0-440-59881-8, Delta). Dell.

Yonnondio: from the Thirties. Tillie Olsen. LC 73-15555. 1974. 5.95. Delacorte Press.

Yoppy: The Autobiography of a Monkey. Mollie Lee Clifford. LC 5-21571. (Illustrated animal autobiographical series). 1905. H.M. Caldwell Co.

Yorke the Adventurer, and Other Stories. Louis Becke. LC 71-37535. (Short story index reprint series). 1972. (ISBN 0-8369-4094-6). Books for Libraries Press.

Yorke the Adventurer: And Other Stories. Louis Becke. LC 25-12252. 1925. J. B. Lippincott Company.

Yorkshire Farm. Vera Murdock Stuart Jervis. LC 44-334040. 1943. Hurst & Blackett Ltd.

Yorkshire Farm. Vera Murdock Stuart Jervis. LC 44-398394. 1944. Arcadia House, Inc.

Yorkshire Moorland Murder. Joseph Smith Fletcher. LC 30-12991. 1930. A. A. Knopf.

Yorkshire Ripper. Roger Cross. (Illus.). 255p. 1981. pap. 2.95 (ISBN 0-440-19802-X). Dell.

Yorktown. Burke Davis. LC 52-9600. 1952. Rinehart.

Yorktown: An Historical Romance... Eliza Lanesford Foster Cushing. LC 9-3847. 1826. Wells and Lilly.

Yorkville Yankee. Edward Edgar Fuchs. LC 50-13517. 1950.

Yosemite Valley Romance. William Lee Popham. LC 11-32418. 1.00. The World Supply Company.

Yoshar, the Soldier. William Harrington. LC 66-128322. 1966. 4.50. Dial.

Yoshe Kalb. Israel Joshua Singer. Tr. by Maurice Samuel from Yiddish. LC 73-78157. 246p. 1976. 10.00 (ISBN 0-8149-0730-X). Vanguard.

Yoshe Kalb. Israel Joshua Singer. 1968. pap. 0.75 o.p. (33-027). Lancer.

Yoshe Kalb. Introd. by Isaac Bashevis Singer. Tr. from Yiddish by Maurice Samuel. Israel Joshua Singer. Tr. by Maurice Samuel. LC 65-20988. 1965. 4.95. Harper.

Yoshko the Dumbell. 1982. 5.95; pap. 3.95 (ISBN 0-87306-246-9). Feldheim.

You. Gladys Sheila Donisthrope. LC 27-24578. 1927. Duffield & Company.

You. Magdeleine Legendre Paz. Tr. by Seltzer, Adele Szold. LC 21-22103. 1921. T. Seltzer.

You. Henry L. Slaughter. 1969. 3.00 o.p. (ISBN 0-8059-1353-X). Dorrance.

You. 320p. (Orig.). 1981. pap. 2.95 (ISBN 0-553-14478-2). Bantam.

You and I. Myron Brinig. LC 45-9227. 1945. Farrar & Rinehart, Inc.

You and I. Olive Wadsley. LC 25-308729. 1924. Cassell and Company, Ltd.

You and I. Olive Wadsley. LC 25-7833. 1925. Dodd, Mead and Company.

You & I, & Love. Terry Rowe. (O.si.). 1977. 5.95 o.s.i. (ISBN 0-8037-9859-8). Dial.

You & I & Yesterday. Marjorie Holmes. (Adult Ser.). 295p. 1974. Repr. lib. bdg. 7.95 o.p. (ISBN 0-8161-6178-X, Large Print Bks). G K Hall.

You and Me, Babe. Chuck Barris. LC 73-17635. 1974. 6.95 (ISBN 0-06-120342-4). Harper's Magazine Press.

You Are France, Lisette. Eileen Jeanette Lyttle Garrett. LC 43-17616. 1943. Creative Age Press, Inc.

You Are Hiding God from Me. Albert H. Van Den Heuvel. LC 72-91519. (Open, 8). (Illus.). 1973. 2.50 (ISBN 0-8006-0146-7). Fortress Press.

You Are My Love. Leonard McCombe. LC 52-7639. 1952. Sloane.

You Are Not the Target. Laura Archera Huxley. pap. 4.00 (ISBN 0-87980-175-1). Wilshire.

You Are the One. Rob Eden. LC 45-391844. 1945. Gramercy Publishing Company.

You Are the One. Berta Ruck. LC 45-3499. 1945. Dodd, Mead & Company.

You Are the Rain. R. Rozanne Knudson. 1978. pap. 1.25 (ISBN 0-440-99898-0, LFL). Dell.

You Asked for It, Charlie Brown: Selected Cartoons from "You're the Guest of Honor, Charlie Brown", Vol. II. Charles M. Schulz. (Peanuts Ser.). (Illus.). 1978. pap. 1.75 (ISBN 0-449-23957-8, Crest). Fawcett.

You Be the Mother Follies. Claire Burch. 1981. 12.50 o.p. (ISBN 0-8482-0219-8); pap. 5.00 o.p. Norwood Edns.

You Belong to Me: A Novel. Sam Ross. LC 55-32837. (Popular library, 657). 1955. Popular Library.

You Bet Your Life. Stuart M Kaminsky. LC 78-4016. 8.95 (ISBN 0-312-89662-X). St. Martin's Press.

You Better Believe It. Dee Hill, pseud. Orig. Title: Three to Make Merry. 1967. pap. 0.50 o.p. (52-591). Paperback Lib.

You Call That a House? A Novel. William Manners. LC 56-7350. 1956. J. Day Co.

You Can Always Blame the Rain. Mike Fredman. LC 79-8446. 8.95 (ISBN 0-312-89667-0). St. Martin's Press.

You Can Die Laughing: By A.A. Fair Pseud. Erle Stanley Gardner. LC 57-6841. (A Morrow mystery). 1957. Morrow.

You Can Have It When I'm Through with It. Betty Webb Mace. LC 76-7813. 4.00 (ISBN 0-913780-12-X). Daughters, Inc.

You Can Hear the Echo. Mary Paula King O'Donnell. LC 65-26255. 1965-1966. Simon and Schuster.

You Can Kiss This Boy Goodbye: A Novella and Eight Stories. Marvin Elkoff. LC 81-409. 12.95 (ISBN 0-671-41145-4). Wyndham Books.

You Cannot Die. Ian Currie. LC 80-83590. 288p. 1981. pap. 2.95 (ISBN 0-86721-024-9). Playboy Pbks.

You Can't Be Too Careful. Herbert George Wells. LC 42-13386. 1942. G. P. Putnam's Sons.

You Can't Beat the Law: A Gripping Story of Love and Adventure, Based on the Motion Picture Story. Herbert Hartwell Van Loan. LC 28-9846. Jacobsen-Hodgkinson-Corporation.

You Can't Believe Your Eyes. Joan Margaret Fleming. LC 57-11042. (Chantecler mystery novel). 1957. I. Washburn.

You Can't Catch Me. Lawrence Lariar. LC 51-14225. 1951. Crown Publishers.

You Can't Come Back. Bruce Beaver. LC 66-17470. 1966. 3.45. Rigby.

You Can't Do That to Svoboda.". John Szekely. LC 43-5437. 1943. The Dial Press.

You Can't Eat Orchids. Nancy Starr. LC 38-5358. 1937. Hillman Curl, Inc.

You Can't Escape. Faith Baldwin. 1976. Repr. of 1943 ed. lib. bdg. 14.10x (ISBN 0-88411-625-5). Amereon Ltd.

You Can't Escape. Faith Baldwin Cuthrell. LC 76-40435. 1976. 6.95 (ISBN 0-88411-625-5). Aeonian Press.

You Can't Escape. Faith Baldwin Cuthrell. LC 43-10322. 1943. Farrar & Rinehart, Incorporated.

You Can't Escape. Faith Baldwin Cuthrell. 1974. (pbk.) 0.95. Warner Paperback Library.

You Can't Escape. Laurence M. Janifer. pap. 0.60 o.p. Lancer.

You Can't Get Away by Running. Elwyn Whitman Chambers. LC 39-8353. 1939. Doubleday, Doran & Co., Inc.

You Can't Get There from Here. Earl Hamner. LC 65-11287. 4.95. Random.

You Can't Get There from Here. Earl Hamner. (Bantam pathfinder editions). 1974. (pbk.) 1.25. Bantam Books.

You Can't Go Home Again. Thomas Wolfe. LC 57-136465. (Grosset's universal library, UL 16). 1957. Grosset & Dunlap.

You Can't Go Home Again. Thomas Wolfe. LC 40-27633. Harper & Brothers.

You Can't Go Home Again. Thomas Wolfe. LC 45-32786. 1942. The Sun Dial Press.

You Can't Go Home Again. With an Introd. by Edward C. Aswell. Thomas Wolfe. LC 58-3057. (Harper's modern classics). Harper.

You Can't Have Everything. Kathleen Thompson Norris. LC 37-28522. 1937. Doubleday, Doran & Company, Inc.

You Can't Ignore Murder. Ruth Townsend Mills Teague & Teague, Walter Dorwin, 1883- Joint Author. LC 42-36244. 1942. G. P. Putnam's Sons.

You Can't Keep a Good Woman Down: Stories. Alice Walker. LC 80-8761. 10.95 (ISBN 0-15-199754-3). Harcourt Brace Jovanovich.

You Can't Keep the Change. Peter Cheyney. LC 44-5201. 1944. Dodd, Mead & Company.

You Can't Keep the Change... Peter Cheyney. LC 46-21821. 1946.

You Can't Kill a Corpse. Louis Trimble. LC 46-20588. 1946. Phoenix Press.

You Can't Kill a Dead Man. Daniel Panger. 208p. (Orig.). 1982. pap. 2.25 (ISBN 0-8439-1057-7, Leisure Bks). Nordon Pubns.

You Can't Learn 'em Nothin' Montague Marsden Glass. LC 30-3868. 1930. Doubleday, Doran & Company, Inc.

You Can't Let the Weeds Grow. Armand Hellersberg. LC 41-20724. Balletto-Sweetman, Inc.

You Can't Live Forever. Harold Q Masur. LC 50-11043. (Inner sanctum mystery). 1951. Simon and Schuster.

You Can't See Around Corners. Jon Cleary. LC 47-31123. 1947. C. Scribner's Sons.

You Can't Sleep Here. Edward Newhouse. LC 34-38718. The Macaulay Company.

You Can't Stop Living. Fern Rives. LC 45-2266. 1945. G. P. Putnam's Sons.

You Can't Tell About Love. Helen Diehl Olds. LC 50-6060. 1950. Messner.

You Can't Unfry an Egg. Robert Pershall. LC 76-13754. 1977. 6.95 (ISBN 0-914090-31-3); pap. 3.95 (ISBN 0-914090-32-1). Chicago Review.

You Could Die Laughing: Or, I Was a Comic for the F.B.I., and The Swingers. Joey Adams. LC 68-27631. 1968. 4.95. Bobbs-Merrill.
You Could Live If They Let You. Wallace Markfield. LC 74-8373. 1974. 5.95 (ISBN 0-394-46056-1). Knopf; Distributed by Random House.
You Did It. Eaton K Goldthwaite. LC 43-82459. 1943. Duell, Sloan and Pearce.
You Didn't Even Try. Philip Whalen. 200p. (Orig.). pap. 1.95 o.p. Coyote.
You Die Next, Jill Baby! Kirby Carr. LC 75-13496. 1.25 (ISBN 0-89041-007-0). Major Books.
You Die Today! Baynard Hardwick Kendrick. LC 52-7500. 1952. Morrow.
You Do Take It with You: By Donald K. MacDonald and Alaric J. Roberts. Donald K MacDonald & Alaric J. Roberts. LC 53-10305. Vantage Press.
You Don't Belong Here. Sally Gibbs. LC 43-9412. 1943. Doubleday, Doran and Company, Inc.
You Don't Have to Slay a Dragon. John Marberger Stuart & Marjorie L. Stuart. LC 75-14540. (Illus.). 1975. 8.95 (ISBN 0-915730-01-4). Marburger Publications.
You Don't Know Charly! Valentine Thomson. LC 30-31595. Brewer and Warren Inc.
You Don't Need an Enemy. Richard Martin Stern. LC 74-162762. 1971. (ISBN 0-684-12581-1). Scribner.
You Fight for Treasure! Edouard A. Stackpole. LC 32-17903. 1932. W. Morrow & Company.
You Get Used to a Place. Vera Randal. LC 72-77964. 1972. 6.95 (ISBN 0-399-11019-4). Putnam.
You Get What You Ask for. Norman Macleod. LC 39-33745. Harrison-Hilton Books, Inc.
You Go Your Way. Katharine Brush. LC 41-9689. Farrar & Rinehart, Inc.
You Gotta Accommodate the Public. Mary Miles Kleinman. LC 68-23553. 1968. Adams Press.
You Have Chosen. Denise Robins. 1972. pap. 0.75 o.p. (94218). Beagle Bks.
You Have to Draw the Line Somewhere. Christie Harris. LC 64-12147. (Illus.). 1964. Atheneum.
You Have Yourself a Deal. Rene Raymond. LC 68-14006. 1968. Walker.
You Haven't Changed. Margaret Culkin Banning. LC 38-103262. 1938. Harper & Brothers.
You Know Charles. Margaret Breuning. LC 21-19845. 1921. 1.60. H. Holt and Company.
You Know Me. W. A. Rocker. 1972. 7.50 (ISBN 0-912090-24-3); pap. 2.45 (ISBN 0-912090-23-5). Sumac Mich.
You Know Me Al. Ring Lardner. 1960. pap. 1.65 o.p. (ISBN 0-684-71835-9, SL156). Scribner.
You Know Me Al: A Busher's Letters. Ring W Lardner. LC 16-15595. 1.25. George H. Doran Company.
You Know Me Al: A Busher's Letters. Ring Wilmer Lardner. LC 25-969332. 1925. C. Scribner's Sons.
You Leave Me Cold! Samuel Rogers. LC 46-72123. 1946. Harper & Brothers.
You Little Match-Maker. Anne Arrington Tyson. LC 31-11914. The Knickerbocker Press.
You Live Once. John Dann MacDonald. 1978. pap. 1.95 (ISBN 0-449-14050-4, GM). Fawcett.
You Lovely People. Bienvenido N. Santos. 1978. pap. text ed. 5.00x (Pub. by Bookmark). Cellar.
You Made Me! Ann Lawrence. LC 36-359972. 1936. Godwin.
You May Be Next: A Personal Message to Everyone Living in the Strange World of Today. 1st Ed. William Michael Higgins. LC 58-141695. Greenwich Book Publishers.
You Mean: A Novel. Lucy R Lippard. LC 78-78257. 1979. 5.95 (ISBN 0-933568-00-2). Chrysalis Books.
You Must Be Sisters: A Novel. Deborah Moggach. LC 78-19432. 1979. 8.95 (ISBN 0-312-89685-9). St. Martin's Press.
You Must Break Out Sometimes, and Other Stories. Thomas Owen Beachcroft. LC 75-113648. (Short story index reprint). 1970. Books for Libraries Press.
You Must Know Everything. Isaak Emmanuilovich Babel. Ed. by Nathalie Babel. Tr. by Max Hayward from Rus. 1969. 10.95 o.p. (ISBN 0-374-29408-9); pap. 6.95 (ISBN 0-374-51580-8). FS&G.
You Must Know Everything: Stories, 1915-1937. Isaak Emmanuilovich Babel. LC 69-11576. 1969. 5.95. Farrar, Straus and Giroux.
You Must Love the Enemy. Lester E. Hood. 5.00 o.p. Carlton.
You Must Never Go Back. Brian Talbot Cleeve. LC 68-28572. 1968. 4.95. Random House.
You, My Brother. Philip Burton. 1973. 10.95 o.p. (ISBN 0-394-48478-9). Random.
You, My Brother: A Novel Based on the Lives of Edmund & William Shakespeare. Philip Burton. LC 73-5009. 1973. 8.95 (ISBN 0-394-48478-9). Random House.
You Need a Complete Rest. Charles Fry Haywood. LC 53-314022. 1953. Nichols-Ellis Press.
You Never Can Tell. Elizabeth Egan Sears. LC 36-243950. Green Circle Books.
You Never Know Your Luck: Being the Story of a Matrimonial Deserter. Gilbert Parker. LC 14-14233. 1914. George H. Doran Company.
You Never Saw Such a Girl. George Weston. LC 19-10465. 1919. Dodd, Mead and Company.
You No Longer Count (Tu N'es Plus Rien!) Rene Boylesve. Tr. by Houghton, Louise (Seymour) LC 18-10962. 1918. C. Scribner's Sons.
You Only Hang Once. Henry Wisdom Roden. LC 43-228620. 1944. Books Inc., Distributed by W. Morrow & Company.
You Only Live Twice. Ian Fleming. pap. 4.50 fr. ed; pap. 2.95 span. ed. French & Eur.
You Only Live Twice. Ian Fleming. pap. 2.50 (ISBN 0-451-12108-2, AE2108, Sig). NAL.
You Only Live Until You Die. Sol Weinstein. LC 68-18315. 1968. Trident Press.
You Pay for Pity: By William Mole Pseud. William Antony Younger. LC 58-6830. (Red badge detective). 1958. Dodd, Mead.
You Play the Black and the Red Comes up. Eric Mowbray Knight. LC 38-104438. 1938. R. M. McBridge and Company.
You Play the Black and the Red Comes up. Eric Mowbray Knight. LC 80-12193. (Gregg Press Mystery Fiction Series). 1980. 13.95 (ISBN 0-8398-2646-X). Gregg Press.
You Remember the Case. Tod Claymore. LC 39-31199. 1939. T. Nelson and Sons Ltd.
You Rolling River. Archie Binns. LC 47-30902. 1947. C. Scribner's Sons.
You Sane Men. Laurence M. Janifer. (Orig.). pap. 0.60 o.p. (72-789). Lancer.
You Say You Saw a Camel. Elizabeth Jane Coatsworth. (Illus.). 1962. 2.95 o.p. (CN). Har-Row.
You Shall Know Them: By Vercors Pseud. Translated by Rita Barisse. 1st Ed. Jean Bruller. LC 52-12650. 1953. Little, Brown.
You Should Only Be Happy. Yuri Suhl. (Orig.). 1969. pap. 0.95 o.p. (ISBN 0-446-65126-5, 65-126). Paperback Lib.
You Should Worry Says John Henry. George Vere Hobart. LC 14-133320. G. W. Dillingham Company.
You Stand Accused. Dana Hughston. LC 37-33114. 1937. Hillman-Curl, Inc.
You Tell My Son. Rex K Pratt. LC 58-10952. 1958. Random House.
You, the Jury. Jean Mayer Liebeler. LC 44-6667. 1944. Farrar & Rinehart, Inc.
You, the Jury: A Novel. 1st American Ed. Mary Borden. LC 52-5646. 1952. Longmans, Green.
You Too. Roger Burlingame. LC 24-54512. 1924. C. Scribner's Sons.
You Ve Got to Show Me: And Other Stories. 1st Ed. Noel Bacchus. LC 53-8087. 1953. Pageant Press.
You Want to Die, Johnny? Gavin Black. LC 66-13934. 1979. pap. 1.95i o.p. (ISBN 0-06-080472-6, P 472, PL). Har-Row.
You Want to Die, Johnny? Oswald Wynd. LC 66-13934. Harper & Row.
You Were Saying, Andy Capp. Smythe. 128p. 1980. pap. text ed. 1.50 (ISBN 0-449-14346-5, GM). Fawcett.
You Will Die Today! R. I. Wakefield, pseud. LC 53-10210. (Red badge detective). 1953. Dodd, Mead.
You Will Like It Here. Nancy Dorer & Frances Dorer. (Orig.). 1979. pap. 1.95 (ISBN 0-532-23257-7). Woodhill.
You Will Live Again. Brad Steiger. pap. 1.95 (ISBN 0-440-09775-4). Dell.
You Will Never Be the Same. Paul Myron Anthony Linebarger. LC 75-424. (Garland Library of Science Fiction). 1975. 11.00 (ISBN 0-8240-1429-4). Garland Pub.
You Will Never Be the Same. Cordwainer Smith, pseud. Ed. by Lester Del Ray. LC 75-429. (Library of Science Fiction). 1975. lib. bdg. 15.00 (ISBN 0-8240-1429-4). Garland Pub.
You Won't Let Me Finnish. Joan Margaret Fleming. LC 76-46516. 1977. 8.95. J. Curley & Associates.
You Would If You Loved Me. Nora Stirling. 176p. (gr. 7-10). 1982. pap. 1.95 (ISBN 0-380-01631-1, 57984, Flare). Avon.
You Wouldn't Believe It. Arthur Frederick Goodrich. LC 36-115586. 1936. D. Appleton-Century Company, Incorporated.
You, You & You! Pete Grafton. 192p. (Orig.). 1982. pap. 5.95 (ISBN 0-86104-360-X). Pluto Pr.
You'd Be Surprised. Clarence T Hubbard. LC 30-5247. The Finlay Brothers.
You'll Be Sorry! Samuel Rogers. LC 45-730212. 1945. Harper & Brothers.
You'll Die Laughing. Marjorie J. Grove. (Mystery Puzzler Ser.: No. 5). (Illus., Orig.). 1978. pap. 1.95 (ISBN 0-89083-408-3). Zebra.
You'll Die Next! Harry Whittington. LC 54-35683. (Ace double novel books, D-63). 1954. Ace Books.
You'll Die Today. Marjorie J. Grove. (Mystery Puzzlers Ser.: No. 22). (Illus., Orig.). 1979. pap. 1.95. Zebra.
You'll Die Tomorrow. Marjorie J. Grove. (Mystery Puzzler Ser.: No. 9). (Illus., Orig.). 1978. pap. 1.95 (ISBN 0-89083-421-0). Zebra.
You'll Die When You Hear This. Marjorie J. Grove. (Mystery Puzzlers Ser.: No. 1). (Illus., Orig.). 1978. pap. 1.95 (ISBN 0-89083-395-8). Zebra.
You'll Die Yesterday. Marjorie J. Grove. (Mystery Puzzlers Ser.: No. 18). (Illus., Orig.). 1979. pap. 1.95 (ISBN 0-89083-453-9). Zebra.
You'll Hang, My Love. Swann & Emerick. pap. 0.60 o.p. Lancer.
You'll Hear Me Laughing. Richard Laurence Gordon. LC 78-69534. 8.95 (ISBN 0-690-01791-X). Crowell.
You'll Like My Mother. Naomi A Hintze. LC 69-17786. 1969. 4.50. Putnam.
You'll Never Come Back. Elizabeth W. Freeman. LC 79-66735. 1979. pap. write for info. (ISBN 0-87930-124-4). Miller Freeman.
You'll Never Fail Me. Rosemary Frances Rees. LC 41-3913. 1939. Arcadia House, Inc.
You'll Never Go Back: A Novel. Kathleen Nevin. LC 47-12041. 1947. B. Humphries.
You'll Never Hang Me. Lee Deighton. 160p. 1981. pap. 1.75 (ISBN 0-345-29119-0). Ballantine.
You'll Never Take Me. Robert Douglas Mead. LC 76-56324. 1978. 6.95 (ISBN 0-385-12090-7). Doubleday.
You'll Pay for This...All of You! Bill Rechin et al. 1979. pap. 1.25 (ISBN 0-449-14121-7, GM). Fawcett.
You'll Remembez. Anne Tedlock Brooks. LC 49-49643. 1949. Arcadia House.
Youma: The Story of a West-Indian Slave. Lafcadio Hearn. LC 74-80890. 1969. AMS Press.
Youma: The Story of a West-Indian Slave. Lafcadio Hearn. LC 78-131738. 1970. Scholarly Press.
Youma: The Story of a West-Indian Slave. Lafcadio Hearn. LC 7-5043. 1890. Harper & Brother.
Young, a Novel. Miriam Colwell. LC 55-5487. 1955. Ballantine Books.
Young Actor: Or, The Solution of a Mystery. William Taylor Adams. LC 5-42964. (On cover: Leather-clad tales, no. 27). United States Book Company.
Young Actresses. Susan Parrish. 1974. (pbk.) 1.25. Ace Books.
Young Adam. Alexander Trocchi. 1982. 12.95 (ISBN 0-7145-3925-2); pap. 5.95 (ISBN 0-7145-3931-7). Riverrun NY.
Young Adolf. Beryl Bainbridge. Date not set. pap. 2.50 (ISBN 0-553-13194-X). Bantam.
Young Adolf. Beryl Bainbridge. LC 78-26174. 208p. 1979. Repr. of 1978 ed. 7.95 (ISBN 0-8076-0910-2). Braziller.
Young Alaskans. Emerson Hough. 1976. lib. bdg. 14.25x (ISBN 0-89968-049-6). Lightyear.
Young Alaskans in the Rockies. Emerson Hough. 1976. lib. bdg. 15.25x (ISBN 0-89968-050-X). Lightyear.
Young Amanda, The Truant Bride & Beggars May Sing. Sara Seale. (Harlequin Romances (3-in-1) Ser.). 576p. 1983. pap. 3.95 (ISBN 0-373-20070-6). Harlequin Bks.
Young America. Samuel Field & Ballard, Frederick, 1884- LC 16-5196. 1916. 1.25. Duffield & Company.
Young Ames. Walter Dumaux Edmonds. LC 41-28075. 1942. Little, Brown and Company.
Young Anal Daughters. Stacey. pap. 1.95 o.p. (ISBN 0-87682-191-3, 7191). Barclay Hse.
Young Anal Lovers. Kaye. pap. 1.95 o.p. (ISBN 0-87056-179-0, 6179). Brandon.
Young Anarchy. Philip Hamilton Gibbs. LC 26-228639. George H. Doran Company.
Young & Black. Ed. by Edith Crocker. 1971. 4.95 o.p. (ISBN 0-448-02816-6); lib. bdg. 4.99 o.p.; pap. 0.95 o.p. G&D.
Young and Dangerous. Peggy Gaddis, pseud. LC 43-8534. 1943. Phoenix Press.
Young and Evil. Charles Henri Ford & Parker Tyler. LC 75-12351. (Homosexuality). 1975. 10.00 (ISBN 0-405-07392-5). Arno Press.
Young and Fair. Laetitia McDonald Irwin. LC 33-2519. 1933. Farrar & Rinehart.
Young and Fair. Laetitia McDonald. LC 33-251990. Farrar & Rinehart, Incorporated.
Young and Fair Is Iowa. Mathias Martin Hoffmann. LC 47-4070. 1946. The Loras College Press.
Young and Healthy. Donald Henderson Clarke. LC 81-22907. The Vanguard Press.
Young and Hungry-Hearted. Stories. James Aswell. LC 55-5863. (Signet book, 1166). 1955. New American Library.
Young and Secret. Alice Grant Rosman. LC 30-18861. 1930. Minton, Balch & Company.
Young and the Immortal. Isabel Currier. LC 41-14543. 1941. A. A. Knopf.
Young and the Restless. Deborah Sherwood. 1976. (pbk.) 1.25. Bantam.
Young Apollo. Anthony Gibbs. LC 29-19023. 1929. Harper & Brothers.
Young April.". Egerton Castle. LC 99-4631. 1899. The Macmillan Company.
Young April. Dorothy Lester Chadwick. LC 36-14934. Arcadia House.
Young Archimedes: And Other Stories. Aldous Leonard Huxley. LC 24-22679. George H. Doran Company.
Young Art and Old Hector. Neil Miller Gunn. LC 77-354454. 1976. 3.00. (ISBN 0-285-62249-8) (ISBN 0-285-62254-4). Souvenir Press.
Young Art and Old Hector. Neil Miller Gunn. LC 44-40219. 1944. G. W. Stewart, Inc.
Young Artist: Or, The Dream of Italy. Timothy Shay Arthur. 1850. M. W. Dodd.
Young Barbarians. John Watson. LC 1-25444. 1901. Dodd, Mead and Co.
Young Beck, a Chip of the Old Block. Matthias McDonnell Bodkin. LC 12-2460. 1912. 1.25. Little, Brown and Company.
Young Bess. Margaret Emma Faith Irwin. LC 45-35025. 1945. Harcourt, Brace and Company.
Young Blockaders; a Story of the Civil War. Everett Titsworth Tomlinson. LC 10-23631. (His War for the union series). 1910. Lothrop, Lee & Shepard Co.
Young Blood. Katina Alexis. 288p. (Orig.). 1982. pap. 2.95 (ISBN 0-523-48028-8). Pinnacle Bks.
Young Blood. Francis Lynde. LC 29-12063. 1929. C. Scribner's Sons.
Young Boys & Their Older Women see Older Women's Young Studs.
Young Bride. George Jordan. 1971. pap. 0.75 o.p. (75-384). Manor Bks.
Young Brown: Or, The Law of Inheritance. Eustace Clare Grenville Murray. (Seaside library, v. 62, no. 1285). 1882. G. Munro.
Young Caesar. Rex Warner. LC 58-6031. 1958. Little, Brown.
Young Can Die Protesting. Stanton Forbes, pseud. LC 77-78691. 1969. 4.50. Published for the Crime Club by Doubleday.
Young Capitalist. Linnie Sarah Harris. LC 7-2900. The Pilgrim Press.
Young Captain Jack; or, Son of a Soldier. Horatio Alger. 267p. 1974. Repr. of 1901 ed. lib. bdg. 15.15x (ISBN 0-88411-808-8). Amereon Ltd.
Young Captains: Or, Prisoners of the King; a Stirring Tale of Philadelphia. Thomas Chalmers Harbaugh. LC 13-805617. (Boys of liberty library) $0.50). D. McKay.
Young Captive Prince: A Tale of Allegory and Fact. P. O Eastman. LC 6-36813. 1870. Register Steam Printing Establishment !
Young Captives: A Story of Judah and Babylon. Erasmus W Jones. LC 7-38606. D. C. Cook Publishing Company.
Young Castaways. Spencer S. Mitsunaga & Erie K. Mitsunaga. 3.95 o.p. Vantage.
Young Castaways: A Novel. Leon Lewis. (On cover: The popular series, no. 18). 1892. R. Bonner's Sons.
Young Catherine: An Historical Novel. Martha Edith Almedingen. LC 38-1970. 1938. Frederick A. Stokes Company.
Young Champion: One Year in Grace Aguilar's Girlhood. Abram Samuel Isaccs. LC 13-126008. 1913. The Jewish Publication Society of America.
Young Chief & the Old Chief of the Secret Indian Mine in Indian Paradise. A. J. Mansfield. (Illus.). 4.50 o.s.i. Mansfield.
Young Claudia. Rose Franken. LC 46-721394. 1946. Rinehart and Company, Inc.
Young Clementina. Dorothy Emily Stevenson. LC 76-118158. 1970. 5.95. Holt, Rinehart and Winston.
Young Clementina. Dorothy Emily Stevenson. 1979. 1.95 (ISBN 0-441-95048-5). Ace Books.
Young Color Guard: Or, Tommy Collins at Santiago. Mary Greene Bonesteel. LC 4-5916. 1902. Benziger Brothers.
Young Concubine. Makhali-Phal & Weismiller, Edward, Tr. LC 42-8909. 1942. Random House.
Young Continentals at Bunker Hill. John Thomas McIntyre. LC 10-107778. 1910. The Penn Publishing Company.
Young Continentals at Trenton. John Thomas McIntyre. 1911. 1.25. The Penn Publishing Company.
Young Crankshaw. Cecil Hemley. LC 63-8092. 1963. Harcourt, Brace & World.
Young Dee of Dundee... Ted Pauter Smith. LC 25-22383.
Young Defenders. Everett Titsworth Tomlinson. LC 13-17001. (Stories of colony and nation) $0.48). Silver, Burdett and Company.
Young Desire. Clement Yore. LC 31-16243. The Macaulay Company.
Young Diana: An Experiment of the Future. Marie Corelli. LC 18-20939. 1.50. George H. Doran Company.
Young Die Good. Nancy Hale. LC 32-5594. 1932. C. Scribner's Sons.
Young Disciple. A Novel. John A. Clark. LC 9-1495. W. B. Smith & Co.

Young Divorcees. Lissa Charell. LC 63-14539. 1963. Macmillan.
Young Dr. Bob. Kathleen Harris, pseud. 1945. Arcadia House, Inc.
Young Dr. Bob. Adelaide Humphries. LC 45-8202. 1945. Arcadia House.
Young Doctor Galahad. Elizabeth Seifert. LC 73-79134. 1973. 5.95. Aeonian Press.
Young Doctor Galahad. Elizabeth Seifert. LC 38-32605. 1938. Dodd, Mead & Company.
Young Doctor Glenn. Cateau De Leeuw. LC 48-3291. 1948. Macrae-Smith-Co.
Young Doctor Hamilton. Mary Ann Fisher. 1908. Cochrane Publishing Co.
Young Doctor Kildare. Max Brand. 1978. 15.00 (ISBN 0-86025-129-2). State Mutual Bk.
Young Dr. Kildare. Max Brand. 1972. pap. 0.95 o.p. (95254). Beagle Bks.
Young Dr. Kildare: By Max Brand. Max Brand. LC 41-3324. 1941. Dodd, Mead & Company.
Young Doctor Merry. Peggy Gaddis, pseud. LC 44-957943. 1944. Arcadia House, Inc.
Young Doctor Randall. Adeline McElfresh. LC 57-126797. 1957. Avalon Books.
Young Doctors in Love. Michael Elias & Michael Eustis. 168p. 1982. pap. 2.75 (ISBN 0-380-80671-1, 80671). Avon.
Young Dogs. Claude Faux. Tr. by T. White. 1962. 4.00x o.p. Verry.
Young Dogs. Tr. from French by Tony White. Claude Faux. 1966. bds., 2.50. Hamish Hamilton.
Young Dragons. J. Bradford Olesker. 1982. pap. 3.50 (ISBN 0-451-11453-1, AE1453, Sig). NAL.
Young Dreamers, Danger, and Strange Powers. Ed. by Roger Elwood. LC 74-19020. 1975. 6.50 (ISBN 0-8019-5958-6). Chilton Book Co.
Young Duck-Shooters in Camp. Frank Eugene Kellogg. LC 10-283321. 1910. Frederick A. Stokes Company.
Young Duke... harper's stereotype ed. Benjamin Disraeli Beaconsfield. LC 6-28751. 1831. J & J. Harper.
Young Duke... Benjamin Disraeli Beaconsfield. (Franklin square library, no. 13). Harper & Brothers.
Young Duke... Benjamin Disraeli Beaconsfield. (Seaside library, v. 46, no. 933). 1881. G. Munro.
Young Duke: A Moral Tale, Though Gay. Benjamin Disraeli. 1853. lib. bdg. 20.00 (ISBN 0-8414-2473-X). Folcroft.
Young Eagles. Ian Cameron, pseud. 1980. 10.00 o.p. (ISBN 0-312-89719-7). St Martin.
Young Eagles: A Novel. Donald Gordon Payne. LC 79-23236. 1979. 10.00 (ISBN 0-312-89719-7). St. Martin's Press.
Young Earnest: The Romance of a Bad Start in Life. Gilbert Cannan. LC 15-2817. 1915. D. Appleton and Company.
Young Elizabeth. Jennette Dowling Letton & Francis Letton. LC 76-9122. 1976. 7.25 (ISBN 0-89244-014-7). Queens House Publishers.
Young Elizabeth: By Jennette and Francis Letton. 1st Ed. Jennette Dowling Letton & Francis Letton. LC 53-536522. 1953. Harper.
Young Emigrants. A Tale Designed for Young Persons. Susan Ann Livingston Sedgwick. LC 45-263484. 1830. Carter and Hendce.
Young Emmanuel. Naomi Ellington Jacob. (Signet Book). 1973. (pbk) 1.25. New American Lib.
Young Emperor: A Novel. Pierre Stephen Robert Payne. LC 50-10496. 1950. Macmillan.
Young Emperor: William the Second of Germany see Collected Works.
Young Enchanted: A Romantic Story. Hugh Walpole. LC 21-27485. George H. Doran Company.
Young Entry: By M.J. Farrell Pseud... Mary Nesta Keane. LC 29-26493. 1929. H. Holt and Company.
Young Fair Maidens. 1st Ed. Naomi Lane Babson. LC 58-8580. 1958. Harcourt, Brace.
Young Family. Robert Hyde. LC 28-225746. Payson & Clarke Ltd.
Young Farmer. George Bradbury Hill. LC 13-7316. 1913. 1.00. The Penn Publishing Company.
Young Fawcett's Mabel. Linn Boyd Porter. (Dillingham's American authors library, no. 10). 1896. G. W. Dillingham.
Young Felix. Frank Arthur Swinnerton. LC 23-16461. George H. Doran Company.
Young Fisherman: Or, The Cruiser of the English Channel. A Story of the Olden Times. Julius Warren Lewis & Till, George Canning, 1825-1898. LC 9-3850. 1853. F. Gleason's Publishing Hall.
Young Flesh and Blood: A Novel. Wilbur Finley Fauley. LC 41-227741. Sheridan House.
Young Folk, Old Folk: A Novel of the Younger Set. Constance Travers Sweatman. LC 26-181636. 1926. W. Morrow and Company, Inc.
Young Folks' Uncle Tom's Cabin. Harriet Elizabeth Beecher Stowe & Boylan, Mrs. Grace (Duffin) Ed. LC 3-27799. 1901. Jamieson-Higgins Co.
Young Folks' Uncle Tom's Cabin. Harriet Elizabeth Beecher Stowe & Boylan, Mrs. Grace (Duffin) Ed. LC 2-22855. 1902. Jamieson-Higgins Co.
Young Forester. Zane Grey. LC 10-228031. 1910. Harper & Brothers.
Young Foresters. William Henry Giles Kingston. (On cover: Lovell's library, v. 7, no. 335). 1884. J. W. Lovell Company.
Young Frankenstein. Gilbert Pearlman. (Illus.). 1974. (pbk.) 1.50 (ISBN 0-345-24268-8). Ballantine Books.
Young Fu of the Upper Yangtze. Elizabeth Foreman Lewis. (Yearling Book). (Illus.). 1974. (pbk.) 0.95. Dell Pub. Co.
Young Gentlemen, Rise. Travis Ingham. LC 35-3245. Farrar, & Rinehart, Incorporated.
Young Girls & Their Doctors. Sue Varian. pap. 1.95 o.p. (ISBN 0-87682-192-1, 7192). Barclay Hse.
Young Girls & Their Older Teachers. Rivers. pap. 1.95 o.p. (ISBN 0-87056-177-4). Brandon.
Young Girl's Love. Pauline Cassin Caro. Tr. by Lorangier, Alexina. LC 6-24230. (On cover: The optimus series, no. 24). 1892. Donohue, Henneberry & Co.
Young Girls Who Seduce Older Men. Richard E. Geis. 192p. pap. 1.95 o.p. (7159). Barclay Hse.
Young Girl's Wooing. Edward Payson Roe. LC 13-17654. (On cover: Cornwall edition). Dodd, Mead and Company.
Young Greek and the Creole: And Other Stories. Philip Freund. LC 44-7918. 1944. Pilgrim House.
Young Greer of Kentucky: A Novel. Eleanor Talbot Kinkead. 1895. Rand, McNally & Company.
Young Hart: A Novel. William Harry Harding. LC 82-15493. 16.95 (ISBN 0-03-062754-0). Holt, Rinehart, and Winston.
Young Hearts. Annie Edith Foster Jameson. LC 20-11074. 1.90. George H. Doran Company.
Young Hearts: A Novel of Modern Israel. David Maletz. LC 50-727600. (Transliterated: Ma galot). 1950. Schocken Rooks.
Young Henry of Navarre. Heinrich Mann & Sutton, Eric, Tr. LC 37-22221. 1937. A. A. Knopf.
Young Hershel Goldberg's Northern Plantation & Other Stories. Larry Detwiler. 1981. 6.95 (ISBN 0-533-04897-4). Vantage.
Young Honesty"--Politician: Being the Story of How a Young Ranchman Helped to Elect His Father Congressman. John Willard Lincoln. LC 12-21403. 1.00. W. A. Wilde Company.
Young Hot Mouth People. Del Val. pap. 1.95 o.p. (ISBN 0-87682-177-8, 7177). Barclay Hse.
Young Howson's Wife. Andrew Edward Watrous. LC 2-8865. 1902. Quail & Warner.
Young Idea, a Comedy of Environment. Frank Arthur Swinnerton. LC 30-6550. 1930. Doubleday, Doran & Company, Inc.
Young Idea: A Neighborhood Chronicle. Parker Hoysted Fillmore. LC 11-147533. 1911. 1.25. John Lane Company.
Young in Heart. Ida Alexa Ross Wylie. LC 40-11454. Triangle Books.
Young in Illinois. Robert Wilson. LC 75-17572. (Illus.). 112p. 1975. pap. 5.95x (ISBN 0-913204-06-4). December Pr.
Young in One Another's Arms. Jane Rule. LC 76-16256. 1977. 6.95 (ISBN 0-385-11660-8). Doubleday.
Young Ireland: A Fragment of Irish History, 1840-1850. Charles Gavan Duffy. LC 21-15364. (Seaside library, v. 44, no. 902). 1880. G. Munro.
Young Is My Love... Ruby Mildred Ayres. LC 41-764486. 1941. Doubleday, Doran and Company, Inc.
Young Islanders. Elisabeth Ogilvie. Repr. lib. bdg. 10.85x (ISBN 0-88411-341-8). Amereon Ltd.
Young Jewess: A Narrative Illustrative of the Polish and English Jews of the Present Century, Exhibiting the Superior Moral Influence of Christianity. From the London Ed. LC 50-47128. 1827. J. Loring.
Young Joe Brody. Marty Brown. LC 59-39621. 1959. Macaulay Co.
Young John: A Novel. 1st Ed. Jim Barbee. LC 54-5746. 1954. Exposition Press.
Young John Takes Over. Elizabeth Garver Jordan. LC 42-111191. 1942. D. Appleton-Century Company, Incorporated.
Young Jonathan. Sophia Cleugh. LC 32-260506. 1932. Houghton Mifflin Company.
Young Joseph. Thomas Mann. Tr. by Helen Tracy Lowe. LC 35-6196. 1935. A. A. Knopf.
Young Kate: Or, The Rescue, A Tale of the Great Kanawha ... LC 9-1193. (On cover: Pocket editions of select novels, no. 2). 1844. Harper & Brothers.
Young Ladies Should Marry. Jessie Benton Fremont & Redfield, Elizabeth Henry. LC 36-29836. R. M. McBride & Company.
Young Lady. Mary Howard, pseud. LC 50-6861. 1950. Arcadia House.
Young Lady of Paris. Sidonie Gabrielle Colette & Gauthier-Villars, Henry. Tr. by Whitall, James. LC 31-17271. A. & C. Boni.
Young Lady with Red Hair. Mary Ann Gibbs, pseud. 1974. pap. 0.95 o.p. (26579-3-095). Beagle Bks.
Young Landlords. Walter D. Meyers. 1980. pap. 1.95 (ISBN 0-380-52191-1, 59378). Avon.
Young Librarian. James Noble Gifford. LC 40-6734. 1940. Gramercy Pub. Co.
Young Librarian. Carol Holliston. LC 40-67347. Gramercy Publishing Co.
Young Life. Jessie Leckie Herbertson. LC 11-637. 1911. Duffield & Company.
Young Life: A Novel. Leo Townsend. LC 58-7463. 1958. J. Day Co.
Young Lion Hunter. Zane Grey. LC 11-27111. 1911. Harper & Brothers.
Young Lions. Irwin Shaw. LC 50-12513. (Signet book, 817 AB). 1950. New American Library.
Young Lions. Irwin Shaw. 1976. 1.95. Dell.
Young Lions. Irwin Shaw. LC 58-6365. (Modern library of the world's best books 112). 1958. Modern Library.
Young Lions. Irwin Shaw. LC 48-8508. 1948. Random House.
Young Lives. Richard Le Gallienne. LC 99-2126. 1899. J. Lane.
Young Livingstones. Denis George Mackail. LC 30-185632. 1930. Houghton Mifflin Company.
Young Lonigan: A Boyhood in Chicago Streets. James Thomas Farrell & Thrasher, Frederic Milton. LC 32-11122. 1932. The Vanguard Press.
Young Lonigan: With a New Introduction Written by the Author for This Edition. James Thomas Farrell. LC 44-1702. 1943. The World Publishing Company.
Young Lord Penrith. A Novel. John Berwick Harwood. (Franklin square library, no. 119). 1880. Harper & Brothers.
Young Lord Stranleigh: A Novel. Robert Barr. LC 8-16950. 1908. D. Appleton and Company.
Young Love. John Gordon Brandon. LC 26-791. Brentano's.
Young Love and Other Infidelities. Stepas Zobarskas. LC 73-153021. 1971. 4.95 (ISBN 0-87141-035-4). Manyland Books.
Young Love. Translated from the Danish by Naomi Walford. 1st American Ed. Johannes Allen. LC 59-542402. 1959. Knopf.
Young Love: Variations on a Theme. John Erskine. LC 36-185557. The Bobbs-Merrill Company.
Young Lovers. Henry Christopher Bailey. LC 29-24681. E. P. Dutton & Co., Inc.
Young Lovers: A Novel. Julian Halevy. LC 55-5943. 1955. Simon and Schuster.
Young Lovers (Frankie and Johnnie) Meyer Levin. LC 52-36195. (Signet book. 911).
Young Low. George A Dorsey. LC 17-183567. George H. Doran Company.
Young Lucretia: And Other Stories. Mary Eleanor Wilkins Freeman. LC 79-106287. (Short story index reprint series). (Illus.). 1970. Books for Libraries Press.
Young Lucretia: And Other Stories. Mary Eleanor Wilkins Freeman. LC 6-40025. 1892. Harper & Brothers.
Young Lucretia & Other Stories by Mary E. Wilkins. Mary Eleanor Wilkins Freeman. LC 79-106287. (Short Story Index Reprint Ser.). 1892. 16.00 (ISBN 0-8369-3324-9). Ayer Co.
Young Lusters. Sylvia Sharon. pap. 1.25 o.p. Lancer.
Young McDermott. Edward McSorley. LC 49-10745. 1949. Harper.
Young Macedonian in the Army of Alexander the Great. Alfred John Church. LC 12-313622. (On cover: The Knickerbocker series). 1912. G. P. Putnam's Sons.
Young Maids and Old. Clara Louise Root Burnham. LC 6-19670. 1889. Ticknor and Company.
Young Malcom. George Blake. LC 27-2654. 1927. Harper & Brothers.
Young Man About to Commit Suicide. INew York: W. Faro, Inc. Anthony Gudaitis. LC 39-7604. 1932. W. Fargo, Inc.
Young Man at Sea. Maxwell Laurie. LC 31-19091. 1931. Doubleday, Doran & Company, Inc.
Young Man for Sale. Dwayne Simpson. pap. 1.25 o.p. Lancer.
Young Man from Lima. John Blackburn. 1977. 5.35 o.p. State Mutual Bk.
Young Man from Middlefield. Jessie Hunter Brown Pounds. LC 1-24951. 1901. Christian Publishing Company.
Young Man from Mount Vernon: A Novel by Arthur Pier. Arthur Stanwood Pier. LC 40-27175. 1940. Frederick A. Stokes Company.
Young Man, I Think You're Dying. Joan Margaret Fleming. LC 76-47542. 1977. 8.95 (ISBN 0-89340-058-0). J. Curley.
Young Man, I Think You're Dying. Joan Margaret Fleming. LC 71-125725. (Red mask mystery). 1970. 4.95. Putnam.
Young Man in a Hurry: And Other Short Stories. Robert William Chambers. LC 71-103504. (Short story index reprint series). (Illus.). 1969. Books for Libraries Press.
Young Man in a Hurry: And Other Short Stories. Robert William Chambers. LC 4-30587. 1904. Harper & Brothers.
Young Man in a Hurry & Other Short Stories. facsimile ed. Robert William Chambers. LC 71-103504. (Short Story Index Reprint Ser). 1904. 17.00 (ISBN 0-8369-3246-3). Ayer Co.
Young Man of Fifty. Rose Caroline Feld. LC 32-28825. E. P. Dutton & Co., Inc.
Young Man of Greenwich Village. Doris Overland. LC 37-19646. L. C. Page & Company.
Young Man of Manhattan. Katharine Brush. LC 49-22495. (Avon, 192). 1949. Avon Pub. Co.
Young Man of Manhattan. Katharine Brush. LC 30-2051. 1930. Farrar & Rinehart, Incorporated.
Young Man of Manhattan. Katharine Brush. LC 42-47441. 1931. Grosset & Dunlap.
Young Man of Paris. Translated from the French by Jacques LeClercq. 1st Ed. Henri Calet. LC 50-9310. 1950. Dutton.
Young Man of the Period. Andre Theuriet & Maury, Max, Pseud.? Tr. LC 8-27735. (library of choice fiction no. 52). 1892. Laird & Lee.
Young Man of the Year: A Novel. Elizabeth Grey Stewart. LC 61-8348. 1961. Putnam.
Young Man on a Dolphin. Thorne, Anthony. LC 52-10931. 1952. Lippincott.
Young Man on a Ledge. 1st Ed. Donald V Hock. LC 51-228. 1950. Pageant Press.
Young Man Who Fled Naked: The Story of Mark, the Defender of the Spirit of Christianity. 1st Ed. William J Luebeck. LC 60-51724. 1960. Exposition Press.
Young Man Who Wrote Soap Operas. Joel Gross. LC 74-13357. 1975. 7.95 (ISBN 0-684-14100-0). Scribner.
Young Man with a Dream: A Novel. Kenneth Sheils Reddin. LC 46-4952. 1946. Current Books, Inc., A.A. Wyn.
Young Man with a Horn. Dorothy Dodds Baker. LC 38-13334. 1938. Houghton Mifflin Company.
Young Man with a Horn. Dorothy Dodds Baker. LC 43-51229. 1943. The Press of the Readers Club.
Young Man with a Scythe. Alan Kennington. LC 51-10346. 1951. Macmillan.
Young Man, Young Man. Eda K. Stertz. (Hearth Ser.). 1979. pap. 1.75 (ISBN 0-310-38672-1). Zondervan.
Young Man, Young Man. Eda K. Stertz. 1972. 3.95 o.p. (10648). Zondervan.
Young Mandarin: A Story of Chinese Life. John A Davis. Congregational Sunday-School and Publishing Society.
Young Manhood of Studs Lonigan. James Thomas Farrell. LC 34-2152. The Vanguard Press.
Young Manhood of Studs Lonigan: With a New Introduction Written by the Author for This Edition. James Thomas Farrell. LC 44-295070. 1944. The World Publishing Company.
Young Man's Fancy. John Thomas McIntyre. LC 25-8270. 1925. Frederick A. Stokes Compnay.
Young Man's Fancy. A Novel. Adrian Bell. LC 56-9851. 1956. Abelard-Schuman.
Young Man's Fancy: And Other Tales. Mrs. Bridges. (On cover: Lovell's library, v. 18, no. 867). 1887. J. W. Lovell Company.
Young Man's Girl. Robert William Chambers. LC 34-23469. 1934. D. Appleton-Century Company, Incorporated.
Young Man's Heart. Cornell Woolrich, pseud. LC 32-433922. 1930. Mason Publishing Co.
Young Man's Year. Anthony Hope Hawkins. LC 15-18107. 1915. 1.35. D. Appleton and Company.
Young Marchesa: A Story of Malta; Illustrated by Victor J. Bertoglio. Sheila Davies. LC 51-13650. 1951. Dodd, Mead.
Young Marrieds. Judith Heiman. LC 61-12855. 1961. Simon and Schuster.
Young Masters. Alan Scholefield. LC 78-151903. 1972. 5.95. Morrow.
Young Mate-Swappers. Nora Pendler. pap. 3.45 o.p. (4015). Cameo.
Young Matriarch. Gladys Bronwyn Stern. LC 42-24042. 1942. The Macmillan Company.
Young Maugars: From the French of Andre Theuriet... Andre Theuriet. LC 8-27734. (Half-title: Collection of foreign authors, no. XVII). 1879. D. Appleton and Company.
Young May Moon. Percy Howard Newby. LC 51-9089. 1951. Knopf.
Young May Moon. Martha Ostenso. LC 29-17089. 1929. Dodd, Mead & Company.
Young Men in Love. Michael Arlen. LC 27-9454. George H. Doran Company.
Young Men in Spats. Pelham Grenville Wodehouse. LC 36-27373. 1936. Doubleday, Doran & Company, Inc.
Young Men in Spats. Pelham Grenville Wodehouse. LC 37-321623. 1937. The Sun Dial Press, Inc.
Young Men May Die. David Craig. LC 73-122430. 1970. 4.95 o.p. (ISBN 0-8128-1314-6). Stein & Day.

Young Men May Die. Allan James Tucker. LC 73-122430. 1970. 4.95 (ISBN 0-8128-1314-6). Stein and Day.

Young Men of Paris. Stephen Longstreet. (9858). 1968. Dell.

Young Men of Paris. Stephen Longstreet. LC 67-18229. 1967. Delacorte Press.

Young Merchant and the Indian Captive. Henry Diffenderffer. LC 77-1966. (Garland Library of Narratives of North American Indian Captivities; V. 64). 1977. 25.00 (ISBN 0-8240-1688-2). Garland Pub.

Young Mischief and the Perfect Pair. Hugh De Selincourt. LC 25-8316. 1925. A. & C. Boni.

Young Miss Giddy. Linn Boyd Porter. LC 7-37758. (On cover: The albatross novels). 1893. G. W. Dillingham.

Young Miss Hubbard. Peggy O'More, pseud. LC 63-6815. 1963. Arcadia House.

Young Mr. Ainslie's Courtship. Francis Charles Philips. LC 7-36065. (On cover: Lovell's international series, no. 40). F. F. Lovell & Company.

Young Mr. Barter's Repentance. David Christie Murray. (On cover: Seaside library. Pocket ed., no. 1102). 1888. G. Munro.

Young Mr. Keefe. Stephen Birmingham. LC 58-5656. 1958. Little, Brown.

Young Mr. X. Elizabeth Garver Jordan. LC 33-263391. 2.00. The Century Co.

Young Mistley. Henry S. Merriman. Ed. by Herbert Van Thal. 1888-1966. 7.95 (ISBN 0-304-93090-3); pap. 4.95. Dufour.

Young Mistley. ... rev. and authorized ed. Hugh Stowell Scott. LC 99-5465. 1899. Dodd, Mead and Company.

Young Mistley. Hugh Stowell Scott. LC 99-528. 1899. A. Mackel & Company.

Young Mistley. Hugh Stowell Scott. LC 530. (On cover: Arrow library, no. 95). 1899. Street & Smith.

Young Mountaineers. facsimile ed. Mary Noailles Murfree. LC 70-98588. (Short Story Index Reprint Ser). 1897. 16.00 (ISBN 0-8369-3162-9). Ayer Co.

Young Mountaineers: Short Stories. Mary Noailles Murfree. LC 70-98588. (Short story index reprint series). (Illus.). 1969. Books for Libraries Press.

Young Mountaineers: Short Stories. Mary Noailles Murfree. LC 4-23689. 1898. Houghton, Mifflin and Company.

Young Mrs. Blennerbassett: A Novel of Early Days in West Virginia. Nellie Whan Peppers. LC 64-1273. (Exposition-Lochinvar book). 1964. Expostion Press.

Young Mrs. Brand. Robert Smythe Hichens. LC 44-8682. 1944. Macrae-Smith Company.

Young Mrs. Burton. Margaret Penn. LC 80-41544. 1981. 8.95 (ISBN 0-521-28298-5). Cambridge University Press.

Young Mrs. Charnleigh. A Novel. Thomas W Hanshew. LC 7-1916. 1883. G.W. Carleton & Co.

Young Mrs. Charnleigh. A Novel. Thomas W Hanshew. (Street & Smith's select series, no. 64). 1890. Street & Smith.

Young Mrs. Cruse. Viola Meynell. LC 25-9144. 1925. Harcourt, Brace and Company.

Young Mrs. Greeley. Booth Tarkington. LC 29-12765. 1929. Doubleday, Doran & Company, Inc.

Young Mrs. Jardine. Dinah Maria Mulock Craik. (On cover: Seaside library Pocket ed., no. 1053). G. Munro.

Young Mrs. Jardine: A Novel. Dinah Maria Mulock Craik. LC 16-937245. (Lettered on cover: Miss Mulock's works). Harper & Brothers.

Young Mrs. Jardine. A Novel. Dinah Maria Mulock Craik. 1880. Harper & Brothers.

Young Mrs. Meigs. Elizabeth Frances Corbett. LC 31-23588. The Century Co.

Young Mrs. Savage: Being an Account of Every-Day Events in the Lives of Mrs. Savage and Her Four Children. Dorothy Emily Stevenson. LC 49-7692. 1949. Rinehart.

Young Muscovite: Or, The Poles in Russia. Frederick Chamier. LC 17-229843. 1834. Harper & Brothers.

Young Musgrave. A Novel. Margaret Oliphant Wilson Oliphant. LC 24-14945. 1878. Harper & Brothers.

Young Navy Man. Belle Burns Gremer. LC 34-7406. 1934. H. C. Kinsey & Company, Inc.

Young New Zealand Poets. Ed. by Arthur Baysting. LC 74-170631. 200p. 1974. 11.00x (ISBN 0-8002-0092-6). Intl Pubns Serv.

Young Nympho. Denise Hutton. pap. 1.95 o.p. (8030). Cameo.

Young O'Briens: Being an Account of Their Sojourn in London. LC 6-14225. 1906. J. Lane.

Young Orland. Herbert Asquith. LC 27-21882. 1927. C. Scribner's Sons.

Young Outlaw: Or Adrift in the Streets. Horatio Alger, Jr. 172p. 1975. pap. 1.25 (ISBN 0-89041-009-7, 3009). Major Bks.

Young Pandora. Ann Chidester. LC 42-194423. 1942. C. Scribner's Sons.

Young Pathbreaker & Other Stories. 1975. pap. 1.95 o.p. (ISBN 0-8351-0446-X). China Bks.

Young Pathbreaker & Other Stories. 1975. pap. 1.95 o.p. (ISBN 0-8351-0446-X). China Bks.

Young Patroon: Or, Christman in 1690. A Tale of New-York. Peter Hamilton Myers. 1849. G. P. Putnam; Etc., Etc.

Young Pattullo. John Innes Mackintosh Stewart. LC 75-25551. 1976. 7.95 (ISBN 0-393-08367-5). Norton.

Young People. John Davys Beresford. LC 24-332. E. P. Dutton & Co., Inc.

Young People. Hans Ernst Kinck & Ten Eyck, Barent, Tr. LC 29-872259. E. P. Dutton & Co., Inc.

Young People. Gertrude Schweitzer. LC 53-8437. 1953. Crowell.

Young People & Adults. Rosenberger. pap. 1.95 o.p. (ISBN 0-87682-178-6, 7178). Barclay Hse.

Young People's Pride: A Novel. Stephen Vincent Benet. LC 22-20536. 1922. H. Holt and Company.

Young Phillips, Reporter. illustrated by sanford strother. ed. Henry Justin Smith. LC 33-22470. Harcourt, Brace and Company.

Young Philosopher: A Novel. Charlotte Turner Smith. LC 73-22132. (Feminist Controversy in England, 1788-1810). 1974. (ISBN 0-8240-0881-2). Garland Pub.

Young Physician. Francis Brett Young. LC 20-8520. E. P. Dutton & Company.

Young Pilgrim, or, Alfred Campbell's Return to the East; and His Travels in Egypt, Nubia, Asia Minor, Arabia Petraea, &C. &C. By Mrs. Hofland... Barbara Wreaks Hoole Hofland. LC 7-6595. 1828. O. A. Roorbach.

Young Pilot Grounded Forever. Bobby Tubbs. 2.75 o.p. Vantage.

Young Pioneers. Rose Wilder Lane. LC 75-46559. (Illus.). 1976. 5.95 (ISBN 0-07-036205-X). McGraw-Hill.

Young Pioneers. Rose Wilder Lane. 1976. (pbk.) 1.25. Bantam.

Young Pioneers: Illustrated by the Author. 1st Ed. Hallie H Holt. LC 55-420314. 1955.

Young Pitcher. Zane Grey. LC 11-3475. 1911. Harper & Brothers.

Young Pitt: A Novel. A. M Maughan. LC 74-9363. 1975. (ISBN 0-381-98276-9). John Day Co.

Young Prey. Hillary Waugh. LC 70-78692. 1969. 4.95. Doubleday.

Young Prima Donna: A Romance of the Opera. Elizabeth Caroline Grey. LC 42-43613. 1840. Lea & Blanchard.

Young Prince: A Fantastic Story Perhaps. Arthur Hamilton Gibbs. LC 38-460. J. B. Lippincott Company.

Young Professor: A Story of Bible Inspiration. Eldridge Burwell Hatcher. LC 1-8301. (The Eva Garvey publishing fund, book no. 2). Sunday School Board, Southern Baptist Convention.

Young Renny. Mazo De La Roche. 1961. Grosset & Dunlap.

Young Renny: Jalna--1906. Mazo De La Roche. LC 35-546420. 1935. Little, Brown, and Company.

Young Renny: Jalna-1906). Mazo De La Roche. 1976. (pbk.) 1.50. Fawcett.

Young Revolutionist. Pearl Sydenstricker Buck. LC 32-610485. Friendship Press.

Young Robert: A Brief History. George Sumner Albee. LC 37-488219. Reynal & Hitchcock.

Young Romantic. Iris Bromige. 1972. pap. 0.75 o.p. (94241). Beagle Bks.

Young Russians: A Collection of Stories About Them. Ed. by Thomas P. Whitney. LC 78-185216. 1972. 5.95. Macmillan.

Young Sam and Sabina. Walter Raymond. (On cover: The "unknown" library no. 31). The Cassell Publishing Co.

Young Scarron. Thomas Mozeen. LC 74-16152. (Flowering of the Novel). 1974. (ISBN 0-8240-1136-8). Garland Pub.

Young School-Teacher. A True Story of Brooklyn. Mary Grace Halpine. LC 7-1200. (On cover: Munro's library, v. 1., no. 407). N. L. Munro.

Young Section-Hand. Burton Egbert Stevenson. LC 5-262237. 1905. L. C. Page & Company.

Young Sharpshooter; a Story of the Peninsular Campaign in 1862. Everett Titsworth Tomlinson. LC 13-19336. 1913. Houghton Mifflin Company.

Young Sin Teacher. Thomas Shire. 192p. (Orig.). 1973. pap. 1.95 o.p. (ISBN 0-87682-330-4, 7330). Barclay Hse.

Young Sinner. Elisabeth Gill. pap. 0.60 o.p. (60-359). Manor Bks.

Young Skipper & Other Stories. 1973. 3.95 o.p. (ISBN 0-8351-0447-8); pap. 1.95 o.p. China Bks.

Young Skipper & Other Stories. 1973. 3.95 o.p. (ISBN 0-8351-0447-8); pap. 1.95 o.p. China Bks.

Young Sleuthe's Victory: Or, A Detective's Adventure. Archie Kutch. LC 22-145626. G. W. Ogilvie.

Young Stagers. Percival Christopher Wren. LC 18-10541. 1917. Longmans, Green and Co.

Young Stagers: Being Further Faites and Gestes of the Junior Curlton Club of Karabad, India, Whereof Some Were Heretofore Set Forth in the Book Yclept Dew and Mildew. Percival Christopher Wren. LC 27-169182. 1926. Frederick A. Stokes Company.

Young Summers. Peter Lake. 4.95 o.p. Vantage.

Young Summers. Peter Lake. 1974. 4.95 (ISBN 0-533-01041-1). Vantage Press.

Young Surgeons. Edith P. Begner. 1971. pap. 0.95 o.p. (ISBN 0-447-75184-0). Lancer.

Young Teacher. Douglas Marshall, pseud. LC 43-597. 1943. Gramercy Publishing Co.

Young Texan. Paul Evan Lehman. 1971. pap. 0.60 o.p. (60-476). Manor Bks.

Young Thing. Murray Pfeffer. LC 72-97390. 1973. 6.95. Thimble Press.

Young Titan. F. Van Wyck Mason. 1976. Repr. of 1959 ed. lib. bdg. 27.20x (ISBN 0-89190-355-0). Am Repr-Rivercity Pr.

Young Titan. 1st Ed. Francis Van Wyck Mason. LC 59-7912. 1959. Doubleday.

Young Torless. Robert Musil. LC 81-19003. 1982. 5.95 (ISBN 0-394-71015-0). Pantheon Books.

"Young Towns" of Lima: Aspects of Urbanization in Peru. Peter Cutt Lloyd. LC 79-41644. (Urbanization in developing countries). (Illus.). 1980. 34.50 (ISBN 0-521-22871-9) (ISBN 0-521-29688-9). Cambridge University Press.

Young Trailers. Joseph Alexander Altsheler. 1976. lib. bdg. 15.30x (ISBN 0-89968-005-4). Lightyear.

Young Vanish. Francis William Stroke. LC 32-22992. 1932. W. Morrow & Co.

Young Vargas Lewis. Robert Brainard Pearsall. LC 68-23029. (Illus.). 1968. 6.95. Houghton Mifflin.

Young Victoria. Michael Sidney Tyler-Whittle. (Illus.). 1973. 1.50. Warner Paperback Lib.

Young Victoria. Tyler-Whittle, Michael Sidney. LC 71-176157. (Illus.). 1971. 6.95. St. Martin's Press.

Young Villain with Wings: A Novel. Rayne Kruger. LC 53-4427. 1953. Longmans, Green.

Young Visiters. Daisy Ashford. (Illus.). 96p. 1972. 4.95 o.p. (ISBN 0-385-01115-6). Doubleday.

Young Visiters: Or, Mr. Salteena's Plan, by Daisy Ashford. Daisy Ashford. LC 19-11363. George H. Doran Company.

Young Visiters: Or, Mr. Salteena's Plan. Illustrated by William Pene Du Bois. Daisy Ashford. LC 51-7997. 1951. Doubleday.

Young Visitors: A Novel. John Barrington Wain. bds., 4.50. Viking.

Young Wallingford. George Randolph Chester. LC 10-23397. The Bobbs-Merrill Company.

Young Wantons. Richard Wilson. pap. 2.25 o.s.i. (Venus). Grove.

Young West: A Sequel to Edward Bellamy's Celebrated Novel "Looking Backward". Solomon Schindler & Edward Bellamy. LC 70-154462. (Utopian Literature). 1971. (ISBN 0-405-03544-6). Arno Press.

Young Widow. Eleanor Cameron, pseud. 1974. (pbk.) 0.95. Dell.

Young Widow. Clarissa Fairchild Cushman. LC 42-7193. 1942. Little, Brown and Company.

Young Wife. Wallace Irwin. LC 36-4465. 1936. D. Appleton-Century Company, Incorporated.

Young Wife's Tale. William Sansom. 224p. 1979. 7.95 o.p. (ISBN 0-7012-0396-X, Pub. by Chatto Bodley Jonathan). Merrimack Pub Cir.

Young Woman. Paul Bodin. LC 71-75058. 1969. 4.95. Crown.

Young Woman in Love. Mary Barrow Linfield. LC 29-2737. The Macaulay Company.

Young Woman of Europe: A Novel. Ruth Feiner. LC 42-51782. 1942. J. B. Lippincott Company.

Young Woman of 1914: Translated from German. Arnold Zweig & Sutton, Eric, Tr. LC 32-338403. 1932. The Viking Press.

Young Woodley: A Novel. John Van Druten. LC 29-9989. 1929. The John Day Company.

Youngblood. John Oliver Killens. LC 66-2277. 1966. 6.95. Trident.

Youngblood. John Oliver Killens. LC 54-71231. 1954. Dial Press.

Youngblood. John Oliver Killens. LC 81-16156. 1982. 20.00 (ISBN 0-8203-0601-0) (ISBN 0-8203-0602-9). University of Georgia Press.

Youngblood Hawke. Herman Wouk. 1975. (pbk.) 2.45 (ISBN 0-671-80149-X). Pocket Books.

Youngblood Hawke: A Novel. Herman Wouk. LC 62-7698. 1962. Doubleday.

Younger & the Older. Scott Rainey. 192p. pap. 1.95 o.p. (7141). Barclay Hse.

Younger Boys & Older Women. Morton Parker. 192p. pap. 1.95 o.p. (7147). Barclay Hse.

Younger Brother. Hal Correll. LC 31-3094. David C. Cook Publishing Co.

Younger Girls with Older Men. Sterling. pap. 1.95 o.p. (ISBN 0-87682-187-5, 7187). Barclay Hse.

Younger Ones: By John Jordan Pseud. 1st Ed. Jean Paul Jordan. LC 53-18612. 1952. Pageant Press.

Younger Set. Robert William Chambers. LC 24-14920. 1907. A. L. Burt Company.

Younger Set. Robert William Chambers. 1907. D. Appleton and Company.

Younger Sister. Kathleen Thompson Norris. LC 32-16972. 1932. Doubleday, Doran & Company, Inc.

Younger Venus: A Tale. Naomi Gwladys Royde-Smith. LC 39-27008. 1939. The Macmillan Company.

Youngerman Guns. Lewis B Patten. LC 69-10967. (A Double D western). 1969. 3.95. Doubleday.

Youngest. Gillian Tindall. LC 68-13254. 1968. Walker.

Youngest Brother: A Socialistic Romance. Ernst Wichert & Kannida, Pseud., Tr. (On cover: The library of choice fiction, no. 17). 1891. Laird & Lee.

Youngest Disciple. Edward John Thompson. LC 38-17823. 1938. E. P. Dutton & Co., Inc.

Youngest Mistress. Karl Rockwood. pap. 1.95 o.p. (ISBN 0-87056-208-8, 6208). Brandon.

Youngest One. Katharine Haviland Taylor. LC 28-16854. 1928. Doubleday, Doran & Company, Inc.

Youngest Profession. Lillian Day. LC 40-30755. 1940. Doubleday, Doran & Co., Inc.

Youngest Soldier of the Grand Armee. Fortune Du Boisgobey. LC 6-34408. (On cover: Idylwild series, v. 1, no. 27). Morrill, Higgins & Co.

Youngest Venus: Or, The Love Story of a Plain Girl. Berta Ruck. LC 28-21888. 1928. Dodd, Mead and Company.

Youngest World: A Novel of the Frontier. Robert Dunn. LC 14-5197. 1914. 1.40. Dodd, Mead and Company.

Young'un. Herbert Best. LC 44-9470. 1944. The Macmillan Company.

Your Body & How It Works. J. D. Ratcliff. 1975. 8.95 o.p. (ISBN 0-440-09896-3). Delacorte.

Your Casket Awaits, Madame. Miriam Lynch. LC 57-9799. 1957. Arcadia House.

Your Cheatin' Heart. Elizabeth Gilchrist. LC 78-23349. 9.95 (ISBN 0-02-543230-3). Macmillan.

Your Child and Mine. Anne Warner French. LC 9-25821. 1909. 1.50. Little, Brown, and Company.

Your Cuckoo Sings by Kind. Valentine Dobree. LC 27-19131. 1927. A. A. Knopf.

Your Daughter and Mine: A Novel of Sorority Life. John Monte Le Noir & Furlong, Jeannette Marie. LC 47-1796. 1946. The William-Frederick Press.

Your Daughter Iris: A Novel. 1st Ed. Jerome Wiedman. LC 55-6484. 1955. Doubleday.

Your Daughter Will Die. James P Cody. (D.C. man). 1975. (pbk.) 0.95 (ISBN 0-425-02820-8). Berkley Pub. Co.

Your Day in the Barrel. Alan Furst. LC 76-4941. 1976. 7.95 (ISBN 0-689-10727-7). Atheneum.

Your Eastern Star. Daniel Logan. (Illus.). 256p. 1973. pap. 1.50 o.p. (532-15103-150). Manor Bks.

Your Exciting Middle Years. John C. Cooper & Rachel C. Wahlberg. LC 76-2858. 1976. pap. 3.95 o.p. (ISBN 0-87680-857-7, 98075). Word Bks.

Your Eyelids Are Growing Heavy. Barbara Paul. LC 80-2462. 1981. 9.95 (ISBN 0-385-17466-7). Published for the Crime Club by Doubleday.

Your Family Is Good for You. Harvey White. 1980. pap. 2.50 (ISBN 0-425-04634-6). Berkley Pub.

Your Father. James L. Weil. 1973. pap. 8.00 (Pub. by Elizabeth Pr). SBD.

Your Friendly Neighborhood Death Pedlar. Jimmy Sangster. 256p. 1972. 5.95 o.p. (ISBN 0-396-06508-2). Dodd.

Your Friendly Neighbourhood Death Pedlar. Jimmy Sangster. LC 77-184188. 1972. 5.95 (ISBN 0-396-06508-2). Dodd, Mead.

Your Golden Jugular. Will Squerent. LC 79-85125. (Cock Robin mystery). 1969. Macmillan.

Your Husband or Mine. Kitty Parsons. (Illus.). 1970. 4.00 (ISBN 0-8233-0158-3). Golden Quill.

Your Life Lies Before You. Harry Hansen. LC 35-223946. Harcourt, Brace and Company.

Your Little Brother James. Caroline H Pemberton. LC 7-36384. 1896. G. W. Jacobs & Co.

Your Loving Mother. Monte Sohn. LC 43-17978. 1943. Dodd, Mead & Company.

Your Money and Your Wife. Ritchie Perry. LC 75-46635. 1976. 6.95 (ISBN 0-395-24346-7). Houghton Mifflin.

Your Money or Your Life: A Story. Edith Carpenter. LC 6-24229. 1896. C. Scribner's Sons.

Your Own Beloved Sons. Thomas Anderson. LC 56-5218. 1956. Random House.

Your Personal Mark Twain. Mark Twain. Ed. by Phoebe Standart. (Orig.). 1970. pap. 1.25 o.p. (ISBN 0-7178-0223-X, N*W-S6). Intl Pub Co.

Your Place or Mine?". Julia Beard. 1974. (pbk.) 1.25. Warner Paperback Library.

Your Pre-Teens Can Be Fun. Jane W. Pugel. (Uplook Ser.). 30p. 1972. pap. 0.75 (ISBN 0-8163-0084-4, 24515-9). Pacific Pr Pub Assn.

Your President Sends You Greetings...". Mary Lou Tritch. LC 73-90101. 1975. 6.95 (ISBN 0-8059-1961-9). Dorrance.

Your Secret Is in a Well. Elaine Turner. 1978. pap. 1.50 (ISBN 0-532-15300-6). Woodhill.

Your Sins and Mine. Taylor Caldwell. LC 59-5483. 1959. Caxton Printers.

Your Sparkle Cavalcade of Death. Robert Shiarella. LC 73-5233. 1974. 7.95 (ISBN 0-670-79588-7). Viking Press.

Your Stewardess. William Arthur Neubauer. LC 45-548477. 1945. Gramercy Publishing Company.

Your Ticket Is No Longer Valid. Romain Gary, pseud. LC 76-16695. 1977. 8.95 (ISBN 0-8076-0838-6). G. Braziller.

Your Uncle Lew, a Natural-Born American: A Novel. Charles Reginald Sherlock. LC 1-31373. Frederick A. Stokes Company.

Your Ups & Downs. Philip B. Knoche. (Uplook Ser.). 32p. 1970. pap. 0.75 (ISBN 0-8163-0085-2, 24535-7). Pacific Pr Pub Assn.

Your Voice Makes My Knees Tickle. Todd Richards. LC 76-186723. 64p. 1972. pap. 2.25 o.p. Valley Sun.

Your Young Life. Marjory Hall, pseud. LC 49-10142. 1949. Houghton Mifflin Co.

You're a Gent, Andy Capp. Smythe. (Andy Capp Ser.). 1978. pap. 1.25 (ISBN 0-449-13964-6, GM). Fawcett.

You're a Hard Man, Jamie Coxman. Kym Allyson, pseud. (Orig.). 1969. pap. 1.75 o.p. (3064). Brandon.

You're a Long Time Dead. Richard Clapperton. LC 68-24318. (Red mask mystery). 1968. Putnam.

You're Best Alone. Norah Robinson Lofts. 160p. 1982. pap. 1.95 (ISBN 0-449-24559-4, Crest). Fawcett.

You're Hired: You're Dead. Kirby Carr. LC 75-21347. 192p. (Orig.). 1975. pap. 1.25 (ISBN 0-89041-034-8, 3034). Major Bks.

You're in the Racket, Too. James Curtis. LC 38-5756. 1938. A. A. Knopf.

You're Lonely When You're Dead: By James Hadley Chase. Rene Raymond. LC 50-12089. 1950. Duell, Sloan and Pearce.

You're Marrying Me. Vivien Grey. LC 52-11391. 1952. Arcadia House.

You're Never Too Old to Die. Arthur D Goldstein. LC 74-9093. 1974. 5.95 (ISBN 0-394-49431-8). Random House.

You're Next on the List: A Satire on Modern Bureaucracy. David Oakes Woodbury. LC 68-5154. 1968. Western Islands.

You're Not Alone: A Doctor's Diary: a Novel. Harry Summerfield Hoff. LC 76-373943. 1976. 3.95 (ISBN 0-333-19655-4). Macmillan.

You're Only Young Once. Margaret Widdemer. LC 18-176103. 1918. H. Holt and Company.

You're the One. Adelaide Humphries. LC 42-203301. 1942. Arcadia House, Inc.

You're Welcome to Ulster. Menna Gallie. LC 71-144191. 1971. 6.95. Harper & Row.

You're Well Out of a Hospital. Rose Franken. LC 66-117336. 2.95. Doubleday.

You're Wrong, Delaney: By Bant Singer Pseud. Charles Shaw. LC 53-5275. 1953. Crown Publishers.

You're Young but Once. Louise Marks Clancy. LC 26-12247. L.C. Page & Company.

Your're a Long Time Dead see No News on Monday.

Yours. Jonathan Street. LC 70-101713. 1970. Doubleday.

Yours, and Mine; Novella and Stories. Judith Rascoe. LC 72-12595. 1973. 6.95 (ISBN 0-316-75634-2). Little, Brown.

Yours Ever. Maysie Greig. LC 48-786119. 1948. Random House.

Yours for Four Years. Paul Hutchens. LC 55-15733. 1954. Van Kampen Press.

Yours for the Asking. Jane Ludlow Drake Abbott. LC 43-1295. 1943. J. B. Lippincott Company.

Yours to Command. Peggy Gaddis, pseud. LC 41-154411. 1941. Arcadia House, Inc.

Yours Truly. Anne Brooks. LC 44-993. 1943. Gramercy Publishing Co.

Yours with Love. Mary Burchell. (Harlequin Romances Ser.). 192p. (Orig.). 1981. pap. 1.25 (ISBN 0-373-02379-0, Pub. by Harlequin). PB.

Yours, with Love. Jean Carew. LC 47-19191. 1947. Arcadia House.

Yourself and the Neighbours. Seumas MacManus. LC 14-16475. The Devin-Adai Company.

Youry Olesha: The Complete Short Stories and the Three Fat Men. Iurii Olesha. Tr. by Aimee Fisher from Rus. 1979. 17.50 (ISBN 0-88233-213-9); pap. 7.00 (ISBN 0-88233-214-7). Ardis Pubs.

Youth. Joseph Conrad. Bd. with Nigger of the Narcissus. 1982. pap. 10.00x (ISBN 0-330-24818-9, Pub. by Pan Bks). State Mutual Bk.

Youth. Marion Hill et al. (Stories from Mc Clure's). (Half-title: Stories from McClure's). 1901. McClure, Phillips & Co.

Youth & Maturity: Twenty Short Stories. James Coulos. 1970. pap. text ed. 8.95x (ISBN 0-02-325260-X, 32526). Macmillan.

Youth and Maturity: 20 Short Stories. Ed. by James S. Coulos. LC 79-92081. 1969. Macmillan.

Youth and the Bright Medusa. Willa Sibert Cather. LC 75-11560. 1975. 2.95 (ISBN 0-394-71684-1). Vintage Books.

Youth and the Bright Medusa. Willa Sibert Cather. LC 23-1653. 1923. A. A. Knopf.

Youth and the Bright Medusa. Willa Sibert Cather. LC 34-38278. 1928. A. A. Knopf.

Youth and The End of the Tether. Joseph Conrad. LC 76-374062. (Penguin modern classics). 1975. 1.95 (ISBN 0-14-004055-2). Penguin.

Youth, and Two Other Stories. Joseph Conrad. LC 16-6826. 1915. Doubleday, Page & Company.

Youth, and Two Other Stories. Joseph Conrad. LC 22-10650. 1920. Doubleday, Page & Company.

Youth, and Two Other Stories. Joseph Conrad. LC 25-21592. 1925. Doubleday, Page & Company.

Youth, and Two Other Stories. Joseph Conrad. LC 3-5183. 1903. McClure, Phillips & Co.

Youth, and Two Other Stories: By Joseph Conrad... Joseph Conrad. LC 17-314268. 1916. Doubleday, Page & Company.

Youth Can't Be Served. Norah Hoult. LC 34-215115. 1934. Harper & Brothers.

Youth Challenges. Clarence Budington Kelland. LC 20-18251. Harper & Brothers.

Youth Cries Out. Bernice Claire Spidelsky. LC 32-8424. W. Godwin, Inc.

Youth Dares All, Anonymous. David Liebovitz. LC 30-21950. 1930. The Macaulay Company.

Youth Demands. Sally Chayes. LC 34-35891. The Halsey Company.

Youth Goes Forth: Unpublished Chapters from an Old-Time Chronicle. Parker Hord. LC 28-244797. Fleming H. Revell Company.

Youth Goes Seeking. Oscar Graeve. LC 19-14353. 1919. 1.60. Dodd, Mead and Company.

Youth, "Heart of Darkness", & "the End of the Tether". Joseph Conrad. 1978. 9.95x (ISBN 0-460-00694-0, Evman); pap. 2.50x (ISBN 0-460-01694-6, Evman). Biblio Dist.

Youth, Heart of Darkness, Typhoon, The Secret Sharer. with Reader's Guide. Joseph Conrad. (AMSCO Literature Program). (gr. 9-12). 1974. pap. text ed. 5.92 (ISBN 0-87720-819-0); tchr's ed. 3.75 (ISBN 0-87720-919-7). AMSCO Sch.

Youth Hostel Murders: By Glyn Carr Pseud. 1st Ed. Showell Styles. LC 53-6088. (Guilt edge mystery). 1953. Dutton.

Youth in Asia: A Novel. 1st Ed. Richard D Ressler. LC 56-7470. Exposition Press.

Youth in Harley. Gordon Hall Gerould. LC 20-142941. 1920. C. Scribner's Sons.

Youth in Hell. Albert Bein. LC 30-14088. J. Cape & H. Smith.

Youth in Love. Walter Marquiss. LC 34-393624. The Macaulay Company.

Youth in Trust. Frederick Stallknecht Wight. LC 37-29163. Farrar & Rinehart, Inc.

Youth Is the Time. Robert Gessner. LC 45-3920. 1945. C. Scribner's Sons.

Youth Must Laugh. Inez Haynes Irwin. LC 32-225399. The Bobbs-Merrill Company.

Youth North. Olof Alfred Hallstrom. LC 36-18876. 1936. The Caxton Printers, Ltd.

Youth of Color, a Novel. Thomason, Caroline Wasson. LC 51-11872. 1951. Exposition Press.

Youth of Jefferson: Or, A Chronicle of College Scrapes at Williamsburg, in Virginia, A. D. 1761... John Esten Cooke. 1854. Redfield.

Youth of Parnassus, and Other Stories. Logan Pearsall Smith. LC 7-3053. 1895. Macmillan and Co.

Youth of the Great Elector. Klara Muller Mundt. Tr. by Smith, Mary Stuart (Harrison) LC 16-1233. (historical romances of Louisa Muhlbach pseud.). D. Appleton and Company.

Youth of the Great Elector: An Historical Romance. Klara Muller Mundt. Tr. by Smith, Mary Stuart (Harrison) LC 7-31821. 1896. D. Appleton and Company.

Youth Plupy: Or, The Lad with a Downy Chin. Henry Augustus Shute. LC 17-23759. 1917. Houghton Mifflin Company.

Youth Rides Out. Beatrice Kean Stapleton Seymour. LC 29-23770. 1929. A. A. Knopf.

Youth Rides West: A Story of the Seventies. William Henry Irwin. LC 25-4856. 1925. A. A. Knopf.

Youth Triumphant. George Fort Gibbs. LC 21-16797. 1921. D. Appleton and Company.

Youth Will Be Served. Dolf Wyllarde. LC 13-21254. 1913. John Lane Company.

Youth Wins. Muriel Hine Coxon. LC 24-23487. 1924. 2.00. Dodd, Mead and Company.

Youth Without Glory: A Novel. Betsey Riddle Hutton Zum Stolzenberg. LC 33-15224. 1938. E. P. Doran & Co., Inc.

Youthful Writings: Cahiers Two. Albert Camus. Tr. by Ellen Kennedy from Fr. 1976. 10.95 (ISBN 0-394-49535-7). Knopf.

Youth's a Stuff Will Not Endure: A Novel. Paul Grabill. LC 78-52915. 1.75 (ISBN 0-380-01938-8). Avon Books.

Youth's Encounter. Compton Mackenzie. LC 13-21705. 1913. D. Appleton and Company.

Youth's Magic Horn: Seven Stories. Jon Wahl. LC 77-29127. 1978. 6.95 o.p. (ISBN 0-525-66582-X). Elsevier-Nelson.

Youth's Way. Cale Young Rice. LC 23-694423. 1923. The Century Co.

Youth's Worship. Hervey White. The Maverick Press.

You've Got It Coming. Rene Raymond. 1973. (pbk) 0.75 (ISBN 0-671-75739-3). Pocket Books.

You've Got to Ride the Subway! Madge Reinhardt. LC 76-4760. 8.95 (ISBN 0-917162-01-3) (ISBN 0-917162-02-1). Back Row Press.

You've Met Mrs. Parrish? Marie Blizard. LC 42-23948. 1942. Arcadia House, Inc.

Yozonde of the Wilderness. Harry Irving Greene. LC 10-20901. 1910. D. Fitzgerald, Inc.

Ypiranga: A Love Tale of the Brazils. Charles Frederick Markell. LC 7-24692. 1897. Printed by J. Murphy & Co.

Ysabel Kid. John Thomas Edson. (Berkley book). 1978. 1.50 (ISBN 0-425-03846-7). Berkley Pub. Corp.

YSSN: Four Words-Four Lives. James Serino. LC 75-43422. 1976. 1.98 (ISBN 0-89144-015-1). Crescent Publications.

Yu-Chi Stone. Edmund Snell. LC 26-647523. The Macaulay Company.

Yu'an 'Hee See Laughs. Arthur Sarsfield Ward. LC 32-10113. 1932. Pub. for the Crime Club, Inc., by Doubleday, Doran & Company, Inc.

Yucay: A Romance of Early Peru. Dorothea Knox Martin. LC 41-3908. Suttonhouse.

Yucay: A Romance of Early Peru. Dorothea Knox Martin. LC 43-7364. Institute Press.

Yucca City Outlaw. William L Hopson. LC 49-489270. 1949. Phoenix Press.

Yudel: A Novel. Rachael Levin Geilich. LC 54-8893. Dorrance.

Yugoslav Short Stories. Tr. by Svetozar Koljevic. (World's Classics Ser: No. 608). 4.50 o.p. (ISBN 0-19-250608-0). Oxford U Pr.

Yugoslav Short Stories: Selected, Translated and with Introduction by Svetozar Koljevic. Ed. by Svetozar Koljevic. LC 66-70847. (World's Classics, 608: B66-7591). 1966. Oxford U.P.

Yukiko. Donald W. Heiney. LC 77-22457. 1977. 8.95. Farrar Straus Giroux.

Yukiko. Donald W Heiney. 1979. 2.25. Avon.

Yuklko. Macdonald Harris. 1977. 8.95 o.p. FS&G.

Yukon Breed. Lee D. Willoughby. (Making of America Ser.: No. 33). (Orig.). 1983. pap. 3.25 (ISBN 0-440-09899-8, Bryans). Dell.

Yukon Drive. Robert Ormond Case. LC 30-6548. 1930. Doubleday, Doran & Company Co., ! Inc.

Yukon Gold. William D Blankenship. LC 76-55733. 9.95. Dutton.

Yukon Kid. James Beardsley Hendryx. LC 76-28247. 1976. 6.95 (ISBN 0-88411-838-X). Aeonian Press.

Yukon Kid. James Beardsley Hendryx. LC 34-8141. 1934. Doubleday, Doran and Company, Inc.

Yukon Kid. James Beardsley Hendryx. LC 43-18197. 1943. Triangle Books.

Yukon Ride. Gene Curry. (Saddler Ser.: No. 7). 192p. (Orig.). 1981. pap. 2.25 (ISBN 0-505-51734-5). Tower Bks.

Yukon Trail. William MacLeod Raine. 1973. (pbk.) 0.75. Popular Library.

Yukon Trail: A Tale of the North. William MacLeod Raine. LC 17-13621. 1917. 1.35. Houghton Mifflin Company.

Yule Log. La Salle Corbell Pickett. (In de miz series, v. 2). 1900. The Neale Co.

Yule-Tide Stories. Ed. by Benjamin Thorpe. LC 68-55557. (Bohn's Antiquarian Library Ser). Repr. of 1853 ed. 24.50 (ISBN 0-404-50024-2). AMS Pr.

Yulika and Iluska. Ilse Varady. LC 49-7974. 1949. Universum Book Pub. Co.

Yuma. Russell Smith. (Leisure Book). (Illus.). 1978. (ISBN 0-8439-0603-0). Nordon Pub, Inc.

Yuma Brand. Dan Roberts. LC 67-6690. 1967. Arcadia House.

Yuma Brand. William Edward Daniel Ross. LC 67-6690. 1967. Arcadia House.

Yuma: Renegade Gold. Russell Smith. 1979. pap. 1.50 o.s.i. (ISBN 0-8439-0660-X, Leisure Bks). Nordon Pubns.

Y'understand. Montague Marsden Glass. LC 25-19525. 1925. Doubleday, Page & Company.

Yurth Burden. Andre Norton, pseud. (Science Fiction Ser.). 1978. pap. 1.75 (ISBN 0-87997-400-1, UE1400). DAW Bks.

Yushka. Aleksandr Ivanovich Kuprin. 26p. 1977. pap. 1.49 (ISBN 0-8285-1256-6, Pub. by Progress Pubs USSR). Imported Pubns.

YV 88: An Eco-Fiction of Tomorrow. Christopher Swan & Chet Roaman. LC 77-7596. 1977. 6.95 (ISBN 0-87156-195-6). Sierra Club Books.

Yvar, Prince of Rus. Richard Cloke. LC 80-80543. 6.75 (ISBN 0-917458-08-7). Cerulean Press.

Yvette--a Novelette: And Ten Other Stories. Guy De Maupassant. Tr. by Ada Cooper Galsworthy. Conrad, Joseph, 1857-1924. 1919. A. A. Knopf.

Yvette--a Novellette: And Ten Other Stories. Guy De Maupassant. Tr. by Ada Cooper Galsworthy. Conrad, Joseph, 1857-1924. LC 16-639420. 1916. A. A. Knopf.

Yvette-a Novelette and Ten Other Stories. Guy De Maupassant. LC 70-150550. (Short story index reprint series). 1971. (ISBN 0-8369-3847-X). Books for Libraries Press.

Yvette and Other Stories. Guy De Maupassant. LC 49-26246. (Avon, 198). 1949. Avon Pub. Co.

Yvonne. Mary Suckit. 1971. pap. 1.45 o.p. (V1010Q, Venus). Grove.

Yvonne of Braithwaite: A Romance of the Mississippi Delta. Marie Bankhead Owen. LC 27-9627. 1927. L. C. Page & Company.

Yvonne, the Confident. Katheryn Kimbrough, pseud. 1.75 (ISBN 0-445-04383-0). Popular Library.

Ywain: The Knight of the Lion. Chretien De Troyes. Tr. by Robert W. Ackerman & Frederick W. Locke. LC 77-10461. (Milestones of Thought Ser.). pap. 3.95 (ISBN 0-8044-6084-1). Ungar.

Z

Z. Vassilis Vassilikos. Tr. by Marilyn Calmann from Ger. LC 68-19010. 1968. 6.95 o.p. (ISBN 0-374-29632-4). FS&G.

Z Document. Nick Carter. (Killmaster spy chiller). 1975. (pbk.) 1.25. Award Books.

Z Effect. Marshall Laurens. (Pocket Book science fiction). 1974. (pbk.) 1.25. Pocket Books.

Z for Zaborra. Eva-Lis Wuorio. LC 66-102866. (Rinehart suspense novel). 1966. bds., 3.50. Holt.

Z. Marcas, Madame De La Chanterie, The Novice. Honore De Balzac. Tr. by George Burnham Ives. LC 42-28. The Neale Company.

"Z" Murders. Joseph Jefferson Farjeon. LC 32-114599. 1932. L. MacVeagh, The Dial Press, Inc.

Z-Papers. Geoffrey S. Simmons. LC 74-31429. 7.95 (ISBN 0-87795-108-X). Arbor House.

Z R. Wins. Fitzhugh Green. LC 24-16567. 1924. D. Appleton and Company.

Z Ray. Edmund Snell. LC 32-101087. 1932. J. B. Lippincott Company.

Z-Sting. Ian Wallace. 1978. 1.95 (ISBN 0-87997-408-7). DAW Books.

Zacchaeus Meets the Savior. Neal Boehlke. 1980. pap. 0.89 (ISBN 0-570-06132-6, 59-1250, Arch Bk). Concordia.

Zachariah, the Congressman: A Tale of American Society. Gilbert Ashville Pierce. LC 7-35907. (On cover: D. G. & L. series). 1880. Donnelley, Gassette & Lloyd.

Zachary. Mike Breen. 1974. (pbk.) 0.95. Popular Library.

Zachary Philps. Edwin Lassetter Bynner. 1892. Houghton, Mifflin and Company.

Zack Jones, Fisherman-Philosopher. Helen Swift. LC 44-874. 1944. A. Kroch and Son.

Zadig see Candide.

Zadig and Other Stories. Francois Marie Arouet De Voltaire. Ed. by H. T. Mason. LC 79-26405. (Clarendon French series). 1971. 0.90 (ISBN 0-19-832376-X). Oxford University Press.

Zadig: Or, The Book of Fate. Francois Marie Arouet De Voltaire. LC 74-16198. (Flowering of the Novel). (Illus.). 1974. (ISBN 0-8240-1124-4). Garland Publishing.

Zadoc Pine and Other Stories. Henry Cuyler Bunner. LC 70-94704. (Short story index reprint series). 1969. Books for Libraries Press.

Zadoc Pine: And Other Stories. Henry Cuyler Bunner. LC 4-15072. 1891. C. Scribner's Sons.

Zadok's Treasure. Margot Arnold, pseud. LC 80-80980. 192p. (Orig.). 1980. pap. 2.50 (ISBN 0-86721-228-4). Playboy Pbks.

Zady Clinton, Trouble-Shooter: A Story of the Great West. Grace C Burnard. LC 66-21149. 1966. Greenwich Book Publishers.

Zafloya; or the Moor: A Romance of the Fifteenth Century, 3 vols, Vol. 8. Charlotte Dacre. LC 73-22763. (Gothic Novels Ser.). 802p. 1974. Repr. of 1806 ed. Set. 66.00x (ISBN 0-405-06014-9). Ayer Co.

Zahara: Or, A Leap for Empire. A Novel. Mansfield Tracy Walworth. LC 12-19553. 1888. G. W. Dillingham.

Zaharan Pursuit. Adam Hamilton. (Peacemaker). (Berkley Medallion book: Vl. 1). 1974. (pbk.) 0.95 (ISBN 0-425-02586-1). Berkley Pub. Co.
Zakhar Berkut. Ivan Franko & Boresky, Theodosia, Tr. LC 44-24563. 1944. Theo. Gaus' Sons, Inc.
Zakhov Mission. Andrei Guliashki. LC 69-20102. 1969. 4.50. Published for the Crime Club by Doubleday.
Zal: An International Romance. Rupert Hughes. 1905. The Century Co.
Zalea: A Psychological Episode and Tale of Love. Rufus Cummins Garland. LC 1-29044. 1900. The Neale Company.
Zaleski's Percentage. Donald MacKenie. (Adult Ser.). 392p. 1974. Repr. lib. bdg. 9.95 o.p. (ISBN 0-8161-6211-5, Large Print Bks). G K Hall.
Zaleski's Percentage. Donald MacKenzie. LC 73-18233. (Midnight novel of suspense). 1974. 5.95 (ISBN 0-395-18465-7). Houghton Mifflin.
Zaleski's Percentage. Donald MacKenzie. LC 74-5034. 1974. (lib. bdg.) 9.95 (ISBN 0-8161-6211-5). G. K. Hall.
Zalmen or the Madness of God. Elie Wiesel. 1975. 6.95 (ISBN 0-394-49637-X). Random.
Zami: A New Spelling of My Name. Audre Lorde. LC 82-15086. 264p. (Orig.). 1982. pap. 7.95 (ISBN 0-930436-15-6). Persephone.
Zamora: Change & Continuity in a Mexican Town. Oriol Pi-Sunyer. LC 73-2369. (Case Studies in Cultural Anthropology). 1973. pap. text ed. 5.95 o.p. (ISBN 0-03-085769-4, HoltC). HR&W.
Zandra. Norma Lee Clark. 224p. (Orig.). 1980. pap. 1.75 (ISBN 0-449-50075-6, Coventry). Fawcett.
Zandra. William Rotsler. LC 77-76258. 1978. 6.95 (ISBN 0-385-13143-7). Doubleday.
Zandrie. Marian Edwards Richards. LC 9-24236. 1909. 1.50. The Century Co.
Zane Grey Omnibus. Zane Grey & Gentles, Ruth Graeme, 1896- Ed. LC 43-4314. 1943. Harper & Brothers.
Zane Grey's Arizona Ames: Gun Trouble in Tonto Basin. Romer Z. Grey. (Orig.). 1980. pap. 1.95 (ISBN 0-505-51479-6). Tower Bks.
Zane Grey's Arizona Ames: King of the Outlaw Horde. Romer Z. Grey. (Orig.). 1980. pap. 1.95 o.s.i. (ISBN 0-505-51509-1). Tower Bks.
Zane Grey's Buck Duane: King of the Range. Romer Z. Grey. (Orig.). 1980. pap. 1.95 (ISBN 0-505-51499-0). Tower Bks.
Zane Grey's Buck Duane: The Rider of Distant Trails. Romer Z. Grey. 1980. pap. 1.95 o.s.i. (ISBN 0-505-51469-9). Tower Bks.
Zane Grey's Greatest Indian Stories. Zane Grey. Ed. by Loren Grey. (O.s.i.). (Orig.). 1975. pap. 1.25 o.s.i. (BT50819). Belmont-Tower.
Zane Grey's Greatest Indian Stories. Zane Grey. Ed. by Loren Grey. 1975. (pbk.) 1.25. Belmont Tower Books.
Zane Grey's Greatest Western Stories. Zane Grey. Ed. by Loren Grey. 1975. (pbk.) 1.25. Belmont Tower Books.
Zane Grey's Laramie Nelson: The Other Side of the Canyon. Romer Z. Grey. 1980. pap. 1.95 (ISBN 0-505-51489-3). Tower Bks.
Zane Grey's Nevada Jim Lacy: Beyond the Mogollon Rim. Romer Z. Grey. (Orig.). 1980. pap. 1.95 o.s.i. (ISBN 0-505-51529-6). Tower Bks.
Zane Grey's: The Big Land. Zane Grey. Ed. by Loren Grey. (O.s.i.). 1976. pap. 1.25 o.s.i. (BT50959). Belmont-Tower.
Zane Grey's Yaqui: Siege at Forlorn River. Romer Z. Grey. (Orig.). 1980. pap. 1.95 o.s.i. (ISBN 0-505-51519-9). Tower Bks.
Zanita: A Tale of the Yo-Semite. Maria Theresa Longworth. 1872. Hurd and Houghton.
Zanoni. Edward George Earle Lytton Bulwer-Lytton Lytton. LC 9-817. G. Routledge and Sons.
Zanoni. Edward George Earle Lytton Bulwer-Lytton Lytton. LC 4-15324. (Half-title: Novels of Sir Edward Bulwer Lytton. Library ed. Romances, vol. III). 1893. Little, Brown, and Company.
Zanoni: A Rosicrucian Tale. Edward George Earle Lytton Bulwer-Lytton Lytton. LC 78-157505. (Steinerbooks, 1723). (Illus.). 1971. 2.45. Rudolph Steiner.
Zanoni, Zicci. Edward George Earle Lytton Bulwer-Lytton Lytton. LC 26-23554. (Half-title: Novels and romances of Edward Bulwer Lytton (Lord Lytton) Handy library edition). 1912. Little, Brown and Co.
Zanoza: A Borzoi Story. Ralph G Kirk. LC 18-18742. 1918. A. A. Knopf.
Zanthar at Moon's Madness. Robert M. Williams. (Orig.). 1968. pap. 0.60 o.p. (73-805). Lancer.
Zanthar at the Edge of Never. easy eye ed. Robert M. Williams. (Orig.). 1968. pap. 0.75 o.p. (74-941). Lancer.
Zanthar at Trip's End. Robert M. Williams. (Orig.). 1969. pap. 0.60 o.p. (73-836). Lancer.
Zanthar of the Many Worlds. Robert M. Williams. (Orig.). 1968. pap. 0.60 o.p. (73-694). Lancer.
Zanthodon. Lin Carter. (Science Fiction Ser.). 1980. pap. 1.75 (ISBN 0-87997-543-1, UE1543). DAW Bks.
Zanthon: A Novel. James Of San Francisco Doran. LC 6-33723. 1891. The Bancroft Company.
Zaos: A Novel. Roe Raymond Hobbs. LC 6-25696. 1906. The Neale Publishing Company.
Zap Gun. Philip K Dick. LC 79-538. (Gregg Press science fiction series). (Illus.). 1979. 12.95 (ISBN 0-8398-2494-7). Gregg Press.
Zaphra: A Story of to-Day. John P Stockton. LC 8-15534. 1894. Arena Publishing Company.
Zapiski Dissidenta. Andrei Amal'ryk. 368p. (Rus.). 1982. 24.50 (ISBN 0-88233-750-5); pap. 14.00. Ardis Pubs.
Zara. Meredith Steinbach. LC 81-9898. 1982. 10.95 (ISBN 0-88001-000-2). Ecco Press.
Zara. Joyce Stranger, pseud. LC 70-104131. 1970. 5.75. Viking Press.
Zarah, the Cruel. Joan Conquest. LC 23-764692. 1823. Cassell and Company, Ltd.
Zarah the Cruel. Joan Conquest. LC 23-118258. The Macaulay Company.
Zarailla: A Novel. Fanny D Bates. 1889. G. W. Dillingham, Successor to G. W. Carleton & Co.
Zarco. Ignacio Manuel Altamirano. Ed. by Raymond L. Grismer & Miguel Ruelas. 1933. 3.95x o.p. (ISBN 0-393-09442-1, NortonC). Norton.
Zardec. Florence Lucinda Carpenter Dieudonne. LC 42-268008. 1885. The Author.
Zarkon, Lord of the Unknown, and His Omega Crew. Lin Carter. 1978. Popular Library.
Zarkon, Lord of the Unknown in Invisible Death: A Case from the Files of Omega. Lin Carter. LC 75-9219. 1975. 5.95 (ISBN 0-385-08768-3). Doubleday.
Zarkon, Lord of the Unknown, in The Earth-Shaker: A Case from the Files of Omega. Lin Carter. LC 76-42320. 1982. 10.95 (ISBN 0-385-12477-5). Doubleday.
Zarkon, Lord of the Unknown in The Nemesis of Evil: A Case from the Files of Omega. Lin Carter. LC 74-25097. 1975. (ISBN 0-385-00583-0). Doubleday.
Zarkon, Lord of the Unknown in the Volcano Ogre: A Case from the Files of Omega. Lin Carter. LC 75-21217. 1976. 5.95 (ISBN 0-385-08807-8). Doubleday.
Zarlah, the Martian. Robert Norman Grisewood. LC 9-22948. 1909. R. F. Fenno & Company.
Zarsthor's Bane. Andre Norton, pseud. (Illus.). 1978. 1.95 (ISBN 0-441-95490-1). Ace Books.
Zashchita Luzhina. Vladimir Vladimirovich Nabokov. (Rus.). 1979. 15.00 (ISBN 0-88233-427-1); pap. 7.00 (ISBN 0-88233-428-X). Ardis Pubs.
Zastrozzi: A Romance. Percy Bysshe Shelley. (Illus.). standard bdg. 20.00 o.p. (ISBN 0-498-08561-9); deluxe ed. 45.00 special bdg. o.p. (ISBN 0-498-07321-1). Golden Cockerel.
Zastrozzi: A Romance and St. Irvyne: or, The Rosicrucian: a Romance. Percy Bysshe Shelley. LC 77-2046. (Gothic Novels III). 1977. 25.00 (ISBN 0-405-10144-9). Arno Press.
Zatthu: A Tale of Ancient Galilee. Edmund Hamilton Sears. LC 25-11004. The Cornhill Publishing Company.
Zavist. IUrii Olesha. (Illus., Rus.). 1977. 15.00 o.p. (ISBN 0-88233-126-4); pap. 4.00 o.p. (ISBN 0-88233-127-2). Ardis Pubs.
Zawis and Kunigunde: A Bohemian Tale. Robert H Vickers. LC 8-32802. 1895. C. H. Keer & Company.
Zazie in the Metro. Raymond Queneau. Tr. by Barbara Wright from Fr. (Riverrun Writers Ser.). 1982. 13.95 (ISBN 0-7145-3872-8); pap. 7.95 (ISBN 0-7145-3923-6). Riverrun NY.
Zazie. Translated by Barbara Wright. 1st Ed. Raymond Queneau. LC 60-10447. 1960. Harper.
Zealot in Tulle: A Novel. Marion White Wildrick. LC 8-37023. 1887. D. Appleton and Company.
Zeb: A Celebrated Schooner Life. new ed. Polly Burroughs. LC 72-80278. (O.s.i). 1972. 14.95 (ISBN 0-85699-050-7). Chatham Pr.
Zeb Harkins. Lillian Opal Hamilton. LC 52-968682. Vantage Press.
Zebadiah Sartwell: The Miller of Whallonsburgh. Samuel Paige Johnson. LC 3-24225. 1903. Broadway Publishing Company.
Zebedee V. By Edith Barnard Delano... Edith Barnard Delano. LC 12-25073. 1.20. Small, Maynard and Company.
Zebina's Mountain. Blair Fuller. LC 74-15872. 1975. 6.95 (ISBN 0-06-011387-1). Harper & Row.
Zebra Derby. Max Shulman. LC 46-607. 1946. Doubleday & Company, Inc.
Zebra-Striped Hearse. Ross Macdonald. LC 79-25722. 1981. 11.50 (ISBN 0-89340-249-4). J. Curley & Associates.
Zebra-Striped Hearse: By Ross Macdonald Pseud. 1st Ed. Kenneth Millar. LC 62-18122. 1962. Knopf.
Zeinab, the Panjabi. A Story Founded on Facts. Elwood Morris Wherry. LC 8-36043. American Tract Society.
Zeit-Geist: A Novel. Lily Dougall. LC 6-33691. 1895. D. Appleton and Company.
Zeit Zu Leben Und Zeit Zu Sterben. Erich Maria Remarque. Ed. by F. G. Goldbert. 1961. pap. text ed. 2.75 o.p. (ISBN 0-442-22071-5). Van Nos Reinhold.
Zelauto: The Fountaine of Fame, 1580. Anthony Munday & Stillinger, Jack, Ed. LC 62-15003. 1963. Southern Illinois University Press.
Zelda. William F McMillan. LC 7-20303. 1895. McMillan Publishing Co.
Zelda Dameron. Meredith Nicholson. LC 4-28205. 1904. The Bobbs-Merrill Company.
Zelda Marsh. Charles Gilman Norris. LC 27-18473. E. P. Dutton & Company.
Zell: A Novel. Harold Hunter Armstrong. LC 21-3814. 1921. A. A. Knopf.
Zelma, the Mystic: Or, White Magic, Versus Black. Alwyn M Thurber. LC 8-19942. 1897. Authors Publishing Co.
Zemindar. Valerie Fitzgerald. LC 81-66606. (Illus.). 1982. 19.95 (ISBN 0-553-05006-0) (ISBN 0-553-01360-2). Bantam Books.
Zen There Was Murder. Henry R. Keating. 1963. pap. 0.85 o.p. (ISBN 0-14-001965-0). Penguin.
Zenaida. Florence Anderson. LC 6-24521. 1858. J. B. Lippincott & Co.
Zenia, the Vestal: Or, The Problem of Vibrations. 2d ed. Margaret Bloodgood Peeke. LC 7-36467. 1893. Arena Publishing Company.
Zenobia: Or, The Fall of Palmyra. In Letters of L. Manlius Piso Pseud. from Palmyra, to His Friend Marcus Curtius at Rome. 9th ed.... ed. William Ware. LC 8-37765. 1854. C. S. Francis and Company.
Zenobia: Or, The Fall of Palmyra. In Letters of L. Manlius Piso Pseud. from Palmyra, to His Friend Marcus Curtius at Rome. 9th ed.... ed. William Ware. LC 8-37764. 1869. J. Miller.
Zenobia: Or, The Fall of Palmyra, in Letters of L. Manlius Piso Pseud. from Palmyra, to His Friend Marcus Curtius at Rome. a new ed.... ed. William Ware. LC 41-33253. T. R. Knox & Co.
Zenobia: Or, The Fall of Palmyra. In Letters of L. Manlius Piso Pseud. from Palmyra, to His Friend Marcus Curtius at Rome. William Ware. (On cover: Seaside library. Pocket ed. no. 709). 1886. G. Munro.
Zenya. E. C. Tubb. (Science Fiction Ser.). 1974. pap. 0.95 o.p. (UQ1126). DAW Bks.
Zenya. E. C Tubb. 1974. (pbk.) 0.95. DAW Books.
Zeph." A Novel. Sallie Branch Miller. LC 7-25966. (On cover: Dixie library, no. 1). 1889. J. P. Bell Company.
Zeph: a Posthumous Story. Helen Maria Fiske Hunt Jackson. LC 75-164569. (American fiction reprint series). 1971. (ISBN 0-8369-7046-2). Books for Libraries Press.
Zeph. A Posthumous Story. Helen Maria Fiske Hunt Jackson. LC 7-9470. 1885. Roberts Brothers.
Zepheria. Ed. by Thomas Corser. LC 72-185712. (Spenser Society Publications Ser: No. 5). 44p. Repr. of 1594 ed. 24.50 (ISBN 0-8337-3920-4). B Franklin.
Zephyr Wile. Mary Louise Rodgers. LC 30-169752. The Christopher Publishing House.
Zeppelin. Lucien Agniel et al. (Orig.). 1971. pap. 0.75 o.p. (ISBN 0-446-64662-8, 64-662). Paperback Lib.
Zeppelin, a Novel. Ronald Florence. LC 81-66959. 14.95 (ISBN 0-87795-327-9). Arbor House.
Zeppelin Coming Down. William Lawson. LC 76-9412. 1976. 5.50. Yardbird Wing Editions.
Zeppelin Nights: A London Entertainment. Violet Hunt & Hueffer, Ford Madox, 1873- Joint Author. LC 16-2220. 1916. 1.25. John Lane.
Zeppelin's Passenger. Edward Phillips Oppenheim. LC 18-18186. 1918. Little, Brown and Company.
Zerah: A Tale of Old Bethlehem. Montanye Perry. LC 15-186966. 0.50. The Abingdon Press.
Zero. H Collinson Owen. LC 27-43190. 1927. Dodd-Mead & Company.
Zero: A Story of Monte Carlo. Rosa Caroline Murray-Prior Praed. (On cover: Seaside library. Pocket ed. no. 428). 1885. G. Munro.
Zero at the Bone. Morna Doris MacTaggart Brown. 1973. (pbk.) 0.75. Dell.
Zero at the Bone. Morna Doris MacTaggart Brown. LC 68-25329. 1968. 3.95. Walker.
Zero Factor. William Oscar Johnson. 2.75 (ISBN 0-671-83261-1). Pocket Books.
Zero Hour. Georg Grabenhorst. LC 29-20791. 1929. Little, Brown, and Company.
Zero Minus X. Karl Zeigfreid, pseud. LC 65-7991. 1965. Arcadia House.
Zero Stone. Andre Norton, pseud. 224p. 1981. pap. 2.25 (ISBN 0-441-95964-4). Ace Bks.
Zero-Sum Society. Lester C. Thurow. 230p. 1981. pap. 4.95 (ISBN 0-14-005807-9). Penguin.
Zero Trap. Paula Gosling. LC 79-25758. 1980. 9.95 (ISBN 0-698-11020-X). Coward, McCann & Geoghegan.
Zero Weather. Ramon S. Morningstar. Ed. by Una King & Delia Moon. LC 80-20072. 367p. (Orig.). 1980. pap. 3.95 (ISBN 0-937770-00-0). Family Pub CA.
Zero Weather: A Future Fantasy. Ramon Sender Morningstar. LC 80-20072. 6.95 (ISBN 0-937770-00-0). Family Pub. Co.
Zerub Throop's Experiment. Adeline Dutton Train Whitney. LC 12-19558. Loring.
Zest. Charles Gilman Norris. LC 33-126497. 1933. Doubleday; Doran & Company, Inc.
Zest for Life. Emile Zola. LC 56-12002. 1956. Indiana University Press.
Zest for Life. Tr. from French by Jean Stewart. Pref. by Angus Wilson. Emile Zola. 1965. bds., 3.95. Elek Bks.
Zeta Conspiracy. Terence L. Moore. 1981. 6.95 (ISBN 0-8062-1844-4). Carlton.
Zeus Bentley: Or, A Love That Conquered Death. Joseph D Parker. LC 34-34579. 1934. Meador Publishing Company.
Zeus Has Two Urns. Charles E Jarvis. LC 76-377748. (Illus.). 4.95 (ISBN 0-915940-01-9) (ISBN 0-915940-01-9). Ithaca Press.
Zeyna el Zegal: The Phantom Lady of the Villa Montinni; the Romance of a Haunted House. Homer P Branch. LC 6-17937. 1890. Pub. by the Author.
Zhenia's Childhood. Boris Leonidovich Pasternak. 128p. 1982. 13.95 (ISBN 0-8052-8128-2, Pub. by Allison & Busby England); pap. 5.95 (ISBN 0-8052-8129-0, Pub. by Allison & Busby England). Schocken.
Zhenskie Rasskazy: Women's Stories. Ruth Zernova. 160p. (Rus.). 1981. pap. 7.50 (ISBN 0-938920-04-9). Hermitage MI.
Zhukov Briefing. Antony Trew. LC 74-83584. 7.95. St. Martin's Press.
Zia. Scott O'Dell. 1978. pap. 1.95 (ISBN 0-440-99904-9, LFL). Dell.
Zibeline. Philippe Massa. Tr. by Dora Knowlton Thompson Ranous. LC 42-1110. 1910. Current Literature Publishing Company.
Zig-Zag Paths of Life: A Novel. Matilda Vance Cooke. 1895. C. H. Kerr and Company.
Zig-Zag, the Clown: Or, The Steel Gauntlets. Fortune Du Boisgobey. LC 6-34407. (On cover: Seaside library. Pocket ed. no. 522). G. Munro.
Zig Zag to Armageddon. Tony Foster. LC 78-110351. (Illus.). 10.95 (ISBN 0-89343-051-X). Ermine Publishers.
Ziggurat. Robert Katz. LC 77-23200. 1977. 7.95 (ISBN 0-395-25352-7). Houghton Mifflin.
Ziggy Faces Life. Tom Wilson. 1982. pap. 1.75 (ISBN 0-451-11428-0, AE1428, Sig). NAL.
Zillah, the Child Medium: A Tale of Spiritualism. LC 8-37863. 1857. Dix, Edwards & Co.
Zilov Bombs. Donald Gabriel Barron. 1977. 6.00 o.p. (ISBN 0-86025-055-5). State Mutual Bk.
Zina's Awaking: A Novel. Lilian Headland Spender. LC 8-14069. (Ledger library. no. 63). 1892. R. Bonner's Sons.
Zinsser Implant: A Novel. Lawrence Kamarck. LC 78-21531. 7.95. Dial Press.
Zinzin Road. Fletcher Knebel. (N3577). 1967. Bantam.
Zinzin Road. Fletcher Knebel. LC 66-20977. 1966. Doubleday.
Zion Road. Henry Gibbs. LC 68-16680. 1968. 3.95. Walker.
Zion Road. Simon Harvester. 1981. 18.95x (Pub. by Remploy England). State Mutual Bk.
Zion Road. Simon Harvester. 208p. 1983. pap. 2.95 (ISBN 0-8027-3013-2). Walker & Co.
Zion Road. Simon Harvester. (Road Ser). 1970. pap. 0.60 o.p. (60-440). Manor Bks.
Zion Road. Simon Harvester. 1968. 3.95 o.p. Walker & Co.
Zip: A Novel of the Left and the Right. Max Apple. LC 77-28363. 1978. 8.95 (ISBN 0-670-79692-1). Viking.
Zipline, River Park. Donald Lloyd Moore. LC 75-22871. 4.95 (ISBN 0-8283-1648-1). Branden Press.
Zippers. James Harvey. 1979. pap. 2.25 o.s.i. (ISBN 0-505-51424-9). Tower Bks.
Ziska. Marie Corelli. pap. 4.95 (ISBN 0-910122-28-8). Amherst Pr.
Ziska: The Problem of a Wicked Soul. Marie Corelli. LC 6-28737. 1897. Stone & Kimball.
Zit and Xoe: Their Early Experiences. Henry Curwen. LC 8-37875. (On cover: Harper's Franklin square library, no. 647). 1889. Harper & Brothers.
Zizi's Career. Evelyn Van Buren. LC 21-1895. The Bobbs-Merrill Company.
Zoan of Zion. Marjorie Sinclair. LC 32-316. Marjorie Sinclaire.
Zodiac. James Dickey. LC 76-2767. 125p. 1976. 6.00 (ISBN 0-385-02065-1); limited edition 30.00 (ISBN 0-385-12781-2). Doubleday.
Zodiac. Dan Lees. LC 72-80524. 1973. 5.95 (ISBN 0-8027-5256-X). Walker.
Zodiac. Dan Lees. 1974. (pbk.) 1.25 (ISBN 0-523-00453-2). Pinnacle Books.

Zodiac Affairs. Hans Holzer. (O.s.i.). 1970. pap. 0.75 o.s.i. (A759S, Award). Univ Pub & Dist.

Zodiak, Translated from the German. Walther Eidlitz & Sutton, Eric, Tr. LC 31-28917. 1931. Harper & Brothers.

Zoe. Geraldine Endsor Jewsbury. LC 75-1518. (Victorian Fiction: Novels of Faith and Doubt). 1975. 35.00 (ISBN 0-8240-1591-6). Garland Pub.

Zoe, or The Martel Papers: A Manuscript of the Conciergerie. LC 9-1340. 1865. Sheldon & Co.

Zoe; or, The Quadroon's Triumph. A Tale for the Times. Elizabeth D Livermore. LC 7-16059. 1855. Truman and Spofford.

Zoe, the Dancer. Ida Wild. LC 11-6002. 1911. John Lane.

Zoe: The History of Two Lives 1845. Geraldine Endsor Jewsbury. Ed. by Robert L. Wolff. LC 75-1518. (Victorian Fiction Ser.). (O.s.i.). 1975. lib. bdg. 66.00 o.s.i (ISBN 0-8240-1591-6). Garland Pub.

Zoe's Book. Gail Pass. 1976. 7.95 o.p. (ISBN 0-395-24350-5). HM.

Zoe's Book: A Novel. Gail Pass. LC 75-45076. 1976. 7.95 (ISBN 0-395-24350-5). Houghton Mifflin.

Zoes Book: A Novel. Gail Pass. 1977. 1.75 (ISBN 0-380-00972-2). Avon Books.

Zoe's Daughter. Anna Hanson McKenney Dorsey. LC 6-33703. 1888. J. Murphy & Co.

Zoe's Daughter. Anna Hanson McKenney Dorsey. LC 43-21544. John Murphy Company.

Zoe's Zodiac. Mary Jo Stephens. LC 71-163169. (Sandpiper book). 1974. (pbk.) 0.95. Houghton Mifflin.

Zokar, Divinity of Love, Peace, Truth and Justice. H Barrington Davis. LC 50-13799. 1950. W. Malliet.

Zollenstein. William Blair Morton Ferguson. 1908. D. Appleton and Company.

Zolotaia Nasha Zhelezka. Vasilii Pavlovich Aksenov. (Rus.). 1979. 15.00 (ISBN 0-88233-479-4); pap. 5.00 o.p (ISBN 0-88233-480-8). Ardis Pubs.

Zolotov Affair. Robert H. Rimmer. (N3687). 1968. Bantam.

Zolotov Affair: A Novel by Robert H. Rimmer. Robert H. Rimmer. LC 67-17561. 1967. bds., 3.95. Sherbourne.

Zolta Configuration. David Quammen. LC 81-43729. 1983. 15.95 (ISBN 0-385-17899-9). Doubleday.

Zomara. A Romance of Spain. Frank Cowan. LC 6-392501. 1873. Stevenson & Foster, Printers.

Zombie: the Living Dead. Rose London. 1977. pap. 2.95 o.p. (ISBN 0-517-52596-8, Bounty Books). Crown.

Zone Null. Herbert W. Franke. LC 73-6414. (Continuum book). 1974. 7.95 (ISBN 0-8164-9159-3). Seabury Press.

Zone of Emptiness. Translated from the French by Bernard Frechtman. 1st Ed. Hiroshi Noma. LC 77-161310. 1971. 7.95 (ISBN 0-8014-0656-0). Cornell University Press.

Zone of the Interior. Clancy Sigal. LC 76-4831. 8.95 (ISBN 0-690-01091-5). Crowell.

Zone of the Interior. Clancy Sigal. 1978. 1.95 (ISBN 0-445-04153-6). Popular Library.

Zoned Man. Anton Gross. LC 44-3534. 1944. The Hobson Book Press.

Zoo Gang. Paul Gallico. 1973. (pbk.) 1.50. Dell.

Zoo Gang. Paul Gallico. LC 75-172621. 1971. 6.95. Coward, McCann & Geoghegan.

Zoo Is Home. Edward William Dolch & Marguerite Pierce Dolch. LC 63-22906. (His A first reading book). 1958. Garrard Pub. Co.

Zoo: Or, Letters Not About Love. Viktor Borisovich Shklovskii. LC 77-161310. 1971. 7.95 (ISBN 0-8014-0656-0). Cornell University Press.

Zoom. Harold Horwood. LC 71-171299. 1972. 5.95 o.p. Doubleday.

Zoom! Peter Townend. 1975. (pbk.) 1.25 (ISBN 0-523-00586-5). Pinnacle Books.

Zoom! Peter Townend. LC 76-188614. 1972. 5.95. St. Martin's Press.

Zoomar: A Novel. 1st Ed. Erine Kovacs. LC 57-11429. 1957. Doubleday.

Zoot-Suit Murders. Thomas Sanchez. 1980. pap. 2.50 (ISBN 0-671-82913-0). PB.

Zoot-Suit Murders: A Novel. Thomas Sanchez. LC 78-15281. (Illus.). 9.95. Dutton.

Zophiel: Or, The Bride of Seven. Maria Brooks. LC 21-2358. 1833. Carter and Hendee.

Zorah. A Love-Tale of Modern Egypt. Elizabeth Balch. LC 6-6861. 1887. Cupples and Hurd.

Zoraida: A Romance of the Harem and the Great Sahara. William Le Queux. LC 7-13130. F. A. Stokes Company.

Zorba the Greek. Nikos Kazantzakis. LC 53-7756. 1953. Simon and Schuster.

Zorba the Greek. Nikos Kazantzakis. 1959. pap. 5.75 (ISBN 0-671-21132-3, Touchstone Bks). S&S.

Zoroaster. Francis Marion Crawford. LC 74-126704. 1970. AMS Press.

Zoroaster. Francis Marion Crawford. LC 76-7815. 1969. Scholarly Press.

Zoroaster. Francis Marion Crawford. LC 6-30882. 1885. Macmillan and Co.

Zoroaster. Francis Marion Crawford. LC 37-32806. 1892. Macmillan and Co.

Zoroaster. Francis Marion Crawford. LC 33-77716. 1893. Macmillan and Co.

Zoroaster. Francis Marion Crawford. LC 4-19012. (On cover: The works of F. Marion Crawford). 1901. The Macmillan Company.

Zoroaster: And Marzio's Crucifix. Francis Marion Crawford. LC 16-191467. (On cover: Works of F. Marion Crawford). 1914. The Macmillan Company.

Zorro, The Gay Blade. Les Dean. (Illus.). 208p (Orig.). 1982. pap. 2.50 (ISBN 0-8439-1007-0). Leisure Bks CT.

Zotz! Walter Karig. LC 47-11135. 1947. Rinehart.

ZR Wins. Fitzhugh Green. LC 77-84232. (Lost Race and Adult Fantasy Fiction). (Illus.). 1978. 18.00 (ISBN 0-405-10980-6). Arno Press.

Zuckerman Unbound. Philip Roth. LC 81-4640. 10.95 (ISBN 0-374-29945-5). Farrar, Straus and Giroux.

Zuckerman Unbound. Philip Roth. LC 81-13158. 1981. 13.95 (ISBN 0-8161-3291-7). G.K. Hall.

Zuleika Dobson. Max Beerbohm. (On cover: Modern library). Boni and Liveright, Inc.

Zuleika Dobson: Or, An Oxford Love Story, By Max Beerbohm. Max Beerbohm. LC 12-149. 1912. John Lane Company.

Zuleika Dobson: Or, An Oxford Love Story. Pref. by Douglas Cleverdon. Illus. by George Him. Max Beerbohm. LC 60-37418. 1960. Printed for the Members of the Limited Editions Club at the Garamond Press.

Zuleika Dobson: Or, An Oxford Love Story. Max Beerbohm. LC 65-1270. 1965. 3.75. Dodd.

Zuleika Dobson: Or, An Oxford Love Story. Max Beerbohm. LC 66-28096. (Signet classic, CT338). 1966. New American Library.

Zuleika Dobson, (or an Oxford Love Story) Max Beerbohm. 1978. 6.95 (ISBN 0-396-07593-2). Dodd.

Zuleika: Or, The Force of Love. Eugene Sue & Brewster, J. P., Tr. LC 8-17669. 1843. Burgess & Stringer.

Zuleka: Being the History of an Adventure in the Life of an American Gentleman, with Some Account of the Recent Disturbance in Dorola. Clinton Ross. LC 8-675. 1897. Lamson, Wolffe and Company.

Zulma, A Story of the Old South. Mary Frances Seibert. LC 8-6447. 1897. Natchez Printing and Stationery Co.

Zulu and the Zeide: Short Stories. 1st Ed. Dan Jacobson. LC 59-7336. 1959. Little, Brown.

Zulu Heart: A Novel. Shirley Graham Du Bois. LC 73-92801. 1974. 7.95 (ISBN 0-89388-132-5). Third Press.

Zulu Moon. Gwen Westwood. (Harlequin Romances Ser.). 192p. 1981. pap. 1.25 (ISBN 0-373-02417-7). Harlequin Bks.

Zury: the Meanest Man in Spring County: A Novel of Western Life. With an Introd. by John T. Flangan. Joseph Kirkland. LC 56-84199. 1956. University of Illinois Press.

Zury: the Meanest Man in Spring County: A Novel of Western Life. Joseph Kirkland. LC 7-12516. 1887. Houghton, Mifflin and Company.

Zury: The Meanest Man in Spring County. Joseph Kirkland. Ed. by John T. Flanagan. LC 71-96665. (American Authors Ser.) 1970. lib. bdg. 27.50 o.s.i. (ISBN 0-512-00446-3). Garrett Pr.

Zury, the Meanest Man in Spring County see Collected Works.

Zut, and Other Parisians. Guy Wetmore Carryl. LC 76-81266. (Short story index reprint series). 1969. Books for Libraries Press.

Zwei Geschichten: Beim Weiden-Josef und Moni der Geissub. Johanna Heusser Spyri & Balduf, Emery W., Ed. LC 18-23389. (Lake German classics). Scott, Foresman and Company.

Zwolf Dichter der Gegenwart. Ed. by Margaret Jeffrey & Volbehr, Johanna Elizabeth. LC 38-1072. (On cover: College German series). H. Holt and Company.

Zyx and His Fairy: Or, The Soul in Search of Peace. Nathan Brown. 1867. Brown and Duer.

Key to Publishers' and Distributors' Abbreviations

A & W Pubs, *(A & W Pubs., Inc.; 0-89479),* 95 Madison Ave., New York, NY 10016 Tel 212-725-4970 (SAN 200-2418) Do Not Confuse with A-W, Addison-Wesley Publishing Co., Inc. *Imprints:* A & W Visual Library (A & W Visual Library).
A & W Visual Library *Imprint of* A & W Pubs
A Bifrost, *(Bifrost, Andrew; 0-916266),* 342 E. 15th St., New York, NY 10003 Tel 212-673-6025 (SAN 208-0656).
A J Garvin, *(Garvin, A. J., & Associates; 0-9607252),* 720 E. Ann St., Ann Arbor, MI 48104 Tel 313-662-2734 (SAN 281-7357); Orders to: P.O. Box 7525, Ann Arbor, MI 48107 (SAN 281-7365).
A James Bks
  See Alicejamesbooks
A Jones, *(Jones, Anson, Press; 0-912432),* P.O. Box 65, Salado, TX 76571 Tel 817-947-5414 (SAN 201-2014).
A McKay, *(McKay, Alice; 0-941474),* 3455 Table Mesa Dr., No. 141d, Boulder, CO 80303 Tel 303-494-7174 (SAN 239-1147).
A Meriwether
  See Meriwether Pub
A R Klinski
  See Paranoid Pubns
A S Barnes, *(Barnes, A.S., & Co., Inc.; 0-498),* 9601 Aero Dr., San Diego, CA 92123 Tel 619-560-5163 (SAN 201-2030).
A-W, *(Addison-Wesley Publishing Co., Inc.; 0-201),* One Jacob Way, Reading, MA 01867 Tel 617-944-3700 (SAN 200-2000).
A Wofsy Fine Arts, *(Wofsy, Alan, Fine Arts; 0-915346),* P.O. Box 2210, San Francisco, CA 94126 Tel 415-986-3030 (SAN 207-6438).
AA *Imprint of* U of Mich Pr
Aaron-Jenkins, *(Aaron-Jenkins Press),* P.O. Box 998, Lawndale, CA 90260 Tel 213-324-9083 (SAN 210-9891).
Abbeville Pr, *(Abbeville Press, Inc.; 0-89659),* 505 Park Ave., New York, NY 10022 Tel 212-888-1969 (SAN 211-4755).
Abelard, *(Abelard-Schuman Ltd.; 0-200),* 10 E. 53rd St., New York, NY 10022 Tel 212-593-7000 (SAN 201-2081); c/o Harper & Row Pubs., Keystone Industrial Park, Scranton, PA 18512 (SAN 215-3742).
Abingdon, *(Abingdon Press; 0-687),* Customer Service Dept., 201 Eight Ave. S., Nashville, TN 37202 Tel 615-749-6301 (SAN 201-0054).
Abrams, *(Abrams, Harry N., Inc.; 0-8109),* Subs. of Times Mirror Co., 110 E. 59th St., New York, NY 10022 Tel 212-758-8600 (SAN 200-2434).

Abyss, *(Abyss Pubns.; 0-911856),* P.O. Box C, Somerville, MA 02143 Tel 617-666-1804 (SAN 201-1859).
Acad Pr, *(Academic Press, Inc.; 0-12),* 111 Fifth Ave., New York, NY 10003 Tel 212-741-6865 (SAN 206-8990).
Acad Therapy, *(Academic Therapy Pubns.; 0-87879),* 20 Commercial Blvd., Novato, CA 94947 Tel 415-883-3314 (SAN 201-2111).
Academy Chi Ltd, *(Academy Chicago, Ltd.; 0-915864),* 425 N. Michigan Ave., Chicago, IL 60611 Tel 312-644-1723 (SAN 213-2001).
Academy-Parliament, *(Academy Pr.; 0-87964),* c/o Parliament News Inc., 21314 Lassen St., Chatsworth, CA 91311 (SAN 201-2154).
Acadian Pub, *(Acadian Publishing Enterprise, Inc.; 0-914216),* Rte. 4 Box 470, Church Point, LA 70525 Tel 318-684-5871 (SAN 202-3199).
Ace Bks, *(Ace Bks.; 0-441),* Div. of Charter Communications, Inc., ; c/o Berkley/Jove Pub., 200 Madison Ave., New York, NY 10016 Tel 212-686-9820 (SAN 169-5800); Dist. by: ICD, 250 W. 55th St., New York, NY 10019 Tel 212-262-7444 (SAN 270-885X).
Acoma Bks, *(Acoma Books; 0-916552),* P.O. Box 4, Ramona, CA 92065 Tel 714-789-1288 (SAN 207-7221).
Acorn OH, *(Acorn; 0-9604194),* 1778 Radnor Rd., Cleveland, OH 44118 (SAN 216-213X).
Acrobat, *(Acrobat Books; 0-918226),* P.O. Box 480820, Los Angeles, CA 90048 (SAN 209-3936).
Acropolis, *(Acropolis Books; 0-87491),* 2400 17th St. N.W., Washington, DC 20009 Tel 202-387-6805 (SAN 201-2227).
Adler, *(Adler's Foreign Books, Inc.; 0-8417),* 162 Fifth Ave., New York, NY 10010 Tel 212-691-5151 (SAN 201-2251).
Adm Nimitz Foun, *(Admiral Nimitz Foundation),* P.O. Box 777, Fredericksburg, TX 78624 Tel 512-997-4379 (SAN 201-1883).
Adonis Pr, *(Adonis Press; 0-932776),* Hawthorne Valley/Harlemville, Ghent, NY 12075 (SAN 218-463X).
Advent, *(Advent Pubs., Inc.; 0-911682),* P.O. Box A3228, Chicago, IL 60690 (SAN 201-2286).
Advent Bk
  See Advent NY
Advent NY, *(Advent Books, Inc; 0-89891),* 141 E. 44th St., Suite 511, New York, NY 10017 Tel 212-697-0887 (SAN 212-9973).

Adventure Pubns, *(Adventure Pubns.; 0-934860),* P.O. Box 96, Staples, MN 56479 Tel 218-894-3591 (SAN 212-7199).
Aeonian Pr
  See Amereon Ltd
Aero-Medical, *(Aero-Medical Consultants, Inc.; 0-912522),* 10912 Hamlin Blvd., Largo, FL 33540 Tel 813-596-2551 (SAN 201-2316).
Aesthetic Realism, *(Aesthetic Realism Foundation & Terrain Gallery; 0-911492),* 141 Greene St., New York, NY 10012 Tel 212-777-4490 (SAN 205-423X).
Africana *Imprint of* Holmes & Meier
Afro-Am, *(Afro-Am Publishing Co., Inc.; 0-910030),* 910 S. Michigan Ave., Rm. 556, Chicago, IL 60605 Tel 312-922-1147 (SAN 201-2332).
Agascha Prods
  See Shabazz Pr
AHM Pub
  See Harlan Davidson
Airmont, *(Airmont Publishing Co., Inc.; 0-8049),* 22 E. 60th St., New York, NY 10022 (SAN 206-8710).
ALA, *(American Library Assn.; 0-8389),* 50 E. Huron St., Chicago, IL 60611 Tel 312-944-6780 (SAN 201-0062).
Aladdin *Imprint of* Atheneum
Alba, *(Alba House; 0-8189),* Div. of the Society of St. Paul, 2187 Victory Blvd., Staten Island, NY 10314 Tel 212-761-0047 (SAN 201-2405).
Albion Am Bks, *(Albion-American Books),* P.O. Box 50011, Tucson, AZ 85703 (SAN 215-7225).
Algol Pr, *(Algol Press; 0-916186),* P.O. Box 4175, New York, NY 10163 Tel 212-643-9011 (SAN 207-9445); Orders to: F&SF Book Co., 740 Delafield Ave., Staten Island, NY 10310 (SAN 207-9453).
Alicejamesbooks, *(Alicejamesbooks; 0-914086),* 138 Mt. Auburn St., Cambridge, MA 02138 Tel 617-354-1408 (SAN 201-1158).
Alinda Pr, *(Alinda Press; 0-933076),* Box 553, Eureka, CA 95501 Tel 707-443-2510 (SAN 212-4734).
Allen Lane, *(Allen Lane),* Dist. by: The Viking Press, 625 Madison Ave., New York, NY 10022 (SAN 282-5066).
Allen Unwin, *(Allen & Unwin, Inc.; 0-04; 0-86861),* 9 Winchester Terrace, Winchester, MA 01890 Tel 617-729-0830 (SAN 210-3362); Orders to: 300 Ratitan Center, Edison, NJ 08818 Tel 201-225-5555 (SAN 210-3370).
Allenson
  See Allenson-Breckinridge

KEY TO PUBLISHERS' AND DISTRIBUTORS' ABBREVIATIONS

Allenson-Breckinridge, *(Allenson-Breckinridge Books; 0-8401),* P.O. Box 447, Geneva, AL 36340 (SAN 162-4903).

Alliance Coll, *(Alliance College),* Cambridge Springs, PA 16403 (SAN 216-0862).

Alpha-Omega Bk, *(Alpha-Omega Book Publishers, Inc.; 0-938764),* 605 W. 113th St. Suite 82, New York, NY 10025 Tel 212-864-4638 (SAN 237-9279).

Alpha-Omega Bks
 See Alpha-Omega Bk

Alpha Printing, *(Alpha Printing Ltd.; 0-937268),* 6301-B Central Ave., N.W., Albuquerque, NM 87105 (SAN 215-6172) Moved, left no forwarding address.

Alphabet MA, *(Alphabet Press, MA; 0-940032),* 60 N. Mina St., Natick, MA 01760 Tel 617-655-9696 (SAN 217-1449).

Alphabet Quincy
 See Alphabet MA

Alyson Pubns, *(Alyson Pubns., Inc.; 0-932870),* P.O. Box 2783, Boston, MA 02208 Tel 617-542-5679 (SAN 213-6546).

Am Canadian, *(American-Canadian Pubs., Inc.; 0-913844),* Drawer 2078, Portales, NM 88130 Tel 505-356-4082 (SAN 201-260X).

Am Heritage, *(American Heritage Publishing Co.; 0-8281),* 10 Rockefeller Plaza, New York, NY 10020 Tel 212-399-8900 (SAN 206-9032).

Am Hist Pr, *(American History Press; 0-89002),* Div. of Northwoods Press, P.O. Box 123, S. Thomaston, ME 04858 (SAN 217-0876).

Am Philos, *(American Philosophical Society; 0-87169),* 104 S. Fifth St., Philadelphia, PA 19106 Tel 215-627-0706 (SAN 206-9016).

Am Repr-Rivercity Pr, *(American Reprint Co./Rivercity Press; 0-89190),* Dist. by: Amereon Ltd., P.O. Box 1200, Mattituck, NY 11952 Tel 516-298-5100 (SAN 201-2413).

Am Samizdat, *(American Samizdat; 0-935500),* 724 Tenth Ave., Apt. 4A, New York, NY 10019 Tel 212-586-5780 (SAN 213-4578).

Am Scandinavian, *(American-Scandinavian Foundation; 0-89067),* 127 E. 73rd St., New York, NY 10021 Tel 212-879-9779 (SAN 201-7075); Orders to: Heritage Resource Center, P.O. Box 26305, Minneapolis, MN 55426 (SAN 201-7083).

Am Stud Pr, *(American Studies Press, Inc.; 0-934996),* 13511 Palmwood Lane, Tampa, FL 33624 Tel 813-961-7200 (SAN 213-2788).

Am Univ Artforms, *(American Universal Artforms Corp.; 0-913632),* P.O. Box 4574, Austin, TX 78765 Tel 512-451-3588 (SAN 202-4772).

Am West
 See Crown

AmCen *Imprint of* **Hill & Wang**

Amata Graphics, *(Amata Graphics; 0-931224),* P.O. Box 12313, Portland, OR 97212 Tel 503-231-8540 (SAN 211-2094).

Amereon Ltd, *(Amereon Ltd.; 0-88411; 0-89190),* P.O. Box 1200, Mattituck, NY 11952 Tel 516-298-5100 (SAN 201-2413).

Amherst Pr, *(Amherst Press),* P.O. Box 296, Amherst, WI 54406 Tel 715-824-5890 (SAN 213-9820).

AMI Pr, *(AMI International Press; 0-911988),* Mountain View Rd., Washington, NJ 07822 Tel 201-689-1700 (SAN 213-6791).

AMS Pr, *(AMS Press, Inc.; 0-404),* 56 E. 13th St., New York, NY 10003 Tel 212-777-4700 (SAN 201-1743).

AMSCO Sch, *(AMSCO School Pubns., Inc.; 0-87720),* 315 Hudson St., New York, NY 10013 Tel 212-675-7000 (SAN 201-1751).

Amuru Pr, *(Amuru Press, Inc.; 0-87976),* 161 Madison Ave., New York, NY 10016 Tel 212-686-5508 (SAN 201-176X).

Ananda, *(Ananda Pubns.; 0-916124),* 14618 Tyler Foote Rd., Nevada City, CA 95959 Tel 916-292-3656 (SAN 201-1778).

Anch *Imprint of* **Doubleday**

Anchor Pr *Imprint of* **Doubleday**

And-or Pr, *(And/Or Press, Inc.; 0-915904),* P.O. Box 2246, Berkeley, CA 94702 Tel 415-849-2665 (SAN 206-9458).

Andante Pub, *(Andante Pubs.; 0-940038),* 175-20 Wexford Terrace, Suite 11L, Jamaica Estates, NY 11432 Tel 212-526-7814 (SAN 220-1992).

Andor Pub, *(Andor Publishing Co., Inc.; 0-89319),* 163 E. Union Ave., E. Rutherford, NJ 07073 Tel 201-460-1495 (SAN 208-5267).

Andrews & McMeel, *(Andrews & McMeel, Inc.; 0-8362),* 4400 Johnson Dr., Fairway, KS 66205 Tel 913-362-1523 (SAN 202-540X).

Angriff Pr, *(Angriff Press; 0-913022),* P.O. Box 2726, Hollywood, CA 90028 Tel 213-386-9826 (SAN 203-4743).

Angst World, *(Angst World Library; 0-914580),* 1160 Forest Creek Rd., Selma, OR 97538 (SAN 201-1786).

Anhinga Pr, *(Anhinga Press; 0-938078),* Apalachee Poetry Ctr., 406 Williams Bldg., Florida State Univ., Tallahassee, FL 32306 (SAN 216-0943).

Anthelion Pr, *(Anthelion Press, Inc.; 0-89185),* P.O. Box 614, Corte Madera, CA 94925 Tel 415-924-5311 (SAN 208-0575).

Anthony, *(Anthony, C & R, Pubs., Inc.; 0-910140),* 300 Park Ave., S., New York, NY 10010 Tel 212-986-7693 (SAN 203-4786) Do Not Confuse with Anthony Pub Co.

Anv *Imprint of* **Van Nos Reinhold**

Anvil Pr, *(Anvil Press; 0-918552),* P.O. Box 37, Millville, MN 55957 (SAN 203-4794).

Apollo Eds, *(Apollo Editions; 0-8152),* C/O Harper & Row Pubs., 10 E. 53rd St., New York, NY 10022 (SAN 211-691X); Dist. by: Harper & Row Pubs., Keystone Industrial Park, Scranton, PA 18512 (SAN 215-3742).

Appel, *(Appel, Paul P., Pub.; 0-911858),* 216 Washington St., Mt. Vernon, NY 10553 Tel 914-667-7365 (SAN 202-3253).

Apple Wood, *(Apple-Wood Books; 0-918222),* Box 2870, Cambridge, MA 02139 Tel 617-923-9337 (SAN 210-3419).

Appleton, *(Appleton-Century-Crofts, Inc.),* Publisher Abbreviation Without Address Are for Titles That Are Out of Print. These Are Obsolete Abbreviations. Publishers Abbreviation Is Now ACC.

Applezaba, *(Applezaba Press; 0-930090),* P.O. Box 4134, Long Beach, CA 90804 Tel 213-591-0015 (SAN 210-7023).

April Pub, *(April Publishing; 0-939122),* P.O. Box 480000, Los Angeles, CA 90048 (SAN 238-0048).

Apt Bks, *(Apt Books, Inc.; 0-86590),* 141 E. 44th St., Suite 511, New York, NY 10017 (SAN 215-7209).

Aqua Educ, *(Aquarian Educational Group; 0-911794),* 30188 Mulholland Hwy., Agoura, CA 91301 Tel 213-889-9678 (SAN 203-4816).

Aragorn Bks, *(Aragorn Books, Inc.; 0-913862),* 14698 Nordhoff St., Panorama City, CA 91402 Tel 213-894-3104 (SAN 203-4832).

Arbor Hse, *(Arbor House Publishing Co.; 0-87795),* 300 E. 44th St., New York, NY 10017 Tel 212-599-3131 (SAN 201-1522).

Arc Bks
 See Arco

Arcadia, *(Arcadia House),* Dist. by: Lenox Hill Press, 419 Park Ave., S., New York, NY 10016 (SAN 201-0801).

Arcana Pub, *(Arcana Publishing; 0-910261),* P.O. Box Two, Wilmot, WI 53192 (SAN 241-3604).

Archer Edns, *(Archer Editions Press; 0-89097),* 318 Fry Branch Rd., Lynnville, TN 38472 Tel 615-527-3643 (SAN 207-7124).

Archival Pr, *(Archival Press, Inc.; 0-915882),* P.O. Box 93, MIT Branch Sta., Cambridge, MA 02139 (SAN 214-283X).

Archon Bks *Imprint of* **Shoe String**

Archway, *(Archway Paperbacks; 0-671),* c/o Pocket Bks., 1230 Ave. of the Americas, New York, NY 10020 Tel 212-246-2121 (SAN 202-5922).

Arco, *(Arco Publishing, Inc.; 0-668),* Div. of Prentice-Hall, Inc., 215 Park Ave., S., New York, NY 10003 Tel 212-777-6300 (SAN 201-0003).

Arden Lib, *(Arden Library; 0-8495),* Mill & Main Sts., Darby, PA 19023 Tel 215-726-5505 (SAN 207-477X).

Ardis Pubs, *(Ardis Pubs.; 0-88233),* 2901 Heatherway, Ann Arbor, MI 48104 Tel 313-971-2367 (SAN 201-1492).

Argo *Imprint of* **Atheneum**

Argos House, *(Argos House; 0-9607082),* Crescent Ave., Saratoga Springs, NY 12866 Tel 518-584-5817 (SAN 238-9428).

Argus Comm, *(Argus Communications; 0-913592; 0-89505),* One DLM Park, Box 5000, Allen, TX 75002 Tel 214-248-6300 (SAN 201-1476).

Ariel OH, *(Ariel Press; 0-89804),* 3391 Edenbrook Ct., Columbus, OH 43220 Tel 614-451-2030 (SAN 219-8460).

Arif, *(Arif; 0-913537),* 2748 Ninth St., Berkeley, CA 94710 Tel 415-848-5386 (SAN 206-944X).

Arkham, *(Arkham House Pubs.; 0-87054),* P.O. Box 546, Sauk City, WI 53583 Tel 608-643-4500 (SAN 206-9741). *Imprints:* Mycroft & Moran (Mycroft & Moran).

Arlin J Brown, *(Brown, Arlin J.),* The Arlin J. Brown Info. Center, P.O. Box 251, Ft. Belvoir, VA 22060 Tel 703-451-8638 (SAN 203-4891).

Arlington Hse *Imprint of* **Crown**

Arno, *(Arno Press Inc., A New York Times Company; 0-405),* Three Park Ave., New York, NY 10016 Tel 212-725-2050 (SAN 265-3508).

Arrowhead Bks
 See Arrowhead Pr

Arrowhead Pr, *(Arrowhead Press; 0-9604152),* 3005 Fulton, Berkeley, CA 94705 Tel 415-548-5110 (SAN 214-2562).

Ars Eterna, *(Ars Eterna Press; 0-9602170),* 7627 Glen Prairie, Houston, TX 77061 (SAN 212-4785).

Arte Publico, *(Arte Publico Press; 0-934770),* Revista Chicano-Riquena, Univ. of Houston Central Campus, Houston, TX 77004 (SAN 213-4594).

Artist-Dealer
 See Davenport

As-Shabazz Pr
 See Shabazz Pr

Ashley Bks, *(Ashley Books, Inc.; 0-87949),* 30 Main St., Port Washington, NY 11050 Tel 516-883-2221 (SAN 201-1409); Orders to: P.O. Box 768, Port Washington, NY 11050 Tel 516-883-2221 (SAN 201-1417).

Ashod
 See Ashod Pr

Ashod Pr, *(Ashod Press; 0-935102),* 620 E. 20th St, 11F, New York, NY 10009 Tel 212-475-0711 (SAN 281-2894); Orders to: P.O. Box 1147 Madison Square Station, New York, NY 10159 (SAN 281-2908).

Asia, *(Asia Publishing House; 0-210),* Dist. by: APT Books, Inc., 141 E. 44th St., Suite 511, New York, NY 10017 Tel 212-697-0887 (SAN 215-7209).

Asian Am Stud, *(Asian American Studies Center, UCLA),* 3232 Campbell Hall, Univ. of California, Los Angeles, CA 90024 Tel 213-825-2974 (SAN 210-7759).

Aspen Art, *(Aspen Art; 0-9601120),* 401 Center, Evanston, WY 82930 Tel 307-789-9879 (SAN 210-167X).

Aspen Pr
 See Rue Morgue

ASPIRATION, *(A S P I R A T I O N; 0-914182),* P.O. Box M, University Sta., Charlottesville, VA 22903 Tel 804-295-7718 (SAN 207-107X).

Assembling Pr, *(Assembling Press; 0-915066),* P.O. Box 1967, Brooklyn, NY 11202 (SAN 201-1360).

Assoc Bk, *(Associated Booksellers; 0-87497),* 147 McKinley Ave., P.O. Box 6361, Bridgeport, CT 06606 Tel 203-366-5494 (SAN 169-0655).

Assoc Creative Writers, *(Associated Creative Writers; 0-933362),* 9231 Molly Woods Ave., La Mesa, CA 92041 (SAN 212-8292).

Aston Hall, *(Aston Hall Pubns, Inc.; 0-89936),* 1835 Hicks Rd., Rolling Meadows, IL 60008 (SAN 213-0068).

Astor-Honor, *(Astor-Honor, Inc.; 0-8392),* 48 E. 43rd St., New York, NY 10017 (SAN 203-5022).

Astro Artz, *(Astro Artz; 0-937122),* 240 S. Broadway, Los Angeles, CA 90012 (SAN 215-6229).

Ata Bks, *(Ata Books; 0-931688),* 1928 Stuart St., Berkeley, CA 94703 Tel 415-841-9613 (SAN 211-4801).

Atheneum, *(Atheneum Pubs.; 0-689),* 597 Fifth Ave., New York, NY 10017 Tel 212-486-2700 (SAN 201-0011); 122 E. 42nd St., New York, NY 10017 (SAN 209-3162); Dist. by: The Scribner Book Companies, 201 Willowbrook Blvd., Wayne, NJ 07470 (SAN 201-002X). *Imprints:* Aladdin (Aladdin Books); Argo (Argo Books).

Athlone Pr *Imprint of* **Humanities**

KEY TO PUBLISHERS' AND DISTRIBUTORS' ABBREVIATIONS

Atlantis-by-the-Sea, *(Atlantis-by-the-Sea, Ltd.; 0-89200),* 745 Seventh Ave., New York, NY 10019 (SAN 211-7193) Moved, left no forwarding address.

Attic Pr, *(Attic Press; 0-87921),* Stony Point, Rte. 2, Greenwood, SC 29646 Tel 803-374-3013 (SAN 201-1328).

Augsburg, *(Augsburg Publishing House; 0-8066),* 426 S. Fifth St., Box 1209, Minneapolis, MN 55440 Tel 612-330-3404 (SAN 169-4081); 57 E. Main St., Columbus, OH 43215 (SAN 156-4951); 5210 N. Lamar, Austin, TX 78765 (SAN 146-3365).

August Hse, *(August House; 0-935304),* 1010 W. 3rd St., Little Rock, AR 72201 Tel 501-376-4516 (SAN 223-7288).

Aum Pubns, *(Aum Pubns.; 0-88497),* P.O. Box 32433, Jamaica, NY 11431 Tel 212-523-3471 (SAN 201-128X).

Auromere, *(Auromere, Inc.; 0-89744),* 1291 Weber St., Pomona, CA 91768 Tel 714-629-8255 (SAN 169-0043).

Aurora Pubs, *(Aurora Pubs.; 0-87695),* P.O. Box 120616, Nashville, TN 37212 Tel 615-254-5842 (SAN 201-1271).

Australia N U P, *(Australia National University Press),* 15601 S.W. 83rd Ave., Miami, FL 33157 Tel 305-251-3934 (SAN 212-0658).

Avant Bks, *(Avant Books; 0-932238),* 3719 Sixth Ave., San Diego, CA 92103 Tel 714-295-0473 (SAN 212-8055).

Avant Garde CR, *(Avant Garde Creations, Inc.; 0-930182),* Box 30160, Eugene, OR 97403 Tel 503-345-3043 (SAN 210-5853) Do Not Confuse with Avant-Garde Media, Inc. in NY.

Avon, *(Avon Books; 0-380),* 1790 Broadway, New York, NY 10019 Tel 212-399-4500 (SAN 201-4009). *Imprints:* Bard (Avon Bard Books); Camelot (Avon Camelot Books); Discus (Avon Discus Books); Flare (Avon Flare Books).

AWM Co, *(A. W. M. Company; 0-89105),* P.O. Box 7643, Ann Arbor, MI 48107 Tel 313-482-7623 (SAN 207-2025).

Ayer Co, *(Ayer Co.; 0-88143),* 99 Main St., Salem, NY 03079 Tel 617-683-8741 (SAN 211-6936).

B & R Samizdat, *(B & R Samizdat Express; 0-915232),* P.O. Box 161, West Roxbury, MA 02132 Tel 617-469-2269 (SAN 207-1037).

B Franklin, *(Franklin, Burt, Pub.; 0-89102),* Dist. by: Lenox Hill Publishing & Distributing Corp., 235 E. 44th St., New York, NY 10017 (SAN 282-597X).

B M Stewart, *(Stewart, B. M.),* 4494 Wausau Rd., Okemos, MI 48864 Tel 517-349-0297 (SAN 202-0548).

B of A, *(B of A Communications Co.; 0-911238),* P.O. Box 22252, Louisiana State Univ., Baton Rouge, LA 70893 Tel 504-272-6600 (SAN 204-6776); Pelican Office Center, 11628 S. Choctaw Dr., Baton Rouge, LA 70815 Tel 504-272-6600 (SAN 200-4208); Orders to: P.O. Box 15809, Broadmoor Sta., Baton Rouge, LA 70893 Tel 504-272-6600 (SAN 200-4216).

B Owens
See Working Pr CA

B Stallard, *(Stallard, Bernard; 0-9606908),* Rt. 2, Box 430-B, Speedwell, TN 37870 (SAN 282-3616)600 Cherakee Rd., Raceland, KY 41169 (SAN 282-3624).

Back Fork Bks, *(Back Fork Books),* Drawer 752, Webster Springs, WV 26288 (SAN 240-4699).

Back Row Pr, *(Back Row Press; 0-917162),* 1803 Venus Ave., St. Paul, MN 55112 Tel 612-633-1685 (SAN 208-5569).

Backdraft, *(Backdraft Pubns.; 0-936174),* P.O. Box 401, Basking Ridge, NJ 07920 Tel 201-766-7937 (SAN 214-1027).

Backeddy Bks, *(Backeddy Books; 0-9603566),* Box 301, Cambridge, ID 83610 (SAN 211-4615).

Baker Bk, *(Baker Book House; 0-8010),* P.O. Box 6287, Grand Rapids, MI 49506 Tel 616-676-9186 (SAN 201-4041).

Balcom, *(Balcom Books; 0-9600008),* 320 Bawden St., Apt. 401, Ketchikan, AK 99901 Tel 907-225-2496 (SAN 202-3725).

Ballantine, *(Ballantine Books, Inc.; 0-345),* Div. of Random House, Inc., 201 E. 50th St., New York, NY 10022 Tel 212-751-2600 (SAN 214-1175); Orders to: 400 Hahn Rd., Westminster, MD 21157 (SAN 214-1183).

Bamboo Ridge Pr, *(Bamboo Ridge Press; 0-910043),* 990 Hahaione St., Honolulu, HI 96825 Tel 808-395-7098 (SAN 241-2071).

Banbury *Imprint of* **Dell**

Bandanna Bks, *(Bandanna Books; 0-942208),* 209 W. De la Guerra, Santa Barbara, CA 93101 Tel 805-962-9996 (SAN 238-7956).

B&N
See B&N Imports

B&N Imports, *(Barnes & Noble Books-Imports; 0-389),* Div. of Littlefield, Adams & Co., 81 Adams Dr., Totowa, NJ 07512 Tel 201-256-8600 (SAN 206-7803).

B&N NY, *(Barnes & Noble Books),* Div. of Harper & Row, 10 E. 53rd St., New York, NY 10022 Tel 212-593-7000 (SAN 238-4906).

Banner *Imprint of* **Exposition**

Bantam, *(Bantam Books, Inc.; 0-553),* 666 Fifth Ave., New York, NY 10019 Tel 212-765-6500 (SAN 201-3975); Orders to: 414 E. Golf Rd., Des Plaines, IL 60016 (SAN 201-3983). *Imprints:* Skylark (Skylark).

Banyan Bks, *(Banyan Books; 0-916224),* P.O. Box 431160, Miami, FL 33143 Tel 305-665-6011 (SAN 208-340X).

Banyan Tree, *(Banyan Tree Books; 0-9604320),* 1963 El Dorado Ave., Berkeley, CA 94707 (SAN 207-3862); Dist. by: Bookpeople, 2940 Seventh St., Berkeley, CA 94710 Tel 415-549-3033 (SAN 168-9517).

Baptist Span
See Casa Bautista

Barah, *(Barah Publishing; 0-930292),* P.O. Box 697, San Anselmo, CA 94960 Tel 415-459-1165 (SAN 209-3480).

Barclay Hse, *(Barclay House; 0-87682),* Div. of American Art Enterprises, Inc., 21322 Lassen St., Chatsworth, CA 91311 Tel 213-882-5900 (SAN 201-7342) Moved, Left No Forwardind Address.

Bard *Imprint of* **Avon**

Bark-Back, *(Bark-Back; 0-9603338),* P.O. Box 235, Glenshaw, PA 15116 Tel 412-364-3743 (SAN 213-4624).

Barn Owl Bks, *(Barn Owl Books; 0-9609626),* 1101 Keeler Ave., Berkeley, CA 94708 Tel 415-549-2149 (SAN 268-2214).

Baronet, *(Baronet Pub. Co.; 0-89437),* 509 Madison Ave., New York, NY 10022 Tel 212-752-7331 (SAN 210-1734) Moved, Left No Forwarding Address.

Barre, *(Barre Publishing Co.),* Dist. by: Crown Publishers, Inc., 1 Park Ave., New York, NY 10016 (SAN 213-4357).

Barrett, *(Barrett & Co., Pubs.; 0-9609396),* 465 City Center Plaza South, P.O. Box 6700, Jackson, MS 39212 Tel 601-373-4400 (SAN 240-8732).

Barron, *(Barron's Educational Series, Inc.; 0-8120),* 113 Crossways Park Dr., Woodbury, NY 11797 Tel 516-921-8750 (SAN 201-453X).

Barth, *(Barth, Robert L.; 0-941150),* 14 Lucas St., Florence, KY 41042 (SAN 238-9126).

Basic, *(Basic Books, Inc.; 0-465),* 10 E. 53rd St., New York, NY 10022 Tel 212-593-7057 (SAN 201-4521).

Basil Blackwell
See Biblio Dist

Bauhan, *(Bauhan, William L., Inc.; 0-87233),* Old County Rd., Dublin, NH 03444 Tel 603-563-8020 (SAN 204-384X).

BBM Assocs
See Calif Street

BC *Imprint of* **Grove**

Beacon
See Beacon Hill

Beacon Hill, *(Beacon Hill Pr. of Kansas City; 0-8341),* Dist. by: Nazarene Pub. Hse., P.O. Box 527, Kansas City, MO 64141 Tel 816-931-1900 (SAN 202-9022).

Beacon Hse, *(Beacon House, Inc.; 0-87648),* P.O. Box 311, Beacon, NY 12508 Tel 914-831-2318 (SAN 202-3830).

Beacon Pr, *(Beacon Press, Inc.; 0-8070),* 25 Beacon St., Boston, MA 02108 Tel 617-742-2110 (SAN 201-4483); Orders to: Harper & Row Pubs., Inc., Keystone Industrial Park, Scranton, PA 18512 Tel 800-238-4175 (SAN 215-3742).

Beacon Presse IA, *(Le Beacon Presse; 0-935954),* 621 Holt, Iowa City, IA 52240 (SAN 281-8736); Orders to: Keith S. Gormezano, 6 Beacon Presse, 2921 E. Madison St., Suite 7 BIP, Seattle, WA 98112 Tel 206-322-1431 (SAN 281-8744).

Bean Assoc
See Bean Pub

Bean Pub, *(Carolyn Bean Publishing, Ltd.; 0-916860),* 120 Second St., San Francisco, CA 94105 Tel 415-957-9574 (SAN 208-5445).

Beanie Bks, *(Beanie Bks.; 0-933530),* 7443 Stanford, St. Louis, MO 63130 (SAN 281-3130).

Beatty, *(Beatty, R. W.; 0-87948),* P.O. Box 26, Arlington, VA 22210 (SAN 206-7110).

Beaufort
See Beaufort SC

Beaufort Bks NY, *(Beaufort Books, Inc.; 0-8253),* 9 E. 40th St., New York, NY 10016 (SAN 281-3149).

Beaufort Book Co
See Beaufort SC

Beaufort SC, *(Beaufort Book Co.; 0-910206),* Box 1127, Beaufort, SC 29902 Tel 803-524-5172 (SAN 202-3873) Do not confuse with Beaufort Bks NY.

Beechcliff Bks, *(Beechcliff Books; 0-9608930),* Number 605, One Hundred Seven, Annapolis, MD 21403 Tel 301-263-3580 (SAN 241-001X).

Beekman Hill, *(Beekman Hill Press; 0-940534),* 342 E. 51st St., Apt. 3A, New York, NY 10022 Tel 212-755-0218 (SAN 222-9919).

Beekman Pubs, *(Beekman Pubs., Inc.; 0-8464),* P.O. Box 888, Woodstock, NY 12498 Tel 914-679-2300 (SAN 201-4467).

Behrman, *(Behrman House, Inc.; 0-87441),* 1261 Broadway, New York, NY 10001 Tel 212-689-2020 (SAN 201-4459).

Being Inc, *(Being Inc.; 0-915412),* P.O. Box 742, Ojai, CA 93023 (SAN 207-2041) Moved, left no forwarding address.

Belier Pr, *(Belier Press, Inc.; 0-914646),* P.O. Box BB Old Chelsea Sta., New York, NY 10113 Tel 212-620-4276 (SAN 206-4766).

Believers Bkshelf, *(Believers Bookshelf; 0-941202),* Box 261, Sunbury, PA 17801 Tel 717-672-2134 (SAN 211-7746).

Bellerophon Bks, *(Bellerophon Books; 0-88388),* 36 Anacapa St., Santa Barbara, CA 93101 Tel 805-965-7034 (SAN 202-392X).

Belmont-Tower
See Tower Bks

Bennet Pub, *(Bennet, Rebecca, Pubns., Inc.; 0-910218),* 5409 18th Ave., Brooklyn, NY 11204 (SAN 206-8443).

Bentley, *(Bentley, Robert, Inc.; 0-8376),* 872 Massachusetts Ave., Cambridge, MA 02139 Tel 617-547-4170 (SAN 213-9839).

Benziger
See Glencoe

Benziger Sis, *(Benziger Sisters Publishers),* 466 E. Mariposa St., Altadena, CA 91001 (SAN 209-5297).

Berg, *(Berg, Norman S., Publisher, Ltd.; 0-910220),* P.O. Box 15232, Atlanta, GA 30333 (SAN 226-8086).

Berg
See Larlin Corp

Berkeley Slavic, *(Berkeley Slavic Specialities; 0-933884),* P.O. Box 3034, Oakland, CA 94609 Tel 415-653-8048 (SAN 212-7245).

Berkley Pub, *(Berkley Publishing Corp.; 0-425),* Affiliate of G. P. Putnam's Sons, 200 Madison Ave., New York, NY 10016 Tel 212-686-9820 (SAN 201-3991); Dist. by: ICD, 250 W. 55th St., New York, NY 10019 Tel 212-262-7444 (SAN 169-5800). *Imprints:* Medallion (Medallion Books); Windhover (Windhover).

Berkshire Traveller, *(Berkshire Traveller Press; 0-912944),* Pine St., Stockbridge, MA 01262 Tel 413-298-3636 (SAN 201-4424).

Bert & I Bks, *(Bert & I Books; 0-9607546),* 35 Mill Rd., Ipswich, MA 01938 Tel 617-356-3509 (SAN 238-2202).

Beta Bk, *(Beta Book Co.; 0-89293),* 10857 Valiente Court, San Diego, CA 92124 Tel 714-293-3832 (SAN 208-0397) Moved, left no forwarding address.

Bethany Fell
See Bethany Hse

Bethany Fellow, *(Bethany Fellowship, Inc.; 0-87123),* 6820 Auto Club Rd., Minneapolis, MN 55438 (SAN 237-9899).

Bethany Hse, *(Bethany House Pubs.; 0-87123),* 6820 Auto Club Rd., Minneapolis, MN 55438 Tel 612-944-2121 (SAN 201-4416).

Bethany Pr, *(Bethany Press; 0-8272),* 2320 Pine Blvd., Box 179, St. Louis, MO 63166 Tel 314-371-6900 (SAN 201-4408).

Bethel Pub, *(Bethel Publishing Co.; 0-934998)*, 1819 S. Main St., Elkhart, IN 46516 Tel 219-293-8585 (SAN 201-7555).

BH Ent, *(BH Enterprises; 0-9604896)*, P.O. Box 216, Midwood Sta., Brooklyn, NY 11230 Tel 212-336-0521 (SAN 220-0562).

Biblio Dist, *(Biblio Distribution Centre)*, 81 Adams Dr., Totowa, NJ 07512 Tel 201-256-8600 (SAN 211-724X).

Bibliotheca, *(Bibliotheca Islamica, Inc.; 0-88297)*, P.O. Box 14474, University Station, Minneapolis, MN 55414 Tel 612-221-9883 (SAN 202-4063).

Biblo, *(Biblo & Tannen Booksellers & Pubs., Inc.; 0-8196)*, 321 Sandbank Rd., P.O. Box 302, Cheshire, CT 06410 Tel 203-272-2308 (SAN 202-4071).

Bieler, *(Bieler Press; 0-931460)*, P.O. Box 3856, St. Paul, MN 55165 Tel 612-292-9936 (SAN 209-7087).

Bilingual Pr, *(Bilingual Press; 0-916950)*, Dept. of Foreign Languages & Bilingual Studies, 217 New Alexander, Eastern Michigan University, Ypsilanti, MI 48197 Tel 313-487-0042 (SAN 208-5526).

Binford, *(Binford & Mort Pubs.; 0-8323)*, 2536 S.E. 11th Ave., Portland, OR 97202 Tel 503-238-9666 (SAN 201-4386).

Birmingham Hist Soc, *(Birmingham Historical Society)*, 1425 22nd Street South, Birmingham, AL 35205 (SAN 240-1347).

BJ Pub Group, *(BJ Publishing Group)*, 200 Madison Ave., New York, NY 10016 Tel 212-686-9820 (SAN 213-2370).

Bk Page, *(Book Page; 0-910266)*, 904 Silver Spur Rd.-Suite 120, Rolling Hills Estate, CA 90274 Tel 213-373-1914 (SAN 158-8869).

Bk Pr Release, *(Book Press Release, Inc.; 0-936114)*, P.O. Box 762, Berkeley, CA 94701 Tel 415-843-5961 (SAN 214-2325).

BkMk, *(BkMk Press, (University of Missouri-Kansas City); 0-933532)*, UMKC, 5100 Rockhill Rd, 107 Cockefair Hall, Kansas City, MO 64110 Tel 816-276-1305 (SAN 207-7914).

Bks Australia
  See Australia N U P

Bks for All Times, *(Books for All Times, Inc.; 0-939360)*, P.O. Box 2, Alexandria, VA 22313 Tel 703-548-0457 (SAN 216-2253).

Bks for Bet Living, *(Books for Better Living; 0-88491; 0-87056)*, Div. of American Art Enterprises, Inc., 21322 Lassen St., Chatsworth, CA 91311 Tel 213-882-5900 (SAN 201-7334) Out of Business.

Bks for Libs, *(Books for Libraries, Inc.; 0-8369; 0-518)*, 1 Dupont St., Plainview, NY 11803 Tel 516-938-8100 (SAN 202-4098).

Black Buzzard, *(Black Buzzard Press; 0-938872)*, 4705 S. Eighth Rd., Arlington, VA 22024 (SAN 216-0196).

Black Letter, *(Black Letter Press; 0-912382)*, 663 Bridge St., N. W., Grand Rapids, MI 49504 Tel 616-454-7300 (SAN 201-436X).

Black River, *(Black River Writers; 0-916692)*, P.O. Box 15853, Sacramento, CA 95813 (SAN 206-4782); Orders to: P.O. Box 2491, East St. Louis, IL 62201 Tel 916-482-0799 (SAN 206-4790) Moved, Left No Forwarding Address.

Black Sparrow, *(Black Sparrow Press; 0-87685)*, P.O. Box 3993, Santa Barbara, CA 93130 Tel 805-687-5014 (SAN 201-4343).

Black Swan CT, *(Black Swan Books Ltd.; 0-933806)*, P.O. Box 327, Redding Ridge, CT 06876 Tel 203-938-9548 (SAN 213-4675).

Blackberry ME, *(Blackberry - Salted in the Shell)*, P.O. Box 186, Brunswick, ME 04011 Tel 207-833-6051 (SAN 207-7949) Do Not Confuse with Blackberry Books.

Blair, *(Blair, John F., Pub.; 0-910244; 0-89587)*, 1406 Plaza Dr., Winston-Salem, NC 27103 Tel 919-768-1374 (SAN 201-4319).

Blind John, *(Blind John Pubns.)*, 2740 Onyx St., Eugene, OR 97403 Tel 217-0906).

Bloch, *(Bloch Publishing Co.; 0-8197)*, 19 W. 21st St., New York, NY 10010 Tel 212-989-9104 (SAN 214-204X).

Blom, *(Blom, Benjamin, Inc.)*, Publisher Abbreviation Without Addresses Are for Titles That Are Out of Print. These Are Obsolete Abbreviations.

Blue Feather, *(Blue Feather Press; 0-932482)*, P.O. Box 5113, Santa Fe, NM 87502 Tel 505-983-2776 (SAN 211-9293).

Blue Lagoon, *(Blue Lagoon Pubs.; 0-9605338)*, 3606 Coldwater Canyon, Studio City, CA 91604 (SAN 215-9899).

Blue Moon Pr, *(Blue Moon Press, Inc.; 0-933188)*, c/o Univ. of Arizona, Dept. of English, Tucson, AZ 85721 (SAN 213-0157).

Blue Mtn Arts
  See Blue Mtn Pr CO

Blue Mtn Pr CO, *(Blue Mountain Press, Inc.; 0-88396)*, P.O. Box 4549, Boulder, CO 80306 Tel 303-449-0536 (SAN 201-4289).

Blue Oak, *(Blue Oak Press; 0-912950)*, P.O. Box 27, Sattley, CA 96124 (SAN 207-0383).

Blue Star, *(Blue Star Press; 0-939602)*, 163 Joralemon St., Suite 1144, Brooklyn, NY 11201 (SAN 216-616X); Dist. by: Caroline House Publishers, 920 W. Industrial Dr., Aurora, IL 60506 Tel 312-897-2050 (SAN 211-2280).

Blue Wind, *(Blue Wind Press; 0-912652)*, P.O. Box 7175, Berkeley, CA 94707 Tel 415-526-1905 (SAN 206-7099).

Bobbs, *(Bobbs-Merrill Co., Inc.; 0-672)*, A Thomas Audel Co., 630 Third Ave., New York, NY 10017 Tel 212-697-7050 (SAN 201-3959).

Bodine, *(Bodine & Associates, Inc.; 0-910254)*, 1101 St. Paul St., Baltimore, MD 21202 Tel 301-385-1103 (SAN 201-4246).

Boise St Univ, *(Boise State Univ.; 0-88430)*, Dept. of English, Boise, ID 83725 Tel 208-385-1246 (SAN 206-7080).

Bond Pub Co, *(Bond Publishing Co.; 0-939296)*, Div. of Progressive Artistic Communications Enterprises Inc., 226 Massachusetts Ave. N.E., Washington, DC 20002 Tel 202-547-3140 (SAN 220-1488).

Book Promo Unltd, *(Book Promotions Unlimited; 0-933586)*, P.O. Box 122, Flushing, MI 48433 Tel 313-659-6683 (SAN 212-7288).

Book Pub Co, *(Book Publishing Co., The; 0-913990)*, 156 Drakes Lane, Summertown, TN 38483 Tel 615-964-3571 (SAN 202-439X).

Bookcraft Inc, *(Bookcraft, Inc.; 0-88494)*, 1848 W. 2300, S., Salt Lake City, UT 84119 Tel 801-972-6180 (SAN 204-3998).

Bookfinger, *(Bookfinger; 0-913774)*, P.O. Box 487, Peter Stuyvesant Sta., New York, NY 10009 (SAN 202-4144).

Bookpeople, *(Bookpeople)*, 2940 Seventh St., Berkeley, CA 94710 Tel 415-549-3030 (SAN 168-9517).

Bookslinger, *(Bookslinger Editions)*, 330 E. Ninth St., St. Paul, MN 55101 Tel 612-221-0429 (SAN 169-4154); Box 16251, St. Paul, MN 55116 Tel 217-1457).

Borden, *(Borden Publishing Co.; 0-87505)*, 1855 W. Main St., Alhambra, CA 91801 Tel 213-283-5031 (SAN 201-419X).

Borgo Pr, *(Borgo Press; 0-89370)*, P.O. Box 2845, San Bernardino, CA 92406 Tel 714-884-5813 (SAN 208-9459).

Borogove Pr, *(Borogove Press; 0-9608246)*, 78 Bay View Ave., Belvedere, CA 94920 Tel 415-435-1152 (SAN 240-3447).

Boulevard, *(Boulevard Books; 0-910278)*, P.O. Box 89, Topanga, CA 90290 Tel 213-445-1036 (SAN 202-4179).

Bouregy, *(Bouregy, Thomas, & Co., Inc.; 0-8034)*, 22 E. 60th St., New York, NY 10022 Tel 212-753-8410 (SAN 201-4173).

Bowker, *(Bowker, R. R., Co.; 0-8352)*, A Xerox Information Co., 205 E. 42nd St., New York, NY 10017 Tel 212-916-1600 (SAN 214-1191); Orders to: P.O. Box 1807, Ann Arbor, MI 48106 (SAN 214-1205).

Bowling Green Univ, *(Bowling Green Univ., Popular Press; 0-87972)*, Bowling Green State Univ., Popular Culture Ctr., Bowling Green, OH 43403 Tel 419-372-2981 (SAN 201-4165).

Bowmar
  See Bowmar-Noble

Bowmar-Noble, *(Bowmar/Noble Pubs.; 0-8372; 0-8107)*, Div. of The Economy Company, 4563 Colorado Blvd., Los Angeles, CA 90039 Tel 213-247-8995 (SAN 201-4157).

Boxwood, *(Boxwood Press; 0-910286; 0-940168)*, 183 Ocean View Blvd., Pacific Grove, CA 93950 Tel 408-375-9110 (SAN 201-4149).

Brady Pr, *(Brady Press; 0-934620)*, Div. of KDI Productions, P.O. Box 10012, Jacksonville, FL 32207 Tel 904-733-8445 (SAN 213-2117).

Branden, *(Branden Press, Inc.; 0-8283)*, Box 843, 21 Sta. St., Brookline Village, MA 02147 Tel 617-734-2045 (SAN 201-4106).

Brandon, *(Brandon Books; 0-87056)*, Div. of American Art Enterprises, Inc., 21335 Roscoe Blvd., Canoga Park, CA 91304 Tel 213-999-4100 (SAN 201-7350).

Brandywine Bks, *(Brandywine Books; 0-9604986)*, 5020 73rd St., Suite B, San Diego, CA 92115 (SAN 216-020X).

Branford, *(Branford, Charles T., Co.; 0-8231)*, P.O. Box 41, Newton Centre, MA 02159 (SAN 201-9302).

Brasch & Brasch, *(Brasch & Brasch, Pubs.; 0-89554)*, 104 W. C St., Ontario, CA 91762 Tel 714-986-3631 (SAN 210-3443) Moved, Left No Forwarding Address.

Brasch & M
  See Brasch & Brasch

Braziller, *(Braziller, George, Inc.; 0-8076)*, One Park Ave., New York, NY 10016 Tel 212-889-0909 (SAN 201-9310).

Breaking Point, *(Breaking Point, Inc.; 0-917020)*, P.O. Box 328, Wharton, NJ 07885 Tel 201-361-7238 (SAN 208-0699).

Breitenbush Pubns, *(Breitenbush Pubns.; 0-932576)*, P.O. Box 02137, Portland, OR 97202 Tel 503-635-8050 (SAN 219-7707).

Brenner Bks, *(Brenner, Conrad, Books; 0-88116)*, 666 West End Ave., New York, NY 10025 Tel 212-724-8200 (SAN 238-2520).

Brethren, *(Brethren Press; 0-87178)*, 1451 Dundee Ave., Elgin, IL 60120 Tel 312-742-5100 (SAN 201-9329).

Brevet Pr, *(Brevet Press; 0-88498)*, Box 1404, Sioux Falls, SD 57101 Tel 605-339-2330 (SAN 201-7563).

Bridge Pub, *(Bridge Publishing Co.)*, 2500 Hamilton Blvd., South Plainfield, NJ 08805 Tel 201-754-0745 (SAN 239-5061).

Bridge Pubns Inc, *(Bridge Pubns. Inc.; 0-88404)*, 1414 N. Catalina St., Los Angeles, CA 90027 Tel 213-382-0382 (SAN 208-3884).

Bridgeberg, *(Bridgeberg Books; 0-915358)*, 7 Oak Ave., Kentfield, CA 94904 Tel 415-457-4963 (SAN 210-3028).

Brighton House, *(Brighton House Pubns.; 0-9603256)*, 3045 Brighton 8th St., Brooklyn, NY 11235 Tel 212-934-1349 (SAN 213-6570).

British Am Bks, *(British American Books; 0-89979)*, P. O. Box 302, Willits, CA 95490 (SAN 209-9353).

British Bk Ctr, *(British Book Center; 0-8277)*, Fairview Park, Elmsford, NY 10523 Tel 914-592-7700 (SAN 201-9361).

Broadman, *(Broadman Press; 0-8054)*, 127 Ninth Ave., N., Nashville, TN 37234 Tel 615-251-2544 (SAN 281-3440).

Broadside, *(Broadside Press Pubns.; 0-910296)*, 74 Glendale Ave., Highland Park, MI 48203 Tel 313-868-1585 (SAN 201-9388).

Brock Pub, *(Brock Publishing Co.; 0-930534)*, P.O. Box 1685, Chico, CA 95927 Tel 714-673-6310 (SAN 201-8616).

Brodart, *(Bro-Dart Publishing Co.; 0-87272)*, 1609 Memorial Ave., Williamsport, PA 17701 Tel 717-326-2461 (SAN 203-6711).

Brookfield Pub Co, *(Brookfield Publishing Co.; 0-604)*, Old Post Rd., Brookfield, VT 05036 Tel 802-276-3355 (SAN 213-4446).

Brown Bk, *(Brown Book Co.; 0-910294)*, 120 Secatogue Ave., Farmingdale, NY 11735 Tel 516-293-6969 (SAN 202-4276).

Bruccoli, *(Bruccoli Clark Books; 0-89723)*, 2006 Sumter St., Columbia, SC 29201 (SAN 209-3987).

Bruce Pub Co
  See Glencoe

Brunswick Pub, *(Brunswick Publishing Co.; 0-931494)*, P.O. Box 555, Lawrenceville, VA 23868 Tel 804-848-3865 (SAN 211-6332).

Bryans Imprint of **Dell**

Buccaneer Bks, *(Buccaneer Books; 0-89966)*, P.O. Box 168, Cutchogue, NY 11935 (SAN 209-1542).

Buddhist Text, *(Buddhist Text Translation Society; 0-917512)*, Box 217, City of Ten Thousand Buddhas, Talmage, CA 95481 Tel 707-462-0939 (SAN 281-3556); Orders to: Box 217, City of Ten Thousand Buddhas, Talmage, CA 94481 Tel 707-462-0939 (SAN 281-3564).

KEY TO PUBLISHERS' AND DISTRIBUTORS' ABBREVIATIONS

Bunkhouse, *(Bunkhouse Pubs., Inc.; 0-918628),* 123 N. Sultana Ave., Ontario, CA 91764 (SAN 215-062X).

Burke's Bk Store, *(Burke's Book Store, Inc.; 0-937130),* 634 Poplar Ave., Memphis, TN 38105 Tel 901-527-7484 (SAN 127-3124).

Burning Deck, *(Burning Deck; 0-930900; 0-930901),* 71 Elmgrove Ave., Providence, RI 02906 (SAN 207-7981).

Butterfly Pub, *(Butterfly Publishing, Inc.; 0-941254),* P.O. Box 30427, Santa Barbara, CA 93105 (SAN 237-935X); Dist. by: Richard Maher Sales, 90 W. Senior Way, Salt Lake City, UT 84115 (SAN 158-8141).

By Hand & Foot, *(By Hand & Foot, Ltd.; 0-938670),* Green River Rd., P.O. Box 611, Brattleboro, VT 05301 (SAN 215-8493).

BYR Imprint of **Random**

C & L Pub Co *(C&L Publishing Co.; 0-9605724),* 2525 Wilson Boulevrad, Arlington, VA 22201 (SAN 216-3462).

C B Pub & Dist
See Caratzas Pub Co

C B Slack
See Slack Inc

C C Thomas, *(Thomas, Charles C., Pub.; 0-398),* 2600 S. First St., Springfield, IL 62717 Tel 217-789-8980 (SAN 201-9485).

C E Tuttle, *(Tuttle, Charles E., Co., Inc.; 0-8048),* P.O. Box 410, 28 S. Main St., Rutland, VT 05701 Tel 802-773-8229 (SAN 213-2621).

C Fredericks, *(Fredericks, Carl),* Orders to: Circle Publications, P.O. Box 53, Lyndhurst, NJ 07071 (SAN 209-2093) Moved, Left No Forwarding Address.

C G Jung Frisco, *(Jung, C.G., Institute of San Francisco; 0-932630),* 2040 Gough St., San Francisco, CA 94109 (SAN 281-8493); Dist. by: Spring Pubs., P.O. Box 222069, Dallas, TX 75222 (SAN 282-6127).

C Horn, *(Horn, Calvin, Pubs., Inc.; 0-910750),* P.O. Box 4204, Albuquerque, NM 87106 Tel 505-268-9226 (SAN 201-9493).

C Jordan, *(Jordan, Carol; 0-9605360),* 654 Jerome St., Davis, CA 95616 (SAN 216-0463).

C N Aronson, *(Aronson, Charles N., Writer-Publisher; 0-915736),* 11520 Bixby Hill Road, Arcade, NY 14009 Tel 716-496-6002 (SAN 207-6144).

C N Potter Bks Imprint of **Crown**

C Woodward, *(Woodward, Claire; 0-9606812),* 10806 Fairway Court W., Sun City, AZ 85351 Tel 602-974-6919 (SAN 217-4618).

CA Assn Older, *(California Association for Older Americans; 0-917154),* Orders to: Volcano Press, 330 Ellis St., San Francisco, CA 94102 Tel 415-775-0918 (SAN 268-5795).

Caballus Pubs
See Printed Horse

Cadmus Eds, *(Cadmus Editions; 0-932274),* P.O. Box 4725, Santa Barbara, CA 93103 (SAN 212-887X); Dist. by: The Subterranean Co., P.O. Box 10233, Eugene, OR 97440 Tel 503-343-6324 (SAN 169-7102).

Caislan Pr, *(Caislan Press; 0-937444),* Box 28371, San Jose, CA 95159 Tel 408-264-5287 (SAN 284-9909); Orders to: Bookpeople Inc., 2940 Seventh St., Berkeley, CA 94710 (SAN 284-9917); Orders to: Baker and Taylor, Six Kibby Ave., Soomerville, NJ 08876 (SAN 284-9925); Orders to: Baker and Taylor, 501 S. Gladiola St., Momence, IL 60954 (SAN 284-9933).

Calamus Bks, *(Calamus Books; 0-930762),* Box 689, Cooper Sta., New York, NY 10276 (SAN 211-7002).

Caledonia Pr, *(Caledonia Press; 0-932282),* P.O. Box 245, Racine, WI 53401 Tel 414-637-6200 (SAN 211-8432).

Calico Pr, *(Calico Press; 0-912714),* P.O. Box 758, Twenty-Nine Palms, CA 92277 Tel 619-367-7661 (SAN 202-4993).

Calif Hist, *(California Historical Society; 0-910312),* P.O. Box 3370, San Diego, CA 92103 (SAN 281-3734); Orders to: 2090 Jackson St., San Francisco, CA 94109 Tel 415-567-1848 (SAN 281-3742).

Calif Pubns, *(California Pubns.; 0-917306),* P.O. Box 14, Calabasas, CA 91302 Tel 213-880-4181 (SAN 208-578X).

Calif Street, *(California Street; 0-915090),* 723 Dwight Way, Berkeley, CA 94710 Tel 415-549-2461 (SAN 207-673X).

Cambridge Bk, *(Cambridge Bk. Co.; 0-8428),* Div. of Esquire, Inc., 888 Seventh Ave., New York, NY 10022 Tel 212-957-5300 (SAN 169-5703).

Cambridge U Pr, *(Cambridge Univ. Press; 0-521),* 32 E. 57th St., New York, NY 10022 Tel 212-688-8888 (SAN 281-3750); Orders to: 510 North Ave., New Rochelle, NY 10801 Tel 914-235-0300 (SAN 281-3769).

Camden Hse, *(Camden House, Inc.; 0-938100),* Drawer 2025, Columbia, SC 29202 (SAN 215-9376).

Camelot Imprint of **Avon**

Cameo Pr, *(Cameo Press; 0-937868),* 373 Fifth Ave., Suite 1102, New York, NY 10016 (SAN 216-1125) Moved, left no forwarding address.

Camward Hse, *(Camward House; 0-936460),* P.O. Box 268, E. Patrick St. Sta., Frederick, MD 21701 (SAN 214-1833).

Canaveral, *(Canaveral Press, Inc.),* 315 Montana Ave., No. 203, Santa Monica, CA 90403 Tel 213-394-0514 (SAN 281-3777).

Canterbury Pr, *(Canterbury Press; 0-933993),* 5540 Vista Del Amigo, Anaheim, CA 92807 (SAN 212-890X).

Canyon Bks, *(Canyon Books; 0-89014),* Div. of American Art Enterprises, Inc., 21322 Lassen St., Chatsworth, CA 91311 (SAN 201-8691).

Capra Pr, *(Capra Press; 0-88496; 0-912264),* P.O. Box 2068, Santa Barbara, CA 93120 Tel 805-966-4590 (SAN 201-9620).

Caratzas Bros
See Caratzas Pub Co

Caratzas Pub Co, *(Caratzas Publishing Co., Inc.; 0-89241),* 481 Main St. (P.O. Box 210), New Rochelle, NY 10801 Tel 914-632-8487 (SAN 201-3134).

Caravan-Maritime, *(Caravan-Maritime Books; 0-917368),* 87-06 168th Place, Jamaica, NY 11432 Tel 212-526-1380 (SAN 201-8705) Do Not Confuse with Caravan Bks.

Carcosa, *(Carcosa; 0-913796),* P.O. Box 1064, Chapel Hill, NC 27514 Tel 919-929-2974 (SAN 202-5124).

Carlton, *(Carlton Press; 0-8062),* 84 Fifth Ave., New York, NY 10011 Tel 212-243-8800 (SAN 201-9655).

Carolina Edns, *(Carolina Editions, Inc.; 0-914056),* P.O. Box 3169, Greenwood, SC 29646 Tel 803-229-3503 (SAN 201-8721).

Carolina Wren, *(Carolina Wren Press, The; 0-932112),* 300 Barclay Rd., Chapel Hill, NC 27514 (SAN 213-0327).

Caroline Hse, *(Caroline Hse., Inc.),* 920 W. Industrial Dr., Aurora, IL 60506 Tel 312-897-2050 (SAN 211-2280).

Carpenter Pr, *(Carpenter Press; 0-914140),* Rte. 4, Pomeroy, OH 45769 Tel 614-992-7520 (SAN 206-4650).

Carroll Coll, *(Carroll College Press; 0-916120),* 100 North East Ave., Waukesha, WI 53186 Tel 414-547-1211 (SAN 208-5879).

Casa Bautista, *(Casa Bautista De Publicaciones; 0-311),* P.O. Box 4255, 7000 Alabama St., El Paso, TX 79914 Tel 915-566-9656 (SAN 220-0139). Imprints: Edit Mundo (Editorial Mundo Hispano).

Cats Pajamas, *(Cat's Pajamas Press; 0-916866),* 527 Lyman Ave., Oak Park, IL 60304 Tel 312-386-5137 (SAN 207-8015).

Causeway, *(Causeway Books; 0-88356),* Div. of Promotional Book Corp., 95 Madison Ave., New York, NY 10016 Tel 212-725-4970 (SAN 205-6100).

Cave Bks MO, *(Cave Books; 0-939748),* 756 Harvard Ave., St. Louis, MO 63130 Tel 314-862-7646 (SAN 216-7220).

Caxton, *(Caxton Printers, Ltd.; 0-87004),* P.O. Box 700, Caldwell, ID 83605 Tel 208-459-7421 (SAN 201-9698).

Cayucos, *(Cayucos Books; 0-9600372),* P.O. Box 2113, Monterey, CA 93940 Tel 408-375-5289 (SAN 208-5887).

CC Imprint of **WSP**

CCPr Imprint of **Macmillan**

Cedar Crest Bks, *(Cedar Crest Books; 0-910291),* P.O. Box 36, Cochituate, MA 01778 Tel 617-491-0683 (SAN 241-2837).

Cedar Rock, *(Cedar Rock Press; 0-930024),* 1121 Madeline, New Braunfels, TX 78130 Tel 512-625-6002 (SAN 213-2699).

Cedarwinds, *(Cedarwinds Publishing Co.),* Drawer A, Cedar Mountain, NC 28718 Tel 904-893-6252 (SAN 212-1700).

Celestial Arts, *(Celestial Arts Publishing Co.; 0-912310; 0-89087),* P.O. Box 7327, Berkeley, CA 94707 (SAN 284-9941); 231 Adrian Rd., Millbrae, CA 94030 Tel 415-692-4500 (SAN 284-995X) (SAN 201-9701).

Cellar, *(Cellar Bk. Shop),* 18090 Wyoming, Detroit, MI 48221 Tel 313-861-1776 (SAN 213-4330).

Centaur, *(Centaur Books, Inc.; 0-87818),* 799 Broadway, New York, NY 10003 Tel 212-677-1720 (SAN 201-7725).

Centaur Pubn VA, *(Centaur Publication Co.; 0-932700),* 7807 Stovall Court, Lorton, VA 22079 (SAN 212-0771).

Centennial, *(Centennial Press; 0-8220),* Div. of Cliff's Notes, Inc., P.O. Box 80728, Lincoln, NE 68501 Tel 402-477-6971 (SAN 206-6339).

Centurion Pr, *(Centurion Press),* Drawer 62, Los Angeles, CA 90028 (SAN 206-4839).

Century Bookbindery, *(Century Bookbindery; 0-89984),* P.O. Box 6471, Philadelphia, PA 19145 (SAN 209-2441).

Century Twenty One
See R & E Res Assoc

Chalfant Pr, *(Chalfant Press, Inc.; 0-912494),* P.O. Box 787, Bishop, CA 93514 Tel 619-873-3535 (SAN 203-6347).

Chandler & Sharp, *(Chandler & Sharp Pubs., Inc.; 0-88316),* 11A Commercial Blvd., Novato, CA 94947 Tel 415-883-2353 (SAN 205-6127).

Chandler Pub, *(Chandler Publishing Co.),* Publisher Abbreviation Without Addresses Are for Titles That Are Out of Print. These Are Obsolete Abbreviations. Publisher Was Aquired by Har-Row College.

Chantry Pr, *(Chantry Press; 0-941608),* P.O. Box 144, Midland Park, NJ 07432 Tel 201-423-2921 (SAN 239-0752).

Charles Pub, *(Charles Publishing Co.; 0-912880),* 12125 Riverside Dr., Suite 201, North Hollywood, CA 91607 Tel 213-762-0633 (SAN 201-9779).

Charles River Bks, *(Charles River Books; 0-89182),* 1 Thompson Square, Boston, MA 02129 Tel 617-242-5111 (SAN 209-2530).

Charterhouse, *(Charterhouse Books, Inc.; 0-88327),* Affiliate of David McKay Co., Inc., 750 Third Ave., New York, NY 10017 (SAN 201-9787).

Chatham Bkseller, *(Chatham Bookseller; 0-911860),* 8 Green Village Rd., Madison, NJ 07940 Tel 201-822-1361 (SAN 203-641X).

Chatham Pr, *(Chatham Press; 0-85699),* 143 Sound Beach, Old Greenwich, CT 06870 Tel 203-637-4531 (SAN 201-9795); Dist. by: The Devin-Adair Co., Old Greenwich, CT 06870 (SAN 213-750X).

Chatto-Bodley-Jonathan
See Merrimack Publishers' Circle

Cheap St, *(Cheap Street; 0-941826),* Route 2, Box 293, New Castle, VA 24127 Tel 703-864-6288 (SAN 239-1783).

Chelsea Hse, *(Chelsea House Pubs.; 0-87754),* 133 Christopher St., New York, NY 10014 Tel 212-924-6414 (SAN 206-7609); Dist. by: Scribner Book Companies, 597 Fifth Ave., New York, NY 10017 Tel 212-486-2700 (SAN 201-002X).

Cherry Valley, *(Cherry Valley Editions; 0-916156),* 2314 Georgian Woods Pl., Wheaton, MD 20902 Tel 301-946-0947 (SAN 208-1482); Dist. by: Writers & Books, 892 S. Clinton Ave., Rochester, NY 14620 (SAN 156-9678).

Cherubim, *(Cherubim; 0-938574),* P.O. Box 75, Ft. Tilden, NY 11695 (SAN 215-8523).

Cheyenne Cor, *(Cheyenne Corral; 0-9609648),* 520 E. 27th St., Cheyenne, WY 82001 Tel 307-638-6846 (SAN 281-4099).

Chicago Review, *(Chicago Review Press, Inc.; 0-914090; 0-914091),* 213 W. Institute Place, Chicago, IL 60610 Tel 312-337-0747 (SAN 213-5744); 820 N. Franklin, Chicago, IL 60610 Tel 312-337-5457 (SAN 213-5744); 215 W. Ohio St., Chicago, IL 60610 Tel 312-337-5457 (SAN 213-764X).

Chick Pubns, *(Chick Pubns.; 0-937958),* P.O. Box 662, Chino, CA 91710 Tel 714-987-0771 (SAN 211-7770).

Child Focus Co, *(Child Focus Co.; 0-933892),* 1230 Keats St., Manhattan Beach, CA 90266 Tel 213-379-4144 (SAN 207-5199).

KEY TO PUBLISHERS' AND DISTRIBUTORS' ABBREVIATIONS

Chilton, *(Chilton Book Co.; 0-8019),* Orders to: School, Library Services, Chilton Way, Radnor, PA 19089 Tel 215-964-4729 (SAN 202-1552).

China Bks, *(China Books & Periodicals, Inc.; 0-8351),* 2929 24th St., San Francisco, CA 94110 Tel 415-282-2994 (SAN 214-1213).

Chong-Donnie, *(Chong-Donnie; 0-938918),* 246 E. 62nd St., New York, NY 10021 (SAN 216-1087) Moved, Left No Forwarding Address.

Choosen Bks Pub
See Chosen Bks Zondervan

Chosen Bks Zondervan, *(Chosen Books of the Zondervan Corp.; 0-912376),* Lincoln, VA 22078 Tel 703-338-4131 (SAN 202-1587); Dist. by: The Zonervan Corp., 1415 Lake Dr. S.E., Grand Rapids, MI 48506 Tel 800-253-1309 (SAN 203-6094).

Chr Classics, *(Christian Classics, Inc.; 0-87061),* P.O. Box 30, Westminster, MD 21157 Tel 301-848-3065 (SAN 203-6525).

Chr Lit, *(Christian Literature Crusade, Inc.; 0-87508),* Pennsylvania Ave., Fort Washington, PA 19034 (SAN 202-1609).

Chris Mass, *(Christopher Publishing House (Mass); 0-8158),* 1405 Hanover St., Box 1014, West Hanover, MA 02339 Tel 617-878-4656 (SAN 202-1625).

Christian Herald, *(Christian Herald Books; 0-915684; 0-86693),* 40 Overlook Dr., Chappaqua, NY 10514 Tel 914-769-9000 (SAN 208-1474).

Christophers Bks, *(Christopher's Books; 0-87922),* 390 62nd St., Oakland, CA 94618 Tel 415-428-1120 (SAN 212-5870).

Chronicle Bks, *(Chronicle Books; 0-87701),* Div. of Chronicle Publishing Co., 870 Market St., Suite 917, San Francisco, CA 94102 Tel 415-777-7240 (SAN 202-165X).

Chthon Pr, *(Chthon Press),* 77 Mark Vincent Dr., Westford, MA 01886 (SAN 208-2438).

Cider Pr, *(Cider Press; 0-914994),* P.O. Box 10115, Columbus, OH 43201 (SAN 207-1088) Moved, Left No Forwarding Address.

Circinatum Pr, *(Circinatum Press; 0-931594),* Box 99309, Tacoma, WA 98499 (SAN 211-5522) Tel 206-588-2503.

Citadel Pr, *(Citadel Press; 0-8065),* Subs. of Lyle Stuart, Inc., 120 Enterprise Ave., Secaucus, NJ 07094 Tel 212-736-0007 (SAN 202-1676).

City Lights, *(City Lights Books; 0-87286),* 261 Columbus Ave., San Francisco, CA 94133 Tel 415-362-8193 (SAN 202-1684); Dist. by: Subterranean Co., P.O. Box 10233, Eugene, OR 97440 Tel 503-343-6324 (SAN 169-7102).

Claitors, *(Claitors Publishing Division; 0-87511),* 3165 S. Acadian at Interstate 10, Box 239, Baton Rouge, LA 70821 (SAN 206-8346).

Clarion Imprint of HM

CLCB Pr, *(CLCB Press),* Div. of CLCBI International, 5901 Plainfield Dr., Charlotte, NC 28215 (SAN 211-2892).

Clearwater Pub, *(Clearwater Publishing Co.; 0-8287; 0-88354),* 1995 Broadway, New York, NY 10023 Tel 212-873-2100 (SAN 201-8969) Primarily microfiche on American Indian & peace studies; microfiche distributor for Alpha Com, The Architectural Press, Bibliotheque Nationale, Centre National de Recherche Scientifique (France), Elsevier Sequoia, France Expansion, Interdocumentation Co., Irish Microfilms, Microdditions Hachette, Microeditions Universitaires, Microform Ltd., Mikropress, Georg Olms Verlag, OECD, Oxford University Press Microfiche Editions, Presses de la Fondation National des Sciences Politiques, Publications Orientalistes de France, K G Saur, World Microfilms Publications, Yushodo Film Publications.

Cliffs, *(Cliff's Notes, Inc.; 0-8220),* 1701 "P" St., Lincoln, NE 68501 Tel 402-477-6971 (SAN 202-1706).

Cloud Ent, *(Cloud Enterprises; 0-911167),* P.O. Box 1006, Orinda, CA 94563 Tel 415-945-1210 (SAN 281-5125); Dist. by: Bookpeople, 2940 Seventh St., Berkely, CA 94710 Tel 415-549-3030 (SAN 168-9517); Dist. by: U.S. Game Systems, 38 E. 32nd St., New York, NY 10016 Tel 212-685-4300 (SAN 282-7336).

CLP Pubs, *(CLP Pubs.; 0-89051),* Subs. Creation-Life Publishers, Inc., P.O. Box 15666, San Diego, CA 92115 Tel 619-449-9400 (SAN 205-6119).

CN Imprint of Har-Row

Coach Hse, *(Coach House Press, Inc.),* 53 W. Jackson Blvd., Chicago, IL 60604 Tel 312-922-8993 (SAN 201-7709).

Cobblesmith, *(Cobblesmith; 0-89166),* Box 191, RFD 1, Freeport, ME 04032 Tel 207-865-6495 (SAN 210-346X).

Coda Pr, *(Coda Press, Inc.; 0-930956),* 700 W. Badger Rd., Suite 101, Madison, WI 53713 (SAN 211-4968) Moved, left no forwarding address.

Colby, *(Colby College Press; 0-910394),* Library, Waterville, ME 04901 Tel 207-873-0311 (SAN 203-5669).

Cole-Outreach, *(Cole, David M./Outreach Books),* P.O. Box 425, Corona, CA 91720 Tel 714-735-8701 (SAN 214-2589).

Coll & U Pr
See New Coll U Pr

Coll Kids Cook, *(College Kids Cookbooks; 0-912848),* 624 N. Bailey Ave., Fort Worth, TX 76107 Tel 817-626-4083 (SAN 201-761X).

Collectors Choice, *(Collector's Choice; 0-9602742),* c/o French-Bray Inc., P.O. Box 698, Glen Burnie, MD 21061 Tel 301-768-6000 (SAN 204-2479).

Collegiate Pub, *(Collegiate Publishing, Inc.; 0-88429),* 1010 Second Ave., Suite 1808, San Diego, CA 92101 Tel 714-234-3231 (SAN 202-1730).

Collier Imprint of Macmillan

Collins Pubs, *(Collins, William, Pubs., Inc.),* 2080 W. 117th St., Cleveland, OH 44111 Tel 216-941-6930 (SAN 205-4930); 200 Madison Ave., Suite 1405, New York, NY 10016 (SAN 205-4949).

Collins-World
See Collins Pubs

Colo Assoc, *(Colorado Associated Univ. Press, Univ. of Colorado; 0-87081),* 1338 Grandview Ave. Box 480, Univ. of Colorado, Boulder, CO 80309 Tel 303-492-7191 (SAN 202-1749).

Colton Bk, *(Colton Book Imports),* P.O. Box 526, San Francisco, CA 94101 (SAN 204-7136).

Columbia U Pr, *(Columbia Univ. Press; 0-231),* 562 W. 113th St., New York, NY 10025 Tel 212-678-6777 (SAN 212-2472); Orders to: 136 S. Broadway, Irvington-on-Hudson, NY 10533 Tel 914-591-9111 (SAN 212-2480).

Commonsense, *(Commonsense Pubns.; 0-911734),* 1925 Vermont Ave., Toledo, OH 43624 (SAN 206-9059).

Commonwealth Pr, *(Commonwealth Press, Inc.; 0-89227),* Box 3547, Radford, VA 24141 Tel 703-639-2475 (SAN 281-515X); Orders to: 415 First St., Radford, VA 24141 Tel 703-639-2476 (SAN 281-5168).

Compass Va, *(Compass Pubns., Inc.; 0-910422),* 1117 N. 19th St., Arlington, VA 22209 Tel 703-524-3136 (SAN 203-5774).

CompCare, *(CompCare Pubns.; 0-89638),* 2415 Annapolis Lane, Minneapolis, MN 55441 Tel 612-559-4800 (SAN 211-464X).

Comstock, *(Comstock Publishing Associates),* Dist. by: Cornell Univ. Press, Sales Manager, 124 Roberts Place, Ithaca, NY 14850 (SAN 281-5672).

Comstock Edns, *(Comstock Editions, Inc.; 0-89174),* 3030 Bridgeway Blvd., Sausalito, CA 94965 Tel 415-332-3216 (SAN 207-6454); Orders to: Comstock Book Distributors Inc., 1380 W. Second Ave., Eugene, OR 97402 Tel 503-686-8001 (SAN 207-6462).

Con Brio, *(Con Brio Press; 0-9602068),* 8708 Morris Rd., Minneapolis, MN 55437 (SAN 212-3428).

Concordia, *(Concordia Publishing House; 0-570),* 3558 S. Jefferson Ave., St. Louis, MO 63118 Tel 314-664-7000 (SAN 202-1781).

Condor Pub Co, *(Condor Publishing Co., Inc.; 0-89516),* 29 E. Main St., Westport, CT 06880 Tel 203-226-9591 (SAN 210-3494) Moved, Left No Forwarding Address.

Confluence Pr, *(Confluence Press, Inc.; 0-917652),* Spalding Hall, Lewis-Clark Campus, Lewiston, ID 83501 Tel 208-746-2341 (SAN 209-5467).

Congdon & Lattes
See Congdon & Weed

Congdon & Weed, *(Congdon & Weed; 0-86553),* 298 Fifth Ave., 7th Fl., New York, NY 10001 Tel 212-736-4883 (SAN 214-3585); Dist. by: St. Martin's Press, 175 Fifth Ave., New York, NY 10010 Tel 212-674-5151 (SAN 200-2132).

Conner & Sanderson, *(Conner-Sanderson Publications; 0-9606904),* Dist. by: Coleman Graphics Inc., 99 Milbar Blvd., Farmingdale, NY 11735 (SAN 238-1508).

Consortium
See McGrath

Consortium Pr, *(Consortium Books),* Publisher Abbreviation Without Addresses Are for Titles That Are Out of Print. These Are Obsolete Abbreviations. Publisher Was Aquired by McGrath.

Contemp Bks, *(Contemporary Books, Inc.; 0-8092),* 180 N. Michigan Ave., Chicago, IL 60601 Tel 312-782-9181 (SAN 202-5493) Formerly Named Henry Regnery Co.

Continent Pub, *(Continental Publishing House; 0-915002),* 2116 N.E. 18th Ave., Portland, OR 97212 Tel 503-282-1383 (SAN 211-3112) Moved, left no forwarding address.

Continuum, *(Continuum Publishing Co.; 0-8264),* 370 Lexington Ave., New York, NY 10017 Tel 212-532-3650 (SAN 213-8220); Dist. by: Scribner Book Co, 201 Willowbrook Blvd, Wayne, NJ 07470 Tel 212-421-4800 (SAN 282-602X).

Cook, *(Cook, David C., Publishing Co.; 0-89191; 0-912692),* 850 N. Grove Ave., Elgin, IL 60120 Tel 312-741-2400 (SAN 206-0981).

Cookie Pr, *(Cookie Press; 0-938236),* 4225 University, Des Moines, IA 50311 Tel 515-255-3552 (SAN 209-7214).

Cooper Sq, *(Cooper Square Pubs., Inc.; 0-8154),* 81 Adams Dr., Totowa, NJ 07512 Tel 201-256-8600 (SAN 281-5621).

Copper Beech, *(Copper Beech Press),* Box 1852, Brown University, Providence, RI 02912 (SAN 212-8063).

Copper Canyon, *(Copper Canyon Press; 0-914742),* P.O. Box 271, Port Townsend, WA 98368 Tel 206-385-4925 (SAN 206-488X).

Copple Hse, *(Copple House Books; 0-932298),* Orders to: Copple House Books, Roads' End, Lakemont, GA 30552 Tel 404-782-2134 (SAN 281-5648).

Coral Reef, *(Coral Reef Pubns., Inc.; 0-914042; 0-86540),* Box 918, Davenport, FL 33837 (SAN 201-775X).

Core Collection, *(Core Collection Books, Inc.; 0-8486),* 11 Middle Neck Rd., Great Neck, NY 11021 Tel 516-466-3676 (SAN 208-6123).

CORE Collection
See Core Collection

Corinth Bks, *(Corinth Books; 0-87091),* 6912 Ridgeway Ave., Chevy Chase, MD 20815 Tel 301-652-1016 (SAN 281-5656); Orders to: Bookslinger, 330 E. Ninth St., St. Paul, MN 55101 (SAN 281-5664).

Cornell Maritime, *(Cornell Maritime Press, Inc.; 0-87033),* P.O. Box 456, Centreville, MD 21617 Tel 301-758-1075 (SAN 203-5901).

Cornell SE Asia, *(Cornell Univ., Southeast Asia Program; 0-87727),* 120 Uris Hall, Ithaca, NY 14853 Tel 607-256-2378 (SAN 206-6416).

Cornell U Pr, *(Cornell Univ. Pr.; 0-8014),* 124 Roberts Pl., P.O. Box 250, Ithaca, NY 14850 Tel 607-257-7000 (SAN 281-5672); Orders to: 714 Cascadila St., Ithaca, NY 14850 Tel 607-277-2211 (SAN 281-5680).

Corner Hse, *(Corner House Pubs.; 0-87928),* 1321 Green River Rd., Williamstown, MA 01267 Tel 413-458-8561 (SAN 203-5936).

Corning, *(Corning Museum of Glass; 0-87290),* Corning Glass Ctr., Corning, NY 14831 Tel 607-937-5371 (SAN 202-1897).

Cornwall Bks, *(Cornwall Books; 0-8453),* 4 Cornwall Dr., East Brunswick, NJ 08816 (SAN 219-7804).

Corona Pub, *(Corona Publishing Co.; 0-931722),* 1037 S. Alamo, San Antonio, TX 78210 Tel 512-227-1771 (SAN 211-8491).

Coronado Pr, *(Coronado Press, Inc.; 0-87291),* P.O. Box 3232, Lawrence, KS 66044 Tel 913-843-5988 (SAN 201-7776).

KEY TO PUBLISHERS' AND DISTRIBUTORS' ABBREVIATIONS

Corwin, *(Corwin Books; 0-89474),* One Century Plaza, 2029 Century Park, E., Los Angeles, CA 90067 Tel 213-552-9111 (SAN 208-614X); Dist. by: Independent News, 75 Rockefeller Plaza, New York, NY 10019 (SAN 208-6158).

Cotton Lane, *(Cotton Lane Press; 0-9604810),* 2 Cotton Lane, Augusta, GA 30902 Tel 404-722-0232 (SAN 281-5699); Dist. by: Pelican Publishing Co., 1101 Monroe St., Gretna, LA 70053 Tel 504-368-1175 (SAN 212-0623); Dist. by: Copple House Books, Road's End, Lakemont, GA 30552 Tel 404-782-2134 (SAN 269-3828).

Country Print, *(Country Printing, Inc.),* P.O. Box 240, Pequot Lakes, MN 56472 Tel 218-568-8521 (SAN 208-189X).

Countryman, *(Countryman Press, Inc.; 0-914378),* Woodstock, VT 05091 Tel 802-457-1049 (SAN 206-4901). *Imprints:* Foul Play (Foul Play Press).

Courthouse Pr, *(Courthouse Press; 0-911736),* P.O. Box 205, Floral Park, NY 11002 Tel 516-437-9463 (SAN 203-6010) Moved, Left No Forwarding Address.

Cove Pub Co
See R H Barnes

Covenant, *(Covenant Press; 0-910452),* 3200 W. Foster Ave., Chicago, IL 60625 Tel 312-478-4676 (SAN 203-6029).

Cow Puddle, *(Cow Puddle Press; 0-9600672),* Sunset Trading Post, Sunset, TX 76270 Tel 817-872-2027 (SAN 206-5282).

Cowley Pubns, *(Cowley Pubns.),* 980 Memorial Dr., Cambridge, MA 02138 (SAN 213-9987).

Coyote, *(Coyote Books; 0-940556),* P.O. Box 629, Brunswick, ME 04011 (SAN 212-6060).

Cramer Bkstore, *(Cramer Bookstore; 0-913118),* P.O. Box 7235, Kansas City, MO 64113 (SAN 203-607X).

Crane-Russak Co, *(Crane, Russak & Co., Inc.; 0-8448),* 3 E. 44th St, New York, NY 10017 Tel 212-867-1490 (SAN 202-1978).

Creation Hse, *(Creation House; 0-88419),* 396 E. St. Charles Rd., Wheaton, IL 60188 Tel 312-653-1472 (SAN 202-2001).

Creation-Life
See CLP Pubs

Creation Sci, *(Creation Science Research Center; 0-88213),* P.O. Box 23195, San Diego, CA 92123 Tel 714-569-8673 (SAN 203-6096).

Creations Unltd, *(Creations Unlimited; 0-938900),* P.O. Box 2591, Farmington Hills, MI 48018 (SAN 216-1109).

Creative Arts Bk, *(Creative Arts Book Co.; 0-916870),* 833 Bancroft Way, Berkeley, CA 94710 Tel 415-848-4777 (SAN 208-4880).

Creative Bk Co, *(Creative Book Co.; 0-88409),* 8210 Varna Ave., Van Nuys, CA 91402-5599 Tel 818-988-2334 (SAN 203-610X).

Creative Ed, *(Creative Education, Inc.; 0-87191),* 123 S. Broad St., PO. Box 227, Mankato, MN 56001 Tel 507-388-6273 (SAN 269-512X).

Creative Lit, *(Creative Literature, Inc.; 0-9609110),* P.O. Box 9975, Phoenix, AZ 85068 Tel 602-274-4151 (SAN 281-5753); 1521 E. Flower St., Phoenix, AZ 85014 (SAN 281-5761).

Creek Hse, *(Creek House; 0-9600490),* P.O. Box 793, Ojai, CA 93023 Tel 805-646-3200 (SAN 203-6126).

Crescent Pubns, *(Crescent Pubns., Inc.; 0-914184),* 5410 Wilshire Blvd., Suite 400, Los Angeles, CA 90036 (SAN 202-2036).

Crest *Imprint of* **Fawcett**

Criterion Bks, *(Criterion Bks., Inc.; 0-200),* c/o Harper & Row, Pubs., 10 E. 53 St., New York, NY 10022 (SAN 215-3734).

Cross Cult, *(Cross-Cultural Communications; 0-89304),* 239 Wynsum Ave., Merrick, NY 11566 Tel 516-868-5635 (SAN 208-6212).

Crossing Pr, *(Crossing Press, The; 0-89594; 0-912278),* Box 640, Trumansburg, NY 14886 Tel 607-387-6217 (SAN 202-2060).

Crossroad NY, *(Crossroad Publishing Co.; 0-8245),* 370 Lexington Ave., New York, NY 10017 Tel 212-532-3650 (SAN 287-0118); Dist. by: Sribner Book Co, 201 Willowbrool Blvd, Wayne, NJ 07670 (SAN 287-0126).

Crossroads Pr, *(Crossroads Press, Inc.),* P.O. Box 833, Honolulu, HI 96808 Tel 808-521-0021 (SAN 218-6950).

Crossway Bks *Imprint of* **Good News**

Crown, *(Crown Pubs., Inc.; 0-517),* 1 Park Ave., New York, NY 10016 Tel 212-532-9200 (SAN 213-4357); 419 Park Ave., New York, NY 10016 (SAN 282-6038). *Imprints:* Arlington Hse (Arlington House); C N Potter Bks (Potter, Clarkson, N. Books); Harmony (Harmony Books).

Crusade Pubs, *(Crusade Pubns),* 11326 Ranchito St., El Monte, CA 91732 (SAN 203-8595) Religious Publications Only.

Cruzada Span Pubns, *(Cruzada Spanish Pubns.; 0-933648),* P.O. Box 650909, Miami, FL 33165 (SAN 214-2376).

Crystal Pr, *(Crystal Press, Ltd.; 0-938108),* P.O. Box 215, Crystal Bay, NV 89402 (SAN 239-5282).

CSS Pub, *(C.S.S. Publishing Co.; 0-89536),* 628 S. Main St., Lima, OH 45804 Tel 419-227-1818 (SAN 207-0707).

CSUN, *(California State Univ., Northridge Library; 0-937048),* 18111 Nordhoff St., Northridge, CA 91330 Tel 213-885-2271 (SAN 203-8722).

Ctr Western Studies, *(Center for Western Studies; 0-931170),* Augustana College, Sioux Falls, SD 57197 Tel 605-336-4007 (SAN 211-4844).

Cultural Pr, *(Cultural Press; 0-910476),* 517 Madison St., Waukesha, WI 53186 (SAN 203-8757).

Cumberland, *(Cumberland Journal),* P.O. Box 2648, Harrisburg, PA 17105 (SAN 219-161X).

Cumberland Pr, *(Cumberland Press; 0-87027),* 136 Main St., Freeport, ME 04032 Tel 207-865-4951 (SAN 203-2090).

Cummington, *(Cummington Press/Cleary House; 0-914026),* Univ. of Nebraska at Omaha, P.O. Box 688, Omaha, NE 68101 (SAN 203-8765).

Curbstone, *(Curbstone Press; 0-915306),* 321 Jackson St., Willimantic, CT 06226 Tel 203-423-9190 (SAN 209-4282); Orders to: Ziesing Brothers, 768 Main St., Willimatic, CT 06226 Tel 203-423-5836 (SAN 200-4232).

Curbstone Pub NY TX, *(Curbstone Publishing; 0-931604),* P.O. Box 1613, New York, NY 10116 (SAN 281-5796); Orders to: P.O. Box 7445, Austin, TX 78712 Tel 512-444-9463 (SAN 281-580X).

Curtis, *(Curtis Books Inc.; 0-502),* 600 Third Ave., New York, NY 10017 (SAN 206-6300).

Curtis Pub Co, *(Curtis Publishing Co., The; 0-89387),* Saturday Evening Post Book Div., 1100 Waterway Blvd., Indianapolis, IN 46206 Tel 317-634-1100 (SAN 216-3624).

Custom Hse, *(Custom House Press; 0-940560),* 2900 Newark Rd., P.O. Box 2369, Zanesville, OH 43701 (SAN 216-3632).

D Brown Bks, *(Brown, D., Books),* 511 Capp St., San Francisco, CA 94110 Tel 415-648-3653 (SAN 209-4290).

D Jenkins, *(Jenkins, Doris),* 4827 Hillside Ave., Lincoln, NE 68506 Tel 402-488-4200 (SAN 208-2624).

D Kermode, *(Kermode, Doug; 0-9602202),* P.O. Box 8087, Long Beach, CA 90808 (SAN 212-3665).

D Landman
See Dennis-Landman

D M Grant, *(Grant, Donald M., Publisher, Inc; 0-937986),* West Kingston, RI 02892 Tel 401-783-3266 (SAN 281-7535); Dist. by: Pacific Comics, Inc., 4887 Ronson Ct., Suite E, San Diego, CA (SAN 169-0124); Dist. by: Bud Plant Inc., 13393 Grass Valley Dr., Suite 7, P.O. Box 1886, Grass Valley, CA 95945 (SAN 268-5086); Dist. by: F. & S.F. Book Co., P.O. Box 415, Staten Island, NY 10302 (SAN 169-6270).

D Ponicsan, *(Ponicsan, Darryl),* P.O. Box 1596, Ojai, CA 93023 Tel 805-646-4215 (SAN 206-8192).

D Van Nostrand
See Van Nos Reinhold

D White, *(White, David, Co.; 0-87250),* One Pleasant Ave., Port Washington, NY 11050 Tel 516-944-9325 (SAN 201-2936).

Da Capo, *(Da Capo Press, Inc.; 0-306),* 233 Spring St., New York, NY 10013 Tel 212-620-8000 (SAN 201-2944).

Dale Books Inc, *(Dale Books, Inc.; 0-89559),* Subs. of Davis Pubns. Inc., 380 Lexington Ave., New York, NY 10017 Tel 212-949-9190 (SAN 211-1918).

Damien-Dutton, *(Damien Dutton Society for Leprosy Aid),* 616 Bedford Ave, Bellmore, NY 11710 (SAN 224-3482).

Dan River Pr, *(Dan River Press; 0-89754),* P.O. Box 123, S. Thomaston, ME 04858 Tel 207-594-4751 (SAN 212-7377).

Dansk Blue Bk, *(Dansk Blue Books; 0-87977),* Dist. by: Parliament News, Inc., 21314 Lassen St., Chatsworth, CA 91311 (SAN 282-6585).

Darby Bks, *(Darby Books; 0-89987),* P.O. Box 148, Darby, PA 19023 Tel 215-583-4550 (SAN 204-2371).

Daring Pr, *(Daring Press; 0-938936),* 1308 Harrison Rd., Canton, OH 44706 (SAN 216-0293).

Daughterayne, *(Daughterayne; 0-942762),* 3844 Third Ave., San Diego, CA 92103 Tel 714-298-4246 (SAN 238-8456).

Daughters, *(Daughters Publishing Co., Inc.; 0-913780),* MS 590, P.O. Box 42999, Houston, TX 77042 (SAN 206-6343).

Davenport, *(Davenport, May, Publishers; 0-9603118; 0-943864),* 26313 Purissima Rd., Los Altos Hills, CA 94022 Tel 415-948-6499 (SAN 212-467X).

David & Charles, *(David & Charles, Inc.; 0-7153),* P.O. Box 57, North Pomfret, VT 05053 Tel 802-457-1911 (SAN 213-8859).

Davis Pubns, *(Davis Pubns., Inc.; 0-89559),* 380 Lexington Ave., New York, NY 10017 Tel 212-557-9100 (SAN 204-2347).

DAW Bks, *(DAW Bks.; 0-87997),* c/o New American Library, 1633 Broadway, New York, NY 10019 Tel 212-397-8000 (SAN 206-8079).

Dawn Horse Pr, *(Dawn Horse Press; 0-913922),* 119 Paul Drive, San Rafael, CA 94903 Tel 707-994-8281 (SAN 201-3029); Dist. by: Dawn Horse Press, P.O. Box 3680, Clearlake Highlands, CA 95422 Tel 707-994-8281 (SAN 201-3029).

Dawn Pr, *(Dawn Press; 0-933704),* 1011 Jeffrey Rd., Wilmington, DE 19810 (SAN 221-2269).

Dawsons, *(Dawson's Book Shop; 0-87093),* 535 N. Larchmont Blvd., Los Angeles, CA 90004 Tel 213-469-2186 (SAN 201-3045).

Dayton Labs, *(Dayton Laboratories; 0-916750),* 3235 Dayton Ave., Lorain, OH 44055 Tel 216-246-1397 (SAN 208-1946).

De Graff, *(De Graff, John, Inc.; 0-8286),* Clinton Corners, NY 12514 (SAN 201-3061); Dist. by: International Marine Publishing Co., 21 Elm St., Camden, ME 04843 Tel 207-236-4342 (SAN 202-716X).

De Gruyter, *(De Gruyter, Walter, Inc.; 3-11; 0-89925),* 200 Saw Mill River Rd., Hawthorne, NY 10532 Tel 914-747-0110 (SAN 201-3088).

De Vorss, *(De Vorss & Co.; 0-87516),* P.O. Box 550, Marina Del Rey, CA 90294 Tel 213-870-7478 (SAN 168-9886).

Dear Kids, *(Dear Kids Pubs.),* Currierville Rd., Newton, NH 03858 Tel 603-382-7503 (SAN 206-4677).

Decatur Hse, *(Decatur House Press, Ltd; 0-916276),* 2122 Decatur Place, N.W., Washington, DC 20008 Tel 202-387-3913 (SAN 208-1539).

December Pr, *(December Press; 0-913204),* 3093 Dato,, Highland Park, IL 60035 Tel 312-432-6804 (SAN 203-8854).

Dee Pub Co, *(Dee Publishing Co.; 0-934476),* 864 S. Commercial, Salem, OR 97302 Tel 503-363-2410 (SAN 206-4685).

Definition, *(Definition Press; 0-910492),* 141 Greene St., New York, NY 10012 Tel 212-777-4490 (SAN 201-310X).

Delacorte, *(Delacorte Press),* c/o Dell Publishing Co., 1 Dag Hammarskjold Plaza, 245 E. 47th St., New York, NY 10017 Tel 212-605-3496 (SAN 201-0097). *Imprints:* E Friede (Eleanor Friede); Sey Lawr (Seymour Lawrence).

Delair, *(Delair Publishing Co., Inc.; 0-8326),* 420 Lexington Ave., Rm. 1621, New York, NY 10170 Tel 212-867-2255 (SAN 213-4349).

Delilah Bks, *(Delilah Books; 0-933328),* 118 E. 25th St., New York, NY 10010 (SAN 238-9339); Dist. by: Putnam Publishing Group, 1050 Wall St. W., Lyndhurst, NJ 07071 (SAN 202-554X).

KEY TO PUBLISHERS' AND DISTRIBUTORS' ABBREVIATIONS

Dell, *(Dell Publishing Co., Inc.; 0-440),* 1 Dag Hammarskjold Plaza, 245 E. 47th St., New York, NY 10017 Tel 212-605-3000 (SAN 201-0097). *Imprints:* Banbury (Banbury); Bryans (Bryans); Dell Trade Pbks (Dell Trade Paperbacks); Delta (Delta Books); LE (Laurel Editions); LFL (Laurel Leaf Library); Standish (Standish); YB (Yearling Books).

Dell Trade Pbks *Imprint of* **Dell**

DeLorme Pub, *(DeLorme Publishing Co.; 0-89933),* P.O. Box 298, Freeport, ME 04032 Tel 207-865-4171 (SAN 220-1208).

Delta *Imprint of* **Dell**

Dembner Bks, *(Dembner Books; 0-934878),* Div. of Red Dembner Enterprises Corp., 1841 Broadway, New York, NY 10023 Tel 212-265-1250 (SAN 211-5573); Dist. by: W.W. Norton & Co., Inc., 500 Fifth Ave., New York, NY 10110 Tel 212-354-5500 (SAN 202-5795).

Dennis-Landman, *(Dennis-Landman Pubs.; 0-930422),* 1150 18th St., Santa Monica, CA 90403 Tel 213-394-8683 (SAN 210-9352).

Dept NE Stud, *(Univ. of Michigan, Dept. of Near Eastern Studies; 0-916798),* 3074 Frieze Bldg., Ann Arbor, MI 48109 Tel 313-764-0314 (SAN 285-1059); Dist. by: Eisenbrauns, P.O. Box 275, Winona Lake, IN 46590 Tel 219-269-2011 (SAN 285-1067); Dist. by: Publications Distribution Service, University of Michigan Press, 839 Greene St., Ann Arbor, MI 48109 Tel 313-764-4394 (SAN 285-1075); Dist. by: Cambridge University Press, Customer Service, 510 North Ave., New Rochelle, NY 10801 (SAN 285-1083); Orders to: Kitab, Dept of Near Eastern Studies, 3085 Frieze Bldg., Ann Arbor, MI 48109 Tel 313-763-1597 (SAN 285-1091).

Derbibooks, *(Derbibooks, Inc.; 0-89009),* Dist. by: Book Sales Inc., 110 Enterprise Ave., Secaucus, NJ 07094 Tel 201-864-6341 (SAN 204-4005).

Deseret Bk, *(Deseret Book Co.; 0-87747),* 40 E. South Temple, P.O. Box 30178, Salt Lake City, UT 84130 Tel 801-534-1515 (SAN 201-3185).

Determined Prods, *(Determined Productions, Inc.; 0-915696),* 315 Pacific Ave. at Battery, P.O. Box 2150, San Francisco, CA 94126 Tel 415-433-0660 (SAN 212-7385).

Deuce, *(Deuce of Clubs Press; 0-9600200),* Rt. 3, Box 178, Arcata, CA 95521 Tel 707-822-2000 (SAN 203-8897).

Devin, *(Devin-Adair Co., Inc.; 0-8159),* 143 Sound Beach Ave., Old Greenwich, CT 06870 Tel 203-637-4531 (SAN 213-750X).

Devon Pr, *(Devon Press; 0-934160),* 820 Miramar, Berkeley, CA 94707 Tel 415-526-1905 (SAN 212-8500).

Dghtrs St Paul, *(Daughters of St. Paul; 0-8198),* 50 St. Paul's Ave., Boston, MA 02130 Tel 617-522-8911 (SAN 203-8900).

Dharma Pub, *(Dharma Publishing; 0-913546; 0-89800),* 2425 Hillside Ave., Berkeley, CA 94704 Tel 415-548-5407 (SAN 201-2723).

Dial, *(Dial Press; 0-8037),* 1 Dag Hammarskjold Plaza, 245 E. 47th St., New York, NY 10017 Tel 212-832-7300 (SAN 201-3231) Adult titles now listed as imprint of Doubleday; juvenile titles listed under Dial Bks Young.

Diana Pr, *(Diana Press, Inc.; 0-88447),* 4400 Market St., Oakland, CA 94608 Tel 415-658-5558 (SAN 206-3549).

Diane Bks, *(Diane Books Publishing, Inc.; 0-88264),* 2808 Oregon CT. No. E, Torrance, CA 90503 Tel 213-320-2591 (SAN 201-2731).

Dickenson, *(Dickenson Publishing Co.; 0-8221),* c/o Wadsworth, Inc., 10 Davis Dr., Belmont, CA 94002 Tel 415-595-2350 (SAN 200-2213).

Dill Ent, *(Dill Enterprises; 0-9606504),* P.O. Box 2627, "O" St., Lincoln, NE 68529 Tel 402-476-1776 (SAN 219-0842).

Diotima Bks, *(Diotima Books; 0-935772),* Box H, Glen Carbon, IL 62034 (SAN 214-3631).

Directed Media, *(Directed Media Inc.; 0-939688),* P.O. Box 3005, Wenatchee, WA 98801 Tel 509-662-7693 (SAN 216-7263).

Discovery Bks, *(Discovery Books; 0-913976),* 351 Broad St., Suite 1704, Newark, NJ 07104 Tel 201-483-7782 (SAN 206-9512).

Discus *Imprint of* **Avon**

Divry, *(Divry, D.C., Inc.; 0-910516),* 293 Seventh Ave., New York, NY 10001 Tel 212-255-2153 (SAN 201-3320).

Dnomro Pubns, *(Dnomro Pubns.),* 40 Fairmont Ave., Waltham, MA 02154 (SAN 201-274X).

Dodd, *(Dodd, Mead & Co.; 0-396),* 79 Madison Ave., New York, NY 10016 Tel 212-685-6464 (SAN 201-3339).

Dolmen Pr *Imprint of* **Humanities**

Dolp *Imprint of* **Doubleday**

Donning Co, *(Donning Co. Pubs.; 0-915442; 0-89865),* 5659 Virginia Beach Blvd., Norfolk, VA 23502 Tel 804-461-8090 (SAN 211-6316). *Imprints:* Starblaze (Starblaze).

Dooryard, *(Dooryard Press; 0-937160),* P.O. Box 221, Story, WY 82842 (SAN 216-1230).

Dorchester Pub Co, *(Dorchester Publishing Co., Inc.; 0-8439),* c/o Winick & Rich, 41 East 60th Street, 5th Floor, New York, NY 10022 Tel 212-935-9360 (SAN 264-0090).

Dorrance, *(Dorrance & Co.; 0-8059),* 828 Lancaster Ave., Bryn Mawr, PA 19010 Tel 215-527-7880 (SAN 201-3363).

Doubleday, *(Doubleday & Co., Inc.; 0-385),* 245 Park Ave., New York, NY 10017 (SAN 281-6075); Orders to: 501 Franklin Ave., Garden City, NY 11530 (SAN 281-6083). *Imprints:* Anch (Anchor Books); Anchor Pr (Anchor Press); Dolp (Dolphin Books); Im (Image Books).

Dover, *(Dover Pubns., Inc.; 0-486),* 31 E. 2nd St., Mineola, NY 11501 Tel 516-294-7000 (SAN 201-338X).

Dow Jones, *(Dow Jones Books; 0-87128),* P.O. Box 300, Princeton, NJ 08540 Tel 609-452-2000 (SAN 201-8055).

Down East, *(Down East Books; 0-89272),* Div. of Down East Enterprise Inc., P.O. Box 679, Camden, ME 04843 Tel 207-594-9544 (SAN 208-6301).

Dragon Gate, *(Dragon Gate; 0-937872),* 508 Lincoln St., Port Townsend, WA 98368 (SAN 217-099X).

Dragons Teeth, *(Dragons Teeth Press; 0-934218),* El Dorado National Forest, Georgetown, CA 95634 (SAN 201-3398).

Dramatists Play, *(Dramatists Play Service, Inc.; 0-8222),* 440 Park Ave. S., New York, NY 10016 (SAN 207-5717).

Dream Garden, *(Dream Garden Press; 0-9604402; 0-942688),* 1199 Iola Ave., Salt Lake City, UT 84104 Tel 801-355-2154 (SAN 217-1007).

Droke-Hallux, *(Droke House/Hallux; 0-8375),* 116 W. Orr St., Box 2027, Anderson, SC 29621 Tel 803-226-7231 (SAN 203-8951) Moved Left No Forwarding Address.

Drollery Pr, *(Drollery Press; 0-940920),* 1516 Oak St., No. 313, Alameda, CA 94501 Tel 415-521-4087 (SAN 223-1808).

Dryad Pr, *(Dryad Press; 0-931848),* 15 Sherman Ave., Takoma Park, MD 20912 Tel 301-891-3729 (SAN 206-197X).

Du Vall Financial, *(Du Vall Press Financial Pubns.; 0-931232),* 920 W. Grand River, Williamston, MI 48895 (SAN 212-0380).

DuBois Zone Pr, *(DuBois Zone Press, The; 0-931498),* 516 Eleventh Ave., Grafton, WI 53024 (SAN 212-8071).

Duck Down, *(Duck Down Press; 0-916918),* P.O. Box 1047, Fallon, NV 89406 Tel 702-423-6643 (SAN 208-502X).

Dufour, *(Dufour Editions, Inc.; 0-8023),* Box 449, Chester Springs, PA 19425 Tel 215-458-5005 (SAN 201-341X).

Dundee Pub, *(Dundee Publishing; 0-935210),* P.O. Box 202, Dundee, NY 14837 Tel 301-432-8079 (SAN 213-6848).

Duquesne, *(Duquesne Univ. Press; 0-8207),* Dist. by: Humanities Press, Inc., Atlantic Highlands, NJ 07716 (SAN 201-9272).

Durrell, *(Durrell Pubns., Inc.; 0-911764),* P.O. Box 743, Kennebunkport, ME 04046 Tel 207-985-3904 (SAN 201-3452).

Dustbooks, *(Dustbooks; 0-913218),* Box 100, Paradise, CA 95969 Tel 916-877-6110 (SAN 204-1871).

Dutton, *(Dutton, E. P.; 0-525),* 2 Park Ave., New York, NY 10016 Tel 212-725-1818 (SAN 201-0070). *Imprints:* Hawthorn (Hawthorn Books).

Dynamic Learn Corp, *(Dynamic Learning Corp.; 0-915890),* 59 Commercial Wharf, Boston, MA 02110 Tel 617-742-9493 (SAN 209-049X). *Imprints:* Telegraph (Telegraph Books).

E & E Enterprises, *(E & E Enterprises; 0-917954),* 1203 Pomelo Court, Longwood, FL 32750 Tel 305-862-2823 (SAN 208-3906).

E Friede *Imprint of* **Delacorte**

E Keys, *(Keys, Elsie),* 1239 E. Marshall Ave., Phoenix, AZ 85014 (SAN 215-2428).

E L Harris, *(Harris, Elbert L.),* Box 43, Rutgers Univ., 5th & Penn Sts., Camden, NJ 08102 (SAN 208-2349).

E Torres & Sons, *(Torres, Eliseo, & Sons; 0-88303),* Box 2, Eastchester, NY 10709 (SAN 207-0235).

Eagle Bks, *(Eagle Books; 0-910971),* Rte. 3, Box 320, Rolla, MO 65401 Tel 314-364-3229 (SAN 263-2160).

Eakin Pubns, *(Eakin Pubns. Inc.; 0-89015),* P.O. Box 23066, Austin, TX 78735 Tel 512-288-1771 (SAN 207-3633).

Eakins, *(Eakins Press Foundation; 0-87130),* 155 E. 42nd St., New York, NY 10017 Tel 212-986-4077 (SAN 201-3541).

Earthwise Pubns, *(Earthwise Pubns.; 0-933494),* P.O. Box 680-536, Miami, FL 33168 (SAN 223-7407).

Ecco Pr, *(Ecco Press; 0-912946; 0-88001),* 18 W. 30th St., New York, NY 10001 Tel 212-685-8240 (SAN 202-5795); Dist. by: W.W. Norton & Co., Inc., Keystone Industrial Park, Scranton, PA 18512 (SAN 281-6202); Orders to: W. W. Norton & Co., 500 Fifth Ave., New York, NY 10110 Tel 212-354-5500 (SAN 202-5795).

Echo Pubs, *(Echo Pubs.; 0-912852),* P.O. Box 7130, West Menlo Park, CA 94025 Tel 415-524-1575 (SAN 201-3592).

Ed Solutions, *(Educational Solutions, Inc.; 0-87825),* 80 Fifth Ave., New York, NY 10011 Tel 212-924-1744 (SAN 205-6186).

Ed Tecnicos
See French & Eur

Edelweiss Pr, *(Edelweiss Press; 0-9600874),* 124 Front St., Massapequa Park, NY 11762 Tel 516-799-1150 (SAN 208-0419).

Eden, *(Eden Publishing House; 0-910532),* 1724 Chouteau Ave., St. Louis, MO 63103 Tel 314-421-1544 (SAN 201-3673).

Eden Co, *(Eden Co.),* South Kortright, NY 13842 (SAN 239-4227).

Ediciones, *(Ediciones Universal; 0-89729),* 3090 S.W. 8th St., Miami, FL 33135 Tel 305-642-3355 (SAN 207-2203).

Ediciones Huracan, *(Ediciones Huracan, Inc.; 0-940238),* Avenida Gonzalez 1002, Rio Piedras, PR 00925 Tel 809-763-7407 (SAN 217-5134).

Ediciones Norte, *(Ediciones Del Norte; 0-910061),* P.O. Box A130L, Hanover, NH 03755 Tel 603-795-2433 (SAN 241-2993).

Edins Hispamerica, *(Ediciones Hispamerica; 0-935318),* 5 Pueblo Court, Gaithersburg, MD 20878 Tel 301-948-3494 (SAN 213-9200).

Edit Mensaje, *(Editorial Mensaje; 0-86515),* 125 Queen St., Staten Island, NY 10314 Tel 212-761-0556 (SAN 214-0063).

Edit Mundo *Imprint of* **Casa Bautista**

Editorial Justa, *(Editorial Justa Pubns. Inc.; 0-915808),* 2831 Seventh St., Berkeley, CA 94710 Tel 415-848-3628 (SAN 208-1962); Orders to: P.O. Box 2131-C, Berkeley, CA 94702 (SAN 208-1970).

EdMart Intl, *(EdMart International; 0-89485),* 177 White Plains Rd., Tarrytown, NY 10591 Tel 914-332-0931 (SAN 210-0770).

Educ Today
See Pitman Learning

Educator Bks, *(Educator Books, Inc.; 0-912092),* Drawer 32, 10 N. Main, San Angelo, TX 76901 Tel 915-653-0152 (SAN 203-8382).

Educator Pubns, *(Educator Pubns.; 0-913558),* 1110 S. Pomona Ave., Fullerton, CA 92632 Tel 714-871-2950 (SAN 201-3746); P.O. Box 333, Fullerton, CA 92632 (SAN 201-3754).

Eerdmans, *(Eerdmans, Wm. B., Publishing Co.; 0-8028),* 255 Jefferson Ave., S.E., Grand Rapids, MI 49503 Tel 616-459-4591 (SAN 220-0058).

Eggplant Pr, *(Eggplant Press; 0-935060),* P.O. Box 18641, Denver, CO 80218 (SAN 211-6030).

El-Shabazz Pr
See Shabazz Pr

Eldridge Pub, *(Eldridge Publishing Co.; 0-912963),* P. O. Drawer 208, Franklin, OH 45005 Tel 513-746-6531 (SAN 204-1553).

KEY TO PUBLISHERS' AND DISTRIBUTORS' ABBREVIATIONS

Elgen Pub Co, *(Elgen Publishing Co.; 0-935774)*, 1004 Taurus Dr., Colorado Springs, CO 80906 (SAN 214-2392).

Elizabeth Pr, *(Elizabeth Press)*, 103 Van Etten Blvd., New Rochelle, NY 10804 (SAN 201-3789).

Elliots Bks, *(Elliot's Books; 0-911830)*, P.O. Box 6, Northford, CT 06472 Tel 203-484-2184 (SAN 204-1529).

ELS Intl, *(ELS International Inc.; 0-89318)*, 5761 Buckingham Pkwy., Culver City, CA 90230 Tel 213-642-0994 (SAN 281-6261); Orders to: Order Fulfillment Center, 14350 N.W. Science Park Dr., Portland, OR 97229 Tel 800-547-1515 (SAN 281-627X).

Elsevier-Nelson
    See Lodestar Bks

Elysium, *(Elysium Growth Press; 0-910550)*, 5436 Fernwood Ave., Los Angeles, CA 90027 Tel 213-465-7121 (SAN 210-5950).

EMC, *(EMC Pub.; 0-88436; 0-912022; 0-8219)*, 300 York Ave., St. Paul, MN 55101 Tel 612-771-1555 (SAN 201-3800).

Emerson Hall, *(Emerson Hall Pubs., Inc.)*, 215 W. 98th St., New York, NY 10025 Tel 212-663-7690 (SAN 203-8404).

Encino Pr, *(Encino Press; 0-88426)*, 510 Baylor St., Austin, TX 78703 Tel 512-476-6821 (SAN 201-3843).

English Lang, *(ELS Pubns.; 0-89285)*, 5761 Buckingham Pkwy., Culver City, CA 90230 Tel 213-642-0994 (SAN 281-6288); Orders to: Imprint of **Pacific Coast** Fulfillment Center, 14350 N.W. Science Park Dr., Portland, OR 97229 Tel 800-547-1515 (SAN 281-6296).

Enitharmon Pr, *(Enitharmon Press)*, Dist. by: SBD: Small Press Distribution, 1636 Ocean View Ave., Kensington, CA 94707 Tel 415-524-2107 (SAN 204-5826).

Entheos, *(Entheos Communications; 0-939750)*, P.O. Box 10696, Bainbridge Island, WA 98110 Tel 206-842-3641 (SAN 216-3209).

Entwhistle Bks, *(Entwhistle Books; 0-9601428; 0-934558)*, P.O. Box 611, Glen Ellen, CA 95442 Tel 707-996-3901 (SAN 211-0113).

Eriksson, *(Eriksson, Paul S., Pubs.; 0-8397)*, Battell Bldg., Middlebury, VT 05753 Tel 802-388-7303 (SAN 201-6702); Dist. by: Independent Publishers Group, 1 Pleasant Ave., Port Washington, NY 11050 Tel 516-944-9325 (SAN 201-6710).

ESPress, *(ESPress; 0-917200)*, P.O. Box 8606, Washington, DC 20011 Tel 202-723-4578 (SAN 206-748X).

Essaye Pub, *(Essaye Publishing Co.; 0-939756)*, 22713 Ventura Blvd., Suite F, Woodland Hills, CA 91364 Tel (SAN 216-3780) Moved, left no forwarding address.

Euclid Pub, *(Euclid Publishing Co., The; 0-935490)*, Dist. by: Bond & Bacon Assocs., P.O. Box 121, Cathedral Sta., New York, NY 10025 (SAN 211-6057).

Evans
    See M Evans

Ever Imprint of **Grove**

EverBC Imprint of **Grove**

Expedition Pr, *(Expedition Press; 0-939924)*, P.O. Box 1198, Kalamazoo, MI 49006 (SAN 216-8111).

Exposition, *(Exposition Press, Inc.; 0-682)*, 325 Rabro Dr., Box 2120, Smithtown, NY 11787 Tel 516-582-6655 (SAN 207-0642).
    Imprints: Banner (Banner); Lochinvar (Lochinvar); University (University).

F Apple, *(Apple, Faye)*, P.O. Box 3036, W. Durham Sta., Durham, NC 27705 Tel 919-286-2250 (SAN 219-953X).

F B Johnson, *(Johnson, Forrest Bryant; 0-9600510)*, 589 Sierra Vista, No. 31, Las Vegas, NV 89109 Tel 702-796-6219 (SAN 205-5694).

F Cass Co
    See Biblio Dist

F Hallman, *(Hallman, Frank)*, Dist. by: SBD: Small Press Distribution, 1636 Ocean View Ave., Kensington, CA 94707 Tel 415-524-2107 (SAN 204-5826).

F M Swan, *(Swan, Frances M.; 0-9602126)*, 11533 Old St. Charles Rd., Bridgeton, MO 63044 (SAN 212-3835).

F Merriwell, *(Merriwell, Frank, Inc.; 0-8373)*, 212 Michael Dr., Syosset, NY 11791 Tel 516-921-8888 (SAN 209-259X).

F Murat, *(Murat, Felix, Co.; 0-9600356)*, 2132 N.W. 11th Ave., Miami, FL 33127 (SAN 205-5724).

Faber & Faber, *(Faber & Faber, Inc.; 0-571)*, 39 Thompson St., Winchester, MA 01890 Tel 617-721-1427 (SAN 218-7256).

Fablewaves, *(Fablewaves Press)*, P.O. Box 7874, Van Nuys, CA 91409 Tel 213-372-2983 (SAN 215-0719).

Fairleigh Dickinson, *(Fairleigh Dickinson Univ. Press; 0-8386)*, Div. of Associated University Presses, 4 Cornwall Dr., East Brunswick, NJ 08816 Tel 201-254-0132 (SAN 201-4718).

Faith Pub Hse, *(Faith Publishing House)*, P.O. Box 518, 920 W. Mansur, Guthrie, OK 73044 Tel 405-282-1479 (SAN 204-1243).

Falcon Printing
    See Falcon Pub Venice

Falcon Pub Venice, *(Falcon Publishing; 0-942764)*, 2000 Strongs, Venice, CA 92091 Tel 213-399-4791 (SAN 212-8322).

Fallen Angel, *(Fallen Angel Press; 0-931598)*, 1981 W. McNichols Cl, Highland Park, MI 48203 Tel 313-864-0982 (SAN 211-8963).

Family Pub CA, *(Family Publishing Co., The; 0-937770)*, P.O. Box 462, Bodega Bay, CA 94923 Tel 707-875-3373 (SAN 215-3092).

Fantasy Pub Co, *(Fantasy Publishing Co., Inc.)*, c/o Borden Publishing Co., 1855 W. Main St., Alhambra, CA 91801 Tel 213-337-7947 (SAN 201-419X).

Far Eastern Pubns, *(Far Eastern Pubns.)*, Box 2505 A, 340 Edwards St., New Haven, CT 06520 Tel 203-436-1075 (SAN 219-0710).

Farallon Imprint of **Pacific Coast**

Farnum Films, *(Farnum Films; 0-915790)*, Executive House, 225 E. 46th St., New York, NY 10017 Tel 212-371-8679 (SAN 206-1988); Orders to: P.O. Box 1094, New York, NY 10017 (SAN 206-1996).

Fawcett, *(Fawcett Book Group; 0-449)*, 201 E. 50th St., New York, NY 10022 Tel 212-751-2600 (SAN 201-4572).
    Imprints: Crest (Crest Books); GM (Gold Medal Books); Juniper (Juniper); Prem (Premier Books).

Fawcett World
    See Fawcett

Fax Collect, *(Fax Collector's Editions, Inc.; 0-913960)*, P.O. Box 851, Mercer Island, WA 98040 Tel 206-232-8484 (SAN 208-6468).

Faxon, *(Faxon, F. W., Co., Inc.; 0-87305)*, 15 Southwest Park, Westwood, MA 02090 Tel 617-329-3350 (SAN 206-4081).

Fearon-Pitman
    See Pitman Learning

FEB, *(First Edition Books/FEB Co.; 0-89502)*, FEB Bldg., 120 Clairton Blvd., Pittsburgh, PA 15236 Tel 412-655-9733 (SAN 210-0827).

Fedora Bks, *(Fedora Books)*, P.O. Box 265, Hopedale, MA 01747 Tel (SAN 207-5628) Moved, Left No Forwarding Address.

Feldheim, *(Feldheim, Philipp, Inc.; 0-87306)*, 96 E. Broadway, New York, NY 10002 Tel 212-925-3180 (SAN 164-9671).

Fell, *(Fell, Frederick, Pubs., Inc.; 0-8119)*, 386 Park Ave. S., New York, NY 10016 Tel 212-685-9017 (SAN 208-2365).

Feminist Pr, *(Feminist Press; 0-912670; 0-935312)*, SUNY/College at Old Westbury, Box 334, Old Westbury, NY 11568 Tel 516-997-7660 (SAN 213-6813).

Fernhill, *(Fernhill House, Ltd.; 0-87522)*, Publisher Abbreviation Without Addresses Are for Titles That Are Out of Print. These Are Obsolete Abbreviations. Publisher Acquired by Humanities Press, Inc.

Fertig, *(Fertig, Howard, Inc.; 0-86527)*, 80 E. 11th St., New York, NY 10003 Tel 212-982-7922 (SAN 201-4777).

Fibonacci Corp, *(Fibonacci Corp.; 0-915494)*, P.O. Box 610, Golden Bridge, NY 10526 Tel 914-232-4293 (SAN 208-2373).

Fiction Coll, *(Fiction Collective; 0-914590)*, Brooklyn Coll., c/o English Dept., Brooklyn, NY 11210 Tel 212-780-5480 (SAN 201-4785); Dist. by: Flatiron Bk. Distributors, 175 Fifth Ave., Suite 814, New York, NY 10010 Tel 212-228-0390 (SAN 240-9917).

Fiction Intl, *(Fiction International; 0-931362)*, St. Lawrence Univ., Canton, NY 13617 Tel 315-379-5961 (SAN 221-1548).

Fictioneer Bks, *(Fictioneer Books, Ltd; 0-934882)*, Box B.I.P, Screamer Mountain, Clayton, GA 30525 Tel 404-782-3318 (SAN 213-3113).

Fidelis Pubs, *(Fidelis Pubs., Inc.)*, P.O. Box 1334, Palm Desert, CA 92261 Tel 714-345-5346 (SAN 212-0895) Moved, left no forwarding address.

Fides, *(Fides Pubs., Inc.)*, Publisher Abbreviation Without Addresses Are for Titles That Are Out of Print. These Are Obsolet E Abbreviations. Publisher's Abbreviationiis Now Fides Claretian.

Fiesta Pub, *(Fiesta Publishing Corp.; 0-88473)*, 6360 N.E. 4th Court, Miami, FL 33138 Tel 305-751-1181 (SAN 201-8470).

Fig Leaf, *(Fig Leaf Creations; 0-918774)*, 1706 Olive Ave., Santa Barbara, CA 93101 Tel 805-962-4987 (SAN 210-4245).

Filter, *(Filter Press; 0-910584; 0-86541)*, P.O. Box 5, Palmer Lake, CO 80133 Tel 303-481-2523 (SAN 201-484X).

Fireside Imprint of **S&S**

Firestein Bks, *(Firestein Books; 0-9602498)*, P. O. Box 17214, El Paso, TX 79917 Tel 915-592-0260 (SAN 212-940X).

Firm Foun Pub, *(Firm Foundation Publishing House; 0-88027)*, P.O. Box 610, Austin, TX 78767 Tel 512-452-7651 (SAN 201-4858).

First Amend, *(First Amendment Lawyers Association)*, 1737 Chestnut St., Philadelphia, PA 19103 (SAN 237-7179).

First East, *(First East Coast Theatre and Publishing Company, Inc.; 0-910829)*, P.O. Box A244, Village Sta., New York, NY 10014 Tel 212-255-4612 (SAN 270-1812).

Fjord Pr, *(Fjord Press; 0-940242)*, P. O. Box 615, Corte Madera, CA 94925 Tel 415-924-9566 (SAN 285-0192); Dist. by: Publishers Services, P.O. Box 3914, San Rafael, CA 94902 (SAN 285-0206).

FL State U Pr, *(Florida State Univ. Press; 0-87307)*, 213 Longmire Bldg., Tallahassee, FL 32306 (SAN 221-9239).

Flare Imprint of **Avon**

Fleet, *(Fleet Press Corp.; 0-8303)*, 160 Fifth Ave., New York, NY 10010 Tel 212-243-6100 (SAN 201-4874).

Flying Buttress, *(Flying Buttress Pubns.; 0-918348)*, P.O. Box 254, Endicott, NY 13760 Tel 607-785-5423 (SAN 210-0835).

Folcroft, *(Folcroft Library Editions; 0-8414)*, P.O. Box 182, Folcroft, PA 19032 (SAN 206-8362).

Folder Edns, *(Folder Editions; 0-913152)*, 103-26 68th Rd., Apt A63, Forest Hills, NY 11375 (SAN 206-6475).

Fontana Pap Imprint of **Watts**

Footsteps, *(Footsteps Press; 0-934796)*, P.O. Box 948, Hobbs, NM 88240 (SAN 213-666X).

Forest Peace, *(Forest of Peace Books, Inc.; 0-939516)*, Route One, Box 247, Easton, KS 66020 Tel 913-773-8255 (SAN 216-6739).

Forrest Bryant
    See F B Johnson

Forrest Printing, *(Forrest Printing; 0-89023)*, P.O. Box 105, Grand Haven, MI 49417 (SAN 239-8524).

Fortress, *(Fortress Press; 0-8006)*, 2900 Queen Lane, Philadelphia, PA 19129 Tel 800-822-3906 (SAN 220-0074).

Forward Movement, *(Forward Movement Pubns.)*, 412 Sycamore St., Cincinnati, OH 45202 Tel 513-721-6659 (SAN 208-3841).

Fotonovel, *(Fotonovel Pubns.; 0-89752)*, 8831 Sunset Blvd., PH-W, Los Angeles, CA 90069 Tel 213-659-8888 (SAN 213-2486); Dist. by: The Independent News Co., 75 Rockefeller Plaza, New York, NY 10019 (SAN 208-6158).

Foul Play Imprint of **Countryman**

Foun Bks, *(Foundation Books; 0-934988)*, P.O. Box 29229, Lincoln, NE 68529 Tel 402-466-4988 (SAN 201-6567).

Foun Hist Rest, *(Foundation for Historic Restoration in Pendleton Area; 0-912462)*, P.O. Box 444, Pendleton, SC 29670 Tel 803-654-2640 (SAN 206-4286).

Foun Human Under, *(Foundation of Human Understanding; 0-933900)*, P.O. Box 34036, Los Angeles, CA 90034 Tel 213-559-3711 (SAN 213-9545).

Found Class Rep
    See Found Class Reprints

Found Class Reprints, *(Foundation for Classical Reprints, The; 0-89901)*, 607 McKnight St. N.W., Albuquerque, NM 87102 (SAN 212-9051).

Fountainhead, *(Fountainhead Pubs., Inc.; 0-87310)*, 475 Fifth Ave., New York, NY 10017 Tel 212-421-1556 (SAN 206-4324).

KEY TO PUBLISHERS' AND DISTRIBUTORS' ABBREVIATIONS

Four D Pub Co, *(Four D Publishing Co.; 0-9610006),* Box 381, Princeton, IL 61356 (SAN 270-3092).
Four Seasons Foun, *(Four Seasons Foundation; 0-87704),* P.O. Box 31190, San Francisco, CA 94131 Tel 415-824-5774 (SAN 201-6591); Dist. by: Subterranean Co., P.O. Box 10233, Eugene, OR 97440 Tel 503-343-6324 (SAN 169-7102).
Foursquare Pr, *(Foursquare Press; 0-930616),* 648 Ransom Rd., Lancaster, NY 14086 Tel 716-681-2586 (SAN 211-8998).
Franciscan Herald, *(Franciscan Herald Press; 0-8199),* 1434 W. 51st St., Chicago, IL 60609 Tel 312-254-4455 (SAN 201-6621).
Free Pr, *(Free Press; 0-02),* Div. of Macmillan Publishing Co., Inc., 866 Third Ave., New York, NY 10022 Tel 212-935-2000 (SAN 201-6656); Dist. by: Macmillan Co., Front & Brown Sts., Riverside, NJ 08370 Tel 609-461-6500 (SAN 202-5582).
Freedom Bks, *(Freedom Books; 0-930374),* P.O. Box 5303, Hamden, CT 06518 Tel 203-281-6791 (SAN 210-9255).
Freeland Pubns, *(Freeland Pubns.; 0-936868),* P.O. Box 18941, Philadelphia, PA 19119 (SAN 215-3130).
French & Eur, *(French & European Pubns., Inc.; 0-8288),* 115 Fifth Ave., New York, NY 10003 Tel 212-673-7400 (SAN 206-8109).
French Lit
    See Summa Pubns
Friend Freedom, *(Friends of Freedom Pubs.),* P.O. Box 6124, Waco, TX 76706 Tel 817-662-4643 (SAN 207-3757).
Friend Pr, *(Friendship Press; 0-377),* 475 Riverside Dr., Rm. 772, New York, NY 10027 Tel 212-870-2497 (SAN 201-5773); Orders to: Friendship Press Distribution, P.O. Box 37844, Cincinnati, OH 45237 Tel 513-761-2100 (SAN 201-5781).
Frog in Well, *(Frog in the Well; 0-9603628),* 430 Oakdale Rd., East Palo Alto, CA 94303 (SAN 207-8295).
From Here, *(From Here Pr.; 0-89120),* P. O. Box 219, Fanwood, NJ 07023 Tel 201-889-7886 (SAN 209-746X).
Frontier Press Calif, *(Frontier Press),* P.O. Box 5023, Santa Rosa, CA 95402 Tel 707-544-5174 (SAN 206-653X).
FS&G, *(Farrar, Straus & Giroux, Inc.; 0-374),* 19 Union Square, W., New York, NY 10003 Tel 212-741-6900 (SAN 206-782X).
    Imprints: Sunburst (Sunburst Books).
Full Court NY, *(Full Court Press, Inc.; 0-916190),* 138-140 Watts St., New York, NY 10013 Tel 212-966-1831 (SAN 211-9021).
Funk & W, *(Funk & Wagnalls Co.; 0-308),* C/O Harper & Row Pubs., 10 E. 53rd St., New York, NY 10022 (SAN 211-6944); Dist. by: Harper & Row Pubs, Keystone Industrial Park, Scranton, PA 18512 (SAN 215-3742).
Funkshunal, *(Funkshunal Features; 0-932442),* P.O. Box 47728, Los Angeles, CA 90047 Tel 213-778-5422 (SAN 212-212X).
Fur Line Pr, *(Fur Line Press; 0-912662),* Dist. by: ManRoot Press, Box 982, South San Francisco, CA 94080 (SAN 217-8710).
Future Pr, *(Future Press; 0-918406),* P. O. Box 73, Canal St., New York, NY 10013 (SAN 210-0886).
Future Shop, *(Future Shop; 0-930490),* P.O. Box 3262, Santa Barbara, CA 93130 Tel 805-687-6684 (SAN 211-2396).
G Barker Bks, *(Barker, Gray, Books; 0-911306),* Box D, Jane Lew, WV 26378 Tel 304-269-2719 (SAN 204-7292).
G D Kieffer, *(Kieffer, George David, ,Pub.; 0-9609344),* P.O. Box 67874, Los Angeles, CA 90067 Tel 213-556-5522 (SAN 260-2156).
G F Edwards, *(Edwards, G. F.; 0-932318),* Box 1461, Lawton, OK 73502 Tel 405-248-6870 (SAN 212-1719).
G J Sneed, *(Sneed, Glenn J.),* P.O. Box 232, Royalton, IL 62983 (SAN 211-4941).
G K Hall, *(Hall, G. K., & Co.; 0-8161),* 70 Lincoln St., Boston, MA 02111 Tel 617-423-3990 (SAN 206-8427).
    Imprints: Gregg (Gregg Press); Large Print Bks (Large Print Books); Twayne (Twayne Publishers).
G K Westgard, *(Westgard, Gilbert, K. II),* 9226 W. Golf Rd., Des Plaines, IL 60016 (SAN 240-5032).

G Stempien, *(Stempien, G., Publishing Co.; 0-930472),* 1213 Edgehill Ave., Joliet, IL 60432 Tel 815-722-4216 (SAN 210-9840).
Gale, *(Gale Research Co.; 0-8103),* Book Tower, Detroit, MI 48226 Tel 313-961-2242 (SAN 213-4373).
Galleon Pubns
    See Galleon-Whitehurst
Galleon-Whitehurst, *(Galleon Pubns.; 0-918602),* 12 Tiffany Rd., No. 6, Salem, NH 03079 (SAN 210-9158).
Galley OR, *(Galley Press),* P.O. Box 892, Portland, OR 97207 Tel 206-693-1397 (SAN 215-3149).
Gallimaufry, *(Gallimaufry; 0-916300),* Dist. by: Apple-Wood Press, P.O. Box 2870, Cambridge, MA 02139 Tel 617-964-5150 (SAN 210-3419).
Gallopade Pub Group, *(Gallopade Publishing Group; 0-935326),* P.O. Box 1537, Tryon, NC 28782 Tel 704-859-9253 (SAN 213-8441).
Galloway, *(Galloway Pubns. Inc.; 0-87874),* 2940 N.W. Circle Blvd., Corvallis, OR 97330 (SAN 201-5854).
Gambit, *(Gambit Inc. Pubs.; 0-87645),* 27 N. Main St., Ipswich, MA 01938 Tel 617-356-2956 (SAN 201-5862).
Gannon, *(Gannon, William; 0-88307),* 143 Sombrio Dr., Santa Fe, NM 87501 Tel 505-983-1579 (SAN 201-5889).
Garber Comm, *(Garber Communications, Inc.; 0-89345),* 7 Garber Hill Rd., Blauvelt, NY 10913 Tel 914-359-9292 (SAN 226-2789).
    Imprints: Spiritual Sci Lib (Spiritual Science Library).
Garland Pub, *(Garland Publishing, Inc.; 0-8240),* 136 Madison Ave. 2nd Floor, New York, NY 10016 Tel 212-686-7492 (SAN 201-5897).
Garrett-Helix, *(Garrett Pubns.-Helix Press; 0-912326),* Orders to: Taplinger Publishing Co., 200 Park Ave., S., New York, NY 10003 Tel 213-6821).
Garrett Pr, *(Garrett Press),* Publisher Abbreviation Without Addresses Are for Titles That Are Out of Print. These Are Obsolete Abbreviations.
Garvin A J
    See A J Garvin
Gaslight, *(Gaslight Pubns.; 0-934468),* 112 E. Second, Bloomington, IN 47401 Tel 812-332-5169 (SAN 213-5019).
Gateway Ed Ltd
    See Regnery-Gateway
Gauntlet Bks, *(Gauntlet Books),* 144 King St., Franklin, MA 02038 Tel 617-528-4414 (SAN 201-5935).
Gaus, *(Gaus, Theo., Ltd.; 0-912444),* P.O. Box 1168, Brooklyn, NY 11202 Tel 212-625-4651 (SAN 203-4174).
Gay Mens Pr, *(Gay Mens Press; 0-907040),* Dist. by: Flatiron Book Distributors, 175 Fifth Ave., New York, NY 10011 (SAN 240-9917).
Gay Pr NY, *(Gay Presses of New York; 0-9604724),* P.O. Box 294, New York, NY 10014 (SAN 215-210X).
Gay Sunshine, *(Gay Sunshine Press; 0-917342),* Box 40397, San Francisco, CA 94140 Tel 415-824-3184 (SAN 208-0915); Dist. by: Bookpeople, 2940 Seventh St., Berkeley, CA 94710 Tel 800-227-1516 (SAN 168-9517).
GB Imprint of **Oxford U Pr**
Geis, *(Geis, Bernard, Associates, Inc.; 0-87035),* 128 E. 56th St., New York, NY 10022 Tel 212-752-1975 (SAN 203-4190).
Gemaia Pr, *(Gemaia Press; 0-9602232),* 209 Wilcox Lane, Sequim, WA 98382 (SAN 214-4238).
Georgetown Pr, *(Georgetown Press; 0-914558),* 483 Francisco St., San Francisco, CA 94133 Tel 415-397-4753 (SAN 206-7463).
Georgetown U Pr, *(Georgetown Univ. Press; 0-87840),* Intercultural Center, Room 111, Washington, DC 20057 Tel 202-625-4824 (SAN 203-4247).
Germinal Pr, *(Germinal Press; 0-918064),* 209 Prospect, San Francisco, CA 94110 Tel 415-824-4795 (SAN 210-2048).
Geron-X, *(Geron-X, Inc.; 0-87672),* P.O. Box 1108, Los Altos, CA 94022 Tel 415-941-1692 (SAN 201-5994).
Ghost Town, *(Ghost Town Pubns.; 0-933818),* P.O. Drawer 5998, Carmel, CA 93921 Tel 408-373-2885 (SAN 209-4401).

Gibson, *(Gibson, C. R., Co.; 0-8378),* Knight St., Norwalk, CT 06856 Tel 203-847-4543 (SAN 281-7446) (SAN 281-7454); Dist. by: Fob-C. R. Gibson, Distribution Center, Beacon Falls, CT 06403 (SAN 281-7462).
Ginn, *(Ginn & Co.; 0-663),* A Xerox Publishing Co., 191 Spring St., Lexington, MA 02173 Tel 617-861-1670 (SAN 201-6486); Orders to: P.O. Box 2649, 1250 Fairwood Ave., Columbus, OH 43216 Tel 614-253-8661 (SAN 201-6494).
Glen Pr, *(Glen Press; 0-9603518),* 2247 Glen Ave., Berkeley, CA 94709 (SAN 215-7667).
Glencoe, *(Glencoe Publishing Co., Inc.; 0-02),* c/o Macmillan Publishing Co., Inc., 866 Third Ave., New York, NY 10022 Tel 212-935-2000 (SAN 202-5574).
Glenson Pub, *(Glenson Publishing; 0-934884),* P.O. Box 298, Sterling Heights, MI 48077 (SAN 214-378X).
Glenwood, *(Glenwood Pubs.; 0-911760),* P.O. Box 880, Felton, CA 95018 Tel 408-335-4406 (SAN 203-431X).
Global Comm, *(Global Communications; 0-938294),* 303 Fifth Ave., Suite 1306, New York, NY 10016 Tel 212-685-4080 (SAN 216-3896).
Globe Pequot, *(Globe Pequot Press; 0-87106),* Old Chester Rd., Box Q, Chester, CT 06412 Tel 203-526-9572 (SAN 201-9892) CT History Ser., Dist. Only by the Center for CT Studies of Eastern CT State College, Willimantic, CT 06226.
Gloucester Art, *(Gloucester Art Press; 0-930582),* P.O. Box 4526, Albuquerque, NM 87196 Tel 505-843-7749 (SAN 205-2865).
Gluxlit Pr, *(Gluxlit Press; 0-930524),* P.O. Box 11165, Dallas, TX 75223 (SAN 211-9528) Moved, Left No Forwarding Address.
GM Imprint of **Fawcett**
God Unltd-U of Healing
    See U of Healing
Godine, *(Godine, David R., Pub., Inc.; 0-87923),* 306 Dartmouth St., Boston, MA 02116 Tel 617-536-0761 (SAN 213-4381).
    Imprints: Nonpareil Bks (Nonpareil Books).
Gold Penny, *(Gold Penny Press, The; 0-87786),* Box 2177, Canoga Park, CA 91306 Tel 213-368-1417 (SAN 281-7470); Orders to: Associated Booksellers, 147 McKinley Ave., Bridgeport, CT 06606 Tel 203-366-5494 (SAN 281-7489).
Golden Bell, *(Golden Bell Press; 0-87315),* 2403 Champa St., Denver, CO 80205 Tel 303-572-1777 (SAN 203-4344).
Golden Cockerel, *(Golden Cockerel Press; 0-498),* P. O. Box 421, Cranbury, NJ 08512 (SAN 203-4352).
Golden Pr Imprint of **Western Pub**
Golden Quill, *(Golden Quill Press, The; 0-8233),* Francestown, NH 03043 Tel 603-547-6622 (SAN 201-6419).
Golden West, *(Golden West Books; 0-87095),* P. O. Box 80250, San Marino, CA 91108-8250 Tel 213-283-3446 (SAN 201-6400).
Goliards Pr, *(Goliards Press),* 3515 18th St., Bellingham, WA 98225 (SAN 206-9903).
Good Gay, *(Good Gay Poets),* P.O. Box 277, Astor Sta., Boston, MA 02123 Tel 617-661-7534 (SAN 207-3536).
Good News, *(Good News Pubs.; 0-89107),* 9825 W. Roosevelt Rd., Westchester, IL 60153 Tel 312-345-7474 (SAN 211-7991).
    Imprints: Crossway Bks (Crossway Books).
Gordon Pr, *(Gordon Press Pubs.; 0-87968),* P.O. Box 459, Bowling Green Sta., New York, NY 10004 (SAN 201-6362).
Gordons & Weinberg, *(Gordons & T. Weinberg; 0-9603484),* Weinberg, 1302 W. Fourth, Coffeyville, KS 67337 (SAN 213-571X).
Gospel Pub, *(Gospel Publishing House; 0-88243),* 1445 Boonville Ave., Springfield, MO 65802 Tel 417-862-2781 (SAN 206-8826).
Gospel Pubns FL, *(Gospel Pubns. Inc. of Jax, Florida; 0-937408),* P.O. Box 16824, Jax, FL 32216 (SAN 215-2479).
Gotham, *(Gotham Book Mart; 0-910664),* 41 W. 47th St., New York, NY 10036 Tel 212-757-0367 (SAN 203-4417).
Grant Dahlstrom, *(Dahlstrom, Grant, /Castle Press),* 516 N. Fair Oaks Ave., Pasadena, CA 91103 (SAN 206-7455).
Graphic Impress, *(Graphic Impressions; 0-914628),* 1939 W. 32nd Ave., Denver, CO 80211 Tel 303-458-7475 (SAN 201-6311).

KEY TO PUBLISHERS' AND DISTRIBUTORS' ABBREVIATIONS

Graphic Pub, *(Graphic Publishing Co.; 0-89279),* 204 N. Second Ave., W., Lake Mills, IA 50450 Tel 515-592-0031 (SAN 202-4306).

Great Basin, *(Great Basin Press; 0-930830),* Box 11162, Reno, NV 89510 Tel 702-826-7729 (SAN 211-1144).

Great Ocean, *(Great Ocean Pubs.; 0-915556),* 1823 North Lincoln Street, Arlington, VA 22207 Tel 703-525-0909 (SAN 207-527X).

Great Outdoors, *(Great Outdoors Publishing Co.; 0-8200),* 4747 28th St., N., St. Petersburg, FL 33714 Tel 813-525-6609 (SAN 201-6273).

Great Raven Pr, *(Great Raven Press),* Box 813, Fort Kent, ME 04743 (SAN 211-9595).

Green Eagle Pr, *(Green Eagle Pr; 0-914018),* 241 W. 97th St., New York, NY 10025 Tel 212-663-2167 (SAN 203-4492).

Green Hill, *(Green Hill Pubs.; 0-916054; 0-89803),* 722 Columbus St., Ottawa, IL 61350 Tel 815-434-7905 (SAN 281-7578); Dist. by: Caroline House Pubs., Inc., 920 W. Industrial Dr., Aurora, IL 60503 (SAN 211-2280).

Green Hut, *(Green Hut Press; 0-916678),* 24051 Rotunda Rd., Valencia Hills, CA 91355 Tel 805-259-5290 (SAN 208-2888).

Green River, *(Green River Press, Inc.; 0-940580),* Saginaw Valley State College, University Center, MI 48710 Tel 517-790-4376 (SAN 207-5881).

Greene, *(Greene, Stephen, Press; 0-8289),* Fessenden Rd. at Indian Flat, P.O. Box 1000, Brattleboro, VT 05301 Tel 802-257-7757 (SAN 201-6222).

Greenfld Rev Pr, *(Greenfield Review Press; 0-912678),* R.D. 1, Box 80, Greenfield Ctr., NY 12833 Tel 518-584-1728 (SAN 203-4506).

Greenlf Bks, *(Greenleaf Books; 0-934676),* Weare, NH 03281 (SAN 203-4514).

Greenwood, *(Greenwood Press; 0-8371; 0-313),* 88 Post Rd. W., P.O. Box 5007, Westport, CT 06881 Tel 203-226-3571 (SAN 213-2028).

Gregg *Imprint of* **G K Hall**

Grey Fox, *(Grey Fox Press; 0-912516),* Box 31190, San Francisco, CA 94131 (SAN 201-6176); Dist. by: Subterranean Co., P.O. Box 10233, Eugene, OR 97440 Tel 503-343-6324 (SAN 169-7102).

Grossman, *(Grossman Pubs., Inc.; 0-670),* c/o Viking Penguin, 625 Madison Ave., New York, NY 10022 (SAN 200-2450).

Grossmont Pr, *(Grossmont Press, Inc.; 0-913182; 0-89543),* 3211 Jefferson St., San Diego, CA 92110 Tel 714-299-2205 (SAN 201-615X).

Grove, *(Grove Press, Inc.; 0-8021; 0-394),* 196 W. Houston St., New York, NY 10014 Tel 212-242-4900 (SAN 201-4890); Orders to: Grove Press Order Dept., 196 W. Houston St., New York, NY 10014 (SAN 201-4904). Imprints: BC (Black Cat Books); Ever (Evergreen Books); EverBC (Evergreen-Black Cat Books); Zebra (Zebra Books).

Guignol Bks, *(Guignol Books; 0-941062),* P.O. Box 247, Rhinebeck, NY 12572 Tel 914-876-6776 (SAN 281-7594).

Guild Bks, *(Guild Books, Catholic Polls, Inc.; 0-912080),* 86 Riverside Dr., New York, NY 10024 Tel 212-799-2600 (SAN 203-4646).

Guild Pr, *(Guild Press; 0-940248),* P.O. Box 22583, Robbinsdale, MN 55422 Tel 612-566-1842 (SAN 220-3340).

Gull Bks, *(Gull Books; 0-940584),* 657 E. 26th St., No. 4S, Brooklyn, NY 11210 Tel 212-434-0094 (SAN 281-7632); Orders to: 1736 E. 53rd St., Brooklyn, NY 11234 (SAN 281-7640).

Guthrie Pub, *(Guthrie Publishing Co.; 0-941064),* P.O. Box 1, Guthrie, MN 56451 Tel 218-224-2118 (SAN 217-3751).

GWP, *(Great Western Publishing; 0-86666),* 416 Magnolia, Glendale, CA 91204 (SAN 220-2492) Do Not Confuse with Great Western Pubns.

H Chase, *(Chase, Herman, Surveyor),* Alstead, NH 03602 (SAN 206-8176).

H Jones, *(Jones, Harry; 0-9601980),* P.O. Box 10054, Austin, TX 78766-1054 Tel 512-451-2644 (SAN 212-615X).

H M Gousha, *(Gousha, H. M., Co., The; 0-88098),* 2001 The Alameda, San Jose, CA 95150 Tel 408-296-1060 (SAN 281-7519); Orders to: Dept. ABI, P.O. Box 6227, San Jose, CA 95150 (SAN 281-7527).

H P Bks, *(H. P. Books; 0-912656; 0-89586),* P.O. Box 5367, Tucson, AZ 85703 Tel 602-888-2150 (SAN 201-6087).

Hal Z Bennett, *(Bennett, Hal Z.),* 124 Ardmore Rd., Kensington, CA 94707 (SAN 212-6052).

Halldin Pub, *(Halldin, A. G., Publishing Co.; 0-935648),* P.O. Box 667, Indiana, PA 15701 Tel 412-463-8450 (SAN 208-208X).

Hallmark, *(Hallmark Card, Inc.; 0-87529),* 25th & McGee Sts., Kansas City, MO 64108 Tel 816-274-5111 (SAN 202-2672).

Halty Ferguson, *(Halty Ferguson; 0-912604),* 376 Harvard St., Cambridge, MA 02138 Tel 617-868-6190 (SAN 202-2699).

Hamber
See BH Ent

Hammond Inc, *(Hammond, Inc.; 0-8437),* 515 Valley St., Maplewood, NJ 07040 Tel 201-763-6000 (SAN 202-2702).

Hammond Records, *(Hammond Records; 0-942874),* P.O. Box 3431 - 874 Chelterham Circle, Thousand Oaks, CA 91360 Tel 805-495-1143 (SAN 239-5517).

Hanging Loose, *(Hanging Loose Press; 0-914610),* 231 Wyckoff St., Brooklyn, NY 11217 Tel 212-643-9559 (SAN 206-4960).

Hapi Pr, *(Hapi Press; 0-913244),* 512 S.W. Maplecrest Dr., Portland, OR 97219 Tel 503-246-9632 (SAN 204-0239).

Har-Row, *(Harper & Row Pubs., Inc.; 0-06),* 10 E. 53rd St., New York, NY 10022 Tel 212-207-7000 (SAN 200-2086); 1700 Montgomery St., San Francisco, CA 94111 Tel 415-989-9000 (SAN 215-3734); Orders to: Keystone Industrial Park, Scranton, PA 18512 (SAN 215-3742). Imprints: CN (Colophon Books); HarpC (Harper's College Division); HarpJ (Juvenile Books); HarpR (Harper Religious Books); HarpT (Harper Trade Books); HW (Harrow Books Paperback Department); PL (Perennial Library); Torch (Torchbooks); TYC-J (Crowell Junior Books).

HarBraceJ, *(Harcourt Brace Jovanovich, Inc.; 0-15),* 1250 Sixth Ave., San Diego, CA 92101 Tel 714-231-6616 (SAN 200-2736); 757 Third Ave., New York, NY 10017 (SAN 200-2299). Imprints: Harv (Harvest Books); HC (Harcourt Brace Jovanovich, Inc., College Dept.); HPL (Harbrace Paperback Library); VoyB (Voyager Books).

Harlan Davidson, *(Davidson, Harlan, Inc.; 0-88295),* 3110 N. Arlington Heights Rd., Arlington Heights, IL 60004 Tel 312-253-9720 (SAN 201-2375).

Harlequin Bks, *(Harlequin Books),* 580 White Plains Rd., Tarrytown, NY 10591 Tel 914-332-1313 (SAN 226-2940).

Harlo Pr, *(Harlo Press; 0-8187),* 50 Victor Ave., Detroit, MI 48203 Tel 313-883-3600 (SAN 202-2745).

Harmony *Imprint of* **Crown**

Harmony & Co
See Buccaneer Bks

Harmony Raine, *(Harmony Raine & Co.; 0-89967),* Box 133, Greenport, NY 11944 (SAN 262-0367).

Harold Hse, *(Harold House, Pubs.; 0-930138),* P.O. Box 59, 203 Walnut St., Marshall, AR 72650 Tel 501-448-5170 (SAN 210-7392).

HarpC *Imprint of* **Har-Row**

Harper Mag Pr, *(Harper's Magazine Press),* 10 E. 53rd St., New York, NY 10022 Tel 212-593-7000 (SAN 202-2753).

HarpJ *Imprint of* **Har-Row**
HarpR *Imprint of* **Har-Row**
HarpT *Imprint of* **Har-Row**

Harrison Hse, *(Harrison House, Inc.; 0-89274),* P.O. Box 35035, Tulsa, OK 74153 Tel 918-582-2126 (SAN 208-676X).

Harrowood Bks, *(Harrowood Books; 0-915180),* 3943 N. Providence Rd., Newtown Square, PA 19073 (SAN 207-1622).

Hart, *(Hart Associates; 0-8055),* 12 E. 12th St., New York, NY 10003 Tel 212-260-2430 (SAN 202-2761).

Hartmore, *(Hartmore House),* Dist. by: Hartmore House, 1363 Fairfield Ave., Bridgeport, CT 06605 (SAN 206-8729).

Hartmus Pr, *(Hartmus Press; 0-915868),* 23 Lomita Dr., Mill Valley, CA 94941 Tel 415-388-0822 (SAN 204-0263).

Harv *Imprint of* **HarBraceJ**

Harvard Common Pr, *(Harvard Common Press; 0-916782),* 535 Albany St., Boston, MA 02172 Tel 617-423-5803 (SAN 208-6778); Orders to: Independent Publishers Group, C/O David White, Inc., One Pleasant Ave., Port Washington, NY 11050 (SAN 208-6786).

Harvard U Pr, *(Harvard Univ. Press; 0-674),* 79 Garden St., Cambridge, MA 02138 Tel 617-495-2600 (SAN 281-7721); Orders to: Customer Service, Harvard Univ. Press, 79 Garden St., Cambridge, MA 02138 Tel 617-495-2480 (SAN 281-773X).

Harvest Hse, *(Harvest House Pubs.; 0-89081),* 1075 Arrowsmith, Eugene, OR 97402 Tel 503-343-0123 (SAN 207-4745).

Haskell, *(Haskell Booksellers, Inc.; 0-8383),* P.O. Box FF, Blythebourne Sta., Brooklyn, NY 11219 Tel 212-435-0500 (SAN 202-2818).

Hastings, *(Hastings House Pubs., Inc.; 0-8038),* 10 E. 40th St., New York, NY 10016 Tel 212-689-5400 (SAN 213-9561).

Hastings Bks, *(Hastings Books),* 111 Coulter Ave., Ardmore, PA 19003 Tel 215-649-1227 (SAN 205-048X).

Haven Corp, *(The Haven Corporation; 0-911361),* 802 Madison Ave., Evanston, IL 60202 Tel 312-869-3434 (SAN 275-9977).

Havertown Bks, *(Havertown Books),* P.O. Box 711, Havertown, PA 19083 (SAN 208-4384).

Hawkes Pub Inc, *(Hawkes Publishing Inc.; 0-89036),* 3775 S. 500 West, Box 15711, Salt Lake City, UT 84115 Tel 801-262-5555 (SAN 205-6232).

Haworth Pr, *(Haworth Press Inc., The; 0-917724; 0-86656),* 28 E. 22nd St., New York, NY 10010 Tel 212-228-2800 (SAN 211-0156).

Hawthorn *Imprint of* **Dutton**

Hayden, *(Hayden Book Co., Inc.; 0-8104),* 50 Essex St., Rochelle Park, NJ 07662 Tel 201-843-0550 (SAN 200-2094).

Hazelden, *(Hazelden Foundation; 0-89486),* Box 176, Center City, MN 55012 Tel 612-257-4010 (SAN 209-4010).

HC *Imprint of* **HarBraceJ**

Headway Pubns, *(Headway Pubns.; 0-89537),* 1700 Port Manleigh Circle, Newport Beach, CA 92660 Tel 714-640-0736 (SAN 210-4342).

Hearth Pub, *(Hearthstone Pubns.; 0-943098),* P.O. Box 2002, Darien, CT 06820 Tel 203-734-5398 (SAN 240-3854).

Hearthside, *(Hearthside Press, Inc.; 0-8208),* Orders to: Ingram Book Co., 347 Redwood Dr., Nashville, TN 37217 (SAN 202-2869) Moved, left no forwarding address.

Heath, *(Heath, D.C., Co.; 0-669),* Div. of Raytheon Co., 125 Spring St., Lexington, MA 02173 Tel 617-862-6650 (SAN 213-7526); Orders to: D. C. Heath & Co., Distribution Ctr., 2700 Richardt Ave., Indianapolis, IN 46219 Tel 317-359-5585 (SAN 202-2885).

Hebrew Pub, *(Hebrew Publishing Co.; 0-88482),* 100 Water St., Brooklyn, NY 11201 Tel 212-858-6928 (SAN 201-5404).

Heian Intl, *(Heian International Publishing, Inc.; 0-89346),* P.O. Box 2402, South San Francisco, CA 94083-2402 Tel 415-467-0222 (SAN 213-2036).

Heidelberg Graph, *(Heidelberg Graphics; 0-918606),* P.O. Box 3606, Chico, CA 95927 (SAN 211-5654).

Heidelberg Pubns, *(Heidelberg Pubns., Inc.; 0-913206),* 1003 Brown Bldg., Austin, TX 78701 (SAN 201-5501).

Heinemann Ed, *(Heinemann Educational Books Inc.; 0-435),* 4 Front St., Exeter, NH 03833 Tel 603-778-0534 (SAN 210-5829).

Heinman, *(Heinman, W.S., Imported Books),* 225 W. 57th St., Rm. 404, New York, NY 10019 Tel 212-757-7628 (SAN 121-6201); P.O. Box, Ansonia Sta., New York, NY 10019 (SAN 121-6201).

Helix Hse, *(Helix House Pubs.; 0-930866),* 9231 Molly Woods Ave., La Mesa, CA 92041 (SAN 211-3171).

Hellcoal Pr, *(Hellcoal Press; 0-916912),* P.O. Box 4, S. A. O. , Brown Univ., Providence, RI 02912 Tel 401-863-2341 (SAN 208-6808).

Hemisphere Hse, *(Hemisphere House Books; 0-930770),* P.O. Box 1934, Corpus Christi, TX 78403 (SAN 211-0717).

KEY TO PUBLISHERS' AND DISTRIBUTORS' ABBREVIATIONS

Hendricks House, *(Hendricks House, Inc.; 0-87532),* Main St., Putney, VT 05346 (SAN 206-9830).

Herald Hse, *(Herald House; 0-8309),* Drawer HH, 3225 S. Noland Rd., Independence, MO 64055 Tel 816-252-5010 (SAN 202-2907).

Herald Pr, *(Herald Press; 0-8361),* 616 Walnut Ave., Scottdale, PA 15683 Tel 412-887-8500 (SAN 202-2915).

Herder & Herder, *(Herder & Herder),* Publisher Abbreviation Without Addresses Are for Titles That Are Out of Print. These Are Obsolete Abbreviations.

Heritage Pr, *(Heritage Press; 0-935428),* P.O. Box 18625, Baltimore, MD 21216 (SAN 221-2684).

Heritage Trails, *(Heritage Trails Press; 0-910083),* 94 Santa Maria Dr., Novato, CA 94947 Tel 415-897-5679 (SAN 240-8589).

Hermes Hse, *(Hermes House Press; 0-9605008),* 127 W.15th St. Apt. 3F, New York, NY 10011 Tel 212-691-9773 (SAN 220-0589).

Hermitage MI, *(Hermitage; 0-938920),* 2269 Shadowood, Ann Arbor, MI 48104 (SAN 239-4413).

Hiawatha Pub, *(Pyramid Pubs. of Iowa),* P.O. Box 400, Perry, IA 50220 Tel 515-465-5010 (SAN 282-1966); Dist. by: Hiawatha Book Co., 7567 N.E. 102nd Ave., Bondurant, IA 50035 Tel 515-967-4025 (SAN 282-6496).

Hidden Hse Imprint of **Music Sales**

Highflyer Pr, *(Highflyer Press; 0-9605010),* 9704 E 26 st, Independence, Kansas City, MO 64052 (SAN 240-1517).

Highland Pr, *(Highland Press; 0-910722),* Rte. 3, Box 3125, Boerne, TX 78006 (SAN 204-0522).

Hill & Wang, *(Hill & Wang, Inc.; 0-8090),* Div. of Farrar, Straus & Giroux, Inc., 19 Union Square W., New York, NY 10003 Tel 212-741-6900 (SAN 201-9299). *Imprints:* AmCen (American Century Series); Mermaid (Mermaid Dramabooks); New Mermaid (New Mermaid Dramabooks).

Hill Hse Pr, *(Hill House Press, Pubs.; 0-915602),* Old Lane & Chester Rd., Chester, VA 23831 Tel 804-262-0228 (SAN 201-5412).

Hillary, *(Hillary House Pubs., Ltd.),* Div. of Humanities Press, Inc., Atlantic Highlands, NJ 07716 (SAN 202-294X).

Hippocrene Bks, *(Hippocrene Books, Inc. B; 0-88254),* 171 Madison Ave., New York, NY 10016 Tel 212-685-4372 (SAN 213-2060).

Hispanic Soc, *(Hispanic Society of America; 0-87535),* 613 W. 155th St., New York, NY 10032 Tel 212-926-2234 (SAN 204-0573).

HM, *(Houghton Mifflin Co.; 0-395),* 2 Park St., Boston, MA 02107 Tel 617-725-5000 (SAN 200-2388); Orders to: Wayside Road, Burlington, MA 01803 Tel 617-272-1500 (SAN 215-3793). *Imprints:* Clarion (Clarion Books); RivEd (Riverside Editions); RivLit (Riverside Literature Series); RRS (Riverside Reading Series); SenEd (Sentry Editions).

Hobart & Wm Smith, *(Hobart & William Smith Colleges Press; 0-934888),* Hobart & William Smith Colleges, Geneva, NY 14456 (SAN 213-3202).

Hogarth, *(Hogarth Press; 0-911776),* P.O. Box 10606, Honolulu, HI 96816 Tel 808-737-4150 (SAN 202-2966).

Holiday, *(Holiday House, Inc.; 0-8234),* 18 E. 53rd St., New York, NY 10022 Tel 212-688-0085 (SAN 202-3008).

Holloway, *(Holloway House Publishing Co.; 0-87067),* 8060 Melrose Ave., Los Angeles, CA 90046 Tel 213-653-8060 (SAN 206-8451). *Imprints:* Melrose Sq (Melrose Square).

Holly Hill, *(Holly Hill Pubs.; 0-9606508),* Holly Hill Box 723, Saluda, NC 28773 (SAN 219-3396).

Hollywood, *(Hollywood Book Service; 0-910738),* 1654 N. Cherokee Ave., Hollywood, CA 90028 Tel 213-464-4164 (SAN 204-0646).

Holmes & Meier, *(Holmes & Meier Pubs., Inc.; 0-8419),* IUB Bldg., 30 Irving Place, New York, NY 10003 Tel 212-254-4100 (SAN 201-9280). *Imprints:* Africana (Africana Pub.).

Holmgangers, *(Holmgangers Press; 0-914974),* 95 Carson Ct. Shelter Cove, Whitethorn, CA 95489 Tel 707-986-7700 (SAN 206-5029).

HoltC Imprint of **HR&W**

Holy Cow, *(Holy Cow! Press; 0-930100),* P.O. Box 618, Minneapolis, MN 55440 (SAN 210-6302).

Holy Cross Orthodox, *(Holy Cross Orthodox Press; 0-916586),* 50 Goddard Ave., Brookline, MA 02146 Tel 617-232-4544 (SAN 208-6840).

Homeward Pr, *(Homeward Press; 0-938392),* P.O. Box 2307, Berkeley, CA 94702 (SAN 220-2522).

Horizon, *(Horizon Press Pubs.; 0-8180),* 156 Fifth Ave., New York, NY 10010 Tel 212-924-9225 (SAN 202-3040).

Horizons, *(Horizons; 0-932960),* P.O. Box 35008, Phoenix, AZ 85069 (SAN 212-2146); Dist. by: Thinking Caps, Inc., P.O. Box 7239, Phoenix, AZ 85011 Tel 602-956-1515 (SAN 239-4960).

Horn Bk, *(Horn Book, Inc.; 0-87675),* Park Square Bldg., 31 St. James Ave., Boston, MA 02116 Tel 617-482-5198 (SAN 202-3059).

Horsebreeder
See **Printed Horse**

Howard U Pr, *(Howard Univ. Press; 0-88258),* 2900 Van Ness St., N.W., Washington, DC 20008 Tel 202-686-6696 (SAN 202-3067).

HPL Imprint of **HarBraceJ**

HR&W, *(Holt, Rinehart & Winston, Inc.; 0-03),* 383 Madison Ave., New York, NY 10017 Tel 212-872-2000 (SAN 200-2108). *Imprints:* HoltC (Holt College Department).

Hse by the Sea, *(House by the Sea Publishing Co.),* 8610 Highway 101, Waldport, OR 97394 (SAN 212-9477).

Hse of Collectibles, *(House of Collectibles, Inc.; 0-87637),* 1900 Premier Row, Orlando, FL 32809 Tel 305-857-9095 (SAN 202-3113).

Hse of One Pub, *(House of One Publishing Co.),* Box 3407, Portland, OR 97208 (SAN 211-3953).

Hudson-Mohawk, *(Hudson-Mohawk Association of Colleges & Universities),* 91 Fiddlers Lane, Latham, NY 12110 Tel 518-785-3219 (SAN 241-5402).

Huh Pubns, *(Huh Pubns.; 0-938642),* P.O. Box 30782, Santa Barbara, CA 93105 (SAN 222-9765).

Humanities, *(Humanities Press, Inc.; 0-391),* Atlantic Highlands, NJ 07716 Tel 201-872-1441 (SAN 201-9272). *Imprints:* Athlone Pr (Athlone Press); Dolmen Pr (Dolmen Press).

Humanity Pubns, *(Humanity Pubns.),* 27 S. Maple St., Shelburne Falls, MA 01370 Tel 413-625-6823 (SAN 209-0430) Moved, Left No Forwarding Address.

Hungarian Rev, *(American Hungarian Review; 0-911862),* 5410 Kerth Rd., St. Louis, MO 63128 Tel 314-487-7566 (SAN 204-0816).

Hunt Inst Botanical, *(Hunt Institute for Botanical Documentation; 0-913196),* Carnegie-Mellon Univ., Pittsburgh, PA 15213 Tel 412-578-2434 (SAN 206-9156).

Huntington Lib, *(Huntington Library Pubns.; 0-87328),* 1151 Oxford Rd., San Marino, CA 91108 Tel 213-792-6141 (SAN 202-313X).

Hutchinson
See **Merrimack Publishers' Circle**

HW Imprint of **Har-Row**

Hwong Pub, *(Hwong Publishing Co.; 0-89260),* 10353 Los Alamitos Blvd., Los Alamitos, CA 90720 Tel 213-431-0868 (SAN 208-2306).

Hyde Park Pr, *(Hyde Park Press; 0-9608454),* P. O. Box 2009, Boise, ID 83701 (SAN 240-4834).

Hydra Bk
See **Warm Wind Bks**

Hyperion Conn, *(Hyperion Press, Inc.; 0-88355; 0-8305),* 47 Riverside Ave., P.O. Box 591, Westport, CT 06880 Tel 203-226-1091 (SAN 202-3148).

Hyst'ry Myst'ry, *(Hyst'ry Myst'ry House; 0-937884),* 1 Brush Court, Garnerville, NY 10923 (SAN 218-4796); Dist. by: Associated Booksellers Inc., P.O. Box 6361, McKinley Ave., Bridgeport, CT 06606 Tel 203-366-5494 (SAN 206-9717).

I & O Pub, *(I & O Publishing Co.; 0-911752),* P.O. Box 906, Boulder City, NV 89005 (SAN 202-3156).

Icarus, *(Icarus Press, Inc.; 0-89651),* P.O. Box 1225, South Bend, IN 46624 Tel 219-233-6020 (SAN 285-0273); Dist. by: Harper & Row, Keystone Industrial Park, Scranton, PA 18512 Tel 800-233-4175 (SAN 285-0281).

Ideals, *(Ideals Publishing Corp.; 0-89542),* 11315 Watertown Plank Rd., Milwaukee, WI 53226 Tel 414-771-2700 (SAN 213-4403).

IDHHB, *(Institute for the Development of the Harmonious Human Being Inc.; 0-89556),* P.O. Box 370, Nevada City, CA 95959 Tel 916-786-7313 (SAN 211-3635).

IHS, *(Information Handling Services; 0-910972; 0-89847),* 15 Inverness Way E., P.O. Box 1154, Englewood, CO 80150 Tel 303-779-0600 (SAN 203-7254) Prepackaged & custom services on 8mm & 16mm roll microfilm & microfiche. Products include federal & military specifications & standards, industry standards, government procurement packages, product & vendor catalog data, scholarly & legal publications for industry, government, libraries & education.

IHS-PDS
See **IHS**

Illum Way Pr
See **IWP Pub**

Illusive Unicorn, *(Illusive Unicorn Pubns.),* P.O. Box 6841, San Jose, CA 95150 Tel 408-279-1520 (SAN 212-7474).

Im Imprint of **Doubleday**

Imp Pr, *(Imp Press; 0-9603008),* P.O. Box 93, Buffalo, NY 14213 Tel 716-881-5391 (SAN 213-0858).

Impact Tenn, *(Impact Books; 0-914850; 0-86608),* Div. of the Benson Co., 365 Great Circle Rd., Nashville, TN 37228 Tel 615-259-9111 (SAN 202-6872); Dist. by: Zondervan Corp., 1415 Lake Dr. S.E., Grand Rapids, MI 49506 Tel 616-698-6900 (SAN 203-2694).

Impermanent Pr, *(Impermanent Press),* 218 Monclay Court, St. Louis, MO 63122 (SAN 209-0414).

Imported Pubns, *(Imported Pubns.; 0-8285),* 320 W. Ohio St., Chicago, IL 60610 Tel 312-787-9017 (SAN 169-1805).

Impress Hse, *(Impress House; 0-913992),* Orders to: Associated Booksellers, 147 McKinley Ave., Bridgeport, CT 06606 (SAN 206-6513).

Incunabula, *(Incunabula Collection; 0-930226),* 277 Hillside Ave., Nutley, NJ 07110 Tel 201-667-8502 (SAN 210-3591).

Ind Sch Pr, *(Independent School Press; 0-88334),* 51 River St., Wellesley Hills, MA 02181 Tel 617-237-2591 (SAN 203-8013).

Ind U Pr, *(Indiana Univ. Press; 0-253),* 1700 Mishawaka Ave.P.O. Box7111, South Bend, IN 44634 Tel 219-237-4214 (SAN 202-5647).

Ind-US Inc, *(Ind-US, Inc.),* Box 56, East Glastonbury, CT 06025 Tel 203-633-0045 (SAN 213-5809).

Index Pubs, *(Index Pubs.; 0-934692),* 26 St. Mark's Pl., New York, NY 10003 (SAN 213-5140); c/o Russica Book & Art Store, 799 Broadway, New York, NY 10003 Tel 212-473-7480 (SAN 212-310X) Moved, left no forwarding address.

Indian Hist Pr, *(Indian Historian Press, Inc.; 0-913436),* 1451 Masonic Ave., San Francisco, CA 94117 Tel 415-626-5235 (SAN 202-6929).

Indigena, *(Indigena Pubns.; 0-9602972),* 133 Brooks Ave., Venice, CA 90291 (SAN 213-0866) Moved, left no forwarding address.

Inner Tradit, *(Inner Traditions International, Ltd.; 0-89281),* 377 Park Ave. S., 6th Fl., New York, NY 10016 Tel 212-889-8350 (SAN 208-6948).

Inspiration Conn, *(Inspiration House Pubs.; 0-918114),* P.O. Box 1, South Windsor, CT 06074 Tel 203-289-7363 (SAN 206-1066).

Inst Adv Philo, *(Institute for the Advancement of Philosophy for Children; 0-916834),* c/o The First Mountain Foundation, P.O. Box 196, Montclair, NJ 07042 Tel 201-893-4277 (SAN 207-2378).

Inst Byzantine, *(Institute for Byzantine & Modern Greek Studies, Inc.; 0-914744),* 115 Gilbert Rd., Belmont, MA 02178 Tel 617-484-6595 (SAN 201-5110).

Inst Dev Harmonious
See **IDHHB**

Inter Am U Pr, *(Inter American Univ. Press; 0-913480),* G.P.O. Box 3255, San Juan, PR 00936 Tel 809-754-8145 (SAN 202-7062).

Inter-Varsity, *(Inter-Varsity Press; 0-87784; 0-8308),* P.O. Box F, Downers Grove, IL 60515 Tel 312-964-5700 (SAN 202-7089).

KEY TO PUBLISHERS' AND DISTRIBUTORS' ABBREVIATIONS

Interbk Inc, *(Interbook, Inc.; 0-913456; 0-89192)*, 611 Broadway, Rm. 227, New York, NY 10012 Tel 212-677-9201 (SAN 202-7070).

Intercult Network
See Intercult Pr

Intercult Pr, *(Intercultural Press, Inc.; 0-933622)*, 70 W. Hubbard St., Chicago, IL 60610 Tel 312-321-0075 (SAN 212-6699).

InterCulture, *(InterCulture Associates; 0-88253; 0-89253)*, Quaddick Rd., P.O. Box 277, Thompson, CT 06277 Tel 203-923-9494 (SAN 202-7097).

Interstate, *(Interstate; 0-8134)*, 19-27 N. Jackson St., Danville, IL 61832 Tel 217-446-0500 (SAN 206-6548).

Interurban, *(Interurban Press; 0-916374)*, P.O. Box 6444, Glendale, CA 91205 Tel 213-240-9130 (SAN 207-9593).

Interurbans
See Interurban

Intl Bk Ctr, *(International Book Centre; 0-917062; 0-86685)*, P.O. Box 295, Troy, MI 48099 Tel 313-879-8436 (SAN 208-7022).

Intl Learn Syst, *(International Learning Systems, Inc.)*, 1715 Connecticut Ave., N.W., Washington, DC 20009 Tel 202-232-4111 (SAN 209-1615).

Intl Polygonics, *(International Polygonics, Ltd.; 0-930330)*, Madison Square, P.O. Box 1563, New York, NY 10159 Tel 212-683-2914 (SAN 211-0210); Dist. by: Academy Chicago, 425 N. Michigan Ave., Chicago, IL 60611 Tel 312-644-1723 (SAN 213-2001).

Intl Print, *(International Print Co.)*, 711 South 50th St., Philadelphia, PA 19143 (SAN 240-8627); Dist. by: Sebastian Ben Giletto, 1127 Watkins St., Philadelphia, PA 19148 (SAN 240-8635).

Intl Pub Co, *(International Pubs. Co.; 0-7178)*, 381 Park Ave., S., Suite 1301, New York, NY 10016 Tel 212-685-2864 (SAN 202-5655).

Intl Pubns Serv, *(International Pubns. Service; 0-8002; 0-85066)*, 114 E. 32nd St., New York, NY 10016 Tel 212-685-9351 (SAN 169-5819).

Intl Schol Bk Serv, *(International Scholarly Book Services, Inc. (ISBS, Inc.); 0-89955)*, P.O. Box 1632, Beaverton, OR 97075 Tel 503-292-2606 (SAN 169-7129).

Intl Univs Pr, *(International Universities Press, Inc.; 0-8236)*, 315 Fifth Ave., New York, NY 10016 Tel 212-684-7900 (SAN 202-7186).

IO Pubns
See North Atlantic

Iowa St U Pr, *(Iowa State Univ. Press; 0-8138)*, 2121 S. State Ave., Ames, IA 50010 Tel 515-294-5280 (SAN 202-7194).

Irego, *(Irego; 0-911732)*, P.O. Box 286, Lenox Hill Sta., 221 E. 70th St., New York, NY 10021 (SAN 215-661X).

Iris Pr, *(Iris Press, Inc.; 0-916078)*, 27 Chestnut St., Binghamton, NY 13905 Tel 607-722-6739 (SAN 207-7566).

Irish Bk Ctr, *(Irish Book Center)*, 245 W. 104th St., New York, NY 10025 Tel 212-866-0309 (SAN 209-1089).

Iron Mtn Pr, *(Iron Mountain Press)*, Box D, Emory, VA 24327 Tel 215-344 217-7994).

Iroquois Hse, *(Iroquois House, Pubs.; 0-931980)*, Haynes Canyon, Mountain Park, NM 88325 Tel 505-682-2751 (SAN 212-8101).

Irvington, *(Irvington Pubs.; 0-89197; 0-8290)*, 551 Fifth Ave., New York, NY 10176 Tel 212-697-8100 (SAN 207-2408).

Island CA, *(Island Press; 0-933280)*, Div. of Round Valley Agrarian Institute, Star Route 1, Box 38, Covelo, CA 95428 Tel 707-983-6432 (SAN 212-5129).

Island Her, *(Island Heritage Ltd.; 0-89610)*, 550 North Nimitz Highway, Honolulu, HI 96817 Tel 808-526-1126 (SAN 211-1403).

ITA
See Pitman Learning

Ithaca Hse, *(Ithaca House; 0-87886)*, 108 N. Plain St., Ithaca, NY 14850 Tel 607-272-1233 (SAN 202-7224).

Ithaca Pr MA, *(Ithaca Press; 0-915940)*, P.O. Box 853, Lowell, MA 01853 Tel 617-453-2177 (SAN 208-709X).

Ivey Pubns, *(Ivey Pubns.; 0-9600864)*, 1845 Arkoe Dr., S.E, Atlanta, GA 30316 (SAN 207-6799).

Ivy Hill, *(Ivy Hill Press; 0-9601542)*, 8817 Greenview Place, Spring Valley, CA 92077 (SAN 212-5145).

IWP Pub, *(IWP Publishing; 0-914766)*, P.O. Box 2449, Menlo Park, CA 94025 Tel 415-321-4468 (SAN 203-798X).

J A Allen, *(Allen, J. A., & Co. Ltd.; 0-85131)*, Dist. by: Sporting Book Center, Inc., Canaan, NY 12029 Tel 518-794-8998 (SAN 222-8734).

J A Lohmann, *(Lohmann, Jeanne A.)*, 722 Tenth Ave., San Francisco, CA 94118 Tel 415-387-7644 (SAN 209-2204).

J & J Dist, *(J. & J. Distributors)*, P.O. Box 247, Raymondville, TX 78580 Tel 512-689-2523 (SAN 213-5256).

J B Burns, *(Burns, J. B.; 0-9602998)*, 4250 Lauderdale Ave., La Crescenta, CA 91214 (SAN 213-473X).

J Custis
See D Brown Bks

J De Graff
See De Graff

J H Hammill, *(Hammill, J. H., III; 0-9600652)*, Diablo Valley College, 321 Golf Club Rd., Pleasant Hill, CA 94523 Tel 415-685-1230 (SAN 203-8986).

J M Bryant, *(Bryant, James M.)*, P.O. Box 412, Normangee, TX 77871 Tel 713-828-4265 (SAN 206-2070).

J P Tarcher, *(Tarcher, J. P., Inc.; 0-87477)*, 9110 Sunset Blvd., Suite 250, Los Angeles, CA 90069 Tel 213-273-3274 (SAN 202-0424); Dist. by: Houghton Mifflin Co., Wayside Rd., Burlington, MA 01803 Tel 800-225-3362 (SAN 200-2388).

J Simon, *(Simon, Joseph; 0-934710)*, Box 4071, Malibu, CA 90265 Tel 213-457-3293 (SAN 213-9669).

J T White, *(White, James T., & Co.; 0-88371)*, 1700 State Hwy. 3, Clifton, NJ 07013 Tel 201-773-9300 (SAN 202-7291).

J V Willis, *(Willis, J. V., Pubs.; 0-913732)*, 825 May St., Hammond, IN 46320 Tel 219-931-2672 (SAN 201-0178).

Jacek, *(Jacek Publishing Co.; 0-9601084)*, 38 Morris Lane, Milford, CT 06460 (SAN 209-4029).

Jacobs Enter
See J & J Dist

Jamestown Pubs, *(Jamestown Pubs., Inc.; 0-89061)*, P.O. Box 6743, Providence, RI 02940 Tel 401-351-1915 (SAN 201-5196).

Janus Bks, *(Janus Book Pubs.; 0-915510)*, 2501 Industrial Pkwy. W., Hayward, CA 94545 Tel 415-887-7070 (SAN 208-0478).

Japan Pubns, *(Japan Pubns. Inc.; 0-87040)*, Dist. by: Kodansha International Inc., C/O Harper & Row Pubs., Inc, Keystone Industrial Park, Scranton, PA 18512 (SAN 215-3742).

Jargon Soc, *(Jargon Society, Inc., The; 0-912330)*, Dist. by: Inland Book Co., 22 Hemingway Ave., East Haven, CT 06512 Tel 203-467-4257 (SAN 200-4151).

Jawbone Pr, *(Jawbone Pr.; 0-918198)*, Waldron Island, WA 98297 (SAN 210-2188).

Jelm Mtn, *(Jelm Mountain Pubns.; 0-936204)*, 209 Park St., Laramie, WY 82070 Tel 307-742-8053 (SAN 216-1419).

Jenkins, *(Jenkins Publishing Co.; 0-8363)*, P.O. Box 2085, Austin, TX 78767 Tel 512-444-6616 (SAN 202-7321).

Jeremy Bks, *(Jeremy Books; 0-89877)*, Dist. by: Successful Living, Inc., 9905 Hamilton Road, Eden Prairie, MN 55344 (SAN 213-0939).

Jewish Pubn, *(Jewish Publication Society of America; 0-8276)*, 1930 Chestnut St., Philadelphia, PA 19103 Tel 215-564-5925 (SAN 201-0240).

JH Pr, *(JH Press; 0-935672)*, P.O. Box 294, Village Sta., New York, NY 10014 (SAN 213-6279).

JLJ Pubs, *(JLJ Pubs.; 0-937172)*, 824 Shrine Rd., Springfield, OH 45504 (SAN 215-322X).

John Day, *(John Day Co., Inc.; 0-381)*, C/O Harper & Row Pubs., 10 E. 53rd St., New York, NY 10022 (SAN 211-6960); Dist. by: Harper & Row Pubs., Keystone Industrial Park, Scranton, PA 18512 (SAN 215-3742).

John Knox, *(John Knox Press; 0-8042)*, 341 Ponce De Leon Ave., N.E., Rm. 416, Atlanta, GA 30365 Tel 404-873-1549 (SAN 271-7956).

John Muir, *(Muir, John, Pubns.; 0-912528)*, P.O. Box 613, Santa Fe, NM 87504-0613 Tel 505-982-4078 (SAN 203-9079); Dist. by: W. W. Norton & Co., 500 Fifth Ave., New York, NY 10110 Tel 212-354-5500 (SAN 202-5795).

Johns Hopkins, *(Johns Hopkins Univ. Press; 0-8018)*, Baltimore, MD 21218 Tel 301-338-7861 (SAN 202-7348).

Johnson Chi, *(Johnson Publishing Co., Inc.; 0-87485)*, 820 S. Michigan Ave., Chicago, IL 60605 Tel 312-322-9248 (SAN 201-0305).

Johnson NC, *(Johnson Publishing Co.; 0-930230)*, P. O. Box 217, Murfreesboro, NC 27855 (SAN 201-0291).

Johnson Repr, *(Johnson Reprint Corp.; 0-384)*, Subs. of Harcourt, Brace & Jovanovich, Inc., 111 Fifth Ave., New York, NY 10003 Tel 212-741-6800 (SAN 285-0362); Orders to: 757 Third Ave., New York, NY 10017 Tel 212-888-2925 (SAN 285-0370).

Jolean Pub Co, *(Jolean Publishing Co.; 0-934284)*, P.O. Box 163, Arverne, NY 11692 (SAN 212-9507).

Jorgensen Pub, *(Jorgensen Publishing Co.; 0-938128)*, 1801 Ave. of the Stars, Los Angeles, CA 90067 (SAN 219-7944).

Joseph Nichols, *(Joseph Nichols Publisher; 0-912484)*, P.O. Box 2394, Tulsa, OK 74101 Tel 918-583-3390 (SAN 203-901X).

Jotarian, *(Jotarian Productions; 0-943454)*, 3976 Warner Ave., No. A-4, Landover Hills, MD 20784 Tel 301-322-2480 (SAN 240-6918).

Jove Pubns, *(Jove Pubns., Inc.; 0-515)*, Div. of Berkley/Jove Publishing Group, 200 Madison Ave., New York, NY 10016 Tel 212-686-9820 (SAN 215-8817); Dist. by: ICD, 250 W. 55th St., New York, NY 10019 Tel 212-262-7444 (SAN 169-5800).

Jubilee Bks, *(Jubilee Books; 0-914300)*, Box 1460, New York, NY 10001 (SAN 209-2549).

Judson, *(Judson Press; 0-8170)*, P.O. Box 851, Valley Forge, PA 19482-0851 Tel 215-768-2111 (SAN 201-0348).

Jungle Garden, *(Jungle Garden Press)*, 47 Oak Rd., Fairfax, CA 94930 Tel 415-456-4884 (SAN 210-8216).

Juniper, *(Juniper Press; 0-910822)*, 41-15 44th St., Long Island City, NY 11104 (SAN 203-9117) Moved, Left No Forwarding Address.

Juniper Imprint of **Fawcett**

Juniper Maine, *(Juniper Press; 0-913977)*, c/o Betts Bookstore, Bangor Mall, Stillwater Ave., Bangor, ME 04401 Tel 207-947-7052 (SAN 212-1077).

Juniper Pr WI, *(Juniper Press; 0-910822)*, 1310 Shorewood Dr., La Crosse, WI 54601 Tel 608-788-0096 (SAN 207-8570).

Jupiter Bks, *(Jupiter Books; 0-935344)*, 7300 Eades Ave., La Jolla, CA 92037 (SAN 213-7658).

K B S Pr, *(K.B.S. Press; 0-942020)*, P.O. Box 665, Kenmore, WA 98028 Tel 206-488-8065 (SAN 237-9686).

K M Gentile, *(K.M. Gentile Publishing/Singing Wind Press; 0-935896)*, 4164 W. Pine, St. Louis, MO 63108 Tel 314-535-2118 (SAN 214-3917).

Kanchenjunga Pr, *(Kanchenjunga Press; 0-913600)*, 22 Rio Vista Lane, Red Bluff, CA 96080 (SAN 202-652X).

Kanthaka, *(Kanthaka Press; 0-916926)*, P.O. Box 696, Brookline Village, MA 02147 Tel 617-734-8146 (SAN 206-4375).

Karoma, *(Karoma Pubns., Inc.; 0-89720)*, 3400 Daleview Dr., Ann Arbor, MI 48103 Tel 313-665-3331 (SAN 213-8131).

Karpat, *(Karpat Pub.; 0-918570)*, 19608 Thornridge Ave., Cleveland, OH 44135 Tel 216-362-0316 (SAN 209-939X).

Kauai Museum, *(Kauai Museum Assn., Ltd.; 0-940948)*, Box 248, Lihue, HI 96766 Tel 808-245-6932 (SAN 213-1013).

Kayak, *(Kayak; 0-87711)*, 325 Ocean View Ave., Santa Cruz, CA 95062 (SAN 203-9168).

Kazi Pubns, *(Kazi Pubns.; 0-935782)*, 1215 W. Belmont Ave., Chicago, IL 60657 Tel 312-327-7598 (SAN 209-6676).

Kelley, *(Kelley, Augustus M., Pubs.; 0-678)*, 1140 Broadway, Room 901, New York, NY 10001 Tel 212-685-7202 (SAN 206-975X); Orders to: 300 Fairfield Rd., P.O. Box 1308, Fairfield, NJ 07006 (SAN 206-9768).

Kendall Whaling, *(Kendall Whaling Museum; 0-937854)*, P.O. Box 297, Sharon, MA 02067 Tel 617-784-5642 (SAN 204-9783).

Kennikat, *(Kennikat Press; 0-8046)*, 90 S. Bayles Ave., Port Washington, NY 11050 Tel 516-883-0570 (SAN 207-3064).

2139

KEY TO PUBLISHERS' AND DISTRIBUTORS' ABBREVIATIONS

Kent Pubns, (Kent Pubns.; 0-917458), 18301 Halstead St., Northbridge, CA 91325 Tel 213-349-2080 (SAN 209-0597).

Kent St U Pr, (Kent State Univ. Press; 0-87338), Kent, OH 44242 Tel 216-672-7913 (SAN 201-0437).

Kesend Pub Co
See Kesend Pub Ltd

Kesend Pub Ltd, (Kesend, Michael, Publishing, Ltd.; 0-935576), 1025 Fifth Ave., New York, NY 10028 Tel 212-249-5150 (SAN 213-6902).

KID Broadcast, (KID Broadcasting Corp.; 0-9607304), P.O. Box 2008, Idaho Falls, ID 83401 (SAN 240-9569).

King Pubns, (King Pubns.; 0-917676), P.O. Box 19332, Washington, DC 20036 Tel 202-332-7079 (SAN 209-2387).

Kings Farspan, (King's Farspan, Inc.; 0-932814), 1473 S. La Luna Ave., Ojai, CA 93023 Tel 805-646-2928 (SAN 211-8084).

Kings Pr
See Kings Farspan

Kirban, (Kirban, Salem, Inc.; 0-912582), 2117 Kent Rd., Huntingdon Valley, PA 19000 Tel 215-947-1330 (SAN 201-047X).

Kitchen Sink, (Kitchen Sink Press; 0-87816), No. 2 Swamp Road, Princeton, WI 54968 Tel 414-295-6922 (SAN 212-7784).

Kjos, (Kjos, Neil A., Music Co.; 0-910842; 0-8497), 4382 Jutland Dr., San Diego, CA 92117 Tel 619-270-9800 (SAN 201-0488).

Kluwer Academic, (Kluwer Academic Publishers), 190 Old Derby St., Hingham, MA 02043 Tel 617-749-5262 (SAN 211-481X).

Kluwer Boston
See Kluwer Academic

Knopf, (Knopf, Alfred A., Inc.; 0-394), Subs. of Random House, Inc., 201 E. 50th St., New York, NY 10022 Tel 212-757-2600 (SAN 202-5825); Orders to: 400 Hahn Rd., Westminster, MD 21157 (SAN 202-5833).

Knowles, (Knowles, Alison; 0-914216), 122 Spring St., New York, NY 10012 (SAN 216-1516).

Kodansha, (Kodansha International USA, Ltd.; 0-87011), C/O Harper & Row Pubs., 10 E. 53rd St., New York, NY 10022 Tel 212-593-7050 (SAN 201-0526); Dist. by: Harper & Row Pubs., Inc., Keystone Industrial Park, Scranton, PA 18512 (SAN 215-3742).

Koheleth Pub, (Koheleth Publishing Co.; 0-913964), 750 Gonzalez Dr., San Francisco, CA 94132 (SAN 203-9230) Moved, Left No Forwarding Address.

Konglomerati, (Konglomerati Florida Foundation for Literature & the Book Arts, Inc.; 0-916906), P.O. Box 5001, Gulfport, FL 33737 Tel 813-323-0386 (SAN 207-8589).

Kraus Intl, (Kraus International Publications; 0-527), Div. of Kraus-Thomson Organization Ltd., Rte. 100, Millwood, NY 10546 Tel 914-762-2200 (SAN 210-7562).

Kraus Repr, (Kraus Reprint; 0-527; 3-601; 3-262), A Div. of Kraus-Thomson Organization, Ltd., Rte. 100, Millwood, NY 10546 Tel 914-762-2200 (SAN 201-0542).

Kregel, (Kregel Pubns.; 0-8254), P.O. Box 2607, Grand Rapids, MI 49501 Tel 616-459-9444 (SAN 206-9792). Imprints: RBDH (Religious Book Discount House Pubns.).

Krishna Pr, (Krishna Press), Div. of Gordon Press, P.O. Box 459, Bowling Green Sta., New York, NY 10004 (SAN 202-6570).

Kronos Pr, (Kronos Press; 0-917994), Glassboro State College, Glassboro, NJ 08028 Tel 609-445-6048 (SAN 210-2226).

Ktav, (Ktav Publishing House, Inc.; 0-87068), 75 Varick St., New York, NY 10013 Tel 212-966-6980 (SAN 201-0038).

KTO Pr
See Kraus Intl

L Gray Pub, (Gray, Lee, Publishing; 0-9603976), 187 James Ave., Red Bluff, CA 96080 (SAN 213-7402) Moved, left no forwarding address.

L Maynard, (Maynard, Louis), 5922 S. Sunnylane Rd., Oklahoma City, OK 73135 Tel 405-799-2148 (SAN 207-2483).

L Olds, (Olds, Lee), P.O. Box 40731, San Francisco, CA 94110 (SAN 206-1597); Dist. by: Book People, 2940 Seventh St., Berkeley, CA 94710 (SAN 168-9517) Moved, Left No Forwarding Address.

L S Brown Pub, (Brown, Lewis, S., Publisher; 0-9608542), 124 W. Pierpont St., Kingston, NY 12401 Tel 914-338-4352 (SAN 240-6047).

La Leche, (La Leche League International, Inc.; 0-912500), 9616 Minneapolis Ave., Franklin Park, IL 60131 Tel 312-455-7730 (SAN 201-0585).

La Siesta, (La Siesta Press; 0-910856), P.O. Box 406, Glendale, CA 91209 Tel 213-244-9305 (SAN 201-0607).

La State U Pr, (Louisiana State Univ. Press; 0-8071), Baton Rouge, LA 70893 Tel 504-388-6666 (SAN 202-6597).

Lacon Pubs, (Lacon Pubs.; 0-930344), Rte. 1, P.O. Box 15, Harrison, ID 83833 Tel 208-689-3467 (SAN 204-9597).

Laddin Pr, (Laddin Press; 0-913806), 2 Park Ave., New York, NY 10016 Tel 212-532-4384 (SAN 201-0615).

Lake View Pr, (Lake View Press; 0-941702), P.O. Box 25421, Chicago, IL 60625 Tel 312-935-2694 (SAN 239-2488).

Lame Johnny, (Lame Johnny Pr.; 0-917624), Div. of Independent Publishing Services, Star Rte. 3, Box 9A, Hermosa, SD 57744 Tel 605-255-4466 (SAN 204-6136).

Lancaster-Miller, (Lancaster-Miller Pubs.; 0-89581), P. O. Box 3056, Berkeley, CA 94703 Tel 415-845-3782 (SAN 213-6503).

Lancer, (Lancer Militaria; 0-935856), P.O. Box 100, Sims, AR 71969 Tel 501-867-2232 (SAN 213-7682).

Landfall Pr, (Landfall Press, Inc.; 0-913428), 5171 Chapin St., Dayton, OH 45429 Tel 513-298-9123 (SAN 202-6627).

Landgrove Pr, (Landgrove Press; 0-9608726), Landgrove, VT 05148 Tel 802-824-5943 (SAN 238-3098).

Lane
See Sunset-Lane

Lanser Pr, (Lanser Press; 0-9603900), P.O. Box 38, Plainfield, VT 05667 (SAN 214-3933).

Large Print Bks Imprint of G K Hall

Larksdale, (Larksdale Press, The; 0-89896), 5400 Memorial Towers, Houston, TX 77007 Tel 713-869-9092 (SAN 220-0643).

Larlin Corp, (Larlin Corp.; 0-910220; 0-89783), P.O. Box 1523, Marietta, GA 30061 Tel 404-424-6210 (SAN 201-4432).

Larousse, (Larousse & Co., Inc.; 0-88332), 572 Fifth Ave., New York, NY 10036 Tel 212-575-9515 (SAN 202-6643).

Lat Am Lit Rev Pr, (Latin American Lit. Rev. Press; 0-935480), Box 8316, Pittsburgh, PA 15218 (SAN 215-2142).

Latitudes Pr, (Latitudes Press), 3215 Lafayette Ave., Austin, TX 78722 Tel 512-478-1454 (SAN 202-6651); Dist. by: SBD: Small Press Distribution, 1636 Oceanview, Kensington, CA 94707 (SAN 204-5826).

Law Arts, (Law-Arts Pubs., Inc.; 0-88238), 2001 Wilshire Blvd., Suite 500, Santa Monica, CA 90043 Tel 213-829-4315 (SAN 201-0712).

Lawrence Hill, (Hill, Lawrence, & Co., Inc.; 0-88208), 520 Riverside Ave., Westport, CT 06880 Tel 203-226-9392 (SAN 214-1221).

Lawton Pr, (Lawton Press; 0-933044), 673 Pelham Rd., Suite 16E, New Rochelle, NY 10805 (SAN 212-2871) Moved, left no forwarding address.

LE Imprint of Dell

Leaf Pr, (Leaf Press; 0-940360), 841 Lucile, No. 3, Los Angeles, CA 90026 (SAN 222-9803).

Lectorum Corp
See Lectorum Pubns

Lectorum Pubns, (Lectorum Pubns.), 137 W. 14th St., New York, NY 10011 (SAN 207-253X).

Leetes Isl, (Leete's Island Books; 0-918172), P.O. Box 1131, New Haven, CT 06505 Tel 203-481-2536 (SAN 210-2285); Dist. by: Independent Publishers Group, One Pleasant Ave., Port Washington, NY 11050 (SAN 210-2293).

Legacy Pub Co, (Legacy Publishing Co.; 0-918784), 2008 Perkins Rd., Baton Rouge, LA 70808 Tel 504-343-0366 (SAN 210-4539).

Leisure Bks CT, (Leisure Books), P.O. Box 270, Norwalk, CT 06852 (SAN 215-2258) Moved, left no forwarding address.

Lemma, (Lemma Publishing Corp.; 0-87696), 509 Fifth Ave., New York, NY 10017 (SAN 202-6694) Moved, Left No Forwarding Address.

Lenox Hill, (Lenox Hill Press), Div. of Crown Publishing, Inc., 235 E. 44th St., New York, NY 10017 Tel 212-687-5250 (SAN 201-0801).

LFL Imprint of Dell

Lib Res, (Library Research Associates; 0-912526), Dunderberg Rd., R.D. 5, Box 41, Monroe, NY 10950 Tel 914-783-1144 (SAN 201-0887).

Liberation Bk, (Liberation Bookstore), P.O. Box 17, Radio City Sta., New York, NY 10019 (SAN 206-4006) Moved, left no forwarding address.

Liberator Pr, (Liberator Press; 0-930720), Box 7128, Chicago, IL 60680 Tel 312-243-3791 (SAN 213-1072).

Libra, (Libra Pubs., Inc.; 0-87212), 391 Willets Rd., Roslyn Heights, L. I., NY 11577 Tel 516-484-4950 (SAN 201-0909).

Library Pr Imprint of Open Court

Life Pubs Intl, (Life Pubs. International; 0-8297), 3360 N.W. 110th St., Miami, FL 33167 Tel 305-685-6334 (SAN 213-5817).

Lifesigns, (Lifesigns: Words & Images; 0-943510), 882 Bates Ave., El Cerrito, CA 94530 Tel 415-527-6722 (SAN 240-7043).

Light & Life, (Light & Life Press (IN); 0-89367), 999 College Ave., Winona Lake, IN 46590 Tel 219-267-7161 (SAN 206-8419).

Lighthouse Pr NY
See Lightyear

Lightyear, (Lightyear Press, Inc.; 0-89968), P.O. Box 507, Laurel, NY 11948 (SAN 213-1102).

Liguori Pubns, (Liguori Pubns.; 0-89243), 1 Liguori Dr., Liguori, MO 63057 Tel 800-325-9521 (SAN 202-6783).

Limited Ed, (Limited Editions Press; 0-8100), 8412 Wilbur Ave., Northridge, CA 91324 Tel 213-885-9961 (SAN 240-9623).

Linden Pr Imprint of S&S

Linden Pubs, (Linden Pubs.; 0-89642), 1750 N. Sycamore, Hollywood, CA 90028 (SAN 206-7218).

Lionhead Pub, (Lionhead Publishing; 0-89018), 2521 East Stratford Court, Shorewood, Milwaukee, WI 53211 Tel 414-332-7474 (SAN 206-5568).

Lion's Head, (Lion's Head Publishing Co.), 4415 Karen Ave., Fort Wayne, IN 46815 (SAN 207-2564).

Lippincott, (Lippincott, J. B., Co.; 0-397), E. Washington Square, Philadelphia, PA 19105 Tel 215-574-4200 (SAN 201-0933); Orders to: 2350 Virginia Ave., Hagerstown, MD 21740 (SAN 215-3742).

Literary Classics, (Literary Classics of the U.S., Inc.; 0-940450), 1 Lincoln Place, New York, NY 10023 Tel 212-595-5449 (SAN 217-1945); Dist. by: Viking Press, 40 W. 23rd St., New York, NY 10010 Tel 212-807-7300 (SAN 282-5074).

Literary Herald, (Literary Herald Press; 0-9602124), 408 Oak St., Danville, IL 61832 (SAN 212-5242).

Literati Pr, (Literati Press, Pubs.; 0-933744), The Olive Bldg., 18 E. Sunrise Hwy., Freeport, NY 11520 (SAN 212-8586).

Little, (Little, Brown & Co.; 0-316), 34 Beacon St., Boston, MA 02106 Tel 617-227-0730 (SAN 281-8884); Orders to: 200 West St., Waltham, MA 02154 Tel 617-890-0250 (SAN 281-8892).

Little Brick Hse, (Little Brick House, The; 0-9601648), 621 Saint Clair St., Vandalia, IL 62471 Tel 618-283-0024 (SAN 209-2069).

Little London, (Little London Press; 0-936564), 716 E. Washington, Colorado Springs, CO 80907 Tel 303-471-1322 (SAN 214-0419).

Liveright, (Liveright Publishing Corp.; 0-87140), Subs. of W. W. Norton Co., Inc., 500 Fifth Ave., New York, NY 10110 Tel 212-354-5500 (SAN 201-0976).

Llewellyn
See Llewellyn Pubns

Llewellyn Pubns, (Llewellyn Pubns.; 0-87542), Div. of Chester-Kent, Inc., P.O. Box 43383, St. Paul, MN 55164 Tel 612-291-1970 (SAN 281-9147); Orders to: P.O. Box 43383, St. Paul, MN 55164 Tel 612-291-1970 (SAN 281-9155).

Lochinvar Imprint of Exposition

Lodestar Bks, (Lodestar Books; 0-525), 2 Park Ave., New York, NY 10016 Tel 212-725-1818 (SAN 212-5013).

Loizeaux, (Loizeaux Brothers, Inc.; 0-87213), 1238 Corlies Ave., Box 277, Neptune, NJ 07753 Tel 201-774-8144 (SAN 202-6848).

KEY TO PUBLISHERS' AND DISTRIBUTORS' ABBREVIATIONS

Longman, *(Longman Inc.),* 1560 Broadway, New York, NY 10036 Tel 212-764-3950 (SAN 202-6856).
LongRiver Bks, *(LongRiver Bks.; 0-942986),* c/o Inland Bk. Co., 22 Hemingway Ave., East Haven, CT 06512 Tel 203-467-4257 (SAN 240-3986).
Longship Pr, *(Longship Press; 0-917712),* Crooked Lane, Nantucket, MA 02554 Tel 207-722-3344 (SAN 209-4576); Orders to: RFD 1, Box 124, Brooks, ME 04921 (SAN 209-4584).
Longwood Pr, *(Longwood Publishing Group, In c.; 0-89341),* 51 Washington St., Dover, NH 03820 Tel 603-742-4662 (SAN 209-3170).
Loompanics, *(Loompanics Unlimited),* P.O. Box 1197, Port Townsend, WA 98368 Tel 206-385-5087 (SAN 206-4421).
Lord John, *(Lord John Press; 0-935716),* 19073 Los Alimos St., Northridge, CA 91326 Tel 213-363-6621 (SAN 213-6333).
Lorien Hse, *(Lorien House; 0-934852),* P.O. Box 1112, Black Mountain, NC 28711 Tel 704-669-6211 (SAN 209-2999).
Lotus, *(Lotus Press, Inc.; 0-916418),* P.O. Box 21607, Detroit, MI 48221 Tel 313-861-1280 (SAN 213-8867).
Lower Cape, *(Lower Cape Publishing; 0-936972),* P.O. Box 901, Orleans, MA 02653 Tel 617-255-2244 (SAN 214-4050).
Lowy Pub, *(Lowy Publishing; 0-9602940),* 5047 Wigton, Houston, TX 77096 Tel 713-723-3209 (SAN 212-9132).
Lucas, *(Lucas Brothers Pubs.; 0-87543),* 909 Lowry St., Missouri Store Bldg., Columbia, MO 65201 Tel 314-442-6161 (SAN 201-1050).
Luce, *(Luce, Robert B., Inc.; 0-88331),* 425 Asylum St., Bridgeport, CT 06610 Tel 203-334-2165 (SAN 201-1069); Orders to: 540 Barnum Ave., Bridgeport, CT 06608 Tel 203-366-1900 (SAN 201-1077).
Lucis, *(Lucis Publishing Co.; 0-85330),* 866 United Nations Plaza, Suite 566-7, New York, NY 10017 Tel 212-421-1577 (SAN 201-1085).
Lunan-Ferguson, *(Lunan-Ferguson Library, Pubs.; 0-911724),* 2219 Clement St., San Francisco, CA 94121 Tel 415-752-6100 (SAN 203-4042).
Lyle Stuart, *(Stuart, Lyle, Inc.; 0-8184),* 120 Enterprise Ave., Secaucus, NJ 07094 Tel 201-866-0490 (SAN 201-1131).
Lynx Hse, *(Lynx House Press; 0-89924),* P.O. Box 800, Amherst, MA 01002 Tel 413-773-7988 (SAN 208-2691).
M Arman, *(Arman, M., Pub. Inc.; 0-933078),* Box 785, Ormond Beach, FL 32074 Tel 904-673-5576 (SAN 212-4777).
M Bibb, *(Bibb, Mary),* 1100 Bellevue Pl., N.W., Grants Pass, OR 97526 Tel 503-474-2581 (SAN 238-0420).
M Evans, *(Evans, M., & Co., Inc.; 0-87131),* 216 E. 49th St., New York, NY 10017 Tel 212-688-2810 (SAN 203-4050); Dist. by: E. P. Dutton, 2 Park Ave., New York, NY 10016 (SAN 201-0070).
M Jones, *(Jones, Marshall, Co.; 0-8338),* Div. of Golden Quill Press, Francestown, NH 03043 (SAN 206-8834).
M McCosh Bkslr, *(McCosh, Melvin, Bookseller),* 26500 Edgewood Rd., Excelsior, MN 55331 Tel 612-474-8084 (SAN 207-4248).
M Molek Inc, *(Molek, M., Inc.; 0-9603142),* P.O. Box 453, Dover, DE 19901 Tel 302-678-1260 (SAN 212-1166).
M O P Pr, *(M.O.P. Press; 0-942432),* Rte. 24, Box 53C, Fort Myers, FL 33908 (SAN 223-0860).
M Robertson
See Biblio Dist
M S Rosenberg, *(Rosenberg, Mary S., Inc.; 0-917324),* 17 W. 60th St., New York, NY 10023 Tel 212-362-4873 (SAN 205-2296).
M Wiener, *(Wiener, Moshe; 0-9605406),* 854 Newburg Ave., North Woodmere, NY 11581 (SAN 215-9856).
Macalester, *(Macalester Park Publishing Co.; 0-910924),* 1571 Grand Ave., St. Paul, MN 55105 Tel 612-698-8877 (SAN 203-9451).
McBooks Pr, *(McBooks Press; 0-935526),* 106 N. Aurora, Ithaca, NY 14850 Tel 607-272-6602 (SAN 213-8573) (SAN 202-2060).
McClain, *(McClain Printing Co.; 0-87012),* 212 Main St., Parsons, WV 26287 Tel 304-478-2881 (SAN 203-9478).

McDougal-Littell, *(McDougal, Littell & Co.; 0-88343),* P.O. Box 1667, Evanston, IL 60204 Tel 312-967-0900 (SAN 202-2532).
McGill-Queens U Pr, *(McGill-Queens Univ. Press; 0-7735),* Orders to: University of Toronto Press, 33 E. Tupper St., Buffalo, NY 14203 Tel 416-667-7791 (SAN 214-2651).
McGrath, *(McGrath Publishing Co.; 0-8434),* P.O. Box 9001, Wilmington, NC 28402 Tel 919-763-3757 (SAN 212-0275).
McGraw, *(McGraw-Hill Book Co.; 0-07),* 1221 Avenue of the Americas,27th Fl., New York, NY 10020 Tel 212-997-6611 (SAN 200-2248); Orders to: Hightstown, NJ 08520 Tel 609-426-5254 (SAN 200-254X); Orders to: 8171 Redwood Hwy., Novato, CA 94947 Tel 415-897-5201 (SAN 200-2566); Orders to: Manchester, MO 63011 Tel 314-227-1600 (SAN 200-2558).
McKay, *(McKay, David, Co., Inc.; 0-679),* 2 Park Ave., New York, NY 10016 Tel 212-340-9800 (SAN 285-046X); Orders to: Fodor's/McKay, O'Neill Hwy., Dunmore, PA 18512 Tel 717-344-2614 (SAN 285-0478). *Imprints:* Weybright (Weybright & Talley, Inc.); Wyden (Wyden, Peter H., Inc.).
Mackinac Island, *(Mackinac Island State Park Commission; 0-911872),* Box 370, Mackinac Island, MI 49757 Tel 906-847-3328 (SAN 202-5981).
Macmillan, *(Macmillan Publishing Co., Inc.; 0-02),* 866 Third Ave., New York, NY 10022 Tel 212-935-2000 (SAN 202-5574); Orders to: Front & Brown Sts., Riverside, NJ 08370 (SAN 202-5582). *Imprints:* Collier (Collier Books); CCPr (Crowell-Collier Press).
McNally, *(McNally, Loftin & West, Publishers; 0-87461),* P.O. Box 1316, Santa Barbara, CA 93102 Tel 805-964-5117 (SAN 281-9643); Orders to: 5390 Overpass Rd., Santa Barbara, CA 93111 (SAN 281-9651).
Macoy Pub, *(Macoy Publishing & Masonic Supply Co., Inc.; 0-910928),* P.O. Box 9759, Richmond, VA 23228 Tel 804-262-6551 (SAN 202-2265).
McPherson & Co, *(McPherson & Company; 0-914232),* P.O. Box 638, New Paltz, NY 12561 Tel 914-255-7084 (SAN 203-0624).
Macrae, *(Macrae Smith Co.; 0-8255),* Rtes. 54 & Old 147, Turbotville, PA 17772 (SAN 202-6007) Moved, Left No Forwarding Address.
Macro Bks, *(Macro Books; 0-913080),* P.O. Box 26661, Tempe, AZ 85282 Tel 602-949-5559 (SAN 207-0480).
MCS, *(MCS; 0-932150),* Box 1774, Morganton, NC 28655 (SAN 239-4529).
Maelstrom, *(Maelstrom Press; 0-917554),* 8 Farm Hill Rd., Cape Elizabeth, ME 04107 (SAN 207-8899).
Mafdet, *(Mafdet Press; 0-918534),* 1313 S. Jefferson Ave., Springfield, MO 65807 Tel 417-866-5141 (SAN 209-9497).
Magic Circle Bk, *(Magic Circle Book Shop),* 10 Grace Ave, Great Neck, NY 11021 (SAN 227-1273) Moved, left no forwarding address.
Magic Unicorn Pubns, *(Magic Unicorn Pubns.; 0-9601836),* Sunrise Country Club, 93 Palma Dr, Rancho Mirage, CA 92270 Tel 619-324-6906 (SAN 222-0636); Dist. by: Bookpeople, 2940 Seventh St., Berkeley, CA 94710 Tel 415-549-3030 (SAN 168-9517).
Magnes Mus, *(Magnes Museum),* 2911 Russell St., Berkeley, CA 94705 Tel 415-849-2710 (SAN 214-2511).
Maize Pr, *(Maize Press; 0-939558),* P.O. Box 8251, San Diego, CA 92102 Tel 714-455-1128 (SAN 216-6852).
Major Bks, *(Major Books; 0-89041),* 21335 Roscoe Blvd., Canoga Park, CA 91304 Tel 213-999-4100 (SAN 207-4117); 18-39 128th St., College Point, NY 11356 Tel 212-939-1119 (SAN 207-4117); Orders to: Kable News, Inc., 777 Third Ave., New York, NY 10017 Tel 212-486-2828 (SAN 207-4109).
Man-Root, *(Man-Root),* P. O. Box 982, South San Francisco, CA 94080 (SAN 207-8635).
Manchester, *(Manchester Univ. Press; 0-7190),* 51 Washington St., Dover, NH 03820 Tel 603-742-4662 (SAN 281-9740).
Mandala
See Irvington

Mandala Bks, *(Mandala Books; 0-9603226),* RFD Box 56, Vershire, VT 05079 (SAN 213-7542) Do Not Confuse with Mandala Press in MA (Mandala) or Mandala Press in NC (Mandala Pr).
Mangan Bks, *(Mangan Books; 0-930208),* 6245 Snowheights Ct., El Paso, TX 79912 Tel 915-584-1662 (SAN 209-3804).
Manifest Destiny, *(Manifest Destiny Books; 0-914852),* P.O. Box 57, Dorchester, MA 02124 Tel 617-288-8765 (SAN 206-7889) Tel 617-423-4340.
Manor Bks
See Woodhill
Manuscript Pr, *(Manuscript Press; 0-936414),* Box 1762, Wayne, NJ 07470 Tel 201-628-1259 (SAN 214-3224); Dist. by: PDA Enterprises, Box 8010, New Orleans, LA 70182 (SAN 222-0989).
Manyland, *(Manyland Books, Inc.; 0-87141),* 84-39 90th St., Woodhaven, NY 11421 Tel 212-441-6768 (SAN 203-963X).
Margoe Jane, *(Margoe Jane Pubns.; 0-9602330),* Sawyer Ave., Apartment No. 45, Malone, NY 12953 Tel 518-483-2020 (SAN 212-2200).
Marlboro Pr, *(Marlboro Pr., the; 0-910395),* Box 157, Marlboro, VT 05344 Tel 802-257-0781 (SAN 281-9813); Dist. by: Inland Bk. Co., P.O. Box 261, E. Haven, CT 06512 Tel 203-467-4257 (SAN 200-4151); Dist. by: New York State Small Pr. Assn., 198 Main St., Nyack, NY 10960 Tel 914-358-1190 (SAN 281-983X); Orders to: Small Press Distribution Inc., 1784 Shattuck Ave., Berkeley, CA 94709 Tel 415-549-3336 (SAN 282-5996).
Marquette, *(Marquette Univ. Press; 0-87462),* 1324 W. Wisconsin Ave., Rm. 409, Milwaukee, WI 53233 Tel 414-224-1564 (SAN 203-9702).
Mars Pubns, *(Mars Pubns.; 0-910759),* 1211 East Altadena Drive, Altadena, CA 91001 (SAN 264-1984).
Mason Charter
See Van Nos Reinhold
Mason-Charter Pub, *(Mason/Charter Publishers,Inc.),* 641 Lex. Ave., New York, NY 10022 (SAN 220-8326).
Master Writer & Pubs, *(Master Writers & Pubs.; 0-941718),* P.O. Box 24, Haddon Heights, NJ 08035 Tel 609-547-7439 (SAN 239-2550).
Mathom, *(Mathom Publishing Co; 0-930000),* 68 E. Mohawk St., Oswego, NY 13126 Tel 315-343-3035 (SAN 285-0508); P.O. Box 362, Oswego, NY 13126 (SAN 285-0516).
Maverick, *(Maverick Pubns.; 0-89288),* P.O. Box 243, Bend, OR 97709 Tel 503-382-6978 (SAN 208-7634).
Maverick Bks, *(Maverick Books (TX); 0-9608612),* 1101 Baylor, Perryton, TX 79070 (SAN 240-7183).
Mazgeen Pr, *(Mazgeen Press; 0-915330),* P.O. Box 70, Key West, FL 33040 Tel 305-294-0734 (SAN 207-1797) Moved, Left No Forwarding Address.
Md Bk Exch, *(Maryland Book Exchange),* 4500 College Ave., College Park, MD 20740 Tel 301-927-2510 (SAN 203-977X).
MD Bks, *(MD Books; 0-9603118),* 26313 Purissima Rd., Los Altos Hills, CA 94022 (SAN 223-1670).
Md Hist, *(Maryland Historical Society; 0-938420),* 201 W. Monument St., Baltimore, MD 21201 (SAN 203-9788).
Meadow Lane, *(Meadow Lane Pubns.; 0-934826),* 530 North Midway Drive, No. 79, Escondido, CA 92027 Tel 619-747-0258 (SAN 213-5361).
Medallion Imprint of **Berkley Pub**
Medieval & Renaissance NY, *(Medieval & Renaissance Texts & Studies; 0-86698),* State Univ. of New York, Binghamton, NY 13901 (SAN 216-6119).
Meher Baba Info, *(Meher Baba Information; 0-940700),* Box 1101, Berkeley, CA 94701 Tel 415-562-1101 (SAN 202-618X); Dist. by: Bookpeople, 2940 Seventh St., Berkeley, CA 94710 Tel 415-549-3033 (SAN 168-9517).
Melrose Sq Imprint of **Holloway**
Memphis St Univ, *(Memphis State Univ. Press; 0-87870),* Memphis State Univ., Memphis, TN 38152 Tel 901-454-2752 (SAN 202-6228).

KEY TO PUBLISHERS' AND DISTRIBUTORS' ABBREVIATIONS

Menorah Pub, *(Menorah Publishing Co., Inc.; 0-932232)*, 15 W. 84th St., New York, NY 10024 Tel 212-787-2248 (SAN 212-1158).
Ment *Imprint of* NAL
Mer *Imprint of* NAL
Meredith, *(Meredith Corp.)*, Publisher Abbreviation Without Addresses Are for Titles That Are Out of Print. These Are Obsolete Abbreviations. Publisher's Abbreviation Is Now BH&G.
Merging Media, *(Merging Media; 0-934536)*, 59 Sandra Circle A3, Westfield, NJ 07090 Tel 201-232-7224 (SAN 206-3662).
Meriwether Pub, *(Meriwether Publishing Ltd.; 0-916260)*, P.O. Box 7710, Colorado Springs, CO 80933 Tel 312-495-0300 (SAN 208-4716).
Mermaid *Imprint of* **Hill & Wang**
Merrill, *(Merrill, Charles E., Publishing Co.; 0-675)*, Div. of Bell & Howell Co., 1300 Alum Creek Dr., Columbus, OH 43216 Tel 614-258-8441 (SAN 200-2116).
Merrimack Bk Serv
  See Merrimack Publishers' Circle
Merrimack Publishers' Circle, *(Merrimack Book Service, Inc.)*, 458 Boston St., Topsfield, MA 01973 Tel 617-887-2440 (SAN 212-193X); Orders to: 99 Main St., Salem, NH 03079 Tel 617-685-4636 (SAN 212-1948).
Metacom Pr, *(Metacom Press; 0-911381)*, 31 Beaver St., Worcester, MA 01603 Tel 617-757-1683 (SAN 272-3581).
Metagam, *(Metagaming)*, Box 15346, Austin, TX 78761 Tel 512-836-4116 (SAN 211-8637).
Meth U Pr
  See SMU Press
Methuen Inc, *(Methuen Inc.; 0-416)*, 733 Third Ave, New York, NY 10017 Tel 212-922-3550 (SAN 213-196X); Dist. by: Transworld Distribution Services, Inc., 80 Northfield Ave., Raritan Center, Edison, NJ 08817 (SAN 213-1978).
Metis Pr Inc, *(Metis Press, Inc.; 0-934816)*, P.O. Box 25187, Chicago, IL 60625 (SAN 213-2575).
Metro Bks, *(Metro Books, Inc.; 0-8411)*, 3110 N. Arlington Heights Rd., Arlington Heights, IL 60004 Tel 312-253-9720 (SAN 203-9893).
Micah Pubns, *(Micah Pubns.; 2-916288)*, 255 Humphrey St., Marblehead, MA 01945 Tel 617-631-7601 (SAN 209-1577).
Mich St U Pr, *(Michigan State Univ. Press; 0-87013)*, 1405 S. Harrison Rd., 25 Manly Miles Bldg., East Lansing, MI 48824 Tel 517-355-9543 (SAN 202-6295).
Michael Joseph
  See Merrimack Publishers' Circle
Miles & Weir, *(Miles & Weir, Ltd.; 0-917300)*, P.O. Box 1906, San Pedro, CA 90731 Tel 213-548-5964 (SAN 208-8541).
Miller Bks, *(Miller Books; 0-912472)*, 2908 W. Valley Blvd., Alhambra, CA 91803 Tel 213-284-7607 (SAN 203-9931).
Miller Freeman, *(Miller Freeman Pubns., Inc.; 0-87930)*, 500 Howard St., San Francisco, CA 94105 Tel 415-397-1881 (SAN 213-6511).
Milwaukee Journal, *(Milwaukee Journal, Public Service Bureau)*, 333 W. State St., Milwaukee, WI 53201 Tel 414-224-2120 (SAN 240-0561).
Minn Rev Pr, *(Minnesota Review Press; 0-936484)*, C/O Dept. of English, Oregon State Univ., Corvalis, OR 97331 Tel 503-752-2536 (SAN 214-0578).
Mirage Pr, *(Mirage Press, Ltd.; 0-88358)*, P.O. Box 28, Manchester, MD 21102 Tel 301-239-8999 (SAN 202-6406).
Missing Link, *(Missing Link Co., The; 0-910149)*, P.O. Box 44014, Phoenix, AZ 85064 Tel 602-265-4753 (SAN 241-2268).
MIT Pr, *(MIT Press; 0-262)*, 28 Carleton St., Cambridge, MA 02142 Tel 617-253-2884 (SAN 202-6414).
MJG Co, *(MJG Co.; 0-932632)*, P.O. Box 7743, Midland, TX 79708-0743 Tel 915-682-3184 (SAN 212-2901).
MN Pubs, *(M. N. Pubs.; 0-932964)*, Rte. 2, Box 55, Bonnerdale, AR 71933 Tel 501-991-3815 (SAN 212-291X) Temporarily out of business.
Mnemosyne, *(Mnemosyne Publishing Co., Inc.)*, 410 Alcazar Ave., Coral Gables, FL 33134 Tel 305-444-8908 (SAN 203-9966).

Mockingbird Bks, *(Mockingbird Books; 0-89176)*, Box 624, St. Simons Island, GA 31522 Tel 912-638-7212 (SAN 207-6470).
Mod LibC *Imprint of* **Modern Lib**
Modern Lib, *(Modern Library, Inc.)*, 201 E. 50th St., New York, NY 10022 Tel 212-751-2600 (SAN 204-5605); Orders to: Order Dept., 400 Hahn Rd., Westminster, MD 21157 (SAN 204-5613). *Imprints:* Mod LibC (Modern Library College Department).
Modernismo, *(Modernismo Pubns., Ltd.; 0-89237)*, 155 Ave. of the Americas, New York, NY 10013 Tel 212-691-7700 (SAN 208-0036).
Mojave Bks, *(Mojave Books; 0-87881)*, 7118 Canby Ave., Reseda, CA 91335 Tel 213-342-3403 (SAN 202-6430).
Molly Yes, *(Molly Yes Press; 0-931308)*, RD3, Box 70B, New Berlin, NY 13411 Tel 607-847-8070 (SAN 217-9075).
Momos, *(Momo's Press; 0-917672)*, 45 Sheridan St., San Francisco, CA 94103 Tel 415-863-3009 (SAN 206-1619).
Mona Pub, *(Mona Publishing Co., Ltd.; 0-938952)*, 79 Wall St., Suite 501, New York, NY 10005 (SAN 215-9716) Moved, Left No Forwarding Address.
Monarch Pr, *(Monarch Press; 0-671)*, Div. of Simon & Schuster, Inc., 1230 Ave. of the Americas, 12th Fl., New York, NY 10020 Tel 212-245-6400 (SAN 204-5621).
Mongolia, *(Mongolia Society, Inc., The; 0-910980)*, P.O. Drawer 606, Bloomington, IN 47402 Tel 812-335-2766 (SAN 204-000X).
Monkey Man, *(Monkey Man Press; 0-9605594)*, 8710 Wonderland Pk. Ave., Los Angeles, CA 90046 Tel 213-654-9154 (SAN 216-1648).
Monthly Rev, *(Monthly Review Press; 0-85345)*, 155 W. 23rd Street, New York, NY 10011 Tel 212-691-2555 (SAN 202-6481).
Moody, *(Moody Press; 0-8024)*, 2101 W. Howard St., Chicago, IL 60645 Tel 312-973-7800 (SAN 202-5604).
Moon Bks, *(Moon Books; 0-931452)*, P. O. Box 9223, Berkeley, CA 94709 (SAN 209-6420); Dist. by: Bookpeople, 2940 Seventh St., Berkeley, CA 94610 (SAN 168-9517).
Moore Pub Co, *(Moore Publishing Co.; 0-87716)*, P.O. Box 3036, W. Durham Sta., Durham, NC 27705 Tel 919-286-2250 (SAN 202-649X).
Moore Pub Co
  See F Apple
Moore-Taylor-Moore
  See MTM Pub Co
Morehouse, *(Morehouse-Barlow Co.; 0-8192)*, 78 Danbury Rd., Wilton, CT 06897 Tel 203-762-0721 (SAN 202-6511).
Morgan-Pacific, *(Morgan-Pacific Press Inc.; 0-89430)*, P. O. Box 456, Lomita, CA 90717 Tel 213-373-1002 (SAN 282-0218); Dist. by: Palos Verdes Book Co., P. O. Box 456, Lomita, CA 90717 (SAN 282-0226).
Morgan Pr CA
  See Morgan-Pacific
Morningland, *(Morningland Pubns., Inc.; 0-935146)*, 2630 E. Seventh St., Long Beach, CA 90804 (SAN 213-6368).
Morrow, *(Morrow, William, & Co., Inc.; 0-688)*, 105 Madison Ave., New York, NY 10016 Tel 212-889-3050 (SAN 202-5760); Orders to: Wilmor Warehouse, 6 Henderson Dr., West Caldwell, NJ 07006 (SAN 202-5779).
Mosaic Pr, *(Mosaic Pr., the; 0-934696)*, P.O. Box 925, Sedona, AZ 86336 Tel 602-282-4234 (SAN 213-4187).
Mosaic Pr OH, *(Mosaic Press; 0-88014)*, 220 W. Blackledge Dr., Tucson, AZ 85705 (SAN 219-6077).
Motheroot, *(Motheroot Pubns.)*, 214 Dewey St., Pittsburgh, PA 15218 (SAN 216-4205).
Mothers Hen, *(Mother's Hen; 0-914370)*, P.O. Box 99592, San Francisco, CA 94109 (SAN 206-1635) Moved, Left No Forwarding Address.
Motiv Methods, *(Motivational Methods, Inc.; 0-933664)*, 8569 Ramblewood Dr., Coral Springs, FL 33065 Tel 305-753-3579 (SAN 212-7687).
Mott Media, *(Mott Media; 0-915134)*, 1000 E. Huron, Milford, MI 48042 Tel 313-685-8773 (SAN 207-1460).
Mountain Pr, *(Mountain Press Publishing Co., Inc.; 0-87842)*, P.O. Box 2399, Missoula, MT 59806 Tel 406-728-1900 (SAN 202-8832).

Mouth of Dragon
  See A Bifrost
Mouton, *(Mouton Pubs.)*, Div. of Walter De Gruyter, Inc., 200 Saw Mill River Rd., Hawthorne, NY 10532 Tel 914-747-0111 (SAN 210-9239).
Mowbray Co, *(Mowbray Co. Pubs.; 0-917218)*, 222 W. Exchange St., Providence, RI 02903 Tel 401-861-1000 (SAN 205-8111).
MTM Pub Co, *(M/T/M Publishing Co.)*, P.O. Box 245, Washougal, WA 98671 (SAN 206-1627).
Mudborn, *(Mudborn Press; 0-930012)*, 301 E. Canon Perdido, Santa Barbara, CA 93101 Tel 805-965-3676 (SAN 210-4660).
Mudra, *(Mudra; 0-914726)*, Dist. by: Bookpeople, 2940 Seventh St., Berkeley, CA 94710 Tel 415-549-3033 (SAN 168-9517).
Multinational Media, *(Multinational Media; 0-917112)*, 228 Burlwood Dr., Scotts Valley, CA 95066 Tel 408-438-0253 (SAN 208-3957).
Museum Mod Art, *(Museum of Modern Art; 0-87070)*, 11 W. 53rd St., New York, NY 10019 Tel 212-956-7216 (SAN 202-5809); Orders to: Trade Sales, 11 W. 53rd St., New York, NY 10019 Tel 212-956-7265 (SAN 202-5817).
Music Sales, *(Music Sales Corp.; 0-8256)*, 799 Broadway, New York, NY 10003 (SAN 282-0277). *Imprints:* Hidden Hse (Hidden House).
Mycroft, *(Mycroft Business Press; 0-910998)*, P.O. Box 579, Branson, MO 65616 Tel 417-334-3436 (SAN 204-0174).
Mycroft & Moran *Imprint of* **Arkham**
Mysterious Pr, *(Mysterious Press; 0-89296)*, 129 W. 56th St., New York, NY 10019 (SAN 208-2152).
N Dak Inst, *(North Dakota Institute for Regional Studies; 0-911042)*, State University Sta., Fargo, ND 58105 Tel 701-237-8338 (SAN 203-1574).
N H Ludlow, *(Ludlow, Norman H.; 0-916706)*, 516 Arnett Blvd., Rochester, NY 14619 Tel 716-235-0951 (SAN 207-5776).
N Point Pr, *(North Point Press; 0-86547)*, 850 Talbot Ave., Berkeley, CA 94706 Tel 415-527-6260 (SAN 220-133X); Orders to: The Scribner Book Companies, 201 Willowbrook Blvd., Wayne, NJ 07470 Tel 201-256-0700 (SAN 201-002X).
Naiad Pr, *(Naiad Press; 0-930044)*, P.O. Box 10543, Tallahassee, FL 32302 Tel 904-539-9322 (SAN 206-801X).
NAL, *(New American Library; 0-451; 0-452; 0-453)*, 1633 Broadway, New York, NY 10019 Tel 212-397-8000 (SAN 206-8079); Orders to: 120 Woodbine St., Bergenfield, NJ 07621 Tel 201-387-0600 (SAN 206-8087). *Imprints:* Ment (Mentor Books); Mer (Meridian Books); Plume (Plume Books); Sig (Signet Books); Sig Classics (Signet Classics).
NAL *Imprint of* **Norton**
Nash Pub, *(Nash Publishing Corp.; 0-8402)*, 1290 Ave. of Americas, Suite 4150, New York, NY 10019 Tel 212-977-9500 (SAN 202-8883).
Nationwide Pr, *(Nationwide Press, Ltd.; 0-917188)*, P.O. Box 1528, Pueblo, CO 81002 Tel 303-543-1382 (SAN 208-7812).
Natl Mat Dev, *(National Materials Development Center for French; 0-911409)*, Dept. of Media Services, Dimond Library, UNH, Durham, NH 03824 (SAN 264-2344).
Natl Writ Pr, *(National Writers Press, the; 0-88100)*, Div. of the National Writers Club, Subs. of Assn. Headquarters, Inc., 1450 S. Havana, Suite 620, Aurora, CO 80012 (SAN 240-320X); Dist. by: Rish-Whit Dist., Box 21, Elwood, NE 68937 (SAN 240-3218).
Naturegraph, *(Naturegraph Pubs., Inc.; 0-911010; 0-87961)*, P.O. Box 1075, Happy Camp, CA 96039 Tel 916-493-5353 (SAN 202-8999).
Nautical & Aviation, *(Nautical & Aviation Publishing Co. of America, The; 0-933852)*, 8 Randall St., Annapolis, MD 21401 Tel 301-267-8522 (SAN 213-3431).
Nautical Avia
  See Nautical & Aviation
Naval Inst Pr, *(Naval Institute Press; 0-87021)*, Annapolis, MD 21402 Tel 301-268-6110 (SAN 202-9006).
Naylor, *(Naylor Co.; 0-8111)*, P.O. Box 1838, San Antonio, TX 78206 (SAN 202-9014).

KEY TO PUBLISHERS' AND DISTRIBUTORS' ABBREVIATIONS

Nazarene, *(Nazarene Publishing House; 0-8341),* P.O. Box 527, Kansas City, MO 64141 Tel 816-931-1900 (SAN 202-9022).

Necronomicon, *(Necronomicon Press),* 101 Lockwood St., West Warwick, RI 02893 Tel 401-828-5319 (SAN 210-315X).

Nefertiti, *(Nefertiti Head Press; 0-918722),* Drawer J. Univ. Sta., Austin, TX 78712 (SAN 209-6749).

Negro U Pr
See Greenwood

NELF Pr, *(National Unity Equality Leadership Fraternity Press),* 78 Maplevale Dr., Woodbridge, CT 06525 Tel 203-393-3913 (SAN 203-7297).

Nelson, *(Nelson, Thomas, Publishers; 0-8407),* P.O. Box 141000, Nelson Place at Elm Hill Pike, Nashville, TN 37214 Tel 615-889-9000 (SAN 209-3820).

Nelson B Robinson, *(Robinson, Nelson B. Bookseller; 0-930352),* P.O. Box 153, Rockport, MA 01966 Tel 617-546-7323 (SAN 209-004X).

Nesbit, *(Nesbit, Norman L.; 0-911746),* 2104 Goddard Place, Boulder, CO 80303 Tel 303-494-6206 (SAN 206-1651).

NESFA Pr, *(New England Science Fiction Assn., Inc.; 0-915368),* P.O. Box G, MIT Branch P.O., Cambridge, MA 02139 (SAN 208-4066).

Nevada Pubns, *(Nevada Pubns.; 0-913814),* 4135 Badger Circle, Reno, NV 89509 Tel 702-747-0800 (SAN 203-7319).

New Age, *(New Age Press, Inc.; 0-87613),* P.O. Box 1216, Black Mountain, NC 28711 Tel 704-669-9788 (SAN 203-7327).

New Albion, *(New Albion Books),* 3002 W. Camelback Rd., No. 10, Phoenix, AZ 85017 (SAN 211-6243) Moved, Left No Forwarding Address.

New Century, *(New Century Pubs., Inc.; 0-8329),* 220 Old New Brunswick Rd., Piscataway, NJ 08854 Tel 201-981-0820 (SAN 217-1201).

New City, *(New City Press; 0-911782),* 206 Skillman Ave., Brooklyn, NY 11211 Tel 212-782-2844 (SAN 203-7335).

New Coll U Pr, *(New College & Univ. Press, The; 0-8084),* 267 Chapel St., New Haven, CT 06513 Tel 203-562-3101 (SAN 203-6223).

New Day NY, *(New Day Pubns.; 0-9605994),* GPO Box 1924, New York, NY 10116 Tel 212-665-4669 (SAN 216-7530).

New Directions, *(New Directions Publishing Corp.; 0-8112),* 80 Eighth Ave., New York, NY 10011 Tel 212-354-5500 (SAN 202-9081); Dist. by: W. W. Norton Co., 500 Fifth Ave., New York, NY 10110 (SAN 202-5795).

New Earth, *(New Earth Books; 0-918258),* 58 St. Marks Place, New York, NY 10003 Tel 212-673-1682 (SAN 209-6277) Moved, left no forwarding address.

New Eng Pr VT, *(New England Press Inc., The; 0-933050),* P.O. Box 575, Shelburne, VT 05482 Tel 802-985-2569 (SAN 213-6376).

New Expressions, *(New Expressions Unltd.),* 30886 Sutherland Dr., Redlands, CA 92373 Tel 714-794-4868 (SAN 209-4053).

New Hope, *(New Hope Publishing Co.; 0-915460),* Dist. by: Midway Copy Services, P.O. Box 378, Lahaska, PA 18931 Tel 212-794-5757 (SAN 202-9103).

New Horizons, *(New Horizons Press; 0-914914),* P.O. Box 1758, Chico, CA 95927 Tel 916-345-0225 (SAN 206-7927).

New Leaf, *(New Leaf Press; 0-89221),* P.O. Box 1045, Harrison, AR 72601 Tel 501-741-2514 (SAN 207-9518).

New London Pr, *(New London Press; 0-89683),* Box 7458, Dallas, TX 75209 Tel 214-742-9037 (SAN 211-4402).

New Mermaid Imprint of **Hill & Wang**

New Orlando, *(New Orlando Pubns.; 0-917608),* Box 103 Village Sta., New York, NY 10014 Tel 212-449-6236 (SAN 205-7115).

New Paradise Bks, *(New Paradise Books; 0-943654),* Suite 206, 3000 N. Atlantic, Cocoa Beach, FL 32931 Tel 305-783-5651 (SAN 238-0765).

New Rivers Pr, *(New Rivers Press; 0-912284; 0-89823),* 1602 Selby Ave., St. Paul, MN 55104 Tel 612-645-6324 (SAN 209-9138).

New South Co, *(New South Co., The; 0-917990),* P.O. Box 24918, Los Angeles, CA 90024 Tel 213-489-5700 (SAN 209-3340).

New Victoria Pubs, *(New Victoria Pubs. Inc.; 0-934678),* 7 Bank St., Lebanon, NH 03766 Tel 603-448-2264 (SAN 212-1204).

New Viewpoints
See Watts

New Voices Pub, *(New Voices Publishing Co.; 0-911024),* 146-47 29th Ave., Flushing, NY 11354 Tel 212-445-4718 (SAN 202-103X).

New Worlds, *(New Worlds Unlimited; 0-917398),* 100 Maple St., No. 53, Garfield, NJ 07026 Tel 201-340-0247 (SAN 207-267X); Orders to: P.O. Box 556, Saddle Brook, NJ 07662 (SAN 207-2688).

Newberry, *(Newberry Library; 0-911028),* 60 W. Walton St., Chicago, IL 60610 Tel 312-943-9090 (SAN 203-7378).

Newbury Hse, *(Newbury House Pubs.; 0-88377; 0-912066),* 54 Warehouse Lane, Rowley, MA 01969 Tel 800-343-1240 (SAN 202-9146).

Newcastle Pub, *(Newcastle Publishing Co., Inc.; 0-87877),* 13419 Saticoy St., North Hollywood, CA 91605 Tel 213-873-3191 (SAN 202-9154); Orders to: P.O. Box 7589, Van Nuys, CA 91409 (SAN 202-9162).

NH Pub Co, *(New Hampshire Publishing Co.; 0-912274; 0-89725),* P.O. Box 70, Somersworth, NH 03878 Tel 603-692-3727 (SAN 202-9189).

Night Horn Books, *(Night Horn Books; 0-941842),* 495 Ellis St., Box 1156, San Francisco, CA 94102 Tel 415-431-6198 (SAN 239-2704).

Nightowl, *(Press of the Nightowl; 0-912960),* 320 Snapfinger Dr., Athens, GA 30605 Tel 404-353-7719 (SAN 205-6364).

Nikki Pr, *(Nikki Press; 0-943148),* 6 Heath St., Eatontown, NJ 07724 Tel 201-222-9343 (SAN 240-7361).

No Country Comm Coll, *(North Country Community College Press; 0-940280),* 20 Winona Ave., Saranac Lake, NY 12983 Tel 518-891-2915 (SAN 217-5479).

No Dead Lines, *(No Dead Lines; 0-931832),* 261 Hamilton, No. 320D, Palo Alto, CA 94301 Tel 415-321-0842 (SAN 211-6103).

Noble, *(Noble & Noble Pubs., Inc.),* Publisher Abbreviation Without Addresses Are for Titles That Are Out of Print. These Are Obsolete Abbreviations. Publisher's Abbreviation Is Now Bowmar-Noble.

Noble
See Bowmar-Noble

Nodin Pr, *(Nodin Press; 0-931714),* c/o The Bookmen, Inc., 525 N. Third St., Minneapolis, MN 55401 (SAN 204-398X).

Noe, *(Noe, Fay; 0-9600208),* Rte. 7, Boiling Springs Rd., Licking, MO 65542 (SAN 203-7424).

Nolo Pr, *(Nolo Press; 0-917316),* P.O. Box 544, Occidental, CA 95465 Tel 707-874-3105 (SAN 206-7935).

Nonpareil Bks Imprint of **Godine**

Noontide, *(Noontide Press; 0-911038; 0-939482),* P.O. Box 1248, Torrance, CA 90505 (SAN 213-1307).

Nordic Trans, *(Nordic Translators; 0-938500),* 1747 Holton St., St. Paul, MN 55113 Tel 612-645-8352 (SAN 239-9199).

Nordland Pub, *(Nordland Publishing International, Inc.; 0-913124),* P.O. Box 454, Woodside, NY 11377 Tel 212-335-1412 (SAN 282-0579); 3009 Plumb St., P.O. Box 25388, Houston, TX 77005 Tel 713-661-6126 (SAN 282-0587).

Nortex Pr
See Eakin Pubns

North Am Pub Co, *(North American Publishing Co.; 0-912920),* 401 N. Broad St., Philadelphia, PA 19108 Tel 215-574-9600 (SAN 203-1647).

North Am Rev, *(North American Review Press; 0-915996),* Cedar Falls, IA 50613 Tel 319-273-2681 (SAN 206-0760).

North Atlantic, *(North Atlantic Books; 0-938190; 0-913028),* 2320 Blake St., Berkeley, CA 94704 (SAN 203-1655).

North Plains, *(North Plains Press; 0-87970),* P.O. Box 1830, Aberdeen, SD 57401 Tel 605-225-5360 (SAN 202-9243).

Northland, *(Northland Press; 0-87358),* P.O. Box N, Flagstaff, AZ 86002 Tel 602-774-5251 (SAN 202-9251).

Northwest Pub, *(Northwestern Publishing House; 0-8100),* 3624 W. North Ave., Milwaukee, WI 53208 Tel 414-442-1810 (SAN 206-7943).

Northwestern, *(Northwestern College, Ramaker Library Art Gallery),* 101 Seventh St. S.W., Orange City, IA 51041 (SAN 279-9227).

Northwoods Pr, *(Northwoods Press; 0-89002),* Div. of Romar, Inc., P.O. Box 246, Stafford, VA 22554 Tel 703-659-7441 (SAN 208-449X).

Norton, *(Norton, W. W., & Co., Inc.; 0-393),* 500 Fifth Ave., New York, NY 10110 Tel 212-354-5500 (SAN 202-5795). Imprints: NortonC (Norton College Division); NAL (New American Library).

NortonC Imprint of **Norton**

Norwood
See Norwood Edns

Norwood Edns, *(Norwood Editions; 0-88305; 0-8482),* P.O. Box 38, Norwood, PA 19074 Tel 215-583-4550 (SAN 206-8613).

Nostalgia Pr, *(Nostalgia Press, Inc.; 0-87897),* 72 Franklin Ave., Franklin Square, NY 11010 Tel 516-488-4748 (SAN 205-3721); Orders to: P.O. Box 293, Franklin Square, NY 11010 (SAN 205-373X).

NY Pub Lib, *(New York Public Library; 0-87104),* Fifth Ave. & 42nd St., New York, NY 10018 Tel 212-260-2010 (SAN 202-926X); Orders to: Publishing Center for Cultural Resources, 625 Broadway, New York, NY 10012 Tel 212-340-0897 (SAN 209-9926) Ordering Address for NYPL Branch Libraries Imprint Only: 455 Fifth Ave., N.Y., N.Y. 10016.

NYU Pr, *(New York Univ. Press; 0-8147),* Dist. by: Columbia University Press, 562 W. 113th St., New York, NY 10025 Tel 212-678-6777 (SAN 212-2472).

O L Holmes, *(Holmes, Opal Laurel, Publisher; 0-918522),* P.O. Box 2535, Boise, ID 83701 Tel 208-344-4517 (SAN 210-1017); Dist. by: Pub. Marketing Group, Baker & Taylor Co., P.O. Box 350, Momence, IL 60954 (SAN 169-2100).

O W Frost, *(Frost, O.W.; 0-930766),* 2141 Lord Baranof Dr., Anchorage, AK 99503 (SAN 211-3163).

Oak Tree Pubns, *(Oak Tree Pubns. Inc.; 0-916392),* 11175 Flintkote Ave., San Diego, CA 92121 Tel 714-457-3200 (SAN 211-4828).

OAS, *(Organization of American States; 0-8270),* Dept. of Publications, 6840 Industrial Rd., Springfield, VA 22151 Tel 703-941-1617 (SAN 206-8877).

Occidental, *(Occidental Press; 0-911050),* P.O. Box 1005, Washington, DC 20013 (SAN 203-7599).

Oceana, *(Oceana Pubns.; 0-379),* 75 Main St., Dobbs Ferry, NY 10522 Tel 914-693-5944 (SAN 202-5744).

Octagon, *(Octagon Books; 0-374),* 19 Union Square W., New York, NY 10003 Tel 212-741-6961 (SAN 202-8123).

Odyssey MA, *(Odyssey Pubns., Inc.; 0-933752),* P.O. Box G-148, Greenwood, MA 01880 (SAN 214-4301).

Odyssey Pr, *(Odyssey Press; 0-8399),* Dist. by: Bobbs-Merrill Co., Inc., 4300 W. 62nd St., P. O. Box 7080, Indianapolis, IN 46206 Tel 317-298-5688 (SAN 201-3959).

O'Hara, *(O'Hara, J. Philip, Inc., Pubs.; 0-87955),* c/o Scroll Press, Inc., 2858 Valerie Court, Merrick, NY 11566 Tel 516-379-4283 (SAN 202-5868).

Ohara Pubns, *(Ohara Pubns., Inc.; 0-89750),* 1813 Victory Place, P.O. Box 7728, Burbank, CA 91510-7728 Tel 213-843-4444 (SAN 205-3632).

Ohio Hist Soc, *(Ohio Historical Society),* Ohio Historical Center, Interstate 71 & 17th Ave., Columbus, OH 43211 Tel 614-466-4664 (SAN 202-1331).

Ohio St U Lib, *(Ohio State Univ. Libraries; 0-88215),* Rm. 001, Main Lib., 1858 Neil Ave. Mall, Columbus, OH 43210 Tel 614-422-4738 (SAN 202-814X).

Ohio St U Pr, *(Ohio State Univ. Press; 0-8142),* Hitchcock Hall, Rm. 346, 2070 Neil Ave., Columbus, OH 43210 Tel 614-422-6930 (SAN 202-8158).

Ohio U Pr, *(Ohio Univ. Press; 0-8214),* Scott Quadrangle, Room 144, Athens, OH 45701 Tel 614-594-5505 (SAN 282-0773); Orders to: Harper & Row Publishers, Inc, Keystone Industrial Park, Scranton, PA 18512 Tel 800-233-4377 (SAN 282-0781).

KEY TO PUBLISHERS' AND DISTRIBUTORS' ABBREVIATIONS

Oil Bks, *(Oil Books),* Box 88, RD 1, Sugar Run, PA 18846 Tel 717-265-8665 (SAN 207-8813).

Okpaku Communications, *(Okpaku Communications; 0-89388),* Div. of Third Press Review of Books Company, 330 Seventh Ave., New York, NY 10001 Tel 212-563-1850 (SAN 202-5701).

Old Time, *(Old Time Bottle Publishing Co.; 0-911068),* 611 Lancaster Dr., N.E., Salem, OR 97301 Tel 503-362-1446 (SAN 203-7718).

Oleander Pr, *(Oleander Press; 0-902675; 0-900891; 0-906672),* 210 Fifth Ave., New York, NY 10010 (SAN 206-1031).

Olivant, *(Olivant Press; 0-87956),* P.O. Box 1409, Homestead, FL 33030 (SAN 205-3578).

Olympia, *(Olympia Press),* 220 Park Ave., S., New York, NY 10003 (SAN 204-5591). *Imprints:* Ophelia (Ophelia Books); Travellers Comp (Travellers Companion Ser.).

Olympus Pub Co, *(Olympus Publishing Co.; 0-913420),* 1670 E. 13th South, Salt Lake City, UT 84105 Tel 801-583-3666 (SAN 202-8204).

Oman Ent, *(Oman Enterprises; 0-917346),* P.O. Box 222357, Carmel, CA 93922 Tel 408-624-4386 (SAN 208-7936).

Omega Pubns OR, *(Omega Pubns.; 0-86694),* P.O. Box 4130, Medford, OR 97501 Tel 503-826-7773 (SAN 220-1534).

Omen Pr, *(Omen Press; 0-912358),* P.O. Box 12457, Tucson, AZ 85711 Tel 602-296-4002 (SAN 202-8212).

OMF Bks, *(OMF Books),* 404 S. Church St., Robesonia, PA 19551 (SAN 211-8351).

Omkara Pr, *(Omkara Press; 0-934094),* 912 Beaver St., Santa Rosa, CA 95404 Tel 707-575-1736 (SAN 212-9558).

Ontario Pr, *(Ontario Press; 0-913254),* 61 W. Ontario St., Chicago, IL 60610 Tel 312-751-1656 (SAN 203-7734).

Ontario Rev NJ, *(Ontario Review Press, The; 0-86538),* Dist. by: Persea Books, Inc., 225 Lafayette St., New York, NY 10012 Tel 212-431-5270 (SAN 212-8233).

Oolp Pr, *(OOLP (Out of London Press) Inc.; 0-915570),* 33 Union Square West, New York, NY 10003 Tel 212-989-3083 (SAN 202-8263).

Open Bk Pubns, *(Open Book Pubns.; 0-940170),* Station Hill Rd., Barrytown, NY 12507 Tel 914-758-5840 (SAN 220-3006).

Open Court, *(Open Court Publishing Co.; 0-87548; 0-89688; 0-8126),* Div. of Carus Corp., P.O. Box 599, LaSalle, IL 61301 Tel 815-223-2520 (SAN 202-5876). *Imprints:* Library Pr (Library Press).

Open Window, *(Open Window Books Inc.; 0-917694),* Box 949, Chickasha, OK 73018 Tel 405-224-3217 (SAN 209-4657).

Ophelia *Imprint of* Olympia

Orange Blossom, *(Orange Blossom Publishers Limited; 0-9608100),* P.O. 2187, Henderson, NE 89015 Tel 805-524-2221 (SAN 238-8553).

Orbis Bks, *(Orbis Books; 0-88344),* Maryknoll, NY 10545 Tel 914-941-7590 (SAN 202-828X).

Orchard, *(Orchard House),* 1281 Burg St., Granville, OH 43023 (SAN 209-407X).

Oreg Hist Soc, *(Oregon Historical Society; 0-87595),* 1230 S.W. Park Ave., Portland, OR 97205 Tel 503-222-1741 (SAN 202-8301).

Orenda-Unity, *(Orenda Publishing/Unity Press; 0-913300),* 61 Camino Alto, Suite 100, Mill Valley, CA 94941 Tel 415-388-0804 (SAN 282-0811); Orders to: Network, Inc., P.O. Box 2246, Berkeley, CA 94702 (SAN 282-082X).

Orient Bk Dist, *(Orient Book Distributors; 0-89684),* P.O. Box 100, Livingston, NJ 07039 Tel 201-992-6992 (SAN 211-819X).

Oriental Bk Store, *(Oriental Book Store, The),* P.O. Box 177, South Pasadena, CA 91030-0177 Tel 213-577-2413 (SAN 285-0818); 630 E. Colorado Blvd., Pasadena, CA 91101 Tel 213-577-2413 (SAN 285-0826).

Orientalia, *(Orientalia Art, Ltd.; 0-87902),* P.O. Box 597, New York, NY 10025 Tel 212-473-9837 (SAN 282-0919); 61 Fourth Ave., New York, NY 10003 (SAN 282-0927).

Our Sunday Visitor, *(Our Sunday Visitor, Inc.; 0-87973),* 200 Noll Plaza, Huntington, IN 46750 Tel 219-356-8400 (SAN 202-8344).

Out of the Ashes, *(Out of the Ashes Press; 0-912874),* P.O. Box 42384, Portland, OR 97242 (SAN 202-8352).

Outbooks, *(Outbooks; 0-89646),* 217 Kimball Ave., Golden, CO 80401 Tel 303-279-9066 (SAN 211-0849).

Overlook Pr, *(Overlook Press; 0-87951),* 667 Madison Ave., Suite 401A, New York, NY 10021 Tel 212-688-0920 (SAN 202-8360); c/o Viking Press, 40 W. 23 St., New York, NY 10010 Tel 212-807-7300 (SAN 200-2469).

Owlswick Pr, *(Owlswick Press; 0-913896),* P.O. Box 8243, Philadelphia, PA 19101 Tel 215-382-5415 (SAN 202-8387).

Oxford U Pr, *(Oxford Univ. Press, Inc.; 0-19),* 200 Madison Ave., New York, NY 10016 Tel 212-679-7300 (SAN 202-5884); Orders to: 16-00 Pollitt Dr., Fair Lawn, NJ 07410 Tel 201-796-8000 (SAN 202-5892) New York Accounts Use 212-564-6680. *Imprints:* GB (Galaxy Books).

Oyez, *(Oyez; 0-911088),* 212 Colgate Ave., Kensington, CA 94707 (SAN 206-877X).

P Arendson, *(Arendson, Peter),* 1151 Xenia St., Denver, CO 80220 Tel 303-320-4448 (SAN 239-586X).

P Downsbrough, *(Downsbrough, Peter; 0-9602192),* 305 E. Houston St, New York, NY 10012 (SAN 212-3460); Dist. by: Printed Matter, 7 Lispenard St., New York, NY 10013 (SAN 169-5924).

P Elek
See Merrimack Publishers' Circle

P-H, *(Prentice-Hall, Inc.; 0-13),* Rte. 9W, Englewood Cliffs, NJ 07632 Tel 201-592-2000 (SAN 200-2175); Orders to: Box 500, Englewood Cliffs, NJ 07632 (SAN 215-3939). *Imprints:* Spec (Spectrum Books).

P Lang Pubs, *(Lang, Peter, Publishing, Inc.),* 34 E. 39th St., New York, NY 10016 Tel 212-692-9009 (SAN 241-5534).

P McIlvaine, *(McIlvaine, Paul, Pub.; 0-9600410),* Sky Village, 124 Scenic Lane, Hendersonville, NC 28739 Tel 704-692-3971 (SAN 203-7890).

Pacific Coast, *(Pacific Coast Pubs; 0-87465),* 4085 Campbell Ave., Menlo Park, CA 94025 (SAN 206-7846) Moved, Left No Forwarding Address. *Imprints:* Farallon (Farallon Island).

Pacific Perceptions, *(Pacific Perceptions, Inc.),* 3718 Vinton Ave., Suite 5, Los Angeles, CA 90034 (SAN 206-3743).

Pacific Perceptions
See Pacific Perceptions

Pacific Pr Pub Assn, *(Pacific Press Publishing Assn.; 0-8163),* P.O. Box 7000, Mountain View, CA 94039 Tel 415-961-2323 (SAN 202-8409).

Pacific Search, *(Pacific Search Press; 0-914718),* 222 Dexter Ave. N., Seattle, WA 98109 Tel 206-682-5044 (SAN 202-8476).

Packrat Pr, *(Packrat Press Books),* P.O. Box 74, Cambridge, ID 83610 (SAN 211-7525).

Paddington, *(Paddington Press, Ltd.),* 95 Madison Ave, New York, NY 10016 Tel 212-689-4801 (SAN 209-4673); Orders to: Grosset & Dunlap, 51 Madison Ave., New York, NY 10010 (SAN 201-4912).

Padre Prods, *(Padre Productions; 0-914598),* P.O. Box 1275, San Luis Obispo, CA 93406 Tel 805-543-5404 (SAN 202-8484).

Pageant-Poseidon, *(Pageant-Poseidon),* 155 W. 15th St., New York, NY 10011 Tel 212-929-5956 (SAN 202-8492) Moved, Left No Fowarding Address.

Pan-Am Publishing Co, *(Pan-American Publishing Co.; 0-932906),* P.O. Box 1505, Las Vegas, NM 87701 (SAN 212-5366).

Panjandrum, *(Panjandrum Books; 0-915572),* 11321 Iowa Ave., Suite 1, Los Angeles, CA 90025 Tel 213-477-8771 (SAN 282-1257); Dist. by: Publisher's Group West, 5855 Beaudry, Emeryville, CA 94608 Tel 415-549-3033 (SAN 202-8522); Dist. by: Bruce Miller, 1936 N. Clark St., Chicago, IL 60614 (SAN 202-8530); Dist. by: Como Sales Inc., 799 Broadway, New York, NY 10013 (SAN 202-8549); Dist. by: Doug Paton, North East Book Sales, 802 Oak Ridge Ave., North Attleboro, MA 02760 (SAN 168-9509); Dist. by: Bookpeople, 2940 Seventh St., Berkeley, CA 94710 (SAN 168-9517); Dist. by: The Distributors, South Bend, IN 46624 (SAN 212-0364); Dist. by: Ingram Book Co., P.O. Box 17266, Nashville, TN 37217 (SAN 169-7978); Dist. by: Henry Walck, Jr., 731 E. Shore Dr., Ithaca, NY 14850 (SAN 282-1338); Dist. by: Inland Book Co., East Haven, CT 46618 (SAN 200-4151).

Panjandrum Pr
See Panjandrum

Pantheon, *(Pantheon Books),* Div. of Random House, Inc., 201 E. 50th St., New York, NY 10022 Tel 212-751-2600 (SAN 202-862X); Orders to: Random House, Inc., 400 Hahn Rd., Westminster, MD 21157 (SAN 202-5515).

Panther Hse, *(Panther House, Ltd.; 0-87676),* Box 3552, GCPO, New York, NY 10017 (SAN 202-8646).

Paper Vision
See Western Tanager

Paperback Lib, *(Warner Paperback Library; 0-446),* 75 Rockefeller Plaza, New York, NY 10019 Tel 212-484-8000 (SAN 207-4079).

Paperback Lib
See Warner Bks

Parable Pr, *(Parable Press; 0-917250),* 136 Gray St., Amherst, MA 01002 Tel 413-253-5634 (SAN 208-4449).

Paragon, *(Paragon Book Reprint Corp.; 0-8188),* 14 E. 38th St., New York, NY 10016 Tel 212-532-4920 (SAN 213-1986).

Paranoid Pubns, *(Paranoid Pubns.),* P.O. Box 152, 108 W. Lincoln, Onarga, IL 60955 Tel 815-268-7621 (SAN 212-7857).

Parchment Pr, *(Parchment Press; 0-88428),* 5345 Atlanta Hwy., Montgomery, AL 36193 Tel 205-272-5820 (SAN 202-8670).

Parent Scene, *(Parent Scene; 0-910529),* P.O. Box 2222, 1280 E. San Bernadino Ave., Redlands, CA 92373 Tel 714-792-2412 (SAN 260-244X).

Paris Pubns, *(Paris Pubns., Inc.; 0-912248),* 2 Haven Ave., Port Washington, NY 11050 Tel 516-883-4650 (SAN 202-8700) Moved, Left No Forwarding Address.

Park View, *(Park View Press, Inc.; 0-87813),* 1066 Chicago Ave., Harrisonburg, VA 22801 Tel 703-434-0765 (SAN 204-9279).

Parker & Son, *(Parker & Son Pubns., Inc.; 0-911110),* Box 60001, Los Angeles, CA 90060 Tel 213-727-1088 (SAN 202-8719).

Parsley Pr, *(Parsley Press; 0-9608222),* Box 94 Turnpike Sta., Shrewsbury, MA 01545 Tel 617-366-2511 (SAN 240-4214).

Pass, *(Pass Press; 0-9601870),* 170 2nd Ave., 2A, New York, NY 10003 (SAN 210-5411).

Path Pr NY, *(Pathfinder Press; 0-87348),* 410 West St., New York, NY 10014 Tel 212-741-0690 (SAN 202-5906).

Pathmark Bks, *(Pathmark Books, Inc.; 0-913390),* P.O. Box 115, Newton Upper Falls, MA 02164 Tel 617-964-2300 (SAN 203-0926).

Pathway Bks, *(Pathway Books; 0-935538),* 700 Parkview Terrace, Golden Valley, MN 55416 Tel 612-377-1521 (SAN 213-4241).

Pathway Pr, *(Pathway Pr.; 0-87148),* 1080 Montgomery Ave., Cleveland, TN 37311 Tel 615-476-4512 (SAN 202-8727).

Patrice Pr, *(Patrice Press; 0-935284),* Box 42, Gerald, MO 63037 Tel 314-764-2801 (SAN 203-1019).

Paulist-Newman
See Paulist Pr

Paulist Pr, *(Paulist Press; 0-8091),* 545 Island Rd., Ramsey, NJ 07446 Tel 201-825-7300 (SAN 202-5159); Orders to: 301 Island Rd., Mahwah, NJ 07430 (SAN 202-5167).

KEY TO PUBLISHERS' AND DISTRIBUTORS' ABBREVIATIONS

PB, *(Pocket Books, Inc.; 0-671),* Div. of Simon & Schuster, Inc., 1230 Ave. of the Americas, New York, NY 10020 Tel 212-246-2121 (SAN 202-5922). *Imprints:* Timescape (Timescape); Wallaby (Wallaby).

Peace & Pieces
  See SF Arts & Letters

Peace on Earth, *(Peace on Earth Press; 0-942992),* P.O. Box 3947, Stanford, CA 94305 (SAN 240-4222); P.O. Box 128, Bedford, MA 01730 (SAN 240-4230).

Peace Pr, *(Peace Press, Inc.; 0-915238),* 3828 Willat Ave., Culver City, CA 90230 Tel 213-838-7387 (SAN 207-1134).

Peachtree Pubs, *(Peachtree Pubs., Ltd.; 0-931948),* 494 Armour Circle, N.E., Atlanta, GA 30324 Tel 404-876-8761 (SAN 212-1999).

Peacock *Imprint of* Penguin

Pee Wee, *(Pee Wee Books; 0-941352),* Tel 707-778-6473; c/o E. F. Hutton & Co., Kaiser Center, 300 Lakeside Dr., Oakland, CA 94612 (SAN 239-0167).

Pelican, *(Pelican Publishing Co., Inc.; 0-911116; 0-88289),* 1101 Monroe St., P.O. Box 189, Gretna, LA 70053 Tel 504-368-1175 (SAN 212-0623).

Pelican *Imprint of* Penguin

Pella Pub, *(Pella Publishing Co., Inc.; 0-918618),* 461 Eighth Ave., New York, NY 10001 Tel 212-279-9586 (SAN 210-6183).

Pemberley Pr, *(Pemberley Pr.; 0-9607830),* 250 W. 54th St. Rm. 800, New York, NY 10019 Tel 212-757-9631 (SAN 238-1052).

Pen-Art, *(Pen-Art Pubs.),* 402 Fairview Ave., Westwood, NJ 07675 Tel 201-664-8412 (SAN 211-3287).

Pendel Hill
  See Pendle Hill

Pendell Pub, *(Pendell Publishing Co.; 0-87812),* 1700 James Savage Rd., P.O. Box 2066 Bip, Midland, MI 48640 Tel 517-496-3333 (SAN 202-8786).

Pendle Hill, *(Pendle Hill Pubns.; 0-87574),* Pendle Hill, 338 Plush Mill Rd, Wallingford, PA 19086 Tel 215-566-4507 (SAN 202-8794).

Pendragon Hse, *(Pendragon House, Inc.; 0-916988),* 2898 Joseph Ave., Campbell, CA 95008 Tel 408-371-2737 (SAN 208-8037).

Pendulum Pr, *(Pendulum Press, Inc.; 0-88301),* Academic Bldg., Saw Mill Rd., West Haven, CT 06516 Tel 203-933-2551 (SAN 202-8808).

Penguin, *(Penguin Books, Inc.; 0-14),* 40 W. 23rd St., New York, NY 10010 Tel 212-807-7300 (SAN 202-5914). *Imprints:* Peacock (Peacock Books); Pelican (Pelican Books); Puffin (Puffin Books).

Penmaen Pr, *(Penmaen Press, Ltd.; 0-915778),* R.D. 2, P.O. Box 145, Great Barrington, MA 01230 Tel 413-528-2749 (SAN 208-1113).

Penmaen Pr & Design
  See Penmaen Pr

Pennington, *(Pennington Trading Post; 0-911120),* c/o Eunice Pennington, Fremont, MO 63941 (SAN 204-9392).

Pennyfarthing, *(Pennyfarthing Press; 0-930800),* 2000 Center St., No. 1226, Berkeley, CA 94704 Tel 415-845-1990 (SAN 211-920X).

Penobscot Bay, *(Penobscot Bay Press, Inc.),* Box 36, Stonington, ME 04681 (SAN 212-2960).

Pentagram, *(Pentagram; 0-915316; 0-937596),* Box 379, Markesan, WI 53946 Tel 414-398-2161 (SAN 207-1789).

Penthouse Pr, *(Penthouse Press, Ltd.; 0-89110),* 909 Third Ave., New York, NY 10022 (SAN 207-4133).

Penumbra Press, *(Penumbra Press, The),* Box 12, Lisbon, IA 52253 Tel 319-455-2182 (SAN 209-858X).

Peoples Pr, *(People's Press; 0-914750),* 2680 21st St., San Francisco, CA 94110 Tel 415-282-0856 (SAN 204-9406) Moved, Left No Forwarding Address.

Pequot
  See Globe Pequot

Pere Marquette, *(Pere Marquette Press; 0-934640),* P.O. Box 495, Alton, IL 62002 (SAN 206-3042).

Peregrine Smith, *(Peregrine Smith Books; 0-87905),* P.O. Box 667, Layton, UT 84041 Tel 801-554-9800 (SAN 201-9906).

Performing Arts, *(Performing Arts Journal Pubns.; 0-933826),* 325 Spring St., Rm 318, New York, NY 10013 Tel 212-243-3885 (SAN 220-2670).

Pergamon, *(Pergamon Press, Inc.; 0-08),* Maxwell House, Fairview Park, Elmsford, NY 10523 Tel 914-592-7700 (SAN 213-9022).

Perigee *Imprint of* **Putnam Pub Group**

Perilous Pr, *(Perilous Press; 0-9609502),* P.O. Box 17914, Tampa, FL 33612 (SAN 262-057X).

Perivale Pr, *(Perivale Press; 0-912288),* 13830 Erwin St., Van Nuys, CA 91401 Tel 213-785-4671 (SAN 201-9922).

Permanent Pr, *(Permanent Press, The; 0-932966),* R. D. 2 Noyac Rd., Sag Harbor, NY 11963 Tel 516-725-1101 (SAN 212-2995).

Persea Bks, *(Persea Bks., Inc.; 0-89255),* 225 Lafayette St., New York, NY 10012 Tel 212-431-5270 (SAN 212-8233).

Persephone, *(Persephone Press, Inc.; 0-930436),* P.O. Box 7222, Watertown, MA 02172 Tel 617-924-0336 (SAN 211-9218).

Persona Pr, *(Persona Press; 0-931906),* P.O. Box 14022, San Francisco, CA 94114 Tel 415-775-6143 (SAN 212-3002).

Perspective, *(Perspective Pubns., Inc.; 0-911130),* 509 Madison Ave., New York, NY 10022 Tel 212-752-2212 (SAN 201-8799) Moved, Left No Forwarding Address.

Peter Pauper, *(Peter Pauper Press, Inc.; 0-88088),* 135 W. 50th St., New York, NY 10020 Tel 914-681-0144 (SAN 204-9449).

Peter Smith, *(Smith, Peter, Publisher Inc.; 0-8446),* 6 Lexington Ave., Magnolia, MA 01930 Tel 617-525-3562 (SAN 206-8885).

Petersen Pub, *(Petersen Publishing Co., Book Division; 0-8227),* 6725 Sunset Blvd., Los Angeles, CA 90028 Tel 213-657-5100 (SAN 201-9949).

Petrocelli-Charter
  See Van Nos Reinhold

Petroglyph, *(Petroglyph Press Ltd.; 0-912180),* 201 Kinoole St., Hilo, HI 96720 (SAN 204-9457).

Petronium Pr, *(Petronium Press; 0-932136),* 1255 Nuuanu Ave., 1813, Honolulu, HI 96817 Tel 808-521-7541 (SAN 217-7541).

Pflaum-Standard, *(Pflaum/Standard; 0-8278),* c/o CEBCO Standard Publishing, 9 Kulick Rd, Fairfield, NJ 07006 (SAN 207-1568) Name Changed to CEBCO-Standard.

Phaidon
  See Dutton

Phantasia Pr, *(Phantasia Press; 0-932096),* 13101 Lincoln, Huntington Woods, MI 48070 (SAN 211-755X); Dist. by: F & SF Book Co., P.O. Box 415, Staten Island, NY 10302 (SAN 169-6270).

Phillips Pub Co, *(Phillips Publishing Co.),* 1562 Main St., Suite 713, Springfield, MA 01103 Tel 413-734-9020 (SAN 201-9981) Moved, Left No Forwarding Address.

Philos Lib, *(Philosophical Library, Inc.; 0-8022),* 200 W. 57th St., New York, NY 10019 Tel 212-265-6050 (SAN 201-999X).

Philos Pub, *(Philosophical Publishing Co.),* P.O. Box 220, Quakertown, PA 18951 Tel 215-536-5168 (SAN 205-3810).

Philos Res, *(Philosophical Research Society, Inc.; 0-89314),* 3910 Los Feliz Blvd., Los Angeles, CA 90027 Tel 213-663-2167 (SAN 205-3829).

Phoenix Bk Shop, *(Phoenix Book Shop; 0-916228),* 22 Jones St., New York, NY 10014 Tel 212-675-2795 (SAN 211-3724).

Phoenix Pub, *(Phoenix Publishing; 0-914016),* Canaan St., NH 03741 Tel 603-523-9902 (SAN 201-8810).

Photopia Pr, *(Photopia Press; 0-942478),* P.O. Box 1844, Corvallis, OR 97339 Tel 503-757-8761 (SAN 238-5562).

Pi Pr, *(Pi Press, Inc.; 0-931420),* Box 23371, Honolulu, HI 96822 (SAN 211-3007).

Pierpont Morgan, *(Pierpont Morgan Library; 0-87598),* 29 E. 36th St., New York, NY 10016 Tel 212-685-0008 (SAN 204-8957).

Pig Iron Pr, *(Pig Iron Press; 0-917530),* P.O. Box 237, Youngstown, OH 44501 Tel 216-744-2258 (SAN 209-0937).

Pigiron Pr
  See Pig Iron Pr

Pikeville Coll, *(Pikeville College Press; 0-933302),* Pikeville, KY 41501 Tel 606-432-9227 (SAN 212-1298).

Pilgrim NY, *(Pilgrim Press, The; 0-8298),* 132 W. 31st St., New York, NY 10001 Tel 212-594-8555 (SAN 212-601X); Dist. by: Seabury Service Center, Somers, CT 06071 Tel 800-243-0004 (SAN 202-5426).

Pinnacle Bks, *(Pinnacle Books; 0-523),* 1430 Broadway, New York, NY 10018 Tel 212-719-5900 (SAN 200-2442).

Pioneer Pub Co, *(Pioneer Publishing Co.; 0-914330),* 8 E. Olive Ave., Fresno, CA 93728 Tel 209-485-2631 (SAN 202-0041).

Pitman, *(Pitman Publishing Corp.),* Publisher Abbreviation Without Addresses Are for Titles That Are Out of Print. These Are Obsolete Abbreviations. Publisher's Abbreviation Is Now Fearon-Pitman.

Pitman
  See Pitman Learning

Pitman Learning, *(Pitman Learning, Inc.; 0-8224),* 19 Davis Dr., Belmont, CA 94002 Tel 415-592-7810 (SAN 212-775X).

Pitt Hist & Landmks Found, *(Pittsburgh History & Landmarks Foundation),* One Landmarks Sq., Pittsburgh, PA 15212 Tel 412-322-1204 (SAN 205-129X).

PL *Imprint of* Har-Row

Planet Drum Books, *(Planet/Drum Foundation; 0-937102),* P.O. Box 31251, San Francisco, CA 94131 Tel 415-285-6556 (SAN 216-437X).

Planetary, *(Planetary Press; 0-938330),* P.O. Box 4641, Baltimore, MD 21212 (SAN 216-0536).

Play Schs, *(Play Schools Assn.; 0-936426),* 19 West 44th St., New York, NY 10017 Tel 212-921-2940 (SAN 202-0076).

Playboy, *(Playboy Press; 0-87223),* Div. of Putnam Publishing Group, 200 Madison Ave., New York, NY 10016 Tel 212-576-8900 (SAN 213-2656); Dist. by: Harper & Row Pubs., Inc., Keystone Industrial Park, Scranton, PA 18512 (SAN 215-3742).

Playboy Pbks, *(Playboy Paperbacks; 0-87216; 0-86721),* Div. of P.E.I. Books, Inc., 200 Madison Ave., New York, NY 10019 Tel 212-576-8900 (SAN 213-2672); Dist. by: ICD, 250 W. 55th St., New York, NY 10019 Tel 212-262-7444 (SAN 169-5800).

Playboy Pr Pbks
  See Playboy Pbks

Playmore & Prestige, *(Playmore & Prestige Pubs.),* 200 Fifth Ave, New York, NY 10159 Tel 212-924-7447 (SAN 219-340X).

Plaza Pubs, *(Plaza Pubs.),* 2010 Empire Blvd., Webster, NY 14580 Tel 716-671-1533 (SAN 202-1544).

Pleasure Trove, *(Pleasure Trove Books; 0-930400),* 2156 Merokee Dr., Merrick, NY 11566 Tel 516-379-2501 (SAN 207-2742).

Plough, *(Plough Publishing House of the Hutterian Society of Brothers; 0-87486),* Rifton, NY 12471 Tel 914-658-3141 (SAN 202-0092).

Plume *Imprint of* NAL

Pluto Pr, *(Pluto Press; 0-86104),* Dist. by: Flatiron Book Distributors Inc., 175 Fifth Ave., Suite 814, New York, NY 10010 Tel 212-228-0390 (SAN 240-0917).

Pocumtuck Valley Mem, *(Pocumtuck Valley Memorial Assn.),* Memorial Hall Museum, Deerfield, MA 01342 Tel 413-773-8929 (SAN 211-2663).

Poet Gal Pr, *(Poet Gallery Press; 0-913054),* 224 W. 29th St., New York, NY 10001 (SAN 204-9015).

Polish Inst Art & Sci, *(Polish Institute of Arts & Sciences),* 59 E 66 St, New York, NY 10021 Tel 212-988-4338 (SAN 225-3747).

Pomegranate, *(Pomegranate Press; 0-915192),* P.O. Box 181, Cambridge, MA 02140 Tel 617-489-3896 (SAN 207-883X).

Pomerica Pr, *(Pomerica Press, Ltd.; 0-918732),* 386 Pararso, New York, NY 10016 Tel 212-685-0808 (SAN 211-0504); Dist. by: Franklin Watts Inc., 730 Fifth Ave., New York, NY 10019 Tel 212-757-4050 (SAN 200-223X).

Poor Souls Pr, *(Poor Souls Pr./Scaramouche Bks.; 0-916296),* P.O. Box 236, Millbrae, CA 94030 Tel 415-588-4163 (SAN 209-679X).

Porcupine Pr, *(Porcupine Press, Inc.; 0-87991),* 1317 Filbert St., Philadelphia, PA 19107 Tel 215-563-2288 (SAN 202-0122).

Porphyrion Pr, *(Porphyrion Press; 0-913884),* R.R. 1, Box 439, Middle Grove, NY 12850 Tel 518-587-9809 (SAN 206-6823).

Portals Pr, *(Portals Press; 0-916620),* P.O. Box 1048, Tuscaloosa, AL 35403 Tel 205-758-1874 (SAN 208-8126).

Porter, *(Porter, Bern; 0-911156),* 22 Salmond Rd., Belfast, ME 04915 (SAN 202-0130).

KEY TO PUBLISHERS' AND DISTRIBUTORS' ABBREVIATIONS

Pourboire, (Pourboire Press), P.O. Box 6881, Providence, RI 02940 Tel 401-331-9800 (SAN 209-8628); Dist. by: Woods Hole Press, P.O. Box 44, Woods Hole, MA 02543 Tel 617-548-9600 (SAN 210-332X).

Pr of Case WR, (Press of Case Western Reserve Univ.; 0-8295), Frank Adgate Quail Bldg., Cleveland, OH 44106 Tel 216-368-3770 (SAN 202-0203).

Pr of Morningside, (Press of Morningside Bookshop; 0-89029), P.O. Box 1087, Dayton, OH 45401 Tel 513-461-6736 (SAN 202-0211).

Pr Pacifica, (Press Pacifica; 0-916630), P.O. Box 47, Waipahu, HI 96734 Tel 808-261-6594 (SAN 169-1635).

Praeger, (Praeger Pubs.; 0-275), Div. of Holt Rinehart & Winston/CBS, 521 Fifth Ave., New York, NY 10175 Tel 212-599-8413 (SAN 202-022X).

Prairie Pub, (Prairie Publishing), R. R. 1, Rushville, NE 69360 (SAN 207-7442).

Prairie Sun, (Prairie Sun Communications, Inc.; 0-936722), 1109 W. Main St., Peoria, IL 61606 Tel 309-673-6624 (SAN 214-218X).

Prem Imprint of Fawcett

Presby & Reformed, (Presbyterian & Reformed Publishing Co.; 0-87552), Box 817, Phillipsburg, NJ 08865 Tel 201-454-0505 (SAN 205-3918).

Prescott St Pr, (Prescott Street Press; 0-915986), 407 Postal Bldg., Portland, OR 97204 Tel 503-254-2922 (SAN 207-4729).

Presence Inc, (Presence Inc.; 0-937296), P.O. Box 3094, Marion, IN 46952 (SAN 240-8813).

Preservation Pr, (Preservation Press, National Trust for Historic Preservation; 0-89133), 1785 Massachusetts Ave., N.W., Washington, DC 20036 Tel 202-673-4000 (SAN 209-3146).

Presidio Pr, (Presidio Press; 0-89141), 31 Pamaron Way, Novato, CA 94947 Tel 415-883-1373 (SAN 214-2759).

Pressworks, (Pressworks Publishing, Inc.; 0-939722), 2800 Routh St., No. 249, Dallas, TX 75201 Tel 214-749-1044 (SAN 216-7581).

Price Stern, (Price, Stern, Sloan, Pubs., Inc.; 0-8431), 410 N. La Cienega Blvd., Los Angeles, CA 90048 Tel 213-657-6100 (SAN 202-0246).

Primary, (Primary Sources; 0-911184), P.O. Box 472, Cooper Sta., New York, NY 10003 (SAN 205-3942).

Princeton Lib, (Princeton Univ. Library; 0-87811), Princeton, NJ 08544 Tel 609-452-3245 (SAN 205-3950).

Princeton U Pr, (Princeton Univ. Press; 0-691), 41 William St., Princeton, NJ 08540 Tel 609-452-4900 (SAN 202-0254).

Prinit Pr, (Prinit Press; 0-932970), Box 65, Dublin, IN 47335 (SAN 212-680X).

Printed Horse, (Printed Horse, The; 0-912830), P.O. Box 1908, Fort Collins, CO 80522 Tel 303-482-2286 (SAN 210-4377).

Printed Matter, (Printed Matter, Inc.; 0-89439), 7 Lispenard St., New York, NY 10013 Tel 212-925-0325 (SAN 169-5924).

Proj Pub & Des, (Project Publishing & Design; 0-915082), 1119 Colorado Ave., Suite 104, Santa Monica, CA 90404 Tel 213-393-9631 (SAN 201-1150).

Proscenium, (Proscenium Press; 0-912262), P.O. Box 361, Newark, DE 19711 Tel 215-255-4083 (SAN 203-0950).

Prospect, (Prospect Books; 0-913710), P.O. Box 57, Prospect, NY 13435 Tel 315-896-2249 (SAN 205-4000).

Proteus Pub NY, (Proteus Publishing Co., Inc.; 0-906071), 9 W. 57th St., New York, NY 10019 (SAN 215-2363); Dist. by Charles Scribner's Sons, 597 Fifth Ave., New York, NY 10017 (SAN 282-6550).

Pruett, (Pruett Publishing Co.; 0-87108), 2928 Pearl St., Boulder, CO 80301 Tel 303-449-4919 (SAN 205-4035).

Pub Aff Pr, (Public Affairs Press; 0-8183), 419 New Jersey Ave., Washington, DC 20003 Tel 202-544-3024 (SAN 202-1471).

Pubn Arts, (Publication Arts, Inc.; 0-86573), 5700 Green Circle Dr., Minnetonka, MN 55343 (SAN 215-1774).

Pubns Organization
See Bridge Pubns Inc

Pubs Inc, (Publishers, Inc.; 0-89163), Drawer P, Del Mar, CA 92014 Tel 714-481-8133 (SAN 207-4222).

Puckerbrush, (Puckerbrush Press; 0-913006), 76 Main St., Orono, ME 04473 Tel 207-866-4868 (SAN 202-0327).

Puddingstone, (Puddingstone Press), P.O. Box 67, Banner Elk, NC 28604 (SAN 205-4019).

Pueblo Pub Pr, (Pueblo Publishing Press; 0-942316), 401 Vandament Ave., Yukon, OK 73099 (SAN 239-5940).

Puffin Imprint of Penguin

Purdue
See Purdue U Pr

Purdue U Pr, (Purdue Univ. Press; 0-911198), S. Campus Courts-D, West Lafayette, IN 47907 Tel 317-494-2035 (SAN 203-4026).

Purple Mouth, (Purple Mouth Press; 0-9603300), 713 Paul St., Newport News, VA 23605 Tel 804-380-6595 (SAN 209-8709).

Pushcart Bk Pr
See Pushcart Pr

Pushcart Pr, (Pushcart Press, The; 0-916366), P.O. Box 380, Wainscott, NY 11975 Tel 516-324-9300 (SAN 202-9871).

Putnam Pub Group, (Putnam Publishing Group, The; 0-399), 200 Madison Ave., New York, NY 10016 Tel 212-576-8908 (SAN 202-5531); Orders to: 1050 Wall St. W., Lyndhurst, NJ 07071 Tel 201-933-9292 (SAN 202-554X). Imprints: Perigee (Perigee Books).

PWS Pubs, (PWS Publishers; 0-87150), Statler Office Bldg., 20 Park Plaza, Boston, MA 02116 Tel 617-482-2344 (SAN 200-2264).

Pyquag, (Pyquag Books, Pubs.; 0-912492), P.O. Box 328, Wethersfield, CT 06109 (SAN 205-4086).

Pyramid Iowa
See Hiawatha Pub

Pyramid Pubns, (Pyramid Pubns., Inc.; 0-515), 9 Garden St, Moonachie, NJ 07074 Tel 201-641-3311 (SAN 202-5523).

Pyramid WV, (Pyramid Press Publishing Co.), 1686 Marshall St., Benwood, WV 26031 (SAN 207-6683).

Pyrotechnics, (Pyrotechnics Guild International, Inc.), 5415 Bangert St., White Marsh, MD 21162 (SAN 260-3098).

Python Pub, (Python Publishing Group; 0-89300), 162 Washington St., Newark, NJ 07102 (SAN 240-057X).

Quadrangle, (Quadrangle/The New York Times Co.), Publisher Abbreviations Without Addresses Are for Titles That Are Out of Print. These Are Obsolete Abbreviations. Publisher's New Abbreviation Is Times Bks.

Quadrangle
See Times Bks

Quail Run, (Quail Run Pubns., Inc.; 0-930380), 3336 N.32nd St., Suite 104, Phoenix, AZ 85018 Tel 602-955-5953 (SAN 210-9476).

Quality Ohio, (Quality Pubns. Inc.; 0-934040), P.O. Box 2633, Lakewood, OH 44107 (SAN 216-2911).

Quality Pubns, (Quality Pubns.; 0-89137), Div. of Quality Printing Co., Inc., P.O. Box 1060, Abilene, TX 79604 Tel 915-677-6262 (SAN 203-0071).

Quarterdeck, (Quarterdeck Press; 0-918546), P.O. Box 134, Pacific Palisades, CA 90272 Tel 213-459-6832 (SAN 209-990X).

Queens Hse, (Queens House; 0-89244), 105 Grovers Ave., Bridgeport, CT 06605 Tel 203-367-1578 (SAN 208-2802).

Quest Imprint of Theos Pub Hse

Quill NY, (Quill; 0-688), 105 Madison Ave., New York, NY 10016 Tel 239-4790).

Quill Pubns, (Quill Pubns.; 0-916608), 1260 Coast Village Circle, Santa Barbara, CA 93108 Tel 805-969-2542 (SAN 208-3442).

Quincunx, (Quincunx; 0-942626), 235 S. 15th St. 3B, Philadelphia, PA 19102 Tel 215-732-0593 (SAN 238-5643).

Quinto Sol Pubns
See Tonatiuh-Quinto Sol Intl

Quist, (Quist, Harlin, Books; 0-8252), Dist. by: Dial/Delacorte Sales, 1 Dag Hammarskjold Plaza, 245 E. 47th St., New York, NY 10017 Tel 212-832-7300 (SAN 282-6178).

R & E Res Assoc, (R & E Research Associates, Inc.; 0-88247), 936 Industrial Ave., Palo Alto, CA 94303 Tel 408-866-6303 (SAN 204-6555).

R C Rapier, (Rapier, Regina C.; 0-9600584), 292 S. Cherokee Rd., Social Circle, GA 30279 Tel 404-464-2582 (SAN 204-6571).

R H Barnes, (Barnes, Robert H.; 0-930480), P.O. Box 418, Grayland, WA 98547 Tel 206-267-3601 (SAN 210-3532).

R H Sang & Son, (Sang, R. H., & Son Pubs. Inc.; 0-932844), 211 E. Delaware Place, Chicago, IL 60611 Tel 312-787-9565 (SAN 212-968X).

R Hart, (Hart, Richard; 0-9602100), P.O. Box 598, Berkeley, CA 94701 (SAN 281-7705)P. O. Box 598, Berkeley, CA 94701 (SAN 281-7713).

R L Bryan, (Bryan, R. L.; 0-934870), 5 Ramblewood Lane, Greenville, SC 29609 (SAN 203-6827).

R L Merriam, (Merriam, Robert L.), Newhall Rd., Conway, MA 01341 (SAN 163-4070).

R Nahass, (Nahass, Rick, Publishing; 0-9608422), P.O. Box 27630, San Francisco, CA 94127 Tel 415-334-7191 (SAN 240-7299).

R S Barnes, (Barnes, Richard S., & Co. Books), 821 Foster St., Evanston, IL 60201 Tel 312-869-2272 (SAN 209-2395).

R Seaver Bks
See Seaver Bks

R W Baron, (Baron, Richard W., Publishing Co.; 0-87777), Orders to: E. P. Dutton & Co., Inc., 210 Park Ave. S., New York, NY 10003 (SAN 201-0070).

R West, (West, Richard; 0-8492; 0-8274), Box 6404, Philadelphia, PA 19145 (SAN 206-8907).

Racz Pub, (Racz Publishing Co.; 0-916546), P.O. Box 287, Oxnard, CA 93032 Tel 805-642-1186 (SAN 208-0265).

Ragnarok
See Merging Media

Rainbow-Betty, (Rainbow Books/Betty Wright; 0-935834), Dept. 1-H, P.O. Box 1069, Moore Haven, FL 33471 Tel 813-946-0293 (SAN 213-5515).

Ramfre, (Ramfre Press; 0-911208), 1206 N. Henderson, Cape Girardeau, MO 63701 Tel 314-335-6582 (SAN 204-6695).

RanC Imprint of Random

Ranch House Pr, (Ranch House Press; 0-88100), Rte. 2, Box 296, Pagosa Springs, CO 81147 Tel 303-264-2647 (SAN 240-1126).

Rand, (Rand McNally & Co.; 0-528), P.O. Box 7600, Chicago, IL 60680 Tel 312-673-9100 (SAN 203-3917).

Randall Hse, (Randall House Pubns.; 0-89265), 114 Bush Rd., P.O. Box 17306, Nashville, TN 37217 Tel 615-361-1221 (SAN 207-5040).

R&M Pub Co, (R&M Publishing Co.; 0-936026), P.O. Box 1276, Holly Hill, SC 29059 Tel 803-531-2053 (SAN 213-6392).

Random, (Random House, Inc.; 0-394), Random House Publicity (11-6), 201 E. 50th St., New York, NY 10022 Tel 212-751-2600 (SAN 202-5507); Orders to: 400 Hahn Rd., Westminster, MD 21157 (SAN 202-5515). Imprints: BYR (Books for Young Readers); RanC (Random House College Division); Vin (Vintage Trade Books).

Rapids Christian, (Rapids Christian Press, Inc.; 0-915374), P.O. Box 487, 810 4th Ave., N., Wisconsin Rapids, WI 54494 Tel 715-423-4670 (SAN 205-0986).

Rapier Pr, (Rapier Press, The; 0-939066), P.O. Box 44911, Tacoma, WA 98444 (SAN 218-5024) Moved, left no forwarding address.

Rational Isl, (Rational Island Pubs.; 0-911214; 0-913937), 719 Second Ave. N., Seattle, WA 98109 Tel 206-284-0311 (SAN 204-6725); Orders to: P.O. Box 2081, Main Office Sta., Seattle, WA 98111 (SAN 204-6733).

Raven Print, (Raven Printing Co., Inc.; 0-89023), 317 S. Beechtree, Grand Haven, MI 49417 Tel 616-525-8005 (SAN 206-6173) Moved, left no forwarding address.

Ravengate Pr, (Ravengate Press; 0-911218), P.O. Box 103, Cambridge, MA 02238 Tel 617-456-8181 (SAN 203-090X).

Rawson Assocs
See Rawson Wade

Rawson Wade, (Rawson, Wade Pubs., Inc.; 0-89256), 597 Fifth Ave., New York, NY 10017 Tel 212-867-6610 (SAN 209-3154); Dist. by: Atheneum Pubs., 122 E. 42nd St., New York, NY 10017 (SAN 209-3162).

RBDH Imprint of Kregel

RC&J
See Reed & Cannon

KEY TO PUBLISHERS' AND DISTRIBUTORS' ABBREVIATIONS

RD Assn, *(Reader's Digest Assn., Inc.; 0-89577),* 750 Third Ave., New York, NY 10017-2797 Tel 212-850-7100 (SAN 282-2083); Orders to: Customer Service, Pleasantville, NY 10570 Tel 914-769-7000 (SAN 282-2091).
RE *Imprint of* **WSP**
Readers Digest Pr, *(Reader's Digest Press; 0-88349),* 200 Park Ave., New York, NY 10017 (SAN 203-3887); Dist. by: McGraw-Hill Book Co., 1221 Ave. of the Americas, New York, NY 10020 (SAN 200-2248).
Red Clay, *(Red Clay Books; 0-911692),* 6366 Sharon Hills Rd., Charlotte, NC 28210 Tel 704-366-9624 (SAN 202-9774) Moved, left no forwarding address.
Red Dust, *(Red Dust Inc.; 0-87376),* P.O. Box 630, Gracie Sta., New York, NY 10028 Tel 212-348-4388 (SAN 203-3860).
Red Herring, *(Red Herring Press; 0-932884),* 1209 W. Oregon, Urbana, IL 61801 Tel 217-359-0067 (SAN 212-2251).
Red Key Pr, *(Red Key Press; 0-943696),* P.O. Box 551, Port St. Joe, FL 32456 (SAN 240-8848).
Red Rose Pr, *(Red Rose Press; 0-9609888),* P.O. Box 24, Encino, CA 91426 Tel 213-981-7638 (SAN 282-2121); Dist. by: Bookpeople, 2940 7th St., Berkeley, CA 94710 Tel 415-549-3030 (SAN 168-9517); Dist. by: Publisher's Group West, 5855 Beaudry St., Emeryville, CA 94609 Tel 415-650-3453 (SAN 202-8522).
Red Rose Studio, *(Red Rose Studio; 0-932514),* 358 Flintlock Dr., Willow Street, PA 17584 (SAN 212-162X).
Red Studio, *(Red Studio Press; 0-916320),* 200 22nd Ave. S., Minneapolis, MN 55454 Tel 612-339-2042 (SAN 208-3434).
Reed & Cannon, *(Reed & Cannon Co.; 0-918408),* 2140 Shattuck Ave., Rm. 311, Berkeley, CA 94704 Tel 415-527-1586 (SAN 282-2393); 285 E. Third St., New York, NY 10009 (SAN 282-2407).
Reed & Youngs Quilt, *(Reed, Ishmael & Al Young's Quilt; 0-931676),* 2140 Shattuck Ave., Rm. 311, Berkeley, CA 94704 Tel 415-527-1586 (SAN 282-2334); Dist. by: Bookpeople, 2940 Seventh St., Berkeley, CA 94710 (SAN 168-9517); Dist. by: Before Columbus Foundation, 1446-D Sixth St., Berkeley, CA 94710 (SAN 219-4651); Dist. by: Small Press, 1784 Shattuck Ave., Berkeley, CA 94709 Tel 415-529-3336 (SAN 204-5826); Dist. by: Bookslinger, 330 E. Ninth St., St. Paul, MN 55101 (SAN 169-4154); Dist. by: Inland Bk. Co., P.O. Box 261, 22 Hemingway Ave., E. Haven, CT 06512 (SAN 282-2385).
Reed Bks, *(Reed Books; 0-89169),* Subs. of Addison House, ; c/o Addison House, Morgan's Run, Danbury, NH 03230 Tel 603-768-3903 (SAN 210-5543).
Regal, *(Regal Books; 0-8307),* Div. of G/L Pubns., 2300 Knoll Dr., Ventura, CA 93003 Tel 805-644-9721 (SAN 203-3852).
Regent House
 See B of A
Regents Pub, *(Regents Publishing Co., Inc.; 0-88345),* Div. of Hachette, 2 Park Ave., New York, NY 10016 Tel 212-889-2780 (SAN 203-3844).
Regnery, *(Regnery, Henry, Co.),* Publisher Abbreviation Without Addresses Are for Titles That Are Out of Print. These Are Obsolete Abbreviations. Publisher's Abbreviation Is Now Contemp Bks.
Regnery
 See Contemp Bks
Regnery-Gateway, *(Regnery Gateway, Inc.; 0-89526),* 360 W. Superior St., Chicago, IL 60610 Tel 312-440-1647 (SAN 210-5578).
Reidel Pub
 See Kluwer Academic
Reilly & Lee, *(Reilly & Lee Co.; 0-8092),* Dist. by: Henry Regnery Co., 180 N. Michigan Ave., Chicago, IL 60601 (SAN 202-5493) Acquired by Henry Regnery.
Reilly & Lee
 See Contemp Bks
Reiner, *(Reiner Pubns.; 0-87377),* Swengel PA 17880 Tel 717-922-3213 (SAN 204-6784).
Religious Soc Friends, *(Philadelphia Yearly Meeting, Religious Society of Friends, Book Services; 0-941308),* 1515 Cherry St., Philadelphia, PA 19102 (SAN 239-3778)

Renaissance Soc Am, *(Renaissance Society of America),* 1161 Amsterdam Ave., New York, NY 10027 Tel 212-280-2318 (SAN 209-4835).
Renouf
 See Brookfield Pub Co
Reprint, *(Reprint Co.; 0-87152),* P.O. Box 5401, 601 Hillcrest Offices, Spartanburg, SC 29304 Tel 803-582-0732 (SAN 203-3828).
Res Publs, *(Research Pubs.; 0-911252),* 108 S. Patton, Arlington Heights, IL 60005 Tel 312-255-1961 (SAN 206-6645).
Resolute Pr, *(Resolute Press; 0-9604382),* 13 Regent Court, Edison, NJ 08817 (SAN 216-0099).
Resource Pubs, *(Resource Pubns.; 0-89390),* 160 E. Virginia St., No. 290, San Jose, CA 95112 Tel 408-286-8505 (SAN 209-3081).
Reston, *(Reston Publishing Co., Inc.; 0-87909; 0-8359),* 11480 Sunset Hills Rd., Reston, VA 22090 Tel 703-437-8900 (SAN 200-2337); Dist. by: Prentice-Hall, Inc., Englewood Cliffs, NJ 07632 (SAN 215-3939).
Revell, *(Revell, Fleming H., Co.; 0-8007),* 184 Central Ave., Old Tappan, NJ 07675 Tel 201-768-8060 (SAN 203-3801). Imprints: Spire Bks (Spire Books).
Review & Herald, *(Review & Herald Publishing Assn.; 0-8280),* 6856 Eastern Ave. NW, Washington, DC 20012 Tel 202-723-3700 (SAN 203-3798).
Revisionist Pr, *(Revisionist Press; 0-87700),* P.O. Box 2009, Brooklyn, NY 11202 (SAN 203-378X).
Reynolds Morse, *(Reynolds Morse Foundation; 0-934236),* 10395 Stafford Rd., Chagrin Fall, OH 44022 (SAN 282-2520); Dist. by: L.D.S. Books, P.O. Box 67, MCS, Dayton, OH 45402 (SAN 282-5864).
Rhinoceros Pr, *(Rhinoceros Press; 0-931376),* Box 1186, El Cerrito, CA 94930 (SAN 211-5166).
RHS Bk Assn, *(R. H. S. Book Assn. to Assist Poverty-Stricken Americans),* 1017 Park St., Lorned, KS 67550 (SAN 203-3771).
Richards Pub, *(Richards, Frank E., Publishing Co., Inc.; 0-88323),* P.O. Box 66, Phoenix, NY 13135 Tel 315-695-7261 (SAN 203-0861).
Richboro Pr, *(Richboro Press; 0-89713),* Box 1, Richboro, PA 18954 (SAN 214-1353).
Ricwalt Pub Co, *(Ricwalt Publishing Co.; 0-933054),* C-3 Bldg., Rm. 110, Fishermen's Terminal, Seattle, WA 98119 Tel 206-282-7545 (SAN 213-1587).
Ridgefield Pub, *(Ridgefield Pub. Co.; 0-86628),* 6925 Canby Ave., Suite 104, Reseda, CA 91335 Tel 213-343-8811 (SAN 215-8035).
Ridgeview Jr High Pr, *(Ridgeview Junior High Press; 0-936920),* 9424 Highlander Court, Walkersville, MD 21793 (SAN 214-4573).
Ridgeway Bks, *(Ridgeway Books),* P. O. Box 6431, Philadelphia, PA 19145 (SAN 207-7485).
Right White Line, *(Right White Line; 0-918926),* 531 N. Inlet, Lincoln City, OR 97367 Tel 503-994-8433 (SAN 209-6536).
Ringa Pr, *(Ringa Press; 0-88100),* 6833 W. Grand Avenue, Chicago, IL 60635 (SAN 264-3529).
Rio Grande, *(Rio Grande Press, Inc.; 0-87380),* P.O. Box 33, Glorieta, NM 87535 Tel 505-757-6275 (SAN 203-3763).
Ritchie, *(Ritchie, Ward, Press; 0-378),* 474 S. Arroyo Pkwy., Pasadena, CA 91105 Tel 213-793-1163 (SAN 212-1879).
Rittenhouse, *(Rittenhouse Book Distributors),* 511 Feheley Dr., King of Prussia, PA 19406 Tel 215-277-1414 (SAN 213-4454).
RivEd *Imprint of* **HM**
Riverrun NY, *(Riverrun Press Inc.; 0-7145),* 175 Fifth Ave., Suite 814, New York, NY 10010 Tel 212-228-0390 (SAN 212-551X); Dist. by: Flatiron Book Distributors, Inc., 175 Fifth Ave., Suite 814, New York, NY 10010 Tel 212-228-0390 (SAN 240-9917).
Riverrun Texas
 See Riverrun NY
RivLit *Imprint of* **HM**
Rizzoli Intl, *(Rizzoli International Pubns., Inc.; 0-8478),* 712 Fifth Ave., New York, NY 10019 Tel 212-397-3740 (SAN 207-7000).
RK Edns, *(RK Editions; 0-932360),* P.O. Box 73, Canal St., New York, NY 10013 (SAN 211-447X).

Roadrunner Tech, *(Roadrunner-Technical Pubns., Inc.; 0-89741),* Div. of Desert Laboratories, Inc., 3136 E. Columbia St., Tucson, AZ 85714 Tel 602-294-3431 (SAN 204-2169).
Roark Pubns, *(Roark Pubns.; 0-939546),* P.O. Box 5973-325, Sherman Oaks, CA 91413 Tel 213-784-7421 (SAN 220-1852).
Roca Pub, *(Roca Publishing, Inc.; 0-88025),* P.O. Box 176, St. David, PA 19087 Tel 215-337-0576 (SAN 217-4243).
Rochester Folk Art, *(Rochester Folk Art Guild),* Rte. 1, Box 10, Middlesex, NY 14507 Tel 716-554-3539 (SAN 210-9492).
Rock Pub, *(Rock Publishing Co.; 0-9601804),* 3667 San Pascual Ave., Las Vegas, NV 89110 (SAN 212-6869) Moved, Left No Forwarding Address.
Rocket Pub Co, *(Rocket Publishing Co.),* P.O. Box 412, Normangee, TX 77871 Tel 713-828-4265 (SAN 204-5699).
Rocking Chair Pr, *(Rocking Chair Press, Inc.; 0-913562),* 2109 Queenswood Dr., Tallahassee, FL 32303 (SAN 204-6938).
Rod & Staff, *(Rod & Staff Pubs., Inc.),* Crockett, KY 41413 Tel 606-522-4348 (SAN 206-7633).
Rodney, *(Rodney Pubns., Inc.; 0-913830),* 349 E. 49th St., New York, NY 10017 Tel 212-421-5444 (SAN 204-6954).
Rogers Bk, *(Rogers Book Service; 0-911268),* 217 W. 18th St, Box V, New York, NY 10011 (SAN 204-6970).
Rongataur, *(Rongataur Press; 0-941006),* P.O. Box 991, Vacaville, CA 95696 Tel 707-447-0739 (SAN 217-4278).
Rook Pr, *(Rook Press; 0-916684),* P.O. Box 144, Ruffsdale, PA 15679 (SAN 208-3353).
Rooney Pubns, *(Rooney Pubns.; 0-9604600),* P.O. Box 44146, Panorama City, CA 91412 Tel 213-894-2585 (SAN 215-1790).
Rosen Group, *(Rosen Pub. Group; 0-8239),* 29 E. 21st St., New York, NY 10010 Tel 212-777-3017 (SAN 203-3720).
Rosen Pr
 See Rosen Group
Rosenbach Found
 See Rosenbach Mus & Lib
Rosenbach Mus & Lib, *(Rosenbach Museum & Library, The),* 2010 De Lancey Place, Philadelphia, PA 19103 Tel 215-732-1600 (SAN 211-9749).
Ross, *(Ross & Haines Old Books Co.; 0-87018),* 639 E. Lake St., Wayzata, MN 55391 Tel 612-473-7551 (SAN 204-7004).
Ross-Erikson, *(Ross-Erikson, Inc.; 0-915520),* 629 State St., Suite 207, Santa Barbara, CA 93101 Tel 805-962-1175 (SAN 208-0494).
Rota Pr, *(Rota Press; 0-87908),* P.O. Box 332, Waverly, IA 50677 (SAN 206-8648).
Routledge & Kegan, *(Routledge & Kegan Paul, Ltd.; 0-7100),* 9 Park St., Boston, MA 02108 Tel 617-742-5863 (SAN 202-5469).
Rowcliff, *(Rowcliff, Norman),* Rte. 1, Box 564, Batavia, IL 60510 (SAN 204-7039).
Rowman, *(Rowman & Littlefield, Inc.; 0-87471; 0-8476),* Div. of Littlefield, Adams, & Co., 81 Adams Dr., Box 327, Totowa, NJ 07511 Tel 201-256-8600 (SAN 203-3704).
Roy, *(Roy Pubs., Inc.; 0-8035),* 30 E. 74th St., New York, NY 10021 Tel 212-879-5935 (SAN 204-7047); Dist. by: Ventura Book Service, 114-20 Rockaway Beach Blvd., Rockaway Park, NY 11694 (SAN 204-7055).
RRS *Imprint of* **HM**
Rue Morgue, *(Rue Morgue Press; 0-915230),* P.O. Box 4119, Boulder, CO 80306 Tel 303-443-8346 (SAN 207-737X).
Running Pr, *(Running Press Book Publishers; 0-89471),* 125 S. 22nd St., Philadelphia, PA 19103 Tel 215-567-5080 (SAN 204-5702).
Rushlight Club, *(Rushlight Club; 0-917422),* P.O. Box 3053, Talcottville, CT 06066 (SAN 207-4958).
Russell, *(Russell & Russell, Pubs.; 0-8462),* Div. of Atheneum Pubs., 597 Fifth Ave., New York, NY 10017 Tel 212-486-2685 (SAN 282-2644); Orders to: Scribner Distribution Center, 201 Willowbrook Blvd., Wayne, NJ 07470 Tel 201-256-0700 (SAN 282-2652).
Russica Bk Art
 See Russica Pubs
Russica Pubs, *(Russica Publishers; 0-89830),* C/O Russica Book & Art Co., 799 Broadway, New York, NY 10003 (SAN 212-310X).

KEY TO PUBLISHERS' AND DISTRIBUTORS' ABBREVIATIONS

Rutgers U Pr, *(Rutgers Univ. Pr.; 0-8135)*, 30 College Ave., New Brunswick, NJ 08903 Tel 201-932-7764 (SAN 203-364X).
Rutledge Pr *Imprint of* **Smith Pubs**
Rydal, *(Rydal Press-The Print; 0-911292)*, P.O. Box 250, Santa Fe, NM 87501 Tel 505-982-2689 (SAN 204-7098).
S & S Pr TX, *(S & S Press; 0-934646)*, P.O. Box 5931, Austin, TX 78763 (SAN 212-6885) Do Not Confuse with Simon & Schuster (S&S).
S Campbell, *(Campbell, Sandy M.; 0-917366)*, 230 Central Park S., New York, NY 10019 Tel 212-582-6286 (SAN 204-7128).
S F Vanni, *(Vanni, S.F.; 0-913298)*, 30 W. 12th St., New York, NY 10011 Tel 212-675-6336 (SAN 220-0031).
S G Phillips, *(Phillips, S. G., Inc.; 0-87599)*, P.O. Box 83, Chatham, NY 12037 Tel 518-392-3068 (SAN 203-3631).
S Ill U Pr, *(Southern Illinois Univ. Press; 0-8093)*, P.O. Box 3697, Carbondale, IL 62901 Tel 618-453-2281 (SAN 203-3623).
S K Chapman, *(Chapman, Sarah K.)*, P.O. Box 3684, Sarasota, FL 33578 (SAN 263-9696).
S Meth U Pr
  See **SMU Press**
Sagarin Pr, *(Sagarin Press; 0-915298)*, Box 251, Sand Lake, NY 12153 Tel 518-674-2998 (SAN 207-396X).
Saguaro, *(Saguaro Publishing; 0-9608864)*, 1302 E. Becker Lane, Phoenix, AZ 85020 (SAN 241-0761).
Saifer, *(Saifer, Albert, Pub.; 0-87556)*, P.O. Box 239 W.O.B., West Orange, NJ 07052 (SAN 204-7225).
Sail Bks, *(Sail Bks., Inc.; 0-914814)*, 34 Commercial Wharf, Boston, MA 02110 (SAN 207-0820).
Salt Lick, *(Salt Lick Press; 0-913918)*, 5107 Martin Ave., Austin, TX 78751 (SAN 202-0823).
Samisdat, *(Samisdat)*, Box 129, Richford, VT 05476 (SAN 207-8929).
Samuel P Co, *(Powell, Samuel, Publishing Co.)*, 2201 I St., Sacramento, CA 95816 (SAN 219-2756).
Sand Dollar, *(Sand Dollar Press)*, 1222 Solano Ave., Albany, CA 94706 Tel 415-527-1931 (SAN 203-2686).
Sandlapper Pub Co, *(Sandlapper Pub. Co., Inc.; 0-87844)*, P.O. Box 1932, Orangeburg, SC 29116 Tel 803-531-1658 (SAN 203-2678).
Sandlapper Store
  See **Sandlapper Pub Co**
S&S, *(Simon & Schuster, Inc.; 0-671)*, 1230 Ave. of the Americas, New York, NY 10020 Tel 212-245-6400 (SAN 200-2450). *Imprints:* Fireside (Fireside Paperbacks); Linden Pr (Linden Press); Touchstone Bks (Touchstone Books).
S&S Co CA
  See **S&S Co OR**
S&S Co OR, *(S&S Co., The)*, 11047 Antiock Rd, Central Point, OR 97502 Tel 503-826-7870 (SAN 212-2588) Moved, left no forwarding address.
Sant Bani Ash, *(Sant Bani Ashram, Inc.)*, Franklin, NH 03235 Tel 603-934-4209 (SAN 209-5114).
Sat Eve Post
  See **Curtis Pub Co**
Sat Rev Pr
  See **Dutton**
Saturday Pr, *(Saturday Press, Inc.; 0-938158)*, P.O. Box 884, Upper Montclair, NJ 07043 Tel 201-256-1731 (SAN 207-5792).
Saturday Review, *(Saturday Review Press)*, 201 Park Ave S, New York, NY 10003 (SAN 226-3807).
Saucerian
  See **G Barker Bks**
SBD
  See **Small Pr Dist**
Scarecrow, *(Scarecrow Press, Inc.; 0-8108)*, Subs. of Grolier Educational Corp., 52 Liberty St., Box 656, Metuchen, NJ 08840 Tel 201-548-8600 (SAN 203-2651).
Sch Living Pr
  See **Wisconsin Bks**
Schalkenbach, *(Schalkenbach, Robert, Foundation; 0-911312)*, 5 E. 44th St., New York, NY 10017 Tel 212-986-8684 (SAN 206-1317).
Schiffer, *(Schiffer Publishing Ltd.; 0-916838)*, P.O. Box E, Exton, PA 19341 Tel 215-363-6889 (SAN 208-8218).

Schocken, *(Schocken Books, Inc.; 0-8052)*, 200 Madison Ave., New York, NY 10016 Tel 212-685-6500 (SAN 213-7585).
Schoenhof, *(Schoenhof's Foreign Books, Inc.; 0-87774)*, 1280 Massachusetts Ave., Cambridge, MA 02138 Tel 617-547-8855 (SAN 200-0062).
Schol Bk Serv
  See **Scholastic Inc**
Schol Facsimiles, *(Scholars' Facsimiles & Reprints; 0-8201)*, P.O. Box 344, Delmar, NY 12054 Tel 518-439-5978 (SAN 203-2627).
Scholarly, *(Scholarly Press Inc.; 0-403)*, P.O. Box 160, Saint Clair Shores, MI 48080 Tel 313-884-0400 (SAN 209-0473).
Scholars Pr
  See **Scholars Pr CA**
Scholars Pr CA, *(Scholars Press; 0-89130)*, 101 Salem St. P.O. Box 2268, Chico, CA 95927 Tel 916-891-4541 (SAN 207-964X).
Scholars Pr MI
  See **Scholars Pr CA**
Scholars Ref Lib, *(Scholar's Reference Library)*, P.O. Box 148, Darby, PA 19023 (SAN 205-1400).
Scholastic Inc, *(Scholastic, Inc.; 0-590)*, 730 Broadway, New York, NY 10003 Tel 212-505-3000 (SAN 202-5442); Orders to: P.O. Box 7502, 2931 E. McCarty St., Jefferson City, MO 65102 (SAN 202-5450).
SCOP Pubns, *(SCOP Pubns., Inc.)*, P.O. Box 376, College Park, MD 20740 (SAN 211-2035).
Scott F, *(Scott, Foresman & Co.; 0-673)*, 1900 E. Lake Ave., Glenview, IL 60025 Tel 312-729-3000 (SAN 200-2140).
Scribner, *(Scribner's, Charles, Sons; 0-684)*, 597 Fifth Ave., New York, NY 10017 Tel 212-486-2703 (SAN 282-2873); Orders to: Shipping & Service Ctr., Vreeland Ave., Totowa, NJ 07512 (SAN 282-6550).
Scrimshaw Calif, *(Scrimshaw Press (California); 0-912020)*, 6040 Claremont Ave., Oakland, CA 94618 Tel 415-658-2323 (SAN 202-5434).
Scrip Pr
  See **Victor Bks**
Sea Horse, *(Sea Horse Press, Ltd., The; 0-933322)*, 307 W. 11th St., New York, NY 10014 Tel 212-691-9066 (SAN 212-4505).
Sea of Storms, *(Sea of Storms; 0-931910)*, P.O. Box 22613, San Francisco, CA 94122 Tel 707-795-2098 (SAN 211-4518).
Seabury, *(Seabury Press, Inc.; 0-8164)*, 815 Second Ave., New York, NY 10017 Tel 212-557-0500 (SAN 202-5418); Orders to: Seabury Service Center, Somers, CT 06071 Tel 800-243-0004 (SAN 202-5426).
Seagull Pubns., *(Seagull Pubns., Inc.; 0-930290)*, 1736 E. 53rd St., Brooklyn, NY 11234 Tel 212-338-6622 (SAN 210-1378).
SeaHorse Pr
  See **Sea Horse**
Seal Pr Feminist, *(Seal Pr.)*, 312 S. Washington, Seattle, WA 98104 Tel 206-624-5262 (SAN 215-3416).
Seal Pr WA
  See **Seal Pr Feminist**
Seattle Bk, *(Seattle Book Co.; 0-915112)*, P.O. Box 9254, Seattle, WA 98109 Tel 206-285-1226 (SAN 207-1835).
Seaver Bks, *(Seaver Books; 0-394)*, 333 Central Park West, New York, NY 10025 Tel 212-866-9278 (SAN 214-4719); Orders to: Grove Press, Inc., 196 W. Houston St., New York, NY 10014 (SAN 201-4890); Dist. by: Arbor House Publishing Company, 300 E. 44th St., New York, NY 10017 (SAN 201-1522).
Seaview Pr, *(Seaview Press; 0-9606048)*, P.O. Box 32, El Cerrito, CA 94530 Tel 415-525-5495 (SAN 216-4477).
Second Chance, *(Second Chance Press; 0-933256)*, RD 2, Box 38AA, Noyac Rd., Sag Harbor, NY 11963 Tel 516-725-1101 (SAN 213-1633).
Second Coming, *(Second Coming Press; 0-915016)*, P.O. Box 31249, San Francisco, CA 94131 Tel 415-647-3679 (SAN 206-376X).
Seed Center, *(Seed Center; 0-916108)*, P.O. Box 658, Garberville, CA 95440 Tel 707-986-7575 (SAN 203-2554).
Select Pub, *(Select Publishing; 0-9606458)*, P.O. Box 85707, Los Angeles, CA 90072 (SAN 215-5970).

Self Therapy *See* **Wingbow Pr**
Senda Nueva, *(Senda Nueva De Ediciones, Inc.; 0-918454)*, 640 W. 231st St., Apt. 3-B, Bronx, NY 10463 (SAN 210-0061).
SenEd *Imprint of* **HM**
Serrell-Simons, *(Serrell & Simons, Publishers; 0-943104)*, Box 64, Winnebago, WI 54985 Tel 414-231-1939 (SAN 240-4400); Dist. by: Baker & Taylor, P.O. Box 458, Commerce, GA 30599 (SAN 169-1503); Dist. by: Baker & Taylor, 501 S. Gladiolus Ave., Momence, IL 60954 (SAN 169-2100); Dist. by: Baker & Taylor, 380 Edison Way, Reno, NV 89564 (SAN 169-4464); Dist. by: Taylor & Baker, 50 Kirby Ave., Somerville, NJ 08876 (SAN 169-4901); Dist. by: The Distributors, 702 S. Michigan, South Bend, IN 46618 Tel 219-232-8500 (SAN 212-0364).
Seven Oaks, *(Seven Oaks Press; 0-932508)*, 405 S. 7th St., St. Charles, IL 60174 Tel 312-584-0187 (SAN 212-1735).
Seven Woods Pr, *(Seven Woods Press; 0-913282)*, P.O. Box 32 Village Sta., New York, NY 10014 (SAN 203-2503).
Sey Lawr *Imprint of* **Delacorte**
SF Arts & Letters, *(San Francisco Arts & Letters Foundation; 0-914024)*, P.O. Box 99394, San Francisco, CA 94109 Tel 415-771-3431 (SAN 202-8751).
Shabazz Pr, *(El-Hajj Malik Shabazz Press; 0-913358)*, 445 Park Rd. N. W., Washington, DC 20010 (SAN 201-2340); Orders to: Liberation Information Distributing Co., 4206 Edson Place N.E., Washington, DC 20019 (SAN 201-2359).
Shalom, *(Shalom, P., Pubns., Inc.; 0-87559)*, 5409 18th Ave., Brooklyn, NY 11204 (SAN 204-5893).
Shambhala Pubns, *(Shambhala Pubns., Inc.; 0-87773)*, 1920 13th St., P.O. Box 271, Boulder, CO 80306 Tel 303-449-6111 (SAN 203-2481); Dist. by: Random House, Inc., 400 Hahn Rd., Westminster, MD 21157 (SAN 202-5515).
Shameless Hussy, *(Shameless Hussy Press; 0-915288)*, Box 3092, Berkeley, CA 94703 Tel 415-548-7800 (SAN 282-3071); Dist. by: Bookpeople, 2940 Seventh St., Berkeley, CA 94710 Tel 415-549-3030 (SAN 168-9517); Dist. by: Bookslinger, 330 East Ninth St., St. Paul, MN 55101 Tel 612-221-0429 (SAN 169-4154); Dist. by: The Crossing Press, Trumansburg, New York, NY 14886 Tel 607-387-6217 (SAN 202-2060); Dist. by: Straight Talk Distributing, P.O. Box 750, Point Reyes Station, CA 94956 Tel 219-232-8500 (SAN 282-311X); Dist. by: The Distributors, 702 S. Michigan, South Bend, IN 46618 (SAN 212-0364).
Shamrock Pubns, *(Shamrock Pubns; 0-9608142)*, 406 Rising Hill Drive, Fairborn, OH 45324 (SAN 240-1584).
Sharon Hill, *(Sharon Hill Books; 0-932062)*, P.O. Box 67, Sharon Hill, PA 19079 (SAN 210-5632).
Sharon Pubns, *(Sharon Pubns. Inc.; 0-89531)*, 105 Union Ave., Cresslill, NJ 07626 Tel 201-568-8800 (SAN 210-4989).
Sharral Pub, *(Sharral Publishing Co.; 0-940978)*, Subs. of Lee Rothchild, Ltd., 13540 E. Boundary Rd., Midlothian, VA 23113 Tel 804-744-3658 (SAN 217-4375).
Shaw Pubs, *(Shaw, Harold, Pubs.; 0-87788)*, Box 567, 388 Gundersen Dr., Wheaton, IL 60189 Tel 312-665-6700 (SAN 203-2473).
Shearer Pub, *(Shearer Publishing; 0-940672)*, 3208 Turtle Grove, Bryan, TX 77801 Tel 713-779-1762 (SAN 218-5989).
Sheep Meadow, *(Sheep Meadow Press, The; 0-935296)*, Dist. by: Persea Bks., Inc., 225 Lafayette St., New York, NY 10012 Tel 212-431-5270 (SAN 212-8233).
Shelter Pubns
  See **Random**
Shengold, *(Shengold Pubs., Inc.; 0-88400)*, 23 W. 45th St., New York, NY 10036 Tel 212-944-2555 (SAN 203-2465).
Sherbourne, *(Sherbourne Press; 0-8202)*, P.O. Box 12037, Nashville, TN 37212 Tel 615-254-5842 (SAN 204-5907).
Sherry Urie, *(Urie, Sherry; 0-9603324)*, RFD, West Glover, VT 05875 (SAN 211-4526).

KEY TO PUBLISHERS' AND DISTRIBUTORS' ABBREVIATIONS

Shoe String, *(Shoe String Press, Inc.; 0-208),* P.O. Box 4327, 995 Sherman Ave., Hamden, CT 06514 Tel 203-248-6307 (SAN 213-2079). *Imprints:* Archon Bks (Archon Books).

Shorey, *(Shorey Pubns.; 0-8466),* 110 Union St., Seattle, WA 98101 Tel 206-624-0221 (SAN 204-5958).

Short Methods, *(Short Methods & Systems; 0-915800),* P.O. Box 247, Claremont, CA 91711 Tel 714-626-3213 (SAN 207-4842).

Sierra, *(Sierra Club Bks.; 0-87156),* 2034 Fillmore St., San Francisco, CA 94115 Tel 415-931-7950 (SAN 203-2406); Dist. by: Random Hse., Inc., Distribution Ctr., 400 Hahn Rd., Westminster, MD 21157 (SAN 202-5515).

Sig *Imprint of* **NAL**

Sig Classics *Imprint of* **NAL**

Sigga Pr, *(Sigga Press; 0-916348),* P.O. Box 25, Nottingham, NH 03290 (SAN 211-2698).

Silvergirl Bks, *(Silvergirl Books),* P.O. Box 4858, Austin, TX 78765 Tel 512-863-2537 (SAN 239-3875).

Silvermine, *(Silvermine Pubs.; 0-87231),* Comstock Hill, Silvermine, Norwalk, CT 06850 Tel 203-847-4732 (SAN 209-6005).

Simonetta Pr, *(Simonetta Press; 0-941594),* 4219 W. Eighth St., Los Angeles, CA 90005 (SAN 239-3883).

Singing Tree, *(Singing Tree Press),* Publisher Abbreviation Without Addresses Are for Titles That Are Out of Print. These Are Obsolete Abbreviations.

Singlejack
See Miles & Weir

Sirius Pubns, *(Sirius Pubns.),* 270 S. La Cienega Blvd., Suite 301, Beverly Hills, CA 90211 (SAN 282-3195); Dist. by: Uri Dowbenko, 2117 14th Ave., San Francisco, CA 94116 Tel 213-706-8838 (SAN 282-3209).

Sitnalta Pr, *(Sitnalta Press; 0-931826),* P.O. Box 2730, San Francisco, CA 94126 (SAN 211-5026).

Sky Pubns NJ, *(Sky Pubns.; 0-941566),* 210 Skylands Rd., Ringwood, NJ 07456 (SAN 239-3123).

Skydog OR, *(Skydog),* 6735 SE 78th St., Portland, OR 97206 (SAN 226-8019).

Skydog WA
See Skydog OR

Skylark *Imprint of* **Bantam**

Slack Inc, *(Slack, Inc.; 0-913590; 0-943432),* 6900 Grove Rd., Thorofare, NJ 08086 Tel 609-848-1000 (SAN 201-8632).

Slavia Lib, *(Slavia Library; 0-918884),* 418 W. Nittany Ave., State College, PA 16801 (SAN 211-0598).

Sleepy Hollow, *(Sleepy Hollow Press; 0-912882),* 150 White Plains Rd., Tarrytown, NY 10591 Tel 914-631-8200 (SAN 202-0750); Dist. by: Independent Publishers Group, One Pleasant Ave., Port Washington, NY 11050 Tel 516-944-9325 (SAN 202-0769).

Slough Pr TX, *(Slough Pr.; 0-941720),* Box 1385, Austin, TX 78767 Tel 512-474-5488 (SAN 239-3131).

Slow Loris, *(Slow Loris Press; 0-918366),* 923 Highview St., Pittsburgh, PA 15206 (SAN 209-6803).

SLUSA, *(SLUSA),* 88 Eastern Ave., Somerville, NJ 08876 (SAN 216-1931).

Small Pr Dist, *(Small Press Distribution, Inc.; 0-914068),* 1784 Shattuck Ave., Berkeley, CA 94709 Tel 415-529-3336 (SAN 204-5826).

Smith Pubs, *(Smith, W. H., Pubs., Inc.; 0-8317),* 112 Madison Ave., New York, NY 10016 Tel 212-532-6600 (SAN 216-3241).
Imprints: Rutledge Pr (Rutledge Press).

Smithsonian, *(Smithsonian Institution Pr.; 0-87474),* Rm. 2280, Arts & Industries Bldg., Washington, DC 20560 Tel 202-357-1912 (SAN 206-8044); Orders to: P.O. Box 1579, Washington, DC 20013 Tel 202-357-1793 (SAN 206-8052) Booksellers Order from: Publications Sales, 1111 N. Capitol St., Washington, DC 20560, Tel- 202-357-1793.

SMU Press, *(Southern Methodist Univ. Press; 0-87074),* Dallas, TX 75275 Tel 214-692-2263 (SAN 203-3615).

Smyrna, *(Smyrna Press; 0-918266),* P.O. Box 1803, GPO, Brooklyn, NY 11202 Tel 212-638-8939 (SAN 207-897X).

Soccer
See Sportshelf

Society Sp & Sp-Am, *(Society of Spanish & Spanish-American Studies; 0-89295),* Dept. of Modern Languages & Literatures, Univ. of Nebraska-Lincoln, Lincoln, NE 68588 Tel 402-472-3842 (SAN 208-3221).

Soft Pr, *(Soft Press; 0-919590),* 1525 McRae Ave., Victoria British Columbia, V8P 1G4, Tel 604-598-2173 (SAN 208-2594).

Solaris Pr, *(Solaris Press, Inc.),* P.O. Box 1009, Rochester, MI 48063 (SAN 262-0820).

Somerset Pub, *(Somerset Pubs.),* Div. of Scholarly Press, Inc., 200 Park Ave., Suite 303E, New York, NY 10017 Tel 313-884-0440 (SAN 204-6105).

Somrie Pr, *(Somrie Press; 0-9603950),* Ryder Street Station; Box 328, Brooklyn, NY 11234 (SAN 214-1450).

South Asia Bks, *(South Asia Books; 0-88386; 0-8364),* P.O. Box 502, Columbia, MO 65205 Tel 314-449-1359 (SAN 207-4044).

Southern U Pr, *(Southern Univ. Press; 0-87651),* 130 S. 19th St., Birmingham, AL 35233 (SAN 204-6148).

Space Age, *(Space Age Press, Ltd.; 0-911412),* P.O. Box 11448, Fort Worth, TX 76109 (SAN 204-6164).

Spec *Imprint of* **P-H**

Speller, *(Speller, Robert, & Sons, Pubs., Inc.; 0-8315),* 30 E. 23rd St., New York, NY 10108 Tel 212-477-5524 (SAN 203-2295); Orders to: P.O. Box 461, Times Square Sta., New York, NY 10036 (SAN 203-2309).

Spilman Pr, *(Spilman Press; 0-918180),* Subs. of Spilman Printing Co., 1801 9th St., Sacramento, CA 95814 Tel 916-444-0411 (SAN 210-2722).

Spindrift, *(Spindrift Press; 0-914864),* P.O. Box 3252, Catonsville, MD 21228 Tel 301-944-3317 (SAN 206-3808).

Spinsters Ink, *(Spinsters, Ink; 0-933216),* 233 Dolores No. 8, San Francisco, CA 94103 Tel 415-431-9082 (SAN 212-6923).

Spire Bks *Imprint of* **Revell**

Spiritual Sci Lib *Imprint of* **Garber Comm**

Sportshelf, *(Sportshelf & Soccer Associates; 0-392),* P.O. Box 634, New Rochelle, NY 10802 Tel 914-235-2347 (SAN 202-5388).

Springtide, *(Springtide Books; 0-910873),* 30 Watkins Rd., Brick, NJ 08723 Tel 201-458-1543 (SAN 262-0871).

Sproing, *(Sproing Books; 0-916176),* 3721 Barcelona St., Tampa, FL 33609 (SAN 206-3816).

St Andrews NC, *(St. Andrews Press; 0-932662),* St. Andrews Presbyterian College, Laurinburg, NC 28352 Tel 919-276-3652 (SAN 207-8902).

St Anthony Mess Pr, *(St. Anthony Messenger Press; 0-912228; 0-86716),* 1615 Republic St., Cincinnati, OH 45210 Tel 513-241-5616 (SAN 204-6237).

St Basil Pr, *(St. Basil Press; 0-9604278),* 4106 N. Ozark Ave., Norridge, IL 60634 (SAN 215-1057).

St Clair Pr
See Wiley

St Edns, *(Street Editions),* 20 Desbrosses St., New York, NY 10013 (SAN 282-373X).

St George Bk Serv, *(St. George Book Service; 0-916786),* P.O. Box 225, Spring Valley, NY 10977 Tel 914-623-7852 (SAN 208-8371).

St Heironymous, *(St. Heironymous Press, Inc.; 0-913718),* P.O. Box 9431, Berkeley, CA 94709 Tel 415-549-1405 (SAN 203-3550).

St Le Macs Pr, *(St. Le Macs, Pierre, Press; 0-913030),* 450 Park Plaza Professional Bldg., Houston, TX 77004 Tel 713-523-8181 (SAN 204-6253); Orders to: 2615 Marilee, No. 1, Houston, TX 77057 Tel 713-783-2721 (SAN 204-6261).

St Luke Pub, *(St. Luke's Publishing Co.; 0-939502),* P.O. Box 1378, South Bend, IN 46624 Tel 219-234-5115 (SAN 216-6925).

St Luke TN, *(St. Luke's Press; 0-918518),* Mid-Memphis Tower, Suite 401, 1407 Union Ave., Memphis, TN 38104 Tel 901-357-5441 (SAN 210-0029).

St Martin, *(St. Martin's Press, Inc.; 0-312),* 175 Fifth Ave., New York, NY 10010 Tel 212-674-5151 (SAN 200-2132).

St Onge, *(St. Onge, Achille J., Pub.; 0-911422),* 7 Arden Rd., Worcester, MA 01606 Tel 617-853-8315 (SAN 204-627X).

Stackpole, *(Stackpole Books, Inc.; 0-8117),* P.O. Box 1831, Cameron & Kelker Sts., Harrisburg, PA 17105 Tel 717-234-5041 (SAN 202-5396).

Standard Edns, *(Standard Editions; 0-918746),* P.O. Box 1297, Stuyvesant Sta., New York, NY 10009 (SAN 212-1646).

Standard Pub, *(Standard Publishing Co.; 0-87239),* 8121 Hamilton Ave., Cincinnati, OH 45231 Tel 513-931-4050 (SAN 220-0147).

Standish *Imprint of* **Dell**

Stanford U Pr, *(Stanford Univ. Press; 0-8047),* Stanford, CA 94305 Tel 415-497-9434 (SAN 203-3526).

Stanton & Lee, *(Stanton & Lee Pubs., Inc.; 0-88361),* 44 E. Mifflin St., Madison, WI 53703 Tel 608-255-3254 (SAN 211-2744).

Stanwix, *(Stanwix House, Inc.; 0-87076),* 3020 Chartiers Ave., Pittsburgh, PA 15204 Tel 412-771-4233 (SAN 206-7706) Book Sizes Are 7 X 10 or 8 1/2 X 11.

Star Pub Fla, *(Star Publishing Co., Inc.),* 609 N. Railroad, P.O. Drawer BB, Boynton Beach, FL 33435 (SAN 207-2904).

Star Rover, *(Star Rover House; 0-932458),* 1914 Foothill Blvd., Oakland, CA 94606 Tel 415-839-6822 (SAN 212-4572).

Starblaze *Imprint of* **Donning Co**

Starmont Hse, *(Starmont House; 0-916732),* Box 851, Mercer Island, WA 98040 Tel 206-232-8484 (SAN 208-8703).

State Hist Soc Wis, *(State Historical Society of Wisconsin; 0-87020),* 816 State St., Madison, WI 53706 Tel 608-262-1368 (SAN 203-350X).

State Mutual Bk, *(State Mutual Book & Periodical Service, Ltd.; 0-89771),* 521 Fifth Ave., 17th Floor, New York, NY 10017 Tel 212-682-5844 (SAN 169-5975).

State Ptg, *(State Printing Co.; 0-917195),* P.O. Box 1388, 1305 Sumter St., Columbia, SC 29202 (SAN 204-6334).

State St Pubns, *(State Street Pubns.; 0-936150),* 2357 State St., Suite C, San Diego, CA 92101 (SAN 213-9677) Moved, left no forwarding address.

Station Hill Pr, *(Station Hill Press; 0-930794),* Div. of Open Books, Station Hill Rd., Barrytown, NY 12507 (SAN 214-1485).

Stay Away, *(Stay Away Joe Pubs.; 0-911436),* Box 2054, Great Falls, MT 59401 (SAN 206-6350).

Steck-V, *(Steck-Vaughn Co.; 0-8114),* P.O. Box 2028, Austin, TX 78768 Tel 512-476-6721 (SAN 203-347X).

Stein & Day, *(Stein & Day; 0-8128),* Scarborough House, Briarcliff Manor, NY 10510 Tel 914-762-2151 (SAN 203-3461).

Stewart, *(Stewart, Henry; 0-911444),* 253 Main St., East Aurora, NY 14052 Tel 716-652-1770 (SAN 204-6407).

Still Point Pr, *(Still Point Press; 0-941660),* P.O. Box 1606, 223 W. First St., Mansfield, OH 44901 Tel 419-526-2227 (SAN 239-3190).

Stone-Marrow Pr, *(Stone-Marrow Press),* Dept. of English, 248 McMicken, Univ. of Cincinnati, Cincinnati, OH 45221 (SAN 203-3429).

Stone Pr Calif, *(Stone Press, The),* 3978 26th St., San Francisco, CA 94131 Tel 415-648-5392 (SAN 210-8623).

Stone Pr MI, *(Stone Press),* 1790 Grand River, Okemos, MI 48864 (SAN 207-902X).

Stonehenge, *(Stonehenge Books; 0-937050),* 1582 S. Parker Rd., Suite 200, Parker Plaza, Denver, CO 80231 Tel 303-695-4710 (SAN 216-454X).

Stonehill Pub Co, *(Stonehill Publishing Co., Inc.; 0-88373),* 1140 Ave. of Americas, 19th Fl., New York, NY 10036 Tel 212-658-5980 (SAN 203-3437); Dist. by: Farrar, Straus & Giroux, Inc., 19 Union Square, New York, NY 10003 Tel 212-741-6900 (SAN 206-782X).

Story Pr, *(Story Press; 0-931704),* P.O. Box 10040, Chicago, IL 60610 Tel 312-456-0300 (SAN 212-6982).

Stratford Pr, *(Stratford Press Inc.),* 11340 W. Olympic Blvd. Suite 340, Los Angeles, CA 90064 Tel 213-530-8292 (SAN 282-3713); Dist. by: Harper & Row, Publishers Inc., 10 E. 53rd St., New York, NY 10022 Tel 212-593-7000 (SAN 282-3721).

Strawberry Hill, *(Strawberry Hill Press; 0-89407),* 2594 15th Ave., San Francisco, CA 94127 Tel 415-664-8112 (SAN 238-8103).

KEY TO PUBLISHERS' AND DISTRIBUTORS' ABBREVIATIONS

Strawberry Pr NY, *(Strawberry Press; 0-936574),* P.O. Box 451, Bowling Green Sta., New York, NY 10004 (SAN 215-9198).

Strawberry Valley, *(Strawberry Valley Press; 0-913612),* P.O. Box 157, Idyllwild, CA 92349 Tel 714-659-2145 (SAN 202-7410).

Street Fiction, *(Street Fiction Press, Inc.; 0-914908),* 130 Touro St., P.O. Box 625, Newport, RI 02840 Tel 401-847-1067 (SAN 207-0863).

Strode, *(Strode Pubs.; 0-87397),* 720 Church St., NW., Huntsville, AL 35801 Tel 205-539-2187 (SAN 202-7429).

Stroker, *(Stroker Press; 0-918154),* 129 Second Ave., No. 3, New York, NY 10003 (SAN 209-6811).

Structures Pub
 See Ideals

Sugden, *(Sugden, Sherwood, & Company; 0-89385),* 1117 Eighth St., La Salle, IL 61301 Tel 815-223-1231 (SAN 210-5659).

Suhrkamp, *(Suhrkamp/Insel Pubs. Boston Inc.; 3-458; 3-518),* 380 Green St., Cambridge, MA 02139 Tel 617-876-2333 (SAN 215-2762).

Sumac, *(Sumac Press; 0-911462),* 613 N. 22nd St., La Crosse, WI 54601 Tel 608-782-1290 (SAN 206-8699).

Sumac Mich, *(Sumac Press; 0-912090),* P.O. Box 39, Fremont, MI 49412 Tel 616-924-3464 (SAN 206-1236).

Summa Pubns, *(Summa Publications; 0-917786),* P.O. Box 20725, Birmingham, AL 35216 Tel 205-823-6923 (SAN 212-0925).

Summit Bks, *(Summit Books),* Subs. of Simon & Schuster, 1230 Ave. of the Americas, New York, NY 10020 Tel 212-246-2471 (SAN 206-1244).

Summit Pub Co
 See Gold Penny

Summit Univ, *(Summit Univ. Press; 0-916766),* Box A, Malibu, CA 90265 Tel 213-991-4751 (SAN 208-4120).

SUN, *(SUN; 0-915342),* 347 W. 39th St., New York, NY 10018 Tel 212-594-8428 (SAN 206-3832).

Sun & Moon MD, *(Sun & Moon Press),* 4330 Hartwick Rd., College Park, MD 20740 Tel 301-864-6921 (SAN 216-3063).

Sun-Scape Pubns, *(Sun-Scape Pubns.; 0-919842),* P.O. Box 42725, Tucson, AZ 85733 Tel 602-325-7424 (SAN 211-870X).

Sunburst *Imprint of* FS&G

Sunburst Pr, *(Sunburst Press; 0-934648),* P.O. Box 14205, Portland, OR 97214 (SAN 206-3840).

Sundance OR, *(Sundance Publishing Co.; 0-942822),* P.O. Box 604, Salem, OR 97308 Tel 503-585-0200 (SAN 240-2858).

Sunflower Ink, *(Sunflower Ink; 0-931104),* Palo Colorado Canyon, Carmel, CA 93923 (SAN 212-9728).

Sunflower U Pr, *(Sunflower Univ. Press; 0-89745),* P.O. Box 1009, Manhattan, KS 66502 Tel 913-532-6733 (SAN 218-5075).

Sunflowers KS, *(Sunflowers; 0-939726),* RR 1, Box 262, Clearwater, KS 67026 Tel 316-545-7587 (SAN 216-7638).

Sunset-Lane, *(Sunset Books/Lane Publishing Co.; 0-376),* Willow & Middlefield Rds., Menlo Park, CA 94025 Tel 415-321-3600 (SAN 201-0658).

Sunstone Pr, *(Sunstone Press, The; 0-913270; 0-86534),* P.O. Box 2321, Santa Fe, NM 87501 Tel 505-988-4418 (SAN 214-2090).

Superior Pub, *(Superior Publishing Co.; 0-87564),* 708 Sixth Ave., N., Box 1710, Seattle, WA 98111 Tel 206-282-4310 (SAN 202-747X).

SW Pks Mnmts, *(Southwest Parks & Monuments Assn.; 0-911408),* P.O. Box 1562, Globe, AZ 85501 Tel 602-425-8183 (SAN 202-750X).

Swallow, *(Swallow Press; 0-8040),* Ohio University Press, Scott Quadrangle Room 144, Athens, OH 45701 Tel 614-594-5852 (SAN 202-5663); Orders to: Harper & Row Publishers, Inc., Order Service Dept., Keystone Industrial Park, Scranton, PA 18512 Tel 800-233-4175 (SAN 202-5671) Tel 800-982-4377.

Sweet, *(Sweet Publishing Co.; 0-8344),* Box 18928, Ft. Worth, TX 78765 Tel 817-595-2667 (SAN 206-8958).

Swordsman Pr, *(Swordsman Press; 0-940018),* 15445 Ventura Blvd., No. 10, Box 5973, Sherman Oaks, CA 91413 Tel 213-342-1422 (SAN 216-860X).

SYDA Found, *(SYDA Foundation; 0-914602),* P.O. Box 600, South Fallsburg, NY 12779 Tel 914-434-2000 (SAN 206-5649).

Syder Pr, *(Syder Press; 0-939470),* 5893 Kahara Court, Sacramento, CA 95822 (SAN 216-4590).

Syncline, *(Syncline; 0-9603794),* 7825 S. Ridgeway, Chicago, IL 60652 (SAN 214-1515).

Synergistic Pr, *(Synergistic Press, Inc.; 0-912184),* 3965 Sacramento St., San Francisco, CA 94118 Tel 415-387-8180 (SAN 205-4116).

Syracuse U Foreign Comp, *(Syracuse Univ., Foreign & Comparative Studies Program; 0-915984),* 119 College Place, Syracuse, NY 13210 Tel 315-423-2552 (SAN 220-0082).

Syracuse U Pr, *(Syracuse Univ. Press; 0-8156),* 1600 Jamesville Ave., Syracuse, NY 13210 Tel 315-423-2596 (SAN 206-9776).

Syzygy Pr, *(Syzygy Press; 0-9608372),* P.O. Box 183, Mill Valley, CA 94942 Tel 415-883-2046 (SAN 240-4508); Dist. by: Subterranean Co., The, P.O. Box 10233, Eugene, OR 97440 (SAN 169-7102).

T L Cannon & N F Whitmore, *(Cannon, Timothy L., & Nancy F. Whitmore; 0-9602816),* 7916 Juniper Dr., Frederick, MD 21701 (SAN 213-4756).

T Weinberg
 See Gordons & Weinberg

T Y Crowell, *(Crowell, Thomas Y., Co.; 0-690),* 10 E. 53rd St., New York, NY 10022 Tel 212-593-3900 (SAN 210-5918); Dist. by: Harper & Row Pubs., Keystone Industrial Park, Scranton, PA 18512 (SAN 215-3742).

T Y Crowell
 See Funk & W

Talisman, *(Talisman Press; 0-934612),* P.O. Box 455, Georgetown, CA 95634 Tel 916-333-4486 (SAN 205-4140).

Tamal Land, *(Tamal Land Press; 0-912908),* 39 Merwin Ave., Fairfax, CA 94930 Tel 415-456-4705 (SAN 207-0162).

Tanam Pr, *(Tanam Press; 0-934378),* 40 White St., New York, NY 10013 (SAN 215-3467).

Tandem Pr, *(Tandem Press Pubs.; 0-913024),* P.O. Box 237, Tannersville, PA 18372 Tel 717-629-2250 (SAN 202-7615).

Taplinger, *(Taplinger Publishing Co., Inc.; 0-8008),* 132 W. 22nd St., New York, NY 10011 Tel 212-741-0801 (SAN 213-6821).

Tarrant, *(Tarrant, Patrick; 0-9608850),* 1907 Castle Ave., Bloomington, IL 61701 (SAN 241-080X).

Tashmoo, *(Tashmoo Press, The; 0-932384),* RFD, Vineyard Haven, MA 02568 (SAN 212-5706).

TBW Bks, *(TBW Books; 0-931474),* Rural Route One, P.O. Box 164, Woolwich, ME 04579 Tel 207-442-7632 (SAN 212-2367).

Telegraph *Imprint of* **Dynamic Learn Corp**

Telegraph Bks, *(Telegraph Books; 0-89760),* Box 38, Norwood, PA 19074 Tel 215-583-4550 (SAN 213-8042).

Telephone Bks, *(Telephone Books Press; 0-916382),* 109 Dunk Rock Rd., Guilford, CT 06437 Tel 203-453-4415 (SAN 208-2462).

Templegate, *(Templegate Pubs.; 0-87243),* 302 E. Adams St., P.O. Box 5152, Springfield, IL 62705 Tel 217-522-3361 (SAN 213-1994).

Tetragrammaton, *(Tetragrammaton Press; 0-937326),* 3594 Sepulveda Blvd., Sherman Oaks, CA 91403 (SAN 214-4778).

Tex A&M Univ Pr, *(Texas A & M Univ. Press; 0-89096),* Drawer "C", College Station, TX 77843 Tel 713-845-1436 (SAN 207-5237).

Tex Christian, *(Texas Christian Univ. Press; 0-912646),* Box 30783, Fort Worth, TX 76129 Tel 817-921-7822 (SAN 202-7690); Dist. by: Texas A & M University Press, Drawer C, College Station, TX 77843-4354 Tel 409-845-1436 (SAN 207-5237).

Tex Ctr Writers, *(Texas Center for Writers Press),* P.O. Box 19876, Dallas, TX 75219 (SAN 208-0257) Moved, left no forwarding address.

Tex Portfolio
 See Cedar Rock

Tex Tech Pr, *(Texas Tech Press; 0-89672),* P.O. Box 4460, Lubbock, TX 79409 Tel 806-742-2781 (SAN 208-1709); Orders to: Sales Office, Texas Tech Univ. Library, Lubbock, TX 79409 Tel 806-742-1569 (SAN 208-1717).

Tex Western, *(Texas Western Press, Univ. of Texas at El Paso; 0-87404),* El Paso, TX 79968 Tel 915-747-5688 (SAN 202-7712).

Texan-Am Pub, *(Texan-American Publisher's Co.; 0-935622),* 3008 West Ohio, Midland, TX 79701 Tel 915-699-1934 (SAN 213-3865).

Texas Month Pr, *(Texas Monthly Press; 0-932012),* 4606 Burleson Rd., Unit N, Austin, TX 78744 Tel 512-476-7085 (SAN 200-2531); Orders to: P.O. Bx 1569 Austin,, Austin, TX 78767 (SAN 200-2531).

Texian, *(Texian Press; 0-87244),* P.O. Box 1684, Waco, TX 76703 Tel 817-754-5636 (SAN 205-4256).

Textile Bk, *(Textile Book Service, Inc.; 0-87245),* P.O. Box 25, Broadway, NJ 08808 Tel 201-689-2230 (SAN 206-7714).

Textile Bridge, *(Textile Bridge Press),* P.O. Box 157, Clarence Center, NY 14032 (SAN 216-0676).

Thales Microuniv, *(Thales Microuniversity Press; 0-914312),* 13761 S. Fern, Glenpool, OK 74033 Tel 918-299-5854 (SAN 202-7739).

Thames Hudson, *(Thames & Hudson; 0-500),* Dist. by: W.W. Norton, & Co., Inc., 500 Fifth Ave., New York, NY 10110 Tel 212-354-3763 (SAN 202-5795).

That New Pub, *(That New Publishing Co.; 0-918270),* 1525 Eielson St., Fairbanks, AK 99701 Tel 907-452-3007 (SAN 209-6862).

The Hemphills, *(Hemphills, The; 0-9600948),* P.O. Box 8302, Nashville, TN 37207 Tel 615-865-7100 (SAN 208-4856).

The Smith, *(Smith, The; 0-912292),* 5 Beekman St., New York, NY 10038 Tel 212-732-4821 (SAN 202-7747); Dist. by: Horizon Press, 156 Fifth Ave, New York, NY 10010 (SAN 202-3040).

Thelema Pubns, *(Thelema Pubns.; 0-913576),* P.O. Box 1093, Kings Beach, CA 95719 Tel 916-546-2160 (SAN 205-4272).

Theos Pub Hse, *(Theosophical Publishing House; 0-8356),* 306 W. Geneva Rd., Wheaton, IL 60187-0270 Tel 312-665-0123 (SAN 202-5698). *Imprints:* Quest (Quest Books).

Theta Bks, *(Theta Books, Inc.; 0-917972),* P.O. Box 600, Clearwater, FL 33517 Tel 813-446-3556 (SAN 209-8946) Moved, Left no Forwarding Address.

Third Pr
 See Okpaku Communications

Third World, *(Third World Press; 0-88378),* 7524 S. Cottage Grove, Chicago, IL 60019 Tel 312-651-0700 (SAN 202-778X).

Thorndike Pr, *(Thorndike Press; 0-89621),* P.O. Box 157, Thorndike, ME 04986 Tel 207-948-2962 (SAN 212-2375).

Thornwood Bk, *(Thornwood Book Publishers; 0-943054),* P.O. Box 1442, Florence, AL 35630 Tel 205-766-4100 (SAN 240-4540).

Thorp Springs, *(Thorp Springs Press; 0-914476),* 803 Red River St., Austin, TX 78701 (SAN 202-781X).

Three Continents, *(Three Continents Press; 0-89410; 0-914478),* 1346 Connecticut Ave., Suite 224, Washington, DC 20036 Tel 202-457-0288 (SAN 212-0070).

Thueson, *(Thueson, James D.; 0-911506),* Box 14474, Univ. Sta., Minneapolis, MN 55414 (SAN 239-4979).

Thunder's Mouth, *(Thunder's Mouth Press; 0-938410),* P.O. Box 780, New York, NY 10025 (SAN 216-4663); 1152 S. East, Oak Park, IL 60304 (SAN 216-4671).

Ticknor & Fields, *(Ticknor & Fields; 0-89919),* 52 Vanderbilt Ave., New York, NY 10017 Tel 212-687-8996 (SAN 282-4043); 383 Orange St., New Haven, CT 06511 Tel 203-776-1878 (SAN 282-4035); Dist. by: Houghton Mifflin Co., 2 Park St., Boston, MA 02108 Tel 617-725-5000 (SAN 200-2388).

Tidal Pr, *(Tidal Press, The),* Cranberry Isles, ME 04625 Tel 207-244-7220 (SAN 211-3783).

KEY TO PUBLISHERS' AND DISTRIBUTORS' ABBREVIATIONS

Tide Bk Pub Co, *(Tide Book Publishing Co.; 0-9602786),* P.O. Box 268, Manchester, MA 01944 (SAN 282-406X); Orders to: The Distributors Inc., 702 S. Michigan, South Bend, IN 46618 Tel 219-232-8500 (SAN 282-4078).

Timber, *(Timber Press; 0-917304; 0-931146; 0-931340),* P.O. Box 1631, Beaverton, OR 97075 Tel 503-292-2606 (SAN 216-082X); Dist. by: International Specialized Book Services, Inc., P.O. Box 1632, Beaverton, OR 97075 Tel 503-292-2606 (SAN 200-4305).

Time Bks
  See Times Bks

Time-Life, *(Time-Life Books; 0-8094),* Div. of Time, Inc., 777 Duke St., Rm. 204, Alexandria, VA 22314 Tel 703-960-5421 (SAN 202-7836); Dist. by: Little, Brown & Co., 34 Beacon St., Boston, MA 02106 (SAN 281-8892); Dist. by: Morgan & Morgan Co., 145 Palisades St., Dobs Ferry, NY 10522 (SAN 202-5620) Lib. & School Orders to: Silver Burdett Co., Morristown, NJ 13664.

Timely Bks, *(Timely Books; 0-931328),* P.O. Box 267, New Milford, CT 06776 Tel 203-744-4719 (SAN 211-3791).

Times Bks, *(Times Books; 0-8129),* The New York Times Book Co., Inc., Three Park Ave., New York, NY 10016 Tel 212-725-2050 (SAN 202-5558); Dist. by: Harper & Row, Keystone Industrial Park, Scranton, PA 18512 (SAN 200-2086).

Times Change, *(Times Change Press; 0-87810),* Publishers Services, P.O. Box 3914, San Rafael, CA 94902 Tel 415-883-3530 (SAN 202-7860).

Timescape Imprint of **PB**

Titan Pub Co, *(Titan Publishing Co.; 0-9603314),* P.O. Box 506, Mesilla, NM 88046 (SAN 211-7142).

Todd & Honeywell, *(Todd & Honeywell Inc.; 0-89962),* 10 Cuttermill Rd., Great Neck, NY 11021 Tel 516-487-9777 (SAN 213-179X).

Todd Tarbox, *(Todd Tarbox Books; 0-89297),* 421 Sharondale, El Paso, TX 79912 Tel 915-749-7219 (SAN 208-2012).

Tombouctou, *(Tombouctou Books),* P.O. Box 265, Bolinas, CA 94924 (SAN 282-4647); Dist. by: Bookpeople, 2940 Seventh St., Berkeley, CA 94710 Tel 415-549-3030 (SAN 168-9517); Dist. by: Bookslinger, P.O. Box 1651, 2163 Ford Pkwy., St. Paul, MN 55116 Tel 612-690-0293 (SAN 169-4154); Dist. by: Dark Horse, 17705 S. Western Ave., Suite 1, Gardenia, CA 90248 Tel 415-843-5796 (SAN 282-4671); Dist. by: Barbary Coast Distribution, 635 Amador, Richmond, CA 94805 Tel 415-236-1197 (SAN 282-468X); Dist. by: Serendipity Books Distribution, 1970 Shattuck Ave., Berkeley, CA 94704 Tel 415-549-3336 (SAN 282-4698); Dist. by: Word Works, 1421 Second Ave., N. Seattle, WA 98109 Tel 206-284-8127 (SAN 282-4698); Dist. by: New York State Small Press Assn., P.O. Box 1264, Radio City Sta., New York, NY 10019 (SAN 219-5127); Dist. by: Publisher Services, P.O. Box 3414, San Rafael, CA 94902 Tel 415-883-3530 (SAN 282-4728).

Tonatiuh Intl
  See Tonatiuh-Quinto Sol Intl

Tonatiuh-Quinto Sol Intl, *(Tonatiuh/Quinto Sol International, Inc.; 0-88412),* P.O. Box 9275, Berkeley, CA 94709 Tel 415-655-8036 (SAN 203-3984).

Toothpaste, *(Toothpaste Press; 0-915124),* P.O. Box 546, West Branch, IA 52358 Tel 319-643-2604 (SAN 282-7123); Dist. by: Bookslinger, 213 E. Fourth St., St. Paul, MN 55101 Tel 612-221-0429 (SAN 217-1457).

Topgallant, *(Topgallant Publishing Co., Ltd.; 0-914916),* Elizabeth Bldg. 845 Mission Lane, Honolulu, HI 96813 Tel 808-524-0884 (SAN 209-4932).

Tor Bks, *(Tor Bks.; 0-8125),* Tom Doherty Associates, Inc., 8-10 W. 36th St., New York, NY 10018 Tel 212-564-0150 (SAN 239-3956); Dist. by: Pinnacle Bks., Inc., 1430 Broadway, New York, NY 10018 Tel 212-719-5900 (SAN 200-2442).

Torch Imprint of **Har-Row**

Touchstone Bks Imprint of **S&S**

Touchstone Pr OR, *(Touchstone Press; 0-911518),* P.O. Box 81, Beaverton, OR 97075 Tel 503-646-8081 (SAN 205-4442).

Tower
  See Tower Bks

Tower Bks, *(Tower Publications, Inc.; 0-505),* 2 Park Ave., Suite 910, New York, NY 10016 Tel 212-679-7707 (SAN 212-016X); Dist. by: Capital Distributing Co., 2 Park Ave. Suite 910, New York, NY 10016 Tel 212-679-7707 (SAN 212-016X).

Tradd St Pr, *(Tradd Street Press; 0-937684),* 38 Tradd St., Charleston, SC 29401 Tel 803-722-4293 (SAN 205-4469).

Transatlantic, *(Transatlantic Arts, Inc.; 0-693),* P.O. Box 6086, Albuquerque, NM 87197 Tel 505-898-2289 (SAN 202-7968).

Trask Hse Bks, *(Trask House Books, Inc.; 0-932264),* 2754 S.E. 27th Ave., Portland, OR 97202 Tel 503-235-1898 (SAN 211-9889).

Traumwald Pr, *(Traumwald Press; 0-913676),* 3550 N. Lake Shore Dr., Suite 10, Chicago, IL 60657 Tel 312-525-5303 (SAN 205-454X).

Travelers Digest Edns, *(Traveler's Digest Editions; 0-936578),* 106 Perry St., New York, NY 10014 Tel 212-214-1531); Dist. by: Small Press Association, P.O. Box 1264, Radio City Sta., New York, NY 10019 (SAN 214-154X).

Travellers Comp Imprint of **Olympia**

Treacle
  See McPherson & Co

Treasure Chest, *(Treasure Chest Pubns.; 0-918080),* 1842 W. Grant Rd., Suite 107, Tucson, AZ 85745 Tel 602-623-9558 (SAN 209-3243); Orders to: P.O. Box 5250, Tucson, AZ 85703 (SAN 209-3251).

Tree Bks, *(Tree Bks.),* Box 9005, Berkeley, CA 94709 (SAN 203-6576).

Tree Line, *(Tree Line Books; 0-931476),* P.O. Box 1062, Radio City Sta., New York, NY 10019 (SAN 212-3886).

Trek-CIR, *(TREK-CIR Pubns.; 0-932464),* Box 898, Valley Forge, PA 19481 Tel 215-337-3110 (SAN 212-2383).

Trends & Events, *(Trends & Events, Inc.; 0-942698),* P.O. Box 158, Fayette, IA 52142 Tel 319-425-4411 (SAN 240-2882).

Tri-Science Pubs, *(Tri-Science Pubs.; 0-935040),* Box 1232, Pico Rivera, CA 90660 (SAN 209-2581).

Tricore Assoc, *(Tricore Associates, Inc.; 0-9607132),* 69 Rte. 23 S., Riverdale, NJ 07457 Tel 201-835-9219 (SAN 239-0469).

Trident, *(Trident Press; 0-671),* Div. of Simon & Schuster, Inc., 630 Fifth Ave., New York, NY 10020 Tel 212-245-6400 (SAN 202-8026).

Trilogy Pubs, *(Trilogy Pubs.; 0-931558),* 2901 Heatherway, Ann Arbor, MI 48104 (SAN 211-4747).

Trinity Pub Hse, *(Trinity Publishing House, Inc.; 0-933656),* 263 W. Fifth St., Winona, MN 55987 (SAN 215-1189).

Trinity U Pr, *(Trinity Univ. Press; 0-911536; 0-939980),* 715 Stadium Dr., San Antonio, TX 78284 Tel 512-736-7619 (SAN 205-4590).

Triton Bks, *(Triton Books; 0-943958),* P.O. Box 27934, Los Angeles, CA 90027 Tel 213-247-4177 (SAN 241-161X).

Troubador Pr, *(Troubador Press; 0-912300; 0-89844),* 385 Fremont St., San Francisco, CA 94105 Tel 415-397-3716 (SAN 285-0931); Dist. by: Price/Stern/Sloan Publishers, 410 N. La Cienega Blvd., Los Angeles, CA 90048 Tel 213-657-6100 (SAN 285-094X).

Tudor, *(Tudor Publishing Co.; 0-8148),* 31 W. 46th St., New York, NY 10036 (SAN 202-571X); Orders to: 225 Secaucus Rd., Secaucus, NJ 07094 (SAN 202-5728) Now Leon Amiel, Pub.

Tundra Bks, *(Tundra Books of Northern New York; 0-912776; 0-89541),* 51 Clinton St., Box 1030, Plattsburgh, NY 12901 (SAN 202-8085); Dist. by: University of Toronto Press, 33 E. Tupper St., Buffalo, NY 14203 (SAN 200-4224).

Turkey Pr, *(Turkey Press; 0-918824),* 6746 Sueno Rd., Isla Vista, CA 93117 Tel 805-685-3603 (SAN 210-5195).

Turtle Isl Foun, *(Turtle Island Foundation; Netzhaulcoyotl Historical Society; 0-913666),* 2845 Buena Vista Way, Berkeley, CA 94708 Tel 415-845-0984 (SAN 205-4639).

Turtles Quill, *(Turtles Quill Scriptorium; 0-937686),* P.O. Box 643, Mendocino, CA 95460 Tel 707-937-4328 (SAN 206-8966).

TUVOTI, *(Unspeakable Visions of the Individual, The; 0-934660),* P. O. Box 439, California, PA 15419 Tel 412-938-8956 (SAN 207-916X).

TVRT, *(TVRT; 0-931106),* 25 E. Fourth St., New York, NY 10003 Tel 212-260-4254 (SAN 206-1341).

Twayne Imprint of **G K Hall**

Twentieth Century, *(Twentieth Century Books; 0-86649),* Div. of Automated Reproductions, 745 Seventh Ave., New York, NY 10019 (SAN 216-3128) Moved, left no forwarding address.

Two Eighteen, *(Two-Eighteen Press),* P.O. Box 218, Village Sta., New York, NY 10014 Tel 212-966-5877 (SAN 207-9127).

Two Horses, *(Two Horses Pr.),* 1950 W. Ruthrauff Rd., Tucson, AZ 85705 (SAN 276-5451).

TYC-J Imprint of **Har-Row**

Tyndale, *(Tyndale House Pubs.; 0-8423),* 336 Gundersen Dr., Wheaton, IL 60187 Tel 312-668-8300 (SAN 206-7749).

Typographeum, *(Typographeum Bookshop, The; 0-930126),* The Stone Cottage, Bennington Rd., Francestown, NH 03043 (SAN 211-3031).

U Delaware Pr, *(Univ. of Delaware Press; 0-87413),* c/o Associated Univ. Presses, Inc., 4 Cornwall Dr., East Brunswick, NJ 08816 Tel 201-254-0132 (SAN 203-4476).

U Maine Orono, *(Univ. of Maine at Orono Press; 0-89101),* PICS Building, Univ. of Maine at Orono, Orono, ME 04469 Tel 207-581-7349 (SAN 207-2971).

U of Ala Pr, *(Univ. of Alabama Press; 0-8173),* Box 2877, University, AL 35486 Tel 205-348-5180 (SAN 202-5272).

U of Ariz Pr, *(Univ. of Arizona Press; 0-8165),* 1615 E. Speedway, Tucson, AZ 85719 Tel 602-621-1441 (SAN 205-468X).

U of Ark Pr, *(Univ. of Arkansas Press; 0-938626),* McIlroy House, Univ. of Arkansas, Fayetteville, AR 72701 Tel 501-575-3246 (SAN 239-3972).

U of Cal Pr, *(Univ. of California Press; 0-520),* 2223 Fulton St., Berkeley, CA 94720 Tel 415-642-6683 (SAN 203-3046).

U of Chicago Pr, *(Univ. of Chicago Press; 0-226),* 5801 Ellis Ave., Chicago, IL 60637 Tel 312-962-7906 (SAN 202-5280); Orders to: 11030 S. Langley Ave., Chicago, IL 60628 Tel 312-568-1550 (SAN 202-5299).

U of Fla Pr, *(Univ. of Florida Press),* Publisher Abbreviation Without Addresses Are for Titles That Are Out of Print. These Are Obsolete Abbreviations. Publisher's Abbreviation Is Now U Presses Fla.

U of Ga Pr, *(Univ. of Georgia Press; 0-8203),* Terrell Hall, Athens, GA 30602 Tel 404-542-2830 (SAN 203-3054).

U of Healing, *(Univ. of Healing Press),* 32750 Hwy. 94, Campo, CA 92006 Tel 619-478-5111 (SAN 211-7983).

U of Ill Pr, *(Univ. of Illinois Press; 0-252),* 54 E. Gregory Dr., Champaign, IL 61820 Tel 217-333-0957 (SAN 202-5310).

U of Iowa Pr, *(Univ. of Iowa Press; 0-87745),* 214 Graphic Services Bldg., Iowa City, IA 52242 Tel 319-353-3181 (SAN 282-4868); Orders to: Oakdale Campus, Univ. of Iowa, Iowa City, IA 52242 Tel 319-353-4171 (SAN 282-4876).

U of Mass Pr, *(Univ. of Massachusetts Press; 0-87023),* P.O. Box 429, Amherst, MA 01004 Tel 413-545-2217 (SAN 203-3089).

U of Miami Pr, *(Univ. of Miami Press; 0-87024),* P.O. Box 4836, Hampden Sta., Baltimore, MD 21211 Tel 301-338-7886 (SAN 203-3119).

U of Mich Pr, *(Univ. of Michigan Press; 0-472),* P.O. Box 1104, Ann Arbor, MI 48106 Tel 313-764-4330 (SAN 282-4884); Orders to: 839 Greene St., Ann Arbor, MI 48106 Tel 313-764-4392 (SAN 282-4892).
Imprints: AA (Ann Arbor Books).

U of Minn Pr, *(Univ. of Minnesota Press; 0-8166),* 2037 University Ave. S.E., Minneapolis, MN 55414 Tel 612-373-3266 (SAN 213-2648).

U of Mo Pr, *(Univ. of Missouri Press; 0-8262),* 200 Lewis, Columbia, MO 65211 Tel 314-882-7641 (SAN 203-3143).

KEY TO PUBLISHERS' AND DISTRIBUTORS' ABBREVIATIONS

U of NC Pr, *(Univ. of North Carolina Press; 0-8078),* P.O Box 2288, Chapel Hill, NC 27514 Tel 919-966-3561 (SAN 203-3151).

U of Nebr Pr, *(Univ. of Nebraska Press; 0-8032),* 901 N. 17th St., Lincoln, NE 68588 Tel 402-472-3581 (SAN 202-5337).

U of Nev Pr, *(Univ. of Nevada Press; 0-87417),* Reno, NV 89557 Tel 702-784-6573 (SAN 203-316X).

U of NM Pr, *(Univ. of New Mexico Press; 0-8263),* Albuquerque, NM 87131 Tel 505-277-2346 (SAN 213-9588).

U of Notre Dame Pr, *(Univ. of Notre Dame Press; 0-268),* P.O. Box L, Notre Dame, IN 46556 Tel 219-239-6346 (SAN 203-3178); Dist. by: Harper & Row Pubs., Keystone Industrial Park, Scranton, PA 18512 (SAN 215-3742).

U of Okla Pr, *(Univ. of Oklahoma Press; 0-8061),* 1005 Asp Ave., Norman, OK 73019 Tel 405-325-5111 (SAN 203-3194).

U of Oreg Bks, *(Univ. of Oregon Books; 0-87114),* Univ. Pubns., 358 Susan Campbell Hall, Univ. of Oregon, Eugene, OR 97403 Tel 503-686-5396 (SAN 206-7757).

U of Pa Pr, *(Univ. of Pennsylvania Press; 0-8122),* 3933 Walnut St., Philadelphia, PA 19104 Tel 215-243-6261 (SAN 202-5345).

U of Pittsburgh Pr, *(Univ. of Pittsburgh Press; 0-8229),* 127 N. Bellefield Ave., Pittsburgh, PA 15260 Tel 412-624-4110 (SAN 203-3216).

U of PR Pr, *(Univ. of Puerto Rico Press; 0-8477),* P.O. Box X, U.P.R. Sta., Rio Piedras, PR 00931 Tel 809-763-0812 (SAN 208-1245).

U of Queensland Pr, *(Univ. of Queensland Press),* P.O. Box 1365, New York, NY 10023 Tel 212-799-3854 (SAN 206-8540); Orders to: 5 S. Union St., Lawrence, MA 01843 Tel 617-685-3306 (SAN 206-8559).

U of SC Pr, *(Univ. of South Carolina Press; 0-87249),* Columbia, SC 29208 Tel 803-777-5243 (SAN 203-3224).

U of Tenn Pr, *(Univ. of Tennessee Press; 0-87049),* 293 Communications Bldg., Knoxville, TN 37996 Tel 615-974-3321 (SAN 212-9930).

U of Tex Hum Res, *(Univ. of Texas, Humanities Research Ctr.; 0-87959),* P.O. Box 7219, Austin, TX 78712 Tel 512-471-9113 (SAN 203-1906).

U of Tex Pr, *(Univ. of Texas Press; 0-292),* P.O. Box 7819, Austin, TX 78712 Tel 512-471-4278 (SAN 212-9876) Tel 512-471-4032.

U of Toronto Pr, *(Univ. of Toronto Press; 0-8020),* 33 E. Tupper St., Buffalo, NY 14203 Tel 416-978-2052 (SAN 214-2651).

U of Utah Pr, *(Univ. of Utah Press; 0-87480),* Salt Lake City, UT 84112 Tel 801-581-6771 (SAN 220-0023).

U of Wash Pr, *(Univ. of Washington Pr.; 0-295),* P.O. Box 85569, Seattle, WA 98105 Tel 206-543-4050 (SAN 212-2502).

U of Wis Pr, *(Univ. of Wisconsin Press; 0-299),* 114 North Murray St., Madison, WI 53715 Tel 608-262-4922 (SAN 203-3259).

U Pr of Amer, *(University Press of America; 0-8191),* 4720 Boston Way, Lanham, MD 20706 Tel 301-459-3366 (SAN 200-2256).

U Pr of Hawaii
See UH Pr

U Pr of Ky, *(Univ. Pr. of Kentucky; 0-8131),* Univ. of Kentucky, 102 Lafferty Hall, Lexington, KY 40506-0024 Tel 606-257-8437 (SAN 203-3275).

U Pr of Va, *(Univ. Press of Virginia; 0-8139),* P.O. Box 3608, University Sta., Charlottesville, VA 22903 Tel 804-924-3468 (SAN 202-5361).

U Presses Fla, *(Univ. Presses of Fla.; 0-8130),* 15 N.W. 15th St., Gainesville, FL 32603 Tel 904-392-1351 (SAN 207-9275).

UC Ctr S&SE Asian, *(University of California, Berkeley, Center for SE Asian Studies),* Orders to: Cellar Book Shop, 18090 Wyoming, Detroit, MI 48221 (SAN 213-4330).

UCLA Chicano Stud, *(Univ. of California, Los Angeles Chicano Studies Research Center, Pubns. Unit; 0-89551),* 3126 Campbell Hall, 405 Hilgard Ave., Los Angeles, CA 90024 Tel 213-825-2642 (SAN 209-097X).

UH Pr, *(Univ. of Hawaii Press, The; 0-8248),* 2840 Kolowalu St., Honolulu, HI 96822 Tel 808-948-8697 (SAN 202-5353).

Ukrainian Acad, *(Ukrainian Academic Press; 0-87287),* Div. of Libraries Unlimited, Inc., P.O. Box 263, Littleton, CO 80160 Tel 303-770-1220 (SAN 203-3305).

Ultramarine Pub, *(Ultramarine Publishing Co., Inc.; 0-89366),* P.O. Box 303, Hastings-on-Hudson, NY 10706 Tel 914-478-2522 (SAN 208-8762).

Unarius, *(Unarius Educational Foundation; 0-932642),* 145 S Magnolia Ave., El Cajon, CA 92021 Tel 714-447-4170 (SAN 168-9614).

Underwood-Miller, *(Underwood/Miller; 0-934438),* P.O. Box 5402, San Francisco, CA 94101 Tel 415-459-3296 (SAN 282-4795); 239 N. Fourth St., Columbia, PA 17512 (SAN 282-4809); Orders to: Underwood/Miller Publishers, 651 Chestnut St., Columbia, PA 17512 Tel 717-684-7335 (SAN 282-4817).

Une Pub, *(Une Publishing),* P.O. Box 140, New Haven, CT 06520 (SAN 217-1368).

Ungar, *(Ungar, Frederick, Publishing Co., Inc.; 0-8044),* 250 Park Ave. S., New York, NY 10003 Tel 212-473-7885 (SAN 202-5256).

Unicorn Pr, *(Unicorn Press; 0-87775),* P.O. Box 3307, Greensboro, NC 27402 Tel 919-852-0281 (SAN 203-3313).

Unique Pubns, *(Unique Pubns.; 0-86568),* 7011 Sunset Blvd., Hollywood, CA 90028 (SAN 214-3313).

United Church, *(United Church Press),* 1505 Race St, Philadelphia, PA 19102 (SAN 227-1206).

United Church Pr
See Pilgrim NY

Unity Pr
See Orenda-Unity

Univ Bks, *(University Books, Inc.; 0-8216),* Div. of Lyle Stuart, Inc., 120 Enterprise Ave., Secaucus, NJ 07094 Tel 201-866-0490 (SAN 203-3348).

Univ Microfilms, *(University Microfilms International; 0-8357),* A Xerox Information Resources Co., 300 N. Zeeb Rd., Ann Arbor, MI 48106 Tel 313-761-4700 (SAN 212-2464) Serials and newspapers in microform, reprints of articles and issues, dissertations published and available on demand. Imprints: Books on Demand, reprinting of out-of-print books, and UMI Research Press, scholarly and professional book publishing.

Univ Place, *(University Place Book Shop; 0-911556),* 821 Broadway, New York, NY 10003 Tel 212-254-5998 (SAN 204-8841).

Univ Pub & Dist, *(Universal Publishing & Distributing Corp.; 0-426),* 235 E. 45th St., New York, NY 10023 Tel 212-683-3000 (SAN 212-0186); Orders to: Award Books, 350 Kennedy Dr., Hauppage, NY 11788 (SAN 212-0194) No Longer Publishing.

Universe, *(Universe Books, Inc.; 0-87663),* 381 Park Ave. S., New York, NY 10016 Tel 212-685-7400 (SAN 202-537X).

University *Imprint of* **Exposition**

Unmuzzled Ox, *(Unmuzzled Ox Press),* 105 Hudson St., New York, NY 10013 Tel 212-226-7170 (SAN 207-9151).

Upper Room, *(Upper Room; 0-8358),* 1908 Grand Ave., P.O. Box 189, Nashville, TN 37202 Tel 615-327-2700 (SAN 203-3364).

Urbanek, *(Urbanek, Mae),* Lusk, WY 82225 Tel 307-334-2473 (SAN 213-9006).

Urizen Bks, *(Urizen Books, Inc.; 0-89396; 0-916354),* 66 W. Broadway, New York, NY 10007 Tel 212-962-3413 (SAN 208-9408).

Utah St U Pr, *(Utah State Univ. Press; 0-87421),* UMC 95, Logan, UT 84322 Tel 801-750-1362 (SAN 202-9294).

V Quade, *(Quade, Vicki; 0-9602604),* 1110 Monroe St.,, Evanston, IL 60202 Tel 312-328-2527 (SAN 213-151X).

V S Morris, *(Morris, Victoria S., Books; 0-914318),* 39 Gleneden Ave., Oakland, CA 94611 Tel 415-652-2013 (SAN 202-2125).

VA Bk, *(Virginia Book Co.; 0-911578),* Box 431, Berryville, VA 22611 Tel 703-955-1428 (SAN 206-7773).

Vagabond Pr, *(Vagabond Press; 0-912824),* 1610 N. Water St., Ellensburg, WA 98926 Tel 509-925-5634 (SAN 203-0535).

Valkyrie Hse, *(Valkyrie Press, Inc.; 0-912760; 0-934616; 0-912589),* 6236-12th St. S., St. Petersburg, FL 33705 Tel 813-822-0515 (SAN 203-1671).

Valkyrie Pr
See Valkyrie Hse

Vallentine Mitchell
See Biblio Dist

Valley Calif
See Western Tanager

Valley Sun, *(Valley of the Sun Publishing Co.; 0-911842),* Box 38, Malibu, CA 90265 Tel 213-456-7361 (SAN 206-8974).

Van Nos Reinhold, *(Van Nostrand Reinhold Co. Inc; 0-442),* Div. of Litton Educational Publishing, Inc., 135 W. 50th St., New York, NY 10020 Tel 212-265-8700 (SAN 202-5183); Orders to: VNR Order Processing, 7625 Empire Dr., Florence, KY 41042 (SAN 202-5191). *Imprints:* Anv (Anvil Books).

Van Vactor & Goodheart, *(Van Vactor & Goodheart; 0-941324),* 24 Lee St., Cambridge, MA 02139 (SAN 282-5007); Orders to: Persea Books, Inc., 225 Lafayette St., New York, NY 10012 (SAN 282-5015).

Vancento Pub, *(Vancento Pub. Co.),* 62 Court St., Reno, NV 89501 (SAN 238-7697).

Vanderbilt U Pr, *(Vanderbilt Univ. Press; 0-8265),* 2505(Rear) West End Ave., Nashville, TN 37203 Tel 615-322-3585 (SAN 202-9308).

Vanguard, *(Vanguard Press, Inc.; 0-8149),* 424 Madison Ave., New York, NY 10017 Tel 212-753-3906 (SAN 202-9316).

Vanity, *(Vanity Press; 0-917938),* P.O. Box 15064, Atlanta, GA 30333 Tel 404-874-5462 (SAN 209-519X) Moved, Left No Forwarding Address.

Vanous, *(Vanous, Arthur, Co.; 0-89918),* 616 Kinderkamack Rd., River Edge, NJ 07661 Tel 201-265-7555 (SAN 202-9324); Orders to: P.O. Box A, River Edge, NJ 07661 (SAN 202-9332).

Vantage, *(Vantage Press, Inc.; 0-533),* 516 W. 34th St., New York, NY 10001 Tel 212-736-1767 (SAN 206-8893).

Vedanta Pr, *(Vedanta Press; 0-87481),* 1946 Vedanta Place, Hollywood, CA 90068-3996 Tel 213-465-7114 (SAN 202-9340) (SAN 202-9359).

Ventura
See Ventura Pr

Ventura Pr, *(Ventura Press; 0-917438),* P.O. Box 1076, Guerneville, CA 95446 (SAN 205-4779).

Vermont Crossroads, *(Vermont Crossroads Press; 0-915248),* P.O. Box 30, Waitsfield, VT 05667 Tel 802-496-2469 (SAN 282-5023); Orders to: Rd 1, Box 147, Plainfield, VT 05667 Tel 802-454-7715 (SAN 282-5031).

Verry, *(Verry, Lawrence, Inc.; 0-8426),* Mystic, CT 06355 Tel 203-536-7373 (SAN 202-5205).

Vicky Bird Bks
See V S Morris

Victor Bks, *(Victor Books; 0-88207; 0-89693),* P.O. Box 1825, Wheaton, IL 60187 Tel 312-668-6000 (SAN 207-7302); Orders to: 1825 College Ave., Wheaton, IL 60187 (SAN 207-7310).

Vida Pubs
See Life Pubs Intl

Viking Pr, *(Viking Press, Inc.; 0-670),* 40 W. 23rd St., New York, NY 10010 Tel 212-807-7300 (SAN 282-5066); Orders to: Viking/Penguin, Inc., 299 Murray Hill Pkwy., East Rutherford, NJ 07073 (SAN 282-5074).

Vin *Imprint of* **Random**

Vistula Pr, *(Vistula Press, The),* 328 Anthony Circle, Charlotte, NC 28211 (SAN 282-5171)328 Anthony Circle, Charlotte, NC 28211 Tel 704-364-0035 (SAN 282-518X).

Visual Impact, *(Visual Impact Pubs., Communicators; 0-913426),* 723 S. Wells St., Chicago, IL 60607 Tel 312-922-2083 (SAN 206-8591).

Visual Studies, *(Visual Studies Workshop),* 31 Prince St., Rochester, NY 14607 (SAN 218-1606).

Volaphon Bks, *(Volaphon Books; 0-916258),* 73 Fox Ridge Crescent, Warwick, RI 02886 (SAN 208-0559).

VoyB *Imprint of* **HarBraceJ**

W A Benjamin
See A-W

W Collins, *(Collins, Wm., Sons, & Co., Ltd.),* Publisher Abbreviation Without Addresses Are for Titles That Are Out of Print. These Are Obsolete Abbreviations. Publisher's Abbreviation Is Now Collins-World.

W J Johnson *See* Walter J Johnson

KEY TO PUBLISHERS' AND DISTRIBUTORS' ABBREVIATIONS

W Perry, *(Perry, Warner; 0-9603962),* 23 Knickerbocker Dr., Newark, DE 19713 (SAN 213-5450).

W Thomas Taylor, *(Taylor, W. Thomas, Bookseller; 0-935072),* 708 Colorado, Austin, TX 78701 Tel 512-478-7628 (SAN 211-1454).

Wadsworth Atheneum, *(Wadsworth Atheneum),* 25 Prospect St., Hartford, CT 06103 (SAN 205-4981).

Wagon & Star, *(Wagon & Star Pubs.),* 4032 W. Century Blvd., Inglewood, CA 90304 (SAN 202-9421).

Wake-Brook, *(Wake-Brook House; 0-87482),* 990 N.W. 53rd St., Fort Lauderdale, FL 33309 Tel 305-776-5884 (SAN 205-5023) June 1st Through October 15th, Contact at: P.O. Box 153, Hyannis, MA 02601, Tel: 617-775-5860.

Walden Pr, *(Walden Press; 0-911938),* 423 S. Franklin Ave., Flint, MI 48503 (SAN 205-5031).

Walker & Co, *(Walker & Co.; 0-8027),* 720 Fifth Ave., New York, NY 10019 Tel 212-265-3632 (SAN 202-5213).

Wallaby Imprint of **PB**

Wallace-Homestead, *(Wallace-Homestead Book Co.; 0-87069),* 1912 Grand Ave., Des Moines, IA 50305 Tel 515-243-6181 (SAN 205-5058).

Walter J Johnson, *(Johnson, Walter J., Inc.; 0-8472),* 355 Chestnut St., Norwood, NJ 07648 Tel 201-767-1303 (SAN 209-1828).

Wampeter Pr, *(Wampeter Press; 0-931694),* P.O. Box 512, Green Harbor, ME 02041 (SAN 212-3231).

Wanderer Bks, *(Wanderer Books; 0-671),* Div. of Simon & Schuster, 1230 Ave. of the Americas, New York, NY 10020 Tel 212-245-6400 (SAN 212-5803).

Warm Wind Bks, *(Warm Wind Books),* Box 813, Forest Grove, OR 97116 (SAN 218-429X).

Warner Bks, *(Warner Books, Inc.; 0-446),* 666 Fifth Ave., New York, NY 10103 Tel 212-484-2900 (SAN 282-5368); Orders to: Warner Publisher Services, 666 Fith Ave., New York, NY 10103 Tel 212-484-2900 (SAN 282-5376).

Warner Pr, *(Warner Press Pubs.; 0-87162),* P.O. Box 2499, 1200 E. Fifth St., Anderson, IN 46018 Tel 317-644-7721 (SAN 202-9472).

Wash Launderan, *(Wash Launderan Press; 0-9605326),* 5804 Ingersoll Ave., Des Moines, IA 50312 Tel 515-279-7774 (SAN 215-9295).

Washburn, *(Washburn, Ives, Inc.),* Subs. of David McKay Co., Inc., 750 Third Ave., New York, NY 10017 Tel 212-661-1700 (SAN 209-9502).

Washingtonian, *(Washingtonian Books; 0-915168),* 1828 L St., N.W. Suite 200, Washington, DC 20036 Tel 202-296-3600 (SAN 207-4206).

Washoe, *(Washoe Press; 0-89376),* P.O. Box 91922, Los Angeles, CA 90009 (SAN 209-0694).

Waterfall Pr, *(Waterfall Press; 0-932278),* 2122 Junction Ave., El Cerritto, CA 94530 Tel 415-232-5539 (SAN 211-7665).

Waterford Pr, *(Waterford Press; 0-9608706),* 32-66 72nd St., Jackson Heights, NY 11370 Tel 212-424-4685 (SAN 238-4124).

Waterfront NJ, *(Waterfront Press; 0-943862),* 52 Maple Ave., Maplewood, NJ 07040 Tel 201-762-1565 (SAN 241-5941).

Waterfront NY
  See Waterfront NJ

Watts, *(Watts, Franklin, Inc.; 0-531),* Subs. of Grolier Inc., 387 Park Ave. South, New York, NY 10016 Tel 212-686-7070 (SAN 285-1156); 730 Fifth Ave., New York, NY 10019 Tel 212-757-4050 (SAN 285-1164). Imprints: Fontana Pap (Fontana Paperbacks).

Wayne St U Pr, *(Wayne State Univ. Press; 0-8143),* The Leonard N. Simons Bldg., 5959 Woodward Ave., Detroit, MI 48202 Tel 313-577-4603 (SAN 202-5221).

Weatherhill, *(Weatherhill, John, Inc.; 0-8348),* 6 E. 39th St., New York, NY 10016 Tel 212-686-2857 (SAN 202-9529); Dist. by: Charles E. Tuttle, Co., Inc., 28 S. Main St., Rutland, VT 05701 (SAN 213-2621).

Wehman, *(Wehman Brothers, Inc.; 0-911604),* Ridgedale Ave., Morris County Mall, Cedar Knolls, NJ 07927 Tel 201-539-6300 (SAN 206-779X).

Weills
  See Berkley Pub

Weiser, *(Weiser, Samuel, Inc.; 0-87728),* P.O. Box 612, York Beach, ME 03910 Tel 207-363-4393 (SAN 202-9588).

West Coast, *(West Coast Poetry Review; 0-915596),* 1335 Dartmouth Dr., Reno, NV 89509 Tel 702-322-4467 (SAN 207-3684).

West End, *(West End Press; 0-931122),* Box 7232, Minneapolis, MN 55407 Tel 612-822-3488 (SAN 211-3406).

West SW Pub Co, *(West Southwest Publishing Co.),* P.O. Box 4064, Redding, CA 96099 (SAN 214-4883).

Westburg, *(Westburg Associates, Pubs.; 0-87423),* 1745 Madison St., Fennimore, WI 53809 Tel 608-822-6237 (SAN 205-5171).

Western Epics, *(Western Epics Publishing Co.; 0-914740),* 254 S. Main St., Salt Lake City, UT 84101 Tel 801-328-2586 (SAN 206-1384).

Western Her Texas, *(Western Heritage Press; 0-89351),* 1530 Bonnie Brae, Houston, TX 77006 Tel 713-522-7158 (SAN 210-9778).

Western Pub, *(Western Publishing Co., Inc.; 0-307),* 850 Third Ave., New York, NY 10022 Tel 212-753-8500 (SAN 202-523X); Orders to: Dept. M, 1220 Mound Ave., Racine, WI 53404 Tel 414-633-2431 (SAN 202-5248) Not to be confused with Western Publisher in Florida. Imprints: Golden Pr (Golden Press).

Western Sun Pubns, *(Western Sun Pubns.; 0-9608146),* P.O. Box 1470, 209 S. First Ave., Suite 300, Yuma, AZ 85364 Tel 602-782-4646 (SAN 240-5067).

Western Tanager, *(Western Tanager Press; 0-934136),* 1111 Pacific Ave., Santa Cruz, CA 95060 Tel 408-425-1111 (SAN 220-0155).

Westernlore, *(Westernlore Pubns.; 0-87026),* 11860 N. Tami Place, Tucson, AZ 85704 Tel 602-297-5491 (SAN 202-9642); Orders to: Westernlore Press, P.O. Box 35305, Tucson, AZ 85740 Tel 602-297-5491 (SAN 202-9650).

Westlake, *(Westlake, Kevin L.; 0-9604862),* RR 2, Montpelier, ID 83254 (SAN 215-7136).

Westminster, *(Westminster Press; 0-664),* 925 Chestnut St., Philadelphia, PA 19107 Tel 215-928-2700 (SAN 202-9669); Orders to: Order Dept., P.O. Box 718 Wm. Penn Annex, Philadelphia, PA 19105 (SAN 202-9677).

Westview, *(Westview Press; 0-89158; 0-86531; 0-8133),* 5500 Central Ave., Boulder, CO 80301 Tel 303-444-3541 (SAN 219-970X).

Weybright, *(Weybright & Talley, Inc.),* Publisher Abbreviation Without Addresses Are For Titles That Are Out of Print. These Are Obsolete Abbreviations. Publisher Was Aquired by McKay.

Weybright
  See McKay

Weybright Imprint of **McKay**

Wheelwright Pr, *(Wheelwright Press; 0-935706),* 300 Page St., San Francisco, CA 94102 (SAN 222-0326).

Wheelwright UT, *(Wheelwright Press, Ltd.; 0-937512),* 1836 Sunnyside Ave., Salt Lake City, UT 84108 Tel 801-582-8158 (SAN 205-9533).

Whispers, *(Whispers Press; 0-918372),* 70 Highland Ave., Binghamtom, NY 13905 Tel 607-729-6920 (SAN 210-6272).

Whitaker Hse, *(Whitaker House; 0-88368),* Pittsburgh & Colfax Sts., Springdale, PA 15144 Tel 412-274-4440 (SAN 203-2104).

White Cross, *(White Cross Press; 0-918186),* Route One, Box 592, Granger, TX 76530 Tel 512-859-2814 (SAN 210-2862).

White Ewe, *(White Ewe Press; 0-917976),* P.O. Box 996, Adelphi, MD 20783 (SAN 209-410X).

White Horse, *(White Horse Productions, Inc.; 0-940376),* 286 Cabot St., Beverly, MA 01915 Tel 617-927-3677 (SAN 219-8355).

White Rabbit, *(White Rabbit Press),* 631 State St., Santa Barbara, CA 93101 Tel 415-548-8204 (SAN 205-5228).

Whitmore, *(Whitmore Publishing Co.; 0-87426),* 35 Cricket Terrace, Ardmore, PA 19003 (SAN 203-2112).

Whitston Pub, *(Whitston Publishing Co., Inc.; 0-87875),* P.O. Box 958, Troy, NY 12181 Tel 518-283-4363 (SAN 203-2120).

Wild Horses, *(Wild Horses Publishing Co.; 0-9601088; 0-937148),* 12310 Concepcion Rd., Los Altos Hills, CA 94022 Tel 415-941-3396 (SAN 211-8289); Dist. by: Bookpeople, 2940 7th St., Berkeley, CA 94710 Tel 415-549-3030 (SAN 168-9517).

Wild Horses Potted Plant
  See Wild Horses

Wildwood, *(Wildwood Press),* 2110 Wood Ave., Colorado Springs, CO 80907 Tel 303-634-8078 (SAN 210-5284).

Wiley, *(Wiley, John, & Sons, Inc.; 0-471),* 605 Third Ave., New York, NY 10158 Tel 212-850-6418 (SAN 200-2272).

William Carey Lib, *(William Carey Library Pubs.; 0-87808),* 1705 N. Sierra Bonita Ave., P.O. Box 40129, Pasadena, CA 91104 Tel 213-798-0819 (SAN 208-2101).

William-F, *(William-Frederick Press; 0-87164),* 308 E. 79th St., New York, NY 10021 Tel 212-628-1995 (SAN 205-5309).

William of Orange, *(William of Orange Publications),* N84 W16033 Menomonee Ave., No. 109, Menomonee Falls, WI 53051 Tel 414-255-4309 (SAN 264-4983).

Williamsburg, *(Colonial Williamsburg Foundation; 0-910412; 0-87935),* Publications Dept., P.O. Box C, Williamsburg, VA 23187 Tel 804-229-1000 (SAN 203-297X); Orders to: Products, P.O. Box C, Williamsburg, VA 23187 (SAN 203-2988).

Willing Pub, *(Willing Publishing Co.),* 251 S. San Gabriel Blvd., San Gabriel, CA 91778 (SAN 205-5325); Dist. by: Devorss & Co., 1641 Lincoln Blvd., Santa Monica, CA 90404 (SAN 168-9886).

Willoughby, *(Willoughby Books),* 14 Hamburg Turnpike, Hamburg, NJ 07419 (SAN 205-5341).

Willow Creek, *(Willow Creek Press; 0-932558),* Div. of Wisconsin Sportsman, P.O. Box 2266, Oshkosh, WI 54903 Tel 414-233-4143 (SAN 211-2825).

Willow Hse, *(Willow House Pubs., Inc.; 0-912450),* Box 155, Aptos, CA 95003 Tel 408-688-4128 (SAN 205-535X).

Willyshe Pub, *(Willyshe Publishing Co., Inc.; 0-936112),* 112 Mountain Rd., Linthicum Heights, MD 21090 (SAN 213-9499).

Wilmar Pubs, *(Wilmar Pubs.),* P.O. Box 5295, Sherman Oaks, CA 91413 Tel 213-762-1234 (SAN 210-9697).

Wilshire, *(Wilshire Book Co.; 0-87980),* 12015 Sherman Rd., North Hollywood, CA 91605 Tel 213-875-1711 (SAN 168-9932).

Winchester Pr, *(Winchester Press; 0-87691),* P.O. Box 1260, Tulsa, OK 74101 Tel 918-663-4220 (SAN 203-2953).

Windhover Imprint of **Berkley Pub**

Window Edns, *(Window Editions; 0-939290),* 350 Old Roaring Brook Rd., Mount Kisco, NY 10549 Tel 212-222-1689 (SAN 216-5201).

Windy Row, *(Windy Row Press; 0-911838),* Peterborough, NH 03458 Tel 603-924-3340 (SAN 203-2929).

Wingbow Pr, *(Wingbow Press; 0-914728),* Dist. by: Bookpeople, 2940 Seventh St., Berkeley, CA 94710 Tel 415-549-3033 (SAN 168-9517).

Wings ME, *(Wings Press; 0-939736),* RFD 2 Box 730, Belfast, ME 04915 Tel 207-338-2005 (SAN 216-7689).

Winston Pr, *(Winston Press, Inc.; 0-86683),* Subs. of CBS Educational Publishing, 430 Oak Grove, Minneapolis, MN 55403 Tel 612-871-7000 (SAN 213-9596).

Wisconsin Bks, *(Wisconsin Bks.),* 2025 Dunn Pl., Madison, WI 53713 Tel 608-257-4126 (SAN 213-8875) Formerly Named School of Living Press.

Wisconsin Hse, *(Wisconsin House Book Pubs.; 0-88361),* P.O. Box 2118, Madison, WI 53701 Tel 608-251-3222 (SAN 203-2899).

Wish Bklets, *(Wish Booklets; 0-913786),* 11909 Blue Spruce Rd, Reston, VA 22091 Tel 703-620-4966 (SAN 205-5430).

Wittenborn, *(Wittenborn, George, Inc.; 0-8150),* 1018 Madison Ave., New York, NY 10021 Tel 212-288-1558 (SAN 203-2880).

Wm C Brown, *(Brown, William C., Publishers; 0-697),* 2460 Kerper Blvd., Dubuque, IA 52001 Tel 319-589-2822 (SAN 203-2864).

KEY TO PUBLISHERS' AND DISTRIBUTORS' ABBREVIATIONS

Woburn Pr *See* Biblio Dist
Wolf Hse, *(Wolf House Books; 0-915046),* P.O. Box 6657, Grand Rapids, MI 49506 Tel 616-245-8812 (SAN 203-2856).
Wolf Run Bks, *(Wolf Run Books),* P.O. Box 9620, Minneapolis, MN 55440 Tel 612-333-7437 (SAN 206-9571).
Woodbine-Volaphon
   See Volaphon Bks
Woodbridge Pr, *(Woodbridge Pr. Pub. Co.; 0-912800; 0-88007),* P.O. Box 6189, Santa Barbara, CA 93160 Tel 805-965-7039 (SAN 212-9892).
Woodhill, *(Woodhill Press, Inc.; 0-532),* 300 W. 43rd St., New York, NY 10036 Tel 212-397-5200 (SAN 202-6066).
Word Bks, *(Word, Inc.; 0-87680; 0-8499),* 4800 W. Waco Drive, Waco, TX 76796 Tel 817-772-7650 (SAN 203-283X).
Word Shop
   See Avant Bks
WorDoctor, *(WorDoctor Pubns.; 0-918248),* P.O. Box 9761, 6516 Ben Ave., North Hollywood, CA 91609 Tel 213-980-3576 (SAN 207-5865).
Working Pr CA, *(Working Press; 0-9602462),* P.O. Box 687, Livermore, CA 94550 Tel 415-447-5943 (SAN 212-7717).
Workman Pub, *(Workman Publishing Co., Inc.; 0-911104; 0-89480),* 1 W. 39th St., New York, NY 10018 Tel 212-398-9160 (SAN 203-2821).
World Light, *(World Light Pubns.; 0-916940),* 1518 Poplar Level Rd., Louisville, KY 40217 Tel 502-634-4185 (SAN 208-9300).
World Pub, *(World Publishing Co.),* Publisher Abbreviation Without Addresses Are for Titles That Are Out of Print. These Are Obsolete Abbreviations. Publisher's Abbreviation Is Now Collins-World.

Wormhoudt, *(Wormhoudt, Arthur, Dr.; 0-916358),* Dept. of Language & Literature, William Penn College, Oskaloosa, IA 52577 Tel 515-673-3091 (SAN 207-5547).
Writers & Readers, *(Writers & Readers),* c/o W.W. Norton Co., 500 Fifth Ave., New York, NY 10110 Tel 212-228-0390 (SAN 216-4795).
Writers West, *(Writers West Books),* Dept. of English, Univ. of Colorado, Colorado Springs, CO 80907 Tel 303-449-2101 (SAN 212-3266); Dist. by: Swallow Press, Inc., 811 W. Junior Terrace, Chicago, IL 60613 Tel 312-871-2760 (SAN 202-5671).
WSP, *(Washington Square Press, Inc.),* Div. of Simon & Schuster, Inc., 1230 Ave. of the Americas, New York, NY 10020 Tel 212-246-2121 (SAN 206-9784).
   Imprints: CC (Collateral Classics Series); RE (Readers Enrichment Series).
Wyden, *(Wyden Books; 0-87223),* Div. of P.E.I. Books, Inc., P.O. Box 151, Ridgefield, CT 06877 Tel 203-438-9631 (SAN 210-9794); Dist. by: Harper & Row, Keystone Indus Pk, Scranton, PA 18512 (SAN 215-3742).
Wyden *Imprint of* McKay
Xerox College, *(Xerox College Publishing; 0-536),* a Xerox Education Co., 191 Spring St., Lexington, MA 02173 Tel 617-861-1670 (SAN 203-2767).
Yale U Pr, *(Yale Univ. Press; 0-300),* 302 Temple St., New Haven, CT 06520 Tel 203-432-4920 (SAN 203-2740); Orders to: 92A Yale Sta., New Haven, CT 06520 Tel 203-432-4969 (SAN 203-2759).
Yama Trans, *(Yama Trans Co.; 0-942512),* 24228 Hawthorne Blvd., Torrance, CA 90505 Tel 213-378-8700 (SAN 238-2105).
Yankee Bks, *(Yankee Books; 0-911658; 0-89909),* A Division of Yankee Publishing Inc., Dublin, NH 03444 Tel 603-563-8111 (SAN 203-2732).

Yankee Inc *See* Yankee Bks
Yankee Peddler, *(Yankee Peddler Book Co.; 0-911660),* Drawer O, Southampton, NY 11968 Tel 516-283-1612 (SAN 205-5570).
Yardbird Wing, *(Yardbird Wing Editions; 0-918412),* Dist. by: Yardbird Pub. Co., Inc., P.O. Box 2370, Station A, Berkeley, CA 94702 Tel 415-527-7426 (SAN 208-9343).
YB *Imprint of* **Dell**
Y'bird
   See Reed & Youngs Quilt
Yellow Jacket, *(Yellow Jacket Press; 0-915626),* 901 Alspaugh Lane, Grand Prairie, TX 75052 (SAN 207-3048).
Z Pr, *(Z Press, Inc.; 0-915990),* Calais, VT 05648 (SAN 207-656X).
Zalozba Prometej, *(Zalozba Prometej; 0-934158),* P.O. Box 8391, New Orleans, LA 70182 Tel 504-283-7177 (SAN 212-8462).
Zebra, *(Zebra Books; 0-89083; 0-8217),* 475 Park Ave. S., New York, NY 10016 Tel 212-889-2299 (SAN 207-9860); Dist. by: Kable News Co., 777 3rd Ave., New York, NY 10017 (SAN 169-5835).
Zebra *Imprint of* Grove
Zeppelin, *(Zeppelin Pub. Co.; 0-915628),* P.O. Box 22252, Louisiana State Univ. Station, Baton Rouge, LA 70893 Tel 504-272-6600 (SAN 204-6776); Pelican Office Center, 11628 S. Choctaw Dr., Baton Rouge, LA 70815 Tel 504-272-6600 (SAN 200-4208); Orders to: P.O. Box 15809, Broadmoor Station, Baton Rouge, LA 70893 Tel 504-272-6600 (SAN 200-4216).
Ziesing Bros, *(Ziesing Bros. Book Emporium),* 768 Main St., Willimantic, CT 06226 (SAN 209-6935).
Zondervan, *(Zondervan Publishing House; 0-310),* 1415 Lake Dr., S.E., Grand Rapids, MI 49506 Tel 616-459-6900 (SAN 203-2694).

Directory of Publishers and Distributors

AAR/Tantalus, Inc., *(AAR-Tantalus; 0-931052)*, 1600 Rio Grande, Suite 203, Austin, TX 78701 Tel 512-476-3225 (SAN 281-2371); Orders to: P.O. Box 893, Austin, TX 78767 (SAN 281-238X).

AA Sales Inc., *(AA Sales Inc; 0-931388)*, 9600 Stone Ave. N., Seattle, WA 98103 (SAN 211-4070).

A & M Books, *(A & M Bks; 0-937150)*, P.O. Box 24112, Richmond, VA 23224 Tel 804-232-3904 (SAN 214-3348).

A & P Books, *(A & P Bks; 0-86550)*, P. O. Box 6639, Oakland, CA 94603 (SAN 237-997X).

A&R Publishing Co., *(A & R Pub; 0-943354)*, 21-B Maplewood Dr., Whiting, NJ 08759 Tel 201-350-8845 (SAN 240-575X).

A & W Pubs., Inc., *(A & W Pubs; 0-89479)*, 95 Madison Ave., New York, NY 10016 Tel 212-725-4970 (SAN 200-2418) Do Not Confuse with A-W, Addison-Wesley Publishing Co., Inc. *Imprints:* A & W Visual Library (A & W Visual Library).

A & W Visual Library See **A & W Pubs., Inc.**

ABA Professional Education Pubns., *(ABA Prof Educ Pubns; 0-89707)*, 1155 E. 60th St., Chicago, IL 60637 (SAN 219-7502).

ABBE Pubns. Assn. of Washington D.C., *(ABBE Pubs Assn; 0-941864; 0-88164)*, 4111 Gallows Rd., Annandale, VA 22003 Tel 703-750-0255 (SAN 239-1430).

ABK Pubns., *(ABK Pubns; 0-9601420)*, P.O. Box 962, Hanover, NH 03755 (SAN 212-6346).

A. C. Libro, *(Libro A C; 0-940538)*, 613 Howard Ave., Pitman, NJ 08071 (SAN 238-7913); Dist. by: Joanne Nobes Hoey, 33 East Centennial Dr., Marlton, NJ 08053 (SAN 238-7921).

AC Pubns., *(AC Pubns; 0-935496)*, P.O. Box 238, Homer, NY 13077 Tel 607-749-4040 (SAN 213-4462).

ACS Publishing Co., *(ACS Pub; 0-9606868)*, P.O. Box 82363, San Diego, CA 92138 Tel 714-223-5331 (SAN 217-3212).

ACTA Foundation, *(ACTA Found; 0-87946; 0-914070)*, 4848 N. Clark St., Chicago, IL 60640 Tel 312-271-1030 (SAN 204-7489).

ADAPTS(Alcohol & Drug Abuse Prevention & Training Services, *(ADAPTS; 0-9606016)*, 932 W. Franklin St., Richmond, VA 23220 Tel 804-358-0408 (SAN 216-9452).

ADC Pubns., *(ADC Pubns; 0-937414)*, Dist. by: Robert Silver Associates, 95 Madison Ave., New York, NY 10016 Tel 212-686-5630 (SAN 241-5801).

A.D.M. Co., Inc., *(ADM Co; 0-937974)*, P.O. Box 10462, Phoenix, AZ 85016 Tel 602-279-2070 (SAN 220-0260).

ADS Press, *(ADS Pr)*, 311 Farmers Bank Building, P.O. Box 395, Jacksonville, IL 62650 (SAN 263-9017).

AEON-Hierophant Communications, Inc., *(AEON-Hierophant; 0-9606110)*, Box 1181, Seattle, WA 98111 Tel 206-324-6801 (SAN 216-7816).

AEVAC, Inc., *(AEVAC; 0-913356)*, 5 Mountain Ave., North Plainfield, NJ 07060 Tel 201-561-0222 (SAN 204-5567).

AFIPS Press, *(AFIPS Pr; 0-88283)*, P.O. Box 9657, 1815 N. Lynn St., Suite 800, Arlington, VA 22209 Tel 703-558-3631 (SAN 204-7470).

AFUA Enterprises, Inc., *(AFUA Ent; 0-918088)*, Box 9026, General Lafayette Sta., Jersey City, NJ 07304 Tel 201-435-7225 (SAN 210-1599).

AG Press, *(AG Pr)*, 16th & Yuma, Box 1009, Manhattan, KS 66502 Tel 913-539-7558 (SAN 204-7632).

AG2 Press, *(Agtwo Pr; 0-9606552)*, 6234 N. Central Ave., Phoenix, AZ 85012 Tel 602-265-9407 (SAN 222-9897).

A. J. Publishing Co., *(A J Pub; 0-914190)*, P.O. Box 3012, Duluth, MN 55803 Tel 218-722-3253 (SAN 201-1840).

ALB Associates, *(ALB Assocs; 0-913405)*, P.O. Box 15243, Pittsburgh, PA 15237 Tel 412-367-3240 (SAN 285-8096).

ALM Associates, Inc., *(ALM Assocs)*, P.O.Box 568, Otisville, NY 10963 (SAN 287-2897).

A M A C O M, Div. of American Management Associations, *(Am Mgmt; 0-8144)*, 135 W. 50th St., New York, NY 10020 Tel 212-586-8100 (SAN 201-1670).

AMCO International, *(AMCO Intl; 0-9602406)*, P.O. Box 347, Staten Island, NY 10301 Tel 518-489-6736 (SAN 212-6354).

AMG Pubs., *(AMG Pubs; 0-89957)*, 6815 Shallowford Rd., Chattanooga, TN 37421 (SAN 211-3074).

AMIGOS Bibliographic Council, *(AMIGOS Biblio; 0-938288)*, 11300 N. Central Expressway, Suite 321, Dallas, TX 75243 Tel 214-750-6130 (SAN 219-7596).

AMI International Press, *(AMI Pr; 0-911988)*, Mountain View Rd., Washington, NJ 07822 Tel 201-689-1700 (SAN 213-6791).

A M O R C, Div. of Supreme Grand Lodge of AMORC, Inc., *(AMORC; 0-912057)*, Rosicrucian Order, Park Naglee, San Jose, CA 95191 Tel 408-287-9171 (SAN 211-3864).

AMR Pub. Co., *(AMR Pub Co; 0-913698; 0-913599)*, 1705 N. 45th St., Seattle, WA 98103 Tel 206-633-3664 (SAN 281-272X); Orders to: P.O. Box 3194, Seattle, WA 98114 Tel 206-633-3664 (SAN 281-2738).

AMS Press, Inc., *(AMS Pr; 0-404)*, 56 E. 13th St., New York, NY 10003 Tel 212-777-4700 (SAN 201-1743).

AMTEC, *(AMTEC; 0-941450)*, 1028 N. Lake Ave., Suite 103, Pasadena, CA 91104 (SAN 239-3557).

A.N., Inc., *(AN Inc)*, P.O. Box 145, Whitefish, MT 59937 (SAN 214-0888).

AOI Corp., *(AOI Corp; 0-936074)*, Box 1109, Ogden Dunes, Portage, IN 46368 (SAN 223-3932).

APLIC International, *(APLIC Intl; 0-933438)*, Population Council Library, One Dag Hamarskjold Plaza, New York, NY 10017 (SAN 205-1486).

APL Press, *(APL Pr; 0-917326)*, 220 California Ave., Suite 201, Palo Alto, CA 94306 Tel 415-327-1700 (SAN 208-5070).

A.P.M. Press, *(A P M Pr; 0-937612)*, 650 Ocean Ave., Brooklyn, NY 11226 (SAN 214-3356).

APSA, *(APSA)*, P.O. Box 5503, Washington, DC 20016 (SAN 212-4009).

ARC Press, *(ARC Pr; 0-9600884)*, 3090 Berkshire Rd., Clev. Hts., OH 44118 (SAN 263-9033).

ARCsoft Pubs., *(ARCsoft; 0-86668)*, P.O. Box 132, Woodsboro, MD 21798 Tel 301-845-8856 (SAN 216-2210).

A.R.E. Press, *(ARE Pr; 0-87604)*, P.O. Box 595, Editorial Dept., Virginia Beach, VA 23451 Tel 804-428-3588 (SAN 201-1484).

ARO Publishing Co., *(ARO Pub; 0-89868)*, Box 193, 398 S. 1100 West, Provo, UT 84601 Tel 801-377-8218 (SAN 212-6370).

A.S.C. Holding Corp., *(ASC Holding; 0-935578)*, 1782 N. Orange Dr., Hollywood, CA 90028 (SAN 287-2889).

ASI Pubs., Inc., *(ASI Pubs Inc; 0-88231)*, 63 W. 38th St., Suite 505, New York, NY 10018 Tel 212-679-5676 (SAN 201-1395).

A to Z Publishing Co., *(A to Z Pub Co)*, 8825 National Boulevard, Culver City, CA 90230 Tel 213-870-1141 (SAN 265-3788).

AVI Publishing Co. Inc., *(AVI; 0-87055)*, 250 Post Rd. E., P.O. Box 831, Westport, CT 06881 Tel 203-226-0738 (SAN 201-4017).

A. W. M. Company, *(AWM Co; 0-89105)*, P.O. Box 7643, Ann Arbor, MI 48107 Tel 313-482-7623 (SAN 207-2025).

A.R.A. See **Administrative Research Associates**

Aames-Allen Publishing Co., *(Aames-Allen; 0-936930)*, 924 Main St., Huntington Beach, CA 92648 Tel 714-536-4926 (SAN 214-4395).

Aaron-Jenkins Press, *(Aaron-Jenkins)*, P.O. Box 998, Lawndale, CA 90260 Tel 213-324-9083 (SAN 210-9891).

Aaron Pubs., Inc., *(Aaron Pubs; 0-936076)*, P.O. Box 2572, Sarasota, FL 33578 (SAN 214-0896).

aatec Pubns., *(aatec Pubns; 0-937948)*, P.O. Box 7119, Ann Arbor, MI 48107 Tel 313-995-1470 (SAN 215-7217).

Aazunna Publishing, *(Aazunna; 0-934444)*, 801 S. Victoria Ave. Suite 106, Ventura, CA 93003 (SAN 213-716X).

Abage Pubns., *(Abage; 0-917350)*, 6430 N. Western Ave., Chicago, IL 60645 Tel 312-761-5917 (SAN 206-3972).

Abak Press, *(Abak Pr; 0-914214)*, 500 Pepper Ridge Rd., Stamford, CT 06905 Tel 203-329-9009 (SAN 201-1166).

Abalache Bookshop Publishing Co., *(Abalache Bkshop; 0-910453)*, 311 S. Klein, Oklahoma City, OK 73108 Tel 405-235-3288 (SAN 260-0110).

Abaris Books, Inc., *(Abaris Bks; 0-913870; 0-89835)*, 24 W. 40th St., New York, NY 10018 Tel 212-354-1313 (SAN 206-4588).

Abbetira Pubns., *(Abbetira Pubns; 0-913407)*, Orders to: P.O. Box 17600, Tucson, AZ 85731 Tel 602-296-9067 (SAN 285-8053).

Abbeville Press, Inc., *(Abbeville Pr; 0-89659)*, 505 Park Ave., New York, NY 10022 Tel 212-888-1969 (SAN 211-4755).

Abbey, Stella K., *(S K Abbey)*, 2840 80th St., N.E., Bellevue, WA 98004 (SAN 204-7152).

Abbincott Publishing Co., *(Abbincott; 0-938490)*, 1501 Broadway, Rm. 1414, New York, NY 10036 (SAN 215-8345).

Abbott, Delila M., *(D M Abbott; 0-9607336)*, 4775 Bon Air St., Salt Lake City, UT 84117 Tel 801-277-2733 (SAN 239-1449); Dist. by: Zion's Book Store, 254 S. Main St., Salt Lake City, UT 84101 (SAN 239-1457); Dist. by: Deseret Book Store, 44 E. South Temple, Salt Lake City, UT 84111 (SAN 200-4097); Dist. by: Country Furniture, Old Gardner Mill, 1050 W. 7800 S., West Jordan, UT 84084 (SAN 200-4100).

Abbott, P.A., Pubns., *(P A Abbott; 0-938564)*, P.O. Box 2085, Kalamazoo, MI 49003 (SAN 220-1410).

Abbott, Langer & Associates, *(Abbott Langer Assocs; 0-916506)*, 548 First St., Crete, IL 60417 Tel 312-672-4200 (SAN 207-9305).

Abbott Loop Christian Center, *(Abbott Loop; 0-911739)*, 2626 Abbott Rd., Anchorage, AK 99507-4299 Tel 907-349-9641 (SAN 263-905X).

ABC-Clio Press See **American Bibliographical Center-Clio Press**

ABC Enterprises, *(ABC Enterprises; 0-9608126)*, 2521-F N. Grand Ave., Santa Ana, CA 92701 Tel 714-835-7389 (SAN 240-0790).

A B C Press of Silicon Valley, *(ABC Pr Silicon; 0-912957)*, 320 Encinal Ave., Menlo Park, CA 94025 Tel 415-329-0256 (SAN 282-7220); Dist. by: William Kaufmann, Inc., 95 First St., Los Altos, CA 94022 Tel 415-948-5810 (SAN 202-9383).

Abelard-Schuman Junior Books See **Harper & Row Pubs., Inc**

Abingdon Press, *(Abingdon; 0-687)*, Customer Service Dept., 201 Eight Ave. S., Nashville, TN 37202 Tel 615-749-6301 (SAN 201-0054). Imprints: Apex Books (Apex); Festival Books (Festival).

Ablex Publishing Corp., *(Ablex Pub; 0-89391)*, 355 Chestnut St., Norwood, NJ 07648 Tel 201-767-8450 (SAN 209-3332).

Abracadabra Press, *(Abracadabra Pr; 0-934542)*, P.O. Box 334, Balboa Island, CA 92662 Tel 714-675-0966 (SAN 238-0099).

Abrams, Harry N., Inc., Subs. of Times Mirror Co., *(Abrams; 0-8109)*, 110 E. 59th St., New York, NY 10022 Tel 212-758-8600 (SAN 200-2434).

Abraxas Press, Inc., *(Abraxas; 0-932868)*, 2518 Gregory St., Madison, WI 53711 Tel 608-238-0175 (SAN 207-7744).

Abraxas Publishing, *(Abraxas Pub WA; 0-939768)*, P.O. Box 312, 439 Kirkland Way, Kirkland, WA 98033 Tel 206-822-6081 (SAN 216-8731).

Abt Books, *(Abt Bks; 0-89011)*, Orders to: 55 Wheeler St., Cambridge, MA 02138 Tel 617-492-7100 (SAN 266-0210).

Abused Womens Aid in Crisis, *(AWAIC)*, GPO Box 1699, New York, NY 10001 Tel 212-686-3628 (SAN 237-2975).

Abyss Pubns., *(Abyss; 0-911856)*, P.O. Box C, Somerville, MA 02143 Tel 617-666-1804 (SAN 201-1859).

Academia Press, *(Academia; 0-911880)*, P.O. Box 125, Oshkosh, WI 54901 Tel 414-235-8362 (SAN 201-2146).

Academic Assoc., *(Acad Assoc; 0-918260)*, P.O. Box 628, Van Nuys, CA 91408 Tel 213-988-2479 (SAN 210-1556).

Academic Book Club, *(Acad Bk Club)*, N. 5411 Post St., Spokane, WA 99208 Tel 509-325-1435 (SAN 213-6058).

Academic Information Service, Inc., *(Acad Info Serv; 0-916018)*, P.O. Box 6296, Washington, DC 20015 (SAN 222-4755).

Academic International, *(Academic Intl; 0-87569)*, P.O. Box 1111, Gulf Breeze, FL 32561 (SAN 201-212X).

Academic Press, Inc., *(Acad Pr; 0-12)*, 111 Fifth Ave., New York, NY 10003 Tel 212-741-6865 (SAN 206-8990).

Academic Publishers of America, *(Acad Pub Amer; 0-911337)*, 6458 Lake Shore Dr., San Diego, CA 92119 Tel 619-698-0066 (SAN 266-0245).

Academic Therapy Pubns., *(Acad Therapy; 0-87879)*, 20 Commercial Blvd., Novato, CA 94947 Tel 415-883-3314 (SAN 201-2111).

Academic World, Div. of Acaworld Corp., *(Academic World; 0-915582)*, Drawer 4037, Greenville, NC 27834 Tel 919-355-6555 (SAN 208-1350).

Academy Books, *(Academy Bks; 0-914960)*, P.O. Box 757, Rutland, VT 05701 Tel 802-773-9194 (SAN 208-4325); Dist. by: Charles E. Tuttle Co., Inc, P.O. Box 410, S. Main St., Rutland, VT 05701 Tel 802-773-8229 (SAN 213-2621).

Academy Chicago, Ltd., *(Academy Chi Ltd; 0-915864)*, 425 N. Michigan Ave., Chicago, IL 60611 Tel 312-644-1723 (SAN 213-2001).

Academy for Educational Development, Inc., *(Acad Educ Dev; 0-89492)*, 680 5th Ave., New York, NY 10019 Tel 212-397-0040 (SAN 210-0185); 1414-22nd St., N.W., Washington, DC 20037 (SAN 215-0379).

Academy Hill Press, *(Academy Hill; 0-932312)*, 292 Academy Hill Rd., Red Hook, NY 12571 Tel 914-758-9042 (SAN 211-4607).

Academy of American Franciscan History, *(AAFH; 0-88382)*, P.O. Box 34440, Washington, DC 20034 Tel 301-365-1763 (SAN 201-1964).

Academy of Management, *(Acad of Mgmt; 0-915350)*, Dept. of Management, College of Business Administration, Wichita State Univ., Wichita, KS 67208 (SAN 207-3463); Orders to: Dennis F. Ray, The Academy of Management College of Business, Mississippi State University, Mississippi State, MS 39762 (SAN 207-3471).

Academy of Motion Picture Arts & Sciences, *(Acad Motion Pic)*, 8949 Wilshire Blvd., Beverly Hills, CA 90211 Tel 213-278-8990 (SAN 210-5471).

Academy of Prison Arts, The, *(Acad Prison Arts; 0-939406)*, P.O. Box 99901, Pittsburgh, PA 15233 Tel 412-761-1955 (SAN 216-5651); Dist. by: Motheroot, 214 Dewey St., Pittsburgh, PA 15218 Tel 412-731-4453 (SAN 216-4205).

Academy of Professional Art Conservation & Science, *(Acad Prof Art; 0-911877)*, 165 W. Napa St., P.O. Box 192, Sonoma, CA 95476 Tel 707-938-3801 (SAN 263-9076).

Academy of the New Church, *(Acad New Church; 0-910557)*, P.O. Box 278, Bryn Athyn, PA 19009 Tel 215-947-5085 (SAN 266-0512).

Academy Press, *(Academy Pr-Santa; 0-912314; 0-89733)*, 5227 Stevens Point, Santa Clara, CA 95051 Tel 408-241-6799 (SAN 201-2162).

Academy Pubns., *(Academy Pubns; 0-931560)*, Box 5224, Sherman Oaks, CA 91413 (SAN 212-1778).

Acadian Genealogy Exchange, *(Acadian Genealogy; 0-939444)*, 863 Wayman Branch Rd., Covington, KY 41015 (SAN 216-325X).

Acadian Publishing Enterprise, Inc., *(Acadian Pub; 0-914216)*, Rte. 4 Box 470, Church Point, LA 70525 Tel 318-684-5871 (SAN 202-3199).

Acadiana Press, The, *(Acadiana Pr; 0-937614)*, P.O. Box 42290, USL, Lafayette, LA 70504 Tel 318-662-3468 (SAN 215-6156).

Accelerated Development Inc., *(Accel Devel; 0-915202)*, 3400 Kilgore Ave., Muncie, IN 47304 Tel 317-284-7511 (SAN 210-3346).

Accelerated Indexing Systems, Inc., *(Accelerated Index; 0-89593)*, 19 W. South Temple, Suite 600 Union Pacific Annex, Salt Lake City, UT 84101 Tel 801-531-0098 (SAN 211-8793).

Accent Books, *(Accent Bks; 0-89636; 0-916406)*, P.O. Box 15337, Lakewood Sta., Denver, CO 80215 Tel 303-988-5300 (SAN 208-5097); 12100 W. Sixth Ave., Denver, CO 80215 (SAN 208-5100).

Accent Editions, *(Accent Edns; 0-942842)*, 446 E. 78th St., New York, NY 10021 Tel 212-737-0072 (SAN 240-1827) Tel 212-956-4215.

Access Press, Ltd., *(Access Pr; 0-9604858)*, 672 S. LaFayette Park Place, Los Angeles, CA 90057 (SAN 263-2500).

Accura Music, Inc., *(Accura; 0-918194)*, Box 887, Athens, OH 45701 Tel 614-594-3547 (SAN 210-1564).

Ace Bks., Div. of Charter Communications, Inc., *(Ace Bks; 0-441)*, c/o Berkley/Jove Pub., 200 Madison Ave., New York, NY 10016 Tel 212-686-9820 (SAN 169-5800); Dist. by: ICD, 250 W. 55th St., New York, NY 10019 Tel 212-262-7444 (SAN 270-885X).

ACETO Bookmen, *(ACETO Bookmen; 0-9607906)*, 5721 Antietam Dr., Sarasota, FL 33581 (SAN 237-9252).

Acheron Press, *(Acheron Pr; 0-941452)*, Bear Creek at the Kettle, Friendsville, MD 21531 Tel 301-689-3774 (SAN 239-0612).

Achievement Institute, The, *(Achievement Inst; 0-936452)*, 3125 Geddes Ave., Ann Arbor, MI 48104 (SAN 214-2783).

Ackerman-Rorex Corp., *(Ackerman-Rorex; 0-942112)*, 930 W. Oak St., Fort Collins, CO 80521 (SAN 239-5266); Dist. by: Jean Ford Assocs, Quail Park F4, 801 S. Rancho Dr., Las Vegas, NV 89106 (SAN 239-5274).

Acme Law Book Co., Inc., *(Acme Law; 0-910012)*, Post Office Bldg., Amityville, NY 11701 Tel 516-799-8686 (SAN 201-2219).

Acoma Books, *(Acoma Bks; 0-916552)*, P.O. Box 4, Ramona, CA 92065 Tel 714-789-1288 (SAN 207-7221).

Acorn, *(Acorn OH; 0-9604194)*, 1778 Radnor Rd., Cleveland, OH 44118 (SAN 216-213X).

Acorn Books See **Macmillan Publishing Co., Inc.**

Acorn Music Press See **Music Sales Corp.**

Acorn Press, *(Acorn NC; 0-89386)*, 1318 Broad St., Box 4007, Duke Sta., Durham, NC 27706 Tel 919-471-3842 (SAN 216-4833).

Acquisition Planning, Inc., *(Acquisition Plan; 0-940694)*, 200 W. Monroe St., Suite 1607, Chicago, IL 60614 Tel 312-332-5361 (SAN 218-5598).

Acre Press, *(Acre Pr)*, C/O Alma C. Reith, 5945 Evergreen, Dearborn Heights, MI 48127 (SAN 213-2737).

Acrobat Books, *(Acrobat; 0-918226)*, P.O. Box 480820, Los Angeles, CA 90048 (SAN 209-3936).

Acropolis Books, *(Acropolis; 0-87491)*, 2400 17th St. N.W., Washington, DC 20009 Tel 202-387-6805 (SAN 201-2227).

A C S Publications, Inc., *(A C S Pubns Inc; 0-917086)*, P.O. Box 16430, San Diego, CA 92116 Tel 714-297-9203 (SAN 208-5380); Dist. by: Para Research, Whistlestop Mall, Rockport, MA 01966 Tel 617-546-3413 (SAN 169-3565).

A.C.T. (Alcohlism, Children, Therapy), *(A C T; 0-9607940)*, P.O. Box 8536, Newport Beach, CA 92660 Tel 714-499-4806 (SAN 240-9488).

Action Link Pubns., *(Action Link; 0-936148)*, 53 Condon Court, San Mateo, CA 94403 (SAN 214-090X).

Action Productions, *(Action Prods; 0-9608868)*, 1102 17th St., N.W., Puyallup, WA 98371 Tel 206-845-3627 (SAN 241-0915).

Actionizing, Inc., *(Actionizing; 0-912137)*, 412 Mayo Bldg., Tulsa, OK 74103 Tel 918-582-5928 (SAN 264-7109).

Active Learning, *(Active Learning; 0-914460)*, P.O. Box 64992, Lubbock, TX 79464 (SAN 201-1174).

Activity Records, Inc, *(Activity Rec; 0-914296; 0-89525)*, 1937 Grand Ave., Baldwin, NY 11510 Tel 516-223-4666 (SAN 209-3405); Dist. by: Educational Activities, Inc., P.O. Box 392, Freeport, NY 11520 Tel 516-223-4666 (SAN 207-4400).

Activity Resources Co., Inc., *(Activity Resources; 0-918932),* P.O. Box 4875, 20655 Hathaway Ave., Hayward, CA 94541 Tel 415-782-1300 (SAN 209-0201).

Ad-Dee Publishers, Inc., *(Ad-dee Pubs Inc; 0-9600982),* Ad-Dee Pub Inc., Drawer 5426-B, Eugene, OR 97405 Tel 503-343-5868 (SAN 208-6638).

Ad-Images Pubs., *(Ad-Images Pub; 0-943154),* Waters Bldg., Suite 208, 161 Ottawa N. W., Grand Rapids, MI 49503 (SAN 240-3293).

Ad-Lib Publications, Div. of Whimsy Toys & Bks, *(Ad-Lib; 0-912411),* P.O. Box 1102, 51 1/2 E. B'way, Fairfield, IA 52556 Tel 515-472-6617 (SAN 265-170X).

Adamas Pubs., *(Adamas Pub; 0-9607892),* P.O. Box 5504, Washington, DC 20016 Tel 301-656-0008 (SAN 238-1362).

Adamiak, Richard Rare, & Scholarly Books, *(Adamiak-Rare; 0-9610650),* 1545 E. 60th St., Chicago, IL 60637 Tel 312-955-4571 (SAN 264-648X).

Adams, Bob, Inc., *(Adams Inc MA),* 2045 Commonwealth Ave., Brighton, MA 02135 Tel 617-782-5707 (SAN 215-2886).

Adams, Charles J. III, *(C J Adams; 0-9610008),* 14 E. 34th St., Reading, PA 19606 Tel 215-779-8173 (SAN 266-0865).

Adams, Thomas Dean, *(T Adams; 0-9609242),* 2817 Darrow Ave, Klamath, OR 90210 Tel 213-271-0938 (SAN 241-2624).

Adams County Historical Society, *(Adams County; 0-934858),* P.O. Box 102, Hastings, NE 68901 Tel 402-463-5838 (SAN 209-1917).

Adams Press, *(Adams Minn; 0-914828),* 59 Seymour Ave., S.E., Minneapolis, MN 55414 Tel 612-378-9076 (SAN 201-1867); Orders to: Lerner Publications Co., 241 First Ave. N., Minneapolis, MN 55401 (SAN 201-0828).

Adams Press, *(Adams Pr),* 30 W. Washington St., Chicago, IL 60602 (SAN 240-1290).

Adamson, Douglas, *(D Adamson),* New Boston Rd., Box 173, Sanbornton, NH 03269 (SAN 208-1288).

Adastra Press, *(Adastra Pr; 0-938566),* 101 Strong St., Easthampton, MA 01027 (SAN 207-7752).

ADCO Enterprises, *(ADCO Enterp; 0-9608870),* 465 Van Duzer St., Staten Island, NY 10304 Tel 212-447-3280 (SAN 241-0923).

Add-Effect Associates, Inc., *(Add-Effect Assoc),* P.O. Box 401, 1093 Radnor Rd., Wayne, PA 19087 Tel 215-688-6489 (SAN 219-0761).

Addiction Research Foundation of Ontario, *(Addict Res Ont; 0-88868),* 33 Russell St., Toronto, Ont. M5S 2S1, .

Addison House, Subs. of American Showcase, Inc., *(Addison Hse; 0-89169),* 724 Fifth Ave., Tenth Floor, New York, NY 10019 Tel 212-586-8036 (SAN 210-5543).

Addison-Wesley Children's Books *See* **Addison-Wesley Publishing Co., Inc.**

Addison-Wesley Publishing Co., Inc., *(A-W; 0-201),* One Jacob Way, Reading, MA 01867 Tel 617-944-3700 (SAN 200-2000). Imprints: Addison Wesley Publishing Co., Inc., Medical/Nursing Division (Med-Nurse); Addison-Wesley Children's Books (A-W Childrens); Advance Book Program (Adv Bk Prog).

Addison Wesley Publishing Co., Inc., Medical, Nursing Division *See* **Addison-Wesley Publishing Co., Inc.**

Addresso'set, *(Addresso'set; 0-916944),* P.O. Box 1530, Vallejo, CA 94590 Tel 707-644-6358 (SAN 208-5127).

Adelantre, *(ADELANTRE; 0-917288),* 4594 Bedford Ave., Brooklyn, NY 11235 (SAN 208-2268).

Adelphi Univ. Press, *(Adelphi Univ; 0-88461),* South Ave., Garden City, NY 11530 Tel 516-663-1120 (SAN 201-6826).

Adenine Press Inc., *(Adenine Pr; 0-940030),* 7 Ashford Dr., Albany, NY 12203 Tel 518-456-7982 (SAN 281-241X); Orders to: P.O. Box 355, Guilderland, NY 12084 (SAN 281-2428).

Adinkra Press, *(Adinkra Pr; 0-9611900),* 431 Coffield Ave., Napa, CA 94558 Tel 707-224-3300 (SAN 286-0279).

Adirondack Mountain Club, Inc., *(ADK Mtn Club; 0-935272),* 172 Ridge St., Glens Falls, NY 12801 Tel 518-793-7737 (SAN 204-7691).

Adirondack Museum, The, *(Adirondack Mus; 0-910020),* Blue Mountain Lake, NY 12812 Tel 518-352-7311 (SAN 201-7105).

Adirondack Trail Improvement Society, *(Adirondack Trail; 0-9600450),* St. Huberts, NY 12943 Tel 518-576-4427 (SAN 281-2436); Orders to: Box 64, Keene Valley, NY 12943 Tel 518-576-4427 (SAN 281-2444).

Adirondack Yesteryears, Inc., *(Adirondack Yes; 0-9601158),* Lake St. Extension-Drawer 209, Saranac Lake, NY 12983 Tel 518-891-3206 (SAN 209-4126).

Adizes Institute, Inc., The, *(Adizes Inst Inc; 0-89074),* 2001 Wilshire Blvd., Santa Monica, CA 90403 Tel 213-453-5593 (SAN 265-3729).

Adler, Alfred, Institute of Chicago, Inc., *(A Adler Inst; 0-918560),* 159 N. Dearborn St., Chicago, IL 60601 Tel 312-346-3458 (SAN 201-1956).

Adler Publishing Co., *(Adler Pub Co; 0-913623),* P.O. Box 9342, Rochester, NY 14604 (SAN 285-6808).

Adlerian Consulting & Counseling Center, *(Adlerian Coun),* 4984 Arboleda Dr., Fair Oaks, CA 95628 (SAN 237-9953).

Adler's Foreign Books, Inc., *(Adler; 0-8417),* 162 Fifth Ave., New York, NY 10010 Tel 212-691-5151 (SAN 201-2251).

Administrative Research Associates, *(ARA; 0-910022),* Irvine Town Ctr., Box 4211, Irvine, CA 92716 Tel 714-499-3939 (SAN 201-1891).

Admiral Nimitz Foundation, *(Adm Nimitz Foun),* P.O. Box 777, Fredericksburg, TX 78624 Tel 512-997-4379 (SAN 201-1883).

Admiralty Publishing House, Ltd., *(Admiralty Pub Hse; 0-913544),* P.O. Box 191, Annapolis, MD 21404 Tel 301-268-5291 (SAN 201-1905).

Adner Productions, *(Adner Prods),* 2500 New York Ave., Melville, NY 11747 (SAN 238-9037).

Adobe House Pubns, *(Adobe Hse Pubns; 0-938062),* 1131 N. Country Club Rd., Tucson, AZ 85716 (SAN 265-3737).

Adobe Press, *(Adobe Pr; 0-933004),* 515 Isleta Blvd. S.W., Box 12334, Albuquerque, NM 87105 Tel 505-873-1155 (SAN 213-022X).

Adonis Press, *(Adonis Pr; 0-932776),* Hawthorne Valley/Harlemville, Ghent, NY 12075 (SAN 218-463X).

Adoption Press, *(Adoption Pr),* P.O. Box 584, Minneapolis, MN 55440 Tel 612-378-1343 (SAN 219-7510).

Adrian Press, *(Adrian; 0-910024),* 157 W. 57th St., New York, NY 10019 Tel 212-265-6637 (SAN 201-226X).

Adrienne Pubns., Inc., *(Adrienne Pubns Inc; 0-9610534),* 123 Cheshire Rd., Bethany, CT 06525 Tel 203-393-2323 (SAN 263-9092).

Advance Book Program *See* **Addison-Wesley Publishing Co., Inc.**

Advance Book Program *See* **Benjamin-Cummings Publishing Co.**

Advance Planning Pubns., *(Advance Planning; 0-9600524),* Rte. 3, St. Croix Cove, Hudson, WI 54016 Tel 715-549-1070).

Advance Press, *(Advance Pr; 0-9609750),* 13905 Braun Rd., Golden, CO 80401 Tel 303-279-1522 (SAN 263-0249).

Advanced Acceptance, *(Adv Accept),* Box 3692, Quincy, IL 62301 (SAN 217-2216).

Advanced Backgammon Enterprises, *(Advanced Back; 0-9608566),* 256 S. Robertson Blvd., Beverly Hills, CA 90211 Tel 213-820-0678 (SAN 238-2210).

Advanced Computer Techniques Corp., Inc., *(Advanced Computer; 0-931336),* 437 Madison Ave., New York, NY 10022 (SAN 211-4089).

Advanced International Studies Institute (AISI), in Association with the Univ. of Miami, *(AISI; 0-933074),* 4330 East-West Highway, Suite 1122, Washington, DC 20014 Tel 301-951-0818 (SAN 201-8675).

Advanced Professional Seminars, Inc., *(Adv Prof Seminars; 0-9604532),* 7033 Ramsgate Place, Suite "A", Los Angeles, CA 90045 (SAN 220-0279); Orders to: P.O. Box 45791, Los Angeles, CA 90045 Tel 213-776-0113 (SAN 220-0287).

Advent Books, Inc, *(Advent NY; 0-89891),* 141 E. 44th St., Suite 511, New York, NY 10017 Tel 212-697-0887 (SAN 212-9973). Imprints: Plutarch Press (Plutarch Pr).

Advent Pubs., Inc., *(Advent; 0-911682),* P.O. Box A3228, Chicago, IL 60690 (SAN 201-2286).

Adventure Pubns., *(Adventure Pubns; 0-934860),* P.O. Box 96, Staples, MN 56479 Tel 218-894-3591 (SAN 212-7199).

Adventures in Living, *(Adventures in Living; 0-9605868),* 500 Vance St., Suite 12-G, Lakewood Park, CO 80226 Tel 303-234-0317 (SAN 216-2148); Dist. by: DeVorss & Company, P.O. Box 550, Marina Del Rey, CA 90291 Tel 213-870-7478 (SAN 168-9886).

Advert Publishing, Inc., *(Advert Pub; 0-9607410),* 120 Oak Brook Ctr. Mall, Oak Brook, IL 60521 Tel 312-355-1100 (SAN 239-1465).

Advertisement Digest, *(AD Digest; 0-939670),* P.O. Box 165, Morton Grove, IL 60053 Tel 312-965-1456 (SAN 216-9460).

Advocacy Press, *(Advocacy Pr; 0-911655),* P.O. Box 236, Santa Barbara, CA 93102 Tel 805-962-2728 (SAN 263-9114).

Advocate House, *(Advocate Hse; 0-910029),* P.O. Box 731, Ben Lomond, CA 95005 Tel 408-338-3354 (SAN 241-1946).

Advocate Press, *(Advocate; 0-911866),* Franklin Springs, GA 30639 Tel 404-245-7272 (SAN 201-2294).

Advocate Publishing Group, Avatar Media Associates, *(Advocate Pub Group; 0-89894),* P.O. Box 351, Reynoldsburg, OH 43068 (SAN 213-0238).

Aegean Park Press, *(Aegean Park Pr; 0-89412),* P.O. Box 2837, Laguna Hills, CA 92653 Tel 714-586-8811 (SAN 210-0231).

Aegis Publishing Co., *(Aegis Pub Co),* 3290 Sixth Ave. lf, San Diego, CA 92103 Tel 619-296-6751 (SAN 213-9030).

Aerial Photography Services, Inc., *(Aerial Photo),* 2300 Dunavant St., Charlotte, NC 28203 (SAN 214-2791).

Aerial Press, Inc., *(Aerial Pr; 0-942344),* P.O. Box 1360, Santa Cruz, CA 95061 Tel 408-425-8619 (SAN 239-7056).

Aero-Medical Consultants, Inc., *(Aero-Medical; 0-912522),* 10912 Hamlin Blvd., Largo, FL 33540 Tel 813-596-2551 (SAN 201-2316).

Aero Press Pubs., *(Aero Pr; 0-936450),* P.O. Box 2091, Fall River, MA 02722 Tel 617-644-2058 (SAN 207-0650).

Aero Products Research, Inc., *(Aero Products; 0-912682),* 11201 Hindry Ave., Los Angeles, CA 90045 Tel 213-641-7242 (SAN 205-5996).

Aero Pubs., Inc., *(Aero; 0-8168),* 329 W. Aviation Rd., Fallbrook, CA 92028 Tel 619-728-8456 (SAN 201-2308).

Aero Visions, Inc., *(Aero Vis; 0-941730),* 14962 Merced Circle, Irvine, CA 92714 Tel 714-559-7113 (SAN 239-1473).

Aerodrome Press, *(Aerodrome Pr; 0-935092),* Box 44, Story City, IA 50248 (SAN 213-4519).

Aerofacts, *(Aerofacts; 0-934268),* P.O. Box 11347, Las Vegas, NV 89111 Tel 702-458-3754 (SAN 213-2087).

Aerofax, Inc., *(Aerofax; 0-942548),* Box 5337, Austin, TX 78763 Tel 512-478-6555 (SAN 240-0642).

Aerographics, *(AeroGraphics; 0-9607814),* P.O. Box 189, Deltona, FL 32725 Tel 904-736-9779 (SAN 238-1370).

AeroTravel Research, *(AeroTravel Res),* P.O. Box 3694, Cranston, RI 02910 Tel 401-941-6140 (SAN 219-3442).

Aesculapius Pubs., Inc., *(Aesculapius Pubs; 0-918228),* Ten W. 66th St., Suite 6D, New York, NY 10023 Tel 212-595-0558 (SAN 210-1572).

Aesthetic Accidents Unltd., *(Aesthetic Accidents; 0-9603458),* 434 Greenwich St., New York, NY 10013 (SAN 213-4527).

Aesthetic Realism Foundation & Terrain Gallery, *(Aesthetic Realism; 0-911492),* 141 Greene St., New York, NY 10012 Tel 212-777-4490 (SAN 205-423X).

Affirmation Books, *(Affirmation; 0-89571),* 456 Hill St., Whitinsville, MA 01588 Tel 617-234-6266 (SAN 209-5211).

Africa Books *See* **Unipub**

Africa Fund, *(Africa Fund; 0-943428),* 198 Broadway, New York, NY 10038 Tel 212-962-1210 (SAN 224-0319).

Africa Research & Publications Project, *(Africa Res; 0-86543),* P.O. Box 1892, Trenton, NJ 08608 (SAN 265-3745).

African-American Institute, *(AAI; 0-87862),* 833 United Nations Plaza, New York, NY 10017 Tel 212-949-5666 (SAN 204-5540).

African American Trading Co., *(African Am Trading),* P.O. Box 43585, Los Angeles, CA 90043 Tel 213-294-2314 (SAN 216-2156).

African Policy Institute, *(African Policy),* 120 Wall St., Suite 1044, New York, NY 10005 (SAN 215-1235).

African Studies Assn., *(African Studies Assn; 0-918456),* Epstein Service Bldg., Brandeis Univ., Waltham, MA 02254 Tel 617-899-3079 (SAN 212-260X). *Imprints:* Crossroads Press (Crossroads).

African Studies Center, Boston Univ., *(Boston U African; 0-915118),* 125 Bay State Rd., Boston, MA 02215 (SAN 223-5927).

Africana Pub. *See* Holmes & Meier Pubs., Inc.

Africana Publishing Co., Div. of Holmes & Meier, *(Africana Pub; 0-8419),* 30 Irving Place, New York, NY 10003 (SAN 219-5828).

Africana Research Pubns., *(Africana Res; 0-933524),* 2580 Seventh Ave., New York, NY 10039 (SAN 212-470X).

Afro-Am Publishing Co., Inc., *(Afro-Am; 0-910030),* 910 S. Michigan Ave., Rm. 556, Chicago, IL 60605 Tel 312-922-1147 (SAN 201-2332).

A. G. Bell Assn. for the Deaf, *(Bell Assn Deaf; 0-88200),* 3417 Volta Place, N.W., Washington, DC 20007 Tel 202-337-5220 (SAN 216-0722).

Agadir Press, *(Agadir Pr; 0-913627),* P.O. Box 2015, Corvallis, OR 97339 Tel 503-929-5918 (SAN 286-0309); 424 S. 17th St., Philomath, OR 97370 (SAN 286-0317).

Agape, *(Agape IL; 0-916642),* 380 S. Main Place, Carol Stream, IL 60188 (SAN 217-2224).

Agathon Press Inc., *(Agathon; 0-87586),* 15 E. 26th St., New York, NY 10010 Tel 212-679-1674 (SAN 201-2367).

Ageless Books, *(Ageless Bks; 0-918482),* P.O. Box 6300, Beverly Hills, CA 90212 Tel 213-933-6338 (SAN 210-0215).

Agnew Tech-Tran, Inc., *(Agnew Tech-Tran),* P.O. Box 789, Woodland Hills, CA 91365 Tel 213-340-5147 (SAN 212-7202).

Agni Review, *(Agni Review),* P.O. Box 349, Cambridge, MA 02138 (SAN 219-4600).

Agni Yoga Society, Inc., *(Agni Yoga Soc; 0-933574),* 319 W. 107th St., New York, NY 10025 Tel 212-864-7752 (SAN 201-7121).

Agri-Fence, *(Agri-Fence),* P.O. Box 521, Rough & Ready, CA 96975 Tel 916-273-5492 (SAN 263-2519).

Agricultural Sciences Pubns. Univ. of California, *(Ag Sci Pubns; 0-931876),* 1422 Harbour Way S., Richmond, CA 94804 Tel 415-642-2431 (SAN 211-4771).

AgriData Resources, Inc., Subs. of Raintree Pubs., *(AgriData; 0-910939),* 2684 Sumac Ridge, White Bear Lake, MN 55110 Tel 612-777-0143 (SAN 266-1578).

Agrinde Pubns., Ltd., *(Agrinde Pubns; 0-9601068),* 820 Second Ave., New York, NY 10017 Tel 212-557-1590 (SAN 281-2452); Dist. by: Everest House, 79 Madison Ave., New York, NY 10016 Tel 212-685-6464 (SAN 281-2460).

Agriware Co., *(Agriware Co; 0-912859),* 3426 Wyndcrest DR., Elko, MN 55020 Tel 612-461-3429 (SAN 282-9614).

Ahday Pubs., Div. of the Neighbor-Link Inc., *(Ahday Pubs; 0-910031),* 5530 E. 79th St., Indianapolis, IN 46250 Tel 317-849-0404 (SAN 241-1954).

Ahsahta Press, *(Ahsahta Pr; 0-916272),* Dept. of English, Boise State Univ., Boise, ID 83725 Tel 208-385-1246 (SAN 207-9461); Orders to: Univ. Bookstore, Boise State Univ., Boise, ID 83725 Tel 208-385-1276 (SAN 207-947X).

Ai, *(Ai; 0-938454),* 118 E. 25th St., New York, NY 10010 Tel 212-674-8366 (SAN 215-8353).

Aid-U Publishing Co., *(Aid-U Pub; 0-940370),* 17220 W. Eight Mile Rd., Bldg. B, Suite 24, Southfield, MI 48075 Tel 313-835-6291 (SAN 217-149X).

Aids For Learning, *(Aids Learning; 0-9609636),* 2684 Sumac Ridge, St. Paul, MN 55110 (SAN 283-2445).

Aiga Pubns., *(AIGA Pubns; 0-943980),* P.O. Box 148, Laie, HI 96762 Tel 808-237-7047 (SAN 241-094X).

Aikido Fed. of California, *(Aikido Fed),* P.O. Box 10962, Costa Mesa, CA 92627 (SAN 263-9122).

Air Age, Inc., *(Air Age; 0-911295),* 837 Post Rd., Darien, CT 06820 Tel 203-655-7736 (SAN 266-1667).

Air-Plus Enterprises, *(Air-Plus Ent; 0-940726),* P.O. Box 367, Glassboro, NJ 08028 Tel 609-881-0724 (SAN 219-7545).

Aircraft Charter & Rental Tariff Information Service of North America, *(Aircraft Chart & Rent; 0-9603908),* Box 3000, Oak Park, IL 60303 Tel 217-546-1491 (SAN 213-9049).

Airman Universal Pubns., *(Airman Universal; 0-941978),* P.O. Box 41004, Atlanta, GA 30331 (SAN 239-5118).

Airmont Publishing Co., Inc., *(Airmont; 0-8049),* 22 E. 60th St., New York, NY 10022 (SAN 206-8710).

Airport Book Press, *(Airport Bk Pr; 0-935866),* 11205 Farmland Dr., Rockville, MD 20852 Tel 301-881-4996 (SAN 213-7178).

Airshow Pubs., *(Airshow Pubs; 0-9601506),* 2014 Homewood Rd., Annapolis, MD 21402 Tel 301-757-1806 (SAN 201-6974).

AJAY Enterprises, *(AJAY Ent; 0-939440),* P.O. Box 2018, Mosby Branch, Falls Church, VA 22042-0018 Tel 703-573-8220 (SAN 211-1209).

Akers, Mona J. Coole, *(Akers; 0-912706),* 219 S. Williams St., Denver, CO 80209 Tel 303-722-1892 (SAN 206-9075).

Akiba Press, *(Akiba Pr; 0-934764),* Box 13086, Oakland, CA 94661 Tel 415-339-1283 (SAN 212-0666).

Akili Books of America, *(Akili Bks of Amer; 0-9607296),* P.O. Box 1291, South Gate, CA 90280 Tel 213-635-7191 (SAN 239-1481).

Al-Anon Family Group Headquarters, Inc., *(Al-Anon; 0-910034),* 1 Park Ave., Second Fl., New York, NY 10016 Tel 212-683-1771 (SAN 201-2391).

AL-DEL Hobbies, Inc., *(AL-DEL; 0-933360),* 1933 Fairgrounds Rd., N.E., Salem, OR 97303 Tel 503-378-7909 (SAN 212-4718).

Al Fresco Enterprise, *(Al Fresco),* Postal Drawer 11530, Pueblo, CO 81001 Tel 303-545-9524 (SAN 211-5832).

Al Kitab Sudan & Rene Productions, *(Al Kitab Sudan; 0-914388),* 9846 A St., Oakland, CA 94603 (SAN 206-7196) Moved,Left No Forwarding Address.

Alabama Law Inst., *(AL Law Inst),* Rm. 326, Law Ctr., P. O. Box 1425, University, AL 35486 (SAN 000-0000).

Aladdin Books *See* Atheneum Pubs.

Alameda Poets, *(Alameda; 0-916734),* P.O. Box 1751, Alameda, CA 94501 (SAN 208-2667).

Alamo Press, *(Alamo Pr; 0-9605140),* 104 Garydale Court, Alamo, CA 94507 (SAN 216-2164).

Alandale Press, *(Alandale Pr; 0-937748),* R.D. 5, Ballston Rd., Amsterdam, NY 12010 Tel 518-842-5189 (SAN 216-0978).

Alaska Historical Commission, *(Alaska Hist; 0-943712),* Dept. of Education, Old City Hall, 524 W. 4th Ave., Suite 207, Anchorage, AK 99501 (SAN 240-9933).

Alaska Natural History Assn., *(Alaska Natural; 0-9602876),* 540 W. Fifth Ave., Anchorage, AK 99501 (SAN 223-5269).

Alaska Northwest Publishing Co., *(Alaska Northwest; 0-88240),* 130 Second Ave. S., Edmonds, WA 98020 Tel 206-774-4111 (SAN 201-2383).

Alaska Pacific Univ. Press, *(Alaska Pacific; 0-935094),* Alaska Pacific University, 4101 University Dr., Anchorage, AK 99508 Tel 907-561-1266 (SAN 215-2908).

Alaska State Council on the Arts, *(Alaska St Coun; 0-910615),* 619 Warehouse Ave., Suite 220, Anchorage, AK 99501 Tel 907-279-1558 (SAN 260-1591).

Alaskabooks, *(Alaskabks),* P.O. Box 1494, Juneau, AK 99802 Tel 907-586-3067 (SAN 201-6990).

Alba House, Div. of the Society of St. Paul, *(Alba; 0-8189),* 2187 Victory Blvd., Staten Island, NY 10314 Tel 212-761-0047 (SAN 201-2405).

Albacore Press, *(Albacore Pr; 0-9601716),* P.O. Box 355, Eastsound, WA 98245 (SAN 223-4181).

Albany County Historical Assn., *(Albany County; 0-89062),* 9 Ten Broeck Place, Albany, NY 12210 (SAN 219-7553); Dist. by: Publishing Center for Cultural Resources, 625 Broadway, New York, NY 10012 Tel 212-260-2010 (SAN 212-6036).

Albany Institute of History & Art, *(Albany Hist & Art),* 125 Washington Ave., Albany, NY 12210 Tel 518-463-4478 (SAN 204-7764).

Albany Public Library, *(Albany Pub Lib; 0-9605090),* 161 Washington Ave., Albany, NY 12210 (SAN 215-8361).

Albert House Publishing, *(Albert Hse Pub; 0-913553),* 30 Ayles Rd., Hyde Park, MA 02136 Tel 617-361-4398 (SAN 285-2071).

Albin, James R., *(Albin; 0-916210),* 431 Bridgeway, Sausalito, CA 94965 Tel 415-332-6438 (SAN 207-4850).

Albion, *(Albion NC; 0-932530),* Dept. of History, Appalachan State Univ., Boone, NC 28608 (SAN 212-2626).

Albion Albums, *(Albion Albums; 0-9604100),* P.O. Box 301, Albion, CA 95410 (SAN 216-2172).

Albion-American Books, *(Albion Am Bks),* P.O. Box 50011, Tucson, AZ 85703 (SAN 215-7225).

Albion Press, *(Albion Pr; 0-9606846),* 582 Stratford Ave., St. Louis, MO 63130 Tel 314-863-9285 (SAN 217-3220).

Alchemist/Light Publishing, *(Alchemist-Light; 0-9600650),* P.O. Box 5530, San Francisco, CA 94101 Tel 415-345-7021 (SAN 201-7164).

Alchemy Books, *(Alchemy Bks; 0-931290),* 681 Market, Suite 755, San Francisco, CA 94105 Tel 415-362-2708 (SAN 211-304X).

Alcoholics Anonymous World Services, Inc., *(AAWS; 0-916856),* 468 Park Ave. S., New York, NY 10016 Tel 212-686-1100 (SAN 210-7678); Orders to: Box 459, Grand Central Sta., New York, NY 10163 (SAN 215-0441).

Alcott Press, Inc., *(Alcott Pr; 0-936998),* P.O. Box 335, Edwardsville, IL 64025 Tel 618-656-7445 (SAN 215-2916).

Aldebaran Review, *(Aldebaran Rev; 0-917744),* 2209 California St., Berkeley, CA 94703 Tel 415-549-2456 (SAN 209-6978).

Alden, Jay, Pubs., *(J Alden; 0-914844),* P.O. Box 1295, 546 S. Hofgaarden St., La Puente, CA 91749 Tel 213-968-6424 (SAN 204-7780).

Alden, John, Bks., *(John Alden Bks; 0-9605818),* 187 Barmont Dr., Rochester, NY 14626 Tel 716-225-8534 (SAN 216-5678).

Alden Electronics & IRE Co. Inc., *(Alden Electronics; 0-96070004),* Washington St., Westboro, MA 01581 Tel 617-366-8851 (SAN 237-9287).

Alder Press Inc., *(Alder Pr; 0-9601940),* P.O. Box 25361, Houston, TX 77005 (SAN 212-0100).

Aldine Publishing Co., Inc., Div. of Walter De Gruyter, Inc., *(Aldine Pub; 0-202),* 200 Saw Mill River Rd., Hawthorne, NY 10532 Tel 914-747-0115 (SAN 212-4726).

Aldredg-Blair Inc., *(Aldredg-Blair; 0-942446),* P.O. Box 7195, Dallas, TX 75209 Tel 214-521-6724 (SAN 238-1389).

Alemany Press, The, *(Alemany Pr; 0-88084),* P.O. Box 5265, San Francisco, CA 94172 (SAN 240-1312).

Alembic Press, *(Alembic Pr; 0-934184),* 1424 Stanley Rd., Plainfield, IN 46168 Tel 317-839-8312 (SAN 281-2479); Dist. by: The Distributors, South Bend, IN 46618 (SAN 212-0364).

Aletheia Books *See* Univ. Pubns. of America, Inc.

Aletheia Pubs., Inc., *(Aletheia Pubs; 0-86717),* P.O. Box 1437, Tempe, AZ 85281 Tel 602-966-9175 (SAN 216-7824).

Alethes, *(Alethes; 0-930254),* P.O. Box 5842, Carmel, CA 93921 (SAN 202-3598).

Aleuthian/Phibil of Islands Association, Inc. (AANG ANGAGIN), *(Aleuthian; 0-9609308),* 1689 C St., Anchorage, AK 99501 Tel 907-276-2700 (SAN 260-0102).

Alexander Collection, The, *(Alex Collection; 0-913629),* P.O. Box 20760, Seattle, WN 98102 (SAN 283-247X).

Alexander Graham Bell Assn. for the Deaf, The, *(Alexander Graham; 0-88200),* 3417 Volta Place N.W., Washington, DC 20007 Tel 202-337-5220 (SAN 203-6924).

NAME INDEX

Alexandria Hse. Bks., Div. of Kephart Communications, Inc., *(Alexandria Hse; 0-932496)*, Kephart Communications, Inc., 901 N. Washington St., Suite 605, Alexandria, VA 22314 Tel 703-836-3313 (SAN 218-8104).

Alfa Sierra Pubns., *(Alfa Sierra; 0-9604728)*, P.O. Box 9636, San Diego, CA 92109 Tel 619-276-6291 (SAN 216-0137).

Alfred & Alfred Co., *(Alfred)*, 5260 Figueroa St., Suite 114, Los Angeles, CA 90037 (SAN 206-9636).

Alfred Publishing Co., Inc., *(Alfred Pub; 0-88284)*, 15335 Morrison St., Suite 235, Sherman Oaks, CA 91403 Tel 213-995-8811 (SAN 201-243X).

Algol Press, *(Algol Pr; 0-916186)*, P.O. Box 4175, New York, NY 10163 Tel 212-643-9011 (SAN 207-9445); Orders to: F&SF Book Co., 740 Delafield Ave., Staten Island, NY 10310 (SAN 207-9453).

Algorithmics, Inc., *(Algorithmics; 0-917448)*, 44 W. 62nd St., New York, NY 10023 Tel 212-246-2366 (SAN 201-2448).

ALI-ABA, *(ALI-ABA)*, 4025 Chestnut St., Philadelphia, PA 19104 Tel 215-243-1600 (SAN 201-5153).

Alicejamesbooks, *(Alicejamesbooks; 0-914086)*, 138 Mt. Auburn St., Cambridge, MA 02138 Tel 617-354-1408 (SAN 201-1158).

Alin Foundation Press, *(Alin Found Pr; 0-9606924)*, 2107 Dwight Way, Berkeley, CA 94704 Tel 415-845-4907 (SAN 212-0682).

Alinda Press, *(Alinda Pr; 0-933076)*, Box 553, Eureka, CA 95501 Tel 707-443-2510 (SAN 212-4734).

Aliotta & Manhart Pubs., *(Aliotta Manhart Pubs; 0-940498)*, P.O. Box 257, Lyons, IL 60534 Tel 312-472-5078 (SAN 217-1503).

Alised Enterprises, *(Alised; 0-913377)*, 7808 Maryknoll Ave., Bethesda, MD 20817 Tel 301-320-3306 (SAN 209-522X).

Alive Polarity Publications, *(Alive Polarity; 0-941732)*, 28779 Vialas Flores, Murrietaa, CA 92362 Tel 714-677-7451 (SAN 239-149X).

Alive Pubns. Ltd., *(Alive Pubns; 0-935572)*, 11 Park Place, New York, NY 10007 Tel 212-962-0316 (SAN 281-2495); Dist. by: Hippocrene Books, 171 Madison Ave., New York, NY 10016 Tel 212-685-4372 (SAN 213-2060).

All in All Alliance, Ltd., *(All in All; 0-912819)*, P.O. Box 910, New York, NY 10003 Tel 212-475-2048 (SAN 262-0006).

All This & Less Pubs., *(All This; 0-915682)*, Regents 509, NMSU, Las Cruces, NM 88003 (SAN 207-7795) Moved, Left No Forwarding Address.

Allanheld & Schram, *(Allanheld & Schram; 0-8390)*, 36 Park St., Montclair, NJ 07042 (SAN 212-7741).

Allanheld, Osmun & Co. Pubs., Inc., Div. of Littlefield, Adams & Co., *(Allanheld; 0-916672; 0-86598)*, 81 Adams Dr., Totowa, NJ 07512 Tel 201-256-8600 (SAN 211-724X).

Allan's, *(Allans; 0-88100)*, P.O. Box 4806, Inglewood, CA 90309 (SAN 265-3753).

Allegany Mountain Press, *(Allegany Mtn Pr; 0-931588)*, 111 N. Tenth St., Olean, NY 14760 Tel 716-372-0935 (SAN 211-5034).

Allegheny Press, *(Allegheny; 0-910042)*, 522 East St., California, PA 15419 (SAN 201-2456).

Allegro Publishing Co., *(Allegro Pub; 0-9601042)*, P.O. Box 39892, Los Angeles, CA 90039 Tel 213-665-6783 (SAN 201-2464).

Alleluia Press, *(Alleluia Pr; 0-911726)*, P.O. Box 103, Allendale, NJ 07401 Tel 201-327-3513 (SAN 202-3601); 672 Franklin Turnpike, NJ 07401 (SAN 202-361X).

Allen, J. A., & Co. Ltd., *(J A Allen; 0-85131)*, Dist. by: Sporting Book Center, Inc., Canaan, NY 12029 Tel 518-794-8998 (SAN 222-8734).

Allen, Milton F., *(M F Allen)*, 2989 McCully Dr. NE, Atlanta, GA 30345 Tel 404-939-1678 (SAN 239-4030).

Allen, Nathan, Publishing Co., *(N Allen Pub; 0-943586)*, 1503 Van Stone Dr., Milford, MI 48042 Tel 313-363-2206 (SAN 240-5806).

Allen & Unwin, Inc., *(Allen Unwin; 0-04; 0-86861)*, 9 Winchester Terrace, Winchester, MA 01890 Tel 617-729-0830 (SAN 210-3362); Orders to: 300 Ratitan Center, Edison, NJ 08818 Tel 201-225-5555 (SAN 210-3370).

Allen Group, Inc., the, *(Allen Group; 0-943402)*, 145 E. Center St., Provo, UT 84061 Tel 801-373-8000 (SAN 240-5792).

Allen Press, Inc., *(Allen Pr; 0-935868)*, P.O. Box 368, Lawrence, KS 66044 (SAN 213-7186).

Allenson-Breckinridge Books, *(Allenson-Breckinridge; 0-8401)*, P.O. Box 447, Geneva, AL 36340 (SAN 162-4903).

Allerton Press, Inc., *(Allerton Pr; 0-89864)*, 150 Fifth Ave., New York, NY 10011 (SAN 239-4049).

Allgood Books, *(Allgood Bks)*, P.O. Box 1329, Jackson, MS 39205 Tel 601-355-5419 (SAN 208-1318).

Alliance College, *(Alliance Coll)*, Cambridge Springs, PA 16403 (SAN 216-0862).

Alliance Pubs., *(Alliance Pubs)*, P.O. Box 25004, Fort Lauderdale, FL 33320 Tel 305-722-5361 (SAN 213-3768).

Allied Enterprises, *(Allied Ent; 0-9605082)*, P.O. Box 8050, Chicago, IL 60680 (SAN 238-9045).

Allied Research Society, Inc., *(Allied Res Soc; 0-912984)*, 11057 New River Circle, Rancho Cordova, CA 95670 Tel 916-635-7728 (SAN 201-2480).

Allison Enterprises, *(Allison Ent; 0-918324)*, P.O. Box 200, Franklin, NJ 07416 Tel 201-827-5104 (SAN 210-024X).

Allison Pubs., *(Allison Pubs)*, 1 La Playa, Box 733, Cochise, AZ 85606 (SAN 207-2009).

Allnut Publishing, *(Allnut Pub; 0-934374)*, P.O. Box 24 7, Indian Hills, CO 80454 (SAN 221-962X).

Allowance, Inc., *(Allowance; 0-9604228)*, 1516 Bonnie Brae, Denton, TX 76201 (SAN 214-2805).

Allwyn Press, *(Allwyn Pr; 0-911768)*, P.O. Box 240, Washington Bridge Sta., New York, NY 10033 Tel 212-796-0498 (SAN 201-2502).

Ally Press, *(Ally Pr; 0-915408)*, P.O. Box 30340, Dept. BP, St. Paul, MN 55175 (SAN 207-7116).

Allyn & Bacon, Inc., Div. of Esquire, Inc., *(Allyn; 0-205)*, 7 Wells Ave., Newton, MA 02159 Tel 617-964-5530 (SAN 201-2510); Orders to: College Division, Link Dr., Rockleigh, NJ 07647 Tel 800-526-4799 (SAN 201-2529).

Alma Historical Society, *(Alma Hist Soc; 0-9604684)*, P.O. Box 87, Alma, WI 54610 (SAN 216-0986).

Almar Press, *(Almar; 0-930256)*, 4105 Marietta Dr., Binghamton, NY 13903 Tel 607-722-6251 (SAN 210-5713) Tel 607-722-0265.

Almo Pubns., *(Almo Pubns; 0-89705)*, 1358 N. La Brea, Hollywood, CA 90028 (SAN 211-6995); Dist. by: Columbia Pictures Pubns., 16333 N.W. 54th Ave., Hialeah, FL 33014 Tel 800-327-7643 (SAN 203-042X).

Aloe Press, Inc., *(Aloe Pr Inc; 0-9604014)*, P.O. Box 52172, Atlanta, GA 30355 Tel 404-351-6779 (SAN 223-4467).

Aloha Press, *(Aloha Pr; 0-943758)*, P.O. Box 26214, Honolulu, HI 96825 Tel 808-395-7369 (SAN 238-0382).

Aloray Inc., *(Aloray; 0-913690)*, 175 W. Carver St., Huntington, NY 11743 Tel 516-549-5746 (SAN 201-1190).

Alpenrose Press, *(Alpenrose Pr; 0-9603624)*, Box 499, Silverthorne, CO 80498 Tel 303-468-6273 (SAN 222-2612).

Alpert, Burt, *(Alpert; 0-9600642)*, 877 26th Ave., San Francisco, CA 94121 (SAN 201-1204).

Alpha Centauri Pubs., *(Alpha Centauri; 0-940332)*, P.O. Box 1011, Highland, NY 12528 Tel 914-691-7014 (SAN 220-3162).

Alpha Communications, *(Alpha Communications; 0-9605662)*, 933 W. Pico Blvd., Santa Monica, CA 90405 Tel 213-450-9777 (SAN 237-9260).

Alpha Gamma Arts, *(Alpha Gamma; 0-941716)*, 2625 Kiowa Court, P.O. Box 4671, Walnut Creek, CA 94596 Tel 415-935-7409 (SAN 281-2517); Dist. by: Bookpeople, 2940 Seventh St, Berkeley, CA 94710 Tel 415-549-3030 (SAN 168-9517); Dist. by: China Books, 2929-24th St., San Francisco, CA 94110 Tel 415-282-2994 (SAN 169-0167); Dist. by: Inland Book Company, P.O. Box 261, East Haven, CT 06512 Tel 203-467-4257 (SAN 200-4151).

Alpha Iota of Pi Lambda Theta, Pubns., *(Alpha Iota; 0-914522)*, 2260 N. Orange Grove Ave., Pomona, CA 91767 Tel 714-626-5065 (SAN 206-3204).

Alpha Omega, *(Alpha and Omega; 0-941734)*, 1530 Stiner, Coeur d'Alene, ID 83814 Tel 208-667-3382 (SAN 239-1503).

Alpha-Omega Book Publishers, Inc., *(Alpha-Omega Bk; 0-938764)*, 605 W. 113th St. Suite 82, New York, NY 10025 Tel 212-864-4638 (SAN 237-9279).

Alpha Press, *(Alpha Pr; 0-914620)*, 3574 Clinton St., Gardenville, NY 14224 Tel 716-674-6183 (SAN 201-1212).

Alpha Pubns., *(Alpha IN; 0-937400)*, P.O. Box 655, Winona Lake, IN 46590 (SAN 216-2180).

Alpha Pubns., Inc., *(Alpha Pubns; 0-912404)*, 1079 De Kalb Pike, Blue Bell, PA 19422 Tel 215-277-6342 (SAN 201-2537).

Alpha Pyramis Publishing Co, Inc., Div. of Bibliotheca Press, *(Alpha Pyramis Pub Co; 0-913597)*, 153 S. Bradford St., Dover, DE 19901 (SAN 282-5694); Orders to: Affinity Publishers Services, Box 600531, Houston, TX 77260 (SAN 282-5708).

Alphabet Press, *(Alphabet Pr; 0-9602690)*, P.O. Box 6180, Boston, MA 02209 Tel 617-323-7942 (SAN 213-2753) Do Not Confuse with Alphabet Quincy.

Alphabet Press, MA, *(Alphabet MA; 0-940032)*, 60 N. Mina St., Natick, MA 01760 Tel 617-655-9696 (SAN 217-1449).

Alpine Enterprises, *(Alpine Ent)*, P. O. Box 766, Dearborn, MI 48121 Tel 313-864-7200 (SAN 210-6973).

Alpine Fine Arts Collection, Ltd., *(Alpine Fine Arts; 0-933516; 0-88168)*, 164 Madison Ave., New York, NY 10016 Tel 212-679-7072 (SAN 214-1809).

Alpine Guild, *(Alpine Guild; 0-931712)*, 508 N. Oak Park Ave., Oak Park, IL 60302 (SAN 281-2541); Orders to: P.O. Box 183, Oak Park, IL 60303 (SAN 281-255X).

Alpine Pubns., *(Alpine Pubns; 0-931866)*, 214 19th St. S.E., Loveland, CO 80537 Tel 303-667-2017 (SAN 211-478X).

Alpine-Tahoe Press, *(Alpine-Tahoe; 0-9604574)*, Box 1484, Tahoe City, CA 95730 Tel 916-583-3273 (SAN 211-2108).

Alta Gaia Books, *(Alta Gaia Bks; 0-933432)*, P.O. Box 541, Millerton, NY 12546 (SAN 222-6642).

Alta Napa Press, *(Alta Napa)*, 1969 Mora Ave., Calistoga, CA 94515 Tel 707-942-4444 (SAN 216-3276).

Altai Publishers, *(Altai Pub; 0-9609710)*, P.O.Box 1972, Flagstaff, AZ 86002 Tel 602-779-0491 (SAN 263-0281).

Altair Press, *(Altair Pr; 0-934768)*, P.O. Box 1286, Boulder, CO 80306 Tel 303-494-6405 (SAN 209-1585).

Altair Publishing Co., *(Altair Pub Co; 0-9604976)*, 217 S. Louis St., Mt. Prospect, IL 60056 (SAN 215-935X).

Altamira/Lascaux Pubs., *(Altamira Lascaux)*, P.O. Box 564, Housatonic, MA 01236 (SAN 210-606X).

Altar Books, Altar Records, Altar Film Productions, *(Altar Bks; 0-941148)*, P.O. Box 404, Luray, VA 22835 (SAN 239-5126).

Altara Group, The, *(Altara Group; 0-9607106)*, Seven Charles Court, P.O. Box 24, N. Haven, CT 06473 Tel 203-239-9400 (SAN 238-9363).

Altarinda Books, *(Altarinda Bks; 0-9607896)*, 13 Estates Dr., Orinda, CA 94563 Tel 415-254-3830 (SAN 238-1397).

Alternate Energy Publishing Co., *(Alternate Energy; 0-930086)*, P.O. Box 26507, Albuquerque, NM 87125 Tel 505-873-2084 (SAN 210-6981).

Alternative Sources of Energy, Inc., *(ASEI; 0-917328)*, 107 S. Central Ave., Milaca, MN 56353 Tel 612-983-6892 (SAN 208-5151).

Alternatives, *(Alternatives; 0-914966),* 4274 Oaklawn Dr., Jackson, MS 39206 Tel 601-366-8468 (SAN 206-8915).

Alternatives in Religious Education, Inc., *(AIRE; 0-86705),* 3945 S. Oneida St., Denver, CO 80237 Tel 303-758-4017 (SAN 216-6534).

Alyson Pubns., Inc., *(Alyson Pubns; 0-932870),* P.O. Box 2783, Boston, MA 02208 Tel 617-542-5679 (SAN 213-6546).

Am-Fem Co., *(AM-FEM Co; 0-9607232),* P.O. Box 93, Cooper Sta., New York, NY 10276 (SAN 239-152X).

Am-Law Publishing Corp., *(Am Law Pub; 0-9606682),* 2 Park Ave., New York, NY 10016 Tel 212-561-8210 (SAN 219-7049).

Amadeo Concha Press, *(Amadeo Concha; 0-939448),* 832 Arkansas St., Lawrence, KS 66044 Tel 913-842-6393 (SAN 216-5864).

Amarta Press, *(Amarta Pr; 0-935100),* P.O. Box 202, West Franklin, NH 03235 Tel 603-934-2420 (SAN 213-2761).

Amaryllis Press, *(Amaryllis Pr; 0-89275; 0-943276),* 212 W. 79 St., New York, NY 10024 Tel 212-496-6460 (SAN 201-4300) Name Formerly Benjamin Blom.

Amata Graphics, *(Amata Graphics; 0-931224),* P.O. Box 12313, Portland, OR 97212 Tel 503-231-8540 (SAN 211-2094).

Amateur Athletic Union of the United States, *(AAU Pubns; 0-89710),* 3400 W. 86th St., Indianapolis, IN 46268 Tel 317-872-2900 (SAN 204-7853).

Amato, Frank, Pubns., *(F Amato Pubns; 0-936608),* P.O. Box 02112, Portland, OR 97202 Tel 503-236-2305 (SAN 214-3372).

Amazon Press, *(Amazon Pr; 0-931458),* 1101 Keeler Ave., Berkeley, CA 94708 (SAN 210-1106); Dist. by: Bookpeople, 2940 Seventh St., Berkeley, CA 94710 Tel 415-549-3033 (SAN 168-9517).

Ambassador Pubns., *(Ambassador Pubns),* P.O. Box 4206, Clearwater, FL 33518 (SAN 202-4780).

Amber Beetle Press, *(Amber Beetle; 0-937432),* 6315 Camac St., Philadelphia, PA 19141 (SAN 240-818X).

Amber Publishing Corp., *(Amber Pub; 0-916788),* 21 Hudson St., New York, NY 10013 Tel 212-431-9675 (SAN 208-5178).

Ambleside Publishers, Inc., *(Ambleside; 0-913011),* 2122 E. Concorda Dr., Tempe, AZ 85282 Tel 602-967-3457 (SAN 283-2887).

Ameco Publishing Corp., *(Ameco; 0-912146),* 275 Hillside Ave., Williston Park, NY 11596 Tel 516-741-5030 (SAN 202-4199).

Amen Publishing Co., *(Amen Pub; 0-941204),* Box 3612, Arcadia, CA 91006 Tel 213-355-9336 (SAN 217-3239).

Amereon Ltd., *(Amereon Ltd; 0-88411; 0-89190),* P.O. Box 1200, Mattituck, NY 11952 Tel 516-298-5100 (SAN 204-2413).

American Academic Assn. for Peace in the Middle East, *(AAAPME; 0-917158),* 330 Seventh Ave. Suite 606, New York, NY 10001 Tel 212-563-2580 (SAN 208-5186).

American Academy & Institute of Arts & Letters, *(Am Acad Inst Arts; 0-915974),* 633 W. 155th St., New York, NY 10032 Tel 212-368-5900 (SAN 204-7888).

American Academy of Advertising, *(Am Acad Advert; 0-931030),* 395 JKB, Institute of Business Management, Brigham Young Univ., Provo, UT 84602 Tel 801-378-2080 (SAN 212-1786).

American Academy of Osteopathy, *(Am Acad Osteopathy; 0-940668),* P.O. Box 750, Newark, OH 43055 Tel 614-349-8701 (SAN 218-5296).

American Academy of Pediatrics, *(AM Acad Pediat; 0-910761),* 1801 Hinman Ave., Evanston, IL 60201 (SAN 265-3540).

American Academy of Political & Social Science, *(Am Acad Pol Soc Sci; 0-87761),* 3937 Chestnut St., Philadelphia, PA 19104 Tel 215-386-4594 (SAN 201-1239); Dist. by: Sage Publications, Inc., 275 S. Beverly Dr., Beverly Hills, CA 90212 Tel 213-274-8003 (SAN 204-7217).

American Accounting Assn., *(Am Accounting),* 5717 Bessie Dr., Sarasota, FL 33583 Tel 813-921-7747 (SAN 204-790X).

American Alliance for Health, Physical Education, Recreation & Dance, Affiliate of National Education Assn., *(AAHPERD; 0-88314),* 1900 Association Dr., Reston, VA 22091 Tel 703-476-3400 (SAN 202-3237).

American Anthropological Assn., *(Am Anthro Assn),* Pubns. Dept., 1703 New Hampshire Ave., N.W., Washington, DC 20009 Tel 202-232-8800 (SAN 202-4284).

American Antiquarian Society, *(Am Antiquarian; 0-912296),* 185 Salisbury St., Worcester, MA 01609 Tel 617-755-5221 (SAN 206-474X); Dist. by: Univ. Press of Virginia, P.O. Box 3608, University Sta., Charlottesville, VA 22903 (SAN 202-5361).

American Arbitration Association, *(Am Arbitration),* 140 W. 51st St., New York, NY 10020 Tel 212-484-4000 (SAN 225-0802).

American Assembly, *(Am Assembly),* Columbia University, New York, NY 10027 (SAN 209-6471).

American Assn. for Adult & Continuing Education, *(A A A C E; 0-88379),* 1201 16th St., N.W., Suite 301, Washington, DC 20036 Tel 202-822-7866 (SAN 201-2278).

American Assn. for Chinese Studies, *(Am Assn Chinese Stud; 0-9606594),* New York Univ., Dept. of Politics, 25 Waverly Pl., New York, NY 10003 Tel 212-598-3275 (SAN 219-757X).

American Assn. for Clinical Chemistry, *(Am Assn Clinical Chem; 0-915274),* 1725 K St., N.W., Suite 1010, Washington, DC 20006 (SAN 214-2813).

American Association for State & Local History, *(AASLH; 0-910050),* 708 Berry Rd., Nashville, TN 37204 (SAN 201-1972).

American Assn. for the Advancement of Science, *(AAAS; 0-87168),* 1515 Massachusetts Ave., N.W., Washington, DC 20005 Tel 202-467-4400 (SAN 201-193X).

American Association for the Advancement of Science, Pacific Division, *(AAASPD; 0-934394),* c/o California Academy of Sciences, Golden Gate Park, San Francisco, CA 94118 (SAN 204-3661).

American Association of Blood Banks, *(Am Assn Blood; 0-914404),* Suite 600, 1117 N. 19th St/, Arlington, VA 22209 Tel 703-528-8200 (SAN 201-1573).

American Assn. of Cereal Chemists, *(Am Assn Cereal Chem; 0-913250),* 3340 Pilot Knob Rd., St. Paul, MN 55121 Tel 612-454-7250 (SAN 204-7934).

American Association of Colleges for Teacher Education, *(AACTE; 0-910052; 0-89333),* One Dupont Circle, Suite 610, Washington, DC 20036 Tel 202-293-2450 (SAN 204-3882).

American Association of Colleges of Osteopathic Medicine, *(Am Assn Coll Osteo Med),* 4720 Montgomery Ln, Washington, DC 20014 Tel 301-654-5600 (SAN 224-4063).

American Association of Community & Junior Colleges, *(Am Assn Comm Jr Coll; 0-87117),* 1 Dupont Circle, N.W., Washington, DC 20036 Tel 202-293-7050 (SAN 201-7253).

American Association of Correctional Officers, *(Am Correctional Officers),* 1474 Willow Ave., Des Plaines, IL 60016 Tel 312-751-6068 (SAN 224-036X).

American Association of Cost Engineers, *(Am Assn Cost Engineers),* 308 Monogahela Bldg., Morgantown, WV 26505 (SAN 214-0942).

American Association of Diabetes Educators, *(Am Assn Diabetes Ed),* Box 56, Pitman, NJ 08071 Tel 609-589-4831 (SAN 224-3091).

American Association of Engineering Societies, *(AAES; 0-87615),* 345 E. 47th St., New York, NY 10017 Tel 212-705-7840 (SAN 201-386X).

American Association of Homes for the Aging, *(Am Assn Homes),* 1050 17th St N.W., Suite 770, Washington, DC 20036 Tel 202-296-5960 (SAN 260-3918).

American Association of School Administrators, *(Am Assn Sch Admin),* 1801 N. Moore St., Arlington, VA 22209 Tel 703-528-0700 (SAN 202-3628).

American Assn. of State Highway & Transportation Officials, *(AASHTO),* 444 N. Capitol St., N. W., Washington, DC 20001 Tel 202-624-5800 (SAN 204-7969).

American Association on Mental Deficiency, *(Am Assn Mental; 0-940898),* 5101 Wisconsin Ave., N.W., Washington, DC 20016 Tel 202-686-5400 (SAN 206-961X).

American Astronautical Society, *(Am Astronaut; 0-87703),* Orders to: Univelt, Inc., P.O. Box 28130, San Diego, CA 92128 Tel 714-746-4005 (SAN 201-2561).

American Atheist Press, *(Am Atheist; 0-911826; 0-910309),* P.O. Box 2117, Austin, TX 78768-2117 Tel 512-458-1244 (SAN 206-7188).

American Automobile Assn., *(AAA; 0-916748),* 8111 Gatehouse Rd., Falls Church, VA 22047 Tel 703-222-6345 (SAN 208-5194).

American Bando Assn., *(Am Bando Assn; 0-9608394),* Catonsville Community College, Catonsville, MD 21228 Tel 301-788-6149 (SAN 240-5830).

American Bankers Assn., *(Am Bankers; 0-89982),* 1120 Connecticut Ave. N.W., Washington, DC 20036 Tel 202-467-6660 (SAN 208-4554).

American Baptist Historical Society, *(Am Baptist; 0-910056),* 1106 S. Goodman St., Rochester, NY 14620 Tel 716-473-1740 (SAN 201-257X).

American Bar Association, *(Amer Bar Assn; 0-89707),* 1155 E. 60th St., Chicago, IL 60637 Tel 312-947-3607 (SAN 211-4798).

American Bar Foundation, *(Am Bar Foun; 0-910058; 0-910059),* 1155 E. 60th St., Chicago, IL 60637 Tel 312-667-4700 (SAN 201-2588).

American Bible Society, *(Am Bible; 0-8267)* 1865 Broadway, New York, NY 10023 Tel 212-581-7400 (SAN 203-5189).

American Bibliographical Center-Clio Press, *(ABC-Clio; 0-87436),* Riviera Campus 2040 Alameda Padre Serra, Box 4397, Santa Barbara, CA 93103 Tel 805-963-4221 (SAN 301-5467).

American Biographical Center, *(Am Biog Ctr; 0-9601168),* P.O. Box 473, Williamsburg, VA 23185 Tel 804-725-2234 (SAN 210-0266).

American Biographical Institute, *(Am Biog Inst; 0-934544),* 205 W. Martin St., P.O. Box 226, Raleigh, NC 27602 Tel 919-832-2001 (SAN 213-0092).

American Blade Book Service, *(Am Blade Bk Serv; 0-911881),* 112 Lee Parkway Dr., Stonewall Bldg. ,Suite 104, Chattanooga, TN 37421 (SAN 265-3559).

American Blood Commission, *(Am Blood Comm; 0-935498),* 1901 N. Fort Myer Dr., Suite 300, Arlington, VA 22209 Tel 703-522-8414 (SAN 213-7194).

American Book Co., Div. of International Thomson Educational Publishing, Inc., *(ABC; 0-278),* 135 W. 50th St., New York, NY 10020 Tel 212-265-8700 (SAN 201-534X); Orders to: 7625 Empire Dr., Florence, KY 41042 Tel 800-354-9815 (SAN 201-5358).

American Bureau of Metal Statistics, *(Am Bur Metal; 0-910064),* 420 Lexington Ave., Rm. 420, New York, NY 10017 Tel 212-867-9450 (SAN 201-1581).

American Business Communication Assn., *(Am Busn Comm Assn; 0-931874),* 100 English Bldg., 608 S. Wright St., Urbana, IL 61801 Tel 217-333-0458 (SAN 211-9382).

American Business Consultants, Inc., *(Am Busn Consult; 0-937152),* 1540 Nuthatch Lane, Sunnyvale, CA 94087 Tel 408-732-8931 (SAN 214-3399).

American Camping Assn., *(Am Camping; 0-87603),* Bradford Woods, Martinsville, IN 46151 Tel 317-342-8456 (SAN 201-2596).

American-Canadian Pubs., Inc., *(Am Canadian; 0-913844),* Drawer 2078, Portales, NM 88130 Tel 505-356-4082 (SAN 201-260X).

American Canal & Transportation Center, *(Am Canal & Transport; 0-933788),* 809 Rathton Rd., York, PA 17403 Tel 717-843-4035 (SAN 212-4750).

American Cancer Society, Colorado Div., Inc., *(Am Cancer Colo),* 1809 E. 18th Ave., Denver, CO 80218 (SAN 217-300X).

American Cancer Society, Iowa Div. Inc., *(Am Cancer Iowa),* Box 980, Mason City, IA 50401 (SAN 217-2771).

American Cancer Society, Maryland Div., Inc., *(Am Cancer MD),* 200 E. Joppa Rd., Towson, MD 21204 (SAN 217-2860).

American Cancer Society, Massachusetts Div., Inc., *(Am Cancer Mass),* 247 Commonwealth Ave., Boston, MA 02116 (SAN 217-278X).

American Cancer Society, Michigan Div., Inc., *(Am Cancer Mich),* 1205 E. Saginaw St., Lansing, MI 48906 (SAN 217-2852).

American Cancer Society, Minnesota Division, Inc., *(Am Cancer Minn)*, 3316 W. 66th. St., Minneapolis, MN 55435 Tel 612-871-2111 (SAN 219-9963).

American Cancer Society, Mississippi Div., Inc., *(Am Cancer MS)*, 345 N. Mart Plaza, Jackson, MS 39206 (SAN 217-2828).

American Cancer Society, Missouri Div., Inc., *(Am Cancer MO)*, P.O. Box 1066, Jefferson City, MO 65102 (SAN 217-2844).

American Cancer Society, New Hampshire Div., Inc., *(Am Cancer NH)*, 686 Mast Rd., Manchester, NH 03102 (SAN 217-2836).

American Cancer Society, New York Div., Inc., *(Am Cancer Forest Hills)*, 111-15 Queens Blvd., Forest Hills, NY 11375 (SAN 217-2763).

American Cancer Society, New York Div., Inc., *(Am Cancer Syracuse)*, 6725 Lyons St., East Syracuse, NY 13057 (SAN 217-2801).

American Cancer Society, Oregon Div., Inc., *(Am Cancer Oreg)*, 910 N.E. Union Ave., Portland, OR 97232 (SAN 217-281X).

American Cancer Society, Wyoming Div., Inc., *(Am Cancer WY)*, 506 Shoshoni, Cheyenne, WY 82001 (SAN 217-2798).

American Casting Education Foundation, Inc., *(Am Casting; 0-9605960)*, 4910 Woodmere Dr., Lakeland, FL 33803 Tel 813-644-3104 (SAN 281-2614); Dist. by: ACEF Publications, P.O. Box 261, Great Falls, VA 22066-0261 (SAN 282-6666); Dist. by: American Casting Assn., 2341 Fifth Ave., San Rafael, CA 94901 (SAN 281-2630).

American Catholic Philosophical Association, *(Am Cath Philo; 0-918090)*, Catholic Univ. of America, Washington, DC 20064 Tel 202-635-5518 (SAN 203-6290).

American Catholic Press, *(Am Cath Pr; 0-915866)*, 1223 Rossell Ave., Oak Park, IL 60302 Tel 312-386-1366 (SAN 202-4411).

American Century Series See Hill & Wang, Inc.

American Ceramic Society, Inc, *(Am Ceramic; 0-916094)*, 65 Ceramic Dr., Columbus, OH 43214 Tel 614-268-8645 (SAN 201-6958).

American Chemical Dependency Society, *(Am Chem Dep)*, 5001 Olson Memorial Hwy., Minneapolis, MN 55422 Tel 612-546-5001 (SAN 277-6537).

American Chemical Society, *(Am Chemical; 0-8412)*, 1155 16th St., N.W., Washington, DC 20036 Tel 202-872-4600 (SAN 201-2626).

American Chiropractic Academic Press, *(Am Chiro Acad; 0-936948)*, 6840 N.W. 16th, Suite 146, Oklahoma City, OK 73127 (SAN 215-6180).

American Chiropractic Assn., *(Am Chiro Assn; 0-9606618)*, 1916 Wilson Blvd., Arlington, VA 22201 Tel 219-7588).

American Christian Press, The Way International, *(Am Christian; 0-910068)*, P.O. Box 328, New Knoxville, OH 45871 Tel 419-753-2523 (SAN 206-9628).

American Classical College Press, *(Am Classical Coll Pr; 0-913314; 0-89266)*, P.O. Box 4526, Albuquerque, NM 87106 Tel 505-843-7749 (SAN 201-2618).

American Coalition of Citizens with Disabilities, Inc., *(Am Coalition Citizens Disabil; 0-933526)*, 1200 15th St., N.W., Suite 201, Washington, DC 20005 Tel 202-785-4265 (SAN 223-677X).

American College of Apothecaries, *(Am Coll Apothecaries; 0-934322)*, 874 Union Ave., Memphis, TN 38163 (SAN 217-0868).

American College of Heraldry, Inc., The, *(Am Coll Heraldry; 0-9605668)*, P.O. Box CG, University, AL 35486 (SAN 216-0994).

American College of Obstetricians & Gynecologists, *(Am Coll Obstetric)*, 600 Maryland Ave., S.W., Washington, DC 20024 Tel 202-638-5577 (SAN 284-9623); 900 Auburn Rd., Pontiac, MI 48057 Tel 313-332-6360 (SAN 284-9631).

American College Testing Program, *(Am Coll Testing; 0-937734)*, 2201 N. Dodge St., P.O. Box 168, Iowa City, IA 52243 Tel 319-337-1409 (SAN 204-8027).

American College, the, *(Amer College; 0-943590)*, 270 Bryn Mawr Ave., Bryn Mawr, PA 19010 Tel 215-896-4548 (SAN 240-5822).

American Community Cultural Center Association, *(Am Community Cultural)*, 19 Foothills Dr, Pompton Plains, NJ 07444 Tel 201-244-4270 (SAN 225-3011).

American Compensation Association, *(Am Compensation)*, P O Box 1176, Scottsdale, AZ 85252 (SAN 227-0080).

American Concrete Institute, *(ACI; 0-87031)*, 22400 W. Seven Mile Rd., P.O. Box 19150, Detroit, MI 48219 Tel 313-532-2600 (SAN 203-1450).

American Consulting Engineers Council, *(Am Consul Eng; 0-910090)*, 1015 15th St., N.W., Washington, DC 20005 (SAN 206-8508).

American Council for Nationalities Service, *(ACNS; 0-915384)*, 20 W. 40th St., New York, NY 10018 (SAN 218-4613).

American Council for the Arts, *(Am Council Arts; 0-915400)*, 570 Seventh Ave., New York, NY 10018 Tel 212-354-6655 (SAN 207-3706).

American Council on Consumer Interests, *(Am Coun Consumer)*, Univ of Missouri, Columbia, MO 62511 Tel 314-822-3817 (SAN 225-641X).

American Council on Education, *(ACE; 0-8268)*, 1 Dupont Circle, Washington, DC 20036 Tel 202-833-4785 (SAN 201-2170).

American Council on Marijuana & Other Psychoactive Drugs, Inc., the, *(Am Council On Marijuana; 0-942348)*, 6193 Executive Blvd., Rockville, MD 20852 Tel 212-758-8060 (SAN 239-7099).

American Craft Council, *(Am Craft; 0-88321)*, 401 Park Ave. South, New York, NY 10016 Tel 212-696-0710 (SAN 201-2634).

American Deafness & Rehabilitation Association, *(Am Deaf & Rehab; 0-914494)*, 814 Thayer Ave., Silver Spring, MD 20910 Tel 301-589-0880 (SAN 201-8918).

American Dental Assn., *(Am Dental; 0-910074)*, 211 E. Chicago Ave., Chicago, IL 60611 Tel 312-440-2741 (SAN 202-4519).

American Developing Industries, *(Am Developing; 0-8187)*, 10520 First Way N., St. Petersburg, FL 33702 (SAN 217-2232).

American Dietetic Association, *(Am Dietetic Assn)*, 430 N. Michigan Ave., Chicago, IL 60611 Tel 312-280-5000 (SAN 228-1341).

American Dynamics Corp., *(Am Dynamics NY; 0-9608962)*, Box 11, Cathedral Sta., New York, NY 10025 Tel 212-749-3546 (SAN 218-6160).

American Educational Research Assn., *(Am Educ Res; 0-935302)*, 1230 17th St., N.W., Washington, DC 20036 Tel 202-223-9485 (SAN 203-1191).

American Elsevier Publishing Co., Inc., *(Am Elsevier; 0-444)*, Orders to: 52 Vanderbilt Ave., New York, NY 10017 Tel 212-867-9040 (SAN 201-2642) Name Changed to Elsevier-North Holland Publishing Co.

American Enterprise Institute for Public Policy Research, *(Am Enterprise; 0-8447)*, 1150 17th St., N.W., Washington, DC 20036 Tel 202-862-5800 (SAN 202-4527).

American Entomological Institute, *(Am Entom Inst)*, 5950 Warren Rd., Ann Arbor, MI 48105 Tel 313-662-8476 (SAN 202-4535).

American Ethnological Society, *(Am Ethnological Soc; 0-942976)*, 1703 N. H. Ave NW, Washington, DC 20009 Tel 202-232-8800 (SAN 240-3331).

American Faculty Press, Inc., *(Am Faculty Pr; 0-912834)*, 44 Lake Shore Dr., Rockaway, NJ 07866 Tel 201-627-2727 (SAN 201-2650).

American Family Communiversity Press, *(Am Family; 0-910574)*, 5242 W. North Ave., Chicago, IL 60639 Tel 312-237-4793 (SAN 210-7708).

American Family Records Assn., *(AFRA; 0-913233)*, 311 E. 12th St., Kansas City, MO 64106 Tel 816-453-1294 (SAN 241-3566).

American Federation of Arts, *(Am Fed Arts; 0-917418)*, 41 E. 65th St., New York, NY 10021 Tel 212-988-7700 (SAN 201-2669).

American Forestry Assn., Book Edit Dept., *(Am Forestry; 0-935050)*, 1319 18th St., N.W., Washington, DC 20036 Tel 202-467-5810 (SAN 204-8175).

American Foundation for the Blind, *(Am Foun Blind; 0-89128)*, 15 W. 16th St., New York, NY 10011 Tel 212-620-2152 (SAN 201-2677).

American Friends Service Committee, *(Am Fr Serv Comm; 0-910082)*, 1501 Cherry St., Philadelphia, PA 19102 Tel 215-241-7000 (SAN 201-2685).

American Geological Institute, *(Am Geol; 0-913312)*, One Skyline Place, 5205 Leesburg Pike, Falls Church, VA 22041 Tel 703-379-2480 (SAN 202-4543).

American Geophysical Union, *(Am Geophysical; 0-87590)*, 2000 Florida Ave. N.W., Washington, DC 20009 Tel 202-462-6903 (SAN 202-4489).

American Guidance Service, Inc., *(Am Guidance; 0-913476; 0-88671)*, Publishers' Bldg., Circle Pines, MN 55014 Tel 612-786-4343 (SAN 201-694X).

American Guide Pubns., *(Am Guide Pubns; 0-932948)*, P.O. Box 1000, Glendale, CA 91209 Tel 213-956-3716 (SAN 215-126X).

American Heart Assn., Inc., *(Am Heart; 0-87493)*, 7320 Greenville Ave., Dallas, TX 75231 Tel 214-750-5468 (SAN 202-4551).

American Heritage Publishing Co., *(Am Heritage; 0-8281)*, 10 Rockefeller Plaza, New York, NY 10020 Tel 212-399-8900 (SAN 206-9032).

American Hispanist, Inc., *(American Hispanist; 0-89217)*, 107 S. College, Bloomington, IN 47401 Tel 812-334-3008 (SAN 209-3944).

American Historical Assn., *(Am Hist Assn; 0-87229)*, 400 "A" St., S. E., Washington, DC 20003 Tel 202-544-2422 (SAN 201-159X).

American Historical Society of Germans from Russia, *(Am Hist Soc Ger; 0-914222)*, 631 "D" St., Lincoln, NE 68502 Tel 402-477-4524 (SAN 204-7543).

American History Press, Div. of Northwoods Press, *(Am Hist Pr; 0-89002)*, P.O. Box 123, S. Thomaston, ME 04858 (SAN 217-0876).

American History Research Associates, *(Am Hist Res; 0-910086)*, P.O. Box 140, Brookeville, MD 20833 Tel 301-774-3573 (SAN 206-717X).

American Home Economics Association, *(Am Home Eco)*, 2010 Massachusetts Ave Nw, Washington, DC 20036 Tel 202-862-8300 (SAN 266-9277).

American Hospital Assn., *(Am Hospital; 0-87258)*, 840 N. Lake Shore Dr., Chicago, IL 60611 Tel 312-280-6235 (SAN 201-1603); Orders to: P.O. Box 9600 Chicago, IL 60693 Tel 312-280-6000 (SAN 201-1611).

American Hungarian Educators Association, *(Am Hungarian Ed)*, Po Box 4103, Silver Springs, MD 20904 Tel 301-384-4657 (SAN 225-8110).

American Hungarian Review, *(Hungarian Rev; 0-911862)*, 5410 Kerth Rd., St. Louis, MO 63128 Tel 314-487-7566 (SAN 204-0816).

American Indian Archaeological Institute, *(Am Indian Arch; 0-936322)*, Box 260, Washington, CT 06793 (SAN 221-2536).

American Indian Pubs., Inc., *(Am Indian Pubs; 0-937862)*, 177 F Riverside Dr., Newport Beach, CA 92663 (SAN 216-3284).

American Industrial Arts Assn., Inc., *(Am Indus Arts)*, 1201 Sixteenth St., N.W., Rm 230, Washington, DC 20036 Tel 202-833-4211 (SAN 207-3293).

American Institute for Marxist Studies, *(Am Inst Marxist; 0-89977)*, 20 E. 30th St., New York, NY 10016 Tel 212-689-4530 (SAN 202-4594).

American Institute for Property & Liability Underwriters, Inc., *(Am Inst Property; 0-89463)*, Providence & Sugartown Rds., Malvern, PA 19355 Tel 215-644-2100 (SAN 210-1629).

American Institute for Psychological Research, The, *(Am Inst Psych; 0-89920)*, 614 Indian School Rd. N.W., Albuquerque, NM 87102 Tel 505-843-7749 (SAN 212-9302).

American Institute for Writing Research, Corp., *(Am Inst Writing Res; 0-917944)*, Box 1364, Grand Central Sta., New York, NY 10163 Tel 212-266-4141 (SAN 210-0290).

American Institute of Architects, *(Am Inst Arch; 0-913962)*, 1735 New York Ave., N.W., Washington, DC 20006 Tel 202-626-7450 (SAN 277-9536).

American Institute of Certified Public Accountants, *(Am Inst CPA; 0-87051)*, 1211 Avenue of the Americas, New York, NY 10036 Tel 212-575-6200 (SAN 202-4578).

American Institute of Chemical Engineers, *(Am Inst Chem Eng; 0-8169)*, 345 E. 47th St., New York, NY 10017 Tel 212-752-6800 (SAN 204-7551).

American Institute of Chemists, (Amer Inst Chem), 7315 Wisconsin Ave NW, Bethesda, MD 20814 Tel 301-652-2447 (SAN 232-6280).

American Institute of Cooperation, (Am Inst Cooperation; 0-938868), 1800 Massachusetts Ave., N. W., Suite 508, Washington, DC 20036 Tel 202-296-6825 (SAN 204-5281).

American Institute of Discussion, (Am Inst Disc; 0-910092), P.O. Box 103, Oklahoma City, OK 73101 Tel 405-235-9681 (SAN 202-4586).

American Institute of Italian Studies, (Am Inst Ital Stud; 0-916322), Villa Walsh, Morristown, NJ 07960 (SAN 220-2298).

American Institute of Maintenance, (Am Inst Maint; 0-9609052), 1120 E. Chevy Chase Dr., P.O. Box 2068, Glendale, CA 92109 Tel 213-244-1176 (SAN 260-3179).

American Institute of Mining Metallurgical & Petroleum Engineers, (Am Inst Mining), 345 E. 47th St., New York, NY 10017 Tel 212-644-7695 (SAN 225-2163).

American Institute of Parliamentarians, (Am Inst Parliamentarians), 229 Army Post Road Suite B, Des Moines, IA 50315 (SAN 225-3690).

American Institute of Physics, (Am Inst Physics; 0-88318), 335 E. 45th St., New York, NY 10017 Tel 212-661-9404 (SAN 201-162X) Micropublisher of scholarly journals, physics & related sciences on 16mm & 35mm microfilm reel & cartridges & mocrofiche. North American distributor of publications from the Institute of physics (UK).

American Institute of Real Estate Appraisers, (Am Inst Real Estate Appraisers; 0-911780), 430 N. Michigan Ave., Chicago, IL 60611 Tel 312-440-8171 (SAN 206-7153); Dist. by: Follett Publishing Co., 1010 W. Washington Blvd., Chicago, IL 60607 Tel 312-666-5858 (SAN 200-2035).

American Institute of the History of Pharmacy, (Am Inst Pharmacy; 0-931292), Pharmacy Bldg., Madison, WI 53706 Tel 608-262-5378 (SAN 204-5257); c/o Glenn Sonnedecker, American Institute of the History of Pharmacy, Pharmacy Building, Madison, WI 53706 (SAN 215-420X).

American Institutes for Research, (Am Inst Res; 0-89785), P.O. Box 1113, Palo Alto, CA 94302 (SAN 202-442X).

American Institutes for Research, Systems Division, (AIR Systems; 0-89785), 41 North Rd., Bedford, MA 01730 Tel 617-275-0800 (SAN 215-9368).

American Iris Society, (Am Iris; 0-9601242), 6518 Beachy Ave., Wichita, KS 67206 Tel 316-686-8734 (SAN 210-3826); Orders to: 226 E. 20th St., Tulsa, OK 74119 Tel 918-582-4932 (SAN 210-3834).

American Italian Historical Assn., Inc., (Am Italian), 29 Roxbury Place, Glen Rock, NJ 07452 (SAN 210-8828).

American Jewish Committee, (Am Jewish Comm; 0-87495), 165 E. 56th St., New York, NY 10022 Tel 212-751-4000 (SAN 201-1638).

American Jewish Historical Society, (Am Jewish Hist Soc; 0-911934), 2 Thornton Rd., Waltham, MA 02154 Tel 617-891-8110 (SAN 202-4608).

American Journal of Nursing Co., Educational Services Div., (Am Journal Nurse), 555 W. 57th St., New York, NY 10019 Tel 212-582-8820 (SAN 202-4616).

American Judicature Society, (Am Judicature), 200 W. Monroe, Suite 1606, Chicago, IL 60606 Tel 312-558-6900 (SAN 201-7202).

American Language Academy, (Am Lang Acad; 0-934270), Materials Dept., 11426 Rockville Pike, Rockville, MD 20852 Tel 301-984-3400 (SAN 281-2665).

American Law Institute, (Am Law Inst; 0-8318), 4025 Chestnut St., Philadelphia, PA 19104 Tel 215-243-1600 (SAN 204-756X).

American Lawn Bowlers' Guide, (Am Lawn Bowlers; 0-9600068), P.O. Box 824, Laguna Beach, CA 92652 Tel 714-494-2606 (SAN 202-3245).

American Librarians' Agency, (Am Librarians; 0-914240), P. O. Box 5764, New York, NY 10017 (SAN 202-4438).

American Library Assn., (ALA; 0-8389), 50 E. Huron St., Chicago, IL 60611 Tel 312-944-6780 (SAN 201-0062).

American Library Publishing Co., Inc., (Am Lib Pub Co; 0-934598), 275 Central Park, W., New York, NY 10024 Tel 212-362-1442 (SAN 201-9868).

American Life Foundation & Study Institute, (Am Life Foun; 0-89257), P.O. Box 349, Watkins Glen, NY 14891 Tel 607-535-4737 (SAN 201-1646).

American Logistics Assn., (Am Logistics Assn), 1133 15th St.N.W. No. 500, Washington, DC 20005 (SAN 225-1027).

American Lung Assn., (Am Lung Assn; 0-915116), 1740 Broadway, New York, NY 10019 (SAN 211-3503).

American Malacologists, Inc., (Am Malacologists; 0-915826), Box 2255, Melbourne, FL 32901 Tel 305-725-2260 (SAN 207-6403).

American Management Associations, (Am Mgmt Assns), Trudeau Rd. Fulfillment Dept., Saranac Lake, NY 12983 (SAN 227-3578).

American Map Corp., (Am Map; 0-8416), 46-35 54th Rd., Maspeth, NY 11378 Tel 212-784-0055 (SAN 202-4634).

American Marketing Assn., (Am Mktg; 0-87757), 250 S. Wacker Dr. No. 200, Chicago, IL 60606 Tel 312-648-0536 (SAN 202-4667).

American Mathematical Society, (Am Math; 0-8218), P.O. Box 6248, Providence, RI 02940 Tel 401-272-9500 (SAN 201-1654); Orders to: P.O. Box 1571, Annex Sta., Providence, RI 02901 (SAN 201-1662).

American Media, (Am Media; 0-912986), 790 Hampshire Rd., Suite H, Westlake Village, CA 91361 Tel 213-889-1231 (SAN 202-4632).

American Medical Association, (AMA; 0-89970), 535 N. Dearborn St., Chicago, IL 60610 Tel 312-751-6000 (SAN 206-8516).

American Medical Publishing Assn., (Am Med Pub; 0-911411), P.O. Box 1900, Santa Barbara, CA 93102 Tel 805-682-7475 (SAN 263-0443).

American Metal Market/Metalworking News, (Am Metal Mkt; 0-910094), Dist. by: Fairchild Pubns., Inc., 7 E. 12th St., New York, NY 10003 (SAN 201-470X).

American Meteorite Laboratory, (Am Meteorite; 0-910096), P.O. Box 2098, Denver, CO 80201 Tel 303-428-1371 (SAN 202-4659).

American Metric Journal, (Am Metric), P.O. Box 847, Tarzana, CA 91356 Tel 805-484-5787 (SAN 209-4134).

American Mideast Research, (Am Mideast), 55 Sutter, Suite 712, San Francisco, CA 94104 Tel 415-921-5002 (SAN 215-0506).

American Mizrachi Women, (Am Mizrachi Wmn), 817 Broadway, New York, NY 10003 (SAN 225-4549).

American Mosquito Control Assn., (Am Mosquito), 5545 E Shields Ave, Fresno, CA 93727 Tel 209-292-5329 (SAN 224-3652).

American Museum of Natural History, (Am Mus Natl Hist; 0-913424), Central Park W. at 79th St., New York, NY 10024 Tel 212-873-1498 (SAN 208-2160).

American Museum Science Books See Natural History Press

American Music Center, Inc., (Am Music Ctr), 250 W 54th St., New York, NY 10019 (SAN 225-3518).

American Music Conference, (American Music; 0-918196), Public Relations Board, Inc., 150 E. Huron St., Chicago, IL 60611 Tel 312-266-7200 (SAN 209-3952); c/o American Music Conference, 1000 Skokie Blvd., Wilmette, IL 60091 Tel 312-251-1600 (SAN 209-3960).

American Mutuality Foundation, (Am Mutuality; 0-938844), 9428 S. Western Ave., Los Angeles, CA 90047 (SAN 216-0153).

American Narcolepsy Association, (Am Narcolepsy), Box 5846, Stanford, CA 94305 (SAN 224-4594).

American National Metric Council, (Am Natl; 0-916148), 5410 Grovenor Lane, Bethesda, MD 20814 Tel 301-530-8333 (SAN 207-9380).

American National Publishing Co., (Am Natl Pub; 0-913514), 237 Plymouth Bldg., 12 S. Sixth Street, Minneapolis, MN 55402 Tel 612-338-3362 (SAN 201-0119).

American National Standards Institute, (ANSI), 1430 Broadway, New York, NY 10018 Tel 212-354-3311 (SAN 203-4778).

American New Church Sunday School Assn., (Am New Church Sunday; 0-917426), 48 Highland St., Sharon, MA 02067 Tel 617-784-5041 (SAN 208-9432); Dist. by: Swedenborg Library, 79 Newbury St., Boston, MA 02116 (SAN 208-9440).

American Nuclear Society, (Am Nuclear Soc; 0-89448), 555 N. Kensington Ave., La Grange Park, IL 60525 Tel 312-352-6611 (SAN 207-5172).

American Numismatic Assn., (American Numismatic; 0-89637), 818 North Cascade, Colorado Springs, CO 80903 Tel 303-473-9142 (SAN 211-3481).

American Numismatic Society, (Am Numismatic; 0-89722), Broadway at 155th St., New York, NY 10032 Tel 212-234-3130 (SAN 201-7067).

American Nurses Assn., (ANA), 2420 Pershing Rd., Kansas City, MO 64108 Tel 816-474-5720 (SAN 204-5176).

American Occupational Therapy Association Inc., (Am Occup Therapy), 1383 Piccard Dr., Rockville, MD 20850 Tel 301-948-9626 (SAN 224-4705).

American Oriental Society, (Am Orient Soc), 329 Sterling Memorial Library, Yale Sta., New Haven, CT 06520 Tel 203-436-1040 (SAN 211-3082).

American Ornithologists Union (AOU) NHB-378, (Am Ornithologists), National Museum Natural History, Washington, DC 20560 Tel 202-381-5286 (SAN 225-2252).

American Personnel & Guidance Assn., (Am Personnel), 2 Skyline Place, Suite 400, 5203 Leeburg Pike, Falls Church, VA 22041 Tel 703-820-4700 (SAN 202-4675).

American Petroleum Institute Pubns., (Am Petroleum; 0-89364), 2101 "L" St., N.W., Washington, DC 20037 Tel 202-833-5790 (SAN 204-5141).

American Pharmaceutical Assn., (Am Pharm Assn; 0-917330), 2215 Constitution Ave., N.W., Washington, DC 20037 Tel 202-628-4410 (SAN 202-4446).

American Philatelic Research Library, (Am Philatelic Res Lib), P.O. Box 338, State College, PA 16801 Tel 814-237-3803 (SAN 225-5863).

American Philosophical Society, (Am Philos; 0-87169), 104 S. Fifth St., Philadelphia, PA 19106 Tel 215-627-0706 (SAN 206-9016).

American Physical Therapy Assn., (Am Phys Therapy Assn; 0-912452), 1156 15th St., N.W., Washington, DC 20005 Tel 202-466-2070 (SAN 202-4683).

American Phytopathological Society, (Am Phytopathol Soc; 0-89054), 3340 Pilot Knob Rd., St. Paul, MN 55121 Tel 612-454-7250 (SAN 212-0704).

American Pine Barrens Pub. Co., (Am Pine Barrens; 0-937438), P.O. Box 22820, 1400 Washington Ave., Albany, NY 12222 (SAN 215-1278).

American Poetry Press, (Am Poetry Pr; 0-933486), P. O. Box 2013, Upper Darby, PA 19082 (SAN 212-6397).

American Political Items Collectors, (Am Political Collect), 1054 Sharpsburg Dr., Huntsville, AL 35803 (SAN 225-5308).

American Powder Metallurgy Institute, (Am Powder Metal), 105 College Road E., Princeton, NJ 08540 (SAN 211-0652).

American Press, (American Pr; 0-89641), 520 Commonwealth Ave., No. 416, Boston, MA 02215 Tel 617-247-0022 (SAN 210-7007).

American Production & Inventory Control Society, (Am Prod & Inventory; 0-935406), 500 W. Annandale Rd., Falls Church, VA 22046 Tel 703-237-8344 (SAN 213-7208).

American Prudential Enterprises, (Am Prudential; 0-9608346), P.O. Box 4506, Salisbury, NC 28144 Tel 704-637-4407 (SAN 238-9053).

American Psychiatric Assn., Subs. of American Psychiatric Assn., (Am Psychiatric; 0-89042), 1400 K. St. N. W., Washington, DC 20005 Tel 202-682-6269 (SAN 202-4691).

American Psychiatric Press See American Psychiatric Assn.

American Psychological Assn., (Am Psychol; 0-912704), 1200 17th St., N.W., Washington, DC 20036 Tel 202-833-7600 (SAN 202-4705).

American Public Health Assn. Pubns., (Am Pub Health; 0-87553), 1015 15th St. N.W., Washington, DC 20005 Tel 202-789-5666 (SAN 202-4713).

American Public Welfare Assn., *(Am Pub Welfare; 0-910106),* 1125 15th St., N.W., Washington, DC 20005 Tel 202-293-7550 (SAN 202-4721).

American Public Works Assn., *(Am Public Works; 0-917084),* 1313 E. 60th St., Chicago, IL 60637 Tel 312-947-2541 (SAN 208-130X).

American Pub., *(Am Pub; 0-916036),* P.O. Box 102, Oxford, IN 47971 (SAN 207-7019).

American Publishing Company, *(Am Pub Co WI),* 2909 Syene Rd., Madison, WI 53713 Tel 608-271-6544 (SAN 210-301X).

American Publishing House, *(Am Pub House),* P.O. Box 256, Union City, NJ 07087 (SAN 240-1320).

American Quality Books, *(Am Quality; 0-936956),* 12415 E. DeSmet, No. 35, Spokane, WA 99216 Tel 509-928-0061 (SAN 214-2821).

American Quilt Study Group, *(Am Quilt; 0-9606590),* 105 Molino Ave., Mill Valley, CA 94941 Tel 415-388-6324 (SAN 219-6867).

American Radio Relay League, Inc., *(Am Radio; 0-87259),* 225 Main St., Newington, CT 06111 Tel 203-666-1541 (SAN 202-473X).

American Record Collectors Exchange, *(Am Record; 0-914652),* P.O. Box 1377, F.D.R. Sta., New York, NY 10022 Tel 212-688-8426 (SAN 201-1689).

American Reprint Co./Rivercity Press, *(Am Repr-Rivercity Pr; 0-89190),* Dist. by: Amereon Ltd., P.O. Box 1200, Mattituck, NY 11952 Tel 516-298-5100 (SAN 201-2413).

American Reprints Co., *(Am Reprints; 0-915706),* 111 W. Dent, P.O. Box 1, Ironton, MO 63650 Tel 314-546-7251 (SAN 207-5008).

American Research Press, *(Am Res Pr; 0-937616),* 5153 Elkmont, Rancho Palos Verdes, CA 90274 (SAN 215-2924) Moved, left no forwarding address.

American Romanian Academy of Arts & Sciences, *(Am Romanian; 0-912131),* 4310 Finley Ave., No. 6, Los Angeles, CA 90027 Tel 916-752-6442 (SAN 211-2116).

American-Scandinavian Foundation, *(Am Scandinavian; 0-89067),* 127 E. 73rd St., New York, NY 10021 Tel 212-879-9779 (SAN 201-7075); Orders to: Heritage Resource Center, P.O. Box 26305, Minneapolis, MN 55426 (SAN 201-7083).

American School Health Assn., *(Am Sch Health; 0-917160),* P.O. Box 708, Kent, OH 44240 Tel 216-678-1601 (SAN 208-5240).

American School of Astrology, *(Am Sch Astrol),* 21 Mellon Ave., West Orange, NJ 07052 Tel 201-731-2255 (SAN 211-2868).

American School of Classical Studies at Athens, *(Am Sch Athens; 0-87661),* c/o Institute for Advanced Study, Princeton, NJ 08540 Tel 609-734-8387 (SAN 201-1697).

American Schools of Oriental Research, *(Am Sch Orient Res; 0-89757),* 4243 Spruce St., Philadelphia, PA 19104 Tel 617-547-9780 (SAN 239-4057); Dist. by: Eisenbrauns, P.O. Box 275, Winona Lake, IN 46590 (SAN 213-4365).

American Science & Engineering, Inc., *(Am Sci & Eng; 0-8339),* 955 Massachusetts Ave., Cambridge, MA 02139 (SAN 206-7145).

American Sciences Press, Inc., *(Am Sciences Pr; 0-935950),* 20 Cross Rd., Syracuse, NY 13224 (SAN 213-8883).

American Scientist, *(American Scientist),* c/o Sigma Xi the Scientific Research Society, 345 Whitney Ave., New Haven, CT 06511 (SAN 275-357X).

American Showcase, Inc., *(Am Showcase; 0-931144),* 724 Fifth Ave., New York, NY 10019 Tel 212-245-0981 (SAN 281-2681); Dist. by: W.H.Smith & Son, 112 Madison Ave., New York, NY 10016 (SAN 281-269X); Dist. by: Fleetbooks, S.A., 100 Park Ave, New York, NY 10017 (SAN 215-0530); Dist. by: Van Nostrand Reinhold, 135 W. 50 St., New York, NY 10020 Tel 212-265-8700 (SAN 202-5183); Dist. by: Robert Silver Assoc., 95 Madison Ave., New York, NY 10016 (SAN 241-5801).

American Society for Education & Religion, Inc., *(Am Soc Ed & Rel; 0-942978),* P.O. Box 458, Springfield, VA 22150 Tel 703-642-5246 (SAN 240-334X).

American Society for Information Science See Knowledge Industry Pubns., Inc.

American Society for Metals, *(ASM; 0-87170),* 9275 Kinsman Rd., Metals Park, OH 44073 Tel 216-338-5151 (SAN 204-7586).

American Society for Microbiology, *(Am Soc Microbio; 0-914826),* 1913 "I" St., N.W., Washington, DC 20006 Tel 202-833-9680 (SAN 202-1153).

American Society for Personnel Administration, *(Am Soc Personnel; 0-939900),* 30 Park Dr., Berea, OH 44017 Tel 216-826-4790 (SAN 224-8964).

American Society for Pharmacology & Experimental Therapeutics, *(Am Phar & Ex),* 9650 Rockville Pike, Bethesda, MD 20014 Tel 301-530-7060 (SAN 267-3223).

American Society for Public Administration, *(Am Soc Pub Admin; 0-936678),* 1120 G St., N.W. No. 500, Washington, DC 20005 (SAN 223-3924).

American Society for Testing & Materials, *(ASTM; 0-8031),* 1916 Race St., Philadelphia, PA 19103 Tel 215-299-5400 (SAN 201-1344).

American Society of Agricultural Engineers, *(Am Soc Ag Eng; 0-916150),* 2950 Niles Rd., St. Joseph, MI 49085 (SAN 223-6087).

American Society of Agronomy, *(Am Soc Agron; 0-89118),* 677 S. Segoe Rd., Madison, WI 53711 Tel 608-274-1212 (SAN 204-5060).

American Society of Appraisers, *(Am Soc Appraisers; 0-937828),* Dulles International Airport, P.O. Box 17265, Washington, DC 20041 Tel 703-620-3838 (SAN 206-2194).

American Society Assn Executives, *(Am Soc Assn Execs),* 1575 Eye St. NW, Washington, DC 20005 Tel 202-626-2723 (SAN 224-8182).

American Society of Cinematographers, *(Am Soc Cine),* P.O. Box 2230, Hollywood, CA 90028 (SAN 202-4756).

American Society of Civil Engineers, *(Am Soc Civil Eng; 0-87262),* 345 E. 47th St., New York, NY 10017 Tel 212-705-7518 (SAN 204-7594).

American Society of Clinical Pathologists Press, *(Am Soc Clinical; 0-89189),* Educational Products Division, 2100 W. Harrison St., Chicago, IL 60612 Tel 312-738-1336 (SAN 207-9429).

American Society of Heating Refrigerating and Air Conditioning Engineers, Inc., *(Am Heat Ref & Air Eng),* 1791 Tullie Cirlce NE, Atlanta, GA 30329 Tel 404-636-8400 (SAN 223-9809).

American Society of Hospital Pharmacists, *(Am Soc Hosp Pharm; 0-930530),* 4630 Montgomery Ave., Washington, DC 20014 Tel 301-657-3000 (SAN 204-5052).

American Society of Journalists & Authors, *(Am Soc Jrnl & Auth),* 1501 Broadway Ste 1907, New York, NY 10036 Tel 212-997-0947 (SAN 225-4441).

American Society of Mammalogists, *(Am Soc Mammalogists; 0-943612),* Vertebrate Museum Shippensburg University, Shippensburg, PA 17257 Tel 717-532-1407 (SAN 225-204X).

American Society of Mechanical Engineers, *(ASME; 0-87053),* 345 E. 47th St., New York, NY 10017 Tel 212-705-7712 (SAN 201-1379).

American Society of Newspaper Editors Foundation, *(Am Soc News; 0-943086),* Box 17004, Washington, DC 20041 (SAN 240-3358).

American Society of Photogrammetry, *(ASP; 0-937294),* 210 Little Falls St., Falls Church, VA 22046 Tel 703-534-6617 (SAN 204-5044).

American Society of Safety Engineers, *(ASSE; 0-939874),* 850 Busse Hwy., Park Ridge, IL 60068 Tel 312-692-4121 (SAN 201-7032).

American Solar Energy Society, Inc., US Section of the Intl Solar Energy Society, *(Am Solar Energy; 0-89553),* 110 W. 34th St., New York, NY 10001 Tel 212-736-8727 (SAN 210-3842).

American Speech-Language Hearing Association, *(Am Speech Lang Hearing),* 10801 Rockville Pike, Rockville, MD 20852 (SAN 224-4608).

American Sports Sales, Inc., *(Am Sports Sales; 0-912354),* P.O. Box 160, Orangeburg, NY 10962 Tel 914-359-5300 (SAN 203-4964).

American Studies Press, Inc., *(Am Stud Pr; 0-934996),* 13511 Palmwood Lane, Tampa, FL 33624 Tel 813-961-7200 (SAN 213-2788).

American Studies Publishing Co., *(Amer Studies; 0-942738),* 19496 Sandcastle Lane, Huntington Beach, CA 92648 Tel 714-960-2117 (SAN 240-1851).

American Teaching Aids, *(Am Teaching; 0-88037),* P.O. Box 1406, Covina, CA 91722 Tel 213-966-1731 (SAN 238-9398).

American Technical Pubs., Inc., *(Am Technical; 0-8269),* 12235 S. Laramie Ave., Alsip, IL 60658 Tel 800-323-3471 (SAN 206-8141).

American Theatre Assn., *(Am Theatre Assoc; 0-940528),* 1010 Wisconsin Ave., N.W. Suite 630, Washington, DC 20007 Tel 202-342-7530 (SAN 206-8133).

American Tinnitus Association, *(Am Tinnitus Assn),* Box 5, Portland, OR 97207 Tel 503-248-9985 (SAN 224-4616).

American Trend Publishing Co., The, *(Am Trend Pub; 0-941388),* 645 Emporia Rd., Boulder, CO 80303 Tel 303-499-4582 (SAN 238-9401).

American Trucking Association, *(Am Trucking Assns; 0-88711),* 1616 P St. N.W., Washington, DC 20036 Tel 202-797-5291 (SAN 224-9693).

American Trust Pubns., *(Am Trust Pubns; 0-89259),* Dist. by: Islamic Book Service, 10900 W. Washington St., Indianapolis, IN 46231 Tel 317-839-8150 (SAN 169-2453).

American Univ. of Beirut Pubns. See Syracuse Univ. Press

American Universal Artforms Corp., *(Am Univ Artforms; 0-913632),* P.O. Box 4574, Austin, TX 78765 Tel 512-451-3588 (SAN 202-4772).

American Veterinary Publications Inc., *(Am Vet Pubns),* Drawer KK, Santa Barbara, CA 93102 Tel 805-965-8859 (SAN 277-6545).

American Visual Aid Books, *(Am Visual),* P.O. Box 28718, Sacramento, CA 95828 (SAN 208-4694).

American Vocational Assn., Inc., *(Am Voc Assn; 0-89514),* 2020 N. 14th St., Arlington, VA 22201 Tel 703-522-6121 (SAN 202-4462).

American Water Works Assn., *(Am Water Wks Assn; 0-89867),* 6666 W. Quincy Ave., Denver, CO 80235 Tel 303-794-7711 (SAN 212-8241).

American Welding Society, *(Am Welding; 0-87171),* 2501 N. W. Seventh St., Miami, FL 33125 Tel 305-642-7090 (SAN 201-1700).

Americana Review, *(Americana Rev; 0-914166),* 10 Socha Lane, Scotia, NY 12302 Tel 518-399-6482 (SAN 206-3220).

Americanist Press, *(Americanist; 0-910120),* 1525 Shenkel Rd., Pottstown, PA 19464 Tel 215-323-5289 (SAN 205-6003).

Americans for Energy Independence, *(Americans Energy Ind; 0-934458),* 1629 K St., N.W., Suite 1201, Washington, DC 20006 Tel 202-466-2105 (SAN 212-999X).

Americas Foundation, *(Americas Found),* Box 3333, Jackson, MS 39207 (SAN 225-6320).

Amethyst, *(Amethyst; 0-912865),* 2800 Woodley Road, N.W., No. 423, Washington, DC 20008 Tel 207-797-9707 (SAN 265-377X).

Amhara Corp., *(Amhara Corp; 0-917450),* 6990 S. 1700 East, Salt Lake City, UT 84121 (SAN 208-063X).

Amherst Media, *(Amherst Media; 0-936262),* 418 Homecrest Dr., Amherst, NY 14226 (SAN 214-0950).

Amherst Press, *(Amherst Pr),* P.O. Box 296, Amherst, WI 54406 Tel 715-824-5890 (SAN 213-9820).

Amiel, Leon, Pub., *(L Amiel Pub; 0-8148),* 31 W. 46th St., New York, NY 10036 Tel 212-575-0010 (SAN 207-0766).

Amigo Press, *(Amigo Pr; 0-935098),* P.O. Box 1882, Laguna Beach, CA 92652 Tel 714-494-2302 (SAN 213-2796).

Amistad Brands, Inc., *(Amistad Brands; 0-9610432),* 22 Division Ave., N.E., Washington, DC 20019 (SAN 263-9165).

Amity Books, *(Amity Bks MO; 0-934864),* 1702 Magnolia, Liberty, MO 64048 (SAN 213-7216).

Amity Hallmark, Ltd., *(Amity Hallmark),* 40-09 149th Place, Flushing, NY 11354 (SAN 210-766X).

Amity Publications, *(Amity Pubns; 0-943814),* 78688 Sears Rd., Cottage Grove, OR 97424 (SAN 285-6794).

Amnesty International of the USA, Inc., *(Amnesty Intl USA; 0-939994),* 304 W. 58th St., New York, NY 10019 (SAN 220-2301).

Amon Carter Museum of Western Art, *(Amon Carter; 0-88360),* P.O. Box 2365, Fort Worth, TX 76113 Tel 817-738-1933 (SAN 204-7608).

Amonics, *(Amonics; 0-918166),* P.O. Box 1045, Norman, OK 73069 Tel 405-321-8076 (SAN 209-3707).

Amory & Pugh, *(Amory & Pugh; 0-9607492),* 79 Raymond St., Cambridge, MA 02140 (SAN 238-0056).

Amos, Winsom, Pub., *(W Amos; 0-9600520),* c/o Soma Press, P.O. Box 416, Yellow Springs, OH 45387 (SAN 222-8858).

Amoskeag Press, Inc., *(Amoskeag Pr),* P.O. Box 666, Hooksett, NH 03106 Tel 603-622-6626 (SAN 208-2721).

Ampersand Editions, *(Ampersand Editions),* Suite 218, 109 Minna St., San Francisco, CA 94105 (SAN 240-0804).

Ampersand Press, *(Ampersand; 0-910128),* P.O. Box 241, Princeton, NJ 08540 (SAN 206-9644) Moved, Left No Forwarding Address.

Ampersand Press, *(Ampersand RI; 0-9604740),* Roger Williams College, Bristol, RI 02809 (SAN 216-2202).

Ampersand Publishing, *(Ampersand Pub; 0-9607234),* 3609 Mukilteo Blvd., Everett, WA 98203 Tel 206-353-7593 (SAN 239-1546).

Amphibian Pubns., *(Amphibian Pubns),* P.O. Box 5352, Athens, GA 30604 (SAN 240-0812).

Amrita Foundation, Inc., *(Amrita Found; 0-937134),* P.O. Box 8080, Dallas, TX 75205 Tel 214-521-1072 (SAN 284-9666); Orders to: P.O. Box 8080, Dallas, TX 75205 Tel 214-521-1072 (SAN 284-9674).

Amsco Music *See* Music Sales Corp.

AMSCO School Pubns., Inc., *(AMSCO Sch; 0-87720),* 315 Hudson St., New York, NY 10013 Tel 212-675-7000 (SAN 201-1751).

Amulefi Publishing Co., *(Amulefi; 0-936360),* 11 E. Utica St., Buffalo, NY 14209 (SAN 214-0969).

Amusement Park Books, Inc., *(Amusement Pk Bks; 0-935408),* 8341 Esther St., Mentor, OH 44060 (SAN 222-7673).

Amward Pubns., Inc., *(Amward Pubns; 0-939676),* P.O. Box 137, Benjamin Franklin Sta., Washington, DC 20044 Tel 202-773-1826 (SAN 216-7131).

Ana-Doug Publishing, *(Ana-Doug Pub; 0-916946),* 1428 Carleton Way, Fullerton, CA 92633 Tel 714-738-1655 (SAN 208-4821).

Anaheim Publishing Co., *(Anaheim Pub Co; 0-88236),* 2632 Saturn St., Brea, CA 92621 Tel 714-993-3700 (SAN 202-4802).

Anais Nin Foundation, The, *(Anais Nin Foun; 0-9611238),* P.O. Box 276, Becket, MA 01223 Tel 413-623-5170 (SAN 283-068X).

Analog Devices, Inc., *(Analog Devices; 0-916550),* P.O. Box 280, Norwood, MA 02062 Tel 617-329-4700 (SAN 210-3389); Orders to: P.O. Box 796, Norwood, MA 02062 (SAN 210-3397).

Analysis Press, Subs. of Merrill Analysis, Inc., *(Analysis; 0-911894),* Box 228, Chappaqua, NY 10514 Tel 914-238-3641 (SAN 210-9549).

Analytech Management Consulting, *(Analytech; 0-9610932),* 215 N. West St., Alexandria, VA 22314 Tel 703-836-7962 (SAN 265-1734).

Analytic Investment Management, Inc., *(Analytic Invest),* 2222 Martin St., No. 230, Irvine, CA 92715 Tel 714-833-0294 (SAN 210-8844).

Analytic Press, The, *(Analytic Pr; 0-88163),* 365 Broadway, Suite 102, Hillsdale, NJ 07642 Tel 201-666-4110 (SAN 267-5455).

Analytical Psychology Club of Los Angeles, *(Analytic Psych; 0-9600936),* 10349 W. Pico Blvd., Los Angeles, CA 90064 (SAN 223-663X); Dist. by: Sigo Press, 2601 Ocean Park Blvd., Suite 210, Santa Monica, CA 90405 (SAN 216-3020).

Ananda Marga Pubns., *(Ananda Marga; 0-88476),* 854 Pearl St., Denver, CO 80203 Tel 303-832-6465 (SAN 206-3239).

Ananda Pubns., *(Ananda; 0-916124),* 14618 Tyler Foote Rd., Nevada City, CA 95959 Tel 916-292-3656 (SAN 201-1778).

Ananse Press, *(Ananse Pr; 0-9605670),* P.O. Box 22565, Seattle, WA 98122 (SAN 216-3292).

Ancestral Historian Society, *(Ancestral Hist; 0-939774),* Postal Unit 529, Evans, GA 30809 Tel 404-863-2863 (SAN 216-8774).

Anchor Books *See* Doubleday & Co., Inc.

Anchor Press *See* Doubleday & Co., Inc.

Anchorage Press, *(Anchorage; 0-87602),* P. O. Box 8067, New Orleans, LA 70182 Tel 504-283-8868 (SAN 203-4727).

Ancient City Press, *(Ancient City Pr; 0-941270),* P.O. Box 5401, Santa Fe, NM 87502 Tel 505-982-8195 (SAN 164-5552).

And Books, *(And Bks; 0-89708),* 702 S. Michigan, Suite 836, South Bend, IN 46618 Tel 219-232-3134 (SAN 213-9502).

And/Or Press, Inc., *(And-or Pr; 0-915904),* P.O. Box 2246, Berkeley, CA 94702 Tel 415-849-2665 (SAN 206-9458).

Andacht, Sandra, Pub., *(S Andacht; 0-9607616),* P.O. Box 94, Little Neck, NY 11363 Tel 212-229-6593 (SAN 238-6402).

Andante Pubs., *(Andante Pub; 0-940038),* 175-20 Wexford Terrace, Suite 11L, Jamaica Estates, NY 11432 Tel 212-526-7814 (SAN 220-1992).

Andersen, Paul, *(P Andersen; 0-9604720),* P.O. Box 2184, Laguna Hills, CA 92653 (SAN 215-1286).

Anderson, David, Gallery, Inc., *(D Anderson; 0-915956),* 521 W. 57th St., New York, NY 10019 (SAN 281-2746).

Anderson, Julian G., *(J G Anderson; 0-9602128),* P.O. Box 1751, Naples, FL 33939 Tel 813-262-5592 (SAN 209-5238).

Anderson, Robert D., Publishing Co., *(Anderson R; 0-942028),* P.O. Box 22324, Sacramento, CA 95822 Tel 916-391-4706 (SAN 238-4434).

Anderson, Velma Irene, *(V I Anderson; 0-89279),* Stanhope, IA 50246 (SAN 283-295X).

Anderson Communications, *(Anderson Comm; 0-9607692),* 508 Colquitt St., Suite A, Houston, TX 77006 (SAN 262-0014).

Anderson Kramer Associates, Inc., *(Anderson Kramer; 0-910136),* 1722 "H" St., N.W., Washington, DC 20006 Tel 202-298-7867 (SAN 203-4735).

Anderson Publications, *(Anderson MI; 0-9610088),* 1421 Wexford Dr., Davison, MI 48423 Tel 313-653-0243 (SAN 267-5633).

Anderson Publishing Co., *(Anderson Pub Co; 0-87084),* 646 Main St., Cincinnati, OH 45201 (SAN 208-2799).

Anderson World, Inc., *(Anderson World; 0-89037),* 1400 Stierlin Rd., Mountain View, CA 94043 Tel 415-965-8777 (SAN 281-2754); Orders to: P.O. Box 366, Mountain View, CA 94042 (SAN 281-2762).

Andor Publishing Co., Inc., *(Andor Pub; 0-89319),* 163 E. Union Ave., E. Rutherford, NJ 07073 Tel 201-460-1495 (SAN 208-5267).

Andover Press, *(Andover Pr; 0-939014),* 516 W. 34th St., New York, NY 10001 (SAN 216-1001).

Andre Deutsch, *(Andre Deutsch; 0-233),* c/o Elsevier Dutton, Two Park Ave., New York, NY 10016 (SAN 201-0070).

Andre's & Co., *(Andre's & Co; 0-936264),* 289 Varick St., Jersey City, NJ 07302 (SAN 214-0977).

Andrew Mountain Press, *(Andrew Mtn Pr; 0-9603840),* P.O. Box 14353, Hartford, CT 06114 (SAN 213-7232).

Andrews & McMeel, Inc., *(Andrews & McMeel; 0-8362),* 4400 Johnson Dr., Fairway, KS 66205 Tel 913-362-1523 (SAN 202-540X).

Andrews Univ. Press, *(Andrews Univ Pr; 0-943872),* Andrews Univ., Berrien Springs, MI 49104 Tel 616-471-3392 (SAN 241-0958).

Andromeda Press, *(Andromeda; 0-9602996),* 111 E. Platt, Maquoketa, IA 52060 (SAN 213-0017).

Anemone Editions, Ltd., *(Anemone Edns; 0-9604818),* P.O. Box 6056, Carmel, CA 93921 (SAN 216-0161).

Angel City Books, *(Angel City; 0-9605416),* 8033 Sunset Blvd., No. 366, Hollywood, CA 90046 (SAN 216-0951).

Angel Press Pubs., *(Angel Pr; 0-912216),* 561 Tyler St., Monterey, CA 93940 Tel 408-372-1658 (SAN 205-3330).

Angers Publishing Corp., *(Angers Pub; 0-939524),* Box H, Lafayette, LA 70502 Tel 318-233-4420 (SAN 216-6542).

Angriff Press, *(Angriff Pr; 0-913022),* P.O. Box 2726, Hollywood, CA 90028 Tel 213-386-9826 (SAN 203-4743).

Angst World Library, *(Angst World; 0-914580),* 1160 Forest Creek Rd., Selma, OR 97538 (SAN 201-1786).

Angus Downs Ltd., *(Angus Downs; 0-910053),* 4101 Lake Ridge Drive, Holland, MI 49423 (SAN 263-2489).

Anhinga Press, *(Anhinga Pr; 0-938078),* Apalachee Poetry Ctr., 406 Williams Bldg., Florida State Univ., Tallahassee, FL 32306 (SAN 216-0943).

Anima Pubns., *(Anima Pubns; 0-89012),* 1053 Wilson Ave., Chambersburg, PA 17201 Tel 717-263-8303 (SAN 281-2770).

Animal Cracker Press, *(Animal Cracker),* 3707 N.E. 65th Ave., Portland, OR 97213 Tel 503-282-0772 (SAN 210-9123).

Animal Owners Motivation Programs, *(Animal Owners; 0-9604576),* P.O. Box 16,, Frankfort, IL 60423 (SAN 215-1294).

Anirt Press, *(Anirt Pr; 0-9605878),* 15707 Eastwood Ave., Lawndale, CA 90260 Tel 213-678-9753 (SAN 216-6550).

Anma Libri, *(Anma Libri; 0-915838),* P.O. Box 876, Saratoga, CA 95071 Tel 415-851-3375 (SAN 212-5889).

Ann Arbor Book Co., *(Ann Arbor Bk; 0-932364),* P.O. Box 8064, Ann Arbor, MI 48107 (SAN 212-0712).

Ann Arbor Books *See* Univ. of Michigan Press

Ann Arbor Pubs., *(Ann Arbor Pr; 0-89039),* P.O. Box 7249, Naples, FL 33940 (SAN 213-8271).

Ann Arbor Science Pubs., *(Ann Arbor Science; 0-250),* c/o Butterworth Publishers, Inc., 10 Tower Office Park, Woburn, MA 01801 Tel 617-935-9361 (SAN 206-3964).

Anna Publishing, Inc., *(Anna Pub; 0-89305),* P.O. Box 218, 8 Bluford Ave., Ocoee, FL 32761 Tel 305-656-6998 (SAN 281-2789); Orders to: Anna Publishing, No. 8 South Bluford Ave., Ocoee, FL 32761 (SAN 281-2797).

Annand Enterprises, Inc., *(Annand Ent),* Ball Hill Rd., Milford, NH 03055 (SAN 240-9666).

Annandale-International, *(Annandale-Intl; 0-9602562),* Box 384, Bronx, NY 10472 Tel 212-292-8067 (SAN 212-8470).

Annegan, Charles, *(C Annegan; 0-9605200),* 1466 Palomar Dr., San Marcos, CA 92069 (SAN 215-8469).

Annual Reviews, Inc., *(Annual Reviews; 0-8243),* 4139 El Camino Way, Palo Alto, CA 94306 Tel 415-493-4400 (SAN 201-1816).

Annuals Publishing Company, *(Annuals Pub Co; 0-912417),* 10 E. 23rd St., New York, NY 10010 Tel 212-475-1620 (SAN 265-1742).

Another View, Inc., *(Another View; 0-913564),* P.O. Box 1921, Brooklyn, NY 11202 Tel 212-624-0939 (SAN 201-4351).

Anozira Agency, *(Anozira),* 1725 Farmer Ave., Tempe, AZ 85281 (SAN 206-4596).

Ansal Pr., *(ANSAL Pr; 0-910455),* 8620 Olympic View Dr., Edmonds, WA 98020 Tel 206-774-4645 (SAN 260-0137).

Answer-Book Library, *(Answer-Bk; 0-9608460),* 2000 Center St., Box 1470, Berkely, CA 94704 Tel 312-871-7859 (SAN 240-5857).

Antelope Island Press, *(Antelope Island; 0-917946),* P.O. Box 220, St. George, UT 84770 Tel 801-673-6093 (SAN 209-2921).

Anthelion Press, Inc., *(Anthelion Pr; 0-89185),* P.O. Box 614, Corte Madera, CA 94925 Tel 415-924-5311 (SAN 208-0575).

Anthoensen Press, *(Anthoesen Pr; 0-9602608),* 37 Exchange St, Portland, ME 04101 (SAN 281-2800); Dist. by: J. S. Moody, 211 Fireside Rd., Falmouth, ME 04105 Tel 207-781-4571 (SAN 282-5872).

Anthology Film Archives, *(Anthology Film; 0-911689),* 491 Broadway, New York, NY 10012 Tel 212-226-0010 (SAN 263-9181).

Anthony, C & R, Pubs., Inc., *(Anthony; 0-910140),* 300 Park Ave., S., New York, NY 10010 Tel 212-986-7693 (SAN 203-4786) Do Not Confuse with Anthony Pub Co.

Anthony, Dorothy Malone, *(Anthony D M; 0-9607944),* 802 S. Eddy, Fort Scott, KS 66701 Tel 316-223-3404 (SAN 239-6130).

Anthony, Travis D., *(T D Anthony; 0-9604686),* P.O. Box 646, Rush Springs, OK 73082 Tel 405-476-2211 (SAN 214-2295).

Anthony Press, *(Anthony Pr CA; 0-9606850),* Box 3722, Alhambra, CA 91803 Tel 213-570-2945 (SAN 217-2240).

Anthony Publishing Co., *(Anthony Pub Co; 0-9603832),* 218 Gleasondale Rd., Stow, MA 01775 Tel 617-897-7191 (SAN 213-9073).

Anthropology Resource Center, Inc., *(Anthropology Res; 0-932978),* 37 Temple Place, Rm 521, Boston, MA 02111 Tel 617-426-9286 (SAN 212-2642).

Anthroposophic Press, Inc., *(Anthroposophic; 0-910142),* 258 Hungry Hollow Rd., Spring Valley, NY 10977 Tel 914-352-2295 (SAN 201-1824).

Anti-Defamation League of B'nai B'rith, *(ADL; 0-88464),* 823 United Nations Plaza, New York, NY 10017 Tel 212-689-7400 (SAN 204-7616).

Antietam Press, *(Antietam Pr; 0-931590),* P.O. Box 62, Boonsboro, MD 21713 Tel 301-432-8079 (SAN 211-5859).

Antiquarium, The, *(Antiquarium),* 66 Humiston Dr., Bethany, CT 06525 Tel 203-393-2723 (SAN 201-6850).

Antiquary Pr., *(Antiquary Pr; 0-937864),* P.O. Box 9523, Baltimore, MD 21237 Tel 301-734-4254 (SAN 220-0309).

Antique Classic Reprints, *(Antique Classic; 0-930088),* 144 Red Mill Rd., Peekskill, NY 10566 Tel 914-528-4074 (SAN 210-7015).

Antique Clocks Publishing, *(Antique Clocks; 0-933396),* P.O. Box 21387, Concord, CA 94521 Tel 415-687-8252 (SAN 284-9682); Dist. by: S. La Rose Inc., P.O. Box 21208, Greensboro, NC 27240 Tel 919-275-0462 (SAN 284-9690).

Antique Collectors' Club, *(Antique Collect; 0-902028),* E9, Sevana Park, Ithaca, NY 14850 (SAN 208-5003).

Antique Doorknob Publishing Company, The, *(Ant Doorknob Pub; 0-9610800),* 3900 Latimer Rd. N., Tallamook, OR 97141 Tel 503-842-2244 (SAN 265-0665).

Antique Pubns., *(Antique Pubns; 0-915410),* P.O. Box 655, Marietta, OH 45750 (SAN 216-3306).

Antiquity Reprints, *(Antiquity Re; 0-937214),* Box 370, Rockeville Centre, NY 11571 Tel 516-766-5585 (SAN 237-9295).

Anura Publishing, *(Anura Pub; 0-9607074),* 12077 Wilshire Blvd., Suite 611, W. los Angeles, CA 90025 Tel 213-464-0300 (SAN 238-941X).

Anvil Books *See* Van Nostrand Reinhold Co. Inc

Anvil Press, *(Anvil Pr; 0-918552),* P.O. Box 37, Millville, MN 55957 (SAN 203-4794).

Aozora Publishing, *(Aozora Pub; 0-9605962),* P.O. Box 95, 131 Ash St., Myrtle Point, OR 97458 Tel 503-572-5089 (SAN 216-714X).

Aperture, Inc., *(Aperture; 0-89381; 0-912334),* Elm St., Millerton, NY 12546 Tel 518-789-4491 (SAN 201-1832); Dist. by: Viking Press, 40 W. 23rd St., New York, NY 10010 Tel 212-807-7300 (SAN 282-5074).

Apex Books *See* Abingdon Press

Apex Univ. Press, *(Apex U Pr; 0-916146),* c/o Castle-Pierce Printing Co., P.O. Box 2247, Oshkosh, WI 54903 (SAN 201-1565).

Apocalypse Publishing Co., *(Apocalypse Pub; 0-941614),* P.O. Box 1, Niagara Falls, NY 14305 (SAN 239-1562).

Apollo, *(Apollo; 0-938290),* 391 South Rd., Poughkeepsie, NY 12601 (SAN 216-101X).

Apollo Computer Systems, Inc., *(Apollo Com; 0-9610582),* 616 14th St., Arcata, CA 95521 Tel 707-822-0318 (SAN 264-651X).

Apollo Editions, *(Apollo Eds; 0-8152),* C/O Harper & Row Pubs., 10 E. 53rd St., New York, NY 10022 (SAN 211-691X); Dist. by: Harper & Row Pubs., Keystone Industrial Park, Scranton, PA 18512 (SAN 215-3742). *Imprints:* Apollo Editions Juvenile Books (AE-J).

Apollo Editions Juvenile Books *See* Apollo Editions

Apostolate for Family Consecration, The, *(AFC; 0-932406),* Box 220, Kenosha, WI 53141 (SAN 223-6702).

Apostolic Formation Center for Christian Renew-All, Inc., *(Apostolic Formation; 0-935488),* Box 355, Somers, CT 06071 Tel 203-749-4895 (SAN 215-6199).

Appalachian Associates, *(Appalach Assoc; 0-940414),* 615 Pasteur Ave., Bowling Green, OH 43402 (SAN 219-760X).

Appalachian Books, *(Appalachian Bks; 0-912660),* P.O. Box 249, Oakton, VA 22124 Tel 703-281-2464 (SAN 204-5524).

Appalachian Consortium, Inc., *(Appalach Consortium),* 202 Appalachian St., Boone, NC 28607 Tel 704-262-2064 (SAN 210-7732).

Appalachian Mountain Club, *(Appalach Mtn; 0-910146),* Five Joy St., Boston, MA 02108 Tel 617-523-0636 (SAN 203-4808).

Appel, Paul P., Pub., *(Appel; 0-911858),* 216 Washington St., Mt. Vernon, NY 10553 Tel 914-667-7365 (SAN 202-3253).

Appellate Publishing, *(Appellate Pub; 0-9603848),* P. O. Box 10687, Edgemont Branch, Golden, CO 80401 (SAN 213-828X) Moved, left no forwarding address.

Applause Pubns., *(Applause Pubns; 0-932352),* 2234 S. Shady Hills Dr., Diamond Bar, CA 91765 (SAN 211-8807).

Apple Computer, Inc., *(Apple Comp; 0-9609780),* 10260 Bandley Dr., Cupertino, CA 95014 Tel 408-996-1010 (SAN 267-6044); 7101 Patterson Dr., Garden Grove, CA 92641 Tel 714-898-9076.

Apple-Gems, *(Apple-Gems; 0-9602122),* P.O. Box 16292, San Francisco, CA 94116 Tel 415-587-9752 (SAN 212-4769).

Apple Hut Publishing Co., *(Apple Hut; 0-931148),* 1047 Park Hill Dr., P. O. Box 2704, Escondido, CA 92025 Tel 714-741-3565 (SAN 211-2159).

Apple Pie Publishing Co., *(Apple Pie Pub Co; 0-911149),* 7521 E. Costilla Ave., Englewood, CO 80112 Tel 303-770-1784 (SAN 267-6052).

Apple Press, *(Apple Pr; 0-9602238),* 5536 S.E. Harlow, Milwaukie, OR 97222 Tel 503-659-2475 (SAN 212-8489).

Apple Publishing Co., *(Apple Pub Co; 0-9604134),* Box 2498, Grand Central Sta., New York, NY 10163 (SAN 215-0549).

Apple Tree Lane, *(Apple Tree Ln; 0-9601602),* 801 La Honda Rd., Woodside, CA 94062 (SAN 211-7177).

Apple Tree Press, Inc., *(Apple Tree; 0-913082),* P.O. Box 1012, Flint, MI 48501 Tel 313-234-5451 (SAN 206-7366).

Apple-Wood Books, *(Apple Wood; 0-918222),* Box 2870, Cambridge, MA 02139 Tel 617-923-9337 (SAN 210-3419).

Applegate Computer Enterprises, *(Applegate Comp Ent),* 470 Slagle Center, Grants Pass, OR 97526 (SAN 285-6840).

Appleman, Robert C., *(R C Appleman),* 7216 57th N.E., Seattle, WA 98115 Tel 206-525-7909 (SAN 211-0520).

Appleseeds, *(Appleseed; 0-9608944),* 4508 W. Ponds View Dr., Littleton, CO 80123 (SAN 240-9674).

Appleton-Century-Crofts, *(ACC; 0-8385),* 25 Van Zant St., East Norwalk, CT 06855 Tel 203-838-4400 (SAN 209-1488); Orders to: Prentice-Hall, Order Dept., Englewood Cliffs, NJ 07632 (SAN 209-1496).

Appleton Davies, Inc., *(Appleton Davies; 0-941022),* 32 S. Raymond Ave., Suite 10, Pasadena, CA 91105 Tel 213-792-3046 (SAN 217-3255).

Applewhite, Karen Miller, *(Applewhite; 0-9603472),* 5702 N. Tenth Ave., Phoenix, AZ 85013 Tel 602-246-8243 (SAN 213-6074).

Appleyard, John, Agency, Inc., *(Appleyard Agency),* Box 1902, Pensacola, FL 32589 Tel 904-432-8396 (SAN 211-2167).

Applezaba Press, *(Applezaba; 0-930090),* P.O. Box 4134, Long Beach, CA 90804 Tel 213-591-0015 (SAN 210-7023).

Application Engineering Corp., *(Application Eng Corp; 0-910447),* 850 Pratt Blvd., Elk Grove Village, IL 60007 Tel 312-593-5000 (SAN 260-0145).

Applied Arts Pubs., Div. of Sowers Printing Co., *(Applied Arts; 0-911410),* Box 479, Lebanon, PA 17042 Tel 717-272-6667 (SAN 204-4838).

Applied Pressure Techniques, Wm. J. Cosmetics, *(Applied Press; 0-685),* P.O. Box 3172, Munster, IN 46321 Tel 219-932-6550 (SAN 205-1532).

Applied Publishing Ltd., *(Applied Pub; 0-915834),* P.O. Box 261, Wilmette, IL 60091 (SAN 207-608X).

Applied Therapeutics, Inc., *(Applied Therapeutics; 0-915486),* P.O. Box 1903, Spokane, WA 99210 Tel 509-448-2816 (SAN 212-2057).

April Enterprises, Inc., *(April Enterp; 0-9608772),* 14136 Janna Way, Sylmar, CA 91342 Tel 213-829-6805 (SAN 238-2385).

April Hill Pubs., *(April Hill),* 79 Elm St., Springfield, VT 05156 (SAN 213-6554).

April Publishing, *(April Pub; 0-939122),* P.O. Box 480000, Los Angeles, CA 90048 (SAN 238-0048).

Apt Books, Inc., *(Apt Bks; 0-86590),* 141 E. 44th St., Suite 511, New York, NY 10017 (SAN 215-7209).

Aqua-Sol Enterprises, *(Aqua-Sol Ent; 0-9604874),* P.O. Box 18646, Fort Worth, TX 76118 Tel 817-284-8003 (SAN 220-0317).

Aquari Corp., *(Aquari Corp; 0-916204),* P.O. Box 1966, Midland, MI 48640 Tel 517-631-5660 (SAN 207-9917).

Aquarian Book Pubs., *(Aquarian Bk Pubs; 0-9605126),* 7011 Hammond Ave., Dallas, TX 75223 (SAN 216-096X).

Aquarian Educational Group, *(Aqua Educ; 0-911794),* 30188 Mulholland Hwy., Agoura, CA 91301 Tel 213-889-9678 (SAN 203-4816).

Aquarian Press, *(Aquarian Pr; 0-902146),* P.O. Box 625, Stockbridge, MA 01262 Tel 413-298-3066 (SAN 212-825X).

Aquarian Research Foundation, *(Aquarian Res; 0-916726),* 5620 Morton St., Philadelphia, PA 19144 Tel 215-849-3237 (SAN 208-5305).

Aquarius Enterprises, *(Aquarius; 0-941200),* 53 Central Ave. 15 Wailuku, Maui, HI 96793 Tel 808-244-7347 (SAN 203-4824).

Aquin Publishing Co., *(Aquin Pub; 0-915352),* 4412 Laurelgrove Ave., Studio City, CA 91604 Tel 213-508-7169 (SAN 203-4085).

Arab Petroleum Research Inst., *(Arab Petro Res; 0-913177),* P.O. Box 535, Shelburne, VT 05482 Tel 802-985-3851 (SAN 282-9584).

Arader, Graham, III, *(W G Arader; 0-934626),* 1000 Boxwood Court, King of Prussia, PA 19406 Tel 215-825-6570 (SAN 212-8497).

Aragorn Books, Inc., *(Aragorn Bks; 0-913862),* 14698 Nordhoff St., Panorama City, CA 91402 Tel 213-894-3104 (SAN 203-4832).

Aramaic Bible Society, Inc., *(Aramaic Bible),* P.O. Box 15307, St. Petersburg, FL 33733 Tel 813-345-1636 (SAN 204-4900).

Ararat Press, Div. of Armenian General Benevolent Union, *(Ararat Pr; 0-933706),* 585 Saddle River Rd., Saddle Brook, NJ 07662 Tel 201-797-7600 (SAN 212-8268).

Arbit Books, Inc, *(Arbit; 0-930038),* 8050 N. Port Washington Rd., Milwaukee, WI 53217 Tel 414-352-4404 (SAN 210-4695).

Arbor House Publishing Co., *(Arbor Hse; 0-87795),* 300 E. 44th St., New York, NY 10017 Tel 212-599-3131 (SAN 201-1522).

Arbor Press, *(Arbor Pr CA; 0-9606345),* 22527 Haynes St., Canoga Park, CA 91307 (SAN 219-7618).

Arbor Press, The, *(Arbor Claremont; 0-9607108),* Box 846, Claremont, CA 91711 Tel 714-624-2698 (SAN 238-9061).

Arbor Pubns., *(Arbor Pubns; 0-9602556),* P.O. Box 8185, Ann Arbor, MI 48107 Tel 313-662-5786 (SAN 212-8276).

Arcadia Pr., *(Arcadia Pr; 0-938186),* 11 Waverly Pl., Penthouse D, New York, NY 10003 (SAN 215-6210).

Arcana Publishing, *(Arcana Pub; 0-910261),* P.O. Box Two, Wilmot, WI 53192 (SAN 241-3604).

Arcane Pubns., *(Arcane Pubns; 0-912240),* Box 36, York Harbor, ME 03911 Tel 207-363-3333 (SAN 203-4840).

Arceneaux, Thelma Hoffman Tyler, *(T H Arceneaux; 0-9600870),* 115 Apricot St., Thibodaux, LA 70301 Tel 504-446-1037 (SAN 207-5342).

Archaeological News, Inc., *(Arch News Inc; 0-943254),* Florida State Univ., Dept. of Classics, Tallahassee, FL 32306 Tel 904-644-3033 (SAN 240-3374).

Archer Editions Press, *(Archer Edns; 0-89097),* 318 Fry Branch Rd., Lynnville, TN 38472 Tel 615-527-3643 (SAN 207-7124).

Archinform, *(Archinform; 0-937254)*, P.O. Box 27732, Los Angeles, CA 90027 Tel 213-662-0216 (SAN 212-3320).

Architectural Book Publishing Co., *(Architectural)*, Dist. by: Hastings House Pubs., Inc., 10 E. 40th St., New York, NY 10016 Tel 212-689-5400 (SAN 213-9561).

Architectural Pubns., *(Arch Pubns; 0-9608208)*, 103 MacDougal St., New York, NY 10012 Tel 212-477-6385 (SAN 240-3382).

Architectural Record Books *See* **McGraw-Hill Book Co.**

Archival Press, Inc., *(Archival Pr; 0-915882)*, P.O. Box 93, MIT Branch Sta., Cambridge, MA 02139 (SAN 214-283X).

Archive Corporation, *(Archive Corp; 0-9608810)*, 3540 Cadillac Ave., Costa Mesa, CA 92626 Tel 714-641-0279 (SAN 238-2393).

Archive Press, The, *(Archive Pr; 0-910720)*, 2101 192nd Ave., S.E., Issaquah, WA 98027 (SAN 217-2259).

Archives Ink, Ltd., *(Archives Ink; 0-915528)*, P.O. Box 1776, 16 Prospect Ave., Haworth, NJ 07641 Tel 201-384-4777 (SAN 207-7132).

Archives of Social History, *(Archives Soc Hist; 0-914924)*, P.O. Box 763, Stony Brook, NY 11790 Tel 516-751-3709 (SAN 204-4889).

Archon Books *See* **Shoe String Press, Inc.**

Archway Paperbacks, *(Archway; 0-671)*, c/o Pocket Bks., 1230 Ave. of the Americas, New York, NY 10020 Tel 212-246-2121 (SAN 202-5922).

Arco Publishing, Inc., Div. of Prentice-Hall, Inc., *(Arco; 0-668)*, 215 Park Ave., S., New York, NY 10003 Tel 212-777-6300 (SAN 201-0003).

Arctinurus Co., *(Arctinurus Co; 0-915386)*, P.O. Box 275, Bellmawr, NJ 08031-0275 Tel 609-933-0212 (SAN 276-9719).

Arden Library, *(Arden Lib; 0-8495)*, Mill & Main Sts., Darby, PA 19023 Tel 215-726-5505 (SAN 207-477X).

Arden Press, Inc., *(Arden Pr; 0-912869)*, P.O. Box 418, Denver, CO 80201 Tel 303-455-7688 (SAN 277-6553).

Ardis Pubs., *(Ardis Pubs; 0-88233)*, 2901 Heatherway, Ann Arbor, MI 48104 Tel 313-971-2367 (SAN 201-1492).

Arena Lettres, *(Arena Lettres; 0-88479)*, 8 Lincoln Place, Waldwick, NJ 07463 Tel 201-445-7154 (SAN 206-3247).

Arendson, Peter, *(P Arendson)*, 1151 Xenia St., Denver, CO 80220 Tel 303-320-4448 (SAN 239-586X).

Ares Pubs., Inc., *(Ares; 0-89005)*, 7020 N. Western Ave., Chicago, IL 60645 Tel 312-743-1405 (SAN 205-6011).

Arete Press, *(Arete Pr; 0-941736)*, 480 W. Sixth St., Claremont, CA 91711 Tel 714-624-7770 (SAN 239-1570).

Arete Pubns., *(Arete Pubns; 0-9602148)*, 8655 E. Vista Dr., Scottsdale, AZ 85253 (SAN 212-2065).

Argee Pub. Co., *(Argee Pub; 0-931084)*, 14569 Benefit, No.205, Sherman Oaks, CA 91403 Tel 213-990-6172 (SAN 211-8815).

Argo Books, *(Argo Bks; 0-912148)*, Main St., Norwich, VT 05055 Tel 802-649-1000 (SAN 203-4867).

Argo Books *See* **Atheneum Pubs.**

Argos House, *(Argos House; 0-9607082)*, Crescent Ave., Saratoga Springs, NY 12866 Tel 518-584-5817 (SAN 238-9428).

Argosy, *(Argosy; 0-87266)*, 116 E. 59th St., New York, NY 10022 (SAN 203-4875).

Argus Archives, *(Argus Archives; 0-916858)*, 228 E. 49th St, New York, NY 10017 Tel 212-355-6140 (SAN 208-4244).

Argus Communications, *(Argus Comm; 0-913592; 0-89505)*, One DLM Park, Box 5000, Allen, TX 75002 Tel 214-248-6300 (SAN 201-1476).

Ariadne Press, *(Ariadne Pr; 0-918056)*, 4817 Tallahassee Ave., Rockville, MD 20853 Tel 301-949-2514 (SAN 210-1661).

Arica Institute Press, *(Arica Inst Pr; 0-916554)*, 101 Fifth Ave., New York, NY 10003 Tel 212-807-9600 (SAN 208-5321).

Ariel Press, *(Ariel OH; 0-89804)*, 3391 Edenbrook Ct., Columbus, OH 43220 Tel 614-451-2030 (SAN 219-8460).

Ariel Pubns., *(Ariel Pubns; 0-917656)*, 14417 S.E. 19th Pl., Bellevue, WA 98007 Tel 206-641-0518 (SAN 207-5334) Do Not Confuse with Ariel Bks, CA; Ariel Pr.

Aries Press, *(Aries Pr; 0-933646)*, P.O. Box 30081, Chicago, IL 60630 Tel 312-545-0717 (SAN 212-7210).

Aries Publishing, *(Aries Pub; 0-911151)*, 24559 Amador, No. 47, Hayward, CA 94544 Tel 415-785-5446 (SAN 267-632X).

Arif, *(Arif; 0-913537)*, 2748 Ninth St., Berkeley, CA 94710 Tel 415-848-5386 (SAN 206-944X).

Arion Press, *(Arion Pr; 0-910457)*, 566 Commercial St., San Francisco, CA 94111 (SAN 267-6346) Tel 415-981-8974.

Aris Books, *(Aris Bks; 0-943186)*, 1635 Channing Way, Berkeley, CA 94703 Tel 415-843-0330 (SAN 219-7626).

Arista Corp., NDE Div., *(Arista Corp NDE; 0-912790; 0-89796; 0-914876; 0-89856)*, P.O. Box 6146, 2440 Estand Way, Concord, CA 94524 Tel 800-227-1616 (SAN 207-7078).

Arithmetic of God, The, *(AOG; 0-940532)*, P.O. Box 573, Kings Mountain, NC 28086 (SAN 219-7642).

Star Publishing Co., Subs. of Pulitzer Pub. Co., *(Ariz Daily Star; 0-9607758)*, P.O. Box 26807, 4850 S. Park Ave., Tucson, AZ 85726 Tel 602-573-4400 (SAN 239-748X).

Arizona Historical Foundation, *(AZ Hist Foun; 0-910152)*, Hayden Memorial Library, Arizona State University, Tempe, AZ 85287 Tel 602-966-8331 (SAN 201-7040).

Arizona Historical Society, *(AZ Hist Soc)*, 949 E. Second St., Tucson, AZ 85719 Tel 602-882-5774 (SAN 201-6982).

Arizona Law Institute College of Law, *(AZ Law Inst; 0-910039)*, Univ of Arizona, Tucson, AZ 85721 Tel 602-621-5522 (SAN 227-3535).

Arizona State Univ., Center for Asian Studies, *(ASU Ctr Asian; 0-939252)*, Tempe, AZ 85287 Tel 602-965-2067 (SAN 220-1623).

Arizona State Univ., Center for Latin American Studies, *(ASU Lat Am St; 0-87918)*, Tempe, AZ 85281 Tel 602-965-5127 (SAN 201-1336).

Ark & Arbor Press, *(Ark & Arbor; 0-9606234)*, Box 901, Little Compton, RI 02837 (SAN 238-907X).

Arkansas Commemorative Commission, Trapnall Hall, *(AR Commemorative; 0-9606278)*, 300 W. Markham, Little Rock, AR 72201 Tel 501-371-1799 (SAN 223-2111).

Arkansas Valley Publications, *(Ark Val Pubns; 0-910625)*, 2628 Mt. Vernon, Springfield, MO 65802 Tel 417-865-1184 (SAN 267-6443).

Arkham House Pubs., *(Arkham; 0-87054)*, P.O. Box 546, Sauk City, WI 53583 Tel 608-643-4500 (SAN 206-9741). *Imprints:* Mycroft & Moran (Mycroft & Moran).

Arlington Enterprises, *(Arlington Ent)*, P.O. Box 4381, Arlington, VA 22204 (SAN 207-6721) Moved, Left No Forwarding Address.

Arlington House *See* **Crown Pubs., Inc.**

Arlotta Press, *(Arlotta; 0-918838)*, 6340 Millbank Dr., Dayton, OH 45459 Tel 513-434-1518 (SAN 210-3877).

Arma Press, *(Arma Pr; 0-9603662)*, Rte. 139, North Branford, CT 06471 (SAN 203-4093).

Armadillo Press, *(Armadillo Pr; 0-912556)*, P.O. Box 8131, Univ. Sta., Austin, TX 78712 (SAN 203-4905).

Armado & Moth, *(Armado & Moth; 0-9603626)*, 2131 Arapahoe, Boulder, CO 80302 Tel 303-442-1415 (SAN 213-4586).

Arman, M., Pub. Inc., *(M Arman; 0-933078)*, Box 785, Ormond Beach, FL 32074 Tel 904-673-5576 (SAN 212-4777).

Arman Enterprises, Inc., *(Arman Ent; 0-915438)*, Rd 1, Box 353a, Woodstock, CT 06281 Tel 203-928-5838 (SAN 207-1673).

Armchair Press, *(Armchair Pr)*, 123 Dorchester, Scarsdale, NY 10583 (SAN 209-7028).

Armenian Numismatic Society, *(ANS; 0-9606842)*, 8511 Beverly Park Place, Pico Rivera, CA 90660 Tel 213-695-0380 (SAN 217-3263).

Armory Pubns., *(Armory Pubns; 0-9604982)*, P.O. Box 44372, Tacoma, WA 98444 Tel 206-531-4632 (SAN 215-725X).

Arms & Armour Press *See* **Stackpole Books, Inc.**

Armstrong, D., Co., Inc., *(D Armstrong; 0-918464)*, 2000-B Governor's Circle, Houston, TX 77092 Tel 713-688-1441 (SAN 210-0320).

Armstrong, Irma M., *(I M Armstrong; 0-9611106)*, 1188 Harrison Ave., Salt Lake, UT 84105 Tel 801-484-7123 (SAN 283-2925); Dist. by: Aztec Copy Inc., 881 E. 3900 S., Salt Lake City, UT 84105 (SAN 283-2933).

Armstrong Books, Inc. *See* **Armstrong Publishing Co.**

Armstrong Browning Library, *(Armstrong Browning; 0-914108)*, P.O. Box 6336, Waco, TX 76706 Tel 817-755-3566 (SAN 206-3263).

Armstrong Press, *(Armstrong Pr)*, Rte. 2, Box 509, Notasulga, AL 36866 (SAN 216-3314).

Armstrong Publishing Co., *(Armstrong Pub; 0-915936)*, 5514 Wilshire Blvd., Los Angeles, CA 90036 Tel 213-937-3600 (SAN 208-533X).

Arner Pubns., *(Arner Pubns; 0-914124)*, P.O. Box 307, Westmoreland, NY 13490 Tel 315-853-6555 (SAN 201-145X).

Arnold, Edward, Publishers Ltd., *(E Arnold; 0-7131)*, 300 North Charles Street, Baltimore, MD 21201 Tel 301-539-1529 (SAN 263-9203).

Arnold, Luis, *(L Arnold; 0-9610434)*, 13 Loma Vista Place, San Rafael, CA 94901 Tel 415-454-5075 (SAN 263-9211).

Arnold-Porter Publishing Co., *(Arnold-Porter Pub; 0-9605048)*, P.O. Box 646, Keego Harbor, MI 48033 Tel 313-338-4478 (SAN 220-0325).

Aronson, Charles N., Writer-Publisher, *(C N Aronson; 0-915736)*, 11520 Bixby Hill Road, Arcade, NY 14009 Tel 716-496-6002 (SAN 207-6144).

Aronson, Jason, Inc., *(Aronson; 0-87668)*, 111 Eighth Ave., New York, NY 10011 Tel 212-924-6663 (SAN 201-0127).

Aronson Publishing, *(Aronson Pub; 0-9604554)*, P.O. Box 3453, San Mateo, CA 94403 Tel 415-726-7134 (SAN 213-9081).

Arriaga Pubns., *(Arriaga Pubns)*, P.O. Box 652, Booneville, AK 72927 (SAN 214-0985).

Arrow Publishing Co., Inc., *(Arrow Pub; 0-913450)*, 1020 Turnpike St., Canton, MA 02021 Tel 617-828-8013 (SAN 201-6753).

Arroway Pubs., *(Arroway; 0-9600284)*, 11760 Roscoe Blvd., Bldg. E, Sun Valley, CA 91352 Tel 213-875-3730 (SAN 203-4913).

Arrowhead Press, *(Arrowhead Pr; 0-9604152)*, 3005 Fulton, Berkeley, CA 94705 Tel 415-548-5110 (SAN 214-2562).

Ars Ceramica, Ltd., *(Ars Ceramica; 0-89344)*, P.O. Box 7366, Ann Arbor, MI 48107 Tel 313-429-7864 (SAN 209-343X); Dist. by: Keramos, P.O. Box 7500, Ann Arbor, MI 48107 (SAN 169-3670).

Ars Edition Inc., *(Ars Edition; 0-86724)*, 38736 Merrick Rd., Seaford, NY 11783 Tel 516-826-6400 (SAN 220-2018).

ARS Electronics, *(Ars Electronics; 0-938630)*, 3030 Pheasant Creek Dr. 402, Northbrook, IL 60062 Tel 312-251-0089 (SAN 238-9088).

Ars Eterna Press, *(Ars Eterna; 0-9602170)*, 7627 Glen Prairie, Houston, TX 77061 (SAN 212-4785).

Ars Publishing Co., *(ARS Pub; 0-941616)*, 6 W. Main St., Suite 1, Stockton, CA 95202 Tel 209-465-8243 (SAN 239-1422).

Arsenal Press, *(Arsenal Pr; 0-9609022)*, Box 12244, Atlanta, GA 30355 Tel 404-261-7696 (SAN 241-2012).

Art Adventures Press, *(Art Adventure; 0-918326)*, 1286 Grizzly Peak, Berkeley, CA 94704 Tel 415-843-6197 (SAN 210-0339).

Art Alliance Press, Div. of Associated University Presses, *(Art Alliance; 0-87982)*, 440 Forsgate Dr., Cranbury, NJ 08512 Tel 609-655-4770 (SAN 205-602X).

Art & Communications, *(Art & Comm; 0-943188)*, 812 N. Edwards, Carlsbad, NM 88220 Tel 505-885-3295 (SAN 240-5865).

Art & Reference House, *(Art & Ref; 0-910156)*, Brownsboro, TX 75756 (SAN 203-4921).

Art Direction Book Co., *(Art Dir; 0-910158)*, Dist. by: Advertising Trade Pubns., Inc., 10 E. 39th St., Sixth Floor, New York, NY 10016 Tel 212-889-6500 (SAN 282-6704).

Art Education, Inc., *(Art Educ; 0-912242)*, 28 E. Erie St., Blauvelt, NY 10913 Tel 914-359-2233 (SAN 203-493X).

Art History Pubs., *(Art History; 0-9600002),* Rte. 2, Red Wing, MN 55066 Tel 612-388-4046 (SAN 203-4948).

Art Institute of Chicago, *(Art Inst Chi; 0-86559),* Michigan Ave. & Adams St., Chicago, IL 60603 Tel 312-443-3540 (SAN 204-479X); Dist. by: Univ. of Chicago Press, 11030 S. Langley Ave., Chicago, IL 60628 Tel 312-568-1550 (SAN 202-5299).

Art Libraries Society of North America, *(Art Libs Soc),* 3775 Bear Creek Cr., Tucson, AZ 85749 Tel 602-749-9112 (SAN 225-3291).

Art Museum & Galleries, CSULB, The, *(Art Mus Gall; 0-936270),* 1250 Bellflower Blvd., Long Beach, CA 90840 Tel 213-498-5761 (SAN 215-1308).

Arte Publico Press, *(Arte Publico; 0-934770),* Revista Chicano-Riquena, Univ. of Houston Central Campus, Houston, TX 77004 (SAN 213-4594).

Artech House, Inc., *(Artech Hse; 0-89006),* 610 Washington St., Dedham, MA 02026 Tel 617-326-8220 (SAN 201-1441).

Artefact Co, the, *(Artefact Co; 0-943190),* 5537 Germantown Ave., Philadelphia, PA 19144 Tel 215-849-0100 (SAN 240-5873).

Artemis Press, *(Artemis Pr; 0-9604664),* P.O. Box 58572, Los Angeles, CA 90058 Tel 213-692-6556 (SAN 220-0333).

Arthritis Is Easy to Stop, *(Arthritis; 0-9601236),* 304 Tenth Ave., Baraboo, WI 53913 Tel 608-356-5652 (SAN 209-5246).

Arthur Owned Publishing, *(Arthur Owned; 0-9602112),* 606A Adams Ave., Philadelphia, PA 19120 (SAN 212-2650).

Arthur Pubns., Inc., *(Arthur Pubns; 0-932782),* P.O. Box 23101, Jacksonville, FL 32241-3101 Tel 904-389-6515 (SAN 211-8823).

Arti Grafiche Il Torchio, *(Arti Grafiche; 0-935194),* 1414 Mar Vista Way, Laguna Beach, CA 92651 (SAN 213-4608).

Artichoke Press, *(Artichoke; 0-9603916),* 3274 Parkhurst Dr., Rancho Palos Verdes, CA 90274 (SAN 213-6562).

Artichoke Pubns., *(Artichoke Pub; 0-910163),* 7410 Baxtershire Dr., Dallas, TX 75230 Tel 214-233-9479 (SAN 241-2020).

Artisan Books, *(Artisan Bks; 0-89528),* Box 37, Pleasantville, NY 10570 Tel 914-747-0710 (SAN 210-3885).

Artisan Press, *(Artisan Pr),* Dist. by: Bookpeople, 2940 Seventh St., Berkeley, CA 94710 Tel 415-549-3033 (SAN 168-9517).

Artisan Sales, *(Artisan Sales; 0-934666),* P.O. Box 1497, Thousand Oaks, CA 91360 Tel 805-482-8076 (SAN 211-8408).

Artistic Endeavors, *(Artistic Endeavors; 0-9604500),* 24 Emerson Place, Boston, MA 02114 Tel 617-227-1967 (SAN 207-5733).

Artists & Alchemists Pubns., *(Artists & Alchemists; 0-915600),* 215 Bridgeway, Sausalito, CA 94965 Tel 415-332-0326 (SAN 207-3978); Dist. by: Swallow Press, 811 Junior Terrace, Chicago, IL 60613 (SAN 202-5671).

Artists Foundation, Inc., The, *(Artists Found; 0-932246),* 110 Broad St., Boston, MA 02110 Tel 617-482-8100 (SAN 212-2073).

Artman's Press, *(Artmans Pr),* 1511 McGee Ave., Berkeley, CA 94703 (SAN 206-8923).

Arts Administration Research Institute, *(Arts Admin Res Inst; 0-915440),* 75 Spark St., Cambridge, MA 02138 (SAN 223-6222).

Arts & Architecture Press, *(Arts & Arch; 0-931228),* 1137 Second St., Suite 200, Santa Monica, CA 90403 (SAN 211-5050).

Arts & Culture of the North, *(Arts & Culture; 0-9605898),* Box 1333, Gracie Square Sta., New York, NY 10028 Tel 212-879-9019 (SAN 216-3322).

Arts & Humanities Council of Tulsa, *(Art & Human Council Tulsa),* 2210 S. Main, Tulsa, OK 74114 (SAN 238-0064).

Arts Books, *(Arts Bks; 0-9607458),* 80 Piedmont Court, Larkspur, CA 94939 Tel 415-924-2633 (SAN 238-003X).

Arts End Books, *(Arts End; 0-933292),* P.O. Box 162, Newton, MA 02168 Tel 617-965-2478 (SAN 213-6082).

Artus Co., The, *(Artus Co),* 19318 Lunn Rd., Cleveland, OH 44136 (SAN 215-6687).

Arvidson, J., Press, *(J Arvidson; 0-9602098),* P.O. Box 4022, Helena, MT 59601 Tel 406-442-0354 (SAN 209-0848).

As Is/So & So Press, *(Asis So&So),* 2864 Folsom, San Francisco, CA 94110 (SAN 219-1148).

Asbury, Francis, Publishing Co., *(F Asbury Pub Co),* P.O. Box 7, Wilmore, KY 40390 (SAN 215-0557).

Asbury Theological Seminary, *(Asbury Theological),* Wilmore, KY 40390 (SAN 208-2616).

Ascension Academy Chinese Project, *(Ascension; 0-9600176),* 4401 W. Braddock Rd., Alexandria, VA 22304 Tel 703-379-6050 (SAN 203-4956).

Aschley Press, The, *(Aschley Pr; 0-940900),* 3329 Grenway Rd., Cleveland, OH 44122 Tel 216-752-3535 (SAN 223-1735).

Ascii, *(Ascii; 0-9603432; 0-939414),* P.O. Box 222, Eagle River, AK 99577 Tel 907-688-9485 (SAN 213-6015).

Asclepiad Pubns., Inc., *(Asclepiad; 0-935718),* 2257 Independence, Ann Arbor, MI 48104 (SAN 213-7240).

Ash-Kar Press, *(Ash-Kar Pr; 0-9605308),* 519 Castro St., San Francisco, CA 94114 (SAN 213-0025).

Ash Lad Press, *(Ash Lad Pr; 0-915492),* P.O. Box 396, Canton, NY 13617 Tel 315-386-8820 (SAN 207-4265).

Ashford Press, *(Ashford Pr CT; 0-937992),* RFD 1, Box 182-A, Willimantic, CT 06226 (SAN 219-7650).

Ashford Pubns., *(Ashford; 0-938260),* Kingsride Lane, Houston, TX 77079 Tel 713-932-0518 (SAN 281-2878); Orders to: Box 61648, Houston, TX 77208 Tel 713-754-1299 (SAN 281-2886) Alternate Name Smith & Assoc.

Ashland Poetry Press, *(Ashland Poetry; 0-912592),* Ashland College, Ashland, OH 44805 Tel 419-289-4096 (SAN 203-4972).

Ashlar Press, *(Ashlar Pr; 0-932534),* Box 120277, Nashville, TN 37212 (SAN 212-4025); Dist. by: Third Century Press,Ltd., 2103 Crestmoor Rd., Nashville, TN 37215 (SAN 200-4119).

Ashlee Publishing Co., Inc., *(Ashlee Pub Co; 0-911993),* 310 Madison Ave., New York, NY 10017 Tel 212-682-7681 (SAN 264-7125).

Ashley Books, Inc., *(Ashley Bks; 0-87949),* 30 Main St., Port Washington, NY 11050 Tel 516-883-2221 (SAN 201-1409); Orders to: P.O. Box 768, Port Washington, NY 11050 Tel 516-883-2221 (SAN 201-1417).

Ashod Press, *(Ashod Pr; 0-935102),* 620 E. 20th St, 11F, New York, NY 10009 Tel 212-475-0711 (SAN 281-2894); Orders to: P.O. Box 1147 Madison Square Station, New York, NY 10159 (SAN 281-2908).

Asia Book Corp. of America, *(Asia Bk Corp; 0-940500),* 94-41 218th St., Queens Village, NY 11426 Tel 212-648-1481 (SAN 214-493X).

Asia Publishing House, *(Asia; 0-210),* Dist. by: APT Books, Inc., 141 E. 44th St., Suite 511, New York, NY 10017 Tel 212-697-0887 (SAN 215-7209).

Asia Society, Inc., *(Asia Soc; 0-87848),* 725 Park Ave., New York, NY 10021 Tel 212-288-6400 (SAN 281-2916); Dist. by: Charles E. Tuttle, Co., P.O. Box 419, Rutland, VT 05701 Tel 802-773-8930 (SAN 213-2621).

Asian American Studies Center, UCLA, *(Asian Am Stud),* 3232 Campbell Hall, Univ. of California, Los Angeles, CA 90024 Tel 213-825-2974 (SAN 210-7759).

Asian Conservation Laboratory, *(Asian Conserv Lab),* Dist. by: Raiko Corp., P.O. Box 597, New York, NY 10003 Tel 212-783-2597 (SAN 240-9542).

Asian Humanities Press See Lancaster-Miller Pubs.

Asian Music Pubns., *(Asian Music Pub; 0-913360),* University of WA, School of Music, Seattle, WA 98195 Tel 206-543-0974 (SAN 201-1387).

Asian Productivity Organization See Unipub

Asigan Limited, *(Asigan Ltd; 0-910333),* P.O. Box 10688, Beverly Hills, CA 90213 Tel 213-550-1982 (SAN 241-2667).

Asociacion Nacional Pro Personas Mayores, *(Assn Personas Mayores; 0-913139),* 1730 W. Olympic Blvd. Suite 401, Los Angeles, CA 90015 Tel 213-487-1922 (SAN 223-7768).

Aspen Art, *(Aspen Art; 0-9601120),* 401 Center, Evanston, WY 82930 Tel 307-789-9879 (SAN 210-167X).

Aspen Center for the Visual Arts, *(Aspen Ctr Visual Arts; 0-934324),* 590 N. Mill St., Aspen, CO 81611 Tel 303-925-8050 (SAN 213-2834).

Aspen Institute for Humanistic Studies, *(Aspen Inst Human; 0-89843),* 717 Fifth Ave., New York, NY 10022 Tel 212-759-1053 (SAN 213-0033); Orders to: Aspen Institute at Wye Plantation, Publications Office, P.O. Box 150, Queenstown, MD 21658 (SAN 213-0041).

Aspen Pubns., *(Aspen Pubns; 0-9603756),* 839 S. 250 West, Orem, UT 84057 Tel 801-225-2403 (SAN 214-2309).

Aspen Systems Corp., *(Aspen Systems; 0-912862; 0-89443),* 1600 Research Blvd., Rockville, MD 20850 Tel 301-251-5000 (SAN 226-2126).

Assembling Press, *(Assembling Pr; 0-915066),* P.O. Box 1967, Brooklyn, NY 11202 (SAN 201-1360).

Assertive Training Institute, *(Assert Train Inst; 0-9603958),* P.O. Box 3201, Flagstaff, AZ 86003 (SAN 221-590X).

Associated Advertisers Services, *(Assoc Advert Serv),* P.O. Box 570122, Houston, TX 77257 (SAN 285-6883).

Associated Air Balance Council, *(Assoc Air Bal),* 1133 15th St. N.W., Washington, DC 20005 Tel 267-7113).

Associated Book Pubs., Inc., *(Assoc Bk Pubs; 0-910164),* P.O. Box 5657, Scottsdale, AZ 85261 Tel 602-998-5223 (SAN 212-2081).

Associated Booksellers, *(Assoc Bk; 0-87497),* 147 McKinley Ave., P.O. Box 6361, Bridgeport, CT 06606 Tel 203-366-5494 (SAN 169-0655).

Associated Creative Writers, *(Assoc Creative Writers; 0-933362),* 9231 Molly Woods Ave., La Mesa, CA 92041 (SAN 212-8292).

Associated Faculty Press, *(Assoc Faculty Pr; 0-86733),* 90 South Bayles Ave., Port Washington, NY 11050 Tel 914-332-4030 (SAN 281-2932); 110 W. 57th Street, New York, NY 10019 (SAN 281-2940). *Imprints:* National University Publications (Natl U).

Associated Grantmakers of Massachusetts, Inc., *(Assoc Grant; 0-912427),* Suite 417, 294 Washington St., Boston, MA 02108 Tel 617-426-2606 (SAN 265-1807).

Associated Music Publishers G. Schirmer, Inc., Subs. of G. Shirmer, Inc., *(Assoc Mus; 0-911320),* 866 Third Ave., New York, NY 10022 (SAN 222-9544).

Associated Printers, *(Assoc Print),* Grafton-Grand Forks, Box 471, Grafton, ND 58237 Tel 701-352-0640 (SAN 209-5254).

Associated Pubns., *(Assoc Pubns; 0-9608806),* P.O. Box 728, Glendora, CA 91740 (SAN 238-2407).

Associated Pubs., *(Assoc Pubs NY; 0-940902),* 40 Fairview Ave., White Plains, NY 10603 Tel 914-997-0671 (SAN 223-1611).

Associated Writing Programs, *(Assoc Writing Progs; 0-936266),* c/o Old Dominion Univ., Norfolk, VA 23508 Tel 804-440-3840 (SAN 214-0993).

Associates in Thanatology, *(Assocs Thanatology; 0-9607928),* 206 Maplewood St., Watertown, MA 02172 (SAN 281-2967); Dist. by: DeVorss and Co., P. O. Box 550, Marina Del Rey, CA 90291 Tel 213-870-7487 (SAN 168-9886); Dist. by: Inland Book Co., P. O. Box 261, East Haven, CT 06512 Tel 203-467-4257 (SAN 200-4151).

Associates of the James Ford Bell Library, *(Assocs James Bell; 0-9601798),* 472 Wilson Library, Univ. of Minnesota, 309 19th Ave. S., Minneapolis, MN 55455 Tel 612-373-2888 (SAN 209-1763).

Association for Brain Tumor Research, *(Assn Brain Tumor),* 6232 N Pulaski Rd, Chicago, IL 60646 (SAN 224-280X).

Assn. for Childhood Education International, *(ACEI; 0-87173),* 3615 Wisconsin Ave., N.W., Washington, DC 20016 Tel 202-363-6963 (SAN 201-2200).

Assn. for Consumer Research, *(Assn Consumer Res; 0-915552),* Grad. Sch. of Business Admin., Univ. of Michigan, Ann Arbor, MI 48109 (SAN 207-3838).

Assn. for Educational Communications & Technology, *(Assn Ed Comm Tech; 0-89240),* 1126 Sixteenth St., N.W., Washington, DC 20036 Tel 202-466-4780 (SAN 207-3277).

Association for Holistic Health Staff, *(Assn Holistic;)*, P.O. Box 9532, San Diego, CA 92109 (SAN 263-9246).

Association for Northern California Records & Research, *(Assn NC Records;)*, P.O. Box 3024, Chico, CA 95927 Tel 916-895-5710 (SAN 267-8063).

Association for Public Justice Education Fund, *(Assn Public Justice; 0-936456)*, 2000 K St., Suite 300, Washington, DC 20006 Tel 202-429-0244 (SAN 214-1000).

Association for Research & Enlightenment, Inc. See A.R.E. Press

Assn. for Supervision & Curriculum Development, *(Assn Supervision; 0-87120)*, 225 N. Washington St., Alexandria, VA 22314 Tel 703-549-9110 (SAN 201-1352).

Assn. for Systems Management, *(Assn Syst Mgmt; 0-934356)*, 24587 Bagley Rd., Cleveland, OH 44138 Tel 216-243-6900 (SAN 201-7091).

Association for the Advancement of Medical Instrumentation, *(Assn Adv Med Instrs; 0-910275)*, 1901 N Fort Myer Dr., Suite 602, Arlington, VA 22209 Tel 703-525-4890 (SAN 224-3407).

Assn. for the Study of Family Living, The, *(Assn Family Living; 0-9602670)*, P.O. Box 130, Brooklyn, NY 11208 Tel 212-647-7406 (SAN 212-8772).

Association of American Colleges, *(Assn Am Coll; 0-911696)*, 1818 R St. N.W., Washington, DC 20009 Tel 202-387-3760 (SAN 224-0572).

Association of American Geographers, *(Assn Am Geographers; 0-89291)*, 1710 16th St., N.W., Washington, DC 20009 Tel 202-234-1450 (SAN 201-6796).

Assn. of American Pubs., Inc., *(AAP; 0-933636)*, 1 Park Ave., New York, NY 10016 Tel 212-689-8920 (SAN 204-4714).

Assn. of Arab-American Univ. Graduates, *(Assn Arab-Amer U Grads; 0-937694)*, 556 Trapelo Rd., Belmont, MA 02178 (SAN 240-0820).

Assn. of Baptist Professors of Religion, *(Assn Baptist Profs; 0-932180)*, Box A, Mercer Univ., Macon, GA 31207 (SAN 211-2175).

Assn. of Christian Librarians, *(Assn Chr Libs;)*, Houghton College - Buffalo Suburban Campus, 910 Union Rd., West Seneca, NY 14224 (SAN 217-2267).

Assn. of Christian Pubs. & Booksellers, Inc., *(Assn Christian Pub; 0-943258)*, 3360 NW 110th St., Miami, FL 33167 (SAN 240-3390).

Assn. of Information Systems Professionals, *(AISP; 0-935220)*, 1015 North York Rd., Willow Grove, PA 19090 Tel 215-657-6300 (SAN 213-5191).

Association of Interpretive Naturalists Incorporated, *(Assn Interp Naturalist;)*, 6700 Needwood Rd., Derwood, MD 20855 Tel 301-948-8844 (SAN 226-6644).

Assn. of School Business Officials of the United States & Canada, *(Assn Sch Busn; 0-910170)*, 720 Garden St., Park Ridge, IL 60068 Tel 312-823-9320 (SAN 204-5478).

Assn. of Sexologists, The, *(Assn Sexologists; 0-939902)*, 1523 Franklin St., San Francisco, CA 94109 (SAN 216-7867); Dist. by: Multi-Media Resource Ctr., 1525 Franklin St., San Francisco, CA 94109 (SAN 206-6017).

Association of Systematics Collections, *(Assn Syst Coll; 0-942924)*, Museum of Natural History, Univ. of Kansas, Lawrence, KS 66045 (SAN 232-5853).

Association of Teacher Educators, Affiliate of National Education Assn., *(Assn Tchr Ed;)*, 1900 Association Dr., Suite ATE, Reston, VA 22091 Tel 703-620-3110 (SAN 203-7904).

Assn. of Trial Lawyers of America Education Fund, *(Assn Trial Ed; 0-941916)*, 1050 31st St. NW, Washington, DC 20007 Tel 202-965-3500 (SAN 238-2156).

Association of University Programs in Health Administration, *(Assn Univ Progs Hlth;)*, One Dupont Circle, Washington, DC 20036 Tel 202-659-4354 (SAN 224-4793).

Association on American Indian Affairs, *(Assn Am Indian;)*, 432 Park Ave., S., New York, NY 10016 Tel 212-689-8720 (SAN 204-4730).

Association for the Study of the Nationalities (USSR) and East Europe, *(Assn Study Nat; 0-910895)*, Coleman Hall 216, Eastern Illinois University, Charleston, IL 61920 (SAN 263-2470).

Assurance Pubs., *(Assurance Pubs; 0-932940)*, P.O. Box 753, Rockville, MD 20851 (SAN 213-005X).

Astara, Inc., *(Astara; 0-918936)*, 800 W. Arrow Hwy., P.O. Box 5003, Upland, CA 91786 Tel 714-981-4941 (SAN 207-6446).

Aston Hall Pubns, Inc., *(Aston Hall; 0-89036)*, 1835 Hicks Rd., Rolling Meadows, IL 60008 (SAN 213-0068).

Astor-Honor, Inc., *(Astor-Honor; 0-8392)*, 48 E. 43rd St., New York, NY 10017 (SAN 203-5022).

Astraea Pubs., Inc., *(Astraea Pub; 0-910285)*, P.O. Box 7903, Atlanta, GA 30357 Tel 404-873-4793 (SAN 241-2675).

Astro Artz, *(Astro Artz; 0-937122)*, 240 S. Broadway, Los Angeles, CA 90012 (SAN 215-6229).

Astro Press, *(Astro Pr TX; 0-9608568)*, P.O. Box 820399, Dallas, TX 75382 (SAN 238-2415).

Astro Psychology Institute, *(Astro Psych; 0-941208)*, 2640 Greenwich, Suite 403, San Francisco, CA 94123 Tel 415-921-1192 (SAN 217-3271).

Astro Pubs., *(Astro Pubs; 0-941272)*, 1332 University Blvd. N., Jacksonville, FL 32211 Tel 904-743-7344 (SAN 238-9096).

Astroart Enterprises, *(Astroart Ent; 0-917814)*, P.O. Box 503, South Houston, TX 77587 Tel 713-649-6601 (SAN 203-5030).

Astrologer on Wheels, Inc., *(Astrol Wheels; 0-940044)*, 141 E. 55th St., New York, NY 10022 (SAN 220-2034); P.O. Box 5255, F. D. R. Sta., New York, NY 10150 (SAN 220-2042).

Astronomical Calendar, *(Astron Cal; 0-934546)*, Dept. of Physics, Furman Univ., Greenville, SC 29613 Tel 803-294-2208 (SAN 209-5602).

Astrosonics Research Institute, *(Astrosonics; 0-939192)*, 11037 1/2 Freeman Ave., Lennox, CA 90304 Tel 213-673-4649 (SAN 220-1631).

Asylum Hill, Inc., *(Asylum Hill; 0-9602952)*, 880 Asylum Ave., Hartford, CT 06105 (SAN 213-0114).

Asylum's Press, *(Asylums Pr; 0-940220)*, 464 Amsterdam Ave., New York, NY 10024 Tel 212-799-4475 (SAN 220-3235).

At Speed Press, *(At Speed Pr; 0-940046)*, P.O. Box 5400, Santa Barbara, CA 93108 Tel 805-966-2814 (SAN 220-2050); Dist. by: Motorbooks International, P.O. Box 2, 729 Prospect Ave., Osceola, WI 54020 Tel 800-826-6600 (SAN 212-3304).

At-Swim Press, *(At-Swim; 0-939254)*, c/o Facsimile Book Shop, 16 W. 55th St., New York, NY 10019 Tel 212-581-2672 (SAN 215-3084).

Ata Books, *(Ata Bks; 0-931688)*, 1928 Stuart St., Berkeley, CA 94703 Tel 415-841-9613 (SAN 211-4801).

Atcom, Inc., *(Atcom; 0-915260)*, 2315 Broadway, New York, NY 10024 (SAN 208-4252).

ATE See Association of Teacher Educators

Athena Press, Inc., *(Athena Pr; 0-9602736)*, P.O. Box 776, Vienna, VA 22180 (SAN 213-0076).

Athena Press, The, *(Athena Pr ND; 0-940730)*, 602 S. Fourth St., Grand Forks, ND 58201 Tel 701-775-9156 (SAN 219-7081).

Athena Pubns., *(Athena Pubns; 0-932950)*, Box 837, 23 Aurora St., Moravia, NY 13118 (SAN 212-7156).

Athenaeum of Philadelphia, *(Athenaeum Phila; 0-916530)*, 219 S. Sixth St., E. Washington Square, Philadelphia, PA 19106 Tel 215-925-2688 (SAN 208-5402).

Atheneum Pubs., *(Atheneum; 0-689)*, 597 Fifth Ave., New York, NY 10017 Tel 212-486-2700 (SAN 201-0011); 122 E. 42nd St., New York, NY 10017 (SAN 209-3162); Dist. by: The Scribner Book Companies, 201 Willowbrook Blvd., Wayne, NJ 07470 (SAN 201-002X). *Imprints:* Aladdin Books (Aladdin); Argo Books (Argo); McElderry Book (McElderry Bk).

Athenian House Pubs., *(Athenian Hse; 0-936038)*, P.O. Box 90968, Nashville, TN 37209 (SAN 213-9103).

Athletic Institute, *(Athletic Inst; 0-87670)*, 200 N. Castlewood Dr., North Palm Beach, FL 33408 Tel 304-842-3600 (SAN 203-5065).

Athletic Press, *(Athletic; 0-87095)*, P.O. Box 50314, Pasadena, CA 91105 Tel 213-283-3446 (SAN 203-5057).

Athletics Congress/USA, The, *(Athletics Cong; 0-939254)*, P.O. Box 120, Indianapolis, IN 46206 Tel 317-638-9155 (SAN 220-164X).

Atkinson, Mary D., *(Atkinson; 0-937436)*, 8712-63rd Ave., College Park, MD 20740 (SAN 215-6091).

Atlanta's Best Buys, *(Atlantas Best; 0-9608196)*, P.O. Box 11662, Atlanta, GA 30355 Tel 404-261-0566 (SAN 240-1878).

Atlantic Pubs., Inc., *(Atlantic Pub NY;)*, 135 W. 50th St., New York, NY 10020 (SAN 237-9910).

Atlantic Reef Committee, The, *(Univ Miami A R C;)*, Univ. of Miami, Fisher Island Sta., Miami Beach, FL 33139 (SAN 239-5134).

Atlantis Editions, *(Atlantis;)*, 11 E. 73rd St., New York, NY 10021 (SAN 209-312X).

Atlantis Editions, *(Atlantis Edns; 0-910174)*, P.O. Box 18326, Philadelphia, PA 19120 (SAN 207-5849).

Atlantis Pub Co., *(Atlantis Pub NY; 0-442)*, 135 W. 50th St., New York, NY 10020 Tel 212-265-8700 (SAN 200-237X).

Atlantis Rising, *(Atlantis Rising; 0-932932)*, 308 Eureka St., San Francisco, CA 94114 (SAN 212-2669) Moved, Left No Forwarding Address.

ATQ (American Transcendental Quarterly), *(ATQ; 0-9607894)*, Department of English, University of Rhode Island, Kingston, RI (SAN 237-9325)02881.

Attention Span Advancement Registry Service, *(ASA; 0-9606990)*, 1940 Fifth Ave., Sacramento, CA 95818 (SAN 238-910X).

Attic Books Ltd., *(Attic Bks; 0-915018)*, 41 E. 57th St., Suite 1210, New York, NY 10022 Tel 212-593-3970 (SAN 206-8931); Orders to: P.O. Box 38, South Salem, NY 10590 (SAN 206-894X).

Attic Press, *(Attic Pr; 0-87921)*, Stony Point, Rte. 2, Greenwood, SC 29646 Tel 803-374-3013 (SAN 201-1328).

Auburn House Publishing Co., Inc., *(Auburn Hse; 0-86569)*, 131 Clarendon St., Boston, MA 02116 Tel 617-247-2650 (SAN 220-0341).

Auburn-Wolfe Publishing, *(Auburn-Wolfe; 0-912385)*, 584 Castro St., No. 351, San Francisco, CA 94114 Tel 415-665-2025 (SAN 265-1823).

Audel, Theodore, *(Audel; 0-672)*, Dist. by: Bobbs-Merrill, 4300 W. 62nd St., P.O. Box 7083, Indianapolis, IN 46206 Tel 317-298-5542 (SAN 201-3959).

Audit Investments Inc., *(Audit Investments; 0-912840)*, 230 Park Ave., New York, NY 10169 Tel 212-661-1710 (SAN 201-1301).

Audubon Publishing Co., *(Audubon Pub Co; 0-910629)*, P.O. Box 581, Owensboro, KY 42302-0581 (SAN 263-2462).

Audubon Society of Portland, *(Audubon Soc Portland; 0-931686)*, 5151 N.W. Cornell Rd., Portland, OR 97210 Tel 211-2132 (SAN 211-2132).

Augsburg Publishing House, *(Augsburg; 0-8066)*, 426 S. Fifth St., Box 1209, Minneapolis, MN 55440 Tel 612-330-3404 (SAN 169-4081); 57 E. Main St., Columbus, OH 43215 (SAN 156-4951); 5210 N. Lamar, Austin, TX 78765 (SAN 146-3365).

August Corp., *(August Corp; 0-933482)*, P.O. Box 582, Scottsdale, AZ 85252 Tel 602-949-7366 (SAN 215-2940).

August House, *(August Hse; 0-935304)*, 1010 W. 3rd St., Little Rock, AR 72201 Tel 501-376-4516 (SAN 223-7288).

Augustana College Library, *(Augustana Coll; 0-910182)*, 35th St. & Seventh Ave., Rock Island, IL 61201 Tel 309-794-7266 (SAN 203-5073).

Augustana Historical Society, *(Augustana; 0-910184)*, Augustana College Library, Rock Island, IL 61201 Tel 309-794-7266 (SAN 206-6378); Orders to: Denkmann Memorial Library, Augustana College, Rock Island, IL 61201 (SAN 206-6386).

Augustin, J. J., Inc., Pub., *(J J Augustin; 0-87439)*, Locust Valley, NY 11560 Tel 516-676-1510 (SAN 204-5451).

Aum Pubns., *(Aum Pubns; 0-88497)*, P.O. Box 32433, Jamaica, NY 11431 Tel 212-523-3471 (SAN 201-128X).

Aunt Lute Book Co., *(Aunt Lute Bk Co; 0-918040),* 529 S. Gilbert St., Iowa City, IA 52240 Tel 319-338-7022 (SAN 210-217X).
Aura Books, *(Aura Bks; 0-937736),* 7911 Willoughby Ave., Los Angeles, CA 90046 (SAN 215-7268).
Aura Publishing Co., *(Aura Pub),* 1747 47th St., Brooklyn, NY 11204 (SAN 237-9317).
Aurea Pubns., *(Aurea; 0-87174),* P.O. Box 176, Allenhurst, NJ 07711 Tel 201-531-4535 (SAN 203-5081).
Aurelian Press, *(Aurelian Pr; 0-918844),* P.O. Box 366, Wilmette, IL 60091 Tel 312-251-6718 (SAN 210-3907).
Aurelon Tales, *(Aurelon; 0-912388),* R.F.D. No. 2, 177 Sarles St., Mt. Kisco, NY 10549 (SAN 203-509X).
Auricle Press, *(Auricle Pr; 0-939904),* 499 Humboldt St., Santa Rosa, CA 95404 (SAN 216-7875).
Aurico Publishing Co., *(Aurico; 0-910186),* 87 Elmwood St., Somerville, MA 02144 Tel 617-491-2565 (SAN 203-1442).
Auriga, *(Auriga; 0-9602738),* Box F, 8 Candlelight Court, Clifton Park, NY 12065 Tel 518-371-2015 (SAN 212-8780).
Auromere, Inc., *(Auromere; 0-89744),* 1291 Weber St., Pomona, CA 91768 Tel 714-629-8255 (SAN 169-0043).
Aurora News Register Publishing Co., *(Aurora News Reg; 0-8300),* 1320 K, Aurora, NE 68818 (SAN 281-2991); Dist. by: Shirley Lueth, 1409 9th St., Aurora, NE 68818 (SAN 282-5910).
Aurora Press, *(Aurora Press; 0-943358),* 205 Third Ave., Apt 2-A, New York, NY 10003 Tel 212-673-1831 (SAN 240-5881).
Aurora Pubs., *(Aurora Pubs; 0-87695),* P.O. Box 120616, Nashville, TN 37212 Tel 615-254-5842 (SAN 201-1271).
Ausonia Press, *(Ausonia Pr; 0-914872),* 1997 Eddy St., San Francisco, CA 94115 Tel 415-931-5553 (SAN 265-1831).
Austin Bilingual Language Editions, *(Austin Bilingual Lang Ed; 0-940048),* P.O. Box 3864, Austin, TX 78764 Tel 512-441-1436 (SAN 220-2069).
Austin Hill Press, Inc., *(Austin Hill Pr; 0-89690),* 2955 Renault Place, San Diego, CA 92122 Tel 619-453-6486 (SAN 211-8831).
Austin Junior Forum, Inc., *(Austin Junior; 0-9607152),* P.O. Box 26628, Austin, TX 78755 Tel 512-345-0704 (SAN 238-9436).
Austin Press, Div. of Lone Star Pubs. Inc., *(Austin Pr; 0-914872),* P.O. Box 9774, Austin, TX 78766 Tel 512-255-2333 (SAN 206-7870).
Australia National University Press, *(Australia N U P),* 15601 S.W. 83rd Ave., Miami, FL 33157 Tel 305-251-3934 (SAN 212-0658).
Australian National Univ. Pr., *(ANU Pr; 0-7081),* P. O. Box 1365, New York, NY 10023 Tel 212-799-3854.
Australiana Pubns., *(Australiana; 0-909162),* 6511 Riviera Dr., Coral Gables, FL 33146 Tel 305-666-9404 (SAN 209-3235) Name Formerly Dryden Press of Australia.
Author Aid/Researh Associates International, Div. of Research Associates International, *(Author Aid; 0-911085),* 340 E. 52nd St., New York, NY 10022 Tel 212-758-4213 (SAN 263-0672).
Authors' Co-op Publishing Co., *(Authors Co-op; 0-931150),* Rte. 4, Box 137, Franklin, TN 37064 Tel 615-646-3757 (SAN 211-5875).
Authors Edition, Inc., *(Authors Edn; 0-918058),* Box 803, Lenox, MA 01240 Tel 413-637-0666 (SAN 210-1696).
Auto Book Press, *(Auto Bk; 0-910390),* 1511 Grand Ave., San Marcos, CA 92069 Tel 619-744-3582 (SAN 201-1263).
Automated Marketing Systems, Inc., *(Automated Mktg; 0-912610),* 310 S. Michigan Ave., Suite 1150, Chicago, IL 60604 Tel 312-663-5580 (SAN 205-7336); Orders to: 424 N. Third St., Burlington, IA 52601 Tel 319-752-5415 (SAN 205-7344).
Automation in Housing, *(Automation in Housing Mag; 0-9607408),* P.O. Box 120, Carpinteria, CA 93014 Tel 805-684-7659 (SAN 239-1589).
Automation Printing, *(Automation Print; 0-9603984),* P.O. Box 12201, El Cajon, CA 92022 (SAN 223-4483).

Automobile Quarterly Pubns., *(Auto Quarterly; 0-915038),* P.O.Box 348, Kutztown, PA 19530 Tel 800-523-0236 (SAN 281-3017); Orders to: 245 W. Main St., Kutztown, PA 19530 Tel 215-683-8352 (SAN 281-3025).
Autonomy House Publications, *(Autonomy Hse),* 417 N. Main St., Monticello, IN 47960 Tel 219-583-8593 (SAN 263-9254).
Autotronic Conversions, *(Autotronic Conversions),* P.O. Box 17249, El Paso, TX 79917 Tel (SAN 208-2241).
Autumn Press, *(Autumn Pr; 0-914398),* 1318 Beacon St., Brookline, MA 02146 Tel 617-738-5680 (SAN 207-043X).
Auvinen, Jewell Shelly, *(J S Auvinen; 0-9610158),* P.O. Box 5185, Santa Cruz, CA 95063 Tel 408-423-7004 (SAN 263-9262).
Auxiliary of Burdette Tomlin Memorial Hospital, *(B T Memorial; 0-9608326),* Cape May Court House, Cape May, NJ 08210 Tel 609-368-5068 (SAN 240-5156).
Auxiliary Univ. Pr., *(Auxiliary U Pr; 0-913034),* Box 772, Barrington, IL 60010 Tel 312-381-7888 (SAN 202-327X); c/o Lea Denory, Box 772, Barrington, IL 60010 Tel 312-381-7888 (SAN 202-327X).
Avalon Communications, Inc., *(Avalon Comm; 0-88041),* 1705 Broadway, Hewlett, NY 11557 Tel 516-599-4555 (SAN 281-3033); Dist. by: Doubleday & Co., Inc., 501 Franklin Ave., Garden City, NY 11530 (SAN 281-6083).
Avalon Hill Game Co., *(Avalon Hill),* 4517 Harford Rd., Baltimore, MD 21214 Tel 301-254-5300 (SAN 204-4633).
Avant Books, *(Avant Bks; 0-932238),* 3719 Sixth Ave., San Diego, CA 92103 Tel 714-295-0473 (SAN 212-8055).
Avant Garde Creations, Inc., *(Avant Garde CR; 0-930182),* Box 30160, Eugene, OR 97403 Tel 503-345-3043 (SAN 210-5853) Do Not Confuse with Avant-Garde Media, Inc. in NY.
Avant-Garde Media, Inc., *(Avant-Garde; 0-913568),* 251 W. 57th St., New York, NY 10019 Tel 212-581-2000 (SAN 206-9563) Do Not Confuse with Avant Garde Creations in OR.
Avatar, *(AVATAR MO; 0-936040),* P.O. Box 16703, Raytown, MO 64133 (SAN 220-2328).
Avatar Book Institute, *(Avatar Bk Inst; 0-941390),* 23131 Canzonet St., Woodland Hills, CA 91367 Tel 213-888-8209 (SAN 238-9444).
Avatar Press, *(Avatar Pr; 0-914790),* P.O. Box 7727, Atlanta, GA 30357 Tel 404-972-7282 (SAN 206-7579).
Avcom International Inc., *(Avcom Intl; 0-941024),* P.O. Box 2398, Wichita, KS 67201 Tel 316-262-1491 (SAN 223-1743).
Ave Maria Institute Press See **AMI International Press**
Ave Maria Press, *(Ave Maria; 0-87793),* Notre Dame, IN 46556 Tel 219-287-2831 (SAN 201-1255).
Avenue Publishing Co., *(Avenue Pub; 0-910977),* 9417 Conant Ave., Hamtramck, MI 48212 Tel 313-875-6635 (SAN 268-1811).
Avery Color Studios, *(Avery Color; 0-932212),* Star Route Box 275, Au Train, MI 49806 Tel 906-892-8251 (SAN 211-1470).
Avery Press, *(Avery Pr),* P.O. Box 7396, Atlanta, GA 30357 (SAN 210-9131).
Avery Pub. Group, Inc., *(Avery Pub; 0-89529),* 142 Fulton Ave., Garden City Park, NY 11040 Tel 516-741-2155 (SAN 281-305X); Orders to: 89 Baldwin Terrace, Wayne, NJ 07470 (SAN 281-3068).
Avian Pubns., *(Avian Pubns; 0-910335),* 310 Maria Dr., Warrsau, WI 54401 Tel 715-845-5101 (SAN 241-2691).
Aviation Book Co., *(Aviation; 0-911720; 0-911721),* 1640 Victory Blvd., Glendale, CA 91201 Tel 213-240-1771 (SAN 120-1530); P.O. Box 4187, Glendale, CA 91202 (SAN 213-4993).
Aviation Language School Inc., *(Aviation Lang Sch; 0-941456),* 4011 Woodridge Rd., Coconut Grove, FL 33133 Tel 305-665-9041 (SAN 239-0639).
Aviation Maintenance Pubns., *(Aviation Maintenance; 0-89100),* P.O. Box 890, Basin, WY 82410 Tel 307-568-2413 (SAN 209-3189).
Aviation Pubns., *(Aviat Pub; 0-87994),* P.O. Box 357, Appleton, WI 54912 (SAN 201-713X).

Aviation Quarterly, *(Aviation Quart; 0-911721),* P.O. Box 606, Plano, TX 75074 (SAN 238-0013).
Avocation Pubs., *(Avocation Pubs; 0-934200),* 50 King St., Suite 3D, New York, NY 10014 (SAN 213-2826).
Avocet, Inc., *(Avocet Inc.; 0-9607236),* Box 7615, Menlo Park, CA 94025 Tel 415-321-8501 (SAN 239-1597).
Avon Bard Books See **Avon Books**
Avon Books, *(Avon; 0-380),* 1790 Broadway, New York, NY 10019 Tel 212-399-4500 (SAN 201-4009). *Imprints:* Avon Bard Books (Bard); Avon Camelot Books (Camelot); Avon Discus Books (Discus); Avon Flare Books (Flare).
Avon Camelot Books See **Avon Books**
Avon Discus Books See **Avon Books**
Avon Flare Books See **Avon Books**
Avons Research Pubns., *(Avons Res; 0-913772),* P.O. Box 40, La Canada, CA 91011 Tel 213-790-5370 (SAN 202-3644).
Awakening Productions Inc., *(Awakening Prods; 0-914706),* 4132 Tuller Ave., Culver City, CA 90230 (SAN 205-6046).
Awani Press, *(Awani Pr; 0-915266),* P.O. Box 881, Fredericksburg, TX 78624 (SAN 206-4626).
Axiom Press, *(Axiom Pr; 0-933800),* P.O. Box 1668, Burlingame, CA 94010 Tel 415-441-1211 (SAN 213-2354); Dist. by: Medical & Technical Books, Inc., 11511 Tennessee Ave., Los Angeles, CA 90064 Tel 213-879-1607 (SAN 168-9800).
Ayer Co., *(Ayer Co; 0-88143),* 99 Main St., Salem, NY 03079 Tel 617-683-8741 (SAN 211-6936).
Ayer Pr., *(Ayer Pr; 0-910190),* 1 Bala Ave., Bala Cynwyd, PA 19004 Tel 215-664-6203 (SAN 204-5427).
Aylesworth, Owen R., *(O R Aylesworth; 0-9609312),* 621 W. Arrellaga St., Santa Barbara, CA 93101 Tel 805-962-4252 (SAN 260-0161).
Aylmer Press, *(Aylmer Pr; 0-932314),* P.O. Box 2735, Madison, WI 53701 Tel 608-251-2506 (SAN 212-6044).
Aylsworth Publishing Co., *(Aylsworth; 0-916572),* P.O. Box 345, Hancock, MI 49930 Tel 906-482-8230 (SAN 208-516X).
Aztec Corp., *(Aztex; 0-89404),* 1126 N. Sixth Ave., P.O. Box 50046, Tucson, AZ 85703 Tel 602-882-4656 (SAN 210-0371).
Azure Coast Publishing Co., *(Azure Coast; 0-942514),* 7480 la Jolla Blvd., La Jolla, CA 92037 Tel 714-459-0122 (SAN 238-1419).
B&B Pubs., *(B & B Pubs; 0-9608674),* P.O. Box 1062, Brookville, FL 33512 Tel 904-796-7712 (SAN 240-5903).
B. & B. Publishing, *(B&B Pub; 0-9607008),* P.O. Box 165, Saugus, CA 91350 Tel 805-255-3422 (SAN 238-9452).
B & E Enterprises, Pubs., *(B & E Ent; 0-915454),* P.O. Box 984, Everett, WA 98206 (SAN 207-7140).
B & G Associates, *(B & G Assoc; 0-9604230),* 408 Larkwood Dr., Montgomery, AL 36109 (SAN 215-0565).
B & R Samizdat Express, *(B & R Samizdat; 0-915232),* P.O. Box 161, West Roxbury, MA 02132 Tel 617-469-2269 (SAN 207-1037).
BCA Publishing Corp., *(BCA Pub; 0-931562),* P.O. Box 87536, Chicago, IL 60680-0536 Tel 312-973-7957 (SAN 211-7215).
BETOM Pubns., *(BETOM Pubns; 0-9605172),* P.O. Box 47, New London, WI 54961 Tel 414-982-3123 (SAN 238-5198).
BH Enterprises, *(BH Ent; 0-9604896),* P.O. Box 216, Midwood Sta., Brooklyn, NY 11230 Tel 212-336-0521 (SAN 220-0562).
BHRA Fluid Engineering, *(BHRA Fluid; 0-900983),* Dist. by: Air Science Co., P.O. Box 143, Corning, NY 14830 Tel 607-962-5591 (SAN 210-7791).
B J Phunn Pubs., *(B J Phunn; 0-931762),* P.O. Box 201, Wild Rose, WI 54984 Tel 414-622-3251 (SAN 212-128X).
BJ Service, *(B J Serv; 0-911535),* 152 S. Reeves Dr., Suite 105, Beverly Hills, CA 90212 Tel 213-276-8945 (SAN 263-9270).
BMA Press, *(BMA Pr; 0-89323),* P.O. Box 12000, St. Louis, MO 63112 (SAN 214-1019).
BMB Publishing Co., *(BMB Pub Co; 0-930924; 0-9600164),* P.O. Box 1622, Boston, MA 02105 Tel 617-492-5762 (SAN 201-4270).

BMDP Statistical Software, *(BMDP Stat; 0-935386),* 1964 Westwood Blvd., Suite 202, Los Angeles, CA 90025 Tel 213-475-5700 (SAN 213-8069).

BMH Books, *(BMH Bks; 0-88469),* P.O. Box 544, Winona Lake, IN 46590 Tel 219-267-7158 (SAN 201-7571).

BNR Press, *(BNR Pr; 0-931960),* 132 E. Second St., Port Clinton, OH 43452 Tel 419-734-2422 (SAN 211-5948).

B of A Communications Co., *(B of A; 0-911238),* P.O. Box 22252, Louisiana State Univ., Baton Rouge, LA 70893 Tel 504-272-6600 (SAN 204-6776); Pelican Office Center, 11628 S. Choctaw Dr., Baton Rouge, LA 70815 Tel 504-272-6600 (SAN 200-4208); Orders to: P.O. Box 15809, Broadmoor Sta., Baton Rouge, LA 70893 Tel 504-272-6600 (SAN 200-4216). *Imprints:* Malibu Publications (Malibu Pubns); Regent House (Regent House).

B.R.K. Enterprises, Inc., *(B R K Ent),* 336 S. Donald Ave., Arlington Heights, IL 60004 Tel 312-259-8376 (SAN 285-6859).

BUC International Corp., *(BUC Intl; 0-911778),* 1881 N.E. 26th St., Suite 95, Fort Lauderdale, FL 33305 Tel 305-565-6715 (SAN 201-9426).

BYLS Press, Div. of Bet Yoatz Library Services, *(BYLS Pr),* 6247 N. Francisco Ave., Chicago, IL 60659 Tel 312-262-8959 (SAN 212-7253).

Babson College Center for Enterpreneurial Studies, *(Babson College; 0-910897),* Babson College, Wellesley, MA 02157 Tel 617-235-1200 (SAN 263-0737).

Bacchus Press, *(Bacchus Pr; 0-940416),* 4225 Candleberry Ave., Seal Beach, CA 90740 Tel 213-430-5245 (SAN 219-7669); Dist. by: Publishers Group West, 5835 Beaudry Ave, Emeryville, CA 94608 (SAN 202-8522); Dist. by: GBC Press, 630 S. 11th St., Las Vegas, NV 89127 Tel 702-382-7555 (SAN 203-414X).

Back Bay Books, Inc., *(Back Bay),* P.O. Box 1396, Newport Beach, CA 92663 (SAN 216-1060).

Back Door Press, *(Back Door Pr),* 111 4th Ave N., Edmonds, WA 98020 (SAN 241-3620).

Back Fork Books, *(Back Fork Bks),* Drawer 752, Webster Springs, WV 26288 (SAN 240-4699).

Back Row Press, *(Back Row Pr; 0-917162),* 1803 Venus Ave., St. Paul, MN 55112 Tel 612-633-1685 (SAN 208-5569).

Back to Eden Books, *(Back to Eden; 0-940676),* P.O. Box 1439, Loma Linda, CA 92354 Tel 714-796-9615 (SAN 218-5318).

Backcountry Pubns., Inc., *(Backcountry Pubns; 0-942440),* P.O. Box 175, Woodstock, VT 05091 Tel 802-457-1049 (SAN 238-1427).

Backdraft Pubns., *(Backdraft; 0-936174),* P.O. Box 401, Basking Ridge, NJ 07920 Tel 201-766-7937 (SAN 214-1027).

Backeddy Books, *(Backeddy Bks; 0-9603566),* Box 301, Cambridge, ID 83610 (SAN 211-4615).

Backroads, *(Backroads; 0-933294),* Box 370, Wilson, WY 83014 (SAN 213-831X).

Backstreet Editions, Inc., *(Backstreet),* Box 555, Port Jefferson, NY 11777 Tel 516-584-5455 (SAN 240-3404).

Backwards & Backwards, *(Backwards & Backwards; 0-910253),* 101 S. Rocky River Dr., Suite 407, Berea, OH 44017 Tel 800-621-0443 (SAN 241-4724).

Backwoods Pubns., Div. of Backwoods Films, *(Backwoods Pubns; 0-911997),* P.O. Box 1831, Kettering, OH 45429 Tel 513-293-5299 (SAN 263-9289).

Bacon Street Press, *(Bacon St Pr),* One Bacon St., Newton Corner, MA 02158 (SAN 238-0390).

Badger Books, *(Badger Bks; 0-930478),* P.O. Box 40336, San Francisco, CA 94140 Tel 415-285-2708 (SAN 211-0008).

Badger Press, *(Badger; 0-9601264),* P.O. Box 25, Cross Plains, WI 53528 Tel 608-798-4168 (SAN 210-3923).

Badlands Natural History Assn., *(Badlands Natl Hist; 0-912410),* P.O. Box 6, Interior, SD 57750 Tel 605-433-5361 (SAN 202-3695).

Baha'i Publishing Trust, *(Baha'i; 0-87743),* 415 Linden Ave., Wilmette, IL 60091 Tel 312-251-1854 (SAN 213-7496).

Bahm, Archie J., *(Bahm; 0-911714),* 1915 Las Lomas Rd., N.E., Albuquerque, NM 87106 Tel 505-242-9983 (SAN 212-5854).

Baier, Paul M., *(Baier Pubns; 0-9602276),* 114 Canton St., Troy, PA 16947 (SAN 223-4947).

Baikie, Kenneth, *(K Baikie),* 4613 N. 74th Pl., Scottsdale, AZ 85251 Tel 602-994-4083 (SAN 207-6985).

Bailey, William, Pub., *(W Bailey Pub; 0-9604196),* P.O. Box 331, West Point, CA 95255 Tel 209-293-4303 (SAN 214-2317).

Bailey Pubns., *(Bailey Pubns; 0-933246),* 225 South Blvd., Nyack, NY 10960 Tel 914-358-3631 (SAN 211-7223).

Bailliere-Tindall *See* **Saunders, W. B., Co.**

Bainbridge, *(Bainbridge; 0-915234),* 1012 St. Louis St., Edwardsville, IL 62025 Tel 618-656-4817 (SAN 207-1231).

Baja Books, *(Baja Bks; 0-9602838),* Box 229, Woodland Hills, CA 91365 (SAN 213-0122).

Baja Enterprises, *(Baja Enter; 0-9609470),* P.O. Box 11988, Costa Mesa, CA 92627 Tel 714-548-2744 (SAN 260-163X).

Baja Press, *(Baja Pr; 0-910041),* 2829 Nipoma St., San Diego, CA 92106 Tel 714-223-1563 (SAN 241-2055).

Baja Trail Pubns., Inc., *(Baja Trail; 0-914622),* P.O. Box 6088, Huntington Beach, CA 92615 Tel 714-536-8081 (SAN 206-3301).

Bakebooks & Cookbooks, Inc., *(Bakebks & Cookbks; 0-9606686),* P.O. Box 92185, Milwaukee, WI 53202 Tel 414-277-8240 (SAN 219-7111).

Baker, Walter H., Co., *(Baker's Plays; 0-87440),* 100 Chauncy St., Boston, MA 02111 Tel 617-482-1280 (SAN 203-3717).

Baker Book House, *(Baker Bk; 0-8010),* P.O. Box 6287, Grand Rapids, MI 49506 Tel 616-676-9186 (SAN 201-4041).

Baker Co. *See* **Baker Gallery Press**

Baker Gallery Press, *(Baker Gallery; 0-912196),* P.O. Box 1920, Lubbock, TX 79408 Tel 806-763-3431 (SAN 202-3709).

Baker Library *See* **Kelley, Augustus M., Pubs.**

Bala Books, *(Bala Bks; 0-89647),* c/o Joshua M. Greene, 30 W. 60 St., New York, NY 10023 (SAN 284-9747).

Bala Publishing Division, *(Bala Pub Div),* 1500 W. 3rd Ave., Suite 329, Columbus, OH 43212 (SAN 215-0573).

Balaban International Science Services, *(Balaban Intl Sci Serv; 0-86689),* c/o Pomerantz Distributors, 2242 Mt. Carmel Ave., Glenside, PA 19038 Tel 215-885-2880 (SAN 216-5236).

Balamp Publishing, *(Balamp Pub; 0-913642),* 4205 Fullerton Ave., Detroit, MI 48238 Tel 313-491-1950 (SAN 202-4330); Orders to: P.O. Box 02367, North End, Detroit, MI 48202 (SAN 202-4349).

Balassanian, Sonia, *(S Balassanian; 0-9608388),* 81 Murray St., New York, NY 10007 Tel 212-732-3598 (SAN 240-5172).

Balboa Publishing, *(Balboa Pub; 0-935902),* P.O. Box 26427, San Francisco, CA 94126 Tel 415-459-7355 (SAN 220-035X).

Balcom Books, *(Balcom; 0-9600008),* 320 Bawden St., Apt. 401, Ketchikan, AK 99901 Tel 907-225-2496 (SAN 202-3725).

Bale Books, *(Bale Bks; 0-912070),* P.O. Box 2727, New Orleans, LA 70176 Tel 504-895-1371 (SAN 201-405X).

Bales, William J., *(Bales),* P.O. Box 3172, Munster, IN 46321 Tel 219-241-2183 (SAN 211-2183).

Ball State Univ., Ctr. for Environmental Design, Research & Service, *(Ctr Env Des Res; 0-912431),* College of Architecture and Planning /AB104, Munice, IN 47306-1099 Tel 317-285-8393 (SAN 265-1890).

Ball State Univ., *(Ball State Univ; 0-937994),* Muncie, IN 47306 (SAN 239-4081).

Ballantine Books, Inc., Div. of Random House, Inc., *(Ballantine; 0-345),* 201 E. 50th St., New York, NY 10022 Tel 212-751-2600 (SAN 211-1175); Orders to: Westminster, MD 21157 (SAN 214-1183).

Ballena Press, *(Ballena Pr; 0-87919),* 381 First St., Suite 5033, Los Altos, CA 94022 Tel 415-323-9261 (SAN 201-4076).

Balletmonographs, *(Balletmonographs; 0-9604232),* 2545 Pomeroy Court, S. San Francisco, CA 94080 (SAN 214-3054).

Ballinger Publishing Co., Subs. of Harper & Row, Inc., *(Ballinger Pub; 0-88410; 0-88730),* 54 Church St., P.O. Box 281, Harvard Square, Cambridge, MA 02138 Tel 617-492-0670 (SAN 201-4084).

Baltic Cinematographic Research Centre Press, The, *(Baltic Cinema; 0-941618),* 921 Norwood, Melrose Park, IL 60160 Tel 312-343-8857 (SAN 239-1619).

Baltimore County Fire Service Centennial Committee, *(Baltimore CFSCC; 0-9608952),* 800 York Rd., Towson, MD 21204 Tel 301-494-4531 (SAN 241-2063).

Baltimore County Public Library, *(Baltimore Co Pub Lib; 0-937076),* 320 York Rd., Towson, MD 21204 (SAN 214-3429).

Baltimore Museum of Art, *(Baltimore Mus; 0-912298),* Art Museum Dr., Baltimore, MD 21218 Tel 301-396-6316 (SAN 201-7431); Orders to: The Museum Shop, Art Museum Dr., Baltimore, MD 21218 Tel 301-396-6338 (SAN 201-744X).

Baltimore NRHS Pubns., *(Baltimore NRHS; 0-9601320),* 4710 Keswick Rd., Baltimore, MD 21210 Tel 301-467-8849 (SAN 202-4365); Orders to: 2107 N. Charles St., Baltimore, MD 21218 Tel 301-685-6161 (SAN 202-4373).

Baltimore Streetcar Museum, *(Baltimore Streetcar; 0-9609638),* Box 7184, Baltimore, MD 21218 Tel 301-484-7773 (SAN 262-5857).

Bamboo Ridge Press, *(Bamboo Ridge Pr; 0-910043),* 990 Hahaione St., Honolulu, HI 96825 Tel 808-395-7098 (SAN 241-2071).

Banbury *See* **Dell Publishing Co., Inc.**

Banbury Publishing Co., *(Banbury Pub Co; 0-9609598),* P.O. Box 926, 302 W. Jefferson, Effingham, IL 62401 Tel 217-347-7555 (SAN 260-1648).

Bancroft, John C., *(J C Bancroft),* 5855 Sheridan Rd., Apt. 7D, Chicago, IL 60660 Tel 312-271-7747 (SAN 207-6071).

Bancroft Books, *(Bancroft Bks; 0-9600332),* P.O. Box 9348, Berkeley, CA 94709 Tel 415-529-1231 (SAN 206-4510).

Bancroft Parkman Inc., *(Bancroft Parkman; 0-914022),* P.O. Box 236, Washington, CT 06793 (SAN 215-0581).

Bancroft Press, *(Bancroft Pr; 0-914888),* 27 McNear Dr., San Rafael, CA 94901 Tel 415-454-7094 (SAN 206-4634).

Bandanna Books, *(Bandanna Bks; 0-942208),* 209 W. De la Guerra, Santa Barbara, CA 93101 Tel 805-962-9996 (SAN 238-7956).

Bande House Publishing Co., *(Bande Hse Pub; 0-943760),* 1142 Manhattan Ave., Manhattan Beach, CA 90266 Tel 213-379-6924 (SAN 238-2458).

Bandon Historical Society, *(Bandon Hist; 0-932368),* P.O. Box 737, Bandon, OR 97411 Tel 503-347-2164 (SAN 212-2677).

Bankers Press Inc., *(Bankers Pr; 0-9602414),* 5810 S. Green St., Chicago, IL 60621 (SAN 213-0130).

Bankers Publishing Co., *(Bankers; 0-87267),* 210 South St., Boston, MA 02111 Tel 617-426-4495 (SAN 201-4564).

Banks-Baldwin Law Publishing Co., *(Banks-Baldwin; 0-8322),* University Ctr., P.O. Box 1974, Cleveland, OH 44106 Tel 216-721-7373 (SAN 204-5370).

Banner *See* **Exposition Press, Inc.**

Banner of Truth, The, *(Banner of Truth; 0-85151),* P.O. Box 621, Carlisle, PA 17013 Tel 717-249-5747 (SAN 211-7738).

Banner Press, *(Banner Pr IL; 0-916650),* P.O. Box 6469, Chicago, IL 60680 Tel 312-663-1843 (SAN 212-0119).

Banning, Arthur J., Press, *(Banning Pr; 0-938060),* 509 Foshay Tower, Minneapolis, MN 55402 Tel 612-788-9248 (SAN 220-0368).

Banster Press, The, *(Banster Pr; 0-9604620),* 117 Pinon Dr., P.O. Box 7326, Menlo Park, CA 94025 Tel 415-851-8032 (SAN 218-4656).

Bantam Books, Inc., *(Bantam; 0-553),* 666 Fifth Ave., New York, NY 10019 Tel 212-765-6500 (SAN 201-3975); Orders to: 414 E. Golf Rd., Des Plaines, IL 60016 (SAN 201-3983). *Imprints:* Peacock (Peacock); Skylark (Skylark); Windstone (Windstone).

Banyan Books, *(Banyan Bks; 0-916224),* P.O. Box 431160, Miami, FL 33143 Tel 305-665-6011 (SAN 208-340X).

Banyan Pr., *(Banyan Pr; 0-9607706),* 911 W. Webster, Chicago, IL 60614 Tel 312-871-5941 (SAN 238-6410).

Banyan Tree Books, *(Banyan Tree; 0-9604320),* 1963 El Dorado Ave., Berkeley, CA 94707 (SAN 207-3862); Dist. by: Bookpeople, 2940 Seventh St., Berkeley, CA 94710 Tel 415-549-3033 (SAN 168-9517).

Baptist Publishing House, *(Baptist Pub Hse; 0-89114),* 1319 Magnolia, Texarkana, TX 75501 (SAN 281-3092); Orders to: 712 Main, Little Rock, AR 72201 Tel 501-374-2328 (SAN 281-3106).

Bar Guide Enterprises, *(Bar Guide; 0-918338),* P.O. Box 4044, Terminal Annex, Los Angeles, CA 90051 Tel 213-883-5369 (SAN 210-041X).

Barah Publishing, *(Barah; 0-930292),* P.O. Box 697, San Anselmo, CA 94960 Tel 415-459-1165 (SAN 209-3480).

Baranski Pub. Corp., *(Baranski Pub Corp; 0-941974),* 500 Kansas Ave., P.O. Box 4527, Topeka, KS 66604 (SAN 238-0005).

Barber, Lilian, Press, *(Barber Pr; 0-936508),* Box 4224, Grand Central Sta., New York, NY 10163 (SAN 214-1817).

Barber, William A., *(Barber W A),* 42 Simsbury Rd., Stamford, CT 06905 (SAN 240-9186).

Barbour, Clifford E., Library, *(C E Barbour; 0-931222),* Pittsburgh Theological Seminary, 616 N. Highland Ave., Pittsburgh, PA 15206 Tel 412-362-5610 (SAN 209-6560).

Barbour, James L., *(J L Barbour),* P.O. Box 326, Port Tobacco, MD 20677 (SAN 215-6245).

Barclay Bridge Supplies, Inc., *(Barclay Bridge; 0-87643),* Eight Bush Ave., Port Chester, NY 10573 Tel 914-937-4200 (SAN 202-3768).

Bard Press, *(Bard Pr; 0-934776),* 799 Greenwich St., New York, NY 10014 Tel 212-929-3169 (SAN 214-1035) Not to be confused with Avon Imprint.

Bardic Echoes Brochures, *(Bardic; 0-915020),* P.O. Box 5339, Ft. Wayne, IN 46895 (SAN 207-0952).

Barding, L.F., Publishing, *(Barding Pub; 0-9605848),* P.O. Box 06264, Ft. Myers, FL 33906 Tel 813-936-2774 (SAN 216-5880).

Bare Feet & Happy People Press, The, *(Bare Feet; 0-9607238),* P.O. Box 84, Jemez Springs, NM 87025 Tel 505-829-3854 (SAN 239-1627).

Bargara Press, *(Bargara Pr; 0-911087),* 1523 Fillmore St., Lynchburg, VA 24501 Tel 804-332-5147 (SAN 268-2176); Rte. 2, Box 444, Rustburg, VA 24588 Tel 804-332-0961 (SAN 268-2184).

Bark-Back, *(Bark-Back; 0-9603338),* P.O. Box 235, Glenshaw, PA 15116 Tel 412-364-3743 (SAN 213-4624).

Barker, Gray, Books, *(G Barker Bks; 0-911306),* Box D, Jane Lew, WV 26378 Tel 304-269-2719 (SAN 204-7292).

Barker, Joseph, *(J Barker),* 4000 N. 7th St., S-102, Dept. 133, Phoenix, AZ 85014 Tel 602-955-7326 (SAN 248-8775).

Barksdale Foundation, *(Barksdale Foun; 0-918588),* P.O. Box 187, Idyllwild, CA 92349 Tel 714-659-4676 (SAN 210-1718).

Barlenmir House, Pubs., *(Barlenmir; 0-87929),* 413 City Island Ave., New York, NY 10464 Tel 212-885-2120 (SAN 201-4556).

Barleycorn Books, *(Barleycorn; 0-935566),* 290 S.W. Tualatin Loop, West Linn, OR 97068 Tel 503-225-0234 (SAN 213-6104).

Barn Owl Books, *(Barn Owl Bks; 0-9609626),* 1101 Keeler Ave., Berkeley, CA 94708 Tel 415-549-2149 (SAN 268-2214).

Barnaby Books, *(Barnaby Bks; 0-940350),* 3290 Pacific Heights Rd., Honolulu, HI 96813 Tel 808-531-5255 (SAN 217-5010).

Barnard, Roberts & Co., Inc., *(Barnard Roberts; 0-934118),* 305 Gun Rd., Baltimore, MD 21227 Tel 301-247-2242 (SAN 213-4632).

Barnegat Light Press, *(Barnegat; 0-937996),* Box 305, Barnegat Light, NJ 08006 (SAN 215-6253).

Barnes, A.S., & Co., Inc., *(A S Barnes; 0-498),* 9601 Aero Dr., San Diego, CA 92123 Tel 619-560-5163 (SAN 201-2030).

Barnes, C. Virginia, *(C V Barnes),* P.O. Box 112, Cathedral Sta., New York, NY 10025 (SAN 218-6438).

Barnes, John W., Publishing, Inc., *(Barnes Pub; 0-914822),* P.O. Box 323, Scarsdale, NY 10583 (SAN 223-6281).

Barnes, Richard S., & Co. Books, *(R S Barnes),* 821 Foster St., Evanston, IL 60201 Tel 312-869-2272 (SAN 209-2395).

Barnes, Robert H., *(R H Barnes; 0-930480),* P.O. Box 418, Grayland, WA 98547 Tel 206-267-3601 (SAN 210-3532).

Barnes & Noble Books, Div. of Harper & Row, *(B&N NY),* 10 E. 53rd St., New York, NY 10022 Tel 212-593-7000 (SAN 238-4906). *Imprints:* College Outline Series (COS); Everyday Handbooks (EH).

Barnes & Noble Books-Imports, Div. of Littlefield, Adams & Co., *(B&N Imports; 0-389),* 81 Adams Dr., Totowa, NJ 07512 Tel 201-256-8600 (SAN 206-7803).

Barney Press, *(Barney Pr; 0-9607888),* 8300 Kern Canyon Rd., Bakersfield, CA 93306 Tel 805-395-4433 (SAN 238-1441).

Barnstable Books, *(Barnstable; 0-918230),* 799 Broadway, Rm. 506A, New York, NY 10003 Tel 212-473-8681 (SAN 210-1726).

Barnwood Press Cooperative, The, *(Barnwood Pr; 0-935306),* River House, R.R. 2, Box 11C, Daleville, IN 47334 (SAN 223-7245).

Baron/Scott Enterprises, Inc., *(Baron-Scott Enterp; 0-943588),* 8804 Monard Dr., Silver Spring, MD 20910 Tel 301-587-2444 (SAN 240-5938).

Barone & Co., *(Barone & Co; 0-940702),* Box 32392, Washington, DC 20007 Tel .202-337-0076 (SAN 218-5326).

Barre Publishing Co., *(Barre),* Dist. by: Crown Publishers, Inc., 1 Park Ave., New York, NY 10016 (SAN 213-4357).

Barrett & Co., Pubs., *(Barrett; 0-9609396),* 465 City Center Plaza South, P.O. Box 6700, Jackson, MS 39212 Tel 601-373-4400 (SAN 240-8732).

Barrett Book Co., *(Barrett Bk; 0-932684),* 1123 High Ridge Rd., Stamford, CT 06905 (SAN 211-5883).

Barrier & Kennedy, ESL, *(Barrier & Kennedy; 0-911743),* P. O. Box 58273, Raleigh, NC 27658 Tel 919-847-1079 (SAN 276-9689).

Barrington Hall Pr., *(Barrington IA; 0-942066),* Box 118, Greeley, IA 52050 Tel 319-925-2962 (SAN 238-6429).

Barron's Educational Series, Inc., *(Barron; 0-8120),* 113 Crossways Park Dr., Woodbury, NY 11797 Tel 516-921-8750 (SAN 201-453X).

Barrows Co., Inc., *(Barrows Co; 0-89069),* 9 E. 53rd St., New York, NY 10022 Tel 212-355-1090 (SAN 203-137X).

Bartco Ltd., *(Bartco; 0-936374),* P.O. Box 26634, St. Louis, MO 63122 (SAN 215-059X).

Bartleby Press, *(Bartleby Pr; 0-910155),* 11141 Georgia Ave. No. A Six, Silver Spring, MD 20902 Tel 301-593-8650 (SAN 241-2098).

Barter Publishing Co., *(Barter Pub; 0-911617),* 323 Franklin Bldg., No. B-216, Suite 804, Chicago, IL 60606-7093 (SAN 281-3114); Orders to: Affinity Publishers Services, Box 600531, Houston, TX 77260 (SAN 281-3122).

Barth, Robert L., *(Barth; 0-941150),* 14 Lucas St., Florence, KY 41042 (SAN 238-9126).

Bartle, Jim, *(Bartle; 0-933982),* 771 W. Dry Creek Rd., Healdsburg, CA 95448 (SAN 216-3330).

Baruch, Bernard M., College Alumni Assn., Inc., *(Alumni Assn; 0-9606858),* 17 Lexington Ave., College Box 280, New York, NY 10010 (SAN 217-2275).

Baseball Facts, *(Baseball Facts; 0-939906),* P.O. Box 3529, Trenton, NJ 08629 (SAN 216-7883).

Baseball Histories, Incorporated, *(Baseball Hist; 0-9608534),* P.O. Box 15168, St. Louis, MO 63110 Tel 314-535-4215 (SAN 240-5954).

Bash Educational Services, Inc., *(Bash Educ Serv; 0-938408),* P.O. Box 2115, San Leandro, CA 94577 Tel 415-352-5420 (SAN 218-4664).

Basic Books, Inc., *(Basic; 0-465),* 10 E. 53rd St., New York, NY 10022 Tel 212-593-7057 (SAN 201-4521).

Basic English Revisited, *(Basic Eng Rev),* 275 Robins Row, Burlington, WI 53105 (SAN 215-2959).

Basic Science Preparation Center, *(Basic Science Prep Ctr; 0-9604722),* 55 Willow Tree Lane, Irvine, CA 92715 (SAN 215-7276); Orders to: 1601 Vivian Lane, Louisville, KY 40205 (SAN 215-7284).

Basic Science Press, *(Basic Sci Pr; 0-917410),* 1608 Via Lazo, Palos Verdes Estates, CA 90274 Tel 213-375-6740 (SAN 209-6498) Formerly Named Lucknow Publishing Co.

Basin Publishing Co., *(Basin Pub),* 168 Weyford Terrace, Garden City, NY 11530 Tel 516-741-0668 (SAN 208-4562).

Baskin Pubs., *(Baskin Pubs; 0-935854),* P.O. Box 3127, San Diego, CA 92103 (SAN 214-1043).

Bass, Clarence, Ripped Enterprises, *(Clarence Bass; 0-9609714),* 528 Chama N.E., Albuquerque, NM 87108 Tel 505-266-5858 (SAN 268-229X).

Bassett & Brush, *(Bassett & Brush; 0-9605548),* W. 4108 Francis Ave., Spokane, WA 99205 Tel 216-3349).

Bastian, Marlene Y., *(M Y Bastian; 0-9609058),* 240 SE 87th, Portland, OR 97216 Tel 503-252-0989 (SAN 241-2101).

Basu, Romen, *(R Basu),* 345 E. 69th St., New York, NY 10021 (SAN 276-9670).

Bataan Book Pubs, *(Bataan Bk Pubs; 0-9608294),* 135 Slater Drive, Pittsburgh, PA 15236 Tel 412-653-4658 (SAN 240-1339).

Bath Street Press, *(Bath St Pr; 0-937618),* 1016 Bath, Ann Arbor, MI 48103 Tel 313-663-2071 (SAN 215-2967).

Battelle Press, Div. of Columbus Laboratories of Batelle Memorial Institute, *(Battelle; 0-935470),* 505 King Ave., Columbus, OH 43201 Tel 614-424-4448 (SAN 213-4640); Dist. by: Springer-Verlag New York, 175 Fifth Ave., New York, NY 10010 Tel 212-460-1515 (SAN 203-2228).

Battery Park Book Co., *(Battery Pk; 0-89782),* Box 710, Forest Hills, NY 11375 (SAN 211-5891).

Battery Press, *(Battery Pr; 0-89839),* P.O. Box 3107, Uptown Sta., Nashville, TN 37219 Tel 615-298-1401 (SAN 212-5897).

Battle, Dennis M., Pubns., *(D M Battle Pubns; 0-933464),* P.O. Box 67, Elyria, OH 44036 Tel 216-323-1729 (SAN 212-8748).

Baublitz, Jacinth Ivie, *(J I Baublitz; 0-9610316),* 3708 Westbrier Terrace, Midland, MI 48640 Tel 517-835-6351 (SAN 263-9327).

Bauer, Rosemarie, *(Bauer),* Rte. 1, Box 1438, Granite City, IL 62040 (SAN 217-2984).

Bauhan, William L., Inc., *(Bauhan; 0-87233),* Old County Rd., Dublin, NH 03444 Tel 603-563-8020 (SAN 204-384X).

Bawden Bros, Inc., *(Bawden Bros),* 400 S. 14th Ave., Eldridge, IA 52748 Tel 319-285-4800 (SAN 212-0585).

Bay Area Gallery Guidebook, *(Bay Area Gallery; 0-9607460),* 4141 Fruitvale Ave., Oakland, CA 94602 Tel 415-530-6821 (SAN 238-6321).

Bay Press, *(Bay Pr; 0-941920),* 3710 Discovery Rd., Port Townsend, WA 98368 (SAN 237-9902).

Bayard Pubns., Inc., *(Bayard Pubns; 0-933268),* 1234 Summer St., Stamford, CT 06905 Tel 203-327-0800 (SAN 214-4033).

Bayer, Constance Pole, *(Bayer; 0-9600276),* 400 Walmer Rd., Apt. 2129, Toronto, Ontario, M5P 2X7, Tel 416-961-7697 (SAN 202-3792).

Bayland Publishing, Inc., *(Bayland Pub; 0-934018),* P.O. Box 25386, Houston, TX 77005 Tel 713-524-3000 (SAN 214-1051).

Baylor Univ. Press, *(Baylor Univ Pr; 0-918954),* Orders to: Book Dept., Baylor Book Store, P.O. Box 6325, Waco, TX 76706 Tel 817-755-2161 (SAN 204-4404).

Bayou Cuisine, *(Bayou Cuisine),* P.O. Box 1005, Indianola, MS 38751 Tel 601-887-1218 (SAN 208-0613).

Bayou Publishing Co., *(Bayou Pub Co; 0-9602570),* 5200 Bon Air Dr., Monroe, LA 71203 Tel 318-343-1964 (SAN 213-2850).

Bayshore Books, *(Bayshore Bks; 0-9602314),* Box 848, Nokomis, FL 33555 Tel 813-485-2564 (SAN 212-7237).

Bayside Publishing Co., *(Bayside; 0-913794),* 1350 77th Ave., N., St. Petersburg, FL 33702 (SAN 202-3806).

Baywood Publishing Co., Inc., *(Baywood Pub; 0-89503),* 120 Marine St., P.O. Box D, Farmingdale, NY 11735 Tel 516-293-7130 (SAN 206-9326).

BCS Educational Aids, Inc., *(BCS Educ Aids; 0-938416),* P.O. Box 100, Bothell, WA 98011 Tel 206-485-4110 (SAN 239-9326).

BDR Learning Products Inc. *(BDR Learn Prods; 0-934698),* P. O. Box 3356, Annapolis, MD 21403 Tel 301-956-4411 (SAN 212-2227).

Be All Books, *(Be All Bks; 0-9601848),* P.O. Box 941, Sonoma, CA 95476 (SAN 212-1476).

Beach Associates, *(Beach Assocs; 0-910339),* P.O. Box 2010, Orlando, FL 32802 Tel 305-843-4919 (SAN 241-2721).

Beacham, Roger, Pub., *(Beacham; 0-911796),* 4509 Balcones Dr., Austin, TX 78731 Tel 512-451-4572 (SAN 202-3814).

Beachcomber Books, *(Beachcomber Bks; 0-913076),* 3829 N. Oracle Rd., Tucson, AZ 85705 (SAN 202-3822).

Beacon Hill Pr. of Kansas City, *(Beacon Hill; 0-8341),* Dist. by: Nazarene Pub. Hse., P.O. Box 527, Kansas City, MO 64141 Tel 816-931-1900 (SAN 202-9022).

Beacon House, Inc., *(Beacon Hse; 0-87648),* P.O. Box 311, Beacon, NY 12508 Tel 914-831-2318 (SAN 202-3830).

Beacon Press, Inc., *(Beacon Pr; 0-8070),* 25 Beacon St., Boston, MA 02108 Tel 617-742-2110 (SAN 201-4483); Orders to: Harper & Row Pubs., Inc., Keystone Industrial Park, Scranton, PA 18512 Tel 800-233-4175 (SAN 215-3742).

Beaconsfield, C., *(Beaconsfield; 0-910202),* 1360 N. Rowell Ave., Fresno, CA 93703 (SAN 202-3849).

Bead Society, The, *(Bead Society; 0-939678),* 6500 Romaine St., No.7, Los Angeles, CA 90038 Tel 213-467-8982 (SAN 216-7166).

Beale, B. Deroy, *(B D Beale; 0-9602132),* 8529 Spalding Dr., Richmond, VA 23229 Tel 803-741-1836 (SAN 223-4971).

Beanie Bks., *(Beanie Bks; 0-933550),* 7443 Stanford, St. Louis, MO 63130 (SAN 281-3130).

Bear & Co., Inc., *(Bear & Co; 0-939680),* Drawer 2860, Santa Fe, NM 87501 Tel 505-983-5968 (SAN 216-7174).

Bear Creek Publishing Co., *(Bear Creek Pub; 0-941026),* P.O. Box 254, Ohray, CO 81427 Tel 303-325-4700 (SAN 217-3298).

Bear Pubns., *(Bear; 0-912934),* P.O. Box 95, Cambridge, NY 12816 Tel 518-677-2766 (SAN 202-3857).

Bear State Books, *(Bear State),* 304 High St., Santa Cruz, CA 95060 Tel 408-426-3272 (SAN 213-6112).

Bear Stone, *(Bear Stone),* 421 Queen No. J, Minneapolis, MN 55405 (SAN 277-5859).

Bear Tribe Publishing Co., *(Bear Tribe; 0-943404),* P.O. Box 9167, Spokane, WA 99209 Tel 509-258-7755 (SAN 207-8643).

Bearly Ltd., *(Bearly Ltd; 0-943456),* 149 York St., Buffalo, NY 14213 Tel 716-883-4571 (SAN 239-3549).

Beatitude Press, *(Beatitude),* 2940 Claremont Ave., Apt. 6, Berkeley, CA 94705 (SAN 209-5270).

Beatty, R. O., & Assocs., *(R O Beatty Assocs; 0-916238),* P.O. Box 763, Boise, ID 83701 Tel 208-343-4949 (SAN 207-9909).

Beatty, R. W., *(Beatty; 0-87948),* P.O. Box 26, Arlington, VA 22210 (SAN 206-7110).

Beau Lac Pubs., *(Beau Lac; 0-911980),* P.O. Box 248, Chuluota, FL 32766 Tel 305-365-3830 (SAN 202-3865).

Beau Rivage Press, *(Beau Rivage; 0-931174),* 7 E. 14th St., Suite 1112, New York, NY 10003 Tel 212-989-1625 (SAN 211-3090).

Beaufort Book Co., *(Beaufort SC; 0-910206),* Box 1127, Beaufort, SC 29902 Tel 803-524-5172 (SAN 202-3873) Do not confuse with Beaufort Bks NY.

Beaufort Books, Inc., *(Beaufort Bks NY; 0-8253),* 9 E. 40th St., New York, NY 10016 (SAN 281-3149).

Beaufort County Open Land Trust, Inc., *(Beaufort County),* Box 75, Beaufort, SC 29902 (SAN 217-2879).

Beaulieu, Beth Sea, *(B S Beaulieu; 0-9608796),* 22 Wells Ave., Chicopee, MA 01020 Tel 413-598-8551 (SAN 241-0001).

Beautiful America Publishing Co., *(Beautiful Am; 0-89802; 0-915796),* P.O. Box 608, Beaverton, OR 97075 Tel 503-641-2272 (SAN 211-4623).

Beautiful Day Books, *(Beautiful Day; 0-930296),* 5008 Berwyn Rd., College Park, MD 20740 Tel 301-345-2121 (SAN 210-587X).

Beauty Without Cruelty, *(Beauty Without Cruelty),* 175 W 12 St, New York, NY 10011 (SAN 225-896X).

Beaux Arts, Inc., *(Beaux Arts; 0-9607010),* c/o Lowe Art Museum, 1301 Stanford Dr., Coral Gables, FL 33146 Tel 305-667-9346 (SAN 279-4357).

Beaver Publications, *(Beaver Pubns; 0-9611234),* 15605 N.W. Cornell Rd., Beaverton, OR 97006 Tel 503-645-8425 (SAN 282-8286).

Beavers, *(Beavers; 0-910208),* Star Rte., Box 537, Laporte, MN 56461 Tel 218-224-2182 (SAN 202-389X).

Becker, Beverly, *(B Becker; 0-9602000),* P.O. Box 360, Park Ridge, IL 60068 Tel 312-635-0306 (SAN 212-2693).

Beckman, Steven D., *(S D Beckman; 0-9609434),* 621 Palm Ave., Lodi, CA 95240 Tel 209-369-3903 (SAN 284-9755); Orders to: 621 Palm Ave., Lodo, CA 95240 Tel 209-369-3903 (SAN 284-9763).

Beckman, Tom, & Assoc., *(T Beckman & Assoc; 0-937204),* P.O. Box 20081, Cincinnati, OH 45219 (SAN 213-2710).

Beckwith, Burnham Putnam, *(Beckwith; 0-9603262),* 656 Lytton Ave., (C430), Palo Alto, CA 94301 Tel 415-324-0342 (SAN 211-884X).

Beddoe Publishing, *(Beddoe Pub; 0-9606106),* 430 Closter Dock Rd., Closter, NJ 07624 (SAN 220-2344).

Bede Press & Bede Records, Inc., *(Bede; 0-911970),* Box 36m32, 5350 Wilshire Blvd., Los Angeles, CA 90036 (SAN 206-7358).

Bedell, Clyde, *(Bedell),* 2390-3e Mariposa W., Laguna Hills, CA 92653 Tel 714-586-2088 (SAN 216-2237).

Bedous Press, *(Bedous; 0-918094),* P.O. Box K, Beaverton, OR 97075 Tel 503-649-7844 (SAN 210-1742).

Bedrick, Peter, Books, *(P Bedrick Bks; 0-911764),* 239 Central Park w., New York, NY 10024 Tel 212-362-5535 (SAN 263-9335).

Beeberry Books, *(Beeberry Bks; 0-9601996),* 230 Maclane, Palo Alto, CA 94306 Tel 415-494-2969 (SAN 216-017X).

Beech Hill Publishing, *(Beech Hill; 0-933786),* Box 229, Mt. Desert, ME 04660 Tel 207-244-3931 (SAN 212-6419).

Beech Leaf Press, *(Beech Leaf; 0-939294),* Dist. by: Kalamazoo Nature Ctr., Inc., 7000 N. Westnedge Ave., Kalamazoo, MI 49007 (SAN 268-2478).

Beech Tree Farm Publications, *(Beech Tree; 0-910210),* 11 Ravensworth Rd., Taylors, SC 29687 Tel 803-268-7888 (SAN 201-4475).

Beechcliff Books, *(Beechcliff Bks; 0-9608930),* Number 605, One Hundred Seven, Annapolis, MD 21403 Tel 301-263-3580 (SAN 241-001X).

Beecher, Willard & Marguerite, Foundation, *(Beecher Found; 0-942350),* 8400 Westchester, Ste. 300, Dallas, TX 75225 (SAN 281-3165); c/o Dewey G. Williams, P.O. Box 2759, Dallas, TX 75221 (SAN 281-3173).

Beechwood Books, *(Beechwood; 0-912221),* P.O. Box 20484, Birmingham, AL 35216 Tel 205-823-2376 (SAN 265-0797).

Beekman Hill Press, *(Beekman Hill; 0-940534),* 342 E. 51st St., Apt. 3A, New York, NY 10022 Tel 212-755-0218 (SAN 222-9919).

Beekman Pubs., Inc., *(Beekman Pubs; 0-8464),* P.O. Box 888, Woodstock, NY 12498 Tel 914-679-2300 (SAN 201-4467).

Beeline Publications, *(Beeline Bks; 0-9611020),* P.O. Box 6121, Albany, NY 12206 Tel 518-434-3236 (SAN 285-127X); Four Central Ave., Albany, NY 12210 (SAN 285-1288).

Beer Flat Music, *(Beer Flat; 0-911999),* P.O. Box 99052, San Diego, CA 92109 Tel 619-272-2514 (SAN 264-6021).

Beginner Books, Div. of Random House, Inc., *(Beginner),* 201 E. 50th St., New York, NY 10022 (SAN 202-3288); Orders to: 400 Hahn Rd., Westminster, MD 21157 (SAN 202-3296).

Behavior Modification Technology, Inc., *(Behavior Mod Tech; 0-89025),* 1379 Sautern Dr., S.W., Ft. Myers, FL 33907 Tel 318-489-1478 (SAN 205-6054).

Behavioral Publishing Co., Div. of Behavioral Therapy Institute, *(Behavioral Pub; 0-940904),* 1736 Old Grove Rd., Pasadena, CA 91109 Tel 213-792-3596 (SAN 217-3301).

Behavioral Research Council, *(Behavioral Mass; 0-913610),* Division St., Great Barrington, MA 01230 Tel 413-528-1216 (SAN 201-7458).

Behavioral Studies Press, *(Behavioral Studies; 0-911958),* P.O. Box 5323, Beverly Hills, CA 90210 Tel 202-3903).

Behavioral Systems, Inc., *(Behavorial Sys Inc; 0-9610136),* Rt. 2, Box 630, Marshall, VA 22115 Tel 703-435-8181 (SAN 268-2559); Dist. by: The Book Carrier, Inc., 9121 Industrial Ct., Gaithersburg, MD 20877 (SAN 200-4046).

Behemoth Publishing, *(Behemoth Pub; 0-9606782),* Star Rte., Oasis, UT 84650 Tel 801-864-2842 (SAN 217-331X).

Behrman House, Inc., *(Behrman; 0-87441),* 1261 Broadway, New York, NY 10001 Tel 212-689-2020 (SAN 201-4459).

Beil, Frederic C., *(Beil),* 321 E. 43rd St., New York, NY 10017 Tel 212-682-5519 (SAN 240-9909). Imprints: Sandstone Press (Sandstone Pr).

Beinfeld Publishing, Inc., *(Beinfeld Pub; 0-917714),* 12767 Saticoy St., North Hollywood, CA 91605 (SAN 215-6261).

Being Books, *(Being Bks),* 19834 Gresham St., Northridge, CA 91324 Tel 213-341-0283 (SAN 215-7292).

Being Pubns, *(Being Pubns),* 1530 Valley Ave. N.W., Grand Rapids, MI 49504 (SAN 207-7876).

Beitzel, Edwin W., *(E W Beitzel; 0-9604502),* P.O. Box 107, Abell, MD 20606 Tel 301-769-3279 (SAN 204-4374).

Bek Technical Pubns., Inc., *(Bek Tech; 0-912884),* 1700 Painters Run Rd., Pittsburgh, PA 15243 Tel 412-221-0900 (SAN 202-3911).

Bel-Air Publishing Co., *(Bel-Air),* 249 S. Camden Drive, Beverly Hills, CA 90212 (SAN 263-2454).

Bel Esprit Press, *(Bel Esprit; 0-9607118),* 10 E. 23rd St., New York, NY 10010 (SAN 239-409X).

Belier Press, Inc., *(Belier Pr; 0-914646),* P.O. Box BB Old Chelsea Sta., New York, NY 10113 Tel 212-620-4276 (SAN 206-4766).

Believers Bookshelf, *(Believers Bkshelf; 0-941202),* Box 261, Sunbury, PA 17801 Tel 717-672-2134 (SAN 211-7746).

Believers Faith Center, *(Believers Faith; 0-912573),* 15762-B Tustin Village Way, Tustin, CA 92680 Tel 714-953-0134 (SAN 277-657X).

Bell, D. Rayford, *(D R Bell; 0-9604820),* 1225 McDaniel Ave., Evanston, IL 60202 (SAN 215-8388).

Bell, James W., Publisher, *(J W Bell; 0-939130),* 7611 Briarwood Dr., Little Rock, AR 72205 (SAN 216-1044); Dist. by: Publishers Distribution Service, 7509 Cantrell Rd., Little Rock, AR 72207 (SAN 216-1052).

Bell, Robert L., *(R L Bell; 0-9602450),* 669 Main St., Melrose, MA 02176 (SAN 211-8866).

Bell Books, *(Bell Bks),* 4649 Yarmouth Lane, Youngstown, OH 44512 (SAN 217-2283) Moved, left no forwarding address.

Bell Enterprises, Inc., *(Bell Ent; 0-918340),* P.O. Box 9054, Pine Bluff, AR 71611 Tel 501-247-1922 (SAN 209-1895).

Bell Publishing, *(Bell Pub; 0-943064),* 15 Surrey Lane, East Brunswick, NJ 08816 Tel 201-257-7793 (SAN 240-1266).

Bell Springs Pub, *(Bell Springs Pub; 0-917510),* P.O. Box 640, Laytonville, CA 95454 Tel 707-984-6746 (SAN 209-3138).

Bell Telephone Laboratories, Inc., *(Bell Telephone; 0-932764),* 600 Mountain Ave., Rm. 6G-301A, Murray Hill, NJ 07974 (SAN 223-6346).

Belldan Pubns, *(Belldan Pubns; 0-940562),* P.O. Box C, Sausalito, CA 94966 (SAN 263-9343).

Belle Mead Press, *(Belle Mead Pr; 0-9610346),* 306 Dutchtown Rd., Belle Mead, NJ 08502 Tel 201-359-5683 (SAN 263-9351).

Belle Pubns., *(Belle Pubs; 0-9605732),* 172 Pathway Lane, W. Lafayette, IN 47906 Tel 317-463-6361 (SAN 216-1036).

Bellefontaine Books, *(Bellefontaine Bks; 0-932786),* P.O. Box 501, Arroyo Grande, CA 93420 Tel 805-489-6242 (SAN 212-5900).

Belleridge Press, *(Belleridge; 0-938632),* P.O. Box 970, Rancho Santa Fe, CA 92067 Tel 619-756-3756 (SAN 220-1291).

Bellerophon Books, *(Bellerophon Bks; 0-88388),* 36 Anacapa St., Santa Barbara, CA 93101 Tel 805-965-7034 (SAN 202-392X).

Bellevue Art Museum, *(Bellevue Art; 0-942342),* 10310 NE Fourth St., Bellevue, WA 98004 (SAN 237-9341).

Bellevue Press, *(Bellevue Pr; 0-933466),* 60 Schubert St., Binghamton, NY 13905 Tel 607-729-0819 (SAN 207-7884).

Bellflower Press, *(Bellflower; 0-934958),* Dept. of English, Case Western Reserve University, Cleveland, OH 44106 Tel 216-368-2340 (SAN 213-2346).

Bellman Publishing Co., *(Bellman; 0-87442),* P.O. Box 164, Arlington, MA 02174-0164 Tel 617-648-7243 (SAN 202-3938).

Bellwether, *(Bellwether Inv; 0-9605770),* Box L, Inverness, CA 94110 Tel 415-982-6655 (SAN 216-5430).

Bellwether Books, *(Bellwether CA; 0-89475),* 15910 Ventura Blvd., Encino, CA 91436 Tel 213-990-1239 (SAN 210-1750).

Bellwether Publishing Co., *(Bellwether Pub; 0-913144),* 167 E. 67th St., New York, NY 10021 (SAN 209-0880).

Belmary Press, *(Belmary; 0-910214),* 4652 E. Pinewood, Mobile, AL 36618 Tel 205-342-7171 (SAN 202-3946).

Belnice Books, *(Belnice Bks; 0-941274),* Box 1325, Claremont, CA 91711 Tel 714-626-1167 (SAN 239-4103).

Ben Royal Press, *(B Royal Pr; 0-9603198),* 19 Highland Ave., Randolph, VT 05060 (SAN 222-2817).

Benbow, Doris R., *(D R Benbow),* 441 Clairmont Ave., Apt. 1014, Decatur, GA 30030 Tel 404-378-7028 (SAN 206-7293).

Bench Mark Publications, *(Bench Mark IL; 0-9610892),* P.O. Box 755, Charleston, IL 61920 Tel 217-345-7581 (SAN 265-0819).

Bench Press, *(Bench Pr; 0-916534),* P.O. Box 24635, Oakland, CA 94623 Tel 415-652-3953 (SAN 208-2217).

Benchmark Books, *(Benchmark Bks; 0-942246),* 2600 Mission St., Suite 203, San Marino, CA 91108 Tel 213-799-1111 (SAN 240-0839); Dist. by: Publishers Group West, 5835 Beaudry St., Emeryville, CA 94608 Tel 415-658-3453 (SAN 202-8522).

Bender, Matthew, & Co., Inc., Subs. of Times Mirror Co., *(Bender; 0-87571),* Attn: Rudolph Sommer, 235 E. 45th St., New York, NY 10017 (SAN 202-330X).

Bender, R. James, Publishing, *(Bender Pub CA; 0-912138),* P.O. Box 23456, San Jose, CA 95123 Tel 408-225-5777 (SAN 201-7296).

Benedictine Convent of Perpetual Adoration, *(Benedict Con Adoration; 0-913108),* 3888 Paducah Dr., San Diego, CA 92117 Tel 619-274-1030 (SAN 204-5346).

Benefield, M.E., Publishing, *(M E Benefield Pub; 0-9607326),* P.O. Box 395, 200 Jennifer, Jonesboro, AR 72401 Tel 501-972-1376 (SAN 239-1635).

Bengal Press, Inc., *(Bengal Pr; 0-935650),* P.O. Box 1128, Grand Rapids, MI 49501 (SAN 213-7259).

Bengor Pubns., Inc., *(Bengor Pubns; 0-913799),* 3827 N.E. 100th, Seattle, WA 98125 Tel 206-622-4090 (SAN 286-0473).

Benin Press, Ltd., *(Benin; 0-910216),* 5225 S. Blackstone Ave., Chicago, IL 60615 (SAN 202-3962).

Beninda Books, *(Beninda; 0-931868),* P.O. Box 9251, Canton, OH 44711 (SAN 211-8874).

Benjamin Co., Inc., *(Benjamin Co; 0-87502),* 1 Westchester Plaza, Elmsford, NY 10523 Tel 914-592-8088 (SAN 202-3970).

Benjamin-Cummings Publishing Co., Subs. of Addison-Wesley Publishing Co., *(Benjamin-Cummings; 0-8053),* 2727 Sand Hill Rd., Menlo Park, CA 94025 Tel 415-854-6020 (SAN 200-2353); Orders to: South St., Reading, MA 01867 (SAN 206-7862). *Imprints:* Advance Book Program (Adv Bk Prog).

Benjamins, John, North America, *(Benjamins North Am; 90-272),* One Buttonwood Sq-202, Philadelphia, PA 19130 Tel 215-564-6379 (SAN 219-7677).

Bennet, Rebecca, Pubns., Inc., *(Bennet Pub; 0-910218),* 5409 18th Ave., Brooklyn, NY 11204 (SAN 206-8443).

Bennett, Hal Z., *(Hal Z Bennett),* 124 Ardmore Rd., Kensington, CA 94707 (SAN 212-6052).

Bennett, Robert, Architect & Engineer, *(Bennett Arch & Eng; 0-9601718),* 6 Snowden Rd., Bala Cynwyd, PA 19004 (SAN 211-657X).

Bennett Publishing Co., *(Bennett Il; 0-87002),* 809 W. Detweiller Dr., Peoria, IL 61615 Tel 309-691-4454 (SAN 201-4440).

Bennington, Ed, Jr., *(E Bennington),* 1604 Argonne Ave. N., Sterling, VA 22170 Tel 703-430-8579 (SAN 207-5482).

Benshaw Pubns., *(Benshaw Pub; 0-9607508),* 940 Princeton Dr., Marina Del Rey, CA 90291 Tel 213-821-7871 (SAN 238-633X).

Benson, W. S., & Co., Inc., *(Benson; 0-87443),* P.O. Box 1866, Austin, TX 78767 Tel 512-476-5050 (SAN 202-3989).

Bentley, Robert, Inc., *(Bentley; 0-8376),* 872 Massachusetts Ave., Cambridge, MA 02139 Tel 617-547-4170 (SAN 213-9839).

Bentley Press, The, *(Bentley Pr; 0-9608572),* 2542 Camino Alfredo, Santa Fe, NM 87501 Tel 505-471-5668 (SAN 238-2490).

Benziger Publishing Co., Div. of Glencoe Publishing Co., *(Benziger Pub Co; 0-02; 0-8460),* c/o Macmillan Publishing Co., Inc., 866 Third Ave., New York, NY 10022 Tel 212-935-2000 (SAN 202-5574).

Benziger Sisters Publishers, *(Benziger Sis),* 466 E. Mariposa St., Altadena, CA 91001 (SAN 209-5297).

Berg, Norman S., Publisher, Ltd., *(Berg; 0-910220),* P.O. Box 15232, Atlanta, GA 30333 (SAN 226-8086).

Berger, Margaret L., *(M L Berger; 0-9605914),* c/o W. F Humphrey Press, 4375 Rte. 21 N., Canandaigua, NY 14424 Tel 716-394-7100 (SAN 281-3181).

Bergerie, Maurine, *(M Bergerie; 0-9604234),* 201 Pollard Ave., New Iberia, LA 70560 (SAN 214-2848).

Bergin & Garvey Publishers, Inc., *(Bergin & Garvey),* 670 Amherst Rd., S. Hadley, MA 01075 Tel 413-467-3114 (SAN 277-707X).

Berke, Carl, *(C Berke),* 20 Simmons Dr., Milford, MA 01757 Tel 617-473-8034 (SAN 216-2105).

Berkel, Boyce N., M.D., *(B Berkel; 0-9603184),* 2245 McMullen Booth Rd., Clearwater, FL 33519 (SAN 213-4667).

Berkeley Art Center, *(Berkeley Art; 0-942744),* 1275 Walnut St., Berkeley, CA 94709 Tel 415-644-6893 (SAN 240-1916).

Berkeley Poets' Workshop & Press (BPW & P), *(BPW & P; 0-917658),* P.O. Box 459, Berkeley, CA 94701 Tel 415-658-9278 (SAN 208-5488).

Berkeley Scientific Pubns., Div. of Scientific Newsletters, Inc., *(Berkeley Sci),* P.O. Box 4546, Anaheim, CA 92803 (SAN 217-7231).

Berkeley Slavic Specialities, *(Berkeley Slavic; 0-933884),* P.O. Box 3034, Oakland, CA 94609 Tel 415-653-8048 (SAN 212-7245).

Berkley Publishing Corp., Affiliate of G. P. Putnam's Sons, *(Berkley Pub; 0-425),* 200 Madison Ave., New York, NY 10016 Tel 212-686-9820 (SAN 201-3991); Dist. by: ICD, 250 W. 55th St., New York, NY 10019 Tel 212-262-7444 (SAN 169-5800). *Imprints:* Medallion Books (Medallion); Windhover (Windhover).

Berkshire Press, Inc., *(Berkshire Pr),* 30 Butler St., Cos Cob, CT 06807 (SAN 285-6832).

Berkshire Traveller Press, *(Berkshire Traveller; 0-912944),* Pine St., Stockbridge, MA 01262 Tel 413-298-3636 (SAN 201-4424).

Berkshire Writers, Inc., *(Berkshire Writ; 0-9609540),* Box 1672, Lenox, MA 01240 Tel 413-637-2486 (SAN 260-1664).

Berlitz See **Macmillan Publishing Co., Inc.**

Bermont Books, *(Bermont Bks; 0-930686),* 815 15th St., N.W., Suite 1108, Washington, DC 20005 Tel 202-737-6437 (SAN 211-1705).

Bermuda Biological Station, *(Bermuda Bio; 0-917642),* c/o Prof. James A. Butler, Pierce Hall, 29 Oxford St., Cambridge, MA 02138 Tel 617-495-2845 (SAN 206-4995).

Bern, Karl, Pubs., *(Karl Bern Pubs; 0-9601524),* 9939 Riviera Dr., Sun City, AZ 85351 Tel 602-933-0854 (SAN 211-1497).

Bernard, Ros, Pubns., *(R Bernard; 0-935872),* 17 Minell Place, Teaneck, NJ 07666 Tel 201-833-0805 (SAN 281-319X); Orders to: P.O. Box 2177, Teaneck, NJ 07666 (SAN 281-3203).

Berot Book, Inc., The, *(Berot Bk; 0-940372),* 220 E. Hillsdale St., Lansing, MI 48933 Tel 517-371-4647 (SAN 217-1589).

Berrick, R., Engineering Co., Inc., *(R Berrick),* 2312 Tilbury Ave., Pittsburgh, PA 15213 (SAN 241-3639).

Berry Patch Press, *(Berry Patch; 0-9609912),* 3350 N.W. Luray Terrace, Portland, OR 97210 Tel 503-224-3350 (SAN 268-2729); Dist. by: Far West Book Service, 3515 NE Hassalo, Portland, OR 97232 (SAN 282-6429).

Berry Publishing, *(Berry Pub; 0-942556),* Box 33, Hazel Crest, IL 60429 Tel 312-335-0347 (SAN 240-0669).

Bert & I Books, *(Bert & I Bks; 0-9607546),* 35 Mill Rd., Ipswich, MA 01938 Tel 617-356-3509 (SAN 238-2202).

Berwyn-London Pubs., *(Berwyn-London; 0-916536),* 2401 Calumet St., Flint, MI 48503 (SAN 208-550X).

Bess Press, *(Bess Pr; 0-935848),* P.O. Box 22388, Honolulu, HI 96822 (SAN 239-4111).

Bessandy Publications, *(Bessandy Pubns; 0-9610936),* 49 N. Main, P.O. Box 87, Clawson, UT 84516 Tel 801-384-2608 (SAN 265-1912).

Best Books, Inc., *(Best Bks; 0-910228),* 28 Madison St., Oak Park, IL 60302 (SAN 202-4012).

Best Cellar Press, *(BCP NY; 0-932874),* 51 Marilyn Pkwy., Rochester, NY 14624 (SAN 212-4041).

Best Western Press, *(Best West Pr; 0-941192),* P.O. Box 494, Bakersfield, CA 93302 (SAN 238-9134).

Bet-Ken Productions, *(Bet-Ken Prods; 0-9603698),* 4363 Cherry Ave., San Jose, CA 95118 Tel 408-267-3425 (SAN 213-683X).

Beta Phi Mu, *(Beta Phi Mu),* Pittsburgh, PA 15260 (SAN 228-8087).

Beth Jacob Hebrew Teachers College Inc., *(B J Hebrew Tchrs; 0-934390),* 1213 Elm Ave., Brooklyn, NY 11230 (SAN 222-741X).

Bethany College Pubns. - Kansas, *(Bethany Coll KS; 0-916030),* P.O. Box 111, Lindsborg, KS 67456 (SAN 211-8882).

Bethany House Pubs., *(Bethany Hse; 0-87123),* 6820 Auto Club Rd., Minneapolis, MN 55438 Tel 612-944-2121 (SAN 201-4416).

Bethany Press, *(Bethany Pr; 0-8272),* 2320 Pine Blvd., Box 179, St. Louis, MO 63166 Tel 314-371-6900 (SAN 201-4408).

Bethel Publishing Co., *(Bethel Pub OR; 0-9600096),* Rte One, Box One, Lyons, OR 97358 Tel 503-859-2228 (SAN 241-273X).

Bethel Publishing Co., *(Bethel Pub; 0-934998),* 1819 S. Main St., Elkhart, IN 46516 Tel 219-293-8585 (SAN 201-7555).

Bethesda Books, *(Bethesda; 0-9601308),* P.O. Box 34567, Bethesda, MD 20034 Tel 301-320-4675 (SAN 209-5025).

Bethlen Press, Inc., *(Bethlen Pr; 0-917718),* P.O. Box 637, Ligonier, PA 15658 Tel 412-238-9244 (SAN 209-2190).

Better Baby Press, The, *(Better Baby; 0-936676),* 8801 Stenton Ave., Philadelphia, PA 19118 (SAN 215-7314).

Better Books Pub., *(Better Bks),* Rte. 2, Box 2574, Vale, OR 97918 Tel 503-473-2133 (SAN 215-7322).

Better Homes & Gardens Books, Div. of Meredith Corp., *(BH&G; 0-696),* 1716 Locust St., Des Moines, IA 50336 Tel 515-284-2844 (SAN 202-4055).

Betterway Pubns, *(Betterway Pubns; 0-932620),* White Hall, VA 22987 Tel 804-823-5661 (SAN 215-2975); Dist. by: Berkshire Traveller Press, Pine St., Stockbridge, MA 01262 Tel 413-298-3636 (SAN 201-4424).

Between Hours Press, *(Between Hours; 0-910232),* 29 E. 63rd St., New York, NY 10021 (SAN 202-4039).

Betz Publishing Co., Inc., *(Betz Pub Co Inc; 0-941406),* P.O. Box 34631, Bethesda, MD 20817 Tel 301-340-0030 (SAN 238-9886).

Betzold, Michael, *(Betzold; 0-9602452),* 150 W. Nevada, Detroit, MI 48203 (SAN 211-6170).

Beulah Records & Publishing Co., *(Beulah; 0-911870),* Rte. 1, Crossville, IL 62827 Tel 618-966-3405 (SAN 202-4047).

Beverage Media, Ltd., *(Beverage Media; 0-9602566),* 161 Sixth Ave., New York, NY 10013 (SAN 214-106X).

Bewick Editions, *(Bewick Edns; 0-935590),* 1443 Bewick, Detroit, MI 48214 (SAN 213-6139).

Beyond Baroque Foundation Pubns., *(Beyond Baroque),* 1639 W. Washington Blvd., Venice, CA 90291 Tel 213-392-5763 (SAN 208-4708) Moved, left no forwarding address.

Bezalel Art, *(Bezalel Art; 0-914734),* 11 Essex St., New York, NY 10002 Tel 212-228-5982 (SAN 204-0719).

Bezkorovainy, Anatoly, *(Bezkorovainy),* 6801 N. Kilpatrick, Lincolnwood, IL 60646 Tel 312-942-5429 (SAN 218-4672).

Bhaktivedanta Book Trust, *(Bhaktivedanta; 0-912776),* 3764 Watseka Ave., Los Angeles, CA 90034 Tel 213-559-4455 (SAN 203-8560).

Bi World Industries, Inc., *(Bi World Indus; 0-89557),* P.O. Box 1143, Orem, UT 84057 Tel 801-224-5803 (SAN 210-5888).

Bibb, Mary, *(M Bibb),* 1100 Bellevue Pl., N.W., Grants Pass, OR 97526 Tel 503-474-2581 (SAN 238-0420).

Bible Club Movement, Inc., *(BCM Inc; 0-86508),* 237 Fairfield Ave., Upper Darby, PA 19082 Tel 215-352-7177 (SAN 211-7762).

Bible Light Pubns., *(Bible Light; 0-937078),* P.O. Box 168, Jerome Ave. Sta., Bronx, NY 10468 (SAN 214-3445).

Bible Literature Pubns., *(Bible Lit; 0-910236),* 937 Lassen View Dr., Lake Almanor Peninsula, CA 96137 Tel 916-259-3906 (SAN 201-7318).

Bible Press, *(Bible Pr; 0-914936),* 7600 N.E. Glisan, Portland, OR 97213 Tel 503-253-3460 (SAN 206-1953); Dist. by: Bible & Gift Shop, 7545 N.E. Glisan St., Portland, OR 97213 Tel 503-253-9020 (SAN 206-1961).

Bible-Speak Enterprises, *(Bible-Speak; 0-911423),* 1940 Mount Vernon Ct., No. 4, Mountain View, CA 94040 Tel 415-965-9020 (SAN 268-2931).

Bible Study Press, *(Bible Study Pr; 0-9600154),* 9017 N. 70 St., Milwaukee, WI 53223 Tel 414-354-3504 (SAN 281-3211); Dist. by: Omnibook Co., N 57 W 136 88 Carmen Ave., Menomonee Falls, WI 53051 Tel 414-781-2866 (SAN 281-322X).

Bible Voice, Inc., *(Bible Voice; 0-89728),* P.O. Box 7491, Van Nuys, CA 91409 Tel 213-781-2900 (SAN 211-7843); Dist. by: Unilit, 5600 N.E. Hassalo St., Portland, OR 97213 Tel 800-547-8020 (SAN 211-7851).

Bibli O'Phile Publishing Co., *(Bibli O'Phile Pub Co; 0-942104),* 156 E. 61st., New York, NY 10021 Tel 212-421-9177 (SAN 238-6437); Dist. by: E.P. Dutton & Co., 2 Park Ave., New York, NY 10016 Tel 212-725-1818 (SAN 201-0070).

Biblical Research Associates Inc., *(Biblical Res Assocs; 0-935106),* The College of Wooster, Wooster, OH 44691 Tel 216-263-2000 (SAN 211-2876).

Biblical Research Press, *(Bibl Res Pr; 0-89112),* 1334 Ruswood, Abilene, TX 79601 Tel 915-672-6702 (SAN 207-1681).

Biblically Based Developmental Training Books, Inc., *(Bibl Based Develop; 0-937442),* P.O. Box 15124, Atlanta, GA 30333 (SAN 216-0188).

Biblio Distribution Centre, *(Biblio Dist),* 81 Adams Dr., Totowa, NJ 07512 Tel 201-256-8600 (SAN 211-724X).

Biblio Press, *(Biblio NY; 0-9602036),* P.O. Box 22, Fresh Meadows, NY 11365 Tel 212-361-3141 (SAN 217-0892).

Bibliographical Society of America, *(Biblio Soc Am),* Po Bx 397 Grand Central Sta, New York, NY 10017 (SAN 225-333X).

Bibliophile Legion Books, Inc., *(Bibliophile; 0-918184),* P.O. Box 612, Silver Spring, MD 20901 Tel 301-498-7824 (SAN 207-6322).

Biblioteca Siglo de Oro, *(Biblio Siglo),* 530 N. First St., Charlottesville, VA 22901 Tel 804-295-1021 (SAN 208-2705).

Bibliotheca Chrysostomica, *(Biblio Chrysos; 0-943684),* Box 8091, Portland, ME 04104 Tel 207-774-2006 (SAN 238-2504).

Bibliotheca Islamica, Inc., *(Bibliotheca; 0-88297),* P.O. Box 14474, University Station, Minneapolis, MN 55414 Tel 612-221-9883 (SAN 202-4063).

Bibliotheca Press, Inc., *(Biblio Pr GA; 0-9605246; 0-939476),* P.O. Box 98378, Atlanta, GA 30359 Tel 404 281-3335); Dist. by: Bibliotheca Press S. W., Richell Ctr., P.O. Box 570122, Houston, TX 77257 (SAN 281-3327).

Biblo & Tannen Booksellers & Pubs., Inc., *(Biblo; 0-8196),* 321 Sandbank Rd., P.O. Box 302, Cheshire, CT 06410 Tel 203-272-2308 (SAN 202-4071).

Bibulophile Press, *(Bibulophile Pr; 0-911153),* P.O. Box 399, Bantam, CT 06750-0399 Tel 203-567-5543 (SAN 268-2990).

Bicentennial Era Enterprises, *(Bicent Era; 0-9605734),* P.O. Box 1148, Scappoose, OR 97056 Tel 503-226-2785 (SAN 216-2245).

Bielawski, Maxwell, *(Bielawski; 0-9600014),* 320 Lakeshore Dr., Dunkirk, NY 14048 Tel 716-366-2241 (SAN 204-5338).

Bieler Press, *(Bieler; 0-931460),* P.O. Box 3856, St. Paul, MN 55165 Tel 612-292-9936 (SAN 209-7087).

Big Bend Natural History Association, Inc., *(Big Bend; 0-912001),* Box 68, Big Bend National Park, TX 79834 Tel 915-477-2236 (SAN 268-3075).

Big Island Club Hawaii, Inc., *(Big Island; 0-9608396),* P.O. Box 344, Paauilo, HI 96776 Tel 808-775-7331 (SAN 240-5962).

Big Moose Press, *(Big Moose; 0-914692),* P.O. Box 180, Big Moose, NY 13331 Tel 315-357-2821 (SAN 206-3336).

Big Morning Press, *(Big Morning Pr; 0-935056),* Box 3342, Lawrence, KS 66044 Tel 913-843-4801 (SAN 211-4100).

Big Sky Books, *(Big Sky Bks),* 151 Hampton Rd., Southampton, NY 11968 (SAN 207-7892).

Big Toad Press, *(Big Toad Pr; 0-940536),* 617 25th St., Sacramento, CA 95816 Tel 916-446-7363 (SAN 209-5300).

Biggs, Marge, *(M Biggs; 0-9603218),* 12475 Willet, Grand Terrace, CA 92324 (SAN 213-2400).

Bigoni Books, *(Bigoni Bks; 0-938996),* 4121 NE Highland, Portland, OR 97211 Tel 503-288-0997 (SAN 216-3357).

Bilingual Books Inc., Div. of Outdoor Empire, *(Bilingual Bks; 0-916682),* 511 Eastlake Ave. E., Seattle, WA 98109 Tel 206-624-5344 (SAN 220-2352).

Bilingual Educational Services, Inc., *(Bilingual Ed Serv; 0-86624),* 2514 S. Grand Ave., Los Angeles, CA 90007 (SAN 218-4680).

Bilingual Press, *(Bilingual Pr; 0-916950),* Dept. of Foreign Languages & Bilingual Studies, 217 New Alexander, Eastern Michigan University, Ypsilanti, MI 48197 Tel 313-487-0042 (SAN 208-5526).

Billboard Bks. See **Watson-Guptill Pubns., Inc.**

Binford & Mort Pubs., *(Binford; 0-8323),* 2536 S.E. 11th Ave., Portland, OR 97202 Tel 503-238-9666 (SAN 201 4386).

Binney & Smith, Inc., *(Binney & Smith; 0-86696),* P.O. Box 431, Easton, PA 18042 (SAN 216-5899).

Binns, Joseph J., *(J J Binns; 0-89674),* 6919 Radnor Rd., Bethesda, MD 20034 Tel 301-320-3327 (SAN 213-2095); Dist. by: Robert B. Luce, Inc., 540 Barnum Ave., Bridgeport, CT 06610 Tel 203-334-2165 (SAN 201-1077).

Bio Energy Council, *(Bio Energy),* 1625 I St., N.W., Suite 825A, Washington, DC 20006 Tel 202-833-5656 (SAN 209-6145).

Biobehavioral Press, *(Biobehavioral Pr; 0-938176),* 10603 Grant Rd., Houston, TX 77251 Tel 713-890-8575 (SAN 214-4875).

Biofeedback & Advanced Therapy Institute, Inc., (BATI), 5979 West Third St., Suite 205, Los Angeles, CA 90036 Tel 213-938-0478 (SAN 239-6181).

Biofeedback Press, *(Biofeed Pr),* 3428 Sacramento St., San Francisco, CA 94118 Tel 415-921-5455 (SAN 212-8187).

Biofeedback Research Institute Inc., *(Biofeedback Research; 0-930758),* 6399 Wilshire Blvd., Suite 900, Los Angeles, CA 90048 Tel 213-933-9451 (SAN 208-2225).

Biograf Pubns. See **Garber Communications, Inc.**

Biohydrant, *(Biohydrant; 0-918562),* R.F.D. 3, St. Albans, VT 05478 Tel 802-524-6307 (SAN 209-6374).

Biokinesiology Institute, *(Biokinesiology Institute; 0-937216),* P.O. Box 1158, Shady Cove, OR 97539 Tel 503-878-2080 (SAN 214-3437).

Biomedical Pubns., *(Biomed Pubns; 0-931890),* P.O. Box 495, Davis, CA 95617 Tel 916-756-8453 (SAN 211-5913).

Bionomic Publishers, Inc., *(Bionomic; 0-912987),* 28306 Industrial Blvd. Ste. M., Hayward, CA 94545 (SAN 283-2879).

Bios Publishers, *(Bios Pubs; 0-9610636),* Box 159, Aransas Pass, TX 78336 Tel 512-758-2105 (SAN 264-6528).

BioService Corp., *(BioServ Corp; 0-938278),* 500 S. Racine Ave., Suite 302, Chicago, IL 60607 (SAN 215-7330).

Biostim, Inc., *(Biostim; 0-912863),* P.O. Box 3138, Clarksville Rd. & Everett Dr., Princeton, NJ 08540 Tel 609-799-2996 (SAN 282-9819).

Birch Run Publishing, *(Birch Run Pub; 0-931964),* 19 Sycamore Lane, Madison, CT 06443 (SAN 211-5921).

Birch Tree Press, *(Birch Tree Pr; 0-9603124),* 315 S. San Gabriel Blvd., Pasadena, CA 91107 Tel 213-991-2600 (SAN 213-9111).

Birchfield Books, *(Birchfield Bks; 0-912871),* P.O. Box 1305, N. Conway, NH 03860 Tel 603-447-3086 (SAN 277-6510).

Birds' Meadow Publishing Co., Inc., *(Birds' Meadow Pub),* 2914 Parkwood Dr., Rogers, AR 72756 (SAN 208-0710).

Birdseed, *(Birdseed; 0-933006),* 1219 Pearl St., Alameda, CA 94501 (SAN 212-3339).

Birkhauser Boston Inc., *(Birkhauser; 0-8176),* 380 Green St., Cambridge, MA 02139 Tel 617-876-2334 (SAN 213-2869).

Birmingham Historical Society, *(Birmingham Hist Soc),* 1425 22nd Street South, Birmingham, AL 35205 (SAN 240-1347).

Birth Day Publishing Co., *(Birth Day; 0-9600958),* P.O. Box 7722, San Diego, CA 92107 Tel 619-296-3194 (SAN 208-5542).

Bisbee Press Collective, *(Bisbee Pr; 0-938196),* Drawer HA, Bisbee, AZ 85603 (SAN 215-8418).

Bishop Graphics, Inc., *(Bishop Graphics; 0-9601748),* 5388 Sterling Center Dr., Westlake Village, CA 91359 (SAN 211-7258) Tel 213-991-2600.

Bishop Museum Press, *(Bishop Mus; 0-910240),* P.O. Box 19000-A, Honolulu, HI 96819 Tel 808-847-3511 (SAN 202-408X).

Bishop Press, The, *(Bishop Pr; 0-911329),* P.O. Box 2522, Del Mar, CA 92014 Tel 619-755-6514 (SAN 268-3334).

Bissette, Yoma V., *(Y V Bissette),* Dist. by: Historical Research Associates, 705 Yuma Trail, Bisbee, AZ 85603 (SAN 240-1355).

Biting Idge Press, the, *(Biting Idge; 0-942352),* 410 Cental Ave. No. 6, Sandusky, OH 44870 (SAN 239-7153).

Bits Press, *(Bits Pr; 0-933248),* Dept. of English, Case Western Reserve Univ., Cleveland, OH 44106 Tel 216-795-2810 (SAN 212-5927).

Bitteroot-West of Boston, *(Bitterroot-West; 0-911155),* 14 Bayfield Rd., Wayland, MA 01778 Tel 617-653-7241 (SAN 284-9771); Orders to: West of Boston, Cochituate Sta., P.O. Box 2, Wayland, MA 01778 (SAN 284-978X).

Biviano, Ronald, *(Biviano; 0-9605476),* 909 Charles, Crete, IL 60417 (SAN 215-9880).

Biworld Pubs., *(Biworld Pubs; 0-89557),* P.O. Box 1144, 671 North State, Orem, UT 84057 Tel 801-224-5803 (SAN 219-3531).

Bixler, Herbert E., *(H E Bixler; 0-9610066),* South Hill Rd., Jaffrey Center, NH 03454 Tel 603-532-6918 (SAN 268-3415).

Bjoerling, Jussi Memorial Archive, Inc., the, *(J Bjoerling; 0-9608546),* P.O. Box 2638, Indianapolis, IN 46206 Tel 317-635-2021 (SAN 240-5989).

BkMk Press, (University of Missouri-Kansas City), *(BkMk; 0-933532),* UMKC, 5100 Rockhill Rd, 107 Cockefair Hall, Kansas City, MO 64110 Tel 816-276-1305 (SAN 207-7914).

Black, Sidney T., *(S T Black),* Box 522, Simsbury, CT 06070 (SAN 213-8344).

Black, Tzvi, *(T Black; 0-9609752),* 1392 Lively Ridge Rd., Atlanta, GA 30329 (SAN 283-2968).

Black-A-Moors, Inc., The, *(Black-A-Moors; 0-933886),* 2339 N. Fairhill St., Philadelphia, PA 19133 (SAN 223-7180).

Black & Red, *(Black & Red; 0-934868),* P.O. Box 02374, Detroit, MI 48202 (SAN 208-5550).

Black & White Publishing, *(Black & White; 0-940050),* 18 Cogswell Ave., Cambridge, MA 02140 Tel 617-864-0134 (SAN 220-2077).

Black Buzzard Press, *(Black Buzzard; 0-938872),* 4705 S. Eighth Rd., Arlington, VA 22024 (SAN 216-0196).

Black Cat Books See Grove Press, Inc.

Black Caucus of the ALA, *(Black Caucus),* Universities Libraries, Howard University, Washington, DC 20059 (SAN 224-0858).

Black Ice Pubs., *(Black Ice),* 100 Prescott St., Worcester, MA 01605 Tel 617-753-1243 (SAN 216-0889).

Black Letter Press, *(Black Letter; 0-912382),* 663 Bridge St., N. W., Grand Rapids, MI 49504 Tel 616-454-7300 (SAN 201-436X).

Black Light Fellowship, *(Black Light Fellow; 0-933176),* P.O. Box 5369, Chicago, IL 60680 Tel 312-722-1442 (SAN 212-3347).

Black Mountain Books, *(Black Mntn),* P.O. Box 601, State College, PA 16801 Tel 814-234-1967 (SAN 216-3365).

Black Oak Press, *(Black Oak; 0-930674),* Box 4663, University Place Sta., Lincoln, NE 68504 (SAN 212-7261).

Black Oak Pubs, *(Black Oak NY; 0-9608834),* Lloyd Harbor Rd., Huntington, NY 11743 Tel 516-421-5646 (SAN 241-0044).

Black Oyster Press, *(Black Oyster; 0-9605966),* 14 August Alley, San Francisco, CA 94133 Tel 415-552-7162 (SAN 216-7182).

Black Plankton Press, *(Black Plankton; 0-9611236),* P.O. Box 9812, Berkeley, CA 94709 (SAN 277-6588).

Black Resource Guide Incorporated, *(Black Resource),* 501 Oneida Place, N.W., Washington, DC 20011 Tel 202-291-4373 (SAN 240-1363).

Black Scholar Press, *(Black Scholar Pr; 0-933296),* P.O. Box 7106, San Francisco, CA 94120 (SAN 222-5816).

Black Sparrow Press, *(Black Sparrow; 0-87685),* P.O. Box 3993, Santa Barbara, CA 93130 Tel 805-687-5014 (SAN 201-4343).

Black Stallion Country Press, *(Black Stallion Ctry Pr; 0-9607694),* P.O. Box 2250, Culver City, CA 90230 (SAN 237-9376).

Black Star Publishing Co., *(Black Star Pub; 0-9605426),* 450 Park Ave., S., New York, NY 10016 Tel 212-679-3288 (SAN 204-4153).

Black Star Series, *(Black Star),* 16 Clipper St., San Francisco, CA 94114 (SAN 219-4848).

Black Stone Press, *(Black Stone; 0-937002),* 865 Florida St., San Francisco, CA 94110 Tel 415-282-8806 (SAN 209-5319).

Black Swan Books Ltd., *(Black Swan CT; 0-933806),* P.O. Box 327, Redding Ridge, CT 06876 Tel 203-938-9548 (SAN 213-4675).

Black Swan Press/Surrealist Editions, *(Black Swan Pr; 0-941194),* 1726 W. Jarvis Ave., Chicago, IL 60626 (SAN 211-593X).

Black Thorn Books, *(Black Thorn Bks; 0-932366),* 186 Willow Ave., Somerville, MA 02144 (SAN 213-2877).

Black Willow Poetry, *(Black Willow; 0-910047),* 3214 Sunset Ave., Norristown, PA 19403 Tel 215-584-5461 (SAN 240-9682).

Blackberry Books, *(Blackberry Bks),* P.O. Box 1009, Bolinas, CA 94924 (SAN 208-4201) Do Not Confuse with Blackberry-Salted in the Shell.

Blackberry - Salted in the Shell, *(Blackberry ME),* P.O. Box 186, Brunswick, ME 04011 Tel 207-833-6051 (SAN 207-7949) Do Not Confuse with Blackberry Books.

Blacksmith Corp., *(Blacksmith Corp; 0-941540),* P.O. Box 424, Southport, CT 06490 Tel 203-367-4041 (SAN 239-0671).

Blackwater Publishing Co., Inc., *(Blackwater Pub Co; 0-910341),* 530 Allison Ave., S.W., Roanoke, VA 24016 Tel 703-362-4810 (SAN 241-2756).

Blackwell Scientific Pubns., Inc., *(Blackwell Sci; 0-86542),* 52 Beacon St., Boston, MA 02108 Tel 617-720-0761 (SAN 215-2029).

Blagrove Pubns., *(Blagrove Pubns; 0-9604466; 0-939776),* 80 Pitkin St., P.O. Box 584, Manchester, CT 06040 Tel 203-647-1785 (SAN 215-1316).

Blair, John, *(J Blair; 0-9601880),* P.O. Box 1584, Riverside, CA 92502 Tel 714-686-7523 (SAN 211-8858).

Blair, John F., Pub., *(Blair; 0-910244; 0-89587),* 1406 Plaza Dr., Winston-Salem, NC 27103 Tel 919-768-1374 (SAN 201-4319).

Blair Publishing Co., *(Blair Pub; 0-9607782),* P.O. Box 329-B, Bandon, OR 97411 (SAN 237-9392).

Blake, William, Press, Inc., The, *(W Blake Pr; 0-942868),* 140 Tenn. Ave. NE, Washington, DC 20002 Tel 202-546-3237 (SAN 238-843X).

Blakely, Richard P., *(R P Blakely; 0-9607110),* Rte. 6, Box 163, Astoria, OR 97103 Tel 503-458-6849 (SAN 238-9517).

Blalock, Jack, *(J Blalock; 0-9605156),* P.O. Box 8746, Pembroke Pines, FL 33084-0746 (SAN 215-8396).

Blanck, Helen E., *(H E Blanck; 0-9603700),* 1228 108 Ave., N.E., Minneapolis, MN 55434 Tel 612-757-5374 (SAN 208-0702).

Bland, Charles, *(C L Bland; 0-9610804),* 154 Delamere Rd., Williamsville, NY 14221 Tel 716-631-3193 (SAN 265-0886).

Blaney, Warren W., *(W W Blaney; 0-9607156),* 26412 Jacinto Dr., Mission Viejo, CA 92692 (SAN 237-9805).

Blarney Books, *(Blarney Bks; 0-935420),* 6129 Shenandoah Dr., Sacramento, CA 95841 (SAN 213-4683).

Blazing Flowers Press, *(W T Pancoast; 0-9610562),* 358 Willowdell, Mansfield, OH 44906 Tel 419-529-2649 (SAN 263-9318).

Blazon Books, *(Blazon Bks; 0-913017),* 1934 W. Belle Plaine, Chicago, IL 60613 Tel 312-274-3000 (SAN 283-2860).

Bleecker Street Publishing Corp., *(Bleecker St Pub; 0-941376),* Suite 104, Six Koger Executive Center, Norfolk, VA 23502 Tel 804-461-1212 (SAN 238-9525).

Blind Beggar Press, *(Blind Beggar; 0-940738),* 2059 McGraw Ave., Suite 12G, Bronx, NY 10462 (SAN 219-7154) Moved, left no forwarding address.

Blind John Pubns., *(Blind John),* 2740 Onyx St., Eugene, OR 97403 (SAN 217-0906).

Blis Press, *(Blis Pr),* 138 Concourse East, Brightwaters, NY 11718 (SAN 237-9384).

Bliss, Beatrice, *(Bliss; 0-9600504),* 17195 Poblado Way, San Diego, CA 92127 (SAN 202-411X).

Blitz Publishing Co., *(Blitz Pub Co),* 1600 Verona St., Middleton, WI 53562 Tel 608-836-7550 (SAN 215-1324).

Bloch & Co., *(Bloch & Co OH),* P.O. Box 18058, Cleveland, OH 44118 Tel 216-371-0979 (SAN 201-7261).

Bloch Publishing Co., *(Bloch; 0-8197),* 19 W. 21st St., New York, NY 10010 Tel 212-989-9104 (SAN 214-204X).

Block Pubs., *(Block; 0-916864),* Box 34223, Dallas, TX 75234 Tel 214-242-0069 (SAN 208-5577).

Blood-Horse, The, Pubns. of Thoroughbred Owners & Breeders Assn., *(Blood-Horse),* P.O. Box 4038, Lexington, KY 40544 Tel 606-278-2361 (SAN 203-5294).

Blood Information Service, *(Blood Info; 0-914508),* 508 Getzville Rd., Buffalo, NY 14226 Tel 716-832-7997 (SAN 206-3344).

Bloom Books Inc., *(Bloom Bks; 0-935000),* 1020 Broad St., Newark, NJ 07102 (SAN 215-1332).

Blooming Prarie Warehouse, Education/Outreach Project, *(Blooming; 0-9608298),* 1155 So. Riverside Dr., Iowa City, IA 52240 Tel 319-337-6448 (SAN 240-3420).

Blossom Valley Press, *(Blossom Valley; 0-939894),* P.O. Box 4044, Blossom Valley Sta., Mountain View, CA 94040 Tel 415-941-7525 (SAN 216-7905).

Blue Cross & Blue Shield Assn., *(Blue Cross & Shield; 0-914818),* 676 N. St. Clair, Chicago, IL 60611 Tel 312-440-6182 (SAN 223-629X).

Blue Diamond Press, The, *(Blue Diamond; 0-930856),* 801 Tilden St., Bronx, NY 10467 (SAN 220-4142).

Blue Dolphin Enterprises, Inc., *(Blue Dolphin; 0-943128),* c/o Pacific Comics, 8423 Production Ave., San Diego, CA 92121 Tel 619-566-3290 (SAN 239-3573).

Blue Dragon Press, *(Blue Dragon),* 1515 Poplar Ave., Richmond Heights, CA 94805 Tel 415-235-0361 (SAN 214-3453).

Blue Engine Express, The, *(Blue Engine; 0-9611370),* 173 E. Iroquois, Pontiac, MI 48053 Tel 313-338-3275 (SAN 283-2852).

Blue Feather Press, *(Blue Feather; 0-932482),* P.O. Box 5113, Santa Fe, NM 87502 Tel 505-983-2776 (SAN 211-9293).

Blue Flower, *(Blue Flower; 0-9603924),* Dist. by: Han Books, 3607 Baring St., Philadelphia, PA 19104 Tel 215-382-1410 (SAN 214-2864).

Blue Goose, Incorporated, *(Blue Goose MA; 0-9611512),* 1835 Pennsylvania Ave., P.O. Box 1118, Hagerstown, MD 21740 (SAN 285-6816).

Blue Harbor Press, *(Blue Harbor; 0-9605278),* P.O. Box 1028, Lomita, CA 90717 (SAN 215-8442).

Blue Haven Area Foundation, Inc., *(Blue Haven; 0-9609210),* Rte. 3, Box 629, Marble Falls, TX 78654 Tel 512-598-5524 (SAN 241-2764).

Blue Heron Press, Inc., *(Blue Heron; 0-939198),* 1728 Herrick N.E., Grand Rapids, MI 49505 Tel 616-363-7810 (SAN 220-0376).

Blue Horizon Press, *(Blue Horizon),* 1517 Crestwood Dr., Greenville, TN 37743 Tel 615-639-1264 (SAN 213-0254).

Blue Lagoon Pubs., *(Blue Lagoon; 0-9605338),* 3606 Coldwater Canyon, Studio City, CA 91604 (SAN 215-9899).

Blue Leaf Editions, *(Blue Leaf; 0-915206),* P.O. Box 857, New London, CT 06320 Tel 203-445-7391 (SAN 207-205X).

Blue Moon Press, Inc., *(Blue Moon Pr; 0-933188),* c/o Univ. of Arizona, Dept. of English, Tucson, AZ 85721 (SAN 213-0157).

Blue Mountain Press, *(Blue Mtn MI; 0-9602408),* 511 Campbell St., Kalamazoo, MI 49007 Tel 616-349-3924 (SAN 207-7965).

Blue Mountain Press, Inc., *(Blue Mtn Pr CO; 0-88396),* P.O. Box 4549, Boulder, CO 80306 Tel 303-449-0536 (SAN 201-4289).

Blue Mouse Studio, The, *(Blue Mouse; 0-9609640),* P.O. Box 312, Union, MI 49130 Tel 616-641-5468 (SAN 268-3725).

Blue-Note Press, *(Blue Note; 0-9610658),* 54 Cherrywood Lane, Erie, PA 16509 Tel 814-864-9759 (SAN 264-7168).

Blue Oak Press, *(Blue Oak; 0-912950),* P.O. Box 27, Sattley, CA 96124 (SAN 207-0383).

Blue Pacific Books, *(Blue Pacific; 0-915520),* 426 E. Pennsylvania Ave., San Diego, CA 92103 Tel 714-298-9701 (SAN 214-347X).

Blue Ridge Press of Boone, Inc., *(Blue Ridge; 0-938980),* P.O. Box 1693, Boone, NC 28607 (SAN 216-3373).

Blue River Publishing Co., *(Blue River; 0-936324),* P.O. Box 882, Sheboygan, WI 53081 (SAN 215-627X).

Blue Sky Marketing, Inc., *(Blue Sky; 0-911493),* 2006 Arkwright Street, St. Paul, MN 55117 (SAN 263-9394).

Blue Star Press, *(Blue Star; 0-939602),* 163 Joralemon St., Suite 1144, Brooklyn, NY 11201 (SAN 216-616X); Dist. by: Caroline House Publishers, 920 W. Industrial Dr., Aurora, IL 60506 Tel 312-897-2050 (SAN 211-2280).

Blue Unicorn, *(Blue Unicorn; 0-9608574),* 22 Avon Rd., Kensington, CA 94707 Tel 415-254-0669 (SAN 238-0447).

Blue Wind Press, *(Blue Wind; 0-912652),* P.O. Box 7175, Berkeley, CA 94707 Tel 415-526-1905 (SAN 206-7099).

Bluejay Press, *(Bluejay Pr; 0-939132),* 5900 Dartmouth Ct., Kokomo, IN 46901 (SAN 216-3381); Orders to: P.O. Box 6134, Kokomo, IN 46901 (SAN 216-339X).

Bluestem Productions, *(Bluestem Prod; 0-9609064),* Box 334, 2327 Lafayette Rd., Wayzata, MN 55391 (SAN 240-9747); Dist. by: Bluestem & the Bookmen, Inc., 525 N. Third St., Minneapolis, MN 55401 Tel 612-471-7795 (SAN 169-409X).

Bluestocking Books, *(Bluestocking; 0-931458),* 1732 20th Ave., Seattle, WA 98122 Tel 206-323-8556 (SAN 212-4823); Dist. by: Bookpeople, 2940 Seventh St., Berkeley, CA 94710 (SAN 168-9517).

Bluetick Publishing, *(Bluetick Pub),* 2014 Carroll Ave., San Francisco, CA 94124 (SAN 285-6824).

Blustein/Geary Associates, *(Blustein-Geary; 0-9605248),* 46 Glen Circle, Waltham, MA 02154 (SAN 215-8450).

Blyden, Edward W., Press, Inc., *(Blyden Pr; 0-914110),* P.O. Box 621, Manhattanville Sta., New York, NY 10027 Tel 212-222-6000 (SAN 206-4804).

Blythe - Pennington, Ltd., *(Blythe-Pennington; 0-943778),* P.O. Box 338, Croton-on-Hudson, NY 10520 Tel 914-271-4905 (SAN 241-0060).

BM Consumer Pubns, *(BM Consumer Pubns; 0-942662),* Suite 118, 1885 The Alameda, San Jose, CA 95126 Tel 408-727-7771 (SAN 239-6165).

B'nai B'rith Hillel Foundations, *(B'nai B'rith-Hillel; 0-9603058),* 1640 Rhode Island Ave., N.W., Washington, DC 20036 Tel 202-857-6564 (SAN 204-4080).

Bo-Tree Productions, Inc., *(Bo-Tree Prods; 0-933714),* 1137 San Antonio Rd., Suite E, Palo Alto, CA 94303 Tel 415-967-1817 (SAN 216-7050).

Boa Editions, *(Boa Edns; 0-918526),* 92 Park Ave., Brockport, NY 14420 Tel 716-637-3844 (SAN 281-3351); Dist. by: Writers & Books, 892 S. Clinton Ave., Rochester, NY 14620 (SAN 156-9678).

Board for Publications of The Evangelical Lutheran Synod, *(Board Pub Evang; 0-89279),* 734 Marsh St., Mankato, MN 56001 (SAN 262-0030).

Board of Jewish Education of Greater New York, *(Board Jewish Educ),* 426 W. 58th St, New York, NY 10019 Tel 212-245-8200 (SAN 213-0165).

Board of Pubn., LCA, *(Bd of Pubn LCA),* 2900 Queen Lane, Philadelphia, PA 19129 (SAN 213-1110).

Board of Publicatons of the Christian Reformed Church, *(Bd of Pubns CRC; 0-933140),* 2850 Kalamazoo Ave. S.E., Grand Rapids, MI 49560 Tel 616-241-1691 (SAN 212-727X).

Boardman, Clark, Co., Ltd., *(Boardman; 0-87632),* 435 Hudson St., New York, NY 10014 Tel 212-929-7500 (SAN 202-4136).

Boardroom Books, Div. of Boardroom Reports, Inc., *(Boardroom; 0-932648; 0-88723),* 330 West 42nd St., New York, NY 10136 Tel 212-239-9000 (SAN 211-5956).

Boar's Head Press, *(Boars Head; 0-932114),* P.O. Box 16413, St. Louis, MO 63125 Tel 314-846-2694 (SAN 211-1489).

Boatner Norton Press, *(Boatner-Norton; 0-9606654),* c/o The Million Year Picknick, 99 Mt. Auburn St., Cambridge, MA 02138 Tel 617-492-7896 (SAN 219-7162).

Bobbi Enterprises, *(Bobbi Ent; 0-9603200),* Rte. 1, Box 44, Mt. Iron, MN 55768 Tel 218-735-8364 (SAN 213-2885).

Bobbs-Merrill Co., Inc., A Thomas Audel Co., *(Bobbs; 0-672),* 630 Third Ave., New York, NY 10017 Tel 212-697-7050 (SAN 201-3959).

Bobets Publishing Co., *(Bobets; 0-9609782),* P.O. Box 8385, Scottsdale, AZ 85251 (SAN 263-2446).

Bobley Publishing Corp., Subs. of Illustrated World Encyclopedia, Inc., *(Bobley; 0-8324),* 311 Crossways Park Dr., Woodbury, NY 11797 Tel 516-364-1800 (SAN 202-3334).

Bodima, *(Bodima; 0-88875),* Dist. by: Altarinda Books, 13 Estates Dr., Orinda, CA 94563 Tel 415-254-3830 (SAN 238-1397).

Bodine & Associates, Inc., *(Bodine; 0-910254),* 1101 St. Paul St., Baltimore, MD 21202 Tel 301-385-1103 (SAN 201-4246).

Body Enterprises, *(Body Enterprises; 0-941460),* P.O. Box 80577, Lincoln, NE 68501 Tel 402-474-2100 (SAN 239-068X).

Boehm, Edward Marshall, Inc., *(E M Boehm; 0-918096),* 25 Fairfacts St., P.O. Box 5051, Trenton, NJ 08638 Tel 609-392-2207 (SAN 210-1777).

Bogden, George A., & Sons, Inc., *(Bogden & Son; 0-942068),* 45 Hudson St., Ridgewood, NJ 07450 Tel 201-444-1422 (SAN 237-9813).

Bohemica, *(Bohemica; 0-935504),* Columbia Univ. Dept. of Slavic Languages, New York, NY 10027 (SAN 223-7148).

Boian Books, *(Boian Bks; 0-9604420),* 780 Riverside Dr., Apt. 5E, New York, NY 10032 Tel 212-234-0173 (SAN 220-1305).

Boise State Univ., *(Boise St Univ; 0-88430),* Dept. of English, Boise, ID 83725 Tel 208-385-1246 (SAN 206-7080).

Bola Press, *(Bola Pr; 0-9608062),* P.O. Box 96, Village Sta., New York, NY 10014 Tel 212-431-5067 (SAN 206-4812).

Bola Pubns., *(Bola Pubns; 0-943118),* 8769 Devon Ave., Hesperia, CA 92345 Tel 619-244-6050 (SAN 240-3439).

Bolchazy-Carducci Pubs., *(Bolchazy-Carducci; 0-86516),* 8 S. Michigan Ave., Chicago, IL 60603 (SAN 219-7685).

Bold Blue Jay Pubns., *(Bold Blue Jay Pubns; 0-9608182),* 229 Moonlite Dr., Circle Pines, MN 55014 Tel 612-784-7522 (SAN 238-0412).

Bold Strummer, Ltd, *(Bold Strummer Ltd; 0-933224),* 1 Webb Rd., Westport, CT 06880 Tel 203-226-8230 (SAN 213-0262).

Bolder Landry, *(Bolder Landry),* 8925 San Salvador Circle, Buena Park, CA 90620 (SAN 210-9344).

Boldt Publishing Co., *(Boldt Pub; 0-941252),* P.O. Box 3065, San Rafael, CA 94912 (SAN 238-9142).

Bolton, D. Joyce, *(D J Bolton; 0-9602368),* 700 Paseo De Peralta, Santa Fe, NM 87501 Tel 505-982-4953 (SAN 211-2922).

Bon Chance Enterprises, *(Bon Chance Ent; 0-941922),* 14547 Titus St. Suite 102, Panorama City, CA 91412 Tel 213-785-3149 (SAN 238-6356).

Bon Mot Pubns., *(Bon Mot Pubns; 0-9601044),* RD 7 Box 394, Sevierville, TN 37862 (SAN 209-3472).

Bond, Dorothy, *(D Bond; 0-9606086),* 34706 Row River Rd., Cottage Grove, OR 97424 Tel 503-942-3235 (SAN 216-7913).

Bond, James O., *(J O Bond; 0-9608520),* Box 141, Williamsport, MD 21795 (SAN 240-6004).

Bond Publishing Co., Div. of Progressive Artistic Communications Enterprises Inc., *(Bond Pub Co; 0-939296),* 226 Massachusetts Ave. N.E., Washington, DC 20002 Tel 202-547-3140 (SAN 220-1488).

Bone Books, *(Bone Bks; 0-9611174),* 709 Kearney, Laramie, WY 82070 Tel 307-742-6727 (SAN 277-6596); Dist. by: Missouri Archaeological Society, P.O. Box 958, Columbia, MO 65205 (SAN 238-8316).

Bonney, Orrin H., *(Bonney; 0-931620),* 625 E. 14th St., Houston, TX 77008 Tel 713-864-8697 (SAN 206-7072) Tel 713-363-1243.

Bons Amis, *(Bons Amis; 0-941886),* 32-71 37th St, Long Island City, NY 11103 (SAN 237-9821).

Bonsall Pubns., *(Bonsall Pub; 0-9602066),* 4339 Holly Lane, Bonsall, CA 92003 (SAN 223-4939).

Boojum Pr., *(Boojum Pr; 0-9610186),* 18758 Bryant St., Northridge, CA 91324 (SAN 268-3989).

Book & Tackle Shop, *(Book & Tackle; 0-910258),* 29 Old Colony Rd., Chestnut Hill, MA 02167 Tel 617-965-0459 (SAN 208-0389).

Book Company, The, Subs. of Arrays, Inc., *(Bk Co; 0-912003),* 11223 S. Hindry Ave., Los Angeles, CA 90045 Tel 213-410-9466 (SAN 264-603X).

Book Department, The, *(Book Dept; 0-9606080),* P.O. Box 241, Hartford, CT 06141-0241 Tel 203-728-3470 (SAN 216-7921).

Book Distribution Center, *(Book Dist Ctr; 0-941722),* P.O. Box 31669, Houston, TX 77235 Tel 713-721-1980 (SAN 226-2770).

Book Industry Study Group, *(Bk Industry Stud),* 160 Fifth Ave., New York, NY 10010 (SAN 216-793X).

Book Industry Study Group, Inc., *(Bk Indus Study; 0-940016),* 160 Fifth Ave., New York, NY 10010 Tel 212-929-1393 (SAN 216-793X).

Book-Lab, Inc., *(Book-Lab; 0-87594),* 500 74 St., North Bergen, NJ 07047 Tel 201-861-6763 (SAN 201-422X).

Book Nest, The, *(Book Nest),* 366 Second St., Los Altos, CA 94022 (SAN 214-1086).

Book Page, *(Bk Page; 0-910266),* 904 Silver Spur Rd.-Suite 120, Rolling Hills Estate, CA 90274 Tel 213-373-1914 (SAN 158-8869).

Book Pools Ltd., *(Bk Pools),* 77 W. 55th St., Suite 3-H, New York, NY 10019 (SAN 284-9607); Orders to: P.O. Box 123, Corona, CA 91720 Tel 714-279-2233 (SAN 284-9615).

Book Press Release, Inc., *(Bk Pr Release; 0-936114),* P.O. Box 762, Berkeley, CA 94701 Tel 415-843-5961 (SAN 214-2325).

Book Promotions Unlimited, *(Book Promo Unltd; 0-933586),* P.O. Box 122, Flushing, MI 48433 Tel 313-659-6683 (SAN 212-7288).

Book Publishers of Texas, *(Book Texas; 0-910779),* P.O. Box 8262, Tyler, TX 75711-8262 Tel 214-597-1416 (SAN 260-1672).

Book Publishing Co., The, *(Book Pub Co; 0-913990),* 156 Drakes Lane, Summertown, TN 38483 Tel 615-964-3571 (SAN 202-439X).

Book Searchers, *(Book Searchers; 0-932484),* 2622 15th Ave., Forest Grove, OR 97116 Tel 503-357-6948 (SAN 212-0739).

Bookcraft, Inc., *(Bookcraft Inc; 0-88494),* 1848 W. 2300, S., Salt Lake City, UT 84119 Tel 801-972-6180 (SAN 204-3998).

Bookery, *(Bookery; 0-930822),* 8193 Riata Dr., Redding, CA 96002 Tel 916-365-8068 (SAN 211-8904).

Bookfinger, *(Bookfinger; 0-913774),* P.O. Box 487, Peter Stuyvesant Sta., New York, NY 10009 (SAN 202-4144).

Booklegger Press, *(Booklegger Pr; 0-912932),* 555 29th St., San Francisco, CA 94131 Tel 415-647-9074 (SAN 206-2232).

Bookling Pubs., The, *(Bookling Pub; 0-910717),* Flat Swamp Rd., Newton, CT 06470 Tel 203-426-3021 (SAN 268-4047).

Booklore Pubs., Inc., *(Booklore Pubs; 0-931110),* P.O. Drawer 3679, Sarasota, FL 33578 Tel 813-758-1533 (SAN 212-6427).

Bookmaker Publishing, *(Bookmaker; 0-934778),* 1212 E. 131st St., Burnsville, MN 55337 (SAN 213-2907).

Bookman Dan!, *(Bookman Dan; 0-934780),* P.O. Box 13492, Baltimore, MD 21203 Tel 202-234-1242 (SAN 213-2915).

Bookmark, Div. of Mayhill Pubns, *(Bookmark),* P.O. Box 74, Knightstown, IN 46148 Tel 317-345-5335 (SAN 203-5278).

Bookmates International, Inc., *(Bookmates Intl; 0-933082),* P.O. Box 9883, Fresno, CA 93795 Tel 209-298-3308 (SAN 212-8799).

Bookpeople, *(Bookpeople),* 2940 Seventh St., Berkeley, CA 94710 Tel 415-549-3030 (SAN 168-9517).

Books, *(Books; 0-910268),* 635 N. Elmwood Avenue, Waukegan, IL 60085 Tel 312-623-6963 (SAN 202-4152).

Books Alaska, *(Books AK),* Box 4020-A, Anchorage, AK 99507 (SAN 212-8802).

Books Americana, Inc., *(Bks Americana; 0-89689),* P.O. Box 2326, Florence, AL 35630 Tel 205-757-9966 (SAN 212-1816).

Books by Kellogg, *(Bks by Kellogg; 0-9603972),* P.O. Box 487, Annandale, VA 22003 Tel 703-256-2483 (SAN 214-0454).

Books for All Times, Inc., *(Bks for All Times; 0-939360),* P.O. Box 2, Alexandria, VA 22313 Tel 703-548-0457 (SAN 216-2253).

Books for Business, Inc., *(Bks Business; 0-89499),* 1100 Seventeenth St., N.W., Washington, DC 20036 Tel 202-466-2372 (SAN 210-0436).

Books for Professionals, *(Bks for Profs; 0-935422),* 4600 Valley Hi Dr., Sacramento, CA 95823 Tel 916-428-5984 (SAN 212-3355).

Books for Young Readers See Random House, Inc.

Books in Focus, Inc., *(Bks in Focus; 0-916728),* 160 E. 38th St., Suite 31B, New York, NY 10016 Tel 212-490-0334 (SAN 208-5607).

Books International of DH-TE International, Inc., *(Bks Intl DH-TE),* P.O. Box 14487, St. Louis, MO 63178 Tel 314-721-8787 (SAN 202-4101).

Books Marcus, *(Books Marcus; 0-916020),* P.O. Box 788, Ojai, CA 93023 (SAN 207-9763).

Books of Value, *(Bks of Value; 0-9603174),* 2458 Chislehurst Dr., Los Angeles, CA 90027 Tel 213-664-8981 (SAN 210-5896).

Bookslinger Editions, *(Bookslinger),* 330 E. Ninth St., St. Paul, MN 55101 Tel 612-221-0429 (SAN 169-4154); Box 16251, St. Paul, MN 55116 (SAN 217-1457).

Bookstore Press, *(Bookstore Pr; 0-912846),* Box 191, RFD 1, Freeport, ME 04032 (SAN 201-4211).

Bookthrift, Inc., Div. of Simon & Schuster, *(Bookthrift; 0-89673),* 45 W. 36th St., New York, NY 10018 Tel 212-947-0909 (SAN 158-8109) Hardcover & paperback remainders & special promotional book publishing, hardcover reprints & imports, paperback promotional assortments (quality & trade).

Bookworks, *(Bookworks),* Dist. by: Random House, Inc., 400 Hahn Rd., Westminster, MD 21157 (SAN 202-5515).
Bookworld Communications Corp., *(Bookworld Comm; 0-914242),* P.O. Box 4081, Louisville, KY 40204 Tel 201-4203).
Bookworm Pub., *(Bookworm NY; 0-9609624),* 86 S. Union St., Apt. 409, Rochester, NY 14607 Tel 716-325-2671 (SAN 268-4098).
Bookworm Publishing Co. Inc., *(Bookworm Pub; 0-916302),* P.O. Box 1792, Russelville, AR 72801 Tel 501-284-4153 (SAN 207-978X).
Boomerang Pubs., *(Boomerang; 0-9605900),* 6164 W. 83rd Way, Arvada, CO 80003 Tel 303-423-6643 (SAN 216-3403) Tel 303-431-0831.
Boone & Crockett Club, *(Boone & Crockett; 0-940864),* 205 S. Patrick St., Alexandria, VA 22314 (SAN 219-7693).
Boone-Thomas Enterprises, *(Boone-Thomas; 0-9611780),* Box 761, Hyattsville, MD 20783 Tel 301-935-5348 (SAN 285-2225); 8801 35th Ave., College Park, MD 20740 (SAN 285-2233).
Boonin, Joseph, Inc. See **European American Music**
Boosey & Hawkes, Inc., *(Boosey & Hawkes; 0-913932),* P.O. Box 130, Oceanside, NY 11572 Tel 516-678-2500 (SAN 213-6805).
Bootsrap Economic, *(Bootstrap Eco)* 292 W. Wahington Pl., Pasadena, CA 91103 (SAN 265-3818).
Borden Publishing Co., *(Borden; 0-87505),* 1855 W. Main St., Alhambra, CA 91801 Tel 213-283-5031 (SAN 201-419X).
Borf Books, *(Borf Bks; 0-9604894),* Brownsville, KY 42210 Tel 502-597-2187 (SAN 214-3496).
Borgo Press, *(Borgo Pr; 0-89370),* P.O. Box 2845, San Bernardino, CA 92406 Tel 714-884-5813 (SAN 208-9459).
Bork Research, *(Bork Res; 0-939258),* 23 E. Elm Ave., Quincy, MA 02170 Tel 617-472-5608 (SAN 220-1658).
Born-Hawes Pub. Ltd., *(Born-Hawes Pub; 0-85667),* 55 Vandam St., New York, NY 10013 Tel 212-929-5275 (SAN 211-2213).
Bornstein Memory Training Schools, *(Bornstein Memory; 0-9602610),* 11693 San Vicente Blvd., W. Los Angeles, CA 90049 Tel 213-478-2056 (SAN 213-0181).
Borogove Press, *(Borogove Pr; 0-9608246),* 78 Bay View Ave., Belvedere, CA 94920 Tel 415-435-1152 (SAN 240-3447).
Boss Books, *(Boss Bks; 0-932430),* P.O. Box 370, Madison Square Sta., New York, NY 10159 Tel 212-683-3274 (SAN 211-8920).
Boston Athenaeum Library, *(Boston Athenaeum; 0-934552),* 10 1/2 Beacon St., Boston, MA 02108 (SAN 213-019X).
Boston College, *(Boston Coll)* Chestnut Hill, MA 02167 (SAN 202-3342); Dist. by: Consortium Press, 821 15th St., N.W., Washington, DC 20005 (SAN 202-3350).
Boston College Mathematics Institute, *(Boston Coll Math; 0-917916),* Boston College, Chestnut Hill, MA 02167 Tel 617-969-0100 (SAN 209-9551).
Boston Music Company, The, *(Boston Music),* 116 Boylston St., Boston, MA 02116 Tel 617-426-5100 (SAN 201-7326).
Boston Public Library, *(Boston Public Lib; 0-89073),* P.O. Box 286, Boston, MA 02117 Tel 617-536-5400 (SAN 204-3971).
Boston Publishing Co., *(Boston Pub Co; 0-939526),* 314 Dartmouth St., Boston, MA 02116 Tel 617-267-8800 (SAN 281-3394); Dist. by: Addison-Wesley Publishing Co., Reading, MA 01867 Tel 617-944-3700 (SAN 200-2000).
Boston Risk Management Corp., *(Boston Risk Mgmt; 0-9607398),* 79 Milk St., Boston, MA 02109 (SAN 239-5142).
Boston Street Railway Assn., *(Boston St Rwy; 0-917012),* P.O. Box 102, Cambridge, MA 02138 (SAN 239-5150).
Boston Univ. School of Theology, *(Boston U Sch of Theology; 0-87270),* Orders to: Mueller Festschrift, School of Theology, 745 Commonwealth Ave., Box 27, Boston, MA 02215 Tel 617-353-3062 (SAN 213-9138).
Bottom Line Press, *(Bottom Line Pr; 0-943020),* P.O. Box 31420, San Francisco, CA 94131 Tel 415-661-1040 (SAN 240-3455).
Boulevard Books, *(Boulevard; 0-910278),* P.O. Box 89, Topanga, CA 90290 Tel 213-445-1036 (SAN 202-4179).

Bouregy, Thomas, & Co., Inc., *(Bouregy; 0-8034),* 22 E. 60th St., New York, NY 10022 Tel 212-753-8410 (SAN 201-4173).
Bovin Publishing, *(Bovin; 0-910280),* 68-36 108th St., Forest Hills, NY 11375 Tel 212-268-2292 (SAN 202-4187).
Bowdoin College Museum of Art, *(Bowdoin Coll),* College Editor, Bowdoin College, Brunswick, ME 04011 Tel 207-725-8731 (SAN 201-7210).
Bowen, F A., Reports, *(F A Bowen; 0-9602830),* P.O. Box 213, Janesville, WI 53545 Tel 608-752-6333 (SAN 212-8810).
Bowen, Glen, Communications, *(G Bowen Comm; 0-910173),* 2117 Linneman St., Glenview, IL 60025 Tel 312-724-3076 (SAN 241-2772).
Bowen, Robert Goss, Jr., *(R G Bowen; 0-9607512),* 31 Cobb Rd., Mountain Lakes, NJ 07046 (SAN 237-983X).
Bowen's Publishing Division, *(Bowens Pub Div.; 0-942354),* P.O. Box 270, Bedford, MA 01730-0270 Tel 617-275-1660 (SAN 239-717X).
Bowers, John D., *(J D Bowers; 0-9601360),* P.O. Box 101, Radnor, PA 19087 Tel 215-688-5541 (SAN 208-0028).
Bowers, Sampson, *(Sampson Bowers; 0-916448),* P.O. Box 731, Carmel Valley, CA 93924 (SAN 208-4058).
Bowers & Ruddy Galleries, Research Facility, *(Bowers & Ruddy; 0-914490),* 5525 Willshire Blvd., Los Angeles, CA 90036 (SAN 168-9746).
Bowery Publishing, *(Bowery Pub; 0-9602038),* P.O. Box 12784, Reno, NV 89510 (SAN 212-484X).
Bowker, R. R., Co., A Xerox Information Co., *(Bowker; 0-8352),* 205 E. 42nd St., New York, NY 10017 Tel 212-916-1600 (SAN 214-1191); Orders to: P.O. Box 1807, Ann Arbor, MI 48106 (SAN 214-1205).
Bowling Green State Univ., Dept. of Philosophy, *(BGSU Dept Phil; 0-935756),* Bowling Green State Univ., Bowling Green, OH 43403 Tel 419-372-2117 (SAN 213-2923).
Bowling Green State Univ., Social Philosophy & Policy Center, *(Soc Phil Pol; 0-912051),* Social Philosophy & Policy Center, Bowling Green, OH 43403 Tel 419-372-2536 (SAN 264-6048).
Bowling Green Univ., Popular Press, *(Bowling Green Univ; 0-87972),* Bowling Green State Univ., Popular Culture Ctr., Bowling Green, OH 43403 Tel 419-372-2981 (SAN 201-4165).
Bowmar/Noble Pubs., Div. of The Economy Company, *(Bowmar-Noble; 0-8372; 0-8107),* 4563 Colorado Blvd., Los Angeles, CA 90039 Tel 213-247-8995 (SAN 201-4157).
Box 21, Inc., *(Box Twenty One; 0-918846),* Tucson, AZ 85702 Tel 602-325-9602 (SAN 210-394X).
Boxwood Press, *(Boxwood; 0-910286; 0-940168),* 183 Ocean View Blvd., Pacific Grove, CA 93950 Tel 408-375-9110 (SAN 201-4149).
Boy Scouts of America, *(BSA; 0-8395),* 1325 Walnut Hill Lane, Irving, TX 75062 Tel 214-659-2285 (SAN 284-9798); Orders to: Eastern Distribution Ctr., 2109 Westinghouse Blvd., P.O. Box 7143, Charlotte, NC 28217 Tel 704-588-4260 (SAN 284-9801).
Boyar Books, *(Boyar; 0-9608464),* 2802 E. Locust St., Davenport, IA 52803 Tel 319-355-7246 (SAN 240-6039).
Boyars, Marion, Ltd., *(M Boyars; 0-7145),* 457 Broome St., New York, NY 10013 Tel 212-431-9368 (SAN 284-981X); Dist. by: Scribner Book Company, 201 Willowbrook Blvd., Wayne, NJ 07470 (SAN 284-9828).
Boyd, Ima Gene (Guthery), *(Ima Boyd; 0-9600502),* 370 Archwood Ave., Akron, OH 44301 Tel 216-773-1757 (SAN 203-7998).
Boyd, Philip L., Deep Canyon Desert Research Center of the Univ. of California, *(Boyd Deep Canyon),* Riverside, CA 92521 Tel 714-787-5917 (SAN 210-8852).
Boyd & Fraser Publishing Co., *(Boyd & Fraser; 0-87835),* 3627 Sacramento St., San Francisco, CA 94118 Tel 415-346-0686 (SAN 201-4130).
Boyer, Carl, *(C Boyer, 0-936124),* P.O. Box 333, Newhall, CA 91322 (SAN 215-7349).

Boykin, James H., *(Boykin; 0-9603342),* 1260 N.W. 122nd St, Miami, FL 33167 Tel 305-681-7663 (SAN 215-0603).
Boyle, Michael, Publisher, *(M Boyle Pub; 0-911097),* 155 Afleck St., Hartford, CT 06106 Tel 203-728-3828 (SAN 268-4284).
Boynton & Associates, *(Boynton & Assoc; 0-933168),* Clifton House, Clifton, VA 22024 (SAN 212-9310).
Boynton Cook Pubs., Inc., *(Boynton Cook Pubs; 0-86709),* P.O. Box 860, 52 Upper Montclair Plaza, Upper Montclair, NJ 07043 Tel 201-783-3310 (SAN 216-6186).
Boys' Clubs of America, *(Boys Clubs),* 771 First Ave., New York, NY 10017 Tel 212-557-7755 (SAN 204-3920).
Boys Town, N.E. Center, The, *(Boys Town Ctr; 0-938510),* Boys Town, NE 68010 Tel 402-498-1570 (SAN 215-8477).
Bozo Press, *(Bozo Pr; 0-936774),* P.O. Box 6207, Hilton Head Island, SC 29938 (SAN 216-3411).
BR-Three Press, *(Br-Three Pr; 0-9607566),* 1709 Ferndale Pl., Ann Arbor, MI 48104 Tel 313-663-0998 (SAN 238-4469).
Bracale & Associates, Inc., *(Bracale & Assoc),* 4710 Beidler Rd., Willoughby, OH 44094 (SAN 263-2438).
Brace, Beverly W., *(B W Brace),* 455 Crescent Dr., No. 27, Sunnyvale, CA 94087 Tel 408-737-1304 (SAN 210-3435).
Brace-Park Press, *(Brace-Park),* P.O. Box 526, Lake Forest, IL 60045 (SAN 239-412X).
Bradbury Press, *(Bradbury Pr; 0-87888),* 2 Overhill Rd., Scarsdale, NY 10583 Tel 914-472-5100 (SAN 201-4114); Dist. by: MacMillan Publishing Co., Inc., Riverside, NJ 08370 (SAN 202-5582).
Bradford, Leroy, *(L Bradford),* 3511 S. 172nd, Seattle, WA 98188 (SAN 238-9150).
Bradford Co., The, *(Bradford Co),* P.O. Box 256, Scituate, MA 02066 (SAN 263-242X).
Bradford Publishing Co., *(Bradford Pub; 0-931716),* P.O. Box 6363, Woodland Hills, CA 91365 (SAN 211-5972) Moved, left no forwarding address.
Bradford's Directory of Marketing Research Agencies & Management Consultants, *(Bradfords VA; 0-910290),* P.O. Box 276, Dept. B-15, Fairfax, VA 22030 Tel 703-631-1500 (SAN 204-2754).
Bradgate Centennial Committee, *(Bradgate Cent; 0-89279),* Bradgate, IA 50520 (SAN 283-9342).
Bradley CPA Study Aids, Inc., *(Bradley CPA; 0-932788),* 21146 Ventura Blvd., Suite 203, Woodland Hills, CA 91364 Tel 213-340-3779 (SAN 212-338X).
Bradley David Associates, Ltd., *(Bradley David Assocs; 0-9601694),* Box 5279, 909 Third Ave., New York, NY 10150 Tel 212-246-1114 (SAN 211-7282).
Bradley-Nord Sun Enterprises, *(Bradley-Nord; 0-941278),* Rte. 1 Box 30, Coldwater, KS 67029 (SAN 238-9169); 323 Pacific St., Bakersfield, CA 93305 (SAN 238-9177).
Bradley Publishing, *(Bradley Pub; 0-940716),* P.O. Box 7383, Little Rock, AR 72217 Tel 501-224-0692 (SAN 219-6891).
Bradson Press, *(Bradson; 0-9603574),* 120 Longfellow St., Thousand Oaks, CA 91360 Tel 805-496-8212 (SAN 213-7267).
Bradt Enterprises Pubns., *(Bradt Ent; 0-933982; 0-9505797),* 93 Harvey St., Apt. 8, Cambridge, MA 02140 Tel 617-492-8776 (SAN 169-328X).
Brady, Robert J., Co., Subs. of Prentice Hall, Inc., *(R J Brady; 0-87618; 0-87619; 0-89303),* Rtes. 197 & 450, Bowie, MD 20715 Tel 301-262-6300 (SAN 204-5656).
Braemar Books, *(Braemar Bks; 0-911159),* 127 E. 59th St., No. 201, New York, NY 10022 Tel 212-421-1950 (SAN 268-4373).
Bragg, Emma White, Ph. D., *(E W Bragg; 0-9611930),* 707 Ringgold Dr., Nashville, TN 37207 Tel 615-227-8923 (SAN 286-0732).
Brain-Image Power Press, *(Brain-Image; 0-9609246),* P.O. Box 1723, Hollywood, CA 90078 (SAN 260-0218).
Brain Research Pubns., *(Brain Res; 0-916088),* Highbridge Terrace, Fayetteville, NY 13066 (SAN 207-9666).
Brainerd Art Gallery, *(Brainerd; 0-942746),* State University College of Arts & Sciences, Potsdam, NY 13676 Tel 315-267-2254 (SAN 240-1959).

BRANCALEONE EDUCATIONAL

Brancaleone Educational Co, *(Brancaleone Educ; 0-9601186),* 169 Wildwood Ave., Upper Montclair, MI 48224 (SAN 209-6218).

Branch-Smith, Inc., *(Branch-Smith; 0-87706),* P.O. Box 1868, Fort Worth, TX 76101 Tel 817-332-6377 (SAN 201-7237); 120 St. Louis Ave., Fort Worth, TX 76101 (SAN 201-7245).

Branchemco, Inc., *(Branchemco; 0-9610178),* 8286 Western Way Circle, C-2, Jacksonville, FL 32216 Tel 904-737-0984 (SAN 268-442X).

Brandeis-Bardin Institute Pubns., The, *(Brandeis-Bardin Inst; 0-916952),* Brandeis, CA 93064 Tel 213-348-7201 (SAN 208-5666).

Branden Press, Inc., *(Branden; 0-8283),* Box 843, 21 Sta. St., Brookline Village, MA 02147 Tel 617-734-2045 (SAN 201-4106).

Brandon House, Inc., *(Brandon Hse; 0-913412),* P.O. Box 240, Bronx, NY 10471 (SAN 201-4092).

Brandywine Books, *(Brandywine Bks; 0-9604986),* 5020 73rd St., Suite B, San Diego, CA 92115 (SAN 216-020X).

Brandywine Conservancy, *(Brandywine Conserv; 0-940540),* P.O. Box 141, Chadds Ford, PA 19317 Tel 215-388-7601 (SAN 214-3518).

Brandywine Press, Inc., The, *(Brandywine; 0-89616),* c/o E. P. Dutton, 2 Park Ave, New York, NY 10016 (SAN 201-0070).

Branford, Charles T., Co., *(Branford; 0-8231),* P.O. Box 41, Newton Centre, MA 02159 (SAN 201-9302).

Brant, Michelle, *(Brant; 0-9611346),* P.O. Box 68, Port Richmond, CA 94807 Tel 415-237-2813 (SAN 283-2518); Dist. by: Bookpeople, 2940 Seventh St., Berkeley, CA 94710 (SAN 168-9517); Dist. by: L & S Distributors, 11611 Post St., San Francisco, CA 94109 (SAN 169-0213).

Brason-Sargar Pubns., *(Brason-Sargar; 0-9602534),* P.O. Box 872, Reseda, CA 91335 Tel 213-851-1229 (SAN 281-3416); Dist. by: DeVorss & Co., P.O. Box 550, Marina Del Rey, CA 90291 Tel 213-870-7478 (SAN 168-9886); Dist. by: CompCare Pubns, 2415 Annapolis Lane, Minneapolis, MN Tel 612-559-4800 (SAN 211-464X).

Brass Press, *(Brass Pr; 0-914282),* 136 Eighth Ave., Nashville, TN 37203 Tel 615-254-8969 (SAN 201-8608).

Brattle Pubns., *(Brattle; 0-918938),* 4 Brattle St., Suite 306, Cambridge, MA 02138 Tel 617-661-7467 (SAN 210-3958).

Brayden Books, *(Brayden; 0-9610994),* 719 Post Rd. E., Westport, CT 06880 Tel 203-227-9667 (SAN 265-1939).

Braynard, Frank O., *(F O Braynard; 0-9606204),* 98 Du Bois Ave., Sea Cliff, NY 11579 Tel 516-676-0733 (SAN 223-2138).

Braziller, George, Inc., *(Braziller; 0-8076),* One Park Ave., New York, NY 10016 Tel 212-889-0909 (SAN 201-9310).

B R E Pubs., *(B R E Pub),* 339 E. Laguna Drive, Tempe, AZ 85282 (SAN 265-380X).

Breaking Point, Inc., *(Breaking Point; 0-917020),* P.O. Box 328, Wharton, NJ 07885 Tel 201-361-7238 (SAN 208-0699).

Breese, Gerald, *(G Breese),* Princeton Univ., Princeton, NJ 08540 (SAN 206-1007).

Breise, Frederic H., *(F H Breise; 0-938576),* 5750 Severin Dr., La Mesa, CA 92041 (SAN 215-8485).

Breitenbush Pubns., *(Breitenbush Pubns; 0-932576),* P.O. Box 02137, Portland, OR 97202 Tel 503-635-8050 (SAN 219-7707).

Bren-Tru Press, *(Bren-Tru Pr; 0-936194),* 666 Grandview Ave., Ridgewood, NY 11385 (SAN 240-0847).

Brentwood Publishing Corp., *(Brentwood Pub; 0-939442),* 825 S. Barrington Ave., Los Angeles, CA 90049 (SAN 216-3438).

Breslau, Nathan, Publishing Co., *(N Breslau; 0-9610716),* 918 A. Savannas Point Dr., Fort Pierce, FL 33450 Tel 305-466-3439 (SAN 264-6544).

Brethren Press, *(Brethren; 0-87178),* 1451 Dundee Ave., Elgin, IL 60120 Tel 312-742-5100 (SAN 201-9329).

Brethren Publishing Co., *(Brethren Ohio; 0-934970),* 524 College Ave., Ashland, OH 44805 Tel 419-289-1708 (SAN 201-730X) Do Not Confuse with Brethren Press (Brethren) in Elgin IL.

Breton Pubs., Div. of Wadsworth Publishing Co., Inc., *(Breton Pubs),* P.O. Box 446, North Scituate, MA 02060 (SAN 213-4691); Dist. by: Wadsworth Publishing Co., Inc., 7625 Empire Dr., Florence, KY 41042 Tel 606-525-2230 (SAN 200-2213).

Brevet Press, *(Brevet Pr; 0-88498),* Box 1404, Sioux Falls, SD 57101 Tel 605-339-2330 (SAN 201-7563).

Brevity Press, *(Brevity; 0-917838),* P.O. Box 120622, Nashville, TN 37212 Tel 615-292-0211 (SAN 209-3979).

Brian's House, Inc., *(Brian's Hse; 0-9606970),* Box 802, West Chester, PA 19380 (SAN 238-9185).

Briarcliff Pub. Co., *(Briarcliff; 0-915754),* 8111 Timberlodge Trail, Dayton, OH 45459 (SAN 210-573X); Orders to: 3640 N. Briarcliff Rd., Kansas City, MO 64116 (SAN 210-5748).

Bric-a-Brac Bookwks., *(Bric-A-Brac),* Box 887, Forked River, NJ 08731 (SAN 282-6364).

Brick House Publishing Co., *(Brick Hse Pub; 0-931790),* 34 Essex St., Andover, MA 01810 Tel 617-475-9568 (SAN 213-201X).

Brickel, Estelle D. & Stephen B., *(E & S Brickel; 0-9609844),* c/o Donovan & Green, 18 E. 53rd St., New York, NY 10022 (SAN 284-9836).

Bricker's International Directory, *(Bricker's Intl; 0-916404),* 425 Family Farm Rd., Woodside, CA 94062 Tel 415-851-3090 (SAN 208-5682).

Bride Guide Enterprises, *(Bride Guide; 0-939884),* 15301 Ventura Blvd., Suite 500, Sherman Oaks, CA 91403 Tel 213-907-0218 (SAN 216-8804); Dist. by: United Book Service, 1310 S. San Fernando Rd., Los Angeles, CA 90025 (SAN 168-986X).

Bridge Pubns. Inc., *(Bridge Pubns Inc; 0-88404),* 1414 N. Catalina St., Los Angeles, CA 90027 Tel 213-382-0382 (SAN 208-3884).

Bridge Publishing Co., *(Bridge Pub),* 2500 Hamilton Blvd., South Plainfield, NJ 08805 Tel 201-754-0745 (SAN 239-5061).

Bridgeberg Books, *(Bridgeberg; 0-915358),* 7 Oak Ave., Kentfield, CA 94904 Tel 415-457-4963 (SAN 210-3028).

Bridgehead Press, *(Bridgehead Pr; 0-912543),* P.O. Box 847, 7214 St. Charles Ave., New Orleans, LA 70118 Tel 504-899-7669 (SAN 265-1963).

Bridges Pr., Div. of Pragmatix Management Resources, *(Bridges Pr),* c/o Pragmatix Management Resources, 408 S.W. 2nd Ave., Suite 425, Portland, OR 97204 Tel 503-223-7524 (SAN 217-2623).

Bridges to the Sound Publishing Corp., *(Bridges Sound; 0-938316),* P.O. Box 260607, Tampa, FL 33615 (SAN 215-7357).

Brigadoon Pubns., Inc., *(Brigadoon; 0-938512),* 52 Otis Ave., Staten Island, NY 10306 (SAN 216-0218).

Brigham Street House, *(Brigham St Hse; 0-912482),* 7050 Chris Lane, Salt Lake City, UT 84121 Tel 801-943-6800 (SAN 202-4225).

Brigham Young Univ. Press, *(Brigham; 0-8425),* 218 University Press Bldg., Provo, UT 84602 Tel 801-378-6599 (SAN 201-9337); Orders to: 205 University Press Bldg, Provo, UT 84602 Tel 801-378-2809 (SAN 201-9345).

Brigham Young University J Reuben Clark Law School, *(BYU Clark Law),* Provo, UT 84602 (SAN 226-4188).

Brigham Young Univ. Law Library, *(BYU Law Lib),* Brigham Young University, Provo, UT 84602 (SAN 268-4640).

Bright Books, *(Bright Bks; 0-9605968),* P.O. Box 428, Akron, IN 46910 Tel 219-893-4684 (SAN 216-7204).

Brighton House Pubns., *(Brighton House; 0-9603256),* 3045 Brighton 8th St., Brooklyn, NY 11235 Tel 212-934-1349 (SAN 216-6570).

Brighton Pubns., *(Brighton Pubns; 0-918420),* P.O. Box 12706, New Brighton, MN 55112 Tel 612-636-2220 (SAN 210-0452).

Brighton Publishing Co., *(Brighton Pub Co; 0-89832),* P.O. Box 6235, Salt Lake City, UT 84106 Tel 801-466-4044 (SAN 213-0475).

Brighton Street Press, The, *(Brighton St Pr; 0-9609642),* 53 Flastaff Rd., Rochester, NY 14609 Tel 716-889-5564 (SAN 268-4667).

PUBLISHERS AND DISTRIBUTORS

Brill, E. J., Pubs., *(E J Brill),* Dist. by: Expediters of the Printed Word, Ltd., P.O. Box 1305, Long Island City, NY 11101 (SAN 282-6399).

Brillig Works Pub., Co., *(Brillig Works; 0-89681),* 1322 College Ave., Boulder, CO 80302 (SAN 211-5999).

Brinkerhoff & Rippy, *(Brinkerhoff & Rippy),* P.O. Box 444, Salem, IL 62881 (SAN 238-0455).

Brinser, Marlin, *(M Brinser; 0-9602298),* 643 Stuyvesant Ave., Irvington, NJ 07111 (SAN 212-6079).

Brinton, William F., Jr., *(W F Brinton; 0-9603554),* P.O. Box 215, Phoenixville, PA 19460 Tel 215-933-3621 (SAN 213-4713); Orders to: Woods End Agriculture Institute, Temple, ME 04984 (SAN 213-4721).

British American Books, *(British Am Bks; 0-89979),* P. O. Box 302, Willits, CA 95490 (SAN 201-9353).

Brittany Press, *(Brittany Pr; 0-912749),* 1567 Mt. Vernon Rd., Dunwoody, GA 30338 (SAN 283-9350).

Brittany Pubns., Ltd., *(Brittany Pubns; 0-941394),* 664 Michigan Ave., Chicago, IL 60611 Tel 312-787-9248 (SAN 238-9541).

Britton, Inc., *(Britton Inc; 0-9611782),* 507 Main St., Hingham, MA 02043 Tel 617-749-9175 (SAN 285-225X).

Britton Publishing Co., *(Britton Pub; 0-938318),* Box 9628, North Hollywood, CA 91609 Tel 213-506-4682 (SAN 216-0226).

Bro-Dart Foundation, *(Bro-Dart Found; 0-912654),* 1807 Pembroke Rd., Greensboro, NC 27408 Tel 919-275-7336 (SAN 204-3890); c/o Brodart, Inc., 500 Arch St., Williamsport, PA 17705 Tel 717-326-2461 (SAN 204-3904).

Bro-Dart Publishing Co., *(Brodart; 0-87272),* 1609 Memorial Ave., Williamsport, PA 17701 Tel 717-326-2461 (SAN 203-6711).

Broadcast Information Bureau, Inc., *(Broadcast Info; 0-943174),* 100 Lafayette Dr., Syosset, NY 11791 Tel 516-496-3355 (SAN 240-3463).

Broadman Press, *(Broadman; 0-8054),* 127 Ninth Ave., N., Nashville, TN 37234 Tel 615-251-2544 (SAN 281-3440).

Broadsheet Pubns, *(Broadsheet Pubns; 0-941142),* P.O. Box 616, McMinnville, OR 97128 Tel 503-472-5524 (SAN 223-1751).

Broadside Press Pubns., *(Broadside; 0-910296),* 74 Glendale Ave., Highland Park, MI 48203 Tel 313-868-1585 (SAN 201-9388).

Broadway Play Publishing, *(Broadway Play; 0-88145),* 249 W. 29th St., New York, NY 10001 Tel 212-563-3820 (SAN 260-1699).

Brock Publishing Co., *(Brock Pub; 0-930534),* P.O. Box 1685, Chico, CA 95927 Tel 714-673-6310 (SAN 201-8616).

Brockton Art Museum/Fuller Memorial, *(Brockton Art Fuller; 0-934358),* Oak St., Brockton, MA 02401 Tel 617-588-6000 (SAN 262-0049).

Brodsky & Treadway, *(B&T; 0-9610914),* 63 Dimick St., Sommerville, MA 02143 Tel 617-666-3372 (SAN 265-0924).

Broken Moom Press, *(Broken Moon; 0-913089),* 330 Del Monte Ave., Tacoma, WA 98466 (SAN 283-2844).

Broken Whisker Studio, *(Broken Whisker; 0-932220),* P.O. Box 1303, Chicago, IL 60690 Tel 312-987-0906 (SAN 209-0856).

Brokering Press, *(Brokering Pr; 0-942562),* 11641 Palmer Rd., Bloomington, MN 55437 Tel 612-888-5281 (SAN 239-622X).

Brolet Press, *(Brolet; 0-910298),* 33 Gold St., New York, NY 10038 Tel 212-227-6280 (SAN 202-425X).

Bronx County Historical Society, The, *(Bronx County; 0-941980),* 3266 Bainbridge Ave., Bronx, NY 10467 Tel 212-881-8900 (SAN 238-4485).

Brookdale Press, *(Brookdale Pr; 0-912650),* 184 Brookdale Rd., Stamford, CT 06903 Tel 203-322-2474 (SAN 208-3744).

Brookes, Paul H., Pubs., *(P H Brookes; 0-933716),* P.O. Box 10624, Baltimore, MD 21204 Tel 301-433-8100 (SAN 219-7693).

Brookfield Publishing Co., *(Brookfield Pub Co; 0-604),* Old Post Rd., Brookfield, VT 05036 Tel 802-276-3355 (SAN 213-4705).

Brookings Institution, *(Brookings; 0-8157),* 1775 Massachusetts Ave., N.W., Washington, DC 20036 Tel 202-797-6254 (SAN 201-9396).

Brooklyn Botanic Garden, *(Bklyn Botanic),* 1000 Washington Ave., Brooklyn, NY 11225 Tel 212-622-4433 (SAN 203-1094).

Brooklyn College Conservatory of Music, *(Bklyn Coll Music; 0-9600976),* Brooklyn College, Brooklyn, NY 11210 Tel 212-780-5286 (SAN 208-4813).

Brooklyn College Press, *(Brooklyn Coll Pr; 0-930888),* 2227 Boylan Hall, Society In Change, Brooklyn, NY 11210 (SAN 281-3467); Orders to: 136 S. Broadway, Irvington-on-Hudson, NY 10533 Tel 914-591-9111 (SAN 281-3475).

Brooklyn Educational & Cultural Alliance, *(Bklyn Educ; 0-933250),* Brooklyn Rediscovery, 517 Willoughby St., Brooklyn, NY 11201 Tel 212-852-6200 (SAN 212-4858).

Brooklyn Museum, *(Bklyn Mus; 0-87273; 0-913696),* Pubns. & Marketing Services, Eastern Pkwy., Brooklyn, NY 11238 Tel 212-638-5000 (SAN 206-3387).

Brooks, Stanley J., Co., *(S J Brooks; 0-941806),* 1460 Westwood Blvd.Suite 303, Los Angeles, CA 90024 (SAN 213-7275).

Brooks/Cole Publishing Co., Div. of Wadsworth, Inc., *(Brooks-Cole; 0-8185),* 555 Abrego St., Monterey, CA 93940 Tel 408-373-0728 (SAN 202-3369); Orders to: Wadsworth, Inc., Customer Service Ctr., 7625 Empire Dr., Florence, KY 41042 Tel 800-354-9706 (SAN 200-2213).

Brooks Publishing Co., *(Brooks Pub Co; 0-932370),* 2740 Fulton Ave., Suite 113, Sacramento, CA 95821 Tel 916-972-0633 (SAN 212-8829); Orders to: P.O. Box 1066, Carmichael, CA 95609 Tel 916-972-0633 (SAN 212-8837).

Brooks-Sterling Co., *(Brooks-Sterling; 0-914418),* P.O. Box 265, Danville, CA 94526 Tel 415-837-1318 (SAN 206-4820).

Broome Closet, the, *(Broome Closet; 0-9608130),* 12433 Cumpston St., N. Hollywood, CA 91607 (SAN 238-8340).

Brotherhood of Life, Inc., *(Bro Life Inc; 0-914732),* 110 Dartmouth, S.E., Albuquerque, NM 87106 Tel 505-255-8980 (SAN 204-4233).

Broude Brothers Ltd., Music, *(Broude; 0-8450),* 170 Varick St., New York, NY 10013 Tel 212-242-7001 (SAN 281-3483); 141 White Oaks Rd., Williamstown, MA 01267 (SAN 281-3491).

Broude International Editions, Inc., *(Broude Intl Edns; 0-89371),* 141 White Oaks Rd., Williamstown, MA 01267 Tel 413-458-8131 (SAN 208-9483).

Brown, Arlin J., *(Arlin J Brown),* The Arlin J. Brown Info. Center, P.O. Box 251, Ft. Belvoir, VA 22060 Tel 703-451-8638 (SAN 203-4891).

Brown, C. C., Publishing Co., *(C C Brown Pub; 0-9600378),* Box 462, Airway Heights, WA 99001 Tel 509-244-5807 (SAN 203-6789).

Brown, D., Books, *(D Brown Bks),* 511 Capp St., San Francisco, CA 94110 Tel 415-648-3653 (SAN 209-4290).

Brown, James L., *(J L Brown; 0-921214),* Orders to: Old Town News, 308 N. Irwin St., Hanford, CA 93230 (SAN 223-1646).

Brown, Lewis S., Publisher, *(L S Brown Pub; 0-9608542),* 124 W. Pierpont St., Kingston, NY 12401 Tel 914-338-4352 (SAN 204-6047).

Brown, P.S., *(P S Brown; 0-9604148),* 2306 Union St., San Francisco, CA 94123 (SAN 215-2983).

Brown, William C., Publishers, *(Wm C Brown; 0-697),* 2460 Kerper Blvd., Dubuque, IA 52001 Tel 319-589-2822 (SAN 203-2864).

Brown Book Co., *(Brown Bk; 0-910294),* 120 Secatogue Ave., Farmingdale, NY 11735 Tel 516-293-6969 (SAN 202-4276).

Brown Cherry Pubns, *(Brown Cherry Pub; 0-910515),* 738 Plum Ave., Hamton, VA 23661 Tel 804-247-3230 (SAN 260-1702).

Brown House Galleries Ltd., *(Brown Hse Gall; 0-9604534),* 5717 Hammersley Rd., P.O. Box 4243, Madison, WI 53711 (SAN 215-7365).

Brown Penny Press, *(Brown Penny),* 18130 Hwy. 36, Blachly, OR 97412 Tel 503-927-6141 (SAN 209-5335).

Brown Rabbit Press, *(Brown Rabbit; 0-933988),* P.O. Box 19111, Houston, TX 77024 Tel 713-465-1168 (SAN 213-0246).

Browning Pubns., *(Browning Pubns; 0-933718),* P.O. Box 81306, Atlanta, GA 30366 Tel 404-455-3430 (SAN 212-8845).

Brownlow Publishing Co. Inc., *(Brownlow Pub Co; 0-915720),* 2821 Vaughn, P.O. Box 50545, Fort Worth, TX 76105 Tel 817-531-1401 (SAN 207-5105).

Brown's Studio, *(Brown's Studio; 0-9604822),* 4004 Seven Springs Blvd., New Port Richey, FL 33552 Tel 813-376-5711 (SAN 215-6288).

Brownstone Books, *(Brownstone Bks; 0-941028),* 1711 Clifty Dr., Madison, IN 47250 Tel 812-273-6908 (SAN 217-3387).

B'ruach HaTorah Pubns., *(Bruach HaTorah; 0-89655),* 7617 Reading Rd., Cincinnati, OH 45237 Tel 513-821-8941 (SAN 284-9844); P.O. Box 37366, Cincinnati, OH 45222 (SAN 284-9852).

Brubaker, E. S., *(Brubaker),* 645 N. President Ave., Lancaster, PA 17603 Tel 717-397-3120 (SAN 209-5343).

Bruccoli Clark Books, *(Bruccoli; 0-89723),* 2006 Sumter St., Columbia, SC 29201 (SAN 209-3987).

Bruce, Martin M., Pubs., *(M M Bruce; 0-935198),* 50 Larchwood Rd., Box 248, Larchmont, NY 10538 Tel 914-834-1555 (SAN 203-6819).

Brun Press Inc., *(Brun Pr; 0-932574),* 701 N.E. 67th St., Miami, FL 33138 Tel 305-756-6249 (SAN 212-033X).

Brune, Gunnar, *(G Brune),* 2014 Royal Club Court, Arlington, TX 76017 Tel 817-465-3171 (SAN 215-0611).

Bruner, William T., *(Bruner),* 3848 Southern Pkwy., Louisville, KY 40214 Tel 502-367-7089 (SAN 211-2884).

Brunner, Mazel, Inc., *(Brunner-Mazel; 0-87630),* 19 Union Square W., New York, NY 10003 Tel 212-924-3344 (SAN 164-9167).

Brunswick Historical Society, *(Brunswick Hist Soc),* P.O. Box 1776, Cropseyville, NY 12052 (SAN 213-0289).

Brunswick Publishing Co., *(Brunswick Pub; 0-931494),* P.O. Box 555, Lawrenceville, VA 23868 Tel 804-848-3865 (SAN 211-6332).

Bryan, R. L., *(R L Bryan; 0-934870),* 5 Ramblewood Lane, Greenville, SC 29609 (SAN 203-6827).

Bryans *See* Dell Publishing Co., Inc.

Bryant, James M., *(J M Bryant),* P.O. Box 412, Normangee, TX 77871 Tel 713-828-4265 (SAN 206-2070).

Bryant, Lawrence C., *(L C Bryant),* 467 Palmetto Pkwy., N.E., Orangeburg, SC 29115 Tel 803-536-1305 (SAN 201-0550).

Bryden Press, *(Bryden; 0-9603510),* P.O. Box 364, Muncie, IN 47305 (SAN 213-7283).

Bryn Ffyliaid Pubns., *(Bryn Ffyliaid; 0-9611114),* 5600 Bellaire Dr., New Orleans, LA 70124 Tel 504-486-7036 (SAN 283-2720).

B2C Adventures, *(B-TwoC; 0-939368),* 2 Carvel Rd., Annapolis, MD 21401 Tel 301-974-0642 (SAN 212-2103).

Bubba Press, *(Bubba Pr; 0-9607240),* P.O. Box 5215, Modesto, CA 95352 (SAN 239-4138).

Buber, Martin, Press, *(M Buber Pr),* G.P.O. Box 2009, Brooklyn, NY 11202 (SAN 212-7318).

Buccaneer Books, *(Buccaneer Bks; 0-89966),* P.O. Box 168, Cutchogue, NY 11935 (SAN 209-1542).

Buchanan, Laurie, *(Buchanan L; 0-943102),* 2140 N. Iris Lane, Escondido, CA 92026 (SAN 240-8236).

Buchs, J., Pubns., *(J Buchs),* 5301 Richmond, No. 24B, Houston, TX 77027 (SAN 208-256X).

Buck Hill Associates, *(Buck Hill; 0-917420),* Garnet Lake Rd., Johnsburg, NY 12843 Tel 518-251-2743 (SAN 202-4403).

Buck Publishing Co., *(Buck Pub; 0-934530),* 2409 Vestavia Dr., Birmingham, AL 35216 Tel 205-979-2296 (SAN 213-0203); Orders to: Buck Pub. Co., 2409 Vestavia Dr., Birmingham,.

Buckley Pubns., Inc., *(Buckley Pubns; 0-915388),* 233 E. Erie St., Suite 402, Chicago, IL 60611 Tel 312-943-2066 (SAN 208-1954).

Buckminster Press, *(Buckminster Pr; 0-9610094),* 159A Heritage Hills, Somers, NY 10589 Tel 914-277-3807 (SAN 268-506X).

Bucknell Univ. Press, Div. of Associated University Presses, *(Bucknell U Pr; 0-8387),* 440 Forsgate Dr., Cranbury, NJ 08512 Tel 609-655-4770 (SAN 201-9434).

Bucks County Historical Society, *(Bucks Co Hist; 0-910302),* Pine & Ashland Sts., Doylestown, PA 18901 Tel 215-345-0210 (SAN 203-6835).

Bucyrus-Erie Co., *(Bucyrus-Erie Co; 0-9604136),* P.O. Box 56, S. Milwaukee, WI 53172 (SAN 214-1825).

Buddhist Association of The U.S., The, *(Buddhist Assn US; 0-915078),* Dist. by: Institute for Advanced Studies of World Religions, 2150 Center Ave., Fort Lee, NJ 07024 (SAN 265-3885).

Buddhist Books International, *(Buddhist Bks; 0-914910),* 9701 Wilshire Blvd., Suite 850, Beverly Hills, CA 90212 (SAN 281-3548).

Buddhist Study Center, The, *(Buddhist Study; 0-938474),* c/o Press Pacifica, P.O. Box 47, Kailua, HI 96734 (SAN 284-9860); Offices of Buddhist Education, 1727 Pali Hwy., Honolulu, HI 96813 (SAN 284-9879).

Buddhist Text Translation Society, *(Buddhist Text; 0-917512),* Box 217,City of Ten Thousand Buddhas, Talmage, CA 95481 Tel 707-462-0939 (SAN 281-3556); Orders to: Box 217, City of Ten Thousand Buddhas, Talmage, CA 94481 Tel 707-462-0939 (SAN 281-3564).

Budgate Press, *(Budgate Pr; 0-9610746),* 1358 Levona St., Ypsilanti, MI 48197 Tel 313-483-5365 (SAN 264-7192).

Budlong Press Co., *(Budlong; 0-910304),* 5915 N. Northwest Hwy., Chicago, IL 60631 (SAN 202-4837).

Buffalo Fine Arts Academy, *(Buffalo Acad; 0-914782),* Albright-Knox Art Gallery, 1285 Elmwood Ave., Buffalo, NY 14222 Tel 716-882-8700 (SAN 202-4845).

Builders of the Adytum, Ltd., *(Builders of Adytum),* 5105 N. Figueroa St., Los Angeles, CA 90042 Tel 213-255-7141 (SAN 202-4853); Orders to: P.O. Box 42278, Dept., O, Los Angeles, CA 90042 (SAN 202-4861).

Building Blocks, *(Building Blocks; 0-943452),* 314 Liberty St., Dundee, IL 60118 Tel 312-426-6919 (SAN 240-6063).

Building Cost File, Inc., *(Building Cost File; 0-942564),* 17 W. John St., Hicksville, NY 11801 Tel 516-822-5010 (SAN 238-0293).

Building Institute, The, *(Building Inst),* River Rd., Piermont, NY 10968 Tel 914-359-0299 (SAN 241-3655).

Bull, Donald, *(D Bull; 0-9601190),* P.O. Box 106, Trumbull, CT 06611 Tel 203-261-2398 (SAN 211-4097).

Bull City, *(Bull City; 0-933974),* 3425 B. Randolph Rd., Durham, NC 27705 Tel 222-7223).

Bull Publishing Co., *(Bull Pub; 0-915950),* P.O. Box 208, Palo Alto, CA 94302 Tel 415-322-2855 (SAN 208-5712).

Bullock Publishing Co., *(Bullock Pub Co; 0-912875),* P.O. Box 350, 5142 Auriesville St., Hazelwood, MO 63042 Tel 314-739-4671 (SAN 283-2941).

Bumann, Richard L., *(Bumann Spec Works; 0-9607112),* 2139 Ranch View Terrace, Olivenhain, CA 92024 Tel 714-753-7279 (SAN 238-9568).

Bunkhouse Pubs., Inc., *(Bunkhouse; 0-918628),* 123 N. Sultana Ave., Ontario, CA 91764 (SAN 215-062X).

Bunting & Lyon, Inc., *(Bunting; 0-913094),* 238 N. Main St., Wallingford, CT 06492 Tel 203-269-3333 (SAN 202-487X).

Burdette & Co., Inc., *(Burdette; 0-910306),* 63 Commercial Wharf, Boston, MA 02210 Tel 617-523-3505 (SAN 202-4888).

Burdick Ancestry Library, The, *(Burdick Ancestry Lib; 0-9609100),* 5022 N. Austin Ave., Chicago, IL 60630 Tel 312-763-1336 (SAN 241-2802).

Bureau Issues Assn., *(Bureau Issues; 0-930412),* 7215 13th Ave., Takoma Park, MD 20012 (SAN 213-0483).

Bureau of Business Practice, Inc., Div. of Prentice-Hall, Inc., *(Bur Busn Prac; 0-87622),* 24 Rope Ferry Rd., Waterford, CT 06386 Tel 203-442-4365 (SAN 204-3742).

Bureau of Business Research, *(Bureau Busn Re Sch; 0-942650),* School of Business Administration, Wayne State University, Prentis Bldg. 209, Detroit, MI 48202 (SAN 240-9178).

Bureau of Business Research, Univ. of Nebraska-Lincoln, *(Bur Busn Res U Nebr),* 200 CBA Bldg., Univ. of Nebr., Lincoln, NE 68588 Tel 402-472-2334 (SAN 209-262X).

Bureau of Economic Geology, Div. of Univ. of Texas at Austin, *(Bur Econ Geology),* University Sta., Box X, Austin, TX 78712 Tel 512-471-1534 (SAN 207-432X).

Bureau of Health & Hospital Careers Counseling, *(Bur Health Hosp; 0-917364),* Lincoln Hospital Medical Ctr., P.O. Box 238, Scarsdale, NY 10583 Tel 914-241-0610 (SAN 208-5720).

Bureau of International Affairs, *(Bur Intl Aff),* 1613 Chelsea Rd., San Marino, CA Tel 213-793-2841 (SAN 201-9442).

Bureau of National Affairs, Inc., *(BNA; 0-87179),* 1231 25th St., N.W., Washington, DC 20037 Tel 202-452-4402 (SAN 201-4262).

Bureau of Public Secrets, *(Bur Public Secrets; 0-939682),* P.O. Box 1044, Berkeley, CA 94701 (SAN 216-2261).

Burger, Joanne, *(J Burger; 0-916188),* 57 Blue Bonnet Court, Lake Jackson, TX 77566 (SAN 211-2191).

Burgess, Jack K., Inc., *(J K Burgess),* 2175 Lemoine Ave., Fort Lee, NJ 07024 Tel 201-592-0739 (SAN 220-1356).

Burgess, Jack K. Inc., -International Ideas Inc., *(Burgess-Intl Ideas),* Orders to: Jack K. Burgess, Inc., 2175 Lemoine Ave., Fort Lee, NJ 07024 Tel 201-592-0739 (SAN 220-1356); Orders to: International Ideas Inc., 1627 Spruce St., Philadelphia, PA 19103 Tel 215-546-0392 (SAN 210-6043).

Burgess Publishing Co., *(Burgess; 0-8087),* 7108 Ohms Lane, Minneapolis, MN 55435 Tel 612-831-1344 (SAN 212-6001). *Imprints:* Feffer & Simons (Feffer & Simons).

Burgundy Press, *(Burgundy Pr; 0-917574),* P.O. Box 313, Southampton, PA 18966 (SAN 212-1859).

Burk, Margaret, *(M Burk),* P.O. Box 22, Ambassador Sta., Los Angeles, CA 90070 (SAN 214-2880).

Burkehaven Press, *(Burkehaven Pr; 0-914062),* Penacook Rd., Contoocook, NH 03229 Tel 603-746-3625 (SAN 202-4896).

Burke's Book Store, Inc., *(Burke's Bk Store; 0-937130),* 634 Poplar Ave., Memphis, TN 38105 Tel 901-527-7484 (SAN 127-3124).

Burn, Hart & Co., Pubs., *(Burn-Hart; 0-918060),* 632 Calle Yucca, Box 1772, Thousand Oaks, CA 91360 Tel 805-498-3985 (SAN 210-1823).

Burnett Family Genealogical Association, Inc., *(Burnett Family Gen; 0-9608266),* 3891 Commander Dr., Chamblee, GA 30341 Tel 404-881-2343 (SAN 240-3471).

Burning Bush Pubns., *(Burning Bush; 0-937528),* 103 Middleton Pl., Jeffersonville, PA 19403 Tel 215-630-8839 (SAN 215-1340).

Burning Deck, *(Burning Deck; 0-930900; 0-930901),* 71 Elmgrove Ave., Providence, RI 02906 Tel 207-7981).

Burns, H. Keith, Publishing, *(H Keith Burns; 0-943842),* 6026 Mesa Ave., Los Angeles, CA 90042 Tel 213-256-5436 (SAN 241-0079).

Burns, J. B., *(J B Burns; 0-9602998),* 4250 Lauderdale Ave., La Crescenta, CA 91214 (SAN 213-473X).

Burntcoat Corp., *(Burntcoat Corp),* Box 350, Hampden, ME 04444 (SAN 216-3454).

Burr, Betty Fagan, *(B F Burr; 0-911619),* 613 Bostwick, Nacogdoches, TX 75961 Tel 713-564-7478 (SAN 263-9491).

Burr Pubns., Ltd., *(Burr Pubns; 0-911994),* RD 1, Rte. 33, Box 429, Hightstown-Freehold Rd., Hightstown, NJ 08520 (SAN 207-2068).

Burrell Center, Inc., *(Burrell Ctr Inc; 0-9606362),* P.O. Box 1611SSS, Springfield, MO 65805 (SAN 223-7520).

Burrill-Ellsworth Assoc., *(Burrill-Ellsworth; 0-935310),* 26 Birchwood Place, Tenafly, NJ 07670 (SAN 281-3602); Orders to: Box 295, Tenafly, NJ 07670 (SAN 281-3610).

Burrows, Hal D., (Dba Inner Press), *(H D Burrows; 0-916886),* 429 E. 98th St., No. 1, Inglewood, CA 90301 Tel 213-671-5959 (SAN 211-0180).

Burrows & Baker, *(Burrows & Baker; 0-930414),* 201 E. 21st St., New York, NY 10010 (SAN 223-2618).

Burtis Enterprises, Pubs., *(Burtis Ent; 0-939530),* 23651 Gerrad Way, Canoga Park, CA 91307 Tel 213-346-8534 (SAN 216-6593).

Burton Gallery, The, *(Turn The Pg; 0-931540),* 203 Baldwin Ave., Roseville, CA 95678 Tel 916-444-7933 (SAN 281-3629); Dist. by: Turn the Page Press, 203 Baldwin Street, Roseville, CA 95678 Tel 916-444-7933 (SAN 265-9832).

Bush, Elsie R. & Dale L., *(D & E Bush; 0-9609440),* 29222 Highway 41, Coarsegold, CA 93614 Tel 209-683-6387 (SAN 260-0234).

Business & Professional Books, Inc., *(Busn Pro Bks; 0-9608576),* Westgate Station, P.O. Box 9671, San Jose, CA 95157 Tel 415-992-7771 (SAN 238-2539).

Business & Professional Div. *See* Prentice-Hall, Inc.

Business Communications Co. Inc. (BCC), *(BCC; 0-89336),* P.O. Box 2070C, 9 Viaduct Rd., Stamford, CT 06906 Tel 203-325-2208 (SAN 207-706X).

Business Information Display, Inc., *(Busn Info; 0-938596),* 4202 Sorrento Valley Blvd. Suite J, San Diego, CA 92121 (SAN 238-6879).

Business Management Sciences, Inc., *(Busn Mgmt Sci; 0-918128),* 95-20 63rd, Rego Park, NY 11374 Tel 212-275-2874 (SAN 209-3669).

Business News Publishing Co., *(Busn News; 0-912524),* P.O. Box 2600, Troy, MI 48007 Tel 313-362-3700 (SAN 201-9450).

Business Press, *(Busn Pr),* Dist. by: Taplinger Publishing Co., 132 W. 22nd St., New York, NY 10011 (SAN 213-6821).

Business Psychology International, *(Busn Psych; 0-931918),* P. O. Box 235-6, Boston, MA 02159 Tel 617-332-3820 (SAN 281-6014).

Business Pubns., Inc., Subs. of Richard D. Irwin, Inc., *(Business Pubns; 0-256),* 200 Chisholm Place, Suite 240, Plano, TX 75075 Tel 214-422-4389 (SAN 202-4926).

Business Sale Institute, *(Busn Sale Inst; 0-933808),* 170 Park Center Plaza, Suite 202, San Jose, CA 95113 Tel 408-286-4850 (SAN 212-8853).

Business Travelers Inc. *See* Watts, Franklin, Inc.

Business Trend Analysts, *(Busn Trend),* 2171 Jericho Turnpike, Commack, NY 11725 Tel 516-462-5454 (SAN 217-2313).

Buten Museum of Wedgwood, *(Buten Mus; 0-912014),* 246 N. Bowman Ave., Merion, PA 19066 Tel 215-664-6601 (SAN 202-4942).

Buteo Books, *(Buteo; 0-931130),* P.O. Box 481, Vermillion, SD 57069 Tel 605-624-4343 (SAN 212-0054).

Butler, Doug, *(Doug Butler; 0-916992),* P.O. Box 370, Maryville, MO 64468 Tel 816-582-3202 (SAN 206-3999).

Butterfly Press, *(Butterfly Pr; 0-918766),* P.O. Box 19571, Houston, TX 77024 Tel 713-464-7570 (SAN 209-7133) Formerly Terzarima System.

Butterfly Publishing, Inc., *(Butterfly Pub; 0-941254),* P.O. Box 30427, Santa Barbara, CA 93105 (SAN 237-935X); Dist. by: Richard Maher Sales, 90 W. Senior Way, Salt Lake City, UT 84115 (SAN 158-8141).

Butterworth Co. of Cape Cod, Inc., The, *(Butterworth of Cape Cod; 0-937338),* 350 Main St., West Yarmouth, MA 02673 (SAN 239-524X).

Butterworth Legal Pubs., Inc., *(Butterworth Legal Pubs; 0-88063),* 381 Elliot St., Newton Upper Falls, MA 02164 Tel 617-964-5333 (SAN 238-1451).

Butterworth's, *(Butterworth),* 10 Tower Office Park, Woburn, MA 01801 Tel 617-933-8260 (SAN 206-3964). *Imprints:* Newnes-Butterworth (Newnes-Butterworth).

Buxbaum, Edwin C., *(Buxbaum; 0-9600494),* P.O. Box 465, Wilmington, DE 19899 Tel 302-994-2663 (SAN 201-7482).

Buyer's Directory, *(Buyer's Directory),* R.D. 3, Box 533, Olean, NY 14760 Tel 716-372-0514 (SAN 214-1108).

Buyout Publications, *(Buyout; 0-9610806),* 91 Paradise Lane, Halifax, MA 02338 Tel 617-293-6655 (SAN 265-0959).

By By Productions, *(By By Prods; 0-938826),* P.O. Box 1743, Glendora, CA 91740 (SAN 216-0242).

By Hand & Foot, Ltd., *(By Hand & Foot; 0-938670),* Green River Rd., P.O. Box 611, Brattleboro, VT 05301 (SAN 215-8493).

Byline Books, *(Byline Books; 0-943996),* 5805-C N. Grand Blvd., Oklahoma City, OK 73118 (SAN 240-9690).

Byram Hilltop Press, *(B Hilltop Pr; 0-9605876),* P.O. Box Z, Andover, NJ 07821 Tel 201-786-6264 (SAN 216-3934).

Byrd, Harold E., *(Byrd; 0-9601972),* 8801 S. Western Ave., Los Angeles, CA 90047 Tel 213-753-1495 (SAN 212-2707).

BYTE Books *See* McGraw-Hill Book Co.

Byzantine Press, *(Byzantine Pr; 0-913168),* 115 N. Seventh St., Las Vegas, NV 89101 Tel 702-384-4200 (SAN 204-3785).

CAK Associates, *(CAK Assocs Inc; 0-911245),* P.O. Box16042, Albuquerque, NM 87191 Tel 505-293-2293 (SAN 268-5612).

C.A.M Co., *(C A M Co; 0-942752),* P.O. Box 352, Hortonville, WI 54944 (SAN 281-3645); Dist. by: The Distributors, 702 S. Michigan, South Bend, IN 46618 Tel 219-232-8500 (SAN 212-0364); Dist. by: Baker & Taylor, Momence, IL 60954 Tel 815-472-2444 (SAN 169-2100).

C.A.P.P. Books, *(CAPP Bks),* P.O. Box 416, Williamsburg, VA 23187 Tel 804-253-1393 (SAN 209-1984).

CAYC Learning Tree, *(CAYC Learning Tree; 0-940908),* 9998 Ferguson Rd., Dallas, TX 75228 Tel 214-321-6484 (SAN 212-8861).

C & E Enterprise, Publishers, *(C & E Ent Pub; 0-9610096),* 980 West St., San Louis Obispo, CA 93401 Tel 805-543-8187 (SAN 268-5620).

C & G Publishing, *(C&G Pub; 0-941030),* 941 Sherwood Ave., Los Altos, CA 94022 Tel 415-941-4082 (SAN 217-3395).

C&L Publishing Co., *(C & L Pub Co; 0-9605724),* 2525 Wilson Boulevard, Arlington, VA 22201 (SAN 216-3462).

C&M Pubns., *(C&M Pubns; 0-938934),* 2505 Stratford Dr., Austin, TX 78746 (SAN 216-227X).

C & S Enterprises, *(C & S Ent; 0-9609028),* 5169 Wheelis Dr., Memphis, TN 38117 Tel 901-767-7961 (SAN 281-367X); Dist. by: Slegman/Laner, 3000 W. 64th St., Shawnee Mission, KS 60208 (SAN 282-5988).

CBH Publishing, Inc., *(CBH Pub),* Box 236, Glencoe, IL 60022 Tel 312-835-0060 (SAN 216-2288).

CBI Publishing Co. Inc., Division of the International Thompson Organisation, *(CBI Pub; 0-8436),* 51 Sleeper St., Boston, MA 02210 Tel 617-426-2224 (SAN 201-9515).

CC Pubs., *(C C Pubs; 0-9603766),* P.O. Box 4044, Clearwater, FL 33518 (SAN 223-5471).

CELESTIAL GEMS, *(Celestial Gems; 0-914154),* 404 State St., Centralia, WA 98531 Tel 206-736-5083 (SAN 201-1948).

C. E. M. Co., *(C E M Comp; 0-930004),* 3154 Coventry Dr., Bay City, MI 48706 Tel 517-686-4208 (SAN 209-5378).

CEPA Gallery, *(CEPA Gall; 0-939784),* 700 Main St., 4th Fl., Buffalo, NY 14202 Tel 716-856-2717 (SAN 216-8839).

CE Publishing, *(C E Pub; 0-912227),* P.O. Box 488, Plantsville, CT 06479 Tel 203-621-6811 (SAN 265-0983).

CERA, *(CERA; 0-936706),* P.O. Box 18103, San Francisco, CA 94118 (SAN 215-8515).

C. E. R. I. Press, Subs. of Communication & Education Resources, Inc., *(C E R I Pr; 0-941822),* 5513 Forrestal Ave., Alexandria, VA 22311 Tel 703-820-7459 (SAN 239-1678).

CHAMH Pubs., *(CHAMH Pub; 0-938666),* 78 Pearl St., New York, NY 10004 (SAN 215-9430).

CHCUS, Inc., *(CHCUS Inc; 0-937256),* P.O. Box 444, Oak Park, IL 60303 Tel 312-848-2210 (SAN 215-2401).

C J Books, *(C J Bks; 0-942878),* P.O. Box 922, Gig Harbor, WA 98335 Tel 206-858-3768 (SAN 263-9548).

CLCB Press, Div. of CLCBI International, *(CLCB Pr),* 5901 Plainfield Dr., Charlotte, NC 28215 (SAN 211-2892).

CLP Pubs., Subs. Creation-Life Publishers, Inc., *(CLP Pubs; 0-89051),* P.O. Box 15666, San Diego, CA 92115 Tel 619-449-9420 (SAN 205-6119). *Imprints:* Institute of Creation Research (Inst Creation); Master Books (Master Bks).

C M Publishing, *(C M Pub; 0-9607514),* 330 Eubank, El Paso, TX 79902 (SAN 237-9856).

COM Press, Inc., *(COMPress; 0-933694),* P.O. Box 102, Wentworth, NH 03282 Tel 603-764-5831 (SAN 284-9887); 286 Congress St., Boston, MA 02110 Tel 617-426-2240 (SAN 284-9895).

C. P. Ela, *(C P Ela; 0-9607464),* 1841 Massachusetts Ave., Lexington, MA 02173 (SAN 240-8163).

CPL Bibliographies, *(CPL Biblios),* 1313 E. 60th St., Merriam Ctr., Chicago, IL 60637 Tel 312-947-2007 (SAN 210-3516).

C. P. Press, *(C P Pr; 0-9600452),* 31 Woodmont Rd., Upper Montclair, NJ 07043 (SAN 202-4985).

CRB Research, *(CRB Res; 0-939780),* P.O. Box 56, Commack, NY 11725 Tel 516-543-7486 (SAN 216-8812).

CRC Press, *(CRC Pr; 0-87819; 0-8493),* 2000 Corporate Blvd., Boca Raton, FL 33431 Tel 305-994-0555 (SAN 202-1994).

CRCS Pubns., *(CRCS Pubns NV; 0-916360),* P.O. Box 20850, Reno, NV 89515 Tel 702-358-2850 (SAN 501-3240) Do Not Confuse with CRC Pr, Florida.

CRS Consultants Press, *(CRS Con; 0-911127),* P.O. Box 490175, Key Biscayne, FL 33149 Tel 305-361-9573 (SAN 268-5663).

CSG Press, Subs. of Capital Systems Group, Inc., *(CSG Pr; 0-9611784),* 11301 Rockville Pike, Kensington, MD 20895 Tel 301-881-9400 (SAN 215-241X).

CS Pubns., *(CS Pubns; 0-934206),* 1791 Primrose Dr., El Cajon, CA 92020 (SAN 213-0459).

CSSEAS Pubns. Center for S. and SE Asian Studies, *(CSSEAS; 0-89148),* University of Michigan, 240 Lane Hall, Ann Arbor, MI 48109 (SAN 263-9556).

C.S.S. Publishing Co., *(CSS Pub; 0-89536),* 628 S. Main St., Lima, OH 45804 Tel 419-227-1818 (SAN 207-0707).

CTB/McGraw Hill, Div. of McGraw Hill, *(CTB McGraw Hill; 0-07),* Del Monte Research Park, Monterey, CA 93940 Tel 408-649-8400 (SAN 204-370X).

CWS Group Press, *(CWS Group Pr; 0-9604324),* P.O. Box 543, 807 W. 15th St., Vinton, IA 52349 Tel 319-472-3552 (SAN 214-3526).

Caann Verlag Gmbtt, *(Caann Verlag),* Dist. by: Associated Booksellers, 147 McKinley Ave., Bridgeport, CT 06606 (SAN 206-9717).

Cabala Press, *(Cabala Pr; 0-941542),* 6424 N. Sacramento, Chicago, IL 60645 Tel 312-761-0682 (SAN 239-071X).

Caballero Press, *(Caballero Pr; 0-9601346),* 1936 Caballero Way, Las Vegas, NV 89109 Tel 702-735-3406 (SAN 210-6825).

Cabat Studio Pubns., *(Cabat Studio Pubns; 0-913521),* 627 N. Fourth Ave., Tucson, AZ 85705 Tel 602-622-6362 (SAN 285-1539).

Cable Television Information Ctr., the, *(Cable TV Info Ctr; 0-943336),* 1800 N. Kent St., Suite 1007, Arlington, VA 22209 Tel 703-528-6846 (SAN 240-6071).

Caboose Press, *(Caboose Pr; 0-9608064),* 499 Embarcadero, Oakland, CA 94606 Tel 415-465-6323 (SAN 240-1983).

Cachalot Books, *(Cachalot Bks; 0-913023),* 6309 Hollywood Blvd., Suite 207, Hollywood, CA 90028 Tel 213-387-3560 (SAN 283-0000).

Cache Valley Newsletter Publishing Co., *(Cache Valley; 0-941462),* Rte. 3 Box 273, Preston, ID 83263 Tel 208-852-3167 (SAN 239-0728).

CAD-CAM Decisions, *(Cad Cam; 0-938800),* P.O. Box 76042, Atlanta, GA 30328 (SAN 240-012X); Dist. by: OnLine Pubns., .

Cadillac Publishing Co., Inc., *(Cadillac; 0-87445),* 709 S. Skinker Blvd., St. Louis, MO 63105 Tel 314-862-7560 (SAN 201-8659); 6611 Clayton Rd., St. Louis, MO 63117 (SAN 201-8667).

Cadmus Editions, *(Cadmus Eds; 0-932274),* P.O. Box 4725, Santa Barbara, CA 93103 (SAN 212-887X); Dist. by: The Subterranean Co., P.O. Box 10233, Eugene, OR 97440 Tel 503-343-6324 (SAN 169-7102).

Caedmon, Div. of Raytheon Co., *(Caedmon; 0-9601156; 0-89845),* 1995 Broadway, New York, NY 10023 Tel 212-580-3400 (SAN 206-278X).

CAFH Foundation, Inc., *(CAFH Found Inc; 0-9609102),* P.O. Box 4665, Berkeley, CA 94704 Tel 805-642-2548 (SAN 281-3696); Dist. by: Bookpeople, 2940 Seventh St., Berkeley, CA 94710 Tel 415-599-3030 (SAN 168-9517).

Cagg, Richard D., *(Cagg),* 423 W. Fourth, Cameron, MO 64429 (SAN 215-6296).

Cahill Publishing Co., *(Cahill Pub Co),* P.O. Box 91053, Houston, TX 77088 Tel 713-447-7932 (SAN 263-9572).

Cain, Katherine, *(K Cain; 0-9603188),* P.O. Box 434, Los Gatos, CA 95030 Tel 408-354-8557 (SAN 213-4748).

Cain, Mike, *(M Cain; 0-9601458),* 192 Terra Manor Dr., Wintersville, OH 43952 Tel 614-264-3687 (SAN 211-2221).

Caislan Press, *(Caislan Pr; 0-937444),* Box 28371, San Jose, CA 95159 Tel 408-264-5287 (SAN 284-9909); Orders to: Bookpeople Inc., 2940 Seventh St., Berkeley, CA 94710 (SAN 284-9917); Orders to: Baker and Taylor, Six Kibby Ave., Soomerville, NJ 08876 (SAN 284-9925); Orders to: Baker and Taylor, 501 S. Gladiola St., Momence, IL 60954 (SAN 284-9933).

Calabrese Pubns., *(Calabrese Pubns; 0-911699),* P.O. Box 7138, Hicksville, NY 11801 Tel 516-997-6683 (SAN 263-9580).

Calaloux Pubns., *(Calaloux Pubns; 0-911565),* P.O. Box 6803, Ithaca, NY 14850 (SAN 263-9599); 470 Broome St., New York, NY 10013 Tel 212-799-7749 (SAN 263-9602).

Calamus Books, *(Calamus Bks; 0-930762),* Box 689, Cooper Sta., New York, NY 10276 (SAN 211-7002).

Calao Publishers, *(Calao Pubs),* 302 West 5400 South, Ste 104, Salt Lake City, UT 84107 (SAN 240-8724).

Calapooia Pubns., *(Calapooia Pubns; 0-934784),* 27006 Gap Rd., Brownsville, OR 97327 (SAN 223-7040).

Calapooya Books, *(Calapooya Bks; 0-935004),* 2182 Cal Young Rd., Eugene, OR 97401 Tel 503-344-4301 (SAN 263-6147).

Calcon Press, *(Calcon Pr; 0-9600740),* P.O. Box 536, Bruce, MS 38915 (SAN 201-8683).

Caledonia Press, *(Caledonia Pr; 0-932282),* P.O. Box 245, Racine, WI 53401 Tel 414-637-6200 (SAN 211-8432).

Caliban Books, *(Caliban Bks; 0-904573),* 51 Washington St., Dover, NH 03820 (SAN 287-2730).

Calibre Books, *(Calibre Bks; 0-9605800),* 2953 Fort St., Wyandotte, MI 48192 Tel 313-671-1599 (SAN 223-7032).

Calibre Press, Inc., *(Calibre Pr; 0-935878),* 666 Dundee Rd., Suite 1607, Northbrook, IL 60062 Tel 312-498-5680 (SAN 213-9146).

Calico Mouse, *(Calico Mse Pubns; 0-943134),* 924 Sespe Ave. W., Fillmore, CA 93015 Tel 805-524-0172 (SAN 240-5210).

Calico Papers, The, *(Calico Papers),* Rte. 1, Cochecton, NY 12726 Tel 914-932-8309 (SAN 210-8925).

Calico Press, *(Calico Pr; 0-912714),* P.O. Box 758, Twenty-Nine Palms, CA 92277 Tel 619-367-7661 (SAN 202-4993).

California Academy of Sciences Pubns., *(Calif Acad Sci; 0-940228),* Golden Gate Park, San Francisco, CA 94118 Tel 415-221-5100 (SAN 204-3661).

California Association for Older Americans, *(CA Assn Older; 0-917154),* Orders to: Volcano Press, 330 Ellis St., San Francisco, CA 94102 Tel 415-775-0918 (SAN 268-5795).

California Books, *(Calif Books; 0-934112),* Box 9551, Stanford, CA 94305 (SAN 212-8888).

California Books, *(Calif Irvine; 0-939478),* 7 Bridgewood, Irvine, CA 92714 Tel 714-551-2795 (SAN 216-5910).

California Cambrian Press, *(Calif Cam; 0-911247),* P.O. Box 2331, Carlsbad, CA 92008 Tel 714-729-0050 (SAN 268-5817).

California Childrens Publication, *(Calif Child Pubns; 0-9610442),* P.O. Box 91102, Long Beach, CA 90809-1102 (SAN 285-6867).

California Continuing Education of the Bar, *(Cal Cont Ed Bar),* 2150 Shattuck Ave., Berkeley, CA 94704 (SAN 237-6105).

California Department of Consumer Affairs Co-Op Development Project, *(Calif Dept Co; 0-910427),* 1020 "N" St., Rm. 500, Sacramento, CA 95814 (SAN 262-0057).

California. Department of Highway Patrol, *(CHiPS),* 2555 First Ave., Sacramento, CA 95804 (SAN 268-5884).

California Financial Pubns. See California Health Pubns.

California Health Pubns., *(Calif Health; 0-930926),* Box 220, Carlsbad, CA 92008 (SAN 211-6588). *Imprints:* California Financial Pubns. (CA Finan Pubns).

California Historical Society, *(Calif Hist; 0-910312),* P.O. Box 3370, San Diego, CA 92103 (SAN 281-3734); Orders to: 2090 Jackson St., San Francisco, CA 94109 Tel 415-567-1848 (SAN 281-3742).

California Institute of International Studies, *(Cal Inst Intl; 0-912098),* 766 Santa Ynez, Stanford, CA 94305 Tel 415-322-2026 (SAN 206-8532).

California Institute of Public Affairs, Affiliate of the Claremont Colleges, *(Cal Inst Public; 0-912102),* P.O. Box 10, Claremont, CA 91711 Tel 714-624-5212 (SAN 202-2087).

California Institute of Technology. Munger Africana Library, *(Munger Africana Lib; 0-934912),* Pasadena, CA 91125 Tel 213-356-4469 (SAN 211-1195).

California Journal Press, *(Cal Journal; 0-930302),* 1714 Capitol Ave., Sacramento, CA 95814 Tel 916-444-2840 (SAN 210-1122).

California Lawyer's Press, Inc., *(Cal Lawyers Pr),* P.O. Box 2435, Los Angeles, CA 90051 (SAN 219-7715); Orders to: Living Books, Inc., 12155 Magnolia Ave., Bldg. 11B, Riverside, CA 92503 Tel 800-854-4745 (SAN 219-7723).

California Living Books, *(Cal Living Bks; 0-89395),* The Hearst Bldg., Suite 501, Third & Market Sts., San Francisco, CA 94103 Tel 415-543-5981 (SAN 211-4208).

California Native Plant Society, the, *(Calif Native; 0-943460),* 2380 Ellsworth St., Suite D, Berkeley, CA 94704 Tel 415-841-5575 (SAN 240-6098).

California Pubns., *(Calif Pubns; 0-917306),* P.O. Box 14, Calabasas, CA 91302 Tel 213-880-4181 (SAN 208-578X).

California State Univ., Center for Business & Economic Research, *(CSU Ctr Busn Econ; 0-9602894),* Chico, CA 95929 (SAN 215-9481).

California State Univ. Fullerton, Oral History Program, *(CSUF Oral Hist; 0-930046),* Fullerton, CA 92634 Tel 714-773-3580 (SAN 210-3982).

California State Univ., Fullerton, Visual Arts Center, *(CSU Art Gallery; 0-935314),* 800 N. State College Blvd., Fullerton, CA 92634 (SAN 223-7059).

California State Univ., Northridge Library, *(CSUN; 0-937048),* 18111 Nordhoff St., Northridge, CA 91330 Tel 213-885-2271 (SAN 203-8722).

California State Univ. at Fullerton Foundation, *(CSU Fullerton),* Fullerton, CA 92634 (SAN 215-1952); Dist. by: Hackett Publishing Co., Inc., P.O. Box 55573, 4047 N. Pennsylvania St., Indianapolis, IN 46205 Tel 317-283-8187 (SAN 201-6044).

California Street, *(Calif Street; 0-915090),* 723 Dwight Way, Berkeley, CA 94710 Tel 415-549-2461 (SAN 207-673X).

California Theatre Council, *(Cal Theatre; 0-934782),* 849 S. Broadway, Suite 621, Los Angeles, CA 90014 Tel 213-623-5793 (SAN 263-9629).

California Tomorrow, *(Calif Tomorrow),* 512 Second St., San Francisco, CA 94107 (SAN 216-3470).

California Weekly Explorer, Inc., *(Calif Weekly; 0-936778),* 631 Paularino, Costa Mesa, CA 92626 (SAN 217-0914).

Callaghan & Co., *(Callaghan; 0-8366),* 3201 Old Grenview Rd., Wilmette, IL 60091 Tel 312-256-7000 (SAN 206-9393).

Callahan's Guides, *(Callahans Guides; 0-910967),* 20 Main St., P.O. Box 116, Essex Junction, VT 05452 (SAN 263-2411).

Callaloo Journal, *(Callaloo Journ; 0-912759),* Dept. of English University of Kentucky, Lexington, KY 40506 Tel 606-257-3114 (SAN 282-7654).

Callarman House, *(Callarman Hse; 0-930092),* 2582 Anchor, Port Hueneme, CA 93041 Tel 805-985-9500 (SAN 210-7066).

Callaway Editions, *(Callaway Edns; 0-935112),* 421 Hudson St., New York, NY 10014 Tel 212-929-5212 (SAN 213-2931).

Calligraphy by Donna, *(Calligraphy Donna; 0-9604308),* 565 SE Airpark Dr., Bend, OR 97702 Tel 503-382-8215 (SAN 216-0250).

Calliope Music, *(Calliope Music; 0-9605912)*, P.O. Box 1460, Ansonia Sta., New York, NY 10023 (SAN 216-6607).

Calliope Press, *(Calliope Pr; 0-939684)*, P.O. Box 2273, N. Hollywood, CA 91602 Tel 213-845-5809 (SAN 216-7212).

CalMedia, *(CalMedia; 0-939782)*, P.O. Box 156, La Mirada, CA 90637 Tel 714-522-7575 (SAN 216-8820).

Calvary Episcopal Church, *(Calvary Episcopal)*, Box 67, Cleveland, MS 38732 (SAN 217-2895).

Calvary Missionary Press, Div. of Calvary Missionary Fellowship, *(Calvary Miss Pr; 0-912375)*, P.O. Box 13532, Tucson, AZ 85732 Tel 602-745-3822 (SAN 265-2021).

Calvert, Mary, *(M Calvert; 0-9609914)*, Lincoln St., E. Boothbay, ME 04544 Tel 207-633-3693 (SAN 268-6120).

Calwood Pubns., *(Calwood Pubns)*, P.O. Box 284, Monsey, NY 10952 Tel 914-352-7760 (SAN 210-9557).

Cam-Tri Productions, *(Cam-Tri Prods; 0-9606218)*, 1895 Tigertail Rd., Eugene, OR 97405 Tel 503-344-0118 (SAN 217-5045).

Camaro Publishing Co., *(Camaro Pub; 0-913290)*, Worldway Postal Sta., P.O. Box 90430, Los Angeles, CA 90009 Tel 213-837-7500 (SAN 201-7865).

Camberleigh & Hall, Pubs., *(Camberleigh & Hall; 0-935880)*, P.O. Box 18914, N. Hills Sta., Raleigh, NC 27619 (SAN 214-1116).

Cambita Books, *(Cambita Bks; 0-9610444)*, P.O. Box 09230, Milwaukee, WI 53209 Tel 414-462-4508 (SAN 263-9637).

Camblos-Winger, *(Camblos-Winger; 0-9602706)*, P.O. Box 15424, Asheville, NC 28813 Tel 704-274-2794 (SAN 212-8896).

Cambrian Pubns., *(Cambrian; 0-912548)*, P.O. Box 191, Little River Sta., Miami, FL 33138 Tel 305-751-1122 (SAN 202-5019).

Cambric Press, *(Cambric; 0-918342)*, 901 Rye Beach Rd., Huron, OH 44839 Tel 419-433-5560 (SAN 210-0460).

Cambridge Bk. Co., Div. of Esquire, Inc., *(Cambridge Bk; 0-8428)*, 888 Seventh Ave., New York, NY 10022 Tel 212-957-5300 (SAN 169-5703).

Cambridge Information & Research Services, Ltd. See Unipub

Cambridge Scientific Abstracts, *(Cambridge Sci)*, Bk; 0-8428; 0-88387), 5161 River Rd., Bethesda, MD 20816 Tel 301-951-1400 (SAN 201-2995).

Cambridge Univ. Press, *(Cambridge U Pr; 0-521)*, 32 E. 57th St., New York, NY 10022 Tel 212-688-8888 (SAN 281-3750); Orders to: 510 North Ave., New Rochelle, NY 10801 Tel 914-235-0300 (SAN 281-3769).

Camda, *(Camda; 0-9600434)*, P.O. Box 2467, Staunton, VA 24401 (SAN 202-5027).

Camden House, Inc., *(Camden Hse; 0-938100)*, Drawer 2025, Columbia, SC 29202 (SAN 215-9376).

Camelot Publishing, *(Camelot Pub MN; 0-942450)*, 1551 Camelot Ln. N.E., Fridley, MN 55432 (SAN 240-0855).

Camelot Publishing Co., *(Camelot Pub; 0-89218)*, P.O. Box 1357, Ormond Beach, FL 32074 Tel 904-672-5672 (SAN 202-5035).

Cameo Publishing Company, *(Cameo Pub; 0-9610814)*, P.O. Box 657, Belgrade, MT 59714 Tel 406-284-6641 (SAN 265-2048).

Cameron & Co., *(Cameron & Co; 0-918684)*, Russ Bldg., Suite 440, 235 Montgomery St., San Francisco, CA 94104 Tel 415-981-1135 (SAN 210-9700).

Camm Publishing Co., *(Camm Pub; 0-9608400)*, P.O. Box 640358, Uleta Branch, Miami, FL 33164 Tel 305-949-7536 (SAN 240-6101).

Camp Denali Publishing, *(Camp Denali; 0-9602792)*, P.O. Box 67, McKinley Park, AK 99755 (SAN 213-0297).

Campaign for Political Rights, *(Campaign Political)*, 201 Massachusetts Ave. NE, Washington, DC 20002 (SAN 237-627X).

Campana Art Co. Inc., *(Campana Art; 0-939608)*, 721 W. Wilks St., Pampa, TX 79065 Tel 806-665-3618 (SAN 204-3572).

Campbell, Lucile M., *(L M Campbell; 0-9607114)*, c/o Mrs. Joe Richardson, 615 Sixth Ave. SW, Decatur, AL 35601 Tel 205-355-8895 (SAN 238-9592).

Campbell, Sandy M., *(S Campbell; 0-917366)*, 230 Central Park S., New York, NY 10019 Tel 212-582-6286 (SAN 204-7128).

Campus Crusade for Christ, International, *(Campus Crusade; 0-918956)*, c/o Heres Life Publisher, P.O. Box 1576, San Bernardino, 92402 Tel 714-886-7981 (SAN 212-4254).

Campus Pubs., *(Campus; 0-87506)*, 713 W. Ellsworth Rd., Ann Arbor, MI 48104 Tel 313-663-4033 (SAN 201-9558).

Campus Scope Press, *(Campus Scope)*, 2928 Dean Parkway, Apt. 4D, Minneapolis, MN 55416 (SAN 216-0269).

Camward House, *(Camward Hse; 0-936460)*, P.O. Box 268, E. Patrick St. Sta., Frederick, MD 21701 (SAN 214-1833).

Can-Do-Books, *(Can-Do Bks; 0-9604192)*, 2119 Lone Oak Ave., Napa, CA 94558 (SAN 214-1841).

Can Do Pubns., *(Can Do Pubns; 0-943024)*, 514 Skyline Dr., Great Falls, MT 59404 (SAN 240-3501).

Can-to-Pan Cookery, *(Can-to-Pan; 0-9605536)*, 143 Benson Ave., Vallejo, CA 94590 Tel 707-557-0578 (SAN 240-9461).

Canaveral Press, Inc., *(Canaveral)*, 315 Montana Ave., No. 203, Santa Monica, CA 90403 Tel 213-394-0514 (SAN 281-3777).

Cancer Care, Inc., *(Cancer Care)*, One Park Ave, New York, NY 10016 Tel 212-679-5700 (SAN 225-9087).

Cancer Control Society, *(Cancer Control Soc)*, 2043 N. Berendo St., Los Angeles, CA 90027 Tel 213-663-7801 (SAN 216-2296).

Candle Books, Inc., *(Candle Bks; 0-9609644)*, 1010 Grey Oak, San Antonio, TX 78213 (SAN 262-0065).

Canner, J. S., & Co., Div. of Plenum Publishing Corp., *(Canner; 0-910324)*, 49-65 Lansdowne St., Boston, MA 02215 Tel 617-437-1923 (SAN 202-5094) Microcards; also microfilm of Plenum journals only.

Canning Pubns, Inc., *(Canning Pubns; 0-938516)*, 925 Anza Ave., Vista, CA 92083 (SAN 215-9384).

Cannon, Timothy L., & Nancy F. Whitmore, *(T L Cannon & N F Whitmore; 0-9602816)*, 7916 Juniper Dr., Frederick, MD 21701 (SAN 213-4756).

Canon Law Society of America, *(Canon Law Soc; 0-943616)*, Catholic Univ., Washington, DC 20064 Tel 202-269-3491 (SAN 237-6296).

Canter & Associates, *(Canter & Assoc; 0-9608978)*, P.O. Box 64517, Los Angeles, CA 90064 (SAN 240-8716).

Canterbury Press, *(Canterbury Pr; 0-933993)*, 5540 Vista Del Amigo, Anaheim, CA 92807 (SAN 212-890X).

Canticle Press, *(Canticle Pr; 0-941396)*, 1986 S. 2600 E., Salt Lake City, UT 84106 Tel 801-466-4028 (SAN 238-9606).

Cantine & Kilpatrick, Pubns., *(Cantine & Kilpatrick; 0-940548)*, P.O. Box 798, Huntington, NY 11743 Tel 516-271-8990 (SAN 222-9927).

Cantor, B.G., Art Foundation, *(Cantor Art Found; 0-939912)*, 1 World Trade Ctr., 105th Fl., New York, NY 10048 Tel 212-938-5136 (SAN 216-7964).

Cantor, Daniel J., And Company, *(D J Cantor)*, Suburban Station Bldg., Philadelphia, PA 19103 (SAN 237-630X).

Canyon Publishing Co., *(Canyon Pub Co; 0-942568)*, 8561 Eatough Ave., Canoga Park, CA 91304 Tel 213-702-0171 (SAN 240-0685).

Cap & Gown Press, Inc., *(Cap & Gown; 0-88105)*, Box 58825, Houston, TX 77258 Tel 409-763-3410 (SAN 240-611X).

Capability's Books, *(Capability's; 0-913643)*, P.O. Box 114, Hwy. No. 46, Deer Park, WI 54007 Tel 715-269-5346 (SAN 286-0759).

Capablanca See Imprint Editions

Capital Bird Dog Enterprises, *(Capital Bird; 0-9601034)*, 10 N. Helderberg Pkwy., Slingerlands, NY 12159 Tel 518-439-2606 (SAN 208-1881).

Capital Planning Information Ltd., *(Capital Plan Info; 0-906011)*, 12 Castle St., Edinburgh EH2 3AT, .

Capital Pubs., Inc., *(Capital Pub DC; 0-87277)*, P.O. Box 6235, Washington, DC 20015 (SAN 202-5108).

Capital Publishing Corp., *(Capital Pub Corp; 0-914470)*, P.O. Box 348, Two Laurel Ave., Wellesley Hills, MA 02181 Tel 617-235-5405 (SAN 206-2240).

Capital Technology, Inc., *(Capital Tech; 0-9603460)*, 2 Fairview Plaza, Suite 116, 5950 Fairview Rd., Charlotte, NC 28210 (SAN 213-294X).

Capitalist Press, *(Capitalist Pr OH)*, P.O. Box 1911, Akron, OH 44309 (SAN 215-9392).

Capitalist Reporter Press, *(Capitalist Reporter; 0-933722)*, 1501 Broadway, Suite 810, New York, NY 10036 (SAN 213-0319).

Capitol Enquiry, *(Capitol Enquiry; 0-917982)*, P.O. Box 22246, Sacramento, CA 95822 Tel 916-428-3271 (SAN 211-5077).

Capra Press, *(Capra Pr; 0-88496; 0-912264)*, P.O. Box 2068, Santa Barbara, CA 93120 Tel 805-966-4590 (SAN 201-9620).

Capricorn Books, *(Capricorn Bks)*, 2 Aztec Court, H.C.B. Toms River, NJ 08757 Tel 201-349-0725 (SAN 260-0013).

Capricorn Corporation, *(Capricorn Corp; 0-910719)*, 4961 Rebel Trail NW, Atlanta, GA 30327 (SAN 262-0073).

Capricornus Press, *(Capricornus Pr; 0-9608544)*, P.O. Box 1023, Boulder, CO 80306 Tel 303-442-2663 (SAN 240-6128); Dist. by: Caroline House Inc., 920 W. Industrial Dr., Aurora, IL 60506 Tel 312-897-2050 (SAN 211-2280).

Caprock Press, *(Caprock Pr; 0-912570)*, 4806 17th St., Lubbock, TX 79416 Tel 806-795-7599 (SAN 201-9639).

Capstone Editions, *(Capstone Edns; 0-9610662)*, P.O. Box 13143, Tucson, AZ 85732 Tel 602-745-6750 (SAN 264-6552).

Captain Stanislaus Mlotkowski Memorial Brigade Society, *(Cptn Stanislaus; 0-9600814)*, 247 Philadelphia Pike, Wilmington, DE 19809 (SAN 207-124X).

Captain's Lady Collections, The, *(Captains Lady; 0-9609534)*, 65-69 High St., Springfield, MA 01105 Tel 413-739-6655 (SAN 260-1729).

Carabelle Books, *(Carabelle; 0-938634)*, Box 2711, Reston, VA 22091 (SAN 281-3785); Orders to: Rte. 3, Box 589, Harpers Ferry, WV 25425 (SAN 281-3793).

Carabis, Anne J., *(Carabis; 0-9605802)*, 25 Nelson Ave., Latham, NY 12110 Tel 518-783-9807 (SAN 216-5600).

Caratzas Publishing Co., Inc., *(Caratzas Pub Co; 0-89241)*, 481 Main St. (P.O. Box 210), New Rochelle, NY 10801 Tel 914-632-8487 (SAN 201-3134).

Caravan Books, *(Caravan Bks; 0-88206)*, P.O. Box 344, Delmar, NY 12054 Tel 518-439-5978 (SAN 206-7323).

Caravan-Maritime Books, *(Caravan-Maritime; 0-917368)*, 87-06 168th Place, Jamaica, NY 11432 Tel 212-526-1380 (SAN 201-8705) Do Not Confuse with Caravan Bks.

Caravan Press, *(Caravan Pr; 0-912159)*, 343 S. Broadway, Los Angeles, CA 90013 Tel 213-479-8115 (SAN 264-7222).

CARBEN Surveying Reprints, *(CARBEN Survey)*, 274 Winthrop Rd., Columbus, OH 43214 (SAN 209-5327) Formerly Named BM Surveying Book Reprints.

Carcosa, *(Carcosa; 0-913796)*, P.O. Box 1064, Chapel Hill, NC 27514 Tel 919-929-2974 (SAN 202-5124).

Cardamom Press, *(Cardamon; 0-9611118)*, P.O. Box D, Richmond, ME 04357 Tel 207-666-5645 (SAN 283-2836).

Cardamone, Helen M., Publisher, *(H M Cardamone; 0-9608330)*, 2108 Genesee St., Utica, NY 13502 Tel 315-735-0363 (SAN 240-5229).

Cardiff-By-The-Sea Publishing Co., *(Cardiff; 0-9608038)*, P.O. Box 909, Cardiff-by-the-Sea, CA 92007 Tel 714-753-1655 (SAN 240-2009).

Cardinal Press, Inc., *(Cardinal Pr; 0-943594)*, 76 N. Yorktown, Tulsa, OK 74110 Tel 918-583-3651 (SAN 219-1385).

Cardinal Pubs., *(Cardinal Pubs; 0-912930)*, P.O. Box 207, Davis, CA 95616 (SAN 201-9647).

Cardot Enterprises, *(Cardot Entpr Inc; 0-9607516)*, 214 Avenida Barbera, Sonoma, CA 95476 (SAN 238-6283).

Cardoza School of Blackjack, *(Cardoza Sch Blackjk; 0-9607618),* P.O. Box 5267, Santa Cruz, CA 95063 (SAN 281-3904); Dist. by: Bookazine, 303 West 10th St., New York, NY 10014 (SAN 169-5665); Dist. by: Book Dynamics, 836 Broadway, New York, NY 10003 (SAN 169-5649); Dist. by: Koen Distributors, 510 B North Bellview, Cinnaminson, NJ 08077 (SAN 169-4642); Dist. by: Publishers Group West, 5855 Beaudry Street, Emeryville, CA 94608 (SAN 202-8522).

Career Institute, Inc., Div. of Singer Communications Corp., *(Career Inst; 0-911744),* 1500 Cardinal Dr., Little Falls, NJ 07424 Tel 201-256-4512 (SAN 202-5132).

Career Planning Pubs., *(Career Plan; 0-910595),* 7101 York Ave. S. No. 200, Edina, MN 55435 Tel 612-831-6459 (SAN 260-0242).

Career Publishing, Inc., *(Career Pub; 0-89262),* 931 N. Main St., P.O. Box 5486, Orange, CA 92667 Tel 800-854-4014 (SAN 208-581X).

Cargo Service Inc., *(Cargo Serv Inc; 0-9610616),* Box 466, Middletown, OH 45042 Tel 513-746-3991 (SAN 276-959X).

Carib House (USA), *(Carib Hse; 0-936378),* P. O. Box 38834, Hollywood, CA 90038 Tel 213-466-6924 (SAN 214-1124).

Carib Pubns. *See* **Casa Bautista De Publicaciones**

Carillon Bks., Div. of Catholic Digest, *(Carillon Bks; 0-89310),* 2115 Summit Ave., St. Paul, MN 55105 Tel 612-647-5251 (SAN 208-5828).

Carlinshar & Assoc. Applied Research Corp., *(Carlinshar; 0-934872),* 519 E. Briarcliff, Bolingbrook, IL 60439 Tel 312-759-9028 (SAN 212-8918).

Carlisle Industries, *(Carlisle Indus; 0-9600344),* P.O. Box 3700, Visalia, CA 93278 Tel 209-798-1544 (SAN 202-5140).

Carlisle Pub., Inc., *(Carlisle Pub; 0-910177),* P.O. Box 112, Hartsdale, NY 10530 Tel 914-725-0408 (SAN 240-9739).

Carlton Press, *(Carlton; 0-8062),* 84 Fifth Ave., New York, NY 10011 Tel 212-243-8800 (SAN 201-9655).

Carlton Pubns.,Inc., *(Carlton Pubns CA; 0-937348),* 10949 Fruitland Dr., Studio City, CA 91604 (SAN 215-9414).

Carlyle Associates, *(Carlyle Assocs; 0-935084),* 1236 Ninth St., P.O. Box 3391, Santa Monica, CA 90403 Tel 213-393-3323 (SAN 213-4764).

Carma Press, *(Carma; 0-918328),* Box 12633, St. Paul, MN 55112 Tel 612-633-6845 (SAN 209-5351).

Carmel, Simon J., *(S Carmel; 0-9600886),* 10500 Rockville Pike, Apt. 1028, Rockville, MD 20852 (SAN 209-536X).

Carmonelle Pubns., *(Carmonelle Pubns; 0-943334),* P.O. Box 74, 304 Main St., Cameron, WI 54822 Tel 715-458-2684 (SAN 240-5237).

Carnation Press, *(Carnation; 0-87601),* P.O. Box 101, State College, PA 16801 Tel 814-238-3577 (SAN 203-5103).

Carnegie Endowment for International Peace, *(Carnegie Endow; 0-87003),* 30 Rockefeller Plaza, New York, NY 10112 Tel 212-572-8200 (SAN 281-3955); Orders to: 11 Dupont Circle, Washington, DC 20036 Tel 202-797-6424 (SAN 281-3963).

Carnegie Foundation for the Advancement of Teaching, The, *(Carnegie Found Adv Teach; 0-931050),* Five Ivy Lane, Princeton, NJ 08540 Tel 609-452-1780 (SAN 239-4146); Dist. by: Princeton University Pr., 3175 Princeton Pike, Lawrenceville, NJ 08648 Tel 609-896-1346 (SAN 202-0254).

Carnegie Institute, Board of Trustees, The, *(Carnegie Board; 0-911239),* 4400 Forbes Ave., Pittsburg, PA 15213 Tel 412-622-3132 (SAN 268-6686).

Carnegie Institution of Washington, *(Carnegie Inst; 0-87279),* 1530 "P" St., N.W., Washington, DC 20005 Tel 202-387-6411 (SAN 201-9663).

Carnegie-Mellon Univ. Pr., *(Carnegie-Mellon; 0-915604),* Carnegie-Mellon Univ., Box 21, Pittsburgh, PA 15213 (SAN 211-2329); Dist. by: Univ. of Pittsburgh Pr., 127 N. Bellefield Ave., Pittsburgh, PA 15260 Tel 412-624-4110 (SAN 203-3216).

Carnegie Press, Inc., *(Carnegie Pr; 0-935506),* 100 Kings Rd., Madison, NJ 07940 (SAN 223-7032).

Carnival Press, Inc., *(Carnival Pr; 0-940742),* P.O. Box 19087, Minneapolis, MN 55419 Tel 612-823-3614 (SAN 219-7200).

Carnot Press, *(Carnot Pr; 0-917308),* P.O. Box 1544, Lake Oswego, OR 97034 Tel 503-636-6894 (SAN 208-5852).

Carnton Association, Inc., *(Carnton Assn; 0-78290),* Rte. 2, Lewisburg Pike, Franklin, TN 37064 (SAN 277-5794).

Carolando Press, *(Carolando),* 6545 W. North Ave., Oak Park, IL 60302 (SAN 219-3426).

Carolina Academic Press, *(Carolina Acad Pr; 0-89089),* P.O. Box 8795, Forest Hills Stations, Durham, NC 27707 Tel 919-489-7486 (SAN 210-7848).

Carolina Art Assn., *(Carolina Art; 0-910326),* 135 Meeting St., Charleston, SC 29401 Tel 803-722-2706 (SAN 203-512X).

Carolina Biological Supply Co., *(Carolina Biological; 0-89278),* 2700 York Rd., Burlington, NC 27215 Tel 919-584-0381 (SAN 208-5860).

Carolina Editions, Inc., *(Carolina Edns; 0-914056),* P.O. Box 3169, Greenwood, SC 29646 Tel 803-229-3503 (SAN 201-8721).

Carolina Population Center, The Univ. of North Carolina at Chapel Hill, *(Carolina Pop Ctr; 0-89055),* Population Pubns., University Sq. 300A, Chapel Hill, NC 27514 Tel 919-966-2152 (SAN 201-7687).

Carolina Wren Press, The, *(Carolina Wren; 0-932112),* 300 Barclay Rd., Chapel Hill, NC 27514 (SAN 213-0327).

Caroline Hse., Inc., *(Caroline Hse),* 920 W. Industrial Dr., Aurora, IL 60506 Tel 312-897-2050 (SAN 211-2280).

Caroline House Pubs., Inc. *See* **Green Hill Pubs.**

Carolrhoda Books, Inc., *(Carolrhoda Bks; 0-87614),* 241 First Ave., N., Minneapolis, MN 55401 Tel 612-332-3344 (SAN 201-9671).

Carolyn Bean Publishing, Ltd., *(Bean Pub; 0-916860),* 120 Second St., San Francisco, CA 94105 Tel 415-957-9574 (SAN 208-5445).

Carothers Co., *(Carothers; 0-943026),* Box 2518, Escondido, CA 92025 Tel 619-741-2755 (SAN 240-3536).

Carousel Press, *(Carousel Pr; 0-917120),* P.O. Box 6061, Albany, CA 94706 Tel 415-527-5849 (SAN 209-2646).

Carpatho-Rusyn Research Center, *(Carpatho-Rusyn Res Ctr; 0-917242),* University of Toronto, 100 St. George St., Toronto, M5S 1A1, (SAN 213-5779); Orders to: 355 Delano Place, Fairview, NJ 07022 (SAN 213-5787).

Carpenter Center for the Visual Arts & the Peabody Museum, *(Carpenter Ctr; 0-674199),* c/o Harvard Univ. Pr., 79 Garden St., Cambridge, MA 02138 (SAN 200-2043).

Carpenter Press, *(Carpenter Pr; 0-914140),* Rte. 4, Pomeroy, OH 45769 Tel 614-992-7520 (SAN 206-4650).

Carrera International, Inc., *(Carrera Intl; 0-910597),* RFD 1682, Laurel Hollow, NY 11791 Tel 516-487-1616 (SAN 263-967X).

Carrey, Dixeann W., *(D W Carrey; 0-931882),* 800 W. Oakland Park Blvd., Suite 309, Fort Lauderdale, FL 33311 Tel 305-561-9667 (SAN 212-4068).

Carrier Pigeon, *(Carrier Pigeon; 0-932870),* P.O. Box 2783, Boston, MA 02208 Tel 617-542-5679 (SAN 169-3301); Orders to: 75 Kneeland St., 1506, Boston, MA 02111 (SAN 156-6857).

Carrier's Beekeeping Supplies, *(Carriers Bees; 0-9607550),* 601 S. Baywood Ave., San Jose, CA 95128 Tel 408-296-6100 (SAN 238-6291).

Carrol Gate Press, the, *(Carrol Gate Pr; 0-9608714),* 951 W. Liberty Dr., Wheaton, IL 60187 Tel 312-690-8574 (SAN 238-048X).

Carroll & Graf Publishers, *(Carroll & Graf; 0-88184),* 260 Fifth Ave., New York, NY 10001 Tel 212-741-1986 (SAN 264-6560); Dist. by: Publishers Group West, 5855 Beaudry St., Emeryville, CA 94608 Tel 415-658-3453 (SAN 202-8522).

Carroll College Press, *(Carroll Coll; 0-916120),* 100 North East Ave., Waukesha, WI 53186 Tel 414-547-1211 (SAN 208-5879).

Carroll Press, *(Carroll Pr; 0-910328),* P.O. Box 8113, 43 Squantum St., Cranston, RI 02920 Tel 401-942-1587 (SAN 203-6231).

Carrollton Press, Inc., U.S. Historical Documents Institute, *(Carrollton Pr; 0-8408),* 1911 Fort Meyer Dr., Arlington, VA 22209 Tel 703-525-5942 (SAN 201-7946).

Carron, L.P., Pubs., *(Carron Pubs),* 205 Ridgewood Rd., Easton, PA 18042 (SAN 238-9207).

Carson, H. Glenn, Enterprises, Ltd., *(H G Carson Ent; 0-941620),* Drawer 71, Deming, NM 88031 Tel 505-546-6100 (SAN 239-1716).

Carson, Ray, *(R Carson),* 711 E. Camden Ave., El Cajon, CA 92102 Tel 619-440-7647 (SAN 206-8222).

Carson Press, *(Carson Pr; 0-934360),* 733 W. Carson St., Torrance, CA 90502 Tel 213-328-3180 (SAN 213-2958).

Carstens Pubns., Inc., *(Carstens Pubns; 0-911868),* P.O. Box 700, Newton, NJ 07860 Tel 201-383-3355 (SAN 281-3971); Orders to: UPS, Purolator Etc., Fredon Township, Newton, NJ 07860 (SAN 281-398X).

Carter, Virginia B., *(V B Carter; 0-9603862),* 5 Geyerwood Lane, St. Louis, MO 63131 Tel 314-965-0577 (SAN 214-1132).

Carter, *(Carter),* P.O. Box 138, Monmouth Junction, NJ 08852 Tel 215-968-6891 (SAN 213-4772).

Carter Craft Doll House, *(Carter Craft; 0-9604404),* 5505 42nd Ave., Hyattsville, MD 20781 Tel 301-277-3051 (SAN 203-624X).

Cartwright, Nellie Parodi, Mrs., *(N P Cartwright; 0-9601482),* 4348 Via Frascati, Rancho Palos Verdes, CA 90274 Tel 213-833-7586 (SAN 210-9883).

Carver Publishing, Inc., *(Carver Pub; 0-915044),* P.O. Box 6002, Hampton Institute, Hampton, VA 23668 Tel 804-727-5000 (SAN 201-0143).

Carves Cards, *(Carves),* 179 South St., Brookline, MA 02167 Tel 617-469-9175 (SAN 209-4177).

Casa Bautista De Publicaciones, *(Casa Bautista; 0-311),* P.O. Box 4255, 7000 Alabama St., El Paso, TX 79914 Tel 915-566-9656 (SAN 220-0139). *Imprints:* Carib Publications (Carib Pubns); Editorial Mundo Hispano (Edit Mundo).

Casavis, James N., *(J N Casavis),* 32 Twin Lakes Dr., Monsey, NY 10952 (SAN 206-4561).

Cascade Photographics, *(Cascade Photo; 0-935818),* 6906 Martin Way, Olympia, WA 98506 Tel 206-491-5473 (SAN 213-7291).

Cascade Publishing Co., The, *(Cascade Pub; 0-9610664),* P.O. Box 27343, Seattle, WA 98125 Tel 206-668-2467 (SAN 264-7249).

CaseCo, *(CaseCo),* 101 Lafayette, Spartanburg, SC 29302 Tel 803-585-3298 (SAN 240-1371).

Casino Gaming Seminars, *(Casino Gam Seminars),* P.O. Box 718, Solvang, CA 93463 (SAN 239-5304).

Casino Publishing, *(Casino; 0-9611120),* P.O. Box 54081, San Jose, CA 95154 (SAN 277-6626).

Caspers Wine Press, *(Caspers Wine; 0-933298),* 15222 Magnolia Blvd., Suite 107, Sherman Oaks, CA 91403 Tel 213-788-1481 (SAN 212-1492).

Cassell Communications Inc., *(Cassell Commun Inc; 0-942980),* 214 Solaz Ave., Port St. Lucie, FL 33452 Tel 305-878-2328 (SAN 240-138X).

Cassizzi, Vic, *(Cassizzi),* P.O. Box 8788, 710 Town Mtn. Rd., Asheville, NC 28804 Tel 704-253-5016 (SAN 217-0922).

Cassone Press, *(Cassone Pr; 0-9610082),* 2838 James Ave. S., Minneapolis, MN 55408 Tel 612-721-7486 (SAN 268-6813).

Castalia Publishing Co., *(Castalia Pub; 0-916154),* P.O. Box 1587, Eugene, OR 97440 (SAN 208-2403).

Castelli Graphics/Artspace, *(Castelli-Artspace; 0-9604140),* 4 E. 77th St., New York, NY 10021 (SAN 214-1140).

Castenholz & Sons, *(Castenholz Sons; 0-9603498),* 1055 Hartzell St., Pacific Palisades, CA 90272 (SAN 237-9449).

Castle Designs, *(Castle Designs; 0-942844),* 2717 Teakwood Ln., Plano, TX 75075 Tel 214-867-0067 (SAN 240-0863).

Castle Distributors, *(Castle Dist),* 316 Estes Dr., Chapel Hill, NC 27514 Tel 919-967-6439 (SAN 239-3530).

Castle Press *See* **Dahlstrom, Grant, , Castle Press**

Castle Pubns., Ltd., *(Castle Pubns; 0-943178),* P.O. Box 580, Van Nuys, CA 91408 Tel 213-629-7823 (SAN 240-3544).

Castle Publishing Co., *(Castle Pub Co; 0-9603372),* P.O. Box 188, Portland, ME 04112 Tel 207-772-7851 (SAN 209-2565).

Castle Publishing Co., Ltd., *(Castle CT),* 50 West Hill Circle, Stamford, CT 06902 Tel 203-324-7923 (SAN 213-0343).

Castlemarsh Pubns, *(Castlemarsh; 0-942250),* P.O. Box 5740, Savannah, GA 31414 (SAN 240-8708).

Castro, Mercedes, *(Castro; 0-9604748),* 78-10 147th St., Apt. 3D, Flushing, NY 11367 (SAN 215-6113).

Catalyst, *(Catalyst; 0-89584),* 14 E. 60th St., New York, NY 10022 (SAN 203-6258).

Catan, Omero C., *(Catan; 0-9600618),* 1901 S.W. 87th Terrace, Ft. Lauderdale, FL 33324 (SAN 203-6266).

Cataract Press, *(Cataract Pr; 0-914764),* P.O. Box 4875, Chicago, IL 60680-4875 Tel 416-638-0659 (SAN 201-8748).

Cathedral of Knowledge, *(Cathedral of Knowledge),* 235 N.E. 84th Ave., Portland, OR 97220 Tel 503-255-3859 (SAN 211-6022).

Catholic Authors Press, *(Cath Authors; 0-910334),* 1201 S. Kirkwood Rd., Kirkwood, MO 63122 Tel 314-965-4801 (SAN 203-6274).

Catholic Biblical Association of America, *(Catholic Biblical; 0-915170),* 620 Michigan Ave. NE, the Catholic Univ. of America, Washington, DC 20064 Tel 202-635-5519 (SAN 268-7038).

Catholic Book Publishing Co., *(Catholic Bk Pub; 0-89942),* 257 W. 17th St., New York, NY 10011 Tel 212-243-4515 (SAN 204-3432).

Catholic Health Association, The, *(Cath Health; 0-87125),* 4455 Woodson Rd., St. Louis, MO 63134 Tel 314-427-2500 (SAN 201-968X).

Catholic Library Assn., *(Cath Lib Assn; 0-87507),* 461 W. Lancaster Ave., Haverford, PA 19041 Tel 215-649-5251 (SAN 203-6282).

Catholic News Publishing Co., *(Cath News Pub Co; 0-010635),* 80 West Broad St., Mt. Vernon, NY 10552 (SAN 268-7240).

Catholic Peace Fellowship, *(Cath Peace Fell),* 339 Lafayette St, New York, NY 10012 Tel 212-673-8990 (SAN 225-6932).

Catholic Press Assn., *(Cath Pr Assn),* 119 N. Park Ave., Rockville Centre, NY 11570 Tel 516-766-3400 (SAN 204-3335).

Catholic Univ. of America Press, *(Cath U Pr; 0-8132),* 620 Michigan Ave., N.E., Washington, DC 20064 Tel 202-635-5052 (SAN 203-6290); Orders to: P.O. Box 4852, Hampden Sta., Baltimore, MD 21211 Tel 301-338-7817 (SAN 203-6304).

Cato Institute, *(Cato Inst; 0-932790),* 224 Second St. S.E., Washington, DC 20003 Tel 202-546-0200 (SAN 212-6095).

Cat's Pajamas Press, *(Cats Pajamas; 0-916866),* 527 Lyman Ave., Oak Park, IL 60304 Tel 312-386-5137 (SAN 207-8015).

Catskill Art Supply, *(Catskill Art; 0-9600350),* 35 Mill Hill Rd., Woodstock, NY 12498 (SAN 205-4663).

Cauce, Cesar, Pubs. & Distributors, *(Cauce Pubs; 0-86686),* P.O. Box 389, 39 Bowery, New York, NY 10002 Tel 212-789-0737 (SAN 216-5287).

Cauldron Press, *(Cauldron),* 8347 Delmar, No. 1-S, St. Louis, MO 63124 (SAN 210-914X).

Cavalier Press, *(Cavalier; 0-910338),* P.O. Box 111, Matteson, IL 60443 (SAN 203-6312).

Cave Books, *(Cave Bks MO; 0-939748),* 756 Harvard Ave., St. Louis, MO 63130 Tel 314-862-7646 (SAN 216-7220).

Cave Books, *(Cave Bks TN),* 901 Buford Pl, Nashville, TN 37204 Tel 615-269-3921 (SAN 287-0002); P.O. Box 613, Newburgh, IN 47630 Tel 812-853-0828 (SAN 287-0010).

Cave Canem Books, *(Cave Canem Bks; 0-9607244),* 120 E. 46th St. No. 98, New York, NY 10003 (SAN 239-1732) Moved, left no forwarding address.

Cavendish, Marshall, Corporation, *(M Cavendish Corp),* 147 W. Merrick Rd., Freeport, NY 11520 (SAN 238-437X).

Caxton Club, *(Caxton Club; 0-940550),* 60 W. Walton St., Chicago, IL 60610 (SAN 216-3195).

Caxton Printers, Ltd., *(Caxton; 0-87004),* P.O. Box 700, Caldwell, ID 83605 Tel 208-459-7421 (SAN 201-9698).

Cay-Bel, *(Cay-Bel; 0-941216),* Thompson-Lyford Bldg. 2nd. Fl., 45 Center St., Brewer, ME 04412 (SAN 238-9215).

Cayo Del Grullo Press, *(C Del Grullo; 0-9611604),* c/o History Department, Texas A & I University, Kingsville, TX 78363 Tel 512-595-3603 (SAN 284-9313).

Cayucos Books, *(Cayucos; 0-9600372),* P.O. Box 2113, Monterey, CA 93940 Tel 408-375-5289 (SAN 208-5887).

CB City International, *(CB City Intl; 0-943132),* P.O. Box 31500, Phoenix, AZ 85046 Tel 602-996-9650 (SAN 240-5199).

CDS Publishing Co., Subs. of Man-Computer Systems, Inc., *(CDS Pub; 0-916376),* 84-13 168th St., Jamaica, NY 11432 Tel 212-739-4242 (SAN 208-5755).

Cedar Creek Press, *(Cedar Creek OK; 0-935286),* P.O. Box 1051, Stillwater, OK 74074 (SAN 213-2966).

Cedar Creek Pubs., *(Cedar Creek IN; 0-935316),* 2310 Sawmill Rd., Fort Wayne, IN 46825 Tel 219-637-3856 (SAN 213-4780).

Cedar Crest Books, *(Cedar Crest Bks; 0-910291),* P.O. Box 36, Cochituate, MA 01778 Tel 617-491-0683 (SAN 241-2837).

Cedar Rock Press, *(Cedar Rock; 0-930024),* 1121 Madeline, New Braunfels, TX 78130 Tel 512-625-6002 (SAN 213-2699).

Cedars Press, *(Cedars Pr; 0-936326),* P.O. Box 29351, Columbus, OH 43229 (SAN 223-3835).

Cedarwinds Publishing Co., *(Cedarwinds),* Drawer A, Cedar Mountain, NC 28718 Tel 904-893-6252 (SAN 212-1700).

Cedarwood Press, *(Cedarwood Pr),* 1115 E. Wylie St., Bloomington, IN 47401 Tel 812-332-3017 (SAN 268-750X).

Celcom Press, *(Celcom Pr),* 901 Boren Ave., Cabrini Medical Tower, Suite 1036, Seattle, WA 98104 (SAN 208-2411).

Celebration Press, *(Celebration Pr; 0-933010),* P.O. Box 76, Nobleboro, ME 04555 Tel 207-563-8269 (SAN 211-8440).

Celebrity Press Inc., *(Celebrity Pr; 0-9607412),* 6656 W. Fifth St., Los Angeles, CA 90048 Tel 213-653-4012 (SAN 239-1759).

Celebrity Publishing, Inc., *(Celebrity Pub; 0-943406),* Six Doe Dr., Suffern, NY 10901 Tel 914-354-3595 (SAN 240-6152).

Celestial Arts Publishing Co., *(Celestial Arts; 0-912310; 0-89087),* P.O. Box 7327, Berkeley, CA 94707 (SAN 284-9941); 231 Adrian Rd., Millbrae, CA 94030 Tel 415-692-4500 (SAN 284-995X) (SAN 201-9701).

Celestial Gifts, *(Celestial Gifts),* 3413 Tulane Drive, No. 34, Hyattsville, MD 20783 Tel 301-422-1982 (SAN 219-1431).

Celestial Press, *(Celestial Pr; 0-910340),* 441 N.E. 24th St., Boca Raton, FL 33432 Tel 305-368-1309 (SAN 203-6320).

Cellar Bk. Shop, *(Cellar),* 18090 Wyoming, Detroit, MI 48221 Tel 313-861-1776 (SAN 213-4330).

Celo Press, *(Celo Pr; 0-914064),* Rte. 5, Burnsville, NC 28714 Tel 704-675-4925 (SAN 201-971X).

Celorio, Cesar Alberto, *(C A Celorio; 0-918168),* 23-42 37th St., Long Island City, NY 11105 Tel 212-278-7890 (SAN 210-1858).

Cembura, Al, *(Cembura; 0-912454),* 139 Arlington Ave., Berkeley, CA 94707 Tel 415-524-0478 (SAN 201-9728).

Centaur Books, Inc., *(Centaur; 0-87818),* 799 Broadway, New York, NY 10003 Tel 212-677-1720 (SAN 201-7725).

Centaur Publication Co., *(Centaur Pubn VA; 0-932700),* 7807 Stovall Court, Lorton, VA 22079 (SAN 212-0771).

Centennial Photo Service, *(Centennial Photo Serv; 0-931838),* Rte. 3, Box 1125, Grantsburg, WI 54840 Tel 715-689-2153 (SAN 212-6443).

Centennial Press, Div. of Cliff's Notes, Inc., *(Centennial; 0-8220),* P.O. Box 80728, Lincoln, NE 68501 Tel 402-477-6971 (SAN 203-6339).

Centennial Reproductions, *(Centennial Repros; 0-9606474),* 27 E. Cache la Poudre, Colorado Springs, CO 80707 (SAN 239-4162).

Center for Afro-American Studies (UCLA), *(Ctr Afro-Am Stud; 0-934934),* 3111 Campbell Hall, 405 Hilgard Ave., Los Angeles, CA 90024 Tel 213-825-3528 (SAN 214-2899).

Center for American Archeology Press, *(Ctr Amer Arche; 0-942118),* P.O.Box 1499, Evanston, IL 60204 (SAN 237-9457).

Center for Analysis of Public Issues, *(Ctr Analysis Public Issues; 0-943136),* 16 Vandeventer Ave., Princeton, NJ 08540 Tel 609-924-9750 (SAN 209-3227).

Center for Applications of Psychological Type, Inc., *(Ctr Applications Psych; 0-935652),* 414 S.W. Seventh Terrace, Gainesville, FL 32601 Tel 904-375-0160 (SAN 213-9162).

Center for Applied Linguistics, *(Ctr Appl Ling; 0-87281),* 3520 Prospect St. NW, Washington, DC 20007 Tel 202-298-9292 (SAN 281-3998)P.O. Box 4866, Hampden Station, Baltimore, MD 21211 (SAN 281-4005).

Center for Applied Research in Education, Inc., The, Subs. of Prentice-Hall, *(Ctr Appl Res; 0-87628),* C/o Prentice-Hall, Englewood Cliffs, NJ 07632 Tel 201-592-2483 (SAN 206-6424); Orders to: P.O. Box 130, W. Nyack, NY 10994 Tel 201-767-5195 (SAN 206-6432).

Center for Archaeological Investigations, *(Center Archaeo; 0-88104),* Southern Illinois University at Carbondale, Carbondale, IL 62901 Tel 618-536-5529 (SAN 240-916X).

Center for Arts Information, *(Ctr for Arts Info; 0-935654),* 625 Broadway, New York, NY 10012 Tel 212-677-7548 (SAN 282-7034); Dist. by: Publishing Center, 625 Broadway, New York, NY 10012 (SAN 274-9025).

Center for Black Studies, *(Ctr Black Stud; 0-939242),* Wayne State University, Detroit, MI 48202 Tel 313-577-2187 (SAN 216-5171).

Center for Business Development & Research, College of Business & Economics, *(Ctr Bus Devel & Res),* Univ. of Idaho, Moscow, ID 83843 Tel 208-885-6611 (SAN 205-9673).

Center for Business Information, *(Ctr Busn Info; 0-936936),* P.O. Box 2404, Meriden, CT 06450 Tel 203-235-1441 (SAN 214-2902).

Center for Communications Management, The (CCMI), *(C C M I),* 76 Arch St., Ramsey, NJ 07446 Tel 201-825-3311 (SAN 239-5185).

Center for Computer/Law, *(Ctr Comp Law; 0-935200),* P.O. Box 54308 T.A., Los Angeles, CA 90054 (SAN 223-7008).

Center for Conflict Resolution, *(Ctr Conflict Resol; 0-941492),* 731 State St., Madison, WI 53703 Tel 608-255-0479 (SAN 239-0736).

Center for Connecticut Studies, *(Ctr Conn Stud),* Eastern Connecticut State University, Willimantic, CT 06226 Tel 203-456-2231 (SAN 212-4874).

Center for Contemporary Poetry, *(Ctr Cont Poetry),* Murphy Library, Univ. of Wisconsin at La Crosse, La Crosse, WI 54601 (SAN 201-906X).

Center for Creative Educational Services, *(Center Creative Ed; 0-940366),* 10101 W. Jefferson, Culver City, CA 90320 Tel 213-558-3100 (SAN 209-5386).

Center for Creative Leadership, *(Ctr Creat Leader; 0-912879),* P.O. Box P-1, 5000 Laurinda Dr., Greensboro, NC 27402-1660 Tel 919-288-7210 (SAN 282-9924).

Center for Defense Information, *(CDI),* 303 Capitol Gallery West, 600 Maryland Ave., SW, Washington, DC 20024 Tel 202-484-9490 (SAN 260-3322).

Center for Economic Analysis, George Mason Univ., *(Ctr Econ Analysis; 0-933588),* Box 1329, Cullowhee, NC 28723 Tel 704-293-5433 (SAN 211-8459).

Center for Education & Research in Free Enterprise, *(Ctr Educ Res; 0-86599),* Texas A&M University, College Station, TX 77843 (SAN 215-0646).

Center for Educational Alternatives, *(Ctr Ed Alternatives; 0-943346),* 8679 Valley Flores Dr., Canoga Park, CA 91304 Tel 213-348-6403 (SAN 240-5245).

Center for Educational Policy & Management, *(Ctr Educ Policy Mgmt),* College of Education, Univ. of Oregon, Eugene, OR 97403 Tel 503-686-5077 (SAN 211-223X).

Center for Family Business, The, *(Ctr Family Busn),* P.O. Box 24268, Cleveland, OH 44124 Tel 216-442-0800 (SAN 222-9706).

Center for Health & Healing, *(Center Health; 0-933320),* 8631 W. Third St., Suite 1140E, Los Angeles, CA 90048 Tel 213-652-9659 (SAN 212-6451).

Center for Holocaust Studies, Documentation and Research, *(Ctr for Holo; 0-9609970),* 1610 Ave. J, Brooklyn, NY 11230 Tel 212-338-6494 (SAN 268-7755).

Center for Independent Living, Inc., *(Center Independent; 0-942846),* Access Project, 2539 Telegraph Ave., Berkeley, CA 94704 Tel 415-841-4776 (SAN 240-2025).

Center for Information on America, *(Ctr Info Am; 0-913172),* Washington, CT 06793 Tel 203-868-2602 (SAN 201-9078).

Center for Information Sharing, *(Ctr Info Sharing; 0-939532),* 77 N. Washington St., Boston, MA 02114 (SAN 216-3489).

Center for International Education, Univ. of Massachusetts, *(Ctr Intl Ed U of MA; 0-932288),* 285 Hills House South, Univ. of Massachusetts, Amherst, MA 01003 (SAN 212-9329).

Center for International Studies, Duke Univ., *(Ctr Intl Stud Duke),* Durham, NC 27706 (SAN 213-5795).

Center for International Training & Education, *(CITE; 0-938960),* 777 United Nations Plaza, Suite 9-A, New York, NY 10017 (SAN 217-0957).

Center for Korean Studies, Univ. of Hawaii at Manoa, *(Ctr Korean U HI at Manoa; 0-917536),* 1881 East-West Rd., Honolulu, HI 96822 Tel 808-949-1833 (SAN 208-0044).

Center for Land Grant Studies, The, *(Ctr Land Grant; 0-9605202),* 136 Grant Ave., Santa Fe, NM 87501 (SAN 216-3497).

Center for Law and Education, Guttman Library, *(Ctr Law & Ed),* 6 Appian Way Third Floor, Cambridge, MA 02138 (SAN 237-6431).

Center for Marital & Sexual Studies, *(Ctr Marital Sexual; 0-9600626),* 5199 E. Pacific Coast Hwy., Long Beach, CA 90804 Tel 213-597-4425 (SAN 203-8587).

Center for Migration Studies, *(Ctr Migration; 0-913256),* 209 Flagg Place, Staten Island, NY 10304 Tel 212-351-8800 (SAN 281-4013).

Center for Modern Psychoanalytic Studies, *(Ctr Mod Psych Stud; 0-916850),* 16 W. 10th St., New York, NY 10011 Tel 212-260-7050 (SAN 208-7537).

Center for National Security Studies, *(Ctr Natl Security; 0-86566),* 122 Maryland Ave. NE, Washington, DC 20002 (SAN 215-2991).

Center for Neo-Hellenic Studies, *(Ctr Neo Hellenic; 0-932242),* 1010 W. 22nd St., Austin, TX 78705 Tel 512-477-5526 (SAN 211-8467).

Center for Professional Advancement, *(Ctr Prof Adv; 0-86563),* 197 Rt. 18, P.O. Box H, E. Brunswick, NJ 08816 Tel 201-249-1400 (SAN 214-185X).

Center for Professional Development, *(Center Prof; 0-9608190),* P.O. Box 1283, USU, Logan, UT 84322 Tel 601-750-1812 (SAN 240-2033).

Center for Public Advocacy Research, Inc., *(Ctr Pub; 0-943138),* 12 W. 37th St., New York, NY 10018 Tel 212-736-7440 (SAN 240-5253).

Center for Reformation Research, *(Center Reform; 0-910345),* 6477 San Bonita Ave., St. Louis, MO 63105 Tel 314-727-6655 (SAN 241-2845).

Center for Research in Ambulatory Health Care Administration, *(Ctr Res Ambulatory; 0-933948),* 4101 E Louisiana Av, Denver, CO 80222 (SAN 230-9459).

Center for Research in Social Change, *(F Roberts Crawford; 0-89937),* Emory University, Atlanta, GA 30322 Tel 404-329-7525 (SAN 211-5247); Dist. by: Fred Roberts Crawford Witness to the Holocaust Project, Emory Univ., Atlanta, GA 30322 (SAN 264-5025).

Center for Research Libraries, *(Ctr Res Lib),* 5060 S. Kenwood Avenue, Chicago, IL 60637 Tel 312-955-4545 (SAN 225-3348).

Center for Research on Criminal Justice, *(Ctr Res Criminal; 0-917404),* 2701 Folsom, San Francisco, CA 94110 (SAN 240-0634); Dist. by: Synthesis Pubns, P.O. Box 40099, San Francisco, CA 94140 Tel 415-282-5272 (SAN 282-3896).

Center for Responsive Psychology, *(Ctr Respon Psych),* Brooklyn Coll Cuny, Brooklyn, NY 11210 Tel 212-780-5960 (SAN 225-7165).

Center for Science in the Public Interest, *(Ctr Sci Public; 0-89329),* 1755 S St., N.W., Washington, DC 20009 Tel 202-332-9110 (SAN 207-6543).

Center for SEAsian Studies, Northern Illinois Univ., *(North Ill U Ctr SE Asian),* Dist. by: Cellar Book Shop, 18090 Wyoming, Detroit, MI 48221 Tel 313-861-1776 (SAN 213-4330).

Center for Self Sufficiency, Inc., *(Center Self; 0-910811),* Center for Self-Sufficiency Distribution Center, P.O. Box 7234, Houston, TX 77248 (SAN 262-0081).

Center for Southern Folklore, *(Ctr South Folklore; 0-89267),* 1216 Peabody Ave., P.O. Box 40105, Memphis, TN 38104 Tel 901-726-4205 (SAN 209-2247).

Center for Strategic & International Studies, *(CSI Studies; 0-89206),* 1800 "K" St. N.W., Washington, DC 20006 Tel 202-877-0200 (SAN 281-4021).

Center for Study of Multiple Birth, The, *(Ctr Multiple Birth; 0-932254),* Suite 463-5, 333 E. Superior St., Chicago, IL 60611 Tel 312-266-9093 (SAN 211-9307).

Center for Study of Responsive Law, *(Ctr Responsive Law),* P.O. Box 19367, Washington, DC 20036 (SAN 281-403X); Dist. by: Education Exploration Center, P.O. Box 7339, Minneapolis, MN 55407 (SAN 217-717X).

Center for Technology, Environment, & Development, *(Ctr Tech Environ; 0-939436),* Clark Univ., 950 Main St., Worcester, MA 01610 (SAN 216-5708).

Center for Telecommunications Studies, The George Washinton Univ., *(CTS-GWU; 0-932768),* 2000 G Street, Bldg. H, Washington, DC 20052 Tel 202-676-7494 (SAN 212-4491).

Center for Thanatology Research & Education, *(Ctr Thanatology; 0-930194),* 391 Atlantic Ave., Brooklyn, NY 11217 Tel 212-858-3026 (SAN 210-7414); Orders to: P.O. Box 989, Brooklyn, NY 11202 (SAN 215-0425).

Center for the Art of Living, *(Ctr Art Living; 0-9602552),* P.O. Box 788, Evanston, IL 60204 Tel 312-864-8664 (SAN 212-8926).

Center for the Scientific Study of Religion, *(Ctr Sci Study; 0-913348),* 5757 University Ave., Chicago, IL 60637 Tel 312-752-5757 (SAN 203-8749).

Center for the Study of Elephants, The, *(Ctr Study Elephants; 0-942074),* P.O. Box 4444, Carson, CA 90749 (SAN 239-5177).

Center for the Study of Services, *(Ctr Study Serv),* 1518 K St. N.W., Suite 406, Washington, DC 20005 Tel 202-347-9612 (SAN 287-2862).

Center for the Study of the Presidency, *(Ctr Study Presidency; 0-938204),* 208 E. 75 St., New York, NY 10021 Tel 212-249-1200 (SAN 225-6339).

Center for Traditionalist Orthodox Studies, *(Ctr Trad Orthodox; 0-911165),* P. O. Box 398, Etna, CA 96027 (SAN 287-0029); c/o St. Gregory Palamas Monastery, P.O. Box 398, Etna, CA 96027 (SAN 287-0037).

Ctr. for Urban Policy Research, *(Ctr Urban Pol Res),* Rutgers Univ., Kilmer Campus, Bldg. 4051, New Brunswick, NJ 08903 Tel 201-932-3122 (SAN 206-6297).

Center for Western Studies, *(Ctr Western Studies; 0-931170),* Augustana College, Sioux Falls, SD 57197 Tel 605-336-4007 (SAN 211-4844).

Center on Minorities & Criminal Justice, *(Ctr Minorities; 0-940826),* School of Criminal Justice, State Univ. of New York at Albany, Albany, NY 12222 (SAN 239-4170).

Center Press, *(Center Pr; 0-934320),* 2045 Francisco St., Berkeley, CA 94709 (SAN 213-0351).

Center Pubns., *(Center Pubns; 0-916820),* 905 S. Normandie Ave., Los Angeles, CA 90006 Tel 213-387-2351 (SAN 208-9386); Dist. by: Great Eastern Book Co., P.O. Box 271, Boulder, CO 80302 Tel 303-449-6111 (SAN 211-6391).

Centerline Press, *(Centerline; 0-913111),* 7603 E. Firestone Blvd., Suite 166, Downey, CA 90241 (SAN 283-9369).

Central Committee for Conscientious Objectors, An Agency for Military & Draft Counseling, *(CCCO; 0-933368),* 2208 South St., Philadelphia, PA 19146 (SAN 207-9852).

Central Conference of American Rabbis, *(Central Conf; 0-916694),* 21 E. 40th St., New York, NY 10016 Tel 212-684-4990 (SAN 204-3262).

Central Electric Railfans' Assn., *(Central Electric; 0-915348),* P.O. Box 503, Chicago, IL 60690 (SAN 207-3110).

Central Florida Voters Congress, *(Central FL Voters),* P.O. Box 1172, Orlando, FL 32802 (SAN 214-4882).

Centralia Press, *(Centralia Pr; 0-9611008),* P.O. Box 607, Floral Park, NY 11002 (SAN 283-9857).

Centre Enterprise, The, *(Centre Ent; 0-932876),* Box 99506, Station "O", San Francisco, CA 94109 Tel 415-239-4892 (SAN 212-3401).

Centro De Investigaciones Regionales De Mesoamerica, *(Centro Invest; 0-910443),* P.O. Box 38, S. Woodstock, VT 05071 (SAN 260-0269).

Century Bookbindery, *(Century Bookbindery; 0-89984),* P.O. Box 6471, Philadelphia, PA 19145 (SAN 209-2441).

Century Communications, Inc., *(Century Comm; 0-930264),* 5520 W. Touhy, Suite G, Skokie, IL 60077 Tel 312-676-4060 (SAN 208-1911).

Century House Pubs., *(Century Hse; 0-87282),* Old Irelandville, Watkins Glen, NY 14891 Tel 607-535-4004 (SAN 201-9736).

Century One Press, *(Century One; 0-937080),* 2325 E. Platte Ave., Colorado Springs, CO 80909 Tel 303-471-1322 (SAN 214-3534).

Century Press, *(Century Pr; 0-915680),* 412 N. Hudson, Oklahoma City, OK 73102 (SAN 207-382X).

Century Three Press, *(Century Three; 0-933400),* 304 S. 13th St., Lincoln, NE 68508 (SAN 213-2125).

Cerberus Book Co., The, *(Cerberus; 0-933590),* P.O. Box 70899, Ft. Bragg, NC 28307 (SAN 213-8352).

Ceres Press, *(Ceres Pr; 0-9606138),* Box 87, Woodstock, NY 12498 (SAN 217-0949).

Cerred Books, Company, *(Cerred Bks Co; 0-912231),* P.O. Box 796, Laurel, MD 20707 Tel 301-490-5949 (SAN 265-105X).

Cerulean Pr., *(Cerulean Pr; 0-917458),* c/o Kent Pubns., 18301 Halsted St., Northbridge, CA 91325 Tel 213-349-2080 (SAN 209-0597).

CES Industries, Inc., *(CES Industries; 0-86711),* 130 Central Ave., Farmingdale, NY 11735 (SAN 237-9864).

C F S Publishing Corp., *(C F S Pub Corp; 0-913095),* 300 Mercer, Suite 32M, New York, NY 10003 Tel 212-460-8000 (SAN 282-9894).

Chadwick House Pubs., Ltd., *(Chadwick Hse; 0-938122),* 25 W. Portola, Los Altos, CA 94022 (SAN 214-1167).

Chadwyck-Healey Inc., *(Chadwyck-Healey; 0-85964),* 623 Martense Ave., Teaneck, NJ 07666 (SAN 216-3500).

Chaffey Communities Cultural Center, *(Chaffey Commun Cult Ctr; 0-9603586),* P.O. Box 772, Upland, CA 91786 (SAN 213-8360).

Chain Store Publishing Company, *(Chain Store),* 2 Park Ave., New York, NY 10016 (SAN 237-5478).

Chalfant Press, Inc., *(Chalfant Pr; 0-912494),* P.O. Box 787, Bishop, CA 93514 Tel 619-873-3535 (SAN 203-6347).

Challenge Expedition Company, *(Challenge Exp; 0-9608120),* Box 1852, Boise, ID 83701 Tel 208-454-2738 (SAN 240-0871).

Challenge Press, Book Div. of Economic Research Center, Inc., *(Challenge Pr; 0-89421),* 1107 Lexington Ave., Dayton, OH 45407 Tel 513-275-8637 (SAN 210-0509).

Chalmers, Irena, Cookbooks, Inc., *(I Chalmers; 0-941034),* 23 E. 92nd St., New York, NY 10028 Tel 212-289-3105 (SAN 217-3425).

Chamber of Commerce, *(COC),* P.O. Box 51, Philadelphia, MS 39350 (SAN 217-2968).

Chamber of Commerce of the U. S., Special Publications Dept., *(Chamber Comm US; 0-89834),* 1615 "H" St., N.W., Washington, DC 20062 Tel 202-463-5567 (SAN 204-3254).

Chamberlain, Mildred Mosher, *(M M Chamberlain; 0-9604142),* 128 Potters Ave., Warwick, RI 02886 (SAN 215-0654).

Chameleon Pubns., *(Chameleon; 0-939988),* 706 Bunker Hill St., Fredericksburg, VA 22401 (SAN 216-7972).

Champaign County Historical Archives, *(Champaign County; 0-9609646),* The Urbana Free Library, 201 S. Race St., Urbana, IL 61801 Tel 217-328-2665 (SAN 268-8476).

Champion Athlete Publishing Co., *(Champion Athlete; 0-938074),* Box 2936, Richmond, VA 23235 Tel 804-794-6034 (SAN 215-6148).

Champion Press, *(Champion Pr),* P.O. Box 1969, Scottsdale, AZ 85252 Tel 602-949-0786 (SAN 218-4710).

Champlin Museum Press, *(Champlin Museum; 0-912173),* 4636 Fighter Aces Dr., Mesa, AZ 85205 Tel 602-830-4540 (SAN 264-7257).

Chan Shal Imi Society Press, *(Chan Shal Imi; 0-936380),* P.O. Box 1365, Stone Mountain, GA 30086 (SAN 213-2974).

Chancery Pubs., Inc., *(Chancery Pubs; 0-940024),* 102 W. Pennsylvania Ave., Baltimore, MD 21204 Tel 301-821-5143 (SAN 217-0655).

Chandler & Sharp Pubs., Inc., *(Chandler & Sharp; 0-88316),* 11A Commercial Blvd., Novato, CA 94947 Tel 415-883-2353 (SAN 205-6127).

Chandonnet, Ann, *(A Chandonnet),* P.O. Box A, Chugiak, AK 99567 Tel 907-688-3591 (SAN 212-8195).

Change Magazine Press, *(Change Mag; 0-915390),* P.O. Box 2023, New Rochelle, NY 10802 Tel 914-235-8700 (SAN 207-1347).

Changing Times Education Service, A Div. of EMC Corporation, *(Changing Times; 0-89247),* 300 York Ave., St. Paul, MN 55101 Tel 612-771-1555 (SAN 208-4015).

Channing Books & Whaleship Plans, *(Channing Bks; 0-9600496),* P.O. Box 552, 35 Main St., Marion, MA 02738 Tel 617-748-0087 (SAN 203-6363).

Chan's Corp., *(Chans Corp; 0-914322),* 230 S. Garfield Ave., Monterey Park, CA 91754 Tel 213-572-0425 (SAN 201-8764).

Chanteyman Press, *(Chanteyman; 0-9601250),* 42 Crocus St., Woodbridge, NJ 07095 Tel 201-634-4123 (SAN 210-4008).

Chanticleer Press, Inc., *(Chanticleer; 0-918810),* 424 Madison Ave., New York, NY 10017 Tel 212-888-1234 (SAN 201-5749).

Chantry Press, *(Chantry Pr; 0-941608),* P.O. Box 144, Midland Park, NJ 07432 Tel 201-423-2921 (SAN 239-0752).

Chapin PTO, *(Chapin PTO; 0-9611640),* Rte. 3, Box 384, Chapin, SC 29036 Tel 803-345-3590 (SAN 284-9348).

Chapman, Sarah K., *(S K Chapman),* P.O. Box 3684, Sarasota, FL 33578 (SAN 263-9696).

Chapter & Cask, *(Chapter & Cask; 0-940056),* P.O. Box 3604, Glyndon, MD 21071 Tel 301-667-4093 (SAN 217-0663).

Character Books, *(Character Bks; 0-942056),* P.O. Box 22073, San Diego, CA 92122 Tel 714-566-7300 (SAN 238-6305).

Character Research Press, *(Character Res; 0-915744),* 266 State St., Schenectady, NY 12305 Tel 518-370-6012 (SAN 209-1240).

Charioteer Press, *(Charioteer; 0-910350),* P.O. Box 57223, Washington, DC 20037 Tel 202-965-5046 (SAN 203-6371).

Charisma Press, *(Charisma Pr; 0-933402),* P.O. Box 263, 459 River Rd., Andover, MA 01810 Tel 617-851-7910 (SAN 212-6478).

Charisma Pubns., Inc., *(Charisma Pubns; 0-937008),* P.O. Box 40321, Indianapolis, IN 46240 Tel 317-844-0719 (SAN 214-3542).

Charismatic Bookshelf, *(Charismatic; 0-943878),* 10205 N. W. 25th Place, Gainesville, FL 32606 Tel 241-1016).

Chariton Review Press, *(Chariton Review; 0-933428),* Northeast Missouri State Univ., Kirksville, MO 63501 Tel 816-785-4499 (SAN 212-4890).

Charland, Thomas C., *(T C Charland; 0-9610754),* P.O. Box 7112, Falls Church, VA 22046-1268 Tel 703-534-1039 (SAN 264-7265).

CharLee Press, *(CharLee Pr; 0-910815),* P.O. Box 5015, Richmond, CA 94805 Tel 415-237-1194 (SAN 262-4583).

Charles, Joseph J., Publishing Co., *(J Charles Pub; 0-9607080),* 130 Sherwood Dr., Hilton, NY 14468 (SAN 238-9223).

Charles & Co., Inc., *(Charles & Co; 0-933318),* P.O. Box 606, Southport, CT 06490 (SAN 212-9337).

Charles Pr. Pubs., Div. of Robert J. Brady, Co., *(Charles; 0-913486; 0-89303),* Rtes. 197 & 450, Bowie, MD 20715 Tel 301-262-6300 (SAN 203-638X).

Charles Publishing Co., *(Charles Pub; 0-912880),* 12125 Riverside Dr., Suite 201, North Hollywood, CA 91607 Tel 213-762-0633 (SAN 201-9779).

Charles River Books, *(Charles River Bks; 0-89182),* 1 Thompson Square, Boston, MA 02129 Tel 617-242-5111 (SAN 209-2530). *Imprints:* Charles River Reprints (CRR).

Charles River Reprints See Charles River Books

Charlotte Pubns., *(Charlotte Pubs; 0-914878),* P.O. Box 57126, Los Angeles, CA 90057 (SAN 203-4107).

ChartGuide Ltd., *(ChartGuide Ltd; 0-938206),* 300 N. Wilshire Ave., Suite 5, Anaheim, CA 92801 Tel 714-533-1423 (SAN 215-7373).

Chartrand, Robert Lee, *(Chartrand),* 5406 Dorset Ave., Chevy Chase, MD 20015 (SAN 211-1152).

Chartwell House, Inc., *(Chartwell; 0-910354),* P.O. Box 166, Bowling Green Sta., New York, NY 10004 (SAN 203-6398).

Chase, Don M., *(D M Chase; 0-918634),* 8569 Lawrence Lane, Sebastopol, CA 95472 Tel 707-823-7670 (SAN 209-4215).

Chase Trade Information Corp., *(Chase Trade; 0-916006),* 1 World Trade Ctr., Suite 7800, New York, NY 10048 (SAN 208-1903).

Chasse Pubns., *(Chasse Pubns; 0-913930),* P.O. Box 906, Denver, CO 80201 Tel 303-757-0160 (SAN 203-6401).

Chateau Publishing, Inc., *(Chateau Pub; 0-88435),* P.O. Box 20432, Herndon Sta., Orlando, FL 32814 Tel 305-898-1641 (SAN 201-7814).

Chateau Thierry Press, *(Chateau Thierry; 0-935046),* 1668 W. Olive Ave., Chicago, IL 60660 (SAN 281-4056); c/o Joan Thing, 7348 N. Ridge Blvd., Chicago, IL (SAN 281-4064).

Chatham Bookseller, *(Chatham Bkseller; 0-911860),* 8 Green Village Rd., Madison, NJ 07940 Tel 201-822-1361 (SAN 203-641X).

Chatham Communicators, Inc., *(Chatham Comm Inc; 0-910347),* 320 Chatham Road, P.O. Box 14091, Columbus, OH 43214 Tel 614-268-8989 (SAN 241-2861).

Chatham House Pubs., Inc., *(Chatham Hse Pubs; 0-934540),* Box 1, Chatham, NJ 07928 Tel 201-635-2059 (SAN 281-4072); Orders to: Chatham House Distributors, 540 Barnum Ave., Bridgeport, CT 06608 Tel 203-366-1900 (SAN 281-4080).

Chatham Press, *(Chatham Pr; 0-85699),* 143 Sound Beach, Old Greenwich, CT 06870 Tel 203-637-4531 (SAN 201-9795); Dist. by: The Devin-Adair Co., Old Greenwich, CT 06870 (SAN 213-750X).

Chatham Publishing Co., *(Chatham Pub CA; 0-89685),* P.O. Box 283, Burlingame, CA 94010 Tel 415-348-0331 (SAN 210-4016).

Chatham Square Press, Inc., *(Chatham Sq; 0-89456),* 401 Broadway, 23rd Fl., New York, NY 10013 Tel 212-226-3368 (SAN 210-1874).

Chatterton Press, *(Chatterton Pr; 0-930574),* 2471 Berthbrook Dr., Cincinnati, OH 45231 (SAN 211-4631).

Cheap Street, *(Cheap St; 0-941826),* Route 2, Box 293, New Castle, VA 24127 Tel 703-864-6288 (SAN 239-1783).

Chedney Press, *(Chedney; 0-910358),* P.O. Box 1148, Auburn, ME 04210 (SAN 203-6428).

Cheever Publishing, Inc., *(Cheever Pub; 0-915708),* P.O. Box 700, Bloomington, IL 61701 Tel 309-378-2961 (SAN 207-9410).

Chelsea House Pubs., *(Chelsea Hse; 0-87754),* 133 Christopher St., New York, NY 10014 Tel 212-924-6414 (SAN 206-7609); Dist. by: Scribner Book Companies, 597 Fifth Ave., New York, NY 10017 Tel 212-486-2700 (SAN 201-002X).

Chelsea-Lee Books, *(Chelsea-Lee Bks; 0-913974),* P.O. Box 66273, Los Angeles, CA 90066 (SAN 201-9817).

Chelsea Publishing Co., *(Chelsea Pub; 0-8284),* 432 Park Ave. S., Rm. 503, New York, NY 10016 Tel 212-889-8095 (SAN 201-9825).

Chem-Orbital, *(Chem-Orbital; 0-930376),* 2405 Bond St., Park Forest South, IL 60466 Tel 312-534-1770 (SAN 213-3466).

Chemical Economic Services, *(Chem Econ; 0-912060),* P.O. Box 468, Palmer Square, Princeton, NJ 08540 Tel 609-921-8468 (SAN 201-9833).

Chemical Engineering See McGraw-Hill Book Co.

Chemical Information Management, Inc., *(CIMI),* P.O. Box 2740, Cherry Hill, NJ 08034 Tel 609-795-6767 (SAN 212-9345).

Chemical Publishing Co., Inc., *(Chem Pub; 0-8206),* 80 8th Ave., New York, NY 10014 Tel 212-255-1950 (SAN 203-6444).

Chen Chi Studio, *(Chen Chi Studio; 0-9604652),* 15 Gramercy Park, New York, NY 10003 (SAN 215-1359).

Chen Fu Tien, *(Chen Fu),* P.O. Box 1854, Norwalk, CA 90650 (SAN 287-2870).

Cheney, Donna B., *(D B Cheney),* 607 Sunset, McCook, NE 69001 (SAN 212-646X).

Cheng & Tsui Co., *(Cheng & Tsui; 0-917056; 0-88727),* 25-31 West St., Boston, MA 02111 Tel 617-277-1769 (SAN 169-3387).

Cherniak/Damele Publishing Co., *(Cherniak-Damele; 0-911093),* P.O. Box 19077, Oakland, CA 94619 Tel 415-533-1598 (SAN 268-8670); Dist. by: Infomedia, 103 Godwin Ave., Midland Park, NJ 07432 Tel 201-447-2569 (SAN 268-8689).

Cherry Lane Music Co., Inc., Div. of Cherry Lane Music Co., Inc., *(Cherry Lane; 0-89524),* 110 Midland Ave., Port Chester, NY 10573 Tel 914-937-8601 (SAN 219-0788).

Cherry Valley Editions, *(Cherry Valley; 0-916156),* 2314 Georgian Woods Pl., Wheaton, MD 20902 Tel 301-946-0947 (SAN 208-1482); Dist. by: Writers & Books, 892 S. Clinton Ave., Rochester, NY 14620 (SAN 156-9678).

Cherubim, *(Cherubim; 0-938574),* P.O. Box 75, Ft. Tilden, NY 11695 (SAN 215-8523).

Chesbro Press, *(Chesbro; 0-938006),* 14976 Tahoe Way, P.O. Box 1326, Morgan Hill, CA 95037 Tel 408-779-5930 (SAN 220-0392).

Cheshire Books, *(Cheshire; 0-917352),* 514 Bryant St., Palo Alto, CA 94301 Tel 415-321-2449 (SAN 208-5925); Dist. by: Kampmann & Co., Inc., 9 E. 40th St., New York, NY 10016 Tel 212-685-2928 (SAN 202-5191).

Chess Enterprises, Inc., *(Chess Ent Inc; 0-931462),* 107 Crosstree Rd., Coraopolis, PA 15108 (SAN 277-5808).

Chess Visions, Inc., *(Chess Visions; 0-939786),* P.O. Box 430372, S. Miami, FL 33143 (SAN 216-8847).

Chester-Leeds Co., *(Chester-Leeds; 0-931624),* P.O. Box 191, Middlesex, NJ 08846 Tel 201-463-0004 (SAN 211-5085).

Chestnut Hill Press, *(Chestnut Hill Pr; 0-9608132),* 5320 Groveland Rd., Geneseo, NY 14454 Tel 716-243-3616 (SAN 238-0498).

Cheval Books, *(Cheval Bks),* P.O. Box 2783, Hollywood, CA 90028 Tel 213-657-7311 (SAN 208-306X).

Cheyenne Corral, *(Cheyenne Cor; 0-9609648),* 520 E. 27th St., Cheyenne, WY 82001 Tel 307-638-6846 (SAN 281-4099).

Chicago Board of Trade, *(Chicago Bd Trade; 0-917456),* 141 W. Jackson, Chicago, IL 60604 Tel 312-435-3556 (SAN 203-6460).

Chicago Center for Afro-American Studies & Research, Inc., *(Chi Ctr Afro-Am Stud; 0-937954),* P.O. Box 7610, Chicago, IL 60680 (SAN 215-9449).

Chicago Historical Society, *(Chicago Hist; 0-913820),* Clark St. at North Ave., Chicago, IL 60614 Tel 312-642-4600 (SAN 203-6479).

Chicago Horticultural Society, *(Chi Horticult; 0-939914),* P.O. Box 400, Glencoe, IL 60022 Tel 312-835-5440 (SAN 216-7980).

Chicago Institute for Psychoanalysis, *(Chicago Psych; 0-918568),* 180 N. Michigan Ave., Chicago, IL 60601 Tel 312-726-6300 (SAN 210-1432).

Chicago Institute of Theology & Culture, The, *(Chicago Theology & Culture; 0-936978),* 5401 S. Cornell Ave., Chicago, IL 60645 (SAN 213-9928).

Chicago Publishing Co., *(Chicago Publishing; 0-9603264),* P.O. Box 635, Chicago, IL 60690 Tel 312-461-1053 (SAN 209-5394).

Chicago Review Press, Inc., *(Chicago Review; 0-914090; 0-914091),* 213 W. Institute Place, Chicago, IL 60610 Tel 312-337-0747 (SAN 213-5744); 820 N. Franklin, Chicago, IL 60610 Tel 312-337-5457 (SAN 213-5744); 215 W. Ohio St., Chicago, IL 60610 (SAN 213-764X).

Chicago Talent, Inc., *(Chicago Talent; 0-942454),* 212 W. Superior., Chicago, IL 60610 Tel 312-446-6190 (SAN 238-1494).

Chicago Tribune Books Today, *(Chicago Trib),* 435 N. Michigan Ave., Chicago, IL 60611 Tel 312-222-3232 (SAN 204-2959).

Chicago Visual Library See **Univ. of Chicago Press**

Chick Pubns., *(Chick Pubns; 0-937958),* P.O. Box 662, Chino, CA 91710 Tel 714-987-0771 (SAN 211-7770).

Chickasaw Bayou Press, *(Chickasaw Bayou; 0-9606372),* 103 Trace Harbor Rd., Madison, MS 39110 Tel 601-354-7705 (SAN 217-1651).

Child & Family Enterprises, Inc., *(Child & Family Ent; 0-935202),* 7 Leonard Place, Albany, NY 12202 (SAN 213-8379).

Child & Waters Incorporated, *(Child & Waters; 0-9611200),* 516 Fifth Ave., New York, NY 10036 Tel 212-840-1935 (SAN 283-2569).

Child Care Information Exchange, *(Child Care; 0-942702),* C44, Redmond, WA 98052 Tel 206-882-1066 (SAN 240-3072).

Child Evangelism Fellowship Press, *(CEF Press),* Warrenton, MO 63383 (SAN 211-7789).

Child Focus Co., *(Child Focus Co; 0-933892),* 1230 Keats St., Manhattan Beach, CA 90266 Tel 213-379-4144 (SAN 207-5199).

Child Health Assn. of Sewickley, Inc., *(Child Health Assoc; 0-9607634),* 1108 Ohio River Blvd., Sewickley, PA 15143 Tel 412-741-3221 (SAN 240-088X).

Child Study Assn. of America/Wel-Met, Inc., *(Child Study; 0-87183),* 853 Broadway, New York, NY 10003 Tel 212-889-3450 (SAN 203-6487).

Child Welfare League of America, Inc., *(Child Welfare; 0-87868),* 67 Irving Place, New York, NY 10003 Tel 212-254-7410 (SAN 201-9876).

Childbirth Graphics, Ltd., *(Childbirth Graphics; 0-943114),* P.O. Box 17025 Irondequoit, Rochester, NY 14617 Tel 716-244-7215 (SAN 240-3587).

Children First Press, *(Children First; 0-9603696),* Box 8008, Ann Arbor, MI 48107 Tel 313-668-8056 (SAN 212-4904).

Children's Art Foundation, Inc., *(Childrens Art; 0-89409),* Box 83, Santa Cruz, CA 95063 Tel 408-426-5557 (SAN 210-0533).

Children's Book Press/Imprenta de Libros Infantiles, *(Childrens Book Pr; 0-89239),* 1461 9th Ave., San Francisco, CA 94122 Tel 415-664-8500 (SAN 210-7864).

Children's Defense Fund, *(Children's Defense; 0-938008),* 1520 New Hampshire Ave., NW, Washington, DC 20036 (SAN 216-1133).

Children's Learning Center, The, *(Children Learn Ctr; 0-917206),* 4660 E. 62nd St., Indianapolis, IN 46220 Tel 317-251-6241 (SAN 208-5933).

Children's Memorial Hospital, The, *(Children's Memorial; 0-9607400),* 2300 Children's Plaza, Chicago, IL 60614 Tel 312-239-4189).

Children's Museum of Indianapolis, *(Child Mus),* 30th and Meridian, Indianapolis, IN 46208 (SAN 268-9057).

Children's Museum of Oak Ridge, *(Children's Mus; 0-9606832),* P.O. Box 3066, Oak Ridge, TN 37830 Tel 615-482-1075 (SAN 219-7227).

Childrens Press, *(Childrens; 0-516),* 1224 W. Van Buren St., Chicago, IL 60607 Tel 312-666-4200 (SAN 201-9264).
Imprints: Elk Grove Books (Elk Grove Bks); Golden Gate (Golden Gate).

Children's Theatre Assn. of America, Div. of American Theatre Assn., *(Childrens Theatre; 0-940528),* 1010 Wisconsin Ave., N.W., Suite 630, Washington, DC 20007 Tel 202-342-7530 (SAN 239-3581).

Child's World, Inc., The, *(Childs World; 0-89565; 0-913778),* 980 N. McLean Blvd., P. O. Box 989, Elgin, IL 60120 Tel 312-741-7591 (SAN 211-0032); Orders to: P.O. Box 989, Elgin, IL 60120 (SAN 211-0040).

Childwrite, Inc., *(Childwrite; 0-943194),* 2522 South 30th, La Crosse, WI 54601 Tel 608-788-7579 (SAN 240-527X).

Chilmark House, *(Chilmark Hse; 0-937532),* 4224 38th St. N.W., Washington, DC 20016 (SAN 215-9457).

Chilton Book Co., *(Chilton; 0-8019),* Orders to: School, Library Services, Chilton Way, Radnor, PA 19089 Tel 215-964-4729 (SAN 202-1552).

China Books & Periodicals, Inc., *(China Bks; 0-8351),* 2929 24th St., San Francisco, CA 94110 Tel 415-282-2994 (SAN 214-1213).

China Phone Book Co., Ltd., The, *(China Phone),* P.O. Box 2385-N, Menlo Park, CA 94025 (SAN 268-9146).

China Research, *(China Res; 0-9605190),* 1500 N.W. 103rd Lane, Coral Springs, FL 33065 Tel 305-752-6274 (SAN 223-1654).

China West Books, *(China West; 0-941340),* P.O. Box 2804, San Francisco, CA 94126 Tel 415-755-3715 (SAN 238-9231).

Chinese Art Appraisers Assn., *(Chinese Art App; 0-930940),* Box 734, 625 Post St., San Francisco, CA 94109 Tel 415-673-6023 (SAN 211-495X).

Chinkapin Press, Inc., *(Chinkapin; 0-938874),* P.O. Box 10565, Eugene, OR 97401 (SAN 220-2360).

Chirich, Nancy, *(N Chirich),* 305 Euclid Ave., Apt. 405, Oakland, CA 94610 Tel 415-763-3510 (SAN 209-5408).

Chiron Press, Inc., *(Chiron Pr; 0-913462),* 24 W. 96th St., New York, NY 10025 Tel 212-662-5486 (SAN 202-1560); Orders to: Publishers Storage & Shipping Corp., 2352 Main St., Concord, MA 01742 Tel 617-897-9332 (SAN 202-1579).

Chlorine Institute, *(Chlorine Inst),* 342 Madison Ave., New York, NY 10173 Tel 212-682-4324 (SAN 204-2983).

Chogie Publishers, *(M K Cox; 0-9610818),* 123 Virginia Road, Oak Ridge, TN 37830 Tel 615-482-7320 (SAN 285-1199); Orders to: Box 884, Clarksville, TN 37040 Tel 615-648-1647 (SAN 285-1202).

Choice, *(Choice),* 1501 Cherry St, Philadelphia, PA 19102 (SAN 260-3969).

Choice Centered Astrology & Tarot, *(Choice Astro; 0-9609650),* P.O. Box 31816, Seattle, WA 98103 (SAN 262-0103).

Chosen Books of the Zondervan Corp., *(Chosen Bks Zondervan; 0-912376),* Lincoln, VA 22078 Tel 703-338-4131 (SAN 202-1587); Dist. by: The Zonervan Corp., 1415 Lake Dr. S.E., Grand Rapids, MI 48506 Tel 800-253-1309 (SAN 203-2694).

Chou-Chou Press, *(Chou-Chou),* P.O. Box 152, Shoreham, NY 11786 (SAN 220-2379).

Christ Episcopal Church, *(Christ Episcopal),* P.O. Box 836, New Bern, NC 28560 (SAN 217-295X).

Christ for the Nations, Inc., *(Christ Nations; 0-899985),* 3404 Conway St., Box 24910, Dallas, TX 75224 Tel 214-376-1711 (SAN 211-7800).

Christ Foundation, The, *(Christ Found; 0-910315),* P.O. Box 10, Port Angeles, WA 98362 Tel 206-452-5249 (SAN 241-4872).

Christendom College Press See **Christendom Pubns.**

Christendom Pubns., *(Christendom Pubns; 0-931888),* Rt. 3, Box 87, Front Royal, VA 22630 Tel 703-636-2908 (SAN 214-2570).
Imprints: Christendom College Press (Chr Coll Pr).

Christian Academy of Success, *(Chr Acad Success; 0-941280),* 5428 W. Barbara Ave., Glendale, AZ 85302 (SAN 238-924X).

Christian Bks., *(Christian Bks; 0-940232),* P.O. Box 1092, Goleta, CA 93116 Tel 805-685-2412 (SAN 201-8942).

Christian Booksellers Assn., *(Chr Bksellers),* 2620 Venetucci Blvd., P.O. Box 200, Colorado Springs, CO 80901 (SAN 216-3519).

Christian Classics, Inc., *(Chr Classics; 0-87061),* P.O. Box 30, Westminster, MD 21157 Tel 301-848-3065 (SAN 203-6525).

Christian Conciliation Service, *(Chr Concil Serv),* P.O. Box 2069, Oak Park, IL 60303 (SAN 277-6634).

Christian Education Research Institute, *(Chr Educ Res Inst; 0-943708),* Box 888-747, Atlanta, GA 30356 Tel 404-972-3888 (SAN 238-0501).

Christian Fellowship Pubs., Inc., *(Christian Fellow Pubs; 0-935008),* 11515 Allecingie Pkwy., Richmond, VA 23235 Tel 804-794-5333 (SAN 207-4885).

Christian Herald Books, *(Christian Herald; 0-915684; 0-86693),* 40 Overlook Dr., Chappaqua, NY 10514 Tel 914-769-9000 (SAN 208-1474).

Christian International Pubs., *(Chr Intl Pubs; 0-939868),* P.O. Box 27398, Phoenix, AZ 85061 (SAN 281-4102).

Christian Legal Society, *(Chr Legal),* P.O. Box 2069, Oak Park, IL 60303 Tel 312-848-6335 (SAN 224-0947).

Christian Light Pubns., Inc., *(Christian Light; 0-87813),* P.O. Box 1126, Harrisonburg, VA 22801 Tel 703-434-0768 (SAN 206-7315).

Christian Literature Crusade, Inc., *(Chr Lit; 0-87508),* Pennsylvania Ave., Fort Washington, PA 19034 (SAN 202-1609).

Christian Marriage Enrichment, *(Chr Marriage; 0-938786),* 8000 E. Girard, No. 301, Denver, CO 80231 (SAN 216-1141).

Christian Pubns., Inc., *(Chr Pubns; 0-87509),* 25 S. 10th St. P.O. Box 3404, Harrisburg, PA 17105 Tel 717-233-6728 (SAN 202-1617).

Christian Publishing Services, Inc., *(Christian Pub; 0-88144),* P.O. Box 55388, Tulsa, OK 74155 Tel 918-451-0774 (SAN 260-0285).

Christian Science Pub. Society, *(Chr Science; 0-87510),* Pub & Media Dept., 1 Norway St., Boston, MA 02115 Tel 617-262-2300 (SAN 203-6541); Orders to: P.O. Box 1875, Boston, MA 02117 (SAN 203-655X).

Christian Studies Center, *(Chr Stud Ctr; 0-939200),* P.O. Box 11110, Memphis, TN 38111 Tel 901-458-0738 (SAN 220-0406).

Christian Success Publishing House, *(Christian Success; 0-934178),* P.O. Box 10871, Yakiman, WA 98909 (SAN 213-0386).

Christian Zion Advocate, *(Christian Zion),* P.O. Box 971, Port Angeles, WA 98362 Tel 206-457-4731 (SAN 203-6568).

Christianica Center, *(Christianica; 0-911346),* 6 N. Michigan Ave., Chicago, IL 60602 Tel 312-782-4230 (SAN 204-739X).

Christian's Library Press, Inc., *(Chr Lib Pr; 0-934874),* P.O. Box 2226, Grand Rapids, MI 49501 (SAN 222-7061).

Christopher Publishing House (Mass), *(Chris Mass; 0-8158),* 1405 Hanover St., Box 1014, West Hanover, MA 02339 Tel 617-878-4656 (SAN 202-1625).

Christopher Resources, Inc., *(Christopher Res; 0-9610034),* P.O. Box E., Frankfort, IL 60423 Tel 312-655-4923 (SAN 268-9707).

Christopher's Books, *(Christophers Bks; 0-87922),* 390 62nd St., Oakland, CA 94618 Tel 415-428-1120 (SAN 212-5870).

Christ's Mission, *(Christs Mission; 0-935120),* Box 176, Hackensack, NJ 07602 Tel 201-342-6202 (SAN 211-7819).

Christward Ministry, *(Christward; 0-910378),* Rte. 5, Box 206, Escondido, CA 92025 Tel 619-744-1500 (SAN 202-1633).

Chromatic Communications, Inc., *(Chromatic Comm; 0-912673),* P.O. Box 3249, Walnut Creek, CA 94598 Tel 415-945-1602 (SAN 277-6642).

Chrome Yellow Private Press, *(Chrome Yellow; 0-935656),* 125 Central Ave., Cresent City, FL 32012 Tel 904-698-2430 (SAN 213-6597).

Chronicle Books, Div. of Chronicle Publishing Co., *(Chronicle Bks; 0-87701),* 870 Market St., Suite 917, San Francisco, CA 94102 Tel 415-777-7240 (SAN 202-165X).

Chronicle Guidance Pubns., *(Chron Guide; 0-912578),* Moravia, NY 13118 Tel 315-497-0330 (SAN 202-1641).

Chrysalis Publishing, Ltd., *(Chrysalis),* P.O. Box 10690, Phoenix, AZ 85064 Tel 602-943-9475 (SAN 218-4729).

Chrysler Museum Library, *(Chrysler Museum; 0-940744),* Olney Rd., & Mowbray Arch, Norfolk, VA 23510 Tel 804-622-1211 (SAN 281-4110); Dist. by: University Press of Virginia, Box 3608 University Station, Charlottesville, VA 22903 (SAN 202-5361).

Chthon Press, *(Chthon Pr)* 77 Mark Vincent Dr., Westford, MA 01886 (SAN 208-2438).

Chulainn Press, Inc., *(Chulainn Press; 0-917600),* 1040 Butterfield Rd., P.O. Box 770, San Anselmo, CA 94960 (SAN 209-3286).

Church & Synagogue Library Assn., *(CSLA; 0-915324),* P.O. Box 1130, Bryn Mawr, PA 19010 Tel 215-853-2870 (SAN 210-7872).

Church History Research & Archives, *(Church History; 0-935122),* 220 Graystone Dr., Gallatin, TN 37066 Tel 615-452-7027 (SAN 211-7827).

Church Library Council, *(Church Lib; 0-9603060),* 5406 Quintana St., Riverdale, MD 20737 Tel 301-864-9308 (SAN 210-5322).

Church of Light, *(Church of Light; 0-87887),* Box 76862, Sanford Sta., Los Angeles, CA 90076 Tel 213-487-6070 (SAN 209-150X).

Church of St. Leo the Great Press, *(Church St. Leo; 0-9607014),* 227 S. Exeter St., Baltimore, MD 21202 Tel 301-727-8600 (SAN 238-9630).

Church of Scientology Information Service-Pubns., *(Church of Scient Info; 0-915598),* c/o Bridge Publications, Inc., 4833 Fountain Ave., Los Angeles, CA 90029 (SAN 268-9774).

Church of Scientology of New York, The, *(Church Scient NY),* 227 W. 46th St., New York, NY 10036 (SAN 211-786X).

Church of the Cross, *(Church Cross; 0-9601178),* 4068 S. Willow Way, Denver, CO 80237 Tel 303-770-2272 (SAN 210-055X).

Churches Alive, *(Churches Alive; 0-934396),* P.O. Box 3800, San Bernardino, CA 92413 Tel 714-886-5361 (SAN 213-2982).

Churchill Livingstone Inc., *(Churchill; 0-443),* 1560 Broadway, New York, NY 10036 Tel 212-921-0430 (SAN 281-501X); Dist. by: J.A. Majors Co., 3770 Zip Industrial Blvd., Atlanta, GA 30354 (SAN 169-8117); Dist. by: Brown & Connolly, Inc., 2 Keithway, Hingham, MA 02043 Tel 617-749-8570 (SAN 169-3298); Dist. by: Login Brothers Books Co, Inc., 1450 W. Randolph St., Chicago, IL 60607 (SAN 169-183X); Dist. by: J.A. Majors Co., 2221 Walnut Hill Lane, Irving, TX 75061 (SAN 169-8117); Dist. by: J.A. Majors Co., 1806 Southgate Blvd., Houston, TX 77025 (SAN 281-5060); Dist. by: Eliot Books, Inc., 35-53 24th St., Long Island City, NY 11106 (SAN 281-5079); Dist. by: J.A. Majors Co., 3909 Bienville St., New Orleans, LA 70119 (SAN 169-2984); Dist. by: Rittenhouse Book Distributors, Inc., 251 S. 24th St., Philadelphia, PA 19103 (SAN 169-7560); Dist. by: Medical & Technical Books, Inc., 11511 Tennessee Ave., Los Angeles, CA 90064 (SAN 168-9800).

Churchilliana Co., *(Churchilliana; 0-917684),* 4629 Sunset Dr., Sacramento, CA 95822 (SAN 211-2248) Tel 916-448-7053.

C I B A Medical Education Division, Div. of CIBA-Geigy Corp., *(CIBA Med; 0-914168),* 14 Henderson Dr., West Caldwell, NJ 07006 (SAN 207-2084); Orders to: P.O. Box 12832, Newark, NJ 07101 (SAN 207-2092).

Cibbarelli & Associates, Inc., *(Cibbarelli & Assocs; 0-913203),* 11684 Ventura Blvd., No.295, Studio City, CA 91604 Tel 213-760-8110 (SAN 283-2775).

Cichy, Helen J., Mrs., *(H J Cichy; 0-9601852),* Brandon, MN 56315 (SAN 211-190X).

Cider Mill Press, *(Cider Mill; 0-910380),* P.O. Box 211, Stratford, CT 06497 Tel 203-378-4066 (SAN 201-7792).

Ciga Press, *(Ciga Pr; 0-942574),* Box 654, Fallbrook, CA 92028 Tel 714-728-9308 (SAN 239-6289).

Cilren Co., *(Cilren Co; 0-917096),* 9912 Fair Oaks Blvd., Fair Oaks, CA 95628 Tel 916-961-4830 (SAN 208-5976).

Cimarron Press, Inc., *(Cimarron Pr; 0-9609106),* P.O. Box 851, Amarillo, TX 79105 Tel 806-372-2364 (SAN 241-2888).

Cincinnati Post, *(Cin Post; 0-933002),* 800 Broadway, Cincinnati, OH 45202 Tel 513-352-2000 (SAN 220-4703).

Cinnamon Press Ltd., *(Cinnamon Pr; 0-930612),* Box 426, Denver, CO 80201 (SAN 211-9404).

Circinatum Press, *(Circinatum Pr; 0-931594),* Box 99309, Tacoma, WA 98499 (SAN 211-5522) Tel 206-588-2503.

Circle Fine Art Corp., *(Circle Fine Art; 0-932240),* 232 E. Ohio St., Chicago, IL 60611 (SAN 216-1168).

CIRI-BETH, *(CIRI-BETH; 0-9609834),* 8 Sandy Point West, Gig Harbor, WA 98335 Tel 206-884-4404 (SAN 268-9936).

Cistercian Pubns., Inc., *(Cistercian Pubns; 0-87907),* WMU Sta., Kalamazoo, MI 49008 Tel 616-383-4985 (SAN 202-1668).

Citadel Press, Subs. of Lyle Stuart, Inc., *(Citadel Pr; 0-8065),* 120 Enterprise Ave., Secaucus, NJ 07094 Tel 212-736-0007 (SAN 202-1676).

Citation Press *See Scholastic, Inc.*

Citizen Involvement Training Project, *(Citizen Involve; 0-934210),* c/o Univ. of Massachusetts, 225 Schl. of Education, Amherst, MA 01003 Tel 413-545-2038 (SAN 203-3089).

Citizens Committee for Children of New York, *(Citizens Comm Arms),* 1601 114st S.E., Ste. 151, New York, NY 10010 (SAN 225-9176).

Citizens' Energy Project, *(Citizens Energy; 0-89988),* 1110 Sixth St. N.W., No. 300, Washington, DC 20001 (SAN 213-4799).

Citizens in Defense of Civil Liberties, *(Citizens Defense; 0-9608328),* Suite 918, 343 S. Dearborn St., Chicago, IL 60604 Tel 312-939-2492 (SAN 240-5288).

Citizens Law Library, *(Citizens Law; 0-89648),* 6 W. Loudoun St., P.O. Box 1745, Leesburg, VA 22075 (SAN 211-1543) Moved, left no forwarding address.

City in Print Bibliography, *(City in Print-Bibl Proj; 0-918010),* P.O. Box 40157, Tucson, AZ 85717 (SAN 209-231X); Dist. by: ICU Publisher, P.O. Box 40157, Tucson, AZ 85717 (SAN 219-368X).

City Lights Books, *(City Lights; 0-87286),* 261 Columbus Ave., San Francisco, CA 94133 Tel 415-362-8193 (SAN 202-1684); Dist. by: Subterranean Co., P.O. Box 10233, Eugene, OR 97440 Tel 503-343-6324 (SAN 169-7102).

City Miner Books, *(City Miner Bks; 0-933944),* P.O. Box 176, Berkeley, CA 94701 Tel 415-841-1511 (SAN 222-7010).

City of Edina, *(City Edina; 0-9605054),* 4801 W. 50th St., Edina, MN 55424 Tel 612-927-8861 (SAN 219-774X).

City of Hope, *(City Hope),* 1500 E. Duarte Rd., Duarte, CA 91010 Tel 213-359-8111 (SAN 209-1267).

Civic Data Corp., *(Civic Data; 0-937628),* P.O. Box 54045, Los Angeles, CA 90054 Tel 213-481-1226 (SAN 204-3351).

Civic Education Association, *(Civic Educ Assn; 0-939136),* P.O. Box 1767, Tustin, CA 92681 Tel 714-730-5136 (SAN 239-6823).

Civil War Round Table of New York, *(Civil War; 0-910382),* 168 Weyford Terr., Garden City, NY 11530 (SAN 202-3490).

Claitors Publishing Division, *(Claitors; 0-87511),* 3165 S. Acadian at Interstate 10, Box 239, Baton Rouge, LA 70821 (SAN 206-8346).

Clancy Pubns., Inc., *(Clancy Pubns; 0-940058),* 2505 N. Alvernon Way, Tucson, AZ 85712 Tel 602-327-3476 (SAN 220-2107).

Clare Company, *(Clare Co; 0-918848),* 8001 Lockwood Ave., Skokie, IL 60077 (SAN 210-4040).

Claremont Graduate School, Center for Developmental Studies in Education, *(Claremont Grad; 0-941742),* Harper Hall 200, Claremont, CA 91711 Tel 714-621-8075 (SAN 239-1813).

Claremont House, *(Claremont House; 0-913860),* 231 E. San Fernando St., No. 1, San Jose, CA 95112 Tel 408-293-8650 (SAN 203-3606).

Claremont Press, *(Claremont CA; 0-941358),* P.O. Box 4976, Thousand Oaks, CA 91359 (SAN 240-8694).

Claremont Research and Publications, Inc., *(Claremont; 0-912439),* 160 Claremont Ave., New York, NY 10027 Tel 212-662-0707 (SAN 265-2196).

Claremont Press, *(Claremont Pr),* Box 177, Cooper Sta., New York, NY 10003 (SAN 219-466X).

Clarence House Pubs., *(Clarence Hse; 0-933810),* 2115 Van Ness Ave., San Francisco, CA 94109 Tel 415-441-7745 (SAN 212-8934).

Claretian Pubns., *(Claretian Pubns; 0-89570),* 221 W. Madison St., Chicago, IL 60606 Tel 312-236-7782 (SAN 207-5598).

Clarion Books *See Houghton Mifflin Co.*

Clarity Publishing, *(Clarity Pub; 0-915488),* CRUX 75 Champlain St., Albany, NY 12204 Tel 518-465-4591 (SAN 211-5093); 800 North Pearl, Albany, NY 12204 (SAN 211-5107).

Clark, Arthur H., Co., *(A H Clark; 0-87062),* P.O. Box 230, Glendale, CA 91209 Tel 213-245-9119 (SAN 201-2006).

Clark, I.E., Inc., *(I E Clark; 0-88680),* St. Johns Rd., Schulenburg, TX 78956 Tel 409-743-3232 (SAN 282-7433).

Clark, Merrian E., *(M Clark; 0-910384),* 22151 Clarendon St., P.O. Box 505, Woodland Hills, CA 91365 Tel 213-347-1677 (SAN 203-9419).

Clark County Historical Society, *(Clark County Hist Soc),* 300 W. Main St., Springfield, OH 45504 Tel 513-324-0657 (SAN 204-3378).

Clark Publishing Co., *(Clark Pub; 0-931054),* Dist. by: The Caxton Printers, Ltd., P.O. Box 700, Caldwell, ID 83605 Tel 208-459-7421 (SAN 201-9698).

Clark Publishing, Inc., *(Clark Inc; 0-913821),* P.O. Box 11003, Tacoma, WA 98411 Tel 206-472-4469 (SAN 286-0481); P.O. Box 5603, Tacoma, WA 98405 (SAN 286-049X).

Clark Univ. Press, *(Clark U Pr; 0-914206),* 950 Main St., Worcester, MA 01610 Tel 617-793-7206 (SAN 205-6135).

Clarus Music, Ltd., *(Clarus Music; 0-86704),* 340 Bellevue Ave., Yonkers, NY 10703 Tel 914-591-7715 (SAN 216-6615).

Class Media Productions, *(Class Media Prod; 0-942098),* P.O. Box 2436, Seattle, WA 98111 Tel 206-525-9596 (SAN 237-9961).

Classic *See Exposition Press, Inc.*

Classic Car Club of America, *(Classic Car),* P O Box 443, Madison, NJ 07940 (SAN 225-5057).

Classic Furniture Kits, *(Classic Furn Kits),* 343 Lantana St., Camarillo, CA 93010 (SAN 203-6614).

Classic Nonfiction Library, *(Classic Nonfic; 0-9606540),* Woodward, PA 16882 (SAN 203-6622).

Classic Publishers/Louisville, *(Classic Pub; 0-937222),* Prospect, KY 40059 Tel 502-228-4446 (SAN 215-0662).

Classical Folia, *(Classical Folia),* College of the Holy Cross, Worcester, MA 01610 (SAN 207-5369).

Classics Unlimited, Inc., *(Classics Unltd; 0-936660),* 2121 Arlington Ave., Caldwell, ID 83605 (SAN 214-1868).

Clatworthy Colorvues, *(Clatworthy; 0-918290),* 111 1/2 Riverview, Santa Cruz, CA 95062 Tel 408-426-6401 (SAN 209-5424).

Clausen, Muriel C., *(M C Clausen; 0-9603664),* 780 W. Grand Ave., Oakland, CA 94612 (SAN 213-7305).

Claussen Books, *(Claussen Bks; 0-9603266),* 434 Arballo Dr., San Francisco, CA 94132 Tel 415-585-0716 (SAN 211-9412).

Clawson Printing Co., *(Clawson),* 107 W. 2nd, Frankfort, KS 66427 (SAN 215-1367).

Claymont Communications, *(Claymont Comm; 0-934254),* Box 112, Charles Town, WV 25414 Tel 304-725-4437 (SAN 211-7010).

Clayton Publishing House, Inc., *(Clayton Pub Hse; 0-915644),* 6901 Manchester Ave., St. Louis, MO 63143 Tel 314-781-1070 (SAN 158-6807).

Cleaning Consultant Services, Inc., *(Cleaning Consul; 0-9601054),* 1512 Western Ve., Seattle, WA 98101 Tel 206-682-9748 (SAN 208-2179).

Clear Creek Pubs., Inc., *(Clear Creek; 0-9609318),* P.O. Box 8008, Boulder, CO 80306 Tel 303-449-1278 (SAN 260-1753).

Clear Light Pubns., Inc., *(Clear Light; 0-940666),* Box 2520, New York, NY 10163 (SAN 219-7758).

Clear Marks, *(Clear Marks; 0-9602388),* 2219 Grant St., Berkeley, CA 94703 Tel 415-548-3466 (SAN 212-5285).

Clear View Pubns., *(Clear View Pubns; 0-941156),* P.O. Box 3008, Fox Valley Mall, Aurora, IL 60505 (SAN 237-9929).

Clearview Press, *(Clearview Pr; 0-9606976),* 37 Greenway Lane, Port Chester, NY 10573 (SAN 238-9258).

Clearwater Press, *(Clearwater OR; 0-9605512),* 1115 V Ave., La Grande, OR 97855 (SAN 216-1176).

Clearwater Publishing Co., *(Clearwater Pub; 0-8287; 0-88354),* 1995 Broadway, New York, NY 10023 Tel 212-873-2100 (SAN 201-8969) Primarily microfiche on American Indian & peace studies; microfiche distributor for Alpha Com, The Architectural Press, Bibliotheque Nationale, Centre National de Recherche Scientifique (France), Elsevier Sequoia, France Expansion, Interdocumentation Co., Irish Microfilms, Microdditions Hachette, Microeditions Universitaires, Microform Ltd., Mikropress, Georg Olms Verlag, OECD, Oxford University Press Microfiche Editions, Presses de la Fondation National des Sciences Politiques, Publications Orientalistes de France, K G Saur, World Microfilms Publications, Yushodo Film Publications.

Cleis Press, *(Cleis Pr; 0-939416),* P.O. Box 8933, Pittsburg, PA 15221 Tel 612-871-4567 (SAN 284-9968); P.O. Box 14684, San Francisco, CA 94114 (SAN 284-9976).

Clement, David D. & Dorothy Z., , *(D Clement; 0-9601618),* 3931 Villa Ct., Fair Oaks, CA 95628 Tel 916-966-1666 (SAN 210-7112).

Clementine Press, *(Clementine Pr; 0-943880),* 590 Fenelon Pl., Dubuque, IA 52001 Tel 319-588-1828 (SAN 241-1024).

Clene Publications, *(Clene Pubns),* 620 Michigan Ave., N.E. Washington, DC 20064 (SAN 277-6650).

Cleveland-Cliffs, *(Cleveland Cliffs; 0-9607174),* 1460 Union Congress Bldg., Cleveland, OH 44115 Tel 216-241-2356 (SAN 239-0760).

Cleveland Landmarks Press, Inc., *(Cleveland Landmarks; 0-936760),* P.O. Box 9152, Cleveland, OH 44137 (SAN 214-2929).

Cleveland State Univ. Poetry Center, *(Cleveland St Univ Poetry Ctr; 0-914946),* Cleveland State Univ., Cleveland, OH 44115 Tel 216-687-3986 (SAN 209-2816); Dist. by: Nacscorp, Inc. (Poetry Ser. Only), Oberlin, OH 44074 Tel 216-775-1561 (SAN 209-2824); Dist. by: Field (Poetry Ser. only), Oberlin College, Oberlin, OH 44074 Tel 216-775-8408 (SAN 209-2832).

Cleworth, Charles W., Pub., *(C W Cleworth),* 1129 E. 17th Ave., Denver, CO 80218 Tel 303-832-1022 (SAN 212-7326).

Clifford E. Barbour Library, Pittsburgh Theological Seminary, *(Pitts Theolog),* 616 N. Highland Ave., Pittsburgh, PA 15206 Tel 412-362-5610 (SAN 240-981X).

Cliff's Notes, Inc., *(Cliffs; 0-8220),* 1701 "P" St., Lincoln, NE 68501 Tel 402-477-6971 (SAN 202-1706).

Climate Books, *(Climate Bks),* 204 Greens Grove, Washington, GA 30673 Tel 404-678-1823 (SAN 208-2187) Formerly Named Garland Press, Point Blanc Press.

Cline-Sigmon Pubs., *(Cline-Sigmon; 0-914760),* P.O. Box 367-T, Hickory, NC 28601 Tel 704-322-5090 (SAN 205-6151).

Clinical Cardiology Publishing Co., Inc., *(Clinical Cardiology; 0-933682),* The JBI Bldg., Box 521, Mahwah, NJ 07430 (SAN 215-2770).

Clinical Psychology Publishing Co., Inc., *(Clinical Psych; 0-88422),* 4 Conant Square, Brandon, VT 05733 Tel 802-247-6871 (SAN 201-7679).

Clinitemp, Inc., *(Clinitemp; 0-937450),* P.O. Box 40273, Indianapolis, IN 46240 Tel 317-872-4155 (SAN 215-1375).

Clipboard Pubns., *(Clipboard; 0-9606084),* 606 Pine St., Coulee Dam, WA 99116 Tel 509-633-1546 (SAN 216-8006).

Cliveden Press, The, *(Cliveden Pr; 0-941694),* 1629 K St. N.W., Suite 520, Washington, DC 20006 (SAN 277-6669).

Clodele Enterprises, Inc., *(Clodele; 0-930416),* 2004 Vaugine Ave., Pine Bluff, AR 71601 Tel 501-534-8804 (SAN 209-5432).

Clone Records, Inc., *(Clone Records; 0-9606222),* 44 Maple Rd., Rocky Point, NY 11778 Tel 219-7766).

Cloud Enterprises, *(Cloud Ent; 0-911167),* P.O. Box 1006, Orinda, CA 94563 Tel 415-945-1210 (SAN 281-5125); Dist. by: Bookpeople, 2940 Seventh St., Berkely, CA 94710 Tel 415-549-3030 (SAN 168-9517); Dist. by: U.S. Game Systems, 38 E. 32nd St., New York, NY 10016 Tel 212-685-4300 (SAN 282-7336).

Cloud 10 Creations Inc., *(Cloud Ten; 0-910349),* P.O. Box 99, Cazenovia, NY 13035 Tel 315-655-8285 (SAN 241-2896).

Cloudcrest, *(Cloudcrest),* Box 333, Nashville, IN 47448 (SAN 263-9726).

Clyde Press, The, *(Clyde Pr; 0-933190),* 373 Lincoln Pkwy, Buffalo, NY 14216 Tel 716-834-1254 (SAN 213-8395).

Clymer Pubns., *(Clymer Pubns; 0-89287),* 12860 Muscatine St., Arleta, CA 91331 Tel 213-767-7660 (SAN 204-3416).

Coach House Press, Inc., *(Coach Hse),* 53 W. Jackson Blvd., Chicago, IL 60604 Tel 312-922-8993 (SAN 201-7709).

Coalition on Women & Religion, *(Coalition Women-Relig; 0-9603042),* 4759 15th Ave. N.E, Seattle, WA 98105 Tel 206-525-1213 (SAN 210-7880).

Coast Aire Pubns., *(Coast Aire; 0-9606874),* P.O. Box 61, San Luis Obispo, CA 93406 Tel 805-541-3428 (SAN 217-3433).

Coast to Coast Books, *(Coast to Coast; 0-9602664),* 2934 N.E. 16th Ave., Portland, OR 97212 Tel 503-282-5891 (SAN 212-7334).

Coast to Coast Pubns., Inc., *(Coast Pubns NY; 0-915816),* 679A Hempstead Turnpike, Franklin Square, NY 11010 Tel 516-485-4234 (SAN 223-3053).

Coastal Plains Publishing Co., *(Coastal Plains; 0-9607300),* P.O. Box 1101, Danville, VA 24541 Tel 919-379-8778 (SAN 239-183X).

Coates, Pamela, Antiques, *(P Coates; 0-9600678),* 1506 Harvey Rd., Ardencroft, DE 19810 (SAN 207-3919).

Cobbers, Div. of Martensen Co., Inc., *(Cobbers; 0-934680),* P.O. Box 261, Williamsburg, VA 23185 Tel 804-220-2828 (SAN 213-4802).

Cobblesmith, *(Cobblesmith; 0-89166),* Box 191, RFD 1, Freeport, ME 04032 Tel 207-865-6495 (SAN 210-346X).

Cobblestone Publishing, Inc., *(Cobblestone Pub; 0-9607638),* 28 Main St., Peterborough, NH 03458 (SAN 237-9937).

Cobra Press, *(Cobra Pr; 0-9600384),* 15381 Chelsea Dr., San Jose, CA 95124 Tel 408-377-2319 (SAN 203-6657).

Cochrun, Inc., *(Cochrun; 0-9601050),* 11933 72nd Ave., N., Seminole, FL 33542 (SAN 209-0627).

Cocinero Press, *(Cocinero Pr; 0-9606366),* Box 11583, Phoenix, AZ 85061 (SAN 219-7774).

Cockle, George R., Associates, *(G R Cockle; 0-916160),* P.O. Box 1224, Downtown Sta., Omaha, NE 68101 (SAN 211-3104).

Coffee Break Press, *(Coffee Break),* P.O. Box 103, Burley, WA 98322 Tel 206-857-4329 (SAN 212-341X).

Coffeetable Pubns., *(Coffeetable; 0-938252),* P.O. Box 8236, Montgomery, AL 36110 (SAN 215-739X).

Cognition Books, *(Cognition; 0-912881),* P.O. Box 329, Princeton Junction, NJ 08550 Tel 201-545-1286 (SAN 283-281X); 127 Ainsworth Ave., E. Brunswick, NJ 08816 (SAN 283-2828).

Cohasco, Inc., Div. of Snyder Graphics, *(Cohasco; 0-940746),* P.O. Drawer 821, Yonkers, NY 10702 Tel 914-476-8500 (SAN 219-7243).

Coin & Currency Institute, Inc., *(Coin & Curr; 0-87184),* 102 Linwood Plaza, Fort Lee, NJ 07024 Tel 201-461-2626 (SAN 203-5650).

Coker Publishing House, *(Coker Pub; 0-933012),* P.O. Box 70194, Houston, TX 77270 (SAN 284-9984); Orders to: Rt. One, P.O. Box 229J, Gordonville, TX 76245 (SAN 284-9992).

Colburn & Tegg, *(Colburn & Tegg; 0-9600594),* 19709 Hollis Ave., Hollis, NY 11412 Tel 212-468-3278 (SAN 209-1003).

Colby College Press, *(Colby; 0-910394),* Library, Waterville, ME 04901 Tel 207-873-0311 (SAN 203-5669).

Cold Spring Harbor Laboratory, *(Cold Spring Harbor; 0-87969),* P.O. Box 100, Cold Spring Harbor, NY 11724 Tel 516-367-8351 (SAN 203-6185).

Cole, David M./Outreach Books, *(Cole-Outreach),* P.O. Box 425, Corona, CA 91720 Tel 714-735-8701 (SAN 214-2589).

Cole, Jim, *(J Cole; 0-9601200),* c/o Ed & Janet Reynolds, 37 Lomita Dr., Mill Valley, CA 94941 Tel 415-388-1621 (SAN 269-0713).

Cole & Cole Pubns., *(Cole & Cole Pubns; 0-942956),* 941-D McGlincey Lane, Campbell, CA 95008 Tel 408-867-7735 (SAN 240-2084).

Coleman, Candy, Enterprises, *(C Coleman; 0-943768),* 1309 Main St., Suite 103, Dallas, TX 75202 Tel 214-747-0429 (SAN 238-2628).

Coleman, Dorothy S., *(D S Coleman; 0-910396),* 4315 Van Ness St., Washington, DC 20016 Tel 202-966-2655 (SAN 203-8811).

Coleman, Earl M., Enterprises, Inc., *(E M Coleman Ent; 0-930576),* P.O. Box T, Crugers, NY 10521 (SAN 211-1381).

Colgate Univ. Press, *(Colgate U Pr; 0-912568),* 304 Lawrence Hall, Hamilton, NY 13346 Tel 315-824-1000 (SAN 204-3181).

Colgin Publishing, *(Colgin Pub; 0-9604582),* Box 301, Manlius, NY 13104 (SAN 240-0898).

Collaborative Learning Systems, *(Collaborative Learn; 0-910817),* P.O. Box 37043, Tucson, AZ 85740 Tel 602-626-1019 (SAN 269-0721).

Collage, Inc., *(Collage Inc.; 0-938728),* 1200 S. Willis Ave., Wheeling, IL 60090 Tel 312-541-9290 (SAN 238-7298).

Collamore Press See Heath, D.C., Co.

Colleasius Press, *(Colleasius Pr; 0-941036),* P.O. Box 25066, Colorado Springs, CO 80936 Tel 303-599-3083 (SAN 212-1522).

Collector, *(Collector; 0-914638),* P.O. Box 253, Claremont, CA 91711 Tel 714-621-2461 (SAN 203-6193).

Collector Books, *(Collector Bks; 0-89145),* 5801 Kentucky Dam Rd., Paducah, KY 42001 Tel 502-898-6211 (SAN 157-5368).

Collector Circle, *(Collector Circle),* P.O. Box 12600, 1313 S. Killian Dr., Lake Park, FL 33403 (SAN 225-5319).

Collector's Choice, *(Collectors Choice; 0-9602742),* c/o French-Bray Inc., P.O. Box 698, Glen Burnie, MD 21061 Tel 301-768-6000 (SAN 204-2479).

Collectors Club, Inc., *(Collectors; 0-912574),* 22 E. 35th St., New York, NY 10016 Tel 212-683-0559 (SAN 202-1722); Dist. by: Moretus Press, Inc, 274 Madison Ave., New York, NY 10016 Tel 212-685-2250 (SAN 211-2531).

College Administration Publications Incorporated, *(Coll Admin Pubns; 0-912557),* Box 8492, Asheville, NC 28814 Tel 704-253-9851 (SAN 240-8155).

College Board, The, *(College Bd; 0-87447),* 888 Seventh Ave., New York, NY 10106 Tel 212-582-6210 (SAN 203-5677); Orders to: College Board Pubns, P.O. Box 886, New York, NY 10101 (SAN 203-5685).

College-Hill Press, Inc., *(College-Hill; 0-933014),* 4580-E Alvarado Canyon Rd., San Diego, CA 92120 Tel 714-563-8899 (SAN 220-0414).

College Kids Cookbooks, *(Coll Kids Cook; 0-912848),* 624 N. Bailey Ave., Fort Worth, TX 76107 Tel 817-626-4083 (SAN 201-761X).

College of Community Health Sciences, *(Coll Comm Health; 0-817301),* P.O. Box 6291, University, AL 35486 (SAN 287-2684); Dist. by: University of Alabama Press, P.O. Box 2877, University, AL 35486 (SAN 287-2692).

College of Wooster, Office of Pubns., *(Coll Wooster; 0-9604658),* Wooster, OH 44691 Tel 216-263-2000 (SAN 203-5707).

College Outline Series See Barnes & Noble Books

College Outline Series See Harper & Row Pubs., Inc.

College Placement Council, Inc., *(Coll Placement; 0-913936),* 62 Highland Ave., Bethlehem, PA 18017 Tel 215-868-1421 (SAN 201-7822).

College Press Publishing Co., Inc., *(College Pr Pub; 0-89900),* Box 1132, 205 N. Main, Joplin, MO 64802 Tel 417-623-6280 (SAN 211-9951).

College Readings, Inc., *(College Readings; 0-916580),* P.O. Box 168, Clifton, VA 22024 (SAN 206-8354).

College Store, *(Coll Store; 0-910408),* Middlebury College, 5 Hillcrest Rd., Middlebury, VT 05753 Tel 802-388-3711 (SAN 203-5693).

College Survival, Inc., *(Coll Survival; 0-942456),* P.O. Box 8306, Rapid City, SD 57701 Tel 605-394-4847 (SAN 238-1516).

Collegiate Publishing, Inc., *(Collegiate Pub; 0-88429),* 1010 Second Ave., Suite 1808, San Diego, CA 92101 Tel 714-234-3231 (SAN 202-1730).

Collegiate Visitors Guides, *(Collegiate Visitors; 0-9600260),* 170 Bridge Rd., Hillsborough, CA 94010 (SAN 203-5723).

Collegium Book Pubs., Inc., *(Collegium Bk Pubs; 0-89669),* 525 Executive Blvd., Elmsford, NY 10523 (SAN 214-2341).

Collier, Robert, Pub., Inc., *(R Collier; 0-912576),* P.O. Box 3684, Indialantic, FL 32903 (SAN 204-2908).

Collier Books *See Macmillan Publishing Co., Inc.*

Collings, Adam Randolph, Inc., *(A R Collings; 0-933692),* 1201 W. Cerritos, No. 66, Anaheim, CA 92802 (SAN 220-4851).

Collins, William, Pubs., Inc., *(Collins Pubs),* 2080 W. 117th St., Cleveland, OH 44111 Tel 216-941-6930 (SAN 205-4930); 200 Madison Ave., Suite 1405, New York, NY 10016 (SAN 205-4949).

Colman Pubs., *(Colman Pubs; 0-9602456),* 1147 Elmwood, Stockton, CA 95204 Tel 209-946-2148 (SAN 212-4939).

Cologne Press, *(Cologne Pr; 0-9602310),* P.O. Box 682, Cologne, NJ 08213 Tel 609-965-5163 (SAN 214-2937).

Colonial Society of Massachusetts *See Univ. Press of Virginia*

Colonial Williamsburg Foundation, *(Williamsburg; 0-910412; 0-87935),* Publications Dept., P.O. Box C, Williamsburg, VA 23187 Tel 804-229-1000 (SAN 203-297X); Orders to: Products, P.O. Box C, Williamsburg, VA 23187 (SAN 203-2988).

Colophon Book Shop, The, *(Colophon),* P.O. Box E, Epping, NH 03042 Tel 603-679-8006 (SAN 213-8409).

Colophon Books *See Harper & Row Pubs., Inc.*

Color Coded Charting & Filing Systems, *(Color Coded Charting; 0-9605902),* 7759 California Ave., Riverside, CA 92504 Tel 714-688-0800 (SAN 211-1888).

Color Market, Inc., The, *(Color Market; 0-940014),* 3177 MacArthur Blvd., Northbrook, IL 60062 Tel 312-564-3770 (SAN 216-8049).

Colorado Associated Univ. Press, Univ. of Colorado, *(Colo Assoc; 0-87081),* 1338 Grandview Ave. Box 480, Univ. of Colorado, Boulder, CO 80309 Tel 303-492-7191 (SAN 202-1749).

Colorado Big Game Trophy Records, Inc., *(Colo Big Game; 0-9611376),* 2707 Holiday Lane, Colorado Springs, CO 80909 (SAN 283-9385).

Colorado Classics, *(Colo Classics; 0-9607198),* Rt. One, P.O. Box 434, Calhoun, LA 71225 Tel 318-396-1457 (SAN 239-0779).

Colorado College Music Press, *(Colo Coll Music; 0-933894),* Colorado Springs, CO 80903 Tel 303-473-2233 (SAN 213-6600).

Colorado Creative Supply, Inc., *(Colo Creat Supply; 0-911613),* 2900 Cherryridge Rd., Englewood, CO 80110 Tel 303-761-1798 (SAN 263-9734).

Colorado Fiber Center, Inc., *(Colo Fiber; 0-937452),* P.O. Box 2049, Boulder, CO 80306 (SAN 215-1383).

Colorado Railroad Museum, *(CO RR Mus; 0-918654),* P.O. Box 10, Golden, CO 80402 Tel 303-279-4591 (SAN 201-7830).

Colorado River Press, *(Colo River Pr; 0-931302),* Box 8004, Austin, TX 78712 (SAN 211-1179).

Colorado School of Mines, *(Colo Sch Mines; 0-918062),* Publications Dept./Sales, Golden, CO 80401 Tel 303-273-3607 (SAN 201-7962).

Colorado Springs Fine Arts Center, *(CO Springs Fine Arts),* 30 W. Dale St., Colorado Springs, CO 80903 Tel 303-634-5581 (SAN 240-9372).

Colorist Press, The, *(Colorist Pr; 0-9609086),* 25 Colborne Rd., Brighton, MA 02135 Tel 617-254-2458 (SAN 241-4848).

Colourpicture Pubs., Inc., *(Colourpicture; 0-938440),* 76 Atherton St., Boston, MA 02130 (SAN 216-2318); Dist. by: Smith Novelty Co., 460 Ninth St., San Francisco, CA 94103 (SAN 216-2326).

Coltharp Publishing Company, *(Coltharp Pub),* P.O. Box 7461, Amarillo, TX 79109 (SAN 240-1398).

Colton Book Imports, *(Colton Bk),* P.O. Box 526, San Francisco, CA 94101 (SAN 204-7136).

Coltsfoot Press, Inc., *(Coltsfoot; 0-917372),* 234 Fifth Ave., Third Fl., New York, NY 10001 (SAN 208-6042).

Columbia Bookkeeping Systems, Inc., *(Columbia Bookkeeping; 0-9604828),* 21 George St., Lowell, MA 01852 Tel 617-459-2573 (SAN 215-8531).

Columbia Books Inc., Pubs., *(Columbia Bks; 0-910416),* 777 14th St., N.W., Suite 236, Washington, DC 20005 Tel 202-737-3777 (SAN 202-1757).

Columbia College Chicago, *(Columbia College Chi; 0-932026),* c/o Columbia College, 600 S. Michigan Ave., Chicago, IL 60605 Tel 312-663-1600 (SAN 204-3041).

Columbia County Historical Society, *(Columbia County Hist Soc.; 0-88023),* P.O. Box 197, Orangeville, PA 17859 Tel 717-683-6011 (SAN 217-345X).

Columbia House Publishing Corp., *(Columbia Hse Pub; 0-942200),* P.O. Box 1711, Clemson, SC 29633 (SAN 237-9422).

Columbia Language Services, *(Columbia Lang Serv; 0-9604126),* P.O. Box 28365, Washington, DC 20005 Tel 301-587-4979 (SAN 213-9936).

Columbia Pictures Pubns., *(Columbia Pictures; 0-913650),* 16333 N. W. 54th Ave., Hialeah, FL 33014 Tel 412-322-5100 (SAN 203-042X).

Columbia Publishing Co., Inc., *(Columbia Pub; 0-914366),* Drawer AA, Frenchtown, NJ 08825 Tel 201-996-2141 (SAN 201-8977); Dist. by: Vanguard Press, Inc., 424 Madison Ave., New York, NY 10017 Tel 212-753-3906 (SAN 202-9316).

Columbia Scholastic Press Assn., *(Columbia Scholastic; 0-916084),* Box 11, Central Mailroom, Columbia Univ., New York, NY 10027 (SAN 127-9750).

Columbia Univ., Graduate Program in Public Policy & Administration, *(Grad Program; 0-910955),* 420 W. 118th St., New York, NY 10027 (SAN 269-1183).

Columbia Univ., Center for the Social Sciences, *(Columbia U Ctr Soc Sci; 0-938436),* 420 W. 118th St., 814 I.A.B., New York, NY 10027 Tel 212-280-3621 (SAN 215-7403).

Columbia Univ., East Asian Institute, *(Columbia U E Asian Inst; 0-913418),* 420 W. 118th St., New York, NY 10027 Tel 212-280-2591 (SAN 204-1790).

Columbia Univ. Libraries, *(Columbia U Libs),* 535 W. 114th St., New York, NY 10027 (SAN 211-1896).

Columbia Univ., Oral History Research Office, *(Columbia U Oral Hist Res; 0-9602492),* Box 20, Butler Library, New York, NY 10027 Tel 212-280-2273 (SAN 223-4742).

Columbia Univ. Press, *(Columbia U Pr; 0-231),* 562 W. 113th St., New York, NY 10025 Tel 212-678-6777 (SAN 212-2472); Orders to: 136 S. Broadway, Irvington-on-Hudson, NY 10533 Tel 914-591-9111 (SAN 212-2480).

Columbine Press, *(Columbine Pr; 0-9609108),* Box 845, Aspen, CO 81612 Tel 303-925-6025 (SAN 241-483X).

Columella Press, *(Columella Pr; 0-9605972),* 5040 N. 15th Ave., Phoenix, AZ 85015 Tel 602-254-5015 (SAN 216-7427).

Colwell Co., *(Colwell Co),* 201 Kenyon Rd., Champaign, IL 61820 Tel 217-351-5400 (SAN 208-1431).

Colwyn-Tangno, *(Colwyn-Tangno),* 96 Old River Rd., Wilkes Barre, PA 18702 (SAN 215-7411).

Combustion Engineering Power Systems Group, *(Combustion Eng; 0-9605974),* 1000 Prospect Hill Rd., Dept. 7021-1904, Windsor, CT 06095 Tel 203-688-1911 (SAN 216-7255).

Comedy Ctr., The, *(Comedy Ctr),* 700 Orange St., Wilmington, DE 19801 Tel 302-656-2209 (SAN 276-9751).

Comedy Writings & Co., *(Comedy Writ; 0-9609224),* 2034 Grace Ave., Los Angeles, CA 90068 (SAN 240-9771).

Comenius World Council, *(Comenius World; 0-916824),* 247 S. St., Hartford, CT 06114 Tel 203-524-5741 (SAN 208-6050).

Comicana Inc. Book Divison, *(Comicana; 0-940420),* Rfd 2 Box 242 Hickory Kingdom Rd., Bedford, NY 10506 (SAN 219-7782).

Command Productions, *(Command Prods; 0-933132),* Box 26348, San Francisco, CA 94126 (SAN 223-3150).

Commerce Clearing House, Inc., *(Commerce; 0-8080),* 4025 W. Peterson Ave., Chicago, IL 60646 Tel 312-583-8500 (SAN 202-3504).

Commission for the Advancement of Public Interest Organizations, *(Comm Adv Public Interest; 0-9602744),* 1875 Connecticut Ave. N.W., No. 1013, Washington, DC 20009 (SAN 213-0408).

Commission on Chicago Historical & Architectural Landmarks, *(Comm Chi Hist & Arch; 0-934076),* 320 N. Clark, Chicago, IL 60610 (SAN 213-7313); Dist. by: Chicago Review Press, 820 N. Franklin, Chicago, IL 60610 Tel 312-337-5457 (SAN 213-5744).

Commission to Study the Organization of Peace, *(Comm Peace),* 866 United Nations Plaza, New York, NY 10017 (SAN 203-5324).

Committee for Biological Pest Control, *(Comm Bio Pest),* P.O. Box 2810, San Ysidro, CA 92173 Tel 714-234-1492 (SAN 203-574X) Moved, Left No Forwarding Address.

Committee for Economic Development, *(Comm Econ Dev; 0-87186),* 477 Madison Ave., New York, NY 10022 Tel 212-688-2063 (SAN 202-1765).

Committee for Nuclear Responsibility, Inc., *(Comm Nuclear Respon; 0-932682),* Main P.O. Box 11207, San Francisco, CA 94101 Tel 415-776-8299 (SAN 212-1530).

Committee, The, *(Committee IL; 0-937352),* P.O. Box 1082, Evanston, IL 60204 Tel 312-324-4100 (SAN 217-0965).

Committee to Abolish Prison Slavery, *(Comm Abol Prison; 0-910007),* P.O. Box 3207, Washington, DC 20010 Tel 202-797-7721 (SAN 241-3280).

Commodity Research Bureau, Inc., *(Commodity Res; 0-910418),* 1 Liberty Plaza, 47th Floor, New York, NY 10006 Tel 212-267-3600 (SAN 204-3092).

Common Cause, *(Common Cause),* 2030 M St., N.W., Washington, DC 20036 Tel 202-833-1200 (SAN 219-7790).

Common Knowledge Press, Subs. of Commonweal, *(Common Knowledge; 0-943004),* P.O. Box 316, Bolinas, CA 94924 Tel 415-868-0970 (SAN 240-3080).

Common Sense Ltd., *(Com Sense Ltd),* 8060 W. Catherine, Norwood Park, IL 60656 Tel 312-457-0811 (SAN 285-0028); P.O. Box 353, Des Plaines, IL 60016 (SAN 285-0036).

Common Sense Press, Inc., *(Common Sense Pr; 0-917572),* 711 West 17th St. G-4, Costa Mesa, CA 92627 (SAN 209-424X).

Common Women Collective, *(Common Women; 0-9601122),* c/o Women's Center, 46 Pleasant St., Cambridge, MA 02139 Tel 617-354-8807 (SAN 210-1890).

Commonground Press, *(Commonground Pr),* 546 Albany Post Rd., New Paltz, NY 12561 (SAN 211-1187).

Commonwealth Books, Inc., *(Comwealth Bks NJ; 0-940390),* P.O. Box 66, Palisades Park, NJ 07650 (SAN 217-1635).

Commonwealth Press, *(Commonweth Pr; 0-914274),* 44 Portland St., Worcester, MA 01608 Tel 617-755-4391 (SAN 204-3076).

Commonwealth Press, Inc., *(Commonweth Pr; 0-89227),* Box 3547, Radford, VA 24141 Tel 703-639-2475 (SAN 281-515X); Orders to: 415 First St., Radford, VA 24141 Tel 703-639-2476 (SAN 285-5168).

Communication Consultants International, *(Comm Consultants; 0-938320),* P.O. Box 1212, San Diego, CA 92112 (SAN 215-742X).

Communication Creativity, *(Comm Creat; 0-918880),* P.O. Box 213, Saguache, CO 81149 Tel 303-655-2504 (SAN 210-3478).

Communication Materials Center, *(Comm Materials; 0-940912),* 110 Rices Mill Rd., Wyncote, PA 19095 Tel 215-884-0928 (SAN 207-9356).

Communication Press, *(Comm Pr CA; 0-918850),* Box 22541, Sunset Sta., San Francisco, CA 94122 Tel 415-566-3921 (SAN 210-4067).

Communication Skill Builders, Inc., *(Communication Skill; 0-88450),* 3130 N. Dodge Blvd., P.O. Box 42050, Tucson, AZ 85733 Tel 602-323-7500 (SAN 201-7768).

Communication Skills, Inc., *(Comm Skills),* 89 Poinsettia Ave., San Mateo, CA 94403 Tel 415-341-6881 (SAN 263-9742).

Communication Studies, *(Comm Stud; 0-931814),* 6145 Anita St., Dallas, TX 75214 Tel 214-823-1981 (SAN 211-5530).

Communications Media Center, *(Comm Media; 0-941888),* New York Law School School, 57 Worth St., New York, NY 10013 Tel 212-966-2053 (SAN 238-227X).

Communications Press, Inc., *(Comm Pr Inc; 0-89461),* 1346 Connecticut Ave., N.W., Washington, DC 20036 Tel 202-785-0865 (SAN 210-3486).

Communications Research, *(Comm Res; 0-9611910),* P.O. Box 11143, Oakland, CA 94611 Tel 415-339-3550 (SAN 286-0813).

Communications Research Institute, *(CRI),* 25 Central Park West, New York, NY 10023 Tel 212-752-5566 (SAN 211-9420).

Communications Technology, Inc., *(Comm Tech; 0-918232),* Greenville, NH 03048 Tel 603-878-1441 (SAN 210-1912).

Communicative Arts Group, Div. of Beautiful You, Inc., *(Comm Arts; 0-941874),* 1343 Columbia Suite 405, Richardson, TX 75081 Tel 214-690-1200 (SAN 239-1848).

Communicatons Unlimited, *(Comm Unltd),* 11032 Pinyon Dr., Northglenn, CO 80234 (SAN 209-5459).

Community & Family Study Center, *(Comm & Family; 0-89836),* 1411 E. 60th St., Chicago, IL 60637 Tel 312-753-2518 (SAN 212-6486).

Community Builders, *(Comm Builders; 0-9604422),* Canterbury, NH 03224 (SAN 215-3009).

Community Collaborators, *(Comm Collaborators; 0-930388),* P.O. Box 5429, Charlottesville, VA 22905 Tel 804-977-1126 (SAN 213-3008).

Community Council of Greater New York, *(Comm Coun Great NY),* 225 Park Ave., S., New York, NY 10003 Tel 212-777-5000 (SAN 203-0047).

Community for Conscious Evolution, The, *(Comm Con Ev; 0-9607066),* 171 Jackson St., Newton, MA 02159 Tel 617-964-7448 (SAN 238-9657).

Community for Creative Non-Violence, *(Comm Creat Non-Violence; 0-9611972),* 1345 Euclid St. N.W., Washington, DC 20009 Tel 202-332-4332 (SAN 277-6677).

Community Publishing Co., *(Community Pub),* 103 Lewis St., Perth Amboy, NJ 08861 (SAN 201-8993).

Community Service Foundation, *(Comm Serv Found; 0-9608066),* P.O. Box 70, Sellersville, PA 18960 Tel 215-257-4131 (SAN 240-2092).

Community Service, Inc., *(Comm Serv; 0-910420),* P.O. Box 243, Yellow Springs, OH 45387 Tel 513-767-2161 (SAN 203-5758).

Community Service Society of New York, *(Comm Serv Soc NY),* Office of Information 105 E. 22nd St., New York, NY 10010 Tel 212-254-8900 (SAN 204-3149).

Comox Books, Div. of Eric Duncan Literary Properties, *(Comox; 0-912676),* 2611-H San Diego Ave., San Diego, CA 92110 Tel 714-291-4200 (SAN 202-1773).

Compact Books, Inc., *(Compact Bks; 0-936320),* 3014 Willow Lane, Hollywood, FL 33021 Tel 305-983-6464 (SAN 215-3483).

Compact Books, Inc., *(Compact Bks Inc; 0-936320),* 3014 Willow Lane, Hollywood, FL 33021 (SAN 215-0670).

Compass Pubns., *(Compass Pubns NY),* 115 E. 87th St., Box 12-F, New York, NY 10028 Tel 212-289-2368 (SAN 220-3286).

Compass Pubns., Inc., *(Compass Va; 0-910422),* 1117 N. 19th St., Arlington, VA 22209 Tel 703-524-3136 (SAN 203-5774).

CompCare Pubns., *(CompCare Pubns; 0-89638),* 2415 Annapolis Lane, Minneapolis, MN 55441 Tel 612-559-4800 (SAN 211-464X).

Competence Assurance Systems, *(CAS; 0-89147),* Harvard Square, P. O. Box 81, Cambridge, MA 02138 Tel 617-661-9151 (SAN 208-0001).

Competency Press, *(Comp Pr; 0-9602800),* P.O.. Box 95, White Plains, NY 10605 (SAN 223-5579).

Competent Associates, *(Competent Assocs),* P.O. Box 6745, Washington, DC 20020 (SAN 239-5207).

Compose, *(Compose; 0-940042),* P.O. Box 40375, Ft. Worth, TX 76140 Tel 817-457-5252 (SAN 217-1643).

Compsco Publishing Co., *(Compsco; 0-911788),* 663 Fifth Ave., New York, NY 10022 Tel 212-355-5633 (SAN 203-5782).

Compton Press, *(Compton Pr; 0-9607302),* P.O. Box 871, Cathedral Sta., New York, NY 10025 Tel 212-749-5377 (SAN 239-1856).

Compu-Sultants, *(Compu-Sul; 0-9610734),* P.O. Box 17164, Washington, DC 20041 (SAN 264-6609); 2145 Oram Pl., Herndon, VA 22070 Tel 703-471-5541 (SAN 264-6617).

CompuSoft Publishing, Div. of CompuSoft, Inc., *(CompuSoft; 0-932760),* 535 Broadway,, El Cajon, CA 92021 Tel 619-588-0996 (SAN 287-0045); Dist. by: Micromedia Marketing, P. O. Box 4509, Pasadena, CA 91106 (SAN 287-0053); Dist. by: Ingram Book, 347 Reedwood Dr., Box 17266, Nashville, TN 37217 (SAN 287-0061); Dist. by: Golden-Lee Book Distributors, 1000 Dean St., Brooklyn, NY 11238 (SAN 287-007X); Orders to: CompuSoft Publishing, 535 Broadway, El Cajon, CA 92021 Tel 800-854-6505 (SAN 287-0088).

Compute! Publications, Inc., Subs. Of American Broadcasting Companies, Inc., *(Compute Pubns),* Dealer Sales Department, P.O. Box 5406, Greensboro, NC 27403 Tel 800-334-0868 (SAN 284-320X).

Computeach Press, Inc., *(Computeach; 0-9607864),* P.O. Box 20851, San Jose, CA 95160 Tel 408-268-4240 (SAN 238-1532).

Computer Catalog Corp., *(Computer Cat Corp; 0-940562),* P.O. Box C, Sausalito, CA 94966 (SAN 285-6875).

Computer Directions for Schools, *(Computer Direct; 0-912007),* P.O. Box 1136, Livermore, CA 94550 Tel 415-443-0227 (SAN 264-6072); 714 Alban Lane, Livermore, CA 94550 Tel 415-443-0227 (SAN 264-6080).

Computer Language Co., Inc., The, *(Computer Lang; 0-941878),* 140 W. 30th St., New York, NY 10001 Tel 212-736-8364 (SAN 239-1864).

Computer Science Press, Inc., *(Computer Sci; 0-914894),* 11 Taft Court, Rockville, MD 20850 Tel 301-251-9050 (SAN 200-2361).

Computer Strategies, *(Computer Strat; 0-9603584; 0-913505),* 10218 Chimney Hill, Dallas, TX 75243 Tel 214-644-0222 (SAN 213-6589).

Computing Trends, *(Computing Trends),* 6925 56th Ave. S., Seattle, WA 98118 (SAN 212-2111).

Comstock Bonanza Press, *(Comstock Bon; 0-933994),* 18919 William Quirk Memorial Dr., Grass Valley, CA 95945 (SAN 223-694X).

Comstock Editions, Inc., *(Comstock Edns; 0-89174),* 3030 Bridgeway Blvd., Sausalito, CA 94965 Tel 415-332-3216 (SAN 207-6454); Orders to: Comstock Book Distributors Inc., 1380 W. Second Ave., Eugene, OR 97402 Tel 503-686-8001 (SAN 207-6462).

Comstock Publishing Associates, *(Comstock),* Dist. by: Cornell Univ. Press, Sales Manager, 124 Roberts Place, Ithaca, NY 14850 (SAN 281-5672).

Comware Publishing, *(Comware Pub; 0-912441),* 17777 Main St., Suite B-242, Irvine, CA 92714 Tel 714-838-8876 (SAN 265-2226); Dist. by: Publishers Group West, 5855 Beaudry St., Emeryville, CA 94608 Tel 415-658-3453 (SAN 202-8522).

Con Brio Press, *(Con Brio; 0-9602068),* 8708 Morris Rd., Minneapolis, MN 55437 (SAN 212-3428).

Conarc, *(Conarc),* P.O. Box 339, Bethel Island, CA 94511 Tel 415-684-3362 (SAN 241-368X).

Concept Publishing, *(Concept Pub; 0-930726),* P.O. Box 203, York, NY 14592 Tel 716-243-3148 (SAN 211-5549).

Concept Spelling,Inc., *(Concept Spelling; 0-935276),* 630 Skyview, Costa Mesa, CA 92626 Tel 714-966-2382 (SAN 213-909X).

Concepts, *(Concepts),* P.O. Box 6750, Ithaca, NY 14850 Tel 607-272-3346 (SAN 240-821X).

Concepts by Claire, Inc., *(Concepts by Claire; 0-942356),* 174 Popodickon Dr., Boyertown, PA 19512 Tel 215-367-5481 (SAN 239-7188).

Concepts Unlimited, *(Concepts Unlmted; 0-88075),* 179 Cascade Drive, Indian Head Park, IL 60525 (SAN 237-9414).

Conceptual Design, *(Concept Design; 0-9604902),* 9 Glenmore Rd., Troy, NY 12180 Tel 518-283-6467 (SAN 214-3577).

Concern Counts, *(Concern Counts),* 4049 Pennsylvania, Kansas City, MO 64111 (SAN 263-9777).

Concerned Pubns., Inc., *(Concerned Pubns; 0-939286),* P.O. Box 1024, Clermont, FL 32711 Tel 904-429-3022 (SAN 220-1496).

Conch Magazine Ltd. (Pubs.), *(Conch Mag; 0-914970),* 102 Normal Ave., Buffalo, NY 14213 Tel 716-885-3686 (SAN 206-4855).

Concord Press, *(Concord Pr),* P.O. Box 2686, Seal Beach, CA 90740 Tel 213-431-5711 (SAN 206-4669).

Concord Reference Books, Inc., Subs. of Whitney Communications Corp., *(Concord Ref Bks; 0-940994),* 135 W. 50th St., New York, NY 10020 Tel 212-307-1491 (SAN 219-6530).

Concord Student Journal, *(Concordia Student; 0-911770),* c/o Concordia Seminary, 801 DeMun Ave,, St. Louis, MO 63105 Tel 314-721-5934 (SAN 204-3165).

Concordant Publishing Concern, *(Concordant; 0-910424),* 15570 W. Knochaven Rd., Canyon Country, CA 91351 Tel 805-252-2112 (SAN 203-5790).

Concordia Publishing House, *(Concordia; 0-570),* 3558 S. Jefferson Ave., St. Louis, MO 63118 Tel 314-664-7000 (SAN 202-1781).

Concours Publishing, *(Concours Pub; 0-9602644),* 7271 Jurupa Rd., Riverside, CA 92509 Tel 212-8950).

Conditions, *(Conditions),* P.O. Box 56, Van Brunt Sta., Brooklyn, NY 11215 (SAN 219-0796).

Condo Management Maintenance Corp., *(Cond. Mgmt; 0-910049),* P.O. Box 4908, 65 Highway 22, Ste 4B, Clinton, NJ 08809 (SAN 240-8686).

Condor Publishing, *(Condor MA; 0-9606370),* 7 Macarthur Rd., Ashland, MA 01721 (SAN 219-080X).

Conduit, *(Conduit; 0-9631781),* P.O. Box C, Oakdale, IA 52319 (SAN 214-235X).

Confederate Arms Pubs., *(Confed Arms; 0-87833),* P.O. Box 220802, Charlotte, NC 28222 (SAN 281-5230).

Confederate Calender Works, *(Confed Calendar; 0-943030),* P.O. Drawer 2084, Austin, TX 78768 Tel 512-474-2097 (SAN 240-3625).

Conference Board, Inc., The, *(Conference Bd; 0-8237),* 845 Third Ave., New York, NY 10022 Tel 212-759-0900 (SAN 202-179X).

Conference on Economic Progress, *(Conf Econ Prog; 0-910428),* 2610 Upton St., N.W., Washington, DC 20008 Tel 202-363-6222 (SAN 203-5804).

Confluence Press, Inc., *(Confluence Pr; 0-917652),* Spalding Hall, Lewis-Clark Campus, Lewiston, ID 83501 Tel 208-746-2341 (SAN 209-5467).

Congdon & Weed, *(Congdon & Weed; 0-86553),* 298 Fifth Ave., 7th Fl., New York, NY 10001 Tel 212-736-4883 (SAN 214-3585); Dist. by: St. Martin's Press, 175 Fifth Ave., New York, NY 10010 Tel 212-674-5151 (SAN 200-2132).

Congeros Pubns., *(Congeros Pubns; 0-918628),* 123 N. Sultana Ave., P.O. Box 1387, Ontario, CA 91762 (SAN 213-733X); Orders to: Congeros Publications, P.O. Box 1387, Ontario, CA 91762 Tel 213-733X).

Congregation Shaarai Shomayim, *(Cong Shaarai),* 508 N. Duke St., Lancaster, PA 17602 Tel 717-397-5575 (SAN 215-7438).

Congregation Sons of Israel, *(Congr Sons Israel; 0-9603994),* 116 Grandview Ave., Chambersburg, PA 17201 (SAN 239-5215).

Congress of Racial Equality, *(CORE; 0-917354),* 1916-38 Park Ave., New York, NY 10037 Tel 212-694-9300 (SAN 204-2886).

Congress Square Press, (Congress Sq; 0-9611320), P.O. Box 4060, Portland, ME 04101 Tel 207-772-0181 (SAN 283-2763).

Congressional Information Service, Inc., Subs. of Elsevier US Holdings, Inc., (Cong Info; 0-912380), 4520 East-West Hwy., Suite 800, Bethesda, MD 20814 Tel 301-654-1550 (SAN 206-345X) Federal, state, municipal, foreign & international government documents; doucments from nongovernment sources; statistical data, legislative histories; indexes, abstracts, online & microfiche.

Congressional Quarterly, Inc., (Congr Quarterly; 0-87187), 1414 22nd St., N.W., Washington, DC 20037 Tel 202-887-8620 (SAN 202-1803).

Congressional Staff Directory, Ltd., (Congr Staff; 0-87289), P.O. Box 62, Mount Vernon, VA 22121 Tel 703-765-3400 (SAN 203-5820).

Congreve Publishing Co., Inc., (Congreve Pub; 0-930186), P. O. Box 5241, F. D. R. Station, New York, NY 10150 (SAN 281-5486); Orders to: Educational Distribution Center, The Academic Bldg., Saw Mill Rd., West Haven, CT 06516 Tel 203-933-2551 (SAN 281-5494); Dist. by: Richard R. Ryen Associates, 436 Demarest Ave., Oradell, NJ 07649 Tel 201-261-7450 (SAN 282-731X); Dist. by: Nicholas H. Altwerger Co., 19935 Butterneuet, Southfield, MI 48076 Tel 313-424-8198 (SAN 281-5516); Dist. by: Hand Associates, 1238 Campus Dr., Berkeley, CA 04708 Tel 415-848-1064 (SAN 281-5524); Dist. by: Charles Hensley, 2207 Loftin Rd., Waco, TX 76703 Tel 817-776-5687 (SAN 281-5532).

Conifer Publishing Co., (Conifer Pub; 0-942866), 10149 S.W. Barbur Blvd. Dept 175, Portland, OR 97219 Tel 503-246-7418 (SAN 240-2106).

Conjunctions, (Conjunctions; 0-941964), 33 W. Ninth St., New York, NY 10011 (SAN 239-5169).

Connecticut College Bookshop, (Conn Coll Bkshp), New London, CT 06320 Tel 203-443-0025 (SAN 206-4863).

Connecticut Fireside Press, (Conn Fireside), P. O. Box 5293, Hamden, CT 06518 Tel 203-248-1023 (SAN 207-8090).

Connecticut Historical Commission, (Conn Hist Com; 0-918676), 59 S. Prospect St., Hartford, CT 06106 (SAN 223-3223).

Connecticut Historical Society, (Conn Hist Soc), 1 Elizabeth St., Hartford, CT 06105 Tel 203-236-5621 (SAN 204-2843).

Connecticut Law Tribune, (CT Law Trib), 106 Ann St., Hartford, CT 06103 (SAN 237-675X).

Connecting Link, the, (Connecting Link; 0-9608678), S74 W20850 Field Dr., Muskego, WI 53150 Tel 414-679-2520 (SAN 238-2636).

Connections, (Connections CA), Stations 223, P.O. Box 85330, San Diego, CA 92138 Tel 619-272-6565 (SAN 263-9815).

Conner-Sanderson Publications, (Conner & Sanderson; 0-9606904), Dist. by: Coleman Graphics Inc., 99 Milbar Blvd., Farmingdale, NY 11735 (SAN 238-1508).

Connexions, (Connexions; 0-940546), P.O. Box 30580, Seattle, WA 98103 Tel 206-782-7838 (SAN 218-5369).

Connoisseur Enterprises, (Connoisseur; 0-912605), W. 1117 12th Ave., Spokane, WA 99204 Tel 509-624-6756 (SAN 277-6685).

Conquest Corp., (Conquest Corp MI; 0-936682), 2716 Trafford Rd., Royal Oak, MI 48073 (SAN 219-9734).

Conquest Pubns., (Conquest; 0-930220), 203 Wyntfield Dr., Lewisville, NC 27023 Tel 919-945-9686 (SAN 209-6587).

Conroy, Barbara, (B Conroy), 30 Lynx Rd. Box 520, Tabernash, CO 80478 Tel 303-726-5260 (SAN 214-2961).

Conservation Foundation, (Conservation Foun; 0-89164), 1717 Massachusetts Ave. N.W, Washington, DC 20036 Tel 202-797-4300 (SAN 207-6640).

Conservation Press, (Conserv Pr), Australian Government Trade Commission, 636 Fifth Ave., New York, NY 10111 (SAN 238-0528).

Consortium Books *See* **McGrath Publishing Co.**

Constant Society, (Constant Soc; 0-931894), P.O. Box 5513, 4244 Universe Way N.E., Seattle, WA 98105 (SAN 211-4976).

Construction Industry Pr., (Constr Ind Pr; 0-9605442), 1105-F Spring St., Silver Spring, MD 20910 Tel 301-589-4884 (SAN 240-9151).

Construction Pubns., (Construct Pubns; 0-912324), 4552 E. Palomino Rd., Phoenix, AZ 85018 Tel 602-840-3947 (SAN 201-7970).

Construction Sciences Research Foundation, Inc., The, (Construct Sci Res; 0-9605922), 1150 17th St., NW, Suite 300, Washington, DC 20036 Tel 202-216-3527).

Constructive Action, Inc., (Constructive Action; 0-911956), P.O. Box 4006, Whittier, CA 90607 Tel 213-947-5707 (SAN 203-5839).

Constructive Educational Concepts, Inc., (Construct Educ; 0-934734), 213 Duncaster Rd., Box 667, Bloomfield, CT 06002 (SAN 215-7446).

Consultants Bureau *See* **Plenum Publishing Corp.**

Consultants News, (Consultants News; 0-916654), Templeton Rd., Fitzwilliam, NH 03447 Tel 603-585-2200 (SAN 206-4871).

Consulting Psychologists Press, Inc., (Consulting Psychol; 0-89106), 577 College Ave., Palo Alto, CA 94306 Tel 415-857-1444 (SAN 201-7849).

Consumer Associates, (Consumer Assoc; 0-9602442), P.O. Box 13257, Pittsburgh, PA 15243 Tel 412-344-5560 (SAN 222-9722).

Consumer Awareness Learning Laboratory, (Consumer Aware; 0-910599), Rd. 3, Box 237, Fort Elfsborg Rd., Salem, NJ 08079 Tel 609-935-6705 (SAN 260-1761).

Consumer Communications, Ltd., (Consumer Comm Ltd; 0-940060), 5348 Fairfax Dr. NW, Albuquerque, NM 87114 Tel 505-898-2056 (SAN 217-0671).

Consumer Credit Project, Inc., (Consumer Credit Project), 261 Kimberly, Dept. T, Barrington, IL 60010 (SAN 225-6428).

Consumer Information Pubns., (Consumer Info Pubns), 2245 Curlew Rd., Palm Harbor, FL 33563 Tel 813-784-7795 (SAN 220-2395).

Consumer News Inc., (Consumer News; 0-89696), 813 National Press Bldg., Washington, DC 20045 Tel 202-737-1190 (SAN 208-6077).

Consumer Publications, (Consumer Pubn; 0-914087), P.O. Box 465, Kings Park, NY 11754 (SAN 283-9431).

Consumer Publishing Co., (Consumer Pub; 0-9600270), New & Friendship Rds., Vincentown, NJ 08088 (SAN 206-927X).

Consumer's Advisory Press, (Consumers Advisory; 0-9606340), P.O. Box 77107, Greensboro, NC 27407 (SAN 219-0818).

Consumertronics Co., (Consumertronics; 0-934274), 2011 Crescent Dr., P.O. Drawer 537, Almagordo, NM 88310 (SAN 212-7369).

Contact/II Pubns., (Contact Two; 0-936556), P.O. Box 451, Bowling Green, New York, NY 10004 (SAN 200-4151); Dist. by: Inland Book, 22 Hemingway Ave., E. Haven, CT 06512 (SAN 213-9960).

Contemporary Arts Center, the, (Contemp Arts; 0-917562), 115 E. Fifth St., Cincinnati, OH 45202 Tel 513-721-0390 (SAN 210-5551).

Contemporary Arts Press, Div. of La Mameile, Inc., (Contemporary Arts; 0-931818), P.O. Box 3123, Rincon Annex, San Francisco, CA 94119 (SAN 213-3016).

Contemporary Books, Inc., (Contemp Bks; 0-8092), 180 N. Michigan Ave., Chicago, IL 60601 Tel 312-782-9181 (SAN 202-5493) Formerly Named Henry Regnery Co.

Contemporary Perspectives, Inc., (Contemp Perspectives; 0-675), 223 E. 48th St., New York, NY 10017 (SAN 223-1352); Dist. by: A & P Books, P.O. Box 6639, Oakland, CA 94603 (SAN 237-997X).

Contemporary Publishing Co. of Raleigh, (Contemp Pub Co of Raleigh; 0-89892), 508 St. Marys, Raleigh, NC 27605 Tel 919-821-4566 (SAN 213-0424).

Context Pubns., (Context Pubns; 0-932654), 20 Lomita Ave., San Francisco, CA 94122 Tel 415-664-4477 (SAN 212-8977); Dist. by: Bookpeople, 2940 Seventh St., Berkeley, CA 94710 Tel 415-549-3030 (SAN 168-9517); Dist. by: Publishers Group West, 5855 Beaudry St, Emeryville, CA 94608 Tel 415-658-3453 (SAN 202-8522).

Continental Association of Funeral & Memorial Societies, Inc., (Continent Assn Funeral), 1146 19th St N.W., 3rd Flr., Washington, DC 20036 Tel 202-429-1820 (SAN 202-6201).

Continental Divide Trail Society, (Continent Divide; 0-934326), P.O. Box 30002, Bethesda, MD 20814 (SAN 213-0432).

Continental Editions, (Continent Edns; 0-916868), 2300 Indian Hills Dr., 3-231, Sioux City, IA 51104 Tel 712-239-5954 (SAN 208-192X).

Continental Heritage Press, (Continent Herit; 0-932986), P.O. Box 1620, Tulsa, OK 74101 Tel 918-582-6000 (SAN 212-0348).

Continental Media Company, (Continent Media; 0-912349), P.O. Box 31256, Hartford, CT 06103 Tel 203-247-0300 (SAN 265-1114).

Continental Press, Inc., (Continental Pr; 0-8454), 520 E. Bainbridge St., Elizabethtown, PA 17022 Tel 717-367-1836 (SAN 202-182X).

Continental Pubns. Ltd., (Continental CA; 0-916096), 2270 Camino Vida Roble, P.O. Box 1729, Carlsbad, CA 92008 Tel 714-438-7638 (SAN 208-6093).

Continuing Educaion Division *See* **Wadsworth Publishing Co.**

Continuing Education Systems, Inc., (CES; 0-916780), 112 South Grant St., Hinsdale, IL 60521 Tel 312-654-2596 (SAN 208-6107).

Continuing SAGA Press, (Continuing SAGA), 408 1/2 Greenfield Ave, San Anselmo, CA 94960 Tel 415-454-4411 (SAN 215-7454).

Continuity Press, The, (Continuity Pr; 0-939408), Box 243, Pt. Arena, CA 95468 Tel 415-524-7298 (SAN 216-5724).

Continuum Publishing Co., (Continuum; 0-8264), 370 Lexington Ave., New York, NY 10017 Tel 212-532-3650 (SAN 213-8220); Dist. by: Scribner Book Co, 201 Willowbrook Blvd, Wayne, NJ 07470 Tel 212-421-4800 (SAN 282-602X).

Contraband Press, (Contraband), P.O. Box 4073, Sta. A., Portland, ME 04101 (SAN 209-7206).

Contract Data Pubs., (Contract Data; 0-939260), P.O. Box 366, Alta Loma, CA 91701 Tel 714-987-6850 (SAN 220-1666).

Control Data Education Co., (Control Data; 0-918852), P.O. Box O, (HQA03Y), Minneapolis, MN 55440 Tel 612-853-7340 (SAN 204-2525).

Convention of America Instructors of the Deaf, (Con Am Inst Deaf), 5034 Wisconsin Ave Nw, Washington, DC 20016 (SAN 227-7417) Moved, left no forwarding address.

Convex Industries, Inc., (Convex Indus; 0-913920), 4720 Cheyenne, Boulder, CO 80303 Tel 303-494-4176 (SAN 203-5871).

Conway House, (Conway Hse; 0-914402), P.O. Box 424, Bellaire, MI 49615 (SAN 203-6207).

Conway Pubns., Inc., (Conway Pubns; 0-910436), 1954 Airport Rd. NE., Atlanta, GA 30341 Tel 404-458-6026 (SAN 203-1183).

Cook, Chester L., (C L Cook; 0-9604670), P. O. Box 1511, Slidell, LA 70458 Tel 504-643-3254 (SAN 220-1194).

Cook, David C., Publishing Co., (Cook; 0-89191; 0-912692), 850 N. Grove Ave., Elgin, IL 60120 Tel 312-741-2400 (SAN 206-0981).

Cook, Ray G., (R G Cook; 0-9602002), 366 Hooker Ave., Poughkeepsie, NY 12603 (SAN 223-4009).

Cook-McDowell Pubns., (Cook-McDowell), 1233 Sweeney St., Owensboro, KY 42301 (SAN 217-2321).

Cookbook Factory, The, (Cookbook Fact; 0-910983), P.O. Box 11515, Eugene, OR 97440 Tel 503-344-7759 (SAN 262-012X).

Cookbook Pubs., (Cookbook Pubs; 0-934474), Lenexa, KS 66215 Tel 501-741-7340 (SAN 213-2427); Dist. by: Southern Star, Inc., P.O. Box 968, Harrison, AR 72601 (SAN 213-2435).

Cookbooks, Inc., (Cookbooks Inc), 6 Graham Circle, South Attleboro, MA 02703 (SAN 210-8887).

Cooke City Store, (Cooke City; 0-9608876), Box 1097, Cooke City, MT 59020 Tel 406-838-2234 (SAN 241-1040).

Cookie Press, (Cookie Pr; 0-938236), 4225 University, Des Moines, IA 50311 Tel 515-255-3552 (SAN 209-7214).

Cooper, Lee, *(Cooper; 0-9607116),* P.O. Box 4073, Malibu, CA 90265 Tel 213-457-2832 (SAN 281-5591); Orders to: P.O. Box 80584, Fairbanks, AK 99708 Tel 907-474-7931 (SAN 281-5605); Dist. by: Pacific Pipeline, 19215 66th Ave. S., Kent, WA 98031 (SAN 208-2128); Dist. by: Bookpeople, 2940 Seventh St., Berkeley, CA 94710 Tel 415-549-3030 (SAN 168-9517).

Cooper-Hewitt Museum, Subs. of Smithsonian Museum, *(C H Museum; 0-910503),* 2 E. 91st St., New York, NY 10028 Tel 212-860-6868 (SAN 260-0366).

Cooper-Hewitt Museum of Design, *(Cooper-Hewitt),* 9 E. 90th St., New York, NY 10028 (SAN 219-3590); Dist. by: Smithsonian Institution Press, 2280 A&I Bldg., 900 Jefferson Dr., S.W., Washington, DC 20560 (SAN 206-8044).

Cooper Square Pubs., Inc., *(Cooper Sq; 0-8154),* 81 Adams Dr., Totowa, NJ 07512 Tel 201-256-8600 (SAN 281-5621).

Cooperation in Documentation & Communication, *(CoDoC; 0-914958),* 361 Athol Ave., Oakland, CA 94606 (SAN 207-0685).

Coordinating Council of Literary Magazines, *(Coord Coun Lit Mags),* 33 Park Ave., New York, NY 10016 Tel 212-481-5245 (SAN 225-3410).

Copley Books, *(Copley Bks; 0-913938),* P.O. Box 957, 7776 Ivanhoe Ave., La Jolla, CA 92038 Tel 619-454-1842 (SAN 202-1846).

Coppage, A. Maxim, *(A M Coppage),* 1356 Elderberry Dr., Concord, CA 94521 (SAN 238-0536).

Copper Beech Press, *(Copper Beech),* Box 1852, Brown University, Providence, RI 02912 (SAN 212-8063).

Copper Canyon Press, *(Copper Canyon; 0-914742),* P.O. Box 271, Port Townsend, WA 98368 Tel 206-385-4925 (SAN 206-488X).

Copper Orchid Publishing Co., the, *(Copper Orchid; 0-9608522),* 1966 Westbrook Dr., Jackson, MI 49201 Tel 517-750-4625 (SAN 240-6195).

Copple House Books, *(Copple Hse; 0-932298),* Orders to: Copple House Books, Roads' End, Lakemont, GA 30552 Tel 404-782-2134 (SAN 281-5648).

Copy-Write Artograph Co., *(Copy-Write; 0-912392),* 1865 77th St., Brooklyn, NY 11214 Tel 212-236-1459 (SAN 203-588X).

Coraco, *(Coraco; 0-917628),* 1017 S. Arlington Ave., Los Angeles, CA 90019 Tel 213-737-1066 (SAN 203-5898).

Coral Reef Pubns., Inc., *(Coral Reef; 0-914042; 0-86540),* Box 918, Davenport, FL 33837 (SAN 201-775X).

Corban Productions, *(Corban Prods; 0-9608710),* P.O. Box 215, Worthington, OH 43089 Tel 614-889-0102 (SAN 238-0544).

Corbett, Bayliss, *(Bayliss Corbett; 0-933152),* P.O. Box 1526, Bonita Springs, FL 33923 (SAN 212-5935).

Corbett, H. Roger, Jr., *(Corbett),* 8100 Cardiff St., Lorton, VA 22079 Tel 703-550-7317 (SAN 211-1160).

Corcoran, Lawrence, *(L Corcoran),* R. R. 4, Sturgeon Bay, WI 54235 (SAN 212-6494).

Corcoran Gallery of Art, *(Corcoran),* 17th St. & New York Ave. N.W., Washington, DC 20006 Tel 202-638-3211 (SAN 204-2797).

Cordova Printing, *(Cordova),* 10777 Coloma Rd., Rancho Cordova, CA 95670 (SAN 207-5954).

Core Collection Books, Inc., *(Core Collection; 0-8486),* 11 Middle Neck Rd., Great Neck, NY 11021 Tel 516-466-3676 (SAN 208-6123).

Corinth Books, *(Corinth Bks; 0-87091),* 6912 Ridgewood Ave., Chevy Chase, MD 20815 Tel 301-652-1016 (SAN 281-5656); Orders to: Bookslinger, 330 E. Ninth St., St. Paul, MN 55101 (SAN 281-5664).

Corinth House Pubs., *(Corinth Hse; 0-938280),* 2238 E. Vermont Ave., Anaheim, CA 92806 Tel 714-635-6930 (SAN 214-3607).

Corinthian Press, The, *(Corinthian; 0-86551),* 3592 Lee Rd., Shaker Heights, OH 44120 Tel 216-751-7300 (SAN 216-1214).

Corita Communications, *(Corita Comm; 0-933016),* 1301 N. Kenter Ave., Los Angeles, CA 90049 Tel 212-2723).

Cornell Daily Sun, Inc., The, *(Cornell Daily; 0-938304),* 109 E. State St., Ithaca, NY 14850 Tel 607-273-3606 (SAN 239-8370).

Cornell Maritime Press, Inc., *(Cornell Maritime; 0-87033),* P.O. Box 456, Centreville, MD 21617 Tel 301-758-1075 (SAN 203-5901).

Cornell Modern Indonesia Project, *(Cornell Mod Indo; 0-87763),* 102 West Ave., Ithaca, NY 14850 Tel 607-256-4359 (SAN 203-591X).

Cornell Univ. Pr., *(Cornell U Pr; 0-8014),* 124 Roberts Pl., P.O. Box 250, Ithaca, NY 14850 Tel 607-257-7000 (SAN 281-5672); Orders to: 714 Cascadilla St., Ithaca, NY 14850 Tel 607-277-2211 (SAN 281-5680).

Cornell Univ., School of Hotel Administration, *(Cornell U Sch Hotel; 0-937056),* 327 Statler Hall, Ithaca, NY 14853 Tel 607-256-5093 (SAN 204-2746).

Cornell Univ., Southeast Asia Program, *(Cornell SE Asia; 0-87727),* 120 Uris Hall, Ithaca, NY 14853 Tel 607-256-2378 (SAN 206-6416).

Cornell Widow, Inc., *(Cornell Widow; 0-9605870),* 104 Willard Straight Hall, Cornell University, Ithaca, NY 14853 (SAN 216-356X).

Corner Book Shop, *(Corner; 0-910442),* 102 Fourth Ave., New York, NY 10003 Tel 212-254-7714 (SAN 203-5928).

Corner House Pubs., *(Corner Hse; 0-87928),* 1321 Green River Rd., Williamstown, MA 01267 Tel 413-458-8561 (SAN 203-5936).

Cornerbrook Press, *(CornerBrook Pr; 0-913523),* Box 106, Lansing, NY 14882 Tel 607-533-4056 (SAN 285-1563); 178 N. Lansing School Rd., RD 1, Groton, NY 13073 Tel 607-256-2106 (SAN 285-1571).

Cornerstone Library, Inc., Div. of Simon & Schuster, Inc., *(Cornerstone; 0-346),* Orders to: Simon & Schuster, Inc., 1230 Avenue of the Americas, New York, NY 10020 Tel 212-245-6400 (SAN 200-2442).

Cornerstone Press, *(Cornerstone Pr; 0-918476),* P.O. Box 28048, St. Louis, MO 63119 Tel 314-752-3703 (SAN 210-0584).

Corning Museum of Glass, *(Corning; 0-87290),* Corning Glass Ctr., Corning, NY 14831 Tel 607-937-5371 (SAN 202-1897).

Cornwall Books, *(Cornwall Bks; 0-8453),* 4 Cornwall Dr., East Brunswick, NJ 08816 (SAN 219-7804).

Corona Publishing Co., *(Corona Pub; 0-931722),* 1037 S. Alamo, San Antonio, TX 78210 Tel 512-227-1771 (SAN 211-8491).

Coronado Press, Inc., *(Coronado Pr; 0-87291),* P.O. Box 3232, Lawrence, KS 66044 Tel 913-843-5988 (SAN 201-7776).

Corporation for Enterprise Development, The, *(Corp Ent Dev; 0-9605804),* 2420 K. St. NW, Washington, DC 20037 Tel 202-298-8771 (SAN 216-5619).

Correlan Pubns., *(Correlan Pubns; 0-913842),* P.O. Box 337, Watsonville, CA 95077 Tel 408-724-1991 (SAN 202-0386).

Corroboree Press, *(Corroboree Pr; 0-911169),* 2729 Bloomington Ave. S., Minneapolis, MN 55407 Tel 612-724-1355 (SAN 269-3925).

Corser, Frank Rose, *(F & R Corser; 0-9608636),* 215 Baseline, San Dimas, CA 91773 (SAN 263-984X).

Corvallis Software, Inc., *(Corvallis Software; 0-942358),* P.O. Box 1412, Corvallis, OR 97339 Tel 503-754-9245 (SAN 237-9406).

Corwin Books, *(Corwin; 0-89474),* One Century Plaza, 2029 Century Park, E., Los Angeles, CA 90067 Tel 213-552-9111 (SAN 208-614X); Dist. by: Independent News, 75 Rockefeller Plaza, New York, NY 10019 (SAN 208-6158).

Cosmic Communication Co., *(Cosmic Comm; 0-912038),* 100 Elm Court, Decorah, IA 52101 Tel 319-382-8350 (SAN 201-9043).

Cosmos Of Humanists Press, *(Cosmos Humanists; 0-913429),* P.O. Box 11143, San Francisco, CA 94101 Tel 415-557-1813 (SAN 285-8827).

Cosmos Store, The, *(Cosmos Store; 0-939540),* 2409 Honolulu Ave., Suite 3, Montrose, CA 91020 Tel 213-790-8569 (SAN 216-6666).

Cosmotic Concerns, *(Cosmotic Concerns; 0-938104),* c/o Jacef Relations, P.O. Box 3574, Granada Hills, CA 91344 (SAN 238-0552).

Cosray Research Institute, *(Cosray Res; 0-9606374),* 2505 S. Fourth East, Salt Lake City, UT 84115 (SAN 216-3578).

Costa, *(Costa),* 23 Old Field Pl., Red Bank, NJ 07701 (SAN 263-9858).

Costano Books, *(Costano; 0-930268),* P.O. Box 791, San Anselmo, CA 94960 Tel 707-762-4848 (SAN 210-3508).

Cottage Books, *(Cottage Bks; 0-911253),* P.O. Box 2071, Silver Spring, MD 20902 Tel 301-649-5433 (SAN 285-0044); 8055 Thirteenth St., Suite 305, ; Dist. by: LIDCO, 2849 Georgia Ave., NW, Washington, DC 20001 Tel 202-328-0191 (SAN 285-0052); Orders to: 8055-Thirteenth St., Suite 305, Silver Spring, MD 20910 Tel 301-585-7262 (SAN 285-0060).

Cottage Industries, *(Cottage Indus; 0-938348),* Box 244, Cobalt, CT 06414 (SAN 215-7462).

Cotton Lane Press, *(Cotton Lane; 0-9604810),* 2 Cotton Lane, Augusta, GA 30902 Tel 404-722-0232 (SAN 281-5699); Dist. by: Pelican Publishing Co., 1101 Monroe St., Gretna, LA 70053 Tel 504-368-1175 (SAN 212-0623); Dist. by: Copple House Books, Road's End, Lakemont, GA 30552 Tel 404-782-2134 (SAN 269-3828).

Cottontail Pubns., *(Cottontail Pubns; 0-942124),* 428 N. Bosart, Indianapolis, IN 46181 (SAN 238-6526); P.O. Box 44761, Indianapolis, IN 46201 (SAN 238-6534).

Cougar Books, *(Cougar Bks; 0-917982),* P.O. Box 22246, Sacramento, CA 95822 Tel 916-428-3271 (SAN 209-4266).

Coughlin, Michael E., Pub., *(M E Coughlin; 0-9602574),* 1985 Selby Ave., St. Paul, MN 55104 Tel 612-646-8917 (SAN 211-5220).

Coulee Press, *(Coulee Pr; 0-9611456),* Box 1744, LaCrosse, WI 54601 Tel 608-785-8171 (SAN 283-1171).

Council for Advancement & Support of Education, *(CASE; 0-911966),* 11 Dupont Circle, Suite 400, Washington, DC 20036 Tel 202-328-5900 (SAN 202-4497); Orders to: CASE Publications Order Dept., P.O. Box 298, Alexandria, VA 22313 (SAN 202-4500).

Council for Career Planning, Inc., *(Coun Career Plan; 0-916340),* 310 Madison Ave., New York, NY 10017 Tel 212-687-9490 (SAN 201-2545).

Council for Exceptional Children, *(Coun Exc Child; 0-86586),* 1920 Association Dr., Reston, VA 22091 Tel 703-620-3660 (SAN 203-5952).

Council for Inter-American Security, *(Coun Inter-Am; 0-943624),* 729 8th St. S.E., Suite 200, Washington, DC 20003 Tel 202-543-6625 (SAN 238-2660).

Council for Inter-American Security Educational Institute, *(Coun Inter Ed; 0-910637),* 729 8th St., SE, No. 300, Washington, DC 20003 Tel 202-543-6748 (SAN 269-4174).

Council for Intercultural Studies & Programs, *(CISP; 0-939288),* 777 United Nations Plaza, Suite 9H, New York, NY 10017 (SAN 220-2417).

Council for Social & Economic Studies, Inc., *(Coun Soc Econ),* Suite 520, 1629 K St. N.W., Washington, DC 20006 (SAN 238-0560).

Council of Biology Editors, *(Coun Biology Eds; 0-914340),* 9650 Rockville Pike, Bethesda, MD 20814 (SAN 207-0693).

Council of Europe, European Committee on Crime Problems Publication Section, *(CE Crime Pubns),* 67006 Strasbourg, France, ; Dist. by: Manhattan Publishing Company, 225 Lafayette Street, New York, NY 10012 (SAN 237-6962).

Council of Independent Colleges, *(Coun Indep Colleges; 0-937012),* One Dupont Circle, Suite 320, Washington, DC 20036 Tel 202-466-7230 (SAN 213-3024).

Council of New York Law Associates, *(Coun NY Law),* 36 W 44th St., New York, NY 10036 (SAN 237-6997).

Council of State Governments, *(Coun State Govts; 0-87292),* Iron Works Pike, P.O. Box 11910, Lexington, KY 40578 Tel 606-252-2291 (SAN 225-1264).

Council of State Planning Agencies, The, *(Coun State Plan; 0-934842),* 444 N. Capital St., Washington, DC 20001 Tel 202-624-5386 (SAN 213-3032).

Council of the Americas *See* Unipub

Council on American Affairs, *(Coun Am Affairs; 0-930690),* 1629 K St., N.W., Suite 520, Washington, DC 20006 Tel 202-789-0231 (SAN 210-1130).

Council on Economic Priorities, Inc., *(CEP; 0-87871),* 84 Fifth Ave., New York, NY 10011 Tel 212-691-8550 (SAN 204-269X).

Council on Foundations, Inc., *(Coun Found; 0-913892),* 1828 "L" St., N.W., Washington, DC 20036 (SAN 210-3524).

Council on Interracial Books for Children, Inc., *(CIBC; 0-930040),* 1841 Broadway, New York, NY 10023 Tel 212-757-5339 (SAN 210-7155).

Council on Municipal Performance, *(Coun on Municipal; 0-916450),* 84 Fifth Ave., New York, NY 10011 Tel 212-243-6603 (SAN 208-6166).

Council on Religion & International Affairs, *(Coun Rel & Intl; 0-87641),* 170 E. 64th St., New York, NY 10021 Tel 212-838-4120 (SAN 203-5960).

Counseling & Consulting Services (CCS) Publications, *(Counsel & Consult; 0-910819),* 4020 Moorpark Ave., Suite 204, San Jose, CA 95117 Tel 408-246-1128 (SAN 262-0146).

Counseling & Stress Research Center, *(Counsel & Stress; 0-912561),* 81 Granite St., New London, CT 06320 (SAN 283-9466).

Counter-Propaganda Press, The, *(Counter-Prop Pr; 0-943468),* P.O. Box 365, Park Forest, IL 60466 Tel 312-534-8679 (SAN 240-6217).

Counting House Publishing Co., *(Counting Hse; 0-915026),* 178 S. Main St., Thiensville, WI 53092 Tel 414-242-2460 (SAN 203-5987).

Country Bazaar Publishing & Distributing, *(Country Bazaar; 0-936744),* Honey Inc. Bldg. Rt.2 Box 190, Berryville, AR 72616 Tel 501-423-3131 (SAN 215-1669).

Country Cooking, *(Country Cooking; 0-940750),* P.O. Box 1563, Woodbridge, VA 22193 Tel 703-670-9093 (SAN 223-128X).

Country Dance & Song Society of America, *(Country Dance & Song; 0-917024),* 505 Eighth Ave., Suite 2500, New York, NY 10018 Tel 212-594-8833 (SAN 208-1423).

Country Garden Press, *(Country Garden; 0-9611974),* 4412 McCulloch St., Duluth, MN 55804 Tel 218-525-3294 (SAN 220-2425).

Country House, The, *(Country Hse; 0-940554),* 15 Thomas Ave., Topsham, ME 04086 Tel 207-729-8941 (SAN 216-3586).

Country Journal Publishing Company, Inc., *(Country Journ; 0-918678),* 205 Main St., Brattleboro, VT 05301 Tel 802-223-3363).

Country Music Foundation Press, *(Country Music Found; 0-915608),* 4 Music Square E., Nashville, TN 37203 Tel 615-256-1639 (SAN 207-5121).

Country Press, *(Country Pr CO),* 1700 Hwy. 6 & 24, Grand Junction, CO 81501 (SAN 207-5989).

Country Press, The, *(Country Pr NY; 0-913174),* 2272 Scottsville Rd., Scottsville, NY 14546 Tel 716-889-9790 (SAN 203-5995).

Country Printing, Inc., *(Country Print),* P.O. Box 240, Pequot Lakes, MN 56472 Tel 218-568-8521 (SAN 208-189X).

Country Productions, *(Country Prods; 0-9606224),* 14237 Detroit Ave., Lakewood, OH 44107 Tel 216-221-4614 (SAN 217-5118).

Country Road Press, *(Country Rd; 0-939596),* 414 W. Jonquil Rd., Santa Ana, CA 92706 Tel 714-836-0458 (SAN 216-6194).

Country Squire, The, *(Country Squire; 0-9609228),* Granville, MA 01034 Tel 413-357-8525 (SAN 241-4864).

Countryman Press, Inc., *(Countryman; 0-914378),* Woodstock, VT 05091 Tel 802-457-1049 (SAN 206-4901). *Imprints:* Foul Play Press (Foul Play).

Countryside Books, *(Countryside Bks; 0-88453),* 1845 N. Farwell Ave., Suite 201, Milwaukee, WI 53202 Tel 414-272-6700 (SAN 201-7954).

Countryside Studio, Inc., *(Countryside Studio; 0-9605428),* P.O. Box 88, Hwy. 25 W., Cottontown, TN 37048 Tel 615-206-1222).

Countway, Francis A., Library of Medicine, *(F A Countway),* 10 Shattuck St., Boston, MA 02115 (SAN 206-4057).

Couple to Couple League, *(Couple to Couple; 0-9601036),* P.O. Box 11084, Cincinnati, OH 45211 Tel 513-661-7612 (SAN 208-1490).

Courier of Maine Books, *(Courier of Maine; 0-913954),* 1 Park Dr., Rockland, ME 04841 Tel 207-594-4401 (SAN 203-6002).

Courier Press, *(Courier Pr; 0-917310),* P.O. Box 482, 300 E. Main St., Murfreesboro, TN 37130 (SAN 208-4139).

Courier Press, *(Courier Pr FL; 0-934602),* 428 N.E. 82nd St. Suite 1, Miami, FL 33138 (SAN 212-9949).

Courseware, Inc., *(Courseware; 0-89805),* 10075 Carroll Canyon Rd., San Diego, CA 92131 Tel 619-578-1700 (SAN 212-4955).

Court Scribe, The, *(Court Scribe; 0-9601572),* 2201 Friendly St., Eugene, OR 94705 Tel 503-343-7562 (SAN 210-8879).

Courtroom Compendiums, *(Courtroom Comp; 0-910355),* 22106 Clarendon, P.O. Box 705, Woodland Hills, CA 91365 Tel 213-884-9039 (SAN 260-0374).

Cove View Press, *(Cove View; 0-913896),* Box 810, Arcata, CA 95521 Tel 707-822-7079 (SAN 220-0422).

Covenant Press, *(Covenant; 0-910452),* 3200 W. Foster Ave., Chicago, IL 60625 Tel 312-478-4676 (SAN 203-6029).

Cover Publishing Co., *(Cover Pub; 0-912912),* P.O. Box 1092, Tampa, FL 33601 Tel 813-886-6818 (SAN 203-6037).

Cow Puddle Press, *(Cow Puddle; 0-9600672),* Sunset Trading Post, Sunset, TX 76270 Tel 817-872-2027 (SAN 206-5282).

Cowley Pubns., *(Cowley Pubns),* 980 Memorial Dr., Cambridge, MA 02138 (SAN 213-9987).

Cox, Harold E., *(Cox; 0-911940),* 80 Virginia Terrace, Forty Fort, PA 18704 Tel 717-287-7647 (SAN 202-1943).

Cox, Willis F., *(W F Cox; 0-9610758),* James Store, VA 23080 (SAN 264-7060).

Coyne & Chenoweth, *(Coyne & Chenoweth; 0-941038),* P.O. Box 546, Millerton, NY 12546 Tel 518-329-1522 (SAN 217-3476).

Coyote Books, *(Coyote; 0-940556),* P.O. Box 629, Brunswick, ME 04011 (SAN 212-6060).

Coyote Love Press, *(Coyote Love; 0-913341),* 27 Deering St., Portland, ME 04101 Tel 207-774-8451 (SAN 283-040X); Dist. by: Maine Writers & Pubs. Alliance, P.O. Box 7542, Portlandrpswell, ME 04112 (SAN 283-0418).

Crabtree Publishing, *(Crabtree; 0-937070),* P.O. Box 3451, Federal Way, WA 98003 (SAN 214-3615).

Craftsman Book Co., *(Craftsman; 0-910460),* 6058 Corte Del Cedro Box 6500, Carlsbad, CA 92008 Tel 714-438-7828 (SAN 159-7000).

Craftways Pubns., *(Craftways; 0-9607224),* 1465 Fourth St., Berkeley, CA 94710 Tel 415-527-4561 (SAN 239-0809).

Cragmont Pubns, *(Cragmont Pubns; 0-89666),* 185 Berry St., Suite 5834, San Francisco, CA 94107 Tel 415-546-0646 (SAN 211-4860).

Craig, James D., *(J D Craig; 0-9602042),* P.O. Box 222204, Carmel, CA 93922 (SAN 212-0356).

Craig, James R., *(J R Craig),* 1542 S. Cody, Lakewood, CO 80226 Tel 303-985-0790 (SAN 263-9874).

Crain Books, Div. of Crain Communications, Inc., *(Crain Bks; 0-87251),* 740 Rush St., Chicago, IL 60611 Tel 312-649-5250 (SAN 207-1967).

Crambruck Press, *(Crambruck; 0-87699),* 381 Park Ave. S., New York, NY 10016 Tel 212-532-0871 (SAN 204-2622).

Cramer Bookstore, *(Cramer Bkstore; 0-913118),* P.O. Box 7235, Kansas City, MO 64113 (SAN 203-607X).

Crampton Associates, Inc., *(Crampton Assoc; 0-9610142),* Box 1214, Homewood, IL 60430 Tel 312-798-3710 (SAN 269-5049).

Cranbrook Institute of Science, *(Cranbrook; 0-87737),* 500 Lone Pine Rd., P.O. Box 801, Bloomfield Hills, MI 48013 Tel 313-645-3255 (SAN 203-6088).

Cranbrook Publishing, *(Cranbrook Pub; 0-9604690),* 2815 Cranbrook, Ann Arbor, MI 48104 (SAN 215-7470).

Crane Publishing Co., Div. of MLP, *(Crane Pub Co; 0-89075),* 1301 Hamilton Ave., Box 3713, Trenton, NJ 08629 Tel 609-586-6400 (SAN 207-1053).

Crane, Russak & Co., Inc., *(Crane-Russak Co; 0-8448),* 3 E. 44th St, New York, NY 10017 Tel 212-867-1490 (SAN 202-1978).

Crawford Aviation, *(Crawford Aviation),* P.O. Box 1262, Torrance, CA 90505 (SAN 213-4810); Dist. by: Aviation Book Co., P.O. Box 4187, Glendale, CA 91202 Tel 213-240-1771 (SAN 213-4993).

Crawford Press, Subs of Amer. Companies, Inc., *(Crawford Pr; 0-88103),* Box 1777, Topeka, KS 66601 (SAN 240-365X); c/o Econo-Clad Books, .

Creation House, *(Creation Hse; 0-88419),* 396 E. St. Charles Rd., Wheaton, IL 60188 Tel 312-653-1472 (SAN 202-2001).

Creation Research Society Books, *(Creation Res),* 5093 Williamsport Dr., Norcross, GA 30071 (SAN 216-2873).

Creation Science Research Center, *(Creation Sci; 0-88213),* P.O. Box 23195, San Diego, CA 92123 Tel 714-569-8673 (SAN 203-6096).

Creations Unlimited, *(Creations Unltd; 0-938900),* P.O. Box 2591, Farmington Hills, MI 48018 (SAN 216-1109).

Creative Arts Book Co., *(Creative Arts Bk; 0-916870),* 833 Bancroft Way, Berkeley, CA 94710 Tel 415-848-4777 (SAN 208-4880).

Creative Arts Development, *(Creat Arts Dev; 0-912801),* 144 Viking Court, Soquel, CA 95073 Tel 408-475-2396 (SAN 277-6693).

Creative Arts Rehabilitation Center, *(CARC; 0-9606876),* 251 W. 51st St., New York, NY 10019 Tel 212-246-3113 (SAN 217-3484).

Creative Associates, *(Creative Assoc; 0-941588),* 1911 N. Higley Rd., Mesa, AZ 85205 Tel 602-985-3724 (SAN 239-0817).

Creative Book Co., *(Creative Bk Co; 0-88409),* 8210 Varna Ave., Van Nuys, CA 91402-5599 Tel 818-988-2334 (SAN 203-610X).

Creative Books, *(Creative Bks; 0-914606),* P.O. Box 5162, Carmel, CA 93921 Tel 408-624-7573 (SAN 203-6215).

Creative Communications, *(Creative Comm; 0-939116),* 6719 Highway 101 West, Port Angeles, WA 98362 Tel 206-928-3805 (SAN 239-684X).

Creative Computing, *(Creative Comp; 0-916688),* One Park Avenue, 7th Floor, New York, NY 10016 Tel 212-725-4290 (SAN 281-5737); 39 E. Hanover Avenue, Morris Plains, NJ 07950 Tel 201-540-0445 (SAN 281-5745).

Creative Curriculum, *(Creative Curriculum),* 4302 Rolla Lane, Madison, WI 53711 (SAN 240-8678).

Creative Education Foundation, Inc., *(Creat Educ Found; 0-930222),* c/o State Univ. College at Buffalo, Chase Hall, 1300 Elmwood Ave., Buffalo, NY 14222 Tel 716-878-6221 (SAN 210-7163).

Creative Education, Inc., *(Creative Ed; 0-87191),* 123 S. Broad St., PO. Box 227, Mankato, MN 56001 Tel 507-388-6273 (SAN 269-512X).

Creative Eye Press, *(Creative Eye; 0-916480),* P.O. Box 4191, Modesto, CA 95352 Tel 209-524-8603 (SAN 208-6182).

Creative Genius, *(Creative Gen; 0-911657),* P.O. Box 20,000, Dept. 203, Houston, TX 77021 (SAN 263-9882).

Creative Homeowner Press, Div. of Federal Marketing Corp., *(Creative Homeowner; 0-932944),* 62-70 Myrtle Ave., Passaic, NJ 07055 Tel 800-631-7795 (SAN 213-6627).

Creative Image Associates, *(Creat Image Assocs; 0-912077),* 101 E. Fowling St., Playa del Rey, CA 90291 Tel 213-821-6788 (SAN 264-7281).

Creative Images Ltd., *(Creative Images; 0-941378),* 12000 Windflower Place, Oklahoma City, OK 73120 Tel 405-755-0099 (SAN 238-9266).

Creative Infomatics, Inc., *(Creative Infomatics; 0-917634),* P.O. Box 1607, Durant, OK 74701 Tel 405-924-0643 (SAN 211-5557).

Creative Learning Co., Inc., *(Creat Learning; 0-941802),* 402 Clydebank Court, Louisville, KY 40243 Tel 502-245-0408 (SAN 239-1929).

Creative Learning Press, Inc., *(Creative Learning; 0-936386),* P.O. Box 320, Mansfield Center, CT 06250 Tel 203-281-4036 (SAN 214-2368).

Creative Literature, Inc., *(Creative Lit; 0-9609110),* P.O. Box 9975, Phoenix, AZ 85068 Tel 602-274-4151 (SAN 281-5753); 1521 E. Flower St., Phoenix, AZ 85014 (SAN 281-5761).

Creative Options Publishing Company, *(Creative Options; 0-938106),* P.O.Box 601, Edmonds, WA 98020 (SAN 240-0901).

Creative Programming, Inc., *(Creat Prog Inc; 0-912079),* 1454 Cloverfield Blvd., Santa Monica, CA 90404 Tel 213-829-1654 (SAN 264-7303).

Creative Pubns., Affiliate of Westinghouse Learning Corp., *(Creative Pubns; 0-88488),* P.O. Box 10328, Palo Alto, CA 94303 Tel 415-968-1101 (SAN 206-7617).

Creative Publishing Co., *(Creative Texas; 0-932702),* P.O. Box 9292, College Sta., TX 77840 Tel 713-846-7907 (SAN 209-3499).

Creative Publishing Corp. of America, *(Creative Amer Pub; 0-9608340),* 633 Jefferson Heights Ave., Jefferson, LA 70121 Tel 504-733-1958 (SAN 239-5320).

Creative Research & Educational Systems for Today, *(Creative Res & Educ; 0-935770),* 168-02 Jewel Ave., Flushing, NY 11365 (SAN 213-9170).

Creative Resource Systems, Inc., *(Creat Resource; 0-938772),* P.O. Box 890, 116 Railroad St., Winterville, NC 28590 Tel 919-756-9658 (SAN 238-7301).

Creative Resources, *(Creat Res OH; 0-910601),* 683 Riddle Rd., Cincinnati, OH 45220 Tel 513-559-1481 (SAN 260-1788).

Creative Roots, Inc., *(Creative Roots),* P.O. Box 401, Planetarium Sta., New York, NY 10024 (SAN 218-4737).

Creative Sales Corp., *(Creative Sales; 0-933162),* 762 W. Algonquin Rd., Arlington Heights, IL 60005 Tel 312-2436).

Creative Storytime Press, *(Creative Storytime; 0-934876),* P.O. Box 572, Minneapolis, MN 55440 Tel 612-926-5986 (SAN 211-6634).

Creative Therapeutics, *(Creative Therapeutics; 0-933812),* 155 County Rd., Cresskill, NJ 07626 (SAN 212-6508).

Creative Ventures, Inc., *(Creat Ventures IN; 0-942034),* P.O. Box 2286, West Lafayette, IN 47906 (SAN 239-5231).

Creativity Unlimited Pr., *(Creativity Unltd Pr; 0-912559),* 30819 Casilina, Rancho Palos Verdes, CA 90274 Tel 213-377-7908 (SAN 282-7646).

Creatures at Large, *(Creatures at Large; 0-940064),* 1082 Grand Teton Dr., Pacifica, CA 94044 Tel 415-359-4341 (SAN 281-577X); P.O. Box 687, Pacifica, CA 94044 (SAN 281-5788).

Credence Pub. Hse., *(Credence Pub Hse; 0-9606226),* P. O. Box 6125, Olympia, WA 98502 Tel 206-866-4648 (SAN 217-5126).

Credit Research Foundation, Inc., *(Credit Res Found; 0-939050),* 3000 Marcus Ave., Lake Success, NY 11042 Tel 516-488-1166 (SAN 204-2606).

Credo Pubns., *(Credo Pubns; 0-939612),* P.O. Box 124, West Stockbridge, MA 01266 Tel 413-528-9634 (SAN 216-5894).

Creek House, *(Creek Hse; 0-9600490),* P.O. Box 793, Ojai, CA 93023 Tel 805-646-3200 (SAN 203-6126).

Crehore, John Davenport, *(Crehore; 0-910466),* 1523 E. 28th Ave., No. 2, Oakland, CA 94601 Tel 415-533-2251 (SAN 203-6134).

Crerar, John, Library, *(Crerar Lib),* 35 W. 33rd St., Pubns. Dept., Chicago, IL 60616 Tel 312-225-2526 (SAN 204-2592).

Crescent Heart Publishing, *(Crescent Heart; 0-9609916),* 1991 Garfield St., Eugene, OR 97405 Tel 503-343-2247 (SAN 262-4664).

Crescent Pubns., Inc., *(Crescent Pubns; 0-914184),* 5410 Wilshire Blvd., Suite 400, Los Angeles, CA 90036 (SAN 202-2036).

Cresset Pubs., *(Cresset Pubs; 0-936082),* 519 E. Tabor Rd., Philadelphia, PA 19120 (SAN 215-9473).

Crest Books *See* **Fawcett Book Group**

Crest Challenge Books, *(Crest Challenge; 0-913776),* 42 Dart St., Loma Linda, CA 92354 Tel 714-796-1536 (SAN 203-6142); Orders to: P.O. Box 993, Loma Linda, CA 92354 (SAN 203-6150).

Crestline Publishing Co., *(Crestline; 0-912612),* 1251 N. Jefferson Ave., Sarasota, FL 33577 Tel 813-955-8080 (SAN 212-2044).

Crestwood House, Inc., *(Crestwood Hse; 0-89686; 0-913940),* P.O. Box 3427, Mankato, MN 56001 Tel 507-388-1616 (SAN 206-3492).

Crime and Justice Foundation, *(Crime & Justice),* 31 St. James Ave. Rm 348, Boston, MA 02116 (SAN 237-5931).

Crime & Social Justice, *(Crime & Soc Justice; 0-935206),* 2701 Folsom, San Francisco, CA 94140 (SAN 213-2133); Dist. by: Synthesis Pubns., P.O. Box 40099, San Francisco, CA 94140 Tel 415-282-5272 (SAN 282-3896).

Criminal Justice Center, *(Criminal Jus Ctr; 0-935530),* Sam Houston State Univ., Huntsville, TX 77341 Tel 713-294-1692 (SAN 217-2348).

Crises Research Press, *(Crises Res Pr; 0-86627),* 301 W. 45th St., New York, NY 10036 (SAN 238-9274).

Crispo, Andrew, Gallery, Inc., *(Crispo Gallery; 0-937014),* 41 E. 57th St., New York, NY 10022 (SAN 214-297X).

Crissey, Harrington E., Jr., *(H E Crissey; 0-9608378),* 1806 Benton St., No. One, Philadelphia, PA 19152 Tel 215-745-8503 (SAN 241-1059).

Criterion Music Corp., *(Criterion Mus; 0-910468),* 6124 Selma Ave., Hollywood, CA 90028 Tel 213-469-2296 (SAN 203-6169); Dist. by: Joe Goldfeder Music Enterprises, P.O. Box 660, Lynbrook, NY 11563 (SAN 203-6177).

Criterion Press, *(Criterion Pr; 0-9609428),* P.O. Box 1014, Torrance, CA 90505 Tel 213-326-3503 (SAN 260-0382).

Crittenden Books, Subs. of Crittenden Financing, Inc., *(Crittenden; 0-913153),* P.O. Box 1150, 14 Commercial Blvd., Novato, CA 94948 Tel 415-883-4042 (SAN 283-2771).

Croft, Inc., *(Croft MD; 0-86673),* 4601 York Rd., Baltimore, MD 21212 (SAN 216-2334).

Crofton Publishing Corp., *(Crofton Pub; 0-89020),* 1501 Beacon St., No.1402, Brookline, MA 02146 Tel 617-738-8117 (SAN 206-7560).

Croissant & Co., *(Croissant & Co; 0-912348),* P.O. Box 282, Athens, OH 45701 Tel 614-593-3008 (SAN 204-255X).

Cromwel Press, *(Cromwel; 0-916298),* P.O. Box 335, Santa Margarita, CA 93453 Tel 805-543-1581 (SAN 210-3540).

Cromwell-Smith Services, *(Cromwell-Smith; 0-933086),* 6322 Via Maria, P.O. Box 1714, La Jolla, CA 92038 (SAN 213-2443).

Croner Pubns., *(Croner; 0-87514),* 211-03 Jamaica Ave., Queens Village, NY 11428 Tel 212-464-0866 (SAN 203-8176).

Cronk, Walter, *(Cronk),* 5825 Eldergardens St., San Diego, CA 92120 (SAN 219-3167).

Crop Science Society of America, *(Crop Soc Sci Am),* 677 S. Segoe Rd., Madison, WI 53711 Tel 608-274-1212 (SAN 213-8247).

Crosby County Pioneer Memorial, *(Crosby County),* P.O. Box 386, Crosbyton, TX 79322 Tel 806-675-2331 (SAN 220-116X).

Crosley, *(Crosley; 0-9603268),* 1515 Kitchen, Jonesboro, AR 72401 Tel 501-935-3928 (SAN 212-8985).

Cross Books, *(Cross Bks; 0-9601672),* 50 MacArthur Dr., North Providence, RI 02911 Tel 401-231-0874 (SAN 211-5239).

Cross Country Press, *(Cross Country; 0-916696),* P.O. Box 146 Sta. A, Flushing, NY 11358 Tel 212-445-4199 (SAN 208-3094).

Cross-Cultural Communications, *(Cross Cult; 0-89304),* 239 Wynsum Ave., Merrick, NY 11566 Tel 516-868-5635 (SAN 208-6212).

Cross Harp Press, *(Cross Harp; 0-930948),* 344 Ranch Rd., Visalia, CA 92291 Tel 209-733-1679 (SAN 223-1050).

Crossbar Enterprises, *(Crossbar Ent; 0-9604994),* 9522 Stevebrook Rd., Fairfax, VA 22032 (SAN 215-6326).

Crosscut Saw Press, *(Crosscut Saw; 0-931020),* Orders to: Bookpeople, 2940 7th St., Berkeley, CA 94710 (SAN 212-6060).

Crossing Press, The, *(Crossing Pr; 0-89594; 0-912278),* Box 640, Trumansburg, NY 14886 Tel 607-387-6217 (SAN 202-2060).

Crossroad Publishing Co., *(Crossroad NY; 0-8245),* 370 Lexington Ave., New York, NY 10017 Tel 212-532-3650 (SAN 287-0118); Dist. by: Sribner Book Co, 201 Willowbrool Blvd, Wayne, NJ 07670 (SAN 287-0126).

Crossroads, *(Crossroads; 0-9603672),* 1824 S. Cloverdale, Los Angeles, CA 90019 (SAN 213-6635).

Crossroads Books with the Public Library of Cincinnati & Hamilton County, *(Crossroad Bks Public; 0-9611380),* 485 Wood Ave., Cincinnati, OH 45220 (SAN 283-9490).

Crossroads Press, *(Crossroads MA; 0-918456),* Epstein Bldg., Brandeis Univ., Waltham, MA 02154 (SAN 216-2342).

Crossroads Press *See* **African Studies Assn.**

Crossroads Press, Inc., *(Crossroads Pr),* P.O. Box 833, Honolulu, HI 96808 Tel 808-521-0021 (SAN 218-6950).

Crossway Books, *(Crossway Bks),* 9825 W. Roosevelt Rd., Westchester, IL 60153 (SAN 217-233X).

Crossway Books *See* **Good News Pubs.**

Crow/Lester D., *(L D Crow; 0-932970),* 5300 Washington, Hollywood, FL (SAN 263-9912).

Crowell, Thomas Y., Co., *(T Y Crowell; 0-690),* 10 E. 53rd St., New York, NY 10022 Tel 212-593-3900 (SAN 210-5918); Dist. by: Harper & Row Pubs., Keystone Industrial Park, Scranton, PA 18512 (SAN 215-3742).

Crowell-Collier Press *See* **Macmillan Publishing Co., Inc.**

Crowell Junior Books *See* **Harper & Row Pubs., Inc.**

Crown Pubs., Inc., *(Crown; 0-517),* 1 Park Ave., New York, NY 10016 Tel 212-532-9200 (SAN 213-4357); 419 Park Ave., New York, NY 10016 (SAN 282-6038). *Imprints:* Arlington House (Arlington Hse); Harmony Books (Harmony); Potter, Clarkson, N. Books (C N Potter Bks).

Cruikshank, Eleanor P., *(Cruikshank),* 194 San Carlos Ave., Sausalito, CA 94965 (SAN 215-7489).

Crumpark Publishing Co. *See* **Crumpler, Gus H.**

Crumpler, Gus H., *(G H Crumpler),* 413 N. Center St., Harrison, AR 72601 Tel 501-741-4612 (SAN 209-1658).

Crusade Pubns, *(Crusade Pubs),* 11326 Ranchito St., El Monte, CA 91732 (SAN 203-8595) Religious Publications Only.

Cruzada Spanish Pubns., *(Cruzada Span Pubns; 0-933648),* P.O. Box 650909, Miami, FL 33165 (SAN 214-2376).

Cryptologia, Div. of Mathmatics Rose-Hulman Institute of Technology, *(Cryptologia; 0-9610560),* 5500 Wabash Ave., Terre Haute, IN 47803 Tel 812-877-1511 (SAN 263-9920).

Crysalis Books (WA) *See* **K.B.S. Press**

Crystal Press, Ltd., *(Crystal Pr; 0-938108),* P.O. Box 215, Crystal Bay, NV 89402 (SAN 239-5282).

Crystal Prism Corp., *(Crystal Prism; 0-940236),* P. O. Box 7387, Menlo Park, CA 94025 Tel 415-851-1633 (SAN 223-2154).

Crystal Publications, *(Crystal Pubns; 0-9610820),* 827 Arlington Ave., Berkeley, CA 94707 Tel 415-526-8736 (SAN 265-2269).

C S A, *(CSA; 0-931202),* 309 Great Rd., Bedford, MA 01730 (SAN 283-2712).

CSA Press, *(CSA Pr; 0-87707),* Lakemont, GA 30552 Tel 404-782-3931 (SAN 207-7329).

Csis *See* **Center for Strategic & International Studies**

CSS Pubns, *(CSS Pubns; 0-942170),* P.O. Box 23, Iowa Falls, IA 50126 (SAN 238-0471).

Cucamonga Press, *(Cucamonga; 0-918190),* P.O. Box 632, Cucamonga, CA 91730 Tel 714-985-1921 (SAN 209-5483).

Cuckoo Bird Press, *(Cuckoo Bird Pr; 0-9606826),* P.O. Box 501, Ansonia Sta., New York, NY 10023 Tel 212-757-2186 (SAN 219-7251).

Cuisinart Cooking Club, *(Cuisinart Cooking; 0-936662),* 411 W. Putnam Ave., Greenwich, CT 06830 (SAN 214-2287).

Cuisine Productions, *(Cuisine Prods; 0-910327),* P.O. Box 795217, Dallas, TX 75379 Tel 214-386-6708 (SAN 241-4902).

Cullins & Cullins, *(Cullins; 0-9608386),* P.O. Box 241, Sloughhouse, CA 95683 Tel 916-687-6745 (SAN 240-530X).

Cultivator's Research Service, *(Cultivators Res Serv),* P.O. Box 447, Tesuque, NH 87574 (SAN 237-9473).

Cultural Assistance Center, *(Cultural Assist; 0-912443),* 330 W. 42nd St., New York, NY 10036 Tel 212-947-6340 (SAN 211-8939).

Cultural Press, *(Cultural Pr; 0-910476),* 517 Madison St., Waukesha, WI 53186 (SAN 203-8757).

Cultural Services, Inc., *(Cultural Serv; 0-913169),* 4550 Montgomery Ave., Suite 606N, Bethesda, MD 20814 Tel 301-654-2092 (SAN 283-0469).

Cultural Studies Institute, *(Cultural Stud Inst; 0-9606058),* P.O. Box 5435, San Jose, CA 95150 Tel 408-297-8557 (SAN 216-8863).

Culver City Cannon Co., *(Culver City; 0-910517),* 4220 Irving Place, Culver City, CA 90230 Tel 213-839-6498 (SAN 260-1796).

Cumberland Journal, *(Cumberland),* P.O. Box 2648, Harrisburg, PA 17105 (SAN 219-161X).

Cumberland Press, *(Cumberland Pr; 0-87027),* 136 Main St., Freeport, ME 04032 Tel 207-865-4951 (SAN 203-2090).

Cummington Publishing, Inc., *(Cummington Pub; 0-938350),* 17 Old Orchard Rd., New Rochelle, NY 10804 (SAN 215-7497).

Cumorah Publishing Co., *(Cumorah Pub; 0-940720),* 572 W. 440 S., Orem, UT 84057 (SAN 238-9282).

Cunningham, Eileen S., *(E S Cunningham),* R.R. 2, Carrollton, IL 62016 (SAN 213-0467).

Cunningham Press, *(Cunningham Pr),* 3063 W. Main, Alhambra, CA 91801 Tel 213-283-8838 (SAN 203-8773); Dist. by: Theosophy Co., 245 W. 33rd St., Los Angeles, CA 90007 (SAN 205-4302).

Cunningham Publishing Company, *(Cunningham Pub Co; 0-911659),* 701 Washington, Box 1345, Buffalo, NY 14205 Tel 416-239-5103 (SAN 263-9947).

Curbstone Press, *(Curbstone; 0-915306),* 321 Jackson St., Willimantic, CT 06226 Tel 203-423-9190 (SAN 209-4282); Orders to: Ziesing Brothers, 768 Main St., Willimatic, CT 06226 Tel 203-423-5836 (SAN 200-4232).

Curbstone Publishing, *(Curbstone Pub NY TX; 0-931604),* P.O. Box 1613, New York, NY 10116 (SAN 281-5796); Orders to: P.O. Box 7445, Austin, TX 78712 Tel 512-444-9463 (SAN 281-580X).

Curran, D. F., Productions, *(D F Curran Prods),* RFD No. 1, P.O. Box 40, Hamburg, WI 54438 (SAN 287-2854).

Current Digest of the Soviet Press, The, *(Current Digest; 0-913601),* c/o Ohio State University, 1314 Kinnear Rd., Columbus, OH 43212 Tel 614-422-4234 (SAN 282-7069).

Current Documents & Info., *(Current Documents),* P.O. Box 1134, Langley Park, MD 20787 (SAN 241-3744).

Current Issues Pubns., *(Current Issues; 0-936012),* 2707 Walker St., Berkeley, CA 94705 Tel 415-549-1451 (SAN 213-9189).

Curriculum Information Center, Inc., *(Curriculum Info Ctr; 0-914608; 0-89770),* Ketchum Place, P.O. Box 510, Westport, CT 06881 Tel 203-226-8941 (SAN 206-3506).

Curry County Historical Society, *(Curry County; 0-932368),* 920 S. Ellensburg, Gold Beach, OR 97444 (SAN 215-7500).

Curson House, Inc. Publishers, *(Curson Hse; 0-913694),* Suite 1001, 1346 Chestnut St., Philadelphia, PA 19107 Tel 215-732-7111 (SAN 203-8781).

Curtin & London, Inc., *(Curtin & London; 0-930764),* 6 Vernon St., Somerville, MA 02145 Tel 617-625-1200 (SAN 281-5818); Dist. by: Van Nostrand Reinhold Co., 135 W. 50th St., New York, NY 10020 Tel 212-265-8700 (SAN 202-5183).

Curtis, Donald A., *(D A Curtis; 0-9610284),* 904 W. Main St., E. Palestine, OH 44413 Tel 216-426-4389 (SAN 263-9971).

Curtis, Ralph, Books, *(R Curtis Bks; 0-88359),* 2633 Adams St., Hollywood, FL 33020 Tel 305-920-5778 (SAN 281-5834); Orders to: P.O. Box 3, Hollywood, FL 33022 Tel 305-920-5778 (SAN 281-5834).

Curtis Instruments, Inc., *(Curtis Instruments; 0-939488),* 200 Kisco Ave., Mt. Kisco, NY 10549 Tel 914-666-2971 (SAN 216-3616).

Curtis Publishing Co., The, Saturday Evening Post Book Div., *(Curtis Pub Co; 0-89387),* 1100 Waterway Blvd., Indianapolis, IN 46206 Tel 317-634-1100 (SAN 216-3624).

Cushing, Helen Grant, *(H G Cushing; 0-9603588),* 339 E. 58th St., New York, NY 10022 (SAN 213-9995); Orders to: G. H. Cushing, 16237 Gledhill St., Sepulveda, CA 91343 (SAN 214-0004).

Cushing, W., Co., *(Cushing Co),* North St., Kennebunkport, ME 04046 Tel 207-967-3711 (SAN 217-4693).

Cushman Pubs., *(Cushman Pubs; 0-9607084),* 7720 Brandeis Way, Springfield, VA 22153 Tel 703-243-4960 (SAN 238-9681).

Custer, Marquis, Pubns., *(Custer; 0-9600274),* 1021 S. Lee Ave., Lodi, CA 95240 Tel 209-368-0502 (SAN 206-9261).

Custom Curriculum Concepts, *(Custom Curriculum; 0-9611480),* P.O. Box 2813, Penton, TX 76202 Tel 713-661-0992 (SAN 285-2373).

Custom Cycle Fitments, *(CCF; 0-940558),* 726 Madrone Ave., Sunnyvale, CA 94086 Tel 408-734-9426 (SAN 223-7644).

Custom House Press, *(Custom Hse; 0-940560),* 2900 Newark Rd., P.O. Box 2369, Zanesville, OH 43701 (SAN 216-3632).

Custom House Pubns., *(Custom Hse Pubns; 0-942086),* 5450 Kleberg, Houston, TX 77056 Tel 713-622-5150 (SAN 238-454X).

Custom Publishing Company, *(Custom Pub Co; 0-942728),* P.O. Box 1412, Costa Mesa, CA 92626 (SAN 281-5850); Orders to: P.O. Box 1412, Costa Mesa, CA 92626 Tel 714-545-4653 (SAN 281-5869).

Cutaway Press, *(Cutaway Pr; 0-9610304),* 476 Bluebird Canon Dr., Laguna Beach, CA 92651 Tel 714-494-1370 (SAN 263-998X).

Cybericonics Institutes, *(Cybericonics; 0-9606980),* 1640 East Hale St., Mesa, AZ 85203 (SAN 237-9430).

Cyclopedia Publishing Co., *(Cyclopedia; 0-914226),* 6 Freedom Rd., Pleasant Valley, NY 12569 (SAN 206-6327).

Cykx Books Pubs., *(Cykx; 0-932436),* P.O. Box 299, Lenox Hill Sta., New York, NY 10021 (SAN 212-1557).

Cyometrics, Inc., *(Cyometrics; 0-943284),* 25 W. Courtland St., Bel Air, MD 21014 Tel 301-838-1144 (SAN 240-6225).

Cypress Grove Corporation, Pubs., *(Cypress Grove; 0-942678),* P.O. Box 223103, Carmel, CA 93922 Tel 408-624-0881 (SAN 240-0693).

DAW Bks., *(DAW Bks; 0-87997),* c/o New American Library, 1633 Broadway, New York, NY 10019 Tel 212-397-8000 (SAN 206-8079).

D & A Publishing Co., *(D & A Pub; 0-931578),* 3123 N. 20th St., Phoenix, AZ 85016 Tel 602-955-8469 (SAN 211-4119).

D&S Pubns., *(D&S Pubns; 0-9607090),* 6334 St. Andrews Circle, Fort Myers, FL 33907 (SAN 238-9290).

D and S Publisher, *(D & S Pubs),* 2030 Calumet St, P O Box 5105, Clearwater, FL 33518 Tel 813-441-8933 (SAN 226-983X).

DBA Books, *(DBA Bks; 0-9605276),* 130 Marlborough St., Boston, MA 02116 Tel 617-739-2200 (SAN 281-5877); 77 Gordon St., Brighton, MA 02135 (SAN 281-5885).

DCT Enterprises, *(DCT Ent; 0-9604998),* 2888 Bluff St., Suite 218, Boulder, CO 80301 (SAN 216-0285) Moved, left no forwardilng address.

D Fox Head Press, *(Fox Head; 0-910521),* 28 Vandeventer Ave., Princeton, NJ 08540 Tel 609-924-9316 (SAN 260-1893).

D. I. Y. Books, Inc., *(DIY Bks; 0-9604036),* P.O. Box 2055, Hollywood, CA 90028 (SAN 239-4219).

D.J.A.'s Writing Circle, *(DJA Writ Circle; 0-9608924),* 2900 Country Club Rd., Jacksonville, NC 28540 Tel 919-346-8976 (SAN 241-0117).

DJC, Inc., A Witty Enterprise, *(Costello and Witty; 0-9609894),* P.O. Box 4307, San Pedro, CA 90731 Tel 213-831-0968 (SAN 269-5596).

DMSO News Service, The, *(DMSO News Serv; 0-940530),* 10149 S.W. Barbur Blvd., Suite 103, Portland, OR 97219 (SAN 223-7571).

D. N. R. Press, *(DNR Pr; 0-9604682),* 441 Hillsmont Place, El Cajon, CA 92020 (SAN 216-7107).

DOK Pubs., Inc., *(DOK Pubs; 0-914634),* 71 Radcliffe Rd., Buffalo, NY 14214 Tel 716-837-3391 (SAN 201-3347).

D.P. Enterprises, *(D P Enter; 0-935208),* P.O. Box 23241, Phoenix, AZ 85063 (SAN 213-4837).

DTW Publications Dance Theatre Workshop, *(Dance Theater; 0-9611382),* 219 W. 19th St., New York, NY 10011 Tel 212-691-6500 (SAN 283-121X).

Da Capo Press, Inc., *(Da Capo; 0-306),* 233 Spring St., New York, NY 10013 Tel 212-620-8000 (SAN 201-2944).

Daan Graphics, *(Daan Grap; 0-9609788),* 906 Lincoln Blvd., Middlesex, NJ 08846 Tel 201-469-1887 (SAN 269-5634).

Dabbs, Jack A., *(Dabbs; 0-911494),* 2806 Cherry Lane, Austin, TX 78703 Tel 512-472-7463 (SAN 205-4248).

Dabney, A. L., *(A L Dabney),* 10441 Goodyear Dr., Dallas, TX 75229 (SAN 212-4092).

DaCa Publishing Co., *(DaCa Pub; 0-917904),* 1636 Monaco Dr., St. Louis, MO 63122 Tel 314-966-5678 (SAN 209-3634).

Dada Center Pubns., *(Dada Ctr; 0-930608),* 2319 W. Dry Creek Rd., Healdsburg, CA 95448 Tel 707-433-1237 (SAN 211-1225).

Dadant & Sons, *(Dadant & Sons),* Hamilton, IL 62341 (SAN 224-1137).

Dade Variety Press, *(Dade Variety Pr),* 18154 N. W. Second Ave., Miami, FL 33169 (SAN 206-7005).

D'Agostino, Lena V., *(L V D'Agostino; 0-9601076),* Davenport Center, NY 13751 Tel 607-278-5808 (SAN 209-2085).

Dahlstrom, Grant, /Castle Press, *(Grant Dahlstrom),* 516 N. Fair Oaks Ave., Pasadena, CA 91103 (SAN 206-7455).

Daily Planet Almanac, Inc., The, *(Daily Planet; 0-939882),* P.O. Box 1641, Boulder, CO 80306 Tel 303-440-0268 (SAN 281-5893); Dist. by: Planet Productions, P.O. Box 1641, Boulder, CO 80306 Tel 415-549-3030 (SAN 282-5899).

Daimax Publishing House, *(Daimax Pub Hse),* Dist. by: Press Pacifica, Ltd., P.O. Box 1227, Kailua, HI 96734 (SAN 169-1635).

Dairy Goat Journal, *(Dairy Goat),* P.O. Box 1808, Scottsdale, AZ 85252 Tel 602-991-4628 (SAN 213-6155).

Daisy Press, *(Daisy; 0-935424),* P.O. Box 884, La Mesa, CA 92041 (SAN 213-7089).

Daisy Pub., Inc., *(Daisy Pub WA; 0-943470),* 429 Boren Ave., N., Seattle, WA 98109 Tel 206-624-8921 (SAN 240-6233).

Dakin, H. S., Co., *(H S Dakin; 0-930420),* 3101 Washington St., San Francisco, CA 94115 (SAN 210-5934).

Dakota Press, *(Dakota Pr; 0-88249),* University of South Dakota, Vermillion, SD 57069 Tel 605-677-5281 (SAN 207-7345).

Dallas Publishing, Inc., *(Dallas Pub; 0-941282),* 4560 Belt Line Rd., Suite 200, Dallas, TX 75234 (SAN 238-9304).

Dalmas & Ricour, *(Dalmas & Ricour; 0-940066),* 6322 Cool Shade Dr., Fayetteville, NC 28303 (SAN 220-2433).

Dalton, Pat, *(Dalton),* 410 Lancaster Ave., Haverford, PA 19041 (SAN 215-9902).

Damas Publishing Co., *(Damas Pub; 0-917268),* 6515 Sunset Blvd., Suite 202, Hollywood, CA 90028 Tel 213-851-4653 (SAN 208-4783).

Damascus House, *(Damascus Hse),* Dist. by: Dial Press, Double Day, 501 Franklin Ave., Garden City L.I., New York, NY 11530 (SAN 201-3231).

Dame, Robert F., Inc., *(Dame Inc; 0-936328),* 511 Research Rd., Richmond, VA 23236 (SAN 223-5757).

Dame Pubns., Inc., *(Dame Pubns; 0-931920),* P.O. Box 35556, Houston, TX 77035 Tel 713-995-1000 (SAN 214-3623).

Damerell Publishing, *(Damerell Pub; 0-911343),* 7 W. 14th St., Apt. 6R, New York, NY 10011 Tel 212-242-8945 (SAN 269-5758).

Damgood Books, *(Damgood Bks; 0-912659),* 10500 National Blvd., Los Angeles, CA 90034 Tel 213-838-7445 (SAN 277-6715).

D'amico, Paul M., *(D'amico; 0-9607270),* Main St., Livingston Manor, NY 12758 (SAN 239-4200).

Damien Dutton Society for Leprosy Aid, *(Damien-Dutton),* 616 Bedford Ave., Bellmore, NY 11710 (SAN 224-3482).

Damon Press, Inc., *(Damon Pr; 0-910641),* Box 224, Leonia, NJ 07605 Tel 201-944-3393 (SAN 262-6144).

Dan River Press, *(Dan River Pr; 0-89754),* P.O. Box 123, S. Thomaston, ME 04858 Tel 207-594-4751 (SAN 212-7377).

Danbury Press, *(Danbury Pr),* P.O. Box 613, Suffern, NY 10901 Tel 914-357-0420 (SAN 213-8905).

Danca, Vince, *(V Danca; 0-9602390),* 1191 Roxbury Close, Rockford, IL 61107 (SAN 212-4971).

Dance Films Assn., Inc., *(Dance Films; 0-914438),* 241 E. 34th St., New York, NY 10016 Tel 212-686-7019 (SAN 266-3522).

Dance Horizons, *(Dance Horiz; 0-87127),* 1801 E. 26th St., Brooklyn, NY 11229 Tel 212-627-0477 (SAN 201-2952).

Dance Magazine, Pub. Div. of Dance Magazine, *(Dance Mag Inc; 0-930036),* 33 W. 60th St., New York, NY 10023 Tel 212-245-9050 (SAN 210-4091).

Dance Notation Bureau Press, *(Dance Notation; 0-932582),* 505 Eighth Ave., New York, NY 10018 Tel 212-736-4350 (SAN 212-3452).

Dancin' Bee Co., *(Dancin Bee; 0-933192),* 107 Maple Ave., Box 237, Ridgely, MD 21660 (SAN 213-4845).

Dandelion House, The, Div. of The Child's World, Inc., *(Dandelion Hse; 0-89693),* P.O. Box 989, Elgin, IL 60120 (SAN 240-8910); Dist. by: Scripture Press, 1825 College Ave., Wheaton, IL 60187 (SAN 222-9471).

Dandelion Press, *(Dandelion Pr; 0-89799),* 184 Fifth Ave., New York, NY 10010 Tel 212-929-0090 (SAN 212-0836).

Dandick Co., The, *(Dandick Co; 0-917546),* P.O. Box 55, Scottsdale, AZ 85252 (SAN 223-5765).

Dandy Lion Pubns., *(Dandy Lion; 0-931724),* P.O. Box 190, San Luis Obispo, CA 93406 Tel 805-544-3598 (SAN 211-5565).

Daneco Pubns., *(Daneco Pubns; 0-910519),* 2708 E. Lake St., No. 201, Minneapolis, MN 55406 Tel 714-689-6936 (SAN 260-180X).

Danforth, Edward J., *(E J Danforth; 0-9601174),* 20 Westwood Dr., Orono, ME 04473 Tel 207-866-2846 (SAN 210-0622).

Dangary Publishing Co., *(Dangary Pub; 0-910484),* 920 Washington Blvd., Baltimore, MD 21230 Tel 301-728-3322 (SAN 204-2398).

Daniel, Sherry, *(Sherry Daniel; 0-9611244),* P.O. Box 567, Fredericksburg, TX 78624 (SAN 283-4251).

Dante Univ. of America Press, Inc., *(Dante U Am; 0-937832),* 21 Station St., P.O. Box 843, Brookline Village, MA 02147 Tel 617-734-2045 (SAN 220-150X).

Dantree Press, *(Dantree Pr; 0-89560),* 44 W. 62nd St., Suite 4F, New York, NY 10023 Tel 212-582-4327 (SAN 211-1713); Orders to: ISBS, Box 555, Forest Grove, OR 97116 (SAN 211-1721).

Danube, Inc., *(Danube Inc; 0-9607208),* 428-7 Silver Oaks Dr., Kent, OH 44240 (SAN 238-9312).

Danubian Press, Inc., *(Danubian; 0-87934),* Rte. 1, Box 59, Astor, FL 32002 Tel 904-759-2255 (SAN 201-8047).

Daratech, Inc., *(Daratech; 0-938484),* 16 Myrtle Avenue, Cambridge, MA 02138 Tel 617-354-2339 (SAN 281-5915); Orders to: P.O. Box 410, Cambridge, MA 02238 Tel 617-354-2339 (SAN 281-5923).

Darby Books, *(Darby Bks; 0-89987),* P.O. Box 148, Darby, PA 19023 Tel 215-583-4550 (SAN 204-2371).

Dare, Inc., *(DARE; 0-943690),* 3628 Grant Ave., Rockford, IL 61103 Tel 815-877-8511 (SAN 238-2695).

Darian Books, *(Darian Bks; 0-910899),* 3008 West Angela Dr., Phoenix, AZ 85023 Tel 602-866-1068 (SAN 269-5898).

Darien House Books, *(Darien Hse; 0-88201),* c/o Images Graphiques, 37 Riverside Dr., New York, NY 10023 Tel 212-787-4000 (SAN 210-4415).

Daring Press, *(Daring Pr; 0-938936),* 1308 Harrison Rd., Canton, OH 44706 (SAN 216-0293).

Dark Horse Inc., *(Dark Horse; 0-937762),* 17705 S. Western Ave., Suite 1, Gardenia, CA 90248 Tel 213-575-6488 (SAN 216-2350).

Dark Sun Pr., *(Dark Sun; 0-937968),* c/o MFA Photography, Rochester Institute of Technology, 1 Lomb Mem. Dr., Rochester, NY 14623 Tel 716-475-2616 (SAN 220-0430).

Darrah, William Culp, *(W C Darrah; 0-913116),* 2235 Baltimore Pike, Gettysburg, PA 17325 Tel 717-334-2272 (SAN 205-4922).

Darrow, Frank M., *(Darrow; 0-912636),* P.O. Box 305, Trona, CA 93562 (SAN 201-4661); 82194 7th St., Argus, CA 93562 (SAN 201-467X).

Dartnell Corp., *(Dartnell Corp; 0-85013),* 4660 Ravenswood Ave., Chicago, IL 60640 Tel 312-561-4000 (SAN 207-5407).

Darvill Outdoor Pubns., *(Darvill Outdoor; 0-915740),* 1819 Hickox Rd., Mt. Vernon, WA 98273 Tel 206-424-1298 (SAN 207-5423).

Darwin Press, Inc., *(Darwin Pr; 0-87850),* P.O. Box 2202, Princeton, NJ 08540 Tel 609-924-3938 (SAN 201-2987).

Darwin Pubns., *(Darwin Pubns; 0-933506),* 850 N. Hollywood Way, Burbank, CA 91505 Tel 213-848-0944 (SAN 207-4370).

Data Dynamics Technology, *(Data Dynamics; 0-86672),* 16704 Marquardt, Cerritos, CA 90701 (SAN 240-9011).

Data Financial Press, *(Data Financial; 0-933088),* P.O. Box 668, Menlo Park, CA 94025 (SAN 212-4106); Dist. by: Caroline House, P.O. Box 801, Menlo Park, CA 94025 Tel 415-321-4553 (SAN 212-4114).

Data House Publishing Co., Inc., *(Data Hse; 0-935922),* 5724 N. Pulaski Ave.,, Chicago, IL 60646 Tel 312-478-0900 (SAN 214-0020).

Data Notes Publishing Co., Div. of A. C. Doyle Publishing, Inc., *(Data Notes Pub),* Box 7234, Houston, TX 77248-7234 (SAN 262-0162).

Database Services, *(Database Serv; 0-939920),* 885 N. San Antonio Rd., Suite H, Los Altos, CA 94022 Tel 415-948-8339 (SAN 216-8073); Dist. by: Online, Inc., 11 Tannery Lane, Weston, CT 06883 Tel 203-227-8466 (SAN 218-8864).

Datamost, Inc., *(Datamost; 0-88190),* 8943 Fullbright Ave., Chatsworth, CA 91311 Tel 213-709-1202 (SAN 264-7311).

Datanet Publishing Group, Inc., *(Datanet Pub; 0-911345),* 575 Madison Ave., Suite 1006, New York, NY 10022 Tel 212-605-0308 (SAN 269-5936).

Datar Publishing Co., *(Datar Pub; 0-931572),* 9351 Ewers Dr., Crestwood, MO 63126 Tel 314-843-5343 (SAN 211-4135).

Datarule Publishing Co., Inc., *(Datarule; 0-911740),* P.O. Box 448, New Canaan, CT 06840 Tel 914-533-2263 (SAN 201-2693).

Daughterayne, *(Daughterayne; 0-942762),* 3844 Third Ave., San Diego, CA 92103 Tel 714-298-4246 (SAN 238-8456).

Daughters of St. Paul, *(Dghtrs St Paul; 0-8198),* 50 St. Paul's Ave., Boston, MA 02130 Tel 617-522-8911 (SAN 203-8900).

D'Aurora Press, *(DAurora Pr; 0-933022),* 190 Cascade Dr., Mill Valley, CA 94941 (SAN 212-4122).

Davenport, Donald Jordan, *(D J Davenport; 0-9606640),* 619 E. Nine Mile Rd., Hazel Park, MI 48030 Tel 313-541-1000 (SAN 219-7278).

Davenport, May, Publishers, *(Davenport; 0-9603118; 0-943864),* 26313 Purissima Rd., Los Altos Hills, CA 94022 Tel 415-948-6499 (SAN 212-467X).

Davey, Daniel, & Co., Inc., Pubs., *(Davey; 0-8008),* P. O. Box 6088, Hartford, CT 06106 Tel 203-525-4334 (SAN 203-882X).

David, Deborah, Press, *(D David Pr; 0-930890),* 11 Arthur's Round Table, Wynnewood, PA 19096 Tel 215-649-0998 (SAN 211-2914).

David & Charles, Inc., *(David & Charles; 0-7153),* P.O. Box 57, North Pomfret, VT 05053 Tel 802-457-1911 (SAN 213-8859).

Davida Pubns., *(Davida Pubns; 0-9603022),* 604 Agana Drive, Grand Junction, CO 81504 Tel 303-434-8538 (SAN 212-1565); Dist. by: Devorss & Co., Marina Del Rey, CA 90291 (SAN 168-9886).

Davidson, Harlan, Inc., *(Harlan Davidson; 0-88295),* 3110 N. Arlington Heights Rd., Arlington Heights, IL 60004 Tel 312-253-9720 (SAN 201-2375).

Davidson, Mary Frances, *(M F Davidson),* Rte. 3, Gatlinburg, TN 37738 Tel 615-436-5429 (SAN 203-8668).

Davis, Duane D., *(D D Davis; 0-9605658),* 123 E. Idaho, Sandpoint, ID 83864 Tel 208-263-3014 (SAN 238-1273).

Davis, Elsie Spry, *(E S Davis; 0-9605618),* 710 Second St., Coronado, CA 92118 (SAN 216-129X).

Davis, F. A., Co., *(Davis Co; 0-8036),* 1915 Arch St., Philadelphia, PA 19103 Tel 215-568-2270 (SAN 200-2078).

Davis, Grant, Co., Inc., *(G Davis; 0-934786),* P.O. Box 692, Lewisville, TX 75067 (SAN 213-2141).

Davis, H.B., Co., *(H B Davis; 0-942016),* 480 Canal Street, New York, NY 10013 (SAN 239-5223).

Davis, K. C., Pub. Co., *(K C Davis),* Univ. of San Diego, San Diego, CA 92110 (SAN 238-0609).

Davis, L., Press, Inc., *(Davis Pr; 0-9607902),* 1125 Oxford Pl., Schenectady, NY 12308 Tel 518-374-5636 (SAN 238-1540).

Davis, O. K., *(O K Davis; 0-9610262),* P.O. Box 1427, Ruston, LA 71270 Tel 318-255-3990 (SAN 264-0015).

Davis, Steve, Publishing, *(S Davis Pub; 0-911061),* P.O. Box 190831, Dallas, TX 75219 Tel 214-522-3174 (SAN 268-8422).

Davis Pubns., Inc., *(Davis Mass; 0-87192),* 50 Portland St., Worcester, MA 01608 Tel 617-754-7201 (SAN 201-3002).

Davis Publishing Co., Inc., *(Davis Pub Co; 0-89368),* 250 Potrero St., Santa Cruz, CA 95060 Tel 408-423-4968 (SAN 201-8152); Orders to: P.O. Box 841, Santa Cruz, CA 95061 (SAN 201-8160).

Davison, Marguerite P., *(M P Davison; 0-9603172),* P.O. Box 263, Swarthmore, PA 19081 Tel 215-769-6254 (SAN 212-498X).

Davison Publishing Co., Inc., *(Davison; 0-87515),* P.O. Box 477, Ridgewood, NJ 07451 Tel 201-445-3135 (SAN 204-2339).

Dawn Heron Press, *(Dawn Heron; 0-939790),* 537 Jones St., No. 9207, San Francisco, CA 94102 Tel 415-564-7021 (SAN 216-8871).

Dawn Horse Press, *(Dawn Horse Pr; 0-913922),* 119 Paul Drive, San Rafael, CA 94903 Tel 707-994-8281 (SAN 201-3029); Dist. by: Dawn Horse Press, P.O. Box 3680, Clearlake Highlands, CA 95422 Tel 707-994-8281 (SAN 201-3029).

Dawn Ministries, *(Dawn Ministries; 0-9605892),* 2789 Mendel Way, Sacramento, CA 95833 (SAN 216-5937).

Dawn Press, *(Dawn Pr; 0-933704),* 1011 Jeffrey Rd., Wilmington, DE 19810 (SAN 221-2269).

Dawn Valley Press, *(Dawn Valley; 0-936014),* P.O. Box 58, New Wilmington, PA 16142 Tel 412-946-2948 (SAN 208-9734).

Dawnfire Books, *(Dawnfire; 0-942058),* 1804 Grant, Berkeley, CA 94703 (SAN 239-4332).

Dawson's Book Shop, *(Dawsons; 0-87093),* 535 N. Larchmont Blvd., Los Angeles, CA 90004 Tel 213-469-2186 (SAN 201-3045).

Day Book Company, *(Day Bk Co; 0-9611310),* 3641 N Maple Ave., Fresno, CA 93726 (SAN 277-6723).

Day-by-Day Books, *(Day-by-Day; 0-941926),* P.O. Box 6376, Bossier City, LA 71111 Tel 318-949-2193 (SAN 238-6216).

Day Care Council of America, Inc., *(Day Care Coun; 0-936746),* Dist. by: Day Care Council of America, Inc., 1602 17th St. NW, Washington, DC 20009 Tel 202-745-0220 (SAN 203-4581).

Day Star, *(Day Star NV; 0-939614),* P.O. Box 14052, Las Vegas, NV 89114 Tel 702-361-3022 (SAN 216-6208).

Day Star Pubs., *(Day Star; 0-932994),* 707 Graham Hill Rd., Santa Cruz, CA 95060 (SAN 212-4130).

Daybreak Press, *(Daybreak Pr; 0-940916),* 646 Dale Court S., St. Paul, MN 55112 (SAN 217-2372).

Dayspring Pubns. of California, *(Dayspring CA),* P.O. Box 1667, Whittier, CA 90609 Tel 213-943-2320 (SAN 219-0826).

Daystar Publishing Co., *(Daystar Pub Co; 0-938962),* P.O. Box 707, Angwin, CA 94508 Tel 707-965-2085 (SAN 281-5974); Dist. by: Bookpeople, 2940 Seventh St., Berkeley, CA 94710 Tel 415-549-3030 (SAN 168-9517); Dist. by: Publisher's Group West, 5855 Beaudry, Emeryville, CA 94608 Tel 415-658-3453 (SAN 202-8522); Dist. by: Distributors, the, 702 S. Michigan, South Bend, IN 46618 Tel 219-232-8500 (SAN 212-0364).

Dayton Hudson Foundation, *(Dayton Hudson; 0-9607450),* 777 Nicollet Mall, Minneapolis, MN 55402 Tel 612-370-6555 (SAN 238-2326).

Dayton Laboratories, *(Dayton Labs; 0-916750),* 3235 Dayton Ave., Lorain, OH 44055 Tel 216-246-1397 (SAN 208-1946).

D.B. Music Company, *(DB Music; 0-942760),* P.O. Box 953, Ojai, CA 93023 Tel 805-646-0086 (SAN 240-2130).

DBC, *(DBC; 0-9608798),* 1164 Mall Rd., Webster, NY 14580 Tel 716-872-0393 (SAN 241-0109).

DBI Books, Inc., *(DBI; 0-910676),* 1 Northfield Plaza, Northfield, IL 60093 Tel 312-441-7010 (SAN 202-9960).

DCA, The Darien Community Assn., Inc., *(DCA),* Orders to: Tory Hole, 274 Middlesex Rd., Darien, CT 06820 (SAN 208-4902).

D'Carlin Publishing, *(DCarlin Pub; 0-939342),* 2729 Carlsbad Blvd.s, Carlsbad, CA 92008 Tel 619-729-7758 (SAN 216-2369).

De Bussy, Carvel, *(C de Bussy; 0-9602260),* 3801 Connecticut Ave. N.W., Washington, DC 20008 (SAN 212-6516).

De Graff, John, Inc., *(De Graff; 0-8286),* Clinton Corners, NY 12514 (SAN 201-3061); Dist. by: International Marine Publishing Co., 21 Elm St., Camden, ME 04843 Tel 207-236-4342 (SAN 202-716X).

De Gruyter, Walter, Inc., *(De Gruyter; 3-11; 0-89925),* 200 Saw Mill River Rd., Hawthorne, NY 10532 Tel 914-747-0110 (SAN 201-3088).

De Karsan Publishing Co., *(De Karsan; 0-9602308),* P.O. Box 28404, San Diego, CA 92128 Tel 714-280-3334 (SAN 210-8941).

De La Ree, Gerry, Publisher, *(De La Ree; 0-938192),* 7 Cedarwood Lane, Saddle River, NJ 07458 Tel 201-327-6621 (SAN 207-8309).

De Serio, Louis F., *(De Serio; 0-9603568),* 1744 N. 93rd St., Mesa, AZ 85207 Tel 602-986-4226 (SAN 213-6163).

De Vorss & Co., *(De Vorss; 0-87516),* P.O. Box 550, Marina Del Rey, CA 90294 Tel 213-870-7478 (SAN 168-9886).

De Young Press, *(De Young Pr; 0-936128),* Box 14, Rte. 2, Hull, IA 51239 (SAN 212-7652).

Deacon Press, The, *(Deacon Pr; 0-940684),* 1244 Brian St., Placentia, CA 92670 Tel 714-524-0939 (SAN 218-5415).

Dead Angel, *(Dead Angel; 0-911757),* 1206 Lyndale Dr. SE, Atlanta, GA 30316 (SAN 264-0031).

Deago Enterprises, *(Deago Ent; 0-910723),* 2017 Murchison Dr., No. 15, Burlingame, CA 94010 Tel 415-829-8634 (SAN 269-6088).

Deal, S., Associates, *(S Deal Assoc; 0-930000),* 1629 Guizot St., San Diego, CA 92107 (SAN 210-4105).

Dean & Associates, *(Dean & Assoc; 0-933370),* P.O. Box 2943, Eugene, OR 97402 (SAN 212-6524).

Dean Co. of Washington, *(Dean Co WA; 0-934256),* 300 Centec Building, 11260 Roger Bacon Dr., Reston, VA 22090 Tel 703-471-1725 (SAN 216-2385).

Dean Pubns., *(Dean Pubns; 0-939052),* 2204 El Canto Circle, Rancho Cordova, CA 95670 (SAN 217-0744).

Deanne II, Incorporated, *(Deanne Inc; 0-9611584),* Rt. Four, Country Club Rd., Carthage, MO 64836 (SAN 285-6654).

Dear Kids Pubs., *(Dear Kids),* Currierville Rd., Newton, NH 03858 Tel 603-382-7503 (SAN 206-4677).

Death Valley 49ers, Inc., *(Death Valley Fortyniners; 0-936932),* c/o Chalfant Press, Box 787, Bishop, CA 93514 Tel 619-873-3535 (SAN 203-6347).

Debron Enterprises, *(Debron; 0-911347),* P.O. Box 8242, Witchita, KS 67208 Tel 316-687-1020 (SAN 269-6118).

DeBruyn & Assoc., Robert L., *(R L DeBruyn),* Leadership Lane, P.O. Box 1207, Manhattan, KS 66502 Tel 240-9046).

Decade Media Books, Inc., *(Decade Media; 0-91036500),* 30 E. 42nd St., Rm. 1110, New York, NY 10017 (SAN 263-2152).

Decatur House Press, Ltd., *(Decatur Hse; 0-916276),* 2122 Decatur Place, N.W., Washington, DC 20008 Tel 202-387-3913 (SAN 208-1539).

DECCOM, *(Deccom; 0-9608350),* P.O. Box 35278, Phoenix, AZ 85069 Tel 602-866-0559 (SAN 240-6241).

December Press, *(December Pr; 0-913204),* 3093 Dato,, Highland Park, IL 60035 Tel 312-432-6804 (SAN 203-8854).

Decibel Books, *(Decibel; 0-914672),* P.O. Box 358, Norman, OK 73070 (SAN 205-616X).

Deciduous, *(Deciduous; 0-9601640),* 1456 W. 54th St., Cleveland, OH 44102 Tel 216-651-7725 (SAN 211-4143).

Decker Press, Inc., *(Decker Pr Inc; 0-933724),* P.O. Box 3838, Grand Junction, CO 81502 Tel 303-241-6193 (SAN 216-115X).

Deco-Press Publishing Co., *(Deco-Pr Pub; 0-937016),* 500 E. 84th Ave., Box 29489, Denver, CO 80229 (SAN 220-2441).

Decorative Design Studio, Inc., *(Deco Design Studio; 0-941284),* Rte. 3, Box 155, Smithsburg, MD 21783 Tel 301-824-7592 (SAN 238-9320).

Dectur Corp., *(Dectur Corp; 0-9602228),* 2878 Forest St., Denver, CO 80207 (SAN 212-4149).

Dee Publishing Co., *(Dee Pub Co; 0-934476),* 864 S. Commercial, Salem, OR 97302 Tel 503-363-2410 (SAN 206-4685).

DEEJ Publishing Co., *(Deej Pub; 0-9608832),* Box A, Stilwell, KS 66085 Tel 816-474-8120 (SAN 241-0133).

Deep River Press, *(Deep River Pr; 0-935232),* 51141/2 E. Second St., P.O. Box 3444, Long Beach, CA 90803 Tel 213-433-8738 (SAN 213-8425).

Deepak, A., Publishing, *(A Deepak Pub; 0-937194),* P.O. Box 7390, 17 Research Dr., Hampton, VA 23666 Tel 804-865-1894 (SAN 240-1606).

Deepstar Pubns., *(Deepstar Pubns; 0-918888),* P.O. Box 1266, Crestine, CA 92325 Tel 714-338-4440 (SAN 210-4121).

Deer Crossing Press, *(Deer Crossing; 0-932792),* Rte. 1, Box 18, Paducah, KY 42001 (SAN 212-1867).

Deere & Co. Technical Services, *(Deere & Co; 0-86691),* Dept. 333, John Deere Rd., Moline, IL 61265 (SAN 216-3659).

Deerfield Enterprises, Inc., *(Deerfield Ent; 0-932002),* 1 Adler Dr., E. Syracuse, NY 13057 Tel 315-463-8875 (SAN 221-2226).

Deermouse Press, *(Deermouse; 0-900596),* 4 Berkeley Place, Cambridge, MA 02138 Tel 617-876-0836 (SAN 201-8039).

Defenders Pubns., *(Defenders Pubns; 0-910643),* P.O. Box 11134, Las Vegas, NV 89111 Tel 702-451-5773 (SAN 269-6207).

Defense & Foreign Affairs Publications Ltd., *(Defense & Foreign Aff; 0-9605932),* 1777 "T" St. N.W., Washington, DC 20009 Tel 202-223-4934 (SAN 216-3551).

Definition Press, *(Definition; 0-910492),* 141 Greene St., New York, NY 10012 Tel 212-777-4490 (SAN 201-310X).

Defoggi, Ernest, *(E Defoggi; 0-9602372),* Rt. 1, Box 514-A, Newport, NC 28570 (SAN 211-3120).

Dehack Effort, *(Dehack),* P. O. Box 922, Campbell, CA 95008 Tel 408-265-8799 (SAN 208-1512).

Deinotation-7 Press, *(Deinotation Seven; 0-9602044),* 220 Exchange St., P.O. Box 194, Susquehanna, PA 18847-0204 (SAN 243-4661).

Dekker, Marcel, Inc., *(Dekker; 0-8247),* 270 Madison Ave., New York, NY 10016 Tel 212-696-9000 (SAN 201-3118).

Del Casa Educational Productions, *(Del Casa Educ),* 175 Fifth Ave., New York, NY 10010 Tel 212-677-2200 (SAN 238-132X).

Del Mar Press, *(Del Mar Pr; 0-9611124),* P.O. Box 2508, Del Mar, CA 92014 Tel 619-481-1808 (SAN 283-2682).

Del Oeste Press, *(Del Oeste; 0-89632),* P.O. Box 397, Tarzana, CA 91356 (SAN 211-6642).

Delacorte Press, *(Delacorte),* c/o Dell Publishing Co., 1 Dag Hammarskjold Plaza, 245 E. 47th St., New York, NY 10017 Tel 212-605-3496 (SAN 201-0097). *Imprints:* Eleanor Friede (E Friede); Seymour Lawrence (Sey Lawr).

Delafield Press, *(Delafield Pr; 0-916872),* P.O. Box 335, Suttons Bay, MI 49682 Tel 616-271-3826 (SAN 208-3817).

Delair Publishing Co., Inc., *(Delair; 0-8326),* 420 Lexington Ave., Rm. 1621, New York, NY 10170 Tel 212-867-2255 (SAN 213-4439).

Delanie Way Pub., *(Delanie Way; 0-9602290),* 685 Delanie Way, Stone Mountain, GA 30083 Tel 404-292-9121 (SAN 212-8993).

Delapeake Publishing Co., *(Delapeake Pub Co; 0-911293),* P.O. Box 1148, Wilmington, DE 19899 Tel 302-658-7831 (SAN 269-6274).

Delaware Valley Poets, *(Del Valley; 0-937158),* P.O. Box 6203, Lawrenceville, NJ 08648 Tel 609-737-0222 (SAN 215-1391).

Delbridge Publishing Co., *(Delbridge Pub Co; 0-88232),* P.O. Box 2989, Stanford, CA 94305 Tel 408-446-3131 (SAN 207-2122).

Delcon Corp., *(Delcon; 0-934856),* P.O. Box 323, Harlan St. Rte., Eddyville, OR 97343 (SAN 213-4853).

DeLethein Press, The, *(DeLethein Pr),* Dept. BP, 4605 Holborn Ave., Annandale, VA 22003 (SAN 287-2846).

Delford Press, *(Delford Pr; 0-931726),* P.O. Box 27, Oradell, NJ 07649 Tel 201-262-0647 (SAN 209-7311).

Delgren Books, *(Delgren Bks),* P.O. Box 36023, Tuscon, AZ 85740 (SAN 240-4702).

Delilah Books, *(Delilah Bks; 0-933328),* 118 E. 25th St., New York, NY 10010 (SAN 238-9339); Dist. by: Putnam Publishing Group, 1050 Wall St. W., Lyndhurst, NJ 07071 (SAN 202-554X).

Dell Publishing Co., Inc., *(Dell; 0-440),* 1 Dag Hammarskjold Plaza, 245 E. 47th St., New York, NY 10017 Tel 212-605-3000 (SAN 201-0097). *Imprints:* Banbury (Banbury); Bryans (Bryans); Dell Trade Paperbacks (Dell Trade Pbks); Delta Books (Delta); Laurel Editions (LE); Laurel Leaf Library (LFL); Standish (Standish); Yearling Books (YB).

Dell Trade Paperbacks See **Dell Publishing Co., Inc.**

Dellen Publishing Co., *(Dellen Pub; 0-89517),* 3600 Pruneridge Ave., Santa Clara, CA 95051 Tel 408-246-4215 (SAN 219-0834).

Delmar Company, The, Subs. of Republic Corp., *(Delmar Co; 0-912081),* P.O. Box 220025, 9601 Monroe Rd., Charlotte, NC 28222 Tel 704-847-9801 (SAN 264-732X).

Delmar Pubns., Div. of International Thomson Educational Publishing Inc., *(Delmar; 0-8273),* 2 Computer Dr. West, P.O. Box 15015, Albany, NY 12212 Tel 518-459-1150 (SAN 206-7544); Orders to: 7625 Empire Dr., Florence, KY 41042 Tel 606-525-6600 (SAN 206-7552).

DeLong & Associates, *(DeLong & Assocs; 0-9603414),* P.O. Box 1732, Annapolis, MD 21404 Tel 301-263-5592 (SAN 213-215X).

DeLorme Publishing Co., *(DeLorme Pub; 0-89933),* P.O. Box 298, Freeport, ME 04032 Tel 207-865-4171 (SAN 220-1208).

Delphi Press, *(Delphi Pr WA; 0-939202),* 1346 Coonecticut Ave. N.W., Suite 310, Washington, DC 20036 Tel 202-466-7951 (SAN 220-1674).

Delta Books See **Dell Publishing Co., Inc.**

Delta Group Press, *(Delta G Pr; 0-913787),* 1523 Montane Dr. E., Golden, CO 80401 Tel 303-526-1172 (SAN 286-0902).

Delta Sales, *(Delta Sales; 0-931626),* 399 Southgate Ave., Daly City, CA 94015 (SAN 212-2510).

Delta Systems Co., Inc., *(Delta Systems; 0-937354),* 215 N. Arlington Hts. Rd., Arlington Hts, IL 60004 Tel 312-394-5760 (SAN 220-0457).

Deltiologists of America, *(Deltiologists Am),* 10 Felton Ave., Ridley Park, PA 19078 (SAN 225-607X).

Deluxe Co., The, *(Deluxe Co; 0-938012),* P.O. Box 4246, Shreveport, LA 71104 (SAN 215-7527).

Demarais Studio Press, Inc., *(Demarais Studio; 0-9607462),* 64 Lawn Park Ave., Trenton, NJ 08648 Tel 609-833-1737 (SAN 238-6224).

Dembner Books, Div. of Red Dembner Enterprises Corp., *(Dembner Bks; 0-934878),* 1841 Broadway, New York, NY 10023 Tel 212-265-1250 (SAN 211-5573); Dist. by: W.W. Norton & Co., Inc., 500 Fifth Ave., New York, NY 10110 Tel 212-354-5500 (SAN 202-5795).

Demecon Pubns., *(Demecon; 0-943700),* P.O. Box 3759, Laureldale, PA 19605 Tel 215-929-8336 (SAN 212-8314).

Demeter Press See **Times Books**

DeMos Music Pubns., *(DeMos Music; 0-940026),* P.O. Box 14125, Houston, TX 77021 Tel 713-433-5235 (SAN 217-0698).

Demou, Morris, & Associates, *(M Demou & Assocs; 0-9604794),* 2013 Big Oak Dr., Burnsville, MN 55337 Tel 612-890-3579 (SAN 209-1798).

Denco International, *(Denco Intl),* P.O. Box 2001, Hialeah, FL 33012 Tel 305-822-6666 (SAN 213-6171).

Dendle & Schraibman, *(Dendle & Schraibman; 0-9608168),* 272 S. Hanover, Lexington, KY 40502 (SAN 240-4729).

Denhamwood, Inc., *(Den Hamwood; 0-931544),* 4069 Hayvenhurst Ave., Encino, CA 91436 (SAN 223-3665).

Denison, T. S., & Co., Inc., *(Denison; 0-513),* 9601 Newton Ave. S., Minneapolis, MN 55431 Tel 612-888-1460 (SAN 201-3142) Do Not Confuse with Dennison Pubns.

Denlingers Pubs., Ltd., *(Denlingers; 0-87714),* P.O. Box 76, Fairfax, VA 22030 Tel 703-631-1501 (SAN 201-3150).

Dennis-Landman Pubs., *(Dennis-Landman; 0-930422),* 1150 18th St., Santa Monica, CA 90403 Tel 213-394-8683 (SAN 210-9352).

Dennison Pubns., *(Dennison),* Dist. by: Borden Publishing Co., 1855 W. Main St., Alhambra, CA 91801 (SAN 201-419X).

Denoyer-Geppert Co., *(Denoyer; 0-87453),* 5235 N. Ravenswood Ave., Chicago, IL 60640 Tel 312-561-9200 (SAN 204-2215).

Dental Control Products, Inc., *(Dental Control),* 590 Valley Rd., Upper Montclair, NJ 97043 (SAN 208-3132).

Dental-Info, *(Dental-Info; 0-9607518),* 2509 N. Campbell, No. 262, Tucson, AZ 85719 Tel 602-432-3081 (SAN 239-4340).

Dentan Press, *(Dentan Pr; 0-9610080),* 1404 Buchanan St.,P.O. Box 1745, Novato, CA 94948 Tel 415-897-1483 (SAN 269-6738).

Denton Senior Center, *(Denton Senior Ctr; 0-9606146),* 509 N. Bell Ave., Denton, TX 76201 (SAN 218-4745).

Denver Art Museum, *(Denver Art Mus; 0-914738),* Museum Shop, 100 W. 14th Ave. Pkwy., Denver, CO 80204 Tel 303-575-5582 (SAN 206-3530).

Denver Museum of Natural History, *(Denver Mus Natl Hist; 0-916278),* City Park, Denver, CO 80205 Tel 303-575-3931 (SAN 204-2193).

Denver Public Library, *(Denver Public),* 3840 York St., Denver, CO 80205 Tel 303-571-2367 (SAN 208-1504).

Department Of History Organization of Historical Studies, *(Dept Hist Org),* The American University Massachusetts & Nebraska Avenues N.W., Washington, DC 20016 (SAN 283-2666).

Department of Mechanical Engineering, *(Dept Mech E CA; 0-9607348),* Stanford University, Stanford, CA 94305 (SAN 265-9778).

Depot Press, *(Depot Pr),* P.O. Box 60072, Nashville, TN 37206 (SAN 240-1401).

Der Angriff Pubns., *(Der Angriff; 0-9604770),* 743 11th Ave., Huntington, WV 25701 (SAN 215-8558).

Derby Assocs., *(Derby Assoc; 0-9604692),* 601 Capitol Ctr., 344 W. Dayton St., Madison, WI 53703 (SAN 215-2010).

Derby Publishing Co., *(Derby Pub; 0-940424),* P.O. Box 221474, Charlotte, NC 28222 Tel 704-366-7029 (SAN 217-1716).

Dermody, Gail R. & Eugene M., *(Dermody),* P.O. Box 324, Lakewood, CA 90714 (SAN 212-0860).

Derrick, Sara M., *(S M Derrick; 0-89279),* 1313 Johnson St., Sandusky, OH 44870 (SAN 283-9881).

Derring-Do Press, *(Derring-Do; 0-9606638),* P.O. Box 1233, Mountainside, NJ 07092 Tel 201-654-6930 (SAN 223-7652).

DeRu's Fine Art Books, *(DeRu's Fine Art; 0-939370),* 9100 E. Artesia Blvd., Bellflower, CA 90706 Tel 213-920-1312 (SAN 216-3667).

Deseret Book Co., *(Deseret Bk; 0-87747),* 40 E. South Temple, P.O. Box 30178, Salt Lake City, UT 84130 Tel 801-534-1515 (SAN 201-3185).

Desert Botanical Garden, *(Desert Botanical),* 1201 N. Galvin Parkway, Phoenix, AZ 85008 Tel 602-941-1217 (SAN 212-9000).

Desert First Works, Inc., *(Desert First; 0-916556),* 3870 N. Vine Ave., Tucson, AZ 85719 Tel 602-326-1041 (SAN 208-6263).

Desert Light Pub., *(Desert Light; 0-942128),* 14041 N. 39th Ave., Phoenix, AZ 85283 Tel 602-829-0038 (SAN 238-6550).

Desert Press, The, *(Desert Pr; 0-937764),* Box K, Boude, AZ 85325 (SAN 215-6342).

Desert Publishing, *(Desert Pub CA),* 255 N. El Cielo Rd., Suite 164, Palm Springs, CA 92262 (SAN 216-1265).

Design Enterprises of San Francisco, *(Design Ent SF; 0-932538),* P.O. Box 14695, San Francisco, CA 94114 Tel 415-282-8813 (SAN 211-6359).

Design Methods Group, The, *(Design Meth; 0-910821),* P.O. Box 5, San Luis Obispo, CA 93406 Tel 805-546-1321 (SAN 269-6886).

Design Schools, The, *(Design Schools; 0-9607016),* Pan Am Bldg., East Mez., 200 Park Ave., Rm. 256, New York, NY 10166 Tel 212-972-1505 (SAN 238-969X).

Designs III Pubs., *(Designs Three),* 515 W. Commonwealth Ave., Fullerton, CA 92632 (SAN 209-2336).

Desperation Press, *(Desperation Pr; 0-9609112),* Los Alamos Technical Equipment Co., P.O. Box 659, Los Alamos, NM 87544 Tel 505-662-4815 (SAN 241-4929).

Desserco Publishing, *(Desserco Pub; 0-916698),* P.O. Box 2433, Culver City, CA 90230 Tel 213-827-4600 (SAN 208-3914).

Destiny Books & Astrologer's Library, Div. of Inner Traditions, *(Destiny Bks),* 377 Park Ave. S., New York, NY 10016 Tel 212-889-8350 (SAN 239-8516).

Destiny Pubs., *(Destiny; 0-910500),* 43 Grove St., Merrimac, MA 01860 Tel 617-364-9311 (SAN 203-8889).

Determined Productions, Inc., *(Determined Prods; 0-915696),* 315 Pacific Ave. at Battery, P.O. Box 2150, San Francisco, CA 94126 Tel 415-433-0660 (SAN 212-7385).

Detroit Institute of Arts, *(Detroit Inst Arts; 0-89558),* 5200 Woodward Ave., Detroit, MI 48202 Tel 313-833-7960 (SAN 204-2150).

Deuce of Clubs Press, *(Deuce; 0-9600200),* Rt. 3, Box 178, Arcata, CA 95521 Tel 707-822-2000 (SAN 203-8897).

Devco Press, *(Devco Pr; 0-9611790),* P.O. Box 842, Golden, CO 80402 Tel 303-278-0736 (SAN 285-2330).

Development of Research & Human Services, *(Develop Res; 0-9609114),* 12707 Duenes S.E., Suite A, Albuquerque, NM 87123 Tel 505-293-1700 (SAN 241-4937).

Development Systems Corporation, *(Develop Sys Corp; 0-88462),* 500 N. Dearborn St., Chicago, IL 60610 Tel 312-836-0466 (SAN 201-3622). *Imprints:* Real Estate Education Company (Real Estate Ed).

Developmental Arts, *(Developmental Arts),* P.O. Box 389, Arlington, MA 02174 (SAN 215-8566).

Developmental Learning Materials, *(Develop Learn; 0-937018),* 1 DLM Park, Allen, TX 75002 (SAN 216-2393).

Developmental Reading Distributors, *(Develop Read Dist),* 1944 Sheridan Ave., Laramie, WY 82070 Tel 307-745-9027 (SAN 201-8187).

Devida Pubns., *(Devida Pubns; 0-9607498),* 9115 Reisterstown Rd., Owings Mills, MD 21117 Tel 301-363-2093 (SAN 238-7964)P.O. Box 761, Princeton, NJ 08550 Tel 201-363-2093 (SAN 238-7972).

Devin-Adair Co., Inc., *(Devin; 0-8159),* 143 Sound Beach Ave., Old Greenwich, CT 06870 Tel 203-637-4531 (SAN 213-750X).

DeVito Enterprises, *(De Vito; 0-910506),* 28 Dean St., Box 11, East Windsor, CT 06088 Tel 203-623-3152 (SAN 203-8846).

Devon Press, Inc., *(Devon Pr; 0-934160),* 820 Miramar, Berkeley, CA 94707 Tel 415-526-1905 (SAN 212-8500).

Devon Publishing Co., The, *(Devon Pub; 0-941402),* 2700 Virginia Ave. NW, Washington, DC 20037 Tel 202-233-6240 (SAN 238-9703).

DeWaters, Lillian, Pubns., *(L De Waters),* Old Greenwich, CT 06870 Tel 203-637-0658 (SAN 203-8633).

DeWitt Historical Society, *(DeWitt Hist; 0-942690),* Clinton House, 116 N. Cayuga, Ithaca, NY 14850 (SAN 264-004X).

Dews, Robert Porter, *(R P Dews; 0-940184),* P.O. Box 302, Edison, GA 31746 Tel 912-835-2282 (SAN 213-652X).

Dexter, Lincoln A., *(L A Dexter; 0-9601210),* R. F. D. No. 1, Box N-53, Brookfield, MA 01506 Tel 617-867-9708 (SAN 207-057X).

DFM Associates, *(DFM Assoc),* 15560-A Rockfield Blvd., Irvine, CA 92714 (SAN 239-8508).

Dharma Drum Publications, *(Dharma Drum Pubs; 0-9609854),* 90-31 Corona Ave., Elmhurst, NY 11373 Tel 212-592-6593 (SAN 269-6967).

Dharma Publishing, *(Dharma Pub; 0-913546; 0-89800),* 2425 Hillside Ave., Berkeley, CA 94704 Tel 415-548-5407 (SAN 201-2723).

Di-Tri Books, *(Di-Tri Bks; 0-9603374),* 261 Waubesa St., Madison, WI 53704 (SAN 209-1712).

Diablo Books, *(Diablo Bks; 0-9607520),* 1317 Cayonwood Ct., No. 1, Walnut Creek, CA 94595 Tel 415-939-8644 (SAN 238-6232).

Diablo Press, *(Diablo; 0-87297),* P. O. Box 7042, Berkeley, CA 94707 Tel 415-527-1177 (SAN 201-3223).

Diablo Western Press, *(Diablo West Pr; 0-932438),* P.O. Box 5364, Walnut Creek, CA 94596 (SAN 211-9471).

Dial Books for Young Readers, Div. of E. P. Dutton, *(Dial Bks Young),* 2 Park Ave., New York, NY 10016 Tel 212-725-1818 (SAN 264-0058).

Dial Press, *(Dial; 0-8037),* 1 Dag Hammarskjold Plaza, 245 E. 47th St., New York, NY 10017 Tel 212-832-7300 (SAN 201-3231) Adult titles now listed as imprint of Doubleday; juvenile titles listed under Dial Bks Young.

Dial Press *See* Doubleday & Co., Inc.

Dialog Press, *(Dialog Pr; 0-936390),* P.O. Box 5626, Hilton Head Island, SC 29928 (SAN 214-2384).

Dialogue House Library, *(Dialogue Hse; 0-87941),* 80 E. 11th St., New York, NY 10003 Tel 212-673-5880 (SAN 201-8195).

Dialogue Press of Man & World, The, *(Dialogue Pr Man World; 0-932540),* 246 Sparks Bldg., University Park, PA 16802 Tel 814-865-6397 (SAN 211-9447).

Diamond Communications, Inc., *(Diamond Communications; 0-912083),* P.O. Box 94, Notre Dame, IN 46556 Tel 219-287-9561 (SAN 264-7346).

Diamond Heights Publishing Co., Inc., *(Diamond Heights; 0-936182),* 25 Grand View Ave., San Francisco, CA 94114 (SAN 215-3017).

Diamond Pubs., *(Diamond Pubs; 0-936510),* 23818 Twin Pines Lane, Diamond Bar, CA 91765 (SAN 216-0307).

Diana Press, Inc., *(Diana Pr; 0-88447),* 4400 Market St., Oakland, CA 94608 Tel 415-658-5558 (SAN 206-3549).

Diana's Bimonthly Press, *(Dianas Bimonthly; 0-933442),* 71 Elmgrove Ave., Providence, RI 02906 Tel 401-274-5417 (SAN 207-8147).

Diane Books Publishing, Inc., *(Diane Bks; 0-88264),* 2808 Oregon CT. No. E, Torrance, CA 90503 Tel 213-320-2591 (SAN 201-2731).

Dianic Pubns., *(Dianic Pubns; 0-9610450),* P.O. Box 4231, San Francisco, CA 94101 (SAN 240-4710) Moved, Left no Forwarding Address.

Dick, J., & Company, *(J Dick; 0-943692),* 500 Hyacinth Place, Highland Park, IL 60035 Tel 312-433-0824 (SAN 238-2717).

Dickay Publishing, *(Dickay Pub; 0-9611068),* P.O. Box 664, Buckeye Lake, OH 43008 Tel 614-928-4566 (SAN 282-8596).

Dickey, Grover C., *(G C Dickey),* 200 Gill Dr., Midwest City, OK 73110 (SAN 238-3612).

Diction Books, *(Diction Bks; 0-9609198),* P.O. Box 1727, St. Paul, MN 55117 Tel 612-483-5679 (SAN 241-4945).

Dicul Publishing, *(Dicul Pub; 0-938784),* P.O. Box 091111, Columbus, OH 43209-7111 (SAN 216-0315).

Didactic Systems Inc., *(Didactic Syst; 0-89401),* P.O. Box 457, Cranford, NJ 07016 Tel 212-789-2194 (SAN 209-1739).

Diehl, Kathryn, *(K Diehl; 0-9603552),* 554 N. McDonel, Lima, OH 45801 Tel 419-223-7207 (SAN 285-0079); Orders to: 554 N. Mcdonel, Lima, OH 45801 Tel 419-228-3584 (SAN 285-0087).

Diemar, Eleanor, *(E Diemar; 0-9601046),* P.O. Box 24, Cedarhurst, NY 11516 Tel 516-374-2020 (SAN 202-4969).

Diemer, Smith Publishing Co., Inc., *(Diemer-Smith; 0-941138),* 3377 Solano Ave., Suite 322, Napa, CA 94558 (SAN 238-874X).

Diet Teaching Programs, Inc., The, *(Diet Teach Progs; 0-941040),* P.O. Box 1832, Sun City, AZ 85372 Tel 602-977-6677 (SAN 217-3522).

Dietary Research, *(Dietary Res),* 5201 16th N.E, Seattle, WA 98105 (SAN 206-989X).

Dietz Press, *(Dietz; 0-87517),* 109 E. Cary, Richmond, VA 23219 Tel 804-648-0195 (SAN 201-3258).

Different Drummer Press, *(Different Drum; 0-9609580),* 333 5th. St., W. Des Moines, IA 50265 Tel 515-279-2969 (SAN 262-6217).

Digital Press/Digital Equipment Corp., *(Digital Pr; 0-932376),* 12 Crosby Dr., E/44, Bedford, MA 01730 Tel 617-276-4444 (SAN 212-2529); Orders to: 12-A Esquire Rd., North Billerica, MA 01862 (SAN 212-2537).

Dignatus Co., *(Dignatus Co; 0-9605820),* P.O. Box 2254, Mission Viejo, CA 92690 Tel 714-493-0710 (SAN 216-5732).

Dignity, Inc., *(Dignity Inc; 0-940680),* 1500 Massachusetts Ave., NW, No. 11, Washington, DC 20005 Tel 202-861-0017 (SAN 223-7431).

Dilithium Press, *(Dilithium Pr; 0-918398; 0-88056),* 8285 S.W. Nimbus St., Suite 151, Beaverton, OR 97005 Tel 503-646-2713 (SAN 210-0649); Orders to: P.O. Box 606, Beaverton, OR 97075 (SAN 210-0657).

Dill Enterprises, *(Dill Ent; 0-9606504),* P.O. Box 2627, "O" St., Lincoln, NE 68529 Tel 402-476-1776 (SAN 219-0842).

Dillon-Donnelly, *(Dillon-Donnelly; 0-933508),* 7058 Lindell Blvd., St. Louis, MO 63130 Tel 314-862-6239 (SAN 208-4589).

Dillon/Liederbach, Inc., *(Dillon-Liederbach; 0-913228),* 4870 Thales Road-O, Winston-Salem, NC 27104 Tel 919-768-7014 (SAN 201-3274).

Dillon Press, Inc., *(Dillon; 0-87518),* 500 S. Third St., Minneapolis, MN 55415 Tel 612-333-2691 (SAN 201-3266).

Dillon-Tyler Pubs., *(Dillon-Tyler Pubs; 0-916280),* 1544 Estee Ave., Napa, CA 94558 Tel 707-224-2525 (SAN 208-1075).

Dimension Books, *(Dimension Bks; 0-87193),* P.O. Box 811, Denville, NJ 07834 (SAN 211-7916).

Dimension Press, The, *(Dimension Pr; 0-911173),* 4205 Far West BLvd., P.O. Box 26673, Austin, TX 78755 Tel 512-345-0622 (SAN 269-7114).

Dimensional Graphics International, Ltd., *(Dimen Graphics Intl; 0-941444),* 925 Bethel St., Suite 308, Honolulu, HI 96813 Tel 808-538-7441 (SAN 238-9711).

Dimensionist Press, *(Dimensionist Pr; 0-9602374),* 5931 Stanton Ave., Highland, CA 92346 Tel 714-862-7767 (SAN 212-2545).

Dime's Group, Inc., The, *(Dimes Group; 0-934192),* 2300 Leghorn St., Mountain View, CA 94043 Tel 415-493-1885 (SAN 218-4753).

Dimond Pubs., *(Dimond Pubs),* 3431 Fruitvale Ave., Oakland, CA 94602 (SAN 215-1405).

Dinograph Southwest, Inc., *(Dinograph SW; 0-932680),* P.O. Box 1600, Alamogordo, NM 88310 (SAN 212-1573).

Dinosaur Press, The, *(Dinosaur; 0-9605458),* 86 Leverett Rd., Amherst, MA 01002 Tel 413-549-0404 (SAN 213-618X).

Diocese of Armenian Church, *(D O A C; 0-934728),* 630 Second Ave., New York, NY 10016 (SAN 216-0625).

Diotima Books, *(Diotima Bks; 0-935772),* Box H, Glen Carbon, IL 62034 (SAN 214-3631).

DiPaul, H. Bert, *(DiPaul; 0-9605418),* 1066 Brennan Dr., Warminster, PA 18974 (SAN 216-0323).

Diplomatic Press, *(Diplomatic IN; 0-910512),* Goodbody Hall 344, Indiana Univ., Bloomington, IN 47405 Tel 812-335-1605 (SAN 201-3290).

Direct Market Designs, *(Direct Market; 0-9607990),* P.O. Box 142, Island Lake, IL 60042 Tel 312-526-5141 (SAN 269-7149).

Directed Media Inc., *(Directed Media; 0-939688),* P.O. Box 3005, Wenatchee, WA 98801 Tel 509-662-7693 (SAN 216-7263).

Directions Press, *(Directions Pr; 0-940564),* P.O. Box 1811, Thousand Oaks, CA 91360 (SAN 215-6350).

Directories, *(Directories; 0-9607992),* 436 E. 88th St., New York, NY 10028 Tel 212-348-0025 (SAN 238-5635).

Directories International, Inc., *(Directories Intl; 0-912794),* 1718 Sherman Ave., Evanston, IL 60201 Tel 312-491-0019 (SAN 201-3312) Moved, left no forwarding address.

Directories Publishing Co., Inc., *(Directories Pub),* P.O. Box 1372, Ormond Beach, FL 32075-1372 Tel 904-673-1241 (SAN 203-8919).

Directory of Directors Co., Inc., *(DODC; 0-936612),* P.O. Box 462, Southport, CT 06490 Tel 203-255-8525 (SAN 204-2037).

Directory Systems, Inc., *(Directory Systems Inc; 0-942036),* 215 Shore Rd., Greenwich, CT 06830 Tel 203-661-3988 (SAN 238-6240).

Discipleship Resources, Subs. of Board of Discipleship of the United Methodist Church, *(Discipleship Res; 0-88177),* P.O. Box 840, 1908 Grand Ave., Nashville, TN 37202 Tel 615-327-2700 (SAN 264-0074).

Discount America Guide, *(Discount America; 0-942528),* 51 E. 42 St., Rm 417, New York, NY 10017 Tel 212-687-0810 (SAN 239-6343).

Discoveries Publishing Co., *(Discoveries),* P.O. Box 424, Glastonbury, CT 06033 (SAN 212-7393).

Discovery Books, *(Discovery Bks; 0-913976),* 351 Broad St., Suite 1704, Newark, NJ 07104 Tel 201-483-7782 (SAN 206-9512).

Discovery Pubns., *(Discov Pubns; 0-939490),* 2091 Business Ctr. Dr., Suite 100, Irvine, CA 92715 (SAN 219-7812).

Discovery Publishing Co., *(Discovery Pub; 0-932422),* 404 W. Chestnut, Yakima, WA 98902 (SAN 212-1581) Moved, left no forwarding address.

Discovery Stuff, *(Discovery Stuff; 0-930484),* 5328 W. 67th St., Shawnee Mission, KS 66208 (SAN 211-0636).

Displays for Schools, Inc., *(Displays Sch; 0-9600962),* P.O. Box 163, Gainesville, FL 32602 Tel 904-373-2030 (SAN 157-9711).

Distributors, The, *(Distributors),* 702 S. Michigan Ave., South Bend, IN 46618 Tel 219-232-8500 (SAN 212-0364).

District of Columbia Bar Association, *(DC Bar Assn),* 1426 H St NW, Rm. 840, Washington, DC 20005 (SAN 226-7314).

Div. of G.P. Enterprises *See* Job Hunters Forum

Div. of Manson Western Corp. *See* Western Psychological Services

Diversified Enterprises, Inc., *(Diversified Ent; 0-9601790),* Box 15, Posen, MI 49776 Tel 517-379-4678 (SAN 211-6367).

Diversified Pub. Co, *(Diversified Pub Co; 0-942306),* 5301-44, Lubbock, TX 79414 (SAN 239-8494).

Diversity Press, *(Diversity Pr; 0-941906),* 2738 N. Racine St., Chicago, IL 60614 Tel 312-472-5662 (SAN 239-197X).

Divesports Publishing, *(Divesports Pub; 0-9611522),* SR Two, Box 390, Branson, MO 65616 Tel 417-334-1949 (SAN 285-2462).

Divine Science Federation International, *(Divine Sci Fed),* 1819 E. 14th Ave., Denver, CO 80218 Tel 303-322-7730 (SAN 204-1103).

Divisions, *(Divisions; 0-934276),* P.O. Box 18647, Cleveland Heights, OH 44118 (SAN 223-579X).

Divorce Research Center, *(Divorce Res),* 961 G Ave., Coronado, CA 92118 (SAN 287-5373).

Divry, D.C., Inc., *(Divry; 0-910516),* 293 Seventh Ave., New York, NY 10001 Tel 212-255-2153 (SAN 201-3320).

D K Halcyon Group, Div. of Thom Doran & Partners, Inc., *(DK Halcyon; 0-939550),* 2640 Lance Dr., Dayton, OH 45409 Tel 513-435-6162 (SAN 216-678X).

D L M/C P A, *(DLM CPA; 0-935730),* P.O. Box 70125, Sunnyvale, CA 94086 (SAN 223-1662).

D. M. R. Pubns., Inc., *(DMR Pubns; 0-89552),* 1410 E. Capitol Dr., Milwaukee, WI 53211 Tel 414-961-0120 (SAN 205-325X).

Dnomro Pubns., *(Dnomro Pubns),* 40 Fairmont Ave., Waltham, MA 02154 (SAN 201-274X).

Do-It-Yourself Legal Publishers, *(Do It Yourself Legal Pubs; 0-932704),* 150 Fifth Ave., New York, NY 10011 Tel 212-242-2840 (SAN 214-1876).

Doane Publishing, *(Doane Pub; 0-932250),* 11701 Borman Dr., St. Louis, MO 63146 Tel 314-569-2700 (SAN 207-2149).

Dobbins, Joan H., *(J H Dobbins; 0-9610540),* 419 Windover Circle, Meridian, MS 39301 Tel 601-483-5081 (SAN 264-0082).

Dobbins, Murrell F., *(M F Dobbins; 0-9607176),* 624 Kelly Ln., Glenside, PA 19038 Tel 215-884-8057 (SAN 239-0841).

Doctor Jazz Press, *(Doctor Jazz; 0-934002),* 925 13 St., Tuscaloosa, AL 35401 (SAN 215-6369).

Doctrine of Christ Pubns., *(Doctrine Christ; 0-940068),* 2215 Bourbon St., Beaumont, TX 77705 (SAN 220-2131).

Documan Press Ltd., *(Documan; 0-932076),* 3201 Lorraine Ave., Kalamazoo, MI 49008 Tel 616-344-0805 (SAN 281-6032); Orders to: Box 387, Kalamazoo, MI 49005 Tel 616-344-0805 (SAN 281-6040).

Documentary Pubns., *(Documentary Pubns; 0-89712),* Rte. 12, Box 480, Salisbury, NC 28144 (SAN 211-559X).

Dodd, Mead & Co., *(Dodd; 0-396),* 79 Madison Ave., New York, NY 10016 Tel 212-685-6464 (SAN 201-3339).

Doe, John Press, *(J Doe Pr; 0-9609476),* 420 13th Ave. E., Seattle, WA 98105 Tel 206-525-7901 (SAN 263-2233).

Dog Ear Press, The, *(Dog Ear; 0-937966),* P.O. Box 143, South Harpwell, ME 04079 (SAN 216-3675).

Dog-Eared Pubns., *(Dog Eared Pubns; 0-941042),* 16230 S.E. 35th Place, Bellvue, WA 98008 Tel 202-746-5212 (SAN 281-6059); Dist. by: Pacific Pipeline, Inc., Kent, WA (SAN 208-2128).

Dog-Master Systems, Div. of Environmental Research Labs, *(Dog Master),* 606 Wilshire Blvd., Santa Monica, CA 90401 Tel 213-451-1601 (SAN 209-181X).

Doggeral Press, *(Doggeral Pr; 0-933726),* 417 Seaview, Santa Barbara, CA 93108 (SAN 216-3683).

Doll Collectors of America, Inc., *(Doll Collect Am; 0-9603210),* Dist. by: Patry/Edgar, 11 Charlemont Rd., Medford, MA 02155 (SAN 282-695X).

Doll Works, The, *(Doll Works; 0-940070),* 177 Riverside Ave., Suite F, Newport Beach, CA 92663 (SAN 220-214X).

Dolly Ridge Press, Inc., *(Dolly Ridge; 0-940702),* 3000 Third Ave. S., Birmingham, AL 35233 (SAN 219-7294).

Dolly Varden Pubns., *(D Varden Pubns),* P.O. Box 15380, Rio Rancho, NM 87124 Tel 505-892-8635 (SAN 214-171X).

Dolphin Aquatics, *(Dolphin Aquatics; 0-9602982),* 97 Parry Rd., Stamford, CT 06907 Tel 203-322-7944 (SAN 201-3355) Do Not Confuse with Dolphin, Imprint of Doubleday.

Dolphin Books *See* Doubleday & Co., Inc.

Doma Press, *(Doma; 0-917816),* P.O. Box 1995, Chicago, IL 60690 Tel 312-969-0734 (SAN 210-0681).

Dome Press, *(Dome Pr),* 1169 Logan Ave., Elgin, IL 60120 Tel 312-697-0320 (SAN 211-9323).

Domesday Books, *(Domesday Bks; 0-912195),* P.O. Box 734 Peter Stuyvesant Station, New York, NY 10009 Tel 212-254-1004 (SAN 264-6102).

Dominion Press, *(Dominion Pr; 0-912132),* P.O. Box 37, San Marcos, CA 92069-0025 Tel 619-746-9430 (SAN 203-8935).

Domjan Studio, *(Domjan Studio; 0-933652),* West Lake Rd., Tuxedo Park, NY 10987 Tel 914-351-4596 (SAN 212-6532); Dist. by: Wind, Sun & Stars, Pheasant Ridge Rd., W. Redding, CT 06896 Tel 203-938-9476 (SAN 212-6540).

Domus Books *See* Quality Books Inc.

Don Bosco Multimedia, Div. of Salesian Society, Inc., *(D Bosco Multimedia; 0-89944),* 457 North Ave, Box T, New Rochelle, NY 10802 Tel 914-576-0122 (SAN 213-2613). *Imprints:* Patron Books (Patron); Salesiana Publishers (Salesiana).

Don Quixote Publishing Co., Inc., *(D Quixote Pub; 0-943078),* P.O. Box 9442, Amarillo, TX 79105 (SAN 240-3676).

Donaghey, John, Pubns., *(J Donaghey; 0-9604298),* P.O. Box 402021, Garland, TX 75046 (SAN 214-364X).

Donahoe, Edward D., Pubs., *(Donahoe Pubs; 0-938400),* P.O. Box 22011, Louisville, KY 40222 Tel 502-423-9638 (SAN 217-0973).

Donaldson, Belzano & Associates, *(D B Assoc; 0-9611386),* 2102 Business Ctr. Dr., Suite 203, Irvine, CA 92715 Tel 714-752-2322 (SAN 285-2519).

Doneve Designs, Inc., *(Doneve Designs; 0-89715),* P.O. Box 1072, Saratoga, CA 95070 Tel 408-867-7556 (SAN 211-4895) Moved, left no forwarding address.

Dong Nam P & C Inc., *(Dong Nam P & C; 0-914524),* 2946 N. Lincoln Ave., Chicago, IL 60657 Tel 312-549-4660 (SAN 206-3557).

Donnar Pubns., *(Donnar Pubns; 0-9608068),* 21790 Ybarra Rd., Woodland Hills, CA 91364 Tel 213-883-5633 (SAN 238-0587).

Donnelly, Mary Louise, *(Donnelly),* P.O. Box 306, Burke, VA 22015 Tel 703-455-2401 (SAN 214-0039).

Donning Co. Pubs., *(Donning Co; 0-915442; 0-89865),* 5659 Virginia Beach Blvd., Norfolk, VA 23502 Tel 804-461-8090 (SAN 211-6316). *Imprints:* Starblaze (Starblaze); Unilaw (Unilaw).

Donoghue Organization, Inc., The, *(Donoghue Organ Inc; 0-913755),* Box 540, 360 Woodland St., Holliston, MA 01746 (SAN 285-2365).

Doodly-Squat Press, The, *(Doodly-Squat),* P.O. Box 480740, Los Angeles, CA 90048 (SAN 219-3353).

Doolco, Inc., *(Doolco Inc; 0-914626),* 2016 Canton St., Dallas, TX 75201 Tel 214-741-3607 (SAN 205-6178).

Dooryard Press, *(Dooryard; 0-937160),* P.O. Box 221, Story, WY 82842 (SAN 216-1230).

Dorchester Publishing Co., Inc., *(Dorchester Pub Co; 0-8439),* c/o Winick & Rich, 41 East 60th Street, 5th Floor, New York, NY 10022 Tel 212-935-9360 (SAN 264-0090).

Dorison House Pubs., Inc., *(Dorison Hse; 0-916752),* 824 Park Square Bldg., Boston, MA 02116 Tel 617-426-1715 (SAN 208-3140).

Dorje Ling Pubs., *(Dorje Ling; 0-915880),* P.O. Box 287, Lagunitas, CA 94938 (SAN 208-2144).

Dorland, Wayne E., Publishing Co., *(Dorland Pub Co; 0-9603250),* Box 264, Mendham, NJ 07945 Tel 201-543-2694 (SAN 213-2451).

Dormac, Inc, *(Dormac; 0-86575),* P.O. Box 752, Beaverton, OR 97075 Tel 503-641-3128 (SAN 209-3502).

Dormant Brain Research & Development Laboratory, *(Dormant Brain Res),* Laughing Coyote Mountain, Box 10, Black Hawk, CO 80422 (SAN 219-7820).

Dorrance & Co., *(Dorrance; 0-8059),* 828 Lancaster Ave., Bryn Mawr, PA 19010 Tel 215-527-7880 (SAN 201-3363).

Dorset Press, Subs. of Marborough Books, *(Dorset Pr; 0-88029),* (SAN 223-1794); c/o Marborough Books, 122 Fifth Ave., New York, NY 10003 Tel 212-924-8395 (SAN 287-6663).

Dorsey Press, Div. of Richard D. Irwin, Inc., *(Dorsey; 0-256),* 1818 Ridge Rd., Homewood, IL 60430 Tel 312-798-6000 (SAN 203-8943).

Dos Reals Publishing, *(Dos Reals Pub; 0-915004),* 2490 Channing Way, Berkeley, CA 94704 Tel 415-548-6810 (SAN 207-2157).

Dos Tejedoras, *(Dos Tejedoras; 0-932394),* 3036 N. Snelling Ave., St. Paul, MN 55113 Tel 612-636-0205 (SAN 213-4861).

Dot Gibson Publications, *(D Gibson; 0-941162),* 1603 Rainbow Dr., Waycross, GA 31501 (SAN 241-3760).

Dots Pubns., *(Dots Pubns),* P.O. Box 563, Ventura, CA 93002 Tel 805-643-7021 (SAN 215-7535).

Double C Inc., *(Double C Inc; 0-943288; 0-937844),* 333 S. Front St., Burbank, CA 91502 Tel 213-848-7767 (SAN 240-6292).

Double Crown, *(Double Crown; 0-935010),* 51995 Hernley Road, Aguanga, CA 92302 Tel 714-763-5174 (SAN 212-0372).

Double Decker Pubns., *(Double Decker; 0-938888),* 2800 Neilson Way, Suite 814, Santa Monica, CA 90405 (SAN 217-0981).

Double Helix Press, *(Double Helix; 0-930578),* 1300 Tigertail Rd., Los Angeles, CA 90049 Tel 213-472-6452 (SAN 211-0083); Dist. by: International Universities Press, Inc., 315 Fifth Ave., New York, NY 10016 (SAN 202-7186); Dist. by: Penguin Books, 40 W. 23rd St., New York, NY 10010 Tel 212-807-7300 (SAN 202-5914).

Double Lee Productions, *(Double Lee; 0-9607540),* 401 First Ave., New York, NY 10010 (SAN 239-5339).

Double M Press, *(Double M Pr; 0-916634),* 16455 Tuba St., Sepulveda, CA 91343 Tel 213-366-1056 (SAN 213-9510).

Doubleday & Co., Inc., *(Doubleday; 0-385),* 245 Park Ave., New York, NY 10017 (SAN 281-6075); Orders to: 501 Franklin Ave., Garden City, NY 11530 (SAN 281-6083). *Imprints:* Anchor Books (Anch); Anchor Press (Anchor Pr); Dial Press (Dial); Dolphin Books (Dolp); Echo Books (Echo); Galilee (Galilee); Image Books (Im); Made Simple Books (Made); Virago (Virago); Zenith Books (Zenith); Zephyr (Zephyr).

DoubLeo Pubns., *(DoubLeo Pubns; 0-936560),* 227 E. 11th St., New York, NY 10003 Tel 212-473-2739 (SAN 214-0047).

Doubleshoe Pubs., *(Doubleshoe; 0-9603270),* 5131 E. Shea Blvd., Scottsdale, AZ 85253 Tel 602-948-0355 (SAN 212-937X).

Douglas-West Pubs., Inc., *(Douglas-West; 0-913264),* Dist. by: Book Pool International, P.O. Box 249, Corona, CA 91270 (SAN 269-7513).

Douglass Publishers, Inc., *(Douglass Pubs; 0-935392),* P.O. Box 3270, Alexandria, VA 22302 Tel 703-522-4000 (SAN 211-7037).

Dover Pubns., Inc., *(Dover; 0-486),* 31 E. 2nd St., Mineola, NY 11501 Tel 516-294-7000 (SAN 201-338X).

Doves Publishing Co., *(DOVES Pub Co; 0-911561),* P.O. Box 821, 6414 S.W. Gallery, Lincoln City, OR 97367 Tel 503-996-4279 (SAN 269-7521).

Dovetail Press, *(Dovetail; 0-935468),* 250 W. 94th St., New York, NY 10025 Tel 212-865-9216 (SAN 209-6609).

Dow Jones-Irwin, *(Dow Jones-Irwin; 0-87094; 0-256),* 1818 Ridge Rd., Homewood, IL 60430 Tel 312-798-6000 (SAN 220-0236).

Dowler, Warren L., *(W L Dowler; 0-930188),* 526 Camillo St., Sierra Madre, CA 91024 Tel 213-355-9707 (SAN 210-721X).

Dowling College Press, *(Dowling; 0-917428),* Oakdale L. I., NY 11769 Tel 516-589-6100 (SAN 208-9521).

Down East Books, Div. of Down East Enterprise Inc., *(Down East; 0-89272),* P.O. Box 679, Camden, ME 04843 Tel 207-594-9544 (SAN 208-6301).

Down There Press, *(Down There Pr; 0-940208),* P.O. Box 2086, Burlingame, CA 94010 Tel 415-342-9867 (SAN 212-3312).

Downey, Joel, *(J Downey; 0-9601284),* 1105 S. Braddock Ave., Pittsburgh, PA 15218 Tel 412-371-5880 (SAN 210-4156).

Downey Place Publishing House, Inc., *(Downey Place; 0-910823),* P.O. Box 1352, El Cerrito, CA 94530-1352 Tel 415-529-1012 (SAN 269-753X).

Downsbrough, Peter, *(P Downsbrough; 0-9602192),* 305 E. Houston St, New York, NY 10012 (SAN 212-3460); Dist. by: Printed Matter, 7 Lispenard St., New York, NY 10013 (SAN 169-5924).

Downtown Book Center, Inc., *(Downtown Bk; 0-941010),* 247 S.E. First St., Suites 236-237, Miami, FL 33131 Tel 305-377-9941 (SAN 217-3549).

Downtown Poets Co-Op, *(Downtown Poets; 0-917402),* GPO Box 1720, Brooklyn, NY 11202 Tel 212-625-4245 (SAN 208-9653).

Downtown Research & Development Center, *(Downtown Res; 0-915910),* 270 Madison Ave., Suite 1505, New York, NY 10016 Tel 212-889-5666 (SAN 207-9658).

Doxey, W. S., *(Doxey),* 550 N. White, Carrollton, GA 30117 (SAN 211-8955).

Doyle, Howard A., Publishing Co., *(Howard Doyle; 0-87299),* P.O. Box 555, East Dennis, MA 02641 Tel 617-385-2000 (SAN 204-0751).

Dr.-Ing. Roderich W. Graeff, *(Graeff; 0-9604570),* 607 Church, Ann Arbor, MI 48104 Tel 313-769-6588 (SAN 215-2126).

Dr. Pepper Co., The, *(Dr Pepper; 0-9607448),* P.O. Box 225086, Dallas, TX 75231 Tel 214-824-0331 (SAN 239-1996).

Dragon Co., *(Dragon Co; 0-937456),* P.O. Box 14682, Houston, TX 77021 (SAN 215-7543).

Dragon Enterprises, *(Dragon Ent),* P.O. Box 200, Genoa, NV 89411 Tel 702-782-2486 (SAN 215-3025).

Dragon Gate, *(Dragon Gate; 0-937872),* 508 Lincoln St., Port Townsend, WA 98368 (SAN 217-099X).

Dragon Tree Press, The, *(Dragon Tree; 0-940918),* 118 Sayles Blvd., Abilene, TX 79605 Tel 915-672-8261 (SAN 217-3557).

Dragons Teeth Press, *(Dragons Teeth; 0-934218),* El Dorado National Forest, Georgetown, CA 95634 (SAN 201-3398).

Dragonwyck Publishing Inc., *(Dragonwyck Pub; 0-9606148),* Burrage Rd., Contoocook, NH 03229 Tel 603-746-5606 (SAN 281-6113); Orders to: P.O. Box 385, Contoocook, NH 03229 (SAN 281-6121).

Drain Enterprise, The, *(Drain Enterprise),* 309 First St, Drain, OR 97435 (SAN 240-902X).

Drake's Printing & Pub., *(Drake's Ptg & Pub),* 225 N. Magnolia Ave., Orlando, FL 32801 Tel 305-841-3491 (SAN 216-1249).

Drama Book Publishers, *(Drama Bk; 0-910482; 0-89676),* 821 Broadway, New York, NY 10003 Tel 212-228-3400 (SAN 213-5752).

Dramabooks *See* Hill & Wang, Inc.

Dramatika, *(Dramatika; 0-9604000),* 429 Hope St., Tarpon Springs, FL 33589 Tel 813-937-0109 (SAN 207-8155).

Dramatists Play Service, Inc., *(Dramatists Play; 0-8222),* 440 Park Ave. S., New York, NY 10016 Tel 212-206-5717).

Drayson, James E., *(J E Drayson; 0-934318),* 3642 Dustin Drive, Rte. 9, Billings, MT 59101 (SAN 264-0120).

Dream Garden Press, *(Dream Garden; 0-9604402; 0-942688),* 1199 Iola Ave., Salt Lake City, UT 84104 Tel 801-355-2154 (SAN 217-1007).

Dream Place Pubns., *(Dream Place; 0-930486),* P.O. Box 9416, Stanford, CA 94305 (SAN 211-7053).

Dreaming Spring Press, The, *(Dreaming; 0-9611336),* 2440 Canton Rd., Marietta, GA 30066 (SAN 283-2658).

Dreams Unlimited, *(Dreams Unltd; 0-939878),* P.O. Box 247, Middleton, WI 53562 Tel 608-238-6575 (SAN 215-7551).

Dreenan Press, Ltd., *(Dreenan Pr; 0-88376),* P.O. Box 385, Croton-on-Hudson, NY 10520 Tel 914-271-5085 (SAN 201-808X).

Drelwood Pubns., *(Drelwood Pubns; 0-937766),* P.O. Box 10605, Portland, OR 97210 (SAN 215-756X); Dist. by: Communication Creativity, 5644 La Jolla Blvd., La Jolla, CA 92037 Tel 714-459-4489 (SAN 210-3478).

Dremel, Div. of Emerson Electric Co., *(DREMEL; 0-9606512),* 4915 21st St., Racine, WI 53406 Tel 414-554-1390 (SAN 223-1530).

Driscoll, Robert Bruce, *(R B Driscoll; 0-9601374),* P.O. Box 637, Oakland, CA 94604 Tel 415-451-4870 (SAN 204-1936).

Drivers License Guide Co., *(Drivers License),* 1492 Oddstad Dr., Redwood City, CA 94063 (SAN 215-949X).

Drollery Press, *(Drollery Pr; 0-940920),* 1516 Oak St., No. 313, Alameda, CA 94501 Tel 415-521-4087 (SAN 223-1808).

Drug Abuse Council, *(Drug Abuse),* 1828 "L" St., N.W., Washington, DC 20036 Tel 202-785-5200 (SAN 203-8609).

Drug Intelligence Pubns., *(Drug Intl Pubns; 0-914768),* 7752 Woodmont Ave., Washington, DC 20814 Tel 301-654-8736 (SAN 201-2804); Orders to: 1241 Broadway, Hamilton, IL 62341 Tel 217-847-2504 (SAN 201-2812).

Drug Store Market Guide, *(Drug Store Mkt; 0-9606064),* 1739 Horton Ave., Mohegan Lake, NY 10547 Tel 914-528-7147 (SAN 216-888X).

Druid Books, *(Druid Bks; 0-912518),* Ephraim, WI 54211 Tel 414-854-4875 (SAN 210-797X).

Druid Heights Books, *(Druid Heights),* 685 Camino del Canyon, Muir Woods, Mill Valley, CA 94941 Tel 415-388-2111 (SAN 264-4693).

Drum Associates, *(Drum Assocs; 0-9611024),* W. 201 Sumner, Spokane, WA 99204 Tel 509-838-8167 (SAN 277-674X).

Dryad Press, *(Dryad Pr; 0-931848),* 15 Sherman Ave., Takoma Park, MD 20912 Tel 301-891-3729 (SAN 206-197X).

Dryden Press, Div. of Holt, Rinehart & Winston, Inc., *(Dryden Pr; 0-8498),* 901 N. Elm, Hinsdale, IL 60521 Tel 312-325-2985 (SAN 281-613X); Orders to: CBS College Publishing, 383 Madison Ave., New York, NY 10017 Tel 212-872-2219 (SAN 281-6148).

Dryfus International Publications, Div. of Accord Diversified Corp., *(Dryfus Pubns; 0-911661),* 8 Spring St., Woodland, ME 04694-0699 Tel 207-427-3225 (SAN 264-0147).

DSN See **National Assn. of School Nurses**

Du Sable Museum Press, *(Du Sable Mus),* 740 E. 56th Place, Chicago, IL 60637 Tel 312-947-0600 (SAN 201-8004).

Du Vall Press Financial Pubns., *(Du Vall Financial; 0-931232),* 920 W. Grand River, Williamston, MI 48895 (SAN 212-0380).

Duane Shinn Pubns., *(Duane Shinn; 0-912732),* 5090 Dobrot, Central Point, OR 97501 Tel 503-664-2317 (SAN 204-5931).

Dubis Associates, Inc., *(Dubis Assoc; 0-942076),* 2043 West Rock Rd., Perkasie, PA 18944 Tel 904-756-4937 (SAN 238-4558).

Dublin Press, *(Dublin Pr; 0-9604238),* P.O. Box 2131, Sunnyvale, CA 94087 (SAN 214-3658).

DuBois Zone Press, The, *(DuBois Zone Pr; 0-931498),* 516 Eleventh Ave., Grafton, WI 53024 (SAN 212-8071).

DuBose Publishing, *(DuBose Pub; 0-938072),* P.O. Box 924, Atlanta, GA 30301 (SAN 215-7586).

Duck Down Press, *(Duck Down; 0-916918),* P.O. Box 1047, Fallon, NV 89406 Tel 702-423-6643 (SAN 208-502X).

Duck Press, *(Duck Pr; 0-9604364),* Box 1024, New York, NY 10009 (SAN 214-3666); Orders to: Energy Earth Communications Inc., Box 1141, Galveston, TX 77553 (SAN 214-3674).

Duck Tale Productions, *(Duck Tale Prods; 0-9610374),* P.O. Box 11159e Rd., Memphis, TN 38111 Tel 901-682-9725 (SAN 264-0155).

Ducky, B. K., Enterprises, *(Ducky Ent),* 8836 S. Vermont Ave., No. 2, Los Angeles, CA 90044 Tel 213-377-0216 (SAN 215-1413).

Dudley, Linda, *(Dudley),* 89 Surrey Lane, Hempstead, NY 11550 Tel 516-489-8564 (SAN 210-1459).

Duende Pr, *(Duende; 0-915008),* 6434 Raymond St, Oakland, CA 94609 (SAN 207-8163).

Dufour Editions, Inc., *(Dufour; 0-8023),* Box 449, Chester Springs, PA 19425 Tel 215-458-5005 (SAN 201-341X).

Dugdale, Kathleen, *(Dugdale; 0-9600028),* C/O Indiana University Foundation, P.O. Box 500, Bloomington, IN 47402 Tel 812-335-8311 (SAN 201-3428).

Duke, David A., *(D A Duke; 0-9605056),* P.O. Box 725, Whitehouse, TX 75791 Tel 214-839-4837 (SAN 220-0465).

Duke Press, *(Duke Pr IL; 0-931234),* 8917 W. Cermak Rd., N. Riverside, IL 60546 (SAN 211-9455).

Duke Univ. Press, *(Duke; 0-8223),* 6697 College Sta., Durham, NC 27708 Tel 919-684-2173 (SAN 201-3436).

Dultz, Ron, *(R Dultz; 0-9601636),* P.O. Box 985, Reseda, CA 91335 Tel 213-993-7932 (SAN 211-5603).

Dumbarton Oaks, *(Dumbarton Oaks; 0-88402),* 1703 32nd St., N.W., Washington, DC 20007 Tel 202-342-3259 (SAN 215-5907).

Dun & Bradstreet, Inc., *(Dun),* 299 Park Ave., New York, NY 10007 (SAN 287-0134); Orders to: 99 Church St., New York, NY 10007 (SAN 287-0142).

Duna Studios, *(Duna Studios; 0-942928),* P.O. Box 24051, Minneapolis, MN 55424 (SAN 240-1428).

Dunbar Publishing Co., *(Dunbar Pub; 0-931680),* P.O. Box 13368, Jamaica, NY 11413 (SAN 221-2048).

Duncan-Holmes Publishing Company, *(Duncan-Holmes; 0-9609480),* P.O. Box 481, Syracuse, IN 46567 (SAN 269-7750).

Duncliff's International, *(Duncliffs Intl; 0-911663),* 3662 Katella Ave., Los Alamitos, CA 90720 (SAN 264-018X).

Dunconor Books, *(Dunconor Bks; 0-918820),* Box 17324, Denver, CO 80217 (SAN 208-1776).

Dundee Publishing, *(Dundee Pub; 0-935210),* P.O. Box 202, Dundee, NY 14837 Tel 301-432-8079 (SAN 213-6848).

Dune Pubns., Ltd., *(Dune Pubns; 0-914938),* 150 E. 35th St., Suite 920, New York, NY 10016 Tel 212-684-2997 (SAN 207-0332).

Dunes Enterprises, *(Dunes),* P.O. Box 371, Beverly Shores, IN 46301 Tel 219-872-5943 (SAN 207-0146).

Dunlap Society, *(Dunlap Soc; 0-89481),* Lake Champlain Rd., Essex, NY 12936 Tel 518-963-7373 (SAN 281-6156); Orders to: Princeton University Press, 41 Williams St., Princeton, NJ Tel 609-452-4879 (SAN 281-6164).

Dunnigan, Dorothy, & Patricia Dunnigan Rowley, *(D Dunnigan; 0-9607954),* P.O. Box 8494, Newport Beach, CA 92660 Tel 714-644-7900 (SAN 239-636X); Dist. by: Baker & Taylor, 380 Edison Way, Reno, NV 89564 Tel 702-786-6700 (SAN 169-4464); Dist. by: Dot Gibson Publications, Waycross, GA 31501 Tel 912-285-2848 (SAN 200-4143).

Duobooks, Inc., *(Duobooks; 0-918394),* 154 W. 57th St., New York, NY 10019 Tel 212-757-4438 (SAN 210-0703); Orders to: 300 Fairfield Rd., Fairfield, NJ 07006 (SAN 210-0711).

Duquesne Publishing Co., *(Duquesne Pub; 0-89653),* P.O. Box 222, West Brookfield, MA 01585 Tel 617-867-9341 (SAN 211-1233).

Duquesne Univ. Press, *(Duquesne; 0-8207),* Dist. by: Humanities Press, Inc., Atlantic Highlands, NJ 07716 (SAN 201-9272).

Durand International, *(Durand Intl; 0-9604056),* P.O. Box 925, Lynwood, CA 90262 (SAN 214-1884).

Durant Publishing Co., *(Durant Pub; 0-9606128),* 1208 Tatum Dr., Alexandria, VA 22307 Tel 703-765-4311 (SAN 217-488X).

Durbin Associates, *(Durbin Assoc; 0-936786),* 3711 Southwood Dr., Easton, PA 18042 (SAN 215-0697).

Durrell Pubns., Inc., *(Durrell; 0-911764),* P.O. Box 743, Kennebunkport, ME 04046 Tel 207-985-3904 (SAN 201-3452).

Durst, Sanford J., *(S J Durst; 0-912561; 0-942666),* 29-28 41st Ave., Long Island City, NY 11101 Tel 212-706-0303 (SAN 211-6987).

Dushkin Publishing Group, Inc., *(Dushkin Pub; 0-87967),* Sluice Dock, Guilford, CT 06437 Tel 203-453-4351 (SAN 201-3460).

Dustbooks, *(Dustbooks; 0-913218),* Box 100, Paradise, CA 95969 Tel 916-877-6110 (SAN 204-1871).

Dutch Fork Press, *(Dutch Fork Pr; 0-9611610),* P.O. Box 21766-A, Columbia, SC 29221 Tel 803-772-6919 (SAN 285-2640).

Dutton, E. P., *(Dutton; 0-525),* 2 Park Ave., New York, NY 10016 Tel 212-725-1818 (SAN 201-0070). *Imprints:* Hawthorn Books (Hawthorn).

Duverus Publishing Corp., *(Duverus Pub; 0-918700),* Duverus Bldg., 1906 Lowell Rd., Springdale, AR 72764 Tel 501-756-2002 (SAN 209-1305).

Dvorion Books, *(Dvorion Bks),* 730 NW 95th St., Apt. 22, Miami, FL 33150 (SAN 265-3575).

Dwapara Herald Pubs., Inc., *(Dwapara; 0-917952),* P.O. Box 267, Marble Hill, MO 63764 (SAN 209-5513).

Dwyer, Jeffrey P., *(J P Dwyer),* 30 Pleasant St., Box 426, Northampton, MA 01061 Tel 413-584-7909 (SAN 209-5521).

Dyco, Inc., *(Dyco Inc; 0-937224),* 6702 E. Cactus Rd., Scottsdale, AZ 85254 (SAN 216-1257).

Dynamic Information Publishing, *(Dynamic Info; 0-941286),* 8311 Greeley Blvd., Springfield, VA 22152 (SAN 240-091X).

Dynamic Learning Corp., *(Dynamic Learn Corp; 0-915890),* 59 Commercial Wharf, Boston, MA 02110 Tel 617-742-9493 (SAN 209-049X). *Imprints:* Telegraph Books (Telegraph).

Dynamics of Christian Living Inc., *(Dynamics Chr Liv; 0-940386),* Box 1053, Akron, OH 44309 (SAN 219-7839).

E & C Books, *(E & C Bks; 0-935126),* P.O. Box 6, Massapequa Park, NY 11762 (SAN 213-8433).

E & E Enterprises, *(E & E Enterprises; 0-917954),* 1203 Pomelo Court, Longwood, FL 32750 Tel 305-862-2823 (SAN 208-3906).

E & E Publishing Co., *(E & E Pub),* 27 Franklin Ave., Souderton, PA 18964 Tel 215-723-6689 (SAN 211-3546).

E & L Instruments, *(E & L Instru; 0-89704),* 61 First St., Derby, CT 06418 (SAN 211-4151).

EBHA Press, *(EBHA Pr; 0-935662),* 5919 Cullen Dr., Lincoln, NE 68506 Tel 402-488-0684 (SAN 213-6201).

EBSCO Industries, Inc., *(EBSCO Ind; 0-913956),* First Ave., N. at 13th St., Birmingham, AL 35203 Tel 205-252-1212 (SAN 201-3584).

ECA Associates, *(ECA Assoc; 0-938818),* P.O. Box 15004, Great Bridge Sta., Chesapeake, VA 23320 Tel 804-547-5542 (SAN 215-9503); P.O. Box 57, Lefferts Sta., Brooklyn, NY 11225 (SAN 215-9511).

ECR Associates, *(ECR Assocs; 0-9600352),* 2441 Hassell Place, Charlotte, NC 28209 Tel 704-372-3227 (SAN 201-9752).

EDC Publishing, *(EDC; 0-88110),* 8141 E. 44th St., Tulsa, OK 74145 (SAN 226-2134).

EDITS Pubs., *(EDITS Pubs),* P.O. Box 7234, San Diego, CA 92107 Tel 714-488-1666 (SAN 208-4600).

EGM Enterprises, *(EGM Ent; 0-9604586),* P.O. Box 192, Berkeley Heights, NJ 07922 Tel 201-464-0486 (SAN 215-1448).

EHUD International Language Foundation, *(EHUD),* 1755 Trinity Ave., No. 79, Walnut Creek, CA 94596 Tel 415-937-4841 (SAN 281-6172); Orders to: Box 2082, Dollar Ranch Sta., Walnut Creek, CA 94595 Tel 415-937-4841 (SAN 281-6180).

E-Heart Press, Inc., *(E-Heart Pr; 0-935014),* 3700 Mockingbird Lane, Dallas, TX 75205 (SAN 216-3691).

EIC/Intelligence, *(EIC Intell; 0-89947),* 48 W. 38th St., New York, NY 10018 Tel 212-944-8500 (SAN 211-1276) Tel 800-223-6275.

EKS Publishing Co., *(EKS Pub Co; 0-939144),* 5336 College Ave., Oakland, CA 94618 Tel 415-653-5183 (SAN 216-1281).

EMC Pub., *(EMC; 0-88436; 0-912022; 0-8219),* 300 York Ave., St. Paul, MN 55101 Tel 612-771-1555 (SAN 201-3800).

EMR Pubns., *(EMR Pubns; 0-930308),* P.O. Box 4007, Bryan, TX 77805 Tel 713-779-5060 (SAN 209-5556).

EPICA Task Force, *(EPICA; 0-918346),* 1470 Irving St., N.W., Washington, DC 20010 Tel 202-332-0292 (SAN 207-8244).

EPM Pubns, *(EPM Pubns; 0-914440),* 1003 Turkey Run Rd., McLean, VA 22101 Tel 703-356-5111 (SAN 206-7498); Orders to: P.O. Box 490, McLean, VA 22101 (SAN 206-7501).

E R A Press, Subs. of The New East Magazine, *(Era Pr NC; 0-918234),* Box 1673, Greenville, NC 27834 Tel 919-752-7829 (SAN 210-1971).

E R S See **Educational Research Service**

ESE California, *(ESE Calif; 0-912076),* 509 N. Harbor Blvd., La Habra, CA 90631 Tel 213-691-0737 (SAN 201-4629).

ETC Associates, *(ETC Assocs; 0-910565),* Box 118, Oneida, NY 13421 Tel 315-363-7262 (SAN 269-9796).

ETC Pubns., *(ETC Pubns; 0-88280),* 700 E. Vereda del Sur, Palm Springs, CA 92262 Tel 619-325-5352 (SAN 201-4637); Orders to: Order Dept., Box ETC, Palm Springs, CA 92261-1608 (SAN 201-4645).

EW Engineering, Inc., *(EW Eng; 0-931728),* P.O. Box 28, Dunn Loring, VA 22027 (SAN 212-3487).

E-Z Learning Methods, *(E-Z Learning; 0-931924),* P.O. Box 2582, Pomona, CA 91766 Tel 714-622-6835 (SAN 212-3495).

E.T.T.A. See **Evangelical Teacher Training Assn.**

Eagle Books, *(Eagle Bks; 0-910971),* Rte. 3, Box 320, Rolla, MO 65401 Tel 314-364-3229 (SAN 263-2160).

Eagle Communications, *(Eagle Comm; 0-9605462),* 340 W. Main St., Missoula, MT 59806 (SAN 216-1303).

Eagle Press, Inc., *(Eagle Pr),* P. O. Box 64935, Baton Rouge, LA 70806 Tel 504-344-7443 (SAN 208-158X).

Eagles View Publishing, Subs. of Eagle Feather Trading Post, Inc., *(Eagles View; 0-943604),* 706 W. Riverdale Rd., Ogden, UT 84463 Tel 801-393-3991 (SAN 240-6330).

Eakin Pubns. Inc., *(Eakin Pubns; 0-89015),* P.O. Box 23066, Austin, TX 78735 Tel 512-288-1771 (SAN 207-3633).

Eakins Press Foundation, *(Eakins; 0-87130),* 155 E. 42nd St., New York, NY 10017 Tel 212-986-4077 (SAN 201-3541).

Eardley Pubns., *(Eardley Pubns; 0-937630),* P.O. Box 281, Rochelle Park, NJ 07662 (SAN 215-6377).

Earl Enterprises, *(Earl Ent; 0-9602504),* P.O. Box 1254, 7400 Cutting Blvd., El Cerrito, CA 94530 (SAN 223-4645).

Earle, Arthur, *(A Earle; 0-9600788),* 45 Tulip Circle, Southampton, PA 18966 Tel 215-357-5957 (SAN 207-4648).

Early Educators Press, *(Early Educators; 0-9604390),* P.O. Box 1177, Lake Alfred, FL 33850 Tel 813-956-1569 (SAN 216-2407).

Early Stages Press, Inc., *(Early Stages; 0-915786),* P.O. Box 31463, San Francisco, CA 94131 Tel 415-282-2526 (SAN 209-0155).

Early Winters Press, *(Early Winters; 0-941984),* 110 Prefontaine S., Seattle, WA 98104 (SAN 238-0110).

Earpacker Press, *(Earpacker Pr; 0-9611304),* P.O. Box 5029, Philadelphia, PA 19111 (SAN 277-6766).

Earth Basics Press, *(Earth Basics; 0-910361),* P.O. Box 11742, Palo Alto, CA 94306 Tel 415-852-2280 (SAN 260-0463).

Earth Science Publishing Co., *(Earth Science; 0-940566),* P.O. Box 1815, Colorado Springs, CO 80901 Tel 303-634-7345 (SAN 206-6440).

Earth-Song Press, *(Earth-Song; 0-9605170),* 202 Hartnell Place, Sacramento, CA 95825 Tel 916-927-6863 (SAN 220-0473).

Earth-Space Innovations, *(Earth Space),* P.O. Box 43, Van Etten, NY 14889 (SAN 241-3779).

Earth View, Inc, *(Earth View; 0-932898),* Star Rte., Ashford, WA 98304 Tel 206-569-2261 (SAN 213-0491).

Earthlight Pubs., *(Earthlight; 0-935128),* 5539 Jackson, Kansas City, MO 64130 (SAN 213-3059).

Earthquake Engineering Research Institute, *(Quake Eng),* 2620 Telegraph Ave, Berkeley, CA 94704 (SAN 225-2457).

Earthstewards Publications, *(Earthstewards Pubns),* Box 873, Monte Rio, CA 95462 (SAN 240-1436).

Earthwise Pubs., *(Earthwise Pubs; 0-933494),* P.O. Box 680-536, Miami, FL 33168 (SAN 223-7407).

Easi-Bild Directions Simplified, Inc., *(Easi-Bild; 0-87733),* 529 N. State Rd., P.O. Box 215, Briarcliff Manor, NY 10510 Tel 914-941-6600 (SAN 201-3304).

East & West Pubns., New York, *(East & West Pubns; 0-935886),* P.O. Box 17421, West Hartford, CT 06117 (SAN 206-099X).

East Dennis Publishing Co., *(East Dennis; 0-87299),* P.O. Box 555, East Dennis, MA 02641 Tel 617-385-2000 (SAN 210-8011).

East Eagle Press, *(East Eagle; 0-9605738),* P.O. Box 812, Huron, SD 57350 (SAN 216-3705).

East European Quarterly, *(East Eur Quarterly; 0-914710),* Dist. by: Columbia Univ. Press, 136 S. Broadway, Irvington, NY 10533 Tel 914-591-9111 (SAN 212-2480).

East Palace Publishing Company, Inc., *(East Palace; 0-943628),* 32 West 40 St., Suite 5E, New York, NY 10018 Tel 505-988-3008 (SAN 238-2741).

East Ridge Press, *(East Ridge Pr; 0-914896),* Hankins, NY 12741 Tel 914-887-5499 (SAN 201-2871); Dist. by: Ridge Book Service, 161 Ridge Rd., Hankins, NY 12741 (SAN 282-6453).

East River Anthology, *(East River Anthol; 0-917238),* 75 Gates Ave., Montclair, NJ 07042 Tel 201-746-5941 (SAN 208-6344).

East-West Center, *(E W Center HI),* 1777 East-West Rd., Honolulu, HI 96848 Tel 808-948-6583 (SAN 210-802X).

East-West Cultural Center, *(E-W Cultural Ctr; 0-930736),* 2865 W. 9th St., Los Angeles, CA 90006 Tel 213-480-8325 (SAN 211-0121).

East West Culture Exchange, *(East West Cult; 0-9601274),* 3402 Leicester Dr., Muncie, IN 47304 Tel 317-289-3123 (SAN 210-3559).

East West Journal Dept., Part of Kushi Foundation, Inc., *(East West Journ; 0-936184),* 17 Station St., Box 1200, Brookline, MA 02147 Tel 617-232-1000 (SAN 221-1939).

East-West Press, *(East-West Pr; 0-9606090),* P.O. Box 4315, Minneapolis, MN 55414 Tel 612-379-2049 (SAN 216-809X).

East/West Publishing Co., *(E-W Pub Co; 0-934788),* 838 Grant Ave., Suite 307, San Francisco, CA 94108 Tel 415-781-3194 (SAN 215-8574).

East Windsor Historical Society, Inc., *(E Windsor; 0-910506),* P.O. Box 232, East Windsor, CT 06088 Tel 203-623-8579 (SAN 218-7116).

East Woods Press, Inc., Subs. of Fast & McMillan, Pubs., *(East Woods; 0-914788),* 429 E. Blvd., Charlotte, NC 28203 Tel 704-334-0897 (SAN 206-3565).

Eastern Acorn Press, Div. of Eastern National Park & Monument Assn., *(Eastern Acorn; 0-915992),* 339 Walnut St., Philadelphia, PA 19106 Tel 215-597-7129 (SAN 219-9793).

Eastern Connecticut State College Foundation, *(Eastern CT St Coll Fdn; 0-915884),* P.O. Box 431, Willimantic, CT 06226 Tel 203-456-2231 (SAN 207-4834).

Eastern Mountain Sports, *(Eastern Mount),* 11312 Vose Farm Rd., Peterborough, NH 03458 Tel 603-924-9571 (SAN 213-3067); Dist. by: Appalachian Mountain Club, 5 Joy St., Boston, MA 02108 Tel 617-523-0636 (SAN 203-4808).

Eastern Orthodox Books, *(Eastern Orthodox; 0-89981),* P.O. Box 302, Willits, CA 95490 (SAN 201-355X).

Eastern Press, *(Eastern Pr; 0-939758),* 426 E. 6th Street, Bloomington, IN 47401 (SAN 216-3713).

Eastern Washington State Historical Society, *(Eastern Wash; 0-910524),* W. 2316 First Ave., Spokane, WA 99204 Tel 506-456-3931 (SAN 203-8293).

Eastham Editions, *(Eastham Edns; 0-915102),* P.O. Box 10, Prospect, NY 13435 Tel 315-896-6388 (SAN 207-1258).

Eastland Press, *(Eastland; 0-939616),* P.O. Box 4910, Chicago, IL 60680 Tel 312-726-4742 (SAN 216-6216).

Eastman Kodak Co., *(Eastman Kodak; 0-87985),* 343 State St., Bldg. 16, 2nd Fl., Dept. 373, Rochester, NY 14650 Tel 716-722-2599 (SAN 201-3568).

Eastview Editions, Inc., *(Eastview; 0-89860),* P.O. Box 783, Westfield, NJ 07091 Tel 201-233-0474 (SAN 169-4952).

Eastwest Center Press *See* **Univ. of Hawaii Press, The**

Ebaesay-Namreplican (EBN) Pubns., *(Ebaesay; 0-9608212),* 210 W. Lemon Ave. No. 22, Monrovia, CA 91016 Tel 213-358-1763 (SAN 240-3692).

Ebe, John, *(Ebe),* 445 Grand St., Brooklyn, NY 11211 (SAN 238-8758).

Ebenezer Center for Aging & Human Development, Subs. of Ebenezer Society, *(Ebenezer Ctr; 0-938846),* 2722 Park Ave., Minneapolis, MN 55407 Tel 612-871-7112 (SAN 240-0162).

Eberly Press, *(Eberly Pr; 0-932296),* 430 N. Harrison, East Lansing, MI 48823 Tel 517-351-7299 (SAN 214-0055).

Ebonics Publishers Internationale, *(Ebonics),* P.O. Box 36518, Atlanta, GA 30032 (SAN 240-9038).

Ecclesia Pubns. *See* **William Carey Library Pubs.**

Ecco Press, *(Ecco Pr; 0-912946; 0-88001),* 18 W. 30th St., New York, NY 10001 Tel 212-685-8240 (SAN 202-5795); Dist. by: W.W. Norton & Co., Inc., Keystone Industrial Park, Scranton, PA 18512 (SAN 281-6202); Orders to: W. W. Norton & Co., 500 Fifth Ave., New York, NY 10110 Tel 212-354-5500 (SAN 202-5795).

Echenian Church, The, *(Echenian Church; 0-9603134),* P.O. Box 11893, Reno, NV 89510 (SAN 212-4998) Moved, Left No Forwarding Address.

Echo Books *See* **Doubleday & Co., Inc.**

Echo Pubs., *(Echo Pubs; 0-912852),* P.O. Box 7130, West Menlo Park, CA 94025 Tel 415-524-1575 (SAN 201-3592).

Echo Stage Co., Ltd., *(Echo Stage Co),* 250 W. 16th St., Suite 1A, New York, NY 10011 (SAN 239-5347) Tel 212-243-6805.

Echoes and Shadows, *(Echoes & Shadows; 0-942130),* P.O. Box 241, Elm Grove, WI 53122 (SAN 238-0129).

Eckhardt, Fred, Associates, *(F Eckhardt Assocs),* P.O. Box 546, Portland, OR 97207 Tel 503-289-7596 (SAN 211-2930).

Eckman Center, *(Eckman Ctr; 0-934752),* P.O. Box 621, Woodland Hills, CA 91365 Tel 213-347-4445 (SAN 207-219X).

Eclectic Press, *(Eclectic Pr; 0-9605920),* P.O. Box 984, Ansonia Sta., New York, NY 10023 Tel 212-874-2867 (SAN 216-6682).

Eclectical Publishing Co., *(Eclectical; 0-912447),* P.O. Box 7326, New Orleans, LA 70186 Tel 504-246-1978 (SAN 265-346X).

Economic Information Systems, Div. of Control Data Corporation, *(Econ Info Syst; 0-86692),* 310 Madison Ave., New York, NY 10017 (SAN 216-3721).

Economics Press, Inc., *(Economic Pr),* 12 Daniel Rd., Fairfield, NJ 07006 Tel 201-227-1224 (SAN 204-1774).

Economy Co., *(Economy Co; 0-87892; 0-8332),* 1901 N. Walnut, P.O. Box 25308, Oklahoma City, OK 73125 Tel 405-528-8444 (SAN 201-3606).

ed-it Productions, *(ed-it prods; 0-912761),* 1615 Broadway, Rm. 316, Oakland, CA 94612 (SAN 277-6774); Dist. by: Strawberry Hill Press, 2594 15th Ave., San Francisco, CA 94127 Tel 415-664-8112 (SAN 238-8103).

Ed-U Press, Inc., *(Ed-U Pr; 0-934978),* P.O. Box 583, Fayetteville, NY 13066 Tel 315-637-9524 (SAN 221-1866).

EdCom-Jean Wiley Huyler Communications, Div. of Wagener News Service, *(EdCom; 0-941554),* 922 N. pearl A-27, Tacoma, WA 98406 Tel 206-759-1579 (SAN 264-021X).

Edelson, Mary Beth, *(Edelson; 0-9604650),* 110 Mercer St., New York, NY 10012 Tel 212-226-0832 (SAN 215-7594).

Edelweiss Press, *(Edelweiss Pr; 0-9600874),* 124 Front St., Massapequa Park, NY 11762 Tel 516-799-1150 (SAN 208-0419).

Eden Co., *(Eden Co),* South Kortright, NY 13842 (SAN 239-4227).

Eden Press, *(Eden Pr; 0-920792; 0-88831),* Dist. by: University of Toronto Press, 33 E. Tupper St., Buffalo, NY 14203 Tel 716-852-0342 (SAN 214-2651).

Edenite Society, Inc., *(Edenite; 0-938520),* P.O. Box 115, Rt. 526, Imlaystowwn, NJ 08526 Tel 609-259-7517 (SAN 239-9040).

Eden's Work, *(Eden's Work; 0-937226),* RFD 1, Box 540A, Franklin, ME 04634 Tel 207-565-3533 (SAN 219-998X).

Edenwood House, *(Edenwood Hse),* P.O. Box 607, Garner, NC 27529 Tel 919-772-0107 (SAN 263-2179).

Edery, David, *(D E Pubns; 0-9610756),* P.O. Box 351024, Los Angeles, CA 90035 Tel 213-859-3974 (SAN 264-6137).

Edgar, Betsy J., *(B J Edgar),* Rt. 4, P.O. Box 130, Lewisburg, WV 24901 Tel 304-653-4242 (SAN 204-174X).

Edgemoor Publishing Co., *(Edgemoor; 0-88204),* 721 Durham Dr., Houston, TX 77007 Tel 713-861-3451 (SAN 201-3681); Orders to: P.O. Box 13612, Houston, TX 77019 (SAN 201-369X).

Edgepress, *(Edgepress; 0-918528),* P.O. Box 69, Point Reyes, CA 94956 Tel 415-663-8430 (SAN 209-6625).

Edgerton, William H., *(Edgerton; 0-9601172),* Box 88, Darien, CT 06820 Tel 203-655-9510 (SAN 210-0738).

Edgewater Book Distributors, *(Edgewater),* P.O. Box 586, Cleveland, OH 44107 Tel 216-671-1030 (SAN 215-3033).

Edgewood Press, *(Edgewood; 0-9602472),* 2865 East Rock Rd., Clare, MI 48617 (SAN 212-6559).

Ediciones Alba, *(Edns Alba; 0-9600714),* Encarnacion 1573, Caparra Heights, San Juan, PR 00920 Tel 809-781-5984 (SAN 206-3581).

Ediciones Del Norte, *(Ediciones Norte; 0-910061),* P.O. Box A130L, Hanover, NH 03755 Tel 603-795-2433 (SAN 241-2993).

Ediciones Hispamerica, *(Ediciones Hispamerica; 0-935318),* 5 Pueblo Court, Gaithersburg, MD 20878 Tel 301-948-3494 (SAN 213-9200).

Ediciones Huracan, Inc., *(Ediciones Huracan; 0-940238),* Avenida Gonzalez 1002, Rio Piedras, PR 00925 Tel 809-763-7407 (SAN 217-5134).

Ediciones Universal, *(Ediciones; 0-89729),* 3090 S.W. 8th St., Miami, FL 33135 Tel 305-642-3355 (SAN 207-2203).

Edison Institute, The, *(Edison Inst; 0-933728),* 20900 Oakwood Blvd., Dearborn, MI 48121 (SAN 216-4841). *Imprints:* Henry Ford Museum Press (Ford Mus).

EDITIONS DES   PUBLISHERS AND DISTRIBUTORS

Editions Des Deux Mondes, *(Edns Des Deux Mondes; 0-939586),* P.O. Box 56, Newark, DE 19711 Tel 301-398-2834 (SAN 216-373X).

Editions Limited, *(Editions Ltd; 0-9607938),* 111 Royal Circle, Honolulu, HI 96816 Tel 808-734-0340 (SAN 239-6378).

Editions Orphee, Inc., *(Edit Orphee; 0-936186),* P.O. Box 364, Prudential Ctr., Boston, MA 02115 (SAN 221-1890).

Editions Vilo, Inc., *(Edns Vilo; 0-86710),* 500 Fifth Ave., Suite 1423, New York, NY 10110 Tel 212-398-1723 (SAN 216-7271).

Editorial Asol, *(Edit Asol),* Box 21942, Univ. of Puerto Rico, Rio Piedras, PR 00931 (SAN 238-8766).

Editorial Betania, Div. of Bethany Fellowship, Inc., *(Edit Betania; 0-88113),* 6820 Auto Club Rd., Minneapolis, MN 55431 Tel 612-944-2121 (SAN 240-6349).

Editorial Caribe, *(Edit Caribe; 0-89922),* 3934 S. W. 8th St., Suite 303, Miami, FL 33134 Tel 305-445-0564 (SAN 215-1421).

Editorial Consultants, Inc., *(Edit Consult; 0-917636),* 3221 Pierce, San Francisco, CA 94123 Tel 415-931-7239 (SAN 212-6567).

Editorial Doble Omega, *(Editorial D O; 0-88696),* P.O. Box 650712, Miami, FL 33165 Tel 305-554-4865 (SAN 283-0590); 13895 S.W. 22nd St., Miami, FL 33175 (SAN 283-0604).

Editorial Experts, Inc., *(Edit Experts; 0-935012),* 5905 Pratt St., Alexandria, VA 22310 Tel 703-971-7350 (SAN 216-3748).

Editorial Justa Pubns., *(Editorial Justa; 0-915808),* 2831 Seventh St., Berkeley, CA 94710 Tel 415-848-3628 (SAN 208-1962); Orders to: P.O. Box 2131-C, Berkeley, CA 94702 (SAN 208-1970).

Editorial Mensaje, *(Edit Mensaje; 0-86515),* 125 Queen St., Staten Island, NY 10314 Tel 212-761-0556 (SAN 214-0063).

Editorial Mundo Hispano *See* Casa Bautista De Publicaciones

Editorial Research Service, *(Edit Res Serv; 0-933592),* P.O. Box 1832, Kansas City, MO 64141 (SAN 212-7407).

Editorial Services Co., *(Edit Services; 0-933406),* 1140 Ave. of the Americas, New York, NY 10036 Tel 212-741-4280 (SAN 212-419X).

Editors & Engineers, Ltd., *(Editors; 0-672),* Dist. by: Bobbs-Merrill Co., Inc., 4300 W. 62nd St.,P.O. Box 7080, Indianapolis, IN 46206 Tel 317-298-5595 (SAN 201-3959).

Editors Press Service, Inc., Div. of Charleston Post Pub. Co., *(Edit Pr Serv; 0-89971),* 60 E. 42nd St., New York, NY 10017 Tel 212-682-2888 (SAN 204-1715).

Edmunds, Adeline, *(A Edmunds; 0-9605846),* 421 N. Sixth Ave., Sturgeon Bay, WI 54235 Tel 414-743-9433 (SAN 216-3756).

EDPRESS *See* Educational Press Assn. of America

EduCALC Pubns, *(EduCALC Pubns; 0-936356),* P.O. Box 974, Laguna Beach, CA 92652 Tel 714-497-3600 (SAN 281-6229); Dist. by: Publishers Group West, 5855 Beaudry St., Emeryville, CA 94608 Tel 415-658-6296 (SAN 202-8522).

Education & Training Consultants Co., *(Ed & Training; 0-87657),* Box 2085, Sedona, AZ 86336-2085 Tel 602-282-3009 (SAN 201-3665).

Education & Training Consultants Pubns., Subs. of Education & Training Dev. Consultants, *(Educ & Trainin; 0-937196),* P.O. Box 28165, Detroit, MI 48228 Tel 313-835-3363 (SAN 282-3780).

Education Assocs., *(Ed Assocs; 0-918772),* P.O. Box 8021, Athens, GA 30603 Tel 404-542-4244 (SAN 210-4180).

Education Associates, Inc., *(Ed Assocs KY; 0-940428),* P.O. Box Y, 45 Fountain Place, Frankfort, KY 40602 (SAN 223-0674).

Education Commission of the States, *(Ed Comm States),* Suite 300. 1860 Lincoln St., Denver, CO 80295 (SAN 224-120X).

Education Development Center, Inc., *(Educ Dev Ctr; 0-89292),* Orders to: EDC Distribution Center, 55 Chapel St., Newton, MA 02160 Tel 617-969-7100 (SAN 207-821X).

Education Foundation, Inc., *(Educ Found),* P.O. Box 1187, Charleston, WV 25324 Tel 304-342-0855 (SAN 204-1685).

Education Guide, Inc., *(Educ Guide; 0-914880),* P.O. Box 421, Randolph, MA 02368 Tel 617-961-2217 (SAN 201-4580).

Education Industries, Inc., *(Educ Indus; 0-86652),* P.O. Box 52, Madison, WI 53701 (SAN 216-1273).

Education Press, The, *(Educ Pr CA; 0-9601706),* Box 2358, Huntington Beach, CA 92647 (SAN 213-1323).

Education Research Associates, *(Educ Res MA; 0-913636),* P.O. Box 767, Amherst, MA 01004 Tel 413-253-3582 (SAN 215-3068).

Education Services, *(Education Serv; 0-936394),* P.O. Box 5281, Atlanta, GA 30307 (SAN 221-1920).

Education System Publisher, *(Ed Sys Pub; 0-915676),* 501 Salem Dr., Ithaca, NY 14850 (SAN 207-4028).

Educational Book Pubs., *(Ed Bk Pubs OK; 0-932188),* P.O. Box 1219, Guthrie, OK 73044 (SAN 215-8582).

Educational Book Pubs., Inc., *(Educ Bk Pubs),* 1175 N.E. 125th St., Suite 303, North Miami, FL 33161 Tel 305-891-7471 (SAN 204-1650).

Educational Communications, Inc., *(Educ Comm; 0-915130),* 721 N. McKinley, Lake Forest, IL 60045 Tel 312-295-6650 (SAN 216-6540).

Educational Design, Inc., *(Ed Design Inc; 0-87694),* 47 W. 13th St., New York, NY 10011 Tel 212-255-7900 (SAN 204-1588).

Educational Direction, Inc., *(Educ Direction; 0-940432),* 181 Post Rd. W., Westport, CT 06680 Tel 203-227-3350 (SAN 217-1724).

Educational Directories Inc., *(Ed Direct; 0-910536),* P.O. Box 199, Mt. Prospect, IL 60056 Tel 312-392-1811 (SAN 201-3614).

Educational Editions, *(Educ Editions; 0-933092),* MS-293, P.O. Box 420240, Houston, TX 77243 Tel 713-467-2241 (SAN 212-6575).

Educational Facilities Laboratories, *(Ed Facilities; 0-88481),* c/o Academy for Educational Development, 680 Fifth Ave., New York, NY 10019 Tel 212-397-0040 (SAN 210-0185).

Educational Factors, Inc., *(Ed Factors; 0-936864),* 1261 Lincoln Ave., P.O. Box 6389, San Jose, CA 95150 (SAN 221-9204).

Educational Film Library Assn., *(EFLA; 0-87520),* 43 W. 61st St., New York, NY 10023 Tel 212-246-4533 (SAN 201-8233).

Educational Foundation for Nuclear Science, Inc., *(Educ Found for Nucl Sci),* 5801 S.Kenwood, Chicago, IL 60637 Tel 312-363-5225 (SAN 218-7175).

Educational Insights, *(Educ Insights; 0-88679),* 150 W. Carob St., Compton, CA 90220 (SAN 283-8745).

Educational Institute of the American Hotel & Motel Assn., *(Educ Inst Am Hotel; 0-86612),* 1407 S. Harrison Rd., East Lansing, MI 48823 Tel 517-353-5500 (SAN 215-8590).

Educational Institute Press, *(Ed Inst Pr),* P.O. Box 2537, Laguna Beach, CA 92653 Tel 714-830-0972 (SAN 203-8331) Moved, Left No Forwarding Address.

Educational Leadership and Counseling Department, *(Educ Leadership; 0-911467),* Office of Community Ed. researh, 34F Boone Hall, Eastern Michigan University, Ypsilanti, MI 48197 (SAN 264-0228).

Educational Media & Information Systems, *(Ed Med & Info Sys; 0-913470),* P.O. Box 2411, Fort Collins, CO 80522 (SAN 203-834X) Moved, left no forwarding address.

Educational Media Corp., *(Ed Media Corp; 0-932796),* P.O. Box 21311, Minneapolis, MN 55421 (SAN 212-4203).

Educational Medical Pubs., *(Educ Medical; 0-930728),* 18 Kling St., West Orange, NJ 07052 (SAN 211-1268).

Educational Ministries, Inc., *(Ed Ministries; 0-940754),* 765 Penarth Ave., Walnut, CA 91789 Tel 714-594-2060 (SAN 219-7316).

Educational Planning Services Corporation, *(Educ Plan Serv; 0-9609720),* Box 182, Newton Highlando, MA 02161 Tel 617-964-9509 (SAN 263-2187).

Educational Press Assn. of America, *(Educ Pr Assn; 0-89972),* Glassboro State College, Glassboro, NJ 08028 Tel 609-445-7349 (SAN 204-1634).

Educational Program Development Associates, Inc., *(Educ Prog Dev),* 2103 Crestmoor Rd., Nashville, TN 37215 Tel 615-269-5755 (SAN 240-9895).

Educational Pubns, Inc., *(Ed Pubns; 0-942930),* P.O. Box 41870, Tuscon, AZ 85717 Tel 602-791-9690 (SAN 240-3706).

Educational Research Service, *(Ed Research),* 1800 N. Kent St., Arlington, VA 22209 Tel 703-527-5331 (SAN 203-7912).

Educational Resources Unlimited, Inc., *(Ed Resources; 0-915912),* P.O. Box 43, Baker, NV 89311 Tel 702-234-7213 (SAN 208-6352).

Educational Science Consultants, *(Ed Sci; 0-912990),* P.O. Box 1674, San Leandro, CA 94577 (SAN 201-3657).

Educational Service, Inc., *(Educ Serv; 0-89273),* P.O. Box 219, Stevensville, MI 49127 Tel 616-429-1451 (SAN 206-9423).

Educational Service Publications, *(Educ Serv Pub; 0-9608250),* Box 205, Boones Mill, VA 24065 Tel 703-334-2269 (SAN 240-3714).

Educational Solutions, Inc., *(Ed Solutions; 0-87825),* 80 Fifth Ave., New York, NY 10011 Tel 212-924-1744 (SAN 205-6186).

Educational Studies Press, *(Educ Stud Pr; 0-934328),* Quadrangle, Iowa State Univ., Ames, IA 50011 Tel 515-294-7327 (SAN 213-3083).

Educational Technology Pubns, Inc., *(Educ Tech Pubns; 0-87778),* 140 Sylvan Ave., Englewood Cliffs, NJ 07632 Tel 201-871-4007 (SAN 201-3738).

Educational Testing Service, *(Educ Testing Serv),* ATP: Services for Handicapped Students, Box 2891, Princeton, NJ 08541 Tel 609-921-9000 (SAN 238-034X) Administers Scholastic Aptitude Test and Test of Standard Written English in Large Type Editions.

Educative Services, Inc., *(Educative Serv; 0-939494),* P.O. Box 3787, Thousand Oaks, CA 91359 Tel 213-991-1348 (SAN 216-6690).

Educator Books, Inc., *(Educator Bks; 0-912092),* Drawer 32, 10 N. Main, San Angelo, TX 76901 Tel 915-653-0152 (SAN 203-8382).

Educator Pubns., *(Educator Pubns; 0-913558),* 1110 S. Pomona Ave., Fullerton, CA 92632 Tel 714-871-2950 (SAN 201-3746); P.O. Box 333, Fullerton, CA 92632 (SAN 201-3754).

Educator's Academy, *(Ed Acad; 0-9607160),* P.O. Box 75, Dayton, OH 45402 Tel 513-274-1662 (SAN 238-9738).

Educators Progress Service, Inc., *(Ed Prog; 0-87708),* 214 Center St., Randolph, WI 53956 Tel 414-326-3126 (SAN 201-3649).

EduTech Press, *(Edutech; 0-9610102),* 22158 Ramona, Apple Valley, CA 92307 Tel 619-247-7633 (SAN 269-865X).

Edward De Bono School of Thinking, The, *(E De Bono; 0-942580),* 205 E. 78th St., New York, NY 10021 Tel 212-249-9450 (SAN 239-6319).

Edward Press, *(Edward Pr; 0-9606020),* 62 Brighton St., Rochester, NY 14607 Tel 716-271-4272 (SAN 216-8898).

Edwards, Elmer Eugene, *(Elmer Edwards),* P.O. Box 584, Miami, FL 33161 (SAN 215-143X).

Edwards, Ernest P., *(E P Edwards; 0-911882),* P.O. Box AQ, Sweet Briar, VA 24595 Tel 804-381-5442 (SAN 201-3525).

Edwards, G. F., *(G F Edwards; 0-932318),* Box 1461, Lawton, OK 73502 Tel 405-248-6870 (SAN 212-1719).

Edwards, Lowell E., *(L E Edwards; 0-936024),* P.O. Box 255714, Sacramento, CA 95825 (SAN 213-7348).

Edwards, Thomas Clarke, *(Reverend Clarke; 0-9611840),* 147 Midwood Rd., Paramus, NJ 07652 Tel 201-444-8580 (SAN 286-1925).

Edwards Brothers, Inc., *(Edwards Bros; 0-910546),* 2500 S. State St., P.O. Box 1007, Ann Arbor, MI 48106 Tel 313-769-1000 (SAN 206-9814).

Edwards Publishing Co., *(Edwards Pub Co; 0-911935),* P.O. Box 42218, Tacoma, WA 98442 (SAN 264-0236).

Eerdmans, Wm. B., Publishing Co., *(Eerdmans; 0-8028),* 255 Jefferson Ave., S.E., Grand Rapids, MI 49503 Tel 616-459-4591 (SAN 220-0058).

Effective Learning Inc., *(Effective Learn; 0-915474),* 7 N. MacQuesten Pkwy., P.O. Box 2212, Mount Vernon, NY 10550 (SAN 208-4791).

Effective Learning Pubns., *(Effect Learning GA; 0-933594),* 111 Holly Dr., Statesboro, GA 30458 (SAN 213-487X).

Effective Learning Systems, Inc., *(Effect Learn Sys; 0-913261),* P.O. Box 85, Moraga, CA 94556 Tel 415-376-6162 (SAN 283-0620).

2204

Effective Management Resources Corp., *(Effect Mgmt; 0-939740),* 2229 Nyon Ave., Anaheim, CA 92806 (SAN 216-3764).

Effectiveness Training Associates, *(Effectiveness Train; 0-918460),* 321 River St., Manistee, MI 49660 Tel 616-723-8422 (SAN 209-553X).

Effie's Books, *(Effies Bks),* 1420 45th St., Emeryville, CA 94608 (SAN 209-5548).

Eggplant Press, *(Eggplant Pr; 0-935060),* P.O. Box 18641, Denver, CO 80218 (SAN 211-6030).

Eggs Press, *(Eggs Pr; 0-9602914),* 3038 41st Ave. S., Minneapolis, MN 55406 (SAN 213-6228).

Ego Books, *(Ego Bks; 0-933540),* 6011 Meadowbrook Lane, Lincoln, NE 68510 Tel 402-489-6982 (SAN 212-159X).

Ehde Publishing Co., *(Ehde Pub Co; 0-936188),* Sontag, MS 39665 (SAN 214-0071).

Ehling Clifton Books, *(Ehling Clifton Bks),* 2401 Clifton Ave., Cincinnati, OH 45219 (SAN 240-1444).

EHM Publishing, *(EHM Pub; 0-9609828),* Box 3173, Tallahassee, FL 32315 Tel 904-539-9767 (SAN 262-0170).

Eide, Lucille, *(L Eide; 0-9610668),* Box 2575, Sacramento, CA 95812 (SAN 264-7370).

Eidolon Press, *(Eidolon Pr),* P.O. Box 8204, Pensacola, FL 32505 (SAN 241-3787).

Eighties Press, *(Eighties Pr; 0-87390),* 308 First St., Moose Lake, MN 55767 (SAN 204-5869); Dist. by: Bookpeople, 2940 Seventh St., Berkeley, CA 94710 (SAN 168-9517).

Eilean Ban Publishing Co., *(Eilean Ban Pub; 0-918702),* 4329 Sano St., Alexandria, VA 22312 Tel 703-354-8771 (SAN 211-416X).

Eisenberg Educational Enterprises, *(Eisenberg Ed; 0-930080),* 2 Hamill Rd., Suite 327, Village of Cross Keys, Baltimore, MD 21210 Tel 301-435-8351 (SAN 210-5942).

Eisenbrauns, *(Eisenbrauns; 0-931464),* P.O. Box 275, Winona Lake, IN 46590 Tel 219-269-2011 (SAN 213-4365).

Eisenhower, Dwight D., Library, *(Eisenhower Lib; 0-9605728),* Abilene, KS 67410 Tel 913-263-4751 (SAN 217-1015).

Eiteljorg, Harrison, Pubns., *(Eiteljorg Pubns; 0-9607596),* 4567 Cold Spring Rd., Indianapolis, IN 46208 (SAN 239-4359); Dist. by: Independent Publishers Group, One Pleasant Ave., Port Washington, NY 11050 (SAN 239-4367).

Either-or Press, *(Either-or Pr; 0-910931),* 122 North St., Pittsfield, MA 01201 (SAN 262-0189).

Eko Pubns., *(Eko Pubns),* P.O. Box 5492, Philadelphia, PA 19143 (SAN 201-4599).

El Camino Pubs., *(El Camino; 0-942060),* 4010 Calle Real, Suite 4, Santa Barbara, CA 93110 Tel 805-682-9340 (SAN 238-6151).

El-Hajj Malik Shabazz Press, *(Shabazz Pr; 0-913358),* 445 Park Rd. N.W., Washington, DC 20010 (SAN 201-2340); Orders to: Liberation Information Distributing Co., 4206 Edson Place N.E., Washington, DC 20019 (SAN 201-2359).

Elan Northwest Pubs., *(Elan NW Pubs; 0-9603272),* P.O. Box 5442, Eugene, OR 97405 Tel 503-485-3462 (SAN 206-4707).

Elar Publishing Co.,Inc., *(Elar Pub Co; 0-914130),* 1120 Old Country Rd., Plainview, NY 11803 Tel 516-433-6530 (SAN 215-952X).

Elder, Charles & Randy, Pubs., *(C Elder; 0-918450),* 2115 Elliston Place, Nashville, TN 37203 Tel 615-327-1867 (SAN 201-8292).

Eldridge Publishing Co., *(Eldridge Pub; 0-912963),* P. O. Drawer 208, Franklin, OH 45005 Tel 513-746-6531 (SAN 204-1553).

Eleanor Friede *See* **Delacorte Press**

Electret Scientific Co., *(Electret Sci; 0-917406),* P.O. Box 4132, Star City, WV 26505 Tel 304-594-1639 (SAN 206-4715).

Electro-Optical Research Co., *(Electro-Optical),* Suite 422, 2029 Century Park E., Los Angeles, CA 90067 Tel 213-277-7422 (SAN 207-2211).

Electrodata, Inc., *(Electrodata; 0-943890),* P.O. Box 206, Glen Echo, MD 20812 Tel 301-229-2477 (SAN 241-1083).

Electronic Courseware Systems, Inc., *(Electron Course; 0-942132),* 309 Windsor Rd., Champaign, IL 61820 Tel 217-359-7099 (SAN 238-6577).

Electronic Flea Market, *(Electronic Flea),* 2020 Girard Ave., S., Minneapolis, MN 55405 (SAN 206-4529).

Eleutherian Mills-Hagley Foundation, *(Eleutherian Mills-Hagley; 0-914650),* Box 3630, Greenville, DE 19807 Tel 302-658-2400 (SAN 204-1545).

Elevation Pr., *(Elevation Pr; 0-932624),* 704 N. Beaver, Flagstaff, AZ 86001 Tel 602-779-3019 (SAN 212-1875).

11th Hour Gospel, *(Eleventh Hour; 0-9608662),* Box 190, Prosser, WA 99350 Tel 509-786-4230 (SAN 240-6365).

Elgen Publishing Co., *(Elgen Pub Co; 0-935774),* 1004 Taurus Dr., Colorado Springs, CO 80906 (SAN 214-2392).

Elghund Publishing Company, *(Elghund Pub),* P.O. Box 158, Simpsonville, MD 21150 (SAN 283-2631).

Eli Mail-Order House, Inc., *(Eli Mail; 0-9602230),* P.O. Box 81, Brooklyn, NY 11208 (SAN 212-3509).

Elijah Press, *(Elijah Pr; 0-9608472),* 24 1/2 Center St., Rutland, VT 05701 Tel 802-773-7215 (SAN 240-6381).

Eliopoulos, *(Eliopoulos),* P.O. Box 65, Oak Park, IL 60303 (SAN 220-0856).

Elizabeth Press, *(Elizabeth Pr),* 103 Van Etten Blvd., New Rochelle, NY 10804 (SAN 201-3789).

Elk Grove Books *See* **Childrens Press**

Elk Grove Village Public Library, *(Elk Grove Vill; 0-9605940),* 101 Kennedy Blvd., Elk Grove Village, IL 60007 Tel 312-439-0447 (SAN 216-6224).

Ell Ell Diversified, Inc., *(Ell Ell Diversified; 0-937428),* P.O. Box 1702, Santa Rosa, CA 95402 Tel 707-542-8663 (SAN 215-3076).

Ellingsworth Press, *(Ellingsworth; 0-9605698),* 20 E. Main St., Rm. 338, Waterbury, CT 06702 (SAN 211-1519).

Elliot Press, *(Elliot Pr),* 27 Camden Rd., Auburndale, MA 02166 (SAN 262-4702).

Elliot's Books, *(Elliots Bks; 0-911830),* P.O. Box 6, Northford, CT 06472 Tel 203-484-2184 (SAN 204-1529).

Elliott, J. R., *(J R Elliott),* 9 Country Manor, Fergus Falls, MN 56537 (SAN 238-2380).

TEP, *(TEP; 0-911759),* 44-A Joy St., Suite 8, Boston, MA 02114 Tel 617-227-7277 (SAN 264-0252).

Ellis, Edward, *(E Ellis; 0-9611126),* P.O. Box 661, Rangeley, ME 04970 (SAN 283-2429); 123 Welsh Rd., Ambler, PA 19002 Tel 215-646-3839 (SAN 283-2437).

Ellis & Stewart Publishers, *(Ellis & Stewart Pub; 0-942532),* 270 N. Canon Dr., Suite 103, Beverly Hills, CA 90210 Tel 213-276-5424 (SAN 239-6386).

Ellis Press, The, *(Ellis Pr; 0-933180),* P.O. Box 1443, Peoria, IL 61655 (SAN 214-008X).

Ellison Enterprises, *(Ellison Ent; 0-930580),* 1919 Purdy Ave., Miami Beach, FL 33139 Tel 305-534-4454 (SAN 211-0091).

Elm Pubns., *(Elm Pubs; 0-911175),* P.O. Box 23192, Knoxville, TN 37933-1192 Tel 615-966-5703 (SAN 269-8986).

Elmer, William B., *(Elmer; 0-9601028),* 2 Chestnut St., Andover, MA 01810 Tel 617-475-1020 (SAN 208-1571).

Elmo, Francis, Pub., *(F Elmo; 0-9607590),* 504 E. Palace Ave., Santa Fe, NM 87501 Tel 505-983-1960 (SAN 238-6607).

Elmwood Publishing Co., The, *(Elmwood Pub Co; 0-931396),* 1509 Norman Ave., San Jose, CA 95125 Tel 408-267-2498 (SAN 211-6650).

Elon College Alumni Assn., *(Elon College Alum Assoc; 0-9605976),* Elon College, NC 27244 Tel 919-584-2380 (SAN 216-7298).

ELS International Inc., *(ELS Intl; 0-89318),* 5761 Buckingham Pkwy., Culver City, CA 90230 Tel 213-642-0994 (SAN 281-6261); Orders to: Order Fulfillment Center, 14350 N.W. Science Park Dr., Portland, OR 97229 Tel 800-547-1515 (SAN 281-627X).

ELS Pubns., *(English Lang; 0-89285),* 5761 Buckingham Pkwy., Culver City, CA 90230 Tel 213-642-0994 (SAN 281-6288); Orders to: Order Fulfillment Center, 14350 N.W. Science Park Dr., Portland, OR 97229 Tel 800-547-1515 (SAN 281-6296).

Elsah Landing Restaurant, The, *(Elsah Landing; 0-9606150),* 42 Hillvale Dr., St. Louis, MO 63117 Tel 314-993-4843 (SAN 285-0095); Orders to: W. B. Design & Development, Inc., 10041 Conway Rd., St. Louis, MO 63124 Tel 314-726-6924 (SAN 285-0109); Orders to: Elsah Landing Restaurant Cookbook, P.O. Box 98, Elsah, IL 62028 (SAN 285-0117).

Elsevier North-Holland Biomedical Press *See* **Elsevier Science Publishing Co., Inc.**

Elsevier Science Publishing Co., Inc., Div. of Biomedical Division, *(Elsevier; 0-444; 0-7204),* 52 Vanderbilt Ave., New York, NY 10017 Tel 212-867-9040 (SAN 200-2051). *Imprints:* Elsevier North-Holland Biomedical Press (Biomedical Pr); Excerpta-Medica (Excerpta Medica); North-Holland (North Holland); Thomond Press (Thomond Pr).

Elysian Press, *(Elysian Pr; 0-941692),* P.O. Box 94, Cold Spring Harbor, NY 11724 Tel 212-724-8500 (SAN 239-2844).

Elysium Growth Press, *(Elysium; 0-910550),* 5436 Fernwood Ave., Los Angeles, CA 90027 Tel 213-465-7121 (SAN 210-5950).

Emami, Mary Lou & Suzanne Coulson, *(Emami-Coulson; 0-9602316),* 1691 Dickinson Dr., Wheaton, IL 60187 (SAN 213-9197).

Embee Press, *(Embee Pr; 0-89816),* 82 Pine Grove, Kingston, NY 12401 (SAN 212-1603).

EMC Controls, Inc., *(EMC Controls; 0-9609256),* P.O. Box 242, Cockeysville, MD 21030 Tel 301-667-8162 (SAN 260-0455).

Emerald House, *(Emerald Hse; 0-936958),* P.O. Box 1769, Sand Point, ID 83864 (SAN 214-3682).

Emergence Pubns., *(Emergence; 0-89465),* 185 Beacon Hill, Ashland, OR 97520 Tel 503-482-0666 (SAN 210-6299).

Emergency Service Products & Productions, *(Emerg Service Products & Prod; 0-9606144),* P.O. Box 1363, Chico, CA 95926 Tel 916-894-7150 (SAN 217-5142).

Emeritus, Inc., Publisher, *(Emeritus Inc; 0-943694),* 15 Jade Lane, Cherry Hill, NJ 08202 Tel 609-667-4278 (SAN 238-2768).

Emerson Books, Inc., *(Emerson; 0-87523),* Madelyn Ave., Verplanck, NY 10596 Tel 914-739-3506 (SAN 201-3819).

Emissary Pubns., *(Emissary Pubns; 0-941380),* P.O. Box 642, S. Pasadena, CA 91030 Tel 213-794-3400 (SAN 238-9746).

Emmett Pub. Co., *(Emmett; 0-934682),* 2861 Burnham Blvd., Minneapolis, MN 55416 (SAN 210-556X).

Emmons-Fairfied Publishing Co., *(Emmons-Fairfied Pub; 0-9607956),* 18674 Fairfield, Detroit, MI 48221 Tel 313-284-0180 (SAN 240-0707).

Emotions Anonymous International, *(Emotions Anony Intl; 0-9607356),* P.O. Box 4245, St. Paul, MN 55104 (SAN 239-5495).

Empire Books, *(Empire Bks; 0-88015),* 527 Madison Ave., New York, NY 10022 Tel 212-752-6451 (SAN 219-7324); Dist. by: Harper & Row Pubs., Inc., 10 E. 53rd St., New York, NY 10022 (SAN 200-2086).

Empire Games Press, Div. of Empire Games, Inc., *(Empire Games Pr; 0-913037),* P.O. Box 5462, Arlington, TX 76011 Tel 817-261-3666 (SAN 283-0663); 700 E. Aleram, Arlington, TX 76010 (SAN 283-0671).

Employee Benefit Research Institute, *(Employee Benefit; 0-86643),* 2121 K St., N.W., Suite 860, Washington, DC 20037 Tel 202-659-0670 (SAN 216-2423).

Employee Relocation Council, *(Employee; 0-912614),* 1627 "K" St., N.W., Washington, DC 20006 Tel 202-857-0857 (SAN 201-3827).

Emporia State Press, *(Emporia State),* 1200 Commercial St., Emporia, KS 66801 Tel 316-343-1200 (SAN 207-9771).

Emporium Pubns., *(Emporium Pubns; 0-88278),* 28 Sackville St., Charlestown, MA 02129 Tel 617-241-9549 (SAN 201-3835).

En Passant Poetry Press, *(En Passant Poet; 0-9605098),* 4612 Sylvanus Dr., Wilmington, DE 19803 Tel 302-774-4571 (SAN 212-4211).

Enabling Systems, Inc., *(Enabling Syst; 0-917688),* P.O. Box 2813, Honolulu, HI 96803 Tel 808-536-6528 (SAN 207-2440).

Encino Press, *(Encino Pr; 0-88426),* 510 Baylor St., Austin, TX 78703 Tel 512-476-6821 (SAN 201-3843).

Encyclopaedia Britannica Educational Corp., Affiliate of Encyclopaedia Britannica, Inc., *(Ency Brit Ed; 0-87827),* 425 N. Michigan Ave., Chicago, IL 60611 Tel 312-321-6800 (SAN 201-3851).

Encyclopaedia Britannica, Inc., *(Ency Brit Inc; 0-85229),* 310 S. Michigan Ave., Chicago, IL 60604 Tel 312-347-7000 (SAN 204-1464).

Endurance Press, *(Endurance; 0-910552),* 5695 Lumley St., Detroit, MI 48210 Tel 313-877-3596 (SAN 203-8412).

Energize, *(Energize; 0-940576),* 5450 Wissahickon Ave., Lobby A, Philadelphia, PA 19144 Tel 215-438-8342 (SAN 223-7660).

Energy Blacksouth Press, *(Energy Blacksouth),* Box 441, Howard University, Washington, DC 20059 (SAN 208-1393); 2805 Southmore, Houston, TX 77004 (SAN 208-1407).

Energy Education Pubs., *(Energy Educ),* P.O. Box 6488, Grand Rapids, MI 49506 Tel 616-454-8264 (SAN 211-0105).

Energy Self-Sufficiency, *(Energy Self Suff; 0-9608402),* P.O. Box 999, Siloam Springs, AR 72761 Tel 501-524-9495 (SAN 240-639X).

Energy Textbooks International, Inc., *(Energy Textbks; 0-910649),* 700 Citizens Tower, 2200 Classen Blvd., Oklahoma City, OK 73106 (SAN 262-0200); Dist. by: I E D Publisher House, 1111 N. Robinson, P.O. Box 1167, Oklahoma City, OK 73136 Tel 405-232-2801 (SAN 227-0056).

Engelmeier, Philip A., *(Engelmeier; 0-9605002),* 909 Geary-517, San Francisco, CA 94109 (SAN 215-6415).

Enger, Ronald L., *(R L Enger; 0-9601742),* 1853 Shadowbrook Dr., Merced, CA 95340 (SAN 211-948X).

Engineering Foundation, *(Eng Found; 0-939204),* 345 E. 47th St., New York, NY 10017 (SAN 216-3772).

Engineering Information Inc., *(Eng Info; 0-911820),* 345 E. 47th St., New York, NY 10017 Tel 212-705-7615 (SAN 203-8420).

Engineering Press, Inc., *(Eng Pr; 0-910554),* P.O. Box 1, San Jose, CA 95103 Tel 408-258-4503 (SAN 201-3878).

Engineering Pubns., *(Eng Pubns; 0-9605004),* P.O. Box 302, Blacksburg, VA 24060 (SAN 220-0481).

Engineer's Press, *(Engineers Pr; 0-930644),* P.O. Box 1651, Coral Gables, FL 33134 Tel 305-856-0031 (SAN 201-5668).

English Educational Services International, Inc., *(Eng Educ Serv; 0-936808),* 139 Massachusetts Ave., Boston, MA 02115 Tel 617-267-8063 (SAN 215-160X).

English Factory, The, *(English Fact; 0-911349),* 4225 N. 36th St., No. 20, Phoenix, AZ 85018 Tel 602-957-6592 (SAN 269-9257).

English Language Services, Div. of Washington Educational Research Associates, Inc., *(Eng Language; 0-87789),* 5761 Buckingham Pkwy., Culver City, CA 90230 Tel 213-642-0994 (SAN 281-6326)14350 N.W. Science Park Dr., Portland, OR 97229 Tel 800-547-1515 (SAN 281-6334).

Eno River Press, Inc., *(Eno River Pr; 0-88024),* P.O. Box 4900, Duke Sta., Durham, NC 27706 Tel 604-856-7460 (SAN 217-3573).

Enoch Pratt Free Library, *(Enoch Pratt; 0-910556),* 400 Cathedral St., Baltimore, MD 21201-4484 Tel 301-396-5494 (SAN 201-3916).

Enquiry Press, *(Enquiry Pr; 0-941494),* 799 Broadway, Suite 325, New York, NY 10003 Tel 212-982-2406 (SAN 239-0876).

Enrichment Enterprises, *(Enrichment; 0-9609612),* 1424 Hacienda Place, Pomona, CA 91768 Tel 714-622-4887 (SAN 264-0260).

Enslow, Ridley, Pubs See **Enslow Pubs. Inc.**

Enslow Pubs. Inc., *(Enslow Pubs; 0-89490),* Bloy St. & Ramsey Ave., Box 777, Hillside, NJ 07205 Tel 201-964-4116 (SAN 213-7518); Box 301, Short Hills, NJ 07078 (SAN 209-0651).

Ensminger Publishing Co., *(Ensminger; 0-941218),* 648 W. Sierra Ave., P.O. Box 429, Clovis, CA 93612 (SAN 239-4375).

Entelek, Inc., *(Entelek; 0-87567),* Ward-Whidden House, The Hill, P. O. Box 1303, Portsmouth, NH 03801 Tel 603-436-0439 (SAN 201-3924).

Enterline, J.R., *(J R Enterline),* 144 W. 95th St., New York, NY 10025 Tel 212-865-9648 (SAN 208-399X).

Enterprise Press, *(Enterprise Pr),* Box 108, Bath, MI 48808 Tel 517-332-2134 (SAN 214-2406).

Enterprise Pubns., *(Enterprise Calif; 0-918558),* P.O. Box 4001, Downey, CA 90241 (SAN 207-222X).

Enterprise Publishing Assn., *(Enterprise Pub; 0-939542),* Box 29, W. Second St., Coudersport, PA 16915 Tel 814-274-8044 (SAN 216-6704).

Enterprise Publishing, Inc., *(Enterprise Del; 0-913864),* 725 Market St., Wilmington, DE 19801 Tel 302-654-0110 (SAN 201-3932).

Entertainment Factory, The, *(Entertainment Factory; 0-936086),* P.O. Box 407, Cave Creek, AZ 85331 Tel 602-488-2510 (SAN 214-0098).

Entheos Communications, *(Entheos; 0-939750),* P.O. Box 10696, Bainbridge Island, WA 98110 Tel 206-842-3641 (SAN 216-3209).

Entity Publishing Co., *(Entity Pub Co; 0-89913),* 1314 Larmor Ave., Rowland Heights, CA 91748 Tel 714-598-1755 (SAN 213-3091).

Entomological Reprint Specialists, *(Entomological Repr; 0-911836),* P.O. Box 77224, Dockweiler Sta., Los Angeles, CA 90007 Tel 213-227-1285 (SAN 201-4602).

Entomological Society of America, *(Entomol Soc),* 4603 Calvert Rd., College Park, MD 20740 Tel 301-864-1334 (SAN 201-3940).

Entrepreneurs' Library, Inc., *(Entrepreneurs),* P.O. Box 17729, Fountain Hills, AZ 85268 (SAN 262-0219).

Entrepreneurs Productions, *(Entre Prods; 0-911665),* 5 White Street, New York, NY 10013 (SAN 264-0279).

Entropy Ltd., *(Entropy Ltd),* South Great Rd., Lincoln, MA 01773 (SAN 215-6423).

Entry Publishing Co., Inc., *(Entry Pub; 0-941342),* 27 W. 96th St., New York, NY 10025 Tel 212-662-9703 (SAN 238-9754).

Entwhistle Books, *(Entwhistle Bks; 0-9601428; 0-934558),* P.O. Box 611, Glen Ellen, CA 95442 Tel 707-996-3901 (SAN 211-0113).

Entwood Publishing, *(Entwood Pub; 0-9605978),* P.O. Box 268, Wausau, WI 54401 Tel 715-842-7250 (SAN 216-7301).

Enviro Press, *(Enviro Pr; 0-937976),* P.O. Box 40284, Nashville, TN 37204 Tel 615-794-0110 (SAN 220-049X); Dist. by: CBI Publishing, 51 Sleeper St., Boston, MA 02210 (SAN 201-9515).

Environmental Design & Research Ctr., *(Environ Design; 0-915250),* 261 Port Royal Ave., Foster City, CA 94404 (SAN 285-0125).

Environmental Design Research Assn., *(EDRA; 0-939922),* L'Enfant Plaza Sta., P.O. Box 23129, Washington, DC 20024 Tel 301-657-2651 (SAN 216-8103).

Environmental Law Institute, *(Environ Law Inst),* 1346 Conn Ave N.W., Suite 620, Washington, DC 20036 (SAN 225-0853).

Environmental Press, *(Environ Pr; 0-936960),* P.O. Box 701, Buffalo, NY 14205 Tel 301-942-0119 (SAN 214-3003).

Environmental Pubns. Assocs., Ltd, *(Environ Pubns),* 275 Broad Hollow Rd., Melville, NY 11747 Tel 516-752-9191 (SAN 209-5564).

Environmental Research Institute of Michigan, *(Environ Res Inst; 0-9603590),* P.O. Box 8618, Ann Arbor, MI 48107 (SAN 213-2176).

Environmental Science Services, Div. of Park Publishing Co., *(Environ Sci Serv),* 333 Hudson St., New York, NY 10013 (SAN 206-9407) Moved, Left No Forwarding Address.

Envision Communications, *(Envision Comm; 0-9605942),* 17 Elk St., Albany, NY 12207 Tel 518-462-1135 (SAN 216-6232).

Eo Press, *(EO Pr; 0-935830),* RR 1, Box 353-A Minuet Lane, Kingston, NY 12401 Tel 914-336-8797 (SAN 221-1858).

Epic Pubns., Inc., *(Epic Pubs; 0-914244),* 4420 Westover Dr., Orchard Lake, MI 48033 Tel 313-626-6217 (SAN 203-8439).

Epicurean Traveler Press, *(Epicurean),* 229-A Upper Terrace, San Francisco, CA 94117 Tel 415-731-0475 (SAN 281-6741); Dist. by: Book Dynamics, 836 Broadway, New York, NY 10003 Tel 212-254-7798 (SAN 169-5649); Dist. by: Bookpeople, 2940 7th St., Berkeley, CA 94704 Tel 415-549-3030 (SAN 168-9517); Dist. by: Cogan Books, 4332 Artesia, Fullerton, CA 92633 Tel 714-523-0309 (SAN 168-9649); Dist. by: Inland Books, P.O. Box 261, 22 Hemingway Ave., E. Haven, CT 06512 Tel 203-467-4257 (SAN 200-4151); Dist. by: L&S Distributors, 1161 Post St., San Francisco, CA 94109 Tel 415-771-0330 (SAN 281-6792); Dist. by: Publishers Group West, 5855 Beaudry, Emeryville, CA 94608 Tel 415-658-3453 (SAN 202-8522); Dist. by: Bookazine, 303 W. 10th St., New York, NY 10014 Tel 212-675-8877 (SAN 169-5665).

Epimetheus Press, Inc., *(Epimetheus Pr; 0-88008),* P.O. Box 565, Gracie Square Sta., New York, NY 10028 Tel 212-879-0553 (SAN 285-0133); P.O. Box 4508, Sunrise Station, Ft. Lauderdale, FL 33338 Tel 305-522-4496 (SAN 285-0141).

Epiphany Press, *(Epiphany Pr; 0-916700),* P.O. Box 14606, San Francisco, CA 94114 Tel 415-431-1917 (SAN 206-5037).

Episcopal Center for Evangelism, *(Episcopal Ctr),* P. O. Box 920, Live Oak, FL 32060 (SAN 208-1598).

EPOC See **Equity Policy Center (EPOC)**

Epsilon Pi Tau, *(Epsilon Pi Tau),* Technology Building, Bowling Green State Univ., Bowling Green, OH 43403 (SAN 224-5140).

Epstein, Max C., *(Epstein M C; 0-9612046),* One Montgomery Place, Brooklyn, NY 11215 Tel 212-783-1605 (SAN 286-7796).

Epstein, Vivian Sheldon, *(V S Epstein; 0-9601002),* 212 S. Dexter St., Denver, CO 80222 Tel 303-322-7450 (SAN 208-6425).

Equal Employment Advisory Council, *(Equal Employ; 0-937856),* 1015 Fifteenth St., N.W., Suite 1220, Washington, DC 20005 (SAN 220-0511).

Equipment Guide Book, Div. of Dataquest, *(Equipment Guide),* 2800 W. Bayshore Rd., Palo Alto, CA 94303 Tel 415-856-9100 (SAN 201-825X).

Equity Policy Center (EPOC), *(Equity Policy; 0-941696),* 1525 18th St., N.W., Washington, DC 20036 Tel 202-232-3465 (SAN 239-4235).

Equity Publishing Corp., *(Equity Pub NH; 0-87454),* Main St., Orford, NH 03777 Tel 603-351-4374 (SAN 204-1383).

Era Press, *(Era Davidson; 0-9605270),* Box 548, Davidson, NC 28036 (SAN 215-8612).

Erens, Patricia, *(P Erens; 0-9603920),* 2920 Commonwealth Ave., Chicago, IL 60657 (SAN 213-7356); Dist. by: Chicago Review Press, 820 North Franklin St., Chicago, IL 60610 Tel 312-644-5457 (SAN 213-5744).

Ergo Business Books, *(ERGO Business Bks; 0-941046),* 1401 Pasadena Ave., Fillmore, CA 93015 Tel 805-524-2944 (SAN 217-359X).

Eric's Press, *(Eric's Pr; 0-911985),* 20250 Wilder Ct., Salinas, CA 93907 Tel 408-663-0633 (SAN 264-6668); Box 349, Tahoe City, CA 95730 (SAN 264-6676).

Ericson, *(Ericson; 0-9605868),* 215 Foster Dr., Des Moines, IA 50312 Tel 515-255-0798 (SAN 220-1682).

Ericson Books, *(Ericson Bks; 0-911317),* 1614 Redbud St., Nacogdoches, TX 75961 Tel 409-564-3625 (SAN 263-0923).

Erie Street Pr., The, *(Erie St Pr; 0-942582),* 642 S.Clarence Ave., Oak Park, IL 60304 Tel 312-848-5716 (SAN 285-015X); Orders to: 642 S. Clarence Ave., Oak Park, IL 60304 Tel 312-848-5716 (SAN 285-0168).

Eriksson, Paul S., Pubs., *(Eriksson; 0-8397),* Battell Bldg., Middlebury, VT 05753 Tel 802-388-7303 (SAN 201-6702); Dist. by: Independent Publishers Group, 1 Pleasant Ave., Port Washington, NY 11050 Tel 516-944-9325 (SAN 201-6710).

Erin Hills Pubs., *(Erin Hills; 0-9600754),* 1390 Fairway Dr., San Luis Obispo, CA 93401 Tel 805-543-3050 (SAN 206-4537).

Erlbaum, Lawrence, Assocs., Inc., (L Erlbaum Assocs; 0-89859), 365 Broadway, Hillsdale, NJ 07642 Tel 201-666-4110 (SAN 213-960X).

Erskine, Kathryn A., (Erskine; 0-9605058), Box 398, Hurricane, WV 25526 (SAN 215-9538).

Escortguide: The People Connection To New Mexico, (Escortguide; 0-9607818), 535 Cordova Rd. Suite 125, Santa Fe, NM 87501 Tel 505-988-7099 (SAN 238-1583).

Esoteric Pubns., (Esoteric Pubns; 0-89861), P.O. Box 27291, Phoenix, AZ 85061 Tel 602-249-1953 (SAN 211-7932).

ESP Corp., (ESP Corp; 0-9601610), 195 Cortlandt St., Belleville, NJ 07109 (SAN 211-4194).

ESP, Inc., (ESP; 0-8209), P.O. Drawer 5037, 1201 E. Johnson Ave., Jonesboro, AR 72401 Tel 800-643-0280 (SAN 241-497X).

Esperanto League for North America, Inc., (Esperanto League North Am), P.O. Box 1129, El Cerrito, CA 94530 Tel 415-653-0998 (SAN 201-8241).

ESPress, (ESPress; 0-917200), P.O. Box 8606, Washington, DC 20011 Tel 202-723-4578 (SAN 206-748X).

Essai Seay Publishing Co., (Essai Seay Pubns; 0-9607958), P.O. Box 55, East St. Louis, IL 62202 (SAN 240-0715).

Essays in Literature, (Essays in Lit W Ill U; 0-934312), Dept. of English, Western Illinois Univ., Macomb, IL 61455 Tel 309-298-1113 (SAN 212-6583).

Essence Pubns., (Essence Pubns), 168 Woodbridge Ave., Highland Park, NJ 08904 Tel 201-572-3120 (SAN 211-4909).

Essex County History, (Essex County MA), P.O. Box 418, West Newbury, MA 01985 Tel 617-465-5397 (SAN 203-3731).

Essex Institute, (Essex Inst; 0-88389), 132 Essex St., Salem, MA 01970 Tel 617-744-3390 (SAN 203-8447).

Essex Publishing, Ltd., (Essex Pub Ltd; 0-912889), P.O. Box 317, Ada, MI 49301 Tel 616-676-2000 (SAN 283-2585).

Estacado Books, (Estacado Bks), P.O. Box 4516, Lubbock, TX 79409 Tel 806-742-3115 (SAN 207-6756).

Estate Book Sales, (Estate Bk), 2824 Pennsylvania Ave., N.W., Washington, DC 20007 Tel 202-965-4274 (SAN 207-6373).

Estes, Hiawatha, & Associates, (H Estes; 0-911008), P.O. Box 404-RR, Northridge, CA 91328 Tel 213-885-6588 (SAN 206-8389).

Estrada, Billie, (B Estrada; 0-9690490), c/o Mrs. C. Danielson, 14015 28th N. E., Seattle, WA 98125 (SAN 201-4025).

Estrela Press, (Estrela Pr; 0-943632), 2318 2nd Ave., Box 23, Seattle, WA 98121 Tel 206-322-4596 (SAN 238-2792).

Estuarine Research Federation, (Estuarine Res; 0-9608990), Belle Baruch Institute, Univ. of South Carolina, Columbia, SC 29208 Tel 803-777-3916 (SAN 241-3027).

ETC See **Education & Training Consultants Co.**

Eterna Press, (Eterna Pr; 0-934670), P. O. Box 1344, Oak Brook, IL 60521 (SAN 221-1807).

Eternal Enterprises, (Eternal Ent; 0-917578), P.O. Box 60913, Sacramento, CA 95860 (SAN 206-4383) Name Formerly L P Price.

Ethics & Public Policy Center, Inc., (Ethics & Public Policy; 0-89633), 1030 15th St., N.W., Suite 300, Washington, DC 20005 Tel 202-328-7400 (SAN 216-132X).

Ethics Resource Center, Inc., (Ethics Res Ctr; 0-916152), 1730 Rhode Island Ave., N.W., Suite 717, Washington, DC 20036 Tel 202-223-3411 (SAN 201-6893).

Ethnographic Arts Pubns., (Ethnographic Arts Pubns; 0-9611006), 1040 Erica Rd., Mill Valley, CA 94941 Tel 415-383-2998 (SAN 282-8650).

Ethridge, Blaine, Books, (Ethridge; 0-87917), 13977 Penrod St., Detroit, MI 48223 Tel 313-838-3363 (SAN 201-4327).

Euclid Publishing Co., The, (Euclid Pub; 0-935490), Dist. by: Bond & Bacon Assocs., P.O. Box 121, Cathedral Sta., New York, NY 10025 (SAN 211-6057).

Eupsychian Press, The, (Eupsychian; 0-939344), 950 Roadrunner Rd., Austin, TX 78746 Tel 512-327-2214 (SAN 216-5627).

Eurail Guide Annual, (Eurail Guide; 0-912442), 27540 Pacific Coast Hwy, Malibu, CA 90265 Tel 213-457-7286 (SAN 207-9704).

Euramerica Press, (Euramerica Pr; 0-916876), 381 N. Main St., Pittston, PA 18640 Tel 717-655-6637 (SAN 208-1563).

Eurasia Press, (Eurasia Pr NY; 0-932030), 302 Fifth Ave., New York, NY 10001 (SAN 222-7886).

Eureka Press, Inc., (Eureka Pr; 0-89803), 140 Main St., Gloucester, MA 01930 Tel 617-283-3459 (SAN 238-4299).

Eureka Pubns., (Eureka Pubns; 0-942848), Box 372, Mantua, NJ 08051 Tel 609-468-4145 (SAN 240-2165).

Euro-Dutch, Pubs., (Euro-Dutch Pub), P.O. Box 1070, Buffalo, NY 14221-1070 (SAN 265-3826).

Eurolingua, (Eurolingua; 0-931922), P.O. Box 101, Bloomington, IN 47402-0101 (SAN 222-7894).

Europa, (Europa; 0-905118), c/o Unipub, 1180 Ave. of the Americas, New York, NY 10036 Tel 212-764-2791 (SAN 202-5264).

European American Music, (Eur-Am Music; 0-913574), 11 West End Rd.,, Totowa, NJ 07512 Tel 201-256-7100 (SAN 201-7393).

Eustace, Herbert W., C.S.B., (Eustace CSB), P.O. Box 7328, Berkeley, CA 94707 Tel 415-524-0846 (SAN 276-9743).

Evanel Associates, (Evanel; 0-918948), Box 42, Northfield, OH 44067 Tel 216-467-1750 (SAN 209-4347).

Evangel Press, (Evangel Indiana), 301 N. Elm, Nappanee, IN 46550 (SAN 211-7940).

Evangelical & Reformed Historical Society, (Evang & Ref; 0-910564), 555 W. James St., Lancaster, PA 17603 (SAN 281-6849).

Evangelical Sisterhood of Mary, (Evang Sisterhood Mary), 9849 N. 40th St., Phoenix, AZ 85028 Tel 602-996-4040 (SAN 211-8335).

Evangelical Teacher Training Assn., (Evang Tchr; 0-910566), 110 Bridge St., P.O. Box 327, Wheaton, IL 60189 Tel 312-668-6400 (SAN 203-8471).

Evangelist Assn., (Evang Assn; 0-9603014), 1855 W. 63rd St., Chicago, IL 60636 (SAN 217-2380).

Evans, M., & Co., Inc., (M Evans; 0-87131), 216 E. 49th St., New York, NY 10017 Tel 212-688-2810 (SAN 203-4050); Dist. by: E. P. Dutton, 2 Park Ave., New York, NY 10016 (SAN 201-0070).

Evans, Norma P., (N P Evans; 0-937418), 2211 Liberty, Beaumont, TX 77701 Tel 409-835-7175 (SAN 213-2184).

Evans, Robert L., (R L Evans), 2500 St. Anthony Blvd., Minneapolis, MN 55418 Tel 612-781-7384 (SAN 208-3450).

Evans Pubns., (Evans Pubns), P.O. Box 520, Perkins, OK 74059 Tel 405-547-2882 (SAN 212-9019).

Everest, F. Alton, (F A Everest; 0-9608352), 6275 S. Roundhill Dr., Whittier, CA 90601 Tel 213-698-8831 (SAN 281-6857); Dist. by: SIE Pub., 31121 Via Colinas, Suite 10003, Westlake Village, CA 91361 Tel 213-991-3400 (SAN 240-9054).

Everest House Pubs., (Everest Hse; 0-89696), 79 Madison Ave., New York, NY 10016 Tel 212-685-6464 (SAN 287-0150); Dist. by: Dodd Mead Co., 79 Madison Ave., New York, NY 10016 (SAN 287-0169); Orders to: P. O. Box 141000, Nashville, TN 37214 (SAN 287-0177).

Everett/Edwards, Inc., (Everett-Edwards; 0-912112), P.O. Box 1060, DeLand, FL 32720 Tel 904-734-7458 (SAN 201-4653).

Evergreen Book Distributors, (Evergreen Dist; 0-903729), 6513 Lankershim Blvd., Suite 37, N. Hollywood, CA 91606 (SAN 223-1522).

Evergreen Books See **Grove Press, Inc.**

Evergreen Communications, Inc., (Evergreen Comm; 0-943782), 301 W. Washington, Bloomington, IL 61701 Tel 309-829-9411 (SAN 241-192X).

Evergreen Pacific, (Evergreen Pacific; 0-9609036), 4535 Union Bay Place N.E., Seattle, WA 98105 (SAN 240-9119).

Evergreen Paddleways, (Evergreen Paddleways; 0-916166), 1416 21st St., Two Rivers, WI 54241 Tel 414-794-8485 (SAN 205-6208).

Evergreen Press, (Evergreen Pr; 0-913056), P.O. Box 1711, Oceanside, CA 92054 Tel 714-757-5976 (SAN 206-9415).

Evergreen Press, Inc., (Evergreen; 0-914510), P.O. Box 4971, Walnut Creek, CA 94596 Tel 415-825-7850 (SAN 206-3638).

Evergreen Publishing Co., (Evergreen Pub; 0-9601070), 277 Farnum St., North Andover, MA 01845 Tel 617-683-1128 (SAN 221-5594).

Everlast Pr., (Everlast Pr; 0-9607262), 365 Maple St., W. Hempstead, NY 11552 Tel 516-483-8581 (SAN 239-0884).

Eversaul, George A., (G A Eversaul; 0-9601978), Box 19420, Las Vegas, NV 89132 Tel 702-733-8476 (SAN 212-2553).

Everybody's Press, (Everybodys Pr), Fame Ave.,, Hanover, PA 17331 Tel 717-632-3535 (SAN 237-949X).

Everyday Handbooks See **Barnes & Noble Books**

Everyday Handbooks See **Harper & Row Pubs., Inc.**

Everything In The Universe, (Every Univ; 0-913399), 429 43rd St., Oakland, CA 94609 Tel 415-547-6523 (SAN 285-8576).

Evolutionary Press, (Evolutionary; 0-943408), 2418 Clement St., San Francisco, CA 94121 Tel 415-221-9222 (SAN 240-642X).

Evolving Pubns., (Evolving Pubns; 0-912389), 2531 Sawtelle Blvd., No. 42, Los Angeles, CA 90064 Tel 213-390-5993 (SAN 265-2390).

Ewing Pubns., (Ewing Pubns), 114 Main St., Kingston, NJ 08528 (SAN 212-9388).

Ex Libris, (Ex Libris ID; 0-9605212), Box 225, Sun Valley, ID 83353 Tel 208-622-8174 (SAN 215-7608).

Exanimo Press, (Exanimo Pr; 0-89316), P.O. Box 18, 23520 Hwy. 12, Segundo, CO 81070 (SAN 209-0910).

Excel, Inc., (Excel), Suite 101, 600 Enterprise Dr., Oak Brook, IL 60521 Tel 312-382-7272 (SAN 237-9503).

Excel Press, (Excel Pr), Box 123, Riverdale, NJ 07457 (SAN 262-0227).

Exceptional Parent Press, The, (Exceptional Parent; 0-930958), 296 Boylston St., 3rd Fl., Boston, MA 02116 (SAN 211-5611).

Excerpta-Medica See **Elsevier Science Publishing Co., Inc.**

Excerpta Medica-Princeton, (Excerpta Princeton), 3131 Princeton Pike, Lawrenceville, NJ 08648 (SAN 209-5041).

Execucom Systems Corporation, (Execucom Sys Corp; 0-911941), Box 9758, Austin, TX 78766 Tel 512-346-4980 (SAN 264-0325).

Executive Communications, (Executive Comm; 0-917168), 919 Third Ave, New York, NY 10022 Tel 212-421-3713 (SAN 208-3043).

Executive Computer, (Exec Computer; 0-943892), Box 222178, Carmel, CA 93922 (SAN 241-1091).

Executive Education Press, (Exec Ed Pr; 0-9606022), 114 Liberty St., New York, NY 10006 Tel 212-620-4060 (SAN 216-8928).

Executive Enterprises, (Executive Ent), 5811 La Jolla Corona Dr., La Jolla, CA 92037 Tel 619-459-4901 (SAN 209-1259) Do Not Confuse with Executive Enterprises Pubns. in NY.

Executive Enterprises Pubns. Co., Inc., Div. of Executive Enterprises, Inc., (Exec Ent; 0-917386), 33 W. 60th St., Ninth Fl.,, New York, NY 10023 Tel 212-489-2671 (SAN 208-953X).

Executive Publishing (MO), (Executive Pub; 0-943338), Box 3155, Springfield, MO 65804 Tel 417-883-0950 (SAN 206-6438).

Executive Reports Corp., Subs. of Prentice-Hall, Inc., (Exec Reports; 0-13), 210 Sylvan Ave., Englewood Cliffs, NJ 07632 Tel 201-592-2075 (SAN 204-1294); Orders to: Dept. 200-B, Englewood Cliffs, NJ 07632 Tel 201-767-5059 (SAN 204-1308).

Executive Salary Research Co., (Exec Sal; 0-912716), 1685 Sunrise Dr., Lima, OH 45805 Tel 419-991-3936 (SAN 201-8268); Orders to: P.O. Box 832, Lima, OH 45802 (SAN 201-8276).

Executive Standards, Inc., (Exec Stand; 0-917818), 811 East St., New Britain, CT 06051 Tel 203-224-3357 (SAN 210-0797).

Executives West Publishing Co., (Exec West), 4250 E. Camelback, Suite 180K, Phoenix, AZ 85018 (SAN 219-9742).

Exelrod Press, (Exelrod Pr; 0-917388), P. O. Box 2303, Pleasant Hill, CA 94523 Tel 415-934-3357 (SAN 208-1555).

Exhibit Press, (Exhibit Pr; 0-9607908), P.O. Box 44844, Los Olivos Station, MA 02130 Tel 413-528-4894 (SAN 238-0315).

Exhorters, Inc., The, (Exhorters), P.O. Box 492, Vienna, VA 22180 (SAN 241-3825).

Exhorters, Inc.,The, *(Exhorters Inc; 0-9609260),* P.O. Box 492, Vienna, VA 22180 Tel 703-698-6880 (SAN 260-0536).

Existential Books, *(Existential Bks; 0-89231),* 1816 Stevens Ave.,S., Suite 25, Minneapolis, MN 55403 Tel 612-871-7275 (SAN 208-1547).

Exordium Press, *(Exordium Pr; 0-912784),* P.O. Box 635, Akron, OH 44309 (SAN 203-8501).

Expedited Publishing Co., Div. of Patent Rights, Inc., *(Expedited; 0-9603122),* P.O. Box 67, Scarborough, NY 10510 (SAN 213-490X).

Expedition Press, *(Expedition Pr; 0-939924),* P.O. Box 1198, Kalamazoo, MI 49006 (SAN 216-8111).

Expertise, The, *(Expertise; 0-9605184),* 14426 Kingsdale, Lawndale, CA 90260 (SAN 239-3891).

Exploration Press, *(Exploration Pr; 0-913552),* Chicago Theological Seminary, 5757 S. Univ. Ave., Chicago, IL 60637 Tel 312-752-5757 (SAN 203-851X).

Explorations Institute, *(Explorations Inst; 0-918600),* P.O. Box 1254, 1711-A Grave St., Berkeley, CA 94701 (SAN 210-8968).

Explorer Books, *(Explorer Bks; 0-9605938),* 601 LeGrand Route Six, Panama City Beach, FL 32407 Tel 904-234-1378 (SAN 216-6240).

Exponent Ltd., *(Exponent; 0-935722),* Box 862, Walnut, CA 91789 (SAN 214-3038).

Exporters' Encyclopaedia, Div. of Dun & Bradstreet Intl., *(Exporters Encyc; 0-942526),* One Exchange Place, Suite 715, Jersey City, NJ 07302 Tel 201-547-6053 (SAN 219-8800).

Exposition Press, Inc., *(Exposition; 0-682),* 325 Rabro Dr., Box 2120, Smithtown, NY 11787 Tel 516-582-6655 (SAN 207-0642). *Imprints:* Banner (Banner); Classic (Classic); Lochinvar (Lochinvar); University (University).

Express Publications, *(Express; 0-932956),* P.O. Box 1373, Richmond, CA 94802 Tel 415-236-5496 (SAN 208-6433).

ExPressAll, *(ExPressAll; 0-936190),* 260 Dean Rd., Brookline, MA 02146 Tel 617-734-1297 (SAN 207-5903).

Expression Co., *(Expression),* P.O. Box 153, Londonderry, NH 03053 Tel 603-432-5232 (SAN 203-8536).

Extequer Press, *(Extequer),* 1441 North Altadena Dr., Pasadena, CA 91107 Tel 213-797-3627 (SAN 281-6873); Orders to: P.O. Box 4193, Pasadena, CA 91106 Tel 213-797-3627 (SAN 281-6881).

External Representation of the Ukrainian Helsinki Group, *(ERUHG; 0-86725),* P.O. Box 770, Cooper Sta., New York, NY 10003 Tel 212-564-4334 (SAN 217-0701).

Eyecontact, *(Eyecontact; 0-938112),* 465 Lexington Ave., New York, NY 10017 Tel 212-683-1641 (SAN 281-692X); Dist. by: Golden Lee, 664 Bergen St., Brooklyn, NY 11238 Tel 212-857-6333 (SAN 169-5126); Dist. by: Publishers Group West, 5855 Beaudry St., Emeryville, CA 94608 Tel 415-658-3453 (SAN 202-8522).

EZ Cookin' Book Co., *(EZ Cookin),* 9925 Currant Ave., Fountain Valley, CA 92708 (SAN 240-9364).

FAIR-Federation for American Immigration Reform, *(F A I R; 0-935776),* 2028 P St., N.W., Washington, DC 20036 (SAN 213-7372).

FAS Pubs., *(FAS Pubs),* P.O. Box 5453, Madison, WI 53705 Tel 608-274-1733 (SAN 201-4750).

F & L Associates, *(F & L Assocs),* P.O. Box 8034, Long Beach, CA 90808 (SAN 238-8359).

F&S Press, Div. of Frost & Sullivan, *(F&S Pr; 0-86621),* 106 Fulton St., New York, NY 10038 Tel 212-233-1080 (SAN 220-0538).

F.D.C. Publishing Co., *(FDC Pub; 0-89794),* P.O. Box 206, Stewartsville, NJ 08886 (SAN 212-2758).

F. I. Communications, *(F I Comm; 0-89533),* 45 Alhambra, Portola Valley, CA 94025 Tel 415-851-0254 (SAN 201-8489); Orders to: P.O. Box 3121, Stanford, CA 94305-0036 (SAN 201-8497).

F. I. G. Ltd., *(FIG Ltd; 0-9601452),* P.O. Box 23, Northbrook, IL 60062 (SAN 211-8971).

FM Atlas Pub. Co., *(F M Atlas; 0-917170),* P.O. Box 24, Adolph, MN 55701 Tel 308-237-7953 (SAN 207-6764).

Faber & Faber, Inc., *(Faber & Faber; 0-571),* 39 Thompson St., Winchester, MA 01890 Tel 617-721-1427 (SAN 218-7256).

Fablewaves Press, *(Fablewaves),* P.O. Box 7874, Van Nuys, CA 91409 Tel 213-372-2983 (SAN 215-0719).

Fabmath, *(Fabmath; 0-937138),* P.O. Box 568, Warrington, PA 18976 (SAN 214-3690).

Facsimile Book Shop, Inc., *(Facsimile Bk),* 16 W. 55th St., New York, NY 10019 (SAN 215-3084).

Factory Outlet Shopping Guide, *(FOSG Pubns; 0-913464),* Box 239, Oradell, NJ 07649 Tel 201-384-2500 (SAN 201-6559).

Facts, *(Facts FL; 0-910991),* 727 Granada Dr.,, Boca Raton, FL 33432 (SAN 263-2209).

Facts on File, Inc., *(Facts on File; 0-87196; 0-87103),* 460 Park Ave. S., New York, NY 10016 Tel 212-683-2244 (SAN 201-4696).

Fade in Pubs., *(Fade In; 0-936748),* 312 S. 6th, Bozeman, MT 59715 (SAN 215-0727).

Fag Rag Books, *(Fag Rag; 0-915480),* P.O. Box 331, Kenmore Sta., Boston, MA 02215 (SAN 207-3498).

Fainshaw Pr., Subs. of B. R. Smith & Assoc., *(Fainshaw Pr; 0-943290),* Box 961, Westmoreland, NH 03467 Tel 603-585-6654 (SAN 240-6454).

Fairborn Observatory, *(Fairborn Observ),* 1247 Folk Rd., Fairborn, OH 45324 Tel 513-879-4583 (SAN 270-0255).

Fairchild Books & Visuals, *(Fairchild; 0-87005),* 7 E. 12th St., New York, NY 10003 Tel 212-741-4280 (SAN 201-470X).

Fairfax, C. H., Co., Inc., *(C H Fairfax; 0-935132),* P. O. Box 502, Columbia, MD 21045 (SAN 221-170X).

Fairfax County, *(Fairfax County),* 4100 Chain Bridge Rd., Fairfax, VA 22030 (SAN 212-632X).

Fairfield House, *(Fairfield Hse; 0-9602048),* 3 Fairfield Dr., Baltimore, MD 21228 Tel 301-747-6590 (SAN 209-374X).

Fairfield Press, Inc., *(Fairfield; 0-913158),* 128 E. 62nd St., New York, NY 10021 Tel 212-838-7424 (SAN 206-4049).

Fairisher Press, *(Fairisher Pr; 0-943900),* P.O. Box 2007, Rapid City, SD 57709 (SAN 262-0235).

Fairleigh Dickinson Univ. Press, Div. of Associated University Presses, *(Fairleigh Dickinson; 0-8386),* 4 Cornwall Dr., East Brunswick, NJ 08816 Tel 201-254-0132 (SAN 201-4718).

FairMail Service, Inc., *(FairMail Serv; 0-9601202),* 417 Cleveland Ave., Plainfield, NJ 07060 Tel 201-754-7770 (SAN 210-4210)07060.

Fairmont Press, Inc., The, *(Fairmont Pr; 0-915586),* 425 Pleasantdale Rd., N.E. Suite 340, Atlanta, GA 30340 Tel 404-447-5314 (SAN 207-5946).

Fairway House, *(Fairway Hse; 0-9603180),* P.O. Box 6344, Bakersfield, CA 93386 (SAN 213-6856).

Fairy Publications, *(Fairy Pubns; 0-9611088),* P.O. Box 450, Laguna Beach, CA 92652 Tel 714-661-7533 (SAN 282-8669); Dist. by: Cogan Books, 4332 W. Artesia Ave., Fullerton, CA 92633 (SAN 168-9649); Dist. by: Book Dynamics, 830 Broadway, New York, NY 10003 (SAN 169-5649); Dist. by: The Distributors, 702 S. Michigan, South Bend, IN 46618 Tel 219-232-8500 (SAN 212-0364).

Faith & Life Press, *(Faith & Life; 0-87303),* 718 Main St., Box 347, Newton, KS 67114 Tel 316-283-5100 (SAN 204-4726).

Faith Messenger Pubns., *(Faith Messenger; 0-938544),* 428 S. Brea Blvd., Suite B, Brea, CA 92621 (SAN 281-7012); Orders to: P.O. Box 641, Upland, CA 91786 Tel 714-989-8531 (SAN 281-7020).

Faith Publishing House, *(Faith Pub Hse),* P.O. Box 518, 920 W. Mansur, Guthrie, OK 73044 Tel 405-282-1479 (SAN 204-1243).

FaithAmerica Foundation, *(FaithAmerica; 0-942770),* Suite 212, 4120 N. 70th St., Scottsdale, AZ 85251 (SAN 240-1452).

Falcon Head Press, Ltd., *(Falcon Head Pr; 0-914802),* P.O. Box 913, Golden, CO 80401 (SAN 206-4065).

Falcon Hill Press, *(Falcon Hill Pr; 0-936332),* Box 1431, Sparks, NV 89431 Tel 702-359-5893 (SAN 221-1718).

Falcon Press, *(Falcon Pr Az; 0-941404),* 3660 N. 3rd St., Phoenix, AZ 85012 (SAN 262-0243).

Falcon Press Publishing Co., Inc., *(Falcon Pr MT; 0-934318),* 324 Fuller, P.O. Box 731, Helena, MT 59624 Tel 406-442-6597 (SAN 281-7039); Orders to: P.O. Box 279, Billings, MT 59103 (SAN 281-7047).

Falcon Publishing, *(Falcon Pub Venice; 0-942764),* 2000 Strongs, Venice, CA 92091 Tel 213-399-4791 (SAN 212-8322).

Falk-Leeds International, *(Falk-Leeds Intl; 0-940926),* 49 Hancock St., Boston, MA 02114 Tel 617-227-7063 (SAN 217-3603).

Fallen Angel Press, *(Fallen Angel; 0-931598),* 1981 W. McNichols Cl, Highland Park, MI 48203 Tel 313-864-0982 (SAN 211-8963).

Falley, Margaret Dickson, *(M D Falley),* 1500 Sheridan Rd., Wilmette, IL 60091 Tel 312-251-4588 (SAN 208-1989).

Falling Wall, *(Falling Wall Press; 0-905046),* Dist. by: Flatiron Book Distributors, 175 Fifth Ave., Suite 814, New York, NY 10010 (SAN 240-9917).

Falls of the Tar Pubns., *(Falls Tar),* P.O. Box 4194, Rocky Mount, NC 27801 (SAN 240-0189) Tel 919-442-7423.

Family Album, ABAA, The, *(Family Album; 0-934630),* RD 1, Box 42, Glen Rock, PA 17327 (SAN 212-5021).

Family & Health Improvement Society, *(Family Health; 0-9606024),* P.O. Box 952, Cambridge, OH 43725 Tel 614-432-3007 (SAN 211-3562).

Family Friends Publications, *(Family Friends; 0-9609324),* 1423 2nd S.E., Mason City, IA 50408 Tel 515-424-9976 (SAN 240-849X).

Family Health International, *(Fam Health Intl; 0-939704),* Triangle Dr., Research Triangle Park, NC 27709 Tel 919-549-0517 (SAN 216-7409).

Family History Foundation, *(Family History; 0-943162),* 811 E. 29th St., P.O. Drawer 4464, Bryan, TX 77805 Tel 713-775-0809 (SAN 240-3749).

Family Press, *(Family Pr; 0-9600666),* P. O. Box 16005, St. Paul, MN 55116 Tel 612-699-9108 (SAN 205-5740).

Family Pubns., *(Family Pubns; 0-931128),* P.O. Box 398, Maitland, FL 32751 Tel 305-894-7060 (SAN 211-3147).

Family Publishing Co., The, *(Family Pub CA; 0-937770),* P.O. Box 462, Bodega Bay, CA 94923 Tel 707-875-3373 (SAN 215-3092).

Family Relations Learning Center, *(Family Relations; 0-9672500),* 450 Ord Dr., Boulder, CO 80303 Tel 303-499-1171 (SAN 239-4243).

Family Service Assn. of America, *(Family Serv; 0-87304),* 44 E. 23rd St., New York, NY 10010 Tel 212-674-6100 (SAN 206-4073).

Family Tree Pony Farm, Pubns. Div. *(Family Tree Pony Farm; 0-940074),* 1708 Burwell, Bremerton, WN 98310 Tel 206-373-0589 (SAN 220-2174).

Family World Publishing House, Inc., *(Family World Pub Hse; 0-934176),* P.O. Box 1040, Media, PA 19063 Tel 215-353-3555 (SAN 213-0521).

Famous Press Publishing, *(Famous Pr Pub; 0-942010),* P.O. Box 1673, 200 N. Diamond St., Mansfield, OH 44901 (SAN 238-2377).

Fandom Unlimited Enterprises, *(Fandom Unltd; 0-9607178),* P.O. Box 70868, Sunnyvale, CA 94086 (SAN 239-0906).

Fannin County Historical Commission, *(Fannin County; 0-9609602),* P.O. Box 338, Bonham, TX 75418 Tel 214-583-2832 (SAN 260-1842).

Fant, Freeman, Madson, *(Fant-Freeman-Madson; 0-87518),* 209 Shady Oak Rd., Hopkins, MN 55343 (SAN 223-0682); Dist. by: Alver R. Freeman, 8315 Dupont Ave., Minneapolis, MN 55420 (SAN 223-0690).

Fantaco Pubns., *(Fantaco; 0-938782),* Orders to: Fantaco Enterprises, Inc., 21 Central Ave., Albany, NY 12210 (SAN 270-0379).

Fantasy Publishing Co., Inc., *(Fantasy Pub Co),* c/o Borden Publishing Co. 1855 W. Main St., Alhambra, CA 91801 Tel 213-337-7947 (SAN 201-419X).

Far Eastern Pubns., *(Far Eastern Pubns),* Box 2505 A, 340 Edwards St., New Haven, CT 06520 Tel 203-436-1075 (SAN 219-0710).

Far Eastern Research & Pubns. Center, *(Far Eastern Res; 0-912580),* P.O. Box 31151, Washington, DC 20031 (SAN 205-5759).

Far West Editions, *(Far West Edns; 0-914480),* 3231 Pierce St., San Francisco, CA 94123 Tel 415-563-0399 (SAN 207-0456).

Far Western Philosophy of Education Society, *(Far Western Phil; 0-931702),* Arizona State Univ., College of Education, Hiram Bradford Farmer Education Bldg., Rm. 412, Tempe, AZ 85281 Tel 602-965-3674 (SAN 210-8062).

Faraday Press, *(Faraday; 0-939762),* 1487 Noe St., San Francisco, CA 94131 Tel 415-821-0341 (SAN 216-731X).

Farm & Ranch Vacations, Inc., *(Farm & Ranch; 0-913214),* 36 E. 57th St., New York, NY 10022 Tel 212-355-6334 (SAN 201-4734).

Farm Journal, Inc., *(Farm Journal; 0-89795),* 230 W. Washington Square, Philadelphia, PA 19105 Tel 215-574-1336 (SAN 212-0887).

Farmer, W. D., Residence Designer, Inc., *(W D Farmer; 0-931518),* P.O. Box 450025, Atlanta, GA 30345 Tel 404-934-7380 (SAN 204-1219).

Farmer, Wesley M., Enterprises,Inc., *(Farmer Ent; 0-937772),* P.O. Box 15661, San Diego, CA 92115 (SAN 215-6431).

Farmington Cookbook, the, *(Farmington Cookbook; 0-9602646),* 3033 Bardstown Rd., Louisville, KY 40205 (SAN 218-4486).

Farnsworth Publishing Co., Inc., *(Farnswth Pub; 0-910580; 0-87863),* 78 Randall Ave., Rockville Ctr., NY 11570 Tel 516-536-8400 (SAN 201-4742).

Farnum Films, *(Farnum Films; 0-915790),* Executive House, 225 E. 46th St., New York, NY 10017 Tel 212-371-8679 (SAN 206-1988); Orders to: P.O. Box 1094, New York, NY 10017 (SAN 206-1996).

Farrah, Upland, Westmoreland & Granger, *(Farrah Upland; 0-943568),* 704 Broadway, 7th Fl., New York, NY 10003 Tel 212-260-5291 (SAN 240-6470).

Farrar Publishing, *(Farrar Pub; 0-9605588),* 25 Library Ave., Warrensburg, NY 12885 Tel 518-623-4551 (SAN 216-1311).

Farrar, Straus & Giroux, Inc., *(FS&G; 0-374),* 19 Union Square, W., New York, NY 10003 Tel 212-741-6900 (SAN 206-782X).

Farwell, Brice, *(B Farwell; 0-9600484),* 330 Heidi Court, Morgan Hill, CA 95037 (SAN 206-7129).

Fashion Imprints Associates, *(Fashion Imprints; 0-9602860),* Box 3523, Merchandise Mart, Chicago, IL 60654 Tel 312-821-5922 (SAN 213-0548).

Fathom Eight, *(Fathom Eight; 0-910651),* P.O. Box 80505, San Marino, CA 91108 Tel 213-223-0777 (SAN 270-0611).

Fathom Enterprises, Inc., *(Fathom Ents),* Box 2284, Rancho Palos Verdes, CA 90274 Tel 213-519-8944 (SAN 206-7285).

Fathom Publishing Company, *(Fathom Pub; 0-9607358),* Box 821, Cordova, AK 99574 Tel 907-424-7770 (SAN 239-7684).

Faubus, Orval E., *(Faubus),* 114 E. 2nd St., Little Rock, AR 72203 (SAN 220-1526); c/o Pioneer Pr., P.O. Box 191, Little Rock, AR 72201 Tel 501-374-0271 (SAN 220-1518).

Fault Pubns., *(Fault Pubns; 0-930646),* 33513 6th St., Union City, CA 94587 Tel 415-487-1383 (SAN 207-8252).

Fawcett Book Group, *(Fawcett; 0-449),* 201 E. 50th St., New York, NY 10022 Tel 212-751-2600 (SAN 201-4572). *Imprints:* Crest Books (Crest); Gold Medal Books (GM); Juniper (Juniper); Premier Books (Prem).

Fax Collector's Editions, Inc., *(Fax Collect; 0-913960),* P.O. Box 851, Mercer Island, WA 98040 Tel 206-232-8484 (SAN 208-6468).

Faxon, F. W., Co., Inc., *(Faxon; 0-87305),* 15 Southwest Park, Westwood, MA 02090 Tel 617-329-3350 (SAN 206-4081).

Fay, Loren V., *(L V Fay; 0-942238),* 87 Edgewood Ave., Albany, NY 12203 (SAN 215-2509).

Fay-West Heritage Pubns., *(Fay-West Her; 0-9609326),* 247 Ironshire South, Laurel, MD 20707 Tel 301-725-1908 (SAN 260-1850).

Fayova Publications, *(Fayova Pubns),* P.O. Box 29065, Indianapolis, IN 46229 (SAN 277-6790).

FDW Arts, *(FDW Arts; 0-9608354),* P.O. Box 2540, Fallschurch, VA 22042 Tel 303-979-6707 (SAN 240-6446).

Feather & Good, *(Feather & Good; 0-9607642),* Box 141, Radnor, PA 19087 (SAN 239-8532).

Feather Press, *(Feather Pr; 0-9607960),* Box 1255, Dumas, TX 79029 Tel 806-935-4348 (SAN 240-0723).

F E B Press, *(F E B Pr; 0-9610144),* P.O. Box 2431, Ann Arbor, MI 48106 Tel 313-665-3210 (SAN 270-0662).

Feder, T. H., Books, Div. of Editorial Photo Color Archives, *(T H Feder Bks; 0-933772),* 65 Bleecker St., New York, NY 10012 Tel 212-697-1136 (SAN 212-9396).

Federal Aviation Exams Co., *(Fed Aviation; 0-938706),* Box 718, Solvang, CA 93463 Tel 805-688-0022 (SAN 215-8620).

Federal Bar Association, *(Federal Bar),* 1815 H St. NW, Washington, DC 20006 Tel 202-638-0252 (SAN 223-7784).

Federal Employees News Digest, Inc., *(Fed Employees; 0-910582),* P.O. Box 457, Merrifield, VA 22116 Tel 703-533-3031 (SAN 204-1170).

Federal Legal Pubns., Inc., *(Fed Legal Pubn; 0-87945),* 157 Chambers St., New York, NY 10007 Tel 212-243-5775 (SAN 201-4769).

Federal Publications Incorporated, *(Fed Pubns Inc),* 1120 20th St., N.W., Washington, DC 20036 (SAN 237-7071).

Federal Reserve Bank of Minneapolis, *(Fed Res Bank MN; 0-915484),* Research Dept., 250 Marquette Ave., Minneapolis, MN 55480 Tel 612-340-2355 (SAN 281-7063); Orders to: Office of Public Information, 250 Marquette Ave., Minneapolis, MN 55480 Tel 612-340-2443 (SAN 281-7071).

Federation of American Societies for Experimental Biology, *(FASEB; 0-913822),* 9650 Rockville Pike, Bethesda, MD 20814 Tel 301-530-7030 (SAN 205-5767).

Federation of Societies for Coatings Technology, *(Fed Soc Coat Tech; 0-934010),* 1315 Walnut St., Suite 832, Philadelphia, PA 19107 Tel 215-545-1506 (SAN 212-9035).

Federlin, Tom, *(Federlin; 0-9603136),* 106 Macdougal St., New York, NY 10012 (SAN 213-4934).

FEELGREAT, *(FEELGREAT; 0-942106),* 1370 Windsor Rd., Teaneck, NJ 07666 Tel 201-833-0068 (SAN 239-5363).

Feffer & Simons *See* Burgess Publishing Co.

Fein, Jess, *(J Fein; 0-9604366),* 118 Massachusetts Ave., Boston, MA 02115 (SAN 215-0735).

Feinsot, Bernice B., *(B B Feinsot; 0-915526),* 330 W. 28th St., Apt. 1F, New York, NY 10001 Tel 212-929-2918 (SAN 207-351X).

Feist Pubns., *(Feist Pubns),* 2827 Seventh St., Berkeley, CA 94710 Tel 415-841-5771 (SAN 204-1138).

Fejer, Paul Haralyi, *(P H Fejer; 0-9607422),* 23 Lodewyck St., Mount Clemens, MI 48043 Tel 313-465-1026 (SAN 237-9511).

Feldco Enterprises, *(Feldco Ent; 0-9603550),* Woodward Bldg., Suite 100, Birmingham, AL 35203 (SAN 213-0564).

Feldheim, Philipp, Inc., *(Feldheim; 0-87306),* 96 E. Broadway, New York, NY 10002 Tel 212-925-3180 (SAN 164-9671).

Feldman, Mildred L. B., *(Feldman),* 1424 S. Alameda Dr., Baton Rouge, LA 70815 Tel 504-925-9666 (SAN 209-1135).

Feldspar, *(Feldspar),* P.O. Box 2375, Stanford, CA 94305 (SAN 239-5312).

Felicity Press, *(Felicity; 0-9603846),* Box 14382, University Sta., Gainesville, FL 32604 Tel 904-475-2963 (SAN 215-0743).

Felis-Hadiken Publications, *(Felis Hadiken; 0-9609262),* 16c Division St., Glen Falls, NY 12801 (SAN 260-0552).

Fell, Frederick, Pubs., Inc., *(Fell; 0-8119),* 386 Park Ave. S., New York, NY 10016 Tel 212-685-9017 (SAN 208-2365). *Imprints:* Pegasus Rex (Pegasus Rex).

Fellows of Contemporary Art, *(Fellows Cont Art; 0-911291),* 333 S. Hope St. 48th Fl., Los Angeles, CA 90071 Tel 213-620-1780 (SAN 215-0751).

Fellowship of the Crown, *(Fellowship Crown),* P.O. Box 3743, Carmel, CA 93921 Tel 408-624-5600 (SAN 206-4103).

Fellowship Press, *(Fellowship Pr PA; 0-914390),* 5820 Overbrook Ave., Philadelphia, PA 19131 Tel 215-879-8604 (SAN 201-6117).

Fels & Firn Press, *(Fels & Firn; 0-918704),* 944 Sir Francis Drake Blvd., Apt. 7, Kentfield, CA 94904 Tel 415-457-4361 (SAN 211-237X).

Felsun Press, *(Felsun Pr; 0-940928),* 1800 Old Meadow Rd., Suite 305, McLean, VA 22102 Tel 703-356-7799 (SAN 217-3611).

Feltus, Peter R., *(P R Feltus),* 5709 Keith Ave., Oakland, CA 94618 (SAN 215-3106).

Feminist Committee Press, The, *(Feminist Comm; 0-9603330),* 1957 Westminster Way, NE, Atlanta, GA 30307 Tel 404-636-6436 (SAN 211-1292).

Feminist Press, *(Feminist Pr; 0-912670; 0-935312),* SUNY/College at Old Westbury, Box 334, Old Westbury, NY 11568 Tel 516-997-7660 (SAN 213-6813).

Feminist Writers Guild-Milwaukee Chapter, *(Fem Writers Guild; 0-9606982),* c/o The Womens Coalition, 2211 E. Kenwood Blvd., Milwaukee, WI 53211 (SAN 238-0595).

Fenimore Bk. Store, *(Fenimore Bk),* Lake Rd., Cooperstown, NY 13326 Tel 607-547-2533 (SAN 285-0176); Orders to: P.O. Box 800, Lake Rd., Cooperstown, NY 13326 Tel 607-547-2533 (SAN 285-0184).

Fenn Galleries Publishing, *(Fenn Gall Pub; 0-937634),* 1075 Paseo De Peralta, Santa Fe, NM 87501 (SAN 215-2436).

Fennwyn Press, *(Fennwyn Pr),* 920 E., St. Patrick, Rapid City, SD 57701 (SAN 207-1177); Dist. by: Honor Books, P.O. Box 94, Spearfish, SD 57783 (SAN 208-0877).

Fergeson, F., Productions, *(F Fergeson; 0-935510),* 423 Exeter, Marina, CA 93933 Tel 408-384-6202 (SAN 214-3704).

Ferguson, George Wright, *(G W Ferguson; 0-9606982),* 2000 W. Henderson Rd., P. O. Box 20334, Columbus, OH 43220 Tel 614-459-0372 (SAN 208-3183).

Ferguson-Florissant School District/Early Education, *(Ferguson-Florissant; 0-939418),* 655 January Ave., Ferguson, MO 63135 (SAN 216-5740).

Fermata Press, *(Fermata; 0-939792),* 40 Harriett Rd., Gloucester, MA 01930 Tel 617-283-5849 (SAN 216-8936).

Ferment Pr., *(Ferment Pr; 0-9605318),* P.O. Box 1866, Oakland, CA 94604 Tel 415-893-4696 (SAN 239-9938); Dist. by: Bookpeople, 2940 Seventh St., Berkeley, CA 94710 Tel 415-549-3030 (SAN 168-9517).

Ferrari Pubns., *(Ferrari Pubn; 0-942586),* P.O. Box 35575, Phoenix, AZ 85011 Tel 602-264-5811 (SAN 239-6424).

Ferri, Roger C., & Associates, *(Ferri; 0-9605928),* 261 W. 22nd St., New York, NY 10011 Tel 212-929-8192 (SAN 216-6712).

Ferrucci, Tony F., *(Ferrucci; 0-911489),* 551 South Concord Street, Seattle, WA 98108 (SAN 264-035X).

Fertig, Howard, Inc., *(Fertig; 0-86527),* 80 E. 11th St., New York, NY 10003 Tel 212-982-7922 (SAN 201-4777).

Festival Books *See* Abingdon Press

Festival Pubns., *(Festival Pubns; 0-930828),* P.O. Box 10180, Glendale, CA 91209 Tel 213-222-8626 (SAN 211-1527).

Fevertree Press, *(Fevertree Pr; 0-911027),* Box 64, RR No. 2, Pine Plains, NY 12567 Tel 518-398-7764 (SAN 270-1405).

Fibar Designs, *(Fibar Designs; 0-932086),* The Fannings, 632 Bay Rd., Menlo Park, CA 94025 (SAN 211-6847); Orders to: P.O. Box 2634, Menlo Park, CA 94025 (SAN 211-6855).

Fibonacci Corp., *(Fibonacci Corp; 0-915494),* P.O. Box 610, Golden Bridge, NY 10526 Tel 914-232-4293 (SAN 208-2373).

Fichter Enterprises *See* Menaid Press International

Fiction Collective, Inc., *(Fiction Coll; 0-914590),* Brooklyn Coll., c/o English Dept., Brooklyn, NY 11210 Tel 212-780-5498 (SAN 201-4785); Dist. by: Flatiron Bk. Distributors, 175 Fifth Ave., Suite 814, New York, NY 10010 Tel 212-228-0390 (SAN 240-9917).

Fiction International, *(Fiction Intl; 0-931362),* St. Lawrence Univ., Canton, NY 13617 Tel 315-379-5961 (SAN 221-1548).

Fictioneer Books, Ltd, *(Fictioneer Bks; 0-934882),* Box B.I.P, Screamer Mountain, Clayton, GA 30525 Tel 404-782-3318 (SAN 213-3113).

Fideler Co., *(Fideler; 0-88296),* 31 Ottawa Ave., N. W., Grand Rapids, MI 49503 Tel 616-456-8577 (SAN 201-4793).

Fidelio Press, *(Fidelio Pr; 0-912681),* 2440 Adams Ave., Columbus, OH 43202 Tel 614-267-4030 (SAN 283-2577).

Fidelity Publishing Corp. of America, The, *(Fidelity Pub; 0-942496),* 2021 Business Center Drive, Suite 107, Irvine, CA 92715 Tel 714-752-5544 (SAN 238-1591).

Fides/Claretian, *(Fides Claretian; 0-8190),* 221 W. Madison St., Chicago, IL 60606 Tel 312-236-7783 (SAN 201-4807).

Field Museum of Natural History, *(Field Mus; 0-914868),* Roosevelt Rd., at Lake Shore Dr., Chicago, IL 60605 Tel 312-922-9410 (SAN 211-3554).

Field Translations Series/Oberlin College, *(Field Oberlin; 0-932440),* Rice Hall, Oberlin College, Oberlin, OH 44074 Tel 216-775-8407 (SAN 212-1883).

Fielding Pubns., *(Fielding),* 105 Madison Ave., New York, NY 10016 Tel 212-889-3050 (SAN 201-4823); Dist. by: William Morrow & Co., 6 Henderson Dr., West Caldwell, NJ 07006 (SAN 202-5779).

Fieldstead Institute, *(Fieldstead Inst; 0-940240),* Box Cv, Irvine, CA 92716 Tel 714-975-0117 (SAN 220-3324).

Fieldston Press, *(Fieldston; 0-912166),* P.O. Box 3413, New York, NY 10163 (SAN 205-5783).

Fiesta City Pubs., *(Fiesta City; 0-940076),* P.O. Box 5861, Santa Barbara, CA 93108 (SAN 217-071X).

Fiesta Publishing Corp., *(Fiesta Pub; 0-88473),* 6360 N.E. 4th Court, Miami, FL 33138 Tel 305-751-1181 (SAN 201-8470).

Fifth Wave Press, *(Fifth Wave Pr; 0-911761),* P.O. Box 9355, San Rafael, CA 94912 Tel 415-457-2019 (SAN 264-0368).

Fig Leaf Creations, *(Fig Leaf; 0-918774),* 1706 Olive Ave., Santa Barbara, CA 93101 Tel 805-962-4987 (SAN 210-4245).

Fig Leaf Press, *(Fig Leaf Pr; 0-912235),* 87 E. Olive Ave Suite 2-D, Fresno, CA 93728 Tel 209-442-1259 (SAN 264-0376).

Figures, The, *(Figures; 0-935724),* 2016 Cedar, Berkeley, CA 94709 (SAN 209-2468).

Fila's Designs Unlimited, Inc., *(Filas Des Unltd; 0-9610588),* 1013 Big Baer Dr., Glan Burnie, MD 21061 Tel 301-761-1471 (SAN 264-7338).

Filipino Information Service, *(Filipino Info; 0-941124),* P.O. Box 12215, San Francisco, CA 94112 Tel 415-433-3024 (SAN 217-362X).

Fill the Gap Pubns., *(Fill the Gap; 0-89858),* P.O. Box 53817, Lafayette, LA 70505 Tel 318-234-0678 (SAN 211-9978).

Film Classic Exchange, *(Film Classics; 0-9610916),* P.O. Box 77568 Dockweiler Stn., Los Angeles, CA 90007 Tel 213-731-3854 (SAN 265-1351).

Film Communicators, *(Film Communicators; 0-9606702),* 11136 Weddington St., N. Hollywood, CA 91601 Tel 213-766-3747 (SAN 219-7359).

Film Instruction Co. of America, *(FICOA; 0-931974),* 2901 S. Wentworth Ave., Milwaukee, WI 53207 (SAN 206-2003).

Filmquest Books, *(Filmquest Bks; 0-9610670),* 857 Partridge Ave., No. 1, Menlo Park, CA 94025 (SAN 264-7397).

Filmrow Pubns., *(Filmrow Pubns),* 8272 Sunset Blvd., W. Hollywood, CA 90046 Tel 213-654-8310 (SAN 281-708X); 12349 Milbank St., Studio City, CA 91604 Tel 213-761-2627 (SAN 281-7098).

Filsinger & Co., Ltd., *(Filsinger & Co; 0-916754),* 150 Waverly Place, New York, NY 10014 Tel 212-243-7421 (SAN 208-3574).

Filson Club, Inc., *(Filson Club; 0-9601072),* 118 W. Breckinridge St., Louisville, KY 40203 Tel 502-582-3727 (SAN 205-5791).

Filter Press, *(Filter; 0-910584; 0-86541),* P.O. Box 5, Palmer Lake, CO 80133 Tel 303-481-2523 (SAN 201-484X).

Financial Accounting Standards Board, *(Finan Acct; 0-910065),* High Ridge Park, Stamford, CT 06905 Tel 203-329-9401 (SAN 241-3051).

Financial Aid Assistance Service, *(Financial Aid; 0-9610018),* P.O. Box 1497, Springfield, OR 97477 Tel 503-726-2205 (SAN 270-1561).

Financial Data Corp., *(Finan Data Corp; 0-940758),* P.O. Box 9524, Washington, DC 20016 Tel 202-364-8700 (SAN 219-7367).

Financial Executives Research Foundation, *(Finan Exec; 0-910586),* 10 Madison Ave., P.O. Box 1938, Morristown, NJ 07960 Tel 201-898-4600 (SAN 206-4111).

Financial Freedom Publishers, *(Finan Freedom; 0-942360),* 9260 E. Colonville Rd., Clare, MI 48617 Tel 517-386-7729 (SAN 281-7101); Dist. by: Financial Freedom Consultants, P.O. Box 268, Clare, MI 48617 Tel 517-386-7720 (SAN 281-711X).

Financial Press, Inc., *(Financial Pr)* 4975 S.W. 82nd St., Miami, FL 33143 (SAN 206-4545).

Financial Publishing Co., *(Finan Pub; 0-87600),* 82 Brookline Ave., Boston, MA 02215 Tel 617-262-4040 (SAN 205-5805).

Fine Arts Museums of San Francisco, The, *(Fine Arts Mus; 0-88401),* M.H. De Young Memorial Museum, Golden Gate Park, San Francisco, CA 94118 Tel 415-558-2887 (SAN 206-524X).

Fine Arts Society, *(Fine Arts Soc; 0-932192),* 50459 N. Portage Rd., South Bend, IN 46628 Tel 219-272-9290 (SAN 211-3902); Orders to: 2314 W. Sixth St., Mishawaka, IN 46544 Tel 219-255-8606 (SAN 211-3910).

Fineline Co., *(Fineline; 0-917520),* 303 Fifth Ave., New York, NY 10016 Tel 212-684-3369 (SAN 206-4723).

Fineline Pubns., *(Fineline Pubns; 0-932492),* 2517 Quincy N.E., Albuquerque, NM 87110 Tel 505-884-3367 (SAN 211-9331).

Finn Hill Arts, *(Finn Hill; 0-917270),* P.O. Box 542, Silverton, CO 81433 Tel 303-387-5729 (SAN 208-5054).

Finnerty, Mary T., *(M T Finnerty; 0-9602222),* 33 Johnson, West Roxbury, MA 02132 (SAN 212-2766); Orders to: P.O. Box 591, Astor Sta., Boston, MA 02123 (SAN 212-2774).

Finney Co., *(Finney Co; 0-912486),* 3350 Gorham Ave., Minneapolis, MN 55426 Tel 612-929-6165 (SAN 206-412X).

Finnish American Literary Heritage Foundation, *(Finnish Am Lit; 0-943478),* P.O. Box 1838, Portland, OR 97207 Tel 503-229-3064 (SAN 240-6497).

FinnRoots, Inc., *(FinnRoots; 0-940034),* 1290 Ave. of the Americas, New York, NY 10004 Tel 212-489-0888 (SAN 220-2190).

Fintzenberg Pubns., *(Fintzenberg; 0-914928),* 3700 Gulf Dr. No. 216, Holmes Beach, FL 33510 Tel 813-778-1825 (SAN 206-7951).

Fire Engineering Book Department, Div. of Technical Publishing Co., A Dun & Bradstreet Co., *(Fire Eng),* 875 Third Ave., New York, NY 10022 (SAN 281-7128); Orders to: Fire Engineering Book Service, P.O. Box C-757, Brooklyn, NY 11205 (SAN 281-7136).

Fire Press, The, *(Fire Pr; 0-912607),* P.O. Box 327, Metuchen, NJ 08840 Tel 201-964-8476 (SAN 283-2593).

Firebird Press, *(Firebird Pr; 0-912019),* P.O. Box 69, Dunlap, IL 61525 (SAN 265-3834).

FireBuilders, The, *(FireBuilders; 0-9601794),* RR1, Box 620, Stetson Rd., Brooklyn, CT 06234 Tel 203-774-4824 (SAN 210-5977).

Fireside Books, Div. of Warren H. Green, Inc., *(Fireside Bks; 0-87527),* 8356 Olive Blvd., St. Louis, MO 63132 Tel 314-991-1335 (SAN 201-8500).

Fireside Paperbacks See Simon & Schuster, Inc.

Fireside Press, *(Fireside Pr),* Box 5293, Hamden, CT 06518 Tel 203-248-1023 (SAN 209-7400).

Firestein Books, *(Firestein Bks; 0-9602498),* P.O. Box 17214, El Paso, TX 79917 Tel 915-592-0260 (SAN 242-940X).

Fireweed Press, *(Fireweed; 0-912683),* P.O. Box 6011, Falls Church, VA 22046 Tel 703-560-0810 (SAN 277-6839).

Firey, Walter, *(Firey; 0-9603066),* 1307 Wilshire Blvd., Austin, TX 78722 Tel 512-454-2418 (SAN 209-5572).

Firm Foundation Publishing House, *(Firm Foun Pub; 0-88027),* P.O. Box 610, Austin, TX 78767 Tel 512-452-7651 (SAN 201-4858).

First Amendment Lawyers Association, *(First Amend),* 1737 Chestnut St., Philadelphia, PA 19103 (SAN 237-7179).

1st American Bank for Savings, *(First Am Bank),* 572 Columbia Rd., Dorchester, MA 02125 (SAN 207-5164).

First Baptist Church Archives, Subs. of Sandifer, *(First Bapt Arch; 0-910653),* P.O. Box 65, Blanchard, LA 71009 Tel 318-929-2213 (SAN 270-1774).

First Baptist Church of Steinhatchee, *(First Baptist),* P.O. Box 113, Steinhatchee, FL 32359 Tel 904-498-1754 (SAN 240-1754).

First Choice, *(First Choice; 0-9606704),* P.O. Box 3914, Santa Barbara, CA 93130 Tel 805-682-3815 (SAN 219-7375).

First Church of Christ Scientist, *(First Church),* 1 Norway St., Boston, MA 02115 Tel 617-262-2300 (SAN 206-6467).

First Commonwealth Press, *(First Commonwealth; 0-912709),* 1300 N.E. 157th St., N. Miami Beach, FL 33162 Tel 305-949-7797 (SAN 283-0280).

First East Coast Theatre and Publishing Company, Inc., *(First East; 0-910829),* P.O. Box A244, Village Sta., New York, NY 10014 Tel 212-255-4612 (SAN 270-1812).

First Edition Books/FEB Co., *(FEB; 0-89502),* FEB Bldg., 120 Clairton Blvd., Pittsburgh, PA 15236 Tel 412-655-9733 (SAN 210-0827).

First Encounter Press, The, *(First Encounter; 0-912609),* P.O. Box 946, No. Eastham, Cape Cod, MA 02651 Tel 617-255-3389 (SAN 282-7697).

First Impressions Publishing Co., *(First Impressions; 0-934794),* P.O. Box 9073, Madison, WI 53715 Tel 608-238-6254 (SAN 213-0572).

First Ozark Press, The, *(First Ozark Pr; 0-911559),* P.O. Box 1137, Harrison, AR 72601 (SAN 217-734X).

First Person, *(First Person; 0-916452),* Box 604, Palisades, NY 10964 Tel 914-359-2995 (SAN 208-0508).

First Pubns., Inc., *(First Pubns; 0-912891),* P.O. Box 1832, Evanston, IL 60204 Tel 312-328-2913 (SAN 283-2607).

Firsthand Press, *(Firsthand; 0-939620),* 1207 Second St., Douglas, AK 99824 Tel 907-364-3461 (SAN 216-6259).

Firth, Robert H., *(Firth; 0-9605060),* 20351 Lake Erie Dr., Walnut, CA 91789 (SAN 216-1338).

Fischer, Carl, Inc., *(Fischer Inc NY; 0-8258),* 62 Cooper Square, New York, NY 10003 (SAN 215-1979).

Fischer, Inge, *(I Fischer; 0-9610238),* 1620 Keeaumoku Street, No. 404, Honolulu, HI 96822 (SAN 264-0406).

Fish, Harriet, *(H U Fish),* P.O. Box 135, Carlsborg, WA 98324 (SAN 287-1726) (SAN 287-1734).

Fishelis, Avraham, Pub., *(A Fishelis; 0-9605560),* 577 Grand St., New York, NY 10002 Tel 212-260-1760 (SAN 240-0006).

Fisher, Clay C., *(C C Fisher),* 702 Tenth St., N.E., Massillon, OH 44646 (SAN 202-4977).

Fisher Institute, The, *(Fisher Inst; 0-933028),* 6350 LBJ Freeway, Suite 183E, Dallas, TX 75240 (SAN 213-4942).

Fishergate Publishing Co., Inc., *(Fishergate; 0-942720),* 2521 Riva Rd., Annapolis, MD 21401 Tel 301-841-6646 (SAN 240-2181).

Fisheries Communications, Inc., *(Fisheries Comm; 0-9608932),* Box 37, Dept B, Stonington, ME 04681 Tel 207-367-2396 (SAN 241-0184).

Fishing News Books, Ltd. See Unipub

Fishner Books, *(Fishner Bks; 0-9606848),* P.O. Box 445, Vienna, VA 22180 Tel 703-281-4255 (SAN 217-3638).

Fitness Alternatives Press, *(Fitness Alt Pr),* Box 761, Evergreen, CO 80439 (SAN 240-1096).

Fitness Pubns., *(Fitness; 0-918278),* P.O. Box 1786, Poughkeepsie, NY 12601 Tel 914-463-1626 (SAN 209-3995).

FitzGerald, Jerry, & Associates, *(FitzGerald & Assocs; 0-932410),* 506 Barkentine Lane, Redwood City, CA 94065 Tel 415-591-5676 (SAN 214-0128).

FitzSimons, H. T., Co., Inc., *(FitzSimons; 0-912222),* 357 W. Erie St., Chicago, IL 60610 Tel 312-944-1841 (SAN 206-4200).

Five Star Pubs., *(Five Star Pubs),* Box 1398, Tupelo, MS 38801 Tel 601-844-5036 (SAN 211-7959).

Five Starr Productions, *(Five Starr Prods; 0-9606026),* 1610 Christine, Wichita Falls, TX 76302 Tel 301-838-8059 (SAN 216-8944).

Five Windmills Pub. Co., *(Five Windmills; 0-9609600),* P.O. Box 5841, Scottsdale, AZ 85258 Tel 602-998-0713 (SAN 260-1877).

Fjord Press, *(Fjord Pr; 0-940242),* P. O. Box 615, Corte Madera, CA 94925 Tel 415-924-9566 (SAN 285-0192); Dist. by: Publishers Services, P.O. Box 3914, San Rafael, CA 94902 (SAN 285-0206).

Flame International Inc., *(Flame Intl; 0-933184),* P. O. Box 305, Quantico, VA 22134 (SAN 215-3114).

Flashmaps Publications, Inc., *(Flashmaps Pubns; 0-942226),* P.O. Box 13, Chappaqua, NY 10514 (SAN 239-8540).

Flatiron Book Distributors Inc., *(Flatiron Book Dist),* 175 Fifth Ave., No. 814, New York, NY 10010 (SAN 240-9917).

Flayderman, N., & Co., Inc., *(Flayderman; 0-910598),* Squash Hollow Rd., New Milford, CT 06776 Tel 203-354-5567 (SAN 205-5813).

Fleet Academic Editions, Inc. *See* **Fleet Press Corp.**

Fleet Press Corp., *(Fleet; 0-8303),* 160 Fifth Ave., New York, NY 10010 Tel 212-243-6100 (SAN 201-4874).

Fleming, Don, Seminars Publishing Co., *(D Fleming Sem; 0-9609264),* 1827 E. Rowland Ave., W. Covina, CA 91791 Tel 213-382-7226 (SAN 260-0560).

Fleschner Publishing, *(Fleschner; 0-937878),* 41 Village Lane, Bethany, CT 06525 Tel 203-393-2170 (SAN 216-1346).

Fleur-Di-Lee, *(Fleur-Di-Lee; 0-911579),* 5969 Donna, Tarzana, CA 91356 (SAN 264-0422).

Flightshops, *(Flightshops; 0-939158),* St. Petersburg-Clearwater Airport, Clearwater, FL 33520 (SAN 240-9127).

Flint Hills Book Co., *(Flint Hills),* 1735 Fairview, Manhattan, KS 66502 (SAN 208-1806).

Flint Institute of Arts, *(Flint Inst Arts; 0-939896),* 1120 E. Kearsley St., Flint, MI 48503 Tel 313-234-1695 (SAN 216-812X).

Flora & Fauna Pubns., *(Flora & Fauna; 0-916846),* 2406 NW 47th Terrace, Gainesville, FL 32606 Tel 904-371-9858 (SAN 220-2468).

Floraprint U.S.A., Div. of American Printers & Lithographers, *(Floraprint USA),* 6701 W. Oakton St., Chicago, IL 60648 Tel 312-966-6500 (SAN 216-7069); Dist. by: International Scholarly Book Services, Inc., 2130 Pacific Ave., Forest Grove, OR 97116 Tel 503-357-7192 (SAN 205-4728).

Florham Park Press, Inc., *(Florham; 0-912598),* P.O. Box 303, Florham Park, NJ 07932 Tel 201-377-3670 (SAN 206-4219).

Florida Classics Library, *(Florida Classics; 0-912451),* P.O. Drawer 1657, Port Salerno, FL 33492-1657 Tel 305-287-8910 (SAN 265-2404).

Florida State Bar Association, *(Fla Bar),* 600 Apalachee Pkwy., Tallahassee, FL 32304 (SAN 237-7209).

Florida State Univ. Foundation, *(Florida State U Found; 0-9606708),* 361 Bellamy Bldg, Florida State Univ., Tallahassee, FL 32306 (SAN 219-7405).

Florida State University, Geology Dept., *(FSU Geology; 0-938426),* Tallahassee, FL 32306 Tel 904-644-3208 (SAN 239-9350).

Flourtown Publishing Co., *(Flourtown Pub; 0-9603376),* P.O. Box 148, Flourtown, PA 19031 (SAN 207-6381).

Flower Mound Writing Company, *(Flower Mound Writ; 0-910655),* Box 22984, TWU Sta., Denton, TX 76204 Tel 817-566-3995 (SAN 262-6632).

Flower of Truth Publishing Co., *(Flower Truth; 0-9608164),* P.O. Box 763, Anchorage, AK 99587 (SAN 240-2203).

Flower Press, *(Flower Pr),* 10332 Shaver Rd., Kalamazoo, MI 49002 (SAN 217-7358).

Flowerpot Mountain Press, *(Flowerpot Mtn Pr; 0-9610768),* P.O. Box 3711, Lawrence, KS 66044 (SAN 264-6153).

Fly Tyer Inc., *(Fly Tyer; 0-9607522),* P.O.Box 1231, North Conway, NH 03860 Tel 603-356-5091 (SAN 238-6178).

Flying Books, *(Flying Bks; 0-911139),* 3850 Coronation Rd., Eagan, MN 55122 Tel 612-454-2493 (SAN 270-2185).

Flying Buttress Pubns., *(Flying Buttress; 0-918348),* P.O. Box 254, Endicott, NY 13760 Tel 607-785-5423 (SAN 210-0835).

Flying Diamond Books, *(Flying Diamond Bks; 0-918532),* Rte. 2, Box D301, Hettinger, ND 58639 Tel 701-567-2646 (SAN 209-5580).

Flying Enterprises, Inc, *(Flying Ent; 0-912470),* Box 7000, Dallas, TX 75209 Tel 214-358-3456 (SAN 201-4882).

Flynn, George, *(G Flynn),* 145 W. Twelfth St., New York, NY 10011 (SAN 211-3929).

FMA Business Books, *(FMA Bus; 0-930566),* 3928 Iowa ST, San Diego, CA 92104 (SAN 221-1483).

Focal Pr., *(Focal Pr),* 10 Tower Office Pk., Woburn, MA 01801 Tel 617-933-8260 (SAN 220-0066).

Focus Pub. Co., *(Focus Pub; 0-938442),* 29175 Oak Point Dr., Farmington Hills, MI 48018 Tel 313-553-0298 (SAN 281-7160); Dist. by: The Distributor, 702 S. Michigan, South Bend, IN 46618 Tel 219-232-8500 (SAN 212-0364).

Focus Quality Games Corp., *(Focus Quality; 0-915236),* P.O. Box 114, Blythebourne Sta., Brooklyn, NY 11219 (SAN 207-1266).

Fogg Art Museum, Div. of Harvard University, *(Fogg Art; 0-916724),* 32 Quincy St., Cambridge, MA 02138 Tel 617-495-2387 (SAN 208-6530).

Folcroft Library Editions, *(Folcroft; 0-8414),* P.O. Box 182, Folcroft, PA 19032 (SAN 206-8362).

Foldabook Publishing Co., *(Foldabook Pub; 0-89726),* 111 N. Fuller Ave., Los Angeles, CA 90036 Tel 213-933-3009 (SAN 217-2399).

Folder Editions, *(Folder Edns; 0-913152),* 103-26 68th Rd., Apt A63, Forest Hills, NY 11375 (SAN 206-6475).

Folger Books, *(Folger Bks; 0-918016),* 440 Forsate Dr., Cranburynswick, NY 08512 Tel 201-254-0132 (SAN 210-2013).

Folio Magazine Pub. Corp., *(Folio; 0-918110),* P.O. Box 697, 125 Elm St., New Canaan, CT 06840 Tel 203-972-0761 (SAN 210-2021).

Folio Pubs., *(Folio Pubs; 0-939454),* 1121 Ridgeview Dr., Nashville, TN 37220 Tel 615-373-1675 (SAN 281-7187); Dist. by: Folio Publications, 1121 Ridgeview Dr., Nashville, TN 37220 (SAN 281-7195).

Folk Art Studios, *(Folk Art; 0-930310),* 608 E. First St., Tustin, CA 92680 Tel 714-761-3355 (SAN 207-5601).

Folk-Legacy Records, Inc., *(Folk-Legacy),* Sharon Mountain Rd., Sharon, CT 06069 Tel 203-364-5661 (SAN 207-3390).

Folkestone Press, *(Folkestone; 0-910600),* P.O. Box 3142, St. Louis, MO 63130 Tel 314-725-2767 (SAN 206-4227).

Folklorica Press, Inc., *(Folklorica Pr; 0-939544),* 301 E. 47th St., New York, NY 10017 Tel 212-840-6885 (SAN 216-6720).

Folks Pubns., *(Folks Pubns; 0-941628),* P.O. Box 1121, N. Highland, CA 95660 Tel 916-331-2106 (SAN 239-2089).

Folksay Press, *(Folksay Pr; 0-933710),* 67131 Mills Rd., R.R. 3, St. Clairsville, OH 43950 Tel 614-695-3348 (SAN 208-6514); Dist. by: Bookpeople, 2940 Seventh St., Berkeley, CA 94710 Tel 415-549-3033 (SAN 168-9517).

Folksmedia Publishing Co., *(Folksmedia Pub; 0-9608526),* P.O. Box 9206, Palm Springs, CA 92263 Tel 714-320-6826 (SAN 240-6500).

Folkstone Press, The, *(Folkstone Pr),* P.O. Box 3142, St. Louis, MO 63130 (SAN 285-6778); Dist. by: Paperback Supply, 4121 Forest Park Blvd., St. Louis, MO 63108 (SAN 285-6786).

Fontana, John M., Pub., *(J M Fontana; 0-9600034),* 4 Walnut Place, Huntington, NY 11743 Tel 516-549-0892 (SAN 206-4235).

Fontastic, *(Fontastic; 0-9603596),* 157 Judd St., Madison, WI 53714 Tel 608-249-8701 (SAN 222-3368).

Food & Agriculture Organization *See* **Unipub**

Food First *See* **Institute for Food & Development Policy**

Food for Thought Pubns., *(Food for Thought),* P.O. Box 331, Amherst, MA 01004 Tel 413-253-5432 (SAN 209-4363).

Food Processors Institute, The, *(Food Processors; 0-937774),* 1133 20th St. NW, Washington, DC 20036 (SAN 215-3122).

Food Research & Action Center Inc., *(Food Res Action; 0-934220),* 1319 F St. NW, Washington, DC 20004 (SAN 215-9937).

Fool Court Press, The, *(Fool Court),* P.O. Box 25824, Charlotte, NC 28212 (SAN 240-8503).

Foot Trails Pubns., Inc., *(Foot Trails; 0-933710),* The Pottingshed, Bedford Rd., Greenwich, CT 06830 (SAN 213-2389); Dist. by: Simon & Schuster, Inc., 1230 Ave. of the Americas, New York, NY 10020 Tel 212-245-6400 (SAN 200-2450).

Football Hobbies, Pubs., *(Football Hobbies; 0-912122),* 4216 McConnell, El Paso, TX 79904 Tel 915-565-7354 (SAN 204-1057).

Foothills Press, *(Foothills Pr; 0-917284),* P.O. Box 458, Pittsfield, MA 01202 Tel 413-499-4687 (SAN 208-4171).

Footloose Press, *(Footloose Pr),* P.O. Box 3353, Hayward, CA 94540 Tel 415-538-1197 (SAN 207-7639).

Footsteps Press, *(Footsteps; 0-934796),* P.O. Box 948, Hobbs, NM 88240 (SAN 213-666X).

Foran Pubn., *(Foran Pubn; 0-912941),* P.O. Box 356, Elsie, MI 48831 (SAN 283-2615); Dist. by: Publishers Marketing Group, P.O. Box 170008, Overland Plaza, Richardson, TX 75081 (SAN 262-0995).

Forbes, George F., *(G F Forbes; 0-910604),* 9813 Monogram Ave., Sepulveda, CA 91343 Tel 213-894-6882 (SAN 281-7209).

Force Pub. Co., *(Force Pub; 0-942362),* P.O. Box 4037, Salinas, CA 93912 Tel 408-663-0537 (SAN 239-8559).

Ford Associates, *(Ford Assocs),* 824 E. Seventh St., Auburn, IN 46706 (SAN 201-6508).

Ford Foundation, *(Ford Found; 0-916584),* 320 E. 43rd St., New York, NY 10017 Tel 212-573-4812 (SAN 222-9730).

Ford, Sondra & Assoc., *(S Ford & Assoc; 0-913043),* 478 Hamilton Ave., No.173, Campbell, CA 95008 (SAN 283-0809).

Fordham Equipment & Publishing Co., *(Fordham Pub; 0-913308),* 3308 Edson Ave., Bronx, NY 10469 Tel 212-379-7300 (SAN 207-2254).

Fordham Univ. Press, *(Fordham; 0-8232),* University Box L, Bronx, NY 10458 Tel 212-579-2319 (SAN 201-6516).

Fords Travel Guides, *(Fords Travel; 0-916486),* Box 505, 22151 Clarendon St., Woodland Hills, CA 91365 Tel 213-347-1677 (SAN 212-9418).

Forecaster Publishing Co., Inc., *(Forecaster Pub),* 19623 Ventura Blvd., Tarzana, CA 91356 Tel 213-345-4421 (SAN 218-7272).

Foreign Policy Assn., *(Foreign Policy; 0-87124),* 205 Lexington Ave., New York, NY 10016 Tel 212-481-8450 (SAN 212-9426).

Foreign Policy Research Institute, *(For Policy Res),* 3508 Market St., Suite 350, Philadelphia, PA 19104 Tel 215-382-2054 (SAN 218-7280).

Foreman, Gloria, Publishing Co., *(G Foreman; 0-915198),* P.O. Box 405, Oklahoma City, OK 73101 Tel 918-723-5415 (SAN 203-4263).

Foremost Pubs., Inc., *(Foremost Pubs; 0-940078),* W. Main Rd., Little Compton, RI 02837 Tel 401-635-2900 (SAN 220-2204).

Forest Hill Press, *(Forest Hill; 0-9605472),* 3974 Forest Hill Ave., Oakland, CA 94602 (SAN 215-9945).

Forest History Society, Inc., *(Forest Hist Soc; 0-89030),* 109 Coral St., Santa Cruz, CA 95060 Tel 408-426-3770 (SAN 201-6524).

Forest of Peace Books, Inc., *(Forest Peace; 0-939516),* Route One, Box 247, Easton, KS 66020 Tel 913-773-8255 (SAN 216-6739).

Forest Press Division Lake Placid Education Foundation, *(Forest Pr; 0-910608),* 85 Watervliet Ave., Albany, NY 12206 Tel 518-489-8549 (SAN 210-8070).

Forest Products Research Society, *(Forest Prod; 0-935018),* 2801 Marshall Court, Madison, WI 53705 Tel 608-231-1361 (SAN 211-4216).

Forest Publishing, *(Forest Pub; 0-9605118),* 222 Wisconsin, Suite 201, Lake Forest, IL 60045 (SAN 215-7624).

Foreworks, *(Foreworks; 0-943292),* Box 9747, North Hollywood, CA 91609 Tel 213-982-0467 (SAN 240-6519).

Foris Pubns., USA, *(Foris Pubns),* Orders to: Box C-50, Cinnaminson, NJ 08077 Tel 609-829-6830 (SAN 220-1151).

Forkner Publishing Corp., Subs. of Gage Publishing Ltd., *(Forkner; 0-912036),* 164 Commander Blvd.,Agincourt, Ontario, M1S 3C7, Tel 416-298-8188 (SAN 206-426X).

Forkuo, Peter C., World Enterprises, *(P C Forkuo World Ent; 0-941928),* P.O. Box 402, Worchester, MA 01613 Tel 617-753-1769 (SAN 238-6186).

Forman Publishing, *(Forman Pub),* 11661 San Vicente Blvd., Suite 206, Los Angeles, CA 90049 Tel 213-820-8672 (SAN 216-776X).

Formur International, *(Formur Intl; 0-89378),* 4200 Laclede Ave., St. Louis, MO 63108 (SAN 207-5768).

Forrest Printing, *(Forrest Printing; 0-89023),* P.O. Box 105, Grand Haven, MI 49417 (SAN 239-8524).

Forster, Reginald Bishop, Associates Inc., *(R B Forster; 0-931398),* 3287 Ramos Circle, Sacramento, CA 95827 Tel 916-362-3276 (SAN 211-2388).

Forsyth Gallery, *(Forsyth Gall; 0-9601560),* P.O. Box 525, Cooper Sta., New York, NY 10003 Tel 212-925-6697 (SAN 211-6677).

Forsythe & Cromwell, *(Forsythe & Cromwell; 0-940390),* P.O. Box 217, Andover, NJ 07821 Tel 201-625-1989 (SAN 217-3646).

Fort Concho Sketches Publishing Co., *(Fort Concho),* P.O. Box 5262, San Angelo, TX 76902 (SAN 206-4731).

Fort Sullivan Chapter (Daughters of the American Revolution), *(Fort Sullivan),* P.O. Box 33055, Charleston, SC 29407 (SAN 209-4371).

Forte, Robert L., , Jr., *(R Forte; 0-9609328),* P.O. Box 1051, Flint, MI 48501 Tel 313-789-0244 (SAN 260-1885).

Fortress Press, *(Fortress; 0-8006),* 2900 Queen Lane, Philadelphia, PA 19129 Tel 800-822-3906 (SAN 220-0074).

Fortuna Book Sales, *(Fortuna; 0-910610),* 8035 Fairlane Ave., Brooksville, FL 33512 (SAN 206-4278).

Fortunato, Donald J., *(D J Fortunato),* Millstone Rd., Clarksburg, NJ 08510 Tel 609-259-2137 (SAN 213-0599).

40 Whacks Press, *(Forty Whacks; 0-939264),* P.O. Box 591, Shelton, CT 06484 Tel 203-366-8060 (SAN 220-1542) Moved, left no forwarding address.

Forum for Death Education & Counseling, *(Forum for Death Educ; 0-9607394),* 8823 Cunningham, College Park, MD 20740 Tel 803-777-3859 (SAN 237-952X).

Forum Press, Inc., *(Forum Pr IL; 0-88273),* 3110 N. Arlington Heights Rd, Arlington Heights, IL 60004 (SAN 208-3256). *Imprints:* Piraeus Publishers (Piraeus).

Forum Quorum, *(Forum Quorum; 0-9606778),* P.O. Box 43, Waldwick, NJ 07463 Tel 201-444-0499 (SAN 219-7413).

Forward Movement Pubns., *(Forward Movement),* 412 Sycamore St., Cincinnati, OH 45202 Tel 513-721-6659 (SAN 208-3841).

Forward Press, The, *(Forward Pr; 0-941262),* 30 S. First Ave., Suite 301, Arcadia, CA 91006 Tel 213-445-7204 (SAN 239-426X).

Fotonovel Pubns., *(Fotonovel; 0-89752),* 8831 Sunset Blvd., PH-W, Los Angeles, CA 90069 Tel 213-659-8888 (SAN 213-2486); Dist. by: The Independent News Co., 75 Rockefeller Plaza, New York, NY 10019 (SAN 208-6158).

Foul Play Press *See* **Countryman Press, Inc.**

Foundation Books, *(Foun Bks; 0-934988),* P.O. Box 29229, Lincoln, NE 68529 Tel 402-466-4988 (SAN 201-6567).

Foundation Center, The, *(Foundation Ctr; 0-87954),* 888 Seventh Ave., New York, NY 10019 Tel 212-975-1120 (SAN 207-5687).

Foundation Church of the New Birth, Inc., *(Foun Church New Birth),* P.O. Box 996, Benjamin Franklin Sta., Washington, DC 20044 (SAN 211-7967).

Foundation for American Christian Education, *(Found Am Christ; 0-912498),* 2946 25th Ave., San Francisco, CA 94132 Tel 415-661-1775 (SAN 205-5856).

Foundation for American Communications, *(Foun Am Comm; 0-910755),* 3383 Barham Blvd., Los Angeles, CA 90068 Tel 213-851-7372 (SAN 270-2746).

Foundation for Auditability Research & Education, Inc. *See* **Institute of Internal Auditors, Inc.**

Foundation for Better Living, *(Foun Better; 0-89506),* P.O. Box 2339, Reston, VA 22090 Tel 703-620-9830 (SAN 210-0843).

Foundation for Christian Self-Government, *(Foun Chr Self Govt; 0-941370),* P.O. Box 1087, Thousand Oaks, CA 91360 Tel 213-991-9592 (SAN 238-9800).

Foundation for Christian Services Inc., *(Foun Christ Serv),* P.O. Box 18108, Orlando, FL 32860 (SAN 264-0457).

Foundation for Classical Reprints, The, *(Found Class Reprints; 0-89901),* 607 McKnight St. N.W., Albuquerque, NM 87102 (SAN 212-9051).

Foundation for Economic Education, Inc., *(Foun Econ Ed; 0-910614),* 30 S. Broadway, Irvington-on-Hudson, NY 10533 Tel 914-591-7230 (SAN 311-3515).

Foundation for Historic Restoration in Pendleton Area, *(Foun Hist Rest; 0-912462),* P.O. Box 444, Pendleton, SC 29670 Tel 803-654-2640 (SAN 206-4286).

Foundation for Human Understanding, *(Foun Human GA; 0-936396),* Box 5712, Athens, GA 30604 (SAN 214-3720).

Foundation for Inner Peace, *(Found Inner Peace),* P.O. Box 635, Tiburon, CA 94920 Tel 415-435-2255 (SAN 212-422X).

Foundation for National Progress, *(Foun Natl Prog; 0-938806),* Housing Information Ctr., P.O. Box 8271, Green Bay, WI 54308 (SAN 215-9554).

Foundation for the Advancement of Artists, *(Foun Adv Artists; 0-912916),* 1315 Walnut St. Bldg., Philadelphia, PA 19107 Tel 215-546-3336 (SAN 201-1425).

Foundation for the Advancement of Man, *(Foun Adv Man; 0-939794),* P.O. Box 2876, Escondido, CA 92025 (SAN 218-4761).

FCA Books for the Arts, *(FCA Bks; 0-933032),* 280 Broadway, Suite 412, New York, NY 10007 Tel 212-227-3770 (SAN 212-2782).

Foundation of Human Understanding, *(Foun Human Under; 0-933900),* P.O. Box 34036, Los Angeles, CA 90034 Tel 213-559-3711 (SAN 213-9545).

Foundation Press, Inc., *(Foundation Pr; 0-88277),* P.O. Box 3056, Textbook Department, St. Paul, MN 55165 Tel 612-228-2561 (SAN 281-7217); Orders to: 170 Old Country Rd., Mineola, NY 11501 Tel 516-248-5580 (SAN 281-7225).

Foundation Pubns., Inc., *(Foun Pubns; 0-910618),* P.O. Box 6439, Anaheim, CA 92806 Tel 714-630-6450 (SAN 206-4294).

Foundation Publishing, *(Found Pub; 0-932032),* P.O. Box 3243, Burlington, VT 05401 Tel 802-862-7386 (SAN 211-6189).

Fountain House East, *(Fountain Hse East; 0-914736),* Box 99298, Jeffersontown, KY 40299 Tel 502-267-5414 (SAN 206-6262).

Fountain Press, Inc., *(Fountain Pr; 0-89350),* Dist. by: Inspirational Marketing Inc., Box 301, Indianola, IA 50125 (SAN 208-6557).

Fountain Pubns., *(Fountain Publications Oregon; 0-911376),* 3728 N.W. Thurman St., Portland, OR 97210 Tel 503-223-2232 (SAN 205-5880).

Fountain Publishing Co., Inc., *(Fountain Pub Co NY; 0-916184),* 509 Madison Ave., Rm. 712, New York, NY 10022 Tel 212-838-9215 (SAN 205-5864); Dist. by: Harper & Row, Scranton, PA 18512 (SAN 215-3742).

Fountainhead Pubs., Inc., *(Fountainhead; 0-87310),* 475 Fifth Ave., New York, NY 10017 Tel 212-421-1556 (SAN 206-4324).

Four D Publishing Co., *(Four D Pub Co; 0-9610006),* Box 381, Princeton, IL 61356 (SAN 270-3092).

Four Seasons Book Pubs., *(Four Seas Bk; 0-9605400),* Greenwood Hall Farm, Rte. 1, Box 278, Grasonville, MD 21638 Tel 301-827-7350 (SAN 215-8639).

Four Seasons Foundation, *(Four Seasons Foun; 0-87704),* P.O. Box 31190, San Francisco, CA 94131 Tel 415-824-5774 (SAN 201-6591); Dist. by: Subterranean Co., P.O. Box 10233, Eugene, OR 97440 Tel 503-343-6324 (SAN 169-7102).

Four Star Press, The, *(Four Star),* 815 N. Labrea Ave., P.O. Box 301, Los Angeles, CA 90302 (SAN 217-1031).

Four Winds Press, *(Four Winds Pr),* Box 126, Bristol, FL 32321 (SAN 209-7435).

Four Winds Press *See* **Scholastic, Inc.**

Four Zoas Night House, Ltd., *(Four Zoas Night Ltd; 0-939622),* Po Box 111, Ashvelot Village, NH 02129 Tel 617-241-9817 (SAN 216-6267).

Fournies, F., & Associates, Inc., *(F Fournies; 0-917622),* 129 Edgewood Dr., Bridgewater, NJ 08807 Tel 201-526-2442 (SAN 205-5708).

Foursquare Press, *(Foursquare Pr; 0-930616),* 648 Ransom Rd., Lancaster, NY 14086 Tel 716-681-2586 (SAN 211-8998).

Fowler & Wells, Publisher, *(Fowler & Wells; 0-937776),* 2175 Hudson Terrace, No. 6P, Fort Lee, NJ 07024 (SAN 277-6804); Dist. by: Inland Book Co., P.O. Box 261, E. Haven, CT 06512 (SAN 200-4151).

Fowler Music Enterprises, *(Fowler Music; 0-943894),* 808 S. Alkire St., Lakewood, CO 80228 Tel 303-986-7309 (SAN 241-113X).

Fox, Sanford, *(S Fox; 0-9603854),* 41-41 Christine Court, Fairlawn, NJ 07410 (SAN 214-0152).

Fox, Wesley, *(W Fox; 0-9604122),* 55710 Park Meadow Dr., Naperville, IL 60540 (SAN 214-3739).

Fox Hills Press, The, *(Fox Hills; 0-914932),* 2676 Cunningham Hole Rd., Annapolis, MD 21401 Tel 301-266-6626 (SAN 211-139X).

Fox Hollow Fibres, *(Fox Hollow; 0-9608074),* Rt. 1, Box 161a, Glasgow, VA 24555 (SAN 240-0928).

Fox Reading Research Co., *(Fox Reading Res),* P.O. Box 1059, Coeur D'Alene, ID 83814 Tel 208-772-4524 (SAN 213-0602).

Fox River Publishing Co., *(Fox River; 0-939398),* Box 54, Princeton, WI 54968 (SAN 216-3802).

Fox Thoughts Pubns., *(Fox Thoughts; 0-912403),* 2640 East Twelfth Ave., Department 571, Denver, CO 80206 Tel 303-377-7053 (SAN 265-4040).

Foxhall Press, *(Foxhall Pr; 0-9611128),* P.O. Box 9629, Washington, DC 20016 Tel 202-362-5870 (SAN 282-9061).

Foxhound Enterprises, *(Foxhound Ent; 0-940502),* 25 Tazewell St., Fredericksburg, VA 22405 Tel 703-371-7498 (SAN 223-1034); Dist. by: P. D. Berry, Box 68, Louisa, KY 41230 (SAN 223-1042).

Foxman, L. D., *(Foxman; 0-9610946),* c/o Cambridge Human Resource Group, Inc., 20 N. Clark St., Chicago, IL 60602 Tel 312-444-9860 (SAN 265-2439).

Foxmoor Press, *(Foxmoor; 0-938604),* Box 47, Rte. 2, Tahlequah, OK 74464 (SAN 215-8647).

Fragments/The Valentine Press, *(Fragments Valentine),* P.O. Box 16966, Irvine, CA 92713 (SAN 219-1725).

Framo Publishing, *(Framo Pub; 0-936398),* 561 W. Diversey Pkwy., Chicago, IL 60614 Tel 312-477-1485 (SAN 214-0160).

Franas Press, *(Franas Pr; 0-9600482),* 1116 Ocean Ave., Mantoloking, NJ 08738 (SAN 205-5899).

Franchise Group Pubs., *(Franchise Group; 0-936898),* 4350 E. Camelback, Suite B-140, Phoenix, AZ 85018 (SAN 214-3747).

Franciscan Herald Press, *(Franciscan Herald; 0-8199),* 1434 W. 51st St., Chicago, IL 60609 Tel 312-254-4455 (SAN 201-6621).

Franciscan Institute Pubns., *(Franciscan Inst),* Drawer F, St. Bonaventure University, St. Bonaventure, NY 14778 Tel 716-375-2105 (SAN 201-8543).

Franje, Inc., *(Franje; 0-9601078),* 1175 Barbara Dr., Vista, CA 92083 Tel 619-726-7129 (SAN 205-5902).

Frank, Leonard Roy, *(L R Frank; 0-9601376),* 2300 Webster St., San Francisco, CA 94115 Tel 415-922-3029 (SAN 212-0917).

Frank Pubns., *(Frank Pubns; 0-942952),* 60 E 42nd St., Suite 757, New York, NY 10017 (SAN 240-4737).

Franklin, Burt, Pub., *(B Franklin; 0-89102),* Dist. by: Lenox Hill Publishing & Distributing Corp., 235 E. 44th St., New York, NY 10017 (SAN 282-597X).

Franklin, Chas., Press, The, *(C Franklin Pr; 0-9603516),* 18409 90th Ave. W., Edmonds, WA 98020 Tel 206-774-6979 (SAN 213-4969).

Franklin, Donald, *(Donald Franklin; 0-914714),* 7852 Ducor Ave., Canoga Park, CA 91304 Tel 213-883-4247 (SAN 201-2758).

Franklin, *(Franklin CT; 0-9604424),* 203 Broad St., No. 2, New London, CT 06320 (SAN 214-3755).

Franklin and Marshall College, *(Franklin & Marshall; 0-910626),* P O Box 3003, Lancaster, PA 17604 Tel 717-291-3981 (SAN 226-3408).

Franklin Book Co., *(Franklin Bk; 0-917522),* P.O. Box 208, East Millstone, NJ 08873 Tel 201-873-2156 (SAN 209-2042).

Franklin Institute Press, The, *(Franklin Inst Pr; 0-89168),* Box 2266, Philadelphia, PA 19103 Tel 215-448-1551 (SAN 209-5599).

Franklin Press, The, *(Franklin Pr OH; 0-933034),* P.O. Box 437, 166 S. Franklin St., Chagrin, OH 44022 (SAN 211-7320) Moved, left no forwarding address.

Franks, Ray, Publishing Ranch, *(R Franks Ranch),* P.O. Box 7068, Amarillo, TX 79109 Tel 806-355-6417 (SAN 218-7329).

Franzak & Foster Co., *(Franzak & Foster; 0-942588),* 4012 Bridge Ave., Cleveland, OH 44113 Tel 216-961-4134 (SAN 240-0731).

Fraser, Worden, Pubs., *(W Fraser Pubs; 0-936582),* Box 2032, Stanford, CA 94305 (SAN 214-3763).

Fraser Publishing Co., Div. of Fraser Management Assocs., Inc., *(Fraser Pub Co; 0-87034),* 309 S. Willard St., Burlington, VT 05401 Tel 802-658-0322 (SAN 213-9529); Orders to: Box 494, Burlington, VT 05402 (SAN 213-9537).

Fredericks Publishing Co., *(Fredericks Pub; 0-939690),* P.O. Box 97, Mertztown, PA 19539 Tel 215-682-7784 (SAN 216-7328).

Fredonia, *(Fredonia; 0-940204),* Suite 9490, 29169 W. Heathercliff, Malibu, CA 90265 (SAN 217-104X).

Fredriksen, John C., *(Fredriksen),* 69 Flamingo Dr., Warwick, RI 02886 Tel 401-737-7983 (SAN 213-6864).

Free-Bass Press, *(Free-Bass; 0-8256),* Box 563, Eugene, OR 97440 Tel 206-329-9808 (SAN 217-1058); Dist. by: Music Sales Corp., 79 Broadway, New York, NY 10003 (SAN 209-0988).

Free Church Pubns., *(Free Church Pubns; 0-911802),* 1515 E. 66th St., Minneapolis, MN 55423 Tel 612-866-3343 (SAN 206-4146).

Free Enterprise Institute, Subs. of Amway Corp., *(Free Ent Inst; 0-940434),* 7575 E. Fulton Rd., Ada, MI 49355 Tel 616-676-6986 (SAN 217-1767).

Free Enterprises Services, Inc., *(Free Ent System; 0-943636),* 2120 Beneva Rd., Sarasota, FL 33582 Tel 813-924-4211 (SAN 238-2849).

Free Library of Philadelphia, *(Phila Free Lib; 0-911132),* Rare Book Dept., Logan Square, Philadelphia, PA 19103 Tel 215-686-5416 (SAN 205-3837).

Free Market Bks., *(Free Market; 0-930902),* P.O. Box 298, Dobbs Ferry, NY 10522 Tel 914-591-7769 (SAN 209-1143).

Free Press, Div. of Macmillan Publishing Co., Inc., *(Free Pr; 0-02),* 866 Third Ave., New York, NY 10022 Tel 212-935-2000 (SAN 201-6656); Dist. by: Macmillan Co., Front & Brown Sts., Riverside, NJ 08370 Tel 609-461-6500 (SAN 202-5582).

Freedeeds Books *See Garber Communications, Inc.*

Freedman, Jacob, Liturgy Research Foundation, *(J Freedman Liturgy),* P.O. Box 317, Forest Park Sta., Springfield, MA 01108 (SAN 207-7582).

Freedom Books, *(Freedom Bks; 0-930374),* P.O. Box 5303, Hamden, CT 06518 Tel 203-281-6791 (SAN 210-9255).

Freedom from Religion Foundation, *(Freedom Rel Found),* P.O. Box 750, Madison, WI 53701 Tel 608-256-8900 (SAN 276-9484).

Freedom House, *(Freedom Hse; 0-932088),* 20 W. 40th St., New York, NY 10018 Tel 212-730-7744 (SAN 211-7339).

Freedom Press, *(Freedom Pr; 0-941630),* P.O. Box 5503, Scottsdale, AZ 85261 Tel 607-991-5414 (SAN 239-2100).

Freedom Seminary Press, *(Freedom Sem Pr),* 5927 Windhover Dr., Orlando, FL 32805 Tel 305-351-0898 (SAN 209-505X).

Freedom Unlimited, *(Freedom Unltd; 0-938014),* P.O. Box 599, Garden Grove, CA 92642 (SAN 215-644X).

Freelance Pubns. Ltd, *(Freelance Pubns; 0-9602050),* P.O. Box 8, Bayport, NY 11705 Tel 516-472-1799 (SAN 213-0734).

Freeland Pubns., *(Freeland Pubns; 0-936868),* P.O. Box 18941, Philadelphia, PA 19119 (SAN 215-3130).

Freelandia Institute, *(Freelandia; 0-914674),* Star Rte., Cassville, MO 65625 (SAN 205-6216).

Freeman, H. P., , Publisher, *(Freeman Sr; 0-9609920),* 318 Monroe ST.,P.O. Box 93, Red Bluff, CA 96080 Tel 916-527-1679 (SAN 270-3408).

Freeman, W. H., & Co., Subs. Scientific American, Inc., *(W H Freeman; 0-7167),* 41 Madison Ave., 37th Fl., New York, NY 10010 Tel 212-576-9400 (SAN 200-2302).

Freeman, Cooper & Co., *(Freeman C; 0-87735),* 1736 Stockton St., San Francisco, CA 94133 Tel 415-362-6171 (SAN 201-6672).

Freeman Mutuels Management, *(Freeman Mutuels; 0-9608022),* P.O. Box 622, Henderson, LA 70517 Tel 318-228-2028 (SAN 239-6432).

Freeman Publishing Company, *(Freeman Pub Co; 0-911939),* P.O. Box 703, Van Nuys, CA 91408 Tel 213-990-7482 (SAN 264-049X); 13524 Rye St., No. 4, Sherman Oaks, CA 91423 Tel 213-990-2576 (SAN 264-0503).

Freemen Institute, The, *(Freemen Inst; 0-88080),* P.O. Box 31776, Salt Lake City, UT 84131 Tel 801-566-9864 (SAN 240-074X) Tel 801-973-1776.

Freeperson Press, *(Freeperson; 0-918236),* 455 Ridge Rd., Novato, CA 94947 Tel 415-897-0336 (SAN 209-438X).

Freer Gallery of Art, Smithsonian Institution, *(Freer; 0-934686),* 12th & Jefferson Dr., S.W., Washington, DC 20560 Tel 202-357-2102 (SAN 201-856X).

Freestone Publishing Co., *(Freestone Pub Co; 0-913512),* Box 398, Monroe, UT 84754 Tel 801-527-3738 (SAN 206-4154); Dist. by: Bookpeople, 2940 Seventh St., Berkeley, CA 94710 Tel 415-549-3033 (SAN 168-9517).

Freidus, Robert, Gallery, *(Freidus Gallery),* 158 Lafayette St., New York, NY 10013 Tel 212-925-0113 (SAN 223-2065).

French, Samuel, Inc., *(French; 0-573),* 25 W. 45th St., New York, NY 10036 Tel 212-582-4700 (SAN 206-4170).

French & European Pubns., Inc., *(French & Eur; 0-8288),* 115 Fifth Ave., New York, NY 10003 Tel 212-673-7400 (SAN 206-8109).

French Forum Pubs., Inc., *(French Forum; 0-917058),* P.O. Box 5108, Lexington, KY 40505 Tel 606-299-9530 (SAN 208-4996).

French Institute-Alliance Francaise, *(French Inst; 0-933444),* 22 E. 60th St., New York, NY 10022 Tel 212-355-6100 (SAN 204-207X).

Freneau, Philip, Press, *(Freneau; 0-912480),* 18 Valentine St., Box 116, Monmouth Beach, NJ 07750 Tel 201-222-6458 (SAN 201-6680).

Frenkle, Helga, Publisher, *(Frenkle H. Pub; 0-912406),* 75 Montgomery St., No.3-D, New York, NY 10002 Tel 212-227-7957 (SAN 204-0875).

Fresh Press, *(Fresh Pr; 0-9601398),* 774 Allen Court, Palo Alto, CA 94303 Tel 415-493-3596 (SAN 210-6000).

FreshCut Press, *(FreshCut),* 133 Clara Ave., Ukiah, CA 95482 (SAN 215-8655); 45 N. Prospect, Oberlin, OH 44074 (SAN 215-8663).

Freshet Press, Inc., *(Freshet Pr; 0-88395),* 90 Hamilton Rd., Rockville Centre, NY 11570 Tel 516-766-3011 (SAN 205-5929).

Freshman, Samuel K., *(S K Freshman; 0-9600708),* 700 S. Flower St., Suite 2600, Los Angeles, CA 90017 Tel 213-629-1100 (SAN 206-5266).

Freshwater Logistics, *(Freshwater Logistics; 0-9603006),* 418 Fremont Rd., Port Clinton, OH 43452 Tel 419-734-1430 (SAN 213-0610).

Freshwater Press, Inc., *(Freshwater; 0-912514),* P.O. Box 14009, Cleveland, OH 44114 Tel 216-241-0373 (SAN 201-6699).

Freundlich Books, *(Freundlich; 0-88191),* 80 Madison Ave., Penthouse B, New York, NY 10016 Tel 212-532-9666 (SAN 287-0312); Dist. by: The Scribner Book Companies, Inc., (SAN 264-7419).

Friede Pubns., *(Friede Pubns; 0-9608588),* 510 N. Lapeer St., Davison, MI 48423 Tel 313-658-1955 (SAN 238-2865).

Friedman, Ira J., Div. of Associated Faculty Press, Inc., *(Friedman; 0-87198),* 90 S. Bayles Ave., Port Washington, NY 11050 Tel 516-883-0570 (SAN 206-4189).

Friend of the Library, *(N C Wesleyan Friends Lib; 0-933598),* 3400 Wesleyan College, Rocky Mount, NC 27801 (SAN 240-0456).

Friendly City Publishing Co., *(Friendly City; 0-938212),* 1125 Cedar Springs Road, Athens, TN 37303 Tel 615-745-2960 (SAN 215-6458).

Friendly Fairways of America, *(Friendly Fairways),* P.O. Box 237-A, Royal Oak, MI 48068 Tel 313-652-8099 (SAN 211-9005).

Friendly Press, *(Friendly Oregon; 0-938070),* 2744 Friendly St., Eugene, OR 97405 (SAN 215-8671).

Friends for Long Island's Heritage, *(Friends Long Island; 0-911357),* 1864 Muttontown Rd., Syosset, NY 11791 Tel 516-364-1050 (SAN 270-3564).

Friends Historical Association, *(Friends Hist Assn),* Quaker Collection Haverford College Library, Haverford, PA 19041 Tel 215-896-1161 (SAN 225-4492).

Friends of City Park, *(Friends City Park; 0-9610062),* City Park Administration Bldg., New Orleans, LA 70119 Tel 504-561-8989 (SAN 262-8643).

Friends of Florida State Univ. Library, *(Friends Fla St),* Florida State Univ., Tallahassee, FL 32306 (SAN 205-5937).

Friends of Freedom Pubs., *(Friend Freedom),* P.O. Box 6124, Waco, TX 76706 Tel 817-662-4643 (SAN 207-3757).

Friends of Israel Gospel Ministry, Inc, *(Friends Israel),* P.O. Box 123, W. Collingswood, NJ 08107 Tel 215-922-3030 (SAN 225-445X).

Friends of Nature, Inc., *(Friends Nature; 0-910636),* Brooksville, MA 04617 (SAN 205-5945).

Friends of Photography, The, *(Friends Photography; 0-933286),* P.O. Box 500, Sunset Ctr., Carmel, CA 93921 Tel 408-624-6330 (SAN 212-5064).

Friends of Refugees of Eastern Europe, *(Friends Refugees; 0-86639),* 1383 President St., Brooklyn, NY 11213 Tel 212-467-0860 (SAN 215-9953).

Friends of the Aberdeen Public Library, *(Friends Aberdeen; 0-9605152),* 121 E. Market St., Aberdeen, WA 98520 (SAN 215-7632).

Friends of the Earth, *(Friends Earth; 0-905966),* 9 Poland St., London, W1V 3DG, ; Dist. by: Publications Distribution Co-Operative, 27 Clerkenwell Close, London, EC1R OAT, .

Friends of the Towson Library, Inc., *(Friends Towson Lib; 0-9602326),* 320 York Rd., Towson, MD 21204 (SAN 213-4977).

Friends of the Tucson Public Library, *(Friends Tucson; 0-9608370),* c/o The Poetry Project, Tuscon Public Library, Box 27470, Tuscon, AZ 85726 (SAN 240-3765).

Friends of the Univ. of Toledo Libraries, *(Friends Univ Toledo; 0-918160),* The University of Toledo Library, 2801 W. Bancroft St., Toledo, OH 43606 Tel 419-537-2326 (SAN 208-1792).

Friends of World Teaching, *(Friends World Teach; 0-9601550),* P.O. Box 1049, San Diego, CA 92112 Tel 619-274-5282 (SAN 212-906X).

Friends Peace Committee, Nonviolence & Children Program, *(Friends Peace Comm; 0-9605062),* 1515 Cherry St., Philadelphia, PA 19102 (SAN 215-868X).

Friends United Press, *(Friends United; 0-913408),* 101 Quaker Hill Dr., Richmond, IN 47374 Tel 317-962-7573 (SAN 201-5803).

Friendship Press, *(Friend Pr; 0-377),* 475 Riverside Dr., Rm. 772, New York, NY 10027 Tel 212-870-2497 (SAN 201-5773); Orders to: Friendship Press Distribution, P.O. Box 37844, Cincinnati, OH 45237 Tel 513-761-2100 (SAN 201-5781).

Friendship Publishing Co., *(Friend Pub; 0-9608556),* P.O. Box 27266, Escondido, CA 92027 (SAN 264-6535).

Friis-Pioneer Press, *(Friis-Pioneer Pr; 0-943480),* 1611 S. Minnie St., Santa Ana, CA 92707 Tel 714-835-3456 (SAN 202-1498).

Frisch Howard, *(Frisch H; 0-910638),* P.O. Box 128, Village Station, New York, NY 10014 (SAN 220-5610).

Frog in the Well, *(Frog in Well; 0-9603628),* 430 Oakdale Rd., East Palo Alto, CA 94303 (SAN 207-8295).

From Here Pr., *(From Here; 0-89120),* P. O. Box 219, Fanwood, NJ 07023 Tel 201-889-7886 (SAN 209-746X).

From Me to You, *(From Me; 0-9608590),* 811 Sioux Ave., Box 38, Mapleton, IA 51034 Tel 712-882-1517 (SAN 238-2873).

Fromm International Publishing Co., *(Fromm Intl Pub; 0-88064)*, 560 Lexington Ave., New York, NY 10022 Tel 212-308-4010 (SAN 239-7269); Dist. by: Independent Pubs. Grp., Port Washington, NY 11050 Tel 516-944-9325 (SAN 239-7277).

Frommer-Pasmantier Pubs., *(Frommer-Pasmantier; 0-671)*, 1230 Ave. of the Americas, New York, NY 10020 Tel 212-245-6400 (SAN 205-2725).

Frompovich, C. J., Pubns., *(C J Frompovich; 0-935322)*, R.D. 1, Chestnut Rd., Coopersburg, PA 18036 Tel 215-346-8461 (SAN 213-3121).

Front Row Experience, *(Front Row; 0-915256)*, 540 Discovery Bay Blvd., Byron, CA 94514 Tel 415-634-5710 (SAN 207-1274).

Front Street Pubs., *(Front St; 0-931502)*, 129 Front St., Rm. 301, New York, NY 10005 (SAN 212-3517).

Frontal Lobe, *(Frontal Lobe; 0-931400)*, 836 Starlite Lane, Los Altos, CA 94022 (SAN 211-9013).

Frontier Press, *(Frontier Press Calif)*, P.O. Box 5023, Santa Rosa, CA 95402 Tel 707-544-5174 (SAN 206-653X).

Frontier Press Co., *(Frontier Pr Co; 0-912168)*, P.O. Box 1098, Columbus, OH 43216 Tel 614-864-3737 (SAN 205-5953).

Frontline Pubns., *(Frontline; 0-910657)*, P.O. Box 1104, El Toro, CA 92630 Tel 714-837-6258 (SAN 260-1907).

Frontrunner Pubns., *(Frontrunner; 0-936090)*, P.O. Box 5823, 2309 Wesley Circle, Bossier City, LA 71111 (SAN 214-0187).

Frost, O.W., *(O W Frost; 0-930766)*, 2141 Lord Baranof Dr., Anchorage, AK 99503 (SAN 211-3163).

Frost & Sullivan, Inc., *(Frost & Sullivan)*, 106 Fulton St., New York, NY 10038 Tel 212-233-1080 (SAN 215-8698).

Frost Art Distributors, *(Frost Art; 0-9604802)*, 781 S. Kohler St., Los Angeles, CA 90021 Tel 213-626-3830 (SAN 220-0546).

Fruition Pubns., Inc., *(Fruition Pubns; 0-939926)*, Box 103, Blawenburg, NJ 08504 Tel 609-466-3196 (SAN 216-8146).

Fruitlands Museums, Inc., *(Fruitlands Mus; 0-941632)*, R.Rte. 2, Box 87, Prospect Hill Rd., Harvard, MA 01451 Tel 617-456-3924 (SAN 239-2119).

Fruth, Florence Knight, *(F K Fruth)*, 64 St. Andrews Dr., Beaver Falls, PA 15010 Tel 412-846-5282 (SAN 211-156X).

Fry, L. John, *(L J Fry; 0-9600984)*, 1223 N. Nopal St., Santa Barbara, CA 93103 Tel 805-965-6891 (SAN 208-6565).

Fudge, Edward, Publishing, *(E Fudge)*, P.O. box 218026, Houston, TX 77218 Tel 713-578-7837 (SAN 211-7975).

Full Count Press, *(Full Count Pr OK; 0-936908)*, 223 N. Broadway, Edmond, OK 73034 (SAN 215-1456).

Full Court Press, Inc., *(Full Court NY; 0-916190)*, 138-140 Watts St., New York, NY 10013 Tel 212-966-1831 (SAN 211-9021).

Full Gospel Business Men's Fellowship International, *(Full Gospel; 0-86595)*, P.O. Box 5050, Costa Mesa, CA 92626 (SAN 220-2476).

Fuller, Buckminster, Institute, *(Buckminster Fuller; 0-911573)*, 3501 Market St., Philadelphia, PA 19104 (SAN 264-0511).

Fuller Goldeen Gallery, *(Fuller Golden Gal; 0-9607452)*, 228 Grant Ave., San Francisco, CA 94108 Tel 415-982-6177 (SAN 239-7749).

Fuller Publishing Co., *(Fuller Pub; 0-9605850)*, 1060 Cragmont, Berkeley, CA 94708 Tel 415-527-4412 (SAN 216-5953).

Fuller Theological Seminary, *(Fuller Theol Soc; 0-9602638)*, 84 N. los Robles, Pasadena, CA 91101 (SAN 221-8259).

Fulness House, Inc., *(Fulness Hse; 0-937778)*, P.O. Box 79350, Fort Worth, TX 76179 (SAN 215-9961).

Fulton County Arts Council, *(Fulton Coun Art; 0-9606650)*, 501 William-Oliver Bldg., 32 Peachtree St., N.W., Atlanta, GA 30303 Tel 404-577-7378 (SAN 223-1328).

Fun Publishing Co., *(Fun Pub; 0-918858)*, P.O. Box 2049, Scottsdale, AZ 85252 Tel 602-946-2093 (SAN 210-4261).

Fun Reading Co., *(Fun Reading; 0-9608466)*, 2409 Glenwood Rd., Brooklyn, NY 11210 Tel 212-453-5582 (SAN 240-6055).

Fund for Multinational Management Education *See* Unipub

Fundaburk, Emma Lila, Pub., *(Fundaburk; 0-910642)*, Luverne, AL 36049 (SAN 205-597X).

Funding Exchange, *(Fund Exchange; 0-9601974)*, 4111 24th St., San Francisco, CA 94114 Tel 415-285-2005 (SAN 211-9919); Orders to: Bookpeople, 2940 Seventh St., Berkeley, CA 94710 Tel 800-227-1516 (SAN 212-6060).

Funk & Wagnalls Co., *(Funk & W; 0-308)*, C/O Harper & Row Pubs., 10 E. 53rd St., New York, NY 10022 (SAN 211-6944); Dist. by: Harper & Row Pubs, Keystone Industrial Park, Scranton, PA 18512 (SAN 215-3742).

Funkshunal Features, *(Funkshunal; 0-932442)*, P.O. Box 47728, Los Angeles, CA 90047 Tel 213-778-5422 (SAN 212-212X).

Funky, Punky & Chic, *(Funky-Punky-Chic; 0-940762)*, 103 Second Ave., New York, NY 10003 (SAN 219-7448).

FunPrax Associates, *(FunPrax; 0-9609972)*, 711 Skinner Bldg., Seattle, WA 98101 (SAN 270-4005).

Furman Univ. Bookstore, *(Furman U Bkstr)*, Greenville, SC 29613 Tel 803-294-2164 (SAN 211-240X).

Fusion Energy Foundation, *(Fusion Energy Found; 0-938460)*, 250 W. 57th St. Suite 1711, New York, NY 10019 (SAN 237-9538).

Fusion Groups, Inc., *(Fusion Groups; 0-912778)*, Indian Brook Rd., Garrison, NY 10524 (SAN 205-5988) Name Formerly Sonja.

Futura Pub. Co., Inc., *(Futura Pub; 0-87993)*, P.O. Box 330, 295 Main St., Mount Kisco, NY 10549 Tel 914-666-3505 (SAN 201-582X).

Future Arts, Inc., *(Future Arts; 0-943122)*, Rt 2, Box 691, Baileys Harbor, WI 54202 (SAN 240-3781).

Future Press, *(Future Pr; 0-918406)*, P. O. Box 73, Canal St., New York, NY 10013 (SAN 210-0886).

Future Publishing Co., *(Future Pub TN)*, Jump Off Rd., St. Andrews, TN 37372 (SAN 223-081X).

Future Science Research Publishing Co., *(Future Sci Res; 0-941292)*, P.O. Box 06392, Portland, OR 97206 (SAN 239-4278).

Future Shop, *(Future Shop; 0-930490)*, P.O. Box 3262, Santa Barbara, CA 93130 Tel 805-687-6684 (SAN 211-2396).

Future Systems/TLH Associates, *(Future Syst-TLH; 0-941506)*, Minnesota Bldg., Suite 900, St. Paul, MN 55101 Tel 612-227-8866 (SAN 239-0922).

Futures Group, The, *(Futures Group; 0-9605196)*, 76 Eastern Blvd., Glastonbury, CT 06033 (SAN 215-8701).

Futures Unlimited, Inc., *(Futures Unlimited Inc.; 0-940082)*, 5200 W. 73rd St., Minneapolis, MN 55435 Tel 612-835-7729 (SAN 220-2220).

G & G Pubs., *(G&G Pubs; 0-937534)*, Route 7, No. 63, Hopewell Junction, NY 12533 (SAN 215-2444).

GBC Publishing, *(GBC Pub; 0-9606228)*, Radio Centre Plaza, 9355 Joliet Rd., La Grange, IL 60525 Tel 312-579-1995 (SAN 217-5207).

G B H Publishing, *(G B H Pub)*, 825 32nd Ave., Santa Cruz, CA 95062 Tel 408-462-4916 (SAN 270-4153).

GBS Pubs., Div. of Gordon's Booksellers, *(GBS Pubs; 0-939928)*, 8 E. Baltimore St., Baltimore, MD 21202 (SAN 216-8154).

G. D. A. Pubns., *(GDA Pubns)*, P.O. Box 30119, Lafayette, LA 70503 (SAN 215-2452).

GDE Pubns., Div. of Glen Eley Enterprises, *(GDE Pubns OH; 0-940934)*, P.O. Box 304, Lima, OH 45802 (SAN 222-9749).

GE-PS Cancer Memorial, *(GE-PS Cancer; 0-9601644)*, 519 Austin Ave., Park Ridge, IL 60068 Tel 312-823-5425 (SAN 215-7659).

GGL Publishing Co., Inc., *(G G L Pub Co; 0-9610198)*, 322 Hancock Street, Henderson, KY 42420 (SAN 264-0538).

G-Jo Institute/Falkynor Books, The, *(Falkynor Bks; 0-916878)*, 4950 S.W. 70th Ave., Davie, FL 33314 Tel 305-581-4950 (SAN 208-645X).

G K Press, *(G K Pr; 0-910067)*, 415 Sheffield Rd., Cherry Hill, NJ 08034 Tel 609-877-9115 (SAN 241-3078).

G. L. A. Press, *(GLA Pr; 0-912854)*, P. O. Box 5312, Irving, TX 75062 Tel 214-721-5390 (SAN 203-4271).

GLGLC Music, *(GLGLC Music; 0-9607558)*, P.O. Box 147, Cardiff by the Sea, CA 92007 (SAN 238-6194).

GMG Publishing, *(GMG Pub; 0-939456)*, 25 W. 43rd St., New York, NY 10036 (SAN 216-3888).

GNU Publishing, *(GNU; 0-915914)*, P.O. Box 6820, San Francisco, CA 94101 (SAN 203-5367).

GSE Pubns., *(G S E Pubns; 0-915668)*, P.O. Box 35499, Los Angeles, CA 90035 Tel 213-559-7101 (SAN 207-6772).

Gabriel Books, *(Gabriel Bks; 0-9)*, P.O. Box 224, Mankato, MN 56001 Tel 507-387-4964 (SAN 214-2627); Dist. by: Independent Publishers Group, One Pleasant Ave., Port Washington, NY 11050 (SAN 214-2635).

Gabriel House, Inc., *(Gabriel Hse; 0-936192)*, 5045 W. Oakton St., Suite 7, Skokie, IL 60077 Tel 312-675-1146 (SAN 213-9219).

Gabriel Press, *(Gabriel Pr; 0-937938)*, P.O. Box 6483, Ithaca, NY 14851 Tel 607-273-8506 (SAN 281-7292); Dist. by: Bookpeople, 2940 Seventh Ave., Berkeley, CA 94710 Tel 415-549-3030 (SAN 168-9517); Dist. by: Inland Book, 22 Hemingway Ave., East Haven, CT 06512 (SAN 281-7314); Dist. by: Samuel Weiser, Inc., P.O. Box 612, York Beach, ME 03910 (SAN 202-9588).

Gabrielle Press, *(Gabrielle Pr FL; 0-9608656)*, 6105 Beechwood Ave., Sarasota, FL 33581 Tel 813-922-5317 (SAN 240-7663); Dist. by: Magna Books (Nancy Olds), Sannibel, FL 33957 Tel 813-472-6777 (SAN 200-4267).

Gabriel's Horn Publishing Co., *(Gabriel's Horn; 0-911861)*, P.O. Box 141, Bowling Green, OH 43402 (SAN 283-4219).

Gach, John, Books, *(Gach Bks)*, 5620 Waterloo Rd., Columbia, MD 21045 (SAN 214-0195).

GAF International, *(GAF Intl; 0-942176)*, P.O. Box 1722, Vista, CA 92083 (SAN 238-8367).

Gain Pubns., *(Gain Pubns; 0-910725)*, P.O. Box 2204, Van Nuys, CA 91404 Tel 213-785-1895 (SAN 270-4218).

Gaines, P., Co., The, *(P Gaines Co; 0-936284)*, P.O. Box 2253, Oak Park, IL 60303 Tel 312-996-7829 (SAN 214-0209).

Gajda, George J., *(G Gajda)*, P.O. Box 1846, Santa Monica, CA 90406 (SAN 209-4398).

Galactic Central Pubns., *(Galactic Central; 0-912613)*, 414 Wisconsin, N.E., Albuquerque, NM 87108 Tel 505-266-3141 (SAN 282-7689).

Galahand Press, The, *(Galahand Pr; 0-940578)*, P.O. Box 951, Austin, TX 78767 Tel 512-459-9384 (SAN 223-7687).

Galaxy Books *See* Oxford Univ. Press, Inc.

Galaxy Press, *(Galaxy Pr; 0-916566)*, P.O. Box 1640, Loma Linda 92354, Escondido, CA 92027 Tel 714-746-1170 (SAN 208-0729).

Galaxy Pubns., *(Galaxy Pubns)*, 706 First St., Miami Beach, FL 33139 (SAN 239-362X).

Gale, Hoyt Rodney, *(H R Gale)*, 669 Sturtevant Dr., Sierra Madre, CA 91024 Tel 714-751-1716 (SAN 212-8209) Tel 213-355-2988.

Gale Research Co., *(Gale; 0-8103)*, Book Tower, Detroit, MI 48226 Tel 313-961-2242 (SAN 213-4373).

Galilee *See* Doubleday & Co., Inc.

Galileo Press, *(Galileo; 0-943442)*, P.O. Box 16129, Baltimore, MD 21218 Tel 301-771-4544 (SAN 240-6543).

Gall Pubns., *(Gall Pubns; 0-88904)*, 2965 Weston Ave., Niagara Falls, NY 14305 (SAN 212-6117).

Gallaudet College Press, *(Gallaudet Coll; 0-913580)*, Kendall Green, Washington, DC 20002 Tel 202-651-5595 (SAN 205-261X).

Galleon Pubns., *(Galleon-Whitehurst; 0-918602)*, 12 Tiffany Rd., No. 6, Salem, NH 03079 (SAN 210-9158).

Galleries of the Claremont Colleges, *(Galleries Coll; 0-915478)*, Claremont, CA 91711 Tel 714-621-8000 (SAN 158-0515).

Gallery Graphics Press, *(Gallery Graphics; 0-943294)*, P.O. Box 7403, Carmel, CA 93923 Tel 408-625-0226 (SAN 240-6551).

Gallery Press, *(Gallery Pr; 0-913622)*, 117 N. Main St., Essex, CT 06426 Tel 203-767-0313 (SAN 207-0936).

Gallery West, Inc., *(Gallery West; 0-9610550),* P.O. Box 1589, Taos, NM 87571 Tel 505-776-2355 (SAN 262-026X).

Galley Press, *(Galley OR),* P.O. Box 892, Portland, OR 97207 Tel 206-693-1397 (SAN 215-3149).

Galliard Press, *(Galliard Pr; 0-936616),* P.O. Box 296, Claremont, CA 91711 (SAN 214-2422).

Gallimaufry, *(Gallimaufry; 0-916300),* Dist. by: Apple-Wood Press, P.O. Box 2870, Cambridge, MA 02139 Tel 617-964-5150 (SAN 210-3419).

Gallo, Cristino, *(C Gallo; 0-9604174),* 1107 E. Ocean View Ave. No. 9, Norfolk, VA 23503 Tel 804-587-7744 (SAN 214-3062); Dist. by: Book Service of Puerto Rico, 102 Avenida De Diego, Santurce, PR 00907 (SAN 214-3070) Moved, left no forwarding address.

Gallopade Publishing Group, *(Gallopade Pub Group; 0-935326),* P.O. Box 1537, Tryon, NC 28782 Tel 704-859-9253 (SAN 213-8441).

Galloway Pubns. Inc., *(Galloway; 0-87874),* 2940 N.W. Circle Blvd., Corvallis, OR 97330 (SAN 201-5854).

Gambit Inc. Pubs., *(Gambit; 0-87645),* 27 N. Main St., Ipswich, MA 01938 Tel 617-356-2956 (SAN 201-5862).

Gamblers Anonymous Pub. Co., *(Gamblers Anon),* P.O. Box 17173, Los Angeles, CA 90017 (SAN 201-5870).

Gambler's Book Club/GBC Press, *(Gamblers; 0-911996; 0-89650),* 630 S. 11th St., P.O. Box 4115, Las Vegas, NV 89127 Tel 702-382-7555 (SAN 203-414X).

Gambling Times, Inc., *(Gambling Times; 0-89746),* 1018 N. Cole Ave., Hollywood, CA 90038 (SAN 211-6383).

Game Marketing Co., *(Game Market; 0-941052),* 3355 Birch Circle, Allentown, PA 18103 Tel 215-437-3622 (SAN 217-3662).

Gamesmasters Pubs. Assn., *(Gamesmasters; 0-935426),* 20 Almont St., Nashua, NH 03060 (SAN 213-5000).

Gamma Books, *(Gamma Bks; 0-933124),* 400 Nelson Rd., Ithaca, NY 14850 (SAN 212-4688).

Gamma Psi Chapter, Phi Alpha Theta, *(Gamma Psi; 0-9606168),* History Dept., Washington State Univ., Pullman, WA 99163 Tel 509-335-8676 (SAN 217-5525).

Gamut Music Co., *(Gamut Music; 0-910648),* P.O. Box 454, Dedham, MA 02026 Tel 617-244-3305 (SAN 205-2598).

Gan-Tone Publishing Co., *(Gan-Tone Pub; 0-939458),* Carnegie Hall, 881 Seventh Ave., Studio 1105-6, New York, NY 10019 Tel 212-265-5690 (SAN 216-5961).

G&G Publishing Co., *(G&G Pub),* P.O. Box 49231, Atlanta, GA 30359 (SAN 262-0251).

Ganis & Harris, Inc., *(Ganis & Harris; 0-9605188),* 119 W. 57th St., New York, NY 10019 (SAN 216-0897).

Gannett, Guy, Publishing Co., *(G Gannett; 0-930096),* 390 Congress St., Portland, ME 04104 (SAN 210-7295).

Gannon, William, *(Gannon; 0-88307),* 143 Sombrio Dr., Santa Fe, NM 87501 Tel 505-983-1579 (SAN 201-5889).

Ganong, W.L., Co., *(Ganong W L Co; 0-933036),* Homestead House, P. O. Box 2727, Chapel Hill, NC 27514 (SAN 221-1351).

Gant, Margaret Elizabeth, *(M E Gant; 0-9603138),* 7500 Deer Track Dr., Raleigh, NC 27612 Tel 919-848-8062 (SAN 212-7415).

Garabed Books, *(Garabed),* 23 Leroy St., New York, NY 10014 Tel 212-243-0768 (SAN 281-7330); Orders to: Zareh, Inc., 65 State St., Boston, MA 02109 Tel 617-227-6464 (SAN 281-7349).

Garber Communications, Inc., *(Garber Comm; 0-89345),* 7 Garber Hill Rd., Blauvelt, NY 10913 Tel 914-359-9292 (SAN 226-2789). *Imprints:* Biograf Pubns. (Biograf Pubns); Freedeeds Books (Freedeeds Bks); Spiritual Science Library (Spiritual Sci Lib); Steinerbooks (Steinerbks).

Garcia, Robert T., *(R T Garcia; 0-9610352),* P.O. Box 41714, Chicago, IL 60641 Tel 312-777-6853 (SAN 264-0562).

Garcia River Press, *(Garcia River; 0-932708),* P.O. Box 527, Point Arena, CA 95468 (SAN 212-2790).

Gard & Co., *(Gard & Co; 0-9603316),* P.O. Box 34579, N.W. Sta., Omaha, NE 68134 Tel 402-493-1352 (SAN 209-0198).

Garden City Historical Society, *(Garden City; 0-9604654),* Box 179, Garden City, NY 11530 (SAN 215-1472).

Garden Consultant, *(Garden Consul),* 555 Townsend, Birmingham, MI 48012 (SAN 207-2270).

Garden Publishing Co., *(Garden Pub; 0-939330),* 6833 Creston Rd., Minneapolis, MN 55435 Tel 612-926-1327 (SAN 220-1690).

Garden Way Publishing Co., *(Garden Way Pub; 0-88266),* Charlotte, VT 05445 Tel 802-425-2171 (SAN 203-4158).

Gardner, Arthur C., *(A C Gardner; 0-9602152),* 601 Eastview Ave., Somerset, MA 02726 (SAN 212-3525).

Gardner Press, Inc., *(Gardner Pr; 0-89876),* 19 Union Square W., New York, NY 10003 Tel 212-924-8293 (SAN 214-1906).

Gardnor House, *(Gardnor Hse; 0-943602),* P.O. Box 1928, Spring, TX 77383 (SAN 240-6578); Dist. by: D. Armstrong Co., Inc., 2000B Governors Circle, Houston, TX 77092 (SAN 210-0320).

Garfield, Ray, *(R Garfield; 0-9609856),* P.O. Box 4125, Clearlake, CA 95422 Tel 707-994-2732 (SAN 270-4382).

Garland Publishing, Inc., *(Garland Pub; 0-8240),* 136 Madison Ave., 2nd Floor, New York, NY 10016 Tel 212-686-7492 (SAN 201-5897).

Garland STPM Press *See* Garland Publishing, Inc.

Garlic Press, *(Garlic Pr; 0-932798),* 24 Wellington Ave., Rochester, NY 14611 (SAN 212-095X).

Garlinghouse, L.F., Co. The, *(L F Garlinghouse Co; 0-938708),* P.O. Box 299, 320 S.W. 33rd St., Topeka, KS 66601 Tel 913-267-2490 (SAN 238-7077).

Garrard Publishing Co., *(Garrard; 0-8116),* 29 Goldsborough St., Easton, MD 21601 (SAN 201-5900); Orders to: 1607 N. Market St., Champaign, IL 61820 Tel 217-352-7685 (SAN 201-5919).

Garrett Park Press, *(Garrett Pk; 0-912048),* Garrett Park, MD 20896 Tel 301-946-2553 (SAN 201-5927).

Garric Press, *(Garric Pr; 0-9609922),* P.O. Box 517, Glen Ellen, CA 95442 Tel 707-938-3625 (SAN 270-4404).

Garvin, A. J., & Associates, *(A J Garvin; 0-9607252),* 720 E. Ann St., Ann Arbor, MI 48104 Tel 313-662-2734 (SAN 281-7357); Orders to: P.O. Box 7525, Ann Arbor, MI 48107 (SAN 281-7365).

Gaslight Pubns., *(Gaslight; 0-934468),* 112 E. Second, Bloomington, IN 47401 Tel 812-332-5169 (SAN 213-5019).

Gateway Press, Inc., Div. of Genealogical Publishing Co., *(Gateway Pr; 0-9608106),* 111 Water St., Baltimore, MD 21202 Tel 301-837-8271 (SAN 205-3047).

Gathering Place Productions, *(Gathering Place; 0-9611772),* P.O. Box 18464, Milwaukee, WI 53218 Tel 414-871-9765 (SAN 285-2624).

Gaunt, Wm. W., & Sons, Inc., *(W W Gaunt; 0-912004),* 3011 Gulf St., Holmes Beach, FL 33510-2199 Tel 813-778-5211 (SAN 202-9413).

Gauntlet Books, *(Gauntlet Bks),* 144 King St., Franklin, MA 02038 Tel 617-528-4414 (SAN 201-5935).

Gauquier, Anthony V., *(A Gauquier; 0-9609574),* P.O. Box 1215, Plymouth, MA 02360 (SAN 260-1915).

Gaus, Theo., Ltd., *(Gaus; 0-912444),* P.O. Box 1168, Brooklyn, NY 11202 Tel 212-625-4651 (SAN 203-4174).

Gavea-Brown Pubns., *(Gavea-Brown),* Box O, Brown Univ., Providence, RI 02912 (SAN 240-4788).

Gay Mens Press, *(Gay Mens Pr; 0-907040),* Dist. by: Flatiron Book Distributors, 175 Fifth Ave., New York, NY 10011 (SAN 240-9917).

Gay Presses of New York, *(Gay Pr NY; 0-9604724),* P.O. Box 294, New York, NY 10014 (SAN 215-210X).

Gay Sunshine Press, *(Gay Sunshine; 0-917342),* Box 40397, San Francisco, CA 94140 Tel 415-824-3184 (SAN 208-0915); Dist. by: Bookpeople, 2940 Seventh St., Berkeley, CA 94710 Tel 800-227-1516 (SAN 168-9517).

Gaylord Professional Pubns., Div. of Gaylord Bros., Inc., *(Gaylord Prof Pubns; 0-915794),* P.O. Box 4901, Syracuse, NY 13221 Tel 315-457-5070 (SAN 208-421X).

Gazelle Pubns., *(Gazelle Pubns; 0-930192),* 5580 Stanley Dr., Auburn, CA 95603 (SAN 209-5610).

Gazette Press, Inc., *(Gazette Pr; 0-933390),* 225 Hunter Ave., North Tarrytown, NY 10591 Tel 914-631-8866 (SAN 203-4182).

Gazin, Patricia, *(P Gazin),* 1250 First St., Hermosa Beach, CA 90254 Tel 213-376-5765 (SAN 211-4410).

G B M Books, Div. of God's Broadcaster Ministries, Inc., *(GBM Bks; 0-912695),* P.O. Box 4895, 4850 Whisett Ave., N. Hollywood, CA 91607 Tel 213-763-0942 (SAN 277-6820).

G.D.L., Inc., *(G D L Inc; 0-937358),* P.O. Box 1248, Birmingham, MI 48011 (SAN 215-1464).

Geankoplis, Christie J., *(Geankoplis; 0-9603070),* 140 W. 19th Ave., Columbus, OH 43210 Tel 614-422-2508 (SAN 209-5629); Dist. by: Ohio State Univ. Bookstores, 1315 Kinnear Rd., Columbus, OH 43212 (SAN 209-5637).

Gearhart-Edwards Press, *(Gearhart-Edwards),* 2917 N. Summit Ave., Milwaukee, WI 53211 (SAN 214-0217).

Gebhardt, Chuck, *(C Gebhardt; 0-9601410),* P.O. Box 6821, San Jose, CA 95150 Tel 211-1934).

Gee Tee Bee, *(Gee Tee Bee; 0-917232),* 11901 Sunset Blvd., No. 102, Los Angeles, CA 90049 Tel 213-476-2622 (SAN 206-9652).

Geer, Corinne C., *(C C Geer; 0-9601508),* 2222 Wallington Dr., Albany, GA 31707 (SAN 211-3937).

Gehry Press, *(Gehry Pr; 0-935020),* 1319 Pine St., Iowa City, IA 52240 (SAN 213-0629).

Geistenblumen Press, *(Geistenblumen; 0-913125),* RFD 145, West Lebanon, ME 04027 Tel 207-658-9715 (SAN 283-264X).

Gem City College Press, *(Gem City Coll; 0-910222),* 700 State St., Po.Box 179, Quincy, IL 62306 Tel 217-222-0391 (SAN 202-4004).

Gem-O-Lite Plastics Co., *(Gem O Lite; 0-911888),* P.O. Box 985, N. Hollywood, CA 91603 Tel 213-877-3491 (SAN 203-4204).

Gem Pubns., *(Gem Pubns; 0-941832),* P.O. Box 2499, Melbourne, FL 32901 Tel 305-727-3034 (SAN 239-2143).

Gemaia Press, *(Gemaia Pr; 0-9602232),* 209 Wilcox Lane, Sequim, WA 98382 (SAN 212-4238).

Gemak Publishing, *(Gemak Pub),* 3084 S. Gavilan, Las Vegas, NV 89122 Tel 702-736-7615 (SAN 262-0278).

Gembooks, *(Gembooks; 0-910652),* P. O. Box 687, Mentone, CA 92359 (SAN 201-5943).

Gemini Books, *(Gemini Bks),* P.O. Box 10313, Eugene, OR 97440 (SAN 215-1480).

Gemini Press, *(Gemini Pr; 0-9601690),* 625 Pennsylvania Ave., Oakmont, PA 15139 Tel 412-828-3315 (SAN 211-4933).

Gemini Press, *(Gemini Pr DC; 0-940246),* Box 5154, Greensboro, NC 27435 (SAN 217-5215).

Gemini Publishing Co., *(Gemini Pub Co; 0-937164),* 18301 Upper Bay Rd Suite 118C, Houston, TX 77058 Tel 713-333-2868 (SAN 215-2460).

Gemini Smith, Inc., *(Gemini Smith; 0-935022),* 5858 Desert View Dr., La Jolla, CA 92037 Tel 619-454-4321 (SAN 212-6125).

Gemmeg Press, *(Gemmeg Pr; 0-9608076),* P.O. Box 322, Parkville Station, Brooklyn, NY 11204 Tel 212-259-5379 (SAN 240-4796).

Gemological Institute of America, *(Gemological; 0-87311),* 1660 Stewart St., Santa Monica, CA 90404 Tel 213-829-2991 (SAN 203-4212).

Gena Rose Press, *(G Rose Pr; 0-9604178),* 2424 Franklin, No. B, Denver, CO 80205 (SAN 215-0751).

Genaway, David C., & Associates, Inc., *(D C Genaway; 0-943970),* 530 W. Regency Circle, Canfield, OH 44406 (SAN 241-3833) Trade name: Business Technical Information Service.

Genealogical Assn. of Southwestern Michigan, *(Genealog Assn SW),* P.O. Box 573, St. Joseph, MI 49085 Tel 616-983-5791 (SAN 223-0364).

Genealogical Books in Print, *(GBIP; 0-89157),* 6818 Lois Dr., Springfield, VA 22150 Tel 703-971-5877 (SAN 220-2484).

Genealogical Institute, *(Genealog Inst),* Dist. by: Family History World, 57 W. South Temple, Suite 255, Salt Lake City, UT 84101 Tel 801-532-3327 (SAN 207-1959).

Genealogical Publishing Co., Inc., *(Genealog Pub; 0-8063),* 111 Water St., Baltimore, MD 21202 Tel 301-837-8271 (SAN 206-8370).

Genealogical Sources, Unlimited, *(Genealog Sources; 0-913857),* 7914 Gleason, C-1136, Knoxville, TN 37919 Tel 615-974-3422 (SAN 286-7583).

General Agreement on Tariffs & Trade See Unipub

General Aviation Press, *(Gen Aviation Pr),* P.O. Box 916, Winston Field, Snyder, TX 79549 Tel 915-573-6318 (SAN 212-9078); Dist. by: Aviation Book Co., 1640 Victory Blvd., Glendale, CA 91201 Tel 213-240-1771 (SAN 212-0259).

General Education Pubns., *(General Educ; 0-914504),* 99 S. Van Ness Ave., San Francisco, CA 94103 Tel 415-621-5410 (SAN 209-2182).

General Electric Co., Technical Promotion & Training Services, *(GE Tech Prom & Train; 0-932078),* 1 River Rd., Bldg. 22, Rm. 232, Box MK, Schenectady, NY 12345 (SAN 206-9911).

General Electric Co., Technology Marketing Operation, *(GE Tech Marketing; 0-931690),* 120 Erie Blvd., Schenectady & Ordering Address, NY 12305 (SAN 213-4247).

General Hall, Inc., *(Gen Hall; 0-930390),* 23-45 Corporal Kennedy St., Bayside, NY 11360 Tel 212-423-9397 (SAN 211-1306).

General Means, Inc., *(General Means; 0-9608852),* P. O. Box 3546, City of Industry, CA 91744 Tel 213-336-7763 (SAN 241-0222).

General Society of Mayflower Descendants, *(Mayflower; 0-930270),* Orders to: Mayflower Families, P.O. Box 297, Plymouth, MA 02361 Tel 617-746-3188 (SAN 209-5823) Do Not Confuse with Mayflower Books, Inc.

General Studies Research, *(General Stud Res; 0-89372),* Institutional Studies, Bowling Green State Univ., Bowling Green, OH 43403 Tel 419-372-2681 (SAN 217-7373); Orders to: Institutional Studies, Bowling Green Stat e Uuniv., Bowling Green, OH 43403 Tel 419-372-2681 (SAN 281-7381).

General Technical Services, Inc., *(Gen Tech Serv; 0-914780),* 8794 W. Chester Pike, Upper Darby, PA 19082 Tel 215-449-2333 (SAN 201-5951).

General Welfare Publications, *(Gen Welfare Pubns; 0-87312),* Box 19098, Sacramento, CA 95819 Tel 916-677-1610 (SAN 240-4753).

Generations Publishing Co., *(Generations Pub; 0-9606392),* 901 Post Oak Lane, Charleston, IL 61920 Tel 217-258-2568 (SAN 222-9978).

Genesis Project, The, *(Genesis Project; 0-86702),* P.O. Box 37282, Washington, DC 20013 Tel 703-998-0800 (SAN 216-6747).

Genesis Pubns., Inc., *(Genesis Pubns; 0-904351),* 1613 Spear St. Tower, One Market Plaza, San Francisco, CA 94105 (SAN 239-4286).

Geneva Divinity School Press, *(Geneva Divinity; 0-939404),* 708 Hamvassy Rd., Tyler, TX 75701 Tel 214-592-0620 (SAN 216-5759).

Genie Enterprises, *(Genie Ent; 0-9608594),* Terwilliger Rd. Extension, Hyde Park, NY 12538 Tel 914-229-8730 (SAN 238-289X).

Genny Smith Books, *(Genny Smith Bks; 0-931378),* 1304 Pitman Ave., Palo Alto, CA 94301 Tel 415-321-7247 (SAN 211-3570); Dist. by: William Kaufmann Inc., 95 First St., Los Altos, CA 94022 Tel 415-948-5810 (SAN 202-9383).

Genotype, *(Genotype; 0-936618),* 15042 Montebello Rd., Cupertino, CA 95014 (SAN 214-3089).

Genre Communications, *(Genre Comms; 0-9610948),* 5697 Xenon Ct., Arvada, CO 80002 Tel 303-425-4214 (SAN 265-2463).

Gentle Press, the, *(Gentle Pr),* P.O. Box 47, Medina, OH 44258 (SAN 240-1460).

GeoBooks, *(GeoBooks; 0-914462),* 171 2nd St. Rm. 401, San Francisco, CA 94107 (SAN 206-7471).

Geographics, *(Geographics; 0-930722),* Box 133, Easton, CT 06612 (SAN 211-1810).

Geologic Pubns, Div. of Geology & Earth Resources, *(Geologic Pubns),* Department of Natural Resources, Olympia, WA 98504 (SAN 240-0936).

Geological Society of America, Inc., *(Geol Soc; 0-8137),* 3300 Penrose Place, Boulder, CO 80301 Tel 303-447-2020 (SAN 201-5978).

Geophysical Institute, *(Geophysical Inst; 0-915360),* 301L C.T. Elvey Bldg., Univ. of Alaska, Fairbanks, AK 99701 Tel 907-474-7798 (SAN 216-2482).

George E. Gifford Memorial Committee, *(G E Gifford Memorial),* Calvert School, Rising Sun, MD 21911 (SAN 281-739X); Orders to: Frances M. Hubis, 24 Hubis Lane, Rising Sun, MD 21911 Tel 301-658-6479 (SAN 281-7403).

George Shumway Publisher, *(Shumway; 0-87887),* R.D. 7, Box 388B, York, PA 17402 Tel 717-755-1196 (SAN 203-2422).

Georgetown Press, *(Georgetown Pr; 0-914558),* 483 Francisco St., San Francisco, CA 94133 Tel 415-397-4753 (SAN 206-7463).

Georgetown Univ., Clinical Sociology Assn., *(GU Clin Soc; 0-942756),* Dept. of Sociology, Rhode Island College, Providence, RI 02902 Tel 401-456-8026 (SAN 285-0214); c/o Jonathan Freedman, Hutchings Psychiatric Center, P.O. Box 27, Syracuse, NY 13210 Tel 315-473-7532 (SAN 285-0222).

Georgetown Univ. Press, *(Georgetown U Pr; 0-87840),* Intercultural Center, Room 111, Washington, DC 20057 Tel 202-625-4824 (SAN 203-4247).

Georgetown Univ., School for Summer & Continuing Education, *(GU-Sch Summer & Cont Ed; 0-939998),* Washington, DC 20057 (SAN 216-8162).

Georgetown Univ. School of Foreign Service, *(Geo U Sch for Serv; 0-934742),* Georgetown Univ., Washington, DC 20057 Tel 202-625-3784 (SAN 221-1580).

Georgia Assn. of Historians, *(GA Assn Hist; 0-939346),* Kennesaw College, History Department, Marietta, GA 30061 Tel 404-429-2945 (SAN 216-5643).

Georgia Department of Archives & History, *(GA Dept Archives),* 330 Capitol Ave., Atlanta, GA 30334 Tel 404-656-2393 (SAN 218-7426).

Georgia State Univ., College of Business Administration, *(Ga St U Busn Pub; 0-88406),* Business Publishing Div., Univ. Plaza, Atlanta, GA 30303 Tel 404-658-4253 (SAN 201-5838).

Georgian Press Co., The, *(Georgian Pr; 0-9603408),* 2620 S. W. Georgian Place, Portland, OR 97201 (SAN 213-9766); Dist. by: Pacific Pipeline, Inc., P.O. Box 3711, Seattle, WA 98124 Tel 206-682-8820 (SAN 169-8834).

Geoscience Analytical, *(Geoscience Analytical; 0-941054),* Chemistry UCLA, Los Angeles, CA 90024 Tel 213-825-7675 (SAN 217-3670).

Geothermal Resources Council, *(Geothermal; 0-934412),* P.O. 135098, Davis, CA 95617 (SAN 213-0637).

Gerard, Leona B., *(L B Gerard; 0-9606394),* 534 1/2 15th Ave., Eugene, OR 97401 Tel 503-345-3029 (SAN 218-5482).

Geraventure Corp., *(Geraventure; 0-938524),* P.O. Box 2131, Melbourne, FL 32902-2131 (SAN 216-0331).

Geri-Rehab, Inc., *(Geri-Rehab; 0-941930),* Box 170, Hibbler Rd., Lebanon, NJ 08833 (SAN 239-4383).

Gerlinger/Lorena, *(L Gerlinger),* 4666 Pratt Rd., Hadley, MI 48440 Tel 313-797-4833 (SAN 207-9291).

Germainbooks, *(Germainbooks; 0-914142),* 91 St. Germain Ave., San Francisco, CA 94114 Tel 415-731-8155 (SAN 201-5916).

German American Chamber of Commerce, Inc., *(German Am Chamber; 0-86640),* 666 Fifth Ave., New York, NY 10103 (SAN 216-3845).

Germinal Press, *(Germinal Pr; 0-918064),* 209 Prospect, San Francisco, CA 94110 Tel 415-824-4795 (SAN 210-2048).

Geron-X, Inc., *(Geron-X; 0-87672),* P.O. Box 1108, Los Altos, CA 94022 Tel 415-941-1692 (SAN 201-5994).

Gerosota Pubns., *(Gerosota Pub; 0-9609126),* P.O. Box 15914, Sarasota, FL 33579 Tel 813-924-3251 (SAN 241-5046).

Gestalt Journal, *(Gestalt Journal; 0-939266),* P.O. Box 275, Highland, NY 12528 Tel 914-691-7192 (SAN 216-5317).

Get Happy Books, *(Get Happy),* 2085 Hayes St. No. 2, San Francisco, CA 94117 (SAN 262-0286).

Getty, J. Paul, Museum, *(J P Getty Mus; 0-89236),* 17985 Pacific Coast Hwy., Malibu, CA 90265 Tel 213-459-2306 (SAN 208-2276).

G H C Business Books, *(GHC; 0-9609046),* 4214 N. Post Rd., Omaha, NE 68112 (SAN 241-3183).

Ghirardelli Chocolate Co., *(Ghirardelli Choc; 0-9610218),* 1111 139th Ave., San Leandro, CA 94578 Tel 415-483-6970 (SAN 270-5028).

Ghosh, A., *(Ghosh A; 0-9611614),* 5720 W. Little York, Suite 216, Houston, TX 77091 Tel 713-445-5526 (SAN 285-2780).

Ghost Dance Press, *(Ghost Dance; 0-939520),* ATL EBH MSU, East Lansing, MI 48824 Tel 517-351-5977 (SAN 207-8317).

Ghost Pony Press, *(Ghost Pony Pr; 0-941160),* 2518 Gregory St., Madison, WI 53711 (SAN 237-9546).

Ghost Town Pubns., *(Ghost Town; 0-933818),* P.O. Drawer 5998, Carmel, CA 93921 Tel 408-373-2885 (SAN 209-4401).

G.I.A. Pubns., Inc., *(GIA Pubns),* 7404 S. Mason Ave., Chicago, IL 60638 Tel 312-496-3800 (SAN 205-3217).

Gibbelins Gazette Publications/Silver EEL Press, The, *(Gibbelin's Gazette; 0-9610452),* 4900 Jonquil Lane, Knoxville, TN 37919 Tel 615-584-3884 (SAN 264-0589).

Gibbs Publishing Co., *(Gibbs Pub OH; 0-932924),* P.O. Box 2345, Toledoa, OH 03246 Tel 419-874-1136 (SAN 212-2138).

Gibes Art Gallery See Carolina Art Assn.

Gibraltar Press, *(Gibraltar),* P.O. Box 121425, Nashville, TN 37212 (SAN 216-3853); 171 Fuller St., Brookline, MA 02146 (SAN 216-3861).

Gibson, C. R., Co., *(Gibson; 0-8378),* Knight St., Norwalk, CT 06856 Tel 203-847-4543 (SAN 281-7446) (SAN 281-7454); Dist. by: Fob-C. R. Gibson, Distribution Center, Beacon Falls, CT 06403 (SAN 281-7462).

Gibson, Charles Dana, *(C D Gibson; 0-9608996),* P.O. Box 840, Boca Grande, FL 33921 (SAN 240-866X).

Gibson-Hiller Co., *(Gibson Hiller; 0-918892),* P.O. Box 22, Dayton, OH 45406 Tel 513-277-2427 (SAN 210-427X).

Gick Publishing Inc., *(Gick; 0-918170),* 23152 Verdugo Dr., Laguna Hills, CA 92653 Tel 714-581-5830 (SAN 209-6641).

Gielow, Fred C., *(Gielow; 0-9603938),* 33 Park Dr., Woodstock, NY 12498 Tel 914-385-4474 (SAN 215-0778).

Gift & Decorative Accessories Association, *(Gift & Deco Access),* 372 Park Ave. S., New York, NY 10010 (SAN 224-7704).

Gift Pubns., *(Gift Pubns; 0-86595),* 3150 Bear St., Costa Mesa, CA 92626 (SAN 216-387X).

Gilbert, Skeet, *(S Gilbert; 0-9600548),* Fuquay-Varina, NC 27526 Tel 919-552-4623 (SAN 204-7144).

Gilchem Corp., *(Gilchem Corp; 0-917122),* Woodlawn Rd., Suite 112, Bldg. 3, Woodlawn Green, Box 11291, Charlotte, NC 28209 Tel 704-523-2889 (SAN 208-659X).

Gilfer Associates, Inc., *(Gilfer; 0-914542),* P.O. Box 239, Park Ridge, NJ 07656 Tel 201-391-7887 (SAN 208-3981).

Gilgamesh Press Ltd., *(Gilgamesh Pr IL; 0-936684),* 1059 W. Ardmore Ave., Chicago, IL 60660 Tel 312-334-0327 (SAN 219-9882).

Gilgamesh Publishing Co., *(Gilgamesh Pub; 0-914246),* 6050 Blvd. East, West New York, NJ 07093 (SAN 203-6916).

Giligia Press, *(Giligia; 0-87791),* P.O. Box 626, Aurora, OR 97002 Tel 503-651-2090 (SAN 203-4255).

Gillespie, Charles A., *(C A Gillespie; 0-9609974),* 3 Lynwood Ave., Titusville, FL 32780 Tel 305-269-0643 (SAN 263-1032).

Gilmar Enterprises, *(Gilmar Pr; 0-936402),* P.O. Box 597, Newcastle, CA 95658 (SAN 214-2430).

Gindick, Jon, *(J Gindick),* 344 Ranch Rd., Visalia, CA 93291 Tel 209-733-1679 (SAN 211-0741); Orders to: 344 Ranch Rd., Visalia, CA 93291 (SAN 211-075X).

Gingery, David J., (D J Gingery; 0-9604330), 2045 Boonville, Springfield, MO 65803 (SAN 214-3771).

Ginkgo Hut, (Ginkgo Hut; 0-936620), 13 Augusta Dr., Lincroft, NJ 07738 Tel 201-530-9572 (SAN 215-3157).

Ginn Custom Publishing, Div. of Ginn & Co., (Ginn Custom; 0-536), 191 Spring St., Lexington, MA 02173 Tel 617-861-1670 (SAN 214-0225).

Ginseng Press, (Ginseng Pr; 0-932800), Rte. 2, Box 1105, Franklin, NC 28734 Tel 704-369-9735 (SAN 211-4224).

Giorno Poetry Systems, (Giorno Poetry), 222 Bowery, New York, NY 10012 Tel 212-925-6372 (SAN 207-8325).

Girl Scouts of the USA, (GS; 0-88441), 830 Third Ave., New York, NY 10022 Tel 212-940-7500 (SAN 203-4611).

Girs Press, (Girs Pr), Streeter Hill Rd., West Chesterfield, NH 03466 Tel 603-256-8484 (SAN 206-202X); Orders to: P.O. Box 91, West Chesterfield, NH 03466 (SAN 206-2038).

Gita-Nagari Press, (Gita-Nagari; 0-911233), Rd. 1, Box 163, Port Royal, PA 17082 Tel 717-527-2282 (SAN 262-8759).

Glacier Natural History Assn., Inc., (Glacier Nat Hist Assn; 0-916792), Glacier National Park, West Glacier, MT 59936 Tel 406-888-5441 (SAN 208-6603).

Glanville, Inc., (Glanville; 0-87802), 75 Main St., Dobbs Ferry, NY 10522 Tel 914-693-1320 (SAN 201-6478).

Glaser, Anton, (A Glaser; 0-9600324), 1237 Whitney Rd., Southampton, PA 18966 (SAN 201-1999).

Glass Art Pubns., (Glass Art; 0-9608356), P.O. Box 2244, Van Nuys, CA 91404 Tel 213-769-6410 (SAN 240-6594).

Glass Works Press, (Glass Works; 0-934280), P.O. Box 81782, San Diego, CA 92138 Tel 619-563-8165 (SAN 207-2297).

Glassbooks, (Glassbooks Mo; 0-913074), Rte. 1, Box 357a, Ozark, MO 65721 (SAN 237-9554).

Glazier, Michael, Inc., (M Glazier; 0-89453), 1723 Delaware Ave., Wilmington, DE 19806 Tel 302-654-1635 (SAN 210-2056).

Glen-Bartlett Publishing Co., (Glen-Bartlett; 0-9602802), 105 W. Main St., Westboro, MA 01581 Tel 617-366-7669 (SAN 213-0645).

Glen-L Marine Design, (Glen-L Marine), 9152 Rosecrans, Bellflower, CA 90706 (SAN 203-428X).

Glen Press, (Glen Pr; 0-9603518), 2247 Glen Ave., Berkeley, CA 94709 (SAN 215-7667).

Glencoe Publishing Co., Inc., (Glencoe; 0-02), c/o Macmillan Publishing Co., Inc., 866 Third Ave., New York, NY 10022 Tel 212-935-2000 (SAN 202-5574).

Glendale Adventist Medical Center, (Glendale Advent Med; 0-87313), P.O. Box 871, Glendale, CA 91209 Tel 213-240-2819 (SAN 203-4298).

Glendon House, (Glendon Hse; 0-932124), 3649 Glendon Ave., Los Angeles, CA 90034 (SAN 212-3533); Orders to: Rancho Park Sta., Box 67900A, Los Angeles, CA 90067 (SAN 212-3541).

Glenmary Research Center, (Glenmary Res Ctr; 0-914422), 750 Piedmont Ave., N.E., Atlanta, GA 30308 Tel 404-876-6518 (SAN 201-6443).

Glenn, Peter, Pubns., Inc., (Peter Glenn; 0-87314), 17 E. 48th St., New York, NY 10017 Tel 212-688-7940 (SAN 201-9930).

Glenson Publishing, (Glenson Pub; 0-934884), P.O. Box 298, Sterling Heights, MI 48077 (SAN 214-378X).

Global Communications, (Global Comm; 0-938294), 303 Fifth Ave., Suite 1306, New York, NY 10016 Tel 212-685-4080 (SAN 216-3896).

Global Engineering Documents, Div. of Information Handling Services, (Global Eng; 0-912702), 2625 Hickory St., P.O. Box 2504, Santa Ana, CA 92707 Tel 714-540-9870 (SAN 205-2873).

Global Press, The, (Global Pr CO; 0-911285), 2239 E. Colfax Ave., Suite 202, Denver, CO 80206 Tel 303-393-7647 (SAN 263-1059).

Global Pubns., Inc., (Global Pubns CA; 0-9604752), P.O. Box 2112, Palm Springs, CA 92263 Tel 619-323-4204 (SAN 215-2207).

Globe Pequot Press, (Globe Pequot; 0-87106), Old Chester Rd., Box Q, Chester, CT 06412 Tel 203-526-9572 (SAN 201-9892) CT History Ser., Dist. Only by the Center for CT Studies of Eastern CT State College, Willimantic, CT 06226.

Globe Press, The, (Globe Pr; 0-910321), 18803 North Park Blvd., Cleveland, OH 44122 (SAN 241-5062).

Globe Pubs. International, (Globe Pubs Texas), 2205 Maryland St., Baytown, TX 77520 Tel 713-427-7740 (SAN 203-4328).

Globus Publishers, (Globus Pubs; 0-88669), P.O. Box 27086, San Francisco, CA 94127 (SAN 265-1416); 332 Balboa St., San Francisco, CA 94118 Tel 415-668-4723 (SAN 265-1424).

Gloria Pubs., (Gloria Pubs; 0-9604080), 2489 East Lake Rd., Livonia, NY 14487 (SAN 221-6132).

GloryPatri, (GloryPatri; 0-9607468), 2891 Richmond Rd., Suite 202, Lexington, KY 40509 (SAN 239-4391).

Gloucester Art Press, (Gloucester Art; 0-930582), P.O. Box 4526, Albuquerque, NM 87196 Tel 505-843-7749 (SAN 205-2865).

Gloucester Press *See* **Watts, Franklin, Inc.**

Glover Pubns., (Glover Pubns; 0-9602328), P.O. Box 21745, Seattle, WA 98111 (SAN 221-8275).

Glyphic Press, (Glyphic Pr; 0-935964), 665 Killarney Dr., Morgantown, WV 26505 (SAN 213-9235).

GMI Pubns, (GMI Pub; 0-937408), P.O. Box 16824, Jacksonville, FL 32216 (SAN 240-8511).

Gneiss Books, (Gneiss Bks), P.O. Box 92, 283 Jackson St., Spring Grove, PA 17362 (SAN 240-1479).

GNK Press, Div. of Good Natured Kitchen, (GNK Pr; 0-9609266), 453 Half Hollow Rd., Dix Hills, NY 11746 Tel 516-271-9565 (SAN 260-0587).

Gnomon Press, (Gnomon Pr; 0-917788), P.O. Box 106, Frankfort, KY 40602-0106 Tel 502-223-1858 (SAN 209-0104).

Gnosis Pubns., (Gnosis Pubns; 0-940988), 1440 Tyler Ave., San Diego, CA 92103 Tel 619-296-1628 (SAN 223-7709).

Goat Rock Pubns., (Goat Rock; 0-9610240), P.O. Box 21, Jenner, CA 95450 Tel 707-865-2762 (SAN 264-0600).

Godine, David R., Pub., Inc., (Godine; 0-87923), 306 Dartmouth St., Boston, MA 02116 Tel 617-536-0761 (SAN 213-4381). *Imprints:* Nonpareil Books (Nonpareil Bks).

Godiva Publishing, (Godiva Pub; 0-938018), P.O. Box 42305, Portland, OR 97242 Tel 503-233-1228 (SAN 214-3097).

Gods of the Universe, (Gods Universe; 0-9607228), P.O. Box 1543, Highland, IN 46322 Tel 219-924-8200 (SAN 239-0957).

Godwin, George, Ltd., (G Godwin UK; 0-7114), Trade Counter P. O. Box 87, 1-3 Pemberton Row, Red Lion Ct., Fleet St., London EC4P 4H, ; Dist. by: Macdonald & Evans Ltd Estover Plymouth, PL6 7PZ, .

Goehringer & Sons Associates, (Goehringer & Sons; 0-9601704), Box 9626, Pittsburgh, PA 15226 Tel 412-531-9549 (SAN 211-562X); 1022 Berkshire Ave., Pittsburgh, PA 15226 (SAN 211-5638).

Goethe, Meredyth, Pubs. Ltd., (Goethe Pubs; 0-9606714), 3200 Lenox Rd., N.E., E411, Atlanta, GA 30324 Tel 404-237-3735 (SAN 223-7636).

Gold Circle Productions, (Gold Circle; 0-943986), P.O. Box 586, Nevada City, CA 95959 Tel 916-273-6363 (SAN 241-3841).

Gold Crest Publishing, (Gold Crest; 0-941790), 832 Swallow St., Deerfield, IL 60015 (SAN 239-4294).

Gold Hill Publishing Co., Inc., (Gold Hill; 0-940936), Drawer F, Virginia City, NV 89440 Tel 702-847-0449 (SAN 217-3697).

Gold Horse Publishing Inc., (Gold Horse; 0-912923), 1981 Moreland Pkwy., Annapolis, MD 21401 Tel 301-269-0680 (SAN 285-3957); Dist. by: Frederick Fell Publisher, Inc., 386 Park Ave. S., New York, NY 10016 Tel 212-685-9017 (SAN 285-3965).

Gold/Kane Enterprises, (Gold-Kane Ent; 0-9604430), 1580 Garfield St., Denver, CO 80206 Tel 303-333-9659 (SAN 220-0554).

Gold Medal Books *See* **Fawcett Book Group**

Gold Penny Press, The, (Gold Penny; 0-87786), Box 2177, Canoga Park, CA 91306 Tel 213-368-1417 (SAN 281-7470); Orders to: Associated Booksellers, 147 McKinley Ave., Bridgeport, CT 06606 Tel 203-366-5494 (SAN 281-7489).

Gold Rush Sourdough Co., Inc., (Gold Rush; 0-912936), 122 E. Grand Ave. South, San Francisco, CA 94080 Tel 415-871-0340 (SAN 203-4336).

Gold Star Pubns., (Gold Star Pubns; 0-941508), P.O. Box 1451, Sioux Falls, SD 57101 Tel 605-332-4582 (SAN 239-0965).

Goldberg, James M., (J M Goldberg; 0-9603074), 1735 "K" St., N.W., Suite 200, Washington, DC 20006 (SAN 211-4321).

Golden Aires, Inc., (Golden Aires; 0-9607910), 615 W. Deer St., Glenrock, WY 82637 Tel 307-634-3391 (SAN 239-6513).

Golden Bell Press, (Golden Bell; 0-87315), 2403 Champa St., Denver, CO 80205 Tel 303-572-1777 (SAN 203-4344).

Golden Coast Publishing Co., (Golden Coast; 0-932958), 22 Waite Dr., Savannah, GA 31406 (SAN 212-355X).

Golden Door, Inc., (Gold Door Inc; 0-9610790), P.O. Box 1567, Escondido, CA 92025 Tel 619-295-5791 (SAN 265-1203); 3085 Reynard Way, San Diego, CA 92103 (SAN 265-1211).

Golden Dragon Pubs, Inc., (Golden Dragon Pub; 0-910295), P.O. Box 1529, Princeton, NJ 08540 Tel 609-896-1332 (SAN 241-5070).

Golden Eagle Pubs., (Golden Eagle Pubs; 0-912129), 2706 W. Alameda Ave., Denver, CO 80219 (SAN 265-3850).

Golden Gambit Books, (Golden Gambit; 0-918862), Eight Hayes Ave., Attleboro, MA 02703 Tel 617-222-0176 (SAN 210-1181) Moved, Left No Forwarding Address.

Golden Gate *See* **Childrens Press**

Golden Gate Productions/Kqed, Inc., (Golden Gate Prod; 0-912333), 500 Eighth St., San Francisco, CA 94103 Tel 415-553-2221 (SAN 265-1246).

Golden Gate Univ. Press, (Golden Gate; 0-943864), 536 Mission St., San Francisco, CA 94105 Tel 415-442-7204 (SAN 241-0249).

Golden Glow Publishing, (Golden Glow; 0-933072), Box 488, Sturgeon Bay, WI 54235 Tel 414-743-7322 (SAN 212-3568).

Golden Hill Books, (Golden Hill; 0-9605364), 2456 Broadway, San Diego, CA 92102 (SAN 216-1354).

Golden Key Pubns., (Golden Key; 0-9602166), 123 N. Sirrine, Suite 201, Mesa, AZ 85201 (SAN 212-3576).

Golden Keys Success Seminar, Inc., (Gold Key Succ), P.O. Box 9358, Salt Lake City, UT 84109 (SAN 240-852X).

Golden-Lee Book, Div. of Golden-Lee Book Distributors, Inc., (Golden-Lee Bk; 0-912331), 1000 Dean St., Brooklyn, NY 11238 Tel 212-857-6333 (SAN 265-1254).

Golden Light Press, (Golden Light; 0-940086), 14 Old Cow Path, Miller Place, NY 11764 Tel 516-473-8904 (SAN 217-0728).

Golden Mean Pubs., The, (Golden Mean; 0-937698), 42 E. Main St., Ashland, OR 97520 Tel 503-482-9771 (SAN 216-2490).

Golden Mountain Press, (Golden Mtn; 0-935062), P.O. Box 2387, Ithaca, NY 14850 (SAN 209-1976).

Golden Owl Pubs., (Golden Owl Pub; 0-9601258), 182 Chestnut Rd., Lexington Park, MD 20653 Tel 301-863-9253 (SAN 210-4288).

Golden Phoenix Press, (Golden Phoenix; 0-910727), 1300 LaPlaya No. 1, San Francisco, CA 94122 Tel 415-681-1563 (SAN 262-6772).

Golden Press *See* **Western Publishing Co., Inc.**

Golden Puffer Press, (Golden Puffer; 0-9607022), 1614 N. McKinley Ave., Tucson, AZ 85712 (SAN 238-8774).

Golden Quill Press, The, (Golden Quill; 0-8233), Francestown, NH 03043 Tel 603-547-6622 (SAN 201-6419).

Golden Quill Pubs., Inc., (Gold Quill Pubs CA; 0-933904), P.O. Box 1278-R, Colton, CA 92324 Tel 714-783-0119 (SAN 213-0726).

Golden Rainbow Press, (Golden Rainbow Pr), P.O. Box 106, Houston, TX 77001 (SAN 212-6605).

Golden Seal Research Headquarters, *(Golden Seal; 0-912368),* P.O. Box 27821, Hollywood, CA 90027 (SAN 201-8365).

Golden State Dance Teachers Assn *(Golden St Dance Teach Assn; 0-932980),* 11120 Downey Ave., Downey, CA 90241 Tel 213-861-6933 (SAN 212-6613).

Golden State Industries Corp., *(Golden State Indus),* 5042 E. Third St., Los Angeles, CA 90022 (SAN 211-9536).

Golden West Books, *(Golden West; 0-87095),* P.O. Box 80250, San Marino, CA 91108-8250 Tel 213-283-3446 (SAN 201-6400).

Golden West Historical Pubns., *(Golden West Hist; 0-930960),* P.O. Box 1906, Ventura, CA 93002 (SAN 212-6621).

Golden West Pubs., *(Golden West Pub; 0-914846),* 4113 N. Longview, Phoenix, AZ 85014 Tel 602-265-4392 (SAN 207-5652).

Goldermood Rainbow, *(Goldermood Rainbow; 0-916402),* 331 W. Bonneville St., Pasco, WA 99301 Tel 509-547-5525 (SAN 207-835X).

Goldfield Publishing, *(Goldfield Pub),* 8400 Melrose Ave., Los Angeles, CA 90069 (SAN 241-385X).

Golem Press, *(Golem; 0-911762),* P.O. Box 1342, Boulder, CO 80306 Tel 303-444-0841 (SAN 203-4379).

Golembe Associates, Inc., *(Golembe Assocs),* 1800 M St., N.W., Suite 900-N, Washington, DC 20036 Tel 202-296-5305 (SAN 238-8235).

Golf Associates, *(Golf Assoc; 0-9607140),* P.O. Box 1113, Pebble Beach, CA 93953 Tel 415-323-3582 (SAN 238-9835).

Golf Digest/Tennis, Inc., *(Golf Digest; 0-914178),* 495 Westport Ave., Norwalk, CT 06856 Tel 203-847-5811 (SAN 212-7431); Dist. by: Simon & Schuster, 1230 Ave. of the Americas, New York, NY 10020 Tel 212-245-6400 (SAN 200-2450).

Goliards Press, *(Goliards Pr),* 3515 18th St., Bellingham, WA 98225 (SAN 206-9903).

Goll, Reinhold W., *(R W Goll),* 1942B Mather Way, Elkins Park, PA 19117 (SAN 212-4246).

Gondwana Books, Div. of Alta Napa Press, *(Gondwana Bks; 0-931926),* 1969 Mora Ave., Calistoga, CA 94516 Tel 707-942-4444 (SAN 212-0208).

Gonzaga Univ. Press, *(Gonzaga U Pr),* Spokane, WA 99202 (SAN 206-4480).

Gonzalez, Fernando L., *(F L Gonzalez; 0-9601090),* P.O. Box 1812, Flushing, NY 11352 Tel 212-762-4593 (SAN 210-0924).

Good Apple, Inc., *(Good Apple; 0-916456; 0-86653),* P.O. Box 299, Carthage, IL 62321 Tel 217-357-3981 (SAN 208-6646).

Good Books, *(Good Bks PA; 0-934672),* Dist. by: People's Place Booklets, Main St., Intercourse, PA 17534 Tel 717-768-7171 (SAN 270-5389).

Good Food Books, *(Good Food Bks; 0-932398),* 17 Colonial Terrace, Maplewood, NJ 07040 Tel 201-762-0841 (SAN 212-8535).

Good Gay Poets, *(Good Gay),* P.O. Box 277, Astor Sta., Boston, MA 02123 Tel 617-661-7534 (SAN 207-3536).

Good Hope Press, *(Good Hope GA; 0-9608596),* 75 Silverwood Rd., N.E., Atlanta, GA 30342 Tel 404-255-7416 (SAN 240-6608).

Good Hope Publishing Co., the, *(Good Hope Pub; 0-9608562),* 16541 Warwick, Detroit, MI 48219 Tel 313-532-2531 (SAN 240-6616).

Good Ideas Co., *(Good Ideas; 0-9603940),* Box 296, Berea, OH 44017 Tel 216-234-5411 (SAN 212-5072).

Good Life Press, Div. of Charing Cross Publishing Co., *(Good Life; 0-89074),* 658 S. Bonnie Brae St., Los Angeles, CA 90057 Tel 213-483-5832 (SAN 206-4944).

Good Life Publishers, *(Good Life VA; 0-917374),* 14200 Nash Rd., Chesterfield, VA 23832 Tel 804-794-4954 (SAN 208-6654).

Good News Pubs., *(Good News; 0-89107),* 9825 W. Roosevelt Rd., Westchester, IL 60153 Tel 312-345-7474 (SAN 211-7991). *Imprints:* Crossway Books (Crossway Bks).

Good Sign Pubns., *(Good Sign; 0-937730),* 457 Ruthven Ave., Palo Alto, CA 94301 (SAN 215-6482).

Goodale Publishing, *(Goodale Pub),* 1903 Kenwood Pkwy, Minneapolis, MN 55405 (SAN 262-0294).

Goodfellow Catalog Press, *(Goodfellow; 0-936016),* P.O. Box 4520, Berkeley, CA 94704 Tel 415-428-0142 (SAN 206-4499).

Goodheart-Willcox Co., Inc., *(Goodheart; 0-87006),* 123 W. Taft Dr., South Holland, IL 60473 Tel 312-333-7200 (SAN 203-4387).

Goodkind, Estate of Herbert K., *(H K Goodkind; 0-9600498),* 25 Helena Ave., Larchmont, NY 10538 Tel 914-834-1448 (SAN 203-4700).

Goodlife Resources, Inc., *(Good Life Resources),* 5764 Mill St., Erie, PA 16509 Tel 814-868-3349 (SAN 241-3868).

Goodman, Thomas H., *(T H Goodman; 0-9601252),* 3218 Shelburne Rd., Baltimore, MD 21208 Tel 301-358-2817 (SAN 210-4296).

Goose Pond Press, *(Goose Pond Pr; 0-910835),* 11600 Southwest Freeway, Suite 179, Houston, TX 77031 Tel 617-259-9842 (SAN 270-5419).

Goranson Press, *(Goranson Pr),* 7624 W. Raschen, Chicago, IL 60656 (SAN 207-2300).

Gordian Press, Inc., *(Gordian; 0-87752),* 85 Tompkins St., Staten Island, NY 10304 Tel 212-273-4700 (SAN 201-6389).

Gordon, Harry G., *(H G Gordon),* 711 Coleridge Dr., Greensboro, NC 27410 (SAN 287-2935).

Gordon, Marilyn, ,Pub., *(M Gordon Pub; 0-9609542),* 2153 Westchester Ave., Bronx, NY 10462 Tel 212-829-0830 (SAN 260-1923).

Gordon, William R., *(W R Gordon; 0-910662),* 232 Beresford Rd., Rochester, NY 14610 Tel 716-288-8549 (SAN 202-9405).

Gordon & Breach Science Pubs., Inc., *(Gordon; 0-677),* 1 Park Ave., New York, NY 10016 Tel 212-689-0360 (SAN 201-6370).

Gordon-Cremonesi Book, *(Gordon-Cremonesi),* Dist. by: Atheneum Pubs., 597 Fifth Ave., New York, NY 10017 Tel 212-486-2700 (SAN 201-002X).

Gordon Press Pubs., *(Gordon Pr; 0-87968),* P.O. Box 459, Bowling Green Sta., New York, NY 10004 (SAN 201-6362).

Gordons & T. Weinberg, *(Gordons & Weinberg; 0-9603484),* Weinberg, 1302 W. Fourth, Coffeyville, KS 67337 (SAN 213-571X).

Gordonstown Press, *(Gordonstown; 0-9603942),* Box U, Dillon, CO 80435 (SAN 214-3100).

Gordy Press, *(Gordy Pr; 0-936472),* 330 Pine Ridge Rd., Jackson, MS 39206 Tel 601-362-6518 (SAN 216-1362).

Gorsuch Scarisbrick, Pubs., *(Gorsuch Scarisbrick; 0-89787),* 576 Central, Dubuque, IA 52001 Tel 319-588-2303 (SAN 220-5920).

Gos Inc., *(Gos Inc; 0-942258),* P.O. Box 3912, Missoula, MT 59806 (SAN 237-9562).

Gospel Advocate Co., Inc., *(Gospel Advocate; 0-89225),* P.O. Box 150, Nashville, TN 37202 Tel 615-254-8781 (SAN 205-2792).

Gospel Place, The, *(Gospel Place),* P.O. Box 110304, Nashville, TN 37211 (SAN 277-6847).

Gospel Publishing House, *(Gospel Pub; 0-88243),* 1445 Boonville Ave., Springfield, MO 65802 Tel 417-862-2781 (SAN 206-8826).

Gospic Realty Corp., *(Gospic Realty; 0-943898),* 63 Little Clove Rd., Staten Island, NY 10301 Tel 212-981-6361 (SAN 241-1172).

Goss & Co., Pubs., *(Goss; 0-912010),* 396 Redwood Dr., Pasadena, CA 91105 Tel 213-257-1773 (SAN 203-4409).

Gotham Book Mart, *(Gotham; 0-910664),* 41 W. 47th St., New York, NY 10036 Tel 212-757-0367 (SAN 203-4417).

Gothic Press, *(Gothic Pr; 0-913045),* 4998 Perkins Rd., Baton Rouge, LA 70808 Tel 504-766-2906 (SAN 283-0949).

Gottlieb & Allen, *(Gottlieb & Allen; 0-930768),* 200 E. 27th St., New York, NY 10016 (SAN 211-4232).

Gotuit Enterprises, *(Gotuit Ent; 0-931490),* 1300-9C Golden Rain Rd., P.O. Box 2568, Seal Beach, CA 90740 Tel 213-430-5198 (SAN 211-3597).

Gould, Bruce, Publications, *(B Gould Pubns; 0-918706),* P.O. Box 16, Seattle, WA 98111 (SAN 210-9964).

Gould, Jay, Enterprises, *(J Gould; 0-9608332),* 7840 Old Auburn Rd., Fort Wayne, IN 46825 Tel 219-489-4441 (SAN 240-5334).

Gould Pubns., *(Gould; 0-87526),* 199 State St., Binghamton, NY 13901 Tel 607-724-3000 (SAN 201-6354).

Gourmet Books, Inc., *(Gourmet Bks; 0-933166),* 560 Lexington Ave., New York, NY 10022 Tel 212-371-1330 (SAN 205-2768).

Gourmet Guides, *(Gourmet Guides; 0-937024),* 1767 Stockton St., San Francisco, CA 94133 (SAN 214-3798).

Gourmet Publications, *(Gourmet Pubns),* 1401 W. Calle Kino, Tucson, AZ 85704 (SAN 283-9024).

Gousha, H. M., Co., The, *(H M Gousha; 0-88098),* 2001 The Alameda, San Jose, CA 95150 Tel 408-296-1060 (SAN 281-7519); Orders to: Dept. ABI, P.O. Box 6227, San Jose, CA 95150 (SAN 281-7527).

Government Data Pubns., *(Gov Data Pubns),* 1120 Connecticut Ave., N.W., Washington, DC 20036 (SAN 207-3439).

Government Institutes, Inc., *(Gov Insts; 0-86587),* 966 Hungerford Dr., No. 24, Rockville, MD 20850 (SAN 214-3801).

Government Printing Office, *(Gov Printing Office),* 710 N. Capitol St. NW., Washington, DC 20402 Tel 202-783-3238 (SAN 213-9243).

Government Product News, *(Gov Prod News; 0-9611182),* 1111Chester Ave., Cleveland, OH 44114 Tel 216-696-7000 (SAN 277-6855).

Government Requirement Kit, *(Govt Requirement Kits; 0-941058),* 1801 N. Meridian, Suite A, Tallahassee, FL 32303 Tel 904-385-9467 (SAN 217-3700).

Government Research Pubns., *(Gov Res Pubns; 0-931684),* Box 122, Newton Center, MA 02159 (SAN 211-4674).

Governmental Research Assn., Inc., *(GRA; 0-931684),* One Federal St., Austin, TX 02110 Tel 617-357-8500 (SAN 205-275X).

Gowan, J.C., *(Gowan),* 1426 Southwind, Westlake Village, CA 91361 Tel 818-991-0342 (SAN 202-0343).

Gower Publishing Ltd., *(Gower Pub Ltd; 0-566),* Old Post Rd., Brookfield, VT 05036 Tel 802-276-3355 (SAN 262-0308).

Grace Fellowship Church, *(Grace Fellow; 0-943436),* 8621 S. Memorial Dr., Tulsa, OK 74133 Tel 918-252-1611 (SAN 240-6624).

Grace Pubns., *(Grace Pubns; 0-911925),* P.O. Box 1383, San Marcos, CA 92069 Tel 619-722-4161 (SAN 264-0635).

Grace Publishing Co., *(Grace Pub Co),* P.O. Box 23385, Tampa, FL 33622 Tel 813-884-8003 (SAN 211-8017).

Grace Publishing House, *(Grace Pub House; 0-9605576),* 10505 Cole Rd., Whittier, CA 90604 Tel 213-944-7372 (SAN 238-3543).

Gracelaine Pubns., *(Gracelaine; 0-932984),* 3001 Ashley Ave., Montgomery, AL 36109 (SAN 212-2804).

Graceway Publishing Co., *(Graceway; 0-932126),* P.O. Box 159, Station "C", Flushing, NY 11367 Tel 212-261-0759 (SAN 212-0976).

Gracie Enterprises, Inc., *(Gracie Ent; 0-9606398),* P.O. Box 506, Chula Vista, CA 92012 Tel 619-421-8055 (SAN 226-7934).

Grade Finders, Inc., *(Grade Finders),* 642 Lancaster Ave., Berwyn, PA 19312 Tel 215-644-4159 (SAN 208-2322); Orders to: P.O. Box 444, Bala-Cynwyd, PA 19004 (SAN 208-2330).

Graduate School of Business & Public Administration, Cornell Univ., *(Grad Scl Bus),* Orders to: Partners for Livable Places, 1429 21 St., Washington, DC 20036 (SAN 200-402X).

Graduate School Press, *(Grad School),* U.S. Dept. Agriculture, Room 133, 600 Maryland Ave., S.W., Washington, DC 20024 Tel 202-447-7123 (SAN 203-4425).

Graham, C P, Press, *(C P Graham),* Box 5, Keswick, VA 22947 Tel 804-293-5980 (SAN 209-7230).

Graham, Josephine, *(J Graham),* c/o Suggin Productions, 7710 Choctaw Rd., Little Rock, AR 72205 (SAN 209-8911).

Graham Conley Press, *(Graham Conley; 0-912087),* 2509 N. Campbell Ave., No. 284, Tucson, AZ 85719 Tel 602-626-5223 (SAN 264-746X).

Graham Publishing Company, *(Graham Pub Co; 0-942404),* 4881 S. Main St., Akron, OH 44319 Tel 216-644-5144 (SAN 238-1621).

Gramercy Books Press, Inc., *(Gramercy Bks; 0-935134),* 354 George St, New Brunswick, NJ 08901 (SAN 213-845X).

Grammatical Sciences, *(Grammatical Sci),* 1236 Jackson St., Santa Clara, CA 95050 (SAN 203-4433).

Granberg, Ronald Scott, *(R S Granberg),* c/o Law Distributors, 14415 S. Main St., Gardena, CA 90248 (SAN 212-3681).

Grand Canyon Natural History Assn., *(GCNHA; 0-938216),* P.O. Box 399, Grand Canyon, AZ 86023 (SAN 215-7675).

Granger Book Co., Inc., *(Granger Bk; 0-89609),* P.O. Box 406, Great Neck, NY 11022 Tel 516-466-3676 (SAN 210-9735).

Granite Hill Corp., *(Granite Hill),* RFD No. 1, P.O. Box 210, Hallowell, ME 04347 (SAN 287-1718).

Granite Pubns., *(Granite Pubns; 0-914102),* Box 1367, Southampton, NY 11968 (SAN 201-6346).

Grant, Donald M., Publisher, Inc, *(D M Grant; 0-937986),* West Kingston, RI 02892 Tel 401-783-3266 (SAN 281-7535); Dist. by: Pacific Comics, Inc., 4887 Ronson Ct., Suite E, San Diego, CA (SAN 169-0124); Dist. by: Bud Plant Inc., 13393 Grass Valley Dr., Suite 7, P.O. Box 1886, Grass Valley, CA 95945 (SAN 268-5086); Dist. by: F. & S.F. Book Co., P.O. Box 415, Staten Island, NY 10302 (SAN 169-6270).

Grant, R.W., *(R W Grant; 0-9601218),* P.O. Box 2060, Hanover, MA 02339 (SAN 210-119X).

Grape Hill Press, *(Grape Hill Pr; 0-9610320),* P.O. Box 1402, Greensboro, NC 27402 (SAN 264-066X).

Grape Press, the, *(Grape Pr; 0-9608228),* 142 Citizens Bank Center, Richardson, TX 75080 (SAN 240-3110).

Grapetree Productions, Inc., *(Grapetree Prods; 0-941374),* Box 10cn, 600 Grapetree Dr., Key Biscayne, FL 33149 Tel 305-361-2060 (SAN 239-3638).

Graphic Artists Guild, *(Graphic Artists; 0-932102),* 30 E. 20th St., New York, NY 10010 Tel 212-982-9298 (SAN 221-1203).

Graphic Arts Center Publishing Co., *(Graphic Arts Ctr; 0-912856),* P.O. Box 10306, Portland, OR 97210 Tel 503-224-7777 (SAN 201-6338).

Graphic Arts Trade Journals, *(Graph Arts Trade; 0-910762),* 399 Conklin St., Suite 306, P.O. Box 81, Farmingdale, NY 11735 Tel 516-694-4842 (SAN 206-8281).

Graphic Communications Center, *(Graphic Comm Ctr),* P.O. Bx 357 Appleton, WI 54911 (SAN 201-632X).

Graphic Crafts, Inc., *(Graphic Crafts),* P.O. Box 248, 300 Beaver Valley Pike, Willow Street, PA 17584 Tel 717-464-2733 (SAN 209-3294).

Graphic Dimensions, *(Graphic Dimensions; 0-930904),* 8 Frederick Rd., Pittsford, NY 14534 Tel 716-381-3428 (SAN 213-067X).

Graphic Image Pubns., S, *(Graphic Image; 0-912457),* P.O. Box 1740, La Jolla, CA 92038 Tel 619-457-0344 (SAN 265-4059).

Graphic Impressions, *(Graphic Impress; 0-914628),* 1939 W. 32nd Ave., Denver, CO 80211 Tel 303-458-7475 (SAN 201-6311).

Graphic Learning Corp., *(Graphic Learning; 0-943068),* 2574 Seagate Drive, Tallahassee, FL 32301 Tel 516-671-1245 (SAN 240-3803).

Graphic Publishing Co., *(Graphic Pub; 0-89279),* 204 N. Second Ave., W., Lake Mills, IA 50450 Tel 515-592-0031 (SAN 202-4306).

Graphics-Communication Associates, *(Graphics Comm),* P.O. Drawer 10549, Tallahassee, FL 32302 Tel 904-224-9356).

Graphics Press, *(Graphics Calif; 0-937536),* 3010 Santa Monica Blvd. Suite 406, Santa Monica, CA 90404 Tel 213-395-2676 (SAN 215-2487).

Grassdale, Inc., *(Grassdale; 0-939798),* 1102 Lincoln Green, Norman, OK 73069 Tel 405-329-7071 (SAN 216-8960).

Grassroots Educational Service, *(Grassroots Ed Serv; 0-933426),* 102 1/2 Broadway, Glendale, CA 91205 Tel 213-240-1683 (SAN 212-5099).

Grastorf & Lang, Ltd., *(Grastorf & Lang; 0-933408),* 920 Broadway, New York, NY 10010 Tel 212-677-3470 (SAN 215-0786).

Grauer, Jack, *(J Grauer; 0-930584),* 2005 S.E. 58th, Portland, OR 97215 Tel 503-232-5596 (SAN 208-0885).

Gravel-Kellogg Publishing Co., *(Gravel-Kellogg; 0-9608684),* 235 W. 20th St., Fremont, NE 68025 Tel 402-727-4859 (SAN 238-292X).

Gravesend Press, *(Gravesend Pr; 0-9608508),* 4392 Bussey Rd., Syracuse, NY 13215 (SAN 240-6632).

Gravity Research Pubns., *(Gravity Research; 0-913001),* 1237 Camino Del Mar, Suite C-131, Del Mar, CA 92014 (SAN 283-0981).

Gray, Edgar, Pubns., *(Gray Pubns),* P.O. Box 181, Kalamazoo, MI 49005 Tel 616-344-7070 (SAN 205-3306).

Gray, Herbi, *(H Gray; 0-9608406),* P.O. Box 2343, Olympia, WA 98507 Tel 206-491-4138 (SAN 240-6640).

Gray & Associates, *(Gray Assoc; 0-937636),* P.O. Box 961, Madison, WI 53701 Tel 608-274-7458 (SAN 215-2118).

Gray Beard Publishing, *(Gray Beard; 0-933686),* 107 W. John St., Seattle, WA 98119 (SAN 212-8543).

Gray Moose Press, The, *(Gray Moose; 0-9608018),* 19 Elmwood Ave., Rye, NY 10580 Tel 914-967-0665 (SAN 239-4308).

Graylock Press, *(Graylock; 0-910670),* 428 E. Preston St., Baltimore, MD 21202 Tel 301-528-4105 (SAN 203-445X).

Graywolf Press, *(Graywolf; 0-915308),* P.O. Box 142, Port Townsend, WA 98368 Tel 206-385-1160 (SAN 207-1665).

Grdinic, Eva, *(Grdinic; 0-9604176),* 6661 Vista del Mar, Playa del Rey, CA 90291 (SAN 214-2449).

Great American Books, *(Great Am Bks; 0-936790),* 256 S. Robertson Blvd., Beverly Hills, CA 90211 (SAN 215-1499).

Great Basin Press, *(Great Basin; 0-930830),* Box 11162, Reno, NV 89510 Tel 702-826-7729 (SAN 211-1144).

Great Commission Pubns., *(Great Comm Pubns; 0-934688),* 7401 Old York Rd., Philadelphia, PA 19126 Tel 215-635-6510 (SAN 215-1502).

Great Eastern Book Co., *(Great Eastern; 0-87773),* P.O. Box 271, Boulder, CO 80306 Tel 303-449-6113 (SAN 211-6391).
Imprints: Prajna Press (Prajna).

Great Lakes Books, *(G Lakes Bks; 0-9606400),* P.O. Box 164, Brighton, MI 48116 Tel 313-227-7471 (SAN 222-9994).

Great Northwest Publishing & Distributing Co., *(Great Northwest; 0-937708),* P.O. Box 103902, Anchorage, AK 99510 (SAN 219-9890).

Great Oak Press of Virginia, *(Great Oak Pr VA; 0-9608234),* Box 6541, Falls Church, VA 22046 Tel 703-560-6347 (SAN 240-3129).

Great Ocean Pubns., *(Great Ocean; 0-915556),* 1823 North Lincoln Street, Arlington, VA 22207 Tel 703-525-0909 (SAN 207-527X).

Great Outdoors Publishing Co., *(Great Outdoors; 0-8200),* 4747 28th St., N., St. Petersburg, FL 33714 Tel 813-525-6609 (SAN 201-6273).

Great Pyramid Press, *(Great Pyramid; 0-9605822),* P.O. Box 2745, Augusta, GA 30904 Tel 404-736-3514 (SAN 220-1704).

Great Raven Press, *(Great Raven Pr),* Box 813, Fort Kent, ME 04743 (SAN 211-9595).

Great Star Press, *(Great Star),* 1117 High Court, Berkeley, CA 94708 (SAN 209-1534).

Great Western Publishing, *(GWP; 0-86666),* 416 Magnolia, Glendale, CA 91204 (SAN 220-2492) Do Not Confuse with Great Western Pubns.

Great Western Pubns., *(Great Western; 0-9604572),* 1842 W. 169th St., Gardena, CA 90247 Tel 213-323-7606 (SAN 213-070X).

Great Wine Grapes, *(Great Wine Grapes),* 157 24th Ave., San Francisco, CA 94121 (SAN 211-5271); Dist. by: CBI Publishing Co., Inc., 51 Sleeper St., Boston, MA 02210 Tel 617-426-2224 (SAN 201-9515).

Greater Golden Hill Poetry Express, The, *(Greater Gold; 0-9611842),* 4607 Muir Ave., San Diego, CA 92107 Tel 619-224-5951 (SAN 286-195X).

Greater National Society of Poets, Inc., *(Great Nat Soc Poet; 0-940088),* 3023 W. Hillsborough Ave., Tampa, FL 33614 Tel 813-626-0225 (SAN 214-3828).

Greater Philadelphia Chamber of Commerce, *(Greater Phila; 0-918942),* 1617 John F. Kennedy Blvd., Suite 1960, Philadelphia, PA 19103 Tel 215-568-4040 (SAN 210-3567).

Greater Philadelphia women's Yellow Pages, The, *(Greater PWYP; 0-9611844),* P.O. box 42397, Philadelphia, PA 19101 Tel 215-235-4042 (SAN 286-1968).

Greater Portland Landmarks, Inc., *(Greater Portland; 0-9600612),* 165 State St., Portland, ME 04101 Tel 207-774-5561 (SAN 203-4484).

Greatest Graphics, Inc., *(Greatest Graphics; 0-936120),* 1904 B East Meadowmere, Springfield, MO 65804 (SAN 213-7410); Orders to: P.O. Box 4467gs, Springfield, MO 65804 Tel 417-862-6500 (SAN 213-7429).

Green, Adolph, Publishing Co., *(Adolph Green; 0-9602198),* P.O. Box 337, Arlington, TX 76010 (SAN 212-7164).

Green, Robert Alan, *(R A Green; 0-9600266),* 214 Key Haven Rd., Key West, FL 33040 Tel 305-296-6736 (SAN 204-6563).

Green, Sherwood, *(S Green),* 219 S. D St Po Box 1019, Madera, CA 93637 (SAN 226-3947).

Green, Warren H., Inc., *(Green; 0-87527),* 8356 Olive Blvd., St. Louis, MO 63132 Tel 314-991-1335 (SAN 201-4939).

Green, Wayne, Inc., *(Green Pub Inc; 0-88006),* Book Department, Peterborough, NH 03458 Tel 603-924-9471 (SAN 219-7855).

Green Acres School, *(Green Acres Schl),* 11701 Danville Dr., Rockville, MD 20852 Tel 301-881-4100 (SAN 206-2046).

Green Block Publishing, *(Green Block; 0-9609748),* Rte. 2, Carthage, TN 37030 (SAN 263-1520).

Green Dolphin Bookshop, *(Green Dolphin; 0-911904),* 1300 S.W. Washington St., Portland, OR 97205 Tel 503-224-3060 (SAN 205-3268).

Green Eagle Press, *(Green Eagle Pr; 0-914018),* 241 W. 97th St., New York, NY 10025 Tel 212-663-2167 (SAN 203-4492).

Green Hill Pubs., *(Green Hill; 0-916054; 0-89803),* 722 Columbus St., Ottawa, IL 61350 Tel 815-434-7905 (SAN 281-7578); Dist. by: Caroline House Pubs., Inc., 920 W. Industrial Dr., Aurora, IL 60503 (SAN 211-2280).

Green Hut Press, *(Green Hut; 0-916678),* 24051 Rotunda Rd., Valencia Hills, CA 91355 Tel 805-259-5290 (SAN 208-2888).

Green Key Press, *(Green Key Pr; 0-910783),* P.O. Box 3801, Seminole, FL 33542 (SAN 264-0708).

Green Leaf Press, *(Green Leaf CA; 0-938462),* P.O. Box 6880, Alhambra, CA 91802 Tel 213-281-6800 (SAN 239-3646); 20 W. Commonwealth Ave., Alhambra, CA 91801 Tel 213-281-6809 (SAN 239-3654).

Green Note Music Pubns., *(Green Note Music; 0-912910),* P.O. Box 519, Pt. Reyes Sta., CA 94956 Tel 415-663-1453 (SAN 201-6249); Dist. by: Warner Bros. Pubns., Inc., 75 Rockefeller Plaza, New York, NY 10019 (SAN 203-0586).

Green Oak Press, *(Green Oak Pr; 0-931600),* 9339 Spicer Rd., Brighton, MI 48116 Tel 313-449-4802 (SAN 211-9544).

Green Oak Township Historical Society, *(Green Oak Township; 0-936702),* P.O. Box 84, Brighton, MI 48116 (SAN 218-477X).

Green River Press, Inc., *(Green River; 0-940580),* Saginaw Valley State College, University Center, MI 48710 Tel 517-790-4376 (SAN 207-5881).

Green Tiger Press, The, *(Green Tiger Pr; 0-914676),* Box 3000, La Jolla, CA 92038 (SAN 219-4775).

Greenberg Publishing Co., *(Greenberg Pub Co; 0-89778),* 729 Oklahoma Rd., Sykesville, MD 21784 Tel 301-795-7447 (SAN 211-9552).

Greenbriar Books, *(Greenbriar Bks; 0-932970),* 5906 Hodgman Dr., Parma Heights, OH 44130 (SAN 264-0716).

Greencrest Press, Inc., *(Greencrest; 0-939800),* P.O. Box 7745, Winston-Salem, NC 27109 Tel 919-722-6463 (SAN 216-8979).

Greene, Bill, *(B Greene; 0-934668),* Box 810, Mill Valley, CA 94942 (SAN 213-0149).

Greene, J. R., *(J R Greene; 0-9609404),* 33 Bearsden Rd., Athol, MA 01331 Tel 617-249-9376 (SAN 262-6845).

Greene, Robert E., *(R E Greene; 0-9603320),* 120 "U" St. N.W., Washington, DC 20001 (SAN 213-313X).

Greene, Stephen, Press, *(Greene; 0-8289),* Fessenden Rd. at Indian Flat, P.O. Box 1000, Brattleboro, VT 05301 Tel 802-257-7757 (SAN 201-6222).

Greene, Stephen, Press/Lewis Publishing Company, *(Lewis Pub Co; 0-86616; 0-8289),* Fessenden Rd., Brattleboro, VT 05301 (SAN 276-9379).

Greene Pubns., *(Greene Pubns; 0-9608892),* 1412 Glendale Blvd., Los Angeles, CA 90026 Tel 213-413-2150 (SAN 241-1180).

Greenfield Press, *(Greenfield Pr; 0-9611846),* P.O. Box 176, Southport, CT 06490 Tel 203-371-6523 (SAN 286-1798).

Greenfield Pubns., *(Greenfield Pubns; 0-9606666),* 8720 E. Forrest Dr., Scottsdale, AZ 85257 Tel 602-994-1452 (SAN 223-7717).

Greenfield Review Press, *(Greenfld Rev Pr; 0-912678),* R.D. 1, Box 80, Greenfield Ctr., NY 12833 Tel 518-584-1728 (SAN 203-4506).

Greenhaven Press, *(Greenhaven; 0-912616; 0-89908),* 577 Shoreview Park Rd., St. Paul, MN 55112 Tel 612-482-1582 (SAN 201-6214).

Greenleaf Books, *(Greenlf Bks; 0-934676),* Weare, NH 03281 (SAN 203-4514).

Greenleaf Co., *(Greenleaf Co; 0-940582),* P.O. Box 11393, Chicago, IL 60611 Tel 312-288-2205 (SAN 223-0011).

Greenleaf Pubns., *(Greenlf Pubns; 0-9608812),* P.O. Box 50357, Pasadena, CA 91105 (SAN 238-2938).

Greenpeace Center for Investigative Reporting, *(Greenpeace-Ctr Invest Re; 0-9607166),* 54 Mint St., 4th Fl., San Francisco, CA 94103 Tel 415-543-1200 (SAN 239-0973).

Greenprint Press, Project of Earthweal Great Lakes, *(Greenprint Pr; 0-943806),* P.O. Box 561, Traverse City, MI 49684 Tel 616-947-6515 (SAN 239-3689).

Green's Creek Press, *(Greens Creek; 0-9609406),* Route 5, Dublin, TX 76446 (SAN 262-0316).

Greenvale Press, *(Greenvale; 0-911876),* P.O. Box 242, Kopperl, TX 76652 Tel 817-772-8576 (SAN 203-4522).

Greenview Pubns., *(Greenview Pubns; 0-9606994),* Box 7051, Chicago, IL 60680 (SAN 238-8782).

Greenwich Design, *(Greenwich Des; 0-9603892),* Box 611, Hopkins, MN 55343 Tel 612-935-2574 (SAN 210-7333); 910 1/2 Excelsior Ave W., Hopkins, MN 55343 (SAN 210-7341).

Greenwich Press Ltd., *(Greenwich CT; 0-86713),* 30 Lindeman Dr., Trumbull, CT 06641 Tel 203-371-6568 (SAN 216-8170).

Greenwillow Books, Div. of William Morrow & Co., Inc., *(Greenwillow; 0-688),* 105 Madison Ave., New York, NY 10016 Tel 212-889-3050 (SAN 207-5741); Orders to: William Morrow & Co., Inc., Wilmor Warehouse, 6 Henderson Dr., West Caldwell, NJ 07006 (SAN 202-5779).

Greenwood House, *(Greenwood Hse; 0-9601982),* 1655 Flatbush Ave., Brooklyn, NY 11210 (SAN 212-3584).

Greenwood Press, *(Greenwood; 0-8371; 0-313),* 88 Post Rd. W., P.O. Box 5007, Westport, CT 06881 Tel 203-226-3571 (SAN 213-2028). *Imprints:* Quorum Books (Quorum Bks).

Greetings Publishing Co., *(Greetings Pub Co; 0-9611848),* 2903 Sunset Ave., Asbury Park, NJ 07712 Tel 201-222-6908 (SAN 286-1844).

Gregg, Newton K., Pub., *(N K Gregg; 0-87962; 0-912318),* P.O. Box 1459, Rohnert Park, CA 94928 Tel 707-584-9446 (SAN 206-9709).

Gregg-Hamilton, *(Gregg-Hamilton; 0-934800),* Meridian, Monroe & Maple, Aberdeen, MS 39730 Tel 601-369-8120 (SAN 211-9560).

Gregg Press *See* **Hall, G. K., & Co.**

Gregory, Howard, Associates, *(H Gregory; 0-9607086),* 640 The Village No. 209, Redondo Beach, CA 90277 (SAN 206-4502).

Gregory Pubns., *(Gregory Pubns; 0-917224),* Gateway Sta., Box 440950, Aurora, CO 80044 (SAN 208-6689).

Gregory Publishing Co., *(Gregory Pub),* 806 N. Maple St., Itasca, IL 60143 (SAN 211-5646).

Grenridge Publishing, *(Grenridge Pub; 0-943410),* P.O. Box 4587, Greenville, SC 29608 Tel 803-294-2207 (SAN 240-6659).

Grey Book, *(Grey Bk; 0-912021),* P.O. Box 1237, Flagstaff, AZ 86002 Tel 602-774-2923 (SAN 264-617X).

Grey Fox Press, *(Grey Fox; 0-912516),* Box 31190, San Francisco, CA 94131 (SAN 201-6176); Dist. by: Subterranean Co., P.O. Box 10233, Eugene, OR 97440 Tel 503-343-6324 (SAN 169-7102).

Grey House Publishing, Inc., *(Grey Hse Pub; 0-939300),* 229 E. 79th St., New York, NY 10021 (SAN 216-390X).

Greyfalcon House, *(Greyfalcon Hse; 0-914870),* 124 Waverly Place, New York, NY 10011 Tel 212-777-9042 (SAN 207-0723).

G R F Ltd., *(GRF Ltd; 0-939964),* P.O. Box 715, Roosevelt, UT 84066 (SAN 222-9757).

Grid Publishing, Inc., *(Grid Pub; 0-88244),* 2950 N. High St.,Box 14466, Columbus, OH 43214 Tel 614-261-6565 (SAN 201-8403).

Griffin, Boyd, Inc., *(Boyd Griffin; 0-941726),* 425 E. 51st St., New York, NY 10022 Tel 212-688-8193 (SAN 239-2194).

Griffon House Pubns., *(Griffon Hse; 0-918680),* P.O. Box 81, Whitestone, NY 11357 Tel 212-767-8380 (SAN 211-6685).

Griggs Printing & Publishing, *(Griggs Print; 0-918292),* Box 1351, 426 First St., Havre, MT 59501 Tel 406-265-7431 (SAN 209-441X).

Grinnell College, *(Grinnell Coll),* Grinnell, IA 50112 (SAN 216-3918).

Grinning Idiot Press, *(Grinning; 0-88100),* P.O. Box 1577, Brooklyn, NY 11202 (SAN 283-2674).

Grist Mill, *(Grist Mill; 0-917820),* Energy Conservation Services, 90 Depot Rd., Eliot, ME 03903 Tel 207-439-3873 (SAN 207-4710).

Grolier Club, *(Grolier Club; 0-8139),* Dist. by: Univ. Press of Virginia, Univ. Sta., P.O. Box 3608, Charlottesville, VA 22903 Tel 804-924-3131 (SAN 202-5361).

Grolier Educational Corp., Subs. of Grolier, Inc., *(Grolier Ed Corp; 0-7172),* Sherman Turnpike, Danbury, CT 06816 Tel 203-797-3500 (SAN 205-3195).

Groome Center, *(Groome Ctr; 0-916964),* 5225 Loughboro Rd., N.W., Washington, DC 20016 Tel 202-362-7644 (SAN 208-6697).

Gros Ventre Treaty Committee, *(Gros Ventre Treaty),* Ft. Belknap Agency, Harlem, MT 59526 Tel 210-900X).

Gross, Mrs. Ruth T., *(R T Gross),* 1815 Tigertail Ave., Miami, FL 33133 (SAN 210-0402).

Grossman, David, Press, *(D Grossman Pr; 0-910563),* 212 E. 47th St., Apt. 33a, New York, NY 10017 Tel 212-486-9598 (SAN 260-1958).

Grossman Stamp Co., Inc., *(Grossman Stamp; 0-912618),* 860 Broadway, New York, NY 10003 Tel 212-254-6100 (SAN 206-6963).

Group Books, *(Group Bks; 0-936664),* P.O. Box 481, 425 E. Eisenhower, Loveland, CO 80537 Tel 303-669-3836 (SAN 214-4689).

Group Health Assn. of America, Inc., *(Group Health Assoc of Amer; 0-936164),* 624 9 St.,N.W., Washington, DC 20001 (SAN 221-2811).

Groupwork Today Inc., *(Groupwork Today; 0-916068),* P.O. Box 258, South Plainfield, NJ 07080 Tel 201-755-4803 (SAN 208-0370).

Grove Press, Inc., *(Grove; 0-8021; 0-394),* 196 W. Houston St., New York, NY 10014 Tel 212-242-4900 (SAN 201-4890); Orders to: Grove Press Order Dept., 196 W. Houston St., New York, NY 10014 (SAN 201-4904). *Imprints:* Black Cat Books (BC); Evergreen Books (Ever).

Groves Dictionaries of Music, Inc., *(Groves Dict Music; 0-943818),* 15 E. 26th St., Suite 1503, New York, NY 10010 Tel 212-532-4811 (SAN 211-9579) Tel 800-221-2123.

Growing Pains Press, *(Growing Pains Pr; 0-941834),* 22 Fifth St., Stamford, CT 06905 Tel 203-348-6860 (SAN 239-2208).

Growing Together Press, *(Growing Together; 0-9604118),* P.O. Box 2983, Stanford, CA 94305 (SAN 215-7683).

Growth Associates, *(Growth Assoc; 0-918834),* P.O. Box 8429, Rochester, NY 14618 Tel 716-244-1225 (SAN 210-430X).

Growth Unlimited, *(Growth Unltd; 0-9601334),* 31 East Ave., S., Battle Creek, MI 49017 Tel 616-964-4821 (SAN 210-8976).

Grune & Stratton, *(Grune; 0-8089),* c/o Academic Press, 111 Fifth Ave., 12th Fl., New York, NY 10003 Tel 212-741-6865 (SAN 206-8990).

Gryphon House, Inc., *(Gryphon Hse; 0-87659),* 3706 Otis St., P.O. Box 275, Mt. Rainier, MD 20712 Tel 301-779-6200 (SAN 169-3190).

Gryphon West Pubs., *(Gryphon West Pubs),* 801 E. Harrison St. No. 105, Seattle, WA 98102 (SAN 240-4818).

Guadalupe River Press, *(Guadalupe River Pr),* c/o Trinity University Bookstore, 715 Stadium Rd., San Antonio, TX 78284 (SAN 238-0617).

Guappone's Pubs., *(Guappones Pubs),* R.D. One, Box Ten, McClellantown, PA 15458 Tel 412-737-5172 (SAN 209-4428).

Guarionex Press Ltd., *(Guarionex Pr; 0-935966),* 201 W. 77th St., New York, NY 10024 Tel 212-724-5259 (SAN 216-1370).

Guastella Pubns., *(Guastella Pubns; 0-9607230),* P.O. Box 6082, Tallahassee, FL 32301 (SAN 239-0981).

Guffey Books, Inc., *(Guffey Bks),* 6634 S. Broadway, Littleton, CO 80120 Tel 303-798-6406 (SAN 203-462X).

Guggenheim, Solomon R., Foundation, *(S R Guggenheim; 0-89207),* 1071 Fifth Ave., New York, NY 10028 Tel 212-860-1300 (SAN 205-3152).

Guggenheim Research Association, *(Guggenheim; 0-910377),* 1021 Oregon National Building, 610 S.W. Alder, Portland, OR 97205 (SAN 262-0324); Dist. by: Salem Press of Oregon, 1021 Oregon National Building, 610 S.W. Alder, Portland, OR 97205 (SAN 262-0332).

Guide Press, *(Guide Pr; 0-915472),* 7101 Glenbrook Rd., Bethesda, MD 20814 Tel 301-654-3572 (SAN 207-5709).

Guide to Reprints, Inc., *(Guide to Reprints; 0-918080),* P.O. Box 249, Main St., Kent, CT 06757 Tel 203-927-3523 (SAN 210-2080).

Guide to Richmond, *(Guide to Rich; 0-9607442),* P.O. Box 242, Midlothian, VA 23113 Tel 804-794-8068 (SAN 239-2216).

Guideline Publishing Co., *(Guideline Pub; 0-917474),* 336 S. Occidental Blvd., Los Angeles, CA 90057 Tel 213-382-4500 (SAN 203-4638).

Guidelines Press, *(Guidelines Pr; 0-932570),* 1307 S. Killian Dr., Lake Park, FL 33403 Tel 305-842-9411 (SAN 212-0984).

Guides to Multinational Business, Inc., *(Guides Multinatl Busn; 0-931000),* P.O. Box 92, Harvard Square, Cambridge, MA 02138 (SAN 212-2561).

Guifford-Hill Publishing Co., *(Guifford-Hill),* Rte. 8, Box 264, London, KY 40741 (SAN 211-5123).

Guignol Books, *(Guignol Bks; 0-941062),* P.O. Box 247, Rhinebeck, NY 12572 Tel 914-876-6776 (SAN 281-7594).

Guild Books, Catholic Polls, Inc., *(Guild Bks; 0-912080),* 86 Riverside Dr., New York, NY 10024 Tel 212-799-2600 (SAN 203-4646).

Guild Press, *(Guild Pr; 0-940248),* P.O. Box 22583, Robbinsdale, MN 55422 Tel 612-566-1842 (SAN 220-3340).

Guildhall Pubs., Ltd., *(Guildhall Pubs; 0-940518),* P.O. Box 325, Peoria, IL 61651 (SAN 219-838X).

Guilford Press, The, Div. of Guilford Pubns. Inc., *(Guilford Pr; 0-89862),* 200 Park Ave. S., New York, NY 10003 (SAN 212-9442).

Guinea Hollow Press/Films, *(Guinea Hollow; 0-916344),* 190 Waverly Place, New York, NY 10014 Tel 212-924-4586 (SAN 281-7616); Orders to: P.O. Box 59, Stanhope, NJ 07874 (SAN 281-7624).

Guitar Player Productions, Div. of Guitar Player Magazine, *(Guitar Player; 0-89122),* Dist. by: Music Sales Corp., 79 Broadway, New York, NY 10003 Tel 212-246-0325 (SAN 209-0988).

Gulf Coast Educators Press, *(Gulf Coast Ed),* 4430 Piedmont Rd., Pensacola, FL 32503 (SAN 262-0340).

Gulf Publishing Co., *(Gulf Pub; 0-87201),* P.O. Box 2608, Houston, TX 77001 Tel 713-529-4301 (SAN 201-6125).

Gull Books, *(Gull Bks; 0-940584),* 657 E. 26th St., No. 4S, Brooklyn, NY 11210 Tel 212-434-0094 (SAN 281-7632); Orders to: 1736 E. 53rd St., Brooklyn, NY 11234 (SAN 281-7640).

Gun Hill Publishing Co., *(Gun Hill; 0-9600228),* P.O. Box 187B, Yazoo City, MS 39194 Tel 601-746-3196 (SAN 203-4654).

Gun Room Press, *(Gun Room; 0-88227),* 127 Raritan Ave., Highland Park, NJ 08904 Tel 201-545-4344 (SAN 201-8357).

Gundersen, Dr. Richard O., *(Gunderson; 0-9608080),* 350 W. 66th St., Yuma, AZ 85364 Tel 602-726-9229 (SAN 240-2270).

Gusto Press, *(Gusto Pr; 0-933906),* P.O. Box 1009, 2960 Philip Ave., Bronx, NY 10465 Tel 212-931-8964 (SAN 212-9450).

Gutenberg-Museum, Weltmuseum der Druckkunst, *(Gutenberg),* P.O. box 26345, San Francisco, CA 95126 (SAN 287-0185).

Guthrie, Al, *(A Guthrie; 0-9606526),* P.O. Box 443, Carmichael, CA 95608 Tel 916-483-6543 (SAN 209-4436).

Guthrie Publishing Co., *(Guthrie Pub; 0-941064),* P.O. Box 1, Guthrie, MN 56451 Tel 218-224-2118 (SAN 217-3751).

Gutman Library, Harvard University, *(Gutman Lib; 0-943484),* Appian Way, Cambridge, MA 02138 Tel 617-495-4225 (SAN 240-6675).

Gwethine Publishing Co., *(Gwethine Pub Co),* 201 N. Wells St., Chicago, IL 60606 Tel 312-372-8105 (SAN 220-0007).

Gwinnett, Button, Publishers, Inc., *(Button Gwin; 0-938386),* 125 Scott Street, P.O. Box 508, Buford, GA 30518 (SAN 264-0732).

Gygi, Robert N., *(Gygi),* 1338 N.E. 28th St., Portland, OR 97232 Tel 503-249-8231 (SAN 239-4316).

Gypsum Association, *(Gypsum Assn),* 1603 Orrington Ave., Suite 1210, Evanston, IL 60201 (SAN 224-8808).

H & H Enterprises, Inc., *(H & H Ent; 0-89079),* P.O. Box 1070, 946 Tennessee, Lawrence, KS 66044 Tel 913-843-4793 (SAN 201-5420).

H & H Pubns., *(H & H Pubns CA; 0-910197),* 1524 Hudson St., Redwood City, CA 94061 Tel 415-364-3402 (SAN 241-5364).

H & H Publishing, *(H & H Publish),* P.O. Box 547, Springfield, IL 62705 (SAN 286-3499).

H&H Pub. Co., Inc., *(H & H Pub; 0-943202),* 1117 Webb Dr., Clearwater, FL 33515 Tel 813-447-0835 (SAN 240-5350).

H & S Publishing Co., *(H & S Pub Co; 0-9609268),* P.O. Box 304, Allenhurst, NJ 07711 Tel 201-775-3251 (SAN 260-0641).

H. B. C., *(HBC; 0-9601276),* Box 626, Lansing, IL 60438 Tel 312-474-7999 (SAN 210-4318).

HCP Research, *(HCP Res; 0-941210),* 20655 Sunrise Dr., Cupertino, CA 95014 Tel 408-446-1565 (SAN 217-376X).

HHH Horticultural, *(HHH Horticultural),* 68 Brooktree Rd., Hightstown, NJ 08520 (SAN 213-1951).

HIT Pubns., *(HIT pubns; 0-910993),* P.O. Box 11198, Costa Mesa, CA 92627 Tel 714-851-3936 (SAN 270-6482).

HMB Pubns., *(HMB Pubns; 0-937086),* 7406 Monroe Ave., Hammond, IN 46324 Tel 219-932-1798 (SAN 214-3836).

H. P. Books, *(H P Bks; 0-912656; 0-89586),* P.O. Box 5367, Tucson, AZ 85703 Tel 602-888-2150 (SAN 201-6087).

H R A F Press *See* **Human Relations Area Files Press, Inc.**

HRM Communications, Inc., *(H R M Comm Inc; 0-9611254),* 201 E. 77th St., New York, NY 10021 Tel 212-734-4958 (SAN 282-8723).

HTH Pubs., *(HTH Pubs; 0-916658),* P.O. Box 468, Freeland, WA 98249 (SAN 208-1148).

H3 Enterprises, *(H Three; 0-943578),* 7 Victoria Vale, Monterey, CA 93940 (SAN 240-8317).

Haas, Frederick C., *(Haas; 0-9601180),* Rte. 2 Box 78A, Blackstone, VA 23824 Tel 804-292-4726 (SAN 210-0932).

Haas Enterprises, *(Haas Ent NH; 0-9605552),* 7 N. Main, Box 218, Ashland, NH 03217 Tel 603-968-7177 (SAN 216-034X).

Haase-Mumm Pub Co., Inc., *(Haase-Mumm Pub Co; 0-940114),* 100 E. Ohio St., Rm. B-20, Chicago, IL 60611 Tel 312-951-5267 (SAN 220-2867); Dist. by: Amart Bk. & Catalog Dist. Co., Inc., 100 E. Ohio St., Rm. B-20, Chicago, IL 60611 (SAN 276-9778).

Habel, Robert E., *(Habel; 0-9600444),* 1529 Ellis Hollow Rd., Ithaca, NY 14850 Tel 607-272-3199 (SAN 203-4719).

Hach, Phila, *(Hach; 0-9606192),* 1601 Madison St., Clarksville, TN 37040 Tel 615-647-4084 (SAN 217-0736).

Hacker Art Books, *(Hacker; 0-87817),* 54 W. 57th St., New York, NY 10019 Tel 212-757-1450 (SAN 201-6052).

Hackett Publishing Co., *(Hackett Pub; 0-915144),* P.O. Box 44937, Indianapolis, IN 46204 Tel 317-635-9250 (SAN 201-6044).

Hadady Pubns., Inc., *(Hadady Pubns; 0-611390),* P.O. Box 90490, 61 S. Lake Ave. No. 309, Pasadena, CA 91109-0490 Tel 213-795-1957 (SAN 285-290X).

Haddad's Fine Arts, Inc., *(Haddad's Fine Arts; 0-88445),* P.O. Box 3016 C, Anaheim, CA 92803 Tel 714-996-2100 (SAN 206-5312); 3855 E. Mira Loma Ave., Anaheim, CA 92803 (SAN 206-5320).

Hadley, R. G., Co., *(R G Hadley; 0-9600988),* P.O. Box 5306, Salem, OR 97304 Tel 503-873-4241 (SAN 207-1282).

Hadronic Press, Inc., *(Hadronic Pr Inc; 0-911767),* Nonantum, MA 02195 Tel 617-864-9859 (SAN 264-0740).

Hady, Edmund Carl, *(E C Hady; 0-9600794),* 128 N. Main St., Ashley, PA 18706 (SAN 201-3509).

Haer Institute for Electro/Physiological Research, *(Haer Inst; 0-940090),* 21 Stanwood St., Brunswick, ME 04011 (SAN 220-2255).

Haffenreffer Museum of Antrhopology, *(Haffenreffer Mus Anthro; 0-912089),* Brown University, Mt. Hope Grant, Bristol, RI 02809 Tel 401-253-8388 (SAN 278-9817).

Hafner, Div. of Macmillan Publishing Co., Inc., *(Hafner; 0-02),* 866 Third Ave., New York, NY 10022 Tel 212-935-7616 (SAN 201-6001) Tel 800-343-2806; Dist. by: Collier-Macmillan Distribution Ctr., Riverside, NJ 08075 (SAN 202-5582).

Hagin, Kenneth, Ministries, Inc., *(Hagin Ministries; 0-89276),* P.O. Box 50126, Tulsa, OK 74150 Tel 918-258-1588 (SAN 208-2578).

Hagley Volunteers Cookbook Committee, *(Hagley Vol Ckbk; 0-9610990),* 603 Northside Dr., North Hills, Wilmington, DE 19809 Tel 302-764-7123 (SAN 265-2501).

Hagstrom Map Company, Inc., Subs. of American Map Corp., *(Hagstrom Map; 0-910684),* 4635 54th Rd., Maspeth, NY 11378 Tel 212-784-0055 (SAN 203-543X).

Haimo, Oscar, *(Haimo),* 252 E. 61st St., New York, NY 10021 Tel 212-838-6627 (SAN 202-2664).

Haimowoods Press, *(Haimowoods; 0-917790),* 1101 Forest Ave., Evanston, IL 60202 Tel 312-864-7209 (SAN 210-296X).

Haines, Ben M., *(B Haines; 0-9600586),* Box 1111, Lawrence, KS 66044 Tel 816-525-2579 (SAN 202-3660).

Haitian Society of Pubns., *(Haitian Soc; 0-914280),* 359 Nostrand Ave., Brooklyn, NY 11216 Tel 212-789-4192 (SAN 201-9094).

Haker Books, *(Haker Books; 0-9609964),* 2707 First Ave. N., Great Falls, MT 59401 Tel 406-454-1487 (SAN 262-0359).

Hake's Americana & Collectibles, *(Hake; 0-918708),* P.O. Box 1444, York, PA 17405 Tel 717-843-3731 (SAN 210-3575).

Hakim's Pubs., *(Hakims Pubs),* 210 S. 52nd St., Philadelphia, PA 19139 (SAN 207-2327).

Halbur Publishing, *(Halbur; 0-9603520),* P.O. Box 11354, Santa Rosa, CA 95406 Tel 707-544-7537 (SAN 212-9469).

Halcyon House *See* **National Book Co.**

Halcyon Press of Ithaca, *(Halcyon Ithaca; 0-9604006),* 111 Halcyon Hill Rd., Ithaca, NY 14850 Tel 607-257-1864 (SAN 215-1510).

Haldon Pubns., Inc., *(Haldon Pubns),* 1204 N. 20th Ave., Hollywood, FL 33020 Tel 305-929-1956 (SAN 213-5051); Orders to: P.O. Box 2226, Hollywood, FL 33022 (SAN 213-506X) Moved, Left No Forwarding Address.

Haljan Pubns., *(Haljan Pubns; 0-910907),* P.O. Box 291, 136 S. Main St., LaMoille, IL 61330 Tel 815-638-2152 (SAN 270-6571).

Hall, C. Mitchel, *(C M Hall; 0-914574),* 3401 Bangor St., S.E., Washington, DC 20020 Tel 202-583-3297 (SAN 206-5339).

Hall, Clarence H., *(C H Hall; 0-9604084),* 3409 Altwater Rd., Avon Park, FL 33825 (SAN 214-3119).

Hall, Eva Litchfield, *(E L Hall; 0-9604398),* 1400 S. Plymouth Ave., Apt. 321, Rochester, NY 14611 (SAN 207-2181).

Hall, G. K., & Co., *(G K Hall; 0-8161),* 70 Lincoln St., Boston, MA 02111 Tel 617-423-3990 (SAN 206-8427). *Imprints:* Gregg Press (Gregg); Hall Library Catalogs (Hall Library); Hall Reference Books (Hall Reference); Hall, G. K., Medical Pubs. (Hall Medical); Large Print Books (Large Print Bks); Twayne Publishers (Twayne); University Books (Univ Bks).

Hall, G. K., Medical Pubs. *See* **Hall, G. K., & Co.**

Hall, H. W., *(H W Hall; 0-935064),* 3608 Meadow Oaks Lane, Bryan, TX 77802 Tel 713-845-2316 (SAN 207-2181).

Hall Library Catalogs *See* **Hall, G. K., & Co.**

Hall Press, *(Hall Pr; 0-932218),* P.O. Box 5375, San Bernardino, CA 92412 Tel 714-887-3466 (SAN 211-7061).

Hall Reference Books *See* **Hall, G. K., & Co.**

Hallberg, Charles, & Co., Inc., *(C Hallberg; 0-87319),* P.O. Box 547, Delavan, WI 53115 Tel 414-728-2331 (SAN 205-3063).

Halldin, A. G., Publishing Co., *(Halldin Pub; 0-935648),* P.O. Box 667, Indiana, PA 15701 Tel 412-463-8450 (SAN 208-208X).

Hallmark Books, *(Hallmark Bks; 0-942322),* 12 Jennings Ct., Shelby, OH 44875 (SAN 239-5509).

Halls of Ivy Press, *(Halls of Ivy; 0-912256),* 4545 Industrial St. Unit 5r, Simi Valley, CA 93063 Tel 805-527-0525 (SAN 204-0204).

Hallum, Boen, *(B Hallum; 0-9608854),* 4977 Lockbourne Rd., Columbus, OH 43207 Tel 614-491-3886 (SAN 241-0265).

Halpern & Simon, *(Halpern & Simon; 0-942898),* 117-50 228th St., Queens, NY 11411 Tel 212-525-8795 (SAN 240-3137).

Halsted Press, Div. of John Wiley & Sons, Inc., *(Halsted Pr),* 605 Third Ave., New York, NY 10158 Tel 212-850-6418 (SAN 202-2680).

Halty Ferguson, *(Halty Ferguson; 0-912604),* 376 Harvard St., Cambridge, MA 02138 Tel 617-868-6190 (SAN 202-2699).

Halycon House, Publishers, Inc., *(Halycon Hse; 0-911311),* P.O. Box 9547, Kansas City, MO 64133 Tel 816-737-0064 (SAN 270-6555).

Hamaker-Weaver Publishers, *(Hamaker-Weaver; 0-941550),* Box 457, Potterville, MI 48876 Tel 517-645-2212 (SAN 239-2224).

HamanD Publishing Co., *(HamanD Pub),* 525 B St., Suite 342, San Diego, CA 92101 Tel 714-234-8393 (SAN 208-1172).

Hamba Books, *(Hamba Bks; 0-9606152),* 1901 Creekwood Dr., Conway, AR 72032 Tel 501-329-6147 (SAN 217-5223).

Hamilton, Alexander, Institute, Inc., *(Hamilton Inst),* 1633 Broadway, New York, NY 10019 Tel 212-397-3580 (SAN 205-311X).

Hamilton House, *(Hamilton Hse; 0-917908),* 936 N. 5th, Philadelphia, PA 19123 Tel 215-923-9161 (SAN 209-3308).

Hamilton Press, *(Hamilton Pr; 0-89648),* 4720 Hancock Dr., Boulder, CO 80303 (SAN 219-0869); Dist. by: Chapter & Cask, P.O. Box 113, Glenshaw, PA 15116 (SAN 219-0877).

Hamilton's, *(Hamiltons; 0-9608598),* P.O. Box 932, Bedford, VA 24523 Tel 703-586-5592 (SAN 264-0759).

Hamlet House, *(Hamlet Hse; 0-913861),* P.O. Box 791044, New Orleans, LA 70179-1044 Tel 504-482-4903 (SAN 286-7699); 631 N. Carrollton Ave., New Orleans, LA 70119 (SAN 286-7702).

Hamline University School of Law Advanced Legal Education, *(Hamline Law),* 1536 Hewitt Ave, St Paul, MN 55104 (SAN 227-2636).

Hammill, J. H., III, *(J H Hammill; 0-9600652),* Diablo Valley College, 321 Golf Club Rd., Pleasant Hill, CA 94523 Tel 415-685-1230 (SAN 203-8986).

Hammond, Rick, Photography, *(Hammond Photo; 0-935330),* 2925 "B" Freedom Blvd, Watsonville, Visalia, CA 95076 (SAN 213-5078).

Hammond-Harwood House Assn., Inc., *(Hammond-Harwood; 0-910688),* Orders to: Maryland's Way, Hammond Harwood House, 19 Maryland Ave., Annapolis, MD 21401 Tel 301-267-6891 (SAN 204-0220).

Hammond, Inc., *(Hammond Inc; 0-8437)*, 515 Valley St., Maplewood, NJ 07040 Tel 201-763-6000 (SAN 202-2702).

Hammond Records, *(Hammond Records; 0-942874)*, P.O. Box 3431 - 874 Chelterham Circle, Thousand Oaks, CA 91360 Tel 805-495-1143 (SAN 239-5517).

Hamoroh Press, *(Hamoroh Pr; 0-9604754)*, P.O. Box 48862, Los Angeles, CA 90048 (SAN 215-6512).

Hampol Publishing Co., *(Hampol Pub Co; 0-9609330)*, Box 36, 47 Harvard Ave., Boston, MA 02134 Tel 617-232-2430 (SAN 260-1990).

Hampshire Pacific Press, *(Hampshire Pacific; 0-939930)*, 3043 SW Hampshire St., Portland, OR 97201 (SAN 216-8189).

Hampton Court Pubs., *(Hampton Court Pub; 0-910569)*, P.O. Box 655, Lake Mahopac, NY 10541 Tel 914-628-6155 (SAN 264-0767).

Hampton Press, *(Hampton Pr MI; 0-938352)*, P.O. Box 805, Rochester, MI 48063 Tel 313-852-0980 (SAN 216-0358).

Hancock House Publishers, *(Hancock House; 0-88839)*, 1431 Harrison Ave., Blaine, WA 98230 (SAN 240-8546).

Hancraft Studios, *(Hancraft)*, 248-250 Pomona Mall W., Pomona, CA 91766 Tel 714-623-9555 (SAN 219-9556).

Hand Press, *(Hand Pr; 0-9605620)*, 12015 Coyne St., Los Angeles, CA 90049 Tel 213-472-9691 (SAN 218-4788); Dist. by: Ross Erikson,Inc.,Pubs, 629 State St. Suite 222, Santa Barbara, CA 93101 Tel 805-962-1175 (SAN 208-0494).

Handel & Sons Publishing, Inc., *(Handel & Sons; 0-917080)*, c/o Ambit Publications, Inc., 4227 Herschel, Suite 107, Dallas, TX 75219 Tel 214-522-0102 (SAN 216-5260).

Hands off, *(Hands off; 0-9609596)*, P.O. Box 68, Tacoma, WA 98401 Tel 206-752-2525 (SAN 260-2016).

Hands on Pubns., *(Hands on Pubns; 0-931178)*, 451 Silvera Ave., Long Beach, CA 90803 Tel 213-596-4738 (SAN 213-9286).

Haney Books, *(Haney Bks; 0-99609552)*, P.O. Box 545, Salem, IL 62881 (SAN 283-9059).

Hang Gliding Press, *(Hang Gliding; 0-938282)*, Box 22552, San Diego, CA 92122 Tel 619-452-1768 (SAN 215-6520).

Hanging Loose Press, *(Hanging Loose; 0-914610)*, 231 Wyckoff St., Brooklyn, NY 11217 Tel 212-643-9559 (SAN 206-4960).

Hanna, J. S., House, *(J S Hanna, 0-9607024)*, 183 Gifford Way, Sacramento, CA 95825 (SAN 238-986X).

Hannon, Douglas, *(D Hannon; 0-937866)*, Rte. 2, Box 991, Odessa, FL 33556 (SAN 215-7705); Dist. by: Great Outdoors Publishing Co., St. Petersburg, FL 33714 (SAN 201-6273).

Hansen, Arne B., *(A B Hansen; 0-9600842)*, P.O. Box 10638, Glendale, CA 91209 Tel 213-244-3036 (SAN 207-3811).

Hansen, Mack, *(M Hansen; 0-9606672)*, 207 Hill Blvd., Petaluma, CA 94952 Tel 707-763-1489 (SAN 219-7499).

Hansen & Miller, *(Hansen & Miller; 0-9601312)*, P.O. Box 1 Kenwood, Lower Lake, CA 95452 (SAN 211-0709).

Hansen Publishing Co., *(Hansen Pub MI; 0-930098)*, P.O. Box 1723, East Lansing, MI 48823 Tel 517-332-5946 (SAN 210-735X); Dist. by: Holley International Co., 63 Kercheval, Suite 204A, Grosse Pointe Farms, MI 48236 Tel 313-882-0405 (SAN 210-7368).

Hansi Ministries, Inc., *(Hansi; 0-932878)*, P.O. Box 552, Huntington Beach, CA 92648 Tel 714-894-7559 (SAN 213-5086).

Hanson, Margaret B., *(Hanson; 0-9605834)*, Mayoworth Rte., Kaycee, WY 82639 Tel 307-738-2215 (SAN 216-4884).

Hapi Press, *(Hapi Pr; 0-913244)*, 512 S.W. Maplecrest Dr., Portland, OR 97219 Tel 503-246-9632 (SAN 204-0239).

Happiness Press, *(Happiness Pr; 0-916508)*, 160 Wycliff Way, Drawer ADD, Magalia, CA 95954 Tel 916-873-0294 (SAN 208-6719); Orders to: P.O. Box Add, Magalia, CA 95954 (SAN 208-6727).

Happiness Unlimited Pubns., *(Happiness Unltd; 0-939372)*, 122 the Maine, Williamsburg, VA 23185 Tel 804-220-3378 (SAN 220-1550).

Happy Hands Publishing Co., *(Happy Hands; 0-941468)*, 4949 Byers, Ft. Worth, TX 76107 Tel 817-732-7494 (SAN 264-0775).

Happy Health Pubs., *(Happy Health)*, P.O. Box 2702, Seal Beach, CA 90740 Tel 213-431-0069 (SAN 206-4979).

Happy History, Inc., *(Happy History; 0-918430)*, P.O. Box 2160, Boca Raton, FL 33432 Tel 305-483-8093 (SAN 210-0940).

Happy Thoughts & Rainbow Company, The, *(Happy Thoughts & Rainbow; 0-9608686)*, Rte. One, Box 419C, Aurora, MN 55705 Tel 218-229-3116 (SAN 238-2954).

Haralson Publishing Co., *(Haralson Pub Co; 0-934534)*, Buchanan, GA 30113 Tel 404-646-3858 (SAN 221-1076).

Harben Publishing Company, *(Harben Pub; 0-9608158)*, P.O. Box 1055, Safety Harbor, FL 33572 (SAN 238-8375).

Harbinger Press Library, *(Harbinger Pr; 0-936092)*, 347 Willow Ave., Corte Madera, CA 94925 Tel 415-924-6490 (SAN 213-7437).

Harbor Hill Books, *(Harbor Hill Bks; 0-916346)*, P.O. Box 407, Harrison, NY 10528 Tel 914-698-3495 (SAN 201-9159).

Harbor House Books Ltd., Subs. of Louis J. Martin & Associates, Inc., *(Harbor Hse Bk; 0-916800)*, 95 Madison Ave., New York, NY 10016 Tel 212-725-2157 (SAN 208-6735) Moved, Left No Forwarding Address.

Harbor Publishing Inc., *(Harbor Pub CA; 0-936602)*, 1668 Lombard, San Francisco, CA 94123 Tel 415-775-4740 (SAN 215-3173); Dist. by: Kampmann and Co., 9 E.40th St., New York, NY 10016 (SAN 201-3800).

Harbrace Paperback Library See **Harcourt Brace Jovanovich, Inc.**

Harco, D. W., Inc., *(Harco Inc; 0-9607570)*, 11719 Jones Rd. Suite 103, Houston, TX 77070 (SAN 239-4405).

Harcourt Brace Jovanovich, Inc., *(HarBraceJ; 0-15)*, 1250 Sixth Ave., San Diego, CA 92101 Tel 714-231-6616 (SAN 200-2736); 757 Third Ave., New York, NY 10017 (SAN 200-2299). *Imprints:* Harbrace Paperback Library (HPL); Harcourt Brace Jovanovich, Inc., College Dept. (HC); Harvest Books (Harv); Voyager Books (VoyB).

Harcourt Brace Jovanovich, Inc., College Dept. See **Harcourt Brace Jovanovich, Inc.**

Hard Press, *(Hard Pr)*, 340 E. 11th St., New York, NY 10003 (SAN 219-1849).

Hard Press'd, *(Hard Press'd; 0-9604180)*, 1110 Buffalo St., Box 444, Franklin, PA 16323 (SAN 214-2457).

Hardin, Albert N., Jr., *(Hardin; 0-9601778)*, 5414 Lexington Ave., Pennsauken, NJ 08109 (SAN 210-9026).

Hardin-Simmons University Press, *(Hardin-Simmons; 0-910075)*, Box 896 HSU, Abilene, TX 79698 Tel 915-677-7281 (SAN 241-3205).

Harding, A. R., Publishing Co., *(A R Harding Pub)*, 2878 E. Main St., Columbus, OH 43209 Tel 614-231-9585 (SAN 206-4936).

Hardscrabble Books, *(Hardscrabble Bks; 0-915056)*, Rte. 2, Box 285, Berrien Springs, MI 49103 Tel 616-473-5570 (SAN 207-0960).

Hardwood Books, *(Hardwood Bks; 0-935332)*, 75 Algonquin Park, Plattsburgh, NY 12901 (SAN 218-4370).

Hardwood Plywood Manufacturers Association, *(Hardwd Ply)*, Box 2789, 1825 Faraday Dr., Reston, VA 22090 (SAN 224-7569).

Hardy, Arthur, & Associates, *(A Hardy & Assocs; 0-930892)*, P.O. Box 8058, New Orleans, LA 70182 Tel 504-282-2326 (SAN 210-9913).

Hardy, Max, *(M Hardy; 0-939460)*, 14484 S. Yukon, Hawthorne, CA 90250 Tel 213-973-4389 (SAN 216-597X).

Hardy House Pub. Co., A Hardy-Roberts Enterprise, *(Hardy Hse; 0-917844)*, P.O. Box 705, S. Laguna Beach, CA 92677 Tel 714-497-2670 (SAN 210-0959).

Hare Editions, *(Hare Ed; 0-916740)*, The Kensington House, Apt. 616, 200 W. 20th St., New York, NY 10011 (SAN 208-6751).

Hargreaves Co., Inc., *(Hargreaves; 0-910690)*, P.O. Box 895, Kailua, HI 96734 Tel 808-262-7320 (SAN 204-0247).

Hari Kari Products Co., *(Hari Kari; 0-913809)*, P.O. Box 610053, Houston, TX 77208 Tel 713-827-1651 (SAN 283-9598).

Harian Books, *(Harian; 0-87036)*, 1 Vernon Ave., Floral Park, NY 11001 (SAN 202-2729).

Harian Creative Press, *(Harian Creative; 0-911906)*, 47 Hyde Blvd., Ballston Spa, NY 12020 Tel 518-885-6699 (SAN 204-0255).

Harlequin Books, *(Harlequin Bks)*, 580 White Plains Rd., Tarrytown, NY 10591 Tel 914-332-1313 (SAN 226-2940).

Harlin Jacque, *(Harlin Jacque; 0-940938)*, 89 Surrey Lane, Hempstead, NY 11550 Tel 516-489-8564 (SAN 281-7659); Orders to: P.O. Box 808, Medford, NY 11763 (SAN 281-7667).

Harlo Press, *(Harlo Pr; 0-8187)*, 50 Victor Ave., Detroit, MI 48203 Tel 313-883-3600 (SAN 202-2745).

Harmon-Meek Gallery, *(Harmon-Meek Gal; 0-911431)*, 1258 Third Street S., Naples, FL 33940 (SAN 264-0791).

Harmonious Circle Press, *(Harmonious Pr; 0-9610544)*, 15 Ozone Ave., Apt. 2, Venice, CA 90291 (SAN 264-0813).

Harmonious Pubns., *(Harmonious Pubns; 0-912687)*, 7745 E. Redfield Dr., No. 100, Scottsdale, AZ 85260 Tel 602-996-1289 (SAN 282-7840).

Harmony Books See **Crown Pubs., Inc.**

Harmony Press, Inc., *(Harmony Pr)*, P.O. Box 122, North Granby, CT 06060 (SAN 238-8790).

Harmony Raine & Co., *(Harmony Raine; 0-89967)*, Box 133, Greenport, NY 11944 (SAN 262-0367).

Harmony Society Press, *(Harmony Soc; 0-937640)*, Box A 57, Clark University, Worcester, MA 01610 (SAN 215-6539).

Harmsen Publishing Co., *(Harmsen; 0-9601322)*, 1331 E. Alameda Ave., Denver, CO 80209 (SAN 213-0742).

Haroldsen, Mark O., *(M O Haroldsen; 0-932444)*, 1831 E. Fourth Union Blvd., Salt Lake City, UT 84121 (SAN 281-7675).

Harp & Thistle Ltd., *(Harp & Thistle)*, P.O. Drawer BO, Agana, GU 96910 Tel 617-477-8831 (SAN 262-4885).

Harp Press, *(Harp Pr; 0-9610456)*, 822 Magdelaine Dr., Madison, WI 53704 Tel 608-249-3458 (SAN 264-0821).

Harper & Row Pubs., Inc., *(Har-Row; 0-06)*, 10 E. 53rd St., New York, NY 10022 Tel 212-207-7000 (SAN 200-2086); 1700 Montgomery St., San Francisco, CA 94111 Tel 415-989-9000 (SAN 215-3734); Orders to: Keystone Industrial Park, Scranton, PA 18512 (SAN 215-3742). *Imprints:* Abelard-Schuman Junior Books (AbS-J); College Outline Series (COS); Colophon Books (CN); Crowell Junior Books (TYC-J); Everyday Handbooks (EH); Harper Religious Books (HarpR); Harper Trade Books (HarpT); Harper's College Division (HarpC); International Department (IntlDept); J.B. Lippincott/Harper & Row Medical Division (Harper Medical); John Day Junior Books (JD-J); Juvenile Books (HarpJ); Lippincott Junior Books (JBL-J); Perennial Library (PL); School Department (SchDept); Torchbooks (Torch); Trophy (Trophy).

Harper Medical See **Lippincott, J. B., Co.**

Harper Religious Books See **Harper & Row Pubs., Inc.**

Harper Square Press, *(Harper Sq Pr; 0-933908)*, 401 W. Ontario St., Chicago, IL 60610 Tel 312-751-1650 (SAN 212-9086).

Harper Trade Books See **Harper & Row Pubs., Inc.**

Harper's College Division See **Harper & Row Pubs., Inc.**

Harpswell Press, *(Harpswell Pr; 0-88448)*, P.O. Box 266, Brunswick, ME 04011 Tel 207-865-4512 (SAN 208-1199).

Harriet's Kitchen, *(Harriet's Kitchen; 0-938592)*, P.O. Box 424, Forest Hills, NY 11375 (SAN 216-2520).

Harris, Barbara, *(B Harris; 0-9601060)*, P.O. Box 2992, Portland, OR 97208 Tel 503-223-6434 (SAN 281-7691).

Harris, Frank, *(F Harris; 0-9610458)*, 1171 West Iowa Ave., Sunnyvale, CA 94086 (SAN 264-0848).

NAME INDEX

Harris, H. E., & Co., Inc., *(Harris & Co; 0-937458),* 645 Summer St., Boston, MA 02210 Tel 617-269-5200 (SAN 202-1137); Orders to: Box A, Boston, MA 02117 (SAN 215-3866).

Harris, Walter J., *(W J Harris; 0-9608156),* 1099 Rolling Hills Dr., Fayetteville, AK 72701 Tel 501-442-5255 (SAN 201-5366).

Harris Learning Academy, *(Harris Learning; 0-911181),* 2402 S. Newberry Court, Denver, CO 80222 (SAN 264-0856).

Harris Publishing Co., *(Harris Pub; 0-916512),* 2057-2 East Aurora Rd., Twinsburg, OH 44087 Tel 216-425-9143 (SAN 208-3280).

Harrison, E. Bruce, Co., *(E B Harrison; 0-9609130),* 605 14th St., NW, Washington, DC 20005 (SAN 241-5119).

Harrison Co., *(Harrison Co GA; 0-910694),* 3110 Crossing Park, Norcross, GA 30071 Tel 404-447-9150 (SAN 205-0536).

Harrison Education Motivation Enterprises, (HEMECO), 21863 Brill Rd., Riverside, CA 92508 Tel 714-653-4779 (SAN 212-744X).

Harrison House, Inc., *(Harrison Hse; 0-89274),* P.O. Box 35035, Tulsa, OK 74153 Tel 918-582-2126 (SAN 208-676X).

Harrow & Heston, *(Harrow & Heston),* Box 5434, Roessleville Station, NY 12205 (SAN 264-0872).

Harrowood Books, *(Harrowood Bks; 0-915180),* 3943 N. Providence Rd., Newtown Square, PA 19073 (SAN 207-1622).

Hart, R. S., *(R S Hart),* 6636 Wash. Blvd., Box 53, Elkridge, MD 21227 (SAN 214-2465).

Hart, Richard, *(R Hart; 0-9602100),* P.O. Box 598, Berkeley, CA 94701 (SAN 281-7705)P. O. Box 598, Berkeley, CA 94701 (SAN 281-7713).

Hart Associates, *(Hart; 0-8055),* 12 E. 12th St., New York, NY 10003 Tel 212-260-2430 (SAN 202-2761).

Hart Brothers Publishing, *(Hart Bro Pub; 0-910077),* P.O. Box 205, Williston, VT 05495 Tel 802-879-4670 (SAN 240-8562).

Hart Graphics, *(Hart Graphics; 0-9605422),* P.O. Box 968, Austin, TX 78767 (SAN 217-1074).

Hartley Enterprises, *(Hartley Ent),* P.O. Box 701, Rancho Mirage, CA 92270 (SAN 209-3278).

Hartley House, *(Hartley Hse; 0-937518),* P.O. Box 1352, Hartford, CT 06143 Tel 203-525-2376 (SAN 220-0570).

Hartline Publications, *(Hartline Pub),* P. O. Box 16782, Phoenix, AZ 85011 (SAN 270-6830).

Hartmore House, *(Hartmore),* Dist. by: Hartmore House, 1363 Fairfield Ave., Bridgeport, CT 06605 (SAN 206-8729).

Hartnell Pubns., *(Hartnell Pubns; 0-9605754),* 195 Hartnell Place, Sacramento, CA 95825 (SAN 219-7863).

Hart's Spring Works, *(Harts Spring Wks; 0-943096),* Box 1609, Suite 200, 533 Sutter, San Francisco, CA 94102 Tel 415-982-8043 (SAN 240-3846).

Hartung, Marion T., *(Hartung; 0-913910),* 814 Constitution St., Emporia, KS 66801 Tel 316-342-6200 (SAN 206-5355).

Harvard Business School, Division of Research, *(Harvard Busn; 0-87584),* Soldiers Field, Boston, MA 02174 (SAN 202-277X); Dist. by: Harvard University Press, 79 Garden St., Cambridge, MA 02138 Tel 617-495-2480 (SAN 200-2043).

Harvard Common Press, *(Harvard Common Pr; 0-916782),* 535 Albany St., Boston, MA 02172 Tel 617-423-5803 (SAN 208-6778); Orders to: Independent Publishers Group, C/O David White, Inc., One Pleasant Ave., Port Washington, NY 11050 (SAN 208-6786).

Harvard East Asian Institute, *(Harvard E Asian),* Harvard University, 1737 Cambridge St., Cambridge, MA 02138 (SAN 286-6900); Dist. by: Harvard University Press, 79 Garden St., Cambridge, MA 02138 (SAN 286-6919).

Harvard Educational Review, *(Harvard Educ Rev; 0-916690),* 13 Appian Way, Cambridge, MA 02138 Tel 617-495-3432 (SAN 208-3426).

Harvard Group, Inc., The, *(Harvard Group; 0-942408),* Harvard Sq., P.O. Box 223, Cambridge, MA 02138 Tel 201-778-0162 (SAN 238-163X).

Harvard Law School, International Tax Program, *(Harvard Law Intl Tax; 0-915506),* Harvard Law School, Cambridge, MA 02138 Tel 617-495-4407 (SAN 207-3803).

Harvard Ukrainian Research Institute, *(Harvard Ukrainian; 0-916458),* 1583 Mass. Ave., Cambridge, MA 02138 Tel 617-495-3692 (SAN 208-967X).

Harvard Univ., Ctr. for International Affairs, *(Harvard U Intl Aff; 0-87674),* Coolidge Hall-International Studies, 1737 Cambridge St., Cambridge, MA 02138 Tel 617-495-2137 (SAN 204-0271).

Harvard Univ., Dept. of Romance Languages & Literatures, *(Harvard U Romance Lang & Lit; 0-940940),* Cambridge, MA 02138 Tel 617-495-2546 (SAN 217-3786); 201 Boylston Hall, Cambridge, ; c/o French Forum, Inc., P.O. Box 5108, Lexington, KY 40505 Tel 606-299-9530 (SAN 208-4996).

Harvard Univ. Press, *(Harvard U Pr; 0-674),* 79 Garden St., Cambridge, MA 02138 Tel 617-495-2600 (SAN 281-7721); Orders to: Customer Service, Harvard Univ. Press, 79 Garden St., Cambridge, MA 02138 Tel 617-495-2480 (SAN 281-773X).

Harvest Books See Harcourt Brace Jovanovich, Inc.

Harvest House Pubs., Inc., *(Harvest Hse; 0-89081),* 1075 Arrowsmith, Eugene, OR 97402 Tel 503-343-0123 (SAN 207-4745).

Harvest Moon Books, *(Harvest Moon; 0-9602886),* P.O. Box 172, Riverside, CA 92502 Tel 714-682-4907 (SAN 213-0750).

Harvest Press, *(Harvest Pr; 0-917332),* 480 Nelson Road, Santa Cruz, CA 95066 Tel 408-335-5015 (SAN 208-6794).

Harvest Press, Inc., *(Harvest Pr Texas; 0-930718),* P.O. Box 7971, Waco, TX 76701 Tel 817-752-5544 (SAN 211-4038).

Harvest Pubns., *(Harvest Pubns; 0-939074),* Box 1337, Goleta, CA 93116 Tel 805-685-1358 (SAN 209-2964).

Harvestman & Associates, *(Harvestman),* P.O. Box 271, Menlo Park, CA 94025 Tel 415-327-4190 (SAN 212-1662).

Harvey, Arnold, Associates, *(A Harvey; 0-913014),* P.O. Box 89, Commack, NY 11725 Tel 516-543-2738 (SAN 204-028X).

Harvey House, Pubs., *(Harvey; 0-8178),* 20 Waterside Plaza, New York, NY 10010 Tel 212-889-9520 (SAN 202-2796); Orders to: 128 W. River St., Chippewa Falls, WI 54729 Tel 715-723-2814 (SAN 202-280X).

Harvey Woman's Club, *(Harvey Womans; 0-9611654),* P.O. Box 1058, Palestine, TX 75801 Tel 214-723-4103 (SAN 285-306X).

Harwal Publishing Co., *(Harwal Pub Co; 0-932036),* 207 W. Baker St., Media, PA 19063 Tel 215-566-7560 (SAN 285-0230); Orders to: 330 W. State St., Media, PA 19063 Tel 215-565-0746 (SAN 285-0249).

Harwood Academic Pubs., *(Harwood Academic; 3-7186),* P.O. Box 786, Cooper Sta., New York, NY 10276 Tel 212-242-4464 (SAN 213-9294).

Haskell Booksellers, Inc., *(Haskell; 0-8383),* P.O. Box FF, Blythebourne Sta., Brooklyn, NY 11219 Tel 212-435-0500 (SAN 202-2818).

Haskett Specialties, *(Haskett Spec; 0-9609724),* P.O. Box 143, Mooresville, IN 46158 Tel 317-831-1668 (SAN 270-6946).

Hass, Ed, *(E Hass; 0-9611166),* 966 Ponderosa Ave., Sunnyvale, CA 94086 Tel 408-735-7188 (SAN 277-6758).

Hastings Books, *(Hastings Bks),* 111 Coulter Ave., Ardmore, PA 19003 Tel 215-649-1227 (SAN 205-048X).

Hastings Center, Institute of Society, Ethics & Life Sciences, *(Hastings Ctr Inst Soc; 0-916558),* 360 Broadway, Hastings-on-Hudson, NY 10706 Tel 914-478-0500 (SAN 211-2426).

Hastings House Pubs., Inc., *(Hastings; 0-8038),* 10 E. 40th St., New York, NY 10016 Tel 212-689-5400 (SAN 213-9561).

Hatfield, Glen, *(Hatfield; 0-9600216),* P.O. Box 329, Kankakee, IL 60901 Tel 815-939-1818 (SAN 204-0298).

Haunted Bookshop, The, *(Haunted Bk Shop; 0-940882),* 214 Ste. Francis St., Mobile, AL 36602 Tel 205-432-6606 (SAN 223-1344).

Haupt, Rudy, & Co., *(R Haupt; 0-935274),* 231 Hay Ave., Johnstown, PA 15902 Tel 814-536-7536 (SAN 213-3164).

Havemeyer Books, *(Havemeyer Bks; 0-911397),* 12 Havemeyer Place, Greenwich, CT 06830 Tel 203-661-3823 (SAN 270-6962).

Haverford House, *(Haverford; 0-910702),* 34 West Ave., Wayne, PA 19087 Tel 215-688-5191 (SAN 204-0301).

Havertown Books, *(Havertown Bks),* P.O. Box 711, Havertown, PA 19083 (SAN 208-4384).

Hawaiian Service, Inc., *(Hawaiian Serv; 0-930492),* P.O. Box 2835, Honolulu, HI 96803 Tel 808-841-0134 (SAN 205-0463).

Hawk-Island Associates, *(Hawk-Island; 0-937342),* 2630 N. 8th St., Sheboygan, WI 53081 (SAN 215-0794).

Hawkes Publishing Inc., *(Hawkes Pub Inc; 0-89054),* 3775 S. 500 West, Box 15711, Salt Lake City, UT 84115 Tel 801-262-5555 (SAN 205-6232).

Hawkins, Beverly, Studio & Gallery, Inc., *(B Hawkins Studio; 0-9608084),* 102 Old St., Petersburg, VA 23803 (SAN 240-1495).

Hawkins, Robert L., *(R L Hawkins),* 525 S. 13 Hiway, Lexington, MO 64067 Tel 816-259-6551 (SAN 212-6648).

Hawkline Books, *(Hawkline Bks; 0-9609860),* 520 Military Way, Palo Alto, CA 94306 Tel 415-493-4387 (SAN 270-7020).

Hawkshead Book Distribution Co., *(Hawkshead Bk),* P.O. Box 294, Old Westbury, NY 11568 Tel 516-333-6325 (SAN 212-8217).

Hawley, W. M., *(Hawley; 0-910704),* 8200 Gould Ave., Hollywood, CA 90046 Tel 213-654-1573 (SAN 204-0328).

Hawley, Cooke, & Orr Pubs., *(Hawley Cooke Orr; 0-937246),* P.O. Box 6052, Louisville, KY 40207 Tel 502-893-0133 (SAN 214-3844).

Haworth Press Inc., The, *(Haworth Pr; 0-917724; 0-86656),* 28 E. 22nd St., New York, NY 10010 Tel 212-228-2800 (SAN 211-0156).

Hawthorn Books See Dutton, E. P.

Hayden Book Co., Inc., *(Hayden; 0-8104),* 50 Essex St., Rochelle Park, NJ 07662 Tel 201-843-0550 (SAN 200-2094).

Hayden House Publishing Co., *(Hayden Hse; 0-937602),* 68 Mitchell Blvd., San Rafael, CA 94903 Tel 415-472-5233 (SAN 215-224X).

Hayes, Gordon, *(G H Hayes; 0-9605880),* 3626 Meyler St., San Pedro, CA 90731 Tel 213-833-7066 (SAN 216-6798).

Hayes Publishing Co., Inc., *(Hayes; 0-910728),* 6304 Hamilton Ave., Cincinnati, OH 45224 (SAN 277-6154).

Hayfield Publishing Co., *(Hayfield Pub; 0-913856),* Box 11, Hayfield, MN 55940 Tel 507-477-2511 (SAN 204-0336).

Haymark Pubns., *(Haymark; 0-933910),* P.O. Box 243, Fredericksburg, VA 22401 Tel 703-373-1144 (SAN 213-2508).

Haynes Pubns., Inc., *(Haynes Pubns),* 861 Lawrence Dr., Newbury Park, CA 91320 Tel 805-498-6703 (SAN 212-1611).

Hays, Rolfes & Assocs., *(Hays Rolfes; 0-9602448),* P.O. Box 11465, Memphis, TN 38111 Tel 901-682-8128 (SAN 212-6656).

Haywire Press, *(Haywire Pr),* 44 S. Mountain Rd., New City, NY 10956 Tel 914-634-5214 (SAN 210-8100).

Haywood Press, *(Haywood Pr; 0-9609892),* Box 176, Brooklyn, NY 11205 Tel 212-891-6460 (SAN 270-7055).

Hazardous Materials Control Research Institute, *(Hazardous Mat Control),* 9300 Columbia Boulevard, Silver Spring, MD 20910 Tel 301-587-9390 (SAN 276-9433).

Hazelden Foundation, *(Hazelden; 0-89486),* Box 176, Center City, MN 55012 Tel 612-257-4010 (SAN 209-4010).

Hazlett Printing & Publishing, Inc., *(Hazlett Print; 0-940588),* 2135 1st Ave., SO, St. Petersburg, FL 33712 (SAN 264-0902).

Headwaters Press, *(Headwaters Pr; 0-932428),* P.O. Box 727, Staunton, VA 24401 Tel 703-885-8077 (SAN 211-9609).

Headway Pubns., *(Headway Pubns; 0-89537),* 1700 Port Manleigh Circle, Newport Beach, CA 92660 Tel 714-640-0736 (SAN 210-4342).

Heahstan Press, The, *(Heahstan Pr; 0-9604244),* P.O. Box 954, Denton, TX 76202 (SAN 214-3127).

Healing Yourself, *(Healing Yourself),* P.O. Box 952, Vashon, WA 98070 (SAN 209-0287); Orders to: P.O. Box 752, Vashon, WA 98070 (SAN 209-0287).

Health Administration Press, *(Health Admin Pr; 0-914904)*, 1021 E. Huron St., Univ. of Michigan, Ann Arbor, MI 48109 Tel 313-764-1380 (SAN 207-0464).

Health Communications, Inc., *(Health Comm; 0-932194)*, 2119-A Hollywood Blvd., Hollywood, FL 33020 Tel 305-920-9435 (SAN 212-100X).

Health Education Aids, *(Health Ed Aids; 0-89829)*, 8 S. Lakeview Dr., Goddard, KS 67052 Tel 316-794-2216 (SAN 220-6323).

Health Education & Life Expansion Research, *(Health Ed & Life Exp Res; 0-9607142)*, Box 70027, Los Angeles, CA 90070 Tel 213-383-8606 (SAN 238-9878).

Health Education Training and Administration Consortium, Inc., The, *(Health Ed Train; 0-911067)*, 1764 Bising Ave., No. 4, North College Hill, OH 45239 Tel 513-931-9227 (SAN 270-711X).

Health Information Library, Div. of Krames Communication, *(Health Info Lib; 0-911931)*, 312 90th St., Daly City, CA 94015 Tel 415-994-8800 (SAN 264-2816).

Health Plus, Pubs., *(Health Plus; 0-932090)*, P.O. Box 22001, Phoenix, AZ 85028 Tel 602-992-0589 (SAN 211-4984).

Health Research Services & Analysis, Inc., *(Health Res Serv; 0-9607292)*, 6208 Montgomery Blvd. NE, Albuquerque, NM 87109 Tel 505-884-4172 (SAN 239-2240).

Health Science, *(Health Sci; 0-87790)*, P.O. Box 7, Santa Barbara, CA 93102 Tel 805-968-1028 (SAN 208-1016).

Health Science Pr., *(Health Sci Pr; 0-909337)*, 515 Madison Ave., New York, NY 10022 (SAN 214-1795).

Health Sciences Communications Association, *(Health Sci Comm)*, 2343 N 115 St, Wauwatosa, WI 53226 (SAN 224-2915).

Healthcare Financial Management Assn., *(Healthcare Fin Man Assn; 0-930228)*, 1900 Spring Rd., Suite 500, Oak Brook, IL 60521 Tel 312-655-4600 (SAN 207-5911).

Healthful Living Publishers, *(Healthful Liv Pubs; 0-913047)*, 17848 C.R. 126 P.O. Box 563, Goshenox 563, IN 46526 (SAN 283-913X).

HealthRight Publishing, *(HealthRight; 0-911433)*, 1230 Grant Ave., No.552, San Francisco, CA 94133 Tel 415-391-2141 (SAN 270-7209).

Healthstyles Pubns., *(Healthstyles Pubns; 0-941344)*, 4005 W. 65th St., Edina, MN 55435 Tel 612-926-8600 (SAN 238-9894).

Healthworks, Inc., *(Healthworks; 0-938480)*, 31582 S. Coast Hwy., S. Laguna, CA 92677 (SAN 215-7721).

Hearne-Books U.S.A., *(Hearne Bks; 0-918760)*, 22 River St., Braintree, MA 02184 Tel 617-843-5702 (SAN 210-4350).

Hearst Books, Div. of the Hearst Corp., *(Hearst Bks; 0-910992; 0-87851; 0-910990)*, 224 W. 57th St., Rm. 307, New York, NY 10019 Tel 212-262-8605 (SAN 202-2842); Orders to: P.O. Box 1406, Radio City Sta., New York, NY 10019 (SAN 202-2850).

Heart of America Press, *(Heart Am Pr; 0-913902)*, P.O. Box 9808, 10101 Blue Ridge Blvd., Kansas City, MO 64134 Tel 816-761-0080 (SAN 204-0379).

Heart of the Lakes Publishing, *(Heart of the Lakes; 0-932334)*, Interlaken, NY 14847-0299 Tel 607-532-4204 (SAN 213-0769).

Hearthstone Press, *(Hearthstone; 0-937308)*, 708 Inglewood Dr., Broderick, CA 95605 Tel 916-372-0250 (SAN 209-4460).

Hearthstone Pubns., *(Hearth Pub; 0-943098)*, P.O. Box 2002, Darien, CT 06820 Tel 203-734-5398 (SAN 240-3854).

Heartwork Press, *(Heartwork Pr; 0-935598)*, 220 Redwood Hwy., Mill Valley, CA 94941 (SAN 214-025X).

Heath, D.C., Co., Div. of Raytheon Co., *(Heath; 0-669)*, 125 Spring St., Lexington, MA 02173 Tel 617-862-6650 (SAN 213-7526); Orders to: D. C. Heath & Co., Distribution Ctr., 2700 Richardt Ave., Indianapolis, IN 46219 Tel 317-359-5585 (SAN 202-2885). *Imprints:* Collamore Press (Collamore).

Heathcote Pubs., *(Heathcote; 0-9602350)*, P.O. Box 135, Monmouth Jct., NJ 08852 Tel 201-297-4891 (SAN 212-5358).

Heather Foundation, *(Heather Foun; 0-9600300)*, P.O. Box 48, San Pedro, CA 90733 Tel 213-831-6269 (SAN 204-0387).

Heatherdown Press, *(Heatherdown Pr; 0-9610038)*, 3450 Brantford Rd., Toledo, OH 43606 Tel 419-877-0073 (SAN 270-7284).

Hebraeus Press, *(Hebraeus Pr; 0-910511)*, 1217 Cedar Ave., Provo, UT 84604 Tel 801-347-8839 (SAN 260-0692).

Hebrew Publishing Co., *(Hebrew Pub; 0-88482)*, 100 Water St., Brooklyn, NY 11201 Tel 212-858-6928 (SAN 201-5404).

Hebrew Union College Press, *(Hebrew Union Coll Pr; 0-87820)*, Clifton Ave., Cincinnati, OH 45220 (SAN 220-6358).

Hebrew Union College Press See Ktav Publishing House, Inc.

Hedgehog Press, *(Hedgehog Pr; 0-943486)*, 3041 Lopez, Pebble Beach, CA 93953 Tel 408-649-3415 (SAN 240-6705).

Hedman Stenotype, *(Hedman Steno; 0-939056)*, 1158 W. Armitage Ave., Chicago, IL 60614 Tel 312-871-6500 (SAN 239-7579).

Heffron, Dan, Enterprises, *(Heffron Ent; 0-9605104)*, P.O. Box 9019, Cleveland, OH 44137 (SAN 216-0366).

Heian International Publishing, Inc., *(Heian Intl; 0-89346)*, P.O. Box 2402, South San Francisco, CA 94083-2402 Tel 415-467-0222 (SAN 213-2036).

Heidelberg Graphics, *(Heidelberg Graph; 0-918606)*, P.O. Box 3606, Chico, CA 95927 (SAN 211-5654).

Heidelberg Pubs., Inc., *(Heidelberg Pubs; 0-913206)*, 1003 Brown Bldg., Austin, TX 78701 (SAN 201-5501).

Heidenreich House, *(Heidenreich; 0-9600428)*, 5012 Oak Point Way, Fair Oaks, CA 95628 Tel 916-961-3297 (SAN 204-0395).

Heimburger House Publishing Co., *(Heimburger Hse Pub; 0-911581)*, 310 Lathrop Ave., River Forest, IL 60305 Tel 312-366-1973 (SAN 264-0929).

Hein, William S., & Co., Inc., *(W S Hein; 0-89941; 0-930342)*, Hein Bldg. 1285 Main St., Buffalo, NY 14209 Tel 716-882-2600 (SAN 210-9212).

Heineman, James H., Inc., Pub., *(Heineman; 0-87008)*, 475 Park Ave., New York, NY 10022 Tel 212-688-2028 (SAN 204-0409).

Heinemann Educational Books Inc., *(Heinemann Ed; 0-435)*, 4 Front St., Exeter, NH 03833 Tel 603-778-0534 (SAN 210-5829).

Heinle & Heinle Pubs., Inc., *(Heinle & Heinle; 0-8384)*, 286 Congress St., Boston, MA 02210 Tel 617-451-1940 (SAN 216-0730).

Heinman, W.S., Imported Books, *(Heinman)*, 225 W. 57th St., Rm. 404, New York, NY 10019 Tel 212-757-7628 (SAN 121-6201); P.O. Box, Ansonia Sta., New York, NY 10019 (SAN 121-6201).

Heirlomm Pubns. Ltd., *(Heirloom Pubns; 0-9609488)*, P.O. Box 667, Cedar Rapids, IA 52406 Tel 319-366-4690 (SAN 270-7403).

Heironymous Tuesday Press, *(Hieronymous Tues Pr; 0-9610086)*, P.O. Box 914, Danville, CA 94526 Tel 415-820-4289 (SAN 270-7411).

Heirs International, *(Heirs Intl; 0-915970)*, 3562 18 St., San Francisco, CA 94110 Tel 415-861-8375 (SAN 207-8414).

Helander, Joel E., *(Helander; 0-935600)*, 36 Norton Ave., Guilford, CT 06437 Tel 203-453-6626 (SAN 213-7445).

Heldref Pubns., *(Heldref Pubns; 0-916882)*, 4000 Albemarle St., N.W., Washington, DC 20016 Tel 202-362-6445 (SAN 208-0788).

Helicon House, *(Helicon House)*, P. O. Box 1254, La Jolla, CA 92038 (SAN 221-0983).

Helikon Press, *(Helikon NY; 0-914496)*, 120 W. 71st St., New York, NY 10023 Tel 212-873-6884 (SAN 201-9175).

Helios, *(Helios Vt; 0-87931)*, Pawlet, VT 05761 Tel 802-325-3360 (SAN 204-0425).

Helios Book Publishing Co., Div. of International Media, Inc., *(Helios; 0-87037)*, 127 Madison Ave., Fourth Fl., New York, NY 10016 Tel 212-679-3111 (SAN 206-8397).

Helix House Pubs., *(Helix Hse; 0-930866)*, 9231 Molly Woods Ave., La Mesa, CA 92041 (SAN 211-3171).

Hellcoal Press, *(Hellcoal Pr; 0-916912)*, P.O. Box 5, S.A.O., Brown Univ., Providence, RI 02912 Tel 401-863-2341 (SAN 208-6808).

Hellenes-English Biblical Foundation, *(Hellenes; 0-910710)*, P.O. Box 10412, Jackson, MS 39209 (SAN 204-0433).

Hellenic College Press, Div. of Holy Cross Orthodox Press, *(Hellenic Coll Pr; 0-916586)*, 50 Goddard Ave., Brookline, MA 02146 (SAN 213-6694).

Heller, Marjorie K., *(M K Heller; 0-915362)*, Box 78, Bayside, NY 11361 Tel 212-229-7715 (SAN 209-066X).

Helm Publishing, *(Helm Pub)*, 4316 Hilldale Ave., Las Vegas, NV 89104 Tel 702-456-1580 (SAN 211-4240).

H.E.L.P Books, Inc., *(HELP Bks; 0-918500)*, 1201 E. Calle Elena, Tucson, AZ 85718 Tel 602-297-6452 (SAN 209-665X).

Hemenway Corp., *(Hemenway; 0-935026)*, 101 Tremont St., Suite 208, Boston, MA 02108 Tel 617-426-1931 (SAN 213-3172).

Hemingway, Donald W., *(D W Hemingway)*, 309 S. Tenth W., Salt Lake City, UT 84104 (SAN 220-2506); Dist. by: George Mc. Co. Inc., P.O. Box 15671, Salt Lake City, UT 84115 (SAN 220-2514).

Hemisphere House Books, *(Hemisphere Hse; 0-930770)*, P.O. Box 1934, Corpus Christi, TX 78403 (SAN 211-0717).

Hemisphere Pubns., *(Hemisphere NY; 0-917292)*, 20 Elm St., Franklinville, NY 14737 Tel 716-676-2462 (SAN 208-6816).

Hemisphere Publishing Corp., *(Hemisphere Pub; 0-89116)*, 1010 Vermont Ave., N.W., Washington, DC 20005 Tel 202-783-3958 (SAN 207-4001); Orders to: 19 W. 44th St., New York, NY 10036 Tel 212-921-0606 (SAN 207-401X).

Hemlock Press, *(Hemlock Pr)*, Rte. 1, Box 549, Alburtis, PA 18011 Tel 215-682-7332 (SAN 208-0842).

Hemlock Society, *(Hemlock Soc; 0-9606030)*, P.O. BOX 66218, Los Angeles, CA 90066 Tel 213-391-1871 (SAN 216-8995).

Hemphill Publishing Co., *(Hemphill; 0-914696)*, 1400 Wathen Ave., Austin, TX 78703 Tel 512-476-9422 (SAN 204-0441).

Hemphills, The, *(The Hemphills; 0-9600948)*, P.O. Box 8302, Nashville, TN 37207 Tel 615-865-7100 (SAN 208-4856).

Hempstead House, *(Hempstead House; 0-940094)*, 1019 Jerome St., Houston, TX 77009 Tel 713-864-6130 (SAN 220-2271).

Hendel & Reinke, *(Hendel; 0-918656)*, 2800 Route St., Suite 247A, Dallas, TX 75201 (SAN 209-4479).

Hendershot Bibliography, *(Hendershot; 0-911832)*, 4114 Ridgewood Dr., Bay City, MI 48706 Tel 517-684-3148 (SAN 204-045X).

Henderson, T. Emmett, *(T E Henderson; 0-940590)*, 130 W. Main St., Middletown, NY 10940 Tel 914-343-1038 (SAN 208-0834).

Hendrick-Long Publishing Co., *(Hendrick-Long; 0-937620)*, 4811 W. Lovers Lane, Dallas, TX 75209 (SAN 281-7748); P.O. Box 12311, Dallas, TX 75225 (SAN 281-7756).

Hendricks House, Inc., *(Hendricks House; 0-87532)*, Main St., Putney, VT 05346 (SAN 206-9830).

Hendricks Publishing, *(Hendricks Pub; 0-943764)*, P.O. Box 724026, Atlanta, GA 30339 (SAN 264-0945).

Henke, Mary Alice, *(Henke M A; 0-9611032)*, Box 351, Enders, NE 69027 Tel 308-882-4004 (SAN 282-8782).

Hennepin Hall Publications, *(Hennepin Hall; 0-912243)*, P.O. Box 84, Rockford, IL 61105 Tel 815-877-5345 (SAN 265-1289).

Hennessey & Ingalls, Inc., *(Hennessey; 0-912158)*, 10814 W. Pico Blvd., Los Angeles, CA 90064 Tel 213-474-2541 (SAN 213-9855).

Henry Art Gallery, *(Henry Art; 0-935558)*, DE-15, Univ. of Washington, Seattle, WA 98195 Tel 206-543-2280 (SAN 213-6708).

Henry Ford Museum Press See Edison Institute, The

Henry John & Co., *(Henry John & Co; 0-937028)*, P.O. Box 10235, Dillingham, AK 99576 Tel 907-842-5458 (SAN 214-3909).

Hen's Publishing Co., *(Hen's Pub; 0-9607820)*, P.O. Box 13112, Portland, OR 97213 (SAN 239-5533).

Heptangle Books, *(Heptangle; 0-935214)*, P.O. Box 283, Berkeley Heights, NJ 07922 Tel 201-647-4449 (SAN 210-6329).

Her Publishing Co., Inc., *(Her Pub Co; 0-930676)*, P.O. Box 1168, Oakwood Shopping Ctr., Gretna, LA 70053 (SAN 211-0164).

Herald Books, *(Herald Bks; 0-910714),* P.O. Box 17, Pelham, NY 10803 Tel 914-576-1121 (SAN 202-2893).

Herald House, *(Herald Hse; 0-8309),* Drawer HH, 3225 S. Noland Rd., Independence, MO 64055 Tel 816-252-5010 (SAN 202-2907).

Herald Press, *(Herald Pr; 0-8361),* 616 Walnut Ave., Scottdale, PA 15683 Tel 412-887-8500 (SAN 202-2915).

Herbal Perception, the, *(Herbal Perception; 0-943638),* Box 143, Mt. Clemens, MI 48043 Tel 313-652-0597 (SAN 238-2997).

Herbert Pubs., *(Herbert Pubs; 0-935780),* P.O. Box 162, Mount Laurel, NJ 08054 (SAN 214-0268).

Here's Life Pubs., Inc., *(Heres Life; 0-89840),* P.O. Box 1576, San Bernardino, CA 92402 Tel 714-886-7981 (SAN 212-4254).

Heresy Press, *(Heresy Pr; 0-9603276),* 713 Paul St., Newport News, VA 23605 (SAN 213-2516).

Heretic Books, *(Heretic Bks),* 175 Fifth Ave., Ste 814, New York, NY 10010 (SAN 240-8570); Dist. by: Flatiron Book Distributors, Inc., 175 Fifth Ave., Suite 814, New York, NY 10010 (SAN 240-9917).

Heritage Arts, *(Heritage Arts; 0-911029),* 1807 Prarie Ave., Downers Grove, IL 60515 Tel 312-964-1194 (SAN 270-7543).

Heritage Associates, Inc., *(Heritage Assocs; 0-910467),* 5409 Eakes Rd. Nw, Albuquerque, NM 87107 Tel 505-344-2621 (SAN 260-0706).

Heritage Books, *(Heritage Kansas),* Rte. 6 Box 25, Salina, KS 67401 Tel 913-827-7861 (SAN 212-0410).

Heritage Books, Inc., *(Heritage Bk; 0-917890),* 3602 Maureen Lane, Bowie, MD 20715 Tel 301-464-1159 (SAN 209-3367).

Heritage Foundation, *(Heritage Found; 0-89195),* 513 "C" St., N.E., Washington, DC 20002 Tel 202-546-4400 (SAN 209-3758).

Heritage Press, *(Heritage Pr; 0-935428),* P.O. Box 18625, Baltimore, MD 21216 (SAN 221-2684).

Heritage Press of Pacific, *(Heritage Pac; 0-9609132),* 1279-203 Ala Kapuna St., Honolulu, HI 96819 (SAN 264-0961).

Heritage Recording, *(Heritage Rec; 0-9602888),* Box 8132, St. Paul, MN 55113 Tel 612-484-7481 (SAN 211-1942).

Heritage Trails Press, *(Heritage Trails; 0-910083),* 94 Santa Maria Dr., Novato, CA 94947 Tel 415-897-5679 (SAN 240-8589).

Herman Publishing, Inc., *(Herman Pub; 0-89046; 0-89047),* 45 Newbury St., Boston, MA 02116 Tel 617-536-5810 (SAN 213-2044).

Hermes House Press, *(Hermes Hse; 0-9605008),* 127 W.15th St. Apt. 3F, New York, NY 10011 Tel 212-691-9773 (SAN 220-0589).

Hermitage, *(Hermitage MI; 0-938920),* 2269 Shadowood, Ann Arbor, MI 48104 (SAN 234-4413).

Hermosa Pubs., *(Hermosa; 0-913478),* P.O. Box 8172, Albuquerque, NM 87198 Tel 505-262-0440 (SAN 203-0012).

Herndon House, *(Herndon Hse; 0-915542),* P.O. Box 19938, Philadelphia, PA 19143 (SAN 281-7764); Dist. by: Lawrence-Hill Publishers, 520 Riverside Dr., Westport, CT 06880 Tel 203-226-9392 (SAN 214-1221).

Heron Books, *(Heron Bks; 0-89739),* P.O. Box 563, Portland, OR 97207 Tel 503-843-4939 (SAN 216-2539).

Heron House Pubs., *(Heron Hse; 0-916920),* 9610 Manitou Beach Dr., N.E., Bainbridge Island, WA 98110 Tel 206-842-3768 (SAN 208-4767).

Heron Press, The, *(Heron Pr; 0-931246),* 36 Bromfield St., Boston, MA 02108 Tel 617-482-3615 (SAN 206-5002).

Hershel Shanks, Publisher, *(Hershel Shanks Pubs; 0-9607092),* 3111 Rittenhouse St. NW, Washington, DC 20015 (SAN 237-9570).

Hershey, Virginia Sharpe, *(Hershey; 0-9605320),* 5325 Wikiup Bridgeway, Santa Rosa, CA 95404 (SAN 216-2024).

Hershey Foods Corporation, *(Hershey Foods; 0-943296),* 14 E. Chocolate Ave., Hershey, PA 17033 Tel 717-534-4912 (SAN 240-6713).

Herzl Press, *(Herzl Pr; 0-930832),* 515 Park Ave., New York, NY 10022 Tel 212-752-0600 (SAN 201-5374).

Hesher Publishing, *(Hesher Publ; 0-914013),* P.O. Box 402, Grand Island, NY 14072 Tel 716-773-1321 (SAN 286-7745).

Hesperian Foundation, The, *(Hesperian Found),* P.O. Box 1692, Palo Alto, CA 94302 (SAN 239-8567).

Heuristicus Publishing Co., *(Heuristicus; 0-934016),* 401 Tolbert St., Brea, CA 92621 (SAN 212-8551).

Heyday Books, *(Heyday Bks; 0-930588),* P.O. Box 9145, Berkeley, CA 94709 Tel 415-549-3564 (SAN 207-2351).

Heyden & Son, Inc., *(Heyden),* 247 S. 41st St., Philadelphia, PA 19104 Tel 215-382-6673 (SAN 213-2052).

Heyeck Press, The, *(Heyeck Pr),* 25 Patrol Court, Woodside, CA 94062 (SAN 217-7692).

Hi-Country Pubs., *(Hi Country Pubs; 0-938354),* P.O. Box 2362, Littleton, CO 80161 (SAN 216-0374).

Hi-Tech Publishing House, Inc., *(Hi Tech Pub; 0-912619),* P.O. Box 19656, Atlanta, GA 30325 (SAN 282-8006).

Hi Willow Research & Publishing, *(Hi Willow; 0-931510),* Box 1801, Fayetteville, AR 72702 Tel 501-575-5477 (SAN 211-3945).

Hiawatha Press, *(Hiawatha Pr; 0-930276),* 3505 St. Paul Ave., Minneapolis, MN 55416 (SAN 211-1799).

Pyramid Pubs. of Iowa, *(Hiawatha Pub),* P.O. Box 400, Perry, IA 50220 Tel 515-465-5010 (SAN 282-1966); Dist. by: Hiawatha Book Co., 7567 N.E. 102nd Ave., Bondurant, IA 50035 Tel 515-967-4025 (SAN 282-6496).

Hice, Bethell Whitley, *(B'W Hice; 0-9608046),* 1344 Fairview Ave., Bridgeport, WA 98813 (SAN 240-1509).

Hidden Assets, *(Hidden Assets),* P.O. Box 22011, Seattle, WA 98122 (SAN 239-4324).

Hidden House See Music Sales Corp.

Hidden Studio, *(Hidden Studio; 0-942722),* P.O. Box 55, Cornish, NH 03746 Tel 603-675-2770 (SAN 238-8480).

Hidden Valley Press, *(Hidden Valley; 0-935710),* 7051 P.O. Box 606, Poole Jones Rd., Frederick, MD 21701 Tel 301-662-6745 (SAN 213-5094).

Hiddigeigei Books, *(Hiddigeigei; 0-915560),* P.O. Box 5031, San Francisco, CA 94101 Tel 415-922-6114 (SAN 207-981X).

High Museum of Art, The, *(High Mus Art; 0-939802),* 1280 Peachtree St., Atlanta, GA 30309 Tel 304-892-3600 (SAN 216-9002).

High Pubs., *(High Pubs; 0-9604216),* 65 MacAlester Rd., Pueblo, CO 81001 Tel 303-542-7028 (SAN 281-7780); Orders to: P.O. Box 11411, Pueblo, CO 81001 (SAN 281-7799).

High Q Pubns., *(High Q; 0-931820),* P. O. Box 40H, Scarsdale, NY 10583 (SAN 207-3900).

High Rockies Enterprises, Inc., *(High Rockies; 0-937166),* P.O. Box 4809, Dept. 2002, Boulder, CO 80306 (SAN 215-1529).

High-Scope Educational Research Foundation, *(High-Scope; 0-931114),* 600 N. River St., Ypsilanti, MI 48197 (SAN 211-9617).

High Score, Inc., *(High Scores; 0-940182),* Box 522, Long Beach, MS 39560 (SAN 220-228X).

High Valley Press, *(High Valley Pr; 0-943640),* P.O. Box 63, Monte Vista, CO 81144 Tel 303-655-2504 (SAN 238-3012).

Highflyer Press, *(Highflyer Pr; 0-9605010),* 9704 E 26 st, Independence, Kansas City, MO 64052 (SAN 240-1517).

Highland Enterprises, *(Highland Ent; 0-913490),* Box 7000, Dallas, TX 75209 Tel 214-358-3456 (SAN 204-0514).

Highland House Pubs., Inc., *(Highland Hse; 0-918712),* 814 "H" St., N.W., Washington, DC 20001 (SAN 210-3583).

Highland House Publishing, Inc., *(Highland NY; 0-938988),* 74 Hunters Lane, Westbury, NY 11590 Tel 516-334-6497 (SAN 217-1082).

Highland Press, *(Highland Pr; 0-910722),* Rte. 3, Box 3125, Boerne, TX 78006 (SAN 204-0522).

Highlander Research & Education Center, *(Highlander; 0-9602226),* Rte. 3 Box 370, New Market, TN 37820 (SAN 212-6664).

Highlands Pub. Co., *(Highlands Pub; 0-943328),* 424 N.W. Lakeview Dr., Sebring, FL 33870 (SAN 240-4826).

Highlights for Children, Inc., *(Highlights; 0-87534; 0-87534),* 803 Church St., Honesdale, PA 18431 (SAN 281-7802)2300 W. Fifth Ave., P.O. Box 269, Columbus, OH 43216 (SAN 281-7810).

Hilarian Books, *(Hilarian Bks; 0-937168),* 535 Cordova Rd., Suite 422, Santa Fe, NM 87501 (SAN 238-8820).

Hilary House Pubs., Inc., *(Hilary Hse Pubs; 0-934464),* 1033 Channel Dr., Hewlett, NY 11557 Tel 213-2524).

Hill, Grace, *(G Hill; 0-9604506),* 3 Haskins Rd., Hanover, NH 03755 Tel 603-643-4059 (SAN 213-0785); Orders to: Fitness First, P.O. Box 279, Hanover, NH 03755 Tel 603-643-4059 (SAN 213-0793).

Hill, Lawrence, & Co., Inc., *(Lawrence Hill; 0-88208),* 520 Riverside Ave., Westport, CT 06880 Tel 203-226-9392 (SAN 214-1221).

Hill & Wang, Inc., Div. of Farrar, Straus & Giroux, Inc., *(Hill & Wang; 0-8090),* 19 Union Square W., New York, NY 10003 Tel 212-741-6900 (SAN 201-9299). *Imprints:* American Century Series (AmCen); Dramabooks (Drama); Mermaid Dramabooks (Mermaid); New Mermaid Dramabooks (New Mermaid); Terra Magica Books (Terra Magica)

Hill House Press, Pubs., *(Hill Hse Pr; 0-915602),* Old Lane & Chester Rd., Chester, VA 23831 Tel 804-262-0228 (SAN 201-5412).

Hill Junior College Press, *(Hill Jr Coll; 0-912172),* P.O. Box 619, Hillsboro, TX 76645 Tel 817-582-2555 (SAN 201-5463).

Hill Monastic Manuscript Library, *(Hill Monastic; 0-940250),* Bush Ctr., St. John's Univ., Collegeville, MN 56321 (SAN 238-8839).

Hill Pubns., *(Hill Pubns; 0-9602704),* P.O. Box 1236, Boca Raton, FL 33433 (SAN 213-0831).

Hillel Jewish Student Center, *(Hillel Jewish; 0-9611580),* 2615 Clifton Ave., Cincinnati, OH 45220 Tel 513-621-6459 (SAN 285-3175).

Hillhouse Press, *(Hillhouse; 0-910724),* Rutgers Center of Alcohol Studies. P.O. Box 969, Piscataway, NJ 08854 (SAN 204-0557).

Hills Medical/Sports, The, *(Hills Med),* 4615 Bee Cave Road, Austin, TX 78746 (SAN 264-097X).

Hillsdale Educational Pubs., *(Hillsdale Educ; 0-910726),* 39 North St., Box 245, Hillsdale, MI 49242 Tel 517-437-3179 (SAN 159-8759).

Hillside Books, *(Hillside Bks; 0-9611350),* P.O. Box 601, Lynnfield, MA 01940 (SAN 283-2364).

Hillside Press, *(Hillside; 0-918462),* P.O. Box 785, Vista, CA 92083 Tel 619-724-1853 (SAN 209-5661).

Hillside Press, The, *(Hillside Pr; 0-941066),* P.O. Box 42, Carversville, PA 18913 Tel 215-297-5800 (SAN 217-3808).

Hilltop Press, *(Hilltop Pr CA; 0-941470),* P.O. Box 14592, San Francisco, CA 94114 (SAN 239-1007).

Hilltop Pubns., Inc., *(Hilltop Pubns; 0-937782),* 127 E. 69th St., New York, NY 10021 (SAN 215-6547).

Hilltop Publishing Co. (PA), *(Hilltop Publishing; 0-913397),* P.O. Box 148, 446 Monroe Rd., Sarver, PA 16055-0148 Tel 412-353-1411 (SAN 285-8487).

Hilltop Publishing Company, *(Hilltop Pub Co; 0-912133),* P.O. Box 654, Sonoma, CA 95476 Tel 707-938-1846 (SAN 264-6706).

Hilmarton Manor Press, *(Hilmarton Manor),* 27 Harrison St., Bridgeport, CT 06604 (SAN 210-9751).

Himalaya House, *(Himalaya Hse; 0-89654),* P.O. Box 792, Wheat Ridge, CO 80033 Tel 303-423-3170 (SAN 211-1969).

Himalayan Publishers, *(Himalayan Intl Inst; 0-89389),* Rd 1, Box 88-A, Honesdale, PA 18431 Tel 717-253-3022 (SAN 207-5067).

Himmah, Gael, Publishing Co., *(Gael Himmah; 0-9600488),* P.O. Box 4591, Walnut Creek, CA 94596 Tel 415-939-3555 (SAN 203-4123).

Hinckley, Clive, *(C Hinckley; 0-9602984),* 106 E. Sunset Dr., S., Redlands, CA 92373 (SAN 207-480X).

Hine's Legal Directory Incorporated, *(Hines Legal Dir),* 443 Duane St, P O Box 71, Glen Ellyn, IL 60137 (SAN 226-4331).

Hinman, Marjory B., *(M B Hinman),* P. O. Box 345, Windsor, NY 13865 Tel 607-655-2011 (SAN 208-1237).

Hippocrene Books, Inc. B, *(Hippocrene Bks; 0-88254),* 171 Madison Ave., New York, NY 10016 Tel 212-685-4372 (SAN 213-2060).

Hired Hand Press, *(Hired Hand; 0-9602256),* P.O. Box 426, Dover, MA 02030 Tel 617-325-8155 (SAN 212-4262).

Hispanic Seminary of Medieval Studies, *(Hispanic Seminary),* 3734 Ross St., Madison, WI 53705 (SAN 207-9836).

Hispanic Society of America, *(Hispanic Soc; 0-87535),* 613 W. 155th St., New York, NY 10032 Tel 212-926-2234 (SAN 204-0573).

Historic Baltimore Society, Incorporated, *(Hist Balt Soc; 0-942460),* 4 Willow Brook Ct., Randallstown, MD 21133 Tel 301-922-3649 (SAN 285-0257); Orders to: Sydney Bragg, P.O. Box 19958, Hampden Station, Baltimore, MD 21211 Tel 301-338-7806 (SAN 285-0265).

Historic Cherry Hill, *(Hist Cherry Hill; 0-943366),* 523 1/2 South Pearl St., Albany, NY 12202 Tel 518-434-4791 (SAN 240-6721).

Historic Denver Inc., *(Hist Denver; 0-914248),* 770 Pennsylvania St., Denver, CO 80203 (SAN 220-651X).

Historic Heartland Assn., Inc., *(Hist Heart Assoc Inc; 0-910623),* P.O. Box 1, Brainerd, MN 56401 Tel 218-963-2218 (SAN 260-2024).

Historic Kansas City Foundation, *(Hist Kansas City; 0-913504),* 20 W. Ninth St., Kansas City, MO 64105 (SAN 239-4421).

Historic Key West Preservation Board, *(Hist Key West; 0-943528),* 500 Whitehead, Monroe County Courthouse, Key West, FL 33040 Tel 305-299-7511 (SAN 240-6748).

Historic New Orleans Collection, The, *(Historic New Orleans; 0-917860),* 533 Royal St., New Orleans, LA 70130 Tel 504-523-4662 (SAN 281-7829); Orders to: Susan R. Laudeman, the Shop at the Collection, 533 Royal St., New Orleans, LA 70130 Tel 504-523-4662 (SAN 281-7837).

Historic Photos, *(Historic Photos; 0-933206),* 3460 St. Helena Hwy. N., St. Helena, CA 94574 Tel 707-963-3117 (SAN 212-6672).

storic Preservation Assn. of Bourbon County, Inc., *(Historic Pres Bourbon; 0-9601568),* 502 S. National Ave., Fort Scott, KS 66701 Tel 316-223-3300 (SAN 211-528X).

Historic Pubns. of Fredericksburg, *(Hist Pubns; 0-9608408),* 300 Princess Anne St., Fredericksburg, VA 22401 Tel 703-371-0585 (SAN 240-673X).

Historic Savannah Foundation, Inc., *(Historic Sav; 0-9610106),* P.O. Box 1983, Savannah, GA 31402 Tel 912-233-7787 (SAN 270-7802).

Historical Airplanes, *(Hist Airplanes; 0-941068),* 10231 Slater Ave., No.216, P.O. Box 8394, Fountain Valley, CA 92708 Tel 714-979-7292 (SAN 217-3816).

Historical Aviation Album, *(Hist Aviation; 0-911852),* P.O. Box 33, Temple City, CA 91780 Tel 213-286-7655 (SAN 213-5108).

Historical Society of Baldwin Park, The, *(Historical Soc; 0-9607306),* 13009 Amar Rd., P.O. Box 1, Baldwin Park, CA 91706 Tel 213-337-3285 (SAN 239-2267).

Historical Society of Greater Lansing & Livingston County Historical Society, *(Hist Soc Lansing & Livingston Cnty Hist Soc; 0-9602844),* Box 12095, Lansing, MI 48901 Tel 517-321-1746 (SAN 213-0807).

Historical Society of Long Beach, The, *(Hist Soc Long Beach; 0-9610250),* 4600 Virginia Rd., Long Beach, CA 90807 Tel 213-426-2620 (SAN 264-0988).

Historical Society of Pennsylvania, *(Pa Hist Soc; 0-910732),* 1300 Locust St., Philadelphia, PA 19107 Tel 215-732-6200 (SAN 202-8441).

Historical Society of Rockland County, *(Rockland County Hist),* 20 Zukor Rd., New City, NY 10956 (SAN 211-4488).

Historical Society of Seattle & King County, *(Hist Soc Seattle; 0-939806),* 2161 E. Hamlin St., McCurdy Park, Seattle, WA 98112 Tel 206-324-1125 (SAN 216-7360).

Historical Society of Western Pennsylvania, *(Hist Soc West Pa; 0-936340),* 4338 Bigelow Blvd., Pittsburgh, PA 15213 (SAN 214-0276).

Historical Tales Ink, *(Hist Tales; 0-938404),* 7344 Rich St., Reynoldsburg, OH 43068 Tel 215-7748).

Hit Enterprises, *(Hit Ent; 0-935938),* 2945 Leticia Dr., Hacienda Heights, CA 91745 (SAN 213-7453).

Hive Publishing Co., *(Hive Pub; 0-87960),* P.O. Box 1004, Easton, PA 18042 Tel 215-258-6663 (SAN 202-2958).

H.K.R. Publishing CO., Inc., *(HKR Pub Co; 0-9609550),* Red Fox Trail, Hidden Valley, Rte.3, Box 344, Trinty, NC 27370 (SAN 270-7888).

H.Mark/Corbett, *(H Mark-Corbett; 0-9608152),* 34 Janet Dr., North Haven, CT 06473 (SAN 240-1487).

Ho, Steve, *(S Ho),* 4295 Okemos Rd., P.O. Box 99, Okemos, MI 48864 Tel 517-349-0795 (SAN 241-5372).

Ho, Van H., Assocs., *(V H Ho; 0-9602904),* P.O. Box 130, Harbor City, CA 90710 (SAN 213-5124).

Hobart & William Smith Colleges Press, *(Hobart & Wm Smith; 0-934888),* Hobart & William Smith Colleges, Geneva, NY 14456 (SAN 213-3202).

Hobbit House Press, *(Hobbit Hse; 0-9604300),* 5920 Dimmway, Richmond, CA 94805 (SAN 214-3852).

Hobby Horse Publishing, *(Hobby Horse; 0-935138),* 10091 Hobby Horse Lane, Box 54, Mentor, OH 44060 Tel 216-255-3434 (SAN 213-5132).

Hobby House Press, *(Hobby Hse; 0-87588),* 900 Frederick St., Cumberland, MD 21502 Tel 301-759-3770 (SAN 204-059X).

Hobby Publishing Service, *(Hobby Pub Serv; 0-917922),* 1318 Seventh St., N.W., Albuquerque, NM 87102 Tel 505-242-9465 (SAN 207-6330).

Hochberg, Bette, *(B Hochberg; 0-9600990),* 333 Wilkes Circle, Santa Cruz, CA 95060 Tel 408-427-2127 (SAN 281-7845); Dist. by: Textile Artists Supplies, 3006 San Pablo Ave., Berkeley, CA 94702 (SAN 282-6461).

Hoehler, Richard S., *(R S Hoehler; 0-930590),* P.O. Box 240, Conifer, CO 80433 Tel 303-838-4046 (SAN 204-6628).

Hoffman, Irwin J., Inc., *(I J Hoffman; 0-9604082),* 5734 S. Ivanhoe St., Denver, CO 80111 (SAN 214-0284).

Hoffman Enterprises, *(Hoffman Enter; 0-942662),* P.O. Box 2091, Manteca, CA 95336 Tel 209-239-5576 (SAN 241-5380).

Hoffman Pubns., Inc., *(Hoffman Pubns; 0-934890),* P.O. Box 11299, Fort Lauderdale, FL 33339 Tel 305-566-8401 (SAN 203-1264).

Hoffman Research Services, *(Hoffman Res; 0-910203),* P.O. Box 342, Rillton, PA 15678 (SAN 240-8597).

Hofmann, Margret, *(Hofmann; 0-9600166),* 2706 Nottingham Lane, Austin, TX 78704 Tel 512-444-8877 (SAN 204-0603).

Hogarth Press, *(Hogarth; 0-911776),* P.O. Box 10606, Honolulu, HI 96816 Tel 808-737-4150 (SAN 202-2966).

Hogfiddle Press, *(Hogfiddle Pr; 0-9608842),* 14 Mountain View, Rural Route 3, Box 43, Chester, VT 05143 Tel 802-875-2272 (SAN 262-0383).

Hogrefe, C. J., Inc., *(C J Hogrefe; 0-88937),* P.O. Box 51, Lewiston, NY 14092 (SAN 240-8600).

Holbrook Research Institute, *(Holbrook Res; 0-931248),* 57 Locust St., Oxford, MA 01540 Tel 617-987-0881 (SAN 211-1551).

Holden-Day, Inc., *(Holden-Day; 0-8162),* 4432 Telegraph Ave., Oakland, CA 94609 Tel 415-428-9400 (SAN 202-2990).

Holden Travel Research, *(Holden Pac; 0-910571),* 207 1/2 1st Ave. S., Seattle, WA 98104 Tel 206-624-3622 (SAN 260-0714).

Holiday House, Inc., *(Holiday; 0-8234),* 18 E. 53rd St., New York, NY 10022 Tel 212-688-0085 (SAN 202-3008).

Holland House Press, *(Holland Hse Pr; 0-913042),* Box 42, 6215 Six Mile Rd., Northville, MI 48167 Tel 313-836-0286 (SAN 204-0611).

Hollander Co., *(Hollander Co; 0-943032),* 12320 Wayzata Blvd., Minnetonka, MN 55343 Tel 612-544-4111 (SAN 240-3870).

Hollibaugh, Hiltrud, *(Hollibaugh; 0-939114),* P.O. Box 18753, Wichita, KS 67218 (SAN 219-7871).

Hollow Spring Press, *(Hollow Spring Pr),* R.D. 1, Chester, MA 01011 (SAN 213-8468).

Holloway House Publishing Co., *(Holloway; 0-87067),* 8060 Melrose Ave., Los Angeles, CA 90046 Tel 213-653-8060 (SAN 206-8451). *Imprints:* Melrose Square (Melrose Sq).

Holly Hill Pubs., *(Holly Hill; 0-9606508),* Holly Hill Box 723, Saluda, NC 28773 (SAN 219-3396).

Holly-Pix Music Publishing Co., *(Holly-Pix; 0-910736),* 4931 Alcove Ave N. Hollywood, Sherman Oaks, CA 91607 Tel 213-788-3668 (SAN 204-062X); Orders to: WIM, 2859 Holt Ave., Los Angeles, CA 90034 (SAN 204-0638).

Holly Press, The, *(Holly Pr; 0-935968),* P.O. Box 306, Hockessin, DE 19707 Tel 302-239-2416 (SAN 214-0292).

Hollybrooke Press, *(HollyBrooke Hse Inc; 0-933356),* 1605 E. Charleston Blvd., Las Vegas, NV 89110 (SAN 221-0932).

HollyDay Books, *(HollyDay; 0-943786),* 130 Ashley Rd., Hopkins, MN 55343 Tel 612-935-4562 (SAN 241-0281).

Hollym International Corp., *(Hollym Intl; 0-930878),* 18 Donald Place, Elizabeth, NJ 07208 (SAN 211-0172).

Hollywood Book Service, *(Hollywood; 0-910738),* 1654 N. Cherokee Ave., Hollywood, CA 90028 Tel 213-464-4164 (SAN 204-0646).

Hollywood Film Archive, *(Hollywd Film Arch; 0-913616),* 8344 Melrose Ave., Hollywood, CA 90069 Tel 213-933-3345 (SAN 206-7447).

Holman, A.J., Co., *(Holman; 0-87981),* 127 Ninth Ave., N., Nashville, TN 37234 Tel 615-251-2611 (SAN 202-3016).

Holmes, Oakley N., *(O N Holmes),* c/o Black Artists in America, Macgowan Enterprises, 39 Wilshire Dr., Spring Valley, NY 10977 (SAN 270-8000).

Holmes, Opal Laurel, Publisher, *(O L Holmes; 0-918522),* P.O. Box 2535, Boise, ID 83701 Tel 208-344-4517 (SAN 210-1017); Dist. by: Pub. Marketing Group, Baker & Taylor Co., P.O. Box 350, Momence, IL 60954 (SAN 169-2100).

Holmes & Meier Pubs., Inc., *(Holmes & Meier; 0-8419),* IUB Bldg., 30 Irving Place, New York, NY 10003 Tel 212-254-4100 (SAN 201-9280). *Imprints:* Africana Pub. (Africana).

Holmes Book Co., *(Holmes; 0-910740),* 274 14th St., Oakland, CA 94612 Tel 415-893-6860 (SAN 204-0654).

Holmes/Stacey, Enterprises, *(S Holmes Enter; 0-910681),* 6520 Selma Ave., Box 556, Hollywood, CA 90028 (SAN 264-0996).

Holmgangers Press, *(Holmgangers; 0-914974),* 95 Carson Ct. Shelter Cove, Whitethorn, CA 95489 Tel 707-986-7700 (SAN 206-5029).

Holocaust Library, *(Holocaust Lib; 0-89604),* 216 W. 18th St., New York, NY 10011 (SAN 215-0808); Dist. by: Schocken Books, 200 Madison Ave., New York, NY 10016 (SAN 213-7585).

Holsen Pubns., *(HolSen Pubns; 0-912897),* 125 E. 32nd St., Box 216, Durango, CO 81301 Tel 303-385-4800 (SAN 283-0434).

Holsinger, T. W., *(T W Holsinger; 0-9607966),* 150 S. Magnolia No.231, Anaheim, CA 92804 Tel 714-776-9362 (SAN 239-6548).

Holt-Atherton Pacific Center for Western Studies, *(Holt-Atherton; 0-931156),* Univ. of the Pacific, Stockton, CA 95211 Tel 209-946-2404 (SAN 203-1884).

Holt College Department *See* Holt, Rinehart & Winston, Inc.

Holt Information Systems *See* Holt, Rinehart & Winston, Inc.

Holt, Rinehart & Winston, Inc., *(HR&W; 0-03),* 383 Madison Ave., New York, NY 10017 Tel 212-872-2000 (SAN 200-2108). *Imprints:* Holt College Department (HoltC); Holt Information Systems (HIS).

Holtzman Press, Inc., *(Holtzman Pr; 0-941372),* 1225 Forest Ave., Evanston, IL 60202 Tel 312-475-4573 (SAN 238-8847).

Holy Cow! Press, *(Holy Cow; 0-930100),* P.O. Box 618, Minneapolis, MN 55440 (SAN 210-6302).

Holy Cross Orthodox Press, *(Holy Cross Orthodox; 0-916586),* 50 Goddard Ave., Brookline, MA 02146 Tel 617-232-4544 (SAN 208-6840).

Holy Trinity Monastery, *(Holy Trinity; 0-88465),* Jordanville, NY 13361 Tel 315-858-0940 (SAN 207-3501).

Home & School Press, *(Home & Sch; 0-910742),* P.O. Box 2055, Sun City, AZ 85372 Tel 602-974-3063 (SAN 204-0662).

Home-Business Press, *(Home-Busn Pr; 0-939626),* 10855 S. Western Ave., Chicago, IL 60643 (SAN 216-3942).

Home Company, The, *(Home Co),* 1717 Madison Ave., Loveland, CO 80537 Tel 303-669-2277 (SAN 283-2348).

Home Economics Education Assn., *(Home Econ Educ),* 1201 Sixteenth St., N.W., Rm. 232, Washington, DC 20036 Tel 202-822-7844 (SAN 207-3307).

Home Economist Consulting Services, *(Home Ec Consult; 0-941294),* P.O. Box 13112, Arlington, TX 76013 (SAN 238-8855).

Home Equity Co., *(Home Equity),* 600 S.W. Tenth St., Room 502, Portland, OR 97205 Tel 503-224-4522 (SAN 204-6670).

Home Index Pubns., *(Home Index Pubns; 0-912023),* P.O. Box 93, Clovis, CA 93613 Tel 209-224-5674 (SAN 281-7861); 4672 N. Barton, Fresno, CA 93726 (SAN 281-787X).

Home Mission Board of the Southern Baptist Convention, *(Home Mission; 0-937170),* 1350 Spring St., N.W., Atlanta, GA 30367 Tel 404-873-4041 (SAN 207-5318).

Home of Frosted Sunshine, The, *(Home Frosted; 0-937118),* R.R. 1, Box 612, Shermans Dale, PA 17090 Tel 717-432-8596 (SAN 215-7756).

Home on Arrange, *(Home on Arrange),* 2044 Paradise Dr., Tiburon, CA 94920 (SAN 216-2547).

Home Planners, Inc., *(Home Planners; 0-918894),* 23761 Research Dr., Farmington Hills, MI 48024 Tel 313-477-1850 (SAN 201-5382).

Home-Science Pubs., Subs. of Mitchell & Webb Inc., *(Home-Science; 0-943440),* 839 Beacon St., Boston, MA 02215 Tel 617-262-6980 (SAN 240-6756).

Homefront Graphics, *(Homefront Graphics; 0-939374),* P.O. Box 4114, Santa Barbara, CA 93103 Tel 805-965-7347 (SAN 216-4892).

Homestead Book Co., *(Homestead Bk; 0-930180),* 6101 22 Ave., N.W., Seattle, WA 98107 Tel 206-782-4532 (SAN 210-5365).

Homestead Books, *(Homestead NY),* Brookfield, NY 13314 (SAN 210-7422).

Homestead Publishers, *(Homestead MI; 0-913529),* 10084 Rushton Rd., S. Lyon, MI 48178 Tel 313-437-6782 (SAN 285-1679).

Homestead Publishers, *(Homestead Pub; 0-912714),* P.O. Box 219, Twentynine Palms, CA 92277 Tel 619-367-7726 (SAN 262-0391).

Homestead Publishing, *(Homestead WY; 0-943972),* Box 193, Moose, WY 83012 Tel 307-733-6287 (SAN 241-029X).

Homeward Press, *(Homeward Pr; 0-938392),* P.O. Box 2307, Berkeley, CA 94702 (SAN 220-2522).

Homosexual Information Center, Inc., *(Homosexual Info),* 6758 Hollywood Blvd., No. 208, Los Angeles, CA 90028 Tel 213-464-8431 (SAN 210-8127).

Hondale, Inc., *(Hondale; 0-942462),* 553 Auburndale Ave., Akron, OH 44313 Tel 216-836-3660 (SAN 238-1664).

Honduras Information Service, *(Honduras Info; 0-937538),* 501 Fifth Ave., Suite 1611, New York, NY 10017 Tel 212-490-0766 (SAN 213-084X).

Honey Hill Publishing Co., *(Honey Hill; 0-937642),* 1022 Bonham Terrace, Austin, TX 78704 Tel 512-442-4177 (SAN 220-0600).

Honnold Library for the Associated Colleges, *(Honnold Lib; 0-937368),* Claremont, CA 91711 (SAN 264-1011).

Honor Books, *(Honor Bks; 0-931446),* P.O. Box 641, Rapid City, SD 57709 Tel 605-348-9734 (SAN 208-0877).

Hood, Alan C., Publisher, *(A C Hood Pub; 0-911469),* P.O. Box 1218, Brattleboro, VT 05301 Tel 802-257-4151 (SAN 270-8221); Dist. by: Backcountry Publications, Inc., P.O. Box 175, Woodstock, VT 05091 (SAN 238-1427).

Hooper, Doug, *(D Hooper; 0-9604702),* P.O. Box 792, Danville, CA 94526 (SAN 217-2402).

Hoover Institution Press, *(Hoover Inst Pr; 0-8179),* Stanford University, Stanford, CA 94305 Tel 415-497-3373 (SAN 202-3024) Micropublishing of 20th-century works on social, political & economic change.

Hope Enterprises of Jacksonville, Florida, Inc., *(Hope Ent Fla; 0-932650),* Box 8401, Jacksonville, FL 32211 (SAN 211-5298).

Hope Farm Press & Bookshop, *(Hope Farm; 0-910746),* Strong Rd., Cornwallville, NY 12418 Tel 518-239-4745 (SAN 204-0697).

Hope Publishing Co., *(Hope Pub; 0-916642),* 380 S. Main Place, Carol Stream, IL 60187 Tel 312-665-3200 (SAN 208-3361).

Hopewell Books, Inc., *(Hopewell; 0-910839),* 1670 Sturbridge Dr., Rd. 1, Sewickley, PA 15143 Tel 412-366-3287 (SAN 270-8264).

Hopewood Press, *(Hopewood Pr; 0-936286),* P.O. Box 27541, Minneapolis, MN 55427 (SAN 215-0816).

Hopkins Syndicate, Inc., *(Hopkins; 0-910748),* Hopkins Bldg., Mellott, IN 47958 Tel 317-295-2253 (SAN 204-0700).

Hopkinson & Blake, Pubs., *(Hopkinson; 0-911974),* 50 W. 34th St., New York, NY 10001 Tel 212-947-8282 (SAN 202-3032).

Horizon Books, *(Horizon Bks CA; 0-938840),* P.O. Box 3083, Fremont, CA 94539 Tel 415-657-6439 (SAN 216-0390).

Horizon House, *(Horizon Hse),* 610 Washington St., Dedham, MA 02026 Tel 617-326-8220 (SAN 204-8388).

Horizon Press Pubs., *(Horizon; 0-8180),* 156 Fifth Ave., New York, NY 10010 Tel 212-924-9225 (SAN 202-3040).

Horizon Pubs. & Distributors, Inc., *(Horizon Utah; 0-88290),* P.O. Box 490, 50 S. 500 West, Bountiful, UT 84010 Tel 801-295-9451 (SAN 159-4885).

Horizons, *(Horizons; 0-932960),* P.O. Box 35008, Phoenix, AZ 85069 (SAN 212-2146); Dist. by: Thinking Caps, Inc., P.O. Box 7239, Phoenix, AZ 85011 Tel 602-956-1515 (SAN 239-4960).

Horn Book, Inc., *(Horn Bk; 0-87675),* Park Square Bldg., 31 St. James Ave., Boston, MA 02116 Tel 617-482-5198 (SAN 202-3059).

Hornbeam Press, *(Hornbeam Pr; 0-917496),* 6520 Courtwood Dr., Columbia, SC 29206 Tel 803-782-7667 (SAN 209-0325).

Horse & Bird Press, The, *(Horse & Bird; 0-9602214),* P.O. Box 67C89, Los Angeles, CA 90067 Tel 213-823-4364 (SAN 281-7888); Dist. by: Publisher's Group West, 5855 Beaudry St., Emeryville, CA 94608 Tel 415-658-3453 (SAN 202-8522); Dist. by: The Distributors, 702 S. Michigan St., South Bend, IN 46618 Tel 219-232-8500 (SAN 212-0364); Dist. by: Inland Book Co, P.O. Box 261, East Haven, CT 06512 Tel 203-467-4257 (SAN 200-4151); Dist. by: Book People, 2940 Seventh St., Berkeley, CA 94710 Tel 415-549-3030 (SAN 168-9517).

Horticultural Books, Inc., *(Horticult FL; 0-9600046),* P.O. Box 107, Stuart, FL 33495 Tel 305-287-1091 (SAN 204-0735).

Horticultural Pubns., *(Horticult Pubns; 0-938378),* 3906 N.W. 31st Place, Gainesville, FL 32601 Tel 904-732-5077 (SAN 216-1389).

Horticultural Research Institute, Inc., *(Horticult Research; 0-935336),* 230 Southern Bldg., Washington, DC 20005 Tel 202-737-4060 (SAN 213-3210).

Horton, Thomas, & Daughters, *(T Horton & Dghts; 0-913878),* 22 Appleton Place, P.O. Box 3, Glen Ridge, NJ 07028 Tel 201-748-8095 (SAN 201-5331).

Hospital Compensation Service, *(Hosp Compensation),* 115 Watching Dr., P.O. Box 321, Hawthorne, NJ 07507 (SAN 217-1090).

Hospital, Institution, & Educational Food Service Society, *(Hosp Inst Ed Food),* 4410 W Roosevelt Rd, Hillside, IL 60162 (SAN 224-3903).

Hospital Research & Educational Trust, *(Hosp Res & Educ; 0-87914),* 840 N. Lake Shore Dr., Chicago, IL 60611 Tel 312-280-6381 (SAN 206-9121).

Host, Jim, & Associates, Inc., *(Host Assoc; 0-934554),* 120 Kentucky Ave., Suite A-1, Lexington, KY 40502 (SAN 216-1400).

Hot off the Press, *(Hot off Pr; 0-9605904),* 7212 S. Seven Oaks, Canby, OR 97013 (SAN 216-3977).

Hot Water Publishing Co., *(Hot Water Pubs; 0-941904),* 131 E. McKenzie, Stockton, CA 95204 Tel 209-948-4404 (SAN 239-2283).

Hotchkiss House, Inc., *(Hotchkiss House; 0-912220),* 18 Hearthstone Rd., Pittsford, NY 14534 (SAN 204-0743).

Hotline Multi-Enterprises, *(Hotline Multi-Ent; 0-935864),* 2709 Georgetown Rd., Mechanicsville, VA 23111 (SAN 214-3860).

Houghton Mifflin Co., *(HM; 0-395),* 2 Park St., Boston, MA 02107 Tel 617-725-5000 (SAN 200-2388); Orders to: Wayside Road, Burlington, MA 01803 Tel 617-272-1500 (SAN 215-3793). *Imprints:* Clarion Books (Clarion); Piper Books (Piper); Riverside Editions (RivEd); Sentry Editions (SenEd).

Housatonuc Bookshop, *(Housatonuc; 0-910756),* Main St., Salisbury, CT 06068 Tel 203-435-2100 (SAN 201-5447).

House, Deanna, Specialties, Inc., *(Deanna Hse; 0-9610752),* Box 492, Portage, MI 49081 Tel 616-327-4571 (SAN 264-7508).

House by the Sea Publishing Co., *(Hse by the Sea),* 8610 Highway 101, Waldport, OR 97394 (SAN 212-9477).

House of Charles, *(Hse of Charles; 0-9605344),* 4833 NE 238th Ave., Vancouver, WA 98662 Tel 206-892-1589 (SAN 215-8728).

House of Collectibles, Inc., *(Hse of Collectibles; 0-87637),* 1900 Premier Row, Orlando, FL 32809 Tel 305-857-9095 (SAN 202-3113).

House of Print, *(House of Print),* 322 Benzel Ave., Madelia, MN 56062 Tel 507-642-3298 (SAN 211-0687).

House of York, *(Hse of York; 0-916660),* 1992 Borchers Dr., San Jose, CA 95124 Tel 408-377-8472 (SAN 208-2357).

House ov Day Vid, *(Hse ov Day Vid; 0-912672),* 978 Amherst St., Apt. 6, Buffalo, NY 14216 Tel 716-873-8856 (SAN 204-0778).

Housesmith's Press, *(Housesmith; 0-918238),* P.O. Box 157, Kittery Point, ME 03905 Tel 207-439-0638 (SAN 210-2102).

Housing Connection, The, *(Housing Connect; 0-9609586),* P.O. Box 5536, Arlington, VA 22205 Tel 703-243-6805 (SAN 262-0405).

Houston, Charles S., *(Houston C; 0-930410),* 77 Ledge Rd., Burlington, VT 05401 Tel 802-863-6441 (SAN 220-2727).

Hover Co., The, *(Hover; 0-934414),* 14713 La Mesa Dr., La Mirada, CA 90638 Tel 714-521-3046 (SAN 213-747X).

Hovnanian, Ralph R., *(Hovnanian; 0-9607774),* 2128 Prospect Ave., Evanston, IL 60201 (SAN 241-5399).

How-to Press, *(How-to Pr; 0-938356),* P.O. Box 483, Arlington, TX 76010 (SAN 215-7764).

Howard, Allen, Enterprises, Inc., *(Howard Allen; 0-914576),* P.O. Box 76, Cape Canaveral, FL 32920 (SAN 203-4662).

Howard, Barney, *(B Howard; 0-935602),* 10114 Tracy, Kansas City, MO 64131 Tel 816-942-2934 (SAN 214-0314).

Howard, Daniel L., *(D L Howard; 0-936144),* P.O. Box 41432, Los Angeles, CA 90041 Tel 213-258-2121 (SAN 213-9316).

Howard Univ. Press, *(Howard U Pr; 0-88258),* 2900 Van Ness St., N.W., Washington, DC 20008 Tel 202-686-6696 (SAN 202-3067).

Howe Brothers, *(Howe Brothers; 0-935704),* Box 6394, Salt Lake City, UT 84106 (SAN 222-0318).

Howe Street Press, The, *(Howe St Pr; 0-9609666),* 212 E. Howe St., Seattle, WA 98102 (SAN 270-8507).

Howell, John, Books, *(J Howell; 0-910760),* 434 Post St., San Francisco, CA 94102 Tel 415-781-7795 (SAN 203-8994).

Howell, Susan P., Enterprises, *(S P Howell; 0-9603076),* Box 116 B, Hebron, CT 06248 (SAN 212-7458).

Howell, Will C., *(W C Howell; 0-9601140),* 185 E. Norton, Sherwood, OR 97140 Tel 503-625-7409 (SAN 210-2110).

Howell Book House Inc., *(Howell Bk; 0-87605),* Helmsley Bldg., 230 Park Ave., New York, NY 10169 Tel 212-986-4488 (SAN 202-3075).

Howell-North Books, Inc., Div. of Darwin Pubns., *(Howell North; 0-8310),* 850 N. Hollywood Way, Burbank, CA 91505 Tel 213-848-0944 (SAN 202-3083).

HP Publishing Co., Inc., *(HP Pub Co; 0-913800),* 575 Lexington Ave., New York, NY 10022 Tel 212-421-7320 (SAN 207-1738).

HTC Publishing Co. (Hot Tub Cooks), *(HTC Pub; 0-9605582),* 10636 Main St., Suite 284, Bellevue, WA 98004 Tel 206-453-5569 (SAN 239-8230).

Hubbard Scientific, *(Hubbard Sci; 0-8331),* P.O. Box 104, 1946 Raymond Dr., Northbrook, IL 60062 Tel 312-272-7810 (SAN 202-3121).

Hudson Hills Press, Inc., *(Hudson Hills; 0-933920),* 220 Fifth Ave, Suite 301, New York, NY 10001 (SAN 213-0815); Dist. by: Viking Penguin, Inc., 625 Madison Ave., New York, NY 10022 Tel 212-755-4330 (SAN 200-2442).

Hudson-Mohawk Association of Colleges & Universities, *(Hudson-Mohawk),* 91 Fiddlers Lane, Latham, NY 12110 Tel 518-785-3219 (SAN 241-5402).

Hudson Review, The, *(Hudson Rev),* 684 Park Ave., New York, NY 10021 Tel 212-650-0020 (SAN 209-2859).

Huebner, S. S., Foundation for Insurance Education, *(Huebner Foun Insur),* 3641 Locust Walk CE, Philadelphia, PA 19104 Tel 215-898-5644 (SAN 211-6405); Dist. by: Richard D. Irwin, Inc., 1818 Ridge Rd., Homewood, IL 60430 (SAN 206-8400).

Huenefeld Co., Inc., *(Huenefeld Co; 0-931932),* P.O. Box U, Bedford, MA 01730 Tel 617-861-9650 (SAN 211-5662).

Huffman Press, *(Huffman Pr),* 805 N. Royal St., Alexandria, VA 22314 Tel 703-683-1695 (SAN 208-0826).

Hughes, Clarence, *(C Hughes),* P.O. Box 451, Annawan, IL 61234 Tel 309-935-6715 (SAN 208-1229).

Hughes Press, *(Hughes Pr; 0-912560),* 500 23rd St., N.W., Box B203, Washington, DC 20037 Tel 202-293-2686 (SAN 210-9360).

Hughley Pubns., *(Hughley Pubns; 0-9605150),* P.O. Box 261, Springfield Gardens, NY 11413 Tel 212-528-0391 (SAN 215-8078).

Huguley, John, Co., Inc., *(Huguley Co; 0-9605064),* 269 King St., Charleston, SC 29401 (SAN 215-8736).

Huh Pubns., *(Huh Pubns; 0-938642),* P.O. Box 30782, Santa Barbara, CA 93105 (SAN 222-9765).

Hui-Hanai, Queen Lilioukalani Childrens Center, *(Hui-Hanai-Queen),* Dist. by: Press Pacifica, P.O. Box 1227, Kailua, HI 96734 (SAN 169-1635).

Hull, Harry A., *(Hull; 0-9606118),* 1710 Del Webb Blvd., Sun City Center, FL 33570 Tel 813-634-4967 (SAN 281-7942); c/o Albert E. Deeds Associates, 1300 Benedum-Trees Bldg., Pittsburgh, PA 15222 Tel 412-281-1616 (SAN 281-7950).

Human Behavior Research Group, Inc., *(Human Behavior; 0-939552),* P.O. Box 17122, Irvine, CA 92713 Tel 714-559-6946 (SAN 216-6801).

Human Conservancy Press, *(Human Conserv Pr; 0-9612052),* 374 Holly St., Denver, CO 80220 Tel 303-388-1691 (SAN 283-9164).

Human Development Press, *(Human Dev Pr; 0-938024),* 10701 Lomas NE, 210, Albuquerque, NM 87112 Tel 505-292-0370 (SAN 215-6555).

Human Development Training Institute, *(Human Dev Train; 0-86584),* 1727 Fifth Ave., San Diego, CA 92101 Tel 714-233-7023 (SAN 206-7439).

Human Ecology Research Foundation of the South West, *(Human Eco Res; 0-941962),* 12110 Webb Chaple Rd. Suite E305, Dallas, TX 75234 Tel 214-620-0620 (SAN 238-2474).

Human Kinetics Pubs., *(Human Kinetics; 0-931250),* P.O. Box 5076, Champaign, IL 61820 Tel 217-351-5076 (SAN 211-7088).

Human Policy Press, *(Human Policy Pr; 0-937540),* P.O. Box 127, Syracuse, NY 13210 (SAN 213-8476).

Human Potential Pubns., *(Human Potential; 0-939268),* 17330 Warrington Dr., Detroit, MI 48221 Tel 313-341-0492 (SAN 215-0832).

Human Relations Area Files Press, Inc., *(HRAFP; 0-87536),* P.O. Box 2015, Yale Sta., New Haven, CT 06520 Tel 203-777-2334 (SAN 202-3091).

Human Resource Communications Group, *(Human Res Comm; 0-9609088),* 2355 E. Stadium Blvd., Ann Arbor, MI 48104 Tel 313-994-9285 (SAN 264-102X).

Human Resource Development Press, *(Human Res Dev Pr; 0-914234),* 22 Amherst Rd., Amherst, MA 01002 Tel 413-253-3488 (SAN 201-9213).

Human Resources Center, *(Human Res Ctr),* Iuwillts Rd, Albertson, NY 11507 (SAN 227-0323).

Human Resources Research Organization, *(Human Resources),* 300 N. Washington St., Alexandria, VA 22314 Tel 703-549-3611 (SAN 207-3692).

Human Sciences Press, Inc., *(Human Sci Pr; 0-87705; 0-89885),* 72 Fifth Ave., New York, NY 10011 Tel 212-243-6000 (SAN 200-2159); Dist. by: Independent Publishers Group, One Pleasant Ave., Port Washington, NY 11050 (SAN 215-4870) Formerly Named Behavioral Pubns. Inc.

Human Services Development Center, *(Human Serv Dev; 0-938850),* P.O. Box 161809, Sacramento, CA 95816 (SAN 219-788X).

Human Services Press, *(Human Serv Pr; 0-9610834),* 200 E. 24th, New York, NY 10010 (SAN 277-688X).

Humana Press, The, *(Humana; 0-89603),* Crescent Manor, P.O. Box 2148, Clifton, NJ 07015 Tel 201-773-4389 (SAN 212-3606).

Humanics Associates, *(Humanics Assoc),* Publisher Abbreviations Without Addresses Are for Titles That Are Out of Print. These Are Obsolete Abbreviations.

Humanics Ltd., *(Humanics Ltd; 0-89334),* P.O. Box 7447, Atlanta, GA 30309 (SAN 208-3833).

Humanities Press, Inc., *(Humanities; 0-391),* Atlantic Highlands, NJ 07716 Tel 201-872-1441 (SAN 201-9272).

Humbird Enterprise, *(Humbird Ent; 0-914128),* P.O. Box 1197, San Francisco, CA 94101 Tel 415-861-2333 (SAN 206-9148).

Humbird Hopkins Inc., Pubs., *(Humbird Hopkins; 0-931854),* P.O. Box 49813, Los Angeles, CA 90049 Tel 213-828-3617 (SAN 211-4992).

Humble Hills Books, *(Humble Hills; 0-935858),* P.O. Box 7, Kalamazoo, MI 49004 Tel 616-343-2211 (SAN 209-8466).

Humble Publishing Co., *(Humble Pub Co; 0-9611756),* 33 Ivy Trail N.E., Atlanta, GA 30342 Tel 404-261-3243 (SAN 285-2950).

Hummingbird Press, *(Hummingbird; 0-912998),* 2400 Hannett, N.E., Albuquerque, NM 87106 Tel 505-268-6277 (SAN 204-0794).

Humorhouse Pubs., *(Humorhouse),* 4077 W. Third St., No. 106, Los Angeles, CA 90020 (SAN 223-1425).

Humphreys Academy Patrons, *(Humphreys Acad; 0-9610058),* P.O. Box 717, Belzoni, MS 39038 Tel 601-247-1572 (SAN 262-9070).

Huna Research Inc., *(Huna Res Inc; 0-910764),* 126 Camellia Dr., Cape Girardeau, MO 63701 Tel 314-334-3478 (SAN 201-548X).

Hungarian Alumni Assn., *(Hungarian Alumni; 0-910539),* P.O. Box 174, New Brunswick, NJ 08903 Tel 201-249-7921 (SAN 260-0722).

Hungarian Cultural Foundation, *(Hungarian Cultural; 0-914648),* P.O. Box 364, Stone Mountain, GA 30086 Tel 404-377-2600 (SAN 205-6240).

Hungness, Carl, Publishing, *(C Hungness; 0-915088),* P.O. Box 24308, Speedway, IN 46224 Tel 317-244-4792 (SAN 207-1193).

Hunt Institute for Botanical Documentation, *(Hunt Inst Botanical; 0-913196),* Carnegie-Mellon Univ., Pittsburgh, PA 15213 Tel 412-578-2434 (SAN 206-9156).

Hunter Books, *(Hunter Bks; 0-917726),* 201 McClellan Rd., Kingwood, TX 77339 Tel 713-358-7575 (SAN 209-2611).

Hunter House, Inc., *(Hunter Hse; 0-89793),* Box 1302, Claremont, CA 91711 Tel 714-624-2277 (SAN 281-7969); c/o Publisher's Services, Box 3914, San Rafael, CA 94901 Tel 415-883-3530 (SAN 281-7977).

Hunter Publishing Co., *(Hunter Ariz; 0-918126),* P.O. Box 9533, Phoenix, AZ 85068 Tel 602-944-1022 (SAN 209-2980).

Hunter Textbooks, Inc., *(Hunter Textbks; 0-88725),* 823 Reynolds Rd., Winston-Salem, NC 27104 Tel 919-725-0608 (SAN 209-567X).

Hunterdon County Board of Agriculture, *(Hunterdon County Bd; 0-9606584),* R.D. 6, Box 48, Flemington, NJ 08822 Tel 201-236-2022 (SAN 223-7695).

Hunterdon House, *(Hunterdon Hse; 0-912606),* 38 Swan St., Lambertville, NJ 08822 Tel 609-397-2523 (SAN 204-0824).

Huntington House, Inc., *(Huntington Hse Inc; 0-910311),* 1200 N. Market St., G, Shreveport, LA 71107 Tel 318-996-7408 (SAN 241-5208).

Huntington Library Pubns., *(Huntington Lib; 0-87328),* 1151 Oxford Rd., San Marino, CA 91108 Tel 213-792-6141 (SAN 202-313X).

Huntleigh House, *(Huntleigh; 0-918354),* P.O. Drawer 20602, Oklahoma City, OK 73156 Tel 405-751-8444 (SAN 209-4487).

Hurricane Co., The, *(Hurricane Co; 0-933272),* P.O. Box 426, Jacksonville, NC 28540 (SAN 212-7466).

Husher & Welch, *(Husher & Welch; 0-9603944),* 50 Nahant Rd., Nahant, MA 01908 (SAN 215-6563).

Huston, Harvey, *(Huston; 0-9600048),* 860 Mount Pleasant St., Winnetka, IL 60093 Tel 312-446-1594 (SAN 204-0840).

Hutar Growth Management Institute, *(Hutar; 0-918896),* 1701 E. Lake Ave. Suite 270, Glenview, IL 60025 (SAN 210-4385).

Hutchinson, Ted, *(T Hutchinson; 0-9601366),* 14 Devries Ave., N. Tarrytown, NY 10591 Tel 914-631-1848 (SAN 209-0449).

Hutchinson Ross Publishing Co., *(Hutchinson Ross; 0-87933),* 523 Sarah St., Box 699, Stroudsburg, PA 18360 Tel 717-421-4060 (SAN 201-2707); Dist. by: SAE/VNR Order Processing, 7625 Empire Dr., Florence, KY 41042 Tel 606-525-6600 (SAN 206-8990).

Hutchinsons, *(Hutchinsons; 0-943368),* 26 Main St., Orleans, MA 02653 Tel 617-255-8458 (SAN 240-6764).

Hutson, Martha, Associates, *(Hutson Assoc; 0-9606126),* P.O. Box 185, Orefield, PA 18069 Tel 215-776-1421 (SAN 215-7772).

Hwong Publishing Co., *(Hwong Pub; 0-89260),* 10353 Los Alamitos Blvd., Los Alamitos, CA 90720 Tel 213-431-0868 (SAN 208-2306).

Hyde, Arnout, *(A Hyde; 0-9604590),* 418 Lehigh Terrace, Charleston, WV 25302 (SAN 219-9750).

Hyde, Floy S., *(F S Hyde; 0-9600528),* 65 Elm St., Oneonta, NY 13820 (SAN 205-5732).

Hyde Collection, The, *(Hyde Collect; 0-9606718),* 161 Warren St., Glens Falls, NY 12801 Tel 518-792-1761 (SAN 219-6638).

Hyde Park Press, *(Hyde Park Pr; 0-9608454),* P. O. Box 2009, Boise, ID 83701 (SAN 240-4834).

Hyde School, The, *(Hyde Sch; 0-9607904),* 616 High St., Bath, ME 04530 (SAN 238-1672).

Hydraulic Institute, *(Hydraulic Inst),* 712 Lakewood Ctr. N., 14600 Detroit Ave., Cleveland, OH 44107 (SAN 224-7984).

Hykes, Susan S., *(S S Hykes; 0-9608894),* 2610 Leo Dr., Colorado Springs, CO 80906 Tel 303-636-3467 (SAN 241-1202).

Hymnary Press, The, *(Hymnary Pr; 0-942466),* 1317 Sorenson Rd., Helena, MT 59601 Tel 406-458-6227 (SAN 239-6564).

HyperDynamics, *(HyperDynamics),* P.O. Box 392, Santa Fe, NM 87501 Tel 505-988-2416 (SAN 208-290X).

Hyperion Press, Inc., *(Hyperion Conn; 0-88355; 0-8305),* 47 Riverside Ave., P.O. Box 591, Westport, CT 06880 Tel 203-226-1091 (SAN 202-3148).

Hypnos Press, *(Hypnos Pr; 0-939628),* 3000 Connecticut Ave. NW, Suite 308, Washington, DC 20008 Tel 202-462-0221 (SAN 216-6283).

Hyst'ry Myst'ry House, *(Hyst'ry Myst'ry; 0-937884),* 1 Brush Court, Garnerville, NY 10923 (SAN 218-4796); Dist. by: Associated Booksellers Inc., P.O. Box 6361, McKinley Ave., Bridgeport, CT 06606 Tel 203-366-5494 (SAN 206-9717).

IAM Enterprises, Inc., *(IAM Ent; 0-910469),* 8930 Foster Lane, Overland Park, KS 66212 Tel 913-649-3695 (SAN 260-0730).

I A R Press (Institute of Applied Research), *(IAR Press),* P.O. Box 31308, St. Louis, MO 63131 (SAN 262-4958).

I & O Publishing Co., *(I & O Pub; 0-911752),* P.O. Box 906, Boulder City, NV 89005 (SAN 202-3156).

IBC Pubns., *(I B C Pubns),* Illinois Benedictine College, Lisle, IL 60532 (SAN 265-3877).

IBM Corp., *(IBM Armonk; 0-933186),* Armonk, NY 10504 Tel 914-765-1900 (SAN 214-1914).

NAME INDEX

IBMS Inc., *(IBMS Inc; 0-933738),* 105 Winthrop Rd., Hillside, NJ 07642 Tel 201-666-0909 (SAN 212-9094).

IBR Publishing, Inc., *(IBR Pub; 0-911693),* 2414 Forsyth Rd., Orlando, FL 32807 (SAN 264-1054).

ICA Pubs., *(ICA Pubs; 0-941472),* 303 W. Pleasantview Ave., Hackensack, NJ 07601 Tel 201-836-9595 (SAN 239-3662).

ICARE Press Inc., *(ICARE Pr),* 193-12 Nero Ave., Jamaica, NY 11423 Tel 212-465-2843 (SAN 270-8809).

I C E A *See* **International Childbirth Education Assn., Inc.**

I C S Books, Inc., *(ICS Bks; 0-934802),* P.O. Box 8002, Merrillville, IN 46410 Tel 219-769-0585 (SAN 213-3237).

ICS Pr., *(ICS Pr),* Institute for Contemporary Studies, 260 California St., San Francisco, CA 94111 Tel 415-398-3010 (SAN 276-9735).

I.C.S. Pubns., Institute of Carmelite Studies, *(ICS Pubns; 0-9600876; 0-935316),* 2131 Lincoln Rd., N.E., Washington, DC 20002 Tel 202-832-6622 (SAN 201-5285).

ICTL Pubns., *(ICTL Pubns),* P.O. Box 82233, San Diego, CA 92138 (SAN 262-0413).

I Can See Clearly Now, *(I Can See; 0-9609532),* P.O. Box 784, Coupeville, WA 98239 Tel 206-678-4606 (SAN 260-2059).

IDTTC, *(IDTTC; 0-916922),* Fairview St., Antrim, NH 03440 Tel 617-588-2990 (SAN 202-3172).

I Dare You Committee, *(I Dare You; 0-9602416),* P.O. Box 1606, St. Louis, MO 63188 Tel 314-351-4456 (SAN 210-9034).

IGBE, *(IGBE; 0-941234),* 2049 Century Park E., Los Angeles, CA 90067 (SAN 239-3670).

IJG, Inc., *(IJG Inc; 0-936200),* 1953 W. 11th St., Upland, CA 91786 (SAN 214-0322).

ILR Pr., *(ILR Pr; 0-87546),* New York State School of Industrial Relations, Cornell Univ., Box 1000, Ithaca, NY 14853 Tel 607-256-3061 (SAN 270-8825).

I Like Me Publishing Co., the, *(I Like Me Pub; 0-9608516),* P.O. Box 43287, Chicago, IL 60628 Tel 312-445-6497 (SAN 240-6772).

IMM/North American Pubns. Center, *(IMM North Am),* Old Post Rd., Brookfield, VT 05036 (SAN 219-791X).

IMS Pr., *(IMS Pr; 0-910190),* 426 Pennsylvania Ave., Fort Washington, PA 19034 Tel 215-628-4920 (SAN 204-5427).

IMTEC, *(IMTEC; 0-943494),* P.O. Box 1402, Bowie, MD 20716 Tel 301-266-4731 (SAN 240-6780).

INFORM, *(INFORM; 0-918780),* 381 Park Ave. South, New York, NY 10016 Tel 212-689-4040 (SAN 210-4423).

IR Pubns. Ltd., *(IR Pubns),* 35 W. 38th St. No. 3W 903, New York, NY 10018 Tel 212-730-0518 (SAN 216-2113).

ISI Press, Subs. of Institute for Scientific Information, *(ISI Pr; 0-89495),* 3501 Market St., Philadelphia, PA 19104 Tel 215-386-0100 (SAN 209-9349).

I-74 Press, *(I-Seventy-Four; 0-940096),* Estes Park 4F, Carrboro, NC 27510 (SAN 217-0752).

IWP Publishing, *(IWP Pub; 0-914766),* P.O. Box 2449, Menlo Park, CA 94025 Tel 415-321-4468 (SAN 203-798X).

I. C. E. R. Press *See* **International Center for Environmental Research**

Iapetus Press, *(Iapetus Pr; 0-941602),* 2009 Tidewater Lane, Madison, MS 39110 Tel 601-987-5950 (SAN 239-1023).

I.B.S. Internacional, *(IBS Intl; 0-89564),* 3144 Dove St., San Diego, CA 92103 Tel 714-298-5061 (SAN 210-3001).

Icarus Press, Inc., *(Icarus; 0-89651),* P.O. Box 1225, South Bend, IN 46624 Tel 219-233-6020 (SAN 285-0273); Dist. by: Harper & Row, Keystone Industrial Park, Scranton, PA 18512 Tel 800-233-4175 (SAN 285-0281).

ICUC Press, *(ICUC Pr; 0-910205),* P.O. Box 1447, Springfield, VA 22151 Tel 703-323-8065 (SAN 241-5216).

Idaho Museum of Natural History, *(Idaho Mus Nat Hist; 0-939696),* Campus Box 8096, Idaho State Univ., Pocatello, ID 83209 Tel 208-236-3168 (SAN 201-5315).

Idaho State Historical Society, *(Idaho State Soc; 0-931406),* 610 N. Julia Davis Dr., Boise, ID 83706 (SAN 221-0827).

Ide House, Inc., *(Ide Hse; 0-86663),* 4631 Harvey Dr., Mesquite, TX 75150 (SAN 216-146X).

Ideal World Publishing Co., *(Ideal World; 0-915068),* P.O. Box 1237-EG, Melbourne, FL 32935 Tel 305-254-6003 (SAN 201-923X).

Ideals, Inc., *(Ideals PA; 0-932990),* P. O. Box 391, State College of Penn, PA 16801 (SAN 221-0770).

Ideals Publishing Corp., *(Ideals; 0-89542),* 11315 Watertown Plank Rd., Milwaukee, WI 53226 Tel 414-771-2700 (SAN 213-4403).

Ideas Unlimited Press, *(Ideas Unltd; 0-9606574),* 1632 Berkley Circle, Chattanooga, TN 37405 (SAN 219-7898); Dist. by: The Plum Nelly Shop, 1201 Hixson Pike, Chattanooga, TN 37405 (SAN 216-1745).

Identity Institute, The, *(Identity Inst; 0-912093),* P.O. Box 11039, Honolulu, HI 96828 (SAN 277-6898).

IEM-HOTEP Assn., *(IEM-HOTEP; 0-932806),* 250 N.W. 9 St., Boca Raton, FL 33432 Tel 305-392-8514 (SAN 212-4270).

Igaku-Shoin Medical Pubs., *(Igaku-Shoin; 0-89640),* 1140 Ave. of the Americas, New York, NY 10036 Tel 212-944-7540 (SAN 211-5689).

Ignatius Press, *(Ignatius Pr; 0-89870),* P.O. Box 18990, San Francisco, CA 94118 Tel 415-387-2324 (SAN 285-029X); Orders to: Distribution Division, 15 Oakland Ave., Harrison, NY 10528 (SAN 285-0303).

Igram Press, *(Igram Pr; 0-911119),* 2020 16th Ave. SW, Cedar Rapids, IA 52404 Tel 319-366-5335 (SAN 263-1709).

II Editions, *(Two Edit),* 488 Madison Ave., New York, NY 10022 (SAN 276-9417).

Ili-Cor Pubns., *(Ili-Cor Pubns),* 53 Storz Rd., Sacramento, CA 95823 Tel 916-393-3021 (SAN 240-1525).

Ilkon Press, *(Ilkon Pr; 0-916832),* 210 Riverside Dr., Apt 6-G, New York, NY 10025 Tel 212-663-2579 (SAN 208-6883).

Illinois Labor History Society, *(Ill Labor Hist Soc; 0-916884),* 20 E. Jackson Blvd., Chicago, IL 60604 Tel 312-663-4107 (SAN 281-8019); Dist. by Charles H. Kerr Pub. Co., P. O. Box 914, Chicago, IL 60690 Tel 312-663-4107 (SAN 207-7051); Dist. by: C.H. Kerr, 1740 W. Greenleaf, Chicago, IL 60626 (SAN 207-7043).

Illinois South Project, *(Illinois South; 0-943724),* 116 1/2 W. Cherry, Herrin, IL 62948 Tel 618-942-6613 (SAN 241-0303).

Illinois State Historical Library, *(Ill St Hist Lib; 0-912154),* Old State Capitol, Springfield, IL 62706 Tel 217-782-4836 (SAN 203-7963).

Illinois State Historical Society, *(Ill Hist Soc; 0-912226),* Old State Capitol, Springfield, IL 62706 Tel 217-782-4836 (SAN 203-7971).

Illinois State Museum Society, *(Ill St Museum; 0-89792; 0-932336),* Spring & Edwards, Springfield, IL 62706 Tel 217-782-7386 (SAN 201-5137).

Illuminati, *(Illuminati; 0-89807),* 8812 W. Pico Blvd., Suite 204, Los Angeles, CA 90035 Tel 213-273-8372 (SAN 212-856X).

Illumination Engineering Society of North America, *(Illum Eng; 0-87995),* 345 E. 47th St., New York, NY 10017 Tel 212-644-7920 (SAN 202-3180).

Illuminations Press, *(Illum Pr),* P.O. Box 126, St. Helena, CA Tel 707-963-9342 (SAN 241-5445).

Illuminations Press, *(Illuminations Pr; 0-941442),* 2110 Ninth St., Apt. B, Berkeley, CA 94710 Tel 415-849-2102 (SAN 209-8172).

Illusive Unicorn Pubns., *(Illusive Unicorn),* P.O. Box 6841, San Jose, CA 95150 Tel 408-279-1520 (SAN 212-7474).

Ilse, Sherokee, & Associates, *(Sherokee; 0-9609456),* 4105 Oak St., Long Lake, MN 55356 Tel 612-476-1303 (SAN 260-0749).

IMA Education & Research Foundation, *(IMA Ed; 0-918486),* P.O. Box 526, Newtonville, NY 12128 Tel 518-434-3859 (SAN 210-105X).

Image & Idea, Inc., *(Image & Idea; 0-934570),* Box 1991, Iowa City, IA 52240 (SAN 213-3229); Dist. by: Iowa State Univ. Press, 2121 S. State Ave., Ames, IA 50010 (SAN 202-7194).

Image Awareness Corp., *(Image Awareness; 0-9604592),* P.O. Box 3307, Auburn, CA 95604 (SAN 215-1545).

Image Books *See* **Doubleday & Co., Inc.**

IMPRINT EDITIONS

Image Gallery, *(Image Gallery; 0-918362),* 1017 S. W. Morrison St., Rm. 307, Portland, OR 97205 Tel 503-224-9629 (SAN 210-1068).

Image Makers of Pittsford, *(Image Makers; 0-911705),* 6 Wood Gate, Pittsford, NY 14534 Tel 716-385-4567 (SAN 264-1070).

Image Pubns., *(Image Pubns; 0-942772),* 6409 Appalachian Way, P.O. Box 5016, Madison, WI 53705 Tel 608-233-5033 (SAN 238-8499).

Image West Press, *(Image West; 0-918966),* P.O. Box 5511, Eugene, OR 97405 Tel 503-342-3797 (SAN 210-4407).

Images Graphiques, Inc., *(Images Graphiques; 0-89545),* 37 Riverside Dr., New York, NY 10023 Tel 212-787-4000 (SAN 210-4415).

Images, Ink, Inc., *(Images Ink; 0-942088),* P.O. Box 12685, 9135 Spearhead Way, Reno, NE 89506 Tel 702-972-3361 (SAN 238-6119).

Images of Key West, *(Images Key; 0-9609272),* P.O. Box 1237, Key West, FL 33040 (SAN 260-0757).

Imagesmith, *(Imagesmith; 0-938700),* P.O. Box 1524, Bellevue, WA 98009 (SAN 216-0420).

Imaginart Press, *(Imaginart Pr; 0-9609464),* 8726 S. Sepulveda Blvd., No. 2641, Los Angeles, CA 90045 Tel 213-645-6016 (SAN 260-2067).

Imibooks Pubns., *(Imibooks Pubns; 0-918066),* P.O. Box 165, Roslyn, NY 11576 Tel 212-423-0722 (SAN 209-3766).

Immer Brothers Books, *(Immer Brothers Bks; 0-939144),* 4210 B. F. Goodrich Blvd., Memphis, TN 38118 (SAN 237-9589).

Imp Press, *(Imp Pr; 0-9603008),* P.O. Box 93, Buffalo, NY 14213 Tel 716-881-5391 (SAN 213-0858).

Impact, *(Impact IN; 0-9611220),* P.O. Box 455, Muncie, IN 47305 (SAN 283-2305); c/o Precision Printing, Inc., P.O. Box 118, Muncie, IN 47305 Tel 317-249-9281 (SAN 283-2313).

Impact Books, Div. of the Benson Co., *(Impact Tenn; 0-914850; 0-86608),* 365 Great Circle Rd., Nashville, TN 37228 Tel 615-259-9111 (SAN 202-6872); Dist. by: Zondervan Corp., 1415 Lake Dr. S.E., Grand Rapids, MI 49506 Tel 616-698-6900 (SAN 203-2694).

Impact Books, Inc., *(Impact Bks MO; 0-89228),* 137 W. Jefferson, Kirkwood, MO 63122 (SAN 214-0330).

Impact Press, *(Impact Pr IL),* 6424 N. Sacramento Ave., Chicago, IL 60645 Tel 312-761-0682 (SAN 213-9782).

Impact Pubns., *(Impact Pubns IL; 0-9607474),* 203 N. Wabash Ave., Chicago, IL 60601 Tel 312-475-5748 (SAN 238-6127).

Impact Pubns., *(Impact VA; 0-942710),* 5201 Leesburg Pike, Suite 900, Falls Church, VA 22041 Tel 703-379-2900 (SAN 240-1142).

Impact Pubs., Inc., *(Impact Pubs Cal; 0-915166),* P.O. Box 1094, San Luis Obispo, CA 93406 Tel 805-543-5911 (SAN 202-6864).

Impact Publishing Co., *(Impact Pub; 0-9601530),* 2110 Omega Rd., Suite A, San Ramon, CA 94583 Tel 415-831-1655 (SAN 211-3651).

Imperial Publishing Co., *(Imperial Pub Co; 0-9602960),* 190 S. Florida Ave., P.O. Box 120, Bartow, FL 33830 Tel 813-533-4183 (SAN 213-9871).

Imperio, Leroy, *(L Imperio; 0-9609302),* 39 15th St., Elkins, WV 26241 Tel 304-636-3434 (SAN 241-5224).

Impermanent Press, *(Impermanent Pr),* 218 Monclay Court, St. Louis, MO 63122 (SAN 209-0414).

Impresora Sahuaro, *(Impresora Sahuaro),* 7575 Sendero De Juana, Tucson, AZ 85718 Tel 602-297-3089 (SAN 218-7760).

Impress House, *(Impress Hse; 0-913992),* Orders to: Associated Booksellers, 147 McKinley Ave., Bridgeport, CT 06606 (SAN 206-6513).

Impressions, *(Impressions),* P.O. Box 6191, Harrisburg, PA 17112 (SAN 213-2192).

Impressions Publishing Co., *(Impress Pub; 0-913049),* P.O. Box 3286, Boise, ID 83703 (SAN 283-9784).

Imprimis Press, *(Imprimis; 0-937600),* 8809 Stonewall Rd., Manassas, VA 22110 (SAN 215-3203).

Imprint Editions, *(Imprint Edns),* 1520 South College, Fort Collins, CO 80524 (SAN 216-485X). *Imprints:* Capablanca (Capablanca).

2229

Imrie/Risley Miniatures, Inc., *(Imrie-Risley; 0-912364),* P.O. Box 89, Burnt Hills, NY 12027 Tel 518-885-6054 (SAN 206-6521).

In Between Books, *(In Between; 0-935430),* Box T, Sausalito, CA 94965 (SAN 213-6236).

In Sight Press, *(In Sight Pr NM; 0-942524),* Suite 228, 535 Cordova Rd., Santa Fe, NM 87501 Tel 505-982-9117 (SAN 238-1680).

In-the-Valley-of-the-Wichitas House, *(In Valley Wichitas; 0-941634),* P.O. Box 6741, Lawton, OK 73506 (SAN 239-2321).

Incentive Pubns., Inc., *(Incentive Pubns; 0-913916; 0-86530),* 2400 Crestmoor Rd., Nashville, TN 37215 Tel 615-385-2934 (SAN 203-8005).

Incentive Publishing, *(Incent Pub; 0-912715),* P.O. Box 15060, Sacramento, CA 95851 (SAN 283-0515).

Incremental Motion Control Systems Society, *(Incremental Motion; 0-931538),* P.O. Box 2772, Sta. A, Champaign, IL 61820 Tel 217-356-1523 (SAN 211-4259).

Ind-US, Inc., *(Ind-US Inc),* Box 56, East Glastonbury, CT 06025 Tel 203-633-0045 (SAN 213-5809).

Independence Press, *(Ind Pr; 0-910122),* Rte. One, Waupaca, WI 54981 (SAN 283-2690).

Independence Press, Div. of Herald House, *(Ind Pr MO; 0-8309),* Drawer HH, Independence, MO 64055 Tel 816-252-5010 (SAN 202-6902).

Independence Unlimited, *(Independence Unltd; 0-931040),* 27 Gardner St., Portsmouth, NH 03801 (SAN 213-8484).

Independent Battery Manufacturers Assn., *(IBMA Pubns; 0-912254),* 100 Larchwood Dr., Largo, FL 33540 Tel 813-586-1408 (SAN 206-9180).

Independent Cambridge Enterprises, *(Ind Cam Ent; 0-9609138),* 12881 Western Ave., Suite A, Garden Grove, CA 92641 Tel 714-891-8002 (SAN 241-5240).

Independent Pubs., *(Indep Pubs; 0-9608134),* 415 Medical Dr., Bountiful, UT 84010 Tel 801-298-2471 (SAN 240-2327).

Independent School Press, *(Ind Sch Pr; 0-88334),* 51 River St., Wellesley Hills, MA 02181 Tel 617-237-2591 (SAN 203-8013).

Index to Jewish Periodicals, *(IJP; 0-939698),* P.O. Box 18570, Cleveland Heights, OH 44118 Tel 216-321-7296 (SAN 204-8566).

Indian Feather Publishing, *(Indian Feather; 0-937962),* 7218 SW Oak, Portland, OR 97223 (SAN 215-9996).

Indian Historian Press, Inc., *(Indian Hist Pr; 0-913436),* 1451 Masonic Ave., San Francisco, CA 94117 Tel 415-626-5235 (SAN 202-6929).

Indian Pubns., *(Indian Pubns; 0-934170),* 1869 Second Ave., New York, NY 10029 Tel 212-370-2187 (SAN 212-808X).

Indian Univ. Press, *(Indian U Pr; 0-940392),* Bacone College, Muskogee, OK 74401 Tel 918-683-4581 (SAN 217-1821).

Indian Women's Pocahontas Club, *(Indian Pocahontas Club),* 323 N. Choctaw, Claremore, OK 74017 (SAN 208-3272).

Indiana University, African Studies Program, *(Indiana Africa; 0-941934),* 221 Woodburn Hall Indiana University, Bloomington, IN 47405 (SAN 238-6135).

Indiana Univ., Bureau of Business Research, *(Ind U Busn Res; 0-87925),* Bloomington, IN 47405 Tel 812-335-5507 (SAN 202-6880).

Indiana University, Dept. of Health & Safety Education, Office of Pubns. & Editorial Services, *(IN U Dept Health; 0-941636),* HPER Bldg., Rm. 116, Bloomington, IN 47405 Tel 812-335-7975 (SAN 239-233X).

Indiana Univ. Press, *(Ind U Pr; 0-253),* 1700 Mishawaka Ave.P.O. Box7111, South Bend, IN 44634 Tel 219-237-4214 (SAN 202-5647).

Indiana Univ. Research Institute for Inner Asian Studies, *(Ind U Res Inst; 0-933070),* Goodbody Hall 344, Bloomington, IN 47405 Tel 812-335-1605 (SAN 215-1553).

Indianapolis Museum of Art, *(Ind Mus Art; 0-936260),* 1200 W. 38th St., Indianapolis, IN 46208 (SAN 215-6571).

Indigenous Pubns., *(Indigenous Pubns; 0-930740),* P.O. Box 1614, Aptos, CA 95003 Tel 209-529-5087 (SAN 210-8801).

Indigo Press, *(Indigo Pr; 0-9604060),* 5950 Fern Flat Rd., Aptos, CA 95003 (SAN 239-443X); Dist. by: Straw into Gold, 3006 San Pablo, Berkeley, CA 94702 (SAN 239-4448).

Indisota Publishers, *(Indisota Pubs; 0-9603420),* 3166 Ridge Court, Placerville, CA 95667 (SAN 213-8492).

Individual Learning Systems, Inc., Southwest Offset, Inc., *(Individual Learn; 0-86589),* P.O. Box 225447, Dallas, TX 75265 Tel 214-630-0313 (SAN 203-8021).

Indochina Curriculum Group, *(Indochina Curriculum Grp; 0-9607794),* 11 Garden St., Cambridge, MA 02138 Tel 617-354-6583 (SAN 217-7854).

Industrial Development Div., Institute of Science & Technology, *(Indus Dev Inst Sci; 0-938654),* Univ. of Michigan, 2200 Bonisteel Blvd., Ann Arbor, MI 48105 Tel 313-764-5260 (SAN 204-8590).

Industrial Press Inc., *(Indus Pr; 0-8311),* 200 Madison Ave., New York, NY 10157 Tel 212-889-6330 (SAN 202-6945).

Industrial Relations Counselors, Inc. (IRC), *(Indus Rel; 0-87330),* P.O. Box 1530, New York, NY 10101 Tel 212-541-6086 (SAN 203-8048).

Industrial Research Service, Inc., *(Indus Res Serv),* 132 Concord Rd., Dover, NH 03820 Tel 603-868-2593 (SAN 204-8612).

Industrial Research Unit-The Wharton School, *(Indus Res Unit-Wharton; 0-89546),* Univ. of Pennsylvania, Vance Hall/CS, 3733 Spruce St., Philadelphia, PA 19104 Tel 215-898-5606 (SAN 206-0744).

Industrial Training Consultants, Inc., *(Indus Training; 0-9603702),* P.O. Box 3213, Richmond, VA 23235 (SAN 215-1561).

Industrial Workers of the World, *(Indus Workers World; 0-917124),* 3435 N. Sheffield, Chicago, IL 60657 Tel 312-549-5045 (SAN 209-1909).

Industry Book Publishing, Inc., *(Indus Bk Pub; 0-939554),* 1437 Tuttle Ave., Wallingford, CT 06492 Tel 203-269-9184 (SAN 220-1720).

Indytype, Inc., *(Indytype; 0-9607968),* P.O. Box 68110, Indianapolis, IN 46268 Tel 317-293-1500 (SAN 238-0463).

Infernal Artists Scribes Publishers, *(Infernal Artists),* 185 Butler St., Hamden, CT 06511 Tel 203-787-4376 (SAN 209-4495); P.O. Box 4034, Hamden, CT 06514 (SAN 209-4509).

Infomap, Incorporated, *(Infomap Inc),* 3300 Arapahoe No. 207, Boulder, CO 80303 (SAN 262-0421).

Information Alternative, *(Info Alternative; 0-936288),* P.O. Box 5571, Chicago, IL 60680 (SAN 215-8744).

Information Clearing House, Inc., *(Info Clearing House; 0-931634),* 500 Fifth Ave., New York, NY 10110 (SAN 212-6680).

Information Coordinators, Inc., *(Info Coord; 0-911772; 0-89990),* 1435-37 Randolph St., Detroit, MI 48226 (SAN 206-7641).

Information Gatekeepers, Inc., *(Info Gatekeepers),* 167 Corey Road, Brookline, MA 02146 Tel 617-739-2022 (SAN 237-9597).

Information Handling Services, *(IHS; 0-910972; 0-89847),* 15 Inverness Way E., P.O. Box 1154, Englewood, CO 80150 Tel 303-779-0600 (SAN 203-7254) Prepackaged & custom services on 8mm & 16mm roll microfilm & microfiche. Products include federal & military specifications & standards, industry standards, government procurement packages, product & vendor catalog data, scholarly & legal publications for industry, government, libraries & education.

Information Industry Association, *(Info Indus),* 316 Pennsylvania Ave, SE, Ste. 400, Washington, DC 20003 (SAN 224-7070).

Information Management Press, *(Info Mgmt Pr; 0-9606408),* P.O. Box 19166, Washington, DC 20037 Tel 202-293-5519 (SAN 218-5563).

Information Press, The, *(Info Pr; 0-911927),* P.O. Box 957, Sisters, OR 97759 Tel 503-549-5181 (SAN 264-1127).

Information Products, *(Info Prods; 0-937978),* 30917 Rue de la Pierre, Rancho Palos Verdes, CA 90274 (SAN 214-0349).

Information Reduction Research, *(Info Reduction; 0-919621),* P.O. Box 488, New Canaan, CT 06840 (SAN 240-9763).

Information Research, *(Info Res MI; 0-910085),* 10367 Paw Paw Lake Dr., Mattawan, MI 49071 Tel 616-668-2049 (SAN 241-3159).

Information Resources, Inc., *(Info Res Inc; 0-912864),* P.O. Box 417, Lexington, MA 02173 Tel 617-861-7996 (SAN 203-1434).

Information Resources Press, Div. of Herner & Co., *(Info Resources; 0-87815),* 1700 N. Moore St., Suite 700, Arlington, VA 22209 Tel 703-558-8270 (SAN 202-6961).

Information Services, Inc., *(Info Serv),* Suite 735, 4733 Bethesda Ave., Bethesda, MD 20814 (SAN 286-3464).

Information Sources, Inc., *(Info Sources; 0-943906),* 1807 Glenview Rd., Glenview, IL 60025 Tel 312-724-9285 (SAN 241-1210).

Information Store, Inc., The, *(Info Store; 0-940004),* 140 Second St.,Fifth Floor, San Francisco, CA 94105 Tel 415-543-4636 (SAN 216-8219).

Information Systems Development, *(Info Systems; 0-931738),* 1100 E. Eighth, Austin, TX 78702 (SAN 213-6244).

Information Transfer Inc., *(Info Transfer; 0-937398),* 9300 Columbia Blvd., Silver Springs, MD 20910 Tel 301-587-9390 (SAN 213-2532).

Informed Performer, The, *(TIP),* P.O. Box 793, Ansonia Station, New York, NY 10023 (SAN 237-9600).

Infosources Publishing, *(Infosources; 0-939486),* 118 W. 79th St., New York, NY 10024 Tel 212-595-3161 (SAN 216-3985).

Ingham Publishing, Inc., *(Ingham Pub; 0-9611804),* P.O. Box 12642, St. Petersburg, FL 33733 Tel 813-343-4811 (SAN 286-1127).

Ingleside Publishing, *(Ingleside; 0-9603502),* 410 Grove Ave., Barrington, IL 60010 Tel 312-381-4312 (SAN 213-5221).

Inglewood Public Library, *(Inglewood CA; 0-913578),* 101 W. Manchester Blvd., Inglewood, CA 90301 Tel 213-649-7397 (SAN 201-5145); Orders to: Inglewood Finance Dept., P.O. Box 6500, Inglewood, CA 90301 (SAN 215-0018).

Ingram, Rose S., *(Ingram; 0-9606230),* P.O. Box 31895, Lafayette, LA 70503 Tel 318-984-3395 (SAN 217-5290).

Ink Arts Pubns., *(Ink Art Pubns),* P.O. Box 36070, Indianapolis, IN 46236 Tel 317-897-5793 (SAN 213-0874).

Ink Slinger Publishing Company, *(Ink Slinger Pub; 0-941956),* P.O. Box 2425, Bellingham, WA 98227 Tel 206-734-2123 (SAN 239-7757).

Inka Dinka Ink, *(Inka Dinka Ink; 0-939700),* 4741 Guerley Rd., Cincinnati, OH 45238 Tel 513-471-0825 (SAN 281-8086); Dist. by: Baker & Taylor, Gladiola Ave., Momence, IL 60954 (SAN 169-4901); Dist. by: Baker & Taylor, Commerce, GA 30599 (SAN 169-1503); Dist. by: Baker & Taylor, 50 Kirby Ave., Somerville, NJ 08876 (SAN 169-4901).

Inkspot Press, *(Inkspot Pr; 0-9611590),* 635 Staats, Bloomington, IN 47401 Tel 812-336-0375 (SAN 285-323X).

Inkstone Books, *(Inkstone Books; 0-9604542),* P.O. Box 22172, Carmel, CA 93922 Tel 408-375-3296 (SAN 262-043X).

Inkworks Press, *(Inkworks; 0-930712),* 4220 Telegraph Ave., Oakland, CA 94609 Tel 415-652-7111 (SAN 281-8124); Orders to: 2943 Seventh St., Berkeley, CA 94710 Tel 415-549-3030 (SAN 281-8132).

Inky Press Productions, *(Inky Pr; 0-930810),* Box 92595, Rochester, NY 14692 (SAN 283-3840).

Inman, W. Richard, *(W R Inman),* 996-C Ponderoso Ave., Sunnyvale, CA 94086 (SAN 208-4198).

Inner Circle Publishing Co., *(Inner Circle; 0-938284),* P.O. Box 1617, Detroit, MI 48231 (SAN 215-7780).

Inner Light Publishing, *(Inner Light Pub; 0-911717),* 21 Crest Road, Fairfax, CA 94930 Tel 415-456-6176 (SAN 264-1143).

Inner Traditions International, Ltd., *(Inner Tradit; 0-89281),* 377 Park Ave. S., 6th Fl., New York, NY 10016 Tel 212-889-8350 (SAN 208-6948).

Innersphere Music Studio, *(Innersphere; 0-942542),* Brandywine Valley, Headquarters, P.O. Box 7333, Wilmington, DE 19803 (SAN 239-6599).

Innovations Press, *(Innovations Pr; 0-949438),* P. O. Box 13158, Pittsburgh, PA 15243 Tel 412-341-4863 (SAN 219-967X).

Innovative Education Publishing Co., *(Innovative Pub),* P.O. Box 5066, Milford, CT 06460 Tel 203-874-6046 (SAN 287-2927).

Innovative Educational Affairs, Inc., *(Innovative Ed; 0-914394),* 16 Tain Dr., Great Neck, NY 11021 Tel 516-466-2498 (SAN 202-697X).

Innovative Informations Inc., *(Innovative Inform; 0-910661),* P.O. Box 408, Greenbelt, MD 20770 Tel 301-345-4372 (SAN 262-7302).

Innovex Press, *(Innovex; 0-9609906),* 11 Stone Root Lane, Sudbury, MA 01776 Tel 617-443-4771 (SAN 271-0129).

InPrint, *(InPrint; 0-937362),* P.O. Box 687, Farmingdale, NJ 07727 (SAN 262-0448).

Inquiry Press, *(Inquiry Pr; 0-918112),* 4925 Jefferson Ave, Midland, MI 48640 Tel 517-631-0009 (SAN 208-1164).

Inscape Corp., *(Inscape Corp; 0-87953),* 1629 "K" St., N.W., Suite 5107, Washington, DC 20006 Tel 301-469-7788 (SAN 207-0731); Orders to: Inscape Customer Service, P.O. Box 978, Edison, NJ 08817 (SAN 207-074X) Moved, Left No Forwarding Address.

Insearch Press, *(Insearch Pr; 0-943902),* 408 W. Main, Lexington, IL 61753 Tel 309-365-8746 (SAN 241-1229).

Insiders' Publishing Group, *(Insiders Pub; 0-932338),* 349 W. Bute St., Room C-5, Norfolk, VA 23510 Tel 804-627-9925 (SAN 213-3245).

Insiders Software Consultants, Inc., *(Insiders Software; 0-939462),* P.O. Box 7086, Alexandria, VA 22307 (SAN 216-3993).

Insight Books See Van Nostrand Reinhold Co. Inc

Insight Press, *(Insight Pr CA; 0-935218),* 614 Vermont St., San Francisco, CA 94107 (SAN 213-0955).

Insight Press, Inc., *(Insight Pr; 0-914520),* P.O. Box 8369, New Orleans, LA 70182 (SAN 202-6988).

Insights Books, *(Insight Bks; 0-910087),* P.O. Box 1784, Ann Arbor, MI 48106 Tel 313-663-9645 (SAN 240-8252).

Inspiration Co., *(Inspiration MI),* P. O. Box 17, Birmingham, MI 48012 (SAN 221-0738).

Inspiration House Pubs., *(Inspiration Conn; 0-918114),* P.O. Box 1, South Windsor, CT 06074 Tel 203-289-7363 (SAN 206-1066).

Inspirational Books, *(Inspirational Bks),* 5104 Glenwood, Chicago, IL 60640 Tel 312-649-5316 (SAN 213-3261).

Institute for Advanced Studies of World Religions, The, *(Inst Adv Stud Wld; 0-915078),* 2150 Center Ave., Fort Lee, NJ 07024 (SAN 265-3885); Dist. by: Melville Memorial Library, State University of New York at Stony Brook, Stony Brook, NY 11794 (SAN 200-4275).

Institute for American Research, *(Inst Am Res; 0-911773),* 300 No. Los Carneros Rd., Goleta, CA 93117 (SAN 264-116X).

Institute for Architecture & Urban Studies, The, *(IAUS; 0-932628),* 8 W. 40th St., New York, NY 10018 Tel 212-398-9474 (SAN 213-5167).

Institute for Business Planning, Inc., *(Inst Busn Plan; 0-87624),* 210 Sylvan Ave., Englewood Cliffs, NJ 07632 Tel 201-592-2015 (SAN 202-7003).

Institute for Byzantine & Modern Greek Studies, Inc., *(Inst Byzantine; 0-914744),* 115 Gilbert Rd., Belmont, MA 02178 Tel 617-484-6595 (SAN 201-5110).

Institute for Contemporary Studies, *(Inst Contemporary; 0-917616),* 260 California St., Suite 811, San Francisco, CA 94111 Tel 415-398-3010 (SAN 209-2638).

Institute for Contemporary Studies See ICS Pr.

Institute for Cross-Cultural Research, *(ICR; 0-911976),* 4000 Albermarle St., N.W., Washington, DC 20016 (SAN 206-6505).

Institute for Cultural Progress, *(Inst Cult Prog; 0-942776),* 2913 29th St., N. W., Washington, DC 20008 Tel 202-234-1616 (SAN 219-8398); Dist. by: Publishing Center for Cultural Resources, 625 Broadway, New York, NY 10012 Tel 212-260-2010 (SAN 212-6036).

Institute for Ecological Policies, *(Inst Ecological; 0-937786),* 9208 Christopher St., Fairfax, VA 22031 (SAN 215-6598).

Institute for Econometric Research, *(Inst Econometric; 0-917604),* 3471 N. Federal Hwy., Suite 350, Fort Lauderdale, FL 33306 Tel 305-563-9000 (SAN 209-2174).

Institute for Economic & Financial Research, *(Inst Econ Finan; 0-918968),* Dist. by: American Classical College Press, P.O. Box 4526, Albuquerque, NM 87196 Tel 505-843-7749 (SAN 201-2618).

Institute for Economic & Political World Strategic Studies, *(Inst Econ Pol; 0-930008; 0-86722),* P.O. Box 4526, Sta. A, Albuquerque, NM 87196 Tel 505-843-7749 (SAN 210-4431).

Institute for Educational Leadership, *(Inst Educ Lead),* 1001 Connecticut Ave, N.W., Ste. 310, Washington, DC 20036 Tel 202-676-5900 (SAN 225-7823).

Institute for Educational Leadership, Inc., *(Inst Ed Leadership),* 1001 Connecticut Ave. N.W., Suite 310, Washington, DC 20036 (SAN 287-2749).

Institute for Educational Management, *(Inst Ed Management; 0-934222),* Harvard University, 337 Gutman Library, Appian Way, Cambridge, MA 02138 Tel 617-495-2655 (SAN 213-5175).

Institute for Effective Management, *(Inst Effect Mgmt; 0-914804),* Chapman Rd., Fountainville, PA 18923 Tel 215-345-0265 (SAN 206-4553).

Institute for Environmental Action, *(Inst for Environ Action; 0-936020),* 81 Leonard St., New York, NY 10013 (SAN 213-7623).

Institute for Environmental Studies, *(Inst Environ),* 3400 Walnut St, Philadelphia, PA 19104 (SAN 226-5648).

Institute for Evolutionary Research, *(Inst Evolutionary; 0-938710),* 200 Park Ave., New York, NY 10166 (SAN 215-8760).

Institute for Food & Development Policy, *(Inst Food & Develop; 0-935028),* 1885 Mission St., San Francisco, CA 94103 Tel 415-864-6620 (SAN 213-327X).

Institute for Foreign Policy Analysis, Inc., *(Inst Foreign Policy Anal; 0-89549),* 675 Massachusetts Ave., Central Plaza Bldg. 10th Fl., Cambridge, MA 02139 Tel 617-492-2116 (SAN 210-444X).

Institute for Historical Review, *(Inst Hist Rev; 0-939484),* P. O. Box 1306, Torrance, CA 90505 Tel 213-326-4504 (SAN 220-1275).

Institute for Human Growth & Awareness, The, *(Inst Human Growth; 0-87852),* P.O. Box 6695, San Jose, CA 95150 Tel 408-275-1911 (SAN 202-3636).

Institute for Human Studies, *(Inst Human NY; 0-932340),* Box 240, Gardiner, NY 12525 (SAN 211-710X); Orders to: 14 South Division St., Peekskill, NY 10566 (SAN 211-7118) Moved, Left No Forwarding Address.

Institute for Humane Studies, Inc., *(Inst Humane; 0-89617),* 1177 University Dr., Menlo Park, CA 94025 Tel 415-323-2464 (SAN 214-123X); Orders to: P.O. Box 2256, Wichita, KS 67201 Tel 316-832-5604 (SAN 214-1248).

Institute for Independent Social Journalism, *(IISJ; 0-917654),* 33 W. 17th St., New York, NY 10011 Tel 212-691-0404 (SAN 201-842X).

Institute for Information Policy & Research, *(Inst. for Info),* 6200 N. Capitol St. N.W., P.O. Box 60381, Washington, DC 20039 (SAN 238-0625).

Institute for Information Studies, *(Inst Info Stud; 0-935294),* 200 Little Falls St., Suite 104, Falls Church, VA 22046 (SAN 215-6601).

Institute for International Economics, *(Inst Intl Eco; 0-88132),* 11 Dupont Circle N.W., Washington, DC 20036 Tel 202-328-0583 (SAN 241-5259).

Institute for Local Self-Reliance, *(Inst Local Self Re),* 1717 18th St., N.W., Washington, DC 20009 (SAN 217-7919).

Institute for Mining & Minerals Research, *(Inst Mining & Minerals; 0-86607),* Iron Works Pike, Box 13015, Lexington, KY 40583 Tel 606-252-5535 (SAN 239-4456).

Institute for Palestine Studies, *(Inst Palestine; 0-88728),* P.O. Box 19449, Washington, DC 20036 (SAN 207-611X).

Institute For Peace & Justice, Inc., *(Inst Peace; 0-912765),* 4144 Lindell Blvd., Suite 400, St. Loius, MO 63108 Tel 314-423-1834 (SAN 282-7891).

Institute for Personality & Ability Testing, Inc., *(Inst Personality & Ability; 0-918296),* P. O. Box 188, Champaign, IL 61820 Tel 217-352-4739 (SAN 209-3197).

Institute for Policy Studies, *(Inst Policy Stud; 0-89758),* 1901 "Q" St., N.W., Washington, DC 20009 Tel 202-234-9382 (SAN 212-1026).

Institute for Polynesian Studies, The, *(Inst Polynesian; 0-939154),* Brigham Young Univ.-Hawaii Campus, Laie, HI 96762 (SAN 219-8606).

Institute for Product Safety, *(Inst Product; 0-938830),* 1410 Duke University Rd., Durham, NC 27701 (SAN 216-0439).

Institute for Public Management, *(Inst Pub Mgmt),* Suite 365, 550 W. Jackson Blvd., Chicago, IL 60606 Tel 312-559-0515 (SAN 238-8251).

Institute for Quality in Human Life, *(Inst Qual Hum Life; 0-939630),* 6335 N. Delaware Ave., Portland, OR 97217 Tel 503-289-6136 (SAN 206-4367).

Institute for Rational-Emotive Therapy, *(Inst Rational-Emotive; 0-917476),* 45 E. 65th St., New York, NY 10021 Tel 212-535-0822 (SAN 210-3079).

Institute for Rational Living, *(Inst Rat Liv),* 1162 Beacon St., Brookline, MA 02146 Tel 617-739-5063 (SAN 209-5068).

Institute for Responsive Education, *(Inst Responsive; 0-917754),* 605 Commonwealth Ave., Boston, MA 02215 (SAN 216-1451).

Institute for Social Research Univ. of Michigan, *(Inst Soc Res; 0-87944),* Box 1248, Ann Arbor, MI 48106 Tel 313-764-7509 (SAN 210-6035).

Institute for Socioeconomic Studies, *(Inst Socioecon),* Airport Rd, White Plains, NY 10604 (SAN 235-6023).

Institute for Software Engineering, *(Inst Software Eng; 0-931900),* 510 Oakmead Parkway, Sunnyvale, CA 94086 Tel 408-749-0133 (SAN 209-0686).

Institute for Southern Studies, *(Inst Southern Studies),* P.O. Box 531, Durham, NC 27702 (SAN 226-0107).

Institute for Studies in American Music, *(Inst Am Music; 0-914678),* Conservatory of Music, Brooklyn College, Brooklyn, NY 11210 Tel 212-780-5655 (SAN 202-6996).

Institute for Studies in Pragmaticism, *(Inst Stud Prag; 0-936842),* Rm 304K, Library, Texas Tech. Univ., Lubbock, TX 79409 (SAN 214-3135).

Institute for the Advancement of Philosophy for Children, *(Inst Adv Philo; 0-916834),* c/o The First Mountain Foundation, P.O. Box 196, Montclair, NJ 07042 Tel 201-893-4277 (SAN 207-2378).

Institute for the Analysis, Evaluation & Design of Human Action, *(Inst Analysis; 0-938526),* 44 Clifford Ave., Pelham, NY 10803 (SAN 215-8752).

Institute for the Arts, Rice Univ., *(Inst for the Arts; 0-914412),* P.O. Box 1892, Houston, TX 77001 Tel 713-527-4858 (SAN 207-4435).

Institute for the Development of the Harmonious Human Being Inc., *(IDHHB; 0-89556),* P.O. Box 370, Nevada City, CA 95959 Tel 916-786-7313 (SAN 211-3635).

Institute for the Study of Animal Problems, *(Inst Study Animal; 0-937712),* 2100 L St., N.W., Washington, DC 20037 (SAN 215-2088).

Institute for the Study of Human Issues (ISHI), *(Inst Study Human; 0-89727; 0-915980),* 3401 Market St., Philadelphia, PA 19104 Tel 215-387-9002 (SAN 207-6608).

Institute for the Study of Human Knowledge, *(Ins Study Human),* P. O. Box 176, Los Altos, CA 94022 Tel 415-948-9428 (SAN 226-4536).

Institute for the Study of Man, Inc., *(Inst Study Man),* 1629 K St., N.W., Suite 520, Washington, DC 20006 Tel 202-789-0231 (SAN 213-523X).

Institute for Urban & Regional Studies, Washington Univ., *(Inst for Urban & Regional),* P.O. Box 1051, St. Louis, MO 63130 (SAN 212-2812).

Institute for Urban Design, *(Inst Urban Des; 0-042468),* Main P.O. Box 105, Purchase, NY 10577 (SAN 264-1178).

Institute in Basic Youth Conflicts, *(Inst Basic Youth; 0-916888),* P.O. Box 1, Oak Brook, IL 60521 Tel 312-323-9800 (SAN 208-6972).

Institute of Arab Studies, *(Inst Arab Stud; 0-912031),* 556 Trapelo Rd., Belmont, MA 02178 (SAN 265-3583).

Institute of Certified Travel Agents, *(Inst Cert Trav Agts; 0-931202),* 148 Linden St., Wellesley, MA 02181 (SAN 238-7700).

Institute of Creation Research *See* **CLP Pubs.**

Institute of Dowsing, The, *(Inst Dowsing; 0-931740),* 414 Biscayne Dr., Wilmington, NC 28405 (SAN 211-643X).

Institute of Early American History & Culture, *(Inst Early Am; 0-910776),* P.O. Box 220, Williamsburg, VA 23187 Tel 804-229-2771 (SAN 201-5161).

Institute of Electrical & Electronics Engineers, *(Inst Electrical; 0-87942),* 345 E. 47th St., New York, NY 10017 Tel 212-705-7558 (SAN 203-8064); Orders to: IEEE Ctr., 445 Hoes Lane, Piscataway, NJ 08854 Tel 201-981-0060 (SAN 203-8072).

Institute of Electrical Engineers, *(Inst Elect Eng; 0-85296),* PPL/IEEE Service Center, 445 Hoes Lane, Piscataway, NJ 08854 Tel 201-981-0060 (SAN 213-0882).

Institute of General Semantics, *(Inst Gen Semantics; 0-910780),* R.R. 1, P.O. Box 215, Lakeville, CT 06039 Tel 203-435-9174 (SAN 203-8080).

Institute of Industrial Engineers, *(Inst Indus Eng; 0-89806),* 25 Technology Park-Atlanta, Norcross, GA 30092 Tel 404-449-0460 (SAN 213-2338).

Institute of Internal Auditors, Inc., *(Inst Inter Aud; 0-89413),* 249 Maitland Ave., Altamonte Springs, FL 32701 Tel 305-830-7600 (SAN 213-4411). *Imprints:* Foundation for Auditability Research & Education, Inc. (Found Audit Res).

Institute of International Education, *(Inst Intl Educ; 0-87206),* 809 United Nations Plaza, New York, NY 10017 Tel 212-883-8279 (SAN 202-702X).

Institute of Jesuit Sources, The, *(Inst Jesuit; 0-912422),* Fusz Memorial, St. Louis Univ., 3700 W. Pine Blvd., St. Louis, MO 63108 Tel 314-652-5737 (SAN 202-7038).

Institute of Management & Labor Relations, *(Inst Mgmt & Labor),* Public Education Dept., Ryders Lane, Cook Campus, New Brunswick, NJ 08903 (SAN 215-8779).

Institute of Mediaeval Music, *(Inst Mediaeval Mus; 0-912024; 0-931902),* (SAN 206-6955); c/o L.A. Dittmer, P.O. Box 295, Henryville, PA 18332 Tel 717-629-1278 (SAN 285-0311).

Institute of Middle Eastern & North African Affairs, *(Inst Mid East & North Africa; 0-934484),* P.O. Box 1674, Hyattsville, MD 20788 (SAN 213-8506).

Institute of Modern Languages, Inc., *(Inst Mod Lang; 0-88499),* P.O. Box 1087, Silver Spring, MD 20910 Tel 301-565-2580 (SAN 206-9598).

Institute of Paper Chemistry, *(Inst Paper Chem; 0-87010),* P.O. Box 1039, Appleton, WI 54912 Tel 414-734-9251 (SAN 203-8099).

Institute of Psychorientology, *(Inst Psych Inc; 0-913343),* P.O. Box 2249, 1110 Cedar, Laredo, TX 78041 Tel 512-722-6391 (SAN 283-118X).

Institute of Real Estate Management, *(Inst Real Estate; 0-912104),* 430 N. Michigan Ave., Chicago, IL 60611-4090 Tel 312-661-1930 (SAN 202-7046).

Institute of Sino-American Research, *(Inst Sino-Amer; 0-913973),* 108 Shady Dr., Indiana, PA 15701 Tel 412-463-0513 (SAN 241-5453).

Institute of Society, Ethics & Life Sciences-The Hastings Center, *(Inst Soc Ethics; 0-916558),* 360 Broadway, Hastings-on-Hudson, NY 10706 Tel 914-478-0500 (SAN 208-6980).

Institute of Urban Studies, the Univ. of Texas at Arlington, *(Inst Urban Studies),* P.O. Box 19588, Arlington, TX 76019 Tel 817-273-3071 (SAN 207-5253).

Institute Press, *(Inst Pr; 0-931976),* 2210 Wilshire Blvd., Suite 171, Santa Monica, CA 90403 Tel 213-828-6541 (SAN 211-321X).

Institute Press, Div. of Int'l Loss Control Institute, *(Inst Pr Ga),* Highway 78, Loganville, GA 30249 Tel 404-466-2208 (SAN 240-9887).

Institutes for Energy Development, Inc., *(Inst Energy; 0-89419),* P.O. Box 19243, Oklahoma City, OK 76133 Tel 405-691-4449 (SAN 209-9322).

Institution for Tuberculosis Research, Univ. of Illinois, Medical Ctr., *(Inst Tuberculosis; 0-915314),* 904 W. Adams St., Chicago, IL 60607 Tel 312-996-4688 (SAN 207-1428).

Institutional Development and Economic Affairs Service, Inc., *(Inst Dev & Econ),* Magnolia Star Rte, Nederland, CO 80466 Tel 303-443-8789 (SAN 225-6681).

Instructional Aides, Inc., *(Instruct Aides TX; 0-936474),* X1401 Windy Meadow Dr., Plano, TX 75023 (SAN 220-2557).

Instructional Objectives Exchange, *(Instruct Object; 0-932166),* 11411 W. Jefferson Blvd., Culver City, CA 90230 Tel 213-391-6295 (SAN 211-1322).

Instructional Resources Inc., *(Instruct Res),* P.O. Box 3452, Tallahassee, FL 32315 Tel 904-385-2546 (SAN 215-7799).

Instrument Society of America, *(Instru Soc; 0-87664),* P.O. Box 12277, 67 Alexander Dr., Research Triangle Park, NC 27709 Tel 919-549-8411 (SAN 202-7054).

Instrumentalist Co., *(Instrumental Co)* 1418 Lake St., Evanston, IL 60204 Tel 312-328-6000 (SAN 203-7033).

Insurance Achievement, Inc., *(Insurance Achiev; 0-88171),* 7330 Highland Rd., Baton Rouge, LA 70808 Tel 800-535-3042 (SAN 264-1186).

Insurance Institute of America, Inc., *(IIA; 0-89462),* Providence & Sugartown Rds., Malvern, PA 19355 Tel 215-644-2100 (SAN 210-2129).

Insurance Research Service, *(Ins Res Svc),* 571 E. Main St., Brevard, NC 28712 Tel 704-883-9333 (SAN 213-3288).

Inswinger, Inc., *(Inswinger; 0-9608170),* 5580 la Jolla Blvd., Suite 418, La Jolla, CA 92037 (SAN 238-826X).

Integral Yoga Pubns., *(Integral Yoga Pubns),* Satchidananda Ashram-Yogaville, P.O. Box 108, Rt. 97, Pomfret Ctr., CT 06259 Tel 203-974-1008 (SAN 285-032X); c/o Satchidananda Ashram-Yogaville, P.O. Box 172, Buckingham, VA 23921 Tel 804-969-4801 (SAN 285-0338).

Integrated Education Associates, *(Integrated Ed Assoc; 0-912008),* Univ. of Massachusetts School of Education, Amherst, MA 01003 Tel 413-545-0327 (SAN 203-8129).

Integrated Energy Systems, *(Integ Energy; 0-9608358),* Rt 2, Box 61A1, Monroe, GA 30655 Tel 404-267-3534 (SAN 240-6802).

Integrated Press, *(Integrated Pr),* 526 Comstock Dr., Tiburon, CA 94920 (SAN 263-2403).

Integration Pr., *(Integ Pr; 0-9609928),* c/o H. Newton Malony, 177 N. Madison, Pasadena, CA (SAN 271-1257).

Integrity Press, *(Integrity; 0-918048),* 3888 Morse Rd., Columbus, OH 43219 Tel 614-471-2759 (SAN 210-2145).

Intentional Educations, Inc., *(Intentional Ed; 0-9607970),* 341 Mt. Auburn St., Watertown, MA 02172 Tel 617-923-7707 (SAN 239-6610).

Inter-American Tropical Tuna Commission, *(Inter-Am Tropical; 0-9603078),* P.O. Box 1529, La Jolla, CA 92093 (SAN 214-3143).

Inter American Univ. Press, *(Inter Am U Pr; 0-913480),* G.P.O. Box 3255, San Juan, PR 00936 Tel 809-754-8145 (SAN 202-7062).

Inter-Crescent Publishing Co., Inc., *(Inter-Crescent; 0-916400),* P.O. Box 31413, Dallas, TX 75231 Tel 214-341-4792 (SAN 208-7006).

Inter-Optics Pubns., Inc., *(Inter-Optics Pubns; 0-935726),* 90 Bagby Dr., Suite 222, Birmingham, AL 35209 Tel 205-942-5232 (SAN 214-0403).

Inter-Religious Task Force for Social Analysis, *(Inter-Religious Task; 0-936476),* 361 Athol Ave., Oakland, CA 94606 (SAN 216-2563).

Inter-Ski Services, Inc., *(Inter-Ski; 0-931636),* P. O. Box 3635, Georgetown Sta., Washington, DC 20007 (SAN 221-0622).

Inter-university Consortium for Political & Social Research, *(ICPSR; 0-89138),* P.O. Box 1248, Ann Arbor, MI 48106 Tel 313-763-5010 (SAN 207-7450).

Inter-Varsity Press, *(Inter-Varsity; 0-87784; 0-8308),* P.O. Box F, Downers Grove, IL 60515 Tel 312-964-5700 (SAN 202-7089).

Interbook, Inc., *(Interbk Inc; 0-913456; 0-89192),* 611 Broadway, Rm. 227, New York, NY 10012 Tel 212-677-9201 (SAN 202-7070).

Intercontinental Press, *(Intercont Press; 0-933142),* P.O. Box 565, Auburn, AL 36830 Tel 205-887-5297 (SAN 281-8167); Orders to: Raj P. Mohan, Box 565, Auburn, AL 36830 Tel 205-887-5297 (SAN 281-8175).

Intercultural Press, Inc., *(Intercult Pr; 0-933622),* 70 W. Hubbard St., Chicago, IL 60610 Tel 312-321-0075 (SAN 212-6699).

Interdependent Learning Model, *(ILM; 0-939632),* Fordham Univ., Keating Hall, B24, Bronx, NY 10458 Tel 212-579-2495 (SAN 216-6305).

INTEREG *See* **International Regulations Publishing & Distributing Organization**

Interfacia, Inc., Div. of Creative Informatics, *(Interfacia Inc; 0-917634),* P.O. Box 4422, Chicago, IL 60680 Tel 312-643-9050 (SAN 213-6724).

Intergalactic Publishing Co., *(Intergalactic NJ),* P.O. Box 188, Clementon, NJ 08021 Tel 609-854-0499 (SAN 213-988X).

Interhouse Publishing, *(Interhouse Pub; 0-932380),* 457 Highland, Elmhurst, IL 60126 (SAN 221-0576).

Interior Design Books, A Division of Whitney Communications Corp., *(Inter Design; 0-943370),* 850 Third Ave., New York, NY 10022 Tel 212-715-2680 (SAN 240-6810); Dist. by: Van Nostrand Reinhold, Co., 135 W. 50th St., New York, NY 10020 Tel 212-265-8700 (SAN 202-5183).

Interiors by Arden, *(Interiors; 0-934892),* 8131 Lemon, No. 8, La Mesa, CA 92041 Tel 714-460-7998 (SAN 213-2540).

Interland Publishing, Inc., *(Interland Pub; 0-87989),* 799 Broadway, New York, NY 10003 Tel 212-673-8280 (SAN 203-8145).

Interlingual Institute, *(Interlingual; 0-917848),* Box 126, Canal St. Sta., New York, NY 10013 Tel 212-349-3679 (SAN 209-9330).

InterMed Communications, Inc., *(InterMed Comm; 0-916730),* 1111 Bethlehem Pike, Springhouse, PA 19477 Tel 215-646-8700 (SAN 208-1202).

Intermedia, Inc., *(Intermedia; 0-910788),* 434 Woodward Rd., Nassau, NY 12123 (SAN 206-6947).

Intermediate Technology Development Group of North America, *(Intermediate Tech; 0-942850),* P.O. Box 337, Croton-on-Hudson, NY 10520 Tel 914-271-6500 (SAN 218-4303).

Intermountain Air Press, *(Intermtn Air; 0-914680),* 171 S. Second E., Preston, ID 83263 (SAN 206-5428).

Intermountain Arts & Crafts, *(Intermntn Arts; 0-9605840),* Rte. 2 Box 2042, Burney, CA 96013 Tel 916-335-4330 (SAN 216-5996).

International Art Alliance, *(Intl Art Alliance; 0-943488),* P.O. Box 1608, Largo, FL 34294 Tel 813-581-7328 (SAN 240-6829).

International Assn. of Assessing Officers, *(Intl Assess; 0-88329),* 1313 E. 60th St., Chicago, IL 60637 Tel 312-947-2069 (SAN 205-0277).

International Assn. of Chiefs of Police, *(Intl Assn Chiefs Police; 0-88269),* 11 Firstfield Rd., Gaithersburg, MD 20760 Tel 301-948-0922 (SAN 211-5301).

International Assn. of Fish & Wildlife Agencies (IAFWA), *(IAFWA; 0-932108),* 1412 16th St., N.W., Washington, DC 20036 Tel 202-232-1652 (SAN 213-5205).

International Assn. of Schools of Social Work, (Intl Assn Schools; 0-931638), C/O CSWE, 345 E. 46th St., Rm 615, New York, NY 10017 (SAN 212-7482) No Longer in the U.S.

International Association of Business Communicators, (Intl Assn Busn Comm), 870 Market St Ste 940, San Francisco, CA 94102 Tel 415-433-3400 (SAN 224-893X).

International Atomic Energy Agency See **Unipub**

International Aviation Consultants, Inc., (Intl Av Consult; 0-9609000), 301 S.W. 30th Court, Miami, FL 33135 (SAN 240-9798).

International Book Centre, (Intl Bk Ctr; 0-917062; 0-86685), P.O. Box 295, Troy, MI 48099 Tel 313-879-8436 (SAN 208-7022).

International Book Co., (Intl Bk Co IL; 0-910790), 332 S. Michigan Ave., Chicago, IL 60604 Tel 312-427-4545 (SAN 205-0250).

International Book Distributors, (Intl Bk Dist), P.O. Box 180, Murray Hill Sta., New York, NY 10016 (SAN 210-6337).

International Business & Publishing Consultants, (I B P C Inc), P.O. Box 11225, San Francisco, CA 94101 (SAN 239-5541).

International Business Education & Research Program, Graduate School of Business Administration, (Intl Busn Educ; 0-939322), IBEAR/GSBA, Univ. of Southern California, Los Angeles, CA 90089-1421 Tel 213-743-2272 (SAN 216-5562).

International Center for Environmental Research, (Intl Ctr Environment; 0-914704), ICER Press, P.O. Box 877, Claremont, CA 91711 (SAN 205-6267).

International Center for Law in Development, (Intl Ctr Law), 777 United Nations Plaza, New York, NY 10017 (SAN 221-0592).

International Center of Photography, (Intl Ctr Photo; 0-933642), 1130 Fifth Ave., New York, NY 10028 Tel 212-860-1777 (SAN 213-3296).

International Childbirth Education Assn., Inc., (ICEA; 0-934024), P.O. Box 20048, Minneapolis, MN 55420 Tel 612-854-8660 (SAN 210-7430).

International City Management Assn., (Intl City Mgt; 0-87326), 1120 G St., N.W., Washington, DC 20005 Tel 202-626-4600 (SAN 204-9120).

International Co-Operative Publishing House, (Intl Co-Op; 0-89974), P.O. Box 245, Burtonsville, MD 20866 (SAN 213-6260).

International Commercial Service, (Intl Comm Serv; 0-935402), P.O. Box 4082, Irvine, CA 92716 Tel 714-552-8494 (SAN 281-8183); Dist. by: International Business & Management Institute University Town Centre, P.O. Box 4082, Irvine, CA 92716 Tel 714-552-8494 (SAN 282-647X).

International Commission on Radiation Units & Measurements, (Intl Comm Rad Meas; 0-913394), 7910 Woodmont Ave., Suite 1016, Bethesda, MD 20814 Tel 301-657-2652 (SAN 202-7127); Orders to: ICRU Publishers, Bethesda, MD 20814 (SAN 207-7135).

International Communication Center, (Intl Comm Ctr; 0-933236), School of Communications DS-40, Univ. of Washington, Seattle, WA 98195 (SAN 212-3614).

International Community of Christ, (Intl Comm Christ; 0-936202), Pub. Dept. Chancellery, 643 Ralston St., Reno, NV 89503 (SAN 214-0373).

International Computer Programs, Inc., (Intl Computer; 0-88094), 9000 Keystone Crossing, Indianapolis, IN 46240 Tel 317-844-7461 (SAN 218-7949).

International Conference of Building Officials, (Intl Conf Bldg off), 5360 S Workman Mill Rd, Whittier, CA 90601 (SAN 225-0713).

International Council of Scientific Unions-Abstracting Board of Pubns. See **Unipub**

International Council of Shopping Centers, (Intl Coun Shop; 0-913598), 665 Fifth Ave., New York, NY 10022 Tel 212-421-8181 (SAN 206-7412).

International Council on the Future of the Univ., (Intl Coun Future of the Univ; 0-930160), 745 Fifth Ave., New York, NY 10022 Tel 212-421-0170 (SAN 210-7465).

International Cultural Foundation Pr., (ICF Pr; 0-89226), GPO Box 1311, New York, NY 10116 Tel 212-947-1756 (SAN 210-3087).

International Department See **Harper & Row Pubs., Inc.**

International Development Institute, (Intl Development; 0-89249), 400 E. Seventh St., Bloomington, IN 47405 Tel 812-335-8596 (SAN 208-7030).

International Development Research Centre See **Unipub**

International Dialogue Press, (Intl Dialogue Pr; 0-89881; 0-931364), P.O. Box 1257, Davis, CA 95617 Tel 916-758-6500 (SAN 212-3827).

International Economy Pubns, (Intl Econ Pubns; 0-942368), P.O. Box 10897, Bakersfield, CA 93389 Tel 805-831-3094 (SAN 239-7358).

International Educational Development, Inc., (Intl Educ Dev; 0-939420), P.O. Box 7066, Silver Spring, MD 20910 (SAN 216-2571).

International Educational Systems, Inc., (Intl Educ Systems), 5521 W. 110th St., Oak Lawn, IL 60653 Tel 312-423-1717 (SAN 210-6248).

International Evangelism Crusade, Inc., (Intl Evang), 7970 Woodman Ave., Suite 103, Van Nuys, CA 91402 Tel 213-781-7704 (SAN 203-8153).

International Exhibitions Foundation, (Intl Exhibit Foun; 0-88397), 1729 "H" St., N.W., Suite 310, Washington, DC 20006 Tel 202-298-7010 (SAN 204-0964).

International Federation on Ageing, (Intl Fed Ageing), 1909 K St Nw, Washington, DC 20049 Tel 202-728-4719 (SAN 225-8889).

International Fertilizer Development Center, (Intl Fertilizer; 0-88090), P.O. Box 2040, Muscle Shoals, AL 35660 Tel 205-381-6600 (SAN 240-1150).

International Film Bureau, Inc., (Intl Film; 0-8354), 332 S. Michigan Ave., Chicago, IL 60604 Tel 312-427-4545 (SAN 207-4931).

International Fire Service Training Assn., (Intl Fire Serv; 0-87939), Oklahoma State Univ., Stillwater, OK 74078 Tel 405-624-5723 (SAN 204-1111).

International Foundation for Biosocial Development & Human Health, (Intl Found Biosocial Dev; 0-934314), 6 Lomond Ave., Spring Valley, NY 10977 (SAN 214-0381).

International Foundation of Employee Benefit Plans, (Intl Found Employ; 0-89154), P.O. Box 69, 18700 W. Bluemound Rd., Brookfield, WI 53005 Tel 414-786-6700 (SAN 207-429X).

International Friendship, (Intl Friend; 0-935340), P.O. Box 248, Waxhaw, NC 28173 Tel 704-843-3168 (SAN 213-5183).

International General, (Intl General; 0-88477), P.O. Box 350, New York, NY 10013 (SAN 206-5436).

International Health Pubns., (Intl Health Pub), P.O. Box 17535, San Diego, CA 92117 (SAN 286-3472).

International Human Resources Development Corp., (Intl Human Res; 0-934634), 137 Newbury St., Boston, MA 02116 (SAN 220-2549).

International Ideas Inc., (Intl Ideas; 0-89563), 1627 Spruce St., Philadelphia, PA 19103 Tel 215-546-0392 (SAN 210-6043).

International Imports, (Intl Imports), Box 2010, Toluca Lake, CA 91602 Tel 213-761-3991 (SAN 209-8202).

International Information Management Congress, (Intl Info; 0-940496), P.O. Box 34404, Bethesda, MD 20817 Tel 301-983-0604 (SAN 217-1856).

International Institute for Advanced Studies, (Intl Inst Adv Stud), 8015 Forsyth Blvd., Clayton, MO 63105 Tel 314-218-4818).

International Institute of Garibaldian Studies, Inc., (Intl Inst Garibaldian), 1025 Shadowlawn Way, Sarasota, FL 33581 Tel 813-349-0585 (SAN 238-0137).

International Institute of Natural Health Sciences, Inc., (Intl Inst Nat Health; 0-86664), 7422 Mountjoy Dr., Huntington Beach, CA 92648 (SAN 216-258X).

International Institute of Preventive Psychiatry, (Intl Inst Psych; 0-939210), 11445 Dona Dolores Place, Studio City, CA 91604 (SAN 220-2565).

International Institute of Refrigeration See **Unipub**

International Intertrade Index Printing Consultants, Pubs., (Intl Intertrade; 0-910794), P.O. Box 636, Federal Square, Newark, NJ 07101 Tel 201-686-2382 (SAN 202-7143).

International Labour Office, (Intl Labour Office; 92-2), Washington Branch, 1750 New York Ave., N.W., Suite 311, Washington, DC 20006 (SAN 203-817X).

International Law Institute, (Intl Law Inst), Georgetown Univ. Law Ctr, 600 New Jersey Ave. N.W., Washington, DC 20001 Tel 202-624-8330 (SAN 224-1676).

International Learning Systems, Inc., (Intl Learn Syst), 1715 Connecticut Ave., N.W., Washington, DC 20009 Tel 202-232-4111 (SAN 209-1615).

International Library-Book Pubs., (Intl Lib; 0-914250), 3865 Wilson Blvd., Suite 100-A, Arlington, VA 22203 Tel 703-538-4211 (SAN 202-7151).

International Linguistics Corp., (Intl Linguistics; 0-939990), 401 W. 89th St., Kansas City, MO 64114 Tel 816-941-9797 (SAN 220-2573).

International Marine Publishing Co., (Intl Marine; 0-87742), 21 Elm St., Camden, ME 04843 Tel 207-236-4342 (SAN 202-716X).

International Marketing Institute, (Intl Mktg), Univ. of New Orleans, New Orleans, LA 70148 (SAN 239-4464).

International Marriage Encounter, Inc., (Intl Marriage; 0-936098), 955 Lake Dr., St. Paul, MN 55120 (SAN 215-6830).

International Monetary Fund, (Intl Monetary; 0-939934), 700 19th St., N.W., Washington, DC 20431 Tel 202-477-3086 (SAN 203-8188).

International Museum of Photography at George Eastman House, (Intl Mus Photo; 0-935398), 900 East Ave., Rochester, NY 14607 Tel 716-271-3361 (SAN 205-0153).

International Myopia Prevention Association, (Intl Myopia; 0-9608476), Rd 5 Box 171, Ligonier, PA 15658 Tel 412-238-2101 (SAN 228-1848).

International Ozone Assn., (Intl Ozone; 0-918650), 301 Maple Ave., Suite 510, Vienna, VA 22180 Tel 703-255-2210 (SAN 271-5082); Orders to: 301 Maple Ave., W., Suite 510, Vienna, VA 22180 Tel 703-255-2210 (SAN 271-5082).

International Peace Academy, (Intl Peace), 777 United Nations Plaza, New York, NY 10017 (SAN 225-6940).

International Personnel Management Assn., (Intl Personnel Mgmt; 0-87373), 1850 "K" St. N.W., Suite 870, Washington, DC 20006 Tel 202-833-5860 (SAN 203-8196); 485-487 National Press Bldg., 14 & "F" Sts., N.W., Washington, DC 20004 Tel 202-833-1545 (SAN 203-820X).

International Pictorical Pubns., (Intl Pict Pubns; 0-916722), 49 S. Baldwin, Sierra Madre, CA 91024 Tel 213-355-8205 (SAN 208-4732).

International Polygonics, Ltd., (Intl Polygonics; 0-930330), Madison Square, P.O. Box 1563, New York, NY 10159 Tel 212-683-2914 (SAN 211-0210); Dist. by: Academy Chicago, 425 N. Michigan Ave., Chicago, IL 60611 Tel 312-644-1723 (SAN 213-2001).

International Postal Marketing Corp., (Intl Postal Mkting; 0-9606786), 128 Passaic Ave., Fairfield, NJ 07006 Tel 201-288-5404 (SAN 223-1867).

International Print Co., (Intl Print), 711 South 50th St., Philadelphia, PA 19143 (SAN 240-8627); Dist. by: Sebastian Ben Giletto, 1127 Watkins St., Philadelphia, PA 19148 (SAN 240-8635).

International Program of Laboratories for Population Statistics, (Intl Program Labs; 0-89383), NCNB Plaza, Suite 400, 136 E. Rosemary St., Chapel Hill, NC 27514 Tel 919-966-1131 (SAN 211-0229).

International Psychological Press, Inc., (Intl Psych Pr; 0-915662), 1850 Hanover Dr., No. 69, Davis, CA 95616 Tel 916-758-0685 (SAN 207-3722).

International Publishing Corp., (Intl Pub Corp OH; 0-941712), 4026 April Dr., Uniontown, OH 44685 Tel 216-896-2485 (SAN 239-2356).

International Pubns. Service, (Intl Pubns Serv; 0-8002; 0-85066), 114 E. 32nd St., New York, NY 10016 Tel 212-685-9351 (SAN 169-5819).

International Pubs. Co., (Intl Pub Co; 0-7178), 381 Park Ave., S., Suite 1301, New York, NY 10016 Tel 212-685-2864 (SAN 202-5655).

International Reading Assn., (Intl Reading; 0-87207), 800 Barksdale Rd., Box 8139, Newark, DE 19711 Tel 302-731-1600 (SAN 203-8218).

International Regulations Publishing & Distributing Organization, (INTEREG; 0-940394), Dist. by: Labelmaster, 5724 N. Pulaski Rd., Chicago, IL 60646 (SAN 218-480X).

International Research & Evaluation, (Intl Res Eval; 0-930318), Research Pubns. Div., 21098 IRE Control Ctr., Eagan, MN 55121 Tel 612-888-9635 (SAN 209-6668).

International Research Center for Energy & Economic Development, (Intl Res Ctr Energy; 0-918714), 216 Economics Bldg., Univ. of Colo., Boulder, CO 80309 (SAN 211-3643).

International Research Institute for Political Science, (Intl Res Inst), Box 199, College Park, MD 20740 (SAN 210-1203).

International Research Service, Inc., (Intl Research Serv; 0-934366), P.O. Box 225, Blue Bell, PA 19422 (SAN 213-1935).

International Resources Development Inc., (Intl Res Dev), 30 High Street, Norwalk, CT 06851 (SAN 264-1208).

International Review Service, (Intl Review; 0-87138), 15 Washington Place, New York, NY 10003 Tel 212-751-0833 (SAN 202-3539); UN Bureau: Rm. 301, United Nations, New York, NY 10017 (SAN 202-3547).

International Scholarly Book Services, Inc. (ISBS, Inc.), (Intl Schol Bk Serv; 0-89955), P.O. Box 1632, Beaverton, OR 97075 Tel 503-292-2606 (SAN 169-7119).

International School Psychology Association, (Intl Schl Psych; 0-917668), 1367 E. Main St., Columbus, OH 43205 (SAN 209-2913).

International Schools Services, (Intl School Servs; 0-913663), P.O. Box 5910 126 Alexander St., Princeton, NJ 08540 Tel 609-921-9110 (SAN 225-8196).

International Science & Technology Institute, Inc., (Intl Sci Tech; 0-936130), 2033 M St. N.W., Suite 300, Washington, DC 20036 Tel 202-466-7290 (SAN 212-5110).

International Self-Counsel Press, (ISC Pr; 0-88908), 306 West 25th St. North Vancouver BC, V7N 2G1, .

International Society for Artificial Organs, (Intl Soc Artifical Organs; 0-936022), 8937 Euclid Ave., Cleveland, OH 44106 (SAN 214-039X).

International Society for General Semantics, (Intl Gen Semantics; 0-918970), P.O. Box 2469, San Francisco, CA 94126 Tel 415-543-1747 (SAN 203-8161).

International Society of Certified Employees Benefit Specialists, (Intl Soc Cert Emp; 0-911731), 18700 W. Bluemound Rd., Brookfield, WI 63005 Tel 414-786-6700 (SAN 264-1216).

International Tree Crops Institute U.S.A., Inc., (Intl Tree Crops; 0-938240), P.O. Box 666, Winters, CA 95694 (SAN 216-2598).

International Typface Corp., (Intl Typeface; 0-9608034), 2 Hammarskjold Pl. 3rd Fl., New York, NY 10017 (SAN 239-6637); c/o Robert Silver Assocs., 95 Madison Ave., New York, NY 10016 Tel 212-686-5630 (SAN 241-5801).

International Union for Conservation of Nature & Natural Resources See Unipub

International Universities Press, Inc., (Intl Univs Pr; 0-8236), 315 Fifth Ave., New York, NY 10016 Tel 212-684-7900 (SAN 202-7186).

International Univ., The, (Intl Univ MO), 1301 S. Noland Rd., Independence, MO 64055 (SAN 241-1938).

International Wealth Success, Inc., (Intl Wealth; 0-914306), 24 Canterbury Rd., Rockville Center, NY 11570 Tel 516-766-5850 (SAN 201-5129).

International Wine Society, (Intl Wine Soc; 0-89219), 304 E. 45th St., New York, NY 10017 Tel 212-661-2700 (SAN 209-083X).

Interperson Press, (Interperson Pr; 0-940942), 913 N. Shore Dr., Crystal Lake, IL 60014 Tel 815-459-1795 (SAN 217-3832).

Interpersonal Communication Programs, Inc., (Interpersonal Comm; 0-917340), 1925 Nicollet Ave., Minneapolis, MN 55403 Tel 612-871-7388 (SAN 208-7057).

Interpharm Press, (Interpharm; 0-935184), P.O. Box 530, Prairie View, IL 60069 (SAN 213-5248).

Interpretive Pubns., (Interpretive Pubns; 0-936478), Box 1384, Arlington, VA 22210 (SAN 221-4830).

Interservice Publishing Co., Inc., (Interserv Pub; 0-86695), P.O. Box 5437 Dept. X, San Francisco, CA 94101 Tel 415-465-0187 (SAN 216-6003).

Intersociety Committee Pathology Information, (Intersoc Comm Path Info; 0-937888), 4733 Bethesda Ave., Suite 735, Bethesda, MD 20814 Tel 301-656-2944 (SAN 205-0072).

Interstate, (Interstate; 0-8134), 19-27 N. Jackson St., Danville, IL 61832 Tel 217-446-0500 (SAN 206-6548).

Interstate Piano Co., (Interstate Piano; 0-9604092), 4001 N. Interstate Ave., Portland, OR 97227 Tel 503-288-2600 (SAN 214-0829).

Intersystems Pubns, (Intersystems Pubns; 0-914105), P.O. Box 624, Seaside, CA 93955 (SAN 237-9619).

Interurban Press, (Interurban; 0-916374), P.O. Box 6444, Glendale, CA 91205 Tel 213-240-9130 (SAN 207-9593).

Intervale Publishing Co., Inc., (Intervale Pub Co; 0-932400), Box 777, Meredith, NH 03253 Tel 603-284-7726 (SAN 211-9633).

Interweave Press, Inc., (Interweave; 0-934026), 306 N. Washington Ave., Loveland, CO 80537 Tel 303-669-7672 (SAN 214-3151).

Intrepid Press, (Intrepid), P.O. Box 1423, Buffalo, NY 14214 Tel 716-886-7136 (SAN 207-8503).

Investigations Institute, (Investigations; 0-9607876), 53 W. Jackson Blvd., Chicago, IL 60604 Tel 312-939-6050 (SAN 205-0064).

Investment & Tax Publications, Inc., (Invest Tax Pubn), P.O. Bx 1201, Orem, UT 84057 (SAN 240-978X).

Investment Evaluations Corp., (Invest Eval; 0-9603282), 2000 Goldenvue Dr., Golden, CO 80401 Tel 303-278-3464 (SAN 210-9042).

Investor Pubns., Inc., (Investor Pubns; 0-914230), 219 Parkade, Cedar Falls, IA 50613 Tel 319-277-6341 (SAN 281-8205); Sales/Marketing: 250 S. Wacker Dr., Suite 250, Chicago, IL 60606 Tel 312-977-0999 (SAN 281-8213).

Investor's Systems, Inc., (Investor's Syst; 0-915610), P.O. Box 1422, Dayton, OH 45401 Tel 513-223-6870 (SAN 207-3420).

Investrek Publishing, (Investrek; 0-9604914), 419 Main St., No. 160, Huntington Beach, CA 92648 Tel 714-536-8360 (SAN 216-1443).

Involvement Group Press, (Involve Group Pr), 1512 N. Nicholas St., Arlington, VA 22205 Tel 703-241-2879 (SAN 264-1240).

IO Pub. Co., (IO; 0-9609334), P. O. Box 192, Santa Rosa, CA 95402 Tel 707-544-0784 (SAN 260-2075).

Iona Press Company, The, (Iona Pr; 0-910789), P.O. Box C-3181, Wooster, OH 44691 Tel 216-263-2470 (SAN 271-6666).

Iota Press, (Iota Pr; 0-936412), 361 Burgundy Square, No. 102, East Lansing, MI 48823 (SAN 214-3895).

Iowa State Univ. Press, (Iowa St U Pr; 0-8138), 2121 S. State Ave., Ames, IA 50010 Tel 515-294-5280 (SAN 202-7194).

Ipse Dixit Press, Inc., (Ipse Dixit Pr; 0-9602468), Box 4277, St. Paul, MN 55104 Tel 612-690-0980 (SAN 212-8098).

Ipswich Press, The, (Ipswich Pr; 0-938864), P.O. Box 291, Ipswich, MA 01938 Tel 617-426-3900 (SAN 218-4826).

Irego, (Irego; 0-911732), P.O. Box 286, Lenox Hill Sta., 221 E. 70th St., New York, NY 10021 (SAN 215-661X).

Ireland Educational Corp., (Ireland Educ; 0-89103), 7076 S. Alton Way, Bldg. C, Englewood, CO 80112 (SAN 207-9488).

Iris Press, Inc., (Iris Pr; 0-916078), 27 Chestnut St., Binghamton, NY 13905 Tel 607-722-6739 (SAN 207-7566).

Irish Book Center, (Irish Bk Ctr), 245 W. 104th St., New York, NY 10025 Tel 212-866-0309 (SAN 209-1089).

Irish Books & Media, (Irish Bks Media; 0-937702), 683 Osceola Ave., St. Paul, MN 55105 (SAN 215-1987).

Irish Family Names Society, The, (Irish Family Names; 0-9601868), P. O. Box 2095, La Mesa, CA 92041 Tel 619-466-8739 (SAN 221-3567).

Irish Genealogical Foundation, (Irish Genealog; 0-940134), P.O. Box 7575, Kansas City, MO 64116 (SAN 218-4834).

IRL Press, (IRL Pr; 0-917000; 0-904147), Suite 907, 1911 Jefferson Davis Hwy., Arlington, VA 22202 Tel 703-998-2980 (SAN 208-693X).

Iron & Steel Society of AIME, (Iron & Steel), 410 Commonwealth Dr., Warrendale, PA 15086 (SAN 224-876X).

Iron Mountain Press, (Iron Mtn Pr), Box D, Emory, VA 24327 (SAN 217-7994).

Iron Press, The, (Iron Pr; 0-912363), P.O. Box 176, Franklin, MI 48025 Tel 313-626-1075 (SAN 265-1548).

Ironwood Press, (Ironwood Calif; 0-936800), 11251 Macmurray St., Garden Grove, CA 92641 Tel 714-539-9830 (SAN 221-9379).

Iroquois House, Pubs., (Iroquois Hse; 0-931980), Haynes Canyon, Mountain Park, NM 88325 Tel 505-682-2751 (SAN 212-8101).

Irresistible Books, (Irresistible; 0-918464), P.O. Box 1059, Angleton, TX 77515 (SAN 283-3816).

Irrigation Assn., The, (Irrigation; 0-935030), 13975 Connecticut Ave., Silver Spring, MD 20906 Tel 301-871-1200 (SAN 202-0807).

Irvington Historical Society, (Irvington Hist; 0-9611394), 35 Clinton Terrace, Irvington, NJ 07111 Tel 201-994-4210 (SAN 285-3280).

Irvington Pubs., (Irvington; 0-89197; 0-8290), 551 Fifth Ave., New York, NY 10176 Tel 212-697-8100 (SAN 207-2408).

Irwin, Richard D., Inc., (Irwin; 0-256), 1818 Ridge Rd., Homewood, IL 60430 Tel 312-798-6000 (SAN 206-8400).

Irwinton Pubs., (Irwinton), 9685 Anderson Rd., Mercersburg, PA 17236 (SAN 202-7208).

Isaacs, Harold, (H Isaacs; 0-9601406), Dist. by: Peanut Brigade, P.O. Box 237, Plains, GA 31780 Tel 912-924-8287 (SAN 210-976X).

Isabella Stewart Gardner Museum, (I S Gardner Mus; 0-914660), 2 Palace Rd., Boston, MA 02115 Tel 617-566-1401 (SAN 201-9221).

ISC Pubns, (ISC Pubns; 0-942916), P.O. Box 10857, Costa Mesa, CA 92627 (SAN 240-1169).

ISHI Publications See Institute for the Study of Human Issues (ISHI)

Isis Press, (Isis Pr; 0-940944), 1516 Morton Ave., Ann Arbor, MI 48104 Tel 313-665-4740 (SAN 223-1883).

Islamic Center of Detroit, The, (Islamic Ctr; 0-942778), 15571 Joy Rd., Detroit, MI 48228 Tel 313-582-7442 (SAN 240-2335).

Islamic Productions International, (Islamic Prods; 0-934894), 739 E. Sixth St., Tucson, AZ 85719 Tel 602-791-3989 (SAN 203-8625).

Islamic Seminary, The, (Islamic Seminary; 0-941742), 50-11 Queens Blvd., Woodside, NY 11377 Tel 212-458-0924 (SAN 239-2372).

Island Heritage Ltd., (Island Her; 0-89610), 550 North Nimitz Highway, Honolulu, HI 96817 Tel 808-526-1126 (SAN 211-1403).

Island Press, Div. of Round Valley Agrarian Institute, (Island CA; 0-933280), Star Route 1, Box 38, Covelo, CA 95428 Tel 707-983-6432 (SAN 212-5129).

Island Press, (Island Pr; 0-87208), 175 Bahia Via, Fort Myers Beach, FL 33931 Tel 813-463-9482 (SAN 202-7216).

Island Publishing House, (Island Pub; 0-916424), P.O. Drawer 758, Manteo, NC 27954 Tel 919-473-2838 (SAN 208-0362).

Island Writers Publishing Co., (Island Writers; 0-9604798), Box 25382, Honolulu, HI 96825 Tel 808-395-2615 (SAN 220-0619).

Isle of Guam International Publishers, (Isle of Guam; 0-942780), P.O. Box 21119, Guam Main Facility, GU 96921 Tel 808-845-9672 (SAN 240-2343).

Ism Press, Inc., (Ism Pr), Box 150, 2440 - 16th St., San Francisco, CA 94103 Tel 415-285-9085 (SAN 241-5496).

Issues in Cooperation & Power, Subs. of Cooperation Corporation, (IC&P), P.O. Box 5039, Berkeley, CA 94705 (SAN 210-7473).

Italimuse, Inc., *(Italimuse; 0-910798),* 3128 Burr St, Fairfield, CT 06430 Tel 203-259-5788 (SAN 203-8242).

ITEC, Inc., *(ITEC; 0-943908),* Box 464, Beaver, PA 15009 Tel 412-728-4318 (SAN 241-1237).

Ithaca College, *(Ithaca Coll; 0-9610556),* South Hill Campus, Ithaca, NY 14850 Tel 607-274-3452 (SAN 264-1267).

Ithaca House, *(Ithaca Hse; 0-87886),* 108 N. Plain St., Ithaca, NY 14850 Tel 607-272-1233 (SAN 202-7224).

Ithaca Press, *(Ithaca Pr MA; 0-915940),* P.O. Box 853, Lowell, MA 01853 Tel 617-453-2177 (SAN 208-709X).

Ivan Publishing, Inc., *(Ivan Pub; 0-9602578),* P.O. Box 17947, San Antonio, TX 78217 Tel 512-828-7995 (SAN 212-6702).

Ivans Publishing Co., *(Ivans Pub NY; 0-9607476),* 211-10 23rd Ave., Bayside, NY 11360 Tel 212-423-4307 (SAN 238-6143).

Iverna Tompkins Ministry, *(I Tompkins; 0-9611260),* 2945 Pheasant Drive, Decatur, GA 30034 (SAN 283-2240).

Ivey Pubns., *(Ivey Pubns; 0-9600864),* 1845 Arkoe Dr., S.E, Atlanta, GA 30316 (SAN 207-6799).

Ivory House, *(Ivory Hse; 0-9608896),* P.O. Box 676, 121 Randolph Rd., Freehold, NJ 07728 Tel 201-462-1620 (SAN 241-1245).

Ivory Palaces Music Publishing Co., Inc., *(Ivory Pal; 0-943644),* 3141 Spottswood Ave., Memphis, TN 38111 Tel 901-323-3509 (SAN 238-3020).

Ivory Scroll Books, Pubs., *(Ivory Scroll),* P.O. Box 7526, Philadelphia, PA 19101 (SAN 205-003X).

Ivosevic, Stanley W., *(S W Ivosevic; 0-9611352),* 207 World Savings Bldg., 12221 West Alameda Pkwy., Denver, CO 80228 Tel 303-988-6050 (SAN 283-2267).

Ivy Club, The, *(Ivy Club; 0-934756),* 43 Prospect Ave., Princeton, NJ 08540 (SAN 213-0904).

Ivy Hill Press, *(Ivy Hill; 0-9601542),* 8817 Greenview Place, Spring Valley, CA 92077 (SAN 212-5145).

Ivy Press Inc., The, *(Ivy Pr; 0-933372),* 2121 N. Akard, Dallas, TX 75201 Tel 800-527-9250 (SAN 212-9108).

J. A. Enterprises, *(J A Ent; 0-9606722),* 2417 House Ave., Cheyenne, WY 82001 (SAN 219-6654).

JA Micropublishing, Inc., *(JA Micropublishing; 0-912127),* 274 White Plains Rd., Box 218, Eastchester, NY 10707 Tel 914-793-2100 (SAN 264-6730).

J&A Enterprises, *(J & A Enterprises; 0-934368),* 5522 W. Acoma Rd., Glendale, AZ 85306 (SAN 212-9116).

J&B Pubs., *(J & B Pubs; 0-943498),* Box 2866, Toas, NM 87571 Tel 505-776-2355 (SAN 240-6861).

J & J Books, Inc., *(J & J Bks; 0-914464),* 1004 Springhill Dr., Angola, IN 46703 Tel 219-665-5346 (SAN 202-7232); Orders to: Ulrich's Books Inc., 549 E. University Ave., Ann Arbor, MI 48104 Tel 313-662-3201 (SAN 204-8779).

J. & J. Distributors, *(J & J Dist),* P.O. Box 247, Raymondville, TX 78580 Tel 512-689-2523 (SAN 213-5256).

J&J Pubns., *(J&J Pubns MI; 0-9605786),* Box 1424, Traverse City, MI 49684 (SAN 216-4000).

J & J Publishing, *(J & J Pub),* 1088 Madison Ave., New York, NY 10028 Tel 212-535-7399 (SAN 211-1950).

J&M Publishing Co., *(J&M Pub; 0-930630),* 11 Matthews Ave., Riverdale, NJ 07457 Tel 201-838-9434 (SAN 211-1411).

J & R Enterprises, *(J & R Enter; 0-9608550),* P.O. Box 8264, Anchorage, AK 99508 Tel 907-333-4442 (SAN 240-687X).

J&W Tex-Mex, *(J&W Tex-Mex; 0-9604842),* P.O. Box 983, Arlington, VA 22216 (SAN 215-6628).

J-B Publishing Co., *(J-B Pubs; 0-916170),* 430 Ivy Ave., Crete, NE 68333 Tel 402-826-3356 (SAN 207-2424).

JCL House, *(JCL Hse; 0-9610274),* P.O. Box 1821, East Lansing, MI 48823 (SAN 264-1305).

JCP Corp. of Virginia, *(JCP Corp VA; 0-938694),* P.O. Box 814, Virginia Beach, VA 23451 Tel 804-422-5426 (SAN 220-1313).

J. C. Printing Co., *(J C Print),* 3493 N. Main St., College Park, GA 30337 (SAN 211-0245).

J. E. B. Pub. Co., *(JEB Pub),* Rte. 2 Box 400, Franklin, GA 30217 (SAN 281-8396); Orders to: Groover Medical Bldg., Ambulance Dr., Carrollton, GA 30117 Tel 404-832-6861 (SAN 281-840X).

JED, *(JED; 0-9602200),* P.O. Box 7143 RC, Toledo, OH 43615 Tel 419-885-2932 (SAN 212-3622).

JH Press, *(JH Pr; 0-935672),* P.O. Box 294, Village Sta., New York, NY 10014 (SAN 213-6279).

JJ Publishing, *(JJ Pub FL; 0-9604610),* 1312 Arthur St., Hollywood, FL 33019 Tel 305-929-3559 (SAN 220-0090).

JLA Pubns., *(JLA Pubns; 0-940374),* 50 Follen St., Suite 507, Cambridge, MA 02138 (SAN 223-1441).

JLJ Pubs., *(JLJ Pubs; 0-937172),* 824 Shrine Rd., Springfield, OH 45504 (SAN 215-322X).

J L Productions, *(J L Prods; 0-9610564),* 1366 Broadway, Somerville, MA 02144 Tel 617-623-5030 (SAN 264-1321).

JMB Pubns., *(JMB Pubns; 0-9606834),* 10810 Cherry Grove Court, Louisville, KY 40299 (SAN 217-2410).

JMP Mfg. Corp., *(JMP Mfg; 0-9608898),* 4467 Eaton-Gettysburg Rd., Eaton, OH 45320 (SAN 264-133X).

JM Productions, *(J M Prods; 0-939298),* Box 837, Brentwood, TN 37027 (SAN 216-4019); Dist. by: Spring Arbor Distributors, 772 Airport Blvd., P.O. Box 985, Ann Arbor, MI 48106 Tel 313-994-4053 (SAN 158-9016); Dist. by: Ingram Book Co., 347 Reedwood Dr., Box 17266, Nashville, TN 37217 Tel 615-361-5000 (SAN 169-7978); Dist. by: East Coast Christian Distributors, 35 Readington Rd., Somerville, NJ 08876 Tel 201-722-5050 (SAN 169-491X).

JP Pubns., *(JP Pubns WI; 0-9602978),* P.O. Box 4173, Madison, WI 53711 Tel 608-231-2373 (SAN 214-0411).

J P Pubns., *(JP Pubns CA; 0-910703),* 2952 Grinnel, Davis, CA 95616 (SAN 260-2083).

J.R.&G. Co., *(J R and G; 0-9608844),* 4165 Greenwood Dr., Bethleham, PA 18017 Tel 215-694-0860 (SAN 241-0311).

J. R. Pubns., *(J R Pubns; 0-913952),* 170 N.E. 33rd St., Ft. Lauderdale, FL 33334 Tel 305-563-1844 (SAN 202-7283).

J.W.B., *(JWB; 0-914820),* 15 E. 26th St., New York, NY 10010 Tel 212-532-4949 (SAN 203-9060).

J.B. Lippincott, Harper & Row Medical Division *See* **Harper & Row Pubs., Inc.**

Ja-Mar Pubs., *(Ja-Mar Pubs; 0-941556),* P.O. Box 296, Huntsville, TX 77340 Tel 713-295-2389 (SAN 239-2380).

Jaal Productions, *(Jaal Product; 0-9611908),* 9953 La Tuna Canyon Rd., Sun Valley, CA 91352 Tel 213-767-6164 (SAN 286-1240).

Jacbar Pubns., *(Jacbar Pubns; 0-9606154),* Box 103, Randolph, OH 44265 (SAN 217-1120).

Jacek Publishing Co., *(Jacek; 0-9601084),* 38 Morris Lane, Milford, CT 06460 (SAN 209-4029).

Jack Mack Paperbacks, *(Jack Mack; 0-910391),* 612 E. Manning, Apt. 3, Reedley, CA 93654 Tel 209-638-3392 (SAN 260-0994).

Jackpine Press, *(Jackpine Pr; 0-917492),* 1878 Meadowbrook Dr., Winston-Salem, NC 27104 Tel 919-725-8828 (SAN 208-273X).

Jackson, G. B., *(Jackson G B),* 1030 Edgewater Ave. W., St. Paul, MN 55112 (SAN 287-2757).

Jackson, G. Don, Associate, *(G D Jackson; 0-913211),* One Penn Plaza, Suite 100, New York, NY 10119 Tel 212-774-2041 (SAN 283-1228).

Jacobs Publishing Co., *(Jacobs; 0-918272),* 3334 E. Indian School Rd., Suite C, Phoenix, AZ 85018 Tel 602-954-6581 (SAN 209-4525).

Jacobsen, Anita, *(A Jacobsen; 0-9604456),* 963 Post Ave., Staten Island, NY 10302 (SAN 214-2473).

Jacqueline Enterprises, Inc., *(Jacqueline Enter; 0-932446),* 1660 S. Albion St., Writers Towers Two, No. 409, Denver, CO 80222 Tel 303-691-9781 (SAN 221-0487).

Jade House Pubns., *(Jade Hse Pubns; 0-942596),* P.O. Box 155, Bryans Rd., MD 20616 Tel 301-283-2489 (SAN 239-6653).

Jadestone Publishing Corp., *(Jadestone),* 3341 West Peoria Avenue, Phoenix, AZ 85029 (SAN 264-1348).

Jaeger, Julia, Mrs., *(Jaeger),* The Tenth Muse, P.O. Box 1417, Pacifica, CA 94044 (SAN 211-2957).

Jai Pr., Inc., *(Jai Pr; 0-89232),* 36 Sherwood Pl., Greenwich, CT 06836 Tel 203-661-7602 (SAN 208-4082).

Jaks Publishing Co., *(Jaks Pub Co; 0-935674),* 1106 N. Washington St., P.O. Box 5625, Helena, MT 59601 (SAN 214-042X).

Jakubowsky, *(Jakubowsky; 0-932588),* 1565 Madison St., Oakland, CA 94612 Tel 415-763-4324 (SAN 212-1034).

Jalamap Pubns., Inc., *(Jalamap; 0-934750),* 833 Scenic Dr., Charleston, WV 25311 (SAN 216-1478).

Jalapeno Press, *(Jalapeno Pr; 0-935342),* Rte. 2, Box 600, Bandon, OR 97411 (SAN 213-8514).

Jalmar Press, *(Jalmar Pr; 0-915190),* 45 Hitching Post Dr., Bldg. 2, Rolling Hills Estate, CA 90274 Tel 213-539-6430 (SAN 281-8302); Orders to: Product Developer, 25851 S. Frampton Ave., Harbor City, CA 90710 (SAN 281-8310).

Jam Jar Press, *(Jam Jar; 0-9606276),* 201 Chestnut St., P.O. Box 348, Towanda, PA 18848 Tel 717-265-9601 (SAN 217-5304).

Jama Books, *(Jama Bks; 0-934130),* 1120 Beach St., Flint Barbara, MI 48502 (SAN 281-8329).

James, Timothy A, *(James T A; 0-9608478),* 5770 Hoagland-Blackstub Rd., Cortland, OH 44410 Tel 216-637-5520 (SAN 285-0346); 1319 Newport Gap Pike, Wilmington, DE 19804 Tel 800-441-7596 (SAN 285-0354).

James Bond 007 Fan Club, The, *(Bond Double-O Seven; 0-9605838),* P.O. Box 414, Bronxville, NY 10708 Tel 914-961-3440 (SAN 216-5902).

James Madison Research Institute, The, *(J Madison Research),* Box 2134, Stephens College, Columbia, MO 65215 (SAN 285-676X).

James Publishing Co., *(James Pub),* Rte. 1, Box 114-K, Winchester, VA 22601 (SAN 211-0768).

Jameson, E. W., Jr., *(E W Jameson Jr),* 13 Oakside, Davis, CA 95616 (SAN 207-5148).

Jamestown Pubs., Inc., *(Jamestown Pubs; 0-89061),* P.O. Box 6743, Providence, RI 02940 Tel 401-351-1915 (SAN 201-5196).

Jamison Station Press, *(Jamison Stn),* 7115 Pembroke Dr., Reno, NE 89502 (SAN 277-691X).

Jan Publications Inc., *(Jan Pubns Inc; 0-934896),* Box 156, Oaklyn, NJ 08107 Tel 600-667-0291 (SAN 213-2222).

Jane Reynolds, *(J Reynolds; 0-930114),* P.O. Box 2623, Del Mar, CA 92014 Tel 619-942-1025 (SAN 210-6604).

Janeric Press, *(Janeric Pr; 0-911373),* P.O. Box 477, Banner Elk, NC 28604 Tel 704-898-5500 (SAN 271-7182).

Jane's Publishing Inc., *(Jane's Pub Inc),* 286 Congress St., Boston, MA 02210 Tel 617-542-6564 (SAN 286-357X).

Janevar Publishing Co., *(Janevar Pub; 0-937174),* R. R. 11, Box 129, Muncie, IN 47302 Tel 317-289-3137 (SAN 215-157X).

Janice Porter Books, *(J Porter Bks; 0-9607670),* P.O. Box 2367, Reston, VA 22090 (SAN 240-0979).

Janova Press, Inc., *(Janova Pr; 0-917294),* 3833 Barker Rd., Cincinnati, OH 45229 Tel 513-861-0511 (SAN 208-3671).

Jansen Publishing, *(Jansen Pub; 0-931212),* P.O. Box 105, Coarsegold, CA 93614 Tel 209-683-5883 (SAN 210-6051).

Jantz, Virginia C., *(V C Jantz; 0-9607170),* Rte. 1 Box 1453, Waco, TX 76710 Tel 817-848-4786 (SAN 239-1031).

Janus Book Pubs., *(Janus Bks; 0-915510),* 2501 Industrial Pkwy. W., Hayward, CA 94545 Tel 415-887-7070 (SAN 208-0478).

Janus Press, *(Janus Pr; 0-916172),* P.O. Box 578, Rogue River, OR 97537 Tel 503-582-1520 (SAN 207-5806); Dist. by: Caroline House Publishers, 920 W. Industrial Dr., Aurora, IL 60506 Tel 312-897-2050 (SAN 211-2280).

Janzen, P., Associates, *(Janzen Assoc; 0-9604458),* P.O. Box 231, Libertyville, IL 60048 (SAN 215-1588).

Japan Pubns. Inc., *(Japan Pubns; 0-87040),* Dist. by: Kodansha International Inc., C/O Harper & Row Pubs., Inc, Keystone Industrial Park, Scranton, PA 18512 (SAN 215-3742).

Japan Society, *(Japan Soc; 0-913304),* 333 East 47 St, New York, NY 10017 (SAN 225-3259).

Japanese American Anthology Committee, *(Japan Amer Anthlgy Com; 0-9603222),* P.O. Box 5024, San Francisco, CA 94101 (SAN 222-3643).

Jarchow, Michael, Publications, *(M Jarchow Pubns; 0-9608204),* P.O. Box 3238, Seal Beach, CA 90740 (SAN 238-8278).

Jargon Society, Inc., The, *(Jargon Soc; 0-912330),* Dist. by: Inland Book Co., 22 Hemingway Ave., East Haven, CT 06512 Tel 203-467-4257 (SAN 200-4151).

Jarrett, Richard Buhler, *(Jarrett; 0-9606884),* P.O. Box 6007, Suite 250, Redding, CA 96099 (SAN 217-3840).

Jasper County Abstract Co., *(Jasper County; 0-9604474),* Kellner at Van Rensselaer St., Rensselaer, IN 47978 (SAN 215-0840).

Jawbone Pr., *(Jawbone Pr; 0-918116),* Waldron Island, WA 98297 (SAN 210-2188).

Jay, Robert, Publishing, *(R J Pub),* P.O. Box 1171, Madison, WI 53701 Tel 608-255-3420 (SAN 215-6636).

Jay & Associates, Pubs., *(Jay & Assoc; 0-939422),* P.O. Box 13898, Arlington, TX 76013 Tel 817-273-2876 (SAN 281-837X); Orders to: Marketing Department, P. O. Box 19469, Arlington, TX 76019 (SAN 281-8388).

Jay Pubns., *(Jay Pubns; 0-916666),* P.O. Box 1141, San Andreas, CA 95249 Tel 209-754-4520 (SAN 208-3922).

Jay Publishing Co., *(Jay Pub; 0-930140),* P.O. Box 454, Lakewood, CA 90714 Tel 714-893-0326 (SAN 209-4533).

Jayanel Publishing Company, *(Jayanel Pub; 0-9608088),* 6961 Wide Valley Dr, Brighton, MI 48116 (SAN 238-8170).

Jayco Pub. Co., *(Jayco Pub),* P.O. Box 1511, South Bend, IN 46634 Tel 219-291-2291 (SAN 237-9627).

Jaye, Gail C., *(G C Jaye),* 4 Chalet Dr., Bay Minette, AL 36507 (SAN 217-2941).

Jaynes, Thomas L., *(T L Jaynes; 0-935514),* P.O. Box 651038, Miami, FL 33265-1038 (SAN 213-8522).

Jazz Press, *(Jazz Pr; 0-937310),* 2409 Mission St., Santa Cruz, CA 95060 (SAN 215-1596).

JC/DC Cartoons Ink, *(JC-DC Cartoons; 0-934574),* 5536 Fruitland Rd N.E., Salem, OR 97301 (SAN 213-0963).

Jeanies Classics, *(Jeanies Classics; 0-9609672),* 2123 Oxford St., Rockford, IL 61103 Tel 815-968-4544 (SAN 271-7395); Dist. by: Jeanies Classics Publishing, P.O. Box 5164, Rockford, IL 61125 (SAN 271-7409).

Jeanne's Dreams, *(Jeannes Dreams; 0-9604694),* P.O. Box 211, La Farge, WI 54639 Tel 608-625-2425 (SAN 213-6872).

Jebco Books Division, *(Jebco Bks; 0-9609494),* P.O. Box 268, Harrison, OH 45030 Tel 513-385-5986 (SAN 262-7574).

Jedick, Peter, Enterprises, *(Jedick Ent; 0-9605568),* 3637 W. 47th St., Cleveland, OH 44102 (SAN 216-0455).

Jeffers-Carr Associates, *(Jeffers-Carr; 0-9603954),* 307 E. 44th St., New York, NY 10017 Tel 212-599-2327 (SAN 281-8418).

Jefferson County Office of Historic Preservation & Archives, *(Jefferson County Office Hist Pres Arch; 0-9607612),* 100 Fiscal Court Building, Louisville, KY 40202 (SAN 237-9635).

Jefferson National Expansion Historical Assn., *(Jefferson Natl; 0-931056),* 11 N. 4th St., St. Louis, MO 63102 (SAN 213-0912).

Jefferson Pubns., Inc., *(Jefferson Pubns),* Monticello Books Div., 44 S. Old Rand Rd., Box 19, Lake Zurich, IL 60047 Tel 312-438-4114 (SAN 207-639X).

Jefren Pub. Co., *(Jefren Pub; 0-917244),* 1513 Auburn Ave., Rockville, MD 20850 (SAN 208-7138).

Jelm Mountain Pubns., *(Jelm Mtn; 0-936204),* 209 Park St., Laramie, WY 82070 Tel 307-742-8053 (SAN 216-1419).

Jemta Press, *(Jemta Pr),* 11313 Beech Daly, Redford Township, MI 48239 Tel 313-937-1986 (SAN 209-1372).

Jen House Publishing Co., *(Jen Hse Pub Co; 0-910841),* 119 Cherry Valley Rd., Reisterstown, MD 21136 Tel 301-833-8931 (SAN 262-7604).

Jenfred Press, *(Jenfred Pr),* P.O. Box 767, Trinidad, CA 95570 (SAN 215-6644).

Jenkins, Doris, *(D Jenkins),* 4827 Hillside Ave., Lincoln, NE 68506 Tel 402-488-4200 (SAN 208-2624).

Jenkins Publishing Co., *(Jenkins; 0-8363),* P.O. Box 2085, Austin, TX 78767 Tel 512-444-6616 (SAN 202-7321).

Jensen, Bernard, Publisher, *(B Jensen; 0-9608604),* Route One, Box 52, Escondido, CA 92025 (SAN 240-690X).

Jeppesen Sanderson, Affiliate of Times Mirror Co., *(Jeppesen Sanderson; 0-88487),* 55 Inverness Dr. E., Englewood, CO 80112 Tel 303-779-5757 (SAN 201-0224).

Jepson Herbarium, *(Jepson Herbarium; 0-935628),* Botany Dept., Univ. of California, Berkeley, Berkeley, CA 94720 Tel 415-642-2465 (SAN 214-2112); Dist. by: Lubrecht & Cramer, RFD 1, Box 227, Monticello, NY 12701 Tel 914-794-8539 (SAN 214-1256).

Jeremy Books, *(Jeremy Bks; 0-89877),* Dist. by: Successful Living, Inc., 9905 Hamilton Road, Eden Prairie, MN 55344 (SAN 213-0939).

Jesuit Books, *(Jesuit Bks; 0-913452),* Seattle University, Seattle, WA 98122 Tel 206-775-7545 (SAN 201-0232).

Jesuit Historical Institute, *(Jesuit Hist),* c/o Loyola Univ. Pr., 3441 N. Ashland Ave., Chicago, IL 60657 (SAN 211-6537).

Jesuits of Holy Cross College, Inc., *(Jesuits Holy Cross),* College of the Holy Cross, Worcester, MA 01610 Tel 617-793-2011 (SAN 210-1211).

Jesus-First Pubs., Inc., *(Jesus-First; 0-9602440),* 1116-4th St., N.W, Ruskin, FL 33570 Tel 813-645-5726 (SAN 212-3630).

Jet'iquette, *(Jet'iquette; 0-9600786),* 510 Michigan Ave., Charlevoix, MI 49720 Tel 616-547-6443 (SAN 202-733X).

Jetsand Pubs., *(Jetsand Pubs Ltd; 0-933374),* Box 17052, W. Hartford, CT 06117 (SAN 212-8349).

Jewel Pubns., *(Jewel Pubns; 0-917728),* 2417 Hazelwood Ave., Fort Wayne, IN 46805 Tel 219-483-6625 (SAN 209-3049).

Jewelers' Circular-Keystone, *(Jewelers Circular; 0-931744),* Chilton Way, Radnor, PA 19089 Tel 215-964-4480 (SAN 210-9050).

Jewell-Johnson & Co. Inc., *(Jewell-Johnson),* 502 Benton St., Port Townsend, WA 98368 Tel 206-385-4342 (SAN 210-9077).

Jewish Board of Family & Children's Services, Inc., *(Jewish Bd Family),* 120 W. 57th St., New York, NY 10019 Tel 212-582-9100 (SAN 211-9080).

Jewish Community Center of Greater Boston, *(Jewish Comm Ctr; 0-9605624),* 72 Franklin St., Boston, MA 02110 (SAN 218-4842).

Jewish Historical Society of New York, Inc., *(Jewish Hist; 0-916790),* 8 W. 70th St., New York, NY 10023 Tel 212-873-0300 (SAN 208-7146).

Jewish Publication Society of America, *(Jewish Pubn; 0-8276),* 1930 Chestnut St., Philadelphia, PA 19103 Tel 215-564-5925 (SAN 201-0240).

Jimora Associated Publishing Co., *(Jimora Assoc; 0-918392),* MPO Box 7047, Chicago, IL 60680 Tel 312-994-4846 (SAN 210-0355) Formerly Named Associated Publishing Co.

Jinro Publishing Co., *(Jinro Pub; 0-940772),* 432 Board of Trade Bldg., 127 W. Tenth St., Kansas City, MO 84105 Tel 816-221-6640 (SAN 219-6670).

JML Enterprises, *(JML Ent; 0-9607096),* P.O. Box 13167, Albuquerque, NM 87192 Tel 505-296-4667 (SAN 238-9932).

JML Enterprises, Inc., *(JML Enter MD; 0-938464),* P.O Box 488, Bel Air, MD 21014 Tel 301-879-8552 (SAN 238-5279).

JMT Pubns., *(JMT Pubns),* P.O. Box 603, Camp Hill, PA 17011 (SAN 238-8189).

Jo-Jo Pubns., *(Jo-Jo Pubns; 0-9602266),* 208 N. Sparrow Rd., Chesapeake, VA 23325 (SAN 212-5153).

Joan Kahn Book, A *See* **St. Martin's Press, Inc.**

Joanna Taylor Books, *(J Taylor Bks),* 2461 el Pavo Way, Rancho Cordova, CA 95670 (SAN 238-8227).

Job Hunters Forum, *(Job Hunters Forum; 0-918350),* 132 Pinecrest Dr., Annapolis, MD 21403 Tel 301-268-6425 (SAN 209-178X).

Jobeco Books, *(Jobeco Bks; 0-9607572),* P.O. Box 3323, Humble, TX 77347 (SAN 237-9651).

Joby Books, *(Joby Bks),* Box 2603, San Rafael, CA 94901 (SAN 209-1518); Dist. by: Bookpeople, 2940 Seventh St., Berkeley, CA 94710 Tel 415-549-3033 (SAN 168-9517).

Jochum, Helen Parker, *(Jochum),* 79 Huntington Rd., Garden City, NY 11530 (SAN 215-8787); Dist. by: Skills, 24 S. Prospect St., Amherst, MA 01002 Tel 413-253-9500 (SAN 215-8795).

Johannes Press, *(Johannes; 0-910810),* c/o Galerie St. Etienne, 24 W. 57th St., New York, NY 10019 Tel 212-245-6734 (SAN 206-9806).

Johannes Schwalm Historical Assn., Inc., *(Johannes Schwalm Hist),* 4983 S. Sedgewick Rd., Lyndhurst, OH 44124 (SAN 209-5076).

John, Edna S., *(E S John),* 1481 "D" St., Springfield, OR 97477 (SAN 209-2050).

John & Mabel Ringling Museum of Art *See* **John & Mable Ringling Museum of Art Foundation**

John & Mable Ringling Museum of Art Foundation, *(Ringling Mus Art; 0-916758),* 5401 Bayshore Rd., Sarasota, FL 33578 Tel 813-355-5101 (SAN 208-7154) Self-Pub & Self-Dist.

John Clancy's Kitchen Workshop, *(Clancys Kitchen),* 324 W. 19th St., New York, NY 10011 Tel 212-243-0958 (SAN 213-5264); Orders to: Johnson Press, 49 Sheridan Ave., Albany, NY 12210 (SAN 213-5272).

John Day Junior Books *See* **Harper & Row Pubs., Inc.**

John Jay Press, *(John Jay Pr; 0-89444),* 444 W. 56th St., New York, NY 10019 Tel 212-489-3515 (SAN 210-2196).

John Knox Press, *(John Knox; 0-8042),* 341 Ponce De Leon Ave., N.E., Rm. 416, Atlanta, GA 30365 Tel 404-873-1549 (SAN 271-7956).

Johnny Reads, Inc., *(Johnny Reads; 0-910812),* P.O. Box 12834, St. Petersburg, FL 33733 Tel 813-867-7647 (SAN 201-0283).

Johns Hopkins Univ., Dept. of International Health, *(Dept Intl Health; 0-912888),* 615 N. Wolfe St., Baltimore, MD 21205 (SAN 202-3520).

Johns Hopkins Univ. Press, *(Johns Hopkins; 0-8018),* Baltimore, MD 21218 Tel 301-338-7861 (SAN 202-7348).

John's Press, *(Johns Pr; 0-9607730),* Box 3405 CRS, Roch Hill, SC 29731 Tel 803-366-7392 (SAN 238-7948).

Johnson, Barbara Mary, *(B M Johnson),* 7381 Webb Rd., Chatsworth, CA 91311 Tel 213-703-1594 (SAN 263-2381).

Johnson, Forrest Bryant, *(F B Johnson; 0-9600510),* 589 Sierra Vista, No. 31, Las Vegas, NV 89109 Tel 702-796-6219 (SAN 205-5694).

Johnson, Joe Donald, *(Joe D Johnson; 0-915960),* P.O. Box 31, Eureka, CA 95502 (SAN 207-3366).

Johnson, John, *(J Johnson; 0-910914),* R.D. 2, N. Bennington, VT 05257 Tel 802-442-6738 (SAN 208-4910).

Johnson, LTC Thomas M., *(T M Johnson; 0-9600906),* P.O. Box 7152, Alexandria, VA 22307 Tel 703-373-9150 (SAN 208-7162).

Johnson, Mabel, *(M Johnson; 0-9600838),* P.O. Box 7, Boring, OR 97009 Tel 503-663-3428 (SAN 206-1015).

Johnson, Merwyn S., *(M S Johnson; 0-9601590),* P.O. Box 368, Due West, SC 29639 Tel 803-379-8193 (SAN 212-3649).

Johnson, Walter J., Inc., *(Walter J Johnson; 0-8472),* 355 Chestnut St., Norwood, NJ 07648 Tel 201-767-1303 (SAN 209-1828).

Johnson & Johnson Baby Products Co., *(Johnson & Johnson; 0-931562),* 220 Centennial Ave., Piscataway, NJ 08854 (SAN 211-5131).

Johnson Books, *(Johnson Bks; 0-933472),* P.O. Box 990, 1880 S. 57th Court, Boulder, CO 80301 Tel 303-443-1576 (SAN 201-0313).

Johnson Publishing Co., *(Johnson NC; 0-930230),* P. O. Box 217, Murfreesboro, NC 27855 (SAN 201-0291).

Johnson Publishing Co., Inc., *(Johnson Chi; 0-87485),* 820 S. Michigan Ave., Chicago, IL 60605 Tel 312-322-9248 (SAN 201-0305).

Johnson Reprint Corp., Subs. of Harcourt, Brace & Jovanovich, Inc., *(Johnson Repr; 0-384),* 111 Fifth Ave., New York, NY 10003 Tel 212-741-6800 (SAN 285-0362); Orders to: 757 Third Ave., New York, NY 10017 Tel 212-888-2925 (SAN 285-0370).

Johnston Publishing, Inc., *(Johnston Pub; 0-942934),* Box 96, Afton, MN 55001 Tel 612-436-7344 (SAN 240-3900).

Joint Center for Political Studies, *(Jt Ctr Pol Studies),* 1301 Pennsylvania NW, Suite 400, Washington, DC 20004 Tel 202-626-3500 (SAN 233-2558).

Joint Center for Urban Studies of MIT and Harvard Univ., *(Joint Cen Urban; 0-943142),* 53 Church St., Cambridge, MA 02138 (SAN 240-5385).

Joint Commission on Accreditation of Hospitals, *(Joint Comm Hosp; 0-86688),* Dept. of Pubns., 875 N. Michigan Ave., Chicago, IL 60611 Tel 312-642-6061 (SAN 210-8194).

Joint Committee on Law Study Programs, *(Jt Comm Law Study),* New England School of Law, 154 Stuart St, Boston, MA 02116 (SAN 238-7670).

Jolean Publishing Co., *(Jolean Pub Co; 0-934284),* P.O. Box 163, Arverne, NY 11692 (SAN 212-9507).

Jolex, Inc., *(Jolex; 0-89149),* Dist. by: John Olson Co., 294 W. Oakland Ave., Oakland, NJ 07436 Tel 201-337-3355 (SAN 208-4104).

Jolly, David C., *(D C Jolly; 0-911775),* P.O. Box 931, Brookline, MA 02146 Tel 617-232-6222 (SAN 264-1380).

Jon-Juan, Inc., *(Jon-Juan),* P.O. Box 239, Guilderland, NY 12084 (SAN 237-966X).

Jonathan David Pubs., Inc., *(Jonathan David; 0-8246),* 68-22 Eliot Ave., Middle Village, NY 11379 Tel 212-456-8611 (SAN 201-0321).

Jonathan Pubns., *(Jonathan Pubns; 0-9603348),* 660 Prospect Ave., Hartford, CT 06105 (SAN 213-330X).

Jonathan Publishing Co., *(Jonathan LA; 0-940718),* 1152 Ingleside, Baton Rouge, LA 70806 (SAN 219-7936).

Jones, Anson, Press, *(A Jones; 0-912432),* P.O. Box 65, Salado, TX 76571 Tel 817-947-5414 (SAN 201-2014).

Jones, Arnold, & Associates, *(Arnold Jones; 0-943036),* 3400 Ben Lomand Pl. No. 123, Los Angeles, CA 90027 Tel 213-662-6580 (SAN 240-3919).

Jones, Bob University Press, *(Bob Jones Univ Pr; 0-89084),* Greenville, SC 29614 (SAN 284-5490).

Jones, Edward-Lynn, & Associates, *(Ed-Lynne Jones; 0-9602458),* 5517 17th Ave. NE, Seattle, WA 98105 (SAN 263-2195).

Jones, Ernest R., *(E R Jones; 0-9600934),* 2104 Apache Place, N.E., Albuquerque, NM 87112 Tel 505-292-7688 (SAN 208-0214).

Jones, Harry, *(H Jones; 0-9601980),* P.O. Box 10054, Austin, TX 78766-1054 Tel 512-451-2644 (SAN 212-615X).

Jones, Lowell, *(L Jones; 0-9602074),* 11832 Brookmont Dr., Maryland Heights, MO 63043 (SAN 212-2847).

Jones, Marshall, Co., Div. of Golden Quill Press, *(M Jones; 0-8338),* Francestown, NH 03043 (SAN 206-8834).

Jones, Stan, Publishing, Inc., *(Jones Pub; 0-939936),* 3421 E. Mercer St., Seattle, WA 98112 (SAN 216-8243).

Jones, Wendy, *(W Jones),* Box 7186, Canyon Lake, CA 92380 (SAN 264-1410).

Jones International Ltd., *(Jones Intl; 0-935910),* 5275 DTC Parkway, No. 44, Englewood, CO 80111 Tel 303-740-9700 (SAN 213-8530).

Jones Library, *(Jones Lib),* 43 Amity St., Amherst, MA 01002 Tel 413-256-0246 (SAN 204-9872).

Jones Medical Pubns., *(Jones Med; 0-930010),* 355 Los Cerros Dr., Greenbrae, CA 94904 Tel 415-461-3749 (SAN 210-4466).

Jonsalvania Publishing Co., *(Jonsalvania),* Russell Rd., Canton, NY 13617 Tel 315-386-4007 (SAN 214-1671).

Jordan, Carol, *(C Jordan; 0-9605360),* 654 Jerome St., Davis, CA 95616 (SAN 216-0463).

Jordan, Thomas, F., *(T F Jordan; 0-9602762),* 2249 Dunedin Ave., Duluth, MN 55803 (SAN 240-0944).

Jordan Associates, Ltd., *(Jordan Assoc; 0-9610354),* P.O. Box 814, Virginia Beach, VA 23451 (SAN 264-1437).

Jordan Publishing, *(Jordan Pub),* 360 West Pine St., Cedar Springs, MI 49319 (SAN 240-9712).

Jordan Valley Heritage House, *(Jordan Valley; 0-939810),* 43502 Hwy. 226, Stayton, OR 97383 Tel 503-859-3144 (SAN 216-7425).

Jordan-Volpe Gallery, The, *(Jordan-Volpe Gall),* 457 W. Broadway, New York, NY 10012 Tel 212-533-3900 (SAN 214-0438); Dist. by: Peregrine Smith, Inc., P.O. Box 667, Layton, UT 84041 (SAN 201-9906).

Jorgensen Pubns., Inc., *(Jorg Pubns CA; 0-943340),* P.O. Box 68, Saratoga, CA 95070 Tel 408-252-3820 (SAN 240-5393).

Jorgensen Publishing Co., *(Jorgensen Pub; 0-938128),* 1801 Ave. of the Stars, Los Angeles, CA 90067 (SAN 219-7944).

Jory Pubns, *(Jory Pubns; 0-9607732),* 12535 Sunview Dr., St. Louis, MO 63141 Tel 314-434-0066 (SAN 238-0935).

Joseph Nichols Publisher, *(Joseph Nichols; 0-912484),* P.O. Box 2394, Tulsa, OK 74101 Tel 918-583-3390 (SAN 203-901X).

Joseph Publishing Co., *(Joseph Pub Co; 0-915878),* P.O. Box 770, San Mateo, CA 94401 Tel 415-345-4100 (SAN 207-8538).

Joshua Publishing Company, *(Joshua Pub Co; 0-910665),* 8033 Sunset Blvd., Suite 306, Los Angeles, CA 90046 Tel 213-650-8127 (SAN 262-7639).

Joslyn Art Museum, *(Joslyn Art; 0-936364),* 2200 Dodge St., Omaha, NE 68102 (SAN 281-8442); Orders to: Joslyn Museum Shop, 2200 Dodge St., Omaha, NE 68102 Tel 402-342-3300 (SAN 281-8450).

Jossey-Bass Inc., Pubs., *(Jossey-Bass; 0-87589),* 433 California St., San Francisco, CA 94104 Tel 415-433-1740 (SAN 201-033X).

Jostens Pubns., *(Jostens; 0-88136),* P.O. Box 1903, Topeka, KS 66601 Tel 913-266-3300 (SAN 241-5313).

Jotarian Productions, *(Jotarian; 0-943454),* 3976 Warner Ave., No. A-4, Landover Hills, MD 20784 Tel 301-322-2480 (SAN 240-6918).

Journal Herald, The, *(Journal Herald; 0-938492),* 37 S. Ludlow St., Dayton, OH 45342 (SAN 215-5809).

Journal of Chemical Education, *(Chem Educ; 0-910362),* 238 Kent Rd., Springfield, PA 19064 (SAN 203-6436).

Journal of Irreproducible Results, Inc., *(JIR; 0-9605852),* 2405 Bond St., Park Forest South, IL 60466 Tel 312-534-1770 (SAN 282-7077)P.O. Box 234, Chicago Heights, IL 60411 Tel 312-534-1770 (SAN 282-7085).

Journal of Spanish Studies: Twentieth Century, *(Journal Span Stud; 0-89294),* The University of Nebraska-Lincoln, Dept. of Modern Languages, Oldfather Hall, Lincoln, NE 68588 Tel 402-472-3745 (SAN 209-4541); Dist. by: Society of Spanish & Spanish-American Studies, Dept. of Modern Languages & Literatures, Univ. of Nebraska-Lincoln, Lincoln, NE 68588 (SAN 208-3221).

Journal of the West, *(Journal of the West),* Box 1009, Manhattan, KS 66502 Tel 913-532-6733 (SAN 224-2141).

Journey Books, Inc., *(Journey Bks; 0-933156),* P.O. Box 100, Clarksville, MD 21029 (SAN 212-2839).

Journey Press, *(Journey Pr; 0-918572),* 1828 Virginia St., Berkeley, CA 94703 Tel 415-540-5500 (SAN 281-8469); Dist. by: Bookpeople, 2940 Sedente St., Berkeley, CA 94710 (SAN 168-9517); Dist. by: And/Or Press, Inc., P. O. Box 2246, Berkeley, CA 94702 Tel 415-849-2665 (SAN 206-9458).

Journey Pubns., *(Journey Pubns; 0-918038),* P.O. Box 423, Woodstock, NY 12498 Tel 914-679-2250 (SAN 209-570X).

Jove Pubns., Inc., Div. of Berkley/Jove Publishing Group, *(Jove Pubns; 0-515),* 200 Madison Ave., New York, NY 10016 Tel 212-686-9820 (SAN 215-8817); Dist. by: ICD, 250 W. 55th St., New York, NY 10019 Tel 212-262-7444 (SAN 169-5800).

Joy-Co Press, *(Joy-Co; 0-9605984),* 2636 Burgener Blvd., San Diego, CA 92110 Tel 714-276-9760 (SAN 216-7433).

Joy Publishing Co., *(Joy Pub CA; 0-933376),* 450 Sutter St., Suite 930, San Francisco, CA 94108 (SAN 221-4733).

Joy Publishing Co., *(Joy Pub Co; 0-9601758),* P.O. Box 2532, Boca Raton, FL 33432 Tel 305-276-5879 (SAN 211-0806).

Joybug Teaching Aids, Inc., *(Joybug; 0-931218),* P.O. Box 2138, 1125 E. Wayne, Salina, KS 67401 Tel 913-825-1589 (SAN 212-1050); Dist. by: Liberty Publishing Co., 50 Scott Adam Rd., Cockeysville, MD Tel 301-667-6680 (SAN 211-030X).

Joyce Media Inc., *(Joyce Media; 0-917002),* 8753 Shirley Ave., P.O. Box 458, Northridge, CA 91328 Tel 213-885-7181 (SAN 208-7197).

Joyful Noise Productions, International, *(Joyful Noise; 0-936874),* 109 Minna St., Suite 153, San Francisco, CA 94105 (SAN 215-0883).

Ju, I-Hsiung, *(Ju I Hsiung; 0-9611726),* RFD Five, Box 85, Lexington, VA 24450 Tel 703-463-7961 (SAN 285-3361).

Jubilee Committee See **Rabinowitz, Solomon, Hebrew Book Store, Inc.**

Jubilee Press, Inc., *(Jubilee Pr; 0-9609674),* 7906 Hillside Ave., Los Angeles, CA 90046 Tel 213-851-5893 (SAN 262-7663).

Judaica Press, Inc., *(Judaica Pr; 0-910818),* 521 Fifth Ave., New York, NY 10017 Tel 212-260-0520 (SAN 204-9856).

Judson Press, *(Judson; 0-8170),* P.O. Box 851, Valley Forge, PA 19482-0851 Tel 215-768-2111 (SAN 201-0348).

Judy Publishing Co., *(Judy; 0-87702),* Main P.O., Box 5270, Chicago, IL 60680 Tel 312-787-7233 (SAN 202-7372).

Jukebox Collector Newsletter, *(Jukebox Coll New; 0-912789),* 2545 S.E. 60th Ct., Des Moines, IA 50317 Tel 515-265-8324 (SAN 282-809X).

Jung, C. G., Foundation Publications, *(C G Jung Foun; 0-913430),* 28 E. 39th St., New York, NY 10016 Tel 212-697-6430 (SAN 207-0391).

Jung, C.G., Institute of Los Angeles, Inc., *(C G Jung Inst; 0-918608),* 10349 W. Pico Blvd., Los Angeles, CA 90064 (SAN 220-6927).

Jung, C.G., Institute of San Francisco, *(C G Jung Frisco; 0-932630),* 2040 Gough St., San Francisco, CA 94109 (SAN 281-8493); Dist. by: Spring Pubs., P.O. Box 222069, Dallas, TX 75222 (SAN 282-6127).

Jungle Garden Press, *(Jungle Garden),* 47 Oak Rd., Fairfax, CA 94930 Tel 415-456-4884 (SAN 210-8216).

Jungle Video, *(Jungle Video; 0-9602756),* 2013 Lincoln Apartment Three, Berkeley, CA 94709 (SAN 221-8038).

Junior Board of the Tri-City Symphony Orchestra, *(Jr Bd Tri-City Symph; 0-9606524),* P. O. Box 67, Davenport, IA 52805 (SAN 218-5601).

Junior Committee of The Cleveland Orchestra, The, *(Jr Comm Cleveland; 0-9609142),* Severance Hall, Cleveland, OH 44106 Tel 216-231-7300 (SAN 241-5321).

Junior League of Amarillo Texas, Inc., The, *(Jr League Amarillo; 0-9604102),* P.O. Box 381, Amarillo, TX 79105 (SAN 215-0891).

Junior League of Asheville Publications, *(Jr League Asheville; 0-9608444),* P.O. Box 8723, Asheville, NC 28814 Tel 704-258-2098 (SAN 240-6926).

Junior League of Austin, Texas, *(Jr League Austin; 0-9605906),* P.O. Box 165, Austin, TX 78767 Tel 512-472-3753 (SAN 216-6828).

Junior League of Beaumont, Inc., *(Jr League Beau; 0-9609604),* P.O. Box 7031, Beaumont, TX 77706 Tel 713-835-7180 (SAN 260-2105).

Junior League of Binghamton Publishing Co., *(Jr League Binghamton; 0-9607710),* 85 Walnut St., Binghamton, NY 13905 (SAN 238-4310).

Junior League of Charleston, S.C., Inc., *(Jun League Charl SC),* P.O. Box 177, Charleston, SC 29402 Tel 803-722-0679 (SAN 218-8031).

Junior League of Charleston West Virginia, Inc., *(Jr League Charleston; 0-9606232),* P.O. Box 1924, Charleston, WV 25327 Tel 304-343-2190 (SAN 220-3359).

Junior League of Chicago, Inc., The, *(JLC Inc; 0-9611622),* 1447 N. Astor St., Chicago, IL 60610 Tel 312-251-0043 (SAN 238-8863).

Junior League of Colorado Springs, Inc., The, *(Jr League Colo Spgs; 0-9609930),* 1600 N. Cascade Ave., Colorado Springs, CO 80907 Tel 303-632-2702 (SAN 271-8332).

Junior League of Corpus Christi, Inc., *(Jr League Corpus Christi; 0-9609144),* P.O. Box 837, Corpus Christi, TX 78403 Tel 512-883-9351 (SAN 241-533X).

Junior League of El Paso, Inc, *(Jr League El Paso; 0-9607974),* 520 Thunderbird, El Paso, TX 79912 (SAN 240-9518).

Junior League of Elmira, Inc., *(Jr League Elmira; 0-9609980),* 500 Roe Ave., Elmira, NY 14901 Tel 607-732-9075 (SAN 271-8413).

Junior League of Eugene Pubs., *(Jr League Eugene; 0-9607976),* 2839 Willamette St., Eugene, OR 97405 Tel 503-345-7370 (SAN 238-5341).

Junior League of Fort Lauderdale, *(Jr League Ft Lauderdale; 0-9604158),* 2510 N.E. 15th Ave., Fort Lauderdale, FL 33305 Tel 305-566-3736 (SAN 214-2481).

Junior League of Gainesville Florida, Inc., *(Jr League Gainesville; 0-9606616),* P.O. Box 422, Gainesville, FL 32602 Tel 904-372-1710 (SAN 219-6697).

Junior League of Greensboro, Inc., The, *(Jr League Green; 0-9605788),* 113 S. Elm St., Greensboro, NC 27401 Tel 919-275-9292 (SAN 216-5333).

Junior League of Jackson, Mississippi, *(Jr League Jackson; 0-9606886),* P.O. Box 4553, Jackson, MS 39216 Tel 601-981-2505 (SAN 217-3867).

Junior League of Jacksonville Inc.,The, *(Jr League FL; 0-9609338),* 2165 Park St., Jacksonville, FL 32204 Tel 904-389-2176 (SAN 260-2113).

Junior League of Kalamazoo, Inc., *(Jr League Kalamazoo; 0-9606506),* 309 E. Water St., Kalamazoo, MI 49007 Tel 616-344-9814 (SAN 217-1880).

Junior League of Kansas City Missouri, Inc., *(Jr League KC; 0-9607076),* 4509 Troost, Kansas City, MO 64110 Tel 816-531-1535 (SAN 238-9959).

Junior League of Lafayette, The, *(Jr League Lafayette; 0-935032),* P.O. Box 52387, Oil Ctr Sta., Lafayette, LA 70505 Tel 318-233-2063 (SAN 212-3657).

Junior League of Memphis, Inc.,The, *(Jr League Memphis; 0-9604222),* 2711 Union Ave. Extended, Memphis, TN 38112 Tel 901-452-2151 (SAN 214-316X).

Junior League of Monroe, *(Jun League Mon; 0-9602364),* P.O. Box 7138, Monroe, LA 71203 Tel 318-322-3863 (SAN 208-1822).

Junior League of Montclair-Newark, Inc., *(Jr League Montclair-Newark; 0-9605328),* P.O. Box 825, Upper Montclair, NJ 07043 Tel 201-746-2499 (SAN 220-1577).

Junior League of New Orleans, Inc., *(Jr League New Orleans; 0-9604774),* 4319 Carondelet, New Orleans, LA 70115 (SAN 215-6652).

Junior League of Newport Harbor, Inc., *(Jun League NH; 0-9608306),* One Park Newport, Newport, CA 92660 Tel 714-646-5595 (SAN 240-5407).

Junior League of Northern Westchester, Inc., *(Jr League N Westchester; 0-9604314),* P.O. Box 214, Chappaqua, NY 10514 (SAN 265-4067).

Junior League of Peoria, Inc., *(Jr League Peoria; 0-9608206),* 256 N.E. Randolph Ave., Peoria, IL 61606 (SAN 238-8286).

Junior League of Rochester, Inc., *(Jr League Rochester; 0-9605612),* 33 S. Washington St., Rochester, NY 14608 (SAN 216-1486).

Junior League of San Antonio, The, *(Jr League Antonio; 0-9610416),* 819 Augusta Street, San Antonio, TX 78205 Tel 512-264-1461).

Junior League of Shreveport, Inc., *(Jr League Shreveport; 0-9602246),* P.O. Box 4648, Shreveport, LA 71104 Tel 318-868-7866 (SAN 212-4297).

Junior League of South Bend, Inc., *(Jr League S Bend; 0-9607120),* c/o Nutbread & Nostalgia, P.O. Box 305, South Bend, IN 46624 Tel 219-291-4036 (SAN 238-9967).

Junior League of the Palm Beaches, Inc., the, *(Jr League Palm Beaches; 0-9608090),* Post Box 168, Palm Beach, FL 33480 (SAN 240-1177).

Junior League of Tulsa Pubns., *(Jr League Tulsa),* 167 London Square, Tulsa, OK 74105 Tel 918-743-9767 (SAN 219-9718).

Junior League of Tyler, Inc., The, *(Jr League Tyler; 0-9607122),* 4500 S. Broadway, Suite C, Tyler, TX 75703 Tel 214-593-1134 (SAN 238-9975).

Junior League of Wichita Falls, *(Jr League Wichita; 0-9608308),* Two Eureka Circle, Wichita Falls, TX 76308 Tel 817-538-5846 (SAN 240-5415).

Junior Welfare League of Enid, Oklahoma, Inc., *(Jr Welfare Enid; 0-9609340),* P. O. Box 5877, Enid, OK 73702 Tel 405-234-2665 (SAN 276-9700).

Juniper *See* **Fawcett Book Group**

Juniper House, *(Juniper Hse; 0-931870),* P.O. Box 2094, Boulder, CO 80306 Tel 303-449-7757 (SAN 212-1891).

Juniper Press, *(Juniper Maine; 0-913977),* c/o Betts Bookstore, Bangor Mall, Stillwater Ave., Bangor, ME 04401 Tel 207-947-7052 (SAN 212-1077).

Juniper Press, *(Juniper Pr WI; 0-910822),* 1310 Shorewood Dr., La Crosse, WI 54601 Tel 608-788-0096 (SAN 207-8570).

Juniper Pubs., *(Juniper Pubs; 0-9605986),* P.O. Box 11872, Lexington, KY 40511 Tel 606-266-4675 (SAN 207-2432).

Junius, Inc., *(Junius Inc; 0-9603932),* 842 Lombard St., Philadelphia, PA 19147 Tel 215-627-8298 (SAN 214-0934).

Junius-Vaughn Press, The, *(Junius-Vaughn; 0-940198),* P.O. Box 85, Fairview, NJ 07022 (SAN 217-1139).

Jupiter Books, *(Jupiter Bks; 0-935344),* 7300 Eades Ave., La Jolla, CA 92037 (SAN 213-7658).

Jupiter Press, *(Jupiter Pr; 0-933104),* P.O. Box 101, Lake Bluff, IL 60044 Tel 312-234-3997 (SAN 212-5161).

Jupiter Pubns., *(Jupiter Pubns; 0-939270),* 118 W. 74th St., New York, NY 10023 Tel 212-873-3132 (SAN 216-5341).

Jurgensen Publishing Co., *(Jurgensen Pub; 0-9610112),* 14713 E. Caspian Pl., Aurora, CO 80014 Tel 303-755-9716 (SAN 271-8421).

Just Above Midtown, Inc., *(Just Above Midtown; 0-9605830),* 178-80 Franklin St., New York, NY 10013 Tel 212-966-7020 (SAN 211-4704).

Just Another Asshole, *(Just Another; 0-913803),* Eight Spring St., 4 EF, New York, NY 10012 Tel 212-966-0623 (SAN 286-1291).

Just Clare Corporation, *(Just Clare; 0-9608092),* 1825 Union St. No. 377, San Francisco, CA 94123 Tel 415-563-6313 (SAN 240-2386).

Just in Time Publishing, *(Just in Time Pub; 0-943208),* 2031 36th Ave., Longview, WA 98632 Tel 206-425-4678 (SAN 240-5423).

Justice Pubs., *(Justice Pubs; 0-941348),* P.O. Box 35360, Los Angeles, CA 90035 Tel 213-995-3329 (SAN 238-9991).

Juul, Peter, Press, Inc., *(P Juul Pr; 0-915456),* P.O. Box 40605, Tucson, AZ 85717 Tel 602-622-3409 (SAN 207-513X).

Juvenescent Research Corp., *(Juvenescent; 0-9600148),* 807 Riverside Dr., New York, NY 10032 Tel 212-795-8765 (SAN 206-7250).

Juvenile Books *See* **Harper & Row Pubs., Inc.**
Juvenile Books *See* **Simon & Schuster, Inc.**

Jym Enterprises, *(Jym Ent),* P.O. Box 73, Batavia, OH 45103 (SAN 210-5373).

K & K Enterprises, *(K & K Enter; 0-935346),* 4572 Via Marina, Suite 309, Marina Del Rey, CA 90291 (SAN 221-4652).

K&K Pubs., *(K & K Pubs; 0-9604218),* 216 N. Batavia Ave., Batavia, IL 60510 Tel 312-879-6214 (SAN 214-3186).

KCE Publishing, *(KCE Pub; 0-940686),* 40 Cordone Dr., San Anselmo, CA 94960 (SAN 239-555X).

KC Pubns., *(KC Pubns; 0-916122; 0-88714),* P.O. Box 14883, 2901 Industrial Rd., Las Vegas, NV 89114 Tel 702-731-3123 (SAN 201-0364).

KEL Pubns., *(KEL Pubns; 0-9605710),* 443 Schley Rd., Annapolis, MD 21401 Tel 301-268-9704 (SAN 216-1508).

KEND Publishing, *(KEND Pub; 0-938218),* 15 Dorchester Rd., Emerson, NJ 07630 (SAN 217-2429).

KET, *(KET; 0-910475),* Network Center, 600 Cooper Drive, Lexington, KY 40502 Tel 606-233-3000 (SAN 264-147X).

KID Broadcasting Corp., *(KID Broadcast; 0-9607304),* P.O. Box 2008, Idaho Falls, ID 83401 (SAN 240-9569).

KMG Pubns., *(KMG Pubns OR; 0-938928),* 290 E. Ashland Lane, P.O. Box 1055, Ashland, OR 97520 Tel 503-488-2826 (SAN 215-9562).

KMS Press, *(KMS Pr CO),* P.O. Box 6516, Denver, CO 80206 (SAN 215-9570).

KOSMOS, *(KOSMOS; 0-916426),* 381 Arlington St., San Francisco, CA 94131 Tel 415-586-7255 (SAN 208-029X).

K/P Medical Systems, *(KP Med),* P.O. Box 8900, Stockton, CA 95208 Tel 209-466-6761 (SAN 209-5726).

K-Q Associates Inc., *(K Q Assocs; 0-941988),* P.O. Box 2132, Cedar Rapids, IA 52406 (SAN 238-4655).

KRC Development Council, *(K R C Dev; 0-917440),* 431 Valley Rd., New Canaan, CT 06840 Tel 203-972-0401 (SAN 207-9690).

Kabyn Books, *(Kabyn; 0-940444),* 5643 El Cajon Blvd., San Diego, CA 92115 Tel 619-287-3883 (SAN 217-1902).

KaChunk Press, *(KaChunk Pr; 0-9604292),* Box 1043, Iowa City, IA 52244 (SAN 214-3194).

Kagg Press, *(Kagg Pr; 0-912200),* 9910 Columbus Circle, Nw, Albuquerque, NM 87114 Tel 505-898-4541 (SAN 203-9133).

Kahn, Hannah, *(H Kahn; 0-9602340),* 3301 N.E. Fifth Ave., Suite 318, Miami, FL 33137 Tel 305-576-1499 (SAN 208-1342).

Kahn, Joan, Books *See* **Ticknor & Fields**

Kahn & Kahan Publishing Co., Inc., *(Kahn & Kahan; 0-9604286),* 31 South St., P.O. Box 661, Morristown, NJ 07960 (SAN 214-2597).

Kaihong Books, *(Kaihong Bks; 0-940446),* P.O. Box 527, Whittier, CA 90608 (SAN 218-4850).

Kairos Books, Inc., *(Kairos Bks; 0-9608410),* P.O. Box 708, Libertyville, IL 60048 Tel 312-362-1898 (SAN 240-6942).

Kalamazoo Institute of Arts, *(Kalamazoo Inst Arts; 0-933742),* 314 S. Park St., Kalamazoo, MI 49007 Tel 616-349-7775 (SAN 221-4660).

Kalimat Press, *(Kalimat; 0-933770),* 10889 Wilshire Blvd., Suite 700, Los Angeles, CA 90024 Tel 213-208-8559 (SAN 213-7666).

Kalium, Inc., *(Kalium; 0-9610114),* 141 Mt. Horeb Rd., Warren, NJ 07060 Tel 201-647-6016 (SAN 271-8480).

Kallman Publishing Co., *(Kallman; 0-910824),* 1614 W. University Ave., Box 14076, Gainesville, FL 32601 Tel 904-376-6066 (SAN 203-9141).

Kalmbach Publishing Co., *(Kalmbach; 0-89024),* 1027 N. Seventh St., Milwaukee, WI 53233 Tel 414-272-2060 (SAN 201-0399).

Kalum Press, *(Kalum Pr; 0-937788),* 596 Joey Ave., El Cajon, CA 92020 (SAN 215-6660).

Kambrina, *(Kambrina; 0-9605742),* P.O. Box 1331, Newport, OR 97365 (SAN 216-2601).

Kan, Johnny, Inc., *(Kan J; 0-9608900),* 708 Grant Ave., San Francisco, CA 94108 Tel 415-982-2388 (SAN 241-127X).

Kanchenjunga Press, *(Kanchenjunga Pr; 0-913600),* 22 Rio Vista Lane, Red Bluff, CA 96080 (SAN 202-652X).

Kanegis, James, *(Kanegis; 0-9600226),* 3907 Madison St., Hyattsville, MD 20781 Tel 301-699-5064 (SAN 201-0402).

Kaneshiro, Hansel S., *(Kaneshiro; 0-9600670),* 1524 N. Hoyne Ave., Chicago, IL 60622 Tel 312-276-8024 (SAN 203-915X).

Kansas Arts Commission, *(Kansas Arts Com; 0-9607978),* 112 W. 6th St. Suite 401, Topeka, KS 66603 Tel 913-296-3335 (SAN 239-9393).

Kansas Bar Association CLE, *(KS Bar CLE),* Box 1037, Topeka, KS 66601 (SAN 237-7314).

Kansas State Historical Society, *(Kansas St Hist; 0-87726),* Memorial Bldg., 120 W. 10th St., Topeka, KS 66612 Tel 913-296-3251 (SAN 207-0014).

Kansas State Univ., *(KSU),* Orders to: Library Publications, Kansas State Univ. Library, Manhattan, KS 66506 (SAN 210-1483).

Kanthaka Press, *(Kanthaka; 0-916926),* P.O. Box 696, Brookline Village, MA 02147 Tel 617-734-8146 (SAN 206-4375).

Kapilla, Cleo & Simons, Eleanor, *(K & S; 0-9611466),* P.O. Box 4995, Ocala, FL 32678 Tel 904-622-4914 (SAN 277-6928).

Kappeler Institute Publishing, *(Kappeler Inst Pub; 0-942958),* 2019 Delaware Ave., Wilmington, DE 19806 (SAN 240-1185).

Kar-Ben Copies, Inc., *(Kar Ben; 0-930494),* 11216 Empire Lane, Rockville, MD 20852 Tel 301-984-8733 (SAN 210-7511).

Karger, S., AG, *(S Karger; 3-8055),* 150 5th Ave., Suite 1103, New York, NY 10011 Tel 212-924-9222 (SAN 281-8531); Dist. by: Albert J. Phiebig, P. O. Box 352, White Plains, NY 10602 (SAN 281-854X).

Karma Publishing Co., *(Karma Pub),* 4404 Pennsylvania Ave., Pittsburgh, PA 15224 (SAN 238-888X).

Karoma Pubs., Inc., *(Karoma; 0-89720),* 3400 Daleview Dr., Ann Arbor, MI 48103 Tel 313-665-3331 (SAN 213-8131).

Karpat Pub., *(Karpat; 0-918570),* 19608 Thornridge Ave., Cleveland, OH 44135 Tel 216-362-0316 (SAN 209-939X).

Karwyn Enterprises, *(Karwyn Ent; 0-939938),* 17227 17th Ave. W., Lynnwood, WA 98036 Tel 206-743-0722 (SAN 216-8251).

Karz-Cohl Pubs., Inc., *(Karz-Cohl Pub; 0-943828),* 24 Brookstone Dr., Princeton, NJ 08540 Tel 609-683-1016 (SAN 238-3063).

Kashong Pubns., *(Kashong Pubns),* P.O. Box 90, Bellona, NY 14415 Tel 315-789-9574 (SAN 218-8074).

Katahdin Press, *(Katahdin; 0-939212),* P.O. Box 231, Campbell, CA 95009 (SAN 216-261X).

Katanya Pubns., *(Katanya Pubns; 0-912101),* P.O. Box 5355, Takoma Park, MD 20912 Tel 301-589-8263 (SAN 264-7575).

Katonah Gallery, *(Katonah Gal),* 28 Bedford Rd., Katonah, NY 10536 (SAN 279-2680).

Kauai Museum Assn., Ltd., *(Kauai Museum; 0-940948),* Box 248, Lihue, HI 96766 Tel 808-245-6932 (SAN 213-1013).

Kauf Pubs., *(Kauf Pubs; 0-936804),* 715 38th St., W. Des Moines, IA 50265 (SAN 238-793X).

Kaufman, Alvin B., Pubs., *(Kaufman A B Pubs; 0-9607736),* 22420 Philiprimm St., Woodland Hills, CA 91367 Tel 213-340-8945 (SAN 239-5568).

Kaufman House Pubs., *(Kaufman Hse; 0-9602500),* 366 Terrace Ave., Cincinnati, OH 45220 Tel 513-751-6381 (SAN 212-517X).

Kaufmann, William, Inc., *(W Kaufmann; 0-913232; 0-86576),* 95 First St., Los Altos, CA 94022 Tel 415-948-5810 (SAN 202-9383).

Kavanagh, Peter, Hand Press, *(Kavanagh; 0-914612),* 250 E. 30th St., New York, NY 10016 Tel 212-686-5099 (SAN 205-6291).

Kay, L.E., Publishing Co., *(L E Kay; 0-9611256),* P.O. Box 333, Fogelsville, PA 18051 (SAN 283-3026); 2 Woodsbluff Run, Fogelsville, PA 18051 Tel 215-398-0107 (SAN 283-3034).

Kay Publishing Co., Inc., *(KAY Pub; 0-940708),* Box 550, Beverly Farms, MA 01915 Tel 617-927-1387 (SAN 223-1212).

Kayak, *(Kayak; 0-87711),* 325 Ocean View Ave., Santa Cruz, CA 95062 (SAN 203-9168).

Kaye's & Knight Pub. Co., *(K K Pub Co),* P.O. Box 2065, Fargo, ND 58107 (SAN 287-2765).

Kazi Pubns., *(Kazi Pubns; 0-935782),* 1215 W. Belmont Ave., Chicago, IL 60657 Tel 312-327-7598 (SAN 209-6676).

K.B.S. Press, *(K B S Pr; 0-942020),* P.O. Box 665, Kenmore, WA 98028 Tel 206-488-8065 (SAN 237-9686).

KDK Publications, *(KDK Pubns; 0-910165),* 1892 Fell St., San Francisco, CA 94117 Tel 415-386-9656 (SAN 241-2144).

Kearney Publishing Co., *(Kearney; 0-9604688),* 2515 Peachtree Lane, Northbrook, IL 60062 Tel 312-732-6307 (SAN 212-7612).

Keats Publishing, Inc., *(Keats; 0-87983),* 27 Pine St., Box 876, New Canaan, CT 06840 Tel 203-966-8721 (SAN 201-0410).

Keeble Press, The, *(Keeble Pr; 0-933144),* 3634 Winchell Rd., Shaker Heights, OH 44122 (SAN 214-249X).

Keech, Andy, *(A Keech; 0-9503341),* 6339 31st. Place N.W., Washington, DC 20015 Tel 202-966-5186 (SAN 207-5385); Orders to: Skies Call, P.O. Box 57238, Washington, DC 20037 (SAN 207-5393).

Keech, John, *(J Keech; 0-9607200),* P.O. Box 43, State University, AR 72467 Tel 501-935-2573 (SAN 239-1058).

Keegan Press, *(Keegan Pr; 0-9607328),* 412 E. Bloomington St., Iowa City, IA 52240 Tel 319-338-7129 (SAN 239-2445).

Keene, J. Calvin, *(J Calvin Keene; 0-9603084),* 134 Verna Rd., Lewisburg, PA 17837 (SAN 211-9099).

Keene, Sherman, Publications, *(Sherman Keene; 0-942080),* 1626 N. Wilcox, No. 677, Hollywood, CA 90028 Tel 213-708-2933 (SAN 238-6046).

Kegan Paul International See **Routledge & Kegan Paul, Ltd.**

Keim, Abe, *(A Keim; 0-9608214),* P.O. Box 18, Mt. Hope, OH 44660 (SAN 240-3161).

Keithwood Publishing Co., *(Keithwood),* 6835 Greenway Ave., Philadelphia, PA 19142 Tel 215-727-0883 (SAN 213-9324).

Kelane Pubns., *(Kelane Pub; 0-9609394),* 6005 121 St. SE, Bellevue, WA 98006 Tel 206-747-9849 (SAN 281-8558); P.O. Box 5556, Bellevue, WA 98006 (SAN 281-8566).

Keller, J. J., Associates, Inc., *(J J Keller; 0-934674),* 145 W. Wisconsin Ave., Neenah, WI 54956 Tel 414-722-2848 (SAN 201-5056).

Keller, Burns & McGuirk Pub. Co., *(Keller-Burns & McGuirk; 0-9602506),* c/o James P. Gould, Colony Park Bldg., 37th & Woodland, West Des Moines, IA 50265 Tel 515-225-3122 (SAN 213-2230).

Kelley, Augustus M., Pubs., *(Kelley; 0-678),* 1140 Broadway, Room 901, New York, NY 10001 Tel 212-685-7202 (SAN 206-975X); Orders to: 300 Fairfield Rd., P.O. Box 1308, Fairfield, NJ 07006 (SAN 206-9768). Imprints: Baker Library (Baker Library); Reference Book Pubs. (Reference Bk Pubs).

Kellner/McCaffery Associates, Inc., *(Kellner-McCaffery; 0-911069),* 150 Fifth Ave., Suite 322, New York, NY 10011 Tel 212-741-0280 (SAN 271-8782).

Kellogg, Edward P., Jr., *(Kellogg; 0-9603914),* 1755 Trinity Ave., No. 79, Walnut Creek, CA 94596 Tel 415-937-4841 (SAN 213-6880); Orders to: EHUD International Language Foundation, P.O. Box 2082, Dollar Ranch Sta., Walnut Creek, CA 94595 Tel 415-937-4841 (SAN 214-2988).

Kelly, Thomas, *(Kelly; 0-910832),* 227 Midland Ave., East Orange, NJ 07017 Tel 201-672-9238 (SAN 206-7242).

Kelner, A., & Associates, *(A Kelner; 0-939812),* 1201 First Ave., Salt Lake City, UT 84103 Tel 801-359-5387 (SAN 213-2249).

Kelsey Publishing, *(Kelsey Pub; 0-9605824),* 310 E. 950 S., Springville, UT 84663 Tel 801-489-6666 (SAN 216-5775).

Kelsey St. Press, *(Kelsey St Pr; 0-932716),* P.O. Box 9235, Berkeley, CA 94709 Tel 415-843-7060 (SAN 212-6729).

Kelso Manufacturing Co., *(Kelso),* Rt. 2, Box 499, Greenville, MS 38701 (SAN 210-1491).

Kemery, Phil/Jeff Yentz, *(Kemery-Yentz; 0-939940),* 8771 Southwestern Blvd., Apt. 1151, Dallas, TX 75206 Tel 214-748-8407 (SAN 216-826X).

Kemnitz, Milton N., *(M N Kemnitz),* 1180 Bird Rd., P.O. Box 7390, Ann Arbor, MI 48107 Tel 313-668-9895 (SAN 211-1586).

Kempfer, Lester L., *(L Kempfer),* P.O. Box 317, Marysville, OH 43040 (SAN 201-0569).

Kempler Institute, *(Kempler Inst),* P.O. Box 1692, Costa Mesa, CA 92626 (SAN 207-6284).

Ken-Books, *(Ken-Bks; 0-913164),* 1932 Ocean Ave., San Francisco, CA 94127 Tel 415-584-0799 (SAN 201-0429).

Ken Kra Pubs., *(Ken Kra Pubs; 0-941522),* 1657 Thornwood Dr., Concord, CA 94521 Tel 415-676-9184 (SAN 239-0000).

Ken Orr & Associates, Inc., *(Orr & Assocs; 0-9605884),* 1725 Gage Blvd., Topeka, KS 66604 (SAN 216-4280) Tel 913-273-0653.

Kendall Books, *(Kendall Bks; 0-935678),* 1212 N.W. 12th Ave., Gainesville, FL 32601 (SAN 221-4563).

Kendall/Hunt Publishing Co., *(Kendall-Hunt; 0-8403),* 2460 Kerper Blvd., Dubuque, IA 52001 Tel 319-589-2870 (SAN 203-9184).

Kendall Whaling Museum, *(Kendall Whaling; 0-937854),* P.O. Box 297, Sharon, MA 02067 Tel 617-784-5642 (SAN 204-9783).

Kenilworth Press, *(Kenilworth; 0-9603876),* 421 W. Grant Ave., Eau Claire, WI 54701 Tel 715-832-2161 (SAN 204-9775).

Kennedy, Byron, & Co., *(Kennedy & Co; 0-941072),* P.O. Box 10937, St. Petersburg, FL 33733 Tel 813-822-3738 (SAN 217-3875).

Kennedy, David M., International Center,Brigham Young Univ., *(D M Kennedy Ctr Brigham; 0-912575),* Box 61 Faculty Office Building, Provo, UT 84602 Tel 801-378-6528 (SAN 283-2895).

Kennedy, M., *(M Kennedy),* 310 Franklin St., No. 285, Boston, MA 02110 (SAN 239-5576).

Kennedy Galleries, *(Kennedy Gall; 0-87920),* 40 W. 57th St., New York, NY 10019 (SAN 207-3226).

Kennedy Publishing, *(Kennedy Pub; 0-9605088),* P.O. Box 2, Chatsworth, CA 91311 Tel 213-883-7939 (SAN 220-0627).

Kennikat Press, *(Kennikat; 0-8046),* 90 S. Bayles Ave., Port Washington, NY 11050 Tel 516-883-0570 (SAN 207-3064).

Kensington Press, *(Kensington; 0-89626),* P.O. Box 99621, San Diego, CA 92109 (SAN 213-8921).

Kent, Carol Miller, *(C M Kent; 0-9604886),* 929 E. 50th, Austin, TX 78751 (SAN 212-5188).

Kent, Earl, Welding Consultant, *(E Kent; 0-918782),* 9809 Spruce Court, Cypress, CA 90630 Tel 714-828-8064 (SAN 210-4482).

Kent Popular Press, *(Kent Popular; 0-933522),* P.O. Box 73, Kent, OH 44240 (SAN 213-6295).

Kent Pubns., *(Kent Pubns; 0-917458),* 18301 Halstead St., Northbridge, CA 91325 Tel 213-349-2080 (SAN 209-0597).

Kent Publishing Co., Div. of Wadsworth, Inc., *(Kent Pub Co; 0-534),* 20 Parl Plaza, Boston, MA 02116 Tel 617-542-1629 (SAN 215-3491).

Kent State Univ. Press, *(Kent St U Pr; 0-87338),* Kent, OH 44242 Tel 216-672-7913 (SAN 201-0437).

Kentucky Arts Council, *(Kentucky Arts; 0-939058),* Berry Hill, Frankfort, KY 40601 (SAN 218-4869).

Kentucky Historical Society, *(Kentucky Hist; 0-916968),* Old-State-House, Box H, Frankfort, KY 40602 Tel 502-564-3016 (SAN 204-9759).

Kenyon Pubns., *(Kenyon; 0-934286),* 361 Pin Oak Lane, Westbury, NY 11590 Tel 516-333-3236 (SAN 201-5072); Dist. by: G. Schirmer, Inc., 866 Third Ave., New York, NY 10022 Tel 212-702-5500 (SAN 222-9544).

Kepley, Ray R., *(Kepley; 0-9604248),* Rte. 2 Box 128A, Ulysses, KS 67880 Tel 316-356-1568 (SAN 214-3208).

Kepner-Tregoe, Inc., *(Kepner-Tregoe),* P.O. Box 704, Research Road, Princeton, NJ 08540 (SAN 264-1496).

Keramos Bks., Subs. of Westwood Ceramic Supply Co., *(Keramos Bks; 0-935066),* P.O. Box 2305, Bassett, CA 91746 Tel 213-330-0631 (SAN 207-5571); 14400 Lomitas Ave., City of Industry, CA 91746 (SAN 207-558X).

Kern County Historical Society, *(Kern Historical; 0-943500),* P.O. Box 141, Bakersfield, CA 93302 Tel 805-322-4962 (SAN 240-6969).

Kerning Arts Press, The, *(Kerning Arts; 0-9606956),* 719 S. Elm Blvd., Champaign, IL 61820 Tel 217-359-2575 (SAN 239-4472).

Kerr, Charles, Enterprises, Inc., *(C Kerr Ent; 0-936002),* 129 N. Main St., New Hope, PA 18938 Tel 215-862-9618 (SAN 213-7674).

Kerr, Charles H., Publishing Co., *(C H Kerr; 0-88286),* 1740 W. Greenleaf Ave., Chicago, IL 60626 Tel 312-663-4107 (SAN 207-7043); 1740 W. Greenleaf, Chicago, IL 60626 (SAN 207-7043); Orders to: P.O. Box 914, Chicago, IL 60690 (SAN 207-7051).

Kerr Associates, Inc., *(Kerr Assoc; 0-937890),* 1942 Irving Ave., S., Minneapolis, MN 55403 Tel 612-374-5438 (SAN 220-0635).

Kersenbrock, Paul, *(Paul's Pubns; 0-9606032),* 1424 Grove, Crete, NE 68333 Tel 402-826-2003 (SAN 216-9010).

Kerth, A. L., *(A L Kerth; 0-9601188),* Jericho Run, Buckland Valley Farms, Washington Crossing, PA 18977 (SAN 207-3773).

Kesend, Michael, Publishing, Ltd., *(Kesend Pub Ltd; 0-935576)*, 1025 Fifth Ave., New York, NY 10028 Tel 212-249-5150 (SAN 213-6902).

Kesher Press, *(Kesher; 0-9602394)*, 1817 21 Ave. S., Nashville, TN 37212 (SAN 212-6761).

Kester, J. J., *(J J Kester; 0-9602084)*, 416 Pine Grove Circle, Scotch Plains, NJ 07076 Tel 201-889-7077 (SAN 212-8357).

Keturah Press, *(Keturah Pr; 0-942546)*, 350-A Quincy St., Brooklyn, NY 11216 Tel 212-636-1437 (SAN 240-0774).

Key Book Service, Inc., *(Key Bk Serv; 0-934636)*, 425 Asylum St., Bridgeport, CT 06610 Tel 203-334-2165 (SAN 169-0671).

Key Books, *(Key Bks)*, Dist. by: Associated Booksellers, 147 McKinley Ave., Bridgeport, CT 06606 (SAN 206-9717).

Key Curriculum Project, *(Key Curr Proj; 0-913684)*, P.O. Box 2304, Berkeley, CA 94702 Tel 415-548-2304 (SAN 202-6538).

Key of David Pubns., *(Key of David; 0-943374)*, 222 N. 17th, Philadelphia, PA 19103 Tel 215-587-3750 (SAN 239-4480).

Keyline Pubs., Div. of LTP, Inc., *(Keyline Pubs)*, P.O. Box 31534, Billings, MT 59107 Tel 406-245-0187 (SAN 215-2517).

Keys, Elsie, *(E Keys)*, 1239 E. Marshall Ave., Phoenix, AZ 85014 (SAN 215-2428).

Keystone Pubns., Inc., *(Keystone Pubns; 0-912126)*, 1657 Broadway, 2nd Fl., New York, NY 10019 Tel 212-582-2254 (SAN 204-9708).

Khaneghah & Maktab of Maleknia Naseralishah, *(Khaneghah & Maktab; 0-917220)*, P.O. Box 665, Palisades, NY 10964 Tel 914-359-7547 (SAN 208-5046).

KhaniQahi-Nimatullahi, *(KhaniQahi-Nimatullahi; 0-933546)*, 306 W. 11th St., New York, NY 10014 Tel 212-924-7739 (SAN 212-3673).

Khedcanron Publishing, *(Khedcanron Pub; 0-9610264)*, 126 Westward Dr., Corte Madera, CA 94925 Tel 415-924-1944 (SAN 264-150X).

Khiralla, T. W., *(T W Khiralla; 0-9601752)*, 12400 Rye St., Studio City, CA 91604 Tel 213-763-2679 (SAN 211-531X).

Kibo Books, *(Kibo Bks; 0-941266)*, P.O. Box 1442, Main Post Office, Brooklyn, NY 11202 (SAN 239-5584).

Kici, Gasper, *(G Kici)*, P.O. Box 1855, Washington, DC 20013 Tel 703-560-6467 (SAN 203-4115).

Kickapoo Press, *(Kickapoo; 0-933180)*, P.O. Box 1443, Peoria, IL 61655 (SAN 214-2503).

Kid-Love Unlimited, *(kid-love Unltd; 0-912249)*, 1649 D. Iowa St., Costa Mesa, CA 92626 Tel 714-751-4330 (SAN 265-1572).

Kids Come in Special Flavors Co., *(Kids Special)*, Box 562, Forest Park Sta., Dayton, OH 45405 Tel 513-299-1308 (SAN 216-2628).

Kieffer, George David, ,Pub., *(G D Kieffer; 0-9609344)*, P.O. Box 67874, Los Angeles, CA 90067 Tel 213-556-5522 (SAN 260-2156).

Kilgore, *(Kilgore; 0-9609280)*, 1424 Acacia Dr., Colorado Springs, CO 80907 Tel 303-598-2410 (SAN 260-0870).

Kilkerrin House, *(Kilkerrin House; 0-9611728)*, P.O. Box 60155, Santa Barbara, CA 93160 Tel 805-967-1903 (SAN 285-3647).

Kilmarnock Press, The, *(Kilmarnock Pr; 0-937982)*, P.O. Box 1302, South Pasadena, CA 91030 (SAN 265-3893).

Kiltie, Ordean, & Co., *(Kiltie)*, 2445 Fairfield, A201, Ft. Wayne, IN 46807 Tel 219-745-9139 (SAN 209-5718).

Kimbell Art Museum, *(Kimbell Art; 0-912804)*, 3333 Camp Bowie Blvd., P.O. Box 9440, Fort Worth, TX 76107 Tel 817-332-8451 (SAN 208-0516).

Kimberly, Jones Publishing Co., *(Kimberly-Jones; 0-941412)*, 2828 S. 94th St., P.O. Box 14213, Omaha, NE 68124 Tel 402-393-8121 (SAN 238-8898); Dist. by: International Scholarly Book Services, Inc., 2130 Pacific Ave., Forest Grove, OR 97116 Tel 503-357-7192 (SAN 205-4728).

Kindler, Leonard, *(Kindler; 0-943502)*, P.O. Box 12328, Philadelphia, PA 19119 Tel 215-843-4487 (SAN 240-6977).

Kindred Joy Pubns., *(Kindred Joy; 0-911141)*, 554 W. 4th, Coquille, OR 97423 Tel 503-396-4154 (SAN 262-9275).

Kindred Press, *(Kindred Pr)*, Box L, Hillsboro, KS 67063 Tel 316-947-3966 (SAN 205-8634).

King, C. D., Ltd., *(C King; 0-9608862)*, 311 12th St., Huntington Beach, CA 92648 Tel 714-960-5285 (SAN 241-0397).

King, Carl R., *(C R King; 0-9610786)*, 124 Webster Rd., Spencerport, NY 14559 Tel 716-352-5152 (SAN 265-1580).

King, Joseph A., *(J A King; 0-9608500)*, 1161 Nogales St., Lafayette, CA 94549 Tel 415-934-8196 (SAN 240-5431).

King, Lary, Company The, *(L King Co; 0-9611450)*, P.O. Box 1247, Hollywood, CA 90078 Tel 213-765-8920 (SAN 283-1503).

King, Phil, *(Phil King; 0-911739)*, 3005 Woodlawn Ave., Wesleyville, PA 16510 Tel 814-899-3532 (SAN 211-9641).

King & Mary, *(King & Mary; 0-9601890)*, 4709 Comita, Fort Worth, TX 76132 Tel 817-292-1295 (SAN 211-8602).

King Books, *(King Bks; 0-9611532)*, 817 S. 265th St., Kent, WA 98032 Tel 206-941-2992 (SAN 285-368X).

King Freedom Pubns., *(King Freedom; 0-911435)*, Box 962, Glenwood Springs, CO 81602 Tel 303-945-8847 (SAN 271-888X).

King Pubns., *(King Pubns; 0-917676)*, P.O. Box 19332, Washington, DC 20036 Tel 202-332-7079 (SAN 209-2387).

Kingdom of God, *(Kingdom God; 0-9607702)*, P.O. Box 7123, Minneapolis, MN 55407 Tel 612-823-1783 (SAN 238-6704).

Kingdom Press, *(Kingdom; 0-910840)*, 105 Chestnut Hill Rd., Amherst, NH 03031 Tel 603-673-3208 (SAN 201-0461).

King's Court Communications, Inc., *(Kings Court; 0-89139)*, 590 Pearl Rd., Box 224, Brunswick, OH 44212 Tel 216-273-2100 (SAN 207-3730).

King's Farspan, Inc., *(Kings Farspan; 0-932814)*, 1473 S. La Luna Ave., Ojai, CA 93023 Tel 805-646-2928 (SAN 211-8084).

Kingsfield Publishing Co., *(Kingsfield; 0-938494)*, 10405 Town & Country Way, Suite 100, Houston, TX 77024 (SAN 215-8825).

Kingston Press, Inc., The, *(Kingston Pr; 0-940670)*, P.O. Box 1456, Princeton, NJ 08540 Tel 201-359-6415 (SAN 226-7950).

Kinkead, Eugene, *(E Kinkead; 0-940476)*, Colebrook, CT 06021 Tel 203-379-6843 (SAN 203-8277).

Kino Pubns., *(Kino Pubns; 0-9607366)*, 6625 N. First Ave., Tucson, AZ 85718 Tel 602-297-7278 (SAN 238-2547).

Kiowa Press, *(Kiowa Pr)*, P.O. Box 555, Woodburn, OR 97071 Tel 503-981-3017 (SAN 222-9773).

Kiracofe & Kile, *(Kiracofe & Kile; 0-913327)*, 955 14th St., San Francisco, CA 94114 Tel 415-431-1222 (SAN 283-2275).

Kirban, Salem, Inc., *(Kirban; 0-912682)*, 2117 Kent Rd., Huntingdon Valley, PA 19000 Tel 215-947-1330 (SAN 201-047X).

Kirby, Walter, W., *(W W Kirby)*, 1351 N Austin Ave, Chicago, IL 60657 (SAN 237-7411).

Kirin Books & Art, *(Kirin Bks & Art; 0-935034)*, 4620 N. Pegram St., Alexandria, VA 22304 Tel 703-751-3141 (SAN 213-5280).

Kirk Press, *(Kirk Pr)*, 1811 Hammond Ave., Superior, WI 54880 (SAN 211-4275).

Kirk Publishing, Div. of Kirksite Enterprises, Inc., *(Kirk Pub; 0-911821)*, One E. First St., No. 1400, Reno, NV 89501 Tel 415-826-1005 (SAN 264-1518).

Kiryat Sefer, Ltd., *(K Sefer; 965-17)*, c/o Ridgefield Pub. Co., 6925 Canby Ave., Suite 104, Reseda, CA 91335 Tel 213-343-8811 (SAN 215-8035).

Kisaku, Inc., *(Kisaku)*, 920 Prospect St., Honolulu, HI 96822 (SAN 285-6603).

Kiser, Clyde V., & Alna L., *(C & A Kiser; 0-9611920)*, P.O. Box 154, Bessemer City, NC 28016 Tel 704-629-4674 (SAN 286-1275).

Kitchen Harvest Press, *(Kitchen Harvest; 0-917234)*, 3N 681 Bittersweet Dr., St. Charles, IL 60174 Tel 312-584-4084 (SAN 207-2467).

Kitchen Sink Press, *(Kitchen Sink; 0-87816)*, No. 2 Swamp Road, Princeton, WI 54968 Tel 414-295-6922 (SAN 212-7784).

Kitchen Treasures, *(Kitchen Treas; 0-9609282)*, 810 First Ave. South, P.O. Box 142, Escanaba, MI 49829 Tel 906-786-1531 (SAN 260-0897).

Kitten Pubns., *(Kitten Pub; 0-9608722)*, 240 Indian Hills, Corydon, IN 47112 Tel 812-738-8452 (SAN 238-3071).

Kjos, Neil A., Music Co., *(Kjos; 0-910842; 0-8497)*, 4382 Jutland Dr., San Diego, CA 92117 Tel 619-270-9800 (SAN 201-0488).

Klamath Pioneer Publishing, *(Klamath Pioneer Pub; 0-9605120)*, 132 S. 7th St., Klamath Falls, OR 97601 Tel 503-882-1821 (SAN 239-8443).

Klang, Innerer, *(I Klang; 0-911623)*, 7 Sherman St., 2B, Charlestown, MA 02129 (SAN 264-1542).

Klassen, Beatrice C. Harris, *(Klassen)*, P.O. Box 794, La Conner, WA 98257 (SAN 215-8833).

Klein, B., Pubns., *(B Klein Pubns; 0-87340)*, P.O. Box 8503, Coral Springs, FL 33065 Tel 305-752-1708 (SAN 210-7554).

Klein, Elizabeth Pfahning, *(E P Klein; 0-9604250)*, 11041 S.W. 46th St., Miami, FL 33165 (SAN 214-3216).

Klein Publications, *(Klein Pubns; 0-913051)*, 12225 Magdalena, Los Altos, CA 94022 Tel 415-948-5398 (SAN 283-1287).

Kleinsinger, Irene J., *(Kleinsinger; 0-9605146)*, 16 Holbrooke Rd., White Plains, NY 10605 Tel 914-948-5785 (SAN 215-7829).

Klemm, Edwin O., *(E O Klemm)*, 303 S. Jefferson St., Saginaw, MI 48607 Tel 313-755-3559 (SAN 203-8285).

Kline, Charles H., & Co., Inc., *(Kline; 0-917148)*, 330 Passaic Ave., Fairfield, NJ 07006 Tel 201-227-6262 (SAN 202-6546).

Klock & Klock Christian Pubs., *(Klock & Klock; 0-86522)*, 2527 Girard Ave. N., Minneapolis, MN 55411 Tel 612-522-2244 (SAN 212-0003).

Klutz Press, *(Klutz Pr; 0-932592)*, P.O. Box 2992, Stanford, CA 94305 Tel 415-857-0888 (SAN 212-7539).

Kluwer Academic Publishers, *(Kluwer Academic)*, 190 Old Derby St., Hingham, MA 02043 Tel 617-749-5262 (SAN 211-481X).

Kluwer-Nijhoff Publishing, *(Kluwer-Nijhoff; 0-89838)*, Dist. by: Kluwer Boston, Inc., 190 Old Derby St., Hingham, MA 02043 Tel 617-749-5262 (SAN 211-481X).

K.M. Gentile Publishing/Singing Wind Press, *(K M Gentile; 0-935896)*, 4164 W. Pine, St. Louis, MO 63108 Tel 314-535-2118 (SAN 214-3917).

Knapp Press, The, Div. of Knapp Communications Corp., *(Knapp Pr; 0-89535)*, 5900 Wilshire Blvd., Los Angeles, CA 90036 Tel 213-937-3454 (SAN 210-4490).

Knauff, Thomas, *(Knauff)*, Julian, PA 16844 (SAN 216-1524).

Knees Paperback Publishing Co., *(Knees Pbk; 0-9600978)*, 4115 Marshall St., Dallas, TX 75210 Tel 214-948-3613 (SAN 208-760X).

Knickerbocker Publishing Co., *(Knickerbocker; 0-911635)*, P.O. Box 863, Southbridge, MA 01550 (SAN 264-1569).

Knife World Pubns., *(Knife World; 0-940362)*, P.O. Box 3395, Knoxville, TN 37917 Tel 615-523-3339 (SAN 218-5628).

Knighttime Pubns., *(Knighttime Pubns; 0-942902)*, P.O. Box 591, Cupertino, CA 95014 Tel 408-996-0668 (SAN 240-317X).

Knoedler Publishing Inc., *(Knoedler; 0-937608)*, 19 E. 70th St., New York, NY 10021 (SAN 215-2177).

Knollwood Publishing Co., *(Knollwood Pub; 0-915614)*, P.O. Box 735, 513 Benson Ave. E., Willmar, MN 56201 Tel 612-235-4950 (SAN 207-5504).

Knopf, Alfred A., Inc., Subs. of Random House, Inc., *(Knopf; 0-394)*, 201 E. 50th St., New York, NY 10022 Tel 212-757-2600 (SAN 202-5825); Orders to: 400 Hahn Rd., Westminster, MD 21157 (SAN 202-5833). *Imprints:* Knopf College Department (KnopfC).

Knopf College Department *See* Knopf, Alfred A., Inc.

Know How Pubns., *(Know How; 0-910846)*, Box 7126, Landscape Sta., Berkeley, CA 94717 Tel 415-526-5400 (SAN 207-0359).

Know, Inc., *(Know Inc; 0-912786)*, P.O. Box 86031, Pittsburgh, PA 15221 Tel 412-241-2844 (SAN 201-050X).

Knowledge Bank Publishers, Inc., *(Knowledge Bank)*, P.O. Box 2364, Falls Church, VA 22042 (SAN 224-1765)Box 2364, Falls Church, VA 22042 Tel 703-938-6431 (SAN 224-1773).

Knowledge Builders, Inc., *(Knowledge Builders; 0-940950),* 744 E. Green Briar, Lake Forest, IL 60045 Tel 312-295-2099 (SAN 217-3883).

Knowledge Industry Pubns., Inc., *(Knowledge Indus; 0-914236; 0-86729),* 701 Westchester Ave., White Plains, NY 10604 Tel 914-328-9157 (SAN 214-2082). *Imprints:* American Society for Information Science (ASIS).

Knowledge Investments Pubns., *(Know Investments Pubns; 0-941488),* 705 N. Wilson, Fresno, CA 93728 Tel 209-486-3955 (SAN 239-0019).

Knowles, Alison, *(Knowles; 0-914162),* 122 Spring St., New York, NY 10012 (SAN 216-1516).

Knox, Daryl K., *(D Knox),* P.O. Box 38, Fortuna, ND 58844 Tel 701-834-2292 (SAN 216-4035).

Kober Press, The, *(Kober Pr; 0-915034),* P.O. Box 2194, San Francisco, CA 94126 Tel 415-362-1231 (SAN 207-0758).

Kobro Pubns., Inc., *(Kobro Pubns; 0-9604676),* 192 Lexington Ave., New York, NY 10016 (SAN 215-6695).

Kodansha International USA, Ltd., *(Kodansha; 0-87011),* C/O Harper & Row Pubs., 10 E. 53rd St., New York, NY 10022 Tel 212-593-7050 (SAN 201-0526); Dist. by: Harper & Row Pubs., Inc., Keystone Industrial Park, Scranton, PA 18512 (SAN 215-3742).

Koester, Arthur R., Books, *(A R Koester Bks; 0-9602558),* P.O. Box 344, Burbank, CA 91503-0344 (SAN 213-0971).

Koinonia Productions, *(Koinonia Prods; 0-86635),* 5920 Dante, Stockton, CA 95207 (SAN 238-0633).

Kokono, *(Kokono; 0-916956),* 540 Discovery Bay Blvd., Byron, CA 94514 Tel 415-634-5710 (SAN 208-6026); Dist. by: Front Row Experience, 540 Discovery Bay Blvd., Byron, CA 94514 (SAN 207-1274).

Konglomerati Florida Foundation for Literature & the Book Arts, Inc., *(Konglomerati; 0-916906),* P.O. Box 5001, Gulfport, FL 33737 Tel 813-323-0386 (SAN 207-8589).

Konocit, Sipapu *See* Sipapu, Konocti Books

Korakas, Roberts & Kirby, *(Korakas-Roberts-Kirby),* 600 N.W. 46th St., Oklahoma City, OK 73118 Tel 405-524-5985 (SAN 216-1532).

Korea Development Institute *See* Univ. of Hawaii Press, The

Korn, Alfred, Jr., *(Korn; 0-917498),* 324 Coolidge Dr., Kennilworth, NJ 07033 (SAN 209-0589).

Kornberg, Patti, *(P Kornberg; 0-9609240),* 650 N. Atlantic Ave., Cocoa Beach, FL 32931 Tel 305-783-7079 (SAN 241-5356).

Korpalski, Adam, *(A Korpalski),* Ferry Bridge Rd., Washington, CT 06793 Tel 203-868-2503 (SAN 211-1977).

Kosciuszko Foundation, Inc., *(Kosciuszko; 0-917004),* 15 E. 65th St., New York, NY 10021 Tel 212-734-2130 (SAN 208-7251).

Kosikowski, F. V., & Assocs., *(F V Kosikowski; 0-9602322),* P.O. Box 139, Brooktondale, NY 14817 Tel 607-272-7779 (SAN 211-6693).

Kovanda, William James, *(Kovanda; 0-9606658),* Box 27, Albion, CA 95410 Tel 707-937-4919 (SAN 223-1190).

Kovar, Milo, *(Milo Kovar),* 2640 Greenwich, No. 403, San Francisco, CA 94123 (SAN 239-5592); Dist. by: Capital Distributing Co., Derby, CT 06418 (SAN 169-068X).

Krag Pubns., *(Krag Pubns),* 1217-8th St., S.E., Minneapolis, MN 55414 (SAN 213-098X).

Kramer, Justin, Inc., *(J Kramer),* 1028 W. 8th Place, Los Angeles, CA 90017 (SAN 209-1224).

Krank Press, *(Krank Pr; 0-940056),* P.O. Box 16271, St. Louis, MO 63105 (SAN 222-9781).

Kraus International Publications, Div. of Kraus-Thomson Organization Ltd., *(Kraus Intl; 0-527),* Rte. 100, Millwood, NY 10546 Tel 914-762-2200 (SAN 210-7562).

Kraus Reprint, A Div. of Kraus-Thomson Organization, Ltd., *(Kraus Repr; 0-527; 3-601; 3-262),* Rte. 100, Millwood, NY 10546 Tel 914-762-2200 (SAN 201-0542).

Krause Pubns., Inc., *(Krause Pubns; 0-87341),* 700 E. State St., Iola, WI 54990 Tel 715-445-2214 (SAN 202-6554).

Krebs, John E., *(J E Krebs; 0-9607026),* 711 Santa Fe Dr., Apt. 232, Weatherford, TX 76086 Tel 817-594-6135 (SAN 239-0027).

Kregel Pubns., *(Kregel; 0-8254),* P.O. Box 2607, Grand Rapids, MI 49501 Tel 616-459-9444 (SAN 206-9792).

Kreitman Publishing, Inc., *(Kreitman Pub; 0-935492),* 9665 Wilshire Blvd., Suite 410, Beverly Hills, CA 90212 Tel 213-858-1048 (SAN 213-5310).

Krejcarek, Philip, *(P Krejcarek),* 1735 N. 57th, Milwaukee, WI 53208 (SAN 212-2863).

Kreysa, Francis John, *(Kreysa; 0-9611398),* 18742 Curry Powder Lane, Germantown, MD 20874 Tel 301-349-5001 (SAN 285-3752).

Krieger, Robert E., Pub. Co., Inc., *(Krieger; 0-88275; 0-89874),* P.O. Box 9542, Melbourne, FL 32902-9542 Tel 305-724-9542 (SAN 202-6562).

Kripalu Pubns., *(Kripalu Pubns; 0-940258),* Box 120,, Summit Station, PA 17979 Tel 717-754-3051 (SAN 217-5320) New Address as of Nov. 1, 1983: Rt. 183, Box 793, Lennox, MA 01240, 413-637-3280.

Krishna Press, Div. of Gordon Press, *(Krishna Pr),* P.O. Box 459, Bowling Green Sta., New York, NY 10004 (SAN 202-6570).

Kronos Press, *(Kronos Pr; 0-917994),* Glassboro State College, Glassboro, NJ 08028 Tel 609-445-6048 (SAN 210-2226).

KronOscope Press, *(KronOscope; 0-9608768),* 44 Brannan St., San Francisco, CA 94107 Tel 415-543-6251 (SAN 238-308X).

Krumwiede, Grace I., *(G I Krumwiede),* 3713 S. George Mason Dr., No. 608W, Falls Church, VA 22041 Tel 703-998-0251 (SAN 213-0998).

Ktav Publishing House, Inc., *(Ktav; 0-87068),* 75 Varick St., New York, NY 10013 Tel 212-966-6980 (SAN 201-0038). *Imprints:* Hebrew Union College Press (HUC Pr).

Kudzu-Ivy, *(Kudzu-Ivy; 0-9605142),* P.O. Box 52743, Atlanta, GA 30355 Tel 404-351-4827 (SAN 215-9589).

Kukla Press, *(Kukla Pr),* 855 Morse Ave., Elk Grove Village, IL 60007 (SAN 213-3318); Dist. by: Common Sense Ltd., P.O. Box 353, Des Plaines, IL 60016 (SAN 213-2990).

Kulchur Foundation, *(Kulchur Foun; 0-936538),* 888 Park Ave., New York, NY 10021 Tel 212-988-5193 (SAN 207-2475).

Kumarian Press, *(Kumarian Pr; 0-931816),* 29 Bishop Rd., West Hartford, CT 06119 Tel 203-232-4360 (SAN 212-5978).

Kuppinger, Roger, *(R Kuppinger),* 77 Woodland Lane, Arcadia, CA 91006 Tel 213-489-3900 (SAN 212-677X).

Kurian, George, Reference Books, *(G Kurian; 0-914746),* P.O. Box 519, Baldwin Place, NY 10505 Tel 914-962-3287 (SAN 203-1981).

Kurios Foundation, *(Kurios Found; 0-932210),* P.O. Box 946, Bryn Mawr, PA 19010 Tel 215-527-4923 (SAN 213-1005).

Kurios Press, *(Kurios Pr; 0-916588),* P.O. Box 946, Bryn Mawr, PA 19010 Tel 215-527-4635 (SAN 207-7159).

Kusel, George, *(Kusel; 0-9604476),* 600 Lakevue Dr., Willow Grove, PA 19090 (SAN 215-7837).

Kwik Sew Pattern Co., Inc., *(Kwik Sew; 0-931212),* 300 Sixth Ave. N., Minneapolis, MN 55401 Tel 612-339-9348 (SAN 209-1380).

Kylix Press, *(Kylix Pr; 0-914408),* 1485 Maywood, Ann Arbor, MI 48103 Tel 313-761-5399 (SAN 206-5525).

L. A. Pop Books, *(L A Pop),* Box 24941, Los Angeles, CA 90024 Tel 213-466-7127 (SAN 211-0814) Moved, Left No Forwarding Address.

L B J School of Public Affairs, Office of Publications, *(LBJ Sch Public Affairs),* Univ. of Texas Austin, Austin, TX 78712 Tel 512-471-4962 (SAN 206-2216).

L.C.D. Pub., *(LCD; 0-941414),* 663 Calle Miramar, Redondo Beach, CA 90277 Tel 213-375-6336 (SAN 239-0035).

LDA Pubs., *(L D A Pubs; 0-935912),* 42-36 209th St., Bayside, NY 11361 (SAN 221-4423).

LEHI Publishing Co., *(LEHI Pub Co; 0-934486),* 303 Gretna Green Way, Los Angeles, CA 90049 Tel 213-476-6024 (SAN 213-4101).

LJB Foundation, *(LJB Found),* 933 Overlook Rd., Whitehall, PA 18052 Tel 215-433-7667 (SAN 210-9107).

LJ Pubns., *(L J Pubns),* 359 San Miquel, Newport Beach, CA 92660 (SAN 264-1623).

LJR, Inc., *(LJR Inc; 0-936624),* 200 Joseph Square, Columbia, MD 21044 Tel 301-730-5365 (SAN 215-2541).

LL Co., *(LL Co; 0-937892),* 1647 Manning Ave., Los Angeles, CA 90024 Tel 213-475-3664 (SAN 203-0314).

LOM Press, Inc., *(LOM Pr),* 1 Plaza Place, Suite 1008, St. Petersburg, FL 33701 (SAN 217-2453).

L P Pubns., *(L P Pubns; 0-916192),* P. O. Box 7601, San Diego, CA 92107 Tel 619-225-0133 (SAN 207-2513).

L Pubns., *(L Pubns; 0-917824),* 34 Fransiscan Way, Kensington, CA 94707 (SAN 209-5734).

LUISA Productions, *(LUISA Prods; 0-939584),* P.O. Box 6836-AB, Santa Barbara, CA 93111 (SAN 216-4108).

La Car Publishing Co., *(La Car Pub),* 2109 Broadway, New York, NY 10023 (SAN 207-7272).

La Cumbre Publishing Co., *(La Cumbre; 0-935222),* P.O. Box 30959, Santa Barbara, CA 93105 (SAN 221-4431).

La Grange Press, *(La Grange; 0-931324),* 7732 Guenivere Way, Citrus Heights, CA 95610 Tel 916-967-7997 (SAN 211-0601).

La Jolla Institute, *(La Jolla Inst; 0-943256),* P.O. Box 1434, La Jolla, CA 92038 Tel 714-454-8831 (SAN 240-3935).

La Jolla Museum of Contemporary Art, *(La Jolla Mus Contemp Art; 0-934418),* 700 Prospect St., La Jolla, CA 92037 Tel 714-454-3541 (SAN 210-8232).

La Leche League International, Inc., *(La Leche; 0-912500),* 9616 Minneapolis Ave., Franklin Park, IL 60131 Tel 312-455-7730 (SAN 201-0585).

La Luz Press, The, *(La Luz Pr),* P.O. Box 444, La Luz, NM 88337 Tel 505-437-0789 (SAN 219-8525).

La Morenita Pubs., Inc., *(La Morenita; 0-941812),* 25-A Hill St., San Francisco, CA 94110 Tel 415-282-3532 (SAN 239-2461).

La Pice, Margaret, *(M La Pice; 0-9604508),* 210 Montcalm, San Francisco, CA 94110 (SAN 212-1093).

LA-RAN Publishing Co., *(La-Ran Pub Co; 0-9610842),* 187 W. End Ave., Newark, NJ 07106 Tel 201-373-5216 (SAN 265-2641).

La Siesta Press, *(La Siesta; 0-910856),* P.O. Box 406, Glendale, CA 91209 Tel 213-244-9305 (SAN 201-0607).

La Stampa Calligrafica, *(La Stampa Calligrafica; 0-9606630),* P.O. Box 19079, Detroit, MI 48219 Tel 313-531-3805 (SAN 281-8582); Dist. by: Bookpeople, 2940 Seventh St., Berkeley, CA 94710 (SAN 168-9517); Dist. by: Inland Book Company, P. O. Box 261, 22 Hemingway Ave., East Haven, CT 06512 Tel 203-467-4257 (SAN 200-4151).

La Tienda El Quetzal, *(La Tienda; 0-913129),* Box 246, Troy, NY 12186 Tel 518-271-7629 (SAN 283-1295).

Laal Companies, *(Laal Co; 0-910211),* Research Group, 9 Kaufman Dr., Westwood, NJ 07675 (SAN 241-3892).

LaBarre, George H., Galleries, Inc., *(G H laBarre; 0-941538),* P.O. Box 746, Hollis, NH 03049 Tel 603-882-2411 (SAN 239-1066).

Labor Arts Books, *(Labor Arts; 0-9603888),* 1064 Amherst St., Buffalo, NY 14216 Tel 716-873-4131 (SAN 213-8158).

Laboratory Data Control, *(Lab Data Control; 0-9504833),* P.O. Box 10235, Interstate Industrial Park, Riviera Beach, FL 33404 (SAN 210-9085).

Laboratory for Applied Behavioral Science, *(LAB; 0-943300),* 47 Unami Terrace, Westfield, NJ 07090 Tel 201-233-4260 (SAN 239-4499).

Labyrinth Press, Inc., The, *(Labyrinth Pr; 0-939464),* P.O. Box 2124, Durham, NC 27702-2124 Tel 919-489-5678 (SAN 281-8612); 2814 Chapel Hill Rd., Durham, NC 27707 (SAN 281-8620).

Lacis Pubns., *(Lacis Pubns; 0-916896),* 2982 Adeline St., Berkeley, CA 94703 Tel 415-843-7178 (SAN 202-9901).

Lacon Pubs., *(Lacon Pubs; 0-930344),* Rte. 1, P.O. Box 15, Harrison, ID 83833 Tel 208-689-3467 (SAN 204-9597).

Lacret Publishing Co., *(Lacret Pub; 0-943144),* 601 12th St., Union City, NJ 07087 Tel 201-866-5257 (SAN 240-3927).

Lacrosse Foundation, Inc., *(Lacrosse Found; 0-9610654),* 301 Homewood, Baltimore, MD 21218 Tel 301-235-6882 (SAN 285-0389); P.O. Box 5680, Baltimore, MD 21218 (SAN 285-0397); Orders to: 107 E. 25th St., Baltimore, MD 21218 Tel 301-235-2000 (SAN 285-0400).

Laddin Press, *(Laddin Pr; 0-913806),* 2 Park Ave., New York, NY 10016 Tel 212-532-4384 (SAN 201-0615).

Ladies Philoptochos Society Chapter Four Hundred & Fifty One, *(Ladies Philo; 0-9611164),* Nativity of Christ Church 1110 Dickson Dr., Novato, CA (SAN 283-3581); P.O. Box 543, Novato, CA 94948 Tel 415-883-1998 (SAN 283-359X).

Lafayette Museum Association, Inc., the, *(Lafayette Mus; 0-9608412),* 1122 Lafayette St., Lafayette, LA 70501 (SAN 240-7000).

LaFray Pub. Co., *(LaFray Pub; 0-942084),* P.O. Box 7326, St. Petersburg, FL 33704 Tel 813-821-3233 (SAN 281-8639); 3210-9th St. N., St. Petersburg, FL 33704 (SAN 281-8647).

Laguna Beach Museum of Art, *(Laguna Beach; 0-940872),* 307 Cliff Dr., Laguna Beach, CA 92651 Tel 714-494-6531 (SAN 219-676X).

Lake, A. V., & Co., *(Lake; 0-910860),* P.O. Box 1595, Beverly Hills, CA 90213 Tel 213-271-4386 (SAN 201-0623).

Lake End Graphics Ltd., *(Lake End; 0-943998),* 21 Prince St., New York, NY 10012 Tel 212-226-7086 (SAN 241-2152).

Lake Erie College Press, *(Lake Erie Col Pr; 0-935518),* Lake Erie College, Painesville, OH 44077 Tel 216-352-3361 (SAN 204-9562).

Lake Forest College Holography Workshops, *(Lake Forest; 0-910535),* Lake Forest, IL 60045 Tel 312-234-3100 (SAN 260-0900).

Lake Lure Press, *(Lake Lure Pr; 0-9610172),* RR 32, Box 316, Terre Haute, IN 47803 Tel 812-877-2204 (SAN 271-9444).

Lake Press, *(Lake Pr; 0-9608446),* P.O. Box 7934, Peducah, KY 42001 Tel 502-443-8425 (SAN 240-544X).

Lake View Press, *(Lake View Pr; 0-941702),* P.O. Box 25421, Chicago, IL 60625 Tel 312-935-2694 (SAN 239-2488).

Lakes & Prairies Press, *(Lakes & Prairies Pr; 0-9607780),* 6334 N. Sheridan Rd, Chicago, IL 60660 (SAN 239-5614).

Lakeside-Charter Books, *(Lakeside Chart; 0-918206),* 5466 S. Everett, Chicago, IL 60615 Tel 312-955-0521 (SAN 210-2234).

Lakeside Publishing Co., *(Lakeside Pub Co; 0-913053),* P.O. Box 129, Pewaukee, WI 53072 Tel 414-691-0963 (SAN 283-1317).

Lakstun Press, *(Lakstun Pr; 0-9603706),* P.O. Box 429, Bensalem, PA 19020 (SAN 213-6309).

Lal Pubs., *(LAL Pub),* P.O. Box 1225, Denison, TX 75020 (SAN 238-0641).

Lalvani, Haresh, *(H Lalvani),* P.O. Box 1538, New York, NY 10116 (SAN 211-3228).

Lamagna, Joseph, *(J Lamagna; 0-9610464),* P.O. Box 572, Yonkers, NY 10702 Tel 914-963-3260 (SAN 238-065X).

Lamb, Howard, *(H Lamb; 0-9609150),* P.O. Box 796, Mill Valley, CA 94942 Tel 415-388-1163 (SAN 241-3906).

Lambert Book House, Inc., *(Lambert Bk; 0-89315),* 133 Kings Hwy., Box 4007, Shreveport, LA 71104 Tel 318-861-3140 (SAN 208-7278).

Lambert Pubns., Inc., *(Lambert Pubns; 0-939304),* 1000 Connecticut Ave. NW, Washington, DC 20036 (SAN 216-4043).

Lambeth, James, *(Lambeth; 0-9601678),* 1591 Clark St., Fayetteville, AR 72701 Tel 501-521-1304 (SAN 211-9102).

Lambeth Press, *(Lambeth Pr; 0-931186),* 143 E. 37th St., New York, NY 10016 Tel 212-679-0163 (SAN 240-0421).

Lame Johnny Pr., Div. of Independent Publishing Services, *(Lame Johnny; 0-917624),* Star Rte. 3, Box 9A, Hermosa, SD 57744 Tel 605-255-4466 (SAN 207-6136).

Lamm-Morada Publishing Co., Inc., *(Lamm-Morada; 0-932128),* Box 7607, Stockton, CA 95207 Tel 209-931-1056 (SAN 212-520X).

Lamont-Doherty Geological Observatory, *(Lamont-Doherty),* Columbia University, Palisades, NY 10964 (SAN 287-2609).

Lampkin, J. G., Publishing, *(Lampkin Pub; 0-9604918),* 15346 Stone Ave. N., Seattle, WA 98133 (SAN 215-6725).

Lamplight Publishing Inc., *(Lamplight Pub; 0-88308),* 548 W. 26th St., New York, NY 10001 Tel 212-695-8222 (SAN 287-0193); c/o Scroll Press, 2858 Valerie Court, Merrick, NY 11566 Tel 516-379-4283 (SAN 287-0207).

Lamplighter Press, *(Lamplighter; 0-912870),* P.O. Box 258, Carlinville, IL 62626 (SAN 201-0631).

Lampus Press, *(Lampus Pr; 0-9609002),* P.O. Box 541, Cape May, NJ 08204 Tel 609-884-4906 (SAN 240-8643).

Lancaster House Press, *(Lancaster Hse Pr; 0-914356),* 36 Freshmeadow Dr., Lancaster, PA 17603 (SAN 202-6619) Moved, Left No Forwarding Address.

Lancaster-Miller Pubs., *(Lancaster-Miller; 0-89581),* P. O. Box 3056, Berkeley, CA 94703 Tel 415-845-3782 (SAN 213-6503). *Imprints:* Asian Humanities Press (Asian Humanities).

Lancer Militaria, *(Lancer; 0-935856),* P.O. Box 100, Sims, AR 71969 Tel 501-867-2232 (SAN 213-7682).

Land Design Publishing, *(Land Design; 0-9605988),* P.O. Box 857, San Dimas, CA 91773 Tel 714-599-7452 (SAN 216-745X).

Land Values, *(Land Values),* 2821 Frontier Dr., Midland, TX 79701 Tel 915-683-2922 (SAN 206-6270); Orders to: P.O. Box 1533, Midland, TX 79702 (SAN 206-6289) Moved, left no forwarding address.

Landau Book Co., Inc., *(Landau; 0-910864),* P.O. Box 570, Long Beach, NY 11561 Tel 516-889-0616 (SAN 201-064X).

Landes, Burton R., *(B R Landes; 0-915568),* 11 College Ave., Trappe, PA 19426 Tel 215-489-2908 (SAN 207-3625).

Landfall Press, Inc., *(Landfall Pr; 0-913428),* 5171 Chapin St., Dayton, OH 45429 Tel 513-298-9123 (SAN 202-6627).

Landgrove Press, *(Landgrove Pr; 0-9608726),* Landgrove, VT 05148 Tel 802-824-5943 (SAN 238-3098).

Landing Press, the, *(Landing Pr; 0-943912),* 17 Sherwood Way, Landing, NJ 07850 Tel 201-398-7027 (SAN 241-1296).

Landmark Book Co., *(Landmark NY),* 119 W. 57th St., New York, NY 10019 (SAN 216-4051).

Landmark Books, Inc., *(Landmark Bks; 0-934400),* 7847 12th Ave. S., Bloomington, MN 55420 Tel 612-854-3345 (SAN 213-280X).

Landmark Enterprises, *(Landmark Ent; 0-910845),* 10324 Newton Way, Rancho Cordova, CA 95670 (SAN 271-955X).

Landmark Press, *(Landmark Pr; 0-911439),* Box 13547, 1461 Dunn Rd., St. Louis, MO 63138 Tel 314-355-7650 (SAN 271-9568).

Landmark Publishing Corp., Div. of Clearwater Corp., *(Landmark Pub; 0-918200),* Box 3287, Burlington, VT 05402 Tel 802-372-4522 (SAN 210-2242).

Landmarks Preservation Commission, *(Landmarks Preserv Comm),* 20 Vesey St., New York, NY 10007 (SAN 240-0413).

Landown House, *(Landown Hse; 0-936562),* 5816 Esrig Way, Sacramento, CA 95841 (SAN 281-8655); Orders to: P.O. Box 176, N. Highlands, CA 95660 (SAN 281-8663).

Landrum, Jeff, Publishing, *(J Landrum Pub; 0-9611894),* Box 98, Burkburnett, TX 76354 Tel 817-569-2580 (SAN 285-3299).

Lands End Books, *(Lands End Bks; 0-9603558),* Rte. 3, Box 998, Gloucester, VA 23061 Tel 804-693-4262 (SAN 203-9281).

Lane, Joe, Publishing Co, *(Joe Lane Pub; 0-9603378),* P.O. Box 2646, Evergreen, CO 80439 Tel 303-674-5314 (SAN 211-0784).

Lane & Associates, *(Lane & Assoc; 0-89882),* Box 3063, La Jolla, CA 92037 (SAN 220-7419).

Lane Press, *(Lane Pr; 0-935606),* P. O. Box 7822, Stanford, CA 94305 (SAN 221-4326).

Lang, Peter, Publishing, Inc., *(P Lang Pubs),* 34 E. 39th St., New York, NY 10016 Tel 212-692-9009 (SAN 241-5534).

Lang Pubns, *(Lang Pubns; 0-942242),* 490 North 31st St. Suite 100, Billings, MT 59101 (SAN 238-4337); Dist. by: World Bible Publishers, Iowa Falls, IA 50126 Tel 800-247-5111 (SAN 215-2797).

Langdon, Larry Pubns., *(Langdon Pubns; 0-943726),* 34735 Perkins Creek Rd., Cottage Grove, OR 97424 Tel 503-942-7496 (SAN 241-0427).

Lange Medical Pubns., *(Lange; 0-87041),* Drawer L, Los Altos, CA 94022 Tel 415-948-4526 (SAN 202-6635).

Langenscheidt Pubs., *(Langenscheidt),* 46-35 54th Rd., Maspeth, NY 11378 Tel 212-784-0055 (SAN 276-9441).

Langford, Bill, Publisher, *(B Langford; 0-943504),* 2525 Freeport Rd., Harmarville, PA 15238 Tel 414-466-0391 (SAN 240-7019).

Langley, Ray, *(Langley),* 3664 Scorpio Dr., Sacramento, CA 95827 (SAN 215-6733).

Langley Press, *(Langley Pr; 0-911607),* 821 Georgia Street, Key West, FL 33040 (SAN 264-164X).

Langman Incorporated, *(Longman Inc; 0-582),* 19 W 44 St, New York, NY 10036 (SAN 227-0315).

Language Innovations, Inc., *(Lang Innovations; 0-931746),* 2112 Broadway, Rm. 515, New York, NY 10023 Tel 212-873-9476 (SAN 208-1326).

Language Press, *(Language Pr; 0-912386),* P.O. Box 342, Whitewater, WI 53190 Tel 414-473-6055 (SAN 201-0674).

Language Research Educational Series, *(Research Lang; 0-9609446),* P.O. Box 29512, Washington, DC 20017 Tel 202-635-7907 (SAN 260-0927).

Language Service, Inc., Pubns. Div., *(Lang Serv; 0-913942),* P.O. Box 8, Hastings-on-Hudson, NY 10706 Tel 212-687-4183 (SAN 201-0666).

Language Services, *(Lang Svcs CA),* 6453 Gem Lake Ave., San Diego, CA 92119 Tel 619-698-7999 (SAN 214-3925).

Lankey Pub. Co., Subs. of Huber Enterprises, Inc., *(Lankey; 0-918300),* Huber Enterprises, Inc., R.D. One, Box 205, West Newton, PA 15089 Tel 412-722-3507 (SAN 209-9446).

Lanks, Herbert, *(H C Lanks),* Inter-American Features, Jenkintown, PA (SAN 265-3869).

Lansdowne Edition, *(Lansdown Ans; 0-7018),* 14 Lansdowne St. Melbourne Vic. 3002, .

Lanser Press, *(Lanser Pr; 0-9603900),* P.O. Box 38, Plainfield, VT 05667 (SAN 214-3933).

Lantern Press, Inc. Pubs., *(Lantern; 0-8313),* 354 Hussey Rd., Mount Vernon, NY 10552 Tel 914-668-9736 (SAN 201-0682).

Lantz, Walter D., *(W D Lantz; 0-9610364),* 1424 Marietta St., Lancaster, PA 17603 Tel 717-299-2943 (SAN 264-1666).

Laranmark Press, Div. of Laranmark, Inc., *(Laranmark; 0-910937),* Box 253, Neshkoro, WI 54960 Tel 414-293-8216 (SAN 271-9606).

Larchmont Books, *(Larchmont Bks; 0-915962),* 390 Fifth Ave., New York, NY 10018 Tel 212-613-9700 (SAN 203-8641).

Large Print Books *See* **Hall, G. K., & Co.**

Laridae Press, *(Laridae Pr; 0-9606094),* 3012 Wesley Ave., Ocean City, NJ 08226 Tel 609-399-3222 (SAN 216-8278).

Larimi Communications, *(Larimi Comm; 0-935224),* 151 E. 50th St., New York, NY 10022 Tel 212-935-9262 (SAN 210-8259).

Lark Books, *(Lark Bks; 0-937274),* 50 College St, Asheville, NC 28801 Tel 704-253-0468 (SAN 219-9947).

Larkin, Larry, Pub., *(Larkin; 0-9605748),* 762 S. Lake Shore Dr., Lake Geneva, WI 53147 Tel 414-248-2569 (SAN 240-0219).

Larksdale Press, The, *(Larksdale; 0-89896),* 5400 Memorial Towers, Houston, TX 77007 Tel 713-869-9092 (SAN 220-0643).

Larkspur Pubns., *(Larkspur; 0-939942),* P.O. Box 211, Bowmansville, NY 14026 Tel 716-337-2758 (SAN 216-8286).

Larlin Corp., *(Larlin Corp; 0-910220; 0-89783),* P.O. Box 1523, Marietta, GA 30061 Tel 404-424-6210 (SAN 201-4432).

Larousse & Co., Inc., *(Larousse; 0-88332),* 572 Fifth Ave., New York, NY 10036 Tel 212-575-9515 (SAN 202-6643).

Larren Pubns., *(Larren Pubns; 0-9604370),* P.O. Box 594, Nevada, MO 64772 Tel 417-667-3706 (SAN 220-0651).

Larsen, J., Publishing, *(J Larsen; 0-9602474),* P.O. Box 586, Deer Lodge, MT 59722 Tel 406-846-2610 (SAN 212-1107).

Larson Pubns., Inc., Subs. of Bokforlaget Robert Larson Sweden, *(Larson Pubns Inc; 0-943914),* 4936 Rte 414, Burdett, NY 14818 Tel 607-546-9342 (SAN 241-130X); Dist. by: Kampman & Co., 9 E. 40th St., New York, NY 10016 (SAN 202-5191).

Las Campanas Pubns., *(Las Campanas; 0-938476),* P.O. Box 357, Bernalillo, NM 87004 Tel 505-867-3210 (SAN 239-9369).

Las Palomas De Taos, *(Las Palomas),* P.O. Box 3194, Taos, NM 87571 (SAN 264-1682).

Lasenda Pubs., *(Lasenda; 0-918916),* 32331 Coast Hwy., S. Laguna, CA 92677 Tel 714-499-1301 (SAN 210-4504).

Laser Institute of America, *(Laser Inst; 0-912035),* 5151 Monroe St., Ste. 103 W., Toledo, OH 43623 Tel 419-882-8706 (SAN 225-2007).

Lash Pubns., *(Lash Pubns; 0-9607150),* P.O. Box 32873, Detroit, MI 48232 Tel 313-886-0555 (SAN 239-0043).

Lateiner Publishing, *(Lateiner; 0-911722),* Atrium Tower I-A-2, 3400 S Ocean Blvd., Palm Beach, FL 33480 Tel 305-585-1818 (SAN 201-0690).

Lathrop, Norman, Enterprises, *(Lathrop; 0-910868),* P.O. Box 198, Wooster, OH 44691 Tel 216-262-5587 (SAN 285-0419); Orders to: P.O. Box 198, Wooster, OH 44691 Tel 216-262-5587 (SAN 285-0427).

Latin, R. R., Associates, Inc., *(Latin Assoc; 0-940106),* 404 E. 55th St., New York, NY 10022 Tel 212-758-6389 (SAN 220-2832).

Latin American Center, UCLA See Univ. of California, Latin American Center

Latin American Lit. Rev. Press, *(Lat Am Lit Rev Pr; 0-935480),* Box 8316, Pittsburgh, PA 15218 (SAN 215-2142).

Latin American Studies, Univ. of Houston, *(Lat Am Stud),* 401 Hoffman Hall, Univ. of Houston, Houston, TX 77004 Tel 713-749-4885 (SAN 207-7191) Not to be confused with Mexican American Studies, Univ. of Houston.

Latitudes Press, *(Latitudes Pr),* 3215 Lafayette Ave., Austin, TX 78722 Tel 512-478-1454 (SAN 202-6651); Dist. by: SBD: Small Press Distribution, 1636 Oceanview, Kensington, CA 94707 (SAN 204-5826).

Latona Press, *(Latona Pr; 0-932448),* Box 154, RFD 2, Ellsworth, ME 04605 (SAN 216-406X).

Laughing Sam's Press, *(Laughing Sams Pr; 0-9607824),* 5243 San Feliciano Dr., Woodland Hills, CA 91364 Tel 213-340-4175 (SAN 238-0188).

Laughing Waters Press, The, *(Laughing Waters; 0-939634),* 1416 Euclid Ave., Boulder, CO 80203 (SAN 216-6313).

Laughlin Enterprises, *(Laughlin Enter; 0-933604),* 1845 Oak Terrace, Newcastle, CA 95658 Tel 916-663-2295 (SAN 213-5329).

Laurel Editions See Dell Publishing Co., Inc.

Laurel Entertainment, Inc., *(Laurel Enter; 0-930392),* 928 Broadway, New York, NY 10010 Tel 212-674-3800 (SAN 211-0296).

Laurel Hill Press, *(Laurel Hill Pr; 0-9608688),* 107 Wildcat Creek, Chapel Hill, NC 27514 Tel 919-962-6945 (SAN 238-3101).

Laurel Leaf Library See Dell Publishing Co., Inc.

Laurida Book Publishing Co., *(Laurida; 0-934810),* P.O. Box 2061, Hollywood, CA 90028 Tel 213-466-1707 (SAN 203-9303).

L'Avant Studios, *(L'Avant Studios; 0-914570),* P.O. Box 1711, Tallahassee, FL 32302 Tel 904-224-1411 (SAN 205-6038).

Lavin Associates, *(Lavin Assocs; 0-941890),* 12 Promontory Dr., Cheshire, CT 06410 Tel 203-272-9121 (SAN 239-779X).

Law, Rod, *(Rod Law; 0-9601730),* P. O. Box 24025, Los Angeles, CA 90024 (SAN 222-0555).

Law & Capital Dynamics, *(Law & Cap Dynamics; 0-9600708),* 700 S. Flower St. Suite 2600, Los Angeles, CA 90017 Tel 213-629-1100 (SAN 213-7690).

Law & Justice Pubs., *(Law & Justice),* P.O. Box 6111, San Diego, CA 92106 (SAN 212-8578).

Law & Psychology Press, *(Law & Psych; 0-9603630),* 4150 Via Dolce, No. 236, Marina Del Rey, CA 90291 Tel 213-823-4460 (SAN 281-871X); Orders to: P. O. Box 9489, Venice, CA 90291 (SAN 281-8728).

Law & Technology Press, *(Law & Tech Pr; 0-910215),* P.O. Box 4658 T. A., Los Angeles, CA 90051 Tel 213-748-9416 (SAN 241-3914).

Law-Arts Pubs., Inc., *(Law Arts; 0-88238),* 2001 Wilshire Blvd., Suite 500, Santa Monica, CA 90043 Tel 213-829-4315 (SAN 201-0712).

Law Enforcement Ordnance Co., *(Law Enf Ord Co; 0-943850),* Box 1547, Athens, GA 30603 Tel 404-549-6976 (SAN 241-0435).

Law Enforcement Reference Manual, *(Law Enforce Ref; 0-916104),* P.O. Box 7333, Trenton, NJ 08628 Tel 609-883-1886 (SAN 206-1678); Orders to: 240 Mulberry St., Newark, NJ 07101 Tel 201-642-0075 (SAN 206-1686).

Lawkits, Inc., *(Lawkits; 0-937464),* 26339 Monte Verde, Carmel, CA 93923 Tel 408-373-3067 (SAN 215-2282); Dist. by: Publishers Group West, 5855 Beaudry St., Emeryville, CA 94608 Tel 415-658-3453 (SAN 202-8522).

Lawler, Louise, *(L Lawler; 0-931706),* 407 Greenwich St., New York, NY 10013 (SAN 211-7363).

Lawrence House, *(Lawrence Hse; 0-9609436),* 718 Sherwood St., N. Woodmere, NY 11581 Tel 516-791-5725 (SAN 260-0935).

Lawson's Psychological Services, *(Lawson's Psych; 0-9611668),* 2051 W. Brichta Dr., Tucson, AZ 85745 Tel 602-792-3181 (SAN 285-3418).

Lawton, Elise Timmons, *(Lawton E T),* 4521 Joyce Blvd., Houston, TX 77084 (SAN 240-9615).

Lawton-Teague Pubns., *(Lawton-Teague; 0-932516),* P.O. Box 12353, Oakland, CA 94604 (SAN 211-2485); Dist. by: Bookpeople, 2940 Seventh St., Berkeley, CA 94710 (SAN 168-9517).

Lawyers & Judges Publishing Co., *(Lawyers & Judges; 0-913875),* 8950 Villa la Jolla Dr., Suite 1200, La Jolla, CA 92037 Tel 619-456-2701 (SAN 202-2354).

Lawyers Co-Operative Publishing Co., *(Lawyers Co-Op),* 1 Graves St., Rochester, NY 14694 Tel 716-546-5530 (SAN 202-6678).

Lawyers for the Creative Arts, *(Lawyers Creative Arts; 0-936122),* 220 S. State, Suite 1404, Chicago, IL 60604 (SAN 213-7704); Dist. by: Chicago Review Press, 820 N. Franklin, Chicago, IL 60610 Tel 312-337-0747 (SAN 213-5744).

Lazuli Productions, Inc., *(Lazuli Prod; 0-9600522),* P.O. Box 125, Beaverton, OR 97075 (SAN 211-738X).

Lazy Press, The, *(Lazy Pr),* 2520 N. Lincoln Ave., Box One, Chicago, IL 60614 Tel 312-934-8451 (SAN 285-1210); Orders to: 2520 Lincoln Ave., Box 1, Chicago, IL 60614 Tel 312-934-8451 (SAN 285-1229).

LBS Productions, *(lbs Productions),* 2389 Sherwood Rd., Columbus, OH 43209 (SAN 240-0472).

Le Beacon Presse, *(Beacon Presse IA; 0-935954),* 621 Holt, Iowa City, IA 52240 (SAN 281-8736); Orders to: Keith S. Gormezano, 6 Beacon Presse, 2921 E. Madison St., Suite 7 BIP, Seattle, WA 98112 Tel 206-322-1431 (SAN 281-8744).

Lea & Febiger, *(Lea & Febiger; 0-8121),* 600 S. Washington Square, Philadelphia, PA 19106 Tel 215-922-1330 (SAN 201-0747).

Leadership Dynamics, *(Leadership Dyn; 0-911777),* 119 Longs Peak Dr., P.O. Box 320, Lyons, CO 80540 Tel 303-823-5146 (SAN 264-1704).

Leadership Press, *(Leadership Pr; 0-936626),* Box 1144, Claremont, CA 91711 Tel 714-624-6242 (SAN 214-3941).

League Books, *(League Bks),* P.O. Box 6055, Cleveland, OH 44101 (SAN 209-0406).

League of Women Voters of Minnesota, *(LWV MN; 0-939816),* 555 Wabasha St., Suite 212, St. Paul, MN 55102 Tel 612-224-5445 (SAN 216-9045).

League of Women Voters of NYS, *(LWV NYS; 0-938588),* 817 Broadway, New York, NY 10003 (SAN 216-1591).

League of Women Voters of Pennsylvania, *(LWVPA; 0-931370),* Strawbridge & Clothier, 8th & Market Sts., Philadelphia, PA 19105 Tel 215-627-7937 (SAN 207-0588).

League of Women Voters of the City of New York, *(LWV NYC; 0-916130),* 817 Broadway, New York, NY 10003 (SAN 207-2602).

League of Women Voters of the U.S., *(LWV US; 0-89959),* 1730 M. St. N.W., Washington, DC 20036 Tel 202-296-1770 (SAN 207-5288).

Leahy, Barbara, *(B Leahy; 0-9610312),* 415 Paddock St., Watertown, NY 13601 Tel 315-788-5846 (SAN 264-1720).

Lear Enterprises, *(Lear; 0-941990),* P.O. Box 649, Woodland Hills, CA 91365 Tel 213-340-8800 (SAN 238-6062).

Learn, *(Learn Mich; 0-9604634),* 827 CNB Bldg., Detroit, MI 48226 (SAN 215-2533).

Learned Information, Inc., *(Learned Info; 0-938734),* 143 Old Marlton Pike, Medford, NJ 08055 (SAN 215-8841).

Learned Pubns., Inc., *(Learned Pubns; 0-912116),* 83-53 Manton St., Jamaica, NY 11435 Tel 212-441-8084 (SAN 201-0755).

Learning Concepts, Inc., *(Learn Concepts OH; 0-934902),* 7601 Mentor Ave., Mentor, OH 44060 Tel 216-946-6437 (SAN 213-411X) Not affiliated with San Diego Learning Concepts.

Learning Concepts, Inc., *(Learning Concepts; 0-89384),* Orders to: Learning Concepts/Univ. Associates, 8517 Production Ave., P.O. Box 26240, San Diego, CA 92126 Tel 800-854-2143 (SAN 272-006X).

Learning House Pubs., *(Learning Hse; 0-9602730),* 38 South St., Roslyn Heights, NY 11577 Tel 516-621-5755 (SAN 214-3968); Dist. by: Liberty Publishing Co., 50 Scott Adam Rd., Cockeysville, MD 21030 (SAN 211-030X).

Learning Inc., *(Learning Inc.; 0-913692),* Learning Place, Manset, ME 04656 Tel 207-244-5015 (SAN 201-5714).

Learning Line, The, *(Learning Line; 0-8449),* P.O. Box 577, Palo Alto, CA 94302 Tel 415-854-4400 (SAN 220-018X); Orders to: P.O. Box 1200, Palo Alto, CA 94302 (SAN 220-0198).

Learning Pubns., Inc., *(Learning Pubns; 0-918452),* 3030 S. Ninth St., Kalamazoo, MI 49009 Tel 616-372-1045 (SAN 208-1695).

Learning Resource Institute, *(LRI; 0-940952),* 2552 Moraga Dr., Pinole, CA 94564 Tel 415-758-0846 (SAN 217-3905); Dist. by: Educational Book Distributor, 222 Madrone Ave., Larkspur, CA 94939 (SAN 158-2259).

Learning Resources in International Studies, *(Learn Res Intl Stud; 0-936876),* P.O. Box 337, Croton-on-Hudson, NY 10520 (SAN 281-8752); Orders to: 777 United Nations Plaza, New York, NY 10017 Tel 212-972-9877 (SAN 281-8760).

Learning Works, Inc., The, *(Learning Wks; 0-88160),* P.O. Box 6187, Santa Barbara, CA 93111 Tel 805-964-4220 (SAN 272-0078).

Learntech Pubns., *(Learntech Pubns; 0-940108),* 8808 Hidden Hill Lane, Rockville, MD 20854 Tel 301-499-7142 (SAN 220-2840).

Leaseway Transportation Corp, *(Leaseway Trans Corp; 0-9610146),* 3700 Park East Dr., Cleveland, OH 44122 Tel 216-464-3300 (SAN 272-0086).

Leaves of Grass Press, Inc., *(Leaves of Grass; 0-915070),* Publishers Services, P.O. Box 3914, San Rafael, CA 94902 Tel 415-833-3530 (SAN 207-9321).

Lebanese Cuisine, *(Lebanese Cuisine; 0-9603050),* P.O. Box 66395, Portland, OR 97266 Tel 503-774-6126 (SAN 213-103X).

Lebhar-Friedman Books, Subs. of Lebhar-Friedman, Inc., *(Lebhar Friedman; 0-912016; 0-86730),* 425 Park Ave, New York, NY 10022 Tel 212-371-9400 (SAN 201-9744).

Lectorum Pubns., *(Lectorum Pubns),* 137 W. 14th St., New York, NY 10011 (SAN 207-253X).

Lederer Enterprises, *(Lederer Enterprises; 0-9608040),* Box 506, Lake Oswego, OR 97034 (SAN 238-0668).

Lee, J. & L., Co., *(J & L Lee; 0-934904),* P.O. Box 5575, Lincoln, NE 68505 Tel 402-467-4416 (SAN 213-8557).

Lee, Ralph E., *(R E Lee; 0-9606268),* 5698 Hollyleaf Lane, San Jose, CA 95118 Tel 408-266-1440 (SAN 220-3367); Orders to: Pro/Press Publishing Co., 5698 Hollyleaf Lane, San Jose, CA 95130 Tel 408-266-1440 (SAN 220-3375).

Lee, Shyh-Yuan David, *(D L Shyh Yuan; 0-9611810),* P.O. Box 1170, Eisless, TX 76039 Tel 214-638-1270 (SAN 285-3329).

Lee Books, *(Lee Bks; 0-939818),* P.O. Box 906, Novato, CA 94948 Tel 415-897-3550 (SAN 216-2636).

Lee Enterprises, Inc., *(Lee Enterprises; 0-910847),* 130 E. Second St., Davenport, IA 52801 Tel 319-383-2208 (SAN 262-7892).

Lee Pubns., *(Lee Pubns; 0-910872),* 105 Suffolk Rd., Wellesley Hills, MA 02181 (SAN 203-932X) Moved, Left No Forwarding Address.

Lee Ward Institute, The, *(Lee Ward Inst; 0-932474),* Rte. 2, Box 62, Piggott, AR 72454 Tel 501-598-3911 (SAN 210-5837).

Leeco, Inc., *(Leeco; 0-941222),* 201 Benton Ave., Linthicum, MD 21090 (SAN 238-0676).

Leeger Press, *(Leeger Pr; 0-9609706),* P.O. Box 371, Norwalk, CT 06851 (SAN 262-7914); 29 Lockwood Lane, Norwalk, CT 06851 (SAN 262-7922).

Lees-Haley, Paul R., Associates, Inc., *(P R Lees-Haley; 0-938124),* 4025 Piedmont Dr., Huntsville, AL 35802 Tel 205-883-5364 (SAN 215-658X).

Leete's Island Books, *(Leetes Isl; 0-918172),* P.O. Box 1131, New Haven, CT 06505 Tel 203-481-2536 (SAN 210-2285); Dist. by: Independent Publishers Group, One Pleasant Ave., Port Washington, NY 11050 (SAN 210-2293).

LeFax Publishing Co., *(LeFax; 0-87684),* 2867 E. Allegheny Ave., Philadelphia, PA 19134 (SAN 210-0771).

Left Bank Books, *(Left Bank; 0-939306),* 92 Pike St., Box B, Seattle, WA 98101 Tel 206-622-0195 (SAN 216-5368).

Lega Books, Div. of Charing Cross Pub. Co., *(Lega Bks),* 658 S. Bonnie Brae St., Los Angeles, CA 90057 Tel 213-483-5832 (SAN 212-5218).

Legacy Books, *(Legacy Bks; 0-913714),* Box 494, 12 Meetinghouse Rd., Hatboro, PA 19040 Tel 215-675-6762 (SAN 202-2389).

Legacy House, *(Legacy Hse; 0-9608008),* Box 786, Orofino, ID 83544 (SAN 238-0684).

Legacy Of Love, A, *(Legacy Of Love),* 1638 Daniels Dr., North Fort Meyers, FL 33903 (SAN 283-2992).

Legacy Publishing (CA), *(Legacy Publish; 0-9611902),* 2920 Buchanan St., Suite 5, San Francisco, CA 94123 Tel 415-563-1263 (SAN 286-1577).

Legal Book Co., *(Legal Bk Co; 0-910874),* 316 W. Second St., Los Angeles, CA 90012 Tel 213-626-3494 (SAN 201-0798).

Legal First Aid, *(Legal First Aid),* 899 Ellis St., San Francisco, CA 94109 Tel 415-441-4044 (SAN 206-4391) Moved, left no forwarding address.

Legal Management Services, Inc., *(Legal Mgmt Serv; 0-937542),* 250 W. 94th St., New York, NY 10025 Tel 212-864-6169 (SAN 220-066X); Dist. by: LMS Distribution Center, P.O. Box 2614, LaCrosse, WI 54601 (SAN 220-0678).

Legal Pubns. Inc., *(Legal Pubns CA)* 6931 Van Nuys Blvd., P.O. Box 3723, Van Nuys, CA 91407 Tel 213-873-4939 (SAN 210-8267).

Legal Research Bureau, *(Legal Res Bureau; 0-9609346),* P.O. Box 374, Kew Gardens, NY 11415 Tel 212-846-4544 (SAN 260-2164).

Leibowitz, Herbert, *(Leibowitz),* 205 W. 89th St., New York, NY 10024 (SAN 239-4502).

Leider & Harding Enterprises, *(Leider & Harding; 0-9607504),* 7101 York Ave. S., Minneapolis, MN 55435 Tel 612-831-2371 (SAN 239-7803).

Leisure Books, *(Leisure Bks CT),* P.O. Box 270, Norwalk, CT 06852 (SAN 215-2258) Moved, left no forwarding address.

Leisure Data Inc., *(Leisure Data; 0-913979),* 35104 Euclid Ave., Suite 2A, Willoughby, OH 44094 Tel 216-942-9002 (SAN 283-9652).

Leisure Press, *(Leisure Pr; 0-918438; 0-88011),* P.O. Box 3, West Point, NY 10996 Tel 914-446-7110 (SAN 210-1513).

Lem, Dean, Associates, Inc., *(D Lem Assocs; 0-914218),* 1526 Pontius Ave.,Suite C, Los Angeles, CA 90025 Tel 213-478-0092 (SAN 201-5005); Orders to: P.O. Box 25920, Los Angeles, CA 90025 (SAN 201-5013).

Lemma Publishing Corp., *(Lemma; 0-87696),* 509 Fifth Ave., New York, NY 10017 (SAN 202-6694) Moved, Left No Forwarding Address.

Lemur Musical Research Corp., *(Lemur; 0-9606888),* P.O. Box 121, Bloomington, IN 47402 Tel 812-333-1009 (SAN 201-5706).

Len Beach Press, *(Len Beach Pr),* P.O. Box 7269 R.C., Toledo, OH 43615 (SAN 213-1048).

Lenape Publishing, Ltd., *(Lenape Pub; 0-917178),* 4657 Dartmoor Dr., Wilmington, DE 19803 Tel 302-652-7847 (SAN 208-7324).

LenChamps Publishers, *(LenChamps Pubs; 0-917230),* 607 Fourth St., S.W., Washington, DC 20024 Tel 202-484-3571 (SAN 208-7332).

Lenox Books, *(Lenox Bks; 0-9605872),* P.O. Box 104, Little Falls, NJ 07424 (SAN 216-4078).

Lenox Library Assn. *See SnO Pubns.*

Leo Press, *(Leo Pr; 0-931580),* Allen Park, MI 48101 (SAN 212-4300).

Leo Victor Press, *(L Victor Pr; 0-9606562),* 2203 Brandenburg Way, King of Prussia, PA 19406 (SAN 213-3970).

Leonaitis, Joseph Felix, *(Leonaitis; 0-9601272),* 3323 S. Lowe Ave., Chicago, IL 60616 Tel 312-376-7524 (SAN 210-4547).

Leonard, Cliff R., & Duke Coleman, *(C R Leonard & D Coleman; 0-9603818),* 1007 N. Noyes Dr., Silver Spring, MD 20910 (SAN 213-9804); Dist. by: Nothing New, P.O. Box 714, Silver Spring, MD 20901 (SAN 213-9812).

Leonard's Associates, *(Leonard Assocs; 0-936692),* 2423 North 2nd St., Harrisburg, PA 17110 (SAN 221-4318).

Leone Pubns., *(Leone Pubns; 0-942786),* 2721 Lyle Ct., Santa Clara, CA 95051 Tel 415-948-8077 (SAN 238-8510).

Leonine Press, *(Leonine Pr; 0-942228),* 2317 Outlook St., Kalamazoo, MI 49001 Tel 616-345-2740 (SAN 240-0405).

Leopold-Littlebear Press, *(Leopold; 0-941756),* 2124 Kittredge, Box 52, Berkeley, CA 94704 Tel 415-845-2206 (SAN 239-2518).

L'Epervier Press, *(L'Epervier Pr; 0-934332),* 762 Hayes, No. 15, Seattle, WA 98109 Tel 206-283-4952 (SAN 281-8779); Dist. by: Small Press Distribution Inc., 1784 Shattuck Ave., Berkeley, CA 94709 (SAN 204-5826).

Leprechaun Pr., *(Leprechaun Pr; 0-9607368),* 808 W. End Ave., No. 408, New York, NY 10025 Tel 212-666-3357 (SAN 240-0391).

Lerner Law Book Co., *(Lerner Law; 0-87342),* 53 "E" St., N. W., Washington, DC 20001 Tel 202-628-5785 (SAN 201-081X).

Lerner Publications Co., *(Lerner Pubns; 0-8225),* 241 First Ave., N., Minneapolis, MN 55401 Tel 612-332-3344 (SAN 201-0828).

Les Femmes Publishing, *(Les Femmes Pub; 0-89087),* P.O. Box 7327, Berkeley, CA 94707 (SAN 207-7353).

Leslie Press, Inc., *(Leslie Pr; 0-913816),* 111 Leslie St., Dallas, TX 75207 Tel 214-748-0566 (SAN 202-6708).

Lesly, Philip, Co., The, *(Lesly Co; 0-9602866),* 130 E. Randolph St., Chicago, IL 60601 (SAN 222-2086).

Letellier, Phyllis M., *(P M Letellier; 0-9611138),* Shell Rte. Box 23, Greybull, WY 82426 (SAN 283-2976) Tel 307-765-2109.

Levada Services, *(Levada; 0-9605014),* P.O. Box 686, 11300 Eastside Rd., Fort Jones, CA 96032 (SAN 215-9597).

Levenson Press, *(Levenson Pr; 0-914442),* P.O. Box 19606, Los Angeles, CA 90019 (SAN 202-6716).

Levi Publishing Co., Inc., *(Levi Pub; 0-910876),* P.O. Box 730, Sumter, SC 29150 (SAN 203-9338).

Levine, Samuel P., *(S P Levine; 0-9602906),* P.O. Box 174, Canoga Park, CA 91305 Tel 213-343-0550 (SAN 213-1056).

Levine Press, *(Levine Pr),* P.O. Box 517, Cascade, CO 80809 (SAN 209-0309) Moved, Left No Forwarding Address.

Levinson Institute Inc., *(Levinson Inst; 0-916516),* Box 95, Cambridge, MA 02138 Tel 617-489-3040 (SAN 208-7359).

Lewis, A. F., & Co., Inc., *(Lewis; 0-910880),* 79 Madison Ave., New York, NY 10016 Tel 212-679-0770 (SAN 201-0844).

Lewis Carroll Society of North America, *(Lewis Carroll Soc; 0-930326),* 617 Rockford Rd., Silver Spring, MD 20902 (SAN 213-1064).

Lewis-Sloan Publishing Co., *(Lewis-Sloan; 0-915114),* 2546 Etiwan Ave., Charleston, SC 29407 Tel 803-766-4735 (SAN 201-0852).

Lex-Cal-Tex Press, *(Lex-Cal-Tex Pr; 0-912558),* P.O. Box 5512, Walnut Creek, CA 94596 Tel 415-863-1598 (SAN 201-0860).

Lexigrow International Corp., *(Lexigrow Intl),* 9202 North Meridian St., P.O. Box 1491, Indianapolis, IN 46206 Tel 317-844-5691 (SAN 262-0464).

Lexik House Pubs., *(Lexik Hse; 0-936368),* 75 Main St., P.O. Box 247, Cold Spring, NY 10516 Tel 914-265-2822 (SAN 214-3984).

Lexikos Publishing, *(Lexikos; 0-938530),* 208 Central Tower, 703 Market St., San Francisco, CA 94103 Tel 415-495-3493 (SAN 219-8517).

Lexington Book Co., *(Lex Bk Co CA; 0-9604372),* 4872 Old Cliffs Rd., San Diego, CA 92120 Tel 619-583-8348 (SAN 214-3992).

Lexington Books, Div. of D. C. Heath & Co., *(Lexington Bks; 0-669),* Dist. by: D. C. Heath & Co., 125 Spring St., Lexington, MA 02173 Tel 617-862-6650 (SAN 213-7526).

Lexington Data, Inc., *(Lexington Data; 0-914428; 0-88178),* Box 371, Ashland, MA 01721 Tel 617-881-2576 (SAN 202-6724).

Lexington-Fayette County Historic Commission, *(Lexington-Fayette; 0-912839),* 253 Market St., Lexington, KY 40508 Tel 606-255-8312 (SAN 277-6936).

Leyerle, William D., *(W D Leyerle; 0-9602296),* 28 Stanley St., Mt. Morris, NY 14510 Tel 716-658-2193 (SAN 211-5700); Orders to: Vocal Development Through Organic Imagery, or Leyerle Pubns., Box 384, Geneseo, NY 14454 (SAN 211-5719).

Liberation Publications, Inc., *(Liberation Pubns; 0-917076),* P.O. Box 5847, San Mateo, CA 94402 Tel 415-573-7100 (SAN 208-7367).

Liberian Studies, *(Liberian Studies),* Dept. of Anthropology, Univ. of Delaware, Newark, DE 19711 (SAN 207-5032).

Libertarian Books, *(Libertarian Bks),* P.O. Box 22026, Tampa, FL 33622 (SAN 208-3418).

Libertarian Pr., *(Libertarian Press; 0-910884),* P.O. Box 218, 366 E. 166th St., South Holland, IL 60473 Tel 312-333-0031 (SAN 201-0895).

Liberty Bell Associates, *(Libty Bell Assoc; 0-918940),* P.O. Box 51, Franklin Park, NJ 08823 Tel 201-297-3051 (SAN 206-4405).

Liberty Bell Press, *(Liberty Bell Pr; 0-914053),* P.O. Box 32, Florissant, MO 63033 Tel 314-837-5343 (SAN 202-2435).

Liberty Book Co., *(Liberty Bk),* 374 Morris St., Albany, NY 12208 Tel 518-463-0483 (SAN 204-3734).

Liberty Communications House, *(Libty Comm Hse; 0-934334),* 3331 Liberty St., St. Louis, MO 63111 Tel 314-351-2846 (SAN 213-4128).

Liberty Lobby, *(Liberty Lobby; 0-935036),* 300 Independence Ave., S.E., Washington, DC 20003 Tel 202-546-5611 (SAN 202-2524).

Liberty Press, *(Liberty Pr; 0-936860),* 350 W. 500 S., Provo, UT 84601 Tel 264-1747).

Liberty Press, *(Libty Pr IA; 0-939272),* 905 Leroy St., Muscatine, IA 52761 (SAN 216-4086).

Liberty Press/Liberty Classics, *(Liberty Clas; 0-913966; 0-86597),* 7440 N. Shadeland Ave., Indianapolis, IN 46250 Tel 317-842-0880 (SAN 202-6740).

Liberty Publishing Co., Inc., *(Liberty Pub; 0-89709),* 50 Scott Adam Rd., Cockeysville, MD 21030 Tel 301-667-6680 (SAN 211-030X).

Libra Press, *(Libra Pr),* 2316 E. Porter, Los Angeles, CA 90021 Tel 213-627-5264 (SAN 241-1326).

Libra Pubs., Inc., *(Libra; 0-87212),* 391 Willets Rd., Roslyn Heights, L. I., NY 11577 Tel 516-484-4950 (SAN 201-0909).

Libraries Unlimited, Inc., *(Libs Unl; 0-87287),* P.O. Box 263, Littleton, CO 80160 Tel 303-770-1220 (SAN 202-6767).

Library Co. of Philadelphia, *(Lib Co Phila; 0-914076),* 1314 Locust St., Philadelphia, PA 19107 Tel 215-546-3181 (SAN 201-4955).

Library of Armenian Studies, *(Library of Armenian; 0-910154),* 129 Robbins Rd., Watertown, MA 02172 (SAN 209-1232).

Library of Congress, *(Lib Congress; 0-8444),* Washington, DC 20540 Tel 202-287-5093 (SAN 205-6593).

Library of Psychological Anthropology, *(Lib Psychol Anthrop; 0-914434),* 2315 Broadway, New York, NY 10024 (SAN 212-5226).

Library of Social Science, *(Lib Soc Sci; 0-915042),* 475 Amsterdam Ave., New York, NY 10024 Tel 212-749-3567 (SAN 207-589X).

Library Press *See* **Open Court Publishing Co.**

Library Reports & Research Service, Inc., *(Library Reports; 0-912717),* 4140 W. 80th Place, Westminster, CO 80030 (SAN 285-659X).

Library Research Associates, *(Lib Res; 0-912526),* Dunderberg Rd., R.D. 5, Box 41, Monroe, NY 10950 Tel 914-783-1144 (SAN 201-0887).

Library Services Inc., *(Lib Serv Inc),* Box 711, Havertown, PA 19083 (SAN 210-5381).

Licht, Lilla M., *(L M Licht; 0-9607184),* R.D. 1, Woods Rd., Remsen, NY 13438 Tel 315-831-5463 (SAN 239-1074).

Lichtner, Schomer, *(Lichtner; 0-941074),* 2626A N. Maryland Ave., Milwaukee, WI 53211 Tel 414-962-7519 (SAN 223-1891).

Lidiraven Books, *(Lidiraven Bks; 0-936162),* Box 5567, Sherman Oaks, CA 91413 Tel 213-892-0059 (SAN 213-9340).

Lieber-Atherton, Inc., *(Lieber-Atherton; 0-88311),* 1841 Broadway, New York, NY 10023 Tel 212-586-2118 (SAN 202-5639).

Liebert, Mary Ann,, Inc., *(M Liebert; 0-913113),* 157 E. 86th St., New York, NY 10028 Tel 212-289-2300 (SAN 283-2259).

Liederbach, Robert J., Co., *(R J Liederbach; 0-934906),* 4870 Thales Rd.-O, Winston-Salem, NC 27104 Tel 919-768-7014 (SAN 213-1080).

Life Arts Publishing, *(Life Arts; 0-937894),* 116 Curryer S., Santa Maria, CA 93454 (SAN 220-0686).

Life Enrichment Pubs., *(Life Enrich; 0-938736),* Box 526, Canton, OH 44701 (SAN 215-9600).

Life-Long Learning Library, *(Life Long Learn),* P.O. Box 7361, Atlanta, GA 30309 (SAN 209-0384).

Life Management Systems, *(Life Mgmt IL; 0-9606788),* 636 Church St., No. 419, Evanston, IL 60201 Tel 312-869-2775 (SAN 223-1905).

Life Office Management Assn., *(LOMA; 0-915322),* 100 Colony Square, Atlanta, GA 30361 Tel 404-892-7272 (SAN 207-2548); Orders to: Professional Book Distributors, P.O. Box 02055, Columbus, OH 43202 Tel 800-848-0773 (SAN 207-2556).

Life Pubs. International, *(Life Pubs Intl; 0-8297),* 3360 N.W. 110th St., Miami, FL 33167 Tel 305-685-6334 (SAN 213-5817).

Life Science Institute, *(Life Science; 0-9609802),* P.O. Box 1057, Ft. Pierce, FL 33454 Tel 305-461-5292 (SAN 263-1830).

Life Skills Training Associates, *(Life Skills; 0-9604510),* P.O. Box 48133, Chicago, IL 60648 Tel 312-823-0650 (SAN 220-0694).

Life Sustaining Press, *(Life Sustaining; 0-9608946),* 167 N. Eastman Ave., Los Angeles, CA 90063 Tel 213-265-4512 (SAN 241-3310).

Life Understanding Foundation, *(Life Understanding; 0-88234),* P.O. Box 30305, 741 Rosarita Lane, Santa Barbara, CA 93105 Tel 805-682-5151 (SAN 203-8390).

Lifecraft, *(Lifecraft; 0-911505),* Box 1, Heisson, WA 98622 (SAN 264-1755).

Lifeline, *(Lifeline),* 3500 N. Hayden Rd., No. 1705, Scottsdale, AZ 85251 Tel 602-941-8094 (SAN 281-8817); Orders to: 1421 S. Park St., Madison, WI 53715 (SAN 281-8825).

Lifesigns: Words & Images, *(Lifesigns; 0-943510),* 882 Bates Ave., El Cerrito, CA 94530 Tel 415-527-6722 (SAN 240-7043).

Lifestyle One, Inc., *(Lifestyle One; 0-9603016),* P.O. Box 630668, Miami, FL 33163 (SAN 213-1099).

Lifestyle Press, *(Lifestyle Pr; 0-9606860),* 10023 Main St., Bellevue, WA 98004 (SAN 223-1913).

Lifetime Learning Pubns., Div. of Wadsworth Inc., *(Lifetime Learn; 0-534),* 10 Davis Dr., Belmont, CA 94002 Tel 415-595-2350 (SAN 211-7398).

Light & Life Press (IN), *(Light & Life; 0-89367),* 999 College Ave., Winona Lake, IN 46590 Tel 219-267-7161 (SAN 206-8419).

Light & Life Pub. Co., *(Light&Life Pub Co MN; 0-937032),* 3450 Irving Ave. S., Minneapolis, MN 55408 Tel 612-925-3888 (SAN 213-8565).

Light Impressions Corp., *(Light Impressions; 0-87992),* P.O. Box 940, 439 Monroe Ave., Rochester, NY 14603 Tel 716-271-8960 (SAN 169-619X).

Lightbooks, *(Lightbooks; 0-934420),* P.O. Box 1268, Twain Harte, CA 95383 (SAN 214-400X).

Lighthouse Hill Publishing, *(Lighthouse Hill Pub; 0-9608690),* 279 Edinboro Rd., Lighthouse Hill, Staten Island, NY 10306 Tel 212-987-7586 (SAN 238-0706).

Lightning Tree, *(Lightning Tree; 0-89016),* P.O. Box 1837, Santa Fe, NM 87501 Tel 505-983-7434 (SAN 206-555X).

Lighton Pubns., *(Lighton Pubns; 0-910892),* 73223 Sunnyvale Dr., Twentynine Palms, CA 92277 Tel 619-367-7386 (SAN 201-0917).

LightSong, *(LightSong),* 1325 Rimrock Dr., San Jose, CA 95120 (SAN 209-1607).

Lightyear Press, Inc., *(Lightyear; 0-89968),* P.O. Box 507, Laurel, NY 11948 (SAN 213-1102).

Liguori Pubns., *(Liguori Pubns; 0-89243),* 1 Liguori Dr., Liguori, MO 63057 Tel 800-325-9521 (SAN 202-6783).

Lilien, M., *(M Lilien; 0-9607652),* 68-50 Burns Street, Forest Hills, NY 11375 (SAN 264-1763).

Lillian & M. E., *(Lillian; 0-918174),* 11 Tudor Dr., Northport, NY 11788 Tel 516-757-5615 (SAN 209-5742).

Lim Press, *(LIM Press CA; 0-942714),* P.O. Box 363, Belmont, CA 94002 Tel 415-591-9056 (SAN 240-2424).

Lime Rock Press, Inc., *(Lime Rock Pr; 0-915998),* Mount Riga Rd., Box 363, Salisbury, CT 06068 Tel 203-435-2236 (SAN 208-2055).

Limestone Press, *(Limestone Pr; 0-919642),* P.O. Box 1604, Kingston, Ontario, Canada K7l 5c8, (SAN 209-0120); Dist. by: A. S. Donnelly, 125 Southwood Dr., Vestal, NY 13850 (SAN 209-0139).

Limited Editions Press, *(Limited Ed; 0-8100),* 8412 Wilbur Ave., Northridge, CA 91324 Tel 213-885-9961 (SAN 240-9623).

Linch Corp., *(Linch Corp; 0-913455),* P.O. Box 75, Orlando, FL 32802 Tel 305-647-3025 (SAN 285-1792).

Lincoln, James F., Arc Welding Foundation, *(Lincoln Arc Weld; 0-937390),* P.O. Box 17035, Cleveland, OH 44117 Tel 216-481-4300 (SAN 202-2443).

Lincoln County Historical Society, *(Lincoln Coun Hist; 0-911443),* 545 S.W. 9th St., Newport, OR 97365 Tel 503-265-7509 (SAN 272-0663).

Lincoln-Herndon Pr., the, *(Lincoln-Herndon Pr),* One Old State Capitol Plaza, Suite 503, Springfield, IL 62701 Tel 217-522-2732 (SAN 240-3188).

Lincoln Institute of Land Policy, *(Lincoln Inst Land),* 26 Trowbridge St., Cambridge, MA 02138 Tel 617-661-3016 (SAN 209-2506).

Lincoln Press, *(Lincoln Pr MI),* 4610 Delemere Blvd., Royal Oak, MI 48073 Tel 313-549-1900 (SAN 211-7401).

Lincoln Publishing, *(Lincoln Pub; 0-918898),* 3434 Janice Way, Palo Alto, CA 94303 Tel 415-494-7448 (SAN 209-6730).

Lincoln's Leadership Library, *(Lincoln's Leadership; 0-89764),* 5902 E. Fourth Terrace, Tulsa, OK 74112 (SAN 215-675X).

Lind Graphics Publications, *(Lind Grap Pubns; 0-910389),* 192 Third Ave., Westwood, NJ 07675 Tel 201-666-7313 (SAN 260-0951).

Lindahl, Judy, *(Lindahl; 0-9603032),* 3211 N.E. Siskiyou, Portland, OR 97212 Tel 503-288-0772 (SAN 210-6086).

Lindbrook Press, *(Lindbrook Pr; 0-942882),* P.O. Box 1082, 15243 la Cruz Dr., Pacific Palisades, CA 90272 (SAN 238-0692).

Lindell Pubs., *(Lindell Pubs; 0-9604940),* P.O. Box 28, Bucks County, Springtown, PA 18081 (SAN 215-9619).

Linden, Millicent, *(M Linden NY; 0-912628),* 500 E. 74th St., New York, NY 10021 (SAN 207-0596).

Linden Books, *(Linden Bks; 0-9603288),* Interlaken, NY 14847 Tel 607-387-9398 (SAN 209-6692).

Linden Press *See* **Simon & Schuster, Inc.**

Linden Pubs., *(Linden Pubs; 0-89642),* 1750 N. Sycamore, Hollywood, CA 90028 (SAN 206-7218).

Linden Publishing Co., *(Linden Pub Fresno; 0-941936),* 3845 N. Blackstone, Fresno, CA 93726 Tel 209-227-2901 (SAN 238-6089).

Lindenhof Press, *(Lindenhof Pr; 0-9609678),* P.O. Box 18513, Irvine, CA 92714 Tel 714-545-6984 (SAN 262-7981).

Linder, Herbert, *(H Linder; 0-917396),* 55 Park Ave., New York, NY 10016 Tel 212-685-2571 (SAN 206-8605).

Linder, William A., Co., Pubs., *(W A Linder; 0-934844),* P.O. Box 443, Lindsborg, KS 67456 Tel 913-227-2514 (SAN 205-4892).

Lindisfarne Press, The, *(Lindisfarne Pr; 0-940262),* R.D.2, West Stockbridge, MA 01266 Tel 413-232-4377 (SAN 217-5347).

Lindon Pubns., *(Lindon Ent; 0-939820),* Box 1162, Southold, NY 11971 Tel 516-765-3584 (SAN 216-9053).

Lindsay Newspapers, Inc., *(Lindsay News; 0-910713),* Postal Drawer 1719, Sarasota, FL 33578 Tel 813-746-2178 (SAN 260-2172).

Lindsay Pubns., *(Lindsay Pubns; 0-917914),* P. O. Box 12, Bradley, IL 60915 (SAN 209-9462); 152 W. Baker, Manteno, IL 60950 (SAN 209-9470).

Lineal/Cleworth Books, Inc., *(Lineal Cleworth; 0-916628),* 23 Leroy Ave., Darien, CT 06820 Tel 203-655-7676 (SAN 208-4848).

Lingore Press, *(Lingore Pr; 0-9607146),* Back Hanawa Rd., RFD 4, Potsdam, NY 13676 Tel 315-265-6163 (SAN 239-0051); Dist. by: Charles E. Tuttle Co., Inc., P.O. Box 410, 28 S. Main St., Rutland, VT 05701 Tel 802-773-8229 (SAN 213-2621).

Lingua Press, *(Lingua Pr),* Box 481, Ramona, CA 92065 Tel 714-789-8389 (SAN 215-6083).

Lingual House Publishing Co., *(Lingual Hse Pub; 0-940264),* P.O. Box 3537, Tucson, AZ 85722 Tel 602-299-5562 (SAN 220-3383).

Linju-Ryu Karate Assn., Inc., *(LKA Inc; 0-917098),* P.O. Box 102, 7 Putter Lane, Middle Island, NY 11953 Tel 516-924-3888 (SAN 208-7375).

Linn, Jo White, *(J W Linn; 0-918470),* Box 1948, Salisbury, NC 28144 Tel 704-633-3575 (SAN 209-9489).

Linnaea Graphics, Div. of Best Printing Co., *(Linnaea; 0-912467),* 3218 Manor Rd., P.O. Box 1548, Austin, TX 78767 Tel 512-477-9733 (SAN 265-2692).

Linscott, William D., *(W D Linscott; 0-9604920),* 40 Glen Dr., Mill Valley, CA 94941 Tel 415-681-3344 (SAN 214-4018).

Linstok Press, Inc., *(Linstok Pr; 0-932130),* 9306 Mintwood St., Silver Spring, MD 20901 Tel 301-585-1939 (SAN 207-6195).

Lintel, *(Lintel; 0-931642),* P.O. Box 8609,, Roanoke, VA 24014 (SAN 213-6325).

Linwood Pubs., *(Linwood Pub; 0-943512),* P.O. Box 70152, N. Charleston, SC 29405 Tel 803-873-2719 (SAN 240-7051).

Lion Books, *(Lion Bks; 0-87460),* Dist. by: Sayre Publishing, Inc., 111 E. 39th St., New York, NY 10016 Tel 212-661-2680 (SAN 201-0925).

Lion Enterprises, *(Lion Ent; 0-930962),* RR3 Box 127, Walkerton, IN 46574 Tel 219-369-9498 (SAN 211-3678).

Lionhead Publishing, *(Lionhead Pub; 0-89018),* 2521 East Stratford Court, Shorewood, Milwaukee, WI 53211 Tel 414-332-7474 (SAN 206-5568).

Lionheart Books, U.S.A., *(Lionheart; 0-949894),* Box 2820, Chula Vista, CA 92012 (SAN 277-6944).

Lion's Head Publishing Co., *(Lion's Head),* 4415 Karen Ave., Fort Wayne, IN 46815 (SAN 207-2564).

Liplop Press, *(Liplop; 0-936016),* P.O. Box 4520, Berkeley, CA 94704 Tel 415-428-0142 (SAN 281-885X); Dist. by: Bookpeople, 2940 Seventh St., Berkeley, CA 94710 Tel 415-549-3033 (SAN 168-9517); Dist. by: Publishers Group West, 5855 Beaudry St., Emeryville, CA 94608 Tel 415-658-6296 (SAN 202-8522).

Lippa, Erik A., *(EA Lippa; 0-9607980),* 1960 N. Lincoln Pk. W., Apt. 1504, Chicago, IL 60614 Tel 312-883-9465 (SAN 238-5481).

Lippincott, J. B., Co., *(Lippincott; 0-397),* E. Washington Square, Philadelphia, PA 19105 Tel 215-574-4200 (SAN 201-0933); Orders to: 2350 Virginia Ave., Hagerstown, MD 21740 (SAN 215-3742). *Imprints:* Harper Medical (Harper Medical); Lippincott Nursing (Lippincott Nursing).

Lippincott Junior Books See **Harper & Row Pubs., Inc.**

Lippincott Nursing See **Lippincott, J. B., Co.**

Liss, Alan R., Inc., *(A R Liss; 0-8451),* 150 Fifth Ave., New York, NY 10011 Tel 212-741-2515 (SAN 207-7558).

Literacy Council of Montgomery County Maryland, Inc., *(Lit Council Mont; 0-9609392),* 401 Fleet St., Rockville, MD 20850 Tel 301-762-6800 (SAN 260-096X).

Literary Herald Press, *(Literary Herald; 0-9602124),* 408 Oak St., Danville, IL 61832 (SAN 212-5242).

Literary Renewal Books, *(Lit Renewal; 0-940774),* P.O. Box 8639, San Marino, CA 91108 Tel 213-355-6683 (SAN 219-6778).

Literary Sketches, *(Literary Sketches; 0-915588),* P.O. Box 711, Williamsburg, VA 23187 Tel 804-229-2901 (SAN 205-6305).

Literati Press, Pubs., *(Literati Pr; 0-933744),* The Olive Bldg., 18 E. Sunrise Hwy., Freeport, NY 11520 (SAN 212-8586).

Literations, *(Literations; 0-943514),* P.O. Box 1845, Pittsfield, MA 01201 Tel 413-494-6325 (SAN 240-706X).

Literature of the Bible, Inc., *(Lit Bible; 0-932816),* 8265 Felch St., P.O. Box 138, Zeeland, MI 49464 Tel 616-772-4766 (SAN 212-8594).

Lithuanian Library Press, *(Lithuanian Lib; 0-932042),* 3001 W. 59th St., Chicago, IL 60629 Tel 312-778-6872 (SAN 213-8166).

Litmus, Inc., *(Litmus; 0-915214),* 350 S. Palouse, Walla Walla, WA 99362 (SAN 207-8619).

Litoral Arts Press, *(Litoral Arts Pr; 0-940612),* 1063 31st St., San Pedro, CA 90731 Tel 213-547-4526 (SAN 222-9854).

Little, Ruth, *(R Little; 0-9600062),* 3430 34th St., Lubbock, TX 79410 (SAN 204-6598).

Little Bayou Press, *(Little Bayou; 0-9609804),* 148 Central Ave., St. Petersburg, FL 33701 Tel 813-822-3270 (SAN 272-085X).

Little Books & Co., *(Little Bks Co; 0-9604656),* 5892 E. Jefferson Ave., Denver, CO 80237 (SAN 217-247X).

Little Brick House, The, *(Little Brick Hse; 0-9601648),* 621 Saint Clair St., Vandalia, IL 62471 Tel 618-283-0024 (SAN 209-2069).

Little, Brown & Co., *(Little; 0-316),* 34 Beacon St., Boston, MA 02106 Tel 617-227-0730 (SAN 281-8884); Orders to: 200 West St., Waltham, MA 02154 Tel 617-890-0250 (SAN 281-8892).

Little Cajun Books, *(Little Cajun; 0-931108),* 4182 Blecker Dr., Baton Rouge, LA 70809 Tel 504-925-0355 (SAN 212-5250).

Little Feat, *(Little Feat; 0-940112),* P.O. Box 150, Water Mill, NY 11976 Tel 516-726-9535 (SAN 217-0760).

Little Glass Shack, *(Little Glass; 0-911508),* 3161 56th St., Sacramento, CA 95820 Tel 916-455-8197 (SAN 201-0968).

Little Lady's Press, Inc., The, *(Little Lady's Pr; 0-941356),* P.O. Box 10, Park Ridge, IL 60068 (SAN 238-8928).

Little London Press, *(Little London; 0-936564),* 716 E. Washington, Colorado Springs, CO 80907 Tel 303-471-1322 (SAN 214-0489).

Little People Productions, *(Little People; 0-910219),* Kennedy Design Center, 111 S. Lincoln St., Warsaw, IN 46580 Tel 219-269-3823 (SAN 241-3930).

Little Red Hen, Inc., *(Little Red Hen; 0-933046),* P.O. Box 4260, Pocatello, ID 83201 Tel 208-212-7571).

Little Simon See **Simon & Schuster, Inc.**

Littlebee Press, *(Littlebee; 0-940674),* 791 Boulevard E., Weehawken, NJ 07087 Tel 201-867-2595 (SAN 239-4510).

Littlebird Pubns., *(Littlebird; 0-937896),* 126 Fifth Ave., New York, NY 10011 (SAN 215-7853).

Littlefield, Adams & Co., *(Littlefield; 0-8226),* 81 Adams Dr., Box 327, Totowa, NJ 07512 Tel 201-256-8600 (SAN 202-6791).

Littleman Press, *(Littleman; 0-9608264),* Box 7262, Seattle, WA 98133 (SAN 240-9534).

Litton Educational Publishing International See **Atlantic Pubs., Inc.**

Littoral Development Co., *(Littoral Develop; 0-914770),* 252 S. Van Pelt St., Philadelphia, PA 19103 Tel 215-546-3285 (SAN 202-2427).

Liturgical Conference, The, *(Liturgical Conf; 0-918208),* 806 Rhode Island Ave. N.E., Washington, DC 20018 Tel 202-529-7400 (SAN 205-6488).

Liturgical Press, *(Liturgical Pr; 0-8146),* St. John's Abbey, Collegeville, MN 56321 Tel 612-363-2213 (SAN 202-2494).

Live Free Inc., *(Live Free),* P.O. Box 743, Harvey, IL 60426 Tel 312-468-8805 (SAN 209-830X).

Live Oak Media, *(Live Oak Media; 0-941078),* P.O. Box 116, Somers, NY 10589 Tel 914-277-4454 (SAN 217-3921).

Live-Oak Press, *(Live-Oak Pr),* P.O. Box 99444, San Francisco, CA 94109 (SAN 214-4026).

Live Oak Pubns., *(Live Oak Pubns; 0-911781),* 6003 N. 51st St., P.O. Box 2193, Boulder, CO 80306 Tel 303-530-1087 (SAN 264-1798).

Lively Hills Publishing Corp., *(Lively Hills; 0-938194),* P.O. Box 1186, St. Charles, MO 63301 (SAN 216-1559).

Lively MInd Books, *(Lively Mind),* Box 3212, Chap Hill, NC 27514 Tel 919-929-2095 (SAN 283-2984).

Liveright Publishing Corp., Subs. of W. W. Norton Co., Inc., *(Liveright; 0-87140),* 500 Fifth Ave., New York, NY 10110 Tel 212-354-5500 (SAN 201-0976).

Living Flame Press, *(Living Flame Pr; 0-914544),* P.O. Box 74, Locust Valley, NY 11560 Tel 516-676-4265 (SAN 202-6805).

Living Hand, *(Living Hand),* Millis Rd., Box 252, Stanfordville, NY 12581 (SAN 207-2572).

Living Historical Museum, *(Living Histori; 0-933960),* 826 Goodrich Ave., St. Paul, MN 55105 (SAN 221-4199).

Living Love Pubns., *(Living Love; 0-9600688; 0-915972),* 790 Commercial Ave., Coos Bay, OR 97420 Tel 503-267-4232 (SAN 281-9082); Dist. by: DeVorss & Company, P.O. Box 550, Marina Del Rey, CA 90291 Tel 213-870-7478 (SAN 168-9886); Dist. by: Ingram Book Co., 347 Reedville Dr., Nashville, TN 37217 Tel 800-251-5900 (SAN 169-7978); Dist. by: Bookpeople, 2940 Seventh St., Berkeley, CA 94710 Tel 800-227-1516 (SAN 168-9517); Dist. by: Book Dynamics, 836 Broadway, New York, NY Tel 212-254-7798 (SAN 169-5649); Dist. by New Leaf Distributing Co., 1081 Memorial Dr. S.E., Atlanta, GA 30316 Tel 800-241-3829 (SAN 169-1449); Dist. by: Publishers Group West, 5855 Beaudry, Emeryville, CA 94608 Tel 415-658-3453 (SAN 202-8522).

Living Poets Press, *(Living Poets; 0-915726),* 139 7th Ave., Brooklyn, NY 11217 Tel 212-622-4900 (SAN 207-3854).

Living Skills Press, *(Living Skills; 0-941510),* 408 S. Live Oak Park Rd., Fallbrook, CA 92028 Tel 714-723-0188 (SAN 239-1082); Dist. by: Children Press, P.O. Box 3066, Oak Ridge, TN 37830 Tel 615-482-1075 (SAN 239-1090); Dist. by: Celestial Arts Pub Co., 231 Adrian Rd., Millbrae, CA 94030 Tel 415-692-4500 (SAN 201-9701).

Living Spring Pubns., *(Living Spring Pubns; 0-941598),* 790 Metro Dr., Monterey Park, CA 91754 Tel 213-572-9468 (SAN 239-1112).

Livingston Press, *(Livingston Pr; 0-915772),* 820 Hartford Rd., Waterford, CT 06385 Tel 203-442-3383 (SAN 207-6802); Orders to: Independent Pubs. Group, One Pleasant Ave., Port Washington, NY 11050 Tel 207-6810).

Livingston Publishing Co., *(Livingston; 0-87098; 0-915180),* 18 Hampstead Circle, Wynnewood, PA 19096 (SAN 202-6821); Orders to: Harrowood Books, 3943 N. Providence Rd., Newtown Sq., PA 19073 Tel 215-353-5585 (SAN 207-1622).

LLanerch Books, *(LLanerch Bks),* Box 711, Haverton, PA 19083 (SAN 208-4546).

Llewellyn Pubns., Div. of Chester-Kent, Inc., *(Llewellyn Pubns; 0-87542),* P.O. Box 43383, St. Paul, MN 55164 Tel 612-291-1970 (SAN 281-9147); Orders to: P.O. Box 43383, St. Paul, MN 55164 Tel 612-291-1970 (SAN 281-9155).

Lloyd, D. K., & M. Lipow, *(Lloyd & Lipow; 0-9601504),* 201 Calle Miramar, Redondo Beach, CA 90277 Tel 213-217-3848 (SAN 211-0318).

Lloyd, Joseph, Corp., *(J Lloyd Corp; 0-916490),* 2009 Thornwood, Wilmette, IL 60091 (SAN 281-9163).

LLoyd O'Enterprises/Publishers, *(Lloyd O'Ent Pubs; 0-9609886),* P.O. Box 6665, Woodland Hills, CA 91365 Tel 213-883-4058 (SAN 272-0957).

Locare Research Group, *(Locare; 0-913986),* 910 N. Fairfax Ave., Los Angeles, CA 90046 Tel 213-656-4420 (SAN 202-246X).

Lochinvar See **Exposition Press, Inc.**

Lockhart Press, The, *(Lockhart Pr; 0-911783),* Box 1207, Port Townsend, WA 98368 Tel 206-385-6413 (SAN 264-1801).

Locus-Book Division, Div. of T-Track Security Systems, *(LOCUS; 0-943812),* 4311 Atlantic Ave., Suite 200, Long Beach, CA 90807 Tel 213-426-2368 (SAN 238-3128).

Locust Enterprises, *(Locust Ent; 0-9606730),* W. 174 N. 9422, Devonwood Rd., Menomonee Falls, WI 53051 Tel 414-251-1415 (SAN 219-6786).

Lodestar Books, *(Lodestar Bks; 0-525),* 2 Park Ave., New York, NY 10016 Tel 212-725-1818 (SAN 212-5013).

Lodima Press, *(Lodima; 0-9605646),* Revere, PA 18953 Tel 215-847-2005 (SAN 216-1567).

Loewenthal Press, *(Loewenthal Pr; 0-914382),* P.O. Box 1107, New York, NY 10009 (SAN 206-5576).

Loft, Barnell, Ltd., *(B Loft; 0-87965),* 958 Church St., Baldwin, NY 11510 Tel 516-868-6064 (SAN 202-3679).

Log Boom Brewing, *(Log Boom; 0-9604130),* Box 1825, Boulder, CO 80306 (SAN 214-4034).

Logan County Heritage Foundation, *(Logan County; 0-9611816),* P.O. Box 396, Lincoln, IL 62656 Tel 217-732-8878 (SAN 285-0435); Lincoln Public Library, 725 Pekin St., Lincoln, IL 62656 (SAN 285-0443).

Logan Design Group, *(Logan Design; 0-9603856),* P. O. Box 997, N. Hollywood, CA 91603-0997 Tel 213-761-2319 (SAN 213-9359).

Logan Hill Press, *(Logan Hill; 0-918610),* 204 Fairmount Ave., Ithaca, NY 14850 Tel 607-273-0707 (SAN 207-5520).

Logbridge-Rhodes, Inc., *(Logbridge-Rhodes; 0-937406),* P.O. Box 3254, Durango, CO 81301 (SAN 215-0905).

Logical Solutions, Incorporated, *(Logical Sols; 0-912253),* 1799 S. Winchester Blvd., Suite 201, Campbell, CA 95008 Tel 408-374-3650 (SAN 265-1602).

Lohmann, Jeanne A., *(J A Lohmann),* 722 Tenth Ave., San Francisco, CA 94118 Tel 415-387-7644 (SAN 209-2204).

Loizeaux Brothers, Inc., *(Loizeaux; 0-87213),* 1238 Corlies Ave., Box 277, Neptune, NJ 07753 Tel 201-774-8144 (SAN 202-6848).

Lollipop Power, Inc., *(Lollipop Power; 0-914996),* P.O. Box 1171, Chapel Hill, NC 27514 Tel 919-929-4857 (SAN 206-9733).

Lomond Pubns., *(Lomond; 0-912338),* P.O. Box 88, Mt. Airy, MD 21771 Tel 301-829-1496 (SAN 206-765X).

Lond Pubns., *(Lond Pubns),* Pomona, NY 10970 (SAN 208-127X).

London Book Co, *(London Bk),* 212 N. Orange, Glendale, CA 91203 Tel 213-224-0828 (SAN 207-2580).

Lone Eagle Productions, Inc., *(Lone Eagle Prods; 0-943728),* 9903 Santa Monica Blvd., No. 204, Beverly Hills, CA 90212 Tel 213-277-9616 (SAN 241-032X).

Lone Oak Bks., *(Lone Oak; 0-936550),* 10,000 Old Georgetown Rd., Bethesda, MD 20814 Tel 301-656-3360 (SAN 216-1540).

Lone Raven Publishing Co., Inc., *(Lone Raven; 0-933914),* P.O. Box 1739, Anchorage, AK 99510 (SAN 213-5337).

Lone Star Pubs. Inc., *(Lone Star Pubs; 0-914872),* P.O. Box 9774, Austin, TX 78766 Tel 206-352-8622 (SAN 210-8283).

Long, Robert P., *(R P Long; 0-9600064),* 445 Glen Court, Cutchogue, NY 11935 Tel 516-734-5368 (SAN 204-661X); Dist. by: Hastings House Pubs., Inc., 10 E. 40th St., New York, NY 10016 Tel 212-689-5400 (SAN 213-9561).

Long Beach Island Press, *(Long Beach Isl Pr; 0-941418),* P.O. Box 151, Tempe, AZ 85281 Tel 602-968-3414 (SAN 239-006X).

Long Beach Pubns., *(Long Beach Pubns; 0-941910),* P.O. Box 14807, Long Beach, CA 90803 Tel 213-439-8962 (SAN 239-782X).

Long Haul Press, *(Long Haul; 0-9602284),* P.O. Box 592, Van Brunt Sta., Brooklyn, NY 11215 Tel 212-965-3639 (SAN 212-5986).

Long House, Inc., *(Long Hse; 0-912806),* P.O. Box 3, New Canaan, CT 06840 Tel 203-966-3808 (SAN 201-4947).

Long Island Univ. Press, *(LIU Univ; 0-913252),* University Plaza, Brooklyn, NY 11201 Tel 212-834-6064 (SAN 211-688X).

Long Life Center, *(Long Life Ctr; 0-913613),* 3010 Santa Monica Blvd., Suite 239, Santa Monica, CA 90404 Tel 213-396-0976 (SAN 285-3353).

Longanecker Books, *(Longanecker; 0-9601126),* P.O. Box 127, Brewster, WA 98812 Tel 509-689-2441 (SAN 210-2323).

Longfellow National Historic Site, Div. of Nat'l Pk Service, *(Longfellow; 0-9610844),* 105 Brattle St., Cambridge, MA 02138 Tel 617-876-4491 (SAN 265-2706).

Longhorn Pr., *(Longhorn Pr; 0-914208),* Box 150, Cisco, TX 76437 (SAN 206-6920) Tel 817-442-2530.

Longleaf Pubns., *(Longleaf Pubns),* P.O. Box 4282, Tallahassee, FL 32315 Tel 904-385-0383 (SAN 216-4094).

Longman Inc., *(Longman),* 1560 Broadway, New York, NY 10036 Tel 212-764-3950 (SAN 202-6856).

Longone, Jan, *(J Longone),* 1207 W. Madison, Ann Arbor, MI 48103 (SAN 238-8405).

LongRiver Bks., *(LongRiver Bks; 0-942986),* c/o Inland Bk. Co., 22 Hemingway Ave., East Haven, CT 06512 Tel 203-467-4257 (SAN 240-3986).

Longshanks Bk., *(Longshanks Bk; 0-9601000),* 30 Church St., Mystic, CT 06355 Tel 203-536-8656 (SAN 208-7391).

Longship Press, *(Longship Pr; 0-917712),* Crooked Lane, Nantucket, MA 02554 Tel 207-722-3344 (SAN 209-4576); Orders to: RFD 1, Box 124, Brooks, ME 04921 (SAN 209-4584).

Longwood Publishing Group, In c., *(Longwood Pr; 0-89341),* 51 Washington St., Dover, NH 03820 Tel 603-742-4662 (SAN 209-3170).

Lonstein Pubns., *(Lonstein Pubns),* 1 Terrace Hill, Box 351, Ellenville, NY 12428 (SAN 215-0913).

Loo, C. & R., Inc., *(C & R Loo),* 1550 62nd St., P.O. Box 8397, Emeryville, CA 94662 (SAN 211-366X).

Looking Glass Pubns., *(Looking Glass; 0-937646),* P.O. Box 3604, Quincy, IL 62305 (SAN 238-8936).

Loompanics Unlimited, *(Loompanics),* P.O. Box 1197, Port Townsend, WA 98368 Tel 206-385-5087 (SAN 206-4421).

LoonBooks, *(LoonBooks),* P.O. Box 901, Northeast Harbor, ME 04662 (SAN 219-2098).

Lopez, Eddie, *(E Lopez; 0-9606120),* 615 S. 20th, Donna, TX 78537 Tel 512-464-2658 (SAN 216-8316).

Lord, William H., *(W H Lord),* 9210 N. College Ave., Indianapolis, IN 46240 Tel 317-846-3907 (SAN 214-0497).

Lord Americana & Research, Inc., *(Lord Americana; 0-916492),* 1521 Redwood Dr., W. Columbia, SC 29169 Tel 803-794-7104 (SAN 207-5261).

Lord John Press, *(Lord John; 0-935716),* 19073 Los Alimos St., Northridge, CA 91326 Tel 213-363-6621 (SAN 213-6333).

Lord Publishing, *(Lord Pub; 0-930204),* 46 Glen St., Dover, MA 02030 Tel 617-785-1575 (SAN 210-5403).

Lord's Line, *(Lords Line; 0-915952),* 1734 Armour Lane, Redondo Beach, CA 90278 Tel 213-542-5575 (SAN 207-7086).

Lore Unlimited, Inc., *(Lore Unlim; 0-941838),* 4850 Regents Park Lane, Fremont, CA 94538 Tel 415-657-6331 (SAN 239-2534).

Lorenz & Herweg Pubs., *(Lorenz & Herweg; 0-916494),* P.O. Box 7764, Long Beach, CA 90807 Tel 213-422-0059 (SAN 208-7405).

Lorenz Press, Inc., Div. of Lorenz Industries, Subs. of Internat'l Entertainment Corp., *(Lorenz Pr; 0-89328),* 501 E. Third St., Dayton, OH 45401 Tel 513-228-6118 (SAN 208-7413); Dist. by: Independent Publishers Group, 14 Vanderventer Ave., Port Washington, NY 11050 (SAN 208-7421).

Lorenzen, Violet, *(V A Lorenzen; 0-9602174),* 606 S. Mentor Ave., Pasadena, CA 91106 (SAN 221-7961).

Lorian Press, *(Lorian Pr; 0-936878),* P.O. Box 147, Middleton, WI 53562 (SAN 214-4042).

Lorien House, *(Lorien Hse; 0-934852),* P.O. Box 1112, Black Mountain, NC 28711 Tel 704-669-6211 (SAN 209-2999).

Loru Co, The, *(Loru Co; 0-915710),* P.O. Box 396, North Webster, IN 46555 (SAN 220-7923).

Los Alamos Historical Society, *(Los Alamos Hist Soc; 0-941232),* P.O. Box 43, Los Alamos, NM 87544 (SAN 276-9603); Dist. by: University of Mexico Press, Albuquerque, NM 87131 (SAN 213-9588).

Los Angeles County Museum of Art, *(LA Co Art Mus; 0-87587),* 5905 Wilshire Blvd., Los Angeles, CA 90036 Tel 213-857-6043 (SAN 201-0577).

Los Arboles, *(Los Arboles Pub; 0-941992),* 820 Calle De Arboles, Redondo Beach, CA 90277 (SAN 238-020X).

Los Ninos International Adoption & Information Center, *(Los Ninos; 0-935366),* 1106 Randam Circle, Austin, TX 78745 Tel 512-443-2833 (SAN 211-9129).

Lost Data Press, *(Lost Data; 0-937468),* 4410C Burnett Rd., Austin, TX 78756 (SAN 281-935X); Orders to: Weare News Co., Baker Hill Rd., Sutton, NH 03221 (SAN 281-9368); Orders to: The Distributors, 702 S. Michigan, South Bend, IN 46618 (SAN 212-0364); Orders to: Whole Earth Bookstore, Fort Mason Center, Bldg. D, San Francisco, CA 94123 (SAN 281-9384); Orders to: Back to Basics Books, The Mother Earth News, 105 Stony Mountain Rd., Hendersonville, NC 28739 (SAN 281-9392); Orders to: Lindsay Publications, 152 W. Baker St., Mantieno, IL 60950 (SAN 281-9406).

Lost Pleiade Press, *(Lost Pleiade; 0-915270),* P.O. Box 587, Lake Oswego, OR 97034 Tel 503-288-0400 (SAN 207-3358).

Lost Roads Pubs., *(Lost Roads; 0-918786),* P.O. Box 5848, Weybosset Hill Sta., Providence, RI 02903 (SAN 281-9511); Dist. by: Before Columbus, 1446-D Sixth St., Berkeley, CA 94710 (SAN 219-4651); Dist. by: St. Luke's Pr., Mid-Memphis Tower, Suite 401, 1407 Union Ave., Memphis, TN 38104 (SAN 210-0029); Dist. by: Spring Church Bk. Co., P.O. Box 127, Spring Church, PA 15686 (SAN 212-7075); Dist. by: Bookslinger, 2163 Ford Pkwy., St. Paul, MN 55116 Tel 612-690-0293 (SAN 169-4154).

Lothrop, Lee & Shepard Books, Div. of William Morrow & Co., Inc., *(Lothrop; 0-688),* 105 Madison Ave., New York, NY 10016 Tel 212-889-3050 (SAN 201-1034); Orders to: William Morrow & Co., Inc., Wilmor Warehouse, 6 Henderson Dr., West Caldwell, NJ 07006 (SAN 202-5779).

Lotsawa, Inc., *(Lotsawa; 0-932156),* 140 E. 92nd St., New York, NY 10028 Tel 212-534-3384 (SAN 213-893X); Dist. by: Book Dynamics, 836 Broadway, New York, NY 10003 (SAN 169-5649); Dist. by: Bookpeople, 2940 Seventh St., Berkeley, CA 94710 Tel 415-549-3030 (SAN 213-8956); Dist. by: De Vorss & Co., P.O. Box 550, Marina del Rey, CA 90291 Tel 213-870-7478 (SAN 168-9886).

Lotus Light Pubns., *(Lotus Light; 0-941524),* P.O. Box 2, Wilmot, WI 53192 Tel 414-862-6968 (SAN 239-1120).

Lotus Press, Inc., *(Lotus; 0-916418),* P.O. Box 21607, Detroit, MI 48221 Tel 313-861-1280 (SAN 213-8867).

Louis, R., Publishing, *(R Louis Pub; 0-9605410),* 940 Poplar Ave., Boulder, CO 80302 Tel 303-444-6030 (SAN 238-7409).

Louis Foundation, *(Louis Found; 0-9605492),* Box 210, Eastsound, WA 98245 Tel 206-376-2259 (SAN 216-1575).

Louisiana State Univ., Paul M. Hebert Law Center Pubns. Institute, *(LSU Paul M Hebert Law Cen Pub Inst; 0-940448),* LSU Law Ctr., Rm 310, Baton Rouge, LA 70803 (SAN 217-1953).

Louisiana State Univ. Press, *(La State U Pr; 0-8071),* Baton Rouge, LA 70893 Tel 504-388-6666 (SAN 202-6597).

Louisville & Jefferson County Heritage Corporation, *(Louisville & Jefferson; 0-9603278),* 300 W. Liberty St., Louisville, KY 40202 Tel 502-582-2421 (SAN 213-3350).

Louvin Publishing Co., *(Louvin Pub; 0-914471),* Box 5181, Poughkeepsie, NY 12602 (SAN 217-2496).

Love, *(Love; 0-9608692),* Box 9, Prospect Hill, NC 27314 Tel 919-562-3380 (SAN 238-3136).

Lovett School, The (The Lovett Mothers Club), *(Lovett Sch; 0-9610846),* 4075 Paces Ferry Rd., Atlanta, GA 30327 (SAN 265-2714).

Loving Pubs., *(Loving Pubs; 0-938134),* 4576 Alla Rd., Los Angeles, CA 90066 (SAN 215-6768).

Low, Jennie, *(J Low; 0-9602820),* Dist. by: Altarinda Bks., 13 Estates Dr., Orinda, CA 94563 (SAN 238-1397).

Low-Tech Press, *(Low-Tech; 0-9605626),* 30-73 47th St., Long Island City, NY 11103 Tel 212-721-0946 (SAN 216-1583).

Lowe, George L., *(G L Lowe),* 401 E. 32nd St., Chicago, IL 60616 (SAN 217-1155).

Lowe, Joseph D., Publisher, *(Lowe Pub; 0-9605506),* 2518 Clement St. Apt. 6, San Fransico, CA 94121 Tel 415-221-1070 (SAN 240-0227).

Lowe, Thomas E., Ltd., *(T E Lowe; 0-913926),* 2 Penn Plaza, Suite 1500, New York, NY 10001 Tel 212-222-1869 (SAN 206-5592).

Lowell & Lynwood, Ltd., *(Lowell & Lynwood; 0-8484),* 958 Church St., Baldwin, NY 11510 (SAN 208-8430).

Lowell Conference on Industrial History, The, *(Lowell Conf Ind Hist; 0-9607478),* 204 Middle St., Lowell, MA 01852 Tel 617-458-7653 (SAN 238-468X).

Lowell Museum Corporation, *(Lowell Museum; 0-942472),* P.O. Box 8415, Lowell, MA 01853 Tel 617-459-6782 (SAN 239-9423).

Lowell Press, *(Lowell Pr; 0-913504),* 115 E. 31st St., Box 1877, Kansas City, MO 64141 Tel 816-753-4545 (SAN 207-0774).

Lowell Publishing Co., Inc., *(Lowell Pub; 0-943730),* P.O. Box 8515, Lowell, MA 01853 (SAN 241-0338).

Lower Cape Publishing, *(Lower Cape; 0-936972),* P.O. Box 901, Orleans, MA 02653 Tel 617-255-2244 (SAN 214-4050).

Lowry & Volz Pubs., *(Lowry & Volz; 0-9601740),* 2163 Greenspring Dr., Timonium, MD 21093 (SAN 211-6219).

Lowry Hill, *(Lowry Hill; 0-9606416),* 1770 Hennepin Ave., No 42, Minneapolis, MN 55403 Tel 612-374-1579 (SAN 223-0062).

Lowy Publishing, *(Lowy Pub; 0-9602940),* 5047 Wigton, Houston, TX 77096 Tel 713-723-3209 (SAN 212-9132).

Loyola University of Chicago, Center fora Urban Policy, *(Loyola U Ctr Urban; 0-911531),* 820 N. Michigan Ave., Chicago, IL 60611 Tel 312-670-3112 (SAN 214-1836).

Loyola Univ. Press, *(Loyola; 0-8294),* 3441 N. Ashland Ave., Chicago, IL 60657 Tel 312-281-1818 (SAN 211-6537).

Lu, J. L., M.D., *(J L Lu; 0-9601768),* P.O. Box 4276, Sta. A., Dallas, TX 75208 (SAN 211-9137).

Lubavitch Women's Organization Jr. Division, *(Lubavitch Women; 0-930178),* 770 Eastern Pkwy., Brooklyn, NY 11213 Tel 212-771-6033 (SAN 210-6345).

Lubrecht & Cramer, *(Lubrecht & Cramer),* RFD 1, Box 227, Monticello, NY 12701 Tel 914-794-8539 (SAN 214-1256).

Lucas, Elizabeth H., *(E H Lucas),* 518 Monrovia Avenue, Long Beach, CA 90814 (SAN 272-1228).

Lucas Brothers Pubs., *(Lucas; 0-87543),* 909 Lowry St., Missouri Store Bldg., Columbia, MO 65201 Tel 314-442-6161 (SAN 201-1050).

Lucas Pubs., *(Lucas Pubs CA; 0-9604806),* 58 Arden Way, P.O. Box 15224, Sacramento, CA 95813 (SAN 215-6776).

Luce, Robert B., Inc., *(Luce; 0-88331),* 425 Asylum St., Bridgeport, CT 06610 Tel 203-334-2165 (SAN 201-1069); Orders to: 540 Barnum Ave., Bridgeport, CT 06608 Tel 203-366-1900 (SAN 201-1077).

Lucis Publishing Co., *(Lucis; 0-85330),* 866 United Nations Plaza, Suite 566-7, New York, NY 10017 Tel 212-421-1577 (SAN 201-1085).

Lucky Literature, *(Lucky Lit; 0-9611860),* P.O. Box 21043, Woodhaven, NY 11421 Tel 212-296-5252 (SAN 286-1402).

Lucky Pubns., *(Lucky Pubns; 0-932342),* P.O. Box 19307, Las Vegas, NV 89119 Tel 702-564-3895 (SAN 211-741X) Moved, Left No Forwarding Address.

Ludlow, Norman H., *(N H Ludlow; 0-916706),* 516 Arnett Blvd., Rochester, NY 14619 Tel 716-235-0951 (SAN 207-5776).

Luebbers, David J., *(D Luebbers),* 78 S. Jackson, Denver, CO 80209 Tel 303-388-8534 (SAN 209-5777).

Luff, Moe, *(M Luff; 0-9600162),* 12 Greene Rd., Spring Valley, NY 10977 Tel 914-356-4855 (SAN 205-2466).

Lukas & Sons Pubs., *(Lukas & Sons; 0-930994),* 4179 Fairmount Ave., San Diego, CA 92105 (SAN 211-2507).

Lukman, Mphahlele, *(M Lukman; 0-9602660),* 9110 Avenue "A", Brooklyn, NY 11236 (SAN 214-1922).

Lumeli Press, *(Lumeli Pr; 0-930592),* P.O. Box 909, San Carlos, CA 94070 Tel 415-593-7181 (SAN 211-0326).

Lumen Christi Press, *(Lumen Christi; 0-912414),* P.O. Box 13176, Houston, TX 77019 Tel 713-827-0181 (SAN 201-1093).

Lumen Series, *(Lumen Series; 0-9611722),* 224 Washington St., Brighton, MA 02135 Tel 617-254-9073 (SAN 285-3183).

Luna Bisonte Prods., *(Luna Bisonte; 0-935350),* 137 Leland Ave., Columbus, OH 43214 Tel 614-846-4126 (SAN 209-8326).

Luna Pubns., *(Luna Pubns; 0-930346),* 655 Orchard St., Oradell, NJ 07649 (SAN 212-288X).

Lunan-Ferguson Library, Pubs., *(Lunan-Ferguson; 0-911724),* 2219 Clement St., San Francisco, CA 94121 Tel 415-752-6100 (SAN 203-4042).

Lunar & Planetary Institute, *(Lunar & Planet Inst; 0-942862),* 3303 Nasa Rd. One, Houston, TX 77058 Tel 713-486-2161 (SAN 238-0730).

Lunchroom Press, The, *(Lunchroom Pr; 0-938136),* Box 36027, Grosse Pointe Farms, MI 48236 (SAN 215-6784).

Lurie, Hannah Ross, *(H R Lurie; 0-9600728),* 23 Derwen Rd., Bala Cynwyd, PA 19004 Tel 215-667-1350 (SAN 201-6079).

Lust, Benedict, Pubns., *(Lust; 0-87904),* 25 Dewart Rd., Greenwich, CT 06830 Tel 203-661-0980 (SAN 201-1107); Orders to: P.O. Box 404, New York, NY 10156 (SAN 201-1115).

Lustrum Pr., *(Lustrum Pr; 0-912810),* 714 Broadway, New York, NY 10003 (SAN 281-9562); Dist. by: Van Nostrand Reinhold Co., 135 W. 50th St., New York, NY 10020 Tel 212-265-8700 (SAN 202-5183).

Lutheran Academy for Scholarship, *(Luth Acad; 0-913160),* (SAN 206-8184); c/o Richard Jungkuntz, 6310 Hillcrest Dr., S.W., Tacoma, WN 98499 (SAN 285-0451).

Lutheran Council in the U.S.A., Div. of Campus Ministry & Educations Services, *(Luth Coun IL; 0-9609438),* 35 E. Wacker Dr., Suite 1847, Chicago, IL 60601 Tel 312-726-3791 (SAN 272-135X).

LYCO Publishing, *(LYCO Pub; 0-918464),* 3636 Drummond, Houston, TX 77025 Tel 713-668-0194 (SAN 240-9631).

Lydette Publishing Co., *(Lydette; 0-910918),* P.O. Box 654, Cedar Falls, IA 50613 (SAN 203-9400).

Lydian Press, *(Lydian Pr),* P.O. Box 991, Kaneohe, HI 96744 (SAN 212-8365); Dist. by: Press Pacifica, P.O. Box 1227, Kailua, HI 96734 (SAN 169-1635).

Lynch, Marietta & Perry, Patricia, *(M Lynch; 0-9610962),* 240 Atlantic Rd., Gloucester, MA 01930 Tel 617-283-6322 (SAN 265-2722).

Lynch Group Publishing, *(Lynch Group Pub; 0-911671),* P.O. Box 18012, Cleveland, OH 44118 (SAN 264-1852).

Lyndon B. Johnson School of Public Affairs, *(LBJ Sch Pub Aff),* The Univ. of Texas at Austin, Drawer DY, University Sta., Austin, TX 78712 Tel 512-471-5713 (SAN 223-0410).

Lynell Marketing, Inc., *(Lynell Mkting),* 1432 County Line Rd., Huntingdon Valley, PA 19006 (SAN 238-4353).

Lynn, Robinson, Pub., *(Rob Lynn Pub),* 100 Walnut Place, Brookline, MA 02186 (SAN 287-2722).

Lynx House Press, *(Lynx Hse; 0-89924),* P.O. Box 800, Amherst, MA 01002 Tel 413-773-7988 (SAN 208-2691).

Lyons, David, *(D Lyons),* General Delivery, Merrimack, NH 03054 (SAN 212-9515); Orders to: 16 Hampshire Dr., Room C, Nashua, NH 03060 (SAN 212-9523) Moved, Left No Forwarding Address.

Lyons, Emily Bradley, *(E B Lyons; 0-9604374),* 22175 Shoreline Dr., Marshall, CA 94940 (SAN 214-4069).

Lyons/Nick, Book, *(N Lyons Bks),* 212 Fifth Ave., New York, NY 10010 (SAN 264-1860).

Lytton Publishing Co., *(Lytton Pub; 0-915728),* Drawer "G", College Station, TX 77841 Tel 409-845-2246 (SAN 207-4257).

M.A.D. House, *(MAD Hse; 0-9606732),* P.O. Box 1716, Sanford, FL 32771 Tel 305-323-5159 (SAN 219-6794).

M/A Press, *(M-A Pr; 0-930206),* 8285 S.W. Nimbus, Suite 151, Beaverton, OR 97005 Tel 503-646-2713 (SAN 210-6353); Orders to: P.O. Box 606, Beaverton, OR 97075 (SAN 210-6361).

MARC, Missions Advanced Research & Communication Center, *(MARC; 0-912552),* 919 W. Huntington Dr., Monrovia, CA 91016 Tel 213-357-7979 (SAN 203-9656).

MARKCO, *(MARKCO; 0-9606158),* 203 E. 10th St., Julesburg, CO 80737 (SAN 218-4907).

M & B Publishing Co., *(M & B; 0-930496),* 1 Emerald St., Norwalk, CT 06850 Tel 202-846-4294 (SAN 212-1905).

M & R Pubns., *(M and R Pubns; 0-9607424),* P.O. Box 2056, Turlock, CA 95381 Tel 209-892-6282 (SAN 239-7838).

M&S Enterprises, *(M & S Ent; 0-943732),* Box 42978, Tucson, AZ 85733 Tel 602-746-7154 (SAN 241-0346).

M & S Press, *(M&S Pr; 0-87730),* Box 311, Weston, MA 02193 Tel 617-891-5650 (SAN 203-9591).

MBO, Inc., *(MBO Inc; 0-9602950),* 157 Pontoosic Rd., P.O. Box 10, Westfield, MA 01085 (SAN 213-4136).

MCA, *(MCA),* P.O. Box 1775, Quantico, VA 22134 (SAN 218-4923).

MCL Associates, *(MCL Assocs; 0-930696),* 6916 Rosemont Drive., P.O. Box 26, McLean, VA 22101 Tel 703-356-5979 (SAN 281-9589); Orders to: MCL Associates, P.O. Box 26, McLean, VA 22101 Tel 703-356-5979 (SAN 281-9597).

MCP Books, *(MCP Bks; 0-9603926),* P.O. Box 273, Germantown, MD 20874 (SAN 241-1930).

M C Productions, *(MC Prods; 0-9609862),* P.O. Box 2402, Saugatuck Sta., Westport, CT 06880 (SAN 264-1879).

M-C Pubns., *(M-C Pubns; 0-9603850),* 449 N. Lamer St., Burbank, CA 91506 (SAN 214-0500).

MCS, *(MCS; 0-932150),* Box 1774, Morganton, NC 28655 (SAN 239-4529).

MDK, Inc., *(MDK Inc; 0-934580),* P.O. Box 2831, Chapel Hill, NC 27514 Tel 919-929-4260 (SAN 213-6341).

MD Pubns., *(MD Pubns; 0-910922),* 30 E. 60th St., New York, NY 10022 (SAN 206-7668).

MEDA Pubns., *(MEDA Pubns; 0-9610200),* 107 Elena Drive, Scotts Valley, CA 95066 (SAN 264-1887).

M. E. D. S. Corp., *(MEDS Corp; 0-916420),* 97-99 Stuyvesant Ave., Newark, NJ 07106 Tel 201-899-7856 (SAN 207-7094).

MEP Pubns., *(MEP Pubns; 0-930656),* Univ. of Minnesota, Anthropology Dept., 215 Ford Hall, 224 Church St. SE, Minneapolis, MN 55455 Tel 612-922-7993 (SAN 276-9727).

META Pubns., *(META Pubns; 0-916990),* P.O. Box 565, Cupertino, CA 95015 Tel 415-326-6465 (SAN 208-7448).

M. G. Bookgraphics, *(M G Book Graphics; 0-933484),* Los Angeles, CA 90033 (SAN 281-9600); Dist. by: Alfred Publishing Co., Inc., 15335 Morrison, Sherman Oaks, CA 91403 (SAN 201-243X).

M G L S Publishing, *(M G L S Pub; 0-9601682),* 700 S. First St., Marshall, MN 56258 Tel 507-532-3553 (SAN 212-2170).

MGT Information Publishing, *(MGT Info; 0-9610848),* Box 3732, Arcadia, CA 91006 Tel 714-594-5611 (SAN 265-2730).

MINMOR Publishing Co., *(MINMOR; 0-918976),* 14 Germain St., Worcester, MA 01602 Tel 617-757-8463 (SAN 210-4652).

MIR, *(MIR PA; 0-935352),* 845 Suismon Dr., Pittsburgh, PA 15212 Tel 412-322-1319 (SAN 213-5825); Orders to: P.O. Box 962, Pittsburgh, PA 15230 (SAN 213-5833).

MIT Outing Club, *(MIT Outing; 0-9601698),* W20-461, MIT, Cambridge, MA 02139 Tel 617-253-2988 (SAN 210-8291).

MIT Press, *(MIT Pr; 0-262),* 28 Carleton St., Cambridge, MA 02142 Tel 617-253-2884 (SAN 202-6414).

MJB Books, *(MJB Bks; 0-9609680),* P.O. Box 3246, Merced, CA 95344 Tel 209-384-0322 (SAN 272-4731).

MJB Pub., *(MJB Pub; 0-9605990),* 7209 Skyway, No. 13, Paradise, CA 95969 (SAN 216-7468).

MJG Co., *(MJG Co; 0-932632),* P.O. Box 7743, Midland, TX 79708-0743 Tel 915-682-3184 (SAN 212-2901).

MJK Enterprises, *(MJK Ent; 0-9610996),* P.O. Box 5571, San Antonio, TX 78201 Tel 512-344-4348 (SAN 265-2749).

MJ Pubns., *(MJ Pubns; 0-9605144),* 6363 Lynwood Hill Rd., McLean, VA 22101 (SAN 215-790X).

MLB Pub., *(MLB Pub; 0-941794),* P.O. Box 1732, Chesapeake, VA 23320 Tel 804-424-5238 (SAN 239-2542).

MLM Pubs., *(MLM Pubs; 0-939102),* 515 S. We-Go Trail, Suite 139, Mt. Prospect, IL 60056 Tel 312-392-7145 (SAN 216-1613).

MLP Enterprises, *(MLP Ent; 0-939020),* 236 E. Durham St., Philadelphia, PA 19119 Tel 215-248-3218 (SAN 214-4077).

M-L Publishing Co., Ltd., *(M-L Pub; 0-915512),* 157 Devonshire Rd., Wilmington, DE 19803 Tel 302-655-2849 (SAN 207-1746).

MNP Star Enterprises, *(MNP Star; 0-938880),* P.O. Box 8267, S.F. International Airport, San Francisco, CA 94128 (SAN 215-9708).

M. N. Pubs., *(MN Pubs; 0-932964),* Rte. 2, Box 55, Bonnerdale, AR 71933 Tel 501-991-3815 (SAN 212-291X) Temporarily out of business.

M.O.P. Press, *(M O P Pr; 0-942432),* Rte. 24, Box 53C, Fort Myers, FL 33908 (SAN 223-0860).

MRDC Educational Institute, *(MRDC Educ Inst),* P.O. Box 15127, Dallas, TX 75201 (SAN 214-4085).

M-R-K Publishing, *(M R K; 0-9601292),* 448 Seavey Lane, Petaluma, CA 94952 Tel 707-763-0056 (SAN 210-461X).

MTI Teleprograms Inc., *(MTI Tele; 0-916070),* 3710 Commercial Ave., Northbrook, IL 60062 Tel 312-291-9400 (SAN 211-0350).

M/T/M Publishing Co., *(MTM Pub Co),* P.O. Box 245, Washougal, WA 98671 (SAN 206-1627).

MUMPS Users' Group, *(MUMPS; 0-918118),* c/o The Mitre Corp., 4321 Hartwich Rd., Rm. 308, College Park, MD 20740 Tel 301-779-6555 (SAN 207-6993).

MWS Pubns, *(MWS Pubns; 0-939640),* 2241/2 Ridgewood Ave., San Francisco, CA 94127 Tel 415-585-8604 (SAN 216-6340).

Maat Publishing Co., *(Maat Pub; 0-917650),* P.O. Box 281, Bronx, NY 10462 (SAN 209-2239).

Mac Publishing, Inc., *(MAC Pub Inc; 0-936206),* P.O. Box 7037, Colorado Springs, CO 80933 (SAN 221-4148).

Macalester College, *(Mac Col MN; 0-9606844),* Weyerhaeuser Library, St. Paul, MN 55105 Tel 612-696-6346 (SAN 213-2567).

NAME INDEX

Macalester Park Publishing Co., *(Macalester; 0-910924),* 1571 Grand Ave., St. Paul, MN 55105 Tel 612-698-8877 (SAN 203-9451).

McAllister Bks., *(McAllister; 0-910930),* 410 Lake Ct., Waukegan, IL 60085 Tel 312-662-1929 (SAN 203-946X).

MacArthur Memorial, *(MacArthur Memorial; 0-9606418),* MacArthur Square, Norfolk, VA 23510 Tel 804-441-2965 (SAN 215-8876).

McBee Sports Enterprises, Inc., *(McBee Sports; 0-9609500),* P.O. Box 79, Elon College, NC 27244-0079 (SAN 264-1895).

McBogg, Bruce, *(B McBogg; 0-941400),* 3405 Alcott St., Denver, CO 80211 (SAN 237-9848).

McBooks Press, *(McBooks Pr; 0-935526),* 106 N. Aurora, Ithaca, NY 14850 Tel 607-272-6602 (SAN 213-8573) (SAN 202-2060).

McCabe, Donald L., *(McCabe; 0-9605856),* 3221 Greenwood Ave., Sacramento, CA 95821 Tel 916-334-4810 (SAN 216-6054).

Maccabee Publishing Co., Inc., *(Maccabee Pub; 0-942500),* 14 W. Forest Ave., Englewood, NJ 07631 Tel 201-569-8700 (SAN 226-207X).

McCafferty, Jane R., *(McCafferty; 0-9606920),* 613 Rosier Rd., Fort Washington, MD 20744 Tel 301-839-5812 (SAN 217-4022).

McCahan Foundation, *(McCahan Found; 0-937094),* 270 Bryn Mawr Ave., Bryn Mawr, PA 19010 Tel 215-896-4548 (SAN 215-0921).

McCain, John & Maureen, *(McCain; 0-9607050),* 905 Leatzow Rd., Three Lakes, WI 54562 (SAN 238-8952).

McCain Publishing, *(McCain Pub; 0-9608314),* P.O. Box 63, Fort Recovery, OH 45846 Tel 419-375-4226 (SAN 240-5490).

McCalden, David, *(D McCalden; 0-910607),* P.O. Box 3849, Manhattan Beach, CA 90266 Tel 213-546-3689 (SAN 264-1909).

McCartan & Root, Pubs., *(McCartan & Root; 0-935786),* 325 E. 57th St., New York, NY 10022 Tel 212-421-2641 (SAN 214-2546).

McClain Printing Co., *(McClain; 0-87012),* 212 Main St., Parsons, WV 26287 Tel 304-478-2881 (SAN 203-9478).

McClelland & Stewart, Ltd., *(McClelland),* 25 Hollinger Rd., Toronto, Ontario, M4B 3G2, Tel 416-751-4520.

McClure Press/McClure Printing Co., Inc., *(McClure Printing),* P.O. Box 936, Verona, VA 24482 Tel 703-885-0884 (SAN 205-8065).

McConnell, R.A., *(R A McConnell),* 430 Kennedy Ave., Pittsburgh, PA 15214 (SAN 272-1600).

McCormick, D. C., *(D C McCormick),* 1 Isabel St., Massena, NY 13662 (SAN 206-7013).

McCutchan Publishing Corp., *(McCutchan; 0-8211),* P.O. Box 774A, 2526 Grove St., Berkeley, CA 94701 (SAN 415-841-8616) (SAN 203-9486).

McDaniel House Publishing, *(McDaniel House; 0-943650),* P.O. Box 13265, Portland, OR 97213 Tel 503-287-7378 (SAN 238-3152).

McDonald, Paul R., *(McDonald P R; 0-9611258),* 1417 Starview Dr., Cedar Falls, IA 50613 Tel 319-277-6075 (SAN 283-3425).

McDonnell Douglas Automation Co., *(McDonnell Douglas),* Bx 516, St. Louis, MO 63166 (SAN 241-5585).

McDougal, Littell & Co., *(McDougal-Littell; 0-88343),* P.O. Box 1667, Evanston, IL 60204 Tel 312-967-0900 (SAN 202-2532).

McDowell, L. Jerry, *(L J McDowell; 0-9611818),* 6408 Dixon Dr., Raleigh, NC 27609 Tel 919-782-9568 (SAN 286-1496).

Macduff Press, *(Macduff Pr; 0-9606272),* 110 Sutter St., Rm. 1015, San Francisco, CA 94104 Tel 415-981-0970 (SAN 220-3405).

McElderry Book *See* **Atheneum Pubs.**

McFarland & Co., Inc., *(McFarland & Co; 0-89950),* Box 611, Jefferson, NC 28640 Tel 919-246-4460 (SAN 215-093X).

McGill Pubns., *(McGill Pubns),* 163 Ironia Rd., Flanders, NJ 07836 Tel 201-927-0993 (SAN 241-5593).

McGill-Queens Univ. Press, *(McGill-Queens U Pr; 0-7735),* Orders to: University of Toronto Press, 33 E. Tupper St., Buffalo, NY 14203 Tel 416-667-7791 (SAN 214-2651).

McGilvery, Laurence, *(McGilvery; 0-910938),* P.O. Box 852, La Jolla, CA 92037 Tel 714-454-4443 (SAN 203-9494).

McGinnis & Marx, Music Pubs., *(McGinnis & Marx),* Box 229, Planetarium Sta., New York, NY 10024 Tel 212-799-5214 (SAN 281-9627); Dist. by: Pietro Deiro Music Headquarters, 123 Greenwich Ave., New York, NY 10014 Tel 212-675-5460 (SAN 282-5880).

McGlynn, June A., *(McGlynn; 0-9601350),* 1529 Meadowlark Dr., Great Falls, MT 59404 Tel 406-452-3486 (SAN 210-6094).

McGrath Publishing Co., *(McGrath; 0-8434),* P.O. Box 9001, Wilmington, NC 28402 Tel 919-763-3757 (SAN 212-0215). *Imprints:* Consortium Books (Consortium).

McGraw-Hill Book Co., *(McGraw; 0-07),* 1221 Avenue of the Americas, 27th Fl., New York, NY 10020 Tel 212-997-6611 (SAN 200-2248); Orders to: Hightstown, NJ 08520 Tel 609-426-5254 (SAN 200-254X); Orders to: 8171 Redwood Hwy., Novato, CA 94947 Tel 415-897-5201 (SAN 200-2566); Orders to: Manchester, MO 63011 Tel 314-227-1600 (SAN 200-2558). *Imprints:* Architectural Record Books (Architectural Rec Bks); BYTE Books (BYTE Bks); Chemical Engineering (Chem Eng); Shepard's/McGraw-Hill (Shepards-McGraw).

McGraw-Hill Book Co., Health Professions Division, PreTest Series, *(McGraw-Pretest),* P.O. Box 330, 71 S. Turnpike, Wallingford, CT 06492 Tel 203-265-5604 (SAN 207-4176); Orders to: P.O. Box 400, Hightstown, NJ 08520 (SAN 207-4184).

McGraw-Hill Company of Canada Ltd., *(McGraw-Hill Canada),* Grange Park, Toronto M5T 1G4, .

Macgregor, Scotty, Pubns., *(Macgregor; 0-912546),* 10 Pineacre Dr., Smithtown, NY 11787 Tel 516-269-6532 (SAN 206-6912).

Machinery & Allied Products Institute, *(M & A Products),* 1200 18th St., N.W., Washington, DC 20036 (SAN 205-8014).

McIlvaine, Paul, Pub., *(P McIlvaine; 0-9600410),* Sky Village, 124 Scenic Lane, Hendersonville, NC 28739 Tel 704-692-3971 (SAN 203-7890).

Mack Publishing Co., *(Mack Pub; 0-912734),* 20th & Northampton Sts., Easton, PA 18042 Tel 215-258-9111 (SAN 203-9508).

McKay, Alice, *(A McKay; 0-941474),* 3455 Table Mesa Dr., No. 141d, Boulder, CO 80303 Tel 303-494-7174 (SAN 239-1147).

McKay, David, Co., Inc., *(McKay; 0-679),* 2 Park Ave., New York, NY 10016 Tel 212-340-9800 (SAN 285-046X); Orders to: Fodors/McKay, O'Neill Hwy., Dunmore, PA 18512 Tel 717-344-2614 (SAN 285-0478). *Imprints:* Wyden, Peter H., Inc. (Wyden).

McKee, Christian H., *(C H McKee; 0-9611046),* 210 Main St., Rm. No.1, Landisville, PA 17538 Tel 717-898-7109 (SAN 282-9290).

MacKenzie-Koch Associates, *(MacKenzie-Koch; 0-931094),* P.O. Box 240392, Charlotte, NC 28224 Tel 919-842-9308 (SAN 239-4537).

Mackey, Cleo, Publishing, *(C Mackey; 0-9608176),* 6435 Seco Blvd., Dallas, TX 75217 Tel 214-391-5597 (SAN 240-2467).

Mackinac Island State Park Commission, *(Mackinac Island; 0-911872),* Box 370, Mackinac Island, MI 49757 Tel 906-847-3328 (SAN 202-5981).

McKinzie Publishing Co., *(McKinzie Pub; 0-86626),* 11000 Wilshire Blvd., P.O. Box 24339, Los Angeles, CA 90024 (SAN 216-2644).

McKnight Publishing Co., *(McKnight),* 808 I.A.A. Dr., P.O. Box 2854, Bloomington, IL 61701 Tel 309-663-1341 (SAN 202-5957); Dist. by: Taplinger Publishing Co., 200 Park Ave., S., New York, NY 10003 (SAN 213-6821).

Maclay & Associates, *(Maclay Assoc; 0-940776),* P.O. Box 16253, Baltimore, MD 21210 Tel 301-235-7985 (SAN 219-6808).

McLean County Historical Society, *(McLean County; 0-943788),* 201 E. Grove St., Bloomington, IL 61701 Tel 309-827-0428 (SAN 241-0362).

McMaster, Linda, Ms, *(L McMaster),* War Cycles Institute, P.O. Box 1673, Kalispell, MT 59901 (SAN 211-7428).

McMillan, Dennis, *(D McMillan; 0-9609986),* 1353 4th Ave., San Francisco, CA 94122 Tel 415-681-1156 (SAN 272-1686).

Macmillan Information, Div. of Macmillan Publishing Co., Inc., *(Macmillan Info; 0-02),* 866 Third Ave., New York, NY 10022 Tel 212-935-2000 (SAN 202-599X).

McMillan Pubns., Inc., *(McMillan Pubns; 0-934228),* 3208 Halsey Dr., Woodridge, IL 60517 Tel 312-968-3933 (SAN 213-1137).

Macmillan Publishing Co., Inc., *(Macmillan; 0-02),* 866 Third Ave., New York, NY 10022 Tel 212-935-2000 (SAN 202-5574); Orders to: Front & Brown Sts., Riverside, NJ 08370 (SAN 202-5582). *Imprints:* Acorn Books (Acorn); Berlitz (Berlitz); Collier Books (Collier); Crowell-Collier Press (CCPr).

McMillion Pubns., *(McMillion Pubns; 0-942792),* 2333 Emery, Denton, TX 76201 Tel 817-382-6669 (SAN 240-2521).

MCN Press *See* **Military Collectors News Press**

McNally & Loftin, Pubns., Inc., *(McNally NC),* 510 W. 4th St., Charlotte, NC 28202 Tel 704-372-5784 (SAN 214-2600).

McNally, Loftin & West, Publishers, *(McNally; 0-87461),* P.O. Box 1316, Santa Barbara, CA 93102 Tel 805-964-5117 (SAN 281-9643); Orders to: 5390 Overpass Rd., Santa Barbara, CA 93111 (SAN 281-9651).

McNamara Pubns., Inc., *(McNamara Pubns; 0-932770),* 741 Overlook St., Box 27277, Escondido, CA 92027 Tel 619-743-4942 (SAN 212-2189).

McNutt, Randy, Publications, *(McNutt Pubns; 0-940152),* P.O. Box 455, Fairfield, OH 45014 Tel 513-868-9910 (SAN 217-0841).

Macon Junior League Pubns., *(Jr League Macon),* 345 Spring St., Macon, GA 31201 (SAN 223-1697).

Macor, Alida, & Sew On, *(Alida Macor),* P.O. Box 71, Martinsville, NJ 08836 (SAN 264-1925).

Macoupin County Homemakers, *(MCH),* 210 N. Broad St., Carlinville, IL 62626 (SAN 217-2933).

Macoy Publishing & Masonic Supply Co., Inc., *(Macoy Pub; 0-910928),* P.O. Box 9759, Richmond, VA 23228 Tel 804-262-6551 (SAN 202-2265).

McPhail, David, *(D McPhail),* 242 Trinity Ave. Berkeley, CA 94708 (SAN 207-6586).

McPherson & Company, *(McPherson & Co; 0-914232),* P.O. Box 638, New Paltz, NY 12561 Tel 914-255-7084 (SAN 203-0624).

McQueen & Son Publishing Co., *(McQueen & Son; 0-9609354),* 6720 Lincoln Oaks, Fair Oak, CA 95628 Tel 916-967-9515 (SAN 260-2245).

McQueen Publishing Co., *(McQueen; 0-917186),* P.O. Box 198, Tiskilwa, IL 61368 (SAN 203-9516).

McQuerry, Mary Noble, Orchid Books, *(McQuerry-Orchid; 0-913928),* 5700 W. Salerno Rd., Jacksonville, FL 32244 Tel 904-387-5044 (SAN 203-9427).

MacRae, Julia *See* **Watts, Franklin, Inc.**

MacRae's Blue Book, Inc., *(MacRaes Blue Bk; 0-89910),* 817 Broadway, New York, NY 10003 (SAN 241-5569).

Macro Books, *(Macro Bks; 0-913080),* P.O. Box 26661, Tempe, AZ 85282 Tel 602-949-5559 (SAN 207-0480).

Macromedia Inc., *(Macromedia Inc; 0-9601170),* P.O. Box 1025, Lake Placid, NY 12946 Tel 518-523-9683 (SAN 209-3790).

McVicker Sutcliffe Hand Press, *(McVicker Sutcliffe; 0-943164),* 2216 Cliff Dr., Santa Barbara, CA 93109 Tel 805-966-7563 (SAN 240-7191).

Macy, Josiah, Jr. Foundation, *(J Macy Foun; 0-914362),* One Rockefeller Plaza, New York, NY 10020 Tel 212-246-8830 (SAN 201-0151); Dist. by: Independent Publishers Group, One Pleasant Ave., Port Washington, NY 11050 Tel 516-944-9325 (SAN 201-2936).

Macys of Ellinwood, *(Macys Ellinwood),* 606 N. Main St., Ellinwood, KS 67526 (SAN 217-250X).

Mad River Press, *(Mad River; 0-916422),* Rte. 2, Box 151-B, Eureka, CA 95501 Tel 707-443-2947 (SAN 207-530X).

Madden, Robert, *(R Madden; 0-9608256),* 5292 Rosamond Lane, Pontiac, MI 48054 Tel 313-681-3354 (SAN 240-4028).

Made Simple Books *See* **Doubleday & Co., Inc.**

Madhatter Press, *(Madhatter; 0-941082),* 3101 12th Ave. S., No. 5, Minneapolis, MN 55407 Tel 612-722-8951 (SAN 217-3964).

Madis, Valdemar, *(Madis; 0-941350),* 375 Huyler St., South Hackensack, NJ 07606 (SAN 239-4545).
Madison & Polk, *(Madison Polk; 0-910915),* P.O. Box 8447, Asheville, NC 28814 Tel 704-254-0351 (SAN 272-1708).
Madison Financial Services, Inc., *(Madison Financial; 0-913885),* 3930 Knowles Ave., Kensington, MD 20895 Tel 608-257-0158 (SAN 286-7893).
Madison Park Press, *(Madison Park Pr; 0-942178),* 3816 E. Madison St., Seattle, WA 98112 (SAN 238-7867).
Madison Square Press, *(Madison Square; 0-942604),* 10 E. 23rd. St., New York, NY 10010 Tel 212-475-1620 (SAN 238-5384).
Madrona Press, Inc., *(Madrona Pr; 0-89052),* P.O. Box 3750, Austin, TX 78764 Tel 512-327-2683 (SAN 202-6015).
Madrona Pubs., Inc., *(Madrona Pubs; 0-914842),* P.O. Box 22667, Seattle, WA 98122 Tel 206-325-3973 (SAN 281-966X); 113 Madrona Place East, Seattle, WA 98112 (SAN 281-9678).
Maelstrom Press, *(Maelstrom; 0-917554),* 8 Farm Hill Rd., Cape Elizabeth, ME 04107 (SAN 207-8899).
Mafex Associates, Inc., *(Mafex; 0-87804),* 90 Cherry St., Johnstown, PA 15902 Tel 814-535-3597 (SAN 202-2591).
Magaru Enterprises, *(Magaru Enterprises; 0-9609154),* P.O. Box 10271, Waialae Kahala Stn., Honolulu, HI 96816 (SAN 262-0472).
Magazines for Industry, Inc., Subs. of Hardourt Brace Jovanovich, Inc., *(Mag Indus; 0-89451),* 747 Third Ave., New York, NY 10017 Tel 212-838-7778 (SAN 205-7921).
Magee, John, Inc., *(Magee; 0-910944),* 103 State St., Boston, MA 02109 (SAN 206-6556).
Magi Books, Inc., *(Magi Bks; 0-87343),* 33 Buckingham Dr., Albany, NY 12208 Tel 518-482-7781 (SAN 202-6023).
Magic, *(Magic; 0-9607810),* 2212 20th Ave. S., Birmingham, AL 35223 Tel 205-870-5590 (SAN 239-7382).
Magic Carpet Press, The, *(Magic Carpet; 0-935808),* P.O. Box 168, Syosset, NY 11791 Tel 516-367-4865 (SAN 213-7739).
Magic Limited-Lloyd E. Jones, *(Magic Ltd; 0-915926),* P.O. Box 3186, San Leandro, CA 94578 Tel 415-352-1854 (SAN 208-7480); 4064 39th Ave., Oakland, CA 94619 Tel 415-531-5490 (SAN 208-7499).
Magic Unicorn Pubns., *(Magic Unicorn Pubns; 0-9601836),* Sunrise Country Club, 93 Palma Dr, Rancho Mirage, CA 92270 Tel 619-324-6906 (SAN 222-0636); Dist. by: Bookpeople, 2940 Seventh St., Berkeley, CA 94710 Tel 415-549-3030 (SAN 168-9517).
Magical Rainbow Pubns., *(Magical Rainbow; 0-911281),* Box 717, Ojai, CA 93023 Tel 805-646-0364 (SAN 272-1775).
Magickal Childe Inc., *(Magickal Childe; 0-939708),* 35 W. 19th St., New York, NY 10011 (SAN 216-4124).
Magna Carta Book Co., *(Magna Carta Bk; 0-910946),* 5502 Magnolia Ave., Baltimore, MD 21215 Tel 301-466-8191 (SAN 203-9532).
Magna Publishing Co., *(Magna Pub Co; 0-912150),* 607 N. Sherman Ave., Madison, WI 53704 Tel 608-249-2455 (SAN 203-9540).
Magnaflux Corp., *(Magnaflux),* 7300 W. Lawrence St., Chicago, IL 60656 Tel 312-867-8000 (SAN 205-907X).
Magnamusic-Baton, Inc., *(Magnamusic; 0-918812),* 10370 Page Industrial Blvd, St. Louis, MO 63132 Tel 314-427-5660 (SAN 210-4601).
Magnes Museum, *(Magnes Mus),* 2911 Russell St., Berkeley, CA 94705 Tel 415-849-2710 (SAN 214-2511).
Magnet Publishing Co., *(Magnet Pub; 0-9609410),* P.O. Box 612, Goleta, CA 93116 Tel 805-964-3306 (SAN 272-1783).
Magnolia House Publishing, *(Magnolia Hse Pub; 0-913145),* 2843 Thorndyke Ave. W., Seattle, WA 98199 Tel 206-283-0609 (SAN 265-3915).
Magnolia Laboratory, *(Magnolia Lab),* 701 Beach Blvd., Pascagoula, MS 39567 Tel 601-762-1643 (SAN 206-2127).

Magnolia Pubns., Inc., *(Magnolia Pubns Inc; 0-943516),* 380 Lexington Ave., New York, NY 10168 Tel 212-682-2514 (SAN 240-7116).
Magoo's Umbrella, *(Magoos Umbrella; 0-932904),* 18581 Devon Ave., Saratoga, CA 95070 Tel 408-379-7354 (SAN 212-2197).
Magpie Pubns., *(Magpie Pubns; 0-936480),* P.O. Box 636, Alamo, CA 94507 (SAN 221-4091).
Maguey Press, The, *(Maguey Pr; 0-930778),* Box 3395, Tucson, AZ 85722 (SAN 211-3686).
Mah-Tov Pubns., *(Mah-Tov Pubns; 0-917274),* 1680 45th St., Brooklyn, NY 11204 Tel 212-871-5337 (SAN 208-7502).
Maher Ventriloquist Studios, *(Maher Ventril Studio),* P.O. Box 420, Littleton, CO 80160 Tel 303-798-6830 (SAN 208-1385).
Mahoney, Will, *(W Mahoney; 0-9608462),* P.O. Box 6877, Denver, CO 80206 Tel 303-399-9264 (SAN 240-592X).
Maiden Books, *(Maiden Bks; 0-931138),* 300 Washington St., Newark, NJ 07102 (SAN 211-2515).
Maiden Lane Press, *(Maiden Lane; 0-9605688),* P.O. Box 3724, Charlottesville, VA 22903 Tel 703-456-8323 (SAN 216-2652).
Mail Order U.S.A., *(Mail Order; 0-914694),* 3100 Wisconsin Ave. N.W., Washington, DC 20016 Tel 202-686-9521 (SAN 205-6321); Orders to: P.O. Box 19083, Washington, DC 20036 (SAN 205-633X).
Mailbox Club, The, *(Mailbox; 0-9603752),* 404 Eager Rd., Valdosta, GA 31601 Tel 912-244-6812 (SAN 281-9686); Dist. by: Spring Arbor, 772 Airport Blvd., Ann Arbor, MI 48104 (SAN 158-9016).
Maimes, S. L., *(Maimes; 0-917246),* 3726 Virden Ave, Oakland, CA 94619 (SAN 208-1830).
Main, Zilpha P., *(Z Main; 0-9601584),* 2701 Wilshire Blvd., Los Angeles, CA 90057 (SAN 222-0644).
Main Track Pubns., *(Main Track; 0-933866),* 12435 Ventura Court, Studio City, CA 91604 Tel 213-980-5900 (SAN 212-758X).
Maine Antique Digest, Inc., *(Maine Antique; 0-917312),* P.O. Box 358, Waldoboro, ME 04572 Tel 207-832-7534 (SAN 208-3949).
Maine Historical Society, *(Maine Hist; 0-915592),* 485 Congress St., Portland, ME 04111 Tel 207-774-1822 (SAN 202-2605).
Maine State Bar Association, *(Maine St Bar),* 124 State St, P O Box 788, Augusta, ME 04330 Tel 207-622-7523 (SAN 227-0412).
Maine State Museum Pubns., *(Maine St Mus; 0-913764),* State House, Sta. 83, Augusta, ME 04333 Tel 207-289-2301 (SAN 203-9567).
Mainspring Press, *(Mainspring),* Box 82, Stonington, ME 04681 Tel 207-367-2484 (SAN 209-8342).
Maisner & Mason, *(Maisner & Mason; 0-9611406),* 2163 Ronsard Rd., San Pedro, CA 90732 (SAN 283-9709); Dist. by: Premart, Inc., 1948 S. La Cienega Blvd., Los Angeles, CA 90034 (SAN 283-9717).
Maize Press, *(Maize Pr; 0-939558),* P.O. Box 8251, San Diego, CA 92102 Tel 714-455-1128 (SAN 216-6852).
Majestic Books, *(Majestic Bks; 0-9604968),* 2338 Henderson Mill Court, Atlanta, GA 30345 (SAN 215-6792).
Major Books, *(Major Bks; 0-89041),* 21335 Roscoe Blvd., Canoga Park, CA 91304 Tel 213-999-4100 (SAN 207-4117); 18-39 128th St., College Point, NY 11356 Tel 212-939-1119 (SAN 207-4117); Orders to: Kable News, Inc., 777 Third Ave., New York, NY 10017 Tel 212-486-2828 (SAN 207-4109).
Majority Press, The (MA), *(Majority Pr; 0-912469),* P.O. Box 538, Dover, MA 02030 Tel 617-533-4052 (SAN 265-2757).
Makepeace Colony Press, The, *(Makepeace Colony; 0-87741),* P.O. Box 111, Stevens Point, WI 54481 Tel 715-344-2636 (SAN 203-9575).
Makor Publishing, *(Makor Pub; 0-9608310),* 4910 Della Pl., San Diego, CA 92117 Tel 213-273-3306 (SAN 240-5458).
Malaga, Rose C., *(Malaga; 0-939642),* 334 Livingston Ave., Babylon, NY 11702 Tel 516-422-2405 (SAN 216-6356).

Malamud-Rose, Publishers, *(Malamud-Rose; 0-9610466),* 38 Stonywood Road, Commack, NY 11725 (SAN 285-0486); Box 194, Smithtown, NY 11787 (SAN 285-0494).
Malcolm House, *(Malcolm Hse),* 805 Malcolm Dr., Silver Spring, MD 20901 Tel 301-439-4358 (SAN 209-0368).
Maledicta Press, *(Maledicta; 0-916500),* 331 S. Greenfield Ave., Waukesha, WI 53186 Tel 414-542-5853 (SAN 208-1083).
Malhotra, S., *(Malhotra),* 20 Acorn Park, Cambridge, MA 02140 (SAN 203-8676); Orders to: 16 Cooke Rd., Lexington, MA 02173 (SAN 203-8684).
Malibu Publications *See* **B of A Communications Co.**
Malki Museum Press, *(Malki Mus Pr),* Dept. of Linguistics, Univ. of California, Los Angeles, CA 90024 Tel 213-474-0169 (SAN 281-9724); Orders to: 11-795 Fields Rd., Morongo Indian Reservation, Banning, CA 92220 Tel 714-849-7289 (SAN 281-9732).
Mallon, Peter F., Inc., *(P F Mallon),* 45-29-31 Court Sq., Long Island City, NY 11101 (SAN 262-1126).
Malvaux, Ets J., *(Malvaux),* Orders to: Dillon-Donnelly Publishing, 7058 Lindell Blvd., St. Louis, MO 63130 Tel 314-862-6239 (SAN 208-4589).
Mammoth Press, *(Mammoth Pr; 0-937902),* 40-B Grecian Garden Dr., Rochester, NY 14626 (SAN 216-4132).
Man in the Northeast, *(Man NE),* Box 241, NH 03751 (SAN 216-3810).
Man-Root, *(Man-Root),* P. O. Box 982, South San Francisco, CA 94080 (SAN 207-8635).
Management Advisory Associates, Inc., *(Mgmt Advisory Assoc Inc),* P.O. Box 703, Bowling Green, OH 43402 Tel 419-352-7782 (SAN 203-9907).
Management Advisory Pubns., *(Management Advisory Pubns),* Box 151, 44 Washington St., Wellesley Hills, MA 02181 Tel 617-235-2895 (SAN 203-8692).
Management & Industrial Research Pubns., *(Mgmt & Indus Res Pubns; 0-933684),* P.O. Box 7133, Kansas City, MO 64113 Tel 816-444-6622 (SAN 214-0535).
Management Club Consultants, *(Management Club; 0-9609350),* P.O. Box 40028, Garland, TX 75040 Tel 214-276-8742 (SAN 260-2199).
Management Education Ltd., *(Management Ed),* 12326 Riverview Rd., Tantallon, MD 20744 (SAN 238-8197).
Management Information Services, *(Mgmt Info Ser),* 19722 E. Nine Mile Rd., St. Clair Shores, MI 48080 (SAN 206-6564).
Management Press, Inc., *(Management Pr),* P.O. Box 34965, Memphis, TN 38134 (SAN 212-1123).
Manas Pubns., *(Manas; 0-911804),* 1868 Shore Dr. S., No. 205, St. Petersburg, FL 33707 Tel 813-343-1428 (SAN 203-9605).
Manas-Systems, *(Manas-Sys; 0-9610076),* Box 3106, Newport Beach, CA 92663 Tel 714-646-0648 (SAN 272-2062).
Manchaca Publishing Co., *(Manchaca Pub; 0-88408),* P.O. Box 783, Manchaca, TX 78652 (SAN 239-4553).
Manchester Group, Ltd., The, *(Manchester Group; 0-9605792),* 3501 26th Place W., No. 422, Seattle, WA 98199 Tel 206-292-2057 (SAN 220-1747).
Manchester Univ. Press, *(Manchester; 0-7190),* 51 Washington St., Dover, NH 03820 Tel 603-742-4662 (SAN 281-9740).
Mancini, Genevieve, *(G Mancini),* 176 Moffit Blvd., Islip, NY 11751 Tel 516-277-9547 (SAN 213-1145).
Mandala Books, *(Mandala Bks; 0-9603226),* RFD Box 56, Vershire, VT 05079 (SAN 213-7542) Do Not Confuse with Mandala Press in MA (Mandala) or Mandala Press in NC (Mandala Pr).
Mandala Holistic Health, *(Mandala Holistic; 0-939410),* P.O. Box 1233, Del Mar, CA 92014 Tel 619-481-7751 (SAN 216-5783).
Mandala Press, *(Mandala Pr; 0-933158),* 5010 Randall Dr., Wilmington, NC 28403 Tel 919-791-5719 (SAN 212-9159) Do Not Confuse with Mandala Books in VT (Mandala Bks) or Mandala Press in MA (Mandala).
Mandarin Press, *(Mandarin; 0-931514),* 210 Fifth Ave., New York, NY 10010 (SAN 211-514X).

Mandekic, A. V., Enterprise, *(Mandekic; 0-9608312)*, P.O. Box 649, Wrightwood, CA 92397 Tel 619-249-5105 (SAN 240-5466).

Mandel Pubns., *(Mandel Pubns; 0-941420)*, P.O. Box 16432, San Antonio, TX 78216 Tel 512-344-1991 (SAN 239-0094).

Manderino, Ned, Associates, *(N Manderino Assocs; 0-9601194)*, 854 Kodak Drive, Los Angeles, CA 90026 Tel 213-665-0123 (SAN 209-5793).

Manessier Publishing Co., *(Manessier; 0-910950)*, Box C, Bryn Mawr, CA 92318 (SAN 203-9621).

Manet Guild, *(Manet Guild; 0-9602418)*, 310 Franklin St., Dept. 535, Boston, MA 02110 Tel 617-449-3792 (SAN 212-7601).

Mangan Books, *(Mangan Bks; 0-930208)*, 6245 Snowheights Ct., El Paso, TX 79912 Tel 915-584-1662 (SAN 209-3804).

Manhattan, Ltd., Pubs., *(Manhattan Ltd NC; 0-932046)*, P.O. Box 18865, Raleigh, NC 27619 Tel 919-833-2121 (SAN 211-8114).

Mankind Publishing Co., *(Mankind Pub; 0-87687)*, 8060 Melrose Ave., Los Angeles, CA 90046 Tel 213-653-8060 (SAN 208-4422).

Manley, Ray, Commercial Photography, Inc., *(R Manley; 0-931418)*, 238 S. Tucson Blvd., Tucson, AZ 85716 Tel 602-623-0307 (SAN 208-7456).

Mann, Paul, Publishing Co., *(Paul Mann; 0-8184)*, 1517 Rexford Pl., Las Vegas, NV 89104 Tel 702-385-1585 (SAN 204-9341).

Mann Foundation, Inc., *(Mann Found; 0-9608904)*, 7111 Glass Slipper Way, Citrus Heights, CA 95610 Tel 916-725-4488 (SAN 241-1334).

Mann Pubs., *(Mann Pubs; 0-936632)*, P.O. Box 7 AK, Jersey City, NJ 07307 Tel 201-659-8324 (SAN 214-0543).

Mannix Clinic, The, *(Mannix Clinic; 0-399)*, 2021 Pontius Ave., Los Angeles, CA 90025 (SAN 219-0893).

Manor Publishing Co., *(Manor Pub Co)*, G.P.O. Box 194, Staten Island, NY 10314 (SAN 217-2488).

Mansell, *(Mansell; 0-7201)*, 950 University Ave., Bronx, NY 10452 Tel 617-685-8149 (SAN 209-5807).

Manufacturing Confectioner, *(Manufacturing Confectioner)*, 175 Rock Rd., Glen Rock, NJ 07452 Tel 201-652-2655 (SAN 205-8979).

Manuscript Press, *(Manuscript Pr; 0-936414)*, Box 1762, Wayne, NJ 07470 Tel 201-628-1259 (SAN 214-3224); Dist. by: PDA Enterprises, Box 8010, New Orleans, LA 70182 (SAN 222-0989).

Manuscript Press (TN), *(Man Pr TN; 0-910159)*, P.O. Box 40206, Nashville, TN 37204 Tel 615-242-4366 (SAN 240-8651).

Manyland Books, Inc., *(Manyland; 0-87141)*, 84-39 90th St., Woodhaven, NY 11421 Tel 212-441-6768 (SAN 203-963X).

Manzanita Press, *(Manzanita Pr; 0-931644)*, P.O. Box 4027, San Rafael, CA 94903 Tel 415-479-9636 (SAN 211-0342).

Map World Pubns., *(Map World; 0-89414)*, Box 2187, Dublin, CA 94566 Tel 415-829-2728 (SAN 209-6714).

Maplegrove & Montgrove Press, *(Maple Mont)*, 4055 N. Keystone Ave., Chicago, IL 60641 Tel 312-286-2655 (SAN 202-2303).

Maplewood Press, *(Maplewood; 0-914048)*, P.O. Box 90, Meadville, PA 16335 Tel 814-336-1768 (SAN 203-9648).

Mar Vista Publishing Co., *(Mar Vista; 0-9604064)*, 11917 Westminster Place, Los Angeles, CA 90066 (SAN 215-255X).

Mara Books, Inc., *(Mara; 0-87787)*, 1318 Second Street, Santa Monica, CA 90401 Tel 213-394-3429 (SAN 202-6074).

Maran Publishing Co., *(Maran Pub; 0-916526)*, 320 N. Eutaw St., Baltimore, MD 21201 Tel 301-837-3634 (SAN 208-7545).

Maranatha Baptist Press, *(Maranatha Baptist; 0-937136)*, Maranatha Baptist Bible College, 745 W. Main St., Watertown, WI 53094 Tel 414-261-9300 (SAN 220-2581).

Marathon International Publishing Co., *(Marathon Intl Pub Co; 0-915216)*, P.O. Box 33008, Louisville, KY 40232 Tel 502-245-1566 (SAN 206-443X).

Marburger Pubns., *(Marburger; 0-915730)*, P.O. Box 422, Manhasset, NY 11030 (SAN 208-0443).

Marcella Press, *(Marcella; 0-938468)*, P.O. Box 1105, Palm Desert, CA 92261 (SAN 215-8884).

Marco & Johnson, *(Marco & Johnson; 0-910097)*, P.O. Box 4264, Los Angeles, CA 90051 Tel 213-962-9280 (SAN 241-3973).

Marco Polo Pubs., *(Marco Polo; 0-932820)*, 8024 Valley Dr., N. Richland Hills, TX 76180 Tel 817-485-8307 (SAN 212-2898).

Marconi Press, *(Marconi Pr; 0-9605434)*, 3027 N.W. 72nd St., Seattle, WA 98117 Tel 206-784-8813 (SAN 218-4893).

Marcor Publishing, *(Marcor Pub; 0-932248)*, P.O. Box 1072, Port Hueneme, CA 93041 (SAN 220-8237).

Marcourt Press, *(Marcourt Pr; 0-9608748)*, 7465 Beverly Blvd., Los Angeles, CA 90036 Tel 213-852-2025 (SAN 241-0354).

Mardi Press, *(Mardi Pr)*, P.O. Box 4173, Arlington, VA 22204 (SAN 240-0952).

Marduk Manumit, *(Marduk Manumit; 0-940452)*, P.O. Box 9202, Birmingham, AL 35213 Tel 205-879-5383 (SAN 217-1961).

Margarita's Books for Brown Eyes, *(Margaritas Bks Brown; 0-918536)*, 1203 23rd Ave., San Diego, CA 92120 Tel 714-239-4621 (SAN 209-9543).

Marginal Media, *(Marginal Med; 0-942788)*, P.O. Box 241, Fredonia, NY 14063 Tel 716-679-0462 (SAN 240-2475).

Margoe Jane Pubns., *(Margoe Jane; 0-9602330)*, Sawyer Ave., Apartment No. 45, Malone, NY 12953 Tel 518-483-2020 (SAN 212-2200).

Mari-Lyn Publishing, *(Mari-Lyn; 0-912719)*, 71 Wyndham Ave., Providence, RI 02908 Tel 401-272-3606 (SAN 283-0787).

Marianist Communication Center, *(Marianist Com Ctr; 0-9608124)*, 1223 Maryhurst Dr., St. Louis, MO 63122 Tel 314-965-5634 (SAN 240-2483).

Marianna Junior Woman's Club Inc., *(Marianna Jr; 0-939114)*, P.O. Box 6, Marianna, FL 32446 (SAN 264-1968).

Marin Publishing Co., *(Marin Pub; 0-9607482)*, P.O. Box 436, San Rafael, CA 94901 Tel 415-883-4219 (SAN 238-4701).

Marine Biological Laboratory, *(Marine Bio; 0-912544)*, Woods Hole, MA 02543 (SAN 203-9664).

Marine Corps Assn., *(Marine Corps; 0-940328)*, Box 1775, M.C.B., Quantico, VA 22134 Tel 703-640-6161 (SAN 205-8952).

Marine Education Textbooks, *(Marine Educ; 0-934114)*, 124 N. Van Ave., Houma, LA 70360 (SAN 215-9651).

Mariner Press, *(Mariner; 0-910954)*, Route 2, Box A 45, Flat Rock, NC 28731 Tel 704-693-8045 (SAN 203-9672).

Mariner Press, *(Mariner Pr; 0-911920)*, P.O. Box 99, Somerset, NJ 08873 (SAN 206-6904).

Mariner Publishing Co., Inc., *(Mariner Pub; 0-936166)*, 10927 N. Dale Mabry, Tampa, FL 33618 Tel 813-962-8136 (SAN 221-4059).

Mariners Press, Inc., The, *(Mariners Boston; 0-913352)*, P.O. Box 540, Boston, MA 02117-0540 (SAN 203-9680).

Marion County Library, *(Marion Cnty Lib; 0-9603086)*, 101 E. Court St., Marion, SC 29571 Tel 803-423-2244 (SAN 211-2973).

Maris, Stella Books, *(S Maris Bks; 0-912103)*, P.O. Box 11483, Fort Worth, TX 76110 Tel 817-924-7221 (SAN 264-7613).

Mark, J, Press, *(J Mark Pr; 0-912658)*, 22 Allen's Point, Bay Shore, NY 11706 Tel 516-666-0043 (SAN 208-7553); Orders to: Box 33, Islip, NY 11751 (SAN 208-7561).

Mark-Age Inc., *(Mark-Age; 0-912322)*, P.O. Box 290368, Fort Lauderdale, FL 33329 Tel 305-578-5555 (SAN 202-6090).

Mark Foster Music Co., *(Mark Foster Mus; 0-916656)*, P.O. Box 4012, Champaign, IL 61820 Tel 217-398-2760 (SAN 208-2861).

Mark III Productions, *(Mark III Prods; 0-9609982)*, P.O. Box 586, Yuba City, CA 95992 Tel 916-674-7377 (SAN 217-2461).

Mark Victor Publishing Co., *(M Victor Pub; 0-9606258)*, 10855 Whipple St. No. 207, N. Hollywood, CA 91602 (SAN 217-2479).

Market Communications, Inc., *(Market Comm; 0-930820)*, 225 E. Michigan St., Milwaukee, WI 53202 Tel 414-276-6600 (SAN 211-3694).

Market Ed Inc., *(Market Ed; 0-937470)*, P.O. Box 45181, Westlake, OH 44145 Tel 216-779-4689 (SAN 215-3246).

Marketing Economics Institute, Ltd., *(Marketing Econs; 0-914078)*, 108 W. 39th St., New York, NY 10018 Tel 212-869-8260 (SAN 202-6104).

Marketing Effectiveness, Advisory Publishing Service, *(Marketing Effect; 0-910797)*, P.O. Box 1786, Lafayette, CA 95718 Tel 916-525-7951 (SAN 272-2550).

Marketing for Profit, Inc., *(Marketing for Profit; 0-9603370)*, Box 624, St. Charles, IL 60174 (SAN 221-7457).

Markewich, Reese, *(Markewich; 0-9600160)*, Bacon Hill Rd., Pleasantville, NY 10570 Tel 212-674-2979 (SAN 203-9699).

Markham Press Fund, Div. of Baylor Univ. Press, *(Markham Pr Fund; 0-918954)*, Orders to: Book Dept., Baylor Book Store, P.O. Box 6325, Waco, TX 76706 Tel 817-755-2161 (SAN 213-5345).

Markow, Herbert L., *(H L Markow; 0-934108)*, P.O. Box 011451, Miami, FL 33101 Tel 305-858-0200 (SAN 281-9759); Dist. by: Banyan Books, Inc., P.O. Box 431160, Miami, FL 33143 Tel 305-665-6011 (SAN 208-340X); Dist. by: William W. Gaunt & Sons, Inc., 3011 Gulf Dr., Holmes Beach, FL 33510 Tel 813-778-5211 (SAN 202-9413).

Marlboro Pr., the, *(Marlboro Pr; 0-910395)*, Box 157, Marlboro, VT 05344 Tel 802-257-0781 (SAN 281-9813); Dist. by: Inland Bk. Co., P.O. Box 261, E. Haven, CT 06512 Tel 203-467-4257 (SAN 200-4151); Dist. by: New York State Small Pr. Assn., 198 Main St., Nyack, NY 10960 Tel 914-358-1190 (SAN 281-983X); Orders to: Small Press Distribution Inc., 1784 Shattuck Ave., Berkeley, CA 94709 Tel 415-549-3336 (SAN 282-5996).

Marlborough Press, Div. of Brooke Evans Associates, *(Marlborough Pr; 0-910793)*, 14 Washington Ave., Morganville, NJ 07751 Tel 201-536-8207 (SAN 262-8082).

Marlin Pubns. International, Inc., *(Marlin; 0-930624)*, 485 Fifth Ave., New York, NY 10017 Tel 212-986-7752 (SAN 210-9824).

Marling Associates, *(Marling; 0-912818)*, Orders to: Altarinda Books, 13 Estates Dr., Orinda, CA 94563 Tel 415-254-3830 (SAN 206-6890).

Marlor Press, *(Marlor Pr; 0-943400)*, 4304 Brigadoon Dr., St. Paul, MN 55112 Tel 612-483-1588 (SAN 240-7140); Dist. by: Contemporary Books, Inc., 180 North Michigan Avenue, Chicago, IL 60601 Tel 312-782-9181 (SAN 202-5493).

Marmac Publishing Co., *(Marmac Pub; 0-939944)*, 6303 Barfield Rd., No. 208, Atlanta, GA 30328 Tel 404-257-1481 (SAN 216-8324).

Mron Pubns., *(Maron Pubns; 0-941944)*, 7900 Old Branch Ave., No. 106, Clinton, MD 20735 Tel 301-868-5700 (SAN 264-1976).

Marquest Colorguide Books, *(Marquest Colorguide; 0-916240)*, P.O. Box 132, Palos Verdes Estates, CA 90274 Tel 213-373-4301 (SAN 208-4406).

Marquette County Historical Soc., Inc., *(Marquette Cnty; 0-938746)*, 213 N. Front St., Marquette, MI 49855 Tel 906-226-3571 (SAN 205-6874).

Marquette Univ. Press, *(Marquette; 0-87462)*, 1324 W. Wisconsin Ave., Rm. 409, Milwaukee, WI 53233 Tel 414-224-1564 (SAN 203-9702).

Marquis Who's Who, Inc., *(Marquis; 0-8379)*, 200 E. Ohio St., Chicago, IL 60611 Tel 312-787-2008 (SAN 202-6120); Orders to: 4300 W. 62nd St., Indianapolis, IN 46206 Tel 800-428-3898 (SAN 202-6139).

Marr, Jack, Publishing Co., *(J Marr; 0-9605854)*, 350 Ridgefield Rd., Hauppauge, NY 11787 Tel 516-234-4927 (SAN 216-6046).

Marr Pubns., *(Marr Pubns; 0-938712)*, P.O. Box 1421, New York, NY 10101 Tel 516-822-7744 (SAN 213-1242).

Marriage & Family Living Publications, Div. Of Abbey Press, *(Marriage; 0-87029)*, St. Meinrad, IN 47577 Tel 812-357-8011 (SAN 260-0021).

Mars Pubns., *(Mars Pubns; 0-910759)*, 1211 East Altadena Drive, Altadena, CA 91001 (SAN 264-1984).

Marshall, Walter H., *(W H Marshall),* 931 Knight, Helena, MT 59601 (SAN 264-1992).

Marshland Publishing Co., *(Marshland Pub; 0-941512),* P.O. Box 3241, Stony Creek, CT 06405 (SAN 239-1139).

Martin, B. B., Books, *(B B Martin Bks; 0-935682),* 6512 Libyan, Austin, TX 78745 (SAN 213-7755).

Martin, Charles Fontaine, *(C F Martin; 0-9609984),* P.O. Box 57, Wayland, MA 01778 Tel 617-358-2045 (SAN 272-2631).

Martin, Edward A., *(E A Martin),* 550 North Ave., Grand Junction, CO 81501 Tel 303-243-1538 (SAN 210-6108).

Martin, Louis J., & Associates, Inc., *(L J Martin; 0-916800),* 432 Park Ave. S., New York, NY 10016 Tel 212-725-2157 (SAN 209-0945).

Martin Consultants, Inc., *(Martin Consult; 0-9609060),* P.O. Box 1076, Golden, CO 80402 Tel 303-278-0955 (SAN 241-3353).

Martin Genealogical Services, *(Martin Genealog; 0-9611862),* P.O. Box Drawer 2147, Warner Robins, GA 31099 Tel 912-923-1261 (SAN 286-1771).

Martin Gordon, Inc., *(Martin Gordon; 0-931036),* 25 E. 83rd St., New York, NY 10028 Tel 212-249-7350 (SAN 211-1608).

Martin Motorsports Publishing, *(Martin Motorsports; 0-9605068),* P.O. Box 12654, Fort Wayne, IN 46864 (SAN 215-7861).

Martin Press, *(Martin Pr; 0-914976),* P.O. Box 25464, Los Angeles, CA 90025 (SAN 207-4761) Moved,Left No Forwarding Address.

Martin Press, The, *(Martin Pr CA; 0-941018),* 2711 Toledo St., Suite 516, Torrance, CA 90503 Tel 800-421-1212 (SAN 217-4014).

Martin Pubns., *(Martin Pubns; 0-9610182),* P.O. Box 480672, Los Angeles, CA 90048 Tel 213-552-1000 (SAN 272-2658).

Martingale Manuscripts, *(Martingale),* Box 17, North Pitcher, NY 13124 Tel 315-653-4401 (SAN 212-8020).

Marty-Nagy Bookworks, *(Marty-Nagy; 0-917296),* 624 Rhode Island St., San Francisco, CA 94107 Tel 415-824-8274 (SAN 208-757X).

Marvanco Enterprises, *(Marvanco; 0-9604336),* Box 21, Peekskill, NY 10566 (SAN 214-4093).

Marxist-Leninist Pubns., *(Marxist-Leninist; 0-86714),* P.O. Box 11972, Ontario St. Sta., Chicago, IL 60611 (SAN 216-8332).

Mary & Leigh Block Gallery, Northwestern Univ., *(M&L Block; 0-941680),* 1967 Sheridan Rd., Evanston, IL 60201 Tel 312-492-5209 (SAN 239-1643).

Mary Ellen Books, *(Mary Ellen Bks),* P.O. Box 7589-Rincon Annex, San Francisco, CA 94120 Tel (SAN 210-6388).

Mary Ellen Enterprises, *(Mary Ellen Ent),* 6414 Cambridge St., St. Louis Park, MN 55426 Tel 612-922-6166 (SAN 212-0429).

Mary, Inc., *(Mary Inc; 0-915872),* 72 Waterman St., Providence, RI 02906 Tel 401-751-0566 (SAN 207-5938).

Maryben Books, *(Maryben Bks; 0-913184),* 619 Warfield Dr., Rockville, MD 20850 Tel 301-762-5291 (SAN 205-6313).

Maryland Book Exchange, *(Md Bk Exch),* 4500 College Ave., College Park, MD 20740 Tel 301-927-2510 (SAN 203-977X).

Maryland Hall of Records Commission, *(MD Hall Records),* P.O. Box 828, Annapolis, MD 21404 Tel 301-269-3915 (SAN 205-8855).

Maryland Historical Press, *(Maryland Hist Pr; 0-917882),* 9205 Tuckerman St., Lanham, MD 20706 Tel 301-577-2436 (SAN 202-6147).

Maryland Historical Society, *(Md Hist; 0-938420),* 201 W. Monument St., Baltimore, MD 21201 (SAN 203-9788).

Maryland Publishing Co., *(Maryland Pub; 0-911071),* 10 Jack Frost Lane, Baltimore, MD 21204 Tel 301-823-3460 (SAN 272-2690).

M.A.S. de Reinis, Div. of Polymath, Inc., *(M.A.S. De Reinis; 0-937370),* Box 1500, Grand Central Sta., New York, NY 10163 Tel 212-625-4336 (SAN 220-0708).

MAS-Press, *(MAS Pr; 0-9607984),* 1129 New Hampshire Ave., Apt. 610, Washington, DC 20037 Tel 202-659-9580 (SAN 238-5392).

Masda Publishing Co., *(Masda),* 31 Milk St., Boston, MA 02109 (SAN 202-6155).

Mason, James H., *(J H Mason; 0-9609032),* 116 N. Belmont St., Glendale, CA 90206 (SAN 240-9704).

Mason Clinic, The, *(Mason Clinic; 0-9601944),* 1100 Ninth Ave., P.O. Box 900, Seattle, WA 98111 Tel 206-223-6985 (SAN 213-8972).

Mason Publishing Co., *(Mason Pub; 0-917126; 0-86678),* 366 Wacouta St., St. Paul, MN 55101 Tel 612-227-4200 (SAN 205-8839).

Massachusetts Bar Association, *(Mass Bar Assn),* 1 Center Plaza, Boston, MA 02108 (SAN 226-9473).

Massachusetts Coalition for Occupational Safety & Health, *(Mass Coalition; 0-9608416),* 718 Huntington Ave., Boston, MA 02115 Tel 617-277-0097 (SAN 240-7159).

Massachusetts Continuing Legal Education-New England Law Institute Incorporated, *(Mass CLE),* 133 Federal St, Boston, MA 02110 (SAN 226-3033).

Massachusetts Historical Society, *(Mass Hist Soc),* 1154 Boylston St., Boston, MA 02215 Tel 617-536-1608 (SAN 202-2133) Microfilm editions & reproductions of historical manuscripts & journals.

Massachusetts Institute of Technology *See MIT Press*

Massachusetts Institute of Technology, Center For Advanced Engineering Study, *(Ctr Adv Eng Stud; 0-911379),* 77 Mass. Ave. Rm. 9-234, Cambridge, MA 02139 Tel 617-253-7443 (SAN 272-2771).

Massachusetts Medical Society, The, *(MA Med Soc; 0-9608238),* 1440 Main St., Waltham, MA 02254 (SAN 240-4044).

Massachusetts Poverty Law Center, *(MA Poverty Law; 0-910001),* 2 Park Square, Boston, MA 02116 (SAN 241-5577).

Massachusetts State Council Knights of Columbus, *(Mass State; 0-9608258),* 10 Kearney Rd., Needham, MA 02194 Tel 617-793-2011 (SAN 240-4060).

Masson Publishing U.S.A., Inc., *(Masson Pub; 0-89352),* 133 E. 58th St., New York, NY 10022 Tel 212-838-8510 (SAN 211-1764).

Masspac Publishing Co., *(Masspac Pub; 0-918020),* 48855 N. Gratiot, Mt. Clemens, MI 48045 Tel 313-949-9222 (SAN 209-2948).

Mast, C. L., Jr. & Associates, *(C L Mast),* 2041 Vardon Lane, Flossmoor, IL 60422 Tel 312-798-1817 (SAN 205-8804).

Master Books, *(Master Bks; 0-89051),* P.O. Box 15666, San Diego, CA 92115 Tel 714-449-9420 (SAN 214-4107).

Master Books *See CLP Pubs.*

Master Designer, *(Master Design),* 343 S. Dearborn St., Chicago, IL 60604 Tel 312-922-9075 (SAN 205-8782).

Master Key Pubns., *(Master Key; 0-935434),* P.O. Box 519, Bonita, CA 92002 Tel 619-475-5554 (SAN 213-4152).

Master Press, *(Master Pr; 0-9600818),* P. O. Box 432, Dayton, OR 97114 Tel 503-864-2987 (SAN 209-8369).

Master Writers & Pubs., *(Master Writer & Pubs; 0-941718),* P.O. Box 24, Haddon Heights, NJ 08035 Tel 609-547-7439 (SAN 239-2550).

Masterco Press, Inc., *(Masterco Pr; 0-912164),* P.O. Box 7382, Ann Arbor, MI 48107 Tel 313-428-8300 (SAN 205-8774).

Masterson Pubs., *(MasterSon Pub; 0-9608418),* 4025 N. Harmon Ave., Peoria, IL 61614 Tel 309-682-9222 (SAN 240-7175).

Masterwork Press, *(Masterwork Pr; 0-912156),* P.O. Box 302, Pottersville, NJ 07979 Tel 201-439-3816 (SAN 206-720X).

Mastery Education Corp., *(Mastery Ed; 0-935508; 0-88106),* 85 Main St., Watertown, MA 02172 Tel 617-926-4600 (SAN 204-8486).

Matacia, Louis J., *(Matacia),* P.O. Box 32, Oakton, VA 22124 Tel 703-560-8993 (SAN 206-8486).

Matagiri Sri Aurobindo Center, Inc., *(Matagiri; 0-89071),* Mt. Tremper, NY 12457 Tel 914-679-8322 (SAN 214-2058).

Mater Dei Provincialate, *(Mater Dei Provincialate; 0-9605784),* 9400 New Harmony Rd., Evansville, IN 47712 (SAN 216-2679).

Maternity Center Assn., *(Maternity Ctr; 0-912758),* 48 E. 92nd St., New York, NY 10028 Tel 212-369-7300 (SAN 203-9729).

Matez Fielden Pubns., Inc., *(Matez Fielden; 0-933048),* 6618 Michaeljohn Dr., La Jolla, CA 92037 (SAN 212-761X).

Math Counseling Institute Press, *(Math Counsel Inst; 0-9605756),* 4518 Corliss Ave. N., Seattle, WA 98103 (SAN 216-1605).

Math House, Div. of Mosaic Media, Inc., *(Math Hse; 0-917792),* P.O. Box 711, Glen Ellyn, IL 60138 Tel 312-790-1117 (SAN 209-2956).

Math-Sci Press, *(Math Sci Pr; 0-915692),* 53 Jordan Rd., Brookline, MA 02146 Tel 617-738-0307 (SAN 207-415X).

Mathco, *(Mathco; 0-912938),* 84 Main St., Rockport, MA 01966 Tel 617-546-7101 (SAN 203-9745).

Mathematical Alternatives, Inc., *(Math Alternatives; 0-916060),* 101 Park Ave., New York, NY 10178 Tel 212-486-1775 (SAN 207-6578).

Mathematical Assn. of America, *(Math Assn; 0-88385),* 1529 Eighteenth St., N.W., Washington, DC 20036 Tel 202-387-5200 (SAN 203-9737).

Mathom Publishing Co, *(Mathom; 0-930000),* 68 E. Mohawk St., Oswego, NY 13126 Tel 315-343-3035 (SAN 285-0508); P.O. Box 362, Oswego, NY 13126 (SAN 285-0516).

Matiasz, George Z., Editor & Pub., *(Matiasz),* 445 Mariposa, Ventura, CA 93001 Tel 805-643-3661 (SAN 207-6047).

Matrix Press, *(Matrix Pr MA; 0-9610964),* P.O. Box 740, Cambridge, MA 02139 Tel 617-491-5800 (SAN 265-2773).

Matrix Pubns., Inc., *(Matrix Pubns; 0-936554),* 222 Williams St., Providence, RI 02906 Tel 401-421-2068 (SAN 215-1618).

Matrix Pubs., Inc., *(Matrix Pub; 0-916460),* 8285 S.W. Nimbus, Suite 151 E, Beaverton, OR 97005 Tel 503-243-1150 (SAN 216-0757).

Matthew Pubs., *(Matthew Pubs; 0-941366),* P.O. Box 18152, Lansing, MI 48901 Tel 713-229-8668 (SAN 238-8960).

Matthews, Robert T., *(R T Matthews; 0-9601150),* 2400 Pfefferkorn Rd., West Friendship, MD 21794 (SAN 210-2358).

Mattingly & Butler Pubs., Ltd., *(Mattingly & Butler),* 2110 Powers Ferry Rd., Suite 430, Atlanta, GA 30339 Tel 404-952-0678 (SAN 218-4915).

Mattole Press, *(Mattole Pr; 0-916854),* P.O. Box 22324, San Francisco, CA 94122 Tel 707-523-2959 (SAN 208-7626).

Maureen Points, *(Maureen Points),* 2905 Van Ness Ave., No. 101, San Francisco, CA 94109 (SAN 211-3236).

Maverick Books (TX), *(Maverick Bks; 0-9608612),* 1101 Baylor, Perryton, TX 79070 (SAN 240-7183).

Maverick Pubns., *(Maverick; 0-89288),* P.O. Box 243, Bend, OR 97709 Tel 503-382-6978 (SAN 208-7634).

Mawa Publishing Co., *(Mawa Pub; 0-935053),* Box 22525, Makiki, HI 96822 (SAN 220-1453).

Maxim Publishing, *(Maxim Pub; 0-936696),* P.O. Box 42126, Los Angeles, CA 90042 (SAN 215-1626).

Maxima Communications, Inc., *(Maxima; 0-918612),* 5029 Sherborne Dr., St Louis, MO 63128 Tel 314-894-0370 (SAN 210-122X).

Maxwell, Harvey C., *(H C Maxwell),* P.O. Box 824, Laguna Beach, CA 92652 (SAN 217-2518).

May, George W., *(G W May; 0-9605566),* Rte. 1 Box 221, Metropolis, IL 62960 Tel 618-524-4029 (SAN 216-0471).

May Day Press, *(May Day Pr; 0-9602420),* P.O. Box 1351, Bellflower, CA 90706 Tel 213-439-8423 (SAN 212-1131).

May-Murdock, *(May Murdock; 0-932916),* Box 343, 90 Glenwood Ave., Ross, CA 94957 Tel 415-454-1771 (SAN 212-7628).

Maya Press, The, *(Maya Pr; 0-910997),* 1716 Ocean Ave., Box 181, San Francisco, CA 94112 (SAN 272-2933).

Maya Publishing Co. *See Univ. Press of Virginia*

Mayapple Press, *(Mayapple Pr; 0-932412),* P.O. Box 3185, Kent, OH 44240 Tel 216-678-2775 (SAN 212-1913).

Mayer Associates International, *(Mayer Assocs; 0-9609092),* 6009 Walnut St., Pittsburgh, PA 15206 Tel 516-921-7876 (SAN 241-399X).

Mayer-Johnson, *(Mayer-Johnson; 0-9609160),* Box 86, Stillwater, MN 55082 Tel 612-430-1122 (SAN 241-4007).

Mayers, Joseph, & Co., Inc., *(Mayers-Joseph; 0-9604860),* 50 Park Place, Suite H, Newark, NJ 07102 Tel 201-622-7854 (SAN 214-4115).

Mayfair Press, The, *(Mayfair Pr; 0-9607426),* 1102 Mayfair Rd., Champaign, IL 61821 Tel 217-351-8409 (SAN 239-4588).

Mayfield Printing and Office Equipment,Pubs., *(Mayfield Printing; 0-910513),* 810 Keyser, Natchitoches, LA 71457 Tel 318-357-0054 (SAN 260-1028).

Mayfield Publishing Co., *(Mayfield Pub; 0-87484),* 285 Hamilton Ave., Palo Alto, CA 94301 Tel 415-326-1640 (SAN 202-8972).

Mayflower Books See **Smith, W. H., Pubs., Inc.**

Maynard, Louis, *(L Maynard),* 5922 S. Sunnylane Rd., Oklahoma City, OK 73135 Tel 405-799-2148 (SAN 207-2483).

Maywood Publishing, *(Maywood Pub; 0-9609004),* 2509 N. Campbell, Ste. 227, Tuscon, AZ 85719 Tel 602-327-0823 (SAN 241-3388).

Mazda Pubs., *(Mazda Pubs; 0-939214),* 6375 Shier-Rings Rd., Suite G, Dublin, OH 43017 Tel 614-766-2552 (SAN 285-0524); Orders to: P.O. Box 136, Lexington, KY 40501 (SAN 285-0532).

Maznaim Publishing Corp., *(Maznaim; 0-940118),* 4407-15th Ave., Brooklyn, NY 11219 Tel 212-438-7680 (SAN 214-4123).

Mazzulla, Fred & Jo, *(F&J Mazzulla),* 2060 Dunes Cir., Reno, NV 89509 (SAN 205-8723).

MBM Books, *(MBM Bks; 0-942144),* P.O. Box 1087, Valley Center, CA 92082 Tel 619-749-2380 (SAN 238-4418).

M C I Publishing, *(M C I Pub; 0-911445),* 1028 N. Cherry, Wheaton, IL 60187 Tel 312-653-4500 (SAN 272-2968).

MCSA-Medical Communications & Services Assn., *(Med Communications; 0-917054),* 10223 NE. 58th St., Kirkland, WA 98033 Tel 206-828-4263 (SAN 203-9796).

MD Books, *(MD Bks; 0-9603118),* 26313 Purissima Rd., Los Altos Hills, CA 94022 (SAN 223-1670).

Me Pubns., *(Me Pubns; 0-937706),* P.O. Box 14009, Minneapolis, MN 55414 (SAN 215-6814).

Mead Co., The, *(Mead Co; 0-934422),* 21176 S. Alameda St., Long Beach, CA 90810 (SAN 213-1153).

Meadow Lane Pubns., *(Meadow Lane; 0-934826),* 530 North Midway Drive, No. 79, Escondido, CA 92027 Tel 619-747-0258 (SAN 213-5361).

Meadowbrook Press, *(Meadowbrook Pr; 0-915658; 0-88166),* 18318 Minnetonka Blvd., Deephaven, MN 55391 Tel 612-473-5400 (SAN 207-3404).

Meadowlark Press, *(Meadowlark; 0-941126),* P.O. Box 8172, Prairie Village, KS 66208 (SAN 238-8979).

Meagher, Walter L., *(W L Meagher; 0-913115),* P.O. Box 382, Roosevelt, NJ 08555 (SAN 283-2011).

Meals for Millions/Freedom from Hunger Foundation, *(Meals for Millions; 0-9607124),* 815 Second Ave., Suite 1001, New York, NY 10017 (SAN 239-0108).

Means, Robert Snow, Co., Inc., *(Means; 0-911950),* 100 Construction Plaza, Kingston, MA 02364 Tel 617-747-1270 (SAN 202-6163).

Meckler Publishing, *(Meckler Pub; 0-930466),* 520 Riverside Ave., P.O. Box 405, Saugatuck Sta., Westport, CT 06880 Tel 203-226-6967 (SAN 211-0334).

Med-Ed, Inc., *(Med-Ed; 0-9609222),* P.O. Box 738, Atlanta, GA 30301 Tel 912-435-1636 (SAN 241-4015).

Medallion Books See **Berkley Publishing Corp.**

Medallion Press, *(Medallion Pr),* 906 Shadowlawn Dr., Tallahassee, FL 32312 (SAN 265-3591).

Medi Comp Press, *(Medi-Comp; 0-9600704),* 41 Tunnel Rd., Berkeley, CA 94705 Tel 415-548-1188 (SAN 207-2610).

Medi-Publishing Group, *(Medi-Pub),* 1975 E. Sunrise Blvd., Box 327, Fort Lauderdale, FL 33302 Tel 305-467-0189 (SAN 215-3262).

Media America, Inc., *(Media America; 0-916474),* 12 E. Market St., Bethlehem, PA 18018 Tel 215-866-2207 (SAN 208-1040) Moved, left no forwarding address.

Media Awards Handbook, *(Media Awards; 0-910744),* 621 Sheri Lane, Danville, CA 94526 Tel 415-837-7562 (SAN 205-8707).

Media Concepts Press, *(Media Concepts; 0-935608),* 331 N. Broad St., Philadelphia, PA 19107 Tel 215-923-2545 (SAN 215-3254).

Media Form International, *(Media Forum; 0-912460),* P.O. Box 8, Fleetwood, Mount Vernon, NY 10552 Tel 914-667-6575 (SAN 204-5559).

Media Institute, The, *(Media Inst; 0-937790),* 3017 M St., N.W., Washington, DC 20007 (SAN 215-966X).

Media Productions & Marketing, Inc., *(Media Prods & Mktg; 0-939644),* 344 N. 27th St., Lincoln, NE 68503 Tel 402-474-2676 (SAN 216-6372).

Media Pubns., *(Media Pubns; 0-943214),* 8920 N. First St., P.O. Box 1504, Phoenix, AZ 85001 (SAN 240-5504).

Media Referral Service, *(Media Ref; 0-911125),* P.O. Box 3586, Minneapolis, MN 55403 Tel 612-933-2819 (SAN 272-3123).

Media Unlimited Inc., *(Media Unltd; 0-930394),* Dist. by: A-A-AA Publications, P.O. Box I, Alameda, CA 94501 (SAN 210-6124).

Media Ventures, Inc., *(Media Ventures; 0-89645),* 11167 Main St., Cincinnati, OH 45241 Tel 513-563-1222 (SAN 212-114X).

Media West, *(Media West; 0-939216),* 527 N. Prospect Ave., Redondo Beach, CA 90277 Tel 213-376-7087 (SAN 281-9880).

Mediaor Co., *(Mediaor Co; 0-942206),* Box 631, Prineville, OR 97754 (SAN 238-7859).

Mediax, Inc., *(Mediax; 0-912056),* 21 Charles St., Westport, CT 06880 Tel 203-226-2332 (SAN 205-8685).

Medic Pub. Co., *(Medic Pub),* P.O. Box 89, Redmond, WA 98052 Tel 206-881-2883 (SAN 210-8313).

Medical Administration Corp., *(MAC Book Dept; 0-910223),* 1850 High St., Denver, CO 80218 Tel 303-321-2651 (SAN 241-4031).

Medical Arts Publishing Co., *(Medical Arts; 0-913092),* P.O. Box 8627, Detroit, MI 48224 Tel 313-886-5160 (SAN 202-2184).

Medical/Behavioral Associates, Inc., *(Med-Behavior; 0-936514),* 666 Park Ave. W., Mansfield, OH 44906 (SAN 214-4131).

Medical Economics Books, *(Med Economics; 0-87489),* 680 Kinderkamack Rd., Oradell, NJ 07649 Tel 201-262-3030 (SAN 202-2613); Orders to: Box 157, Florence, KY 41042 (SAN 202-2621).

Medical Education Consultants, *(Med Educ; 0-937142),* Box 67101, Century City, Los Angeles, CA 90067 Tel 213-475-5141 (SAN 209-2891).

Medical Examination Publishing Co., Inc., *(Med Exam; 0-87488),* 3003 New Hyde Park Rd., New Hyde Park, NY 11042 Tel 516-328-6200 (SAN 206-7897).

Medical Group Management Assn., *(Med Group Mgmt),* 4101 E. Louisiana Ave., Denver, CO 80222 Tel 303-753-1111 (SAN 216-2695).

Medical Group Management Association, *(Medical Group; 0-933948),* 4101 E. Louisiana Ave., Denver, CO 80222 (SAN 221-3982).

Medical Library Assn., Inc., *(Med Lib Assn; 0-912176),* 919 N. Michigan Ave., Suite 3208, Chicago, IL 60611 Tel 312-266-2456 (SAN 203-980X).

Medical Manor Books, *(Med Manor Bks; 0-934232),* 3501 Newberry Rd., Philadelphia, PA 19154 (SAN 217-2526).

Medical Media Pubs., *(Med Media Pubs; 0-939450),* 4320 Centre Ave., Pittsburgh, PA 15213 (SAN 216-4159); Dist. by: American Hospital Publishing, Inc., 211 E. Chicago Ave., Chicago, IL 60611 (SAN 216-5872).

Medical Software Company, *(Med Software; 0-88672),* Box 874, 328 Main St., Center Moriches, NY 11934 (SAN 265-1661); 860 5th Ave., Suite, 10E, New York, NY 10021 Tel 516-878-2076 (SAN 265-167X).

Medical Student Publishers, *(Med Student Pubs; 0-910015),* c/o McGookey, P.O. Box 190291, Dallas, TX 75219 Tel 214-522-5549 (SAN 241-340X).

Medicavto, Inc., *(Medicanto; 0-931210),* 283 Greenwich Ave., Greenwich, CT 06830 Tel 203-869-5732 (SAN 211-2574).

Medieval Academy of America, *(Medieval Acad; 0-910956),* 1430 Massachusetts Ave., Cambridge, MA 02138 Tel 617-491-1622 (SAN 203-9826).

Medieval & Renaissance Texts & Studies, *(Medieval & Renaissance NY; 0-86698),* State Univ. of New York, Binghamton, NY 13901 (SAN 216-6119).

Medieval Institute Pubns., *(Medieval Inst; 0-918720),* Western Michigan Univ., Kalamazoo, MI 49008 Tel 616-383-6096 (SAN 212-2928).

Medina Univ., Press International, *(Medina Pr; 0-914456),* P.O. Box 614, Wilmette, IL 60091 Tel 312-328-7890 (SAN 206-5932).

MedMaster, Inc., *(MedMaster; 0-940780),* 17500 N.E. Ninth Ave., N. Miami Beach, FL 33162 Tel 305-653-3480 (SAN 219-7960).

Medusa, *(Medusa; 0-9601714),* 4112 Emery Place, N.W., Washington, DC 20016 Tel 202-244-1239 (SAN 215-9678).

Meeker Publishing Co., *(Meeker Pub; 0-935068),* 2605 Virginia St., N.E., Albuquerque, NM 87110 Tel 505-299-6406 (SAN 205-8650).

Megan's World, *(Megans Wld; 0-9610150),* 124 W. Wilshire, P.O. Box 3399, Fullerton, CA 92634 Tel 714-871-1369 (SAN 272-3239).

Megden Publishing, *(Megden Pub; 0-9603676),* P.O. Box 217, Huntington Beach, CA 92648 Tel 714-536-7785 (SAN 214-414X).

Meher Baba Information, *(Meher Baba Info; 0-940700),* Box 1101, Berkeley, CA 94701 Tel 415-562-1101 (SAN 202-618X); Dist. by: Bookpeople, 2940 Seventh St., Berkeley, CA 94710 Tel 415-549-3033 (SAN 168-9517).

Mehetabel & Co., *(Mehetabel & Co; 0-936094),* P.O. Box 151, Tiburon, CA 94920-0151 Tel 415-472-0467 (SAN 281-9902).

Meiklejohn Civil Liberties Institute, *(Meiklejohn Civ Lib; 0-913876),* 1715 Francisco St., Berkeley, CA 94703 Tel 415-848-0599 (SAN 203-9834); Orders to: Box 673, Berkeley, CA 94701 (SAN 203-9842).

Melbourne Univ. Pr., *(Melbourne U Pr; 0-522),* P. O. Box 278, Carleton, South Victoria 3053, .

Mele Loke Publishing Co., *(M Loke; 0-930932),* P.O. Box 7142, Honolulu, HI 96821 Tel 808-734-8611 (SAN 211-1330).

Melek, Jacques, *(J Melek; 0-942330),* P.O. Box 901, Upland, CA 91786 (SAN 241-5607).

Mellen, Edwin Press, *(E Mellen; 0-88946),* P.O. Box 450, Lewiston, NY 14092 Tel 716-754-8566 (SAN 207-110X).

Melodious Pubns., *(Melodious Pubns),* Box 343-X, Brockport, NY 14420 Tel 716-637-4622 (SAN 219-7979).

Melodyland Pubs., Div. of Melodyland Christian Center, *(Melodyland; 0-918818),* P.O. Box 6000, Anaheim, CA 92806 Tel 714-635-6391 (SAN 210-4628).

Melrose Publishing Co., *(Melrose Pub Co; 0-934972),* 384 N. San Vicente Blvd., Los Angeles, CA 90048 Tel 213-655-5177 (SAN 211-7436).

Melrose Square See **Holloway House Publishing Co.**

Membrane Press, *(Membrane Pr; 0-87924),* P.O. Box 11601, Shorewood, Milwaukee, WI 53211 (SAN 202-621X).

Memento Pubns., Inc., *(Memento; 0-89436),* 901 Washington St., Wilmington, DE 19801 Tel 302-654-5511 (SAN 210-1246).

Memorial Sloan-Kettering Cancer Ctr., *(Memorial Sloan-Kettering; 0-911315),* 1275 York Ave., New York, NY 10021 Tel 212-794-7727 (SAN 272-3271).

Memorial Union Corporation, *(Memorial Union; 0-934068),* Emporia State University, 1200 Commercial St., Emporia, KS 66801 (SAN 264-2050).

Memphis Junior League Publications, *(Memphis Jr League Pubns; 0-9604222),* 2711 Union Ave., Memphis, TN 38112 Tel 901-452-2151 (SAN 238-7840).

Memphis State Univ. Press, *(Memphis St Univ; 0-87870),* Memphis State Univ., Memphis, TN 38152 Tel 901-454-2752 (SAN 202-6228).

Menaid Press International, Div. of Fichter Enterprises, *(Menaid; 0-918424),* P.O. Box 25008, Colorado Springs, CO 80936 Tel 303-598-8058 (SAN 209-9578).

Menasha Ridge Press, *(Menasha Ridge; 0-89732)*, Six Grampian Hills, Chapel Hill, NC 27514 (SAN 262-0685).

Mendel, Carol, *(Carol Mendel; 0-9607696)*, P.O. Box 6022, San Diego, CA 92106 Tel 619-226-1406 (SAN 219-3329).

Mendoza, Carlos R., *(C Mendoza; 0-9608420)*, 613 Point Caiman Court, Chula Vista, CA 92011 Tel 714-421-8848 (SAN 240-7205).

Menil Foundation, *(Menil Found; 0-939594)*, c/o Harvard Univ. Pr., 79 Garden St., Cambridge, MA 02138 (SAN 200-2043).

Menorah Publishing Co., Inc., *(Menorah Pub; 0-932232)*, 15 W. 84th St., New York, NY 10024 Tel 212-787-2248 (SAN 212-1158).

Menses, *(Menses; 0-9605700)*, Box 192, Croton-on-Hudson, NY 10520 (SAN 216-2466).

Mental Health Materials Center, *(Mental Health)*, 419 Park Ave S, New York, NY 10016 (SAN 228-068X).

Mentor Books *See* **New American Library**

Mentors, Inc., *(Mentors)*, 8817 Greenview Place, Spring Valley, CA 92077 Tel 714-464-4235 (SAN 241-5615).

Meola, Edward A., *(Meola; 0-9606008)*, 5806 Circle H Place, Tucson, AZ 85713 (SAN 216-4175).

Mercadante, J. L., *(J L Mercadante)*, P.O. Box 1028, New Hyde Park, NY 11040 (SAN 211-0830).

Mercantine Press, *(Mercantine Pr; 0-933962)*, 4351 Washington St., Lincoln, NE 68506 Tel 402-489-2626 (SAN 212-9175).

Mercer House Press, *(Mercer Hse; 0-89080)*, Clover Leaf Farm, Old Rte. 9, Rfd No. 1, Biddeford, ME 04005 Tel 207-282-7116 (SAN 207-1754); Orders to: P.O. Box 681, Kennebunkport, ME 04046 (SAN 207-1762).

Mercer Univ. Press, *(Mercer Univ Pr; 0-86554)*, Macon, GA 31207 Tel 912-744-2880 (SAN 220-0716).

Merchandising Concepts Specialists, *(Merchandising; 0-943038)*, 132 S. Bedford Dr. No 206, Beverly Hills, CA 90212 Tel 213-276-9813 (SAN 240-4087).

Merck & Co., Inc., *(Merck; 0-911910)*, P.O. Box 2000, Rahway, NJ 07065 Tel 201-574-5403 (SAN 202-6236).

Merck Sharp & Dohme International, *(Merck-Sharp-Dohme; 0-911910)*, Professional Communications Dept., West Point, PA 19486 (SAN 212-1921).

Mercury Books, *(Mercury Bks; 0-910963)*, P.O. Box 442, Yardley, PA 19067 Tel 215-482-8404 (SAN 272-3492).

Mercury Press (MO), *(Mercury Pr; 0-912393)*, P.O. Box 811, Columbia, MO 65205-0811 Tel 314-474-4079 (SAN 264-2069).

Mercury Printing Co., *(Mercury Print; 0-9606880)*, 2929 Convair Rd., Memphis, TN 38116 (SAN 238-809X).

Meredith, H. V., *(H V Meredith; 0-9603120)*, Orders to: The State Printing Company, P.O. Box 1388, Columbia, SC 29202 Tel 803-799-9550 (SAN 204-6334).

Meredith, Joseph N., *(J N Meredith; 0-9609300)*, Lewisburg Manor, Apt. 127, 344 N. Court St., Lewisburg, WV 24901 Tel 304-645-6505 (SAN 241-404X).

Meredith Corp., *(Meredith Corp; 0-696)*, Orders to: Better Homes & Gardens Books, 1716 Locust, Des Moines, IA 50336 (SAN 202-4055).

Merganzer Press, *(Merganzer Pr; 0-9602648)*, 659 Northmoor Rd., Lake Forest, IL 60045 (SAN 212-7636).

Merging Media, *(Merging Media; 0-934536)*, 59 Sandra Circle A3, Westfield, NJ 07090 Tel 201-232-7224 (SAN 206-3662).

Meridian Books *See* **New American Library**

Meridian Editions, *(Meridian Ed)*, 9905 Lorain Ave., Silver Spring, MD 20901 (SAN 209-5831).

Meridian Hill Pubns., *(Meridian Hill; 0-940206)*, P.O. Box 416, 1446 Burland Dr., Bailey, CO 80421 Tel 303-838-4877 (SAN 220-3413).

Meridian Press, Subs. of Center for Help for Agoraphobia/Anxiety Through New Growth Experiences, *(Meridian; 0-9609462)*, 1339 S. Wendover Rd., Charlotte, NC 28211 Tel 704-364-5026 (SAN 260-2253).

Meridian Publishing, *(Meridian Pub; 0-86610)*, 2643 Edgewood Rd., Utica, NY 13501 (SAN 215-2568).

Meridional Pubns., *(Meridional Pubns; 0-939710)*, Rte. 2 Box 28a, Wake Forest, NC 27587 Tel 919-556-2940 (SAN 216-7484).

Merit Pubns., Inc., *(Merit Pubns; 0-87803)*, 610 NE 124th St., N. Miami, FL 33161 (SAN 211-4380).

Merit Pubs., *(Merit Calif; 0-910962)*, P.O. Box 1344, Beverly Hills, CA 90213 Tel 213-474-1888 (SAN 203-9869).

Meriwether Publishing Ltd., *(Meriwether Pub; 0-916260)*, P.O. Box 7710, Colorado Springs, CO 80933 Tel 312-495-0300 (SAN 208-4716).

Merk, *(Merk)*, 377 Merk Rd., Watsonville, CA 95076 (SAN 215-8892).

Merlin Engine Works, *(Merlin Engine Wks)*, 548 Elm, San Bruno, CA 94066 (SAN 217-8915).

Merlin Press, *(Merlin Pr; 0-930142)*, P.O. Box 5602, San Jose, CA 95150 (SAN 209-584X).

Mermaid Dramabooks *See* **Hill & Wang, Inc.**

Mermelstein, Mel, *(M Mermelstein; 0-9606534)*, c/o Auschwitz Study Foundation, 7422 Cedar St., P.O. Box 2232, Huntington Beach, CA 92647 Tel 213-592-5550 (SAN 214-4158).

Merriam, Robert L., *(R L Merriam)*, Newhall Rd., Conway, MA 01341 (SAN 163-4070).

Merriam-Eddy Co., Inc., *(Merriam-Eddy; 0-914562)*, P.O. Box 25, South Waterford, ME 04009 (SAN 202-6252).

Merriam-Webster Inc., Subs. of Encyclopaedia Britannica, Inc., *(Merriam-Webster Inc; 0-87779)*, 47 Federal St. P.O. Box 281, Springfield, MA 01101 Tel 413-734-3134 (SAN 202-6244).

Merrill, Charles E., Publishing Co., Div. of Bell & Howell Co., *(Merrill; 0-675)*, 1300 Alum Creek Dr., Columbus, OH 43216 Tel 614-258-8441 (SAN 200-2116).

Merrill, Perry H., *(P H Merrill; 0-9605806)*, 200 Elm St., Montpelier, VT 05602 Tel 802-223-2697 (SAN 220-1755).

Merrimack Book Service, Inc., *(Merrimack Publishers' Circle)*, 458 Boston St., Topsfield, MA 01973 Tel 617-887-2440 (SAN 212-193X); Orders to: 99 Main St., Salem, NH 03079 Tel 617-685-4636 (SAN 212-1948).

Merrimack Publishing Corp., *(Merrimack)*, Dist. by: Associated Booksellers, 214 McKinley Ave., Bridgeport, CT 06606 (SAN 206-9717).

Merrimack Valley Textile Museum, *(Merrimack Vall Textile; 0-937474)*, 800 Massachusetts Ave., North Andover, MA 01845 Tel 617-686-0191 (SAN 205-8537).

Merritt Co., *(Merritt Co; 0-930868)*, 1661 Ninth St., Santa Monica, CA 90406 (SAN 203-8110).

Merritt Pubs., *(Merritt Pubs Texas; 0-930238)*, 718 Westwood, Richardson, TX 75080 Tel 214-644-5765 (SAN 210-6132).

Merriwell, Frank, Inc., *(F Merriwell; 0-8373)*, 212 Michael Dr., Syosset, NY 11791 Tel 516-921-8888 (SAN 209-259X).

Merry Thoughts, *(Merry Thoughts; 0-88230)*, 380 Adams St., Bedford Hills, NY 10507 Tel 914-241-0447 (SAN 206-6882).

Merton House Travel and Tourism Publishers, Inc., *(Merton Hse; 0-916032)*, 937 W. Liberty Dr., Wheaton, IL 60187 Tel 312-668-7410 (SAN 207-9739).

Mesa Press, *(Mesa Pr IL)*, 5835 Kimbark Ave, Chicago, IL 60637 Tel 312-962-1583 (SAN 215-3270).

Mesa Pubns., Div. of Mesa International, Inc., *(Mesa Pubns; 0-931984)*, 6266 N. Swan Rd., Tucson, AZ 85718 (SAN 211-8629).

Mesa Verde Press, *(Mesa Verde; 0-9607220)*, 144 Mesa Verde St., Santa Fe, NM 87501 Tel 505-982-5470 (SAN 239-1163).

Mesorah Pubns., Ltd., *(Mesorah Pubns; 0-89906)*, 1969 Coney Island Ave., Brooklyn, NY 11223 Tel 212-339-1700 (SAN 213-1269).

Messenger Communications, *(Messenger Comm; 0-939336)*, 18706 25th Ave. S.E., Bothell, WA 98011 Tel 206-481-9399 (SAN 216-5392).

Messner, Julian, A Simon & Schuster Div. of Gulf & Western Corp., *(Messner; 0-671)*, 1230 Ave. of the Americas, New York, NY 10020 Tel 212-245-6400 (SAN 202-6260).

Metacom Press, *(Metacom Pr; 0-911381)*, 31 Beaver St., Worcester, MA 01603 Tel 617-757-1683 (SAN 272-3581).

Metagaming, *(Metagam)*, Box 15346, Austin, TX 78761 Tel 512-836-4116 (SAN 211-8637).

Metal Building Dealers Assn., *(Metal Building; 0-9603678)*, 1406 Third National Bldg., Dayton, OH 45402 Tel 513-223-0489 (SAN 213-7763).

Metal Powder Industries Federation, *(Metal Powder; 0-918404)*, 105 College Rd. E., Princeton, NJ 08540 Tel 609-452-7700 (SAN 209-6250).

Metamorphosis Press, *(Metamorphosis Pr)*, 220 Miramonte Ave., Palo Alto, CA 94306 (SAN 209-5858).

Metamorphous Press, *(Metamorphous Pr)*, P.O. Box 1712, Lake Oswego, OR 97034 (SAN 264-2077).

Metascience Corp., *(Metascience; 0-935436)*, Box 747, Franklin, NC 28734 Tel 704-524-5103 (SAN 213-4179).

Metatron Press, *(Metatron Pr; 0-931412)*, P. O. Box 10356, Milwaukee, WI 53210 Tel 414-444-2442 (SAN 211-142X).

Metcut Research Associates, Inc., *(Metcut Res Assocs; 0-936974)*, 3980 Rosslyn Dr., Cincinnati, OH 45209 (SAN 214-4166).

Methodius Press, *(Methodius Pr; 0-9611866)*, 7878 Twin Pines Lane, Sebastopol, CA 95472 Tel 707-823-0978 (SAN 286-1437).

Methuen Inc., *(Methuen Inc; 0-416)*, 733 Third Ave., New York, NY 10017 Tel 212-922-3550 (SAN 213-196X); Dist. by: Transworld Distribution Services, Inc., 80 Northfield Ave., Raritan Center, Edison, NJ 08817 (SAN 213-1978).

Methuselah Books, *(Methuselah Bks; 0-937092)*, Rt. 1 Spindle Rd., Ellsworth, ME 04605 (SAN 214-4174).

Metis Press, Inc., *(Metis Pr Inc; 0-934816)*, P.O. Box 25187, Chicago, IL 60625 (SAN 213-2575).

Metric Media Book Pubs., Div. of Abbey Books, *(Metric Media Bk)*, P.O. Box 266, Somers, NY 10589 Tel 914-248-5522 (SAN 209-147X).

Metro Books, Inc., *(Metro Bks; 0-8411)*, 3110 N. Arlington Heights Rd., Arlington Heights, IL 60004 Tel 312-253-9720 (SAN 203-9893).

Metron Press, *(Metron Pr)*, St. Anthony Falls Sta., Box 4202, Minneapolis, MN 55414 (SAN 220-259X).

Metron Pubns., *(Metron Pubns; 0-940268)*, P.O. Box 1213, Princeton, NJ 08540 Tel 609-921-1617 (SAN 217-5401).

Metropolitan Futures, Inc., *(Metro Futures; 0-915218)*, P.O. Box 1151, New York, NY 10017 (SAN 207-1444).

Metropolitan Museum of Art, *(Metro Mus Art; 0-87099)*, 5th Ave. and 82nd St., New York, NY 10028 Tel 212-879-5500 (SAN 202-6279).

Mettler Studios, Inc., *(Mettler Studios; 0-912536)*, Tucson Creative Dance Ctr., 3131 N. Cherry Ave., Tucson, AZ 85719 Tel 602-327-7453 (SAN 206-1589).

Metzger Press, *(Metzger Pr; 0-9608750)*, 303 W. Glenoaks Blvd., Suite 208, Glendale, CA 91202 Tel 213-244-0365 (SAN 241-0370).

Mexican American Legal Defense & Educational Fund, *(Mex Am Legal)*, 28 Geary, San Francisco, CA 94108 (SAN 232-3362).

Mexican Museum, The, *(Mexican Museum; 0-905194)*, Fort Mason Center, Building D, Laguna & Marina Blvd., San Francisco, CA 94123 Tel 415-441-0404 (SAN 238-7832).

Mey-House Books, *(Mey-Hse Bks; 0-9611140)*, P.O. Box 794, Stroudsburg, PA 18360 (SAN 285-6670).

Meyer, Leo A., Associates, Inc., *(L A Meyer; 0-88069)*, 23850 Clawiter Rd., Hayward, CA 94545 Tel 415-785-1091 (SAN 238-0951).

Meyerbooks, *(Meyerbooks; 0-916638)*, P.O. Box 427, 235 W. Main St., Glenwood, IL 60425 Tel 312-757-4950 (SAN 208-998X).

Mezquita Editorial, *(Mezquita Edit; 0-930174)*, 20 W. 22nd St., Rm 1000, New York, NY 10010 Tel 212-865-4067 (SAN 210-640X).

MH Cap and Company, *(M H Cap; 0-911375)*, P.O. Box 3584, Bakersfield, CA 93385 Tel 213-961-2796 (SAN 272-3972).

M H Enterprises, *(M H Enterprises; 0-9611044),* 420 W. 4th St., Hominy, OK 74035 Tel 918-885-2913 (SAN 282-924X); Dist. by: Centennial Distributors, P.O. Box 424, Deadwood, SD 57732 (SAN 200-4321).

Mho & Mho Works, *(Mho & Mho),* Dist. by: Bookpeople, 2940 Seventh Ave., Berkeley, CA 94710 Tel 415-549-3033 (SAN 168-9517).

Miami Univ. Art Museum, *(Miami Univ Art; 0-940784),* Patterson Ave., Oxford, OH 45056 Tel 513-529-2232 (SAN 219-6042).

Micah Pubns., *(Micah Pubns; 2-916288),* 255 Humphrey St., Marblehead, MA 01945 Tel 617-631-7601 (SAN 209-1577).

Micelle Press, Inc., *(Micelle Pr; 0-9608752),* P.O. Box 653, Cranford, NJ 07016 Tel 201-272-9041 (SAN 241-0443).

Michael, Pansy D., *(P D Michael; 0-9602460),* R.R. 2, South Whitley, IN 46787 Tel 219-839-3135 (SAN 212-8624).

Michael, Prudence Groff, *(P G Michael; 0-9600932),* 64472 U.S.H 31, Lakeville, IN 46536 Tel 219-291-0454 (SAN 208-7669).

Michelin Guides & Maps, Dept. of Michelin Tire Corp., *(Michelin),* P.O. Box 1007, New Hyde Park, NY 11042 Tel 212-895-2342 (SAN 202-6309).

Michie Co., The, *(Michie Co; 0-87215; 0-672),* P.O. Box 7587, Charlottesville, VA 22906 Tel 804-295-6171 (SAN 202-6317).

Michigan Natural Resources Magazine, *(Mich Nat Res; 0-941912),* Box 30034, Lansing, MI 48909 (SAN 239-4596).

Michigan Publications on East Asia *See* **Univ. of Michigan, Center for Chinese Studies**

Michigan Romance Studies, *(Mich Romance; 0-939730),* Dept. of Romance Languages, Univ. of Michigan, Ann Arbor, MI 48109 Tel 313-764-5386 (SAN 216-7654).

Michigan Slavic Pubns, *(Mich Slavic Pubns; 0-930042),* Dept. of Slavic Languages & Literatures, Univ. of Michigan, Ann Arbor, MI 48109 Tel 313-763-4496 (SAN 210-4636).

Michigan State Univ., Community Development, *(MSU-Inst Comm Devel),* S. Harrison Rd., East Lansing, MI 48824 Tel 517-355-0100 (SAN 202-2583).

Michigan State Univ. Press, *(Mich St U Pr; 0-87013),* 1405 S. Harrison Rd., 25 Manly Miles Bldg., East Lansing, MI 48824 Tel 517-355-9543 (SAN 202-6295).

Michigan United Conservation Clubs, *(Mich United Conserv; 0-933112),* P.O. Box 30235, Lansing, MI 48909 Tel 517-371-1041 (SAN 208-1091).

Michilander Industries, *(Michilander Indust; 0-941640),* 1100 State St., St. Joseph, MI 49085 Tel 616-983-4972 (SAN 238-7816).

Mickler House Pubs., The, *(Mickler Hse; 0-913122),* P.O. Box 38, Chuluota, FL 32766 Tel 305-365-3636 (SAN 206-6874).

Micro Information Publishing, *(Micro Info; 0-912603),* 15420 Eagle Creek Ave., Prior Lake, MN 55372 Tel 612-447-6959 (SAN 282-7867).

Micro Ink, Inc., *(Micro Ink; 0-938222),* Ten Northern Blvd., P.O. Box 6502, Amherst, NH 03031 Tel 603-889-4330 (SAN 217-2542).

Micro Magic Cooking Co., *(Micro Magic; 0-9606096),* 145 N. 46th St., Lincoln, NE 68503 Tel 402-475-4536 (SAN 216-8367).

Micro Text Pubns., Inc., *(Micro Text Pubns; 0-942412),* 1 Lincoln Plaza, Suite 27C, New York, NY 10023 Tel 212-877-8539 (SAN 238-1753).

Microcomputer Applications, *(Microcomputer Appns; 0-935230),* 827 Missouri St., Fairfield, CA 94533 (SAN 285-0540); Orders to: P.O. Box E, Suisun City, CA 94595 Tel 707-422-1465 (SAN 285-0559).

Microfilming Corp. of America, *(Microfilming Corp; 0-88455; 0-667),* 1620 Hawkins Ave., P.O. Box 10, Sanford, NC 27330 Tel 919-775-3451 (SAN 202-6325) Microforms of newspapers, periodicals, books, curriculum materials, documents & archival materials for research.

Microform Review, *(Microform Rev; 0-913672),* 520 Riverside Ave., Westport, CT 06880 Tel 203-226-6967 (SAN 202-6333).

Microscope Pubns., Div. of McCrone Research Institute, *(Microscope Pubns; 0-904962),* 2508 S. Michigan Ave., Chicago, IL 60616 Tel 312-842-7100 (SAN 209-9594).

Microtraining Associates, Inc., *(Microtraining Assocs; 0-917276),* P.O. Box 641, North Amherst, MA 01059 Tel 413-256-0200 (SAN 208-7677).

Microwave Helps, *(Microwave Helps; 0-9602930),* P.O. Box 32223, Minneapolis, MN 55432 Tel 612-571-6091 (SAN 212-9531).

Mid-America Press, *(Mid Am Pr; 0-9604672),* P.O. Box 21241, Columbia Heights, MN 55421 Tel 612-781-5166 (SAN 220-0724).

Mid-Atlantic Solar Energy Assn., *(MASEA; 0-9601884),* 2233 Gray's Ferry Ave., Philadelphia, PA 19146 (SAN 220-2603).

Mid East Publishing Co., *(Mid East Pub Co)* P.O. Box A 3777, Chicago, IL 60690 Tel 312-545-0478 (SAN 212-7644).

Mid-Lifelines, *(Mid-Life; 0-9609806),* 267 Firestone Dr., Walnut Creek, CA 94598 Tel 415-933-5481 (SAN 272-4103).

Mid-South Scientific Pubs., *(Mid South Sci Pubs; 0-935974),* Box FM, Hwy. 82 E., Mississippi State Univ., Mississippi State, MS 39762 (SAN 213-7771).

Midcoast Pubns., *(MidCoast Pubns; 0-910025),* 1982 Karlin Dr., St. Louis, MO 63131 Tel 314-966-3023 (SAN 285-0613); Dist. by: Quality Books Inc., 400 Anthony Trail, St. Louis, MO 60642 (SAN 285-0621); Dist. by: Paperback Supply Inc., 4121 Forest Park Ave., St. Louis, MO 63108 (SAN 285-063X); Orders to: 201 S. Central, Suite 310, St. Louis, MO 63105 Tel 314-726-2525 (SAN 285-0648); Orders to: P.O. Box 16880, St. Louis, MO 63105 (SAN 285-0656).

Middle Atlantic Planetarium Society, *(Mid Atlantic Planetarium),* 3911 Sonora Pl, Alexandria, VA 22309 (SAN 225-8609) Moved, left no forwarding address.

Middle East Editorial Associates, *(Middle East Edit; 0-918992),* 1717 Massachusetts Ave., NW, Suite 100, Washington, DC 20036 Tel 202-797-7900 (SAN 210-4644).

Middle East Institute, *(Mid East Inst; 0-916808),* 1761 "N" St., N.W., Washington, DC 20036 Tel 202-785-1141 (SAN 202-2168).

Middle East Review *See* **American Academic Assn. for Peace in the Middle East**

Middleburg Press, The, *(Middleburg Pr; 0-931940),* Box 166, Orange City, IA 51041 (SAN 212-9183).

Midlothian Mirror, *(Midlothian),* Box 1140, Midlothian, TX 76065 (SAN 205-8464).

Midmarch Assocs., *(Midmarch Assocs; 0-9602476),* Box 3304, Grand Central Sta., New York, NY 10163 (SAN 213-3393).

Midnight Call, *(Midnight Call; 0-937422),* P.O. Box 864, Columbia, SC 29202 (SAN 211-8130).

Midnight Sun, *(Midnight Sun; 0-935292),* 223 E. 28th St., 1RE, New York, NY 10016 (SAN 213-537X).

Midway Pubs., *(Midway Pubs; 0-938300),* Box 8088, Naples, FL 33941 (SAN 217-2534).

Midwest Alliance in Nursing, Inc., *(Midwest Alliance Nursing; 0-942146),* Room 108 Br, Indiana University, 1226 W. Michigan St., Indianapolis, IN 46223 (SAN 238-0226).

Midwest Heritage Publishing Co., *(Midwest Heritage; 0-934582),* 108 Pearl St., Iowa City, IA 52240 Tel 319-351-2364 (SAN 213-1161).

Midwest Plan Service, *(Midwest Plan Serv; 0-89373),* 122 Davidson Hall, Iowa State Univ., Ames, IA 50011 Tel 515-294-4337 (SAN 209-0295).

Midwest Pubns. Co., Inc., *(Midwest Pubns; 0-910974; 0-89455),* P.O. Box 448, Pacific Grove, CA 93950 Tel 408-375-2455 (SAN 207-0510).

Midwest Publishing Co., *(Midwest Pub IN; 0-935728),* P.O. Box 33247, 2057 Sloan Ave., Indianapolis, IN 46203 (SAN 214-252X).

Midwest Taekwon-Do Assn. *(Midwest Taekwon-Do; 0-937314),* P.O. Box 281, Grand Blanc, MI 48439 (SAN 214-4182).

Mih Pubns., *(Mih),* 15 Arnold Place, New bedford, MA 02740 Tel 617-993-0156 (SAN 207-8651).

Milady Publishing Corp., *(Milady; 0-87350),* 3839 White Plains Rd., Bronx, NY 10467 Tel 212-881-3000 (SAN 202-635X).

Milagro Press, Inc., *(Milagro Pr Inc; 0-9608504),* P.O. Box 1804, Santa Fe, NM 87501 Tel 505-988-1166 (SAN 240-7221).

Miles, James F., *(J F Miles; 0-9600480),* P.O. Box 1041, Clemson, SC 29631 Tel 803-654-2410 (SAN 203-8978).

Miles & Weir, Ltd., *(Miles & Weir; 0-917300),* P.O. Box 1906, San Pedro, CA 90731 Tel 213-548-5964 (SAN 208-8541).

Miles, R. and E., *(R&E Miles; 0-936810),* Box 1916, San Pedro, CA 90733 (SAN 221-3834).

Milford, Richard, *(R Milford; 0-936292),* 22 Gerdes Ave., Verona, NJ 07044 (SAN 214-056X).

Milford Historical Society, *(Milford Hist Soc; 0-9607742),* 124 E. Commerce, Milford, MI 48042 (SAN 238-7905).

Milford House, Div. of Longwood Pub. Group, *(Milford Hse; 0-87821),* 51 Washington St., Dover, NH 03820 (SAN 202-6368).

Military Affairs (Aerospace Historian Puplishing.), *(MA-AH Pub; 0-89126),* Eisenhower Hall, Kansas State University, Manhattan, KS 66506 Tel 913-532-6733 (SAN 208-0230).

Military Collectors News Press, *(MCN Pr; 0-912958),* P.O. Box 7582, Tulsa, OK 74170 Tel 918-743-6048 (SAN 281-9961); Dist. by: Baker & Taylor, Gladiola Ave., Momence, IL 60945 (SAN 169-2100); Dist. by: Key Book Service, 425 Asylum St., Bridgeport, CT 06610 (SAN 209-6404); Dist. by: Midwest Library Service, 11400 Dorsett Rd., Maryland Heights, MO 63043 (SAN 226-3211).

Military Marketing Services, Inc., *(Military Marketing; 0-914862),* P.O. Box 4010, Arlington, VA 22204 Tel 703-237-0203 (SAN 207-365X).

Mill Books, *(Mill Bks),* Mill & Main St., Darby, PA 19032 (SAN 210-6140).

Millenium House Pubs., *(Millenium Hse; 0-916538),* P.O. Box 85, Agoura, CA 91301 Tel 213-889-3711 (SAN 203-9923).

Millennial Productions, *(Millennial Prods; 0-9602626),* 2455 Calle Roble, Thousand Oaks, CA 91360 (SAN 213-3407).

Miller, Charlotte, *(Miller; 0-9606646),* 1008 Sansome Ct, Modesto, CA 95350 Tel 209-267-1357 (SAN 219-6050).

Miller, Edmund, *(Edmund Miller; 0-9600486),* 61-07 Woodside Ave., Apt. 5J, Woodside, NY 11377 Tel 212-424-0480 (SAN 203-8374).

Miller, Neil, *(N Miller; 0-9601444),* 747 Bruce Dr., East Meadow, NY 11554 Tel 516-292-9569 (SAN 211-0393).

Miller, Oscar R., *(O R Miller; 0-9600552),* P.O. Box 229, Berlin, OH 44610 Tel 216-893-2870 (SAN 203-7556).

Miller, Roger Photo, Ltd., *(R Miller Photo; 0-911897),* 1411 Hollins St., Baltimore, MD 21223 Tel 301-624-5253 (SAN 264-6781).

Miller, Sandra Lake, *(S L Miller; 0-9609448),* 1024 W. Main St., Leesburg, FL 32748 Tel 904-787-3272 (SAN 262-8236).

Miller Books, *(Miller Bks; 0-912472),* 2908 W. Valley Blvd., Alhambra, CA 91803 Tel 213-284-7607 (SAN 203-9931).

Miller Enterprises, *(Miller Ent; 0-89566),* P.O. Box 395, Boulder Creek, CA 95006 Tel 408-338-6780 (SAN 210-6426).

Miller Enterprises, *(Miller OH),* P.O. Box 353, Athens, OH 45701 (SAN 241-5631).

Miller Freeman Pubns., Inc., *(Miller Freeman; 0-87930),* 500 Howard St., San Francisco, CA 94105 Tel 415-397-1881 (SAN 213-6511).

Millers River Publishing Co, *(Millers River Pub Co),* Box 159, Athol, MA 01331 (SAN 265-3605); Dist. by: Inland Book Co., P.O. Box 261, East Haven, CT 06512 Tel 203-467-4257 (SAN 200-4151).

Mills, Charles P., *(C P Mills),* 952 Old Huntingdon Pike, Huntingdon Valley, PA 19006 (SAN 201-8640).

Mills Publishing Co., *(Mills Pub Co; 0-935356),* King Sta., P.O. Box 6158, Santa Ana, CA 92706 Tel 714-541-5750 (SAN 272-4464).

Milton Bradley Company, *(Milton Bradley Co; 0-88049),* 443 Shaker Road, East Longmeadow, MA 01028 (SAN 238-7891).

Milwaukee Books, *(Milwaukee Bks; 0-942608),* 2147 N. 56th St., Milwaukee, WI 53208 Tel 414-257-3750 (SAN 238-5422).

Milwaukee County Historical Society, *(Milwaukee County; 0-938076),* 910 N. Third St., Milwaukee, WI 53203 Tel 414-273-8288 (SAN 205-8383).

Milwaukee Journal, Public Service Bureau, *(Milwaukee Journal),* 333 W. State St., Milwaukee, WI 53201 Tel 414-224-2120 (SAN 240-0561).

Milwaukee Public Museum, *(Milwaukee Pub Mus; 0-89326),* 800 W. Wells St., Milwaukee, WI 53233 Tel 414-278-2787 (SAN 202-229X).

Milwaukee Sentinel, The, *(Milwaukee Sentinel),* 918 N. 4th St., P.O. Box 371, Milwaukee, WI 53201 Tel 414-224-2120 (SAN 215-2827).

Mimir Pubs., Inc., *(Mimir; 0-912084),* P.O. Box 5011, Madison, WI 53705 Tel 608-231-1667 (SAN 202-6376).

Mina Press Publishing, Inc., *(Mina Pr; 0-942610),* P.O. Box 854, Sebastopol, CA 95472 Tel 707-829-0854 (SAN 238-5430).

Mindbody, Inc., *(Mindbody Inc),* 50 Maple Place, Manhasset, NY 11030 Tel 516-365-7722 (SAN 214-0365).

Mindbody Press, *(Mindbody; 0-939508),* 1749 Vine St., Berkeley, CA 94703 Tel 415-843-2766 (SAN 216-4183); Dist. by: Bookpeople, 2940 Seventh St., Berkeley, CA 94710 Tel 415-549-3030 (SAN 168-9517).

Mineralogical Society of America, *(Mineral Soc Ari; 0-910011),* P.O. Box 902, Phoenix, AZ 85001 Tel 602-833-3305 (SAN 241-2241).

Mini-Word Editions, *(Mini-Word; 0-935358),* P.O. Box 3314, Champaign, IL 61820 (SAN 213-5388).

Ministers Life Resources, *(Ministers Life),* 3100 W. Lake St., Minneapolis, MN 55416 Tel 612-927-7131 (SAN 217-2550).

Ministries, Christian, Publications, *(Christian Mini; 0-911567),* 173 Woodland Ave., Lexington, KY 40502 (SAN 264-2115).

Ministry Pubns., *(Ministry Pubns; 0-938234),* P.O. Box 276, Redlands, CA 92373 (SAN 215-787X).

Minkus Pubns., Inc., *(Minkus; 0-912236),* c/o Minkus Stamp Journal, 41 W. 25th St., New York, NY 10010 (SAN 207-6233).

Minneapolis Institute of Arts, *(Minneapolis Inst Arts; 0-912964),* 2400 Third Ave., S., Minneapolis, MN 55404 Tel 612-870-3029 (SAN 202-2567).

Minneapolis Riverfront Development Coordination Board, *(Minneapolis Riverfront; 0-9604360),* 235 City Hall, Minneapolis, MN 55415 (SAN 215-0956).

Minneapolis Star & Tribune Co., The, *(Minneapolis Tribune; 0-932272),* 425 Portland Ave., Minneapolis, MN 55488 Tel 612-372-4420 (SAN 220-2611); Dist. by: The Bookmen, Inc., 525 N. Third St., Minneapolis, MN 55401 (SAN 169-409X).

Minnesota Geological Survey, *(Minn Geol Surv; 0-934938),* 2642 University Avenue, St. Paul, MN 55114 Tel 612-373-3372 (SAN 203-994X).

Minnesota Historical Society, *(Minn Hist; 0-87351),* 690 Cedar St., St. Paul, MN 55101 Tel 612-296-2264 (SAN 202-6384); Orders to: 1500 Mississippi St., St. Paul, MN 55101 (SAN 202-6392).

Minnesota Library Assn., *(Minn Library; 0-939098),* P.O. Box 484, Rosemount, MN 55068 Tel 612-432-2833 (SAN 239-6947).

Minnesota Medical Foundation, Inc., *(Minn Med Found; 0-940210),* Univ. of Minn, P.O. Box 73 Mayo Bldg., 420 Delaware St. S. E., Minneapolis, MN 55455 Tel 612-373-7933 (SAN 217-541X).

Minnesota Scholarly Press, Inc., *(Minn Scholarly; 0-933474),* P.O. Box 224, Mankato, MN 56001 Tel 507-387-4964 (SAN 282-0005); Dist. by: Independent Pubs. Group, 14 Vanderventer Ave., Port Washington, NY 11050 (SAN 282-0013).

Minobras-Mining Services & Research, *(Minobras),* P.O. Box 262, Dana Point, CA 92629 Tel 714-493-6066 (SAN 215-9694).

Miracle Publishing Co., *(Miracle Pub Co),* 18 Charleston North, Sugarland, TX 77478 (SAN 262-0480).

Mirage Press, Ltd., *(Mirage Pr; 0-88358),* P.O. Box 28, Manchester, MD 21102 Tel 301-239-8999 (SAN 202-6406).

Mishler & King Publishing, *(Mishler & King),* 406 Reo St., No. 227, Tampa, FL 33609 (SAN 260-2288).

Miss Jackie Music, *(Miss Jackie; 0-939514),* 10001 El Monte, Overland Park, KS 66207 (SAN 216-4191).

Missing Link Co., The, *(Missing Link; 0-910149),* P.O. Box 44014, Phoenix, AZ 85064 Tel 602-265-4753 (SAN 241-2268).

Mission Dolores Pubs., *(Mission Dolores; 0-912748),* 193 Los Robles Dr., Burlingame, CA 94010 (SAN 203-7882).

Mission Press, *(Mission Pr CA; 0-918418),* 124 Treehaven Court, Suite B-330, Box 614, Kenwood, CA 95452 Tel 707-833-5588 (SAN 209-9624).

Mission Publishing Co., *(Mission Pub; 0-916910),* 346 North St., Greenwich, CT 06830 Tel 203-661-2372 (SAN 209-1836).

Missionary Internship, *(Missionary Intern; 0-942726),* 36200 Freedom Rd., P.O. Box 457, Farmington, MI 48024 Tel 313-474-9110 (SAN 240-253X).

Missions Advanced Research & Communication Center, *(Missions Adv Res Com Ctr; 0-912552),* 919 W. Huntington Dr., Monrovia, CA 91016 (SAN 240-0529).

Mississippi Dept. of Archives & History, *(Mississippi Dept Arch),* P.O. Box 571, Jackson, MS 39205 (SAN 279-618X).

Mississippi Ornithological Society, *(Mississippi Orni),* Box Z, Mississippi State, MS 39762 (SAN 262-0499).

Mississippi Research & Development Center, *(MS Res & Dev Ctr),* Public Information Office, Drawer 2470, Jackson, MS 39205 Tel 601-982-6334 (SAN 202-2109).

Missouri Archaeological Society, *(MO Arch Soc),* P. O. Box 958, Columbia, MO 65205 (SAN 238-8316).

Missouri Basketball, *(MO Basketball; 0-9605092),* 364 Hearnes Bldg., Columbia, MO 65211 (SAN 215-7888).

Mistaire Laboratories, *(Mistaire; 0-9602490),* 152 Glen Ave., Millburn, NJ 07041 Tel 201-376-0915 (SAN 204-2762).

Mr. Cogito Press, *(Mr Cogito Pr),* P.O. Box 66124, Portland, OR 97266 (SAN 212-9191).

Mist'er Rain, Inc., *(Mist'er Rain; 0-916970),* 8411 Pacific Hwy E., Tacoma, WA 98424 Tel 206-927-7333 (SAN 208-7685).

Mitchell, Ralph, *(R Mitchell; 0-9604106),* 18018 Horton Rd., Kenosha, WI 53142 Tel 414-857-2163 (SAN 214-4190).

Mitchell Publishing, Inc., *(Mitchell Pub; 0-938188),* 915 River Street, Santa Cruz, CA 95060 Tel 408-425-3851 (SAN 215-7896).

Mittman, Edward A., & Associates, *(E A Mittman),* 311 Ruby, Balboa Island, CA 92662 Tel 714-673-0188 (SAN 238-8200).

Mitzi Books, Div. of Sinai-Christian Pubns., *(Mitzi Bks; 0-940958),* P.O. Box 160452, Mobile, AL 36616 Tel 404-834-4044 (SAN 223-1948).

Mizan Press, *(Mizan Pr; 0-933782),* P.O. Box 4065, Berkeley, CA 94704 Tel 415-549-1634 (SAN 213-117X).

Mjb, *(M J B CA),* P.O. Box 68, Point Richmond, CA 94807 (SAN 241-5550).

MLW Foundation, The, *(MLW Found; 0-9609348),* Box 525, Greenacres, WA 99016 Tel 509-922-4839 (SAN 260-2180).

Mnemosyne Publishing Co., Inc., *(Mnemosyne),* 410 Alcazar Ave., Coral Gables, FL 33134 Tel 305-444-8908 (SAN 203-9966).

Mobile Junior League Pubns., *(Junior League Mobile; 0-9603054),* P.O. Box 7091, Mobile, AL 36607 Tel 205-479-5133 (SAN 212-1069).

Mockingbird Books, *(Mockingbird Bks; 0-89176),* Box 624, St. Simons Island, GA 31522 Tel 912-638-7212 (SAN 207-6470).

Model Agency Press, the, *(Model Agency; 0-942794),* 7021 Vicky Ave., Canoga Park, CA 91307 Tel 213-340-7268 (SAN 240-2548).

Model Cities Research Institute, *(Model Cities),* 11126 National Blvd., Los Angeles, CA 90064 Tel 213-479-7394 (SAN 208-1296).

Modell, Tod, *(Modell T; 0-9608292),* P.O. Box 3047, San Jose, CA 95156 Tel 408-258-4931 (SAN 240-4095).

Modern Books & Crafts, Inc., *(Modern Bks; 0-913274),* Dist. by: Associated Booksellers, 147 McKinley Ave., Bridgeport, CT 06606 (SAN 206-9717).

Modern Curriculum Press, Div. of Esquire, Inc., *(Modern Curr; 0-87895; 0-8136),* 13900 Prospect Rd., Cleveland, OH 44136 Tel 216-238-2222 (SAN 206-6572).

Modern Day Topics Publishing House, Inc., *(Modern Day Topics; 0-931648),* P.O. Box 9702, Savannah, GA 31412 Tel 912-234-0611 (SAN 211-8645).

Modern Education Pubs., *(Modern Ed),* P.O. Box 93, Saratoga, CA 95070 Tel 408-354-2264 (SAN 206-6580).

Modern Guides Co., *(Modern Guides; 0-940788),* P.O. Box 1340, Old San Juan, PR 00902 Tel 809-723-9105 (SAN 219-6069).

Modern Handcraft, Inc., *(Mod Handcraft; 0-86675),* 4251 Pennsylvania Ave., Kansas City, MO 64111 (SAN 216-1621).

Modern Images Poets Committee, *(Mod Images Poets; 0-915284),* P.O. Box 1544, Toms River, NJ 08753 (SAN 282-0021); Box 912, Mattoon, IL 61938 (SAN 282-003X).

Modern Language Assn. of America, *(Modern Lang; 0-87352),* 62 Fifth Ave., New York, NY 10011 Tel 212-741-5588 (SAN 202-6422).

Modern Library College Department See **Modern Library, Inc.**

Modern Library, Inc., *(Modern Lib),* 201 E. 50th St., New York, NY 10022 Tel 212-751-2600 (SAN 204-5605); Orders to: Order Dept., 400 Hahn Rd., Westminster, MD 21157 (SAN 204-5613). *Imprints:* Modern Library College Department (Mod LibC).

Modern Liturgy See **Resource Pubns.**

Modern Media Institute, *(Mod Media Inst; 0-935742),* 556 Central Ave., St. Petersburg, FL 33701 Tel 813-821-9494 (SAN 214-0586).

Modern Schools of America, *(Modern Schls; 0-917130),* 2538 N. Eight St., Phoenix, AZ 85006 Tel 602-990-8346 (SAN 208-4074).

Modern Signs Press, *(Modern Signs; 0-916708),* 3131 Walker Lee Dr., Rossmoor, CA 90720 (SAN 282-0048); Orders to: P.O. Box 1181, Los Alamitos, CA 90720 Tel 213-596-8548 (SAN 282-0056).

Modern World Publishing Co., *(Modern World; 0-910978),* 3460 Division St., Los Angeles, CA 90065 Tel 213-221-8044 (SAN 203-9982).

Modernismo Pubns., Ltd., *(Modernismo; 0-89237),* 155 Ave. of the Americas, New York, NY 10013 Tel 212-691-7700 (SAN 208-0036).

Moffat Publishing Co., Inc., *(Moffat Pub; 0-86670),* 920 Broadway, New York, NY 10010 (SAN 217-2569).

Moffett Publishing Co., *(Moffett),* Rt. 3, Box 175A, Cushing, OK 74023 (SAN 215-6822).

Mogul Book and Filmworks, *(Mogul Bk; 0-9610404),* P.O. Box 2773, Pittsburgh, PA 15230 (SAN 264-2131).

Moira Books, *(Moira; 0-9600204),* 1460 Heights Blvd., Winona, MN 55987 (SAN 203-9990).

Mojave Books, *(Mojave Bks; 0-87881),* 7118 Canby Ave., Reseda, CA 91335 Tel 213-342-3403 (SAN 202-6430).

Mole Publishing Co., *(Mole Pub Co; 0-9604464),* Route 1, Box 618, Bonners Ferry, ID 83805 Tel 208-267-7349 (SAN 212-8608).

Mollica Stained Glass Press, *(Mollica Stained Glass; 0-9601306),* 10033 Broadway Terr., Oakland, CA 94611 Tel 415-655-5736 (SAN 209-2220).

Molly Yes Press, *(Molly Yes; 0-931308),* RD3, Box 70B, New Berlin, NY 13411 Tel 607-847-8070 (SAN 217-9075).

Momentum Books See **Van Nostrand Reinhold Co. Inc**

Momo's Press, *(Momos; 0-917672),* 45 Sheridan St., San Francisco, CA 94103 Tel 415-863-3009 (SAN 206-1619).

Mona Lisa Precision, *(M Lisa Precision; 0-87643),* Dist. by: Barclay Bridge Supplies, 8 Bush Ave., Port Chester, NY 10573 (SAN 202-3768).

Monad Press, *(Monad Pr; 0-913460),* Dist. by: Pathfinder Press, 410 West St., New York, NY 10014 Tel 212-741-0690 (SAN 202-5906).

Monarch Press See **Monarch Press**

Monarch Press, Div. of Simon & Schuster, Inc., *(Monarch Pr; 0-671),* 1230 Ave. of the Americas, 12th Fl., New York, NY 10020 Tel 212-245-6400 (SAN 204-5621). *Imprints:* Monarch (Monarch).

Monday Books, *(Monday Bks; 0-918510),* 910A Slater St., Santa Rosa, CA 95404 Tel 707-575-7027 (SAN 209-6552).

Mondiello, Anthony S., *(Mondiello; 0-939658),* 20008 N. 28th, Phoenix, AZ 85024 (SAN 218-4931).

Mongeon, Ltd., *(Monegon Ltd; 0-940520),* 4 Professional Dr., No. 130, Gaithersburg, MD 20879 Tel 301-258-7540 (SAN 238-8049).

Money-Maker Publishing Co., *(Money-Maker; 0-910481),* 311 Gruenther Ave., Rockville, MD 20851 Tel 301-762-1385 (SAN 260-1060).

Money Making Methods, *(Money Methods; 0-9605094),* 7920 Miramar Rd., Suite 123, San Diego, CA 92126 Tel 619-566-1080 (SAN 276-9697).

Money Market Directories, Inc., *(Money Mkt; 0-939712),* 300 E. Market St., Charlottesville, VA 22901 Tel 800-446-2810 (SAN 216-7492).

Moneymatters Publishing, *(Moneymatters; 0-912913),* 2616 Juniper Ave. Suite 5, Boulder, CO 80302 Tel 303-449-6689 (SAN 283-3050).

Mongolia Society, Inc., The, *(Mongolia; 0-910980),* P.O. Drawer 606, Bloomington, IN 47402 Tel 812-335-2766 (SAN 204-000X).

Monitor Book Co., Inc., *(Monitor; 0-9600252),* 195 S. Beverly Dr., Beverly Hills, CA 90212 Tel 213-271-5558 (SAN 204-0018).

Monkey Joe Enterprises, Inc., *(Monkey Joe Ent; 0-933208),* 3310 Lebanon Rd., Suite 104, Hermitage, TN 37076 (SAN 212-4319).

Monkey Man Press, *(Monkey Man; 0-9605594),* 8710 Wonderland Pk. Ave., Los Angeles, CA 90046 Tel 213-654-9154 (SAN 216-1648).

Monkey Sisters Inc., the, *(Monkey Sisters; 0-933660),* 22971 Via Cruz, Laguna Niguel, CA 92677 Tel 714-496-1445 (SAN 212-7660).

Monks of New Skete, *(Liturgy & Art),* Cambridge, NY 12816 Tel 518-677-3928 (SAN 218-8228).

Monks of New Skete, *(Monks of New Skete; 0-9607924),* Cambridge, NY 12816 Tel 518-677-3928 (SAN 240-0553).

Monnonite Publishing House, *(Monnonite Pub),* Scottsdale, PA 15683 (SAN 285-6697).

Mono Basin Research Group, The, *(Mono Basin Res; 0-939714),* Box 66, Lee Vining, CA 93541 Tel 714-647-6496 (SAN 285-0664); Forestry Sciences Lab, 3200 Jefferson Way, Corvalles, OR 97331 Tel 503-757-4633 (SAN 285-0672).

Mono Lake Committee, The, *(Mono Lake Comm; 0-939716),* Box 29, Lee Vining, CA 93541 Tel 714-647-6386 (SAN 282-0064); Dist. by: Bookpeople, 2940 Seventh Street, Berkeley, CA 94710 Tel 415-549-3030 (SAN 168-9517); Dist. by: Publishers Group West, 5855 Beaudry St., Emeryville, CA 94608 (SAN 202-8522).

Monocacy Book Co., *(Monocacy; 0-913186),* P.O. Box 765, Redwood City, CA 94064 Tel 415-369-8934 (SAN 202-6473).

Monogram Aviation Pubns., *(Monogram Aviation; 0-914144),* 625 Edgebrook Dr., Boylston, MA 01505 Tel 617-869-6836 (SAN 206-5983).

Monograph Series in World Affairs, Graduate School of International Studies, *(Monograph Series; 0-87940),* University of Denver, Denver, CO 80208 Tel 303-753-2802 (SAN 205-4701).

Monona-Driver Book Co., *(Monona; 0-910982),* 110 Henuah Cir., Madison, WI 53716 Tel 608-222-1973 (SAN 204-0026).

Monongahela Publishing Co., Inc., *(Monongahela Pub),* 106 Morningside Dr., New York, NY 10027 Tel 212-666-5187 (SAN 209-3545); Orders to: 78 B Stony Rd., Fairmont, WV 26554 (SAN 209-3553).

Monroe County Library System, *(Monroe County Lib; 0-940696),* 3700 S. Custer Rd., Monroe, MI 48161 Tel 313-241-5277 (SAN 213-5396).

Monson Productions, *(Monson Product; 0-942796),* P.O. Box 5324, Madison, WI 53705 Tel 608-271-2016 (SAN 240-2556).

Montaigne Publishing, Inc., *(Montaigne; 0-917430),* 99 El Toyonal, Orinda, CA 94563 Tel 208-9602).

Montana Council for Indian Education, *(MT Coun Indian; 0-89992),* 517 Rimrock Rd., Billings, MT 59102 Tel 406-252-1800 (SAN 202-2117).

Montana Historical Society Press, *(MT Hist Soc; 0-917298),* 225 N. Roberts St., Helena, MT 59620 Tel 406-449-2694 (SAN 208-7693).

Montana Magazine, Inc., *(MT Mag; 0-938314),* Box 5630, Helena, MT 59601 Tel 406-443-2842 (SAN 220-0732).

Montana Reconnaissance Project, *(MRP; 0-939872),* P.O. Box 8507, Missoula, MT 59807 Tel 406-543-7357 (SAN 216-9118).

Monte Publishing Co., *(Monte Pub; 0-9606942),* P.O. Box 361, Underwood, WA 98651 (SAN 238-8987).

Montemora Foundation, Inc., The, *(Montemora Found; 0-935528),* Box 336, Cooper Sta., New York, NY 10276 (SAN 213-9383).

Montfort Pubns., *(Montfort Pubns; 0-910984),* 26 S. Saxon Ave., Bay Shore, NY 11706 Tel 516-665-0726 (SAN 205-8227).

Montgomery Communications, *(Montgomery Comm; 0-937096),* 18733, P.O. Box 55545, Seattle, WA 98155 Tel 206-682-4260 (SAN 214-4204).

Montgomery County Historical Society, *(Montgomery Hist; 0-9608694),* Fort Johnson, NY 12070 Tel 518-864-5772 (SAN 238-3179).

Montgomery Museum of Fine Arts, *(Montgomery Mus; 0-89280),* 440 S. McDonough St., Montgomery, AL 36104 Tel 205-834-3490 (SAN 208-3299).

Monthly Review Press, *(Monthly Rev; 0-85345),* 155 W. 23rd Street, New York, NY 10011 Tel 212-691-2555 (SAN 202-6481).

Monticello Press, *(Monticello Pr; 0-9607056),* 1330 Camp St., New Orleans, LA 70130 Tel 504-521-6744 (SAN 239-0124).

Monza Fels *See Plantin Press*

Moody Press, *(Moody; 0-8024),* 2101 W. Howard St., Chicago, IL 60645 Tel 312-973-7800 (SAN 202-5604).

Moon Over the Mountain Publishing Co., *(Moon Over Mntn; 0-9602970),* 6700 W. 44th Ave., Wheatridge, CO 80033 Tel 303-420-4272 (SAN 213-3415).

Moon Publications, *(Moon Pubns CA; 0-9603322),* P. O. Box 1696, Chico, CA 95927 (SAN 221-7406).

Mooney, Tom, *(Mooney; 0-9601240),* 3410 Balt-Som Rd., Millersport, OH 43046 Tel 614-862-8159 (SAN 210-1270).

Moonlight Editions *See Schocken Books, Inc.*

Moonlight Press, *(Moonlight FL; 0-913545),* 3407 Crystal Lake Dr., Orlando, FL 32806 Tel 305-855-7707 (SAN 264-2158).

Moonlight Press, The, *(Moonlight Pr; 0-941818),* 611 Pawling Ave., Troy, NY 12180 (SAN 239-2607).

Moonlight Pubns., *(Moonlight Pubns; 0-931350),* Box 671, La Jolla, CA 92038 (SAN 211-2566).

Moonmad Press, *(Moonmad Pr; 0-917918),* P.O. Box 757, Terre Haute, IN 47808 Tel 812-235-2947 (SAN 209-3537).

Moonraker Pubns., *(Moonraker; 0-940620),* 24452B Alta Vista, Dana Point, CA 92629 Tel 714-661-9172 (SAN 222-9862).

Moons Quilt Press, *(Moons Quilt Pr; 0-943216),* 619 Anastasia, No. 2, Miami, FL 33134 (SAN 240-5512).

Moonstone Press, *(Moonstone; 0-940410),* P.O. Box 661-RB, Anaheim, CA 92805 Tel 714-956-2246 (SAN 282-017X); Orders to: Publisher's Group West, 5855 Beaudry St., Emeryville, CA 94608 (SAN 282-0188); Dist. by: Book Dynamics, 836 Broadway, Ny, NY 10003 (SAN 169-5649); Dist. by: Creative Book Co., 8210 Varna Ave., Van Nuys, CA 91402 (SAN 203-610X).

Moontree Press, *(Moontree Pr),* 3719 4th St., N.W., Albuquerque, NM 87107 (SAN 241-5666).

Moore, Diane M., *(D M Moore; 0-9604030),* P.O. Box 1073, New Iberia, LA 70560 (SAN 214-0608).

Moore, Donna J., Publisher, *(Moore D; 0-9605466),* P.O. Box 723, Bainbridge Is., WA 98110 Tel 206-842-2170 (SAN 240-0243).

Moore, Milton T., Jr., *(M T Moore; 0-9608138),* P.O. Box 140280, Dallas, TX 75214 Tel 214-821-0407 (SAN 240-2564).

Moore Memorial Hospital Auxiliary, *(Moore Memorial),* P.O. Box 704, Pinehurst, NC 28374 (SAN 217-2909).

Moore Pubns., *(Moore Pubns; 0-9602616),* P.O. Box 2530, Redmond, WA 98052 (SAN 238-4396).

Moore Publishing Company, Inc. (II), *(Moore Pub IL; 0-935610),* P.O. Box 709, Oak Park, IL 60303 (SAN 222-643X).

Moosehead Products, *(Moosehead Prods; 0-9609208),* Rte. 1-4710, Corinna, ME 04928 Tel 207-278-3556 (SAN 241-4090).

Mor-Mac Publishing Co., *(Mor-Mac; 0-912178),* P.O. Box 985, Daytona Beach, FL 32015 Tel 904-255-4427 (SAN 204-0042).

Moran/Andrews, Inc., *(Moran Andrews; 0-912286),* 535 N. Michigan Ave., Chicago, IL 60611 Tel 312-644-2793 (SAN 202-6503).

Moran Publishing Co., *(Moran Pub FL),* 9125 Bachman Road, Orlando, FL 32859 (SAN 264-2166).

Moran Publishing Corp., *(Moran Pub Corp; 0-86518),* 5425 Florida Blvd., P.O. Box 66538, Baton Rouge, LA 70896 Tel 504-923-2550 (SAN 214-0616); Dist. by: Aviation Book Co., 1640 Victory Blvd., Glendale, CA 91201 Tel 213-240-1771 (SAN 212-0259).

More, Thomas, Press, *(Thomas More; 0-88347),* 225 W. Huron St., Chicago, IL 60610 Tel 312-951-2100 (SAN 203-0675).

Moreau, Xavier, Inc., *(Xavier Moreau; 0-937950),* 111 West 57th Street, New York, NY 10019 (SAN 264-2174).

Morehouse-Barlow Co., *(Morehouse; 0-8192),* 78 Danbury Rd., Wilton, CT 06897 Tel 203-762-0721 (SAN 202-6511).

Morel Books, *(Morel Bks; 0-9607370),* 2918 Hillegass Ave., Suite C, Berkeley, CA 94705 (SAN 239-460X).

Moretus Press, Inc. The, *(Moretus Pr; 0-89679),* 274 Madison Ave., New York, NY 10016 Tel 212-685-2250 (SAN 211-2523); Orders to: P.O. Box 530, Harrisburg, PA 17108 Tel 717-545-2097 (SAN 211-2531).

Morgan & Morgan, Inc., *(Morgan; 0-87100),* 145 Palisades St., Dobbs Ferry, NY 10522 Tel 914-693-9303 (SAN 202-5620).

Morgan State Univ., *(Morgan State; 0-9610324),* Cold Spring Ln., Baltimore, MD 21239 Tel 301-444-3165 (SAN 264-2182).

Morgantown Printing & Binding Co., *(Morgantown Print & Bind; 0-930284),* P.O. Box 850, Morgantown, WV 26505 Tel 304-292-3368 (SAN 213-1188).

Moriarty, Dan, Associates, *(D Moriarty),* 1410 Second Ave., Newport, MN 55055 Tel 612-459-1857 (SAN 211-6448).

Morning Glory Press, *(Morning Glory; 0-930934),* 6595 San Haroldo Way, Buena Park, CA 90620 Tel 714-828-1998 (SAN 211-2558).

Morningland Pubns., Inc., *(Morningland; 0-935146),* 2630 E. Seventh St., Long Beach, CA 90804 Tel 213-6368).

Morningstar, Jim, *(Morningstar; 0-9604856),* 2728 N. Prospect Ave., Milwaukee, WI 53211 (SAN 215-8906).

Morningsun Pubns., *(Morningsun Pubns; 0-9603424),* 692 Edna Way, San Mateo, CA 94402 Tel 415-341-4491 (SAN 211-6235).

Morris, Victoria S., Books, *(V S Morris; 0-914318),* 39 Gleneden Ave., Oakland, CA 94611 Tel 415-652-2013 (SAN 202-2125).

Morris County Historical Society, *(M C H S; 0-910301),* P.O. Box 170 M, Morristown, NJ 07960 Tel 201-267-3465 (SAN 241-4104).

Morris Genealogical Library, *(Morris Genealog Lib),* P.O. Box 63, Allenhurst, NJ 07711 (SAN 207-6012).

Morris Publishing Co., Subs. of Facemetrics, Inc., *(Morris Pub; 0-9606890),* 3 Blue Ridge Rd., Plymouth Meeting, PA 19462 Tel 215-828-4865 (SAN 282-0234); Orders to: Box 124, Plymouth Meeting, PA 19462 (SAN 282-0242).

Morrison, Butterfield & Boyle Publishing, Ltd., *(MBB Pub; 0-936062),* P.O. Box 4759, Santa Barbara, CA 93103 (SAN 238-8944).

Morrison Publishing Company, *(Morrison Pub Co),* 14 Brown Street, Warren, RI 02885 (SAN 264-2190).

Morrison, Raven-Hill Co., *(Morrison Rav; 0-912189),* 9466 Hidden Valley Pl., Beverly Hills, CA 90210 (SAN 277-6952).

Morristown Historical Society, *(Morristown Hist Soc; 0-9607288),* P.O. Box 838, Morrisville, VT 05661 (SAN 238-0242).

Morrow, William, & Co., Inc., *(Morrow; 0-688),* 105 Madison Ave., New York, NY 10016 Tel 212-889-3050 (SAN 202-5760); Orders to: Wilmor Warehouse, 6 Henderson St., West Caldwell, NJ 07006 (SAN 202-5779).

Morse, Albert L., *(A L Morse; 0-918320),* 320 Miller Ave., Mill Valley, CA 94941 Tel 415-332-3571 (SAN 209-4614).

Morse Press, Inc., *(Morse Pr; 0-933350),* 417 E. Pine, Seattle, WA 98122 Tel 206-323-1820 (SAN 211-8165).

Mortal Press, *(Mortal Pr)* 316 Rue Flambeau 412, South Bend, IN 46615 Tel 219-233-2732 (SAN 211-254X).

Morten Publishing Co., Inc., *(Morten Pub; 0-9607848),* 811 Ridgeway Ave., Signal Mountain, TN 37377 (SAN 238-1788).

Mortgage Bankers Association of America, *(Mortgage Bankers),* 1125 15 St Nw, Washington, DC 20005 (SAN 224-8212).

Morton, Julia F., *(J F Morton; 0-9610184),* 20534 S. W. 92nd Ct., Miami, FL 33189 Tel 305-284-3741 (SAN 272-5185).

Morton Publishing Co., *(Morton Pub; 0-89582),* 295 W. Hampden, Suite 104, Englewood, CO 80110 Tel 303-761-4805 (SAN 210-9174).

Mosaic Press, *(Mosaic Pr OH; 0-88014),* 220 W. Blacklidge Dr., Tucson, AZ 85705 (SAN 219-6077).

Mosaic Pr., the, *(Mosaic Pr; 0-934696),* P.O. Box 925, Sedona, AZ 86336 Tel 602-282-4234 (SAN 213-4187).

Mosby, C. V., Co., *(Mosby; 0-8016),* 11830 Westline Industrial Dr., St. Louis, MO 63141 Tel 314-872-8370 (SAN 200-2280).

Moss, Mary Foy, *(M F Moss),* 1158-63rd St., Apt. 3, Oakland, CA 94608 (SAN 216-2709).

Moss Pubns., *(Moss Pubns VA; 0-943522),* Box 729, Orange, VA 22960 Tel 703-672-5921 (SAN 214-4220).

Mossart, *(Mossart; 0-9606162),* Box 929, Weaverville, CA 96093 Tel 916-623-5406 (SAN 217-1171).

Mossy Rock Publishing Co., *(Mossy Rock WA; 0-936938),* 808 106th N.E., Bellevue, WA 98004 (SAN 215-2134).

Mostly Movement Ltd., *(Mostly Movement; 0-934848),* 58-15 211th St.,, Bayside, NY 11364 (SAN 222-6456).

Motamed Medical Pub, Inc., *(Motamed Med Pub; 0-910161),* 7141 N. Kedzie Ave. Suite 1504, Chicago, IL 60645 Tel 312-761-6667 (SAN 241-2276).

Moth House Pubns., *(Moth Hse; 0-936718),* 3967 S. 2200 W., Salt Lake City, UT 84119 (SAN 222-6375).

Mother Duck Press, *(Mother Duck Pr; 0-934600),* Rte. 1, Box 25A, McNeal, AZ 85617 (SAN 213-1196).

Mother Earth News, The, *(Mother Earth; 0-938432),* P.O. Box 70, Hendersonville, NC 28791 (SAN 215-7918).

Motheroot Pubns., *(Motheroot),* 214 Dewey St., Pittsburgh, PA 15218 (SAN 216-4205).

Motivational Aids, *(Motiv Aids; 0-9607372),* 524 Dickson St., Endicott, NY 13760 (SAN 239-4626).

Motivational Methods, Inc., *(Motiv Methods; 0-933664),* 8569 Ramblewood Dr., Coral Springs, FL 33065 Tel 305-753-3579 (SAN 212-7687).

Motivators Unlimited, *(Motiv Unltd; 0-9609084),* P.O. Box 35922, Tucson, AZ 85740-5922 Tel 602-299-5166 (SAN 241-4112).

Motor Cities Publishing Co., *(Motor Cities),* 10405 Rushton Rd., South Lyon, MI 48178 (SAN 205-8146).

Motor Transportation Association of South Carolina, *(MTASC; 0-9608140),* P.O. Box 50166, Columbia, SC 29205 Tel 803-799-4306 (SAN 240-2580).

Motor Vehicle Manufacturing Association of the United States, *(Motor Veh Man),* Orders to: Technical Affairs Division, 300 New Center Building, Detroit, MI 48202 (SAN 272-5312).

Motorbooks International, Pubs. & Wholesalers, Inc., *(Motorbooks Intl; 0-87938),* P.O. Box 2, 729 Prospect Ave., Osceola, WI 54020 Tel 800-826-6600 (SAN 169-9164).

Motorcycle Safety Foundation, *(Motorcycle Safety),* P.O. Box 120, Chadds Ford, PA 19317 (SAN 224-9413).

Motormatics Pubns., *(Motormatics; 0-930968),* c/o Beach Cities Enterprises, P.O. Box 91051, Long Beach, CA 90809 Tel 213-434-6701 (SAN 211-1349).

Mott Media, *(Mott Media; 0-915134),* 1000 E. Huron, Milford, MI 48042 Tel 313-685-8773 (SAN 207-1460).

Mount St. Mary's College, *(Mount St Marys; 0-9606972),* Emmitsburg, MD 21727 Tel 301-447-6122 (SAN 223-1964).

Mountain, *(Mountain Calif; 0-9605992),* Box 1408, Lower Lake, CA 95457 (SAN 216-7522).

Mountain & Sea, *(Mntn & Sea),* P.O. Box 126, Redondo Beach, CA 90277 Tel 213-379-9321 (SAN 207-5679).

Mountain & Sea Publishing, *(Mountain Sea; 0-911449),* Box 126, Redondo Beach, CA 90277 Tel 213-379-9321 (SAN 272-5371).

Mountain Elegance, *(Mntn Elegance),* P.O. Box 8723, Asheville, NC 28814 (SAN 240-964X).

Mountain House Publishing, Inc., *(Mntn Hse Pub; 0-939274),* Rte. 1 Box 433 A, Waitsfield, VT 05673 (SAN 216-4213).

Mountain Laurel Publications, *(Mountain Laurel; 0-911687),* P.O. Box 1621, Harrisburg, PA 17105 (SAN 264-2239).

Mountain Press Publishing Co., Inc., *(Mountain Pr; 0-87842),* P.O. Box 2399, Missoula, MT 59806 Tel 406-728-1900 (SAN 202-8832).

Mountain View Publishing Co., *(Mountain View),* Tin Cup Rd., Darby, MT 59829 (SAN 212-8381).

Mountain West Publishing Co., *(Mountain West; 0-9610690),* P.O. Box 1841, Grand Junction, CO 81502 Tel 303-242-5035 (SAN 265-2838).

Mountaineers-Books, *(Mountaineers; 0-916890; 0-89886),* 715 Pike St., Seattle, WA 98101 Tel 206-682-4636 (SAN 212-8756).

Mountcastle Corp., The, *(Mountcastle; 0-913063),* P.O. Box 1688, Redondo Beach, CA 90278 (SAN 285-6689).

Mouse Press, *(Mouse Pr; 0-913968),* P.O. Box 5381, Beverly Hills, CA 90210 Tel 213-858-1666 (SAN 203-1795); Dist. by: Light Impressions Corp., P.O. Box 3012, Rochester, NY 14614 (SAN 169-619X).

Mouton Pubs., Div. of Walter De Gruyter, Inc., *(Mouton),* 200 Saw Mill River Rd., Hawthorne, NY 10532 Tel 914-747-0111 (SAN 210-9239).

Mouvement Pubns., *(Mouvement Pubns; 0-932392),* 109 E. State St., Ithaca, NY 14850 Tel 607-272-2157 (SAN 211-7460).

Movement Shorthand Society, Inc., *(Move Short Soc; 0-914336),* P.O. Box 7344, Newport Beach, CA 92660 Tel 714-644-8342 (SAN 203-154X).

Moving Parts Press, *(Moving Parts; 0-939952),* 419-A Maple St., Santa Cruz, CA 95060 Tel 408-427-2271 (SAN 216-8383).

Mowbray Co. Pubs., *(Mowbray Co; 0-917218),* 222 W. Exchange St., Providence, RI 02903 Tel 401-861-1000 (SAN 205-8111).

Mowry Press, *(Mowry Pr; 0-9605368),* Box 405, Wayland, MA 01778 (SAN 215-9724).

Mr. Coach, Inc., *(Mr Coach; 0-9607324),* P.O. Box 1502, Downers Grove, IL 60515 Tel 312-964-3090 (SAN 239-2631).

Mr. D's the Poetic Experience Publishing Company, *(MrD's Poetic Exp; 0-9607748),* 3208 Cahuensa Blvd., West Hollywood, CA 90068 (SAN 240-1274).

Mu Alpha Theta, National High School Mathematics Club, *(Mu Alpha Theta),* 601 Elm Ave., Rm. 423, Norman, OK 73019 (SAN 240-0077).

Mudborn Press, *(Mudborn; 0-930012),* 301 E. Canon Perdido, Santa Barbara, CA 93101 Tel 805-965-3676 (SAN 210-4660).

Mudra, *(Mudra; 0-914726),* Dist. by: Bookpeople, 2940 Seventh St., Berkeley, CA 94710 Tel 415-549-3033 (SAN 168-9517).

Muir, John, Pubns., *(John Muir; 0-912528),* P.O. Box 613, Santa Fe, NM 87504-0613 Tel 505-982-4078 (SAN 203-9079); Dist. by: W. W. Norton & Co., 500 Fifth Ave., New York, NY 10110 Tel 212-354-5500 (SAN 202-5795).

Mulberry Avenue Books, *(Mulberry Ave Bks; 0-938036),* 133 E. Mulberry Ave., San Antonio, TX 78212 (SAN 240-0510).

Mulberry Tree Press, The, *(Mulberry Tree; 0-9610684),* P.O. Box 169, Winchester, VA 22601 Tel 703-636-1126 (SAN 264-7672).

Mulch Press, *(Mulch Pr; 0-913142),* 4837 17th St., San Francisco, CA 94117 (SAN 206-5061).

Mulford Colebrook Publishing Co., *(Mulford Colebrook; 0-930144),* Box 289, Mifflinburg, PA 17844 Tel 814-349-8165 (SAN 210-6434).

Multi Dimensional Communications, Inc., *(Multi Dimen; 0-89507),* 7 Delano Dr., Bedford Hills, NY 10507 (SAN 209-9632).

Multi Media Arts, *(Multi Media TX; 0-86617),* Box 14486, Austin, TX 78761 Tel 512-837-5503 (SAN 214-4239).

Multi-Media Publishing, Inc., *(Multi Media CO; 0-940122),* 1393 S. Inca St., Denver, CO 80223 Tel 303-778-1404 (SAN 220-2913).

Multi Media Resource Center, *(MMRC; 0-9603968; 0-914684),* 1525 Franklin St., San Francisco, CA 94109 Tel 415-673-5100 (SAN 206-6017).

Multi-Spectral Press, *(Multi Spectral; 0-918210),* 4948 Meadowbrook Rd., Buffalo, NY 14221 Tel 716-632-0921 (SAN 210-2412).

Multnomah Press, *(Multnomah; 0-930014; 0-88070),* 10209 S.E. Division St., Portland, OR 97266 Tel 503-257-0526 (SAN 282-0250); Orders to: 10209 SE Division St., Portland, OR 97266 Tel 800-547-5890 (SAN 282-0269).

Mundus Artium Press, *(Mundus Artium; 0-939378),* P.O. Box 688, Richardson, TX 75080 Tel 214-690-2092 (SAN 206-6866).

Munger Oil Information Service, *(Munger Oil),* 9800 S. Sepulveda Blvd., Los Angeles, CA 90045 Tel 213-776-3990 (SAN 205-7867).

Municipal Art Society of New York, The, *(Municipal Art Soc; 0-9606892),* 457 Madison Ave., New York, NY 10022 Tel 212-935-3960 (SAN 217-4065).

Municipal Finance Officers Assn. of the U. S. & Canada, *(Municipal; 0-89125),* 180 N. Michigan Ave., Suite 800, Chicago, IL 60601 Tel 312-977-9700 (SAN 202-2540).

Munro, J Alex, *(J Alex Munro; 0-9601670),* 304 Saxon Dr., Springfield, IL 62704 Tel 217-787-6621 (SAN 212-1174).

Munro, John A., Associates, Inc., *(Munro Assocs; 0-911553),* 16 E. 41st St., New York, NY 10017 Tel 212-689-8787 (SAN 272-555X).

Murach/Mike, & Assoc., Inc., *(M Murach & Assoc; 0-9116250),* 4222 W. Alamos, Suite 101, Fresno, CA 93711 Tel 209-275-3335 (SAN 264-2255).

Murat, Felix, Co., *(F Murat; 0-9600356),* 2132 N.W. 11th Ave., Miami, FL 33127 (SAN 205-5724).

Muratore Agency, Inc., *(Muratore),* 766 W. Shore Rd., P.O. Box 486, Warwick, RI 02889 Tel 401-737-6460 (SAN 205-6356).

Murphy, Dennis D., *(D D Murphy; 0-918788),* 3404 N. Romero Rd., Tucson, AZ 85705 (SAN 210-3125).

Murphy, Eileen M., *(E M Murphy; 0-9609792),* 16901 S. Jonesville Rd., Columbus, IN 47201 Tel 812-522-4079 (SAN 269-8684).

Murphy, Thomas A., Pub., *(T A Murphy),* 414 B Suite Buck Ave., Vacaville, CA 95688 (SAN 218-4958).

Murphy & Broad Publishing Co., *(Murphy & Broad; 0-940792),* 425 30th St., Suite 8, P.O. Box 3208, Newport Beach, CA 92663 Tel 714-673-3348 (SAN 219-6085).

Murphy Publishing Co., *(Murphy Pub Co),* P.O. Box 64, Timonium, MD 21093 Tel 301-377-5083 (SAN 205-7840).

Murrison Co., The, *(Murrison Co; 0-9602110),* 3879 Northstrand Dr., Decatur, GA 30035 Tel 404-289-5012 (SAN 216-1656).

Murton Press, the, *(Murton Pr; 0-9608042),* 26 Anderson Rd., Greenwich, CT 06830 (SAN 240-0960).

Murvin, H. L., Publisher, *(H L Murvin; 0-9608498),* 500 Vernon St., Oakland, CA 94610 Tel 415-658-7517 (SAN 240-7264).

Murzin Publishing, *(Murzin Pub; 0-911199),* Box 8527, Deerfield Beach, FL 33441 Tel 305-427-3060 (SAN 272-5584).

Muscle Games, *(Muscle Games; 0-9603864),* P.O. Box 51, Fairview Village, PA 19409 (SAN 213-9391).

Muse-Ed Company, *(Muse-Ed Comp; 0-9604434),* 14141 Margate St., Van Nuys, CA 91401 (SAN 283-3514).

Museum Books, Inc., *(Museum Bks; 0-87544),* 6 W. 37th St., New York, NY 10018 Tel 212-563-2770 (SAN 204-0131).

Museum Graphics, *(Mus Graphics; 0-913832),* 2643-B Fair Oaks Ave., Redwood City, CA 94063 Tel 415-368-5531 (SAN 201-8454); Orders to: Little, Brown & Co., 200 West St., Waltham, MA 02154 (SAN 201-8462).

Museum of African Art, Smithsonian Institution, *(Mus African Art),* Washington, DC 20002 Tel 202-287-3490 (SAN 213-1250).

Museum of Art, Carnegie Institute, *(Mus Art Carnegie; 0-88039),* 4400 Forbes Ave., Pittsburgh, PA 15213 Tel 412-622-3228 (SAN 239-1171).

Museum of Art, Pennsylvania State Univ., *(Penn St Art; 0-911209),* The Pennsylvania State University, University Park, PA 16802 Tel 814-863-0111 (SAN 274-4953).

Museum of Art Rhode Island School of Design, *(Mus of Art RI),* 224 Benefit St., Providence, RI 02903 Tel 401-331-3511 (SAN 204-0107); Dist. by: Milford House, Inc., 85 Newbury St., Boston, MA 02116 (SAN 204-0115).

Museum of Fine Arts, *(Mus Fine Arts Gal),* P.O. Box 2826, Houston, TX 77005 (SAN 279-7240).

Museum of Modern Art, *(Museum Mod Art; 0-87070),* 11 W. 53rd St., New York, NY 10019 Tel 212-956-7216 (SAN 202-5809); Orders to: Trade Sales, 11 W. 53rd St., New York, NY 10019 Tel 212-956-7265 (SAN 202-5817).

Museum of New Mexico Press, *(Museum NM Pr; 0-89013),* P.O. Box 2087, Santa Fe, NM 87503 Tel 505-827-6457 (SAN 202-2575).

Museum of Northern Arizona, *(Mus Northern Ariz; 0-89734),* Rte. 4, Box 720, Flagstaff, AZ 86001 Tel 602-774-5211 (SAN 204-0093).

Museum of Science & History, The, *(Mus Sci & Hist; 0-9604642),* MacArthur Park, Little Rock, AR 72202 (SAN 215-7926).

Museum of the American China Trade, *(Mus Am China Trade; 0-937650),* 215 Adams St., Milton, MA 02186 Tel 617-696-1815 (SAN 204-1030).

Museum of the American Indian, *(Mus Am Ind; 0-934490),* Broadway at 155th St., New York, NY 10032 Tel 212-283-2420 (SAN 204-0085).

Museum of the City of Mobile, *(Museum Mobile; 0-914334),* 355 Government St., Mobile, AL 36602 Tel 205-438-7569 (SAN 213-1218).

Museum of the City of New york, *(Mus City NY; 0-910961),* 5th Ave. at 103rd St., New York, NY 10029 Tel 212-534-1672 (SAN 272-5630).

Museum of the Great Plains, Pubns. Dept., *(Mus Great Plains; 0-911728),* 601 Ferris, P.O. Box 68, Lawton, OK 73502 Tel 405-353-5675 (SAN 205-7794).

Museum Systems, *(Mus Sys; 0-941094),* 817 N. La Cienaga Blvd., Los Angeles, CA 90069 Tel 213-657-5811 (SAN 204-0123).

Museums at Stony Brook, The, *(Mus Stony; 0-943924),* 1208 Rte. 25A, Stony Brook, NY 11790 Tel 516-751-0066 (SAN 241-1385).

Museums Collaborative, Inc., *(Mus Collaborative),* 15 Grammercy Park S., New York, NY 10003 Tel 212-674-0030 (SAN 219-7987).

Mushroom Cave, Inc., The, *(Mushroom Cave; 0-9601516),* P.O. Box 894, Battle Creek, MI 49016 Tel 616-962-3497 (SAN 211-6723).

Mushrooms, Etc., *(Mushrooms Etc; 0-9606236),* 1853 Winfield Dr., Lakewood, CO 80215 Tel 303-233-6238 (SAN 220-343X).

Music Education Publications, *(Music Educ Pubns; 0-943988),* P.O. Box 3402, Fullerton, CA 92634 Tel 714-525-1397 (SAN 241-5674).

Music Educators National Conference, *(Music Ed),* 1902 Association Dr., Reston, VA 22091 Tel 703-860-4000 (SAN 204-014X).

Music Press, *(Music Pr; 0-918318),* 155 W. 68th St., New York, NY 10023 Tel 212-877-3175 (SAN 209-0899).

Music Sales Corp., *(Music Sales; 0-8256),* 799 Broadway, New York, NY 10003 (SAN 282-0277). *Imprints:* Acorn Music Press (Acorn); Amsco Music (Amsco Music); Hidden House (Hidden Hse); Oak Pubns. (Oak).

Music Treasure Pubns., *(Music Treasure; 0-912028),* 620 Fort Washington Ave., 1-F, New York, NY 10040 (SAN 204-0158).

Musica Publishing Co., *(Musica; 0-9600964),* Box 1266, Edison, NJ 08818 (SAN 208-9696).

Musical Box Society International, The, *(Musical Box Soc; 0-915000),* 19 Colony Dr., Summit, NJ 07901 (SAN 215-9732).

Musical Scope Pubns., *(Musical Scope; 0-913000),* P.O. Box 125, Audubon Sta., New York, NY 10032 (SAN 202-8867).

Musicdata, Inc., *(Musicdata; 0-88478),* 3 Maplewood Mall, Philadelphia, PA 19144 Tel 215-842-0555 (SAN 203-1566).

Musicgraphics, *(Musicgraphics; 0-941814),* 124 Atlantic Ave., Lynbrook, NY 11563 Tel 516-599-5990 (SAN 239-264X).

Mustang Pubns., Inc., *(Mustang Pubns; 0-941596),* 410 Brannen Rd., P.O. Box 5917, Lakeland, FL 33803 (SAN 239-118X).

Mustardseed Press, Subs. of Interuniverse, *(Mustardseed; 0-917920),* 707 N. Carolina Ave., Cocoa, FL 32922 Tel 305-632-2769 (SAN 209-9659).

Muste, A. J., Memorial Institute, *(Muste; 0-9608096),* 339 Lafayette St., New York, NY 10012 Tel 212-533-4335 (SAN 240-2599).

MIND, *(MIND; 0-9605358),* RD 4, Box 455A1, Pleasantville, NJ 08232 Tel 605-646-7757 (SAN 239-8818).

Mutual Press, *(Mutual Pr IL; 0-9605628),* 664 N. Michigan, Suite 1010, Chicago, IL 60611 (SAN 216-2717).

Mutual Publishing, *(Mutual Pub HI; 0-935180),* 2055 N. King St., Honolulu, HI 96819 (SAN 222-6359).

Mutualist Press, The, *(Mutualist Pr),* GPO Box 2009, Brooklyn, NY 11202 (SAN 213-1226).

MVR Books, *(MVR Bks),* 7809 S. LaPorte Ave., Burbank, IL 60459 Tel 312-636-7412 (SAN 210-4709).

Myco Publishing House, *(Myco Pub Hse; 0-936634),* P.O. Box 1237, Arcadia, CA 91006 Tel 714-661-4957 (SAN 214-2538).

Mycological Society of San Francisco, Inc., *(Mycological; 0-918942),* Box 11321, San Francisco, CA 94101 Tel 415-234-7904 (SAN 210-3621).

Mycroft & Moran See Arkham House Pubs.

Mycroft Business Press, *(Mycroft; 0-910998),* P.O. Box 579, Branson, MO 65616 Tel 417-334-3436 (SAN 204-0174).

Myers, Albert E., *(A E Myers; 0-9602156),* 900 South Arlington Ave., Rm. 100, Harrisburg, PA 17109 (SAN 213-1234).

Myers, Anna Dell Fillingim, *(A D F Myers),* Box 4055, Mountain View, CA 94040 (SAN 212-954X).

Myers, S. D., Inc., *(Myers Inc; 0-939320),* P.O. Box 3575, Akron, OH 44310 (SAN 216-2725).

Myles, Ralph, Pub., Inc., *(R Myles; 0-87926),* P.O. Box 1533, Colorado Springs, CO 80901 Tel 303-634-3206 (SAN 204-6601).

Mynabird Publishing, *(Mynabird Pub; 0-917758),* 20 Shoshone Place, Portola Valley, CA 94025 Tel 415-851-8554 (SAN 209-1550).

Myriad Moods, *(Myriad; 0-911843),* 1530 Larkspur, Suite No. 2, San Antonio, TX 78213 Tel 512-342-1652 (SAN 264-2271).

Myriade Press, Inc., The, *(Myriade; 0-918142),* Seven Stony Run, New Rochelle, NY 10804 Tel 914-235-8470 (SAN 212-2439).

Myrin Institute, Inc., *(Myrin Institute; 0-913098),* 136 E. 64th St., New York, NY 10021 Tel 212-758-6475 (SAN 204-0182).

Myrtle Bank Press, *(Myrtle Bank; 0-9606978),* 408 N. Pearl St., Natchez, MS 39120 (SAN 238-8995).

Mysterious Press, *(Mysterious Pr; 0-89296),* 129 W. 56th St., New York, NY 10019 (SAN 208-2152).

Mystic Seaport Museum, Inc., *(Mystic Seaport; 0-913372),* Mystic, CT 06355 Tel 203-572-0711 (SAN 213-7550).

Mythos Press, *(Mythos Pr),* P.O. Box 589, Kalamazoo, MI 49005 (SAN 264-2301).

NACAC, *(NACAC),* 1346 Connecticut Ave., N.W., Suite 229, Washington, DC 20036 (SAN 219-8002).

NAMAC, *(NAMAC; 0-936916),* P.O. Box 963, Ingleside, TX 78362 Tel 512-776-2305 (SAN 216-0498); Dist. by: Astrology & Spiritual Center, 4535 Hohman Ave., Hammond, IN 46327 Tel 219-931-8050 (SAN 159-0456); Dist. by: Devorss, Box 550, Marina Del Rey, CA 90291 (SAN 168-9886); Dist. by: Starlite, Box 20729, Reno, NV 89515 (SAN 169-0299); Dist. by: Parapsychology Education Ctr., P.O. Box 6240, Little Rock, AR 72216 (SAN 200-4186); Dist. by: Walden Book Co., 201 High Ridge Rd., Stanford, CT (SAN 203-1752); Dist. by: The Distributors, 702 S. Michigan, South Bend, IN 46618 (SAN 212-0364); Dist. by: PEP Distributor, 630 Skyview Dr., West Carrollton, OH 45449 (SAN 200-4194); Dist. by: Macoy Publishing, Box 9759, Richmond, CA 23228 (SAN 202-2265).

N&N Publishing, *(N & N Pub; 0-9606036),* Lydia Dr., Wappinger, NY 12590 (SAN 216-4221).

N & N Resources, *(N & N Resources),* P.O. Box 332, Troy, ID 83871 Tel 208-835-2012 (SAN 209-0376).

NCEMMH, *(NCEMMH),* 356 Arps Hall, 1945 N. High St., Columbus, OH 43210 (SAN 262-1118).

NCJW, Inc., *(NCJW; 0-941840),* 15 E. 26th St., New York, NY 10010 Tel 212-532-1740 (SAN 239-2658).

NCRP Pubns., *(NCRP Pubns),* 7910 Woodmount Ave., Ste. 1016, Bethesda, MD 20814 (SAN 218-4974).

NMSEA, *(NMSEA),* P.O. Box 2004, Santa Fe, NM 87504 (SAN 240-0502).

NOK Pubs., Intl., *(NOK Pubs; 0-88357),* 150 Fifth Ave., New York, NY 10011 Tel 212-675-5785 (SAN 205-7522).

NORC, National Opinion Research Center, *(NORC; 0-932132),* 6030 S. Ellis Ave., Chicago, IL 60637 Tel 312-753-1487 (SAN 205-7735).

NPA, *(NPA; 0-88806),* 1606 New Hampshire Ave. NW, Washington, DC 20009 (SAN 239-538X).

NPC Publishing Co., *(NPC Pub Co; 0-932634),* 17217 Hiawatha St., Granada Hills, CA 91344 Tel 213-363-8458 (SAN 212-7814).

NPP Books, *(NPP Bks; 0-916182),* P.O. Box 1491, Ann Arbor, MI 48106-1491 (SAN 208-1067).

N. S. Wait, *(N S Wait; 0-911588),* Box 407, Valparaiso, IN 46383 (SAN 206-6491) Formerly H. H. Wait Pub.

N W R Pubns., *(NWR Pubns; 0-916972),* 162 Madison Ave., Third Floor, New York, NY 10016 Tel 212-696-4765 (SAN 208-4686).

Na Pali Publishing Co., *(Na Pali Pub; 0-917132),* P.O. Box 88082, Honolulu, HI 96815 Tel 213-889-1657 (SAN 208-3876).

Naamikika Publishing, *(Naamikika Pub Co; 0-943146),* c/o Daimyo, Schribner & Hart Co., 90 Spruce St., Glacier Ave., No. 303, Juneau, AK 99801 Tel 907-586-4425 (SAN 240-7280).

Nader, Ralph, *(R Nader; 0-936486),* P.O. Box 19367, Washington, DC 20036 Tel 202-387-8030 (SAN 282-0285); Dist. by: Learning Research Project, P.O. Box 19312, Washington, DC 20036 (SAN 282-5961).

Nadller Concepts, *(Nadller Concepts; 0-9606038),* 150-10 79th Ave., Flushing, NY 11367 Tel 212-591-4167 (SAN 216-9742).

Nahass, Rick, Publishing, *(R Nahass; 0-9608422),* P.O. Box 27630, San Francisco, CA 94127 Tel 415-334-7191 (SAN 240-7299).

Naiad Press, *(Naiad Pr; 0-930044),* P.O. Box 10543, Tallahassee, FL 32302 Tel 904-539-9322 (SAN 206-801X).

Nameless Press, *(Nameless; 0-9603608),* P.O. Box 538, Jonestown, TX 78641 Tel 512-267-1961 (SAN 213-4195).

Nanny Goat Productions, *(Nanny Goat; 0-918440),* P. O. Box 845, Laguna Beach, CA 92652 Tel 714-494-7930 (SAN 209-9675).

Nantucket Historical Assn., *(Nantucket Hist Assn; 0-9607340),* P.O. BOX 1451, Nantucket, MA 02554 Tel 617-228-1894 (SAN 239-2666) In cooperation with Nantucket Historical Trust.

Nantucket Nautical Pubs., *(Nantucket Nautical),* 5 New Mill St., Nantucket, MA 02554 (SAN 215-8914).

Napa Landmarks, *(Napa Landmarks; 0-935360),* P.O. Box 702, Napa, CA 94558 Tel 707-255-1836 (SAN 213-5418).

Napsac Reproductions, *(Napsac Reprods; 0-934426),* Rte. 1 Box 300, Marble Hill, MO 63764 Tel 314-238-2010 (SAN 222-4607).

Narconon, *(Narconon; 0-917958),* 6425 Hollywood Blvd., Suite 206, Hollywood, CA 90028 Tel 213-469-8347 (SAN 209-9683).

Narcotics Education, Inc., *(Narc Ed),* 6830 Laurel St., N.W., Box 4390, Washington, DC 20012 Tel 202-723-4774 (SAN 205-7727).

Nass, Sylvan & Ulla, *(Nass; 0-9606468),* 220 Sunnybrook Rd., Flourtown, PA 19031 Tel 215-836-4884 (SAN 215-9740).

Nassau Press, *(Nassau Pr; 0-911491),* 228 Alexander St., Princeton, NJ 08540 Tel 609-921-1058 (SAN 272-5959).

National Academy of Gallaudet College, The, *(Natl Acad Gallaudet Coll; 0-934336),* Kendall Green, Washington, DC 20002 Tel 202-651-5595 (SAN 213-3423).

National Academy of Sciences, *(Natl Acad Sci; 0-309),* 2101 Constitution Ave, Washington, DC 20418 (SAN 226-6334).

National Academy Press, *(Natl Acad Pr; 0-309),* 2101 Constitution Ave., Washington, DC 20418 Tel 202-334-3113 (SAN 202-8891).

National Accreditation Council for Agencies Serving the Blind & Visually Handicapped, *(NACASBVH; 0-912948),* 79 Madison Ave., Suite 1406, New York, NY 10016 Tel 212-683-8581 (SAN 203-7076).

National Aeronautic Assn., *(Natl Aero),* 821 15th St., N.W., Suite 430, Washington, DC 20005 Tel 202-347-2808 (SAN 210-6167).

National Alliance, *(Natl Alliance; 0-937944),* Box 3535, Washington, DC 20007 Tel 703-979-1886 (SAN 220-0759).

National Archives & Records Service, *(Natl Archives),* Publications Division, Washington, DC 20408 (SAN 210-363X) Official records of the federal government on microfilm; facsimiles & reproductions of important historical documents, census records from 1790 to 1900 on microfilm. Catalog of National Archives Microfilm Publications, Black Studies, Indian Studies, immigration & judicial records. Catalog of Federal Population Census,1790 to1910.

National Art Education Assn., *(Natl Art Ed; 0-937652),* 1916 Association Dr., Reston, VA 22091 Tel 703-860-8000 (SAN 203-7084).

National Art Services, Inc., *(Natl Art Serv Inc; 0-911977),* P.O. Box 24339, Tampa, FL 33623 Tel 813-858-6034 (SAN 276-9492).

National Association for Hispanic Elderly See **Asociacion Nacional Pro Personas Mayores**

National Association for Physical Education in Higher Education, *(NAPEHE),* Department of Human Performance San Jose State University, San Jose, CA 95192 (SAN 224-0033).

National Assn. for Public Continuing & Adult Education, *(Natl Assn Con Adult Ed),* 1201 Sixteenth St., N.W., Washington, DC 20036 Tel 202-833-5486 (SAN 207-0286).

National Association for the Advancement of Humane Education, *(NAAHE; 0-941246),* P.O. Box 362, East Haddam, CT 06423 (SAN 285-0680); P.O. Box 98, East Haddam, CT 06423 (SAN 285-0699).

National Assn. for the Education of Young Children, *(Natl Assn Child Ed; 0-912674),* 1834 Connecticut Ave., N.W., Washington, DC 20009 Tel 202-232-8777 (SAN 202-8905).

National Assn. for Women Deans, Administrators & Counselors, *(Natl Assn Women; 0-943302),* 1625 I St., N.W., Washington, DC 20006 Tel 202-659-9330 (SAN 202-1080).

National Assn. of Accountants, *(Natl Assn Accts),* 919 Third Ave., New York, NY 10022 Tel 212-754-9715 (SAN 207-2637).

National Association of Biology Teachers, Inc., *(Natl Assn Bio Tchrs; 0-941212),* 11250 Roger Bacon Dr., Reston, VA 22090 Tel 703-471-1134 (SAN 217-4073).

National Assn. of College & University Business Officers, *(Natl Assn Coll; 0-915164),* 1 Dupont Circle, Suite 510, Washington, DC 20036 Tel 202-861-2534 (SAN 207-1479).

National Assn. of Counties, *(Natl Assn Counties; 0-911754),* 1735 New York Ave., N.W., Washington, DC 20006 Tel 202-783-5113 (SAN 205-7565).

National Assn. of Credit Management, *(NACM; 0-934914),* Book Edit Dept., 475 Park Ave., S., New York, NY 10016 Tel 212-578-4431 (SAN 205-7573).

National Assn. of Educational Broadcasters, *(NAEB; 0-8105),* 1346 Connecticut Ave., N.W., Washington, DC 20036 Tel 202-785-1100 (SAN 220-0112).

National Assn. of Home Builders, *(Natl Assn Home; 0-86718),* 15th & M St., N.W., Washington, DC 20005 Tel 202-452-0200 (SAN 207-7035).

National Assn. of Independent Schools, *(NAIS; 0-934388),* 18 Tremont St., Boston, MA 02108 Tel 617-723-6900 (SAN 202-0920).

National Assn. of Intercollegiate Athletics, *(NAIA Pubns),* 1221 Baltimore St., Kansas City, MO 64105 Tel 816-842-5050 (SAN 201-9574).

National Assn. of Parents & Prof. for Safe Alternatives in Childbirth, International, *(NAPSAC; 0-917314),* P.O. Box 267, Marble Hill, MO 63764 Tel 314-238-2010 (SAN 208-7766); Dist. by: Napsac Reproductions, Rt.1, Box 300, Marble Hill, MO 63764 Tel 314-238-4273 (SAN 222-4607).

National Association Of Personnel Consultants, *(NAPC; 0-9611608),* 1432 Duke St., Alexandria, VA 22314 Tel 703-684-0180 (SAN 285-2926).

National Association of Printing Ink Manufacturers, Inc., *(Natl Assn Print Ink),* 550 Mamaroneck Ave., Harrison, NY 10528 (SAN 224-2370).

National Assn. of Recycling Industries, *(Natl Recycling; 0-941096),* 330 Madison Ave., New York, NY 10017 Tel 212-867-7330 (SAN 205-7603).

National Assn. of School Nurses, Affiliate of National Education Assn., *(Natl Assn Sch Nurses),* Statler Hilton Hotel, Suite 104, Seventh Ave. & 33rd St., New York, NY 10014 Tel 212-594-0767 (SAN 203-7920).

National Association of Social Workers, *(Natl Assn Soc Wkrs; 0-87101),* Orders to: Publications Sales, NASW, 7981 Eastern Ave., Silver Springs, MD 20910 Tel 301-565-0333 (SAN 202-893X).

National Assn. of the Deaf, *(Natl Assn Deaf; 0-913072),* 814 Thayer Ave., Silver Spring, MD 20910 Tel 301-587-1788 (SAN 203-7092).

National Assn. of Trade & Tech. Schools, *(Natl Assn Trade Tech Schl; 0-942426),* 2021 K St. N.W., Washington, DC 20006 (SAN 238-406X).

National Assn. of Underwater Instructors, *(NAUI; 0-916974),* P.O. Box 630, Colton, CA 92324 Tel 714-824-5440 (SAN 208-1024).

National Audio-Visual Assn., Inc., *(Natl A-V Assn; 0-939718),* 3150 Spring St., Fairfax, VA 22031 Tel 703-273-7200 (SAN 205-7638).

National Audubon Society, *(Natl Audubon; 0-930698),* 950 Third Ave., New York, NY 10022 Tel 212-546-9139 (SAN 282-0307); Orders to: Service Dept., 950 Third Ave., New York, NY 10022 Tel 212-546-9112 (SAN 282-0315).

National Behavior Systems, *(Natl Behavior; 0-937654),* 11601 Balboa Blvd., Granada Hills, CA 91344 Tel 213-363-7160 (SAN 282-0323); Dist. by: Bookpeople, 2940 Seventh St., Berkeley, CA 94710 Tel 415-549-3030 (SAN 168-9517); Dist. by: Baker & Taylor Co., 50 Kirby Ave., Somerville, NJ 08876 (SAN 169-4901).

National Bellamy Award, *(Natl Bellamy),* 265 Hatton St., Portsmouth, VA 23704 (SAN 208-337X).

National Biomedical Research Foundation, *(Natl Biomedical; 0-912466),* Georgetown Univ. Medical Ctr, 3900 Reservoir Rd., N.W., Washington, DC 20007 Tel 202-625-2121 (SAN 203-7106).

National Book Co., Div. of Educational Research Associates, *(Natl Book; 0-89420),* 333 S.W. Park Ave., Portland, OR 97205 Tel 503-228-6345 (SAN 212-4661). *Imprints:* Halcyon House (Halcyon).

National Bureau of Economic Research, Inc., *(Natl Bur Econ Res; 0-87014),* 1050 Massachusetts Ave., Cambridge, MA 02138 (SAN 203-7114); Dist. by: Ballinger Publishing Co., 54 Church St., Cambridge, MA 02138 Tel 617-492-0670 (SAN 201-4084); Dist. by: Columbia University Press, 136 S. Broadway, Irvington-on-Hudson, New York, NY 10533 Tel 914-591-9111 (SAN 212-2472); Dist. by: Harvard University Press, 79 Garden St., Cambridge, MA 02138 Tel 617-495-2600 (SAN 281-7721); Dist. by: The M.I.T. Press, 28 Carleton St., Cambridge, MA 02142 Tel 617-253-2884 (SAN 202-6414); Dist. by: Princeton University Press, P.O. Box AAA, Princeton, NJ 08540 Tel 609-452-4913 (SAN 202-0254); Dist. by: University of Chicago Press, Order Dept., 11030 S. Langley Ave., Chicago, IL 60628 Tel 312-753-2587 (SAN 202-5299).

National Business Clearinghouse, *(NBC; 0-941176),* Box 327, Croton Plaza, Croton, NY 10520 (SAN 238-9010).

National Cable Television Assn., *(Natl Cable),* 1724 Massachusetts Ave., N.W., Washington, DC 20036 (SAN 215-7934).

National Catholic Development Conference, *(Natl Cath Dev; 0-9603196),* 119 N. Park Ave., Rockville Centre, NY 11570 Tel 516-764-6700 (SAN 209-0872).

National Catholic Educational Assn., *(Natl Cath Educ),* 1 Dupont Circle, Suite 350, Washington, DC 20036 Tel 202-293-5954 (SAN 205-7662).

National Catholic Pharmacists Guild of the United States, *(Natl Cath Pharm),* 1012 Surrey Hills Dr, St Louis, MO 63117 (SAN 224-4209).

National Catholic Reporter Publishing Co., Inc., *(Natl Cath Reporter; 0-934134),* 115 E. Armour, Box 281, Kansas City, MO 64141 Tel 816-531-0538 (SAN 207-7396).

National Center for Educational Brokering, *(Natl Ctr Educ Broker; 0-935612),* 325 Ninth St., San Francisco, CA 94103 (SAN 211-7479).

National Center for Faculty Development, *(Natl Ctr Faculty; 0-938540),* 1320 S. Dixie Hwy., No. 900A, Coral Gables, FL 33146 (SAN 216-423X).

National Center for Health Statistics, *(Natl Ctr Health Stats; 0-8406),* Federal Center Bldg., Rm. 1-57, 3700 East-West Hwy., Hyattsville, MD 20782 Tel 301-436-8586 (SAN 206-6033).

National Center for Job-Market Studies, *(Natl Ctr Job Mkt; 0-935234),* P.O. Box 3651 BN, Washington, DC 20007 Tel 202-229-4885 (SAN 213-5841).

National Center for Paralegal Training, *(Natl Ctr PT),* 1271 Ave of the Americas, Rm 777, New York, NY 10020 (SAN 227-0005).

National Center for Policy Analysis, *(Natl Ctr Pol; 0-943802),* 413 Carillon Plaza, Dallas, TX 75240 (SAN 241-0869).

National Center for Public Productivity, *(Natl Ctr Public Prod; 0-942942),* John Jay College, CUNY, 445 W. 59th St., New York, NY 10019 Tel 212-489-5030 (SAN 210-7929).

National Center for State Courts, *(Natl Ctr St Courts; 0-89656),* 300 Newport Ave., Williamsburg, VA 23185 Tel 804-253-2000 (SAN 210-928X).

National Center for the Diaconate, *(Natl Ctr Diaconate; 0-9605798),* 14 Beacon St., Rm. 103, Boston, MA 02108 Tel 617-742-1460 (SAN 220-1763).

National Center for Urban Ethnic Affairs, *(NCUEA; 0-940798),* 1523 O St., N.W., Washington, DC 20005 (SAN 219-8010).

National Chamber Foundation, *(Natl Chamber Foun; 0-89834),* 1615 H St., N.W., Washington, DC 20062 (SAN 238-0757).

National Christian Press, Inc., *(Natl Christian Pr; 0-934916),* P. O. Box 49118, Algood, TN 38501 Tel 615-537-9434 (SAN 212-1182).

National Clearinghouse for Bilingual Education, *(Natl Clearinghse Bilingual Ed; 0-89763),* 1555 Wilson Blvd., Suite 605, Rosslyn, VA 22209 Tel 800-336-4560 (SAN 212-839X).

National Commission on Resources for Youth, Subs. of Institute for Responsive Education, *(Natl Comm Res Youth; 0-912041),* 605 Commonwealth Ave., Boston, MA 02215 Tel 617-353-3309 (SAN 225-7785).

National Committee for Citizens in Education, *(NCCE; 0-934460),* Wilde Lake Village Green, Suite 410, Columbia, MD 21044 Tel 301-997-9300 (SAN 206-1023).

National Computer Graphics Assn. *(Natl Comp Graphics; 0-941514),* 2033 M St. NW, Suite 330, Washington, DC 20036 (SAN 239-1201).

National Consumer Research, *(Natl Consumer),* 6 E. 45th St., New York, NY 10017 (SAN 208-1377) Moved, Left No Forwarding Address.

National Council for Alternative Work Patterns, *(Natl Coun Alt; 0-911583),* 1925 K Street, NW, Suite 308, Washington, DC 20006 Tel 202-466-4467 (SAN 264-231X).

National Council for the Social Studies, *(Coun Soc Studies; 0-87986),* Social Education, 3501 Newark St., NW, Washington, DC 20016 Tel 202-966-7840 (SAN 202-1900).

National Council for US-China Trade, *(Natl Coun US-China; 0-935614),* 1050 17th St., NW, Washington, DC 20036 (SAN 222-4631).

National Council of Architectural Registration Boards, *(NCARB; 0-9607310),* Suite 700, 1735 New York Ave., N.W., Washington, DC 20006 (SAN 240-1282).

National Council Of Jewish Women, Omaha Section, *(Omaha Sec Nat),* 9009 Farnam Rd., Omaha, NE 68114 (SAN 283-3484).

National Council of Teachers of English, *(NCTE; 0-8141),* 1111 Kenyon Rd., Urbana, IL 61801 Tel 217-328-3870 (SAN 202-9049).

National Council of Teachers of Mathematics, *(NCTM; 0-87353),* 1906 Association Dr., Reston, VA 22091 Tel 703-620-9840 (SAN 202-9057).

National Council on Compensation Insurance, *(Natl Comp Ins),* One Penn Plaza, New York, NY 10001 (SAN 224-8360).

National Council on Crime & Delinquency, *(Natl Coun Crime),* 2125 Center Ave., Fort Lee, NJ 07024 (SAN 236-9095).

National Council on the Aging, Inc., *(Natl Coun Aging; 0-910883),* 600 Maryland Ave., S. W., West Wing 100,, Washington, DC 20024 (SAN 262-0502).

National Decision Systems, Inc., *(Natl Decision; 0-911871),* 9968 Hibert St., Suite 100, San Diego, CA 92131 Tel 619-695-0060 (SAN 264-2336).

National District Attorney's Assn., *(Natl Dist Atty),* 708 Pendleton St., Alexandria, VA 22314 Tel 703-549-9222 (SAN 205-7484).

National Education Assn., *(NEA; 0-8106),* 1201 16th St., N.W., Washington, DC 20036 Tel 202-833-4233 (SAN 203-7262); Orders to: The Academic Bldg., Saw Mill Rd., West Haven, CT 06516 Tel 203-934-2669 (SAN 203-7270).

National Education Standards, *(Natl Ed Stand; 0-918192),* One Wilshire Bldg., Suite 1210, 624 S. Grand Ave., Los Angeles, CA 90017 Tel 213-623-9135 (SAN 210-3141).

National Educational Laboratory Pubs. Inc., *(NELP; 0-916542; 0-89965),* P.O. Box 1003, Austin, TX 78767 Tel 512-385-7084 (SAN 208-7782); Orders to: 813 Airport Blvd., Austin, TX 78702 Tel 512-385-7084 (SAN 208-7790).

National Educational Resources, Inc., *(Natl Ed Res; 0-89498),* P.O. Box 536, Mooresville, IN 46158 Tel 317-831-6296 (SAN 209-9691).

National Employment Listing Service, Criminal Justice Center Sam Houston State University, *(Natl Employment; 0-935530),* Huntsville, TX 77341 (SAN 222-6278).

National Entertainment Research & Advisory Services *See* NERAS Systems

National Federation of Abstracting & Information Services, *(NFAIS),* 112 S. 16th St., 12th Fl., Philadelphia, PA 19102 Tel 215-563-2406 (SAN 203-7394).

National Fire Protection Assn., *(Natl Fire Prot; 0-87765),* Batterymarch Park, Quincy, MA 02269 Tel 617-482-8755 (SAN 202-8948).

National Forensic Center, *(Natl Forensic),* 6 Ashburn Place, Fair Lawn, NJ 07410 (SAN 212-7792).

National Foundation-March of Dimes, *(March of Dimes),* 1275 Mamaroneck Ave., White Plains, NY 10605 Tel 914-428-7100 (SAN 205-7441).

National Foundation to Fight Political Corruption, Inc., *(Natl Found Fight; 0-911901),* 816 Galer Place, Glendale, CA 91206 Tel 916-366-0774 (SAN 264-6803).

National Fuchsia Society, *(Natl Fuchsia),* Box 1153, Fort Bragg, CA 95437 (SAN 210-1289).

National Gallery of Art, *(Natl Gallery Art; 0-89468),* Sixth St. & Constitution Ave., N.W., Washington, DC 20565 Tel 202-737-4215 (SAN 203-5545).

National Genealogical Society, *(Natl Genealogical; 0-915156),* 1921 Sunderland Place, N.W., Washington, DC 20036 Tel 202-785-2123 (SAN 202-1056).

National Geographic Society, *(Natl Geog; 0-87044),* 17th & "M" Sts., N.W., Washington, DC 20036 Tel 202-857-7000 (SAN 202-8956).

National Guild of Community Schools of the Arts, Inc., *(NGCSA),* P.O. Box 583, Teaneck, NJ 07666 (SAN 218-4966).

National Heritage, *(Natl Heritage; 0-913188),* P.O. Box 84, Saint James, Beaver Island, MI 49782 Tel 616-448-2299 (SAN 205-7425).

National Housing Law Project, *(Natl Housing Law; 0-9606098),* 1950 Addison St., Berkeley, CA 94704 Tel 415-548-2600 (SAN 216-8391).

National Institute for Burn Medicine, *(Natl Inst Burn; 0-917478),* 909 E. Ann St., Ann Arbor, MI 48104 Tel 313-769-9000 (SAN 209-0570).

National Institute of Career Planning, Inc., *(Natl Inst Career; 0-917592),* 521 Fifth Ave., New York, NY 10017 Tel 212-682-5844 (SAN 208-0206).

National Institute of Judicial Dynamics, *(Natl Judicial Dynamics),* 411 Lakewood Circle, Suite B711, Colorado Springs, CO 80910 Tel 303-574-2082 (SAN 224-2311).

National Institute of Reboundology & Health Inc., *(NIRH; 0-938302),* 7416 212th S.W., Edmonds, WA 98020 Tel 206-774-6403 (SAN 215-0964).

National Intelligence Study Center, *(NISC; 0-938450),* 1015 Eighteenth St., NW, Suite 805, Washington, DC 20036 (SAN 216-0005).

National Iridology Research, Assn., *(Natl Iridology; 0-9602636),* 1590 Canyon Rd., Santa Fe, NM 87501 Tel 505-982-3038 (SAN 282-0420); Dist. by: Sunflower Books, 328 McKenzie St, Santa Fe, CA 87501 Tel 505-988-9272 (SAN 282-0439).

National Law Publishing Corporation, *(Natl Law),* 99 Painters Mill Rd., Owings Mills, MD 21117 Tel 301-363-6400 (SAN 281-1634).

National Lawyers Guild, *(Natl Lawyers Guild; 0-9602188),* 853 Broadway, Rm. 1705, New York, NY 10003 (SAN 212-5307); Dist. by: National Lawyers Guild Report, P.O. Box 14023, Washington, DC 20044 (SAN 212-5315).

National League for Nursing, Inc., *(Natl League Nurse),* 10 Columbus Circle, New York, NY 10019 Tel 212-582-1022 (SAN 203-7130).

National Learning Corp., *(Natl Learning; 0-8373; 0-8293),* 212 Michael Dr., Syosset, NY 11791 Tel 516-921-8888 (SAN 206-8869).

National Maritime Museum Association, *(Natl Maritime; 0-9605182),* Bldg. E, Third Floor, Fort Wilson, San Francisco, CA 94123 Tel 415-556-9872 (SAN 239-9385).

National Materials Development Center for French, *(Natl Mat Dev; 0-911409),* Dept. of Media Services, Dimond Library, UNH, Durham, NH 03824 (SAN 264-2344).

National Mental Health Association, *(Natl Mental Health),* 1800 N. Kent St., Arlington, VA 22209 Tel 703-528-6405 (SAN 223-9159).

National Micrographics Assn., *(Assn Inform Image; 0-89258),* 8719 Colesville Rd., Silver Spring, MD 20910 Tel 301-587-8202 (SAN 202-1021).

National Notary Assn., *(Natl Notary; 0-9600158; 0-933134),* 23012 Ventura Blvd., Woodland Hills, CA 91364 Tel 213-347-2035 (SAN 202-8964).

National Nursing Review, Inc., *(Natl Nursing; 0-917010),* P. O. Box 806, 342 State St., No. 6, Los Altos, CA 94022 Tel 415-941-5784 (SAN 208-7804).

National Paperback Books, Inc., *(Natl Paperback; 0-89826),* 224 Sarvis Dr., Knoxville, TN 37920 Tel 617-577-9943 (SAN 211-5336); Orders to: P.O. Box 146, Knoxville, TN 37901 Tel 615-588-6293 (SAN 211-5344).

National Planning Assn., *(Natl Planning),* 1606 New Hampshire Ave N.W., Washington, DC 20009 Tel 202-265-7685 (SAN 207-0030).

National Poetry Foundation, *(Natl Poet Foun; 0-915032),* Univ. of Maine, 303 English-Math Bldg, Orono, ME 04469 (SAN 206-5088).

National Practice Institute, *(Natl Prac Inst),* 510 First Ave. N., Suite 205, Minneapolis, MN 55403 Tel 800-328-4444 (SAN 217-2577).

National Publishers of the Black Hills, Inc., *(Natl Pub Black Hills; 0-935920),* 521 Kansas City St., Rapid City, SD 57709 (SAN 222-6227).

National Railway Historical Society, Intermountain Chapter, *(Natl Railway Hist; 0-917884),* P.O. Box 5181, Terminal Annex, Denver, CO 80217 Tel 303-623-6747 (SAN 206-1643).

National Railway Historical Society, Rio Grande Chapter, *(Natl Rail Rio Grande; 0-939646),* Box 3381, Grand Junction, CO 81502 Tel 303-242-3304 (SAN 220-1771).

National Railway Historical Society, Rochester Chapter, *(Natl Rail Rochester; 0-9605296),* 169 Gregory St., Rochester, NY 14620 Tel 716-244-6438 (SAN 282-0447); Orders to: P.O. Box 664, Rochester, NY 14603 (SAN 282-0455).

National Railway Historical Society, Washington D.C. Chapter, *(Natl Rail Hist Soc DC Chap; 0-933954),* P.O. Box 3512, Central Sta., Arlington, VA 22203 (SAN 212-8403).

National Register Publishing Co. Inc., Subs. of Standard Rate & Data Inc., *(Natl Register; 0-87217),* 5201 Old Orchard Rd., Skokie, IL 60077 Tel 312-470-3100 (SAN 207-5180).

National Research and Information Center, *(Nat Res Info; 0-9608220),* 1614 Central St., Evanston, IL 60201 Tel 312-328-6545 (SAN 240-4125).

National Research Council, *(Natl Res Coun; 0-309),* 2101 Constitution Ave., Washington, DC 20418 (SAN 223-923X).

National Research Group, *(Natl Res Group),* P.O. Box 93, Valdosta, GA 31601 (SAN 262-0510).

National Retail Merchants Assn., *(Natl Ret Merch; 0-87102),* 100 W. 31st St., New York, NY 10001 Tel 212-244-8780 (SAN 203-7149).

National Retired Teachers Association, *(Natl Ret Teachers),* 1909 K St N.W., Washington, DC 20049 (SAN 236-5928).

National Reunion Association, *(Natl Reunion Assn; 0-9610470),* P.O. Box 295, Nevada City, CA 95959 Tel 916-265-6644 (SAN 264-2360).

National Rifle Assn., *(Natl Rifle Assn; 0-935998),* 1600 Rhode Island Ave. N.W., Washington, DC 20036 Tel 202-828-6000 (SAN 213-859X); Dist. by: A B & C Sales., 2010 Eisenhower Ave, Alexandria, VA 22314 Tel 703-960-6600 (SAN 282-6607).

National Rural Electric Cooperative Assn., *(Natl Rural),* 1800 Massachusetts Ave., N.W., Washington, DC 20036 Tel 202-857-9500 (SAN 205-7328).

National Safety Council, *(Natl Safety Coun; 0-87912),* 444 N. Michigan Ave., Chicago, IL 60611 Tel 312-527-4800 (SAN 203-7157).

National Sanitation Foundation, *(Natl Sanit Foun; 0-940006),* P.O. Box 1468, 3475 Plymouth Rd., Ann Arbor, MI 48106 Tel 313-769-8010 (SAN 216-8413).

National School Boards Assn., *(Natl Sch Boards; 0-88364),* 1055 Thomas Jefferson St., N.W., Washington, DC 20007 Tel 202-337-7666 (SAN 205-731X).

National School of Public Relations Assn., *(Natl Sch PR; 0-87545),* 1801 N. Moore St., Arlington, VA 22209 Tel 703-528-5840 (SAN 203-7165).

National Science Teachers Assn., Affiliate of American Association for the Advancement of Science, *(Natl Sci Tchrs; 0-87355),* 1742 Connecticut Ave., N.W., Washington, DC 20009 Tel 202-328-5846 (SAN 203-7173).

National ShareGraphics, Inc., *(Natl ShareGraphics; 0-88107),* 1931 No. Industrial Blvd. Suite 105, Dallas, TX 75207 Tel 214-651-1025 (SAN 240-7310).

National Shorthand Reporters Association, *(Natl Shorthand Rptr),* 118 Park St Se, Vienna, VA 22180 Tel 703-224-9588).

National Square Dance Directory, *(Natl Sq Dance; 0-9605494),* P.O. Box 54055, Jackson, MS 39208 Tel 601-825-6831 (SAN 215-2576).

National Student Educational Fund, *(Natl Stud Ed; 0-940624),* Suite 305, 2000 P St. N.W., Washington, DC 20036 Tel 202-785-1856 (SAN 218-5199).

National Support Center for Families of the Aging, *(Natl Support Ctr; 0-910227),* Box 245, Swarthmore, PA 19081 Tel 215-544-3605 (SAN 241-4147).

National Technical Information Service, U.S. Dept. of Commerce, *(Natl Tech Info),* U.S. Dept. of Commerce, 14th & Constitution Ave., Room 1067, Washington, DC 20230 Tel 202-377-0365 (SAN 205-7255); Orders to: U.S. Dept of Commerce, 5285 Port Royal Rd., Springfield, VA 22161 Tel 703-487-4650 (SAN 205-7263).

National Textbook Co., *(Natl Textbk; 0-8442),* 4255 W. Touhy Ave., Lincolnwood, IL 60646 Tel 312-679-4210 (SAN 169-2208).

National Tooling & Machining Association, *(Natl Tool & Mach),* 9300 Livingston Rd., Fort Washington, MD 20022 Tel 301-248-6200 (SAN 224-232X).

National Trust for Historic Preservation, *(Natl Trust Hist),* 1785 Massachusetts N W, Washington, DC 20036 Tel 202-673-4000 (SAN 233-0911).

National Trust for Historic Preservation *See* Preservation Press, National Trust for Historic Preservation

National Underwriter Co., *(Natl Underwriter; 0-87218),* 420 E. Fourth St., Cincinnati, OH 45202 Tel 513-721-2140 (SAN 205-7247).

National Unity Equality Leadership Fraternity Press, *(NELF Pr),* 78 Maplevale Dr., Woodbridge, CT 06525 Tel 203-393-3913 (SAN 203-7297).

National University Publications *See* Associated Faculty Press

National Urban League, *(Natl Urban),* 500 E. 62nd St., New York, NY 10021 (SAN 215-2290).

National Video Clearinghouse, Inc., The, *(Natl Video; 0-935478),* 100 Lafayette Dr., Syosset, NY 11791 Tel 516-364-3686 (SAN 213-4209).

National Waterways Conference, Inc., *(Natl Waterways; 0-934292),* 1130 17th St. N.W., No. 200, Washington, DC 20036 (SAN 203-719X).

National Wildlife Federation, *(Natl Wildlife; 0-912186),* 8925 Leesburg Pike, Vienna, VA 22180 Tel 703-790-4227 (SAN 202-8980).

National Women's Hall of Fame, *(Natl Wmns Hall Fame),* 76 Falls St. P.O. Box 335, Seneca Falls, NY 13148 Tel 315-568-8060 (SAN 223-9299).

National Writers Club, *(Natl Writers Club),* 1450 S Havana Suite 620, Aurora, CO 80012 (SAN 225-3992).

National Writers Press, the, Div. of the National Writers Club, Subs. of Assn. Headquarters, Inc., *(Natl Writ Pr; 0-88100),* 1450 S. Havana, Suite 620, Aurora, CO 80012 (SAN 240-320X); Dist. by: Rish-Whit Dist., Box 21, Elwood, NE 68937 (SAN 240-3218).

Nationwide Press, Ltd., *(Nationwide Pr; 0-917188),* P.O. Box 1528, Pueblo, CO 81002 Tel 303-543-1382 (SAN 208-7812).

Natural History Museum of Los Angeles County, *(Nat Hist Mus; 0-938644),* 900 Exposition Blvd., Los Angeles, CA 90007 Tel 213-744-3330 (SAN 238-6925).

Natural History Press, *(Natural Hist),* Dist. by: Doubleday & Co., Inc., 501 Franklin Ave., Garden City, NY 11530 (SAN 281-6083). *Imprints:* American Museum Science Books (AMS).

Natural History Publishing Co., *(Nat Hist Pub Co; 0-9603144),* P.O. Box 962, La Jolla, CA 92038 Tel 714-459-0835 (SAN 207-7515).

Natural Hygiene Press, Div. of American Natural Hygiene Society, Inc., *(Natural Hygiene; 0-914532),* 698 Brooklawn Ave., Bridgeport, CT 06604 Tel 203-366-6229 (SAN 202-4314).

Natural Learning Resources, *(Nat Learn Res; 0-936214),* 5151 Monroe, P.O. Box 8443, Toledo, OH 43623 (SAN 214-0640).

Natural Press, Div. of Natural Enterprises, *(Natural Pr; 0-939956),* P.O. 2107, Manitowoc, WI 54220 Tel 414-682-0738 (SAN 287-0215); Dist. by: Contemporary Books, 180 N. Michigan Ave., Chicago, IL 60601 (SAN 287-0223).

Natural Resources Enterprises, Inc., *(Natural Res Ent; 0-939870),* P.O. Box 4523, Lincoln, NE 68504 Tel 402-472-1519 (SAN 216-9150).

Natural Science for Youth Foundation, *(Natural Sci Youth; 0-916544),* 763 Silvermine Rd., New Canaan, CT 06840 Tel 203-966-5643 (SAN 208-2039).

Natural Therapy Foundation Press, The, *(Nat Therapy; 0-937792),* 5 Greenleaf, Irvine, CA 92714 Tel 714-551-0381 (SAN 215-6849).

Natural World Press, *(Natural World; 0-939560),* 251 Baldwin Ave.,Suite 246, San Mateo, CA 94401 Tel 415-775-1490 (SAN 216-6879).

Nature Books Pubs., *(Nature Bks Pubs; 0-912542),* P.O. Box 12157, Jackson, MS 39211 Tel 601-956-5686 (SAN 203-7211).

Nature Life, Div. of McGill-Jensen, *(Nature Life; 0-918134),* 655 Fairview Ave. N., St. Paul, MN 55104 Tel 612-645-3129 (SAN 209-3596).

Nature Study Guild, *(Nature Study; 0-912550),* P.O. Box 972, Berkeley, CA 94701 (SAN 203-722X).

Nature Trails Press, *(Nature Trails; 0-937794),* 933 Calle Loro, Palm Springs, CA 92262 Tel 714-323-9420 (SAN 207-3609).

Naturegraph Pubs., Inc., *(Naturegraph; 0-911010; 0-87961),* P.O. Box 1075, Happy Camp, CA 96039 Tel 916-493-5353 (SAN 202-8999).

Nature's Medicine Chest, *(Gluten Co; 0-935596),* 509 E. 2100 N., Box 482, Provo, UT 84601 Tel 801-377-6390 (SAN 213-0653).

Nauful, Eli S., *(Nauful),* P.O. Box 1260, Lynchburg, VA 24502 (SAN 209-6269).

Nautical & Aviation Publishing Co. of America, The, *(Nautical & Aviation; 0-933852),* 8 Randall St., Annapolis, MD 21401 Tel 301-267-8522 (SAN 213-3431).

Nautical Books, *(Nautical Bks; 0-931284),* P.O. Box 331, Stoughton, WI 53589 Tel 608-873-5003 (SAN 209-1216).

Nautilus Books, *(Nautilus Bks; 0-916388),* 6 Elmridge Rd., Princeton, NJ 08540 Tel 609-466-0800 (SAN 203-7238).

Navajo Community College Press, *(Navajo Coll Pr; 0-912586),* Navajo Community College, Tsaile, AZ 86556 (SAN 201-9582).

Navajo Curriculum Center Press, *(Navajo Curr; 0-936008),* Rough Rock Demonstration School, Star Rte. 1, Rough Rock, AZ 86503 (SAN 203-1604).

Naval Fighters, *(Naval Fighters; 0-942612),* 1754 Warfield Cir., Simi Valley, CA 93063 Tel 805-527-9732 (SAN 238-5457).

Naval Institute Press, *(Naval Inst Pr; 0-87021),* Annapolis, MD 21402 Tel 301-268-6110 (SAN 202-9006).

Navpress, A Ministry of The Navigators, *(NavPress; 0-89109),* P.O. Box 6000, Colorado Springs, CO 80934 Tel 303-598-1212 (SAN 211-5352).

NAWDAC *See* National Assn. for Women Deans, Administrators & Counselors

Neal, Clarke L., *(C L Neal),* 456 Skeel, Mountain Lakes, NJ 07046 (SAN 239-4634) Moved, left no forwarding address.

Neal, Richard, Associates, *(Neal Assoc; 0-9605018),* Box 23, Manassas, VA 22110 (SAN 215-6857).

Neal Pubns., *(Neal Pubns; 0-9609006),* P.O. Box 451, Perrysburg, OH 43551 (SAN 240-8198).

Neal-Schuman Pubs., Inc., *(Neal-Schuman; 0-918212),* 23 Cornelia St., New York, NY 10014 Tel 212-620-5990 (SAN 210-2455).

Neale Watson Academic Pubns. Inc., *(N Watson; 0-88202),* 156 Fifth Ave., Suite 229, New York, NY 10010 Tel 212-675-7480 (SAN 207-7337). *Imprints:* Prodist (Prodist).

Near, Jean, *(J Near; 0-9609166),* 14909 Tomki Road, Redwood Valley, CA 95470 Tel 707-485-8598 (SAN 264-2409).

Nebraska Art Association, *(Nebraska Art; 0-9602018),* Sheldon Memorial Art Gallery, Univ. of Nebraska, Lincoln, NE 68588 Tel 402-472-2461 (SAN 212-1972).

Nebraska Review, *(Nebraska Review; 0-937796),* Southeast Community College, 924 K St., Fairbury, NE 68352 (SAN 220-262X).

Nebraska State Historical Society, *(Nebraska Hist),* 1500 R St, Lincoln, NE 68503 Tel 402-471-3270 (SAN 209-4630).

Necronomicon Press, *(Necronomicon),* 101 Lockwood St., West Warwick, RI 02893 Tel 401-828-5319 (SAN 210-315X).

Neechee Associates, Inc., *(Neechee Assoc; 0-9602582),* 6664 Paseo Dorado, Tucson, AZ 85715 (SAN 215-6865).

Needlemania, Inc., *(Needlemania),* P.O. Box 123, Franklin, MI 48025 (SAN 240-9208).

Nefertiti Head Press, *(Nefertiti; 0-918722),* Drawer J. Univ. Sta., Austin, TX 78712 (SAN 209-6749).

Negative Capability Press, *(Negative Capability Pr; 0-942544),* 6116 Timberly Rd. N, Mobile, AL 36609 Tel 205-661-9114 (SAN 238-5465).

Neihardt-Smith Publishing Co., *(Neihardt-Smith; 0-9608910),* P.O. Box 217, Medford, OR 97501 (SAN 262-0790).

Neild/Kuvet Publishing Co., *(Neild-Kuvet; 0-912945),* P.O. Box 9184, Berkeley, CA 94709 Tel 415-527-9645 (SAN 283-1015).

Nellen Publishing Co. Inc., *(Nellen Pub; 0-8424),* Box 18, Newton, NJ 07860 Tel 201-383-0114 (SAN 211-2590) Moved, Left No Forwarding Address.

Nelson, G. L., Publishing, Inc./KidsLife Books, *(Nelson G L; 0-937416),* 664 N. Michigan Ave., Suite 1010, Chicago, IL 60611 (SAN 287-2714).

Nelson, Irene J., *(I J Nelson; 0-9601464),* P.O. Box 28, Tuskegee Institute, AL 36088 (SAN 211-0725).

Nelson, Ted, Publisher, *(T Nelson; 0-89347),* Box 3, Schooleys Mountain, NJ 07870 Tel 312-352-8796 (SAN 208-7820); Dist. by: The Distributors, 702 S. Michigan, South Bend, IN 46618 (SAN 212-0364).

Nelson, Thomas, Publishers, *(Nelson; 0-8407),* P.O. Box 141000, Nelson Place at Elm Hill Pike, Nashville, TN 37214 Tel 615-889-9000 (SAN 209-3820).

Nelson, Vera Joyce, *(V J Nelson),* 5558 S.E. Aldercrest Lane, Milwaukie, OR 97222 Tel 503-654-3060 (SAN 207-6829).

Nelson-Atkins Museum of Art, The, *(Nelson-Atkins; 0-942614),* 4525 Oak St., Kansas City, MO 64111 Tel 816-561-4000 (SAN 238-5473).

Nelson-Hall Inc., *(Nelson-Hall; 0-911012; 0-88229; 0-8304),* 111 N. Canal St., Chicago, IL 60606 Tel 312-930-9446 (SAN 202-9065).

Nembutsu Press, *(Nembutsu Pr; 0-912624),* 6257 Golden West Ave., Temple City, CA 91780 (SAN 208-0060).

Nemeth, Doris I., *(Nemeth; 0-932192),* 2314 W. Sixth St., Mishawaka, IN 46544 (SAN 217-118X).

Neo-American Church, *(Neo-Am Church),* Box 4351, Arcata, CA 95521 (SAN 225-4751).

Neo-Medical Publishing, *(Neo Med Pub; 0-9611870),* P.O. Box 1357, New Milford, CT 06776 Tel 203-775-7184 (SAN 286-1356).

Neo Press, *(Neo Pr; 0-911014),* P.O. Box 32, Peaks Island, ME 04108 (SAN 203-7300).

Neptune Books *See* Tail Feather

NERAS Systems, *(NERAS Syst),* 425 N. Doheny Dr., Suite 8, Beverly Hills, CA 90210 Tel 213-278-8584 (SAN 211-1616).

Nesbit, Norman L., *(Nesbit; 0-911746),* 2104 Goddard Place, Boulder, CO 80303 Tel 303-494-6206 (SAN 206-1651).

Nesbitt Enterprises, *(Nesbitt Ent),* 5220 N.E. Roselawn, Portland, OR 97218 Tel 503-287-0306 (SAN 219-8029).

NESFA Press *See* New England Science Fiction Assn., Inc.

Netherton, H. Eugene, *(Netherton),* 1035 Park Blvd., West Sacramento, CA 95691 (SAN 238-9029).

Nettleton House, *(Nettleton Hse),* 737 Fifth Ave., San Francisco, CA 94118 (SAN 214-4263).

Network Project, *(Network Project),* Columbia Univ., 101 Earl Hall, New York, NY 10027 Tel 212-923-3900 (SAN 206-166X).

Network Pubns., *(Network Pubns; 0-941816),* 1700 Mission, Suite 203, Santa Cruz, CA 95065 Tel 408-429-9822 (SAN 216-2881).

Neuberger, Phyllis J., *(P J Neuberger; 0-9610050),* 5855 Sheridan Rd., Chicago, IL 60660 (SAN 262-9607); c/o Ten Plus, Inc., Thomas Graphics, Inc., 412 S. Wells St., Chicago, IL 60607 (SAN 262-9615).

Neuffer, Claude Henry, *(C H Neuffer),* U. S. C. English Dept., Columbia, SC 29208 Tel 803-787-3823 (SAN 207-2076).

Nev Multimedia Pubns., *(NEV Multimedia Pubs; 0-9606426),* 259 Walnut St., Newtonville, MA 02160 Tel 617-332-4953 (SAN 218-5709).

Nevada Historical Society, *(Nevada Hist Soc),* Southern Nevada Office, 1555 E. Flamingo, Suite 238, Las Vegas, NV 89109 Tel 702-734-9716 (SAN 211-2582).

Nevada Pubns., *(Nevada Pubns; 0-913814),* 4135 Badger Circle, Reno, NV 89509 Tel 702-747-0800 (SAN 203-7319).

Nevin, Mark, *(M Nevin),* 1860 Ala Moana (704), Honolulu, HI 96815 (SAN 285-6751).

New Age Action Group, *(New Age Action),* 910 Crescent Dr., Alexandria, VA 22302 Tel 703-836-4930 (SAN 213-1293).

New Age Business Books, *(New Age Bus Bks; 0-911201),* 587 Ave. C, Boulder City, NV 89005 Tel 702-293-4665 (SAN 263-1687).

New Age Press, Inc., *(New Age; 0-87613),* P.O. Box 1216, Black Mountain, NC 28711 Tel 704-669-9788 (SAN 203-7327).

New Age Press Inc., *(New Age Pr NM),* 320 Artist Rd., Santa Fe, NM 87501 Tel 505-982-1500 (SAN 215-7942) Moved, left no forwarding address.

New Age Publishing Center, *(New Age Pub Ctr),* 405 N. Frances, Apt. A, Chicago, IL 60606 Tel 608-251-4828 (SAN 217-1198).

New American Library, *(NAL; 0-451; 0-452; 0-453),* 1633 Broadway, New York, NY 10019 Tel 212-397-8000 (SAN 206-8079); Orders to: 120 Woodbine St., Bergenfield, NJ 07621 Tel 201-387-0600 (SAN 206-8087). *Imprints:* Mentor Books (Ment); Meridian Books (Mer); Plume Books (Plume); Signet Books (Sig); Signet Classics (Sig Classics).

New Bedford Press, *(New Bedford; 0-931656),* 5800 W. Century Blvd., Dept. 91502, Los Angeles, CA 90009 Tel 213-837-2961 (SAN 219-9688).

New Benjamin Franklin House, The, *(New Benjamin; 0-933488),* 304 W. 58th St., 5th Fl., New York, NY 10019 Tel 212-247-7484 (SAN 212-6168).

New Canaan Historical Society, *(New Canaan; 0-939958),* 13 Oenoke Ridge, New Canaan, CT 06840 Tel 203-966-1776 (SAN 216-843X).

New Capernaum Works, *(New Capernaum; 0-938792),* 4615 N.E. Emerson St., Portland, OR 97218 Tel 503-281-1307 (SAN 215-8922).

New Century Pubs., Inc., *(New Century; 0-8329),* 220 Old New Brunswick Rd., Piscataway, NJ 08854 Tel 201-981-0820 (SAN 217-1201).

New Circle Pubns., Art Research Ctr., *(New Circle),* 922 E. 48th St., Kansas City, MO 64110 Tel 816-531-2067 (SAN 274-0044).

New City Press, *(New City; 0-911782),* 206 Skillman Ave., Brooklyn, NY 11211 Tel 212-782-2844 (SAN 203-7335).

New Classics Library, Inc., *(New Classics Lib; 0-932750),* P.O. Box 1618, Gainesville, GA 30503 Tel 404-536-0309 (SAN 212-1190).

New Collage Press, *(New Collage; 0-936814),* 5700 N. Tamiami Trail, Sarasota, FL 33580 Tel 813-355-7671 (SAN 210-6159).

New College & Univ. Press, The, *(New Coll U Pr; 0-8084),* 267 Chapel St., New Haven, CT 06513 Tel 203-562-3101 (SAN 203-6223). *Imprints:* Twayne's U.S. Author Series (Twayne).

New Community Projects, Inc., *(New Community; 0-9603468),* 449 Cambridge St., Union Square, Allston, MA 02134 Tel 617-783-3060 (SAN 207-2645).

New Day Pr., *(New Day Pr; 0-913678),* c/o Karamu Hse., 2355 E. 89th St., Cleveland, OH 44106 (SAN 279-2664).

New Dimension Studio, *(New Dimen Studio; 0-916928),* 3872 Augusta Dr., Rm. 1, Nashville, TN 37209 Tel 615-876-6371 (SAN 208-385X); Orders to: P.O. Box 90492, Nashville, TN 37209 (SAN 208-3868).

New Directions for Young Women, Inc., *(New Dir Young Women; 0-9608696),* 738 N. 5th Ave., Tucson, AZ 85705 Tel 602-623-3677 (SAN 240-7337).

New Directions Press, *(New Dir Pr; 0-9609616),* Rd. Four, Box 343, Newton, NJ 07860 Tel 201-579-1277 (SAN 260-2326).

New Directions Publishing Corp., *(New Directions; 0-8112),* 80 Eighth Ave., New York, NY 10011 Tel 212-354-5500 (SAN 202-9081); Dist. by: W. W. Norton Co., 500 Fifth Ave., New York, NY 10110 (SAN 202-5795).

New England Board of Higher Education, *(NE Board Higher Ed; 0-916220),* 40 Grove St., Wellesley, MA 02181 (SAN 220-9365).

New England History Press, *(NE History; 0-89725),* P.O. Box 70, Somersworth, NH 03878 (SAN 264-2433).

New England Press, *(New England Pr; 0-931060),* 45 Tudor City, No. 1903, New York, NY 10017 (SAN 211-9196).

New England Press Inc., The, *(New Eng Pr VT; 0-933050),* P.O. Box 575, Shelburne, VT 05482 Tel 802-985-2569 (SAN 213-6376).

New England Pub. Co., *(New Eng Pub; 0-932268),* 200 Glendale Rd., Stratford, CT 06497 Tel 203-375-3252 (SAN 212-2499).

New England Science Fiction Assn., Inc., *(NESFA Pr; 0-915368),* P.O. Box G, MIT Branch P.O., Cambridge, MA 02139 (SAN 208-4066).

New English Art Gallery, *(New English Art; 0-913064),* Charles & Liberty Sts., Rochester, NH 03867 Tel 603-332-1761 (SAN 203-7343).

New Era Press, *(New Era; 0-937590),* P.O. Box 124, Weaverville, CA 96093 Tel 916-623-5966 (SAN 215-8930).

New Era Pubns. See World Merchandise-Import Center

New Expressions Unltd., *(New Expressions),* 30886 Sutherland Dr., Redlands, CA 92373 Tel 714-794-4868 (SAN 209-4053).

New Hampshire Publishing Co., *(NH Pub Co; 0-912274; 0-89725),* P.O. Box 70, Somersworth, NH 03878 Tel 603-692-3727 (SAN 202-9189).

New Harbinger Pubns., *(New Harbinger; 0-934986),* 2200 Adeline, Suite 305, Oakland, CA 94607 (SAN 205-0587).

New Hope Books See Revell, Fleming H., Co.

New Hope Publishing Co., *(New Hope; 0-915460),* Dist. by: Midway Copy Services, P.O. Box 378, Lahaska, PA 18931 Tel 212-794-5757 (SAN 202-9103).

New Horizons Press, *(New Horizons; 0-914914),* P.O. Box 1758, Chico, CA 95927 Tel 916-345-0225 (SAN 206-7927).

New House Pubs., *(New House; 0-913516),* 413 Guilford Ave., Queensboro, NC 27401 (SAN 212-2936).

New Image, *(New Image; 0-9609168),* 310 Colima Ct., La Jolla, CA 92037 Tel 714-456-2122 (SAN 241-4163).

New Impressions, *(New Impressions; 0-9611606),* Box 558, 118 Middle St., Lancaster, NH 03584 Tel 603-788-4492 (SAN 285-2942).

New Issues Press, *(New Issues MI; 0-932826),* Dept. of Political Science, Western Michigan Univ., Kalamazoo, MI 49008 Tel 616-383-1886 (SAN 206-2321).

New Issues Press, Inc., *(New Issues Pr; 0-913944),* 1024 Alachua St., Tallahassee, FL 32302 Tel 904-222-4972 (SAN 203-7351) Moved, Left No Forwarding Address.

New Jersey Associates, *(NJ Assocs; 0-911273),* Box 505, Montclair, NJ 07042 Tel 201-746-2000 (SAN 285-0702); Orders to: New Jersey Associates, Box 505, Montclair, NJ 07042 Tel 201-746-2000 (SAN 285-0710).

New Jersey Conservation Foundation, *(NJ Cons Foun; 0-913234),* 300 Mendham Rd., Morristown, NJ 07960 (SAN 206-9725).

New Jersey Historical Society, *(NJ Hist Soc; 0-911020),* 230 Broadway, Newark, NJ 07104 Tel 201-483-3939 (SAN 205-7131).

New Jersey Institute for Continuing Legal Education, *(NJ Inst CLE),* 15 Washington St, Newark, NJ 07101 Tel 201-648-5571 (SAN 226-997X).

New Jersey School Boards Association, *(NJ Schl Bds; 0-912337),* 407 W. State St., Trenton, NJ 08618 (SAN 226-1847).

New Jersey State Museum, *(NJ State Mus; 0-938766),* 205 W. State St., Trenton, NJ 08625 (SAN 220-2638).

New Leaf Press, *(New Leaf; 0-89221),* P.O. Box 1045, Harrison, AR 72601 Tel 501-741-2514 (SAN 207-9518).

New Letters Books, *(New Letters; 0-938652),* 5346 Charlotte, Kansas City, MO 64110 Tel 816-276-1168 (SAN 209-8458).

New Lifestyle Publishing, *(New Lifestyle; 0-941256),* P.O. Box 4419, Los Angeles, CA 90051 (SAN 239-4642).

New London County Historical Society, *(New London County),* 11 Blinman St., New London, CT 06320 Tel 203-443-1209 (SAN 207-0049).

New London Press, *(New London Pr; 0-89683),* Box 7458, Dallas, TX 75209 Tel 214-742-9037 (SAN 211-4402).

New Meridian Press, *(New Meridian Pr; 0-914882),* P.O. Box 229, Clifton Park, NY 12065 Tel 518-877-5845 (SAN 206-5045).

New Mermaid Dramabooks See Hill & Wang, Inc.

New Mexico St. Univ. - Studies in Latin Amer. Popular Culture, *(New Mexico St Univ; 0-9608664),* Dept. of Foreign Languages, Box 3L, Las Cruces, NM 88003 Tel 505-646-2942 (SAN 239-5428).

New Music Times, The, *(New Music Times; 0-9606830),* P.O. Box 8573, Albany, NY 12208 Tel 518-438-4815 (SAN 219-6115).

New Nativity Press, *(New Nativity; 0-940128),* P.O. Box 6223, Leawood, KS 66206 Tel 913-341-8369 (SAN 217-0779).

New Nurse, Pub., The, *(New Nurse; 0-914698),* P.O. Box 803, Plattsburgh, NY 12901 (SAN 206-6041) Name Formerly Hanton.

New Orlando Pubns., *(New Orlando; 0-917608),* Box 103 Village Sta., New York, NY 10014 Tel 212-449-6236 (SAN 205-7115).

New Orleans Museum of Art, *(New Orleans Mus Art; 0-89494),* P. O. Box 19123, New Orleans, LA 70179 Tel 504-488-2631 (SAN 209-9713).

New Orleans Poetry Journal Press, The, *(New Orleans Poetry; 0-938498),* 2131 General Pershing St., New Orleans, LA 70115 (SAN 215-8949).

New Outlook Pubs. & Distributors, *(New Outlook; 0-87898),* 235 W 23 St., New York, NY 10011 (SAN 202-9111).

New Pages Press, *(New Page Pr; 0-941644),* 4426 S. Belsay Rd., Grand Blanc, MI 48439 Tel 313-742-9583 (SAN 239-2682).

New Paradigm Press, *(New Paradigm Pr; 0-911511),* P.O. box 160081, Miami, FL 33116 Tel 305-596-4523 (SAN 264-2468).

New Paradise Books, *(New Paradise Bks; 0-943654),* Suite 206, 3000 N. Atlantic, Cocoa Beach, FL 32931 Tel 305-783-5651 (SAN 238-0765).

New Pen Publishing Co., *(New Pen Pub Co; 0-9609808),* P.O. Box 1690, Newark, NJ 07101 (SAN 264-2476).

New Pittsburgh Pubns., *(New Pittsburgh; 0-9608484),* P.O. Box 16150, Pittsburgh, PA 15242 (SAN 240-7345).

New Plays-Books Incorporated, *(New Plays Bks; 0-932720),* Box 273, Rowayton, CT 06853 (SAN 220-9411).

New Poets Series, *(New Poets; 0-932616),* 541 Piccadilly Rd., Baltimore, MD 21204 Tel 301-321-2868 (SAN 209-4622).

New Puritan Library, Inc., *(New Puritan; 0-932050),* Rte. 1, Lytle Rd., Fletcher, NC 28732 (SAN 213-4217).

New Renaissance Workshop, *(New Renaissance; 0-9600464),* P.O. Box 421, Ojai, CA 93023 (SAN 202-912X).

New Republic Books, *(New Republic; 0-915220),* 1220 19th St. N.W., Suite 205, Washington, DC 20036 Tel 202-331-1250 (SAN 207-2653).

New Research Pubns., *(New Research; 0-910891),* P.O. Box 231, Greenvale, NY 11548 Tel 274-0389; 135 Eileen Way, Syosset, NY 11791 (SAN 274-0397).

New Rivers Press, *(New Rivers Pr; 0-912284; 0-89823),* 1602 Selby Ave., St. Paul, MN 55104 Tel 612-645-6324 (SAN 202-9138).

New Seed Press, *(New Seed; 0-938678),* 1665 Euclid Ave., Berkeley, CA 94709 (SAN 282-0501); Dist. by: Bookpeople, 2940 Seventh St., Berkeley, CA 94710 (SAN 168-9517); Dist. by: The Crossing Press, Trumansburg, NY 14886 (SAN 202-2060).

New Sibylline Books, Inc., *(New Sibylline; 0-9603352),* Box 266, Village Sta., New York, NY 10014 (SAN 214-4271).

New Society Pubs., *(New Soc Pubs; 0-86571),* 4722 Baltimore Ave., Philadelphia, PA 19143 Tel 215-726-6543 (SAN 213-540X).

New South Co., The, *(New South Co; 0-917990),* P.O. Box 24918, Los Angeles, CA 90024 Tel 213-489-5700 (SAN 209-3340).

New Star Press, *(New Star Pr; 0-9607428),* P.O. Box 75, Bedford, NY 10506 Tel 914-234-7167 (SAN 239-7846).

New Tide MTL Publishers, *(New Tide; 0-88100),* Box 21 Contra Station Six, 1525 Sherman St., Denver, CO 80203 (SAN 264-2492).

New University Press, *(New Univ Pr; 0-89044),* 520 N. Michigan Ave., Chicago, IL 60611 Tel 312-828-0420 (SAN 206-8028); Orders to: Precedent Publishing, Inc., P.O. Box 1005, South Holland, IL 60473 Tel 312-877-5490 (SAN 205-1591).

New Victoria Pubs. Inc., *(New Victoria Pubs; 0-934678),* 7 Bank St., Lebanon, NH 03766 Tel 603-448-2264 (SAN 212-1204).

New View Press, *(New View Pr; 0-943066),* 5370 Manhttan Circle, Suite 205, Boulder, CO 80303 Tel 303-494-1004 (SAN 240-4133).

New Visions Press, *(New Visions Pr; 0-934340),* P.O. Box 2025, Gaithersburg, MD 20760 Tel 301-869-1888 (SAN 212-9213).

New Vista Press, *(New Vista; 0-936544),* 10 Oak Tree Dr., P.O. Box 736, Sebastopol, CA 95472 (SAN 214-0667).

New Wave Consultants, *(New Wave; 0-943172),* P.O. Box 5169, Santa Monica, CA 90405 Tel 714-274-2030 (SAN 240-415X).

New Woman Press, *(New Woman),* 2000 King Mountain Trail, Sunny Valley, OR 97497-9799 (SAN 209-8474).

New World Alliance, *(New World Alliance),* 733 15th St., N.W., No. 1131, Washington, DC 20005 Tel 202-347-6082 (SAN 216-2733).

New World Books, *(New World Bks; 0-917480),* 4515 Saul Rd, Kensington, MD 20795 (SAN 208-3388).

New World Cup Press, *(New World Cup CA; 0-9604636),* 9061 Madison Ave., Westminster, CA 92683 (SAN 215-1634).

New World Press, *(New World Press NY; 0-911026),* P.O. Box 416, New York, NY 10017 Tel 212-682-1154 (SAN 203-736X).

New Worlds Unlimited, *(New Worlds; 0-917398),* 100 Maple St., No. 53, Garfield, NJ 07026 Tel 201-340-0247 (SAN 207-267X); Orders to: P.O. Box 556, Saddle Brook, NJ 07662 (SAN 207-2688).

New Writers Guild Press, *(New Writers Guild; 0-913459),* 6323 Rimpau Blvd., Los Angeles, CA 90043 Tel 213-293-1281 (SAN 277-6960).

New York Academy of Sciences, *(NY Acad Sci; 0-89072; 0-89766),* Pubns. Dept., 2 E. 63rd St., New York, NY 10021 Tel 212-838-0230 (SAN 203-753X).

New York Botanical Garden, Pubns. Office, *(NY Botanical; 0-89327),* Bronx, NY 10458 Tel 212-220-8721 (SAN 205-7085).

New York Bound, *(NY Bound; 0-9608788),* 43 W. 54th St., New York, NY 10019 Tel 212-245-8503 (SAN 238-3195).

New York Chiropractic College, *(NY Chiro Coll; 0-938470),* P.O. Box 167, Glen Head, NY 11545 (SAN 216-1680).

New York City Commission on the Status of Woman, *(NYC Comm Woman),* 52 Chambers St., Suite 207, New York, NY 10007 Tel 212-566-3830 (SAN 240-9224); Dist. by: Golden Lee, 1000 Dean St., Brooklyn, NY 11238 Tel 212-857-6333 (SAN 282-5805).

New York Graphic Society Books, *(NYGS; 0-8212),* 34 Beacon St., Boston, MA 02106 Tel 617-227-0730 (SAN 202-5841); Dist. by: Little, Brown & Co., 200 West St., Waltham, MA 02154 (SAN 281-8892).

New York Hunting & Fishing Guide, Inc., *(NY Hunting; 0-937328),* 328 E. Main, Rm 300, Rochester, NY 14604 Tel 716-325-1636 (SAN 215-6873).

New York Institute of Finance, *(NY Inst Finance),* 70 Pine St., New York, NY 10270 (SAN 239-3697).

New York Labor News, *(NY Labor News; 0-935534),* 914 Industrial Ave., Palo Alto, CA 94303 Tel 415-494-1532 (SAN 202-0947).

New York Law Journal Seminars Press, *(NY Law Pub),* 233 Broadway, New York, NY 10007 Tel 212-761-8300 (SAN 226-2800).

New York Library Assn., *(NY Lib Assn; 0-931658),* 60 E. 42nd St., Suite 1242, New York, NY 10017 (SAN 211-6758).

New York Literary Forum, *(NY Lit Forum; 0-931196),* 21 E. 79th St., New York, NY 10021 (SAN 212-9221).

New York Literary Press, *(NY Lit Pr; 0-930910),* 417 W. 56th St., New York, NY 10019 (SAN 211-5379).

New York-New Jersey Trail Conference, Inc., *(NY-NJ Trail Confer; 0-9603966),* 20 W. 40th St., New York, NY 10018 (SAN 213-9421).

New York Production Manual, Inc. Publishing Co., *(NY Prod Manual; 0-935744),* 611 Broadway, Suite 807, New York, NY 10012 Tel 212-777-4002 (SAN 213-6384).

New York Public Library, *(NY Pub Lib; 0-87104),* Fifth Ave. & 42nd St., New York, NY 10018 Tel 212-260-2010 (SAN 202-926X); Orders to: Publishing Center for Cultural Resources, 625 Broadway, New York, NY 10012 Tel 212-340-0897 (SAN 209-9926) Ordering Address for NYPL Branch Libraries Imprint Only: 455 Fifth Ave., N.Y., N.Y. 10016.

New York Review of Books, Inc., The, *(NY Rev Bks; 0-940322),* 250 W. 57th St., New York, NY 10019 Tel 212-757-8070 (SAN 220-3448).

New York State Bar Association, *(NYS Bar; 0-942954),* 1 Elk St., Albany, NY 12207 Tel 518-463-3200 (SAN 226-1952).

New York State College of Agriculture & Life Sciences, *(NY St Coll Ag; 0-9605314),* Media Services, 400 Roberts Hall, Cornell Univ., Ithaca, NY 14853 Tel 607-256-3126 (SAN 282-0536); Orders to: 7 Research Park, Cornell Univ., Ithaca, NY 14850 Tel 607-256-2080 (SAN 282-0544).

New York State Council on the Arts, *(NYSCA),* 80 Center St., New York, NY 10013 (SAN 220-0767).

New York State English Council, *(NY St Eng Coun; 0-930348),* P.O. Box 2397, Liverpool, NY 13089 Tel 315-652-1118 (SAN 211-0377).

New York State Library, *(NYS Library),* State Education Bldg., Albany, NY 12224 Tel 418-474-2121 (SAN 205-7034).

New York Times, *(NY Times),* 229 W. 43rd St., New York, NY 10036 Tel 212-556-1234 (SAN 208-3027).

New York Univ. Press, *(NYU Pr; 0-8147),* Dist. by: Columbia University Press, 562 W. 113th St., New York, NY 10025 Tel 212-678-6777 (SAN 212-2472).

New York Zoetrope, *(NY Zoetrope; 0-918432),* 80 E. 11th St., New York, NY 10003 (SAN 209-6293).

New You Publishing Co., *(New You Pub; 0-917762),* 609 Santa Cruz Ave., Menlo Park, CA 94025 Tel 415-322-9959 (SAN 209-0317).

Newark Beth Israel Medical Center, *(Newark Beth; 0-937714),* 201 Lyons Ave., Newark, NJ 07410 (SAN 215-3297).

Newark Museum Assn., *(Newark Mus),* P.O. Box 540, Newark, NJ 07101 Tel 201-733-6600 (SAN 205-700X).

Newaves Publishing, *(Newaves Pub; 0-930946),* P.O. Box 5169, Santa Monica, CA 90405 (SAN 211-3422).

Newberry Library, *(Newberry; 0-911028),* 60 W. Walton St., Chicago, IL 60610 Tel 312-943-9090 (SAN 203-7378).

Newbold Publishing Inc., *(Newbold Pub; 0-910945),* 406 W. 31st St., New York, NY 10001 Tel 212-463-2862 (SAN 264-2514).

Newbury Books, *(Newbury Bks; 0-912728; 0-912729),* Box 29, Topsfield, MA 01983 Tel 617-887-5082 (SAN 203-7386).

Newbury House Pubs., *(Newbury Hse; 0-88377; 0-912066),* 54 Warehouse Lane, Rowley, MA 01969 Tel 800-343-1240 (SAN 202-9146).

Newcastle Publishing Co., Inc., *(Newcastle Pub; 0-87877),* 13419 Saticoy St., North Hollywood, CA 91605 Tel 213-873-3191 (SAN 202-9154); Orders to: P.O. Box 7589, Van Nuys, CA 91409 (SAN 202-9162).

Newhouse Press, *(Newhouse Pr; 0-918050),* 146 N. Rampart Blvd., Los Angeles, CA 90026 Tel 213-383-1089 (SAN 209-2689); Orders to: P.O. Box 76145, Los Angeles, CA 90076 (SAN 209-2697).

Newman, Albert M., Enterprises, *(A M Newman),* P.O. Box 88196, Honolulu, HI 96815 Tel 808-923-4489 (SAN 209-0864).

Newman, Isadore, *(I Newman; 0-917180),* Univ. of Akron, Dept. of Educational Foundations, Akron, OH 44325 Tel 216-867-7519 (SAN 208-7863).

Newman, S.B., Co., *(S B Newman; 0-942268),* Box 2029, Knoxville, TN 37901 Tel 615-524-7581 (SAN 238-0986).

Newmarket Press, *(Newmarket; 0-937858),* 3 E. 48th St., New York, NY 10017 Tel 212-832-3575 (SAN 282-0552); Dist. by: Scribner Book Companies, 201 Willowbrook Blvd., Wayne, NJ 07470 Tel 201-256-0700 (SAN 201-002X).

Newnes-Butterworth *See* Butterworth's

Newport Beach Pubs, *(Newport Beach; 0-9602980),* 3901 MacArthur Blvd., Suite 211, Newport Beach, CA 92660 Tel 714-752-2268 (SAN 213-1730).

Newport Beach Rentals/Tours Inc., *(Newport Bch Rent; 0-933796),* P.O. Bx 7223, Newport Beach, CA 92660 (SAN 222-402X).

Newport Publishing Co., *(Newport Pub; 0-940008),* 3990 Westerly Place, No. 100, Newport Beach, CA 92660 Tel 714-673-3096 (SAN 216-8448).

News & Letters Committees, *(News & Letters),* 2832 E. Grand Blvd., Detroit, MI 48211 Tel 313-873-8969 (SAN 217-989X).

News and Observer, The, *(News & Observer; 0-935400),* 215 S. McDowell St., Raleigh, NC 27602 (SAN 222-6189).

News Circle, *(News Circle; 0-915652),* P.O. Box 74637, Los Angeles, CA 90057 Tel 213-483-5111 (SAN 206-510X); 2007 Wilshire Blvd., Suite 900, Los Angeles, CA 90057 (SAN 206-5118) Moved, left no forwarding address.

News Group Publications, In., *(News G Pubns; 0-913385),* 730 Third Ave., New York, NY 10017 Tel 212-557-9200 (SAN 285-824X).

News Review Pub. Co., *(News Rev Pub; 0-9607506),* 409 S. Jackson, P.O. Box 8187, Moscow, IL 83843 Tel 208-882-5561 (SAN 239-7854).

News-Tribune, The, *(News-Tribune; 0-939348),* P.O. Box 1116, Fort Worth, TX 76101 Tel 817-338-1055 (SAN 220-178X).

Newspaper Agency, Inc., The, *(Newspaper Agcy; 0-9607254),* 35 W. Main St., Suite 5, Smithtown, NY 11787 (SAN 239-2690).

Newspaper Book Service, *(Newspaper Bk; 0-936294),* P.O. Box 88974, Atlanta, GA 30356 (SAN 214-0675).

Newspaper Enterprise Assn., Inc., *(Newspaper Ent; 0-915106),* 200 Park Ave., New York, NY 10017 Tel 212-557-9651 (SAN 212-0615).

Newspaper Services, *(Newspaper Serv; 0-918488),* P.O. Box 330, Friendship, WI 53934 (SAN 209-6757).

Newsweek, *(Newsweek; 0-88225),* 444 Madison Ave., New York, NY 10022 Tel 212-350-2528 (SAN 202-9170).

Newton, Fred P., *(Newton),* 319 E. California, Gainesville, TX 76240 (SAN 217-2593).

Nexus Press, *(Nexus Pr; 0-932526),* 360 Fortune St., N.E., Atlanta, GA 30312 Tel 404-577-3579 (SAN 213-2265).

Nexus Press (Wa), *(Nexus WA; 0-936666),* Box 437, Kirkland, WA 98033 (SAN 218-4621); Dist. by: Pacific Pipeline, 19215 66th Ave S., Kent, WA 98031 Tel 800-426-4727 (SAN 208-2128).

NFS Press, *(NFS Pr; 0-917986),* P.O. Box 31040, San Francisco, CA 94131 Tel 415-647-4290 (SAN 210-1831).

Niagara University Press, *(Niagara U Pr; 0-937656),* Niagara University, NY 14109 Tel 716-285-1212 (SAN 214-2139).

Nichols, Joseph, *(J Nichols Pub; 0-912484),* P.O. Box 2394, Tulsa, OK 74101 Tel 918-583-3390 (SAN 223-0453).

Nichols Publishing Co., *(Nichols Pub; 0-89397),* P.O. Box 96, New York, NY 10024 Tel 212-580-8079 (SAN 212-0291).

Nicholson, Mary John, *(M J Nicholson; 0-9607974),* 6805 N. Rockwell, Chicago, IL 60645 (SAN 281-9848); Orders to: MJN Pub., P.O. Box 1351, Skokie, IL 60076 (SAN 281-9856).

Nicolas-Hays, Inc., *(Nicolas-Hays),* Dist. by: Samuel Weiser Inc., P.O. Box 612, York Beach, ME 03910 Tel 207-363-4393 (SAN 202-9588).

Niemi, Helens Ruth, *(H R Niemi; 0-9607800),* 47726 W. 2nd St., Oakridge, OR 97463 (SAN 240-0537).

Nieves Press, *(Nieves Pr; 0-9612008),* P.O. Box 2205, Station One, Kingsville, TX 78363 Tel 512-477-3910 (SAN 286-8385).

Night Horn Books, *(Night Horn Books; 0-941842),* 495 Ellis St., Box 1156, San Francisco, CA 94102 Tel 415-431-6198 (SAN 239-2704).

Nighthawk Press, *(Nighthawk Pr; 0-936518),* Box 813, Forest Grove, OR 97116 (SAN 214-428X).

Nightingale Press,The, *(Nightingale Pr; 0-910705),* P.O. Box 6586, Gulfport, MS 39501 Tel 601-896-6819 (SAN 260-2350).

Nightmare Alley Productions, *(Nightmare Alley),* P.O. Box 10806, South Lake Tahoe, CA 95731 (SAN 207-642X).

Nikki Press, *(Nikki Pr; 0-943148),* 6 Heath St., Eatontown, NJ 07724 Tel 201-222-9343 (SAN 240-7361).

Nikmal Publishing, *(Nikmal Pub),* 698 River St., Mattapan, MA 02126 (SAN 219-2241).

Nilgiri Press, *(Nilgiri Pr; 0-915132),* P.O. Box 477, Petaluma, CA 94953 Tel 707-878-2369 (SAN 207-6853) Name Formerly Sadhana Pr.

Nin-Ra Enterprises, *(Nin-Ra Ent; 0-933276),* 1721 La Barranca Rd., La Canada, CA 91011 (SAN 214-1957).

910 Press, *(Nine Hundred-Ten Pr; 0-9606736),* P.O. Box 22361, San Francisco, CA 94122 Tel 415-752-6684 (SAN 219-659X).

Nineteenth Century Club, *(Nineteenth Cent),* 1433 Union, Memphis, TN 38104 (SAN 217-2925).

Ninth Sign Pubns., *(Ninth Sign; 0-930840),* M-525, Hoboken, NJ 07030 (SAN 210-9301).

Nishan Grey Inc., *(N Grey Inc; 0-9605652),* P.O. Box 8368, Salt Lake City, UT 84108 Tel 801-466-9578 (SAN 238-1303).

Nitty Gritty Productions, *(Nitty Gritty; 0-911954),* P.O. Box 5457, Concord, CA 94524 Tel 415-682-3144 (SAN 202-9197).

Nixdorf/Bert, *(B Nixdorf),* 9 Randolph Drive, Mt. Holly, NJ 08060 (SAN 264-2530).

No Dead Lines, *(No Dead Lines; 0-931832),* 261 Hamilton, No. 320D, Palo Alto, CA 94301 Tel 415-321-0842 (SAN 211-6103).

Noble, Gilbert W., *(G W Noble; 0-911036),* P.O. Box 931, Winter Park, FL 32789 Tel 305-647-2431 (SAN 206-4472).

Noble, Robert, *(R Noble),* 5431 N. 12th St., Philadelphia, PA 19141 Tel 215-528-4192 (SAN 277-7029).

Noble, T., *(T Noble; 0-9607144),* 1650 Argonne Place NW, Washington, DC 20009 Tel 202-483-8713 (SAN 239-0132).

Noble House Publishing, *(Noble Hse; 0-9603490),* 256 S. Robertson, Beverly Hills, CA 90211 Tel 213-659-4210 (SAN 213-4225).

Nodin Press, *(Nodin Pr; 0-931714),* c/o The Bookmen, Inc., 525 N. Third St., Minneapolis, MN 55401 (SAN 204-398X).

Noe, Fay, *(Noe; 0-9600208),* Rte. 7, Boiling Springs Rd., Licking, MO 65542 (SAN 203-7424).

Noell's Ark Pub., *(Noells Ark; 0-9602422),* P.O. Box 396, Tarpon Springs, FL 35589 Tel 813-937-8683 (SAN 213-7801).

Noise Control Foundation, *(Noise Control),* P.O. Box 3469, Arlington Branch, Poughkeepsie, NY 12603 Tel 914-462-6719 (SAN 215-2193).

Noit Amrofer Publishing Co., *(Noit Amrofer; 0-932998),* Box 15176, Seattle, WA 98115 (SAN 212-3738); 5706 30th Ave. N.E., Seattle, WA 98105 (SAN 212-3746).

Nolo Press, *(Nolo Pr; 0-917316),* P.O. Box 544, Occidental, CA 95465 Tel 707-874-3105 (SAN 206-7935).

Non-Fiction Publications Corporation, *(Non Fiction Pubns; 0-913279),* P.O. Box 129, Island Park, NY 11558 Tel 516-889-7429 (SAN 285-9106); Dist. by: Icea Bk. Center, P.O. Box 20048, Minneapolis, MN 55420 Tel 612-854-8660 (SAN 285-9114).

Non-Stop Books, *(Non-Stop Bks; 0-936816),* P.O. Box 18073, San Francisco, CA 94118 (SAN 214-4298).

Noname Press, *(Noname Pr),* 5200 Klingle St., N.W., Washington, DC 20016 Tel 202-244-6243 (SAN 203-1639).

Nonpareil Books *See* Godine, David R., Pub., Inc.

Noon Rock, *(Noon Rock; 0-9602934),* Station Hill Rd., Barrytown, NY 12507 Tel 914-758-6682 (SAN 213-8611).

Noontide Press, *(Noontide; 0-911038; 0-939482),* P.O. Box 1248, Torrance, CA 90505 (SAN 213-1307).

Noor Health Foundation, *(Noor Health; 0-9608754),* 2929 Mossrock Dr., Suite 205, San Antonio, TX 78230 Tel 512-340-2266 (SAN 241-046X).

Nopoly Press, Inc., *(Nopoly Pr; 0-930950),* Box 1930, Dept. M-10, Wilmington, DE 19899 Tel 302-764-2126 (SAN 212-1220).

Norawell Pubs., *(Norawell Pubs; 0-9602118),* 1229 Golden Gate Blvd., Mayfield Heights, OH 44124 (SAN 212-3754).

Norbu, Thinley, *(T Norbu; 0-9607000),* P.O. Box 146, New York, NY 10002 (SAN 241-5879).

Nordic Books, *(Nordic Bks; 0-933748),* P.O. Box 1941, Philadelphia, PA 19105 Tel 215-464-4186 (SAN 212-5323).

Nordic Ski Press, *(Nordic Ski),* Box 36, Norden, CA 95724 (SAN 239-4650).

Nordic Translators, *(Nordic Trans; 0-938500),* 1747 Holton St., St. Paul, MN 55113 Tel 612-645-8352 (SAN 239-9199).

Nordland Heritage Foundation, *(Nordland Her Found; 0-9604816),* Humanities Box 2170, Augustana College, Sioux Falls, SD 57197 (SAN 276-9662).

Nordland Publishing International, Inc., *(Nordland Pub; 0-913124),* P.O. Box 454, Woodside, NY 11377 Tel 212-335-1412 (SAN 282-0579); 3009 Plumb St., P.O. Box 25388, Houston, TX 77005 Tel 713-661-6126 (SAN 282-0587).

Norfolk Port & Industrial Authority, *(Norfolk Port; 0-9605682),* Norfolk International Airport, Norfolk, VA 23518 (SAN 216-2741); Dist. by: International Society for General Semantics, 834 Mission St., San Francisco, CA 94103 (SAN 203-8161).

Norman & Sandra, *(Norman & Sandra; 0-936520),* P.O. Box 218, Orient, NY 11957 Tel 516-323-3602 (SAN 220-0252).

Norman Publishing Co., *(Norman Pub; 0-9601788),* 21 Almroth Dr., Wayne, NJ 07470 Tel 201-942-3637 (SAN 212-2944).

Normandie Publishing Co., The, *(Normandie; 0-9602986),* 225 W. 86th St., Suite 805, New York, NY 10024 Tel 212-873-5433 (SAN 213-1315).

Normark Corp., *(Normark Corp),* 1710 E. 78th St., Minneapolis, MN 55423 Tel 612-869-3293 (SAN 209-3006).

Norns Publishing Co., The, *(Norns Pub Co; 0-939960),* P.O. Box 1172, Marathon, FL 33050 Tel 305-743-2796 (SAN 216-8456).

Norse Press, *(Norse Pr; 0-9602692),* 909 E. 35th St, Sioux Falls, SD 57105 (SAN 221-7686).

North, Christina Bolt, *(C B North),* 41-06 12th St., Long Island City, NY 11101 Tel 212-784-7705 (SAN 239-5487).

North, Gloria, *(G North; 0-931758),* 15 Estelle Ave., Larkspur, CA 94939 (SAN 211-5115).

North American Congress on Latin America, *(N Am Congress Latin; 0-916024),* 151 W. 19th St., New York, NY 10011 Tel 212-989-8890 (SAN 218-0022).

North American Consumer's Group Press, *(North Am Consumer),* 3747 S.E. Washington, Portland, OR 97124 (SAN 214-0683).

North American Falconry & Hunting Hawks, *(North Am Fal Hunt; 0-912510),* P.O. Box 1484, Denver, CO 80201 Tel 303-651-1472 (SAN 203-7440).

North American, Inc., *(North American Inc; 0-930244),* P.O. Box 65, New Brunswick, NJ 08903 Tel 201-246-8546 (SAN 210-6469).

North American International, *(North Am Intl; 0-88265),* 1801 Columbia Rd. N.W., Suite 101, Washington, DC 20009 Tel 202-462-1441 (SAN 202-9200).

North American Manufacturing Company, *(North Am Mfg Co; 0-9601596),* 4455 E. 71st St., Cleveland, OH 44105 (SAN 222-0946).

North American Publishing Co., *(North Am Pub Co; 0-912920),* 401 N. Broad St., Philadelphia, PA 19108 Tel 215-574-9600 (SAN 203-1647).

North American Review Press, *(North Am Rev; 0-915996),* Cedar Falls, IA 50613 Tel 319-273-2681 (SAN 206-0760).

North Atlantic Books, *(North Atlantic; 0-938190; 0-913028),* 2320 Blake St., Berkeley, CA 94704 (SAN 203-1655).

North Carolina Central Univ., Dept. of Political Science, *(NC Central Pol Sci),* Durham, NC 27707 (SAN 206-1708).

North Carolina Division of Archives & History, *(NC Archives; 0-86526),* 109 E. Jones St., Raleigh, NC 27611 Tel 919-733-7442 (SAN 203-7246).

North Carolina Genealogical Society, Inc., *(N C Genealogical; 0-936370),* P. O. Bx 1492, Raleigh, NC 27602 (SAN 222-4003).

North Carolina Museum of Art, *(NCMA; 0-88259),* 2110 Blue Ridge Blvd., Raleigh, NC 27607 Tel 919-833-1935 (SAN 202-9030).

North Carolina State Museum of Natural History, *(NC Natl Hist; 0-917134),* 102 N. Salisbury St., P.O. Box 27647, Raleigh, NC 27611 Tel 919-733-7450 (SAN 208-788X).

North Castle Books, Inc., *(North Castle; 0-911040),* 212 Bedford Rd., Greenwich, CT 06830 Tel 203-869-7766 (SAN 202-9219).

North Central Conference on Summer Schools, *(North Central Assn Colls & Schls),* 1221 University Ave, Boulder, CO 80302 (SAN 225-7661).

North Coast Publishing, *(North Coast Pubs; 0-9112269),* P.O. Box 1119, Shaker Heights, OH 44120 Tel 216-491-8699 (SAN 265-0703).

North Country Books, Inc., *(North Country; 0-932052),* P.O. Box 506, Sylvan Beach, NY 13157 Tel 315-762-5140 (SAN 287-0231); 18 Irving Pl., Utica, NY 13501 (SAN 287-024X).

North Country Community College Press, *(No Country Comm Coll; 0-940280),* 20 Winona Ave., Saranac Lake, NY 12983 Tel 518-891-2915 (SAN 217-5479).

North Dakota Council On The Arts, *(N Dak Coun Arts; 0-911205),* Black Bldg., Suite 811, Fargo, ND 58102 Tel 701-237-8959 (SAN 274-1741).

North Dakota Institute for Regional Studies, *(N Dak Inst; 0-911042),* State University Sta., Fargo, ND 58105 Tel 701-237-8338 (SAN 203-1574).

North Foster Baptist Church, *(N Foster Baptist),* Old Killingly Rd., Foster, RI 02903 (SAN 282-0595); Dist. by: Rhode Island Publications Society, Old State House, 150 Benefit St., Providence, RI 02903 Tel 402-272-1776 (SAN 219-9696).

North-Holland *See* Elsevier Science Publishing Co., Inc.

North Lake Productions, *(North Lake Prod; 0-9601722),* 9732 Boucher Dr., Otter Lake, MI 48464 Tel 517-795-2250 (SAN 212-1980).

North Light Pubs., *(North Light Pub; 0-89134),* P.O. Box 489, Westport, CT 06881 Tel 203-336-4225 (SAN 287-0258); 32 Berwick Court, Fairfield, CT 06430 (SAN 287-0266); Dist. by: Writer's Digest Books, 9933 Alliance Rd., Cincinatti, OH 45242 Tel 513-984-0717 (SAN 287-0274).

North Pacific Pubs., *(North Pacific; 0-913138),* P.O. Box 13255, Portland, OR 97213 Tel 503-236-9343 (SAN 203-7467).

North Plains Press, *(North Plains; 0-87970),* P.O. Box 1830, Aberdeen, SD 57401 Tel 605-225-5360 (SAN 202-9243).

North Point Historical Society, *(N Point Hist Soc; 0-9606072),* Box 557, Milwaukee, WI 53201 Tel 414-271-2395 (SAN 216-9177).

North Point Press, *(N Point Pr; 0-86547),* 850 Talbot Ave., Berkeley, CA 94706 Tel 415-527-6260 (SAN 220-133X); Orders to: The Scribner Book Companies, 201 Willowbrook Blvd., Wayne, NJ 07470 Tel 201-256-0700 (SAN 201-002X).

North River Press, Inc., *(North River; 0-88427),* P.O. Box 241, Croton-on-Hudson, NY 10520 Tel 914-941-7175 (SAN 202-1048).

North-South Publishing Co., Inc., The, *(NS Pub Co Inc; 0-913897),* P.O. Box 610, Lanham, MD 20706 Tel 301-552-1098 (SAN 286-8423); 7011 Ren Lane, Lanham, MD 20706 (SAN 286-8431).

North Star Press, *(North Star; 0-87839),* P.O. Box 451, St. Cloud, MN 56301 Tel 612-253-1636 (SAN 203-7491).

North Stonington Press, *(N Stonington; 0-938538),* 2500 Johnson Ave., Riverdale, NY 10463 Tel 212-884-3300 (SAN 282-0633).

North Texas State Univ., Professional Development Institute, *(N Texas St U Pro Devel Inst; 0-940966),* P.O. Box 13288, Denton, TX 76203 Tel 817-565-2483 (SAN 223-1980).

North Valley Diver Publications, *(North Valley; 0-911615),* Suite No. 166, P.O. Box 6007, Redding, CA 96099 (SAN 264-2557).

North West International Trading, Inc., *(NW Intl),* P.O. Box 11483, Eugene, OR 97440 Tel 503-484-7060 (SAN 264-2565).

Northcountry Publishing Co., *(Northcountry Pub; 0-930366),* 216 N. Main St., Sauk Centre, MN 56378 Tel 612-352-6793 (SAN 211-061X).

Northeast Academic Services, *(Northeast A S; 0-913811),* Ten Lydia Dr., Wappingers, NY 12590 Tel 914-297-6389 (SAN 286-1372).

Northeast Books, *(NE Bks; 0-937374),* 401 Clark St., Clarks Green, PA 18504 Tel 717-586-0077 (SAN 215-2665).

Northeast Conference on the Teaching of Foreign Languages, *(NE Conf Teach Foreign; 0-915432),* P.O. Box 623, Middlebury, VT 05753 Tel 802-388-2598 (SAN 207-5113).

Northeast Outdoors, Inc., *(NE Outdoors; 0-936216),* P.O. Box 2180, Waterbury, CT 06722 (SAN 214-0691).

Northeast Regional Center for Rural Development, *(NE Regional Ctr; 0-9609010),* 293 Roberts Hall, Cornell Univ., Ithaca, NY 14853 (SAN 241-3418).

Northeast Sportsman's Press, *(Northeast Sportsmans),* P.O. Box 188, Tarrytown, NY 10591 (SAN 238-8219).

Northeastern Political Science Association, *(NE Poli Sci),* Univ of Massachusetts, Thompson Hall, Amherst, MA 01002 (SAN 226-9279).

Northeastern Univ. Press, *(NE U Pr; 0-930350),* 360 Huntington Ave., 17 Cushing Hall, Northeastern Univ., Boston, MA 02115 Tel 617-437-2783 (SAN 282-065X); Orders to: P.O. Box 116, Boston, MA 02117 (SAN 282-0668).

Northern Arizona University, Dept. of Anthroplgy, *(N Arizona U; 0-910953),* Box 15200, Flagstaff, AZ 86011 Tel 602-523-3180 (SAN 264-2573).

Northern California Grantmakers, *(Northern Cal),* 334 Kearny St., San Francisco, CA 94108 (SAN 287-2706).

Northern Cartographic Inc., *(NCI),* P.O. Box 133, Burlington, VT 05402 (SAN 219-8037).

Northern Illinois Univ. Press, *(N Ill U Pr; 0-87580),* DeKalb, IL 60115 Tel 815-753-1826 (SAN 202-8875).

Northern Illinois University Center for Governmental Studies, *(NIU Ctr Govmt),* 146 Carroll Ave, DeKalb, IL 60115 Tel 815-753-1000 (SAN 227-0439).

Northern Michigan Univ. Press, *(Northern Mich; 0-918616),* 607 Cohodas Administrative Center, Marquette, MI 49855 Tel 906-227-2720 (SAN 205-3748); Orders to: NMU Bookstore, Don H. Bottum University Center, Marquette, MI 49855 Tel 906-227-2480 (SAN 205-3756).

Northern Nut Growers Assn., *(N Nut Growers; 0-9602248),* 13 Broken Arrow Rd., Hamden, CT 06518 Tel 203-288-1026 (SAN 206-9695).

Northern Press, *(Northern Pr),* 18 Cedar St., Potsdam, NY 13676 (SAN 211-7495).

Northernaire Pubns., *(Northernaire; 0-9603380),* 717 Arlington Way, Martinez, CA 94553 (SAN 212-7806).

Northland Press, *(Northland; 0-87358),* P.O. Box N, Flagstaff, AZ 86002 Tel 602-774-5251 (SAN 202-9251).

Northland Publications, *(Northland Pubns WA),* P.O. Box 12157, Seattle, WA 98102 (SAN 210-931X).

Northland Publishing Co., *(Northland WI; 0-939834),* Rte. 4 Box 110, Menomie, WI 54751 Tel 715-235-9434 (SAN 216-9193).

Northlands Press, *(Northlands MI; 0-918808),* 2723 Lake Lansing Rd., East Lansing, MI 48823 Tel 517-332-4274 (SAN 210-3176).

Northstar Commemoratives, Inc., *(Northstar Comm Inc; 0-910667),* P.O. Box 803, Lakeville, MN 55044 Tel 612-469-5433 (SAN 274-1911).

Northwest Historical Consultants, *(NW Hist Cons; 0-9609562),* 2780 26th St., Clarkston, WA 99403 Tel 509-758-5773 (SAN 274-1989).

Northwest Illustrated, *(Northwest Illust; 0-86519),* 745 Fifth Ave., New York, NY 10151 (SAN 239-5371) Moved, left no forwarding address.

Northwest Learning Associates, Inc., *(Northwest Learn; 0-931836),* 8903 188th Southwest, Edmonds, WA 98020 (SAN 211-6251).

Northwest Regional Educational Laboratory, *(Northwest Regional; 0-89354),* 300 S. W. Sixth Ave., Portland, OR 97204 Tel 503-248-6800 (SAN 208-9998).

Northwest Review Books, *(NW Review Bks; 0-918402),* 369 PLC, Univ. of Oregon, Eugene, OR 97403 Tel 503-686-3957 (SAN 209-9721).

Northwest Silver Press, *(NW Silver Pr; 0-9610202),* 3 Lummi Key, Bellevue, WA 98006 Tel 206-643-0143 (SAN 264-2581).

Northwestern College, Ramaker Library Art Gallery, *(Northwestern),* 101 Seventh St. S.W., Orange City, IA 51041 (SAN 279-9227).

Northwestern Memorial Hospital, *(Northwest Memorial; 0-9605996),* Superior St. & Fairbanks Court, Chicago, IL 60611 Tel 312-649-7432 (SAN 216-7549).

Northwestern Publishing House, *(Northwest Pub; 0-8100),* 3624 W. North Ave., Milwaukee, WI 53208 Tel 414-442-1810 (SAN 206-7943).

Northwestern University, Dept. of Astronomy, *(NWU Astro; 0-939160),* Dept. of Astronomy, Evanston, IL 60201 (SAN 217-2305).

Northwestern Univ. Traffic Institute, *(Traffic Inst; 0-912642),* 555 Clark St., P.O. Box 1409, Evanston, IL 60201-1409 Tel 312-492-3033 (SAN 202-7909).

Northwood Institute Press, *(Northwood Inst; 0-87359),* 3225 Cook St., Midland, MI 48640 Tel 517-631-1600 (SAN 202-098X).

Northwoods Press, Div. of Romar, Inc., *(Northwoods Pr; 0-89002),* P.O. Box 246, Stafford, VA 22554 Tel 703-659-7441 (SAN 208-449X).

Northword, *(Northword; 0-942802),* P.O. Box 5634, Madison, WI 53705 Tel 608-231-2355 (SAN 240-4842).

Norton, Jeffrey, Pubs., Inc., *(J Norton Pubs; 0-88432),* 96 Broad St., Guilford, CT 06437 Tel 203-453-9794 (SAN 213-957X). *Imprints:* Speechphone Institute (Speechphone).

Norton, R. W., Art Gallery, *(Norton Art; 0-913060; 0-9600182),* 4747 Creswell Ave., Shreveport, LA 71106 Tel 318-865-4201 (SAN 213-7569).

Norton, W. W., & Co., Inc., *(Norton; 0-393),* 500 Fifth Ave., New York, NY 10110 Tel 212-354-5500 (SAN 202-5795). *Imprints:* Norton College Division (NortonC).

Norton College Division See **Norton, W. W., & Co., Inc.**

Norwalk Press See **O'Sullivan, Woodside & Co.**

Norway Books, *(Norway Bks; 0-939648),* P.O. Box 2010, Sparks, NV 89431 (SAN 216-4248).

Norwegian-American Historical Assn., *(Norwegian-Am Hist Assn; 0-87732),* St. Olaf College, Northfield, MN 55057 Tel 507-663-3221 (SAN 203-1086).

Norwood Editions, *(Norwood Edns; 0-88305; 0-8482),* P.O. Box 38, Norwood, PA 19074 Tel 215-583-4550 (SAN 206-8613).

Nosbooks, *(Nosbooks; 0-911046),* 42 W. 88th St., New York, NY 10024 (SAN 203-7513).

Nostalgia Press, Inc., *(Nostalgia Pr; 0-87897),* 72 Franklin Ave., Franklin Square, NY 11010 Tel 516-488-4748 (SAN 205-3721); Orders to: P.O. Box 293, Franklin Square, NY 11010 (SAN 205-373X).

Nourishing Thoughts Enterprises, *(Nourishing Thoughts; 0-9601198),* 1837 Beech St., Stow, OH 44224 (SAN 210-9298).

Nova Univ. Press, *(Nova-NYIT U Pr),* College Ave., Fort Lauderdale, FL 33314 Tel 305-475-7300 (SAN 211-6111).

Nova Press, *(Nova Pr; 0-914220),* Orders to: Phoenix Inc., 4518 Burnet Rd., Austin, TX 78756 Tel 512-459-0252 (SAN 200-4062).

Novel Ideas Inc., *(Novel Ideas; 0-914059),* 3499 Bunker Ave., Wantagh, NY 11793 Tel 516-783-8833 (SAN 277-6979).

November Books, *(November Bks; 0-941098),* P.O. Box 6173, Santa Barbara, CA 93111 Tel 805-967-3185 (SAN 217-409X).

Nowell, Eppler, *(E Nowell; 0-9611454),* 46 Cragmont Ave., San Franciso, CA 94116 (SAN 283-9229); Dist. by: Bookpeople, 2940 Seventh St., Berkeley, CA 94710 Tel 415-549-3030 (SAN 168-9517).

Nowfel Pubns., *(Nowfel),* Dist. by: Intercontinental Enterprises Co., 69 Stewart Ave., Eastchester, NY 10707 Tel 914-337-2477 (SAN 218-7914).

Noyes Data Corp., *(Noyes; 0-8155),* Mill Rd. at Grand Ave., Park Ridge, NJ 07656 Tel 201-391-8484 (SAN 209-2840). *Imprints:* Noyes Press (NP).

Noyes Press See **Noyes Data Corp.**

N.P.D. Corp., *(NPD Corp; 0-937230),* P.O. Box 10161, Austin, TX 78766 (SAN 282-0676); 7701 N. Lamar Blvd., Austin, TX 78752 Tel 512-453-6154 (SAN 282-0684).

NTL Institute, *(NTL Inst),* P.O. Box 9155, Rosslyn Sta., Arlington, VA 22209 (SAN 223-9485).

Nu-Diet Enterprises, *(Nu-Diet; 0-9609896),* 1739 Blue Ash Place, P.O. Box 29250, Columbus, OH 43229 Tel 614-846-1423 (SAN 274-2101).

Nuance Press Inc., *(Nuance Pr; 0-917924),* 542 N. High St., Columbus, OH 43215 (SAN 209-9748).

Numarc Book Corp., *(Numarc Bk Corp; 0-88471),* 50 Alcona Ave., Buffalo, NY 14226 Tel 716-834-1390 (SAN 206-8702).

Numen Chapbooks, *(Numen Chapbks; 0-939162),* 3202 Ellerslie Ave., Baltimore, MD 21218 (SAN 216-4256).

Numismata Orientalia, *(Numismata Orient),* P.O. Box 212, Tenafly, NJ 07676 (SAN 211-674X).

Numismatic Fine Arts, Inc., *(Numismatic Fine Arts),* 342 N. Rodeo Dr., Beverly Hills, CA 90212 Tel 213-278-1535 (SAN 205-9029); Orders to: P.O. Box 3788, Beverly Hills, CA 90212 (SAN 205-9037).

Nunes, Leslie K., *(Nunes; 0-9604190),* 613 Kaimalino Place, Kailua, HI 96734 (SAN 219-9769).

Nur-I-Alam Pubns., *(Nur Pubns; 0-9608440),* 2331 N. Dunn St., Bloomington, IN 47401 Tel 812-339-5615 (SAN 240-5555); Dist. by: David J. Smith, Worldwide Evangelization Crusade, 709 Pennsylvania Ave., Box A, Fort Washington, PA 19034 (SAN 276-8577).

Nurseco, Inc., *(Nurseco; 0-935236),* P.O. Box 145, Pacific Palisades, CA 90272 (SAN 215-689X).

Nurtury Family School, The, *(Nurtury Fam),* 374 West Baltimore, Larkspur, CA 94939 Tel 415-924-9675 (SAN 264-262X).

Nutri-Kinetic Dynamics Inc., *(Nutri-Kinetic; 0-938478),* 850 Kam Hwy., Pearl City, HI 96782 (SAN 216-2768).

Nutrition Foundation, Inc., *(Nutrition Found),* Office of Education 888 Seventeeth St., N.W., Washington, DC 10017 (SAN 234-3911).

Nuttall Ornithological Club, *(Nuttall Ornith),* Harvard Univ, Cambridge, MA 02138 (SAN 232-9123).

Nuzum, David G., *(D G Nuzum; 0-9609538),* 201 D. St., Keyser, WV 26726 Tel 304-788-3549 (SAN 260-2377).

Nyerges, Anton N., *(Nyerges; 0-9600954),* 201 Langford Ct., Richmond, KY 40475 Tel 606-623-7153 (SAN 208-791X).

O. ARS, *(O ARS; 0-942030),* P.O. Box 179, Cambridge, MA 02238 Tel 617-497-0965 (SAN 238-6011).

O & B Books, Inc., *(O & B Bks; 0-9601586),* 1215 N.W. Kline Place, Corvallis, OR 97330 Tel 503-752-2178 (SAN 210-9328).

ODS Pubns., Inc., *(ODS Pubns; 0-9602516),* 6415 N. Lemai Ave., Chicago, IL 60646 Tel 312-774-6550 (SAN 212-842X).

OGAB Publishing, Subs. of Midwest Pub., *(Ogab Pubs; 0-912477),* 49 Grandview Dr., S. Zanesville, OH 43701 Tel 614-443-5574 (SAN 265-3109).

OMF Books, *(OMF Bks),* 404 S. Church St., Robesonia, PA 19551 (SAN 211-8351).

Oak Cottage Press, *(Oak Cottage; 0-940840),* 2 Forest St., Brattleboro, VT 05301 (SAN 219-8045).

Oak Grove Pubns., *(Oak Grove Pubns; 0-9607162),* P.O. Box 521, Menlo Park, CA 94025 Tel 415-328-4041 (SAN 239-0140).

Oak Hill Publishers, *(Oak Hill KS; 0-911391),* P.O. Box 25024, Corporate Woods, Overland Park, KS 66225 Tel 913-888-4236 (SAN 274-2357).

Oak Knoll Books, *(Oak Knoll; 0-938768),* 414 Delaware St., New Castle, DE 19720 (SAN 216-2776).

Oak Leaf Press, *(Oak Leaf; 0-935370),* 33 Union Square W., New York, NY 10003 (SAN 213-4233).

Oak Park Michigan, *(Oak Park; 0-938968),* 24443 Roanoke, Oak Park, MI 48237 (SAN 216-1427).

Oak Pubns. See Music Sales Corp.

Oak Ridge Associated Universities, *(Oak Ridge; 0-930780),* P.O. Box 117, Oak Ridge, TN 37830 Tel 615-576-3152 (SAN 211-3716).

Oak Tree Pubns. Inc., *(Oak Tree Pubns; 0-916392),* 11175 Flintkote Ave., San Diego, CA 92121 Tel 714-457-3200 (SAN 211-4828).

Oak Valley Pr., *(Oak Valley; 0-9609170),* 228 Virginia Ave., San Mateo, CA 94402 Tel 415-343-3397 (SAN 241-418X).

Oaklawn Press, Inc., *(Oaklawn Pr; 0-916198),* 1318 Fair Oaks Ave.uite 200, S. Pasadena, CA 91030 Tel 213-799-0880 (SAN 208-0621).

Oakview Book Press, *(Oakview; 0-9601104),* P.O. Box 990, Adelphi, MD 20783 Tel 301-434-8106 (SAN 210-0088).

Oasis Bks., *(Oasis Bks; 0-940626),* P.O. Box 1543, S. Pasadena, CA 91030-1543 Tel 213-441-3563 (SAN 218-5202).

Ober Publishing, *(Ober Pub; 0-911785),* 9514-9 Reseda Blvd., No. 478, Northridge, CA 91324 Tel 213-368-0396 (SAN 264-2654).

Oberlin College, Allen Memorial Art Museum, *(Ober Coll Allen; 0-942946),* Oberlin College, Main & Lorain Sts., Oberlin, OH 44074 Tel 216-775-8669 (SAN 240-3226).

Oberlin College Conservatory Library, *(Oberlin Con Lib; 0-9611434),* Oberlin, OH 44074 Tel 216-775-8280 (SAN 283-3042).

Oblate Fathers, *(Oblate),* P.O. Box 96, San Antonio, TX 78291 Tel 512-736-1685 (SAN 209-5890).

Obol International, Div. of Unigraphics Inc., *(Obol Intl; 0-916710; 0-86723),* 8 S. Michigan Ave., Chicago, IL 60603 Tel 312-267-3662 (SAN 282-0692); Orders to: 4747 N. Spaulding, Chicago, IL 60625 (SAN 282-0706).

Obolensky, Helene, Enterprises, Inc., *(Helene Obolensky Ent; 0-9609736),* P.O. Box 87, 909 Third Ave., New York, NY 10150 Tel 212-838-4722 (SAN 274-2381).

Obranoel Press, *(Obranoel Pr),* 63 Franklin Sq., New York, NY 11010 (SAN 208-4473).

O'Brien, F. M., Bookseller, *(O'Brien),* 34 & 36 High St., Portland, ME 04101 (SAN 203-7580).

Observational Research Publications Co., *(Observational; 0-942884),* Buckfield Building-1K, 25 Hillside Ave., White Plains, NY 10601 Tel 914-428-5343 (SAN 240-2629).

Occasional Papers/Reprints Series in Contemporary Asian Studies, Inc., *(Occasional Papers),* Univ. of Maryland Law School, 500 W. Baltimore St., Baltimore, MD 21201 Tel 301-528-3870 (SAN 226-2894).

Occasional Productions, *(Occasional Prods; 0-933264),* 54 Los Gatos Blvd., Los Gatos, CA 95030 Tel 211-6863).

Occidental Press, *(Occidental; 0-911050),* P.O. Box 1005, Washington, DC 20013 (SAN 203-7599).

Ocean East Publishing Co., *(Ocean East; 0-9607028),* 1655 71st St., Vero Beach, FL 32960 Tel 305-567-0960 (SAN 239-0159).

Ocean, Inc., *(Ocean Inc; 0-912043),* P.O. Box 2331, Springfield, VA 22152-0331 Tel 703-323-1928 (SAN 264-6838).

Ocean Tree Books, *(Ocean Tree Bks; 0-943734),* P.O. Box 1295, Santa Fe, NM 87501 Tel 505-983-1412 (SAN 241-0478).

Oceana Pubns., *(Oceana; 0-379),* 75 Main St., Dobbs Ferry, NY 10522 Tel 914-693-5944 (SAN 202-5744).

Ocelot Press, *(Ocelot Pr; 0-912434),* P.O. Box 504, Claremont, CA 91711 Tel 714-624-2439 (SAN 203-7602).

Ocotillo Press, *(Ocotillo; 0-918380),* 215 N. 51st St., Seattle, WA 98103 (SAN 209-4061).

Octagon Books, *(Octagon; 0-374),* 19 Union Square W., New York, NY 10003 Tel 212-741-6961 (SAN 202-8123).

Octameron Associates, *(Octameron Assocs; 0-917760),* 820 Fontaine St., Alexandria, VA 22302 Tel 703-836-1019 (SAN 282-0714); Orders to: P.O. Box 3437, Alexandria, VA 22302 (SAN 282-0722).

Octavia Press, *(Octavia Pr; 0-9605882),* 2611 Octavia St., San Francisco, CA 94123 Tel 415-922-4127 (SAN 282-0730); Orders to: P.O. Box 42493, San Francisco, CA 94101 Tel 415-922-4127 (SAN 282-0749).

October House, *(October; 0-8079),* P.O. Box 454, Stonington, CT 06378 Tel 203-535-3725 (SAN 203-7610).

October Press, Inc., The, *(October Pr; 0-935440),* 1801 N. Lamar, Suite 444, Dallas, TX 75202 Tel 220-1216).

Oda, James, *(Oda),* 7054 Vanscoy Ave., N. Hollywood, CA 91605 (SAN 216-4264).

Oddo Publishing, Inc., *(Oddo; 0-87783),* Storybook Acres-Box 68, Fayetteville, GA 30214 Tel 404-461-7627 (SAN 282-0757); Orders to: Box 68, Fayetteville, GA 30214 Tel 404-461-7627 (SAN 282-0765).

Odens, Peter R., *(P R Odens; 0-9609484),* P.O. Box 222,, El Centro, CA 92244 (SAN 274-2438).

Odin Press, *(Odin Pr; 0-930500),* P.O. Box 536, New York, NY 10021 Tel 212-744-2538 (SAN 211-3244).

Odium, *(Odium),* P.O. Box 65594, Los Angeles, CA 90065 Tel 213-794-1959 (SAN 218-4982).

O'Dwyer, J. R., Company Incorporated, *(J R O'Dwyer),* 271 Madison Ave, New York, NY 10016 (SAN 226-3386).

Odyssey Enterprises, Ltd., *(Odyssey Ent; 0-939006),* P.O. Box 1686, Norman, OK 73070 Tel 405-364-9811 (SAN 216-2784).

Odyssey Press, *(Odyssey Pr; 0-8399),* Dist. by: Bobbs-Merrill Co., Inc., 4300 W. 62nd St., P.O. Box 7080, Indianapolis, IN 46206 Tel 317-298-5688 (SAN 201-3959).

Odyssey Pubns., Inc., *(Odyssey MA; 0-933752),* P.O. Box G-148, Greenwood, MA 01880 (SAN 214-4301).

Oelgeschlager, Gunn & Hain, Inc., *(Oelgeschlager),* 1278 Massachusetts Ave., Cambridge, MA 02138 Tel 617-876-5100 (SAN 213-6937).

OES Pubns., *(OES Pubns; 0-89779),* College of Engineering, Univ. of KY, Lexington, KY 40506-0046 Tel 606-257-3343 (SAN 212-1255).

Off Off Broadway Alliance, *(Off off Broadway; 0-933750),* 162 W. 56th St., Room 206, New York, NY 10019 Tel 212-757-4473 (SAN 213-134X).

Office Pubns., Inc., *(Office Pubns; 0-911054),* 1200 Summer St., P.O. Box 1231, Stamford, CT 06904 Tel 203-327-9670 (SAN 203-7637).

Office Research Institute, *(Office Res; 0-911056),* 1517 Sparrow St., Longwood, FL 32750 Tel 305-339-8527 (SAN 203-7645).

Official Corp., The, *(Official Corp; 0-9605074),* 240 Newport Ctr. Dr., Suite 200, Newport Beach, CA 92660 (SAN 216-2792).

Offshoot Pubns., *(Offshoot Pub; 0-910013),* 1280 Goodpasture Island Rd., Eugene, OR 97401 Tel 503-686-8266 (SAN 241-3426).

Ogham House, Inc., *(Ogham Hse; 0-916590),* 6 Sherri Lane, Spring Valley, NY 10977 (SAN 208-0486).

O'Hara, Betsy, *(B O'Hara; 0-9604188),* 2562 26th Ave., San Francisco, CA 94116 (SAN 219-9777).

O'Hara, J. Philip, Inc., Pubs., *(O'Hara; 0-87955),* c/o Scroll Press, Inc., 2858 Valerie Court, Merrick, NY 11566 Tel 516-379-4283 (SAN 202-5868).

Ohara Pubns., Inc., *(Ohara Pubns; 0-89750),* 1813 Victory Place, P.O. Box 7728, Burbank, CA 91510-7728 Tel 213-843-4444 (SAN 205-3632).

Ohio Academy of Science, The, *(Ohio Acad Sci; 0-933128),* 445 King Ave., Columbus, OH 43201 Tel 614-424-6045 (SAN 212-3762).

Ohio Antique Review, Inc., *(Ohio Antique Rev; 0-9603290),* P.O. Box 538, Worthington, OH 43085 Tel 614-885-9757 (SAN 213-344X).

Ohio Biological Survey, *(Ohio Bio Survey; 0-86727),* 980 Biological Sciences Bldg., Ohio State Univ., 484 W. 12th Ave., Columbus, OH 43210 Tel 614-422-9645 (SAN 217-0787).

Ohio Historical Society, *(Ohio Hist Soc),* Ohio Historical Center, Interstate 71 & 17th Ave., Columbus, OH 43211 Tel 614-466-4664 (SAN 202-1331).

Ohio Library Association, *(Ohio Lib Assn; 0-911060),* 40 S. 3rd St., Suite 409, Columbus, OH 43215 Tel 614-221-9057 (SAN 203-7653).

Ohio Psychology Publishing Co., *(Ohio Psych Pub; 0-910707),* 5 E. Long St., Suite 610, Columbus, OH 43215 Tel 513-293-5225 (SAN 260-2385).

Ohio Review, The, *(Ohio Review; 0-942148),* Ellis Hall, Ohio University, Athens, OH 45701 Tel 614-594-5889 (SAN 239-9687).

Ohio Savings Assn, *(Ohio Savings),* 13109 Shaker Square, Cleveland, OH 44120 Tel 216-752-7000 (SAN 211-0555).

Ohio State Univ., College of Administrative Science, *(Ohio St U Admin Sci; 0-87776),* 220 W. 12th Ave., Columbus, OH 43210 Tel 614-422-2061 (SAN 203-7661); Orders to: O.S.U. Press, The Ohio State Univ., 2070 Neil Ave., Columbus, OH 43210 (SAN 202-8158).

Ohio State Univ. Libraries, *(Ohio St U Lib; 0-88215),* Rm. 001, Main Lib., 1858 Neil Ave. Mall, Columbus, OH 43210 Tel 614-422-4738 (SAN 202-814X).

Ohio State Univ. Press, *(Ohio St U Pr; 0-8142),* Hitchcock Hall, Rm. 346, 2070 Neil Ave., Columbus, OH 43210 Tel 614-422-6930 (SAN 202-8158).

Ohio University, Center for Afro-American Studies, *(Ctr Afro Stud Ohio; 0-911393),* Athens, OH 45701 Tel 614-594-5475 (SAN 274-2586).

Ohio Univ. Press, *(Ohio U Pr; 0-8214),* Scott Quadrangle, Room 144, Athens, OH 45701 Tel 614-594-5505 (SAN 282-0773); Orders to: Harper & Row Publishers, Inc, Keystone Industrial Park, Scranton, PA 18512 Tel 800-233-4377 (SAN 282-0781).

Ohsawa, George, Macrobiotic Foundation, *(G Ohsawa; 0-918860),* 902 14th St., Oroville, CA 95965 Tel 916-533-7702 (SAN 207-7663).

Oil Books, *(Oil Bks),* Box 88, RD 1, Sugar Run, PA 18846 Tel 717-265-8665 (SAN 207-8813).

Oil Daily, *(Oil Daily; 0-918216),* 850 Third Ave., New York, NY 10022 Tel 212-715-2680 (SAN 210-2498).

Ojai Printing & Publishing, *(Ojai; 0-943134),* 111 N. Blanche, Ojai, CA 93023 (SAN 240-9216).

Okefenokee Press, *(Okefenokee Pr; 0-9601606),* Rte. 3, Box 142-C, Folkston, GA 31537 Tel 912-496-7401 (SAN 208-3752).

Oklahoma State University Press, *(Okla State Univ Pr; 0-914956),* North Monroe St., Stillwater, OK 74078 (SAN 221-9514).

Okpaku Communications, Div. of Third Press Review of Books Company, *(Okpaku Communications; 0-89388),* 330 Seventh Ave., New York, NY 10001 Tel 212-563-1850 (SAN 202-5701).

Ol' Attic Books, *(Ol' Attic Bks; 0-9611264),* RTE 1, Box 137A, Pennsboro, WV 26415 Tel 304-659-2212 (SAN 282-9398).

Olam Pubns., *(OLAM; 0-916222),* 2101 N. Court Hse. Rd., Arlington, VA 22201 Tel 703-527-7688 (SAN 207-933X).

Old Adobe Press, *(Old Adobe Pr),* P.O. Box 115, Penngrove, CA 94251 (SAN 203-7696).

Old Army Press, *(Old Army; 0-88342),* P.O. Box 2243, Fort Collins, CO 80521 Tel 303-484-5535 (SAN 202-1307).

Old Dominion Univ. Gallery, *(Old Dominion U Gall),* Hampton Blvd., Norfolk, VA 23508 (SAN 279-9693).

Old Fields Pubs., *(Old Fields Pubs; 0-942434),* P.O. Box 6154, Tallahassee, FL 32301 (SAN 239-5398).

Old House Journal Corp., The, *(Old Hse Journ Corp; 0-942202),* 69A Seventh Ave., Brooklyn, NY 11217 Tel 212-636-4515 (SAN 238-6801); Dist. by: Overlook Pr., .

Old Iron Book Company, *(Old Iron Bk Co; 0-942804),* R.R. 1, Box 28-A, Atkins, IA 52206 (SAN 238-8324).

Old Main Books, *(Old Main Bks; 0-940166),* 74 W. Main St., Mechanicsburg, PA (SAN 238-3586); Dist. by: Berkshire Traveller Press, Pine St., Stockbridge, MA 01262 Tel 413-298-3636 (SAN 201-1424).

Old Mill Press, *(Old Mill; 0-934700),* P.O. Box 388, Old Chelsea Sta., New York, NY 10113 Tel 212-929-4958 (SAN 214-0705).

Old New York Book Shop Press, *(Old NY Bk Shop; 0-937036),* 1069 Juniper St., NE, Atlanta, GA 30309 (SAN 215-6903).

Old Oaktree Motor Co., *(Old Oaktree; 0-9603194),* 2012 Hyperion Ave., Los Angeles, CA 90027 (SAN 213-2273).

Old Sparta Press, *(Old Sparta Pr; 0-9608344),* P.O. Box 6363, Raleigh, NC 27628 Tel 919-832-1358 (SAN 239-5401).

Old Sturbridge, Inc., *(Old Sturbridge; 0-913387),* Old Sturbridge Village, Sturbridge, MA 01566 Tel 617-347-3362 (SAN 203-0004).

Old Time Bottle Publishing Co., *(Old Time; 0-911068),* 611 Lancaster Dr., N.E., Salem, OR 97301 Tel 503-362-1446 (SAN 203-7718).

Old Town Press, *(Old Town Pr; 0-9610140),* 833 S. Main, St. Charles, MO 63301 (SAN 274-2764).

Old Ursuline Convent Cookbook, *(Old Ursuline; 0-9604718),* P.O. Box 7491, Metairie, LA 70010 (SAN 215-7977).

Old Violin-Art Publishing, *(Old Violin; 0-918554),* Box 500, 225 S. Cooke, Helena, MT 59624 (SAN 209-9756).

Old Warren Road Press, *(Old Warren),* 141 W. 17th St., 5th Fl., New York, NY 10011 Tel 212-242-5762 (SAN 264-2697).

Old West Publishing Co., *(Old West; 0-912094),* 1228 E. Colfax Ave., Denver, CO 80218 Tel 303-832-7190 (SAN 202-8174).

Oleander Press, *(Oleander Pr; 0-902675; 0-900891; 0-906672),* 210 Fifth Ave., New York, NY 10010 (SAN 206-1031).

Olearius Editions, *(Olearius Edns; 0-917526),* P.O. Box H, Kemblesville, PA 19347 Tel 215-255-4335 (SAN 207-2696).

Olin Ski Co., Inc., Subs. of Olin Corp., *(Olin Ski Co; 0-9606740),* 475 Smith St., Middletown, CT 06457 Tel 203-632-2000 (SAN 219-6158).

Olivant Press, *(Olivant; 0-87956),* P.O. Box 1409, Homestead, FL 33030 (SAN 205-3578).

Olive Press Pubns., *(Olive Pr Pubns; 0-933380),* P.O. Box 99, Los Olivos, CA 93441 Tel 805-688-2445 (SAN 212-5331).

Oliver, Lawrence, Book, *(L Oliver Bk; 0-9606432),* 815 Armada Terrace, San Diego, CA 92106 Tel 606-7226).

Oliver Press, *(Oliver Pr; 0-914400),* Dist. by: Charles Scribner's Sons, Shipping & Billing Depts., Vreeland Ave., Totowa, NJ 70512 (SAN 282-6550).

Olivet College Press, *(Olivet; 0-911070),* Dist. by: Bill Whitney, P.O. Box 20, Mott Academic Ctr., Olivet, MI 49076 (SAN 282-6801).

Olivia & Hill Press Inc., The, *(Olivia & Hill; 0-934034),* P.O. Box 7396, Ann Arbor, MI 48107 Tel 313-663-0235 (SAN 212-923X).

Olken Pubns., *(Olken Pubns; 0-934818),* 2830 Kennedy St., Livermore, CA 94550 Tel 415-447-5177 (SAN 203-7939).

Oll Korrect Press, *(Oll Korrect),* 119 W. Ocotillo Vista, Tucson, AZ 85704 Tel 602-742-2070 (SAN 209-8512).

Ololon Pubns., *(Ololon Pubns; 0-9607332),* P.O. Box 569, Lumberton, NC 28358 Tel 919-738-9396 (SAN 239-2712).

G&T Enterprises, *(G Olshevsky; 0-943348),* P.O. Box 11021, San Diego, CA 92111 (SAN 240-4761); Dist. by: Pacific Comics, 8423 Production Avenue, San Diego, CA 92121 (SAN 169-0124).

Olson, David V., Q M D, Inc., *(Olson QMD; 0-9609690),* 1740 Stanbridge, St. Paul, MN 55113 Tel 612-633-2914 (SAN 282-079X).

Olympic Media Information, *(Olympic Media; 0-88367),* 70 Hudson St., Hoboken, NJ 07030 Tel 201-963-1600 (SAN 202-8190).

Olympic Press, *(Olympic Pr; 0-930784),* P.O. Box 999, Montclair, NJ 07043 Tel 201-678-4453 (SAN 210-6175) Moved, Left No Forwarding Address.

Olympics Made Easy, *(Olympics Made; 0-910935),* 904 Silver Spur Road, Suite 184, Rolling Hills Estates, CA 90274 Tel 213-541-2842 (SAN 274-2810).

Olympus Publishing Co., *(Olympus Pub Co; 0-913420),* 1670 E. 13th South, Salt Lake City, UT 84105 Tel 801-583-3666 (SAN 202-8204).

Omaha Printing Company, *(Omaha Print; 0-9609116),* 4700 F. Street, Omaha, NE 68117 (SAN 264-2700).

O'Malley, Martin J., *(M J O'Malley),* 222 Paulison Ave., Passaic, NJ 07055 Tel 201-473-4643 (SAN 207-4702).

Oman, Robert, Pubns., *(R Oman Pubns; 0-931660),* 204 Fair Oaks Park, Needham, MA 02192 (SAN 211-7509).

Oman Enterprises, *(Oman Ent; 0-917346),* P.O. Box 222357, Carmel, CA 93922 Tel 408-624-4386 (SAN 208-7936).

Ombudsman Press, *(Omb),* 470 W. Highland Ave., Sierra Madre, CA 91024 Tel 213-355-1325 (SAN 210-3184).

Omega Center, *(Omega Ctr; 0-938726),* 21166 N. Pheasant Trail, Barrington, IL 60010 (SAN 219-8061).

Omega Communications, *(Omega Comms; 0-886780),* 110 Hillside Ave., Springfield, NJ 07081 Tel 201-467-3010 (SAN 277-6987).

Omega Press, *(Omega Pr NM; 0-930872),* 1570 Pacheco St., Santa Fe, NM 87501 Tel 505-988-4411 (SAN 214-1493).

Omega Pubns., *(Omega Pubns OR; 0-86694),* P.O. Box 4130, Medford, OR 97501 Tel 503-826-7773 (SAN 220-1534).

Omenana, *(Omenana; 0-943324),* 116 Howland St., Roxbury, MA 02121 Tel 617-445-0161 (SAN 240-5571).

Omkara Press, *(Omkara Pr; 0-934094),* 912 Beaver St., Santa Rosa, CA 95404 Tel 707-575-1736 (SAN 212-9558).

Ommation Press, *(Ommation Pr; 0-941240),* 5548 N. Sawyer Ave., Chicago, IL 60625 (SAN 216-2997); Dist. by: Word Works, Inc., P.O. Box 42164, Washington, DC 20015 Tel 202-554-3014 (SAN 211-6294).

Omni Pubs., *(Omni Pubs; 0-89127),* 218 E. Grand Ave., No. 201, Escondido, CA 92025 Tel 714-746-5833 (SAN 207-7027).

Onaway Pubns., *(Onaway; 0-918900),* 28 Lucky Dr., San Rafael, CA 94904 Tel 415-924-0884 (SAN 210-4768).

Once Upon A Planet, *(OUP; 0-88020),* 65-42 Fresh Meadow Lane, Fresh Meadows, NY 11365 Tel 212-961-9240 (SAN 218-5733).

Onchiota Books, *(Onchiota Bks; 0-934620),* Onchiota, NY 12951 Tel 518-891-3249 (SAN 213-1366).

Ondine Press, *(Ondine Pr; 0-910795),* 6318 Vesper Ave., Van Nuys, CA 91401 Tel 213-781-4360 (SAN 262-8449).

One Candle Press, *(One Candle; 0-914032),* Dist. by: One Candle Press, P.O. Box 888681, Atlanta, GA 30356 Tel 404-394-3482 (SAN 202-7364) Formerly Judson Press of Ga.

101 Productions, *(One Hund One Prods; 0-912238; 0-89286),* 834 Mission St., San Francisco, CA 94103 Tel 415-495-6040 (SAN 202-8220); Dist. by: Scribner Book Co., 201 Willowbrook Blvd., Wayne, NJ 07470 (SAN 201-002X).

120 Creative Corner, *(One Hund Twenty Creat; 0-912773),* Box 12341, St. Paul, MN 55112 Tel 612-784-8375 (SAN 283-1252).

101st Airborne Division Assn., *(One Hund First Air),* P.O. Box 101 Ab, Parchment, MI 49004 Tel 616-388-5801 (SAN 210-1297).

One Percent Publishing, *(One Percent; 0-935442),* 2888 Bluff St., Suite 143, Boulder, CO 80301 (SAN 216-1702).

One Shot Press, *(One Shot),* P.O. Box 1077, Middletown, CT 06457 Tel 203-349-8626 (SAN 203-1167).

One Ten Records, *(One Ten Records; 0-9605778),* 110 Chambers St., New York, NY 10007 Tel 212-964-2296 (SAN 216-5066).

1000 Ways Pubns., *(One Thousand Ways; 0-940324),* Heacock Literary Agency, 1523 Sixth St., Santa Monica, CA 90401 (SAN 220-3502).

One World Press, *(One World Pr; 0-910485),* 31 Chestnut St., Rhinebeck, NY 12572 Tel 914-876-2911 (SAN 260-1117).

O'Neill, Eugene, Theater Center, *(E O'Neill),* 305 Great Neck Rd., Waterford, CT 06385 Tel 203-443-5378 (SAN 211-2612).

O'Neill Press, *(O'Neill Pr; 0-930970),* 305 Great Neck Rd., Waterford, CT 06385 (SAN 212-1239).

Oneiric Press, *(Oneiric Pr),* Dist. by: Bookpeople, 2940 Seventh St., Berkeley, CA 94710 Tel 415-549-3033 (SAN 168-9517).

Online, Inc., *(Online; 0-910965),* 11 Tannery Lane, Weston, CT 06883 Tel 203-227-8466 (SAN 264-2735).

Onset Pubns., *(Onset Pubns; 0-89411),* 692 Elkader St., Ashland, OR 97520 Tel 503-482-0088 (SAN 209-3561).

Ontario Review Press, The, *(Ontario Rev NJ; 0-86538),* Dist. by: Persea Books, Inc., 225 Lafayette St., New York, NY 10012 Tel 212-431-5270 (SAN 212-8233).

OOLP (Out of London Press) Inc., *(Oolp Pr; 0-915570),* 33 Union Square West, New York, NY 10003 Tel 212-989-3083 (SAN 202-8263).

Open Bible Pubs., *(Open Bible),* 2020 Bell Ave., Des Moines, IA 50315 Tel 515-288-6761 (SAN 238-8545).

Open Book Pubns., *(Open Bk Pubns; 0-940170),* Station Hill Rd., Barrytown, NY 12507 Tel 914-758-5840 (SAN 220-3006).

Open Books, *(Open Books; 0-931416),* 1631 Grant St., Berkeley, CA 94703 (SAN 211-7517).

Open Connections Inc., *(Open Connections; 0-9606434),* 312 Bryn Mawr Ave., Bryn Mawr, PA 19010 Tel 215-527-1504 (SAN 216-2806).

Open Court Publishing Co., Div. of Carus Corp., *(Open Court; 0-87548; 0-89688; 0-8126),* P.O. Box 599, LaSalle, IL 61301 Tel 815-223-2520 (SAN 202-5876). *Imprints:* Library Press (Library Pr).

Open Door Foundation, The, *(Open Door Foun; 0-911335),* Box 3703, Carmel, CA 93921 Tel 408-625-3307 (SAN 274-2969).

Open Door, Inc., The, *(Open Door Inc; 0-940136),* P. O. Box 855, Charlottesville, VA 22902 Tel 804-784-3951 (SAN 217-0795).

Open-Door Press, *(Open-Door; 0-912162),* P.O. Box 6161, Shirlington Sta., Arlington, VA 22206 Tel 703-379-8655 (SAN 203-7742).

Open Door Society of Connecticut, Inc., *(Open Door Soc; 0-918416),* Box 478, Hartford, CT 06101 (SAN 209-3839).

Open Hand Publishing Inc., *(Open Hand; 0-940880),* 5 Securities Bldg. 1904 3 Ave, Seattle, WA 98101 Tel 206-624-5875 (SAN 219-6174).

Open My World Pub, *(Open My World; 0-941996),* 1300 Lorna St., El Cajon, CA 92020 (SAN 238-602X).

Open Path, The, *(Open Path; 0-9602722),* 703 N. 18th St., Boise, ID 83702 Tel 208-342-0208 (SAN 215-9759).

Open Places, *(Open Places; 0-913398),* Box 2085, Stephens College, Columbia, MO 65215 Tel 314-442-2211 (SAN 205-356X).

Open Window Books Inc., *(Open Window; 0-917694),* Box 949, Chickasha, OK 73018 Tel 405-224-3217 (SAN 209-4657).

Opera West Foundation, *(Opera West; 0-9601270),* 361 Dolores St., San Francisco, CA 94110 Tel 415-621-2112 (SAN 210-4776).

Ophir International, *(Ophir Intl),* 15070 Astoria St., Sylmar, CA 91342 (SAN 216-4272).

Opportunities for Learning, Inc., *(Opportunities Learn; 0-86703),* 8950 Lurline Ave., Chatsworth, CA 91311 Tel 213-341-2535 (SAN 216-6895).

Opportunity Knocks Publishers, *(Opportunity Knocks; 0-938908),* P.O. Box 785, Vienna, VA 22180 Tel 703-938-8237 (SAN 238-4965).

Optical Resolution Information Center, *(Optical Resolution; 0-9601918),* Manhattan College, Riverdale, NY 10471 Tel (SAN 212-3770).
Optical Society of America, *(Optical Soc; 0-9600380),* 1816 Jefferson Place, Washington, DC 20036 Tel 202-223-8130 (SAN 203-7750).
Optimum Resource, Inc., *(Optimum Res Inc; 0-911787),* Greenwoods Rd. East, Norfolk, CT 06058 Tel 203-543-5070 (SAN 264-2743).
Options Publishing Co., *(Options; 0-917400),* P.O. Box 311, Wayne, NJ 07470 Tel 201-694-2327 (SAN 208-9629).
Optosonic Press, *(Optosonic Pr; 0-87739),* P.O. Box 883, Ansonia Sta., New York, NY 10023 Tel 212-724-9687 (SAN 202-8271).
Oracle Books, *(Oracle Bks; 0-943434),* P.O. Box 24084, Los Angeles, CA 90024 Tel 213-279-1521 (SAN 240-7388).
Oracle Press, *(Oracle Pr LA; 0-88127),* 5323 Heatherstone Dr., Baton Rouge, LA 70808 Tel 504-766-5577 (SAN 241-3434).
Orafa Pub. Co., Inc., *(Orafa Pub Co; 0-912273),* 1314 S. King, Suite 1064, Honolulu, HI 96814 Tel 808-531-6431 (SAN 285-0753); 3055 La Pietra Circle, Honolulu, HI 96815 Tel 808-922-5177 (SAN 285-0761); Dist. by: Hippocrene Books, Inc., 171 Madison Ave., New York, NY 10016 (SAN 285-077X); Dist. by: Pacific Trade Group, P.O. Box 1227, Kailua, HI 96734 (SAN 285-0788).
Oral History Research Office, *(Oral History; 0-9602492),* Box 20, Butler Library, Columbia University, New York, NY 10027 (SAN 239-5827).
Orange Blossom Publishers Limited, *(Orange Blossom; 0-9608100),* P.O. 2187, Henderson, NE 89015 Tel 805-524-2221 (SAN 238-8553).
Orange Bowl Committee, The, *(Orange Bowl Comm; 0-9610552),* P.O. Box 350748, Miami, FL 33135 Tel 305-642-1515 (SAN 264-2751).
Orange County Genealogical Society, *(Orange County Genealog; 0-9604116),* 101 Main St., Goshen, NY 10924 (SAN 220-021X).
Orbis Books, *(Orbis Bks; 0-88344),* Maryknoll, NY 10545 Tel 914-941-7590 (SAN 202-828X).
Orbis Publications, Inc., *(Orbis Pubns; 0-933146),* 1105 Lantana Dr., Los Angeles, CA 90042 (SAN 221-9697).
Orchard House, *(Orchard),* 1281 Burg St., Granville, OH 43023 (SAN 209-407X).
Orchard House, Inc., *(Orchard Hse MA; 0-933510),* 46 Love Lane, Concord, MA 01742 Tel 617-369-0467 (SAN 285-0796); Orders to: Ball's Hill Rd., Concord, MA 01742 Tel 617-363-0467 (SAN 285-080X).
Ordeman, John T., *(J T Ordeman),* St. Paul's School, Brooklandville, MD 21022 (SAN 265-3613).
ORDINA *See* **Unipub**
Oregon Historical Society, *(Oreg Hist Soc; 0-87595),* 1230 S.W. Park Ave., Portland, OR 97205 Tel 503-222-1741 (SAN 202-8301).
Oregon State Bar Committee on Continuing Legal Education, *(OR Bar CLE),* 808 Sw 15th Ave, Portland, OR 97205 (SAN 227-2563).
Oregon State Univ. Book Stores, Inc., *(Oreg St U Bkstrs; 0-88246),* P.O. Box 489, Corvallis, OR 97339 Tel 503-754-4323 (SAN 100-5189).
Oregon State Univ. Press, *(Oreg St U Pr; 0-87071),* 101 Waldo Hall, Oregon State University, Corvallis, OR 97331 Tel 503-754-3166 (SAN 202-8328).
Orenda Publishing/Unity Press, *(Orenda-Unity; 0-913300),* 61 Camino Alto, Suite 100, Mill Valley, CA 94941 Tel 415-388-0804 (SAN 282-0811); Orders to: Network, Inc., P. O. Box 2246, Berkeley, CA 94702 (SAN 282-082X).
Organ Literature Foundation, The, *(Organ Lit; 0-913746),* 45 Norfolk Rd, Braintree, MA 02184 Tel 617-848-1388 (SAN 203-7769).
Organization Development Services, Inc. *See* **ODS Pubns., Inc.**
Organization for Economic Cooperation & Development, *(OECD),* 1750 Pennsylvania Ave., Suite 1207, N.W., Washington, DC 20006 Tel 202-724-1857 (SAN 202-1277).

Organization of American States, *(OAS; 0-8270),* Dept. of Publications, 6840 Industrial Rd., Springfield, VA 22151 Tel 703-941-1617 (SAN 206-8877).
Organizational Measurement Systems Press, *(Organizat Meas; 0-917926),* Box 81, Atlanta, GA 30301 Tel 404-355-9472 (SAN 209-9764).
Oribello, William Alexander, Ltd., *(Oribello W; 0-910433),* 6309 Hollywood Blvd., Suite No. 173, Hollywoodhia, CA 90028 Tel 213-871-1903 (SAN 260-1494).
Oriel Press, *(Oriel Pr; 0-938628),* P.O. Box 12373, Portland, OR 97212 Tel 503-222-5809 (SAN 282-0870); Orders to: P. O. Box 12373, Portland, OR 97212 (SAN 282-0889); Dist. by: Bookpeople, 2940 Seventh St., Berkeley, CA 94710 Tel 415-549-3030 (SAN 282-0897); Dist. by: Far West Book Service, 3515 N. E. Hasselo, Portland, OR 97232 Tel 503-234-7664 (SAN 282-6429).
Oriel Press *See* **Routledge & Kegan Paul, Ltd.**
Orient Book Distributors, *(Orient Bk Dist; 0-89684),* P.O. Box 100, Livingston, NJ 07039 Tel 201-992-6992 (SAN 211-819X).
Oriental Book Store, The, *(Oriental Bk Store),* P.O. Box 177, South Pasadena, CA 91030-0177 Tel 213-577-2413 (SAN 285-0818); 630 E. Colorado Blvd., Pasadena, CA 91101 Tel 213-577-2413 (SAN 285-0826).
Oriental Institute of the Univ. of Chicago, *(Oriental Inst; 0-918986),* 1155 E. 58th St., Chicago, IL 60637 Tel 312-753-2478 (SAN 210-4784).
Oriental Research Partners, *(Orient Res Partners; 0-89250),* P.O. Box 158, Newtonville, MA 02160 Tel 617-965-4399 (SAN 208-2764).
Orientalia Art, Ltd., *(Orientalia; 0-87902),* P.O. Box 597, New York, NY 10003 Tel 212-473-9837 (SAN 282-0919); 61 Fourth Ave., New York, NY 10003 (SAN 282-0927).
Original Press, Div. of Throckmorton Publishing Co., *(Original Pr; 0-935812),* 561 Milltown Rd., North Brunswick, NJ 08902 (SAN 213-9618).
Original Pubns., Subs. of Jamil Prods. Corp., *(Original Pubns; 0-942272),* 2486 Webster Ave., Bronx, NY 10058 Tel 212-367-9589 (SAN 238-1001).
Orion Editions, *(Orion Ed),* 1317 Filbert St., Philadelphia, PA 19107 Tel 215-563-2288 (SAN 286-3529).
Orion Press, *(Orion Pr; 0-912971),* Box 20-184, Columbus, OH 43220 (SAN 283-3387).
Orirana Press, *(Orirana Pr; 0-938364),* 19737 Covello St., Canoga Park, CA 91306 (SAN 214-0713).
Orlando Publications, *(Orlando Pubns; 0-913065),* 192 Link Ave., Pittsurg, PA 15237 Tel 412-366-4112 (SAN 283-233X).
Orleans County Historical Society, *(Orleans; 0-9610860),* 5 Cliff St., Brownington, VT 05680 (SAN 265-1297).
Ormsby, John R., Jr., *(Ormsby; 0-943736),* Drawer 2429, Greenville, NC 27834 (SAN 240-9232).
Orovan Books, *(Orovan Bks; 0-913748),* P.O. Box 6082, Honolulu, HI 96818 Tel 808-422-6297 (SAN 203-7793).
Orpheus Press, *(Orpheus Pr; 0-915648),* P.O. Box 48423, Los Angeles, CA 90048 Tel 213-653-5800 (SAN 207-3714).
Orphic Press, *(Orphic Pr; 0-9606894),* Box 2072, Glenview, IL 60025 Tel 312-827-1715 (SAN 217-4111).
Orr, Leonard, *(L Orr),* Orders to: Creative Source, P.O. Box 224, Sierraville, CA 96126 Tel 916-994-3552 (SAN 207-2505).
Orr, William N. & Elizabeth, *(W&E Orr; 0-9606502),* P.O. Box 5286, Eugene, OR 97405 (SAN 226-2053).
Ortho Bks., Div. of Chevron Chemical Co., Subs. of Standard Oil Co. of Calif., *(Ortho; 0-917102),* c/o Chevron Chemical Co., 575 Market St., Rm. 546, San Francisco, CA 94105 Tel 415-894-0277 (SAN 218-6780).
Ortho Diagnostic Systems, Inc., *(Ortho Diag; 0-910771),* Room B-50, Raritan, NJ 08869 Tel 201-524-2181 (SAN 260-2393).
Orthodox Christian Education Society, *(Orthodox Chr; 0-938366),* 1916 W. Warner Ave., Chicago, IL 60613 Tel 312-549-0584 (SAN 215-1642).

Oryx Press, *(Oryx Pr; 0-912700; 0-89774),* 2214 N. Central Ave., Phoenix, AZ 85004 Tel 602-254-6156 (SAN 220-0201).
Orzano Publishing Co., *(Orzano Pub Co; 0-936668),* P.O. Box 394, Islip, NY 11751 (SAN 214-2155).
Osborne/McGraw-Hill, *(Osborne-McGraw; 0-931988),* 2600 Tenth St., Berkeley, CA 94710 Tel 415-548-2805 (SAN 274-3450).
Osgood, Merle, Productions, *(M Osgood; 0-913067),* 720 Eleventh St., Bellingham, WN 98225 (SAN 283-975X); Dist. by: Pacific Pipeline, Inc., 19215 66th Ave. S., Kent, WN 98031 (SAN 208-2128).
Osowitz, B. M., *(B M Osowitz),* 1118 S. Broad St., Trenton, NJ 08611 (SAN 211-6766); Orders to: 1111 N.W. 40th Ave., Pompano, FL 33066 (SAN 211-6774).
Osprey Books, *(Osprey Bks; 0-943738),* P.O. Box 965, Huntington, NY 11743 Tel 516-549-0143 (SAN 241-0508).
Ossi Pubns., *(Ossi Pubns; 0-930912),* P.O. Box 141, Fern Park, FL 32730 Tel 305-862-2392 (SAN 211-0415).
Osteen, Ike, *(I Osteen; 0-9602724),* 380 Kansas St., Springfield, CO 81073 Tel 303-523-6580 (SAN 212-9248).
O'Sullivan, Woodside & Co., *(O'Sullivan Woodside; 0-89019),* 2218 E. Magnolia, Phoenix, AZ 85034 Tel 602-244-1000 (SAN 207-4052); Dist. by: Caroline House Pubs., Inc., 236 Forest Park Place, Ottawa, IL 61350 Tel 815-434-7905 (SAN 207-6705). *Imprints:* Norwalk Press (Norwalk Pr).
Otafra Press, *(Otafra; 0-9605220),* P.O. Box 814, Mesilla, NM 88046 (SAN 220-1224).
Other Books, *(Other Bks),* 1412 Spruce St., Berkeley, CA 94709 Tel 415-841-6359 (SAN 209-0813).
O T O (Society Ordo Templi Orientis in America), *(O T O),* P.O. Box 90144, Nashville, TN 37209 (SAN 219-9610); Dist. by: Bookpeople, 2940 Seventh St., Berkeley, CA 94710 Tel 415-549-3030 (SAN 168-9517); Dist. by: The Distributors, 702 S. Michigan, South Bend, IN 46618 Tel 219-232-8500 (SAN 212-0364).
Otstot, Charles M., *(C M Otstot; 0-9603808),* 5124 N. 33rd St., Arlington, VA 22207 Tel 703-538-5446 (SAN 206-9539).
Otterden Press, *(Otterden; 0-918868),* 111 Plymouth Rd., Hillsdale, NJ 07642 Tel 201-664-2583 (SAN 210-4792).
Ouabache Pr., *(Ouabache Pr; 0-9609026),* Box 2076, W. Lafayette, IN 47906 Tel 317-463-9857 (SAN 240-9240).
Our Baby's First Seven Years, *(Our Baby's),* c/o Mothers' Aid of Chicago Lying-in Hospital, 5841 Maryland Ave., Chicago, IL 60637 Tel 312-962-6595 (SAN 287-2951).
Our Sunday Visitor, Inc., *(Our Sunday Visitor; 0-87973),* 200 Noll Plaza, Huntington, IN 46750 Tel 219-356-8400 (SAN 202-8344).
Ourobourus Institute/Unlimited Publishing, *(Ourobourus; 0-918538),* 324 E. 35th St., New York, NY 10016 Tel 212-679-0669 (SAN 209-9772).
Out & Out Books, *(Out & Out; 0-918314),* 476 Second St., Brooklyn, NY 11215 Tel 212-499-9227 (SAN 209-4665).
Out of the Ashes Press, *(Out of the Ashes; 0-912874),* P.O. Box 42384, Portland, OR 97242 (SAN 202-8352).
Out of the Sky Press, *(Out Sky Pr; 0-9603292),* P.O. Box 998, Saratoga, CA 95070 (SAN 218-446X).
Outbooks, *(Outbooks; 0-89646),* 217 Kimball Ave., Golden, CO 80401 Tel 303-278-1491 (SAN 211-0849).
Outdoor Associates, *(Outdoor Assocs; 0-9605556),* 1279 Dean St., Schenectady, NY 12309 Tel 518-372-4585 (SAN 207-270X).
Outdoor Books, Nature Series, Inc., *(Outdoor Bks; 0-942806),* 3813 Fenchurch Rd., Baltimore, MD 21218 Tel 301-243-1179 (SAN 238-8561).
Outdoor Circle, The, *(Outdoor Circle),* 200 N. Vineyard Blvd., Suite 502, Honolulu, HI 96817 Tel 808-521-0074 (SAN 241-4228).
Outdoor Empire Publishing, Inc., *(Outdoor Empire; 0-916682),* 511 Eastlake Ave., P.O. Box C-19000, Seattle, WA 98109 Tel 206-624-3845 (SAN 207-1312).
Outdoor Pictures, *(Outdoor Pict; 0-911080),* P.O. Box 277, Anacortes, WA 98221 Tel 206-293-3200 (SAN 203-7815).

Outdoor Pubns., *(Outdoor Pubns),* P.O. Box 355, Ithaca, NY 14850 Tel 607-273-0061 (SAN 202-1250).

Outdoor Skills Bookshelf, *(Outdoor Skills; 0-940022),* P.O. Box 111501, Nashville, TN 37211 Tel 615-776-5276 (SAN 216-8472).

Outdoors Inc., *(Outdoors Inc; 0-9605254),* Box 999, Brainerd, MN 56401 (SAN 215-8965).

Outer Straubville Press, *(Outer Straubville),* Box 470, Occidental, CA 95465 (SAN 203-7823); Dist. by: Bookpeople, 2940 Seventh St., Berkeley, CA 94710 Tel 415-549-3033 (SAN 168-9509).

Outermost Press, *(Outermost Pr; 0-940282),* Leverett Rd., Shutesbury, MA 01072 Tel 413-256-0735 (SAN 217-5509).

Outlet Book Company, Div. of Crown Publishers, Inc., *(Outlet Bk Co),* One Park Ave., New York, NY 10016 Tel 212-532-9200 (SAN 200-2620) Promotional books of all kinds; remainders, reprints, imports, original publications.

Outlook Bk. Service, Inc., *(Outlook; 0-911082),* 512 E. Main St., Richmond, VA 23219 (SAN 206-684X).

Outre House, *(Outre House; 0-9605404),* 1622 N. St., No. 302, Sacramento, CA 95814 Tel 916-442-6354 (SAN 238-7093).

Outside Enterprise Press, *(Outside Ent; 0-937232),* P.O. Box 2650, College Sta., Pullman, WA 99163 (SAN 215-0972).

Overbrook House, *(Overbrook Hse; 0-910773),* P.O. Box 7688, Mountain Brook, AL 35253 Tel 205-879-8222 (SAN 260-2407).

Overcomer Press, Inc., *(Overcomer Pr; 0-942504),* 310 W. Main St. P.O. Box 70, Owosso, MI 48867 Tel 517-725-9550 (SAN 238-1834).

Overlook Hospital Auxiliary, *(Overlook Hosp; 0-9604560),* Morris Ave., Summit, NJ 07901 Tel 201-522-2004 (SAN 215-0980).

Overlook Press, *(Overlook Pr; 0-87951),* 667 Madison Ave., Suite 401A, New York, NY 10021 Tel 212-688-0920 (SAN 202-8360); c/o Viking Press, 40 W. 23 St., New York, NY 10010 Tel 212-807-7300 (SAN 200-2469).

Overseas Development Council, *(Overseas Dev Council),* 1717 Massachusetts Ave., N.W., Washington, DC 20036 Tel 202-234-8701 (SAN 215-2711).

Overshiner Press, *(Overshiner; 0-937480),* 92 Buckwood Place, Santa Rosa, CA 95405 Tel 707-538-0181 (SAN 215-6911).

Overstreet Pubns., Inc., *(Overstreet; 0-911903),* 780 Hunt Cliff Dr. NW, Cleveland, OH 37311 Tel 615-472-4135 (SAN 216-4302).

Oviedo Publishing Co., *(Oviedo Pub Co; 0-9603034),* P.O. Box 837, Oviedo, FL 32765 (SAN 213-1331).

Owen-Jenkins, Inc., *(Owen & Jenkins; 0-918144),* 1112 Richview Rd., Tallahassee, FL 32301 Tel 904-877-3330 (SAN 209-326X).

Owen Press, *(Owen Pr; 0-9607988),* 212 Grand Ave., Ojai, CA 93023 Tel 805-646-5364 (SAN 238-5511).

Owl Press, *(Owl Pr; 0-911084),* P.O. Box 709, Annapolis, MD 21404 Tel 301-267-6456 (SAN 203-7858).

Owl Press, Inc., *(Owl Pr NV),* 312 Almond Tree Lane, Las Vegas, NV 89104 (SAN 219-0915).

Owlswick Press, *(Owlswick Pr; 0-913896),* P.O. Box 8243, Philadelphia, PA 19101 Tel 215-382-5415 (SAN 202-8387).

Owlswood Productions, *(Owlswood Prods; 0-915942),* 1355 Market St., San Francisco, CA 94103 Tel 415-626-2480 (SAN 207-7264).

Owner-Builder Pubns., *(Owner-Builder; 0-910225),* P.O. Box 817, North Fork, CA 93643 (SAN 207-1894).

Ox Bow Press, *(Ox Bow; 0-918024),* P.O. Box 4045, Woodbridge, CT 06525 Tel 203-387-5900 (SAN 210-2501).

Oxbridge Communications, Inc., *(Oxbridge Comm; 0-917460),* 150 Fifth Ave., Suite 301, New York, NY 10011 Tel 212-741-0231 (SAN 209-0724).

Oxfam America, *(Oxfam Am),* 115 Broadway, Boston, MA 02116 Tel 617-247-3304 (SAN 213-7828).

Oxford Univ. Press, Inc., *(Oxford U Pr; 0-19),* 200 Madison Ave., New York, NY 10016 Tel 212-679-7300 (SAN 202-5884); Orders to: 16-00 Pollitt Dr., Fair Lawn, NJ 07410 Tel 201-796-8000 (SAN 202-5892) New York Accounts Use 212-564-6680. *Imprints:* Galaxy Books (GB).

Oxmoor House, Inc., *(Oxmoor Hse; 0-8487),* P.O. Box 2262, Birmingham, AL 35201 Tel 205-877-6000 (SAN 205-3462); Dist. by: Harper & Row, Pubs., Inc., Keystone Industrial Park, Scranton, PA 18512 Tel 800-233-4175 (SAN 215-3742).

Oxymora Book Press, *(Oxymora Bk Pr; 0-911109),* P.O. Box 429, Venice, CA 90291 Tel 213-399-1524 (SAN 262-9755).

Oyez, *(Oyez; 0-911088),* 212 Colgate Ave., Kensington, CA 94707 (SAN 206-877X).

Oyster Press, *(Oyster Pr; 0-933114),* 103 S. Soledad St., Santa Barbara, CA 93103 (SAN 212-7849).

Ozark Mountain Pubs., *(Ozark Mtn Pubs; 0-915394),* P.O. Box 4718 G.S., Springfield, MO 65804 Tel 417-881-3060 (SAN 207-3595).

Ozark Society, *(Ozark Soc; 0-912456),* P.O. Box 725, Hot Springs, AR 71901 (SAN 203-7874).

Ozark Society Foundation, *(Ozark Soc Found),* P.O. Box 3503, Little Rock, AR 72203 (SAN 282-096X).

Ozer, Jerome S., Pub., Inc., *(Ozer; 0-89198),* 340 Tenafly Rd., Englewood, NJ 07631 Tel 201-567-7040 (SAN 202-8395).

PAGL Press, *(P A G L; 0-913105),* 2854 N. Santiago Blvd. No. 100, Orange, CA 92667 Tel 714-974-9471 (SAN 283-2372); Dist. by: Hunter House Inc., Box 3914, San Rafael, CA 94901 Tel 415-883-3530 (SAN 281-7977).

PAK Enterprises, *(PAK Ent; 0-9610252),* P.O. Box 25421, Richmond, VA 23260 Tel 804-343-1944 (SAN 264-2794).

PAM Pubs., *(PAM Pubs; 0-932724),* 51 Carmel Ave., Salinas, CA 93901 (SAN 212-534X).

PASE Inc., *(PASE),* 90 Carroll Place, New Brunswick, NJ 08901 (SAN 264-2808).

PAX Tapes, Inc., *(PAX Tapes),* 611 Rosetta, Florissant, MO 63031 (SAN 265-3923).

P & K Enterprises, *(P & K Ent; 0-918176),* 2502 Cecile St., Kissimmee, FL 32741 Tel 305-846-6995 (SAN 210-251X).

PBBC Press, *(PBBC Pr),* 315 S. Grove St., Owatonna, MN 55060 Tel 507-451-2710 (SAN 207-2734).

PEM Press, Div. of Pathescope Educational Media, Inc., *(PEM Pr),* 71 Weyman Ave., P.O. Box 719, New Rochelle, NY 10802 Tel 914-235-0800 (SAN 214-0721).

PEN American Center, *(Pen Am Ctr; 0-934638),* 47 Fifth Ave., New York, NY 10003 (SAN 214-4328).

P. F. C. Publishing Co., *(PFC; 0-9603830),* 525 W. 26th St., New York, NY 10001 Tel 212-242-0179 (SAN 206-8338).

PJD Pubns., Ltd., *(PJD Pubns; 0-9600290; 0-915340),* P.O. Box 966, Westbury, NY 11590 Tel 516-626-0650 (SAN 202-0068).

PMA, *(PMA; 0-941562),* Montgomery Prof. Bldg., Rte. 206, Belle Mead, NJ 08502 (SAN 264-2824).

P-M Enterprises, *(PM Ent; 0-9601846),* P.O. Box 782, Hendersonville, NC 28793 Tel 704-697-2261 (SAN 210-3192).

PMF Research Co., *(PMF Research; 0-934036),* P.O. Box 424, Kenilworth, IL 60043 (SAN 212-9574).

P/P Pubns., *(P-P Pubns; 0-9608316),* 500 N. Dearborn, Suite 900, Chicago, IL 60610 (SAN 240-4850).

PRESCOB Publishing Co., *(PRESCOB),* 5110 S. 67th E. Place, Tulsa, OK 74145 Tel 918-664-6717 (SAN 211-612X).

PROMIS Laboratory, *(PROMIS Lab),* MCHV-MFU, Adams Residence, Burlington, VT 05401 Tel 802-656-3946 (SAN 213-2680).

PR Publishing Co., Inc., *(P R Pub Co),* P.O. Box 600, Exeter, NH 03833 Tel 603-778-0514 (SAN 205-3438).

PSI Research, Subs. of Publishing Services, Inc., *(PSI Res; 0-916378),* 1287 Lawrence Station Rd., Sunnyvale, CA 94086 Tel 408-745-7093 (SAN 208-7928).

P.S.I. Rhythms, Inc., *(PSI Rhythms; 0-918882),* P. O. Box 1838, Ormond Beach, FL 32074 Tel 904-255-6444 (SAN 210-4806); 2085 South Halofax, Daytona Beach, FL 32018 (SAN 210-4814).

PTL Pubns., *(PTL Pubns; 0-915420),* Box 1277, Tustin, CA 92680 Tel 714-838-7715 (SAN 211-8203).

Pace Gallery/The, *(Pace Gallery Pubns; 0-938608),* 32 E. 57th St., New York, NY 10022 (SAN 220-2646).

Pace Publishing, Inc., *(Pace Pub; 0-940138),* 6009 Wayzata Blvd., Suite 105, Minneapolis, MN 55416 Tel 612-546-3111 (SAN 220-3014).

Pacesetter Press, Div. of Gulf Publishing Co., *(Pacesetter Pr; 0-88415),* P.O. Box 2608, Houston, TX 77001 Tel 713-529-4301 (SAN 202-845X).

Pacesetter Pub. Hse., Div. of Pacesetter Enterprises, Inc., *(Pacesetter Pub Hse OH; 0-9603826),* P.O. Box 33430, Cleveland, OH 44133-0430 (SAN 218-4990).

Pachart Publishing House, *(Pachart Pub Hse; 0-88126; 0-912918),* P.O. Box 35549, Tucson, AZ 85740 Tel 602-297-4797 (SAN 204-9139).

Pachyderm Press, *(Pachyderm Pr; 0-910403),* Suite 2806, 15 Charles Plaza, Baltimore, MD 21201 Tel 301-547-0184 (SAN 260-1133).

Pacific/Asian American Mental Health Research Center, *(Pacific-Asian; 0-934584),* 1001 W. Van Buren St., Chicago, IL 60607 Tel 312-226-0117 (SAN 214-4336).

Pacific Book Supply Co., *(Pacific Bk Supply; 0-911090),* P.O. Box 337, Farmersville, CA 93223 Tel 209-594-4155 (SAN 202-1366).

Pacific Books, Pubs., *(Pacific Bks; 0-87015),* P.O. Box 558, Palo Alto, CA 94302 Tel 415-856-0550 (SAN 202-8468).

Pacific District Mennonite Brethren Churches, Family Commission, *(Pacific Dist Mennonite; 0-9606436),* 4812 E. Butler, Fresno, CA 93727 Tel 209-251-8681 (SAN 219-807X).

Pacific Editions, *(Pacific Edns; 0-938226),* 350 Arballo Dr., No. 5d, San Francisco, CA 94132 Tel 415-334-5716 (SAN 220-0813).

Pacific Gallery Pubs., *(Pacific Gallery; 0-938942),* P.O. Box 19494, Portland, OR 97219 Tel 503-244-2300 (SAN 220-2654).

Pacific Institute, *(Pacific Inst; 0-9609174),* P.O. Box 33111, San Diego, CA 92103 Tel 714-276-3475 (SAN 241-4236).

Pacific International Publishing Co., *(Pacific Intl; 0-918074),* Box 21814, Seattle, WA 98111 Tel 206-784-0187 (SAN 210-2528).

Pacific Medical Press, *(Pacific Med Pr; 0-9608102),* P.O. Box 553, San Anselmo, CA 94960 Tel 415-921-4868 (SAN 238-8332).

Pacific Northwest Labor History Assn., *(Pacific NW Labor; 0-932942),* P.O. Box 25048, Northgate Sta., Seattle, WA 98125 (SAN 216-1710).

Pacific Pipeline, Inc., *(Pacific Pipeline),* 19215 66th Ave. S., Kent, WA 98032 Tel 206-872-5523 (SAN 208-2128); P.O. Box 3711, Seattle, WA 98124 (SAN 169-8834).

Pacific Press Publishing Assn., *(Pacific Pr Pub Assn; 0-8163),* P.O. Box 7000, Mountain View, CA 94039 Tel 415-961-2323 (SAN 202-8409).

Pacific Press Santa Barbara, *(Pacific Santa Barbara; 0-911094),* P.O. Box 219, Pierce City, MO 65723 Tel 417-476-2034 (SAN 202-1161).

Pacific Publishing House, *(Pacific Pub Hse; 0-918872),* 2430 Kirkham St., San Francisco, CA 94122 Tel 415-566-2988 (SAN 210-3214).

Pacific Rim Research, *(Pacific Rim Res),* P.O. Box 4538, North Hollywood, CA 91607 Tel 213-995-7042 (SAN 282-0986)CA (SAN 282-0994).

Pacific Scientific Press, Inc., *(Pacific Scientific; 0-943792),* P.O. Box 878, Kelso, WA 98626 Tel 206-425-8592 (SAN 241-0532).

Pacific Search Press, *(Pacific Search; 0-914718),* 222 Dexter Ave. N., Seattle, WA 98109 Tel 206-682-5044 (SAN 202-8476).

Pacific Sports Actualities, *(Pacific Sports; 0-910405),* Box 2443, Berkeley, CA 94702 Tel 415-848-5423 (SAN 260-1141).

Pacific Sun Press, *(Pacific Sun; 0-9602908),* 52 R. Arroyo Sorrento Dr., Del Mar, CA 92014 Tel 714-755-4422 (SAN 214-073X).

Pacifica House, Inc., Pubs., *(Pacifica; 0-911098)*, c/o Borden Publishing Co., 1855 W. Main St., Alhambra, CA 91801 (SAN 201-419X).

Package Publicity Service, Inc., *(Package Publ; 0-911100)*, 1501 Broadway, Rm. 1314, New York, NY 10036 Tel 212-354-1840 (SAN 206-8621).

Packard, Rosa Covington, *(R C Packard)*, 208 W. Old Mill Rd., Greenwich, CT 06830 Tel 203-661-8946 (SAN 211-089X).

Packard Publishing, *(Packard; 0-941710)*, P.O. Box 307, Topanga, CA 90290 Tel 213-461-1346 (SAN 239-2895).

Packrat Press Books, *(Packrat Pr)*, P.O. Box 74, Cambridge, ID 83610 (SAN 211-7525).

Paddlewheel Press, *(Paddlewheel; 0-938274)*, 15100 SW 109th, Tigard, OR 97223 (SAN 215-8973).

Padilla, Francisco, *(Padilla; 0-9605292)*, P.O. Box 517, Westminster, CO 80030 Tel 303-629-2425 (SAN 216-2814).

Padma Press, *(Padma; 0-917960)*, P.O. Box 56, Oatman, AZ 86433 (SAN 209-4088).

Padre Productions, *(Padre Prods; 0-914598)*, P.O. Box 1275, San Luis Obispo, CA 93406 Tel 805-543-5404 (SAN 202-8484).

Pagan Press, *(Pagan Pr; 0-943742)*, 26 St. Marks Place, New York, NY 10003 Tel 212-674-3321 (SAN 241-0540).

Paganiniana Pubns., Inc. Div. of T.F.H Pubns., Inc., *(Paganiniana Pubns; 0-87666)*, P.O. Box 427, Neptune, NJ 07753 Tel 201-988-8400 (SAN 209-309X).

Page One Pubns., *(Page One; 0-9607274)*, P.O. Box 2674, La Mesa, CA 92041 (SAN 239-3700).

Page Publishing, *(Page Pub)*, 609-613 Chetco Ave., P. O. Box 1091, Brookings, OR 97415 (SAN 209-6307).

Page Publishing Co., *(Page Pub WI; 0-89769)*, Box 432, Brookfield, WI 53005 (SAN 239-3719).

Pageant Publishing Co., *(Pageant Pub Co)*, P.O. Box 240334, Memphis, TN 38124 (SAN 287-296X).

Pagen, Dennis, *(D Pagen; 0-936310)*, P.O. Box 601, State College, PA 16801 (SAN 238-0250).

Pages to Go!!, *(Pages to Go; 0-943102)*, 2140 N. Iris Lane, Escondido, CA 92026 Tel 619-747-8644 (SAN 240-4206).

Pagurian Press, *(Pagurian; 0-88932; 0-919364)*, Dist. by: Baker & Taylor, 1515 Broadway, New York, NY 10036 Tel 212-673-6600 (SAN 169-5606) Moved, left no forwarding address.

Pair-O'-Dice Press, *(Pair O Dice; 0-943446)*, 525 S. E. 16th Ave., Portland, OR 97214 Tel 503-236-2931 (SAN 240-740X).

Pajarito Pubns, *(Pajarito Pubns; 0-918358)*, 2633 Granite N. W., Albuquerque, NM 87104 Tel 505-242-8075 (SAN 209-8555).

Pakin, Sandra & Associates, Inc., *(Pakin Assocs; 0-9608178)*, 6007 N. Sheridan Rd., Chicago, IL 60660 Tel 312-271-2848 (SAN 240-2637).

Pal, J. B., & Co., Inc., *(J B Pal; 0-916836)*, 904 W. Castlewood Terrace, Chicago, IL 60640 Tel 312-271-0123 (SAN 208-0567).

P.A.L. Press, *(PAL Pr; 0-938034)*, P.O. Box 487, San Anselmo, CA 94960 Tel 805-453-8547 (SAN 220-0791).

Pal Pub., *(Pal Pub; 0-918104)*, Witter Springs, CA 95493 Tel 707-275-2777 (SAN 282-1001); P. O. Box 807, Northridge, CA 91328 Tel 213-360-0600 (SAN 282-101X); 10755 Bachelor Valley Rd., Witter Springs, CA 95493 (SAN 282-1028).

Palace Mission, Incorporated, *(Palace Mission)*, 1622 Spring Mill Rd., Gladwyne, PA 19035 Tel 215-525-5598 (SAN 238-0773); Dist. by: A D F D Pubns., Suite 104, 20 S. 36th St., Philadelphia, PA 19104 Tel 215-662-5381 (SAN 282-6615).

Paladin House Pubs., *(Paladin Hse; 0-88252)*, 2623 Kaneville Rd., Geneva, IL 60134 Tel 312-232-2711 (SAN 203-7041).

Paladin Press, *(Paladin Pr; 0-87364)*, P.O. Box 1307, Boulder, CO 80306 Tel 303-443-7250 (SAN 212-0305).

Paladium Press, *(Paladium Pr; 0-9694090)*, 4413 Tonquil St., Beltsville, MD 20705 (SAN 214-4344).

Palasam Pubs., *(Palasam Pub; 0-9607430)*, 6808 Bowlingdr., Sacramento, CA 95823 (SAN 239-7889).

Palatine Pubns., Inc., *(Palatine Pubns)*, P.O. Drawer 1265, Ruston, LA 71273 (SAN 214-0748).

Pale Horse Press, *(Pale Horse; 0-914720)*, 433 Fair Ave., NE, New Philadelphia, OH 44663 Tel 216-364-3715 (SAN 206-6092).

Paleontological Research Institution, *(Paleo Res; 0-87710)*, 1259 Trumansburg Rd., Ithaca, NY 14850 Tel 607-273-6623 (SAN 204-918X).

Palisades Pubs., *(Palisades Pub; 0-913530)*, P.O. Box 744, Pacific Palisades, CA 90272 Tel 213-454-0826 (SAN 204-9198).

Palm Books, *(Palm Bks; 0-9608036)*, 2301 Sycamore Dr., Dept. 34, Antioch, CA 94509 Tel 415-754-1264 (SAN 239-3727).

Palm Tree Library, *(Palm Tree Lib; 0-933266)*, P.O. Box 84268, Los Angeles, CA 90073 (SAN 212-3789).

Palmer, A. N., Co., The, *(A N Palmer; 0-914268; 0-913941)*, 1720 W. Irving Park Rd., Schaumburg, IL 60193 Tel 800-323-9563 (SAN 202-1374).

Palmer, Birch, *(B Palmer; 0-9610168)*, 1729 Grant Ave., Ogden, UT 84404 (SAN 264-2840).

Palmer, J., Pub., *(J Palmer)*, 155 W. Clark St., No. 5, Manchester, NH 03104 Tel 603-625-5103 (SAN 206-2097).

Palmer Enterprises, *(Palmer Ent)*, P.O. Box 966, Orangevale, CA 95662 Tel 916-988-8435 (SAN 215-1650).

Palmer-Pletsch Associates, *(Palmer-Pletsch; 0-935278)*, P.O. Box 8422, Portland, OR 97207 Tel 503-231-4908 (SAN 209-1933).

Palmer Publications at Amherst, *(Palmer Pubns WI)*, W250 N5467 Hwy. J, Sussex, WI 53089 (SAN 265-9859); Dist. by: Book Services, P.O. Box 94, Sussex, WI 53089 (SAN 265-9867).

Palomar Books, *(Palomar Bks; 0-932882)*, P.O. Box 445, Palmdale, CA 93550 Tel 805-947-5093 (SAN 212-2952).

Palomar Publishing Co., *(Palomar)*, P.O. Box 4444, Whittier, CA 90607 (SAN 204-9201).

Palomino Press, *(Palomino Pr)*, 86-07 144 St., Briarwood, NY 11435 Tel 212-297-5053 (SAN 241-5739).

Palos Verdes Book Company, *(Palos Verdes; 0-936848)*, P. O. Box 456, Lomita, CA 90717 Tel 213-373-1002 (SAN 218-4532).

Pambili Books, *(Pambili Bks; 0-917336)*, 105 Gates St., San Francisco, CA 94110 Tel 415-821-9717 (SAN 208-8010).

Pan-Am Books *See* **Pan-American Publishing Co.**

Pan Am Pubns., *(Pan Am Pubns; 0-87582)*, Pan Am Bldg., New York, NY 10017 (SAN 204-9228).

Pan American Navigation Service, Inc., *(Pan Am Nav; 0-87219)*, P.O. Box 9046, Van Nuys, CA 91409 Tel 213-345-2744 (SAN 202-8506).

Pan-American Publishing Co., *(Pan-Am Publishing Co; 0-932906)*, P.O. Box 1505, Las Vegas, NV 87701 (SAN 212-5366).

Pan/Ishtar Unlimited, *(Pan Ishtar; 0-941698)*, 7559 Santa Monica Blvd., Los Angeles, CA 90046 Tel 213-876-9984 (SAN 239-2747).

Pan Productions, *(Pan Prods; 0-9606100)*, Box 72, Coronado, CA 92118 Tel 619-435-6042 (SAN 216-8480).

Panache Productions, *(Panache Prods; 0-9610596)*, 1388 Moorpark Rd., Thousand Oaks, CA 91360 Tel 805-497-2544 (SAN 264-2859).

Pancake Press, *(Pancake Pr; 0-942908)*, 163 Galewood Circle, San Francisco, CA 94131 Tel 415-665-9215 (SAN 218-0448).

Panda Programs, *(Panda Programs)*, 1872 W. Lotus Place, Brea, CA 92621 (SAN 219-2403).

Pandora's Treasures, *(Pandora's Treasures; 0-9605236)*, 1609 Eastover Terrace, Boise, ID 83706 Tel 208-342-4002 (SAN 282-1036); Orders to: P.O. Box 9051, Boise, ID 83707 (SAN 282-1044).

Panel Pubs., *(Panel Pubs; 0-916592)*, 14 Plaza Rd., Greenvale, NY 11548 Tel 516-484-0006 (SAN 204-921X).

Panjandrum Books, *(Panjandrum; 0-915572)*, 11321 Iowa Ave., Suite 1, Los Angeles, CA 90025 Tel 213-477-8771 (SAN 282-1257); Dist. by: Publisher's Group West, 5855 Beaudry, Emeryville, CA 94608 Tel 415-549-3033 (SAN 202-8522); Dist. by: Bruce Miller, 1936 N. Clark St., Chicago, IL 60614 (SAN 202-8530); Dist. by: Como Sales Inc., 799 Broadway, New York, NY 10013 (SAN 202-8549); Dist. by: Doug Paton, North East Book Sales, 820 Oak Ridge Ave., North Attleboro, MA 02760 (SAN 168-9509); Dist. by: Bookpeople, 2940 Seventh St., Berkeley, CA 94710 (SAN 168-9517); Dist. by: The Distributors, South Bend, IN 46624 (SAN 212-0364); Dist. by: Ingram Book Co., P.O. Box 17266, Nashville, TN 37217 (SAN 169-7978); Dist. by: Henry Walck, Jr., 731 E. Shore Dr., Ithaca, NY 14850 (SAN 282-1338); Dist. by: Inland Book Co., East Haven, CT 46618 (SAN 200-4151).

Panoptic Enterprises, *(Panoptic Ent; 0-912481)*, P.O. Box 1099, Woodbridge, VA 22193-0099 Tel 703-670-2812 (SAN 265-3141).

Panorama West Books, *(Panorama West; 0-914330)*, 8 E. Olive Ave., Fresno, CA 93728 (SAN 216-0501).

Pantheon Books, Div. of Random House, Inc., *(Pantheon)*, 201 E. 50th St., New York, NY 10022 Tel 212-751-2600 (SAN 202-862X); Orders to: Random House, Inc., 400 Hahn Rd., Westminster, MD 21157 (SAN 202-5515).

Paolino, Adele, *(A Paolino; 0-9611448)*, 50 Bedford Ave., Brezzy Point, NY 11697 Tel 212-945-2142 (SAN 277-6995).

Papa's Pr., *(Papa's Pr; 0-9601968)*, P.O. Box 81555, San Diego, CA 92138 Tel 619-582-6294 (SAN 207-6292).

Paper Bag Players, *(Paper Bag)*, 50 Riverside Dr., New York, NY 10024 (SAN 212-9566).

Paper Pile Press of San Anselmo, *(Paper Pile)*, 20 Woodland Ave., San Anselmo, CA 91090 (SAN 287-3087);P.O. Box 337, San Anselmo, CA 94960 (SAN 287-3095).

Paper Tiger Paperbacks, Inc., *(Paper Tiger Pap; 0-933334)*, 1512 N.W. Seventh Place, Gainesville, FL 32603 Tel 904-373-2383 (SAN 212-5374); Orders to: P.O. Box 14015, Gainesville, FL 32604 (SAN 212-5382).

Paper Vision Press *See* **Western Tanager Press**

Paperback Quarterly Pubns., *(Paperback Quarterly; 0-941858)*, 1710 Vincent St., Brownwood, TX 76801 (SAN 239-4669); Dist. by: Borgo Press, P.O. Box 2845, San Bernardino, CA 92406 (SAN 208-9459).

Paperbacks Plus Press, *(Paperbacks Plus; 0-942186)*, 108 East Davis, Mesquite, TX 75149 (SAN 262-0545).

Paperweight Press, *(Paperweight Pr; 0-933756)*, 761 Chestnut St., Santa Cruz, CA 95060 (SAN 212-5390).

Papillon Press, *(Papillon Pr)*, 1232 Vallecito Rd., Carpinteria, CA 93013 Tel 805-684-5038 (SAN 213-1447).

Papillon Pubns., *(Papillon Pubns; 0-938750)*, P.O. Box 7197, San Jose, CA 95150 Tel 408-972-8215 (SAN 238-7468).

Pappani, Debra Ann, *(Pappani; 0-9606062)*, 1990 Hurst Ave., San Jose, CA 95125 Tel 408-264-9907 (SAN 216-9207).

Papyrus Pubs., *(Papyrus Pubs; 0-943698)*, P.O. Box 466, Yonkers, NY 10704 Tel 914-664-0840 (SAN 238-079X).

Para Pub., *(Para Pub; 0-915516)*, P.O. Box 4232-R, Santa Barbara, CA 93101 Tel 805-968-7277 (SAN 282-1451); Dist. by: Baker & Taylor, 50 Kirby Ave., Somerville, NJ 08876 (SAN 169-4901); Dist. by: Bookpeople, 2940 Seventh St., Berkeley, CA 94710 (SAN 200-4151); Dist. by: Inland Book Co., P.O. Box 261, East Haven, CT 06512 Tel 203-467-4257 (SAN 282-1486); Dist. by: Publishers Group/West, 5855 Beaudry St., Emeryville, CA 94608 (SAN 202-8522).

Para Research, Inc., *(Para Res; 0-914918)*, 85 Eastern Ave., Glouster, MA 01930 Tel 617-283-3438 (SAN 213-4438).

Parable, *(Parable)*, 38 N. Austin Blvd., Oak Park, IL 60302 (SAN 283-9792).

Parable Press, *(Parable Pr; 0-917250)*, 136 Gray St., Amherst, MA 01002 Tel 413-253-5634 (SAN 208-4449).

Parabolic Press, Inc., *(Parabolic Pr; 0-915760),* P.O. Box 3032, Stanford, CA 94305 Tel 415-328-1084 (SAN 207-5814).
Parachuting Resources, *(Parachuting Res; 0-933382),* MC P.O. Box 1291, Dayton, OH 45402 Tel 513-256-2676 (SAN 212-5404).
Paraclete Press, *(Paraclete Pr; 0-941478),* Box 1568, 5 Bayview Dr., Orleans, MA 02653 Tel 617-255-4685 (SAN 282-1508).
Paradigm Press, *(Paradigm Pr; 0-937572),* 127 Greenbrae Boardwalk, Greenbrae, CA 94904 Tel 415-461-5457 (SAN 220-0821); Dist. by: Bookpeople, 2940 Seventh St., Berkeley, CA 94710 (SAN 168-9517).
Paradise Press, *(Paradise Pr; 0-940806),* P.O. Box 5306, Santa Monica, CA 90405 Tel 213-392-4098 (SAN 219-6190).
Paradox Publishing Co., *(Paradox Pub Co; 0-89422),* 2476 Buttonwood Court, Florissant, MO 63031 Tel 314-838-0241 (SAN 209-5416).
Paragon Associates, Inc., *(Paragon Assocs; 0-89477),* P. O. Box 23618, Nashville, TN 37202 Tel 615-327-2835 (SAN 209-9780); Dist. by: Alexandria House, P.O. Box 300, Alexandria, IN 46001 (SAN 209-9799).
Paragon Book Reprint Corp., *(Paragon; 0-8188),* 14 E. 38th St., New York, NY 10016 Tel 212-532-4920 (SAN 213-1986).
Paragon Press/Dynapress, *(Paragon-Dynapress; 0-942910),* P.O. Box 866, Fern Park, FL 32730 Tel 305-695-3083 (SAN 240-3234).
Paragon Productions, *(Paragon Prods; 0-9602184),* 817 Pearl St., Denver, CO 80203 Tel 303-832-7687 (SAN 213-2702).
Paragon-Reiss, Div. of National Paragon Corp., *(Paragon-Reiss; 0-910199),* 57-07 31st Ave., Woodside, NY 11377 Tel 212-728-5300 (SAN 241-4244).
Paragraph Press, *(Paragraph Pr; 0-915462),* 204 Circle Dr., P.O. Box 1107, Felton, CA 95018 Tel 408-335-4406 (SAN 207-4974).
Parameter Press, *(Parameter Pr; 0-88203),* 705 Main St., Wakefield, MA 01880 Tel 617-245-9290 (SAN 202-8662).
Paramount Publishing, *(Paramount; 0-918668),* 800 Roosevelt Rd., Suite 413, Bldg. B, Glen Ellyn, IL 60137 Tel 312-790-2483 (SAN 212-6796).
Paramount Publishing, *(Paramount TX; 0-942376),* P. O. Box 3730, Amarillo, TX 79106 Tel 806-355-1040 (SAN 238-1028).
Paranoid Pubns., *(Paranoid Pubns),* P.O. Box 152, 108 W. Lincoln, Onarga, IL 60955 Tel 815-268-7621 (SAN 212-7857).
Parapsych Press, *(Parapsych Pr; 0-911106),* P.O. Box 6847, College Sta., Durham, NC 27708 Tel 919-688-8241 (SAN 204-9252).
Parapsychology Foundation, Inc., *(Parapsych Foun; 0-912232),* 228 E. 71st St., New York, NY 10021 Tel 212-628-1550 (SAN 203-6851).
Parchment Press, *(Parchment Pr; 0-88428),* 5345 Atlanta Hwy., Montgomery, AL 36193 Tel 205-272-5820 (SAN 202-8670).
Pardo Press, The, *(Pardo Pr; 0-9609204),* Northgate Apts. 110-H, One Mile Rd., Cranbury, NJ 08512 Tel 609-443-8533 (SAN 241-4252).
Parent-Child Press, *(Parent-Child Pr; 0-9601016),* P.O. Box 767, 4201 Second Ave., Altoona, PA 16603 Tel 814-946-5213 (SAN 208-4333).
Parent Scene, *(Parent Scene; 0-910529),* P.O. Box 2222, 1280 E. San Bernadino Ave., Redlands, CA 92373 Tel 714-792-2412 (SAN 260-244X).
Parenthesis Press, *(Parenthesis Pr; 0-9601580),* P.O. Box 114, Bridgewater College, Bridgewater, VA 22812 Tel 703-828-6656 (SAN 202-8689).
Parenting Press, *(Parenting Pr; 0-9602862; 0-943990),* 7750 31st Ave. N.E., Seattle, WA 98115 (SAN 215-6938).
Parents Anonymous, *(Parents Anon),* 22330 Hawthorne Blvd., Suite 208, Torrance, CA 90505 (SAN 217-2607).
Parents Magazine Press, *(Parents; 0-8193),* 685 Third Ave., New York, NY 10017 Tel 212-878-8611 (SAN 202-8697); Dist. by: Elsevier-Dutton Publishing Co., 2 Park Ave., Dept. JH, New York, NY 10016 Tel 212-725-1818 (SAN 282-6348).
Parents' Pointers Pubns., *(Parents Pointers; 0-9608756),* Route 1, Box 238, Lawrenceburg, TN 38464 Tel 615-762-2663 (SAN 241-063X).

Parey, Paul, Scientific Pubs., *(Parey Sci Pubs),* 35 W. 38th St., No. 3W, New York, NY 10018 Tel 212-730-0518 (SAN 216-0021).
Park, S.H., *(S H Park; 0-9604440),* P.O. Box 7474, Trenton, NJ 08628 Tel 609-883-3551 (SAN 215-1685).
Park Avenue Books, Inc., *(Park Ave Bks; 0-942418),* GPO Box 1886, New York, NY 10116 Tel 212-689-0269 (SAN 238-1850).
Park City Press, Div. of Sunflower Publishing, Inc, *(Park City Pr),* P.O. Box 25, Glenwood Landing, NY 11457 (SAN 287-2838).
Park Press Co., *(Park Pr Co; 0-941226),* 2612 N. Mattis Ave., Champaign, IL 61820 (SAN 239-4685).
Park Publishing, Inc., *(Park Pub; 0-9603294),* 1999 Shepard Rd., St. Paul, MN 55116 Tel 612-698-1667 (SAN 204-9260).
Park View Press, Inc., *(Park View; 0-87813),* 1066 Chicago Ave., Harrisonburg, VA 22801 Tel 703-434-0765 (SAN 204-9279).
Parker, Clayton A., Publications, *(Parker Pubns; 0-9606438),* 450 Wendell Dr., Salt Lake City, UT 84115 Tel 801-266-2292 (SAN 218-5768).
Parker, D. Coffey, *(D C Parker),* 28 Abbot Rd., Springfield, IL 62704 Tel 217-787-7620 (SAN 216-003X).
Parker, Gertrude M., *(G M Parker; 0-89279),* Southview, Apt. 4, Stanhope, IA 50246 (SAN 286-3480).
Parker & Son Pubns., Inc., *(Parker & Son; 0-911110),* Box 60001, Los Angeles, CA 90060 Tel 213-727-1088 (SAN 202-8719).
Parker Brothers Publishing, Div. of Parker Brothers, *(Parker Bro; 0-910313),* 50 Dunham Rd., Beverly, MA 01915 Tel 617-927-7600 (SAN 241-4260).
Parker Engineering Publishing, *(Parker Engine Pub; 0-9611048),* 1727 Conestoga St. Unit G, Boulder, CO 80301 Tel 303-443-4758 (SAN 283-3417).
Parker Press, The, *(Parker Pr; 0-939562),* 31 Marlboro St., Newburyport, MA 01950 Tel 617-462-3427 (SAN 216-4310).
Parker Publishing Co. *See* Prentice-Hall, Inc.
Parkhurst/Little Rock, *(Parkhurst-Little; 0-941780),* 1010 W. Third St., Little Rock, AR 72201 Tel 501-376-4516 (SAN 239-2755).
Parkhurst Press, *(Parkhurst; 0-939500),* P.O. Box 143, Laguna Beach, CA 92652 (SAN 216-4329).
Parkhurst Pubns., Inc., *(Parkhurst Pubns; 0-911471),* 1545 Promenade Bank Tower, Richardson, TX 75080 Tel 214-231-7181 (SAN 274-4562).
Parkside Press, *(Parkside; 0-941180),* 2026 Parkside Court, West Linn, OR 97068 (SAN 239-3735).
Parkside Press Publishing Co., *(Parkside Pub Co; 0-911585),* P.O. Box 11585, Santa Ana, CA 92711 Tel 714-541-5160 (SAN 264-2883).
Parkway Press, *(Parkway; 0-9610176),* P.O. Box 161, Roslyn Heights, NY 11577 Tel 516-621-1827 (SAN 274-4570).
Parkway Press, Inc., *(Parkway Pr; 0-930408),* 3347 E. Calhoun Pkwy., Minneapolis, MN 55408 Tel 612-827-3347 (SAN 211-0474).
Parkway Pubns., *(Parkway Pubns; 0-9608398),* 5616 W. Rita Drive, West Allis, WI 53219 (SAN 238-0803).
Parkwest Publications, *(Parkwest Pubns; 0-88186),* 400 Central Pk. W., New York, NY 10025 Tel 212-222-6100 (SAN 264-6814).
Parliamentary Publishing, *(Parliamentary Pub; 0-942302),* 2230 Stokes St., No. 4, San Jose, CA 95128 Tel 408-293-9319 (SAN 238-0811).
Parnassos, Greek Cultural Soc. of NY, Inc., *(Parnassos NY; 0-933824),* Box 2928, Grand Central Sta., New York, NY 10163 Tel 203-464-2511 (SAN 210-6493).
Parnassus Imprints, *(Parnassus Imprints; 0-940160),* 21 Canal Rd., Box 335, Orleans, MA 02653 Tel 617-225-2932 (SAN 217-0809).
Parnassus Press, *(Parnassus; 0-87466),* 6421 Regent St., Oakland, CA 94618 Tel 415-654-1368 (SAN 202-1412); Orders to: Houghton Mifflin Co., Wayside Rd., Burlington, MA 01803 (SAN 215-3793).
Parpaglion & Co., *(Parpaglion; 0-9604252),* 1241 Folkstone Way, Cherry Hill, NJ 08034 (SAN 214-4360).

Parr Publishing Co., Inc., *(Parr Pub; 0-89473),* 1200 S. Post Oak Rd., Suite 428, Houston, TX 77056 Tel 713-626-7830 (SAN 209-6315).
Parrish Art Museum, the, *(Parrish Art; 0-943526),* 25 Jobs Lane, Southampton, NY 11968 Tel 516-283-2118 (SAN 240-7418).
Parrot Mountain, Inc., *(Parrot Mntn),* P.O. Box 246, Ranchita, CA 92066 Tel 714-782-3335 (SAN 215-2215).
Parsley Press, *(Parsley Pr; 0-9608222),* Box 94 Turnpike Sta., Shrewsbury, MA 01545 Tel 617-366-2511 (SAN 240-4214).
Part-Ease, *(Part-Ease; 0-9607664),* P.O. Box 144, New Milford, NJ 07646 (SAN 238-082X).
Parthenon Press, *(Parthenon Pr; 0-942276),* 51 E. 42nd St., Suite 517, New York, NY 10017 Tel 212-361-7400 (SAN 239-5835).
Parthenon Pubns., *(Parthenon Pubns),* 139 Santa Fe Ave., El Cerrito, CA 94530 Tel 415-527-1374 (SAN 214-4379).
Partington, Paul G., *(P G Partington; 0-9602538),* 7320 S. Gretna Ave., Whittier, CA 90606 (SAN 212-3797).
Partisan Press, Inc., *(Partisan Pr; 0-935150),* P.O. Box 31387, Seattle, WA 98103 (SAN 215-6946).
Partner Press, *(Partner Pr; 0-933212),* Box 124, Livonia, MI 48152 (SAN 217-7865).
Partners for Livable Places, *(Partners Livable; 0-941182),* 1429 21 St., N.W., Washington, DC 20036 Tel 202-887-5990 (SAN 200-402X); Dist. by: Publishing Center for Cultural Resources, 625 Broadway, New York, NY 10012 (SAN 212-6036).
Partners in Publishing, *(PIP; 0-937660),* P.O. Box 50347, Tulsa, OK 74150 Tel 918-584-5906 (SAN 209-6323).
Partners Press, *(Partners Pr NJ; 0-942676),* Canal Rd., R.D.1, Princeton, NJ 08540 (SAN 239-8656).
Partnership Foundation, the, *(Partnership Foundation; 0-934538),* C/O Capon Springs & Farms, Capon Springs, WV 26823 (SAN 220-9918).
Partridge Pair, Inc., The, *(Partridge Pair; 0-9606440),* P.O. Box 61, Sandy Springs, SC 29677 Tel 803-261-8430 (SAN 218-5776).
Pasadena Art Alliance, *(Pasadena Art; 0-937042),* 314 S. Mentor Ave., Pasadena, CA 91106 Tel 213-795-9276 (SAN 213-5434).
Pascal Pubs, *(Pascal Pubs; 0-938836),* 21 Sunnyside Ave., Wellesley, MA 02181 (SAN 215-3319).
Pass Press, *(Pass; 0-9601870),* 170 2nd Ave., 2A, New York, NY 10003 (SAN 210-5411).
Passive Solar Institute, *(Passive Solar; 0-933490),* 1625 Curtis St., Berkeley, CA 94702 Tel 415-526-1549 (SAN 282-1516)Solar Usage Now, P.O. Box 306, Bascom, OH 44809 (SAN 282-1524).
Passport Press, *(Passport Pr; 0-930016),* Box 596, Moscow, VT 05662 Tel 802-253-9387 (SAN 211-7533).
Past in Glass, *(Past in Glass; 0-9600212),* 515 Northridge Dr., Boulder City, NV 89005 (SAN 204-9317).
Pastore Press, *(Pastore),* Seven Shetland Lane, Stony Brook, NY 11790 Tel 516-751-2254 (SAN 209-4703).
Pata Pubns., *(Pata Pubns; 0-940808),* P.O. Drawer F, Foresthill, CA 95631 Tel 916-367-3479 (SAN 219-841X).
Patch As Patch Can, *(Patch As Patch; 0-9601896),* P.O. Box 843, Port Washington, NY 11050 Tel 516-883-2885 (SAN 239-8575).
Patchwork Pubns., *(Patchwork Pubns; 0-930628),* 2961 Industrial Rd., Las Vegas, NV 89109 Tel 702-732-4541 (SAN 211-3430).
Patelson, Joseph, Music House , Ltd., *(J Patelson Mus; 0-915282),* 160 W. 56th St., New York, NY 10019 Tel 212-757-5587 (SAN 203-9028).
Patent Data Pubns., Inc., *(Patent Data; 0-935714),* 901 N. President St., Wheaton, IL 60187 (SAN 213-9448).
Pathfinder Press, *(Path Pr NY; 0-87348),* 410 West St., New York, NY 10014 Tel 212-741-0690 (SAN 202-5906).

Pathfinder Pubns., *(Pathfinder Pubns; 0-9603354),* 4704 Wilford Way, Minneapolis, MN 55435 Tel 612-835-1128 (SAN 212-9264).

Pathfinder Pubns., Inc., *(Path Pubns NJ; 0-939888),* 210 Central Ave., Madison, NJ 07940 Tel 201-822-2395 (SAN 216-9215).

Pathway Books, *(Pathway Bks; 0-935538),* 700 Parkview Terrace, Golden Valley, MN 55416 Tel 612-377-1521 (SAN 213-4241).

Pathway Pr., *(Pathway Pr; 0-87148),* 1080 Montgomery Ave., Cleveland, TN 37311 Tel 615-476-4512 (SAN 202-8727).

Pathway Pubns., Inc., *(Pathway Pubns; 0-9606442),* 1632 Seventh Ave. W., Birmingham, AL 35208 Tel 205-785-9584 (SAN 218-5784).

Pathways Press, *(Pathway Pr CA; 0-9605022),* P.O. Box 11196-A, Palo Alto, CA 94306 (SAN 283-4367).

Patio Pubns., *(Patio Pubns; 0-9696040),* 850 Woodhollow Lane, Buffalo Grove, IL 60090 Tel 312-259-8500 (SAN 216-9223).

Patmos Press, The, *(Patmos Pr; 0-915762),* P.O. Box V, Shepherdstown, WV 25443 Tel 304-876-2086 (SAN 207-4192).

Patrice Press, *(Patrice Pr; 0-935284),* Box 42, Gerald, MO 63037 Tel 314-764-2801 (SAN 203-1019).

Patriotic Education, Inc., *(Patriotic Educ; 0-912530),* P.O. Box 2121, Daytona Beach, FL 32015 Tel 904-252-3414 (SAN 204-9325).

Patriotic Publishers, *(Patriotic Pubs; 0-9608188),* 159 Woodland Ave., Verona, NJ 07044 (SAN 240-124X).

Patron Books *See* **Don Bosco Multimedia**

Pattecky Music Pubs., *(Pattecky Music; 0-9602178),* Box T, College Park, MD 20740 (SAN 213-7844).

Patterns Ltd., *(Patterns Ltd; 0-9609874),* 1341 Ocean Ave., Suite 181, Santa Monica, CA 90401 (SAN 274-4708); Dist. by: Hunter House Inc., Box 3914, San Rafael, CA 94901 Tel 415-883-3530 (SAN 281-7977).

Patterson, Eleanora, Pr., *(E Patterson Pr; 0-9607432),* P.O. Box 343, Putney, VT 05346 (SAN 239-5355).

Patterson, Richard, *(R Patterson; 0-936004),* 3829 William Penn Blvd., Virginia Beach, VA 23452 (SAN 213-8638).

Patterson, W. B., *(W B Patterson; 0-9606968),* 3080 Alaneo Place, Wailuku, Maui, HI 96793 Tel 808-244-5437 (SAN 205-4914).

Pattie Properties, Inc., *(Pattie Prop Inc; 0-911789),* 1403 Springdale Rd., Zephyrhills, FL 33599 Tel 813-782-9187 (SAN 264-2891).

Patton Creative Associates, *(Patton Creative; 0-911003),* 21 Tulip Circle, Salinas, CA 93905 Tel 408-422-4192 (SAN 274-4716).

Pau Hana Press, *(Pau Hana Pr; 0-912921),* 1314 S. King, Suite 1258, Honolulu, HI 96814 (SAN 283-9245).

Paul, Louis, Publishing Co., *(L Paul Pub; 0-9608890),* P.O. Box 27266, Escondido, CA 92027 Tel 714-747-7598 (SAN 241-1156).

Paulette Publishing Co., *(Paulette Pub),* P.O. Box 545, La Canada, CA 91011 (SAN 217-1228).

Paulist Press, *(Paulist Pr; 0-8091),* 545 Island Rd., Ramsey, NJ 07446 Tel 201-825-7300 (SAN 202-5159); Orders to: 301 Island Rd., Mahwah, NJ 07430 (SAN 202-5167).

Paumalu Press, *(Paumalu Pr; 0-9602354),* P.O. Box 3788, San Clemente, CA 92672 Tel 714-496-5922 (SAN 212-7873).

Paunch, *(Paunch; 0-9602478),* 123 Woodward Ave., Buffalo, NY 14214 (SAN 209-1461).

Pauper Press, Inc., *(Pauper Pr; 0-9601144),* Box 303, Two Rivers, WI 54241 Tel 414-794-8817 (SAN 210-2560).

Pavan Pubs., *(Pavan Pubs; 0-915944),* P.O. Box 1661, Palo Alto, CA 94302 Tel 415-327-3960 (SAN 207-5695).

Pavillion of Fashion, *(Pavillion Fashion),* Golden Cove Center, 31244 Palos Verdes Dr., W., Rancho Palos Verdes, CA 90274 Tel (SAN 211-299X).

Paw-Print Press, *(Paw-Print; 0-9608958),* 9012 Spring Hill Lane, Chevy Chase, MD 20815 Tel 301-656-5793 (SAN 241-3469).

Pawnee Publishing Co., Inc., *(Pawnee Pub; 0-913688),* P.O. Box 630, Higginsville, MO 64037 Tel 816-394-2424 (SAN 207-4036).

Pawson, John R., *(Pawson; 0-9602080),* Box 411, Willow Grove, PA 19090 (SAN 213-229X).

Paycock Pr., *(Paycock Pr; 0-9602424),* P.O. Box 3567, Washington, DC 20007 Tel 202-333-1544 (SAN 212-5420).

PDA Publishers Corp., *(PDA Pubs; 0-914886),* 1725 E. Fountain, Mesa, AZ 85203 Tel 602-835-9161 (SAN 207-0340).

Peabody, Robert S., Foundation for Archaeology, *(Peabody Found; 0-939312),* P. O. Box 71, Andover, MA 01810 Tel 617-475-0248 (SAN 207-0006).

Peabody Museum of Archaeology & Ethnology, Harvard Univ., *(Peabody Harvard; 0-87365),* 11 Divinity Ave., Cambridge, MA 02138 Tel 617-495-3938 (SAN 203-1426); Dist. by: Harvard Univ. Pr., 79 Garden St., Cambridge, MA 02138 Tel 617-495-2600 (SAN 200-2043).

Peabody Publishing Co., *(Peabody Pub),* 361 Moraine St., Brockton, MA 02401 Tel 617-588-0860 (SAN 207-2718).

Peace & Gladness Press, *(Peace & Gladness; 0-940460),* P.O. Box 11478, San Francisco, CA 94101 Tel 415-346-0135 (SAN 219-8088).

Peace on Earth Press, *(Peace on Earth; 0-942992),* P.O. Box 3947, Stanford, CA 94305 (SAN 240-4222); P.O. Box 128, Bedford, MA 01730 (SAN 240-4230).

Peace Press, Inc., *(Peace Pr; 0-915238),* 3828 Willat Ave., Culver City, CA 90230 Tel 213-838-7387 (SAN 207-1134).

Peace Ways Pubns., *(Peace Ways; 0-912730),* 11261 Alger St., Warren, MI 48093 (SAN 206-6610).

Peach Mountain Press Ltd., *(Peach Mount Pr; 0-931850),* Rte. 2 Box 195, Charlevoix, MI 49720 Tel 616-547-4701 (SAN 220-9942).

Peach Pubns., *(Peach; 0-918240),* 580 Bridgeport Ave., Milford, CT 06460 Tel 203-877-1411 (SAN 209-472X).

Peachtree Pubs., Ltd., *(Peachtree Pubs; 0-931948),* 494 Armour Circle, N.E., Atlanta, GA 30324 Tel 404-876-8761 (SAN 212-1999).

Peacock, F. E., Pubs., Inc., *(Peacock Pubs; 0-87581),* 115 N. Prospect Ave., Itasca, IL 60143 Tel 312-773-1155 (SAN 202-876X).

Peacock *See* **Bantam Books, Inc.**

Peanut Butter Publishing, *(Peanut Butter; 0-89716),* 2445 76th Ave. S. E., Mercer Island, WA 98040 Tel 206-236-1982 (SAN 212-7881).

Pearl Press, *(Pearl Pr; 0-914566),* 835 West 19th St, Portales, NM 88130 Tel 505-359-0308 (SAN 202-8778).

Pearl-Win Publishing Co., *(Pearl-Win),* Rte. 1 Box 300, Hancock, WI 54943 (SAN 217-1236).

Pearson, Bob, Enterprises, Inc., *(B Pearson; 0-9608378),* Box 9901, Birmingham, AL 35220-0901 Tel 205-854-5657 (SAN 240-4249).

Pearson, J. Michael, *(J M Pearson; 0-916528),* P.O. Box 402844, Ocean View Sta., Miami Beach, FL 33140 Tel 305-538-0346 (SAN 202-1536).

Pearson Museum, The, *(Pearson Museum),* Southern Illinois School of Medicine, P.O. Box 3926, Springfield, IL 62708 (SAN 241-5755).

Peasant Cottage Press, *(Peasant Cottage Pr; 0-9602698),* P. O. Bx 276, Cambria, CA 93428 (SAN 222-237X).

Peat Marwick Mitchell and Company, *(Peat Marwick),* 345 Park Ave, New York, NY 10022 (SAN 226-7071).

Pecalhen, *(Pecalhen; 0-938910),* 14401 S.W. 85th Ave., Miami, FL 33158 Tel 305-235-3858 (SAN 216-0048).

PECCI Educational Pubs., *(Pecci Educ Pubs; 0-943220),* 440 Davis Ct., No. 405, San Francisco, CA 94111 Tel 415-391-8579 (SAN 240-558X).

Peddlers Wagon, *(Peddlers Wagon; 0-9601048),* 610 Spruce St., Dowagiac, MI 49047 Tel 616-782-3270 (SAN 204-9309).

Pediatric Projects, Inc., *(Pediatric Projects; 0-912599),* P.O. Box 1880, Santa Monica, CA 90406 Tel 213-459-7710 (SAN 282-8146).

Pee Wee Books, *(Pee Wee; 0-941352),* Tel 707-778-6473; c/o E. F. Hutton & Co., Kaiser Center, 300 Lakeside Dr., Oakland, CA 94612 (SAN 239-0167).

Peebles Press International Inc., *(Peebles Pr; 0-85690),* 1865 Broadway, New York, NY 10023 Tel 212-586-2800 (SAN 207-0529); Dist. by: Farrar, Straus & Giroux, Inc., 19 Union Square, New York, NY 10003 Tel 212-741-6900 (SAN 206-782X).

Peek Pubns., *(Peek Pubns; 0-917962),* 574 Weddell Dr., Suite 4, Sunnyvale, CA 94086 (SAN 202-1382); Orders to: P.O. Box 50123, Palo Alto, CA 94303 Tel 408-745-1125 (SAN 202-1390).

Peeples, Edwin A., *(Peeples; 0-9600080),* Vixen Hill, R.D. 2, Phoenixville, PA 19460 Tel 215-827-7241 (SAN 204-9368).

Peer-Southern Pubns., *(Peer-Southern),* 1740 Broadway, New York, NY 10019 (SAN 206-3034).

Peerless Pub. Co., *(Peerless; 0-930234),* 2745 Lafitte Ave., New Orleans, LA 70119 Tel 504-486-6225 (SAN 210-3222).

Pegasus, Affiliated with Bobbs-Merrill Co., Inc., *(Pegasus),* 4300 W. 72nd St., P.O. Box 7080, Indianapolis, IN 46206 Tel 317-298-5686 (SAN 202-5752).

Pegasus Company, *(Pegasus Co SC; 0-9602144),* Rt. 1, Rambling Path, Anderson, SC 29622 (SAN 221-7562).

Pegasus Pubns., *(Pegasus Pubns; 0-936552),* 834 N. Occidental, Los Angeles, CA 90026 (SAN 222-1101).

Pegasus Rex *See* **Fell, Frederick, Pubs., Inc.**

Pegasus Rex Press, Inc., The, *(Pegasus Rex NJ; 0-937484),* 695 Bloomfield Ave., Montclair, NJ 07042 Tel 201-744-3774 (SAN 215-2061).

Pegus Press, *(Pegus Pr; 0-941218),* 648 W. Sierra Ave., Box 429, Clovis, CA 93612 (SAN 241-5763).

Pejepscot Press, *(Pejepscot; 0-917638),* 10 Mason St., Brunswick, ME 04011 Tel 207-729-3442 (SAN 202-1447).

Pelican Books, *(Pelican Bks; 0-941998),* 22632 Claude Circle, El Toro, CA 92630 (SAN 239-4707).

Pelican Books *See* **Penguin Books, Inc.**

Pelican Hill Publishing Company Incorporated the, *(Pelican Hill),* 923 Lincoln Ave., Stuart, FL 33497 Tel 305-286-3387 (SAN 226-8299).

Pelican Publishing Co., Inc., *(Pelican; 0-911116; 0-88289),* 1101 Monroe St., P.O. Box 189, Gretna, LA 70053 Tel 504-368-1175 (SAN 212-0623).

Pella Publishing Co., Inc., *(Pella Pub; 0-918618),* 461 Eighth Ave., New York, NY 10001 Tel 212-279-9586 (SAN 210-6183).

Peloquin Pubns., *(Peloquin Pubns; 0-936448),* P.O. Box 121, Richland, WA 99352 (SAN 214-0845).

Pelton, Charles L., *(C L Pelton; 0-931470),* 201 S. Lloyd, Suite 230 Physician's Plaza, Aberdeen, SD 57401 (SAN 211-965X).

Pemberley Pr., *(Pemberley Pr; 0-9607830),* 250 W. 54th St. Rm. 800, New York, NY 10019 Tel 212-757-9631 (SAN 238-1052).

Pen & Booth, *(Pen & Booth; 0-9605686),* 1608 "R" St. N.W., Washington, DC 20009 (SAN 213-1439).

Pen & Ink Pr., *(Pen & Ink; 0-9607544),* c/o Banyan Books, Inc., P.O. Box 431160, Miami, FL 33143 Tel 305-665-6011 (SAN 208-340X).

Pen & Podium, Inc., *(Pen & Podium; 0-9603982),* 40 Central Park South, New York, NY 10019 (SAN 214-0756).

Pen-Art Pubs., *(Pen-Art),* 402 Fairview Ave., Westwood, NJ 07675 Tel 201-664-8412 (SAN 211-3287).

Pen Notes Inc., *(Pen Notes; 0-939564),* 134 Westside Ave., Freeport, NY 11520 (SAN 216-4337).

Pendell Publishing Co., *(Pendell Pub; 0-87812),* 1700 James Savage Rd., P.O. Box 2066 Bip, Midland, MI 48640 Tel 517-496-3333 (SAN 202-8786).

Pendle Hill Pubns., *(Pendle Hill; 0-87574),* Pendle Hill, 338 Plush Mill Rd, Wallingford, PA 19086 Tel 215-566-4507 (SAN 202-8794).

Pendragon House, Inc., *(Pendragon Hse; 0-916988),* 2898 Joseph Ave., Campbell, CA 95008 Tel 408-371-2737 (SAN 208-8037).

Pendragon Press, *(Pendragon NY; 0-918728),* 162 W. 13th St., New York, NY 10011 Tel 212-243-3494 (SAN 213-1463).

Pendragon Press, *(Pendragon Oregon; 0-914010),* P.O. Box 14834, Portland, OR 97214 Tel 503-232-0869 (SAN 204-9376).

Pendulum Books, (Pendulum Bks; 0-941760), P.O. Box 3627, 615 Garnet St., Redondo Beach, CA 90277 Tel 213-372-0925 (SAN 239-2771).

Pendulum Press, Inc., (Pendulum Pr; 0-88301), Academic Bldg., Saw Mill Rd., West Haven, CT 06516 Tel 203-933-2551 (SAN 202-8808).

Penelope Press, (Penelope Pr; 0-9607018), P.O. Box 31882, Seattle, WA 98103 (SAN 239-4723).

Penfield Press, (Penfield; 0-9603858; 0-941016), 215 Brown St., Iowa City, IA 52240 Tel 319-337-9998 (SAN 221-6671).

Penguin Books, Inc., (Penguin; 0-14), 40 W. 23rd St., New York, NY 10010 Tel 212-807-7300 (SAN 202-5914). *Imprints:* Pelican Books (Pelican); Peregrine Books (Peregrine); Puffin Books (Puffin).

Peninsula Press, (Peninsula NY; 0-9609012), Water's Edge, Fishers Island, NY 06390 Tel 515-788-7868 (SAN 241-3485).

Peninsula Publishing, (Peninsula; 0-932146), P.O. Box 867, Los Altos, CA 94022 Tel 415-948-2511 (SAN 212-257X).

Peninsula Publishing, Inc., (Peninsula WA; 0-918146), P.O. Box 412, Port Angeles, WA 98362 Tel 206-457-7550 (SAN 210-1300).

Peninsula Pubns., (Peninsula Pubns; 0-914372), 26030 New Bridge Dr., Los Altos Hills, CA 94022 Tel 415-857-0381 (SAN 202-8816).

Penmaen Press, Ltd., (Penmaen Pr; 0-915778), R.D. 2, P.O. Box 145, Great Barrington, MA 01230 Tel 413-528-2749 (SAN 208-1113).

Pennacook-Sokoki Inter-Tribal Nation New Hampshire Indian Nation, (Pennacook-Sokoki; 0-9601834), c/o New Hampshire Indian Council, Inc., 913 Elm St., Manchester, NH 03101 Tel 603-274-4929).

Pennant Press, (Pennant Pr; 0-913458), 7620 Miramar Rd. No. 4100, San Diego, CA 92126 Tel 619-695-1810 (SAN 201-9884).

Pennington Trading Post, (Pennington; 0-911120), c/o Eunice Pennington, Fremont, MO 63941 (SAN 204-9392).

Penns Valley Pubs., (Penns Valley; 0-931992), 1298 S. 28th St., Harrisburg, PA 17111 Tel 717-232-5844 (SAN 202-1455).

Pennsylvania Academy of Fine Arts, (Penn Acad Art; 0-943836), Broad & Cherry Sts., Philadelphia, PA 19102 (SAN 280-0748).

Pennsylvania Academy of Science, (Penn Science; 0-9606670), Dept. of Biology, Lafayette College, Easton, PA 18042 Tel 215-250-5464 (SAN 219-6220).

Pennsylvania Assoc. of Notaries, (Penn Assoc Not), 625 Stanwix St., Pittsburgh, PA 15222 Tel 412-281-0678 (SAN 264-2921).

Pennsylvania Crime Commission, (Penna Crime), 523 E Lancaster Ave, St Davids, PA 19087 (SAN 226-7101).

Pennsylvania German Society, (Penn German Soc; 0-911122), R.D. 4, Box 71, New Oxford, PA 17350 Tel 717-627-4106 (SAN 205-1958); Orders to: Box 97, Breinigsville, PA 18031 (SAN 205-1966).

Pennsylvania Historical & Museum Commission, (Pa Hist & Mus; 0-911124; 0-89271), Division of History, Box 1026, Harrisburg, PA 17120 Tel 717-783-9868 (SAN 282-1532); Orders to: Publication Sales Program, Box 1026, Harrisburg, PA 17120 Tel 717-783-2618 (SAN 282-1540).

Pennsylvania State Univ. Press, (Pa St U Pr; 0-271), 215 Wagner Bldg., University Park, PA 16802 Tel 814-865-1327 (SAN 213-5760).

Pennwell Publishing Co., Div. of Pennwell Books, (Pennwell Pub; 0-87814), P.O. Box 1260, Tulsa, OK 74101 Tel 918-663-4220 (SAN 282-1559); Orders to: P.O. Box 21288, Tulsa, OK 74121 Tel 918-663-4225 (SAN 282-1567).

Pennyfarthing Press, (Pennyfarthing; 0-930800), 2000 Center St., No. 1226, Berkeley, CA 94704 Tel 415-845-1990 (SAN 211-920X).

Pennypress, The, (Pennypress; 0-937604), 1100 23rd Ave., E., Seattle, WA 98112 Tel 206-325-1419 (SAN 215-6954); Dist. by: Madrona Publishers, Inc., 113 Madrona Place East, Seattle, WA 98112 Tel 206-624-6840 (SAN 281-9678).

Penobscot Bay Press, Inc., (Penobscot Bay), Box 36, Stonington, ME 04681 (SAN 212-2960).

Penokie Press, (Penokie Pr; 0-9611052), 404 Neipsic Rd., Glastonbury, CT 06033 (SAN 282-8332).

PenOwl Press, (PenOwl Pr; 0-9610680), P.O. Box 1011, Jamaica, NY 11431 (SAN 283-9253).

Penrith Publishing Co., (Penrith; 0-936522), P.O. Box 18070, Cleveland Heights, OH 44118 (SAN 214-2163).

Pensacola Historical Society, (Pensacola Hist; 0-939566), 405 S. Adams St., Pensacola, FL 32501 Tel 204-433-1559 (SAN 216-6909).

Penseur Press, (Penseur Pr; 0-9604044), P.O. Box 659, El Cerrito, CA 94530 (SAN 214-0764).

Penso Pubns., Inc., (Penso Pubns; 0-943796), P.O. Box 10635, Houston, TX 77292 Tel 713-861-9785 (SAN 241-0656).

Pentagram, (Pentagram; 0-915316; 0-937596), Box 379, Markesan, WI 53946 Tel 414-398-2161 (SAN 207-1789).

Pentangle Press, (Pentangle Pr; 0-914748), P. O. Box 5001, 132 Lasky Dr., Beverly Hills, CA 90212 Tel 213-278-4996 (SAN 206-6114).

Pente Games, Inc., (Pente Games; 0-9609414), P.O. Box 1546, Stillwater, OK 74076 Tel 405-624-2910 (SAN 262-8619).

Pentelic Press, (Pentelic Pr; 0-913110), 1032 Cambridge Crescent, Norfolk, VA 23508 (SAN 204-9414).

Penumbra, Inc., (Penumbra Inc; 0-9602030), 302 Termino Ave., Long Beach, CA 90814 (SAN 281-1575); Orders to: 3001 W. Big Beaver Rd., Ste. 620, Troy, MI 48084 (SAN 282-1583).

Penumbra Press, The, (Penumbra Press), Box 12, Lisbon, IA 52253 Tel 319-455-2182 (SAN 209-858X).

People for Open Space, (PFOS; 0-9605262), 512 Second St., San Francisco, CA 94107 (SAN 215-899X).

People Places, Inc., (People Places; 0-9604068), P.O. Box 110, Verona, VA 24482 (SAN 214-0772).

People's Computer Co., (Peoples Computer; 0-918790), P.O. Box E, 1263 El Camino, Menlo Park, CA 94025 Tel 415-323-3111 (SAN 210-4830).

People's Yellow Pages Press, The, (People's Yellow Pages), P.O. Box 31291, San Francisco, CA 94131 Tel 415-641-4011 (SAN 216-4345).

Pepper Publishing, (Pepper Pub; 0-914468), 2901 E. Mabel, Tucson, AZ 85716 Tel 602-881-0783 (SAN 201-8780).

Peppercorn *See* Putnam Publishing Group, The

Pepperdine Univ. Press, (Pepperdine U Pr), Malibu, CA 90265 Tel 213-456-4138 (SAN 219-8096).

Peppertree Publishing, (Peppertree; 0-936822). Box 1712, Newport Beach, CA 92663 Tel 714-642-3669 (SAN 214-4387).

Pepys Press, The, (Pepys Pr; 0-9602270), 1270 Fifth Ave., Apt. 5G, New York, NY 10029 Tel 212-348-6847 (SAN 212-4343).

Pequod Press, (Pequod Press; 0-937912), P.O. Box 122, Northridge, CA 91328 (SAN 262-0553).

Per, (PER), Suite 918, 818 Olive St., St. Louis, MO 63101 Tel 314-241-1445 (SAN 239-5843).

Per Ardua Press, (Per Ardua; 0-917252), 6216 Ellenview Ave., Canoga Park, CA 91307 Tel 213-888-1421 (SAN 208-8053).

Per. Inc., (Per Inc; 0-9602446), P. O. Bx 11465, Memphis, TN 38111 (SAN 282-7107); Dist. by: The Collection, P.O. Box 11465, Memphis, TN 38111 (SAN 282-7115).

Peradam Pub. Hse., (Peradam Pub Hse; 0-930434), 1204 11th St., Bellingham, WA 98825 (SAN 274-5089).

Perception Press, (Perception; 0-930176), P.O. Box 265, Port Bolivar, TX 77650 Tel 713-684-3880 (SAN 209-4738).

Perception Pubns., (Perception Pubns; 0-940406), 1814 W. Seldon Lane, Phoenix, AZ 85021 (SAN 265-3931).

Perdido Bay Press, The, (Perdido Bay; 0-933776), Rte. 2 Box 323, Pensacola, FL 32506 (SAN 215-1693).

Pere Marquette Press, (Pere Marquette; 0-934640), P.O. Box 495, Alton, IL 62002 (SAN 206-3042).

Peregrine Associates, (Peregrine Assoc), P.O. Box 22292, Fort Lauderdale, FL 33316 Tel 305-987-2423 (SAN 239-5851).

Peregrine Books *See* Penguin Books, Inc.

Peregrine Press, (Peregrine Pr; 0-933614), Box 751, Old Saybrook, CT 06475 Tel 203-388-0285 (SAN 213-3474).

Peregrine Smith Books, (Peregrine Smith; 0-87905), P.O. Box 667, Layton, UT 84041 Tel 801-544-9800 (SAN 201-9906).

Perennial Library *See* Harper & Row Pubs., Inc.

Perfect Graphic Arts, (Perfect Graphic; 0-911126), 14 Dearborn Dr., Old Tappan, NJ 07675 Tel 201-767-8575 (SAN 204-9430).

Perfect Productions, (Perfect Prods; 0-941648), P.O. Box 396, Larkspur, CA 94939 Tel 415-924-0850 (SAN 239-278X).

Performance Dynamics, Inc., (Perf Dynamics; 0-912940), 400 Lanidex Plaza, Parsippany, NJ 07054 Tel 201-887-8800 (SAN 201-9914).

Performance Management Pub. Inc., (Perf Manage; 0-937100), 3531 Habersham at Northlake, Tucker, GA 30084 (SAN 262-0561).

Performance Programs, Inc., (Perf Progs), 1660 N. LaSalle, Suite 4211, Chicago, IL 60614 (SAN 215-6962).

Performance Resource Press, Inc., (Perf Resource Pr; 0-9610026), 2145 Crooks Rd. No. 103, Troy, MI 48084 Tel 313-528-1252 (SAN 274-5127).

Performing Arts Journal Pubns., (Performing Arts; 0-933826), 325 Spring St., Rm 318, New York, NY 10013 Tel 212-243-3885 (SAN 220-2670).

Performing Arts Network, (Perf Arts Network; 0-942230), 9025 Wilshire Blvd., Beverly Hills, CA 90211 (SAN 240-9259).

Pergamon Press, Inc., (Pergamon; 0-08), Maxwell House, Fairview Park, Elmsford, NY 10523 Tel 914-592-7700 (SAN 213-9022).

Periday Co., (Periday), Box 583, Woodland Hills, CA 91365 (SAN 216-051X).

Perigee Books *See* Putnam Publishing Group, The

Perilous Press, (Perilous Pr; 0-9609502), P.O. Box 17914, Tampa, FL 33612 (SAN 262-057X).

Perimeter Press Inc., (Perimeter Pr; 0-937486), 356 West Huron, Chicago, IL 60610 (SAN 264-2964).

Periscope Press, (Periscope Pr; 0-914083), P.O. Box 6926, Santa Barbara, CA 93160 Tel 805-964-1749 (SAN 286-8652).

Perish Press, (Perish Pr; 0-934038), P.O. Box 75, Mystic, CT 06355 Tel 203-536-2304 (SAN 212-789X).

Perivale Press, (Perivale Pr; 0-912288), 13830 Erwin St., Van Nuys, CA 91401 Tel 213-785-4671 (SAN 201-9922).

Periwinkle Press, (Periwinkle Pr; 0-9602584), P.O. Box 1305, Woodland Hills, CA 91365 Tel 213-346-3415 (SAN 212-2235).

Periwinkle Pubns., (Periwinkle Pubns; 0-942886), 6015 S.W. 187th Dr., Aloha, OR 97006 Tel 503-642-5009 (SAN 240-2651).

Perkins, Dorothy J., (D J Perkins; 0-9604742), Box 194, Moylan, PA 19065 (SAN 215-6970).

Perkins, E. Stuart, & Associates, (Perkins & Assoc; 0-9606444), Box 362, Wellington, OH 44090 (SAN 219-810X).

Perkins, Percy H. Jr., (P H Perkins Jr.; 0-9603090), 5430 Peachtree-Dunwoody Rd., Atlanta, GA 30342 Tel 404-261-1740 (SAN 212-2987).

Perkins Pubns., (Perkins Pubns; 0-934974), 1442 A Walnut St., Suite 165, Berkeley, CA 94709 Tel 415-644-2190 (SAN 213-5442).

Perkiomen Pubns. Co., Inc., (Perkiomen; 0-9605598), P.O. Box 36, Schwenksville, PA 19473 (SAN 218-5008).

Permanent Press, The, (Permanent Pr; 0-932966), R. D. 2 Noyac Rd., Sag Harbor, NY 11963 Tel 516-725-1101 (SAN 212-2995).

Perry, Warner, (W Perry; 0-9603962), 23 Knickerbocker Dr., Newark, DE 19713 (SAN 213-5450).

Perry Enterprises, (Perry Enterprises; 0-941518), 2666 N. 650 E., Provo, UT 84604 Tel 801-375-9529 (SAN 239-0175).

Perry-Omega Pub. Inc., (Perry Omega; 0-9602586), P.O. Box 27097, Escondido, CA 92027 (SAN 213-1420).

Perry Publishing, (Perry Pub), 1252-20th Place, Yuma, AZ 85364 (SAN 213-2303).

Persea Bks., Inc., (Persea Bks; 0-89255), 225 Lafayette St., New York, NY 10012 Tel 212-431-5270 (SAN 212-8233).

Persephone Press, Inc., *(Persephone; 0-930436),* P.O. Box 7222, Watertown, MA 02172 Tel 617-924-0336 (SAN 211-9218).

Perseus Press, *(Perseus Pr; 0-918026),* P.O. Box 1221, Pacific Palisades, CA 90272 Tel 213-208-7991 (SAN 207-2726).

Perseverance Press, *(Perseverance Pr; 0-9602676),* P.O. Box 384, Menlo Park, CA 94025 Tel 415-323-5572 (SAN 212-9272).

Persona Press, *(Persona LA; 0-940142),* 612 Saint Phillip St., New Orleans, LA 70116 Tel 504-522-0661 (SAN 220-3030).

Persona Press, *(Persona Pr; 0-931906),* P.O. Box 14022, San Francisco, CA 94114 Tel 415-775-6143 (SAN 213-3002).

Personabooks, *(Personabks; 0-932456),* 434-66th St., Oakland, CA 94609 Tel 415-658-2482 (SAN 215-1707).

Personal Achievement Institute, *(Personal Achievement; 0-9606744),* 225 Santa Monica Blvd., Suite 305, Santa Monica, CA 90401 Tel 213-393-3230 (SAN 219-6247).

Personal Achievement Library See Telecom Library, The

Personal Christianity, *(Personal Christianity; 0-938148),* Box 549, Baldwin Park, CA 91706 Tel 213-338-7333 (SAN 211-8211).

Personal Development Center, *(Personal Dev Ctr; 0-917828),* P.O. Box 251, Windham Center, CT 06280 Tel 203-423-4785 (SAN 209-164X).

Personal Planning Programs, Inc., *(Personal Planning),* 6550 York Ave. S., Suite 205, Minneapolis, MN 55435 Tel 612-920-0453 (SAN 217-2615).

Personal Power Potential, *(Personal Power; 0-9607312),* 1850 Goodwin Dr., Palatine, IL 60074 Tel 312-934-1177 (SAN 239-2798).

Personal Pr., *(Personal Press; 0-9605634),* P.O. Box 789, Pt. Reyes Station, CA 94956 (SAN 219-9807).

Personal Responsibility, *(Personal Resp; 0-9610488),* 314 Eighth St. SE, Washington, DC 20003 Tel 202-546-0492 (SAN 264-2972).

Personal Security Systems, *(Personal Security; 0-918384),* P.O. Box 152, River Forest, IL 60305 Tel 312-336-7330 (SAN 207-2793).

Perspective Press, *(Perspective Chicago; 0-9603382),* 629 Deming Place, Rm. 401, Chicago, IL 60614 Tel 312-871-4820 (SAN 208-3191).

Perspective Pubns., Inc., *(Perspective; 0-911130),* 509 Madison Ave., New York, NY 10022 Tel 212-752-2212 (SAN 201-8799) Moved, Left No Forwarding Address.

Perspectives Press, *(Perspect Indiana; 0-9609504),* 905 West Wildwood Ave., Fort Wayne, IN 46807 Tel 219-456-8411 (SAN 262-5059).

Perspicilli Press, *(Perspicilli Pr; 0-936064),* 1916 Oak Knoll Dr., Belmont, CA 94002 (SAN 213-8646).

Persson, R. J., Enterprises, *(R J Persson Ent; 0-9608486),* P.O. Box 338, Olathe, CO 81425 Tel 303-249-7900 (SAN 240-7426).

Perth, J. M., Publishing, Inc., *(Perth Pub; 0-9606546),* P.O. Box 82, Delaplane, VA 22025 Tel 703-347-3620 (SAN 218-5806).

Peter Li, Inc., *(Peter Li; 0-89837),* 2451 E. River Rd., Dayton, OH 45439 Tel 513-294-5785 (SAN 238-7980).

Peter Pauper Press, Inc., *(Peter Pauper; 0-88088),* 135 W. 50th St., New York, NY 10020 Tel 914-681-0144 (SAN 204-9449).

Petereins Press, The, *(Petereins Pr; 0-9606102),* P.O. Box 10446, Glendale, CA 91209 Tel 213-244-9776 (SAN 215-9007).

Peters, Ferguson E., Co., *(F E Peters; 0-918214),* P.O. Box 21587, Fort Lauderdale, FL 33335 Tel 305-463-1776 (SAN 210-2579).

Peters, Paul, Studio, *(P Peters Studio; 0-9607030),* 2305 Park Ave., Bay City, TX 77414 (SAN 239-0183).

Peters, Ted H., *(T H Peters; 0-9601466),* Box 1299, Greenville, TX 75401 (SAN 222-1144).

Petersburg Press, *(Petersburg Pr; 0-902825),* 17 E. 74th St., New York, NY 10021 (SAN 240-1819).

Petersen Publishing Co., Book Division, *(Petersen Pub; 0-8227),* 6725 Sunset Blvd., Los Angeles, CA 90028 Tel 213-657-5100 (SAN 201-9949).

Peterson, Arthur J., *(A G Peterson),* P.O. Box 252, DeBary, FL 32713 Tel 305-668-6587 (SAN 214-0780).

Peterson, John C. & Doris M., *(J & D Peterson; 0-9604376),* R R 1, Box 25, Delphi, IN 46923 Tel 317-564-2855 (SAN 216-0056).

Peterson's Guides Inc., *(Petersons Guides; 0-87866),* 166 Bunn Dr., P.O. Box 2123, Princeton, NJ 08540 Tel 609-924-5338 (SAN 282-1591); Orders to: P.O. Box 978, Edison, NJ 08817 (SAN 282-1605).

Petervin Press, the, *(Petervin Pr),* 4414 San Ramon Drive, Davis, CA 95616 (SAN 238-0838).

Petheric Press, *(Petheric Pr; 0-919380),* Box 1102, Halifax N.S. B3J 2X1, .

Petrie House Publications, *(Petrie Hse; 0-936824),* 2140 W. Olympic Blvd., Los Angeles, CA 90006 (SAN 218-4540).

Petroage Publishing Co., *(Petroage; 0-939172),* P.O. Box 134, Fairfield, IA 52556 (SAN 216-2849).

Petrocelli Books, *(Petrocelli; 0-89433),* 1101 State Rd., Princeton, NJ 08540 Tel 609-924-5851 (SAN 211-3848).

Petroglyph Press Ltd., *(Petroglyph; 0-912180),* 201 Kinoole St., Hilo, HI 96720 (SAN 204-9457).

Petroleum Extension Service (PETEX), *(PETEX; 0-88698),* Industrial & Busn. Training Bur., Univ. of Texas at Austin, Box S, Univ. Sta., Austin, TX 78712 (SAN 208-3892).

Petronium Press, *(Petronium Pr; 0-932136),* 1255 Nuuanu Ave., 1813, Honolulu, HI 96817 (SAN 211-7541).

Pfeiffer, Philip A., *(Pfeiffer; 0-9601038),* 1617 N. Baylen St., Pensacola, FL 32501 Tel 904-433-2906 (SAN 208-3205).

Pflaum/Standard, *(Pflaum-Standard; 0-8278),* c/o CEBCO Standard Publishing, 9 Kulick Rd, Fairfield, NJ 07006 (SAN 207-1568) Name Changed to CEBCO-Standard.

Phaeton Press, Inc., *(Phaeton; 0-87753),* Orders to: Gordian Press, 85 Tompkins St., Staten Island, NY 10304 Tel 212-273-4700 (SAN 201-6389).

Phantasia Press, *(Phantasia Pr; 0-932096),* 13101 Lincoln, Huntington Woods, MI 48070 (SAN 211-755X); Dist. by: F & SF Book Co., P.O. Box 415, Staten Island, NY 10302 (SAN 169-6270).

Pharmaceutical Technology, *(Pharm Tech; 0-943330),* 320 North A St., Springfield, OR 97477 (SAN 240-4869).

Ph.D. Publishing Co., *(PhD Pub; 0-932010),* 10860 Arizona Ave., Culver City, CA 90230 Tel 213-204-1604 (SAN 201-9565).

Pheasant Run Pubns., *(Pheasant Run; 0-936978),* Box 14043, St. Louis, MO 63178 Tel 314-291-3439 (SAN 215-1715).

Phelan, Helene C., *(Phelan; 0-9605836),* 114 S. Main St., Almond, NY 14804 Tel 607-276-6166 (SAN 216-4922).

Phelon, Sheldon & Marsar, Inc., *(P S & M Inc),* 32 Union Square, New York, NY 10003 Tel 212-473-2590 (SAN 205-1869).

Phenix Pubns., Div. of Phenix Technology, Inc., *(Phenix Pub; 0-910105),* 800 S. el Camino Real, Suite 208, San Clemente, CA 92672 Tel 714-492-3324 (SAN 241-4279).

Philadelphia Maritime Museum, *(Phila Maritime Mus; 0-913346),* 321 Chestnut St., Philadelphia, PA 19106 Tel 215-925-5439 (SAN 203-6975).

Philadelphia Museum of Art, *(Phila Mus Art; 0-87633),* P.O. Box 7646, Philadelphia, PA 19101 Tel 215-763-8100 (SAN 203-0969).

Philadelphia Patristic Foundation, Ltd., *(Phila Patristic; 0-915646),* 99 Brattle St., Cambridge, MA 02138 Tel 617-868-3450 (SAN 208-3507).

Philadelphia Yearly Meeting, Religious Society of Friends, Book Services, *(Religious Soc Friends; 0-941308),* 1515 Cherry St., Philadelphia, PA 19102 (SAN 239-3778).

Philam Book Distributors, *(Philam Bk),* 50 Rizal St., San Francisco, CA 94107 (SAN 210-6191).

Philatelic Foundation,, *(Philatelic Found; 0-911989),* 270 Madison Ave, New York, NY 10016 Tel 212-889-6483 (SAN 235-3253).

Phileas Deigh Corp., *(Phileas Deigh; 0-9604200),* 600 Old Country Rd., Suite 321, Garden City, NY 11530 (SAN 214-2171).

Philemon Foundation, *(Philemon Found; 0-9601434),* Dist. by: Selzer Books, 705 Willow Ave., Ukiah, CA 95482 Tel 707-462-1630 (SAN 211-6146).

Philgor Publishing, *(Philgor Pub),* 1555 Winona Court, Denver, CO 80204 (SAN 240-107X).

Philippine Ancestors, *(Philippine Anc; 0-9608528),* P.O. Box 18042, Denver, CO 80218 Tel 303-341-2307 (SAN 240-7434).

Phillipps, John, *(John Philipps; 0-9611412),* 1111 Belair Dr., Fallbrook, CA 92028 (SAN 285-6743).

Phillips, A.J., *(A J Phillips; 0-9605268),* 245-38 W. Bobier Dr., Vista, CA 92083 Tel 619-724-0967 (SAN 215-9023).

Phillips, James M., *(J M Phillips; 0-932572),* P.O. Box 168, Williamstown, NJ 08094 Tel 609-567-0695 (SAN 208-3523).

Phillips, Jean, Publishing Co., *(J Phillips Pub Co; 0-911305),* R.R. 2, Box 135, West Liberty, IA 52776 Tel 319-627-4556 (SAN 274-5968).

Phillips, S. G., Inc., *(S G Phillips; 0-87599),* P.O. Box 83, Chatham, NY 12037 Tel 518-392-3068 (SAN 203-3631).

Phillips Collection, *(Phillips Coll),* 1600-1612 21st St., N.W., Washington, DC 20009 Tel 202-387-2151 (SAN 280-1094) Self-Pub & Self-Dist.

Phillips Exeter Academy Press, The, *(Phillips Exeter Academy; 0-939618),* Phillips Exeter Academy, Exeter, NH 03833 (SAN 216-4353).

Phillips-Neuman, *(Phillips Neuman; 0-910107),* Box 125, Glen Echo, MD 20812 (SAN 240-8244).

Phillips Publications for Holter, Wayne V., *(Holter; 0-932572),* 125 Lakin Ave., Boonsboro, MD 21713 (SAN 264-2999).

Phillips Publishing Co., *(Phillips Pub Co),* 1562 Main St., Suite 713, Springfield, MA 01103 Tel 413-734-9020 (SAN 201-9981) Moved, Left No Forwarding Address.

Philmar Publishers, *(Philmar Pub; 0-88100),* P.O. Box 402, Diablo, CA 94528 (SAN 262-0596).

Philmay Enterprises, Inc., *(Philmay; 0-942894),* 300 W. Wienca Rd. N. E., Atlanta, GA 30342 (SAN 240-8260).

Philmer Enterprises, *(Philmer; 0-918836),* No. 4 Hunter's Run, Spring House, PA 19477 Tel 215-643-2976 (SAN 209-4746).

Philo Press, *(Philo Pr; 0-941650),* Box 277, Youngstown, NY 14174 Tel 716-285-2355 (SAN 239-2801).

Philosophical Library, Inc., *(Philos Lib; 0-8022),* 200 W. 57th St., New York, NY 10019 Tel 212-265-6050 (SAN 201-999X).

Philosophical Publishing Co., *(Philos Pub),* P.O. Box 220, Quakertown, PA 18951 Tel 215-536-5168 (SAN 205-3810).

Philosophical Research Society, Inc., *(Philos Res; 0-89314),* 3910 Los Feliz Blvd., Los Angeles, CA 90027 Tel 213-663-2167 (SAN 205-3829).

Philosophy Documentation Center, *(Philos Document; 0-912632),* Bowling Green State University, Bowling Green, OH 43403 Tel 419-372-2419 (SAN 202-134X).

Philosophy of Science Association, *(Philos Sci Assn; 0-917586),* 18 Morrill Hall, Philosophy Dept., Michigan State Univ., East Lansing, MI 48824 Tel 517-353-9392.

Philosophy Press, The, *(Philos Pr; 0-940284),* P.O. Box 1600, Uniontown, PA 15401 Tel 412-329-8727 (SAN 218-4311).

Phipps Pub. Co., Subs. of New England Mfgr. Co., *(Phipps Pub; 0-918442),* 66 Bridge St., Norwell, MA 02061 Tel 617-659-7003 (SAN 209-9829).

Phoenix Art Museum, *(Phoenix Art; 0-910407),* 1625 N. Central Ave., Phoenix, AZ 85004 Tel 602-257-1880 (SAN 280-1140).

Phoenix Associates Inc., *(Phoenix Assocs; 0-915222),* P.O. Box 693, Boulder, CO 80306 Tel 303-449-3750 (SAN 211-4429).

Phoenix Book Shop, *(Phoenix Bk Shop; 0-916228),* 22 Jones St., New York, NY 10014 Tel 212-675-2795 (SAN 211-3724).

Phoenix Books Pubs., *(Phoenix Bks; 0-914778),* P.O. Box 32008, Phoenix, AZ 85064 Tel 602-952-0163 (SAN 282-1613); P. O. Box 32008, Phoenix, AZ 85064 (SAN 282-1621).

Phoenix Projects, The, *(Phoenix Projects; 0-910109),* 1819 Eaton Rd., Terre Haute, IN 47802 Tel 812-234-3607 (SAN 241-4295).

Phoenix Publishing, *(Phoenix Pub; 0-914016),* Canaan St., NH 03741 Tel 603-523-9902 (SAN 201-8810).

Phoenix Publishing Co., *(Phoenix Pub WA; 0-919345),* P.O. Box 10, Custer, WA 98240 (SAN 215-9422).

Phoenix Publishing Co., The, *(Phoenix FL; 0-940810),* P.O. Box 430733, Miami, FL 33143 Tel 305-253-7411 (SAN 219-8428).

Phoenix Rising, *(Phoenix Rising; 0-9610314),* 601 Dale Dr., Silver Spring, MD 20910 Tel 703-442-3815 (SAN 264-3014).

Pholiota Pr., Inc., *(Pholiota; 0-910231),* P.O. Box DB, Garden Grove, CA 92642-5047 Tel 714-537-5355 (SAN 240-8783).

Photo-Go Press, *(Photo-Go Pr; 0-931662),* P.O. Drawer BB, El Paso, TX 79952 Tel 915-581-6218 (SAN 211-7576).

Photo Survey, *(Photo Survey; 0-960981209),* Box 9157, Akron, OH 44305 (SAN 262-5075).

Photographic Arts Center, The, *(Photo Arts Ctr; 0-913069),* 127 E. 59th St., New York, NY 10022 (SAN 283-9261).

Photographic Book Co., The, Div. of Alemar's America, Inc., *(Photo Bk Co; 0-86636),* 34 W. 32 St., New York, NY 10001 Tel 212-563-4610 (SAN 223-1476); Dist. by: Robert Silver Assocs., 95 Madison Av., New York, NY 10016 (SAN 241-5801).

Photographic Memorabila, *(Photo Memorabila; 0-9604352),* P. O. Box 351, Lexington, MA 02173 Tel 617-862-1222 (SAN 282-163X).

Photographic Research Pubns., *(Photo Res; 0-934918),* P.O. Box 333, Seven Oaks, Detroit, MI 48235 Tel 313-493-3503 (SAN 213-9456).

Photographit, *(Photographit; 0-9605168),* 12 S. Gallatin Ave., Uniontown, PA 15401 (SAN 215-7985).

Photography Media Institute, Inc., *(PMI Inc; 0-936524),* P.O. Box 78, Staten Island, NY 10304 Tel 212-447-3280 (SAN 216-1729).

Photopia Press, *(Photopia Pr; 0-942478),* P.O. Box 1844, Corvallis, OR 97339 Tel 503-757-8761 (SAN 238-5562).

Physicians' Record Co., *(Physicians Rec; 0-917036),* 3000 S. Ridgeland Ave., Berwyn, IL 60402 Tel 312-749-3111 (SAN 205-3853).

Physsardt Pubs., *(Physsardt; 0-916062),* Dist. by: Bloomington Distribution Group, P.O. Box 841, Bloomington, IN 47402 (SAN 282-6828).

P.I. Industries, *(P I Industries; 0-916976),* 243M Griffith Rd., P.O. Box 949, Loveland, CO 80537 Tel 303-669-2980 (SAN 208-7995).

Pi Press, Inc., *(Pi Pr; 0-931420),* Box 23371, Honolulu, HI 96822 (SAN 211-3007).

Pi Yee Press, *(Pi Yee Pr; 0-935926),* 7910 Ivamhoe Ave. No. 34, La Jolla, CA 92037 (SAN 214-0799).

Pica Press See **Universe Books, Inc.**

Pica Special Studies See **Universe Books, Inc.**

Picayune Press, Ltd., *(Picayune Pr; 0-937430),* 326 Picayune Place, New Orleans, LA 70130 (SAN 215-1723).

Picchione, Richard, *(R Picchione; 0-9602840),* Box 5534, Reno, NV 89513 (SAN 213-1471).

Pick Publications, Inc., *(Pick Pub MI; 0-936526),* 8543 Puritan Ave., Detroit, MI 48238 (SAN 282-1648); Dist. by: Manufacturers News, Inc., 4 E. Huron, Chicago, IL 60611 Tel 312-337-1084 (SAN 282-1656); Dist. by: Pick Publications, Inc., 8543 Puritan, Detroit, MI 48238 Tel 313-864-9388 (SAN 282-1648).

Pick Publishing Corp., *(Pick Pub; 0-87551),* 21 West St., New York, NY 10006 Tel 212-425-0591 (SAN 202-0009).

Pickleweed Press, *(Pickleweed; 0-9607890),* 212 Del Casa Dr., Mill Valley, CA 94941 (SAN 238-1885).

Pickwick Pubns., *(Pickwick; 0-915138),* 4137 Timberlane Dr., Allison Park, PA 15101 Tel 412-487-2159 (SAN 210-1319).

Pictorial Histories Publishing Co., *(Pictorial Hist; 0-933126),* 713 South 3rd W., Missoula, MT 59801 (SAN 212-4351).

Picturama Pubns., *(Picturama; 0-918506),* Box 50, 350 Ledo Place, Arroyo Grande, CA 93420 Tel 805-481-0550 (SAN 209-9837).

Picture Book Studio USA, *(Picture Bk Studio USA; 0-907234),* c/o Alphabet Press, 60 N. Main St., Natick, MA 01760 Tel 617-655-9696 (SAN 217-1449).

Pieceful Pleasures, *(Pieceful Pleasures; 0-933758),* 566 30th Ave., San Mateo, CA 94403 Tel 415-573-9243 (SAN 212-7954).

Piedmont Press, Inc., *(Piedmont; 0-912680),* P.O. Box 3605, Georgetown, Washington, DC 20007 Tel 703-549-3980 (SAN 205-3861).

Piequet Press, *(Piequet Pr; 0-914275),* 615 N. Euclid Ave., Suite 207, Ontario, CA 91762 Tel 714-988-5933 (SAN 286-6889).

Pier Press, *(Pier Pr; 0-943306),* 38 Riverdell Dr., Saunderstown, RI 02874 Tel 401-456-1024 (SAN 240-7442).

Pierce, Clayton C., *(C C Pierce; 0-9601564),* 325 Carol Dr., Ventura, CA 93003 Tel 805-653-5979 (SAN 210-9336).

Pierce, Ken, *(K Pierce Inc; 0-912277),* Box 322, Park Forest, IL 60466 Tel 312-672-4457 (SAN 265-0835).

Pierce Pubs., *(Pierce Pubs; 0-9603980),* 309 High St., Chestertown, MD 21620 Tel 301-778-1121 (SAN 214-0802).

Pierian Press, *(Pierian; 0-87650),* P.O. Box 1808, Ann Arbor, MI 48106 Tel 313-434-5530 (SAN 204-8949).

Pierpont Morgan Library, *(Pierpont Morgan; 0-87598),* 29 E. 36th St., New York, NY 10016 Tel 212-685-0008 (SAN 204-8957).

Pig Iron Press, *(Pig Iron Pr; 0-917530),* P.O. Box 237, Youngstown, OH 44501 Tel 216-744-2258 (SAN 209-0937).

Pigeon Roost Press, *(Pigeon Roost Pr),* 739 Clematis Dr., Nashville, TN 37205 (SAN 211-8661).

Pig's Whisker Music, *(Pigs Whisker; 0-9602874),* P. O. Bx 27522, Los Angeles, CA 90027 (SAN 218-4583).

Piirisild & Treumut Partnership, *(Piirisild & Treumut),* P.O. Box 2562, Van Nuys, CA 91404 Tel 213-765-2587 (SAN 216-2857).

Pika Press, *(Pika Pr; 0-935160),* P.O. Box C-9, Mammoth Lakes, CA 93546 (SAN 213-4628).

Pikestaff Press, The, Div. of Pikestaff Publications, Inc., *(Pikestaff Pr; 0-936044),* P.O. Box 127, Normal, IL 61761 Tel 309-452-4831 (SAN 213-8654).

Pikeville College Press, *(Pikeville Coll; 0-933302),* Pikeville, KY 41501 Tel 606-432-9227 (SAN 212-1298).

Pilgrim Books, *(Pilgrim Bks OK; 0-937664),* P.O. Box 2399, Norman, OK 73070 (SAN 215-6989).

Pilgrim Books, *(Pilgrim NJ; 0-9610624),* P.O. Box 385, 26 Georgia, Medford, NJ 08055 Tel 609-953-0404 (SAN 265-4075).

Pilgrim Hall Museum Shop, *(Pilgrim Hall),* 75 Court St., Plymouth, MA 02360 Tel 617-746-1620 (SAN 216-4361).

Pilgrim Press Corp., *(Pilgrim Pr Corp NY; 0-932256),* 36-01 43rd Ave., Long Island City, NY 11101 (SAN 211-9226).

Pilgrim Press, The, *(Pilgrim NY; 0-8298),* 132 W. 31st St., New York, NY 10001 Tel 212-594-8555 (SAN 212-601X); Dist. by: Seabury Service Center, Somers, CT 06071 Tel 800-243-0004 (SAN 202-5426).

Pilgrim Press, The, *(Pilgrim Pr; 0-933476),* 39 University Place, Princeton, NJ 08540 Tel 609-924-9095 (SAN 211-2647).

Pilgrim Pubns., *(Pilgrim Pubns),* P.O. Box 66, Pasadena, TX 77501 Tel 713-477-2329 (SAN 206-3069).

Pilgrim Publishing Co., *(Pilgrim Pub; 0-916034),* 3109 14th Ave., P.O. Box 2181, Chattanooga, TN 37409-0181 Tel 615-698-5545 (SAN 207-4893).

Pilgrimage, Inc., Div. of Anderson Publishing Co., *(Pilgrimage Inc; 0-932930),* P.O. Box 2676, Cincinnati, OH 45201 Tel 800-543-1315 (SAN 285-0834); RTE. 11, Box 553, Jonesboro, TN 37659 Tel 615-753-4887 (SAN 285-0842).

Pilgrimage Press, *(Pilgrimage; 0-918550),* 2398 Telegraph Ave., Berkeley, CA 94704 Tel 415-548-2626 (SAN 210-1327).

Pillman, K., Pubs., *(K Pillman; 0-9608620),* 4704 Calif. Ave. S.W., Seattle, WA 98116 Tel 206-932-3050 (SAN 238-339X).

Pilot Books, *(Pilot Bks; 0-87576),* 103 Cooper St., Babylon, NY 11702 Tel 516-422-2225 (SAN 202-0017).

Pilot Light, *(Pilot Light; 0-9608376),* 1014 S. Indian Creek Dr., P.O. Box 305, Stone Mountain, GA 30086 Tel 404-296-3294 (SAN 240-8791).

Pilot Pubns., *(Pilot Pubns),* P.O. Box 9307, Mobile, AL 36691 Tel 205-666-0577 (SAN 215-0999); Dist. by: Aviation Book Co., 1640 Victory Blvd., Glendale, CA 91201 Tel 213-240-1771 (SAN 212-0259).

Pimmit Press, *(Pimmit Pr; 0-9606042),* Box 4815, Washington, DC 20008 (SAN 216-9231).

Pin Oak Publishing Co., *(Pin Oak Pub Co; 0-910157),* P.O. Box 10471 G. S., Springfield, MO 65804 Tel 417-883-9957 (SAN 241-242X).

Pin Prick Press, The, *(Pin Prick; 0-936424),* 2664 S. Green Rd., Shaker Hts., OH 44122 Tel 216-932-2173 (SAN 214-1965).

Pinchpenny Press, Subs. of Holt Associates, *(Pinchpenny Pr; 0-913677),* c/o Holt Associates, 729 Boylston St., Boston, MA 02116 Tel 617-437-1550 (SAN 286-1119).

Pine Hill Press, *(Pine Hill Pr),* Freeman, SD 57029 (SAN 211-0873).

Pine Mountain Press, Inc., *(Pine Mntn; 0-89769),* P.O. Box 19746, West Allis, WI 53219 Tel 414-546-2310 (SAN 282-1664); Orders to: Douglas Eads, Rt. 2, Box 525, Georgetown, IN 47122 (SAN 282-1672).

Pine Press, *(Pine Pr; 0-930502),* Box 530, R.D. 1, Landisburg, PA 17040 (SAN 211-2655).

Pine Row Pubns., *(Pine Row; 0-935238),* P.O. Box 428, Washington Crossing, PA 18977 Tel 215-493-4259 (SAN 214-0810).

Pine Street Press, *(Pine St Pr; 0-915224),* 872 Pine St., Winnetka, IL 60093 (SAN 212-1301).

Pine Tree Press, *(Pine Tree Pr; 0-932196),* P. O. Box 2353, Orange, CA 92669 Tel 714-639-0706 (SAN 208-4937); Dist. by: Rampart Institute, Box 4, Fullerton, CA 92704 (SAN 282-6410).

Pineapple Press, Inc., The, *(Pineapple Pr; 0-910923),* 202 Pineapple St., Englewood, FL 33533 (SAN 285-0850); Orders to: P.O. Box 314, Englewood, FL 33533 Tel 813-475-2238 (SAN 285-0869).

Pinebrook Press, Div. of Pinebrook Educational Group, Inc., *(Pinebrook Pr; 0-910859),* 2 East Ave., Larchmont, NY 10538 (SAN 262-0618).

Pinecrest Fund, The, *(Pinecrest Fund; 0-9601858),* 204 Tower Park Bldg., 7447 Holmes St., Kansas City, MO 64131 Tel 816-444-9400 (SAN 212-3010).

Pinecrest Publishing Co., *(Pinecrest Pub Co; 0-913287),* 3505 Pinecrest Dr., Kilgore, TX 75662 Tel 214-984-5695 (SAN 283-9288).

Pinerideg Publishing Co., *(Pine Ridge; 0-9607480),* P.O. Box 234, Amesbury, MA 01913 Tel 617-388-0969 (SAN 238-4698).

Pineridge Publishing House, *(Pineridge Pub; 0-9610490),* P.O. Box 289 Gedney, White Plains, NY 10605 Tel 914-761-8962 (SAN 264-3057).

Pinewood Press, *(Pinewood; 0-9604498),* P.O. Box 79104, Houston, TX 77279 (SAN 215-9058).

Pink House Publishing Co., *(Pink Hse Pub; 0-915946),* 410 Magellan Ave., Penthouse 1002, Honolulu, HI 96813 Tel 808-537-1875 (SAN 204-8965).

Pinnacle Books, *(Pinnacle Bks; 0-523),* 1430 Broadway, New York, NY 10018 Tel 212-719-5900 (SAN 200-2442). *Imprints:* Tor Books (Tor Bks).

Pinter, Frances, Publishers, Ltd., *(F Pinter Pubs; 0-86187),* 51 Washington St., Dover, NH 03820 (SAN 241-5771).

Pintores Press, *(Pintores Pr; 0-934116),* Box 1597, Roswell, NM 88201 (SAN 213-1412).

Pioneer Book Pubs., *(Pioneer Bk TX; 0-933512),* Box 426, Seagraves, TX 79359 Tel 806-546-2498 (SAN 209-4762).

Pioneer Press, Inc., *(Pioneer Pr; 0-913150),* P.O. Box 684, Union City, TN 38261 Tel 901-885-0374 (SAN 204-8973).

Pioneer Publishing Co., *(Pioneer Pub Co; 0-914330),* 8 E. Olive Ave., Fresno, CA 93728 Tel 209-485-2631 (SAN 202-0041).

Piper Books See **Houghton Mifflin Co.**

Piper Publishing, Inc., *(Piper; 0-87832),* Blue Earth, MN 56013 Tel 612-377-8100 (SAN 202-005X).

Piraeus Publishers See **Forum Press, Inc.**

Pisapia, John, Associates, *(J Pisapia Assocs; 0-917964),* 0 Seneca Dr., Elkview, WV 25311 Tel 304-965-6842 (SAN 209-9845).

Pisces' Eye, The, *(Pisces Eye; 0-9604470),* P.O. Box 12642, Seattle, WA 98111 (SAN 219-9815).

Pisces Press, *(Pisces Pr TX; 0-938328),* P.O. Box 4075, Lubbock, TX 79409 (SAN 215-7993).

Pisces Printer, The, *(Pisces Print; 0-9604206),* Box 4625, Irvine, CA 92716 (SAN 214-4409).

Pitcairn Press, Inc., *(Pitcairn Pr; 0-914874),* 388 Franklin St., Cambridge, MA 02139 (SAN 207-4087).

Pitkin Press, *(Pitkin; 0-9606332),* 353 W. 56th St., Apt.4-I, New York, NY 10019 Tel 212-582-5125 (SAN 222-9811); Dist. by: Caroline House, 920 W. Industrial Dr., Aurora, IL 60506 Tel 312-897-2050 (SAN 211-2280).

Pitman Books Ltd., *(Pitman UK; 0-273),* 39 Parker St., London WC2B 5PB, ; Orders to: Weald Publishing Agency, High St., Tunbridge Well, Kent, TN1 1XV, .

Pitman Learning, Inc., *(Pitman Learning; 0-8224),* 19 Davis Dr., Belmont, CA 94002 Tel 415-592-7810 (SAN 212-775X).

Pitman Publishing Corp., *(Pitman),* Publisher Abbreviation Without Addresses Are for Titles That Are Out of Print. These Are Obsolete Abbreviations. Publisher's Abbreviation Is Now Fearon-Pitman.

Pitman Publishing, Inc., *(Pitman Pub MA; 0-273),* 1020 Plain St., Marshfield, MA 02050 Tel 617-837-1331 (SAN 220-2697).

Pittore Euforico, *(Pittore Euforico; 0-934376),* P.O. Box 1132, Peter Stuyvesant Sta., New York, NY 10009 (SAN 213-5469).

Pittsburgh History & Landmarks Foundation, *(Pitt Hist & Landmks Found),* One Landmarks Sq., Pittsburgh, PA 15212 Tel 412-322-1204 (SAN 205-129X).

Pittsburgh Jewish Pubn. & Education Foundation, *(Pitt Jewish Foun),* 315 S. Bellefield Ave., Pittsburgh, PA 15213 (SAN 206-3077).

Pixie Press, *(Pixie Pr AZ; 0-9607128),* P.O. Box 13383, Phoenix, AZ 85002 Tel 602-253-7259 (SAN 239-0205).

Pizzazz Press, *(Pizzazz Pr; 0-939390),* 6702 Fairfax Ave., Lincoln, NE 68505 Tel 402-466-5311 (SAN 220-1801).

Pizzuto, Ltd., Pubs., *(Pizzuto Ltd Pub; 0-910441),* 6979 Ferncroft Ave., San Gabriel, CA 91775 Tel 213-285-5131 (SAN 241-4325).

Place of Herons Press, *(Place Herons; 0-916908),* P.O. Box 1952, Austin, TX 78767 (SAN 208-8088).

Plain Talk Press, *(Plain Talk),* Box 16023, Irvine, CA 92714 (SAN 213-9464).

Plain View Press, *(Plain View; 0-911051),* 1509 Dexter, Austin, TX 78704 Tel 512-441-2452 (SAN 264-3073).

Plamen Publishing Co., *(Plamen Pub; 0-9602138),* P.O. Box 3088, Steinway Sta., Astoria, NY 11103 (SAN 212-3029).

Planet Books, *(Planet Bks),* 65-42 Fresh Meadow Lane, Fresh Meadows, NY 11365 Tel 212-961-9240 (SAN 282-5759).

Planet/Drum Foundation, *(Planet Drum Books; 0-937102),* P.O. Box 31251, San Francisco, CA 94131 Tel 415-285-6556 (SAN 216-437X).

Planetary Press, *(Planetary Pr; 0-938330),* P.O. Box 4641, Baltimore, MD 21212 (SAN 216-0536).

Planned Parenthood Assn. of Idaho, Inc., *(Planned Parent; 0-9611762),* 4301 Franklin Rd., Boise, ID 83705 Tel 208-345-0839 (SAN 285-3574).

Planned Parenthood Federation of America, Inc., *(Plan Parent; 0-934586),* 810 Seventh Ave, New York, NY 10019 Tel 212-541-7800 (SAN 205-1281).

Planned Parenthood of Fresno, *(Plan Par Fresno; 0-9610122),* 633 N. Van Ness Ave., Fresno, CA 93728 Tel 209-486-2411 (SAN 274-6662).

Planned Parenthood of Northwest New Jersey, Inc., *(NW Plan Parent; 0-9609366),* 195 Speedwell Ave., Morristown, NJ 07960 Tel 201-539-5838 (SAN 260-2482).

Planners Press, *(Planners Pr; 0-918286),* 1313 E. 60th St., Chicago, IL 60637 Tel 312-955-9100 (SAN 209-3928).

Planning Executives Institute, *(Plan Execs Inst; 0-912841),* 5500 College Corner Pike, Oxford, OH 45056 Tel 513-523-4185 (SAN 230-8673).

Plant Press, The, *(Plant Pr MA; 0-940960),* P.O. Box 133, Halifax, MA 02338 Tel 617-293-3163 (SAN 274-4162).

Plantagenet House, Inc., *(Plantagenet Hse; 0-940812),* P.O. Box 271, Blackshear, GA 31516 Tel 912-449-6601 (SAN 219-6271).

Plantation Press, *(Plantation; 0-911150),* Davies Plantation Rd., Brunswick, Memphis, TN 38134 Tel 901-386-2015 (SAN 205-1273).

Plantin Press, *(Plantin Pr),* 1052 Manzanita, Los Angeles, CA 90029 Tel 213-666-1340 (SAN 205-1265).

Platform Studio, *(Platform Studio; 0-942812),* P.O. Box 247, Kenmore Station, Boston, MA 02215 (SAN 240-4885).

Platinum Pen Publishers, Inc., *(Platinum Pen Pubs; 0-912815),* P.O. Box 11127, 4810 NE Vivion Rd., Kansas City, MO 64119 Tel 816-741-2894 (SAN 265-394X).

Platt & Munk Pubs., Div. of Grosset & Dunlap, *(Platt; 0-448),* 200 Madison Ave., New York, NY 10010 Tel 212-576-8900 (SAN 211-9668).

Plaut, Mordecai, *(Mordecai; 0-9612088),* 1480 E. Tenth St., Brooklyn, NY 11223 Tel 212-339-2817 (SAN 286-8512).

Play Schools Assn., *(Play Schs; 0-936426),* 19 West 44th St., New York, NY 10017 Tel 212-921-2940 (SAN 202-0076).

Playboy Paperbacks, Div. of P.E.I. Books, Inc., *(Playboy Pbks; 0-87216; 0-86721),* 200 Madison Ave., New York, NY 10019 Tel 212-576-8900 (SAN 213-2672); Dist. by: ICD, 250 W. 55th St., New York, NY 10019 Tel 212-262-7444 (SAN 169-5800).

Playette Corp., *(Playette Corp),* P.O. Box 5, Roslyn, NY 11576 Tel 516-883-2825 (SAN 203-1000).

Plays, Inc., *(Plays; 0-8238),* 8 Arlington St., Boston, MA 02116 Tel 617-536-7497 (SAN 202-0084).

Playspaces-International, *(Playspaces; 0-85953),* 31D Union Ave., Sudbury, MA 01776 Tel 617-443-7146 (SAN 216-2121).

Plaza Pubs., *(Plaza Pubs),* 2010 Empire Blvd., Webster, NY 14580 Tel 716-671-1533 (SAN 202-1544).

Pleasant Hill Press, *(Pleasant Hill),* 2600 Pleasant Hill Rd., Sebastopol, CA 95472 Tel 707-823-6583 (SAN 207-1630).

Please Press Ltd., *(Please Pr),* Box 3036, Flint, MI 48502 (SAN 215-8000).

Pleasure Dome Press, Div. of L.I. Poetry Collective, Inc., *(Pleasure Dome; 0-918870),* Box 773, Huntington, NY 11743 Tel 516-691-2376 (SAN 210-4849).

Pleasure Trove Books, *(Pleasure Trove; 0-930400),* 2156 Merokee Dr., Merrick, NY 11566 Tel 516-379-2501 (SAN 207-2742).

Pleneurethic International, *(Pleneurethic Intl),* Earth Light Bookstore, 113 E. Main, Walla Walla, WA 99362 Tel 509-525-4983 (SAN 209-116X).

Plenum Press *See* **Plenum Publishing Corp.**

Plenum Publishing Corp., *(Plenum Pub; 0-306),* 233 Spring St., New York, NY 10013 Tel 212-620-8485 (SAN 201-9248). *Imprints:* Consultants Bureau (Consultants); Plenum Press (Plenum Pr); Plenum Rosetta (Rosetta).

Plenum Rosetta *See* **Plenum Publishing Corp.**

Plexus Publishing, Inc., *(Plexus Pub; 0-937548),* 143 Old Marlton Pike, Medford, NJ 08055 Tel 609-654-6500 (SAN 212-436X).

Plezia, Valerie, *(V Plezia; 0-9609368),* 14009 Mohawk Trail, Cleveland, OH 44130 Tel 216-842-4581 (SAN 260-2490).

Ploss, Douglas A., *(D A Ploss; 0-9603632),* 38822 N. Gratton Rd., Lake Villa, IL 60046 Tel 312-356-5944 (SAN 213-7852).

Plough Publishing House of the Hutterian Society of Brothers, *(Plough; 0-87486),* Rifton, NY 12471 Tel 914-658-3141 (SAN 202-0092).

Ploughshare Press, *(Ploughshare Pr; 0-912396),* P.O. Box 123, Sea Bright, NJ 07760 Tel 201-842-0336 (SAN 205-6380).

Plowshare Press, Inc., *(Plowshare; 0-87368),* P.O. Box 2252, Boston, MA 02107 (SAN 204-899X).

Plum Hall Inc., *(Plum Hall; 0-911537),* 1 Spruce Ave., Cardiff, NJ 08232 Tel 605-927-3770 (SAN 264-3103).

Plum Nelly Shop, Inc., The, *(Plum Nelly),* 1201 Hixson Pike, Chattanooga, TN 37405 Tel 615-266-0585 (SAN 216-1745).

Plumbers Ink Books, *(Plumbers Ink Bks; 0-935684),* P.O.Box 233, Cerrillos, NM 87010 Tel 505-438-3662 (SAN 213-8662).

Plumbing Pubns., *(Plumbing Pubns; 0-9603462),* 1700 N. "H" St., Midland, TX 79701 Tel 915-683-5574 (SAN 213-3148); Orders to: P.O. Box 5461, Midland, TX 79701 Tel 915-682-3249 (SAN 213-3156).

Plume Books *See* **New American Library**

Pluribus Press, Inc., Div. of Teach'em, Inc., *(Pluribus Pr; 0-931028),* 160 E. Illinois St., Chicago, IL 60611 Tel 312-467-0424 (SAN 238-8413).

Plus One Publishing, Inc, *(Plus One Pub; 0-934822),* 625 N. Mansfield Ave., Hollywood, CA 90036 Tel 213-936-1783 (SAN 213-1404).

Plus Seven Books, *(Plus Seven Bks; 0-943416),* 4 Trafford Rd., Hampton, NH 03842 Tel 603-926-5174 (SAN 240-7469).

Plutarch Press *See* **Advent Books, Inc**

Pluto Press, *(Pluto Pr; 0-86104),* Dist. by: Flatiron Book Distributors Inc., 175 Fifth Ave., Suite 814, New York, NY 10010 Tel 212-228-0390 (SAN 240-9917).

Plycon Press, *(Plycon Pr; 0-916434),* P.O. Box 220, Redondo Beach, CA 90277 Tel 213-379-9725 (SAN 201-8829); Dist. by: Burgess Publishing Co., 7108 Ohms Lane, Minneapolis, MN 55435 (SAN 212-6001).

Plymouth Colony Research Group, *(Plymouth Col; 0-910233),* 128 Massasoit Dr., Warwick, RI 02888 Tel 401-781-6759 (SAN 241-4376).

Plymouth Press, *(Plymouth Pr; 0-935540),* P. O. Box 390205, Miami, FL 33119 (SAN 212-9612).

Plymouth Rock Foundation, *(Plymouth Rock Found; 0-942516),* 6 McKinley Circle, Marlborough, NH 03455 (SAN 239-8583).

P'Nye Press, *(P'Nye Pr; 0-9602402),* The Printers Shop, 4047 Transport, Palo Alto, CA 94303 Tel 415-494-6802 (SAN 212-5463).

Pocket Books, Inc., Div. of Simon & Schuster, Inc., *(PB; 0-671),* 1230 Ave. of the Americas, New York, NY 10020 Tel 212-246-2121 (SAN 202-5922). *Imprints:* Poseidon Press (Poseidon); Timescape (Timescape); Wallaby (Wallaby).

Pocumtuck Valley Memorial Assn., *(Pocumtuck Valley Mem),* Memorial Hall Museum, Deerfield, MA 01342 Tel 413-773-8929 (SAN 211-2663).

Podesta Fishing Co., Pubs., *(Podesta Fishing),* 140 S. Peter Dr., Campbell, CA 95008 Tel 408-377-7700 (SAN 211-0881).

Podiatric Educational Pubns., *(Podiatric Educ; 0-9600302),* 28 Prospect St., Waltham, MA 02154 Tel 617-894-1985 (SAN 204-9007).

Poet Gallery Press, *(Poet Gal Pr; 0-913054),* 224 W. 29th St., New York, NY 10001 (SAN 204-9015).

Poet Papers, *(Poet Papers; 0-9600288),* P.O. Box 528, Topanga, CA 90290 (SAN 209-4770).

Poetasumanos Press, *(Poetasumanos; 0-938254),* 949 Capp St., No. 10, San Francisco, CA 94110 (SAN 215-6997).

Poetry, *(Poetry; 0-9607750),* P.O. Box 1117, New York, NY 10028 (SAN 239-5886).

Poetry Eastwest, *(Poetry Eastwest; 0-912206),* P.O. Box 391, Sumter, SC 29150 Tel 803-773-5170 (SAN 202-0106).

Poets & Writers, *(Poets & Writers; 0-913734),* 201 W. 54th St., New York, NY 10019 Tel 212-757-1766 (SAN 204-8981).

Pohl, J., Associates, *(Pohl Assoc; 0-939332),* 461 Spring Run Rd., Coraopolis, PA 15108 Tel 412-457-6300 (SAN 220-181X).

Point, *(Point Calif),* Box 428, Sausalito, CA 94966 Tel 415-332-1716 (SAN 210-7139).

Point Loma Pubns., Inc., *(Point Loma Pub; 0-913004),* P.O. Box 6507, 3727 Charles St., San Diego, CA 92106 Tel 714-222-3291 (SAN 204-9023).

Point Press, *(Point Pr; 0-9601474),* Box 14, Point Pleasant, NJ 08742 Tel 201-892-9480 (SAN 210-9468).

Point Publishing Co., *(Point Pub Co; 0-911909),* P.O. Box 1309, Point Pleasant, NJ 08742 (SAN 265-4083).

Point Two Publications, *(Point Two; 0-911073),* P.O. Box 725, R.C.U., New York, NY 10185 Tel 212-719-9045 (SAN 274-6948).

Poirot, H. M., & Co., *(Poirot & Co; 0-936318),* P.O. Box 3432, Amarillo, TX 79106 Tel 806-374-8558 (SAN 214-0837); Orders to: The Viking Press, 625 Madison Ave., New York, NY 10022 (SAN 200-2450).

Pokeberry Publications, *(Pokeberry Pubns; 0-911111),* P.O. Box 421, Luquillo, PR 00673 (SAN 274-6956).

Polamerica Press, *(Polamerica Pr; 0-914310),* P.O. Box 36415, Los Angeles, CA 90036 (SAN 206-8672).

Polanie Publishing Co., *(Polanie; 0-911154),* 643 Madison St., N.E., Minneapolis, MN 55413 Tel 612-379-9134 (SAN 204-9031).
Polaris Press, *(Polaris Pr; 0-930504),* 16540 Camellia Terrace, Los Gatos, CA 95030 (SAN 204-904X).
Polestar Pubns., *(Polestar; 0-942044),* 620 S. Minnesota Ave., Sioux Falls, SD 57104 Tel 605-338-2888 (SAN 239-474X).
Police Beat Press, *(Police Beat Pr; 0-942724),* 723 N. 53rd St., Milwaukee, WI 53208 (SAN 240-1231).
Police Foundation, *(Police Found),* 1909 K St. NW, Washington, DC 20006 (SAN 237-8280).
Police Press, *(Police Pr; 0-89415),* P.O. Box 2187, Dublin, CA 94568 Tel 415-829-2728 (SAN 209-9853).
Police Training Foundation, *(Police Train),* 3412 Ruby St., Franklin Park, IL 60131 Tel 312-678-4325 (SAN 262-0626).
Policy Studies Associates, *(Pol Stud Assocs; 0-936826),* P.O. Box 337, Croton-on-Hudson, NY 10520 Tel 914-271-6500 (SAN 214-4417).
Policy Studies Organization, *(Policy Studies; 0-918592),* 361 Lincoln Hall, Univ. of Illinois at Urbana-Champaign, Urbana, IL 61801 Tel 217-359-8541 (SAN 210-1343).
Polish American Historical Association, *(Polish American; 0-940962),* 984 Milwaukee Ave., Chicago, IL 60622 (SAN 212-3037).
Polish Institute of Arts & Sciences, *(Polish Inst Art & Sci),* 59 E 66 St, New York, NY 10021 Tel 212-988-4338 (SAN 225-3747).
Polk, Donice, *(D Polk; 0-9605430),* 1973 Reedy, Highland, CA 92346 (SAN 215-9767).
Polk, James K., Memorial Auxilary, *(James K Polk; 0-9607668),* Box 741, Columbia, TN 38401 Tel 615-388-2354 (SAN 239-5908).
Polk, Lewis, *(Polk; 0-911399),* 314 5th Ave., New York, NY 10001 (SAN 264-312X).
Pollnow, James L., *(J L Pollnow; 0-9603708),* 1310 Aldersgate Rd., Little Rock, AR 72205 (SAN 213-8670).
Pollux Press, *(Pollux Pr; 0-913933),* P.O. Box 12, Victor, CO 80860 Tel 303-689-3000 (SAN 286-8687).
Poltergeist Press, *(Poltergeist; 0-9603918),* 706 S. Morain St., Kennewick, WA 99336 Tel 509-783-8695 (SAN 213-5477).
Poly Tone Press, *(Poly Tone; 0-933830),* 16027 Sunburst St., Sepulveda, CA 91343 Tel 213-892-0044 (SAN 210-6515).
Polyanthos, Inc., *(Polyanthos),* Drawer 51359, New Orleans, LA 70151 Tel 504-566-7406 (SAN 205-180X).
Polycrystal Book Service, *(Polycrystal Bk Serv; 0-9601304),* P.O. Box 27, Western Springs, IL 60558 Tel 312-246-3818 (SAN 212-6753).
Polygonal Publishing House, *(Polygonal Pub; 0-936428),* 80 Passaic Ave., Passaic, NJ 07055 Tel 201-779-0166 (SAN 218-4559).
Polymers & Plastics Technical Publishing House, *(Polymers & Plastics Tech Pub Hse; 0-942378),* 33 Salrite Ave., Waldwick, NJ 07463 (SAN 239-8591).
PolyScience Corp., *(PolyScience; 0-913106),* 7800 Merrimac Ave., Niles, IL 60648 Tel 312-965-0611 (SAN 209-0740).
Pomegranate Pubns., *(Pomegranate Calif; 0-917556),* Box 748, Corte Madera, CA 94925 Tel 415-924-8141 (SAN 211-0857).
Pomegranate Press, *(Pomegranate; 0-915192),* P.O. Box 181, Cambridge, MA 02140 Tel 617-489-3896 (SAN 207-883X).
Ponchie & Co., *(Ponchie; 0-9604418),* W.V.U., Dept of Foreign Languages, Morgantown, WV 26506 (SAN 214-4425).
Pond Woods Press, *(Pond Woods),* P.O. Box 82, Stony Brook, NY 11790 Tel 516-751-3232 (SAN 212-4378).
Ponderosa Pubs., *(Ponderosa; 0-913162),* Rte. 1, Box 68, Saint Ignatius, MT 59865 Tel 406-745-4455 (SAN 204-9058).
Pong, Ted, *(Pong),* P.O. Box 321, Freeland, WA 98249 (SAN 216-0544).
Pontine Pr., *(Pontine Pr),* 1153 N. Orange, Hollywood, CA 90038 (SAN 201-8845).
Pony X Press, *(Pony X Pr; 0-939428),* 915 Shorepoint Court, E303, Alameda, CA 94501 Tel 415-522-4928 (SAN 204-9074).
Pool Pubns., *(Pool Pubns; 0-9609588),* Box 3362, Enfield, CT 06082 Tel 203-745-9162 (SAN 274-7332).

Poor Richard's Press, *(Poor Richards; 0-917212),* Box 189, Forest Lake, MN 55025 (SAN 208-2519).
Poor Souls Pr./Scaramouche Bks., *(Poor Souls Pr; 0-916296),* P.O. Box 236, Millbrae, CA 94030 Tel 415-588-4163 (SAN 209-679X).
Popcorn Pubs, *(Popcorn Pubs; 0-930506),* P.O. Box 1308, Pittsfield, MA 01202 Tel 413-443-5601 (SAN 211-044X).
Pope John Center, *(Pope John Ctr; 0-935372),* 4455 Woodson Rd., St. Louis, MO 63134 Tel 314-428-2424 (SAN 282-1729); Dist. by: Franciscan Herald Press, 1434 W. 51st St., Chicago, IL 60609 Tel 312-254-4455 (SAN 201-6621); Dist. by: Saint Mary's Press, Terrace Heights, Winona, MN 55987 Tel 800-533-8095 (SAN 203-073X).
Pope John XXIII Medical-Moral Research & Education Center See **Pope John Center**
Popejoy, Charles L. "Jack", *(Popejoy),* 620 Seatter St., Juneau, AK 99801 Tel 907-586-1203 (SAN 211-7592).
Poplar Books, *(Poplar Bks),* P.O. Box 62, Shiloh, TN 38376 (SAN 287-2595).
Population Council Pues & Information Office, *(Population Coun),* One Dag Hammarskjoid Plaza, New York, NY 10017 (SAN 225-1582).
Population Reference Bureau, *(Population Ref; 0-917136),* 1337 Connecticut Ave., N.W, Washington, DC 20036 Tel 202-785-4664 (SAN 205-1230).
Population Review Publication, A, *(Chandrasekhar; 0-9609080),* 8976 Cliffridge Ave., La Jolla, CA 92307 Tel 714-455-6093 (SAN 241-4341).
Porch Pubns., *(Porch Pubns; 0-932968),* 5310 E. Taylor, Phoenix, AZ 85008 (SAN 282-1753).
Porch Swing Press, Inc., *(Porch Swing; 0-9606550),* P.O. Box 15014, Nashville, TN 37215 (SAN 219-8118).
Porcupine Press, Inc., *(Porcupine Pr; 0-87991),* 1317 Filbert St., Philadelphia, PA 19107 Tel 215-563-2288 (SAN 202-0122).
Porphyrion Press, *(Porphyrion Pr; 0-913884),* R.R. 1, Box 439, Middle Grove, NY 12850 Tel 518-587-9809 (SAN 206-6823).
Port Authority of New York and New Jersey, Police Division, *(PANY Pol Div),* One Path Plaza, Jersey City, NJ 07306 (SAN 237-8078).
Port Press, *(Port Pr; 0-9606104),* 16 Ridge Dr., Port Washington, NY 11050 (SAN 216-8502).
Port Quarters Publishing, *(Port Quarters; 0-9608536),* Los Angeles, CA 90049 Tel 213-207-0122 (SAN 282-1761).
Portals Press, *(Portals Pr; 0-916620),* P.O. Box 1048, Tuscaloosa, AL 35403 Tel 205-758-1874 (SAN 208-8126).
Porter, Bern, *(Porter; 0-911156),* 22 Salmond Rd., Belfast, ME 04915 (SAN 202-0130).
Porter Sargent Pubs., Inc., *(Porter Sargent; 0-87558),* 11 Beacon St., Boston, MA 02108 Tel 617-523-1670 (SAN 208-8142).
Portfolio Press, *(Portfolio Pr; 0-942620),* RD 1, Huntington, NY 11743 Tel 212-989-8700 (SAN 238-5554).
Portland Cement Assn., *(Portland Cement; 0-89312),* 5420 Old Orchard Rd., Skokie, IL 60077 Tel 312-966-6200 (SAN 207-6004).
Portland Symphony Orchestra Women's Committee, *(Portland Symphony Cookbook; 0-9601266),* Box 32, Downtown Sta., Portland, ME 04112 Tel 207-773-8191 (SAN 206-9881).
Portner, Hal, *(Portner; 0-913149),* 67 Westhampton Rd., Northampton, MA 01060 Tel 413-584-1285 (SAN 283-4162).
Portola Pr., *(Portola Pr; 0-9605998),* P.O. Box 1225, Santa Barbara, CA 93102 Tel 805-682-7974 (SAN 216-7573).
Portolan Press, *(Portolan; 0-916762),* 825 Rathjen Rd., Brielle, NJ 08730 Tel 201-528-8264 (SAN 208-8134).
Portrayal Press, *(Portrayal; 0-938242),* P.O. Box 1913, Bloomfield, NJ 07003 (SAN 215-9066).
Portriga Pubns., *(Portriga Pubns; 0-9602274),* 823 N. Edinburg Ave., Los Angeles, CA 90046 (SAN 212-4386).
Poseidon Press See **Pocket Books, Inc.**
Poseidon Pubns., *(Poseidon Pubns; 0-937378),* 1340 N. Alameda, Las Cruces, NM 88001 (SAN 215-1731).
Posey Pubns., *(Posey Pubns),* P.O. Box 338, Orem, UT 84057 (SAN 220-2700).

Posey Pubns., *(Posey Pubns CA; 0-910115),* P.O. Box 2512, Fairfield, CA 94533 Tel 707-864-2010 (SAN 241-435X).
Positive Publishing, *(Positive Pub),* P.O. Box 3372, Pinedale, CA 93650 Tel 209-435-3110 (SAN 215-174X).
Post-Apollo Press, The, *(Post Apollo Pr; 0-942996),* 35 Marie St., Sausalito, CA 94965 Tel 415-332-1458 (SAN 240-429X).
Post-Era Books, *(Post-Era; 0-911160),* Box 150, 119 S. First Ave., Arcadia, CA 91006 Tel 213-446-5000 (SAN 205-1672).
Post Parade Pubs., *(Post Parade; 0-943808),* 6828-3 Quebec Ct., San Diego, CA 92139 Tel 714-267-4135 (SAN 238-3411).
Postilion Pubns., Div. of Roger Koerber Inc., *(Postilion Pubns; 0-941480),* 605 Northland Towers W., Southfield, MI 48075 Tel 313-569-1411 (SAN 239-1260).
Postroad Press Inc, *(Postroad Pr Inc; 0-912691),* P.O. Box 1212, Roanoke, VA 24006 (SAN 283-9318); 635 Day Ave., SW Roanoke, VA 24016 (SAN 283-9326).
Postscript Productions, *(Postscript; 0-9604850),* P.O. Box 307, Suisun, CA 94585 Tel 707-864-8414 (SAN 215-7004).
Posy Pubns., *(Posy Pubns; 0-9603526),* 115 Shasta Ct., Charlottesville, VA 22903 Tel 804-293-8506 (SAN 213-3490).
Pot of Gold Pubns., *(Pot of Gold),* 1152 11th St., Manhattan Beach, CA 90266 (SAN 216-0552).
Potala Corporation, *(Potala; 0-9611474),* 801 Second Ave. Suite 703, New York, NY 92028 Tel 619-723-9126 (SAN 283-1570)10017 Tel 212-867-8721.
Potentials Development, Inc., *(Potentials Development; 0-932910),* 775 Main St., Suite 321, Buffalo, NY 14203 (SAN 239-5916).
Potomac Appalachian Trail Club, *(Potomac Appalach; 0-915746),* 1718 N St., N.W., Washington, DC 20036 Tel 202-638-5307 (SAN 208-1121).
Potomac Books, Inc., Pubs., *(Potomac; 0-87107),* P.O. Box 40604, Palisades Sta., Washington, DC 20016 Tel 202-338-5774 (SAN 202-0149); Orders to: P.O. Box 40604, Palisades Sta., Washington, DC 20016 Tel 202-333-6779 (SAN 202-0157).
Potomac Enterprises, *(Potomac Ent; 0-939836),* Box 146, Fort Branch, IN 47648 Tel 812-753-4977 (SAN 216-924X); Dist. by: Sanford J. Durst, 170 E. 61st St., New York, NY 10021 (SAN 211-6987).
Potomac Press, *(Potomac Pr; 0-917262),* P.O. Box 31086, Washington DC-Temple Hills, MD 20031 Tel 202-582-4064 (SAN 208-8150).
Potpourri Ventures, *(Potpourri; 0-9611150),* Box 303, N. Chelmsford, MA 01863 (SAN 283-8893).
Potter, Bill, Golf Professional, *(B Potter),* P.O. Box 12-606, Albany, NY 12212 (SAN 265-3796).
Potter, Clarkson, N. Books See **Crown Pubs., Inc.**
Potter Pubns., *(Potter Pubns),* 3108 S. Oakhurst Ave., Los Angeles, CA 90034 Tel 213-838-8425 (SAN 283-9830).
Pottle, Ralph R., *(Pottle; 0-911162),* 407 N. Magnolia St., Hammond, LA 70401 Tel 504-345-2105 (SAN 204-9066).
Poudre Press, Div. of Poudre Publishing Co., *(Poudre Pr; 0-935240),* P.O. Box 181, La Porte, CO 80535 Tel 303-482-0758 (SAN 213-3504).
Poulin, Clarence J., *(Poulin; 0-9600084),* 87 High St., Penacook, NH 03301 Tel 603-753-4480 (SAN 204-9074).
Pourboire Press, *(Pourboire),* P.O. Box 6881, Providence, RI 02940 Tel 401-331-9800 (SAN 209-8628); Dist. by: Woods Hole Press, P.O. Box 44, Woods Hole, MA 02543 Tel 617-548-9600 (SAN 210-332X).
Poverty Bay Publishing Co., *(Poverty Bay; 0-936528),* 529 S.W. 294, Federal Way, WA 98003 (SAN 214-1973).
Poverty Hill Press, *(Poverty Hill Pr; 0-88083),* P.O. Box 7376, Reno, NV 89510 Tel 702-747-1219 (SAN 238-5570).
Poway Historical & Memorial Society, *(Poway Hist; 0-914317),* P.O. Box 19, Poway, CA 92064 Tel 619-291-7311 (SAN 287-2978).
Powell, James Wooldridge, *(J W Powell; 0-941518),* 1025 Arno Rd., Kansas City, MO 64113 Tel 816-361-9796 (SAN 211-3988).

Powell, Robert Blake, *(R B Powell; 0-9600680),* P.O. Box 833, Hurst, TX 76053 Tel 817-284-8145 (SAN 203-3968).

Powell, Samuel, Publishing Co., *(Samuel P Co),* 2201 I St., Sacramento, CA 95816 (SAN 219-2756).

Power & Systems Training, Inc., *(Power & Sys; 0-910411),* P.O. Box 388, Prudential Station, Boston, MA 02199 Tel 617-437-1640 (SAN 260-1184).

Power Books *See* **Revell, Fleming H., Co.**

Power Mad Press, *(Power Mad; 0-935444),* 156 W. 27th St., No. 5W, New York, NY 10001 (SAN 213-4292).

Powers, M. J., & Co. Pubs., *(M J Powers & Co; 0-913323),* 374 Millburn Ave., Millburn, NJ 07041 (SAN 283-9660).

Powers, Nancy, & Co. Pubs., Inc., *(N Powers; 0-941684),* 241 Central Park W., New York, NY 10024 Tel 212-877-3262 (SAN 239-281X).

Powley, Mark, Associates, Inc., *(M Powley; 0-943378),* 88 Main St., New Canaan, CT 06840 Tel 203-972-1902 (SAN 240-7485).

Powner, Charles T., Co., Inc., *(Powner; 0-911164),* 407 S. Dearborn St., Chicago, IL 60605 (SAN 204-9082).

Practical Pubns., *(Practical Pubns; 0-912914),* 6272 W. North Ave., Chicago, IL 60639 Tel 312-237-2986 (SAN 204-9090).

Practising Law Institute, *(PLI; 0-87224),* 810 Seventh Ave., New York, NY 10019 Tel 212-765-5700 (SAN 203-0136).

Praeger Pubs., Div. of Holt Rinehart & Winston/CBS, *(Praeger; 0-275),* 521 Fifth Ave., New York, NY 10175 Tel 212-599-8413 (SAN 202-022X).

Praestant Press, *(Praestant; 0-930112),* P.O. Box 43, Delaware, OH 43015 Tel 614-363-1458 (SAN 210-6523).

Praetorius Books, *(Praetorius Bks),* P.O. Box 167, Valhalla, NY 10595 (SAN 217-1244).

Pragmatic Publications, *(Pragmatic Pubns; 0-939962),* P.O. Box 30082, St. Paul, MN 55175 Tel 612-457-0831 (SAN 216-8464).

Pragmatix Management Resources, *(Pragmatix Mgmt),* 408 S.W. Second, No. 425, Portland, OR 97204 Tel 217-2623).

Prairie Book Co., *(Prairie Bk; 0-915518),* P.O. Box 1244, Plainview, TX 79072 (SAN 206-8575) Moved, Left No Forwarding Address.

Prairie Craftsman, *(Prairie Craft; 0-9603788),* Box 424, Hoopeston, IL 60942 (SAN 221-6701).

Prairie House, Inc., *(Prairie Hse; 0-911007),* 509 S. 10th St., Bismark, ND 58501 Tel 701-223-8605 (SAN 262-9844).

Prairie Publishing, *(Prairie Pub),* R. R. 1, Rushville, NE 69360 (SAN 207-7442).

Prairie Rambler Press, *(Prairie Ramb; 0-912279),* P.O. Box 505, Claremont, CA 91711-0505 Tel 714-621-8109 (SAN 265-0843).

Prairie School Pr., *(Prairie Sch; 0-87370),* c/o Prairie Avenue Bookshop, 711 S. Dearborn, Chicago, IL 60605 Tel 312-922-8311 (SAN 274-7723).

Prairie Sun Communications, Inc., *(Prairie Sun; 0-936722),* 1109 W. Main St., Peoria, IL 61606 Tel 309-673-6624 (SAN 214-218X).

Prajna Press *See* **Great Eastern Book Co.**

Prakken Pubns., Inc., *(Prakken; 0-911168),* P.O. Box 8623, 416 Longshore Dr., Ann Arbor, MI 48107 Tel 313-769-1211 (SAN 204-9112).

Prayer Book Press, Inc., *(Prayer Bk; 0-87677),* 389 Second Ave., New York, NY 10010 (SAN 282-1788); Orders to: 1363 Fairfield Ave., Bridgeport, CT 06605 (SAN 282-1796).

Pre-School Learning Corp., *(Pre-School Learn),* P.O. Box 6244, 10206 Rosewood, Overland Park, KS 66207 (SAN 207-6241).

Precedent Publishing, Inc., *(Precedent Pub; 0-913750),* 520 N. Michigan Ave., Chicago, IL 60611 Tel 312-828-0420 (SAN 205-1583); Orders to: P.O. Box 1005, South Holland, IL 60473 Tel 312-877-5490 (SAN 205-1591).

Precious Resources, *(Precious Res; 0-937836),* Box 259A, Rt. 1, Union, KY 41091 Tel 606-586-9943 (SAN 213-3512).

Precision Models, *(Precision Mod; 0-9605414),* 9801 E. Bush Lake Rd., No. 224, Minneapolis, MN 55435 Tel 612-835-1807 (SAN 240-8805).

Precision Publishing Co., *(Precision Pub Co),* P.O. Box 172, Fort Myers, FL 33902 (SAN 215-3343).

Predicasts, *(Predicasts),* 11001 Cedar Ave., Cleveland, OH 44106 Tel 216-795-3000 (SAN 202-148X) Tel 800-321-6388.

Prelude Press, *(Prelude Press; 0-931580),* P.O. Box 69773, Los Angeles, CA 90069 (SAN 262-0642).

Prema Books, *(Prema Bks; 0-941122),* 310 West End Ave., No. 17C, New York, NY 10023 Tel 212-840-3300 (SAN 217-4170).

Premier Books *See* **Fawcett Book Group**

Premier Press, *(Prem Press; 0-912722),* 2914 Domingo Ave., Berkeley, CA 94705 Tel 415-841-2091 (SAN 282-180X); Orders to: P.O. Box 4428, Berkeley, CA 94704 (SAN 282-1818).

Premier Publishing Co., *(Premier Pub; 0-942622),* 1200 Pillsbury Center, Minneapolis, MN 55402 Tel 612-339-8551 (SAN 282-1826); Dist. by: Mailhouse, Inc., 210 N. Second St., Minneapolis, MN 55401 Tel 612-339-8701 (SAN 282-6194).

Prentice-Hall, Inc., *(P-H; 0-13),* Rte. 9W, Englewood Cliffs, NJ 07632 Tel 201-592-2000 (SAN 200-2175); Orders to: Box 500, Englewood Cliffs, NJ 07632 (SAN 215-3939). *Imprints:* Business & Professional Div. (Busn); Parker Publishing Co. (Parker); Reward Books (Reward); Spectrum Books (Spec).

Presbyterian & Reformed Publishing Co., *(Presby & Reformed; 0-87552),* Box 817, Phillipsburg, NJ 08865 Tel 201-454-0505 (SAN 205-3918).

Presbyterian Historical Society, *(Presby Hist; 0-912686),* 425 Lombard St., Philadelphia, PA 19147 Tel 215-627-1852 (SAN 205-1575).

Prescott/Durrell, & Company, *(Prescott Durrell & Co; 0-9609506),* P.O. Box 393, Richmond, VA 23202 Tel 804-643-8141 (SAN 274-7855).

Prescott Street Press, *(Prescott St Pr; 0-915986),* 407 Postal Bldg., Portland, OR 97204 Tel 503-254-2922 (SAN 207-4729).

Presence Inc., *(Presence Inc; 0-937296),* P.O. Box 3094, Marion, IN 46952 (SAN 240-8813).

Preservation Ink, *(Preserv Ink; 0-9605294),* P.O. Box 92314, Milwaukee, WI 53202 Tel 414-272-1193 (SAN 239-9962).

Preservation League of New York State, *(Pres League NYS; 0-942000),* 307 Hamilton St., Albany, NY 12210 Tel 518-462-5658 (SAN 238-5945).

Preservation Press, *(Preserv Pr CA; 0-9611016),* 109 Miramonte Rd., Walnut Creek, CA 94596 (SAN 277-7002).

Preservation Press, National Trust for Historic Preservation, *(Preservation Pr; 0-89133),* 1785 Massachusetts Ave., N.W., Washington, DC 20036 Tel 202-673-4000 (SAN 209-3146).

Preservation Publishing Company, *(Preserv Pub Co; 0-911515),* P.O. Box 567, 719 State St., Grinnell, IA 50112-0567 Tel 515-236-5575 (SAN 264-3162).

Preservation Society of Newport County, The, *(Preserv Soc Newport),* Dist. by: Rhode Island Pubns Society, The Old State House, 150 Benefit St., Providence, RI 02903 (SAN 219-9696).

Presidential Accountability Group, *(Presidential Acct; 0-936486),* Box 19312, Washington, DC 20036 (SAN 239-5924).

Presidial Press, *(Presidial; 0-935978),* P.O. Box 5248, Austin, TX 78763 Tel 512-459-9265 (SAN 209-4789).

Presidio Press, *(Presidio Pr; 0-89141),* 31 Pamaron Way, Novato, CA 94947 Tel 415-883-1373 (SAN 214-2759).

Press at California State University, Fresno, The, *(Cal State Pr; 0-912201),* Shaw and Maple, Fresno, CA 93740 Tel 209-294-3056 (SAN 264-6307).

Press at Vision Studios, The, *(Pr Vision Studios; 0-936888),* P.O. Box 241, La Grange, IL 60525 (SAN 214-4433).

Press De la Plantz, *(Press Plantz; 0-942002),* 899 Bayside Cutoff, Bayside, CA 95524 Tel 707-822-6009 (SAN 282-1842); Dist. by: Textile Artists Supplies, 3006 San Pablo Ave., Berkeley, CA 94702 (SAN 282-6461).

Press 451, *(Press Four Fifty One; 0-917796),* 905 S. Walter Reed Dr., Arlington, VA 22204 (SAN 262-0707).

Press in Tuscany Alley, *(Pr Tuscany; 0-915918),* One Tuscany Alley, San Francisco, CA 94133 Tel 415-986-0641 (SAN 208-8185).

Press of Arden Park, *(Pr Arden Park),* 861 Los Molinos Way, Sacramento, CA 95825 Tel 916-481-7881 (SAN 209-8644).

Press of Circumstances, *(Pr Circumstances),* Box 2357, Central Valley, CA 96019 Tel 916-246-1092 (SAN 219-8126).

Press of Morningside Bookshop, *(Pr of Morningside; 0-89029),* P.O. Box 1087, Dayton, OH 45401 Tel 513-461-6736 (SAN 202-0211).

Press of The Langdon Associates, The, *(Langdon Assoc; 0-916704),* 41 Langdon St., Cambridge, MA 02138 Tel 617-864-4518 (SAN 209-2379).

Press of the Nightowl, *(Nightowl; 0-912960),* 320 Snapfinger Dr., Athens, GA 30605 Tel 404-353-7719 (SAN 205-6364).

Press of the Nova Scotia College of Art & Design, *(Pr of Nova Scotia),* Dist. by: Jaap Rietman, Inc., 157 Spring St., New York, NY 11012 (SAN 205-2105).

Press of the Pegacycle Lady, *(Press Pegacycle; 0-915148),* P.O. Box 69812, Los Angeles, CA 90069 Tel 213-658-8515 (SAN 207-1819).

Press Pacifica, *(Pr Pacifica; 0-916630),* P.O. Box 47, Waipahu, HI 96734 Tel 808-261-6594 (SAN 169-1635).

Press West, *(Press West; 0-914592),* 4947 E. Tanqueray, St. Louis, MO 63129 Tel 314-982-2616 (SAN 202-988X).

Pressure Vessel Handbook Publishing, Inc., *(Pressure; 0-914458),* P.O. Box 35365, Tulsa, OK 74135 Tel 918-742-9637 (SAN 206-6149).

Pressworks Publishing, Inc., *(Pressworks; 0-939722),* 2800 Routh St., No. 249, Dallas, TX 75201 Tel 214-749-1044 (SAN 216-7581).

Prestige Pubns., *(Prestige Pubns; 0-911009),* P.O. Box 2157, Princeton, NJ 08540 Tel 609-921-7403 (SAN 274-791X).

Presto Books, *(Presto Bks; 0-943224),* P.O. Box 818, Shoreham, NY 11786 (SAN 240-4893).

Preston-Hill, Inc., *(Preston-Hill; 0-914616),* P.O. Box 572, Chapel Hill, NC 27514 Tel 919-967-7904 (SAN 201-8861).

Preston Publications Inc., *(Preston Pubns; 0-912474),* P.O. Box 48312, Niles, IL 60648 Tel 312-965-0566 (SAN 205-3926).

Preston Publishing Co., Inc., *(Preston),* 100 Ave. of the Americas, New York, NY 10013 Tel 212-966-5529 (SAN 205-3896).

Preston Publishing Co., Inc., *(Preston Ca),* 391 Springtown Rd., New Paltz, NY 12561 (SAN 216-5090).

Preston Street Press, *(Preston St Pr; 0-939382),* 6 Preston St., Rye, NY 10580 Tel 914-765-2178 (SAN 220-1232).

Prestressed Concrete Institute, *(Prestressed Concrete),* 201 N. Wells St., Chicago, IL 60606 Tel 312-346-4071 (SAN 202-1528).

Prestwick Publishing Co., *(Prestwick Pub; 0-9607812),* P.O. Box 90277, 1277 Grant Ave., San Diego, CA 92109-0780 Tel 714-456-2366 (SAN 239-5932).

Presznick, Rose M., *(R M Presznick; 0-912000),* RD 1, 7810 Avon Lake Rd., Lodi, OH 44254 (SAN 205-1524).

Priam Press Inc, *(Priam Pr; 0-911180),* 134 S. La Salle St., Chicago, IL 60603 Tel 312-726-0569 (SAN 207-690X).

Price, David L., *(D L Price; 0-9604482),* 1954 Old Hickory Blvd., Brentwood, TN 37027 Tel 615-373-0946 (SAN 215-3351).

Price, Chirstine, *(C Price; 0-9603654),* C/O Esalen Institute, Big Sur, CA 93920 (SAN 221-7252).

Price Guide Pubs., *(Price Guide; 0-911182),* P.O. Box 525, Kenmore, WA 98028 Tel 206-362-6670 (SAN 205-3934).

Price, Polly S., *(P S Price; 0-9604012),* 3614 Betsy Ross, San Antonio, TX 78230 (SAN 221-6639).

Price-Pottenger Nutrition Foundation, *(Price-Pottenger; 0-916764),* P.O. Box 2614, La Mesa, CA 92041 Tel 619-582-4168 (SAN 208-1849).

Price, Stern, Sloan, Pubs., Inc., *(Price Stern; 0-8431),* 410 N. La Cienega Blvd., Los Angeles, CA 90048 Tel 213-657-6100 (SAN 202-0246).

Prickly Pear Press, *(Prickly NY; 0-9605794),* P.O. Box 221, Old Chelsea Sta., New York, NY 10113 (SAN 216-5449).

Prickly Pear Press, *(Prickly Pear; 0-933384),* 2132 Edwin St., Fort Worth, TX 76110 (SAN 212-4394).

Primary Press, *(Primary Pr),* Box 105a, Parker Ford, PA 19457 Tel 215-495-7529 (SAN 216-1753).

Primary Sources, *(Primary; 0-911184),* P.O. Box 472, Cooper Sta., New York, NY 10003 (SAN 205-3942).

Primavera, *(Primavera; 0-916980),* Ida Noyes Hall, Univ. of Chicago, 1212 E. 59th St., Chicago, IL 60637 Tel 312-684-2742 (SAN 208-2527).

Primavera Productions, *(Primavera Prods; 0-9607990),* 1063 N. Cove, Union, OR 97883 Tel 503-562-5091 (SAN 238-5597).

Prime National Publishing Co., *(Prime Natl Pub; 0-932834),* 470 Boston Post Rd., Weston, MA 02193 Tel 617-899-2702 (SAN 212-3053).

Prime Press, Ltd., *(Prime Pr AZ; 0-911539),* 3003 W. Northern, No. 1, Phoenix, AZ 85021 Tel 602-995-8803 (SAN 264-3197).

Primer Press, *(Primer Pr CA; 0-910617),* 12 Sherman Bridge Rd., Wayland, MA 01778 Tel 617-358-2660 (SAN 260-2512).

Primer Pubs., *(Primer Pubs; 0-935810),* 5738 N. Central, Phoenix, AZ 85012 Tel 602-266-1043 (SAN 220-0864); Dist. by: Many Feathers, 5738 N. Central, Phoenix, AZ 85012 (SAN 210-9824).

Primrose Press, *(Primrose Pr),* 2131 S. Primrose Ave., Alhambra, CA 91803 (SAN 212-9620).

Prince, Derek, Ministries Publications, *(Derek Prince; 0-934920),* P.O. Box 300, Fort Lauderdale, FL 33302 Tel 305-763-5202 (SAN 211-822X).

Prince George's County Genealogical Society, *(Prince Georges County Gen Soc),* Box 819, Bowie, MD 20715 (SAN 218-9135).

Princeton Architectural Press, *(Princeton Arch; 0-910413),* 158 Valley Rd., Princeton, NJ 08540 Tel 609-924-8462 (SAN 260-1176).

Princeton Book Co., *(Princeton Bk Co),* P.O. Box 109, Princeton, NJ 08540 (SAN 208-404X).

Princeton Opinion Press, *(Princeton Opinion),* 53 Bank St., Princeton, NJ 08540 Tel 609-924-9600 (SAN 205-3969).

Princeton Research Institute, *(Princeton Res Inst; 0-913354),* P.O. Box 363, Princeton, NJ 08540 Tel 609-396-0305 (SAN 207-4478).

Princeton Univ. International Finance Section, Dept. of Economics, *(Princeton U Int Finan Econ),* Dickinson Hall, Princeton University, Princeton, NJ 08544 Tel 609-452-5493 (SAN 205-1109) Tel 609-453-4048.

Princeton Univ. Library, *(Princeton Lib; 0-87811),* Princeton, NJ 08544 Tel 609-452-3245 (SAN 205-3950).

Princeton Univ. Press, *(Princeton U Pr; 0-691),* 41 William St., Princeton, NJ 08540 Tel 609-452-4900 (SAN 202-0254).

Princeton Urban & Regional Research Center, *(PURRC; 0-938882),* Woodrow Wilson School, Princeton University, Princeton, NJ 08544 Tel 609-452-5315 (SAN 282-1869); Orders to: Transaction Books, Rutgers University, New Brunswick, NJ 08903 Tel 201-932-2280 (SAN 282-1877).

Principia Press, *(Principia Pr; 0-911188),* 5743 Kimbark Ave., Chicago, IL 60637 Tel 312-643-8295 (SAN 205-3888).

Prinit Press, *(Prinit Pr; 0-932970),* Box 65, Dublin, IN 47335 (SAN 212-680X).

Prinroad Pubs., *(Prinroad Pubs; 0-911629),* 5717 E. Thomas Rd., Scottsdale, AZ 85251 Tel 602-941-5760 (SAN 264-3200).

Print Media Services, Ltd., *(Print Med Serv Ltd; 0-942398),* 1521 Jarvis Ave., Elk Grove, IL 60007 Tel 312-981-0100 (SAN 238-1109).

Printed Editions, *(Printed Edns; 0-914162),* 122 Spring St., New York, NY 10012 Tel 212-966-5232 (SAN 206-5851); Dist. by: New York Small Press Assn., P.O. Box 1264, Radio City Sta., New York, NY 10019 (SAN 206-586X).

Printed Horse, The, *(Printed Horse; 0-912830),* P.O. Box 1908, Fort Collins, CO 80522 Tel 303-482-2286 (SAN 210-4377).

Printed Matter, Inc., *(Printed Matter; 0-89439),* 7 Lispenard St., New York, NY 10013 Tel 212-925-0325 (SAN 169-5924).

Printed Matter Publishing Co., Inc., *(Print Mat; 0-943084),* 15 N. Arlington Heights Rd., Arlington Heights, IL 60004 Tel 312-870-8742 (SAN 169-5924).

Printed Word Publishing, *(Printed Word),* 22834 Tomball Cemetary Rd., Tomball, TX 77375 Tel 713-351-4577 (SAN 211-0458).

Printek, *(Printek; 0-938042),* 6989 Oxford St., Minneapolis, MN 55426 (SAN 215-7012).

Printing, Mailing Services, Inc., *(Print Mail Serv),* 126 N. Ontario St., Toledo, OH 43624 Tel 419-241-4266 (SAN 216-0064).

Printing Press, Inc., The, *(Print Pr CA; 0-9606840),* 523 Clipper St., San Francisco, CA 94114 Tel 415-648-9416 (SAN 217-4189).

Printworld, Inc., *(Printworld; 0-943606),* P.O. Box 785, Bala Cynwyd, PA 19004 Tel 215-649-5140 (SAN 240-7515).

Prism Press, *(Prism Pr; 0-938774),* 11706 Longleaf Lane, Houston, TX 77024 (SAN 216-4388).

Prisma Books, Inc., *(Prisma Bks; 0-910235),* Box 375, Audubon Station, New York, NY 10032 Tel 212-568-4591 (SAN 241-4384).

Pritchett & Hull Associates, Inc., *(Pritchett & Hull; 0-939838),* 3440 Oakcliff Rd, N.E., Suite 110, Atlanta, GA 30340 Tel 404-451-0602 (SAN 216-9258).

Privacy Journal, *(Privacy Journal; 0-930072),* Box 8844, Washington, DC 20003 Tel 202-547-2865 (SAN 216-6531).

Private Books, *(Private Bks; 0-9606471),* 500 19th Ave., San Francisco, CA 94121 Tel 415-751-2338 (SAN 216-8510).

Private Carrier Conference, Inc., *(Private Carrier),* 1616 P St., N.W., Washington, DC 20036 (SAN 217-264X).

P.R.N. Corp., *(P R N Corp; 0-910757),* 397 Forest Dr. SE, Cedar Rapids, IA 52403 (SAN 240-2415).

Pro-Ed, *(Pro Ed; 0-936104),* 5341 Industrial Oaks Blvd., Austin, TX 78735 Tel 512-892-3142 (SAN 222-1349).

Pro Libris Press, *(Pro Libris Pr; 0-943530),* Ten Third St., Bangor, ME 04401 Tel 207-942-3019 (SAN 240-7523).

Pro Lingua Associates, *(Pro Lingua; 0-86647),* 15 Elm St., Brattleboro, VT 05301 Tel 802-257-7779 (SAN 216-0579).

Pro-Search, *(Pro-Search; 0-9602540),* 3256 Ridge Rd., P.O. 24, Lansing, IL 60438 Tel 312-895-8800 (SAN 213-148X).

Pro West, *(Pro West),* 5745 Via los Ranchos, Paradise Valley, AZ 85253 Tel 602-991-3183 (SAN 215-1758); Dist. by: Motorbooks International, P.O. Box 2, 729 Prospect Ave., Osceola, WI 54020 Tel 715-294-3345 (SAN 212-3304).

ProActive Press, *(ProActive Pr; 0-914158),* P.O. Box 296, Berkeley, CA 94701 Tel 415-549-0839 (SAN 201-1888).

Procedures Unlimited, Inc, *(Procedures),* P.O. Box 66, Palos Park, IL 60464 Tel 312-448-8695 (SAN 287-2811).

Process Press, *(Process Pr; 0-9605378),* 2322 Haste, No. 31, Berkeley, CA 94704 Tel 415-548-6510 (SAN 215-9074).

Proctor, Jones Publishing Co., *(P Jones Pub Co; 0-9606860),* 3401 Sacramento St., San Francisco, CA 94118 Tel 415-922-9222 (SAN 241-0389).

Prodist *See Neale Watson Academic Pubns. Inc.*

Product Structuring Enterprises, *(PSE; 0-940964),* P.O. Box 17723, San Diego, CA 92117 Tel 714-451-1427 (SAN 217-4197).

Production House Corp., *(Prod Hse; 0-932638),* 4307 Euclid Ave., San Diego, CA 92115 Tel 619-287-2560 (SAN 201-1018).

Productivity International, Inc., *(Prod Intl),* Forest Central Dr., Suite 317, Dallas, TX 75243 Tel 214-341-9606 (SAN 217-2658).

Professional Book Center, Inc., *(Prof Bk Ctr Inc; 0-943226),* 5211 N.E. Sandy Blvd., Portland, OR 97213 Tel 503-288-1255 (SAN 240-5601).

Professional Books, *(Prof Bks; 0-933478),* P.O. Box 3494, Jackson, TN 38303 Tel 901-424-4665 (SAN 205-3977).

Professional Books Service, *(Prof Bks Serv; 0-9601052),* Box 366, Dayton, OH 45401 Tel 513-223-3734 (SAN 165-6309).

Professional Business Services, Co., *(Prof Busn Serv; 0-935154),* 5 Grandview Ave., Pittsburgh, PA 15211 Tel 412-381-8010 (SAN 213-3520).

Professional Development Services, *(Prof Dev Serv; 0-941944),* P.O. Box 750, Harrisonburg, VA 22801 (SAN 239-4758).

Professional Education Pubns., *(Prof Educ IL; 0-89707),* 1155 E. 60th St., Chicago, IL 60637 (SAN 214-445X).

Professional Engineering Registration Program, *(Prof Engine; 0-932276),* P.O. Box 911, San Carlos, CA 94070 Tel 415-593-9731 (SAN 282-1915); c/o Professional Publications, Inc., P.O. Box 199, San Carlos, CA 94070 (SAN 282-1923) (SAN 264-6315).

Professional Press, Inc., *(Prof Press; 0-87873),* 11 E. Adams St., Suite 1209, Chicago, IL 60603 (SAN 205-3985).

Professional Pubns., *(Prof Pubns CA; 0-9605954),* P.O. Box 17115, Bixby Sta., Long Beach, CA 90807 (SAN 216-4396).

Professional Pubns., Div of MetaData, Inc., *(Prof Pubns NY; 0-932836),* 441 Lexington Ave., New York, NY 10017 (SAN 213-3539); Orders to: P.O. Box 319, Huntington, NY 11743 (SAN 213-3547).

Professional Pubns., Inc., *(Prof Pubns Ohio; 0-934706),* 1609 Northwest Blvd., Columbus, OH 43212 Tel 614-488-8236 (SAN 203-0942).

Professional Real Estate Pubs., *(Prof Real Estate; 0-89764),* Orders to: Lincoln's Leadership Library, 5902 E. Fourth Terrace, Suite 100, Tulsa, OK 74112 Tel 918-622-7737 (SAN 214-4476).

Professional Research Publication, *(Prof Research; 0-931066),* P.O. Box 20081, San Diego, CA 92120 Tel 619-291-9659 (SAN 262-0677).

Professional Resource Exchange, Inc., *(Pro Resource; 0-943158),* 635 S. Orange Ave., Suites 4-5, Sarasota, FL 33577 (SAN 240-1223).

Profile Press, *(Profile Pr),* 245 Seventh Ave., New York, NY 10001 (SAN 214-1272).

Profit Ideas, *(Profit Ideas; 0-940398),* 8361 Vickers St., Suite 304, San Diego, CA 92111 (SAN 219-8436).

Profit Sharing Research Foundation, *(Profit Sharing; 0-911192),* 1718 Sherman Ave., Evanston, IL 60201 Tel 312-869-8787 (SAN 205-3993).

Progeny Press, Inc., *(Progeny Pr; 0-934168),* P.O. Box 206, Villanova, PA 19085 Tel 215-296-0595 (SAN 213-6740).

Program for Cincinnati, the, *(Prog Cincinnati; 0-9608200),* 230 E. 9th St., Cincinnati, OH 45202 Tel 513-721-5522 (SAN 238-8588).

Programmed Press, *(Prog Pr; 0-916106),* 2301 Baylis Ave., Elmont, NY 11003 Tel 516-775-0933 (SAN 203-0993).

Programmed Studies, Inc., *(Prog Studies; 0-917194),* P.O. Box 113, Stow, MA 01775 Tel 617-897-2130 (SAN 207-7434).

Programs & Pubns., *(Progs & Pubns; 0-934382),* 321 Queen St., Philadelphia, PA 19147 Tel 215-467-5291 (SAN 213-3555).

Programs for Achievement in Reading - P.A.R., Inc., *(PAR Inc; 0-913310; 0-89702),* 274 Weybosset St., Abbot Park Place, Providence, RI 02903 Tel 401-331-0130 (SAN 203-0209).

Programs in Communication Press, *(Programs Comm),* P.O. Box 970, Monument, CO 80132 Tel 303-443-5514 (SAN 218-9186).

Programs on Change, *(Progs on Change; 0-9606012),* 784 Columbus Ave., Suite 1c, New York, NY 10025 Tel 212-222-4606 (SAN 216-759X).

Progresiv Publishr, *(Progresiv Pub; 0-89670),* 401 E. 32nd St., No. 1002, Chicago, IL 60616 Tel 312-225-9181 (SAN 212-6818).

Progress Press, *(Progress Pr WA; 0-935792),* P.O. Box 5019, Seattle, WA 98105 (SAN 214-1280).

Progressive Baptist Publishing House, *(Prog Bapt Pub; 0-819175),* 850 N. Grove Ave., Elgin, IL 60120 (SAN 277-7010).

Progressive Concepts, Inc., *(Prog Concepts; 0-940010),* 2541 Lakewood Lane, Chesapeake, VA 23321 Tel 804-465-0646 (SAN 285-0877); Dist. by: Career Management Concepts, Inc., 2541 Lakewood Lane, Chesapeake, VA 23321 Tel 804-465-0646 (SAN 285-0885).

Progressive Education, *(Prog Educ; 0-935396),* P.O. Box 120574, Nashville, TN 37212 (SAN 239-4766).

Progressive Electronics Pubs., *(Progressive Elect Pubs; 0-912633),* 119 Mason Ave., Room H, Nashville, TN 37205 (SAN 283-8974).
Progressive Found., *(Prog Found; 0-942046),* 315 W. Gorham St., Madison, WI 53703 Tel 608-256-4146 (SAN 238-5961).
Progressive Grocer, *(Prog Grocer; 0-911790),* 708 Third Ave., New York, NY 10017 Tel 212-490-1000 (SAN 202-0270).
Proletarian Pubs, *(Proletarian Pubs; 0-89380),* P.O. Box 3925, Chicago, IL 60654 (SAN 209-2158); Orders to: Vanguard Books, P.O. Box 3566, Chicago, IL 60654 Tel 312-342-3425 (SAN 213-8212).
Prologue Pubns, *(Prologue; 0-930048),* P.O. Box 640, Menlo Park, CA 94025 Tel 415-322-1663 (SAN 210-1351).
Promark Asociates, *(Promark Assocs; 0-9607930),* Box 222, High Falls, NY 12440 Tel 914-687-7230 (SAN 238-5619).
Promethean Arts, *(Promethean Arts; 0-942624),* P.O. Box 2619, Toledo, OH 43606 Tel 419-536-4257 (SAN 238-5627).
Prometheus Books, *(Prometheus Bks; 0-87975),* 700 E. Amherst St., Buffalo, NY 14215 Tel 716-837-2475 (SAN 202-0289).
Prometheus Nemesis Book Co., Inc., *(Prometheus Nemesis; 0-9606954),* P.O. Box 2082, Del Mar, CA 92014 Tel 714-755-5980 (SAN 215-7020).
Promise Corp., *(Promise Corp; 0-936982),* P.O. Box 1534, Pawtucket, RI 02862 (SAN 214-4484).
Promised Land Publications, Inc., Div. of Eagle Systems International, *(Promised Land),* 5600 N. University Ave., Provo, UT 84601 Tel 801-225-2293 (SAN 204-3130) Tel 801-225-9000.
Promotions Ltd. Publishing, *(Promotions Ltd; 0-913679),* 6069 Bonnie Bern Ct., Burke, VA 22015 Tel 703-451-0884 (SAN 286-178X).
Proof Press, *(Proof Pr; 0-935070),* P. O. Box 1256, Berkeley, CA 94701 Tel 415-521-8741 (SAN 209-8687).
Prophecy Pressworks See **Sufi Islamia, Prophecy Pubns.**
Proprietary Assn., *(Proprietary Assn),* 1700 Pennsylvania Ave., N. W., Washington, DC 20006 Tel 202-393-1700 (SAN 209-2034).
Proscenium Press, *(Proscenium; 0-912262),* P.O. Box 361, Newark, DE 19711 Tel 215-255-4083 (SAN 203-0950).
ProSeminar Press, Inc., *(ProSeminar Pr),* 3330 NE 135th Ave., Portland, OR 97230 (SAN 214-4492).
Prospect Books, *(Prospect; 0-913710),* P.O. Box 57, Prospect, NY 13435 Tel 315-896-2249 (SAN 205-4000).
Prospect Hill, *(Prospect Hill; 0-941526),* 216 Wendover Rd., Baltimore, MD 21218 (SAN 239-3743).
Prospect Press, *(Prospect Pr; 0-937562),* 14427 Pebble Hill Lane, Gaithersburg, MD 20878 (SAN 282-194X); Orders to: Box 3069, Gaithersburg, MD 20878 Tel 301-251-4746 (SAN 282-1958).
Prosperity Press, *(Prosperity Pr; 0-935686),* Drawer 210, Queens Village, NY 11429 Tel 212-454-7268 (SAN 214-1299).
Proteus Press, Subs. of Proteus Design, Inc., *(Proteus; 0-918150),* 9225 Baltimore Blvd., College Park, MD 20740 Tel 301-441-2928 (SAN 210-2617).
Proteus Press, The, *(Proteus Calif; 0-932864),* 250 Thunderbird Dr., Aptos, CA 95003 (SAN 212-3800).
Proteus Publishing Co., Inc., *(Proteus Pub NY; 0-906071),* 9 W. 57th St., New York, NY 10019 (SAN 215-2363); Dist. by: Charles Scribner's Sons, 597 Fifth Ave., New York, NY 10017 (SAN 282-6550).
Providence Journal Company, *(Providence Journ),* 75 Fountain St., Providence, RI 02901 (SAN 264-3243).
Providence Press, The, *(Providence AL; 0-9604378),* P.O. Box 253, Florence, AL 35631 (SAN 216-289X).
Provident Press, The, *(Provident; 0-9603298),* P.O. Box 1112, Covina, CA 91722 Tel 213-339-9407 (SAN 213-6767).
Providential Press, *(Providential Pr),* P.O. Box 218026, Houston, TX 77218 Tel 713-578-9837 (SAN 276-9794).
Province, C. M., *(C M Province; 0-932348),* 11307 Vela Dr., San Diego, CA 92126 Tel 714-271-6517 (SAN 211-4445).

Provincial Press, *(Provincial Pr),* P.O. Box 2311, Chapel Hill, NC 27514 Tel 919-493-2240 (SAN 205-1079).
Provision House, *(Provision; 0-935446),* P.O. Box 5487, Austin, TX 78763 Tel 512-452-1417 (SAN 213-5485).
Provost, C. Antonio & Worth Blaney, *(Provost & Blaney),* 26412 Jacinto Dr., Mission Viejo, CA 92692 (SAN 239-3751).
Prow Books/Franciscan Marytown Press, *(Prow Bks-Franciscan; 0-913382),* 1600 W. Park Ave., Libertyville, IL 60048 (SAN 205-1060).
Prudential Publishing Company, *(Prudent Pub Co; 0-934432),* P.O. Box 10751, South Lake Tahoe, CA 95731 Tel 916-541-5029 (SAN 213-1498).
Pruett Publishing Co., *(Pruett; 0-87108),* 2928 Pearl St., Boulder, CO 80301 Tel 303-449-4919 (SAN 205-4035).
Pryor Pettengill, *(Pryor Pettengill; 0-933462),* Box 7074, Ann Arbor, MI 48107 (SAN 213-8697).
Prytaneum Press, *(Prytaneum Pr; 0-907152),* P.O. Box 7161, Amarillo, TX 79114 (SAN 214-4506).
P. S. Ltd. Publishing, *(P S Publishing; 0-912727),* 3857 Birch, Suite 570, Newport Beach, CA 92660 Tel 714-640-8003 (SAN 283-3093).
Psych Graphic Pubs., *(Psych Graphic; 0-932382),* 470 Nautilus St., Suite 303, La Jolla, CA 92037 Tel 619-459-0531 (SAN 210-6213).
Psychenutrition, Inc., *(Psychenutrition; 0-939466),* P.O. Box 3184, Manhattan Beach, CA 90266 Tel 213-545-7012 (SAN 216-440X).
Psychic Books, *(Psychic Bks),* 440 Avalon Pl., Oxnard, CA 93033 (SAN 219-2586).
Psychic Forum, The, *(Psychic Forum; 0-941762),* 921-A Paradise Rd., P.O. Box 2464, Modesto, CA 95351 Tel 209-576-7472 (SAN 239-2852).
Psychoanalytic Quarterly, Inc., *(Psych Qtly; 0-911194),* 57 W. 57th St., New York, NY 10019 (SAN 205-4043).
Psychogenic Disease Publishing Co., *(Psychogenic Disease; 0-87312),* P.O. Box 19098, Sacramento, CA 95819 Tel 916-677-1610 (SAN 203-4239).
Psychohistory Press, Div. of Atcom, Inc., Pubs., *(Psychohistory Pr),* 2315 Broadway, New York, NY 10024 Tel 212-873-5900 (SAN 201-8926).
Psychological Assessment Resources, *(Psych Assess; 0-911907),* P.O. Box 98, Odessa, FL 33556 Tel 813-977-3395 (SAN 264-6897).
Psychological Development Pubns., *(Psych Dev Pubns; 0-912397),* P.O. Box 3198, Aspen, CO 81612 Tel 303-925-9272 (SAN 265-1904).
Psychological Dimensions, Inc., *(Psych Dimensions; 0-88437),* 10 W. 66th St., Suite 4H, New York, NY 10023 Tel 212-877-2313 (SAN 204-3866).
Psychological Press, *(Psych Pr WA; 0-937668),* Box 45435, Seattle, WA 98105 Tel 206-323-5753 (SAN 215-1766).
Psychological Processes, Incorporated, *(Psych Processes Inc; 0-912149),* 1675 Visalia Ave., Berkeley, CA 94707 Tel 415-526-2591 (SAN 264-7788).
Psychology & Consulting Associates Press, *(Psych & Consul Assocs; 0-930626),* P.O. Box 1837, La Jolla, CA 92038 Tel 714-459-1135 (SAN 211-3856).
Psychometric Affiliates, *(Psychometric; 0-9606044),* P.O. Box 3167, Munster, IN 46321 Tel 219-836-1661 (SAN 203-1205).
Psychoneurologia Press, *(Psychoneurologia; 0-935688),* P.O. Box 7542, Shawnee Mission, KS 66207 Tel 913-381-8564 (SAN 213-6945).
Psyon Pubns., *(Psyon Pubns),* 220 Redwood Highway, No. 102, Mill Valley, CA 94941 Tel 415-459-5501 (SAN 241-578X).
P T L Enterprises, *(PTL Enterprises; 0-912275),* Charlotte, NC 28279 (SAN 283-3085).
Ptolemy Press Ltd., *(Ptolemy Pr; 0-933550),* P.O. Box 243, Grove City, PA 16127 Tel 412-458-5145 (SAN 211-2671).
Ptolemy/The Browns Mills Review Press, *(Ptolemy Brown; 0-911851),* P.O. Box 905, Browns Mills, NJ 08015 (SAN 217-3123).
Public Affairs Clearinghouse See **California Institute of Public Affairs**

Public Affairs Committee, Inc., *(Pub Affr Comm; 0-88291),* 381 Park Ave., S., New York, NY 10016 Tel 212-683-4331 (SAN 205-4027).
Public Affairs Press, *(Pub Aff Pr; 0-8183),* 419 New Jersey Ave., Washington, DC 20003 Tel 202-544-3024 (SAN 202-1471).
Public Citizen Inc., *(Pub Citizen Inc; 0-937188),* 2000 P St. NW, No. 708, Washington, DC 20036 (SAN 239-4774).
Public Information Press, Inc., *(Public Info Pr; 0-934954),* P.O. Box 402611, Miami Beach, FL 33140 Tel 305-538-5308 (SAN 213-1390).
Public Insights Press, *(Public Insights; 0-9608776),* Box 242, Drexel Hill, PA 19026 Tel 215-626-8944 (SAN 238-3438).
Public Management Associates, *(Pub Mgmt Assoc; 0-939968),* 2014 Siegle Dr., Lemon Grove, CA 92045 Tel 714-575-2395 (SAN 216-8537).
Public Management Institute, *(Public Management; 0-916664),* 358 Brannan St., San Francisco, CA 94107 Tel 415-896-1900 (SAN 208-6964).
Public Press, *(Public Pr; 0-9611738),* c/o St. Clements Church, 423 W. 46th St., New York, NY 10036 Tel 212-246-7277 (SAN 219-4546).
Public Relations Publishing Co., Inc., *(Public Relations; 0-913046),* 888 Seventh Ave., New York, NY 10106 Tel 212-582-7373 (SAN 202-957X).
Public Sector Labor Relations Conference Board, *(Pub Sect Lab Rel; 0-913400),* Univ. of Maryland, Division of Behavorial and Social Sciences, College Park, MD 20742 (SAN 205-4051).
Public Securities Assn., *(Pub Securities),* 1 World Trade Ctr., Suite 5271, New York, NY 10048 (SAN 216-2903).
Public Service Materials Center, *(Public Serv Materials),* 111 N. Central Ave., Hartsdale, NY 10530 (SAN 211-9676).
Public Service Pubns., Inc., *(Public Serv Pubns),* 1523 W. 8th St., Los Angeles, CA 90017 Tel 213-484-1088 (SAN 212-1328).
Pub. Arts, *(Pubn Arts NJ; 0-942190),* 5 Schoon Ave., Hawthorne, NJ 07506 Tel 201-427-1333 (SAN 239-9717).
Publication Arts, Inc., *(Pubn Arts; 0-86573),* 5700 Green Circle Dr., Minnetonka, MN 55343 (SAN 215-1774).
Publication Board of the American Society of Landscape Architects, *(Am Soc Landscape; 0-911241),* 1190 E. Broadway, Louisville, KY 40204 Tel 502-589-1167 (SAN 274-8975).
Pubns. Devel. Co. of Texas, *(Pubns Devl Co TX; 0-930396),* P.O. Box 1075, Crockett, TX 75835 Tel 713-544-7481 (SAN 211-0490).
Pubns. for Living, *(Pubns Living; 0-912128),* 11224 Big Bend Blvd., St. Louis, MO 63122 Tel 314-821-6177 (SAN 205-1044).
Pubns. of the Pennsylvania-Yale Expedition to Egypt, Yale Univ., *(Penn-Yale Expedit),* c/o Pubns. Off., Peabody Museum of Natural History, 170 Whitney Ave., P.O. Box 6666, New Haven, CT 06511 (SAN 205-177X).
Publicity in Print, *(Publicity; 0-915716),* 935 Thornton Way, San Jose, CA 95128 Tel 408-293-3997 (SAN 207-2750).
Publish or Perish, Inc., *(Publish or Perish; 0-914098),* 901 Washington St., Wilmington, DE 19801 (SAN 202-0319).
Publisher Vaidava, *(Pub Vaidava; 0-936302),* 1621 S. 21st St., Lincoln, NE 68502 (SAN 214-2198).
Publishers, *(Publishers),* The World of Astrological Research, 890-B-So. 6th St, Las Vegas, NV 89101 (SAN 205-406X).
Publishers Agency, Inc., Subs. of Pubco Corp., McLean, Va, *(Pubs Agency; 0-87781),* 1411 Ford Rd., Bensalem, PA 19020 Tel 215-638-7000 (SAN 209-0953).
Publishers Consultants, *(Publishers Consult; 0-88310),* Box 1908, Ft. Collins, CO 80522 (SAN 203-2449) Formerly Shields Publishing Co., Inc.
Publishers Guild, *(Publishers Guild),* P.O. Box 754, Palatine, IL 60067 Tel 312-991-0255 (SAN 212-7180).
Publishers Media, *(Publishers Media; 0-934064),* 5507 Morella Ave., N. Hollywood, CA 91607 (SAN 213-5493).
Publishers of Truth, *(Pubs of Truth; 0-930682),* 1509 Bruce Rd., Oreland, PA 19075 Tel 215-576-1450 (SAN 211-0423).

PUBLISHERS' PRESS

Publishers' Press, *(Publishers Pr; 0-943592),* 1935 S. E. 59th Ave., Portland, OR 97215 Tel 503-232-9293 (SAN 240-7558).

Pubs Unlimited, *(Pub Unlimited; 0-942232),* 6155 Westerville Rd. Box 239, Westerville, OH 43081 (SAN 239-8648).

Publishing Center for Cultural Resources, *(Pub Ctr Cult Res),* 625 Broadway, New York, NY 10012 Tel 212-260-2010 (SAN 274-9025).

Publishing Enterprises, Inc., *(Pub Enterprises; 0-941368),* P.O. Box 66344, Seattle, WA 98166 Tel 206-838-2997 (SAN 239-0248).

Publishing Horizons, Inc., *(Pub Horizons; 0-942280),* 623 High St., Worthington, OH 43085 Tel 614-261-6565 (SAN 239-7439).

Publishing Services Center, *(Pub Serv Ctr)*, Dist. by: William Kaufmann, Inc., 95 First St., Los Altos, CA 94022 Tel 415-948-5858 (SAN 202-9383).

Publishing Ward, Inc., The, *(Pub Ward Inc; 0-911631),* P.O. Box 9077, Fort Collins, CO 80525 Tel 303-226-5107 (SAN 264-3308).

Puckerbrush Press, *(Puckerbrush; 0-913006),* 76 Main St., Orono, ME 04473 Tel 207-866-4868 (SAN 202-0327).

Puddingstone Press, *(Puddingstone),* P.O. Box 67, Banner Elk, NC 28604 (SAN 205-4019).

Pueblo Publishing Co., Inc., *(Pueblo Pub Co; 0-916134),* 1860 Broadway, New York, NY 10023 Tel 212-541-7665 (SAN 211-7606).

Pueblo Publishing Press, *(Pueblo Pub Pr; 0-942316),* 401 Vandament Ave., Yukon, OK 73099 (SAN 239-5940).

Pueo Press, *(Pueo Pr; 0-917850),* P.O. Box 2066, San Rafael, CA 94912 (SAN 209-6331).

Puerto Rico Almanacs, Inc., *(Puerto Rico Almanacs; 0-934642),* P.O. Box 9582, Santurce, PR 00908 Tel 809-724-2402 (SAN 213-1382).

Puffin Books *See* **Penguin Books, Inc.**

Puissance Pubns., Inc., *(Puissance Pubns; 0-940634),* 2802 N. Patton St., Arlington Heights, IL 60004 Tel 314-870-1840 (SAN 218-5229).

Pulmac Enterprises Inc., *(Pulmac Ent; 0-936346),* Middlesex Star Route, Montpelier, VT 05602 Tel 802-223-6326 (SAN 214-1302) Books Can Be Ordered from: Megalon Publications, P.O. Box 705, Goleta, Ca 93116.

Pulp, *(Pulp; 0-9603092),* c/o Howard Sage, 720 Greenwich St., New York, NY 10014 Tel 212-989-0190 (SAN 218-3404).

Pulsar Pubns., *(Pulsar Pub; 0-9609442),* Box 714, Lafayette, CA 94549 (SAN 260-1206); Dist. by: Strawberry Hill Press, 2594 15th Ave., San Francisco, CA 94127 Tel 415-664-8112 (SAN 238-8103).

Pulse-Finger Press, *(Pulse-Finger; 0-912282),* P.O. Box 488, Yellow Springs, OH 45387 Tel 513-376-9033 (SAN 206-6785).

Punch Poster, Inc., *(Punch Poster Inc; 0-941714),* 7540 Little River Tnpke., Annandale, VA 22003 Tel 703-642-8490 (SAN 239-2860).

Punster's Press, *(Punster's Pr; 0-9601402),* 3834 Joanne Dr., Glennview, IL 60025 Tel 312-564-4342 (SAN 211-3449).

Puppet Masters, The, *(Puppet Masters),* P.O. Box 11162, Palo Alto, CA 94306 Tel 415-493-3339 (SAN 218-9259).

Purcell Productions, Inc., *(Purcell Prods; 0-9610742),* 300 W. 55th St., New York, NY 10019 Tel 212-757-5300 (SAN 264-780X).

Purcells, Inc., *(Purcells; 0-931068),* 305 S. 10th, Box 190, Broken Bow, NE 68822 Tel 308-872-2471 (SAN 211-1357).

Purchase Press, The, *(Purchase Pr; 0-938266),* P.O. Box 5, Harrison, NY 10528 Tel 212-986-7355 (SAN 215-9090); Dist. by: Book Dynamics, 836 Broadway, New York, NY 10003 Tel 212-254-7798 (SAN 169-5649).

Purdue Univ., *(Purdue Univ; 0-931682),* Bldg. D, South Campus Courts, West Lafayette, IN 47907 Tel 317-494-2035 (SAN 215-2649).

Purdue Univ. Press, *(Purdue U Pr; 0-911198),* S. Campus Courts-D, West Lafayette, IN 47907 Tel 317-494-2035 (SAN 203-4026).

Purnell Reference Books, Product Line of Raintree Publishers, Inc., *(Purnell Ref Bks; 0-8393),* 205 W. Highland Ave., Milwaukee, WI 53203 Tel 414-273-0873 (SAN 210-5616).

Purple Mouth Press, *(Purple Mouth; 0-9603300),* 713 Paul St., Newport News, VA 23605 Tel 804-380-6595 (SAN 209-8709).

Purple Unicorn Books, *(Purple Unicorn; 0-931998),* P.O. Box 1056, Dania, FL 33004 Tel 305-920-9972 (SAN 212-3061).

Pursifull, Carmen M., *(C M Pursifull; 0-9607856),* 809 W. Maple, Champaign, IL 61820 (SAN 237-9880).

Pushcart Press, The, *(Pushcart Pr; 0-916366),* P.O. Box 380, Wainscott, NY 11975 Tel 516-324-9300 (SAN 202-9871).

Pushkin Press, the, *(Pushkin Pr; 0-943046),* 1930 Columbia Rd. N.W., Washington, DC 20009 Tel 202-265-1871 (SAN 240-4338).

Putnam Publishing Group, The, *(Putnam Pub Group; 0-399),* 200 Madison Ave., New York, NY 10016 Tel 212-576-8908 (SAN 202-5531); Orders to: 1050 Wall St. W., Lyndhurst, NJ 07071 Tel 201-933-9292 (SAN 202-554X). *Imprints:* Peppercorn (Peppercorn); Perigee Books (Perigee).

Putterin Pr., *(Putterin; 0-938946),* P.O. Box 72, Burlingame, CA 94010 Tel 415-343-8426 (SAN 238-7212); Dist. by: Publishers Group West, 5855 Beaudry St., Emeryville, CA 94608 (SAN 202-8522).

PW Pubns., *(PW Pubns),* 37 Ramparts Court, P.O. Box 35311, Colorado Springs, CO 80936 (SAN 239-5959).

PWS Publishers, *(PWS Pubs; 0-87150),* Statler Office Bldg., 20 Park Plaza, Boston, MA 02116 Tel 617-482-2344 (SAN 200-2264).

Pygmalion Press, *(Pygmalion Pr; 0-915242),* 609 El Centro, So. Pasadena, CA 91030 (SAN 206-8206); 2104 Holly Dr., Hollywood, CA 90028 Tel 213-461-2557 (SAN 206-8214).

Pylon Press, Inc., *(Pylon; 0-918524),* 108-19 67th Rd., Forest Hills, NY 11375 Tel 212-261-2533 (SAN 209-9888).

Pym-Randall Press, *(Pym-Rand Pr; 0-918524),* 73 Cohasset St., Roslindale, MA 02131 Tel 617-547-5602 (SAN 218-2793).

Pyquag Books, Pubs., *(Pyquag; 0-912492),* P.O. Box 328, Wethersfield, CT 06109 (SAN 205-4086).

Pyramid Press Publishing Co., *(Pyramid WV),* 1686 Marshall St., Benwood, WV 26031 (SAN 207-6683).

Pyramid Systems, *(Pyramid Systems; 0-942888),* 2800 Corona Drive, Davis, CA 95616 Tel 916-756-2242 (SAN 240-4907).

Python Publishing Group, *(Python Pub; 0-89300),* 162 Washington St., Newark, NJ 07102 (SAN 240-057X).

Pyxidium Press, *(Pyxidium Pr; 0-936568),* Box 462, Old Chelsea Sta., New York, NY 10011 Tel 212-242-5224 (SAN 214-4514).

PZA Enterprises, *(PZA Enterp; 0-943304),* One Anders Tower, Box 12852, Dallas, TX 75225 Tel 214-696-5291 (SAN 240-7396).

QBLH Pubns., *(QBLH Pubns; 0-9603680),* Box 1166, Ramona, CA 92065 (SAN 214-1310).

QDP Inc., *(QDP Inc; 0-9610044),* 701 Erie St., Muskegon, MI 49441 Tel 616-726-6229 (SAN 262-9887).

Q.E.D. Information Sciences, Inc., *(QED Info Sci; 0-89435),* 170 Linden St., Wellesley, MA 02181 Tel 617-237-5656 (SAN 210-136X).

Quade, Vicki, *(V Quade; 0-9602604),* 1110 Monroe St.,, Evanston, IL 60202 Tel 312-328-2527 (SAN 213-151X).

Quadrant Press, *(Quadrant Pr; 0-915276),* 19 W. 44th St., New York, NY 10036 (SAN 211-5727).

Quail Productions, *(Quail Prods; 0-9610764),* Box 312, Roseland, NJ 07068 Tel 212-593-8963 (SAN 264-6323); 37 Belmont Dr., Livingston, NJ 07039 Tel 201-992-5865 (SAN 264-6331).

Quail Ridge Press, Inc., *(Quail Ridge; 0-937552),* P.O. Box 123, Brandon, MS 39042 (SAN 214-2201).

Quail Run Pubns., Inc., *(Quail Run; 0-930380),* 3336 N.32nd St., Suite 104, Phoenix, AZ 85018 Tel 602-955-5953 (SAN 210-9476).

Quaker City Books, *(Quaker City),* P.O. Box 6404, Philadelphia, PA 19145 (SAN 209-1178).

Quaker Press, *(Quaker; 0-911200),* 3218 O St. N.W., Washington, DC 20007 Tel 202-338-3391 (SAN 204-6547).

PUBLISHERS AND DISTRIBUTORS

Quality Books Inc., *(Quality Bks IL; 0-89196),* 400 Anthony Trail, Northbrook, IL 60062 Tel 312-498-4000 (SAN 169-2127) Wholesalers of remainders. Warehouse open for walk-through buyers. *Imprints:* Domus Books (Domus Bks).

Quality Books of Kansas City, Missouri, *(Quality MO; 0-9606586),* P.O. Box 8487, Kansas City, MO 64114 Tel 913-383-2160 (SAN 219-0923).

Quality Circle Institute, *(Quality Circle; 0-937670),* 1425 Vista Way, Airport Industrial Park, P. O. Box Q, Red Bluff, CA 96080 (SAN 220-0880).

Quality Educators, Ltd., *(Quality Educ),* 1236 S.E. Fourth Ave., Ft. Lauderdale, FL 33316 Tel 305-522-2249 (SAN 212-9280).

Quality Hill Books, *(Quality Hill; 0-9605044),* 674 Church St., San Luis Obispo, CA 93401 (SAN 216-0595).

Quality Library Editions, *(Quality Lib),* P.O. Box 148, Darby, PA 19023 (SAN 209-1186).

Quality Pubns., *(Quality OR),* 12180 S.W. 127th, Tigard, OR 97223 Tel 503-639-5977 (SAN 219-8134).

Quality Pubns., Div. of Quality Printing Co., Inc., *(Quality Pubns; 0-89137),* P.O. Box 1060, Abilene, TX 79604 Tel 915-677-6262 (SAN 203-0071).

Quality Pubns. Inc., *(Quality Ohio; 0-934040),* P.O. Box 2633, Lakewood, OH 44107 (SAN 216-2911).

Quality Services, Inc., *(Quality Serv; 0-9608966),* P.O. Box 2848, Gillette, WY 82716 Tel 307-686-2428 (SAN 240-9801).

Quam, Martin, Press, *(Quam Pr),* 1515 Columbia Dr., Cedar Falls, IA 50613 Tel 319-266-6242 (SAN 213-3571); Orders to: 201 Rio St., Rio, WI 53960 (SAN 213-358X).

Quantal Publishing Co., *(Quantal; 0-936596),* P.O. Box 1598, Goleta, CA 93116 Tel 805-964-7293 (SAN 215-1014).

Quantum Publications, Inc., *(Quantum Pubns; 0-9611548),* P.O. Box 1039, Orange, CT 06477-7039 Tel 203-934-3945 (SAN 285-2578); 88 Canton St., W. Haven, CT 02516 (SAN 285-2586).

Quantum Pubs., *(Quantum Pubs; 0-934644),* 94 Rugby Rd., Brooklyn, NY 11226 Tel 212-856-3116 (SAN 207-2777).

Quarterdeck Press, *(Quarterdeck; 0-918546),* P.O. Box 134, Pacific Palisades, CA 90272 Tel 213-459-6832 (SAN 209-990X).

Quarterly Review of Literature Poetry Series, *(Quarterly Rev),* 26 Haslet Ave., Princeton, NJ 08540 Tel 609-921-6976 (SAN 282-1982); Dist. by: B. Deboer, 113 E. Centre St., Nutley, NJ 07110 Tel 201-667-9300 (SAN 282-1990).

Quarterman Pubns., Inc., *(Quarterman; 0-88000),* 5 S. Union St., Lawrence, MA 01843 Tel 617-259-8047 (SAN 203-3992).

Quartuccio, Anthony, *(A Quartuccio; 0-9606934),* 4819 Kingdale Dr., San Jose, CA 95124 (SAN 239-5460).

Quartus Books, Div. of The Quartus Foundation, *(Quartus Bks; 0-942082),* P.O. Box 26683, Austin, TX 78755 Tel 512-452-9237 (SAN 238-0080).

Quartz Press, The, *(Quartz Pr; 0-911455),* P.O. Box 465, Ashland, OR 97520 (SAN 274-9246).

Quasem, M. Adul, *(Quasem),* Dist. by: Habibur Rahman, 502 N. Elm St., Centralia, IL 62801 (SAN 209-5939).

Que Corp., *(Que Corp; 0-88022),* 7960 Castleway Dr., Indianapolis, IN 46250 Tel 317-842-7162 (SAN 219-6298).

Queen Anne Press, The, Div. of Wye Institute, Inc., *(Queen Anne Pr; 0-937692),* Cheston-on-Wye, Queenstown, MD 21658 Tel 301-827-7401 (SAN 215-272X); Orders to: P.O. Box 50, Queenstown, MD 21658 (SAN 215-2738).

Queen of the Missions Publishing Co., *(Queen Missions; 0-941428),* 1503 la Coronilla Dr., Santa Barbara, CA 93109 (SAN 239-376X).

Queens College Press, *(Queens Coll Pr; 0-930146),* Editorial Services, Flushing, NY 11367 Tel 212-520-7599 (SAN 203-1973).

Queens House, *(Queens Hse; 0-89244),* 105 Grovers Ave., Bridgeport, CT 06605 Tel 203-367-1578 (SAN 208-2802).

Quest Books *See* **Theosophical Publishing House**

Quest Editions, *(Quest Edns),* P.O. Box 67, Sharon Hill, PA 19079 (SAN 209-1194).

Quest Products, Inc., *(Quest Prods; 0-9608002),* 11920 Cragwood Way, Potomac, MD 20854 (SAN 264-3332).
Quest Publishing, *(Quest Pub IL; 0-940286),* 2018 29th St., Rock Island, IL 61201 Tel 309-794-0505 (SAN 217-5584).
Quest Publishing Co., *(Quest Pub; 0-930844),* 1351 Titan Way, Brea, CA 92621 Tel 714-738-6400 (SAN 211-3740).
Quest Publishing Inc., *(Quest Utah; 0-938662),* P.O. Box 27317, Salt Lake City, UT 84127 (SAN 215-9775).
Quicksilver Productions, *(Quicksilver Prod; 0-930356),* P.O. Box 340, Ashland, OR 97520 Tel 503-482-5343 (SAN 211-9684).
Quigley Publishing Co. Inc., *(Quigley Pub Co; 0-900610),* 159 W. 53rd. St., New York, NY 10019 Tel 212-247-3100 (SAN 205-1141).
Quill, *(Quill NY; 0-688),* 105 Madison Ave., New York, NY 10016 (SAN 239-4790).
SI, *(Quill and Brush Pr; 0-9610494),* 7649 Old Georgetown Rd., Bethesda Square, Bethesda, MD 20814 Tel 301-951-0290 (SAN 264-3340).
Quill Books, *(Quill Bks; 0-943536),* Box 842, Minot, ND 58701 Tel 701-839-7232 (SAN 274-9300).
Quill Pubns., *(Quill Pubns; 0-916608),* 1260 Coast Village Circle, Santa Barbara, CA 93108 Tel 805-969-2542 (SAN 208-3442).
Quincunx, *(Quincunx; 0-942626),* 235 S. 15th St. 3B, Philadelphia, PA 19102 Tel 215-732-0593 (SAN 238-5643).
Quinn-Gallagher Press, *(Quinn-Gallagher; 0-935282),* 6372 Forward Ave., Pittsburgh, PA 15217 Tel 412-521-1863 (SAN 213-3598).
Quintessence Pubns., *(Quintessence; 0-918466),* 356 Bunker Hill Mine Rd., Amador City, CA 95601 Tel 209-267-5470 (SAN 209-5947).
Quintessence Publishing Co., Inc., *(Quint Pub Co; 0-931386; 0-86715),* 8 S. Michigan Ave., Suite 2301, Chicago, IL 60603 Tel 312-782-3221 (SAN 215-9783).
Quixote Press, *(Quixote; 0-9600306),* P.O. Box 70013, Allen Sta., Houston, TX 77270 Tel 713-529-7944 (SAN 202-1463).
Quorum Books *See* Greenwood Press
RAMCO Pubns., *(RAMCO Pubns; 0-939844),* 224 Harding Ave., Libertyville, IL 60048 Tel 312-362-4948 (SAN 216-9282).
R & D Press, *(R & D Pr; 0-88274),* 885 N. San Antonio Rd., Los Altos, CA 94022 Tel 415-948-0370 (SAN 203-0896).
R & D Pubns., Inc., *(R & D Pubns; 0-938152),* Box 1032, New York, NY 10028 (SAN 282-2008); Orders to: Box 351, Spring Valley, NY 10977 (SAN 282-2016).
R&D Pubs., *(R&D Pubs),* P.O. Box 1584, Los Gatos, CA 95031 (SAN 223-1689).
R & D Services, *(R & D Serv; 0-89511),* P.O. Box 644, Des Moines, IA 50303 Tel 515-288-8391 (SAN 209-6765).
R & E Research Associates, Inc., *(R & E Res Assoc; 0-88247),* 936 Industrial Ave., Palo Alto, CA 94303 Tel 408-866-6303 (SAN 204-6555).
R & H Publishers, *(R & H Pubs; 0-935246),* Box 3587, Georgetown Sta., Washington, DC 20007 Tel 703-524-4226 (SAN 210-5691).
R&M Publishing Co., *(R&M Pub Co; 0-936026),* P.O. Box 1276, Holly Hill, SC 29059 Tel 803-531-2053 (SAN 213-6392).
R & R Newkirk Co. Inc., *(R & R Newkirk; 0-912169),* P.O. Box 1727, Indianapolis, IN 46206 (SAN 287-7635).
RBA Press, *(RBA Pr; 0-9610236),* P.O. Box 991, Vallejo, CA 94590 (SAN 264-4359).
R. B. H. Publishing Enterprises, Div. of Advertising Unlimited Ltd., *(RBH Pub; 0-939842),* 4528 W. Charleston Blvd., Las Vegas, NV 89102 Tel 702-878-8534 (SAN 282-2024); Orders to: 4263 Powell Ave, Las Vegas, NE 89121 Tel 702-878-8534 (SAN 282-2032).
RBX Research, *(RBX Res; 0-917038),* P.O. Box 15, Stanton, TN 38069 (SAN 208-4155).
RCA Distributor & Special Products, *(RCA Dist Spec Prods),* Deptford, NJ 08096 (SAN 208-1210).
RCA Solid State Div., *(RCA Solid State; 0-913972),* P.O. Box 3200, Somerville, NJ 08876 (SAN 205-115X).
RCM Pubns., *(RCM Pubns),* P.O. Box 33565, San Diego, CA 92103 (SAN 215-2584).
RCP Pubns., *(RCP Pubns; 0-89851),* P.O. Box 3486, Merchandise Mart, Chicago, IL 60654 Tel 312-663-5920 (SAN 212-4408).

R. C. Press, *(R C Pr; 0-943854),* 7140 Madison Ave. W., Golden Valley, MN 55427 Tel 612-537-4065 (SAN 241-0613).
R C Pubns., *(R C Pubns; 0-915734),* 6400 Goldsboro Rd., Bethesda, MD 20817 Tel 301-229-9040 (SAN 209-1119).
R. C. Pubns., *(R C Pubns OR; 0-942152),* 1828 NE Stanton, Portland, OR 97212 Tel 503-287-1009 (SAN 239-5967).
RDC Pubs., *(RDC Pubs; 0-9600576),* 4741 School St., Yorba Linda, CA 92686 Tel 714-777-3376 (SAN 207-0154).
R. G. Enterprises, *(R G Enterprises; 0-910575),* 2000 Center St., No. 1067, Berkeley, CA 94704 (SAN 274-9327).
R. H. M. Press, *(R H M Pr; 0-89058),* 172 Forest Ave, Glencove, NY 11542 Tel 516-759-2904 (SAN 206-9873).
RIF Marketing, *(RIF Mktg; 0-9606000),* 912 Five Points Rd., P.O. Box 3055, Virginia Beach, VA 23454 Tel 804-481-0776 (SAN 216-7611).
R/J Associates, *(RJ Assocs; 0-9602090),* 564 Tyler Ave., Livermore, CA 94550 Tel 415-443-7140 (SAN 212-1352).
RK Editions, *(RK Edns; 0-932360),* P.O. Box 73, Canal St., New York, NY 10013 (SAN 211-447X).
RMP Financial Consultants, *(RMP Finan Consul; 0-931664),* 10 Petit Bayou Lane, New Orleans, LA 70129 Tel 504-254-2766 (SAN 211-9692).
ROMARC, Inc., *(ROMARC Inc; 0-940522),* 3738 14 Mile Rd., Stockton, CA 95209 (SAN 219-8150).
RPR, Inc. Public Finance-California Division, *(R P R Inc; 0-9611718),* One California St. No. 2750, San Francisco, CA 94111 Tel 415-989-2300 (SAN 285-2616).
R.P.W. Publishing Corp., *(R P W Pub; 0-9608450),* P.O. Box 729, Lexington, SC 29072 Tel 803-359-9941 (SAN 240-561X).
R.R.P. Pubs., *(RRP Pub; 0-9607034),* 12 W. 17th St., New York, NY 10011 Tel 212-924-4127 (SAN 239-0264).
RSC Pubs., Div. of Research Services Corp., *(RSC Pubs; 0-915074),* 5268 Trail Lake Dr., P.O. Drawer 16549, Ft. Worth, TX 76133 Tel 817-292-4272 (SAN 238-8294).
R.S.V. Publishing, Inc., *(RSV Pub; 0-933514),* Box 182, Times Plaza, Brooklyn, NY 11217 (SAN 212-6184).
RWS Books, *(RWS Bks; 0-939400),* 4296 Mulholland St., Salt Lake City, UT 84117 Tel 801-272-1722 (SAN 220-1593).
RWU Parachuting Pubs., *(R WU Parachuting Pubns),* 1656 Beechwood Ave., Fullerton, CA 92635 Tel 714-990-0369 (SAN 209-1879).
Rabinowitz, Solomon, Hebrew Book Store, Inc., *(Rabinowitz Hebrew Book; 0-87374),* 30 Canal St., New York, NY 10002 Tel 212-267-2406 (SAN 205-1176).
Racquet Sports Information Service, *(Racquet Sports; 0-914934),* P.O. Box 1710, Easton, MD 21601 (SAN 207-0308).
Racz Publishing Co., *(Racz Pub; 0-916546),* P.O. Box 287, Oxnard, CA 93032 Tel 805-642-1186 (SAN 208-0265).
Rada Pr., *(Rada Pr; 0-9604212),* 11930 Mississippi Dr., Champlin, MN 55108 Tel 612-427-4482 (SAN 214-4522).
Radicus Communications, *(Radicus Comm; 0-941564),* 9356 Home Circle, Des Plaines, IL 60016 Tel 312-299-0912 (SAN 239-2917).
Radio City Book Store, *(Radio City; 0-911202),* 324 W. 47th St., New York, NY 10036 Tel 212-245-5754 (SAN 204-6644).
Radio Pubns., Inc., *(Radio Pubns; 0-933616),* Box 149, Wilton, CT 06897 Tel 914-967-5774 (SAN 215-336X).
Radius Pr., *(Radius Pr; 0-942154),* P.O. Box 1271, FDR Sta., New York, NY 10022 Tel 212-988-4715 (SAN 239-5975).
Radix Books Inc., *(Radix Bks),* P.O. Box 171, Beaver Falls, PA 15010 Tel 412-843-2806 (SAN 209-1364).
Radke, George E., *(G E Radke; 0-9607994),* 41 Harvard Rd., Havertown, PA 19083 Tel 215-446-0786 (SAN 238-8308).
Rae John Pubs., *(Rae John; 0-9605226; 0-939438),* Drawer S, Susanville, CA 96130 (SAN 220-1739).
Raemsch Pubns., *(Raemsch Pubns; 0-9605398),* Box 149, West Oneonta, NY 13861 (SAN 214-4530).

Ragan, Lawrence, Communications, Inc., *(Ragan Comm; 0-931368),* 407 S. Dearborn St., Chicago, IL 60605 Tel 312-922-8245 (SAN 212-2243).
Ragnar Press, Inc., *(Ragnar Pr; 0-912735),* P.O. Box 92, West Carrollton, OH 45449 Tel 513-859-8661 (SAN 283-216X).
Ragusan Press, *(Ragusan Pr; 0-918660),* 936 Industrial Ave., Palo Alto, CA 94303 Tel 415-494-1112 (SAN 212-0445).
Rahamah Pubns., *(Rahamah Pubns; 0-9603634),* P.O. Box 135, Lowell, MA 01853 (SAN 216-292X).
Rahija Associates, *(Rahija; 0-942670),* Dist. by: ACLD, 4156 Library Rd., Pittsburgh, PA 15234 (SAN 282-6674).
Raiko Corp., *(Raiko; 0-910263),* P.O. Box 597, New York, NY 10003 Tel 212-783-2597 (SAN 240-9542).
Rail-Europe/Baxter Guides, *(Rail-Europe-Baxter; 0-913384),* P.O. Box 3255, Alexandria, VA 22302 (SAN 203-3933).
Railhead Pubns., *(Railhead Pubns; 0-912113),* P.O. Box 526, Canton, OH 44701 Tel 216-454-7519 (SAN 264-7826).
Railroadians of America, Inc., *(Railroadians; 0-941652),* 18 Okner Pkwy., Livingston, NJ 07039 Tel 201-487-3719 (SAN 239-2925).
Railsearch Publishing, Inc., *(Railsearch; 0-937060),* P.O. Box 84, Chalfont, PA 18914 (SAN 214-4549).
Raimi, Ralph A., *(Raimi),* Dept. of Mathematics, University of Rochester, Rochester, NY 14627 Tel 716-275-4411 (SAN 240-8295).
Rainbow Books/Betty Wright, *(Rainbow-Betty; 0-935834),* Dept. 1-H, P.O. Box 1069, Moore Haven, FL 33471 Tel 813-946-0293 (SAN 213-5515).
Rainbow Books, Inc., *(Rainbow Bks; 0-89508),* 725 Dell Rd., Carlstadt, NJ 07072 Tel 201-935-3309 (SAN 209-9918).
Rainbow Children's Books, *(Rainbow Child; 0-9608784),* Box 513, 311 E. Madison, Goshen, IN 46526 Tel 219-533-4232 (SAN 238-3470).
Rainbow Collection, *(Rainbow Collect; 0-935448),* P.O. Box 75, Akron, OH 44309 (SAN 213-7860).
Rainbow Enterprises, *(Rainbow Ent),* P.O. Box 267, West Friendship, MD 21794 (SAN 239-5983).
Rainbow Press, *(Rainbow Pr NY; 0-943156),* 222 Edwards Dr., Fayetteville, NY 13066 (SAN 240-4354).
Rainbow Press, The, *(Rainbow Pr CA),* 5901 Warner Ave., Huntington Beach, CA 92649 (SAN 217-1260).
Rainbow Pubns., *(Rainbow WA; 0-940364),* 1493 S. Columbian Way, Suite 111, Seattle, WA 98144 (SAN 217-1279).
Rainbow Publishing Co., *(Rainbow Pub Co; 0-936218),* P.O. Box 397, Chesterland, OH 44026 (SAN 219-9912).
Rainbow Spirit Press, *(Rainbow Spirit; 0-9611054),* Box 421528, Rm.425, San Francisco, CA 94142-1528 Tel 415-441-5141 (SAN 283-3077).
Rainbow's End Co., *(Rainbows End; 0-9608780),* P.O. Box 173, Baden, PA 15005 (SAN 238-3489).
Raintree, George Philip, Subs. of Raintree Pubs. Group, *(G P Raintree; 0-8393),* 205 W. Highland Ave., Milwaukee, WI 53203 Tel 414-273-0873 (SAN 209-6706).
Raintree Pubs., Inc., Raintree Childrens Books, *(Raintree Pubs; 0-8172),* 205 W. Highland Ave., Milwaukee, WI 53203 Tel 414-273-0873 (SAN 207-9607).
Rainville Rose Pubns., *(Rainville Rose; 0-938066),* 2505 E. Thousand Oaks Blvd., Suite 266, Thousand Oaks, CA 91360 (SAN 216-2938).
Rainy Day Press, *(Rainy Day Oreg; 0-931742),* P.O. Box 3035, Eugene, OR 97403 Tel 503-484-4626 (SAN 211-397X).
Rainy Day Press, *(Rainy Day Pr; 0-918796),* Box 471, Sausalito, CA 94965 (SAN 209-102X); Dist. by: Bookpeople, 2940 Seventh St., Berkeley, CA 94710 Tel 415-549-3033 (SAN 168-9517).
Raja Press, *(Raja Pr CA; 0-9605926),* 5534 Fremont St., Oakland, CA 94608 (SAN 217-1287).
Rajah Press, *(Rajah; 0-911204),* P.O. Box 23, Summit, NJ 07901 (SAN 204-6679).

Rajneesh Foundation International, *(Rajneesh Found Intl; 0-88050),* Zarathustra Bldg., Zarathustra Rd., P.O. Box Nine, Rajneeshpuram, OR 97741 Tel 503-489-3462 (SAN 240-0987).

Ralston-Pilot, Inc., Pubs., *(Ralston-Pilot; 0-931116),* P.O. Box 1357, Cedar City, UT 84720 Tel 801-586-7395 (SAN 282-2067); Orders to: P.O. Box 10173, Costa Mesa, CA 92627 (SAN 282-2075).

Ram Associates, Ltd., *(Ram Assoc; 0-943308),* Box 2277, Poquoson, VA 23662 Tel 804-868-8970 (SAN 240-1118).

Ram Publishing Co., *(Ram Pub; 0-915920),* P.O. Drawer 38649, Dallas, TX 75238 Tel 214-278-8439 (SAN 203-0837).

Ram Publishing, Inc., *(Ram Pub Inc; 0-941966),* 4133 S. 3165 W., Salt Lake City, UT 84119 (SAN 238-2687).

Ramaker Library Art Gallery *See* **Northwestern College, Ramaker Library Art Gallery**

Ramakrishna-Vivekananda Ctr., *(Ramakrishna; 0-911206),* 17 E. 94th St., New York, NY 10028 Tel 212-534-9445 (SAN 204-6687).

Rambler Press, *(Rambler Pr; 0-9609754),* P.O. Box 184, Weiser, ID 83672 (SAN 264-3375).

Ramfre Press, *(Ramfre; 0-911208),* 1206 N. Henderson, Cape Girardeau, MO 63701 Tel 314-335-6582 (SAN 204-6695).

Ramico Pubns., *(Ramico Pubns; 0-9607272),* P.O. Box 5218, N. Hollywood, CA 91607 Tel 213-985-3675 (SAN 239-2933).

Rampant Lion Pubs, *(Rampant Lion Pubs; 0-942872),* 130 S. Fourth St. No. 19, Las Vegas, NV 89101 (SAN 240-1215).

Rampart Publishing, *(Rampart Pub; 0-9606446),* 869 Paramount Rd., Oakland, CA 94610 Tel 415-835-8268 (SAN 218-5830).

Ramparts Press, *(Ramparts; 0-87867),* P.O. Box 50128, Palo Alto, CA 94303 Tel 415-325-7861 (SAN 203-3925).

RAMSCO Publishing Co., *(Ramsco Pub; 0-943596),* P.O. Box N, Laurel, MD 20707 Tel 301-953-3699 (SAN 240-7582).

Rana House, *(Rana Hse; 0-930172),* Box 2997, St. Louis, MO 63130 (SAN 210-542X).

Ranch House Press, *(Ranch House Pr; 0-88100),* Rte. 2, Box 296, Pagosa Springs, CO 81147 Tel 303-264-2647 (SAN 240-1126).

Rancho Bernardo Junior Woman's Club, Inc., *(Rancho Bern; 0-9608548),* 12652 Gibraltar Dr., San Diego, CA 92128 Tel 714-485-0210 (SAN 240-7590).

Rancho Santa Ana Botanic Garden, *(Rancho Santa Ana; 0-9605808),* 1500 N. College, Claremont, CA 91711 Tel 714-626-3489 (SAN 220-1836).

Ranck, Joyce H., *(Ranck; 0-9606006),* 1103 Fairacres Rd., Richmond, IN 47374 Tel 317-962-4683 (SAN 216-4426).

Rand Corp., The, *(Rand Corp; 0-8330),* 1700 Main St., Santa Monica, CA 90406 Tel 213-393-0411 (SAN 218-9291).

Rand Editions/Tofua Press, *(Rand-Tofua; 0-914488),* P.O. Box 2610, Leucadia, CA 92024 Tel 619-753-2500 (SAN 206-8001).

Rand McNally & Co., *(Rand; 0-528),* P.O. Box 7600, Chicago, IL 60680 Tel 312-673-9100 (SAN 203-3917).

Randall, Peter E., *(P E Randall Pub; 0-914339),* 500 Market Street, Box 4726, Portsmouth, NH 03801 Tel 603-431-5667 (SAN 223-0496).

Randall House Pubns., *(Randall Hse; 0-89265),* 114 Bush Rd., P.O. Box 17306, Nashville, TN 37217 Tel 615-361-1221 (SAN 207-5040).

Randelle Pubns., *(Randelle Pubns; 0-910445),* 1527 First Ave., Charleston, WV 25312 Tel 304-344-4494 (SAN 260-1222).

Random House College Division *See* **Random House, Inc.**

Random House, Inc., *(Random; 0-394),* Random House Publicity (11-6), 201 E. 50th St., New York, NY 10022 Tel 212-751-2600 (SAN 202-5507); Orders to: 400 Hahn Rd., Westminster, MD 21157 (SAN 202-5515). *Imprints:* Books for Young Readers (BYR); Random House College Division (RanC); Vintage Trade Books (Vin).

Ranger Assocs., Inc., *(Ranger Assocs; 0-934588),* P.O. Box 1357, Manassas, VA 22110 Tel 703-369-5336 (SAN 213-5523).

Ranieri, Helene, *(H Ranieri),* 2760 Devonshire Place, N.W., Washington, DC 20008 (SAN 212-8128).

Ranney Pubns., *(Ranney Pubns),* Ranney Enterprise, 1501 H.N. Tustin Ave., Santa Ana, CA 92701 Tel 714-541-5374 (SAN 211-867X).

Ransom Hill Pr., *(Ransom Hill; 0-9604342),* 3601 Main St., Ramona, CA 92065 (SAN 215-9104).

Raphael, Morris, Books, *(M Raphael; 0-9608866),* 1404 Bayou Side Dr., New Iberia, LA 70560 (SAN 241-0737).

Rapid Response, *(Rapid Respon; 0-943936),* 9528 Miramar Rd., No. 164, San Diego, CA 92126 Tel 714-695-3110 (SAN 241-1431).

Rapides Symphony Guild, *(Rapides Symphony; 0-9603758),* P.O. Box 4172, Alexandria, LA 71301 Tel 318-443-7786 (SAN 213-8700).

Rapids Christian Press, Inc., *(Rapids Christian; 0-915374),* P.O. Box 487, 810 4th Ave., N., Wisconsin Rapids, WI 54494 Tel 715-423-4670 (SAN 205-0986).

Rapier, Regina C., *(R C Rapier; 0-9600584),* 292 S. Cherokee Rd., Social Circle, GA 30279 Tel 404-464-2582 (SAN 204-6571).

Rapollo Books, *(Rapollo Bks; 0-9603670),* 1362 Banyan Dr., Fallbrook, CA 92028 (SAN 213-6066); Dist. by: Caroline House Publishers, 2 Ellis Place, Ossining, NY 10562 (SAN 211-2299).

Raquette Press, *(Raquette Pr; 0-916136),* Box 1, Star Route, Canton, NY 13617 Tel 315-386-8354 (SAN 206-6187).

Rare Publishing, *(Rare Pub; 0-939024),* 23352 Erwin St., Woodlawn, CA 91367 Tel 805-526-7616 (SAN 238-1311).

Rare Reprints, Inc., *(Rare Repr; 0-89592),* 610 N.E. 124th St., Miami, FL 33161 (SAN 211-2027).

Rassela Press, *(Rassela Pr; 0-9609180),* 13505 Lucca Dr., Pacific Palisades, CA 90272 Tel 213-937-6250 (SAN 241-4422).

Rateavers, *(Rateavers; 0-9600698; 0-915966),* 9049 Covina St., San Diego, CA 92126 Tel 619-566-8994 (SAN 205-6402).

Rather Press, *(Rather Pr),* 3200 Guido St., Oakland, CA 94602 Tel 415-531-2938 (SAN 209-8792).

Rational Island Pubs., *(Rational Isl; 0-911214; 0-913937),* 719 Second Ave. N., Seattle, WA 98109 Tel 206-284-0311 (SAN 204-6725); Orders to: P.O. Box 2081, Main Office Sta., Seattle, WA 98111 (SAN 204-6733).

Rave Reviews Publications, Div. of Junior League of North Little Rock, *(Rave Reviews; 0-9611224),* P.O. Box 15753, N. Little Rock, AR 72231 Tel 501-372-1436 (SAN 283-3069).

Raven Press, Pubs., *(Raven; 0-89004),* 1140 Ave. of the Americas, New York, NY 10036 Tel 212-575-0335 (SAN 203-3909).

Raven Printing Co., Inc., *(Raven Print; 0-89023),* 317 S. Beechtree, Grand Haven, MI 49417 Tel 616-525-8005 (SAN 206-6173) Moved, left no forwarding address.

Raven Pubs. AKA, Inc., *(Raven Pubs AKA),* 425 Stocking, N.W., Grand Rapids, MI 49504 Tel 616-459-3377 (SAN 215-3378).

Raven Publishing Co., *(Raven Pub Co; 0-9605486),* 911 E. Mahanoy Ave., Mahanoy City, PA 17948 Tel 717-773-1586 (SAN 215-2622).

Ravengate Press, *(Ravengate Pr; 0-911218),* P.O. Box 103, Cambridge, MA 02238 Tel 617-456-8181 (SAN 203-090X).

Rawson, Wade Pubs., Inc., *(Rawson Wade; 0-89256),* 597 Fifth Ave., New York, NY 10017 Tel 212-867-6610 (SAN 209-3154); Dist. by: Atheneum Pubs., 122 E. 42nd St., New York, NY 10017 (SAN 209-3162).

Raycol Products, *(Raycol Prods; 0-9605176),* 5346 E. 9th St., Tucson, AZ 85711 (SAN 215-8019).

Raye's Eclectic Craft Yarns, Inc., *(Rayes Eclec; 0-9601282),* P.O. Box 2356, 8157 Commercial St., La Mesa, CA 92041 Tel 714-460-0721 (SAN 210-3672).

Rayline Company, *(Rayline),* 1413 Edinger, Santa Ana, CA 92705 (SAN 210-6566).

Raymond's Quiet Press, *(Raymonds Quiet Pr; 0-943228),* 6336 Leslie N.E., Albuquerque, NM 87109 Tel 505-821-3627 (SAN 240-7604).

Raymont Pubs., Inc., *(Raymont Pubs; 0-943126),* P.O. Box 780., Orem, UT 84057 (SAN 214-1329); Dist. by: Richard Maher Sales, 5180 S. 300 W., Murray, UT 84107 Tel 800-453-6417 (SAN 158-8141).

Re, Frank M., *(F M Re),* 68 Palm Club, Pompano Beach, FL 33062 Tel 305-946-1234 (SAN 208-0818).

Re-Entry, *(Re-Entry; 0-9605826),* P.O. Box 13535, Portland, OR 97213 Tel 503-222-6461 (SAN 216-5821).

Re-Geniusing Project, The, *(Re-Geniusing; 0-941386),* 1432 Spruce St., Berkeley, CA 94709 Tel 415-841-4903 (SAN 239-0272).

Re/Search Publications, *(Re Search Pubns; 0-940642),* 20 Romolo No. B, San Francisco, CA 94133 Tel 415-362-1465 (SAN 218-5849).

Read, Elizabeth, R. D., *(E Read; 0-9600996),* 4429 East 46th Place, Tulsa, OK 74135 Tel 918-627-0213 (SAN 208-8274).

Reader's Digest Assn., Inc., *(RD Assn; 0-89577),* 750 Third Ave., New York, NY 10017-2797 Tel 212-850-7100 (SAN 282-2083); Orders to: Customer Service, Pleasantville, NY 10570 Tel 914-769-7000 (SAN 282-2091).

Reader's Digest Press, *(Readers Digest Pr; 0-88349),* 200 Park Ave., New York, NY 10017 (SAN 203-3887); Dist. by: McGraw-Hill Book Co., 1221 Ave. of the Americas, New York, NY 10020 (SAN 200-2248).

Readers Enrichment Series *See* **Washington Square Press, Inc.**

Reader's Press, *(Readers Pr CA; 0-930166),* P.O. Box 3136, Newport Beach, CA 92663 Tel 714-631-4911 (SAN 210-6574).

Readex Microprint Corp., *(Readex Bks; 0-918414),* 101 Fifth Ave., New York, NY 10003 Tel 212-243-3822 (SAN 209-9926) Conventional reference works in reduced size (compact editions), research & reference collections in microprint (opaque), microfiche & reel microfilm.

Reading Gems, *(Reading Gems; 0-915988),* P.O. Box 806, Madison, WI 53701 (SAN 207-6934).

Reading House, The, *(Reading Hse; 0-9604388),* Box 2975, Seal Beach, CA 90740 (SAN 282-2105) Box 2748, Mission Viejo, CA 92692 (SAN 282-2113).

Reading Tutorum, The, *(Reading Tutor; 0-910609),* P.O. Box 1586, 9121A Centreville Rd., Manassas, VA 22110 (SAN 240-8309).

Readon Publishing, *(Readon Pub; 0-9604638),* P.O. Box 57142, Webster, TX 77598 Tel 713-333-3269 (SAN 215-2843).

Ready Reference Press, *(Ready Ref Pr; 0-916270),* P.O. Box 5169, Santa Monica, CA 90405 (SAN 218-9305).

Real Comet Press, The, Div. of Such A Deal Corp., *(Real Comet; 0-941104),* 932 18th Ave. E, Seattle, WA 98112 Tel 206-328-1801 (SAN 217-4227).

Real Computers & Intelligence, *(Real Comp & Int; 0-934190),* P.O. Box 74, Santa Clara, CA 95050 (SAN 212-9639).

Real Equity Publishing, Inc., *(Real Equity Pub; 0-9607164),* 655 Broadway, Suite 1000, Denver, CO 80203 Tel 303-861-1614 (SAN 239-0280).

Real Estate Education Company *See* **Development Systems Corporation**

Real Estate Investor Information Center, The, *(Real Estate Investor; 0-939224),* 45 LaSalle Dr., Moraga, CA 94556 Tel 415-376-1362 (SAN 220-1844).

Real Estate Publishing Co., *(Real Estate Pub; 0-914256),* P.O. Box 41177, Sacramento, CA 95841 Tel 916-677-3864 (SAN 202-9782).

Real People Press, *(Real People; 0-911226),* P.O. Box F, Moab, UT 84532 Tel 801-259-7578 (SAN 203-3879).

Real World Pubns., *(Real World; 0-931204),* P.O. Box 176, Niwot, CO 80544 (SAN 212-4424); Dist. by: Caroline House, P.O. Box 161, Thornwood, NY 10594 (SAN 212-4432).

Realities Library, *(Realities; 0-916982),* 2745 Monterey Rd., No. 76, San Jose, CA 95111 (SAN 208-0761).

Reality Productions, *(Reality Prods; 0-9608622),* 9978 Holder St., Buena Park, CA 90620 (SAN 238-3497).

Realm Books, Ltd., *(Realm Bks; 0-941654),* P.O. Box 2831, Phoenix, AZ 85002 (SAN 239-2941).

Realtors National Marketing Institute, *(Realtors Natl; 0-913652),* 430 Michigan Ave., Chicago, IL 60611 Tel 312-440-8514 (SAN 202-0963).

Realty Training Service Co., *(Realty Train; 0-89493),* Elseden Bldg.-Tanner's Lane, Florence, KY 41042 Tel 606-525-8005 (SAN 209-9942).

Realvest American Publishing Co., Div. of Charter Management Associates, Inc., *(Realvest Am Pub Co; 0-933928),* 79 S. Pleasant St., Amherst, MA 01002 Tel 413-253-2554 (SAN 212-9647).

Rearick, Ron & Marg., Publishers, *(Rearick; 0-9609206),* 14601 N.E. 50th Place E-Z, Bellevue, WA 98006 (SAN 241-4430).

Rebel Montgomery Temple, *(Rebel Mont Tem; 0-89279),* 110 1/2 N. St. Marys, Albert Lea, MN 56007 (SAN 265-3680).

Rebel Publishing Co., Inc., *(Rebel Pub; 0-9605666),* Rte. 5 Box 347-M, Texarkana, TX 75503 (SAN 239-4804).

Recipe Press, *(Recipe Pr; 0-939796),* 2307 W. 28th Ave., Eugene, OR 97405 Tel 503-687-0294 (SAN 216-9290).

Recipes Unlimited, Inc., *(Recipes Unltd; 0-918620),* P.O. Box 1271, Burnsville, MN 55337 Tel 612-890-6655 (SAN 209-0058).

Recognition Technologies Users Association, *(Recog Tech; 0-943072),* P.O. Box 2016, Manchester Center, VT 05255 (SAN 240-4362).

Recon Pubns., *(Recon Pubns; 0-916894),* P.O. Box 14602, Philadelphia, PA 19134 (SAN 207-8880).

Reconciliation Associates, *(Reconciliation; 0-932270),* 8 Burnside Rd., Newton, MA 02161 Tel 617-244-7384 (SAN 211-0903).

Record-Rama, *(Record-Rama; 0-910925),* P.O. Box 150, Allison Park, PA 15101 (SAN 264-3391).

Record Research Inc., *(Record Research; 0-89820),* P.O. Box 200, Menomonee Falls, WI 53051 (SAN 212-9655); Dist. by: Gale Research Co., Book Tower, Detroit, MI 48226 Tel 313-961-2242 (SAN 213-4373).

Recorded Sound Research, *(Recorded Sound; 0-916262),* 1627 Moody Court, Peoria, IL 61604 Tel 309-674-2008 (SAN 207-6535).

Recreation Vehicle Industry Association, *(RV Indus Assn),* P O Box 204, Chantilly, VA 22021 (SAN 231-3928).

Recro Products Corp., *(Recro Products; 0-911275),* 565 Fifth Ave., Suite 702, New York, NY 10017 Tel 212-687-1228 (SAN 274-9904).

Rector, L, T., Publishing, *(Rector Pub; 0-9606170),* 310 E. 25th St., Minneapolis, MN 55404 (SAN 223-0704).

Red Alder Books, *(Red Alder; 0-914906),* P.O. Box 2992, Santa Cruz, CA 95063 Tel 408-426-7082 (SAN 206-6181).

Red Cedar Press, *(Red Cedar; 0-937190),* English Dept., Michigan State Univ., East Lansing, MI 48824 Tel 517-351-4313 (SAN 211-6812); Dist. by: Stone Press, 1790 Grand River, Okemos, MI 48864 Tel 517-349-0552 (SAN 207-902X).

Red Dragon Pr., *(Red Dragon; 0-942384),* P.O. Box 9898, Madison, WI 53715 Tel 608-271-8684 (SAN 239-6009).

Red Dust Inc., *(Red Dust; 0-87376),* P.O. Box 630, Gracie Sta., New York, NY 10028 Tel 212-348-4388 (SAN 203-3860).

Red Earth Press, *(Red Earth; 0-918434),* 9247 Cordoba Ct., St. Louis, MO 63126 Tel 314-849-0395 (SAN 209-9268) Formerly Named Yarbrough Mountain Press.

Red Feather Pub. Co., *(Red Feather; 0-936430),* P.O. Drawer 2007, Lubbock, TX 79408 Tel 806-795-7272 (SAN 215-1030).

Red Herring Press, *(Red Herring; 0-932884),* 1209 W. Oregon, Urbana, IL 61801 Tel 217-359-0067 (SAN 212-2251).

Red Hill, *(Red Hill; 0-88031),* P.O. Box 2853, San Francisco, CA 94126 Tel 415-527-1018 (SAN 205-6429).

Red Key Press, *(Red Key Pr; 0-943696),* P.O. Box 551, Port St. Joe, FL 32456 (SAN 240-8848).

Red Lake Books, *(Red Lake Bks; 0-9611678),* P.O. Box 1315, Flagstaff, AZ 86002 (SAN 284-9526).

Red Lion Books, *(Red Lion; 0-940162),* 609 Rte. 109, Suite 2-B, W. Babylon, NY 11704 Tel 516-888-5800 (SAN 217-4898).

Red Lotus Press, *(Red Lotus Pr; 0-943014),* 1442A Walnut St., Suite 140, Berkeley, CA 94709 (SAN 240-4370).

Red Lyon Pubns., *(Red Lyon Pubns; 0-941894),* 6940 NW Oak Creek Dr., Corvallis, OR 97330 Tel 503-753-5019 (SAN 239-295X).

Red Mountain Editions, *(Red Mtn; 0-911234),* P.O. Box 95, Burnsville, NC 28714 Tel 704-682-3735 (SAN 204-675X).

Red River Press, *(Red River; 0-938898),* 4806 Danberry, Wichita Falls, TX 76308 (SAN 216-1788).

Red River Publishing Co., *(Red River Pub Co; 0-938794),* P.O. Box 3055, Wichita Falls, TX 76309 (SAN 240-8856).

Red Rose Press, *(Red Rose Pr; 0-9609888),* P.O. Box 24, Encino, CA 91426 Tel 213-981-7638 (SAN 282-2121); Dist. by: Bookpeople, 2940 7th St., Berkeley, CA 94710 Tel 415-549-3030 (SAN 168-9517); Dist. by: Publisher's Group West, 5855 Beaudry St., Emeryville, CA 94609 Tel 415-650-3453 (SAN 202-8522).

Red Rose Studio, *(Red Rose Studio; 0-932514),* 358 Flintlock Dr., Willow Street, PA 17584 (SAN 212-162X).

Red Studio Press, *(Red Studio; 0-916320),* 200 22nd Ave. S., Minneapolis, MN 55454 Tel 612-339-2042 (SAN 208-3434).

Red Sun Press, *(Red Sun Pr; 0-932728),* 94 Green St., Jamaica Plain, MA 02130 Tel 617-542-4821 (SAN 212-3819).

Red-Tape Publication, *(Red Tape; 0-9608154),* P.O. Box 1236, Ft. Collins, CO 80522 Tel 303-484-1007 (SAN 240-2718).

Redbird Press, *(Redbird; 0-9606046),* 3838 Poplar Ave., Memphis, TN 38111 Tel 901-323-2233 (SAN 216-9304).

Redcor Book Publishing Co., *(Redcor Bk; 0-939588),* 501 W. Port Royale Lane, Phoenix, AZ 85023 Tel 602-863-1415 (SAN 216-4434).

Redd, Charles, Center for Western Studies, *(C Redd Ctr),* 4069 Harold B. Lee Library, Brigham Young Univ., Provo, UT 84602 (SAN 287-2900); Dist. by: Signature Books, 942 E. 7145 S., No. 106, Midvale, UT 84047 (SAN 287-2919).

Reddy Communications, Inc., *(Reddy Comm; 0-9603716),* 537 Steamboat Rd., P.O. Box 1310, Greenwich, CT 06836 Tel 203-661-4800 (SAN 213-6406).

Redencion Viva, *(Redencion Viva; 0-9607576),* Box 141167, Dallas, TX 75214 (SAN 239-6017).

Redgrave Publishing Co., Div. of Docent Corp., *(Redgrave Pub Co; 0-913178),* P.O. Box 67, South Salem, NY 10590 Tel 914-769-3629 (SAN 212-9663).

Redwood Press, The, *(Redwood Pr; 0-941196),* P.O. Box 3323, San Mateo, CA 94403 Tel 415-342-4411 (SAN 239-4812).

Redwood Pubs., *(Redwood; 0-917928),* P.O. Box 7424, Menlo Park, CA 94025 Tel 415-854-3723 (SAN 209-4827) Do Not Confuse with Redwood Publishing Co. in San Luis Obispo, CA.

Redwood Publishing Co., *(Redwood Pub Co; 0-937316),* 3860 S. Higuera, Space 105, San Luis Obispo, CA 93401 (SAN 213-4314) Do Not Confuse with Redwood Publishers in Menlo Park, CA.

Redwood Records, *(Redwood Records; 0-9608774),* 476w. MacArthur Blvd., Oakland, CA 94609 Tel 415-428-9191 (SAN 218-3080).

Reebie Associates, Inc., *(Reebie Assoc; 0-9604776),* P.O. Box 1278, Greenwich, CT 06836 Tel 203-661-8661 (SAN 220-0899).

Reed, Ishmael & Al Young's Quilt, *(Reed & Youngs Quilt; 0-931676),* 2140 Shattuck Ave., Rm. 311, Berkeley, CA 94704 Tel 415-527-1586 (SAN 282-2334); Dist. by: Bookpeople, 2940 Seventh St., Berkeley, CA 94710 (SAN 168-9517); Dist. by: Before Columbus Foundation, 1446-D Sixth St., Berkeley, CA 94710 (SAN 219-4651); Dist. by: Small Press, 1784 Shattuck Ave., Berkeley, CA 94709 Tel 415-529-3336 (SAN 204-5826); Dist. by: Bookslinger, 330 E. Ninth St., St. Paul, MN 55101 (SAN 169-4154); Dist. by: Inland Bk. Co., P.O. Box 261, 22 Hemingway Ave., E. Haven, CT 06512 (SAN 282-2385).

Reed, James H., *(J H Reed; 0-9601314),* 1315 Melrose, Richardson, TX 75080 Tel 214-826-8835 (SAN 209-0031).

Reed, R., *(R Reed),* P.O. Box 1106, Laguna Beach, CA 92652 (SAN 207-5644).

Reed, Robert D., *(R D Reed),* 18581 McFarland Ave., Saratoga, CA 95070 (SAN 212-8632).

Reed & Cannon Co., *(Reed & Cannon; 0-918408),* 2140 Shattuck Ave., Rm. 311, Berkeley, CA 94704 Tel 415-527-1586 (SAN 282-2393); 285 E. Third St., New York, NY 10009 (SAN 282-2407).

Reed Pubs., *(Reed Pubs HI; 0-917064),* P.O. Box 10667, Honolulu, HI 96816 Tel 808-732-1515 (SAN 208-483X).

Reef Dwellers Press, *(Reef Dwellers; 0-9602530),* Jenkintown Plaza, Jenkintown, PA 19046 Tel 215-887-6700 (SAN 213-1528); Orders to: Bryn Athyn, PA 19009 (SAN 213-1536).

Reel Research, *(Reel Res),* P.O. Box 6037, Albany, CA 94706 Tel 415-549-0923 (SAN 209-0066).

Reeves, Emma B., *(E B Reeves; 0-911013),* 1614 Redbud St., Nacogdoches, TX 75961 Tel 713-564-0130 (SAN 274-9971).

Reference & Guide Books Pub. Co., *(Ref Guide Bks; 0-9607942),* 4963 Elmhurst, Box 3581, Ventura, CA 93006 Tel 805-644-8672 (SAN 240-0650).

Reference Book Pubs. See Kelley, Augustus M., Pubs.

Reference Books Inc., *(Ref Bks; 0-933618),* P.O. Box 7866, Chicago, IL 60680 Tel 312-248-9251 (SAN 212-4440).

Reference Pubns., Inc., *(Ref Pubns; 0-917256),* 218 St. Clair River Dr. P. O. Box 344, Algonac, MI 48001 Tel 313-794-5722 (SAN 208-4392).

Reference Service Press, *(Ref Serv Pr; 0-918276),* 9023 Alcott, Suite 201, Los Angeles, CA 90035 Tel 213-271-1955 (SAN 210-2633).

Reflexology Research Project, *(RRP; 0-9606070),* P.O. Box 35820, Station D, Albuquerque, NM 87176 Tel 505-344-9392 (SAN 216-9312).

Reformation Research Press, Inc., *(Reformation Res; 0-936592),* 233 W. Apsley St., Philadelphia, PA 19144 Tel 215-843-2258 (SAN 214-1981).

Reformed Church Press, Reformed Church in America, *(Reformed Church; 0-916466),* 475 Riverside Dr., 18th Fl., New York, NY 10027 Tel 212-870-3020 (SAN 207-4508).

Regal American Marketing Corp., *(Regal Am Mktg),* 13910 Josey Ln., Dallas, TX 75232 Tel 214-241-0576 (SAN 216-4442).

Regal Books, Div. of G/L Pubns., *(Regal; 0-8307),* 2300 Knoll Dr., Ventura, CA 93003 Tel 805-644-9721 (SAN 203-3852).

Regal Publishing Co., *(Regal Pub Co; 0-9604598),* P.O. Box 76846, Atlanta, GA 30328 (SAN 215-1782) Moved, left no forwarding address.

Regenbogen-Verlag, *(Regenbogen-Verlag),* Box 6214, Silver Spring, MD 20906 Tel 301-933-8521 (SAN 216-0072).

Regency Press, *(Regency Pr; 0-933324),* 32 Ridge Dr., Port Washington, NY 11050 Tel 516-935-1143 (SAN 211-8688).

Regent Graphic Services, *(Regent Graphic Serv; 0-912710),* P.O. Box 8372, Swissvale, PA 15218 Tel 412-371-7128 (SAN 204-6768).

Regent House See B of A Communications Co.

Regents Publishing Co., Inc., Div. of Hachette, *(Regents Pub; 0-88345),* 2 Park Ave., New York, NY 10016 Tel 212-889-2780 (SAN 203-3844).

Reggie The Retiree Co., *(Reggie the Retiree; 0-9609960),* R.R. 2, Box 754, Wells, ME 04090 (SAN 262-9925).

Regina Books, *(Regina Bks; 0-941690),* P.O. Box 280, Claremont, CA 91711 Tel 714-624-8466 (SAN 239-2968).

Regina Press, The, *(Regina Pr GA; 0-9609236),* 422 E. Gaston St., Savannah, GA 31401 Tel 912-234-0886 (SAN 241-4449).

Regional Center for Educational Training, *(Regional Ctr Educ; 0-915892),* 45 Lyme Rd., Hanover, NH 03755 Tel 603-643-5666 (SAN 208-8282).

Regional Publishing Co., Affiliate of Genealogical Publishing Co., *(Regional),* 111 Water St., Baltimore, MD 21202 Tel 301-837-8271 (SAN 206-8842).

Regional Science Research Institute, *(Regional Sci Res Inst),* Wentworth Bldg., 256 N. Pleasant St., Amherst, MA 01002 Tel 413-256-8526 (SAN 239-3794).

Regional Young Adult Project, *(Regional Young; 0-9606198),* 944 Market St., Rm. 705, San Francisco, CA 94102 Tel 415-543-0890 (SAN 220-3049).

Register Press, *(Register Pr; 0-911242),* Yarmouth Port, MA 02675 Tel 617-362-2111 (SAN 205-2237).

Registry of Interpreters for the Deaf, Inc., *(RIFD; 0-9602220),* 814 Thayer Ave., Silver Spring, MD 20910 (SAN 216-1796).

Registry Pubns., Ltd., *(Registry Pubns),* 425 Huehl Rd., No. 15B, Northbrook, IL 60062 Tel 312-498-4010 (SAN 204-2932).

Regmar Publishing Co., Inc., *(Regmar Pub; 0-914338),* P.O. Box 11358, Memphis, TN 38111 Tel 901-323-7442 (SAN 203-2015).

Regnery, Henry, Co. See **Contemporary Books, Inc.**

Regnery Gateway, Inc., *(Regnery-Gateway; 0-89526),* 360 W. Superior St., Chicago, IL 60610 Tel 312-440-1647 (SAN 210-5578).

Regnier, Susan L., *(Regnier; 0-9606266),* 5011 Turtle Lane W., Shoreview, MN 55112 Tel 612-483-0390 (SAN 220-3480).

Regular Baptist Press, *(Reg Baptist; 0-87227),* 1300 N. Meacham Rd., P.O. Box 95500, Schaumburg, IL 60195 Tel 312-843-1600 (SAN 205-2229).

Rehabilitation International, *(Rehab Intl; 0-9605554),* 432 Park Ave. S., New York, NY 10016 Tel 212-679-6520 (SAN 216-0080).

Reichner, Herbert, *(H Reichner; 0-9601520),* Shaker Hill, Enfield, NH 03748 Tel 603-632-7725 (SAN 205-2210).

Reid, Hazel E., *(H E Reid; 0-9601892),* P.O. Box 317, Manhattanville, New York, NY 10027 Tel 212-490-0077 (SAN 211-0148).

Reid, Hugh B., *(H B Reid; 0-911244),* Dist. by: Edwards Bros., 2500 S. State St., Ann Arbor, MI 48104 Tel 313-769-1000 (SAN 282-6321).

Reidmore Books Oregon, *(Reidmore Bks; 0-939284),* P.O. Box 2598, Eugene, OR 97402 (SAN 216-2946).

Reiff Press, *(Reiff Pr; 0-911246),* 120 South Eighth St., Apt 3, Indiana, PA 15701 Tel 412-349-3347 (SAN 207-3552).

Reignbow, *(Reignbow; 0-942334),* Box 26174, Phoenix, AZ 85068 (SAN 239-8605).

Reilly, William A., Awareness Techniques, *(W A Reilly; 0-934258),* P.O. Box 63, 6 Crest Dr., Dover, MA 02030 Tel 617-785-0401 (SAN 212-8640).

Reiman Associates, *(Reiman Assocs; 0-89821),* 5400 S. 60th St., Greendale, WI 53129 Tel 414-423-0100 (SAN 208-4368); Orders to: P.O. Box 572, Milwaukee, WI 53201 (SAN 208-4376).

Reiner Pubns., *(Reiner; 0-87377),* Swengel, PA 17880 Tel 717-922-3213 (SAN 204-6784).

Reisner Publishing, *(Reisner Pub; 0-9611680),* 2101 Nuuanu Ave., No. 2502, Honolulu, HI 96817 Tel 808-531-7937 (SAN 284-9542).

Reiss Games, Inc. See **Reiss Pub.**

Reiss Pub., Subs. of National Paragon Corp., *(Reiss Pub; 0-89515),* 230 Fifth Ave., New York, NY 10001 Tel 212-679-2440 (SAN 209-9969); Dist. by: E. P. Dutton Co., 201 Park Ave., S., New York, NY 10003 Tel 212-674-5900 (SAN 201-0070).

Rekalb Press, *(Rekalb Pr; 0-9604614),* 6203 Jane Lane, Columbus, GA 31904 Tel 404-324-1392 (SAN 282-2415).

Rel-Psych, Incorporated, *(Rel Psych; 0-9611682),* P.O. Box 8088, Bangor, ME 04401 Tel 207-945-5997 (SAN 285-1415); 151 Lancaster Ave., Bangor, ME 04401 (SAN 285-1423).

Relevant Pubns., Ltd., *(Relevant Pub),* 14241 Mango, Del Mar, CA 92014 (SAN 202-974X).

Reliance Publishing Co., *(Reliance Pub; 0-937740),* 380 Steinwehr Ave., Gettysburg, PA 17325 Tel 717-334-1103 (SAN 220-0910).

Religion & Ethics Institute, *(REI; 0-914384),* P.O. Box 664, Evanston, IL 60204 Tel 312-328-4049 (SAN 202-9731).

Religious Activities Press, *(Religious Activ),* Rte. 2, Box 343, Mt. Juliet, TN 37122 Tel 615-758-5036 (SAN 212-7911).

Religious Education Press, Inc., *(Religious Educ; 0-89135),* 1531 Wellington Rd., Birmingham, AL 35209 Tel 205-879-4040 (SAN 207-3951). *Imprints:* REP Books (REP Bks).

Remarkable Pubns., *(Remarkable Pubns; 0-9605346),* 8005 Bleriot Ave., Westchester, CA 90045 Tel 213-641-0567 (SAN 282-2431); Dist. by: DeVorss & Co., P.O. Box 550, Marina Del Rey, CA 90291 Tel 213-870-7478 (SAN 168-9886); Orders to: Remarkable Pubns., 8005 Bleriot Ave., Westchester, CA 90045 Tel 213-641-0507 (SAN 282-2431).

Remi Books, *(Remi Bks; 0-943362),* 205 E. 78th St., New York, NY 10021 (SAN 240-9267).

Renaissance Books, *(Renaissance Bks; 0-932476),* 834 N. Plankinton Ave., Milwaukee, WI 53203 Tel 414-271-6850 (SAN 211-9722).

Renaissance Pubs., *(Renaissance Pubs; 0-916560),* 2485 N.E. 214th St., N. Miami Beach, FL 33180 Tel 305-931-3392 (SAN 207-5091).

Renaissance Society of America, *(Renaissance Soc Am),* 1161 Amsterdam Ave., New York, NY 10027 Tel 212-280-2318 (SAN 209-4835).

Rendina, Dave, Publishing Co., *(D Rendina),* 1 Lake Rd., Newfield, NJ 08344 (SAN 212-0461).

Renfro, Nancy, Studios, *(Renfro Studios; 0-931044),* 1117 W. 9th St., Austin, TX 78703 Tel 512-472-2140 (SAN 211-9730).

Renner Pub., *(Renner Pub; 0-942922),* 17811 Davenport Rd. No. 42, Dallas, TX 75252 (SAN 240-1134).

REP Books See **Religious Education Press, Inc.**

R.E.P. Pubs., *(REP Pubs; 0-9604876),* 12703 Red Fox Court, Maryland Hgts., MO 63043 (SAN 239-3786).

Reprint Co., *(Reprint; 0-87152),* P.O. Box 5401, 601 Hillcrest Offices, Spartanburg, SC 29304 Tel 803-582-0732 (SAN 203-3828).

Research, *(Research; 0-930442),* 2444 Charlemagne Ave., Long Beach, CA 90815 Tel 213-597-3718 (SAN 210-6590).

Research Advisory Services, Pubns., Inc., *(Res Adv Serv; 0-931602),* P.O. Box 8151, 286 N. McCarrons Blvd., St. Paul, MN 55113 (SAN 211-3759).

Research & Education Assn., *(Res & Educ; 0-87891),* 505 Eighth Ave., New York, NY 10018 Tel 212-695-9487 (SAN 204-6814).

Research & Service Institute, Inc., *(Res & Serv Inst; 0-942660),* 1504 Dresden Circle, Nashville, TN 37215 Tel 615-373-4996 (SAN 238-5678).

Research Associates, Inc., *(Res Assocs; 0-943928),* 1024 Boyle Bldg., Little Rock, AK 72201 Tel 501-372-7361 (SAN 241-144X).

Research Center for Language & Semiotic Studies, *(Res Ctr Lang Semiotic; 0-87750),* Dist. by: Humanities Press, Inc., Atlantic Highlands, NJ 07716 (SAN 201-9272).

Research Centre of Kabbalah, *(Res Ctr Kabbalah),* 200 Park Ave., Suite 303 E., New York, NY 10017 Tel 212-986-2515 (SAN 210-9484) Moved, Left No Forwarding Address.

Research Institute for Studies in Education, *(Res Inst Stud; 0-943206),* The Quadrangle, Iowa State University, Ames, IA 50011 Tel 515-294-7009 (SAN 240-9275).

Research Institute Management Reports, Inc., *(Res Inst Man Rep),* 589 Fifth Avenue, New York, NY 10017 (SAN 265-4091).

Research Press Co., *(Res Press; 0-87822),* 2612 N. Mattis Ave., Champaign, IL 61820 Tel 217-352-3273 (SAN 282-2482); Orders to: Box 31773, Champaign, IL 61820 (SAN 282-2490) Not to be confused with Res Pr KS in Prairie Village, KS.

Research Press, Inc., *(Res Pr KS),* 4500 W. 72nd Terrace, Prairie Village, KS 66208 Tel 913-362-9667 (SAN 240-1207) Not to be confused with Res Press in Champlain, IL.

Research Pubns., *(Research Pubns; 0-9600478),* P.O. Box 801, Glen Rock, NJ 07452 (SAN 204-6830).

Research Pubs., *(Res Publs; 0-911252),* 108 S. Patton, Arlington Heights, IL 60005 Tel 312-255-1961 (SAN 206-6645).

Research Pubns., Inc., *(Res Pubns Conn; 0-89235),* 12 Lunar Dr., Woodbridge, CT 06525 Tel 203-397-2600 (SAN 203-1159).

Research Services Unlimited, *(Res Serv Unltd),* P.O. Box 562, Toms River, NJ 08753 (SAN 265-4105).

Research Studies Pr., Inc., Div. of John Wiley & Sons, Ltd., *(Res Stud Pr; 0-89355),* c/o John Wiley & Sons, 605 Third Ave., New York, NY 10158 Tel 212-850-6418 (SAN 200-2272).

Researcher Pubns., Inc., *(Res Pubns WA; 0-938428),* 18806-40th Ave., W., Lynnwood, WA 98036 (SAN 216-180X).

Resolute Press, *(Resolute Pr; 0-9604382),* 13 Regent Court, Edison, NJ 08817 (SAN 216-0099).

Resource Center, The, *(Resource Ctr; 0-911213),* Box 4726, Albuquerque, NM 87196 (SAN 275-0570).

Resource Press, Subsidiary of Decision Models, Inc., *(Resource Pr; 0-9609182),* P.O. Box 774, 433 Belle Grove, Richardson, TX 75080 Tel 214-458-1466 (SAN 241-4457).

Resource Pubns., *(Resource Pubns; 0-89390),* 160 E. Virginia St., No. 290, San Jose, CA 95112 Tel 408-286-8505 (SAN 209-3081).

Resources, *(Resources; 0-933342),* P.O. Box 134, Harvard Sq., Cambridge, MA 02138 (SAN 209-0457).

Resources for Children in Hospitals, *(Resources Children; 0-9608150),* P.O. Box 10, Belmont, MA 02178 Tel 617-492-6220 (SAN 240-2734).

Resources for the Future, *(Resources Future),* Johns Hopkins Univ. Press, Baltimore, MD 21218 (SAN 213-1544).

Reston Publishing Co., Inc., *(Reston; 0-87909; 0-8359),* 11480 Sunset Hills Rd., Reston, VA 22090 Tel 703-437-8900 (SAN 200-2337); Dist. by: Prentice-Hall, Inc., Englewood Cliffs, NJ 07632 (SAN 215-3939).

Restoration Research, *(Restoration Re; 0-942284),* P.O. Box 547, Bountiful, UT 84010 Tel 801-298-4058 (SAN 238-1133).

Resurgens Pubns., Inc., *(Resurgens Pubns; 0-89583),* P.O. Box 49321, Atlanta, GA 30329 Tel 404-834-1343 (SAN 211-0539).

Retail Reporting Bureau, *(Retail Report; 0-934590),* 101 Fifth Ave., New York, NY 10003 Tel 212-255-9595 (SAN 213-1552).

Retirement Research, *(Retirement Res),* Box 401, Appleton, WI 54912 Tel 414-734-6610 (SAN 204-6849).

Retriever Books, *(Retriever; 0-9604628),* 250 W. 87th St., New York, NY 10024 Tel 212-874-5579 (SAN 213-5531).

Reunions, Joseph & Mary Ray, *(J & M R Reunions),* 6740 Velasco, Dallas, TX 75214 Tel 214-821-4456 (SAN 203-8250).

Revelation House Pubs., Inc., *(Revelation Hse; 0-9604852),* P.O. Box 73175, Metairie, LA 70033 (SAN 217-1295).

Revell, Fleming H., Co., *(Revell; 0-8007),* 184 Central Ave., Old Tappan, NJ 07675 Tel 201-768-8060 (SAN 203-3801). *Imprints:* New Hope Books (New Hope); Power Books (Power Bks); Spire Books (Spire Bks).

Reverchon Press, *(Reverchon Pr; 0-9601902),* P.O. Box 19647, Dallas, TX 75219 Tel 214-528-6540 (SAN 212-9671).

Review & Herald Publishing Assn., *(Review & Herald; 0-8280),* 6856 Eastern Ave. NW, Washington, DC 20012 Tel 202-723-3700 (SAN 203-3798).

Reviewer, The, *(Reviewer; 0-9606796),* 2197 Berkeley, Salt Lake City, UT 84109 Tel 801-487-4274 (SAN 207-2815).

Revisionary Press, *(Revisionary; 0-9603726),* Box 158A, St. James, NY 11780 Tel 516-862-9296 (SAN 209-5955).

Revisionist Press, *(Revisionist Pr; 0-87700),* P.O. Box 2009, Brooklyn, NY 11202 (SAN 203-378X).

Revolutionary Pubns, *(Revolutionary Pubns),* P.O. Box 4787, Santa Barbara, CA 93103 (SAN 239-6025).

Reward Books See **Prentice-Hall, Inc.**

Reward Publishing, *(Reward Pub; 0-9610280),* P.O. Box 124, Eugene, OR 97440 (SAN 264-343X).

Reymont Associates, *(Reymont; 0-918734),* 6556 Sweet Maple Lane, Boca Raton, FL 33433 Tel 305-483-4343 (SAN 204-6857).

Reyn Publishing Co., *(Reyn Pub Co.; 0-936366),* 14240 E. 14th St., San Leandro, CA 94578 (SAN 214-1345).

Reynal & Co., *(Reynal; 0-688),* 105 Madison Ave., New York, NY 10016 Tel 212-889-3050 (SAN 204-6865); Dist. by: William Morrow & Co., Order Dept., 6 Henderson Dr., W. Caldwell, NJ 07006 (SAN 202-5779).

Reynard House, *(Reynard Hse; 0-932998),* 5706 30th NE, Seattle, WA 98105 (SAN 216-2954).

Reynolds, Bryan P., *(B P Reynolds; 0-9606448),* P.O. Box 186, Palos Park, IL 60464 Tel 312-425-8342 (SAN 215-8027).

Reynolds, Hazel Wright, *(H W Reynolds; 0-9608106),* 11707 Stocksdale Rd., Kingsville, MD 21087 Tel 301-592-8173 (SAN 238-8618).

Reynolds Morse Foundation, *(Reynolds Morse; 0-934236),* 10395 Stafford Rd., Chagrin Fall, OH 44022 (SAN 282-2520); Dist. by: L.D.S. Books, P.O. Box 67, MCS, Dayton, OH 45402 (SAN 282-5864).

Rhema Bible Church *See* Hagin, Kenneth, Ministries, Inc.

Rhineburgh Press Inc., *(Rhineburgh Pr; 0-9604746),* 595 Madison Ave., New York, NY 10022 Tel 212-355-0162 (SAN 215-3394).

Rhino's Press, The, *(Rhinos Pr; 0-937382),* P.O. Box 3520, Laguna Hills, CA 92654 Tel 714-997-3217 (SAN 214-4565).

Rho-Delta Press, *(Rho-Delta Pr; 0-913770),* P.O. Box 69540, Los Angeles, CA 90069 Tel 213-657-1925 (SAN 204-6881).

Rhode Island Genealogical Society, *(RI Genealogical; 0-946144),* 128 Massasoit Dr., Warwick, RI 02888 Tel 401-781-6759 (SAN 216-4450).

Rhode Island Historical Society, *(RI Hist Soc; 0-932840),* 52 Power St., Providence, RI 02906 Tel 401-331-8575 (SAN 203-0829).

Rhode Island Mayflower Society, *(RI Mayflower; 0-930272),* 128 Massasoit Dr., Warwick, RI 02888 Tel 401-781-6759 (SAN 209-4843).

Rhode Island Pubns. Society, *(RI Pubns Soc; 0-917012),* Old State House, 150 Benefit St., Providence, RI 02903 Tel 401-272-1776 (SAN 219-9696).

Rhodes Geographic Library, Inc., *(Rhodes Geo Lib; 0-933768),* 3225 Rum Row, Naples, FL 33940 Tel 813-262-6713 (SAN 212-792X).

Rhythmic Aerobex, *(Rhythmic Aerobex; 0-9610234),* 3308 Midway Dr., No. 680, San Diego, CA 92110 (SAN 264-3456).

Rice, James K., *(J K Rice),* 715 Ratton St., Stockton, CA 95205 (SAN 287-1742).

Rice Univ. Studies, *(Rice Univ; 0-89263),* Rice Univ. Studies P.O. Box 1892, Houston, TX 77251 Tel 713-527-8101 (SAN 204-689X); Dist. by: Texas A&M Univ. Pr., Drawer C, College Station, TX 77843 Tel 409-845-1436 (SAN 207-5237).

Rich Concepts Enterprises, *(Rich Concepts; 0-938582),* P.O. Box 2322, La Jolla, CA 92038 Tel 714-273-1033 (SAN 239-9954).

Rich-Errington, *(Rich-Errington; 0-915898),* P.O. Box 546, Bay City, MI 48706 Tel 517-893-6730 (SAN 207-6691).

Rich Pubs., *(Rich SC),* P.O. Box 1185, Clemson, SC 29633 Tel 803-654-2507 (SAN 207-5857).

Rich Pub. Co., *(Rich Pub Co; 0-9607256),* 10611 Creektree, Houston, TX 77070 Tel 713-469-9165 (SAN 239-300X).

Richards, Frank E., Publishing Co., Inc., *(Richards Pub; 0-88323),* P.O. Box 66, Phoenix, NY 13135 Tel 315-695-7261 (SAN 203-0861).

Richards, John Thomas, *(J T Richards; 0-9605980),* 309 W. Ninth St., Rolla, MO 65401 Tel 402-648-7641 (SAN 220-1917); Orders to: New Frontiers Foundation, Inc., Fellowship Farm, Route 1, Oregon, WI 53575 Tel 608-835-3795 (SAN 214-0659).

Richards, Peter, Co., The, *(Richards Co)* 3 Parkview Plaza, Morristown, NJ 07960 (SAN 239-4820).

Richards, S.P., *(S P Richards; 0-9608224),* Box 501, New Providence, NJ 07974 (SAN 240-1193).

Richards House-FACTS, *(Richards Hse; 0-930702),* P.O. Box 208, Wellesley Hills, MA 02181 Tel 617-235-2152 (SAN 211-0547).

Richardson, Lenore Hennessey, *(L H Richardson; 0-9602958),* Box 281, Berkeley, CA 94701 (SAN 213-1579).

Richardson & Snyder, *(Rich & Snyder; 0-943940),* 25 Broad St., New York, NY 10004 Tel 212-344-1200 (SAN 241-1458); Dist. by: E.P. Dutton, 2 Park Ave., New York, NY 10016 Tel 212-725-1818 (SAN 201-0070).

Richboro Press, *(Richboro Pr; 0-89713),* Box 1, Richboro, PA 18954 (SAN 214-1353).

Richcraft Engineering Ltd., *(Richcraft Eng),* Drawer 1065, No. 1 Wahmeda Industrial Park, Chautauqua, NY 14722 Tel 716-753-2654 (SAN 219-0931).

Richelieu Court Publications, Inc., *(Richelieu Court; 0-911519),* Aspen Heights, Slingerlands, NY 12159 Tel 518-439-7942 (SAN 264-3480).

Richman Publishing, *(Richman Pub; 0-941846),* P.O. Box 11307, Salt Lake City, UT 84147 Tel 801-377-9456 (SAN 239-3018).

Richmond County Historical Society, *(Richmond Cty Hist Soc),* c/o Reese Library, Augusta Coll., 2500 Walton Way, Augusta, GA 30904 Tel 404-828-4566 (SAN 203-0802).

Richwood Pub., Co., *(Richwood Pub; 0-915172),* P.O. Box 381, Scarsdale, NY 10583 Tel 914-723-1286 (SAN 207-3250).

Ricwalt Publishing Co., *(Ricwalt Pub Co; 0-933054),* C-3 Bldg., Rm. 110, Fishermen's Terminal, Seattle, WA 98119 Tel 206-282-7545 (SAN 213-1587).

Ridge Row Press, Univ. of Scranton, *(Ridge Row; 0-940866),* Dept. of Theology & Religious Studies, Scranton, PA 18510 Tel 717-961-7449 (SAN 223-1123).

Ridgefield Bicentennial Commission, *(Ridgefield Bicen Com; 0-9601114),* 400 Main St., Ridgefield, CT 06877 Tel 203-438-7218 (SAN 209-9985).

Ridgefield Pub. Co., *(Ridgefield Pub; 0-86628),* 6925 Canby Ave., Suite 104, Reseda, CA 91335 Tel 213-343-8811 (SAN 215-8035).

Ridgeview Junior High Press, *(Ridgeview Jr High Pr; 0-936920),* 9424 Highlander Court, Walkersville, MD 21793 (SAN 214-4573).

Ridgeview Publishing Co., *(Ridgeview; 0-917930),* Box 686, Atascadero, CA 93423 Tel 805-466-7252 (SAN 209-9993).

Ridgeway Books, *(Ridgeway Bks),* P. O. Box 6431, Philadelphia, PA 19145 (SAN 207-7485).

Ridgeway Press, *(Ridgeway Pr; 0-943230),* 12032 Montecito Road, Los Alamitos, CA 90720 (SAN 240-4915).

Rieker Communications, *(Rieker Communications; 0-941656),* 52 Groveland Terr., No. 413, Minneapolis, MN 55408 Tel 612-922-4142 (SAN 239-3026).

Rietman, Jaap, *(Jaap Rietman; 0-930034),* 167 Spring St., New York, NY 10012 Tel 212-966-7044 (SAN 205-2105).

Rigel, Inc., *(Rigel; 0-937234),* 131 Asl Lane, Elkton, MD 21921 (SAN 214-4581).

Riggers Bible, *(Riggers Bible; 0-9600992),* P.O. Box 3302, Glenstone Sta., Springfield, MO 65804 Tel 417-869-9236 (SAN 207-2823).

Riggs, Karen B., *(Riggs),* Rte. 4, Box 359-R, Mechanicsville, VA 23111 Tel 804-779-3557 (SAN 275-0899).

Right to Life League of Southern California, *(Right to Life),* 1616 W. Ninth St., Suite 220, Los Angeles, CA 90015 (SAN 219-8142).

Right White Line, *(Right White Line; 0-918926),* 531 N. Inlet, Lincoln City, OR 97367 Tel 503-994-8433 (SAN 209-6536).

Riley, Maurice W., *(M W Riley; 0-9603150),* 512 Roosevelt Blvd., Ypsilanti, MI 48197 (SAN 213-3628).

Riling, Ray, Arms Books, *(Ray Riling; 0-9603096),* P.O. Box 18925, 6844 Gorsten St., Philadelphia, PA 19119 Tel 215-438-2456 (SAN 205-2385).

RIM Classroom Plays *See* Stevens & Shea Publishers

Rinehart, Roberts, Inc. Publishers, *(R Rinehart Inc; 0-911797),* P. O. Box 3161, Boulder, CO 80303 Tel 303-492-7191 (SAN 264-3510).

Ringa Press, *(Ringa Pr; 0-88100),* 6833 W. Grand Avenue, Chicago, IL 60635 (SAN 264-3529).

Rio Grande Press, Inc., *(Rio Grande; 0-87380),* P.O. Box 33, Glorieta, NM 87535 Tel 505-757-6275 (SAN 203-3763).

Rip off Press, *(Rip off; 0-89620),* P.O. Box 14158, San Francisco, CA 94114 Tel 415-863-5359 (SAN 207-7671).

Risale i Nur Institute of America, *(Risale i Nur Inst; 0-933552),* 2506 Shattuck Ave., Berkeley, CA 94704 Tel 415-845-4355 (SAN 212-6192).

Rising Star Press, *(Rising Star; 0-933670),* 557 Wellington Ave., San Carlos, CA 94070 Tel 415-592-2459 (SAN 213-3636).

Rising Wolf Inc., *(Rising Wolf; 0-936710),* 1304 Jackson, Missoula, MT 59802 (SAN 214-459X).

Risk Analysis & Research Corp., *(Risk Analysis; 0-932056),* P.O. Drawer DPFC, Monterey, CA 93942 (SAN 211-6464).

Risk & Insurance Mgt. Society, Inc., *(Risk & Ins; 0-937802),* 205 E. 42nd St., New York, NY 10017 Tel 212-286-9292 (SAN 215-8043).

Risk Enterprises, *(Risk Ent),* 1133 Curtis, Laramie, WY 82070 (SAN 213-1560).

Ritchie, George F., *(G F Ritchie; 0-9604392),* 665 Pine St., No. 503, San Francisco, CA 94108 Tel 415-433-6115 (SAN 212-6834).

Ritner, George, *(G Ritner),* 411 Broadway, Suite 203, San Diego, CA 92101 (SAN 211-268X).

Rittenhouse Book Distributors, *(Rittenhouse),* 511 Feheley Dr., King of Prussia, PA 19406 Tel 215-277-1414 (SAN 213-4454).

Rival Pubs., *(Rival Pubs; 0-9607100),* P.O. Box 5628, Everett, WA 98206 Tel 206-334-3965 (SAN 239-0302).

River Basin Publishing Co., *(River Basin; 0-936106),* P.O. Box 30573, St. Paul, MN 55175 Tel 612-291-0980 (SAN 213-7887).

River Bend Publishing, *(River Bend; 0-9605162),* 1222 Vista Court, No. 2, Muscatine, IA 52761 (SAN 215-9112).

River City Pubs., Ltd., *(River City MO),* P.O. Box 28665, St. Louis, MO 63141 (SAN 222-982X).

River Falls Univ. Press, *(River Falls),* 113 E. Hathorn, River Falls, WI 54022 Tel 715-425-3100 (SAN 203-6983).

River Forest Community Center, *(River Forest C C; 0-9606314),* River Forest Community Center, 414 Jackson, River Forest, IL 60305 (SAN 239-8613).

River House, *(River Hse; 0-940644),* 2213 Pennington Bend, Nashville, TN 37214 Tel 615-889-2968 (SAN 216-2962).

River Sedge Press, *(RiverSedge Pr),* P.O. Box 3185, Edinburg, TX 78539 Tel 512-381-3429 (SAN 218-3269).

River West Books, *(River W Bks; 0-9607192),* 663 S. 11th St., Coosbay, OR 97420 Tel 503-269-1363 (SAN 239-1287).

Riverhouse Pubns., *(Riverhouse Pubns; 0-933258),* 20 Waterside Plaza, New York, NY 10010 Tel 212-685-2376 (SAN 212-6850).

Riverrun Press Inc., *(Riverrun NY; 0-7145),* 175 Fifth Ave., Suite 814, New York, NY 10010 Tel 212-228-0390 (SAN 212-551X); Dist. by: Flatiron Book Distributors, Inc., 175 Fifth Ave., Suite 814, New York, NY 10010 Tel 212-228-0390 (SAN 240-9917).

Riverside Editions *See* Houghton Mifflin Co.

Riverside Press, The, *(River Side Pr; 0-912285),* P.O. Box 133, Riverside, CT 06878 Tel 203-637-3084 (SAN 265-0932).

Riverstone Press, *(Riverstone; 0-9601130),* 1851 N. Fremont, Chicago, IL 60614 Tel 312-280-1641 (SAN 210-2641).

Riverstone Press of the Foothills Art Center, *(Riverstone Foothills; 0-936600),* 809 15th St., Golden, CO 80401 (SAN 214-0144).

Riverwood Pubs., Ltd., *(Riverwood Pubs; 0-914762),* 500 E. 77th St., Suite 1204, New York, NY 10162 Tel 212-737-9304 (SAN 206-5185); Dist. by: E.P. Dutton & Co., Inc., 201 Park Ave., S., New York, NY 10003 (SAN 201-0070).

Rizzoli International Pubns., Inc., *(Rizzoli Intl; 0-8478),* 712 Fifth Ave., New York, NY 10019 Tel 212-397-3740 (SAN 207-7000).

Rmi Corporation, *(RMI; 0-910117),* 341 Broadway, Cambridge, MA 02139 (SAN 240-835X).

Ro-Mar Publishing Co., *(Ro-Mar; 0-9609566),* 11325 Valley Oak Dr., Oakdale, CA 95361 (SAN 275-102X).

Road Street Press, The, *(Road St Pr; 0-9609536),* P.O. Box 9605, Washington, DC 20016 (SAN 275-1062); Dist. by: Mary Mitchell, 2810 R St. N.W., Washington, DC 20007 Tel 202-333-2401 (SAN 200-4100).

Roadrunner-Technical Pubns., Inc., Div. of Desert Laboratories, Inc., *(Roadrunner Tech; 0-89741)*, 3136 E. Columbia St., Tucson, AZ 85714 Tel 602-294-3431 (SAN 204-2169).

Roan Horse Press, *(Roan Horse; 0-933234)*, 2509 N. Campbell Ave., Suite 277, Tucson, AZ 85719 (SAN 215-9120).

Roan Press, *(Roan Pr; 0-935546)*, P.O. Box 785, Pearl River, NY 10965 Tel 914-735-8805 (SAN 213-5558).

Roanoke Island Studio, Inc., *(Roanoke Isld; 0-912367)*, P.O. Box 308, Manteo, NC 27954 Tel 919-473-2746 (SAN 265-0940).

Roark Pubns., *(Roark Pubns; 0-939546)*, P.O. Box 5973-325, Sherman Oaks, CA 91413 Tel 213-784-7421 (SAN 220-1852).

Robert Morris Associates, The, *(Robt Morris Assocs)*, 1616 Philadelphia National Bank Bldg., Philadelphia, PA 19107 Tel 215-665-2850 (SAN 224-6473).

Robert Silver Associates, *(R Silver; 0-937414)*, 95 Madison Ave., New York, NY 10016 (SAN 241-5801).

Roberts, A., *(A Roberts)*, 714 Andover Lane, Albany, GA 31705 (SAN 239-4839).

Roberts, F.M., Enterprises, *(F M Roberts; 0-912746)*, P.O. Box 608, Dana Point, CA 92629 Tel 714-493-1977 (SAN 201-4688).

Roberts, Ken, Publishing Co., *(K Roberts; 0-913602)*, P.O. Box 151, Fitzwilliam, NH 03447 Tel 603-585-6612 (SAN 203-0888).

Roberts, Ransom, *(R Roberts; 0-9607834)*, P.O. Box 11146, Glendale, CA 91206-7146 Tel 213-244-3817 (SAN 238-1958).

Roberts, Richard O., *(R O Roberts)*, 205 E. Kehoe Blvd., Wheaton, IL 60187 (SAN 239-4847).

Roberts Enterprises, *(Roberts Ent; 0-9604184)*, 7350 N. Montero Dr., No. 1406, Tucson, AZ 85741 (SAN 214-4603).

Roberts Publishing Corp., *(Roberts Pub; 0-936492)*, 45 John St., New York, NY 10038 Tel 212-233-3768 (SAN 203-0772).

Robertson, Donald W., *(Robertson)*, 3811 Marquette Pl., No. 2 G, San Diego, CA 92106 Tel 619-226-8150 (SAN 211-0911).

Robertson, James E., *(J E Robertson; 0-9600756)*, 5213 Don Pio Dr., Woodland Hills, CA 91364 Tel 213-347-8576 (SAN 202-7267); Orders to: P.O. Box 2227, North Hollywood, CA 91602 (SAN 202-7275).

Robin, Eddie, Publishing, *(E Robin Pub; 0-936362)*, P.O. Box 70688, Las Vegas, NE 89170-0688 Tel 702-798-5029 (SAN 214-4611).

Robin & Russ Handweavers, *(Robin & Russ)*, 533 N. Adams St., McMinnville, OR 97128 Tel 503-472-5760 (SAN 207-284X).

Robinson, Alma, *(A Robinson)*, 196 Dover Rd., Warrenton, VA 22186 (SAN 211-6308).

Robinson, Nelson B. Bookseller, *(Nelson B Robinson; 0-930352)*, P.O. Box 153, Rockport, MA 01966 Tel 617-546-7323 (SAN 209-004X).

Robinson, Peggy, *(P Robinson)*, 1326 Fell St., San Francisco, CA 94117 Tel 415-387-9339 (SAN 215-2223); Dist. by: Far West Book Service, 3515 N.E. Hassalo, Portland, OR 97232 (SAN 282-6429).

Robinson, Ruth E., Books, *(Robinson Bks; 0-9603556)*, Rte. 7, Box 162A, Morgantown, WV 26505 Tel 304-594-3140 (SAN 213-4322).

Robinson & Watkins, *(Robinson & Wat; 0-7224)*, c/o Jenks, 1462 N. Stanley Ave., Rm. 206, Los Angeles, CA 90046 Tel 213-876-3250 (SAN 262-0693).

Robinson Newspapers, *(Robinson News)*, 207 SW 150th St., Burien, WA 98166 Tel 206-242-0100 (SAN 263-2268).

Roblin Enterprises Inc., *(Roblin Enterprises)*, 23 Rosedale Road, Yonkers, NY 10710 Tel 914-337-4576 (SAN 264-3561).

Robotics Press, *(Robotics Pr; 0-89661)*, 8285 S.W. Nimbus, Suite 151, Beaverton, OR 97005 Tel 503-646-2713 (SAN 282-2563); Orders to: P.O. Box 606, Beaverton, OR 97075 Tel 800-547-1842 (SAN 282-2571).

Roca Publishing, Inc., *(Roca Pub; 0-88025)*, P.O. Box 176, St. David, PA 19087 Tel 215-337-0576 (SAN 217-4243).

Rochester Folk Art Guild, *(Rochester Folk Art)*, Rte. 1, Box 10, Middlesex, NY 14507 Tel 716-554-3539 (SAN 210-9492).

Rocin Press, *(Rocin; 0-9608304)*, 8 E. 62 St., New York, NY 10021 (SAN 240-9550).

Rock Harbor Press, *(Rock Harbor; 0-932260)*, P.O. Box 1206, Hyannis, MA 02601 (SAN 214-199X).

Rock Point Community School, *(Rock Point; 0-910675)*, Chinle, AZ 86503 Tel 602-659-4246 (SAN 262-8910).

Rock Spring Pubns., *(Rock Spring)*, 610 South View Terrace, Alexandria, VA 22314 Tel 703-536-8339 (SAN 206-846X).

Rockdale Ridge Press, *(Rockdale Ridge; 0-9602338)*, 8501 Ridge Rd., Cincinnati, OH 45236 Tel 513-891-9900 (SAN 212-4459).

Rockefeller Univ. Press, *(Rockefeller; 0-87470)*, 1230 York Ave., Box 291, New York, NY 10021 Tel 212-570-8571 (SAN 203-3747); Orders to: Box 269, 1230 York Ave., New York, NY 10021 Tel 212-570-8572 (SAN 203-3755).

Rocket Publishing Co., *(Rocket Pub Co)*, P.O. Box 412, Normangee, TX 77871 Tel 713-828-4265 (SAN 204-5699).

Rockets, *(Rockets; 0-912468)*, P.O. Box 591, Corona, CA 91720 Tel 714-735-0169 (SAN 204-692X).

Rockfall Press, *(Rockfall Pr; 0-9601502)*, Cider Mill Rd., Rockfall, CT 06481 (SAN 212-1638).

Rocking Chair Press, Inc., *(Rocking Chair Pr; 0-913562)*, 2109 Queenswood Dr., Tallahassee, FL 32303 (SAN 204-6938).

Rocking Horse Press, *(Rocking Horse; 0-932306)*, 32 Ellise Rd., Storrs, CT 06268 Tel 203-429-1474 (SAN 212-4467).

Rockland Research Institute, *(Rockland Research; 0-936934)*, Information Sciences Division, Orangeburg, NY 10962 (SAN 239-6041).

Rockwell Pubns., *(Rockwell; 0-913208)*, 60 N. Monterey St., Mobile, AL 36604 Tel 205-471-5276 (SAN 206-6742) Formerly Named Thomas-Hull.

Rocky Mountain Books, *(Rocky Mtn Bks)*, P.O. Box 10663, Denver, CO 80210 (SAN 215-7047).

Rocky Mountain Writers Guild, *(Rocky Mtn Writer; 0-937050)*, 2969 Baseline Rd., Boulder, CO 80303 (SAN 240-9658).

Rod & Staff Pubs., Inc., *(Rod & Staff)*, Crockett, KY 41413 Tel 606-522-4348 (SAN 206-7633).

Rodale Press, Inc., *(Rodale Pr Inc; 0-87857)*, 33 E. Minor St., Emmaus, PA 18049 Tel 215-967-5171 (SAN 200-2477).

Rodney Pubns., Inc., *(Rodney; 0-913830)*, 349 E. 49th St., New York, NY 10017 Tel 212-421-5444 (SAN 204-6954).

Roehrs Co., *(Roehrs; 0-911266)*, P.O. Box 125, 227A Paterson Ave., East Rutherford, NJ 07073 Tel 201-939-0090 (SAN 204-6962).

Roerick Music Company, *(Roerick Music)*, 4046 Davana Rd., Sherman Oaks, CA 91423 (SAN 239-8621).

Rogers, Gay Ann, *(G A Rogers)*, Box 181, Claremont, CA 91711 (SAN 287-301X).

Rogers, Helga M., *(H M Rogers; 0-9602294)*, 3806 48th Ave., S., St. Petersburg, NY 33711 Tel 813-864-3292 (SAN 207-0316).

Rogers, Millicent, Museum, *(M Rogers Mus; 0-9609818)*, P.O. Box A, Taos, NM 87571 Tel 505-758-2462 (SAN 264-3588).

Rogers Book Service, *(Rogers Bk; 0-911268)*, 217 W. 18th St, Box V, New York, NY 10011 (SAN 204-6970).

Rogers House Museum Gallery, *(Rogers Hse Mus; 0-9600686)*, 102 E. Main South, Ellsworth, KS 67439 Tel 914-472-3255 (SAN 204-6989).

Rojan Music Pubns., *(RoJan Mus; 0-912151)*, 951 N. 45th, P.O. Box 31475, Seattle, WA 98103 Tel 206-634-1320 (SAN 264-7869).

Role Training Associates of California, *(Role Train Assocs)*, 1750 E. Ocean Blvd., Apt.1105, Long Beach, CA 90802 (SAN 208-0931).

Rolf's Gallery, *(Rolfs Gall; 0-910579)*, P.O. Box 9, Montevideo, MN 56265 Tel 612-269-8409 (SAN 260-2571).

Rolling Block Press, *(Rolling Block; 0-940028)*, P.O. Box 5357, Buena Park, CA 90622 (SAN 217-0817).

Rolling Hills Press, *(Rolling Hills Pr; 0-943978)*, 40 Pilgrim Park, San Rafael, CA 94903 Tel 415-479-5772 (SAN 282-2601); Dist. by: De Fremery & Co., 74 Tehama St., San Francisco, CA 94106 (SAN 282-6097).

Rolling Meadows Library, *(Rolling Meadows; 0-9602782)*, 3110 Martin Lane, Rolling Meadows, IL 60008 Tel 312-259-6050 (SAN 213-7895).

Romaine Pierson Pubs., *(Pierson Pubs; 0-935466)*, 80 Shore Rd., Port Washington, NY 11050 Tel 516-883-6350 (SAN 213-3660).

Roman Enterprises, *(Roman Enter; 0-9606642)*, 16548 Lynch Path, Lakeville, MN 55044 Tel 612-435-5024 (SAN 217-426X).

Romance Books & People, *(Romance Bks & People)*, 5633 Colfax Ave., Suite 312, N. Hollywood, CA 91601 (SAN 263-2276).

Romance Monographs, Inc., *(Romance)*, P.O. Box 7553, University, MS 38677 Tel 601-234-0001 (SAN 209-4878).

Romantic Times, Inc., *(Romantic Times; 0-940338)*, 163 Joralemon St., Brooklyn Heights, NY 11201 (SAN 218-5032).

Romney Press, *(Romney Pr; 0-9604640)*, 308 Fourth Ave., Iowa City, IA 52240 (SAN 215-7055); Dist. by: Eble Music Co., P.O. Box 2570, Iowa City, IA 52244 (SAN 282-6275).

Rongataur Press, *(Rongataur; 0-941006)*, P.O. Box 991, Vacaville, CA 95696 Tel 707-447-0739 (SAN 217-4278).

Rookfield Press, *(Rookfield; 0-917610)*, P.O. Box 45, Deer, AR 72628 Tel 501-446-5793 (SAN 209-3065).

Rooney Pubns., *(Rooney Pubns; 0-9604600)*, P.O. Box 44146, Panorama City, CA 91412 Tel 213-894-2585 (SAN 215-1790).

Root, A. I., Co., *(A I Root; 0-936028)*, Box 706, Medina, OH 44258 Tel 216-725-6677 (SAN 205-230X).

Roper Center User Services, The, *(Roper Ctr User)*, University of Connecticut, Box U-164, Storrs, CT 06268 (SAN 287-2617).

Rorge Publishing Co., *(Rorge Pub Co)*, P.O. Box 130, Evergreen, CO 80439 Tel 303-674-4220 (SAN 202-9715).

Rosallen Pubns, *(Rosallen Pubns; 0-9607486)*, P.O. Box 927, North Hollywood, CA 91603 Tel 213-766-6045 (SAN 239-605X).

Rose Deeprose Press, *(Rose Deeprose; 0-937738)*, 1661 Oak St., San Francisco, CA 94117 Tel 415-552-0991 (SAN 215-3408); Dist. by: Subterranean Co., P.O. Box 10233, Eugene, OR 97440 Tel 503-343-6324 (SAN 169-7102).

Rose Garden Press, The, *(Rose Garden; 0-9611684)*, P.O. Box 749, Pittsburg, CA 94565 Tel 415-427-5994 (SAN 284-933X).

Rose Hill Press, *(Rose Hill; 0-917264)*, 12368 Old Pen Mar Rd., Waynesboro, PA 17268 Tel 717-762-7072 (SAN 208-8312).

Rose Press, *(Rose Pr)*, 1442A Walnut, No. 373, Berkeley, CA 94709 (SAN 240-8767).

Rose Pubns., *(Rose Pubns)*, 3828 Ben Lomond Ct., Toledo, OH 43607 (SAN 209-5963).

Rose Publishing Co., *(Rose Pub MI; 0-937320)*, 4676 Morningside Dr., S.E., Grand Rapids, MI 49508 Tel 616-698-8282 (SAN 211-8378).

Rose Publishing Co., Inc., *(Rose Pub; 0-914546)*, 301 Louisiana, Little Rock, AR 72201 Tel 501-372-1666 (SAN 203-3739).

Rosebud Press, *(Rosebud; 0-9606194)*, P.O. Box 40, Van Brunt Sta., Brooklyn, NY 11215 (SAN 217-0825).

Rosen, Pauline, *(P Rosen; 0-9600214)*, 658 Main St., Placerville, CA 95667 (SAN 206-8303).

Rosen Pub. Group, *(Rosen Group; 0-8239)*, 29 E. 21st St., New York, NY 10010 Tel 212-777-3017 (SAN 203-3720).

Rosenbach Museum & Library, The, *(Rosenbach Mus & Lib)*, 2010 De Lancey Place, Philadelphia, PA 19103 Tel 215-732-1600 (SAN 211-9749).

Rosenberg, Mary S., Inc., *(M S Rosenberg; 0-917324)*, 17 W. 60th St., New York, NY 10023 Tel 212-362-4873 (SAN 205-2296).

Rosenberg, Vivian Graff, *(V G Rosenberg)*, R.D. 2 Box 274, Walkers Mill Rd., Germantown, NY 12526 Tel 518-537-6159 (SAN 212-1360).

Rosenberg Pubns., *(Rosenberg Pubns; 0-9607052)*, Box 1351, Lafayette, CA 94549 (SAN 239-3808).

Rosenblatt, Emil, *(E Rosenblatt; 0-9610060)*, 64 Sunset Dr., Croton-on-Hudson, NY 10520 Tel 914-271-3211 (SAN 275-1267).

Roserich Designs, Ltd., *(Roserich Ltd; 0-913289)*, P.O. Box 1030, Carpinteria, CA 93013 Tel 805-962-0862 (SAN 285-8401).

Rosetta Publishing Co., The, *(Rosetta Pub Co; 0-935850),* P.O. Box 17942, Raleigh, NC 27619 (SAN 213-7909) Moved, Left No Forwarding Address.

Rosey-Royce Publishing Co., *(Rosey-Royce; 0-934138),* 436 W. Ostrander Ave., Syracuse, NY 13205 (SAN 217-2666).

Rosholt House, *(Rosholt Hse; 0-910417),* Box 104, Rosholt, WI 54473 Tel 715-677-4722 (SAN 260-1249).

Ross, Betsy, Pubns., *(Betsy Ross Pub; 0-943232),* 3057 Betsy Ross Dr., Bloomfield Hills, MI 48013 Tel 313-646-5357 (SAN 240-7612).

Ross, Sidney Scott, *(Sidney Scott Ross; 0-9602028),* 1020 Meridian Ave., Miami Beach, FL 33139 Tel 305-538-1442 (SAN 212-1379).

Ross & Haines Old Books Co., *(Ross; 0-87018),* 639 E. Lake St., Wayzata, MN 55391 Tel 612-473-7551 (SAN 204-7004).

Ross/Back Roads Press, *(Ross-Back Roads; 0-931272),* P.O. Box 4340, Berkeley, CA 94704 (SAN 211-2000).

Ross Books, *(Ross Bks; 0-89496),* P.O. Box 4340, Berkeley, CA 94704 Tel 415-841-2474 (SAN 209-5912).

Ross-Erikson, Inc., *(Ross-Erikson; 0-915520),* 629 State St., Suite 207, Santa Barbara, CA 93101 Tel 805-962-1175 (SAN 208-0494).

Ross Valley Book Co., Inc., The, *(Ross Valley),* 1407 Solano Ave., Albany, CA 94706 Tel 415-526-6400 (SAN 216-4868).

Rossel Books, *(Rossel Bks; 0-940646),* 44 Dunbow Dr., Chappaqua, NY 10514 Tel 914-238-8954 (SAN 213-6414).

Rossi Pubns., *(Rossi Pubns; 0-935618),* P.O. Box 2001, Beverly Hills, CA 90213 Tel 213-556-0337 (SAN 213-6414).

Rostrum Books, *(Rostrum Bks),* P.O. Box 1191, Miami, FL 33101 Tel 305-573-5900 (SAN 205-227X).

Rosywick Press, *(Rosywick Pr; 0-9608712),* 175 W. 12th St., New York, NY 10011 (SAN 238-356X).

Rotary Club of Marquette, Michigan, *(Rotary Club; 0-9609764),* c/o Marquette Area Chamber of Commerce, 501 S. Front Street, Marquette, MI 49855 (SAN 264-3618); Dist. by: Marquette County Historical Society, 213 N. Front St., Marquette, MI 49855 (SAN 205-8871).

Rotary International, *(Rotary Intl; 0-915062),* 1600 Ridge Ave., Evanston, IL 60201 Tel 312-328-0100 (SAN 207-9585).

Roth Publishing, *(Roth Pub; 0-87957),* 125 Mineola Ave., Roslyn Hts., NY 11577 Tel 516-621-7242 (SAN 203-0810).

Rothman, Fred B., & Co., *(Rothman; 0-8377),* 10368 W. Centennial Rd., Littleton, CO 80127 Tel 303-979-5657 (SAN 159-9437).

Rothstein, Evelyn, Associates/Creative Communication Resources, *(E Rothstein Assoc; 0-9606172; 0-913935),* P.O. Box 650, Nyack, NY 10960 Tel 914-358-3991 (SAN 217-5622).

Rotz, Anna Overcash, *(Rotz; 0-9605108),* Box 266, 12182 Main St., Fort Loudon, PA 17224 (SAN 215-9139).

Rough Notes Co., Inc., The, *(Rough Notes),* 1200 N. Meridial St., P.O. Box 564, Indianapolis, IN 46206 Tel 317-634-1541 (SAN 203-5588).

Roundtable Press, *(Roundtable; 0-934512),* 4 Linden Square, Wellesley, MA 02181 Tel 617-235-5320 (SAN 282-2628); Orders to: Roundtable Press, 4 Linden Square, Wellesley, MA 02181 (SAN 282-2636).

Rouse Real Estate Finance, Inc., *(Rouse Real Estate; 0-9603790),* P.O. Box 905, Columbia, MD 21044 Tel 301-992-6147 (SAN 213-8174).

Roush, John H., Jr., *(J H Roush; 0-9600830),* 27 Terrace Ave., Kentfield, CA 94904 Tel 415-453-7130 (SAN 217-1827).

Roush Books, *(Roush Bks),* Box 4203, Valley Village, North Hollywood, CA 91607 (SAN 219-2705).

Routledge & Kegan Paul, Ltd., *(Routledge & Kegan; 0-7100),* 9 Park St., Boston, MA 02108 Tel 617-742-5863 (SAN 202-5469). *Imprints:* Kegan Paul International (Kegan Paul); Oriel Press (Oriel).

Rovern Press, *(Rovern Pr; 0-943150),* 185 Birch St., Willimantic, CT 06226 Tel 203-423-6387 (SAN 240-7620).

Rovi Pubns., Inc., *(Rovi; 0-911282),* P.O. Box 259, Belvedere, CA 94920 Tel 415-435-3174 (SAN 204-7020).

Roving Press Pubns., *(RoVing Pr Pub; 0-910449),* Box 2870-MCCA, Estes Park, CO 80517 Tel 800-525-5304 (SAN 260-1257).

Rowan Tree Press, Ltd., *(Rowan Tree; 0-937672),* 124 Chestnut St., Boston, MA 02108 (SAN 214-4638).

Rowland, Ralph & Star, *(R & S Rowland),* 4209 San Juan Dr., Fairfax, VA 22030 Tel 703-273-4891 (SAN 209-4800).

Rowman & Allanheld, Div. of Littlefield, Adams & Co., *(Rowman & Allanheld),* 81 Adams Dr., Totowa, NJ 07512 Tel 201-256-8600 (SAN 282-7921).

Rowman & Littlefield, Inc., Div. of Littlefield, Adams, & Co., *(Rowman; 0-87471; 0-8476),* 81 Adams Dr., Box 327, Totowa, NJ 07511 Tel 201-256-8600 (SAN 203-3704).

Roxbury Data Interface, *(Roxbury Data; 0-89902),* Box 1100, Verdi, NV 89439 Tel 702-747-4448 (SAN 212-8659).

Roxbury Pub. Co., *(Roxbury Pub Co; 0-935732),* 6458 Lake Shore Dr., San Diego, CA 92119 Tel 619-283-8616 (SAN 213-6422); Orders to:

Royal Court Reports, Pubs., *(Royal Court),* 3720 NE 28 Ter., Ocala, FL 32670 (SAN 219-8177).

Royal Publishing, *(Royal Calif; 0-930440),* P.O. Box 5027, Beverly Hills, CA 90210 (SAN 215-7071).

Royal Pub. Co., Div. of Recipes-of-the-Month Club, *(Royal Pub Co; 0-930440),* P.O. Box 5027, Beverly Hills, CA 90210 Tel 213-277-7220 (SAN 210-9190).

Royale Pubs., *(Royale Pubs; 0-9601378),* 9119 Blair River Circle, Fountain Valley, CA 92708 Tel 714-963-4419 (SAN 211-9757).

Royalty Publishing Co., *(Royalty Pub; 0-910487),* P.O. Box 2016, Manassas, VA 22110 Tel 703-368-9878 (SAN 260-1265).

Rpi/Kroll Pubns., Inc., *(RPI Kroll; 0-943424),* 733 Third Ave., New York, NY 10017 Tel 212-661-2222 (SAN 240-7566).

Rube, Ned J., Publisher, *(N J Rube; 0-930562),* 68 Marion Dr., New Rochelle, NY 10804 (SAN 211-0385).

Ruben Publishing, *(Ruben Pub; 0-917434),* P.O. Box 414, Avon, CT 06001 Tel 203-673-0740 (SAN 208-9645).

Rubenstein, Steve, *(Rubenstein; 0-941228),* 1445 Union St., No. 1, San Francisco, CA 94109 (SAN 239-3816).

Rubicon Books, *(Rubicon Bks; 0-913791),* 11627 N. 49th Dr., Glendale, AZ 85304 Tel 602-978-0546 (SAN 286-1895); P.O. Box 37103, Phoenix, AZ 85069 (SAN 286-1909).

Rubio-Boitel, Fr. Fernando, *(Rubio-Boitel),* Our Lady of Belen Church,10th and Church Sts., Belen, NM 87002 Tel 505-865-4455 (SAN 212-5528).

Ruborge Pubs., *(Ruborge Pubs),* Rte. 2, Box 867, Pompano Beach, FL 33067 Tel 305-427-8898 (SAN 212-226X).

Rubric Press, the, *(Rubric Pr; 0-943234),* 776 Warburton Ave., Yonkers, NY 10701 (SAN 240-4923).

Rucker Press, Inc., *(Rucker Pr),* 118 S. Broadway, Sta. B, Box 7025, Dayton, OH 45407 (SAN 208-3051).

Rudolf Dreikurs Institute of Colorado Pubns., *(RDIC Pubns; 0-933450),* P.O. Box 3118, Boulder, CO 80307 Tel 303-499-4500 (SAN 213-5566).

Rue Morgue Press, *(Rue Morgue; 0-915230),* P.O. Box 4119, Boulder, CO 80306 Tel 303-443-8346 (SAN 207-737X).

Ruffer, Eileen, *(E Ruffer),* 318 S. 3rd Ave., Bellwood, IL 60104 (SAN 262-0715); Dist. by: The Temple of Kriya Yoga, 2414 N. Kedzie, Chicago, IL 60647 Tel 312-342-4600 (SAN 240-9348).

Ruffled Feathers Publishing Co., *(Ruffled Feathers; 0-9603582),* 2700 Fourth St., Boulder, CO 80302 Tel 303-442-2660 (SAN 213-7917).

Ruffner, Tacey, *(T Ruffner; 0-9610424),* 2208 Grove Street No. 6, Berkeley, CA 94704 (SAN 264-3634).

Rugged, B., *(B Rugged; 0-9612018),* 11 S. Adelaide Ave., Highland Park, NJ 08904 Tel 201-828-6098 (SAN 277-6561).

Rumbleseat Press, Inc., *(Rumbleseat; 0-913444),* Front & County St., Drawer 288, Greensboro, PA 15338 Tel 412-943-3702 (SAN 205-6437).

Runaway Pubns., *(Runaway Pubns; 0-943662),* Box 1172, Ashland, OR 97520 (SAN 238-3608).

Runnels, Tom, Pubns., *(T Runnels Pubns; 0-9603710),* Marble Hill, MO 63764 Tel 314-238-2824 (SAN 213-8719).

Runner's Log, *(Runner's Log; 0-933872),* 10-50 Jackson Ave., Long Island City, NY 11101 (SAN 216-2970).

Running Press Book Publishers, *(Running Pr; 0-89471),* 125 S. 22nd St., Philadelphia, PA 19103 Tel 215-567-5080 (SAN 204-5702).

Running Wild, *(Running Wild; 0-939350),* P.O. Box 1211, Lafayette, CA 94549 Tel 415-283-7363 (SAN 216-4930).

Rural Development Committee, Center for International Studies, *(RDC Ctr Intl Stud; 0-86731),* 170 Uris Hall, Ithaca, NY 14853 Tel 607-256-6370 (SAN 217-510X).

Rural Life, *(Rural Life),* Rte. 1, Box 183-C, Whitewater, WI 53190 (SAN 206-6769).

Rush, James E., Assoc., Inc., *(Rush Assoc; 0-9128030),* 22 Carriage Rd., Powell, OH 43065 (SAN 200-2744).

Rush-Presbyterian-St. Luke's Medical Center, Dept. of Preventive Medicine, *(Rush-Presby-St Lukes),* 1743 W. Harrison St., Tenth Floor, Chicago, IL 60612 (SAN 219-094X).

Rushlight Club, *(Rushlight Club; 0-917422),* P.O. Box 3053, Talcottville, CT 06066 (SAN 207-4958).

Rusoff Books, *(Rusoff Bks; 0-917932),* 1302 S.E. 4th St., Minneapolis, MN 55414 Tel 612-331-3335 (SAN 209-3057).

Russell, John, *(J Russell),* 19 Doughty Lane, Fair Haven, NJ 07701 (SAN 262-0731).

Russell, Martin, Publisher, *(M Russell NY; 0-912209),* 61 Kincaid Dr., Yonkers, NY 10710 Tel 914-793-5296 (SAN 265-0967).

Russell & Russell, Pubs., Div. of Atheneum Pubs., *(Russell; 0-8462),* 597 Fifth Ave., New York, NY 10017 Tel 212-486-2685 (SAN 282-2644); Orders to: Scribner Distribution Center, 201 Willowbrook Blvd., Wayne, NJ 07470 Tel 201-256-0700 (SAN 282-2652).

Russell Pubns., *(Russell Pubns; 0-933558),* P.O Box 2461, Tampa, FL 33601 Tel 813-879-8580 (SAN 210-5764) Do No Confuse with Russell & Russell in NY (Russell).

Russell Sage Foundation, *(Russell Sage; 0-87154),* 112 E. 64th St., New York, NY 10021 Tel 212-750-6000 (SAN 203-3674); Orders to: Basic Books, Inc., 10 E. 53rd St., New York, NY 10022 (SAN 201-4521).

Russian Book Chamber Abroad, *(Rus Bk Chamber; 0-912306),* P.O. Box 126, Cathedral Sta., New York, NY 10025 (SAN 204-7071).

Russian Hill Hse. Bks., *(Russian Hill; 0-9608968),* P.O. Box 157, San Francisco, CA 94101 Tel 415-931-7249 (SAN 282-2709); Dist. by: Publishers Group West, 5855 Beaudry St., Emeryville, CA 94608 Tel 415-658-3453 (SAN 202-8522); Dist. by: Bookpeople, 2940 Seventh St., Berkeley, CA 94710 Tel 415-549-3030 (SAN 282-2725); Dist. by: L-S, P.O. Box 3063, Riwcon Station, San Francisco, CA 94119 Tel 415-771-0330 (SAN 169-0213).

Russian Numismatic Society, *(Russian Numis; 0-912671),* P.O. Box 3013, Alexandria, VA 22302 Tel 703-920-2043 (SAN 277-7053).

Russian Review, *(Russian Rev; 0-918444),* 1737 Cambridge St., Cambridge, MA 02138 Tel 617-495-4037 (SAN 210-0002).

Russica Publishers, *(Russica Pubs; 0-89830),* C/O Russica Book & Art Co., 799 Broadway, New York, NY 10003 (SAN 212-310X).

Rusthoi Soul Winning Pubns., *(Rusthoi; 0-911288),* P.O. Box 595, Montrose, CA 91020 Tel 213-241-7244 (SAN 204-708X).

Rutan Publishing, *(Rutan Pub; 0-936222),* 2717 Lyndale Ave. S., Minneapolis, MN 55408 (SAN 215-9147).

Rutgers Ctr. of Alcohol Studies Pubns., *(Rutgers Ctr Alcohol; 0-911290),* Smithers Hall, Rutgers Univ., New Brunswick, NJ 08903 Tel 201-932-3510 (SAN 203-3658); Orders to: P.O. Box 969, Piscataway, NJ 08854 Tel 201-932-2190 (SAN 203-3666).

Rutgers Univ., Graduate School of Library & Information Studies, *(Rutgers U SLIS),* Four Huntington St., New Brunswick, NJ 08903 Tel 201-932-7362 (SAN 205-9738).

Rutgers Univ. Pr., *(Rutgers U Pr; 0-8135),* 30 College Ave., New Brunswick, NJ 08903 Tel 201-932-7764 (SAN 203-364X).

Rutledge Press *See* **Smith, W. H., Pubs., Inc.**

Ryan Co., *(Ryan Co; 0-914202),* 2188 Latimer Lane, Los Angeles, CA 90024 Tel 213-474-4175 (SAN 202-9707).

Ryan Research International, *(Ryan Research; 0-942158),* 1593 Filbert Ave., Chico, CA 95926 Tel 916-343-2373 (SAN 239-9776).

Rydal Press-The Print, *(Rydal; 0-911292),* P.O. Box 250, Santa Fe, NM 87501 Tel 505-982-2689 (SAN 204-7098).

Ryder Geosystems, *(Ryder Geo; 0-941784),* 445 Union, Suite 304, Lakewood, CO 80228 Tel 303-988-4853 (SAN 239-3042).

Ryder Press, *(Ryder Pr; 0-916816),* 3307 Chadbourne Rd., Shaker Heights, OH 44120 Tel 216-921-7975 (SAN 208-8339).

Rymer Books, *(Rymer Bks; 0-9600792),* P.O. Box 104, Tollhouse, CA 93667 Tel 209-298-0761 (SAN 207-1010).

Rynders, B., Pubns., *(B Rynders Pubns; 0-9601872),* 1514-21 Ave., N.W., New Brighton, MN 55112 (SAN 212-4475).

SAE, *(SAE; 0-89883),* 400 Commonwealth Dr., Warrendale, PA 15096 Tel 412-776-4841 (SAN 216-0811).

SAS Institute Inc., *(SAS Inst; 0-917382),* SAS Circle, Cary, NC 27511 Tel 919-467-8000 (SAN 208-8347).

S & A Pubns., *(S&A Pubns; 0-9600768),* P.O. Box 2660, Sta. "A", Champaign, IL 61820 Tel 217-359-4222 (SAN 204-7101).

S&J Books, *(S&J Books; 0-9609608),* 387 Ocean Pkwy, Brooklyn, NY 11218 Tel 212-941-1833 (SAN 260-2598).

S & S Press, *(S & S Pr TX; 0-934646),* P.O. Box 5931, Austin, TX 78763 (SAN 212-6885) Do Not Confuse with Simon & Schuster (S&S).

SBS Publishing, Inc., *(SBS Pub; 0-89961),* 14 W. Forest Ave., Englewood, NJ 07631 Tel 201-569-8700 (SAN 213-3695).

SCB Photographics, *(SCB Photos; 0-940468),* P.O. Box 2991, Seal Beach, CA 90740 Tel 213-438-4731 (SAN 223-1581).

SCOAL Press, *(SCOAL Pr; 0-933556),* 53 Pondview Circle, Brockton, MA 02401 Tel 617-587-4275 (SAN 213-3717).

SCOP Pubns., Inc., *(SCOP Pubns),* P.O. Box 376, College Park, MD 20740 (SAN 211-2035).

SJB Publishing Co., *(SJB Pub Co; 0-912287),* 26632 Valpariso Rd., Mission Viejo, CA 92691 Tel 714-768-7238 (SAN 265-0975).

S J S Publishing, Inc., *(SJS Pub Inc),* 2314 S. Vineyard Ave. "E", Ontario, CA 91761 Tel 714-947-8035 (SAN 265-363X).

SLUSA, *(SLUSA),* 88 Eastern Ave., Somerville, NJ 08876 (SAN 216-1931).

S-P I, Inc., *(S-P I; 0-943418),* 1051 Clinton St., Buffalo, NY 14206 Tel 716-856-8029 (SAN 240-7701).

SP Medical & Scientific Books, Div. of Spectrum Publications, Inc., *(SP Med & Sci Bks; 0-89335),* 175-20 Wexford Terrace, Jamaica, NY 11432 Tel 212-658-0888 (SAN 213-5574).

SRS Co., *(S R S Co; 0-9610766),* No. 160, 2554 Lincoln Blvd., Marina del Rey, CA 90291 Tel 213-397-2600 (SAN 264-634X).

S. T. & A., *(ST&A; 0-936702),* P.O. Box 480530, Los Angeles, CA 90048 (SAN 214-4646).

SYDA Foundation, *(SYDA Found; 0-914602),* P.O. Box 600, South Fallsburg, NY 12779 Tel 914-434-2000 (SAN 206-5479).

S.H.C. Publishing *See* **Steinlitz-Hammacher Co.**

SAA Publishing, *(SAA Pub; 0-937922),* P.O. Box 7378, Ann Arbor, MI 48107 (SAN 240-9194).

Sabbagh Management Corporation, *(Sabbagh Manage; 0-912369),* 3310 45th St., NW, Washington, DC 20016 Tel 202-966-2651 (SAN 265-0991).

Sabbot, Rudolph Wm., - Natural History Books, *(Sabbot-Natural Hist Bks),* 5239 Tendilla Ave., Woodland Hills, CA 91364 Tel 213-346-7164 (SAN 213-2583).

Sachem Pr., *(Sachem Pr; 0-937584),* P.O. Box 9, Old Chatham, NY 12136 Tel 518-794-8077 (SAN 215-6075).

Sadler, John M., & Co., *(J M Sadler; 0-930250),* 215 Commonwealth Ave., Massapequa, NY 11758 Tel 516-798-9059 (SAN 210-6620).

Sadlier, William H., Inc., *(Sadlier; 0-8215),* 11 Park Place, New York, NY 10007 Tel 212-227-2120 (SAN 204-0948).

Sadtler Research Laboratories, Inc., *(Sadtler Res; 0-8456),* 3316 Spring Garden St., Philadelphia, PA 19104 Tel 215-382-7800 (SAN 203-0063).

Safe Harbor Press, *(Safe Harbor Pr; 0-913221),* West Ave. J, P.O. Box 4345, Lancaster, CA 93534 (SAN 283-9040).

Safety Consultants, Inc., *(Safety Consul),* 3140 Kingsley Dr., Florissant, MO 63033 Tel 314-921-6776 (SAN 206-3735).

Safety Now Co., Inc., *(Safety Now; 0-917066),* P.O. Box 567, Jenkintown, PA 19046 Tel 215-884-0210 (SAN 208-8355).

Sage Pubns., Inc., *(Sage; 0-8039),* 275 S. Beverly Dr., Beverly Hills, CA 90212 Tel 213-274-8003 (SAN 204-7217).

Sagebrush Press, *(Sagebrush Pr; 0-930704),* P.O. Box 87, Morongo Valley, CA 92256 Tel 211-4496).

Sagittarian Scriptory Enterprises, *(Sag Scriptory; 0-931908),* 2674 Laurel Drive, Fairfield, CA 94533 Tel 707-427-3446 (SAN 212-4483).

Sagittarius Rising, *(Sag Rising; 0-933620),* P.O. Box 252, Arlington, MA 02174 Tel 617-646-2692 (SAN 282-2741).

Saguaro Publishing, *(Saguaro; 0-9608864),* 1302 E. Becker Lane, Phoenix, AZ 85020 (SAN 241-0761).

Saifer, Albert, Pub., *(Saifer; 0-87556),* P.O. Box 239 W.O.B., West Orange, NJ 07052 (SAN 204-7225).

Sail Bks., Inc., *(Sail Bks; 0-914814),* 34 Commercial Wharf, Boston, MA 02110 (SAN 207-0820).

Sail Sales Publishing, *(Sail Sale Pub; 0-943798),* P.O. Box 1028, Aptos, CA 95003 Tel 408-662-2456 (SAN 214-077X).

St. Alban Press, *(St Alban Pr; 0-918980),* 10525 Downey Ave., Apt. F, Downey, CA 90241 Tel 213-861-7569 (SAN 210-492X); Orders to: P.O. Box 598, Ojai, CA 93023 Tel 805-646-6790 (SAN 210-4938).

St. Alban's Episcopal Church, *(St Albans Episcopal; 0-9606174),* 1803 N. Gold Point Circle, P.O. 1104, Hixson, TN 37343 Tel 615-842-1342 (SAN 217-1309).

St. Andrews Press, *(St Andrews NC; 0-932662),* St. Andrews Presbyterian College, Laurinburg, NC 28352 Tel 919-276-3652 (SAN 207-8902).

St. Anthony Messenger Press, *(St Anthony Mess Pr; 0-912228; 0-86716),* 1615 Republic St., Cincinnati, OH 45210 Tel 513-241-5616 (SAN 204-6237).

St. Augeo Publishing Co., *(St Augeo Pub; 0-9606900),* P.O. Box 567, Cross Keys Rd., R.D. 1, Glassboro, NJ 08028 Tel 609-881-4958 (SAN 217-4308).

St. Basil Press, *(St Basil Pr; 0-9604278),* 4106 N. Ozark Ave., Norridge, IL 60634 (SAN 215-1057).

St. Bede's Pubns., *(St Bedes Pubns; 0-932506),* P.O. Box 132, Still River, MA 01467 Tel 617-456-8138 (SAN 222-9692).

St. Cuthbert's Treasury Press, *(St Cuthberts; 0-914724),* 1290 Maricopa Dr., Oshkosh, WI 54901 Tel 414-235-2057 (SAN 206-1287).

Saint Edward's Univ., *(St Edwards Univ; 0-938472),* 3001 S. Congress Ave., Austin, TX 78704 (SAN 215-9155).

St. Genesius Press, Ltd., *(St Genesius Pr Ltd; 0-911673),* 522 Seventh St., Rapid City, SD 57701 Tel 605-348-1890 (SAN 264-3669).

St. George Book Service, *(St George Bk Serv; 0-916786),* P.O. Box 225, Spring Valley, NY 10977 Tel 914-623-7852 (SAN 208-8371).

St. George Press, *(St George Pr; 0-932104),* 3500 N. Coltrane Rd., Oklahoma City, OK 73121 Tel 405-427-5005 (SAN 209-6773).

Saint George Press, The, *(St George IA; 0-939846),* 1516 Delaware Ave., Ames, IA 50010 Tel 309-676-4799 (SAN 216-2989).

Saint Giles Press, *(St Giles; 0-9607382),* Box 1416, Lafayette, CA 94549 (SAN 239-4901).

St. Heironymous Press, Inc., *(St Heironymous; 0-913718),* P.O. Box 9431, Berkeley, CA 94709 Tel 415-549-1405 (SAN 203-3550).

St. James Press, *(St James Pr),* 213 W. Institute Place, Suite 305, Chicago, IL 60610 Tel 312-944-7592 (SAN 205-9258).

Saint Joans Press, *(St Joans Pr),* 325 Spring St., New York, NY 10013 (SAN 226-2797).

St. John, John, Gallery, *(St John Gallery; 0-9605946),* 1683 Copenhagen Dr., Solvang, CA 93463 (SAN 216-6445).

St. Johns - Oklawaha Rivers Trading Co., *(St Johns-Oklawaha; 0-941948),* 110 S. Woodland Blvd. 130, Deland, FL 32720 Tel 904-738-1210 (SAN 238-4809).

St. Joseph's University Press, *(St Joseph),* 54th St. & City Line Ave., Philadelphia, PA 19131 (SAN 240-8368).

St. Le Macs, Pierre, Press, *(St Le Macs Pr; 0-913030),* 450 Park Plaza Professional Bldg., Houston, TX 77004 Tel 713-523-8181 (SAN 204-6253); Orders to: 2615 Marilee, No. 1, Houston, TX 77057 Tel 713-783-2721 (SAN 204-6261).

St. Louis Public Library, Pubns. Dept., *(St Louis Pub Lib),* 1301 Olive St., St. Louis, MO 63103 Tel 314-241-2288 (SAN 205-9215).

St. Luke's Press, *(St Luke TN; 0-918518),* Mid-Memphis Tower, Suite 401, 1407 Union Ave., Memphis, TN 38104 Tel 901-357-5441 (SAN 210-0029).

St. Luke's Publishing Co., *(St Luke Pub; 0-939502),* P.O. Box 1378, South Bend, IN 46624 Tel 219-234-5115 (SAN 216-6925).

St. Margaret's Hospital, *(St Margaret's),* Administrator's Office, 90 Cushing Ave., Boston, MA 02125 (SAN 207-5156).

St. Mark Coptic Orthodox Church, *(St Mark Coptic Orthodox; 0-932098),* P.O. Box 692, Troy, MI 48094 Tel 313-764-0350 (SAN 240-1533).

St. Martin's Press, Inc., *(St Martin; 0-312),* 175 Fifth Ave., New York, NY 10010 Tel 212-674-5151 (SAN 200-2132). *Imprints:* Joan Kahn Book, A (J Kahn).

St. Mary's Press, *(St Mary's; 0-88489),* Winona, MN 55987 Tel 507-452-9090 (SAN 203-073X).

Saint Matthew's Episcopal Church, *(St Matthew's),* 1401 W. Broad St., Savannah, GA 31401 (SAN 219-0966).

St. Michaels Historical Museum, *(St Michaels),* St. Michaels Mission, St. Michaels, AZ 86511 Tel 602-871-4171 (SAN 239-5290).

St. Nectarios Press, *(St Nectarios; 0-913026),* 10300 Ashworth Ave. N., Seattle, WA 98133 Tel 206-522-4471 (SAN 203-3542).

St. Paul Area Chapter, American Red Cross, *(St Paul Area; 0-9605584),* 100 S. Robert St., St. Paul, MN 55107 (SAN 240-8392).

Saint Paul the Apostle Church, *(St Paul the Apostle; 0-9602352),* 202 E. Washington St., Greencastle, IN 46135 (SAN 212-6206).

St. Peters College Press, *(St Peters Coll; 0-930568),* Jersey City, NJ 07306 (SAN 222-4240).

St. Peter's Press, *(St Peters Pr),* Consulate/Rio A.P.O., Miami, FL 34030 (SAN 240-8376).

St. Petersburg Times Publishing Co., *(St Petersburg Times; 0-9605382),* P.O. Box 1121, St. Petersburg, FL 33731 (SAN 216-0617).

St. Scholastica Priory, *(St Scholastica),* Duluth, MN 55811 Tel 218-728-1817 (SAN 206-1309).

St. Sophia Religious Assn. of Ukrainian Catholics, *(St Sophia Religious),* 7911 Whitewood Rd., Philadelphia, PA 19117 Tel 215-635-1555 (SAN 204-949X).

St. Thomas Press, *(St Thomas; 0-940648),* P.O. Box 35096, Houston, TX 77235 Tel 713-666-3111 (SAN 204-6288).

Saint Thomas Seminary, *(St Thomas Seminary; 0-9608630),* 1300 S. Steele St., Denver, CO 80210 Tel 303-722-4687 (SAN 219-0974).

St. Vincent Hospital, *(St Vincent Hosp),* Dept. D., P.O. Box 2107, Santa Fe, NM 87501 (SAN 211-4003).

St. Vladimir's Seminary Press, *(St Vladimirs; 0-913836; 0-88141),* 575 Scarsdale Rd., Crestwood, NY 10707 Tel 914-961-8313 (SAN 204-6296).

Sakura/Dragon Corp., *(Sakura-Dragon Corp; 0-86568),* c/o Unique Publications, 7011 Sunset Blvd., Los Angeles, CA 90028 (SAN 214-3313).

Sal Magundi Enterprises, *(Sal Magundi Ent; 0-9609024),* 6919 S. W. Canyon Lane, P.O. Box 25625, Portland, OR 97225 Tel 503-297-6658 (SAN 241-2470).

Salaam, Yusef A., *(Y A Salaam),* 167 W. 136th, Suite 5, New York, NY 10030 (SAN 287-3001).

Salant, Michael Alan, *(M A Salant; 0-9609288),* 2412 19th St. N.W., Apt. 9, Washington, DC 20009 Tel 202-332-2368 (SAN 260-129X).

Salem Press, Inc., *(Salem Pr; 0-89356)*, Box 1097, Englewood Cliffs, NJ 07632 Tel 201-871-3700 (SAN 208-838X)
Salem Press of Oregon, *(Salem Pr OR)*, 1021 Oregon National Building, 610 SW Alder, Portland, OR 97205 (SAN 262-0332).
Sales, Billee, *(B Sales; 0-9605244)*, 2638 N.W. 59th Ave., Margate, FL 33063 (SAN 215-8051).
Sales and Marketing Executives International, *(Sales & Mktg Execs)*, 380 Lexington Ave, New York, NY 10017 Tel 212-986-9300 (SAN 224-9480).
Salesiana Publishers See **Don Bosco Multimedia**
Salesman's Guide, Inc., *(Salesmans; 0-87228)*, 1140 Broadway, New York, NY 10001 Tel 212-684-2985 (SAN 203-3593).
Salitore, Edward V., & Evelyn D., *(E V Salitore)*, P.O. Box 500, Temecula, CA 92390 Tel 714-676-6355 (SAN 201-2847).
Salt Lick Press, *(Salt Lick; 0-913918)*, 5107 Martin Ave., Austin, TX 78751 (SAN 202-0823).
Salvation Army, *(Salvation Army)*, 120 W 14 Th St, New York, NY 10011 (SAN 237-2649).
Salyer Publishing Co., *(Salyer; 0-911298)*, 3111 19th St., N.W., Oklahoma City, OK 73107 (SAN 204-725X).
Sam Houston State University Institute of Contemporary Corrections and the Behavioral Sciences, *(S Houston Corrections)*, Huntsville, TX 77340 (SAN 226-3726).
SamHar Press, Div. of Story House Corp., *(SamHar Pr)*, Charlotteville, NY 12036 Tel 607-397-8725 (SAN 203-3585).
Samisdat, *(Samisdat)*, Box 129, Richford, VT 05476 (SAN 207-8929).
Sams, Howard W., & Co., Inc., Subs. of ITT, *(Sams; 0-672)*, 4300 W. 62nd St., Indianapolis, IN 46206 Tel 317-298-5400 (SAN 203-3577).
Samuel Stevens & Co., *(Samuel Stevens; 0-89522)*, P.O. Box 3899, Sarasota, FL 33578 Tel 813-924-8441 (SAN 208-1873).
San Anselmo Publishing Co., *(San Anselmo Pub; 0-943264)*, P.O. Box 2299, Norman, OK 73070 Tel 405-275-2415 (SAN 240-5644).
San Bernardino County Bar Association, *(San Bernardino Bar)*, 364 N Arrowhead Ave, San Bernardino, CA 92401 (SAN 226-3734).
San Diego Historical Society, *(San Diego Hist; 0-918740)*, P.O. Box 81825, San Diego, CA 92138 Tel 714-297-3258 (SAN 210-5438).
San Diego Publishing Co., *(San Diego Pub Co; 0-912495)*, 6226 Lake Shore Dr., San Diego, CA 92119 Tel 619-698-5105 (SAN 265-1971).
San Diego State Univ., The, *(SDSU Press; 0-916304)*, 5300 Campanile Dr., San Diego, CA 92182 Tel 714-265-6220 (SAN 202-0637).
San Diego State University Press See **San Diego State Univ., The**
San Francisco Arts & Letters Foundation, *(SF Arts & Letters; 0-914024)*, P.O. Box 99394, San Francisco, CA 94109 Tel 415-771-3431 (SAN 202-8751).
San Francisco Bay Guardian, *(SF Bay Guardian; 0-913192)*, 2700 19th St., San Francisco, CA 94110 Tel 415-824-7660 (SAN 215-2746).
San Francisco Book Co., Inc., *(SF Bk Co; 0-913374)*, Box 3760, San Francisco, CA 94119 Tel 415-681-1166 (SAN 202-0815) Moved, left no forwarding address.
San Francisco Center for Visual Studies, *(SF Center Vis Stud; 0-930976)*, 49 Rivoli St., San Francisco, CA 94117 Tel 415-564-7920 (SAN 209-5106).
San Francisco Historic Records, *(SF Hist Records; 0-911792)*, 1204 Nimitz Dr., Colma, CA 94015 Tel 415-755-2204 (SAN 204-5885).
San Francisco Institute of Automotive Ecology, *(SF Inst Auto Ecol; 0-9603356)*, 124 Anderson St., San Francisco, CA 94110 Tel 415-285-7403 (SAN 207-3188); Dist. by: Bookpeople, 2940 Seventh St., Berkeley, CA 94710 (SAN 168-9517).
San Francisco Mime Troupe, Inc., *(SF Mime; 0-9606902)*, 855 Treat, San Francisco, CA 94110 Tel 415-285-1717 (SAN 217-4316).

San Francisco Study Center, *(SF Stud Ctr; 0-936434)*, 1095 Market St., San Francisco, CA 94101 Tel 415-626-1650 (SAN 214-4654).
San Francisco Yesterday, *(SF Yesterday)*, P.O.Box 4343, San Rafael, CA 94903 Tel 415-479-1550 (SAN 209-4886).
San Jacinto Publishing Co., *(San Jacinto; 0-911982)*, c/o Texas A&M University Press, Drawer C, College Station, TX 77843 Tel 713-845-1436 (SAN 207-5237).
San Juan County Book Company, *(San Juan County; 0-9608000)*, P.O. Box 1, Silverton, CO 81433 Tel 303-387-5477 (SAN 238-5775).
San Luis Quest Press, *(San Luis Quest; 0-935320)*, Box 998, San Luis Obispo, CA 93406 Tel 805-543-8500 (SAN 213-4306).
San Marcos Press, *(San Marcos; 0-88235)*, P.O. Box 53, Cerrillos, NM 87010 (SAN 206-3751).
San Pedro Bay Historical Society, *(San Pedro Hist; 0-9611556)*, P.O. Box 1568, San Pedro, CA 90733 Tel 213-548-3208 (SAN 285-1377); 1159 Amar St., San Redro, CA 90732 Tel 213-833-2872 (SAN 285-1385).
Sanatana Publishing Society, *(Sanatana; 0-933116)*, 830 Bryant St., Palo Alto, CA 94301 Tel 415-326-4232 (SAN 212-7946).
Sanchiz Press, *(Sanchiz Pr; 0-9607384)*, 1500 Massachusetts Ave. NW, No. 409, Washington, DC 20005 (SAN 239-6076).
Sand, George, , Books, *(George Sand; 0-942498)*, 9011 Melrose Ave., Los Angeles, CA 90069 Tel 213-858-1648 (SAN 239-6084); Dist. by: Capra Press, P.O. Box 2068, Santa Barbara, CA 93120 Tel 805-966-4590 (SAN 201-9620).
Sand Pond Pubs., *(Sand Pond)*, Shady Lane, Handcock, NH 03449 Tel 603-525-6615 (SAN 203-0713).
Sandcrab Press, *(Sandcrab; 0-9609870)*, P.O. Box 1479, Corpus Cristi, TX 78411 Tel 512-852-5359 (SAN 264-3685); Dist. by: Publishers' Marketing Group, 1343 Columbia, Suite 405, Richardson, TX 75081 Tel 262-0995).
Sanderson, T. K., Organization, *(T K Sanderson)*, 200 E. 25th St., Baltimore, MD 21218 Tel 301-235-3383 (SAN 202-0785).
Sandifer/Kevin W., *(K W Sandifer; 0-910653)*, First Baptist Church Archives, P.O. Box 65, Blanchard, LA 71009 (SAN 263-2241).
Sandlapper Pub. Co., Inc., *(Sandlapper Pub Co; 0-87844)*, P.O. Box 1932, Orangeburg, SC 29116 Tel 803-531-1658 (SAN 203-2678).
Sandollar Press, *(Sandollar Pr)*, P.O. Box 4157, Santa Barbara, CA 93103 Tel 805-963-7077 (SAN 202-9952).
Sandpiper Press, *(Sandpiper CA; 0-940356)*, P.O.Box 128, Solana Beach, CA 92075 Tel 714-481-5259 (SAN 217-5657).
Sandpiper Press, *(Sandpiper OR; 0-9603748)*, P.O. Box 286, Brookings, OR 97415 Tel 503-469-5588 (SAN 213-5582).
Sandrock & Foster, *(Sandrock & Foster)*, Memorial Foundation, Box 841, Winona, MN 55987 Tel 507-452-1859 (SAN 210-9514).
Sandstone Press See **Beil, Frederic C.**
Sang, R. H., & Son Pubs. Inc., *(R H Sang & Son; 0-932844)*, 211 E. Delaware Place, Chicago, IL 60611 Tel 312-787-9565 (SAN 212-968X).
Sangamon State University, *(Sangamon St U)*, Shepherd Rd, Springfield, IL 62708 Tel 217-786-6600 (SAN 226-2215).
Sanguinaria Publishing, *(Sanguinaria)*, 85 Ferris St., Bridgeport, CT 06605 (SAN 215-806X).
Sankaty Head Press, *(Sankaty Head; 0-9606626)*, Box 18, Siasconset, MA 02564 (SAN 223-114X).
Sant Bani Ashram, Inc., *(Sant Bani Ash)*, Franklin, NH 03235 Tel 603-934-4209 (SAN 209-5114).
Santa Barbara Botanic Garden, *(Santa Barb Botanic; 0-916436)*, 1212 Mission Canyon Rd., Santa Barbara, CA 93105 Tel 805-682-4726 (SAN 208-8398).
Santa Barbara Museum of Art, *(Santa Barb Mus Art; 0-89951)*, 1130 State St., Santa Barbara, CA 93101 Tel 805-963-4364 (SAN 213-3687).
Santa Barbara Museum of Natural History, *(Santa Barbara; 0-936494)*, 2559 Puesta del Sol Rd., Santa Barbara, CA 93105 Tel 805-963-4364 (SAN 224-2176).

Santa Barbara Pro Life Education, *(Santa Barb Pro; 0-9609902)*, P.O. Box 30815, Santa Barbara, CA 93130 (SAN 262-9992).
Santa Fe Community School, *(Santa Fe Comm Sch)*, P.O. Box 2241, Santa Fe, NM 87501 Tel 505-471-9977 (SAN 211-5743).
Santa Fe East Gallery Pubns., *(Santa Fe E Gallery; 0-86534)*, 200 Old Santa Fe Trail, Santa Fe, NM 87501 (SAN 239-3824).
Santa Monica Publishing Co., *(Santa Monica Pub; 0-917640)*, 414 Camino de las Animas, Santa Fe, NM 87501 Tel 505-983-4138 (SAN 209-3855).
Santa Susana Press, *(Santa Susana; 0-937048)*, California State Univ. Library, 18111 Nordhoff St., Northridge, CA 91330 (SAN 217-2674).
Santam Two, Ltd., *(Santam)*, Box 11642, Phoenix, AZ 85017 (SAN 215-1812).
Santarasa Pubns., *(Santarasa Pubns; 0-935548)*, 937 Broadway, Boulder, CO 80302 (SAN 213-7925).
Santiago Press, Inc., *(Santiago Pr; 0-940470)*, 3616 Hyde Park, Midland, TX 79703 (SAN 219-0958).
Santiam Books, *(Santiam Bks; 0-9609936)*, 744 Mader Ave. SE, Salem, OR 97302 Tel 503-362-7471 (SAN 263-0001).
Santilli, Al, Jr., *(A Santilli)*, P.O. Box 2492, Dept.-5M, La Habra, CA 90631 (SAN 213-585X).
Santora, Charles G., *(C G Santora)*, P.O. Box 2223, Ventnor, NJ 08406 (SAN 240-494X).
Saphrograph Co., *(Saphrograph; 0-87557)*, 4910 Fort Hamilton Parkway, Brooklyn, NY 11219 Tel 212-925-7840 (SAN 204-7276).
Sarasota Opera Society, The, *(Sarasota Opera; 0-9605844)*, P.O. Box 1393, Sarasota, FL 33578 (SAN 216-3012).
Sargent, Porter, Pubs., Inc. See **Porter Sargent Pubs., Inc.**
Sarmen Books, *(Sarmen Bks; 0-9610394)*, Yarmouth Port, MA 02675 Tel 617-362-2518 (SAN 283-2550).
SarSan Pub Co, *(SarSan Pub; 0-940336)*, Box 984, Brawley, CA 92227 Tel 714-344-9593 (SAN 217-5665).
Sasco Associates, *(Sasco; 0-912980)*, P.O. Box 335, Southport, CT 06490 (SAN 204-7284).
Sasquatch Publishing Co., *(Sasquatch Pub; 0-912365)*, 1932 First Ave. Suite 605, Seattle, WA 98101 Tel 206-623-3700 (SAN 239-6106); Dist. by: Madrona Publishers, 113 Madrona Place East, Seattle, WA 98112 (SAN 281-9678).
Sassafras Pr., *(Sassafras Pr; 0-930528)*, P.O. Box 1366, Evanston, IL 60204 Tel 312-649-0888 (SAN 214-4662).
Sassafras Pr., The, *(Sassafras MS; 0-9609692)*, (SAN 264-3715); c/o Mijo Lithographing Co., Inc., P.O. Box 1104, Yazoo City, MS 39194 Tel 601-746-4693 (SAN 282-275X).
Satellite Continuing Education Inc., *(Satellite Cont; 0-9609184)*, 706 Second Ave., Charles City, IA 50616 Tel 515-228-5558 (SAN 241-4503).
Satellite World, *(Satellite; 0-910419)*, P.O. Box 74874, Los Angeles, CA 90004 Tel 213-666-1014 (SAN 260-1303).
Saturday Press, Inc., *(Saturday Pr; 0-938158)*, P.O. Box 884, Upper Montclair, NJ 07043 Tel 201-256-1731 (SAN 207-5792).
Saturn Press, *(Saturn Pr IL; 0-9606452)*, P.O. Box 465, Skokie, IL 60076 Tel 312-588-1169 (SAN 218-5946).
Sauk Valley, *(Sauk)*, Irish Hills, Brooklyn, MI 49230 Tel 517-467-2061 (SAN 209-5122).
Saunders, W. B., Co., Subs. of Columbia Broadcasting System, *(Saunders; 0-7216)*, W. Washington Square, Philadelphia, PA 19105 Tel 215-574-4792 (SAN 203-266X). *Imprints:* Bailliere-Tindall (Bailliere-Tindall).
Saunders College Publishing, Div. of CBS College Publishing, *(SCP)*, W. Washington Square, Philadelphia, PA 19105 (SAN 282-2768); 0-03, ; Orders to: 383madison Ave., New York, NY 10017 Tel 212-750-1330 (SAN 282-2776).
Saur, K. G., Publishing, Inc., *(K G Saur; 0-89664)*, 175 Fifth Ave., New York, NY 10010 Tel 201-652-6360 (SAN 214-1264).
Saurian Press, *(Saurian Pr; 0-930830)*, New Mexico Tech, Socorro, NM 87801 Tel 505-835-5445 (SAN 215-1065).
Sauvie Island Press, *(Sauvie Island; 0-9606752)*, Rte. One, Box 526, Portland, OR 97231 Tel 503-621-3357 (SAN 219-6344).

Savannah Junior Auxiliary, The, *(Savannah Jr Aux; 0-939114)*, P.O. Box 434, Savannah, TN 38372 (SAN 262-0758).

Save on Shopping, *(S O S Pubns)*, P.O. Box 10482, Jacksonville, FL 32207 Tel 904-733-8477 (SAN 204-7160); Dist. by: Putnam Publishing Group, 200 Madison Ave., New York, NY 10016 (SAN 202-554X).

Sawan Kirpal Pubns., *(Sawan Kirpal Pubns; 0-918224)*, 115 S. "O" St., Lake Worth, FL 33460 Tel 305-588-1287 (SAN 211-0571); Orders to: Rte. 1, Box 24, Bowling Green, VA 22427 Tel 804-633-5789 (SAN 211-058X).

Saylor, Lee, Inc., *(Saylor; 0-931708)*, 1855 Olympic Blvd., Walnut Creek, CA 94596 (SAN 211-5751).

Scala Books, *(ScalaBooks; 0-935748)*, 1035 Fifth Ave., New York, NY 10028 (SAN 282-2784); Orders to: Harper & Row Pubs, Keystone Industrial Park, Scranton, PA 18512 (SAN 282-2792).

Scandia Pubs., *(Scandia Pubs; 0-937242)*, P.O. Box 1044, Lyons, CO 80540 Tel 303-823-5440 (SAN 282-2806) (SAN 214-4670).

Scanner Master Publishing Co., *(Scanner Master; 0-939430)*, 36 Theodore Rd., Newton Center, MA 02159 Tel 617-332-8444 (SAN 216-583X).

Scanning Electron Microscopy, Inc., *(Scanning Electron; 0-931288)*, P.O. Box 66507, AMF O'Hare, Chicago, IL 60666 Tel 312-529-6677 (SAN 213-5868).

Scarab Press, *(Scarab Pr; 0-912962)*, 63 Bates Blvd., Orinda, CA 94563 (SAN 204-7306).

Scarecrow Press, Inc., Subs. of Grolier Educational Corp., *(Scarecrow; 0-8108)*, 52 Liberty St., Box 656, Metuchen, NJ 08840 Tel 201-548-8600 (SAN 203-2651).

Scarf Press, *(Scarf Pr; 0-934386)*, 58 E. 83rd St., New York, NY 10028 Tel 212-744-3901 (SAN 212-9698).

Scat Pubns., *(Scat Pubns; 0-9606124)*, 32 W. 40th St., Suite 11-B, New York, NY 10018 Tel 212-730-1033 (SAN 213-5876).

Scenographic Media, *(Scenographic; 0-913868)*, Box 2122, Norwalk, CT 06851 (SAN 205-1443).

Scentouri, *(Scentouri)*, Box 600531, Houston, TX 77260 (SAN 283-9016).

Scepter Pubs., *(Scepter Pubs; 0-933932)*, 481 Main St., New Rochelle, NY 10801 Tel 914-636-3377 (SAN 207-2858).

Schaffer, Frank, Pubns., Inc., *(Schaffer Pubns; 0-86734)*, 19771 Magellan Drive, Torrance, CA 90502 Tel 213-532-5420 (SAN 217-5827).

Schafler Enterprises, *(Schafler Ent; 0-9603154)*, 257 Ricardo Rd., Mill Valley, CA 94941 Tel 415-383-0830 (SAN 212-5536).

Schalaco Publishing Co., *(Schalaco Pub; 0-9608560)*, 5123 E. McDonald Dr., Paradise Valley, AZ 85253 Tel 602-279-2885 (SAN 240-768X).

Schalit, Michael, *(M Schalit; 0-9604630)*, 451 Bell Ave., Livermore, CA 94550 Tel 415-443-2456 (SAN 213-7933).

Schalkenbach, Robert, Foundation, *(Schalkenbach; 0-911312)*, 5 E. 44th St., New York, NY 10017 Tel 212-986-8684 (SAN 206-1317).

Schar Publishing Co., *(Schar Pub Co; 0-9611830)*, 2541 W. Ainslie St., Chicago, IL 60625 Tel 312-784-2186 (SAN 240-8279); Dist. by: K. V. Schar, 2541 W. Ainslie St., Chicago, IL 60625 (SAN 240-8287).

Schaumburg Pubns., Inc., *(Schaumburg Pubns; 0-935690)*, 1432 S. Mohawk, Roselle, IL 60172 (SAN 214-221X).

Schenkman Publishing Co., Inc., *(Schenkman; 0-87073)*, 3 Mt. Auburn Place, Cambridge, MA 02138 Tel 617-492-4952 (SAN 203-2643).

Scherer, John L., Jr., *(J L Scherer)*, 4900 18th Ave. S., Minneapolis, MN 55417 Tel 612-722-2947 (SAN 209-1429).

Schiedt, Duncan P., *(D Schiedt; 0-9603528)*, R.R.1, Box 217A, Pittsboro, IN 46167 Tel 317-852-8528 (SAN 211-3996).

Schiffer Publishing Ltd., *(Schiffer; 0-916838)*, P.O. Box E, Exton, PA 19341 Tel 215-363-6889 (SAN 208-8428).

Schiptfeir Enterprises, *(Schpitfeir; 0-9607330)*, P.O. Box 1426, Minnetonka, MN 55343 (SAN 240-8864).

Schirmer, E. C., Music Co., *(E C Schirmer; 0-911318)*, 112 South St., Boston, MA 02111 Tel 617-426-3137 (SAN 201-3517).

Schmul Publishing Co. Inc., *(Schmul Pub Co)*, P.O. Box 4068, Salem, OH 44460 (SAN 211-8246).

Schneider, Claire, *(Claire Schneider; 0-9601982)*, 1655 Flatbush Ave., Apt. B1902, Brooklyn, NY 11210 Tel 217-2682).

Schneider, Coleman, *(C Schneider)*, P.O. Box 762, Tenafly, NJ 07670 Tel 201-567-9157 (SAN 211-4186).

Schneider, R., Pubs., *(Schneider Pubs; 0-936984)*, 312 Linwood Ave., Stevens Point, WI 54481 (SAN 217-1317).

Schneider Ent., Inc, *(Schneider Ent)*, 1386 E. Main St., Salem, VA 24153 Tel 703-389-9005 (SAN 212-6214).

Schnell Publishing Co., Inc., *(Schnell Pub; 0-9606454)*, 100 Church St., New York, NY 10007 Tel 212-732-9820 (SAN 205-1435).

Schocken Books, Inc., *(Schocken; 0-8052)*, 200 Madison Ave., New York, NY 10016 Tel 212-685-6500 (SAN 213-7585). *Imprints:* Moonlight Editions (Moonlight Edns).

Schoenhof's Foreign Books, Inc., *(Schoenhof; 0-87774)*, 1280 Massachusetts Ave., Cambridge, MA 02138 Tel 617-547-8855 (SAN 212-0062).

Schoepfer, G. R., *(G R Schoepfer; 0-931436)*, Farmingdale Garden Apts., Bldg. 9-O, Farmingdale, NJ 07727 (SAN 211-1659).

Schofield Publishing Co., *(Schofield Pub; 0-9608720)*, 29928 Lilac Rd., Valley Center, CA 92082 Tel 714-749-1325 (SAN 238-3659).

Schola Press, *(Schola Pr TX; 0-931016)*, P.O. Box 16064, Ft. Worth, TX 76133 (SAN 216-4469).

Scholarly Press Inc., *(Scholarly; 0-403)*, P.O. Box 160, Saint Clair Shores, MI 48080 Tel 313-884-0400 (SAN 209-0473).

Scholarly Pubns., *(Scholarly Pubns; 0-88065)*, Dist. by: Scholarly Pubns, 7310 el Cresta Dr., Houston, TX 77083 Tel 713-879-8319 (SAN 226-2975).

Scholarly Resources Inc., *(Scholarly Res Inc; 0-8420)*, 104 Greenhill Ave., Wilmington, DE 19805 Tel 302-654-7713 (SAN 203-2619) Source materials on 35mm microfilm & microfiche. Subjects: ethnic studies, genealogy, history, law, military studies & political science. Government documents, journals, manuscript collections & newspapers.

Scholars Book Co., *(Scholars Bk; 0-914348)*, 4431 Mt. Vernon, Houston, TX 77006-5889 Tel 713-528-4395 (SAN 205-1419).

Scholars' Facsimiles & Reprints, *(Schol Facsimiles; 0-8201)*, P.O. Box 344, Delmar, NY 12054 Tel 518-439-5978 (SAN 203-2627).

Scholars Portable Pubns., *(Scholars Portable; 0-9604778)*, 1459 Southfield Rd., Evansville, IN 47715 Tel 812-476-6697 (SAN 211-3465).

Scholars Press, *(Scholars Pr CA; 0-89130)*, 101 Salem St. P.O. Box 2268, Chico, CA 95927 Tel 916-891-4541 (SAN 207-964X).

Scholars' Press, Ltd., *(Scholars Pr Ltd; 0-914044)*, P.O. Box 7231, Roanoke, VA 24019 (SAN 203-2600).

Scholar's Reference Library, *(Scholars Ref Lib)*, P.O. Box 148, Darby, PA 19023 (SAN 205-1400).

Scholars Studies Press, *(Scholars Studies; 0-89177)*, 109 E. Ninth St., New York, NY 10003 Tel 212-674-5296 (SAN 208-3795).

Scholastic, Inc., *(Scholastic Inc; 0-590)*, 730 Broadway, New York, NY 10003 Tel 212-505-3000 (SAN 202-5442); Orders to: P.O. Box 7502, 2931 E. McCarty St., Jefferson City, MO 65102 (SAN 202-5450). *Imprints:* Citation Press (Citation); Four Winds Press (Four Winds); Scholastic Paperbacks (Schol Pap).

Scholastic Paperbacks *See* **Scholastic, Inc.**

Scholastic Testing Service, Inc., *(Schol Test; 0-936224)*, 480 Meyer Rd., Bensenville, IL 60106 Tel 312-766-7150 (SAN 200-2183).

Scholasticus Pub., *(Scholasticus)*, P.O. Box 2727, Springfield, VA 22152 (SAN 211-450X).

Scholium International, Inc, *(Scholium Intl; 0-87936)*, 265 Great Neck Rd., Great Neck, NY 11021 Tel 516-466-5181 (SAN 212-8764).

Schon, Kurt E., Ltd., *(K E Schon; 0-9603880)*, 510 Saint Louis St., New Orleans, LA 70130 Tel 504-524-5462 (SAN 214-1361).

School Aid Co., *(Sch Aid; 0-87385)*, 911 Colfax Dr., P.O. Box 123, Danville, IL 61832 (SAN 158-3719).

School Department *See* **Harper & Row Pubs., Inc.**

School of American Research Press, *(Schol Am Res; 0-933452)*, P.O. Box 2188, Santa Fe, NM 87501 Tel 505-984-0741 (SAN 216-6222).

School of Architecture & Interior Design, *(Sch Arch Interior Des; 0-939592)*, Univ. of Cincinnati, Cincinnati, OH 45221 Tel 513-475-6485 (SAN 216-650X).

School of Journalism, West Virginia Univ., *(Sch Journal WVU; 0-930362)*, Morgantown, WV 26506 (SAN 213-1617).

School of Library Science, Emporia State University, *(Sch Lib Sci)*, 1200 Commercial, Emporia, KS 66801 Tel 316-343-1200 (SAN 209-598X).

School Projectionist Club of America, *(Sch Proj Club; 0-911328)*, P.O. Box 44, State College, PA 16801 (SAN 204-7322).

School Science & Mathematics Association, Inc., *(Sch Sci Math)*, 126 Life Science Bldg, Bowling Green State Univ., Bowling Green, OH 43403 (SAN 275-228X).

Schoolhouse Press, *(Schoolhouse Pr; 0-942018)*, 6899 Cary Bluff, Pittsville, WI 54466 (SAN 239-8044).

Schroder Music Co., *(Schroder Music; 0-915620)*, 1409-Fifth St., Berkeley, CA 94710 Tel 415-524-5804 (SAN 207-3935).

Schroeder Prints, Inc., *(Schroeder Prints; 0-931766)*, P.O. Drawer 580, Chestertown, MD 21620 Tel 301-778-1192 (SAN 211-6472).

Schroeppel, Tom, *(Schroeppel; 0-9603718)*, P.O. Box 521110, Miami, FL 33152 (SAN 213-7941).

Schulak, Bernard, & Assoc. Architects, Pub., *(Schulak & Assoc; 0-9602186)*, 6889 W. Maple Rd., West Bloomfield, MI 48033 (SAN 212-2278).

Schumacher Publications, *(Schumacher Pubns; 0-917378)*, 9229 Lawn St., Proctor, MN 55810 Tel 218-624-7728 (SAN 208-8436).

Schwartz, Bob, *(B Schwartz)*, 604 William, Oakland, CA 94602 Tel 415-531-8494 (SAN 240-4958).

Schwartz, J. H., Rev., *(J H Schwartz)*, 1633 N. Missouri, Peoria, IL 61603 (SAN 208-1644).

Schwenkfelder Library, *(Schwenkfelder Lib; 0-935980)*, 1 Seminary St., Pennsburg, PA 18073 Tel 215-679-7175 (SAN 213-795X).

Science & Behavior Books, Inc., *(Sci & Behavior; 0-8314)*, P.O. Box 11457, Palo Alto, CA 94306 Tel 415-326-6465 (SAN 204-7349).

Science & Technology Press, *(Sci & Tech Pr; 0-912291)*, P.O. Box 614, Latham, NY 12110 Tel 518-785-8517 (SAN 203-2597).

Science Associates/International, Inc., *(Sci Assoc Intl; 0-87837)*, 1841 Broadway, New York, NY 10023 Tel 212-265-4995 (SAN 204-7357).

Science Enterprises, Inc., *(Sci Ent; 0-930116)*, Box 88443, Indianapolis, IN 46208 Tel 317-259-1054 (SAN 210-6639).

Science Fiction Resources, *(Sci Fiction; 0-918364)*, 101 Summit Rd., Port Washington, NY 11050 Tel 516-883-9142 (SAN 210-0037); 148 E. 74th St., New York, NY 10021 Tel 212-988-7526 (SAN 210-0045).

Science for the People, *(Sci People; 0-9607314)*, 897 Main St., Cambridge, MA 02139 (SAN 218-3544).

Science Man Pr., Div. of TSM Marketing, Inc., *(Science Man Pr; 0-936046)*, 4741 N. Harlem Ave., Harwood Heights, IL 60656 (SAN 213-7968).

Science of Identity Foundation, *(Science Identity; 0-88187)*, P.O. Box 27450, Honolulu, HI 96827 Tel 808-949-6966 (SAN 264-6900).

Science of Mind Pubns., *(Sci of Mind; 0-911376)*, P.O. Box 75127, Los Angeles, CA 90075 Tel 213-388-2181 (SAN 203-2570); Dist. by: Devorss & Co., P.O. Box 550, Marina Del Rey, CA 90291 (SAN 168-9886).

Science Press, *(Sci Pr; 0-89500),* 8 Brookstone Dr., Princeton, NJ 08540 Tel 609-921-3405 (SAN 210-0053).

Science Research Associates, Inc., Subs. of IBM, *(SRA; 0-574),* 1540 Page Mill Rd, P.O. Box 10021, Palo Alto, CA 94304 Tel 415-493-4700 (SAN 282-2849); 155 N. Wacker Dr., Chicago, IL 60606 Tel 800-621-0476 (SAN 282-2857); Orders to: 155 N. Wacker Dr., Chicago, IL 60606 (SAN 282-2865).

Science Research Associates, Inc., College Division, *(Sci Res Assoc Coll)* 1540 Page Mill Rd., P.O. Box 10021, Palo Alto, CA 94303 Tel 415-493-4700 (SAN 215-207X).

Science Software Systems, Inc., *(Science Software; 0-937292),* 11899 W. Pico Blvd., West los Angeles, CA 90064 Tel 213-477-8541 (SAN 240-155X).

Science Tech, Inc., *(Sci Tech Inc; 0-910239),* 1227 Dartmouth Rd., Madison, WI 53705 Tel 608-238-5050 (SAN 241-4511).

Science, Technology, & Human Values, *(STHV; 0-932564),* Rm. E51-8 Massachusetts Institute of Technology, Cambridge, MA 02139 Tel 617-253-4010 (SAN 212-2286).

Scienspot Pubns., *(Scienspot; 0-937926),* 39 Brunswick Ave., Troy, NY 12180 (SAN 216-1850).

Scientific-American Illustrated Library, Subs. of W. H. Freeman & Co., *(Sci Am Illus Lib; 0-89454),* 415 Madison Ave., New York, NY 10017 Tel 212-754-0561 (SAN 210-2676).

Scientific Newsletters, Inc., *(Sci Newsletters; 0-930914),* P.O. Box 4546, Anaheim, CA 92803 Tel 714-828-1371 (SAN 212-2294).

Scientific Peace Builders Foundation, *(Sci Peace Builders),* P.O. Box 3037, Santa Monica, CA 90403 Tel 213-394-4111 (SAN 204-7373).

Scientific Press, The, *(Scientific Pr; 0-89426),* 540 University Ave., Palo Alto, CA 94301-1985 Tel 415-322-5221 (SAN 210-2684).

Scissortail Pubs., *(Scissortail; 0-939504),* P.O. Box 16098, Pensacola, FL 32507 Tel 904-478-6551 (SAN 220-1860).

Scoper, Vincent, Jr., *(V Scoper; 0-9600514),* P.O. Box 2366, Laurel, MS 39440 (SAN 205-4736).

Scorpion Press, *(Scorpion Pr),* P.O. Box 764, Bellingham, WA 98227 (SAN 240-8759).

Scott, Beverly A., Pub., *(B A Scott),* P.O. Box 114, Chandler, AZ 85224 Tel 602-963-5787 (SAN 207-6101).

Scott & Daughters Publishing, *(Scott & Daughters; 0-911113),* 1545 Wilcox Ave., No. 204, Hollywood, CA 90028 (SAN 275-2395).

Scott, Foresman & Co., *(Scott F; 0-673),* 1900 E. Lake Ave., Glenview, IL 60025 Tel 312-729-3000 (SAN 200-2140).

Scott Protective Resources, Inc., *(Scott Protective; 0-930788),* Philadelphia, PA 19126 Tel 215-782-1300 (SAN 211-3767).

Scott Pubns., *(Scott Pubns CA; 0-935930),* P.O. Box 3277, Chico, CA 95926 (SAN 214-4697).

Scott Pubns, *(Scott Pubns MI),* 30595 W. 8 Mile Rd., Livonia, MI 48152 (SAN 240-8872).

Scott Publishing Co., *(Scott Pub Co; 0-89487),* 3 E. 57th St., New York, NY 10022 Tel 212-371-5700 (SAN 205-9770).

Scream/Press, *(Scream Pr; 0-910489),* P.O. Box 8531, Santa Cruz, CA 95061 Tel 408-425-0233 (SAN 260-132X).

Scribbles Inc., *(Scribblers; 0-943386),* 3618 Noble, Suite 203, Dallas, TX 75204 Tel 214-522-0405 (SAN 240-7698).

Scribe, B. C., Pubns., *(B C Scribe; 0-930548),* P.O. Box 2453, Providence, RI 02906-0453 Tel 401-831-5069 (SAN 212-1727).

Scribe Publishing Corp., *(Scribe Pub Corp; 0-915748),* 1219 Westlake Ave. N., Suite 108, Seattle, WA 98109 Tel 206-284-9747 (SAN 209-5130).

Scribe's Chamber Pubns., *(Scribe'S Cham; 0-912293),* P.O. Box 2123, E. Peoria, IL 61611 Tel 309-669-6034 (SAN 265-2005).

Scribner's, Charles, Sons, *(Scribner; 0-684),* 597 Fifth Ave., New York, NY 10017 Tel 212-486-2703 (SAN 282-2873); Orders to: Shipping & Service Ctr., Vreeland Ave., Totowa, NJ 07512 (SAN 282-6550).

Scripps Institution of Oceanography, Univ of California, San Diego, *(Scripps Inst Ocean; 0-9603078),* A007, La Jolla, CA 92093 (SAN 213-1625).

Scriptural Living Ministries, *(Scriptual Living Min; 0-9607316),* 12012 Craigview Dr., St. Louis, MO 63141 (SAN 239-3077).

Scripture Press Pubns., Inc., *(SP Pubns; 0-88207; 0-89693),* 1825 College Ave., Wheaton, IL 60187 Tel 312-668-6000 (SAN 222-9471).

Scripture Union Publishing, *(Scripture U Pub; 0-913585),* 1716 Spruce St., Philadelphia, PA 19103 Tel 215-732-2079 (SAN 285-3817).

Scroll Pr., Inc., *(Scroll Pr; 0-87592),* 2858 Valerie Ct., Merrick, NY 11566 Tel 516-379-4283 (SAN 206-796X).

Sculpt-Nouveau, *(Sculpt-Nouveau; 0-9603744),* 21 Redwood Dr., San Rafael, CA 94901 (SAN 213-9634).

Sea Challengers, *(Sea Chall; 0-930118),* 1851 Don Ave., Los Osos, CA 93402 Tel 805-528-0529 (SAN 210-5446).

Sea Crest Publishing Co., *(Sea Crest Pubn; 0-943050),* Box 991, Cape Canaveral, FL 32920 Tel 305-783-6733 (SAN 240-4389).

Sea History Press, Div. of National Maritime Historical Society, *(Sea Hist Pr; 0-930248),* 2 Fulton St., Brooklyn, NY 11201 Tel 212-858-1348 (SAN 210-6647).

Sea Horse Press, Ltd., The, *(Sea Horse; 0-933322),* 307 W. 11th St., New York, NY 10014 Tel 212-691-9066 (SAN 212-4505).

Sea Jay Publishing, *(Sea Jay Pub),* 3778 S. 6670 West, Salt Lake City, UT 84120 (SAN 214-4700).

Sea Lion Pubns., *(Sea Lion; 0-939880),* 1716 India St., San Diego, CA 92101 Tel 619-232-2626 (SAN 216-9320).

Sea of Storms, *(Sea of Storms; 0-931910),* P.O. Box 22613, San Francisco, CA 94122 Tel 707-795-2098 (SAN 214-4518).

Sea Shore Publications, *(Sea Shore Pubn; 0-9611342),* 211 S. Sea Shore Ave., Long Beach, MS 39560 Tel 312-520-1675 (SAN 283-3107).

Sea Urchin Press, *(Sea Urchin; 0-9605208),* P.O. Box 10503, Oakland, CA 94610 (SAN 215-8086).

Sea-Wind Press, *(Sea-Wind Pr; 0-9607436),* P.O. Box 222964, Carmel, CA 93922 Tel 408-624-4760 (SAN 239-8036).

Seablom Design, *(Seablom; 0-918800),* 151 Aloha St., Seattle, WA 98109 Tel 206-285-2308 (SAN 210-4962).

Seabury Press, Inc., *(Seabury; 0-8164),* 815 Second Ave., New York, NY 10017 Tel 212-557-0500 (SAN 202-5418); Orders to: Seabury Service Center, Somers, CT 06071 Tel 800-243-0004 (SAN 202-5426). *Imprints:* Vineyard (Vineyard).

Seacliffe, Ltd., *(Seacliffe; 0-911017),* 6338 Otis, Detroit, MI 48210 Tel 313-895-7158 (SAN 263-0028).

Seaforth Pubns., *(Seaforth Pubns; 0-933496),* 12211 Coit Rd., Bratenahl, OH 44108 Tel 216-681-4561 (SAN 212-5552); Orders to: 117 Pine Acres Dr., Spartanburg, SC 29302 Tel 803-579-1666 (SAN 212-5560).

Seagulls Artistic Pubns., *(Seagulls Artistic; 0-941110),* 1608 Nogales St. No. 177, Rowland Heights, CA 91748 Tel 213-964-7070 (SAN 217-4359).

Seahawk Press, *(Seahawk Pr; 0-913008),* 6840 S.W. 92nd St., Miami, FL 33156 Tel 305-667-4051 (SAN 204-7411).

Seajay Pubns., *(Seajay; 0-9609014),* P.O. Box 2176, Dearborn, MI 48124 Tel 313-274-9731 (SAN 241-2489).

Seal Press, *(Seal Pr; 0-930364),* P.O. Box 3027, Seal Beach, CA 90740 Tel 714-894-4856 (SAN 210-9522).

Seal Pr., *(Seal Pr Feminist),* 312 S. Washington, Seattle, WA 98104 Tel 206-624-5262 (SAN 215-3416).

Seals, Evelyn Johnson, *(E J Seals; 0-9608268),* N. 7th St., Middlesboro, KY 40965 Tel 606-248-5939 (SAN 240-4397).

Seals, Howard E., *(H E Seals; 0-9600232),* 3831 S. Michigan Ave., Rear Bldg., Chicago, IL 60653 Tel 312-285-3256 (SAN 203-4697).

Seapen Books, Inc., *(Seapen Bks; 0-932200),* 580 Fifth Ave., Suite 821, New York, NY 10036 Tel 212-877-8240 (SAN 212-4513).

Seaport Poets & Writers Press, *(Seaport Poets & Writers; 0-942856),* 94 Fulton St. 4th Floor, New York, NY 10038 (SAN 240-1568).

Search & Rescue Magazine, *(Search & Rescue; 0-9603392),* P.O. Box 641, Lompoc, CA 93438 Tel 805-733-3986 (SAN 204-5745).

Search Publications, *(Search Public; 0-910715),* 2000 Old Stage Rd., Florissant, CO 80816 (SAN 262-0766).

Searchers Pubns., *(Searchers Pubns),* 4314 Island Crest Way, Mercer Island, WA 98040 (SAN 212-5579).

Searchlight Books *See* Van Nostrand Reinhold Co. Inc

Seashell Press, *(Seashell Pr; 0-935378),* P.O. Box 747, El Cajon, CA 92022 (SAN 213-9642); Dist. by: Communication Creativity, 5644 La Jolla Blvd., La Jolla, CA 92037 Tel 714-459-4489 (SAN 213-0478).

Seattle Airplane Press, *(Seattle Air; 0-917196),* 6727 Glen Echo Lane, Tacoma, WA 98499 Tel 206-584-7307 (SAN 209-0775).

Seattle Art Museum, *(Seattle Art; 0-932216),* 14th E. & E. Prospect, Seattle, WA 98112 Tel 206-447-4710 (SAN 205-9762).

Seattle Audubon Society, *(Seattle Audubon Soc; 0-941516),* 619 Joshua Green Bldg, 1425 Fourth Ave., Seattle, WA 98101 Tel 206-622-6695 (SAN 203-2562).

Seattle Book Co., *(Seattle Bk; 0-915112),* P.O. Box 9254, Seattle, WA 98109 Tel 206-285-1226 (SAN 207-1835).

Seattle Publishing Co., Inc., *(Seattle Pub Co),* RR One Box 1035, Johnson, VT 05656 Tel 902-635-7440 (SAN 212-8667).

Seaver Books, *(Seaver Bks; 0-394),* 333 Central Park West, New York, NY 10025 Tel 212-866-9278 (SAN 214-4719); Orders to: Grove Press, Inc., 196 W. Houston St., New York, NY 10014 (SAN 201-4890); Dist. by: Arbor House Publishing Company, 300 E. 44th St., New York, NY 10017 (SAN 201-1522).

Seaview Press, *(Seaview Pr; 0-9606048),* P.O. Box 32, El Cerrito, CA 94530 Tel 415-525-5495 (SAN 216-4477).

Secker, Martin, & Warburg Ltd., *(Secker & Warburg; 0-436),* 54 Poland St., London, W1V 3DF, ; Orders to: Windmill Press, Kingwood, Tadworth Surrey KT20 6TG, .

Second Chance Press, *(Second Chance; 0-933256),* RD 2, Box 38AA, Noyac Rd., Sag Harbor, NY 11963 Tel 516-725-1101 (SAN 213-1633).

Second Coming Press, *(Second Coming; 0-915016),* P.O. Box 31249, San Francisco, CA 94131 Tel 415-647-3679 (SAN 206-376X).

Second Hand, The, *(Second Hand; 0-9605858),* P.O. Box 204, Plymouth, WI 53073 Tel 414-893-5226 (SAN 220-1879).

Second Language Pubns., *(Second Lang),* P.O. Box 1700, Blaine, WA 98230 (SAN 206-3778).

Second Society Foundation, *(Second Soc Foun),* 333 N. Michigan Ave., Suite 707, Chicago, IL 60601 (SAN 203-204X).

Second Thoughts, *(Second Thoughts; 0-9601286),* 63 W. Burton Place, Chicago, IL 60610 Tel 312-337-6044 (SAN 210-4970).

Second Thoughts Press, *(Sec Thoughts OR; 0-9607036),* P.O. Box 10741, Eugene, OR 97440 Tel 503-344-3491 (SAN 239-3832).

Second Thoughts Publishing, *(Second T Pub; 0-913587),* 202 Halsted, Chicago Heights, IL 60411 Tel 312-756-7500 (SAN 285-3825).

Secretarial Pubns., *(Secretarial Pubns; 0-943544),* P.O. Box 672, Santa Barbara, CA 93102 Tel 805-682-5706 (SAN 238-3667).

Secure Futures Pubns., *(Secure Futures; 0-938064),* P.O. Box 3362, San Diego, CA 92103 Tel 714-692-0588 (SAN 215-708X).

Secureware, *(Secureware; 0-912639),* P.O. Box 1074, Wheeling, IL 60090 (SAN 283-3123).

Security, *(Security MA; 0-409),* 10 Tower Office Park, Woburn, MA 01801 (SAN 217-2690).

Security Letter, Inc., *(Security Let; 0-9609820),* 166 E. 96th St., New York, NY 10028 (SAN 262-1134); Dist. by: Butterworths, 10 Tower Office Park, Woburn, MA 01801 (SAN 206-3964).

Security Press, Inc., *(Security Pr; 0-939568),* Box 854, McLean, VA 22101 Tel 703-734-1326 (SAN 216-6933).

See-Do Press, *(See Do Pr; 0-9607836),* P.O. Box 815, Lower Lake, CA 95457 Tel 707-994-5204 (SAN 238-1974).

Seed Center, *(Seed Center; 0-916108),* P.O. Box 658, Garberville, CA 95440 Tel 707-986-7575 (SAN 203-2554).

Seek-It Pubns., *(Seek-It Pubns; 0-930706),* P.O. Box 1074, Birmingham, MI 48012 (SAN 215-3424).
Seemann, E. A., Publishing, Inc., *(E A Seemann; 0-912458; 0-89530),* P.O. Box K, Miami, FL 33156 Tel 305-233-5852 (SAN 201-3495).
Seer Ox, *(Seer Ox; 0-916064),* 807 Prospect Ave. No. 107, South Pasadena, CA 91030 (SAN 207-8945).
Sekoni Pubs., *(Sekoni Pubs; 0-9606958),* P.O. Box 15007, Durham, NC 27704 Tel 919-688-5983 (SAN 217-4367).
Selbstverlag Press, *(Selbstverlag; 0-911706),* P.O. Drawer 606, Bloomington, IN 47402 Tel 812-335-2766 (SAN 204-5761).
Select Books, *(Select Bks; 0-910458),* Rte. 1 Box 129C, Mountain View, MO 65548 Tel 417-934-6775 (SAN 202-0602).
Select Publishing, *(Select Pub; 0-9606458),* P.O. Box 85707, Los Angeles, CA 90072 (SAN 218-5970).
Selective Pubs, Inc., *(Selective; 0-912584),* P.O. Box 1140, Clearwater, FL 33517 Tel 813-442-5440 (SAN 204-577X).
Selene Books, *(Selene Bks; 0-9609866),* P.O. Box 136, Kew Gardens, NY 11415 Tel 212-847-5184 (SAN 275-276X).
Self-Counsel Press, Inc., *(Self Counsel Pr),* 1303 N. Northgate Way, Seattle, WA 98133 Tel 206-522-8383 (SAN 240-9925).
Self Defense Kaleidoscope Pubns, *(Self Defense),* 3607 Maple Ave., Oakland, CA 94602 (SAN 240-8880).
Self-Motivated Careers, *(Self-Motiv Careers; 0-381),* 3589 Hermitage Plantation, Duluth, GA 30136 (SAN 220-2743).
Self-Programmed Control Press, *(Self-Prog Control; 0-9601926),* P.O. Box 49939, Los Angeles, CA 90049 Tel 213-826-1959 (SAN 212-2308).
Self Realization Fellowship, *(Self Realization; 0-87612),* 3880 San Rafael Ave., Los Angeles, CA 90065 Tel 213-225-2471 (SAN 204-5788).
Self Reliance Foundation, *(Self Reliance; 0-941580),* P.O. Box 1, Las Trampas, NM 87576 Tel 505-689-2250 (SAN 239-3085).
Sellens, *(Sellens; 0-9612068),* 134 Clark St., Augusta, KS 67010 Tel 316-775-5540 (SAN 212-3843).
Sellers Pubns, *(Sellers Pubns; 0-9608122),* 1120 S. Wolff St., Denver, CO 80219 (SAN 238-8383).
Seluzicki, Charles, Fine Books, *(Seluzicki Poetry; 0-931356),* Box 12367, Salem, OR 97309 Tel 503-364-9346 (SAN 211-9773).
Seminal Publishing House, *(Sem Pub Hse),* P.O. Box 213, Northhampton, MA 01060 (SAN 209-2018).
Seminary Co-Operative Bookstore, Inc., *(Seminary Co-Op; 0-912182),* 5757 S. University Ave., Chicago, IL 60637 Tel 312-752-4381 (SAN 204-5818).
Seminary Press, *(Seminary Pr; 0-912832),* P.O. Box 2218, Univ. Sta., Enid, OK 73702 Tel 405-237-4433 (SAN 203-2546).
Senda Nueva De Ediciones, Inc., *(Senda Nueva; 0-918454),* 640 W. 231st St., Apt. 3-B, Bronx, NY 10463 (SAN 210-0061).
Seneca Books, Inc., *(Seneca Bks; 0-89092),* Dist. by: Ruth E. Robinson Books, Rte. 6, Box 81-B, Morgantown, WV 26505 Tel 304-594-3140 (SAN 213-4322).
Senkers' Whim Enterprises, *(Senkers Whim Ent; 0-9610506),* P.O. Box 797, Devon, PA 19333 Tel 215-293-1044 (SAN 264-3820).
Senna & Shih, Inc., *(Senna & Shih; 0-89460),* P.O. Box 1091, 21 Beacon St., Boston, MA 02103 Tel 617-491-0858 (SAN 210-2692).
Sensei's DoJo Supply, *(Senseis DoJo),* P.O. Box 1164, Hollywood, CA 90028 (SAN 208-3213).
Senterfitt, Arnold, Pubns., *(Senterfitt; 0-937260),* Drawer 27310, Escondido, CA 92027 Tel 714-489-0590 (SAN 205-9487).
Sentinel Star Co., *(Sentinel Star; 0-9605772),* P.O. Box 2833, Orlando, FL 32802 Tel 305-420-5535 (SAN 206-3786).
Sentry Books, Inc., *(Sentry; 0-913194),* 10781 White Oak Ave., Granada Hills, CA 91344 Tel 213-368-2012 (SAN 205-9460); Dist. by: Aviation Book Co., 1640 Victory Blvd., Glendale, CA 91201 Tel 213-240-1771 (SAN 212-0259).
Sentry Editions *See Houghton Mifflin Co.*
Sepher-Hermon Press, Inc., *(Hermon; 0-87203),* 53 Park Place, Suite 503, New York, NY 10007 Tel 212-349-1860 (SAN 204-0506).

Sequoia Press, *(Sequoia Pr),* P.O. Box 9889, Berkeley, CA 94703 Tel 415-849-4703 (SAN 286-3456).
Seraphim Press, *(Seraphim Pr; 0-942632),* Suite 263, 7475 La Palma Ave., Buena Park, CA 90620 Tel 714-527-4475 (SAN 238-5791).
Sercolab, *(Sercolab; 0-918332),* P.O. Box 78, Arlington, MA 02174 (SAN 209-5165).
Serina Press, *(Serina; 0-911952),* 70 Kennedy St., Alexandria, VA 22305 Tel 703-548-4080 (SAN 204-5834).
Serrell & Simons, Publishers, *(Serrell-Simons; 0-943104),* Box 64, Winnebago, WI 54985 Tel 414-231-1939 (SAN 240-4400); Dist. by: Baker & Taylor, P.O. Box 458, Commerce, GA 30599 (SAN 169-1503); Dist. by: Baker & Taylor, 501 S. Gladiolus Ave., Momence, IL 60954 (SAN 169-2100); Dist. by: Baker & Taylor, 380 Edison Way, Reno, NV 89564 (SAN 169-4464); Dist. by: Taylor & Baker, 50 Kirby Ave., Somerville, NJ 08876 (SAN 169-4901); Dist. by: The Distributors, 702 S. Michigan, South Bend, IN 46618 Tel 219-232-8500 (SAN 212-0364).
Servant Publications, *(Servant; 0-89283),* 840 Airport Blvd., Ann Arbor, MI 48107 Tel 313-761-8505 (SAN 208-9238); Orders to: Customer Service Dept., Box 8617, Ann Arbor, MI 48107 Tel 313-761-8983 (SAN 208-9246) Formerly Named Word of Life.
Service League of Lutheran General Hospital, *(Serv League IL; 0-9609292),* 1775 Dempster St., Park Ridge, IL 60068 Tel 312-696-6105 (SAN 260-1338).
Service League of Natchitoches, Inc., *(Service League; 0-9607674),* P.O. Box 2206, Natchitoches, LA 71457 (SAN 226-7993).
Service Publishing Co., *(Service Pub; 0-913104),* Washington Bldg., 15th & New York Ave., N.W., Washington, DC 20005 Tel 202-628-1397 (SAN 204-5842).
Servicios Internacionales, *(Servicios Intles),* P. O. Box 51, La Marque, TX 77568 (SAN 214-137X).
SES Development Corporation, *(SES Development; 0-943982),* Dist. by: The Book Carrier, Inc., 9121 Industrial Court, Gaithersburg, MD 20877 Tel 301-258-1177 (SAN 200-4046).
Sesnon, Mary P., Art Gallery, *(Sesnon Art Gall; 0-939982),* College V, Univ. of California, Santa Cruz, CA 95064 Tel 408-429-2314 (SAN 216-8669).
Sessions Pubs., *(Sessions; 0-911366),* 48 Nassau Dr., New Hyde Park, NY 11040 Tel 516-747-3144 (SAN 204-5850).
Settles Books, *(Settles Bks),* Box 1121, Aurora, IL 60507 (SAN 240-1576).
Seven Arts Press, Inc., *(Seven Arts; 0-911370),* 6253 Hollywood Blvd., No. 1100, Hollywood, CA 90028 Tel 213-469-1095 (SAN 203-2538).
Seven Hills Books, Div. of Books for the Decorative Arts Inc., *(Seven Hills Bks; 0-911403),* 519 W. Third St., Cincinnati, OH 45202 Tel 513-381-3881 (SAN 169-6629) Reference books on art & antiques, juveniles, cookbooks.
Seven Locks Press, *(Seven Locks Pr; 0-932020),* P.O. Box 72, Cabin John, MD 20818 Tel 202-638-1598 (SAN 211-9781).
Seven Oaks, *(Seven Oaks GA; 0-9605514),* 206 Winchester Dr., Savannah, GA 31410 Tel 912-897-1563 (SAN 239-894X).
Seven Oaks Press, *(Seven Oaks; 0-932508),* 405 S. 7th St., St. Charles, IL 60174 Tel 312-584-0187 (SAN 212-1735).
Seven Palms Press, *(Seven Palms; 0-912593),* 4226 Irving Circle, Tucson, AZ 85711 Tel 602-325-9528 (SAN 283-3115).
Seven Seasons Service Co., *(Seven Seasons Serv Co; 0-9610868),* 8865 Hillery Dr., San Diego, CA 92126 (SAN 283-9105).
Seven Springs Center, Inc., *(Seven Springs; 0-943006),* RD 2, Oregon Rd., Mount Kisco, NY 10549 Tel 914-241-1880 (SAN 240-3269).
Seven Woods Press, *(Seven Woods Pr; 0-913282),* P.O. Box 32 Village Sta., New York, NY 10014 (SAN 203-2503).
SevenSeas Press, Inc., *(Seven Seas; 0-915160),* 524 Thames St., Newport, RI 02840 Tel 401-847-1683 (SAN 206-8737).
Seventh Trumpet Publishing Company, *(Seventh Trumpet; 0-9610268),* P.O. Box 18, Schiller Park, IL 60176 (SAN 264-3847).

Seventy-Six Press, *(Seventy-Six; 0-89245),* P.O. Box 725, Seal Beach, CA 90740 Tel 213-596-3491 (SAN 208-2004).
Seville Publishing Co., *(Seville Pub; 0-930990),* 6740 Kester Ave., Second Floor, Van Nuys, CA 91405 Tel 213-501-5200 (SAN 222-9323).
Sew/Fit Pub. Co., *(Sew-Fit),* 905 Hillgrove, No. 6, La Grange, IL 60525 Tel 312-579-3222 (SAN 212-1387).
Sew Wonderful, Inc., *(Sew Wonderful; 0-943704),* 2320 N. 53rd, Seattle, WA 98103 Tel 206-634-1930 (SAN 238-3675).
Sewing Knits Inc., *(Sewing Knits; 0-9605860),* 634 W. Huntington Dr., No.12, Arcadia, CA 91006 Tel 513-435-8069 (SAN 216-6089).
Sex Information & Education Council of the U.S., *(SIECUS),* 80 5th Ave., Suite 801, New York, NY 10011 Tel 212-929-2300 (SAN 224-2435).
Sexauer, Charles F., Publishing Co., *(C F Sexauer; 0-9607148),* 13909 Old Harbor Lane, No. 102, Marina Del Rey, CA 90291 Tel 213-821-2164 (SAN 239-0337).
Seybold Pubns., Inc., *(Seybold; 0-918514),* Box 644, Media, PA 19063 Tel 215-565-2480 (SAN 210-007X).
Seyer, Herman D., *(H D Seyer; 0-9600784),* 6534 No. Bungglow Lane, Fresno, CA 93704 Tel 209-734-7537 (SAN 207-3749).
Seymour, Dale, Pubns., *(Seymour Pubns; 0-86651; 0-9604812),* P.O. Box 10888, Palo Alto, CA 94303 Tel 415-493-2512 (SAN 216-0110).
Seymour Lawrence *See Delacorte Press*
Shacor, *(Shacor Inc; 0-943748),* 223 Katonah Ave., Katonah, NY 10536 Tel 914-232-8108 (SAN 241-0680).
Shade Tree Books, *(Shade Tree; 0-930742),* P.O. Box 2268, Huntington Beach, CA 92647 Tel 714-846-3869 (SAN 211-0954).
Shadow Press, U.S.A, *(Shadow Pr; 0-937724),* Box 8803, Minneapolis, MN 55408 Tel 612-823-1319 (SAN 218-3617); Dist. by: Midwest Distributors, P.O. Box 4642, Kansas City, MO 64109 (SAN 219-5038).
Shadwold Press, *(Shadwold; 0-9603024),* P.O. Box 706, Kennebunkport, ME 04046 Tel 207-967-4400 (SAN 212-5587); Dist. by: Omni Books, 3040 Charlevoix Dr., S.E., Grand Rapids, MI 49506 Tel 800-253-8144 (SAN 238-1826).
Shadyside Press, *(Shadyside),* 320 Brooks Ave., Venice, CA 90291 (SAN 265-9808); Dist. by: Bookpeople, 2940 Seventh St., Berkeley, CA 94710 Tel 800-227-1516 (SAN 168-9517); Dist. by: The Distributors, 702 S. Michigan, South Bend, IN 46618 Tel 219-232-8500 (SAN 212-0364).
Shaffer, Dale E., *(D E Shaffer; 0-915060),* 437 Jennings Ave., Salem, OH 44460 Tel 216-337-3348 (SAN 206-9067).
Shah, Kirit N., *(K N Shah; 0-9609614),* 980 Moraga Ave., Piedmont, CA 94611 Tel 415-658-6970 (SAN 260-2628).
Shaker Museum Foundation Inc., *(Shaker Mus; 0-937942),* Shaker Museum Rd., Old Chatham, NY 12136 Tel 518-794-9100 (SAN 206-7684).
Shaker Prairie Publication, *(Shaker Prairie),* R.R. One, Oaktown, IN 47561 Tel 812-745-3153 (SAN 209-5173).
Shaker Press, The, *(Shaker Pr ME; 0-915836),* Sabbathday Lake, Poland Spring, ME 04274 Tel 207-926-4597 (SAN 214-1388).
Shallway Foundation, *(Shallway Foun; 0-934392),* 125 S. Fourth St., Connellsville, PA 15425 (SAN 213-1641).
Shalom, P., Pubns., Inc., *(Shalom; 0-87559),* 5409 18th Ave., Brooklyn, NY 11204 (SAN 204-5893).
Shamal Books, Inc., *(Shamal Bks; 0-917886),* G.P.O. Box 16, New York, NY 10116 Tel 212-622-4426 (SAN 209-3618).
Shaman Books, *(Shaman Bks; 0-9611274),* 1033 W. Loyola Ave. No. 1007, Chicago, IL 60626 Tel 312-262-4888 (SAN 283-1627).
Shamar Book, A, *(Shamar Bk; 0-9607058),* 9215 N. Concho Lane, Phoenix, AZ 85028 (SAN 239-3840).
Shambhala Pubns., Inc., *(Shambhala Pubns; 0-87773),* 1920 13th St., P.O. Box 271, Boulder, CO 80306 Tel 303-449-6111 (SAN 203-2481); Dist. by: Random House, Inc., 400 Hahn Rd., Westminster, MD 21157 (SAN 202-5515).

Shameless Hussy Press, *(Shameless Hussy; 0-915288),* Box 3092, Berkeley, CA 94703 Tel 415-548-7800 (SAN 282-3071); Dist. by: Bookpeople, 2940 Seventh St., Berkeley, CA 94710 Tel 415-549-3030 (SAN 168-9517); Dist. by: Bookslinger, 330 East Ninth St., St. Paul, MN 55101 Tel 612-221-0429 (SAN 169-4154); Dist. by: The Crossing Press, Trumansburg, New York, NY 14886 Tel 607-387-6217 (SAN 202-2060); Dist. by: Straight Talk Distributing, P.O. Box 750, Point Reyes Station, CA 94956 Tel 219-232-8500 (SAN 282-311X); Dist. by: The Distributors, 702 S. Michigan, South Bend, IN 46618 (SAN 212-0364).

Shamrock Press & Publishing Co., *(Shamrock Pr; 0-910583),* P.O. Box 7256, Alexandria, VA 22307 Tel 703-683-3114 (SAN 260-2636).

Shamrock Pubns, *(Shamrock Pubns; 0-9608142),* 406 Rising Hill Drive, Fairborn, OH 45324 (SAN 240-1584).

Shane Press, *(Shane Pr; 0-942998),* 4719 S.E. Woodstock, Portland, OR 97206 Tel 503-775-1665 (SAN 240-4419).

Shanken, M., Communications, Inc., *(M Shanken Comm; 0-918076),* 400 East 51st Street, New York, NY 10022 Tel 212-751-6500 (SAN 210-2773).

Shapian/Morrell Productions, *(Shapian-Morrell; 0-9610992),* 9110 Sunset Blvd., No. 240, Los Angeles, CA 90069 Tel 213-276-1005 (SAN 265-2056).

Shapiro, Leonard, *(Shapiro; 0-9607318),* 1567 N. Prospect Ave., Apt. 416, Milwaukee, WI 53202 (SAN 239-3093).

Shapiro, Robert B., *(R B Shapiro; 0-9609172),* 276 Acton St., Daly City, CA 94014 Tel 415-584-4484 (SAN 241-4201).

Sharain Books, *(Sharain Bks; 0-9609740),* 774 Allen St., Palo Alto, CA 94303 Tel 415-493-3596 (SAN 262-0782).

Share Publishing Co., *(Share Pub Co; 0-933344),* P.O. Box 3453, Annapolis, MD 21403 (SAN 212-5595).

Shared Care, *(Shared Care; 0-9608702),* 6102 N. 14th St., Phoenix, AZ 85014 Tel 602-279-2619 (SAN 238-3683).

Sharing Co., The, *(Sharing Co),* P.O. Box 2224, Austin, TX 78768-2224 Tel 512-452-4366 (SAN 211-0563).

Sharon Hill Books, *(Sharon Hill; 0-932062),* P.O. Box 67, Sharon Hill, PA 19079 (SAN 210-5632).

Sharon Pubns. Inc., *(Sharon Pubns; 0-89531),* 105 Union Ave., Cresslill, NJ 07626 Tel 201-568-8800 (SAN 210-4989).

Sharpe, John K., Incorporated, *(J K Sharpe Inc),* Box 442, Wilmette, IL 60091 Tel 312-256-2086 (SAN 276-9395).

Sharpe, M. E., Inc., *(M E Sharpe; 0-87332),* 80 Business Park Dr., Armonk, NY 10504 Tel 914-273-1800 (SAN 202-7100).

Sharral Publishing Co., Subs. of Lee Rothchild, Ltd., *(Sharral Pub; 0-940978),* 13540 E. Boundary Rd., Midlothian, VA 23113 Tel 804-744-3658 (SAN 217-4375).

Sharratt & Company, *(Sharratt & Co; 0-912295),* 3713 E. Easter Circle N., Littleton, CO 80122 Tel 303-773-3967 (SAN 277-7061).

Shasta Abbey Pr., *(Shasta Abbey; 0-930066),* P.O. Box 199, Mt. Shasta, CA 96067 Tel 916-926-4208 (SAN 210-6655); Dist. by: Bookpeople, 2940 Seventh St., Berkeley, CA 94710 Tel 415-549-3030 (SAN 168-9517).

Shasta Pubns., *(Shasta Pubns; 0-9608202),* 1062 Tahoe Terr., Cincinnati, OH 45238 Tel 513-451-2774 (SAN 240-2793).

ShaunTar Enterprises, *(ShaunTar Ent; 0-910241),* P.O. Box 11784, Santa Rosa, CA 95406 Tel 707-544-1478 (SAN 241-4546).

Shaw, Harold, Pubs., *(Shaw Pubs; 0-87788),* Box 567, 388 Gundersen Dr., Wheaton, IL 60189 Tel 312-665-6700 (SAN 203-2473).

Shaw, Li Kung, Publisher, *(Li Kung Shaw),* 2530 33rd Ave., San Francisco, CA 94116 (SAN 240-0480).

Shaw, Mara Lynn, Inc., *(Shaw Inc; 0-9605602),* 165 E. 72nd St., Suite 12n, New York, NY 10021 Tel 212-861-1664 (SAN 216-1664).

Shawnee County Historical Society, *(Shawnee County Hist; 0-916934),* 1205 W. 29th St., Rm. 430, Topeka, KS 66611 Tel 913-267-0309 (SAN 282-3136); P.O. Box 56, Topeka, KS 66601 (SAN 282-3144).

Shawnee Press, Inc., *(Shawnee Pr; 0-9603394),* Delaware Water Gap, PA 18327 Tel 717-476-0550 (SAN 202-084X).

Shayna Ltd., *(Shayna Ltd; 0-9604208),* 100 Andrew St., Newton, MA 02161 Tel 617-244-1870 (SAN 214-4727).

Shearer Publishing, *(Shearer Pub; 0-940672),* 3208 Turtle Grove, Bryan, TX 77801 Tel 713-779-1762 (SAN 218-5989).

Shearwater Press, *(Shearwater; 0-938050),* Box 417, Wellfleet, MA 02667 (SAN 216-1923).

Sheba Pubns., *(Sheba Pub; 0-9608430),* P.O. Box 409, Kirkland, WA 98033 Tel 206-451-8697 (SAN 240-7728).

Sheba Review, Inc., *(Sheba Rev; 0-9610626),* P.O. Box 1623, Jefferson City, MO 65102 Tel 314-893-5834 (SAN 264-6927).

Shedd Aquarium Society, *(Shedd Aquarium; 0-9611074),* 1200 S. Lake Shore Dr., Chicago, IL 60605 (SAN 283-4359).

Sheep Meadow Press, The, *(Sheep Meadow; 0-935296),* Dist. by: Persea Bks., Inc., 225 Lafayette St., New York, NY 10012 Tel 212-431-5270 (SAN 212-8233).

Sheephead Books, *(Sheephead Bks; 0-9604644),* P.O. Box 562, Vidalia, GA 30474 Tel 912-537-2852 (SAN 215-8094).

Sheer Press, *(Sheer Pr; 0-9601254),* P.O. Box 4071, Walnut Creek, CA 94596 Tel 415-932-1144 (SAN 210-4997); 3601 Valley Vista Rd., Walnut Creek, CA 94598 (SAN 210-5004).

Shelburne Museum, Inc., *(Shelburne; 0-939384),* Shelburne, VT 05482 Tel 802-985-3346 (SAN 205-941X).

Sheldon, Marc, Publishing, *(M Sheldon Pub; 0-932262),* P.O. Box 272, 777 N. Loren Ave., Azusa, CA 91702 Tel 213-969-1866 (SAN 211-9234).

Shell Cabinet, *(Shell Cab; 0-913792),* P.O. Box 29, Falls Church, VA 22046 Tel 703-256-0707 (SAN 122-8455).

Shellie Press, *(Shellie Pr; 0-9607038),* 420 Wisteria Rd., Venice, FL 33595 (SAN 239-8639).

Shelter Pubns., *(Shelter Pubns; 0-936070),* P.O. Box 279, Bolinas, CA 94924 Tel 415-868-0280 (SAN 212-4521); Dist. by: Random House, 400 Hahn Rd., Westminster, MD 21157 (SAN 202-5515).

Shelton Pubns., *(Shelton; 0-918742),* P.O. Box 391, Sausalito, CA 94966 Tel 415-332-1165 (SAN 210-4733).

Shenandoah History, *(Shenandoah Hist; 0-917968),* P.O. Box 98, Edinburg, VA 22824 Tel 703-459-4598 (SAN 210-0118).

Shengold Pubns., Inc., *(Shengold; 0-88400),* 23 W. 45th St., New York, NY 10036 Tel 212-944-2555 (SAN 203-2465).

Shenson, Howard L., Inc., *(H L Shenson; 0-910549),* 20121 Ventura Blvd., No. 245, Woodland Hills, CA 91354 Tel 213-703-1415 (SAN 260-1346).

Shep, R. L., *(R L Shep; 0-914046),* Box C-20, Lopez Island, WA 98261 (SAN 215-3432).

Shepard, Dennis D., *(D D Shepard; 0-9601234),* 1414 E. Main St., Santa Maria, CA 93454 Tel 805-925-2637 (SAN 210-5012).

Shepard's, McGraw-Hill See **McGraw-Hill Book Co.**

Shepherd-Moore, Marie, Educational Foundation, *(Shepherd-Moore Ed Foun; 0-9603948),* 692 E. 40th St., Brooklyn, NY 11210 (SAN 221-6582).

Shepherd Pubns., Inc., *(Shepherd Pubns; 0-935814),* P.O. Box 20665, Bloomington, MN 55420 Tel 612-835-4423 (SAN 213-7992).

Shepherd Pubs., *(Shepherd Pubs VA; 0-9607308),* 100 Sheriffs Place, Williamsburg, VA 23185 Tel 804-229-0661 (SAN 240-1622).

Sheppard, W. L., *(W L Sheppard),* 923 Old Manoa Rd., Havertown, PA 19083 Tel 215-449-2167 (SAN 216-3225).

Sheriar Press, Inc., *(Sheriar Pr; 0-913078),* 1414 Madison St. S., N. Myrtle Beach, SC 29582 Tel 803-272-5333 (SAN 203-2457).

Sheridan House, Inc., *(Sheridan; 0-911378),* 145 Palisade St., Dobbs Ferry, NY 10522 Tel 914-693-2410 (SAN 204-5915).

Sherman, Faith, *(F Sherman; 0-9607286),* Rte. 1 Box 81 J.S., Tygh Valley, OR 97063 Tel 503-544-3742 (SAN 239-3107).

Sherman, Harvey, *(Sherman),* 4011 Garden Ave., Los Angeles, CA 90039 (SAN 210-3680).

Sherrod, Paul, *(P Sherrod),* 3323 19th St., Lubbock, TX 79410 (SAN 212-1395).

Sherwood Co., The, *(Sherwood Co; 0-933056),* P.O. Box 21645, Denver, CO 80221 Tel 303-423-6481 (SAN 212-8136).

Shetal Enterprises, *(Shetal Ent; 0-932888),* 1787 "B" W. Touhy, Chicago, IL 60626 Tel 312-262-1133 (SAN 213-9553).

Shieldalloy Corp.-Metallurg Alloy Corp., *(Shieldalloy; 0-9606196),* N West Blvd., Newfield, NJ 08344 Tel 609-692-4200 (SAN 220-3065).

Shields Pubns., *(Shields WI; 0-9600102; 0-914116),* P.O. Box 669, Eagle River, WI 54521 Tel 715-479-4810 (SAN 204-5923).

Shifra Stein Productions, *(S Stein Prods; 0-9609752),* 3733 Pennsylvania, Kansas City, MO 64111 (SAN 263-2284).

Shillelagh Books, Inc., *(Shillelagh; 0-9607838),* 8104 Wisner St., Niles, IL 60648 Tel 312-937-4257 (SAN 238-1982).

Shilo Publishing House, Inc., *(Shilo Pub Hse; 0-88328),* 73 Canal St., New York, NY 10002 Tel 212-925-3468 (SAN 205-9894).

Shim, Sang Kyu, Publisher, *(S K Shim Pub; 0-942062),* 17625 W. 7 Mile, Detroit, MI 48235 (SAN 238-5929).

Shinn, Duane, *(D Shinn Pubns; 0-912732),* P.O. Box 192, Medford, OR 97501 (SAN 213-991X).

Shintaido of America, *(Shintaido; 0-942634),* 145 Judah, No. 6, San Francisco, CA 94122 Tel 415-731-9364 (SAN 238-5805).

Shipley, Alice M., *(A M Shipley; 0-9610918),* 217 W. Roma Ave., Phoenix, AZ 85013 (SAN 265-1076).

Shire Press, *(Shire Pr; 0-918828),* P.O. Box 1728, Santa Cruz, CA 95061 Tel 408-425-0842 (SAN 207-6357).

Shirjieh Pubs., *(Shirjieh Pubs; 0-912496),* P.O. Box 259, Menlo Park, CA 94025 (SAN 204-594X).

Shirley's Publishing, Ltd., *(Shirleys Pub; 0-9609868),* 1608 Shenstone Ct., Virginia Beach, VA 23455 Tel 804-460-3668 (SAN 275-3197).

Shiver Mountain Press, Inc., *(Shiver Mntn; 0-89488),* Washington Depot, CT 06794 Tel 203-868-0533 (SAN 210-0134).

Shoaf, Mary Jo Davis, *(M J D Shoaf; 0-9602520),* 310 Forest Hill Rd., Lexington, NC 27292 Tel 704-249-8015 (SAN 212-6893).

Shoal Creek Pubs., *(Shoal Creek Pub; 0-88319),* 3208 Turtle Grove, Bryan, TX 78801 Tel 512-451-7545 (SAN 203-2430).

Schockley Pr., *(Shockley Pr; 0-942048),* P.O. Box 36012, Los Angeles, CA 90036 Tel 213-933-4198 (SAN 238-5937).

Shoe String Press, Inc., *(Shoe String; 0-208),* P.O. Box 4327, 995 Sherman Ave., Hamden, CT 06514 Tel 203-248-6307 (SAN 213-2079). *Imprints:* Archon Books (Archon Bks).

Shoemaker, Rhoda, *(R Shoemaker; 0-9600474),* 1141 Orange Ave., Menlo Park, CA 94025 Tel 415-854-5768 (SAN 204-6636).

Shondo-Shando Press, *(Shondo-Shando; 0-9601754),* P.O. Box 887, Quincy, IL 62301 Tel 217-214-4192 (SAN 212-2596).

Shopen, Sylvia Ames, *(S A Shopen),* Norwich, VT 05055 (SAN 212-7024).

Shopping Experience, Inc., The, *(Shopping Experience; 0-934758),* 2 Grace Court, Brooklyn, NY 11201 Tel 212-522-0762 (SAN 213-9472).

Shore, Michael, Associates, *(M Shore Assocs; 0-910243),* 24 Westfield Rd., Milford, CT 06460 Tel 203-877-9218 (SAN 241-4554).

Shoreland Press, *(Shoreland Pr; 0-913479),* 32 Bayberry Lane, Mountainside, NJ 07092 Tel 201-232-0246 (SAN 285-8509).

Shoreline Publishing, *(Shoreline Pub; 0-938306),* 212-08 75th Ave., Bayside, NY 11364 (SAN 215-8108).

Shorewood Fine Art Books, Inc., *(Shorewood Fine Art; 0-87230),* 475 Tenth Ave., New York, NY 10018 (SAN 219-9637). *Imprints:* Woodbine Books, Inc. (Woodbine Bks).

Shorey Pubns., *(Shorey; 0-8466),* 110 Union St., Seattle, WA 98101 Tel 206-624-0221 (SAN 204-5958).

Short Methods & Systems, *(Short Methods; 0-915800),* P.O. Box 247, Claremont, CA 91711 Tel 714-626-3213 (SAN 207-4842).

Showcase Pubns., *(Showcase Pubns; 0-917800),* P.O. Box 40165, Pasadena, CA 91104 Tel 213-794-7782 (SAN 213-5906).

Showcase Publishing Co., *(Showcase Fairfield; 0-88205),* 1125 Missouri St., Fairfield, CA 94533 Tel 707-427-3130 (SAN 213-6430); Dist. by: Elsevier-Dutton, Inc., Showcase Publishing, 1125 misoduki St. Fairfield,, New York, CA 94533 Tel 707-427-3130 (SAN 282-6348).

Shreveport Publishing Corp., *(Shreveport Pub; 0-939042),* P.O. Box 31110, Shreveport, LA 71130 (SAN 216-1842).

Shrine of the Eternal Breath of Tao, The, *(SEBT; 0-937064),* 117 Stonehaven Way, Los Angeles, CA 90049 (SAN 217-2704).

Shroud of Turin Research Project, Inc., *(Shroud of Turin; 0-9605516),* P.O. Box 7, Amston, CT 06231 (SAN 216-1834).

Shrout, Beatrice Lentz, *(B L Shrout; 0-9609070),* 513 Riverside Dr., Welch, WV 24801 Tel 304-436-3411 (SAN 241-2500).

Shulsinger Sales, Inc., *(Shulsinger Sales; 0-914080),* 50 Washington St., Brooklyn, NY 11201 Tel 212-852-0042 (SAN 205-9851).

Siamese Imports Co., Inc., *(Siamese Imports; 0-940202),* 148 Plandome Rd., Manhasset, NY 11030 Tel 516-365-8867 (SAN 220-3545).

Sibyl-Child Press, *(Sibyl-Child),* Box 1773, Hyattsville, MD 20788 (SAN 211-1675).

Sibyl Jarvis Pischke, *(Sibyl; 0-9608532),* 1401 N. E. 35th St., Ft. Lauderdale, FL 33334 Tel 305-566-5078 (SAN 240-7736).

Siegel, Kenneth L., Publishing, *(Siegel; 0-939848),* 301 E. Balboa Blvd., Newport Beach, CA 92661 Tel 714-673-5410 (SAN 216-762X).

Siegmond, W. E., Enterprises, *(W E Siegmond; 0-916610),* 382 Central Park West, New York, NY 10025 (SAN 208-225X).

Siemens Communication Graphics, *(Siemens Com Graphics; 0-936226),* 1501 Greenleaf, Evanston, IL 60602 (SAN 221-9956).

Siepierski, Gerald E., *(G E Siepierski; 0-9611278),* 20257 Ecorse Rd., Taylor, MI 48180 Tel 313-382-4816 (SAN 283-1643).

Sierra Club Bks., *(Sierra; 0-87156),* 2034 Fillmore St., San Francisco, CA 94115 Tel 415-931-7950 (SAN 203-2406); Dist. by: Random Hse., Inc., Distribution Ctr., 400 Hahn Rd., Westminster, MD 21157 (SAN 202-5515).

Sierra Pubns., *(Sierra Pubns CA; 0-932848),* P.O. Box 3504, San Jose, CA 95156-3504 Tel 408-251-3799 (SAN 211-6154).

Sierra Trading Post, *(Sierra Trading; 0-9605890),* P.O. Box 2497, San Francisco, CA 94126 Tel 415-456-9378 (SAN 216-6097).

SIETAR See **Society for Intercultural Education, Training & Research**

Sigga Press, *(Sigga Pr; 0-916348),* P.O. Box 25, Nottingham, NH 03290 (SAN 211-2698).

Sightseer Pubns., *(Sightseer; 0-937928),* 7400 N. Kendall Dr., Miami, FL 33156 (SAN 220-1240).

Sigma Press, *(Sigma Pr NY),* P.O. Box 264, Manhasset, NY 11030 (SAN 240-9577).

Sigma Press Inc., *(Sigma Pr; 0-9604516),* P.O. Box 379, South Bound Brook, NJ 08880 (SAN 215-8116).

Signature Books, Inc., *(Signature Bks; 0-941214),* 942 E. 7145 S. No. 106, Midvale, UT 84047 Tel 801-355-6499 (SAN 217-4391).

Signet Books See **New American Library**

Signet Classics See **New American Library**

Signmaker Press, *(Signmaker; 0-9605774),* Box 967, Ashland, OR 97520 Tel 503-482-2575 (SAN 216-549X).

Signpost Book Publishing Co., *(Signpost Bk Pub; 0-913140),* 8912 192nd St. S.W., Edmonds, WA 98020 Tel 206-776-0370 (SAN 204-5966).

Signpost Press, *(Signpost Pr; 0-9609592),* N 56 W21414 Silver Spring Rd., Menomonee Falls, WI 53501 (SAN 275-3596).

Signs of the Times Publishing Co., *(Signs of Times; 0-911380),* 407 Gilbert Ave., Cincinnati, OH 45202 Tel 513-421-2050 (SAN 204-5974).

Sigo Press, *(Sigo Pr; 0-938434),* 77 N. Washington St., No. 201, Boston, MA 02114 Tel 617-523-2321 (SAN 216-3020).

Sijthoff & Noordhoff International Publishing Co., *(Sijthoff & Noordhoff),* 1600 Research Blvd., Rockville, MD 20850 Tel 301-251-0950 (SAN 210-8542).

Silberman, Leonard, *(L Silberman; 0-9605080),* P.O. Box 12519, Santa Ana, CA 92712 (SAN 238-0854) Moved, left no forwarding address.

Silbert & Bress Pubns., *(Silbert Bress; 0-89544),* P.O. Box 68, Mahopac, NY 10541 Tel 914-628-7910 (SAN 210-5020).

Silma Delta Research, *(Silma Inc; 0-913223),* 4804 N.W. 79th Ave., No.302, Miami, FL 33166 Tel 305-594-4696 (SAN 283-4081).

Silver Age Publishing, *(Silver Age Pub; 0-940294),* P.O. Box 384, Rego Park, NY 11374 Tel 212-897-6938 (SAN 217-5835).

Silver Apples Press, *(Silver App Pr; 0-943710),* P.O. Box 292, Hainesport, NJ 08036 (SAN 238-3721).

Silver Burdett Co., *(Silver; 0-382),* 250 James St., Cn 018, Morristown, NJ 07960 (SAN 204-5982).

Silver D. Investments, Inc., *(Silver D Invest Inc; 0-912497),* P.O. Box 3038, Richardson, TX 75252 Tel 214-699-0431 (SAN 265-315X).

Silver Dollar City, Inc., *(Silver Dollar),* Silver Dollar City, MO 65616 Tel 417-388-2611 (SAN 210-3699).

Silver Fox Connections, *(Silver Fox; 0-9605910),* 1244 S.W. 301st St., Federal Way, WA 98003 Tel 206-839-3784 (SAN 216-4485).

Silver Pennies Press, *(Silver Pennies; 0-9607040),* 1365 E. 30th Ave., Eugene, OR 97405 Tel 503-345-6286 (SAN 239-0353).

Silver Seal Books, *(Silver Seal Bks; 0-910867),* P.O. Box 106, Fox Island, WA 98333 (SAN 264-3871).

Silverado Publishing Co., *(Silverado; 0-87938),* St. Helena, CA 94574 (SAN 213-3725); Dist. by: Motorbooks International, Pubs. & Wholesalers, P.O. Box 2, 729 Prospect Ave., Osceola, WI 54020 Tel 715-294-3345 (SAN 212-3304).

Silverfish Review Press, *(Silverfish Rev Pr; 0-9610508),* P.O. Box 3541, Eugene, OR 97403 (SAN 264-388X).

Silvergirl Books, *(Silvergirl Bks),* P.O. Box 4858, Austin, TX 78765 Tel 512-863-2537 (SAN 239-3875).

Silvermine Pubns., *(Silvermine; 0-87231),* Comstock Hill, Silvermine, Norwalk, CT 06850 Tel 203-847-4732 (SAN 209-6005).

Simile II, *(Simile II),* 218 Twelfth St., P.O. Box 910, Del Mar, CA 92014 Tel 714-755-0272 (SAN 208-8525).

Simon, Joseph, *(J Simon; 0-934710),* Box 4071, Malibu, CA 90265 Tel 213-457-3293 (SAN 213-9669).

Simon & Schuster, Inc., *(S&S; 0-671),* 1230 Ave. of the Americas, New York, NY 10020 Tel 212-245-6400 (SAN 200-2450). Imprints: Fireside Paperbacks (Fireside); Juvenile Books (Juveniles); Linden Press (Linden Pr); Little Simon (Little Simon); Touchstone Books (Touchstone Bks); Wallaby (Wallaby).

Simonetta Press, *(Simonetta Pr; 0-941594),* 4219 W. Eighth St., Los Angeles, CA 90005 (SAN 239-3883).

Simons Bks., Inc., *(Simons Bks; 0-937812),* P.O. Box 2145, Oceanside, CA 92054 (SAN 216-4493).

Simontsits, Atilla L., *(Simontsits; 0-920004),* 4118 Ridge Rd., Apt. 6, Brooklyn, OH 44144 Tel 216-661-4319 (SAN 283-409X).

Simplex Communications, Inc., *(Simplex Comm; 0-935248),* P.O. Box 9133, Fort Wayne, IN 46783 Tel 219-672-3702 (SAN 213-3741).

Simplicity Pattern Co., Inc., *(Simplicity; 0-918178),* 200 Madison Ave., New York, NY 10016 Tel 212-576-0537 (SAN 282-3179); Orders to: Simplicity Educational Div., 901 Wayne St., Niles, MI 49121 (SAN 282-3187).

Simplified Regulations, *(Simplified Reg; 0-9607866),* W. 137 N 8235 Parkview Dr., Menomonee Falls, WI 53051 Tel 414-255-2204 (SAN 238-1990).

Simply Elegant, *(Simply Elegant Company; 0-9600492),* 3801 N. Mission Hills Rd., Northbrook, IL 60062 Tel 312-564-2221 (SAN 204-5990); Orders to: P.O. Box 74, Winnetka, IL 60093 (SAN 204-6008).

Simpson, Jeanne R., Gallery of Fine Art Ltd., *(J R Simpson; 0-9611558),* 2811 W. 67 Terrace, Shawnee Mission, KS 66208 Tel 913-831-1902 (SAN 284-9127).

Simpson, Ruth M. Rasey, *(R M R Simpson; 0-9604048),* 286 Goundry St., North Tonawanda, NY 14120 Tel 716-692-1830 (SAN 212-971X).

Simpson, J. B. & Associates, *(J B Simpson; 0-9603882),* 2345 Oglesby Bridge Rd., Conyers, GA 30208 (SAN 221-6590).

Simpson Publishing Co., *(Simpson Pub),* 1115 S. Franklin St., Kirksville, MO 63501 Tel 816-665-7251 (SAN 202-9928).

Simtek, Inc., *(Simtek; 0-933836),* P.O. Box 109, Cambridge, MA 02139-0109 Tel 617-232-5020 (SAN 212-6907).

Simulation Learning Institute, Inc., *(Simul Learn; 0-918640),* 15 Duke of Gloucester, Manhassett, NY 11030 Tel 516-627-3839 (SAN 210-3702); Orders to: P.O. Box 1014, Manhasset, NY 11030 (SAN 210-3710).

Sinauer Associates, Inc., *(Sinauer Assoc; 0-87893),* N. Main St, Sunderland, MA 01375 Tel 413-665-3722 (SAN 203-2392).

Singer Island Press, *(Singer Island; 0-935860),* 2649 Lake Dr., Singer Island, FL 33404 (SAN 213-800X).

Singer Press, *(Singer Pr; 0-9610922),* 1540 Rollins Dr., Los Angeles, CA 90063 Tel 213-263-2640 (SAN 265-1106).

Singh, Swayam, *(S Singh; 0-935380),* 2311 Meadow Croft Dr., Lansing, MI 48912 (SAN 213-5914).

Singing Horse Press, *(Singing Horse),* 825 Morris Rd., Blue Bell, PA 19422 (SAN 219-2810).

Singing River Pubs., *(Singing River),* 4310 Twin Oaks Ave., Pascagoula, MS 39567 (SAN 239-4855).

Single Impressions, *(Single Impressions; 0-938562),* 642 W. Zia Dr., Tucson, AZ 85704 (SAN 215-8132).

Single Vision Publications, *(Single Vision; 0-9608960),* 2485-Stoltzhill Rd., Lebanon, OR 97355 Tel 503-258-5888 (SAN 241-2519).

Singles World Publishing Co., *(Singles World; 0-936890),* 1094 Cudahy, No. 102, San Diego, CA 92110 (SAN 214-4735); Dist. by: Communication Creativity, P.O. Box 213, Saguache, CO 81149 Tel 303-655-2502 (SAN 210-3478).

Singletary, Milly, *(Singletary; 0-9601256),* 1655 Makaloa St., Suite 906, Honolulu, HI 96814 Tel 808-949-1968 (SAN 210-5039); Dist. by: Press Pacifica, P. O. Box 1227, Kailua, HI 96734 (SAN 169-1635).

Singular Speech Press, *(Singular Speech Pr; 0-9607756),* 507 Dowd Ave., Canton, CT 06019 Tel 203-693-6059 (SAN 238-115X).

Sipapu/Konocti Books, *(Sipapu-Konocti Bks; 0-914134),* Rte. 1, Box 216, Winters, CA 95694 Tel 916-662-3364 (SAN 206-5517).

Sirius League, The, *(Sirius Leag; 0-9610762),* P.O. Box 40507, Albuquerque, NM 87196 Tel 505-262-0720 (SAN 264-6366).

Sirius Pubns., *(Sirius Pubns),* 270 S. La Cienega Blvd., Suite 301, Beverly Hills, CA 90211 (SAN 282-3195); Dist. by: Uri Dowbenko, 2117 14th Ave., San Francisco, CA 94116 Tel 213-706-8838 (SAN 282-3209).

Sister Kenny Institute, *(Sis Kenny Inst; 0-88440),* 800 E. 28th St., Minneapolis, MN 55407 Tel 612-874-4175 (SAN 203-0705).

Sisters, *(Sisters; 0-9610930),* 2205 Minneapolis Ave., Minneapolis, MN 55414 Tel 612-339-9575 (SAN 265-2080).

Sisters' Choice Press, *(Sisters Choice; 0-932164),* 1409Fifth St., Berkeley, CA 94710 Tel 415-524-5804 (SAN 211-7126).

Sisyphus Editions See **Slow Loris Press**

Sitare, Inc., *(Sitare Inc; 0-940178),* 1888 Century Park E., No. 10, Los Angeles, CA 90067 (SAN 217-0833).

Sitnalta Press, *(Sitnalta Pr; 0-931826),* P.O. Box 2730, San Francisco, CA 94126 (SAN 211-5026).

6 Press, *(Six Pr; 0-943310),* 11889 Dogwood Ave., Fountain Valley, CA 92708 Tel 714-839-1857 (SAN 240-7752).

Sixth House Press, Inc., The, *(Sixth House Pr Inc; 0-913911),* P.O. Box 10458, ST. Petersburg, FL 33733 Tel 813-864-1630 (SAN 286-8741).

SK Pubns., *(SK Pubns; 0-936306),* 7149 Natalie Blvd., Northfield Center, OH 44067 (SAN 214-1396).

Skandia America Group, *(Skandia; 0-9609050),* 280 Park Ave., New York, NY 10017 (SAN 240-9062).

Skillcorp Pubs, *(Skillcorp; 0-88085),* 203 Eighth St., Honesdale, PA 18431 Tel 717-253-4558 (SAN 240-2807).
Skillman, Penny, *(P Skillman; 0-9603396),* 487 Prentiss St., San Francisco, CA 94110 (SAN 212-0488).
Skills Improvement, *(Skills Improvement; 0-939570),* P.O. Box 595, Aurora, CO 80040 Tel 303-695-6187 (SAN 216-6968).
Skinny Books, *(Skinny Bks; 0-912499),* Box A 94, New York, NY 10272 Tel 212-732-0358 (SAN 265-2110); 44 Ann St., New York, NY 10038 (SAN 265-2129).
Skipworth Press, Inc., *(Skipworth Pr; 0-931804),* P.O. Box 9367, Richmond, VA 23227 Tel 804-730-1384 (SAN 211-6480).
Skribent Press, *(Skribent),* 9700 S.W. Lakeside Dr., Tigard, OR 97223 (SAN 283-2542).
Sky Pubns., *(Sky Pubns NJ; 0-941566),* 210 Skylands Rd., Ringwood, NJ 07456 (SAN 239-3123).
Sky Publishing Corp., *(Sky Pub; 0-933346),* 49 Bay State Rd., Cambridge, MA 02238 Tel 617-864-7360 (SAN 212-4556).
Skybridge Publishing, Inc., *(Skybridge Pub Inc; 0-911675),* 11 Beltown Rd., P.O. Box 9, Stamford, CT 06905 Tel 203-323-7245 (SAN 264-391X).
Skydog, *(Skydog OR),* 6735 SE 78th St., Portland, OR 97206 (SAN 226-8019).
Skye Terrier Club of America, *(Skye Terrier; 0-9600722),* 2222 S. 12th St., St. Louis, MO 63104 Tel 314-367-4444 (SAN 206-5681).
Skyer Consultation Center, *(Skyer Consul; 0-943106),* P.O. Box 121, Rockaway Park, NY 11694 Tel 212-634-7206 (SAN 240-4427).
Skyflight International, *(Skyflight Intl),* 1505 11th St., Manhattan Beach, CA 90266 (SAN 264-3928).
Skylark *See* **Bantam Books, Inc.**
Skylight Press, Inc., *(Skylight),* 3603 Hamilton St., Philadelphia, PA 19104 (SAN 240-9070).
Skylite Books, *(Skylite Bks; 0-9607770),* 625 N. Michigan Ave., Suite 500, Chicago, IL 60611 Tel 312-922-5522 (SAN 226-8000).
Skyview Publishing, *(Skyview Pub; 0-934618),* Drawer L, Bellmore, NY 11710 Tel 212-255-5550 (SAN 214-2015).
Slack, Inc., *(Slack Inc; 0-913590; 0-943432),* 6900 Grove Rd., Thorofare, NJ 08086 Tel 609-848-1000 (SAN 201-8632).
Slate Services, *(Slate Servs; 0-913448),* P.O. Box 80, Westminster, CA 92683 Tel 714-892-0889 (SAN 203-2384).
Slater, Jaye, Publisher, *(Slater Pub; 0-9607454),* 12911 Newhope St., Garden Grove, CA 92640 Tel 714-530-8825 (SAN 239-801X).
Slavia Library, *(Slavia Lib; 0-918884),* 418 W. Nittany Ave., State College, PA 16801 (SAN 211-0598).
Slavica Publishers Inc., *(Slavica; 0-89357),* P.O. Box 14388, Columbus, OH 43214 Tel 614-268-4002 (SAN 208-8576).
S.L.E. Pubns., *(SLE; 0-9608230),* P.O. Box 52, Kingston, RI 02881 Tel 401-783-4503 (SAN 240-3250).
Sleepy Hollow Press, *(Sleepy Hollow; 0-912882),* 150 White Plains Rd., Tarrytown, NY 10591 Tel 914-631-8200 (SAN 202-0750); Dist. by: Independent Publishers Group, One Pleasant Ave., Port Washington, NY 11050 Tel 516-944-9325 (SAN 202-0769).
Slingerland Comstock Co., *(Slingerland),* RD 1, Box 195, Homer, NY 13077 (SAN 265-4156).
Sloan, M. Ismail, Publishers, *(M Ismail Sloan Pubs),* 917 Old Trents Ferry Rd., Lynchburg, VA 24503 Tel 804-384-1207 (SAN 240-1592).
Slohm, Natalie, Associates, Inc., *(Slohm Assoc; 0-916840),* 49 W. Main St., Cambridge, NY 12816 Tel 518-677-3040 (SAN 282-3217); P.O. Box 273, Cambridge, NY 12816 (SAN 282-3225).
Slough Pr., *(Slough Pr TX; 0-941720),* Box 1385, Austin, TX 78767 Tel 512-474-5488 (SAN 239-3131).
Slovak Institute of Cleveland, Ohio, *(Slov Ins; 0-9610908),* 2900 E. Blvd., Cleveland, OH 44107 Tel 216-721-5300 (SAN 265-1122).
Slow Loris Press, *(Slow Loris; 0-918366),* 923 Highview St., Pittsburgh, PA 15206 (SAN 209-6803).

Slurry Transport Assn., *(Slurry Transport; 0-932066),* 490 L'Enfant Plaza East., S.W. Suite 3210, Washington, DC 20024 (SAN 211-7134).
Small Business Pubns., Inc., *(Small Busn Pubns; 0-9605436),* Box 5 S C 800 Bearses Way, 800beaerses Way Hyannis, MA 02601 (SAN 215-9163).
Small Press Distribution, Inc., *(Small Pr Dist; 0-914068),* 1784 Shattuck Ave., Berkeley, CA 94709 Tel 415-529-3336 (SAN 204-5826).
Small-Scale Master Builder, The, *(Small Master; 0-911215),* P.O. Box Five, San Luis Obispo, CA 93406 (SAN 283-3395).
Smart, *(Smart; 0-942912),* Central Missouri State Univ., Dept. of English, Warrensburg, MO 64093 (SAN 240-3242).
Smith, Allen, Co., Inc., *(A Smith Co; 0-87473),* 1435 N. Meridian St., Indianapolis, IN 46202 Tel 317-634-4098 (SAN 203-0691).
Smith, Carolyn A., *(C A Smith),* 12901 Twisted Oak Rd., Oklahoma City, OK 73120 Tel 405-751-3166 (SAN 214-140X).
Smith, Cortland Gray, *(C G Smith),* 248 Circle Dr., Plandome, NY 11030 Tel 516-627-5856 (SAN 209-1771).
Smith, Doug, *(D Smith; 0-9602728),* P.O. Box 260, Corvallis, OR 97330 Tel 503-754-3434 (SAN 212-8144).
Smith, Harley, Investments, Inc., *(Harley Smith Invest; 0-916350),* 740 West Willow, Stockton, CA 95203 Tel 209-943-1650 (SAN 208-1679).
Smith, Leonard H., Jr., *(L H Smith),* P.O. Box 6745, Clearwater, FL 33518 Tel 813-581-4444 (SAN 205-9819).
Smith, M. Lee, And Associates, *(M L Smith),* 415 Church St, Crescent Bldg, Third Floor, Nashville, TN 37219 (SAN 226-403X).
Smith, Patterson, Publishing Corp., *(Patterson Smith; 0-87585),* 23 Prospect Terrace, Montclair, NJ 07042 Tel 201-744-3291 (SAN 202-8735).
Smith, Peter, Publisher Inc., *(Peter Smith; 0-8446),* 6 Lexington Ave., Magnolia, MA 01930 Tel 617-525-3562 (SAN 206-8885).
Smith, Phoebe, *(P Smith; 0-9602976),* 764 North Ave., Hapeville, GA 30354 (SAN 213-1676).
Smith, Ruth, *(R Smith; 0-9601182),* Box 327, Cooper Sta., New York, NY 10003 Tel 212-260-4374 (SAN 210-0177).
Smith, Toby, *(T Smith; 0-9608762),* 10601 Apache N.E., Albuquerque, NM 87112 Tel 505-294-2865 (SAN 240-0710).
Smith, W. H., Pubs., Inc., *(Smith Pubs; 0-8317),* 112 Madison Ave., New York, NY 10016 Tel 212-532-6600 (SAN 203-3241). *Imprints:* Mayflower Books (Mayflower Bks); Rutledge Press (Rutledge Pr).
Smith, W. R. C., Publishing Co., *(W R C Smith; 0-912476),* 1760 Peachtree Rd., N.W., Atlanta, GA 30357 Tel 404-874-4462 (SAN 202-9391).
Smith, Warren Hunting, Library, *(Smith Lib; 0-939624),* Hobart & William Smith Colleges, Geneva, NY 14456 Tel 315-789-5500 (SAN 216-6275).
Smith & Associates, *(Smith & Assoc; 0-938260),* Box 61648, Houston, TX 77208 Tel 713-932-0518 (SAN 215-8140).
Smith & Smith Publishing Company, *(Smith & Smith Pub; 0-9609230),* 337 Oak Grove, Carriage House, Minnesota, MN 55403 (SAN 241-4570).
Smith College Museum of Art, *(Smith Coll Mus Art),* Elm at Bedford Terrace, Northampton, MA 01063 Tel 413-584-2700 (SAN 282-3233); Dist. by: University of Chicago Press, 5801 Ellis Ave., Chicago, IL 60637 (SAN 202-5280).
Smith College, Pubns., *(Smith Coll; 0-87391),* College Hall 32, Northampton, MA 01063 Tel 413-584-2700 (SAN 204-6032); Dist. by: Neilson Library, Cffice of the Director of Technical Services, Northampton, MA 01063 (SAN 204-6040).
Smith, Frank E., Inc., *(Smith F E; 0-9602288),* 12846 Ironwood Circle, Beacon Woods, Bayonet Point, FL 33567 (SAN 222-3791).
Smith/Nicholas T., *(N T Smith; 0-935164),* P.O. Box 66, Bronxville, NY 10708 Tel 914-337-2794 (SAN 213-6457).
Smith, Smith & Smith Publishing Co., *(S S S Pub Co; 0-913626),* 17515 S.W. Blue Heron Rd., Lake Oswego, OR 97034 Tel 503-636-2979 (SAN 203-3607).

Smith, The, *(The Smith; 0-912292),* 5 Beekman St., New York, NY 10038 Tel 212-732-4821 (SAN 202-7747); Dist. by: Horizon Press, 156 Fifth Ave, New York, NY 10010 (SAN 202-3040).
Smithsonian Books, *(Smithsonian Bks; 0-89599),* 475 L'enfant Plaza, Rm. 2800, Washington, DC 20560 (SAN 216-1974); Dist. by: W. W. Norton & Co., 500 Fifth Ave., New York, NY 10036 Tel 212-354-5500 (SAN 202-5795); Dist. by: Harmony Books, One Park Ave., 17th Floor, New York, NY 10016 Tel 212-532-9200 (SAN 282-7360).
Smithsonian Institution Pr., *(Smithsonian; 0-87474),* Rm. 2280, Arts & Industries Bldg., Washington, DC 20560 Tel 202-357-1912 (SAN 206-8044); Orders to: P.O. Box 1579, Washington, DC 20013 Tel 202-357-1793 (SAN 206-8052) Booksellers Order from: Publications Sales, 1111 N. Capitol St., Washington, DC 20560, Tel- 202-357-1793.
Smoke Shop Press, The, *(Smoke Shop; 0-939572),* 108 Waterman St., No. 2A, Providence, RI 02906 (SAN 216-4515).
Smoley, C. K., & Sons, Inc., *(Smoley; 0-911390),* P.O. Box 274, Grand Haven, MI 49417 Tel 616-842-9449 (SAN 204-6059).
Smoloskyp Pubs., *(Smoloskyp; 0-914834),* P.O. Box 561, Ellicott, MD 21043 Tel 301-461-1764 (SAN 206-1260).
Smugglers Cove Pub., *(Smugglers; 0-918484),* Ben Dennis & Assoc., 107 W. John St., Seattle, WA 98119 Tel 206-285-3171 (SAN 209-8857).
Smyrna Press, *(Smyrna; 0-918266),* P.O. Box 1803, GPO, Brooklyn, NY 11202 Tel 212-638-8939 (SAN 207-897X).
Sneek-A-Peek Books, *(Sneak-A-Peek Bks; 0-943944),* Fontenelle Dam, Kemmerer, WY 83101 Tel 307-877-9615 (SAN 241-1512).
Snipe International, *(Snipe; 0-938740),* 210 Crystal Park Rd., Manitou Springs, CO 80829 Tel 303-685-9044 (SAN 238-7514) Tel 913-841-1773.
SnO Pubns., *(SnO Pubns; 0-937814),* Stockbridge, MA 01262 (SAN 217-1325). *Imprints:* Lenox Library Assn. (Lenox Lib Assn).
Snohomish Publishing, *(Snohomish Pub),* P. O. Box 2188, Soldotna, AK 99669 (SAN 262-0804).
Snow, Helen F., *(H F Snow; 0-911392),* 148 Mungertown Rd., Madison, CT 06443 Tel 203-245-9714 (SAN 206-3131).
Snow Press, *(Snow Pr; 0-9601148),* 9300 Home Court, Des Plaines, IL 60016 Tel 312-299-7605 (SAN 210-3729).
Snowco-Publishing, *(SNOWCO; 0-939230),* 266 N. El Camino Real, Suite D-12, Oceanside, CA 92054 (SAN 216-5112).
Snowstorm Pubns., *(Snowstorm; 0-9605366),* Box 2310, Breckenridge, CO 80424 (SAN 216-194X).
Snug Harbor Cultural Center, *(Snug Harbor NY; 0-9604254),* 914 Richmond Terrace, Staten Island, NY 10301 Tel 212-448-2500 (SAN 214-4751).
Snyder, Walter, Printer, Inc., *(Snyder Inc; 0-9601556),* Troy, NY 12180 (SAN 239-5789).
Snyder Institute of Research, *(Snyder Inst Res),* 508 N. Pacific Coast Hwy., Redondo Beach, CA 90277 Tel 213-372-4469 (SAN 204-9694).
Snyder Publishing Co., *(Snyder Pub Co; 0-9609526),* No. 250, 1275 Fourth St., Santa Rosa, CA 95404 Tel 707-538-7606 (SAN 260-2660).
So & So Press, *(So&So Pr; 0-918842),* 1003 Kieth Ave., Berkeley, CA 94708 Tel 415-525-2781 (SAN 210-3893).
Soap & Detergent Association, *(Soap & Detergent),* 475 Park Ave. South at 32nd St., New York, NY 10016 Tel 212-725-1262 (SAN 224-7089).
Soaring Symposia, *(Soaring Symposia; 0-914600),* Route 1, Box 157-F, Keyser, WV 26726 Tel 301-786-4697 (SAN 202-991X).
Soccer for Americans, *(Soccer for Am; 0-916802),* P.O. Box 836, Manhattan Beach, CA 90266 Tel 213-372-9000 (SAN 208-3787) Do Not Confuse with Sport-Shelf.
Soccer Publications, Inc., *(Soccer Pub Inc; 0-94?752),* 3530 Greer Rd., Palo Alto, CA 94303 (SAN 287-2374).

Social Change Press, *(Soc Change Pr; 0-9609376)*, Box 2212, Sun City, AZ 85372 Tel 602-972-8356 (SAN 260-1370).

Social Interest Press, Inc., The, *(Social Interest; 0-939654)*, 670 Northwestern Ave., Wooster, OH 44691 Tel 216-262-6976 (SAN 216-6453).

Social Issues Resources Series, Inc., *(Soc Issues; 0-89777)*, Box 2507, 4324 Holland Dr., Boca Raton, FL 33431 Tel 305-994-0079 (SAN 222-8920).

Social Matrix Research, Inc., *(Social Matrix; 0-89995)*, P.O. Box 9128, Boston, MA 02114 Tel 617-247-2181 (SAN 213-5922).

Social Science & Sociological Resources, *(Soc Sci & Soc Res; 0-915574)*, P.O. Box 241, Aurora, IL 60507 (SAN 203-235X).

Social Science Education Consortium, Inc, *(Soc Sci Ed; 0-89994)*, 855 Broadway, Boulder, CO 80302 Tel 303-492-8154 (SAN 213-1684).

Social Science Institute, *(Soc Sci Inst; 0-911394)*, Harborside, ME 04642 (SAN 206-3158).

Social Science Press, Inc., *(Soc Sci Pr; 0-911396)*, 100 Oakdale Rd., Athens, GA 30606 Tel 404-542-4581 (SAN 204-6083).

Society for American Baseball Research, *(Soc Am Baseball Res)*, P O Box 323, Cooperstown, NY 13326 Tel 607-547-9988 (SAN 224-5434).

Society for Animal Rights, Inc., *(Soc Animal Rights; 0-9602632)*, 421 S. State St., Clarks Summit, PA 18411 Tel 717-586-2200 (SAN 214-1418).

Society for Common Insights Press, Inc., *(Soc Common Insights; 0-940888)*, 481 Eighth Ave., Suite 926, New York, NY 10001 Tel 212-947-1657 (SAN 223-1158).

Society for Computer Simulation, *(Soc Computer Sim)*, 1010 Pearl St., Ste. Three, P.O. Box 2228, Lajolla, CA 92038 Tel 714-459-3888 (SAN 225-1973).

Society for Individual Liberty OF Genesee Valley, *(Society Indiv Lib; 0-9608490)*, P.O. Box 10224, Rochester, NY 14610 Tel 716-381-1476 (SAN 240-7760).

Society for Industrial & Applied Mathematics, *(Soc Indus-Appl Math; 0-89871)*, 1405 Architects Bldg., 117 S. 17th St., Philadelphia, PA 19103 Tel 215-564-2929 (SAN 206-5207).

Society for Intercultural Education, Training & Research, *(Soc Intercult Ed Train & Res; 0-933934)*, George Washington University, Washington, DC 20057 (SAN 214-1426) Moved, Left No Forwarding Address.

Society for International Development, *(Soc Intl Dev; 0-911402)*, 1834 Jefferson Place, Washington, DC 20036 Tel 202-293-2903 (SAN 204-6075).

Society for New Language Study, Inc., *(Soc New Lang Study; 0-9502699; 0-936072)*, P.O. Box 10596, Denver, CO 80210 Tel 303-777-6115 (SAN 203-2368).

Society for Nutrition Education, *(Soc Nutrition Ed)*, 1736 Franklin St., Oakland, CA 94612 Tel 415-444-7133 (SAN 225-8552).

Society for Technical Communication, *(Soc Tech Comm; 0-914548)*, 815 15th St. N.W., Suite 506, Washington, DC 20005 Tel 202-737-0035 (SAN 206-569X); Dist. by: Univelt, Inc., P.O. Box 28130, San Diego, CA 92128 Tel 714-746-4005 (SAN 204-8868).

Society for the Advancement of Materials & Process Engineering (S.A.M.P.E.), *(Soc Adv Material)*, Box 613, Azusa, CA 91702 Tel 213-334-1810 (SAN 207-2866).

Society for the Promotion of Science & Scholarship, Inc., *(SPOSS; 0-930664)*, 4139 el Camino Way, Palo Alto, CA 94306 Tel 415-493-4400 (SAN 211-3473).

Society for the Scientific Study of Religion, *(Soc Sci Stud Rel; 0-932566)*, Box U-68A, Univ. of Connecticut, Storrs, CT 06268 (SAN 212-1670).

Society for Visual Education, Inc., *(Soc for Visual; 0-89290)*, 1345 W. Diversey Pkwy., Chicago, IL 60614 Tel 312-525-1500 (SAN 208-3930).

Society of American Archivists, *(Soc Am Archivists; 0-931828)*, 330 S. Wells St., Suite 810, Chicago, IL 60606 Tel 312-922-0140 (SAN 211-7614).

Society of American Foresters, *(Soc Am Foresters; 0-939970)*, 5400 Grosvenor Lane, Bethesda, MD 20014 Tel 301-897-8720 (SAN 216-8561).

Society of Economic Paleontologists and Mineralogists, *(SEPM)*, Box 4756, Tulsa, OK 74159 Tel 918-743-9765 (SAN 260-3462).

Society of Exploration Geophysicists, *(Soc Exploration; 0-931830)*, P.O. Box 3098, Tulsa, OK 74101 Tel 918-743-1365 (SAN 206-2844).

Society of Fire Protection Engineers, *(Society Fire Protect)*, 60 Batterymarch St., Boston, MA 02110 Tel 617-482-0686 (SAN 209-3863).

Society of Industrial Realtors Educational Fund, Div. of National Associaton of Realtors, *(Soc Industrial Realtors)*, 777 14th St., N.W., Washington, DC 20005 Tel 202-383-1150 (SAN 202-0718).

Society of Manufacturing Engineers, *(SME; 0-87263)*, P.O. Box 930, One SME Dr., Dearborn, MI 48128 Tel 513-271-1080 (SAN 203-2376).

Society of Mining Engineers of A. I. M. E., *(Soc Mining Eng; 0-89520)*, Caller No. D, Littleton, CO 80127 Tel 303-973-9550 (SAN 203-1485).

Society of Motion Picture and Television Engineers, *(Soc Motion Pic & TV Engrs)*, 862 Scardale Ave, Scarsdale, NY 10583 Tel 914-472-6600 (SAN 224-0173).

Society of Naval Architects & Marine Engineers, *(Soc Naval Arch; 0-9603048)*, One World Trade Center, 1369, New York, NY 10048 Tel 212-432-0310 (SAN 202-0572).

Society of North American Goldsmiths, *(SNAG; 0-9604446)*, 2849 St. Ann Dr., Green Bay, WI 54301 (SAN 215-1081).

Society of Nuclear Medicine, Inc., *(Soc Nuclear Med; 0-932004)*, 475 Park Ave. S., New York, NY 10016 Tel 212-889-0717 (SAN 212-5625).

Society of Photo-Optical Instrumentation Engineers, *(Photo-Optical; 0-89252)*, P.O. Box 10, 405 Fieldston Rd., Bellingham, WA 98225 Tel 206-676-3290 (SAN 205-3845).

Society of Photographic Scientists & Engineers, *(Soc Photo Sci & Eng; 0-89208)*, 1411 "K" St., N.W., Suite 930, Washington, DC 20005 Tel 202-347-1140 (SAN 203-5626).

Society of Pragmatic Mysticism, *(Soc Pragmatic; 0-89369)*, 200 W. 58th St., Apt. 9B, New York, NY 10019 Tel 212-246-5464 (SAN 207-2874) Moved, Left No Forwarding Address.

Society of Spanish & Spanish-American Studies, *(Society Sp & Sp-Am; 0-89295)*, Dept. of Modern Languages & Literatures, Univ. of Nebraska-Lincoln, Lincoln, NE 68588 Tel 402-472-3842 (SAN 208-3221).

Society of the Descendants of Washington's Army at Valley Forge, *(SDWA; 0-9606828)*, P.O. Box 915, Valley Forge, PA 19481 (SAN 239-3913).

Society of Wood Science & Technology, *(Soc Wood)*, Box 5062, Madison, WI 53705 (SAN 260-3470).

Sociology Press, *(Sociology Pr)*, P.O. Box 400, Mill Valley, CA 94942 (SAN 212-7962).

S O C O Pubns., *(S O C O Pubns)*, 115 Willis Ave., Box 733, Herkimer, NY 13350 (SAN 241-5720).

Softalk Publishing, Inc., *(Softalk Pub; 0-88701)*, 11160 McCormick, Box 60, North Hollywood, CA 91603 Tel 213-980-5074 (SAN 283-4111).

Software House, *(Software Hse; 0-912055)*, 1105 Mass. Ave., Cambridge, MA 02138 Tel 617-661-9440 (SAN 264-6374).

Software Supply, *(Software Supply; 0-9603792)*, 4618 E. Sixth St., Long Beach, CA 90814 (SAN 214-1434).

Soggy Cracker Press, *(Soggy Cracker Pr; 0-9607934)*, 1136 S.E. 32nd Terrace, Cape Coral, FL 33904 (SAN 239-863X).

Soho Bodhi, *(Soho Bodhi; 0-9605096)*, 242 Lafayette St., New York, NY 10012 (SAN 216-1958).

Soil Conservation Society of America, *(Soil Conservation; 0-935734)*, 7515 N.E. Ankeny Rd., Ankeny, IA 50021 (SAN 213-6961).

Soil Science Society of America, *(Soil Sci Soc Am)*, 677 S. Segoe Rd., Madison, WI 53711 Tel 608-274-1212 (SAN 206-2879).

Sokoloff, Valentin A., *(Sokoloff; 0-9607438)*, 773 Cypress Ave., San Bruno, CA 94066 Tel 415-589-4511 (SAN 239-4863).

Sol Press *See* **Wisconsin Bks.**

Solar Age Press, *(Solar Age Pr; 0-914304)*, Indian Mills, WV 24949 (SAN 208-8630).

Solar Energy Information Services (SEIS), *(Solar Energy Info; 0-930978; 0-89934)*, P.O. Box 19475, Sacramento, CA 95819 Tel 916-739-1376 (SAN 282-5902).

Solar Energy Institute of North America, *(SEINAM)*, 1110 6th St., N.W., Washington, DC 20001 (SAN 211-3015).

Solar Studio, The, *(Solar Studio; 0-932320)*, 178 Cowles Rd., Woodbury, CT 06798 Tel 203-263-3147 (SAN 222-8823).

Solar Training Pubns., *(Solar Training; 0-940894)*, 10921 W. Exposition Dr., Lakewood, CO 80226 Tel 303-989-1611 (SAN 219-6360).

Solaris Press, Inc., *(Solaris Pr)*, P.O. Box 1009, Rochester, MI 48063 (SAN 262-0820).

SolarVision Publications, *(SolarVision; 0-918984)*, Church Hill, Harrisville, NH 03450 Tel 603-827-3347 (SAN 210-508X).

Soldier Creek Press, *(Soldier Creek; 0-936996)*, Box 863, Lake Crystal, MN 56055 Tel 507-726-2985 (SAN 215-9171).

S.O.L.E. Pubns., *(S O L E Pubns; 0-9608626)*, P. O. Box 2063, Beaverton, OR 97075 (SAN 238-3624).

Solidarity Pubns., *(Solidarity; 0-942638)*, P.O. Box 40874, San Francisco, CA 94140 Tel 415-626-6626 (SAN 238-5724).

Solipaz Publishing Co., *(Solipaz Pub Co; 0-913999)*, P.O. Box 623, Stockton, CA 95201 Tel 209-368-1595 (SAN 286-8814).

Solo Music, Inc., *(Solo; 0-913754)*, 4708 Van Noord Ave., Sherman Oaks, CA 91423 Tel 213-762-2219 (SAN 206-7692).

Solo Press, *(Solo Pr)*, 7975 Ssan Marcos, Atascadero, CA 93422 Tel 805-466-0947 (SAN 206-3794).

Solo Press, *(Solo Press MA; 0-941866)*, 1009 Mass. Ave., Lexington, MA 02173 Tel 617-861-1340 (SAN 239-3158).

Solo Publishing, Inc., *(Solo Inc; 0-9610216)*, 14450 N. E. 29th Pl., Suite 115, Bellevue, WA 98007 Tel 206-882-3303 (SAN 275-6595).

Solobooks, *(Solobooks; 0-939004)*, P.O. Box 2292, Modesto, CA 95351 (SAN 216-4523) Moved, Left No Forwarding Address.

Solpub Co., *(Solpub; 0-931912)*, 10707 Odyssey, Houston, TX 77099 Tel 713-879-5932 (SAN 212-7970).

Solus Impress, *(Solus Impress)*, Porthill, ID 83853 (SAN 262-0839).

Soma Press, *(Soma Pr; 0-932510)*, P.O. Box 416, Yellow Springs, OH 45387 (SAN 222-8858).

Soma Press of California, *(Soma Pr Cal; 0-943564)*, P.O. Box 3682, Pinedale, CA 93650 Tel 209-439-4829 (SAN 238-3772).

Somerset Hse., *(Somerset Hse; 0-914146; 0-89887; 0-85964)*, 206 N. Alfred St., Alexandria, VA 22314 Tel 703-549-7369 (SAN 282-3306); Orders to: 623 Martense Ave., Teaneck, NJ 07666 Tel 201-692-1801 (SAN 282-3314).

Somerset Press, *(Somerset Pr IL; 0-916642)*, Executive Dr., Carol Stream, IL 60187 Tel 312-665-3200 (SAN 214-3267).

Somerset Pubs., Div. of Scholarly Press, Inc., *(Somerset Pub)*, 200 Park Ave., Suite 303E, New York, NY 10017 Tel 313-884-0440 (SAN 204-6105).

Sometime Press, Inc., *(Sometime Pr; 0-936230)*, 216 Pleasant St., Marblehead, MA 01945 (SAN 214-1442).

Somrie Press, *(Somrie Pr; 0-9603950)*, Ryder Street Station; Box 328, Brooklyn, NY 11234 (SAN 214-1450).

Sonica Press, *(Sonica Pr)*, P.O. Box 42720, Los Angeles, CA 90042 Tel 213-666-7197 (SAN 216-1966).

Sono Pubs., *(Sono Pubs; 0-916898)*, 554 N. Arden Blvd., Los Angeles, CA 90004 Tel 213-467-3597 (SAN 208-8649).

Sonoma County Bike Trails, *(Sonoma County)*, 50 Crest Way, Penngrove, CA 94951 (SAN 215-7098).

Sonoran Press, *(Sonoran; 0-943332)*, Box 423, Youngtown, AZ 85363 Tel 602-974-0720 (SAN 240-5687).

SONrise Productions, *(Sonrise Prods)*, 746 E. 79th St., Box 186, Chicago, IL 60619 (SAN 215-8159).

NAME INDEX

Sons of Liberty, Div. of New Christian Crusade Church, *(Sons Lib; 0-89562)*, Box 214, Metairie, LA 70004 Tel 504-887-3217 (SAN 210-6663).

Sooty-Face Publishing Co., *(Sooty-Face; 0-9602366)*, P.O. Box 26, Clairton, PA 15025 Tel 412-233-6141 (SAN 212-5633).

Sophia Press, *(Sophia Pr; 0-9609378)*, P.O. Box 533, Durham, NH 03824 Tel 603-868-2318 (SAN 260-1397).

Soque Publishers, *(Soque; 0-9608770)*, Rt 3, Clarkesville, GA 30523 Tel 404-947-3440 (SAN 238-3780).

Sorger Associates Inc., *(Sorger Assocs; 0-9604072)*, 229 Humphrey St., Marblehead, MA 01945 (SAN 214-1469).

Soules, Gordon, Economic Marketing Research, *(Gordon Soules Econ; 0-919574)*, 507 Third Ave., Suite 1240, Seattle, WA 98104 (SAN 208-2845).

Sound Advice Enterprises, *(Sound Advice; 0-943668)*, 25 W. Dunes Lane, Port Washington, NY 11050 Tel 516-883-4400 (SAN 238-3799).

Sound Nutrition, *(Sound Nut; 0-9609226)*, 55 S. 100 East, Payson, UT 84651 Tel 801-465-2657 (SAN 241-4597).

Sound Publishing Co., *(Sound Pub)*, 156 E. 37th St., New York, NY 10016 Tel 212-685-3480 (SAN 206-2909).

Soup to Nuts Press, *(Soup to Nuts; 0-9604780)*, 582 Fernando Dr., Novato, CA 94947 (SAN 215-918X).

Sourcebook Project, The, *(Sourcebook; 0-9600712; 0-915554)*, P.O. Box 107, Glen Arm, MD 21057 Tel 301-668-6047 (SAN 201-7652).

Sourcebook Pubns., Inc., *(Sourcebook Pubns FL; 0-939412)*, P.O. Box 1586, Winter Park, FL 32790 Tel 305-628-0545 (SAN 213-5930).

Sourcebooks, *(Sourcebooks CA; 0-933422)*, 18758 Bryant St., Northridge, CA 91324 (SAN 213-1692).

Sources, *(Sources; 0-9603232)*, 26 Hart Ave., Hopewell, NJ 08525 Tel 609-466-0051 (SAN 211-5182).

Sourdough Enterprises, *(Sourdough; 0-911803)*, 16301 3rd Ave. SW, Seattle, WA 98166 Tel 206-244-8115 (SAN 264-3987).

South Asia Books, *(South Asia Bks; 0-88386; 0-8364)*, P.O. Box 502, Columbia, MO 65205 Tel 314-449-1359 (SAN 207-4044).

South Carolina Educational Communications, Inc., *(South Carolina; 0-943274)*, 19 Springdale Lane, Spartanburg, SC 29302 (SAN 240-6314).

South Carolina Magazine of Ancestral Research (SCMAR), *(S C M A R; 0-913363)*, P.O. Box 21766, Columbia, SC 29221 Tel 803-772-6919 (SAN 285-8525).

South Dakota Peace Officers Assn., *(SD Peace Officers; 0-9608456)*, 3102 Pine Tree Trail, Sturgis, SD 57785 Tel 605-677-5242 (SAN 240-5695).

South End Press, *(South End Pr; 0-89608)*, 302 Columbus Ave, Boston, MA 02116 Tel 617-266-0629 (SAN 211-979X).

South Group Pubs., Ltd., *(South Group; 0-940842)*, 30 Main St., Port Washington, NY 11050 Tel 516-944-6161 (SAN 219-6379).

South Pass Press, *(South Pass Pr; 0-932068)*, 8338 E. Gilbert, Wichita, KS 67207 (SAN 204-6121).

South Platte Press, *(South Platte; 0-9609568)*, P.O. Box 163, David City, NE 68632 Tel 402-367-4734 (SAN 262-0855).

South Salem News, *(S Salem News; 0-9610326)*, 178 Harvard Ct. SE, Salem, OR 97302 (SAN 264-4002).

South Street Seaport Museum, *(South St Sea Mus; 0-913344)*, 203 Front St., New York, NY 10038 Tel 212-766-9020 (SAN 282-3322).

South-Western Publishing Co., *(SW Pub; 0-538)*, 5101 Madison Rd., Cincinnati, OH 45227 Tel 513-271-8811 (SAN 202-7518).

SouthArt, Inc., *(SouthArt Inc)*, P.O. Box 5304, Hilton Head Island, SC 29938 Tel 803-671-2576 (SAN 264-7931).

Southeast Acoustics Institute, *(Southeast Acoustics; 0-89671)*, P.O. Box 590, Madison, GA 30650 Tel 912-212-6915).

Southeast Asia Resource Center, *(SE Asia Res Ctr; 0-9604518)*, 198 Broadway, Room 302, New York, NY 10038 Tel 415-548-2546 (SAN 207-7647).

Southern Appalachian Resource Catalog, *(S Appalachian Res)*, Rt. 1, Box 71A, Warne, NC 28909 Tel 704-389-8323 (SAN 215-109X).

Southern California Committee for the Olympic Games, *(S CA Committee; 0-9606628)*, 626 Wilshire Blvd., Suite 1000, Los Angeles, CA 90017 (SAN 219-6387).

Southern Center for International Studies, Inc., *(Southern Ctr Intl Stud; 0-935082)*, 3400 Peachtree Rd., N.E., Suite 1239, Lenox Towers, Atlanta, GA 30326 Tel 404-261-5763 (SAN 213-375X).

Southern Historical Press, *(Southern Hist Pr; 0-89308)*, P.O. Box 738, Easley, SC 29640 Tel 803-859-2336 (SAN 208-8657).

Southern Illinois Univ. Press, *(S Ill U Pr; 0-8093)*, P.O. Box 3697, Carbondale, IL 62901 Tel 618-453-2281 (SAN 203-3623).

Southern-Lite Publishing Co., *(Southern-Lite; 0-942050)*, P.O. Box 12187, Atlanta, GA 30355 Tel 239-4871).

Southern Methodist Univ. Press, *(SMU Press; 0-87074)*, Dallas, TX 75275 Tel 214-692-2263 (SAN 203-3615).

Southern Ohio Genealogical Society, *(S Ohio Genealog; 0-941000)*, P.O. Box 414, Hillsboro, OH 45133 Tel 513-393-2452 (SAN 219-6395).

Southern Oregon Historical Society, *(South Oregon; 0-943388)*, P.O. Box 480, 206 N. Fifth St., Jacksonville, OR 97530 Tel 503-899-1847 (SAN 240-7779).

Southern Regional Education Board, *(S Regional Ed)*, 130 Sixth St., N.W., Atlanta, GA 30313 Tel 404-875-9211 (SAN 206-1783).

Southern Research Institute, *(S Res Inst)*, 2000 Ninth Ave., S., Birmingham, AL 35255 Tel 205-323-6592 (SAN 206-1791).

Southern Univ. Press, *(Southern U Pr; 0-87651)*, 130 S. 19th St., Birmingham, AL 35233 (SAN 204-6148).

Southland Specialty Publications Companies, *(Southland Spec; 0-911041)*, 2170 W. Broadway, No. 202, Anaheim, CA 92804 Tel 714-635-0251 (SAN 263-0087).

Southwest American Publishing Co., *(SW Amer Pub Co; 0-911217)*, 5720 North 1-35 Industrial Blvd., Edmond, OK 73034 (SAN 264-4010).

Southwest Missouri State Univ., Dept. of English, *(S M S U; 0-913785)*, Springfield, MO 65804 Tel 417-836-5107 (SAN 286-1992).

Southwest Museum, *(Southwest Mus)*, P.O. Box 128, Highland Park Sta., Los Angeles, CA 90042 Tel 213-221-2164 (SAN 203-0683).

Southwest Natural History Association, The, *(SW Nat Hist Assn; 0-9610126)*, P.O. Box 35141, Phoenix, AZ 85069 Tel 602-973-0591 (SAN 275-7214).

Southwest Parks & Monuments Assn., *(SW Pks Mnmts; 0-911408)*, P.O. Box 1562, Globe, AZ 85501 Tel 602-425-8183 (SAN 202-750X).

Southwest Scientific Publishing, *(SW Sci Pub; 0-9606246)*, P.O. Box 10, Dalhart, TX 79022 Tel 806-249-4727 (SAN 220-3553).

Southwestern Art Assn., *(SW Art Assn)*, P.O. Box 52510, Tulsa, OK 74152 (SAN 215-9015).

Southwestern Mission Research Center, *(SW Mission; 0-915076)*, Arizona State Museum, Tucson, AZ 85721 (SAN 215-8167).

Sovereign Bks., Div. of Simon & Schuster, *(Sovereign Bks)*, c/o Cornerstone Library, 1230 Ave. of the Americas, New York, NY 10020 Tel 212-245-6400 (SAN 200-2442).

Sovereign Press, *(Sovereign Pr; 0-914752)*, 326 Harris Rd., Rochester, WA 98579 Tel 206-273-5109 (SAN 206-1279).

Soviet Studies, *(Soviet Studies; 0-930232)*, P.O. Box 16, Hayward, CA 94543 (SAN 210-6671).

Sowa Books, *(Sowa Bks; 0-9605638)*, 4923 Brandeis Circle, San Antonio, TX 78249 (SAN 216-1826).

Soyfoods Center, *(Soyfoods Center; 0-933332)*, P.O. Box 234, Lafayette, CA 94549 Tel 415-283-2991 (SAN 212-8411).

Space/Time Designs, Inc., *(Space-Time; 0-9603570)*, P.O. Box 1989, Sedona, AZ 86336 Tel 602-282-3639 (SAN 213-3776).

SPAFASWAP, *(SPAFASWAP)*, 1070 Ahern Dr., La Puente, CA 91746 Tel 213-962-3910 (SAN 209-7737).

Spangler, Richard J.,, *(R J Spangler)*, 9000 Keystone Crossing, P.O. Box 40946, Indianapolis, IN 46240 (SAN 265-3621).

Spanish Literature Pubns. Co., Inc., *(Spanish Lit Pubns; 0-938972)*, Box 707, York, SC 29745 (SAN 216-3039).

Spanish Publicity, *(Spanish Pub; 0-9607386)*, 200 Prairie Dell, Austin, TX 78752 (SAN 239-488X).

Sparhawk Books, Inc., *(Sparhawk; 0-9605776)*, Pierce Crossing Rd., Jaffrey, NH 03452 Tel 603-532-9337 (SAN 216-5538).

Sparks Press, *(Sparks Pr; 0-916822)*, 900 W. Morgan St., P.O. Box 26747, Raleigh, NC 27611 Tel 919-834-8283 (SAN 208-8673).

Sparrow Press, *(Sparrow Pr; 0-935552)*, 103 Waldron St., West Lafayette, IN 47906 Tel 317-743-1991 (SAN 205-0730).

Sparrow Pubns., *(Sparrow Pub NY; 0-9611460)*, 799 Ave.of the Americas, New York, NY 10036 Tel 212-741-0254 (SAN 285-1296); Orders to: P.O. Box 1980, Rockefeller Center Sta., New York, NY 10020 (SAN 285-130X).

Sparrow Publishing, *(Sparrow Pub; 0-942818)*, W. 308 S. 7144 Hwy One, Mukwonago, WI 53149 Tel 414-968-2803 (SAN 238-8634).

Spears, W. H., Jr., *(Spears; 0-9600146)*, 426 N. Kennicott, Arlington Heights, IL 60004 (SAN 204-6180).

Special Aviation Pubns., *(Spec Aviation; 0-915376)*, Rte. One, Box 730, China Spring, TX 76633 Tel 817-836-4269 (SAN 208-8681).

Special Child Pubns., *(Spec Child; 0-87562)*, P.O. Box 33548, Seattle, WA 98133 Tel 206-771-5711 (SAN 203-2317).

Special Features Workshop, *(Spec Features Wkshp; 0-917466)*, 32 Warnock Dr., Westport, CT 06880 Tel 203-226-9370 (SAN 209-0767).

Special Learning Corp., *(Spec Learn Corp; 0-89568)*, P.O. Box 306, Guilford, CT 06437 Tel 203-453-6525 (SAN 211-4542).

Special Libraries Assn., *(SLA; 0-87111)*, 235 Park Avenue S., New York, NY 10003 Tel 212-477-9250 (SAN 204-6024).

Special Literature Press, *(Spec Lit Pr)*, P.O. Box 4397, Benson Sta., Omaha, NE 68104 (SAN 215-8175).

Specialist Publishing Co., The, *(Specialist; 0-911416)*, 109 La Mesa Dr., Burlingame, CA 94010 Tel 415-344-4958 (SAN 204-6199).

Specialty Books, International, *(Specialty Bks; 0-89445)*, P.O. Box 1785, Ann Arbor, MI 48106 Tel 517-456-4764 (SAN 210-2714).

Specialty Press, Inc., *(Spec Pr NJ; 0-913556)*, P.O. Box 2187, Ocean, NJ 07712 Tel 201-774-8447 (SAN 202-0831).

Specialty Press Pubs. & Wholesalers, Inc., *(Specialty Pr; 0-933424)*, Box 426, 729 Prospect Ave., Osceola, WI 54020 Tel 715-294-2090 (SAN 212-6230).

Specialty Publishing Co., *(Spec Pub; 0-939850)*, P.O. Box 1355, La Crosse, WI 54601 Tel 608-783-6470 (SAN 216-9339).

Spectromini, *(Spectromini; 0-943946)*, P.O. Box 177, 168 Genesee Street, Utica, NY 13503 Tel 315-735-2406 (SAN 241-1520).

Spectrum Books See **Prentice-Hall, Inc.**

Spectrum Financial Press, *(Spectrum Fin Pr; 0-911711)*, 1225 Crane St., Box 1146, Menlo Park, CA 94025 Tel 415-321-9111 (SAN 264-4037).

Spectrum Productions, *(Spectrum Prods; 0-914502)*, 979 Casiano Rd., Los Angeles, CA 90049 Tel 213-476-4543 (SAN 202-9898) Do Not Confuse with Spectrum Publications or Spectrum Books.

Speech Foundation of America, *(Speech Found Am; 0-933388)*, P.O. Box 11749, Memphis, TN 38111 (SAN 282-3330); 5139 Klingle St., Washington, DC 20016 (SAN 282-3349).

Speech Science Publications, *(Speech Science)*, 889 Sanford Court, Santa Barbara, CA 93111 (SAN 262-0863).

Speechphone Institute See **Norton, Jeffrey, Pubs., Inc.**

Speedball Publications, *(Detroit Guide; 0-9600448)*, 15365 Glastonbury, Detroit, MI 48223 (SAN 218-4567).

Speer Books, *(Speer Bks; 0-917832)*, 333 Ash St., Red Bluff, CA 96080 (SAN 208-3566).

Speleo Press, *(Speleo Pr; 0-914092)*, P.O. Box 7037, Austin, TX 78712 Tel 512-847-2709 (SAN 206-5754).

Speller, Robert, & Sons, Pubs., Inc., *(Speller; 0-8315)*, 30 E. 23rd St., New York, NY 10108 Tel 212-477-5524 (SAN 203-2295); Orders to: P.O. Box 461, Times Square Sta., New York, NY 10036 (SAN 203-2309).

Spencer Butte Press, *(S Butte Pr; 0-9609420)*, 84889 Harry Taylor Rd., Eugene, OR 97405 Tel 503-345-3962 (SAN 262-916X)

Spencer Institute, The, *(Spencer Inst)*, Eight Burnside Rd., Newton, MA 02161 Tel 617-244-7384 (SAN 205-5651).

Spencer Judd, Publishers, *(S Judd Pubs; 0-911805)*, 6 University Ave., Sewanee, TN 37375 Tel 615-598-5353 (SAN 264-4045).

Spevack, Jerome M., Inc., *(Spevack; 0-9604480)*, 104 N. E. Lakeview Dr., No. 12, Sebring, FL 33870 Tel 813-382-1761 (SAN 215-1103).

Spex International, Ltd., *(Spex Intl; 0-943816)*, 51 E. 42nd St., Suite 517, New York, NY 10017 Tel 212-490-0077 (SAN 238-3802).

Sphinx Pr., *(Sphinx Pr)*, c/o International Universities Pr., Inc., 315 Fifth Ave., New York, NY 10016 (SAN 202-7186).

Spice West Co., *(Spice West; 0-9602812)*, Box 2044, Pocatello, ID 83201 (SAN 214-476X).

Spilman Press, Subs. of Spilman Printing Co., *(Spilman Pr; 0-918180)*, 1801 9th St., Sacramento, CA 95814 Tel 916-444-0411 (SAN 210-2722).

Spin-A-Test Pub. Co., *(Spin-A-Test Pub; 0-915048)*, 404 Old Orchard Ct., Danville, CA 94526 Tel 415-837-4532 (SAN 282-3500); Dist. by: J.R. Holcomb Co., 3000 Quigley Rd., Cleveland, OH 44113 Tel 216-621-6580 (SAN 282-5856); Dist. by: The Black & Taylor Co., 50 Kirby Ave., Somerville, NJ 08876 Tel 201-722-8000 (SAN 169-4901); Dist. by: Educational Exchange, 600 35th Ave., San Francisco, CA 94101 Tel 415-752-3302 (SAN 282-3535).

Spindrift Press, *(Spindrift; 0-914864)*, P.O. Box 3252, Catonsville, MD 21228 Tel 301-944-3317 (SAN 206-3808).

Spinning Spool, *(Spinning Spool)*, P.O. Box 1425, East Lansing, MI 48823 Tel 517-332-3729 (SAN 207-2890).

Spinsters, Ink, *(Spinsters Ink; 0-933216)*, 233 Dolores No. 8, San Francisco, CA 94103 Tel 415-431-9082 (SAN 212-6923).

Spire Books See Revell, Fleming H., Co.

Spirit Mountain Press, *(Spirit Mount Pr; 0-910871)*, P.O. Box 1214, Fairbanks, AK 99707 (SAN 283-9156).

Spirit That Moves Us, The, *(Spirit That Moves; 0-930370)*, P.O. Box 1585, Iowa City, IA 52244 Tel 319-338-5569 (SAN 210-8585).

Spiritual Advisory Press, *(Spiritual Advisory; 0-939386)*, P.O. Box 6344, Santa Barbara, CA 93160-6344 (SAN 216-3047).

Spiritual Community Pubns., *(Spiritual Comm; 0-913852)*, P.O. Box 1067, Berkely, CA 94701 Tel 415-644-3229 (SAN 203-2287).

Spiritual Renaissance Press, *(Spiritual Renaissance; 0-938380)*, P.O. Box 347, Berkeley, CA 94701 Tel 415-540-8366 (SAN 220-1259); Dist. by: Bookpeople, 2940 Seventh St., Berkeley, CA 94710 Tel 415-549-3030 (SAN 168-9517).

Spiritual Science Library See Garber Communications, Inc.

Spiritwarrior Publishing Co., *(Spiritwarrior Pub; 0-940298)*, 306 Cecil St., Waynoka, OK 73880 (SAN 217-5851).

Spiritwood Publishers, *(Spiritwood Pub; 0-9611928)*, 421 Queen N., Minneapolis, MN 55405 Tel 612-377-4259 (SAN 283-3409).

Spizzirri Pub. Co., Inc., *(Spizzirri; 0-86545)*, P.O. Box 664, Medinah, IL 60157 Tel 312-529-1181 (SAN 215-2851).

Spohler/Albert A., *(A A Spohler; 0-9606580)*, P.O. Box 2322, Palos Verdes, CA 90274 Tel 213-375-7775 (SAN 207-1983); 5417 Littlebow Rd., Palos Verdes, CA 90274 (SAN 207-1991).

Spoken Language Services, Inc., *(Spoken Lang Serv; 0-87950)*, P.O. Box 783, Ithaca, NY 14850 Tel 607-257-0500 (SAN 203-2279).

Spoon River Poetry Press, *(Spoon Riv Poetry; 0-933180)*, P.O. Box 1443, Peoria, IL 61655 Tel 309-676-7611 (SAN 210-8593) Do Not Confuse with the Spoon River Press.

Spoon River Press, The, *(Spoon River; 0-930358)*, P.O. Box 3635, Peoria, IL 61614 Tel 309-673-2266 (SAN 211-5190) Do Not Confuse with Spoon River Poetry Press.

Spoonwood Pr., *(Spoonwood Pr)*, 99 Pratt St., Suite 408, Hartford, CT 06103 Tel 203-246-7200 (SAN 219-855X).

Spore Prints, *(Spore Prints; 0-9612020)*, 2985 Scaramento Dr., Redding, CA 96001 Tel 916-246-4834 (SAN 283-3433).

Sporting News Publishing Co., *(Sporting News; 0-8297)*, 1212 N. Lindbergh Blvd. P.O.Box 56, St. Louis, MO 63166 Tel 314-997-7111 (SAN 203-2260).

Sports Fishing Institute, *(Sport Fishing; 0-9602382)*, 608 13th St. N.W., Suite 801, Washington, DC 20005 Tel 202-737-0668 (SAN 210-9719).

Sportsbooks, *(Sportsbks; 0-939468)*, Box 494, Bolivar, NY 14715 Tel 716-928-2825 (SAN 220-1887).

Sportsguide, Inc., *(Sportsguide; 0-935644)*, P.O. Box 1417, Princeton, NJ 08542 Tel 609-921-8599 (SAN 213-5590).

Sportshelf & Soccer Associates, *(Sportshelf; 0-392)*, P.O. Box 634, New Rochelle, NY 10802 Tel 914-235-2347 (SAN 202-5388).

SPOSS, Inc. See Society for the Promotion of Science & Scholarship, Inc.

Spriggle, Howard, *(H Spriggle)*, Rte 2, Box U160, Lewes, DE 19958 (SAN 211-271X).

Spring Hill Center, *(Spring Hill; 0-932676)*, Box 288, Wayzata, MN 55391 (SAN 212-2332).

Spring Manufacturers Institute, Inc., *(Spring Manufac; 0-9604120)*, 1211 W. 22nd St., Oak Brook, IL 60521 (SAN 218-4451).

Spring Pubns., Inc., *(Spring Pubns; 0-88214)*, P.O. Box 222069, Dallas, TX 75222 Tel 214-698-0933 (SAN 203-2244).

Springer Publishing Co., Inc., *(Springer Pub; 0-8261)*, 200 Park Ave., S., New York, NY 10003 Tel 212-475-6580 (SAN 203-2236).

Springer-Verlag New York, Inc., *(Springer-Verlag; 0-387)*, 175 Fifth Avenue, New York, NY 10010 Tel 212-460-1500 (SAN 203-2228).

Springfield Art Museum, *(Springfield; 0-934306)*, 1111 E. Brookside Dr., Springfield, MO 65807 Tel 417-866-2716 (SAN 213-5957).

Springfield Historical Commission, *(Spring Historical; 0-943572)*, Planning Dept., Springfield City Hall, Springfield, OR 97477 Tel 503-686-9961 (SAN 240-7787).

Springfield Library & Museum Assn., *(Springfield Lib & Mus)*, 220 State St., Springfield, MA 01103 (SAN 214-2228).

Springfield Publishing Co., *(Springfield Pub Co; 0-937500)*, 213-701-6821, Northridge, CA 91328 Tel 213-886-2317 (SAN 220-0937).

Springfield Research Service, *(Springfield Res Serv; 0-9603306)*, P. O. Bx 4181, Silver Spring, MD 20904 (SAN 221-7058).

Springhill Press, The, *(Springhill Pr MD; 0-939972)*, P.O. Box 1762, Silver Spring, MD 20902 Tel 301-649-6666 (SAN 216-857X).

Springtide Books, *(Springtide; 0-910873)*, 30 Watkins Rd., Brick, NJ 08723 Tel 201-458-1543 (SAN 262-0871).

Springtime Pubns., *(Springtime)*, 11832 Timmy Lane, Garden Grove, CA 92640 Tel 213-542-3990 (SAN 218-5067).

Sproing Books, *(Sproing; 0-916176)*, 3721 Barcelona St., Tampa, FL 33609 (SAN 206-3816).

Sprout Pubns. Inc., *(Sprout Pubns; 0-932972)*, P.O. Box 4064, Sarasota, FL 33578 Tel 813-349-6535 (SAN 212-6931).

Spurr, John, Design, *(Spurr Design; 0-931312)*, P.O. Box 11249, Palo Alto, CA 94306 (SAN 211-2043).

Sputz, David, *(Sputz; 0-9604312)*, 611 Bedford Ave., Brooklyn, NY 11211 (SAN 215-1847).

Spuyten Duyvil, *(S Duyvil)*, 520 Cathedral Parkway, New York, NY 10025 (SAN 237-9481).

Squadron Signal Pubns., *(Squad Sig Pubns; 0-89747)*, 1115 Crowley Dr., Carrolton, TX 75006 Tel 214-242-1485 (SAN 400-3748).

Squalor Productions, *(Squalor Prod; 0-9611426)*, 510 E. 46th St., Chicago, IL 60653 Tel 312-373-5916 (SAN 284-9208).

Squantum Press, *(Squantum Pr; 0-9607532)*, 39 Knollwood Rd., Quincy, MA 02171 Tel 617-328-0164 (SAN 238-4817).

Squarebooks, *(Squarebooks; 0-916290)*, P.O. Box 1000, Mill Valley, CA 94942 Tel 415-383-0202 (SAN 209-1062)Publishers Group West, 5855 Beaudry St, Emeryville, CA 94608 (SAN 202-8522).

Squeezer Press, *(Squeezer; 0-9608270)*, P.O. Box 421662, San Francisco, CA 94142-1662 Tel 415-282-9597 (SAN 240-4451).

Squire, Ron, *(Squire)*, Orders to: Shirley Squire, 174 Calle Cuervo, San Clemente, CA 92672 Tel 714-492-7068 (SAN 204-8728).

Sri Rama Publishing, *(Sri Rama; 0-918100)*, 161 Robles Dr., Santa Cruz, CA 95060 Tel 408-426-8468 (SAN 282-3578); Orders to: P.O. Box 2550, Santa Cruz, CA 95063 (SAN 282-3586).

Sri Shirdi Sai Pubns., *(Sri Shirdi Sai; 0-938924)*, P.O. Box 2272, Morgantown, WV 26505 (SAN 220-2751).

SRL Publishing Co., *(SRL Pub Co; 0-918152)*, P.O. Box 2277, Sta. A, Champaign, IL 61820 Tel 217-356-1523 (SAN 209-3871).

Sroda, George, *(G Sroda; 0-9604486)*, Amherst Jct., WI 54407 Tel 715-824-3868 (SAN 210-8607).

Sroge, Maxwell, Publishing, Inc., *(Sroge M; 0-942674)*, The Sroge Bldg. 731 N. Cascade, Colorado Springs, CO 80903 Tel 303-633-5556 (SAN 238-5732).

St Francis Hospital Dr William G Eckert Laboratory, *(St Francis Hosp)*, Wichita, KS 67214 (SAN 226-7403).

ST Pubns. See Signs of the Times Publishing Co.

ST2, *(ST Two; 0-943542)*, 203 Si Town Rd., Castle Rock, WA 98611 Tel 206-636-2645 (SAN 238-3810).

Stabell, Brenda B., *(B B Stabell; 0-9610872)*, 10827 Overbrook, Houston, TX 77042 (SAN 264-407X).

Stack the Deck, Inc., *(Stack the Deck; 0-933282)*, 9126 Sandpiper Ct., Orland Park, IL 60462 Tel 312-349-8345 (SAN 212-5668).

Stackpole Books, Inc., *(Stackpole; 0-8117)*, P.O. Box 1831, Cameron & Kelker Sts., Harrisburg, PA 17105 Tel 717-234-5041 (SAN 202-5396). Imprints: Arms & Armour Press (Arms & Armour Pr).

Stafford, Shirley, *(S Stafford; 0-9607580)*, 4231 Casa De Machado, La Mesa, CA 92041 (SAN 239-9806).

Staked Plains Press, *(Staked Plains; 0-918028)*, P.O. Box 779, Canyon, TX 79015 Tel 806-655-7121 (SAN 209-360X).

Stallard, Bernard, *(B Stallard; 0-9606908)*, Rt. 2, Box 430-B, Speedwell, TN 37870 (SAN 282-3616)600 Cherakee Rd., Raceland, KY 41169 (SAN 282-3624).

Stamp Journals Index Co., The, *(Stamp Journal; 0-9608004)*, 177 Columbia Heights, Brooklyn, NY 11201 Tel 212-834-8193 (SAN 238-5740).

Standard & Poor's Corp., *(Standard Poors)*, 25 Broadway, New York, NY 10004 Tel 212-248-2525 (SAN 205-0900).

Standard Arts Press, *(Standard Arts; 0-911426)*, 2324 Butler Rd., Butler, MD 21023 Tel 301-472-4698 (SAN 204-6318).

Standard Editions, *(Standard Edns; 0-918746)*, P.O. Box 1297, Stuyvesant Sta., New York, NY 10009 (SAN 212-1646).

Standard Educational Corp., *(Standard Ed; 0-87392)*, 200 W. Monroe, Chicago, IL 60606 Tel 312-346-7440 (SAN 204-6326).

Standard Publishing Co., *(Standard Pub; 0-87239)*, 8121 Hamilton Ave., Cincinnati, OH 45231 Tel 513-931-4050 (SAN 220-0147).

Standing Orders, Inc., *(Standing Orders; 0-8491)*, 156 5th Ave., Suite 1122, New York, NY 10010 Tel 212-243-0370 (SAN 214-2066); Orders to: P.O. Box 183, Patterson, NY 12563 (SAN 214-2074).

Standish See Dell Publishing Co., Inc.

Stanford Univ. Press, *(Stanford U Pr; 0-8047)*, Stanford, CA 94305 Tel 415-497-9434 (SAN 203-3526).

Stanford University School of Law, *(Stanford U Law)*, Stanford, CA 94305 (SAN 226-3483).

Stanger, Robert A., Co., *(R A Stanger; 0-943570)*, 623 River Rd., Fair Haven, NJ 07701 Tel 201-747-7566 (SAN 262-0898).

StanGib Ltd., *(StanGib Ltd; 0-85259)*, 601 Franklin Ave., Garden City, NY 11530 Tel 516-746-4666 (SAN 213-3784).

Stanley Foundation, The, *(Stanley Found; 0-9603112)*, 420 E. Third St., Muscatine, IA 52761 (SAN 221-7066).

Stanoff, Jerrold G., *(J G Stanoff)*, P.O. Box 1599, Aptos, CA 95003 Tel 408-724-4911 (SAN 213-1706).

Stanton Allaben Production, (Stanton Production; 0-913109), 70 Little Pond Road, Londonderry, UT 05148 (SAN 283-3441).
Stanton & Lee Pubs., Inc., (Stanton & Lee; 0-88361), 44 E. Mifflin St., Madison, WI 53703 Tel 608-255-3254 (SAN 211-2744).
Stanwix House, Inc., (Stanwix; 0-87076), 3020 Chartiers Ave., Pittsburgh, PA 15204 Tel 412-771-4233 (SAN 206-7706) Book Sizes Are 7 X 10 or 8 1/2 X 11.
Star Press, (Star Pr; 0-937038), Box 835, Friday Harbor, WA 98250 (SAN 226-8035).
Star Pubns., (Star Pubns MO; 0-932356), 1211 W. 60th Terrace, Kansas City, MO 64113 Tel 816-523-8228 (SAN 212-4564).
Star Publishing Co., (Star Pub CA; 0-89863), P.O. Box 68, Belmont, CA 94002 (SAN 212-6958).
Star Rover House, (Star Rover; 0-932458), 1914 Foothill Blvd., Oakland, CA 94606 Tel 415-839-6822 (SAN 212-4572).
Star System Press, (Star System; 0-932890), P.O. Box 15202, Wedgwood Sta., Seattle, WA 98115 Tel 206-522-2589 (SAN 207-5059).
Star Tree Press, (Star Tree; 0-940506), 114 Honeyspot Rd., Stratford, CT 06497 (SAN 219-0982).
Starblaze See Donning Co. Pubs.
Starbright Books, (Starbright; 0-9606248), P.O. Box 353, Freeland, WA 98249 Tel 206-321-6138 (SAN 282-3632); Orders to: 1611 E. Dow Rd., Freeland, WA 98249 Tel 206-321-6138 (SAN 282-3640).
Starchand Press, (Starchand Pr; 0-910425), Box 468, Wainscott, NY 11975 Tel 516-324-2632 (SAN 260-1419).
Starfire Books, (Starfire Bks; 0-9608006), P.O. Box 5529, Santa Fe, NM 87502 Tel 505-988-3952 (SAN 238-5759).
Starform, Inc., (Starform; 0-9604946), 1775 Old County Rd., No, 9, Belmont, CA 94002 (SAN 216-1818).
Starkey Laboratories, Inc., (Starkey Labs; 0-9601970), 6700 Washington Ave. S., Eden Prairie, MN 55344 Tel 800-328-8602 (SAN 215-1111).
Starlight Press, (Starlight Pr; 0-9605438), Box 3102, Long Island City, NY 11103 (SAN 216-0633).
Starlog Press, (Starlog; 0-931064), 475 Park Ave. So., New York, NY 10016 Tel 212-689-2830 (SAN 212-1247).
Starmark Publishing, Div. of Starmark, Inc., (Starmark; 0-936572), 706 N. Dearborn St., Chicago, IL 60610 (SAN 214-2236).
Starmont House, (Starmont Hse; 0-916732), Box 851, Mercer Island, WA 98040 Tel 206-232-8484 (SAN 208-8703).
Starogubski Press, (Starogubski; 0-9603234), 345 Riverside Dr., Suite 5J, New York, NY 10025 Tel 212-222-5070 (SAN 207-2912).
Starosciak, Kenneth, Bookseller, (K Starosciak), 117 Wilmot, San Francisco, CA 94115 (SAN 201-0372).
Starpath School of Navigation, (Starpath; 0-914025), 2101 N. 34th St., Seattle, WA 98103 Tel 206-632-1293 (SAN 286-889X).
Starrett Publishing Co., (Starrett Pub Co; 0-911983), 550 Hilbar Lane, Palo Alto, CA 94303 Tel 415-327-1472 (SAN 276-9409).
State Bar of Texas, (State Bar TX; 0-938160), P.O. Box 12487, Capitol Sta., Austin, TX 78711 (SAN 216-4531).
State Historical Society of Iowa, (State Hist Iowa; 0-89033), 402 Iowa Ave., Iowa City, IA 52240 Tel 319-353-6689 (SAN 206-5770).
State Historical Society of Wisconsin, (State Hist Soc Wis; 0-87020), 816 State St., Madison, WI 53706 Tel 608-262-1368 (SAN 203-350X).
State Mutual Book & Periodical Service, Ltd., (State Mutual Bk; 0-89771), 521 Fifth Ave., 17th Floor, New York, NY 10017 Tel 212-682-5844 (SAN 169-5975).
State Univ. of N.Y. at Albany, Univ. Art Gallery, (SUNY Albany U Art; 0-910763), 1400 Washington Ave., Albany, NY 12222 Tel 518-457-3375 (SAN 260-2679).
State Univ. of New York, College of Environmental Science & Forestry, (SUNY Environ), Room 123 Bray Hall, Syracuse, NY 13210 Tel 315-470-6647 (SAN 205-0633).

State Univ. of New York Press, (State U NY Pr; 0-87395; 0-88706), State University Plaza, Albany, NY 12246 Tel 518-473-7602 (SAN 203-3488); Orders to: 300 Ratitan Center Pkwy., Edison, NJ 08818 Tel 201-225-5555 (SAN 203-3496).
Staten Island Historical Society, (Staten Island), 441 Clarke Ave., Richmondtown, NY 10306 Tel 212-351-1611 (SAN 205-0641).
Station Hill Press, Div. of Open Books, (Station Hill Pr; 0-930794), Station Hill Rd., Barrytown, NY 12507 (SAN 214-1485).
Statistical Press, (Statistical Pr; 0-9610700), P.O. Box 11019, San Francisco, CA 94101 Tel 415-922-1267 (SAN 264-7958).
Stay Away Joe Pubs., (Stay Away; 0-911436), Box 2054, Great Falls, MT 59401 (SAN 204-6350).
Steam Press, (Steam Pr MA; 0-942820), 16 Walden St., Cambridge, MA 02140 Tel 617-492-7224 (SAN 238-8642).
Steamship Historical Society of America, Inc., (Steamship Hist Soc; 0-913423), 414 Pelton Ave, Staten Island, NY 10310 Tel 212-727-9583 (SAN 285-0915); Orders to: HC Hall Bldg., 345 Blackstone Blvd., Providence, RI 02906 (SAN 285-0923).
Steel Founders' Society of America, (Steel Founders; 0-9604674), 455 State Street, Des Plauos, OH 60016 (SAN 215-2002).
Steelstone Press, (Steelstone; 0-9605678), 4607 Claussen Lane, Valparaiso, IN 46383 Tel 219-464-1792 (SAN 216-1877).
Steffanides, George F., (Steffanides; 0-9600114), 66 Lourdes Dr., W.D., Fitchburg, MA 01420 Tel 617-342-1997 (SAN 204-6369).
Steffen Publishing Co., (Steffen Pub Co; 0-911913), Main St., Holland Patent, NY 13354 Tel 315-865-4132 (SAN 283-9199).
Stehsel, Donald, (Stehsel), 2600 S. Third Ave., Arcadia, CA 91006 Tel 213-446-3679 (SAN 206-3824).
Stein & Day, (Stein & Day; 0-8128), Scarborough House, Briarcliff Manor, NY 10510 Tel 914-762-2151 (SAN 203-3461).
Stein Publishing House, (Stein Pub; 0-911440), 526 S. State St., Chicago, IL 60605 (SAN 204-6377).
Steinerbooks See Garber Communications, Inc.
Steinlage Products, (Steinlage; 0-914754), 4766 Kremer Hoying Rd, St. Henry, OH 45883 Tel 419-678-4125 (SAN 206-1295).
Steinlitz-Hammacher Co., (Steinlitz-Hammacher; 0-917208), P.O. Box 187, Hasbrouck Heights, NJ 07604 Tel 201-667-1429 (SAN 208-8738).
Steinway & Sons, (Steinway; 0-9607196), Steinway Place, Long Island City, NY 11105 Tel 212-721-2600 (SAN 239-1325).
Stel-Mar, (Stel-Mar; 0-935456), 329 Rhoda Dr., Lancaster, PA 17601 (SAN 215-1855).
Stella, Albert A. M., (A Stella), 220 Exchange St., Susquehanna, PA 18847 (SAN 212-1417); Orders to: Deinotation-7 Press, Box 194, Susquehanna, PA 18847 (SAN 212-1425).
Stella, Joseph G., (J G Stella; 0-9600908; 0-8390), P.O. Box 2158, Fort Lauderdale, FL 33303 Tel 305-463-3545 (SAN 208-8746); Dist. by: Abner Schram, 36 Park St., Montclair, NJ 07042 (SAN 169-4766).
Stelle Group, (Stelle; 0-9600308), Administration Bldg., Stelle, IL 60919 Tel 815-256-2200 (SAN 204-6385).
Stemmer House Pubs., Inc., (Stemmer Hse; 0-916144), 2627 Caves Rd., Owings Mills, MD 21117 Tel 301-363-3690 (SAN 207-9623).
Stempien, G., Publishing Co., (G Stempien; 0-930472), 1213 Edgehill Ave., Joliet, IL 60432 Tel 815-722-4216 (SAN 210-9840).
Step, Inc., (Step Inc; 0-939974), P.O. Box 887, Mukilteo, WA 98275 (SAN 216-8588).
Stephens Engineering Associates, Inc., (Stephens Eng Assocs; 0-911677), 7030 220th SW, Mountlake Terrace, WA 98043 Tel 206-771-2182 (SAN 264-4126).
Stephens Press, (Stephens Pr), Drawer 1441, Spokane, WA 99210 Tel 509-838-8222 (SAN 210-9573).
Stereopticon Press, (Stereopticon Pr; 0-9608824), 534 Wahlmont Dr., Webster, NY 14580 Tel 716-671-2342 (SAN 238-3829).

Sterling, A. James, Jr. Architect Photographer, (A J Sterling; 0-9607042), 2500 North Lakeview Ave., Chicago, IL 60614 Tel 312-528-6648 (SAN 241-5828).
Sterling and Francine Clark Art Institute, (S & F Clark Art; 0-931102), Williamstown, MA 01267 (SAN 222-8491).
Sterling Instrument, (Sterling Instru), 55 S. Denton Ave., New Hyde Park, NY 11040 (SAN 207-2920).
Sterling Publications Ltd., (Sterling Pubns Ltd; 0-913339), 6411 Mulberry Ave., Portage, IN 46368 Tel 219-762-5106 (SAN 283-9202).
Sterling Pub. Co., Inc., (Sterling; 0-8069), 2 Park Ave., New York, NY 10016 Tel 212-532-7160 (SAN 211-6324).
Sterling Swift Pub. Co., (Sterling Swift; 0-88408), 7901 South IH-35, Austin, TX 78744 Tel 512-282-6840 (SAN 206-135X).
Stern, Clarence Ames, (Stern; 0-9600116), P.O. Box 2294, Oshkosh, WI 54903 Tel 414-231-6786 (SAN 204-6393).
Stevens, Irving, (Stevens Irving; 0-9609208), R1-4710, Corinna, ME 04928 (SAN 283-4189).
Stevens & Shea Publishers, (Stevens & Shea; 0-89550), P.O. Box 794, Stockton, CA 95201 Tel 209-465-1880 (SAN 206-3670).
Stevenson International, (Stevenson Intl; 0-9606252), 525 Princeton Circle West, Fullerton, CA 92631 (SAN 217-5878).
Stevenson Language Skills, Inc., (Stevenson Lang Skills; 0-941112), 85 Upland Rd., Attleboro, MA 02703 Tel 617-222-1133 (SAN 217-4413).
Stevenson Press, (Stevenson Pr; 0-89482), P.O. Box 10021, Austin, TX 78766 Tel 512-863-2774 (SAN 209-8873).
Steves Wide World Studios, (Steves Wide World), 111 4th Ave. N., Edmonds, WA 98020 (SAN 214-2244).
Steward & Sons, (Steward & Sons; 0-917144), P.O. Box 15282, Long Beach, CA 90815 (SAN 208-8789).
Stewardship Enterprises, (Stewardship Enters; 0-9611282), P.O. Box 540, Moorestown, NJ 08057 Tel 609-764-1601 (SAN 283-3468).
Stewart, B. M., (B M Stewart), 4494 Wausau Rd., Okemos, MI 48864 Tel 517-349-0297 (SAN 202-0548).
Stewart, Henry, (Stewart; 0-911444), 253 Main St., East Aurora, NY 14052 Tel 716-652-1770 (SAN 204-6407).
Stewart, Lois, (L Stewart; 0-9609512), 3657 W. Nichols, Springfield, MO 65803 Tel 417-831-6140 (SAN 262-088X).
Stewart, Tabori & Chang, Pubs., (Stewart Tabori & Chang; 0-941434), 300 Park Ave. S., New York, NY 10010 Tel 212-722-7533 (SAN 239-0361).
Stice, Will, (W Stice; 0-9610512), P.O. Box 12886, Salem, OR 97309 Tel 503-588-0344 (SAN 264-4142).
Stickley, George F., Co., (G F Stickley Co; 0-89313), 210 W. Washington Square, Philadelphia, PA 19106 Tel 215-922-7126 (SAN 209-0783).
Still News Pubns., (Still News; 0-940828), P.O. Box 353, Port Ludlow, WA 98365 (SAN 219-6417).
Still Point Press, (Still Point Pr; 0-941660), P.O. Box 1606, 223 W. First St., Mansfield, OH 44901 Tel 419-526-2227 (SAN 239-3190).
Stillgate Pubs., (Stillgate; 0-938286), Box 67, Alstead, NH 03602 (SAN 216-1885).
Stillhouse Hollow Publishing Co., (Stillhouse Hollow; 0-9602272), Orders to: First Ladies of Texas, P.O. Box 3015, Temple, TX 76502 (SAN 212-4599).
Stilwell Studio, The, (Stilwell Studio; 0-9605862), P.O. Box 50, Carmel, CA 93921 Tel 408-624-0340 (SAN 220-1895).
Stimler Associates, (Stimler Assoc; 0-9600770), 33 W. Second St., Moorestown, NJ 08057 (SAN 206-7994).
Stinson Beach Press, (Stinson Beach; 0-918540), P.O. Box 475, Stinson Beach, CA 94970 Tel 415-868-1424 (SAN 209-8881).
Stipes Publishing Co., (Stipes; 0-87563), P.O. Box 526, Champaign, IL 61820 Tel 217-356-8391 (SAN 206-8664).
Stirrup Associates, Inc., (Stirrup Assoc; 0-937420), 115 Church St., Decatur, GA 30030 (SAN 215-1863).
Stock Drive Products, (Stock Drive), 55 S. Denton Ave., New Hyde Park, NY 11040 (SAN 204-6415).

Stockton Unified School District, The, *(Stockton Unified Schl Dist; 0-9607134),* 303 E. Yorkshire Dr., Stockton, CA 95203 (SAN 239-037X).

Stoeger Publishing Co., *(Stoeger Pub Co; 0-88317),* 55 Ruta Court, South Hackensack, NJ 07606 Tel 201-440-2700 (SAN 206-118X).

Stokes Publishing Co., *(Stokes; 0-914534),* 1125 Robin Way, Sunnyvale, CA 94087 Tel 408-736-4637 (SAN 206-5789).

Stokesville Publishing Co., *(Stokesville Pub; 0-936030),* P.O. Box 14401, Atlanta, GA 30324 Tel 404-658-3075 (SAN 211-3333).

Stoma Press, Inc., *(Stoma Pr; 0-89939),* 13231 42nd Ave., N.E., Seattle, WA 98125 (SAN 222-8432).

Stone, M. J., Co., *(M J Stone; 0-9601888),* P.O. Box 12793, Seattle, WA 98101 Tel 206-682-0350 (SAN 212-6974) Moved, left no forwarding address.

Stone, Michael B., *(M B Stone; 0-9603448),* 8434 55th Ave., S., Seattle, WA 98118 (SAN 213-5973).

Stone Country Press, *(Stone Country; 0-930020),* P.O. Box 132, Menemsha, MA 02522 Tel 617-693-5832 (SAN 209-7788).

Stone-Marrow Press, *(Stone-Marrow Pr),* Dept. of English, 248 McMicken, Univ. of Cincinnati, Cincinnati, OH 45221 (SAN 203-3429).

Stone Press, *(Stone Pr MI),* 1790 Grand River, Okemos, MI 48864 (SAN 207-902X).

Stone/Robert H., *(R H Stone; 0-9609192),* 1439 South Kansas, Springfield, MO 65807 (SAN 264-4169).

Stone Street Press, The, *(Stone St Pr),* 1 Stone St., Staten Island, NY 10304 Tel 212-447-1436 (SAN 219-8185).

Stone Wall Press, Inc., *(Stone Wall Pr; 0-913276),* 1241 30th St. N.W., Washington, DC 20007 Tel 202-333-1860 (SAN 203-3402); Dist. by: Stackpole Books, Cameron & Kelker St., Harrisburg, PA 17105 (SAN 202-5396).

Stonehenge Books, *(Stonehenge; 0-937050),* 1582 S. Parker Rd., Suite 200, Parker Plaza, Denver, CO 80231 Tel 303-695-4710 (SAN 216-454X).

Stonehouse Pubns., *(Stonehouse; 0-9603236),* Sweet, ID 83670 (SAN 206-1058).

Stoneridge Institute of Politico-Socio-Economics Press, *(Stoneridge Inst; 0-937300),* 7703 Baltimore National Pike, Frederick, MD 21701 (SAN 215-112X).

Stoney Brook Publishing Co., *(Stoney Brook; 0-912928),* 186 Main St., W., Chelmsford, MA 01863 (SAN 204-6423).

Stoneydale Press Publishing Company, *(Stoneydale Pr Pub; 0-912299),* 295 Kootenai Creek Rd., Stevensville, MT 59870 Tel 406-777-5269 (SAN 265-3168).

Storm King Art Center, *(Storm King),* Mountainville, NY 10953 (SAN 280-6606).

Story Press, *(Story Pr; 0-931704),* P.O. Box 10040, Chicago, IL 60610 Tel 312-456-0300 (SAN 212-6982).

Stough Institute, Inc., The, *(Stough Inst; 0-940830),* 54 W. 16th St., New York, NY 10011 (SAN 219-8193).

Stowe-Day Foundation, *(Stowe-Day; 0-917482),* 77 Forest St., Hartford, CT 06105 Tel 203-522-9258 (SAN 209-052X).

Strahm, Virgil, *(Strahm; 0-9606050),* P.O. Box 900, Branson, MO 65616 Tel 417-334-4381 (SAN 216-9347).

Strand, Janann, *(J Strand; 0-9600780),* P.O. Box 50325, Pasadena, CA 91105-0325 Tel 213-799-3153 (SAN 213-1722).

Stratford House Publishing Co., *(Stratford Hse; 0-938614),* P.O. Box 7077, Burbank, CA 91510 (SAN 216-1893).

Stratford Press Inc., *(Stratford Pr),* 11340 W. Olympic Blvd. Suite 340, Los Angeles, CA 90064 Tel 213-530-8292 (SAN 282-3713); Dist. by: Harper & Row, Publishers Inc., 10 E. 53rd St., New York, NY 10022 Tel 212-593-7000 (SAN 282-3721).

Stratford Pubns., Inc., *(Stratford Pubns; 0-941568),* 8614 Camden St., Alexandria, VA 22308 Tel 703-780-4104 (SAN 239-3204).

Strathcona Publishing Co., *(Strathcona; 0-931554),* 24 Brookstone Dr., Princeton, NJ 08540 Tel 212-683-1016 (SAN 211-4550).

Straughan's Book Shop, Inc., *(Straughan; 0-911452),* 2168 Lawndale Dr., Greensboro, NC 27408 Tel 919-273-1214 (SAN 206-9555).

Strauss, Daniel, *(D Strauss; 0-9608338),* 2870 Grand Concourse, Bronx, NY 10458 Tel 212-369-0500 (SAN 240-4478).

Stravon Educational Press, *(Stravon; 0-87396),* 845 Third Ave., New York, NY 10022 Tel 212-371-2880 (SAN 207-7402).

Strawberry Hill Press, *(Strawberry Hill; 0-89407),* 2594 15th Ave., San Francisco, CA 94127 Tel 415-664-8112 (SAN 238-8103).

Strawberry Patchworks, *(Straw Patch; 0-9608428),* 517 Northview Dr., Fayetteville, NC 28303 Tel 919-484-4976 (SAN 240-7809).

Strawberry Patchworks, *(Strawberry Works),* Green Mansion, North, VA 23128 (SAN 262-0901).

Strawberry Press, *(Strawberry Pr NY; 0-936574),* P.O. Box 451, Bowling Green Sta., New York, NY 10004 (SAN 215-9198).

Strawberry Valley Press, *(Strawberry Valley; 0-913612),* P.O. Box 157, Idyllwild, CA 92349 Tel 714-659-2145 (SAN 202-7410).

Strawn Studios, Inc., *(Strawn; 0-943548),* 761 Knolls Ct., West Des Moines, IA 50265 Tel 515-394-3018 (SAN 238-3853).

Streamside Publications, *(Streamside Pubns),* Box 553, Manchester Center, VT 05255 Tel 802-457-1049 (SAN 282-5716); Dist. by: Backcountry Publications, Inc., P.O. Box 175, Woodstock, VT 05091 (SAN 238-1427).

Street Editions, *(St Edns),* 20 Desbrosses St., New York, NY 10013 (SAN 282-373X).

Street Fiction Press, Inc., *(Street Fiction; 0-914908),* 130 Touro St., P.O. Box 625, Newport, RI 02840 Tel 401-847-1067 (SAN 207-0863).

Street Press, *(Street Pr; 0-935252),* Box 555, Port Jefferson, NY 11777 Tel 516-584-5455 (SAN 207-9046).

Strether & Swann, *(Strether & Swann; 0-931522),* 1309 Seventh St., New Orleans, LA 70115 (SAN 211-9811).

Strode Pubs., *(Strode; 0-87397),* 720 Church St., NW., Huntsville, AL 35801 Tel 205-539-2187 (SAN 202-7429).

Stroker Press, *(Stroker; 0-918154),* 129 Second Ave., No. 3, New York, NY 10003 (SAN 206-6811).

Stronghold Press, *(Stronghold Pr; 0-910429),* Box 2337, Bismarck, ND 58502 Tel 701-222-0728 (SAN 260-1435).

Stroock, Paul A., *(P A Stroock; 0-9601138),* 35 Middle Lane, P.O. Box 126, Jericho, L. I., NY 11753 Tel 516-433-9018 (SAN 210-2765).

Stropes Editions, Ltd., *(Stropes Editions; 0-9608512),* Dist. by: Thoth Corp., P.O. Box 92413, Milwaukee, WI 53202 (SAN 275-8245).

Strugglers' Community Press, *(Strug Comm Pr; 0-913491),* 2003 W. 67th Pl., Chicago, IL 60636 Tel 312-776-6400 (SAN 285-1970); c/o Neighborhood United Methodist Church, 431 S. 19th Ave., Maywood, IL 60153 Tel 312-681-5887 (SAN 285-1989).

Stryker, William Norman, *(W N Stryker),* 3804 Adrienne Dr., Alexandria, VA 22309 (SAN 212-7989).

Stryker-Post Pubns., Inc., *(Stryker-Post; 0-943448),* 888 17th St., N.W., Washington, DC 20006 Tel 202-298-9233 (SAN 204-6431).

Stuart, Lyle, Inc., *(Lyle Stuart; 0-8184),* 120 Enterprise Ave., Secaucus, NJ 07094 Tel 201-866-0490 (SAN 201-1131).

Stuart Books, *(Stuart Bks; 0-9608716),* P.O. Box 40081, Garland, TX 75040 (SAN 241-1547).

Stubs Pubns., *(Stubs; 0-911458),* 234 W. 44th St., New York, NY 10036 Tel 212-398-8370 (SAN 202-7445).

Student Assn. Press, *(Student Assn; 0-931118),* 901-761-1350, Memphis, TN 38117 Tel 901-761-1353 (SAN 212-5676).

Student Editors Association, *(Student Ed Assoc; 0-910127),* 504 S. Wheaton Ave., Wheaton, IL 60187 Tel 312-668-8690 (SAN 241-4813).

Studia Hispanica Editors, *(Studia Hispanica; 0-934840),* P.O. Box 7304, Univ. Sta., Austin, TX 78712 Tel 512-458-3447 (SAN 214-1639).

Studia Slovenica, Inc., *(Studia Slovenica),* P.O. Box 232, New York, NY 10032 (SAN 213-6996).

Studio J Publishing, Inc., *(Studio J Pub; 0-940002),* 274 North St., Ridgefield, CT 06877 Tel 203-438-7826 (SAN 216-7808).

Studio Press, *(Studio NY; 0-9610514),* 122 Glen Rd. S., Rome, NY 13440 Tel 315-337-9322 (SAN 264-4177).

Studio Press, The, *(Studio Pr CA),* P.O. Box 3479, Hollywood, CA 90078 (SAN 286-3553); 8033 Sunset, Los Angeles, CA (SAN 286-3561).

Studios West Pubns., *(Studios West; 0-939656),* 167 Saxony Rd., Encinitas, CA 92024 Tel 619-753-8186 (SAN 216-6461).

Stugallz, *(Stugallz; 0-9610702),* 339 N. Virgil Ave., Los Angeles, CA 90004 Tel 213-661-8968 (SAN 264-7982).

Stull & Co., Since 1870, Inc., *(Stull & Co),* 120 Wall St., New York, NY 10005 Tel 212-480-9157 (SAN 211-3317).

Sturge, Judi, Mrs., *(J Sturge),* 18 Lodge Pole Rd., Pittsford, NY 14534 (SAN 211-7622).

Sturzebecker, R. L., *(Sturzebecker; 0-9600466),* 503 Owen Rd., West Chester, PA 19380 Tel 215-696-4590 (SAN 206-1228).

Stuttman, H. S., Inc., *(Stuttman; 0-87475),* 333 Post Rd. W., Westport, CT 06889 (SAN 202-7453).

Subs. of International Self-Counsel Press Ltd. See Self-Counsel Press, Inc.

Success Foundation, Inc., The, *(Success Found; 0-913200),* P. O. Box 6302, Louisville, KY 40206 Tel 502-893-3038 (SAN 208-1261).

Success Now, Inc., *(Success Now; 0-912545),* P.O. Box 32530, Tucson, AZ 85751 Tel 602-298-9129 (SAN 265-220X).

Success Press, *(Success Pr; 0-9607858),* 3700 First Ave., N.E., Cedar Rapids, IA 52402 Tel 319-366-0767 (SAN 238-1176).

Success Unlimited, Inc., The Magazine for Achievers, *(Success Unltd; 0-918448),* 401 N. Wabash, Chicago, IL 60611 Tel 312-828-9500 (SAN 209-2867).

Sue Ann, *(Sue Ann; 0-9604172),* Box 2, North Haven, CT 06473 Tel 203-288-1913 (SAN 215-1138).

Suffolk House, *(Suffolk Hse; 0-936066),* 155 E. Main St., Smithtown, NY 11787 (SAN 216-4582).

Sufi Islamia/Prophecy Pubns., *(Sufi Islamia-Prophecy; 0-915424),* 114 Forrest Ave., Fairfax, CA 94930 Tel 415-453-8159 (SAN 282-3748); Orders to: 65 Norwich St., San Francisco, CA 94110 Tel 415-285-0562 (SAN 282-3756). *Imprints:* Prophecy Pressworks (Prophecy Pressworks).

Sufism Reoriented, Inc., *(Sufism Reoriented; 0-915828),* 1300 Boulevard Way, Walnut Creek, CA 94595 Tel 415-938-4822 (SAN 207-4869).

Sugar Marbel Press, *(Sugar Marbel Pr),* 1547 Shenandoah Ave., Cincinnati, OH 45237 Tel 513-761-8000 (SAN 240-1002).

Sugarfree Center, Inc., *(Sugarfree),* 5623 Mantilija Ave., P.O. Box 114, Van Nuys, CA 91408 Tel 213-994-1093 (SAN 241-5836).

Sugden, Sherwood, & Company, *(Sugden; 0-89385),* 1117 Eighth St., La Salle, IL 61301 Tel 815-223-1231 (SAN 210-5659).

Suhrkamp/Insel Pubs. Boston Inc., *(Suhrkamp; 3-458; 3-518),* 380 Green St., Cambridge, MA 02139 Tel 617-876-2333 (SAN 215-2762).

Sukenick, Ronald, *(R Sukenick),* Box 188, Cooper St., New York, NY 10003 (SAN 226-4323).

Sullivan, Dorothy, Production, *(Sullivan Prod; 0-9604928),* P.O. Box 7045, St. Petersburg, FL 33734 Tel 813-525-1089 (SAN 215-9201).

Sullivan, E. M., *(Sullivan; 0-911460),* P.O. Box 5823, Orange, CA 92667 (SAN 204-6458).

Sullivan Books International, *(Sullivan Bks Intl; 0-913620),* 153 MacAlvey, Martinez, CA 94553 (SAN 206-4774).

Sullwold, William S., Publishing, Inc., *(W S Sullwold; 0-88492),* 18 Pearl St., Taunton, MA 02780 Tel 617-823-0924 (SAN 203-1744).

Sultan of Swat/S.O.S. Books, *(S O S Books; 0-911809),* 1821 Kalorama Rd., NW, Washington, DC 20009 Tel 202-638-1956 (SAN 264-4193).

NAME INDEX

Sumac Press, *(Sumac Mich; 0-912090),* P.O. Box 39, Fremont, MI 49412 Tel 616-924-3464 (SAN 206-1236).

Summa Publications, *(Summa Pubns; 0-917786),* P.O. Box 20725, Birmingham, AL 35216 Tel 205-823-6923 (SAN 212-0925).

Summer House Pubns., *(Summer House; 0-935736),* Box 16257, Baltimore, MD 21210 (SAN 213-8026).

Summer Institute of Linguistics, *(Summer Inst Ling; 0-88312),* Academic Pubns., 7500 W. Camp Wisdom Rd., Dallas, TX 75236 Tel 214-298-3331 (SAN 204-6466).

Summer Stream Press, *(Summer Stream; 0-932460),* P.O. Box 6056, Santa Barbara, CA 93160 Tel 805-967-5992 (SAN 212-6990); Orders to: P.O. Box 6056, Santa Barbara, CA 93160 Tel 805-682-4626 (SAN 215-5567).

Summit Books, Subs. of Simon & Schuster, *(Summit Bks; 0-),* 1230 Ave. of the Americas, New York, NY 10020 Tel 212-246-2471 (SAN 206-1244).

Summit County Chapter O G S, *(Summit Cnty OH),* 410 Bonshire Rd., Akron, OH 44319 Tel 216-644-8660 (SAN 219-9823).

Summit Enterprises, Inc., *(Summit Ent; 0-934174),* 13444 N. 32nd St., Suite 19, Phoenix, AZ 85032 Tel 602-992-5372 (SAN 213-6465).

Summit Junior Fortnightly Club, *(Summit Jr Fort; 0-9608052),* 214 Springfield Ave., Summit, NJ 07901 Tel 201-665-1796 (SAN 238-8650).

Summit Publishing Co., *(Summit Pub Co; 0-9609310),* 1800 Stoney Hill Dr., Hudson, OH 44236 Tel 216-650-4321 (SAN 240-8384).

Summit Univ. Press, *(Summit Univ; 0-916766),* Box A, Malibu, CA 90265 Tel 213-991-4751 (SAN 208-4120).

Summy-Birchard Music, *(Summy; 0-87487),* Box 2072, Princeton, NJ 08540 Tel 609-683-0090 (SAN 202-7461).

SUN, *(SUN; 0-915342),* 347 W. 39th St., New York, NY 10018 Tel 212-594-8428 (SAN 206-3832).

Sun & Moon Press, *(Sun & Moon MD),* 4330 Hartwick Rd., College Park, MD 20740 Tel 301-864-6921 (SAN 216-3063).

Sun Books, *(Sun Bks),* P.O. Box 4383, Albuquerque, NM 87196 Tel 505-255-6550 (SAN 216-3055).

Sun Designs, Subs. of Rexstrom Co., Inc., *(Sun Designs; 0-912355),* P.O. Box 206, Delafield, WI 53018 Tel 414-567-4255 (SAN 265-1181); 36802 Genesee Lake Rd., Oconomowoc, WI 53066 (SAN 265-119X).

Sun Features, Inc., *(Sun Features; 0-937238),* 1160 Rockville Pike, Rockville, MD 20852 Tel 301-340-6036 (SAN 282-3764); Orders to: Box 368-P, Cardiff, CA 92007 Tel 619-753-3489 (SAN 282-3772).

Sun Life, *(Sun Life; 0-937930),* Greystone, Thaxton, VA 24174 Tel 703-586-4898 (SAN 240-8333).

Sun Litho-Print/Frazetta Prints, *(Sun Litho Frazetta; 0-9607060),* P.O. Box R, Marshall Creek, PA 18335 Tel 717-424-2692 (SAN 239-0396).

Sun, Man, Moon, Inc., *(Sun Man Moon; 0-917738),* P.O. Box 5084, 9191 Regatta Dr., Huntington Beach, CA 92646 Tel 714-962-8945 (SAN 210-3745).

Sun Press, *(Sun Pr NY; 0-9601260),* 308 E. 94th St., New York, NY 10028 Tel 212-953-4855 (SAN 210-5101).

Sun Publishing Co., *(Sun Pub; 0-914172; 0-89540),* P.O. Box 4383, Albuquerque, NM 87196 Tel 505-255-6550 (SAN 206-1325).

Sun Publishing, Inc., *(Sun Pub GA; 0-942970),* 1447 Peachtree St., Suite 1005, Atlanta, GA 30309 Tel 404-876-3333 (SAN 238-8669).

Sun-Scape Pubns., *(Sun-Scape Pubns; 0-919842),* P.O. Box 42725, Tucson, AZ 85733 Tel 602-325-7424 (SAN 211-870X).

Sun Scope Publishing Co., *(Sun Scope; 0-9609188),* 9 Sunrise Rd., Danbury, CT 06810 Tel 203-743-6943 (SAN 241-4635).

Sun Valley Books, *(Sun Valley; 0-9605212),* Box 1688, Sun Valley, ID 83353 (SAN 240-8406).

Sunbeam Pubns., *(Sunbeam; 0-9609514),* 780 North 2250 West, Provo, UT 84601 Tel 801-374-6987 (SAN 262-0928).

Sunberry Books, *(Sunberry Bks),* P.O. Box 697, West Acton, MA 01720 (SAN 283-4294).

SunBox Press, *(SunBox; 0-930052),* 750 Alta Vista Way, Laguna Beach, CA 92651 Tel 714-494-2203 (SAN 210-511X).

Sunburst, *(Sunburst; 0-9609618),* P.O. Box 1433, Tacoma, WA 98401 Tel 206-847-8063 (SAN 275-8571).

Sunburst Farms Pub. Co., *(Sunburst Farms),* P.O. Box 2278, Salt Lake, UT 84110 Tel 801-363-5109 (SAN 212-8675); Dist. by: Genesis I Builders, P.O. Box 2278, Salt Lake City, UT 84110 Tel 801-363-5109 (SAN 200-4267).

Sunburst Press, *(Sunburst Pr; 0-934648),* P.O. Box 14205, Portland, OR 97214 (SAN 206-3840).

Sunbury Press, *(Sunbury Pr; 0-915548),* P.O. Box 1778, Raleigh, NC 27602 Tel 919-832-6417 (SAN 207-3943).

Sundance Books *See* Sundance Pubns., Ltd.

Sundance Pubns., Ltd., *(Sundance; 0-913582),* 250 Broadway, Denver, CO 80203 Tel 303-777-2880 (SAN 203-0721).

Sundance Publishing Co., *(Sundance OR; 0-942822),* P.O. Box 604, Salem, OR 97308 Tel 503-585-0200 (SAN 240-2858).

Sunday Pubns., Inc., *(Sunday Pubn; 0-941850),* 3003 S. Congress Ave., No. 2e, Lake Worth, FL 33461 Tel 305-968-4100 (SAN 239-3220).

Sundial Books *See* Sunstone Press, The

Sundowner Services, *(Sundowner Serv; 0-932241),* 2559-47th Ave., San Francisco, CA 94116 Tel 415-564-0068 (SAN 215-9228).

Sunfish Productions, *(Sunfish Prods; 0-911829),* P.O. Box 282-K, Essex Fells, NJ 07021 Tel 212-255-1261 (SAN 264-4231).

Sunflower Ink, *(Sunflower Ink; 0-931104),* Palo Colorado Canyon, Carmel, CA 93923 (SAN 212-9728).

Sunflower Univ. Press, *(Sunflower U Pr; 0-89745),* P.O. Box 1009, Manhattan, KS 66502 Tel 913-532-6733 (SAN 218-5075).

Sunflowers, *(Sunflowers KS; 0-939726),* RR 1, Box 262, Clearwater, KS 67026 Tel 316-545-7587 (SAN 216-7638).

SunMoon Press, *(SunMoon Pr; 0-942064),* P.O. Box 1516, Eugene, OR 97440 Tel 503-343-9544 (SAN 238-4825).

Sunnycrest Publishing, *(Sunnycrest Pub; 0-9610012),* Rt. 1, Box 1, Clements, MN 56224 (SAN 264-424X).

Sunnyside Publishing Co., *(Sunnyside; 0-934650),* Box 29, 51 Willow St., Lynn, MA 01903 Tel 617-595-4742 (SAN 213-1757).

Sunnyvale Marketing, *(Sunnyvale Mktng; 0-941662),* 2627 19th St., Rockford, IL 61109 Tel 815-397-6299 (SAN 239-3239).

Sunrise Christian Bks., *(Sunrise Chr Bks; 0-940652),* c/o One Way, Int., 707 "E" St., Eureka, CA 95501 Tel 707-442-4004 (SAN 211-8254).

Sunrise Foundation, Inc., *(Sunrise Found; 0-9607962),* 746 Myrtle Rd., Charleston, WV 25314 (SAN 241-5852).

SunRise House, *(SunRise Hse; 0-915764),* P.O. Box 217, Longwood, FL 32750 Tel 305-830-7333 (SAN 211-6529).

Sunrise Press, *(Sunrise Pr IL; 0-935800),* 2004 Grant St., Evanston, IL 60201 Tel 312-475-3651 (SAN 215-286X).

Sunrise Pubns, *(Sunrise Pubns; 0-942330),* P.O. Box 139, Ontario, CA 91761 Tel 714-982-4476 (SAN 238-0943).

Sunrise Publishing, *(Sunrise Pub OR; 0-9604344),* P.O. Box 38, Lincoln City, OR 97367 Tel 503-994-6723 (SAN 215-1871).

Sunrise Publishing House, *(Sunrise Pub Hse; 0-9607672),* 12021 Wilshire Blvd., Suite 225, West Los Angeles, CA 90025 (SAN 240-1010).

Sunrise Tortoise Books, *(Sunrise Tortoise; 0-932222),* Box 61, Sandpoint, ID 83864 (SAN 212-5684).

Sunset Books/Lane Publishing Co., *(Sunset-Lane; 0-376),* Willow & Middlefield Rds., Menlo Park, CA 94025 Tel 415-321-3600 (SAN 201-0658).

Sunset Pubns., *(Sunset Pubns; 0-9601256; 0-941244),* 1655 Makaloa St., Suite 906, Honolulu, HI 96814 Tel 808-215-1146).

SunShine, *(SunShine; 0-937710),* Box 4351, Austin, TX 78765 Tel 512-459-6717 (SAN 220-0945).

Sunshine Academic Press, Inc., *(Sunshine Acad; 0-933064),* 304 27th St., West Palm Beach, FL 33407 (SAN 212-4602).

Sunshine Arts, *(Sunshine Arts WA),* W. 1018 Shannon, Spokane, WA 99205 (SAN 215-8183).

Sunshine Enterprises, *(Sunshine Entr; 0-943326),* P.O. Box 403, 210 E. Main, Collinsville, IL 62234 Tel 618-345-7022 (SAN 240-5717).

Sunshine Services Corp., *(Sunshine Serv; 0-942236),* 325 Pennsylvania Ave. SE, Washington, DC 20003 Tel 202-544-3647 (SAN 239-9830).

Sunstone Foundation, *(Sunstone Found),* P.O. Box 2272, Salt Lake City, UT 84110 (SAN 213-9693).

Sunstone Press, The, *(Sunstone Pr; 0-913270; 0-86534),* P.O. Box 2321, Santa Fe, NM 87501 Tel 505-988-4418 (SAN 214-2090). *Imprints:* Sundial Books (Sundial Bks).

Sunstone Publications, Div. of Sunstone, Inc., *(Sunstone Pubns; 0-913319),* P.O. Box 585, 21 Glen Ave., Cooperstown, NY 12326 Tel 607-547-8207 (SAN 283-4227).

Sunwise Turn, Ltd., *(Sunwise Turn; 0-88004),* P.O. Box 117, New York, NY 10003 Tel 212-473-2597 (SAN 222-9838).

Superior Pubns., *(Superior WI),* 5510 Tower Ave., Superior, WI 54880 Tel 715-392-8060 (SAN 209-682X).

Superior Publishing Co., *(Superior Pub; 0-87564),* 708 Sixth Ave., N., Box 1710, Seattle, WA 98111 Tel 206-282-4310 (SAN 202-747X).

Superlove, *(Superlove),* 4245 Ladoga Ave., Lakewood, CA 90713 (SAN 211-982X).

Supnick, Mark, *(M Supnick; 0-9611446),* 8424 N.W. Second St., Coral Springs, FL 33065 Tel 305-755-3448 (SAN 283-1694).

Supplies & Services, Government of Canada *See* Unipub

Supreme Court Historical Society, *(Supreme Ct Hist),* 1629 K St, Washington, DC 20006 (SAN 226-3874).

Suratao, Inc., *(Suratao; 0-932286),* 1232 S. Rimpau Blvd., Los Angeles, CA 90019 Tel 213-931-0371 (SAN 212-1441).

Surevelation, *(Surevelation; 0-917302),* P.O. Box 2193, Concord, CA 94521 Tel 415-687-2703 (SAN 208-8800).

Surface Checking Gage Co., *(Surf Chek; 0-911464),* P.O. Box 1912, Prescott, AZ 86302 Tel 602-778-3160 (SAN 204-6482).

Surrey Books, Inc., *(Surrey Bks; 0-9609516),* 500 N. Michigan Ave., Suite 1940, Chicago, IL 60611 Tel 312-661-0050 (SAN 275-8857).

Surrey Press, *(Surrey Pr; 0-9610652),* 224 Surrey Rd., Warminster, PA 18974 Tel 215-675-4569 (SAN 264-696X).

Survey Publishing Co., *(Survey Pub Co; 0-916510),* 600 E. Eighth St., Kansas City, MO 64106 Tel 816-471-8568 (SAN 202-7488).

Survival, *(Survival CT),* Turkey Hills, Haddam, CT 06438 Tel 203-345-9480 (SAN 213-9480).

Survival Education Assn., *(Survival Ed Assoc; 0-913724),* 9035 Golden Givens Rd., Tacoma, WA 98445 Tel 206-531-3156 (SAN 204-6490).

Susquehanna Publishing Co., *(Susquehanna; 0-9609382),* 709 Apache Dr., Independence, MO 64056 Tel 816-257-0280 (SAN 260-2695).

Sussex Prints, Inc., *(Sussex Pri; 0-911145),* P.O. Box 469, Georgetown, DE 19947 Tel 302-856-0026 (SAN 275-8873).

Sutherland Learning Associates, Inc., *(Sutherland Learn Assocs; 0-934100),* 8700 Reseda Blvd., No. 108, Northridge, CA 91324 Tel 213-701-1344 (SAN 212-8152).

Sutter House, *(Sutter House; 0-915010),* 77 Main St., P.O. Box 212, Lititz, PA 17543 Tel 717-626-0800 (SAN 207-1207).

Sutter Publishing Co., *(Sutter; 0-9600120),* 12311 Conway Rd., Creve Coeur, MO 63141 Tel 314-878-9044 (SAN 204-6504).

Sutton, Weldon L., Publisher, *(W Sutton; 0-9607388),* 8595 Conway Dr., Riverside, CA 92504 Tel 714-687-1313 (SAN 239-7994).

Sutton Press, *(Sutton Pr; 0-940300),* 3631-22nd Ave. S., Minneapolis, MN 55407 (SAN 217-1333).

Sverge-Haus Pubs., *(Sverge-Haus; 0-933348),* 11 Indian Spring Rd., Milton, MA 02186 Tel 617-773-2709 (SAN 212-4610).

Swallow Press, *(Swallow; 0-8040),* Ohio University Press, Scott Quadrangle Room 144, Athens, OH 45701 Tel 614-594-5852 (SAN 202-5663); Orders to: Harper & Row Publishers, Inc., Order Service Dept., Keystone Industrial Park, Scranton, PA 18512 Tel 800-233-4175 (SAN 202-5671) Tel 800-982-4377.

Swampgas Press, *(Swampgas; 0-933838),* 3201 St. Charles Ave., No. 313, New Orleans, LA 70115 Tel 504-897-3413 (SAN 212-7008).

Swan, Frances M., *(F M Swan; 0-9602126),* 11533 Old St. Charles Rd., Bridgeton, MO 63044 (SAN 212-3835).

Swan Books, *(Swan Books),* P.O. Box 332, Fair Oaks, CA 95628 Tel 916-961-8778 (SAN 212-7016).

Swanson, Evadene, *(E Swanson; 0-9600862),* 1404 West Lake, Fort Collins, CO 80524 Tel 303-484-4534 (SAN 208-1156).

Swanson, Jack W., *(J W Swanson; 0-9608764),* Box 1877, Ouray, CO 81427 Tel 303-325-4150 (SAN 241-0796).

Swanson Publishing Co., *(Swanson; 0-911466),* P.O. Box 334, Moline, IL 61265 (SAN 204-6520).

Swearingen & Co., *(Swearingen and Co; 0-911237),* BOX 2015, Dusty Bend Sta., Camden, SC 29020 Tel 803-432-3849 (SAN 275-8903).

Swedenborg Foundation, Inc., *(Swedenborg; 0-87785),* 139 E. 23rd St., New York, NY 10010 Tel 212-673-7310 (SAN 202-7526).

Swedenborg Society, *(Swedenborg UK; 0-85448),* 20-21 Bloomsbury Way, London, WC1A 2TA, .

Swedish Council of America, *(Swedish Council),* c/o American Swedish Institute, 2600 Park Ave., Minneapolis, MN 55407 (SAN 277-9668).

Sweet CH'I Press, *(Sweet Ch'i Pr; 0-912059),* 662 Union St., Brooklyn, NY 11215 Tel 212-857-0449 (SAN 264-6382).

Sweet Publishing Co., *(Sweet; 0-8344),* Box 18928, Ft. Worth, TX 78765 Tel 817-595-2667 (SAN 206-8958).

Sweetbrier Press, *(Sweetbrier; 0-936736),* 536 Emerson St., Palo Alto, CA 94301 (SAN 216-1915).

Sweeter Than Honey, *(Sweeter Than Honey; 0-934244),* P.O. Box 7110, Tyler, TX 75711 Tel 214-597-2247 (SAN 211-8262).

Sweetlight Books, *(Sweetlight; 0-9604462),* P.O. Box 307, Arcata, CA 95521 (SAN 215-1154).

Sweetman, Leonard, *(L Sweetman; 0-9600518),* 1712 Fisherville Rd., Coatesville, PA 19320 (SAN 203-9265).

Sweets Corners Press, *(Sweets Corners; 0-9611284),* 1321 Sweets Corners Rd., Penfield, NY 14526 Tel 716-377-2962 (SAN 283-3476).

Sweetser, Albert G., *(A G Sweetser; 0-9605500),* 17 Broadleaf Dr., Clifton Park, NY 12065 Tel 518-371-7674 (SAN 206-1864).

Sweetwater Editions, *(Sweetwater Edns; 0-941438),* 131 E. 66th St., New York, NY 10021 (SAN 239-393X).

Swets North America, *(Swets North Am),* P. O. Box 517, Berwyn, PA 19312 (SAN 220-004X).

Swimming World, *(Swimming; 0-911822),* 1130 W. Florence Ave., Inglewood, CA 90301 Tel 213-641-2727 (SAN 204-6539).

Swollen Magpie Press, *(Swollen Magpie; 0-9609090),* Rt. 2, Box 499, Putnam Valley, NY 10579 Tel 914-526-3392 (SAN 240-933X).

Sword & Stone Press, *(Sword & Stone; 0-939086),* 4330 Windward Circle, Dallas, TX 75252 Tel 214-380-1433 (SAN 216-3071).

Sword of the Lord Pubs., *(Sword of Lord; 0-87398),* P.O. Box 1099, 224 Bridge Ave., Murfreesboro, TN 37130 Tel 615-893-6700 (SAN 203-5642).

Swordsman Press, *(Swordsman Pr; 0-940018),* 15445 Ventura Blvd., No. 10, Box 5973, Sherman Oaks, CA 91413 Tel 213-342-1422 (SAN 216-860X).

Swordsman Pubns., *(Swordsman Pubns; 0-913493),* P.O. Box 111, Burnt Hills, NY 12027 Tel 518-399-0677 (SAN 285-869X).

Sybex, Inc., *(Sybex; 0-89588),* 2344 Sixth St., Berkeley, CA 94710 Tel 415-848-8233 (SAN 211-1667).

Sycamore Press, Inc., *(Sycamore Pr; 0-916768),* P.O. Box 552, Terre Haute, IN 47808 Tel 812-299-2458 (SAN 208-8827).

Syder Press, *(Syder Pr; 0-939470),* 5893 Kahara Court, Sacramento, CA 95822 (SAN 216-4590).

Sydon, Inc, *(Sydon),* Univ. of the Pacific, Drama Dept., Stockton, CA 95211 Tel 209-946-2116 (SAN 202-070X).

Syentek Books Co., Inc., *(Syentek Bks; 0-914082),* P.O. Box 26588, San Francisco, CA 94126 Tel 415-928-0471 (SAN 202-7534).

Sylvan Institute of Mental Health, *(Sylvan Inst),* 7104 NE Hazel Dell Avenue, Vancouver, WA 98665 Tel 206-694-0911 (SAN 212-0089).

Sylvan Press Pubs., Ltd., *(Sylvan Pr VA; 0-935254),* P.O. Box 15125, Richmond, VA 23227 (SAN 213-8034).

Sylvan Pubns., *(Sylvan Pubns; 0-9606678),* 42185 Baintree Circle, Northville, MI 48167 Tel 313-349-4827 (SAN 219-6433).

Syman, A., Pubns., *(A Syman Pubns; 0-941704),* P.O. Box 3988, San Clemente, CA 92672 (SAN 239-541X).

Symbols & Signs, *(Sym & Sign; 0-912504),* P.O. Box 4536, North Hollywood, CA 91607 (SAN 205-4094).

Symmes Systems, *(Symmes Syst; 0-916352),* P.O. Box 8101, Atlanta, GA 30306 Tel 404-876-7260 (SAN 208-3809).

Symphony League of Jackson, Mississippi, *(Sym League; 0-9608552),* P.O. Box 9402, Jackson, MS 39206 Tel 601-960-1565 (SAN 240-7833).

Symphony Press, Inc., *(Symphony),* P.O. Box 515, Tenafly, NJ 07670 (SAN 210-6310).

Symposia Press, *(Symposia Pr; 0-918542),* P.O. Box 418, Moorestown, NJ 08057 Tel 609-235-8439 (SAN 209-892X).

Symposia Specialists, *(Symposia Special; 0-88372),* 1460 N.E. 129th St., Miami, FL 33161 Tel 305-891-0118 (SAN 202-0564).

Symposium Press, The, *(Symposium Pr),* 1620 Greenfield, Los Angeles, CA 90025 (SAN 213-1943).

Synapse Pubns., *(Synapse Pubns; 0-935170),* 1310 Benedum Trees Bldg., Pittsburgh, PA 15222 Tel 412-765-3140 (SAN 214-1507).

Syncline, *(Syncline; 0-9603794),* 7825 S. Ridgeway, Chicago, IL 60652 (SAN 214-1515).

Syndicate Books, *(Syndicate; 0-911474),* 551 Fifth Ave., New York, NY 10176 Tel 212-682-0546 (SAN 205-4108).

Synecology Press, Inc., *(Synecology; 0-931774),* 309 E. 15th St., Tempe, AZ 85281 Tel 602-967-4173 (SAN 212-2359).

Synergetics Press, The, *(Synergetics WV; 0-910217),* Box 2091, Parkersburg, WV 26102 Tel 304-485-0460 (SAN 241-4643).

Synergistic Press, Inc., *(Synergistic Pr; 0-912184),* 3965 Sacramento St., San Francisco, CA 94118 Tel 415-387-8180 (SAN 205-4116).

Synergy House, *(Synergy Hse; 0-934962),* P.O. Box 1827, Costa Mesa, CA 92626 Tel 714-549-4484 (SAN 213-3792).

Synod of North Carolina, Presbyterian Church (U.S.A.), *(Synod NC Church),* 1015 Wade Ave. P.O. Box 10785, Raleigh, NC 27605 Tel 919-834-4379 (SAN 206-2356).

Syntax Pubns., *(Syntax Pubns),* 4419 Driftwood Place, Boulder, CO 80301 (SAN 240-9879).

Synthesis Pubns., *(Synthesis Pubns; 0-89935),* 2703 Folsom St., San Francisco, CA 94110 Tel 415-550-1284 (SAN 282-3888); Orders to: Synthesis Publications, P.O. Box 40099, San Francisco, CA 94140 (SAN 282-3896).

Sypher, Francis, *(F Sypher),* 220 E. 50th St., New York, NY 10022 (SAN 215-0492).

Syracuse Univ., Foreign & Comparative Studies Program, *(Syracuse U Foreign Comp; 0-915984),* 119 College Place, Syracuse, NY 13210 Tel 315-423-2552 (SAN 220-0082).

Syracuse Univ. Press, *(Syracuse U Pr; 0-8156),* 1600 Jamesville Ave., Syracuse, NY 13210 Tel 315-423-2596 (SAN 206-9776). *Imprints:* American Univ. of Beirut Pubns. (Am U Beirut).

Syracuse Univ. Pubns. in Continuing Education, *(Syracuse U Cont Ed; 0-87060),* 224 Huntington Hall, 150 Marshall St., Syracuse, NY 13210 Tel 315-423-3421 (SAN 202-7577).

System Development Corporation, *(System Dev CA; 0-916368),* 2500 Colorado Avenue, Santa Monica, CA 90406 (SAN 222-8246).

System Logistics, Inc., *(System Logistics; 0-9602362),* P.O. Box 25776, 507 Kawaihae St., Honolulu, HI 96825 Tel 808-396-9650 (SAN 212-5692).

Systematic Development, Inc., *(Systematic Dev),* P.O. Box 52, Pasadena, CA 91102 (SAN 218-981X).

Systems Publications, Inc., *(System Pubn; 0-912503),* P.O. Box 318, Haslett, MI 48840 Tel 517-349-4695 (SAN 265-2234).

Systems Publishing Corp., *(Systems Pub; 0-938974),* P.O. Box 2161, West Lafayette, IN 47906 (SAN 216-308X).

Systems Research Institute, *(Systems Res; 0-912352),* Publications Dept., P.O. Box 4568, Los Angeles, CA 90051 (SAN 202-7585).

Syzygy, *(Syzygy; 0-943108),* P. O. Box 18, Rush, NY 14543 Tel 716-226-2127 (SAN 240-1541).

Syzygy Press, *(Syzygy Pr; 0-9608372),* P.O. Box 183, Mill Valley, CA 94942 Tel 415-883-2046 (SAN 240-4508); Dist. by: Subterranean Co., The, P.O. Box 10233, Eugene, OR 97440 (SAN 169-7102).

Szoke, John Graphics, Inc., *(J Szoke Graphics; 0-936598),* 144 E. 57th St., New York, NY 10022 (SAN 222-1748).

Szwede Slavic Books, *(Szwede Slavic),* P.O. Box 1214, Palo Alto, CA 94302 (SAN 202-053X).

Tab Books, Inc., *(TAB Bks; 0-8306),* Monterey Ave., Blue Ridge Summit, PA 17214 Tel 717-794-2191 (SAN 202-568X).

T.A.C.L., *(TACL),* 641 Towle Way, Palo Alto, CA 94306 Tel 415-493-3628 (SAN 211-5778).

TAM Associates, *(TAM Assoc; 0-913005),* 911 Chicago, Oak Park, IL 60302 Tel 312-848-6760 (SAN 283-4235).

T & E Enterprises, *(T & E Ent; 0-9609942),* P.O. Box 14324, Albuquerque, NM 87191 Tel 505-299-7502 (SAN 275-9101).

TBN Enterprises, *(TBN Ent; 0-935554),* Box 55, Alexandria, VA 22313 Tel 703-549-2506 (SAN 206-2380).

TBW Books, *(TBW Bks; 0-931474),* Rural Route One, P.O. Box 164, Woolwich, ME 04579 Tel 207-442-7632 (SAN 212-2367).

T/C Pubns., Div. of Technology Conferences, *(T-C Pubns CA; 0-938648),* P.O. Box 842, El Segundo, CA 90245 Tel 213-938-6923 (SAN 239-491X).

T. E. A. M. Pubs., *(TEAM Pubs; 0-939658),* 4043 N. 15th Ave., Phoenix, AZ 85015 Tel 602-971-1523 (SAN 216-647X).

T. E. L. L. Pubns., *(TELL Pubns; 0-939028),* P.O. Box 9044, Hampton, VA 23670 (SAN 217-2712).

T. F. H. Pubns., *(TFH Pubns; 0-87666),* 211 W. Sylvania Ave., Neptune, NJ 07753 Tel 201-988-8400 (SAN 202-7720).

TG Publishing, *(T G Pub; 0-9611692),* Box 105, Woody Creek, CO 81656 Tel 303-923-4605 (SAN 284-9070).

T. I. Hayes Publishing Co., *(T I Hayes Pub Co; 0-910728),* P.O. Box 17352, Fort Mitchell, KY 41017 Tel 606-341-3201 (SAN 204-0565).

T.I.S., Inc., Div. of T.I.S. Enterprises, *(TIS Inc; 0-89917),* P.O. Box 1998, 1928 Arlington Rd., Bloomington, IN 47402 Tel 812-332-3307 (SAN 169-2313).

TL Enterprises, Inc., *(TL Enterprises; 0-934798),* 29901 Agoura Rd., Agoura, CA 91301 Tel 213-991-4980 (SAN 213-1803).

TPA Publishing Ltd., *(TPA Pub),* 540 West 112th St., Los Angeles, CA 90044 (SAN 263-2349).

T S L Press (Time & Space Ltd.), *(T S L Pr; 0-939858),* 139 W. 22nd St., New York, NY 10011 Tel 212-741-1032 (SAN 216-938X).

T S M Productions, Inc., *(TSM Prods; 0-941316),* 40 Whitney Ave., Syosset, NY 11791 Tel 516-921-0551 (SAN 239-040X).

T. Schroeder, *(J Schroeder; 0-9691002),* P.O. Box 729, Waterloo, ON, N2J 4C2, (SAN 226-8078).

TVRT, *(TVRT; 0-931106),* 25 E. Fourth St., New York, NY 10003 Tel 212-260-4254 (SAN 206-1341).

TW Pubs, *(T W Pubs),* P.O. Box 152, River Forest, IL 60305 (SAN 205-4124).

NAME INDEX

TA Press, Div. of International Transaction Analysis Assn., *(TA Press; 0-89489),* 1772 Vallejo St., San Francisco, CA 94123 Tel 415-885-5992 (SAN 209-6846).

Taber, Thomas T., *(T T Taber; 0-9603398),* Muncy, PA 17756 (SAN 211-9838).

Tafnews Press, Div. of Track & Field News, Inc., *(Tafnews; 0-911520; 0-911521),* P.O. Box 296, Los Altos, CA 94022 Tel 415-948-8188 (SAN 202-7593).

Taft Corporation, *(Taft Corp; 0-914756),* 5125 Macarthur Blvd. N.W., Washington, DC 20016 Tel 202-966-7086 (SAN 206-5215).

Tahrike Tarsile Quran, *(Tahrike Tarsile Quran),* P.O. Box 1115, Elmhurst, NY 11373 (SAN 217-1341).

Tail Feather, *(Tail Feather; 0-911756),* P.O. Box 1106, Moab, UT 84532 Tel 801-259-5303 (SAN 205-4132); Dist. by: Card Lake Services, Channel Islands Harbor, Suite 178, 3600 S. Harbor Blvd., Oxnard, CA 93030 Tel 805-483-0689 (SAN 200-4135). *Imprints:* Neptune Books (Neptune Bks).

Talbert, Robert, *(R Talbert),* 260 W. 72nd St., Suite 5D, New York, NY 10023 Tel 212-724-9246 (SAN 211-9846).

Tales of the Mojave Road Pub., Co., *(Tales Mojave Rd; 0-914224),* P.O. Box 307, Norco, CA 91760 Tel 714-737-3150 (SAN 202-7607).

Talespinner Pubns., Inc., *(Talespinner; 0-934926),* 4543 Pleasant Ave., S., Minneapolis, MN 55409 Tel 612-823-3614 (SAN 213-3814); Orders to: P.O. Box 19087, Minneapolis, MN 55419 Tel 612-825-0087 (SAN 213-3822).

Talisman Literary Research, Inc., *(Talisman Research; 0-934614),* P.O. Box 455, Georgetown, CA 95634 Tel 916-333-4486 (SAN 206-9547).

Talisman Press, *(Talisman; 0-934612),* P.O. Box 455, Georgetown, CA 95634 Tel 916-333-4486 (SAN 205-4140).

Talking Seal Press, *(Talking Seal; 0-9606322),* P.O. Box 4301, Flint, MI 48504 (SAN 218-5083).

Talley Productions, *(Talley Prods; 0-9606588),* 1626 N. Wilcox, Suite 200, Hollywood, CA 90028 (SAN 219-8207).

Tamal Land Press, *(Tamal Land; 0-912908),* 39 Merwin Ave., Fairfax, CA 94930 Tel 415-456-4705 (SAN 207-0162).

Tamal Vista Pubns., *(Tamal Vista; 0-917436),* 222 Madrone Ave., Larkspur, CA 94939 Tel 415-924-7289 (SAN 218-9844).

Tamalpais Press, *(Tamalpais Pr; 0-916596),* P.O. Box 419, Santa Barbara, CA 93102 Tel 805-963-3233 (SAN 209-2573).

Tamarack Editions, *(Tamarack Edns; 0-918092),* 128 Benedict Ave., Syracuse, NY 13210 Tel 315-478-6495 (SAN 210-170X).

Tamarack Press, *(Tamarack Pr; 0-915024),* P.O. Box 5650, Madison, WI 53705 Tel 608-231-2444 (SAN 209-2425).

Tamburitza Press, *(Tamburitza; 0-936922),* 1801 Blvd. of the Allies, Pittsburgh, PA 15219 (SAN 216-065X).

Tam's Books, Inc., *(Tam's Bks; 0-89179),* 3333 S. Hoover St., Los Angeles, CA 90007 Tel 213-746-1141 (SAN 207-6497).

TAN Books & Pubs., Inc., *(TAN Bks Pubs; 0-89555),* 2135 N. Central Ave., Rockford, IL 61105 Tel 815-962-2662 (SAN 282-390X); Orders to: P.O. Box 424, Rockford, IL 61105 Tel 815-962-2662 (SAN 282-3918).

Tanadgusix Corp., *(Tanadgusix Corp; 0-9601948),* St. Paul, AK 99660 (SAN 211-7630).

Tanager Books Inc., Div. of Longwood Pub. Group, *(Tanager Bks; 0-88072),* 51 Washington St., Dover, NH 03820 Tel 603-522-6282 (SAN 238-2016); Dist. by: Flatiron Book Distributors, Inc., 175 Fifth Ave., Suite 814, New York, NY 10010 Tel 212-228-0390 (SAN 240-9917).

Tanam Press, *(Tanam Pr; 0-934378),* 40 White St., New York, NY 10013 (SAN 215-3467).

Tanasi Archaeological Research Associates, *(TARA; 0-940148),* P.O. Box 7262, College Sta., Durhamlle, NC 27708 Tel 919-682-6097 (SAN 220-3081).

Tandem Press Pubs., *(Tandem Pr; 0-913024),* P.O. Box 237, Tannersville, PA 18372 Tel 717-629-2250 (SAN 202-7615).

Tandem Pubs., *(Tandem Pubs VA; 0-9606244),* 5821 Banning Place, Burke, VA 22015 (SAN 218-5091).

Tangents, *(Tangents; 0-9611742),* P.O. Box 965, Kankakee, IL 60901 Tel 815-932-5130 (SAN 285-3809).

Tanner, Grace A., Center for Human Values, *(G A Tanner Ctr; 0-910153),* c/o Southern Utah State College, Cedar City, UT 84720 Tel 801-533-5617 (SAN 280-5782).

Tanner, Ralph, Associates, Inc., *(R Tanner Assocs Inc; 0-942078),* Suite 102, Great Western Bank Bldg., 122 N. Cortez St., Prescott, AZ 86301 Tel 602-778-4162 (SAN 239-9857).

Tantric Press, *(Tantric Pr; 0-9609746),* P.O. Box 126306, San Diego, CA 92112 (SAN 275-9225).

Tao of Wing Chun Do, *(Tao of Wing; 0-918642),* 11023 N.E. 131st, Kirkland, WA 98033 Tel 206-821-1487 (SAN 211-9854).

Taoist Pubs., *(Taoist Pubs),* Dist. by: MRK Enterprizes, P.O. Box 416, Waterford, MI 48095 Tel 313-623-6765 (SAN 239-4928).

Taplinger Publishing Co., Inc., *(Taplinger; 0-8008),* 132 W. 22nd St., New York, NY 10011 Tel 212-741-0801 (SAN 213-6821).

Tara Center, The, *(Tara Ctr; 0-936604),* P.O. Box 6001, N. Hollywood, CA 91603 Tel 213-954-8885 (SAN 282-3950); Orders to: 3404 W. Victory Blvd., Burbank, CA 91505 (SAN 282-3969); Dist. by: Devorss & Co., P.O. Box 550, Marina Del Rey, CA 90291 Tel 213-870-7478 (SAN 168-9886).

Taraxacum, *(Taraxacum; 0-9602822),* 1227 30th St. N.W., Washington, DC 20007 (SAN 213-8255).

Tarcher, J. P., Inc., *(J P Tarcher; 0-87477),* 9110 Sunset Blvd., Suite 250, Los Angeles, CA 90069 Tel 213-273-3274 (SAN 202-0424); Dist. by: Houghton Mifflin Co., Wayside Rd., Burlington, MA 01803 Tel 800-225-3362 (SAN 200-2388).

Tari Book Pubs., *(Tari Bk Pubs),* 2760 Madison, Eugene, OR 97405 (SAN 214-1523).

TarPar, Ltd., *(TarPar),* P.O. Box 3, Kernersville, NC 27284 (SAN 207-494X).

Tarrant, Patrick, *(Tarrant; 0-9608850),* 1907 Castle Ave., Bloomington, IL 61701 (SAN 241-080X).

Tasa Publishing Co., *(Tasa Pub Co; 0-935698),* P.O. Box 35053, Edina, MN 55435 (SAN 216-0668).

Tashmoo Press, The, *(Tashmoo; 0-932384),* RFD, Vineyard Haven, MA 02568 (SAN 212-5706).

Tat's, Inc., *(Tats; 0-911478),* 3100 Airway Ave., Suite 117, Costa Mesa, CA 92626 Tel 714-545-3121 (SAN 205-4167).

Tatsch Associates, *(Tatsch; 0-912890),* 120 Thunder Rd., Sudbury, MA 01776 Tel 617-443-6343 (SAN 202-7623).

TAU Press, *(TAU Pr),* P.O. Box 2283, Rolling Hills, CA 90274 (SAN 209-3022).

Taugus House Pubs., Inc., *(Taugus Hse; 0-938556),* 1890 San Pablo Dr., San Marcos, CA 92069 (SAN 215-9236).

Taunton Press, Inc., *(Taunton; 0-918804),* Box 355, Newtown, CT 06470 Tel 203-426-8171 (SAN 210-5144).

Taurus Editions, *(Taurus Ed; 0-913925),* 96 Grand St., New York, NY 10013 Tel 212-966-1222 (SAN 286-0597).

Taurus Publishing Co., *(Taurus Pub Co; 0-913495),* 56 Doris Road, Box 492, Halifax, MA 02338 Tel 617-293-9110 (SAN 283-8753).

Tax Foundation, Inc., *(Tax Found),* One Thomas Circle, N.W., Suite 500, Washington, DC 20005 (SAN 225-1302).

Tax Information Center, *(Tax Info Ctr),* Rte. 1, New Concord, OH 43762 (SAN 203-1582).

Tax Management, Inc., *(Tax Mgmt),* 1231 25th St., N.W., Washington, DC 20037 (SAN 240-1630).

Taxpayers' Foundation, *(Taxpayers Found),* 325 Pennsylvania Ave. SE, Washington, DC 20003 (SAN 265-3648).

Taylor, Carl B., *(C B Taylor; 0-9605948),* 773 Augusta, Morgantown, WV 26505 Tel 304-292-8190 (SAN 216-6488).

Taylor, Dorothy Loring, *(D L Taylor; 0-9610640),* R. R. 2, Box 152, Virginia, IL 62691 (SAN 265-3567).

Taylor, James, Ltd., *(Taylor James),* P.O. Box 12060, La Crescenta, CA 91214 (SAN 241-5860).

Taylor, Pat, *(P Taylor; 0-9611404),* P.O. Box 391, Hendersonville, NC 28640 (SAN 283-8796).

Taylor, Robert H., *(R H Taylor),* Box 46, Lumberville, PA 18933 (SAN 282-5767).

Taylor, Sally, & Friends, *(Taylor & Friends; 0-9604904),* 756 Kansas St., San Francisco, CA 94107 (SAN 216-1990).

Taylor, W. Thomas, Bookseller, *(W Thomas Taylor; 0-935072),* 708 Colorado, Austin, TX 78701 Tel 512-478-7628 (SAN 211-1454).

Taylor, William M., *(W M Taylor),* 412 Red Hill Ave., San Anselmo, CA 94960 Tel 415-457-2214 (SAN 212-9736).

Taylor & Ng, *(Taylor & Ng),* Box 200, Brisbane, CA 94005 Tel 415-467-2600 (SAN 208-3396).

Taylor-Carlisle, *(Taylor-Carlisle),* 245 Seventh Ave., New York, NY 10001 Tel 212-674-7788 (SAN 205-4175).

Taylor Homestead, *(Taylor Home; 0-9609384),* Star Rt., Box 35, Sanbornton, NH 03269 Tel 603-286-8927 (SAN 260-2709).

Taylor Museum, *(Taylor Museum),* Dist. by: Colorado Springs Fine Arts Ctr., 30 W. Dale St., Colorado Springs, CO 80903 Tel 303-634-5581 (SAN 206-2720).

Taylor Publishing, *(Taylor Pub WA; 0-9609056),* P.O. Box 413, Anacortes, WA 98221 Tel 206-293-5675 (SAN 240-9860).

Taylor Publishing Co., *(Taylor Pub; 0-87833),* P.O. Box 597, Dallas, TX 75221 (SAN 202-7631).

Taylor Street Press, *(Taylor Street; 0-911407),* 60 Taylor Dr., Fairfax, CA 94930 Tel 415-453-2765 (SAN 275-9403).

Tayu Press, *(Tayu Pr; 0-934350),* P.O. Box 11554, Santa Rosa, CA 95406 Tel 707-887-2490 (SAN 213-1773).

T. C. Pubs., *(T C Pubs; 0-920192),* 51 Columbine Ave., Toronto, ON, M4L 1P6, (SAN 209-4916) Moved, Left no Forwarding Address.

Te-Cum-Tom Enterprises, *(Te Cum Tom; 0-913508),* 1725 Shorepines Dr., Coos Bay, OR 97420 Tel 503-888-6363 (SAN 205-4183).

Tea Rose Press, *(Tea Rose Pr; 0-940302),* P.O. Box 591, East Lansing, MI 48823 Tel 517-351-1317 (SAN 217-5800).

Teach'em, Inc., *(Teach'em; 0-931028),* 160 E. Illinois St., Chicago, IL 60611 (SAN 211-2787).

Teacher Tested Materials, *(Tchr Tested Materials),* P.O. Box 67, Putnam, IL 61560 (SAN 216-4604).

Teacher Update, Inc., *(Teacher Update; 0-89780),* Box 205, Saddle River, NJ 07458 Tel 201-327-8486 (SAN 212-3878).

Teachers & Writers Collaborative, *(Tchrs & Writers Coll; 0-915924),* 84 Fifth Ave., New York, NY 10011 Tel 212-691-6590 (SAN 206-3859).

Teachers College Press, Columbia Univ., *(Tchrs Coll; 0-8077),* 1234 Amsterdam Ave., New York, NY 10027 Tel 212-678-3929 (SAN 282-3985); Orders to: Harper & Row, Keystone Industrial Park, Scranton, PA 18512 Tel 800-233-4175 (SAN 282-3993).

Teacher's Load Press, *(Teachers Load; 0-9603750),* 2631 Farber Dr., St. Louis, MO 63136 Tel 314-741-9800 (SAN 213-8735).

Teacher's Tax Service, *(Teachers Tax; 0-912772),* 1303 E. Balboa Blvd., Newport Beach, CA 92661 Tel 714-675-9891 (SAN 202-0394).

Teal Press, *(Teal Pr; 0-913793),* P.O. Box 4346, Portsmouth, NH 03801 Tel 603-431-2319 (SAN 286-2042).

Teaparty, *(Teaparty Bks),* 10 Loring Ave., Box 232, Kingston, MA 02364 Tel 617-585-4666 (SAN 265-3656).

Tech Data Pubns., *(Tech Data; 0-937816),* 6324 W. Fond Du Lac Ave., Milwaukee, WI 53218 (SAN 216-0129).

Techkits, Inc., *(Techkits; 0-918662),* P.O. Box 105, Demarest, NJ 07627 Tel 201-768-7334 (SAN 210-3753).

Technical & Education Center of the Graphic Arts, Rochester Institute of Technology (T&E Center), *(Tech & Ed Ctr Graph Arts RIT; 0-89938),* 1 Lomb Memorial Dr., Rochester, NY 14623 Tel 716-475-2761 (SAN 205-2334).

Technical Assn. of the Pulp & Paper Industry, *(TAPPI; 0-89852),* 1 Dunwoody Park, Atlanta, GA 30338 Tel 404-394-6130 (SAN 212-5714).

Technical Communications Associates, Inc., *(Tech Comm Assoc; 0-9611694),* 1250 Oakmed Pkwy, Suite 210, Sunnyvale, CA 94086 (SAN 284-9097).

Technical Database Corp., *(Tech Data Corp),* P.O. Box 720, Conroe, TX 77310 (SAN 262-0944).

Technical Dictionaries Co., *(Tech Dict; 0-911484),* P.O. Box 144, New York, NY 10031 (SAN 205-4191).

Technical Education Co., Inc., *(Tech Educ Co; 0-939402),* P.O. Box 18738, Irvine, CA 92713 (SAN 216-4612).

Technical Education Press, *(Tech Ed Pr; 0-911908),* P.O. Box 342, Seal Beach, CA 90740 Tel 213-431-8515 (SAN 205-4205).

Technical Education Services, *(Tech Ed Serv; 0-930552),* Univ. of Missouri, School of Journalism, Kappa Alpha Mu, Box 838, Columbia, MO 65201 Tel 314-442-3161 (SAN 213-3849); Dist. by: Running Press, 125 S. 22nd St., Philadelphia, PA 19103 Tel 215-567-5080 (SAN 204-5702).

Technical Handbook Pubns., Inc., *(Tech Handbk; 0-941114),* P.O. Box 2841, Woburn, MA 01888 Tel 617-657-7360 (SAN 282-4000); Orders to: Intercom Corporation, P.O. Box 2841, Woburn, MA 01888 (SAN 282-4019).

Technical Information Project, Inc., *(Tech Info Proj; 0-939578),* 1346 Connecticut Ave. N.W., Suite 217, Washington, DC 20036 Tel 202-466-2954 (SAN 214-2619).

Technico Books, *(Technico Bks; 0-9607678),* Box 20hc-Orangehurst, Fullerton, CA 92633 (SAN 239-5622).

Technicon Pubs., *(Technicon Pubs; 0-915428),* P.O. Box 1413, Novato, CA 94947 Tel 415-897-7638 (SAN 207-3560).

Technocracy, Inc., *(Technocracy; 0-9606470),* P.O. Box 238, Savannah, OH 44874 Tel 419-962-4712 (SAN 209-7842).

Technology Group, The, *(Tech Group; 0-939856),* P.O. Box 93124, Pasadena, CA 91109 Tel 818-794-6013 (SAN 220-195X).

Technology Management, Inc., *(Tech Mgmt),* 57 Kilvert St., Warwick, RI 02886 (SAN 212-0496); Dist. by: Management Associates, Box 230, Chestnut Hill, MA 02167 (SAN 212-050X).

Technology Marketing Corp., *(Tech Marketing),* 17 Park St., Norwalk, CT 06851 Tel 203-846-2029 (SAN 212-4629).

Technology Press, Inc., The, *(Tech Pr Inc; 0-89321),* P.O. Box 125, Fairfax Station, VA 22039 Tel 703-978-5299 (SAN 208-8851).

Technology Recognition Corporation, *(Tech Recog Corp; 0-933980),* 1382 Old Freeport Rd., Pittsburgh, PA 15238 (SAN 213-3857).

Technology Search International, Inc., *(Tech Search Intl; 0-943420),* 516 Sussex Ct., Elk Groove Village, IL 60007 Tel 312-593-2111 (SAN 240-7868).

Technology Transfer Society, *(Tech Trans),* NIAC-USC Demey Research Building, Los Angeles, CA 90007 (SAN 225-252X).

Technomic Publishing Co., *(Technomic; 0-87762),* 851 New Holland Ave., Box 3535, Lancaster, PA 17604 Tel 717-291-5609 (SAN 202-764X).

Techscience, Inc., *(Techscience Inc; 0-918910),* P.O. Box 1100, Hawthorne, CA 90250 Tel 503-926-5739 (SAN 208-1733).

Tecolote Press, Inc., *(Tecolote Pr; 0-915030),* P.O. Box 188, Glenwood, NM 88039 Tel 505-539-2183 (SAN 207-1851).

Tee Loftin Pubs., Inc., *(Tee Loftin; 0-934812),* 3100 R St., N.W., Washington, DC 20007 (SAN 215-9635).

Telamon, *(Telamon; 0-9610974),* P.O. Box 26648, San Francisco, CA 94126-6648 Tel 415-752-2143 (SAN 265-2277).

Tele-Sell Research Institute *See* **Anthony, C & R, Pubs., Inc.**

Telecom Library, The, *(Telecom Lib; 0-936648),* 205 W. 19th St., New York, NY 10011 Tel 212-691-8215 (SAN 211-9862). *Imprints:* Personal Achievement Library (Personal Achievement).

Telecommunications Research & Action Center (TRAC), *(T R A C; 0-9603466; 0-943444),* 1530 P St., N.W., P.O. Box 12038, Washington, DC 20005 Tel 202-462-2520 (SAN 210-9182).

Telegraph Books, *(Telegraph Bks; 0-89760),* Box 38, Norwood, PA 19074 Tel 215-583-4550 (SAN 213-8042).

Telegraph Books *See* **Dynamic Learning Corp.**

Telegraphic Cable & Radio Registrations, Inc., *(Tele Cable; 0-916446),* 1600 Harrison Ave., Mamaroneck, NY 10543 (SAN 208-886X).

Teleometrics International, Inc., *(Teleometrics; 0-937932),* 1755 Woodstead Court, The Woodlands, TX 77380 Tel 713-367-0060 (SAN 220-0953).

Telephone Books Press, *(Telephone Bks; 0-916382),* 109 Dunk Rock Rd., Guilford, CT 06437 Tel 203-453-4415 (SAN 208-2462).

Television & Cable Factbook, *(TV Factbk; 0-911486),* 1836 Jefferson Place, N.W., Washington, DC 20036 Tel 202-872-9200 (SAN 207-2955).

Telos Press Ltd., *(Telos Pr; 0-914386),* Box 3111, St. Louis, MO 63130 Tel 314-361-8472 (SAN 282-4027).

Telshare Publishing Co., Inc., *(TelShare Pub Co; 0-910287),* 109 State St., Boston, MA 02109 Tel 617-723-1980 (SAN 241-4651).

Telstar Inc., *(Telstar Inc; 0-943000),* 366 N. Prior Ave., St. Paul, MN 55104 Tel 612-644-4726 (SAN 240-4524).

Temescal Books, *(Temescal Bks; 0-914289),* P.O. Box 20067, Oakland, CA 94620-0067 Tel 415-655-5240 (SAN 287-5713); 5367 Shafter Ave., Oakland, CA 94618 (SAN 287-5721).

Tempe Pubs., Inc., *(Tempe Pubs; 0-933554),* P.O. Box 28262, Tempe, AZ 85282 Tel 602-838-3974 (SAN 212-6822).

Temple, Ellen C., *(E C Temple; 0-936650),* 32 Sundown Pkwy., Austin, TX 78746 Tel 512-327-4961 (SAN 215-1162).

Temple Bar Bookshop, *(Temple Bar),* 9 Boylston St., Cambridge, MA 02138 Tel 617-876-6025 (SAN 211-0997).

Temple Univ. Press, *(Temple U Pr; 0-87722),* Philadelphia, PA 19122 Tel 215-787-8787 (SAN 202-7666).

Templegate Pubs., *(Templegate; 0-87243),* 302 E. Adams St., P.O. Box 5152, Springfield, IL 62705 Tel 217-522-3361 (SAN 213-1994).

Templeman, Eleanor Lee, *(Templeman; 0-911044),* 3001 N. Pollard St., Arlington, VA 22207 Tel 703-528-1112 (SAN 207-0189).

Templeton, Larry D., *(Templeton; 0-9608914),* 505 E. Palm St., Litchfield Park, AZ 85340 Tel 602-935-4346 (SAN 241-1571).

Temporal Acuity Press, Div. of Temporal Acuity Products, Inc., *(Temporal; 0-911723),* 1535-121st Ave. SE, Bellevue, WA 98005 Tel 206-746-2790 (SAN 264-4274).

Ten Penny Players, Inc., *(Ten Penny; 0-934830),* 799 Greenwich St., New York, NY 10014 Tel 212-929-3169 (SAN 213-8743).

Ten Speed Press, *(Ten Speed Pr; 0-913668; 0-89815),* P.O. Box 7123, Berkeley, CA 94707 Tel 415-845-8414 (SAN 202-7674).

Ten Talents, *(Ten Talents; 0-9603532),* P.O. Box 86A, Rte. 1, Chisholm, MN 55719 Tel 615-396-2164 (SAN 207-9364).

Tenameca, Inc., *(Tenameca; 0-918582),* P.O. Box 44436, Indianapolis, IN 46244 Tel 317-631-6304 (SAN 210-3761).

Tendril, *(Tendril; 0-937504),* P.O. Box 512, Green Harbor, MA 02041 (SAN 215-188X).

Tennessee Amer. Soc. of Interior Designers, (ASID), P.O. Box 15391, Nashville, TN 37215 (SAN 217-2992).

Tennessee Arts Commission, *(Tenn Arts; 0-918518),* 505 Deaderick St., Suite 1700, Nashville, TN 37219 (SAN 239-4936).

Tennessee Federation of Garden Clubs, *(Tenn Fed Garden; 0-939114),* 3325 Lakewood Dr., Memphis, TN 38128 (SAN 219-8215).

Tennis Manual, *(Tennis Manual; 0-9606066),* 600 N. Fig Tree Lane, Ft. Lauderdale, FL 33317 Tel 305-584-3622 (SAN 216-4620); P.O. Box 16781, Ft. Lauderdale, FL 33318 (SAN 216-4639).

Tensleep Publications, *(Tensleep; 0-9610130),* P.O. Box 925, Aberdeen, SD 57401 Tel 605-622-2275 (SAN 262-7477).

Tenth House Enterprises, Inc., *(Tenth Hse Ent; 0-9603310),* P.O. Box 810, Gracie Sta., New York, NY 10028 (SAN 239-4944).

Ter Bear Publishing, *(Ter Bear; 0-910927),* P.O. Box 287B, Santa Rosa, CA 95402 Tel 707-544-7713 (SAN 264-4290).

Ter-Lyn Co., *(Ter-Lyn; 0-939664),* 4090 Jason St., Denver, CO 80211 Tel 303-455-2132 (SAN 220-1011).

Tern, *(Tern Pr; 0-9605388),* 430 SW 206th St., Seattle, WA 98166 Tel 206-824-4042 (SAN 215-9791).

Terra Magica Books *See* **Hill & Wang, Inc.**

Terra Publishing, *(Terra Pub; 0-9603238),* P.O. Box 99103, Jeffersontown, KY 40299 Tel 502-895-0557 (SAN 212-7997).

Terra View Pubns., *(Terra View; 0-9608474),* 1961 Landings Dr., Mountain View, CA 94043 (SAN 240-9089).

Terraspace Inc., *(Terraspace; 0-918990),* 304 N. Stonestreet Ave., Rockville, MD 20850 Tel 301-424-0090 (SAN 210-5152).

Terrell, Bob, *(B Terrell),* P.O. Box 66, Asheville, NC 28802 Tel 704-255-8435 (SAN 209-1941).

Terry, Newton, *(N Terry; 0-912247),* 7709 Briarcliff Courts, Smithfield, TX 76180 (SAN 285-6719).

Terry Publishing Co., *(Terry Pub),* P.O. Box 525, Olympia, WA 98501 Tel 206-491-2055 (SAN 202-7682).

Tesla Book Co., *(Tesla Bk Co; 0-9603536; 0-914119),* 1580 Magnolia Ave., Millbrae, CA 94030 Tel 415-697-4903 (SAN 213-7011).

Test Corporation of America, *(Test Corp; 0-9611286),* 330 W. 47th St., No.205, Kansas City, MO 64112 Tel 816-756-1686 (SAN 283-3492).

Tested Recipe Pubs., Inc., *(Test Recipe; 0-88351),* 6701 Oakton St., Chicago, IL 60648 Tel 312-966-6500 (SAN 202-0467).

Tethys Press, *(Tethys Pr; 0-941446),* 9407 Old Redwood Hwy., Penngrove, CA 94951 Tel 707-795-8345 (SAN 239-0418).

Teton Bookshop Publishing Co., *(Teton Bkshop; 0-933160),* Box 1903, Jackson, WY 83001 (SAN 213-1781).

Teton Publishing House, *(Teton Pub Hse; 0-9606622),* P.O. Box 2870, Jackson, WY 83001 Tel 307-733-4470 (SAN 219-6476).

Tetra Tech, Inc., *(Tetra Tech; 0-916646),* 1911 Ft. Myer Dr., Suite 601, Arlington, VA 22209 (SAN 208-3345).

Tetragrammaton Press, *(Tetragrammaton; 0-937326),* 3594 Sepulveda Blvd., Sherman Oaks, CA 91403 (SAN 214-4778).

Teutsch, Joel & Champion, *(Teutsch),* 2049 Century Park E., Suite 2730, Los Angeles, CA 90067 Tel 213-277-8773 (SAN 206-3867).

Tex-Mex Books Publishers International Texas, *(Tex-Mex; 0-918268),* Box 186, 820 San Antonio Ave., San Juan, TX 78589 Tel 512-781-2186 (SAN 208-0079).

Texan-American Publisher's Co., *(Texan-Am Pub; 0-935622),* 3008 West Ohio, Midland, TX 79701 Tel 915-699-1934 (SAN 213-3865).

Texas A & I University, *(Texas Univ; 0-918464),* Campus Box 127, Kingsville, TX 78363 Tel 512-854-6857 (SAN 283-4340).

Texas A & M Univ. Press, *(Tex A&M Univ Pr; 0-89096),* Drawer "C", College Station, TX 77843 Tel 713-845-1436 (SAN 207-5237).

Texas Assn. of Museums, *(Tex Assn Mus; 0-935260),* P.O. Box 13353, Capitol Sta., Austin, TX 78711 Tel 512-472-0641 (SAN 213-3873).

Texas Christian Univ. Press, *(Tex Christian; 0-912646),* Box 30783, Fort Worth, TX 76129 Tel 817-921-7822 (SAN 202-7690); Dist. by: Texas A & M University Press, Drawer C, College Station, TX 77843-4354 Tel 409-845-1436 (SAN 207-5237).

Texas Congress of Parents & Teachers, *(Tex Congr Parent & Teach),* 408 W. 11th St., Austin, TX 78701 Tel 512-476-6769 (SAN 210-959X).

Texas Consumer Assn., *(Tex Consumer; 0-937606),* 500 W. 13th St., Austin, TX 78701 (SAN 220-0961).

Texas Foundation for Women's Resources, *(Tex Foun Womens Res; 0-9606256),* P.O. Box 4800, Austin, TX 78765 Tel 512-476-1001 (SAN 220-3510).

Texas Instruments Inc., *(Tex Instr Inc; 0-89512),* P.O. Box 225012 MS54, Dallas, TX 75265 Tel 214-995-5516 (SAN 209-6854).

Texas Monthly Press, *(Texas Month Pr; 0-932012),* 4606 Burleson Rd., Unit N, Austin, TX 78744 Tel 512-476-7085 (SAN 200-2531); Orders to: P.O. Bx 1569 Austin,, Austin, TX 78767 (SAN 200-2531).

Texas State Historical Assn., *(Tex St Hist Assn; 0-87611),* 2-306 Richardson Hall, Univ. Sta., Austin, TX 78712 Tel 512-471-1525 (SAN 202-7704); Dist. by: Texas A & M Univ. Press, Drawer "C", College Station, TX 77843-4354 (SAN 207-5237).

Texas Tech Press, *(Tex Tech Pr; 0-89672),* P.O. Box 4460, Lubbock, TX 79409 Tel 806-742-2781 (SAN 208-1709); Orders to: Sales Office, Texas Tech Univ. Library, Lubbock, TX 79409 Tel 806-742-1569 (SAN 208-1717).

Texas Western Press, Univ. of Texas at El Paso, *(Tex Western; 0-87404),* El Paso, TX 79968 Tel 915-747-5688 (SAN 202-7712).

Texas Woman's University Press, *(TX Womans U Pr; 0-9607488),* P.O. Box 23866, Denton, TX 76204 Tel 817-382-1531 (SAN 238-4833).

Texian Press, *(Texian; 0-87244),* P.O. Box 1684, Waco, TX 76703 Tel 817-754-5636 (SAN 205-4256).

Text-Fiche Press, The, *(Text-Fiche; 0-89969),* 540 Drexel Ave., Glencoe, IL 60022 Tel 312-835-4420 (SAN 220-097X); Orders to: Box 382, Glencoe, IL 60022 (SAN 220-0988).

Textbook Specifications, *(Textbk Specif),* P.O. Box 368, Ridgefield, CT 06877 (SAN 226-8043).

Textile Book Service, Inc., *(Textile Bk; 0-87245),* P.O. Box 25, Broadway, NJ 08808 Tel 201-689-2230 (SAN 206-7714).

Textile Bridge Press, *(Textile Bridge),* P.O. Box 157, Clarence Center, NY 14032 (SAN 216-0676).

Textile Museum, *(Textile Mus; 0-87405),* 2320 "S" St., N.W., Washington, DC 20008 Tel 202-667-0441 (SAN 205-4264) Self-Pub. & Self-Dist.

Thadian Pubns., *(Thadian Pubns; 0-930516),* P.O. Box 129, North Haven, CT 06473 (SAN 210-9379).

Thalassa Press, *(Thalassa Pr; 0-939472),* Box 2098, Astoria, NY 11102 (SAN 216-4647).

Thales Microuniversity Press, *(Thales Microuniv; 0-914312),* 13761 S. Fern, Glenpool, OK 74033 Tel 918-299-5854 (SAN 202-7739).

Thames & Hudson, *(Thames Hudson; 0-500),* Dist. by: W.W. Norton, & Co., Inc., 500 Fifth Ave., New York, NY 10110 Tel 212-354-3763 (SAN 202-5795).

That New Publishing Co., *(That New Pub; 0-918270),* 1525 Eielson St., Fairbanks, AK 99701 Tel 907-452-3007 (SAN 209-6862).

That Patchwork Place, Inc., *(That Patchwork; 0-943574),* P.O. Box 118, Bothell, WA 98011 Tel 800-426-3126 (SAN 240-7876).

Thayer & Associates, *(Thayer Assocs; 0-9611000),* 522 Wilcox St., Fort Atkinson, WI 53538 (SAN 283-4278).

Thayer-Jacoby, *(Thayer-Jacoby; 0-9606472),* 1432 E. Ninth St., Brooklyn, NY 11230 (SAN 213-9685).

The Association, *(Association),* 1725 K St NW, Washington, DC 20006 Tel 202-466-6004 (SAN 226-9759).

The Garden, *(The Garden; 0-9602790),* 6605 Rowland Rd., Eden Prairie, MN 55344 Tel 612-944-2404 (SAN 212-9752).

The GED Institute, *(GED Inst; 0-937128),* G Street Northwest, Waterville, WA 98858 (SAN 276-945X).

The Haven Corporation, *(Haven Corp; 0-911361),* 802 Madison, Evanston, IL 60202 Tel 312-869-3434 (SAN 275-9977).

The Little Brown House Publishing Co., *(The Little Brown House; 0-915782),* P.O. Box 46, Harpers Ferry, WV 25425 Tel 304-535-2493 (SAN 207-4230).

Theatre Arts Books, *(Theatre Arts; 0-87830),* 153 Waverly Place, New York, NY 10014 Tel 212-675-1815 (SAN 202-7763).

Theatre Communications Center of the Bay Area, *(Theatre Ctr Bay; 0-9605896),* 2940 16th St., Suite 102, San Francisco, CA 94103 (SAN 216-4655).

Theatre Communications Group, Inc., *(Theatre Comm; 0-930452),* 355 Lexington Ave., New York, NY 10017 (SAN 210-9387).

Thelema Pubns., *(Thelema Pubns; 0-913576),* P.O. Box 1093, Kings Beach, CA 95719 Tel 916-546-2160 (SAN 205-4272).

Theobald, Paul, & Co., *(Theobald; 0-911498),* 5 N. Wabash Ave., Rm. 1406, Chicago, IL 60602 Tel 312-236-3994 (SAN 205-4280).

Theophrastus, *(Theophrastus; 0-913728),* P.O. Box 458, Little Compton, RI 02837 Tel 401-635-4348 (SAN 202-7771).

Theorex, *(Theorex; 0-916004),* 8327 La Jolla Scenic Dr., La Jolla, CA 92037 Tel 619-453-6988 (SAN 207-6632).

Theoscience Foundation Pub., *(Theoscience Found; 0-917802),* 193 Los Robles Dr., Burlingame, CA 94010 (SAN 209-0260).

Theosophical Publishing House, *(Theos Pub Hse; 0-8356),* 306 W. Geneva Rd., Wheaton, IL 60187-0270 Tel 312-665-0123 (SAN 202-5698). Imprints: Quest Books (Quest).

Theosophical Univ. Press, *(Theos U Pr; 0-911500),* P.O. Bin C, Pasadena, CA 91109 Tel 213-798-3378 (SAN 205-4299).

Theosophy Co., *(Theosophy),* 245 W. 33rd St., Los Angeles, CA 90007 Tel 213-748-7244 (SAN 205-4302).

Theotes-Logos Research, Inc., *(Theotes; 0-911806),* 4318 York Ave. S., Minneapolis, MN 55410 Tel 612-922-3202 (SAN 205-4310).

Theta Press International, *(Theta Pr; 0-918244),* 1518 E. Del Rio Dr., Tempe, AZ 85282 (SAN 208-1725).

Thevenin, Tine, *(T Thevenin; 0-9602010),* P.O. Box 16004, Minneapolis, MN 55416 Tel 612-922-4024 (SAN 210-9603).

Thibodaux Service League, *(Thibodaux; 0-9608800),* P.O. Box 305, Thibodaux, LA 70302 Tel 504-446-9818 (SAN 241-0818).

Thieme-Stratton Inc., *(Thieme-Stratton; 0-913258; 0-86577),* 381 Park Ave., S., New York, NY 10016 Tel 212-683-5088 (SAN 202-7399).

Thigpen, S. G., *(Thigpen; 0-911892),* P.O. Box 819, Picayune, MS 39466 (SAN 205-4329).

Thinkers' Press, *(Thinkers Pr; 0-938650),* 423 Brady St., Davenport, IA 52801 (SAN 239-4952).

Thinking Caps, Inc., *(Thinking Caps; 0-910876),* P.O. Box 7239, Phoenix, AZ 85011 Tel 602-956-1515 (SAN 239-4960).

Thinking Ink Pubns., *(Thinking Ink Pubns; 0-9610370),* 7021 W. Lowes Creek Rd., Eau Claire, WI 54701 Tel 715-832-2488 (SAN 264-4320).

Thinking Lizard, *(Thinking Lizard; 0-936498),* 1500 Royal Crest Dr., Apt. 122, Austin, TX 78741 (SAN 222-013X).

Third Century Fund, *(Third Century; 0-9603360),* 1370-C Cabrillo Park Dr., Santa Ana, CA 92701 Tel 714-547-1700 (SAN 212-8004).

Third Party Pub. Co., *(Third Party Pub; 0-89914),* P.O. Box 13306, Montclair Sta., Oakland, CA 94661 (SAN 127-7294).

Third Sector Press, *(Third Sector; 0-939120),* Box 18044, Cleveland, OH 44118 Tel 216-932-6066 (SAN 217-2720).

Third World Press, *(Third World; 0-88378),* 7524 S. Cottage Grove, Chicago, IL 60019 Tel 312-651-0700 (SAN 202-778X).

Thirteenth House, *(Thirteenth Hse; 0-935458),* 71 Vondran St., Huntington Station, NY 11746 (SAN 213-5639).

13th Moon, Inc., *(Thirteenth Moon; 0-9601224),* Drawer F, Inwood Sta., New York, NY 10034 Tel 212-569-7614 (SAN 208-9831).

This 'N That Press, *(This N That; 0-941900),* P.O. Box 329, Pine Grove, CA 95665 Tel 209-296-7963 (SAN 239-8001).

This Press, *(This Pr; 0-935074),* 1004 Hampshire St., San Francisco, CA 94110 Tel 415-821-3452 (SAN 209-7869).

Thistlerose Pubns., *(Thistlerose; 0-9605630),* 5161 E. County Line Rd., White Bear Lake, MN 55110 (SAN 216-3098).

Thomas, Charles C., Pub., *(C C Thomas; 0-398),* 2600 S. First St., Springfield, IL 62717 Tel 217-789-8980 (SAN 201-9485).

Thomas, Ralph L., *(R L Thomas;)* 5023 Frew Ave., Pittsburgh, PA 15213 Tel 412-683-4420 (SAN 207-3315).

Thomas Brothers Maps, *(Thomas Bros Maps; 0-88130),* 17731 Cowan, Irvine, CA 92714 Tel 714-863-1984 (SAN 158-8192).

Thomas-Geale Pubns., Inc., *(Geal T Pubns Inc; 0-912781),* Drawer C, P.O. 223, 1142 Manhattan Ave., Manhattan Beach, CA 90226 Tel 213-379-4405 (SAN 283-3735).

Thomas Henry Publishing Co., *(T Henry Pub; 0-910078),* 606 Yale Ave. N., Seattle, WA 98109 (SAN 262-0979).

Thomas International, *(Thomas Intl DC; 0-9612128),* P.O. Box 6376, Washington, DC 20015 Tel 301-657-2910 (SAN 277-7088).

Thomas Jefferson Research Center, *(T Jefferson Res Ctr; 0-938308),* 1143 N. Lake Ave., Pasadena, CA 91104 Tel 213-798-0791 (SAN 239-670X).

Thomas-Newell, *(Thomas-Newell; 0-9600690),* 1201 Monroe St., P. O. Box 329, Endicott, NY 13760 Tel 607-754-0410 (SAN 205-4337).

Thomas Paine Press, *(Thomas Paine Pr; 0-934162),* 9528 Miramar Rd., Suite 54, San Diego, CA 92126 Tel 619-485-6549 (SAN 212-9760).

Thomas Press, *(Thomas Pr; 0-89732),* 2030 Ferdon Rd., Ann Arbor, MI 48104 Tel 313-662-1275 (SAN 211-7649).

Thomas Publishing Company, *(Thomas Hse; 0-9607680),* P.O. Box 661, Caldwell, TX 77836 (SAN 239-5630) Moved, left no forwarding address.

Thomasson-Grant, Inc., *(Thomasson-Grant; 0-934738),* 2250 Old Ivy Rd., Charlottesville, VA 22901 Tel 804-977-1780 (SAN 239-3948).

Thomond Press See Elsevier Science Publishing Co., Inc.

Thompson, Paul J., *(P J Thompson; 0-9601288),* 2200 Prospect Ave., Rm. 437, Cleveland, OH 44115 Tel 216-241-9039 (SAN 210-5160).

Thompson Publishing Group, *(Thompson Pub Group),* 2120 L St. N.W., Suite 210, Washington, DC 20037 Tel 202-872-1766 (SAN 287-2986).

Thompson, Roberts & Clare, *(Thompson Roberts; 0-918464),* 185 Aldine bender, No. 153, Houston, TX 77060 (SAN 263-2292).

Thopson-Shore, Inc., *(Thomson-Shore),* 7300 W. Joy Rd., Dexter, MI 48130 (SAN 262-429X); Dist. by: B. Stiles, P.O. Box 812, Gautier, MS 39553 (SAN 262-4303).

Thompson's, *(Thompson's),* P.O. Box 550, Albertville, AL 35950 Tel 205-878-2021 (SAN 207-4656).

Thomson, Phillip, *(Thomson; 0-911504),* 836 Georgia St., Williamston, MI 48895 Tel 517-655-2930 (SAN 202-7798).

Thomson Pubns., *(Thomson Pub CA; 0-913702),* P.O. Box 9335, Fresno, CA 93791 Tel 209-435-2163 (SAN 210-377X).

Thor Publishing Co., *(Thor; 0-87407),* P.O. Box 1782, Ventura, CA 93002 Tel 805-648-4560 (SAN 202-7801).

Thoreau Foundation, Inc., *(Thoreau Found; 0-912130),* Thoreau Lyceum, 156 Belknap St., Concord, MA 01742 Tel 617-369-5912 (SAN 205-4353).

Thorn Creek Press, *(Thorn Creek Pr; 0-915664),* Rte. 2, Box 160, Genesee, ID 83832 (SAN 264-4339).

Thorndike Press, *(Thorndike Pr; 0-89621),* P.O. Box 157, Thorndike, ME 04986 Tel 207-948-2962 (SAN 212-2375).

Thornwood Book Publishers, *(Thornwood Bk; 0-943054),* P.O. Box 1442, Florence, AL 35630 Tel 205-766-4100 (SAN 240-4540).

Thorp Springs Press, *(Thorp Springs; 0-914476),* 803 Red River St., Austin, TX 78701 (SAN 202-781X).

Thorsons Publishers, Inc., *(Thorsons Pubs),* 377 Park Ave. S., 6th Fl., New York, NY 10016 Tel 212-889-8350 (SAN 277-7398); Dist. by: Inner Traditions International, Ltd., 377 Park Ave. S., 6th Fl., New York, NY 10016 Tel 212-889-8350 (SAN 268-6948).

Thrash, *(Thrash Pubns; 0-942658),* Rte. 1, Box 273, Seule, AL 36875 (SAN 277-7096).

Thrasher Balloons, *(Thrasher; 0-9601514),* P.O. Box 1111, Homestead, FL 33030 Tel 305-247-8412 (SAN 211-5425).

Three Continents Press, *(Three Continents; 0-89410; 0-914478),* 1346 Connecticut Ave., Suite 224, Washington, DC 20036 Tel 202-457-0288 (SAN 212-0070).

3-D Pubs., *(Three D Pubs; 0-9600500),* P.O. Box 428, Edgerton, OH 43517 (SAN 205-4361).

Three- D D D Publishing, *(Three D Pub; 0-9611764),* 6521 Racquet Club Dr., Lauderhill, FL 33319 Tel 305-733-9900 (SAN 285-3833).

Three Herons Press, *(Three Herons),* P.O. Box 340-A, Rte. 3, Three Rivers, MI 49093 Tel 616-442-2725 (SAN 207-9089).

Three L Press, *(Three L Pr; 0-9601938),* 170 Ninth St., San Francisco, CA 94103 (SAN 212-0518).

Three Meadows Press, *(Three Meadows Pr; 0-942892),* 861 Oak Knoll Dr., Perrysburg, OH 43551 Tel 419-874-8489 (SAN 240-1649).

Three Mountains Press, *(Three Mtn Pr; 0-930986),* P. O. Box 50, Cooper Sta., New York, NY 10003 Tel 212-989-2737 (SAN 209-7885).
Three Rivers Press, *(Three Rivers Pr; 0-915606),* P.O. Box 21, Carnegie Mellon Univ., Pittsburgh, PA 15213 (SAN 207-9097).
Three Star Enterprises, *(Three Star Ent; 0-912507),* 9709 Raymond Dr., Belleville, IL 62223 Tel 618-397-1155 (SAN 265-2293).
Three Tree Press, *(Three Tree Pr; 0-9604198),* P.O. Box 261, Kalamazoo, MI 49005 (SAN 221-5942).
Thresh Pubns., *(Thresh Pubns; 0-9600572; 0-913664),* 3027 Gateway Rd., P.O. Box 580, Bethel Island, CA 94511 (SAN 202-7828).
Threshold Books, *(Threshold VT; 0-939660),* RD 3 Box 208, Putney, VT 05346 Tel 802-387-4586 (SAN 216-6496).
Thrift, Richard, *(R Thrift),* 108 Clarke Court, Charlottesville, VA 22903 (SAN 211-5433).
Through Thick & Thin, *(Through Thick & Thin; 0-9608638),* 6216 Hills Dr., Birmingham, MI 48010 Tel 313-642-4252 (SAN 239-5649).
Throwkoff, G., *(G Throwkoff; 0-942004),* 908 White Pine Circle, Lawrenceville, NJ 08648 Tel 609-882-7001 (SAN 238-4841).
Thueson, James D., *(Thueson; 0-911506),* Box 14474, Univ. Sta., Minneapolis, MN 55414 (SAN 239-4979).
Thum Printing, *(Thum Print; 0-932920),* 116 W. Pierce St., Elburn, IL 60119 (SAN 212-3150).
Thunder City Press, *(Thunder City; 0-918644),* P.O. Box 11126, Birmingham, AL 35202 Tel 205-322-3753 (SAN 209-6048).
Thunder River Press, *(Thunder River; 0-9604274),* P.O. Box 10935, Aspen, CO 81611 (SAN 214-4786).
Thunderbird Press, *(Thunderbird Pr),* 2747 W. Windrose Dr., Phoenix, AZ 85029 (SAN 206-7722).
Thunderchief Corp., *(Thunderchief),* P.O. Box 85, Troutdale, OR 97060 (SAN 212-8683).
Thunder's Mouth Press, *(Thunder's Mouth; 0-938410),* P.O. Box 780, New York, NY 10025 (SAN 216-4663); 1152 S. East, Oak Park, IL 60304 (SAN 214-4671).
Thursday Pubs., *(Thursday Pubs; 0-934502),* 1846N Pine Bluff Rd., Stevens Point, WI 54481 Tel 715-344-6441 (SAN 212-9779).
TIB Pubns., Div. of The Image Builders, *(TIB Pubns; 0-931882),* 800 W. Oakland Park Blvd., Suite 309, Fort Lauderdale, FL 33311 Tel 305-561-9667 (SAN 211-500X).
Tichenor Publishing, *(Tichenor Pub; 0-89917),* P.O. Box 1998, Bloomington, IN 47402 (SAN 283-8818).
Ticknor & Fields, *(Ticknor & Fields; 0-89919),* 52 Vanderbilt Ave., New York, NY 10017 Tel 212-687-8996 (SAN 282-4043); 383 Orange St., New Haven, CT 06511 Tel 203-776-1878 (SAN 282-4035); Dist. by: Houghton Mifflin Co., 2 Park St., Boston, MA 02108 Tel 617-725-5000 (SAN 200-2388). *Imprints:* Kahn, Joan, Books (Kahn Bks).
Tidal Press, The, *(Tidal Pr),* Cranberry Isles, ME 04625 Tel 207-244-7220 (SAN 211-3783).
Tide Book Publishing Co., *(Tide Bk Pub Co; 0-9602786),* P.O. Box 268, Manchester, MA 01944 (SAN 282-406X); Orders to: The Distributors Inc., 702 S. Michigan, South Bend, IN 46618 Tel 219-232-8500 (SAN 282-4078).
Tide Press, *(Tide Pr; 0-912931),* P.O. Box 477, Linden, NJ 07036 Tel 201-862-0762 (SAN 283-3158).
Tidewater Pubs., Div. of Cormell Maritime Press, Inc., *(Tidewater; 0-87033),* P.O. Box 456, Centreville, MD 21617 Tel 301-758-1075 (SAN 202-0459).
Tieck, W. A., *(W A Tieck; 0-9600398),* 3930 Bailey Ave., Bronx, NY 10463 Tel 212-549-5566 (SAN 205-4906).
Tiffany, Jennifer, *(J Tiffany),* 525 S. Danby Rd., Spencer, NY 14883 (SAN 287-2943).
Tiffany Press, *(Tiffany; 0-914800),* P.O. Box 304, Newton, MA 02158 Tel 617-527-9395 (SAN 206-5819).
Tiger Publications, *(Tiger Pubn; 0-9611318),* 32 Friendship Court, Red Bank, NJ 07701 Tel 201-747-9042 (SAN 283-3506).
Tilden Press, *(Tilden Pr; 0-9605750),* 1737 DeSales St. NW, Washington, DC 20036 (SAN 217-135X).

Till Press, *(Till Pr),* P.O. Box 27816, Los Angeles, CA 90027 (SAN 211-4569).
Tillotson, Ira M., *(I M Tillotson),* P.O. Box 3019, Missoula, MT 59801 Tel 312-9299).
Tilman Publications, *(Tillman Pubns; 0-9605752),* P.O. Box 488, Arverne, NY 11692 (SAN 239-8125).
Tilth, *(Tilth; 0-931380),* 4649 Sunnyside No., Seattle, WA 98103 (SAN 220-4096).
Timber Press, *(Timber; 0-917304; 0-931146; 0-931340),* P.O. Box 1631, Beaverton, OR 97075 Tel 503-292-2606 (SAN 216-082X); Dist. by: International Specialized Book Services, Inc., P.O. Box 1632, Beaverton, OR 97075 Tel 503-292-2606 (SAN 200-4305).
Timberline Books, *(Timberline Bks; 0-913488),* 25890 Weld Rd. 53, Kersey, CO 80644 Tel 303-353-3785 (SAN 202-0416).
Timco International, *(Timco Intl; 0-915624),* P.O. Box 431, Berkeley, CA 94701 (SAN 207-3331).
Time-Lee Pubns., *(Time-Lee Pubns; 0-937210),* P.O. Box 116, Melbourne, FL 32901 Tel 305-727-3010 (SAN 214-3275).
Time-Life Books, Div. of Time, Inc., *(Time-Life; 0-8094),* 777 Duke St., Rm. 204, Alexandria, VA 22314 Tel 703-960-5421 (SAN 202-7836); Dist. by: Little, Brown & Co., 34 Beacon St., Boston, MA 02106 (SAN 281-8892); Dist. by: Morgan & Morgan Co., 145 Palisades St., Dobs Ferry, NY 10522 (SAN 202-5620) Lib. & School Orders to: Silver Burdett Co., Morristown, NJ 13664.
Time Museum, The, Div. of United Realty Corp., *(Time Museum; 0-912947),* 7801 E. State St., P.O. Box 5285, Rockford, IL 61125 Tel 815-398-6000 (SAN 283-3522).
Time Out to Enjoy, Inc., *(Time Out; 0-9608010),* 715 Lake St., Suite 100, Oak Park, IL 60301 Tel 312-383-9017 (SAN 238-5864).
Time-Wise Pubns., *(Time-Wise; 0-918826),* P.O. Box 597, Yucca Valley, CA 92234 Tel 619-365-5888 (SAN 208-2543).
Timeless Books, *(Timeless Bks; 0-931454),* P.O. Box 60, Porthill, ID 83853 Tel 604-227-9224 (SAN 211-6502).
Timely Books, *(Timely Bks; 0-931328),* P.O. Box 267, New Milford, CT 06776 Tel 203-744-4719 (SAN 211-3791).
Timely Pubns., *(Timely Pubns; 0-916548),* P.O. Box 81563, San Diego, CA 92138 (SAN 208-4279) Moved, Left No Forwarding Address.
Times Books, The New York Times Book Co., Inc., *(Times Bks; 0-8129),* Three Park Ave., New York, NY 10016 Tel 212-725-2050 (SAN 202-5558); Dist. by: Harper & Row, Keystone Industrial Park, Scranton, PA 18512 (SAN 200-2086). *Imprints:* Demeter Press (Demeter).
Times Change Press, *(Times Change; 0-87810),* Publishers Services, P.O. Box 3914, San Rafael, CA 94902 Tel 415-883-3530 (SAN 202-7860).
Times-Mirror Press, *(Times-M Pr; 0-911510),* P.O. Box 23951, Los Angeles, CA 90023 Tel 213-265-6767 (SAN 207-3765).
Times Press, The, *(Times Pr; 0-9606608),* 11661 San Vicente Blvd., No. 901, Los Angeles, CA 90049 Tel 213-820-8767 (SAN 219-8223).
Timescape See Pocket Books, Inc.
Timetable Press, *(Timetable Pr; 0-87974),* 50 Sagamore Dr., Syosset, NY 11791 Tel 516-921-2137 (SAN 205-440X).
Tin Man Press, *(Tin Man Pr; 0-936110),* Box 219, Stanwood, WA 98292 (SAN 222-0156).
Tinkers Dam Press, *(Tinkers Dam Pr; 0-943608),* 1703 E. Michigan Ave., Jackson, MI 49202 Tel 517-784-6158 (SAN 240-7884).
Tinnon-Brown Publishing Co., *(Tinnon-Brown; 0-87252),* Orders to: Borden Publishing Co., 1855 W. Main St., Alhambra, CA 91801 (SAN 201-419X).
Tioga Pub. Co., *(Tioga Pub Co; 0-935382),* Dist. by: William Kaufmann, Inc., 95 First St., Los Altos, CA 94022 Tel 415-948-5810 (SAN 202-9383).
Tip-top, *(Tip-top; 0-9610000),* Box 442, New York, NY 10025 (SAN 263-2306).
Tipi Workshop Bks., *(Tipi Wkshp Bks; 0-942914),* Allenspark, CO 80510 Tel 303-322-3438 (SAN 240-3277).

Tippers International, *(Tippers Intl),* Box 2351, Oshkosh, WI 54901 (SAN 225-6460).
Tiresias Press, Inc., *(Tiresias Pr; 0-913292),* 116 Pinehurst Ave., New York, NY 10033 Tel 212-568-9570 (SAN 202-7879).
Tirtha, Ranjit, *(R Tirtha),* Eastern Michigan University, Dept. of Geography, Ypsilanti, MI 48197 Tel 313-487-0218 (SAN 214-3283).
Titan Publishing Co., *(Titan Pub Co; 0-9603314),* P.O. Box 506, Mesilla, NM 88046 (SAN 211-7142).
Titus Publishing Co., *(Titus Pub Co; 0-9610792),* 1803 W. Euless Blvd., P.O. Box 1194, Euless, TX 76039 Tel 817-267-4211 (SAN 265-1432).
T L T Pubns., *(TLT; 0-943314),* 202 S. Fifth St., Goshen, IN 46526 Tel 616-361-8013 (SAN 240-7841).
TM Productions, *(TM Prods; 0-937522),* Box 189, Wilmette, IL 60091 (SAN 215-2096).
To Begin With, *(To Begin With; 0-9606764),* c/o Gordon Pledger, 1142 Hornell Dr., Silver Spring, MD 20904 Tel 301-421-9406 (SAN 219-645X).
To-the-Point Press, *(To-the-Point; 0-9606476),* Drawer 546, Dana Point, CA 92629 Tel 714-496-6677 (SAN 223-0127).
Toadwood Publishers, *(Toadwood Pubs; 0-9610878),* R.R.6, Box 63, Edwardsville, IL 62025 Tel 618-397-1155 (SAN 282-5775); Dist. by: Southwestern Stringed Instruments & Accessories, 1228 E. Prince Rd., Tucson, AZ 85719 (SAN 200-4003).
Today in Bible Prophesy, Inc., *(Today Bible; 0-937682),* P.O. Box 5700, Huntington Beach, CA 92615 (SAN 284-2521).
Today News Service, Inc., *(Today News; 0-932746),* National Press Bldg., Washington, DC 20045 Tel 202-628-6999 (SAN 202-7887).
Todd, Richard E., *(R E Todd; 0-9605324),* 3601 Linden Ave., Long Beach, CA 90807 (SAN 215-9805).
Todd & Honeywell Inc., *(Todd & Honeywell; 0-89962),* 10 Cuttermill Rd., Great Neck, NY 11021 Tel 516-487-9777 (SAN 213-179X).
Todd Publishing, Inc., *(Todd Pub; 0-935988),* P.O. Box 5837, Scottsdale, AZ 85261 (SAN 222-0172).
Todd Tarbox Books, *(Todd Tarbox; 0-89297),* 421 Sharondale, El Paso, TX 79912 Tel 915-749-7219 (SAN 208-2012).
Toggitt, Joan, Ltd., *(Toggitt; 0-911514),* 246 Fifth Ave., New York, NY 10001 (SAN 205-4418).
Tokai University Press See Unipub
Token & Medal Society, Inc., *(TAMS; 0-918492),* P.O. Box 951, Colorado Springs, CO 80901 Tel 303-473-9142 (SAN 209-8954); P.O. Box 321, Northbrook, IL 60062 (SAN 209-8962).
Toledo Museum of Art, The, *(Toledo Mus Art; 0-935172),* Box 1013, Toledo, OH 43697 Tel 419-255-8000 (SAN 213-8980); Dist. by: Pennsylvania State Univ. Press, 215 Wagner Bldg., University Park, PA 16802 (SAN 213-5760).
Tolemac, Inc., *(Tolemac; 0-9609520),* P.O. Box 418, Ashland, OR 97520 Tel 503-482-2720 (SAN 263-2314).
Tolff Pubs., Div. of the Trinity of Light Fellowship Foundation, *(Tolff; 0-916498),* 5750 Via Real, No. 230, Carpinteria, CA 93013 Tel 805-684-6363 (SAN 208-8916).
Tolle Pubns., *(Tolle Pubns; 0-915378),* P.O. Box 6243, Beaumont, TX 77705 Tel 713-860-5628 (SAN 211-0970); 7920 Wilcox Lane, Beaumont, TX 77706 (SAN 211-0989).
Tolstoy Foundation, Inc., *(Tolstoy Found),* 250 W. 57th St., New York, NY 10107 (SAN 209-2778) Tel 212-247-2922.
Tolvan Co., *(Tolvan Co; 0-916774),* P.O. Box 1933, Appleton, WI 54911 Tel 414-766-1828 (SAN 208-8924).
Tomash Pubs., *(Tomash Pubs; 0-938228),* P.O. Box 49613, Los Angeles, CA 90049 (SAN 239-4987).
Tomato Pubns., *(Tomato Pubns; 0-934166),* Preston Hollow, NY 12469 (SAN 213-6007).

Tombouctou Books, *(Tombouctou),* P.O. Box 265, Bolinas, CA 94924 (SAN 282-4647); Dist. by: Bookpeople, 2940 Seventh St., Berkeley, CA 94710 Tel 415-549-3030 (SAN 168-9517); Dist. by: Bookslinger, P.O. Box 1651, 2163 Ford Pkwy., St. Paul, MN 55116 Tel 612-690-0293 (SAN 169-4154); Dist. by: Dark Horse, 17705 S. Western Ave., Suite 1, Gardenia, CA 90248 Tel 415-843-5796 (SAN 282-4671); Dist. by: Barbary Coast Distribution, 635 Amador, Richmond, CA 94805 Tel 415-236-1197 (SAN 282-468X); Dist. by: Serendipity Books Distribution, 1970 Shattuck Ave., Berkeley, CA 94704 Tel 415-549-3336 (SAN 282-4698); Dist. by: Word Works, 1421 Second Ave., N. Seattle, WA 98109 Tel 206-284-8127 (SAN 282-4698); Dist. by: New York State Small Press Assn., P.O. Box 1264, Radio City Sta., New York, NY 10019 (SAN 219-5127); Dist. by: Publisher Services, P.O. Box 3414, San Rafael, CA 94902 (SAN 282-4728).

Tompson & Rutter, Inc., *(Tompson & Rutter; 0-936988),* P.O. Box 297, Grantham, NH 03753 Tel 603-863-4392 (SAN 220-1380); Dist. by: Shoe String Press, Inc., P. O. Box 4327, 995 Sherman Ave., Hamden, CT 06514 Tel 203-248-6307 (SAN 213-2079).

Tonatiuh/Quinto Sol International, Inc., *(Tonatiuh-Quinto Sol Intl; 0-88412),* P.O. Box 9275, Berkeley, CA 94709 Tel 415-655-8036 (SAN 203-3984).

Tony Press/Tony B. Enterprises, *(Tony Pr-Ent),* 130 Clifford Terrace, San Francisco, CA 94117 Tel 415-564-8844 (SAN 239-507X).

Toolbox, The, *(Toolbox; 0-9606548),* 8219 Old Petersburg Rd., Evansville, IN 47711 (SAN 223-0135).

Tools for Schools, Inc., *(Tools for Schools; 0-933242),* 164 27th St., San Francisco, CA 94110 Tel 415-282-2526 (SAN 212-9787).

Tooth of Time Bks., *(Tooth of Time; 0-940510),* 634 Garcia St., Santa Fe, NM 87501 (SAN 219-8231).

Toothpaste Press, *(Toothpaste; 0-915124),* P.O. Box 546, West Branch, IA 52358 Tel 319-643-2604 (SAN 282-7123); Dist. by: Bookslinger, 213 E. Fourth St., St. Paul, MN 55101 Tel 612-221-0429 (SAN 217-1457).

Top-Ecol Press, *(Top-Ecol Pr),* 3025 Highridge Rd., La Crescenta, CA 91214 Tel 213-248-6369 (SAN 218-9976).

Topgallant Publishing Co., Ltd., *(Topgallant; 0-914916),* Elizabeth Bldg. 845 Mission Lane, Honolulu, HI 96813 Tel 808-524-0884 (SAN 209-4932).

Tops Learning Systems, *(Tops Learning; 0-941008),* 10978 S. Mulino Rd., Canby, OR 97013 Tel 503-266-6609 (SAN 217-4456).

Tor Bks., Div. of Tom Doherty Associates, Inc., *(Tor Bks; 0-8125),* 8-10 W. 36th St., New York, NY 10018 Tel 212-564-0150 (SAN 239-3956); Dist. by: Pinnacle Bks., Inc., 1430 Broadway, New York, NY 10018 Tel 212-719-5900 (SAN 200-2442).

Tor Books *See* **Pinnacle Books**

Torah Umesorah Pubns., *(Torah Umesorah; 0-914131),* 160 Broadway, New York, NY 10003 Tel 212-674-6700 (SAN 218-9992).

Torchbooks *See* **Harper & Row Pubs., Inc.**

Torey Press, *(Torey Pr; 0-941318),* P.O. Box 2114, Glen Ellyn, IL 60137 Tel 312-620-5481 (SAN 239-0426).

Torosian, Martin, *(M Torosian),* 1010 Hunter Court, Deerfield, IL 60015 (SAN 216-6265).

Torres, Eliseo, & Sons, *(E Torres & Sons; 0-88303),* Box 2, Eastchester, NY 10709 (SAN 207-0235).

Torskript Pubs., *(Torskript Pubs; 0-913048),* P.O. Box 297, San Francisco, CA 94101 Tel 415-584-8813 (SAN 205-4434).

Tortoise Press, The, *(Tortoise Pr; 0-939518),* 1215 Via Coronel, Palos Verdes Estates, CA 90274 Tel 213-378-7061 (SAN 220-1909).

Tosaw Publishing Co., *(Tosaw; 0-9609016),* 2415 Lawrence St., Ste A, P.O. Box 939, Ceres, CA 95307 (SAN 240-9097).

Total Graphics, *(Total Graphics; 0-912860),* 316 W. Mission Rd., San Marcos, CA 92069 Tel 714-744-1108 (SAN 207-0243).

Total Trial System, The, *(Total Trial; 0-9605222),* P.O. Box 3663, St. Paul, MN 55165 (SAN 215-8191).

Total Universe Book Co., *(Total Univ Bk),* P.O. Box 143, Dearborn, MI 48121 (SAN 209-6870).

Touche Ross & Co., *(Touche Co; 0-942640),* 1633 Broadway, New York, NY 10019 Tel 212-489-1600 (SAN 239-5657).

Touchstone Books *See* **Simon & Schuster, Inc.**

Touchstone Center For Children, Inc., The, *(Touchstone Ctr Child),* 141 E. 88th St., New York, NY 10028 (SAN 265-3664).

Touchstone Enterprises, Inc., *(Touchstone Ent ND; 0-939728),* 2108 S. University Dr., Park Place Plaza, Suite 103, Fargo, ND 58103 Tel 701-237-4742 (SAN 216-7646).

Touchstone Press, *(Touchstone Pr OR; 0-911518),* P.O. Box 81, Beaverton, OR 97075 Tel 503-646-8081 (SAN 205-4442).

Tout De Suite A la Microwave, Inc., *(Tout De Suite),* P. O. Box 30121, 305 Wood Bluff, Lafayette, LA 70503 Tel 318-984-2903 (SAN 238-7565).

Tower Enterprises, *(Tower Ent; 0-910431),* 3380 S. Fourth Ave., No. 18, Yuma, AZ 85365 Tel 602-726-0471 (SAN 260-1478).

Tower Hill Press, *(Tower Hill Pr; 0-941668),* P.O. Box 1132, 95 N. Broad St., Doylestown, PA 18901 Tel 215-345-1338 (SAN 239-3298).

Tower Publications, Inc., *(Tower Bks; 0-505),* 2 Park Ave., Suite 910, New York, NY 10016 Tel 212-679-7707 (SAN 212-016X); Dist. by: Capital Distributing Co., 2 Park Ave. Suite 910, New York, NY 10016 Tel 212-679-7707 (SAN 212-016X).

Tower Publishing Co., *(Tower Pub Co; 0-89442),* 34 Diamond St., Portland, ME 04112 Tel 207-774-9813 (SAN 210-2811).

Towers Club Press, *(Towers Club; 0-930668),* P.O. Box 2038, Vancouver, WA 98668 Tel 206-699-4428 (SAN 209-6072).

Town Forum, Inc., *(Town Forum),* P.O. Box 569, Cerro Gordo Ranch, Cottage Grove, OR 97424 Tel 503-942-7720 (SAN 209-7915).

Town of Andover, MA, *(Town of Andover MA; 0-9603160),* Town Clerk, 20 Main St., Andover, MA 01810 Tel 617-475-3205 (SAN 211-4836).

Towncourt Enterprises, Inc., *(Towncourt Ent; 0-9608928),* P.O. Box 9151, Coral Springs, FL 33075 (SAN 281-8671).

Townsend-Beddoes, Peggy, *(P Townsend-Beddoes; 0-9606478),* 365 S. 18th St., Harrisburg, PA 17104 Tel 717-233-1511 (SAN 218-5997).

Townsend Press, *(Townsend Pr; 0-935990),* 767 East Oakwood Blvd., Chicago, IL 60653 (SAN 206-8249).

Toys 'n Things Pr., Div. of Resources for Child Caring, Inc., *(Toys 'n Things; 0-934140),* 906 N. Dale St., St. Paul, MN 55103 Tel 612-488-7284 (SAN 212-8691).

T P A Publishing, *(TPA Publishing; 0-912651),* 2022 Taravel St., Box 5357, San Francisco, CA 94116 Tel 415-564-2055 (SAN 283-3549).

TPR Pub. Co., Inc., *(TPR Pub Inc; 0-918000),* 81 Montgomery St., Scarsdale, NY 10583 Tel 914-472-0366 (SAN 210-282X).

Trackaday, *(Trackaday; 0-9606522),* Rte. 1, Box 330, New Market, VA 22844 (SAN 201-8624).

Tracy, John, Clinic, *(John Tracy Clinic),* 806 W. Adams Blvd., Los Angeles, CA 90007 Tel 213-748-5481 (SAN 203-056X).

Tracy Publishing, *(Tracy Pub),* 1627 Boathouse Circle, Suite No. H-228, Sarasota, FL 33581 Tel 813-966-3797 (SAN 209-5750).

Tradd Street Press, *(Tradd St Pr; 0-937684),* 38 Tradd St., Charleston, SC 29401 Tel 803-722-4293 (SAN 205-4469).

Trade House Publishing Co., *(Trade House; 0-943600),* P.O. Box 17845, Denver, CO 80217 Tel 303-469-7200 (SAN 240-7906).

Trade Ship Publishing Co., *(Trade Ship Pub Co; 0-934592),* 60 State St., 34th Fl. Tower, Boston, MA 02109 (SAN 213-876X).

Trademark Register, *(Trademark Reg; 0-911522),* 454 Washington Bldg., Washington, DC 20005 (SAN 205-4477).

Traders Press, Inc., *(Traders Pr; 0-934380),* P.O. Box 10344, Greenville, SC 29603 Tel 803-288-3900 (SAN 212-9795).

Tradex Pubns., *(Tradex Pubns; 0-931528),* P.O. Box 27561, Houston, TX 77027 Tel 713-961-4432 (SAN 212-1743).

Traditional Studies Press, *(Traditional Stud; 0-919608),* 423 E. 84th St., New York, NY 10028 (SAN 215-2592).

Traditionalist Press, *(Trad Pr; 0-9610736),* P.O. Box 1611, Louisville, KY 40201 Tel 502-636-0959 (SAN 265-4148).

Trado-Medic Books, Div. of Conch Magazine, Ltd., Pubs., *(Trado-Medic; 0-932426),* 102 Normal Ave., Buffalo, NY 14213 (SAN 212-5722).

Traffic Service Corp., *(Traffic Serv; 0-87408),* 1435 "G" St. N.W., Suite 815, Washington, DC 20005 Tel 202-626-4535 (SAN 202-7917).

Trail-R Club of America, *(Trail-R; 0-87593),* 610 W. Ninth Ave., Suite 14, Escondido, CA 92025 Tel 714-743-8648 (SAN 205-4493); Orders to: P.O. Box 1376, Beverly Hills, CA 90213 (SAN 205-4507).

Traina, Robert A., *(R A Traina; 0-9601396),* 505 Bellvue Ave., Wilmore, KY 40390 Tel 606-858-3405 (SAN 207-2785).

Trainex Press, *(Trainex Pr; 0-8463),* P.O. Box 116, Garden Grove, CA 92641 Tel 800-854-2485 (SAN 205-4515).

Training Resource Associates, *(Train Res Assoc; 0-933794),* 5 S. Miller Rd., Harrisburg, PA 17109 Tel 717-652-5993 (SAN 216-0684).

Trans-Media Publishing, Co., Affiliated with Oceana Pubns., *(Trans-Media Pub; 0-913338),* 75 Main St., Dobbs Ferry, NY 10522 Tel 914-693-5956 (SAN 202-7925).

Trans Tech Management Press, *(Trans Tech Mgmt; 0-938398),* P.O. Box 23032, Sacramento, CA 95823 (SAN 216-0692).

Trans Tech Pubns., *(Trans Tech; 0-87849),* 16 Bear Skin Neck, Rockport, MA 01966 Tel 617-546-6426 (SAN 216-0692).

Transaction Books, *(Transaction Bks; 0-87855),* Bldg. 4051, Rutgers-State Univ., New Brunswick, NJ 08903 Tel 201-932-2280 (SAN 202-7941).

Transatlantic Arts, Inc., *(Transatlantic; 0-693),* P.O. Box 6086, Albuquerque, NM 87197 Tel 505-898-2289 (SAN 202-7968).

Transbooks, Inc., *(Transbooks; 0-89192),* 611 Broadway, Rm. 227, New York, NY 10012 Tel 212-677-9201 (SAN 218-5105).

Transculture, Inc., *(Transculture Inc; 0-935862),* Village Box 104, New York, NY 10014 (SAN 213-8050).

Transemantics, Inc., *(Transemantics; 0-930124),* 1828 L St., N.W., No. 400, Washington, DC 20036 Tel 202-659-9640 (SAN 210-5667).

Transformation Pubns., *(Transform Pubns; 0-932462),* 11401 Blucher Ave., Granada Hills, CA 91344 Tel 213-366-4092 (SAN 212-1751).

Transformations Press, *(Transform Berkeley; 0-930162),* 1625 Jaynes St., Berkeley, CA 94703 Tel 415-524-8391 (SAN 210-6744).

Transitions, *(Transitions),* p.o. Box 478, Peoria, AZ 85345 Tel 602-972-7504 (SAN 287-282X).

Transitour Inc., *(Transitour; 0-939108),* 111 St. Charles Ave., New Orleans, LA 70130 Tel 504-524-2626 (SAN 216-2008).

Translation Press, *(Translation Pr; 0-931556),* 2901 Heatherway, Ann Arbor, MI 48104 (SAN 211-4739).

Translation Research Institute, *(Translation Research; 0-917564),* 5914 Pulaski Ave., Philadelphia, PA 19144 Tel 215-848-7084 (SAN 207-2319).

Transmedia, *(Transmedia; 0-912750),* P.O. Box 2847, La Mesa, CA 92041 Tel 619-466-2138 (SAN 205-4531).

Transmediacom, Inc., *(Transmediacom; 0-942696),* 1447 E. Second St., P.O. Box 907, Plainfield, NJ 07061 Tel 201-756-6868 (SAN 239-944X).

Transmedica Inc., *(TransMedica; 0-88137),* 801 Second Ave., Suite 1404, New York, NY 10017 Tel 212-599-3637 (SAN 241-466X).

Transnational Investments, Ltd., *(Transnatl Invest; 0-933678),* P.O. Box 56049, Washington, DC 20011 Tel 202-829-0002 (SAN 219-9726).

Transnational Pubs., Inc., *(Transl Pubs; 0-941320),* P.O. Box 361, Dobbs Ferry, NY 10522 Tel 914-693-0089 (SAN 226-2967).

Transnational Pubs., Inc., *(Transnatl Pubs; 0-941320),* P.O. Box 361, Dobbs Ferry, NY 10522 Tel 914-693-0089 (SAN 239-0434).

Transport Environment, The, *(Transport Env; 0-9608112),* SR 285 Old Squaw Dr., Kitty Hawk, NC 27949 Tel 919-261-2267 (SAN 240-1657).

Transrep/Bibliographics, Div. of Colorado Researchers, Inc., *(Transrep; 0-918370),* 2186 S. Holly, No. 105, P.O. Box 22678, Denver, CO 80222 Tel 303-757-4697 (SAN 209-8997).

Transworld Pubs. *See* **Carpatho-Rusyn Research Center**

Trask House Books, Inc., *(Trask Hse Bks; 0-932264),* 2754 S.E. 27th Ave., Portland, OR 97202 Tel 503-235-1898 (SAN 211-9889).

Traumwald Press, *(Traumwald Pr; 0-913676),* 3550 N. Lake Shore Dr., Suite 10, Chicago, IL 60657 Tel 312-525-5303 (SAN 205-454X).

Travel & Tourism Press, *(Travel & Tourism; 0-935638),* P.O. Box 1188, Santa Cruz, CA 95061 Tel 408-429-1709 (SAN 213-7038).

Travel Digests, Div. of Paul Richmond & Co., Pubs., *(Travel Digests; 0-912640),* 73-465 Ironwood, Palm Desert, CA 92260 Tel 714-346-4792 (SAN 202-7976); Orders to: 30695 Ganado Dr., Rancho Palos Verdes, CA 90274 Tel 213-541-6161 (SAN 202-7984).

Travel Discoveries, *(Travel Discover; 0-930570),* 10 Fenway N., Milford, CT 06460 (SAN 211-0067).

Travel Information Bureau, *(Travel Info; 0-914072),* 44 County Line Rd., Farmingdale, NY 11735 Tel 516-454-0880 (SAN 202-7992).

Travel Interludes, *(Travel Inter; 0-9609388),* P.O. Box 4276, Carmel, CA 93921 Tel 408-624-0928 (SAN 260-2725).

Travel Press, *(Travel Pr; 0-930328),* 16 E. Third Ave., Suite A, San Mateo, CA 94401 Tel 415-342-5591 (SAN 210-6760).

Travel World Pubns., *(Travel World; 0-89416),* Box 2187, Dublin, CA 94568 Tel 415-829-2728 (SAN 210-5462).

Traveler's Digest Editions, *(Travelers Digest Edns; 0-936578),* 106 Perry St., New York, NY 10014 (SAN 214-1531); Dist. by: Small Press Association, P.O. Box 1264, Radio City Sta., New York, NY 10019 (SAN 214-154X).

Travfunish Publishing, *(Trafunish Pub; 0-9612022),* P.O. Box 1018, Decatur, AL 35602 Tel 205-355-2603 (SAN 286-8865).

Travis Piano Service, *(Travis; 0-9600394),* P.O. Box 5359-0359, 8012 Carroll Ave., Takoma Park, MD 20912 Tel 301-439-4111 (SAN 205-4558) Tel 301-431-0870.

Treasure Chest Pubns., *(Treasure Chest; 0-918080),* 1842 W. Grant Rd., Suite 107, Tucson, AZ 85745 Tel 602-623-9158 (SAN 209-3243); Orders to: P.O. Box 5250, Tucson, AZ 85703 (SAN 209-3251).

Treasure Guide Publishing Co., *(Treasure Guide Pub),* P.O. Box 368, Mesilla Park, NM 88047 (SAN 209-1747).

Trebor Press, Ltd., *(Trebor Pr; 0-88030),* P.O. Box 32725, Oklahoma City, OK 73123 Tel 405-789-1714 (SAN 217-4464).

Tree Bks., *(Tree Bks),* Box 9005, Berkeley, CA 94709 (SAN 203-6576).

Tree by the River Publishing, *(Tree by River; 0-935174),* P.O. Box 413, Riverside, CA -92502 Tel 714-682-8942 (SAN 213-389X).

Tree Communications, Inc., *(Tree Comm; 0-934504),* 250 Park Ave. S., New York, NY 10003 Tel 212-674-1480 (SAN 282-714X); Attn: Order Service Dept., Harper & Row, Keystone Industrial Dept., Scranton, PA 18512 Tel 800-233-4175 (SAN 282-7158).

Treehouse Productions, *(Treehouse Prods; 0-926530),* W. 905 Riverside, Suite 305, Spokane, WA 99201 Tel 509-484-6856 (SAN 283-4286).

Treeroots Pr., *(Treeroots; 0-9604450),* P.O. Box 684, Berkeley, CA 94701 (SAN 215-1170); Dist. by: Bookpeople, 2940 Seventh St., Berkeley, CA 94710 Tel 415-549-3030 (SAN 168-9517).

TREK-CIR Pubns., *(Trek-CIR; 0-932464),* Box 898, Valley Forge, PA 19481 Tel 215-337-3110 (SAN 212-2383).

Tremaine Graphic & Publishing, *(Tremaine Graph & Pub; 0-939860),* 2727 Front St., Klamath Falls, OR 97601 Tel 503-884-4193 (SAN 216-9398).

Tremont Press, the, *(Tremont Pr; 0-943954),* P.O. Box 2307, Silver Spring, MD 20902 Tel 301-649-6666 (SAN 241-1601).

Trempealeau Press, *(Trempealeau; 0-912540),* 800 Hillcrest Dr., Santa Fe, NM 87501 Tel 505-983-1947 (SAN 211-9897).

Tremper, W.J., *(Tremper; 0-9604166),* 340 Fairmount Ave., Jersey City, NJ 07306 (SAN 214-4794).

Trend House, Div. of Florida Trend, Inc., *(Trend House; 0-88251),* P.O. Box 611, St. Petersburg, FL 33731 Tel 813-821-5800 (SAN 202-8018).

Trends & Customs, Inc., *(Trends & Custom; 0-910879),* P.O. Box 170008, Overland Plaza, Arlington, TX 76017 (SAN 262-0987); Dist. by: Publishers Marketing Group, 1343 Columbia, Suite 405, Richardson, TX 75081 (SAN 262-0995).

Trends & Events, Inc., *(Trends & Events; 0-942698),* P.O. Box 158, Fayette, IA 52142 Tel 319-425-4411 (SAN 240-2882).

Trends Publishing Co., *(Trends Pub; 0-9602426),* 23100 Providence Dr., Suite 270, Southfield, MI 48075 Tel 313-552-1175 (SAN 206-2445).

Tri-County Special Services, *(Tri-County; 0-943390),* P.O. Box 145, St. Anthony, ID 83445 Tel 208-624-3146 (SAN 241-5887).

Tri-Med Press, *(Tri-Med),* 65 Christopher St., Montclair, NJ 07042 Tel 201-746-9132 (SAN 216-0706).

Tri-Oak Education, *(Tri-Oak; 0-9609732),* 24663 Dry Canyon Colocrk, Calabasas, CA 91302 (SAN 262-1002).

Tri-Science Pubs., *(Tri-Science Pubs; 0-935040),* Box 1232, Pico Rivera, CA 90660 (SAN 209-2581).

Tri State Promotions, *(Tri State Prom; 0-9607868),* P.O. Box 30926, Amarillo, TX 79120 Tel 806-352-1555 (SAN 239-5665).

Tri-State Railway Historical Society Inc., *(Tri-State Rail; 0-9607444),* P.O. Box 2243, Clifton, NJ 07015 Tel 201-857-2987 (SAN 239-3301).

Triad Press, *(Triad Pr TX),* P.O. Box 42006-K, Houston, TX 77242 Tel 713-978-7212 (SAN 214-2023).

Triad Pub. Co., Inc., *(Triad Pub FL; 0-9600472; 0-937404),* 1110 NW Eighth Ave., Gainesville, FL 32601 Tel 904-373-5308 (SAN 205-4574).

Triadoption Library, Inc., *(Triadoption Lib; 0-941770),* P.O. Box 5218, Huntington Beach, CA 92646 Tel 714-892-4098 (SAN 239-331X).

Triangle Pr., *(Triangle Pr; 0-937144),* Rte. 6 Box 327, Kemp, TX 75143 (SAN 216-2016).

Tribal Pr., *(Tribal Pr; 0-9607044),* c/o Lowell Jensen, Rte. 2 Box 599, Cable, WI 54821 Tel 715-794-2247 (SAN 239-0442).

Tribeca Communications, Inc., *(Tribeca Comm; 0-943392),* 401 Broadway, Suite 1907, New York, NY 10013 Tel 212-226-6047 (SAN 240-7922).

Tribune Publishing Co., Inc., *(Tribune Pub; 0-940654),* 18 Okner Pkwy., Livingston, NJ 07039 Tel 201-992-1060 (SAN 219-8258).

Tricor Inc., *(Tricor Inc; 0-9607046),* P.O. Box 386, Penllyn, PA 19422 Tel 215-646-2044 (SAN 239-0450).

Tricore Associates, Inc., *(Tricore Assoc; 0-9607132),* 69 Rte. 23 S., Riverdale, NJ 07457 Tel 201-835-9219 (SAN 239-0469).

Trike Pub., *(Trike; 0-917588),* Box 732, Pismo Beach, CA 93449 Tel 805-489-9218 (SAN 210-3273) Moved, Left No Forwarding Address.

Trilateral Commission, *(Trilateral Comm),* 345 E 46th St, New York, NY 10017 (SAN 225-6703).

Trill Press, *(Trill Pr),* P.O. Box 2608, Sacramento, CA 95812 (SAN 240-1673).

Trillium Press, *(Trillium Pr; 0-89824),* P.O. Box 921, Madison Square Sta., New York, NY 10159 Tel 212-684-7399 (SAN 212-4637).

Trilogy Pubs., *(Trilogy Pubs; 0-931558),* 2901 Heatherway, Ann Arbor, MI 48104 (SAN 211-4747).

Trine Books, *(Trine Bks; 0-912361),* P.O. Box 446, Wallingford, CT 06492 Tel 203-269-6262 (SAN 265-1459).

Trinity Books, *(Trinity Bks; 0-934310),* P.O. Box 8882, East Hartford, CT 06108 Tel 203-528-0408 (SAN 282-8042).

Trinity House, Inc., *(Trinity House; 0-913309),* 5311 Mont Fort Lane, Crestwood, KY 40014 Tel 502-582-6151 (SAN 283-3182).

Trinity Pubns., *(Trinity Pubns; 0-89626),* 1636 N. Curson Ave., Hollywood, CA 90046 Tel 213-876-6226 (SAN 226-8051).

Trinity Publishing House, Inc., *(Trinity Pub Hse; 0-933656),* 263 W. Fifth St., Winona, MN 55987 (SAN 215-1189).

Trinity Univ. Press, *(Trinity U Pr; 0-911536; 0-939980),* 715 Stadium Dr., San Antonio, TX 78284 Tel 512-736-7619 (SAN 205-4590).

Triple B Sales, *(Triple B),* 44 Butternut Dr., Pittsford, NY 14534 Tel 716-381-7767 (SAN 210-3788).

Triple Press, *(Triple Pr; 0-941264),* 33 N. Main St., Medford, NJ 08055 (SAN 239-3964).

Triple "T" Publishing Co., *(Triple T Pub; 0-9606122),* 175 Fifth Ave., New York, NY 10010 Tel 212-677-2200 (SAN 216-8642).

Triplett Enterprises, Ltd., *(Triplett Ents),* Munday-Brohard Rd., Macfarlan, WV 26148 Tel 304-477-3246 (SAN 207-2947).

Trippensee Corp., *(Trippensee Pub),* 301 Cass St., Saginaw, MI 48602 Tel 517-799-8102 (SAN 206-2518).

TriQuarterly Books, *(TriQuarterly; 0-916384),* Northwestern Univ., 1735 Benson Ave., Evanston, IL 60201 Tel 312-492-3490 (SAN 208-8959).

Triton Books, *(Triton Bks; 0-943958),* P.O. Box 27934, Los Angeles, CA 90027 Tel 213-247-4177 (SAN 241-161X).

Triton College Press, *(Triton Coll; 0-931672),* 2000 Fifth Ave., River Grove, IL 60171 (SAN 211-2779).

Tritone Music, *(Tritone Music; 0-9603470),* 155 Montclair Ave., Montclair, NJ 07042 (SAN 213-6023).

Triumph Publishing Co., *(Triumph Pub; 0-917182),* P.O. Box 292, Altadena, CA 91001 (SAN 207-3927).

Trogon Pubns., *(Trogon Pubns; 0-9600578),* 1210 Loucks Ave., Scottdale, PA 15683 Tel 412-887-9436 (SAN 205-4604).

Trojan Books, *(Trojan Bks; 0-9610986),* 1330 Cleveland Ave., Wyomissing, PA 19610 Tel 215-372-8041 (SAN 265-3176).

Trojan Press, Inc., *(Trojan Pr; 0-913914),* 310 E. 18th St., North Kansas City, MO 64116 Tel 816-421-3858 (SAN 202-8069).

Troll Associates, *(Troll Assocs; 0-89375; 0-8167),* 320 Rte. 17, Mahwah, NJ 07430 Tel 201-529-4000 (SAN 209-0503).

Trolley Talk, *(Trolley Talk; 0-914196),* 59 Euclid Ave., Wyoming, OH 45215 (SAN 205-4612).

Trollpost Greetings, *(Trollpost),* 3276 Belmont St., Bellaire, OH 43906 Tel 614-676-1917 (SAN 262-1010).

Trophy *See* **Harper & Row Pubs., Inc.**

Trossbach, J. E., *(J E Trossbach; 0-9608936),* 2608 W. Columbine Rd., Phoenix, AZ 85029 Tel 602-997-2882 (SAN 241-1628).

Troubador Press, *(Troubador Pr; 0-912300; 0-89844),* 385 Fremont St., San Francisco, CA 94105 Tel 415-397-3716 (SAN 285-0931); Dist. by: Price/Stern/Sloan Publishers, 410 N. La Cienega Blvd., Los Angeles, CA 90048 Tel 213-657-6100 (SAN 285-094X).

Troy State University Press, *(TSU Pr; 0-916624),* Wallace Hall, Troy, AL 36082 Tel 205-566-3000 (SAN 208-8967).

Troyanovich, Steve, *(S Troyanovich),* Dist. by: Spring Church Book Co., P.O. Box 127, Spring Church, PA 15686 (SAN 212-7075).

Tru-Faith Publishing Co., *(Tru-Faith; 0-937498),* P.O. Box 2283, Gainesville, GA 30503 (SAN 216-3101).

True Grid Editions, *(True Grid; 0-9610880),* 2600 S. 16th St., No. 729, Arlington, VA 22204 Tel 703-979-2432 (SAN 265-2870).

True Heitz-Thelma Yes Press, *(True Heitz),* 1400 McAndrew Rd., Ojai, CA 93023 (SAN 262-1029).

True Life Foundation, The, *(True Life Found; 0-912753),* 14510 Cordary Ave., Hawthorne, CA 90250 Tel 213-676-5984 (SAN 283-3557).

Truedog Press, *(Truedog; 0-937212),* 216 W. Academy St., Lonoke, AR 72086 (SAN 215-3475).

Trustees for the Complete Writings of Herbert W. Eustace, C.S.B. *See* **Eustace, Herbert W., C.S.B.**

Truth Consciousness, *(Truth Consciousness; 0-933572),* Gold Hill, Salina Star Rte., Boulder, CO 80302 Tel 303-447-1637 (SAN 212-7083).

Truth in Money, Inc., *(Truth in Money),* P.O. Box 16, Chagrin Falls, OH 44022 (SAN 219-8266).

Truth Pubs., *(Truth Pubs; 0-9602182),* P.O. Box 304, La Jolla, CA 92038 Tel 714-459-1470 (SAN 212-3185).

Truth Publishing, Inc., *(Truth Pub MN),* 3802 W. Malapi Dr., Phoenix, AZ 85021 Tel 602-938-9019 (SAN 214-1558).

Truth Seeker Company Inc., *(Truth Seeker),* P.O. Box 2832, San Diego, CA 92112 Tel 619-574-7600 (SAN 226-3645).

Tucker, Grayson L. Jr., *(G L Tucker; 0-9610706),* 2310 Tyler Lane, Louisville, KY 40205 Tel 502-458-2234 (SAN 264-8024).

Tucker Pubns., *(Tucker Pubns),* 409 Hill St., Fayetteville, TN 37334 (SAN 213-6031).

Tucson Creative Dance Center See **Mettler Studios, Inc.**

Tuffy Bks., Inc., *(Tuffy Bks; 0-89828),* 200 Fifth Ave., New York, NY 10010 Tel 212-242-1818 (SAN 213-3903).

Tulane Studies in Political Science, *(Tulane Stud Pol; 0-930598),* Tulane Univ., College of Arts & Sciences, Dept. of Political Science, New Orleans, LA 70118 Tel 504-868-5166 (SAN 207-5660).

Tulane Studies in Romance Languages & Literature, *(Tulane Romance Lang; 0-912788),* Newcomb Coll., Tulane Univ., New Orleans, LA 70118 Tel 504-865-5115 (SAN 206-1333).

Tulane Univ., *(Tulane Univ),* Dist. by: Tulane University, Howard-Tilton Memorial Library, Special Collections Division, New Orleans, LA 70118 Tel (SAN 207-5458).

Tulip Press, *(Tulip Pr; 0-941800),* P.O. Box J, Truckee, CA 95734 Tel 916-587-2995 (SAN 239-3328).

Tulip Press, *(Tulip Pr IL; 0-9608766),* 10622 S. Hamilton, Chicago, IL 60643 Tel 312-864-6747 (SAN 241-0826).

Tullis Productions, *(Tullis Prods),* 4310 Normal Ave., Hollywood, CA 90029 (SAN 209-195X); Orders to: P.O. Box 54119, Los Angeles, CA 90054 (SAN 209-1968).

Tundra Books of Northern New York, *(Tundra Bks; 0-912776; 0-89541),* 51 Clinton St., Box 1030, Plattsburgh, NY 12901 (SAN 202-8085); Dist. by: University of Toronto Press, 33 E. Tupper St., Buffalo, NY 14203 (SAN 200-4224).

Tundra Pubns., *(Tundra Pubns; 0-9606768),* Moraine Rte., Estes Park, CO 80517 Tel 303-586-5794 (SAN 219-6492).

Tuppence, Inc., *(Tuppence; 0-939662),* 2701 S. 35th, Lincoln, NE 68506 Tel 402-488-3655 (SAN 220-1607).

Turbomachinery International Publications, Div. of Business Journals, Inc., *(Turbo Intl Pubn; 0-937506),* P.O. Box 5550, Norwalk, CT 06856 Tel 203-853-6015 (SAN 205-3055).

Turkey Hill Press, *(Turkey Hill Pr; 0-9608050),* 3 Turkey Hill Lane, Westport, CT 06880 (SAN 240-4966); Dist. by: Inland Book Co., 22 Hemingway Ave., East Haven, CT 06512 (SAN 200-4151).

Turkey Press, *(Turkey Pr; 0-918824),* 6746 Sueno Rd., Isla Vista, CA 93117 Tel 805-685-3603 (SAN 210-5195).

Turn of the Century Editions, *(Turn of Cent; 0-940326),* 6 Varick St., New York, NY 10013 Tel 212-925-6587 (SAN 220-3529).

Turning Wheel Press, *(Turning Wheel Pr; 0-9602590),* 4 Washington Square Village, New York, NY 10012 Tel (SAN 214-1566).

Turpin, John C., & Associates, *(Turpin & Assocs; 0-939506),* 7661 Inland Dr., Olmsted Falls, OH 44138 Tel 216-235-9109 (SAN 216-700X).

Turquoise Books, *(Turquoise Bks; 0-917834),* 1202 Austin Bluffs Pkwy., Colorado Springs, CO 80907 Tel 303-634-1556 (SAN 206-5223).

Turret Publishing, *(Turret; 0-931952),* 16240 Ninth Ave., Suite 7B, Whitestone, NY 11357 Tel 212-767-3385 (SAN 211-4577).

Turtle Island Foundation, Netzahualcoyotl Historical Society, *(Turtle Isl Foun; 0-913666),* 2845 Buena Vista Way, Berkeley, CA 94708 Tel 415-845-0984 (SAN 205-4639).

Turtle Press, *(Turtle Pr; 0-916844),* 333 E. 49 St., New York, NY 10017 Tel 212-753-7957 (SAN 208-8975).

Turtles Quill Scriptorium, *(Turtles Quill; 0-937686),* P.O. Box 643, Mendocino, CA 95460 Tel 707-937-4328 (SAN 206-8966).

Tusa-McColloster Publishing Co., *(Tusa McColl; 0-9607062),* 2338 Lake Oaks Pkwy., New Orleans, LA 70122 Tel 504-283-6800 (SAN 239-0477).

Tusayan Gospel Ministries, Inc., *(Tusayan Gospel; 0-9601124),* P.O. Box 9861, Phoenix, AZ 85068 Tel 602-995-9565 (SAN 209-3391).

Tutorial Press, The, *(Tutorial Press; 0-912329),* P.O. Box 10219, Alburquerque, NM 87184 Tel 505-898-7023 (SAN 265-1467).

Tuttle, Charles E., Co., Inc., *(C E Tuttle; 0-8048),* P.O. Box 410, 28 S. Main St., Rutland, VT 05701 Tel 802-773-8229 (SAN 213-2621).

Tuttle, Tom, & Associates, *(Tom Tuttle; 0-930556),* P.O. Box 20081, Cincinnati, OH 45220 Tel 212-475-5114 (SAN 208-2551).

T V Guide, *(TV Guide; 0-9603684),* 4 Radnor Corporate Ctr., Radnor, PA 19088 Tel 215-293-8947 (SAN 214-4808).

T.V. Music Co., *(T V Music; 0-918806),* 1650 Broadway, New York, NY 10019 Tel 212-246-3126 (SAN 210-5136).

Twain Publishing, *(Twain Pub; 0-9609194),* 35 E. St. Nw, Washington, DC 20001 Tel 202-382-3802 (SAN 241-4678).

Twayne Publishers See **Hall, G. K., & Co.**

Twayne's U.S. Author Series See **New College & Univ. Press, The**

Twelvetrees Press, *(Twelvetrees Pr; 0-942642),* P.O. Box 188, Pasadena, CA 91102 Tel 213-798-3556 (SAN 239-9458) Tel 213-798-5207.

Twentieth Century Books, Div. of Automated Reproductions, *(Twentieth Century; 0-86649),* 745 Seventh Ave., New York, NY 10019 (SAN 216-3128) Moved, left no forwarding address.

Twentieth Century Fund, Inc., *(Twentieth Fund; 0-87078),* 41 E. 70th St., New York, NY 10021 (SAN 205-4647).

21st Century Pubns., *(Pubns Twenty First; 0-9610708),* 190 Old Stafford Rd., Tolland, CT 06084 Tel 203-872-4083 (SAN 264-8032).

Twenty First Century Pubns., *(Twen Fir Cent; 0-933278),* P.O. Box 702, 401 N. 4th St., Fairfield, IA 52556 Tel 517-472-5105 (SAN 211-8181).

Twenty-Third Pubns., *(Twenty-Third; 0-89622),* P.O. Box 180, Mystic, CT 06355 Tel 203-536-2611 (SAN 210-9204).

Twesten, Gary, Publisher, *(G Twesten; 0-9602428),* Fox Run, Millstadt, IL 62260 Tel 618-233-5070 (SAN 209-1402).

Twickenham Press, *(Twickenham Pr; 0-936726),* 31 Jane St, Suite 17B, New York, NY 10014 (SAN 214-3291).

Twin City Printery, *(Twin City; 0-9609914),* Box 890, Lewiston, ME 04240 Tel 207-784-9181 (SAN 206-2577).

Twin Oaks Books, *(Twin Oaks Bks)* 4343 Causeway Dr., Lowell, MI 49331 (SAN 238-0862).

Twin Oaks Co., *(Twin Oaks LA),* 26 Marwood St., Albany, NY 12209 Tel 518-489-4009 (SAN 285-0958); P.O. Box 638, Homer, LA 71040 (SAN 285-0966).

Two-Eighteen Press, *(Two Eighteen),* P.O. Box 218, Village Sta., New York, NY 10014 Tel 212-966-5877 (SAN 207-9127).

Two Horses Pr., *(Two Horses),* 1950 W. Ruthrauff Rd., Tucson, AZ 85705 (SAN 276-1351).

Two Riders Pr., *(Two Riders; 0-915860),* P.O. Box 31, Chestnut Hill, MA 02167 Tel 617-232-8819 (SAN 207-6179).

Two Rivers Press, *(Two Rivers; 0-89756),* 28070 S. Meridan Rd., Aurora, OR 97002 Tel 503-651-2090 (SAN 211-6510).

Two's Co. Music, *(Twos Co Music; 0-9604626),* Box 1199, Lawrence, KS 66044 (SAN 239-4995).

Twowindows Press, *(Twowindows Pr; 0-912136),* 2644 Fulton St., Berkeley, CA 94704 (SAN 205-4671).

Tyler Gibson Pubs., *(Tyler Gibson; 0-9605520),* P.O. Box 1266, Boston, MA 02205 Tel 617-423-7929 (SAN 220-1437).

Tyndale House Pubs., *(Tyndale; 0-8423),* 336 Gundersen Dr., Wheaton, IL 60187 Tel 312-668-8300 (SAN 206-7749).

Typographeum Bookshop, The, *(Typographeum; 0-930126),* The Stone Cottage, Bennington Rd., Francestown, NH 03043 (SAN 211-3031).

Typrofile Press, *(Typrofile Pr; 0-943316),* Church Rd., Box 223, Wernersville, PA 19565 Tel 215-678-3886 (SAN 240-7930).

UAH Press, *(UAH Pr; 0-933957),* P.O. Box 1247, Huntsville, AL 35807 (SAN 212-8160).

U&U Pubns., Inc., *(U & U Pubns; 0-912163),* 5061 Sioux Circle, Lilburn, GA 30247 Tel 404-921-7814 (SAN 264-8040).

U-Bild Enterprises, Div. of U-B Newspaper Syndicate, *(U-Bild; 0-910495),* Box 2383, 15233 Stagg St., Van Nuys, CA 91409 Tel 213-785-6368 (SAN 260-1508).

UCLA Tissue Typing Laboratory, *(UCLA Tissue; 0-9604606),* UCLA School of Medicine, Los Angeles, CA 90024 (SAN 282-4752); Orders to: 1000 Veteran Ave., Los Angeles, CA 90024 Tel 213-825-7651 (SAN 282-4760).

UMI Research Press, A Xerox Information Resources Co., *(UMI Res Pr; 0-8357),* 300 N. Zeeb Rd., Ann Arbor, MI 48106 Tel 313-761-4700 (SAN 212-2464) Scholarly and professional book publishing, imprint of University Microfilms International (UMI).

UNIFO Pubs., Ltd., *(UNIFO Pubs; 0-89111),* P.O. Box 37, Pleasantville, NY 10570 Tel 914-747-0710 (SAN 219-8290).

UTAMA Pubns., Inc., *(Utama Pubns; 0-911527),* Tano Rd., Box 236, Santa Fe, NM 87501 Tel 505-988-7321 (SAN 282-4779); Dist. by: Hippocrene Books Inc., 171 Madison Ave., New York, NY 10016 Tel 212-685-4372 (SAN 213-2060).

UWSP Foundation Press, *(UWSP Found Pr; 0-932310),* Univ. of Wisconsin-Stevens Point, Stevens Point, WI 54481 (SAN 213-6775).

Uchill, Ida Libert, *(Uchill; 0-9604468),* P.O. Box 22608, Wellshire Sta., Denver, CO 80222 Tel 303-355-9829 (SAN 214-3305).

UCLA, Grad. School of Management, GSM Pubns. Services, *(UCLA Mgmt; 0-911798),* 405 Hilgard Ave., Los Angeles, CA 90024 Tel 213-825-6474 (SAN 203-0179).

UFO Photo Archives, *(UFO Photo; 0-9608558),* P. O. Box 17206, Tuscon, AZ 85710 Tel 602-296-6753 (SAN 240-7949).

UHL's Publishing Co. (U-L), *(Uhls Pub; 0-943240),* R. D. One, Box 119, Spencer, NY 14883 Tel 607-589-6594 (SAN 240-7957).

Uintah Press, *(Uintah Pr; 0-936234),* P.O. Box 420, Port Townsend, WA 98368 (SAN 214-1574).

SI, *(Ujjaini Pubs; 0-9610134),* 8911 Leamont, Houston, TX 77099 Tel 713-495-5849 (SAN 276-1432).

Ukiyo-e Society of America, Inc., *(Ukiyo-e Soc; 0-9610398),* 1692 Second Ave., New York, NY 10028 (SAN 264-4479).

Ukrainian Academic Press, Div. of Libraries Unlimited, Inc., *(Ukrainian Acad; 0-87287),* P.O. Box 263, Littleton, CO 80160 Tel 303-770-1220 (SAN 203-3305).

Ukrainian Cultural Institute, *(Ukrainian Cult Inst),* Dickinson State College, Dickinson, ND 58601 (SAN 287-2366).

Ukrainian Education Assn. of Maryland, Inc., *(Ukrainian Ed Assn; 0-9606178),* 518 S. Wolfe St., Baltimore, MD 21231 Tel 301-252-3051 (SAN 220-3537).

Ukrainian National Women's League of America, *(UNWLA; 0-9610788),* 108 Second Ave, New York, NY 10003 Tel 212-762-4139 (SAN 234-1298).

Ukrainian Research Foundation, *(Ukrainian Res; 0-934760),* 6931 S. Yosemite St., Englewood, CO 80112 (SAN 213-5647).

Ulrich, H., Corp., *(Ulrich Corp NY; 0-936500),* R.D. 3, Peekskill, NY 10566 (SAN 214-2031).

Ulrich's Bks., Inc., *(Ulrich; 0-914004),* 549 E. University Ave., Ann Arbor, MI 48104 Tel 313-662-3201 (SAN 100-2945).

Ultima Corp. of West Palm Beach, *(Ultima Corp; 0-940656),* P.O. Box 15974, West Palm Beach, FL 33406 Tel (SAN 219-8282).

Ultralight Pubns., *(Ultralight Pubns; 0-938716),* P. O. Box 234, Hummelstown, PA 17036 Tel 717-566-0468 (SAN 220-2786).

Ultramarine Publishing Co., Inc., *(Ultramarine Pub; 0-89366),* P.O. Box 303, Hastings-on-Hudson, NY 10706 Tel 914-478-2522 (SAN 208-8762).

UMI Pubns., Inc., *(UMI; 0-943860; 0-943860),* P.O. Box 30036, Charlotte, NC 28230 Tel 704-374-0420 (SAN 241-0834).

UNABASHED Librarian, *(UNABASHED Lib; 0-916444),* G.P.O. Box 2631, New York, NY 10116 (SAN 208-8983).

Unarius Educational Foundation, *(Unarius; 0-932642),* 145 S Magnolia Ave., El Cajon, CA 92021 Tel 714-447-4170 (SAN 168-9614).

Undena Pubns., *(Undena Pubns; 0-89003),* P.O. Box 97, Malibu, CA 90265 Tel 213-366-1744 (SAN 203-1922).

Underhill, C. S., *(Underhill; 0-9600268),* P.O. Box 127, East Aurora, NY 14052 (SAN 206-670X).

Undersea Resources, Ltd., *(Undersea Res; 0-916630),* P.O. Box 15844, Honolulu, HI 96815 Tel 808-941-5471 (SAN 215-1197).

Underwood/Miller, *(Underwood-Miller; 0-934438),* P.O. Box 5402, San Francisco, CA 94101 Tel 415-459-3296 (SAN 282-4795); 239 N. Fourth St., Columbia, PA 17512 (SAN 282-4809); Orders to: Underwood/Miller Publishers, 651 Chestnut St., Columbia, PA 17512 Tel 717-684-7335 (SAN 282-4817).

Undiscovered Denver Dining, *(Undiscovered; 0-9610064),* 940 Emerson, Denver, CO 80218 (SAN 285-1008); Dist. by: Gordon's, 5450 Valley Hwy., Denver, CO 80216 Tel 303-296-1830 (SAN 285-1016); Dist. by: Dillon's, P.O. Drawer J, Boulder, CO 80306 Tel 303-442-5323 (SAN 285-1024).

Ungar, Frederick, Publishing Co., Inc., *(Ungar; 0-8044),* 250 Park Ave. S., New York, NY 10003 Tel 212-473-7885 (SAN 202-5256).

UNI-SUN, *(Uni-Sun; 0-912949),* P.O. Box 25421, 4005 N.E. 49th Terrace, Kansas City, MO 64119 Tel 816-454-8705 (SAN 283-4332).

Unica, Inc., *(Unica Inc)* P.O. Box 296, Plainfield, IL 60544 Tel 815-436-8438 (SAN 219-1016).

Unicon Enterprises, *(Unicon Ent; 0-912327),* 3602 W. Glen Branch, Peoria, IL 61614 Tel 309-688-3772 (SAN 265-1475).

Unicorn, *(Unicorn VA; 0-9604564),* 808 Charlotte, Fredericksburg, VA 22401 (SAN 214-2643) Not to be confused with Unicorn Press (NC).

Unicorn Enterprises, *(Unicorn Ent; 0-87884),* 1620 Collinsdale Ave., Cincinnati, OH 45230 (SAN 206-6696).

Unicorn Press, *(Unicorn Pr; 0-87775),* P.O. Box 3307, Greensboro, NC 27402 Tel 919-852-0281 (SAN 203-3313).

Unicorn Publishing House, Inc., the, *(Unicorn Pub),* 90 Park Ave., Verona, NJ 07044 Tel 201-239-7088 (SAN 240-4567).

Unicorn Rising Ltd., *(Unicorn Rising; 0-913313),* Rt. 2, P.O. Box 360, Sheridan, OR 97378 Tel 503-843-3902 (SAN 285-8924).

Unification Church Pubns., *(Unification Church),* 4 West 43rd St., New York, NY 10036 (SAN 211-8270).

Unification Theological Seminary, *(Unif Theol Seminary; 0-932894),* 10 Dock Rd., Barrytown, NY 12507 Tel 914-758-8838 (SAN 212-3193); Dist. by: Rose of Sharon Press, Inc., G.P.O. Box 2432, New York, NY 10116 (SAN 212-3207).

Unikorn Magik, *(Unikorn Magik; 0-9604016),* 10 Keys Dr., Peabody, MA 01960 Tel 617-531-1260 (SAN 214-1582).

Unilaw *See Donning Co. Pubs.*

Uniline Division, *(Uniline Div; 0-912904),* John Klein Assocs., Inc., 20700 Miles Ave., Cleveland, OH 44128 Tel 216-587-3070 (SAN 203-0497).

Union & Confederacy Inc., *(Union & Confed Inc.; 0-911679),* Route 1, Box 267, College Grove, TN 37046 (SAN 276-9425).

Union College Press, *(Union Coll; 0-912756),* c/o Syracuse Univ. Press, 1600 Jamesville Ave., Syracuse, NY 13210 Tel 315-423-2596 (SAN 206-9776).

Union Congregational Church, *(UCC UCC; 0-9610366),* 176 Cooper Ave., Upper Montclair, NJ 07043 (SAN 264-4509).

Union League of Philadelphia, *(Union League PA; 0-915810),* 140 S. Broad St., Philadelphia, PA 19102 Tel 215-563-6500 (SAN 207-687X).

Union of American Hebrew Congregations, *(UAHC; 0-8074),* 838 Fifth Ave., New York, NY 10021 Tel 212-249-0100 (SAN 203-3291).

Union Park Press, *(Union Park; 0-9601570),* P.O. Box 2737, Boston, MA 02208 Tel 617-426-8609 (SAN 211-5808).

Union Press, *(Union Pr; 0-9603384),* 3009 Hillegass Ave., Berkeley, CA 94705 Tel 415-845-9658 (SAN 212-3088).

Union Printers Historical Society, *(Union Printers Hist Soc),* 1726 West Jarvis Ave., Chicago, IL 60626 (SAN 240-4990).

Unipub, A Xerox Publishing Co., *(Unipub; 0-89059),* 1180 Ave. of the Americas, New York, NY 10036 Tel 212-764-2791 (SAN 202-5264). Imprints: Africa Books (Africa Bks); Asian Productivity Organization (APO); Cambridge Information & Research Services, Ltd. (CIRS); Council of the Americas (CoA); Fishing News Books, Ltd. (FNB); Food & Agriculture Organization (FAO); Fund for Multinational Management Education (FMME); General Agreement on Tariffs & Trade (GATT); International Atomic Energy Agency (IAEA); International Council of Scientific Unions-Abstracting Board of Pubns. (ICSU); International Development Research Centre (IDRC); International Institute of Refrigeration (IIR); International Union for Conservation of Nature & Natural Resources (IUCN); ORDINA (ORDINA); Supplies & Services, Government of Canada (SSC); Tokai University Press (Tokai); United Nations Educational, Scientific & Cultural Organization (UNESCO); United Nations Fund for Population Activities (UNFPA); United Nations Industrial Development Organization (UNIDO); World Intellectual Property Organization (WIPO); World Meterological Organization (WMO); World Watch (WW).

Unique Books, *(Unique Bks; 0-915286),* P.O. Box 285, Hixson, TN 37343 Tel 615-892-3248 (SAN 203-1949).

Unique Pubns., *(Unique Pubns; 0-86568),* 7011 Sunset Blvd., Hollywood, CA 90028 (SAN 214-3313).

Unitarian Universalist Church, The, *(Unitarian),* E. Main St., Canton, NY 13617 (SAN 213-1838).

United Aloe Technologists Association, Inc., *(United Aloe; 0-911973),* P.O. Box 25007, Phoenix, AZ 85002 Tel 602-241-4848 (SAN 264-701X).

United Bible Societies, *(United Bible),* 1865 Broadway, New York, NY 10023 (SAN 204-8787).

United Business Pubns., Inc., *(United Busn; 0-915616),* 475 Park Ave. S., New York, NY 10016 Tel 212-725-2300 (SAN 211-1012).

United Educators, Inc., *(United Ed; 0-87566),* 801 Green Bay Rd., Lake Bluff, IL 60044 (SAN 204-8795).

United Electrical Radio & Machine Workers of America, *(United Elec R&M; 0-916180),* 11 E. 51st St., New York, NY 10022 Tel 212-753-1960 (SAN 208-3973).

United Methodist Board of Higher Education & Ministry, *(United Meth Educ; 0-938162),* Box 871, Nashville, TN 37202 (SAN 216-3136).

United Methodist Church, Commission on Archives & History, *(United Meth Archives; 0-915466),* P.O. Box 127, Madison, NJ 07940 Tel 201-822-2787 (SAN 203-0578).

United Methodist Church of the Dunes, *(UMCD; 0-9608642),* 943 Lake Ave., Grand Haven, MI 49417 Tel 616-846-5429 (SAN 238-3993).

United Nations, *(UN; 0-680),* Sales Section, Publishing Division, New York, NY 10017 (SAN 206-6718).

United Nations Assn. of the United States of America, Inc., *(UNA-USA; 0-934654),* 300 E. 42nd St, New York, NY 10017 Tel 212-697-3232 (SAN 204-8892).

United Nations Educational, Scientific & Cultural Organization *See Unipub*

United Nations Fund for Population Activities *See Unipub*

United Nations Industrial Development Organization *See Unipub*

United Piece Dye Works, *(United Piece; 0-911546),* 111 W. 40th St., New York, NY 10018 Tel 212-840-0400 (SAN 204-8809).

U.S.A.-International Pubs., *(USA Intl Pub; 0-9608114),* US/P.O. Box 6349, Washington, DC 20015 (SAN 240-2920).

U. S. Catholic Conference, *(US Catholic),* Pubns. Office, 1312 Massachusetts Ave. N.W., Washington, DC 20008 Tel 202-659-6640 (SAN 207-5350).

U. S. Catholic Historical Society, *(US Cath Hist; 0-930060),* St. Joseph's Seminary, Dunwoodie, Yonkers, NY 10704 Tel 914-476-9115 (SAN 210-5470).

United States Coast Guard Auxiliary National Board Inc., *(US Coast Guard; 0-930028),* 306 Wilson Rd., Newark, DE 19711 Tel 302-731-4650 (SAN 210-5217).

U. S. Committee for Refugees, *(US Comm Refugees; 0-936548),* 20 W. 40th St., 7th Floor, New York, NY 10018 (SAN 214-1590).

U. S. Committee for UNICEF, *(US Comm Unicef; 0-935738),* 331 E. 38th St., New York, NY 10016 Tel 212-686-5522 (SAN 202-9286).

United States Department of Commerce-Bureau of the Census, *(US Dept Com-Bureau Census),* Superintendent of Documents, U.S. Government Printing Office, Washington, DC 20402 Tel 202-783-3238 (SAN 240-1053).

U.S. Dept. of Energy, *(DOE; 0-87079),* DOE Technical Information Ctr., P.O. Box 62, Oak Ridge, TN 37830 Tel 615-576-1301 (SAN 210-7996); Dist. by: National Technical Information Service (NTIS), U. S. Department of Commerce, 5285 Port Royal Rd., Springfield, VA 22161 Tel 703-487-4650 (SAN 205-7263).

U.S. Directory Service, Inc., *(US Direct Serv; 0-916524),* P.O. Box 011565, Miami, FL 33101 Tel 305-652-1300 (SAN 282-4825); Orders to: 641 N.W. 183rd St., Miami, FL 33169 (SAN 282-4833).

U.S. Eighteen Sixty Nine Pictorial Research Associates,Inc., *(US Pict Res; 0-9610384),* 720-17 Tramway Lane NE, Albuquerque, NM 87122 Tel 415-846-7083 (SAN 264-4533).

U. S. Federal Judicial Center, *(US Fed Judicial),* 1520 H St NW, Washington, DC 20005 (SAN 226-2541).

U. S. Games Systems, Inc., *(US Games Syst; 0-913866; 0-88079),* 38 E. 32nd St., New York, NY 10016 Tel 212-685-4300 (SAN 158-6483).

United States Golf Association, *(US Golf Assn),* Golf House, Far Hills, NJ 07931 (SAN 224-5663).

U. S. Historical Documents Institute, *(US Hist Doc; 0-88222),* 1911 Fort Myer Dr., Arlington, VA 22209 Tel 703-525-6035 (SAN 201-7938).

U.S. News & World Report Books, *(US News & World; 0-89193),* 2300 "N." St., NW, Washington, DC 20037 Tel 202-861-2000 (SAN 207-9720).

United States Pharmacopeial Convention, Inc., *(USPC),* USP Publication Services Dept., 12601 Twinbrook Pkwy., Rockville, MD 20852 Tel 301-881-0666 (SAN 220-2794).

United States Postal Service, Philatelic Marketing Div., *(USPS; 0-9604756),* 475 L'Enfant Plaza, Washington, DC 20260 Tel 202-245-5778 (SAN 219-8304).

U. S. Pubs. Assn., Inc., *(US Pubs; 0-911548),* 46 Lafayette Ave., New Rochelle, NY 10801 Tel 914-576-1121 (SAN 204-8922).

U. S. School of Professional Paperhanging, Inc., *(US School Prof; 0-9608506),* 16 Chaplin Ave., Rutland, VT 05701 (SAN 240-9852).

U S Screen Print Ind., Inc., *(US Screen; 0-9603530),* 1422 W. 23rd St., Tempe, AZ 85282 (SAN 213-8727).

U.S. Ski Assn., *(US Ski; 0-9604162),* Box 777, Brattleboro, VT 05301 (SAN 214-2252).

US Synchronized Swimming, *(US Synch Swim; 0-911543),* 1750 E. Boulder St., Colorado Springs, CO 80909 Tel 303-578-4585 (SAN 276-3702).

U. S. Tennis Assn., *(USTA),* USTA Pubns., 729 Alexander Rd., Princeton, NJ 08540 Tel 609-452-2580 (SAN 207-6551).

U. S. Trademark Assn., *(US Trademark),* 6 E. 45th St., New York, NY 10017 Tel 212-986-5880 (SAN 203-0527).

U. S. Trotting Assn., *(US Trotting),* 750 Michigan Ave., Columbus, OH 43215 Tel 614-224-2291 (SAN 206-1554).

NAME INDEX

United Synagogue Book Service, Subs. United Synagogue Book Service, *(United Syn Bk; 0-8381),* 155 Fifth Ave., New York, NY 10010 Tel 212-533-7800 (SAN 203-0551).

United Synagogue Commission on Jewish Education, *(United Synagogue; 0-8381),* 155 Fifth Ave., New York, NY 10010 (SAN 236-4174).

Unity Books, *(Unity Bks; 0-87159),* Unity School of Christianity, Unity Village, MO 64065 Tel 816-524-3550 (SAN 204-8817).

Unity Church of Denver, *(Unity Church Denver; 0-942482),* 3021 S. University, Denver, CO 80210 Tel 303-758-5664 (SAN 161-4541).

Unity School of Christianity, *(Unity School; 0-87159),* Unity Village, MO 64065 (SAN 240-9100).

Univ. of Connecticut Library Business Services, U-5B, *(Univ Conn Lib; 0-917590),* Storrs, CT 06268 Tel 203-486-3293 (SAN 209-3901).

Univ. of Missouri, Museum of Art & Archaeology, *(U of Missouri Mus Art Arch; 0-910501),* 1 Pickard Hall, Univ. Of Missouri, Columbia, MO 65211 Tel 314-882-3591 (SAN 260-2733).

Univ. of Wisconsin-Stevens Point, *(U of Wis-Stevens Point; 0-932310),* Stevens Point, WI 54481 (SAN 212-2405).

Univ. Bks *See* Hall, G. K., & Co.

Univ. of Colorado, Colorado Associated Univ. Press *See* Colorado Associated Univ. Press, Univ. of Colorado

Univelt, Inc., *(Univelt Inc; 0-912183; 0-87703; 0-914548),* P.O. Box 28130, San Diego, CA 92128 Tel 619-746-4005 (SAN 204-8868) Publish books & microforms for the American Astronautical Society; microforms for the Society for the Society for Technical Communmication; proceedings for other technical societies.

Universal Autograph Collectors Club, *(Univ Autograph; 0-9608816),* P O Box 467, Rockville Center, NY 11571 Tel 516-766-0093 (SAN 260-3675).

Universal Bk. Co., *(Universal Book Co)* P.O. Box 60943, Terminal Annex, Los Angeles, CA 90060 Tel 213-723-1776 (SAN 219-8983).

Universal Books, Inc., *(Universal Bks; 0-9608856),* 526 Silver Leaf Dr., Oroville, CA 95965 Tel 916-589-3171 (SAN 241-0850).

Universal Coterie of Pipe Smokers, *(Univ Coterie Pipe),* 20-37 120 St., College Point, NY 11356 (SAN 223-8543).

Universal Developments Publishing, *(Universal Develop),* 2855 Velasco Lane, Costa Mesa, CA 92626 Tel 714-540-5452 (SAN 205-9835).

Universal Goddess Center Inc., *(Univ Goddess; 0-937946),* P.O. Box 671, Malibu, CA 90265 Tel 213-457-7119 (SAN 220-0996); Dist. by: The Distributors, 702 S. Michigan, South Bend, IN 46618 (SAN 212-0364).

Universal Great Brotherhood, Inc., *(Univ Great Brother; 0-915594),* P.O. Box 9154, St. Louis, MO 63117 (SAN 207-3447).

Universal Life Bookshelf, *(Univ Life),* 10770 Katella Ave. 25, Anaheim, CA 92804 (SAN 219-3418).

Universal Life Church, Inc., *(Univ Life Church; 0-9608116),* P.O. Box 67752, Los Angeles, CA 90211 (SAN 240-1088) Moved, left no forwarding address.

Universal Ministries, Inc., Publishing House, *(Universal Ministries; 0-942428),* P.O. Box 9017, Pittsburgh, PA 15224 Tel 301-622-9238 (SAN 238-2032).

Universal Press, *(Universal Pr; 0-918950),* 6609 Cherrywood Ave., Bakersfield, CA 93308 Tel 805-393-0381 (SAN 210-5225).

Universal Pubns., *(Univ Pubns; 0-941116),* P.O. Box 117, Fawnskin, CA 92333 Tel 714-585-9630 (SAN 217-4480).

Universal Scientific Pubns. Co., Inc., The, *(TUSPCO; 0-88078),* P.O. Box 60943, Terminal Annex, Los Angeles, CA 90060 Tel 213-723-1776 (SAN 220-309X).

Universal Technology Corp., *(Univ Tech; 0-912426),* 1656 Mardon Dr., Dayton, OH 45432 Tel 513-426-8530 (SAN 204-885X).

Universe Books, Inc., *(Universe; 0-87663),* 381 Park Ave., S., New York, NY 10016 Tel 212-685-7400 (SAN 202-537X). *Imprints:* Pica Press (Pica Pr); Pica Special Studies (Pica Spec Stud).

Universe Publishing Co., *(Universe Pub Co; 0-935484),* 185 W. Demarest Ave., Englewood, NJ 07631 Tel 201-567-4296 (SAN 214-3321).

Universitetsforlaget, *(Universitet; 82-00),* C/O Columbia Univ. Press, 562 W. 113th St., New York, NY 10025 (SAN 204-8876); Dist. by: Columbia Univ. Press, 136 S. Broadway, Irvington-on-Hudson, NY 10533 (SAN 212-2480).

Universities Field Staff International, Inc., *(U Field Staff Intl; 0-910116; 0-88333),* P.O. Box 150, Hanover, NH 03755 Tel 603-643-2110 (SAN 202-4764).

University *See* Exposition Press, Inc.

University Associates, *(Univ Assocs; 0-88390),* 8517 Production Ave., San Diego, CA 92121 Tel 619-578-5900 (SAN 203-333X).

University Book Service, *(Univ Bk Serv),* 21-62 Garrittsen Ave., Brooklyn, NY 11229 Tel 212-280-5066 (SAN 206-4014).

University Books, Inc., Div. of Lyle Stuart, Inc., *(Univ Bks; 0-8216),* 120 Enterprise Ave., Secaucus, NJ 07094 Tel 201-866-0490 (SAN 203-3348).

University Co-Operative Society, *(Univ Co-Op Soc; 0-916048),* P.O. Box 7520, Austin, TX 78712 Tel 512-476-7211 (SAN 207-5083).

University Graphics, *(Univ Graphics; 0-934932),* Southern Illinois University, Carbondale, IL 62901 Tel 618-536-3325 (SAN 204-8825).

University Microfilms International, A Xerox Information Resources Co., *(Univ Microfilms; 0-8357),* 300 N. Zeeb Rd., Ann Arbor, MI 48106 Tel 313-761-4700 (SAN 212-2464) Serials and newspapers in microform, reprints of articles and issues, dissertations published and available on demand. Imprints: Books on Demand, reprinting of out-of-print books, and UMI Research Press, scholarly and professional book publishing.

Univ. Museum, Univ. of Pennsylvania, *(Univ Mus of U PA),* 33rd & Spruce Sts., Philadelphia, PA 19104 Tel 215-898-4090 (SAN 207-9283).

Univ. of Alabama, Center for Business & Economic Research, *(U of Ala Ctr Bus; 0-943394),* Box AK, University, AL 35486 Tel 205-348-6191 (SAN 206-1074).

University of Alabama in Huntsville, Department of Mechanical Engineering, *(U AL Dept Mech Eng; 0-942166),* Huntsville, AL 35899 Tel 205-895-6154 (SAN 239-989X) Tel 205-895-6184.

Univ. of Alabama Press, *(U of Ala Pr; 0-8173),* Box 2877, University, AL 35486 Tel 205-348-5180 (SAN 202-5272).

University of Alabama School of Law, *(U AL Law),* Box 1976, University, AL 35486 (SAN 226-8949).

Univ. of Alaska, Elmer E. Rasmuson Library, *(U Alaska Rasmuson Lib; 0-935792),* Fairbanks, AK 99701 Tel 907-479-7224 (SAN 206-1082).

Univ. of Alaska, Inst of Marine Science, *(U of AK Inst Marine; 0-914500),* Fairbanks, AK 99701 Tel 907-474-7843 (SAN 208-1032).

Univ. of Alaska Institute of Social & Economic Research, *(U Alaska Inst Res; 0-88353),* 707 "A" St., Suite 206, Anchorage, AK 99501 Tel 907-278-4621 (SAN 203-0144).

Univ. of Alaska Press, *(U of Alaska Pr; 0-912006),* University of Alaska, Fairbanks, AK 99701 Tel 907-474-7582 (SAN 203-3011); Dist. by: UA Press, Rm. 2 Bunnell Bldg., Univ. of Alaska, Fairbanks, AK 99701 (SAN 205-4728).

Univ. of Arizona, Arizona Educational Materials Center, *(U of AZ Ed Mat; 0-940870),* College of Education, Box 601, Tucson, AZ 85721 Tel 602-621-3724 (SAN 219-6514).

Univ. of Arizona, Center for Creative Photography, *(U Ariz Ctr Photog; 0-938262),* 843 E. University, Tucson, AZ 85719 (SAN 285-1032); Dist. by: University of Arizona Press, 250 E. Valencia Rd., Tucson, AZ 85706 Tel 602-621-7924 (SAN 285-1040).

Univ. of Arizona Press, *(U of Ariz Pr; 0-8165),* 1615 E. Speedway, Tucson, AZ 85719 Tel 602-621-1441 (SAN 205-468X).

Univ. of Arkansas Press, *(U of Ark Pr; 0-938626),* McIlroy House, Univ. of Arkansas, Fayetteville, AR 72701 Tel 501-575-3246 (SAN 239-3972).

Univ. of British Columbia Press, *(U BC Pr; 0-7748),* 207 S. Westbrook Place. Vancouver, B. C., V6T 1WS, .

Univ. of California, American Indian Studies Center, *(U Cal AISC),* 3220 Campbell Hall, Los Angeles, CA 90024 Tel 213-825-7315 (SAN 220-1283).

University of California at Berkeley Center for Real Estate and Urban Economics, *(UCB Real Estate),* 156 Barrows Hall, Berkeley, CA 94720 (SAN 237-6482).

University of California at Los Angeles School of Law, *(UCLA Law),* Rm 2125c, Los Angeles, CA 90024 (SAN 226-3637).

Univ. of California, Berkeley, Chicano Studies Library, *(UC Chicano; 0-918520),* 3404 Dwinelle Hall, Berkeley, CA 94720 Tel 415-642-3859 (SAN 209-9039).

University of California Berkeley Institute of International Studies, *(UCB Intl Studies; 0-87725),* 215 Moses Hall, Univ. of California, Berkely, CA 94720 Tel 415-642-4065 (SAN 226-9023).

Univ. of California, Div. of Library Automation, *(UCDLA; 0-913248),* 186 University Hall, Berkeley, CA 94720 Tel 415-642-9485 (SAN 207-3617).

Univ. of California, Institute of East Asian Studies, *(IEAS; 0-912966),* Pubns. Office, Institute of East Asian Studies, Univ. of California, Berkeley, CA 94720 Tel 415-642-2816 (SAN 203-8730).

Univ. of California Institute of Governmental Studies, *(Inst Gov Stud Berk; 0-87772),* 109 Moses Hall, Berkeley, CA 94720 Tel 415-642-6722 (SAN 202-7011).

Univ. of California, Institute of Industrial Relations, *(U Cal LA Indus Rel; 0-89215),* 405 Hilgard Ave., Los Angeles, CA 90024 Tel 213-825-9191 (SAN 205-4698).

Univ. of California, Institute of International Studies, *(U of Cal Intl St; 0-87725),* 215 Moses Hall, Berkeley, CA 94720 Tel 415-642-4065 (SAN 203-3038).

Univ. of California, Latin American Center, *(UCLA Lat Am Ctr; 0-87903),* 405 Hilgard Ave., Los Angeles, CA 90024 Tel 213-825-6634 (SAN 201-0704).

Univ. of California, Los Angeles, Business Forecasting Project, *(UCLA Busn Forecasting; 0-913404),* Graduate School of Management, Rm. 4371-C, Los Angeles, CA 90024 Tel 213-825-1623 (SAN 203-0160).

Univ. of California, Los Angeles Chicano Studies Research Center, Pubns. Unit, *(UCLA Chicano Stud; 0-89551),* 3126 Campbell Hall, 405 Hilgard Ave., Los Angeles, CA 90024 Tel 213-825-2642 (SAN 209-097X).

Univ. of California, Los Angeles, Institute of Archaeology, *(UCLA Arch; 0-917956),* 405 Hilgard Ave., Los Angeles, CA 90024 Tel 213-825-1720 (SAN 210-3281).

Univ. of California., Office of History of Science & Technology, *(U Cal Hist Sci Tech; 0-918102),* 470 Stephens Hall, Univ. of California, Berkeley, CA 94720 Tel 415-642-4581 (SAN 210-1394).

Univ. of California, Office of Risk Management & Safety, *(U Cal Risk Management; 0-9602278),* 1942 University Ave., Rm. 208, Berkeley, CA 94720 Tel 415-642-1170 (SAN 212-5765); Orders to: John Morris, 3333 Nutmeg Lane, Walnut Creek, CA 94598 Tel 415-933-3365 (SAN 200-4011).

Univ. of California Press, *(U of Cal Pr; 0-520),* 2223 Fulton St., Berkeley, CA 94720 Tel 415-642-6683 (SAN 203-3046).

Univ. of California, School of Law, *(U of Cal Sch Law; 0-935076),* Davis, CA 95616 (SAN 206-7374); Dist. by: Fred B. Rothman & Co., 10368 W. Centennial Rd., Littleton, CO 80127 Tel 303-979-5657 (SAN 159-9437).

Univ. of Chicago, Center for Policy Study, *(U Chi Ctr Policy),* 5801 S. Ellis Ave., Rm. 200, Chicago, IL 60637 (SAN 220-102X).

Univ. of Chicago, Department of Geography, Research Papers, *(U Chicago Dept Geog; 0-89065),* 5828 S. University Ave., Chicago, IL 60637 Tel 312-962-8314 (SAN 203-3003).

Univ. of Chicago, Dept., of Anthropology, *(U Chi Dept Anthro; 0-916256),* 1126 E. 59 St., Chicago, IL 60637 Tel 312-753-4314 (SAN 208-0583).

Univ. of Chicago Graduate School of Business, (*U Chicago Grad Sch Busn; 0-918584*), 1101 E. 58th St., Chicago, IL 60637 Tel 312-962-7431 (SAN 211-4585).

Univ. of Chicago, Midwest Administration Center, (*U Chicago Midwest Admin; 0-931080*), 5835 S. Kimbark Ave., Chicago, IL 60637 Tel 312-753-3830 (SAN 206-0906).

Univ. of Chicago Press, (*U of Chicago Pr; 0-226*), 5801 Ellis Ave., Chicago, IL 60637 Tel 312-962-7906 (SAN 202-5280); Orders to: 11030 S. Langley Ave., Chicago, IL 60628 Tel 312-568-1550 (SAN 202-5299). *Imprints:* Chicago Visual Library (Chicago Visual Lib).

University of Cincinnati, (*Univ of Cincinnati; 0-9611212*), Department of Geography, Mail Location 131, Cincinnati, OH 45221 (SAN 283-8842).

University of Colorado at Colorado Springs, (*U CO at Colorado Springs; 0-9602992*), P.O. Box 7150, Colorado Springs, CO 80933-7150 Tel 303-599-4023 (SAN 213-392X).

Univ. of Colorado, Business Research Division, (*U CO Busn Res Div; 0-89478*), Campus Box 420, Univ of Colorado, Boulder, CO 80309 Tel 303-492-8227 (SAN 209-9047).

University of Colorado, Economics Institute, (*U Co Econ Inst; 0-88036*), Campus Box 259, Boulder, CO 80309 Tel 303-492-7337 (SAN 239-0493).

Univ. of Connecticut, School of Education, Pubns. Dept., (*Univ Conn Ed*), Storrs, CT 06268 Tel 203-486-4030 (SAN 206-0728).

Univ. of Connecticut School of Law Press, (*U Conn Sch Law; 0-939328*), 1800 Asylum Ave., W. Hartford, CT 06117 Tel 203-241-4638 (SAN 216-5554).

Univ. of Dallas Press, (*U of Dallas Pr; 0-918306*), Irving, TX 75061 Tel 214-438-1123 (SAN 209-4940).

Univ. of Delaware Press, (*U Delaware Pr; 0-87413*), c/o Associated Univ. Presses, Inc., 4 Cornwall Dr., East Brunswick, NJ 08816 Tel 201-254-0132 (SAN 203-4476).

Univ. of Denver, Center for Teaching International Relations Pubns. (CTIR), (*U of Denver Teach; 0-943804*), Univ. of Denver, Graduate School of Int'l Studies, Denver, CO 80208 (SAN 241-0877).

University of Evansville Press, (*U of Evansville Pr; 0-930982*), P.O. Box 329, Evansville, IN 47702 (SAN 265-413X).

University of Georgia, Inst. of Community and Area Development, The, (*Inst Community; 0-911847*), 300 Old College, Athens, GA 30602 Tel 404-542-3350 (SAN 264-4541).

Univ. of Georgia, Institute of Government, (*U of GA Inst Govt; 0-89854*), Terrell Hall, Athens, GA 30602 (SAN 212-8012).

Univ. of Georgia Press, (*U of Ga Pr; 0-8203*), Terrell Hall, Athens, GA 30602 Tel 404-542-2830 (SAN 203-3054).

Univ. of Guelph, (*U of Guelph; 0-88955*), Orders to: L'Esprit Createur, Dept. of French & Italian, Louisiana State University, Baton Rouge, LA 70803 (SAN 214-333X).

Univ. of Hawaii at Manoa, (*U Hawaii*), 2535 the Mall, Honolulu, HI 96822 (SAN 280-8773).

Univ. of Hawaii Press, The, (*UH Pr; 0-8248*), 2840 Kolowalu St., Honolulu, HI 96822 Tel 808-948-8697 (SAN 202-5353). *Imprints:* Eastwest Center Press (Eastwest Ctr); Korea Development Institute (Korea Devel Inst).

Univ. of Healing Press, (*U of Healing*), 32750 Hwy. 94, Campo, CA 92006 Tel 619-478-5111 (SAN 211-7983).

Univ. of IL at Urbana-Champ Archaeological Survey, Inc., (*U IL-Archaeological; 0-942704*), 109 Davenport Hall, 607 S. Mathews Ave., Urbana, IL 61801 (SAN 240-1037).

Univ. of Illinois at Urbana-Champaign, (*U of Ill Lib Info Sci; 0-87845*), Univ. Of Illinois, Grad. School of Library & Info. Science Publications Office, 249 Amory Building, 505 E. Armory St., Champaign, IL 61820 (SAN 277-4917).

Univ. of Illinois Press, (*U of Ill Pr; 0-252*), 54 E. Gregory Dr., Champaign, IL 61820 Tel 217-333-0957 (SAN 202-5310).

Univ. of Illinois School of Music, (*U IL Sch Music*), Univ. of Illinois, Urbana, IL 61801 (SAN 240-5024).

Univ. of Iowa, Center for Educational Experimentation, Development & Evaluation, (*U IA Ctr Ed Experiment; 0-939984; 0-88670*), 218 Lindquist Ctr., Iowa City, IA 52242 Tel 319-353-5400 (SAN 216-8677).

Univ. of Iowa Press, (*U of Iowa Pr; 0-87745*), 214 Graphic Services Bldg., Iowa City, IA 52242 Tel 319-353-3181 (SAN 282-4868); Orders to: Oakdale Campus, Univ. of Iowa, Iowa City, IA 52242 Tel 319-353-4171 (SAN 282-4876).

Univ. of Iowa, School of Social Work, (*U of Iowa Sch Soc Wk; 0-934936*), Iowa City, IA 52242 (SAN 214-1612).

Univ. of Kansas, Independent Study, Div. of Continuing Education, (*U of KS Ind Stud Div; 0-936352*), Lawrence, KS 66045 (SAN 214-1620).

Univ. of Kansas, Museum of Natural History, (*U of KS Mus Nat Hist; 0-89338*), Lawrence, KS 66045 Tel 913-864-4540 (SAN 206-0957).

Univ. of Kansas Pubns., (*U of KS Pubns*), Watson Library, Univ. of Kansas, Lawrence, KS 66045 (SAN 215-7101).

Univ. of Kentucky Library Associates, (*U Ky Lib Assocs; 0-919123*), Lexington, KY 40506 Tel 606-257-3831 (SAN 241-4686).

Univ. of Maine at Orono Press, (*U Maine Orono; 0-89101*), PICS Building, Univ. of Maine at Orono, Orono, ME 04469 Tel 207-581-7349 (SAN 207-2971).

Univ. of Maryland, College of Library & Information Services, (*U of Md Lib Serv; 0-911808*), 1117 Hornbake Library Bldg., College Park, MD 20742 Tel 301-454-3016 (SAN 203-3097); Orders to: Univ. Book Center, College Park, MD 20742 (SAN 203-3100).

Univ. of Maryland, Dept. of Geography, (*U MD Geography; 0-918512*), 1113 Social Sciences Bldg., Univ. of Maryland, College Park, MD 20742 Tel 301-454-2241 (SAN 209-9055).

Univ. of Maryland, School of Medicine-Anatomy Department, (*Univ Maryland; 0-9608786*), 655 W. Baltimore St., Baltimore, MD 21201 Tel 301-528-3532 (SAN 238-4019).

University of Massachusetts, Graduate School, (*Univ Mass Grad; 0-9604712*), Amherst, MA 01003 (SAN 240-9836); Dist. by: Dept. of Geology & Geography, Univ. of Massachusetts, Amherst, MA 01003 (SAN 282-6143).

Univ. of Massachusetts Press, (*U of Mass Pr; 0-87023*), P.O. Box 429, Amherst, MA 01004 Tel 413-545-2217 (SAN 203-3089).

Univ. of Miami, Law & Economics Center, (*Law & Econ U Miami; 0-916770*), P.O. Box 248000, Coral Gables, FL 33124 Tel 305-284-6174 (SAN 208-9017).

Univ. of Miami Press, (*U of Miami Pr; 0-87024*), P.O. Box 4836, Hampden Sta., Baltimore, MD 21211 Tel 301-338-7886 (SAN 203-3119).

Univ. of Miami, Rosenstiel School of Marine & Atmospheric Science, (*U Miami Marine; 0-930050*), Orders to: Pubns. Office, 4600 Rickenbacker Causeway, Miami, FL 33149 Tel 305-350-7518 (SAN 276-4210).

Univ. of Michigan, Center for Chinese Studies, (*U of Mich Ctr Chinese; 0-89264*), 104 Lane Hall, Ann Arbor, MI 48109 Tel 313-763-5888 (SAN 208-2772).

Univ. of Michigan Center for Near Eastern & North African Studies, (*Ctr for NE & North African Stud; 0-932098*), 144 Lane Hall, Univ. of Michigan, Ann Arbor, MI 48109 Tel 313-764-0350 (SAN 211-7150).

Univ. of Michigan, Center for South & Southeast Asian Studies, (*Ctr S&SE Asian; 0-89148*), 240 Lane Hall, Ann Arbor, MI 48109 Tel 313-763-9764 (SAN 206-491X).

Univ. of Michigan, Dept. of Near Eastern Studies, (*Dept NE Stud; 0-916798*), 3074 Frieze Bldg., Ann Arbor, MI 48109 Tel 313-764-0314 (SAN 285-1059); Dist. by: Eisenbrauns, P.O. Box 275, Winona Lake, IN 46590 Tel 219-269-2011 (SAN 285-1067); Dist. by: Publications Distribution Service, University of Michigan Press, 839 Greene St., Ann Arbor, MI 48109 Tel 313-764-4394 (SAN 285-1075); Dist. by: Cambridge University Press, Customer Service, 510 North Ave., New Rochelle, NY 10801 (SAN 285-1083); Orders to: Kitab, Dept of Near Eastern Studies, 3085 Frieze Bldg., Ann Arbor, MI 48109 Tel 313-763-1597 (SAN 285-1091).

Univ. of Michigan, Division of Research, Grad. School of Business Administration, (*U Mich Busn Div Res; 0-87712*), Ann Arbor, MI 48109 Tel 313-764-1366 (SAN 204-8736).

Univ. of Michigan, Museum of Anthropology, Pubns. Dept., (*U Mich Mus Anthro; 0-932206*), 4009 Museums Bldg., 1109 Geddes, Ann Arbor, MI 48109 Tel 313-764-6867 (SAN 203-0489).

Univ. of Michigan Press, (*U of Mich Pr; 0-472*), P.O. Box 1104, Ann Arbor, MI 48106 Tel 313-764-4330 (SAN 282-4884); Orders to: 839 Greene St., Ann Arbor, MI 48106 Tel 313-764-4392 (SAN 282-4892). *Imprints:* Ann Arbor Books (AA).

Univ. of Michigan, Wayne State, Institute of Labor & Industrial Relations, (*U of Mich Inst Labor; 0-87736*), Dist. by: ILIR Publications,Univ. of Michigan, 130 S. First St., Ann Arbor, MI 48109 Tel 313-763-1187 (SAN 203-3127).

University of Minnesota, Div. of Pediatric Nephrology & the Minnesota Medical Foundation, (*U Minn Pediatric; 0-940210*), Box 73 Mayo Bldg., 420 Delaware St. S.E., Minneapolis, MN 55455 (SAN 262-1037).

Univ. of Minnesota, Bell Museum of Pathology, (*U of Minn Bell Mus; 0-912922*), P.O. Box 302, Mayo Memorial Bldg., Minneapolis, MN 55455 (SAN 204-8744).

Univ of Minn. College of Lib. Arts, (*U of MN College Lib Arts; 0-9607884*), 215 Johnston Hall, 101 Pleasant St. S.E., Minneapolis, MN 55455 (SAN 238-4027).

Univ. of Minnesota Computer Center, (*U of Minn Comp Ctr; 0-936992*), University of Minnesota, Duluth, MN 55812 (SAN 215-1200).

University of Minnesota, Department of Anthropology, (*Dept Anthro U Minn; 0-911599*), 215 Ford Hall, 224 Church St. SE, Minnesota, MN 55455 Tel 612-373-4614 (SAN 264-4576).

Univ. of Minnesota Press, (*U of Minn Pr; 0-8166*), 2037 University Ave. S.E., Minneapolis, MN 55414 Tel 612-373-3266 (SAN 213-2648).

Univ. of Minnesota School of Architecture, (*Univ Minn Sch; 0-943352*), Dist. by: Univ. of Minnesota Pr, 2037 University Ave. S.E., Minneapolis, MN 55414 (SAN 213-2648).

Univ. of Mississippi, Bureau of Business & Economic Research, (*U MS Bus Econ*), University, MS 38677 Tel 601-232-7481 (SAN 206-0841).

University of Mississippi Law Center, (*U MS Law Ctr; 0-8377*), University, MS 38677 (SAN 213-3938); Dist. by: Fred B. Rothman & Co., 10368 W. Centennial Rd., Littleton, CO 80123 Tel 303-979-5657 (SAN 159-9437).

Univ. of Missouri-Columbia. Missouri Political Science Assn., (*U MO Poli Sci*), c/o R F Karsch, 118 Middlebush Hall, Columbia, MO 65201 (SAN 285-1105).

Univ. of Missouri-Kansas City, New Letters, (*Univ Missouri; 0-938652*), 5346 Charlotte St., Kansas City, MO 64110 (SAN 238-423X).

Univ. of Missouri, Museum of Anthropology, (*Mus Anthro MO; 0-913134*), 104 Swallow Hall, Columbia, MO 65211 Tel 314-882-3764 (SAN 203-0195).

Univ. of Missouri Press, (*U of Mo Pr; 0-8262*), 200 Lewis, Columbia, MO 65211 Tel 314-882-7641 (SAN 203-3143).

Univ. of Missouri-Saint Louis, (*U MO-St Louis; 0-9601616*), 8001 Natural Bridge Rd., St. Louis, MO 63121 Tel 314-553-5168 (SAN 211-8726).

NAME INDEX

Univ. of Montana Pubns. in History, *(U of MT Pubns Hist),* Missoula, MT 59812 Tel 406-243-2231 (SAN 208-080X).

Univ. of Nebraska Press, *(U of Nebr Pr; 0-8032),* 901 N. 17th St., Lincoln, NE 68588 Tel 402-472-3581 (SAN 202-5337).

Univ. of Nevada Press, *(U of Nev Pr; 0-87417),* Reno, NV 89557 Tel 702-784-6573 (SAN 203-316X).

Univ. of Nevada/Reno Bureau of Business & Economic Research, *(U of Nev Bur Busn; 0-942828),* Reno, NV 89557 (SAN 240-1711).

Univ. of New Mexico, Native American Studies, *(U of NM Nat Am Std; 0-934090),* 1812 Las Lomas N.E., Albuquerque, NM 87131 (SAN 212-8446).

Univ. of New Mexico Press, *(U of NM Pr; 0-8263),* Albuquerque, NM 87131 Tel 505-277-2346 (SAN 213-9588).

Univ. of North Carolina at Chapel Hill, Dept. of Statistics, *(U NC Dept Statistics),* 322 Phillips Hall, Chapel Hill, NC 27514 (SAN 239-5673).

Univ. of NC Dept. of Health Administration, School of Public Health, *(U of NC Dept Health; 0-89055),* Dept. of Health Admin., 263 Rosenau 201-H, Chapel Hill, NC 27514 Tel 919-966-4091 (SAN 207-7574).

Univ. of North Carolina, Institute for Research in Social Science, *(U NC Inst Res Soc Sci; 0-89143),* IRSS Publications, Manning Hall 026A, Chapel Hill, NC 27514 Tel 919-966-3204 (SAN 206-0795).

Univ. of North Carolina, Institute of Government, *(U of NC Inst Gov),* Knapp Bldg. 059A, Chapel Hill, NC 27514 Tel 919-966-4119 (SAN 204-8752).

Univ. of North Carolina Press, *(U of NC Pr; 0-8078),* P.O Box 2288, Chapel Hill, NC 27514 Tel 919-966-3561 (SAN 203-3151).

Univ. of Northern Iowa, Dept. of Art, *(U of NI Dept Art; 0-932660),* Cedar Falls, IA 50613 Tel 319-273-6114 (SAN 212-2391).

Univ. of Notre Dame Press, *(U of Notre Dame Pr; 0-268),* P.O. Box L, Notre Dame, IN 46556 Tel 219-239-6346 (SAN 203-3178); Dist. by: Harper & Row Pubs., Keystone Industrial Park, Scranton, PA 18512 (SAN 215-3742).

Univ. of Oklahoma Bureau of Government Research, *(Univ OK Gov Res),* 455 West Lindsey, Rm. 304, Norman, OK 73019 Tel 405-325-6621 (SAN 209-6102).

Univ. of Oklahoma, Center for Economic & Management Research, *(U OK Ctr Econ; 0-931880),* College of Business Administration, 307 West Brooks St., Rm. 4, Norman, OK 73019 Tel 405-325-2931 (SAN 212-3916).

Univ. of Oklahoma Press, *(U of Okla Pr; 0-8061),* 1005 Asp Ave., Norman, OK 73019 Tel 405-325-5111 (SAN 203-3194).

Univ. of Oregon Books, *(U of Oreg Bks; 0-87114),* Univ. Pubns., 358 Susan Campbell Hall, Univ. of Oregon, Eugene, OR 97403 Tel 503-686-5396 (SAN 206-7757).

University of Oregon Bureau of Governmental Research and Service, *(U OR BGR),* Box 3177, Eugene, OR 97403 (SAN 227-339X).

Univ. of Oregon, Center of Leisure Studies, Dept. of Recreation & Park Management, *(U OR Ctr Leisure; 0-943272),* Esslinger Hall, Rm. 180, Eugene, OR 97403 Tel 503-686-3396 (SAN 219-0249).

Univ. of Oregon ERIC Clearinghouse on Educational Management, *(U of Oreg ERIC),* University of Oregon, Eugene, OR 97403 (SAN 226-806X).

Univ. of Oregon Health Sciences Center Foundation, *(U of Oreg Health Sci),* 3181 S.W. Sam Jackson Park Rd., Portland, OR 97201 (SAN 218-5113); Dist. by: Child Study Clinic, 611 S.W. Campus Dr., Portland, OR 97201 (SAN 218-5121).

Univ. of Pennsylvania, Institute of Contemporary Art, *(U of Pa Contemp Art; 0-88454),* 34th & Walnut Sts., Philadelphia, PA 19104 Tel 215-898-7108 (SAN 203-3208).

University of Pennsylvania Law School, *(U Penn Law),* 3400 Chestnut St, Philadelphia, PA 19174 (SAN 227-3411).

Univ. of Pennsylvania Press, *(U of Pa Pr; 0-8122),* 3933 Walnut St., Philadelphia, PA 19104 Tel 215-243-6261 (SAN 202-5345).

Univ. of Pittsburgh Press, *(U of Pittsburgh Pr; 0-8229),* 127 N. Bellefield Ave., Pittsburgh, PA 15260 Tel 412-624-4110 (SAN 203-3216).

Univ. of Puerto Rico Press, *(U of PR Pr; 0-8477),* P.O. Box X, U.P.R. Sta., Rio Piedras, PR 00931 Tel 809-763-0812 (SAN 208-1245).

Univ. of Queensland Press, *(U of Queensland Pr),* P.O. Box 1365, New York, NY 10023 Tel 212-799-3854 (SAN 206-8540); Orders to: 5 S. Union St., Lawrence, MA 01843 Tel 617-685-3306 (SAN 206-8559).

Univ. of Rhode Island, Marine Advisory Service, *(URI MAS),* Univ. of Rhode Island, Narragansett Bay Campus, Narragansett, RI 02882 Tel 401-792-6211 (SAN 209-0708).

Univ. of Rochester Policy Center Pubns., *(U Rochester Policy; 0-932468),* 105 Dewey Hall, Univ. of Rochester, Rochester, NY 14627 (SAN 212-3924).

Univ. of St. Thomas, *(U of St Thomas),* 3812 Montrose Blvd., Houston, TX 77006 Tel 713-522-7911 (SAN 206-0701).

Univ. of Scranton Ethnic Studies Pgm., *(U Scranton Ethnic; 0-9607870),* Univ. of Scranton, Dept. of Hist. & Political Sci., Scranton, PA 18510 Tel 717-961-7443 (SAN 239-7498).

Univ. of South Carolina Press, *(U of SC Pr; 0-87249),* Columbia, SC 29208 Tel 803-777-5243 (SAN 203-3224).

Univ. of South Dakota, Governmental Research Bureau, *(U of SD Gov Res Bur),* Vermillion, SD 57069 Tel 605-677-5242 (SAN 206-0698).

Univ. of Southern California, Andrus Gerontology Center, *(USC Andrus Geron),* Publications Office, University Park, CA 90007 Tel 213-743-5160 (SAN 282-4906); Dist. by: Lexington Books(D.C. Heath), 125 Spring St., Lexington, MA 02173 (SAN 213-7526).

University of Southern California National Information Center for Educational Media, *(Univ SC Natl Info; 0-89320),* NICEM/USC, 3716 South Hope St., Research Annex-Suite 301, Los Angeles, CA 90007 Tel 213-743-6681 (SAN 208-4570).

Univ. of Southern California Press, *(U of S Cal Pr; 0-88474),* Student Union 400, Univ. of Southern California, Los Angeles, CA 90007 (SAN 203-1892).

Univ. of Southwestern Louisiana, Center for Louisiana Studies, *(U of SW LA Ctr LA Studies; 0-940984),* P.O. Box 40831, Lafayette, LA 70504 Tel 318-231-6029 (SAN 217-4502).

Univ. of Tennessee, Department of Geological Sciences, *(U of Tenn Geo; 0-910249),* Knoxville, TN 37996-1410 Tel 615-974-2366 (SAN 241-4694).

Univ. of Tennessee Press, *(U of Tenn Pr; 0-87049),* 293 Communications Bldg., Knoxville, TN 37996 Tel 615-974-3321 (SAN 212-9930).

Univ. of Tennessee School of Social Work, *(U of Tenn Sch),* 1838 Terrace Ave., Knoxville, TN 37996-3920 (SAN 287-2994).

University of Texas at Arlington Press See UTA Press

Univ. of Texas at Arlington Press, The, *(U of Tex Arlington Pr; 0-87706),* Box 19075, Arlington, TX 76019 (SAN 213-9707); Orders to: 501 Monroe, Arlington, TX 76019 (SAN 213-9715).

University of Texas At Arlington, Texas Humanities Resource Center, *(U TX Arl TX Hum; 0-942484),* Library, P.O. Box 19497, Arlington, TX 76019 Tel 817-273-2767 (SAN 238-5880).

Univ. of Texas at Austin Film Library, *(U Tex Austin Film Lib; 0-913648),* Drawer W, University Sta., Austin, TX 78712 Tel 512-471-3572 (SAN 203-0446).

Univ. of Texas at Austin, General Libraries, *(U TX Austin Gen Libs; 0-930214),* Univ. of Texas at Austin, P.O. Box P, Austin, TX 78712 Tel 512-471-3811 (SAN 210-6795).

Univ. of Texas at Austin, Institute of Latin American Studies, *(U TX Inst Lat Am Stud; 0-86728),* Sid Richardson Hall 1.310, Austin, TX 78712 Tel 512-471-5551 (SAN 220-3103).

Univ. of Texas, Bureau of Business Research, *(Bureau Busn UT; 0-87755),* Univ. of Texas at Austin, P.O. Box 7459, Univ. Sta., Austin, TX 78712 Tel 512-471-1616 (SAN 203-3232).

Univ. of Texas, Bureau of Economic Geology, *(U of Tex Econ Geology),* P.O. Box X, University Sta., Austin, TX 78712 Tel 512-471-1534 (SAN 206-068X).

Univ. of Texas, Dept. of Astronomy, *(U of Tex Dept Astron; 0-9603796),* Astronomy Dept., RLM 15.308, Univ. of Texas, Austin, TX 78712 Tel 512-471-4461 (SAN 214-1647).

Univ. of Texas, Humanities Research Ctr., *(U of Tex Hum Res; 0-87959),* P.O. Box 7219, Austin, TX 78712 Tel 512-471-9113 (SAN 203-1906).

Univ. of Texas, Institute of Texan Cultures, *(U of Tex Inst Tex Culture; 0-933164; 0-86701),* P.O. Box 1226, San Antonio, TX 78294 Tel 512-226-7651 (SAN 213-8778).

Univ. of Texas Press, *(U of Tex Pr; 0-292),* P.O. Box 7819, Austin, TX 78712 Tel 512-471-4278 (SAN 212-9876) Tel 512-471-4032.

Univ. of Texas, Tarlton Law Library, *(U of Tex Tarlton Law Lib; 0-935630),* 727 E. 26th St., Austin, TX 78705 (SAN 214-1655).

University of the South, The, *(Univ South),* SPO 1145, Sewanee, TN 37375 (SAN 287-2676).

Univ. of the Trees Press, *(Univ of Trees; 0-916438),* P.O. Box 644, 13165 Pine St., Boulder Creek, CA 95006 Tel 408-338-2161 (SAN 212-9965).

Univ. of Toronto Press, *(U of Toronto Pr; 0-8020),* 33 E. Tupper St., Buffalo, NY 14203 Tel 416-978-2052 (SAN 214-2651).

University of Utah, Bureau of Economic & Business Research, *(Univ. Utah; 0-942486),* 401 kendall D. Garff Bldg., Salt Lake City, UT 84112 Tel 801-581-7274 (SAN 238-5899).

Univ. of Utah Press, *(U of Utah Pr; 0-87480),* Salt Lake City, UT 84112 Tel 801-581-6771 (SAN 220-0023).

Univ. of Utah, State Arboretum of Utah, *(State Arbor; 0-942830),* Univ. of Utah, Bldg. 436, Salt Lake City, UT 84112 Tel 801-581-5322 (SAN 240-2971).

University of Virginia, Mid-Atlantic Center for Community Education, *(Mid-At Ctr; 0-911525),* 405 Emmet St. - Ruffner 217, Charlottesville, VA 22903 Tel 804-924-0866 (SAN 264-4584).

Univ. of Washington, Graduate School of Business, *(U of Wash Grad Sch Busn),* Mackenzie Hall, DJ-10, Seattle, WA 98195 Tel 206-543-4598 (SAN 203-0187).

Univ. of Washington Pr., *(U of Wash Pr; 0-295),* P.O. Box 85569, Seattle, WA 98105 Tel 206-543-4050 (SAN 212-2502).

Univ. of West Florida, Gulf Coast History & Humanities Conference, *(U of W Fla; 0-940836),* Univ. of West Florida, Bldg. 32, Pensacola, FL 32504 Tel 904-476-9500 (SAN 219-6522).

Univ. of Wisconsin-Madison, Library School, *(U Wis Lib Sch; 0-936442),* 600 N. Park St., Madison, WI 53706 (SAN 219-9874).

Univ. of Wisconsin-Milwaukee, Center for Architecture & Urban Planning Research, *(U of Wis Ctr Arch-Urban),* P.O. Box 413, Milwaukee, WI 53201 Tel 414-963-4014 (SAN 211-9900).

Univ. of Wisconsin-Milwaukee, Center for Latin America, *(Univ of Wis Latin Am; 0-930450),* Univ. of Wisconsin-Milwaukee, Box 413, Milwaukee, WI 53201 Tel 414-963-4401 (SAN 211-0628).

Univ. of Wisconsin Press, *(U of Wis Pr; 0-299),* 114 North Murray St., Madison, WI 53715 Tel 608-262-4922 (SAN 203-3259).

Univ. of Wisconsin Univ Center for Cooperatives, *(U WI Ctr CoOp; 0-942288),* 514 Lowell Hall, Madison, WI 53706 (SAN 240-1681).

Univ. of Wyoming, *(U of Wyoming; 0-941570),* P.O. Box 3315, University Sta., Laramie, WY 82071 Tel 307-766-2379 (SAN 206-0620).

University Park Press, *(Univ Park; 0-8391),* 300 N. Charles St., Baltimore, MD 21201 Tel 301-547-0700 (SAN 204-8833).

University Place Book Shop, *(Univ Place; 0-911556),* 821 Broadway, New York, NY 10003 Tel 212-254-5998 (SAN 204-8841).

University Press, *(University Pr; 0-8418),* Drawer N, Wolfe City, TX 75496 Tel 214-496-2226 (SAN 203-3356).

Univ. Press Books, *(UPB; 0-8295),* 302 Fifth Ave., New York, NY 10001 Tel 212-564-2049 (SAN 207-4907).

Univ. Press, Inc., *(Univ Pr OH; 0-9603614),* P.O. Box 24268, Cleveland, OH 44124 Tel 216-442-0800 (SAN 213-3954).

University Press of America, *(U Pr of Amer; 0-8191),* 4720 Boston Way, Lanham, MD 20706 Tel 301-459-3366 (SAN 200-2256).

Univ. Press of California, *(U Pr of Cal; 0-935048),* 1000 N. Coast Highway, No. 3, Laguna Beach, CA 92651 Tel 714-497-4861 (SAN 212-3215).

Univ. Press of Idaho, Div. of the Idaho Research Foundation, Inc., *(U Pr of Idaho; 0-89301),* University Sta., Box 3368, Moscow, ID 83843 Tel 208-885-7925 (SAN 208-905X).

University Press of Kansas, *(U Pr of KS; 0-7006),* 303 Carruth, Lawrence, KS 66045 Tel 913-864-4154 (SAN 203-3267).

Univ. Pr. of Kentucky, *(U Pr of Ky; 0-8131),* Univ. of Kentucky, 102 Lafferty Hall, Lexington, KY 40506-0024 Tel 606-257-8437 (SAN 203-3275).

Univ. Press of Mississippi, *(U Pr of Miss; 0-87805),* 3825 Ridgewood Rd., Jackson, MS 39211 Tel 601-982-6205 (SAN 203-1914).

Univ. Press of New England, *(U Pr of New Eng; 0-87451),* P. O. Box 979, Hanover, NH 03755 Tel 603-646-3348 (SAN 203-3283).

Univ. Press of Virginia, *(U Pr of Va; 0-8139),* P.O. Box 3608, University Sta., Charlottesville, VA 22903 Tel 804-924-3468 (SAN 202-5361). *Imprints:* Colonial Society of Massachusetts (Colonial Soc MA); Maya Publishing Co. (Maya Pub Co).

Univ. Press of Washington, D.C., *(U Pr of Wash; 0-87419),* University Press Bldg., Delbrook Campus C.A.S., Riverton, VA 22651 Tel 703-635-9562 (SAN 204-8760).

Univ. Press, Univ. of Wisconsin-River Falls, *(U Pr Wisc River Falls;* 113 E. Hawthorn, River Falls, WI 54022 (SAN 214-1663).

Univ. Presses of Fla., *(U Presses Fla; 0-8130),* 15 N.W. 15th St., Gainesville, FL 32603 Tel 904-392-1351 (SAN 207-9275).

University Pubns., *(Univ Pubs NY; 0-911463),* 340 E. 19th Street, New York, NY 10003 (SAN 264-4592).

Univ. Pubns. of America, Inc., *(U Pubns Amer; 0-89093),* 44 N. Market St., Frederick, MD 21701 (SAN 210-5802). *Imprints:* Aletheia Books (Aletheia Bks).

Univ. Publishing Bureau, Div. of Computer Communications Corp., *(Univ Pub Bureau; 0-943960),* 6133 Blue Circle Drive, Minnetonka, MN 55343 (SAN 241-1636).

University Science Books, *(Univ Sci Bks; 0-935702),* 20 Edgehill Rd., Mill Valley, CA 94941 (SAN 213-8085).

University Statistical Tracts, *(Univ Stat Tracts; 0-931316),* 75-19 171st St., Flushing, NY 11366 Tel 212-969-7553 (SAN 211-3341).

Unlimited Marketing Publications, Div. of Unltd. Mktg & Res. Services, Inc., *(Unltd Mktg Pubns; 0-912305),* 190 Angeil St., Box 944 Annex Station, Providence, RI 02901 Tel 401-421-7080 (SAN 265-2897).

Unmuzzled Ox Press, *(Unmuzzled Ox),* 105 Hudson St., New York, NY 10013 Tel 212-226-7170 (SAN 207-9151).

Unspeakable Visions of the Individual, The, *(TUVOTI; 0-934660),* P. O. Box 439, California, PA 15419 Tel 412-938-8956 (SAN 207-916X).

Update Publicare Co., Div. of A.C. Doyle Publishing, Inc., *(Update Pub Co),* Box 570122, Houston, TX 77257-0122 (SAN 264-4606).

Update Pubns., *(Update Pubns AZ; 0-943002),* P.O. Box 31062, Phoenix, AZ 85046 Tel 602-867-6874 (SAN 240-463X).

Updegraff Press, The, *(Updegraff),* 2564 Cherosen Rd., Loiusville, KY 40205 Tel 502-454-3206 (SAN 283-3530).

Upjohn, W.E., Institute for Employment Research, *(Upjohn Inst; 0-911558),* 300 S. Westnedge Ave., Kalamazoo, MI 49007 Tel 616-343-5541 (SAN 206-0558).

Upland Press, *(Upland Pr; 0-932554),* P.O. Box 7390, Chicago, IL 60680 Tel 312-266-2087 (SAN 211-8742).

Uplift Books, *(Uplift Bks; 0-88005),* 428 So. Brea Blvd., Suite B, Brea, CA 92621 Tel 714-529-8406 (SAN 219-8312).

Upper Country People Probe, *(Upper Country),* 204 Andrews Ave., Hartsville, TN 37074 (SAN 239-5002).

Upper Room, *(Upper Room; 0-8358),* 1908 Grand Ave., P.O. Box 189, Nashville, TN 37202 Tel 615-327-2700 (SAN 203-3364).

Uprisings Publishing Co., *(Uprisings Pub Co; 0-9611600),* P.O. Box 2755, Ann Harbor, MI 48106 (SAN 283-8869).

Upsala College, College Relations Office, *(Upsala Coll; 0-9601668),* Prospect St., East Orange, NJ 07019 (SAN 211-545X).

Upstat Publishing Co., *(Upstat; 0-87916),* 1815 19th St. N.W., Washington, DC 20009 Tel 202-667-0065 (SAN 203-3372).

Upstream Press, Inc., *(Upstream Pr; 0-941856),* P.O. Box 2033, Rohnert Park, CA 94928 Tel 707-795-5642 (SAN 239-3360); Dist. by: Publishers Group West, 5855 Beaudry St., Emeryville, CA 94608 Tel 415-658-3453 (SAN 202-8522).

Uptown Books, *(Uptown Bks),* Box 11146, Glendale, CA 91206 (SAN 240-9828).

Uranian Consultants, *(Uranian Consult; 0-9609700),* P.O. Box 40024, Washington, DC 20016 Tel 301-229-8526 (SAN 264-4614).

Uranian Pubns., Inc., *(Uranian Pubns; 0-89159),* P.O. Box 114, Franksville, WI 53126 Tel 414-632-2892 (SAN 210-5705).

URANTIA Foundation, *(URANTIA Foun; 0-911560),* 533 Diversey Pkwy., Chicago, IL 60614 Tel 312-525-3319 (SAN 204-8906).

Uranus Publishing Co., *(Uranus Pub; 0-9601080),* 5050 Calatrana Dr., Woodland Hills, CA 91364 (SAN 207-3544).

Urban & Schwarzenberg, *(Urban & S; 0-8067),* 7 E. Redwood St., Baltimore, MD 21202 Tel 301-539-2550 (SAN 209-6897).

Urban Books, *(Urban Bks),* 295 Grizzly Peak Blvd., Berkeley, CA 94708 Tel 415-524-3315 (SAN 204-8914).

Urban Institute Press, *(Urban Inst; 0-87766),* 2100 "M" St., N.W., Washington, DC 20037 Tel 202-223-1950 (SAN 203-3380).

Urban Land Institute, *(Urban Land; 0-87420),* 1090 Vermont Ave. N. W., Washington, DC 20005 Tel 202-289-8500 (SAN 203-3399).

Urban Research Institute, Inc., *(Urban Res Inst; 0-941484),* 840 E. 87th St., Chicago, IL 60619 Tel 312-994-7200 (SAN 239-0515).

Urbanek, Mae, *(Urbanek),* Lusk, WY 82225 Tel 307-334-2473 (SAN 213-9006).

Urfer, Bill, *(Urfer; 0-9604306),* Box 155, Libby Rte., Heber Springs, AR 72543 Tel 501-362-5209 (SAN 216-3144).

Urie, Sherry, *(Sherry Urie; 0-9603324),* RFD, West Glover, VT 05875 (SAN 211-4526).

Uriel Pubns., *(Uriel Pubns; 0-9603956),* Box 287, Taylor, ND 58656 Tel 701-974-3566 (SAN 213-5655).

Urion Press, *(Urion Pr Oreg; 0-913522),* P.O. Box 2244, Eugene, OR 97402 Tel 408-867-7695 (SAN 282-4930); Orders to: P.O. Box 10085 Westgate Station, San Jose, CA 95157 (SAN 282-4949).

Urizen Books, Inc., *(Urizen Bks; 0-89396; 0-916354),* 66 W. Broadway, New York, NY 10007 Tel 212-962-3413 (SAN 208-9408).

Urquhart, Edward F., *(E Urquhart; 0-9611618),* Box 25092, Northgate Sta., Seattle, WA 98115 Tel 206-523-3200 (SAN 284-902X).

Ursus Press, *(Ursus Pr; 0-910691),* P.O. Box 14220, Chicago, IL 60614 (SAN 262-1045) Moved, left no forwarding address.

U.S. Assn. for the Club of Rome, *(USACOR; 0-942718),* 1525 New Hampshire Ave. N.W., Washington, DC 20036 (SAN 240-5008).

Useful Maps, *(Useful Maps),* Box 92, Collingswood, NJ 08108 (SAN 219-3434).

USS North Carolina Battleship Commission, *(USS North Car; 0-9608538),* P.O. Box 417, Wilmington, NC 28402 Tel 919-762-1829 (SAN 240-7973).

UTA Press, *(UTA Pr; 0-932408),* Box 929, Univ. of Texas at Arlington; Arlington, TX 76019 Tel 817-273-3391 (SAN 212-0542) Tel 817-273-4957.

Utah Division of State History See **Utah State Historical Society**

Utah Museum of Natural History, *(Utah Mus Natural Hist),* University of Utah, Salt Lake City, UT 84112 (SAN 213-5663).

Utah State Historical Society, *(Utah St Hist Soc; 0-913738),* 300 Rio Grande, Salt Lake City, UT 84101 Tel 801-533-6024 (SAN 204-8930).

Utah State Univ. Press, *(Utah St U Pr; 0-87421),* UMC 95, Logan, UT 84322 Tel 801-750-1362 (SAN 202-9294).

Utica House Publishing Co., *(Utica Hse; 0-9609296),* RR No. 1, Utica, IL 61373 Tel 815-223-3200 (SAN 260-1532).

Utopia Press, *(Utopia Pr; 0-911947),* 568 S. Main Square, Cedar City, UT 84720 Tel 619-277-0356 (SAN 264-4622).

Utopian Universe Publishing Co., *(Utopian Universe),* P.O. Box 26, E. Elmhurst, NY 11369 Tel 212-478-3291 (SAN 207-4923).

Uzzano Pr., *(Uzzano Pr; 0-930600),* 511 Sunset Dr., Menomonie, WI 54751 (SAN 211-1020).

VEATU Press, *(VEATU; 0-9610276),* 7126 Morgan Ave. S, Richfield, MN 55423 Tel 612-869-8324 (SAN 264-4649).

V-R Information Systems, Inc., *(V-R Information; 0-937508),* 5818 Balcones Dr., Austin, TX 78731 Tel 512-458-8131 (SAN 209-4959).

VTR Publishing Co., *(VTR Pub; 0-915146),* 23 Eaton Rd., Syosset, NY 11791 Tel 516-938-0878 (SAN 207-0979).

Vadare Publishing Co., *(Vadare; 0-9610782),* 1111 Montauk Hwy, W. Islip, NY 11795 Tel 516-661-3855 (SAN 265-1491).

Vagabond Press, *(Vagabond Pr; 0-912824),* 1610 N. Water St., Ellensburg, WA 98926 Tel 509-925-5634 (SAN 203-0535).

Vail-Ballou Press, Inc., *(Vail Ballou; 0-9600868),* 187 Clinton St., Binghamton, NY 13902 (SAN 239-5681).

Vail Publishing, *(Vail Pub; 0-9607872),* 8285 SW Brookridge, Portland, OR 97225 Tel 503-292-9964 (SAN 240-0766).

Val-House Publishing, *(Val-Hse Pub; 0-936354),* 2903 Carriage Lane, P.O. Box 490443, College Park, GA 30349 Tel 404-344-0300 (SAN 214-4816).

Valencia, Jerry, *(Valencia; 0-9604784),* 7525 Raytheon Rd., San Diego, CA 92111 (SAN 220-1038); Orders to: P.O. Box 758, La Jolla, CA 92038 Tel 619-729-3344 (SAN 220-1046).

Valentine Publishing & Drama Co., *(Valentine Pub; 0-941672),* P.O. Box 461, Rhinebeck, NY 12572 Tel 914-876-3589 (SAN 239-3379).

Valhalla Press, *(Valhalla Pr; 0-9607070),* Box 301, Chicago, IL 60690 (SAN 282-4981); Orders to: 231 S. Green St., Chicago, IL Tel 312-761-1888 (SAN 282-499X).

Valhalla Rehabilitation Publications, Ltd., *(Valhalla Rehab),* P.O. Box 195, Valhalla, NY 10595 (SAN 262-1053).

Valiant Pubns., *(Valiant Pubns; 0-9608244),* 1200 Beneficial Liffe Tower, Salt Lake City, UT 84111 (SAN 240-4656).

Valkyrie Press, Inc., *(Valkyrie Hse; 0-912760; 0-934616; 0-912589),* 6236-12th St. S., St. Petersburg, FL 33705 Tel 813-822-0515 (SAN 203-1671).

Valley Crafts, *(Valley Crafts; 0-915508),* 168 Rainbow Lane, Cary, IL 60013 (SAN 207-6888).

Valley Farms, *(Valley Farms; 0-934318),* 250 Mill Rd., Helena, MT 59601 (SAN 283-3611).

Valley Lights Pubns., *(Valley Lights; 0-9606482),* P.O. Box 355, Oak View, CA 93022 Tel 805-649-3393 (SAN 219-8320).

Valley of the Sun Publishing Co., *(Valley Sun; 0-911842),* Box 38, Malibu, CA 90265 Tel 213-456-7361 (SAN 206-8974).

Valley Presbyterian Hospital, *(Valley Presbyterian; 0-9605718),* 15107 Vanowen St., Van Nuys, CA 91405 Tel 213-981-1300 (SAN 216-4701).

Valley Pubs. See **Western Tanager Press**

Valley View Blueberry Press, *(Valley View; 0-9608432),* 21717 N.E. 68th St., Vancouver, WA 98662 Tel 206-892-2839 (SAN 240-7981).

Valuation Press Inc., *(Valuation; 0-930458),* 661 Washington St., Marina Del Rey, CA 90291 (SAN 210-6809); Orders to: P.O. Box 1080, Marina Del Rey, CA 90291 Tel 213-822-3691 (SAN 210-6817).

Value Communications, Inc., Subs. of Oak Tree Pubns., Inc., *(Value Comm; 0-916392),* 9601 Aero Dr., San Diego, CA 92123 Tel 619-560-5163 (SAN 208-0990).

Valuwrite Pubns., *(ValuWrite; 0-940986),* P.O. Box E, Provo, UT 84603 Tel 801-373-1111 (SAN 223-2022).

Van Dean Educators Inc, *(Van Dean),* Box 1422, Malvern, PA 19355 (SAN 240-8996).

Van der Marck, Alfred, Editions, *(Van der Marck; 0-912383),* 235 Park Ave. S. No. 407, New York, NY 10003 Tel 212-533-5080 (SAN 265-2919).

Van Diver, Bradford B., *(Van Diver; 0-9601106),* The State University College of Arts & Science at Potsdam, Dept. of Geology, Potsdam, NY 13676 Tel 312-267-2288 (SAN 209-908X).

Van Dyk Pubns., *(Van Dyk),* 705 S. Wyoming St., Butte, MT 59701 Tel 406-782-1337 (SAN 209-6129).

Van Lee Guides, *(Van Lee Guides),* P.O. Box 367, Duluth, GA 30136 (SAN 240-8953).

Van Ness LOTCO, *(Van Ness LOTCO; 0-9608648),* 2309 Newmarket Dr., Louisville, KY 40222 Tel 502-425-5118 (SAN 238-4094).

Van Nostrand Reinhold Co. Inc, Div. of Litton Educational Publishing, Inc., *(Van Nos Reinhold; 0-442),* 135 W. 50th St., New York, NY 10020 Tel 212-265-8700 (SAN 202-5183); Orders to: VNR Order Processing, 7625 Empire Dr., Florence, KY 41042 (SAN 202-5191). Imprints: Anvil Books (Anv); Insight Books (IB); Momentum Books (Mtum); Searchlight Books (Srchl).

Van Vactor & Goodheart, *(Van Vactor & Goodheart; 0-941324),* 24 Lee St., Cambridge, MA 02139 (SAN 282-5007); Orders to: Persea Books, Inc., 225 Lafayette St., New York, NY 10012 (SAN 282-5015).

Vance Bibliographies, *(Vance Biblios),* P.O. Box 229, 112 N. Charter St., Monticello, IL 61856 Tel 217-762-3831 (SAN 212-6273).

Vancento Pub. Co., *(Vancento Pub),* 62 Court St., Reno, NV 89501 (SAN 238-7697).

Vanderbilt Univ. Press, *(Vanderbilt U Pr; 0-8265),* 2505(Rear) West End Ave., Nashville, TN 37203 Tel 615-322-3585 (SAN 202-9308).

Vanderstoel, Graeme, *(G Vanderstoel),* P.O. Box 599, El Cerrito, CA 94530 Tel 415-527-2882 (SAN 263-239X).

Vanessa-Ann Collection, The, *(Vanessa-Ann Collec; 0-913921),* P.O. Box 9113, Ogden, UT 84403 (SAN 286-6897).

Vanguard Books, *(Vanguard Bks; 0-917702),* P.O. Box 3566, Chicago, IL 60654 Tel 312-342-3425 (SAN 213-8212).

Vanguard Press, Inc., *(Vanguard; 0-8149),* 424 Madison Ave., New York, NY 10017 Tel 212-753-3906 (SAN 202-9316).

Vanilla Press, *(Vanilla; 0-917626),* 2400 Colfax Ave. S., Minneapolis, MN 55405 Tel 612-374-4726 (SAN 208-9084).

Vanni, S.F., *(S F Vanni; 0-913298),* 30 W. 12th St., New York, NY 10011 Tel 212-675-6336 (SAN 220-0031).

Vanous, Arthur, Co., *(Vanous; 0-89918),* 616 Kinderkamack Rd., River Edge, NJ 07661 Tel 201-265-7555 (SAN 202-9324); Orders to: P.O. Box A, River Edge, NJ 07661 (SAN 202-9332).

Vantage Press, Inc., *(Vantage; 0-533),* 516 W. 34th St., New York, NY 10001 Tel 212-736-1767 (SAN 206-8893).

Vantage Printing Company, *(Vantage Printing; 0-943110),* 2003 Broadway, Houston, TX 77012 Tel 713-644-1994 (SAN 240-4672).

Vardaman Press, *(Vardaman Pr; 0-942648),* 2720 E. 176th St., Tacoma, WA 98445 (SAN 239-9482).

Varfley, Edwin B., *(Varfley; 0-910691),* P.O. Box 2916, Providence, RI 02908 Tel 401-272-8684 (SAN 276-4806).

Vargas, Glenn, *(Glenn Vargas; 0-917646),* 85-159 Ave. 66, Thermal, CA 92274 Tel 619-397-4264 (SAN 203-4301).

Varner, Nick, *(Nick Varner),* P.O. Box 1309, Owensboro, KY 42301 (SAN 239-569X).

Varnes Pubs., *(Varnes Pubs; 0-943584),* 1810 Country Club Lane, P.O. Box 2087, Escondido, CA 92025 Tel 619-489-0940 (SAN 240-8007).

Vassilion, Harry J., *(Vassilion),* 5519 N. Hills Dr., Raleigh, NC 27612 (SAN 216-471X).

Vector Associates, *(Vector Assocs; 0-930808),* P.O. Box 6215, Bellevue, WA 98007 Tel 206-747-5880 (SAN 211-1039).

Vector Counseling Institute, *(Vector Counsel; 0-913596),* P.O. Box 1271, Mt. Vernon, WA 98273 Tel 206-855-0630 (SAN 205-4752).

Vedanta Centre Pubs., *(Vedanta Ctr; 0-911564),* 130 Beechwood St., Cohasset, MA 02025 Tel 617-383-0940 (SAN 206-7781).

Vedanta Press, *(Vedanta Pr; 0-87481),* 1946 Vedanta Place, Hollywood, CA 90068-3996 Tel 213-465-7114 (SAN 202-9340) (SAN 202-9359).

Vedanta Society of St. Louis, *(Vedanta Soc St Louis; 0-916356),* 205 S. Skinker Blvd., St. Louis, MO 63105 Tel 314-721-5118 (SAN 208-1180).

Vedette Printing Co., *(Vedette Print),* Greenfield, MO 65661 (SAN 239-5703).

Vehicle Editions, *(Vehicle Edns; 0-931428),* 238 Mott St., New York, NY 10012 Tel 212-226-1769 (SAN 212-5773).

Veldt Protea Management Services, Inc., *(Veldt Protea; 0-917538),* P.O. Box 152, College Park Sta., Detroit, MI 48221 (SAN 209-3626).

Velo-News, *(Velo-News; 0-941950),* Box 1257, Brattleboro, VT 05301 Tel 802-254-2305 (SAN 239-5711).

VeNard Pubs., *(VeNard Pubs; 0-9610342),* 4812 Folson Blvd. No. H, Sacramento, CA 95819 Tel 916-739-8343 (SAN 264-469X).

Vendome Press, The, *(Vendome; 0-86565),* 515 Madison Ave., Suite 1906, New York, NY 10022 (SAN 215-2347); Dist. by: Viking Press, 40 W. 23rd St., New York, NY 10010 Tel 212-807-7300 (SAN 282-5074).

Venice West Pubs., *(Venice West),* 16814 Los Alimos St., Granada Hills, CA 91344 (SAN 210-2986); Dist. by: Ross-Erikson, 629 State St., Suite 222, Santa Barbara, CA 93101 Tel 805-962-1175 (SAN 208-0494).

Ventnor Pubs., *(Ventnor; 0-911566),* P.O. Box 2078, Ventnor, NJ 08406 (SAN 205-4760).

Ventura Press, *(Ventura Pr; 0-917438),* P.O. Box 1076, Guerneville, CA 95446 (SAN 205-4779).

Venture Books, *(Venture Bks; 0-9600432),* P.O. Box 131, Coopersburg, PA 18036 Tel 215-965-2891 (SAN 205-4787).

Venture Publishing, *(Venture PA),* 1640 Oxford Circle, State College, PA 16801 (SAN 241-5917).

Venture Publishing, *(Venture Pub PA; 0-910251),* 1640 Oxford Circle, State College, PA 16801 (SAN 240-897X).

Venturecraft Kits Co., *(Venturecraft Co; 0-941326),* 1133 Broadway, Suite 607, New York, NY 10010 (SAN 239-5738).

Venus Books, *(Venus Bks),* 3314 Daniel Ave., Suite 17, Dallas, TX 75205 (SAN 216-4728).

Verbatim, *(Verbatim; 0-930454),* Box 668, Essex, CT 06426 Tel 203-767-8248 (SAN 211-1047).

VerDugo Press, *(VerDugo Pr; 0-941140),* 6715 Sunset Blvd, Hollywood, CA 90028 (SAN 239-572X); Dist. by: B. Dalton Booksellers, 1 Corporate Ctr., 7505 Metro Blvd., Minneapolis, MN 55402 (SAN 147-099X).

Veridon Editions, *(Veridon Edns; 0-912061),* P.O. Box 70061, Washington, DC 20088 (SAN 264-7028).

Veritas Foundation, *(Veritas; 0-911568),* P.O. Box 111, West Sayville, NY 11796 (SAN 206-3107) Formerly Named Probe.

Veritas Press, *(Veritas Pr; 0-932208),* 3310 Rochambeau Ave., New York, NY 10467 Tel 212-655-7566 (SAN 212-2413).

Veritas Pubns., *(Veritas Pubns; 0-938264),* P.O. Box 4418, Arlington, VA 22204 Tel 703-979-1159 (SAN 215-9279).

Veritat Foundation, Inc., *(Veritat Found; 0-938760),* 3910 Los Feliz Blvd., Los Angeles, CA 90027 (SAN 205-6348).

Veritie Press, Inc., *(Veritie Pr; 0-915964),* P.O. Box 222, Novelty, OH 44072 Tel 216-338-3374 (SAN 207-6977).

Verlag Chemie International, Inc., *(Verlag Chemie; 0-89573),* 303 N.W.12th Ave., Deerfield Beach, FL 33441 Tel 305-428-5566 (SAN 212-2421).

Vermeer Arts, Ltd., *(Vermeer Arts; 0-934744),* 1676 W. 3rd Ave., Durango, CO 81301 Tel 303-247-3960 (SAN 212-9809).

Vermont Books, Inc., *(Vermont Bks; 0-911570),* 38 Main St., Middlebury, VT 05753 Tel 802-388-2061 (SAN 205-4817).

Vermont Council on the Arts, Inc., *(VT Council Arts; 0-916718),* 136 State St., Montpelier, VT 05602 Tel 802-828-3291 (SAN 208-9092).

Vermont Heritage Press, *(Vermont Herit Pr; 0-911853),* 10 Cleveland Ave., Rutland, VT 05701 Tel 802-773-9194 (SAN 264-472X).

Vermont Historical Society, *(VT Hist Soc; 0-934720),* 109 State St., Montpelier, VT 05602 Tel 802-828-2291 (SAN 206-0442).

Vermont Life Magazine, *(VT Life Mag; 0-936896),* 61 Elm St., Montpelier, VT 05602 (SAN 215-8213).

Vernal Equinox Press, *(Vernal Equinox),* P.O. Box 581, San Anselmo, CA 94960 (SAN 240-1762).

Veronica Press, *(Veronica Pr; 0-9607094),* P.O. Box 42075, Cincinnati, OH 45242 Tel 513-677-0319 (SAN 239-0531).

Verry, Lawrence, Inc., *(Verry; 0-8426),* Mystic, CT 06355 Tel 203-536-7373 (SAN 202-5205).

Versailles, Elizabeth Starr, *(Versailles; 0-9606002),* 42 Nash Hill Rd., Williamsburg, MA 01096 Tel 413-268-7576 (SAN 203-0330).

Vertex Co., *(Vertex),* 4438 Manzanita Dr., San Jose, CA 95129 Tel 408-252-2592 (SAN 209-4096).

Very Best Publishers, The, *(Very Best; 0-911729),* 149 West Newton St., Boston, MA 02118 Tel 617-262-3477 (SAN 264-4746).

Very Serious Business Enterprises, *(VSBE; 0-9605304),* P.O. Box 356, Newark, NJ 07101 (SAN 215-8221).

Vestal Press Ltd., *(Vestal; 0-911572),* P.O. Box 97, 320 N. Jensen Rd., Vestal, NY 13850 Tel 607-797-4872 (SAN 205-4825).

Veterans Information Service, *(Veterans Info),* P.O. Box 111, East Moline, IL 61244 Tel 309-797-1868 (SAN 205-4833).

Veterinary Medicine Publishing Co., *(Veterinary Med; 0-935078),* 690 S. Fourth, Edwardsville, KS 66111 (SAN 209-0074).

Veterinary Textbooks, *(Veterinary Textbks; 0-9601152),* 36 Woodcrest Ave., Ithaca, NY 14850 Tel 607-272-1860 (SAN 207-2998).

Vichitra Press, *(Vichitra Pr; 0-941582),* 10582 Cheviot Dr., Los Angeles, CA 90064 Tel 213-839-8547 (SAN 239-3387); Dist. by: Graeme Vanderstoel, P.O. Box 599, El Cerrito, CA 94530 Tel 415-527-2882 (SAN 239-3395).

Victor Books, *(Victor Bks; 0-88207; 0-89693),* P.O. Box 1825, Wheaton, IL 60187 Tel 312-668-6000 (SAN 207-7302); Orders to: 1825 College Ave., Wheaton, IL 60187 (SAN 207-7310).

Victoria House, Pubs., *(Victoria Hse; 0-918480),* 2218 N.E. 8th Ave., Portland, OR 97212 Tel 503-284-4801 (SAN 209-9101).

Victoria Island Press, The, *(Victoria Isl; 0-938742),* 2951 N. Clark St., Chicago, IL 60657 (SAN 216-4736) Moved, Left No Forwarding Address.

Victorian Design Press, *(Victorian Design; 0-913693),* P.O. Box 5186, Mill Valley, CA 94941 Tel 415-388-4990 (SAN 286-2158); 382 Throckmorton Ave., Mill Valley, CA 94942 (SAN 286-2166).

Victorious Ministry Through Christ, Inc., *(Victorious Ministry; 0-9605178),* P.O. Box 1804, Winter Park, FL 32790 (SAN 215-823X); Dist. by: Impact Books, 137 W. Jefferson, Kirkwood, MO 63122 (SAN 214-0330).

Victory Press, *(Victory Pr; 0-9609908),* Carlton, OR 97111 Tel 503-472-4021 (SAN 276-5063).

Video Athlete Corp., *(Video Athlete),* 120 W. Mifflin, Madison, WI 53703 (SAN 287-2358).

Video-Forum, Div. of Jeffrey Norton Pubs., *(Video-Forum; 0-88432),* 96 Broad St., Guilford, CT 06437 Tel 203-453-9794 (SAN 217-4707).

Video Wizard Co., *(Video Wizard; 0-943320),* 134 St. Charles Ave., San Francisco, CA 94132 Tel 415-952-4990 (SAN 240-8023).

Vienna House, Inc., *(Vienna Hse; 0-8443),* 342 Madison Ave., New York, NY 10017 Tel 212-986-7724 (SAN 202-9367).

Viewpoint Press, *(Viewpoint Pr; 0-943962),* P.O. Box P, Tehachapi, CA 93561 Tel 417-532-6064 (SAN 241-1644).

Vigo Press, *(Vigo Pr; 0-911571),* P.O. Box 2317, Dallas, TX 75221 Tel 214-521-6753 (SAN 211-3384).

Viking Import House, Inc., *(Viking Import; 0-911576),* 412 S.E. Sixth St., Ft. Lauderdale, FL 33301 (SAN 205-485X).

Viking Press, Inc., *(Viking Pr; 0-670),* 40 W. 23rd St., New York, NY 10010 Tel 212-807-7300 (SAN 282-5066); Orders to: Viking/Penguin, Inc., 299 Murray Hill Pkwy., East Rutherford, NJ 07073 (SAN 282-5074).

Village Press, The, *(Village CA; 0-910497),* P.O. Box 310, Fallbrook, CA 92028 Tel 714-728-4305 (SAN 282-5082); Dist. by: Aviation Book Co., 1640 Victory Blvd., Glendale, CA 91201 Tel 213-240-1771 (SAN 212-0259).

Village Press, The, *(Village Pr; 0-940310),* P.O. Box 174, Unionville, CT 06085 Tel 203-673-9827 (SAN 217-5770).

Vincent Campo, *(V Campo),* 1223 Newkirk Ave., Brooklyn, NY 11230 (SAN 237-9945).

Vinco Press, *(Vinco Pr; 0-9603836),* 1553 Woodward, Detroit, MI 48226 (SAN 213-8093).

Vineyard See Seabury Press, Inc.

VinMar Agency, Inc., the, *(VinMar Agency; 0-943964),* P.O. Box 1329, Avon Park, FL 33825 Tel 813-453-7412 (SAN 241-1652).

Vintage America Publishing Co., *(Vintage Am; 0-932330),* P.O. Box 57361, Washington, DC 20037 (SAN 212-1689) Do Not Confuse with Vintage Trade Books, Imprint of Random.

Vintage Book Co., *(Vintage Bk Co; 0-938164),* Box 16182, Elway Sta., St. Paul, MN 55116 Tel 612-690-2363 (SAN 220-1062).

Vintage Image, *(Vin Image; 0-918666),* 1335 Main St., St. Helena, CA 94574 Tel 707-963-3883 (SAN 210-329X).

Vintage Radio Co., *(Vintage Radio; 0-914126),* 26451 Dunwood Rd., P.O. Box 2045, Rolling Hills Estates, CA 90274 Tel 213-375-4272 (SAN 282-5104); Dist. by: McMahon Vintage Radio, P.O. Box 1331, N. Highlands, N. Highlands, CA 95660 Tel 916-332-8262 (SAN 282-6356).

Vintage Trade Books See Random House, Inc.

Vinton Publishing, *(Vinton; 0-7050096),* 1244 Wyoming St., Boulder City, NE 89005 (SAN 277-710X).

Violet Press, *(Violet Pr; 0-912968),* P.O. Box 398, New York, NY 10009 (SAN 203-1701).

Virago See Doubleday & Co., Inc.

Virdon Associates, Inc., *(Virdon Assoc),* P.O. Box 221, Mount Holly Springs, PA 17065 (SAN 211-5468).

Virgin Islands Biological Offices, *(Virgin Islands Biol; 0-9601490),* Box 305, Frederiksted, St. Croix, VI 00840 (SAN 211-4267).

Virginia Book Co., *(VA Bk; 0-911578),* Box 431, Berryville, VA 22611 Tel 703-955-1428 (SAN 206-7773).

Virginia City Restoration Corp., *(VA City Rest),* P.O. Box 221691, Carmel, CA 93922 (SAN 215-1901).

Virginia Museum of Fine Arts, *(VA Mus Fine Arts; 0-917046),* Boulevard & Grove Ave., Richmond, VA 23221 Tel 804-257-0818 (SAN 206-0418).

Virginia Office of the Attorney General, *(VA Atty Genl),* 1101 E Broad St Supreme Court Bldg, Richmond, VA 23219 (SAN 226-7888).

Virginia State Library, *(VA State Lib; 0-88490),* 12th & Capitol Sts., Richmond, VA 23219 Tel 804-786-2312 (SAN 203-0543).

Virginia Surveyors Foundation, *(VA Surveyors; 0-9604076),* 6001 Lakeside Ave., Richmond, VA 23223 (SAN 282-5120); Orders to: P.O. Box 451, Annandale, VA 22003 Tel 703-941-5750 (SAN 282-5139).

Virginia Woolf Quarterly Press, *(Woolf Quarterly; 0-89363),* P.O. Box 4904, San Ysidro, CA 92073 (SAN 209-2484).

Virgo Press, *(Virgo Pr; 0-930558),* P.O. Box 402651, Miami Beach, FL 33140 Tel 305-538-6324 (SAN 211-1063).

Virtue Notagraph Editions, *(Virtue Notagraph; 0-914596),* 4940 Beaumont Dr., La Mesa, CA 92041 Tel 714-469-6634 (SAN 206-1376).

Virtuoso Pubns., Inc., *(Virtuoso; 0-918624),* 206 S.E. 46th Lane, Cape Coral, FL 33904 Tel 813-549-1802 (SAN 210-153X).

Visa Publishing Corp., *(Visa Pub; 0-9606802),* 50 E. 42nd St., New York, NY 10017 (SAN 217-2739); Dist. by: Bookazine Co., Inc., 303 W. Tenth St., New York, NY Tel 212-675-8877 (SAN 169-5665).

Visage Press, Inc., *(Visage Pr; 0-916818),* 2333 N. Vernon St., Arlington, VA 22207 Tel 703-528-8872 (SAN 208-3728).

Vishwa Dharma Pubns., *(Vishwa; 0-942508),* 174 Santa Clara Ave., Oakland, CA 94610 Tel 415-832-2194 (SAN 238-2075).

Visibility Enterprises, *(Visibility Ent; 0-9603740),* 11 W. 81st St., New York, NY 10024 (SAN 214-4832).

Visible Language Workshop, *(Visible Lang; 0-938334),* N51-138 MIT, 275 Massachusetts Ave., Cambridge, MA 02139 (SAN 220-2808).

VisiCorp, *(VisiCorp; 0-912213),* 2895 Zanker Road, San Jose, CA 95134 Tel 408-946-9000 (SAN 264-9837).

Vision Books, *(Vision Bks; 0-942024),* 790 Commercial Ave., Coos Bay, OR 97420 Tel 503-267-4232 (SAN 282-5147).

Vision Foundation, *(Vision Found),* 2 Mt. Auburn St., Watertown, MA 02172 Tel 617-926-4232 (SAN 217-1376).

Vision House, *(Vision Hse; 0-88449),* 2300 Knoll Drive, Ventura, CA 93003 Tel 805-644-9721 (SAN 282-5155); Orders to: Gospel Light Publications, P.O. Box 6309, Oxnard, CA 93031 Tel 800-235-3411 (SAN 282-5163).

Vismar Publishing Co., *(Vismar; 0-9602206),* P.O. Box 29034, Parma, OH 44129 (SAN 212-3932).

Vista Graphics, *(Vista Graphics; 0-9109350),* 1700 S. Vermont Ave., Gardena, CA (SAN 264-4770).

Vista Pubns., *(Vista CA; 0-932740),* 3010 Santa Monica Blvd., Suite 221, Santa Monica, CA 90404 Tel 213-828-3258 (SAN 213-7046) Do Not Confuse with Vista Pubns. in Texas.

Vista Pubns., *(Vista Pubns; 0-930938),* 1108 McAdams Ave., Dallas, TX 75224 (SAN 211-2817) Do Not Confuse with Vista Pubns. in California.

Vistula Press, The, *(Vistula Pr),* 328 Anthony Circle, Charlotte, NC 28211 (SAN 282-5171)328 Anthony Circle, Charlotte, NC 28211 Tel 704-364-0035 (SAN 282-518X).

Visual Arts Productions, *(Visual Art; 0-9610164),* 262 7th St., Hoboken, NJ 07030 Tel 201-792-5608 (SAN 276-525X).

Visual Evangels Publishing Co., *(Visual Evangels; 0-915398),* 1401 Ohio St., Michigan City, IN 46360 Tel 219-874-3902 (SAN 212-002X).

Visual Impact Pubs., Communicators, *(Visual Impact; 0-913426),* 723 S. Wells St., Chicago, IL 60607 Tel 312-922-2083 (SAN 206-8591).

Visual Materials, Inc., *(Visual Materials; 0-88337),* 4170 Grove Ave., Gurnee, CA 60031 Tel 415-321-0800 (SAN 206-0396).

Visual Purple, *(Visual Purple; 0-917198),* Box 996, Berkeley, CA 94701 Tel 415-208-9114); Dist. by: Bookpeople, 2940 Seventh St., Berkeley, CA 94710 Tel 415-549-3033 (SAN 168-9517).

Visual Resources Assn., *(Visual Resources Assn; 0-938852),* Univ. of Missouri-Kansas City, 204 Fine Arts Bldg., Kansas City, MO 64110 Tel 816-276-1501 (SAN 215-9686).

Visual Studies Workshop, *(Visual Studies),* 31 Prince St., Rochester, NY 14607 (SAN 218-1606).

Visually Handicapped Inspiration Library, *(Visually Hand Insp Lib; 0-9608650),* 8010 Petaluma Hill Rd., Penngrove, CA 94951 Tel 707-795-4875 (SAN 213-3679).

Vita Press, *(Vita Pr TN),* 2143 Poplar Ave., Memphis, TN 38104 Tel 901-725-4072 (SAN 214-4840).

Vital Information, Inc., *(Vital Info; 0-941520),* 7899 Mastin Dr., Overland Park, KS 66204 Tel 800-255-5119 (SAN 239-0558).

Vital Press, *(Vital Pr; 0-915660),* Box 38341, Sacramento, CA 95838 (SAN 213-1846).

Vitality Associates, *(Vitality Assocs; 0-930918),* P.O. Box 2154, Saratoga, CA 95070 Tel 408-867-1241 (SAN 211-2809).

Vitullo, Ray, *(Raymond-Nicholas; 0-9607752),* Raymond-Nicholas Adv., 330 Mountain Ave, North Plainfield, NJ 07060 (SAN 239-5754).

Vivekananda Vedanta Society, *(Vivekananda; 0-9600826),* 5423 South Hyde Park Blvd., Chicago, IL 60615 (SAN 222-190X).

Vles, Joseph, M., *(J M Vles; 0-9608452),* 137 Washington Rd., Princeton, NJ 08540 (SAN 240-4982).

Vocational & Career Assessment, *(Voc Career Assess; 0-940150),* P.O. Box 1566, Lakeside, CA 92040 Tel 619-561-2092 (SAN 220-3111).

Vogelsang Press, *(Vogelsang Pr; 0-917742),* 3835 Scott St., Suite 206, San Francisco, CA 94123 Tel 415-931-1461 (SAN 211-1071).

Vogt, Helen, *(H Vogt; 0-9602542),* 121 Blaine Ave., Brownsville, PA 15417 Tel 412-785-3804 (SAN 212-579X).

Voice of Liberty Pubns., *(Voice of Liberty; 0-934762),* 3 Borger Place, Pearl River, NY 10965 Tel 914-735-8140 (SAN 213-568X).

Voigt, Tracy, *(T Voigt),* 111 W. Fifth St., Los Angeles, CA 90013 (SAN 239-5746).

Volan, Leon, *(L Volan),* P.O. Box 15557, San Francisco, CA 94115 Tel 415-929-7659 (SAN 213-8786).

Volaphon Books, *(Volaphon Bks; 0-916258),* 73 Fox Ridge Crescent, Warwick, RI 02886 (SAN 208-0559).

Volcanda Educational Pubns., *(Volcanda Educ),* Rte. 4 Box 764, DeLand, FL 32720 (SAN 213-3368).

Volcano Press, Inc., *(Volcano Pr; 0-912078),* 330 Ellis St., Rm. 518, San Francisco, CA 94102 Tel 415-664-5600 (SAN 220-0015).

Voldstad Enterprise, *(Voldstad Ent; 0-9603906),* 688 S. Hobart Blvd., Los Angeles, CA 90005 (SAN 209-0791).

Voler Publishing Co., *(Voler Pub; 0-943968),* 910 Industry Dr., Seattle, WA 98188 (SAN 241-0885).

Volin, Stan, *(S Volin; 0-9600922),* 19 Steven St., Plainview, NY 11803 Tel 516-681-6040 (SAN 207-7469); Orders to: Box 571-B, Hicksville, NY 11802 (SAN 207-7477).

Volta Press Inc., The, *(Volta Press; 0-910437),* 20 W. Mosholu Pkwy. Suite 26F, Bronx, NY 10468 Tel 212-928-2970 (SAN 241-4732).

Volunteer Management Associates, *(Volunteer Mgmt; 0-9603362),* 279 S. Cedar Brook Rd., Boulder, CO 80302 (SAN 221-6914).

Volunteer Pubns., *(Volunteer Pubns; 0-938310),* P.O. Box 240786, Memphis, TN 38124-0786 Tel 901-685-9577 (SAN 215-9287).

Volunteers in Asia, Inc., *(Volunteers Asia; 0-917704),* P.O. Box 4543, Stanford, CA 94305 Tel 415-497-3228 (SAN 210-9638).

Von-Bogckmann Jones, Printers, *(Von-Bogckmann),* Austin, TX 78742 (SAN 262-1061).

Von Gehr Press, The, *(Von Gehr; 0-9601470),* P.O. Box 7654, Menlo Park, CA 94025 Tel 415-342-2631 (SAN 211-3376).

Vongrutnorv Og Press, *(Vongrutnorv Og; 0-9603504),* Randall Flat Rd. P.O. Box 411, Troy, ID 83871 Tel 208-835-4902 (SAN 211-7169).

Voter Education Project, *(Voter Ed Proj),* 52 Fairlie St Nw, Atlanta, GA 30303 (SAN 235-8336).

Voters Service Education Fund of the League of Women Voters of the Cincinnati Area, The, *(Voters Serv Educ; 0-9608724),* 103 Wm. Howard Taft Rd., Cincinnati, OH 45219 Tel 513-281-8683 (SAN 238-4108).

Voyager Books See Harcourt Brace Jovanovich, Inc.

Voyager Pubns., Inc., *(Voyager Pubns; 0-9603020),* 2604 First National Bank Tower, Atlanta, GA 30303 Tel 404-658-1228 (SAN 213-1854); Orders to: P.O. Box 229, Lansing, NY 14882 Tel 607-257-1648 (SAN 213-1862).

Voyageur Press, Inc., *(Voyageur Pr Inc),* 9337 Nesbitt Rd., Bloomington, MN 55437 (SAN 287-2668).

Voyaging Press, *(Voyaging Pr; 0-910711),* 669 N. 400 W., W. Lafayette, IN 47906 Tel 317-743-2042 (SAN 260-275X).

Vulcan Books, Inc., *(Vulcan Bks; 0-914350),* 12722 Lake City Way, N.E., Seattle, WA 98125 Tel 206-362-2606 (SAN 203-1728); Orders to: P. O. Box 25616, Seattle, WA 98125 (SAN 203-1736).

VUV Associates, *(VUV Assocs),* 1600 Regency Dr., Lincoln, NE 68506 (SAN 282-583X).

W & M Press, *(W & M Pr; 0-942240),* 6301 Colby, Des Moines, IA 50311 Tel 515-277-4354 (SAN 241-5925).

WB Design & Development, Inc., *(WB Design),* 42 Hillvale Dr., St. Louis, MO 63105 (SAN 285-6700).

WELS Board for Parish Education, *(WELS Board; 0-938272),* 3614 W. North Ave., Milwaukee, WI 53208 (SAN 216-3160).

W E Upjohn Institute for Employment Research, *(W E Upjohn),* 300 S Westnedge Ave, Kalamazoo, MI 49007 Tel 616-343-5541 (SAN 236-9486).

W F I Publishing Co., Div. of WFI Corporation, *(WFI Pub Co; 0-933560),* 2049 Century Park E., Los Angeles, CA 90067 Tel 213-553-8700 (SAN 212-9817).

WHO Houston, Inc., *(Who Houston),* 2801 S. Post Oak, Suite 111, Houston, TX 77024 Tel 713-961-2648 (SAN 216-3187).

WIM, *(WIM Oakland; 0-938842),* 6000 Contra Costa Rd., Oakland, CA 94618 (SAN 216-2059).

WIM Pubns., *(WIM Pubns; 0-934172),* Box 367, College Corner, OH 45003 Tel 513-523-5994 (SAN 282-5198); Box, (SAN 282-5201).

WWH Press, *(WWH Pr; 0-939240),* 41 Hampton Rd., Scarsdale, NY 10583 Tel 914-725-3632 (SAN 216-5163).

WWWWW Information Services, *(WWWWW Info Serv; 0-912688),* 1475 Winton Road North, Rochester, NY 14609 Tel 716-482-2022 (SAN 203-2783).

Waddell, Ward, Jr., *(Waddell; 0-9600130),* 495 San Fernando St., San Diego, CA 92106 (SAN 205-4973).

Wade Bks., *(Wade Bks),* P.O. Box 847, Kentfield, CA 94914 (SAN 241-5933).

Wadley Institutes of Molecular Medicine, *(Wadley Inst Molecular Med; 0-935994),* 9000 Harry Hines, Dallas, TX 75235 (SAN 213-8794).

Wadsworth Atheneum, *(Wadsworth Atheneum),* 25 Prospect St., Hartford, CT 06103 (SAN 205-4981).

Wadsworth Publishing Co., *(Wadsworth Pub; 0-534),* 10 Davis Dr., Belmont, CA 94002 Tel 415-595-2350 (SAN 200-2213). *Imprints:* Continuing Educaion Division (Continuing Ed).

Wag On The Wall, *(Wag On Wall; 0-9609628),* 2005 Valle Vista, National City, CA 92050 (SAN 262-4419).

Wagener News Service, *(Wagener News Serv; 0-941554),* 930 National Press Bldg., Washinton, DC 20019 (SAN 238-8014); Dist. by: Jean Wiley Huyler Communications, 922 N. Pearl, A-27, Tacoma, WA 98406 (SAN 238-8022).

Wagon & Star Pubs., *(Wagon & Star),* 4032 W. Century Blvd., Inglewood, CA 90304 (SAN 202-9421).

Wagoner, George, *(Wagoner; 0-9600178),* 4318 Glenridge Dr., Carmichael, CA 95608 Tel 916-967-6988 (SAN 205-5007).

Wahr, George, Publishing Co., *(Wahr; 0-911586),* 304 1/2 S. State St., Ann Arbor, MI 48104 Tel 313-668-6097 (SAN 205-5015).

Waite, Benjamin & Martha, Press, Ltd., *(B & M Waite Pr; 0-934528),* 1126 E. 59th St., Chicago, IL 60637 (SAN 213-3989).

Wake, Harry S., *(H S Wake),* 4171 Stettler Way, San Diego, CA 92122 (SAN 282-5317); Dist. by: Metropolitan Music Co., Mountain Rd., Stowe, VT 05672 (SAN 282-6437); Dist. by: International Violin Co., 4026 W. Belvedere Ave., Baltimore, MD 21215 (SAN 282-728X); Dist. by: International Luthier Supply, Inc., P. O. Box 15444, Tulsa, OK 74112 (SAN 282-5341); Dist. by: Vitali Import Co., P. O. Box 249, Maywood, CA 90270 (SAN 282-535X).

Wake-Brook House, *(Wake-Brook; 0-87482),* 990 N.W. 53rd St., Fort Lauderdale, FL 33309 Tel 305-776-5884 (SAN 205-5023) June 1st Through October 15th, Contact at: P.O. Box 153, Hyannis, MA 02601, Tel: 617-775-5860.

Wake Forest Univ. Press, *(Wake Forest; 0-916390),* Dist. by: UNiversity of North Carolina Press, Box 2288, Chapel Hill, NC 27514 Tel 919-761-5448 (SAN 208-2063).

Wake Forest University School of Law, *(Wake Forest Law),* Winston-Salem, NC 27109 (SAN 237-9074).

Walden Press, *(Walden Pr; 0-911938),* 423 S. Franklin Ave., Flint, MI 48503 (SAN 205-5031).

Waldo Bruce Pubs., *(Waldo Bruce Pubns; 0-9607338),* P.O. Box 140906, Dallas, TX 75214 Tel 214-368-2614 (SAN 239-3409).

Waldorf Press, *(Waldorf Pr; 0-914614),* Dept. of Education, Linen Hall Basement, Adelphi Univ., Cambridge Ave., Garden City, NY 11530 Tel 516-294-8700 (SAN 203-1760).

Waldron, A. James, Enterprises, *(Waldron; 0-911590),* 371 Kings Hwy., W., Haddonfield, NJ 08033 Tel 609-428-3742 (SAN 205-504X).

Waldrop Pubns., *(Waldrop Pubns; 0-9603364),* Box 396, Mt. Baldy, CA 91759 Tel 714-985-6128 (SAN 208-4007).

Walker, David Press, The, *(D Walker Pr; 0-912135),* P.O. Box 741, Brooklyn, NY 11207 Tel 212-788-2044 (SAN 264-8075); 670 Carroll St., Brooklyn, NY 11215 (SAN 264-8083).

Walker, Evans, & Cogswell Co., *(W Evans & Cogswell),* 64 Broad St., P.O. Box 370, Charleston, SC 29402 (SAN 265-4121).

Walker, Frank R., Co., *(F R Walker; 0-911592),* 5030 N. Harlem Ave., Chicago, IL 60656 Tel 312-867-7070 (SAN 206-4022).

Walker & Co., *(Walker & Co; 0-8027),* 720 Fifth Ave., New York, NY 10019 Tel 212-265-3632 (SAN 202-5213).

Walker Educational Book Corp., Affiliate of Walker & Co., *(Walker Educ; 0-8027),* 720 Fifth Ave., New York, NY 10019 Tel 212-265-3632 (SAN 206-1899).

Walker Press, The, *(Walker Pr KY),* P.O. Box 22144, Louisville, KY 40222 (SAN 210-9662).

Walkers Manual Inc., *(Walkers Manual; 0-916234),* 14032 Lake St., Suite 101, Garden Grove, CA 92643 Tel 714-636-2952 (SAN 211-2833).

Walking News, Inc., *(Walking News Inc; 0-915850),* P.O. Box 352 - Canal St. Sta., New York, NY 10012 Tel 212-925-2632 (SAN 239-5436).

Wall, R. A. Investments, Inc., *(R A Wall; 0-916522),* 9465 Wilshire Blvd., Suite 525, Beverly Hills, CA 90212 (SAN 208-032X).

Wallaby *See* Pocket Books, Inc.

Wallaby *See* Simon & Schuster, Inc.

Wallace-Homestead Book Co., *(Wallace-Homestead; 0-87069),* 1912 Grand Ave., Des Moines, IA 50305 Tel 515-243-6181 (SAN 205-5058).

Wallcur, Inc., *(Wallcur Inc; 0-918082),* 3287 F Street, Suite G, San Diego, CA 92102 Tel 619-233-9628 (SAN 209-3642).

Wallflower Press, *(Wallflower; 0-9606260),* P.O. Box 1275, Bridgehampton, NY 11932 (SAN 217-1392).

Wallingford Press, *(Wallingford NJ; 0-930988),* Alpine, NJ 07620 Tel 201-568-5111 (SAN 211-3821).

Wallis, Joe, *(J Wallis; 0-9605950),* P.O. Box 2294, Washington, DC 20013 (SAN 216-4752).

Walloon Press, *(Walloon Pr),* 4260 Ridgecrest Dr., El Paso, TX 79902 Tel 915-533-3166 (SAN 207-5539).

Walmyr Publishing Co., *(Walmyr; 0-942390),* P.O. Box 3554, Leon Sta., Tallahassee, FL 32303 Tel 904-386-5796 (SAN 238-1249).

Walnut Press, *(Walnut AZ; 0-932183),* 12010 Hillcrest Drive, Sun City, AZ 85351 Tel 602-972-5814 (SAN 285-113X); Orders to: Walnut Press, 2809 E. Victor Hugo, Phoenix, AZ 85032 Tel 602-992-4962 (SAN 285-1148).

Walnut Press, *(Walnut Pr),* Tully, NY 13159 Tel 607-842-6668 (SAN 207-9992).

Walsh, Patrick, Pr, *(P Walsh Pr; 0-86700),* 2206 S. Priest Dr., Suite 105, Tempe, AZ 85282 Tel 602-894-1230 (SAN 216-6135).

Walterick Pubs., *(Walterick Pubs; 0-937396),* Box 2216, Kansas City, KS 66110 Tel 913-371-3273 (SAN 211-9366).

Walters Art Gallery, *(Walters Art; 0-911886),* 600 N. Charles St., Baltimore, MD 21201 Tel 301-547-9000 (SAN 202-9448).

Walters Publishing Co., *(Walters Pub),* 1409 Allston Way, Berkeley, CA 94702 Tel 415-549-1412 (SAN 211-1136).

Walthers, Wm. K., Inc., *(W K Walthers; 0-941952),* 5601 W. Florist Ave., Milwaukee, WI 53218 Tel 414-527-0770 (SAN 238-4868).

Wampeter Press, *(Wampeter Pr; 0-931694),* P.O. Box 512, Green Harbor, ME 02041 Tel 212-3231).

Wampler, Joseph Carson, *(J Wampler; 0-935080),* Box 45, Berkeley, CA 94701 (SAN 206-1910).

Wanderer Books, Div. of Simon & Schuster, *(Wanderer Bks; 0-671),* 1230 Ave. of the Americas, New York, NY 10020 Tel 212-245-6400 (SAN 212-5803).

Wanderer Pr, the, *(Wanderer Pr),* 201 Ohio St., St. Paul, MN 55107 Tel 612-224-5733 (SAN 240-8961).

Want Publishing Co., *(Want Pub; 0-942008),* 1511 K St. NW, Washington, DC 20005 Tel 202-783-1887 (SAN 238-7727).

Want Publishing Company, *(Want Pub Co)* 1511 K St Nw, Rm 635, DC 20005 Tel 202-783-1887 (SAN 276-5535).

War Resisters' International, *(War Resisters; 0-9500205; 0-903517),* Dist. by: Housmans Bookshop Ltd., 5 Caledonian Rd., London, N1 9DX, .

Ward, Baldwin H., Pubns., *(B H Ward Pubns; 0-913482),* P.O. Box 380, Petaluma, CA 94953 Tel 707-762-0737 (SAN 203-025X).

Ward Press, The, *(Ward Pr; 0-932142),* P.O. Box 1712, Rochester, NY 14603 Tel 716-467-8400 (SAN 212-6281).

Wards Communications, Inc., *(Wards Comm),* 28 W. Adams, Detroit, MI 48226 Tel 313-962-4433 (SAN 206-3905).

Ware Press, Inc., *(Ware Pr; 0-938552),* 28 Hurlbut St., Cambridge, MA 02138 Tel 617-491-1837 (SAN 238-5155).

Waring & Associates, *(Waring & Assocs; 0-912307),* 845 Heathermoor Lane, Perrysburg, OH 43551 Tel 419-874-6044 (SAN 265-2978).

Warman Publishing Co., Inc., *(Warman; 0-911594),* P.O. Box 26742, Elkins Park, PA 19117 Tel 215-657-1812 (SAN 202-9464).

Warne, Frederick, & Co., Inc., *(Warne; 0-7232),* 2 Park Ave., New York, NY 10016 Tel 212-686-9630 (SAN 212-9884).

Warner Books, Inc., *(Warner Bks; 0-446),* 666 Fifth Ave., New York, NY 10103 Tel 212-484-2900 (SAN 282-5368); Orders to: Warner Publisher Services, 666 Fith Ave., New York, NY 10103 Tel 212-484-2900 (SAN 282-5376).

Warner Press Pubs., *(Warner Pr; 0-87162),* P.O. Box 2499, 1200 E. Fifth St., Anderson, IN 46018 Tel 317-644-7721 (SAN 202-9472).

Warren, M. E., *(M E Warren; 0-9606060),* P.O. Box 1508, Annapolis, MD 21404 (SAN 216-7670).

Warren, Gorham & Lamont, Inc., *(Warren; 0-88262; 0-88712),* 210 South St., Boston, MA 02111 Tel 617-423-2020 (SAN 282-7166); 1633 Broadway, New York, NY 10019 Tel 212-977-7431 (SAN 282-7174).

Warren, McVeigh & Griffin, Inc., *(Warren Mac; 0-941360),* 1420 Bristol St. N., Suite 220, Newport Beach, CA 92660 Tel 714-752-1058 (SAN 239-0566).

Warren Publishing Co., *(Warren Pub; 0-9606004),* 3729 W. 16th St., Indianapolis, IN 46222 Tel 317-632-6601 (SAN 213-5698).

Warrington & Company, *(Warrington; 0-911735),* P.O. Box 907, Orinda, CA 94563 (SAN 264-4827).

Warrior, Betsy, *(B Warrior; 0-9601544),* 46 Pleasant St., Cambridge, MA 02139 (SAN 210-993X).

Warthog Press, *(Warthog Pr),* 29 S. Valley Rd., West Orange, NJ 07052 Tel 201-731-9269 (SAN 219-5399).

Warwick Press *See* Watts, Franklin, Inc.

Wasatch Pubs., Inc., *(Wasatch Pubs; 0-915272),* 4647 Idlewild Rd., Salt Lake City, UT 84117 Tel 801-278-3174 (SAN 207-1576).

Wash Launderan Press, *(Wash Launderan; 0-9605326),* 5804 Ingersoll Ave., Des Moines, IA 50312 Tel 515-279-7774 (SAN 215-9295).

Washburn Press, *(Washburn Pr MN; 0-939862),* 2753 Upland Court, Plymouth, MN 55447 (SAN 216-941X).

Washington, Eliza, *(E Washington; 0-939354),* 614 Wilshire Ave., Waterloo, ID 50701 Tel 319-234-1460 (SAN 216-4957).

Washington Business Information, Inc., *(Wash Busn Info; 0-914176),* 235 National Press Bldg., Washington, DC 20045 Tel 202-737-2232 (SAN 201-890X).

Washington County Historical Society, *(WA County Hist; 0-9608434),* Box 278, Chatom, AL 36518 (SAN 240-8058).

Washington Dolls' House & Toy Museum, *(Wash Dolls Hse),* 5236 44th St., N.W., Washington, DC 20015 Tel 202-244-0082 (SAN 217-2747).

Washington Gasohol Commission, (Wash Gasohol; 0-939864), 103 12th Ave. SW, Ephrata, WA 98823 Tel 509-754-3463 (SAN 216-7735).

Washington History Committee, (Wash Hist Comm), Box 75, Washington, NH 03280 Tel 603-495-3566 (SAN 210-9670).

Washington Independent Writers, (Wash In Writers; 0-912521), 525 National Press Bldg., Washington, DC 20045 Tel 202-347-4973 (SAN 265-2986).

Washington Institute for Values in Public Policy, (Wash Inst DC; 0-88702), 1333 N.H. Ave., N.W., Suite 910, Washington, DC 20036 Tel 202-293-7440 (SAN 283-3328).

Washington International Arts Letter, (Wash Intl Arts; 0-912072), 325 Pennsylvania Ave., S.E., Washington, DC 20003 Tel 202-488-0800 (SAN 205-5066); Orders to: P.O. Box 9005, Washington, DC 20003 (SAN 205-5074).

Washington National Monument Assn., (Wash Natl Monument), 740 Jackson Place, N.W., Washington, DC 20506 Tel 202-842-0806 (SAN 206-2925).

Washington Opera, The, (Wash Opera; 0-9610542), The Kennedy Center, Washington, DC 20037 Tel 202-337-5533 (SAN 264-4835).

Washington Park Press, (Wash Park; 0-9605460), 7 Englewood Place, Albany, NY 12203 (SAN 215-9309).

Washington Researchers, (Wash Res; 0-934940), 918 Sixteenth St. N.W., Washington, DC 20006 Tel 202-833-2230 (SAN 211-6286).

Washington Square Press, Inc., Div. of Simon & Schuster, Inc., (WSP), 1230 Ave. of the Americas, New York, NY 10020 Tel 212-246-2121 (SAN 206-9784). *Imprints:* Readers Enrichment Series (RE).

Washington State Bar CLE, (Wash Bar CLE), 5050 Madison, Seattle, WA 98104 (SAN 237-9155).

Washington State Historical Society, (Wash St Hist Soc; 0-917048), 315 N. Stadium Way, Tacoma, WA 98403 Tel 206-593-2830 (SAN 203-2155).

Washington State Univ. Press, (Wash St U Pr; 0-87422), Pullman, WA 99164 Tel 509-335-3518 (SAN 206-6688).

Washington Univ., Gallery of Art, (Wash U Gallery; 0-936316), Campus Box 1214, St. Louis, MO 63130 Tel 314-889-5490 (SAN 214-4859).

Washington University School of Law, (Wash U Law), St Louis, MO 63130 (SAN 237-9171).

Washington Writers Publishing House, (Wash Writers Pub; 0-931846), P.O. Box 50068, Washington, DC 20004 (SAN 211-9250).

Washoe Press, (Washoe; 0-89376), P.O. Box 91922, Los Angeles, CA 90009 (SAN 209-0694).

Washout Pub. Co., (Washout; 0-918310), P.O. Box 9252, Schenectady, NY 12309 (SAN 209-9128).

Water Foundation, (Water Foun; 0-9603252), 1119 Chapala St., Santa Barbara, CA 93101 Tel 805-963-8739 (SAN 213-3997).

Water Information Center, Inc., (Water Info; 0-912394), The North Shore Atrium, 6800 Jericho Turnpike, Syosset, NY 11791 Tel 516-921-7690 (SAN 202-9510).

Water Mark Press, (Water Mark; 0-931956), 175 East Shore Rd., Huntington Bay, NY 11743 Tel 516-549-1150 (SAN 212-5811).

Water Pollution Control Federation, (Water Pollution), 2626 Pennsylvania Ave., N.W., Washington, DC 20037 Tel 202-337-2500 (SAN 217-1406).

Water Resources Pubns., (WRP; 0-918334), 309 Yoakum Pkwy, No. 1401, Alexandria, VA 22304 Tel 703-370-5588 (SAN 209-9136); Orders to: P.O. Box 2841, Littleton, CO 80161 Tel 303-779-6685 (SAN 209-9144).

Waterfall Press, (Waterfall Pr; 0-932278), 2122 Junction Ave., El Cerrito, CA 94530 Tel 415-232-5539 (SAN 211-7665).

Waterford Press, (Waterford Pr; 0-9608706), 32-66 72nd St., Jackson Heights, NY 11370 Tel 212-424-4685 (SAN 238-4124).

Waterford Publishing Co., (Waterford Pub; 0-942052), 221 Waterford Pkwy. N., Waterford, CT 06385 (SAN 239-5797).

Waterfront Press, (Waterfront NJ; 0-943862), 52 Maple Ave., Maplewood, NJ 07040 Tel 201-762-1565 (SAN 241-5941).

Waterfront Press Co., (Waterfront Pr; 0-937288), 1115 46th, N.W., Seattle, WA 98107 (SAN 215-191X).

Watermill Pubs., (Watermill Pubs; 0-88370), 4 Crescent Dr., Albertson, NY 11507 Tel 516-484-2391 (SAN 206-2941).

Waterside Press, (Waterside; 0-936628), Box 1298, Stuyvesant Sta., New York, NY 10009 (SAN 214-4867).

Watson-Guptill Pubns., Inc., Div. Billboard Publications, Inc., (Watson-Guptill; 0-8230; 0-8174; 0-87165), 1 Astor Plaza, 1515 Broadway, New York, NY 10036 Tel 212-764-7518 (SAN 282-5384); Orders to: 1695 Oak St., Lakewood, NJ 08701 Tel 800-526-3641 (SAN 282-5392). *Imprints:* Billboard Books (Billboard Bks); Whitney Library (Whitney Lib).

Wattles, Gurdon H., Pubns., (Wattles Pubns), P.O. Box 5702, Orange, CA 92667 Tel 714-637-1351 (SAN 219-8347).

Watts, Franklin, Inc., Subs. of Grolier Inc., (Watts; 0-531), 387 Park Ave. South, New York, NY 10016 Tel 212-686-7070 (SAN 285-1156); 730 Fifth Ave., New York, NY 10019 Tel 212-757-4050 (SAN 285-1164). *Imprints:* Business Travelers Inc. (Busn Travel); Gloucester Press (Gloucester Pr); MacRae, Julia (MacRae); Warwick Press (Warwick).

Waumbek Books, (Waumbek; 0-9603106), P.O. Box 573, Ashland, NH 03217 Tel 603-968-7959 (SAN 213-5701).

Waveland Press Inc., (Waveland Pr; 0-917974; 0-88133), P.O. Box 400, Prospect Heights, IL 60070 Tel 312-634-0081 (SAN 209-0961).

Waverly Press, Inc., (Waverly Pr; 0-683), 428 E. Preston St., Baltimore, MD 21202 Tel 301-528-4000 (SAN 206-2968).

Way of Seeing, Inc., A, (Way of Seeing), 2869 Grant Dr., Ann Arbor, MI 48104 Tel 313-973-7717 (SAN 216-3152).

Wayne State Univ., Bur. of Bus. Res. School of Business Administration, (WSU Bur Bus Res; 0-942650), Detroit, MI 48202 Tel 313-577-4213 (SAN 239-9512).

Wayne State Univ. Press, (Wayne St U Pr; 0-8143), The Leonard N. Simons Bldg., 5959 Woodward Ave., Detroit, MI 48202 Tel 313-577-4603 (SAN 202-5221).

Waynor Publishing Co., (Waynor; 0-917070), P.O. Box 94, Orange, MA 01364 Tel 617-544-6751 (SAN 208-9165).

Ways of Caring, Inc., (Ways of Caring), P.O. Box 5362, New York, NY 10017 (SAN 239-510X).

Wayside Press, (Wayside), P.O. Box 475, Cottonwood, AZ 86326 (SAN 209-8024).

Weather Workbook Co., (Weather Wkbk; 0-931778), 827 N.W. 31st St., Corvallis, OR 97330 (SAN 206-393X).

Weatherby, Thomas, Pub., (T Weatherby), 115 Billings St., Sharon, MA 02067 (SAN 212-582X).

Weatherford, R.M., Press, (Weatherford; 0-9604078), 10902 Woods Creek Rd., Monroe, WA 98272 Tel 206-794-4318 (SAN 220-1070).

Weatherhill, John, Inc., (Weatherhill; 0-8348), 6 E. 39th St., New York, NY 10016 Tel 212-686-2857 (SAN 202-9529); Dist. by: Charles E. Tuttle, Co., Inc., 28 S. Main St., Rutland, VT 05701 (SAN 213-2621).

Weatherleaf Press, The, (Waterleaf Pr; 0-938912), 233 S. Second St., DeKalb, IL 60115 Tel 815-758-4841 (SAN 238-7646).

Weatherman, Hazel Marie, (Weatherman; 0-913074), c/o Glassbooks, Inc., Rte. 1, Box 357A, Ozark, MO 65721 Tel 417-485-7812 (SAN 237-9554).

Weathervane Books, (Weathervane CA; 0-943246), P.O. Box 2157, Walnut Creek, CA 94595 (SAN 240-5040).

Weaver, Ruth C., (R C Weaver; 0-9607168), RD 2 Box 218, Canonsburg, PA 15317 Tel 412-745-8907 (SAN 239-1376).

Web Publishing House, Inc., The, (Web Pub Hse), P.O. Box 374, Olney, MD 20832 Tel 301-949-7768 (SAN 216-2032).

Webb & Bower, (Webb & Bower), 521 Fifth Ave., New York, NY 10017 (SAN 239-3999).

Webb-Newcomb Co., Inc., (Webb-Newcomb; 0-935054), 308 N.E. Vance St., Wilson, NC 27893 Tel 919-291-7231 (SAN 213-4004).

Weber, John, Gallery, (J Weber Gall; 0-9608288), 142 Greene St., New York, NY 10012 (SAN 240-4575).

Weber Systems, Inc., (Weber Systems; 0-938862), 8437 Mayfield Rd., Chesterland, OH 44026 Tel 216-729-2808 (SAN 240-8201).

Weckstein, Joyce R., (J R Weckstein; 0-9600980), 28290 Tavistock Trail, Southfield, MI 48034 Tel 313-353-6221 (SAN 208-9173).

Wedge Publishing, (Wedge Pub), c/o Radix Books, Inc., 475 43rd St., Richmond, CA 94805 (SAN 209-1364).

Wedgestone Press, (Wedgestone Pr; 0-911459), P.O. Box 175, Winfield, KS 67156 Tel 316-221-2779 (SAN 276-5888).

Wee Smile Books, (Wee Smile; 0-9605444), P.O. Box 1329, Sparks, NV 89431 Tel 702-356-0216 (SAN 215-983X).

Weed Science Society of America, (Weed Sci Soc), 309 W Clark St, Champaign, IL 61820 (SAN 276-5918).

Weeg Computing Center, (Weeg Comp; 0-937114), Univ. of Iowa, 120 LC, Iowa City, IA 52242 (SAN 215-2630).

Wehawken Book Co., (Wehawken Bk; 0-916386), 4221 45th St., N.W., Washington, DC 20016 Tel 202-362-3185 (SAN 207-5512).

Wehman Brothers, Inc., (Wehman; 0-911604), Ridgedale Ave., Morris County Mall, Cedar Knolls, NJ 07927 Tel 201-539-6300 (SAN 206-779X).

Wehmeyer Printing Co., (Wehmeyer Print), Ste. Genevieve, MO 63670 (SAN 239-5444).

Wei-Chuan's Cooking, (Wei-Chuan's Cooking; 0-941676), 1434 S. Atlantic Blvd., Alhambra, CA 91803 Tel 213-289-8288 (SAN 239-5096).

Weight Control Institute, (Weight Control; 0-9608232), 4225 Wade Way, Salt Lake City, UT 84119 Tel 801-968-4099 (SAN 240-3285).

Weinberg, Alyce T., (A T Weinberg; 0-9604552), Box 16, Braddock Heights, MD 21714 (SAN 215-1928).

Weinberg, Michael Aron, (Weinberg; 0-9601014), P.O. Box 27957, Los Angeles, CA 90027 Tel 213-661-9844 (SAN 208-2314).

Weinstock, Beatrice C., (Weinstock; 0-9600568), 1971 San Marco Blvd., Jacksonville, FL 32207 Tel 904-396-7597 (SAN 205-5139).

Weisberg, Harold, (Weisberg; 0-911606), 7627 Old Receiver Rd., Frederick, MD 21701 Tel 301-473-8186 (SAN 205-5147).

Weiser, Samuel, Inc., (Weiser; 0-87728), P.O. Box 612, York Beach, ME 03910 Tel 207-363-4393 (SAN 202-9588).

Weiss, Sigmund, (Weiss S & D), 11 Lancaster Place, Stony Brook, NY 11790 (SAN 219-3035).

Weiss Publishing Co., Inc., (Weiss Pub; 0-916720), 5309 W. Grace St., Richmond, VA 23226 Tel 804-282-4641 (SAN 208-4775).

Weisser, Thomas, (Tom Weisser; 0-9610710), Box 53, Monmouth, OR 97361 Tel 503-838-3485 (SAN 264-8105).

Weist Publishing Co., The, (Weist Pub OH; 0-938166), P.O. Box 164, Englewood, OH 45322 Tel (SAN 215-8256).

Well Aware About Health, (Well Aware; 0-943562), P.O. Box 43338, Tuscon, AZ 85733 Tel 602-626-3055 (SAN 243-0628).

Well-Being Productions, (Well Being; 0-918912), P.O. Box 1829, Santa Cruz, CA 95061 Tel 408-425-5411 (SAN 210-3796).

Well-Made Products, (Well-Made Prod), 832 N.E. 104th, Seattle, WA 98125 (SAN 238-7719).

Wellbeing Bks., Tapes, Seminars, Subs. of Open Marketing Group, (Wellbeing Bks), Open Marketing Group, P. O. Box 735, Brookline Village, MA 02147 Tel 617-277-5226 (SAN 240-4680).

Wellington Books, (Wellington), Bluenose Boatyard, Chester, Nova Scotia, Canada, ; c/o W. Berkowitz, Box 50, Bluehill, ME 04614 (SAN 201-9302).

Wellington Press, (Wellington Pr; 0-910959), P.O. Box 13503, Tallahassee, FL 32308 Tel 904-878-6500 (SAN 264-4878); Dist. by: Educational Clearinghouse, Inc., P.O. Box 3951, Tallahassee, FL 32304 (SAN 264-4886).

Wells, H. C., *(H C Wells; 0-930666),* P.O. Box 2480, Pasadena, CA 91105 (SAN 211-4682).

Wells of Salvation, *(WOS),* 6821 SR 366, Huntsville, OH 43324 (SAN 217-1414).

Wellspring, *(Wellspring CA),* 2090 Fox Way, Concord, CA 94518 Tel 415-676-7022 (SAN 239-5800).

Wellspring Press, *(Wellspring Pr; 0-914688),* Page Rd., Lincoln, MA 01773 (SAN 203-2171).

Wellton Books, *(Wellton Bks; 0-943678),* P.O. Box 989, Citrus Heights, CA 95610 (SAN 238-4159).

Werner, J. Paul, *(J P Werner; 0-9601368),* 4643 N. Front St., N. Philadelphia, PA 19140 Tel 215-457-4081 (SAN 209-6013).

Wertz Pubns, *(Wertz Pubns),* P.O. Box 263 Bridge Station, Niagara Falls, NY 14305 Tel 716-297-0455 (SAN 240-9003).

Wescott Cove Publishing Co., *(Wescott Cove; 0-918752),* Box 130, Stamford, CT 06904 Tel 203-322-0998 (SAN 210-5810).

Weiss Pubns., *(Wesis Pubns),* 29 Meadowbrook Lane, Cedar Grove, NJ 07009 Tel 201-256-7997 (SAN 209-6153).

Wesley Foundation, The, *(Wesley Found; 0-9606652),* 211 N. School St., Normal, IL 61761 Tel 309-452-1435 (SAN 219-6557).

Wesleyan Univ. Press, *(Wesleyan U Pr; 0-8195),* 110 Mt. Vernon St., Middletown, CT 06457 Tel 203-344-7918 (SAN 282-5414); Orders to: Harper & Row Publishers Inc., Keystone Industrial Park, Scranton, PA 18512 Tel 217-343-4761 (SAN 282-5422).

Wesselhoeft Associates, Inc., *(Wesselhoeft Assoc; 0-941954),* 3885 Lawrence Dr., Oscoda, MI 48750 Tel 517-739-3886 (SAN 238-4884).

West, Bill, *(B West; 0-911614),* 536 E. Ada Ave., Glendora, CA 91740 Tel 213-335-7060 (SAN 202-3687).

West, Mark, Pubs., *(M West Pubs),* P.O. Box 1914, Sandpoint, ID 83864 Tel 708-263-0969 (SAN 215-711X).

West, Richard, *(R West; 0-8492; 0-8274),* Box 6404, Philadelphia, PA 19145 (SAN 206-8907).

West Atlantic Pubns., *(West Atlantic; 0-935262),* 426 Columbia Ave., Mount Joy, PA 17552 Tel 717-653-2296 (SAN 213-4012); Orders to: P.O. Box 273, Mount Joy, PA 17552 Tel 717-653-5619 (SAN 213-4020).

West-Central Kentucky Family Research Assn., *(West Cent KY Family Re Assoc),* P.O. Box 1932, Owensboro, KY 42302 Tel 502-684-4150 (SAN 219-0508).

West Coast Plays, *(West Coast Plays; 0-934782),* P.O. Box 7206, Berkeley, CA 94707 (SAN 211-1446).

West Coast Poetry Review, *(West Coast; 0-915596),* 1335 Dartmouth Dr., Reno, NV 89509 Tel 702-322-4467 (SAN 207-3684).

West End Press, *(West End; 0-931122),* Box 7232, Minneapolis, MN 55407 Tel 612-822-3488 (SAN 211-3406).

West Fourth Street Block Assn., *(W Fourth St Block),* 285 W. 4th St., New York, NY 10014 Tel 212-929-1452 (SAN 208-077X).

West Gate Press, *(West Gate Pr; 0-942836),* P.O. Box 961, Portland, ME 04104 (SAN 240-5059).

West Philadelphia Women's Committee for the Philadelphia Orchestra, *(W Phila Womens Comm),* P.O. Box 685, Bryn Mawr, PA 19010 (SAN 217-2887).

West Publishing Co., *(West Pub; 0-8299; 0-314),* P.O. Box 3526, St. Paul, MN 55165 Tel 612-228-2710 (SAN 202-9618).

West River Press, *(West River; 0-9602190),* 3530 W. Huron River Dr., Ann Arbor, MI 48103 Tel 313-668-8170 (SAN 212-324X).

West Southwest Publishing Co., *(West SW Pub Co),* P.O. Box 4064, Redding, CA 96099 (SAN 214-4883).

West Summit Press, *(West Summit; 0-9601356),* 27 W. Summit St., Chagrin Falls, OH 44022 Tel 216-247-4323 (SAN 210-9409).

West Texas Museum Assn., *(West Tex Mus; 0-911618),* P.O. Box 4499, Lubbock, TX 79409 Tel 806-742-2443 (SAN 206-667X).

West Village Publishing Co., *(West Village; 0-933308),* 2904 E. Vanowen Ave., Orange, CA 92667 Tel 714-633-1420 (SAN 213-1870).

West Virginia Univ. Press, *(West Va U Pr; 0-937058),* Morgantown, WV 26506 Tel 304-293-4040 (SAN 205-5163).

West Virginia University, Center for Extension & Continuing Education, *(W Va U Ctr Exten),* 308 Knapp Hall, Morgantown, WV 26506 (SAN 213-4039).

West Virginia Wesleyan College, *(W VA Wesleyan),* Buckhannon, WV 26201 (SAN 239-5762).

Westburg Associates, Pubs., *(Westburg; 0-87423),* 1745 Madison St., Fennimore, WI 53809 Tel 608-822-6237 (SAN 205-5171).

Westcliff Pubns., *(Westcliff Pubns; 0-932896),* 1441 Avocado No. 408, Newport Beach, CA 92660 (SAN 212-2448).

Westcliffe Publishers Inc., *(Westcliffe Pubs Inc; 0-942394),* 3900 S. Windermere, Englewood, CO 80110 Tel 303-761-3922 (SAN 239-7528).

Westcott Pubs., *(Westcott; 0-911620),* P.O. Box 803, Springfield, MO 65801 Tel 417-466-7455 (SAN 205-518X).

Westergaard, Marjorie, *(M Westergaard; 0-9609578),* 31246 Wagner, Warren, MI 48093 Tel 313-977-8942 (SAN 260-2768).

Western Assn. of Map Libraries, *(Western Assn Map; 0-939112),* University Library, Univ. of California, Santa Cruz, CA 95064 (SAN 216-3179).

Western Educational Services, *(Western Educ Serv; 0-916236),* 168 N. Main St., P.O., 596, Centerville, UT 84014 (SAN 207-7426).

Western Epics Publishing Co., *(Western Epics; 0-914740),* 254 S. Main St., Salt Lake City, UT 84101 Tel 801-328-2586 (SAN 206-1384).

Western Guideways, *(Western Guideways; 0-931788),* Box 15532, Lakewood, CO 80215 Tel 303-237-0583 (SAN 210-6264).

Western Heritage Press, *(Western Her Texas; 0-89351),* 1530 Bonnie Brae, Houston, TX 77006 Tel 713-522-7158 (SAN 210-9778).

Western Horseman, Inc., The, *(Western Horseman; 0-911647),* P.O. Box 7980, Colorado Springs, CO 80933 Tel 303-633-5525 (SAN 264-4894).

Western Illinois Univ., *(Western Ill Univ; 0-934312),* Macomb, IL 61455 (SAN 215-7128).

Western Islands, *(Western Islands; 0-88279),* 395 Concord Ave., Belmont, MA 02178 Tel 617-489-0606 (SAN 206-8435).

Western Marine Enterprises Inc., *(Western Marine Ent; 0-930030),* Box Q, Ventura, CA 93002 Tel 805-644-6043 (SAN 210-525X).

Western Michigan News, *(Western Michigan),* 3810 Roger Chaffee Blvd., Grand Rapids, MI 49508 (SAN 169-3875); P.O. Box 10, 301 S. Rath Ave., Ludington, MI 49431 (SAN 169-3905).

Western Mountain Press, *(Rocky Mtn Pr; 0-911625),* 509 Cardenas S. E., Albuquerque, NM 87108 Tel 505-268-8776 (SAN 275-1143).

Western North Carolina Press, Inc., *(Western NC Pr; 0-915948),* 16 Tahquitz Ct., Camarillo, CA 93010 Tel 805-987-5760 (SAN 208-9181).

Western Psychological Services, Div. of Manson Western Corp., *(Western Psych; 0-87424),* 12031 Wilshire Blvd., Los Angeles, CA 90025 Tel 213-478-2061 (SAN 202-9634).

Western Pubs., *(Western Pubs FL; 0-9602218),* 1711 South Lakeside Drive, Lake Worth, FL 33460 Tel 305-588-6848 (SAN 212-8039) Not to be confused with Western Publishing in New York.

Western Publishing Co., Inc., *(Western Pub; 0-307),* 850 Third Ave., New York, NY 10022 Tel 212-753-8500 (SAN 202-523X); Orders to: Dept. M, 1220 Mound Ave., Racine, WI 53404 (SAN 202-5248) Not to be confused with Western Publisher in Florida. *Imprints:* Golden Press (Golden Pr).

Western Reserve Press, Inc., *(Western Res Pr),* P.O. Box 675, Ashtabula, OH 44004 Tel 216-997-5851 (SAN 205-5201).

Western Search Inc., *(Western Search; 0-9602804),* P.O. Box 334, Seahurst, WA 98062 Tel 206-453-9041 (SAN 213-8808).

Western Social Research Pubs., *(Western Soc Res),* Box 306, Del Mar, CA 92014 (SAN 216-4744).

Western States Arts Foundation, *(Western States; 0-9611710),* 141 E. Palace Ave., Sante Fe, NM 87501 Tel 505-988-1166 (SAN 285-3531).

Western Sun Pubns., *(Western Sun Pubns; 0-9608146),* P.O. Box 1470, 290 S. First Ave., Suite 300, Yuma, AZ 85364 Tel 602-782-4646 (SAN 240-5067).

Western Tanager Press, *(Western Tanager; 0-934136),* 1111 Pacific Ave., Santa Cruz, CA 95060 Tel 408-425-1111 (SAN 220-0155). *Imprints:* Paper Vision Press (Paper Vision); Valley Publishers (Valley Calif).

Western Washington Univ., Center for East Asian Studies, *(West Wash Univ; 0-914584),* Bellingham, WA 98225 Tel 206-676-3041 (SAN 203-218X).

Western World Pubs., *(Western World; 0-931864),* Box 27587, San Francisco, CA 94127 Tel 415-661-2663 (SAN 207-6616).

Western World Review, *(West World Pr),* P.O. Box 366, Sun City, CA 92381 (SAN 219-3043).

Westernlore Pubns., *(Westernlore; 0-87026),* 11860 N. Tami Place, Tucson, AZ 85704 Tel 602-297-5491 (SAN 202-9642); Orders to: Westernlore Press, P.O. Box 35305, Tucson, AZ 85740 Tel 602-297-5491 (SAN 202-9650).

Westgard, Gilbert, K. II, *(G K Westgard),* 9226 W. Golf Rd., Des Plaines, IL 60016 (SAN 240-5032).

Westgate Hse., *(Westgate Hse; 0-9607320),* Suite 75, 1716 Ocean Ave., San Franciso, CA 94112 Tel 415-584-8338 (SAN 239-5819).

Westlake, Kevin L., *(Westlake; 0-9604862),* RR 2, Montpelier, ID 83254 (SAN 215-7136).

Westland, John Henry, *(J H Westland),* P.O. Box 3265, Chico, CA 95927 (SAN 211-7681).

Westland Pubns., *(Westland Pubns; 0-915162),* P.O. Box 117, McNeal, AZ 85617 (SAN 207-1169).

Westmail Press, *(Westmail Pr),* 179 Westmoreland Ave., White Plains, NY 10606 Tel 914-948-1116 (SAN 207-5326).

Westminster Press, *(Westminster; 0-664),* 925 Chestnut St., Philadelphia, PA 19107 Tel 215-928-2700 (SAN 202-9669); Orders to: Order Dept., P.O. Box 718 Wm. Penn Annex, Philadelphia, PA 19105 (SAN 202-9677).

Westmoreland County Museum of Art, *(Westmoreland),* Greensburg, PA 15601 (SAN 264-4916); Dist. by: University of Pittsburgh Press, 127 North Bellefield Ave., Pittsburgh, PA 15260 (SAN 203-3216).

Westphal Pub., *(Westphal Pub),* P.O. Box 19542, Irvine, CA 92713 Tel 714-673-8788 (SAN 262-1088).

Westrail Pubns., *(Westrail Pubns; 0-9602466),* Box 300, Glendora, CA 91740 (SAN 212-7091).

Westridge Press, Ltd., *(Westridge; 0-918832),* 1090 Southridge Pl., S., Salem, OR 97302 Tel 503-363-2422 (SAN 210-5268).

Westrom Co., The, *(Westrom; 0-938230),* P.O. Box 85527, Los Angeles, CA 90072 (SAN 215-8264).

Westroots, *(Westroots; 0-936580),* 3131a Via Alicante, La Jolla, CA 92037 (SAN 222-0296).

Westsea Pub. Co., Inc., *(Westsea Pub; 0-937820),* 149D Allen Blvd., Farmingdale, NY 11735 Tel 516-420-1110 (SAN 215-7144).

Westview Press, *(Westview; 0-89158; 0-86531; 0-8133),* 5500 Central Ave., Boulder, CO 80301 Tel 303-444-3541 (SAN 219-970X).

Westville Pub. Co. Ltd., *(Westville Pub Co; 0-938860),* P.O. Box 81, Old Westbury, NY 11568 (SAN 240-0359).

Westwater Books, *(Westwater; 0-916370),* P.O. Box 365, Boulder City, NV 89005 Tel 702-293-1406 (SAN 208-3698).

Westwind Press, *(Westwind Pr),* Rte.1, Box 208, Farmington, WV 26571 (SAN 215-7152).

Westwood Publishing Co., *(Westwood Pub Co; 0-930298),* 312 Riverdale Dr., Glendale, CA 91204 (SAN 211-8769).

Wetherall Publishing Company, *(Wetherall; 0-936750),* 510 First Ave. N., Suite 212, Minneapolis, MN 55403 Tel 612-339-3363 (SAN 222-1977).

Wetterau, Lynne E., Co., *(Wetterau; 0-940704),* 69 S. Moger Ave., Mount Kisco, NY 10549 Tel 914-241-0850 (SAN 218-6020).

Weyandt, Dorothy, *(Weyandt; 0-917424),* Box 6430, Solon Springs, WI 54873 Tel 715-795-2582 (SAN 208-2780).

Weybridge Publishing Co., *(Weybridge; 0-939356),* 16911 Brushfield Dr., Dallas, TX 75248 Tel 214-931-7770 (SAN 216-4965).

Wff'n Proof Pubs., *(Wffn Proof; 0-911624),* 1490 S. Blvd., Ann Arbor, MI 48104 Tel 313-665-2269 (SAN 205-521X).

Whale & Eagle Publishing Co., *(Whale & Eagle),* P.O. Box 698/239-B Seal Beach Blvd., Seal Beach, CA 90740 Tel 213-596-2210 (SAN 211-5476).

What to Do County Pubns., Inc., Div. of Hardscrabble Pubns., Inc., *(What to Do),* P.O. Box 396, Pleasantville, NY 10570 (SAN 213-5728).

Whatever Publishing Inc., Rising Sun Records, *(Whatever Pub; 0-931432),* P.O. Box 137, Mill Valley, CA 94942 Tel 415-849-2665 (SAN 211-8777); Dist. by: Network, Inc., P.O. Box 2246, Berkeley, CA 94702 Tel 800-227-2400 (SAN 282-0471).

Wheat Forder's Press, *(Wheat Forders; 0-917888),* P.O. Box 6317, Washington, DC 20015 Tel 202-362-1588 (SAN 209-9187).

Wheelchair Bowlers of Southern California, *(Wheelchair Bowlers; 0-9605306),* 6512 Cadiz Circle, Huntington Beach, CA 92647 (SAN 215-9848).

Wheeler, Carol Jean, *(C J Wheeler; 0-9608448),* 420 Carolwood Lane, N.E., Atlanta, GA 30342 Tel 404-252-9157 (SAN 240-5733).

Wheeler, Eva Floy, *(E F Wheeler),* 1199 Margarita Ave., Grover City, CA 93433 (SAN 264-4940).

Wheelwright Press, *(Wheelwright Pr; 0-935706),* 300 Page St., San Francisco, CA 94102 (SAN 222-0326).

Wheelwright Press, Ltd., *(Wheelwright UT; 0-937512),* 1836 Sunnyside Ave., Salt Lake City, UT 84108 Tel 801-582-8158 (SAN 205-9533).

Whimsie Press, the, *(Whimsie Pr; 0-916178),* P.O. Box 70, Mill Creek Rd., Otego, NY 13825 (SAN 239-5770).

Whirlpool Corp., *(Whirlpool; 0-938336),* Home Study Department, La Porte, IN 46350 (SAN 215-8272).

Whispering Sands Pubns., *(Whispering Sands Pubns; 0-9608718),* 1543 Luisa St., P.O. Box 181, Santa Fe, NM 87501 Tel 505-983-5960 (SAN 238-0870).

Whispers Press, *(Whispers; 0-918372),* 70 Highland Ave., Binghamtom, NY 13905 Tel 607-729-6920 (SAN 210-6272).

Whitaker House, *(Whitaker Hse; 0-88368),* Pittsburgh & Colfax Sts., Springdale, PA 15144 Tel 412-274-4440 (SAN 203-2104).

Whitcomb Pubns., *(Whitcomb Pubns),* Rte. 3, Box 251F, Stillwater, OK 74076 (SAN 210-9220).

White, Ann Leon, *(A L White; 0-9608198),* 305 West End Ave., New York, NY 10023 (SAN 240-169X).

White, David, Co., *(D White; 0-87250),* One Pleasant Ave., Port Washington, NY 11050 Tel 516-944-9325 (SAN 201-2936).

White, Eugene V., *(E V White; 0-9602034),* One West Main St., Berryville, VA 22611 Tel 703-955-2280 (SAN 212-5838).

White, Glenn E. F., *(White G E F; 0-9611926),* 101 Buckingham St., Meriden, CT 06450 Tel 203-235-7462 (SAN 286-1011).

White, James T., & Co., *(J T White; 0-88371),* 1700 State Hwy. 3, Clifton, NJ 07013 Tel 201-773-9300 (SAN 202-7291).

White, John A., *(J A White; 0-9603242),* 1200 Toyon Dr, Millbrae, CA 94030 Tel 415-697-1187 (SAN 207-1932).

White, Stephen, Editions, *(White Edns; 0-9606808),* 752 N. la Cienega Blvd., Los Angeles, CA 90069 Tel 213-657-6995 (SAN 217-4545).

White Bear Books, *(White Bear; 0-931884),* Box 402, Occidental, CA 95465 (SAN 212-145X).

White Crane Pubns., *(White Crane Pubns; 0-9604880),* P.O. Box 3081, Eugene, OR 97403 Tel 503-342-2759 (SAN 237-9708).

White Cross Press, *(White Cross; 0-918186),* Route One, Box 592, Granger, TX 76530 Tel 512-859-2814 (SAN 210-2862).

White Eagle Pub, The, *(White Eagle Pub; 0-941804),* P.O. Box 1332, Suite BP-0111, Lowell, MA 01853 (SAN 239-3441).

White Ewe Press, *(White Ewe; 0-917976),* P.O. Box 996, Adelphi, MD 20783 (SAN 209-410X).

White Horse Productions, Inc., *(White Horse; 0-940376),* 286 Cabot St., Beverly, MA 01915 Tel 617-927-3677 (SAN 219-8355).

White House Book Company, *(White House Bk Co; 0-9611884),* 729 Curtis St., Albany, CA 94706 Tel 415-526-2083 (SAN 286-0821).

White Mountain Pub. Co., *(White Mtn Pub; 0-917978),* 13801 N. Cave Creek Rd., Phoenix, AZ 85022 Tel 602-971-2720 (SAN 209-9195).

White Oak Publishing House, *(White Oak; 0-932556),* P.O. Box 3089, Redwood City, CA 94064 Tel 415-363-2103 (SAN 210-9646).

White Pine Press, *(White Pine; 0-934834),* P.O. Box 236, Niagara Square Sta., Buffalo, NY 14201 Tel 716-884-7041 (SAN 209-8067).

White Rabbit Press, *(White Rabbit),* 631 State St., Santa Barbara, CA 93101 Tel 415-548-8204 (SAN 205-5228).

White Rose Marketing, *(White Rose),* 23101 Moulton Pkwy., Suite 110, Laguna Hills, CA 92653 (SAN 216-3233).

White Wing Publishing House & Press, *(White Wing Pub; 0-934942),* P.O. Box 3000, Cleveland, TN 37311 Tel 615-476-8536 (SAN 203-2198).

Whitebrook Books, *(Whitebrook Bks),* P.O. Box 746, Easthampton, MA 01027 (SAN 237-9694).

Whiteford International Enterprise See **Wheat Forder's Press**

Whitehead Photography, *(Whitehead Photo; 0-9603486),* 13 S. Foushee St., Richmond, VA 23220 Tel 804-648-3219 (SAN 213-7054).

Whitehead Publishing, *(Whitehead Pub; 0-911225),* 601 W. 14, Austin, TX 78701 (SAN 283-989X).

Whitenwife Pubns., *(Whitenwife Pubns; 0-9603656),* 149 Magellan St., Capitola, CA 95010 Tel 408-476-2730 (SAN 213-8816).

Whitfield, *(Whitfield; 0-930920),* 1841 Pleasant Hill Rd., Pleasant Hill, CA 94523 Tel 415-934-8054 (SAN 210-6280).

Whitlock, Rosemary, *(Whitlock SC; 0-88100),* Rt. 2, Baker Place, Lancaster, SC 29720 Tel 803-285-2888 (SAN 277-7118).

Whitman, Albert, & Co., *(A Whitman; 0-8075),* 5747 W. Howard St., Niles, IL 60648 Tel 312-647-1355 (SAN 201-2049).

Whitman Publishing Co., *(Whitman Pub),* Dist. by: Western Publishing Co., Inc., 1220 Mound Ave., Racine, WI 53404 (SAN 202-5248).

Whitman-Walker Clinic, Inc., the, *(Whitman-Walker),* 2335 18th St., N.W., Washington, DC 20009 (SAN 237-9775).

Whitmarsh & Co., Div. of Whitmarsh Graphics, *(Whitmarsh; 0-940698),* 6342 Ivarene Ave., Hollywood, CA 90068 Tel 213-463-6747 (SAN 218-6039).

Whitmore Publishing Co., *(Whitmore; 0-87426),* 35 Cricket Terrace, Ardmore, PA 19003 (SAN 203-2112).

Whitney Library See **Watson-Guptill Pubns., Inc.**

Whitston Publishing Co., Inc., *(Whitston Pub; 0-87875),* P.O. Box 958, Troy, NY 12181 Tel 518-283-4363 (SAN 203-2120).

Whittell, George, Memorial Press, *(G Whittell Mem; 0-910781),* 3722 South Ave., Youngstown, OH 44502 Tel 216-783-0645 (SAN 260-2776).

Whitten Publishing Co., *(Whitten Pub Co; 0-9602766),* P.O. Box 513, Flatonia, TX 78941 (SAN 213-1889).

Whittle, E., & F. A. Dockery, *(E Whittle & F A Dockery; 0-9604046),* 795-B Beech Circle N. W., Cleveland, TN 37311 (SAN 214-168X).

Whole Person Associates, Inc./Whole Person Press, *(Whole Person; 0-938586),* P.O. Box 3151, Duluth, MN 55803 (SAN 282-5430); Dist. by: Bookpeople, 2940 Seventh St., Berkeley, CA 94710 Tel 415-549-3030 (SAN 168-9517); Orders to: The Bookman, 519 N. Third St., Minneapolis, MN 55401 Tel 612-341-3333 (SAN 282-5457).

Whole World Publishing, Inc., *(Whole World; 0-938184),* 400 Lake Cook Rd., No. 207, Deerfield, IL 60015 (SAN 217-1422).

Wholeo Books, *(Wholeo Bks; 0-942488),* P.O. Box 796, Monte Rio, CA 95462 Tel 707-865-2542 (SAN 239-9547).

Who's Who Among Black Americans, Inc., *(Who's Who Black Am),* 721 N. McKinley, Lake Forest, IL 60045 Tel 312-295-6650 (SAN 207-9968).

Who's Who Historical Society, *(Who's Who Hist Soc; 0-9603166),* 2022 Calle de Los Alamos, San Clemente, CA 92672 Tel 714-498-0600 (SAN 213-7062).

Who's Who in America's Restaurants, Div. of Who's Who in Restaurants, *(Whos Who Rest; 0-910297),* 1841 Broadway, Suite 902, New York, NY 10023 Tel 212-581-0360 (SAN 241-4775).

Who's Who in Black Corporate America, *(Whos Who Corp; 0-9609458),* 1629 K St. Nw Suite 596, Washington, DC 20006 Tel 202-244-2100 (SAN 260-1567).

Who's Who in Chiropractic International Publishing Co., *(Chiropractic; 0-918336),* P.O. Box 2615, Littleton, CO 80161 Tel 303-333-1581 (SAN 209-9209).

Why Not Creations, *(Why Not),* P.O. Box 1467, Monterey, CA 93940 (SAN 211-383X) Moved, Left No Forwarding Address.

Wibat Pubns., *(Wibat Pubns; 0-935996),* P.O. Box 60, Forestville, CA 95436 (SAN 214-1698).

Wichita Art Museum, *(Wichita Art Mus; 0-939324),* 619 Stackman Dr., Wichita, KS 67203 Tel 316-268-4621 (SAN 205-5260).

Wichita State Univ., History Resource Center, Dept. of History, *(WSU Hist Resources; 0-913070),* Wichita, KS 67208 Tel 316-689-3456 (SAN 206-037X).

Wicker Park Press, *(Wicker Park; 0-911595),* Box 5597, Chicago, IL 60680 Tel 312-486-2191 (SAN 264-4967).

Wide Skies Press, *(Wide Skies),* P.O. Box 7, Rt. 1, Polk, NE 68654 Tel 402-765-3798 (SAN 205-5279).

Wide World Publishing/Tetra House, *(Wide World-Tetra; 0-933174),* P.O. Box 476, San Carlos, CA 94070 Tel 415-593-2839 (SAN 211-1462).

Wider Opportunities for Women, *(WOW Inc; 0-934966),* 1325 G St., N.W., Lower Level, Washington, DC 20005 Tel 202-638-3143 (SAN 213-4047).

Wiener, Markus Publishing, Inc., *(Wiener Pub Inc; 0-910129),* 551 Fifth Ave., Suite 3210, New York, NY 10176 (SAN 282-5465); Dist. by: M & B Fulfillment Services, 540 Barnum St., Bridgeport, CT 06610 (SAN 282-6062).

Wiener, Moshe, *(M Wiener; 0-9605406),* 854 Newburg Ave., North Woodmere, NY 11581 (SAN 215-9856).

Wiese, Michael, Film Production, *(M Wiese Film Prod; 0-941188),* Box 406, Westport, CT 06881 Tel 203-227-2905 (SAN 239-9716).

Wigan Pier Press, *(Wigan Pier; 0-934594),* 1283 Page St., San Francisco, CA 94117 Tel 415-863-6664 (SAN 213-1897).

Wiggins, J. H., Co., *(Wiggins; 0-9600346),* 1650 S. Pacific Coast Hwy., Redondo Beach, CA 90277 (SAN 205-5287).

Wilcord Pubns., Ltd., *(Wilcord Pubns; 0-920986),* c/o Robert Silver Assocs., 95 Madison Ave., New York, NY 10016 Tel 212-686-5630 (SAN 241-5801).

Wild Horses Publishing Co., *(Wild Horses; 0-9601088; 0-937148),* 12310 Concepcion Rd., Los Altos Hills, CA 94022 Tel 415-941-3396 (SAN 211-8289); Dist. by: Bookpeople, 2940 7th St., Berkeley, CA 94710 Tel 415-549-3030 (SAN 168-9517).

Wild West Publishing House, *(Wild West Pub; 0-914006),* P.O. Box 1199, San Francisco, CA 94101 (SAN 203-2201).

Wildcat Canyon Books, *(Wildcat Canyon; 0-936034),* P.O. Box 5115, Richmond, CA 94805 (SAN 285-1172); 1332 Shotwell St., San Francisco, CA 94110 (SAN 285-1180).

Wildcat Publishing Company, Inc., *(Wildcat Pubs; 0-941968),* 14 Greenwood Trail, Westport, CT 06880 Tel 203-255-0707 (SAN 238-2776).

Wilderness House, *(Wilderness Hse; 0-931798),* 11129 Caves Hwy., Cave Junction, OR 97523 Tel 503-592-2106 (SAN 208-0907).

Wilderness House Books, *(Wilder Hse Bks; 0-9611590),* 9350 Gregory Rd., P.O. Box 968, Fowlerville, MI 48836 (SAN 285-6662).

Wilderness Press, *(Wilderness; 0-89997; 0-911824),* 2440 Bancroft Way, Berkeley, CA 94704 Tel 415-843-8080 (SAN 203-2139).

Wilderness Press, The, *(Wilderness Pr; 0-933326),* 2620 F St. Number Five, Sacramento, CA 95816 Tel 916-446-0300 (SAN 212-5846).

Wildfire Publishing Co., *(Wildfire Pub; 0-938444),* 1 S. Fairview, Unit C, Goleta, CA 93117 Tel 805-967-8444 (SAN 216-2040).

Wildflower Press, *(Wildflower; 0-938370),* P.O. Box 255, Topanga, CA 90290 (SAN 215-8280).

Wildlife Education, Ltd., *(Wildlife Educ; 0-937934),* 930 W. Washington, Suite 14, San Diego, CA 92103 (SAN 215-8299).

Wildlife Society, Inc., *(Wildlife Soc; 0-933564),* 5410 Grosvenor Lane, Suite 200, Bethesda, MD 20814 Tel 301-897-9770 (SAN 203-0225).

Wildlife-Wildlands Institute, *(Wildlife-Wildlands; 0-910439),* 5200 Upper Miller Creek Rd., Missoula, MT 59803 Tel 406-251-3867 (SAN 260-1575).

Wildman Press, *(Wildman Pr),* 19 W. 44th St., New York, NY 10036 (SAN 265-3842).

Wildwater Designs Ltd., *(Wildwater Designs),* 230 Penllyn Pike, Penllyn, PA 19422 (SAN 219-8371).

Wildwood Press, *(Wildwood; 0-918944),* 2110 Wood Ave., Colorado Springs, CO 80907 Tel 303-634-8078 (SAN 210-5284).

Wildwood Press, *(Wildwood Pr; 0-9607260),* 209 SW Wildwood, Grants Pass, OR 97526 Tel 503-479-3434 (SAN 239-345X).

Wildwood Pubns., *(Wildwood Pubns MI; 0-914104),* P.O. Box 629, Traverse City, MI 49684 Tel 616-941-7160 (SAN 206-5916).

Wiley, John, & Sons, Inc., *(Wiley; 0-471),* 605 Third Ave., New York, NY 10158 Tel 212-850-6418 (SAN 200-2272).

Wiley, Leonard, *(L Wiley; 0-911742),* 2927 S.E. 75th Ave., Portland, OR 97206 Tel 503-777-3645 (SAN 203-9273).

Wilk Publishing Co., *(Wilk Pub),* P.O. Box 320, Park Ridge, IL 60068 Tel 312-725-4878 (SAN 203-221X).

Wilkerson Associates, *(Wilkerson Assocs),* P.O. Box 711, Gig Harbor, WA 98335 Tel 206-858-9076 (SAN 210-9689).

Wilkinson, Paul H., *(Wilkinson; 0-911710),* 5900 Kingswood Rd., N.W., Washington, DC 20014 Tel 301-530-0888 (SAN 205-5295).

Willamette Press, *(Willamette; 0-913695),* P.O. Box 2065, Beaverton, OR 97075 Tel 503-643-1357 (SAN 286-2174).

Willard/Bower, *(Willard-Bower),* 100 Marilyn Ave., Roseville, CA 95678 (SAN 211-9943).

Willcox, P. J., *(P J Willcox; 0-9608436),* P.O. Box 39, Huntington, IN 46750 Tel 219-356-8946 (SAN 240-8066).

Willcraft Pubs., *(Willcraft; 0-910585),* 5093 Williamsport Dr., Norcross, GA 30071 Tel 404-449-4758 (SAN 260-2784).

Willert, James, *(J Willert; 0-930798),* 12804 S. Graff Dr., La Mirada, CA 90638 (SAN 212-2456).

William & Richards, Pubs., *(William & Rich; 0-9600202),* P.O. Box 2546, San Francisco, CA 94126 (SAN 282-5481).

William & Son Pubs., *(Wm & Son Pubs; 0-9607266),* P.O. Box 184, Trontdale, OR 97060 Tel 503-667-3560 (SAN 239-3476).

William Carey Library Pubs., *(William Carey Lib; 0-87808),* 1705 N. Sierra Bonita Ave., P.O. Box 40129, Pasadena, CA 91104 Tel 213-798-0819 (SAN 208-2101). *Imprints:* Ecclesia Pubns. (Ecclesia).

Indiana Univ. Museum, *(W H Mathers Mus; 0-9605982),* 601 E. Eighth St., Indiana Univ., Bloomington, IN 47405 Tel 812-335-7224 (SAN 216-7379).

William of Orange Publications, *(William of Orange),* N84 W16033 Menomonee Ave., No. 109, Menomonee Falls, WI 53051 Tel 414-255-4309 (SAN 264-4983).

William Tyndale College Press, *(William Tyndale Col Pr),* 35700 W. 12th Mile Road, Farmington Hills, MI 48018 Tel 313-553-7200 (SAN 265-3702).

Williams, Bill, Enterprises, *(Williams Ent; 0-934488),* 188 Merchant St., Honolulu, HI 96809 (SAN 220-1089) Moved, Left No Forwarding Address.

Williams, Ken J., Pubns., *(K J Williams Pubns; 0-9603742),* 881 Tenth Ave., Suite 4C, New York, NY 10019 (SAN 214-4891).

Williams & Wilkins Co., *(Williams & Wilkins; 0-683),* 428 E. Preston St., Baltimore, MD 21202 Tel 301-528-4221 (SAN 202-5175).

Williams Communications, Inc., *(Williams Com),* P.O. Box 1849, Orangeburg, SC 29115 (SAN 263-2365).

Williams Press, *(Williams Pr),* 417 Commerce St., Nashville, TN 37219 (SAN 211-1438).

Williams-Wallace Productions International Inc., *(W W Pro Inter),* 826 Pine St., Second Floor, Niagra Falls, NY 14301 (SAN 287-265X).

Williamson School of Horsemanship, *(Williamson Sch; 0-9600144),* P.O. Box 506, Hamilton, MT 59840 Tel 406-363-2874 (SAN 205-5317).

Willie, Ralph G., D.D.S., *(R G Willie DDS),* 30317 16th Ave. S., Federal Way, WA 98003 Tel 206-839-7270 (SAN 212-7113).

Willing Publishing Co., *(Willing Pub),* 251 S. San Gabriel Blvd., San Gabriel, CA 91778 (SAN 205-5325); Dist. by: Devorss & Co., 1641 Lincoln Blvd., Santa Monica, CA 90404 (SAN 168-9886).

Willis, J. V., Pubs., *(J V Willis; 0-913732),* 825 May St., Hammond, IN 46320 Tel 219-931-2672 (SAN 201-0178).

Willmann-Bell, Inc., *(Willman-Bell; 0-943396),* P.O. Box 3125, Richmond, VA 23235 Tel 804-320-7016 (SAN 240-8074).

Willoughby Books, *(Willoughby),* 14 Hamburg Turnpike, Hamburg, NJ 07419 (SAN 205-5341).

Willoughby Wessington Pub. co., *(Willoughby Wessington; 0-911227),* P.O. Box 91, Mercer Island, WA 98040 (SAN 276-6795).

Willow Creek Press, Div. of Wisconsin Sportsman, *(Willow Creek; 0-932558),* P.O. Box 2266, Oshkosh, WI 54903 Tel 414-233-4143 (SAN 211-2825).

Willow House Pubs., Inc., *(Willow Hse; 0-912450),* Box 155, Aptos, CA 95003 Tel 408-688-4128 (SAN 205-535X).

Willow Publishing Co., *(Willow Pub),* P.O. Box 6636 - AH Sta, San Antonio, TX 78209 Tel 512-822-5263 (SAN 205-9401).

Willow River Press, Ltd., *(Willow River; 0-930602),* 3257 W. Bryn Mawr Ave., Chicago, IL 60659 Tel 312-583-5242 (SAN 211-1128).

Willow Tree Press, *(Willow Tree NY; 0-9606960),* 124 Willow Tree Rd., Monsey, NY 10952 Tel 914-354-9139 (SAN 217-4588).

Willowood Press, *(Willowood Pr; 0-938376),* P.O. Box 22321, Lexington, KY 40522 (SAN 215-8302).

Willows Press, *(Willows Pr; 0-9602924),* P.O. Box 2779, Long Beach, CA 90801 Tel 213-433-6276 (SAN 220-1097).

Willyshe Publishing Co., Inc., *(Willyshe Pub; 0-936112),* 112 Mountain Rd., Linthicum Heights, MD 21090 (SAN 203-9499).

Wilmar Pubs., *(Wilmar Pubs),* P.O. Box 5295, Sherman Oaks, CA 91413 Tel 213-762-1234 (SAN 210-9697).

Wilmington Press, *(Wilmington Pr),* Orders to: 13315 Wilmington Dr., Dallas, TX 75234 Tel 214-620-8431 (SAN 282-549X).

Wilshire Book Co., *(Wilshire; 0-87980),* 12015 Sherman Rd., North Hollywood, CA 91605 Tel 213-875-1711 (SAN 168-9932).

Wilson, Bob, *(B Wilson; 0-9608192),* 1542 Big Horn Ave., Sheridan, WY 82801 . Tel 307-674-8422 (SAN 240-3021).

Wilson, H. W., *(Wilson; 0-8242),* 950 University Ave., Bronx, NY 10452 Tel 212-588-8400 (SAN 203-2961).

Wilson, J.B., Press, Inc., *(J B Wilson; 0-933458),* 1730 Columbia Dr. E., Fresno, CA 93727 Tel 209-251-8751 (SAN 211-769X).

Wilson, John, *(Wilson J; 0-9608494),* Rt. Four, 111 Cranens Terrace, Chattanooga, TN 37409 Tel 615-821-2087 (SAN 240-8082).

Wilson, P., Mailservice, *(P Wilson Mail),* P.O. Box 8142, St. Louis, MO 63156 (SAN 209-3847).

Wilson Brothers Pubns., *(Wilson Bros; 0-934944),* P.O. Box 712, Yakima, WA 98907 Tel 509-457-8275 (SAN 212-2014).

Wilton Enterprises, Book Div., *(Wilton; 0-912696),* 1603 S. Michigan Ave., Chicago, IL 60616 Tel 312-663-5096 (SAN 206-0248).

Wilton Place Communications, *(Wilton Place),* 1013 N. Lima St., Burbank, CA 91505 Tel 213-841-5368 (SAN 282-5503); Orders to: P.O. Box 2020, Burbank, CA 91507 (SAN 282-5511).

Wimbledon Music Inc., *(Wimbledon Music),* 1888 Century Park E., Century City, CA 90067 Tel 213-653-6990 (SAN 219-8444).

Wimmer Brothers Books, *(Wimmer Bks; 0-918544),* P.O. Box 18408, Memphis, TN 38118 Tel 901-362-8900 (SAN 209-6544).

Winch, B. L., & Associates, *(B L Winch; 0-935266),* 45 Hitching Post Dr., Building 2, Rolling Hills Estates, CA 90274 (SAN 214-1728).

Winchell, Jane Neely, , *(J N Winchell; 0-9610978),* P.O. Box 5336, Waco, TX 76708 Tel 817-772-2262 (SAN 265-3478).

Winchester Press, *(Winchester Pr; 0-87691),* P.O. Box 1260, Tulsa, OK 74101 Tel 918-663-4220 (SAN 203-2953).

Wind Chimes, *(Wind Chimes; 0-941190),* P.O. Box 601, Glen Burnie, MD 21061 (SAN 237-9724).

Wind Publishing, *(Wind Pub; 0-933312),* P.O. Box 253, Corona Del Mar, CA 92625 (SAN 212-4645).

Wind River Scribes, Ltd., The, *(Wind River Scri; 0-942652),* 1609 8th St. NE, No. 111, Auburn, WA 98002 Tel 206-939-5780 (SAN 238-5902).

Windflower Press, *(Windflower Pr; 0-931534),* P.O. Box 82213, Lincoln, NE 68501 Tel 402-475-0904 (SAN 208-9211).

Windham Bay Press, *(Windham Bay),* Box 1332, Juneau, AK 99802 (SAN 214-4905).

Windhover See Berkley Publishing Corp.

Windless Orchard Series, *(Windless Orchard; 0-87883),* Indiana Univ., English Dept., Fort Wayne, IN 46805 Tel 219-482-5386 (SAN 206-023X).

Windmill Books, Inc., Div. of Intext, *(Windmill Bks; 0-87807; 0-671),* 1230 Ave of the Americas, New York, NY 10020 Tel 212-245-6400 (SAN 205-5376).

Windmill Publishing Co., *(Windmill Pub Co; 0-933846),* 2147 Windmill View Rd., El Cajon, CA 92020 Tel 619-448-5390 (SAN 212-8047).

Window Editions, *(Window Edns; 0-939290),* 350 Old Roaring Brook Rd., Mount Kisco, NY 10549 Tel 212-222-1689 (SAN 216-5201).

Winds of the World Press, *(Winds World Pr; 0-938338),* 35 Whittemore Rd., Framingham, MA 01701 (SAN 215-8310).

Windsinger Enterprises, Inc., *(Windsinger),* P.O. Box 128, Wellsville, UT 84339 Tel 801-245-4030 (SAN 213-8115).

Windsong Books International, *(Windsong; 0-934846),* P.O. Box 867, Huntington Beach, CA 92648 Tel 714-963-0324 (SAN 213-7143).

Windsor Books Division, *(Windsor),* P.O. Box 280, Brightwaters, NY 11718 (SAN 203-2937).

Windsor House, *(Windsor Hse; 0-911321),* 3308 Midway Drive, Suite 145, San Diego, CA 92110 (SAN 276-6906).

Windsor Press, The, *(Windsor Pr; 0-9608260),* P.O. Box 786, Binghamton, NY 13902-0786 (SAN 240-1703).

Windsor Publications, Inc., *(Windsor Pubns Inc; 0-89781),* 21220 Erwin Street, Woodland Hills, CA 91365 Tel 213-884-4050 (SAN 265-3699).

Windstone See Bantam Books, Inc.

Windward Publishing Inc., *(Windward Pub; 0-89317),* 105 N.E. 25th St., P.O. Box 371005, Miami, FL 33137 Tel 305-576-6232 (SAN 208-3663).

Windyridge Press, *(Windyridge; 0-913366),* P.O. Box 591, Rogue River, OR 97537 (SAN 206-3948); Orders to: Northwest Textbook Depository, P.O. Box 5608, Portland, OR 97228 Tel 503-639-3193 (SAN 206-3956).

Wine, J. F., *(J F Wine),* 924 Woodland Ave., Winchester, VA 22601 Tel 703-662-5735 (SAN 206-0221).

Wine Appreciation Guild, the, *(Wine Appreciation; 0-932664),* 1377 Ninth Ave, San Francisco, CA 94122 (SAN 282-5546); 60 Federal St., San Francisco, CA 94107 (SAN 282-5554).

Wine Books, *(Wine Bks; 0-9604488),* P.O. Box 1015, San Marcos, CA 92069 (SAN 215-1936).

WINE CONSULTANTS

Wine Consultants of California, (Wine Consul Calif; 0-916040), P.O. Box 27187, San Francisco, CA 94127 Tel 415-681-8989 (SAN 207-4214).

Wine Pubns., (Wine Pubns; 0-913840), 96 Parnassus Rd., Berkeley, CA 94708 Tel 415-843-4209 (SAN 205-5392).

Winepress, (Winepress MN; 0-9604416), 408 Wendell St., Paynesville, MN 56362 Tel 612-243-3563 (SAN 215-1219).

Winfoto, (Winfoto; 0-9605522), 1790 Kearney St., Denver, CO 80220 (SAN 216-2067).

Wing, Simon Publishing Co., (S Wing Pub; 0-913315), 2793 Clairmont Rd., N.E. Suite 212, Atlanta, GA 30329 Tel 404-321-0120 (SAN 285-8967).

Wingbow Press, (Wingbow Pr; 0-914728), Dist. by: Bookpeople, 2940 Seventh St., Berkeley, CA 94710 Tel 415-549-3033 (SAN 168-9517).

Winged Lion Publishing Ltd., (Winged Lion; 0-915922), 414 S. Western Ave., P.O. Box 75936, Los Angeles, CA 90075 (SAN 208-0346).

Wings Press, (Wings ME; 0-939736), RFD 2 Box 730, Belfast, ME 04915 Tel 207-338-2005 (SAN 216-7689).

Wings Press, (Wings Pr; 0-930324), P.O. Box 25296, Houston, TX 77005 Tel 713-668-7953 (SAN 209-4975).

Winicorp, (Winicorp; 0-9610634), P.O. Box 3314, San Leandro, CA 94578 Tel 415-278-8365 (SAN 276-9476).

Winmark Press, (Winmark Pr), P.O. Box 148, Stratford, CT 06810 (SAN 240-5083).

Winnen, Jo, (J Winnen; 0-9603404), 624 S. Fancher Rd., Racine, WI 53406 (SAN 207-2416).

Winship Press, (Winship Pr; 0-915430), 2324 Clayton St., Macon, GA 31204 Tel 912-743-0029 (SAN 237-3005).

Winston-Derek Pubs.,Inc., (Winston-Derek; 0-938232), P.O. Box 90883, Pennywell Dr., Nashville, TN 37209 (SAN 214-4760); Dist. by: Baker & Taylor, Gladiola Ave., Momence, IL 60954 (SAN 169-2100).

Winston Press, Inc., Subs. of CBS Educational Publishing, (Winston Pr; 0-86683), 430 Oak Grove, Minneapolis, MN 55403 Tel 612-871-7000 (SAN 213-9596).

Winter Brook Pub. Co., (Winter Brook; 0-9602204), P.O. Box 1106, Covina, CA 91722 Tel 213-243-2049 (SAN 212-7121).

Winter Publishing Co., (Winter Pub Co), P.O. Box 36536, Tucson, AZ 85740 (SAN 220-1100); 5740 N. Camino Padre Isidoro, Tucson, AZ 85718 Tel 602-299-1528 (SAN 220-1119).

Wintergreen & Advance Pubs., (Wintergreen; 0-933460), 845 Via De La Paz, Suite 12, Pacific Palisades, CA 90272 Tel 213-454-5260 (SAN 212-713X).

Winters, David, (D Winters), 103 Van Ness St., Santa Cruz, CA 95060 (SAN 277-6707).

Winterthur Museum, (Winterthur; 0-912724), Winterthur, DE 19735 Tel 302-656-8591 (SAN 205-5406).

Wire Press/The Coffeehouse Magazine, (Wire Pr; 0-918034), 80 Maclaren, Ottawa, Ontario, K2P 0K6, Tel 613-232-6796 (SAN 210-2889).

Wirth, Diane E., (D E Wirth; 0-9602096), 16804 E. Peakview Ave., Aurora, CO 80016 (SAN 212-3940).

Wisconsin Bks., (Wisconsin Bks), 2025 Dunn Pl., Madison, WI 53713 Tel 608-257-4126 (SAN 213-8875) Formerly Named School of Living Press. Imprints: Sol Press (Sol Press).

Wisconsin Education Fund, (Wis Ed Fund; 0-9600358), P.O. Box 321, Port Washington, WI 53074 Tel 414-284-9066 (SAN 205-5414).

Wisconsin Ev. Lutheran Synod Board for Parish Education, (Wis Ev Luth; 0-938272), 3614 W. North Ave., Milwaukee, WI 53208 Tel 414-445-4030 (SAN 220-1127).

Wisconsin Sportsman, (Wisconsin Sptmn; 0-932558), P.O. Box 2266, Oshkosh, WI 54903 Tel 414-233-1327 (SAN 207-3013).

Wisconsin State Genealogical Society, Inc., (Wisconsin Gen), 5049 LaCrosse Lane, Madison, WI 53705 Tel 608-233-8018 (SAN 223-0623).

Wisdom Garden Books, (Wisdom Garden; 0-914794), Box 29448, Los Angeles, CA 90029 Tel 213-380-1968 (SAN 206-5584).

Wisdom House Press, (Wisdom House; 0-932560), 4030 Raleigh Ave. S., Minneapolis, MN 55416 Tel 612-920-0510 (SAN 212-2022).

Wisdom Pubs., (Wisdom; 0-911636), P.O. Box 81, San Diego, CA 92112 (SAN 205-5422).

Wise, Wm. H., & Co., Inc, (W H Wise; 0-8349), 336 Mountain Rd., Union City, NJ 07087 Tel 201-864-5200 (SAN 202-1218).

Wise Publishing Co., (Wise Pub; 0-915766), 5625 Wilhelmina Ave., Woodland Hills, CA 91364 (SAN 203-1876).

Wish Booklets, (Wish Bklets; 0-913786), 11909 Blue Spruce Rd, Reston, VA 22091 Tel 703-620-4966 (SAN 205-5430).

Wistaria Press, (Wistaria Pr; 0-916930), 4373 N.E. Wistaria Dr., Portland, OR 97213 Tel 503-281-5945 (SAN 237-9732).

With Kids, (With Kids; 0-9611292), P.O. Box 353, West Sand Lake, NY 12196 (SAN 283-9903).

Witkower Press, Inc., (Witkower; 0-911638), P.O. Box 2296, Bishop's Corner, West Hartford, CT 06117 Tel 203-232-1127 (SAN 205-5449).

Witness to the Holocaust Project, (Witness Holocaust; 0-912313), Emory University, Atlanta, GA 30322 Tel 404-329-7525 (SAN 264-5025).

Witt, Bud, (B Witt; 0-9604932), P.O. Box 2527, 4212 W. Olive, Fullerton, CA 92633 (SAN 215-7160).

Wittenborn, George, Inc., (Wittenborn; 0-8150), 1018 Madison Ave., New York, NY 10021 Tel 212-288-1558 (SAN 203-2880).

Wizards Bookshelf, (Wizards; 0-913510), Box 6600, San Diego, CA 92106 Tel 619-223-4005 (SAN 203-2872).

Wofsy, Alan, Fine Arts, (A Wofsy Fine Arts; 0-915346), P.O. Box 2210, San Francisco, CA 94126 Tel 415-986-3030 (SAN 207-6438).

Wolcotts, Inc., (Wolcotts; 0-910531), 15124 Downey Ave., Paramount, CA 90723 Tel 213-630-0911 (SAN 260-2792).

Wolf Creek Press, (Wolf Creek Pr; 0-9611886), P.O. Box 327, Canyondam, CA 95923 Tel 916-596-3412 (SAN 286-0848).

Wolf House Books, (Wolf Hse; 0-915046), P.O. Box 6657, Grand Rapids, MI 49506 Tel 616-245-8812 (SAN 203-2856).

Wolf Run Books, (Wolf Run Bks), P.O. Box 9620, Minneapolis, MN 55440 Tel 612-333-7437 (SAN 206-9571).

Wolfe, Ernest, Pubns., (E Wolfe Pubns; 0-9603660), 1655 Sawtelle Blvd., Los Angeles, CA 90025 Tel 213-478-2960 (SAN 236-6481).

Wolfe, Howard H., (H H Wolfe; 0-9600850), 12405 Davis Blvd., S. E., Fort Myers, FL 33905 Tel 813-694-1825 (SAN 206-0167).

Wolfson Publishing Co., Inc., (Wolfson; 0-916114), Seven Wood St., Conestoga Bldg., Pittsburgh, PA 15222 Tel 412-391-6190 (SAN 208-922X).

Womack Associates, (Womack Assoc; 0-9605530), 512 Westwood Dr., Prescott, AZ 86301 (SAN 215-9864).

Womack Educational Pubns - Department OF Womack Mchine Supply Co., (Womack Educ Pubns), 2010 Shea Rd., P.O. Box 35027, Dallas, TX 75235 Tel 214-357-3871 (SAN 205-9657).

Woman Activist, Inc., (Woman Activist; 0-917560), 2310 Barbour Rd., Falls Church, VA 22043 Tel 703-573-8716 (SAN 209-617X).

Woman's Institute for Continuing Jewish Education, (Womans Inst-Cont Jewish Ed; 0-9608054), 4079 54th St., San Diego, CA 92105 (SAN 240-1061).

Womansource, (Woman Source; 0-9608012), 1006 Olive St., Denver, CO 80220 Tel 303-333-5131 (SAN 239-9563).

Wombat Enterprises, Unlimited, (Wombat Ent; 0-9650572), P.O. Box 428, Latham, NY 12110 (SAN 239-5029).

Women & Literature Collective, (Women & Lit; 0-915052), P.O. Box 441, Cambridge, MA 02138 Tel 617-492-1262 (SAN 208-9815) Moved, Left No Forwarding Address.

Women for Sobriety, Inc., (WFS), P.O. Box 618, Quakertown, PA 18951 Tel 215-536-8026 (SAN 216-4779).

Women-in-Literature, Inc., (Women-in-Lit; 0-935634), P.O. Box 60550, Reno, NV 89506 Tel 702-972-1671 (SAN 213-8824).

PUBLISHERS AND DISTRIBUTORS

Women on Words & Images, (Women on Words; 0-9600724), 30 Valley Rd., Princeton, NJ 08540 Tel 609-921-8653 (SAN 206-622X); Orders to: P. O. Box 2163, Princeton, NJ 08540 (SAN 206-6238).

Women Writing Press, (Women Writing; 0-917648), P.O. Box 1035, Cathedral Sta., New York, NY 10025 Tel 212-222-3563 (SAN 208-9874).

Women's Action Alliance, Inc., (Women's Action; 0-9605828), 370 Lexington Ave., New York, NY 10017 Tel 212-532-8330 (SAN 207-6950).

Women's Aglow Fellowship, (Women's Aglow; 0-930756), P.O. Box I, Lynnwood, WA 98036 Tel 206-775-7282 (SAN 211-8297).

Women's Auxiliary of the American Cancer Society, (Womens Auxiliary Cancer; 0-9607282), 241 Fourth Ave., Pittsburgh, PA 15222 (SAN 239-3506).

Women's Club of Farmingdale, (Women's Club Farmingdale), Farmingdale, NY 11735 (SAN 217-2917).

Women's Committee of the Buffalo Philharmonic Orchestra Society, Inc., (Womens Com Buffalo; 0-9607538), 26 Richmond Ave., Buffalo, NY 14222 Tel 716-634-7419 (SAN 239-7986).

Women's Division, Central Sephardic Jewish Community of America, Inc., (Women's Div; 0-9611294), Eight W. 70 St., New York, NY 10023 (SAN 283-9911).

Women's History Research Center, Inc., (Women's Hist; 0-912374), 2325 Oak St., Berkeley, CA 94708 Tel 415-548-1770 (SAN 207-7175).

Women's International Bowling Congress, (WIBC), 5301 S. 76th St., Greendale, WI 53129 Tel 414-421-9000 (SAN 216-4787).

Women's International Network News Quarterly, (Womens Intl; 0-942096), 187 Grant St., Lexington, MA 02173 (SAN 237-9740).

Women's Research Action Project, (Womens Research Act; 0-930522), 72 Cornell St., Roslindale, MA 02131 Tel 617-327-5016 (SAN 209-6900).

Women's Service League of West Feliciana Parish, (Womens Serv; 0-9609422), P.O. Box 904, 205 Pine St., St. Francisville, LA 70775 Tel 504-635-6162 (SAN 276-7589).

Women's Times Publishing, (Womens Times; 0-910259), Sr3, Box 732, Grand Marais, MN 55604 (SAN 240-8945).

Women's Yellow Pages, (Womens Yellow Pgs), P.O. Box 66093, Los Angeles, CA 90066 (SAN 282-5562).

Wonder-Treasure Books, Inc., Div. of Grosset & Dunlap, Inc., (Wonder; 0-448), 51 Madison Ave., New York, NY 10010 Tel 212-689-9200 (SAN 205-5457).

Wood, Debby, (D Wood; 0-9607490), 1417 Venetian Ct., Cape Coral, FL 33904 Tel 813-542-7560 (SAN 239-961X).

Wood, Fern Morrow, (F M Wood; 0-9606922), Rte. 2, Cherryvale, KS 67335 (SAN 217-460X).

Wood, Francis Clark, Institute, (Wood Inst; 0-943060), The College of Physicians of Philadelphia, 19 S. 22nd St., Philadelphia, PA 19103 (SAN 240-4591).

Wood, R. V., (R V Wood), 230 Payson Rd., Belmont, MA 02178 (SAN 217-4715).

Wood, Richard D., (R D Wood; 0-9603898), 76 Stonehenge Rd., Kingston, RI 02881 Tel 401-783-2135 (SAN 207-5873).

Wood & Jones Pubs., (Wood & Jones; 0-9606114), 139 W. Colorado Blvd., Pasadena, CA 91105 Tel 213-449-1144 (SAN 216-8707).

Woodall Publishing Co., (Woodall; 0-912082), 500 Hyacinth Place, Highland Park, IL 60035 (SAN 205-5465).

Woodbine Books, Inc. See Shorewood Fine Art Books, Inc.

Woodbridge Pr. Pub. Co., (Woodbridge Pr; 0-912800; 0-88007), P.O. Box 6189, Santa Barbara, CA 93160 Tel 805-965-7039 (SAN 212-9892).

Woodcock Press, (Woodcock Pr; 0-941674), P.O. Box 4744, Santa Rosa, CA 95402 Tel 707-829-2965 (SAN 239-3514).

Woodcock Pubns., (Woodcock; 0-9605352), P. O. Box 985, Pacific Grove, CA 93950 (SAN 217-1430).

NAME INDEX

Woodcraft Supply Corp., *(Woodcraft Supply; 0-918036),* 41 Atlantic Ave., P.O. Box 4000, Woburn, MA 01888 Tel 617-935-5860 (SAN 210-2900).

Wooden Nutmeg Press, *(Wooden Nutmeg; 0-918164),* 74 Waller Rd., Bridgeport, CT 06606 Tel 203-372-8806 (SAN 210-2919).

Wooden Shoe, *(Wooden Shoe),* P.O. Box 174, Pleasantville, NY 10570 Tel 914-769-5580 (SAN 207-3021).

Woodford Memorial Editions, Inc., *(Woodford Mem; 0-9601574),* P.O. Box 55085, Seattle, WA 98155 Tel 206-364-4167 (SAN 210-9727).

Woodgreene Press, *(Woodgreene Pr; 0-910257),* 6915 Greenfield Way, Salt Lake City, UT 84121 Tel 801-942-0761 (SAN 241-4791).

Woodhead-Faulkner Pubs. Ltd., *(Woodhead-Faulkner; 0-85941),* 8 Market Passage, Cambridge, CB2 3PF, .

Woodhead-Faulkner (Publishers) Ltd., *(Woodhead),* 51 Washington Street, Dover, NM 03820 (SAN 276-7678).

Woodhill Press, Inc., *(Woodhill; 0-532),* 300 W. 43rd St., New York, NY 10036 Tel 212-397-5200 (SAN 202-6066).

Woodland Publishing Co., Inc., *(Woodland; 0-934104),* 230 Manitoba Ave., Wayzata, MN 55391 Tel 612-473-2725 (SAN 213-1900).

Woodmont Press, The, *(Woodmont Pr),* P.O. Box 108, Green Village, NJ 07935 Tel 201-377-6243 (SAN 217-2755).

Woodpile Pubs., *(Woodpile Pub; 0-9608118),* 1046 N. Herbert Ave., Tuscon, AZ 85705 (SAN 240-5091).

Woodrow, Ralph, Evangelistic Assn., Inc., *(R Woodrow; 0-916938),* Box 124, Riverside, CA 92502 Tel 714-686-5467 (SAN 206-3700).

Woods, Alfred L., *(A L Woods; 0-9811160),* 5612 S. Maryland Ave., Chicago, IL 60649 Tel 312-978-6713 (SAN 283-0485).

Woods, Jo, Pubns., *(J Woods Pubns),* P.O. Box 7585, Little Rock, AR 72207 (SAN 213-8832).

Woods Books, *(Woods Bks; 0-9602990),* P.O. Box 29521, Los Angeles, CA 90029 Tel 213-247-4177 (SAN 213-1919).

Woods Hole Press, Subs. of the Job Shop, *(Woods Hole; 0-915176),* P.O. Box 44, Woods Hole, MA 02543 Tel 617-548-9600 (SAN 210-332X).

Woods Library Publishing Co., *(Woods Lib Pub; 0-912304),* 9159 Clifton Park, Evergreen Park, IL 60642 Tel 312-423-5986 (SAN 205-5473).

Woods Pubns., *(Woods Pubns; 0-943168),* 2200 Guadalupe, Austin, TX 78705 (SAN 240-5105).

Woodstock Editions, *(Woodstock Edns; 0-933632),* P.O. Box 277, Woodstock, NY 12498 Tel 914-679-6477 (SAN 212-629X).

Woodstone Books, *(Woodstone Bks; 0-939866),* P.O. Box 40114, Albuquerque, NM 87196 Tel 505-268-7994 (SAN 216-9436).

Woodward, Claire, *(C Woodward; 0-9606812),* 10806 Fairway Court W., Sun City, AZ 85351 Tel 602-974-6919 (SAN 217-4618).

Woodward Books, *(Woodward Bks; 0-916028),* P.O. Box 773, Corte Madera, CA 94925 Tel 415-388-5095 (SAN 208-0737).

Wooley, Rebecca Smith, *(R S Wooley; 0-9601654),* 1250 S. Fairfield, Chicago, IL 60608 (SAN 211-4453).

Woolmer/Brotherson, Ltd., *(Woolmer-Brotherson; 0-913506),* Revere, PA 18953 Tel 215-847-5074 (SAN 205-5481).

Word Aflame Press, *(Word Aflame),* 8855 Dunn Rd., Hazelwood, MO 63042 Tel 314-837-7300 (SAN 212-0046).

Word Beat Press, *(Word Beat; 0-912527),* P.O. Box 10509, Tallahassee, FL 32302-2509 (SAN 265-3060).

Word-Craft Publishing Co., *(Word-Craft Pub; 0-936928),* Suite 2, Bldg. 13, Office Park Circle, Birmingham, AL 35223 (SAN 219-1024).

Word Enterprise, *(Word Ent; 0-938722),* P.O. Box 535, Fairview, NJ 07022 (SAN 215-9325).

Word for Today, The, *(Word for Today; 0-936728),* P.O. Box 8000, Costa Mesa, CA 92626 Tel 714-979-0706 (SAN 214-2260).

Word Foundation, Inc. The, *(Word Foun; 0-911650),* P. O. Box 18235, Dallas, TX 75218 Tel 214-348-5006 (SAN 205-549X).

Word-Fraction Math Aid Co., *(Word-Fraction; 0-911642),* P.O. Box 475, Woodland Hills, CA 91366 (SAN 205-5503).

Word, Inc., *(Word Bks; 0-87680; 0-8499),* 4800 W. Waco Drive, Waco, TX 76796 Tel 817-772-7650 (SAN 203-283X).

Word Merchant Press, *(Word Merchant Pr; 0-931482),* 40 Clinton St., No. 6C, Brooklyn, NY 11201 (SAN 265-4113).

Word of Mouth Press, *(Word of Mouth; 0-910027),* P.O. Box 5395, Takoma Park, MD 20912 Tel 301-270-2646 (SAN 240-8937).

Word Power, Inc., *(Word Power; 0-934832),* Lockbox 17034, Seattle, WA 98107 Tel 206-782-1437 (SAN 213-3881).

Word Publishing, *(Word Pub; 0-8499),* 4800 W. Waco Dr., Waco, TX 76796 (SAN 239-5045).

Word Services & Pied Pubns. Publishing Co., *(Word Serv; 0-918626),* 1927 S. 26th St., Lincoln, NE 68502 (SAN 210-5519).

Word Wheel Books, Inc., *(Word Wheel; 0-913700),* 181 Stanford Ave., Menlo Park, CA 94025 Tel 415-854-2496 (SAN 203-1868).

Word Works, Inc., *(Word Works; 0-915380),* P.O. Box 42164, Washington, DC 20015 Tel 202-554-3014 (SAN 211-6294).

Wordcrafter Pubns., *(Wordcraft MD; 0-941448),* 15804 White Rock Rd., Gaithersburg, MD 20878 Tel 301-948-2539 (SAN 239-0590).

WorDoctor Pubns., *(WorDoctor; 0-918248),* P.O. Box 9761, 6516 Ben Ave., North Hollywood, CA 91609 Tel 213-980-3576 (SAN 207-5865).

Words Press, *(Words Pr; 0-9607390),* P.O. Box 1935, Beaverton, OR 97075 (SAN 239-7951).

WordShop Pubns., *(WordShop Pubns; 0-9606338),* P.O. Box 6213, Laguna Niguel, CA 92677 Tel 714-495-3372 (SAN 282-5619); 27252 Pinocha, Mission Viejo, CA 92692 (SAN 282-5627); Orders to: 27252 Pinocha, Mission Viejo, CA 92692 Tel 714-495-3372 (SAN 282-5635).

Wordsmiths, The, *(Wordsmiths; 0-9606108),* P.O. Box 2231, Evergreen, CO 80439 Tel 303-674-8017 (SAN 216-8715).

Wordtree, The, *(Wordtree; 0-936312),* 7306 Brittany, Shawnee Mission, KS 66203-4699 Tel 913-236-7733 (SAN 214-1752).

Work in America Institute Inc., *(Work in Amer; 0-89361),* 700 White Plains Rd., Scarsdale, NY 10583 Tel 914-472-9600 (SAN 208-9262).

Workers of Our Lady of Mt. Carmel, Inc., the, *(Workers Lady Mt Carmel),* Box 606, Lindenhurst, NY 11757 (SAN 237-9783).

Workers Press, *(Workers Pr; 0-917348),* P.O. Box 3774, Chicago, IL 60654 (SAN 208-9270); Dist. by: Vanguard Bks., P.O. Box 3566, Chicago, IL 60654 Tel 312-342-3425 (SAN 213-8212).

Working Directory of Philadelphia Artists, The, *(Working Dir PA Artists),* 737 E. Passyunk Ave., Philadelphia, PA 19147 Tel 215-625-9367 (SAN 212-3258).

Working Peoples Artists, *(Working Peoples Art),* P.O. Box 2307, Berkeley, CA 94702 (SAN 209-0023).

Working Press of the Nation, *(Working Pr),* Orders to: National Research Bureau, Inc., 424 N. Third St., Burlington, IA 52601 Tel 319-752-5415 (SAN 205-7344).

Working Women Education Fund, *(Work Women Educ; 0-912663),* 1224 Huron Rd., Cleveland, OH 44115 (SAN 283-992X).

Workingmans Press, *(Workingmans Pr; 0-935388),* P.O. Box 12486, Seattle, WA 98111 (SAN 209-2298).

Workman Publishing Co., Inc., *(Workman Pub; 0-911104; 0-89480),* 1 W. 39th St., New York, NY 10018 Tel 212-398-9160 (SAN 203-2821).

Workmen's Circle Education Department, *(Workmen's Circle),* 45 E. 33rd St., New York, NY 10016 (SAN 216-2075).

Workshop Center for Open Education, *(Workshop Ctr; 0-918374),* 6 Shepard Hall, Convent Ave. & 140th St., New York, NY 10031 Tel 212-690-4162 (SAN 209-9233).

Workshops for Innovative Teaching, *(Wkshops Innovative Teach; 0-9604042),* 191 Edgewood Ave., San Francisco, CA 94117 (SAN 214-1744).

World Action Pubs., *(World Action; 0-932742),* 135 Ridge Rd., Wethersfield, CT 06109 (SAN 212-1468).

World Almanac, *(World Almanac; 0-911818),* 200 Park Ave., New York, NY 10017 Tel 212-557-9651 (SAN 211-7703).

World Bank, The, *(World Bank),* 1818 H St., N.W., Washington, DC 20433 Tel 202-477-1234 (SAN 219-0648).

World Bible Pubs., Inc., *(World Bible; 0-529),* 15707 Detroit Ave., Lakewood, OH 44107 Tel 216-221-4370 (SAN 215-2789); Orders to: P. O. Box 1058, Iowa Falls, IA 50126 Tel 800-247-5111 (SAN 215-2797).

World Bk., Inc., A Scott Fetzer company, *(World Bk; 0-7166),* Merchandise Mart Plaza, Rm 510, Chicago, IL 60654 Tel 312-245-3456 (SAN 201-4815).

World Citizens Assembly, *(World Citizens),* P.O. Box 2063, San Francisco, CA 94126 (SAN 209-2719).

World Conference on Religion & Peace, *(World Confer Rel & Peace; 0-932934),* 777 United Nations Plaza, New York, NY 10017 (SAN 213-8840).

World Eagle, Inc., *(World Eagle; 0-9608014),* 64 Washburn Ave., Wellesley, MA 02181 Tel 617-237-1055 (SAN 239-9555).

World Education, *(World Educ; 0-914262),* 1414 Ave. of the Americas, New York, NY 10019 Tel 212-838-5255 (SAN 204-4145).

World Education Project, *(World Educ Proj; 0-918158),* Box U-32, School of Education, Univ. of Conn., Storrs, CT 06268 Tel 203-486-3321 (SAN 209-6358).

World Environment Center, *(World Env Ctr; 0-910499),* 605 Third Ave., 17th Floor, New York, NY 10158 Tel 212-986-7200 (SAN 260-2806).

World Evangelical Fellowship, *(World Evang Fellow; 0-936444),* P.O. Box WEF, Wheaton, IL 60189 Tel 312-668-0440 (SAN 214-1760).

World Exonumia, *(World Exo; 0-912317),* P.O. Box 4143 WY, Rockford, IL 61110-0643 Tel 815-226-0771 (SAN 265-3079).

World Food Press, *(World Food; 0-930922),* 10 Myrtle St., Jamaica Plain, MA 02130 (SAN 211-1098); Dist. by: Bookland, Inc., 56 Suffolk St., Holyoke, MA 01040 Tel 413-533-8475 (SAN 211-1101).

World Free Flight Press, *(World Free Flight; 0-933066),* 7513 Sausalito Ave., Canoga Park, CA 91307 Tel 213-340-1704 (SAN 213-6783).

World Future Society, *(World Future; 0-930242),* 4916 St. Elmo Ave., Bethesda, MD 20814 Tel 301-656-8274 (SAN 210-6892).

World Health Organization, *(World Health),* Dist. by: Q Corp., 49 Sheridan Ave., Albany, NY 12210 Tel 518-436-9686 (SAN 221-6310).

World Intellectual Property Organization *See* Unipub

World International Enterprises, Inc., *(World Intl),* P.O. Box 1611, North Miami, FL 33161 Tel 305-538-2869 (SAN 209-2123).

World Issues Information Bureau, *(World Issues; 0-9605110),* 1234 W. Loyola Ave., Chicago, IL 60626 (SAN 215-7179).

World Light Pubns., *(World Light; 0-916940),* 1518 Poplar Level Rd., Louisville, KY 40217 Tel 502-634-4185 (SAN 208-9300).

World Marketing Systems, Publishing Co., Inc., *(World Mktg Systems; 0-937284),* 256 Robertson Blvd., Beverly Hills, CA 90211 Tel 213-657-1575 (SAN 212-5994).

World Merchandise-Import Center, *(World Merch Import; 0-937514),* 609-613 Chetco Ave., P.O. Box 1389, Brookings, OR 97415 Tel 503-469-3218 (SAN 220-0171); *Imprints:* New Era Publications (New Era).

World Meterological Organization *See* Unipub

World Natural History Pubns., *(World Natural Hist; 0-916846),* P.O. Box 550, Marlton, NJ 08053 Tel 609-654-6500 (SAN 208-9297).

World Neighbors, *(World Neigh; 0-942716),* 5116 N Portland Ave, Oklahoma City, OK 73112 (SAN 276-8283).

World of Modeling, Inc., *(World Model; 0-941330),* P.O. Box 100, Croton-on-Hudson, NY 10520 Tel 914-737-8512 (SAN 239-0604).

World Policy Institute, *(World Policy; 0-911646),* 777 United Nations Plaza, New York, NY 10017 Tel 212-490-0010 (SAN 205-5511).

World Press Ltd., Div. of World News Syndicate, Ltd., *(World Pr Ltd; 0-912171),* 6223 Selma Ave., Suite 201, Los Angeles, CA 90028 Tel 213-469-2333 (SAN 276-9581).

World Record Pubns., Ltd., *(World Rec Pubns; 0-930804),* P.O. Box 41, Williston Park, NY 11596 Tel 516-248-8965 (SAN 211-0059).

World Rehabilitation Association for the Psycho-Socially Disabled, *(World Rehab),* P.O. Box 898, Ansonia Sta., New York, NY 10023 (SAN 223-8713); 1990 Broadway, New York, NY 10023 (SAN 223-8721).

World Rehabilitation Fund, Inc., *(World Rehab Fund; 0-939986),* 400 E. 34th St., New York, NY 10016 Tel 212-679-2934 (SAN 216-8723).

World Today, Inc., *(World Today; 0-942962),* World Center Building, Suite 102, 918 16th St., N. W., Washington, DC 20006 (SAN 240-5113).

World Trade Academy Press, *(World Trade; 0-8360),* 50 E. 42nd St., New York, NY 10017 Tel 212-697-4999 (SAN 203-2813).

World Univ. Press, *(World Univ AZ; 0-941902),* 711 - E. Blacklidge Dr., Tucson, AZ 85719 Tel 602-622-2170 (SAN 239-7943).

World Univ. Pr., *(World Univ Pr; 0-938340),* 1425 Bedford St., Suite 1A, Stamford, CT 06905 (SAN 215-8329).

World View Pubns., *(World View Pubns; 0-933774),* P.O. Box 6057, Chicago, IL 60680 Tel 312-648-0277 (SAN 212-9841).

World View Pubs., *(WV Pubs; 0-89567),* 46 W. 21st St., New York, NY 10010 Tel 212-242-4811 (SAN 210-6906).

World Watch See Unipub

World Wide Distributors Ltd., *(World Wide; 0-931548),* 1132 Auahi St., Honolulu, HI 96814 Tel 808-531-0133 (SAN 211-3392).

World Wide Products, *(World Wide Prods; 0-934062),* 740 Pine St., San Francisco, CA 94108 Tel 415-391-6324 (SAN 212-8721).

World Wide Publishing Corp., *(World Wide OR; 0-930294),* P.O. Box 105, Ashland, OR 97520 Tel 503-482-3800 (SAN 207-4818).

World Wide Pubns., *(World Wide Pubs; 0-89066),* 1303 Hennepin Ave., Minneapolis, MN 55403 Tel 612-336-0940 (SAN 203-185X).

World Without War Council Flatiron Building, *(World Without War),* 175 Fifth Ave 21st Fl, New York, NY 10010 (SAN 235-8190).

Worldwatch Institute, *(Worldwatch Inst; 0-916468),* 1776 Massachusetts Ave., N.W., Washington, DC 20036 Tel 202-452-1999 (SAN 209-2727).

Wormhoudt, Arthur, Dr., *(Wormhoudt; 0-916358),* Dept. of Language & Literature, William Penn College, Oskaloosa, IA 52577 Tel 515-673-3091 (SAN 207-5547).

Wormwood Review Press, *(Wormwood Rev; 0-935390),* P.O. Box 8840, Stockton, CA 95208-0840 Tel 209-466-8231 (SAN 209-8113).

Worth, H. S., Co., *(H S Worth; 0-939248),* P.O. Box 601, Oakridge, OR 97463 Tel 503-782-2703 (SAN 220-1615).

Worth Printing Publishing, *(Worth Print; 0-9609734),* P.O. Box 21201, Cleveland, OH 44121 Tel 216-531-6951 (SAN 263-2373).

Worth Pubs., Inc., *(Worth; 0-87901),* 444 Park Ave. S., New York, NY 10016 Tel 212-689-9630 (SAN 205-5546).

Worthington & Company, *(Worthington Co; 0-911529),* P.O. Box 371, Locust Grove, VA 22508 Tel 703-972-2951 (SAN 264-5076).

Worthy Labor Press, *(Worthy Labor Pr),* 1315 Monterey St., Richmond, CA 94804 (SAN 203-1833).

WRC Publishing, Subs. of William R. Cates, Inc., *(WRC Pub; 0-942320),* 2915 Fenimore Rd., Silver Spring, MD 20902 Tel 301-949-6787 (SAN 239-751X).

Wreden, William P., *(Wreden; 0-9600574),* P.O. Box 56, Palo Alto, CA 94302 Tel 415-325-6851 (SAN 123-4048).

Wright, John, PSG, Inc., *(Wright-PSG; 0-88416; 0-7236),* P.O.Box Six, Littleton, MA 01460 Tel 617-486-8971 (SAN 201-8934).

Wright, Mildred S., G.R.S., *(M S Wright; 0-917016),* 140 Briggs, Beaumont, TX 77707 Tel 409-832-2308 (SAN 208-9335).

Wright, Richard E., *(Wright R E; 0-9604210),* Dist. by: Caucasian Rugs, 5666 Northcumberland St., Pittsburgh, PA 15217 Tel 412-422-0300 (SAN 276-8615).

Wright, Stephen, Press, *(Stephen Wright; 0-9601904),* Box 1341, F.D.R. Post Office Sta., New York, NY 10150 Tel 212-927-2869 (SAN 211-8785).

Wright, Stuart,. Pub./Palaemon Press Ltd., *(S Wright; 0-913773),* P.O. Box 7527, Reynolda Sta., Winston-Salem, NC 27109 Tel 919-725-5985 (SAN 286-2026); 2100 Faculty Dr., Winston-Salem, NC 27106 (SAN 286-2034).

Wright, Zelma H., Jr., *(Z H Wright),* 140 Briggs, Beaumont, TX 77707 Tel 409-832-2308 (SAN 209-133X).

Wright Books, *(Wright Bks; 0-913083),* 54 Vly Rd., Albany, NY 12205 (SAN 283-9938).

Wright Group, The, *(Wright Group; 0-940156),* 7620 Miramar Rd., Suite 4100, San Diego, CA 92126 Tel 619-695-1810 (SAN 217-085X).

Wrightwill Publishing Co., *(Wrightwill Pub),* 256 S. Robertson Blvd., Beverly Hills, CA 90211 Tel 213-926-6994 (SAN 220-1135).

Write-A-Book, *(Write-A-Book; 0-943682),* 3297 Las Vegas Blvd. N., No. L-F, Las Vegas, NV 89030 Tel 702-644-4622 (SAN 238-4205).

Write to Sell, *(Write to Sell; 0-9605078),* P.O. Box 706-A, Carpinteria, CA 93013 Tel 805-684-2469 (SAN 215-7187).

Writer, *(Writer; 0-87116),* 8 Arlington St., Boston, MA 02116 Tel 617-536-7420 (SAN 203-2791).

Writers & Readers, *(Writers & Readers),* c/o W.W. Norton Co., 500 Fifth Ave., New York, NY 10110 Tel 212-228-0390 (SAN 216-4795).

Writers Digest Books, *(Writers Digest; 0-89879; 0-911654),* 9933 Alliance Rd., Cincinnati, OH 45242 Tel 513-984-0717 (SAN 212-064X).

Writers Press, *(Writers Pr; 0-931536),* Box 805, 2000 Connecticut Ave., Washington, DC 20008 Tel 202-232-0440 (SAN 212-2030).

Writer's Publishing House, *(Writers Pub Hse; 0-9606510),* 615 N.E. 15th Court, Ft. Lauderdale, FL 33304 Tel 305-764-4824 (SAN 217-2186).

Writers Publishing Service Co., *(Writers Pub Serv; 0-910303),* 1512 Western Ave., Seattle, WA 98101 (SAN 276-6646).

Writer's Services, Inc., *(Writers Serv FL; 0-911229),* P.O. Box 152, Miami Springs, FL 33266 Tel 305-264-5092).

Writing Consultant, The, *(Writing Con; 0-911683),* 65 W. 96 St., 16D, New York, NY 10025 Tel 212-864-6415 (SAN 264-5122).

Writing Works Inc., Div. of Morse Press, Inc., *(Writing; 0-916076),* 417 E. Pine St., Seattle, WA 98122 Tel 206-323-1820 (SAN 209-4118).

Wrongtree Press, *(Wrongtree Pr),* Box 930, Bolinas, CA 94924 (SAN 207-5822).

Wry Idea Co., *(Wry Idea; 0-9606814),* 3150 Ducommun, San Diego, CA 92122 Tel 619-452-7465 (SAN 223-2049).

Wu, T. H., *(T H Wu; 0-918498),* 160 Brookside Oval E., Worthington, OH 43085 Tel 614-888-0137 (SAN 209-6919).

Wunderle, Outdoor Books, *(Wunderle Outdoor; 0-9611162),* 86 Eight Mile Prairie Rd., Carterville, IL 62918 (SAN 283-426X).

Wychwood Press, *(Wychwood Pr; 0-932386),* P.O. Box 44, College Park, MD 20740 Tel 202-426-6390 (SAN 211-7711) Moved, Left No Forwarding Address.

Wyden, Peter H., Inc. See McKay, David, Co., Inc.

Wyden Books, Div. of P.E.I. Books, Inc., *(Wyden; 0-87223),* P.O. Box 151, Ridgefield, CT 06877 Tel 203-438-9631 (SAN 210-9794); Dist. by: Harper & Row Pubs., Inc., Keystone Industrial Park, Scranton, PA 18512 (SAN 215-3742).

Wynaud Press *(Wynaud Pr; 0-9603312),* 3005 Ronna, Las Cruces, NM 88001 Tel 505-524-3132 (SAN 212-3282).

Wynford House Pubs., *(Wynford Hse),* 7175 W. Alabama Dr., Denver, CO 80226 Tel 303-985-5416 (SAN 208-0591).

Wynnehaven Publishing Co., *(Wynnehaven; 0-9601476),* 212 Ocean St., Beach Haven, NJ 08008 Tel 609-492-3601 (SAN 210-1416).

Wyoming Foundry Studios, Inc., *(Wyoming Foundry; 0-9606916),* 23 E. 26th St., New York, NY 10010 Tel 212-689-5118 (SAN 217-4634).

Wyoming Law Institute, *(Wyoming Law Inst; 0-915876),* P.O. Box 3035, University Sta., Laramie, WY 82071 Tel 307-766-6926).

Wyoming Specialties, Inc., *(Wyoming Specialties),* P.O. Box 721, Gillette, WY 82716 (SAN 209-0082).

Wyoming State Press, *(Wyoming State Archives; 0-943398),* Barrett Building, Cheyenne, WY 82002 Tel 307-777-7518 (SAN 240-8104).

Wysinger, Vossa E., *(V E Wysinger),* P.O. Box 158, Berkeley, CA 94704 Tel 415-655-1742 (SAN 203-1140).

Wyvern Pubns., *(Wyvern; 0-9602404),* P.O. Box 188, Dumfries, VA 22026 Tel 703-670-3527 (SAN 215-9872).

X-Log Corp., *(X-Log; 0-9603162),* 393 Main St., Catskill, NY 12414 Tel 518-943-4771 (SAN 212-3290).

X, Taylor, Henry T., *(H T Taylor; 0-938956),* P.O. Box No. 111, Eggertville, NY 14226 (SAN 264-5149).

Xanadu Enterprises, *(Xanadu Ent; 0-933638),* Box 551, Goochland, VA 23063 (SAN 213-4063).

Xenos Books, *(Xenos Bks; 0-934724),* 13524 Crenshaw Blvd., Gardena, CA 90249 Tel 213-538-5000 (SAN 213-4071).

Xerox Education Pubns., Div. of Xerox Corp., *(Xerox Ed Pubns; 0-8374),* 245 Long Hill Rd., Middletown, CT 06457 Tel 203-349-7251 (SAN 207-060X); Orders to: 1250 Fairwood Ave., Columbus, OH 43216 Tel 614-253-0892 (SAN 207-0618).

Xerox Learning Systems, A Xerox Publishing Co., *(Xerox Learning; 0-935268),* P.O. Box 10211, 1600 Summer St., Stamford, CT 06904 Tel 203-965-8400 (SAN 206-0086).

Yale Concilium on International & Area Studies, *(Yale Concilium; 0-936586),* 85 Trumbull St., New Haven, CT 06520 (SAN 283-9806); Dist. by: Slavica Publishers, Inc., P.O. Box 14388, Columbus, OH 43214 (SAN 208-8576).

Yale University Art Gallery, *(Yale Art Gallery; 0-89467),* 2006 Yale Sta., 1111 Chapel St., New Haven, CT 06520 Tel 203-436-0574 (SAN 209-6927).

Yale Univ. Library Pubns., *(Yale U Lib; 0-8457)* P.O. Box 1603A Yale Sta., New Haven, CT 06520 Tel 203-436-8668 (SAN 202-1226).

Yale Univ. Press, *(Yale U Pr; 0-300),* 302 Temple St., New Haven, CT 06520 Tel 203-432-4920 (SAN 203-2740); Orders to: 92A Yale Sta., New Haven, CT 06520 Tel 203-432-4969 (SAN 203-2759).

Yale Univ. Pubns. in Anthropology, *(Yale U Anthro),* P.O. Box 2114, Yale Sta., New Haven, CT 06520 Tel 203-432-3847 (SAN 205-5562).

Yale Univ. Southeast Asia Studies, *(Yale U SE Asia),* Box 13A, Yale University, New Haven, CT 06520 Tel 203-436-8897 (SAN 206-0027).

Yama Publishing Co., *(Yama Pub; 0-937290),* 2266 Fifth Ave., No. 136, New York, NY 10037 Tel 212-283-5220 (SAN 219-984X).

Yama Trans Co., *(Yama Trans; 0-942512),* 24228 Hawthorne Blvd., Torrance, CA 90505 Tel 213-378-8700 (SAN 238-2105).

Yankee Books, A Division of Yankee Publishing Inc., *(Yankee Bks; 0-911658; 0-89909),* Dublin, NH 03444 Tel 603-563-8111 (SAN 203-2732).

Yankee Peddler Book Co., *(Yankee Peddler; 0-911660),* Drawer O, Southampton, NY 11968 Tel 516-283-1612 (SAN 205-5570).

Yankee Peddler Bookshop, *(Yankee Ped Bkshop; 0-918426),* 94 Mill St., Pultneyville, NY 14538 Tel 315-589-2063 (SAN 209-925X).

Yara Press, *(Yara Pr; 0-913038),* P.O. Box 1295, Mendocino, CA 95460 Tel 707-937-0866 (SAN 205-5589).

Yardbird Wing Editions, *(Yardbird Wing; 0-918412),* Dist. by: Yardbird Pub. Co., Inc., P.O. Box 2370, Station A, Berkeley, CA 94702 Tel 415-527-7426 (SAN 208-9343).

Yards, A., *(A Yards; 0-9629555),* 1241 Wasatch Dr., Mountain View, CA 94040 Tel 415-964-3550 (SAN 209-0902).

Yates, Samuel, *(S Yates; 0-9608652),* 157 Capri-D, Kings Point, Delray Beach, FL 33445 Tel 305-499-0323 (SAN 238-4213).

Ye Galleon Press, *(Ye Galleon; 0-87770),* P.O. Box 25, Fairfield, WA 99012 Tel 509-283-2422 (SAN 205-5597).

Ye Olde Printery, *(Ye Olde Print; 0-932606),* 5815 Cherokee Dr., Cincinnati, OH 45243 Tel 513-561-4338 (SAN 213-408X).

Yeamans, George Thomas, *(G T Yeamans; 0-9601006),* 4507 W. Burton Dr., Muncie, IN 47304 Tel 317-288-4345 (SAN 208-9351); Orders to: Ball State Bookstore, Muncie, IN 47306 (SAN 209-1623).
Year Book Medical Pubs., Inc., *(Year Bk Med; 0-8151),* 35 E. Wacker Dr., Chicago, IL 60601 Tel 800-621-9262 (SAN 205-5600).
Yearling Books *See* **Dell Publishing Co., Inc.**
Yellow Book of Pa. Inc., *(Yellow Bk PA; 0-9604612),* 715 Twining Rd., P.O. Box 7, Dresher, PA 19025 (SAN 219-9858).
Yellow Fox Press, *(Yellow Fox; 0-941020),* 2610 Wilson St., No. 106, Austin, TX 78704 Tel 512-448-2181 (SAN 217-4642).
Yellow Jacket Press, *(Yellow Jacket; 0-915626),* 901 Alspaugh Lane, Grand Prairie, TX 75052 (SAN 207-3048).
Yellow Moon Press, *(Yellow Moon; 0-938756),* 1725 Commonwealth Ave., Brighton, MA 02135 Tel 617-782-3183 (SAN 216-4809).
Yellow Press, *(Yellow Pr; 0-916328),* 2394 Blue Island Ave., Chicago, IL 60608 (SAN 207-9631).
Yellow Springs Computer Camp, Inc., *(Yellow Springs; 0-912529),* P.O. Box 292, Yellow Springs, OH 45387 Tel 513-767-7717 (SAN 265-3087); c/o Antioch College, Yellow Springs, OH 45387 (SAN 265-3095).
Yellow Umbrella Press, *(Yellow Umb Pr; 0-942654),* 501 Main St., Chatham, MA 02633 (SAN 223-1018).
Yellowstone Library & Museum Assn., The, *(Yellowstone Lib; 0-934948),* Yellowstone Park, WY 82190 (SAN 214-4921).
Yesnaby Pubs., *(Yesnaby Pubs; 0-9606262),* P.O. Box 213, R.D. 8, Danville, PA 17821 Tel 717-437-3488 (SAN 220-3499).
Yesod Pubs., *(Yesod Pubs),* 75 Prospect Park W., Brooklyn, NY 11215 Tel 212-768-5591 (SAN 211-8300).
Yesterday/Today/Tomorrow Publishing, *(YTT Pub; 0-911685),* No., 619, 1626 N. Wilcox Ave., Hollywood, CA 90028 Tel 213-786-1202 (SAN 264-5157).
Yiddish Archivist Press, *(Yiddish Arch Pr; 0-942656),* 52 Overlook Dr., Meridin, CT 06450 Tel 203-235-1441 (SAN 239-9571).
Yivo Institute for Jewish Research, *(Yivo Inst; 0-914512),* 1048 Fifth Ave., New York, NY 10028 Tel 212-535-6700 (SAN 207-1614).
YMCA of the USA, *(YMCA USA),* 101 N Wacker Dr., Chicago, IL 60606 Tel 312-997-0031 (SAN 223-8780).
Yoga Pubn. Society, *(Yoga; 0-911662),* P.O. Box 8885, Jacksonville, FL 32211 (SAN 203-2724).
Yoga Research Foundation, *(Yoga Res Foun; 0-934664),* 6111 S.W. 74th Ave., Miami, FL 33143 Tel 305-595-5580 (SAN 209-0279).
Yogi Gupta New York Center, *(Yogi Gupta; 0-911664),* 90-16 51st Ave., Elmhurst, NY 11373 (SAN 205-5619).
Yokefellow Press, *(Yokefellow Pr; 0-932970; 0-914005),* 230 College Ave., Richmond, IN 47374 Tel 317-962-6810 (SAN 276-9336).
Yoknapatawpha Press, *(Yoknapatawpha; 0-916242),* Box 248, Oxford, MS 38655 Tel 601-234-0909 (SAN 213-7593).
Yoon, F. T., Co., *(F T Yoon; 0-931168),* P.O. Box 470, Pebble Beach, CA 93953 Tel 408-646-9499 (SAN 212-873X).
York, C. C., *(C C York),* 9000 E. Jefferson Ave., Apt. 1511, Detroit, MI 48214 (SAN 264-5165).
York Press, Inc., *(York Pr; 0-912752),* 2712 Mt. Carmel Rd., Parkton, MD 21120 Tel 301-343-1121 (SAN 203-2708).
Yorke, Harvey, *(Harvey Yorke; 0-9607598),* 495 Rowland Blvd., Novato, CA 94947 Tel 415-897-4050 (SAN 200-2612); P.O. Box 252, Novato, CA 94948 (SAN 237-9767).
Yorke Medical Books, *(Yorke Med; 0-914316),* 875 Third Ave., New York, NY 10022 Tel 212-605-9620 (SAN 207-155X).
Yorkshire Publishing Co., *(Yorkshire Pub; 0-9604732),* P.O. Box 309, Princeton Jct., NJ 08550 (SAN 215-7195).
Yosef, Aish, Publishers-Distributors, Inc., *(Aish Yosef Pub; 0-942694),* 2 W. 46th St., Rm. 402, New York, NY 10036 Tel 212-921-0544 (SAN 239-9598).
Yosemite-Di-Maggio, *(Yosemite D; 0-911819),* 618 Grand Ave., Oakland, CA 94610 Tel 415-839-9780 (SAN 264-5173).

Yosemite Natural History Association, *(Yosemite Natl Hist),* Box 545, Yosemite Ntl Pk, CA 95389 (SAN 225-2201).
You Can Make It Enterprises, *(You Can Make It Ent; 0-9606328),* P.O. Box 35, Nevada City, CA 95959 Tel 916-265-6756 (SAN 219-1040).
Young, Ione, *(I Young),* 4107 Wildwood Rd., Austin, TX 78722 (SAN 207-6268).
Young, Katherine, *(K Young),* 140 East 40th St., New York, NY 10016 Tel 212-684-0999 (SAN 237-9791).
Young, Robert G., *(R G Young; 0-9611010),* Box 40743, Grand Junction, CO 81504-0743 (SAN 277-7037).
Young, Robert Stephen, *(R S Young; 0-9607068),* 304 State, N.W., Albuquerque, NM 87102 (SAN 241-5968).
Young, Victor A., *(V Young; 0-9603694),* 548 S. Main St., Red Lion, PA 17356 Tel 717-244-6816 (SAN 213-5736).
Young Creations, Inc., *(Young Creations; 0-913703),* 15245 Minnetonka Blvd., Minnetonka, MN 55343 Tel 612-935-5937 (SAN 286-0899).
Young Davis Press, *(Young Davis Pr; 0-931914),* 3043 Darlington Dr., Thousand Oaks, CA 91360 Tel 805-492-8364 (SAN 211-4593).
Young Life National Services, *(Young Life; 0-932856),* Box 520, Colorado Springs, CO 80901 Tel 303-473-4262 (SAN 211-8319).
Young People's Press, *(Young People's Pr),* Box 1005, Avon, CT 06001 (SAN 239-4022).
Young Pine Pr., *(Young Pine Pr; 0-9608280),* c/o International Examiner, 318 6th Ave. S. No. 123, Seattle, WA 98104 Tel 206-782-8666 (SAN 240-5741).
Young Women's Christian Assn., (YWCA), National Board, *(YWCA),* 135 W. 50th St., New York, NY 10020 Tel 212-621-5115 (SAN 207-9674).
Young Women's Christian Organization (yMCO; *(YWCO; 0-9608282),* 201 St. Charles St., Baton Rouge, LA 70802 (SAN 240-4613).
Younghusband Co., *(Younghusband; 0-936358),* P.O. Box 68, Montrose, CA 91020 (SAN 214-1779).
Youngjohn Publications, *(Youngjohn Pubns; 0-912321),* 1275 4th Street, Santa Rosa, CA 95404 (SAN 276-9514).
Yourdon Pr., *(Yourdon; 0-917072),* 1133 Ave. of the Americas, New York, NY 10036 Tel 212-391-2828 (SAN 208-2136).
Youth Challenge Pub., *(Youth Challenge; 0-9606116),* Box 4567, Topeka, KS 66604 Tel 913-273-1126 (SAN 216-4817).
Youth Education Systems, Inc., *(Youth Ed; 0-87738),* 3305 W. Warner Ave., Santa Ana, CA 92704 Tel 714-556-7130 (SAN 205-5635).
Youth Specialties, *(Youth Special),* 1224 Greenfield Dr., El Cajon, CA 92021 Tel 312-668-8690 (SAN 211-8327).
Yuchi Pines Institute, *(Yuchi Pines),* Po Box 319, Seale, AL 36856 (SAN 239-5053).
Yuletide International, *(Yuletide Intl; 0-911049),* 9665 Malad St., Boise, ID 83709 (SAN 264-5181).
Z-Graphic Pubns., *(Z Graphic Pubns; 0-941572),* 833 Joost Ave., San Francisco, CA 94127 Tel 415-584-4048 (SAN 239-3522).
Z Press, Inc., *(Z Pr; 0-915990),* Calais, VT 05648 (SAN 207-656X).
Z Productions, *(Z Prods),* Rt. Three, Box 12, Pavo, GA 31778 Tel 912-859-2861 (SAN 214-1787).
Zachry Pubns., *(Zachry Pubns),* 502 E. N. 16th, Abilene, TX 79601 Tel 915-673-2356 (SAN 203-1825).
Zalo Pubns. & Services, Inc., *(Zalo; 0-931200),* Dist. by: Frangipani Press, Div. of T. I. S. Enterprises, P.O. Box 1998, 1928 Arlington Rd., Bloomington, IN 47402 Tel 812-332-3307 (SAN 169-2313).
Zalozba Prometej, *(Zalozba Prometej; 0-934158),* P.O. Box 8391, New Orleans, LA 70182 Tel 504-283-7177 (SAN 212-8462).
Zanel Pubns., *(Zanel Pubns),* P.O. Box 255867, Sacramento, CA 95865-5867 Tel 916-922-8320 (SAN 212-985X).
Zaner-Bloser, Inc., *(Zaner-Bloser; 0-88309),* 2500 W. 5th Ave., P.O. Box 16764, Columbus, OH 43216 Tel 614-486-0221 (SAN 282-5678) (SAN 282-5686).

Zanon Pubns., *(Zanon Pubns),* 9600 Armley Ave., Whittier, CA 90604 Tel 213-693-4828 (SAN 216-4825).
Zapffe, Carl A., *(C A Zapffe; 0-9601448),* 6410 Murray Hill Rd., Baltimore, MD 21212 (SAN 221-2978).
Zartscorp, Inc. Books, *(Zartscorp),* 333 West End Ave., New York, NY 10023 Tel 212-724-5071 (SAN 209-5017).
Zdenek, Dale, Publications, *(D Zdenek Pubns; 0-916902),* 31352 Via Colinas, Westlake, CA 91360 Tel 213-888-6891 (SAN 208-9378).
Zebra Books, *(Zebra; 0-89083; 0-8217),* 475 Park Ave. S., New York, NY 10016 Tel 212-889-2299 (SAN 207-9860); Dist. by: Kable News Co., 777 3rd Ave., New York, NY 10017 (SAN 169-5835).
Z.E.D Books, *(ZED Bks; 0-940874),* P.O. Box 1668, Burbank, CA 91507 Tel 213-353-4389 (SAN 219-6573).
Zellerbach Family Fund, *(Zellerbach F F),* 260 California St., No. 1010, San Francisco, CA 94111 (SAN 287-2633); Dist. by: Early Single Parenting Project, 1005 Market St., No. 313, San Francisco, CA 94103 (SAN 287-2641).
Zen Center, The, *(Zen Ctr; 0-940306),* 7 Arnold Park, Rochester, NY 14607 Tel 216-473-9180 (SAN 217-569X).
Zenanko, Tom, Outdoors, *(Zenanko Outdoors; 0-9610296),* 5612 No. Lilac Dr., Brooklyn Center, MN 55430 (SAN 276-9352).
Zenger Publishing Co., Inc., *(Zenger Pub; 0-89201),* P.O. Box 9883, Washington, DC 20015 Tel 301-881-1470 (SAN 208-0427).
Zenith Books *See* **Doubleday & Co., Inc.**
Zentner Pubns., *(Zentner Pubns; 0-934950),* 2407 Larkspur Lane, No. 231, Sacto, CA 95825 Tel 916-972-0182 (SAN 213-4098).
Zephyr *See* **Doubleday & Co., Inc.**
Zephyr Press, *(Zephyr Pr; 0-939010),* 13 Robinson St., Somerville, MA 02145 Tel 617-623-2799 (SAN 239-7668).
Zephyr Pubs., *(Zephyr; 0-931782),* P.O. Box 43-1275, South Miami, FL 33143 Tel 305-279-7817 (SAN 205-5678).
Zeppelin Pub. Co., *(Zeppelin; 0-915628),* P.O. Box 22252, Louisiana State Univ. Station, Baton Rouge, LA 70893 Tel 504-272-6600 (SAN 204-6776); Pelican Office Center, 11628 S. Choctaw Dr., Baton Rouge, LA 70815 Tel 504-272-6600 (SAN 200-4208); Orders to: P.O. Box 15809, Broadmoor Station, Baton Rouge, LA 70893 Tel 504-272-6600 (SAN 200-4216).
Ziesing Bros. Book Emporium, *(Ziesing Bros),* 768 Main St., Willimantic, CT 06226 (SAN 209-6935).
Zimmerman, Al, Publishing, *(A Zimmerman; 0-914081),* 843 Van Nest Ave., Bronx, NY 10462 Tel 212-822-7333 (SAN 276-9387).
Zimmerman, Gary, *(Zimmerman; 0-916202),* G.P.O. Box 114, Brooklyn, NY 11202 Tel 212-854-4494 (SAN 208-0982).
Zimmerman, Grady, *(G Zimmerman),* 4508 W. Ponds View Dr., Littleton, CO 80123 Tel 303-798-5860 (SAN 219-6832).
Zimmerman, A. M., & Company, *(A M Zimmermann; 0-912125),* 2210 Jackson St., Suite 404, San Francisco, CA 94115 Tel 415-929-7577 (SAN 238-0897).
Zink, J., Inc., *(J Zink; 0-942490),* 1101 John St., Manhattan Beach, CA 90266 Tel 213-545-1031 (SAN 239-9601).
Zinman's Rapid Writing, *(Zinmans; 0-911672),* 55 Inwood Ave., Dept. Z, Point Lookout, NY 11569 (SAN 205-5686).
Zion Natural History Assn., *(Zion; 0-915630),* Zion National Park, Springdale, UT 84767 Tel 801-772-3256 (SAN 205-9959).
Zoe Pubns., *(Zoe Pubns; 0-89841),* P. O. Box 133, Geneva, IL 60134 Tel 312-584-2628 (SAN 212-7148).
Zondervan Publishing House, *(Zondervan; 0-310),* 1415 Lake Dr., S.E., Grand Rapids, MI 49506 Tel 616-459-6900 (SAN 203-2694).
Zoo Press, *(Zoo Pr; 0-911969),* 805 Homestead St., Baltimore, MD 21218 Tel 301-366-2950 (SAN 264-522X); Dist. by: Book Carrier, 9121 Industrial Center, Gaithersburg, MD 20877 Tel 800-638-4108 (SAN 200-4046); Orders to: Zoo Press, 805 Homestead St., Baltimore, MD 21218 Tel 301-366-2950 (SAN 264-522X).
Zook Consulting & Publishing, *(Zook; 0-933222),* P.O. Box 3643, Lawrence, KS 66044 (SAN 212-3959).

Zoological Society of San Diego, *(Zoological Soc; 0-911461),* P.O. Box 551, San Diego, CA 92112 Tel 714-265-8171 (SAN 276-931X).

Zoom Publishing, *(Zoom),* P.O. Box 730, El Toro, CA 92630 (SAN 264-5238).

Zubal, John T., Inc., *(Zubal Inc; 0-939738),* 2969 W. 25th St., Cleveland, OH 44113 Tel 216-241-7640 (SAN 216-7697).

Zucchini Patch, *(Zucchini Patch; 0-940158),* P.O. Box 1100, Nipomo, CA 93444 Tel 805-929-1718 (SAN 220-3146).

Zucker, Marjorie B., *(M B Zucker),* 333 Central Pk W., NY, NY 10025 (211-335X).

Zybert, Richard, *(Zybert),* 1169 Folsom St., San Francisco, CA 94103 Tel 415-863-7229 (SAN 214-2279).

Zyga Multimedia Research, *(ZYGA; 0-9608438),* 642 El Dorado Ave., Oakland, CA 94611 Tel 415-655-2101 (SAN 240-8112).

Zygote Press, *(Zygote Pr; 0-939358),* 1712 Mount Curve Ave., Minneapolis, MN 55403 Tel 612-871-4184 (SAN 216-4973).